Dictionary of Untranslatables

translation
TRANSNATION

SERIES EDITOR **EMILY APTER**

A list of titles in the series appears at the back of the book.

Dictionary of Untranslatables

A Philosophical Lexicon

EDITED BY **Barbara Cassin**

TRANSLATED BY **Steven Rendall, Christian Hubert, Jeffrey Mehlman, Nathanael Stein, and Michael Syrotinski**

TRANSLATION EDITED BY **Emily Apter, Jacques Lezra, and Michael Wood**

PRINCETON UNIVERSITY PRESS   Princeton and Oxford

First published in France under the title *Vocabulaire européen des philosophies: Dictionnaire des intraduisibles*
© 2004 by Éditions de Seuil / Dictionnaires Le Robert
English translation copyright © 2014 by Princeton University Press
Requests for permission to reproduce material from this work should be sent to Permissions, Princeton University Press
Published by Princeton University Press, 41 William Street, Princeton, New Jersey 08540
In the United Kingdom: Princeton University Press, 6 Oxford Street, Woodstock, Oxfordshire OX20 1TW

press.princeton.edu

Jacket design by Tracy Baldwin.

Library of Congress Cataloging-in-Publication Data

Vocabulaire européen des philosophies. English
  Dictionary of untranslatables : a philosophical lexicon / Edited by Barbara Cassin ; Translated by Steven Rendall, Christian Hubert, Jeffrey Mehlman, Nathanael Stein, and Michael Syrotinski ; Translation edited by Emily Apter, Jacques Lezra, and Michael Wood.
       pages   cm
  "First published in France under the title Vocabulaire européen des philosophies: Dictionnaire des intraduisibles (c) 2004 by Éditions de Seuil."
  Includes bibliographical references and index.
  ISBN-13: 978-0-691-13870-1 (cloth : alk. paper)
  ISBN-10: 0-691-13870-2 (cloth : alk. paper) 1. Philosophy--Encyclopedias. 2. Philosophy—Dictionaries--French. I. Cassin, Barbara, editor of compilation. II. Rendall, Steven, translator III. Apter, Emily S., editor of compilaton. IV. Title.
  B51.V6313 2013
  103—dc23   2013008394

British Library Cataloging-in-Publication Data is available

Publication of this book has been aided by the French Ministry of Culture—Centre National du Livre.

This work received essential support from CNRS (Centre National de la Recherche Scientifique).

The editors thank the following for their assistance: Fondation Charles Léopold Mayer, CNPQ (Conselho Nacional de Desenvolvimento Cientifico), and the European program ECHO (European Cultural Heritage Online).

For their personal and institutional support, the editors also thank Maurice Aymard and the Maison des Sciences de l'Homme, Yves Duroux, the Ministère de la Recherche and the Collège International de Philosophie, Roberto Esposito, Avvocato Marotta and the Istituto per gli Studi Filosofici de Naples, Paolo Fabbri and the Institut Culturel Italien de Paris, Elie Faroult and the Direction Général de la Recherche à la Commission Européene, Michèle Gendreau-Massaloux and the Agence Universitaire de la Francophonie, Yves Hersant and the Centre Europe at EHESS (École des Hautes Études en Sciences Sociales), Yves Mabin and the Direction du Livre au Ministère des Affaires Étrangères, Michel Marian and the Centre National du Livre, Georges Molinié, Jean-François Courtine, and the Université Paris IV–Sorbonne.

The article "Subject" was translated by David Macey and originally appeared in *Radical Philosophy* 138 (July/August 2006). Reprinted with permission.

This book has been composed in Gentium Plus, Myriad Pro, ITC Zapf Dingbats Std, Mathematical Pi LT Std, Times New Roman

Printed on acid-free paper. ∞

Printed in the United States of America

10 9 8 7 6 5 4 3 2 1

Contents

v

Preface

Philosophy in Translation

A massive translation exercise with encyclopedic reach, the *Dictionary of Untranslatables: A Philosophical Lexicon*—first published in French under the title *Vocabulaire européen des philosophies: Dictionnaire des intraduisibles*—belongs in a genealogy that includes Diderot and d'Alembert's *Encylopédie* (1751–66), André Lalande's *Vocabulaire technique et critique de philosophie* (1902–23), Émile Benveniste's *Le Vocabulaire des institutions indo-européennes*, Laplanche and Pontalis's *The Language of Psycho-Analysis* (1967, classified as a dictionary), *The Stanford Encyclopedia of Philosophy* (an online resource inaugurated in 1995), and Reinhart Koselleck's *Geschichtliche Grundbegriffe* (a dictionary of political and social concept-history, 2004). Along another axis, it recalls Raymond Williams's short compendium of political and aesthetic terms, *Keywords*, informed by British Marxism of the 1960s and '70s. Unlike these works, however, the *Dictionary* fully mobilizes a multilingual rubric. Accordingly, entries compare and meditate on the specific differences furnished to concepts by the Arabic, Basque, Catalan, Danish, English, French, German, Greek (classical and modern), Hebrew, Hungarian, Latin, Polish, Portuguese, Romanian, Russian, and Spanish languages.

The book was the brainchild of its French editor, Barbara Cassin, herself a specialist of classical philosophy. In 1998, in the introduction to her translation of Parmenides's poem *On Nature*, Cassin had already ascribed the "untranslatable" to the interminability of translating: the idea that one can never have done with translation. In her writings on the pre-Socratics and the Sophists, she tethered the untranslatable to the instability of meaning and sense-making, the performative dimension of sophistic effects, and the condition of temporality in translation. Translation's "time," in Cassin's usage, was associated with the principle of infinite regress and the vertiginous apprehension of infinitude.

Working with assembled teams of scholars from multiple countries and languages, and drawing on the expertise of more than 150 contributors, Cassin coordinated and supervised the *Dictionary* project over a period of eleven years. Published by Éditions du Seuil in 2004, this curious and immensely ambitious book, weighing in at a million and a half words, was a surprise hit with the public. What made it unique was its attempt to rewrite the history of philosophy through the lens of the "untranslatable," defined loosely as a term that is left untranslated as it is transferred from language to language (as in the examples of *polis, Begriff, praxis, Aufheben, mimesis*, "feeling," *lieu commun, logos*, "matter of fact"), or that is typically subject to mistranslation and retranslation.

Despite the redoubtable scale of its erudition and the range of its philosophical ambition, the French edition of the *Dictionary* resonated with a heterogeneous readership: philosophers, scholars in all fields of the humanities, and everyone interested in the cartography of languages or the impact of translation history on the course of philosophy. The work's international reception was then enlarged by its translations (some still under way) into Arabic, Farsi, Romanian, Russian, and Ukrainian. When Princeton University Press committed to publish an English edition, the editors confronted a daunting and very particular set of challenges: how to render a work, published in French, yet layered through and through with the world's languages, into something intelligible to Anglophone readers; how to translate the untranslatable; how to communicate the book's performative aspect, its stake in what it means "to philosophize in translation" over and beyond reviewing the history of philosophy with translation problems in mind.

A group of three editors supervised and edited the English version: Emily Apter (a specialist in French, comparative literature, translation studies, Continental philosophy, and political theory); Jacques Lezra (a literary comparatist with special strengths in Spanish, early modern literature and philosophy, contemporary theory, and Anglo-American philosophy); and Michael Wood (a British comparatist, distinguished as a critic of literary modernism and contemporary cinema with professional expertise as a staff writer for the *London Review of Books*). Cassin and her close associate, the philosopher Étienne Balibar, were de facto coeditors, because the U.S. editors consulted with them at every stage. The collective affiliated with the U.K.-based journal *Radical Philosophy* was also integral to the project's gestation. The journal published a special issue devoted to the book in 2006, including English translations of selected entries by the late David Macey. We have included Macey's translation of the entry SUBJECT in this volume both because it is a strong translation and because it allowed us to acknowledge, albeit only indirectly, *Radical Philosophy*'s abiding commitment to a practice of philosophical translation that would shake up the teaching of philosophy in departments dominated by the normative strictures of the Angloanalytic philosophical tradition.

The *Dictionary of Untranslatables*, like its French predecessor, and like the editions published or under way in other languages, was a labor of many. The translators—of which there were five (Christian Hubert, Jeffrey Mehlman, Steven Rendall, Nathanael Stein, and Michael Syrotinski)—became contributors on every level. Their queries and suggestions, along with those of the copy editors, each of whom had special language proficiencies, proved crucial to the editing process and served as a constant reminder that to translate is an act of rewriting, and, in this particular instance, of assisting words in their becoming philosophical. A broad network of colleagues and specialists generously provided corrections and revisions, and yet another layer of collaboration was provided by graduate student assistants who checked citations and compiled new bibliographies.

The bibliographical revisions were by no means a minor part of remodeling the French edition for an Anglophone audience. In addition to English translations of canonical philosophical texts and standard reference works in English on concepts and philosophers, we added selections from a critical literature that contributed to the *Dictionary*'s acknowledgment of what is referred to in the Anglophone world as theory. "Theory" is an imprecise catchall for a welter of postwar movements in the human sciences—existentialism, structural anthropology, sociolinguistics, semiotics, history of *mentalités*, post-Freudian psychoanalysis, deconstruction, poststructuralism, critical theory, identity politics, postcolonialism, biopolitics, nonphilosophy, speculative materialism—that has no equivalent in European languages. What is often referred to as "theory" in an Anglophone context would simply be called

"philosophy" in Europe. The *Dictionary of Untranslatables* acknowledges this divergence between "theory" and "philosophy" not at the expense of how the editors of the French edition defined philosophy (which, it must be said, was already noncanonical in the choice of terms deemed philosophical), but as a condition of the work's reception by Anglophone readers accustomed to an eclectic "theory" bibliography that not infrequently places G.W.F. Hegel, Friedrich Nietzsche, Martin Heidegger, Walter Benjamin, Theodore Adorno, Michel Foucault, Jacques Derrida, Jacques Lacan, Gilles Deleuze, Julia Kristeva, Jean-Luc Nancy, Antonio Negri, Hélène Cixous, Kojin Karatani, Alain Badiou, Giorgio Agamben, Jacques Rancière, Bruno Latour, and Slavoj Žižek in the same rubric with Stuart Hall, Homi Bhabha, Donna Haraway, Henry Louis Gates, Judith Butler, Eve Kosofsky Sedgwick, Friedrich Kittler, Gayatri Chakravorty Spivak, Edward Said, Fredric Jameson, and Paul Gilroy.

Bearing in mind, then, that the word "philosophy" in the original French title was already an untranslatable insofar as it defaulted to "philosophies" that might line up more easily with "theory" in an Anglophone (and especially U.S. American) context, one of our initial debates focused on how to translate the book's title. There was a doubling of genre announced in the French. Is it a "vocabulary" or a "dictionary"? For Cassin (following Benveniste's *Le Vocabulaire des institutions indo-européennes*), "vocabulary" underscored a non-exhaustive ensemble of terms chosen for their common linguistic "symptoms," while "dictionary," designating an aspiration to impossible completeness, was meant to stand alongside "vocabulary" as an ironic complement. Together, in Cassin's view, they posed the problem of the form of the work as an oxymoron. Such subtle distinctions could, however, easily be missed. Broadly speaking, a dictionary contains an alphabetical list of words with information about them, whereas a vocabulary, the generic term for sets of words that persons are familiar with in a language, is similarly used to describe alphabetized and explained word ensembles, usually for a pedagogical purpose relating to a special field. In France, the long tradition of dictionaries could be bracketed by Pierre Bayle's seminal *Dictionnaire historique et critique* (1697), which privileged biographies and historical events, and the Presses Universitaires de France dictionaries covering such diverse fields as cinema, psychoanalysis, work, sociology, violence, and the human sciences. Given, then, the relative interchangeability of "vocabulary" and "dictionary," we replaced the former with the latter in the main title, and added "lexicon" to the subtitle in the spirit of the expression "terms entering the lexicon," which captures (in a manner that brings out the original work's underlying intention) how live languages incorporate new or non-native elements.

Although some of us worried about a certain awkwardness in the use of the adjective "untranslatable" as a noun, by foregrounding it in the English title we signaled its important role as an organizing principle of the entire project. We also decided to eliminate the reference to Europe. This was a difficult call, as the European focus of the book is undeniable. Removing the emphasis on "European philosophies" would leave us open to criticism that the *Dictionary* now laid claim to being a work of world philosophy, a tall order that it patently did not fill. Our justification on this score was twofold: so that future editions of the *Dictionary of Untranslatables* might incorporate new entries on philosophy hailing from countries and languages cartographically zoned outside of Europe; and because, philologically speaking, conventional distinctions between European and non-European languages make little or no sense. Moreover, it was our sense that the adjective "European," often assumed to refer to a common legacy of Christendom, humanism, and Enlightenment principles, actually misrepresents the complexity of identifying "Europe" culturally and geopolitically at any given moment in history.

Notwithstanding concerns about the global hegemony of English (and more pointedly still, about those forms of standardized, Internet-inflected, business English commonly dubbed "Globish" that are frequently associated with financial "outcomes" and "deliverables"), we assume that the book, by dint of being in English, will disseminate broadly and reach new communities of readers. The book's diffusion in Asia, South Asia, Africa, the Middle East, and Latin America will lead, we hope, not only to more translations in other languages, but also to spin-off versions appropriate to different cultural sites and medial forms. We hope that the English edition, in its current and future iterations, will help to advance experimental formats in research, data-mining, and pedagogy, as well as models of comparativism that place renewed emphasis on the particularities of idiom. Philosophical importance, in this case, is accorded to how a term "is" in its native tongue, and how it "is" or "is not" when relocated or translated in another language. Idiomatic and demotic nuance are fully recognized as constitutive of philosophy, prompting

a shift from concept-driven philosophical analysis to a new kind of process philosophy, what Cassin calls "philosophizing in languages."

In promoting revivified connections among philosophy, translation, linguistics, and philology, the *Dictionary* encourages curricular initiatives in the form of courses, colloquia, and cross-institutional degree programs. The *Dictionary* proves useful for teaching in myriad ways, especially at advanced undergraduate and graduate levels. In an era in which countries all over the world are adopting policies—often in line with the European Union's endorsement of English as its *lingua franca*—that would make English the official language of instruction in scientific and technical fields (if not the social sciences, area studies, and the humanities as well), students increasingly naturalize English as the singular language of universal knowledge, thereby erasing translation-effects and etymological histories, the trajectories of words in exile and in the wake of political and ecological catastrophes. In the *Dictionary* there is a consistent effort to communicate the political, aesthetic, and translational histories of philosophical keywords. The Russian term *pravda*, for instance, is arrayed alongside the Greek *dikaiosunê*; the Latin *justitia*; and the English "righteousness," "justice," "truth," and "law"—as well as *vérité, droit, istina, mir, postupok, praxis, sobornost'*, and *svet*. The article speculates that *pravda*'s absence in the Russian *Encyclopedia of Philosophy* is attributable to its being too ideologically marked as the name of the USSR's official government-controlled newspaper. *Pravda* thus comes into its own as that which is philosophically off limits in its home country. The article also locates *pravda* in an extremely complex semantic field, in the "hiatus" between legality and legitimacy, justice and truth, ethics and praxis. It is traced to the short-circuiting of pardon by vengeance, and vice versa. The word's geo-philosophical trajectory unfurls into a narrative marked by the themes of exile, solidarity with persecuted minorities and refugees, Russian Saint-Simonianism, and Russophilic worldviews.

Though it is not set up as a concept-history, the *Dictionary* lends itself to pedagogical approaches that explicate how concepts come into existence in, through, and across languages. Using the *Dictionary* as a tool to teach Freud's *Beyond the Pleasure Principle* (*Jenseits des Lustprinzips*), for example, reveals how important the German term *Lust* was to the specificities of Freud's theory, better enabling comprehension of how Freud derived from the word constructs of the death-drive, sublimation, and thought as such. From the *Dictionary*'s entry PLEASURE one gleans a whole new appreciation of the disparate meanings acquired by Freud's fundamental psychoanalytic concepts, depending on their languages of translation:

> The initial meaning of the German word *Lust* does not seem to have been "pleasure." Like the English "lust," it derives from the Indo-European *lutan*, which means "to submit," "to bend" and is supposed to have originally designated only a more or less resistible inclination. But whereas English "lust" has retained the restricted meaning of "unbridled desire," "cupidity," or "craving," the semantic range of the German term extends from "appetite," "sexual desire" . . . or "fantasy" to all the forms of satisfaction. In short, the semantic field of *Lust* extends beyond the sensible affect of pleasure to designate the desire that is *Lust*'s origin and effect.

If the *Dictionary* enhances attunement to linguistic difference in the reading of psychoanalysis or philosophy, it also facilitates a philosophical orientation within literary analysis. While working as an editor on the *Dictionary*, for example, Michael Wood found himself sensitized to the way Proust used the word "justice" when writing about the Dreyfus affair. The *Dictionary* entry RIGHT/JUST/GOOD focuses on semantic discrepancies between English and French. Two French words for good, *bien* and *bon*, have similar meanings; in English, however, *bien* can be translated as either "right" or "good," with distinct meanings. And while French clearly distinguishes between "the good" and "the just," with the former designating individual interest or collective good and the latter universal moral law, English is fuzzier on the difference between these terms.

Bearing this in mind, Wood found the difference between French *justice* and English "justice" all the more striking, because the word looks the same in both languages. Reading Proust, reading Proust scholars, testing words in varying contexts, and questioning native speakers, he began to sense that *justice*, in French, unless otherwise qualified, very often has the primary meaning of fitting the punishment to the crime, as in "to do justice," or "to see that justice is done." Although *justice* in French, as in English, has three main meanings—conformity with the law, the practice of justice (the judiciary branch of government), and justice in the sense of equitableness (justice in the moral sense)—the question is which of these meanings is in play at any given time.

Do we know which? Does the speaker know which? The stakes are serious enough for a major French scholar to say, almost without surprise, that Proust does not believe in the rule of law. How can this be? Proust spent a good portion of his life worrying about the miscarriage of justice in the case of Alfred Dreyfus. Still, at one point he has the narrator of *In Search of Lost Time* say "the sense of justice was absent in me, to the point of complete moral idiocy. In the depths of my heart I was immediately on the side of the underdog, of whoever was unhappy."[1] We may want to say at once that he's obviously not talking about justice. But he is.

What is needed, to get a comparative sense of things, is not a firmer or clearer translation of difficult words, but a feeling for how relatively simple words chase each other around in context. Wood pictures the situation as something like a traffic system. Three or four vehicles carry whatever is needed in any language, but the vehicles circulate differently in different places, and divide their loads differently. Thus, to take a simple example, where (with respect to the Proust translation just cited) English uses the word "law" four times—law court, law school, rule of law, force of law—the original French uses *justice* once, *droit* twice, and *loi* once. The same ideas circulate in each case: law, justice, rights, rightness, fairness, and so on. But it's easy to follow the wrong vehicle.

Wood's example of how to read "justice" in Proust through the lens of the untranslatable (an untranslatability rendered more acute in this case because French *justice* and English "justice" are homonymic "false friends"), opens up a world of literature that is alive to the "abilities" of untranslatability. In this picture, what is lost in translation is often the best that can be found, as readers find their way to a *Denkraum*—a space of thinking, inventing, and translating, in which words no longer have a distinct definition proper to any one language.

This said, it is by no means self-evident what "untranslatability" means. This is how Jacques Derrida's *Monolingualism of the Other* approaches the term (in Patrick Mensah's translation):

> Not that I am cultivating the untranslatable. Nothing is untranslatable, however little time is given to the expenditure or expansion of a competent discourse that measures itself against the power of the original. But the "untranslatable"

---

[1] Marcel Proust, *In Search of Lost Time: The Prisoner / The Fugitive*, trans. Carol Clark (London: Penguin, 2003), 268.

remains—should remain, as my law tells me the poetic economy of the idiom, the one that is important to me, for I would die even more quickly without it, and which is important to me, myself to myself, where a given formal "quantity" always fails to restore the singular event of the original, that is to let it be forgotten once recorded, to carry away its number, the prosodic shadow of its quantum.... In a sense, nothing is untranslatable; but *in another sense*, everything is untranslatable; translation is another name for the impossible. In another sense of the word "translation," of course, and from one sense to the other—it is easy for me always to hold firm between these two hyperboles which are fundamentally the same, and always translate each other.[2]

As Jacques Lezra notes, one sense of the term "translatable," then, is signaled by the articulation between geometry and rhetoric provided by the concept of hyperbole. Here, tendentially, "to translate" means to map one point or quantum onto another according to an algorithm: translation is understood as mechanics, as a function, as measure or common measure. This sort of "translation" requires us to understand natural languages as if they were mapped onto a mathematical, or mathematizable, or quantifiable space: what one might call the monadic or mapping or isomorphic definition of translation. Both word-for-word translation and sense-for-sense translation, those archaic Cain-and-Abel brothers of the translational pantheon, can be imagined according to this sort of mathematical, functional paradigm. But what happens when we "translate" this sort of functional translation from the domain of quanta to the domain of rhetoric, even of philosophical rhetoric, where hyperbole has a quite different sort of standing? Here nothing like a smooth, mathematizable space prevails outside of the fantasy of a certain Neoplatonist.

Editorial Liberties

In shifting the *Dictionary*'s language of address, we felt compelled to plug specific gaps, especially those pertaining to "theory," understood in the Anglophone academic sense of that term. We added material by Kevin

McLaughlin to clarify Walter Benjamin's distinction between *Erinnerung* and *Gedächtnis* in the entry MEMORY; by Leland de la Durantaye on Giorgio Agamben's marked use of the expressions *Homo sacer* and "bare life" in the entry ANIMAL; by Étienne Balibar on Jacques Lacan's fungible use of *instance* as a term for "moment," "instantiation," "agency," in the entry WILL; by Immanuel Wallerstein on Ferdinand Braudel's concept of *longue durée* in MOMENT; by Daniel Hoffman-Schwartz on Alain Badiou's reliance on the "forced" relationship between "forcing" and *forçage* in MACHT; and by Michael LeMahieu on Willard Quine's use of *quine/qualia* in OBJECT. Though the book included passages here and there on fancy, imagination, feeling, passion, emotion, sentiment, affection, senses, and sense, we reinforced these terms with dedicated discussions of "fancy" and "feeling" (both by Susan Wolfson) included in the entries FANCY and SENSE. Topical additions on language, translation, and humanism included supplements on "glossolalia" (by Daniel Heller-Roazen), in the entry LOGOS; Leonardo Bruni's humanist practice of translation (by Jane Tylus) in TO TRANSLATE; and "the humanities" (by Michael Wood) in BILDUNG. These highlights were intended to enhance the *Dictionary*'s relevance to literary theory and comparative literature. In response to a raft of recent interdisciplinary debates around surveillance, security, care, and cure, we solicited an entry on the wildly ramified cognates of SECURITAS by John T. Hamilton. What began as a new supplement by Kenneth Reinhard to MITMENSCH grew into a separate entry, NEIGHBOR. We also felt compelled to do more with the cluster of semes associated with "sex" and "gender." While both terms were represented in the original, and entered into dynamic relation with *genre* and *Geschlecht* (and thus to related concepts discussed in those entries, such as "species," "kind," "race," and "people"), we were able to turn this word grouping into a site of critical cross-examination. In this case, Judith Butler on "gender trouble" and Stella Sandford on the French de-sexing of "sexual difference" in English, invite being read in colloquy with Monique David-Ménard and Penelope Deutscher on GENDER and Geneviève Fraisse on SEX.

Other additions include media theory (there is now an entry, MEDIA/MEDIUM, written by Ben Kafka, with an insert on *ordinateur*/"computer"/*numérique*/"digital" by Antoine Picon); CHÔRA in deconstructive architectural theory and practice (courtesy of Anthony Vidler); postcolonial theory (there are new inserts by Robert Young on *colonia* and *imperium*, and by Emilienne Baneth-Nouailhetas on "postcolonialism,"

[2] Jacques Derrida, *Monolingualism of the Other,* trans. Patrick Mensah (Stanford, CA: Stanford University Press, 1998), 56–67.

in STATO; and by Gayatri Chakravorty Spivak on "planetarity" in WELT); and central keywords in Arabic (Souleymane Bachir Diagne contributed pieces on *rabita*, in SEIN; *Qur'ān*, in TO TRANSLATE; and *ijtihad*, in BELIEF). Though each of these examples could have been supplemented by countless others, we were restricted by page limitation, deadline, and expediency to make certain choices, albeit somewhat arbitrary ones, given certain obvious candidates that we hope will make their way into a future revised and expanded edition. Inevitably, the *Dictionary* lends itself to the parlor game of identifying terms undeservedly left out. But as Cassin has often remarked, if one were to be rigorously inclusive, Greek philosophical terms alone would overflow the entire volume.

If the selection of additional entry topics had a lot to do with the heat of a conversation among the editors or a casual encounter, there was less contingency governing what to delete. We occasionally found ourselves questioning the French editors' choice of untranslatables, some of which struck us as nonphilosophical or whimsically highlighted. Such terms as "multiculturalism," "happening," "judicial review," and "welfare" were interesting samples of what European thinkers might regard as untranslatable, but they struck us as having insufficient traction on this score for English speakers. A term such as *Syntagorem*—important though it was as a conceptual prong of medieval Scholasticism—was sacrificed because it was densely technical and ultimately uneditable. For the most part, however, we preserved original entries even when they were highly resistant to translation.

Though we were dealing with a French text, the extent of our translation task became clear only when we realized that a straightforward conversion of the French edition into English simply would not work. Almost every aspect of the translation had to be rethought, starting with the entry terms themselves. Which ones should remain in their original language? Which should be rendered in English? *Bien-être* was retained in French, but *bonheur*—which also carries French Enlightenment freight—was converted to "happiness." It is difficult to reconstruct the rationale for all these decisions: suffice it to say, we had our reasons, even if they fell short of being airtight justifications. Another extremely thorny issue concerned how to revise entries to reflect an Anglophone orientation without reverting to rank Anglocentricity. To give one example, under the entry for the French term *mot*, we discovered that the English term "word" never appeared. We had to rectify this absence in the English

edition by re-framing the entry for WORD to emphasize why the word *mot* was a French untranslatable. The term *Willkür* presented another kind of problem. The entry focused on a tension, essentially grounded in Kant's reworking of a Cartesian legacy, between *libre arbitre* (a free and independent arbitrator, capable of introducing an outcome neither determined nor necessary) and *(freie) Willkür* ("free will," understood in terms of the highest exercise of reasoning; a "freedom" expressive of the highest autonomy of the will). According to the entry as written by Pierre Osmo, Kant's use of the term included additional connotations in German of "arbitrariness" and "caprice." Osmo argues that when Kant used the expression *freie Willkür* (often rendered in English as "free power of choice"), it retained its capricious potential. But this potential typically failed to register in French, in which, according to Osmo, the expression *libre arbitre*, routinely used to translate both *Willkür* and *freie Willkür*, flattened Kant's intentions and originality.

For the English translator of Osmo's article these points proved particularly difficult to convey. The standard English translation of Kant's *Willkür* was "choice" or "free choice," which deflects Osmo's philosophical point about the lost capriciousness of *Willkür* in French translations of Kant. The tensions articulated by Osmo between French and German philosophy (predating and postdating Kant), over conceptions of volition, freedom of the will, the arbitrary exercise of freedom of choice, and the morally, rationally authorized decision were thrown off course by English. Once English intervened at the level of translating a French translation of German, one could say that "meta" untranslatability reared its head, which is to say, an interference at the level of translating unforeseen by the article's author and at odds with her or his argument about a given term's untranslatability in a specific linguistic context.

Specters of National Subjects

Though the original language of the *Dictionary* was French, and the orientation was toward the Hellenic, Scholastic, Enlightenment, and German European tradition, Cassin was interested in what she called a "metaphysics of particles."[3] She referred here to the

---

[3] Barbara Cassin used this expression in discussing the *Vocabulaire* at New York University's Humanities Initiative, February 11, 2010.

shape-shifting capacities of linguistic particulates within a particular language (as in the way German prefixes and suffixes become operative as building blocks of new words). Each language, she maintained, "contains within itself the rules of its own invention and transgression."[4] The book emphasizes the singular philosophical nuances of discrete languages not because Cassin was committed to resurrecting fixtures of "ontological nationalism" (whereby languages are erected as stand-ins for national subjects), but rather because she wanted to emphasize the mobile outlines of languages assuming a national silhouette or subsiding into diffuse, polyglot worlds.

Opposed to the model of the dictionary as a concept mausoleum, Cassin treated words as free radicals, as *parole in libertà*. She devised the construct of *lemmes* (directionals, or signposts) as navigating mechanisms. The directionals would prompt readers to pursue philological links, logical arguments, and conceptual lines of flight revealed by a term's history of translation that would not be apparent in a cross-referencing index. Sometimes these directionals resemble miniature articles unto themselves. Signaling where terms congregate, form star clusters, or proliferate in multiple languages, they contour preponderant overarching ideas and recurrent story lines. These include (but are obviously not limited to) the logic of classical orders; theologies of the law; metaphysical transcendence; aesthetic and domestic economy; sense and signification; human versus nonhuman; gender and species; materialism (both realist and speculative) and phenomenological experience; orders of sovereignty in the naming of polity and political institutions; utopian theories; dialectical thinking; *Dasein*, self-consciousness, and intersubjectivity; temporality and history; memory, cognition, and the intuition of intelligence; creative originality; free will and moral autonomy; rational self-interest and analytic reason; possessive individualism; and the emergence of the modern liberal subject. Notably underplayed, as Howard Caygill has pointed out, was the "divergence between philosophy and science in the modern period," and more specifically, the impact of natural philosophy, Darwinism, evolutionary theory, and genetics.[5]

What the *Dictionary* does best, perhaps, is produce a cartography (Caygill called it a "geo-philosophy") of

linguistic diaspora, migration, and contested global checkpoints from early empires to the technologically patrolled and surveilled post-9/11 era. National languages are profiled not as static, reified monuments of culture, nor as technologies of signification stripped of political consequence, but as internally transnational units, heterodox micro-worlds.

This said, the *Dictionary* is not without its nationalist hauntings. Nowhere are such hauntings more evident than in the entries devoted to languages themselves. Despite the editors' express intention to undercut national language ontologies, there is recidivism in these entries. PORTUGUESE becomes a hymn to the sensibility of the baroque, with *Fado* (fate, lassitude, melancholia) its emblematic figure. GERMAN hews to the language of Kant and Hegel. GREEK is pinioned by the Athenian efflorescence and Heidegger's homage to Greek as the *Ursprache* of philosophy. ITALIAN remains indebted to Machiavelli's notion of "the effective truth of things," Vico's philological historicism, and clichés of expressive *sprezzatura*. In tracing how French came to be globally identified as a preeminent language of philosophy, Alain Badiou both criticizes and mythifies the national language when he insists that for Descartes, Bergson, Sartre, Deleuze, and Lacan, to philosophize is merely to think openly and democratically. Obscurity itself results (or may result) from the need of French philosophers to be French *writers*. Unlike German, whose truth is attained through verbal and syntactic unraveling, French syntax is notionally transparent to truth. Close to being an Adamic language in Badiou's ascription, it lends itself to logical formalism, axioms, maxims, and universal principles. Above all, for Badiou, the French language is conducive to the politicization of expression, unseating predicates through the play of substitutions and the art of the imperious question (what Lacan called the "denunciatory enunciation"). Though national ontology is, strictly speaking, anathema to Badiou, one could say that because he does not historicize the myth, only playfully deploys it, he backhandedly returns it to linguistic nominalism. Such ontologies are, of course, impossible to purge entirely from language-names, for they lend coherence to the world map of languages; they triage and circumscribe the verbal grammatical protocols that qualify for naming as a discrete language.

Even the term "translation," which signifies language in a state of non-belonging, turns out to be nationally marked. The entry TO TRANSLATE notes that *dolmetschen*, an anachronistic verb whose origins go

---

[4] Barbara Cassin, *Plus d'une langue* (Paris: Bayard Editions, 2012), 43. Translation is my own.

[5] Howard Caygill, "From *Abstraction to Wunch*: The philosophies," *Radical Philosophy* 138 (July/August 2006): 13–14.

back to Martin Luther's translation of the Bible into German, renders "to translate" as, literally, "to render as German" or "to Germanize." Schleiermacher was instrumental in replacing *dolmetschen* with *übersetzung* on the grounds that *dolmetschen* referred to the functional work of the interpreter, whereas *übersetzung* referred to the loftier challenge of rendering thought. From this perspective, *übersetzung* is the name of a disavowed Germanocentrism that clings to the history of the word "translation."

Cassin's dictionary was equipped from its inception to do battle with the ontological nationalism of German theories of the subject even while providing wide berth to entries for terms such as *Aufhebung* or *Dasein*. More pointedly, it offered a direct challenge to the preeminence of Anglo-analytic philosophical traditions. In her introduction, Cassin notes analytic philosophy's inveterate hostility to its Continental counterpart, its zeal for (to borrow Cassin's vivid expression) "the puncturing of the windbags of metaphysics" (dégonfler les baudruches de la métaphysique). One way to approach the *Dictionary* is as an attempt to combat analytic philosophy's dismissiveness toward Continental philosophy. Ordinary language philosophy, along with the names of its avatars—Wittgenstein, Russell, Austin, Quine, and Cavell—was represented in the French edition, to be sure, but in general, the imperium of English thought was strategically curtailed. This was especially evident with respect to the tradition of British empiricism, which has no dedicated entry. "Sensation" or "sensationalism"—bulwarks of British empiricism normally accorded substantial amounts of space in standard histories or encyclopedias of philosophy—were subsumed under entries on SENSE (*sens*), CONSCIOUSNESS (*conscience*), and FEELING. Francis Bacon, Thomas Hobbes, John Locke, George Berkeley, and David Hume received scant attention, especially in contrast to Kant, Hegel, and Husserl. As editors, we decided to preserve this skewed distribution of emphasis because it was clearly an important part of the polemical raison d'être of the French original.

Tasks of the Translators

Over and over, as editors, we confronted the task of "translating the untranslatable." This involved at once a plunge into the Benjaminian problematic of translatability as such, qualified by Samuel Weber in terms of Walter Benjamin's activation of translation's

"-abilities" (the "*barkeit*" part of *Ubersetzbarkeit*), and a trial (*épreuve*, endurance test) requiring the conversion of translation failure into something of value and interest. We became increasingly drawn to the paradoxical premise of the book, namely, that of the untranslatable as the interminably (not) translated. One of the risks of the casual use of "untranslatable" is the suggestion of an always absent perfect equivalence. Nothing is exactly the same in one language as in another, so the failure of translation is always necessary and absolute. Apart from its neglect of the fact that some pretty good equivalencies are available, this proposition rests on a mystification, on a dream of perfection we cannot even want, let alone have. If there were a perfect equivalence from language to language, the result would not be translation; it would be a replica. And if such replicas were possible on a regular basis, there would not be any languages, just one vast, blurred international jargon, a sort of late cancellation of the story of Babel. The untranslatable as a construct makes a place for the private anguish that we as translators experience when confronted with material that we don't *want* to translate or see translated. A certain density or richness or color or tone in the source language seems so completely to defy rendering into another language that we would just as soon not try: the poverty of the result is too distressing, makes us miss the first language as we miss a friend or a child. This may be true at times, but we can make a virtue out of seeing differences, and the constant recourse to the metaphor of loss in translation is finally too easy. We can, in any case, be helped to see what we are missing, and that is what much of this book is about.

Over the course of five years we found ourselves engaged in a hands-on way with an encyclopedic project: one that is built on translation and perforce prompts a rethinking of the relation between translation and knowledge-production at every turn. To work on anything encyclopedic is to encounter frustration and exhilaration. At every moment, we had to balance the temptation of disappearing down the rabbit hole of philosophy against the need to withdraw from content so as to concentrate on the material management of the text. Editing, triage, relaying the right version; such mundane tasks were much harder to master than writing or speaking about the project. At one point we mislaid the translated version of *inconscient*. The irony of "losing" the text's "unconscious" hardly needed comment, as it so closely paralleled the at times very conscious wish to lose the albatross of this massive endeavor.

If there is one thing we have come away with, however, it is a deep excitement about using philosophical translation as a way of doing philosophy or "theory," or literary criticism. We see the book as a major contribution to a renewed philosophical turn in translation theory and practice. It occasions reflection on how "untranslatable" carries within it a philosophy of "languages together." What we find in this book, in a sense, is philosophy cast as a political theory of community, built up through the transference and distribution of irreducible, exceptional, semantic units. The places where languages touch reveal the limits of discrete national languages and traditions. We obtain glimpses of languages in paradoxically shared zones of non-national belonging, at the edge of mutual unintelligibility. Such zones encompass opacities at the edges of the spoken and written, a bilingualism that owns up to the condition of un-ownable, unclaimable language property, and perverse grammatology. Untranslatables signify not because they are essentialist predicates of nation or *ethnos* with no ready equivalent in another language, but because they mark singularities of expression that contour a worldscape according to mistranslation, neologism, and semantic dissonance.

Emily Apter

Acknowledgments

A translation of this breadth and ambition would have been impossible to carry off without the vital help and support of many colleagues, students, friends and editorial professionals. We must first thank Barbara Cassin, whose conception of the *Dictionary of Untranslatables* as a philosophical project and whose constant engagement with every step of the English translation, inspired us from beginning to end. Etienne Balibar, one of the major contributors to the French edition, was also an integral member of our editorial group and crucial to the English edition when it was an emergent and transitional object. Eric Alliez, Peter Osborne, and Stella Sandford of the Centre for Research in Modern European Philosophy, now at Kingston University, London, took the first steps toward an English edition. We thank them, the late David Macey, and the journal *Radical Philosophy* for permission to draw on their inaugural work.

We were fortunate to enjoy the constant support of two editors at Princeton University Press: Hanne Winarsky, who recognized the intrinsic interest of the project and arranged to have the book published in the *Translation/Transnation* series, and Anne Savarese, executive editor, who supervised every stage of the complex production process and offered invaluable suggestions on how to make the volume stronger as a research and reference tool. The corps of editors at Princeton who oversaw revision was exceptionally dedicated and proficient. Our special thanks to Karen Fortgang, senior production editor, who kept all of us on track; Ali Parrington, associate production editor; Beth Gianfagna, Aimee Anderson, Maria den Boer, Gail Schmitt, Linda Truilo, Sherry Wert, copy editors (all of whom gave us the benefit of their diverse linguistic expertise); and Natalie Baan and Laurie Burton, proofreaders.

We are profoundly grateful to all the translators—Steven Rendall, Jeffrey Mehlman, Michael Syrotinski, Christian Hubert, and Nathanael Stein—who had the courage to take on this formidable task by transforming philosophical translation into praxis. We were also lucky to have two remarkable research assistants on board: Manoah Finston, executive editorial assistant, who lent us his skills as an organizational powerhouse, and Kevin McCann, whose reflections on entries and help with German and French translations proved crucial at many turns. Other graduate students made important contributions to translation corrections and bibliography: Zakir Paul, Kathryn Stergiopoulos, and Dora Zhang from Princeton University, and Katherina Natalia Piechocki from New York University. Omar Berrada and Souleymane Bachir Diagne offered generous help with queries pertaining to Arabic.

A special note of gratitude must be expressed to Jane Tylus, who wrote for the English edition and provided a forum for discussions of the *Dictionary of Untranslatables* at the Humanities Initiative of New York University. We would also like to acknowledge institutional support from the Office of the Dean of the Faculty of Arts and Science at NYU, the NYU/ CNRS Center for International Research in the Humanities and Social Sciences, and the Mellon Foundation, which sponsored a two-year graduate seminar on "The Problem of Translation" that allowed us to work pedagogically with many of the entries in the volume.

Finally, to Elena Uribe, Anthony Vidler, and Susanne Wofford, all drawn into this project on so many levels, thanks for your forbearance and *un abrazo*!

Emily Apter
Jacques Lezra
Michael Wood

Introduction

One of the most urgent problems posed by the existence of Europe is that of languages. We may envisage two kinds of solution. We could choose a dominant language in which exchanges will take place from now on, a globalized Anglo-American. Or we could gamble on the retention of many languages, making clear on every occasion the meaning and the interest of the differences—the only way of really facilitating communication between languages and cultures. The *Dictionary of Untranslatables* belongs to this second perspective. But it looks to the future rather than to the past. It is not tied to a retrospective and reified Europe (which Europe would that be, in any case?), defined by an accumulation and juxtaposition of legacies that would only reinforce particularities, but to a Europe in progress, fully active, *energeia* rather than *ergon*, which explores divisions, tensions, transfers, appropriations, contradictions, in order to construct better versions of itself.

Our point of departure is a reflection on the difficulty of translating in philosophy. We have tried to think of philosophy within languages, to treat philosophies as they are spoken, and to see what then changes in our ways of philosophizing. This is why we have not created yet another encyclopedia of philosophy, treating concepts, authors, currents, and systems for their own sakes, but a *Dictionary of Untranslatables*, which starts from words situated within the measurable differences among languages, or at least among the principal languages in which philosophy has been written in Europe—since Babel. From this point of view, Émile Benveniste's pluralist and comparatist *Vocabulary of Indo-European Institutions* has been our model. In order to find the meaning of a word in one language, this book explores the networks to which the word belongs and seeks to understand how a network functions in one language by relating it to the networks of other languages.

We have not explored all the words there are, or all languages with regard to a particular word, and still less all the philosophies there are. We have taken as our object *symptoms* of difference, the "untranslatables," among a certain number of contemporary European languages, returning to ancient languages (Greek, Latin) and referring to Hebrew and Arabic whenever it was necessary in order to understand these differences. To speak of *untranslatables* in no way implies that the terms in question, or the expressions, the syntactical or grammatical turns, are not and cannot be translated: the untranslatable is rather what one keeps on (not) translating. But this indicates that their translation, into one language or another, creates a problem, to the extent of sometimes generating a neologism or imposing a new meaning on an old word. It is a sign of the way in which, from one language to another, neither the words nor the conceptual networks can simply be superimposed. Does one understand the same thing by "mind" as by *Geist* or *esprit*, is *pravda* "justice" or "truth," and what happens when we render *mimesis* as "representation" rather than "imitation"? Each entry thus starts from a nexus of untranslatability and proceeds to a comparison of terminological networks, whose distortion creates the history and geography of languages and cultures. The *Dictionary of Untranslatables* makes explicit in its own domain the principal symptoms of difference in languages.

The selection of entries arises from a double labor of exploration, both diachronic and synchronic. Diachrony allows us to reflect on crossings, transfers, and forks in the road: from Greek to Latin, from ancient Latin to scholastic then humanist Latin, with moments of interaction with a Jewish and an Arab tradition; from an ancient language to a vernacular; from one vernacular to another; from one tradition, system, or philosophical idiom to others; from one field of knowledge and disciplinary logic to others. In this way we reencounter the history of concepts, while marking out the turnings, fractures, and carriers that determine a "period." Synchrony permits us to establish a state of play by surveying the present condition of national philosophical landscapes. We are confronted with the irreducibility of certain inventions and acts of forgetting: appearances without any equivalent, intruders, doublings, empty categories, false friends, contradictions, which register within a language the crystallization of themes and the specificity of an operation. We then wonder, on the basis of the modern works that are both the cause and the effect of the philosophical condition of a given language, why the terms we ordinarily consider as immediate equivalents have neither the same meaning nor the same field of application—what a thought can do in what a language can do.

The space of Europe was our framework from the beginning. The *Dictionary* has, in fact, a political ambition: to ensure that the languages of Europe are taken into account, and not only from a preservationist point of view, as one seeks to save threatened species. In this respect, there are two positions from which we clearly distinguish our own. The first is the all-English one, or rather the all-into-English one—that official English of the European Community and of scientific conferences, which certainly has a practical use but is scarcely a language ("real" English speakers are those that one has the most difficulty in understanding). English has imposed itself today as an "auxiliary international language," as Umberto Eco puts it. It has assumed its place in the chronological sequence of instrumental languages (Greek, Latin, French): it is at once the universal language of the cultured technocracy and the language of the market; we need it, for better or for worse. But the philosophical situation of English as a language deserves a slightly different examination. In this case, English is rather in the line of the *characteristica universalis* that Leibniz dreamed of. Not that English can ever be reduced to a conceptual calculus on the model of mathematics: it is, like any other, a natural language, that is to say the language of a culture, magnificent in the strength of its idiosyncrasies. However, for a certain tendency in "analytic philosophy" (it is true that no terminological precaution will ever suffice here, because the label applies, via the "linguistic turn," even to those who teach us again to question the language, from Wittgenstein to Austin, Quine, or Cavell), philosophy relates only to a universal logic, identical in all times and all places—for Aristotle, for my colleague at Oxford. Consequently, the language in which the concept finds its expression, in this case English, matters little. This first universalist assumption meets up with another. The whole Anglo-Saxon tradition has devoted itself to the exclusion of jargon, of esoteric language, to the puncturing of the windbags of metaphysics. English presents itself, this time in its particularity as a language, as that of common sense and shared experience, including the shared experience of language. The presumption of a rationality that belongs to angels rather than humans and a militant insistence on ordinary language combine to support a prevalence of English that becomes, in the worst of cases, a refusal of the status of philosophy to Continental philosophy, which is mired in the contingencies of history and individual languages.

Neither . . . nor. The other position from which we wish to distinguish our own is the one that has led philosophy from the idea of the spirit of language, with all its clichés, to an "ontological nationalism" (the expression is that of Jean-Pierre Lefebvre). The position finds its image in Herder, at the moment when he determines that translation, as imitation and transplantation, is the true vocation of the German language: "If in Italy the muse converses in song, if in France she narrates and reasons politely, if in Spain she imagines chivalrously, in England thinks sharply and deeply, what does she do in Germany? She *imitates.* To *imitate* would thus be her character. . . . To this end we have in our power an admirable means, *our language*; it can be for us what the *hand* is for the person who imitates art" (Herder, *Briefe*). The position is also represented by a certain Heideggerian tradition of "philosophical language," that is to say, the language best suited to speak faithfully for being, which occupies a predominant place in the history of this so Continental Western philosophy. Martin Heidegger thinks that Western thought is born less in Greece than in Greek and that only the German language rises to the level of Greek in the hierarchy of philosophical languages, so that "untranslatability finally becomes the criterion of truth" (Lefebvre, "Philosophie et philologie"). "The Greek language is philosophical, i.e., . . . it philosophizes in its basic structure and formation. The same applies to every genuine language, in a different degree, to be sure. The extent to which this is so depends on the depth and power of the existence of the people and race who speak the language and exist within it. Only our German language has a deep and creative philosophical character to compare with the Greek" (Heidegger, *Essence of Human Freedom*). Even if it is "true" in one sense (Greek and German words and forms are obligatory places of passage for many articles in the *Dictionary*), this is not the truth we need. Our work is as far as could be from such a sacralization of the untranslatable, based on the idea of an absolute incommensurability of languages and linked to the near-sanctity of certain languages. This is why, marking our distance from a teleological history organized according to a register of gain and loss, we have not conferred a special status on any language, dead or alive.

Neither a logical universalism indifferent to languages nor an ontological nationalism essentializing the spirit of languages: what is our position in relation to these alternatives? If I had to characterize it, I would speak Deleuzian and use the word "deterritorialization." This term plays off geography against history, the semantic network against the isolated concept. We began with the many (our plural form indicates this: "dictionary of untranslatables"), and we remain with the many: we have addressed the question of the untranslatable without aiming at unity, whether it is placed at the origin (source language, tributary words, fidelity to what is ontologically given) or at the end (Messianic language, rational community).

Many languages first of all. As Wilhelm von Humboldt stresses, "language appears in reality solely as multiplicity" (*Uber die Verschiedenheiten des menschlichen Sprachbaues*). Babel is an opportunity, as long as we understand that "different languages are not so many designations of a thing: they are different perspectives on that same thing, and when the thing is not an object for the external senses, those perspectives become so many things themselves, differently formed by each person" (*Fragmente der Monographie über die Basken*).

The perspectives constitute the thing; each language is a vision of the world that catches another world in its net, that performs a world; and the shared world is less a point of departure than a regulatory principle. Schleiermacher throws an exemplary light on the tension that exists between a concept, with its claim to universality, and its linguistic expression, when he asserts that in philosophy, more than in any other domain, "any language . . . encompasses within itself a single system of concepts which, precisely because they are contiguous, linking and complementing one another within this language, form a single whole—whose several parts, however, do not correspond to those to be found in comparable systems in other languages, and this is scarcely excluding 'God' and 'to be,' the noun of nouns and the verb of verbs. For even universals, which lie outside the realm of particularity, are illumined and colored by the particular" ("On Different Methods of Translating"). It is that "scarcely excluding" we must underline: even God and Being are illumined and colored by language; the universality of concepts is absorbed by the singularity of languages.

Multiplicity is to be found not only among languages but within each language. A language, as we have considered it, is not a fact of nature, an object, but an effect caught up in history and culture, and that ceaselessly invents itself—again, *energeia* rather than *ergon*. So the *Dictionary*'s concern is constituted by languages in their works, and by the translations of these works into different languages, at different times. The networks of words and senses that we have sought to think through are networks of datable philosophical idioms, placed by specific authors in particular writings; they are unique, time-bound networks, linked to their address (exoteric or esoteric), to their level of language, to their style, to their relation to tradition (models, references, palimpsests, breaks, innovations). Every author, and the philosopher is an author, simultaneously writes in a language and creates his or her language—as Schleiermacher says of the relation between author and language: "He is its organ and it is his" ("General Hermeneutics"). The untranslatable therefore is also a question of case by case.

Finally, there is multiplicity in the meanings of a word in a given language. As Jacques Lacan says in *L'étourdit*, "A language is, among other possibilities, nothing but the sum of the ambiguities that its history has allowed to persist." The *Dictionary* has led us to question the phenomenon of the homonym (same word, several definitions: the dog, celestial constellation and barking animal) in which homophony (bread, bred) is only an extreme case and a modern caricature. We know that since Aristotle and his analysis of the verb "to be" that it is not so easy to distinguish between homonymy and polysemy: the sense of a word, also called "meaning" in English, the sense of touch, *sens* in French meaning "direction"—these represent traces of the polysemy of the Latin *sensus*, itself a translation from the Greek *nous* (flair, wit, intelligence, intention, intuition, etc.), which from our point of view is polysemic in a very different way. Variation from one language to another allows us to perceive these distortions and semantic fluxes; it permits us to register the ambiguities each language carries, their meaning, their history, their intersection with those of other languages.

In his introduction to Aeschylus's *Agamemnon*, which he considers to be "untranslatable," Humboldt suggests that one should create a work that studies the "synonymy of languages," and records the fact that every language expresses a concept with a difference: "A word is so little the sign of a concept that without it the concept cannot even be born, still less be stabilized; the indeterminate action of the power of thought comes together in a word as a faint cluster of clouds gathers in a clear sky." "Such a synonymy of the principal languages . . . has never been attempted," he adds, "although one finds fragments of it in many writers, but it would become, if it was treated with intelligence, one of the most seductive of works" (*Aeschylos Agamemnon*). This work that is among "the most seductive" is perhaps our *Dictionary*. I hope it will make perceptible another way of doing philosophy, which does not think of the concept without thinking of the word, for there is no concept without a word.

The *Dictionary* aims to constitute a cartography of European and some other philosophical differences by capitalizing on the knowledge and experience of translators, and of those translators (historians, exegetes, critics, interpreters) that we are as philosophers. It is a working implement of a new kind, indispensable to the larger scientific community in the process of constituting itself and also a guide to philosophy for students, teachers, researchers, those who are curious about their language and that of others. It is also the collective work of ten or more years. Around a supervisory team of scholars—Charles Baladier, Étienne Balibar, Marc Buhot de Launay, Jean-François Courtine, Marc Crépon, Sandra Laugier, Alain de Libera, Jacqueline Lichtenstein, Philippe Raynaud, Irène Rosier-Catach—it assembled more than 150 contributors, with the most varied linguistic and philosophical domains of competence. The truly collective work (long, difficult, frustrating, to be redone, to be continued) did in any case seduce each of us, drove us back to the drawing board and to consider from other perspectives what we thought we knew in philosophy, of philosophy. Everyone gave more than his or her share of time, energy, knowledge, inventiveness, for something that expresses both our friendship and our sense of adventure, and that is beyond all possible expression of gratitude.

Barbara Cassin

BIBLIOGRAPHY

Heidegger, Martin. *The Essence of Human Freedom*. Translated by Ted Sadler. London: Continuum, 2002.

Herder, Johann Gottfried. *Briefe zur Beförderung der Humanität*. Berlin: Aufbau, 1971.

Humboldt, Wilhelm von, trans. *Aeschylos Agamemnon*. Leipzig: Fleischer, 1816.

Humboldt, Wilhelm von. *Fragmente der Monographie über die Basken*. In *Gesammelte Schriften*, vol. 2. Berlin: Behr, 1908.

———. *Uber die Verschiedenheiten des menschlichen Sprachbaues*. In *Werke in Fünf Bänden*. Stuttgart: J. G. Cotta'sche Buchhandlung, 1963.

Lacan, Jacques. *L'étourdit*. *Scilicet* 4 (1973).

Lefebvre, Jean-Pierre. "Philosophie et philologie: Les traductions des philosophes allemands." In *Encyclopaedia universalis*, symposium supplement, "Les Enjeux," vol. 1. Paris: Encyclopaedia universalis, 1990.

Schleiermacher, Friedrich. "General Hermeneutics." In *Hermeneutics and Criticism and Other Writings*. Translated by Andrew Bowie. Cambridge: Cambridge University Press, 1998.

———. "On Different Methods of Translating." Translated by Susan Bernovsky. In *The Translation Studies Reader*, edited by Lawrence Venuti. 3rd ed. New York: Routledge, 2012.

Translated by Michael Wood

How to Use This Work

The *Dictionary of Untranslatables* offers three types of entries.

(1) Among the "word-based" entries, some start from a single word in a single language, taken as "untranslatable," revealing a given constellation in time and/or space, such as LEGGIADRIA, which initially expresses the gracefulness of women in the Italian Renaissance and evokes for us the smile of the *Mona Lisa*; or MIR, which in Russian means "peace," "the world," and "peasant commune."

Other of these entries present one or more networks and seek to bring out their particularities: for example, under POLITICS we consider both "politics" and "policy"; with STRUCTURE we proceed to a comparison with "pattern" and *Gestalt*; and under SENSE we treat all the senses of "sense," from their complex Latin thread (the unifying *sensus*, which renders the Greek *nous*, literally "flair, intuition," but also refers to the meaning of a word or a text) to the Anglo-German tangle of *Sinn, Bedeutung*, "sense," and "meaning," which is complicated in French translations as *dénotation* or *référence*. The words in various languages that are listed just below the lemma for an entry make no claim to being translations, good or bad: they are the equivalents, approximations, analogues actually discussed in the article.

(2) The more general, "thematic" entries, metaentries in a fashion, examine the way in which one language or another works overall by starting with a crucial characteristic: for example, the difference between *ser* and *estar* in philosophical Spanish (see SPANISH) or diglossia in Russian (RUSSIAN). Some of them engage a major problem, like the order of words (WORD ORDER) or the mode of expressing time and aspect (ASPECT), which are immersed in the different languages.

The longest entries are generally the result of a collaboration, and the boxes (which are signed when they are not written by the authors of the corresponding articles), represent so many beams of light brought to bear on a text, its translation, a terminology, or a tradition.

(3) Finally, the unsigned "directional" entries serve to guide readers. They point toward the relevant entries in foreign languages (*WORLD* and *PEACE* direct us to the Russian MIR, and *MALAISE* sends us to individual ways of designating the dysfunction of body and soul and its implications for existence, ACEDIA, DESENGAÑO, DOR, MELANCHOLY, SAUDADE, SEHNSUCHT, SORGE). They also propose a synthesis of difficulties and differences (*NOTHING, TIME*). When they are referred to, as correlatives, within other entries, they are marked by italics.

In all these kinds of entries, a web of general cross-references is signaled by the symbol (➤). The terms cross-referenced are listed alphabetically. When appropriate, a distinction is drawn in these lists: the principal cross-references appear first; following these is a second group of terms, more distantly related to the first; and a third group of terms (in brackets) are entries to which the cross-references in either of the first two groups refer when discussing the cross-referenced term. When an asterisk precedes a word in the text, it indicates that the word is reconstructed, rather than directly attested (established by written record).

In addition to the individual bibliographies at the ends of articles and boxes, this volume also contains a separate list of general reference tools. When any work contained in this list is cited in the text, it is preceded by the abbreviation "RT," which indicates that the full reference will be found in the reference tools section at the end of this book.

Principal Collaborators

Coordination

Charles Baladier

Publication

Thierry Marchaisse (Seuil) and Gonzague Raynaud (Le Robert)

Editorial Managers

Charles Baladier
Étienne Balibar
Barbara Cassin
Jean-François Courtine
Marc Crépon
Sandra Laugier
Marc Buhot de Launay
Alain de Libera
Jacqueline Lichtenstein
Philippe Raynaud
Irène Rosier-Catach

International Consultants

Tullio Gregory and Marta Fattori, *Lessico Intellettuale Europeo, Rome*
Manuel Reyes Mate Rupérez, *Instituto de Filosofía, Madrid*
Alan Montefiore and Catherine Audard, *Forum for European Philosophy, London*
Constantin Sigov, *European Humanities Research Center, Kiev*
Heinz Wismann, *Forschungstätte der Evangelischen Studiengemeinschaft, Heidelberg*

Translation (English Edition)

Editors

Emily Apter
Jacques Lezra
Michael Wood

Executive Editorial Assistant

Manoah Avram Finston

Contributors

Authors whose names are preceded by an asterisk contributed material new to this editon.

Alexandre Abensour, *Professor of Philosophy, Lycée Saint-Jean à Douai*
- DRIVE, ES, UNCONSCIOUS, WUNSCH

Mercedes Allendesalazar, *Philosopher (France, Spain)*
- DESENGAÑO

Eric Alliez, *Professor in Philosophy, Center for Research in Modern European Philosophy, Kingston University, London*
- AIÔN

Charles Alunni, *Director of the Laboratory of Scientific Thought, École Normale Supérieure (Ulm)*
- ATTUALITÀ

Catherine Audard, *Chair and Co-founder of Forum for European Philosophy, London School of Economics*
- CARE, FAIR, LIBERAL, PRUDENTIAL, RIGHT/JUST/GOOD, UTILITY

Clara Auvray-Assayas, *Professor of Romance Languages and Literatures, University of Rouen*
- BEGRIFF (Box 1), CONSCIOUSNESS (Box 2), LOGOS, LOVE, MADNESS, PLEASURE, RELIGIO, SPECIES, TO TRANSLATE

Alain Badiou, *René Descartes Chair of Philosophy, European Graduate School ; Co-Founder, International Center for the Study of French Philosophy (CIEPFC), École Normale Supérieure (Ulm)*
- FRENCH

Charles Baladier, *Independent Scholar; Member of Freudian Society*
- DEVIL, DOXA, DRIVE (Box 2), DUTY, EIDÔLON (Box 2), I/ME/MYSELF (Box 3), INGENIUM (Box 3), LOVE, MADNESS, PHANTASIA (Box 3), PLEASURE, SUBLIME (Box 3), TALENT

Jean-François Balaudé, *President, University of Paris–Ouest Nanterre La Défense*
- DAIMÔN, PLEASURE

Étienne Balibar, *Professor of Philosophy, University of Paris–Ouest Nanterre La Défense ; Anniversary Chair, Philosophy, Kingston University, London; Visiting Professor, French and Comparative Literature, Columbia University*
- AGENCY (Box 1), CONSCIOUSNESS, DEMOS/ETHNOS/LAOS, I/ME/MYSELF, PRAXIS, SOUL, SUBJECT, WILL (Box 2)

Françoise Balibar, *Professor of Physics, University of Paris–VII Denis Diderot*
- FORCE, MOMENT, SEX (Box 1)

Isabelle Balza, *Researcher, University of San Sebastian*
- GOGO

*Emilienne Baneth-Nouailhetas, *University Attaché, French Embassy*
- STATO (Box 2)

Marc Baratin, *Professor of Classical Languages and Literatures, University of Lille III*
- ASPECT (Box 4), LANGUAGE (Box 2), PROPOSITION, WORD

Marco Baschera, *Professor of Modern French and Comparative Literatures, University of Zurich*
- ACTOR, ESTI (Box 4)

Jean-Pierre Baud, *Professor of History of Law, University of Paris–Ouest Nanterre La Défense*
- LEX

Ali Benmakhlouf, *Professor of Logical Philosophy and Arabic, University of Paris–Est Créteil Val de Marne; Sciences Po*
- PRINCIPLE

Christian Berner, *Professor of German Philosophy, University of Lille III*
- TO TRANSLATE

Bertrand Binoche, *Professor of Philosophy, University of Paris–I Panthéon-Sorbonne*
- HISTORIA UNIVERSALIS, PERFECTIBILITY

Remo Bodei, *Professor of History of Philosophy, University of Pisa; Professor of History of Philosophy, University of California, Los Angeles*
- ITALIAN

Jean Bollack, *Professor of Greek Literature, University of Lille III* (deceased)
- MEMORY

Olivier Boulnois, *Director of Studies, Medieval Philosophy, École Pratique des Hautes Études*
- OBJECT, RES (Box 3)

Jean-Loup Bourget, *Professor of Film Studies, École Normale Supérieure (Ulm)*

- DESCRIPTION, STRUCTURE

Rémi Brague, *Professor of Medieval and Arabic Philosophy, University of Paris I– Panthéon-Sorbonne; Professor of Philosophy and Arabic, Ludwig Maxmilian University (Munich)*

- BERÎT, BILD (Box 1), EUROPE, GOD, INGENIUM (Box 1), INTENTION (Box 1), LËV, LOGOS (Box 4), OLAM, SOUL (Box 4), TALAṬṬUF, TORAH, TRUTH, VORHANDEN (Box 1)

Fabienne Brugère, *Professor of Philosophy, University of Michel de Montaigne–Bordeaux III*

- BEAUTY, COMMON SENSE, GOÛT, INGENIUM (Box 2), MORAL SENSE, STANDARD

*Judith Butler, *Maxine Elliot Professor of Rhetoric and Comparative Literature, University of California, Berkeley; Hannah Arendt Chair of Philosophy, European Graduate School*

- GENDER (Box 1)

Philippe Büttgen, *Professor of the Philosophy of Religions, University of Paris I–Panthéon-Sorbonne*

- AUFHEBEN, BEGRIFF, BERUF, CONSCIOUSNESS (Box 3), ELEUTHERIA (Box 2), GLAUBE, GUT, LOVE, MOMENT, PERCEPTION (Box 3)

Rémi Camus, *Director of Laboratory of Formal Linguistics, Centre National de la Recherche Scientifique (CNRS) ; Maître de conférences, National Institute of Oriental Languages and Civilizations (INALCO)*

- ASPECT

Fabien Capeillères, *Department of Philosophy, University of Caen*

- PRINCIPLE

Barbara Cassin, *Director of Research, Centre Léon Robin, Centre National de la Recherche Scientifique (CNRS)*

- BEAUTY (Box 1), BILDUNG (Box 1), CATHARSIS, COMMONPLACE (Box 1), COMPARISON (Box 1), CONSCIOUSNESS (Box 1), DESCRIPTION (Box 1), DOXA, EIDÔLON (Box 1), ELEUTHERIA (Box 1), ESTI, FORCE (Box 1), GREEK (Boxes 1 and 4), HEIMAT (Box 2), HOMONYM, I/ME/MYSELF (Box 2), IMPLICATION (Box 1), KÊR (Box 2), LANGUAGE, LEX (Box 1), LIGHT (Box 1), LOGOS, LOVE, MIMÊSIS (Box 1), MOMENT, MORALS, NATURE (Box 1), PARDON, PEOPLE/RACE/NATION, PLEASURE, PRAXIS, PRINCIPLE, PROPOSITION, RES (Box 1), SEHNSUCHT (Box 1), SENSE, SIGN, SIGNIFIER/SIGNIFIED, SOUL (Box 3), SPECIES (Box 1), SPEECH ACT, SUBJECT, SUBLIME (Box 1), THEMIS, TO TRANSLATE, TRUTH, UNDERSTANDING (Box 1), VERGÜENZA, VIRTÙ (Box 1), WELT (Boxes 1 and 2), WORD

Pierre Caussat, *Professor of Philosophy, University of Paris–Ouest Nanterre La Défense*

- LANGUAGE

Dominique Chateau, *Professor of Aesthetics and Film, University of Paris I–Panthéon-Sorbonne*

- ART, TABLEAU

Catherine Chevalley, *Professor, University of François Rabelais (Tours); Center for the Study of the Renaissance, Centre National de la Recherche Scientifique (CNRS)*

- ANSCHAULICHKEIT, EPISTEMOLOGY

Jean-Pierre Cléro, *Professor of Philosophy, University of Rouen*

- CHANCE, ENGLISH, EXPERIMENT, FANCY, FEELING, MOMENT (Box 2), PLEASURE, SENSE (Box 4), SOUL (Box 1), STRENGTH

Danielle Cohen-Levinas, *Professor of Musicology, University of Paris IV–Sorbonne*

- MOMENTE, SPRECHGESANG, STIMMUNG (Box 2)

Jacques Colette, *Professor, University of Paris I–Panthéon-Sorbonne*

- CONTINUITET, EVIGHED, MOMENT (Box 3), NEUZEIT (Box 1), PLUDSELIGHED, PRESENT (Box 2)

Blandine Colot, *Maître de conférences, Latin, University of Angers*

- PIETAS

Alfonso Correa Motta, *Assistant Professor of Philosophy, National University of Colombia , Bogotá*

- SPANISH

Lambros Couloubaritsis, *Professor of Philosophy, Free University of Brussels*

- GREEK, SUBJECT (Box 3)

Dominique de Courcelles, *Director of Research, Institute for the History of Classic Thought, Centre National de la Recherche Scientifique (CNRS); Center for the Study of Rhetoric, Philosophy, and Historical Ideas, École Normale Supérieure (Lyons)*

- LOVE (Box 6)

Jean-François Courtine, *Professor of Philosophy, University of Paris IV–Sorbonne; Director, Archives Husserl of Paris (Centre National de la Recherche Scientifique, École Normale Supérieure, Lyons)*

- ESSENCE, OMNITUDO REALITATIS, PRINCIPLE (Box 2), REALITY, RES, SEIN, TO TI ÊN EINAI, VORHANDEN

Marc Crépon, *Director, Department of Philosophy, École Normale Supérieure; Director of Research, Centre National de la Recherche Scientifique (CNRS)*

- BEGRIFF, GESCHLECHT, HEIMAT, MENSCHHEIT, MORALS, PEOPLE/RACE/NATION

Françoise Dastur, *Professor of Philosophy, University of Nice, Sofia-Antipolis*

- ERSCHEINUNG

Pascal David, *Professor of Philosophy, University of Western Brittany , Brest*

- ANXIETY, BILD, COMBINATION AND CONCEPTUALIZATION (Box 1), DASEIN, DICHTUNG (Box 2), EREIGNIS, ES GIBT, GESCHICHTLICH, LANGUAGE (Box 1), LEIB (Box 1), LIGHT, NATURE, PRESENT, SCHICKSAL, SORGE, STIMMUNG, WELT, WELTANSCHAUUNG, WORK

Monique David-Ménard, *Professor of Philosophy, and Director, Centre des Études de Vivant, University of Paris VII–Denis Diderot; Psychoanalyst*

- GENDER, MADNESS, VERNEINUNG

Élisabeth Décultot, *Center for Germanic History, Culture, and Philosophy, Centre National de la Recherche Scientifique (CNRS); École Normale Supérieure (Ulm)*

- AESTHETICS (Box 1), DICHTUNG, MIMÊSIS, ROMANTIC, STILL

*Leland de la Durantaye, *Associate Professor of English, Claremont McKenna College*

- ANIMAL (Boxes 1 AND 2), SUBJECT (Box 1)

Maryse Dennes, *Professor of Philosophy, University of Michel de Montaigne–Bordeaux III*

- ASPECT

Ilse Depraetere, *Professor of English, University of Lille III*

- ASPECT

Natalie Depraz, *Professor of Phenomenological and German Philosophy, University of Rouen*

- ANIMAL, EPOCHÊ, ERLEBEN, LEIB

Vinciane Despret, *Maître de conférences, Philosophy, University of Liège*

- VERGÜENZA

Penelope Deutscher, *Professor of Philosophy, Northwestern University*

- GENDER

*Souleymane Bachir Diagne, *Professor of French and Romance Philology, Columbia University*

- BELIEF (Box 6), SEIN (Box 2), TO TRANSLATE (Box 4)

Jérôme Dokic, *Director of Studies, École des Hautes Études en Sciences Sociales (EHESS)*

- PRINCIPLE, REPRÉSENTATION

Jean-Pierre Dubost, *Professor of Comparative Literature, University of Blaise Pascal–Clermont-Ferrand II*

- COMBINATION AND CONCEPTUALIZATION, ERZÄHLEN, GEFÜHL

Michel Espagne, *Center for Germanic History, Culture, and Philosophy, Centre National de la Recherche Scientifique (CNRS); École Normale Supérieure (Ulm)*

- BILDUNG

Emmanuel Faye, *Professor of Modern and Contemporary Philosophy, University of Rouen*

- INTELLECT

Gisela Febel, *Professor of Romance Languages and Literatures, University of Bremen*

- NEUZEIT

Michel Fichant, *Professor of History and Modern Philosophy, University of Paris IV–Sorbonne*

- PERCEPTION

Alessandro Fontana, *Professor of Italian (emeritus), École Normale Supérieure (Lyons)*

- VIRTÙ

Geneviève Fraisse, *Director of Research, Center for European Political Discourse, Centre National de la Recherche Scientifique (CNRS)*

- SEX

Jeanne-Marie Gagnebin, *Professor of Philosophy, Pontifical Catholic University of São Paulo; Professor of Literary Theory, State University of Campinas (Brazil)*

- JETZTZEIT

Marie Gaille-Nikodimov, *Philosopher; Researcher, History of Classical Thought, Centre National de la Recherche Scientifique (CNRS)*

- PEOPLE/RACE/NATION (Box 1)

Mildred Galland-Szymkowiak, *Research Fellow, Monash University*

- SIGN

Jean-Claude Gens, *Professor of Contemporary Philosophy and German Philosophy, University of Burgundy*

- GEISTESWISSENSCHAFTEN

Tatyana Golitchenko, *Professor of Political Science, University of Kiev-Mohyla*

- BOGOČELOVEČESTVO

Jean-Jacques Gorog, *Psychiatrist; Psychoanalyst, École de Psychanalyse du Champ Lacanien*

- SIGNIFIER/SIGNIFIED (Box 3)

Francis Goyet, *Professor of French Literature, University Stendhal–Grenoble III*

- ART (Box 1), COMMONPLACE, COMPARISON

Anne Grondeux, *Director of Research, History of Linguistic Theory, Centre National de la Recherche Scientifique (CNRS)*
  - LANGUAGE

Jean-François Groulier, *Professor of Philosophy, National Institute of Telecommunications (France)*
  - ARGUTEZZA, BEAUTY, CONCETTO, GOÛT, MIMÊSIS (Boxes 8 AND 9)

*John T. Hamilton, *Professor of Comparative Literature, Harvard University*
  - SECURITAS

François Hartog, *Director of Studies, École des Hautes Études en Sciences Sociales (EHESS)*
  - HISTORY

*Daniel Heller-Roazen, *Arthur W. Marks '19 Professor of Comparative Literature, Princeton University*
  - LOGOS (Box 7)

Christian Helmreich, *Lecturer in Germanic Studies, University of Paris VIII–Vincennes–Saint-Denis*
  - GLÜCK, SEHNSUCHT

*Daniel Hoffman-Schwartz, *Humanities Instructor, Boğaziçi University*
  - MACHT (Box 2)

Frédérique Ildefonse, *Director of Research, Centre Jean Pépin, Centre National de la Recherche Scientifique (CNRS)*
  - BEGRIFF (Box 1), HOMONYM (Box 3), KÊR (Box 4), LOGOS, PARONYME (Box 2), SIGNIFIER/SIGNIFIED, WORD

Ruedi Imbach, *Professor of the History of Medieval Philosophy, University of Paris IV–Sorbonne*
  - ITALIAN (Box 2)

Marc Jimenez, *Professor of Art, University of Paris I–Panthéon-Sorbonne*
  - AESTHETICS

Pierre Judet de la Combe, *Director of Research, Center for Interdisciplinary German Research, Centre National de la Recherche Scientifique (CNRS); Director of Studies, École des Hautes Études en Sciences Sociales (EHESS)*
  - THEMIS

*Ben Kafka, *Associate Professor of Media, Theory and History, New York University*
  - MEDIA/MEDIUM

Zulfia Karimova, *Lecturer, Teesside University*
  - NAROD, STRADANIE, SVET

Françoise Kerleroux, *Professor of Linguistics, University of Paris–Ouest Nanterre La Défense*
  - WORD ORDER

Carita Klippi, *Professor of Linguistics, University of Tampere*
  - SIGNIFIER/SIGNIFIED

Jean-Louis Labarrière, *Director of Research, Centre Louis Gernet, Centre National de la Recherche Scientifique (CNRS)*
  - OIKEIÔSIS, PHANTASIA, PHRONÊSIS

Jean Lallot, *Professor of Greek Linguistics, École Normale Supérieure (Ulm)*
  - ACTOR (Box 1), ASPECT (Box 2), LOGOS, WORD

Marie-Claude Lambotte, *Professor of Psychopathology, University of Paris XIII*
  - MELANCHOLY

Frédéric Langer, *Asian Century Institute*
  - ECONOMY

Sandra Laugier, *Professor of Philosophy, University of Paris I–Panthéon-Sorbonne; Institute for Humanities and Social Sciences, Centre National de la Recherche Scientifique (CNRS)*
  - AGENCY, BEGRIFF, BEHAVIOR, BELIEF, CLAIM, ENGLISH, LOGOS, MATTER OF FACT, NONSENSE, PEOPLE, PRAXIS, PROPOSITION, SENSE, SIGN, SOUL (Box 6), SPEECH ACT, TO TRANSLATE (Box 3), TRUTH

Marc Buhot de Launay, *Director of Research in Philosophy and Germanic Culture, Centre National de la Recherche Scientifique (CNRS); École Normale Supérieure (Ulm)*
  - HERRSCHAFT, MACHT, MENSCHHEIT, MITMENSCH, SECULARIZATION, SOLLEN, WERT

Jean-Pierre Lefebvre, *Professor of German Literature, École Normale Supérieure (Ulm)*
  - GERMAN, SELBST

*Michael LeMahieu, *Associate Professor of English, Clemson University*
  - OBJECT (Box 1)

Jacqueline Léon, *Director of Research, History of Linguistic Theory, Centre National de la Recherche Scientifique (CNRS)*
  - WORD

Alain de Libera, *Professor of Medieval Philosophy, Collège de France; Professor of Medieval Philosophy, University of Geneva*
  - ABSTRACTION, ANALOGY, CONNOTATION, DICTUM, I/ME/MYSELF (Box 4), IMPLICATION, INTELLECTUS, INTENTION, MERKMAL, PARONYM, PRÉDICABLE, PREDICATION, PROPOSITION, SENSUS

COMMUNIS, SENSE, SIGN, SUBJECT, SUPPOSITION, TERM, TROPE, TRUTH, UNIVERSALS

Jacqueline Lichtenstein, *Research Director and Professor, Department of Philosophy, University of Paris IV–Sorbonne*
- ACTOR, CATHARSIS, COMPARISON (Box 2), DISEGNO, MIMÊSIS, SUBLIME (Box 1)

Catherine Malabou, *Professor of Philosophy, Kingston University, London; Professor of Philosophy, European Graduate School*
- PLASTICITY

Charles Malamoud, *Director of Studies Emerita for the Religions for the India, École Pratique des Hautes Études*
- MIR, RUSSIAN

Jean-Marie Marandin, *Director of Research, Formal Linguistics Laboratory, Centre National de la Recherche Scientifique (CNRS)*
- WORD ORDER

Cécile Margellos, *Translator and Literary Critic*
- GREEK (Box 2)

Fosca Mariani-Zini, *Maître de conférences, Philosophy, University Charles de Gaulle–Lille III*
- LEGGIADRIA

José Miguel Marinas, *Professor of Political Philosophy and Sociology, Complutense University of Madrid*
- ACEDIA, SPLEEN, SUBJECT (Box 8)

Marcos Mateos Diaz, *Essayist*
- VERGÜENZA

John McCumber, *Professor of Germanic Languages, University of California, Los Angeles*
- WORK (Box 1)

*Kevin McLaughlin, *Dean of the Faculty and Nicholas Brown Professor of Oratory and Belles Lettres, Brown University*
- MEMORY (Boxes 2 AND 3)

Sylvie Mellet, *Director of Research, "Bases, Corpus, Language," Centre National de la Recherche Scientifique (CNRS)*
- ASPECT

Christian Michel, *Professor of Art History, University of Lausanne*
- MANIERA

Claude Mignot, *Professor of Art History, University of Paris IV–Sorbonne*
- BAROQUE, CLASSIC

Claudia Moatti, *Professor of the Practice of Classics and Law, University of Southern California*
- PEOPLE/RACE/NATION

Marie-José Mondzain, *Director of Research, Center for Political and Moral Sociology, Centre National de la Recherche Scientifique (CNRS)*
- OIKONOMIA

Alan Montefiore, *Fellow, Balliol College, Oxford; President, Forum for European Philosophy, London School of Economics*
- STAND

Frédéric Nef, *Director of Studies, École des Hautes Études en Sciences Sociales (EHESS)*
- IMPLICATION, PROPERTY, SEMOTICS, SIGN

Georges Nivat, *Professor, University of Geneva; President, Rencontres Internationales de Genève*
- SOBORNOST'

Valentin Omelyantchik, *Director of Research, Institute of Philosophy, National Academy of Sciences (Ukraine)*
- RUSSIAN

Pierre Osmo, *Maître de conférences honoraire, Philosophy, University of Paris–Ouest Nanterre La Défense*
- WILLKÜR

Claude Panaccio, *Professor of Philosophy, University of Quebec, Montreal; Canada Research Chair, Theory of Knowledge*
- CONCEPTUS

André Paul, *Historian of Bible Studies*
- TO TRANSLATE

*Antoine Picon, *G. Ware Travelstead Professor of the History of Architecture and Technology, Co-director of Doctoral Programs, Harvard Graduate School of Design*
- MEDIA/MEDIUM (Box 1)

Jackie Pigeaud, *Professor, University of Nantes; Senior Member, University Institute of France*
- MADNESS

Alain Pons, *Maître de conférences honoraire, Philosophy, University of Paris–Ouest Nanterre La Défense*
- CIVILTÀ, CORSO, DICHTUNG (Box 1), GENIUS, INGENIUM, SPREZZATURA, STATO

Dominique Pradelle, *Maître de conférences, Philosophy, University of Paris IV–Sorbonne*
- GEGENSTAND, SACHVERHALT

François Prost, *Maître de conférences, Latin, University of Paris IV–Sorbonne*
- MENSCHHEIT (Box 1), MORALS

Joëlle Proust, *Director of Research, Institute Jean Nicod, Centre National de la Recherche Scientifique (CNRS)*
- AFFORDANCE, EPISTEMOLOGY (Box 2), QUALE, SOUL (Boxes 2 AND 5), WILL (Box 1)

Pietro Pucci, *Goldwin Smith Professor of Classical Languages and Literatures, Cornell University*
- KÊR, MÊTIS

Philippe Quesne, *Professor of Philosophy, École Normale Supérieure (Tunis)*
- TATSACHE (Box 1)

Solal Rabinovitch, *Psychiatrist; Psychoanalyst, Sigmund Freud School of Psychoanalysis*
- ENTSTELLUNG

Jean-Baptiste Rauzy, *Professor of Philosophy, University of Paris IV–Sorbonne*
- TERM (Box 1)

Philippe Raynaud, *Professor of Political Science, University of Paris II–Panthéon-Assas; Professor of Political Science, École des Hautes Études en Sciences Sociales (EHESS)*
- CIVIL RIGHTS, CIVIL SOCIETY, ELEUTHERIA (Box 1), LAW, LIBERAL, POLITICS, RULE OF LAW, STATE/GOVERNMENT, THEMIS (Box 3), WHIG

*Kenneth Reinhard, *Associate Professor of Comparative Literature, University of California, Los Angeles*
- NEIGHBOR

Albert Rijskbaron, *Professor of Greek Linguistics, University of Amsterdam*
- ASPECT, TO TI ÊN EINAI

Denys Riout, *Professor of Art History, University of Paris I–Panthéon-Sorbonne*
- FAKTURA, IN SITU, KITSCH

Sophie Roesch, *Maître de conférences, Latin, University of François Rabelais (Tours)*
- LOGOS

Claude Romano, *Maître de conférences, Philosophy, University of Paris IV–Sorbonne*
- ELEUTHERIA, WILL

Irène Rosier-Catach, *Director of Research, History of Linguistic Theory, Centre National de la Recherche Scientifique (CNRS)*
- CONNOTATION, DICTUM, HOMONYM, IMPLICATION, ITALIAN (Box 2), LANGUAGE, PRÉDICABLE (Box 1), PREDICATION (Box 4), PROPOSITION, SENSE, SIGN, SIGNIFIER/SIGNIFIED, SPEECH ACT, SUPPOSITION (Box 1), TO TRANSLATE, TRUTH, WORD

Baldine Saint Girons, *Professor of Philosophy, University of Paris–Ouest Nanterre La Défense*
- PLEASURE, SUBLIME

*Stella Sandford, *Reader in Modern European Philosophy, Kingston University, London*
- SEX (Box 2)

Fernando Santoro, *Professor of Philosophy, Federal University of Rio de Janeiro; Researcher, National Council for Scientific and Technical Development (Brazil)*
- FICAR, HÁ, PORTUGUESE, SAUDADE

Luca M. Scarantino, *General Secretary, International Council for Philosophy and Humanities (UNESCO)*
- GEISTESWISSENSCHAFTEN (Boxes 1 AND 2)

Bernard Sesé, *Professor of Spanish Literature, University of Paris–Ouest Nanterre La Défense; Correspondent, Real Academia Española (Spain)*
- DUENDE, TALENT

Gérald Sfez, *Professor of Philosophy, Lycée La Bruyère de Versailles*
- KÊR (Box 3)

Constantin Sigov, *Director, European Center for Research in the Humanities, University of Kiev-Mohyla*
- PRAVDA

Gérard Simon, *Professor of Philosophy, University of Lille III (deceased)*
- EIDÔLON, EPISTEMOLOGY (Box 3), SENSE (Box 1)

Michèle Sinapi, *Philosopher*
- TRUTH

Giulia Sissa, *Professor of Classics and Political Science, University of California, Los Angeles; Director of Research, Laboratory of Social Anthropology, Centre National de la Recherche Scientifique (CNRS)*
- PATHOS

Giacinta Spinosa, *Professor of History and Modern Philosophy, University of Cassino*
- SENSE

*Gayatri Chakravorty Spivak, *University Professor of English and Comparative Literature, Columbia University*
- WELT (Box 4)

Elisabete Thamer, *Psychoanalyst and Independent Scholar*
- ANXIETY (Box 1), CATHARSIS, SIGN (Box 5)

Isabelle Thomas-Fogiel, *Professor of Philosophy, University of Ottawa*
- TATSACHE

Denis Thouard, *Director of Research, Knowledge and Texts, Centre National de la Recherche Scientifique (CNRS)*
- GEMÜT, LOGOS (Box 6), UNDERSTANDING

*Jane Tylus, *Professor of Italian and Comparative Literature, New York University*
- TO TRANSLATE (Box 5)

Maria Tzevelekou, *Director of Research, Institute for Language and Speech Processing (Greece)*
- ASPECT

Anca Vasiliu, *Director of Research, Center for the History of Arabic and Medieval Philosophy and Science, Centre National de la Recherche Scientifique (CNRS)*
- DOR

Andriy Vasylchenko, *Researcher, Institute of Philosophy, National Academy of Sciences (Ukraine); Professor of Philosophy, University of Kiev-Mohyla (Ukraine)*
- DRUGOJ, ISTINA, NAROD, POSTUPOK, SAMOST', STRADANIE, SVET, SVOBODA

Hélène Vérin, *Director of Research, Centre Alexandre Koyré, Centre National de la Recherche Scientifique (CNRS)*
- ENTREPRENEUR

*Anthony Vidler, *Professor of Humanities and History of Art and Architecture, Brown University*
- CHÔRA

Sarah de Voguë, *Maître de conférences, Department of Language Science, University of Paris–Ouest Nanterre La Défense; Formal Linguistics Laboratory, Centre National de la Recherche Scientifique (CNRS)*
- ASPECT

*Immanuel Wallerstein, *Senior Research Scholar, Department of Sociology, Yale University*
- MOMENT (Box 4)

Michael Werner, *Director of Research, Center for Interdisciplinary Research on Germany, Centre National de la Recherche Scientifique (CNRS); Director of Studies, École des Hautes Études en Sciences Sociales (EHESS)*
- HISTORY

Francis Wolff, *Professor of Philosophy, École Normale Supérieure (Ulm)*
- POLIS

*Susan J. Wolfson, *Professor of English, Princeton University*
- FANCY (Box 1), SENSE (Box 5)

*Michael Wood, *Charles Barnwell Straut Class of 1923 Professor of English and Comparative Literature, Princeton University*
- BILDUNG (Box 3)

*Robert J. C. Young, *Julius Silver Professor of English and Comparative Literatures, New York University*
- STATO (Box 1)

Translators

Steven Rendall

ABSTRACTION
ABSURD
ACEDIA
ACT
ACTOR
AFFORDANCE
AGENCY
AIÔN
ALLIANCE
ANALOGY
ANIMAL
ANSCHAULICHKEIT
ANXIETY
APPEARANCE
APPROPRIATION
ARGUTEZZA
ART
ASPECT
ATTUALITÀ
AUFHEBEN
AUTHORITY
AUTRUI
BAROQUE
BEAUTY
BEGRIFF
BEHAVIOR
BELIEF
BERÎT
BERUF
BIEN-ÊTRE
BILD
BILDUNG
BOGOČELOVEČESTVO
ÇA
CARE
CATEGORY
CATHARSIS
CERTITUDE

CHANCE
CIVILITY
CIVILIZATION
CIVIL RIGHTS
CIVILTÀ
CLAIM
CLASSIC
COMBINATION AND
CONCEPTUALIZATION
COMMONPLACE
COMMON SENSE
COMMUNITY
COMPARISON
COMPORTMENT
CONCEPT
CONCEPTUS
CONCETTO
CONCILIARITY
CONNOTATION
CONSCIOUSNESS
CONSENSUS
CONSERVATIVE
CONTINUITET
CONTINUITY
CORSO
CROYANCE
CULTURE
DAIMÔN
DASEIN
DRIVE
ENGLISH
FATHERLAND
FLESH
GERMAN
GOOD/EVIL
HAPPINESS
HEART
LOVE

NAROD
NATURE
NEGATION
NEUZEIT
NONSENSE
NOSTALGIA
NOTHING
OBJECT
OBLIGATION
OIKEIÔSIS
OIKONOMIA
OLAM
OMNITUDO REALITATIS
PARDON
PARONYM
PASSION
PATHOS
PEACE
PEOPLE
PEOPLE/RACE/NATION
PERCEPTION
PERFECTIBILITY
PERFORMANCE
PERSON
PHANTASIA
PHÉNOMÈNE
PHRONÊSIS
PIETAS
PITY
PLASTICITY
PLEASURE
PLUDSELIGHED
POETRY
POLIS
POLITICS
PORTUGUESE
POSTUPOK
POWER

PRAVDA
PRAXIS
PRÉDICABLE
PREDICATION
PRESENT
PRINCIPLE
PROBABILITY
PROGRESS
PROPERTY
PROPOSITION
PROPOSITIONAL CONTENT
PRUDENTIAL
QUALE
QUIDDITY
REALITY
REASON
RÉCIT
REFERENCE
RELIGIO
RELIGION
REPRÉSENTATION
RES
RÉVOLUTION
RIGHT
ROMANTIC
RULE
RUSE
RUSSIAN
SACHVERHALT
SAMOST'
SAUDADE
SCHICKSAL
SECULARIZATION
SEHNSUCHT
SOUL
SPEECH ACT
THING
WORD ORDER

Christian Hubert

LIFE	TO TRANSLATE	VERNEINUNG	WHIG
TABLEAU	TROPE	VIRTÙ	WHOLE
TALAṬṬUF	TRUTH	VIRTUE	WILL
TALENT	UNIVERSALS	VOCATION	WILLKÜR
TATSACHE	UTILE	VOICE	WORK
TERM	UTILITY	VORHANDEN	WUNSCH
THEMIS	VALUE	WELT	
TORAH	VERB	WELTANSCHAUUNG	
TO TI ÊN EINAI	VERGÜENZA	WERT	

Jeffrey Mehlman

CIVIL SOCIETY	SENSUS COMMUNIS	SOUCI	STIMMUNG
MIMÊSIS	SEX	SPECIES	STRADANIE
MIR	SHAME	SPLEEN	STRENGTH
MITMENSCH	SIGN	SPRECHTGESANG	STRUCTURE
SEIN	SIGNIFIER/SIGNIFIED	SPREZZATURA	STYLE
SELBST	SOBORNOST'	STAND	SUBLIME
SELF	SOCIETY	STANDARD	SUPPOSITION
SEMIOTICS	SOLLEN	STATE/GOVERNMENT	SVET
SENS COMMUN	SOPHISM	STATO	SVOBODA
SENSE	SORGE	STILL	

Nathanael Stein

AESTHETICS	DRUGOJ	EXIGENCY	GESCHLECHT
DECEPTION	DUENDE	EXPERIENCE	GLAUBE
DEFORMATION	DUTY	FACT	GLÜCK
DEMON	DYNAMIC	FACTURE	GOD
DÉNÉGATION	ECONOMY	FAIR	GOGO
DESCRIPTION	EIDÔLON	FAITH	GOÛT
DESENGAÑO	ELEUTHERIA	FAKTURA	GOVERNMENT
DÉSINVOLTURE	ÉNONCÉ	FALSE	GRACE
DESIRE	ENTREPRENEUR	FANCY	GREEK
DESSEIN	ENTSTELLUNG	FEELING	GUT
DESSIN	EPISTEMOLOGY	FICAR	HÁ
DESTINY	EPOCHÊ	FICTION	HEIMAT
DEVIL	EREIGNIS	FORCE	HERRSCHAFT
DIALECTIC	ERLEBEN	FORM	HISTORIA UNIVERSALIS
DICHTUNG	ERSCHEINUNG	FRENCH	HISTORY
DICTUM	ERZÄHLEN	GEFÜHL	MADNESS
DISCOURSE	ES	GEGENSTAND	RULE OF LAW
DISEGNO	ES GIBT	GEISTESWISSENSCHAFTEN	SPANISH
DISPOSITION	ESSENCE	GEMÜT	STATE
DOMINATION	ESTI	GENDER	STATE OF AFFAIRS
DOR	ETERNITY	GENIUS	TO BE
DOXA	EVENT	GENRE	UNDERSTANDING
DROIT	EVIGHED	GESCHICHTLICH	

Michael Syrotinski

EUROPE
HOMONYM
I/ME/MYSELF
IDEA
IDENTITY
IL Y A
IMAGE
IMAGINATION
IMITATION
IMPLICATION
INGENIUM
IN SITU
INSTANT
INSTINCT

INTELLECT
INTELLECTUS
INTENTION
INTUITION
ISTINA
ITALIAN
JETZTZEIT
JUSTICE
KÊR
KITSCH
LANGUAGE
LAW
LEGGIADRIA
LEIB

LËV
LEX
LIBERAL
LIBERTY
LIE
LIEU
LIGHT
LOGOS
MACHT
MALAISE
MANIERA
MATTER OF FACT
MELANCHOLY
MEMORY

MENSCHHEIT
MERKMAL
MÊTIS
MOMENT
MOMENTE
MORALS
MORAL SENSE
MOTIONLESS
UNCONSCIOUS
WITTICISM
WORD
WORLD

Dictionary of Untranslatables

ABSTRACTION, ABSTRACTA, ABSTRACT ENTITIES

FRENCH	*abstraction, abstrait*
GERMAN	*Abstraktion, Entbildung*
GREEK	*aphairesis* [ἀφαίρεσις]
LATIN	*abstractio, ablatio, absolutio, abnegatio; separata, abstracta*

➤ CATEGORY, EPOCHÊ, ESSENCE, *FICTION, IMAGINATION*, INTELLECTUS, INTENTION, *NEGATION, NOTHING*, REALITY, RES, SEIN, SUBJECT, UNIVERSALS

While the meaning of the term "abstraction" is not a problem in formal logic, where it refers to the operation that makes it possible to construct, using an "abstractor," a so-called "abstract" expression on the basis of another expression containing one or more free variables, the term's semantic field in philosophy and the theory of knowledge is more difficult to organize. When Condillac (*L'Art de penser* I.viii) denounces "the abuse of constructed abstract notions," and "in order to avoid this problem" asks that we look back to "the generation of all our abstract notions, ... a method that has been unknown to philosophers, ... who have sought to make up for it by means of definitions," his aim is different from that of Aristotle when the latter mentions, under the rubric "abstract entities" or "things that exist in the abstract [τὰ ἐξ ἀφαιρέσεως]," the forms that mathematical science deals with "by abstracting from their inherent matter" (Aristotle, *De anima*, 431b.13–17), and from that of Dionysius the Areopagite when he asks to be raised by thought to the superessential "through the *aphairesis* [ἀφαίρεσις] of all beings." Thus when speaking of "abstraction" we must distinguish the problem of the generation of abstract ideas insofar as it involves that of universals, that of the existence or nonexistence of general objects, and that of the practice of abstractive negation in the diverse fields—logical, epistemological, theological—where it occurs. The broad range of the term "abstraction" is well illustrated by the modern English usage of the terms "abstracta" and "abstract entities," which are more or less synonymous with "universals," and whose extension includes mathematical objects (numbers, classes, sets), geometrical figures, propositions, properties, and relations. Although English-language historiography has a tendency to regard Plato's Ideas or Forms as the first occurrence of real, non-spatio-temporal "abstract" entities, instantiated or participated in by spatio-temporal objects, it seems more precise to reserve this term for "Aristotelian" ontology by distinguishing, as was done during the Middle Ages, separate entities (*separata*) from abstract entities (*abstracta*).

I. *Epagôgê* and *Aphairesis*, Two Models of Abstraction according to Aristotle

There are two models of abstraction in Aristotelianism. The first is that of "abstractive induction" (*epagôgê* [ἐπαγωγή]), which Aristotle describes this way:

> So out of sense-perception comes to be what we call memory, and out of frequently repeated memories of the same thing develops experience; for a number of memories constitute a single experience. From experience again—i.e. from the universal now stabilized in its entirety within the soul, the one beside the many which is a single identity within them all—originate the skill of the craftsman and the knowledge of the man of science, skill in the sphere of coming to be and science in the sphere of being.
>
> (trans. G.R.G. Mure, *Posterior Analytics*, II.§19)

The second model is that of mathematical (chiefly geometrical) abstraction, which consists not in "bringing together" (*epagein* [ἐπάγειν]) similar elements and grouping them under a single concept, but in "stripping" (*aphaireisthai* [ἀφαιρεῖσθαι]) the image or representation of a thing of its individualizing characteristics (essentially material).

The conflict between these two models is a structural given, a major tendency in Aristotelianism, whose effects made themselves felt throughout the Middle Ages. Philosophers have never ceased to vacillate between the registration of resemblances (the basis of "resemblance nominalism") and the neutralization of individualizing characteristics that are not pertinent for the type, though some have sought to find unlikely compromises between these poles.

■ See Box 1.

II. The Peripatetic Theory of *Aphairesis* and Its Medieval Extensions: "Abstractionism"

A. The classification of the sciences

In his treatise *De caelo* (III.§1.299a 15–17), Aristotle uses the term "abstraction" to distinguish between "mathematical objects" (*ta ex aphaireseôs* [τὰ ἐξ ἀφαιρέσεως], lit. "proceeding from a subtraction") and "physical objects" (*ta ek prostheseôs* [τὰ ἐκ προσθέσεως], lit. "proceeding from an addition"). Nonetheless, it is only in *De anima* (III.§7.431b.12–16) that Aristotle explains how the intellect conceives abstractions:

> As for so-called "abstractions" (*ta en aphairesei legomena* [τὰ ἐν ἀφαιρέσει λεγόμενα], the intellect thinks of them as one would think of the snub-nosed (*simon* [σιμόν]): qua snub-nosed, one would think of it not as separate (*ou kechôrismenôs* [οὐ κεχωρισμένως]) but as concave (*koilon* [κοῖλον]), if one thought of it in action (*energeiai* [ἐνεργείᾳ]), one would think of it without the flesh in which the concavity is realized (*aneu tês sarkos an enoei en hêi to koilon* [ἄνευ τῆς σαρκὸς ἂν ἐνόει ἐν ᾗ τὸ κοῖλον]): so is it when the intellect thinks of abstract terms, it thinks of mathematical things as if they were separate, even though they are not separate

1

1

Aphairesis/Entbildung/Abstractive Negation in mystical theology

The term *aphairesis* [ἀφαίρεσις] has a mystical or at least spiritual use in Neoplatonism. Pseudo-Dionysius the Areopagite defines it as the instrument of unknowing knowledge (Nicholas of Cusa's *docta ignorantia*):

> For that is what it means, in truth, to see and know and sing superessentially, in a hymn, the Superessential, *through the abstractive negation of all beings (pantôn tôn ontôn aphaireseôs* [πάντων τῶν ὄντων ἀφαιρέσεως]), just as those who cause to emerge from a block of marble the statue that was latent in it remove all that prevented, by masking it, the pure vision of the hidden form, and cause the hidden beauty to show itself simply by taking away (*kai auto eph' heautou têi aphairesei monêi* [καὶ αὐτὸ ἐφ᾽ ἑαυτοῦ τῇ ἀφαιρέσει μονῇ]).

The example of the "internal statue" is also attested in this context in Plotinus's *Enneads* (I.6, 9):

> But how are you to see into a virtuous soul and know its loveliness? Withdraw into yourself and look. And if you do not find yourself beautiful yet, act as does the creator of a statue that is to be made beautiful: he cuts away here, he smoothes there, he makes this line lighter, this other purer, until a lovely face has grown upon his work. So do you also cut away all that is excessive, straighten all that is crooked, bring light to all that is overcast, labour to make all one glow of beauty and never cease chiselling your statue, until there shall shine out on you from it the godlike splendour of virtue.

> (trans. S. MacKenna, *The Enneads*)

Although the translation of *aphairesis* as "abstractive negation" may seem ambiguous, medieval Latin offers at least four terms—*ablatio, abstractio, absolutio,* and *abnegatio*—that correspond to the meaning of the Greek term. In the Latin versions of *Mystical Theology* (RT: *PG*) the term *ablatio* is used to render (*a*) *pantôn tôn ontôn aphaireseôs* and (*b*) *kai auto eph' heautou têi aphairesei monêi*. Hilduin: (*a*) *per omnium existencium ablacionem* and (*b*) *et hoc in sui ipsius ablacione sola*. John Scotus Erigena: (*a*) *per omnium existentium ablationem* and (*b*) *et ipsam in seipsa ablatione sola*. Jean Sarrazin: (*a*) *per omnium exsistentium ablationem* and (*b*) *et ipsam in se ipsa ablatione sola*. Robert Grosseteste: (*a*) *per omnium entium ablationem* and (*b*) *et ipsam in se ipsa ablatione sola*. The transition to the vernacular was accompanied by a few remarkable formulations. In Master Eckhart, the Latin *ablatio* becomes the Middle High German *Entbildung*. This is less a translation—*ablatio* does not "mean" *Entbildung*—than a transposition of the problematics of *aphairesis* to a new context, that of the image and the "form," through the mediation of the term *ablatio* and its Latin synonyms. The stripping away of all images, the baring of the soul through "negative" askesis, the passage through images and mental copies, all converge under the term *Entbildung*, so confusing for the inquisitors during Eckhart's trial that it was translated by a periphrasis, *imagine denudari*.

(*ou kechôrismena hôs kechôrismena* [οὐ κεχωρισμένα ὡς κεχωρισμένα]).

In Michael Scot's Latin translation of Averroës's long commentary on *De anima*, the expressions used in *De anima* III.§4.429b.18–22 and III.§7.431b.12–16 are rendered respectively by "things that exist in *mathesis*" and "things that are said negatively." Averroës notes that by "things that are said negatively" Aristotle "means mathematical things," the word *negation* meaning "separation from matter." Negation being, along with separation, ablation, suppression, and abstraction, one of the possible meanings of the Greek *aphairesis*, Averroës's exegesis shows that he sees Aristotle's thought as characterized by a kind of equation: things said negatively = beings separated from matter = mathematical entities.

However, mathematical entities are not the only abstract entities. There are also universals, especially the universals of genus, species, and difference. How should we distinguish, from the point of view of abstraction, mathematical entities from universals? This problem occupied Aristotle's commentators and interpreters from antiquity to the Middle Ages.

As they are defined in the *Metaphysics* (VI.§1.1026a.10–16), the theoretical sciences can be classified in a combinatory manner, depending on whether the entities they concern are "movable" or "immovable," on the one hand, and "separable" or "inseparable" from matter, on the other hand.

But if there is something which is eternal and immovable and separable, clearly the knowledge of it belongs to a theoretical science—not, however, to physics (for physics deals with certain movable things) nor to mathematics, but to a science prior to both. For physics deals with things which exist separately (*achôrista* [ἀχώριστα]) but are not immovable, and some parts of mathematics deal with things which are immovable but presumably do not exist separately, but as embodied in matter (*hôs en hulêi* [ὡς ἐν ὕλῃ]); while the first science deals with things which both exist separately and are immovable (*chôrista kai akinêta* [χωριστὰ καὶ ἀκίνητα]).

> (trans. W. D. Ross, *Metaphysics*, in *The Basic Works of Aristotle*)

In the eighteenth century, an anonymous work providing an introduction to philosophy, *Philosophica disciplina*, presents the same tripartite classification in an order that later became standard, an order of increasing "separation" determined by the "ontological value" of its objects: physics, mathematics, metaphysics.

The things . . . dealt with by speculative philosophy are either connected with (*conjuncte*) movement and matter in accord with being and knowledge, or are completely (*omnino*) separate. If they are considered in the first way, then we have natural philosophy; if in the second way, mathematics; if in the third way, metaphysics. And that is why there are only three speculative sciences of things.

(C. Lafleur, ed., *Philosophica disciplina*, in *Quatre Introductions à la philosophie au XIIIe siècle*)

Whatever the classification adopted, one fact emerges: metaphysics deals with "separate" entities (separate substances or "intelligences," God, "thought about thought," even intellects traditionally called "poietic" or "active" and "hylic" or "possible"); mathematics deals with "abstract" entities. Where should universals be located in such a scheme? The answer is given, in an epoch-making manner, by Alexander of Aphrodisias, who formulated a doctrine that was to become part of the common Peripatetic language, and that modern interpreters designate by the term "abstractionism."

B. Abstractionism

Abstractionism's starting point is a thesis (extrapolated from *De anima* III.§7.431b.12–16) stipulating that abstraction is a mental operation that consists in conceiving as separate from matter things that are nonetheless not separate from matter. Two of Alexander's texts, *Peri psuchês* [Περὶ ψυχῆς] (*De anima liber cum mantissa*) and *Quaestiones naturales et morales*, give a precise elaboration of this thesis in the framework of an opposition between "incorporeal forms that are by themselves immaterial" (for Alexander, the separate Intellect, the unmoved First Mover) and "forms embodied in matter." The latter, not being "by themselves" intelligible, become intelligible because an intellect "makes them intelligible by separating them from matter through thought, by apprehending them as if they were [separate] by themselves." Alexander's thesis does not bear *prima facie* on mathematical objects, but rather on all sorts of so-called "material" forms (that is, those that are embodied in matter). This is a generalization of the theory in *De anima* III.§.7, outside the context of mathematics, or rather geometry. This generalization, "abstractionism," is made possible not only because geometrical possibilities are among abstract intelligibles in general, but also because geometrical intelligibles usually function as examples of abstract intelligibles.

Regarding abstract universals' mode of existence, Alexander of Aphrodisias formulates the main theorem of "abstractionism" this way: "The universal [that is] in all [particulars] does not exist in the same way that it is conceived." The universal has two modes of being: one in things, the other as conceived. This distinction corresponds to that established by Scholasticism between the universal *in re* and the universal *post rem*. It seems to be based on a difference between "being" and "existing," whose significance and scope remain to be historically determined, and which Alexander expresses, generally, by saying that universals have "being" (*einai* [εἶναι]) in thought, while *hupostasis* [ὑπόστασις] / *huparxis* [ὕπαρξις] has being in particulars (for *hupostasis*, see *Quaestiones naturales et morales*, 59, 7–8, and his *In Aristotelis Topicorum libros octo commentaria*, II.2, and for *huparxis*, see *De anima liber cum mantissa*, 90; see also SUBJECT and ESSENCE).

At the dawn of the Middle Ages, Boethius, a Latin translator and commentator on Aristotle, formulated the second thesis on which abstractionism is based, explaining that "all concepts derived from things that are not conceived as they are arranged are not necessarily empty and false" (RT: *PG*, t. 64, col. 84B11–14). The problem assumed here is the one that thirteenth-century Aristotelians would later formulate in the Scholastic adage "Abtrahentium non est mendacium" (Abstraction is not a lie). In the context with which Boethius's thesis is concerned, the opposition is the Neoplatonic one between authentic concepts (which have a basic reality) and empty or false concepts. The respective paths of abstraction and fiction thus intersect, in accord with an argumentative schema that continues down to the modern period. For Boethius, there is "false opinion" if and only if things are "composed by thought" that cannot exist "naturally joined." That is the case, for example, when one combines in imagination a man and a horse to produce a Centaur (a traditional example of *phantasia* [φαντασία] among Greek commentators).

> Si enim quis componat atque conjungat intellectu id quod natura jungi non patiatur, illud falsum esse nullus ignorat: ut si quis equum atque hominem jungat imaginatione, atque effigiet Centaurum.
>
> (If in fact something is composed or combined by thought whose junction nature would not allow, everyone knows that it is false: for example, if the imagination combines a horse and a man, a centaur would be obtained [that is, something false = something that does not exist].)
>
> (RT: *PG*, t. 64, col. 84)

But for all that, every concept of a thing "conceived differently from the way it is composed" is not a false concept. Therefore we must distinguish between a false concept and a concept derived from things by abstraction. A false concept, like that of the centaur, does not proceed from a thing conceived in a way different from that in which it is composed. It is not, strictly speaking, a derived concept. On the contrary, resulting from a mental combination of what "cannot" exist combined in nature, one can and must say that it is not derived from any "thing." In contrast, in the case of a concept derived from things by abstraction, we are dealing with a derived concept that proceeds from a "division" or "abstraction" carried out on an authentically existing thing. Boethius's abstraction is thus, as in Alexander of Aphrodisias, a separation or dissociation bearing on "incorporeals" (a Stoic term characteristic of Alexander's syncretic Peripateticism): it is the act carried out by thought when, "receiving the incorporeals mixed with bodies, it divides the former from the latter in order to consider and contemplate them in themselves" (Boethius, ibid.).

C. Discriminating attention: *Intentio/attentio*

In the twelfth century, Peter Abelard introduced a theme that was to become central in modern empiricist and nominalist theories of abstraction: attention (*intentio*, *attentio*). For Abelard, the role of attention is determined on the basis of the hylemorphic ontology inherited from Aristotle, Porphyry, and Boethius. Matter and form never exist in isolation:

they are always "mixed" with one another (Abelard, *Logica, Super Porphyrium*). However, the mind, or rather the reason, can consider them in three ways. It can "consider matter in itself," "focus its attention on the form alone," or "conceive the two as united." The first two types of intellection are carried out "through abstraction," the latter "through junction."

In Abelard, Boethius's "abstractionist" thesis is reformulated: intellection through abstraction is not empty. Two new arguments are advanced: (1) this type of intellection does not attribute to a thing properties other than its own; (2) it limits itself to abstracting from some of them.

> Such understandings by "abstraction" perhaps seemed to be "false" or "empty" because they perceive the thing otherwise than as it subsists. . . . But that is not so. If someone understands a thing otherwise than as it is in the sense that he attends to it in terms of a nature or characteristic that it does not have, that understanding is surely empty. But this does not happen with abstraction.
>
> (P. Abelard, *Logica, Super Porphyrium*, 25.5–22; trans. P. Spade, "Glosses on Porphyry")

Thus here *abstraire* means "abstract from, set aside"; or in ordinary language, "ignore" or "not take into account." This common acceptation of an act that is elsewhere described in terms of the extraction of "incorporeals" from the matter in which they are entangled makes Abelard's descriptions of the act of abstraction look like anticipations of John Stuart Mill's.

Thus Abelard opposes to the model of extraction basing itself on the presentation of abstraction as abstractive induction, a registration of resemblances or a coincidence of images, and surreptitiously drawing on canonical passages of the *Metaphysics* and *Posterior Analytics*, a second model of discriminating attention that is present from the outset in the Peripatetic tradition but has been usually supplanted by the first model. It is clear that the model of attention has played a role in certain non-"inductivist" formulations by medieval philosophers, commentators on Aristotle arguing against the thesis of abstraction-induction and for an act of forming or producing the general "in a single example." This thesis, attested in Averroës, consists in characterizing abstraction as a "neutralization" of a certain set of nonpertinent traits and a "focusing" on a single "pertinent" trait enabling the perception of a "co-specificity" among individuals of the same "type." In this theory, the intelligible is not drawn from the perception of resemblances among images, it is the product of the "stripping-down" of a particular image. I do not produce the concept of man by abstracting from a plurality of images of particular men, but by stripping a particular image of everything that makes it particular. Averroës's theory is continued by all the authors who conceive abstraction as possible "on the basis of a single example." One of its major problems is the obscurity of the analysis of the respective roles of sensation, imagination, the "cogitative" faculty (see INTENTION, Box 2), and the intellect (possible and active) in the process of "stripping down" the sensible "intention." As Abelard describes it, the act of abstraction is simpler and less problematic than it is in the Averroist psychology. Here, for once, Abelard is close to common empirical intuitions. His first observation is that if I consider a given individual man as a substance or as a body, without at the same time considering him as an animal, man, or grammarian, my intellection bears only on characteristics that are part of his nature. However, and this is the second observation, in these cases my intellection does not bear upon all the characteristics present "in": it ignores some of them in order to make itself present "to." Thus for Abelard, abstraction is indeed the product of a movement of "focusing attention," so that "directing one's attention" toward this or that property of a nature implies that "attention is diverted" from others. This movement of attention has no ontological significance:

> When I say that I attend to the nature "only" insofar as it has this or that feature, the term "only" refers to the attention and not to the mode of subsisting.
>
> (P. Abelard, *Logica, Super Porphyrium*, 25; trans. P. Spade, "Glosses on Porphyry")

If the word "only" concerned nothing other than the mode of being, my intellection would be empty. But this is not the case: the way in which my intellection takes place does not imply that a given nature "possesses only" a given quality, it means that I "consider it only" insofar as it possesses that quality.

Thus we can say with Boethius that in a sense abstractive intellection conceives a thing in a certain way other than it is, that is to say, not in the sense in which it would be conceived with another status, that is, another structure than its own, but in the sense in which the mode of its intellection is different from the mode of its subsistence. Now, intellection depends on *my* operation. Therefore we have to distinguish (1) the fact of being considered "separately" from that of being considered as "separate," and (2) the fact of being "considered" separately from that of "existing" separately.

III. The Modern Empiricist Critique of Abstraction

A. Locke's "general triangle"

The problem of the origin of "ideas" or "abstract notions" is one of the special loci for the expression of "resemblance nominalism," which is based on the elaboration of the supposed relationship between the use of "names" and the registration of "resemblances." The standard formulation of resemblance nominalism is given by John Locke in a frequently discussed passage of the *Essay Concerning Human Understanding* (ed., P. H. Nidditch, 415):

> But yet I think we may say, the sorting of them under names is the workmanship of the understanding, taking occasion, from the similitude it observes amongst them, to make abstract general ideas.

To this description David Hume adds the idea of the name's "abbreviative" function in relation to the plurality of particular ideas:

> When we have found a resemblance among several objects, that often occur to us, we apply the same name to all of them, whatever differences we may observe in the degrees of their quantity and quality, and whatever other differences may appear among them. After we have acquired a custom of this kind, the hearing of

that name revives the idea of one of these objects, and makes the imagination conceive it with all its particular circumstances and proportions. But as the same word is suppos'd to have been frequently applied to other individuals, that are different in many respects from that idea, which is immediately present to the mind; the word not being able to revive the idea of all these individuals, but only touches the soul . . . and revives that custom, which we have acquir'd by surveying them. . . . The word raises up an individual idea, along with a certain custom; and that custom produces any other individual one, for which we may have occasion. But as the production of all the ideas, to which the name may be apply'd, is in most cases impossible, we abridge that work by a more partial consideration, and find but few inconveniences to arise in our reasoning from that abridgment.

(*A Treatise of Human Nature*, ed. L. A. Selby-Bigge and P. H. Nidditch)

Thus we can say that Locke and Hume defend the same thesis regarding the empirical origin of general abstract ideas. On the other hand, the two philosophers differ on the second problem: the status of "general objects." In the *Essay*, Locke refers to a "general idea of a triangle" that is supposed to have apparently incompatible properties:

For example, does it not require some pains and skill to form the general Idea of a Triangle (which is yet none of the most abstract, comprehensive, and difficult), for it must be neither Oblique nor Rectangle, neither Equilateral, Equicrural, nor Scalenon; but all and none of these at once.

(*An Essay Concerning Human Understanding*, IV, VII.§9, ed. P. H. Nidditch)

Locke does not claim that such an object exists. On the contrary, he notes that characterized in this way, a general triangle "is something imperfect, that cannot exist," and adds that it is "an Idea wherein some parts of several different and inconsistent Ideas are put together" (it is noteworthy that Coste's French translation of the *Essay* omits this passage). Locke's general abstract triangle, an object that is imperfect in one case, contradictory in another, does not make a claim for existence, to use a concept found both in Leibniz (*ad existentiam pretendere*) and in Bolzano ("Anspruch auf Wirklichkeit machen," in *Paradoxien des Unendlichen*, §13). However, "Locke's general triangle" has become an obligatory philosophical reference point for all theoreticians of abstraction, drawing toward itself the most diverse critiques from Berkeley and Hume to Husserl.

B. Junction, separation / power of representation: Berkeley and John Stuart Mill

In his introduction to the *Principles of Human Knowledge* (§13), George Berkeley transposes the problem raised by Locke's general triangle onto a strictly empirical ground, pretending to inquire whether anyone "has, or can attain to have, an idea that shall correspond with the description that is here given of the general idea of a triangle, which is 'neither oblique nor rectangle, equilateral, equicrural nor scalenon,

but all and none of these at once?'" He replies that "when I demonstrate any proposition concerning triangles, it is to be supposed that I have in view the universal idea of a triangle; which ought not to be understood as if I could frame an idea of a triangle which was neither equilateral, nor scalenon, nor equicrural. . ." (§15), and that it is in any case *impossible* to form an abstract general idea of the triangle on the basis of incompatible elements (§16). There is not and cannot be a general idea of the triangle that is "neither oblique nor rectangle, neither Equilateral, Equicrural, nor Scalenon; but all and none of these at once" because the conjunction "oblique + rectangular + equilateral + isosceles + scalene" is an "inconsistent idea" (§16).

To argue his claim, Berkeley stresses, in the process that Locke incorrectly describes as leading to the formation of a general abstract idea, a different element: attention. We must not confuse "forming a general abstract idea" with paying attention to some quality of a particular figure at the expense of another, producing a theoretical monster by combining the properties of different objects, all of which no one of them could possess, and isolating or setting aside from an object some of the properties that it in fact possesses.

And here it must be acknowledged that a man may consider a figure merely as triangular, without attending to the particular qualities of the angles, or relations of the sides. So far he may abstract; but this will never prove that he can frame an abstract, general, inconsistent idea of a triangle. In like manner we may consider Peter so far forth as man, or so far forth as animal without framing the aforementioned abstract idea, either of man or of animal, inasmuch as all that is perceived is not considered.

(*Principles of Human Knowledge*, §16)

That is, Berkeley acknowledges the existence of

a faculty of imagining, or representing to myself, the ideas of those particular things I have perceived, and of variously compounding and dividing them. I can consider the hand, the eye, the nose, each by itself abstracted or separated from the rest of the body. But then whatever hand or eye I imagine, it must have some particular shape and colour. Likewise the idea of man that I frame to myself must be either of a white, or a black, or a tawny, a straight, or a crooked, a tall, or a low, or a middle-sized man. I cannot by any effort of thought conceive the abstract idea above described.

(Ibid., §10)

The terms "combination" and "separation" refer to the very origins of the notion of abstraction as elaborated in the Middle Ages from Boethius to Abelard, in the wake of Aristotle and Alexander of Aphrodisias. Berkeley's rejection of Lockean abstraction remains in fact immanent in the sphere of what might be called Peripatetic "abstractionism," so that paradoxically, and obviously without his realizing it, Berkeley opposes to abstraction according to Locke a weak version of the theory proposed by Boethius and his medieval successors.

Recognizing that he is capable of abstracting in a certain sense (*Principles*, §10), Berkeley distinguishes between two kinds of abstraction: authentic abstraction and pseudo-abstraction (the latter being, for him, the one that in Locke presides over the formation of general abstract ideas). Authentic abstraction occurs "when I consider some particular parts or qualities separated from others, with which, though they are united in some object, yet it is possible they may really exist without them." Pseudo-abstraction occurs when I claim to abstract one from the other or to represent to myself separately qualities that could not exist separately from one another (*Principles*, §10).

The same theory of attention is adopted, *mutatis mutandis*, by John Stuart Mill. In his book *An Examination of Sir William Hamilton's Philosophy*, Mill explains that abstraction is not a mental act consisting in the separation of certain attributes that are supposed to compose an object in order to conceive them as detached from all others, but rather an act that, assuming these attributes are conceived as parts of a larger whole, focuses attention on them to the detriment of the others with which they are combined. In his *Lectures on Metaphysics and Logic* (III.132–33), Hamilton defines the process of attention as antithetical and complementary to abstraction:

an act of volition, called Attention, concentrates consciousness on the qualities thus recognised as similar; and that concentration, by attention, on them, involves an abstraction of consciousness from these which have been recognised and thrown aside as dissimilar; for the power of consciousness is limited, and it is clear or vivid precisely in proportion to the simplicity or oneness of the object.

For Mill, who prefers to speak of "complex ideas of objects in the concrete," rather than of "general concepts," abstraction consists in attending "exclusively to certain parts of the concrete idea" (*An Examination of Sir William Hamilton's Philosophy*, 42).

Hume's critique of Locke follows more or less the same argument as Berkeley's. However, Hume does not attribute to Locke the whole of the position considered absurd by all the adversaries of the "general triangle." According to Hume, Locke did not maintain that it is possible to form an idea of an object constituted by the conjunction of quantitative or qualitative ideas that are mutually incompatible and represent them all, but rather than since that is impossible, and since there are nonetheless general abstract ideas, we have to accept the second part of the thesis: the possibility of forming an idea of an object stripped of all its characteristics, or rather an idea of an object that represents none of its quantitative or qualitative properties. The abstract idea of a man represents men of all sizes and qualities, and it can do so only by representing at once all possible sizes and qualities, or none of them in particular. Now, since it has been judged absurd to maintain the first proposition, because it implies an infinite capacity of the mind, writers usually have concluded in favor of the second proposition, and it has been supposed that our abstract ideas represent no particular degree of quantity and quality:

The abstract idea of a man represents men of all sizes and all qualities; which 'tis concluded it cannot do, but either by representing at once all possible sizes and all possible qualities, or by representing no particular one at all. Now it having been esteemed absurd to defend the former proposition, as implying an infinite capacity in the mind, it has been commonly infer'd in favour of the latter: and our abstract ideas have been suppos'd to represent no particular degree either of quantity or quality.

(Hume, *A Treatise of Human Nature*, I.§1, chap. 7)

In opposition to this fiction, Hume asserts that while "the mind cannot form any notion of quantity or quality without forming a precise notion of degrees of each," the mind is capable of forming "a notion of all possible degrees of quantity and quality, in such a manner at least, as, however imperfect, may serve all the purposes of reflection and conversation" (*Treatise of Human Nature*, I.§1, chap. 7). The first pseudo-requirement of the general abstract idea is thereby met, on a terrain different from that of Lockean abstraction, whereas, by a kind of mirror effect or reversal, the second is abandoned. Hume takes the opportunity to clarify the problem of the genesis of so-called general ideas, explaining how an idea particular in its nature becomes general in its power of representation. This is the place of custom, designated here by its Latin name *habitus*, through which Hume's thesis connects both with the medieval thesis of "habitual knowledge" (*notitia habitualis*) and with its foundation in Ockhamist nominalism: the role of general terms in language as instruments recalling particular contents established by an enduring association and "re-mobilizable" in the form of the connected term:

'tis certain *that* we form the idea of individuals, whenever we use any general term; *that* we seldom or never can exhaust these individuals; and *that* those, which remain, are only represented by means of that habit, by which we recall them, whenever any present occasion requires it. This then is the nature of our abstract ideas and general terms; and 'tis after this manner we account for the . . . paradox, *that some ideas are particular in their nature, but general in their representation*. A particular idea becomes general by being annex'd to a general term; that is, to a term, which from a customary conjunction has a relation to many other particular ideas, and readily recalls them in the imagination.

(Hume, *Treatise of Human Nature*, I.§1, chap. 7)

Alain de Libera

BIBLIOGRAPHY

Abelard. *Logica, Super Porphyrium*. Edited by B. Geyer. Münster, Ger.: Aschendorff, 1973. Translation by Paul Vincent Spade: "Glosses on Porphyry." In *Five Texts on the Medieval Problem of Universals*. Edited by P. Spade. New York: Hackett, 1994.

Alexander of Aphrodisias. *Peri psuchês* [Περὶ ψυχῆς] (*De anima liber cum mantissa*). Edited by I. Bruns. Berlin: Reimer, 1887.

———. *In Aristotelis Topicorum libros octo commentaria*. Edited by Maximilianus Wallies. Commentaria in Aristotelem Graeca. Berlin: Reimer, 1891.

———. *Quaestiones naturales et morales*. Edited by I. Bruns. Berlin: Reimer, 1892. Translation by R. Sharples: *Quaestiones*. London: Duckworth, 1992.

———. *Metaphysics*. Translated by W. D. Ross. In *The Basic Works of Aristotle*, edited by R. McKeon. New York: Random House, 1941.

———. *Posterior Analytics*. Translated by G.R.G. Mure. In *The Basic Works of Aristotle*, edited by R. McKeon. New York: Random House, 1941.

Berkeley, George. *A Treatise Concerning the Principles of Human Knowledge*. Oxford: Oxford University Press, 1996. First published in 1710–34.

Bolzano, B. *Paradoxien des Unendlichen*. Edited by B. Van Rootselaar. Hamburg: Felix Meiner, 1975.

Condillac, Étienne Bonnot de. *Traité de l'art de penser*. Paris: Vrin, 1981. First published in *Cours d'études*, 1769–73.

———. *Essai sur l'origine des connaissances humaines*. Paris: Alive, 1998. First published in 1748. Translation by Hans Aarsleff: *Essay on the Origin of Human Knowledge*. Cambridge: Cambridge University Press, 2001.

Hamilton, William. *Lectures on Metaphysics and Logic*. 4 vols. Edinburgh: William Blackwood and Sons, 1861–66.

Hume, David. *A Treatise of Human Nature*. Edited by L. A. Selby-Bigge and P. H. Nidditch. Oxford: Clarendon Press, 1978. First published in 1888.

Lafleur, C., ed. *Philosophica disciplina*, in *Quatre Introductions à la philosophie au XIIIe siècle*. Paris: Vrin, 1988.

Locke, John. *An Essay Concerning Human Understanding*. Edited and introduced by P. H. Nidditch. Oxford: Clarendon Press, 1975. First published in 1689.

Mill, John Stuart. *An Examination of Sir William Hamilton's Philosophy*. Vol. 9 in *Collected Works*. Toronto: University of Toronto Press, 1979. *Examination* first published in 1865.

Plotinus. *The Enneads*. Translated by Stephen MacKenna. Burdett, NY: Larson Publications, 1992.

ABSURD

The absurd is what is dissonant or is *not heard* (cf. Lat. *surdus*), and is defined as a discord or disagreement with the understanding or reason, or with meaning, including the meaning of life. The term thus provides access to three main networks—logical, linguistic, and psychological. We will refer first to the English term "nonsense," in which these three networks intersect, because it forces us to think about the positive dimension of this dissonance: see NONSENSE.

I. The Absurd and Reason

The absurd is contrary to reason as a faculty of the mind (see *REASON* and parts of the articles LOGOS and MADNESS). But beyond this general definition, the absurd designates an actual manifestation of the absence of reason; therefore to define it we have to specify the criteria of the rational, regarding either logical requirements (thus arguing "from the absurd" and *reductio ad absurdum* are based on noncontradiction; see PRINCIPLE) or practical values (see PRAXIS, *PRUDENCE,* and parts of PHRONÊSIS). The absurd is thus neither simply the false (see *FALSE,* TRUTH) nor the absence of good sense (see COMMON SENSE). It designates a radical disconnection with the facts (see MATTER OF FACT, SACHVERHALT).

II. The Absurd and Meaning

Beyond the logical question of contradiction there is that of the rules of language and the criteria of meaning (see SENSE, HOMONYM, SIGNIFIER/SIGNIFIED). The possession or endowment of meaning depends in particular on a syntax; apparently correct sentences can be nonsensical (*unsinnig*, as opposed to *sinnlos* [meaningless]). This is the case for metaphysical utterances, according to some philosophers (Wittgenstein, Carnap) who make critical use of nonsense, doing away with propositions and sentences that say nothing (see PROPOSITION).

III. The Absurd and Existence

The absurd, as a sensation of the absence of meaning, is also something experienced (see ERLEBEN). Defined by Albert Camus as the "mystery and strangeness of the world," it belongs to the French vocabulary of existentialism, which we have explored in its German source (see DASEIN). It is an ontological affect broadly described in the works of Schelling, Kierkegaard, Freud, and Heidegger (see ANXIETY and, more generally, *MALAISE*) in connection with "facticity" (see TATSACHE, Box 1).

In a specific, positive way, the three components of the absurd—logical, linguistic, and existential—are at work in the French word *esprit*; "nonsense" refers to a specific form of humor related in English to "wit" and in German to *Witz* (see NONSENSE, *WITTICISM*).

➤ BELIEF, *NOTHING*

ACEDIA (SPANISH)

FRENCH	*tristesse, acédie*
GREEK	*akêdeia* [ἀκήδεια], *akêdia* [ἀκηδία]
LATIN	*taedium*

➤ *MALAISE* [MELANCHOLY, SPLEEN], and DASEIN, DESENGAÑO, OIKEIÔSIS, SORGE, VERGÜENZA

Through the intermediary of monastic Latin, *acedia*, "weariness, indifference" (Cassian, *De institutis coenobiorum*, 10.2.3; RT: *PL*, vol. 49, cols. 363–69), the rich Greek concept of *akêdeia*, a privative formed on *kêdos* [κῆδος], "care," and bearing the twofold meaning of lacking care (negligence) and absence of care (from lassitude or from serenity), established itself in the Spanish language in such a way as to create through three phonetic variations of a single term—*acedia, acidia, accidia*—a concept that belongs simultaneously to the communal and the moral registers. The Greek was originally associated with social rituals; in philosophical Latin from Seneca on, it was related to the moral virtue of intimacy, but its contemporary usage has returned it to a collective dimension.

The Greek *akêdeia* is simultaneously part of the register of the obligations owed to others and part of the register of self-esteem: this breadth of meaning determines the later variations. On the social level, the substantive *kêdos*, "care, concern," is specialized as early as Homer in two particular uses: mourning, the honors rendered to the dead, and union, family relationship through marriage or through alliance; *kêdeia* [κήδεια] (adj. *kêdeos* [κήδεος]) is the attention that must be paid to the dead, as well as the concern and care for allies, characteristic of this relationship of alliance, which is distinct from that of blood and also contributes to *philia* [φιλία], to the well-being of the city-state (Aristotle, *Politics*, 9.1280b 36; see LOVE and POLIS); *ho kêdemôn* [ὁ κηδεμών] refers to all those who protect, for example, tutelary gods (Xenophon, *Cyropaedia*, 3.3.21). *Akêdês* [ἀκηδής] qualifies in an active sense, in a positive way, someone who is exempt from care and anxiety (Hesiod, *Theogony*, 5.489, apropos of the "invincible and impassive" Zeus, but also, negatively, the serving woman or negligent man; Homer, *Odyssey*, 17.319; Plato, *Laws*, 913c); in the passive sense, it designates a person who is neglected (*Odyssey*, 20.130) or abandoned without burial (like Hector, *Iliad*, 24.554). How can the lack of care, *akêdeia*, become a virtue of the reflexive type?

The twofold sense of the term (transitive: care for others; reflexive: care for oneself) is maintained in the meaning of the Spanish word *acedia*. The first movement toward the ethics of intimacy is determined by practical philosophy's reflection on the finitude of human life. The event represented by death produces a sadness that seems to have no consolation. The moral reaction to situations in which one finds oneself fearing such a finitude is presented in an active and critical way in the ethics developed by Seneca in the *Consolations*. Grace and purity can temper sadness ("Marcum blandissimum puerum, ad cujus conspectum nulla potest durare tristitia" [Marcus, this boy, so gentle, before whom no sadness can last]; *De consolatione ad Helviam*, 18.4). But above all, it is the effort of reason and study that can overcome any sadness ("liberalia studia: illa sanabunt vulnus tuum, illa omnem tristitiam tibi evellent" [these studies will heal your wound, will free you from any sadness]; *De consolatione ad Helviam*, 17.3). This view of internal control is foundational for a style rooted in the culture of the South: the sober acceptance of death, and more generally, of finitude. *Acidia* is conceived as having a twofold psychological and theological meaning. First of all, it is a passion of the *animus* and is therefore one of the four kinds of sadness, the other three being *pigritia*, "laziness," *tristitia*, "sadness" properly so called, and *taedium*, "boredom."

In Christian monasticism of the fourth and fifth centuries, especially in Cassian and the eastern desert fathers, *acedia* is one of the seven or eight temptations with which the monks might have to struggle at one time or another. Usually mentioned between sadness and vainglory in a list that was to become that of the "seven deadly sins," it is characterized by a pronounced distaste for spiritual life and the eremitic ideal, a discouragement and profound boredom that lead to a state of lethargy or to the abandonment of monastic life. It was designated by the expression "noonday demon," which is supposed to come from verse 6 of Psalm 91. Thomas Aquinas opposes *acedia* to the joy that is inherent in the virtue of charity and makes it a specific sin, as a sadness with regard to spiritual goods (*Summa theologica*, IIa, IIae, q. 35). Fray Luis de Granada adopted this idea (*Escritos espirituales*, chap. 13), placing *acedia* among the seven deadly sins. If it is equivalent to the more widespread terms *tedio* (*taedium*) and *pereza* (*pigritia*), that is because it is the result of an excess of dispersion or idle chatter, and of the sadness and indifference (*incuria*) produced by the difficulty of obtaining spiritual goods. Thus *desolación* (*desolatio*) is supposed also to be a term related to *acedia*, and is often employed in spiritual and mystical literature—from Saint John of the Cross to Ignatius of Loyola—and it subsists in the vocabulary of moral sentiments.

The secular sense that the word has acquired in modern Spanish can make *acidia* or *acedia* the result of a situation of crisis and social conflict. In his *Historia de España*, Juan de Mariana connects the common sense of *acedia* (derived from the adjective *acedo*, from Lat. *acidus*, "bitter, acid") with the deprivation and need to which the poor are subject. The opposition between *acedia* and *amor* is often found in writers of the golden age, notably Cervantes:

Mírala si se pone ahora sobre el uno, ahora sobre el otro pie, si te repite la respuesta que te diere dos veces, si la muda de blanda en áspera, de aceda en amorosa.

(Should she be standing, observe whether she rests now on one foot and now on the other, if she repeats her reply two or three times, if she passes from gentleness to austerity, from asperity to tenderness.)

Among the Spanish moralists of our time, Miguel de Unamuno and Pío Baroja seem to be the last to use the term *acedia* in this way, while at the same time situating it among those that express collective feelings of distress or spiritual decline: the absence of care for oneself thus appears as a phenomenon of society and culture that does not dare to confront the demands of the transformation of modern identity. This crisis situation makes *acedia* an equivalent of routine, the outcome of a tradition received in an uncritical way, incapable of bringing new personal and collective resources to bear on it. The *tristeza de las cosas*, the "sadness of things," an expression of the feeling of ephemeralness, is a formula that, even though it goes back to late romanticism in Francisco Villaespesa, adds an aesthetic dimension. It involves the naturalization or loss of *aura* discussed by Walter Benjamin, who draws on Baudelaire's notion of "spleen" and on the phenomenology of the consciousness of loss or collective distress that follows the great upheavals of modernization (*Das Passagen-Werk*). The sociological reception of *acedia* moves, starting with the interwar period, in two directions: the first works on the economic causes of contemporary distress and on the forms of revolt that follow from it (Deleito y Piñuela), the other on postmodern aesthetic pleasure (Eugenio d'Ors), with notions such as *tedio opulento* (opulent boredom).

José Miguel Marinas

BIBLIOGRAPHY

Benjamin, Walter. *Das Passagen-Werk*. Vol. 5 of *Gesammelte Schriften*. Edited by R. Tiedemann. Frankfurt: Suhrkamp, 1982. Translation by H. Eiland and K. McLaughlin: *The Arcades Project*. Cambridge, MA: Harvard University Press, 1999.

Cervantes, Miguel de. *Don Quixote*. Translated by John Ormsby, revised by J. R. Jones and K. Douglas. New York: Norton, 1981.

De Granada, Luis. Chap. 13, in *Escritos espirituales*. Vol. 3 of *Obras completas*. Madrid: Fundación Universitaria Española, 1988.

De Mariana, Juan. *Historia de España*. Saragosse: Ebro, 1964. Translation by John Stevens: *The General History of Spain*. London: R. Sare, 1699.

Deleito y Piñuela, José. *El Sentimiento de tristeza en la literatura contemporanea*. Barcelona: Minerva, 1917.

D'Ors, Eugenio. *Oceanografía del tedio*. Barcelona: Calpe, 1920.

Meltzer, Françoise. "Acedia and Melancholia." In *Walter Benjamin and the Demands of History*. Ithaca, NY: Cornell University Press, 1996.

Villaespesa, Francisco. *Tristitiae rerum*. Madrid: Imp. Arroyave, 1906.

ACT

"Act" comes from Latin *actum*, the nominalized passive past participle of *agere*, which means "to push ahead of oneself," like the Greek *agein* [ἄγειν] (cf. *agôn* [ἀγών], struggle, trial); the Latin verb is differentiated, on the one hand, from *ducere*, "walk at the head of" (like Gr. *archêin* [ἄρχειν]; cf. PRINCIPLE), and on the other hand from *facere*, "to do," insofar as it implies duration, activity, and achievement rather than specific, instantaneous action (thus *agere aetatem, vitam*, pass time, life). *Actus*, the fact of moving, an action or the result of action, is a doublet of *actio* (same etymology), but the duality allows significant specializations: *actus* designates the action of a play (which Aristotle designates by the words *prattein* [πράττειν] or *pragmata* [πράγματα]) or its subdivision into acts, whereas *actio* is juridical and rhetorical (court action, oratorical action, pleading). Thus "actor" refers both to the character in a play and the person who plays that character: see ACTOR; cf. MIMÊSIS, *PASSION*.

The vocabulary of "act" is drawn from three great pairs of oppositions—ontological, ethical, and pragmatic—which constantly intersect with each other.

I. Ontology: Potential and Act

1. In Latin, the distinction between *potentia* and *actus* is used to translate the Aristotelian distinction between *dunamis* [δύναμις] and *energeia* [ἐνέργεια]. *Actus* translates the two terms of the Greek differentiation between *ergon* [ἔργον] and *energeia* [ἐνέργεια], which French has difficulty rendering without using two roots, *œuvre* for *ergon* (from *werg-; cf. Ger. *Wirkung*) and *acte* for *energeia*: for the Greek, see FORCE, Box 1, PRAXIS, Box 1, ESSENCE, *TO BE,* WORK.

2. On the ontological gradation between potential and act, see, in addition to the Aristotelian definition of movement (FORCE, Box 1): ESSENCE, ESTI, *TO BE,* PROPERTY; cf. TO TI ÊN EINAI and *DYNAMIC*. It culminates in the conception of god as "pure act"; see INTELLECTUS, and cf. GOD.

    On the way in which the Latin vocabulary of actuality is thus transposed into the register of reality, see REALITY (with the study of the doublet *Realität/Wirklichkeit*) and, for the Italian system, ATTUALITÀ; cf. RES.

3. Moreover, *dunamis* signifies both "potentiality" as the "not yet" of the act, and the "power" that results from it: on this difference, which Latin renders by means of the two terms *potentia* and *potestas*, see *DYNAMIC* and *POWER* [MACHT; cf. HERRSCHAFT].

4. Potentiality can thus become not the absence of the act, but rather its eminent quality and the mark of the human, which makes the act a work. As for the "failed act" whose success depends precisely on the fact that it is failed, see INGENIUM, Box 3; cf. UNCONSCIOUS, *WITTICISM* [NONSENSE].

II. Ethics: Action and Passion

1. The distinction between action and passion has been one of the matrices of ethical thought ever since the philosophical schools of antiquity, which privileged the first term, though they sometimes interpreted it differently (one can be active with regard to oneself in the form of peace of mind); see PATHOS, *PASSION,* and cf. LOVE, *WISDOM*. The emergence of the vocabulary of the will as a desiring faculty intersects with the same problematics; see WILL, WILLKÜR, and *LIBERTY* (ELEUTHERIA, Box 2).

2. An exploration of the main systems valorizing action by extending moral action to historicity and politics will be found under PRAXIS and VIRTÙ. The Russian *postupok* [поступок] designates the ethical act carried out by a person (*ličnost'* [личность]; see RUSSIAN), and is characterized by responsibility and commitment; see POSTUPOK. Finally, the Fichtean neologism *Tathandlung*, which is irreducible to an *Akt*, beyond the simple paradigms of *tun, handeln,* and *wirken* (do, act, work), and beyond the Kantian *Faktum* (fact), reduplicates the posing of an act/fact by the achievement of what is posed, in accord with the equation I = I (see TATSACHE) and opens the way to pragmatics.

III. Pragmatics: Speaking and Acting

1. Contemporary developments, in particular, in analytical philosophy, have led to a reorganization of fields and disciplines around a problematics of action that owes much of its power to the polysemy of the English term "agency"; see AGENCY; see also AFFORDANCE. The domain of thought and language is its necessary condition and element; see SPEECH ACT; cf. INTENTION, SENSE, TRUTH.

2. On the way in which a philosophical idiom tends to develop its own pragmatics, we might refer to the example of Italian, which, even when it translates German idealism, preserves or renews a thematics of the actual (*effetuale*) truth of the thing that refers to its event-character rather than to its universal historicity or the performativity of discourse; see ATTUALITÀ.

➤ DASEIN, *FACT*, SOUL

ACTOR, THESPIAN, COMEDIAN

FRENCH	*acteur, personnage, comédien*
GERMAN	*Schauplatz, Schauspieler, Akteur, Person*
GREEK	*prosôpon* [πρόσωπον], *hupokritês* [ὑποκριτής]
ITALIAN	*attore, comico, maschera*
LATIN	*persona, actor, histrio*

➤ ACT, MIMÊSIS, PATHOS, *PERSON*, PRAXIS, SUBJECT

In seventeenth-century French, the word *acteur* still referred both to the dramatic character who acts and whose actions the play "represents" (in conformity with the notion of *mimêsis praxeôn* [μίμησις πράξεων] in Aristotle's *Poetics*), and to the person who plays the character onstage and whom we call the "actor." The character was subsequently differentiated from the actor. In Italy, it was only in the eighteenth century, under the probable influence of the development in French, that the word *attore*, which up to that point had signified solely the character who acts, took on the meaning of a stage actor, whereas the word *personnaggio* was established to designate what French calls a *personnage* and English a "character." All of these shifts in meaning take place within the semantic field of the Latin language as it was constituted in the domain of rhetoric. The ambiguity and evolution of the word "actor" are in fact related to the term's double heritage, theatrical and rhetorical: on the stage, the actor is the person who puts on a voice-amplifying mask (*prosôpon* [πρόσωπον]) and thus takes on the traits of the character he represents. In this sense, his action is a passion, he is inhabited by a character. But the actor is also an orator, whose *actio*, gestural and vocal, is an esteemed art: he acts out his text and his character, which without him would have no effect. He is then an actor in the active sense of the term, the coauthor of the effect produced.

I. *Actio* and *Hupokrisis*

Latin has several terms to designate the stage actor: *histrio*, *actor*, *comoedus*, *tragoedus*, etc. *Histrio* already includes all the pejorative values of the French word *histrion* or the English "histrionic." It is opposed to *actor*, the stage actor who is trained in the great discipline of rhetoric and who can serve as a model for the orator. We see this in Cicero's esteem for the actor Roscius, for whom he composed a plea. These exchanges between oratory art and dramatic art "reformed" in accord with rhetoric were implied by the identity of the terms that Latin used in referring to the theater and the courtroom. *Actio* designates the art of the actor, that of the orator, and a legal suit; *actor* designates the actor ennobled by his rhetorical training and the plaintiff in a legal case; *agere* is applied both to a procedure (*agere causam*) and to a theatrical role (*agere fabulam*), or to a social role assumed with responsibility and vigor.

Actio (delivery), in the rhetorical sense of the term, belongs to what might be called corporeal eloquence. Cicero defines it this way: "Est enim actio quasi corporis quaedam eloquentia, cum constet e voce atque motu" (In fact, delivery is a kind of elocution of the body, since it consists in voice and gesture, *De oratore* 17.55). Even though delivery is only one of the five parts of rhetoric (the four others being invention, disposition, elocution, and memory), Cicero accords it first place among the means of persuasion: "Actio, inquam, in dicendo una dominatur. Sine hac sumus orator esse in numero nullo potest" (Delivery, I assert, is the dominant factor in oratory; without delivery the best speaker cannot be of any account at all, *De oratore* 3.56.213). It is through *actio* that the orator succeeds in moving his audience, in acting upon it, and thus in winning its support. The role attributed to oratorical *actio* is thus inseparable from the place accorded in Ciceronian rhetoric to *movere*, that is, to emotion or passion. To the emotionally moving body of the orator corresponds the deeply moved body of the audience. In this sense, the orator has much to learn from actors, as Cicero recognizes in speaking of Roscius. But the orator is not only an *actor*, he is also an *auctor*. As the author of his discourse, he is not a simple imitator who limits himself to reproducing gestures and intonations. His *actio* is effective only because it is the expression of a passion whose effects the orator is the first to feel.

In this conception of rhetorical *actio*, we see the mark of Aristotle's influence. As Cicero defines it, *actio* corresponds to what Aristotle calls *hupokrisis* [ὑπόκρισις], the art of the tragic actor. The term comes from *hupo-krinomai* [ὑπο-κρίνομαι], "to reply," which initially designated a rejoinder in a play, then came to indicate declamation and dissimulation:

> [Delivery (*autê*, sc. *hê hupokrisis*)] is, essentially, a matter of the right management of the voice to express the various emotions—of speaking loudly, softly, or between the two; of high, low, or intermediate pitch; of the various rhythms that suit various subjects . . . and just as in drama the actors now count for more than the poets, so it is in the contests of public life, owing to the defects of our political institutions.

> (Aristotle, *Rhetoric* 3.1, 1403b26–35, in *Complete Works*, ed. Barnes)

But this definition concerns only the forms of vocal expression, and not gestures, whose importance Aristotle recognizes, including among the poets:

> The poet should remember to put the actual scenes as far as possible before his eyes [*pro ommatôn* (πρὸ ὀμμάτων)]. . . . As far as may be, too, the poet should even act his story with the very gestures [*tois skêmasin* (τοῖς σχήμασιν)] of his personages. Given the same natural qualifications, he who feels the emotions to be described will be the most convincing; distress and anger, for instance, are portrayed most truthfully by one who is feeling them at the moment.

> (Aristotle, *Poetics* 1455a22–32, in *Complete Works*, ed. Barnes)

This helps to explain a certain hesitation among Latin authors regarding the term best suited to render this form of eloquence specific to rhetorical *actio*. *Pronuntiatio*, Quintilian notes, is generally considered equivalent to *actio*, but the former seems to refer to the voice (*voce*), the latter to gesture (*gestu*), for Cicero defines *actio* sometimes as "a form of speech" (*quasi sermonem*), and sometimes as "a kind of physical eloquence" (*eloquentia quandam corporis*). However, in his *Institutio oratoria* (11.3.1), Quintilian distinguishes within *actio* two elements that are the same as those found in oratorical delivery (*pronuntiationis*): voice and gesture (*vocem atque motum*). Thus the two terms can be used interchangeably. But starting with *De oratore*, Cicero uses chiefly *actio*, a preference that corresponds to the importance he places on visible and thus silent forms of physical eloquence in the techniques of persuasion.

Redeveloped on the basis of a different conception of the action/passion pair that comes out of Descartes, the problematics of the rhetorical delivery were to play a fundamental role in a seventeenth-century theory of art. Theoreticians of art constantly use the word "action" in a technical, rhetorical sense, that is, in the sense of a physical *actio*, as in Charles Le Brun's lecture on the expression of the passions: "Since it is true that most of the passions of the soul produce bodily actions, we must discover what physical actions express the passions, and what an action is" (lecture delivered on 7 April 1668, in Mérot, *Les conférences*).

■ See Box 1.

1

Prosôpon, persona: From theater to grammar

➤ I / ME / MYSELF, Box 1; SUBJECT, Box 6

Since Homer, *prosôpon* [πρόσωπον], etymologically "what is opposite the gaze," has designated the human "face" in particular, and then, metaphorically, the "façade" of a building, and synechdochically, the whole "person" bearing the face. Another remarkable semantic extension is that of the theatrical "mask" (Aristotle, *Poetics* 1449a36), leading in turn to the meaning "character in a drama" (Alexandrian stage directions for dramatic works regularly included the list of the *prosôpa tou dramatos* [πρόσωπα τοῦ δράματος]), and then to a narrative. Its Latin equivalent, *persona*, refers in its turn to the mask that makes the voice resonate (*personare*), before it designates a character, a personality, and a grammatical person (Varro).

The meaning of the compound *prosôpopoiein* [προσωπο-ποιεῖν]—"to compose in direct discourse," that is, to make the characters speak themselves—clearly shows that the dramatic meaning of *prosôpon* had a particularly great influence on the history of the word. In any event, it seems quite likely that when grammarians adopted *prosôpon* to designate the grammatical "person," they were thinking of the dialogue situation characteristic of the theatrical text, which makes use of the alternation "I-you": the face-to-face encounter between person(age)s is rooted in the category of the "person" (see SUBJECT, Box 6).

Whereas terms like "tense" (*chronos* [χρόνος]) and "case" (*ptôsis* [πτῶσις]) are attested before they appear in strictly grammatical texts, this is not the case for *prosôpon* used to refer to the "person" as a linguistic category. On the other hand, in the earliest grammatical texts, and in a way that remains perfectly stable later on, *prosôpon* is adopted to describe both the *protagonists* of the dialogue and the *marks*, both pronominal and verbal, of their inscription in the linguistic material. In fact, the main difficulty encountered by grammarians regarding the notion of *prosôpon* seems to have been how properly to articulate reference to real persons occupying differentiated positions in linguistic exchange (speaker, addressee, other) with reference to the person as a grammatical mark. This difficulty occurs notably in a quarrel about definition. In the *Technê* attributed to Dionysius Thrax (*Grammatici Graeci* 1.1 [chap. 13, p. 51.3 Uhlig = 57.18 Lallot]), the verbal accident of *prosôpon* is defined as follows:

Prosôpa tria, prôton, deuteron, triton; prôton men aph' hou ho logos, deuteron de pros hon ho logos, triton de peri hou ho logos [Πρόσωπα τρία, πρῶτον, δεύτερον, τρίτον· πρῶτον μὲν ἀφ' οὗ ὁ λόγος, δεύτερον δὲ πρὸς ὃν ὁ λόγος, τρίτον δὲ περὶ οὗ ὁ λόγος].

There are three persons: first, second, third. The first is the one from whom the utterance comes, the second, the one to whom it is addressed, the third, the one about whom he is speaking.

This minimal definition clearly sets forth the two protagonists of the dialogue, distinguishing them by their position in the exchange, and introduces without special precaution a third position, characterized as constituting the subject matter of the utterance. The parallelism of the three definitions—a simple pronoun for each "person"—masks the lack of symmetry between the (real) first and second persons and the third person; the latter, as Benveniste pointed out (*Problèmes de linguistique générale*, 228), may very well not be a "person" in the strictest sense.

This definition, which remained canonical for several centuries, was attacked by Apollonius Dyscolus, who completed it as follows (I adopt the formulation in Choeroboscos [*Grammatici Graeci* 4.2 (p. 10.27 Uhlig)], a Byzantine witness to the Alexandrian master):

Prôton men aph' hou ho logos peri emou tou prosphônountos, deuteron de pros hon ho logos peri autou tou prosphônoumenou, triton de peri hou ho logos mête prosphônountos mête prosphônoumenou [πρῶτον μὲν ἀφ' οὗ ὁ λόγος περὶ ἐμοῦ τοῦ προσφωνοῦντος, δεύτερον δὲ πρὸς ὃν ὁ λόγος περὶ αὐτοῦ τοῦ προσφωνουμένου, τρίτον δὲ περὶ οὗ ὁ λόγος μήτε προσφωνοῦντος μήτε προσφωνουμένου].)

The first person is the one from whom the utterance comes *meaning me, the speaker*, the second, the one who to whom the utterance is addressed *meaning the addressee himself*, the third the one about whom the utterance speaks *and who is neither the speaker nor the addressee*.

Apollonius's arrangement contributes useful explanations: (a) each "person," including the first two, can be the subject of the utterance; (b) the third is defined negatively as being neither the first nor the second (which implicitly opens up the possibility that it is a "person" only in an extended sense, insofar as it does not need to be competent as an interlocutor); (c) the overlap of enunciation and enunciated is explicit: there is a first person when the utterance refers to the enunciator-source, a second person when it refers to the addressee, and a third when it refers to someone or something else.

Despite the incontestable advance represented by Apollonius's revision, it nonetheless leaves an ambiguity regarding the *designatum* of *prosôpon*: are we talking about extralinguistic entities, "persons" engaging in dialogue or not, or are we talking about linguistic entities, "accidents" of the conjugated verb and the pronominal paradigm (personal pronouns)? Apparently the former, which is surprising coming from a grammarian who prides himself on correcting another grammarian. In fact, there is hardly any doubt that in Apollonius, the ambiguity I mentioned is still attached to the term *prosôpon*. Consider the following text, taken from Apollonius's *Syntax* 3.59 (*Grammatici Graeci* 2.2 [p. 325.5–7 Uhlig]):

Ta gar meteilêphota prosôpa tou pragmatos eis prosôpa anemeristhê, peripatô, peripateis, peripatei [τά γὰρ μετειληφότα πρόσωπα τοῦ πράγματος εἰς πρόσωπα ἀνεμερίσθη, περιπατῶ, περιπατεῖς, περιπατεῖ].

The persons who take part in the act [of walking] are distributed into persons: I walk, you walk, he/she walks.

We can interpret this to mean that in a group of persons—extralinguistic entities—who are walking, every utterance concerning the walk will elicit the appearance of verb endings distributing the walkers among the three grammatical persons: such is the alchemy of Apollonius's *prosôpon*.

Jean Lallot

BIBLIOGRAPHY

Benveniste, Émile. "Structure des relations de personne dans le verbe." Chap. 18 in *Problèmes de linguistique générale*, 225–36. Paris: Gallimard, 1966. Translation by M. A. Meek: *Problems in General Linguistics*. Coral Gables, FL: University of Miami Press, 1971.

Grammatici Graeci. Edited by A. Hilgard, R. Schneider, G. Uhlig, and A. Lentz. Leipzig: Teubner, 1878–1902. Reprint, Hildesheim, Ger.: Olms, 1965.

Lallot, Jean. *La grammaire de Denys le Thrace*. Paris: Le Centre National de la Recherche Scientifique, 1998.

II. The Actor: Character and Thespian

In seventeenth-century France, an *acteur* was primarily the character who is active, who is involved in a dramatic action (in accord with the etymology: *acteur* is derived from the Latin *agere*, "to do"). He is thus the "dramatic character" as such. It is in this sense that the words *acteur* and *personnage*, used more or less interchangeably, appear at the head of the list of the dramatis personae at the beginning of each play, but with a clear preference for the word *acteur*. In contrast to the imaginary *acteur* conceived by the author, the thespian is the person who mounts the boards and whose craft consists in acting out the drama in the broad sense of a "theatrical play composed in accord with the rules of the art" (RT: Furetière, *Dictionnaire universel*) that the seventeenth century accorded to this expression.

It is striking to see that it is precisely in the seventeenth century that the word *acteur* appears in French—though rarely as a synonym of *comédien* (actor). The word *comédien* remains connected with the profession of representing onstage, whereas the word *acteur* refers to the character involved in the dramatic action as well as to the person who plays him. Pierre Corneille employs both *acteur* and *personnage* in speaking about the characters in his plays, and François Hédelin, abbé d'Aubignac, in his book *La pratique du théâtre*, entitles one of the chapters "Des personnages ou Acteurs, et ce que le Poète doit y observer" (251).

The art of the thespian, the playwright, and theatrical literature in general was greatly stimulated by the rediscovery of Quintilian's *Institutio oratoria* and the cult of Cicero, as well as by the seventeenth-century *renovatio studii*. This powerful network of Jesuit schools, which based its pedagogical activity on a Christianized version of Quintilian's *Institutio oratoria* and on the *Ratio studiorum*, the basic document of Jesuit education, trained an audience familiar with the rhetorical disciplines. Eager to win the esteem of courts and academies, the thespians of the seventeenth century tried to distinguish themselves from more primitive players by emphasizing their complete mastery of oratorical delivery.

A French thespian of the seventeenth century, and especially a tragedian, found himself in a situation analogous to that of the orator: not having a mask, he had to rely solely on the evocative magic of verbal figures to play his role. By studying characters and their bodily expression, gestural expression was also governed by customs of an ethological nature. Moreover, the ascetic simplicity of the tragic stage between 1630 and 1660 coincided with an increasing interest in questions of eloquence and rhetoric. The stage became a testing site for the powers of rhetorical discourse left to its own devices. The thespian's delivery was thus almost as important as the power of the verbal figures that the playwright put into the text for him. This emphasis on delivery reveals the idea of an imminent power in the text that is reflected in the distribution of roles; only an excellent actor would be capable of realizing this potential in performance. But if the character's written part contains a potentiality that has to be actualized, the thespian has to exhibit onstage this passage from written words to his body. Both the character and the thespian are therefore *acteurs* in the strong sense of the term. One of them acts on the other. Thus the fictive unity of the character represented by the thespian onstage is always interrupted by the reminder of the invisible text, and the thespian, by his bodily presence, recites and plays the text of another, absent person—of an author who has created the character.

This vague and troubling difference between the thespian and the character is at the heart of Jean Rotrou's *Véritable Saint Genest* (staged in 1645), a play written in the tradition of the play-within-a-play. A pagan thespian, Genest, plays the role of a Christian martyr, Adrian, in a play. In the scene where he represents Adrian's conversion, the thespian suddenly becomes the character he is playing. "Heaven . . . has made me its actor [*acteur*]," he says, the word *acteur* having here the twofold sense of someone who acts on behalf of an idea or a religious belief, and of a thespian who acts on the scene of the great theater of the world. Struck by grace, the thespian leaves his role to express himself in his own name: "This is no longer Adrian speaking, it is Genest who is expressing himself; / This play is no longer a play, but a truth / . . . Where, myself the object and the actor [*acteur*] of myself, / . . . I profess a law" (vv. 1324–30). The thespian becomes the author of his own text at the very moment in which he is acted upon by another text and speaks in the name of another author, the divine author. Playing on the reflexive structure of the play-within-a-play, Rotrou was able to represent in this drama the indeterminacy that characterizes all relations between the thespian and his character, as well as the considerable stakes that flow from this and that go so far as to involve, as an absent character, the supreme author.

III. The *Inventio* of Italian Actors: *Attore, Comico, Maschera*

At the beginning of the seventeenth century, *attore* still indicated the person who acts, who does things. The *Vocabolario degli accademici della Crusca* (1612) gives *facitore* as a synonym of *attore*, with, on the one hand, a reference to God as the "attore della batitudine" (the author or origin of beatitude), and on the other hand, a reference to the plaintiff, the person who pleads a case—a meaning still in use in modern Italian.

One of the reasons that the Italian language of the sixteenth and seventeenth centuries did not actualize the meaning contained in the Latin word *actor* to designate the thespian has to do with the existence, starting in the middle of the sixteenth century, of troupes of professional thespians who wrote their own texts. The formation of these troupes is connected with the birth of the *commedia dell'arte*. These thespians had left the limited domain of *actio* in order to practice in that of *inventio* as well. In fact, the expression *il comico*, whose initial meaning indicates a relationship to the theater, includes the productive aspect of theatrical texts. In their work, these thespians practiced *dispositio*, *elocutio*, and *memoria*, thus covering the whole range of rhetorical creation. In addition, they were capable of representing on the stage any of the period's theatrical genres. That was what distinguished them from the cruder players called *buffoni*, *mimi*, *istrioni*, and *comedianti*. Several theoretical texts written by professional thespians, such as Francesco Andreini's *Le bravure del Capitano Spavento* (1607) or Niccolò Barbieri's *La supplica* (1634), emphasize this difference, seeking to ennoble the thespian's profession and to present him in a positive light as an expert in the rules of rhetoric.

The constraints of the theater market did not allow these professional thespians to produce the same play at the same place over an extended period of time. They were forced to produce new kinds of show. This is what was called at the time playing *all' improvviso* or *a soggeto*. This technique clearly distinguished the Italians from other European troupes. The Italian thespians were accustomed to raiding and dismembering rhetorical treatises or literary texts in order to extract from them *parti*, roles, which they would then slip into a kind of personal collection that each thespian kept concerning a single type of character (*primo amoroso*, servant, old Venetian merchant, etc.). They distinguished two aspects in the character, one that changed from one play to the next, and another that remained invariable and was called *la maschera*. The use of half-masks in leather emphasized the fixed aspect of characters. The masks determined the way a personage dressed, spoke, gestured, and so on, but not the character traits, which varied in each representation, depending on the different plots and the agreement of the other thespians. The secret of the "masks" of *commedia all'improvviso* resided in a constantly varying, subtle equilibrium between the indetermination of the character of a personage and the rigid predetermination of all the other elements. Thus the thespian becomes the author of a text that is created at the very moment of its representation and vanishes immediately afterward. His representation consists in verbal action similar to that of the orator, where what is said is both subject to strict rules and completely uncertain. We can understand why Molière and Shakespeare took such an interest in the technique of thespians who were able to combine the repetitive elements of dramatic characters with a great versatility of forms.

But soon the creative conjunction of the thespian and the author tended to become no more than an empty form. That is when there emerged a new conception of the thespian as *attore*, that is, as someone whose craft consisted in representing a text given in advance. Thus Carlo Goldoni, in his preface to the first collection of his comedies published in 1750, reproaches "mercenari comici nostri," that is, the professional thespians in Italian troupes, for altering and disfiguring texts "recitandole all'improvviso" (Goldoni, *Commedie*, 66). Goldoni was one of the first to speak of *attori*, clearly distinguishing the latter from *comici*. In his comedies, he reintroduced individual psychology in his characters by doing away with the fixed character traits of the *maschere*. The theatrical reform begun by Goldoni gave the Italian theater a literary and "authorial" orientation; the thespian came after the fact to incarnate and actualize a text written by an author.

From that point on, the word *attore* designates the thespian in general, the expression *il comico* being reserved for actors playing comic roles. Yet the productive aspect of the person who writes a comic theatrical text has remained. This meaning is preserved in the English "comedian," which designates a particular type of actor-author who performs alone on a stage, with "actor" designating those who perform in works made for the theater or the cinema—but there are many actors who lay claim to the tradition of the comedian, such as Woody Allen.

IV. *Schauplatz, Schauspieler, Akteur, Person*

Unlike French and Italian, German accentuates, in the word *Schauspieler*, the idea of the person who creates and shows a play, a theatrical illusion. The word has been used in German since the sixteenth century. In the seventeenth century, the actor was also designated by the expression *die darstellende Person*—the representing person. Starting in the first half of the eighteenth century, in German as in Italian, under the influence of French, the expressions *der Akteur* and *die Aktrice* were used, replacing the word *Komödiant*, which had taken on the pejorative sense of a person who feigns. But this use of the word *Akteur* is lost in modern German, where it still designates the person who is at the head of a political action.

The word *Schauspieler* was definitively established by the beginning of the nineteenth century. It derives from *Schauspiel*, used since the end of the sixteenth century in the general sense of shows presented before an audience, but also in the more restricted sense of theatrical representation. *Schauspiel* is connected with the word *Schauplatz*, which translates the Greek *theatron* [θέατρον], designating a platform set up and intended for juridical activities, plays, or ceremonies. Since the seventeenth century, this word has also had the sense of a dramatic setting. Thus at the beginning of Andreas Gryphius's *Leo Armenius* (1646): "Der Schauplatz ist Constantinopel" (The scene is Constantinople). In the same period, the word *Schaubühne* was used to designate a wooden scaffolding or platform set up for a show. But in the seventeenth century, people spoke simply of *Bühne*. In religious history, *Schauplatz* means "Calvary," and its eschatological sense refers to the earthly site where the end of the world will be revealed. In his *Origin of German Tragic Drama*, Walter Benjamin wrote a few famous pages on this last meaning. The *Schauplatz* of the baroque period is for him the place where history is secularized and where the temporal process settles into a spatial image.

As for the theatrical character, from the beginning of the sixteenth century, it is called *die Person, die spielende Person*. According to the Grimms, this usage derives from translations of the word *persona*, "mask," which appears in Latin comedy (RT: *Deutsches Wörterbuch*, s.v.). German thus does not distinguish between the real person and the fictive person.

Marco Baschera
Jacqueline Lichtenstein (I)

BIBLIOGRAPHY

Aristotle. *Complete Works*. Edited by Jonathan Barnes. 2 vols. Princeton, NJ: Princeton University Press, 1984.

Benjamin, Walter. *Ursprung des deutschen Trauerspiels*. In *Gesammelte Schriften*. Frankfurt: Suhrkamp, 1974. Translation by J. Osborne: *The Origin of German Tragic Drama*. London: NLB, 1977.

Brecht, Bertold. *Schriften zum Theater*. Frankfurt: Suhrkamp, 1957. Translations by J. Willett: "A Dialogue about Acting" and "A Letter to an Actor." In *Brecht on Theatre: The Development of an Aesthetic*. New York: Farrar, Straus and Giroux, 1992.

Fumaroli, Marc. *L'âge de l'éloquence*. Paris: Droz, 1980.

———. "Le statut du personnage dans la tragédie classique." *Revue d'Histoire du Théâtre* (July–Sept. 1972): 223–50.

Goldoni, Carlo. *Commedie*. Edited by N. Magnini. Turin: Unione Tipografica-Editrice Torinese, 1971.

Hédelin, François, abbé d'Aubignac. "Des personnages ou Acteurs, et ce que le Poète doit y observer." In *La pratique du théâtre* [1657], edited by Hans-Jörg Neuschäfe. Darmstadt, Ger.: Wilhelm Fink, 1971.

Lichtenstein, Jacqueline. *La couleur éloquente*. Paris: Flammarion, 1991. Translation by E. McVarish: *The Eloquence of Color: Rhetoric and Painting in the French Rhetorical Age*. Berkeley: University of California Press, 1993.

Mérot, Alain. *Les conférences de l'académie royale de peinture et de sculpture au XVIIe siècle*. Paris: École Nationale Supérieure des Beaux-Arts, 1996.

Rotrou, Jean. *Saint Genest and Venceslas*. Charleston, SC: Nabu, 2011.

Souiller, Didier, and Philippe Baron. *L'acteur en son métier*. Dijon, Fr.: Éditions universitaires de Dijon, 1997.

Stanislavski, Constantin. *An Actor Prepares*. London: Methuen, 1988.

Taviani, Ferdinando. *Il Segreto della commedia dell'arte: La memoria delle compagnie italiane del XVI, XVII et XVIII secolo*. Florence: La Casa Usher, 1982.

| AESTHETICS

FRENCH	*esthétique*
GERMAN	*Ästhetik* (n.), *ästhetisch* (adj.)
GREEK	*aisthêtikos* [αἰσθητικός]
LATIN	*aesthetica*

➤ ART, BEAUTY, EPISTEMOLOGY, ERSCHEINUNG, GOÛT, PERCEPTION, SENSE

Because of its etymology, the term "aesthetics" does not appear to pose any special problem of translation in its transposition from one European language to another. Created by Alexander Gottlieb Baumgarten (1714–1762), the neologism *Ästhetik* seemed, at least in the mind of the German philosopher, not to suffer from any ambiguity, and European philosophers, aware of its Greek origins and its insertion into Latin philosophical vocabulary, spontaneously adopted it widely. However, from the beginning of the nineteenth century, it stirred fascination and mistrust in equal measure. The problems, variable from one language to another and from one country to another, concern both the delimitation of the field of knowledge bearing on art and the beautiful, as well as the specialization of knowledge, methods, and objects relative to the study of the sensible. The epistemological coherence that seems to guarantee the nearly identical circulation of a term that is perfectly identifiable from one language to the next—whether English or Romanian, modern Greek, Spanish, Italian, and so forth—thenceforth appears to be an illusion.

I. Baumgarten and the Epistemology of a Science of the Sensible

Starting from the Platonic and Aristotelian distinction—later taken over by the Church Fathers—between *aisthêta* (sensible things or facts of perception) and *noêta* (intelligible things or fact of intelligibility), A. G. Baumgarten has no doubt, as early as 1735, in his *Meditationes philosophicae de nonnulis ad poema pertinentibus*, of the existence of a science of the perceptible world. "*Noêta* . . . are the objects of Logic, *aisthêta* are the objects of *aisthêtikê*, or Aesthetics" (§116). At least, this is how the philosopher, fifteen years before the publication (in Latin) of his *Aesthetica* (between 1750 and 1758), clarifies the object of a discipline that does not exist yet and that he attempts to define later, with a few variations. These variations aim to determine progressively the epistemological framework of aesthetics. In the first edition of his *Metaphysics* (1739), Baumgarten reconstructs, along the lines of the scholastic tradition, a kind of

trivium on the basis of the modalities of aesthetics, between rhetoric and poetics, which, in another work, he describes as follows: "The science of the mode of sensory knowledge and exposition is aesthetics; to the extent it aims at the slightest perfection of sensory thought and discourse, it is rhetoric; to the extent it aims at their greatest perfection, it is universal poetics" (*Aesthetica*, 533).

▪ See Box 1.

However, as though the project of a universal poetics seemed too restricted, Baumgarten abandons this definition in the subsequent editions of his *Aesthetica*, ending up with, in the same paragraph, a formulation that is supposed to attest to the complete autonomy of aesthetics (7th ed., 1779): "The science of the sensible mode of knowledge and exposition is aesthetics (logic of the lower faculty of knowledge, philosophy of the graces and the muses, lower gnoseology, the art of the beauty of thought, art of the analogon of reason)."

This is more or less the definition with which the *Aesthetica* of 1750 begins: "Aesthetics (or theory of liberal arts, lower gnoseology, art of the beauty of thought, art of the analogon of reason) is the science of sensible knowledge."

II. The Term "Aesthetics" in Latin, Greek, German, and Other Languages

This characterization of aesthetics, which Baumgarten thinks of as global and able to subsume under a single concept not only beauty and artistic taste but also perceptual experience, does a poor job of masking a plurality of definitions whose coherence is, certainly, far from being clear. In fact, Baumgarten reveals the cognitive dimension of aesthetics by playing on the amphibolous character of the word, at the cost of redundancies that come close to pleonasm—"theory," "science of knowledge," "gnoseology." He Latinizes the Greek adjective *aisthêtikos* as *aesthetica*, but he is also thinking of *sentio*, to perceive by the sense and (or) to perceive by the intellect, which is a way of reminding us, following Aristotle, that there are no *aisthêta* without *noêta* and that they cannot be dissociated, as Kant reminds us when he refers to the Greek adage: *aisthêta kai noêta* (the sensible and the intelligible, what can be sensed and what can be understood). But even this notion Baumgarten formulates, in his own way, in Latin: aesthetics is *ars analogi rationis* (art analogous to reason).

Thus, an equivocation affects the term "aesthetics," one which is all the more formidable since it is not evident, which reveals itself to be a source of difficulty and confusion even among those who use it and thus ratify its usage. While translators in European languages overcome their distress at a term with uncertain roots by trusting either Indo-European (*aiein*, to perceive) or Greek (*aisthanomai*, to feel), of which the Latin *sentio* is an acceptable equivalent according to Baumgarten, things are different for philosophers and thinkers who venture out to explore the field of aesthetics, which, as it is badly circumscribed, turns out to be unlimited.

Kant is certainly one of the first to have attracted attention to the specific, typically Germanic usage of the term aesthetics. In the chapter of the *Critique of Pure Reason* (trans. P. Guyer and A. Wood, 1998) devoted to the "Transcendental

1

Ästhetik

It is as a direct transcription of the German *Ästhetik* that the word *esthétique* enters a French dictionary for the first time, at the end of the eighteenth century. The *Supplément à l'Encyclopédie*, which was published in 1776, provides as a "new term" a note "Esthétique," which is simply a quasi-literal translation of the article "Ästhetik" in J. G. Sulzer's dictionary, *Allgemeine Theorie der schönen Künste* (General theory of fine arts) (1771). The word, documented in French as early as 1753, but not to be found in the RT: *Dictionnaire de l'Académie Française* in either the 1740 or 1762 editions, is thus elevated to lexicographical dignity. The translator of the note, who remains anonymous, comes from the milieu of the Berlin Academy, which played a central role in the exchanges between Germany and French encyclopedists. Sulzer may thus be considered a major agent in the linguistic exchanges in the domain of fine arts, and especially in the introduction of the Baumgartian theory into France. His name, somewhat eclipsed by Johann Joachim Winckelmann's coming into fashion, is nevertheless regularly cited by French theorists of art, such as Quatremère de Quincy. Besides this simple lexical importation, it is the whole project of the *Allgemeine Theorie* that is thus presented and transposed in the *Supplément*, since Sulzer had made this note one of the matrices of his dictionary.

The word's presence in French dictionaries was nonetheless a short one. By 1792 it had disappeared from the section of the *Encyclopedie méthodique* devoted to fine arts. It does not make itself at home in French until the mid-nineteenth century, notably with the publication in 1843 of T. Jouffroy's *Cours d'esthétique*. The comparison between the German note "Ästhetik" and its French translation in the *Supplément* also betrays some characteristic displacements of emphasis and interest. Though he remains relatively faithful to the original text, the translator nevertheless tends to attenuate Sulzer's criticisms of J.-B. Du Bos, and, on the other hand, to temper the praise of Baumgarten. Where the German presents Baumgarten as "daring," in a heroic gesture, to lay the first stones of this new science of aesthetics, the French, more skeptically, describes him as "hazardant [sic]". In general, the initial balance of the German note between speculative analysis of the essence of art and concrete examination of its different techniques seems to be turned upside-down in the French version, where the practical part is made much more precise, more dynamic, and more programmatic than in the German version. Aesthetics, in the French version, thus remains, up until the *Supplément*, more directly related to an empiricist and practical approach. It presents itself as an examination of the technical modalities of *the arts*, rather than as a speculative analysis of the foundations of *art*. Thus, from the first crossing of the border, a Franco-German divide emerges with regard to the word "esthétique," which the passage of time quickly accentuates.

Élisabeth Décultot

BIBLIOGRAPHY

Jouffroy, Théodore. *Cours d'esthétique*. Paris: Hachette, 1843.

Quatremère de Quincy, Antoine Chysostome. *An Essay on the Nature, the End, and the Means of Imitation in the Fine Arts.* Translated by J. C. Kent. New York: Garland, 1979.

Saint-Girons, Baldine. *Esthétique du XVIIIe siècle. Le modèle français*. Paris: P. Sers, 1990.

Sulzer, Johann Georg. "Ästhetik." Pp. 35–38 in vol. 1 of *Allgemeine Theorie der schönen Künster*, 4 vols. Edited by F. von Blankenburg. Leipzig: Weidemanns Erben and Reich, 1786–1787. First edition published in 1771.

———. *Aesthetics and the Art of Musical Composition in the German Enlightenment: Selected Writings of Johann Georg Sulzer and Heinrich Christoph Koch.* Edited by N. Kovaleff Baker and T. Christensen. Cambridge: Cambridge University Press, 1995.

Watelet, Claude-Henri, and Pierre-Charles Lévesque. *Dictionnaire des arts de peinture, sculpture et gravure* (Paris: Prault, 1792).

Aesthetic," he indicates the peculiar meaning of the word, which, he points out, only the Germans use to refer to the philosophy of the beautiful. Implicitly, he indicates here the difficulty of a transposition of the word into a foreign language. Kant, hoping to make this particular meaning of aesthetic more precise ("science of all the a priori principles of perception"), notes the following (156):

> The Germans are the only ones who now employ the word "aesthetics" [*Ästhetik*] to designate that which others call the critique of taste [*Kritik des Geschmacks*]. The ground for this is a failed hope, held by the excellent analyst Baumgarten, of bringing the critical estimation of the beautiful under principles of reason, and elevating its rules to a science. But this effort is futile. For the putative rules or criteria are merely empirical as far as their sources are concerned, and can therefore never serve as *a priori* rules according to which our judgment of taste must be directed; rather the latter constitutes the genuine touchstone of the correctness of the former. For this reason it is advisable again to desist from the use of this term and to save it for that doctrine which is true science (whereby one would come closer to the language and the sense of the ancients, among whom the division of cognition into *aisthêta kai noêta* was very well known).

Hegel evinces a similar suspicion regarding the German *Ästhetik* and doubts it can be adequately translated into English or French: "To us Germans the term is familiar; it is not known to other peoples" (*Vorlesungen über Ästhetik* [1935]; trans. Knox, *Aesthetics: Lectures on Fine Art*). He clarifies that the French say *théorie des arts* or *belles-lettres*, while the English, he says, referencing Henry Home's (1690–1782) work *Elements of Criticism*, classify aesthetics under "criticism."

In his *Aesthetics*, Hegel finds the term "aesthetic" improper (*unpassend*) and superficial (*oberflächlig*). He mentions the neologism "callistics," constructed from the Greek *to kallos* (beauty), which some had offered as an alternative, but finds it inadequate (*ungenügend*), since it refers to the beautiful in general and not the beautiful as artistic creation. Restricted to a term that has already "passed over into common speech" (*in die gemeine Sprache übergegangen*), he takes care to clarify that he does not mean to deal with the science of sense or sensation, nor with feelings such as pleasantness or fear, but with the philosophy of art, and notably with the philosophy of fine art (*Philosophie der schönen Kunst*).

Hegel puts himself assuredly and deliberately at the opposite extreme from the Kantian double meaning of "aesthetic," meaning both a study of a priori forms of perception and a critique of taste, the study of the feelings of pleasure and pain related to the faculty of judgment, whose domain of application is, according to Kant, art. Nevertheless, we know the paramount importance he gives to nature to the detriment of art in general and fine arts in particular. Similarly, the Hegelian notion of "aesthetics," a term imposed by use and not fully accepted, distances itself from the sense given to it by the Kantian and Rousseauist Friedrich Schiller, in the *Letters on the Aesthetic Education of Man*, where it is primarily a question of the "aesthetic disposition of the soul" (*ästhetische Stimmung des Gemüts*) in its aspiration to the unity of beauty, morality, and liberty.

Finally, one would search in vain for a commonality of meaning, intention, or project between Hegel's philosophy of art and the aesthetics of Jean Paul, the author of *Vorschule zur Ästhetik* (1804, 1813) (translated into English as *Horn of Oberon: Jean Paul Richter's School for Aesthetics*), where aesthetics is defined by the author himself as a "theory of foretaste" (*Vor-Geschmackslehre*), despite the fact that the term *Geschmackslehre* is deliberately formed as an equivalent of "aesthetics."

There is thus little chance, as Hegel points out, that the simple utterance of the word "aesthetic," used as a noun or adjective, would mean the same thing in English, French, and German. Jean Paul, not without perspicacity and humor, brings up such distortions when he sharply criticizes the pseudoscientific constructions of his contemporaries and compatriots ("the modern transcendental aestheticians") and offers an ambiguous homage to "English and French aestheticians" (he cites Home, Geattie, Fontenelle, and Voltaire), for whom, he adds, "the artist at least gains something." "Each nation has its own aesthetic," Jean Paul seems to lament, and he denounces the division of student-aestheticians of Leipzig (prettily named the "sons of the Muses") according to whether they were French, Polish, Meissenish, or Saxon, on the model of the Parisian Collège des Quatre Nations (*Horn of Oberon*).

III. Aesthetics and *Kunstwissenschaft*

The term "aesthetics" seems from the nineteenth century on to be as necessary on epistemological and scientific levels as it seems superfluous on the linguistic one. Faced with this term, European translators, carried away by the urgency of transposition, can easily follow in Hegel's footsteps and make use of the obvious etymological transposition of *aisthêtikos* into their own languages. However, on pain of missing important theoretical and philosophical issues, the translator must make sure of the field covered by the generic "*aesthetics.*" He has, more or less, the choice between "philosophy of art," "philosophy of the beautiful," "theory of taste," "theory of art," "theory of fine arts," "theory" or "science" or "critique of the beautiful," "theory or science of art," not to mention some of their close equivalents from other languages, such as *théorie des beaux-arts*, *Wissenschaft vom Schönen*, *Kunstlehre*, *Kunstkritik*, or *Kunstwissenschaft*, the last of which is not always fully distinguished from *Kunstgeschichte*.

The same concern with differentiating the domains of knowledge falling under aesthetics prompts twentieth-century philosophers to specify the nature and orientation of their work. "Aesthetics" thus loses its relational and interdisciplinary character, straddling different human sciences, and comes to mean rather a sort of generalist and referential metatheory or metadiscourse. Thus, Theodor Lipps takes care to clarify, as a subtitle, that his *Ästhetik* (1923) should be understood as a psychology of the beautiful and of art (*Psychologie des Schönen und der Kunst*). To be sure, he adopts from the very beginning the classic definition, or at least the most commonly agreed-upon one, of aesthetics as the science of the beautiful:

Aesthetics is the science of the beautiful and thus implicitly also that of the ugly. An object is qualified as beautiful if it is suited to arouse or to attempt to arouse in me a particular feeling, notably that which we have the habit of calling the "feeling of beauty."

Immediately afterward, however, he claims peremptorily that, on one hand, aesthetics may be considered as applied psychology, and on the other, that the historical science of art (*historische Kunstwissenschaft*) ventures into aesthetics only on pain of betraying its most essential scientific calling.

Lipps is coming up against the difficult question of the status of aesthetics, considered sometimes as a general philosophical and theoretical discipline, sometimes as a discipline that is itself a part of another more general one, along with art criticism, art history, sociology, psychology, ethnology, and other disciplines concerning the arts as well as the experience that goes along with them. To mitigate this kind of difficulty, Max Dessoir (1906) attempts in the very title of his book to establish a double name, unlikely to be acceptable in another language: *Ästhetik und allgemeine Kunstwissenschaft* (Aesthetics and the general knowledge of art).

IV. Semantic Indeterminacy

This operation that aims to join two distinct approaches—for example, the Hegelian type of philosophy of art and the more scientific and descriptive theories of a Riegl or a Wölfflin—within one discipline, may be congenial to German-speaking philosophers and aestheticians. The English and especially the French, however, are less convinced as to the pertinence of this doubling up within a rather cumbersome expression, especially since the translation of *allgemeine Kunstwissenschaft* by "general science of art" or *science générale de l'art* does not indicate in English or in French any particular method or definite object.

In *The Essentials of Aesthetics* (1921), George Lansing Raymond dwells, as it happens, on the strangeness of importing the German word *Ästhetik* into English. By analogy with "mathematics," "physics," "mechanics," and "ethics," he justifies the plural use of "aesthetics," rather than the singular "aesthetic"—("this term . . . seems to be out of analogy with the English usage")—by the fact that the word refers to a plurality of disciplines in which similar methods produce "greatly varying results." According to the author, the singular ending "ic" would wrongly relate "aesthetic" with "logic" or "music," specific departments centered on a unique object, in which scientific method produces similar results. From that point on, an expansive definition of "aesthetics" understood in the sense of a "science of beauty exemplified in art" allows the author to devote his reflection to themes and domains that come mostly from what Germans call *Kunstwissenschaft* and *Kunstgeschichte*, and the French *sciences de l'art*, rather than theoretical and philosophical aesthetics.

A pure invention of an eighteenth-century philosopher, the term *aisthêtike*—linguistically irreproachable, as it happens—will no doubt retain some semantic indeterminacy for a long time, despite its apparent translatability. However, though it does not explain by itself how the shift from the Greek verb *aisthanomai* to the philosophy of the beautiful or the science of art came about, it is a continual reminder of the attempt to understand how "humble" sensations, objects of a *gnoseologia inferior*, form in man the ideas that he then reincarnates in what he calls "works of art."

Marc Jimenez

BIBLIOGRAPHY

Baumgarten, Alexander Gottlieb. *Aesthetica*. Hamburg: Meiner, 1983. First published in 1750.

Dessoir, Max. *Ästhetik und allgemeine Kunstwissenschaft*. Stuttgart: Enke, 1906. Second edition published in 1923.

Hegel, Georg Wilhelm Friedrich. *Aesthetics: Lectures on Fine Art*. 2 vols. Translated by T. M. Knox. Oxford: Oxford University Press, 1975.

Jean Paul. *Vorschule zur Ästhetik*. Berlin: Holzinger, 2013. First published in 1804; second edition published in 1813. Translation by M. R. Hale: *Horn of Oberon: Jean Paul Richter's School for Aesthetics*. Detroit: Wayne State University Press, 1973.

Kant, Immanuel. *Kritik der reinen Vernunft*. In vol. 6 of *Kants Werke*. Berlin: Gruyter, 1968. Book first published in 1781. Translation and editing by P. Guyer and A. Wood: *Critique of Pure Reason*. Cambridge: Cambridge University Press, 1998.

Lipps, Theodor. *Ästhetik. Psychologie des Schönen und der Kunst*. Leipzig: Voss, 1923.

Munro, Thomas. "Present Tendencies in American Esthetics." In *Philosophic Thought in France and the United States*. New York: University of Buffalo-Farber, 1950.

Raymond, George Lansing. *The Essentials of Aesthetics*. New York: Putnam, 1921.

Schiller, Friedrich von. *On the Aesthetic Education of Man*. Edited by E. M. Wilkinson and L. A. Willoughby. Oxford: Clarendon Press, 1967.

AFFORDANCE

FRENCH   *disponibilité* [of a resource], *exploitabilité* [of a situation]
GERMAN   *affordanz*

➤ *DISPOSITION* and *ACT*, ANIMAL, BEHAVIOR, CONSCIOUSNESS, LEIB, Box 1, PERCEPTION, REPRÉSENTATION, VORHANDEN

The word "affordance" is a neologism coined by James J. Gibson to account for the way in which every organism perceives its environment.

Ecological psychology (Gibson, *Ecological Approach*) and the theory of knowledge derived from it (Noë, "Experience"), contest the representationalist conception. According to the latter, the perceiving subject must form mental representations because he has access only to fragmentary and changing sense data. The ecological theory maintains on the contrary that what humans and animals perceive is *affordances*, that is, possibilities of acting, that exist objectively

in the world independent of the fact that they are perceived. The perception of *affordances* uses the information provided by perceptual systems because of their privileged resonance with a determinate environment. Action plays a major role in perception insofar as movement makes it possible to extract perceptual constants from the perceptual optical flux to which it gives rise.

The word "affordance" poses a serious problem for the translator. English "to afford" (to do something) has the twofold sense of having access to sufficient resources and being in a position to act without risk. These two meanings are exploited in Gibson's definition: "The *affordances* of the environment are what it provides to animals, what it gives them or furnishes them, for better or for worse" (Gibson, "Theory of Affordances"). Thus "affordances" could be rendered in French by *ressources* insofar as the English term covers both the targets of action and the obstacles or dangers connected with a given situation. The predominant usage is currently to retain the neologism transposed into French.

Joëlle Proust

BIBLIOGRAPHY

Gibson, James. *The Ecological Approach to Visual Perception*. Boston: Houghton Mifflin, 1979.

———. "The Theory of Affordances." In *Perceiving, Acting and Knowing: Toward an Ecological Psychology*, edited by R. E. Shaw and J. Bransford, 67–82. New York: Wiley, 1977.

Noë, Alva. "Experience and the Active Mind." *Synthese* 129, no.1 (2001).

AGENCY

FRENCH   *action, agent, agence, agir*

➤ *ACT*, and ACTOR, ENGLISH, FORCE, INTENTION, *LIBERTY*, PATHOS, PRAXIS, SOUL, SPEECH ACT, SUBJECT

The word "agency" appeared in English in the seventeenth century. When it was introduced into philosophy in the eighteenth century, it was initially used in a classically Aristotelian way, opposing action and passion, agent and patient. "Agency" can designate action (in the physical sense) or what modifies action (in contrast to being the object of action), or what modifies the agent (in contrast to the patient). Thanks to the operation of various expressions in English, "agency" came to sum up the difficulties of defining action and, in the contemporary period, of what makes it possible to act, no longer as a category opposed to passion, but as a "disposition" to action, a disposition that upsets the active/passive opposition. In agency, the agents themselves are no longer only the actors/authors of action; instead, they are also caught up in a system of relations that shifts the place and authority of action and modifies (or even completely muddies, notably in its use in economic theory) the definition of action. In its contemporary uses, "agency" is thus the point where the dualisms action/passion and agent/patient are erased and also where the subject/agent is defined in a new way.

The French translation of "agency" as *agir* (which has now become standard and is made possible by the specificity of the infinitive in French but which introduces a unilaterally active character), or even as *puissance d'agir* (which strengthens still further the classical tonality by implicitly correlating agency/*puissance* with action/*acte*), remains blind to such a development in usage and continues to be linked with a classical view of action and the agent. In many cases, "agent" would be more easily translated by *sujet* (and, in turn, "agency" translates *sujet* better than "subject" does). However, we should note that the French word *agence* is an adequate translation of "agency" when it designates, in a derived usage, an entity or institution endowed with a power of acting. This institutional usage (e.g., Agence nationale pour l'emploi, Central Intelligence Agency) is revealing, in both languages, of a complexity in the mode of action: agency (or the agent) being that which acts, but on behalf of another.

"Agency," which is today widely used in Anglo-Saxon analytical philosophy, especially in America, is probably untranslatable in the primary, strict sense of the term; that is, it is impossible to make it correspond to one and the same term in French translations of the texts in which it figures. This problem is connected to syntactical properties of English that have been systematically exploited in constituting a "semantics of action." Thus, examining this problem, and the more or less satisfactory solutions that translators and commentators have provided, may direct our attention toward a feature peculiar to the way in which a nominalist tradition that goes back at least as far as Hume, and that is illustrated today in the works of the post-Wittgensteinians, deals with the field of subjectivity. As often happens, the existence of alternative "paths" in modern philosophy proves to be inseparable from the interaction between concept and language.

I. Examples of the Polysemy of "Agency"

We can introduce the problem by examining Michael Sandel's book *Liberalism and the Limits of Justice,* which was translated into French by Jean-Fabien Spitz. Sandel devotes a major portion of his work to discussing what he calls two moral "theories," such as those developed in particular by John Rawls: "certain theories of community and agency at the foundation of justice," which Spitz translates (or glosses?) as "certaines théories de la communauté et de la qualité d'agent au fondement même de la théorie de la justice" (*Le libéralisme*). A little further on, Sandel continues his discussion by saying that "[w]e need therefore to assess Rawls' theory of the good, and in particular his accounts of community and agency, not only for their plausibility . . . ," and this time Spitz simplifies, rendering "agency" as *agent*: "Il nous faut donc évaluer la théorie rawlsienne du bien, et en particulier son analyse des notions de communauté et d'agent, non seulement pour apprécier leur plausibilité . . . ." The subhead "Agency and the Role of Reflection" is rendered as "La qualité d'agent et le rôle de la réflexion," the term "agency" once again being simplified to "agent," which makes it possible to achieve the stylistic compression of a hendiadys ("For Rawls, the account of agency and ends falls under the conception of good" [Pour Rawls, l'analyse de l'agent et de ses fins est du ressort de la conception du bien]).

But further on, Spitz has to resort once again to a gloss that makes explicit the position he has taken with regard to the term "agency": "[T]he bounds of the self must be antecedently given . . . in order to assure the agency of the subject, its capacity to choose its ends" is rendered as "[L]es limites du moi doivent être données au préalable . . . pour garantir que le sujet soit bien un agent et qu'il ait la capacité de choisir ses fins." However, immediately afterward, Spitz is forced to completely change his paradigm: "[W]hile the bounds of

the self may seem an undue restriction on agency . . . they are in fact a prerequisite of agency" is translated as "[L]es limites du moi peuvent sans doute nous apparaître comme des restrictions indues de notre pouvoir d'action . . . mais ces limites sont en fait la condition même de l'action." The same fluctuations can be seen throughout the argument.

In this transfer of the contemporary concept of agency into French, we must pay particular attention to the choices made by Paul Ricœur, who has discussed this question on several occasions in a dialogue with analytical philosophers' "semantics." Ricœur began by retaining the word "agency" in its original language:

> Richard Taylor, dans son œuvre récente, *Action and Purpose* (Englewood Cliffs: Prentice Hall, 1966) a développé toutes les implications de cette crise de l'idée de causalité lorsqu'elle est rapportée à l'agent et à son *agency*. L'*agency* de l'agent implique un certain nombre de traits diamétralement opposés à ceux que la notion moderne de cause a conquis.

> (Richard Taylor, in his recent work, *Action and Purpose*, (Englewood Cliffs: Prentice Hall, 1966) has developed all the implications of this crisis of the idea of causality when it is related to the agent and his agency. The *agency* of the agent implies a certain number of characteristics that are diametrically opposed to those that the modern notion of cause has taken on.

> (*La sémantique de l'action*)

This allows Ricœur to move immediately to the apparently substitutable expression "la causalité de l'agent," whose specific characteristics he discusses. On the other hand, in his later works, and especially in *Soi-même comme un autre* (which includes a long discussion on Davidson under the subhead "Troisième étude: une sémantique de l'action sans agent"), he explicitly proposes to translate "agency" by *puissance d'agir*. But he notes: "On pourrait attendre, sous ce titre, une analyse du pouvoir-faire de l'agent. Il n'en est rien; il est seulement question du critère distinctif des actions proprement dites (*deeds and doings*) par rapport aux événements qui ne sont que de simples occurrences (*happenings*), lorsque semble faire défaut le caractère intentionnel [Given the title . . . one might expect an analysis of the agent's power to act. There is nothing of the sort; instead it is solely a matter of the distinguishing criterion of acts in general ("deeds and doing") in relation to events which are but mere happenings, when the intentional character appears to be lacking]."

Ricœur's translations or non-translations are thus always at the same time claims made regarding the essence of the question of the relationships between the "semantics of action" and the "philosophy of 'subjectivity,'" which the uses of "agency" appear to unveil.

An interesting counterexample is provided by reading a more recent essay by Vincent Descombes on "action" ("L'action"). Not only is Descombes familiar with analytical philosophers and discusses their common presuppositions (the pass uniformly given to the psychology of "will" to the advantage of sentences expressing the relationship of the subject to his action) and divergences (the structural point of view versus the causal point of view), but he clearly writes with English expressions in mind. That is why it is tempting to reconstitute behind one or another of his varied formulations the presence of a term like "agency" (which he never mentions) or the possibility of retranslating them by this term. But this is not always the case, and "agency" is here remarkably translated and absorbed into an overall view of the history of thinking about action.

II. "Agency" as a Principle of Action

"Agency" nonetheless has its own history. In *The Invention of Autonomy*, J. B. Schneewind observes that the first occurrence of the term "agency" in its philosophical sense is found in Samuel Clarke's *Lectures*. What Clarke calls the "Power of Agency or Free Choice" is the ability to act in accord with one's knowledge of eternal ideas. Schneewind adds:

> The *Oxford English Dictionary* shows only one earlier use, in 1658, which is not clearly a philosophical one. It then gives a citation from Jonathan Edwards dated 1762, although Berkeley, Hume, and Price had all previously used the term. In 1731 Edmund Law, referring to Clarke, described the word as "generally including the power of beginning Thought as well as Motion." (King, *Essay*, p. 156n).

In classical English thought, "agency" designates a general and undefined property of acting closely connected with causality and efficacy: agency is thus the active force, the effective cause of action (cf. Ger. *Wirkung*, which differs from *Handlung*, action). In Hobbes, for instance, the conception of agency is classically Aristotelian, as is shown by the perfect agent/patient symmetry that structures his whole reflection on action:

> As when one body by putting forwards another body generates motion in it, it is called the AGENT; and the body in which motion is so generated, is called the PATIENT; so fire that warms the hand is the agent, and the hand, which is warmed, is the patient.
>
> (*Elements of Philosophy*, pt. 2, in *Complete English Works*, chap. 9)

Thus agency is what characterizes action and the person who performs it and is related to the real and effective cause of action. For example, God may be the source of the agency of an agent, even if the latter seems to be the one performing it.

> [T]he agency of external objects is only from God; therefore all actions, even of free and voluntary agents, are necessary.
>
> (Hobbes, *Questions concerning Liberty, Necessity, and Chance*, in *Complete English Works*)

Here we find an interesting distinction between the author (as the subject of the will and of responsibility) and agency, the effective cause of action.

It is clear that these classical uses of "agency" are indebted to an action/passion dualism and to a causal interpretation of action (that identifies action with physical efficacy). Hume, who denies the possibility of knowing any causal connection in action, thus clearly asserts the synonymy of agency and force or efficacy, and, even in his skepticism, identifies agency with causality:

> I begin with observing that the terms of efficacy, agency, power, force, energy, necessity, connection, and productive quality, are all nearly synonymous; and therefore it is an absurdity to employ any of them in defining the rest. . . . Upon the whole, we may conclude that it is impossible, in any one instance, to show the principle in which the force and agency of a cause is placed.
>
> (*Treatise of Human Nature*, pt. 1, §3)

In Hume, causal agency is subject to skepticism for the same reason as causal connection: the common error made by philosophers, according to Hume, is to believe that the causal connection is in things and not in the mind (on "mind," see SOUL) and to seek its first nature. Hume and British empiricism thus make possible the first situation of action within anthropology—by showing that it is a matter of mental, and not physical or metaphysical, connections. Such an anthropologization of action marks the term "agency." Nonetheless, Hume closely connects agency and causality, and this has continued to characterize theories of action down to the contemporary period.

> But philosophers, who abstract from the effects of custom . . . , instead of concluding that we have no idea of power or agency, separate from the mind and belonging to causes; I say, instead of drawing this conclusion, they frequently search for the qualities in which this agency consists.
>
> (*Treatise of Human Nature*, pt. 1, §4.)

III. "Agency" as a Decentering of Action

Contemporary thinking about agency questions the possibility of conceiving action in general terms of cause and effect or action and reaction. It is inseparable from an anthropologization, as is shown by the frequency of the expression "human agency" in contemporary philosophy in English (especially the philosophy of action and moral philosophy): agency is supposed to be what characterizes, among the events of the world, what belongs to the order of human action. Davidson posed the problem very clearly in his already classic essays on action and particularly in his article "Agency" (which was translated by P. Engel as "L'Agir," where Engel translates "agency" sometimes by *agir* and sometimes by *action*):

> What events in the life of a person reveal agency; what are his deeds and his doings in contrast to mere happenings in his history: what is the mark that distinguishes his actions?

Agency is a *quality* of events that makes them into actions, but it is not necessarily their material cause (even if Davidson ends up defining action in causal terms and, fundamentally, identifying it with the event). The difficulty of framing a general definition of agency is precisely the difficulty of classifying specific events under the category of action (ibid.):

> Philosophers often seem to think that there must be some simple grammatical litmus of agency, but none has been discovered. I drugged the sentry, I contracted malaria, I danced, I swooned, Jones was kicked by me,

Smith was outlived by me: this is a series of examples designed to show that a person named as subject in sentences in the active or as object in sentences in the passive, may or may not be the agent of the event recorded.

One way of defining action and agency would thus be to introduce the concept of *intention* (see INTENTION), as is done by a whole series of English-language philosophers concerned with action (Anscombe, Geach, Kenny), and to define agency, in structural terms, by intentionality. In Davidson, the question of agency is eliminated in favor of a reflection on the causality of actions and on the articulation of the mental and the physical. The debate between these two main schools of reflection on action bears, as Descombes observes ("L'action"), on the ontological reality of action: is action defined by a corporeal movement describable as an intentional act produced by a mental or physical state of the agent (the causal conception), or by the change intentionally caused in the patient by the agent within a certain narrative structure (the causative or structural conception)? But beyond this very interesting debate, or short of it, the question remains: is there a definition or a criterion of agency?

This question is not only that of the nature of action, but also that of its *subject*: the variety of actions and modes of agency may be the most striking element of the English language (see ENGLISH), inseparable from a specific conception of subjectivity.

This point has been particularly well treated by Austin in his seminal article "A Plea for Excuses," which is an essential source of contemporary reflection on action and acting (it is frequently cited by Davidson in "Agency," for example). Austin challenges precisely the point mentioned earlier by Hume: the idea of a characteristic or general definition of action. The subject of Austin's article, and of the problematics of excuses, is first of all the profound differences between modes of action. The constant recourse to agency among English-language philosophers does not seek, contrary to the French terms used as equivalents (*agir, puissance, agent*), to erase these differences but rather to mark their irreducibility.

Austin emphasizes both the differences between actions ("Is to sneeze to do an action?") and what "doing something" really means. For Austin, we do not know what an action is, and philosophers who reflect on the question in general terms allow themselves to fall prey to the "myth of the verb," according to which there would be some "thing," "doing an action," which makes manifest the essential characteristics of what is classified under the substitute "do an action."

Why excuses, then? Austin wants to invert the classical philosophical approach that begins by positing the action and then examines justifications and causes. In reality, it is excuses—what we say when it appears that we have acted wrongly (clumsily, inadequately, etc.)—that enable us to begin classifying what we bring together under the general expression, the "dummy" action. Excuses can help us define agency: what is common to an action that one has succeeded in doing and a failed action? Between an action done intentionally, deliberately, expressly, etc., and the same action done (as excuses say) unintentionally, not expressly, etc.? The existence of excuses is for Austin essential to the nature

of human action—they do not come, as it were, after the fact, but are implicated in it. The variety of excuses shows the impossibility of defining agency generally, in a way other than in the detail and diversity of our modes of responsibility and explanation.

Excuses show us, in a sense, what an action is. An action is precisely something that one can excuse, something one does not do exactly. Here we should refer to Austin's underestimated article "Three Ways of Spilling Ink" and to the conclusion of his article "Pretending":

> . . . . [i]n the long-term project of classifying and clarifying all the possible ways of *not exactly doing things*, which has to be carried through if we are ever to understand properly what doing things is . . .

The existence of excuses shows, beyond the multiplicity and "humanness" of agency, its passivity, since an excuse always seeks to say in a certain way: "I'm not the agent." As Stanley Cavell says apropos of Austin:

> Excuses are as essentially implicated in Austin's view of human actions as slips and overdetermination are in Freud's. What does it betoken about human actions that the reticulated constellation of predicates of excuse is made for them—that they can be done unintentionally, unwillingly, involuntarily, . . . and so on? It betokens, we might say, the all but unending vulnerability of human action, its openness to the independence of the world and the preoccupation of the mind.

> (*A Pitch of Philosophy*)

We see that the thematics of the excuse complicates rather than simplifies that of agency. Austin notes, for example, that we do not use just any excuse with just any action. One can excuse oneself for lighting a cigarette "out of habit," but a murderer cannot excuse himself by saying that he acted "out of habit." Finally, Austin says ("A Plea for Excuses") there is a limit to the acts for which any given excuse will be accepted: "standards of the unacceptable" are a question intimately related to the nature of agency.

Just as there is no universal excuse, so there is no *type* of the action, and agency is in no way a general qualification of action but rather the mark of its indefinability and its decentering.

The interest of Austin's thought on this point is that in any case it excludes—as does Wittgenstein in his writings on philosophy and psychology—the facile solution that consists in defining action, and a fortiori (human) agency by the presence of a metaphysical or subjective will, or of a "backstage artiste." The problematics of "A Plea for Excuses" consists not only in saying that I am not the master of my actions, but even that I am not their author or subject. Thus agency forms an interesting couple with "performance," another untranslatable term. The duality of success and failure that Austin establishes regarding the very special actions, neither active nor passive, constituted by speech acts, may define action and agency better than the Aristotelian categories that are invoked to explain and translate the word "agency."

Agency upsets the active/passive pair as well as the cause/effect pair. The passive, whose role is much more important in English than in French, thus occupies a crucial place in the work of defining action through the concept of agency. In English, a passive utterance is not always the inversion of the active and does not describe an "undergoing," as is shown by Davidson's remark cited earlier: in the English passive, we often see the pure and simple disappearance of the agent, the passive becoming the privileged form of the exposition of an action. Such an erasure of the agent generalizes the phenomenon of *recessive diathesis* (the loss of the actor) of which Descombes, following Wittgenstein and Anscombe, now makes heavy use in his reflection on action ("L'action").

IV. Specific Uses

A. "Agency" in law and economics

The vocabulary of agency in the domain of law and economics allows us to describe modes of action that are in a sense "by proxy," that is, carried out by someone in place of someone else. This is not the "action without a subject" that Ricœur reproaches Davidson for instituting (through the identification of action and event), but, more radically, it is an action whose subject is not where we think it is, in the agent.

Thus we can describe the relation *principal/agent* in the market as conceived in the theory of economic agency. One of the ways most commonly used today to conceive economic organization is the relation between a principal and an agent (cf., e.g., Kenneth Arrow, "Agency and the Market"). The simplest organization is in fact the one that involves two parties, for example, an employer and a worker, a landowner and a farmer, a lawyer and his client. The principal (or constituent) delegates to the agent an action that may be more or less observable. It is this possibility of non-observability that is at the center of the theory of agency.

> The common element is the presence of two individuals. One (the agent) is to choose an action among a number of alternative possibilities. The action affects the welfare of the other, the principal, as well as that of the agent's self.
>
> (Arrow, "Agency and the Market")

Thus we have the example of an action that has an effect on at least two persons, the agent and the principal, but in which the agent is the author only in an uncertain way. Agency is inseparable from this aspect of uncertainty: "The outcome is affected but not completely determined by the agent's action" (ibid.).

The principal has the additional function of prescribing rules and thus controlling the agent's action. The interest of this model is that agency is not only the action of the agent but also a function of this mini-organization. In general, the action of the agent is only imperfectly visible. In fact, the result observed by the principal is the joint product of chance and an action that is known only to the agent (Laffont, *Economics of Uncertainty*).

The ambiguity of the word "agent" is evident: "agent" has both a passive and an active sense (cf. French usages in *agent du gouvernement*, *agent secret*, *notre agent à Hong Kong*). There may be several agents for one principal. Arrow gives two examples in which the relation between principal and agent

upsets the established relations between active and passive: the doctor/patient relationship, in which the patient is the principal and the doctor the agent (because of the doctor's superior knowledge), and the case of torts, for example in the event of an accident:

> One individual takes an action which results in damage to another, for example, one automobile hitting another. Although it may seem an odd use of language, one has to consider the damager as the agent and the one damaged as the principal.
>
> ("Agency and the Market")

If the usage is odd, that is because in the normal case of agency, the agent is controlled by the principal and depends on him.

B. "Agency" in Peirce

We can see the two senses of "agency," which are interesting in their very difference, in the work of C. S. Peirce: the first classically connected with the idea of cause (Peirce writes: "any cause or agency"). The second, more unusual, sense designates the particular authorities within a plurality of faculties, a usage characterized by the possibility of using the plural "agencies":

> I wish philosophy to be a strict science, passionless and severely fair. I know very well that science is not the whole of life, but I believe in the division of labor among intellectual agencies.
>
> (*Collected Papers*, 5:536–7)

C. The political sense

In addition to the importance of the term in pragmatism, "agency" has acquired, in American English, a concrete political sense, becoming the function of the agent, and then an establishment or institution that has the power to act on behalf of someone ("an establishment for the purpose of doing business for another," RT: *Oxford English Dictionary*). An unexpected sense appears in the eighteenth and nineteenth centuries in the context of the conquest of the American West and the establishment of local authorities, designating their jurisdiction over the Indians: "agency" designates the political power, the office of this power, and by extension, the Indian territory subject to its jurisdiction.

This usage, which shifts agency from the source of power and action to its field of application, clearly shows the tendency in the political uses of "agency" to make concrete and to embody power in the object on which it is exercised, a tendency we also see in the sole French use of *agence*.

Here we find the erasure of the border between active and passive in the definition of agency and of power, which certainly has consequences for the definition of the political subject/agent. Here again we see the ambivalence of the term *agent*, which is central in English (in contrast to *acteur*, which is often preferred in French and is more clearly active).

In any case, we see that it is impossible to set up a correspondence, even a very general one, between the English set "action"/"agency"/"agent" and the French set *action/agir/ acteur* (or the German set *Handlung/Wirkung/Kraft*), a fact all the more surprising because in contemporary philosophy as it is written in these languages, these sets have defined the nature and the domain of subjective and collective action.

- See Box 1.

Étienne Balibar
Sandra Laugier

BIBLIOGRAPHY

Arrow, Kenneth. "Agency and the Market." In *Handbook of Mathematical Economics*, vol. 3, edited by K. Arrow and M. Intriligator. Amsterdam: Elsevier, 1986.

Austin, John L. "A Plea for Excuses." In *Philosophical Papers*, edited by J. O. Urmson and G. J. Warnock. Oxford: Clarendon Press, 1962.

———. "Pretending." In *Philosophical Papers*, edited by J. O. Urmson and G. J. Warnock. Oxford: Clarendon Press, 1962.

Barnes, Jonathan. *Aristotle*. Oxford: Oxford University Press, 1982.

Cavell, Stanley. *A Pitch of Philosophy*. Cambridge, MA: Harvard University Press, 1994.

Cohen, Tom. "Political Thrillers: Hitchcock, de Man and Secret Agency in 'The Aesthetic State.'" In *Material Events: Paul de Man and the Afterlife of Theory*, edited by Tom Cohen, Barbara Cohen, J. Hilis Miller, Andrjez Warminski. Minneapolis: University of Minnesota Press, 2001.

Davidson, Donald. "Agency." In *Essays on Actions and Events*. Oxford: Clarendon Press, 1980. Translation by P. Engel: "L'agir." In *Actions et événements*. Paris: Presses Universitaires de France, 1993.

Descombes, Vincent. "L'action." In *Notions de philosophie*, vol. 2, edited by D. Kambouchner, 103–174. Paris: Gallimard, 1995.

Hobbes, Thomas. *Complete English Works*. London: Molesworth, 1869.

Hume, David. *A Treatise of Human Nature*. Edited by L. A. Selby-Bigge. Oxford: Oxford University Press, 1978. First published in 1739–40.

Laffont, Jean-Jacques. *The Economics of Uncertainty and Information*. Translated by J. P. Bonin and H. Bonin. Cambridge, MA: MIT Press, 1989.

Peirce, Charles Sanders. *Collected Papers*. Edited by C. Hartshorne and P. Weiss. Cambridge, MA: Harvard University Press, 1931–35.

Ricœur, Paul. *From Text to Action: Essays in Hermeneutics II*. Translated by K. Blamey and J. B. Thompson. Evanston, IL: Northwestern University Press, 1991.

———. *La sémantique de l'action*. Paris: Centre National de la Recherche Scientifique, 1977.

———. "Troisième étude: Une sémantique de l'action sans agent." In *Soi-même comme un autre*. Paris: Éditions du Seuil, 1990. Translation by K. Blamey: *Oneself as Another*. Chicago: University of Chicago Press, 1992.

Sandel, Michael J. *Liberalism and the Limits of Justice*. Cambridge: Cambridge University Press, 1998. First published in 1982. Translation by J.-F. Spitz: *Le libéralisme et les limites de la justice*. Paris: Éditions du Seuil, 1999.

Schneewind, Jerome B. *The Invention of Autonomy*. Cambridge: Cambridge University Press, 1998.

1

"Agency"/"instance"

In the 1960s and 1970s, the French philosophers Jacques Lacan and Louis Althusser both used the category "instance" in a manner that became typical of the structuralist moment. Its use was then widely expanded by their common disciples and involved a complex superimposition of notions of agency, demand, insistence, efficiency, decision, and hierarchy that could not be preserved in English translation. This syncretic formation made it possible to combine in various manners a triple legacy of Marx, Freud, and Saussure, drawing on the historical polysemy of the word *instance* in French. The lack of a match between French and English as far as this polysemy is concerned (especially where idiomatic nuances weigh in) brings out fundamental tensions nested in the structuralist paradigm and helps explain, at least to some extent, the paradigm's logical fragility.

Chronologically, the first use of *instance* appears in Lacan's essay "L'instance de la lettre dans l'inconscient ou la raison depuis Freud," published in 1957 (but, as was the case for most of Lacan's scattered œuvre, influential only after its inclusion in the *Écrits* in 1966 and its 1977 English translation). The expression "L'instance de la lettre" in the essay's title is counterposed in the body of the essay to the expression "l'instance du signifiant." Attention is thus called to the model borrowed from Saussure's binary signifier/signified (S/s), with emphasis placed on the paradoxical character of the signifier as something both material and formal. In

English translation (at least the 1977 one published by Alan Sheridan with the title beginning "The Agency of the Letter"; Bruce Fink's 2002 translation opts for "The Instance of the Letter," obviously hewing more closely to the original French), the double character of *signifiant* is complicated by the double character of *instance*. With *instance* here rendered as "agency," the translation privileges one connotation of the French word at the expense of the other. So, for example, in one sense the letter's agency refers to its "efficacy" in producing the place where a subject thinks unconsciously (not the same as the place where it "exists" consciously). This meaning knocks out the sense of agency as an "insisting" of the signifying chain, or more precisely, the coercion of repetition of thoughts or symptoms. What becomes manifest in the latter is the "indestructibility" of unconscious desire of which the subject is the instrument, not the master.

In 1962 Louis Althusser published an essay on Marxist dialectics, "Contradiction and Overdetermination," later incorporated into the volume *For Marx*. For the first time, he there explained his theory of the "overdetermination" of historical causality, a term explicitly borrowed from Freud's analysis of the unconscious genesis of dreams and other symptoms but transferred to the field of history and politics (and applied specifically to the analysis of revolutions). Although *instance* (translated as "instance" by Brewster) plays an important role in Freud's metapsychology, it

was not used by Althusser with reference to psychoanalysis but rather to a phrase used by Engels when commenting on Marx's "materialist conception of history." Historical events and social configurations, he maintained, are determined by economic factors, albeit only "in the last instance" (*in letzter Instanz*). In Althusser's criticism, this yielded the idea that a social formation is composed of several variously articulated "instances" (what Marx called the economic "infrastructure," or "base," as distinct from the ideological and political "superstructure" (*Überbau*). For Althusser, neither economic base nor ideological superstructure was reducible to the other, even if one retained causal primacy. In subsequent expositions of his theory of "structural causality" (particularly in the collective book *Reading Capital*), the "last instance" was defined not as the one that always overrides the other, but as the one that, secretly, distributes the "efficacy" (*efficace* or *indice d'efficace*) of the "dominant cause." Althusser always preferred "instance" to other partial equivalents (such as "level," "region," or even "practice") because none of these alternatives was as effective in combining a "topography" (*topique*) with a "causality." Only "instance" made it possible to erase the Hegelian dialectical category of "moment" (*das Moment*) as used by Engels.

With Lacan there is a recasting of psychoanalytic problems (ultimately deriving from Freud) by extending them through Saussurian linguistic concepts. Thus we arrive at the idea of the discursive structure of the unconscious. With Althusser there is a radical transformation (some would say denaturalization) of Marxian and Marxist dialectical categories, with the key notion of "contradiction" set up in analogy to Freudian models of interpretation. The multivalent connotations of *Instanz* in Freud (translated as *instance* in French, and "agency" in English by the *Standard Edition*), and the polysemy of "instance" in both French and English, are fully activated in both Lacanian and Althusserian discourses.

"Instance" is a quite remarkable semantic unit. Derived from the Latin *instantia*, and therefore ultimately from the verb *instare* (literally "to stay in" or "to stay before"), and echoing the "frequentative" form *insistere* (to apply, to insist), it emerged almost simultaneously in French and English in the fourteenth century with the evolution of the two languages, displaying and hierarchizing four types of usage recorded by dictionaries: (1) "urgency, pressure, urging influence" (including the ideas to act "at the instance of" someone, and of "repeated solicitation"); (2) "instant time" (either in the present or at an indeterminate time); (3) an illustration, supporting argument or, on the contrary, an objection (in rhetoric or logic)—where the French uses *par exemple*, the English normally uses "for instance"; (4) "a process in a court of justice" (or this court itself), understood either institutionally or metaphorically (RT: *Oxford English Dictionary*; RT: Bloch and Wartburg, *Dictionnaire étymologique de la langue française*). The first three uses are less old-fashioned in French than in English. On the other hand, as is typically the case, English has a verb form—"to insist," "insisting"—for what in French exists only as a noun (which is now obsolete or technical). In German, *Instanz* (which is today a purely juridical term, except for its post-Freudian and post-Althusserian uses) also existed originally, but it was rapidly challenged by the quasi-homonymous and synonymous German term *Instand* (from *stehen in*), whence derives in particular the adverb *inständig* (insistently). Perhaps we can submit that the "invariant" running through the various uses is the idea of a repeated demand or contest before a tribunal (itself "instantiated"), whose very insistence produces more or less irreversible effects.

In Freud's writings, *Instanz* became a "systemic" concept only very late, when the results of the speculations on the "second topography" were presented in a pedagogic manner (*Abriss der Psychoanalyse*). This occurred in two steps, each of which calls for different associations and evokes a specific "scheme" of thought, but which never remain entirely separate. Initially (as early as the *Traumdeutung* [*The Interpretation of Dreams*], 1900), Freud occasionally used the word *Instanz* to characterize the function of

censorship, which in dreams and other psychic processes selects and represses some desires, pushing their expression into the unconscious. Freud even used the Kafkaesque metaphor of a "warden" standing at the gate separating the licit from the illicit. When the same function (now including "observation" and even "persecution" of the self) was retrieved in manias and obsessions and came to be associated with the *Über-Ich*, or superego, in 1923, it became the typical name for the instance that "splits" the *Ich*, or ego, in order to "judge" (and even "punish") it from the inside. This is in contrast to punishment from the outside, which is typically carried out by various social authorities, especially the father, or more generally the parents (also called *Elterninstanz*, or "parental instance"). Generally, in the usage of this judiciary metaphor, the name "instance" was applied only to the superego and not to the other "regions" (*Bezirke*) or "systems" of the psyche.

In a second step (essentially the *Neue Folge Vorlesungen zur Einführung in die Psychoanalyse* and the contemporary clinical studies on angst), another guiding metaphor, or scheme, comes into play. A conflict emerges in which the ego/subject is caught between the incompatible exigencies of several "masters." The exigencies of pleasure (libido), originating from an infinite "reservoir" called the *Es* (the "it," but translated as "id" by Strachey), battle the exigencies of the superego, which are linked to the "uneasy" process of moralization and civilization. There is some inconsistency in Freud's presentation because sometimes the ego is the "miserable" common target of opposing masters, and sometimes it is "instantiated" as representative of a third kind of exigency: a potential source of anxiety for the subject, namely that of the "external world," or "reality." In Freud's presentation of this structure of the psychic apparatus as a symmetrical interplay of conflictual forces (reminiscent of Plato), the translation of *Instanz* as "agency," as chosen by James Strachey in the *Standard Edition*, makes more sense, provided the term is "depersonalized." "Instance" in the sense of "urgency" would also be relevant, this time on the side of the id, whose "repeated entreaties" force the ego and the superego to erect interdictions and defenses.

We now return to Althusser and Lacan. It is as if they had exploited opposite aspects of the Freudian metaphoric discourse, combining it with different notions of structure and conflict but opening up the possibility of a conversation that was then realized by their disciples. In Althusser's case, it could seem that "instance" is only a nominal reference, used to bridge the gap between Marxian and Freudian notions of "conflict" or "conflicting forces." The essential idea here was to import the latter's model of complexity ("overdetermination") into the

former's concept of the political. However, the continuous reference to Engels's phrase "determination in last instance," where the judiciary connotations are explicit, could not but evoke in the mind of such an assiduous reader of classical political theory the central question always asked by Hobbes in *Leviathan*, "Who shall be Judge?" This is the defining question of sovereignty, which as a consequence can be said to permanently haunt the discourse of "structural causality" itself. Perhaps it forms the unspeakable side of the "materialist" postulate according to which the productive forces (i.e., mainly the workers themselves) remain the driving motor of history, even if in an aporetic manner ("the lonely hour of the last instance never comes"; *For Marx*). An anonymous multiple sovereign—perhaps powerless—inhabits the Althusserian play of causes. In Lacan's case, the driving motive is more explicitly referred to the idiomatic (and paradoxical) fusion of the judiciary process and the schemes of causal automatism ("L'instance, ai-je dit, de la lettre, et si j'emploie instance, c'est non sans raison [car ce mot] résonne aussi bien au niveau de la juridiction qu'à celui de l'insistance" [The instance, I have said, of the letter; and if I use the word instance it is not without reason, for it resonates just as well at the level of juridical utterance as it does at the level of insistence]; *Je parle aux murs*), but a key indication is also given by the subtitle of the celebrated 1957 essay: "La raison depuis Freud" ("Reason since Freud"). One is reminded that in the Kantian tradition, which towers over our conceptions of the subject, "reason" is presented as a "tribunal" that exercises a "critical" function or a function of judgment. The ultimate tribunal is not that of reason, however; it is that of the unconscious. This said, the unconscious itself is not some purely "irrational" agency. It results from the "other logic" of the signifier (or the "letter") to which the subject is subjected or within which it must find a "place." Agency therefore is only half of a good translation: though it marks the Freudian legacy of subjection by "autonomizing" the power of the signifier, it loses the semantic dimension of "structural causality." In the systematization of Lacan's doctrine proposed by the "Althusserian" Jacques-Alain Miller (author of the detailed index of *Écrits*), this structural element essentially amounted to a flirtation with Marxian notions of "materiality" and "domination." This flirtation was eventually overcome, in Miller's scheme, by Lacan's concept of "the real" as an insistence of the void—the "thing" causing anxiety—that can never become symbolized. Interestingly, although perhaps not surprisingly, the vexed translation of *instance* into

(continued)

(continued)

English reveals in the cases of both Althusser and Lacan the enigma of the relationship between action, or agency, and the aporetic determinations of its subjectification. To discuss them in two languages instead of one adds precision, if not resolution, to the aporia.

Étienne Balibar

BIBLIOGRAPHY

Althusser, Louis. "Contradiction et surdétermination (Notes pour une recherche)." *La Pensée* 106 (1962): 3–22. Translation by B. Brewster: "Contradiction and Overdetermination: Notes for an Investigation." In *For Marx*. London: Verso 2005.

Althusser, Louis, and Étienne Balibar. *Lire le Capital*. Paris: Librairie François Maspero, 1965. Translation by B. Brewster: *Reading Capital*. London: Verso, 2009.

Freud, Sigmund. *Abriss der Psychoanalyse. Einführende Darstellung*. Vol. 17 of *Gesammelte Werke*. Frankfurt: Fischer, 1940. Translation by J. Strachey: *An Outline of Psycho-Analysis*. Vol. 23 of *The Standard Edition of the Complete Psychological Works of Sigmund Freud*. London: Hogarth Press, 1960.

———. *Neue Folge Vorlesungen zur Einführung in die Psychoanalyse*. Vol. 15 of *Gesammelte Werke*. Frankfurt: Fischer, 1940. Translation by J. Strachey: *New Introductory Lectures on Psycho-Analysis*. Vol. 22 of *The Standard*

Edition of the Complete Psychological Works of Sigmund Freud. London: Hogarth Press, 1960.

Lacan, Jacques. "L'instance de la lettre dans l'inconscient ou la raison depuis Freud." In *Écrits*, vol. 1. Paris: Éditions du Seuil, 1966. First published in 1957. Translation by A. Sheridan: "The Agency of the Letter in the Unconscious, or Reason since Freud." In *Écrits: A Selection*. New York: W. W. Norton, 1977. Translation by B. Fink: "The Instance of the Letter in the Unconscious, or Reason since Freud." In *Écrits: A Selection*. New York: W. W. Norton, 2002.

———. *Je parle aux murs: Entretiens de la Chapelle de Sainte-Anne*, edited by Jacques-Alain Miller. Paris: Éditions du Seuil, 2011.

AIÔN [αἰών], CHRONOS [χρόνος] (GREEK)

FRENCH	*fluide vital, durée de vie, vie, âge, durée, génération, éternité/temps*
GERMAN	*Ewigkeit/Zeit*
LATIN	*aevum, aeternitas, perpetuitas, aeviternitas, sempiternitas/tempus*

➤ *ETERNITY, TIME,* and DASEIN, ERLEBEN, EVIGHED, GOD, HISTORIA UNIVERSALIS, HISTORY, LEIB, MOMENT, PRESENT, *WORLD*

If *chronos* [χρόνος], symbolized by Kronos [Κρόνος], the Greek god who devours his children, has all the characteristics of "time," *aiôn* [αἰών], it is, on the other hand, a term without modern equivalent. In the Homeric poems it designates the vital fluid, hence a man's lifespan and destiny, the intensity of a part of time. But when, in the *Timaeus*, Plato relates the *aiôn* to the life of the gods and no longer to the human lifespan, the sense of "eternity" comes in. Aristotle also uses this term for his Unmoved Mover, and Plotinus makes it Being's mode of existence. *Chronos* becomes the "mobile image" of the *aiôn* and, in Neoplatonic interpretations, its "son."

The Greek opposition between *aiôn* and *chronos* thus does not coincide with any of the oppositions with which we are familiar, neither that between subjective experience of time and objective time, nor that between eternity and time. It refers instead to two models of time. There is first the model of the physical *kosmos* [κόσμος], which can be dealt with through mathematics and to which *chronos* belongs, cosmic time, connected with the cyclical movement of the heavenly bodies and the sphere of the fixed stars, which Aristotle defined as a succession of instants ("now," *nun* [νῦν]) and "the number of movement in respect of before and after" (*Physics*, 4). Then there is the model of life and time as experienced, linear, with a beginning and an end.

Aiôn, transliterated in Latin as *aevum*, was adopted and adapted by Christian theology. For Aquinas, for instance, "strictly speaking *aevum* and *aeternitas* differ no more than *anthrôpos* and *homo*." But in the thirteenth century, *aevum* was detached from *aeternitas* to designate an intermediary between time and eternity, a guarantee of "the order and connection of things" suitable for characterizing "eviternal" realities, such as angels, that have a beginning but not an end (*aeternitatis ex parte post*).

Aiôn in the Greek philosophical lexicon, and *aevum* in Scholastic terminology, are among the terms most characteristic of the subtlety of the vocabulary of temporality, in the plurality—difficult for us to understand today—of its registers.

I. *Aiôn*: From Vital Fluid to Eternal Life

A. "Stuff of life" and the duration of an existence

In Homer, the *aiôn* is first of all a vital fluid, "the sweet *aiôn* that flows away" (*Iliad*, 22.58; *Odyssey*, 5.160–61): tears, sweat, and later on, cerebral-spinal fluid, sperm, everything that makes life and strength, that melts when one weeps and disappears with the breath of the soul when one dies ("psuchê te kai aiôn [ψυχή τε καὶ αἰών]," *Iliad*, 16.453)—the "stuff of life," R. B. Onians calls it (*Origins of European Thought*). The temporal meaning of *aiôn*, "lifespan," "existence," is attested in Pindar (*Pythian Odes*, 8.97) and the tragic playwrights, particularly in the combination *moira-aiôn* [μοῖρα-αἰών], indicating the "share of life" assigned to each person, the "lifespan imparted by fate" (Euripides, *Iphigeneia in Aulis*, 1507–8; see KÊR). That is probably the meaning with which Heraclitus is playing when he defines *aiôn* as "a child that gives birth to a child, who plays draughts" (RT: B.52 DK: "aiôn pais esti paizôn, pesseuôn [αἰὼν παῖς ἐστι παίζων, πεσσεύων]"): Bollack and Wismann (*Héraclite ou la séparation*, 182–85) argue that the iteration of the substantive *pais* [παῖς] (child) and the verb *paizô* [παίζω] (whose common meaning is "play like a child") suggests the interpretation of *aiôn* as referring to the time of a "generation," the time it takes for a child to become a father and play his own role. In this sense, *aiôn* is a limitation or delimitation of *chronos* [χρόνος], "time" in general: it is "the *chronos* of an individual life" (Festugière, "Le sens philosophique," 271); thus *aiôn* is, to use Euripides's expression, "the son of *chronos*" ("Aiôn te Chronou pais [Αἰών τε Χρόνου παῖς]," *Heracleidae* 900).

B. The divine *aiôn*: In time or outside time?

1. Time (*chronos*): A moving image of eternity (*aiôn*)?

When the lifespan designated by *aiôn* is no longer that of a mortal but that of a god, the limits recede: that is how, according to Festugière ("Le sens philosophique"), the transition to the meaning "eternity" takes place. That holds for the Homeric gods, who are "always living" (that is how Paul Mazon translates the expression "theoi aien eontes [θεοὶ αἰὲν ἐόντες]," *Iliad*, 1.290), and also for Empedocles's *Sphairos* [Σφαῖρος], whose "ineffable life" (*aspetos aiôn* [ἄσπετος αἰών], RT: B16 DK = 118 Bollack) extends into the past and the future ("It once was, was already, and will be").

But with Plato's *Timaeus*, a new conceptual distinction appears between this type of unlimited temporality, which extends through time, and an "eternity" that is outside time and may even generate time. "Eternity" is the customary translation of *aiôn* on the divine model, from which the demiurge took his inspiration in creating the world. The god is an "eternal living being" ("zôion aidion on [ζῷον ἀίδιον ὄν]," *Timaeus*, 37d2), concerning which we must say— exactly as we must say about Parmenides's Being (8.5)—that it "is," but not that it "was" or that it "will be" (*Timaeus*, 37e6–8). Time, *chronos*, is the name of a supplementary invention of the demiurge to make the world he has just created still more similar to the eternal god: it is, according to the famous expression, "a moving image of eternity" ("eikô . . . kinêton tina aiônos [εἰκὼ . . . κινητόν τινα αἰῶνος]," 37d5–6); but see Brague ("Pour en finir"), for whom this moving image is "heaven" and not time. Instead of remaining in unity, like the god, time moves in a circle according to number ("kat' arithmon kukloumenou [κατ' ἀριθμὸν κυκλουμένου]," 38a7–8) and includes divisions or parts that participate in becoming (days, nights, months, seasons) and to which "was" and "will be" apply.

Thus on the one hand Plato maintains the connection between life and *aiôn*: *aiônios* [αἰώνιος], an adjective he probably created alongside the traditional *aidios* [ἀίδιος], also applies to the living being that is the god-model (*aiônios*, 37d4; cf. *diaiônias* [διαιωνίας], 38b8), as well as to time as an image (*aiônion*) connected with the living beings that are the world and the heavens—but we understand that it is not so simple to translate it by "eternal," and that applied to time it means very literally "what has all the characteristics of the *aiôn*." On the other hand, and at the same time, we move from an *aiôn* that is the son of *chronos*, a lifespan included within (limited) time or coextensive with time, to an *aiôn* that is properly called an "eternity," outside time, for which it constitutes the model—Proclus was even to say that the *aiôn* is the "father of *chronos*" (cf. *In Platonis Rem publicam commentarii*, ed. Kroll, 2:17.10; *Elements of Theology*, prop. 52).

In a rigorously anti-Platonic gesture, Marcus Aurelius reversed, term for term, the relationship between *aiôn* and *chronos*. The infinite time at time's two extremities, abstract, unlimited, and corresponding to the void in its incorporeality close to nonbeing, takes the name of *aiôn* ("apeiron aiônos [ἄπειρον αἰῶνος]," 4.3.7), whereas the limited time of the present, which is always determined by the act that sets its extent (*diastêma* [διάστημα]), is associated with a "materialist" approach to *chronos*—both at the level of duration and insofar as the cosmic period thus torn out of the irreality of the *aiôn* is concerned (cf. Arius Didymus, *Epitome*, 26; RT: *SVF*, 2:509; with Goldschmidt's commentary, *Le système stoïcien et l'idée de temps*, 39–41; see also Deleuze, *Logic of Sense*, 78 and 190–94; and SIGNIFIER/SIGNIFIED, Box 1).

2. Time (*chronos*): The number of movement according to the anterior and the posterior?

Aristotle uses etymology to confirm the extension of the meaning of *aiôn* as "lifespan" from mortals to god (*De caelo*, 1.9.279a22–28): "This word 'duration' [*aiôn*] possessed a divine significance for the ancients." In fact, it is the word itself that encourages the passage from the lifespan of each individual to that of the heavens as a whole—or, more precisely, from "the limit that includes the time of each life" to "the limit that includes all time and infinity" ("to ton panta chronon kai tên apeirian periechon telos [τὸ τὸν πάντα χρόνον καὶ τὴν ἀπειρίαν περιέχον τέλος]"; on *to telos* [τὸ τέλος], "the end," "the limit," see PRINCIPLE, I.A). The life of the heavens is properly named *aiôn* "because it is aiei, always [*apo tou aei einai tên epônumian eilêphôs* (ἀπὸ τοῦ ἀεὶ εἶναι τὴν ἐπωνυμίαν εἰληφώς)] being immortal and divine [*athanatos kai theios* (ἀθάνατος καὶ θεῖος)]." In the *Metaphysics*, the same holds for the Unmoved Mover as well: since the act or transformation of intelligence into an act (*hê nou energeia* (ἡ νοῦ ἐνέργεια)) is life, and since the Unmoved Mover is this transformation into act, "we say therefore that God is a living being, eternal, most good, so that life and duration continuous and eternal belong to God, for this *is* God" (*Metaphysics*, 12.7.1072b28–30).

Aristotle also confirms the break between *aiôn* and *chronos*, with *aiôn* for the world of the heavens, and *chronos* for the plurality of the sublunary world: "Things that are always are not, as such, in time [*ouk estin en chronôi* (οὐκ ἔστιν ἐν χρόνῳ)]" (*Physics*, 4.12.221b4–5). In fact, time-*chronos* belongs to the order of passivity and not of activity: it causes aging, consumes, leads to oblivion. Although indissolubly connected with generation and becoming, "time is by its nature the cause rather of decay, since it is the number of change, and change removes what is" ("arithmos gar kinêseôs, hê de kinêsis existêsi to huparchon [ἀριθμὸς γὰρ κινήσεως, ἡ δὲ κίνησις ἐξίστησι τὸ ὑπάρχον]," *Physics*, 221b1–3). This sentence, which is both arithmetic and existential, deserves closer examination. On the one hand, it refers to the mathematical definition of time: in Aristotle's *Physics*, time is definitively able to be expressed in mathematics because it is definitely spatialized, connected with movement, which is itself connected with place: "For time is just this—number of motion in respect of 'before' and 'after'" (219b1–2). On the other hand, it refers to existence (*existêsi* [ἐξίστησι], from *ex-istêmi* [ἐξίστημι], "move, put outside oneself"; see DASEIN and ESSENCE) of the subject (*to huparchon* [τὸ ὑπάρχον], from *hup-archein* [ὑπ-άρχειν], "rule below, begin, present oneself, be available, be"; see SUBJECT), to the manner in which time acts on beings that are in time and, in particular, on us, humans who know how to count ("Whether if soul did not exist time would exist or not, is a question that may fairly be asked," 223a21–22). *Aiôn* and *chronos* can henceforth no longer be treated in the same way.

C. From Neoplatonism to the Christian appropriation: *Adiotês* and the persistent polysemy of *aiôn*

Plotinus's interpretation of "always" (*aei* [ἀεί]) as rigorously nontemporal (*ou chronikon* [οὐ χρονικόν]: cf. *Enneads*, 1.5.7; 3.7.2), which is justifiably based on Plato, provides the point of departure for a tradition that seeks to maintain the distinction between the adjectives *aiônios* and *aidios* to mark the difference between "eternal" and "perpetual" (*Enneads*, 3.7.3). The Neoplatonic tradition thus introduces on the side of time-*chronos* and at a distance from *aiôn*-eternity, even though it derives from the latter, a perpetuity in becoming for which the term *aidotês* [ἀιδιότης] was used only later on. Thus Damascius gives the name "complete time [*ho sumpas chronos* (ὁ σύμπας χρόνος)]" to "time that always flows." "Since this intermediary is related both to time and to eternity," Simplicius remarks, "some philosophers have called it *chronos* and others *aiôn*" (Simplicius, *Corollary on Place*, ed. Diels, 776.10–12 and 779). And Proclus distinguishes between an eternal sense and a temporal sense of *aidiotês* (*Elements of Theology*, prop. 55), modeled on the double interpretation of *aei*: *to chronikon* [τὸ χρονικόν] and *to aiônion* [τὸ αἰώνιον] (*On the Timaeus*, 1.239.2–3 and 3.3.9). Including the "life of eternity" qua "infinite life" without past or future, the life of the whole being present simultaneously, uniting in the atemporal (*achronos* [ἄχρονος]) life of the *nous* [νοῦς] the characteristics of the perfect living being of the *Timaeus* with those of the total being in the *Sophist* (*pantelôs on* [παντελῶς ὄν], 248e8), Plotinus establishes time in the soul as a "moving image of eternity" (*Enneads*, 3.7.11). An image without resemblance with regard to a divine presence that illuminates in its immanent life the reciprocal relation between "being" and "always" (on the identity of *to on* [τὸ ὄν], cf. ibid., 3.7.6), between the *aiôn* and the Intelligible, which posits the Intellect as a god (ibid., 5.8.3) whose beatitude is eternal because it is the very nature of eternity (*ho ontôs aiôn* [ὁ ὄντως αἰών], ibid., 5.1.4). That is why it is justifiable to call eternity "god who manifests himself and makes himself appear in his nature" (ibid., 3.7.5), in accord with an echo of the "Chaldaic" name of the god *Aiôn* as an *autophanès* [αὐτοφανής] that loses here all cosmological meaning.

"It was precisely this atemporal, 'vertical' notion, connected with the notions of life, presence, and divinity, that was later adopted"—and adapted—"by Christian theology through Augustine, Boethius, Bonaventure . . ." (Leibovich, "*L'AIÔN*," 99). But from a lexicographical point of view, the polysemy of the term *aiôn* remains present in all Greek patristic writing through the Septuagint ("generation": Ws 14:6; "long period": Ps 143 [142]; "Eternity": Eccl 12:5) and the New Testament ("period" in general: Eph 2:7; "present age" in the sense of this world: Mt 13:39—often with strong pejorative connotation—and 1 Tm 6:17; "eternity," especially in the extensive sense of "forever": Jn 12:34 and Gal 1:5). After having referred to this polysemy, John of Damascus nonetheless enumerated six meanings of the word *aiôn*: (1) each individual's lifespan; (2) a period of a thousand years; (3) the total duration of time and the world; (4) future life after the Resurrection; (5) each of the seven eras that constitute the history of the world, to which an eighth should be added, beginning after the Last Judgment; (6) according to a definition adopted by Gregory of Nazianzus (*Orationes*, 38.8, in RT: *PG*, vol. 36, col. 320), the *aiôn* is neither time nor part of time, but what "extends itself" (*diastêma*) with eternal realities, being for the latter what time is for temporal realities (John of Damascus, *Expositio fidei*, 15 [2.1], ed. Kotter, 43–44; the Latin translation renders *aiôn* not by *aevum* but rather by *saeculum* [*translatio Burgundii*, fifteenth century, ed. Buytaert, 66–68]). In the tenth chapter of *Divine Names*,

Pseudo-Dionysius notes with regret that the Scriptures "do not always reserve the epithet *aiônios* for what escapes all engenderment, for what exists in a truly eternal way, and not even for indestructible, immortal, immutable, and identical beings." Even "the beings called eternal [*aiônia* (αἰώνια)] are not . . . coeternal [*sunaidia* (συναΐδια)] with God, who is prior to all eternity [*pro aiônôn* (πρὸ αἰώνων)]; in following the Scriptures with all rigor, we must . . . consider as intermediary between being and becoming everything that participates in both *aiôn* and *chronos*" (Pseudo-Dionysius the Areopagite, *De divinis nominibus*, 10.937C–940A). Knowing that *aiôn* was to be translated by *aevum* (*translatio Saraceni*; *Dionysiaca*, 1:492–93), it will be granted that Pseudo-Dionysius's attempted lexical clarification was far from successful.

II. A Multiplicity of Eternities:
Aevum, Aeternitas, Sempiternitas, Perpetuitas

At first sight, nothing seems simpler than to connect, as did medieval writers themselves, the Latin form *aevum* with the transliteration of the Greek *aiôn*, and thus to differentiate "eternity" from movement-time (*chronos*). According to Aquinas, "strictly speaking, *aevum* and *aeternitas* differ no more than *anthrôpos* and *homo*" (*Liber de causis*, prop. 2, lect. 2). The translation problem arises from the fact that the Scholastic lexicon made a rigorous distinction between *aevum* and *aeternitas*—though it did so belatedly. In the course of the thirteenth century, *aevum* detached itself from *aeternitas*, coming to designate an intermediary between time and eternity and characterizing certain realities called "eviternal" that have a beginning but not an end (*aeternitatis ex parte post*).

But precisely because of the principle of correspondence between the measures of duration and the essence of beings, this purely extensive differentiation is contested. For eternity is not simply defined *ex negativo* as time without limit (from the point of view of its "continuity," *perpetuitas*) or as an eternity of duration (which would be "always," *sempiternitas*): it is first of all, positively, a permanence and presence itself that is atemporal and intensive (*tota simul*), as incommensurable as God himself. From here comes the essential instability of this intermediary figure, which has to include a temporal aspect in order to distinguish itself from atemporal eternity—without, however, being confused with time.

A. *Aeternitas/aevum*: Eternity of God, eternity of angels (Augustine)

Aevum does not designate the eminently simple eternity that is inseparable from the essence of God, but rather a "qualified," "participated" eternity (*aeternitas participata*), which measures the duration of living creatures whose being is not variable and successive (like celestial bodies and separate substances: angels or rational souls), without, however, attaining *immutability* in the full and absolute sense: either it reintroduces a certain type of variability at the level of the operations of which it is the locus, or it reveals itself as potentially incomplete. Consequently, *aevum* signifies an "angelic" eternity that can be said to be eternal only insofar as it participates in divine eternity without being coeternal with God.

In his *De diversis quaestionibus* (qu. 72: "De temporibus aeternis"), Saint Augustine (354–430) distinguishes two forms of eternity: the first belongs only to God through his absolute immutability; the second coincides with the totality of time. It is from this latter point of view that angels can be said to be "eternal," since they have existed for all time, without nonetheless being coeternal with God because his immutability is beyond all time. In comparison with created time, which is susceptible to change (*tempus mutabile*), this derived eternity called *aevum* is thus presented as a "stable" form (*illud stabile*).

In his *City of God* (12.16), Augustine wonders how God can "precede time," or better yet, "precede all times": "It is not in time that God precedes times; in that case, how could he have preceded all times? He precedes them from the height of his always-present eternity. He dominates all times to come, because they are to come and because, when they have come, they will be past. Our years pass and follow each other, and their number will be complete at the very moment when they will cease to be. God's years are like a single day that is always present. It is eternity" (cf. Augustine, *Œuvres*, 745 n. 87). The *aevum* is thus an *aeternitatis ex parte post*, *aeternitatis creata*, or *aeternitatis diminuta*, as it was reformulated in the thirteenth century by Bonaventure and James of Viterbo.

B. *Aeternitas/sempiternitas*: The eternity of God and that of the universe (Boethius)

The second cardinal distinction that runs throughout the Latin Middle Ages is the one introduced by Boethius (470–524) between eternity proper (*aeternitas*) and sempiternity (*sempiternitas*): eternity as the "complete possession, simultaneous and perfect, of a life without limit" ("interminabilis vitae tota simul et perfecta possessio," in *Consolation of Philosophy*, 5.6.4), as opposed to *sempiternitas*, the eternity of the universe, subject to time, even if it knows neither beginning nor end.

■ See Box 1.

The chief distinctions between a temporal "now" and an eternal "now," a temporal "always" (*sempiternitas*) and an eternal "always" (*aeternitas*), were already established in the *De Trinitate*, where Boethius inquires into the *praedicatio in divinis*, the question of what the conversion that affects categories in the application to God must be:

> The expression "God is ever" denotes a single Present, summing up His continual presence in all the past, in all the present—however that term be used—and in all the future. Philosophers say that "ever" may be applied to the life of the heavens and other immortal bodies. But as applied to God it has a different meaning. He is ever [*semper*], because "ever" is with Him a term of present time, and there is this great difference between "now" [*nunc*], which is our present, and the divine present. Our present connotes changing time and sempiternity [nostrum "nunc" quasi currens tempus facit et sempiternitatem]; God's present, unmoved, and immovable, connotes eternity ["nunc" permanens neque movens sese atque consistens aeternitatem facit]. Add *semper* to eternity and you get the constant, incessant, and thereby perpetual course of our present time, that is to say, sempiternity [iugem indefessumque ac per hoc perpetuum cursum quod est sempiternitas].
>
> (*De Trinitate*, 4.28–32)

Thus Boethius establishes in a practically definitive way the distinction between an intensive conception of eternity grasped in the plenitude of its atemporal presence ("plenitudinem totam pariter . . . totam pariter praesentiam"), in the immutable presence of a single instant, and an extensive conception of perpetuity referring to the infinity of a "worldly" time/times that cannot be coeternal with God in any way. The interminable (*interminabilis*) character of eternity, which medieval writers interpreted etymologically as *extra terminos* or *sine termino*, is only the negative (and still worldly) form of the simplicity and perfection that are the positive conditions of its immobility and simultaneity (unitotality). But the quoted definition of eternity implies still more than its atemporal or untemporal being: the eternity of God is a form of life, a life of thought, thought that includes

---

1

Boethius's definition: "What is eternity?"

Eternity, then, is the complete, simultaneous, and perfect possession of everlasting life [*interminabilis vitae tota simul et perfecta perfectio*]; this will be clear from a comparison with creatures that exist in time. Whatever lives in time exists in the present and progresses from the past to the future [id praesens a praeteritis in futura procedit], and there is nothing set in time that can embrace simultaneously the whole extent of its life [totum vitae suae spatium pariter amplecti]: it is in the position of not yet possessing tomorrow when it has already lost yesterday. In this life of today you do not live more fully than in that fleeting and transitory moment. Whatever, therefore, suffers the condition of being in time, even though it never had any beginning, never has any ending and its life extends into the infinity of time, as Aristotle thought was the case of the world, it is still not such that it may properly be considered eternal. Its life may be infinitely long but it does not embrace and comprehend its whole extent simultaneously [interminabilis vitae plenitudinem totam partier comprehendit atque complectitur]. It still lacks the future, while already having lost the past. So that which embraces and possesses simultaneously the future and has lost nothing of the past, that is what may properly be said to be eternal, of necessity it will always be present to itself, controlling itself, and have present the infinity of fleeting time [necesse est et sui compos praesens sibi semper adsistere et infinitatem mobilis temporis habere praesentem].

(Boethius, *The Consolation of Philosophy*, trans. Victor Watts [Cambridge: Cambridge University Press, 2000])

everything that can be included all at once, as opposed to time, the condition of life for weaker minds, which can think things only one after the other. God thus lives in an eternal present, which is the model of the ordinary present (cf. Marenbon, *Boethius*, 134–38).

C. The difficult place of the *aevum* between eternity and time

Under the influence of Neoplatonism and especially of the *Liber de causis*, the term *aevum*, which until the thirteenth century had been commonly used in the sense of *aeternitas* or *aetas perpetua*, came to designate the duration intermediate between time and eternity, "post aeternitatem et supra tempus," as Aquinas put it in his commentary on the *Liber de causis*:

> Omne esse superius aut est superius aeternitate et ante ipsam, aut est cum aeternitate, aut est post aeternitatem et supra tempus.

> Every superior being is either above eternity and before it, or with it, or after it and above time.

> (*Liber de causis*, 2.19)

These three kinds of superior being correspond to the First Cause, the Intelligence, and the Soul, respectively. This classification is adopted, in a modified form, by medieval writers. For example, commenting on the formula "Deus est temporis et aevi causa" (God is the cause of time and the *aevum*), Albert the Great (1200–1280) explains: "Time is the image of the *aevum*, and the *aevum* is the image of eternity" (tempus est imago aevi et aevum est imago aeternitatis). The notion of *aevum*, thus detached from *aeternitas* and having been given an autonomous position intermediary between time and eternity, is perfectly characterized by Nicholas of Strasburg (ca. 1320): "Medio modo se habentibus oportet dare mensuram mediam inter aeternitatem simplicem et tempus. Haec autem non potest esse alia quam aevum" (It is important to give to entities whose status is intermediary a measure intermediary between simple eternity and time. The measure cannot be other than the *aevum*: *On Time*, 215 va.).

This tripartite classification encountered several insurmountable difficulties, however, and did not succeed in establishing itself. For one thing, the fact that the realities measured by the *aevum* are heterogeneous (angels, rational souls, the heavens, and even sometimes first matter) seems to suggest that a single measure would be impossible. But since unity is the mark of perfection, is it conceivable that time would be one, whereas the *aevum* would be multiple? Is the argument that the *aevum* must be considered one in virtue of its cause and its participation in eternity sufficient to avoid any subjective deviation toward an angelic time that might soon come to be seen as a "quid ad placitum" (cf. Suarez-Nani, *Tempo*, 33–35)?

Along with the question of the unity of the *aevum*, the problem of its simplicity and indivisibility was widely debated in the Scholastic literature around the turn of the fourteenth century. We can easily see why: if the *aevum* is absolutely simple and indivisible, its nature no longer differs from that of eternity; if, on the contrary, the *aevum* has extension and is composed of parts, it is a successive quantity in the same way as time. Just as in the case of the problem of unity, the necessity of coping with this dilemma runs throughout the Franciscan and Dominican schools and shapes the temporality of eviternal being.

D. The Scotist break: The extension of *aevum* to permanent existence

In the Scotist school, the notion of *aevum* underwent a fundamental transformation determined by the problems involved in the Aristotelian analysis of time associated with movement (and primarily the problem of the movement of the heavens), in order to account for the *being* of substances. If the *aevum* is a measure of permanent being that is potentially corruptible, isn't it *aevum* that has to account for all forms of permanence, substantial as well as accidental, insofar as they depend in an invariable and uniform way on a single cause—namely, God (Duns Scotus, *Sentences* [*Ordinatio*], 2, dist. 2, p. 1, q. 4)? For movement is what is measured by time—not what precedes and receives it. Using this argument, John Duns Scotus (1266–1308) makes the *aevum* the measure of permanent existence as such, no longer recognizing, from this point of view, any difference between a stone and an angel:

> dico quod exsistentia angeli mensuratur aevo; et etiam exsistentia lapidis et omnis exsistentia quae uniformiter manet, dum manet, mensuratur aevo.

> Whence I say that the existence of angels is measured by the *aevum*; and also that the existence of stones and of all forms of existence that remain the same, while they remain, is measured by the *aevum*.

> (*Sentences* [*Lectura*], dist. 2, p. 1, q. 3)

Thus freed from any essential reference to separate substances or to celestial bodies, the *aevum* can be defined functionally as the measure of the uniformity of permanent things in general, in their dependence on the "first cause," which is alone capable of preserving them in being (*Sentences*, [*Ordinatio*] 2, dist. 3, p. 1, q. 4). This new model of the *aevum* (which coincides with the weakening of the Aristotelian cosmological paradigm to the point of authorizing the idea of a potential time of which the movement of the heavens, in its recognized uniformity, is only the actual representative) challenges the principle of ontological heterogeneity and hierarchy between celestial realities and the sublunary world. It spread far beyond the Scotist school.

E. Ockham's Razor: *Aevum nihil est*, "The *aevum* isn't anything"

Within the nominalist tradition, William of Ockham (1285/90–1347/49) emphasized the impossibility of conceiving the possibility that an angel might be annihilated after its creation, or that the life of one angel might be longer than that of another, without referring to a "coexisting" succession. Angelic duration, like any duration, must be measured only by the ordinary time of succession, the only one appropriate to it: "Time is the measure of the duration of angels, as it is the measure of movement" (tempus est mensura durationis angelorum, sicut est mensura motus, William of Ockham, *Sentences* [*Reportatio*], 3, q. 8 and q. 11; *Tractatus de successivis*, ed. Boehner, 96).

Thus *aevum* passes definitively from its unstable intermediary position, not to eternity (even as a "second" eternity), but to common, heterogeneous time, it being posited that "time properly so called" (tempus proprissime dictum), or "common time" (tempus commune), "no longer refers to the movement of the Unmoved Mover as its cause [ratio causalitatis] qua cause of all other movements, but in virtue of the character of uniformity that belongs to it 'accidentally' [accidit]" (William of Ockham, *Quaestiones super libros physicorum*, q. 45; cf. Duhem, *Le système du monde*, 7:379–92). So there exist only two ways of measuring duration: the clock-time conceived for created realities, and eternity for the divine essence alone—even though divine duration, qua infinite duration, cannot be "represented" without coexisting with the duration we conceive.

Only René Descartes was able to take advantage of this last argument from the *motus cogitationis*, the movement of thought, in which the primacy of the thinking self is established in its persistence; but more broadly, it is the whole of the new physics that invests a conception of time that puts an end to the necessity of the *aevum* in its principle of convertibility between (difference in) being and (difference in) duration, after having invested and broadened all the anti-Aristotelian virtualities.

III. The Paradoxes of Time and Eternity

A. "Time," "duration," and "eternity" in the seventeenth century

Freed from the Aristotelian cosmological paradigm as the idea of an arbitrary plurality of purely subjective times (*ad placitum . . .*), in the seventeenth century time is thus defined on the basis of an objective, functional representation and a universal form. The Cartesian criticism of "Scholastic opinion" (*l'opinion de l'École*) has its place in this movement of conceptual unification; if duration is always only "the way in which we *conceive* a thing insofar as it perseveres in being" (putemus durationem rei cuiusque esse tantum modum, sub quo concepimus rem istam, quatenus esse perseverat, *Principles*, 1.55 [in *Œuvres*, ed. Adam and Tannery, 8-1.26.12–15]), and if time is never more than the "way of conceiving" (modus cogitandi) of duration when we want to measure it (*Principles*, 1.57), then the same duration must be attributed to things that are moved and those that are not moved, because "the before and after of all durations, whatever they might be, appear to me through the before and after of the successive duration that I discover in my thought, with which other things are coexistent" (prius enim et posterius durationis cuiscunque mihi innotescit per prius et posterius durationis successivae, quam in cogitatione mea, cui res aliae coexistunt, deprehendo, Letter to Arnaud, 29 July 1648 [in *Œuvres*, ed. Adam and Tannery, 5.223.17–19]). As for eternity itself, it is *tota simul* "insofar as nothing could ever be added to the nature of God or taken away from it," but "it is not all at once and once and for all insofar as it coexists, for since we can distinguish in it parts since the creation of the world, why could we not also distinguish parts in it before, since it is the same duration?" (sed non est simul et semel, quatenus simul existit, nam cum possimus in ea distinguere partes iam post mundi creationem, quidni illud etiam possemus facere ante eam, cum eadem duratio sit, *Conversation with Burman* [in *Œuvres*, ed. Adam and Tannery, 5.149].

The Cartesian critique allows us to understand why the concept of *aevum* disappears from philosophical speculations in the seventeenth century and does not appear, despite commentators' efforts to implant it there, where it has been thought to reemerge because of the "temporalization of eternity": in Spinoza. In fact, Spinoza's *Ethics* presents the clearest refusal to explain eternity "by continuance or time, though continuance may be conceived without a beginning or end" (*Ethics* 1, expl. of def. 8: "per durationem, aut tempus explicari non potest, tametsi duratio principio, et fine carere concipiatur"). Eternity, which must be understood as "existence itself, insofar as it is conceived necessarily to follow from the definition of that which is eternal" (per aeternitatem intelligo ipsam existentiam quatenus ex sola rei aeternae definitione necessario sequi concipitur, *Ethics*, 1, def. 8), is conceived by Spinoza on the model of eternal truths, whose exemplary form is provided by mathematical truths (insofar as they are valid *ab aeterno et in aeterno*), whereas duration is identified with "the indefinite continuance of existing" (indefinita existendi continuatio, *Ethics*, 2, def. 5), "because it can never be determined on the basis of the nature itself of the existing thing" (*Ethics*, 2, expl. of def. 5). But the fact that duration can be divided into parts when it is measured by this "way of thinking" that is time, in accord with a movement of abstraction establishing "at will" (*ad libitum*) the universal reference-point of all durations (Spinoza, letter 12, ed. Gebhardt, 4:61 and 55) and making it possible in turn to insert them into the system of the laws of nature, does not in any way imply that one of them, an "affection" of things (*duratio*), can be reduced to the other, an imaginary being (*tempus*). For if the force through which a thing perseveres in existence (*conatus*) is nothing other than the power of God expressing itself in a finite, determinate form, the duration of a thing can be understood *sub specie aeternitatis* by conceiving it insofar as it endures "through the essence of God" (Spinoza, *Ethics*, 5, prop. 30, proof). It is by virtue of this immanence of divine power that duration is said to "flow [*fluit*] from eternal things," as Spinoza puts it in letter 12 (ed. Gebhardt, 4:56).

▪ See Box 2.

B. *Ewigkeit* and the ecstasy of time: Schelling

Not until the post-Kantian period, when speculative philosophies of history appeared, and especially Schelling's attempt to establish a "geneaology of time," were the notions of *aiôn* and *aevum* re-represented, in an entirely different theoretical domain. "Eternity" (*Ewigkeit*), "in all eternity" (*von Ewigkeit*), were themselves rearticulated with the different figures of time: the "now," but also the instant or decisive lightning-flash (*Jetzt, Augenblick, Blitz*), "lifetime" (*Lebenzeit*), the time or age of the world (*Weltalter*). It was Schelling who pushed furthest the project of rising to a "superior history," in which a genuinely "historical" God is temporalized distinguishing the "times" or "ages" within it, in accord with a time that is "inner" (*innere Zeit*) and "organic." The revival in a new context of the Augustinian question of the "beginning" ("What does it mean to begin? How can one make a beginning?") leads Schelling to locate in God himself ("God in becoming and God to

2

"Eternity of death" versus "living eternity": The Bergsonian experience of *durée*

It is by starting from Spinoza, namely from the irreducibility of duration (*durée*) to mathematical time, and from a certain "eternalization" of that duration, that we can best understand the notion of duration in Bergson's thought. Beyond the ontological partitions of the *aevum*, the Bergsonian experience of duration rediscovers the vitality of the *aiôn*. Bergson opposes "conceptual eternity, which is an eternity of death" (immutable, immobile eternity) to an "eternity of life," "a living and therefore still moving eternity in which our own particular duration would be included as the vibrations are in light; an eternity which would be the concentration of all duration, as materiality is its dispersion"

(Bergson, "Introduction to Metaphysics" [1903]) . He conceives psychological duration only as an opening onto an ontological duration whose reality condition is that the All is never "given," as differentiated, but is an *élan vital*, a movement of differentiation and duration. *The Two Sources of Morality and Religion* (1932), which continues the argument of *Creative Evolution* (1907), seeks to show that Duration is not called Life without a movement appearing that tends to free "man from the level proper to him to make of him a creator, adequate to the whole movement of creation" (Deleuze, *Le Bergsonisme*, 117). Thus Bergson clearly claims to give us the first and last reasons why "the

measure of time never bears on duration qua duration" (*La pensée*, 3).

BIBLIOGRAPHY

Bergson, Henri. *Creative Evolution*. Translated by Arthur Mitchell. New York: Dover, 1998.
———. *Introduction to Metaphysics*. Translated by T. E. Hulme. Cambridge, MA: Hackett, 1999.
———. *La pensée et le mouvant*. Paris: F. Alcan, 1934.
———. *The Two Sources of Morality and Religion*. Translated by R. Ashley Audra and Cloudesley Brereton. Notre Dame, IN: University of Notre Dame Press, 1977.
Deleuze, Gilles. *Le Bergsonisme*. Paris: Presses Universitaires de France, 1966.

come") the principle of temporalization, that is, the "decisive separation" (*Scheidung*) that engenders the present, which splits off and frees itself from the past by opening up a future: "The future is what is peculiarly temporal in time" (*Aphorismen*, §214). Thus eternity can once again be seen as the "daughter of time": "Eternity is not by itself, it is only through time; time therefore precedes eternity in accord with actuality" (*Urfassungen*, ed. Schröder, 73; *The Ages of the World*, trans. Wirth). Whatever the considerable differences in conceptualization, we can still discern in the term *Ewigkeit*, which etymology derives directly from *aiôn* and *aevum* (which Kluge links with *Lebenzeit*), the mark of the Homeric sense of *aiôn* as "life," the force and duration of life.

Éric Alliez

BIBLIOGRAPHY

Alliez, Éric. *Capital Times: Tales from the Conquest of Time*. Translated by G. Van Den Abbeele. Foreword by G. Deleuze. Minneapolis: University of Minnesota Press, 1996.
Ancona Costa, Cristina. "*Esse quod est supra eternitatem*: La cause première, l'être et l'éternité dans le *Liber de causis* et dans ses sources." *Revue des Sciences Philosophiques et Théologiques*, no. 76 (1992): 41–62.
Aristotle. *Physics*. Translated by Robin Waterfield. Oxford: Oxford University Press, 1996.
Augustine. *The City of God against the Pagans*. Translated by R. W. Dyson. Cambridge: Cambridge University Press, 1998.
———. *De diversis quaestionibus*. Question 72: "De temporibus aeternis" [On the eternal times]. In *Responses to Miscellaneous Questions*, translated by Boniface Ramsey, edited by Raymond Canning. New York: New City Press, 2008.
———. *Œuvres de saint Augustin*. Edited by G. Bardy, J.-A. Beckaert, and J. Boutet. Bibliothéque Augustinienne 10. Paris: Desclée de Brouwer, 1952.
Benveniste, Émile. "Expression indo-européenne de l'éternité." *Bulletin de la Société de Linguistique Française*, no. 38 (1937): 103–12.
———. *Indo-European Language and Society*. Translated by E. Palmer. Coral Gables, FL: University of Miami Press, 1973.
———. "Latin tempus." In *Mélanges de philologie, de littérature et d'histoire anciennes offerts à Alfred Ernout*, 11–16. Paris: Klincksieck, 1940.
Bergson, Henri. *Duration and Simultaneity*. Translated by L. Jacobson. Indianapolis, IN: Bobbs-Merrill, 1965.
———. *Matter and Memory*. Translated by N. M. Paul and W. S. Palmer. New York: Zone Books, 1988.
———. *Œuvres*. Paris: Éditions du Centenaire, Presses Universitaires de France, 1959.
Boethius. *Theological Tractates*. Translated by H. F. Stewart and E. K. Rand. London: Heinemann, 1918.
Bollack, Jean. *Empédocle*. 4 vols. Paris: Minuit, 1965–69.
Bollack, Jean, and Heinz Wismann. *Héraclite ou la séparation*. Paris: Minuit, 1972.
Brague, Rémi. "Pour en finir avec 'le temps, image mobile de l'éternité.'" In *Du temps chez Platon et Aristote*, 11–71. Paris: Presses Universitaires de France, 1982.
Courtine, Jean-François. "Histoire supérieure et système du temps." In *Extase de la raison: Essais sur Schelling*, 237–59. Paris: Galilée, 1990.
———. "Temporalité et révélation." In *Le dernier Schelling: Raison et positivité*, edited by J.-F. Courtine and J.-F. Marquet, 9–30. Paris: Vrin, 1990.
Degani, Enzo. *Aiôn da Omero ad Aristotele*. Padua, It.: Cedam, 1961.
Deleuze, Gilles. *Bergsonism*. Translated by H. Tomlinson and B. Habberjam. New York: Zone Books, 1988.
———. *Logic of Sense*. Translated by M. Lester with C. Stivale. Edited by C. V. Boundas. New York: Columbia University Press, 1990.
Derrida, Jacques. "*Ousia* and *grammè*: Note on a Note from *Being and Time*." In *Margins of Philosophy*, translated by A. Bass, 29–67. Chicago: University of Chicago Press, 1982.
Descartes, René. *Œuvres*. Edited by Charles Adam and Paul Tannery. Paris: Cerf, 1897–1910.
Duhem, Pierre. *Le système du monde*. Vol. 7, *La physique parisienne au XIVème siècle*. Paris: Hermann, 1956.
Empedocles. *The Extant Fragments*. Edited by R. M. Wright. New Haven, CT: Yale University Press, 1981.
Festugière, André. "Le sens philosophique du mot *AIÔN*." *La Parola del Passato* 11 (1949): 172–89. Reprinted in *Études de philosophie grecque*. Paris: Vrin, 1971.
Galpérine, Marie-Claire. "Le temps intégral selon Damascius." *Les Études Philosophiques*, no. 3 (1980): 307–41.
Ganssle, Gregory E., and David M. Woodruff, eds. *God and Time*. Oxford: Oxford University Press, 2002.
Goldschmidt, Victor. *Le système stoïcien et l'idée de temps*. Paris: Vrin, 1969.
———. *Temps physique et temps tragique chez Aristote*. Paris: Vrin, 1982.
Hoffmann, Philippe. "Jamblique exégète du pythagoricien Archytas: Trois originalités d'une doctrine du temps." *Les Études Philosophiques*, no. 3 (1980): 325–41.
Homer. *Iliade*. Translated by Paul Mazon. Paris: Gallimard / La Pléiade, 1975.
Jaquet, Chantal. "*Sub specie aeternitatis*": *Étude de l'origine des concepts de temps, durée et éternité chez Spinoza*. Paris: Kimé, 1997.

John of Damascus. *Exposition fidei [De fide orthodoxa]*. Edited by Bonifatius Kotter. Berlin: De Gruyter, 1969. *Translatio Burgundii* [15th cent.], edited by E. M. Buytaert. New York: St. Bonaventure, 1955.

Leibovich, E. "L'*AIÔN* et le temps dans le fragment B52 d'Héraclite." *Alter* 2 (1994): 87–118.

Leyden, W. [von]. "Time, Number and Eternity in Plato and Aristotle." *Philosophical Quarterly* 14 (1964): 35–52.

Marenbon, John. *Boethius*. Oxford: Oxford University Press, 2003.

Margel, Serge. *Le tombeau du Dieu artisan*. Paris: Éditions de Minuit, 1995.

O'Brien, Denis. "Temps et éternité dans la philosophie grecque." In *Mythes et représentations du temps*, edited by D. Tiffenau, Actes du Colloque CNRS, 59–85. Paris: Édition du CNRS, 1985.

Onians, Richard Broxton. *The Origins of European Thought*. Cambridge: Cambridge University Press, 1988.

Owen, G.E.L. "*Aiôn* and *aiônios*." *Journal of Theological Studies*, no. 37 (1936): 265–83 [*aiôn*] and 390–404 [*aiônios*].

Plato. *Timaeus* and *Critias*. In *Complete Works*, edited by J. Cooper. Indianapolis, IN: Hackett, 1997.

Plotinus. *The Enneads*. Translated by S. MacKenna. London: Faber, 1966.

Porro, Pasquale. *Forme e modelli di durata nel pensiero medievale: L'Aevum, il tempo discreto, la categoria "quando."* Louvain, Belg.: Presses Universitaires de Louvain, 1996.

———. *The Medieval Concept of Time: Studies on the Scholastic Debate and Its Reception in Early Modern Philosophy*. Edited by P. Porro. Leiden, Neth.: Brill, 2001.

Proclus. *Commentary on Plato's* Timaeus. Translated by Harold Tarrant. Cambridge: Cambridge University Press, 2007.

———. *The Elements of Theology*. Translated by E. R. Dodds. Oxford: Oxford University Press, 1992.

———. *In Platonis Rem publicam commentarii*. Edited by Wilhelm Kroll. Amsterdam, Neth.: Hakkert, 1965

Pseudo-Dionysius. *The Complete Works*. Translated by Paul Rorem. Mahwah, NJ: Paulist Press, 1988.

Schelling, Friedrich Wilhelm Joseph. *The Ages of the World*. Translated by J. Wirth. Albany: State University of New York Press, 2000.

———. *Aphorismen zur Einleitung in die Naturphilosophie* [Aphorisms as an introduction to the philosophy of nature]. In *Sämtliche Werke*, edited by K.F.A. Schelling, 1:291–329. Stuttgart: Cotta, 1856–61. First published in 1806.

Simplicius. *In Aristotelis Physicorum libros quattuor priores commentaria*. Edited by H. Diels. Berlin: Königlich Preussischen Akademie der Wissenschaften, 1882. Translation by J. O Urmson: *Corollaries on Place and Time*. Ithaca, NY: Cornell University Press, 1992.

Sorabji, Richard. *Time, Creation and the Continuum*. London: Duckworth, 1983.

Spinoza. *Opera*. Edited by Carl Gebhardt. 5 vols. Heidelberg: Carl Winters, 1925–87.

Suarez-Nani, Tiziana. *Tempo ed essere nell'autunno del medievo: Il* De tempore *di Nicolas de Strasburgo ed il senso del tempo agli inizi del XIV secolo*. Amsterdam, Neth.: B. R. Grüner, 1989.

William of Ockham. *Philosophical Writings*. Translated by Philotheus Boehner. Cambridge, MA: Hackett, 1990.

Wolfson, Harry Austryn. *The Philosophy of Spinoza: Unfolding the Latent Process of His Reasoning*. Cambridge, MA: Harvard University Press, 1934.

| ALLIANCE

This is the traditional French translation of Hebrew *bĕrit* [בְּרִית] which designates the covenant between the people and its god; see BERĪT. Cf. DUTY and EUROPE.

Concerning the terminological networks that make it possible to conceive the relation between humans and the god(s), the entries have been chosen in each language in relation to the values that determine the singularities of each case, in particular: Greek, KÊR, THEMIS, then OIKONOMIA, see *DESTINY, IMAGE*; Latin, PIETAS, RELIGIO, see *OBLIGATION*; Russian BOGOČELOVEČESTVO, SOBORNOST'; German, BERUF, SOLLEN, see *VOCATION*.

➤ *COMMUNITY, CONSENSUS*, GOD, *HUMANITY*, PEOPLE, *VALUE*

| ANALOGY

GREEK	*analogia* [ἀναλογία]
LATIN	*proportio, analogia*

➤ COMPARISON, CONNOTATION, GOD, HOMONYM, *IMAGE*, LOGOS, PARONYM, PREDICATION, SENSE, SIGN, *TO BE*

The term "analogy" poses no translation problem in English, Italian, or German because its primary meaning is that of the Greek *analogia* [ἀναλογία], which was initially rendered in Latin by *proportio*. It refers to a mathematical relationship between quantities or, more precisely, an equation of two relationships by quotient. The obvious meaning of "relationship of two parts to each other and to the whole" is thus found in Littré's French dictionary as well as in Cicero (in his Latin translation of Plato's *Timaeus*) and Varro (*De lingua latina*, 8.32). However, this mathematical meaning of "relationship between relationships" was very soon superseded by that of "resemblance between relationships," so that, as Michel Foucault pointed out, "an old concept, already familiar to Greek science and medieval thought," was resituated in the more general register of "similitudes" and ends up occupying in the seventeenth century a separate site between the field of *convenientia* ("making possible the marvelous confrontation of resemblances across space") and that of ethical and even aesthetic *aemulatio* (speaking of "adjacencies, bonds and joints") and extending from a single given point "to an endless number of relationships" (*Order of Things*, 21). These multiple relationships justify the presence of the word "analogy"—always too easily translated—in a vocabulary of untranslatable words because of the multiplicity of fields that it silently coordinates through a series of power plays continued indefinitely by their very familiarity.

Practically speaking, a translator of Plato's *Timaeus* (31c, 32a–b) will have no difficulty in rendering the term *analogia* Plato uses to designate the "bond" or "mean" that makes it possible to order "in a beautiful composition" two "numbers, masses, or forces of any kind" through a third or "mean" ("which is to the last term what the first term is to it"). Nor will a translator of Aristotle's *Poetics* have any difficulty in rendering the same term used to indicate the type of relationship in which "there are four terms so related that the second (B) is to the first (A), as the fourth (D) is to the third (C)" (*Poetics*, 1457b16–26). But the same can be said about a translator of A. G. Baumgarten's *Aesthetica* when he encounters the expression *analogia rationis*, which allows this disciple of Christian Wolff to bring the domain of sensitivity and judgments of taste into the field of knowledge, or about a translator of the theologian Karl Barth or Paul Tillich, when he encounters the expressions "*analogia fidei seu revelationis*" (taken from Paul's Epistle to the Romans 12:6, where Paul says that the gift of prophecy must be practiced "in proportion to our faith") and "*analogia imaginis*" (analogy of the image). The only translation problem raised by the Greco-Latin term *analogia* proceeds not from the absence of an equivalent in European philosophical languages, but from the consequences and stakes involved in applying it to the "problem of being" outside its original sphere, under the Scholastic title of *analogia entis* (analogy of being or analogy of the existent), and thus, by that very fact, from its "Greco-Latin" character. It is a translation *that has already been made*, and in a very precise field it raises questions for the philosopher and the historian of philosophy; it is a translation that is, in a sense, *too successful*, and functions as a kind of screen between ancient philosophy, especially the Aristotelian tradition, and the various heirs of medieval Scholasticism. As a result, it is for readers of a work in which it does not appear as such—Aristotle's *Metaphysics*—that *analogia* poses a problem whose multiple ambiguities can be dissipated only by a genealogy of an expression that is deliberately "saturated," a genealogy that at the same time produces the "network" that has enabled it to make history. Here lexicography and theoretical innovation are inseparable, so that (and this makes *analogia* a singular, if not really isolated, case) the history of one can be truly written only through a philosophical archeology of the other. Given the importance of the "Thomist" phase in this "twofold" history, that is where we must begin.

I. Forming the Theory of Analogy

The theory known as the "analogy of being" (*analogia entis*) is a central element of Scholastic metaphysics, and is generally presented as an "Aristotelian" or "Aristotelian-Thomist" theory. This appellation should be abandoned. There are several Thomist formulations of the notion of analogy, some of them philosophical, in the commentaries on Aristotle, others theological, in the personal works (*Quaestiones disputatae de veritate, Summa contra gentiles, Summa theologica*). The first of these are intended to resolve the Aristotelian problem of the "multiplicity of the meanings of being," while the second return to the non-Aristotelian problem, raised by Boethius and Pseudo-Dionysius, of the *praedicatio in divinis* as it is set forth in Boethius's *De Trinitate*, 4, or, to put it another way, to the question of the "divine names." In any case, the medieval notion of the "analogy of being" cannot claim to borrow directly from a positive theory that is aleady constituted as such in Aristotle; instead, it appears at the end of a long hermeneutic process that begins, it seems, as early as Alexander of Aphrodisias, and to which the Aristotelian interpretive tradition contributed throughout late antiquity, from Plotinus to Simplicius. Interpreted on the basis of the Aristotelian corpus, the formation of the medieval theory of analogy presents itself as the gradual fusion of at least six texts that differ in inspiration, scope, and meaning: the distinction between synonyms, homonyms, and paronyms in the first chapter of the *Categories*; the distinction between two types of homonymy (derived from things to their definitions) in the *Topics*, 1.15.107b6–12; the distinction among the different modes of error involving homonymy proposed in *Sophistical Refutations*, 17; the problematic distinction of three kinds of intentional homonyms introduced in the *Nicomachean Ethics*, 1.4.1096b26–31—a unity of origin or provenance, a unity of end or tendency, and a unity of analogy, in which "analogy" has its authentic Aristotelian sense of a mathematical proportion with four terms (a/b = c/d) (see HOMONYM); the theory of the unification of the multiplicity of the meanings of being set forth in book 4 of the *Metaphysics* on the basis of the meaning of the terms "healthy" and "medical," itself complemented by the theory of the accident as an inflection of substance suggested by certain passages in book 7 of the *Metaphysics* (1.1028a15–25). The medieval theory of the analogy of being proceeded mainly from the encounter between the *Categories*, 1.1, the *Nicomachean Ethics*, 1.6, and the *Metaphysics*, 4.1. Before this

synthesis, the notion of a reduced homonymy was preferred, being used without any metaphysical preoccupation as a semantic concept connected with the interpretation of two standard logical problems of homonymy according to Aristotle: the elucidation of the distinction between homonyms and synonyms in the *Categories*, 1.1 and the analysis of the semantic mechanisms of *fallacia aequivocationis* in *Sophistical Refutations*, 17. Characteristic of this problem are the analysis of *aequivocatio ex adiunctus* by the *Anonymus cantabrigiensis*, based on three interpretations of the homonymy of *sanum* clearly taken from *Topics*, 1.15.106b34–38 and that of the *Anonymi compendiosus tractatus de fallaciis*, interpreting in terms of "consignification" the semantic variation presiding over the paralogism of "equivocalness *ex adiunctis*," on the basis of the two senses of *sanum* mentioned in *Topics*, 1.15.106a5–9. At this stage of development, the question of homonymy had not yet produced a theory of the analogy of being: it remained within the limits of the fragments of Porphyry's works transmitted by Boethius's commentaries on Aristotle's logic and the Aristotelian sources of the *Logica vetus* and the *Logica nova*. The metaphysical problem of the plurality of the meanings of being was not confronted as such. Neither did the notion of analogy continue to play an assignable role in the Greco-Roman metaphysics of Boethius's time (*aetas boetiana*), in which until the end of the twelfth century the dominant problem was that of the transfer of categories, the *transsumptio rationum*, which marked all theological uses of the ten Aristotelian categories. In this universe of discourse, the Aristotelian question of the plurality of the meanings of being was occulted by that of the applicability of ontological categories in the domain of theology. Abundantly illustrated in the first medieval commentaries on Boethius's *De Trinitate*, notably in Gilbert de Poitiers and the Porretains, the problem then dominant resided in a single question extrapolated from chapter 4 of Boethius's work: given that "categories change meaning when they are applied to God," is there a pure equivocalness, a metaphoric usage or a "transsumption" of categorial language when it is transposed from the natural domain to the divine domain? (see TO TRANSLATE, Box 1).

II. *Denominativa, Convenientia, Analogia*

The Scholastic problem of analogy appears at the beginning of the thirteenth century, when the word and the notion of *analoga* begin, if not directly to replace, at least to overlap with Aristotle's *denominativa* (or paronyms). This overlapping has a long earlier history: Simplicius (whose *Commentary on the Categories* was translated by William of Moerbeke in 1268) tells us that the Hellenophone interpreters of Aristotle very early on "combined in a single mode homonymy *ab uno* and homonymy *ad finem*," and that other writers "posited them as intermediaries between homonyms and synonyms" (*In praedicamenta Aristotelis*). There is no lack of Latin witnesses to the substitution of the sequence homonyms-synonyms-analogues for the triad homonyms-synonyms-paronyms: the shift had been made as early as 1245, with the first university *Lecturae* of Aristotle's *Libri naturales*. Albert the Great's commentaries on the *Logica vetus* enable us to identify the professors' source here: the Arab philosophers who intercalated between *univoca* and *aequivoca* "what they call *convenientia*" in order to master conceptually the problem with the homonymy of *being*. Starting with Albert and the sources he mentions, al-Ghazali and Avicenna, we can call the theory of "the analogy of being" any theory that has the following elements: the interpretation of homonymy *ad unum* in terms of proportion; the application of this relation, which is oriented and not convertible like paronymy, to the relationship between substance and accident understood as a relationship between *prius* and *posterius*, primary (anterior) and secondary (derived, posterior); and the distinction between "three modes of analogy," that is, three types of "relationships" governing the attribution of so-called analogical terms—*proportio ad unum subiectum*, which is equivalent to the term "being," *proportio ad unum efficiens actum*, which is equivalent to the term "medical," and finally *porportio*, which is equivalent to the term "healthy," and is more or less clearly connected with final causality. Avicenna's *Metaphysics* was known to Latins before Aristotle's *Metaphysics*, and was thus for the Latin Middle Ages, according to Albert himself, the main source for the problem of the plurality of the meanings of being. It was Avicenna's work that determined the reading of Aristotle's works and established the view that the unity of the concept of being sought by Aristotle is a "convention in accord with ambiguity" (*convenance selon l'ambiguïté*) legible in terms of the "relation of the anterior to the posterior," that is, in the more or less Platonizing framework of a theory of participation by degrees. Although the conception of analogy "in accord with the anterior and the posterior" in the Avicenna tradition dominated most logical and metaphysical commentaries on Aristotle up to 1250–60 (Nicolas of Paris, *Summae metenses*; Roger Bacon, *Quaestiones alterae supra libros primae philosophiae Aristotelis*, IV, q. 3–4), later theories became increasingly complex.

III. Philosophical Analogy/Theological Analogy

The distinction between philosophical and theological analogies explodes the initially unitary formulation. Since, given the absence of an assignable relationship or proportion, it was not possible to approach the problem of *praedicatio in divinis* in the framework of a theory of analogy "in accord with the anterior and the posterior" between God as creator and as infinite, on the one hand, and created, finite being on the other, Thomas Aquinas introduced, to compensate for this shortcoming, a distinction between analogy of proportion and analogy of proportionality, which has been well described by recent interpreters. Since Boethius's *De institutione arithmetica* (2.40), "proportion" has meant a relationship between two terms, and "proportionality" has meant a relationship between two relationships, whereas by "analogy of proportion" Thomas accounts for what we now call the "focal meaning" of being (or rather of the word "being"): the diverse categorical meanings can be coordinated horizontally like those of the word "healthy." The "analogy of proportionality" seeks to connect two relationships: a cognitive, conceptual relationship (*secundum intentionem*) and an ontological relationship (*secundum esse*). In the sixteenth century, Meister Eckhart virtually exhausts the concept by reducing theological analogy to a simple analogy of extrinsic attribution based on an "analogy" in the strict sense of the term (a proportion with four elements): just as health exists only in an animal, there is no being except in God. The creature is a sign of God, as urine is the sign of health. However, the relationship between the sign and the thing signified being reflected in a relationship between cause and effect, the exact content of the theory of analogy is a theory of "analogical causality": God is the creator and giver of being, hence the creature is; but the latter's being, which is not rooted in itself, can be reduced to that of God and is no more than a sign of the latter. With the appearance of the "univocal concept of being" in Duns Scotus, the theory of analogy gradually evolves in the direction of a theory of the "analogical concept of being," which the Thomists, and then the "Second Scholasticism," tried to oppose to the Scotist theory. This development, which led beyond the Middle Ages, produced more or less syncretic formations of the ideas of analogy used by the Neo-Thomists and Neo-Scholastics: thus the model for Jacques Maritain's notion of analogy is John of St. Thomas more than Thomas Aquinas.

The discursive complex of *analogia entis* does not exhaust the whole of the field of *analogia*. Modern debates about the purely allegorical status of analogy (E. Cassirer) or, on the contrary, the "effect of metaphorical meaning" that surreptitiously plagues medieval theological analogy (P. Ricoeur) are nonetheless situated in the network defined by the encounter between the Aristotelian problem of "the multiplicity of the meanings of being" and the purely theological problem of "the divine names" inherited from late antique and medieval thought. *Analogia* is the heart of a system from which radiate and become relatively autonomous diverse fields that are necessarily connected by the founding act of *inventio analogiae*: metaphor, symbol, and category.

Alain de Libera

BIBLIOGRAPHY

Ashworth, Earline Jennifer. "Analogy and Equivocation in Thirteenth-Century Logic: Aquinas in Context." *Mediaeval Studies* 54 (1992): 94–135.

———. "Suarez and the Analogy of Being: Some Historical Background." *Vivarium* 33 (1995): 50–75.

Aubenque, Pierre. "Sur la naissance de la doctrine pseudo-aristotélicienne de l'analogie de l'être." *Les Etudes Philosophiques* 3–4 (1989): 291–304.

Baumbarten, A. G. *Aesthetica*, I–II. Frankfurt, 1750–58; repr. Hildesheim, Ger.: Olms, 1961.

Brentano, Franz. *Von der mannigfachen Bedeutung des Seienden nach Aristoteles*. Hildesheim. Ger.: Olms, 1960. Translation by R. Georg: *On the Several Senses of Being in Aristotle*. Berkeley: University of California Press, 1981.

Courtine, Jean-François. *Suarez et le système de la métaphysique*. Paris: Presses Universitaires de France, 1990.

Foucault, Michel. *Les mots et les choses*. Paris: Gallimard / La Pléiade, 1966. Translation by A. Sheridan: *The Order of Things*. New York: Vintage, 1994.

Simplicius. "Commentary on Aristotle's Categories." In *In praedicamenta Aristotelis*. Edited by André Pattin and Willem Stuyven. Louvain: Publications Universitaires de Louvain, 1971.

Vuillemin, Jules. *De la logique à la théologie: Cinq études sur Aristote*. Paris: Flammarion, 1967. 44–125.

Wolfson, H. A. "The Amphibolous Terms in Aristotle, Arabic Philosophy and Maimonides." *Harvard Theological Review* 31 (1938): 151–73.

ANIMAL

GERMAN   *Animal, Bestie, Tier, animalisches Wesen*
GREEK   *to zôion* [τὸ ζῷον], *to thêrion* [τὸ θηρίον]
LATIN   *animal*

➤ AFFORDANCE, LEIB, *LIFE/LEBEN*, LOGOS, NATURE, PHANTASIA, SOUL, SUBJECT

Today, we tend to take the triad "human"/"animal"/"plant" for granted: usage in Romance languages generally reserves "animal" for animals that lack reason but are mobile. However, if we take into account its etymological echo of the root *anima*, in the sense of the vital breath, "animal" also has an extended meaning that allows it to designate any living being. The Greek language offers us a still broader semantic configuration: the word *zôion* [ζῷον] (from *zôô* [ζώω], "to live," *zôê* [ζωή], "life"), which is usually rendered as "animal," includes in many texts not only humans but also the stars and the gods, and sometimes plants. Moreover, the usual translation of the term "animal" in German, *das Tier*, refers to still another constellation of meanings. Close to the Greek *thêr* [θήρ] (with its derivative *thêrion* [θηρίον], which means "wild beast," "predator of game"), the etymology of *Tier* reveals a proximity not with the soul, or even with life, but with brutality, savagery, bestial violence, and even death. This kind of inflection, which tends to turn toward a semantic opposition, thus leads French translators to render *das Tier* as *bête* (beast) rather than *animal*. Too narrow or too broad, the French word *animal* involves a projection onto other taxonomies.

I. The Absence of the Animal among the Greeks: The *Zôion*

History of Animals, Parts of Animals, Generation of Animals, and so on—Aristotle's biological treatises seem to support the view that the concept "animal" functioned in the same way for the Greeks as it does for us. But the Greek term we translate, through Latin, as "animal" has a much broader meaning: *to zôion*, a neuter noun formed on *zôô* [ζώω], "to live": "For everything that partakes of life may be truly called a living being" (Plato, *Timaeus*, 77b), even plants, but first of all the world itself (30b), the gods that are stars in the sky and those of Olympus (39e–f), and, of course, humans no less than our "animals."

However, in this hierarchy of the diversity of species, Aristotle often distinguishes *zôia* [ζῷα] proper (noun) from *zôntes* [ζῶντες] (present participle of the verb) and *zôoi* [ζωόι] (nominalized adjective), namely, simple "living beings" situated at a lower rung on the ladder, those whose souls have the faculty of feeding themselves and reproducing (plants), but not of feeling, moving (our "animals"), thinking, or speaking (humans): "For nature passes from lifeless objects [*tôn apsuchôn* (τῶν ἀψύχων)] to *zôia* [ζῷα] in . . . unbroken sequence, interposing between them beings that live [*tôn zôntôn* (τῶν ζώντων)] yet are not *zôia*" (*Parts of Animals*, 681a12–13; see also *On the Soul*, 2.413b1–4). The difficulty in translating *zôion* is here at its greatest. Wolff's suggestion that it be translated in French as *animé* (animate being: Wolff, "L'animal et le dieu," 163) avoids the confusion with our restricted sense of "animal," but it encounters a new problem: in Aristotle there are *animés* (literally, *empsucha* [ἔμψυχα], in contrast to *apsucha*, "inanimate beings" such as stones; cf. *On the Soul*, 2.413a22) that are not *zôia*, "animals" (precisely, plants, *ta phuta* [τα φυτά]), or concerning which it is difficult to decide, so intermediary is their nature (sponges, for instance: *Parts of Animals*, 681a10–17). In any case, a translation as *animé* or "animal" erases the great chain that leads from simple "animate beings" to *zôia*, singular beings well defined by their increasingly differentiated activities.

■ See Box 1.

1

Bare life (It. *la nuda vita*; Ger. *das bloße Leben*)

"Bare life" is a central term in Giorgio Agamben's political philosophy designating a life stripped of all activities, attributes, qualities, and qualifications.

Early in his book *Homo sacer*, Agamben announces that "the protagonist of this book is bare life" (11; trans. Heller-Roazen, 8). That book's reader might well wonder, however, what this "bare life" is and in what sense it is bared. Is it a good thing, on the order of a purification; a bad thing, such as a deprivation; or neither? The answers Agamben gives to these questions are to be found in the subtle genealogy he offers of conceptions—philosophical and other—of "life" from ancient Greece to the present day.

"Bare life" presents a translation difficulty that should be noted—namely, the English translation given in *Homo sacer* for Agamben's expression *la nuda vita*. The history

of this translation is more complicated than it might first appear. In a brief discussion of the idea of the sacred at the end of *Language and Death*, Agamben wrote that "even the sacralization of life derives from sacrifice: from this point of view it simply abandons the naked natural life [*la nuda vita*] to its own violence and its own unspeakableness" (133; trans. Pinkus, 106). This suggestive use of the term *la nuda vita*—literally, "naked life"—does not, however, prepare us for the role it will play in Agamben's later thought. In an essay from 1993, "Bartleby o Della contingenza," Agamben again invokes *la nuda vita*, and in a widely read translation of that essay three years later, the term is again rendered as "naked life." Daniel Heller-Roazen's translation of *Homo sacer* chooses a different translation for *la nuda vita*: "bare life." *Bare* and

naked are indeed often synonymous, and this divergence might seem, at first sight, a negligible one reflecting a mere stylistic preference. It is, however, more than this, as *la nuda vita* is not a term of Agamben's own invention. It, too, is a translation—a quotation without quotation marks from the work of Walter Benjamin.

In "Destiny and Character," Benjamin introduces the term *das bloße Leben*, "bare life," and employs it again in "The Critique of Violence" (see *Gesammelte Schriften*, 2:175 and 2:199–200). That Agamben conceived *la nuda vita* as a translation of Benjamin's *das bloße Leben* is not made clear to his reader in *Language and Death*, in the 1993 "Bartleby o Della contingenza," or in any of the other essays leading up to *Homo sacer*. Nor, for that matter, is it made clear in the opening sections of *Homo sacer*.

At the end of part 1, however, Agamben turns to Benjamin's analyses of law and life and there underlines the relation of the one formulation to the other: "nuda vita [*bloße Leben*]." *Nuda vita*—naked or bare life—is thus, for Agamben, another way of saying *bloße Leben*—bare life—and knowing this allows us to understand better not only Heller-Roazen's translation but also *Homo sacer*'s protagonist. Benjamin's expression *das bloße Leben* designates a life shorn of all qualification and conceived of as independent of its traditional attributes. Although Benjamin does not offer further directions for how it is to be understood, it is clear that "bare life" is not an initial state so much as what becomes visible through a stripping away of predicates and attributes. It is best understood in relation to Agamben's discussion of the two Greek terms for life, *bios* [βίος] and *zôê* [ζωή]. As Agamben observes, for the Greeks the term *zôê* designated "life" in the sense of "the simple fact of living common to all living beings (animals, men, or gods)," and for this reason it tellingly admitted of no plural form (*Homo sacer*, 3; trans. Heller-Roazen, 1). *Zôê*

was then life in its most general sense, a sense every bit as general as "being." The second term, *bios*, referred to the forms our lives take—to "the form or way of living proper to an individual or a group" (*Homo sacer*, 3; trans. Heller-Roazen, 1). In addition to the undifferentiated fact of a thing being alive—*zôê*—there is a specific way of living—*bios*. This distinction corresponded to a fundamental division in the Greeks' political landscape. For them, "simple, natural life" (*zôê*) was not the affair of the city (*polis*), but instead of the home (*oikos*), whereas *bios* was the life that concerned the *polis*. In the very words the Greeks used to express the divisions of their culture, there was a distinction between the life that was the concern of the (city-)state and the private life that lay beyond its province. In Agamben's hands, bare life is linked both to an ideal conception—one where individual lives are not weighed, measured, judged, or valued against their fulfillment of certain criteria (being red, Communist, Italian, etc.)—and to a potentially dangerous one, as in instances where individuals and groups are stripped of all rights associated with such belonging and reduced to a mere

nude or bare life, subjected to unqualified suffering.

Leland De la Durantaye

BIBLIOGRAPHY

Agamben, Giorgio. "Bartleby o Della contingenza." In Giorgio Agamben and Gilles Deleuze, *Bartleby: La formula della creazione*. Macerata, It.: Quodlibet, 1993. Translation by Daniel Heller-Roazen: "Bartleby, or On Contingency." In *Potentialities*, edited by Daniel Heller-Roazen. Stanford, CA: Stanford University Press, 1999.

———. *Homo sacer: Il potere sovrano e la nuda vita*. Turin, It.: Einaudi, 1995. Translation by Daniel Heller-Roazen: *Homo Sacer: Sovereign Power and Bare Life*. Stanford, CA: Stanford University Press, 1998.

———. *Il linguaggio e la morte: Un seminario sul luogo della negatività*. Turin, It.: Einaudi, 1982. Translation by Karen E. Pinkus with Michael Hardt: *Language and Death: The Place of Negativity*. Minneapolis: University of Minnesota Press, 1991.

Benjamin, Walter. *Gesammelte Schriften*. Edited by Rolf Tiedemann and Herman Schweppenhäuser. 7 vols. Frankfurt: Suhrkamp Verlag, 1974–89.

We will have no more success in adequately projecting our concept of "animal" on the Greek *thêr* [θήρ] or its derivative *thêrion* [θηρίον]. Even if it happens that the *thêrion* is said to be "peaceful" (*hêmeron*: Plato, *Republic*, 588c) as well as "ferocious" (*agrion*), the word usually designates a "predator," a "wild beast" that is hostile to humans (lions or boars that hunt and are hunted, and are more terrestrial than fish or birds), in contrast to domestic or tame animals. Although a human is by nature a *zôion*—more precisely, according to Aristotle's related definitions, a *zôion logon echon* [ζῷον λόγον ἔχον], a *rational animal* or living being endowed with language, and a *politikon zôion* [πολιτικὸν ζῷον], a political animal living in a city-state (*Politics*, 1.1253a1–10)—in denaturing himself he becomes a *thêrion*. Thus just as someone who has no need to live in a community is a *theos*, "god," so someone who is incapable of doing so is a *thêrion*, "beast," "monster," and no longer a human (ibid., 27–29). Similarly, *thêriotês* [θηριότης], "bestiality," is something quite different from vice: it is the monstrous degradation of a species, seen, for example, among barbarians (*Nicomachean Ethics*, 7.1; cf. Bodéüs, "Les considérations"). This tripartite classification, which situates man between the animal (*thêrion*) and the god and is constitutive of ethics and politics, structures the continuist ontology of the living, *zôos* and *zôion*, which is determinant in biology and cosmology. But none of the Greek terms correspond to the same portion of the world as our word "animal."

▪ See Box 2.

II. The Invention of the Animal in the Christian Era: "Animal," *Animus, Anima*

In the era when Christianity was emerging, following the lineage of a sacrificial Judaism, animals were both endowed with the status of creatures on an equal footing with humans and devalued because of their alleged lack of a soul. In the context of a discontinuist ontology based on the metaphysical tripartite division matter/life/spirituality, the animal was situated among the living beings deprived of soul or spirit. Saint Augustine was the first to systematize this philosophical position: although refusing them any spiritual principle, he granted them the vital principle (the *anima*, the Greek *psuchê* [ψυχή]), that is, mobility. However, he reserved the *animus* (the soul that knows) and the *pneuma* [πνεῦμα] for humans alone.

The sequence animal / life / living being is constituted, and in the seventeenth century the Cartesians found it easy, on this basis, to define animals in relation to the mind and rationality, whether they were "for" (Gassendi, La Fontaine, Leibniz) or "against" (Descartes himself, La Mettrie, et al.). The debate between mechanism and vitalism (Do animals have souls?) thus has its source in Augustinianism, which connects "animal" and *anima*, and disconnects "animal" and *animus*, thus ratifying for a long time a sharp break between the living and the spiritual.

III. Conceiving the Beast in Relation to the Animal

The humanist position that arises in the Christian era creates this break between the living animal and humans, who have

2

Homo sacer

Homo sacer (sacred man) is a Latin term borrowed from archaic Roman law by Giorgio Agamben to discuss a range of political and philosophical issues. In its original sense, *homo sacer* designated an individual who was banished in response to a grave trespass. From the moment of his ritual pronouncement as *homo sacer*, this person could be killed with impunity, but could not be employed in sacrificial rituals that required the taking of a life. The term is first discussed in Agamben's *Homo sacer: Il potere sovrano e la nuda vita* (1995), where it is presented as a paradigm for understanding contemporary political and biopolitical situations ranging from Nazi concentration camps to everyday life in Western democracies.

The first thing to note about this figure of a "sacred man" in Roman law is that he was not sacred in any reverential sense—in fact, he was far closer to the opposite. Removed from the continuum of social activity and civil legislation, the only law that still applied to him was the one that irrevocably cast him out of the communal sphere. In *Homo sacer* and its sequels, Agamben stresses the enigmatic, paradoxical, and "paradigmatic" status of this figure from archaic Roman law. As Freud, Benveniste, and others have demonstrated, the term "sacred" has displayed in its history a remarkable degree of semantic ambiguity. Emblematically, Agamben's titular figure amply partakes of this ambiguity. To explore the *homo sacer*'s paradoxical status, Agamben turns to Greek conceptions of

"life," beginning with the two Greek words for life, *bios* and *zôê*. The former concerns a life seen in function of its various activities and attributes, the latter refers to the life shared by all the living. It is in light of this distinction that Agamben develops a paradox inherent in the definition of the *homo sacer*. From the perspective of the community that has banished him, the *homo sacer* is stripped of the customary forms or qualifications of a specific life (what the Greeks called *bios*). What remains is an individual utterly without status, seen by the community that cast him out as reduced to bare life (what the Greeks called *zôê*).

Agamben's interest in this figure is not primarily historiographical, and though such banishment was doubtless a terrible fate for an individual, it is not the psychological suffering or sociological implications of this practice that Agamben is endeavoring to understand. For him, this figure from the most remote past of Western legal history bears a message—an ominous one—for today's societies. The explicit goal of the *Homo sacer* project is to explore what Agamben calls "the essential function" of this figure "in modern politics." In the wake of Foucault's studies of "biopolitics" and Arendt's work on related matters, Agamben sees an increasing tendency on the part of societies, both totalitarian and democratic, to discipline and control their subjects through minute observation, definition, and documentation. This subtle control of the activities and attributes

of an individual life (*bios*) is coupled with an extremely disturbing set of cases where individuals are stripped not only of legal rights, but of all attributes except that of their mere physical existence (*zôê*). This process, writ large in the Nazi concentration camps, is one that Agamben sees writ small elsewhere and is the reason why he appeals to his readers' vigilance in the face of contemporary political trends. "If today," Agamben writes in *Homo sacer*, "there is no longer any one clear figure of the sacred man, it is perhaps because we are all virtually [*virtualmente*] *homines sacri*" (*Homo sacer*, 127; trans. Heller-Roazen, 115). This is a "virtually" that commentators such as Slavoj Žižek have tended to ignore; but what bears noting is that for Agamben, the present historical situation shows signs of this exceptional figure returning on a global scale. In sum, Agamben's *homo sacer* is a figure from the remote past that brings into focus a disturbing element in our political present—and points toward a possible future that Agamben sees as our principal duty to avert.

Leland de la Durantaye

BIBLIOGRAPHY

Agamben, Giorgio. *Homo sacer: Il potere sovrano e la nuda vita*. Turin, It.: Einaudi, 1995. Translation by Daniel Heller-Roazen: *Homo Sacer: Sovereign Power and Bare Life*. Stanford, CA: Stanford University Press, 1998.

spirit/mind, and gives birth to the idea that the animal corresponds to a unitary genus that coincides with the category of the living. The presence in German not only of the word *Bestie*, but of two additional terms, *Tier* and *Animal*, that can both be translated into English as "animal" thus poses once again the question, already raised by Greek usage, whether "animal" really refers to a unified category, that is, "a homogeneous genus."

"Animal" is in fact the most common translation of *Tier*, whether we are dealing with a *Haustier* (domestic animal, pet), a *Pelztier* (fur-bearing animal), a *Zugtier* (draft animal), or a *Reittier* (saddle animal). We also speak of the "animal kingdom" (*Tierreich*), the "small animal" (*Tierchen*), and even of "animality" (*Tiernatur, tierisches Wesen*). But the latent Latin root is also used to translate the noun "animality" (*Animalität*) and the corresponding adjective (*animalisch*). In French, there are only two words, *animal* and *bête*. So why is *Tier* usually rendered as *animal* and not as *bête*? Does this reflect, through the Latin lexical connection, a humanist prejudice?

Tier indicates a semantic polarity that is connected etymologically with the Greek *thêrion* (wild beast) and, further back, with the Sanskrit *dheu* (Dastur), which is said to combine in

a single term the original interrelationship of life and death. In some contemporary phenomenological studies, the term *Tier* has been uncritically rendered by *animal* and not by *bête*, even if in the same texts we also find *Animal* and *animalisches Wesen* (Husserl). This kind of translation problem obviously involves the relationship between humans and animals—namely, the problem of the humanization of the animal (if *Tier* is rendered as *animal*, in which the soul is indicated)—as much as it does that of the animalization, or rather the bestialization, of humans (when *Tier* is translated as *bête*, which indicates brutal or savage nature).

Natalie Depraz

BIBLIOGRAPHY

Agamben, Giorgio. *Homo Sacer: Sovereign Power and Bare Life*. Translated by Daniel Heller-Roazen. Stanford, CA: Stanford University Press, 1998.

Augustine. *On Free Choice of the Will* [De libero arbitrio]. Translated by Thomas Williams. Indianapolis, IN: Hackett, 1993.

Bodéüs, Richard. "Les considérations aristotéliciennes sur la bestialité." In *L'Animal dans l'antiquité*, edited by B. Cassin and J.-L. Labarrière, 247–58. Paris: Vrin, 1997.

Cabestan, Philippe. "La constitution de l'animal dans les *Ideen*." *Alter* 3 (1995): 39–81.

Dastur, Françoise. "Pour une zoologie privative." *Alter* 3 (1995): 281–319.

Depraz, Natalie. "Y a-t-il une animalité transcendantale?" *Alter* 3 (1995): 81–115.

Fonenay, Elisabeth de. *Le silence des bêtes: La philosophie à l'épreuve de l'animalité.* Paris: Fayard, 1998.

Heidegger, Martin. *The Fundamental Concepts of Metaphysics: World, Finitude, Solitude.* Translated by William McNeill and Nicholas Walker. Bloomington: Indiana University Press, 1995.

Husserl, Edmund. "La crise de l'humanité européenne et la philosophie." *Alter* 3 (1995): 167–219. Texts by Husserl (appendix 12 of *Ideas* and text no. 35 in *Husserliana* 15).

———. *Ideas Pertaining to a Pure Phenomenology and to a Phenomenological Philosophy.* Book 2: *Studies in the Phenomenology of Constitution,* translated by R. Rojcewicz and A. Schuwer. Dordrecht, Neth.: Kluwer, 1989.

Lotz, Christian. "Psyche or Person? Husserl's Phenomenology of Animals." In *Interdisziplinäre Perspektiven der Phänomenologie,* edited by Dieter Lohmar and Dirk Fonfara, 190–202. Dordrecht, Neth.: Springer, 2006.

Wolff, Francis. "L'animal et le dieu: Deux modèles pour l'homme. Remarques pouvant servir à l'invention de l'animal." In *L'animal dans l'antiquité,* edited by B. Cassin and J.-L Labarrière, 157–80. Paris: Vrin, 1997.

ANSCHAULICHKEIT (GERMAN)

ENGLISH   clarity, openness to view, visualizability
FRENCH   *caractère intuitif*

➤ *INTUITION* and ANALOGY, EPISTEMOLOGY, ERSCHEINUNG, PERCEPTION, REPRÉSENTATION, SACHVERHALT, SIGN

Since the 1930s the German term *Anschaulichkeit* has presented a typical case of untranslatability, to the point that its importance for philosophical reflection on science has only recently been rediscovered. Deriving from the Kantian tradition, the term's meaning has been radically modified by quantum theory.

Although it is not listed in the Kantian lexicon proper (where we find *Anschauung* and *Anschauungsformen*), the term does belong to the tradition inspired by Kant that marks all the work done by German mathematicians, physicists, and physiologists of the second half of the nineteenth century. *Anschaulichkeit* designates what is translated inaccurately in French as the *caractère intuitif* or in English by the "visualizability" or "clarity" of a physical theory, but in fact it refers to the possibility of giving phenomena and objects a "spatiotemporal representation," that is, an image in ordinary space and time. With the appearance of quantum theory, this possibility, and this demand, had to be abandoned, whence a drastic change took place in two stages. First, Niels Bohr abandoned the maintenance, in the atomic physics, of "spatiotemporal representations through which up to this point we have tried to describe natural phenomena" ("Über die Wirkung von Atomen bei Stossen"), introducing instead of *Anschaulichkeit* the notion of "symbolic analogy" (*symbolische Analogie*), the only possible approach to objects that cannot be described in spatio-temporal terms. In a second stage the term *Anschaulichkeit* is taken up again but redefined in a way that emphasizes, on the one hand, the role of experimental procedures in the definition of a theory's fundamental concepts (W. Heisenberg, "Über den anschaulichen Inhalt"), and on the other hand—elaborating the Helmholtzian idea

of *Anschaubarkeit* (translated in English by "intuitability"), which, applied to mathematics, appears in Helmholtz's 1878 lecture entitled "Die Tatsachen in der Wahrnehmung" ("Facts of Perception")—the necessary abstraction that the physicist has to carry out with regard to his usual mental images: "The new system of concepts also gives the intuitive content [*der anschauliche Inhalt*] of the new theory. We must thus ask of an intuitive theory in this sense only that it be in itself free of contradiction and that it allow us to predict without ambiguity the results of all imaginable experiments in its domain" (Born, Heisenberg, and Jordan, "Zur Quantenmechanik").

In the late 1920s these changes in the meaning of the term *Anschaulichkeit* had the effect of breaking out of the original Kantian context. The difficulty of translating the term into other languages can thus be easily explained: to understand it, one has to follow the twofold process of the formation and implosion of a vocabulary specifically associated with the history of German philosophy.

Catherine Chevalley

BIBLIOGRAPHY

Bohr, Niels. "Über die Wirkung von Atomen bei Stossen." *Zeitschrift für Physik* 34 (1925): 142–57, postscriptum.

Born, M., W. Heisenberg, and P. Jordan, "Zur Quantenmechanik." *Zeitschrift für Physik* 35 (1926): 557–615.

Chevalley, Catherine. "Niels Bohr's Words and Atlantis of Kantianism." In *Niels Bohr and Contemporary Philosophy,* edited by J. Faye and H. Folse, 33–57. Dordrecht, Neth.: Kluwer, 1994.

Darrigol, Oivier. *From c-Numbers to q-Numbers. The Classical Analogy in the History of Quantum Theory.* Berkeley: University of California Press, 1992.

Heisenberg, Werner. "Über den anschaulichen Inhalt der quantentheoretischen Kinematik und Mechanik." *Zeitschrift für Physik* 43 (1927): 172–98. "The Physical Content of Quantum Kinematics and Mechanics" in *Quantum Theory and Measurement,* edited by J. A. Wheeler and W. H. Zurek, 62–84. Princeton, NJ: Princeton University Press, 1983.

Heisenberg, Werner, and Max Born. "La mécanique des quanta." In *Electrons et photons,* 143–81. Paris: Gauthier-Villars, 1928.

Helmholtz, Herman von. "The Facts of Perception." In *Selected Writings.* Middletown, CT: Wesleyan University Press, 1971.

Miller, Arthur. "Visualization Lost and Regained: The Genesis of Quantum Theory in the Period 1913–1927." In *On Aesthetics in Science,* edited by J. Wechsler. Cambridge, MA: MIT Press, 1978.

ANXIETY

DANISH   *Angest*
FRENCH   *angoisse*
GERMAN   *Angst*
LATIN   *angustia(e)*
SPANISH   *angustia*

➤ CARE, DASEIN, *IL Y A, MALAISE, NEGATION, NOTHING,* SORGE, *TO BE*

The term "anxiety" is etymologically related to that of "narrowness," or "tightening," as are the corresponding Romance and Germanic words, and this can still be sensed in the works of Friedrich Schelling and Jakob Böhme. However, it is above all its elective relationship with nothingness (as non-being) and the possibility of the pure state that Heidegger, following Kierkegaard, will emphasize. That *Angst,* unlike *Furcht* (fear), is "without object" is no less crucial for psychoanalysis.

In a note in section 40 of *Being and Time*, Heidegger refers to Kierkegaard's 1844 book, *The Concept of Anxiety*, declaring that no one had gone as far as Kierkegaard in the analysis of this phenomenon as it appears in the theological context of a "psychological" exposition of the problem of hereditary sin.

In his book (chap. 2, §1), Kierkegaard himself refers to Schelling's non-anthropomorphic use of *Angst*, seeing in it "the sufferings of the divinity longing for creation." Following Böhme, Schelling understands *Angst* in its relationship with *Enge* ("narrowness," "restriction," from the Gr. *agchô*, "tighten," "constrain," "suffocate," and Lat. *angustia*, usually used in the plural, *angustiae*; cf. the Fr. *angoisse/angine*—"that which oppresses, chokes") as a centrifugal movement peculiar to a being that feels stifled or restricted (*beengt*) within himself:

> The anxiety of life itself pushes man outside the center in which he was created. . . . [T]o be able to live there . . . man is almost necessarily tempted to leave the center to escape toward the periphery.

> (Schelling, *Sämtliche Werke*, vol. 7)

It is less from this concept of anxiety in Schelling's 1809 *Untersuchungen* that Kierkegaard seeks to distance himself than from that in *Die Weltalter* (*Sämtliche Werke*, vol. 8), where "the sufferings of the divinity longing for creation" characterize a *divine* anxiety whose anthropomorphism Kierkegaard stresses. As for the relationship *Angst/Enge*, it still remains present in German, even if it is muted. It is no accident that Heidegger frequently uses the verb *beengen* in analyzing the phenomenon of anxiety: "What oppresses [lit., 'constrains' or 'makes narrow'] . . . is the world itself" (*Was beengt ist . . . die Welt selbst*; *Sein und Zeit*, §40). In Kierkegaard, the relationship *anxiety/constraint* is less determinant than the relationship of anxiety to nothingness and to possibility. Anxiety (*Angst*) is entirely distinct from fear (*aldeles forskjelligt fra Frygt*)—and this distinction *Angst/Frygt* is found in Heidegger as the distinction *Angst/Furcht* (cf. "Was ist Metaphysik?")—for if fear has

to do with something determinate or very precise (*bestemt*), we are anxious "for nothing" (*for Intet*). This leads Kierkegaard to define "anxiety" this way: "Anxiety is the reality [Dan. *Virkelighed* = Ger. *Wirklichkeit*] of freedom as the possibility offered to possibility" (*Angest er Frihedens Virkelighed som Mulighed for Muligheden*; *Begrebet Angest*, chap. 1, §5).

In innocent Adam, in whom the prohibition on eating the fruit of "the tree of the knowledge of good and evil" (Gn 2:17) awakens the possibility of freedom, the "nothingness of anxiety" (*Angestens Intet*) is transformed into "den oenstende Mulighed af at *kunne*" (the dreadful possibility of *power*), not, to be sure, the power to choose good or evil, but simply *to be able*—"*Mulighed er at kunne*" (possibility consists in *being able*; *Begrebet Angest*, chap. 1, §6).

The specific contribution of Heidegger is to have combined Schelling's and Kierkegaard's definitions of anxiety in his concept of *Angst*, understood as constraint and relationship to Nothing. Into the "bright night" of Nothing, which Heidegger recognizes in his 1929 inaugural lecture "What Is Metaphysics?" as an initiatory gateway into metaphysics, pierces Nothing, as non-being.

■ See Box 1.

Pascal David

BIBLIOGRAPHY

Heidegger, Martin. *Sein und Zeit*. Vol. 2 of *Gesamtausgabe*. Frankfurt: Klostermann, 1977. Translation by J. Macquarrie and E. Robinson: *Being and Time*. Oxford: Blackwell, 1967.
———. "Was ist Metaphysik?" In vol. 9 of *Gesamtausgabe*. Frankfurt: Klostermann, 1976. Translation by D. F. Krell: "What Is Metaphysics?" In *Basic Writings*, edited by D. F. Krell. New York: Harper & Row, 1977.
Kierkegaard, Søren. *Begrebet Angest*. Edited by V. Sørensen. Copenhagen: Gyldendal, 1960. Translation by Reidar Thomte: *The Concept of Anxiety*. Princeton, NJ: Princeton University Press, 1980.
Schelling, Friedrich Wilhelm Joseph von. *The Ages of the World*. Translated by J. Wirth. Albany: State University of New York Press, 2000.
———. *Philosophical Investigations into the Essence of Human Freedom*. Translated by J. Love and J. Schmidt. Albany: State University of New York Press, 2006.
———. *Sämtliche Werke*. Munich: Schröter, 1965.

1

Angst and anxiety in psychoanalysis

➤ DRIVE, ES, HEIMAT, Box 2, SUBJECT, VERNEINUNG, WUNSCH

I. The two Freudian theories of anxiety

Sigmund Freud worked out two theories regarding anxiety. The first goes back to the beginning of his work and presents anxiety as a "transformation of the libido" (*Angst als Umwandlung von Libido*). This transformation of the libido into anxiety takes place when "the accumulated psychic tension attains

the threshold that allows it to elicit a psychic affect, but . . . for some reason, the psychic connection that is offered to it remains insufficient; the psychic affect cannot be produced, because certain psychic conditions are partially lacking, whence the transformation into anxiety of the tension which has not been psychically 'bound'" (Manuscript E, "Wie die Angst entsteht," in *Briefe an Wilhelm Fliess*).

Freud's second theory of anxiety is presented in *Hemmung, Symptom und Angst* (1925). Anxiety is conceived first of all as "something felt" (*etwas Empfundenes*), an "affective state" (*Affektzustand*) that appears "as a reaction to a state of danger" (*als Reaktion auf einen Zustand der Gefahr*). It is understood as a "signal" proceeding from the Ego, since only the Ego can judge situations of danger (*Gesammelte Werke*, vol. 14; see ES). Anxiety is a reaction—a signal—confronted with the "danger of losing the object" (*Reaktion auf die Gefahr des Objektverlust*; ibid.). Freud presents several forms of the loss of an object that are merely attenuated versions of the "helplessness" (*Hilflosigkeit*) of trauma and constitute the core of the situation of danger (ibid.). We also note an essential modification of the Freudian development relating to repression: "[I]t is anxiety that produces repression, not, as we thought, the reverse" ("Angst und Triebleben" [1932], in *Gesammelte Werke*, vol. 15).

Freud distinguishes two kinds of anxiety: "anxiety about the real" (*Realangst*) and "neurotic anxiety" (*neurotische Angst*). "Real danger [*Realgefahr*] is a danger we know, and real anxiety [*Realangst*] is anxiety regarding such a known danger. Neurotic danger [*die neurotische Angst*] is anxiety regarding a danger we do not know," and neurotic danger is "a pulsional danger" (*eine Triebgefahr*; *Hemmung, Symptom und Angst*, in *Gesammelte Werke*, vol. 14; see also *Die Angst*, in *Gesammelte Werke*, vol. 11).

So far as the notion of danger is concerned, Freud distinguishes between "real danger" (*Realgefahr*), a threat posed by an external object, and neurotic danger, which proceeds from "pulsional demand" (*Triebanspruch*; ibid.).

II. Translation problems

Freud's texts on anxiety pose a few translation problems because of the twofold meaning of *Angst* in German, which can mean "anxiety," but also "to be afraid of," followed in this case by the preposition *vor* (*Angst haben vor etwas*). Freud himself tried to define the difference between these two meanings:

"Fright," "fear," and "anxiety" are improperly used as synonymous expressions; they are in fact capable of clear distinction in their relation to danger. "Anxiety" describes a particular state of expecting the danger or preparing for it, even though it may be an unknown one. "Fear" requires a definite object of which to be afraid. "Fright," however, is the name we give to the state a person gets into when he has run into danger without being prepared for it; it emphasizes the factor of surprise.

(*Beyond the Pleasure Principle*).

In *Hemmung, Symptom und Angst*, Freud emphasizes that anxiety is "characterized by indetermination [*Unbestimmtheit*] and the absence of an object [*Objektlösigkeit*]; a correct use of the language even changes its name when it has found an object, and replaces it by *fear* [*Furcht*]."

The difficulty persists, despite this remark; neither Freud nor the German language commonly makes this distinction, as is shown by the Duden dictionary (RT: *Duden: Deutsches Universalwörterbuch*) and the RT: *Historisches Wörterbuch der Philosophie*. In the latter dictionary's article "Angst," we read: "A broad distinction between *Angst* as being without object, a free, dispersed feeling, and *Furcht* as something that is attached to an object, is made neither in the literature as a whole nor in common usage." In addition, the article "Obsessions et Phobies," which Freud wrote in French, offers an opportunity to see that the meaning of the word in question is not univocal: Freud uses both the words *angoisse* and *anxiété* to render the German *Angst* and also uses the expression *névrose anxieuse* to render *Angstneurose* (*Gesammelte Werke*, vol. 1). Faced with this problem, French translators use either a version of the original German or an interpretation of the contexts in which Freud used the word *Angst*. Thus the French version of *Hemmung, Symptom und Angst* translates *Angst* and *Angst haben vor etwas* by *angoisse* and *avoir angoisse devant quelque chose*, respectively. On the other hand, the translators of the *Conférences d'introduction à la psychanalyse* and the *Nouvelles conférences d'introduction à la psychanalyse*, for example, translate the term in a different way. The English version makes the same choice, translating *Angst* by "anxiety" or, depending on the context, by "fear," "afraid," "alarm," etc. In *The Standard Edition* (Strachey, vol. 20, translator's note), however, there is some question as to whether the English "anxiety" still retains a semantic connection with the German *Angst*. The Spanish translation renders *Angst* by *angustia* but occasionally resorts to other terms, such as *miedo* (Lopez-Ballesteros y de Torres, *Obras completas*, vol. 2).

III. Jacques Lacan: Anxiety "is not without an object"

Lacan devoted a whole seminar to the subject of anxiety (*L'Angoisse*), but important remarks on this subject are already found in his earlier seminar on identification: "It is not impossible that you encounter the desire of the other as such, of the real Other. . . . It is here that anxiety arises. . . . Anxiety is the sensation of the Other's desire" (*L'Identification*, 4 April). For Lacan as much as for Freud, anxiety is a signal, but a signal of the presence of the Other's desire as "real" and no longer "symbolic." The Other's desire as "symbolic" presupposes the phallus, which is, Lacan says, the "name" of the Other's desire, that is, it is included in the signifier (see SIGNIFIER/SIGNIFIED). At the same time, the phallus is a lack, a "structuring void" around which is established every possibility of signification (cf. "La signification du phallus," *Écrits*, and *L'angoisse*, 12 December). Anxiety makes its appearance at the moment when the phallus, which governs the relations between the subject and the enigma of the Other's desire, is lacking. Lacan declares: "[T]here is a fear of losing the phallus, because only the phallus can give desire its own field" (Lacan, *L'Identification*, 4 April). Thus anxiety corresponds to "the lack of the lack," which implies a direct encounter with the desire of the "real Other" (cf. *L'Angoisse*, 28 November and 5 December). These reflections led Lacan to undertake a "rectification" of the concept of anxiety with respect to the Freudian position and a certain philosophical tradition: anxiety, he says, "is not without an object" (ibid., 9 January 1963) and for that reason it is the only affect that "does not deceive" (ibid., 19 December 1962). The discussion of anxiety thus paves the way for the elaboration of the concept of the *objet petit a*, the "object causing desire," which he was to announce in the following year's seminar (*Les quatre concepts*).

Elisabete Thamer

BIBLIOGRAPHY

Freud, Sigmund. *Beyond the Pleasure Principle*. In *The Freud Reader*, edited by P. Gay, translated by J. Strachey. New York: W. W. Norton, 1989.
———. *Briefe an Wilhelm Fliess*. Edited by Jeffrey Masson. Frankfurt: Fischer, 1999. Translation by Jeffrey Masson: *The Complete Letters of Sigmund Freud to Wilhelm Fliess*. Cambridge, MA: Belknap Press, 1986.
———. *Gesammelte Werke*. 18 vols. Frankfurt: Fischer, 1999. Translation by James Strachey: *The Complete Psychological Works of Sigmund Freud*. New York: Vintage, 2001. Translation by Luis Lopez-Ballesteros y de Torres: *Obras completas*. 17 vols. Madrid: Editorial Biblioteca Nueva, 1968. First published in 1923.
Lacan, Jacques. *L'Angoisse*. Vol. 10 of *Le séminaire*. Paris: Éditions du Seuil, 2004.
———. *L'Identification*. Vol. 9 of *Le séminaire*. Unpublished.
———. *Les quatre concepts fondamentaux de la psychanalyse*. Vol. 11 of *Le séminaire*, edited by J.-A. Miller. Paris: Éditions du Seuil, 1973. Translation by Alan Sheridan: *The Four Fundamental Concepts of Psychoanalysis*. New York: Norton, 1998.

APPEARANCE

The word "appearance" is ambiguous from the outset, since it sometimes points toward the phenomenon, the objectivity of what appears on its own, and sometimes toward illusion and deception.

I. Appearance-Apparition

"Appearance" and "apparition" are modeled on Late Latin *apparentia* and *apparitio* (themselves connected with *appareo*, which means "appear," but also "be in the service of," just as *pareo* means "come forth" and "obey"), synonyms in Church Latin, which uses *apparitio* to render the Greek *epiphaneia* [ἐπιφάνεια] (manifestation, epiphany). "Appearance-apparition" refers to what appears in full light, the manifestation or *phainomenon* [φαινόμενον] in the original sense of the Greek verb *phainô* [φαίνω] (to appear), from the same root as the Greek *phôs* [φῶς] (light): see PHANTASIA, I, LIGHT, Box 1, and PHÉNOMÈNE.

II. Appearance-Illusion

"Appearance" also refers to false appearance or illusion (as in "don't trust appearances"). This illusion may be connected with individual subjectivity and may concern an error made by the senses, imagination, or judgment (see DOXA, PERCEPTION, PHANTASIA, REPRÉSENTATION). It can also be conceived as having to do with a transcendental subjectivity, and it may be connected with the opposition between the phenomenon and the thing-in-itself (see ERSCHEINUNG; REALITY, with the difference *Realität/Wirklichkeit*; see also GEGENSTAND).

III. The Ambiguities of Greek and German

The interweaving of both positive and negative meanings is particularly marked in Greek and German. Consider the breadth of the term *doxa* [δόξα], which refers to the appearance of what appears, to right opinion (*dokei moi* [δοκεῖ μοι], "it seems to me"), and to general opinion, with its rhetorical meaning (see *endoxon* [ἔνδοξον], "acceptable," under DOXA, II.C; cf. COMMONPLACE and EIDÔLON, Box 1), and finally to the glory of God and its radiance; but in opposition to *alêtheia* [ἀλήθεια] (see TRUTH), it continues to designate at the same time mortals' error and illusion.

Similarly, note the proximity in German of *Schein* and *Scheinen*, of simple appearance and deceptive appearance (*Anschein*), and of the appearing of what shows itself in its full radiance, which "has just appeared" (*zum Vorschein kommt*): *die Sonne scheint* (the sun shines) or *der Mondschein* (moonlight) (see ERSCHEINUNG).

To illustrate this connection, we may cite Gorgias and Hegel:

[ἔλεγε δὲ τὸ μὲν εἶναι ἀφανὲς μὴ τυχὸν τοῦ δοκεῖν, τὸ δὲ δοκεῖν ἀσθενὲς μὴ τυχὸν τοῦ εἶναι]

([H]e said that being was invisible if it did not encounter appearance, and the appearance was without power if it did not encounter being.)

(Gorgias, 82.B.26 DK)

Das Wesen muß erscheinen.

([T]he essence must appear [appearance is not inessential, it is part of the essence itself].)

So erscheint das *Wesen*.

(That is how essence appears,)

(Hegel, *Wissenschaft der Logik*, Bk. II, §2).

IV. Aesthetic Meanings

See *IMAGE* and, in part, EIDÔLON and MIMÊSIS.

➤ AESTHETICS, ESSENCE, *IMAGINATION*, OBJECT, RES, SUBJECT, TABLEAU, *TO BE*

APPROPRIATION

1. "Appropriation," borrowed from Late Latin *appropriatio*, was used especially in medicine (in the sense of assimilation) and in chemistry (in the sense of catalysis), before being adopted by philosophy as one of the possible translations of the German word *Ereignis* (from the adjective *eigen*, own, characteristic) as it is used by Heidegger; see EREIGNIS; cf. *DESTINY* and *EVENT*.
2. Moreover, it is also the literal translation of a key term in Stoic ethics, *oikeiôsis* [οἰκείωσις], which designates our (extendable) relationship to that with which nature has made us familiar and which is peculiar to us (*oikeios* [οἰκεῖος], domestic); see OIKEIÔSIS; cf. OIKONOMIA, ECONOMY, and *COMMUNITY*, POLIS, POLITICS.
3. More generally, on ways of expressing what is one's "own" and property, see PROPERTY.
4. Finally, on the propriety of terms and discourses in grammar or rhetoric, see COMMONPLACE, COMPARISON, HOMONYM, MIMÊSIS, Box 6, TROPE; cf. *STYLE*.

➤ RES, *TO BE, WISDOM*

ARGUTEZZA (ITALIAN)

FRENCH	*subtilité ingénieuse*
SPANISH	*agudeza*

➤ *WITTICISM*, AND BAROQUE, COMPARISON, CONCETTO, GENIUS, GOÛT, *IMAGE, IMAGINATION*, INGENIUM, MIMÊSIS

In seventeenth-century Italian theory of art, *argutezza* refers to the activity of the imagination and understanding that tends to show the greatest metaphorical ingenuity. From the outset, the word presents significant translation problems because it designates in a language that is itself metaphorical and ingenious, the necessary conditions for the most "subtle" and "witty" modes of signification, and it is practiced in a very broad domain that ranges from sign systems that are discourses to symbolic figures (allegories, emblems, devices, tableaux).

The problem of *argutezza* is inseparable from the so-called baroque aesthetics that developed in Italy. As it appears in Emanuele Tesauro's *Il cannocchiale aristotelico* (The Aristotelian telescope, 1654), *argutezza* refers to the idea of "ingenious subtlety"; that is, the act par excellence of metaphorical thought, and it implies extremely complex goals that are irreducible to simple "acuity" or "witticism"—although "ingenious subtlety" is accurate enough to render *agudeza* as used by Baltasar Gracián (*Agudeza y arte*), the Spanish remaining closer to the Latin *acutus*.

■ See Box 1.

Like most seventeenth-century theories, Tesauro's draws not only on rhetoric and poetics, but also on Aristotle's whole philosophy, of which it is an application and extension to multiple systems of representation. The network consisting of *argutezza*, *concetto*, and *ingegno* is central in the theory of baroque art: it governs, more or less directly, every conception of metaphor, of the figurability of ideas and inventions, both poetic and graphic. Contrary to the Spanish term *agudeza*, which belongs solely to literary or political discourse, an *argutezza*, in Tesauro's sense, can appear in allegories, verbal enigmas, and devices, in a text and in an architectural work, in an inscription, and in the composition of a picture or the expression of a sculpture.

What is *argutezza* according to Tesauro? "[U]n divin parto dell'ingegno" (a divine part of the mind); the "ultimo sforzo dell'intelletto" (the ultimate effort of the intellect); the "spirito vitale delle morte pagine" (the living spirit of the dead page). Through the power of this divine Pythia, the discourse of ingenious men (*ingegnosi*) differs as much from that of the crowd as the discourse of the angels differs from that of men; these ingenious men have the miraculous power to make mute things to speak, incurable people to revive, and the dead to rise again; this enchantress of souls gives a voice to tombs, to marbles, to statues; and ingenious men who speak ingeniously give them spirit (*spirito*) and movement (*movimento*) (*Il cannocchiale aristotelico*, chap. 1).

In this sense, *argutezza* goes deeper than *concetto*, since it is a faculty of the mind that is between understanding and imagination. One of the essential reasons that the word has no equivalent in other European languages—including Latin, into which the main texts of the period were translated—is that it emphasizes all the metaphorical possibilities of thought by extending it to all the figures peculiar to the visual field, that is, to the plastic arts and to ballet. Thus *argutia* and *argutezza* are in fact the necessary conditions for

the production of any symbolic composition and thus transcend the frameworks of traditional *mimêsis*.

Seventeenth-century French theoreticians, such as Le Moyne or Ménestrier, never translate the Italian word: they render or express it by means of periphrasis, as in the forms *représentation ingénieuse*, *invention spirituelle*, *image savante*. The untranslatability of the word is thus patent; but *argutezza*, like *concetto*, had to be "rendered," that is, transposed by circumlocution, as the project of a philosophy of symbolic images was elaborated in France during the last decades of the seventeenth century. Based in the first place on the primacy of the image and the metaphorical nature of thought, this "philosophy" often shows clearly sophistical tendencies in its conception of language and its rehabilitation of myth, of which we still find echoes in Vico.

The failure of translation was compensated for by many theoretical achievements illustrating what is implied by the very concept of *argutezza*. The empty place left by the untranslatability of the word had the effect of renewing, in European texts, the problem of the image, of invention, and of metaphor and imitation, leading to the elaboration of theories far more rigorous than the preceding ones. Thus, starting in the seventeenth century, a whole semantic sequence was contaminated by this new triumph of *concettism*, ranging from the notions of the image, representation, and the sign as such to that of the figure (the Latin *figura* here recovering its full meaning). This tradition persisted in Europe, especially in Germany, down to Herder, despite the hostile rationalist criticism to which it was subjected by the Enlightenment.

This figurability, which was inherent in *concetto* as well as in *argutezza*, that is, in the creativity of the imagination and the understanding, is one reason that both German and English are put to the test by the act of translation. In German, contemporary philologists and historians encounter a difficulty that sometimes increases their "anti-figurative" prejudices. After having proposed *geistreiche Einfälle* (witty ideas) and *witzige Spielereien* (witty play) as translations of *argutezza*, E. Curtius (RT: *La littérature européenne et le Moyen-Âge latin*) adopts the French word *pointe*, which can only produce further ambiguity. To render *argutezza* as *pointe*—instead of the German *Geistreicheleien* (subtleties), for example—in order to preserve the idea of *acutus* and *argutus* is to return to

---

1

Agudeza and *acutezza/argutezza*

To designate acuity of mind and its ingenious inventions—witticisms, quips, sallies—Spanish has only one word: *agudeza*. Italian has two, which are often difficult to distinguish: *acutezza* and *argutezza*, the former deriving from *acutus*, "sharp," "keen"; the latter from *arguere*, "bring to light," "demonstrate." These two words are almost synonymous for Tesauro and the Italian theoreticians. *Argutezza* also

includes discursive metaphors, the *concetti* that can be found in sermons or inscriptions, as well as figurative representations such as emblems, ballets, and allegories. *Acutezza* is a term that is itself metaphorical, designating the metaphorical activity of the mind as a subtle, ingenious, clever faculty of expression. Although we often find *argutezza* used in the same sense, *acutezza* strongly emphasizes the pointed,

penetrating, and trenchant quality of this subtlety that is peculiar to the spirit of the *concetto*. We also find in Tesauro the term *acuto*, which in his work refers to the idea of a strong, precise expression, contrary to the Latin *acutus*, which designated a simple style without rhetorical figures. As for *argutia*, which Tesauro sometimes writes *arguzia*, it is often used in the sense of subtlety.

the French translation of the seventeenth century, which is extremely reductive since it denies the fecundity of concettism by reducing it to a pure play of the wit, that is, to a certain conception of the mind that is implicitly classical and rationalist, and thus French. As for the untranslatability of *argutezza*, the deep metaphoricity of the language is, after all, only one difficulty among others. This metaphoricity is a site of confrontation and privileged comparison that arose from the eighteenth century's rationalist desire to eliminate concettism.

Must we finally resign ourselves to including *argutezza* among the untranslatables that are a dominant phenomenon of baroque culture? In reality, we have to resituate the concept not only in the semantic networks of European theories of art but also in comparison to other *topoi*: those of the theology of the image (still active in the seventeenth century) and those of theories of language down to Vico, Hamann, and Jean Paul. This presupposes that we find connections among networks that may at first appear historically and theoretically heterogeneous.

Jean-François Groulier

BIBLIOGRAPHY

Gracián, Baltasar. *Agudeza y arte de ingenio en que se explican todos los modos y diferencias*. Mexico City: Universidad Nacional Autónoma de México, 1996. First published in 1648.

Grady, Hugh H. "Rhetoric, Wit and Art in Gracián's *Agudeza*." *Modern Language Quarterly* 41, no. 1 (1980): 21–37.

Kircher, Athanasius. *Oedipus Aegyptiacus*. Rome, 1653.

———. *Polygraphia nova*. Rome, 1663.

Lange, Klaus-Peter. *Theoretiker des literarischen Manierismus*. Munich: Fink, 1968.

Marino, Giambattista. *Dicerie sacre*. Turin: Einaudi, 1960.

Masen, Jakob. *Speculum imaginum veritatis occultae*. Cologne, 1650.

Ménestrier, Claude François. *La philosophie des images*. Paris, 1682.

———. *La philosophie des images énigmatiques*. Lyon, 1694.

Pellegrini, Matteo. *Delle acutezze, che altrimenti spiriti, vivezze e concetti, volgarmente si appellano*. Geneva, 1639.

Proctor, Robert E. "Emanuele Tesauro: A Theory of the Conceit." *Modern Language Notes* 88, no. 1 (1973): 68–94.

Tesauro, Emanuele. *Il cannocchiale aristotelico o sia Idea dell'arguta et ingeniosa elucuzione che serve à tutta l'arte oratoria, lapidaria et simbolica esaminata co'principi del divino Aristotele*. Turin: Einaudi, 1978. First published in 1654.

———. *Idea delle perfette imprese*. 1629.

Vuilleumier-Laurens, Florence. *La raison des figures symboliques à la Renaissance et à l'âge classique*. Geneva: Droz, 2000.

ART

FRENCH	*art*
GERMAN	*Kunst*
GREEK	*technê* [τέχνη]
ITALIAN	*arte*
LATIN	*ars*

➤ AESTHETICS, BEAUTY, BILDUNG, GENIUS, GOÛT, INGENIUM, MIMÊSIS, NATURE, PHANTASIA, TABLEAU

The word "art" has a general sense, that of a way of being or doing ("the art of pleasing"). It becomes more precise when it is associated with the idea of a specialization of know-how implying rules that are peculiar to it ("the art of cooking"); and it is still further specified when it designates a set of human practices, those of artists, "men who have devoted themselves to expression in art" (Baudelaire, *Salon de 1859*). The movement into this lexical funnel was also a historical process, a long sociocultural maturation marked by the influence of the notions of *technê* [τέχνη], *ars*, *art*, and *Kunst*, the transitory influence of the terms "fine arts," *beaux arts*, *schöne Künsten*, and so on, and the return, at the beginning of the nineteenth century, of the term "art" in the singular, the meaning of which had changed in the interim.

I. The Space of *Technê*

A. Know-how

Reflecting on the history of the word "art," Robin Collingwood notes that the "aesthetic sense of the word" is "very recent in origin"; *ars* in Latin and *technê* in Greek, terms that we regularly translate by "art," signify "a craft or specialized form of skill, like carpentry or smithying or surgery" (*Principles of Art*, 5). No distinction is made between the artist and the artisan, or more precisely, the man of art.

■ See Box 1.

The ancient Greeks thus had no term to isolate what we now call "art." *Technê*, like *ars*, covers a much wider field, ranging from know-how in a craft to deception, trickery, and more generally, a way of doing something, a means (RT: *Dictionnaire étymologique de la langue grecque*, s.v.). Nonetheless, the thematics of imitation allows us to approach the "modern" sense of "art"—or at least to project it more or less well in a certain number of contexts. We can delimit the meaning of *technê* by its situation between simple experience or empirical practice (*empeiria* [ἐμπειρία]) on the one hand, and science (*epistêmê* [ἐπιστήμη]) on the other. Plato and Aristotle superimpose a conceptual action on the state of the lexicon. Plato initiates and generalizes the use of adjectives in the feminine (-*ikos*, -*ikê*, -*ikon* indicate relationship) to designate multiple *technai*: in the *Gorgias*, we thus find, alongside weaving or music (*hê huphantikê* [ἡ ὑφαντική], *hê mousikê* [ἡ μουσική], 449d), drawing, arithmetic, reasoning, and geometry (*hê graphikê, arithmêtikê, logistikê, geômetrikê* [ἡ γραφική, ἀριθμητική, λογιστική, γεωμετρική], 450d), and a large number of obvious neologisms: eristic, antilogic, dialectic, sophistic, politics, and rhetoric (*hê eristikê* [ἡ ἐριστική], *hê antilogikê* [ἡ ἀντιλογική], *hê dialektikê* [ἡ διαλεκτική], *hê sophistikê* [ἡ σοφιστική], *hê politikê* [ἡ πολιτική], *hê rhêtorikê* [ἡ ῥητορική]), the last being the one that gives its subtitle to the dialogue, *Peri tês rhêtorikês* [Περὶ τῆς ῥητορικῆς]). It is in this paradoxical dialogue, which deals with the *technê rhetorikê*, the art of speaking, that Plato defines *technê* the most precisely, the better to deny rhetoric the status of *technê*: unlike a simple "routine and a knack" (*empeiria kai tribê* [ἐμπειρία καὶ τριβή], the former meaning literally "rubbing," 463b), art examines the nature and cause (*tên phusin, tên aitian* [τὴν φύσιν, τὴν αἰτίαν]) of that with which it deals, and accounts for them (*logon echei* [λόγον ἔχει], 465a, 501a). Ultimately, rhetoric and cookery are put in the same category, that of the image (*eidôlon* [εἴδωλον]) and flattery (*kolakeia* [κολακεία]), which

1

Art of the Ancients, art of the Moderns: The rules of art

➤ LOGOS, PRAXIS, *VIRTUE*

Modern descriptions of art constantly mix two great conceptual legacies. The legacy of the Ancients is interested in the process of making any object or work; the aesthetics of the Moderns is interested in the sensations that the object produces for the beholder. The two perspectives do not precisely coincide. The "art" of the Ancients includes every kind of making, and thus what we would call "technique" or "technology." The Moderns' aesthetics include every kind of admirable beauty, and thus the beauty of natural phenomena (the sublimity of volcanoes). When studying the art-technique of the Ancients, we have to abandon as false oppositions antinomies that are legitimate from the point of view of Moderns. Art did not have the beautiful as its exclusive domain, and technique was not limited to the useful. Art was not the realm of mysterious things and "artistic" vagueness, as opposed to technique as the realm of serious things, rigorous procedures, and guaranteed results. Clarifying the vocabulary was as important as relativizing, as a dictatorship or caricature, any scientific view of rationality modeled on industry and, later on, techno-science.

The ancient theory of art does not seem to have aroused great debates or challenges, in any case not before the end of the eighteenth century—that is, before the dawn of the industrial revolutions. For the Ancients, and so long as people thought with Latin, art and technique were one and the same thing: Latin *ars* (from the root **er-*, which provides in particular Gr. *arthron* [ἄρθρον], "articulation," and Lat. *armus*, "upper arm," but which also appears in Lat. *ritus*, "rite," and Gr. *arithmos* [ἀριθμός], "number") equals Greek *technê* [τέχνη] (from the root **teks-*, "construct," "make"). Since art and technique are defined by the production of an object, the question is what guarantees the success of the finished product, and the classic answer is the worker's skill, which is the necessary result of long training: "By the work, one knows the worker."

The fundamental concepts of this theory are those of Aristotle, whose presentation is synthesized in a short chapter of the *Nicomachean Ethics* (6.4.1140a1–24). Technical art is concerned with the production of objects or "works of art," Greek *poiêsis* [ποίησις],

Latin *fabricatio* or *fictio*. Thus in Greek, the artist-craftsman is called a "poet," in classical Latin a *faber* or *fictor*, and in Late Latin *factor* or *operator* (cf. the French expression *facteur d'orgues*). Fabrication is the sole specific character of art. Very generally, art is an "excellence" or "virtue" (*arêtê* [ἀρητή]): "a disposition accompanied by a true (or right) rule." The disposition is rendered as *hexis* [εξις] in Greek, *habitus* in Latin. (See "with a rule": *meta logou* [μετὰ λόγου], Gr. *logos* [λόγος], Lat. *ratio*; "true" or "right": Gr. *alêthês* [ἀληθής] or *orthos* [ὀρθός], Lat. *vera* or *recta*.) Finally, technical art moves in the domain of the contingent, of what might be other than what it is. This character is not peculiar to it. The contingent is also the domain of "prudence" (*phronêsis* [φρόνησις]), which is, so to speak, the production of actions, Greek *praxis* [πρᾶξις]. Technical art and prudence are thus opposed to the intellectual virtues, such as science or *epistêmê* [ἐπιστήμη], which seek to know the necessary (for example, geometry or astronomy). As Thomas Aquinas sums it up, technical art is *recta ratio factibilium*, and prudence is *recta ratio agibilium* (*Summa theologica*, 2a–2ae, q. 47, art. 5). To understand what kind of rationality is referred to here, we have to explain the idea of true *logos* or "right reason," *recta ratio*. The word *recta* refers to the idea of a rule, from *regula*, "regulation," that is, etymologically from *regere*, "to rule" (less "to correct" than "to direct"). The rule of art—as of prudence—is not so much a norm as a fixed reference point in a world of movement. This can be seen in the application of the rules as well as in their discovery.

On the one hand, the rule makes it possible to escape from the contingent. The rule of art must be applied if one wants to obtain a specific result. As defined by the Scholastics, it is a "via certa et determinata." From this point of view, there is no uncertainty in the arts and techniques, neither in the rule nor in the product obtained by applying the rule. This holds for the fabrication in accord with the rules of a knife, a ship, or a house. In these domains, uncertainty and the unpredictable can be reduced almost to zero. The adjective *certus* signifies that the rule has been objectified, expressed, visualized by the intelligence, so to speak, and that we are no longer groping our way by means of an instinctive

practice. The *logos alêthês* [λόγος ἀληθής] of the technician-artist is an increasingly clear and distinct awareness of his means. The clearer the rule, the less difficult it is to transmit it and have it applied by others.

On the other hand, the rules of art have to be discovered. As Aristotle insists at the beginning of the *Metaphysics*, it is by observing particulars that one can arrive at general or even universal rules by induction (A.1). Besides the physician, the canonical example of the technician is the ship's pilot. The sea is more powerful than he is, and it is far from being perfectly predictable. Aristotle lived in a maritime world, where nature made people conscious of how much they were neither its masters nor its possessors. However, far from leading to fatalism, this only made the role of the pilot more important. It is not the sea or the world that is rational, but he. If the rule is a stable reference point in a moving world, it is on the side of the subject, the regulating intelligence. It is the formal element in the operation. The moving world is on the side of the object, of that to which the rule is applied: it is the material element. Aristotle attributes contingency to the object alone, not to the subject—to the result, not to the rule. Modern technical triumphs have caused to be considered "true" only those rules that have been validated by the predictability of the results. But in Aristotle and Aquinas, the absence of guaranteed results does not signify an absence of rules, of rationality. To speak of medicine as an art is now considered a way of emphasizing the irreducible contingency of medicine, which cannot achieve the status of a "true" science. For the Ancients, it was instead a way of emphasizing medicine's ability to find rules, something stable. We look for stability in the material, they sought it in the intelligible. For the production of things in which technique triumphs, the two points of view merge. For techniques that remain, like medicine, an art, the divergence is only a matter of emphasis. But for the fine arts, the divergence is at its maximum. They push to the limit a conception of rationality that seems to us paradoxical, and that dares to assert that the absence of guaranteed results goes hand in hand with the presence of infallible rules.

Francis Goyet

impersonate the corresponding *technê* (464c–d). Thus *technê* is characterized by the presence of the semantic trait "knowledge," to the point that one might often hesitate about which noun to add: *hê politikê* [ἡ πολιτική] (*technê*: *Gorgias*, 464b or *Protagoras*, 319a, *Statesman*, 267d; *epistêmê*: *Statesman*, 303e).

It remained for Aristotle—for whom, contrary to Plato, rhetoric is in fact a *technê*, and even a power of "theorizing" (*theôrêsai* [θεωρῆσαι], *Rhetoric*, 1.2.1355b32) and of reflecting on causes and means by distinguishing the true from the apparent (1.1.1355b10–16)—to make the distinction by the criterion of the field of application: art, like action (see PRAXIS for the difference between *praxis* and *poiêsis* [πρᾶξις/ποίησις]), deals with the contingent, whereas science deals with the necessary (see Box 1). Once the orbit of the meanings of *technê* in its original consistency has been sketched, how should we conceive its relationship with what we moderns call "art"? We need to resort to another defining trait: *mimêsis* [μίμησις].

B. Valorizations and devalorizations

Technê and *phusis* [φύσις], art and nature, are conceived in a relationship of imitation or reciprocal representation that is constantly reversed, both regarding the term imitated (Which is primary, nature or art?) and regarding the value of imitation itself, depending on the system in question (see MIMÊSIS).

Something approaching a modern meaning of "art" can found at the end of Plato's *Sophist*. "Mimesis" is defined as the production of images (*poiêsis tis* [ποίησίς τίς], *eidôlôn mentoi* [εἰδώλων μέντοι], 265b) and not of the things themselves. It can be divine or human. In fact, the divine produces not only things in nature (humans, fire), but also the image that accompanies each thing ("to parakolouthoun eidôlon hekastôi [τὸ παρακολουθοῦν εἴδωλον ἑκάστῳ]," 266c, *phantasmata* [φαντάσματα]—dreams, shadows, reflections; see EIDÔLON, PHANTASIA); and even humans produce not only works (the house produced by the mason's art), but also images ("In building it produces an actual house, and in painting [*graphikêi*] a house of a different sort, as it were a manmade dream for waking eyes," 266c); and these images can be identical copies, reproductions (*to eikastikon* [τὸ εἰκαστικόν], or *hê eikastikê* [ἡ εἰκαστική], the art of making *eikones* [εἰκόνες], 235d, 266d), or relative copies, which include point of view or perspective, trompe l'oeil (*to phantastikon* [τὸ φανταστικόν] or *hê phantastikê* [ἡ φανταστική], the art of making *phantasmata*, 236b–c, 266d). Something like visual art is thus isolated in order to serve as a model for the distinctions to be introduced in the art of speaking, but it is not explored as such. Its main characteristic is ontological: in the *Republic* (book 10), the art of illusory appearance, painting (*graphê* [γραφή]), considered as situated at a distance of three degrees from the truth, proves to be ontologically inferior to carpentry, which takes its models directly from ideas (597a). For each "art," the question is whether a principle other than imitation can save it from the regress that it implies: thus music has a privileged place, given its relation to mathematics—though there is a bad kind of music, which, acting on our senses, softens the mind, and a good kind of music, which is regulated by the principles of mathematical *epistêmê* (3.401d; *Protagoras*, 326a–b).

"Art imitates nature [*hê technê mimeitai tên phusin* (ἡ τέχνη μιμεῖται τὴν φύσιν)]." That means that nature is primary, present first, composed of a plurality of beings that have in themselves the principle of their movement (*technê*

consists of bringing into existence things "whose origin is in the maker and not in the thing made," *Nicomachean Ethics*, 6.4.1140a13–14). But that always also implies that art provides the concepts necessary for thinking about nature. Aristotle elaborates his physical theory of the four causes with reference to making and doing things (*Physics*, 2.2 and 3): for each natural being, we will seek, on the model precisely of a statue, what is its matter (*to ex hou* [τὸ ἐξ οὗ]: bronze, the cause of the statue), its form (*to eidos kai to paradeigma* [τὸ εἶδος καὶ τὸ παράδειγμα]: Athena, who serves as a model for the statue), its efficient cause (the sculptor Polykleitos), and its purpose (to adorn a temple, to bring the city into existence). From this comes the famous complement: "Generally art partly completes what nature cannot bring to a finish [*epitelei ha hê phusis adunatei apergasasthai* (ἐπιτελεῖ ἃ ἡ φύσις ἀδυνατεῖ ἀπεργάσασθαι)], and partly imitates her" (*Physics* 2.8.199a15–16). Art displays both its dependency on the model by imitating it, and a certain superiority in realizing what the model, even though it is prior, was not able to produce.

We understand why in his *Poetics* Aristotle regards positively the pleasure that we derive from what we would call the arts, those that represent (imitate in images, *mimountai . . . apeikazontes* [μιμοῦνταί . . . ἀπεικάζοντες], 1.1447a19) with colors and figures, or that use rhythm, melody, or language, in prose or in verse—music, painting, or poetry. Pleasure (*to chairein* [τὸ χαίρειν], see PLEASURE) is of two kinds. First there is an intellectual pleasure: on looking at an image, we learn to know something, to recognize it for what it is ("The reason of the delight in seeing the picture is that one is at the same time learning—gathering the meaning of things" ["*theôrountas manthanein kai sullogizesthai ti hekaston* (θεωροῦντας μανθάνειν καὶ συλλογίζεσθαι τί ἕκαστον)"], *Poetics*, 4.1448b15–17). But there is also what we would call an aesthetic pleasure: "It will be due to the execution or coloring or some such other cause" (4.6).

The field of *technê* can thus include all values from divine demiurgy (*artifex mundi*, the Romans called it) to human power or faculty, which is rational and useful, but obviously susceptible to Promethean excess and trickery. If we try to isolate in it the premises of what we now call art, value judgments are ontologically, as well as politically and socially, amplified:

> The Greeks . . . could say in one and the same breath: "He who has not seen the Zeus of Phidias at Olympia has lived in vain" *and* "People like Phidias, namely sculptors, are unfit for citizenship."
>
> (Arendt, *Between Past and Future*, 216–17)

II. *Ars, Kunst*: The Practical and the Intellectual

The Latin notion of *ars*, and the notion of art (and its European equivalents) up to the seventeenth century, is qualified by the adjunction of antonymic adjectives (liberal/mechanical, noble/servile). *Ars* is largely a matter of "making," but it also covers more intellectual attitudes. Similarly, the German notion of *Kunst* wavers between ability (*können*) and knowing (*kennen*).

Rome never admitted the visual arts into the cycle of the liberal arts, the *artes liberales*, or, in other words, into the body of theoretical knowledge which a freeman was expected to master. The liberal arts remained the corner-stone of Christian education and this implied the exclusion of the visual arts from the higher sphere throughout the Middle Ages.

(Wittkower and Wittkower, *Born under Saturn*, 7–8)

These remarks direct our analysis of the meaning of the terms *ars*, *arte*, *art*, and *Kunst* in two directions: on the one hand, the status of the artist and that of his activity, and on the other, the criterion for his social legitimation. The vocabulary the authors of Latin antiquity used to classify diverse human practices is significant in this regard. They distinguished the *artes liberales* (Pliny, Seneca), *honestae* (Cicero), and *ingenuae* (Quintilian) from the *artes illiberales* or *sordidae* (Cicero). The *artes liberales* are intellectual activities such as grammar and rhetoric, the *studia liberalia* Seneca talks about in his letter 88, which have no goal other than the cultivation of the mind, and are alone worthy of a free man. (In his *Etymologies*, Isidore of Seville derived the word *liberatis* from *liber*.) The *artes illiberales* are manual activities, the *artes mechanicae* are reserved for slaves or are remunerated by wages; they include painting and sculpture, but not music, which is considered a mathematical discipline. In the Middle Ages, the number of the liberal arts was set at seven: grammar, rhetoric, dialectic, arithmetic, geometry, music, and astronomy. The first four constituted the so-called *quadrivium*, the last three the *trivium*. Starting in the Renaissance, painters and sculptors no longer wanted to be confused with artisans. The battle they fought ensured that their activity would no longer be regarded as a mercenary craft, but would gain the dignity that was the privilege of the liberal arts. Far from challenging the distinction between mechanical arts and liberal arts, the battle testifies to the permanence of that division, which persisted at least until the eighteenth century. A definition like that given by Jacques Bénigne Bossuet shows the continuing influence of Greek and Latin notions: "The liberal and mechanical arts are distinguished by the fact that the former work with the mind rather than with the hand; and the others, whose success depends on routine rather than on science, work more with the hand than with the mind" (*Connaissance de Dieu*, 1.15).

In the Latin vocabulary, *ars*, in addition to having the very general meaning of a way of being or behaving, was applied in three domains: that involving the object of a "making," of a manual trade; that which requires know-how; and that which has to do with the application of rules: carpentry, rhetoric, and grammar are thus subsumed under a single category. It is therefore the most specific rules, notably of painting, that make it possible to distinguish the arts in the modern sense. The beginning of *De inventione* (1.1–4), where Cicero takes up, with an intention different from Plato's, the parallel between discourse and painting, offers a significant example of this. Commenting on the commission the inhabitants of Croton gave to Zeuxis for a portrait of Helen, Cicero mentions the "very large number of pictures [*tabulas*]" painted by the artist, and speaks of "embellishing the temple of Juno with unmatched pictures [*picturis*]" and masterpieces (*magna opera*), but he does not use the word *ars*. On the other hand, the word appears in the second part of the analogy, when the process of induction that rises from several real women to the ideal model of the woman is applied to rhetoric, called *ars dicendi*.

As Erwin Panofsky showed in *Idea* (1924), the development of the modern notion of art and artists passed by way of a conjunction of the inductive model of *De inventione* and the deductive model of *Brutus*, in which, this time, Cicero seeks the model for the *ars dicendi* in the example of Phidias sculpting the image of Zeus on the basis of the idea that he forms of him in his mind. Here, *ars* qualifies the activity of the artist turned toward his internal eye (see SPECIES):

contemplabatur aliquem, e quo similitudinem duceret, sed ipsius in mente insidebat species pulchritudinis eximia quaedam, quam intuens in eaque defixus, ad illius similitudinem artem et manum dirigebat.

It was in his own mind that resided a separate vision of beauty that he contemplated and on which he fixed his gaze, guiding his art and his hand by resemblance with this vision.

(Cicero, *Brutus*, 2.7–8)

A crucial aspect of the development of the notion of art thus resides in the appearance in the Renaissance of "a new type of artist . . . essentially different from the artisan of old, in that he was conscious of his intellectual and creative powers" (Wittkower and Wittkower, *Born under Saturn*, 31). The signs of art, which appear in large numbers at that time, no longer have the sporadic character seen in antiquity; they are given concrete form, notably by the inclusion of artists in humanistic culture. The centrifugal force of the process of becoming autonomous is inseparable from the centripetal force that subjects the artist to an intellectual and political dependency. Thus Albrecht Dürer owed his career to the Elector of Saxony, Frederick III, called the Wise, who, through the mediation of the poet and humanist Conrad Celtis, brought him into the Round Table of the learned men of Nuremberg.

The reference to Dürer is particular instructive here. The shift in the meaning of *Kunst* on the basis of its original double meaning allows us to understand how the artisan was transformed into the artist. As Panofsky notes:

Like *ars* in Latin and "art" in English, the German word *Kunst* had originally two different meanings, the second of which is now all but extinct. On the one hand, it denoted "ability" [*können*], that is, man's ability purposely to produce things or effects. . . . On the other hand, it denoted "knowledge" [*kennen*], that is, theoretical knowledge or insight as opposed to practice. . . . In the second, or narrower, sense—which still survives in the expression *Die freien Künste* or "The Liberal Arts"—astronomy could be called *Künst der Sterne* ("art of the stars"); . . . and when Dürer wished to express the idea that a good painter needed both theoretical insight and practical skill he could do it . . . by saying that he had to combine *Kunst* and *Brauch*.

(Panofsky, *The Life and Art of Albrecht Dürer*)

This distinction between *Kunst* and *Brauch* (custom, practical sense) allows us to connect *Kunst* with human activities that more or less imply theoretical foundations. But in other texts, Dürer turns the meaning of *Kunst* in another direction, like a scale that he tips to suit his interest. Thus when he speaks of the rules of art in his *Underweysung der Messung mit dem Zirckel und Richtscheyt* (Four Books on Measurement), it is in the most instrumental sense, as the standard measure of magnitudes.

III. The Arts, the Beaux Arts, and Art in the Modern Sense

In a context in which the opposition, which is Latin in origin, between the liberal arts and the mechanical arts continues to be dominant, the notion of the "fine arts" was used to carry out a transformation of and around the notion of art until the latter was identified with art as such.

Extrinsic legitimation, especially intellectual legitimation through science or philosophy, is a stage in the artist's slow conquest of autonomy. But although this process continued in the seventeenth century, it did so in conjunction with a gradual separation from certain arts whose goals were cognitive. The intellectual criterion made it possible to elevate art, in the hierarchy that governed legitimation, to the dignity of a liberal art: "To judge beauty is to judge order, proportion, and rightness, things that only the mind can perceive," wrote Bossuet in *Connaissance de Dieu et de soi-même* (1670); but this criterion of beauty also made it possible to put into a distinct class some of the arts that benefited from this ennobling. It is important always to keep in mind this twofold movement through which the accession to liberal status was accompanied by a concentration on the specificity of art. More or less concomitantly, the notions of fine arts, beaux arts, *schöne Künste*, and *belle arti*, which had appeared when art began to be institutionalized in the seventeenth century (in the French Académie des Beaux-Arts, for instance), show the convergence of the European vocabulary toward a common concept.

We must also note, however, an inverse process that appeared later on, in RT: *Encyclopédie ou Dictionnaire raisonné des sciences, des arts et des métiers*: the recognition that even the mechanical arts involve mental activity. The latter reflected or led to a rehabilitation of manual trades in the framework of the encyclopedic treatment of human practices sanctioned by the *Encyclopédie* article "Art." In this article, Diderot denounces the incoherence of a definition that assimilates liberal art to a purely mental activity, ignoring the fact that it is an art, that is, an activity that involves making or doing. Precisely to the extent that art assumes the execution of an object, it is distinguished from the pure mental activity expressed in science. Inversely, Diderot rejects the traditional, equally erroneous conception of mechanical art that denies this form of activity any connection with intelligence. In art, execution is based on rules: one can adopt either a practical attitude that consists in operating in accord with the rules without reflecting on them, or a theoretical, "inoperative" attitude that consists in reflecting on the rules. "Every art has its speculation and its practice," Diderot writes (RT: *Encyclopédie ou Dictionnaire*, s.v.), thus restoring to the word "art" a sense rather close to that of the Latin *ars*.

With Immanuel Kant, the philosophical determination of the specificity of art turns in a quite different direction. Taste, he writes in the *Critique of Judgment*, "is merely a judging and not a productive faculty, and what is appropriate to it is therefore not a work of beautiful art [*der schönen Künsten*]. It can only be a product belonging to useful and mechanical art [*nützlichen und mechanischen Kunst*] or even to science [*Wissenschaft*], produced according to definite rules that can be learned and must be exactly followed" (§48). Although a poem, a piece of music, a picture gallery, and so on, belong to the class of the beaux arts, a table service or a sermon is excluded from it. However, this criterion of classification is not sufficient: there is in addition or opposition a notion involving *what art does in the work*, which depends on an entirely different principle. Works allegedly assigned to the beaux arts, Kant says in §49, cannot lack "spirit" (*Geist*), the principle that "animates the soul" ("das belebende Prinzip im Gemüte"): "A poem may be very neat and elegant, but without spirit." The same holds for a narrative, a "festal discourse," or a conversation. In other words, a work of art may lack art, whereas a production that is not a work of art may correspond to the principle of art.

In addition to this chiasmus, there is also the chiasmus of taste and genius: there can be *genius without taste* as well as *taste without genius*. The aesthetic definition of art is thus superimposed upon its artistic determination. The spirit that makes art "is that which purposively sets the mental powers into motion, i.e., into a play that is self-maintaining and even strengthens the powers to that end." It is the free play of the faculties, of the understanding and the imagination, that defines pure aesthetic judgment. The principle that animates art, Kant adds, is "that representation of the imagination that occasions much thinking though without it being possible for any determinate thought, i.e., concept, to be adequate to it, which, consequently, no language fully attains or can make intelligible" (Kant, *Critique of the Power of Judgment*, trans. Guyer and Matthews). The concept dedicates the work to an external or internal goal and manifests the mechanical rules of the art. A work of fine art, instead of being reducible to the concept of a rule, must appear as nature, as the product of genius, that is, "the natural talent [*ingenium*] that gives the rule to art [die angeborene Gemütsanlage (ingenium), durch welche die Natur der Kunst die Regel gibt]" (§46).

■ See Box 2.

At the beginning of the nineteenth century, the meanings associated with the beaux arts gradually passed into the words "art" (French and English), *Kunst*, *arte*, and so on. G.W.F. Hegel put his philosophical signature on this transfer with his famous *Lectures on Aesthetics* (1820–29), which were poorly named, since in fact they concern, as he himself said, not aesthetics, but a philosophy of art (*Philosophie der Kunst*). The discipline that he founded confirms the Kantian rejection of the reduction of art to know-how, but deviates from the theory of taste and separates art from nature. This modern sense of the word "art" and its equivalents in various European languages was then added to an old sense (which persisted, obviously), but also soon rose up to oppose it. Artistic interest could no longer be reduced to a vocational activity, but rather required an individual's total commitment. This figure of the artist inherited from the Renaissance proliferated with Romanticism and the doctrine of art for art's sake:

> Art, for these gentlemen, is everything—poetry, painting, etc.; they are in love with *art*, and scorn anyone who does not work for *art*, spend their lives talking about *art*, speaking *art*.

> (*Revue de Paris*, January 1833)

Dominique Chateau

BIBLIOGRAPHY

Arendt, Hannah. *Between Past and Future: Eight Exercises in Political Thought.* New York: Viking, 2006.

Aristotle. *Nicomachean Ethics.* Translated by D. Ross. Revised by J. L. Ackrill and J. O. Urmson. Oxford: Oxford University Press, 1998.

———. *Poetics.* In *The Complete Works of Aristotle,* edited by J. Barnes, vol. 2. Princeton, NJ: Princeton University Press, 1984.

Aubenque, Pierre. *Le problème de l'être chez Aristote.* Paris: Presses Universitaires de France, 1962.

Baudelaire, Charles. *Le salon de 1859.* Edited by Wolfgang Drost, with Ulrike Riechers. Paris: H. Champion, 2006.

Bossuet, Jacques Bénigne. *Connaissance de Dieu et de soi-même.* In *Œuvres,* vol. 34. Versailles, Fr.: Imprimerie de J. A. Lebel, 1818. First published in 1670.

Collingwood, Robin George. *The Principles of Art.* Oxford: Clarendon, 1938.

Furley, David J., and Alexander Nehamas, eds. *Aristotle's* Rhetoric. Princeton, NJ: Princeton University Press, 1994.

Goldschmidt, Victor. *Temps physique et temps tragique chez Aristote.* Paris: Vrin, 1982.

Hegel, Georg Wilhem Friedrich. *Vorlesungen über die Aesthetik.* In *Werke.* Frankfurt: Suhrkamp Verlag, 1970. First published in 1822–29. Translation by T. M. Knox: *Aesthetics: Lectures on Fine Art.* 2 vols. Oxford: Oxford University Press, 1975.

Husain, Martha. *Ontology and the Art of Tragedy: An Approach to Aristotle's Poetics.* Albany: State University of New York Press, 2001.

Kant, Immanuel. *Critique of the Power of Judgment.* Translated by P. Guyer and E. Matthews. Cambridge: Cambridge University Press, 2001.

Kraut, Richard, ed. *The Cambridge Companion to Plato.* Cambridge: Cambridge University Press, 1992.

Ledbetter, Grace. *Poetics before Plato: Interpretation and Authority in Early Greek Theories of Poetry.* Princeton, NJ: Princeton University Press, 2003.

Michel, Pierre-Henri. *De Pythagore à Euclide.* Paris: Belles Lettres, 1950.

Panofsky, Erwin. *Idea: A Concept in Art Theory.* Translated by J. S. Peake. Columbia: University of South Carolina Press, 1968.

———. *The Life and Art of Albrecht Dürer.* Princeton, NJ: Princeton University Press, 1934–35.

Plato. *Complete Works.* Edited by J. M. Cooper. Indianapolis, IN: Hackett, 1997.

Reinach, Adolphe. *La peinture ancienne.* Recueil Milliet. Paris: Macula, Deucalion Collection, 1985.

Schuhl, Pierre-Maxime. *Platon et l'art de son temps: Arts Plastiques.* Paris: Presses Universitaires de France, 1952.

Wittkower, Rudolph, and Margot Wittkower. *Born under Saturn.* New York: W. W. Norton, 1963.

2

Plastic, the plastic arts, *bildende Künste*

➤ PLASTICITY, and BILD, *FICTION*, HISTORY, TRUTH

Plasticity has long characterized the arts of modeling. The Greek *plassein* [πλάσσειν], "shape, fashion, form," is built on a root that means "spread a thin layer, coat" (whence "plaster"; cf. RT: *Dictionnaire étymologique de la langue grecque,* s.v.). It provides the specific vocabulary for working with clay and modeling, and serves in particular to describe the activity of Prometheus, "of whom it is said that he fashioned us, along with other living beings" (Philemon, 89.1), and also that of Hephaistos shaping Pandora, the very paradigm of deception and trickery, a beautiful virgin molded out of earth dampened with water and unleashed among men to open the jar containing all evils (Hesiod, *Works and Days,* 70ff.). From this comes its use relating to literary creation, to fiction assumed to be capable of deceiving—the plasticity of words: in his *Encomium of Helen* (82.B11 DK, §11), Gorgias mentions all those who "have persuaded and persuade . . . by fashioning a false discourse [*pseudê logon plasantes* (ψευδῆ λόγον πλάσαντες)]." Thus in the vocabulary of the historians, *plasma* [πλάσμα] comes to designate fiction, that is, "things that have not happened, but that are narrated like those that have," the false

recounted as true, in contrast to *muthos* [μῦθος] and *historia* [ἱστορία], myth (the false recounted as false) and history (the true recounted as true); cf. Sextus Empiricus, *Against the Mathematicians,* 263–64. And in the Latin rhetorical terminology, *plasma* becomes *argumentum,* whereas *plassein* is rendered by *fingere* (Quintilian, *Institutio oratoria,* 1.8.18–21). On all of this, see Cassin, *L'effet sophistique,* 470–512.

But until the eighteenth century, the material-formal sense was dominant as the criterion for distinguishing a kind of art, as is shown by the article in the *Encyclopédie* (RT: *Encyclopédie ou Dictionnaire*), alongside which appears, without apparent connection, another article with the curious title "*PLASTIQUE (Métaphysique) nature plastique,* a principle that some philosophers claim serves to form organized bodies, & which is different from the life of animals." However, at the very beginning of the century, Lord Shaftesbury had already established the link. For him, the expression "plastic nature," a concept that emerged from the theosophy of the Cambridge Platonists of the second half of the seventeenth century, designated both the unconscious vegetative state of

the growth of beings (a tree or a fetus) and a human power that was free, internal, and conscious, and reflected the principle of nature while transcending determinism. In his *Advice to an Author* (1710; RT: *Characteristicks of Men,* 1:207), Shaftesbury compares the poet and his ability to shape a unitary, organic work to Prometheus, "that sovereign artist, or Universal Plastic Nature." In his *Plastics or the Original Progress and Power of Designatory Art,* an unfinished work that was published in part, and on which he worked in 1712–13, the idea is applied to the plastic arts explicitly designated as such: the painter, who works *materia plastica,* "begins by working first *within.* Here the imagery! Here the plastic work! First he makes forms, fashions, corrects, amplifies, contracts, unites, modifies, assimilates, adapts, conforms, polishes, refines, etc., forms his *ideas:* then his hand: his strokes" (in Shaftesbury, *Second Characters,* 142).

Thus it happens that the term "plastic arts" makes a fleeting and remarkable appearance. Shaftesbury's intuition was developed much later in France, notably by Lamennais (*Esquisse d'une philosophie* [1840]) and Taine

(continued)

(continued)

(Philosophie de l'art [1864–69]). The expression became part of the French critical and philosophical vocabulary far more than of the English vocabulary, where the notion of plastic art is generally rare (except, at the beginning of the twentieth century, in the context of the discovery of modern French art and African art).

In the Germanic domain, on the other hand, the idea, if not the word, began to establish itself at the end of the eighteenth century: not around "plastic," but rather around *Bild*. The plastic arts are the *bildenden Künste*, about which Thomas Munro observes that "its abstract connotation is broad and vague, coming from a noun [*Bild*] meaning 'image' and a verb [*bilden*] meaning 'to form.' Hence it suggests the forming of visual representations" (*Arts and Their Interrelations* [1949], 401); the term, given its application to architecture (a nonrepresentational art) and to painting (a non-three-dimensional art), to the exclusion of mobile arts, is supposed to cover the "arts of static visual form" (ibid.). In the *Critique of Judgment* (1790), Kant distinguishes the *bildenden Künste*, "those by which expression is found for ideas in *sensible intuition*" (§51), which include the plastic (*die Plastik*, sculpture and architecture) and painting, from *redenden Künste*, the verbal arts, which include eloquence and poetry, and from the *Kunst des schönen Spiels der Empfindung*, that is, the art of the beautiful play of sensations, music and the art of colors (*Farbenkunst*). The occurrence of *Plastik* in this classification signals that the original Greek term is being specialized, considerably enriching the German aesthetic vocabulary. "The Greek genius is the plastic artist [*plastischer Künstler*] who makes stone into a work

of art [*zum Kunstwerk bildet*]," writes Hegel in his *Lectures on the Philosophy of History* (1837).

The richness of the German vocabulary introduces numerous paths for aesthetic thought to follow (Herder, Schelling, Hegel, Nietzsche, Fiedler) that are more or less closed to other languages. The example of Herder is particularly interesting: in *Plastik, Einige Wahrnehmungen über Form und Gestalt aus Pygmalions bildendem Traum*, a text published in 1778, his thought is organized around three poles: the generic notion of *bildenden Künste* and the specific notions of *Skulptur* (versus *Malerei*) and *Plastik* (versus *Piktur*). In addition to a new *paragone* of the arts, what is at work here is a promotion of the plastic and of its (tactile) values as a criterion of beauty ("What is beauty?—Ask the blind man!" we read in the epigraph to *Plastik*). For asserting the superiority of the hand over the eye, by the yardstick of the blind man (Rousseau, Diderot, et al.), the vocabulary formed around *Bild* is welcome: "A blind sculptor [*Bildner*], even who was born blind, would be a wretched painter, but in sculpture [*bilden*] he is not at any disadvantage and would probably even surpass a sighted peer," or again: "Sculpture [*Bildnerei*] is truth, whereas painting is a dream" (Herder, *Sculpture*, trans. Gaiger, 64, 45). *Plastik* thus goes beyond the classificatory meaning of *Skulptur*: as posterity was to show (notably Fiedler, Riegl, Einstein), it is the more general modern notion of plasticity (a criterion for assessing painting itself) that is beginning to be explored here.

BIBLIOGRAPHY

Cassin, B. *L'effet sophistique*. Paris: Gallimard / La Pléiade, 1995.

Chateau, Dominique. *Arts plastiques: Archéologie d'une notion*. Nîmes, Fr.: Jacqueline Chambon, "Rayon-art," 1999.

Fiedler, Konrad. *Schriften über den Kunst*. Posthumous edition. Munich: R. Piper, 1913–14.

Hegel, G.W.F. *The Philosophy of History*. Translated by John Sibree. New York: Dover, 2004.

Herder, Johann Gottfried. *Plastik, Einige Wahrnehmungen über Form und Gestalt aus Pygmalions bildendem Traum*. First published in 1778. In *Werke in fünf Bänden*, edited by W. Dobbek. Weier, Ger.: Volksverlag, 1957. Translation by J. Gaiger: *Sculpture: Some Observations on Shape and Form from Pygmalion's Creative Dream*. Chicago: University of Chicago Press, 2002.

Lamennais, Félicité Robert de. *Esquisse d'une philosophie*. Paris: Pagnerre, 1840.

Larthomas, Jean-Paul. *De Shaftesbury à Kant*. Atelier national de reproduction des thèses. Paris: Didier érudition, 1985.

Munro, Thomas. *The Arts and Their Interrelations*. New York: Liberal Arts Press, 1949.

Riegl, Alois. *Stilfragen, Grundlegungen zu einer Geschichte der Ornamentik*. Munich: Mäander Kunstverlag, 1977. First published in 1893. Translation by E. Kain: *Problems of Style: Foundations for a History of Ornament*. Princeton, NJ: Princeton University Press, 1992.

———. *Spätrömische Kunstindustrie*. Darmstadt, Ger.: Wissenschaftliche Buchgesellschaft, 1973. First published in 1901. Translation by R. Winkes: *Late Roman Art Industry*. Rome: Giorgio Bretschneider, 1985.

Shaftesbury, Anthony Ashley Cooper. *Second Characters, or the Language of Forms*. Edited by Benjamin Rand. Cambridge: Cambridge University Press, 1914.

Taine, Hippolyte. *Philosophie de l'art*. First published in 1864–69. In *Corpus des œuvres de philosophie en langue française*, edited by Michel Serres. Paris: Fayard, 1985.

ASPECT

Aspect, between *Parole, Langues,* and *Langage*

➤ *TIME,* and ESTI, JETZTZEIT, LANGUAGE, MOMENT, PRESENT, SPEECH ACT, *TO BE*

The term "aspect" designates a semantic category of languages, like number, mood, or voice. Traditionally, it is described as referring to the "mode of development" of the process to which the verb refers; more broadly, it concerns the form that this process can take, whether or not the latter is part of some development. This notion is in itself a philosophical object. It appears as such in the history of philosophy, particularly in Greek philosophy, at a time when the concepts that were to serve as the foundation for the linguistic tradition were being worked out. Although the term "aspect," which was introduced later on by analysts of language, is not part of the philosophical vocabulary, a number of other words that are more or less closely associated with it (ranging from the Greek *telos* [τέλος] to the English "performative") were at first philosophical terms. The whole history of thought about aspect, which has been marked by translation issues, as we will see, shows that the words in question are untranslatable.

However, if "aspect" is connected with the untranslatable, it is in a different way. On the material level, the category corresponds to a network of formal differences that is rather heterogeneous but in which we can nonetheless isolate a kind of "hard core" constituted by forms involved in conjugation (at least in languages in which verbs are conjugated, as in Indo-European languages). Between two marks of conjugation taken from two different languages, there will never be a strict equivalence, precisely insofar as each of them is situated in a different system of conjugation that necessarily determines the value it can have. Moreover, these values run through the whole language:

it is not a question of an isolated form but of a whole system that structures the construction of the reference of verbs in that language. As such, they constitute one of the dimensions in which the so-called genius of a language is determined.

However, aspectual events are also outside language. They are aspects insofar as they represent values that can be measured first of all in sentences and discourses, that is, where what Saussure called *parole* is involved, depending as much on the individual thought that the "speaker" elaborates as on the language that conditions this elaboration. On the other hand, they are aspects insofar as they concern a question that involves language generally: the question of the reference of verbs, which is not peculiar to any single language.

Caught both between *langue* and *parole* and between *langues* and *langage*, aspect thus touches in the most acute way on the question of the untranslatable.

Everything about aspect is complicated, heterogeneous, and tumultuous: the types of values concerned, the types of forms involved, and the types of concepts elaborated to account for them. This has in part to do with the very notion of aspect, which is to a large extent problematic, and in part with the history of its conceptualization, which is itself singularly tumultuous.

I. Little Parade of Values

When we speak of aspect, it may initially be a question of the different phases to which reference can be made within a given process: thus we distinguish a phase before this process, when it is merely imminent, its advent proper, its development, its completion, and also the situation that results from it. Languages generally have specific expressions to refer to each of these phases (in French, there are various verbal expressions such as *commencer à, finir de,* etc.). But similar values can be obtained without the mediation of a specific lexical expression. Here are a few examples in French:

— Il sortait quand le téléphone a sonné (He was going to go out).
— À ce moment-là, il neigea (It began to snow).
— Quand elle est entrée, il dormait (He was sleeping).
— Voilà! Il a réparé la voiture (He finished repairing the car; he did all the work, so it should run).
— Désolé, il est sorti (Sorry, he has gone out).

In addition, alongside these "partial" registrations, in which the process is presented at some phase of its development, there is also the possibility of so-called overall registration, in which the process is presented as having happened, without that happening involving a development: that is how, for instance, the following two utterances in French are opposed to each other, the first presenting the overall process, while the latter describes it as it is happening:

— Il répara sa voiture (He repaired his car).
— Il réparait sa voiture (He was repairing his car).

And there is also the matter of the more or less iterative character of the process designated: here we distinguish among isolated processes, intrinsically repetitive processes, reiterated processes, and habitual, recurrent processes.

Finally, alongside the question of phases, differences in "point of view" relative to the way in which the process is envisaged also come into play: certain utterances can stage a kind of reference point from which the process is described, and that may be distinct from the moment of utterance. This point of view can be simultaneous with the unfolding of the process, but it can also be external to it, whether prospective or retrospective. The fact that the point of view can be distinct from the point of registration is demonstrated by the following contrast, in which the same process, registered comprehensively in both cases, is envisaged either retrospectively (from the moment of utterance) or from a point of view presented as simultaneous with its completion:

— Il est entré (He has entered).
— Il entra (He entered).

This variety of phenomena can be explained in part by the empirical diversity of the values that can in fact be marked in languages by procedures that are said to be of an aspectual order. It can also be explained by the complex way in which the concept of aspect itself developed in the history of thought and the history of linguistics.

II. Exchanges among Languages

The concept of aspect developed in an exchange between languages in which it was constantly imported and then re-imported from one language into another, from Greek to Latin, from Romance languages to Germanic languages, from Slavic languages to classical languages, and just as much in the opposite direction, from classical languages to Slavic languages. What is revelatory of this mutual exchange is the history of the word "aspect" itself, which appeared quite late, since it was invented only in the nineteenth century. The word was created in the encounter between East and West, though we do not know whether it was a matter of describing a specific trait of Slavic languages (which were characterized more by aspect than classical languages, or at least more than Romance languages), or of neutralizing what might have been their specificity (by imposing on them a concept of aspect based on classical languages).

■ See Box 1.

For general linguistics, the result is a term used against type: when one thinks about it, the word "aspect" is one of the vaguest for designating what one wants to designate (the mode of development cited by tradition). Naturally, this made the term available for all kinds of reinterpretations: without meaning, it functions as a simple label, ready to cover anything that one might balk at treating under other categories.

This explains why the category of aspect was also able to function as a kind of catchall for the category from which it issued, at least in the Western tradition, namely, the neighboring category of tense.

III. Tense and Aspect

The boundaries between tense and aspect have been debated ever since grammarians began to reflect on aspect.

■ See Box 2.

1

Species, the appearance of words, the appearance of actions, and point of view: The invention of the word "aspect" to designate aspect

The word "aspect" designating a non-chronological verbal category is generally considered a translation of the Russian term *vid* [вид] by C.-P. Reiff (*Grammaire russe*), who introduced the work of N. I. Greč (1787–1867) into France. This attribution obscures earlier attestations of the term outside the Slavic domain: M. de Neuville (1818, cited by Auroux, "Le temps verbal dans la grammaire générale") distinguishes, in addition to the person, number, and tense of a verb, "the aspect, degree, and acceptance"; here, "aspect" designates the duration of the "modification" expressed by the verb, collected in a point or developed to its full extent. The attribution to Reiff also obscures the fact that the translation in question is highly problematic, insofar as the word *vid* itself can be interpreted as "species, division" (in a classification) or as "aspect" (external: what can be seen; cf. the verb *videt'* [видеть], "see")—and insofar as this word already had a grammatical use in traditions before Greč, traditions that used essentially the first meaning (the second is attested chiefly in certain seventeenth-century Czech grammarians). Finally, this attribution obscures the fact that Reiff himself hesitated between these two values in his translation, initially opting for *branche*, which is related to a division. He probably substituted "aspect" for it in the 1828 edition. But the last editions written during his lifetime adopt the term *branche*, and it was the editions reworked by L. Léger (1843–1923) that definitively established the term "aspect," particularly the 1877 edition, which was long considered authoritative, and which served as a basic textbook at the École des langues orientales in Paris.

To be convinced that this translation proceeds from a deviation, if not a betrayal, we need only read Greč's own text, which is given here in a "re-translation" made by J. Fontaine, in which the author has chosen not to translate *vid*:

> in grammatical tenses, that is, in the forms of the language through which times are expressed [in nature], can be expressed a few accessory circumstances through which the meaning and scope of the action are defined more precisely.…
> Forms serving to express these circumstances of the action are called *vidy* [виды].

The very way in which the notion of *vid* is used in Russian grammatical discourse (and no longer in the discourse of French Slavic studies) goes in the same direction: "perfective verb" is *glagol soveršennogo vida* [глагол совершенного вида], literally, "verb *vid* completed," just as "masculine substantive" is *suščestvitel'noe mužskogo roda* [существительное мужского рода], literally, "substantive of the masculine gender." *A contrario*, "substantive in the plural" is *suščestvitel'noe VO množestvennom čisle* [существительное ВО множественном числе], literally, "substantive with/in plural number." In the exercises in textbooks written in Russian we hardly find the equivalent of the French "mettre ce verbe au perfectif" (put this verb in the perfective), and Russian students taking courses in Russian language in France generally do not understand this instruction. In fact, for speakers of Russian, the *glagoly (ne)soveršennogo vida* [глаголы (не)совершенного вида] are nothing more than "verbs of an (in)complete kind," a subset of verbs constituting distinct words and not forms of one and the same word (and if they refused to "conjugate in the present" a "verb of the complete kind," that is because schoolbook grammar associates these forms with the expression of a direction, the "future"). In other words, this translation has only maintained a persistent misunderstanding between the two grammatical traditions.

We see the paradox: the word "aspect," which is supposed to register the specificity of Russian grammar relative to the organization of verbal forms, and which is supposed to draw a lesson from Russian to challenge categories that issued from the classical tradition, is in fact a betrayal of the way in which Russian grammars conceive Russian grammar.

However, another difficulty slips into this operation of translation/betrayal that makes it entirely paradoxical. When the word "aspect" comes to be used to name the division Greč talks about, and also, in a parallel manner (already in Neuville, and to a large extent in the aspectual literature that followed), all the semantic differences, in whatever language, relating to what Greč describes as "the meaning and scope of the action," to what Neuville defines as concerning "the duration of the modification," to what came to be called "the mode of development," and to what has been constantly analyzed since the first descriptions in terms of achievement, perfection, and *telos* [τέλος], it introduces ipso facto a new dimension into the apprehension of the differences in question: the dimension of "seeing," strongly presented in *vid* (formally connected with the verb *videt'*, "see"), and also in *aspect* (derived from *aspicere*, "look at"). Thenceforth, aspect was understood as being a matter of point of view: the notion has been contaminated by the words that name it.

That contamination was doubtless fertile for the general understanding of aspectual events in Russian and other languages, making it possible, for example, to introduce a distinction between the form of a process and the way in which the latter is perceived, or between the way in which it is manifested and the way one chooses to see it: a given aspect and a constructed aspect, which may or may not coincide. We can understand, for example, how the opposition between lexical aspect (which is given) and grammatical aspect (which can be used for enunciatively reconstructing the process) was able to develop within such a problematics. However, it is likely that the conceptual imbroglio was much less fertile for the conception that French Slavic studies developed regarding the way aspectual events play out in Russian. The opposition between several categories of verbs governed by regular properties, discovered by Slavic students of Slavic languages, was made into a matter of marking (since the plural is a matter of marking), whereas it is a matter of categories of verbs. This marking was made the exclusive expression of everything relating to the aspectual event, as if in Russian aspect had a simple, univocal expression, whereas in other languages it is mingled with tense and is constructed over a whole sentence, a whole text. This reduced aspect in Russian to a categorization of verbs, and thus to the opposition that the same non-Slavic students of Slavic called, apparently under the influence of the Neogrammarians, by a Latin name: perfective/imperfective.

This may explain the recent introduction of a new term to designate in Russian all the events relating to the category of aspect. By a precise reversal, this term is a kind of borrowing from the word that translated *vid*: *aspektual'nost'* [аспектуальность] (aspectuality), introduced by A. Bondarko ("Contribution to the problematic of semantic-functional categories") and covering phenomena manifesting themselves in various ways in utterances and texts.

BIBLIOGRAPHY

Archaimbault, Sylvie. *Préhistoire de l'aspect verbal.* Paris: CNRS, 1999.

Auroux, Sylvain. "Le temps verbal dans la grammaire générale." In *Hommages à Jean-Toussaint Desanti,* 55–84. Mauvezin, Fr.: TER, 1991.

Bondarko, Aleksandr Vladimirovič. "K problematike funkcinonal'nosemantičeskix kategorij (glagol'nyj vid aspektual'nost v rsskom jazyke) [Contribution to the problematic of semantic-functional categories (verbal aspect and aspectuality)]." *Voprosy jazykoznanija* 2 (1967).

———. *Functional Grammar: A Field Approach.* Translated by I. S. Chulaki. Amsterdam: J. Benjamins, 1991.

Fontaine, Jacqueline. *Grammaire du texte et aspect du verbe en russe contemporain.* IES, 1983.

Greč, Nicolaj Ivanovic. *Praticeskaja russkaja grammatika.* St. Petersburg, 1827.

L'Hermitte, René. "Les premiers grammairiens techques et la notion d'aspect verbal." *Revue des études slaves* 40, no. 3 (1988): 543–47.

Richardson, Kylie. *Case and Aspect in Slavic.* New York: Oxford University Press, 2007.

Reiff, Charles. *Grammaire russe.* Edited by E. Guilmoto. 2nd ed., 1851; 6th ed. [without an indication of a date, after 1878].

Unbegaun, Boris Ottokar. *Russian Grammar.* Oxford: Clarendon Press, 1960.

2

The emergence of temporal and aspectual categories in the Greek grammatical tradition: How the Greek grammarian understood aspect without knowing how, or wanting, to isolate it from tense

Adopting a classification and a vocabulary that he owes to Plato, Aristotle (*Poetics*, 20.1457a10–18; *De interpretatione*, 2–3,16a 19f., 16b 6f.) opposes the "verb" *rhêma* [ῥῆμα] to the "noun" *onoma* [ὄνομα] by a distinctive trait, the ability to "signify time as well" (*rhêma . . . esti to prosêmainon chronon* [ῥῆμα . . . ἐστι τὸ προσημαῖνον χρόνον]) (*De interpretatione*, 2–3.16b6). As an example, he opposes *badizei* [βαδίζει], "he walks," which "also signifies present time (*ton paronta chronon* [τὸν παρόντα χρόνον])," to *bebadiken* [βεβάδικεν], "he walked," which also signifies "the past" (*ton parelêluthota* [τὸν παρεληλυθότα]) (*Poetics*, 1457a17). Of these initial definitions, grammarians adopted only the idea that the inflectional paradigms of the Greek verb are "times," *chronoi* [χρόνοι], which they named using nominalized adjectives in the masculine (the implied term *chronos* is masculine), several of which designated, in common usage, divisions of time: for instance, *enestôs* [ἐνεστώς], "present," and *mellôn* [μέλλων], "future." If no paradigm is called "past," that is because for referring to the past Greek had several paradigms, each of which was to receive its own label, but none of which could claim for itself alone the name of "past." Here we touch upon a crucial point: what difference could there have been between the different "times" of the past? It seems that the Stoics raised this problem, and more generally recognized that the different "times" of the verb had *complex meanings*, in which chronology with respect to the present was not the only factor. A scholia on Dionysius Thrax's *Tekhnê* tells us that for the four "times" that the grammarians (and following them, we ourselves) called respectively present (*enestôs* [ἐνεστώς]), imperfect (*paratatikos* [παρατατικός]), perfect (*parakeimenos* [παρακείμενος]; literally, "adjacent"), and pluperfect (*hupersuntelikos* [ὑπερσυντελικός]),

the Stoics used the following "double" designations: present extensive (*enestôs paratatikos* [ἐνεστὼς παρατατικός]), past extensive (*parôichêmenos paratatikos* [παρῳχημένος παρατατικός]), present perfective (*enestôs suntelikos* [ἐνεστὼς συντελικός]), and past perfective (*parôichêmenos suntelikos* [παρῳχημένος συντελικός]). Whatever one thinks of the Stoic theory of time that is in the background of these designations (and the question remains very controversial), it is hard not to admit that the second term of each double designation resembles an *aspectual* designation. In other words, whereas Aristotle saw *badizei* and *bebadiken* as illustrating an opposition between the present and the past, the Stoics saw in it an opposition between presents, between extension and achievement—something like "he is now walking" vs. "he has now finished his walk."

Among the Alexandrian grammarians, as we have seen, "times" were given simple designations which, in two cases out of four, can result from a simplification of the Stoic designations: *present extensive→present*, *past extensive→extensive*; whereas in the other two cases, a different term is used: *adjacent* (the Stoic *present perfective*) and *pluperfect* (the Stoic *past perfective*). Thus any suggestion that the four "times" (of the indicative) concerned might involve a complex temporal-aspectual idea disappeared from the terminology. Does that mean that the grammarians had lost all sensitivity to aspectuality? Not really, but it does seem that they resisted giving it an autonomous status that was dissociated from temporality. This resistance is manifested in a particularly clear way in two passages in Apollonius (*Syntax*, 3, §100 and 102). Examining the difference introduced in utterances in the optative of wish (§100) and the imperative (§102) by the variation of the verbal theme—the "present" theme vs. the "aorist"

theme—Apollonius notes that the present theme implies the idea of extension (*paratasis* [παράτασις]), and the aorist theme the idea of achievement (*sunteleia* [συντέλεια]), for example, *graphe* [γράφε] (present), "continues to write," vs. *grapson* [γράψον], "finishes writing"; but, commenting on the wish formula he attributes to Agamemnon (*eitheporthêsaimi* (aor.) *tên Ilion* [εἴθεπορθήσαιμι (aor.) τὴν Ἴλιον]) ([I wish] I could complete the siege of Troy), he glosses it by saying that the wish here is literally aimed at "the *past* and the finished in time (*to parôichêmenon kai suntelès tou chronou* [τὸ παρῳχημένον καὶ συντελὲς τοῦ χρόνου])," as if the aspectual notion of the perfective could not, in his view, be isolated from the temporal notion of the past.

This example shows how the Greek grammarian both "understands" perfectly the expression of aspectuality in his language, and nonetheless presents a "deficient description" of it because he is unable to isolate aspectuality and temporality conceptually. We can also understand why the grammarians abandoned the double designations that reflected the Stoic point of view in which the expression of tense and the expression of aspect were combined, in favor of a more poorly motivated simple designation, the four "times" of the indicative mentioned above. As for the values that they associated with these "times" in their descriptions of them, even the explanations of the scholiast who cites Stoic terminology lead us to think that they could all be formulated in *temporal* terms, the four "times" envisaged being simply arranged on a chronological scale going from the oldest (the *pluperfect*, distant past) to the most present (the *present*, the time of action still full of the future), via the

(continued)

(continued)

adjacent (the recent past, bordering on the present), and the *imperfect* (action mainly past, but still including a small portion of future).

Jean Lallot

BIBLIOGRAPHY

Apollonius Dyscolus. *The Syntax of Apollonius Dyscolus*. Translated by F. W. Householder. Amsterdam: J. Benjamins, 1981.

Aristotle: *De interpretatione*. Edited by L. Minio Paluello, translated by J. L. Ackrill. Oxford: Clarendon Press, 1963.

———. *Poetics*. In *The Complete Works of Aristotle*, edited by J. Barnes, rev. ed., 2 vols. Princeton, NJ: Princeton University Press, 1984. Vol. 2, 2316–3240.

Dionysius Thrax. *La grammaire de Denys le Thrace*. 2nd ed. Edited and translated by J. Lallot. Paris: CNRS, 1998.

However, these boundaries are quite porous, some facts being attributed indiscriminately to one category or the other, and the notions themselves sometimes being defined in equivalent ways. Thus in characterizing aspect, grammarians often speak of a temporality internal to the process.

As for temporal categories, it is as if they were haunted by the aspectual question.

It is generally acknowledged that the linguistic category of tense is organized into three periods around an origin, the present, and that this origin determines the past, the present, and the future tenses.

Such a conception of linguistic tense is debatable.

First of all, there are linguistic forms whose interpretation appears to be unaware of both the problematics of origin and the structure of the periods thus asymmetrically constituted (the past is established, while the future is virtual). This is the case, for example, with generic utterances. It is also one of the things involved in the category the Stoics isolated and described as the *aorist*: a form whose value is supposed to be to refer to a moment taken in an indeterminate relation (*a-oristos* [ἀ-όριστος]) to the moment of utterance. In other words, the aorist offers the possibility of not distinguishing periods of time. In addition, it has been shown that the temporal structuring involved in utterances using the aorist was of a quite different order from that described by the past/present/future scheme: there is no longer an origin separating two periods of time nor the double orientation that that division supposes between retrospection toward a completed past and anticipation of a virtual future. Here the ordering of facts is strictly linear, corresponding to what is described as the sequence of events—unless it is in addition recursive, as in certain cases where the aorist can take on a gnomic value. It turns out in addition that each of the three time periods can give rise to different conceptualizations (see PRESENT) that depend on aspectual oppositions: between a past that has disappeared and a past that has been preserved, between the future and what is to come, between a present that is not limited temporally and a present concomitant with the act of speaking (or thinking, or perceiving), in which it is a matter of what takes place in the simultaneity of that act. Such distinctions occur in languages: consider, on the one hand, the melancholy that can be attached to the French imperfect, and on the other hand the values of achievement that the French *passé composé* can have; or all the marks associated with the expression of the future (e.g., the simple future of the type "je partirai" [I shall leave] and the periphrastic future called "proximate" of the type "je vais partir" [I am going to leave]); or the distinction made in English between the present progressive and the simple present, in particular, with the performative values that the latter can have. The question of the moment—instant, interval, but also point of advent (see MOMENT)—is also shaped by the forms of language, by the different presents on the one hand, and by the aorists on the other—when they ignore duration ("il pleuvra" [it is going to rain]), when they accept duration ("il plut pendant trois jours" [it rained for three days]), and when they say what occurred ("il neigea" [it snowed]).

We can understand, then, why the categories of aspect and tense have been connected throughout the history of linguistics. This may result from a confusion on the part of the describers, who are incapable of truly conceptualizing an autonomous aspectual category. But this confusion is also inevitable because tense is haunted by questions of aspect.

IV. Grammatical Aspect and Lexical Aspect

Although it is inseparable from the temporal question, aspect is distinct from tense in its strongly lexical dimension: in particular, there is the question of how the process is instantiated and the form it can be given. This depends first of all on the type of verbal lexeme involved, and the semantic modalities of the configuration of its reference, whence the necessity of considering alongside so-called grammatical aspect an aspect that is properly lexical.

In the inventory of aspectual facts we have tried to draw up, we did not distinguish a priori between lexical aspect and grammatical aspect. The boundary between them is not absolutely clear, whether from one language to another or within a single language, when similar aspectual configurations might sometimes be attached to oppositions between lexical units constructed with the help of conjugation or through the arrangement of different lexical units within an utterance. Nonetheless, distinctions like those that oppose finalized processes and nonfinalized processes, or those that concern the more or less limited, or more or less intrinsically iterative, character of the process seem at first to correspond to types of processes that are defined lexically. These different dichotomies can refer to types of verbs, distinguishing on the lexical level through the more or less finalized, more or less factual or punctual character of the processes to which they refer. Thus there is a lexical dimension to the aspectual problematics.

Depending on the theory, three, four, or two major categories of process can be enumerated on the lexical level. The classification is based on distinctions that are for the most part borrowed from Aristotle, and in particular from a text that was always to serve as a reference point for theories of lexical aspect: the passage on the two sorts of activity in the *Metaphysics* (Υ.6).

■ See Box 3.

On this basis, an opposition between telic and atelic processes was constructed by the Neogrammarians of the nineteenth century to elaborate the distinction between perfective and imperfective processes, probably in relation to the Slavic opposition then being theorized. The specificity of the Slavic system is that the aspectual system is organized precisely on the basis of a lexical opposition, insofar as it mobilizes classes of verbs, and among these verbs, relationships of derivation.

At the same time, independently of Slavic and any derivational relationship, a typology of processes was worked out that constantly oscillated between ontology and semantics (classes of processes, classes of verbs), and whose touchstone was Vendler's classification, in which the initial dichotomy of the telic and the atelic is simultaneously reanalyzed, completed (there are also verbs that do not refer to a process; there are also properties), and made more complex (there are two distinct types of finalized processes). Vendler proposes four classes, which he calls "states," "activities," "accomplishments," and "achievements."

These four classes continued to be regularly reconstructed and re-evaluated. They seem fated to always follow in the footsteps of another, better established lexical categorization bordering on semantics and syntax: the opposition between transitive and intransitive verbs, with perhaps also middle verbs coming in to complicate matters, and behind them the whole question of diathesis. There is a relation between finalization and transitivity, between the object and the finality relative to that object. There is a relation between the state and the middle verbs, diathesis appearing to be one of the privileged procedures that will cause a verb to move from one category to the other. The fate of this categorization seems thus to intersect with syntax in various ways, to be constantly struggling with the relation between the lexical and the syntactical.

Once again, the dissociation in question, that between the lexical and the grammatical, has turned out to be impossible.

On the one hand, the so-called lexical aspect cannot be conceived as a fixed given. There are verbs that are predetermined in some way for a reference of this or that type (*réparer* is cited for finalized processes, *bricoler* for nonfinalized processes, *savoir* for properties, and *perdre* for events), but in general these oppositions are constructed in the sentence, in a given inflectional form, in a given syntactical environment.

3

Aristotle and *telos*

➤ ESTI, FORCE, PRAXIS, PRINCIPLE

In the *Metaphysics* (Υ.6.1048b18–35), Aristotle discusses the definition of an action (*praxis* [πρᾶξις]). He distinguishes two kinds of activities: *kinêseis* [κινήσεις] and *energeiai* [ἐνέργειαι]:

[Only] that movement in which the end is present is an action. E.g., at the same time we are seeing and have seen (*horai hama <kai heôrake>* [ὁρᾷ ἅμα <καὶ ἑώρακε>]), are understanding and have understood (*phronei <kai pephronêke>* [φρονεῖ <καὶ πεφρόνηκε>]), are thinking and have thought (*noei kai nenoêken* [νοεῖ καὶ νενόηκεν]) (when it is not true that at the same time we are learning and have learnt [*ou manthanei kai memathêken* [οὐ μανθάνει καὶ μεμάθηκεν]], or are being cured and have been cured [*oud' hugiazetai kai hugiastai* [οὐδ᾽ ὑγιάζεται καὶ ὑγίασται]]). At the same time we are living well and have lived well (*eu zêi kai eu ezêken hama* [εὖ ζῇ καὶ εὖ ἔζηκεν ἅμα]), and are happy and have been happy (*eudaimonei kai eudaimonêken* [εὐδαιμονεῖ καὶ εὐδαιμόνηκεν]).... Of these processes, then, we must call the one set

movements (*kinêseis* [κινήσεις]), and the other actualities (*energeiai* [ἐνέργειαι]).

We see that the distinctive properties of these two categories of verbs are provided by relations of inference and semantic compatibility between the form of the present and the form of the perfect. In the case of *energeiai*, there is a relation of inference between the present and the perfect, in the sense that when someone says "I see" we can infer "I have seen." There is also a relation of semantic compatibility since one can very well say "I have seen" and continue to see. Thus the two forms—the present and the perfect—are verifiable at the same time (*hama* [ἅμα], simultaneously).

On the other hand, in the case of *kinêseis*, the present and the perfect are not verifiable at the same time. In fact, when someone says "I am building a house," we cannot infer "I have built a house," at least in the sense in which the house is finished. In addition, once the house is finished, one is no longer constructing it, which means that there is a semantic incompatibility between the present and the perfect.

The term *telos* [τέλος], which means both "complete action," that is, "end," and "limit"

(in competition with *peras* [πέρας]), plays a crucial role in this opposition. In the category of *energeiai*, we have actions proper, that is, activities that are complete (*teleiai* [τέλειαι]) because they have an immanent finality (*enuparchei to telos* [ἐνυπάρχει τὸ τέλος]). In the category of *kinêseis*, we have imperfect activities (*ateleis* [ἀτελεῖς]) that do not carry their own end within themselves but are transitive and aim at realizing something. Thus activities having an external goal that is at the same time a limit (*peras*) do not carry their own goal (*telos*) within themselves; they are directed toward a goal but this goal is not attained during the activity, but is realized at the end of the activity.

BIBLIOGRAPHY

Ackrill, John Lloyd. "Aristotle's Distinction between *energeia* and *kinesis*." In *New Essays in Plato and Aristotle*, edited by R. Bambrough, 121–42. New York: Humanities Press, 1965.

Aristotle. *Poetics*. In *The Basic Works of Aristotle*, edited by R. McKeon and translated by W. D. Ross. New York: Random House, 1941.

Waterlow, Sarah. *Nature, Change, and Agency in Aristotle's* Physics. Oxford: Clarendon Press, 1982.

Thus *manger du poulet* (eat chicken) is not finalized, *manger de la viande* (eat meat) can refer to a property (opposing non-vegetarians to vegetarians), *manger sa viande* (eat one's meat) will be finalized, and *il mangea sa viande* (he ate his meat) is probably factual.

On the other hand, the dichotomies in question shape not only syntax but also, to an equal extent and in a way at least as closely connected, the value of marks considered grammatical that appear in the conjugation of verbs: thus finalization is one of the values that can be associated with aorists or perfects, and nonfinalization is in a certain way involved in the characterization of imperfects.

Distinctions are no doubt required: imperfects are in general wholly compatible with finalized processes ("Il réparait sa voiture quand on lui a téléphoné" [He was repairing his car when he received a phone call]); then they simply mark the fact that the finality in question was not achieved (at least that is one of the values they can have). If we speak of non-finalization for imperfects, then we must understand it not as an absence of finality, but as the nonrealization of this finality.

V. The Imbroglio of Terminologies

The fact that the question of the imperfectivity of the imperfect can be raised is in itself astonishing. The word *imparfait* (imperfect) "translates" (or rather comes from) the Latin word *imperfectum*, from which "imperfective" also derives (and which it also translates). Moreover, at the same time that the word *imperfectum* was invented (see Box 4), we see a hesitation that is precisely the one that causes a problem here, between *imperfectum* and *infectum* (a nonachieved finality, an absence of finality).

The important point is that the whole history of aspectual terminology is constituted by such exchanges. The invention of the words *perfectum* and *imperfectum* itself proceeds from an enterprise of translation, in which it is a question of taking as a model, or rephrasing, the Greek grammarians' opposition between *suntelikos* [συντελικός] and non-*suntelikos*. However, the difference between the two terminologies is noticeable. A supine past participle, *-fectum,* has replaced *telikos*, and hence *telos*, thereby reintroducing, if not tense (was tense really involved in that past participle?), at least the achievement of an act, and consequently merges with the question of the "accomplished." In this operation, the Stoics' opposition between *suntelikos* (which would thus designate the choice of perfects or imperfects) and *paratatikos* [παρατατικός] (the extensive, in which the question of the *telos* is not involved) was made symmetrical, introducing into aspectual terminology a binariness from which we have never recovered. And this symmetricalization, which sought to describe the organization of a conjugation, was then modeled on the distinction introduced by Aristotle (between *teleios* [τέλειος] and *atelês* [ἀτελής]), which was not grammatical but lexical.

This resulted in a new confusion that is not without foundation because it was already implicit in the *montage* constructed by the Greek philosophers, with on the one hand the *telos* used by Aristotle to differentiate types of process, and on the other the same *telos* used by the Stoics to structure conjugation.

And history repeated itself, in the same terms, regarding Slavic languages, with on the one hand the words "perfective" and "imperfective," modeled on the Latin opposition and imported to describe an opposition in which lexicon and grammar are truly interwoven (since it is a question of categories of verbs, which determine the whole organization of conjugation), and on the other hand the Russian words that are used to characterize the same categories of verbs, and that "signify" the accomplished and the unaccomplished.

In the terminological imbroglio, we can once again see the effects of a confusion connected with the inability to acknowledge the autonomy of lexical aspect, or, in the particular case of Slavic languages, the difficulty of isolating the aspectual dimension in the general system of the language. Nevertheless, the same questions, that of the *telos* and that of accomplishment, are at the foundation of the two aspectual dimensions. They are even so prominent that, alongside the heterogeneous inventory from which we began, we also find, and almost simultaneously in the aspectual tradition, a leveling of all differences in favor of two categories that are supposed to be the categories par excellence of grammatical aspect: the perfective on the one hand, and the imperfective on the other. However, there is also the continuing competition of the "perfect," another translation of the same "word," *perfectum*, designating a category that is not exactly the same as that of the perfective, and which is, for its part, always a grammatical category, never a lexical category: one speaks of "perfect" to designate compound tenses in Germanic languages, for example, of the type "I have received " (as opposed to "I received"), which corresponds to the idea that the *telos* is not only achieved, but transcended in the constitution of a fixed state, given as the result of the completion of the process.

Two, or three, grammatical categories that are the same and not the same as the two, three, or four lexical categories. It is in the name of these categories, and literally behind their name, that the aspectual descriptions succeeded in being applicable to all languages, conflating all the "imperfects" of all languages (and also the English progressive and the Russian imperfective), all the "aorists" in all languages, and aligning perfects, perfectives, the English perfect, the German *Perfekt*, the Latin *perfectum* and the Greek "perfect." The facts are different, but the words, and the recurrence of a problematics that seems invariable, are too strong. Although it is a matter of conjugations, the lexicon and the relation to ontological questions are too influential.

VI. The Aspectual Calculation

Lexical aspect and grammatical aspect reduplicate each other. And, in the same movement, the linguistic differences between aspectual categories reduplicate the ontological differences between categories of processes, the former claiming to draw their legitimacy from the latter. And, still in the same movement, metalinguistic differences reduplicate, and then forget, linguistic differences when the term "imperfect" is used in a universal way, to designate a general category of languages, and, at the same time, as a simple morphological label designating forms in a given language.

Such confusions between the world and languages, between words and sentences, between *langues* and metalanguage, between metalanguage and *langage*, are ultimately quite commonplace. But here the situation is too tangled not to see in it a symptom of what is preying on the aspectual question in this case. If all aspects are related to each other, that is because aspect cannot be reduced to distinctions between categories (categories of words, categories of formal procedures, ontological categories). Aspect is constructed in a complex interaction between lexicon and grammar. There are not as many aspectual categories as aspectual operations. And these operations play a role several times, in the lexicon, in syntax, in conjugation—and may even play several roles within conjugation, producing, for example, perfects alongside perfectives, and then also aorists, and finally simple preterites (the return of tense), in which the conversion to the perfective has operated in a different way each time.

Thus these are operations that belong to a calculation. In the transition from the lexicon to conjugations, another displacement is involved. The lexicon is composed of singularities that can sometimes collect, more or less broadly, in categories. Conjugations involve system and regularities: they form paradigms, obey rules, and are constructed on the basis of the differences between them. It is in inflectional systems, and perhaps only in them, if we exclude phonology, that the Saussurean notion of value can find its whole scope and become a veritable formal, calculable object. We have rules, procedures for generating. To move from lexicon to conjugations is thus to move from a logic of categories to a logic of calculation.

That is probably the discovery that was involved in the slight shift that took place when Latin grammarians adopted the discoveries made by Greek grammar (see Box 4): choices (of a category, of a theme) are replaced by combinations (of values, of affixes) in accord with regular relationships of generation (paradigmatics) and coexistence (syntagmatics); thus a calculation is beginning to emerge. For this to happen, themes probably had to have lost their operativity in Latin, and affixation, which makes the aspectual value "calculable," had to have begun to occupy the terrain more clearly. If aspect proceeds from a calculation, then we can understand why it can play a role again and give rise to all distinctions. We can see that with the same oppositions, the same invariant parameters, each language can put into play values that are always singular. Languages do not reproduce, with more or less success, two, or three, or four great, invariant categories; they combine in diverse ways two, three, or four great invariant parameters.

▪ See Box 4.

VII. Aspect and Enunciative Structuration

To the preceding, a final effect of connection will now be added, in which aspect is plunged into a new dimension, that of the types of discourse that configure the utterance. There is a relation between aspect and type of discourse. The connection is more recent. It was made by Benveniste, who discovered the *discours/histoire* dichotomy while reflecting on aspectual oppositions (the description of the *passé simple* and the *passé composé* in French). Weinrich makes it central to the aspectual question: the distinction between the *imparfait* and the *passé simple* or *passé composé*, a distinction that does not

exist in German, is said to be primarily a matter of discursive construction (with the *imparfait* forming the background of a narration, and the past tenses forming the foreground of what develops and occurs). More recently, this area has been dominated by theories that situate aspect in a "theory of discursive representations" (cf. Kamp's discourse representation theory), and try to reduce it to a matter of discursive organization: thus the models currently most discussed make the *imparfait* an anaphoric mark that repeats an element of the context instead of constructing an independent referent.

Once again the relations are inextricably confused: the types of discourse clearly have particular aspectual properties (we have already seen this in connection with aoristic utterances that structure both aspect and tense differently), and yet all or almost all aspectual forms can appear anywhere, in all or almost all types of discursive contexts. Thus we have "foregrounded" *imparfaits*, which have been recorded and are sometimes called "narrative" *imparfaits*—for example, in an utterance like "Trois jours après, il mourait" (Three days later, he was dying), where it is a question of narrating a prominent event, and where the distinction between *imparfait* and *passé simple* becomes more difficult to evaluate. We also find *passé composés* in narratives, where they compete with the *passé simple*: that is why many analysts of the language consider the *passé simple* an archaic form that is being abandoned in favor of the *passé composé*.

The difficulty is clear: it is hard to attach a given formal procedure to a given enunciative structuration, not only because enunciative structures are supposed to be compatible with several aspectual values, but first of all because the formal procedures themselves are all, more or less broadly, polysemous, their value depending precisely on the context and thus on the enunciative structure in which they are situated.

Here again, this is commonplace: polysemy is everywhere in languages. But in this case it affects aspect: it consists precisely in running through aspectual oppositions, the very ones that are also supposed to be associated with some aspectual marker. The case of narrative uses of the *imparfait* seems to indicate that the *imparfait* can have different aspectual values, of which some are more or less apparently perfective. The narrative *passé composés* (for instance, "Il s'est levé et il est sorti" [He got up and went out]) describe the process in its advent and thus do not have the same aspectual properties as those that appear in utterances describing the state resulting from the process (e.g., "Désolé, en ce moment il est sorti" [Sorry, he left just now]). Not to mention the presents, which are highly polysemous in many languages and which, depending on the language, therefore occupy a more or less extensive aspectual terrain. We are obliged to note that aspect is at least partially independent of formal procedures, that it also plays a role elsewhere, in particular, in the enunciative configuration.

VIII. The Theories

Several models of aspect are in circulation in the linguistic literature. We can divide them roughly into four groups corresponding to four conceptions of aspect.

The first group privileges tense. The peculiar feature of verbs is said to be their temporal dimension. Their reference would therefore be fundamentally a matter of situating in

4

Tenses as a system of family relationships in Latin linguistic texts

Very few texts on interpretations of tense in the Latin domain remain extant. These texts are very probably all of Greek origin, but we cannot gauge with precision the inevitable role of adaptation and reorganization resulting from the specificities of the Latin language and the critical freedom of the Latin describers.

The major characteristic of these texts is that tenses are analyzed in relation to each other, in accord with an overall model of the family relations type: relations among tenses are presented in terms of family relations, engenderment, and marriage.

Consider first Varro. In *De lingua latina* (ca. 45 BCE) he was the first to exploit the two axes, aspectual and temporal, which appear in the Greek texts. His presentation of the verbal system is based on an aspectual binary opposition, *infectum/perfectum* (cf. 10.48), built on the semantic opposition between the unachieved (*infectum*) and the achieved (*perfectum*). Moreover, this presentation is based on the properly temporal tripartite classification *praeteritum/praesens/futurum* (in that order, that is, along an axis oriented from the past toward the future), in which each term is a participle of the tense it is supposed to represent (*praeteritum*: past participle of *praeterire*, "pass before, flow away"; *praesens*: present participle of *praeesse*, "to be at the head of," whence "to be there personally, to attend," *futurum*: future participle of *esse*, "to be"). Varro suggests (but does not say explicitly) that the same tripartite temporal classification can be found in the *infectum* and the *perfectum*, which would give us a series with six terms: the *infectum* would have a present, a preterite, and a future, corresponding in our nomenclature to the present, imperfect, and future; and the *perfectum* would have once again a present (see XII.B for the problems raised by such an analysis from the interpretive point of view), a preterite, and a future, corresponding to our perfect, pluperfect, and future anterior.

The forms that appear along these two axes entertain relationships of engenderment. The point of origin is the present: *lego* (I read) engenders both the two other temporal forms of the *infectum* and the form of the *perfectum*, *legi* (I have read), which necessarily governs in turn the two other forms of the *perfectum*. This relationship of engenderment substitutes one order for another. In a first phase, the temporal axis is presented as a realistic progression (from the past to the future), and the aspectual opposition is constructed according to bipolar opposition in which the unachieved seems to be the marked pole in relation to the achieved. On the other hand, engenderment makes the present the source of the past and the future, and it makes the unachieved the source of the achieved, the unmarked pole. This substitution in the form of an inversion is clearly of morphological origin: in the Latin verbal system the form called "present" is unmarked morphologically, which makes the others appear to proceed from it by the simple adjunction of temporal morphemes, just as the form of the *infectum* is generally (and in any case in living formations at the historical period) unmarked with respect to the form of the *perfectum* (on the way this *perfectum* is formed, see XII.B). The form that we would call the present, which is the least marked morphologically, is thus presented as engendering all the others, in accord with a principle (explicit in Varro) of the development of linguistic forms by branching out from a root form.

At the end of antiquity, Priscian (sixth century), in book 8 of his *Institutiones grammaticae*, preserves the principle of this engenderment: his whole presentation of verb tenses is based on the model of *cognatio* (family relationship), but with notable differences. Like the whole Latin academic tradition preceding him, Priscian retains (*Grammatici latini*, 2.414.9–418.21) only one temporal series, with five tenses: three fundamental tenses, the present, past, and future, and a division of the past into three tenses, *imperfectum, perfectum,* and *plusquam perfectum* (imperfect, perfect, and pluperfect). This does not mean that Priscian is unaware of or rejects the opposition between the unachieved and the achieved, but under the influence of Greek classifications, he uses it to connect tenses with one another, not to account for the fundamental morphological opposition of the Latin verb. The mode of engenderment Priscian describes thus proceeds in accord with principle of continuity: the present includes partly the past and partly the future; the past contained by the present corresponds, if it remains unachieved, to the imperfect, but becomes a perfect if it is achieved, and a pluperfect if this achievement is distant. This effect of continuity allows Priscian to preserve the image of engenderment on the basis of the present, and to indicate a realist legitimation: as soon as the present includes a past element and a future element, it contains, as it were, the embryo of the past and the future.

In addition to this family relationship that we could call paradigmatic, Latin texts attest to the existence of a syntagmatic type of family relationship, the *cunjunctio temporum*, or "marriage of times." This is a study of the organization of tenses with respect to one another when there are two verbal forms in an utterance. It was in the work of Diomedes, a fourth-century grammarian/compiler (who was undoubtedly drawing on an earlier author), that this study appeared in the most developed form (*Grammatici latini*, 1.388.11–395.10). This text, and the parallel passages we find in Charisius, another grammarian/compiler of the same period, cannot be creations *ex nihilo*. But it remains that the grammatical tradition abandoned this kind of effort. In fact, properly grammatical analysis was recentered on the isolated minimal utterance that constitutes for grammarians the privileged analytical framework. Then the only original studies on temporal relationships, which Diomedes echoes, were these isolated and largely fragmentary "fossil" texts.

Marc Baratin

BIBLIOGRAPHY

Keil, Heinrich, ed. *Grammatici latini*. 7 vols. Leipzig: Teubner, 1857–80; repr. Hildesheim, Ger.: Olms, 1981.

Priscianus. Vols. 1 and 2 in *Grammatici latini*. 7 vols. Edited by Heinrich Keil. Leipzig: Teubner, 1857–80; repr. Hildesheim, Ger.: Olms, 1981.

Varro, Marcus Terentius. *De lingua latina*. Edited by G. Goetz and F. Schoell. Leipzig: Teubner, 1910.

time and occupying time, aspect having as its object the internal temporality of processes (the time that they endure), whereas (linguistic) tense has as its object their "external" temporality, that is, the period in which they are situated. The consequence is that all aspectual facts are related to the construction of intervals (the interval during which the process is instantiated). These intervals can be of variable dimensions, reduced to a point, limited, or unlimited; they can partially overlap or be included in each other. Above all, they are capable of being structured by an opposition borrowed from the topology relating to the nature of their boundaries: these are either "open" or "closed," the latter having the topological particularity of including a first or a last internal point, which then represents either the point of arrival or the point of finality. This provides a possible representation of the notion of perfectivity.

The second group privileges the oppositions discussed in relation to the lexicon. The matter is based on a rereading of the Aristotelian opposition between *energeia* and *kinesis* in terms of qualitative homogeneity or heterogeneity: there are homogenous processes in which the qualitative properties of what is instantiated are stable throughout the instantiation of the process (*dormir* [sleep] or *voir* [see] are supposed to be qualitatively stable, and, in the area of inflectional values, a generic present or an aorist is supposed each to be in its own way given as stabilized); there are processes based on a qualitative heterogeneity, precisely because they are finalized, and they thus imply a qualitative change, whether this concerns simply the result sought or is continually manifested during the whole time of the instantiation of the process (*réparer* [repairing] or *construire* [constructing] indicate a qualitative evolution aiming at a new state that is differentiated precisely on the qualitative level; a secant *imparfait* is supposed to indicate an ongoing qualitative development; a *parfait* is supposed to indicate a qualitative rupture resulting from the instantiation of the process).

The third group has already been mentioned: here aspect is fundamentally a matter of the type of discourse and the enunciative configuration.

Finally, the fourth group organizes the category around the question of the reference point from which the process is regarded. This involves the double problematic of the registration and the point of view that is emphasized.

A matter of intervals, of quality, of discursive arrangement, or of relations between points of reference: it is enough to make one think that one has no idea what aspect is. To be sure, the models are not mutually exclusive. Often enough several of these ingredients are used in the descriptions. Ultimately, we might even say that the tendency is generally to use all of these resources, aspect then being simultaneously a matter of intervals, of quality, of discourse, and of points of reference. That restores some content to it, though the content is rather heterogeneous, but one would thereby have obtained this thesis regarding aspect: aspect is something that mixes diverse ingredients.

There remains a problem that still makes these theories of aspect unsatisfactory, even if one considers combining them. In the combination of an interval, qualitatively differentiated zones, a discursive arrangement, and diverse reference points, we cover all sorts of characteristics of verbal reference, but on the other hand, we have said nothing about the entities that have these characteristics, nothing about what thus comes to occupy the interval in question, to receive these qualities, to be ordered in these ways, nothing about this event that a point of view has registered. We have an interval of time, but in this interval something is supposed to take place that is precisely not merely time passing. There is a process that is instantiated, and it is its instantiation that has this or that quality that can be registered or diversely situated in this or that sequence.

Consequently, we see what the four models arrive at: emptying the aspectual problematics of what nonetheless constitutes it, namely, the process, in its accomplishment. A paradoxical effect, when we have said everything except what we were supposed to say.

On the empirical level, this leads to theories of aspect abandoning, in just as paradoxical a way, a question that is nonetheless situated at the heart of the problem of aspect, namely, the opposition between process and property. None of the four models truly succeeds in rendering the distinction. Processes and properties can both cover more or less limited intervals, even if there are probably more temporally limited properties than unlimited processes. Properties are by definition qualitatively homogeneous, but processes may be. Properties may even begin, situating themselves in a gradual sequence. Although a point of view is necessary to posit a property, the use of that point of view may involve any kind of process, including procedures, particularly when the latter are the object of a description.

The grammatical tradition encounters this question as soon as, seeking to characterize the category of verbs, it repeats that verbs designate actions, and then has to add that they also sometimes designate states and properties. This shows that the difficulty is central: what these aspectual models and traditional conceptions of the verb lack is a theory of what the referent of a verb can be. Thus they lack precisely what Aristotle set about to elaborate, a theory of what he called "movement," of what in this movement exceeds both time and being: we lack a *physics*, in which what happens is distinguished from what is true.

Thus to deal with the question of aspect we need something that linguists are not, a priori, competent to provide, and which is not their subject: philosophy. Aspect is an subject that is irremediably philosophical.

What happens has to be distinguished from what is true. Because languages distinguish the two, and because this distinction is one of the central dimensions of aspect, we must recognize that processes have a qualitative dimension that makes it possible to distinguish them qualitatively from one another, probably a temporal extension, but also a qualitative extension: verbs refer to something that takes place, or does not take place, that is in time, but is not only time. This thing also has qualitative properties. But that is because it does not have only qualitative properties, but is also accomplishment, because the question of aspect exists and develops.

IX. The Infinite Reversals of the Question of Aspect

This connection between the quantitative and qualitative dimensions in processes' mode of instantiation enables us to consider various things. It also allows us to account for the reversals to which the determination of an aspectual value can lead, reversals with which descriptions constantly collide.

Maria Tzevelekou describes one of these reversals (see Box 5) that is crucial and seems to have determined the whole history of conceptions of lexical aspect. According to her, around the notion of *telos*, between Aristotle's founding distinctions and their reinterpretation in the light of aspectual facts, a veritable misunderstanding emerged that led to a literal inversion of Aristotle's theses.

■ See Box 5.

5

The reasons for a reversal: Aristotle's heirs unwittingly betray him

In the contemporary literature we find the opposition "telic/non-telic." It is obvious that these terms are constructed on the analogy with Aristotle's terms *teleios* [τέλειος] and *atelês* [ἀτελής]. However, their content is reversed. The telic corresponds to Aristotle's a-telic (*a-teles, a* = privative morpheme), whereas the non-telic corresponds to the *teleios*. Thus the term "non-telic" designates predicates that do not include a limit of accomplishment, whereas for Aristotle *atelès* characterizes the predicates that are fully realized only at the end of the interval of time during which these processes are instantiated: it therefore includes a limit of accomplishment that corresponds to the point of perfection, which is, as it were, delayed.

This inversion of the content of the terms used can be explained. It reflects a shift in interest: it seems that the authors who carried out this borrowing and this deviation, which determines our contemporary use of the terms "telic" and "non-telic," were more interested in the way in which the interval corresponding to the process is constituted than in the degree of perfection of the (perfect or imperfect) actualization of a process during its instantiation. As a result, their central question is no longer the mode of realization (actualization) of process, but rather the existence (or non-existence) of a natural end that delimits the temporal interval.

Key to this reversal is the notion of *telos*, which is translated into French by the word *fin*, which is itself ambiguous (meaning both "purpose" and "end"), but which is not sufficiently ambiguous to render what is involved in *telos*. The Greek *telos* can be attained at the beginning of the instantiation of a process: that is the case for *energeiai*, which are perfect as soon as they are instantiated. *Telos* designates the alternation between quantitative and qualitative instantiation. Thus it implies that the two dimensions can be dissociated, while at the same time designating the point where they coincide. To use the word *telos* thus involves referring to both this dissociation and this coincidence. Depending on the process, but also on the points of view adopted, sometimes dissociation, sometimes coincidence will be emphasized. And a process that is a-telic because not finalized will also be telic from another point of view because it has attained immediately its point of perfection (or "achievement," to use Vendler's term).

These reversals explain the constant misunderstandings surrounding the question of aspect. They also explain the subtle aspectual differentiations that may develop in languages when the telic oscillation, operating at different levels, configures each of these levels differently. They also explain the extensive polysemy of most of the aspectual marks, which can be both telic in some of their uses and a-telic in others.

When we consider the way in which the oppositions between perfection and imperfection are constituted through languages, we have to acknowledge that they are infinitely variable. A single process can be considered perfective in one language and imperfective in another. The French verbs *prendre* (take) and *donner* (give) are thus described as fundamentally perfective insofar as they both refer to finalized processes; but one of the corresponding simplexes in Russian, *dat'* [дать] (give), belongs to the category of the perfective, while the other, *brat'* [брать] (take), is considered imperfective, probably because a gift is a gift from the moment it is instantiated, whereas taking implies some delay between the activity it develops and the expected result. Such facts, which multiply when we examine aspectual oppositions in detail, even within a single language, prevent us from considering perfection as a predetermined, stable ontological category: perfection is constructed through diverse articulations of the qualitative and the quantitative, these articulations being not just any articulations, always calculable and explainable, but always and incessantly renegotiable.

The question of the *telos* and perfection is not the only one that gives rise to such reversals. Everything in the dissociation between quantity and quality is perpetually unstable and renegotiable. The fluctuating values of the perfect, the way they reduplicate without reduplicating the perfective, and the shift to which they seem to lead in the evolution of a language (from a value of accomplishment to a value of preterition), are probably another manifestation of these reversals.

Everything about aspect leads to confusions. Only a step-by-step calculation of each aspectual value can restitute what will be the foundation of the distinctions involved.

X. Aspect, Location, and Determination

The distinction between quantity and quality is central to the aspectual question because every instantiation of processes is caught up in the dialectic to which this distinction leads. But that does not mean that aspect can be reduced to the calculation of this distinction. An instantiation is constructed: it also has to be diversely located and determined. Thus there must be two other types of questions, two other calculative elements, in the constitution of aspectual values.

First of all, there are the various relations that points of quantitative and/or qualitative instantiation can entertain with the original reference point of the utterance. The category of the aorist testifies to relations of rupture. And the effects of translation often produced by imperfects testify to a complex relation between differentiation and identification that can certainly not be reduced to a matter of anteriority.

Second, there is the question that aspectual models hardly touch upon, that of the different forms of iteration or genericity that can be associated with an utterance (with the reference to a verb in an utterance). This implies a model of instantiation, whether quantitative or qualitative, which takes into account the fact that instantiation can be singular, plural, or generic. The same problem arises with regard to the reference of nouns (or rather of nouns taken in a nominal group that is itself part of a sentence, which is in turn part of some discursive configuration). That is, the question of iteration shows that aspect is also a matter of determination, the determination in question operating not on nouns, but on verbs.

Aspect is a problem of instantiation. Instantiation turns out to operate in two registers, that of quantities and that of qualities. It proceeds like any instantiation of operations of determination. Through its qualitative dimension it makes use of differentiated points of view that can compete with the speaker's point of view or simply displace it. And because the operations of determination, quantitative and qualitative, are involved several times (verb, conjugation, syntactical construction, context, discourse), the aspectual calculation produces values that may vary infinitely from one language to another or from one utterance to another.

XI. The Question of a Typology of Aspect

If it is true that aspectual calculation runs through all forms of the expression of time, we have to give up the idea that there are languages that are more "aspectual" than others, that is, more attached to the expression of aspect than others that are supposed to be more attached to the expression of time.

There may be less "temporal" languages in the sense that relations between time described and moment of utterance are less determined. That is often said to be true of ancient Greek. It is not clear that this is pertinent. The ancient Greek aorist has a particularly broad range of values, with major variations regarding the moment of utterance. But that is also true of the French present, and even of the French imperfect, where we find not only hypothetical values (not anchored in time), but also present values ("Qu'est-ce qu'elle voulait, la petite dame?" [What did the little lady want?]), and even references to the future ("C'est dommage, il y avait dimanche prochain un joli marathon à courir" [That's too bad, there was a nice marathon to be run next Sunday]). As for the French *passé simple*, it covers a narrower field of values, but it would be difficult to maintain that it refers systematically to the past: the rupture it implies with respect to the sphere of the utterance causes it to be often included in narratives of a fictional kind, for which it makes no real sense to speak of a past (*La belle au bois dormant* [Sleeping Beauty] tells us about something that has nothing to do with the past other than its mythical dimension). What is taken as a temporal affair is simply the fact that these narratives refer to events that are given as both completed (in a register that is that of fiction) and discontinuous with the present.

There is another way of conceiving a typological difference between Greek and French. The system of Greek (ancient and modern) and system of Russian both combine two formal procedures that are largely independent. In Greek, each form of conjugation is characterized in part by the choice of a particular theme, and in part by the choice of an affix. All affixes can, a priori, be combined with any of the three available themes: then we have both imperatives and past tenses or participles in each of the three series. In Russian, there is no theme, but two classes of verbal lexemes. The lexemes of these two classes are compatible with almost all the inflections of the system. In fact, the situation is still more complex: there are a few constraints that are crucial for distinguishing the two classes. It remains that we find also imperatives, infinitives, and past tenses of the two classes. We do not find the same autonomy in French, German, or English, where, even when it is possible to dissociate two types of formal procedures, they are not clearly autonomous. Thus in French, between the base of the present, that of the *passé simple*, and that of the "past participle" there are differences of a thematic order: series like *voit/vit/vu* and even *chante/chanta/chanté* are probably analyzed more on the model of the theme than on that of affixation, to the extent that the vowel that varies cannot be considered as being external to the base (the *oi* in *voir*, and also the *e* in *chante*, are part of the lexical base of the verb). But the inflections that can be associated with each of these bases are for the most part strictly specific to them. In French there is no imperative constructed on a base of the *passé simple* or the "past participle"; and only the "past participle" gives rise to the procedure of auxiliarization that leads to all the system's forms that are called *composées*.

Even from the point of view of the economy of the systems of conjugation, such a contrast is extremely important. It has been proposed to see in this a difference in the treatment of the relation between tense and aspect: Greek and Russian are supposed to dissociate aspectual marking and temporal marking, whereas other languages have marks associating aspectual value with temporal value. If we grant that the opposition between tense and aspect must be reconsidered, such an interpretation can no longer be maintained as such. Nonetheless, the aspectual operations involved in the two types of procedures are not of the same order. It is the question of the articulation between the quantitative and the qualitative instantiations of the process that plagues, in different forms, both the perfective/imperfective opposition in Russian and the series present/preterite-aorist/perfect in non-Slavic languages. On the other hand, affixes and auxiliaries mark operations related to the determination and location of occurrences of constructed processes—determinations and locations whose effects (in terms of iterativity, on the one hand, and variations in point of view, on the other) correspond to the values that traditional analysts identify as either temporal or modal.

Thus we have an (aspectual) calculation related to the quantitative and qualitative dimensions of the occurrence of a constructed process, and on the other hand, a calculation (simultaneously aspectual, temporal, and modal) related to the determination and location of this occurrence. The particularity of Russian and Greek thus seems to be that they dissociate these two types of calculation. That amounts to giving a real autonomy to the strictly aspectual question of the connection between quantity and quality, whereas in other languages the two calculations interfere.

There is another, equally or more important typological difference that intersects with this one, and which this time involves a contrast between Russian and Greek. It concerns the mechanisms at work in the choice of the base subjected to inflexion and auxiliarization.

In Slavic languages, this is a derivational mechanism: to move from one aspectual class to another, another verbal lexeme is constructed using various affixes, and the lexeme so constructed then has a new semantic value, independently of the fact that it is associated with an invariant aspectual value. The system of themes is based on entirely different principles: it is not a question of constructing another verbal lexeme, but simply of varying the aspectual value of a given lexeme. The morphemes of derivation are singular units of the language; the themes have no singularity and are part of a mechanism of regular variation.

The mechanism itself is regular but not generalized. It is in French, where, apart from a few rare defective verbs, all verbs have a present, a *passé simple*, and a past participle. It is not in Greek, where the absence of a morphology of the perfect is a nonmarginal phenomenon: thus there can be verbs whose lexical particularities are opposed to the construction of such a theme. Themes in French, on the other hand, because they are not restricted, are independent of the semantic content of the lexeme: the regularity of the system has taken priority over the singularity of the lexicon.

These differences will necessarily have effects on the mode of calculation with which aspect proceeds in each of these three types of language. In Russian, this calculation appears as a construction associated with regular semantic effects, whereas in Greek it is part of a selection conditioned by semantic singularities, and in French the selection has become as regular as for any kind of inflection. Whereas the Russian aspect is constructed, and the Greek aspect is chosen, we might say that, under the influence of a rule that is blind because unlimited, the French aspect is obtained: it proceeds from a sort of regular deformation operating within the lexeme's semantic field.

That is, aspect is not conceived, and not perceived, in the same way in the three languages. In particular, one of the consequences of the Greek system's defectiveness is that in Greek aspectual categories can be invented (the missing perfect is invented, a new category is invented), and then be shaped by the genius of a thought. In Russian, aspect has to do solely with the semantic genius of the language, the values that that language invents, and that it reinvents anew for each lexeme: for thought, the Russian aspect is a kind of generator of concepts (see Rémi Camus's text below on the noun *poznanie* [познание], which is said to invent a perfective knowledge). In French, the genius has taken on the regularity of a calculatory mechanics, in which nothing is invented, but in which regular effects are produced beyond the lexemes: the French aspect is thus a generator of new points of view on concepts, new insofar as language alone has brought them about. Three different geniuses of aspect: thus we understand better why it has been so hard to export the notion of aspect from one language to another.

XII. When Aspect Serves to Conceive Aspect

There is an aspectual genius in languages, but there is also the genius peculiar to each form, which can make it untranslatable because it is irremediably singular. There are in fact different ways in which a linguistic event can be untranslatable. This holds in particular for aspectual events. To conclude, we consider three examples, each chosen for its exemplarity, each involving a different form of untranslatability.

First, the case of a word constructed aspectually that can only be specific to a language and its aspectual procedures: it is here that the genius of the language is involved, and what that language alone is able to say.

A. First example. Aspects of "knowledge" in contemporary Russian: A perfective knowledge and an imperfective knowledge

In the expression "theory of knowledge," "knowledge" is translated with the help of the de-verbal *poznanie*, corresponding to the verb *poznat'* [познать], "to be familiar with," constituted on the base of *znat'* [знать], "to know, be familiar with" and the prefix *po-*[no], conferring a perfective status on the verb. The simplex *znanie* [знание], from the imperfective *znat'*, would be interpreted here as "to know"—supposing that such a theory is conceived.

Nonetheless, there is no bi-univocal relationship between the oppositions *poznanie/znanie* on the one hand and *connaissance/savoir* on the other (cf. also Ger. *Kennen/Wissen*, which is something else again). Here we seem to find an opposition between an "imperfective" knowledge and a "perfective" knowledge. The originality of this situation is manifest in the articles of the *Dictionnaire encyclopédique de philosophie* (Moscow, 1983), where *poznanie* is described as an activity (*dejatel'nost'* [деятельность]) associated with a movement from the state (*sostojanie* [состояние]) of ignorance (*ne-znanie* [не-знание]) to that of knowledge. Thus one speaks of *protsess poznanija* [процесс познания], "procedure of knowledge," or again of *čuvstvennoe poznanie* [чувственное познание], "sense knowledge" (knowledge gained through the senses), but of *sostojanie znanija* [состояние знания], "state of knowledge."

Speaking of an aspectual opposition in characterizing nouns, even if they are derivatives—as here—of verbs and opposable in an analogous way to the latter, poses problems. In any case, tradition balks at doing so: it tacitly reserves the perfective/imperfective opposition for forms that have the faculty of governing an object complement. In fact, aspect seems to produce very little among Russian de-verbals (unlike Czech or Slovak, for instance). However, at least in the present case, there is no doubt that the pair *znanie/poznanie* reflects certain characteristics of the verbal opposition *znat'/poznat'*.

1. The values of *poznat'* (perfective), or when knowledge becomes an experience

Two main values of *poznat'* emerge (as lexicographic practice confirms) associated with differentiated restrictions on usage:

a. *poznat' istinu* [познать истину], "know the truth": acquire certain, true knowledge
This usage has three characteristics:

— *Poznat'* is indissociable from an (intellectual, physical) investment, from an implication of the subject who accedes to knowledge by himself. Uses in which the complement is located in a teleonomy (the object of knowledge is "to be known") belong to this class.

— The measure of actual knowledge is not provided by the object as a concept, but is circumscribed by the investment (in time and space) of the subject; whence the possibility of an adjustment, a more or less exact agreement, between, on the one hand, the direct object as an object of knowledge and, on the other hand, the subject's investment: "Vy načitalis' grošovyx brošjur evropejskogo kommunizma i dumaete, čto vy poznali istinu! [Вы начитались грошовых брошюр европейского коммунизма и думаете, что вы познали истину!]" (You stuffed yourself on ten-penny European communist pamphlets and you imagine that you know the truth!).

— Attestable complements are terms given as inaccessible to a subject's knowledge: *nevedomoe i zapretnoe* [неведомое и запретное], "what is unknown and forbidden," *tajny bessmertija* [тайны бессмертия], "the secrets of immortality," *smysl žizni* [смысл жизни], "the meaning of life," *real'nost'* [реальность], "reality," *dobro i zlo* [добро и зло], "Good and Evil," *sebja* [себя], "oneself," whence *poznaj samogo sebja* [познай самого себя], "know thyself," and so on.

b. *poznat' plen* [познать плен], "know captivity": to feel and experience captivity
Compared with (a), this use is distinguished less by the "concrete" character of the relation it establishes between the subject and the object of knowledge (the subject having been in captivity) than by the absence of teleonomy: the relation is strictly contingent.

Thus we find in the position of a complement feelings and internal states (*nenavist'* [ненависть], "hatred," *blaženstvo* [блаженство], "beatitude," *gore* [горе], "sorrow," *bol'* [боль], "pain," *veru Xristovu* [веруХристову], "faith in Christ," etc.); states and processes that affect the subject of knowledge against his will and that will thus tend to be interpreted as harmful (*smert'* [смерть], "death," *nevolju* [неволю], "absence of freedom," etc.); and properties predicated of a term (or a process), generally to a greater degree than one might have expected a priori, and whose astonishing intensity is then emphasized (*bednost' žizni* [бедность жизни], "the poverty of life," *čelovečeskoe moguščestvo* [человеческое могущество], "the greatness of man," *prelesti osedloj žizni* [прелести оседлой жизни], "the charms of sedentary life," etc.).

In these two classes of uses, it is a matter of an immediate, experienced knowledge, and thus of a knowledge that is fundamentally intransmissible because it is inseparable from the singular conditions of its acquisition by a subject.

The simple verb *znat'* is certainly not incompatible with the experiential value (glossed as "feel" by the *Dictionnaire de l'Académie*) of (b): *On s detskix let znal gore* [он с детских лет знал горе] (he has [had] felt unhappy since he was a small child). Similarly, a complement of the type *ženščina* [женщина], "woman," is possible in the plural, or with a negative: *ni odnoj ženščiny* [ни одной женщины], "not any woman at all."

But the particularity of *poznat'* is that it can refer to a precise event, a particular experience. Thus *po-* performs a kind of "takeover": knowledge, a nontemporal notion par excellence, is transmuted into an event endowed with a spatio-temporal extension. Knowing becomes an experience. This has in return an effect on the interpretation of the complement of *poznat'*, of whose meaning it retains—in the context of the establishment of a relation to the subject—only what can be envisaged as an interaction in space and time, the woman becoming a sexual partner, the poverty of the world and truth becoming singular experiences. Thus we see that with *poznat'* knowledge is necessarily partial since it is limited to what can be experienced by the subject: the object of knowledge always exceeds what the subject "knows" about it. That is why we find complements after *znat'* that are impossible after *poznat'*: *č'ju-to familiju* [чью-то фамилию], "someone's family name," *nomer rejsa na Moskvu* [номер рейса на Москву], "the number of the flight to Moscow," *pričinu* [причину], "the cause [of]," *svoju ošibku* [свою ошибку], "his error," *parol'* [пароль], "the password." These terms refer to objects of knowledge that are incompatible with partial knowledge.

2. The noun *poznanie* midway between knowledge and knowledge connected with a singular experience

The noun *poznanie* is interpreted in different ways depending on whether it is used in the singular or the plural. In the singular, it is generally given a dynamic, processive value, close to what we have seen at work in *poznat'*: knowledge is often figured as something mobile, or as a mechanism (endowed with a motor), or as a process, even as a path, for example, in the formula *Ternist put' poznanija* [Тернист путь познания], "the path to knowledge is full of thorns."

This processive value denotes the instability of the relation established between the subject and knowledge: the subject does not attain the stable state that constitutes the possession of knowledge. This instability is connected in turn with the actual circumstances of the acquisition of knowledge by the subject(s), with the chance factors encountered, with the difficulties that have to be overcome, with the strategies adopted, and so on. The *teorija poznanija* [теория познания], "theory of knowledge," inquires into the actual conditions under which knowledge is acquired. *Poznanie* also designates knowledge as a human faculty (even if we seldom speak of a "faculty of knowledge"): a faculty manifests itself only if circumstances allow it to do so. Moreover, alongside the negative term *neznanie*, "ignorance," there is no more a **nezpoznanie* than there is a "nonknowledge" or a "nonbirthday": failing to achieve the process of knowledge amounts to remaining in a state of ignorance.

In the plural, on the other hand, we find a resultative interpretation. But then *poznanija* [познания] indicates knowledge acquired through what is once again presented as an individual experience, whence the idea of fragmentary or even superficial knowledge, illustrated by this sentence from Turgeniev: "On byl vsegda vysokogo mnenija o poznanijax Dar'ji Mixajlovny v rossijskom jazyke [он был всегда высокого мнения о познаниях Дарьи Михайловны в российском языке]" (he always had the highest opinion of Daria Mikhaïlovna's knowledge of Russian [superficial, amateur knowledge]).

Inversely, in "Biblioteka soderžala obširnyj svod èzoteričeskix znanij [библиотека содержала обширный свод эзотерических знаний]" (The library held a rich collection of knowledge [znanij]), it is impossible to substitute *poznanija* for *znanija* because the knowledge in question is envisaged independently of the conditions of acquiring it (the library having as its function precisely to make knowledge available to everyone).

3. Knowing life, living knowledge: The Byzantine heritage

We have seen that the opposition between imperfective knowledge (*znanie*) and perfective knowledge (*poznanie*) involves in a crucial way a relationship between knowledge and empirical experience, perfective knowledge (*poznanie*) being a lived or experienced knowledge.

We can inquire into the existing relation between the linguistic pertinence of this lived knowledge and the very special nature of theories of knowledge—of the act of knowing?—in Russia. It seems that we might be able to oppose the Latin tradition, which accords priority to the domain of abstraction and work on concepts, to the "Byzantine" tradition, which emphasizes hypostases: what is in each person is at once a compound of essence (*ousia* [οὐσία]) and energy (*energeia* [ἐνέργεια]), an experience and a movement of life. We have to acknowledge a clear pre-eminence of the Byzantine spiritual heritage in Russian tradition, even if that pre-eminence also has historical and cultural causes.

B. Second example: The Latin perfect and Saint Augustine's attempt to express time and creation

The second example is the Latin *perfectum*, which illustrates a quite different kind of "genius of the language" since it is described as raising no translation problem, and as finding in each of its uses and each of its values possible equivalents, if not in every language, at least in French. Its genius resides only in the sum of these uses and values, in the field covered, which is peculiar to the Latin *perfectum* alone, and which might allow, better than any form in another language, the conception of an achievement outside time. Here, the genius of the language is not of the order of what can be said, but of the objects that a language proposes for thought, and thus of what can be conceived in that language.

The Latin perfect is not untranslatable in French; its translation is rarely found unsatisfactory. On the other hand, to translate the various occurrences of the Latin perfect, we have to resort to the whole arsenal of French past tenses—*passé simple, passé composé, passé antérieur, plus-que-parfait, imparfait*—and sometimes even the present.

In other words, this "tense" is likely to assume very diverse values depending on the contexts in which it is used. This richness of use corresponds to its morphological richness, and in fact the paradigm of the Latin perfect is based on the syncretism of inherited forms that constituted different, independent paradigms in Indo-European (e.g., the reduplicative perfects vs. sigmatic aorists that we find, respectively, in forms of the Latin perfect such as *tegigi*, "I touched," and *scripsi*, "I wrote," and also in alternating vocalizations of the root, the suffix -*u*, etc.).

In this context, the traditional name of the Latin perfect is very ambiguous: it is a translation, both set and amputated of one of its fundamental elements, of the Latin term *praeteritum perfectum*. The explicit indication that we are dealing with a past tense has thus disappeared, and this is not, as we will see, a matter of indifference. The term "perfect" remains, which has the drawback not only of being a not very legible calque of the word *perfectum*, but also of leading to confusion with other terms that belong to the same terminological field but cover very diverse linguistic realities: the Greek perfect, the perfective in Slavic languages, the English perfect—which are all prisms that have prevented a precise perception of the values peculiar to the Latin perfect.

1. The specificity of the enunciative location

Contrary to the two other Latin preterites, and contrary to the French *passé simple*, the Latin perfect is also frequently encountered in the kinds of text where reference is organized around the subject and the moment of utterance; these texts belong to what Benveniste calls "discourse," as contrasted with more neutral texts not connected (*embrayées*) with the situation of utterance, which he puts in the category of "history," where "events seem to narrate themselves."

The Latin perfect itself does not determine the construction of the enunciative reference point that structures the representation of the process. In this respect, it differs from the French *passé composé*, which, by virtue of its etymology, systematically takes the *nunc* of utterance as its basis; with the Latin perfect, this basis is contextual. It also differs from the French *passé composé* insofar as unlike the latter, it is not aoristic; an aoristic configuration necessarily implies a break between the process described and the enunciative source, which is far from being the general case for the perfect, even though it can also adapt to this situation in the context of historical narration. On the contrary, in a "discourse"-type context, its factual value is combined with a strong assertive modality that is incompatible with the aoristic break.

2. The specificity of the aspectual registration of the process

In a general way, the Latin perfect provides an overall view of the process: translating the inscription of this process in time (its realization or, what amounts to the same thing, its achievement), it also accompanies its achievement until the end, thus leaving the field open for taking into account the situation subsequent to the process in question.

This situation can moreover be simply singularized by the fact that the process is no longer instantiated: there is a considerable compatibility between the perfect and negative value. Here is one example among others, taken from the famous chapter on time in Augustine's *Confessions*: "Quam longotempore illud non *vidi*!" (what a long time since I *saw* that!; *Confessions*, 11.28). There was a last process ("seeing") beyond which the contrary ("not seeing") takes over, and what the circumstantial exclamative measures is this *non-p* that has succeeded *p*.

Another, commonplace type is what is usually called the "resultative": the adjacent situation corresponds to the state resulting from the process described. Variations in the degree to which the perfect is lexically fixed can then appear, ranging from entirely set expressions—*memini*, "I remember" (the verb is defective and has no present form: literally, the form means "I have put into memory")—to free creations, which are rather rare, for example: "Exarsit animus meus nosse istuc inplicatissimum aenigma" (My soul is on fire to know this most intricate enigma) (*Confessions*, 28), via expressions that are being lexicalized—"*mihi visum est*" (it seemed to me [morally and/or pragmatically] right, hence I decide, or it seemed to me [intellectually] right, hence, I conclude).

A third realization of this point of view is the one that makes it possible to express what is over and done with, both achieved and "gone," hence past: in the text below, this value is not only used but staged by the description of what is "gone" in this case: "Et ipsa una hora fugitivis particulis agitur: quidquid eius avolavit, praeteritum est, quidquid restat, futurum" (Yea, that one hour passeth away in flying particles. Whatsoever of it hath flown away, is past; whatsoever remaineth, is to come; *Confessions*, 15.20).

The final case is the one in which a different process simply comes to occupy the subsequent situation: this is the case of narrative sequences, where the perfective is usually translated by a *passé simple*, at least if the enunciative fixation is not too marked.

We can consequently understand why the Latin perfect would be a particularly flexible and well-adapted tool for expressing the complexity of our perception of time past. Evoking both the image of the achieved and that of what has disappeared, of what is still present or of what has been definitively lost, it stays very close to the lexical meaning of the verbs that in Augustine try to describe the flight of time and memory traces:

> Quamquam praeterita cum vera narrantur, ex memoria proferuntur non res ipsae, quae praeterierunt, sed verba concepta ex imaginibus earum, quae in animo velut vestigia per sensus praetereundo fixerunt.

> (Although when past facts are related, they are drawn out of the memory, not the things themselves that are past, but words which, conceived by the images of the things, they, in passing, have through the senses left as traces in the mind.)

> (*Confessions*, 23)

With *praeterire*, which recurs three times in this one sentence and also designates simultaneously, as it does in French, the past, what is no longer and what has been, and then with *fixere* (literally, fix, attach), both the paradox of time and the very diversity of the values of the perfect are described.

In addition, we have seen that the perfect showed the situation of the process in time in such a way that one attains and then passes beyond the final boundary of this process, in order, possibly, to be established in the resulting state. Thus it combines the ability to accompany action in a narrative context with the ability to stabilize an achievement: an ideal form for trying to resolve, linguistically at least, the apparent self-contradiction of the divine act of creation as Augustine sees it, and which is moreover the source of his inquiry into time: "Si enim ullus motus in Deo novus extitit et voluntas nova . . . quomodo jam vera aeternitas, ubi oritur voluntas quae non erat?" (For did any new motion arise in God, and a new will to make a creature . . . how then would that be a true eternity, where there ariseth a will, which was not?) (ibid., 12).

We find this resolution realized in the following passage in the text: "Hodiernus tuus aeternitas: ideo coaeternum genuisti, cui dixisti 'Ego hodie genui te.' Omnia tempora tu fecisti et ante omnia tempora es" (Thy To-day is Eternity; therefore didst Thou beget The Coeternal, to whom Thou saidst, This day have I begotten Thee. Thou hast made all things; and before all times Thou art) (ibid., 16).

This passage perfectly illustrates the strong assertive value that the perfect can have: for Augustine, it is a matter of attesting the eternity of God, of making it a credo; for God, it is a matter of promulgating the creation of coeternal Being, that is, the advent of the Son. The creative word—though it is a simple word, it suffices to create—is in the perfect.

It also shows how one and the same form is able to render the founding act of creation as being both past and yet detached from all temporality, true forever, independently of any experience or any passage of time, and thus escaping human deictic locations that would make it a past that has gone and that has not always been.

C. Third example: The function of the perfect in the definitions of *energeia* and *kinêsis*

The third example is Greek, drawn from Aristotle, and illustrates a third kind of untranslatable: a perfect that is supposed to be untranslatable precisely because it does not belong to Greek, since Aristotle is supposed to have invented it.

As we have seen in Box 3 on Aristotle and the *telos*, Aristotle bases his definitions of the key concepts *energeia* and *kinêsis* on an analysis of the compatibilities between forms of the present and forms of the perfect: only *energeiai* have as their characteristic that the indicative present "goes hand in hand" with the indicative perfect. To support his analysis, Aristotle uses a certain number of perfects, in particular, for each of the *energeiai* that he has in mind: *heôrake* [ἑώρακε], *pephronêke* [πεφρόνηκε], *nenoêke* [νενόηκε], *ezêken* [ἔζηκεν], *eudaimonêken* [εὐδαιμόνηκεν], which are respectively the perfects of the forms *horai* [ὁρᾷ] (see), *phronei* (conceive), *noei* (think), *zêi* (live well), *eudaimonei* (enjoy happiness). What is the function of the perfects here with regard to the forms of the present that precede them in the text? How should these perfects be translated?

To explain, and at the same time translate, Aristotle's argument, Gilbert Ryle writes: "Aristotle points out, quite correctly . . . that I can say 'I have seen it' as soon as I can say 'I see it.'" The expression "I can say," which is of course not present in the Greek text, makes it seem that one could in fact use either of these tenses in the Greek language of Aristotle's time, as Aristotle himself does in the text in question. The truth is quite different: Aristotle's use of the perfect in the analysis of what he describes as *energeiai* has nothing to do with contemporary usage of the perfect of these verbs.

First of all, the perfects Aristotle uses in the *Metaphysics* to illustrate *energeiai* are all, with the exception of *heôrake*, extremely rare in Greek; it is even likely that he coined *eudaimonêke* and *ezêke* for the occasion (the normal perfect with *zeî* [ζῇ] being *bebiôke* [βεβίωκε]). *Heôrake*, the only perfect that is regularly found in the texts, never expresses simply the completion of the action of seeing, as it does in Aristotle: its particularity is instead that it continually refers to both the present and the past. For example, in *oude touton heôraka* [οὐδὲ τοῦτον ἑώρακα], taken from Plato's *Ion*, 533b4, which is translated in English by "I never saw one," and means very precisely "one that I have not been able to see on any occasion (past or present)."

This shows that we must not introduce the notion of "saying" into the interpretation of our text (nor, moreover, that of "one can"): it is not what one can say that interests Aristotle here.

Why does Aristotle nonetheless use the perfect *heôrake* to elucidate the ontological status of *horai*? Because the value of the perfect of the other class of verbs, the kinetic verbs, gave him a very convenient tool for this purpose. The perfect of these verbs faithfully reflects common usage: thus *ôikodomêke* [ᾠκοδόμηκε] (to have built) expresses the state at which the action of *oikodomei* [οἰκοδομεῖ] (to build) has (gradually) arrived. Just as Aristotle could use this value to show that "one builds" does not simultaneously (*ouch hama* [οὐχ ἅμα]) express achievement, he could also use it to show that "one sees" does in fact simultaneously express (*hama* [ἅμα]) achievement.

In other words: the perfect is employed to show that the complete nature of *horai* is opposed to the incomplete nature of *oikodomei*. Using modern terms, we might say that what Aristotle is doing here is showing that there is a "relation of implication" between *horai* and *heôrake*, and a relation of "nonimplication" between *oikodomei* and *oikodomêke*. His approach is thus very similar to that of recent commentators who have proposed basing the opposition between telic and non-telic processes on tests of implication between propositions (see, e.g., Dowty's "entailment tests").

As for translation, if the analysis presented above is valid, it would be better to translate *horai hama <kai heôrake>* by "he sees" implying "he has seen" than by "at the same time one sees and one has seen."

Beyond what distinguishes them, these three examples have in common that the question raised by the aspectual form singled out is precisely an aspectual question: in *poznanie* the question of what can be a property (knowledge) is raised when it is connected with a concrete experience that instantiates it; the *perfectum* Saint Augustine employs is used to challenge the temporal anchorage of an achievement; Aristotle's perfect seeks to express the perfection of an *energeia*.

That is, what is untranslatable in aspect is the way in which it conceives itself.

We should never translate an aspectual form: what it thinks is literally in its form, in what this form literally constructs. Thus we must always translate an aspectual form: translate it literally, in the detours of its form, in order to hear what this form says. Although there can be room for some between-two-languages in the case of nouns, here there is no in-between: one cannot pair a Greek perfect with a French *passé composé*, there is only Greek and French, the languages one by one—or, outside languages, the invariant question of aspect.

Sarah de Voguë
Rémi Camus (in collaboration with Maryse Dennes)
Ilse Depraetere
Sylvie Mellet
Albert Rijksbaron
Maria Tzevelekou

BIBLIOGRAPHY

Benveniste, Émile. "Le language et l'expérience humaine." In *Problèmes de linguistique générale*, vol. 1, 67–78. Paris: Gallimard / Le Pléiade, 1966.

———. "Les relations de temps dans le verbe français." Reprinted in *Problèmes de linguistique générale*, vol. 1, 237–50. Paris: Gallimard / Le Pléiade, 1966. First published in 1959.

———. *Problems in General Linguistics*. Translated by M. E. Meek. Coral Gables, FL: University of Miami Press, 1971.

Binnick, Robert. *Time and the Verb: A Guide to Tense and Aspect*. New York: Oxford University Press, 1991.

Bouscaren, Janine, Alain Deschamps, and Catherine Mazodier. "Elements pour une typologie des process." *Cahiers de recherche en grammaire anglaise* 6 (1993): 7–34.

Bybee, Joan L., Revere Perlins, and Wlliam Pagliuca. *The Evolution of Grammar: Tense, Aspect, and Modality in the Languages of the World*. Chicago: University of Chicago Press, 1994.

Comrie, Bernard. *Aspect: An Introduction to the Study of Verbal Aspect and Related Problems*. Cambridge: Cambridge University Press, 1976.

Confais, Jean-Paul. *Temps, Mode, Aspect*. Toulouse: Presses Universitaires du Mirail, 1995.

Culioli, Antoine. "Valeurs aspectuelles et opérations énonciatives: l'aoristique." In *La notion d'aspect*, edited by J. David and R. Martin, 181–93. Paris: Klincksieck, 1980.

Declerck, Renaat. "Aspect and the Bounded/Unbounded (Telic/Atelic) Distinction." *Linguistics* 17 (1979): 761–94.

Dowty, David R. "The Effects of Aspectual Class on the Temporal Structure of Discourse: Semantics or Pragmatics?" *Linguistics and Philosophy* 9 (1986): 37–61.

Fuchs, Catherine. *Les typologies de process*. Paris: Klincksieck, 1991.

Guillaume, Gustave. *Temps et verbe; théorie des aspects, des modes et des temps*. Paris: H. Champion, 1929; repr. 1984.

Hoffman, Philippe. "Paratasis." *Revue des etudes Grecques* 96 (1983): 1–26.

Hopper, Paul J., ed. *Tense-Aspect: Between Semantics and Pragmatics*. Amsterdam: Benjamins, 1982.

Kamp, Hans. "Événements, représentations discursives et référence temporelle." *Language* 64 (1981): 39–64.

Reichenbach, Hans. *Elements of Symbolic Logic*. New York: Macmillan, 1947.

Ryle, Gilbert. *Dilemmas*. Cambridge: Cambridge University Press, 1964.

Thieroff, Rolf, and Joachim Ballweg, eds. *Tense Systems in European Languages*. Tübingen: Niemeyer, 1994.

Vendler, Zeno. *Linguistics in Philosophy*. Ithaca, NY: Cornell University Press, 1967.

Verkuyl, Hendrik Jacob. "Aspectual Classes and Aspectual Composition." *Linguistics and Philosophy* 12, no. 1 (1989): 39–94.

Vetters, Carl. *Temps, aspect et narration*. Amsterdam: Rodopi, 1996.

Weinrich, Harald. *Tempus: Besprochene und erzählte Welt*. Stuttgart: W. Kohlhammer, 1964; repr. 1977).

ATTUALITÀ, ATTUOSITÀ (ITALIAN)

ENGLISH	actuality
FRENCH	*réalité, effectivité, actualité, réalité effective*
GERMAN	*Tat, Handlung, Wirklichkeit, Aktuosität*
GREEK	*energeia* [ἐνέργεια], *ergon* [ἔργον]
LATIN	*actuositas, actus*

➤ *ACT*, and AGENCY, AUFHEBEN, ESSENCE, ESTI, FORCE, ITALIAN, PRAXIS, REALITY, RES, STATO, TATSACHE, *TO BE*, TO TI ÊN EINAI

A set of speculations centered on the notion of the act provided a name for a major philosophical school of the twentieth century: Giovanni Gentile's "actualism." This Italian neo-idealism marks a division that reappears within the body of Hegelianism, following from the first revision of the original doctrines proposed by the Young Hegelians in Germany. It is linked to the decision taken by Bertrando

Spaventa to translate the German *Wirklichkeit,* on the model of *Aktuosität,* as *atttualità.*

The history of ideas that developed was immediately mirrored in a genuine political history: the philosophical apparatus originally worked out by Neapolitan Hegelianism had national reunification as its goal (the Hegelian logico-philosophical program was reconceived as the speculative and political structure of the Risorgimento) before it was transformed again into a speculative apparatus serving the philosophical and political elaboration of a fascist state, for which Gentile himself created the term *Stato totalitario.*

I. Italian Neo-idealism as a Reform of the Hegelian Dialectic and as Translation: The Mediation of Bertrando Spaventa (1817–83)

In a letter dated 5 December 1864, and addressed to the Berlin Hegelian journal *Der Gedanke,* Theodor Straeter, who had just come back from Naples, noted that "if modern philosophy can still really hope to have a future, it will come neither in Germany nor in France, nor in England, but in Italy, and in particular on its marvelous west coast (at Naples) where, at a certain period, the Greek philosophers formulated their immortal thoughts." In the work of Spaventa, the founder of the Neapolitan neo-Hegelian school, we find an idealism that has been both modernized and renewed.

A. The reform of the primary categories of Hegelian logic

1. The pair *pensare/pensato* (*Denken/ Gedanken*): Being as an act of thought

In his *Le prime Categorie della logica di Hegel* (1864), where we find no less than fifty-four occurrences of the term *atto,* Spaventa interprets the inaugural categories of Hegel's logic: Being, Non-Being, Becoming. For Spaventa, Being is nothing other than a thought that is unaware of itself. Within the *act* of thinking (*pensare*) is established, through an abstractive process, the object itself of thought, the thinkable (*il pensabile*).

> *I can,* in thought [*pensiero*], abstract from myself as thought, as simple act, as a function of thinking, and simply *focus* on what is thought [*il pensato*]. Then what is thought is nothing less than Being, the Thinkable, the first Thinkable.
>
> (*Le prime Categorie della logica di Hegel,* 379)

In the *Frammento inedito* (Unpublished fragment [1880–81], published by G. Gentile in his own *Riforma della dialettica hegeliana* [1913]), after having pointed to the four cardinal points of his great "reform," Spaventa radicalized his initial reflections: "Being is essentially the *act* of thought." Being cannot move by itself, for it cannot move outside identity, whence the necessity of a "logical thought":

> The reflection that discovers the deepest determinations in being and non-being is *logical thought* (*das logische Denken*) through which these determinations are engendered not in a contingent but in a necessary manner. . . . The *Gedanke* is thought, we may even say— with or without pleonasm—the content of thought (*Gedankeninhalt*), or, as the translator puts it, *the*

> *speculative content.* . . . Distinct from the *Gedanke, Denken* is in general the *act* of thinking, the *vis cogitans,* so to speak. This *vis* engenders all the determinations, all the *states,* all the logical elements: it is the soul of the logical process. We can rightly describe all its products as *thoughts,* in the sense in which they are engendered by it, that is, by thinking as such. . . . [Henceforth,] the true *entity* of these products will be *Denken,* not only because they are its *products,* but also because they themselves produce nothing without the *Denken* that is immanent in them.
>
> (*Frammento inedito,* 442, 445–47)

But Spaventa adds to this a new solution responding to the interpretive limits of the *Le prime Categorie della logica di Hegel*:

> [I]n a first phase, thought conceived as *the being* itself of being does not yet appear clearly, because it appears practically as a purely subjective function: given that *pure vision* is impossible, etc., I would ask the following question: how can we think the existent? I then retreat into thought, into the *elements* of thought, which do not constitute *concrete* thought (the latter being above all and in the first instance a thought of the existent). And I add: thinking = *distinguishing* (and uniting); being is what can be distinguished [*il distinguible*], what is purely distinguishable [*il puro distinguibile*]. *Non-being* is the pure act of distinguishing: the existent (*Dasein,* what has become) is the *Distinct,* the pure distinct. And *becoming*? Becoming is the distinguishable (being) qua *dis-tinction* (non-being, simply, which is in this respect both identical and non-identical with being).
>
> (*Frammento inedito*)

2. Return to Trendelenburg and the Young Hegelians' first reform

a. Spaventa's criticism of the first categories of Hegel's *Wissenschaft der Logik* (*Science of Logic*) draws upon the objections of the Berlin Aristotelian Adolf Trendelenburg (1802–72):

> What is difficult is not acknowledging the identity of Being and Nothingness, when both of them are the Indeterminate, but rather perceiving and defining their *difference,* a *difference* without which *Becoming* itself is impossible. Most of the old Hegelians have very poorly grasped the difficulty of this position.
>
> Trendelenburg was truly the first to draw the attention of both friends and enemies of Hegel to this point, and particularly that of his enemies. . . . Trendelenburg was quite right.
>
> (B. Spaventa, *Prime Categorie,* 400).

In chapter 3 of his *Logische Untersuchungen* (1840), and under the rubric of *Die dialektische Methode,* Trendelenburg attacked the Hegelian dialectic in its inaugural triad, Being–Non-Being–Becoming (*Sein-Nichtsein-Werden*). His first question concerns the possibility of a pure thought independent of any image or intuition. That is impossible, and *movement* constitutes in fact the *Vorausgetztes* and the actual vehicle of dialectical thought. "Das reine Sein, sich selbst gleich, ist Ruhe; das Nichts—das sich selbst gleich—ist ebenfalls Ruhe" (Pure Being, self-identical, is rest; Nothingness, self-identical, is also rest). Their sought-for unity could never produce anything more than a "static union." How then can movement be introduced into these stagnant waters?

Aus dem reinen Sein, einer zugestandenen Abstraktion, und aus dem Nichts, ebenfalls einer zugestandenen Abstraktion, kann nicht urplötzlich das Werden entstehen, diese concrete, Leben und Tod beherrschende, Anschauung.

(From pure Being, from an admitted abstraction, and from Nothingness, also an admitted abstraction, Becoming, this concrete, life-and-death-dominating intuition, cannot suddenly emerge.)

(Trendelenburg, *Logische Untersuchungen*, chap. 3)

In reality, the much-vaunted "immanent connection" (*immanenter Zusammenhang*) of the system lets us glimpse different fissures, as well as a general discontinuity. The dialectical process, which was supposed to demonstrate the agreement of concept and thing, "stellt im Gegenteil die Entstehung der Sache auf dem Kopf" (on the contrary stands the origin of the matter on its head) (*Logische Untersuchungen*, 37f., 108f.). Then Trendelenburg goes through, in the categories of negation and identity, the logical means that the dialectic uses to produce, from empty Being, the absolute Idea, through the series of intermediate figures. Thus it is pointless to conceal the intuition that is already there, just as it is absurd to keep silent about the difference between "logical contradiction" and a "real opposition" that can never be attained by a purely logical route.

[T]he responses presented by the bravest commentators of Hegel with a view to forestalling this kind of objection have absolutely not convinced me—perhaps that is an error on my part, but I cannot do otherwise than set forth very clearly my thought on this point. I shall nonetheless make a very limited exception for [Karl] Werner and Kuno Fischer.

(B. Spaventa, *Prime Categorie*, 369)

b. Here Spaventa refers to the enterprise of the Young Hegelians, first of all Karl Werner and Kuno Fischer, in response to Trendelenburg's criticisms.

Karl Werner, the first "reformer," replied to the objections in his *Logik. Als Kommentar und Ergänzung zu Hegels W. der L.* (1841). Concentrating his attention, like almost all his successors, on the first triad of categories in Hegel's *Wissenschaft der Logik* as an example of the inability of Hegel's philosophy to produce movement, he grants Trendelenburg that Hegel demonstrated only the identity of Being and Nothingness, asserting that their difference was only an "opinion" (*einen nur gemeinten* [*Unterschied*]). Werner does not accept the Hegelian thesis regarding the "ineffability" of the distinction between Being and Nothingness. The central point is that one should not in any way attack the question in terms of "content," but instead keep to the level

of "form"; that is the axis of the passage from the *Phenomenology of Spirit* to the *Logic*, and the key to understanding the intrinsically negative character of Being, and, consequently, its distinction from Non-Being, from the Nothingness that is its explanation, and thus a "more" than Being which then is distinguished from it. If the Being/Nothingness distinction were only a matter of content, there would be no reason to begin with Being rather than with Nothingness—and inversely. But that is not the case, for as Werner goes on to say,

Nothingness is more profound than Being, it is the very depth of Being . . . as regards *form*. Form means knowledge, because knowledge means *shape* (*gestalten*). Being begins, and Nothingness follows; it is the *impulse* for the process (*Fortgang*) in the beginning (*Anfang*); now, Nothingness is not process as such, in this form of *Nothingness*, but process as such means becoming, for only becoming *is* the beginning. Actual beginning means proceeding, means beginning and process as a single, identical process (*Gang*), as a *return to oneself*—which means, as a passing (*Übergehen*). Nothingness is the immediate precedent of Being. This knowledge is the ulterior determination. That is why we have two forms, that of the original form and that of form; form means distinction. Being and Nothingness are equally distinct, as regards *form*; for each identity, each content *is* only qua distinction, qua form, for they are at once development and manifestation.

(*Logik, Als Kommentar*, 45–46)

Thus we can demonstrate the difference between Being and Nothingness by taking into account the fact that Nothingness is "interiorization-memory" (*Erinnerung*) (see MEMORY) of Being, its negation, and as "negating," that is, "thinking," already a Becoming:

When I say Nothingness, I know more about it than when I say Being—for the latter is something more, it is what reveals itself, tearing away its own veil; for it is *naked* Being, the spirit of Being, Being in Being.

In Nothingness, Being itself breaks the silence in itself. Nothingness is the reflection (*Besinnung*) [which Spaventa translates by *accorgimento*, that is, "penetration," "intelligence-consciousness-perspicacity"] of Being, the opening up in it of its meaning; its look in itself, the point where its originary character emerges. In Nothingness the sacrosanct duplicity of meaning of the emptiness of Being is unveiled. That it is nothing other than Being itself, Being through itself, *full* solely of itself—which says its emptiness, which says Nothingness. Nothingness is thus the knowledge of Being with regard to its plenitude, to its accomplishment on the basis of itself, *with regard to its free action*, to its self-creation;—and in the actuality (*in der Energie*) [= in *energeia* [ἐνέργεια] of this knowledge that moves in itself, Being no longer says Being, but *Becoming*].

(Ibid., 41)

Through this identification of Nothingness with thought, movement, contradiction and necessity are reintroduced into the interior of the Hegelian dialectic. Distinction thus rediscovers its "effability" in what Hegel calls the "*speculative system of the proposition*."

Kuno Fischer, the most imposing of the German "reformers," also lays emphasis on the first categories by observing that already the first one, Being, qua result of an abstraction carried out by thought, assumes "thought in act," that is, the "act of thinking" (*Denkakt*):

That is why logic begins for itself with the willed act of thought (*mit dem Willensakt des Denkens*), and for others, who want to construct (and teach) it, with the postulate of the accomplishment of this *Act*. The postulate says: "*think*."

(*System der Logik und Metaphysik oder Wissenschaftslehre*)

But Being, qua abstract and at rest, denies thought, that is, it denies itself, contradicts itself, and so does Nothingness, which is not pure absence of Being but its negation, that is, its contradiction. Thus they pass into one another, giving rise to Becoming, where the contradiction is dissolved.

Thinking and Being are identical. Thinking and being are non-identical. The identity is explained in the concept of being, the non-identity in the concept of non-being.

(*Logik und Metaphysik oder Wissenschaftslehre*, 194–98)

That is the contradiction internal to Being—to the concept of Being, which permits Fischer to explain Becoming without leaving pure thought. Here everything depends on the act of "abstraction."

In the act of abstraction [*Akt der Abstraktion*], thought withdraws from all external content and every given into its pure activity, thus creating, on the basis of this material, the universal system of pure concepts that produce themselves as necessary actions of thought in the dialectical order. . . . Pure thought contains the preceding stages of the natural and spiritual world as moments that are prominent in itself, and it is thus, by its very nature, full of the essence of things. It is therefore incomprehensible that someone [Trendelenburg!] should reproach Hegel for thinking that acts of pure thought [*die Akte des reinen Denkens*] (the categories) are creations *ex nihilo*.

(Ibid., §28f.)

While Werner was concerned about introducing movement into the inaugural triad by identifying the second category (Nothingness) with thought, Fischer makes the latter retrocede into the first (Being). The 1865 edition radicalizes still further this gnoseological and subjectivist dimension of Hegelian logic by definitively shifting attention from the initial Being/Nothingness relationship to the "unprecedable" (*indevançable*) Being/Thought relationship:

[Thought is] *necessary* Thought, or Thought in which nothing is represented other than what is Thought itself: its necessary function.

(*System der Logik*, 205–6)

B. *Wirklichkeit—Aktuosität* versus *attualità*: Translation's decision

In section 3 of the *Wissenschaft der Logik* (1812 ed.), entitled "Die Wirklichkeit," Hegel introduces, in the third paragraph of "Relation of Substantiality," the notion of *Aktuosität*:

Diese Bewegung der Accidentalität ist die Aktuosität der Substanz als ruhiges Hervorgehen ihrer selbst. Sie ist nicht thätig gegen Etwas, sondern nur gegen sich als einfaches widerstandloses Element.

(This movement of accidentality is the actuosity [*Aktuosität*] of substance as a tranquil coming forth of itself. It is not active against something but only against itself as a simple unresisting element.)

("Die objektive Logik," Part I of *Wissenschaft der Logik*; trans. A. V. Miller, *Hegel's Science of Logic*)

Further on, in the context of the "Relation of Causality," Hegel continues:

Die Substanz geht . . . in ihrem Bestimmen nicht von der Accidentalität aus, als ob diese voraus ein Anderes wäre, und nun erst als Bestimmtheit gesetzt würde, sondern beides ist Eine Aktuosität. . . . So ist die die absolute Aktuosität Ursache.

(Substance proceeds . . . in its determination not from accidentality, as if the latter were formerly something different, and were only now posited as something determined, but rather both are an *Aktuosität*. . . . Thus absolute *Aktuosität* is cause.)

Finally, in the *Zusatz* at paragraph 34 of his *Encyclopedia of the Philosophical Sciences*, Hegel explains the following:

Der Geist ist Tätigkeit, in dem Sinne, in welchem schon die Scholastiker von Gott sagten, er sei absolute Aktuosität.

(Spirit is activity, in the sense in which the Scholastics already said of God that he is absolute *Aktuosität*.)

In short, Hegelian *Aktuosität* (the state of what is "in actuality," that is, that which has force and density) is nothing other than the manifestation of substance's own *Wirklichkeit*, or what constitutes, in the strong sense, the essential "actuality" of a thing—its reality as necessary reality of the self in relation to itself, that is, free. It is a question, in this context, of explaining, against a certain reifying understanding of Kantian thought, that nothing preexists the movement of manifestation conceived as *die sich selbst gleich absolute Wirklichkeit* (absolute self-identical reality) (*Wissenschaft der Logik*, 269).

While the term *Aktuosität* appears once in Johann Gottlieb Fichte's work, it nonetheless is not one of his own categories. It is in response to Friedrich Heinrich Jacobi, and in the context of the accusation of "nihilism"" (where the term

Aktuosität is created for the first time by Jacobi himself!) that this single occurrence is located:

> Was er [Jacobi] von der Freiheit sagt: Wer sie läugne, komme auf eine unbestimmte Aktuosität und Agilität an sich.
>
> (What he [Jacobi] says about freedom: anyone who denied it would arrive at an indeterminate *Aktuosität* and agility in itself.)

(J. G. Fichte, Nachgelassene Werke, 3:390)

It is, moreover, probable that Hegel himself took this term from Jacobi, and more particularly from the following passage in the *Beilagen zu den Briefen über die Lehre des Spinoza*:

> Aus dem Satze: das Werden könne eben so wenig geworden oder enstanden sein, als das Sein oder die Substanz, zog Spinoza die richtige Folge, daß eine ewige unendliche Actuosität der Materie eigen, und ein unmittelbarer Modus der Substanz sein müsse.
>
> (From the proposition: Becoming can no more have become or emerged than Being or substance can, Spinoza drew the right conclusion, that matter must have an eternal, infinite *Actuosität*, and that there must be an immediate mode of substance.)

(F. Jacobi, Werke, 4:2, 137–40)

In reality, through Jacobi, it is the whole speculative apparatus of German idealism that was thus condemned: the question of substance, of the Absolute's self-presentation, and their fatal inscription in Spinozism. Although Spinoza does not use the concept of *actuositas*, the obvious allusion to Jacobi is accompanied by a certain allusion to Spinoza affirming that divine power (*potentia*) is none other than his *essentia actuosa* (God's essence in action) (Spinoza, *Ethics* 2, prop. 3, schol.).

The critics seem never to have inquired into the origin of an act and a translation decision rife with an unprecedented conceptual and doctrinal force, nor into the source of the speculative and "transductive" passage from *Wirklichkeit* to *Attualità*. It is as if philosophers were satisfied with a kind of obviousness of the system delivered in its general economy, in the aftermath of its "monumentalization": Italian neo-idealism, and the "actualism" of Gentile. Although the inscription of this lexical-doctrinal history can be read in the text itself, in Spaventa's pure and simple substitution of the neo-Hegelian *attualità* for every occurrence of the Hegelian *Wirklichkeit* (reality), it seems possible to reinscribe this choice in the Hegelian original as such. Let us note that it is the "intermediary link" of Spaventa's writings that dominated the whole future of this twist, which is simultaneously translational, practical, and speculative, of interiorization-memory (*Erinnerung*) within the "little Hegelian" system peculiar to Italy. It is in fact in the intermediary work of 1867, and in the central chapter of Spaventa's *Doctrine of Essence*, that the decision to translate the Hegelian *Wirklichkeit* by *attualità* was made. The choice of this topic is not accidental: as the "background" of Being, Essence is this internal alterity that defines it as Being. It is a structuring alterity, the very dynamism of its engenderment, the process of its

"actualization," that is, of the movement without origin or end that precedes (logically) all facticity, and which, freeing it from its representative fixity, brings out its potentialities by connecting it with itself as its other.

The present author's hypothesis is thus that seeking to strengthen a radicalization of the "active" and "actualizing" part of the category of *Wirklichkeit*, on the basis of a dynamic return of the resources of the neo-Fichteans, Young Hegelians, and the nascent *Philosophie der Tat* (through the connected notions of *Tat, Handlung, Tathandlung, wirken, Tätigkeit, Akt. . . .* See TATSACHE), the concept of *Aktuosität*, itself radicalized, certainly offered the model for the whole construction leading to the replacement of the master category of *Wirklichkeit* by that of *Attualità*. Its radicalization has in particular to do with its privileged attribution to the Absolute as such, namely God (cf. the previously cited Hegelian *Zusatz*). Let us note in passing that the English translation of Hegel's *Wissenschaft der Logik*, as well as the associated critical literature (McTaggart, Mure, Harris), proposing a parallel solution, were also to establish the term "actuality" as a translation of *Wirklichkeit*. In France, while Eugène Fleischmann hesitates between *réalité agissante* and *actualité* (*La Science universelle ou la Logique de Hegel* [glossary]), André Droz opts for *Wirklichkeit-Actualité* on the basis of a historical and categorial argument (the Hegelian relation to the tradition of Aristotelian onto-theology, around [l'ἐνέργεια], [l'ἔργον], and to Spinozism) (*La Logique de Hegel et les Problèmes traditionels de l'ontologie*, 123, 125–75).

Thus the act of translating set the translated text in movement; it is the translating, that is, the copy, that stimulates and activates the translated, that is, the "original," by thus providing it a "more-than-life," a "sur-vival," a *fort-leben* that is always to come as Life of the Spirit raising/removing itself above Nature (cf. C. Alunni, "La langue en partage," 63). This was, moreover, to become the categorial and speculative paradigm for the whole political/logical system of" the "(Italic) circulation of European ideas."

II. The Actualism of Giovanni Gentile (1817–83)

Actualism is a doctrine from which Martin Heidegger found it necessary to distinguish himself imperatively and explicitly in 1941: "Actualism is the reverse side of Historicism as a philosophy of the pure Act."

A. The act of auto-synthesis

Following Spaventa, Gentile takes into account the same necessity of reforming Hegelianism in a radically "immanentist" sense by founding a concept of Spirit (*Geist*) conceived through and through as an "auto-concept," as well as a synthesis that is through and through an "auto-synthesis."

To speak of dialectic is to speak of autonomy; that is why the dialectical conception of the real no longer accepts the positing of a *Logos* (of the "Idea") alienated outside itself—or Nature—but wants a *Logos* that, on the basis of itself, makes itself an object inside itself: it is spirit as act that *ex se oritur* (originates in itself). That is what Spaventa approached by positing, in the margins of Hegel's text, "Thinking" at the generating center of Being, this Thinking that he described as a "great prevaricator." Gentile mentions that in Spaventa's magisterial work of 1861, *La filosofia italiana nelle sue relazioni con la filosofia europea*, the author noted the necessity of "mentalizing (*mentalizzare*) [Hegel's] logic." But it was in his *Frammento inedito* (449) that Spaventa came closest to a "pre-actualist" textuality:

> Generally, subjective thought is reflection: *Nachdenken* (rethinking); it presupposes *Denken* (thinking), and in this sense is posterior to it. Hence logic, whatever it is, is posterior to the *logos*: Hegel's *Nachdenken* is posterior to *Denken*, whose secret he intended to reveal. . . . For some Hegelians (Gabler, "La droite hégélienne"), thinking (*Denken*) is and remains absolutely and eternally thought and thinking in itself, that is, absolute subject: we could also say *Vordenken*, *Vorsubjekt* (proto-thought, proto-subject); thought or the human subject, reflection, are *Nachdenken*; the absolute subject thinks: as for us, we think again.

Thus for Gentile it is clear that

> Spaventa succeeded in glimpsing the principle of idealism as we now understand it, by sapping the opposition between logic (*Denken*) and reflection (*Nachdenken*), by wholly resolving the dialectical process, on the basis of Being itself, in the pure act of thinking: whence the genuine liquidation of the transcendent, and the *actuation* (*l'inveramento*) [which translates as *Verwirklichung*—trans.]

of Hegelianism as "transcendental dialectic," and, consequently as absolute immanentism.

(*La riforma della dialettica hegeliana*, 37)

It is on this Spaventian basis (and drawing more on the system inaugurated by Kuno Fischer than on Werner's first reform) that Gentile affirms his great principle that was to "reform" the whole of transcendental logic: the true category, the true idea, is act, act in act, this *actus purus* in which the "transcendental ego" consists as a eternal positing of self in the other, of self as an other, the dialectical union of opposites, of subject-object. It thus imposes a sort of transcendental concept of the dialectic—which he describes in Spaventa as "dialectic as *Wissenschaftslehre*" (*La riforma*, 30)—by positing, at the very heart of becoming, the Being-subject of "thinking thought" (*pensiero pensante*), "that *pure act* of thought (*del pensare*), which is eternal." This thought or "universal ego" is beyond time. "Nothing, finally, transcends thought [which is] absolute immanence," and the totality of experience restitutes its process, a veritable productive synthesis of self, or *autoctisi*.

■ See Box 1.

A single task remains: to resolve the object in itself, in the "becoming-act" of thinking, by moving from an analytical categoriality (at the hypostatized level of the *res*) to auto-synthetic categoriality (level of *autoctisi*), of the transcendental dialectic of Being as an auto-concept.

1

"Auto-": "Auto-subject," "auto-concept," "auto-synthesis," *autoctisi*. . .

➤ I/ME/MYSELF, SELBST

For Gentile, Hegel, whom he regarded as having forgotten the very nature of a dialectical logic, did not achieve a full awareness of the fact that the generating center of the circular movement of the Absolute (thesis-antithesis-synthesis) can only be thought itself as a subject that is an "auto-subject" (*autosogetto*), a synthesis that is an *act* of "auto-synthesis" (*autosintesi*). "Auto-concept" (*autoconcetto*) and "auto-synthesis" thus provide the titles for chapters 6 and 8 of the *Sistema di logica come teoria del conoscere* (1:74f. and 153f.). Here the prefix "auto-" is used to express the German *Selbst*, the reflected/reflecting Ego in itself in its objectivization, the "auto-subject":

"Concept" is the thought (*pensamento*) of the truth objectively considered as independent of the act that thinks it (*dell'atto del pensarla*). . . . Auto-concept (*autoconcetto*) is the thought (*pensa-mento*) of the truth that is constituted in the very act of thinking (*pensiero*) that thinks. A thinking intrinsic to the truth which thus thinks itself.

(Ibid., 2:153)

The Self is the Self on one condition: qua *ex se oritur*, qua identical with and different from itself. Its being is neither simple identity nor simple difference, nor simple unity of identity and difference; but this unity qua creative of itself: *autoctisi*: a synthesis that posits its terms in their synthetic relationship.

(Ibid., 2:81)

Autoctisi: Here, Gentile transposes the Greek [αὐτοκτίσις] to designate thought's self-foundation, self-creation:

There is neither any pure thesis nor any pure antithesis: non-being and non-non-being: but the synthesis, that unique act that we ourselves are, Thinking (*il Pensiero*). Being (thesis) in its abstraction (*astrattezza*) is nothingness; nothingness of thinking (*pensiero*) (which is true being). But this thinking, which is eternal, is never preceded by its own nothingness. It is rather this nothingness that is posited by it; and it is, qua nothingness of thinking (*nulla del pensiero*), thinking of nothingness

(*pensiero del nulla*) that is integral thinking. The thesis does not make the synthesis possible; on the contrary, it is the synthesis that makes the thesis possible by creating it with its antithesis, that is, by creating itself. That is why the pure act is *autoctisi*.

(*La riforma della dialettica hegeliana*, 195)

The generic correlative of this autonomic character is the concept of "self-consciousness" (Ger. *Selbstbewusstsein*): the object of the Ego is the Ego itself. Every cognitive process is an act of self-consciousness.

Self-consciousness is neither an abstract identity, nor immobility, but precisely a concrete act. If it were something identical, inert, it would need something else to move. But that would destroy its freedom. Its movement is not something posterior to its being: it coincides with being. Self-consciousness is movement or process as such.

(*La riforma della dialettica hegeliana*, 194)

B. Praxis in translation

1. Complex exchangers

Gentile always considered Spaventa to be an idealist who considered and valued experience, and whose philosophy consequently had no pure theoretical moment. The gain in the objectivity of knowledge, the very one that can constantly dissolve the ever-recurring opposition between the titular subject of this knowledge and the object that is supposed to make this same knowledge "objective," is, for Spaventa, a "*practical* process."

> But all that is impossible in the order of pure theory, without practical activity. . . . This concept, lucidly set forth by Spaventa, is, in my opinion, the key to the new, post-Kantian gnoseology; and it is a great merit in our philosopher to have revealed it in Hegel's *Phenomenology*, and to have brought it to light. It was moreover one of the most profound ideas of one of Hegel's German epigones who was very famous but certainly unknown to Spaventa in this regard: Karl Marx. . . . Man can prove truth in *praxis*, that is, in reality and power, the positivity of his own thought.
>
> (G. Gentile, "Bertrando Spaventa," 111–12)

Gentile thus emphasizes the point where Spaventa's concept, which he shared, of a concrete knowledge conceived as action, intersects with Marxist *praxis*. Gentile's "act" will always have to be grasped as practical activity, *praxis*, that is, as transformative, creative, and revolutionary (fascist) activity (see PRAXIS).

This is the site of the greatest density of the translative exchangers implemented by actualism, the site of their speculative crystallization and their historical-political precipitate. What are its fundamental equations? "Actualism" defined as the "philosophy of the *pure act*" raises, as soon as it is posited, a question concerning the historical-political translation and "traditionalization" of philosophy in general; we must also add the question of what is described, north of the Alps, as cultural or historical hegemony. From the first sequence—the body of texts collected in Gentile's *La riforma della dialettica hegeliana* (particularly "The Act of Thinking as Pure Act," 1911)—to those that were to inaugurate performatively the new era (a new *Zeitalter* in politics, Heidegger said, confronted with a work entitled *Aktualismus, Schellings Abhandlung über das Wesen der menschlichen Freiheit*) in the form: "Everything is in the state, and nothing human or spiritual exists, and less still, has any value, outside the state. In this sense fascism is *totalitarian*." Gentile appeals to the state-pedagogue and his foundational role. (Here we may speak of a certain consequence of Hegel's *Encyclopedia of the Philosophical Sciences*, which is doubly pegged to a "philosophy of action" [*Philosophie der Tat*] and a "role of the scientist." It is noteworthy that both dimensions are largely indebted to a Hegel who has himself been rewritten by the early Fichte.) The translational exchanger connected with the *Philosophie der Tat* refers first of all to Moses Hess and his *European Triarchy* (1841), conceived (against Hegel) as a "holy action of the Spirit" and divided into *subjektive GEISTEStat, absolutes GEISTESphilosophie*, and *absolute GEISTEStat*, where the true theoretical commutator of the sequence appears, here too, as the sovereign "Spirit" of which history is the product. In his *Philosophy of Action* (1842–43), Hess defines the "ego" as "the performance of an act" (see G. Bensussan, *Moses Hess. La philosophie, le socialisme (1836–1845)*, 174). The "I think" is thus designated as the action that includes three moments, which, taken together constitute the ego; and the latter . . . is not a being . . . but the *performance of an act*." Thus here we have the sequence of the concepts *Akt, Tat*, and *Tätigkeit*, which question the Hegelian opposition between the sphere of interiority (*Tätigkeit, Tun*) and the sphere of real exteriority (*Tat*). "Action" represents the integrated unity of thinking (*Denken*) and doing (*Handeln*). Let us add, still apropos of Hess, this other point of contact that is the goal of an essential alterity of the future, of an irreversible novelty that constitutes the background of this prospective view *in actu* as a "praxological" reduplication of the contradiction speculative action/ philosophy. Here the Fichtean operator of the *Tat-Handlung* is still one of those most present.

We must also add to the circle of the exchanger the signatures of A. von Cieszkowski, Bruno Bauer, and Arnold Ruge. Let us note the latter's programmatic imperative:

> In place of the system of abstract and theoretically absolute development, the system of concrete development now offers itself, a system that conceives spirit everywhere in its history, and posits the requirement of its future at the end of every history. Hegel's speculative contemplation has to be awakened by Fichte's active force.
>
> (A. Ruge, *Hallische Jahrbücher*, 1209f.)

Disagreeing with subsistent reality, the representatives of the Hegelian Left thus refer their present to the future, a fundamental leitmotif adopted by Gentile.

2. The return of German translation in Italy

These attempts to reform the Hegelian dialectic are presented as an effort to translate the results of German philosophy into a language adhering to the actual requirements of the civil and speculative life of the Italian nation. At the same time, this practice of translation was accompanied by its actualist theory. Whereas Antonio Rosmini (1797–1855) called Hegel a "speculative smuggler," Spaventa developed, through his theory of the "circulation of European ideas," a general and speculative theory of "translation"/"tradition" by relating different philosophical traditions as contraband, import-export, and then as traditionalization (unless it should be called nationalization). He considered the constellation of German idealism a simple resumption (a pursuit, underground and elsewhere) of a national and philosophical textuality in exile, constituted "originarily" by the purest renascent and modern Italian philosophical tradition.

It is precisely this textuality, first translated into German by Hegel, that Spaventa sought to "repatriate" into an "original" Italic space. Here the (German) "original" is already a translation of the translating language (Italian).

Through the work of these series of conceptual and doctrinal exchangers we see the constitution of a genuinely European philosophical fabric marked by a triangulation of which the mediator, up to that point absent from Franco-German *Begriffsgeschichte*, is none other than what we would describe as the third party excluded from the Franco-German Annals: Italy.

This system, which is extremely innovative for every contemporary theory of the act of translation, is accompanied by an absolutely pioneering text by Gentile: "Il torto e il diritto delle traduzioni" ("Wrongs and Rights of Translation") in *Frammenti di estetica e letteratura*. In 1920, four years before Walter Benjamin published his famous essay "Die Aufgabe des Übersetzers" ("The Task of the Translator"), the founder of actualism had already given a performative dimension to both to what Roman Jakobson was to call "intralinguistic translation" and to Benjamin's notions of an *Ur-Sprache* (originary language) or *Überleben/Fortleben* (survival, afterlife), while at the same time defending (against Benedetto Croce) the idea of a genuine "poetics" of translation.

The necessary condition for such a conception no doubt has to do with the whole complex, self-reflexive history of this translating/traducing of the concept of *Wirklichkeit* into the performative *attualità*. It is through the actualization of this deviation that these views of translation and the theory of translation were able to see the light.

Charles Alunnil

BIBLIOGRAPHY

Alunni, Charles. "Giovanni Gentile-Martin Heidegger. Note sur un point de (non) traduction." *Collège International de Philosophie* 6 (1988): 7–12.

———. "Giovanni Gentile ou l'interminable traduction d'une politique de la pensée." In *Les extrême-droites en France et en Europe*, edited by Michel Surya, 181–94. Paris: Séguier, 1988.

———. "La langue en partage." *Revue de Métaphysique et de morale* 1 (1989): 59–69.

Bensussan, Gérard. *Moses Hess. La philosophie, le socialisme (1836–1845)*. Paris: Presses Universitaires de France, 1985.

Ciezkowski, August von. *Prolegomena zur Historiosophie*. Hamburg: F. Meiner, 1981.

Cubeddu, Italo. *Bertrando Spaventa*, "Pubblicazioni dell'istituto di filosofia dell'Università di Roma." Florence: Sansoni Editore, 1964.

Di Giovanni, Piero, ed. *Il neoidalismo italiano*. Laterza: Bari, 1988.

Droz, André. *La Logique de Hegel et les Problèmes traditionels de l'ontologie*. Paris: Vrin, 1987.

Fichte, Johann Gottlieb. *Nachgelassene Werke*, vol. 3. Edited by I. H. Fichte. Bonn: Adolphus Marcus, 1835.

Fischer, Kuno. *Logik und Metaphysik oder Wissenschaftslehre*. Introduction by H.-G. Gadamer. Heidelberg: Manutius Verlag, 1998. First published in 1852.

———. *System der Logik und Metaphysik oder Wissenschaftslehre*. Frankfurt: Minerva Verlag, 1983. First published in 1865.

Fleischmann, Eugène. *La Science universelle ou la Logique de Hegel*. Paris: Plon, 1968.

———. "Die Wirklichkeit in Hegels' Logik." *Zeitschrift für Philosophische Forschung* 18 (1964): 3–29.

Franchini, Raffaello, ed. *Bertrando Spaventa, Dalla scienza della logica alla logica della scienza*. Salerne: Tullio Pironti Editore, 1986.

Garin, Eugenio. *History of Italian Philosophy*. 2 vols. New York: Rodopi, 2007.

Gentile, Giovanni. "Bertrando Spaventa." In *Opere*, edited by G. Gentile. Florence: Sansoni, 1972. Essay first published in 1899.

———. *Frammenti di estetica e letteratura*. Florence: Lanciano, 1920.

———. *The Philosophy of Art*. Translated by G. Gullace. Ithaca, NY: Cornell University Press, 1972.

———. *La riforma della dialettica hegeliana*. 4th ed. Florence: Sansoni Editore, 1975. First published in 1913.

———. *Sistema Logica come teoria del conoscere*. 5th ed. 2 vols. Florence: Sansoni Editore, 1987. First published in 1917–23.

———. "Teoria generale dello spirito atto puro." In *Opere filosofiche*. Milan: Garzanti, 1991. Essay first published in 1916. Translation by W. W. Carr: *The Theory of Mind as Pure Act*. London: Macmillan, 1922.

———. "Il torto et il diritto delle traduzioni." In *Frammenti di estetica e letteratura*. Florence: Lanciano, 1920.

Hegel, Georg Wilhelm Friedrich. *Wissenschaft der Logik*. Edited by Anton Koch and Friedrike Schick. Berlin: Akademieverlag, 2002. First published in 1812. Translation by A. V. Miller: *Hegel's Science of Logic*. Amherst, NY: Prometheus Books / Humanities Press, 1991.

Labarrière, Pierre-Jean. "De l'actualité en philosophie. Analyse d'un concept." *Les Cahiers de Philosophie* 13, special issue on "L'actualité" (1991): 85–98.

Mangiagalli, Maurizio. *Logica e metafisica nel pensiero di F. A. Trendelenburg*. Milan: CUSL, 1983.

Parasporo, Leone. "Sulla storia della 'Logica' di Hegel. Saggio di confronto tra le due redazioni della 'Dottrina dell'Essere.'" *Annali dell'istituto italiano per gli studi storici* 8 (1983–84): 175–218.

Ruge, Arnold. *Hallische Jahrbücher*. Halle, 1840.

Spaventa, Bertrando. "Dottrina del Trendelenburg sul movimento." In *La cultura italiana tr '800 e '900: Studi e ricerchi*, edited by Eugenio Garin, 76–79. 2nd ed. Bari: Laterza, 1976. Essay first published in 1863.

———. *La filosofia italiana nelle sue relazionicon la filosofia europea (1861–1863)*. In vol. 2 of *Opere*, edited by G. Gentile, 407–719. Florence: Sansoni, 1972. First published in 1908.

———. *Frammento inedito*. In vol. 3 of *Opere*, edited by G. Gentile. Florence: Sansoni, 1972. First published in 1880–81.

———. *Logica e metafisica*. In vol. 3 of *Opere*, edited by G. Gentile. Florence: Sansoni, 1972. First published in 1867.

———. *Le prime Categorie della logica di Hegel*. In vol. 1 of *Opere*, edited by G. Gentile. Florence: Sansoni, 1972. First published in 1864.

Tessitore, Fulvio, ed. *Incidenza di Hegel*. Naples: Morano, 1970.

Vitiello, Vicenzo. *Bertrando Spaventa e il problema del comminciamento*. Naples: Guida Editore, 1970.

Werner, Karl. *Die Italienische des neunzehnten Jarhunderts*. Vienna: G. P. Faesy, 1884.

———. *Logik. Als Kommentar und Ergänzung zu Hegels W. der L.* 1841. Reprint, Hildesheim, Ger.: Gerstenburg, 1977.

AUFHEBEN, AUFHEBUNG (GERMAN)

> FRENCH   supprimer, suppression; abolir, abolition; sursumer, sursomption; assumer, assomption; dépasser, surpasser, abroger, sur-primer, mettre en grange; enlever, enlèvement; relever, relève

➤ DIALECTIC, and GERMAN, MOMENT, NEGATION, PLASTICITY, RUSSIAN, VERNEINUNG

Since 1939, when the first volume of Hegel's *Phenomenology of Mind* translated into French by Jean Hyppolite was published, *aufheben* and *Aufhebung* have been revered as fetishes of the untranslatable. The "double meaning" (to adopt Hegel's term) of a verb, *aufheben*, that means both "maintain, preserve" and "halt, end," has not only been recognized by Hegel's interpreters and specialists in German philosophy but has become simply part of today's philosophical culture. *Aufhebung* refers to a turn of thought that consists in "transcending" a point of view without refuting it, in carrying out a "synthesis" while retaining the best part of the "thesis" and "antithesis" and at the same time "opening" onto broader perspectives. Perhaps aided by academic habits and the practice of the dissertation, and certainly favored by the penetration of Hegelianism in France after 1945, the debate regarding these two words is probably the most long lasting, the most documented, and the best known of all those that concern problems of philosophical translation.

To draw up a complete list of the French translations of *aufheben* and *Aufhebung* would be a project in itself, which several scholars have already undertaken; here we will limit ourselves, in a first phase, to bringing it up to date.

The most recent inventory (Pierre-Jean Labarrière, 1986, following Gilbert Kirscher, 1978) included, for *aufheben*, and in the order of their entrance on stage: *supprimer* (Jean Hyppolite, 1939) and its neologistic variant, *sur-primer* (Jean Wahl, 1966), *abroger* (Albert Baraquin, 1975), *enlever* (André Doz, 1976), *mettre en grange* (Jean-Louis Vieillard-Baron, 1977), *conservé et dépassé* for the past participle *aufgehoben* (Henri Denis, 1984, preceded by Xavier Tilliette, who in 1973 proposed *dépasser* or *surpasser* for the infinitive), *assumer* (Emmanuel Martineau, 1984). The candidates that have remained the most famous are *relever* (Jacques Derrida, 1972, adopted by Jean-Luc Nancy, 1973) and *sursumer* (following Yvon Gauthier, 1967, Pierre-Jean Labarrière and Gwendoline Jarczyk, first for the *Wissenschaft der Logik* that they translated beginning in 1972). In 1991 Jean-Pierre Lefebvre proposed *abolir* and *abolition* for the noun *Aufhebung* in the *Phenomenology of Mind*, while G. Jarczyk and P.-J. Labarrière used *sursumer* and *sursomption* in their translation of the *Phenomenology* in 1993.

These proposals have not all been useful in translations of works or even particular texts by Hegel: it is the Hegelian *Aufhebung* in general, outside any context, that people seek to translate. This provides an initial illustration of the fetish status that *aufheben* and *Aufhebung* very rapidly took on: people debate *one* word (or two words), and everyone feels competent to propose something, without necessarily dealing with a particular textual content. That is what we have to understand first in the numerous declarations that make *Aufhebung* the main difficulty or the key to what is called "Hegelianism" (see, for example, J. Wahl, "Le rôle de A. Koyré").

I. *Aufhebung* and Its Text: The Remark on *Aufheben* in Hegel's *Wissenschaft der Logik* (1812–31)

This decontextualization of *aufheben* has itself to be explained. We can show that it has its origin in Hegel himself. The word is discussed in the *Wissenschaft der Logik* in a note on terminology that has, as was probably inevitable, attracted all the exegesis of the Hegelian *Aufhebung*. We must therefore reread this text without, however, committing ourselves with regard to the translation of the word at issue:

Anmerkung. Aufheben und das Aufgehobene (das Ideelle) ist einer der wichtigsten Begriffe der Philosophie, eine Grundbestimmung, die schlechthin allenthalben wiederkehrt, deren Sinn bestimmt aufzufassen und besonders vom Nichts zu unterscheiden ist.—Was sich aufhebt wird dadurch nicht zu Nichts. Nichts ist das Unmittelbare; ein Aufgehobenes dagegen ist ein Vermitteltes, es ist das Nichtseyende, aber als Resultat, das von einem Seyn ausgegangen *ist; es hat daher* die Bestimmtheit, aus der es herkommt, noch an sich Aufheben hat in der Sprache den gedoppelten Sinn, daß es so viel als aufbewahren, erhalten bedeutet, und zugleich so viel als aufhören lassen, ein Ende machen. Das Aufbewahren selbst schließt schon das Negative in sich, daß etwas seiner Unmittelbarkeit und damit einem den äußerlichen Einwirkungen

offenen Daseyn entnommen wird, um es zu erhalten.—So ist das Aufgehobene ein zugleich Aufbewahrtes, das nur seine Unmittelbarkeit verloren hat, aber darum nicht vernichtet ist.—Die angegebenen zwei Bestimmungen des Aufhebens können lexikalisch als zwei Bedeutungen dieses Wortes aufgeführt werden. Auffallend müßte es aber dabei seyn, daß es eine Sprache dazu gekommen ist, ein und dasselbe Wort für zwei entgegensetzte Bestimmungen zu gebrauchen. Für das spekulative Denken ist es erfreulich, in der Sprache Wörter zu finden, welche eine spekulative Bedeutung an ihnen selbst haben; die deutsche Sprache hat mehrere dergleichen. Der Doppelsinn des lateinischen: *tollere* (der durch den ciceronischen Witz *tollendum esse Octavium*, berühmt geworden), geht nicht so weit, die affirmative Bedeutung geht nur bis zum Emporheben.

(Hegel, *Wissenschaft der Logik*, in *Sämtliche Werke*, 1965, 4:119–20)

(Remarque. *Aufheben* et le *Aufgehobene* [participe passé substantivé] (l'idéel) est l'un des concepts les plus importants de la philosophie, une détermination fondamentale qui revient purement et simplement partout, et dont il convient de saisir le sens de façon déterminée, en particulier en le distinguant du néant [*Nichts*].—Ce qui se *aufhebt* ne devient pas par là néant. Le néant est l'immédiat; en revanche, un *Aufgehobenes* est quelque chose de médiatisé, c'est le non-étant, mais comme résultat sorti d'un être; il a donc encore en lui la détermité [*Bestimmtheit*] dont il provient. *Aufheben* a dans la langue un double sens qui fait qu'il signifie à la fois quelque chose comme conserver [*aufbewahren*], garder [*erhalten*], et quelque chose comme faire s'arrêter [*aufhören lassen*], mettre fin [*ein Ende machen*]. Le fait de garder inclut déjà en soi le négatif, au sens où quelque chose se trouve soustrait à son immédiateté et ainsi à un être-là [*Dasein*] ouvert aux influences extérieures afin de garder son être-là.—Ainsi le *Aufgehobene* est-il en même temps quelque chose de conservé, à ceci près qu'il a perdu son immédiateté, sans pour autant l'avoir anéantie [*vernichtet*].—Les deux déterminations de l'*Aufheben* données plus haut peuvent d'un point de vue lexical être présentées comme deux significations de ce mot. Pourtant, il faut s'étonner qu'une langue en soit venue à employer un seul et même mot pour deux déterminations opposées. Pour la pensée spéculative, il est réjouissant de trouver dans la langue des mots qui ont en eux-mêmes une signification spéculative; la langue allemande en a plusieurs de cette sorte. Le double sens du latin *tollere* (rendu célèbre par le jeu de mots de Cicéron : *tollendum esse Octavium*) ne va pas aussi loin, la détermination affirmative ne va que jusqu'à l'élévation.)

(Hegel, *Science de la logique* [emphasis in original])

(Remark: The expression "To Sublate." To sublate [*aufheben*], and the *sublated* [*aufgehobene*] (that which exists ideally as a moment), constitute one of the most important notions in philosophy. It is a fundamental determination which repeatedly occurs throughout the whole of philosophy, the meaning of which is to be clearly grasped and especially distinguished from *nothing* [*Nichts*]. What is sublated is not thereby reduced to nothing. Nothing is *immediate*; what is sublated [*aufgehobene*], on the other hand, is the result of *mediation*; it is a non-being but as a *result* which had its origin in a being. It still has, therefore, *in itself* the determinateness [*Bestimmtheit*] *from which it originates*. "*To sublate*" has a twofold meaning in the language: on the one hand it means to preserve [*aufbewahren*], to maintain [*erhalten*], and equally it also means to cause to cease [*aufhören lassen*], to put an end to [*ein Ende machen*]. Even "to preserve" includes a negative element, namely, that something is removed from its immediacy and so from an existence [*Dasein*] which is open to external influences, in order to preserve it. Thus what is sublated [*aufgehobene*] is at the same time preserved; it has only lost its immediacy but is not on that account annihilated [*vernichtet*]. The two definitions of "to sublate" [*aufheben*] which we have given can be quoted as two dictionary *meanings* of this word. But it is certainly remarkable to find that a language has come to use one and the same word for two opposite meanings. It is a delight to speculative thought to find in the language words which have in themselves a speculative meaning; the German language has a number of such. The double meaning of the Latin *tollere* (which has become famous through the Ciceronian pun: *tollendum est Octavium*) does not go so far; its affirmative determination signifies only a lifting-up.)

(Hegel, *Science of Logic*, 1:106–7, trans. A.V. Miller)

By reattaching it to its context, that of the beginning of *The Doctrine of Being*, where being and nothingness, far from being fixed points of reflection, merely pass into one another, and where the becoming that succeeds them in the unfolding of objective logic is not the "unity" of being and nothingness, but rather the very movement of their passage, J.-L. Nancy presents the text in its characteristic *chiaroscuro* (Nancy, *La remarque spéculative*, 107). The difficulty can be summed up this way: the effect of displaying the word, elicited by its particular treatment in a terminological note, is countered on the other side by the absence of any definition or even explanation of *aufheben*, whereas according to Hegel it is a "concept," and moreover, "one of the most important in philosophy." Nonetheless, this concept did not wait for the remark that is devoted to it in the text to act and constitute the operator of the dialectic of being and nothingness, but in a way that is itself difficult to assign. Hegel resorts from the outset to various names for action as substitutes for *aufheben*—*übergehen* (pass into), *auflösen* (dissolve), *verschwinden* (disappear)—each of which raises particular difficulties and does not allow us to determine exactly what *aufheben* is, its nature, and the object on which it operates (ibid., 42–58). Inversely, the explanations given in the Remark are not deducible from what precedes it. For Hegel *aufheben* does not mean "annihilate" (*vernichten*); the operation of *Aufhebung* produces something, a "result" that, in virtue of the very fact that it is a result, is something "mediated" (*ein vermitteltes*). From this, however, one cannot conclude that mediation defines

Aufhebung. Rather the reverse (ibid., 62), just as the recourse to the terms of the dialectic of being and nothingness in the Remark (in particular, the distinction that it makes between what is *aufgehoben* and nothingness, *Nichts*) should not lead us to believe that the concept of *Aufhebung* draws all its resources from this dialectic: if that were the case, it could not "recur everywhere" in philosophy. Thus not only is the meaning of *aufheben* made difficult by the coexistence of two meanings "from the lexical point of view" (in natural language) but the "speculative" sense of the word eludes our grasp even in the texts that are supposed to explain it (ibid., 78) and that reveal themselves instead, as Nancy shows, to be incapable of "following the straight line of a discourse" (ibid., 97).

Thus we can better understand the way the debate has proceeded, its obsession with the word, or rather the name *Aufhebung*, whereas it is the verb that Hegel uses most often (in the table of contents of the *Wissenschaft der Logik*, this Remark is listed under the title "The expression [*Ausdruck*] *aufheben*"). As for the difficulty itself that is dealt with in this discussion, it is simple. The best formulation has been provided by J. Wahl, at a time (1966) when the translators' controversies had not yet obscured the stakes: "It is very difficult to say at once 'abolish and preserve'" (*supprimer et conserver*) (J. Wahl, "Le rôle de A. Koyré," 22).

II. *Aufhebung* between Positivity and Negativity

The first question in the debate can be quite rapidly decided with the help of the Remark on *aufheben* in the *Wissenschaft der Logik*: the latter, by virtue of its very generality and its "disconnection" from any precise context (J.-L. Nancy, *La remarque spéculative*, 66) provides at least a good criterion for evaluating translation proposals. This criterion resides in the affirmation of a *positivity* of the process of *aufheben*, which excludes all translations marked by a negative or destructive meaning. The Remark expressly distinguishes *aufheben* from *vernichten* ("annihilate") and from *Nichts* ("nothingness"): we have seen that what is *aufgehoben* is not abolished but remains or rather becomes something that the text calls "mediated" (*ein vermitteltes*). In the lexical network of the Remark, this definition of *Aufhebung* as a process of mediation draws on another distinction between nothingness (*das Nichts*) and the nonexisting (*das Nichtseiende*): there is no nothingness, there is the nonexistence *of* something, in other words, a determinate nonexistent, and not a void of determination, since nothingness in fact cannot be thought. Mediation and determination are thus the two characteristics of the process of *Aufhebung* and found its positivity.

We can grant that here we are dealing with an exegetical achievement. P.-J. Labarrière has particularly emphasized this: "Such a positivity of the negative in the movement itself of its accomplishment—in the becoming that it engenders—is the most direct meaning of *Aufhebung*" ("Sursumer/sursomption," 107). That is why "all translations that privilege the aspect of negativity—*supprimer, abolir, abroger*—will be deficient from a speculative point of view" (ibid., 109). Labarrière then proposes *sursumer* ("sursume"), following Y. Gauthier, who created this neologism by contrast with the Kantian "subsume": in Kant, "subsuming" is defined as the action of "distinguishing whether something does or does not stand under a given rule (*casus datae legis*)" (*Critique of Pure Reason*, "Analytic of Principles," Introduction, B 171), whereas Hegelian *sursumption* would designate, inversely, "the process of totalizing the part" (Y. Gauthier, "Logique hégélienne," 152n5). It is striking that Emmanuel Martineau's violent polemic against the Labarrière-Jarczyk solution was also waged in the name of the positivity of *aufheben*: to "sursume," which is supposed to persist in "referring to *supprimer* and *surmonter*," or again "the idea of an *eviction* of a less elevated term by a more elevated term" (E. Martineau, "Avertissement," 17), we are asked to prefer *assumer* ("assume"), with the edifying and Marial *assomption* ("assumption") for *Aufhebung*.

It is surely here that the debate about *Aufhebung* in French goes astray, where it unveils the most clearly its strangeness: without realizing it, we have come to debate the nuances of a neologism that should have only those that its inventor gave it. But there is no doubt a reason why, once we have granted the common premise according to which *aufheben* has to be rendered by a verb that brings out its positivity, the competition persisted among proposed translations. *Sursumer* and *relever*, the two main candidates in recent Hegelian literature in French, seem to be of equal value, as do *dépasser* and *assumer*, at least insofar as they do not suggest suppression or annihilation (despite what P.-J. Labarrière says ["Sursumer/sursomption," 116], we do not see what *relever* can add in the way of a negative meaning). On the one hand, however, we have a neologism; on the other, dictionary terms are used, taking greater or lesser liberties with what is supposed to be their definition (notably in the case of *relever*). We must now examine this new dividing line.

III. The Idiomaticity of *Aufheben*: Between Natural Language and Peasant Folklore

The point of departure is twofold: French has no word that means "both 'abolish' and 'preserve'" (J. Wahl), and *aufheben* is a word that is, if not exactly everyday, at least perfectly ordinary in the German vocabulary. But we must also ask: what does it mean to say that this German word means "both 'abolish' and 'preserve'"? The comparison Hegel makes with the Latin *tollere* on the basis of a pun (*Witz*, see INGENIUM) made by Cicero (*Ad familiares*, XI, 20) allows us to illustrate this. *Tollere* means either "raise" (to the highest office) or "eliminate, abolish): the *Witz* proceeds from the fact that Cicero succeeds in making this "second meaning," which is threatening, heard in a passage that is apparently favorable to Octavian ("We must praise this young man, adorn him with all the virtues, *tollere* him"). On the other hand, *aufheben* means both "preserve" and "put an end to," both at the same time and "both at once." The first concern of French translators has been to understand how such a thing is possible. They thus set out to find communicative situations in which *aufheben* has both its meanings simultaneously, without leaving what P.-J. Labarrière calls its "'natural' site" ("Sursumer-sursomption," 105). Hence on the basis of the supposedly idiomatic expression "Konfituren für den Winter aufheben," the now famous example of jam jars and their contents, the fruit is *aufgehoben*, that is, modified "by a form of negation" that "makes it apt to subsist under other conditions than those which were

originally its own" (ibid., 106), that is, the negative preservation of immediacy Hegel talks about in the Remark. A still more pronounced interest in the realities of life outside is to be seen in the *mettre en grange* ("store up") suggested by J.-L. Vieillard-Baron for *aufheben*, in the name of "Hegel's Swabian and peasant background" ("Compte rendu," 217). We could give other examples of the same kind (the Grimm brothers mention the ancient expression *Teller aufheben* ("change plates"): one plate disappears, another is set in its place), while at the same time wondering about the necessity of the operation: in German, *speichern* can mean "save a file to disk," that is, "store," and that usage is just as free of peasant motives as when we say in French that a company has *engrangé bénéfices* (stored up profits). We might also wonder about the widespread fascination with Swabia and its supposed influence on Hegel's intellectual development (and on Heidegger's as well, but Hegel, for his part, rather quickly left his native area). It is true that the region borders on France, and that this allows us to feel more at home. Generally speaking, this tendency to exaggerate rusticity betrays the embarrassment of all translation when confronted by catachreses—that is, metaphors made inaudible because they have been "naturalized" (the legs of a table)—in foreign languages. We can always say "both at once" (but there too . . .) so that the German reader no longer hears the barn and the jam in *aufheben* and that he nonetheless hears them a little bit: who can decide here? Moreover, the problem grows still more complicated when we inquire into the meaning of this naturalization regarding a term concerning which Hegel emphasizes that it provides philosophy—or at least his philosophy—with one of its most important concepts. Hegel's statements concerning the relation between *aufheben* and natural language are in fact ambiguous: astonishment that "a language has come to use one and the same word for two opposed determinations" is not thematized by Hegel (though the expression "auffallend müßte es sein" does not deserve the abundant commentary that J.-L. Nancy devotes to it in *La remarque spéculative*, 72–73: the conditional *müßte*, far from being a marker of ambivalence, is called for by the adjective *auffallend*, which usually requires a modal), except to say that speculative thought finds in it a source of joy ("für das spekulative Denken ist es erfreulich"). The new preface Hegel added, a few days before his death, to the 1831 edition of the *Wissenschaft der Logik* appears to speak of a "joy" (*Freude*) that thought feels in noting the existence of a "speculative spirit of the language [*ein spekulativer Geist der Sprache*]" in words that have the "property . . . of having meanings that are not only different [*verschiedene*] but also opposed [*entgegengesezte*]," as is the case with *aufheben*, which is, moreover, not mentioned here (*Wissenschaft der Logik*, 22). The status of the "speculative spirit of the language" is, however, not clear in either of the two texts (cf. J.-L. Nancy, *La remarque spéculative*, 81, on the undecidable question "of the anteriority—or the interiority—of a similar spirit with respect to the linguistic system"), and it is as though this spirit were scarcely able to attach itself except to words, dispersed here and there by a "stroke of luck" and "good fortune" (ibid., 73) that elicit the thinker's "joy." As for the question as to whether this "joy" is felt in some languages more than in others, it is more difficult than one might at first believe. The 1831 preface does say that the coexistence of opposed meanings in several of its words constitutes a "privilege" of the German language "in comparison with other modern languages," and Hegel seems to authorize only reluctantly the borrowing of "a few words" from foreign languages. However, a few pages further on, the Remark on *aufheben* no longer bears any trace of this praise of the German language. Above all, it defends the maintenance, in the "technical language of philosophy," of "Latin expressions," which Hegel regards as more apt to "recall the reflected" (*das reflektierte*, a Latinism precisely for *das vermittelte* given at the outset), than the "immediacy" of the "native language." That is why, later in the Remark, *Aufhebung* itself, or more exactly its product, what is *aufgehoben*, can be described "in an appropriate manner" with the help of the "Latin" word *Moment* (see MOMENT).

All these hesitations on Hegel's part regarding the privilege of German, the use of everyday language, and the necessity of a philosophical terminology—in a word, regarding what a "speculative meaning" might be (J.-L. Nancy, *La remarque spéculative*, 76)—explain the difficulty of translating *aufheben-Aufhebung* as much and perhaps more than the simple observation of the absence of a word that can mean "both 'abolish' and 'preserve'" in French. We will, in fact, always hesitate between a "technical" translation such as P.-J. Labarrière's *sursumer*, which presents *aufheben* in its character as a "conventional logical operator" (*Présentation de La Doctrine de l'essence* [*Science de la logique*, I, 2], 1976, p. 29), and a translation more anchored in the idiom, such as *relever* or *dépasser*. And with these last two candidates we will still have to choose between the one that is in accord with etymology (*heben* in *aufheben* means "lift," whence *relever*) and something more usual: *dépasser*, for example, a point of view, has become established in the language of argumentation without—and that is what constitutes its interest here—becoming a technical term; but on the other hand, *se relever* for *sich aufheben* is perhaps better than *se dépasser*, with its ethical-ascetic connotation. In other words, it is the definition itself of what we deem "idiomatic" that is at issue in each case here. And it is precisely this that the Hegelian use of *aufheben* puts in question in German itself, that is, in a language that he shakes up by bringing an ordinary term into the realm of philosophical terminology. That is very precisely what he does with *Aufhebung*. There is the *Aufhebung* that shares with other words the privilege of revealing the fertile contradiction of "opposite meanings" in the natural language, and there is the one that Hegel brings into the technical language of philosophy and that is thus associated with the "Latin" *Moment*. The difficulty derives from this duality that French is obliged to transpose onto the lexical level, or rather—to be more Hegelian—from the movement within the word that in French produces two words, the neologism (*sursumer*) and the "ordinary" word, which is always overdetermined (*relever*); for in fact it is the same *aufheben*, but that is what one can show only by referring it immediately to the German. Thus the translators' debate can probably not come to a conclusion, if coming to a conclusion means finding *the* word that "corresponds" to *Aufhebung*, and it can do it all the less insofar as it concentrates, beforehand, on *one* word, *aufheben* or *Aufhebung*. However, by showing that it is the economy of Hegelian discourse that, by the simple fact that *aufheben* deserves a particular comment, is the first to carry out this

transformation of the word into a fetish, we have at the same time shown that the understanding of *Aufhebung* depends on that of a Hegelian philosophy of signification whose difficulties have been well known in France for the past thirty years. The translation of *Aufhebung* is thereby sent back to the explication of Hegel's text: depending on the importance accorded to this type of exercise, this will be regarded as a consolation or a makeshift.

Philippe Büttgen

BIBLIOGRAPHY

Denis, Henri. *Logique hégélienne et systèmes économiques*. Paris: Presses Universitaires de France, 1984.

Derrida, Jacques. *Marges de la philosophie*. Paris: Minuit, 1972. Translation by A. Bass: *Margins of Philosophy*. Chicago: University of Chicago Press, 1982.

Gauthier, Yvon. "Logique hégélienne et formalisation." *Dialogue. Revue canadienne de philosophie* 5, no. 1 (1967): 151–65.

Hamacher, Werner. *Pleroma: Reading in Hegel: The Genesis and Structure of a Dialectical Hermeneutics in Hegel*. Translated by N. Walker and S. Jarvis. London: Athlone Press, 1998.

Hegel, Georg Wilhelm Friedrich. *Fenomenologia dello spirito*. Edited by G. Schulze. Translated by A. Novelli. Naples: Rossi-Romano, 1863.

———. *Fenomenologia dello spirito*. Translated by E. de Negri. Rome: Edizioni di storia e letteratura, 2008.

———. *Heidelberg Writings*. Translated by B. Bowman and A. Speight. Cambridge: Cambridge University Press, 2009.

———. *Phénoménologie de l'Esprit*. Translated by J. Hyppolite. Paris: Aubier-Montaigne, 1939–41.

———. *Phénoménologie de l'Esprit*. Translated by J. P. Lefebvre. Paris: Aubier, 1991.

———. *Phénoménologie de l'Esprit*. Translated by G. Jarczyk and P.-J. Labarrière. Paris: Gallimard / La Pléiade, 1993; reedited Folio, 2002.

———. *The Phenomenology of Mind*. Translated by J. B. Baillie. London: Schwan Sonnenstein, 1910.

———. *The Phenomenology of Spirit*. Translated by A. V. Miller, analysis and foreword by J. N. Findlay. Oxford: Oxford University Press, 1977.

———. *Recension des oeuvres de Jacobi*. Translated by A. Droz. Paris: Vrin, 1976.

———. *Sämtliche Werke*. 20 vols. Stuttgart: F. Frommann, 1957.

———. *Science de la logique*. Translated by Jankélévitch. Paris: Aubier-Montaigne, 1949.

———. *Science de la logique*. Vol. 1 [La logique objective]. Book 1: *L'Être*. Translated by P.-J. Labarrière and G. Jarczyk. Paris: Aubier-Montaigne, 1972.

———. *Science de la logique*. Vol. 1 [La logique objective]. Book 2: *La doctrine de l'Essence*. Translated by P.-J. Labarrière and G. Jarczyk. Paris: Aubier-Montaigne, 1976.

———. *Science de la logique*. "Préface de 1831." Translated by C. Malabou. *Philosophie*, no. 21 (1990): 7–26.

———. *The Science of Logic*. Translated by A. V. Miller. Atlantic Highlands, NJ: Humanities Press International, 1969.

Kirscher, Gilbert. "Compte rendu de *G.W.F. Hegel. Recension des Oeuvres de Jacobi* (trans. A. Droz. Paris: Vrin, 1976)." *Hegel Studien* 13 (1978): 290–91.

Labarrière, Jean-Pierre. "Sursumer/sursomption." In *Hegeliana*, edited by G. Jarczyk and P.-J. Labarrière, 102–20. Paris: Presses Universitaires de France, 1986.

Lefebvre, Jean-Pierre. "Philosophie et philologie: La traduction du vocabulaire philosophique allemand." *Encyclopaedia Universalis, Symposium* (1985): 110–19.

Martineau, Emmanuel. "Avertissement du traducteur." In *La phénoménologie de l'esprit de Hegel*, by Martin Heidegger, 13–23. Paris: Gallimard / La Pléiade, 1984.

Marx, Karl. *Critique of Hegel's Philosophy of Right*. Translated by A. Jolin and J. O'Malley. Cambridge: Cambridge University Press, 1970.

Nancy, Jean-Luc. *La remarque spéculative (un bon mot de Hegel)*. Paris: Galilée, 1973. Translation by C. Surprenant: *The Speculative Remark: One of Hegel's bons mots*. Stanford, CA: Stanford University Press, 2001.

Pinkard, Terry. *Hegel's Phenomenology: The Sociality of Reason*. Cambridge: Cambridge University Press, 1994.

Tilliette, Xavier. "Compte-rendu de G.W.F. Hegel *Science de la logique*, v.1, bk. 1, *L'Etre* (trans. P. J. Labarrière and G. Jarczyk. Paris: Aubier-Montaigne, 1972)." *Archives de philosophie* 36, no. 3 (1973): 513–14.

Vieillard-Baron, Jean-Louis. "Compte-rendu de G.W.F. Hegel *Science de la logique*, v.1, bk. 1, *L'Etre*, ed. de 1812 and v.1, bk. 2, *La doctrine de l'essence* (trans. P. J. Labarrière et G. Jarczyk (Paris: Aubier-Montaigne, 1972 et 1976)." *Hegel-Studien* 12 (1977): 215–19.

Wahl, Jean. "Le rôle de A. Koyré dans le développement des études hégéliennes en France." *Hegel-Studien*, suppl. 3 (Bonn: Bouvier) 1966: 15–26.

| AUTHORITY

"Authority" derives from the Latin *auctoritas*, from *augere* (to grow, increase): the *auctor* is a person who "increases confidence" and is the guarantor, the model, the source, the advisor, the founder, before he becomes the "author" in the modern sense of a writer; see ACTOR, and cf. LAW, PIETAS, *RELIGION*; cf. DOXA. Classically, authority (*auctoritas*) is distinguished from power (*potestas*): it is the modality of human command that has its source in a legitimate order and that, by right, dispenses with both constraint and persuasion. Here we find a significant example of the difficulties that modern and contemporary thought encounters in giving a content to this distinction with the analysis of the notion of *Herrschaft*, which translators of Max Weber sometimes render by "authority" and sometimes by "domination": see HERRSCHAFT; cf. *DOMINATION*.

➤ *DROIT*, *POWER*, PRINCIPLE, *WISDOM*

| AUTRUI

Autrui is the complement of *autre*, from Latin *alter*, which first meant, as the suffix of the comparative shows, "the other of two," "one, the other, the second," like the Greek *heteros* [ἕτερος], whereas *alius*, corresponding to the Greek *allos* [ἄλλος], designates "the other of several," and provides the expression of reciprocity (Lat. *alius, alium*; Gr. *allêlôn* [ἀλλήλων]). On the one hand, the you opposed to an I, an "alter ego" whose distance is to be gauged and whose difference is to be understood; on the other hand, a he or it of some kind, an "other" among others, representing a contingent variation of personal identity. The competition between these two ways of expressing alterity, moreover deriving from a single root differently modulated, exists in numerous European languages (cf. Eng. "other"/"else"), even if the difference in usage is not always easy to trace, both being usually finally rendered in French dictionaries by *autrui*.

1. On the Greek difference *allos/heteros*, and the entirely different "heterogeneous" represented by "barbarian," see TO TRANSLATE, Box 1.
2. On the connection between *alius* and *alienus*, "who belongs to an other [in the juridical sense, *alienare* designates the transfer of the property right], foreign, improper, hostile, disadvantageous," and the more modern sense, even if it is still connected with the juridical acceptation, of *aliéné* as irresponsible and foreign to itself, cf. MADNESS. As the RT: *DHLF* notes, *aliénation* began a new career with Sartre and his translation of *Entfremdung*—from *fremd*, "foreign"—in Hegel and Marx: cf. PRAXIS, SECULARIZATION, and *APPROPRIATION*, PROPERTY.
3. But the choice has been made to take up the whole of the network through the difference in German between *Nebenmensch*, which designates the neutral alterity of other individuals or "neighbors" as opposed to a postulated identical universal, and *Mitmensch*, which expresses a singularity irreducible to the tension between particular and universal and constitutes a modality structuring the relationship of an ego to the world: see MITMENSCH and NEIGHBOR; cf. *IDENTITY*, I/ME/MYSELF, MENSCHHEIT, *PERSON*.
4. In Russian, *drugoj* [другой], the "other," in the sense of "second," *heteros*, is terminologically connected with *drug* [друг], "friend, comrade," in a network of relationships in which friendship and familiar proximity reign (*philia* [φιλία]; see LOVE); see DRUGOJ, and cf. SOBORNOST'.

➤ CONSCIOUSNESS, HEIMAT, WELT

BAROQUE

FRENCH	*baroque*
GERMAN	*Barock* (n.), *barock* (adj.)
ITALIAN	*barocco*
PORTUGUESE	*barroco*

➤ AESTHETICS, ARGUTEZZA, CLASSIC, CONCETTO, GOÛT, MANIERA, NEUZEIT, PORTUGUESE, ROMANTIC

The ease of translating the word "baroque" in European languages, whose corresponding words all come from a common Portuguese root, masks its multiple meanings resulting from successive displacements, contractions, and extensions that do not coincide over the five centuries of its trans-European history.

Derived from a Portuguese jeweler's term, *barocco*, which refers to irregular pearls, the term "baroque" initially had, in the seventeenth century, a pejorative connotation. In late nineteenth-century German art history, "baroque" became a neutral adjective referring to the art of the Late Roman Empire and the post-Renaissance, and was subsequently used, coupled with the word "classic," in various attempts to construct a *Kunstwissenschaft*, a general and trans-historical aesthetics.

But the term's limits fluctuated over time, depending on the country and the domains concerned, leading to a great diversity of contents that intersect with, include, or exclude competing or neighboring notions: mannerism, classicism, rococo. During the last two decades of the twentieth century, "baroque" tended to become, like "Romanesque" or "Gothic," a simple chronological adjective designating the seventeenth century, dislodging the term "classic" in French culture.

A floating signifier, a portmanteau word , "baroque" is thus—depending on the context, the domain, the period, or even the speaker—an antonym or a synonym of "classic," just as it can contain or succeed "mannerism" or "rococo." In many texts, the word could be deleted without any loss of meaning, or be replaced by more precise and less ambiguous terms.

However, the connotations associated with the original figurative sense, which is still alive, the realistic illusion, the nominalist temptation, and the always vigorous post-Hegelian resurgences, can lead to a return of repressed meanings. The step-by-step deconstruction of this linguistic palimpsest is probably the only effective antidote against this babelizing confusion.

I. From the Literal to the Figurative Meaning

In the course of five centuries, the word "baroque" traveled all over Europe. From the literal sense, which is attested in sixteenth-century Portuguese and later passed into French (RT: *Dictionnaire universel*, 1690: "jeweler's term, used only for pearls that are not perfectly round"), derives a figurative sense, "irregular, bizarre, uneven," registered in the 1740 edition of the RT: *Dictionnaire de l'Académie Française*, the only meaning listed in the 1873 RT: *Dictionnaire de la langue*

française by Littré and is still used today. In the context of the French aesthetics, both normative and idealist, of "good taste," the word was used in the eighteenth century in the field of the fine arts to designate, with a pejorative connotation, heterodox, bizarre, or libertine forms: "[B]aroque is everything that does not follow norms and proportions, but only the artist's caprice. In Tintoretto's paintings, there is always something strange and unexpected, there is always something baroque" (RT: *Dictionnaire portatif de peinture, sculpture et gravure*, 1757); "baroque music: music whose harmony is confused, full of modulations and dissonances" (Rousseau, in *L'Encyclopédie*, supplement, 1776). In the RT: *Encyclopédie méthodique, Architecture*, vol. 1 (1788), Quatremer de Quincy uses the term with the same normative meaning:

> *Baroque*, adjective. In architecture, the baroque is a nuance of the bizarre. It is, so to speak, a refinement, or, dare we say, an abuse of the bizarre. . . . Borromini provided the greatest models of bizarreness, Guarini can be considered the master of the baroque.

The word passed into Italian and German, where it was used in the same way, a sign of France's cultural domination in Enlightenment Europe.

This first use of the word "baroque" in artistic aesthetics did not refer specifically, and still less generally, to the art of the seventeenth century; it could be used to describe Gothic ornaments and the painting of Tintoretto or El Greco as well as the architecture of Borromini or Guarini, but never the art of Rubens or Bernini. However, the use of the adjective "baroque" with reference to Guarini's fanciful architecture paved the way for anchoring the word "baroque" in the Italian art of the *Seicento*, just as the monarchical propaganda that claimed that the century of Louis XIV equaled those of Pericles and Augustus anticipated the anchorage of the word "classic" in seventeenth-century French culture.

II. From the Figurative to the Historical Meaning(s)

When the discipline of the history of art was founded in Germany at the end of the nineteenth century, after Romanticism's break with the consensus based on "good taste," the word *barock* was adopted to describe the late phases of ancient Roman art (von Sybel 1888) and the art of the Italian Renaissance (Burckhardt 1855, 1878; Gurlitt 1887). "It has become customary to use the term 'baroque' to describe the style into which the Renaissance resolved itself, or, as it is more commonly expressed, into which the Renaissance degenerated" (H. Wölfflin, *Renaissance und Barok*, trans. K. Simon, *Renaissance and Baroque*). Distinguishing a series of formal criteria that form a system (painterly or "picturesque" style, grand style, effects of mass, movement), Heinrich Wölfflin makes the word lose its pejorative connotation.

For Wölfflin, the baroque, a phenomenon peculiar to the Italian fine arts, covers two centuries, from the Renaissance to neoclassicism: it arose around 1520, arrived at full maturity in 1580, entered into a new phase around 1630, and came to an end about 1750, with the triumph of so-called neoclassical aesthetics (Ger. *Klassizismus*). But during the following century its historical and geographical field of application tends to be both restricted by the emergence or resistance of concurrent notions and extended to other countries and other arts.

The example set by German art historians was soon followed by their foreign colleagues, who also used the word "baroque" to designate Italian art. But some of them extended its field of application to other geographical areas and other arts (Schubert 1908; Novák 1915), and some broadened its formal or cultural bases to the flourishing ornamental art (Weisbach 1924), post-Tridentine art (Weisbach 1921), or the art of absolute rule (Friedrich 1952).

But in France the word collided with the idiomatic usage of the terms *classique* and *classicisme* to designate the art of the seventeenth century, a usage with nationalist connotations, whether these were old, in opposition to Italian taste, or, more recently, in opposition to German scholarship. In Spain, though more discreetly, it collided with other terms, such as *siglo de oro* for a somewhat different period (1550–60), or *churriguerismo*, after the name of the Churriguera family of architects active between 1650 and 1740. Later on, "baroque" interfered with "rococo," used in France and Germany to designate not only decorative art but also, by extension, the architecture, painting, and sculpture of the first half of the eighteenth century: according to some scholars (from Wölfflin to Pevsner), rococo is only a late phase of the baroque; for others (from Kimball to Minguet), it is a specific, entirely different formal system. For the earlier period, the emergence of the notions of mannerism and anti-mannerism in painting (Dvorak 1920; Friedlander 1925), and then in architecture (Wittkower 1934), tended to limit baroque to the second phase that Wölfflin originally distinguished (Revel 1963; Zerner 1972). But some scholars, such as Emil Kaufmann, found in the architecture of the Renaissance, from Brunelleschi to Alberti, the bases of the baroque system of composition by gradation and hierarchy, whose extension then turns out to coincide with that of the "classical language of architecture" defined by John Summerson (*The Classical Language of Architecture*, 1963) or with classicism in the broad sense described by Louis Hautecoeur (*Histoire de l'architecture classique en France*, 1943–67).

The word soon entered the field of music, where it designates a form of music that appeared around 1600 and was characterized by the use of *basso continuo* (Clercx 1948). It was also adopted by literary historians, who applied it to the period from 1560–80 to 1640, and defined it according to thematic or stylistic criteria such as the figures of Circe and the peacock or to the intensive use of metaphor (Mourgues 1953; Rousset 1953). All these shifts and overlappings blurred the initial definition proposed by Wölfflin, but they were masked by other new developments in the area of aesthetics.

III. The Aesthetic Category of the Baroque: Realism or Nominalism

After having defined in 1888 the characteristics of the post -Renaissance baroque style, and in 1899 those of the classical art of the high Italian Renaissance, in 1915 Wölfflin attempted, in his *Principles of Art History*, to define a *Kunstwissenschaft* by generalizing the observations made. He distinguished five pairs of fundamental principles of composition: linear/painterly, plane/recession, closed/open form, multiplicity/unity, clearness/unclearness.

The more abstract nature of these concepts, which is illustrated by examples borrowed not only from Italian art but also from the art of Northern Europe, paved the way for a transhistorical broadening that was already anticipated by the initial double historical anchorage that could easily be completed: the classical art of the fifth century BCE / Hellenistic art; Augustan classicism / flamboyant Gothic; Aemilian classicism / the baroque of Rubens; and the transhistorical generalization of the classic / baroque pair that sacrificed the contents.

This thesis and others like it, connected with philosophical-mystical reveries about cyclical history or binary polarity, were able to delude people. They were supported by a return of the represented initial meaning, and by a reduction of Wölfflin's subtle visual analyses to simplistic binary oppositions that intersected with other oppositions belonging to aesthetics (Apollinian/Dionysian) or to ancient stylistics (Atticism/Asianism), or that were based on elementary distinctions (plain/ornamented, simple/complex). The semantic inflation of the word "baroque" was the source of endless confusion that explains its success. Once the word had been launched, it was thought that the baroque was an essence *ante rem*, and people asked whether this or that work was baroque, forgetting that the baroque had no existence outside the corpus that served to define it. When mannerism is evicted from the field of the baroque or, inversely, when it is made to include the French "grand style" or the German rococo, its meaning changes almost completely. The elaborations on the notion of baroque are as about as pertinent for the history of art and culture as are those that can be made on the signs of the Zodiac for human psychology. Like fauvism (Lebensztejn 1999), the baroque is an ill-founded notion conceived sometimes as a synchrony whose limits are very fluctuating, and sometimes as a diachronic stylistic system whose definition changes with the corpus concerned.

French culture, which had specific reasons for developing the notion of a classical seventeenth century, was the last to resist the European triumph of the baroque, basing itself on certain specific features that were opposed to the baroque in the original, figurative sense of the term. The overcoming of this cultural blockage, of which Michel Butor's novel *La modification* (1957) offers a premonitory novelistic expression, closely followed the signature of the Treaty of Rome and the establishment of the Common Market. Victor Tapié's book *Baroque et classicisme* (1957) no doubt played a major role in the substitution of the word "baroque" for the word "classic" in France. Our generation saw Versailles, which had earlier been considered the masterpiece of French classicism, become the great theater of the baroque, and the Maisons-Lafitte château, a classic example of French architecture, perceived as a baroque orchestration of volumes. As the Italian term *gotico* replaced in the seventeenth century the term "modern" that had been used in the sixteenth century to describe the architecture of French cathedrals, the "Baroque Age" replaced the term

"Classic Age" as French aligned itself with other European languages, and we now commonly speak of the "century of the Baroque" as we speak of the "century of the Enlightenment" in referring to the eighteenth century.

Claude Mignot

BIBLIOGRAPHY

Burckhardt, Jakob. *Der Cicerone*. Bâle, Ger., 1855. Translation by A. H. Clough: *The Cicerone: An Art Guide to Painting in Italy for the Use of Travellers and Students*. New York: Scribner, 1908.

———. *Geschichte der Renaissance in Italien*. Stuttgart: Ebner und Subert, 1878.

Butor, Michel. *La modification*. Paris: Éditions de Minuit, 1957.

Clercx, Suzanne. *Le Baroque et la musique: Essai d'esthétique musicale*. Brussels: Éditions de la Librairie Encyclopédique, 1948.

Dvorak, Max. "Über Greco und den Manierismus." In *Kunstgeschichte als Geistgeschichte*. Munich: n.p., 1924. Essay first published in 1920. Translation by J. Hardy: "On El Greco and Mannerism." In *The History of Art as the History of Ideas*. London: Routledge and Kegan Paul, 1984.

Friedlander, Walter. *Mannerism and Anti-Mannerism in Italian Painting*. New York: Schocken Books, 1965. First German edition published in 1925.

Friedrich, Carl J. *The Age of the Baroque*. New York: Harper, 1952.

Gurlitt, Cornelius. *Geschichte des Barockstiles in Italien*. Stuttgart: n.p., 1887.

Hautecoeur, Louis. *Histoire de l'architecture classique en France*. 6 vols. Paris: Picard, 1943–67.

Kaufmann, Emil. *Architecture in the Age of Reason, Baroque and Postbaroque in England, Italy and France*. Cambridge, MA: Harvard University Press, 1955.

Kimball, Fiske. *The Creation of the Rococo*. Philadelphia: Philadelphia Museum of Art, 1943.

Kurz, Otto. "Barocco: Storia di un concetto." In *Barocco europeo e barocco veneziano*, edited by V. Branca. Florence: Sansoni, 1963.

———. *Manierismo, barocco, rococo, concetti e termini*. Rome, 1960.

Lebensztejn, Jean-Claude. "Sol." In *Annexes de l'oeuvre d'art*. Brussels: La Part de l'Oeil, 1999. Essay first published in 1967.

Minguet, Philippe. *Esthétique du rococo*. Paris: Vrin, 1966.

Mourgues, Odette de. *Metaphysical Baroque and Precieux Poetry*. Oxford: Clarendon Press, 1953.

Novák, Arne. *Praha barokní* [Baroque Prague]. Prague: Manes, 1915.

Ors, Eugenio d'. *Lo barroco*. Madrid: Tecnos, Alianza Editorial, 2002.

Pevsner, Nikolaus. *An Outline of European Architecture*. New York: Penguin Books, 1942.

Revel, Jean-François. "Une invention du vingtième siècle, le maniérisme." *L'Oeil* 31 (1963): 2–14, 63–64.

Rousseau, Jean-Jacques. *Dictionnaire de la musique*. Geneva: Minkoff, 1998. First published by Veuve Duchesne Paris in 1768. Translation by W. Waring: *A Complete Dictionary of Music: Consisting of a Copious Explanation of All Words Necessary to a True Knowledge and Understanding of Music*. New York: AMS Press, 1975. First printed in London for J. French, 1775(?). An electronic version is available at http://archive.org/details/RousseausDictionaryOfMusic (last accessed 17 May 2013).

Rousset, J. *La littérature de l'âge baroque en France*. Paris: Corti, 1953.

Schönberger, Arno, and H. Soehner. *The Age of Rococo*. Translated by D. Woodward. London: Thames and Hudson, 1960.

Schubert, O. *Geschichte des Barocks in Spanien*. Esslingen, Ger.: Neff, 1908.

Summerson, John. *The Classical Language of Architecture*. London: British Broadcasting Corporation, 1963.

Sybel, Ludwig von. *Weltgeschichte der Kunst bis zur Erbauung der Sophienkirche*. Marburg, Ger.: Elwert, 1888.

Tapié, Victor Louis. *Baroque et classicisme*. Paris: Pref. M. Fumaroli Librairie Générale Française, 1980. First published by Plon in 1957. Translation by A. Ross Williamson: *The Age of Grandeur: Baroque and Classicism in Europe*. London: Weidenfeld and Nicolson, 1960.

Weisbach, W. *Der Barock als Kunst des Gegenreformation*. Berlin: P. Cassirer, 1921.

———. *Die Kunst des Barock in Italien, Frankreich, Deutchsland und Spanien*, Berlin: Propyläen, 1924.

Wittkower, Rudolph: "Michelangelo's Biblioteca Laurenziana." *Ars Bulletin* (1934): 123–218.

Wölfflin, Heinrich. *Renaissance und Barok*. Bâle, Ger.: Schwabe und Co., 1888. Translation by Kathrin Simon: *Renaissance and Baroque*. Ithaca, NY: Cornell University Press, 1966.

———. *Kunstgeschichtliche Grundbegriffe*. Bâle, Ger.: Schwabe und Co., 1915. Translation by M. D. Hottinger: *Principles of Art History: The Problem of the Development of Style in Later Art*. New York: Dover Publications, 1950.

Zerner, Henri. "Observations on the Use of the Concept of Mannerism." In *The Meaning of Mannerism*, edited by F. W. Robinson and S. G. Nichols, 107–9. Hanover, NH: University Press of New England, 1972.

▌ BEAUTY

FRENCH	*beauté*
GERMAN	*Schönheit*
GREEK	*kallos* [κάλλος], *kalon* [καλόν]
ITALIAN	*bellezza*
LATIN	*pulchritudo*

➤ AESTHETICS, ART, CLASSIC, DISEGNO, GOÛT, *IMAGE*, LEGGIADRIA, LOVE, MIMÊSIS, PLEASURE, SUBLIME, UTILITY

The words *beauté, beauty, bellezza, kallos* [κάλλος], *pulchritudo*, and *Schönheit* present a twofold difficulty. The first difficulty is conceptual and is inherent in the metaphysics of the beautiful from Plato to Ficino, and in the whole history of aesthetics since the eighteenth century. The concept of the beautiful must satisfy the requirements of universality, necessity, and rationality specific to philosophical reflection, and also adequately designate productions that belong to the artistic domain and are multiple, singular, and without common denominator. The second difficulty has to do with the semantic peculiarities of European languages. For more than a millennium, Greek thinking about the beautiful was understood almost exclusively in Latin. Just as the meaning of the word *mimêsis* [μίμησις] has been reconceived in the term *imitatio*, *kalon* [καλόν] has been reinterpreted through *pulchrum* and has been constantly reinterpreted in the context of new theoretical fields. Whereas *pulchritudo* as understood by Albert the Great and Aquinas assumed a specific comprehension of Aristotle, the same word, as it was understood in the Renaissance, clearly asserted a return to Plato, and especially to the *Symposium*.

The transition to the vernacular language led to new transformations. The mingling of the themes and the frequently Neoplatonic inspiration does not allow us to avoid the play of multiple meanings, contradictions that are intentional and developed in accord with the mode of thought characteristic of the Renaissance. *Bellezza* does not truly render the meaning of *pulchritudo* (any more than it corresponds completely to the meaning of *Schönheit*, which is the philosophical and aesthetic reference point for most contemporary Italian theorists). Moreover, *Schönheit* is itself a very polysemous term. Thus Kant's, Hegel's, and Nietzsche's uses of this term are not only dissimilar but incommensurable.

As for the contemporary desire to reduce the beautiful to an axiological concept, and hence to a question of the logic of value judgments (often in order to disqualify both the beautiful and value), it has ended up making the meaning of the word far more complex and often more obscure, without succeeding in producing positive theoretical results.

I. Metaphysics and Rhetoric: *To Kallos, Pulchritudo*

Theorized by Plato and Neoplatonism, the idea of the beautiful was spread throughout Europe by the Latin language, and this means that *to kalon* [τὸ καλόν] (nominalized adjective, "the beautiful") and *to kallos* [τὸ κάλλος] (geminated noun, "beauty"—Chrysippos created the feminine *kalotês* [καλότης]; see RT: Chantraine, *Dictionnaire étymologique de la langue grecque*, s.v.) were understood through Cicero's writings, just as the work of Plotinus and Proclus were interpreted and disseminated by Marsilio Ficino's commentaries. The theory of art was constructed during the Renaissance within the Latin language and then developed in Italian and French. In the theoreticians of Italian art, *bellezza* refers to a Platonism explicitly inspired by Cicero, that is, to a *kalon* entirely reworked on the basis of *pulchrum*.

A. The metaphysical foundations of the beautiful

Greek thought about the beautiful is subject to three essential orientations: (1) Ethical and metaphysical, through the identification of the beautiful, the true, and the good. The latter was amply developed during the Middle Ages (*Pulchrum perfectum est*). (2) Aesthetic, by privileging the visual domain from the outset. This conception was radicalized and fully developed in Renaissance thought, profoundly influencing the meaning of *pulchritudo* and *bellezza* through the primacy of the eye and vision. (3) Artistic. It was especially the latter meaning that was retained by European culture down to the nineteenth century. But the identification of art with the beautiful, which was extremely ambiguous from the start, has always been a source of problems and logical contradictions that led to its being radically challenged by modern aesthetic thought.

The definition of the word that Socrates attributes to the Sophists no doubt reflects common usage in the fifth century: "*to kalon esti to di' akoês te kai di' opseôs hêdu* [τὸ καλόν ἐστι τὸ δι' ἀκοῆς τε καὶ δι' ὄψεως ἡδύ]" (The beautiful is the pleasure procured by hearing and vision; *Hippias Major*, 298a). But *to kalon* is already a generic term, because the Greek language has more technical terms—such as *summetria* [συμμετρία] (commensurability, proportion) to designate all forms of visible beauty, or *harmonia* [ἁρμονία] (adjustment, harmony) to characterize audible beauty—not to mention a large number of descriptive compounds formed with *eu-* [εὐ] (an adverb that expresses abundance, success, or facility, and that is often rendered by "well"; thus *eueidês* [εὐειδής] designates the beautiful as "beautiful to see," as in the grace of a woman or a warrior, and *euprepês* [εὐπρεπής], "what is appropriate," designates the beautiful as decent, suitable, distinguished, glorious). When Plato uses *kalos*, he is drawing on the multiple meanings of the word, so that the sense of "honest," "just," or "pure" can merge with the properly aesthetic sense of the term.

■ See Box 1.

The polysemy of *kalos* is at the heart of *Hippias Major*, in which several definitions of the beautiful are examined, and all turn out to be unsatisfactory. The distinction between beautiful things and the beautiful is also taken up in the *Symposium*, but in a quite different way. The ascending dialectic

---

1

Beautiful and good: *Kalos kagathos*

➤ VIRTÙ

In Homer, the adjective *kalos* [καλός] already designates both what we call physical beauty (Polyphemus tells Ulysses, who has blinded him: "I was expecting a tall, handsome mortal [*megan kai kalon* (μέγαν καὶ καλὸν)]"; *Odyssey*, 9.513) and what we call moral beauty (the swineherd Eumaeus speaking to the suitor who refuses to give Ulysses something to eat because he is dressed in beggar's garb: "What you say is not handsome for a noble [*ou men kala kai esthlos eôn agoreueis* (οὐ μὲν καλὰ καὶ ἐσθλὸς ἐὼν ἀγορεύεις)]"; ibid., 18.381). It is opposed to *aischros* [αἰσχρός], which, like French *vilain*, designates both the ugly, the graceless, the deformed, and the vile, shameful, and dishonorable.

This synergy between the beauty of the body and the beauty of the soul, the inside and the outside, is manifest in the phrase *kalos kagathos* [καλὸς κἀγαθός], which designates a kind of excellence (Xenophon, *Cyropedia*, 4.3.23) that ranges from birth to actions (ibid., 1.5.9) and determines and sums up all the others (RT: LSJ, quoting Herodotus, 1.30, explains that the term "denotes a perfect gentleman." The portmanteau-words formed in the same way, such as *kalokagatheô* [καλονἀγαθέω] and *kalokagathia* [καλονἀγαθία] are part of this same conjunction, which could be called "social," of nature, ethics, and politics; thus in Aristotle nobility or magnanimity (*megalopsuchia* [μεγαλοψυχία]) "is impossible without *kalokagathia* [perfect virtue]" (*Nichomachean Ethics*, 4.71124a; cf. 10.10.1179b 10). Moreover, Aristotle notes, "we may ask about the natural ruler, and the natural subject, whether they have the same or different virtues. For if a noble nature [*kalokagathia*] is equally required in both, why should one of them always rule, and the other always be ruled?" (*Politics* 1.13.1259b 34–36). In turn, *agathos* [ἀγαθός], in opposition to *kakos* [κακός] (bad, mean, cowardly), designates both physical valor, the warrior's bravery, and nobility of birth and behavior: in each case, the outside testifies to the inside, and the inside manifests itself outside.

We can understand why Socrates serves as a counter-model here, since he is an *agalma* [ἄγαλμα], one of the hollow statues given to the gods, an ugly bearded Silenus on the outside and bearing treasures on the inside (Plato, *Symposium*, 216d–e). And we can also see why Nietzsche interprets Platonism, which makes the body the tomb of the soul, as quintessentially anti-Greek: unlike Plato, the Greeks believed in "the whole Olympus of appearance. Those Greeks were superficial— *out of profundity*" (preface to *The Gay Science*).

Barbara Cassin

BIBLIOGRAPHY

Aristotle. *Politics*. Translated by B. Jowett. In *Basic Works of Aristotle*, edited by R. Mckeon. New York: Random House, 1941.

Nietzsche, Friedrich. *The Gay Science*. Translated by W. Kaufmann. Includes "Nietzsche's Preface for the Second Edition" of the original work published in German in 1887. New York: Random House, 1974.

of love rises from the beauty of bodies to that of souls, discourses, actions, and laws, then to the beauty of sciences, and finally attains the beautiful in itself (*auto to kalon* [αὐτὸ τὸ καλὸν]; 211d), the reality that "is the same on every hand [*têi men kalon, têi d'aischron* (τῇ μὲν καλόν, τῇ δ' αἰσχρόν)], the same then as now, here as there, this way as that way, the same to every worshiper as it is to every other," and that is not "something that exists in something else, such as a living creature, or the earth, or the heavens, or anything that is" (211a–b). In addition to this distinction between relative beauties and absolute beauty, Plato repeatedly makes another between the diverse forms of visible beauties, between living bodies, between paintings and geometrical figures, as in the *Philebus*:

> The beauty of figures [*schêmatôn te gar kallos* (σχημάτων τε γὰρ κάλλος)] which I am now trying to indicate is not what most people would understand as such, not the beauty of a living creature or a picture [*ê zôiôn ê tinôn zôgraphêmatôn* (ἢ ζῴων ἤ τινων ζωγραφημάτων)]; what I mean, what the argument points to, is something straight, or round [*euthu ti . . . kai peripheres* (εὐθύ τι . . . καὶ περιφερὲς)], and the surfaces and solids which a lathe, or a carpenter's rule and square, produces from the straight and round.
>
> (*Philebus*, 51c)

Without lingering over the Pythagorean heritage of these geometrical ideas, we must at least recall that the sense of the beauty of forms is inseparable here from their purity, which arises from abstraction from forms perceivable through the senses. The Sophists' sensualist and relativist position, which emphasizes the subjectivity of perception connected with the infinite variety of colors and sensible forms, is opposed to Pythagorean philosophy and its aesthetic of numbers. Although Plato's thought tends toward the latter conception, that does not mean that sensible qualities, colors, precious metals are absolutely without value: it is simply that they participate in a profoundly degraded world that is absorbed in the sensible. In the cosmological myth with which the *Phaedo* ends, the colors of the "real earth," that of the ethereal heights, are described, as "more brilliant and more pure" (*lamproterôn kai katharôterôn* [λαμπροτέρων καὶ καθαρωτέρων]), to the point that this brilliance lends their variegated colors a unity of aspect, of "idea" (*eidos* [εἶδος]):

> There the whole earth is made up of such colors and others far brighter and purer still. One section is a marvelously beautiful [*thaumastên to kallos* (θαυμαστὴν τὸ κάλλος)] purple, and another is golden. All that is white of it is whiter than chalk or snow, and the rest is similarly made up of the other colors, still more and lovelier [*pleionôn kai kallionôn* (πλειόνων καὶ καλλιόνων)] than those which we have seen. Even these very hollows in the earth . . . assume a kind of color as they gleam [*chrômatos ti eidos . . . stilbonta* (χρώματός τι εἶδος . . . στίλβοντα)] amid the different hues around them, so that there appears to be one continuous surface of varied colors.
>
> (*Phaedo*, 110c)

In the myth in the *Phaedrus*, it is in the space of the beyond, that of heaven, that we could contemplate the truth in all its brilliance: "It is there that true being dwells, without color or shape, that cannot be touched" (*hê gar achrômatos te kai aschêmatistos kai anaphês ousia antôs ousa* [ἡ γὰρ ἀχρώματός τε καὶ ἀσχημάτιστος καὶ ἀναφὴς]; 247c), and where "Beauty was ours to see in all its brightness" (*kallos de tot' ên idein lampron* [κάλλος δὲ τότ' ἦν ἰδεῖν λαμπρόν]; 250b), "most manifest to sense and most lovely of them all" (*stilbon enargestata* [στίλβον ἐναργέστατα]; 250d). Clearly, it is by analogy with the intelligible world that the purest figures acquire meaning.

Renaissance philosophers like Ficino and Bruno and the theoreticians of art all thought they were being faithful to the Platonic conception of the beautiful by exemplifying it in symbolic and allegorical representations. In the Renaissance, the theory of art was based on the paradox that consists in sometimes eclipsing, sometimes underestimating the intellectual primacy of the beautiful to the benefit of an analogical procedure constituted by sensible images, from the perfect proportions of geometrical figures to pure colors. The cult of Plato in the fifteenth and sixteenth centuries gave rise to an interpretation of *to kallos* that was all the more important because it continued to spread until the nineteenth century: the *eidos* was gradually transformed into an ideal, and while the purity of geometrical figures has a major paradigmatic value, it does so in the function of the "golden number" and in relation to the Pythagorean heritage. When Marsilio Ficino writes, "Amor enim fruende pulchritudinis desiderium est. Pulchritudo autem splendor quidam est, humanum ad se rapiens" (For love is in fact a desire to enjoy beauty. But beauty is the splendor that attracts the human soul to itself), or again, "Praeterea rationalis anima proxime pendet ex mente divina et pulchritudinis ideam sibi illice impressam servat intus" (In addition, the rational soul is closely dependent on the divine mind and preserves in itself the idea of the beauty that the latter has imprinted upon it; *Plotini Enneadis* 1.66, in *Opera omnia*), his definition of beauty is incontestably Platonic in inspiration. But here *pulchritudo* is not equivalent to *to kallos*. In Ficino, as in many philosophers of the Renaissance, the meaning of *pulchritudo* is all the more difficult to determine because beneath its apparent unity it is deeply conditioned by a syncretism that juxtaposes Plato, Plotinus, Jamblichus, Hermes Trismegistus, and Dionysius the Areopagite. Although the conception according to which love is the necessary mediator for gaining access to the beautiful remains in conformity with Platonic thought, the idea that terrestrial beauties reflect heavenly splendor owes much more to Plotinus than to Plato.

■ See Box 2.

When a Platonist like the artist and theoretician Lorenzo Ghiberti writes in his *Commentarii* (c. 1450): "La proportionalità solamente fa pulchritudine" (Proportionality alone makes beauty), proportion is surely one of the essential attributes of the beautiful, even its essence, but it is not determined by reference to Plato's theory of solid bodies: in reality, it is borrowed from Vitruvius's *De architectura* (first century BCE). Heir to Greek theories of architecture, Vitruvius's aesthetic thought is centered on the concepts of *diathesis*

2

The beautiful as participation in light and interiority: Plotinus

➤ LIGHT

Without breaking with the ancient heritage, Plotinus's philosophy developed a reflection on the beautiful, on *mimêsis* [μίμησις], and art that made it possible for the first time to harmonize the requirements of a metaphysics of the beautiful with those of a philosophy of art.

For Plotinus, in contrast to Plato, the world of ideas is not separate from the visible world; radiant with the purest light, it participates in earthly realities through the mediation of the cosmic order. The divine light spreads over the world and truly gives form to chaotic, formless matter. The consequences are important: Plotinus does not deny that a stone or a tree can be beautiful, but they are beautiful only to the extent that they participate in light. In the material, corporeal order, nothing can be absolutely beautiful if the divine light does not exercise its action in giving form to everything. The other aspect that opposes Plotinus's thought to Plato's on the subject of the beautiful concerns the relations between the idea of the beautiful and the existence of art. For Plotinus, art is a mode of knowledge, and even of metaphysical knowledge insofar as it helps us come closer to the One. The main principle that defines the reality of a work of art is no longer *mimêsis*, doomed as it is to be a skilled and empty reproduction of earthly realities, but rather participation (*methexis* [μέθεξις]), now conceived as the cause of artistic activity. Artists are creative, not because they reproduce the forms of reality, even in accord with perfect proportions and harmony, but because they refer to an internal form within their minds. We must add that this internal

form is not the expression of a creative subjectivity but the reflection of an ideal model of beauty (*archetupon* [ἀρχέτυπον]). In other words, this Neoplatonic metaphysics opened up perspectives that were crucial for thinking about art and the beautiful in the Middle Ages. It was to dominate reflection on art during the Renaissance and continue to be productive until the advent of German idealism and European romanticism.

Plotinus's critique of the idea of proportion was just as innovative and original. If proportion and symmetry are in fact beautiful, they are not beautiful as such, but to the extent to which they have their origin in an internal, ideal, and spiritual form. Then the classical theory of the beautiful, proceeding from harmony and proportion—that is, the conception that the whole of antiquity had developed as an immutable axiom—suddenly found itself transformed from top to bottom. This meant in particular that any realism, any objectivism of the beautiful was rejected in favor of a more spiritual conception: "Again, since the one face, constant in symmetry, appears sometimes fair and sometimes not, can we doubt that beauty is something more than symmetry, that symmetry itself owes its beauty to a remoter principle?" (*Enneads* 1.6.1). Though determinant for the existence of the beautiful, proportion and harmony are not measurable quantities but qualities that can be completely perceptible only through the purifying activity of the inner eye and after a specific kind of ascetic practice. That is why in Plotinus the word *kallos* does not designate a property belonging specifically to a determinate form but indicates a participation in

the intelligible, even if it is apprehended in the contemplation of an imperfect being occupying a modest place in the hierarchy of terrestrial things. Having as its goal the world of ideas and the intelligible, the experience of the beautiful implies the conversion of the whole being with a view to a wholly internal perfection: "Withdraw into yourself and look. And if you do not find yourself beautiful yet, act as does the creator of a statue that is to be made beautiful: he cuts away here, he smoothes there, he makes this line lighter, this other purer, until a lovely face has grown upon his work" (*Enneads*, 1.6.9). From that point on, the experience of the beautiful merges with a metaphysical experience, so that the word "beautiful" applied to an object is meaningful only with a considerable extension that implies for the philosopher another way of life and what Pierre Hadot called a spiritual exercise.

BIBLIOGRAPHY

Bourbon di Petrella, Fiametta. *Il problema dell'arte et della belleza in Plotino*. Florence: Le Monnier, 1956.

Hadot, Pierre. *Philosophy as a Way of Life: Spiritual Exercises from Socrates and Foucault*. Edited by A. Davidson. Translated by M. Chase. Oxford: Blackwell, 1995.

———. *Plotinus, or the Simplicity of Vision*. Translated by M. Chase. Chicago: University of Chicago Press, 2008.

O'Meara, Dominic. *Plotinus: An Introduction to the "Enneads."* Oxford: Clarendon Press; New York: Oxford University Press, 1993.

Plotinus. *Enneads*. Translated by S. MacKenna. Burdett, NY: Larson, 2004.

[διάθεσις] (the charm that arises from the composition of the parts), *euruthmia* [εὐρυθμία], and *summetria* (the agreement between the parts and the work as a whole). Despite their more or less overt Platonism, these determinations of the beautiful are relatively foreign to the speculations in the *Philebus* or the *Timaeus*. But from the Middle Ages and the Renaissance on, they were so closely related to the concept of the beautiful, to its *idea* [ἰδέα], that down to the nineteenth century most theoreticians adopted them as such, though in each case they had to analyze and justify them and ground them in the body of a doctrine. Thus Hegel still defines them as categories constitutive of the beauty of abstract form. As transmitted by Vitruvius, *pulchritudo* claims to restitute all the meanings of *kallos*, and it is in relation to the Latin word that later authors were able to Platonize regarding the ideas of proportion, symmetry, and harmony as specific conditions of the beautiful.

B. The exclusive reign of *pulchritudo*

In reality, from antiquity to the eighteenth century, and even into the nineteenth century, the Platonic idea of the beautiful was often given as a supreme aesthetic argument only to make it say something else, indeed the contrary of what it actually said. One of the most famous authors of this philosophical inversion to the benefit of a conception of art was Cicero, the true father of the theory of art. In *De finibus*, Cicero writes: "Et quoniam haec deducuntur de corpore, quid est cur non recte pulchritudo etiam ipsa propter se expedanta ducatur?" (And since all that belongs to the corporal domain, why shouldn't we consider that beauty deserves to be sought for itself?; 5.47). What does *pulchritudo* mean here? The word implies the twofold meaning of an achieved and perfect corporal beauty—which it expresses more strongly than the term *forma*—and a sort of moral excellence close to the Greek *kalos kagathos*. But the specifically aesthetic sense appears clearly in a passage in *De natura deorum* where Cicero sets forth the Stoic cosmology: what occupies the soul of the world more than anything else, he writes, "is first of all that the world be made as well as possible to last, and then that it lack nothing, and especially that it have within it an eminent beauty [*eximia pulchritudo*] and all ornaments [*omnis ornatus*]" (2.22) (that is the meaning of *kosmos* [κόσμος]; see *WORLD*). Despite their semantic position in Latin, *pulchrum* and *pulchritudo*, unlike *forma, venustus, elegans*, and, naturally, *bellus*, were not taken over into the vocabularies of Romance languages. Nonetheless, it was *pulchrum* that, in classical Latin, was deemed most apt to render the universality and abstract rigor of the idea of the beautiful. In a famous passage in *De oratore*, Cicero defines the beautiful as an ideal:

> [T]here is no human production of any kind, so compleatly beautiful [*tampulchrum*], than which there is not a something still more beautiful, from which the other is copied like a portrait from real life, and which can be discerned neither by our eyes nor ears, nor any of our bodily senses, but is visible only to thought and imagination [*cogitatione tantum et mente complectimur*]. Though the statues, therefore, of Phidias, and the other images above-mentioned, are all so wonderfully charming, that nothing can be found which is more excellent of the kind; we may still, however, suppose a something which is more exquisite, and more compleat [*cogitare tamen possumus pulchriora*]. For it must not be thought that the ingenious artist, when he was sketching out the form of a Jupiter, or a Minerva, borrowed the likeness from any particular object;—but a certain admirable semblance of beauty [*species pulchritudinis eximiae*] was present to his mind [*mente*], which he viewed and dwelt upon, and by which his skill and his hand were guided.

> (*Orator*, 2.7)

Despite its obvious contradiction of Plato's thought, the adulteration of *kallos* by *pulchrum* is crucial, because it was to acquire authority and become a reference point for seventeenth-century theoreticians of art and even for the founder of aesthetics, Baumgarten. By identifying the Platonic idea of the beautiful, the *to kallos*, with the ideal of the beautiful, that is, with a sort of interior model, Cicero gave *pulchrum* a new meaning. From then on, the separation of the beautiful from the mimetic arts that Platonic metaphysics maintained was in large measure surmounted. It no longer subsisted except in Scholastic thought and in Ficino and Nifo.

The meaning of *pulchrum* in Aquinas is determined first of all by his effort to resolve the problems raised by the antagonistic conceptions within Scholastic thought, namely, the realism of Platonic theories and the persistent subjectivism in aesthetic reflection, and especially the various orders in accord with which the word is used: the ontological or metaphysical order, the logical order, the anthropological order, and finally the specifically aesthetic order. Insofar as it assumes a proportional relation between matter and form, *pulchrum* has an ontological status that is inseparable from the structure of reality. Moreover, this conception explicitly excludes any idealist or subjectivist orientation, but this does not mean that aesthetic subjectivity, in the sense of sensual delight in the perception of the object, is rejected:

> Unde pulchrum in debita proportione consistit: quia sensu delectatur in rebus debite proportionatis, sicut in sibi similibus; nam et sensus ratio quaedam est, et omnis virtus cognoscitiva.

> (Hence beauty consists in due proportion; for the senses delight in things duly proportioned, as in what is after their own kind—because even sense is a sort of reason, just as is every cognitive faculty.)

> (Thomas Aquinas, *Summa theologica*)

The peculiar feature of *pulchrum* is that it implies an act of knowing, that is, an effort of judgment to understand the objective aesthetic properties inherent in the structure of reality and the world. *Pulchrum* means intellectual comprehension, including through the senses. Furthermore, qua transcendental, the beautiful possesses what Aquinas calls three properties: *integritas sive perfectio, proportio sive consonantia*, and *claritas*. These properties constitute the most durable meaning of the classical ideal in the arts and determined for a long time the most general categories of aesthetics. But whatever the ulterior meanings of *pulchrum* and *pulchritudo* as "transcendental" might be in Scholastic writers, or as "idea" in the theoreticians of the Renaissance, the words designating beauty in Romance languages remain profoundly marked by the contribution of ancient metaphysics and rhetoric.

II. *Bellezza* in Renaissance Theories of Art

It was by implicitly opposing this metaphysics that Alberti and Leonardo sought to construct the idea of beauty on the basis of a system of rules that had a completely autonomous theoretical value. Among the Renaissance theoreticians, *bellezza* is certainly not a translation of *pulchritudo*. But the considerable effort they made to transfer to the theories of art the theories of light and the Neoplatonic contemplation of the intelligible gave *bellezza* a more intellectual cast that deliberately exalted the primacy of vision, so that *bellezza* surely had a more visual meaning than *beau* or especially *Schönheit* were to have. In reality, contrary to *pulchritudo*, which was almost always used to express a metaphysical idea, even in the field of rhetoric, *bellezza* had to satisfy several contradictory requirements: it had to conform to the *idea* as a superior authority; it had to be realized in the work as an ideal system of proportions and measures, while at the same time exploiting the totality of the forms offered by empirical reality; and, finally, by basing itself on artistic rules set a priori and the actual practice of art, it showed that the work was a second creation of nature, a *natura naturans*, analogous to divine beauty. The word thus crystallized a set of tensions and aspirations that are often incompatible, at the risk of sometimes becoming almost unintelligible. Ficino's cherished idea that beauty is by essence distant from corporeal matter could not be accepted by Alberti and Leonardo, because measure, proportion, and harmony must imperatively be objectified in a perfect work.

■ See Box 3.

3

Bellezza and *vaghezza*

A comparison of the two versions in which Alberti published his own treatise, one in Latin, the other in Italian, allows us to grasp the transformations introduced by the transition to the vernacular. In *De pictura* (bk. 3), Alberti writes regarding the painter Demetrius:

> At ex partibus omnibus non modo similitudinem rerum, verum etiam in primis ipsam pulchritudinem diligat. Nam est pulchritudo in pictura res non minus grata quam expetita. (Let him seek in all parts not only the resemblance of things, but first of all beauty itself. For in painting beauty is no less pleasant than sought.)

The same injunction is expressed in *Della pittura*:

> Edi tutte le parti li piacerà non solo renderne similitudine, ma piu edgiugniervi bellezza; pero che nella pittura la vaghezza non meno è grata che richiesta. (It will please him not only to render all the elements with resemblance, but to add beauty to them; for in painting grace is pleasant as well as required.)

Whereas the Latin uses the same term (*pulchritudinem, pulchritudo*), the Italian resorts to two different words, *bellezza* and then *vaghezza*, the latter of which Spencer, in his English edition of the Italian treatise, translates as "loveliness" (*On Painting*).

Vaghezza is derived from the Latin *vagus*, which means "vague, indeterminate." But it also takes on a positive sense, that of an indefinite charm that is closer to the idea of grace than to that of beauty. It is distinguished from *bellezza*, whose meaning here almost coincides with that of the Latin *concinnitas*, which is used in particular to designate the symmetry and harmony of a discourse (some philologists derive *concinnitas* from the adjective *concinnus*, which means "well-proportioned," while others derive it from the verb *concinnare*, which means "organize, arrange, prepare"). Correggio's figures, and of course the *Mona Lisa*, are the pictorial paradigms of *vaghezza*, whereas the plastic perfection of Raphael's madonnas corresponds very closely to the idea of *bellezza*.

BIBLIOGRAPHY

Alberti, Leon Battista. *De pictura*. 1435. *Della pittura*. 1436. Edited by C. Grayson. Rome: Laterza, 1975.

———. *On Painting*. Edited and translated by J. R. Spencer. New Haven, CT: Yale University Press, 1956.

The *idea della bellezza* remains a metaphysical authority that is recognized as immanent to the artist's consciousness, but becomes intelligible only in the sovereignty of the *regola*. The proper application of the systems of relations and measures that constitute proportion thus becomes an a priori condition, necessary and sufficient, for the accomplishment of the work. As Francesco Scannelli puts it:

> The beauty [*bellezza*] we desire so much is only a reflection of the supreme light, a sort of divine emanation, and it seems to me to be constituted by a harmonious equilibrium of the parts [*buona simmetria di parti*] combined with sweetness [*suavità*] of colors that represent on Earth the relics and promises of heavenly, immortal life.

> (*Microcosmo della pittura*)

Scannelli's definition sums up all the goals of the classical ideal, but it was already anachronistic in the seventeenth century. The teleology of the "simmetria di parti," which had reigned from the Pythagoreans to the Renaissance, the conception of the beautiful as a reflection of heavenly life that was still vigorously defended by Bellori and Poussin, was henceforth threatened. Ficino, Bruno, and the theoreticians of mannerism had already adopted the critique of proportion and, ultimately, of rules that is found in Plotinus. The appearance of taste as a new criterion, of genius, of the diversity of rules, ultimately destabilized the balance of the classical theory of the beautiful, as is shown by the first lines of Crousaz's *Traité du beau*, published in 1715: "There are no doubt few terms that people use more often than 'beautiful,' and yet nothing is less determinate than its meaning, nothing is more vague than its idea."

III. The Process of Subjectivizing the Beautiful: From the Artistic to the Aesthetic

A. *Beau* and *beauté*: Attempts to synthesize the heterogeneous

Before the eighteenth century, the French word *beau* was seldom nominalized, and its semantic diversity, which was very evident in the use of the adjective, was often foreign to any aesthetic preoccupation. In any case, in expressions such as *le beau monde* (high society) and *le bel esprit* (wit), the word expresses a certain idea of perfection and sometimes a nuance of irony. Moreover, compared with Italian, it is much more distant from any metaphysical or theological reference.

It is particularly striking that *beau* has virtually no philosophical content and often tends to be no more than a predicate or even a neutral reference. The word appears in Mersenne in its most abstract usage: "To be sure, it is difficult to find or to imagine anything in the world that is more beautiful than light, since it seems that the beauty of all things depends on it" (*Questions inouyes*). The Neoplatonic connotation of the word is very meager here and depends on a relatively conventional usage. In a letter to Mersenne, Descartes writes:

> Regarding your question whether the reason for the beautiful can be established, it is the same as if you were to ask in advance why one sound is more pleasant than another, if not because the word "beautiful" seems to be more particularly related to the sense of sight. But in general neither the beautiful nor the pleasant signify anything more than a relationship between our judgment and the object; and because human judgments are

so different, we cannot say that either the beautiful or the pleasant have a determinate measure.

(18 March 1630, in *Œuvres*)

In other words, judgments regarding the beautiful are no more than the expression of a person, a subjective preference, and thus cannot be the object of any philosophical discussion. Spinoza is just as explicit when he writes that beauty (*pulchritudo*) "is not so much a quality of the object beheld as an effect [*effectus*] in him who beholds it," narrowly determined by our condition and temperament (letter to Hugo Boxel, 1674). From Descartes to Voltaire, philosophical rationalism tends to make judgments regarding the beautiful, and to make the beautiful itself a product of subjectivity; and this subjectivity necessarily gives rise to an infinite relativism that destroys not only any possible objectivity of the beautiful, but also reduces it to the status of an illusion. In the seventeenth century, even before the birth of aesthetics as a philosophical discipline, the latter's most essential concept was thus already largely invalidated in the name of philosophical rationality.

The first consequence of this is that the intelligibility of the beautiful can no longer be determined by philosophical reflection, and that it will, as it were, move into the field of the theory of art and the nascent art criticism. The word *beau* survives in its essential attributes and its metonymic determinations, namely, perfection, form, and systems of proportion. If the beautiful can no longer be conceived as transcendental in the Scholastic sense, as an idea to which the artist's thought conforms, then it has to be defined in the immanence of the experience of art. Whether it is a matter of the creator or the spectator, each party is obliged to reflect on the criteria of the beautiful as they are given by proportion, harmony, and perfection, that is, in a perceptive experience that necessarily disqualifies a priori reasoning and deductive procedures. Only the exemplarity of the perfection of a picture, a poem, or a work of architecture allows us to verify positively the well-foundedness of the rules, so that the idea of a rule without possible reference, determined a priori as in the Italian theoreticians, is henceforth excluded. But this immanence implied by the attention given to rules and to the ideality of the great models in the relationship to works of art does not imply any kind of realism with regard to artistic properties. The idea that an artistic and aesthetic quality might subsist as a real property inherent in the object, independently of the application of the rule and the exercise of judgment, now appears highly problematic. Even Nicole, who was nonetheless determined to restore the beautiful in as rational a manner as possible, rejects any kind of objectivism and sees no solution other than in a logic of judgment. Humans, he writes, must "form an idea of the beautiful that can serve them as a rule in making judgments" (*Traité de la beauté des ouvrages de l'esprit*). Nicole's precept is based on a theoretical demand that has become exorbitant, namely, the identification of the beautiful and the true, and the primacy of the understanding in the exercise of judgment, so that the theoretical solution he proposes is in real danger of becoming a new source of problems. A demand for the universality of systems of artistic rules was gradually substituted for the universality of the idea of the beautiful. Basing themselves on the rejection of a

purely speculative and thus metaphysical procedure, theoreticians sought nothing less than to reconcile the singularity of the rule of art—modifiable in each of its applications—with the right to aesthetic universality.

■ See Box 4.

If the beautiful could be thus reactivated despite the philosophical crisis of which it was the object, it was by virtue of the intervention of an institutional discourse, that of the Académie de Peinture et de Sculpture, founded in 1648, one of whose functions was to produce artistic and aesthetic categories. Nevertheless, a solution in accord with the requirements of rationalism awaited its theoretician. It was for Boileau to realize this program corresponding to the horizon of expectations elicited by the classical doctrine. He gave the word *beau* a new meaning that was to be decisive for the subsequent development of eighteenth-century aesthetic thought: "Nothing is beautiful except the True, the True alone is pleasing" (*Épître IX*). The truth that must be at the heart of art's beauty is not at all the expression of good sense or of a vague common sense, but rather what the artist's genius should aim at insofar as its goal is to reach the point where reason and beauty, truth and nature, are one. The genius of art is thus to achieve a synthesis of these heterogeneous givens. The overproduction of metaphors, patent in Spain and Italy, was incapable of producing this synthesis because it transgressed the order of nature, and thus of the true, to the advantage of the imagination alone. But although Boileau conceived the beautiful as a diversity of authorities (nature, truth, a rational order) in the unity of the concept, he did not yet see the countless relations that constantly threaten the word's univocal meaning. At the beginning of the eighteenth century, Crousaz formulated the central difficulty that was to confront aesthetics:

> When we ask what the *Beau* is, we are not talking about an object that exists outside us, separate from any other, as we do when we ask what a Horse is, or what a Tree is. A Tree is a Tree, a Horse is a Horse, it is what it is absolutely, in itself, and without any necessity of comparing it with any of the other parts that the Universe contains. This is not the case with *Beauté*; this term is not absolute, but expresses the relationship of objects that we call beautiful with our ideas, or with our feelings, our intellectual abilities, our heart or, finally, with other objects that are different from us. So that to determine the idea of Beauty, we have to determine and examine in detail the relations to which we attach this name.

(*Traité du beau*)

In asserting that the concept of the beautiful is intelligible only through the analysis of a plurality of relations and determinations, Crousaz initiated a process that in the long run threatened to empty the notion of any productive content. In reality, reflections on the word *beau* clearly indicate a process of subjectivization based on psychological considerations. What does *beau* mean? For Abbé Trublet, "We say that anything that pleases us is beautiful, when the feeling of pleasure, although it is received by some bodily organ, is in the mind itself and not in that organ" (*Essais sur divers sujets*). For Voltaire, the subjectivity of the feeling of pleasure

4

Beauty and grace

The specificity of the theory of art, as it developed in the second half of the seventeenth century in France, resides in the will to overcome this tension between an ideality based on rules and an artistic perfection shown by works and empirical practices. Whence the temptation to deviate from purely rational principles and to derive the beautiful from proportion and symmetry as inherent, objective properties of the work, as for example Félibien does when he distinguishes between beauty and grace:

Beauty arises from the proportion and symmetry that is found between the corporeal and material parts. And grace arises from the uniformity of internal movements caused by the affections and feelings of the soul. Thus when there is only a symmetry of the corporeal parts with one another, the resulting beauty is a beauty without grace. But when in addition to this beautiful proportion we see a relationship and a harmony of all the internal movements, which not only unite with the other parts of the body but animate them and make them act with a certain accord and a very exact and uniform cadence, then it engenders the grace that we admire in the most accomplished persons, and without it the most beautiful proportion of the members has not achieved its ultimate perfection.

(*Entretien* no. 1)

As manifested in a beautiful body or in a work of art, proportion and symmetry are constitutive of beauty, but of an abstract, normative, and inanimate beauty. Grace, on the other hand, is inseparable from what seventeenth-century art theorists call "expression," namely, the body's actions that make the movements of the soul visible. Far from being one quality among others, expression is that through which beauty acts on the spectator, touches and moves him or her. That is why it is an essential part of the painter's and sculptor's art. In this sense, we can define grace as the soul of beauty, the beauty of beauty. It consists, Félibien says, in a *je ne sais quoi* "that one cannot well express," and that is "like a secret knot that links these two parts of the body and the mind."

Thus grace has become the necessary condition of aesthetic pleasure. And, unlike beauty, grace cannot be confined within rules: "What pleases," the Chevalier de Méré writes, "consists in almost imperceptible things, such as a wink, a smile, and certain something [*je ne sais quoi*] that very easily escapes us and is not easily found when we look for it" (*Des agréments*).

The debate about art and artistic categories, about the power of rules, thus really begins only with grace, which becomes a condition of the work of art's perfection that requires the implementation of a technique of composing figures and forms, producing harmony and the *je ne sais quoi* without which the language of art remains a dead letter.

BIBLIOGRAPHY

Félibien, André. *Des agréments*. In *Œuvres*. Paris: Les Belles Lettres, 1930.

———. *Entretiens sur les vies et les ouvrages des plus excellents peintres anciens et modernes: Livres I et II*. Edited by René Démoris. Paris: Les Belles Lettres, 1987. First published in 1668–88.

is transformed into a radical relativism: "Ask a toad what beauty, great beauty, the *to kalon* is? He'll answer that it's his female toad, with her big round eyes starting out of her little head. . . . Ask philosophers, finally, and they'll respond with gobbledygook; they have to have something in conformity with the archetype of the beautiful in its essence, with the *to kalon*" (RT: *Dictionnaire philosophique*).

By trying to save the concept by resorting to the imitation of "beautiful nature," Batteux merely eludes the problem by systematically extending *mimêsis* to all the fine arts. For Diderot as for many other theoreticians, only reference to British writers, to the idea of the beautiful as an "inner feeling," could make it possible to preserve an idea that was hard pressed by the hegemony of taste and a certain hostility to metaphysics. But this aesthetic feeling naturally implies a correlate that has to be determined in a system of relations and proportions. Diderot's most precise definition of the beautiful requires him to avoid both La Mettrie's relativism and the classical tradition's objectivism. Aesthetic judgment has to overcome any kind of substantialism of qualities or objects while at the same time maintaining a principle of objectivity. The solution to this problem is entirely dependent on the idea of relationship, which is founded in both judgment and things. The sense of the beautiful has its origin in the perception of relationships:

The beautiful [*Le beau*] that results from the perception of a single relationship is usually less than that which results from the perception of several relationships. . . . Nonetheless, the number of relationships must not be infinitely great; and beauty does not follow this progression: we acknowledge in beautiful things only relationships that a good mind can clearly and easily perceive in them.

("Beau" [1751] in *Œuvres esthétiques*)

Thus the establishment of aesthetics as an exclusively philosophical discipline that gave meaning to the category of "the beautiful" necessarily led to an upheaval in the traditional problematics.

B. "Beauty" and "beautiful": From moral excellence to aesthetic pleasure

"Beauty" and "beautiful" are not reducible to the concept of beauty as it is constructed by the history of philosophy. The association linking beauty with excellence, which issued from the Platonic tradition and which refers to the Greek *to kalon*, is not central to reflection on this network. The use of the word "beauty" is very diverse. It brings in aesthetic and nonaesthetic properties, qualifies the object and its form, and recognizes a specific pleasure felt by the subject. In relation to the object, "beauty" is associated with "simplicity" or "grace"; in relation to the subject, it refers to "design" (intention) or "expression."

At first, the recourse to "beauty" or "beautiful" was inseparable from an analysis of the relation between the beautiful and the good. The idea of moral beauty arose in England around 1700, and combined a sense of beauty with moral discernment. According to Shaftesbury's *Characteristicks of Men, Manners, Opinions, Times* (1711), people approach the absolute character of beauty by devoting themselves to self-knowledge (RT: Cooper, *Characteristicks*). Thus the soliloquy as interior dialogue expresses a proper sense of the beautiful and the good that reveals the depth of the soul, the order of the heart. Winckelmann, Schiller, Hölderlin, and Wieland continued to develop this archetypal form of moral beauty with the notion of the "beautiful soul" (*schöne Seele*). The originality of the English-language tradition lies in other occurrences of the term "beauty." In *A Treatise of Human Nature* (1739–40), Hume introduces two conceptions of beauty, one anthropological or passional—"beauty is a form"—and the other social or practical—"beauty of interest." Beauty is a form that produces pleasure. Closely connected with the ego, it becomes a source of pride and belongs to the domain of the passions. But it is also based on the convenience that provides pleasure: for instance, the functionality of a house, the luxury of a building, or the fertility of a field all belong to the register of beauty. The value of the beauty of objects resides in their use. The contemplation of the beautiful assumes a social interaction between an owner and a spectator, such that the spectator has an interest, through sympathy or through the easy communication of feelings, in an advantage that directly concerns the owner of the object. These two meanings of "beauty" are not based on a specifically artistic view of the term. In his *Theory of Moral Sentiments* (1759), Adam Smith emphasizes the importance of the beauty of self-interest by stressing the arrangement of objects that provides convenience and manifestly produces the feeling of utility in the spectator; such objects effectively satisfy the love of distinction that so promptly furnishes a satisfaction by sympathy with an owner who seems to be fortunately provided.

In addition to Hume's and Smith's anthropological and social approaches, we must also mention more properly intra-aesthetic reflections regarding the determination of the subject or the object of the beautiful. Thus in *Essays on the Nature and Principles of Taste* (1790), Alison does not associate beauty with the qualities of objects. Objects are merely signs that produce an emotion. From the point of view of a history of the progress of the arts, the quality of the "design" (intention) is first of all productive of the feeling of beauty. Uniformity and regularity thus adequately express the existence of the "design" by making it possible to isolate in the object a resemblance of the parts that makes a regular form discernible. But the more the arts are imbued with talent, the more the feeling of beauty they can elicit has to do with the expression of passion and not with intention. The great criterion of excellence in beautiful forms is the character or expression that corresponds to the appearance or perception of a quality that affects us on the basis of the variety of forms. The superiority of "beauty of expression" over "beauty of design" is accompanied by something that can be a peculiarly artistic or even stylistic character of beauty: the contemplation of the free expressiveness of forms. Alison's analyses of the arts can be explained by the painter Hogarth's *The Analysis of Beauty* (1753), a work about what makes a painting beautiful. Beauty is understood on the basis of the rules regarding lines in painting. According to Hogarth, the spirit of painting has always been the victim of prejudices in favor of straight lines, of the geometricalization of space in the representation of the beauty of human forms. He proposes to make the serpentine or curved line central to painting as the line of beauty. Beauty is thus no longer associated with simplicity but rather with "grace," the latter term emphasizing the infinite variety and complexity of forms, the attraction of the *je ne sais quoi*. Reflection on beauty leads to the necessity of defending the autonomy of artistic expression, the expressive development of painting. In addition, "beauty" is used to examine the cognitive and affective process that generates the idea of beauty in the perceiving mind. From this point of view, the conception of beauty and its perception in Hutcheson's *An Inquiry into the Original of Our Ideas of Beauty and Virtue* (1725) proves essential. According to Hutcheson, humans have a faculty of perceiving ideas of beauty and harmony or an internal sense of beauty through which pleasure strikes us at exactly the same time as the idea of beauty. This "internal sense" is a passive faculty of receiving ideas of beauty from all objects in which there is unity in variety. "Regular" and "harmonious" are synonymous with "beautiful." The assessment of beauty requires the functioning of an inner sense, but it also presupposes a rule of the beautiful, the foundation of the beauty of works of art residing in the unity of proportion among the parts and between each part and the whole. Hutcheson's work made possible the emergence of categories specific to the judgment of the beautiful. A value peculiar to beauty could then be recognized. Beauty was increasingly connected with aesthetic value; then it became entirely possible to give beauty a large role in contemporary aesthetic thought (Mothersill, *Beauty Restored*; Zemach, *Real Beauty*).

IV. *Schönheit* and Its Philosophical Goals

It was in Baumgarten's Latin that Kant first found a definition of the beautiful that he rejected in a way decisive for the whole history of aesthetics. The passage from *pulchritudo*, as it was used by Baumgarten, to *Schönheit*, in the sense given it by Kant, constitutes a fundamental break with all earlier conceptions of the beautiful, both those of the metaphysics of the beautiful and those of theories of art.

Baumgarten's project, set forth in his *Metaphysica* and his *Aesthetica*, was to construct a theory in which the beautiful became a genuine object of knowledge, expressing itself in accord with concepts and forms of sensibility specific to it: "Aesthetices finis est perfectio cognitionis sensitivae, qua talis, haec autem est pulchritudo" (The goal of aesthetics is the perfection of sense knowledge as such, that is, beauty; *Aesthetica*, 1.1 §14). This definition is very likely to be unintelligible if it is opposed at the outset to the central theses of Kant's *Critique of the Power of Judgment*. Baumgarten's originality was to seek to provide the beautiful with a metaphysical foundation without at the same time breaking with the rhetorical and humanistic heritage. Defining beauty as the perfection of sense knowledge implies the possibility that the latter can be determined as truth of a certain type, namely, aesthetic truth. Aesthetic truth differs from logical truth but is not opposed to it; it participates in a *cognitio inferior*, that of the senses and perceptions. This explicitly cognitive position excludes any link with an empirical conception and, of course, with any transcendental theory of aesthetic experience. Contrary to what is still often said, Baumgarten's *pulchritudo* in no way constitutes a kind of stage necessarily leading to the solutions in Kant's *Critique of Judgment*; it is the expression of an original thought that maintains the tension between the categories of ancient rhetoric, those of Leibnizian metaphysics and semiology, and philosophical demands.

In Kant, the chief condition for the use of *Schönheit* is the rejection on principle of the word *pulchritudo* and all its philosophical implications. In the third *Critique*, every determination of the beautiful is in a way foreign to aesthetics as Baumgarten and Meier understood it. In Kant, *Schönheit* never refers to an idea of the beautiful or to an intellectualist conception, but rather to the problem of taste or to a critique of taste. One remark in the *Nachlass* clearly illustrates all the difficulties that the analytic of the beautiful had to resolve:

> The sensible form of a cognition pleases [*gefällt*] as a play of sensations, or as a form of intuition, or as a way of conceiving the good. In the first case, it is a matter of attraction [*Reiz*]; in the second, of sensible beauty [*das sinnliche Schöne*]; in the third, of the beautiful in itself [*selbständigen Schönheit*].
>
> (*Nachlass*)

In the analytic of the beautiful, the sole true attribute of the beautiful—that is, what is exclusively predicable of it—is the feeling of aesthetic pleasure itself, and not some possible property of the object. This feeling of pleasure is primary and rigorously irreducible to any rule or aesthetic idea. In order to transcend the aesthetic solipsism to which this conception of the experience of the beautiful threatens to lead, Kant posits a subjective universality inherent in the very form of judgments of taste. But this postulate is still the requirement of a right: the latter has to be expressed in a universal communicability that justifies aesthetic experience but is not its goal. In precritical writings as well as in Kant's *Critique of Judgment*, the specific meaning of *Schönheit* is inseparable from that of *Geschmack* as *judicium* or, more precisely, as reflective judgment, and thus as an affirmation of aesthetic subjectivity (see GOÛT).

The post-Kantians' relationship to Kant is marked by an explicit desire to break with him. In his *System of Transcendental Philosophy* (1800), Schelling shows that philosophical thought has to include art as a specific form of intellectual intuition, that is, as a mediation between freedom and nature. Kant had certainly seen the connections between freedom and nature in the beautiful, but not in the ontogenesis of art itself. This recognition of the functions and the metaphysical necessity of art is central to Hegel's conception of beauty. Hegel seeks to show the internal necessity of the link between the historicity of art, and thus of the beautiful, and the systematic structure of his philosophical thought:

> Thus demonstrating the idea of the beautiful [*die Idee des Schönen*], which we take as our starting point, that is, deriving this idea as a necessary implication of the presuppositions that, for science, precede it and within which it arises, is not our goal here, but is rather a matter for an encyclopedic development of philosophy as a whole and of its particular disciplines. For us, the concept of the beautiful and of art is a presupposition given by the system of philosophy [*Für uns ist der Begriff des Schönen und der Kunst eine durch das System des Philosophie gegebene Voraussetzung*].
>
> (*Vorlesungen über die Aesthetik*)

This passage clearly develops what was already announced in "The Oldest System-Program of German Idealism" (a manuscript Franz Rosenzweig found in 1917 among papers that had belonged to Hegel, and whose attribution remains uncertain): the reconciliation of art and philosophy, the identification of the beautiful and art, of thought and appearance, and especially of art and truth. However, problems inherent in Hegel's aesthetic thought remain: How can the idea of artistic beauty, that is, the sole true beauty, be both rooted in metaphysics and the source from which the creative genius of every artist draws nourishment? And how can this metaphysical idea coincide with modes of appearance and manifestation that are as diverse as those of the work of art? In reality, a complete understanding of the concept of the beautiful would assume an infinite analytical regression of the presuppositions operative in the encyclopedic knowledge of philosophy and an endless analysis of all the forms of expression through which the idea of the beautiful is actualized and manifests itself in the history of art.

In many respects, Nietzsche's aesthetic concepts—appearance, illusion, value as the conditions for preserving life—are derived from, or are rather a kind of distant echo, of Kant's thought.

> Nothing is more conditional—or, let us say, narrower—than our feeling for beauty. Whosoever would think of it apart from man's joy in man would immediately lose any foothold. "Beautiful in itself" is a mere phrase, not even a concept. In the beautiful, man posits himself as the measure of perfection; in special cases he worships himself in it. A species cannot do otherwise but thus affirm itself alone. Its *lowest* instinct, that of self-preservation and self-expansion, still radiates in such sublimities. Man believes the world itself to be overloaded with beauty—and he forgets himself as the cause of this. He alone has presented the world with beauty—alas! only with a very human, all-too-human beauty. . . . [T]he judgment "beautiful" is the *vanity of his species* [*das Urteil "schön" ist seine Gattungs-Eitelkeit*].
>
> (*The Twilight of the Idols*)

Contrary to the last idealist aestheticians, such as Vischer or Lotze, and even to Schopenhauer, Nietzsche clearly distinguishes between art and the beautiful. Modern on this point, he makes the beautiful the effect of a belief, an illusion that is necessary insofar as it stimulates every aesthetic feeling. But this critique of idealism becomes inseparable from a rejection of any intellectualist conception of the idea of the beautiful, and this necessarily leads to the latter losing all content. The question of what the word *Schönheit* might still mean today is dealt with using arguments that belong to logic, sociology, and more rarely aesthetics proper, allowing us to discern a will to eliminate the concept, or else a desire to preserve and sometimes restore a notion that others consider anachronistic or even reactionary. Today, any aesthetics that seeks to give a precise content to the concept of the beautiful is necessarily confronted by a choice: either resort to a metaphysical construction, at the risk of ending up in a position that is difficult to defend, or fulfill the conditions of a logical-semantic procedure that is nonetheless exposed to multiple self-contradictions.

Thus Reinold Schmücker declares: "That art imitates nature, that beauty can be experienced and makes divine perfection perceptible, are no longer plausible claims in the era of waste-management plants and atheism" (*Was ist Kunst?*). Franz von Kutschera replies to these excessive statements with propositions that express the contemporary quandary more subtly: "Beauty is merely one aesthetic concept among others, but because of its vast field of application, it has often been considered the dominant concept of all aesthetic qualities, and aesthetic theory has been defined as the theory of the beautiful. This conception is typical of the old aesthetics" (*Aesthetik*). Given the extreme difficulty of defining exactly what an aesthetic quality is and rigorously theorizing a notion that persists in ordinary discourse as well as in philosophical discourse, we can say that the meaning of the words *beau*, *Schönheit*, "beauty," etc. remains largely indeterminate. But that does not mean that they are empty of content, outdated, or unsuitable for conceptual treatment.

Jean-François Groulier
Fabienne Brugère (III.B)

BIBLIOGRAPHY

Alison, Archibald. *Essays on the Nature and Principles of Taste*. 2nd ed. London, 1811. First published in 1790.

Baumgarten, Alexander Gottlieb. *Aesthetica*. Hamburg: Meiner, 1983. First published in 1750.

Boileau, Nicolas. *Œuvres complètes*. Paris: Gallimard / La Pléiade, 1966. Translation by Des Maizeaux and N. Rowe: *The Works of Monsieur Boileau*. 2nd ed. London: W. Shropshire and Edward Littleton, 1736. Eighteenth Century Collections Online, Gale Digital Collections (by subscription).

Cicero, Marcus Tullius. *On the Ideal Orator*. Translated by J. M. May. Oxford: Oxford University Press, 2001.

———. *Orator*. Translated by E. Jones. In *Cicero's Brutus or History of Famous Orators; also His Orator, or Accomplished Speaker*. London, 1776. Digital text at Project Gutenberg. http://www.gutenberg.org.

Crousaz, Jean-Pierre de. *Traité du beau*. Reprint, Paris: Fayard, 1985. First published in 1715.

Descartes, René. *Oeuvres*. Edited by Charles Adam and Paul Tannery. Paris: Éditions du Cerf, 1897–1913. Reprint, Paris: Librairie Philosophique, J. Vrin, 1983.

Diderot, Denis. *Œuvres esthétiques*. Paris: Garnier, 1956. Translation by J. Goodman: *Diderot on Art*. New Haven, CT: Yale University Press, 1995.

Ficino, Marsilio. *Meditations on the Soul: Selected Letters of Marsilio Ficino*. Edited by C. Salamn. Rochester, VT: Inner Traditions, 1997.

———. *Opera omnia*. Basel, Switz., 1576.

———. *Platonic Theology*. Edited by J. Hankins. Translated by M.J.B. Allen. Cambridge, MA: Harvard University Press, 2001.

———. *Three Books on Life*. Edited and translated by C. V. Kaske and J. R. Clark. Binghamton, NY: Center for Medieval and Early Renaissance Studies, State University of New York at Binghamton, 1989.

Ghiberti, Lorenzo. *I commentarii*. Edited by J. von Schlosser. Berlin: Julius Bard, 1912.

Hegel, Georg Wilhelm Friedrich. *Vorlesungen über die Aesthetik*. Frankfurt: Suhrkamp, 1970. Translation by T. M. Knox: *Aesthetics: Lectures on Fine Arts*. 2 vols. Oxford: Oxford University Press, 1975.

Hogarth, William. *The Analysis of Beauty*. London: J. Reeves, 1753.

Hume, David. *A Treatise of Human Nature*. Oxford: Clarendon Press, 1978. First published in 1739–40.

Hutcheson, Francis. *An Inquiry into the Original of Our Ideas of Beauty and Virtue*. In *Philosophical Writings*. London: Everyman, 1994. First published in 1725.

Kant, Immanuel. *Kritik der Urteilskraft*. Hamburg: Meiner, 1968. Translation by P. Guyer and E. Matthews: *Critique of the Power of Judgment*. Cambridge: Cambridge University Press, 2001. First published in 1790.

———. *Nachlass*. In vol. 21 of *Gesammelte Schriften*. Berlin: Akademia Ausgabe, 1936. Translation by Curtis Bowman, Paul Guyer, and Frederick Rauscher: *Notes and Fragments*, edited by P. Guyer. New York: Cambridge University Press, 2005.

Kutschera, Franz von. *Aesthetik*. Berlin: De Gruyter, 1998.

Lotze, Hermann. *Geschichte der Aesthetik in Deutschland*. Munich: J. G. Cotta, 1868.

———. *Outlines of Aesthetics: Dictated Portions of the Lectures of Hermann Lotze*. Edited and translated by G. T. Ladd. Boston: Ginn, 1886.

Meier, Georg Friedrich. *Anfangsgründe aller schönen Wissenschaften*. Halle, Ger., 1748.

Mersenne, Marin. *Questions inouyes*. In *Corpus des œuvres de philosophie en langue française*. Paris: Fayard, 1985.

Monteil, Pierre. *Le beau et le laid en latin*. Paris: Klincksieck, 1964.

Mothersill, Mary. *Beauty Restored*. Oxford: Clarendon Press, 1984.

Nicole, Pierre. *An Essay on True and Apparent Beauty in Which from Settled Principles Is Rendered the Grounds for Choosing and Rejecting Epigrams*. Translated by J. V. Cunningham. Los Angeles: William Andrews Clark Memorial Library, University of California, 1950.

———. *Traité de la beauté des ouvrages de l'esprit*. Toulouse, 1689.

Nietzsche, Friedrich. *The Twilight of the Idols*. Translated by Walter Kaufmann. In *The Portable Nietzsche*. New York: Viking, 1954.

Norton, Robert E. *The Beautiful Soul*. Ithaca, NY: Cornell University Press, 1995.

Plato. *Hippias Major*. Translated by Benjamin Jowett. In *The Collected Dialogues of Plato*. Edited by E. Hamilton and H. Cairns. Princeton, NJ: Princeton University Press / Bollingen, 1961.

———. *Phaedo*. Translated by Hugh Tredennick. In *The Collected Dialogues of Plato*. Edited by E. Hamilton and H. Cairns. Princeton, NJ: Princeton University Press / Bollingen, 1961.

———. *Phaedrus*. Translated by R. Hackforth. In *The Collected Dialogues of Plato*. Edited by E. Hamilton and H. Cairns. Princeton, NJ: Princeton University Press / Bollingen, 1961.

———. *Philebus*. Translated by R. Hackforth. In *The Collected Dialogues of Plato*. Edited by E. Hamilton and H. Cairns. Princeton, NJ: Princeton University Press / Bollingen, 1961.

———. *Symposium*. Translated by Michael Joyce. In *The Collected Dialogues of Plato*. Edited by E. Hamilton and H. Cairns. Princeton, NJ: Princeton University Press / Bollingen, 1961.

Plotinus. *The Enneads*. Translated by S. Mackenna. Burdett, NY: Published for the Paul Brunton Philosophic Foundation by Larson Publications, 1992.

Pouillon, Henri. "La beauté, propriété transcendantale chez les scolastiques (1220–1270)." *Archives de l'Histoire Doctrinale et Littéraire du Moyen-Âge* 15 (1946).

Scannelli, Francesco. *Microcosmo della pittura*. Cesena, It., 1657.

Schelling, Friedrich Wilhelm Joseph von. *System of Transcendental Philosophy*. Translated by P. Heath. Charlottesville: University Press of Virginia, 1978.

Schmücker, Reinold. *Was ist Kunst?* Munich: Fink Verlag, 1998.

Smith, Adam. *The Theory of Moral Sentiments*. 1759. Oxford: Oxford University Press, 1976.

Spinoza, Baruch. *Chief Works of Spinoza*. Translated by R.H.M. Elwes. New York: Dover, 1951.

Thomas Aquinas, Saint. *Summa theologiae: Questions on God*. Edited by B. Davies and B. Leftow. Cambridge: Cambridge University Press, 2006.

Trublet, Nicolas Charles Joseph. *Essais sur divers sujets de littérature et de morale*. Paris: Briasso, 1735. Translation: *Essays upon Several Subjects of Literature and Morality*. London: J. Osborn, 1744. Eighteenth Century Collections Online, Gale Digital Collections (by subscription).

Vischer, Friedrich Theodor. *Aesthetik oder Wissenschaft des Schönen*. Reutlingen, Ger.: C. Macken, 1847–57. 2nd ed. Edited by R. Vischer. Munich: Meyer and Jessen, 1922–23.

Vitruvius Pollo. *Ten Books on Architecture*. Translated by I. D. Rowland. Cambridge: Cambridge University Press, 1999.

Zemach, Eddy. *Real Beauty*. University Park: Pennsylvania State University Press, 1997.

BEGRIFF (GERMAN)

ENGLISH	concept
FRENCH	*concept*
GREEK	*katalêpsis* [κατάληψις]
LATIN	*comprehensio*

➤ *CONCEPT* [CONCEPTUS, CONCETTO], and AUFHEBEN, GEISTESWISSENSCHAFTEN, INTELLECT, INTELLECTUS, PERCEPTION, PLASTICITY, PREDICATION, *REASON,* SOUL, UNDERSTANDING

In its common usage, the German verb *begreifen* designates an understanding of an intellectual order. It is this sense of the "intellectual grasp of a thing or an idea" (in *begreifen* there are echoes of the verb *greifen*: "to seize, catch, capture") that is found in *Begriff*: "Ich habe keinen Begriff davon" means that one has no access to the thing or idea in question. The inflections to which *Begriff* is subjected in philosophy are related to transformations in theories of knowledge. At first, *Begriff* had the strict sense of a function of understanding (Kant), but then it was given independent reality as a figure of knowledge that acquires consciousness in its journey toward absolute knowledge (Hegel). Finally, on the basis of a definition of *Begriff* that claims to be strictly logical, these different meanings were redefined as still too psychological, to the degree that they still contain something of the ordinary sense of the term (Frege). The current discussion of the possibility of reintellectualizing concepts continues to stumble over the difference in languages between a German *Begriff* that has retained part of its naturalness and an English "concept" that is totally unrelated to ordinary usage.

I. *Begreifen, Verstehen, Konzipieren* (Kant): Varieties of Understanding

It was with Immanuel Kant that *Begriff* acquired a specific philosophical meaning far removed from the general meaning forged by Christian Wolff (cf. Wolff, *Vernünfftige Gedanken*, 1.4: "any representation of a thing in our ideas [*jede Vorstellung einer Sache in unseren Vorstellungen*]"). In his *Logic*, which revised and transformed the vocabulary of German academic philosophy, Kant set this very general meaning of representation against a precise meaning that is part of a classification of the kinds of knowledge in which *begreifen* is distinguished from *verstehen* and *konzipieren*. Here is his definition of the "fifth degree" of knowledge:

> To understand [*verstehen, intelligere*] something, to cognize something through the understanding by means of concepts [*durch den Verstand vermöge der Begriffe*], or to conceive [*konzipieren*]. This is very different from comprehending something [*begreifen*]. One can conceive much, although one cannot comprehend it, e.g., a *perpetuum mobile* whose impossibility is shown by mechanics.
>
> (*Lectures on Logic*, trans. Young, 570)

On the other hand, the seventh degree, "to grasp [*begreifen, comprehendere*] something," means "to know through reason [*durch die Vernunft*] or *a priori*, to the extent that this is suitable for our purposes [*in dem Grade . . . als zu unserer Absicht hinreichend ist*]" (*Logik*, Introduction, §8, in RT: Ak., 9:65; Kant, *Lectures on Logic*, trans. Young, 570).

The classification proposed in the *Logic* is remarkable in that it dissociates the verb *begreifen* from the noun *Begriff*.

Whereas the latter enters easily into the definition of *verstehen* as the fifth degree of knowledge ("cognize something through the understanding by means of concepts"), Kant reserves *begreifen* for the supreme degree of knowledge. It is as if *Begriff* were already neutralized by its technical usage, whereas the meaning of *begreifen* could still be debated. The reason for this is doubtless that the verb *begreifen* still connotes something of the act of grasping, and that Kant can see in it the most complete form of capturing or appropriating the object in question. The phenomenon is further accentuated by the presence in *begreifen* of the prefix *be-*, which signifies transitivity and implies, in this precise case, direct, full contact with the object.

The Kantian classifications may vary, but they never alter this fundamental definition of *begreifen*. Elsewhere, Kant corrects the terminology earlier proposed by the Wolffian Georg Friedrich Meier by refusing to translate *begreifen* with *concipere* (conceive): *begreifen* has to be reserved for *comprehendere*, that is, for a mode of knowledge that makes use of an intuition "per apprehensionem" (*Wiener Logik*, in RT: Ak., 24:845). The detour through Latin is revealing: the idea of *apprehensio*—that is, grasping or capturing—naturally leads Kant to *begreifen*, which contains this idea in its etymology (*greifen*). To be sure, *konzipieren*, which is derived from the Latin *capere*, also includes the idea of capture, but the etymology is blurred, and the determination of *begreifen* passes precisely through a new translation or a new Latin equivalent, *comprehendere*, in which the meaning of prehension, of taking in hand, is more clearly heard.

■ See Box 1.

This is the distinction inherited by the term *Begriff*. In the *Critique of Pure Reason*, the *Begriff* becomes a function of the understanding (as opposed to the object of an intuition)—itself defined as a power of concepts. The *Begriff* is what gathers together, unites, and synthesizes the empirical manifold:

> The knowledge yielded by understanding, or at least by the human understanding, must therefore be by means of concepts, and so is not intuitive, but discursive. Whereas all intuitions, as sensible, rest on affections, concepts rest on functions. By "function" I mean the unity of the act of bringing various representations under one common representation. Concepts are based on the spontaneity of thought, sensible intuitions on the receptivity of impressions.
>
> (*Kritik der reinen Vernunft*, in RT: Ak., 3:85–86, trans. Kemp-Smith, 105)

II. *Der Begriff*: Concepts and the Concept (Hegel)

The relative ease with which the use of the term *Begriff* in the *Critique of Pure Reason* can be translated (unlike its use in passages dealing with definitions, such as the one in the *Logic*) no doubt proceeds from the fact that Kant conceives *Begriffe* in their plurality: there are as many concepts as there are possible functions. On the other hand, the term becomes more difficult to understand when it is used exclusively in the singular—as it is in Hegel, whose philosophy is a philosophy of the Concept, the *Begriff*, without further determination. The passage from the plural to the singular also marks

1

Grasping: *Katalêpsis* and *comprehensio*

➤ CONCEPTUS, PATHOS, PERCEPTION, PHANTASIA, REPRÉSENTATION

The Stoics distinguish among true representations those that are apprehensive (in the active sense of "capable of actively grasping objects or situations") and those that are not. For them, an apprehensive representation, *phantasia katalêptikê* [φαντασία καταληπτική], is the most exact and precise, and the one that represents in the mind the peculiar characteristics of the thing represented:

> An apprehensive one is the one that is from a real thing and is stamped and impressed in accordance with just *that* real thing, and is of such a kind as could not come about from a thing that was not real. For since they trust this appearance to be capable of perfectly grasping the underlying things, and to be skillfully stamped with all the peculiarities attaching to them, they say that it has each of these as an attribute.
>
> (Sextus Empiricus, *Adversus mathematicos*, 8.248–49, trans. Bett, 50)

It is a representation so "plain and striking" that it "all but grabs us by the hair, and draws us into assent" (ibid., 8.257, trans. Bett, 52).

The assent that we irresistibly give to such a representation leads to grasping or comprehension, *katalêpsis* [κατάληψις]:

> Zeno professed to illustrate this by a piece of action; for when he stretched out his fingers, and showed the palm of his hand, "Perception," said he, "is a thing like this." Then, when he had a little closed his fingers, "Assent is like this." Afterwards, when he had completely closed his hand, and held forth his fist, that, he said, was comprehension. From which simile he also gave that state a name which it had not before, and called it *katalêpsis*. But when he brought his left hand against his right, and with it took a firm and tight hold of his fist, knowledge, he said, was of that character; and that was what none but a wise man possessed.
>
> (Cicero, *Academic Questions*, 1.47, trans. Yonge)

The clenched fist illustrates comprehension; the other hand gripping it tightly illustrates science, which stabilizes and preserves this comprehension.

The act of prehension and grasping expressed by the verb *comprehendere* (and the noun *comprehensio*) is discernible in all uses of the term that include sensorial apprehension (e.g., Cicero, *De legibus*, 1.30) and all of the levels of taking possession intellectually: thus discourse is imprinted on the mind of the orator because he has first "grasped" the ideas that he will develop by means of images that remind him of them (Cicero, *De oratore*, 2.359). The words themselves "enclose" the thought that they have "grasped" (*De oratore*, 1.70), just as the oratorical period "includes" and "circumscribes" the thought (*Brutus*, 34). All of these possible translations of *comprehendere* allow us to glimpse the richness of the term that Cicero chose to render the Stoic *katalêpsis*: other terms were acceptable, which the Stoic in the dialogue *De finibus* (3.17) gives as equivalents of *katalêpsis*: *cognitio* and *perceptio*. But by choosing *comprehendere*, Cicero emphasizes the gesture Zeno used to describe the different levels of knowledge (and to illustrate as well the relation between rhetoric and dialectic [*De finibus*, 2.17; *De oratore*, 113]). The importance Cicero accords to this gesture, attested by him alone, gives its full weight to Zeno's bending of the substantive *katalêpsis*, which before him had never been used to designate anything but a concrete grasping or capture. The hand gesture makes it possible to understand the unity of movement from representation (*phantasis-visum*)—the open hand—to comprehension—the closed fist—and then to science—the fist gripped by the other hand (*Academic Questions*, 2.145; see above). The hand is still active, but it exercises its activity on itself: the close interweaving of activity in the course of a process that is also a passive reception is stressed by Cicero's translations of *phantasia katalêptikê*. The adjective *katalêptikê* [καταληπτική], generally interpreted as having an active sense, also has a passive sense: Cicero uses not *katalêptikon* [καταληπτικόν] but *katalêpton* [καταληπτόν], which means "grasp" or "what

can be grasped" (*Academic Questions*, 1.41); he translates this term by *comprehendibile*, so that we understand more clearly, thanks to this translation, that representation is what permits grasping, because it can itself be grasped; the grasp becomes possession only when the representation has received assent and approval ("visum . . . acceptum . . . et approbatum"):

> [Zeno] did not give credit to everything which is perceived, but only to those which contain some especial character of those things which are seen; but he pronounced what was seen, when it was discerned on account of its own power, *comprehensible* . . . after it had been received and approved, then he called it *comprehension*, resembling those things which are taken up [*prehenduntur*] in the hand.
>
> (Cicero, *Academic Questions*, 1.41, trans. Yonge)

Thus strengthened by the explanation given to the Stoic "gesture" of *katalêpsis*, the classical meanings of the Latin *comprehendere* determined its subsequent philosophical uses. In the Middle Ages, the novelty of the Latin *conceptus* had to do with the fact that to the image of capture, still present in the word through the verb *con-capere*, was added another, that of giving birth (as in "conception"). From this resulted an entirely different representation of the system of the faculties and of the activity of knowledge (see CONCEPTUS).

Clara Auvray-Assayas
Frédérique Ildefonse

BIBLIOGRAPHY

Cicero. *Academic Questions*. Translated by C. D. Yonge. London: H. G. Bohn, 1853. Facs. reprint, Charleston, SC: Nabu, 2010.

Sextus Empiricus. *Against the Logicians*. Translated and edited by Richard Bett. Cambridge: Cambridge University Press, 2005.

the passage from a philosophy of knowledge that associates concept and understanding with a philosophy that claims to be a Science, and to that end unites the Concept with Spirit.

In French translations, the capital *C* is probably the most economical way of indicating the emphatic use Hegel makes of the term "Concept"; it would otherwise be difficult to render in French, which is accustomed to the plural (*les concepts*) or the indefinite (*un concept*). Hegel is in fact the philosopher who opposes *the* Concept to concepts in the plural (cf. *Aesthetik* 1, in *Werke*, 13:127: "In recent times, no concept has been as infirm as the Concept itself"). *The* Concept is thus considered to be a figure of knowledge: it is the absolutely simple and pure element in which truth has its existence (*Phänomenologie des Geistes*, in *Werke,* vol. 3), and only its deployment, also called "the work of the concept" (*Arbeit des Begriffs*), provides access to "scientific understanding" (*wissenschaftliche Einsicht*). The *Phenomenology of Mind* makes the *Begriff* almost a dramatic figure by characterizing it as the "movement of knowledge," a movement that is a "self-movement" (*Selbstbewegung*). This movement of the Concept, which can also be called a movement of self-reflection, but is already in the unity of being and reflection (cf. *Wissenschaft der Logik*, in *Werke,* vol. 6), terminates in the unity of knowledge and its object (*Phänomenologie*), which is at the same time division, partition, separation between the different things that are "what they are through the activity of the Concept that dwells in them and reveals itself in them" (die Dinge sind das was sie sind durch die Tätigkeit des innewohnenden und in ihnen sich offenbarenden Begriffs: *Enzyklopädie der philosophischen Wissenschaften* 1, *Die Wissenschaft der Logik*, §163, add. 2, in *Werke,* 8:313). At the end of "Doctrine of the Concept" in *Science of Logic*, the *Begriff* is subsumed by the Idea (see AUFHEBEN), which is also in the singular: the Idea is "the adequate Concept, the objectively true or the true as such" (der adäquate Begriff, das objektive Wahre oder das Wahre als solches, *Die Wissenschaft der Logik*, in *Werke,* vol. 6). Nonetheless, it remains the "principle of philosophy," and in this sense we find it again in the *Philosophy of Mind* in the *Encyclopedia* (cf. *Philosophie des Geistes*, in *Werke,* vol. 10).

This speculative use of the term *Begriff* remains doubly faithful to the common use of the word, however. In the singular, *der Begriff* perhaps suggests above all the act of seizing or grasping, of taking everything to "inhabit" it and be "revealed" in it, as we have seen in Hegel. In addition, when Hegel speaks of the "Begriff des Begriffs" (in *Werke,* vol. 6), he adds to this play on the etymology a completely ordinary use of the word that makes it a synonym of *Bestimmung*, "definition." Despite the inherently speculative aspect of this reduplication of terms, "Begriff des Begriffs" does not mean so much "concept of the concept" as "definition of the concept," that is, its abridged idea, or, as Hegel puts it, its *Abbreviatur*, "abbreviation" (in *Werke,* vol. 5). The extended use of the term, between common language and technical vocabulary, makes it possible to take the same term in two different senses in the same expression.

Thus in Kant and Hegel, the specificity of *Begriff* and *begreifen* resides in each case in grammatical peculiarities: the different uses that make the nominal form (*Begriff*) and the verbal form (*begreifen*) possible in Kant, and the singular and the plural of *Begriff* possible in Hegel. From one author to the other, the play on etymology shifts from the verb (Kant plays mainly on *begreifen*) to the noun (Hegel's play on the majesty of the singular). In both cases, however, the theory of knowledge and the speculative doctrine of science are deployed in a close relationship with ordinary language, or at least with the phantasmal version provided by the etymology. It is this relationship that is lost as soon as the term is translated into French.

III. *Begriff* and the Linguistic Turn

A. *Begriffsschrift* (*Frege*)

Begriff also lends itself to a more strictly *logical* definition, that is, one in which the preceding meanings are contested as connected with a use that is still "psychological." Gottlob Frege's *Begriffsschrift* undertakes a transformation of this kind, and the French translation of his title (*Idéographie*) is for that reason problematic. As Frege points out in his preface:

My goal was to seek first of all to reduce the concept of succession [*den Begriff der Anordnung*] to a series of logical consequences, and then to advance toward the concept of number. To prevent something intuitive [*etwas anschauliches*] from being inadvertently introduced, the absence of gaps in the sequence of deductions had to be assured. . . . That is why I abandoned any attempt to express anything that has no meaning for the deduction. In §3, I have designated as conceptual content [*als begrifflichen Inhalt*] what alone is important to me. This explanation must consequently always be kept in mind if one wants to understand correctly the essence of my formula language [*Formelsprache*]. From this also follows the name *Begriffsschrift*.

The difficulty involved in using "concept" in translating the *Begriffsschrift* comes from the fact that in it, Frege proposes a definition of the concept (and thus of the conceptual content) that is inseparable from his view of logic and his principled antipsychologism. In the preface to *Die Grundlagen der Arithmetik* (The foundations of arithmetic), he defines the three principles guiding his approach: always clearly separate the psychological from the logical, the subjective from the objective; never ask what a word means by itself, but always in context; and never lose sight of the distinction between concept and object (der Unterschied zwischen Begriff und Gegenstand ist im Auge zu behalten: *Die Grundlagen der Arithmetik*, x). The *Begriff* is not a psychological but a logical notion. The distinction between concept and object proceeds entirely from the new logic, according to which simple utterances are analyzed for their function and argument. For example, in the sentence "The Earth is a planet," we can replace "Earth" by other proper nouns, and obtain in this way the sentences "Venus is a planet," "Mars is a planet," and so on. What remains invariant in these sentences is a function, which takes this or that object as its argument. A concept is a function at a place, what can be said of an object. We see that the notion of the concept, thus defined, is in no way psychological, and is independent of any idea of "grasping." Moreover, as Frege explains in "Funktion und Begriff" (Function and concept), the concept thus defined is no longer closed or complete, but in need of an argument; it is "unsaturated" (*ungesättigt*: in *Funktion, Begriff, Bedeutung*, 29).

In his article "Begriff und Gegenstand" (Concept and object), Frege replies to a few objections that had been addressed to him by Benno Kerry regarding his use of the concept of concept:

The term "concept" [*Begriff*] has several uses; it is sometimes taken in the psychological sense, and sometimes in the logical sense, and perhaps also in a confused acceptation that mixes the two. But this freedom has its natural limit; as soon as a certain use of the term is put in play, it is desirable that it should be maintained. For my part, I have chosen to adhere strictly to the purely logical use of the term.

("Begriff und Gegenstand," in *Funktion, Begriff, Bedeutung*, 66)

B. The analytical uses of "concept"

Such a purely logical approach poses a problem, which Frege lucidly outlines in "Begriff und Gegenstand": How can we talk about a concept (for example, when we say that it is clear, simple, general, and so on) without making it an object and thus violating the principles of Frege's approach? The question, which was to obsess many twentieth-century philosophers of language, is that of predication. If an object is anything about which one can say something (and thus, anything one can make "fall under a" concept), we can speak of "a" concept, and that is what we do, very commonly in fact. Frege's redefinitions have thus not eliminated, even in the analytical field, all work on the notion of the concept, and they have even elicited a new line of reflection on individuation and the distinction of concepts. The logicization and depsychologization of the concept of concept accomplished by Frege have certainly led, in a first phase, to a decay of the concept in favor of predication and objects (to which first Rudolf Carnap's work and then W.V.O. Quine's testifies, each in its own way). The term "concept" has been maintained, but in a rather vague sense, notably in the common expression "conceptual scheme" used by Quine (*From a Logical Point of View*, 44ff.) and his successors in the sense of the whole of our conception of the world, or the whole of our knowledge ("the conceptual scheme of science"): the expression acquires a special flavor from the fact that according to Quine, this conceptual scheme is inseparable from a language and an ontology that are themselves untranslatable into another language in an unequivocal way (see SENSE). The idea of a conceptual scheme is thus associated with the whole debate about incommensurability and relativism that has roiled analytical philosophy and epistemology since the 1960s. This is shown not only by Richard Rorty's work, but also by Donald Davidson's famous text, "On the Very Idea of a Conceptual Scheme," in which Davidson vehemently criticizes the idea of a conceptual scheme and a "point of view" on the world as a source of "conceptual relativism" and associates it—following in that respect Quine himself—with the idea of linguistic difference and untranslatability. A conceptual scheme is language conceived as a source of the conception and categorization of the world. We see what difficulties the philosophy of language encounters in seeking to eliminate or resolve the question of conceptualization, difficulties that have led to a massive return, since the end of the twentieth century, to concepts: it was in fact the return of analytical philosophy to the philosophy of mind, against the antipsychological precepts of Frege and Ludwig Wittgenstein, that allowed a resurgence of the term, this time generally in the plural and rementalized: that is the case in English philosopher Christopher Peacocke's *A Study of Concepts*, which has been much discussed since the 1990s. Many recent discussions of concepts bear on the *possession* of concepts, in the sense of "mental representations." There is, for example, current debate about "nonconceptual content," that is, an intrinsic content of experience that is supposed to be a representation independent of concepts.

Peacocke introduces his thought in *A Study of Concepts* this way:

We need to be clear about the subject matter of a theory of concepts. The term "concept" has by now come to be something of a term of art. The word does not have in English a unique sense that is theoretically important.

Peacocke then quotes Woody Allen, who has a character in his film *Annie Hall* say, "Right now it's only a notion, but I think I can get money to make it into a concept . . . and later turn it into an idea." Peacocke implies here, in an interesting way, that the word "concept" in English no longer really has an ordinary use, and that it certainly does not refer, as he says later on, to the Fregean use. Hence he proposes a purely stipulative definition of concepts based on distinguishing them through their propositional content. We can imagine that it is the logicism of the Fregean conceptual notation and definitions that makes constantly possible, in the wake of analytical philosophy, new, more or less arbitrary definitions of the concept; nonetheless, by the roles that he assigns in his definitions to "functions" and their operativity, Frege maintains a naturalness in the use of *Begriff* that is probably lost in later English translations and the most contemporary uses of "concept."

Philippe Büttgen
Marc Crépon
Sandra Laugier

BIBLIOGRAPHY

Davidson, Donald. "On the Very Idea of a Conceptual Scheme." In *Inquiries into Truth and Interpretation*. Oxford: Clarendon, 1984.

Frege, Gottlob. *Begriffschrift und andere Aufsätze*. Edited by I. Angelelli. 2nd ed. Hildesheim, Ger.: Olms, 1964. Translation by T. W. Bynum: *Conceptual Notation, and Related Articles*. Edited by T. W. Bynum. Oxford: Clarendon, 1972.

———. *Collected Papers on Mathematics, Logic, and Philosophy*. Edited by B. McGuinness. Translated by M. Black, V. H. Dudman, P. Geach, H. Kaal, E.-H. W. Kluge, B. McGuinness, and R. H. Stoothoff. Oxford: Blackwell, 1984.

———. *Funktion, Begriff, Bedutung: Fünf logische Studien*. Edited by G. Patzig. 4th ed. Göttingen, Ger.: Vandenhoek and Ruprecht, 1975.

———. *Die Grundlagen der Arithmetik*. Edited by C. Thiel. Hamburg: Meiner, 1988.

———. *Logical Investigations*. Translated by P. T. Geach and R. H. Stoothoff. Oxford: Blackwell, 1977.

———. *Translations from the Philosophical Writings of Gottlob Frege*. Edited and translated by Peter Geach and Max Black. Oxford: Blackwell, 1980.

Hegel, Friedrich Wilhelm Friedrich. *The Hegel Reader*. London: Wiley-Blackwell, 1998.

———. *Werke in zwanzig Bänden*. Edited by E. Moldenhauer and K. M. Michel. 20 vols. Frankfurt: Suhrkamp, 1986.

Kant, Immanuel. *The Cambridge Edition of the Works of Immanuel Kant in Translation*. Cambridge: Cambridge University Press, 1995–.

———. *Critique of Pure Reason*. Translated by N. Kemp-Smith. London: St. Martin's Press, 1929.

———. *Lectures on Logic*. Translated by J. M. Young. Cambridge: Cambridge University Press, 2004.

Peacocke, Christopher. *A Study of Concepts*. Cambridge, MA: MIT Press, 1992.

Quine, W. V. O. *From a Logical Point of View*. Cambridge, MA: Harvard University Press, 1953.

Rorty, Richard. *Objectivity, Relativism, and Truth*. Cambridge: Cambridge University Press, 1991.

BEHAVIOR, BEHAVIORISM

FRENCH *conduite, comportement, béhaviorisme,*
           béhaviourisme, comportementalisme
GERMAN *Verhalten, Behaviorismus*
ITALIAN *comportamento, comportamentismo*

➤ *COMPORTMENT,* and *ACT,* AGENCY, ENGLISH, EPISTEMOLOGY,
   GEISTESWISSENSCHAFTEN, INTENTION, LEIB, MANIERA, PRAXIS,
   SENSE, SOUL, SPEECH ACT, UNCONSCIOUS, *WORLD*

The untranslatable character of the English term "behavior" appears (1) in the hesitation between two translations of the term in French, *conduite* and *comportement,* with the transition (in 1908, with Henri Piéron's reintroduction of the term in psychology) from the former to the latter, manifesting a desire to objectify and make scientific the "observable" notion of behavior; (2) in the contemporary choice of the French term *béhaviorisme* instead of *comportmentalisme* (rarer) to translate "behaviorism." The same can be said of German, which uses "Behaviorism" (*ein verkappter Behaviourist,* "a behaviorist in disguise," [L. Wittgenstein, *Philosophische Untersuchungen,* §307]).

The French term *behaviorisme,* simply copied from the English, designates a given philosophical conception (dating historically from the beginning of the twentieth century in America and in John B. Watson's theories, elaborated at the same time as those of Ivan Pavlov in Russia), according to which only the observation of so-called external behavior can be proved to provide a basis for the description of mental states. The term, introduced in a positive way, has now become pejorative, or at least negative: in French, *behaviourisme,* simplifying and scientistic, tends to be opposed to a possible true theory of behavior (cf. M. Merleau-Ponty, *La Structure du comportement*).

We see that the difficulty also concerns the term *comportement.* This term, which since the fifteenth century has designated a way of acting, does not seem to correspond to the problematizations of behavior that have appeared successively in English-language philosophy, notably in the social and even moral dimensions of the English term, to which its classical translation by *conduite* testifies. It was only the behaviorist redefinition of *comportement* at the beginning of the twentieth century that forcibly united the problematic pair *comportement*/behavior. French reluctance to really translate "behaviorism" may in turn signal this gap with respect to conceptions and descriptions of *comportement* and "behavior."

I. "Empiricism," "Naturalism," "Behaviorism"

The term "behavior" appears in the fifteenth century in English and has had from the outset the moral dimension of "conduct," as is shown by the intransitive use of "to behave" (act in accordance with social norms). Thus in Hobbes we read the following:

By manners, I mean not here, decency of behaviour; as how one man should salute another, or how a man should wash his mouth, or pick his teeth before company, and such other points of the small morals.

(Hobbes, *Leviathan,* Part I, chap. 11)

This normative and social dimension of "behavior" (associated with decency, manners, and morals) is transformed in the empiricists, notably in Hume, where it is complicated

by a descriptive dimension. Hume defines human behavior as an observable physical manifestation, an empirical, experienceable phenomenon. It is this behavioral datum that was to found moral science and "naturalize" it by giving it a certitude comparable to that of the natural sciences.

We must therefore glean up our experiments in this science from a cautious observation of human life, and take them as they appear in the common course of the world, by men's behaviour in company, in affairs, and in their pleasures.

(Hume, *Treatise,* I, Introduction, xxiii.)

Here, "behavior" is immediately translated by *conduite,* which can raise questions since "conduct" is also very frequent in Hume, as well as the pair "behavior and conduct" ("Their whole conduct and behaviour," *Treatise,* Part II, chap. 3). However, the coupling (analogous to that of "belief and assent," see BELIEF) indicates the proximity of behavior and social custom or usage—both objects of observation and experimentation. Behavior thus proves to be the starting point for a naturalization of the social that is not a reduction to physical data but may produce knowledge that is of a quite different kind, and just as certain.

II. "Conduct"/"Behavior": Pragmatism and Behaviorism

In the term "behavior" it becomes difficult to differentiate behavior as such from a problematics of good conduct, a set of social habits, or a product of character, virtues, and so forth. The problematics of "behavior" is very rich among nineteenth-century American pragmatists, and first of all in the work of William James. In his *Talks to Teachers* (1899), he defines the child as a "behaving organism" (rendered by the French translator as "L'enfant comme organisme tourné vers le pratique"). James tries to produce a nonmoral, functionalist, and cognitive concept, thus distinguishing it from conduct (emblematized by Emerson and his "Conduct of Life"). Hume's pair, behavior/conduct, is split apart. "Behavior" is drawn toward a genuine scientific knowledge, and the latter is drawn toward a more socialized set of morals.

But it is obviously the founding texts of behaviorism as a theory of psychology that produced the most explicit redefinition of "behavior," and especially in John B. Watson's famous article "Psychology as the Behaviorist Views It" (1913). This is a naturalistic credo that sought to make psychology a science of which the object and foundation is human (and, indissolubly, animal) behavior.

Psychology as the behaviorist views it is a purely objective experimental branch of natural science. . . . The behaviorist, in his efforts to get a unitary scheme of animal response, recognizes no dividing line between man and brute. The behavior of man, with all of its refinement and complexity, forms only a part of the behaviorist's total scheme of investigation.

Watson, who was influenced by John Dewey's "functional psychology" tried, unlike the pragmatists, to separate the concept of behavior from that of consciousness (see CONSCIOUSNESS) and to associate it with the concepts of reflex arc, stimulus, habit, and disposition, all terms that were gradually to invade scientific psychology and lead it to reject data derived from introspection, common sense, or so-called popular psychology. In this context, linguistic behavior turns out to be an important dimension of behavior (*Verbal Behavior* is the title of an influential work by B. F. Skinner) that refers to language from the point of view of its observable productions (see SPEECH ACT).

> The Behaviorist asks: Why don't we make what we can observe the real field of psychology? Let us limit ourselves to things that can be observed, and formulate laws concerning only the observed things. Now, what can we observe? Well, we can observe behavior—what the organism does or says. And let me make this fundamental point at once: that saying is doing—that is, behaving. Speaking overtly or silently is just as objective a type of behavior as baseball.
>
> (Watson, "Behaviorism,
> the Modern Note in Psychology")

Behaviorism proves to be inseparable from a certain conception of behavior as observable and bodily or organic, denying the dimension of conduct and preserving in habit only the idea of conditioning. The stimulus-response schema thus becomes central to the definition of behavior. It is this apparently caricatural and restrictive conception of behavior that leads people to see in "behaviorism" a theory of behavior observed in the laboratory, whose most famous illustration is found in the experiments on conditioned reflexes conducted by Pavlov and his associates between 1900 and 1917.

However, among some pragmatists, notably Dewey and George Herbert Mead, there is a critique of behaviorism understood in this way, and an attempt to reframe the term "behavior" in a way that remains faithful to Hume's definition: experimentation and observation of behavior involve the environment as much as they do the organism. And the environment includes other human beings and complex social mediations.

> Only by analysis and selective abstraction can we differentiate the actual occurrence into two factors, one called organism and the other, environment. This fact militates strongly against any form of behaviorism that defines behavior in terms of the nervous system or body alone.
>
> (Dewey, "Conduct and Experience")

It is also in Dewey's work that we find an interesting clarification of the necessary "seriality" of behavior, and see the appearance of the English terms "comportment/deportment" and the reappearance of "conduct":

> Although the word "behavior" implies comportment, as well as deportment, the word "conduct" brings out the aspect of seriality better than does "behavior," for it clearly involves the facts both of direction (or a vector property) and of conveying or conducing.
>
> (Ibid.)

In Mead as well there is a shift from the notion of "behavior" to that of "conduct":

The behaviorism which we shall make use of is more adequate than that of which Watson makes use. Behaviorism in this wider sense is simply an approach to the study of the experience of the individual from the point of view of his conduct, particularly, but not exclusively, the conduct as it is observable by others.

> (Mead, *Mind, Self and Society*)

Linguistic behavior is thus no longer a special case, but *the* domain in which the social character of behavior appears, through the necessity of the individual's inclusion in the group of co-locutors:

> We want to approach language not from the standpoint of inner meanings to be expressed, but in its larger context of cooperation in the group. Meaning appears within that process. Our behaviorism is a social behaviorism. . . . Social psychology studies the activity or behavior of the individual as it lies within the social process; the behavior of an individual can be understood only in terms of the behavior of the whole social group of which he is a member.
>
> (Ibid.)

Social behaviorism thus seems to rehabilitate the concept of conduct. In French, the term *conduite* was long preferred in describing behavior as a component of social relationships:

> Thus we see that the most useful observations on human intellectual and moral nature, collected, not by philosophers inclined to theories and systems, but by men truly endowed with the spirit of observation and disposed to grasp the practical side of things—moralists, historians, statesmen, legislators, schoolteachers—, have not in general resulted from solitary contemplation and inward-looking study of events in consciousness, but instead from an attentive study of the conduct (*conduite*) of men placed in various situations, subjected to passions and influences of all kinds from which the observer takes great care to free himself as much as possible.
>
> (A. Cournot, *Essai sur les fondements
> de nos connaissances*, 2:548–49)

Thus *comportement* comes to be associated with a specific (nonsocial) conception of psychology. The introduction of the term *comportement* in a technical sense is exactly contemporaneous with the development of behaviorist psychology without being entirely dependent upon it. Empirical psychology, even before Pavlov's work was known and at a time when American behaviorism was still being elaborated theoretically, was represented in France by Binet's successor, Henri Piéron, who introduced the term *comportement* explicitly as a translation, defining the peculiar object of scientific psychology as

> the activity of beings and their sensory-motor relationships with their environment, what the Americans call "behavior," Germans *das Verhalten*, Italians *il comportamento*, and what we can correctly call *le comportement des organismes*.
>
> (Piéron, "Leçon inaugurale à l'École pratique
> des hautes études," 1908)

Piéron, thus anticipating certain cognitivist conceptions, also corrects Watson's behaviorism by contesting the stimulus-response pair and emphasizing physiological mechanisms. Nonetheless, the term *comportement* was henceforth associated with an empirical approach, and refers precisely to behaviorism, just as the adjective *comportemental*, introduced in French a little later (1949), translates "behavioral."

III. Behaviorism and the Philosophy of Mind: Criticisms of Behaviorism and Behaviorism as Criticism

The resistance to behaviorism on the part of the French, discernible in the refusal to really translate the term, may be a sign of a refusal to extend the objectivist method—that of a pure "external description"—to psychology and to what Vincent Descombes calls "mental phenomena" (*les phénomènes du mental*). Over the past quarter century, behaviorism seems to have become a red flag. The term is clearly pejorative and now coexists in French with the less theoretical *comportementalisme*. Today the latter refers to rather specific ultra-empirical methods involving rigid conditioning (in connection with dog-trainers, internal relationships, managers in business, shock treatment, and the *thérapies comportementalistes* of *cognitivo-comportementalisme*). As for the term *comportement*, its uses extend beyond human behavior: physicists speak of the *comportement des molécules*, and linguists of the *comportement* of this or that verb.

Today the negative connotation of behaviorism is no less current in English: behaviorism is the primary target of the philosophy of mind (see SOUL, Box 6), which since the end of the twentieth century has developed largely by using it as a foil. The problem is that this mentalist backlash also involves a repression of behaviorism's critical dimension, which was initially a challenge to a certain discourse on the mental and to the "myth of interiority." Thus, when Ludwig Wittgenstein alludes to behaviorism and notes the behaviorist flavor of his remarks, he does so in part to draw attention to a "truth" of behaviorism, repeated obsessively in the *Philosophical Investigations*: to gain access to another person's interiority we have nothing to go on other than what that person does and says (his exterior). Behaviorism is thus right insofar as it takes into account the limitation of our discourse on the mental. But it is wrong insofar as it seeks to take behavior as the criterion and foundation for knowledge of human nature, outside of any relationship to others or to society. But contemporary mentalist criticisms of behaviorism sometimes seem to see in it only its narrow scientism and naturalism, repressing the philosophical radicalness of its empiricist position.

Two criticisms of behaviorism that are exact contraries coexist today, and can serve to outline the field of the philosophy of mind. The first, which continues Dewey's and Wittgenstein's line of argument, refers to behavior as institutional and social (cf. Descombes): any acquisition of habits or dispositions is social, and the concept of behavior cannot be reduced to individual behavior. The second criticism is at the basis of neo-mentalism: the mental is irreducible to empirical behavior, the mind is certainly somewhere "inside," even if this inside is physical (or neurophysiological).

At first, behaviorism cohabited with the analytical philosophy that issued from the Austrian emigration, whose logical empiricism could be connected with behaviorism's radical empiricism, at the cost of a few misunderstandings. For example, Clark Hull proposed, in his *System of Behavior* (1952), a reconstruction of the theoretical foundations of behaviorism carried out in collaboration with Otto Neurath. The failure of this attempt at systematization prefigured the crisis of behaviorism, which was displaced by the advent of cognitive psychology, the turning point coming with Noam Chomsky's scathing 1959 review of Skinner's *Verbal Behavior*. We can lament the fact that the justified criticisms of certain aspects of the behaviorist program led to a rejection of the behaviorist critique of mentalism, which was precisely what interested Wittgenstein. In his fascinating article "Whatever Happened to Psychology as the Science of Behavior?" Skinner rightly interpreted the decline of behaviorism as a return of mentalism. Discussing, shortly before his death, the history of behaviorism and the way in which psychology as a science of behavior was eclipsed by the cognitive sciences, Skinner notes, "Everyone could relax. Mind was back."

The philosophical rejection of behaviorism has sometimes led to an uncritical acceptance of a psychology that is just as scientistic, and mentalistic in addition. Willard Van Orman Quine, a central figure in analytical philosophy and the last behaviorist, promoted a minimal behaviorism borrowed from P. Ziff: "Behaviorism is not a metaphysical theory: it is a denial of a metaphysical theory. Consequently it asserts nothing" (*Word and Object*, 265). Behaviorism raises a problem particularly interesting for the philosophy of language: what is at our disposal, in matters of language, other than verbal behavior—ours and that of others? That is, *what we say*? In an unpublished lecture, "The Behavioral Limits of Meaning," Quine noted, "In psychology, we can choose to be behaviorists or not, but in linguistics we don't have that choice." Behaviorism is the recognition of the immanent character of all linguistic research, and of the obligatory character of our starting point: ordinary language, "the social art" par excellence. In Quine or Wittgenstein, behaviorism turns out to be a reflection on the nature of the linguistic given. Thus this minimal behaviorism has to take into account the social character of behavior, which is ultimately coherent with Hume's conception of "behaviour" ("we must therefore glean up our experiments in this science from a cautious observation of human life, and take them as they appear in the common course of the world, by men's behaviour in company, in affairs, and in their pleasures" [*Treatise*, xxiii]). It should also be noted that despite American attempts, it is difficult to rid even the term "behavior" of any moral dimension, as is shown by the still-current use of the verb "to behave" in the sense of "conduct oneself well." The subtle grammatical complications surrounding this usage surface in a famous exchange in G. Cukor's film *Philadelphia Story* (1940). A character pontificates, "A woman has to behave, naturally," and another (played by Cary Grant) retorts, "A woman has to behave naturally." Here the meaning of "behavior" depends on a comma.

Sandra Laugier

BIBLIOGRAPHY

Bouveresse, Jacques. *Le Mythe de l'intériorité*. Paris: Éditions de Minuit, 1976.

Chomsky, Noam. "A Review of Skinner's Verbal Behavior." *Language* 35 (1959), 26–58.

Cournot, Antoine-Augustin. *Essai sur les fondements de nos connaissances*. Paris: Hachette, 1851.

Descombes, Vincent. *La Denrée Mentale*. Paris: Éditions de Minuit, 1995. Translation by S. A. Schwartz *The Mind's Provisions: A Critique of Cognitivism*. Princeton, NJ: Princeton University Press, 2001.

———. *Les Institutions du sens*. Paris: Éditions de Minuit, 1996.

Dewey, John. "Conduct and Experience." In *Later Works*, vol. 5, edited by J. A. Boydston. Carbondale: Southern Illinois University Press, 1981.

Hobbes, Thomas. *Leviathan*. In *The English Works of Thomas Hobbes*, 11 vols., edited by W. Molesworth. London: J. Bohn, 1839–45; reprinted by Routledge in 1992. First published in 1651.

Hume, David. *A Treatise of Human Nature*. Edited by P. Nidditch. Oxford: Oxford University Press, 1978. First published in 1740.

James, William. "The Child as a Behaving Organism." In *Talks to Teachers on Psychology, and to Students on Some of Life's Ideals*, vol. 10 in *The Works of William James*, edited by F. Buckhardt. Cambridge, MA: Harvard University Press, 1983. *Talks to Teachers* was first published in 1899.

Mead, George Herbert. *Mind, Self and Society*. Chicago: Chicago University Press, 1934.

Merleau-Ponty, Maurice. *La structure du comportement*. Paris: Presses Universitaires de France, 1942. Translation by A. L. Fisher: *The Structure of Behavior*. Pittsburgh: Duquesne University Press, 1983.

Quine, Willard Van Orman. *Word and Object*. Cambridge, MA: MIT Press, 1960.

Skinner, Burrhus Frederic. *Science and Human Behavior*. New York: Macmillan, 1953.

———. *Verbal Behavior*. New York: Appleton-Century Crofts, 1957.

———. "Whatever Happened to Psychology as the Science of Behavior?" In *Recent Issues in the Analysis of Behavior*. Columbus, OH: Merrill, 1989. Essay first published in 1987.

Watson, John Broadus. "Behaviorism, the Modern Note in Psychology." In *The Battle of Behaviorism*, edited by J. B. Watson and W. McDougall. London: Kegan Paul, Trench, Trubner, 1928.

———. "Psychology as the Behaviorist Views It." *Psychological Review* 20 (1913): 158–77.

Wittgenstein, Ludwig. *Bemerkungen über die Philosophie der Psychologie*. Edited by G.E.M. Anscombe and G. H. von Wright. Frankfurt: Suhrkamp, 1982. Translation by G.E.M. Anscombe: *Remarks on the Philosophy of Psychology*. Oxford: Blackwell, 1980.

———. *Philosophische Untersuchungen*. Edited by G.E.M. Anscombe, G. H. von Wright, and R. Rhees. Translation by G.E.M. Anscombe: *Philosophical Investigations*. Oxford : Blackwell, 1953; reprinted in 2000.

Wiff, Paul. "About Behaviorism." *Analysis* 18 (1958): 132–36.

BELIEF

| FRENCH | *croyance* |
| GERMAN | *Glaube* |

➤ *CROYANCE, FAITH,* and CLAIM, DOXA, GLAUBE, MATTER OF FACT, PERCEPTION, PROPOSITION, SOUL, TRUTH

"Belief" has undergone an evolution characteristic of certain terms in English that pass from a mental and moral meaning (as affect or feeling) to a cognitive and propositional meaning (belief gradually detached from faith and assent). This process of objectivization was accompanied by major changes in the grammar of belief. The problem raised by the translation of "belief" has to do with the term's lack of definition, which allows it to move from the emotional to the logical and from the epistemic (degree of conviction, subjective) to the cognitive (conditions of validity, objective).

I. "Belief"/"Faith"

"Belief" is related etymologically to German *Glaube* (via *galauben*, thirteenth to fourteenth century, then *ileve-leve*, the prefix *be-* being added by analogy with the verb *bileve*; cf. *Middle English Dictionary*). The first meaning of "belief," which was identical with that of "faith" (cf. *fides*, *pistis*), belonged to the same semantic field as "reliance" and "confidence"; it referred to a mental or affective condition that was connected with *confiding*, passively relying on someone or something. Thus we read this in Hobbes: "Faith is a gift of God, which man can neither give nor take away"), or in Cardinal Newman: "To have faith in God is to surrender oneself to God." In addition to this theological dimension that closely associated the word first of all with faith, "belief" has a psychological or emotional meaning; it refers more to an affect than to a relation with a proposition. In its first meaning, "belief," like *Glaube*, designated a sense of adhesion that did not need to be justified rationally (see GLAUBE). In the seventeenth century, "belief" and "faith" began gradually to diverge. "Faith" supplanted "belief" in the area of religion, the latter designating a process that differentiated itself from faith, on the one hand by a lesser intensity, and on the other hand by a more intellectual dimension, or even a judgment. This intellectualization of belief (which becomes a state or act of mind) that started in the seventeenth and eighteenth centuries developed without abandoning—and this is the interest of the way the semantic field of "belief" was constituted in English, and also a factor contributing to its untranslatability—the first meaning's dimension of affect or passivity. The French term *croyance*, which is still used to translate "belief" even in its most sophisticated recent uses, raises a problem because it accounts for neither the sensible nor the objective dimension of "belief."

II. Belief and Feeling: Hume

Does "belief" refer to a feeling or to a proposition? Is it subjective or objective? The interplay of these elements determines the term's different senses. Thus it would be problematic to use contemporary distinctions to divide "belief" into psychological and propositional elements and to make belief a "mental state" belonging to the category of the propositional attitudes that Russell defines as associating a (mental or emotional) attitude with a "content" (a proposition or statement). For Hume, "belief" designates both a feeling and a judgment, indissolubly linked, and his use of the term has become a constant point of reference for contemporary theories of belief.

■ See Box 1.

The "belief"/"assent" pair defines a set of problems that deviates from the traditional hierarchies of *savoir/croyance* and *Wissen/Glaube*. Thus it would be a mistake to think of "belief" and "assent" as representing degrees of knowledge, even if probabilistic interpretations of belief tend in this direction. Hume's notion of an intensity of belief that is variable though not measurable may be the origin of the term's semantic deviations, along with his formulation of the problem of knowing "matters of fact," which misleadingly associates the definition of "belief" with the problems of skepticism and of confirming empirical knowledge.

1

Hume: "Belief"/"assent"

To define belief, Hume starts out from the difference between idea and impression, the former being derived and copied from the latter, of which it is only a less intense version: belief is "a lively idea related to or associated with a present impression" (*A Treatise of Human Nature*, 96), or else a "feeling or sentiment" (623) identified with the immediacy of the impression: "To believe is to feel an immediate impression of the senses." This immediacy gives belief an assurance that the idea lacks, particularly in the domain of "matters of fact" (see MATTER OF FACT):

> There is a great difference betwixt the simple conception of the existence of an object, and the belief of it, and as this difference lies not in the parts or composition of the idea, which we conceive, it follows, that it must lie in the manner, in which we conceive it.
>
> (Hume, *A Treatise of Human Nature*)

> Belief is a feeling of the existence of its object. Such an "assertion" of existence neither coincides with nor assumes the idea in order to yield a belief: belief is nothing other than a "way" of feeling or conceiving our ideas that gives them more or less force or influence—whence the difficulty of translating *belief* in French as *croyance*, which is closer to the English word "opinion" (cf. "opinion or belief," *Treatise*) and can hardly be seen in French as

an affect: "Belief does nothing but vary the manner in which we conceive any object."

To understand this point, we have to note the essential connection that Hume establishes between belief and assent, that is, the mind's "strong propensity" (265) to affirm what it conceives. "Assent" is naturally connected with French *sentir* (it derives, oddly, from French *assentir*, during the thirteenth to fourteenth centuries), and belongs to the order of feeling (that is, the order of the mind). "Assent"—cf. the associated term "consent," as well as "approval" and "agreement"— designates an individual and collective feeling of acceptance. This assent is not a *fürwahrhalten* (an acceptance of a truth claim) and differs from the logical assent given to a proposition. The "belief"/"assent" pair is wholly defined by the immediacy and vivacity of impression, which can then constitute judgment and establish reasoning from cause to effect.

> Thus it appears that the belief or assent, which always attends the memory and senses, is nothing but the vivacity of those perceptions they present. . . . 'Tis merely the force and liveliness of the perception, which constitutes the first act of the judgment, and lays the foundation of that reasoning, which we build upon it, when we trace the relation of cause and effect.
>
> (Hume, *A Treatise of Human Nature*)

The "belief"/"assent" pair thus defines the semantic field of a sensitive mind difficult to relate to the French use of *croyance* or the German use of *Glaube*. It is all the more remarkable that Hume, in defining "belief"/ "assent," problematizes judgment and inquires into the difference between believing and disbelieving a given proposition regarding matters of fact: "Wherein consists the difference betwixt incredulity and belief?" How can we determine the difference between assenting to a proposition about matters of fact and rejecting it, since this difference is not in the idea itself?

The answer still has to do with the more forceful "manner" of conceiving the idea that is characteristic of belief. The "belief"/"assent" pair defines a feeling of natural and unavoidable belief (183) determined not by reason but by "custom," a mental feeling that we cannot avoid any more than we can wholly elicit it, for it is not active, but passive, and acts on us by causing our actions.

> Nature, by an absolute and uncontroulable necessity has determin'd us to judge as well as to breathe and feel . . . Belief is more properly an act of the sensitive, than of the cogitative part of our natures.
>
> (Hume, *A Treatise of Human Nature*)

III. Belief, Causes, and Consequences

The epistemological problem of the foundation of empirical knowledge, which is at the origin of most contemporary discussions of belief, determines two trends in the redefinition of belief: with regard to its causes, and with regard to its effects.

A. Belief and justification

After Hume, the first trend no longer concerns the empirical causes of belief (habit), but rather its justification, and hence its reasons (cf. the distinction, which has become omnipresent in the philosophical vocabulary, between "cause" and "reason"). The skeptical problem of the cause of our factual beliefs is retranslated into an epistemological problem of the objective conditions of the confirmation of empirical beliefs—in contemporary terms, the problem of induction—and this reintegrates belief into the *croyance/savoir* hierarchy. This is shown not only by the literature on the so-called "problem of induction" and of confirmation by experience, but also by the emergence of new expressions such as "justified belief" and "warranted belief."

■ See Box 2.

Most epistemological theories of belief seek instead to include it within knowledge, to objectify it as Frege did in proposing an objective conception of thoughts (*Gedanken*) as belonging to the mind, not to minds. Beliefs, exactly like Frege's *Gedanken*, are seen as independent of the believer in the framework of a general theory of judgment. Thus Willard Van Orman Quine in his *Pursuit of Truth*:

> A perception is an event in just one percipient; . . . a belief, on the other hand, can have many believers.

Here, belief is propositional: a shareable statement to which one may adhere or not. Such a shift, which may be acrobatic and in any case involves a sharp break with Hume's conception of belief, is illustrated by Russell's procedures. At first, Russell viewed belief as a dual relation between a subject and a proposition conceived as "an objective entity which exists whether or not it is believed." Thus the object of belief is identified with belief itself.

■ See Box 3.

The development that we have sketched here, from a "felt" belief (Hume) to a logical or "propositional" belief

2

Popper and the attempt to separate knowledge and belief

Karl Popper proposes to abandon Hume's concept of belief, which he regards as too "subjectivist," and to separate it from the objective concepts of knowledge and truth. The danger involved in taking belief into account is that knowledge and truth might be seen as "particular cases" of belief, those in which it is justified.

If we start from our subjective experience of believing, and thus look upon knowledge as a special kind of belief, then we may indeed have to look upon truth as

some even more special kind of belief : as one that is well founded and justified.

(Popper, *Conjectures and Refutations*)

For Popper, both verificationist theories (those that emphasize the empirical justification of beliefs, even in terms of probability) and psychologizing theories (those that are concerned with the causes and origins of our beliefs), because they cling to belief and its justification, have to abandon the objectivity of truth.

They all say, more or less, that truth is what we are justified in believing or in accepting.

(Ibid.)

Popper therefore sets out to separate the domain of objective and even conjectural knowledge (which Popper, like Frege, calls "World 3") from that of belief. Popper's point of view is symptomatic, even if it runs counter to the redefinitions of belief (let us recall that he was not a native speaker of English).

3

Wittgenstein and Ramsey: Belief's effects

We can compare the influence of the Frege-Russell conception of belief on F. P. Ramsey and Wittgenstein. Ramsey in his *Foundations* proposes the following definition:

I prefer to deal with those beliefs which are expressed in words, consciously asserted or denied ; for these beliefs are the most proper subject for logical criticism. The mental factors of such a belief I take to be words, . . . connected together and accompanied by a feeling or feelings of belief or disbelief.

A footnote on the same page indicates Ramsey's distance from Hume, but also the complexity of his relationship to empiricism:

I speak throughout as if the differences between belief, disbelief, and mere consideration lay in the presence or absence of "feelings" but any other word may be substituted for "feeling," e.g. "specific quality," "act of assertion" and "act of denial."

Here Ramsey is attacking a logical problem considered in an astonishing way by Wittgenstein, notably in the *Tractatus* (5.54f.). Wittgenstein criticizes Russell's theory of belief as relating a subject A and a proposition *p* in a compound proposition "A believes that *p*." For Wittgenstein, such a conception suggests the possibility (which must be excluded) of thinking or judging nonsense: in the case in which *p* is meaningless, we would then have a meaningless element in a compound proposition that is itself meaningful, which is impossible; therefore the proposition is defective. See *Tractatus* (5.5422): "The correct explanation of the form of the proposition (*Satz*) "A makes the judgment p" (*A urteilt p*) must

show that it is impossible for a judgment to be a piece of nonsense."

Here is the radical solution Wittgenstein proposes in the *Tractatus*:

5542. Es ist aber klar, dass "A glaubt dass p," "A denkt p," "A sagt p" von der Form "'p' sagt p" sind.

(It is clear, however, that "A believes that p," "A has the thought p," and "A says p" are of the form "'p' says p.")

Propositions that bear on a belief do not coordinate a fact and an object (*Gegenstand*) that is the subject A (which would lead to nonsense [*Unsinn*], but instead coordinate *two facts* ("p"—the thought that p—and the fact p). This redefinition of belief (*Glaube*) has sometimes been interpreted in an antisubjectivist sense. Matters are perhaps more complicated: in 5.5421, Wittgenstein explains that his definition shows that "the soul—the subject, etc. as it is conceived in the superficial psychology of the present day" are *ein Unding*, a non-thing. A composite soul would no longer be a soul. In reality, Wittgenstein is challenging the psychological idea of a unified subject—"A"—who is supposed to be the subject of assent: if there were a subject of the thought p, the subject would have himself to be composed, like p (would have to be a *zusammengetzte Seele* [a composite soul]), and decomposable into elements of thought. The principle of Wittgenstein's extensionalism thus leads him to a complete depsychologization of belief and the "mind."

It is on the basis of this radical, nonpsychological conception of thought and belief that Ramsey posits once again, in his article "Facts and Propositions" in *Foundations*, the

untranslatable Humean question of the difference between believing and disbelieving a proposition (see Box 1). After proposing his famous solution to the problem of truth (see TRUTH), Ramsey inquires into the equivalence—logically indispensable if we are still following Wittgenstein—of believing not-p and disbelieving p, "but to determine what we mean by this 'equivalent' is, to my mind, the central difficulty of the subject" (*Foundations*, as reprinted in Ramsey, *Philosophical Papers*, 43). Ramsey continues: "It seems to me that the equivalence between believing 'not-p' and disbelieving 'p' is to be defined in terms of causation."

Ramsey proposes to define belief in terms not of attitude but of causal properties (causes and especially effects of beliefs [*Foundations*]), while at the same time admitting, with a modesty that distinguishes him from his successors, that he scarcely sees how to determine them and that his definition remains imprecise. In "Truth and Probability" (reprinted in *Philosophical Papers*), Ramsey produces a theory of the degrees of belief and probability that played a founding role. Ramsey is not interested in the psychological degree or intensity of belief, but in "a measurement of belief *qua* basis of action" (67), and hence in probability. The connection between belief and probability, or between belief and the "problem of induction," is thus constituted entirely differently from the way it appears in Hume, and separately from any examination or measure of feeling, since Ramsey wants to give a resolutely extensional definition of belief that will lead him to a whole reworking of the classical concept of probability.

(Wittgenstein) would be relatively easy to describe if it were not complicated by the maintenance, and even the strengthening, of an emotional or psychological dimension of assent, since most contemporary thinkers on belief do not want to go as far as Wittgenstein and Ramsey in eliminating "attitude" and mind from belief. This is a rather curious point: the propositional (or enunciative) conception of belief has been able to coexist, and has even been associated in contemporary reflection on the status of beliefs and their relationships (notably in Davidson), with a repsychologization of assent, which brings back into the mental act or state of assent the "mind" or feeling that had been excluded by the logical program (which was perhaps hopeless) of what one might have called "proposition-belief."

B. Belief and propensity: Functionalism

A second trend deals with beliefs as causes of our actions, interpreting beliefs, often in naturalistic terms, as dispositions or propensities to action that are based on habit (see Peirce, who inspired Ramsey). In such a dispositionalist theory, belief is generally conceived as a representation that is, in a sense, rather indeterminate. This view is often defined by referring to Ramsey's fine expression asserting that belief is a "navigational chart" that tells us how to orient ourselves in our environment. Ramsey is obviously very prudent as to the causal determination that our beliefs might exercise on our actions and statements. Quine, a philosopher who was, however, clearly dispositionalist, wrote, "Manifestations of belief vary extravagantly with the belief and the circumstances of the believer" (*The Pursuit of Truth*).

Considering belief as a representation that has past causes, notably sensorial and semantic, and future effects, notably on action and other representations, contemporary cognitivists have taken up and transformed Ramsey's attempts. This "representationalist" point of view is found in the cognitive sciences, particularly in functionalism, which defines belief causally as a state brought about by sensorial inputs associated with dispositions to action, and thus stimulating behavioral outputs. Beliefs are supposed to correspond to concrete cerebral states that are not wholly determined (except in extreme functionalist programs) but can be associated with a set of behaviors that may be semantic. This is not the place to enter into the debates surrounding the question of (mental or semantic) holism. It is clear that since the recent development of the sciences of the brain/mind and their invasion of semantic and philosophical questions, we are now seeing a reformatting of the notion of belief, conceived alternatively, and even simultaneously, as a state that is mental, neurophysiological, physical, and so forth. It remains to discover whether the term "belief" can carry this whole new conceptual load, and whether such uses do not involve, as J. L. Austin would say, an excessive abuse of the ordinary use of the word "belief" by overdetermining its natural ambiguity. Because they insist on the passive character of belief and posit it as a source of action and representations, these redefinitions seem once again to revive Hume's naturalism. But they are problematic. The acknowledged failure of functionalism is only one example of the theoretical difficulties encountered by causal theories of belief. However, that is only a symptom of a fundamental problem that concerns precisely the use

of "belief." The recent evolution of the term leads us to ask whether it is so easy to understand it naturally in a physico-mental sense, for example, as an intermediate state that is neither physical not mental but located at the intersection of the two, and capable of causing our actions and discourses. With "belief," we have a case in which the noncritical transfer into French of contemporary English usage raises a problem (whence the difficulty in translating Ramsey), because the French term *croyance* is still more difficult to interpret as designating a causal state detachable from its object ("propositional" or other) than is "belief."

More generally, the flexibility of the use of "belief" in English makes it easier to use in connection with the vocabulary of action than the corresponding terms in other languages. For example, "to act on a belief" is a common expression in English, but it is difficult to translate into French, and so is the substantive "believer," which is obviously not equivalent to the French *croyant*. French philosophers' recent adoption of the term "belief," conceived simultaneously as a statement, a disposition, a physical or mental state, a cause of action, and so on, was philosophically possible and fertile only because of the multiplicity and naturalness of the uses of "belief" in English. The limits of this creativity are seen when we try to find equally pertinent uses in French or German. We can compare this with the difficulty of translating the expression "philosophy of mind" and even of constituting its field, and draw a parallel between the translation of "mind" by *esprit* and the translation of "belief" by *croyance*: in both cases, the French term suffers from strong associations with a thematics (at once spiritualist and psychologizing) that overdetermines translations and forces us to resort to a whole series of specific definitions, or even to invent an artificial language.

IV. The Grammars of Belief: "Belief"/"Certainty"/*Gewissheit*

Philosophical thought has attempted to divide the Humean conception, to separate assent from belief. In addition to the difficulties raised by causal theories, this has led to a neglect of a fundamental logical problem of belief: that of the nature of *assent*. Is it an adherence of the mind (the first meaning of "assent," synonymous with "faith"), a disposition to assert the truth of what the mind conceives, or a "holding-for-true" (*fürwahrhalten*, usually rendered in translations of Kant and Frege as "assent," or in French, as *assentiment*)? Is assent inseparable from judgment and its function, or is it added to judgment, like Russell's assertion-sign? The grammar of assent is also that of belief, of certainty, and of knowledge (the distinction between *savoir* and *connaissance* does not exist in English; see EPISTEMOLOGY, Box 3). It is this set of language games that has to be examined in order to see that it is really possible to abstract *belief* from the other terms—not only *assent*, but also *certainty* and *knowledge*—with which it is systematically connected.

■ See Box 4.

So is certainty a subjective or an objective state? This question, outlined in Newman, allows us to challenge mentalist and dispositionalist interpretations of certainty, and even of belief, which has a closer grammatical relationship with truth.

■ See Box 5.

4

Newman and the typology of "assents"

J. H. Newman, in his extraordinary work *An Essay in Aid of a Grammar of Assent* (1870), classifies kinds of assent, distinguishing "notional assent" (theological, inferential in nature) and "real assent" ("or belief" [63], which is stronger, involving unconditional acceptance, and is therefore religious in nature). He then differentiates "simple assent" (106; a more or less conscious mental assertion) from complex assent, which is voluntary and the result of thought, hence a judgment: "such assents as must be made consciously and deliberately, and which I shall call complex and reflex assents" (24).

This typology of assents inevitably leads to an examination of the case in which reflective assent involves the assertion of a proposition as true.

Let the proposition to which the assent is given be as absolutely true as the reflex act pronounces it to be, that is, objectively true as well as subjectively—then the assent may be called a perception, the conviction a certitude, the proposition or truth a certainty, or thing known, or a matter of knowledge, and to assent to it is to know.

Here we must note the difference between "certitude" and "certainty," the former designating a subjective state, the latter an objective condition dependent on knowledge. It is indeed a grammar of assent that Newman elaborates in his examination of the "language game" of belief and certitude, placing certitude, that is, reflective and thus indefectible assent, above "simple assent." Religion demands a certitude: "This is why religion demands more than an assent to its truth; it requires a certitude." Certitude is a mental act, subjective but reflective and founded, of adhesion to a truth (for Newman, a divine truth). The concept thus blends faith and truth in a remarkable way. All certitude is not true; however, when it is false, the error is not in the assent but in the reasoning that leads to it. There is no test for determining whether a certitude is "true," whether it is a *savoir*, except the criteria of proof, of intellectual satisfaction and irreversibility.

5

Wittgenstein and certitude: *Über Gewissheit* / "On certainty"

We must start over from Wittgenstein, using his critique of Russell's concept of assertion and his reworking of Moore's paradox. I can believe something that is not true, or not believe something that is true. But I cannot say (or rather, it is meaningless to say), "It's raining, but I don't believe it" (a). One therefore cannot separate, in the proposition "I believe *p*," the proposition *p* and a (mental or logical) act of assertion. This has several consequences. To say "I believe *p*" is not a description of a psychological state or a disposition; otherwise (a) would not be paradoxical. "I believe *p*" is an expression (*Äusserung, Ausdruck* [see CLAIM]; these terms could also be translated by "avowal") like "I hurt." Believing (*croire, glauben*) is therefore neither a state (mental, physical, or any other kind) nor a disposition (we cannot determine all its consequences and expressions). Wittgenstein thus challenges the idea that assent is an assertion added, in some way, to a proposition when I assert its truth. If (a) is paradoxical, that is because the statement *p* somehow produces its own affirmation, and this was already implicit in Ramsey's "redundant" conception of truth, which preceded the definition of "belief" (cf. TRUTH). This observation ends up causing the implosion of the whole tradition summed up in the belief/assent pair, which is extended to interpretations of belief like that of William James (see *Principles of Psychology*, II, and *The Will to Believe*) and that of Russell. According to Wittgenstein, belief is not a feeling or an act of approval with regard to a proposition (no matter how powerful it might be: in James it creates truth), just as an assertion need not be an affirmative supplement, perhaps symbolized by a sign, to a proposition.

> Daß er das und das glaubt, ergibt sich für uns aus der Beobachtung seiner Person, aber die Aussage "Ich glaube" macht er nicht auf Grund der Selbstbeobachtung. Und *darum* kann "Ich glaube p" äquivalent sein der Behauptung von "p."
>
> (That he believes such-and-such, *we* gather from observation of his person, but *he* does not make the statement "I believe. . ." on grounds of observation of himself. And *that* is why "I believe p" may be equivalent to the assertion of "p.")
>
> (Wittgenstein, *Remarks on the Philosophy of Psychology*, I.§504)

More generally, "believe" (*croire-glauben*) is systematically connected with the parent notions of certainty and knowledge, and thus constitute a language game in ordinary language that has to be taken into account. The point is made more precise in Wittgenstein's last text, *Über Gewissheit* [*On Certainty*]. The French *croire*—like "certitude," "certainty," *Gewissheit*—is connected with *savoir*, not because it is a (more subjective or more intense) form of *savoir*, but because of its grammar. There are important grammatical differences between *savoir* and the other verbs. Saying *je sais "p"* does not guarantee that *p* is true, and thus that I really know *p*; I have to prove, in one way or another, that I know it; *je sais "p"* can thus be false or misleading, like *je promets*.

> "Ich weiss," sagt man, wenn mann bereit ist, zwingende Gründe zu geben. "Ich weiss" bezieht sich auf eine Möglichkeit des Darthuns der Wahrheit.
>
> (One says "I know" when one is ready to give compelling grounds. "I know" relates to a possibility of demonstrating the truth.)
>
> (Wittgenstein, *On Certainty* = *Über Gewissheit* [bilingual edition], trans. D. Paul and G.E.M. Anscombe, §243)

On the other hand, "I believe *p*" and "I am certain that *p*" always have a subjective truth, and do not require external justification to be accepted. There is an asymmetry between *glauben* and *wissen* that corresponds in part to the difference between "expression" and "description," which is often found in Wittgenstein.

> Es wäre richtig zu sagen: "Ich glaube . . ." hat subjektive Wahrheit; aber "Ich weiss . . ." nicht. "Ich glaube" ist ein Äusserung, nicht aber "ich weiss."
>
> (It would be correct to say "I believe" has subjective truth, but not "I know.")

(continued)

(continued)

"I believe" is an "expression," but "I know" is not.)

(Ibid., §179-80)

But through its relationship with *wissen* (unlike the French *certitude*, which is closer to *certain* than to *savoir*, and which corresponds to German *Sicherheit* instead), *Gewissheit* has a special status. It is not a mental state, but neither is it a state of things. In *Über Gewissheit*, the term *wissen* (*savoir*) paradoxically acquires a status that is both subjective and objective: I am the one who knows.

Wann aber ist etwas objektiv gewiss? Wenn ein Irrtum nicht möglich ist . . .

Muss der Irrtum nicht *logisch* ausgeschlossen sein?

(But when is something objectively certain? When a mistake is not possible. . . . Mustn't mistake be *logically* excluded?)

(Ibid., §194)

Wittgenstein seems to distinguish *Sichersein* (a grammatically subjective state, but one that is connected with knowledge, §357) from *Gewissheit*. Propositions that are certain (*gewiß*) have a particular form of objectivity; they are the ones we do not doubt, not because they have been proved (one cannot prove them, any more than any empirical proposition), but because they are the "hinges" (*Angeln*) on which our questions and judgments pivot. Propositions that are

certain, even when they are empirical, are part of our logic.

D.h., *die Fragen*, die wir stellen, und unsere *Zweifel* beruhen darauf, dass gewisse Sätze vom Zweifel ausgenommen sind, gleichsam die Angeln, in welchen jene sich bewegen. . . . D.h., es gehört zur Logik unserer wissenschaftlichen Untersuchungen, dass Gewisses in der Tat nicht angezweifelt wird.

(That is to say, the *questions* we raise and our *doubts* depend on the fact that some propositions are exempt from doubt, are as it were like hinges on which those turn. . . . That is to say, it belongs to the logic of our scientific investigations that certain things are in deed not doubted.)

(Ibid., §341–42)

For Wittgenstein, the feeling of certainty attached to "hinge propositions" is not so much a mental state (*Seelenzustand*; in *Über Gewissheit* [*On Certainty*], §356) as a feeling of peace or contentment that is not the unreflective acceptance (*Vorschnellheit*) that philosophers attribute to common sense, but rather a form of life: "*Mein Leben* besteht darin, dass ich mich mit manchem zufrieden gebe" (*My life* consists in my being content to accept many things; trans. D. Paul and G.E.M. Anscombe, *Über Gewissheit = On Certainty* [bilingual edition], §344).

Wittgenstein himself acknowledges having the greatest difficulty in "expressing and thinking" the kind of "lived" certainty (*Sicherheit*) he refers to, which is neither objective nor subjective, and remarks, "Das ist sehr schlecht ausgedrückt, und wohl auch schlecht gedacht" (That is very badly expressed and probably badly thought as well; ibid. §358–59). Finally, Wittgenstein recognizes that the type of certainty he wants to describe is "something animal" (*etwas animalisches*, ibid. §359). This is less a nauralistic notation than a reference to the passive dimension of belief, which is in fact an essential element of *Gewissheit*. To explain it, Wittgenstein has to move into English, using the untranslatable expression "satisfied that": "We are satisfied that the earth is round" (ibid., §299).

Certain propositions' very special status between *Wissen* and belief is complicated by various translation difficulties. In French, *certitude* is closer to *croyance* than to *savoir*, whereas German *Gewissheit* allows Wittgenstein connections with *Wissen*. In English "certain" allows, like "belief," very flexible constructions. For example, we have the curious construction "a person is certain to do something," which means not that the person is (subjectively) certain that he will do something, but that the fact that he is going to do it is certain (cf. "the town is certain to be taken"). Such constructions are possible only in a language game in which "certain" has a vague status located between the subjective and the objective that cannot, any more than "belief," be divided into two functions (assertive and propositional, psychological and logical). It was Wittgenstein who most clearly challenged the neo-Humean dogma of the propositional attitude by showing, through the examination of "I believe" at the intersection of two languages, the genuine subtlety of the grammars of assent.

■ See Box 6.

Sandra Laugier

BIBLIOGRAPHY

Hobbes, Thomas. *Leviathan*. London, 1651.

Hume, David. *A Treatise of Human Nature*. Edited by L. A. Selby-Bigge and P. H. Nidditch. Oxford: Oxford University Press / Clarendon, 1978. First published 1739.

James, William. *The Will to Believe*. New York: Longmans, Green and Company, 1897. Vol. 6 in *The Works of William James*. 8 vols. Edited by F. Burckhardt. Cambridge, MA: Harvard University Press, 1975–88.

———. *Principles of Psychology*. 2 vols. New York: Holt, 1890. Vol. 3 in *The Works of William James*. 8 vols. Edited by F. Burckhardt. Cambridge, MA: Harvard University Press, 1975–88.

Newman, John Henry. *An Essay in Aid of a Grammar of Assent*. Reprint. London: Longman, Green and Company, 1903. First published in 1870.

Popper, Karl R. *Conjectures and Refutations: The Growth of Scientific Knowledge*. 4th ed. rev. London: Routledge and Kegan Paul, 1974. First published in 1963.

Quine, Willard Van Orman. *The Pursuit of Truth*. Cambridge, MA: Harvard University Press, 1990.

Ramsey, Frank P. *Foundations: Essays in Philosophy, Logic, Mathematics and Economics*. Edited by D. H. Mellor. Atlantic Highlands, NJ: Humanities Press, 1978. First published in 1931.

———. *Philosophical Papers*. Edited by D. H. Mellor. Cambridge: Cambridge University Press, 1990.

Wittgenstein, Ludwig. *On Certainty = Über Gewissheit*. Bilingual edition. Edited by G.E.M. Anscombe and G. H. von Wright. Translated by Denis Paul and G.E.M. Anscombe. Reprint. Oxford: Blackwell, 1979.

———. *Remarks on the Philosophy of Psychology*, Edited by G.E.M. Anscombe and G. H. Wright. Translated by G.E.M. Anscombe. Oxford: Basil Blackwell, 1980.

———. *Tractatus Logico-Philosophicus*, Translated by D. F. Pears and B. F. McGuinness. London: Routledge, 1994.

6

Ijtihād [اجتهاد]

The word comes from the verbal radical *jhd* meaning "to apply oneself to," "to strive." The corresponding substantive *jihād*, meaning primarily "effort" and "striving," has also come to be used for "holy war." *Ijtihād* is another derived substantive and is to be translated also as "effort" or "initiative," but it means, above all, "effort of interpretation," especially in jurisprudential matters. Thus the noun *mujtahid* (the person who performs *ijtihād*) designates a scholar who interprets the law in order to apply it or adapt it to new cases and circumstances.

Beyond its technical meaning, the concept of *ijtihād*, especially for reformist modern thinkers, has come to signify the intellectual effort of the Muslim world to reconstruct the religious thought and the law in Islam in order to cope with the challenges of the changed times. In that sense *ijtihād* is the dialectical other of *taqlīd*, which is the blind adherence to and repetition of tradition (or what is constructed as such) simply because it is tradition.

Bachir Diagne

BIBLIOGRAPHY

Kurzman, Charles, ed. *Liberal Islam: A Source Book.* New York: Oxford University Press, 1998.

Mas'ud, Khalid. *Iqbal's Reconstruction of Ijtihad.* Lahore: Iqbal Academy Pakistan, 2003.

Ramadan, Tariq. *Radical Reform: Islamic Ethics and Liberation.* Oxford: Oxford University Press, 2009.

Smock, David R. *Ijtihad: Reinterpreting Islamic Principles for the Twenty-First Century.* Washington, DC: US Institute of Peace, 2004.

BERĪT [בְּרִית] (HEBREW)

ENGLISH	covenant
FRENCH	*alliance*
GERMAN	*Bund*
GREEK	*diathêkê* [διαθήκη]
ITALIAN	*patto*
LATIN	*testamentum, foedus, pactum*

➤ *ALLIANCE*, and BERUF, BOGOČELOVEČESTVO, EUROPE, GOD, LAW, PEOPLE, SOBORNOST'

The word used in the Bible to designate the covenant, *berit*, is certainly related to the Akkadian *birītu*, "bond." Thus the underlying idea is probably the same as that underlying German *Bund*, from *binden*, "to bind." On the other hand, the literal meaning of the usual expression for "conclude," *karat berit* [כָּרַת בְּרִית], is "cut" (cf. Gr. *horkia temnein* [ὅρκια τέμνειν]), whence a semantic paradox: one binds by dividing. The expression no doubt comes from the sacrifice consecrating the covenant, as the Greek equivalent *spondê* [σπονδή] came from the libation that completed it, or the English expression "to strike a bargain" came from the gesture of shaking hands. People passed between the two halves of an animal, calling down on themselves the same fate in the event that they committed treachery (Gn 15:9, 17; Jer 34:18).

A covenant is an oath connected with a curse (Gn 26:28; Dt 29:11). The idea first arises from a contract between humans, such as a soldier's obligation to serve his leader (2 Kgs 11:4). At first, this contract is unequal: a superior imposes duties (Jgs 2:20; Ps 111:9). Later it becomes an agreement among equals (Gn 14:13), brothers (Am 1:9), friends (1 Sm 23:18), or spouses (Mal 2:14). The idea of a covenant may include, as it does in contemporary French, international treaties. Such treaties, beginning with the most ancient, between Egyptians and Hittites (1280 BCE), appeal to the gods as guarantors. In this way, every people that enters into a contract recognizes the power of the other's gods and thus makes a kind of covenant with them as well (Ex 23:32). The novelty of Israel is the idea of a covenant between a people and its own god, a god who chose his people (Ex 19:5f.). The divine was a guarantor; now he becomes a partner. In the Septuagint, the word is not translated by the usual Greek word, *spondê*, but by *diathêkê* [διαθήκη], which designates the last dispositions made by a dying person, and thus a testament. In turn, it was rendered in Latin by *testamentum*—which has remained in the "Old/New Testament." On the other hand, the Vulgate prefers *foedus* or *pactum*—Italian *patto*. English "covenant" comes from French *convenir*, whose semantic field is different. The biblical covenant is historical; there is, however, nothing like it in Islam, which is why the term "covenant" is not used to describe the pact (*mītāq* [ميثاق]) through which humans, miraculously drawn from Adam's loins, recognize Allah's dominion (Qur'ān 7:172). This pact is situated in pre-eternity. Allah commits himself in no way, but man is bound by the pact even before he can ratify it in his temporal life.

Rémi Brague

BERUF (GERMAN)

ENGLISH	profession, vocation, calling
FRENCH	*métier, vocation*
GREEK	*ergon* [ἔργον], *ponos* [πόνος], *klêsis* [κλῆσις]
HEBREW	*tapēqīd* [תַּפְקִיד]
LATIN	*officium, professio, vocatio*

➤ *VOCATION*, and CLAIM, GLAUBE, GOD, LIBERAL, OIKONOMIA, SECULARIZATION, SOLLEN, STAND, STRADANIE, WORK

Beruf became untranslatable relatively recently: it is associated with Max Weber and his 1904–5 study on *The Protestant Ethic and the Spirit of Capitalism*. The problem concerns first the twofold meaning of the word, which oscillates between the secular (trade, profession) and the religious (vocation): whereas German hesitates, French is forced to choose. But *Beruf* has another, remarkable particularity: its untranslatable aspect does not have to do with the genius peculiar to a language, but to the decision made by a translator, Luther, and to a historical development, that of modern capitalism, whose whole novelty is, according to Weber, concentrated in it.

I. The Semantic Development of *Beruf*

By devoting a section of *The Protestant Ethic and the Spirit of Capitalism* to "The Notion of *Beruf* in Luther," Weber gave the philosophical and sociological vocabulary a new term, and at the same time discovered an untranslatable: the French at times also use the word *Beruf*, all the more willingly because for Weber it has the value of an emblem for the whole process of the emergence of modern capitalism. In itself, *Beruf* can be defined as a certain conception of work as "an absolute end in itself, a calling." For Weber, the spirit of capitalism is concentrated in *Beruf*, as is shown by his definition (or at least his "provisional *image*") of a "mentality that seeks, in a systematic, rational way, a legitimate profit through a vocation (*Beruf*)." This quest for profit was accompanied, in the modern period, by a "social ethic" bearing "a specific idea of *vocation* as duty (*Berufspflicht*)" that would confer a moral value on labor and on the vocation in which it is performed. In the French translations of the preceding quotations, the word *Beruf* is rendered by *vocation* and *métier*; the first translator, Jacques Chavy, used in the same passages the terms *vocation, profession*, and *métier, profession*. Here we see the difficulty of the term. In French not every *métier* is a *vocation*, whereas *Beruf* denotes two things at once: a regular, remunerated occupation, and a calling (the word *Beruf* comes from *rufen*, "to call"), the election that leads to this occupation and gives life its ultimate meaning. French translators of Weber can choose among three solutions. The first accepts the necessity of choosing, as Éric de Dampierre, who helped revise the first French translation, explains in a note:

> The translation of *Beruf*, "métier et vocation," a key word for Weber in many regards (cf. *Le savant et le politique*), required that the semantic tension between its two poles be retained. We have rendered it by *métier* (or *profession*) in a religious context, and by *vocation* in an occupational context, in order to emphasize this tension that provides the foundation for the work's thesis. Nonetheless, it would be incorrect to assume that these two complementary meanings are present everywhere, in particular in a Biblical context, where doing so would amount to reintroducing an anachronism: in such cases, we have made do with *besogne*, an old Scriptural word that seemed to us the best suited to render the notion in its undifferentiated state.

The principle of translation is thus a constant inversion: to render the foreignness of *Beruf*, the word *métier*, normally used in secular, occupational contexts, is used in religious ones, and the word *vocation*, which is normally used in religious contexts, is used in occupational ones. This solution is necessarily a makeshift one: the inversion is not carried out systematically, and cannot be, since it has to assume what is in question, namely, the division into the temporal and the spiritual, the occupational and the confessional. The peculiarity of German *Beruf* is that it attenuates this division, and expresses simultaneously what French has to distinguish or even oppose. It is thus dangerous to start from this distinction between the sacred and the profane to translate a term that challenges that distinction.

A second solution consists in coining a portmanteau word that indicates the difficulty: that is what Jean-Pierre Grossein does by using *profession-vocation* in the most recent French translation of *The Protestant Ethic*—after having justified this solution in his selection of Weber's writings on the *Sociologie des religions*, arguing that "awkwardness" must be preferred to "insipidness" in cases where *Beruf* clearly denotes the "interweaving" of the two registers ("Glossaire raisonné"). Translator Isabelle Kalinowski emphasizes that this neologism "is more an explanation than a translation." The choice to really translate, that is, to situate the word in the normal usages of the target language, led her to a third solution, using throughout the word *métier*, which has "the advantage of applying better to the very broad meaning that Weber gives to *Beruf*"—unless, of course, the translator is obliged to leave *Beruf* in German. However, with *métier* one of the two nuances of *Beruf* disappears: the French word has no particular religious resonance. Kalinowski accepts this risk, and even sees in it a confirmation of the starting point of Weber's analysis, namely, "the absence in Luther's time of a term having the connotation of the word 'vocation' *in Romance languages*—and, we might add, in other languages as well" (italics in original). The most faithful French translation of Weber would thus be one that failed, precisely because it is a translation into a Romance language, to render the plurality of the meanings of *Beruf*.

The polemic raging among translators thus opposes two philosophies of translation that are probably irreconcilable. As for the word itself, it would be false to say that *Beruf* spontaneously unites contraries, the sacred and the profane, and that it is in its nature to express something different from what other languages express. Weber very clearly refuses to take into account "any ethnical peculiarity of the languages concerned" or to see in the word "the product of a Germanic spirit" (cf. his refusal to invoke a "national character"). Weber's starting point is in fact linguistic, but his reasons are located outside language:

> And if we trace the history of the word through the civilized languages, it appears that neither the predominantly Catholic peoples nor those of classical antiquity have possessed any expression of similar connotation for what we know as a calling (in the sense of a life-task, a definite field in which to work), while one has existed for all predominantly Protestant peoples.

Beruf does not divide languages qua languages, but it reveals another division separating Protestant peoples from others, and from Catholic peoples in particular. In this sense, *Beruf* is a very special kind of untranslatable: "the idea is new, a product of the Reformation"—in short, it is a confessional untranslatable.

How can *Beruf* lack an equivalent if it is not by virtue of a particular character of the language itself? The first thing to note is that *Beruf* was not initially an untranslatable term, but became one: thus we must assume a historical change. Second, this change takes the typical form of a decision, that of an author, Martin Luther, who according to Weber chose to understand the word in a new sense. Third, this authorial decision is more precisely a translator's decision: for Weber, it was in translating the Bible that Luther created the modern concept of *Beruf* by modifying the earlier use of the word.

Weber's reasoning is set forth in particular in two long notes, veritable textual and linguistic surveys reviewing Hebrew, Greek, Latin, German, English, and Romance languages. The old use of *Beruf* is defined as religious, equivalent to *Berufung* or *Vokation*: it corresponds to French *vocation*, and particularly to ecclesiastical vocation. For Weber, the current sense of the word is thus a "profane" sense, "purely secular": in a remarkable way, Luther is supposed to have secularized the term. According to Weber, the pivotal text that marks the term's transition to its modern use is found in Luther's translation of a passage in Sirach (Ecclesiasticus), 11:20–21, which recommends:

20 Stand by your task, and attend to it, and grow old in your work.

21 Do not wonder at the works of a sinner, but trust in the Lord and keep at your toil; for it is easy in the sight of the Lord to enrich a poor man quickly and suddenly.

The stakes involved in translation seem to multiply infinitely when we consider that the text of Sirach translated by Luther was composed in Hebrew, but transmitted in Greek (the book is, moreover, not part of the Jewish canon). The original Hebrew text was partially rediscovered only in 1896 and finally completed in Qumran, then in 1964: in Weber there are echoes of the first reconstitution (French trans. K.). The Greek translates the first occurrence of the Hebrew *tapĕqîd* [תַּפְקִיד]—rendered here as "task," designating an established occupation—by *diathêkê* [διαθήκη]; "work" (v. 20a) renders *ergon* [ἔργον], and "toil" (v. 21a) *ponos* [πόνος]. It is the last two words that Luther (who knew only the Greek text) translated by *Beruf*: *en tôi ergôi sou palaiôthêti* [ἐν τῷ ἔργῳ σοῦ παλαιώθητι] becomes *beharre in deinem Beruf*, and *emmene toi ponôi sou* [ἔμμενε τῷ πόνῳ σοῦ] becomes *bleibe in deinem Beruf* (on the other hand, in v. 20a, *diathêkê* is oddly rendered by *Gottes Wort*, the Word of God; cf. *Die deutsche Bibel*). Earlier German translations had never resorted to *Beruf*, limiting themselves to a literal translation of *ergon* by *Werk*, "work" (the Vulgate translates this word by *opus*). Luther was also the first to conflate the work and the effort that produces it, *ergon* and *ponos*, in a single term: the verse thus begins to turn around this *Beruf* that the translation repeats twice and elevates to the dignity of a biblical concept.

In itself, however, Luther's new translation of Sirach does not make *Beruf* an untranslatable. We must add that he uses the term to translate another word, which is also Greek, but this time it is not a Hebrew word translated into Greek because it is drawn from the Epistles of Paul. The word in question is *klêsis* [κλῆσις], which a French Bible such as the *Jerusalem Bible* translates by *appel* (call) (1 Cor 1:26; Eph 1:18; 4:1–4) or by *vocation* (Heb 3:1), while the Vulgate makes systematic use of *vocatio*. Thus Luther assimilates into *Beruf* not only *ergon* and *ponos* but also *klêsis*: according to Weber, this is the source of the word's twofold meaning of "occupation" and "vocation." Luther's translation decision appears still more remarkable if we follow not the order of the books of the Bible but the chronology of his translation. Luther began by translating the New Testament in 1522; his complete version of the Bible dates from 1534. When he translated Sirach, he had thus already used *Beruf* in its traditional sense (earlier

German Bibles also used a composite of *rufen, ruffunge*). The choice of *Beruf* to render *ponos/ergon* appears as a deviation of meaning that we are justified in assuming to be deliberate when we consider how much was invested theologically and doctrinally in this whole translation.

Nevertheless, the question remains whether the conflation of occupation and divine vocation has a basis in the text of the Bible. Weber (French trans. K.) locates a passage in 1 Corinthians (7:20) that seems to move in this direction. This passage exhorts every Christian to "stay in that calling in which he was called" (*en têi klêsei hêi eklêthê* [ἐν τῇ κλήσει ᾗ ἐκλήθη]). In the characteristic reduplication of *klêsis/eklêthê*, we seem to find the two senses of *Beruf*, or at least *klêsis* seems likely to have a non-religious meaning. However, Weber notes that here the word is not strictly synonymous with *ergon* in Sirach (French trans. K.), and interprets it as a social status (*Stand*) rather than as a *Beruf* (in the sense, he explains, of a "delimited domain of activity").

There are, nonetheless, certain problems with Weber's thesis. The first is intrinsic: for a speaker of modern German, Luther's *Beruf* is almost as untranslatable as for a speaker of any other language. The two senses of the word seem to have diverged again after Luther: to avoid any ambiguity, the German editions of the Bible that revise Luther's translation now render the Pauline *klêsis* by *Berufung* (vocation). Weber himself hesitated regarding the sense of *Beruf* in modern German. On several occasions he refers to the "current meaning" of the word (French trans. K), taking it for granted that the latter is "profane" (French trans. K.). Thus *Beruf* would signify no more than an occupation in a "neutral" sense (French trans. K.). However, it is striking that a few lines further on, in describing the development of the Latin *opificium*, Weber explains that the word was "morally neutral" and contrasts it with a text by Seneca (*De beneficiis*, 4.18), where it "becomes . . . the equivalent of *Beruf*" (French trans. K.).

Weber's hesitations show that the word's nuances are still difficult to handle—even for a native speaker, if he lingers over it a moment and asks what it really means. They also show that *Beruf*'s semantic development continues—at least if Weber has correctly accounted for it.

Here we encounter a second difficulty: we can ask whether the use of the term owes as much to Luther as Weber assumes. We should note first that Sirach, where Luther is supposed to have invented the modern meaning of *Beruf*, was not included in the canon of the Protestant Bible. Thus it is unlikely that this meaning would have had much influence had it not been spread by Luther's original works as well. On this point, assessments may vary: there is indeed a doctrine of the *Beruf* in Luther's political works, but one may wonder, reducing it to its real proportions, whether the importance accorded to it is not a retrospective illusion produced by reading Weber.

II. The Doctrine of *Beruf*: A Retrospective Illusion?

Luther's 1523 treatise on political authority, *Von weltlicher Oberkeit*, formulates the idea that "everyone must attend to his *Beruf* and his work" (*Denn eyn iglicher muss seins beruffens und wercks warten*). But it does not go much further. Luther's other political works elaborate instead a doctrine of conditions (*Stände*). The latter's content corresponds to what Weber says about *Beruf* and about Luther's sacralization of temporal activity, notably through his refusal to confer a superior value on monastic ways of life: for Luther, God is just as present in the kitchen as in the convent—if not more (see, e.g., *Predigten des Jahres 1534*). Nonetheless, the word *Beruf* is not given special treatment: in particular, it never appears alone, but always in association with *Stände* (see the commentary on Psalm 118, *Das schöne Confitemini*, and the treatise *Vom ehelichen Leben*, which shows that among the *Stände* we must count not only occupations but also marriage). The idea that there is a Lutheran doctrine of the *Beruf* (Gustaf Wingren) is thus more selected from the texts than actually developed in them: it is not that the resulting interpretation is false, but it would take a long investigation into the history of ideas to determine how exegetes finally came to regard the notion of *Beruf* as a central category in Luther's thought. In this investigation, we would have first to determine how Weber himself was persuaded of the importance of the word and idea of *Beruf* for Luther.

The suspicion that Luther has been read retrospectively on the basis of Weber is illustrated by a passage in the chapter on Luther and Calvin in the *History of Political Philosophy* edited by Leo Strauss and Joseph Cropsey. This passage is entitled "Politics as Vocation," but seems in fact to deal with the doctrine of social status. A note added by the French translator recalls, however, the author's main concern at the same time that it returns to the problem of translation:

> The English word "vocation," like the French *vocation*, is a poor translation of the German *Beruf*, and signifies an occupation insofar as one is called to it, the activity that one performs (the text speaks here of the "vocation" of the father or husband). The author is implicitly referring to Max Weber's text on "*Politik als Beruf*."

Many things are in fact left implicit here (except perhaps the title itself, "Politics as Vocation," a literal translation of Weber's book *Politik als Beruf*). American political science is perhaps alone in giving Luther's politics the place it deserves, and its representatives who emigrated from Europe, from Hannah Arendt to Leo Strauss, played some role in that, but because of the constant debate that they carried on with Weber, they probably knew Luther only through the categories of *The Protestant Ethic and the Spirit of Capitalism*. This retrograde movement came in addition to the one carried out by Weber himself, who found his own questions anticipated in Luther—questions of science and politics as *Beruf*, which, as Catherine Colliot-Théllène points out in her translation of *Wissenschaft als Beruf* and *Politik als Beruf*, deal with the "mission" of the scientist and the politician and refer to something quite different from the Protestant sublimation of everyday occupations. However, that does not mean that we are dealing here with a false problem, as is shown by the difficulties Weber encountered in handling the word. The problem of *Beruf* could probably appear only in the question that Weber asks: to what degree, and in what respects, are we still Protestants? Regarding Luther, the *Protestant Ethic* offers a contrasting analysis. So far as *translation* is concerned, Luther's posterity is strongly emphasized: the English Puritans used "calling," modeled on the *rufen* (call) of *Beruf* to denote a simple occupation—but the word had difficulty establishing itself as a translation of *klêsis* in English Bibles (French trans. K.).

On the other hand, so far as *doctrine* is concerned, Weber recognizes Luther's "economic traditionalism" (French trans. K.), and locates—as did Troeltsch later—modernity in the Puritan sects, the first to establish the "secular asceticism" he considered characteristic of the Protestant ethic and the spirit of capitalism (see French trans. K., where this asceticism is contrasted with Luther's "acceptance" of "the fate that God has irremediably determined for everyone").

No doubt we must also take into account the contribution made by Luther's disciples, who may have provided the theoretical mediation that the new use of *Beruf* in translation needed. In any case, Weber remains prudent in examining the Augsburg Confession (see Kalinowski's note in her French translation; she does not see the modern sense of *Beruf* clearly emerging in this text). Here we are close to the core of the problem, which has to do with the partition between the temporal and the spiritual. Luther's decision to bring *Beruf* into his translation of Sirach is open to completely contradictory interpretations depending on the position taken with regard to the problem of secularization: did Luther secularize the word by using it to translate *ergon* and *ponos*, or did he instead give "everyday temporal work" a "religious meaning" (French trans. K.) far removed from the "disenchantment of the world"? Weber's hesitations concerning the modern meaning of *Beruf* (neutral or ethical?) show that the difficulty has not been resolved—if it ever can be: on the contrary, everything suggests that the secularization thesis is connected with the hermeneutic postulate. We might just as well maintain that the translation of *ponos/ergon* by *Beruf* could hardly be more religious. In the history of German translations of the Bible, *Beruf* here replaces *Werk*. This terminological substitution has a theological motivation that Weber, surprisingly, does not mention: even in an Old Testament text, Luther took care to avoid *Werk*, which referred immediately to the execrated doctrine of salvation by works. The *sola fides* doctrine of justification (justification by faith alone), whose connection with the concept of *Beruf* (see French trans. K.) Weber mentions only further on, thus played a role in the translation in a way disproportionate to the relatively small doctrinal importance of the verse. *Beruf* is a theologically overdetermined translation, and it is probably this overdetermination that explains the other translational twist (also ignored by Weber) that led Luther to render by a single term the two distinct Greek words *ergon* and *ponos*: taken out of its traditional use, *Beruf* had the advantage of drawing attention away from both works and the effort (*ponos*) that performs them, that is, from both the adverse theology and the psychology on which it was based.

Moreover, Weber was the first to emphasize that the "import" of his analysis of Luther's *Beruf* was at best "problematic." He thus abandoned the attempt to establish a direct connection between Luther's attitude toward temporal activity and the emergence of capitalism (French trans. K.). Similarly, it is impossible to explain an untranslatable term like *Beruf* as a decision made at a certain point by a translator when this decision seems not to have had a special impact, at least before Weber. It would be more accurate to say that Weber is the sole inventor of *Beruf*, or that the latter is a Weberian and not a Lutheran untranslatable. To be sure, explaining a term by reference to an individual decision, even if it is a translatorial decision, does not necessarily make it less enigmatic: that is the case when *Beruf* is explained solely by Luther's initiative. But the solution ceases to be inaccessible when the study of translatorial decisions is connected with that of their reception: *Beruf* probably came from a question peculiar to Weber, who transformed a translatorial fact into a genuine concept, and in doing so brought out the real difficulty. Untranslatables do not always arise where we expect them—in this case, they arise at the intersection of the philosophical, the religious, the political, and the social.

Philippe Büttgen

BIBLIOGRAPHY

Grossein, Jean-Pierre. "Peut-on lire en français L'Ethique protestante et l'esprit du capitalisme?" *Archives européennes de sociologie* 40 (1999): 125–57.

———. "À propos d'une nouvelle traduction de *L'Éthique protestante et l'esprit du capitalisme*." *Revue française de sociologie* 43 (2003): 653–71.

Luther, Martin. *Das Schöne Confitemini an der Zahl des 118, Psalms*. In *Werke, Kritische Gesamtausgabe* (hereafter WA), vol. 31/I, 68–182. Weimar: Böhlaus Nacht, 1906–61.

———. *Ecclésiastique*, in *Die deutsche Bibel*.

———. *Predigten des Jahres 1534*. In WA, vol. 37, 480, 1.2–8.

———. *Vom ehelichen Leben*. In WA, vol. 10/II, 275–305.

———. *Von weltlicher Oberkeit, wie weit man ihr Gehorsam schuldig sei*. In WA, vol. 11, 229–81.

———. *Works of Martin Luther*. Philadelphia: Muhlenberg Press, 1943.

Strauss, Leo, and Joseph Cropsey, eds. *History of Political Philosophy*. Chicago: Rand McNally, 1963.

Weber, Max. *Die protestantische Ethik und der "Geist" des Kapitalismus*. Edited by K. Lichtblau and J. Weiss. Bodenheim: Athenäum Hain Hanstein, 1993.

———. *Gesammelte Aufsätze zur Religionssoziologie*. Vol. 1. Tübingen: Mohr, 1988.

———. *L'Ethique protestante et l'esprit du capitalisme*. French translation by I. Kalinowski. Flammarion, 2000.

———. *L'Ethique protestante et l'esprit du capitalisme*. French translation by J. Chavy. Plon, 1964; repr. 1990.

———. *L'Ethique protestante et l'esprit du capitalisme*. French translation by J.-P. Grosseain. Gallimard / La Pléiade, 2003.

———. *Max Weber: Political Writings*. Edited by P. Lassman and R. Speirs. Cambridge: Cambridge University Press, 1994.

———. *Protestant Ethics and the Spirit of Capitalism*. Translated by S. Kalberg. Los Angeles: Roxbury, 2002.

———. *The Sociology of Religion*. Introduction by T. Parsons. Boston: Beacon Press, 1993.

———. *Wissenschaft als Beruf*. Translated by Catherine Colliot-Thélénè. Paris: La Découverte, 2003.

———. *Wissenschaft als Beruf (1917–1919), Politik als Beruf (1919-1922) Max Weber Gesamtausgabe*. Edited by M. Reiner Lepsius, W. J. Mommsen, W. Schluchter, and J. Winckelmann. Tübingen: Mohr (Siebeck), 1992.

Wingren, Gustaf. *Luther on Vocation*. Translated by Carl C. Rasmussen. Philadelphia: Muhlenberg Press, 1957.

BIEN-ÊTRE

This term is generally used to translate the English term "welfare," but differs from "well-being" as the objective form differs from the subjective. See CARE, RIGHT/JUST/GOOD, UTILITY (cf. *UTILE*). On the welfare state, its German translation as *Wohlfahrtsstaat*, and the connotations of its French translation as *état providence*, see GLÜCK, IV; cf. *HAPPINESS*.

➤ CIVIL SOCIETY, *GOOD/EVIL*, PLEASURE, POLITICS, *STATE*, *VALUE*

BILD (GERMAN)

FRENCH	*image, tableau, figure, visage*
GREEK	*eidôlon* [εἴδωλον]
HEBREW	*ṣèlèm* [צֶלֶם], *děmût* [דְמוּת]
LATIN	*imago, species*

➤ *IMAGE* [EIDÔLON], and ANALOGY, BILDUNG, DICHTUNG, DOXA, *IMAGINATION*, MIMÊSIS, OIKONOMIA, REPRÉSENTATION, SPECIES, TABLEAU

The vocabulary derived from *Bild* (image) is particularly rich in German: not because there is, as in Greek, a differentiated plurality of terms to designate an image from different points of view, but because there is an especially complex set of words that are modeled on *Bild* and systematically related to it: *Urbild* (paradigm/archetype) and *Abbild* (copy), *Gleichbild* ("copy," as well, but emphasizing resemblance more than fabrication), *Nachbild* ("ectype," "copy," emphasizing its secondary, imitated status), *Bildung* (education, culture), *Einbildungskraft* (imagination), and so on. The development of this system is representative of a large part of the history of German philosophy.

The starting point for thought about the image (*Bild*) was provided by the biblical verse that says God created man "in his own image" (Gn 1:27). Meister Eckhart's speculation that the image and its model are identical was based on this biblical text and left its mark on later philosophies. In each case, *Bild* had to be entirely rethought, indeed retranslated, depending on whether it was associated with its model (whence the *Urbild/Abbild* opposition) or with the faculty that produces the image (*Einbildungskraft*), and on the way in which the force and function of this faculty was conceived, as reproductive or truly productive. In the course of interpretations of Kant from Fichte to Heidegger, the way in which *Bild* was conceived came to concentrate the major opposition between the understanding and sensibility, and thus the conception of the subject, between spontaneity and receptivity.

I. The Avatars of the Biblical Verse

The beginning of Genesis raises the question of the fundamental determination of the human being created in the image and likeness of the creator in the context of the biblical prohibition on images (cf. Heidegger, *Sein und Zeit*, §10). Thus in Luther's translation, *Bild* (*Gottes*) corresponds to the Hebrew *ṣèlèm* [צֶלֶם], the Greek *eidôlon* [εἴδωλον], and the Latin *imago*.

■ See Box 1.

The New Testament says that Christ is *eichôn tou theou tou aoratou* [εἰχὼν τοῦ θεοῦ τοῦ ἀοράτου] ("the image of the invisible God," Col 1:15), and the Vulgate says that he is *imago Dei invisibilis*. Luther renders this as "das Ebenbilde des unsichtbaren Gottes." Luther's translation is more precise than that of the Vulgate; *Bild* leaves open the possibility of a dissemblance (the *dissimilitudo* mentioned by Saint Augustine [*Confessions*, book 7, chap. 10] and later by Saint Bernard [*De diversis*, sermon 42.2]), whereas *Ebenbild* is so to speak on the same footing with its original, a "perfect image" that is not susceptible to degenerating from "the vivacity of the original" (Bossuet). This translation variant shows in an exemplary way the problem raised by the relationship between the image and its model, *Bild* and *Urbild*; in German, the issue was framed by Meister Eckhart, two centuries before Luther.

1

The image in Hebrew (ṣèlèm [צֶלֶם], děmût [דְּמוּת])

The passage in Genesis where it is said that man is made in the image of God is a monologue in which God, addressing himself in the plural, says, "Let us make man in our image, as our likeness" (1:26). The verse presents several difficulties:

a. to whom is this plural addressed? The church fathers saw in it a foreshadowing of the Trinity; the Jews and modern exegetes see in it the chorus of angels;

b. why these two different words, each preceded by a preposition with a different nuance? An almost identical binary formulation, in which the prepositions are inverted, expresses the resemblance between the father and the child (Gn 5:3);

c. what does this resemblance consist of? Is it a physical property, like standing upright? Is it reason? Is it freedom? A poetic formula justifies the inviolability of the person: "whoso sheddeth man's blood, by man shall his blood be shed: for in the image of God made he man" (Gn 9:6);

d. the verse is followed immediately by the reminder of sexual difference: "So God created man in his image (běṣalěmēnû [בְּצַלְמֵנוּ]); in the image of God created him; male and female created he them" (Gn 1:27). What relation is there between the two affirmations?

As for the words for "image," the first comes from a root meaning "to carve" and in the first place designates a sculpted figure, above all for use in a cult—what the prophets call an "idol" once the cult has come to concentrate only on the Temple of Jerusalem. The root of the second means "to be similar," and the word itself designates in the first place a copy, a reproduction.

Furthermore, the first preposition, of which the chief sense is "in," supposes a stable possession; the second, which in the first place means "like," suggests the status of the image is itself metaphorical.

Christian theology distinguishes between the image, which partakes of the nature of man and thus cannot be lost, and the resemblance. Sin disturbed the second, and the economy of salvation must permit its recuperation. The idea is present with the Greek and Latin fathers (Irenaeus, *Against Heresies*, 5.16.2; Saint Augustine, *Of the Trinity*, 14.4.6) before it passes into the Middle Ages (e.g., Saint Bernard, *On the Song of Songs*, 82.7–8). Maimonides explicates the two terms with the principal aim of removing all temptation to make God into a corporeal being (*Guide for the Perplexed*, 1.1).

Rémi Brague

II. *Abbild, Urbild*: Meister Eckhart or the Life of the Image

The term *Bild* underwent a rich theological and mystical development from Meister Eckhart to Angelus Silesius. The originality of Eckhart's doctrine of the *bilde* (Lat. *imago*) has notably to do, on the one hand, with its conception of "being-an-image" (*das Bildsein*) as a relationship of perfect assimilation (*imago est similis*) between the image (*Abbild*) and that of which it is an image (*Urbild*), so that being-an-image is boldly declared to be the whole of the image, which lacks nothing of that of which it is the image: the image is less relative to a model (*Urbild*) than it is the living relationship to this model, which is in turn nothing other than the relationship to the image that constitutes it as a model. On the other hand, Eckhart's doctrine is characterized by his dynamic conception of the image: "*Imago proprie est emanatio simplex, formalis, transfusiva totius essentiae purae nudae*" (Strictly speaking, the image is a simple, typical emanation transfused with the whole essence pure and unadorned), a kind of internal gushing forth and boiling. Eckhart's image is never at rest, but constantly seething, because it is life.

Wackernagel has noted the "prodigious enrichment undergone by the motif of the image through its conversion from Latin into Eckhart's native language," and also the semantic gap between *bilden* and *entbilden* (a term that remained extremely rare: Suso, Tauler, Angelus Silesius): "Between a *bilde* taken sometimes as an image and sometimes as an anti-image, the prefix *ent-* can indicate both difference and its contrary, that is, assimilation" ("Imagine denudari").

With Kant, the term *Bild* embarks upon a philosophical career that is no less rich, if only because of the profusion of terms that it elicited.

III. *Bild, Einbildung*: Kant from the Imaged to the Imaging

Kant clearly understands *Bild* on the basis of the verb *einbilden*, which seems to have been introduced into the German language by mysticism (cf. Grimm, Duden, Kluge), so that it has the meaning of "leaving an imprint on the mind," on the model of terms such as *Einblick* (vision), *Eindruck* (impression), *Einfall* (incidence, idea that occurs to one), and *Einleuchten* (illumination). In this case, the prefix *ein-* indicates a movement of internalization toward the "living source" constituted, according to Meister Eckhart, by "the image of God in the depths of the soul" (*daz gotes bilde in der sêle grunde*), whereas Kant understands it in the sense of a unification. *Einbildung* has in fact been "one of the fundamental terms of Germanic thought since Paracelsus and Böhme, and even since the great mystics of the Rhineland" (Marquet, *Liberté et existence*).

In the "Transcendental Deduction" in the first edition of the *Critique of Pure Reason* (A, 120), Kant writes: "*Die Einbildungskraft soll . . . das Mannigfaltige der Anschauung in ein Bild bringen.*" Kemp-Smith renders this as "imagination has to bring the manifold of intuition into the form of an image," but it might better be translated as "the imagination has to form a *picture* of the manifold of intuition." Jean Beaufret has even interpreted this sentence to mean that imagination "organizes into a *single picture* the manifold provided by intuition," having emphasized that "the literal meaning of *Bild* is 'picture' much more than 'image'" ("Kant et la notion de Darstellung"). The "single picture" (*Bild*) in question is none other than the manifold as it presents itself, not as a jumble of sense impressions, but with the more attractive appearance of a universe—as a *kosmos* [κόσμος] rather than a *chaos* [χάος]. Kant thus conceives *Einbildungskraft*, a German translation of the Latin *vis imaginationis*, on the basis of *Bild*, a picture that is single because unified; but he also conceives it, inversely, as a unifying and synthesizing power of "uni-formation." To qualify the synthesis of the manifold of sense intuition, which is possible and necessary a priori, Kant resorts to the expression "figurative (*figürlich*) synthesis," giving the Latin equivalent, *synthesis speciosa*, in which *species* echoes one of the Latin equivalents of *Bild*. Because it is "figurative," the *synthesis speciosa* is thus ipso facto *bildlich* (Heidegger), which means that it refers to the figuring or rather the configuring power of *Einbildungskraft*. On this "very beautiful Latin expression that Kant uses, however, only once in the *Critique*," see Longuenesse (*Kant et le pouvoir de juger*), who refers to a passage in Kant's 1770 *Inaugural Dissertation* in which space and time are described as *formae seu species* essential to the constitution of our minds (§4). It is a "very beautiful expression" notably in that the Latin terms *forma* and *species* always associate the idea of beauty (esp. *hermosura*, Ital. *formosità*) with that of form and aspect—so that we see here already an anticipation of the *Critique of Judgment*.

If imagination (Gr. *phantasia*, Ger. *Phantasie*), defined classically in accord with an Aristotelian tradition as reproductive imagination (*De anima*, 3.3), is taken up again by *Schulmetaphysik* (e.g., in Wolff, *Psychologia empirica*, §92, and Baumgarten, *Psychologia empirica*), for his part, Kant distinguishes, notably in §28 of his *Anthropology from a Pragmatic Point of View* (*Anthropologie in pragmatischer Hinsicht*), a reproductive imagination that belongs to the domain of psychology, and a productive imagination that belongs to the domain of transcendental philosophy, an *exhibitio derivativa* and an *exhibitio originaria*. The reproductive imagination is still called in German *zurückrufend* (re-calling), and the productive imagination *dichtend* (poetic or creative). Insofar as *imago* (image) is etymologically related to the verb *imitari* (imitate), "imagination" is a not very satisfactory translation of *Einbildungskraft* when the latter, conceived as productive, is seen as an originary configuring power in the service of the understanding, or even, according to the first edition of the *Critique of Pure Reason*, as constituting its essence. The question of *Bild* comes up again in the chapter on the schematism, where Kant feels the need to distinguish *Bild* from schema (*Schema*; A, 140–B, 179), thus emphasizing *a contrario* their proximity to each other. The schema, one of the four figures (with the example, the symbol, and the construction) of *Darstellung*, *exhibitio*, is defined as "the representation [*Vorstellung*] of a universal process of the imagination [*Einbildungskraft*] in providing an image [*Bild*] for a concept." This acceptation provided a springboard for Fichte.

IV. *Bild, Bildung*: Fichte or the Projection of the Ego in Image

Fichte builds on the thetic character of the synthesis of the transcendental imagination, conceiving *Bild* on the basis of *bilden*, the image on the basis of imaging, positing "the image as such" as a "free product of the ego," of a projecting, imaging ego: the image is not a makeshift reflection of the thing that has reached the ego, but a projection (*Reflex*) of the ego producing itself in an image in the course of its free activity. In other words, the sole original to which the image can appeal is the ego. Fichte thus associates the imaginary activity of the ego-projecting-itself-in-an-image (*Bild*) with its formation (*Bildung*) understood as an autonomous genesis: "In the act of producing an image, the ego is entirely free" (*Grundriss des Eigentümlichen der Wissenschaftslehre*).

Fichte thus understands *Bild* on the basis of *bilden*, the formed on the basis of forming, and not the other way around. The *Bild* is the result of the production at work in the absolute ego's self-positing; by projecting itself in an image, the ego gives itself a sort of mirror in which its free productivity is reflected. Thus Fichte has deliberately accentuated and radicalized the thetic character of the synthesis peculiar to the productive imagination, extending the transcendental schematism and its *Schweben* (floating in suspension) that shapes in advance the contours of the thing that the intuition is preparing to take in (Kant) or to capture as part of its sphere of influence (Fichte). When I perceive a house, Kant says, "I draw as it were the outline of the house" (*Critique of Pure Reason*, B, 162), the imagination thus understood being a constitutive ingredient of perception: "This floating (*Schweben*) itself designates imagination by its product; it produces the latter, as it were, in this movement and through this movement itself" (*Fichtes Werke*, vol. 1, *Grundlage der gesamten Wissensschaftslehre*). The Fichtean *Bild* is thus less feigned than freely fashioned in accord with the self-deployment of the absolute ego. *Einbildungskraft*, which Fichte still sometimes calls *Einbildungsvermögen* (shaping power) can thus be defined as "das bildende Vermögen des Ich" (*Fichtes Werke*, vol. 9, *Nachgelassenes zur theoretischen Philosophie*), a "formative power of the ego." Moreover, according to Fichte it would be better termed *Bildungskraft*; here Fichte is pursuing the Kantian enterprise of reappropriating for philosophy a term bequeathed to the German language by the mysticism of the Rhineland.

It was left to other great figures of German idealism, notably Hölderlin and Schelling, to exploit the speculative and poetic resources of *Einbildungskraft* understood as productive imagination, even if Fichte's philosophy is—still more than that of Schelling, with which it is often associated in this respect—the philosophical apotheosis of *Bild*. This phenomenon is probably related to Fichte's concern to anchor in ordinary language the results of his apparently very esoteric research. He is no doubt the philosopher in whose work we find the most occurrences of the term *Bild*. But "the *image*, the correct translation of *Bild*, does not express this inner power that makes *Wissenschaftslehre* (Doctrine of Science) and consequently the self, a being that 'creates itself'" (Philonenko, *L'Œuvre de Fichte*).

V. *Bild, Gleichbild*: Schelling or the Image as Power

Ascribed in turn to Hegel, Schelling, and Hölderlin, the text Franz Rosenzweig titled *The Oldest System-Program of German Idealism* (ca. 1796) seeks to justify the idea of a "sensible religion" made possible, *nolens volens*, by Kant's *Critique of Judgment*, which makes the beautiful the symbol of morality (§59). By maintaining that "the philosopher must have just as much aesthetic power as the poet" (*der Philosoph muss eben so viel ästhetische Kraft besitzen, als der Dichter*), the author of this text, as a reader of Schiller, seems to have grasped the essence of the Kantian analyses by making this "aesthetic power," which is the imagination as *Einbildungskraft*, the poetizing or productive (*dichtend*) source of philosophizing activity, for all that Kant had made the imagination the secret, common root of understanding and sensibility.

Schelling did not fail to emphasize *Einbildungskraft*, "so well-named in German," which he interprets, in §22 of his *Philosophy of Art* (*Philosophie der Kunst*), as "signifying literally the power of making uniform" (*die Kraft der Ineinsbildung*). This uniformizing or *esemplasie* (Coleridge), a term created on the basis of the Greek *eis en plattein* [εἰς ἕν πλάττειν], characterizes the fusion of the finite and the infinite (cf. Tilliette, *Schelling*), or again, *Hineinbildung* (another of Schelling's neologisms), that is, the mutual interpenetration of the ideal and the *real* (distinguished from *reel* to match the ideal and come closer to the Latin *res, realitas*).

A crossroads for Schelling's meditations up to 1815, the term *Bild* also has a Platonic resonance that is linked in particular with the interpretation of the *Timaeus*, in the opposition between *Urbild* (archetype) or *Vorbild* (paradigm) and *Nachbild* (ectype). Two characteristics constitute the *Bild*: not being the object itself, and being "just like" it, as is explained in Lesson XI of the *l'Historisch-kritische Einleitung in die Philosophie der Mythologie* (*Critical-Historical Introduction to the Philosophy of Mythology*): "*Das Bild is nicht der Gegenstand selbst, und doch völlig wie der Gegenstand selbst*" (The image is not the object itself, and yet it is wholly like the object itself). Nonetheless, in mythology Schelling recognized the presence, if not of the "divine Self" in person, the "*image of the true God*" (*das Bild des wahren Gottes*), or at least his *Gleichbild* or "replica," as an anticipation, and almost by proxy, so that it is to the term *Bild* that Schelling resorts here to connect revelation and mythology. Like *Ebenbild* (which we have already encountered in Luther's translation of Paul's Epistle to the Colossians 1:15), *Gleichbild* is almost an oxymoron, or at least the expression of a unity that is conflicted and accepted as such, designating the element of revelation in a mythology that is not yet revelation.

VI. *Bild, Anblick*: Heidegger or the Image Looking at Us

We have examined what Kant's immediate successors said about the question of the transcendental imagination. In a sense, however, nothing was said, at least according to an important note in Heidegger's book on Kant (*Kantbuch*, §27):

> The explicit characterization of the power of imagination as a basic faculty [*Grundvermögen*] must have driven home the meaning of this faculty to Kant's contemporaries. Thus Fichte and Schelling, and in his own way, Jacobi as well, attributed an essential role to the power of imagination. Whether in this way the power of imagination as seen by Kant was recognized, adhered to, and even interpreted in a more original way, cannot be discussed here. The following interpretation of the transcendental power of imagination grows out of another way of questioning and moves, so to speak, in the opposite direction from that of German Idealism.

Such a declaration shows us first of all that the "stone thrown into the pond" of Marburg Neo-Kantianism represented by Heidegger's *Kantbuch* is nonetheless engaging, secretly but no less "athletically" in a debate with all the interpretations of Kant since 1781, and notably the one that the history of ideas has retained under the name of "German idealism" (Hölderlin being quickly excepted), to the point of characterizing Kant's work as "an unconquered fortress behind the new battlefront." Thus it remains to ask in what way "the essence of *Einbildungskraft* as Kant understood it"

could have been so misunderstood and disfigured by his immediate posterity that this question has to be examined all over again from the opposite direction.

We will limit ourselves here to emphasizing that Heidegger's reading of Kant, like his reading of Hölderlin, accentuates the idea of an essential finitude of the human being, who is a "king of finitude" (Hölderlin, hymn "To Freedom"), whereas German idealism emphasized the unconditional nature of the ego of transcendental apperception as *Selbstbewusstsein*, or "self-consciousness." The *Bild* itself thus became the stake in conflicting interpretations that sometimes inscribed it within a spontaneity Kant reserved for the understanding, and sometimes sought to maintain the equal balance of spontaneity and receptivity, of logic and aesthetics. Instead of stressing the thetic character of the Kantian synthesis (Fichte and Schelling), Heidegger underlines the essential part played, in every knowing, by sensibility understood not as passivity but as receptivity.

Referring to Kant's comment cited earlier, Heidegger remarks that

> The term *Bild* is to be taken here truly at the source, as when we say, looking on a landscape, "What a beautiful view!" [*Bild*] (*Anblick*), or again, in the presence of a gloomy group, "What a sad sight!" [*Bild*] (*Anblick*).

> *Kantbuch*, §19

In a way that is strictly the inverse of the formation of Fichte's (or even Schelling's) *Bild*, here the *Bild* presents itself and offers us a presence that is not the result of our imagination or created by the power of the imagination. The narrowness of the *Bild/Anblick* relationship Heidegger establishes will allow a bold reversal (§20):

> One says of a landscape that it is a view (picture), *species* ["*Anblick (Bild)*," species], as if it were looking at us ["*gleich als blicke sie uns an*"].

The *Bild* is in a way "de-subjugated." Here we see that the question of the *Bild*, with its abundant vocabulary, constitutes a major issue in what opposes Kant's immediate posterity, that is, German idealism, to the phenomenological interpretation of the transcendental schematism in an unexpected revival of the impulse provided by Husserl.

Pascal David

BIBLIOGRAPHY

Beaufret, Jean. "Kant et la notion de Darstellung." In *Dialogue avec Heidegger, II, Philosophie moderne*, 77–109. Paris: Éditions de Minuit, 1973.

Fichte, Johann Gottlieb. *Introduction to the Wissenschaftslehre and Other Writings, 1797–1800*. Edited and translated by D. Breazeale. Indianapolis: Hackett, 1994.

———. *Foundations of Transcendental Philosophy (Wissenschaftslehre) nova methodo (1796/99)*. Edited and translated by D. Breazeale. Ithaca, NY: Cornell University Press, 1992.

———. *Grundriss des Eigentümlichen der Wissenschaftslehre*. In *Fichtes Werke*, vol. 1. Berlin: De Gruyer, 1971.

Heidegger, Martin. *Die Frage nach dem Ding*. In *GA*, vol. 41. Translation by W. B. Barton Jr. and V. Deutsch: *What is a Thing*. Chicago: Regnery, 1968.

———. *Kant und das Problem der Metaphysik*. In *GA*, vol. 3. Frankfurt: Klostermann, 1975–. Translation by R. Taft: *Kant and the Problem of Metaphysics*. 5th ed. Bloomington: Indiana University Press, 1997.

———. *Sein und Zeit*. Tübingen: Niemeyer, 2006. Translation by Joan Stambaugh: *Being and Time*. Rev. ed. Buffalo: State University of New York Press, 2010.

Kant, Immanuel. *Critique of Pure Reason*. Translated by Norman Kemp. London: Macmillan, 2003.

———. *Inaugural Dissertation of 1770*. Translated by William Jeckoff. Whitefish, MT: Kessinger, 2004.

Libera, Alain de. "La théologie de l'image . . ." In *La mystique rhénane*. Paris: Éditions du Seuil, 1984.

Longuenesse, Beatrice. *Kant et le pouvoir de juger*. Paris: Presses Universitaires de France, 1993.

Marquet, Jean-François. *Liberté et existence. Étude sur la formation de la philosophie de Schelling*. Paris: Gallimard / La Pléiade, 1973.

Oltmanns, Käte. *Meister Eckhart*. Frankfurt: Klostermann, 1935.

Philonenko, Alexis. *L'Œuvre de Fichte*. Paris: Vrin, 1984.

Schelling, Friedrich Wilhelm Joseph von. *Historical-Critical Introduction to the Philosophy of Mythology*. Translated by Mason Richey et al. Buffalo: State University of New York Press, 2008.

———. *Philosophie der Kunst*. In *Schellings Werke*, vol. 5. Edited by O. Weiss. Leipzig: Eckhardt, 1907.

———. *Schelling's Philosophy of Mythology and Revelation*. Translated by V. C. Hayes. Australian Association for the Study of Religions, 1995.

Schönborn (von), Christoph. *L'Icône du Christ: fondements théologiques*. Paris: Éditions du Cerf, 1986. First published in 1976.

———. *God's Human Face: The Christ-icon*. Translated by L. Krauth. San Francisco: Ignatius Press, 1994.

Tilliette, X. *Schelling*. 2nd ed. Paris: Vrin, 1992.

Wackernagel, Wolfgang. "Imagine denudari." In *Éthique de l'image et métaphysique de l'abstraction chez Maître Eckhart*. Paris: Vrin, 1991.

BILDUNG, KULTUR, ZIVILISATION (GERMAN)

FRENCH	*culture, position, éducation, formation, libération des préjugés, raffinement des moeurs, civilisation*
GREEK	*paideia* [παίδεια]
LATIN	*cultura*

➤ CULTURE, and AUFHEBEN, BEHAVIOR, BILD, CIVILTÀ, CONCETTO, *IMAGE, IMAGINATION,* LIGHT, MORALS, PERFECTIBILITY, PEOPLE, PLASTICITY, PRAXIS, STRUCTURE

Designating alternatively physical beauty, intellectual cultivation, the divine imprint on the human mind, the integration of the individual into society, and the constantly emphasized parallelism between Greek culture and German culture, the term *Bildung* is certainly one of those words whose translation seems the most aleatory. The difficulty also has to do with the persistence of secondary meanings that are not eliminated by the choice of a primary meaning but are always conveyed in the background. Moreover, there is a tension between the term *Bildung* and the term *Kultur* that develops starting in the Enlightenment and designates the progress of mores thanks to civilization and then gradually comes to refer to the organic coherence of a social group. The terms *Bildung*, *Kultur*, and *Zivilisation* thus define each other in a variable relationship, but *Bildung* remains the word most difficult to transpose. Between the universality of the nation or of knowledge and immediate singularity, in the German context *Bildung* represents the element of particularity, which explains why it is usually anchored in the two privileged domains of language and art. This particularity of *Bildung* can have an identity-related dimension only by postulating its difference. The German notion of *Bildung* includes precisely an element of programmed incommunicability with regard to anyone who tries to approach the term from the outside.

I. The Question of Holism

By "culture" we can mean, depending on the context or period, a certain amount of knowledge in the domains of history, literature, art, music, and language that distinguishes a person who possesses it from one who does not, and serves as a sign of recognition among members of a group. The German definition of *Bildung* implies, on the other hand, an actualization of human perfectibility. In this sense, it is not reducible to any definite content. If Humboldt praises the Greeks and advocates imitating them, it is especially in order to posit as a paradigm a principle of self-determination and self-regulation that he perceives as central to Greek culture. In many respects, the Greek reference is interchangeable. Far from being an accumulation of objective knowledge, the theory of *Bildung*, as Humboldt defines it, is constructed on the basis of the observation of a gap between the multiplication of fields of partial knowledge and the moral progress of humanity. The point is to take over the positive sciences in order to subject them to the Rousseauian imperative of moral progress. Reducing external reality to imaginary representations produced by *Einbildungskraft*, art constitutes a way of extending *Bildung* that contributes to the self-determination that places the subject of *Bildung* at the center of the perceived world. It reduces the indefinite multiplicity of phenomena to a small number of symbolic elements referring to the infinite. This self-fashioning of autonomous individuality is nonetheless fully realizable only through the mediation of language, which, better than art, provides a symbolic relationship to the world and enables the subject to appropriate it. But through language we pass from human individuality to the singularity of the group in which a relationship to the world can be expressed. At the same time that it expresses the individual's aspiration to the universal, *Bildung* marks a difference because the modes of appropriation and expression of the world through language are not identical. We have often been struck by the theological dimensions of a theory that makes of the human being involved in the dynamism of *Bildung* a veritable monad. In this respect, we can only approve of the idea that *Bildung* is the expression of a holistic dimension of German culture, whereas in his *Sociology of Religions* Max Weber speaks of an *Einsheitskultur* (homogeneous culture), and in his book on *Der Historismus und seine Probleme* (*Historicism and its Problems*) Ernst Troeltsch aspires to a *Kultursynthese* (cultural synthesis). To develop a theory of *Bildung* is to postulate a coincidence of the singular with the universal in a dynamics that is history envisaged from a German point of view. The degree of generality attained by a term that can then be associated with the totality of the elements of an intellectual tradition arouses distrust. *Bildung* is less a pernicious ideologeme than an empty place in discourse, a *coincidentia oppositorum* whose postulated existence makes it possible to engage in discourses on the singularity of the subject and the coherence of the group. It is certainly in this function of touchstone or interstitial glue between conceptual sets that the term *Bildung* is most untranslatable.

It would in fact be rather absurd to claim that a word designating the acquisition of theoretical or practical knowledge can be translated only if it does not assume an identifying function. The idea of a co-extensiveness of language and human understanding, of a necessary mediation of language in the symbolic appropriation of the world, is not absent from the linguistic thought of eighteenth-century France, whether we think of Condorcet or his posterity among the members of the Société des Idéologues frequented by Humboldt during his stay in Paris and his turn toward linguistics. To a certain extent, the term *Bildung* is thus invested with an arbitrary will to untranslatability. To define the term *Bildung* as an index of a holism peculiar to German culture is thus to accept uncritically a form of intellectual self-perception and the marked-out paths that it implies for anyone who wishes to explore it only from the inside. Whether one thinks the notion of *Bildung* can or cannot be translated ultimately depends only on the arbitrary choice of an intellectual position inside or outside the discourse that it structures.

II. From the Image of God to Human Development

A. Lexical stages

Friedrich Kluge's etymological dictionary (RT: *An Etymological Dictionary of the German Language*) explains that the term *Bildung* (*bildunga* in Old High German), which derives from *Bild*, "image," signified at first creation, fabrication, the fact of giving form. The transition to the idea of intellectual training and then to education is supposed to have proceeded from the language of mysticism, in which *înbilden* designates the acquisition of a figurative representation, establishing a de facto relationship between *Bildung* and *Einbildung* (imagination). The mysticism of the late Middle Ages, like Pietism, maintained that God imprinted his image (*sich einbildet*) on humans. In his 1793 dictionary, Johann Christoph Adelung attributes to the term *Bild* three main meanings: that of the form of a thing, that of the representation of a thing, and finally that of a person or thing considered from the point of view of its apparent form (a man can be designated by the term *Mannsbild*). According to Adelung, the verb *bilden* signifies giving form to something, but also reproducing a thing's form (a meaning that subsists residually in the concept of *bildende Künste*, "plastic arts," "arts of reproduction"; see ART, Box 2). The noun *Bildung* is thus supposed to designate both the action of giving a form and the form itself, notably the form of the human face. Theodor Heinsius's dictionary (1818) lists these two meanings and adds that of a cultivated person's state, as well as that of the ability of the mind to recompose, in a whole that did not previously exist, the singular representations transmitted by the imagination (*Einbildungskraft*). In their dictionary (1860), the Grimm brothers observe that the term *Bildung* is characteristic of the German language, and that it is not found, or found only in forms derived from German, in other Germanic languages. The term is supposed to have designated an image, *imago*, and then, more broadly, a form (*Gestalt*). It is still in this sense that Winckelmann himself knew the term when he wrote that over time, scientific advances taught Etruscan and Greek artists to free themselves from primitive fixed and rigid forms. And, speaking of the Laocoon, Lessing explains that it had "a form [*Bildung*] which inspired pity because it possessed beauty and pain at the same time." The Grimm brothers also note the meaning of *cultus animi, humanitatis*, which they attribute notably to Goethe (see MENSCHHEIT). The numerous compounds into which the word *Bildung* enters can help explain

its meaning. Thus *Bildungsanstalt* (educational institution) refers to the most intellectual sense of the term, whereas the concept of *Bildungstrieb* (formative drive; see DRIVE), borrowed from the anthropologist and anatomist Johann Friedrich Blumenbach, designates nature's aptitude for causing forms to emerge.

Whereas the classical dictionaries of the German language reveal a great wealth of meanings for the term *Bildung*, they are much more circumspect about *Kultur* and *Zivilisation*. Adelung defines *Cultur* (culture), whose roots he recognizes in both French and the agricultural vocabulary, as a purification of the mental and physical strengths of a person or a people, so that *Cultur* can signify both a liberation from prejudices (Enlightenment, *Aufklärung*; see LIGHT) and refinement of manners. The term *Zivilisation* is unknown to Adelung, but he defines "civil" as *bürgerlich*, characteristic of the citizen, and notes that *civilisieren*, borrowed from French *civiliser*, signifies "give good manners." Heinsius adopts these definitions and notes the term *civilisation* in the sense of improvement of manners, derived from the Latin *civilitas, civilis*. The term *civilisation*, in its oldest stratum, refers to the political organization of the city. From this survey we can conclude that the great lexicographical investigations that are chronologically close to German idealism do not give the terms *Kultur* and *Zivilisation* a historical or ethnological sense, but simply designate a process of the purification of manners from the point of view of the Enlightenment. Thus these two terms appear in the Hegelian lexicon, and even then rarely, with a processual value.

B. *Aufklärung* and culture

In *Über die Frage: Was heisst aufklären?* (1784), Moses Mendelssohn complains that the words *Aufklärung*, *Kultur*, and *Bildung* are newcomers in the German language. They belong only to the language of books and the common man does not understand them. Mendelssohn's complaint allows us to note a semantic equivalence or extreme proximity among three terms that moreover belong largely to scholarly language.

From Kant's point of view, the determining term is not *Bildung* but *Kultur*. Starting out from a rude, uncultivated state, humans arrive, thanks to the development of their dispositions, at culture (*"aus der Rohigkeit zur Kultur"*), at the organization of their lives in accord with their goals and with the deployment of their own strengths. Humans elaborate culture in society (*Idea for a Universal History with a Cosmopolitan Purpose* [*Idee zu einer allgemeinen Geschichte in weltbürgerlicher Absicht*], chap. 4). From this point of view, culture is also a duty to oneself and to others. In fact, the transition to culture does not result from a continuous evolution, but is produced instead by a tension, humans being, according to Kant, both social and opposed to sociability, inclined to confine themselves to individual behaviors. Culture, more a process than a result, arises from the effort to discipline the tendencies to reject sociability. However, dissensions are not in principle contrary to culture, and may even serve as its motive force. Culture does violence to nature, but at the same time it develops nature's virtualities. Humans' goal is indeed to develop their natural strengths, *"der Anbau-cultura—seiner Naturkräfte"* (*Metaphysics of Morals* [*Metaphysik der Sitten*], 1797), and these natural strengths are not limited to intellectual and spiritual strengths, but also include physical strengths.

The development of culture culminates in a constitution defined in accord with the concepts of human rights, in an overall refinement of the manners and the intellectual qualities, not of the individual, but of civil society. Thus culture's vocation is to find its full realization in politics. In his *Anthropology from a Pragmatic Point of View* (*Anthropologie in pragmatischer Hinsicht*, 1798) Kant uses the terms *kultivieren, zivilisieren,* and *moralisieren* almost as synonyms. Culture includes education and upbringing and finally obtains a certain aptitude. The term *Zivilisierung* is said to emphasize culture, insofar as culture inclines people to enter into the social whole (*Über Pädagogik*). According to the distinctions made in Kant's posthumously published writings, morality represents a third stage in the progress of humanity toward perfection, following culture and civilization. The relative absence of the term *Bildung* in Kant's work is revelatory of an approach that is comprehensive, collective, and political, without any mystical or organicist dimension.

C. *Bildung* and humanity

The notion of *Bildung* becomes central once again in the language of Herder, who stresses movement and becoming in relation to any fixed situation. In his work, *Bildung* acquires a status that allows it to include the reference both to the biological and organic development of forms and to intellectual education and the refinement of manners. The tension between Kant and Herder is projected in the semantic opposition that leads one of them to prefer to speak of *Kultur* and the other to speak of *Bildung*. Furthermore, *Bildung* applies less to the individual than to humanity as a whole. As a result, it tends to coincide purely and simply with history, a history that would not be solely a history of ideas, but also one of behaviors, feelings, and sense impressions, which is already suggested by the title *Auch eine Philosophie der Geschichte zur Bildung der Menschheit* (*Another Philosophy of History for the Cultivation of Humanity*, 1774). *Bildung* is determined first of all by external conditions and tendencies, by appetites based on the imitation of a model.

> What were these tendencies? What could they be? The most natural, the strongest, the simplest! For every century, the eternal foundation of the education of men [*Menschenbildung*]: wisdom rather than science, the fear of God rather than wisdom, love among children and spouses instead of elegance and extravagances, order of life, domination over a house in conformity with God's order, the primitive image [*das Urbild*] of every order and every civil organization—in all that the simplest and deepest enjoyment of humanity, how could that have been, not conceived [*erbildet*], but even developed [*angebildet*], perfected [*fortgebildet*], except by that eternal power of the model [*Vorbild*] and of a series of models [*Vorbilde*] around us?

This eternal model that is the source of all *Bildung* has a pronounced theological dimension. While *Bildung* is a kind of education, it cannot be limited to an intellectual education transmitted by books and libraries:

> The education [*Bildung*] and improvement [*Fortbildung*] of a nation are nothing other than the work of destiny: the result of countless causes that converge, so to speak the result of the whole element in which they live.

Reasoning and understanding alone cannot in any case be the sole vehicles of this education of humanity that Herder calls for in the context of the Enlightenment. The heart, blood, warmth, life are all elements that are involved in the education of humanity and cannot be reduced to a rational mechanism. In its double meaning of a process of acquisition and a terminal state, culture (*Kultur*) remains in Herder the distinctive trait of a people and even suggests the possibility of outlining hierarchies among peoples. In Herder, the term *Bildung* is applied to humanity and to the nation, but also to language, the vehicle of culture. While he likes to talk about the formation of language (*Bildung einer Sprache*), this is naturally in the trivial sense of the term. In order for a language to take form it must go through a certain number of phases that historians of the language can reconstruct and scan. But here *Bildung* also signifies that the language is enriching itself, that it is accomplishing a process of improvement, ennobling itself:

> Our language is in a phase of formation (*Bildung*)—and the expression "formation (*Bildung*) of the language" is almost a motto that is today on almost everyone's lips: writers, art critics, translators, scientists. Each of them wants to form (*bilden*) it in his own way: and one is often opposed to the other. What should we do if everyone is allowed to form (*bilden*) it: shall I then be authorized to ask what "form" (*bilden*) means? What is a language without formation (*ungebildete Sprache*)? And what revolutions have other languages undergone before they appeared formed (*ausgebildet*)?

This questioning is followed by a series of historical considerations on the best ways of enriching the language among which translation, notably the translation of ancient authors who are distant from German in their mode of expression, plays a central role.

III. Formation or Self-Making

A. Self-Making

The essential dimension that the term *Bildung* acquires around 1800 is that of reflexivity. The development that *Bildung* implies is not only the acquisition of competences with a view to improvement, but corresponds to a process of the self-fashioning of the individual who becomes what he was at the outset, who reconciles himself with his essence. This use of the word is found notably in Hegel, who devotes long passages to *Bildung* in the fourth part of the *Phenomenology of Mind* (*Phänomenologie des Geistes*), the one entitled "Spirit":

> The means, then, whereby the individual gets objective validity and concrete actuality here is the formative process of Culture [*Bildung*]. The estrangement [*Entfremdung*] on the part of spirit from its natural existence is here the individual's true and original nature, his very substance. . . . This individuality moulds itself [*bildet sich*] by culture to what it inherently is, and only

by doing so is it then something per se and possessed of concrete existence. The extent of its culture [*Bildung*] is the measure of its reality and its power.

We can see how difficult it is to express otherwise than by convention the whole of the semantic field covered by the term *Bildung* in its Hegelian acceptation. Individual self-fashioning is at the same time a transition from substance to a reality that makes it alien to consciousness.

The process in which individuality cultivates itself is, therefore, ipso facto, the development of individuality qua universal objective being; that is to say, it is the development of the actual world. This world, although it has come into being by means of individuality, is in the eyes of self-consciousness something that is directly and primarily estranged.

In other words, *Bildung* is a process that both produces and alienates individuality. In order to accede to *Bildung*, individuality distances itself from its Self. A splitting takes place, and the language of this splitting is the perfect language of the world of culture. The overthrow and mutual alienation of reality (*Wirklichkeit*) and of thought define "pure culture" (*reine Bildung*). "The spiritual condition of self-estrangement exists in the sphere of culture as a fact." In the play of the formation of individuality in a process of self-fashioning on the one hand, and of alienation, the estrangement from that same individuality, on the other, thought acquires a content and *Bildung* ceases to be a pure virtuality.

The notion of *Bildung* is important in Fichte's political writings, notably in his *Addresses to the German Nation* (1808), where the education that modifies not only the individual's heritage but his nature itself becomes a kind of glue unifying the people. *Bildung* is no longer a specific education but a "general culture" (*allgemeine Bildung*). Schelling shares with Hegel a comprehensive conception of *Bildung* and in his *Vorlesungen über die Methode des akademischen Studiums* (*On University Studies*) (1808) he explains that "to attain absolute form, the spirit must test itself in all domains, that is the universal law of all free education (*Bildung*)." Nonetheless, in Schelling the term has a much weightier meaning in a passage in his treatise on the essence of human freedom (*Philosophische Untersuchungen über das Wesen der menschlichen Freiheit und die damit zusammenhängenden Gegenstände* [1809]) that illuminates the movement from the *Grund* or initial obscurity to division. According to Schelling, this movement can take place only through a "veritable in-formation (*Ein-Bildung*), things in development being informed (*hineingebildet*) in nature or more precisely by an awakening, the understanding highlighting the unity or *Idea* concealed in the separation from the *Grund*." When Hegel was writing the *Phenomenology of Mind*, *Bildung* still conveyed a mystical meaning inherited from the representation of a form breathed into matter. But this process is henceforth situated strictly within the framework of a self-constituting subjectivity.

B. The indefinite

In many of the contexts in which it is used, *Bildung* includes an element of indetermination that makes it unsuitable for designating solely a process of education, whether it is a matter of intellectual or moral education. The highest form in the hierarchy of forms, the one that would best represent *Bildung*, the forming or shaping with theological roots, would be precisely, in an ever-latent reversal, the absence of form. We encounter this sense of the term *Bildung* notably in the work of Friedrich Schlegel, and particularly in his 1799 novel, *Lucinde*. Carried away by a love without object in the chaos of his inner life, the hero, Julius, feeling that he is destined to be an artist, discovers how far behind he still is in *Bildung* ("*dass er noch so weit zurück sei in der Bildung*"). But the decision to educate himself (*bildete sich*) leads him to forget his century and take his models among the heroes of the past or to project himself into the future, in short, to emancipate himself from temporal determinations. *Bildung* is almost as indeterminate as the state it allows us to leave behind. Schlegel even develops a theory of *Bildung* whose highest degree would be passivity, the abandonment of forms, and the acceptance of idleness. Women are supposed to attain spontaneously this state of openness to the indefinite. Men, on the other hand, should seek to achieve it. "That is why in women's love there are no degrees or stages of *Bildung*." The indefinite dimension of *Bildung*, its openness to a vague infinity and its reversal into a victory over the tyranny of forms, is not peculiar to Romanticism. Paul Natorp, in a very nationalist work entitled *Die Seele des Deutschen* (*The German Soul*, 1918), emphasized the fact that Goethe, beyond his philosophical, aesthetic, and literary qualities, acted as a *Lebensbildner* (shaper of life). After him, "the term *Bildung* should never have been understood in a superficial sense, because for him, and for anyone who remained faithful to his spirit, it meant nothing less than the organization of the whole of life into a living masterpiece." *Bildung* is supposed to be the act of giving life and in that way moving beyond forms. Natorp appeals to the model of Goethe's Prometheus: "I am here and give form to men in accord with my image, to a race that resembles me." Understood in this way, *Bildung* becomes a kind of organic duty to express a German idea that cannot be limited to the individual but includes the collectivity.

C. *Bildung* and philology

Despite its numerous extensions, *Bildung* corresponds to a specific kind of education: the study of antiquity and especially Greek philology. There is a very clear reason for this. The Greeks had an all-encompassing cultural system, *paideia* [παίδεια], whose paradigmatic value in turn permitted the construction of national cultural systems in Europe: "The original Greek creation of culture (*Kultur*) as a system of *paideia* and pure forms that served as its organ produced the effect of an illumination on the peoples of the world" (Jaeger, *Humanistische Reden und Vorträge*).

■ See Box 1.

Transposing the Greek paradigm to German reality required a special familiarity with the ancient Greek language and the texts that transmitted it. *Bildung* became primarily a philological activity. Even before Friedrich August Wolf made in clear in his *Prolegomena ad Homerum* (*Prolegomena to Homer*, 1795) that understanding the *Iliad* and the *Odyssey* required an understanding of how they were transmitted

1

Paideia, cultura, Bildung: Nature and culture

➤ *IMAGE*, LOGOS, RELIGIO, VIRTÙ, *WORLD*

A fragment of Democritus quoted, via Aristotle, by Stobaeus, sums up the importance of *paideia* and its aura: "*Paideia* is the world [*kosmos* [κόσμος]; Diels-Kranz suggests *Schmuck* (ornament)] of those for whom this goes well (*tois eutuchousin* [τοῖς εὐτυχοῦσιν]), and the refuge of those for whom it goes badly (*atuchousin de kataphugion* [ἀτυχοῦσιν δὲ καταφύγιον])" (68 B 180 DK). The word *paideia*, which designates both "youth" and "education, culture," derives from *pais* [παῖς], "child"; not the child as his mother gives birth to him, *teknon* [τέκνον] (from *tiktô* [τίκτω]), engender, and as he is brought up (*trephô* [τρέφω]), feed, cause to grow), like any animal at all, but the human offspring whose body and mind have to be shaped, whence a common phrase, notably in Plato, *paideia kai trophê* [παίδεια καὶ τροφή] (*Phaedo*, 107d, e.g., translated by L. Robin as "formation morale et régime de vie", and "culture et goûts" by M. Dixsaut. *Paideia* is understood in its proximity to *paidia* [παιδιά], "play": thus Plato's *Laws* call for legislation "on *paideia* and *paidia* relative to the Muses" (2.656c). *Paideia* is opposed to *apaideusia* [ἀπαιδευσία], the ignorance of the badly educated, as is shown, for example, by the myth of the cave, which opens like this: "Next, said I, compare our nature in respect of education and its lack to such an experience as this" (*Republic*, 7.514a 1–2). Or again: "By education, then, I mean goodness in the form in which it is first acquired by a child" (tên paragignomenên prôton paisin aretên [τὴν παραγιγνομένην πρῶτον παισὶν ἀρετήν]) (*Laws*, 2.653b 1–2). From Socratic dialectic to the austerities of the laws, everything in Plato is thus persuasive and pedagogical, oriented toward the standard of virtue that would be taught by the philosopher-king and conveyed through institutions.

Everything in Plato, but also everything in Aristotle, for whom *paideia* is a way of fulfilling the definition of man as an animal endowed with *logos* [λόγος]. No one, neither the child, nor, of course, women, nor even slaves, achieves this without *paideia*: each one is in his own way not only a living being, like an ox, but a living being endowed with enough *logos* to acquire more ("Wherefore they are mistaken who forbid us to converse with slaves and say that we should employ command only, for slaves stand even more in need of admonition than children"; *Politics*, 1260b 5–7; cf. Cassin, *Aristote*). No one has *logos* from the outset, totally and once and for all, because *logos* constitutes for us nature's goal (*Politics*, 7.13.1334b 15): to lead

toward *logos* by *logos* is the very essence of *paideia* (Cassin, *Aristote*). In other words, man's nature is his culture. The breadth of *paideia* ranges from politics—it is the *logos* that makes man a "more political" animal than others (*Politics*, 1.1253a 7–10)—to ontology—it is evidence of *apaideusia* (lack of education) to demand that everything be demonstrated (*Metaphysics*, 4.4.1006a 6; cf. 3.1005b 3–4), and, in the case of the principle of noncontradiction, we are then "no better than a vegetable" (*Metaphysics* 4.4.1006a 14–15).

As Hannah Arendt emphasizes, it is a matter of our mode of relation to the things of the world (*Between Past and Future*). To characterize Greek culture in its relationship to the art that is often confused with it, Arendt cites the statement Thucydides puts into the mouth of Pericles in his funeral oration for the latter: "We love beauty within the limits of political judgment, and we philosophize without the barbarous vice of softness" (*philokaloumen te gar met' euteleias kai philosophoumen aneu malakias* [φιλοκαλοῦμέν τε γὰρ μετ᾽ εὐτελείας καὶ φιλοσοφοῦμεν ἄνευ μαλακίας]) (Thucydides, 2.40; Arendt, *Between Past and Future*; cf. Cassin, *L'Effet sophistique*). In opposition to the over-refinement of the barbarians, the political and practical standard of *paideia* defines the Greeks' relation to beauty and wisdom. In relation to the barbarians, and then to the Romans, we see that the *logos* constituted par excellence by the Greek language can become the depository of *paideia* (see GREEK, Box 1), and that in the Hellenistic schools, culture was presented in the form of *mimêsis rhêtorichê* [μίμησις ῥητορική], "literary culture," meaning the appropriation of great authors and of creative imitation, but of culture and no longer of nature (Cassin, *L'Effet sophistique*).

We also see why it is Greek *paideia* and not Roman *cultura* that functions as a model in German *Bildung*. *Cultura* derives from *colere*, "to inhabit, cultivate, practice, maintain," from the root **kwel-*, like *pelomai* [πέλομαι], "to turn around," which we find again in "circle," and the verb designates both humans' relation to the gods—they cultivate them, make them the object of a cult—and that of the gods to humans—they live with them, protect and cherish them (cf. A. Ernout and A. Meillet). Literally and first of all, *cultura* is *agricultura*, "the culture of the earth": the mind is like a field that cannot produce unless it is suitably cultivated and "philosophy is the culture of the mind" (*cultura autem animi philosophia est*; Cicero, *Tusculan Orations*,

2.13). Arendt notes emphatically: "It was in the midst of a primarily agricultural people that the concept of culture first appeared, and the artistic connotations which might have been connected with this culture concerned the incomparably close relationship of the Latin people to nature, the creation of the famous Italian landscape" (*Between Past and Future*). It is precisely here that we see one of the fundamental differences between the Greeks, who conceived cultivating the earth as a Promethean act, almost a rape, and the Romans, who fashioned nature into a habitable place: "The reason why there is no Greek equivalent of the Roman concept of culture resides in the predominance of the arts of fabrication in Greek civilization. Whereas the Romans tended to see even art as a kind of agriculture, as the culture of nature, the Greeks tended to see even agriculture as an element of fabrication, as one of the ingenious and skilful technical artifices through which humans, who are more frightening than anything else that exists, domesticate and dominate nature."

Bildung is located on the side of *technê* [τεχνή], art, of artifice and fabrication, and not on the side of *natura*. Werner Jaeger never ceased to emphasize its relation to plastic activity, the *plassein* [πλάσσειν] through which the sculptor models his creation: "The term culture (*Bildung*) should be reserved for this kind of education (*Art der Erziehung*) alone, the one for which Plato uses the material metaphor of the character that is *fashioned* (*als bildlicher Ausdruck für das erzieherische Tun*). The German word *Tun* indicates very clearly the nature of Greek education in the Platonic sense: it suggests just as much the artist's plastic composition (*das künstlerische Formende, Plastische*) as the guiding model which is always present to the mind of the artist (*dem Bildner innerlich vorschwebende normative Bild*), the *idea* or *typos*" (*Paideia*; see ART and PLASTICITY). And what is thus shaped by the legislator is "the living man": "Other nations have created gods, kings, spirits: only the Greeks have shaped men" (cf. this phrase which we will not try to translate: "Ausbildung, Durchbildung, Vorbildung, Fortbildung, nicht Bildung," Jaeger, *Humanistische Reden und Vorträge*).

Thus it is through humanism and not culture that *Bildung*, which considers humans as works of art, inherits the very action of *paideia*.

Barbara Cassin

(continued)

(continued)

BIBLIOGRAPHY

Arendt, Hannah. "The Crisis in Culture." In *Between Past and Future*. New York: Viking Press, 1961; rev. ed., 1968. 197–226.

Aristotle. *Politics*. In *Basic Works of Aristotle*, edited by R. McKeon and translated by B. Jowett. New York: Vintage, 2001.

Cassin, Barbara. *L'Effet sophistique*. Paris: Gallimard / La Pléiade, 1995.

————. *Aristote et le logos. Contes de la phénoménologie ordinaire*. Paris: Presses Universitaires de France, 1997, chaps. 2 and 3.

Jaeger, Werner. *Humanistische Reden und Vorträge*. Berlin: De Gruyter, 1960.

————. *Paideia. Die Formung der Griechischen Menschen*. Vol. 1. Berlin: De Gruyter, 1934. Translation by G. Highet: *Paideia: The Ideals of Greek Culture*. New York: Oxford University Press, 1945–.

Plato. *Laws*. In *The Collected Dialogues of Plato*, edited by E. Hamilton and H. Cairns,

translated by A. E. Taylor. Princeton, NJ: Bollingen, 1961.

————. *Phaedo*. Translated by M. Dixsaut. Paris: Flammarion, 1991.

————. *Phaedo*. Translated by L. Robin. Paris: Les Belles Lettres, 1926.

————. *Republic*. In *The Collected Dialogues of Plato*, edited by E. Hamilton and H. Cairns, translated by P. Shorey. Princeton, NJ: Bollingen, 1961.

Waterfield, Robin, ed. *The First Philosophers: The Presocratics and Sophists*. Oxford: Oxford University Press, 2009.

during the intellectual history of Greece, Wilhelm von Humboldt had told him that in his opinion there was, alongside the particular forms of intellectual learning, another that federated humans' various modes of expression and gave them their unity.

> This education (*Ausbildung*) is increasingly losing its importance and achieved its highest degree among the Greeks. It can be better promoted, it seems to me, only by studying great and remarkable men from this point of view, or to put it in a word, by studying the Greeks.

> Letter from Humboldt to Wolf, 1 December 1792

In his *Darstellung der Altertumswissenschaft* (1807), Wolf pointed out a radical difference between the ancient peoples of the Orient on the one hand, and the Greeks and Romans on the other:

> One of the most important differences is . . . that the former scarcely rose, or only by a few degrees, above the kind of culture (*Bildung*) that is called politeness (*Policirung*) or civilization (*Civilisation*), in contrast to superior intellectual culture (*Geisteskultur*) properly so called.

The germ of a dichotomy between *Kultur* and *Zivilisation* is already present here. By an obvious paradox, in Wolf's work the term *Kultur* often designates the education of the mind, whereas *Bildung* designates the social condition attained. The conceptual divisions do not exactly coincide with the semantic divisions.

To create a new German culture, to gather together what had been dispersed, to restore a unity comparable to that of the model of *paideia*, Germans had to study Greek. *Bildung* became a kind of substitute for a centralized state at the same time as a humanistic improvement of the individual. This simultaneously educational and political function of *Bildung* was in fact of a very different nature depending on whether the Greek paradigm was invoked to construct a German culture around 1800 or to magnify the German Empire and its subjects' conformism during the Wilhelmine period.

It is chiefly Humboldt who can be considered the theoretician of *Bildung* as a transfer of the Greek paradigm to Germany. Moreover, we find in Humboldt a competing use of the terms *Bildung*, *Ausbildung*, and *Kultur* that challenges the frequently alleged opposition between *Bildung* as intellectual education and *Ausbildung* as practical training. We can show, Humboldt writes in *Über das Studium des Altertums* (*On the Study of Antiquity*), that the attention given to physical and intellectual culture (*Bildung*) was very great in Greece and was guided principally by ideas of beauty, and that "a strong tendency among the Greeks to educate [*auszubilden*] man both in his greatest diversity and in his greatest possible unity is undeniable." The parallel between the fragmentation of Greece and the fragmentation of Germany being obvious in Humboldt's writing, *Bildung* appears as a form of constructive tension between identity and plurality. The *Bildung* of German Hellenist philologists from Wolf to Wilamowitz by way of Philipp August Boeckh, Gottfried Hermann, Otfried Müller, Hermann Usener, and others is also a way the individual participates in the collective.

D. The individual and the collective

The term *Bildungsroman*, generally translated as "novel of education," was introduced into critical terminology by Wilhelm Dilthey, who makes use of it in his *Leben Schleiermachers* (*Life of Schleiermacher*, 1870) to characterize the novels of German classicism. A novel about a young man's coming to awareness of himself and at the same time finding his place in the social world, the *Bildungsroman*, which is often also called the *Entwicklungsroman*, "novel of development," or *Erziehungsroman*, "novel of character development," combines Rousseauist roots (the German reception of *Émile, ou de l'éducation*, 1762) with Pietist roots (Karl-Philipp Moritz's *Anton Reiser*, 1785). This twofold background corresponds to the structural ambiguity of the notion of *Bildung* as both the education of the social individual and an internal education independent of any context. A subset of the *Bildungsroman* genre is the *Künstlerroman* (novel about an artist), in which the hero's discovery of the world of art enables him to succeed in his exploration of both an inner space and a social life.

The main example of the *Bildungsroman* is provided by Goethe's *Wilhelm Meister*, and more particularly by the first volume, *Wilhelm Meisters Lehrjahre* (*Wilhelm Meister's Apprenticeship*, 1795–96). For Goethe and his hero, the notion of *Bildung* implies a shaping of singular existence by the acceptance of outside influences, family relationships, art and especially the theater, Pietistic religious trends, and certain social milieus, especially the nobility. The hero himself explains what he means by *Bildung*: "Let me tell you: ever since I was a boy, my wish and intention has been to educate myself completely as I am." According to Goethe, German bourgeoisie were able to acquire practical training, to develop some of their abilities with a view to being socially useful, and even to acquire a general intellectual education. However, he considers this education inferior to the one he thinks was previously reserved for the nobility, an education of the person taken as a whole, without any amputation. The influence of a complete, unamputated personality can be obtained through a new form of aristocracy whose acquisition depends notably on artistic education. It is easy to show that the various phases of the acquisition of *Bildung* in *Wilhelm Meister* correspond to the phases through which German culture passed in the eighteenth century, thus making the individual development of Wilhelm's personality an allegory of the education of the German people itself. Another notable characteristic of Goethe's conception of *Bildung* has to do with the role accorded to action. Whereas the complete education of the personality, analogous to the education of the people as a whole, transcends the acquisition of separate abilities, it must, when it is once acquired, reconnect with practical activity. *Wilhelm Meisters Wanderjahre* (*Wilhelm Meister's Journeyman Years*, 1821, 1829), a sequel to the first novel, justifies this return to the practical, as if the notion of *Bildung*, in the simple context of Goethe's work, were already evolving and included within itself the necessity of a theoretical reformulation. "In any case, society now forces us to have a general education; therefore we do not need to worry about it anymore, it is the particular that we have to appropriate." Let us note that in his poem *Hermann und Dorothea* Goethe uses the term *Bildung* in an archaic sense of harmonious physical constitution, at the same time that in *Wilhelm Meister* he is developing the theory of *Bildung* as intellectual education.

IV. Resisting Organicism

A. *Bildungsbürgertum*

The French occupation of Germany during the Revolutionary Wars and especially during the Napoleonic Wars was a sort of incubation period during which the concept of *Bildung* acquired its central place in Germany's philosophical self-image. This French period of German history is characterized by a radical reduction of spatial fragmentation and the emergence of the idea of a German state that would be the heir to the Enlightenment, that is, of a pedagogical state. Whereas in old Germany intellectual education was one of the duties of certain social groups, virtually the prerogative of corporate organizations after 1800, and more precisely after the foundation of the Humboldt University in Berlin (1810), it became the distinctive insignia of servants of the state, of a state that was initially virtual or partial but after 1871 included most of the Germanic world. *Bildung*, a reference point that was clearly less important in Alemannic Switzerland and Austria than in Germany proper, was the condition of membership in the universality of the state, just like property. Real property or military office that was not accompanied by cultural capital, that was not legitimized by *Bildung*, even became suspect. Educating a new kind of citizen or subject, the *Bildungsbürger* (roughly, middle-class intellectual) tended to deprive *Bildung*

of its subjective, individual, reflexive dimension and make it a form of property or symbolic capital. In the second half of the nineteenth century the idea of technical, professionalized, socially pertinent training was established, and led to a previously almost imperceptible opposition between general education, culture, *Bildung* and specialized training, even technical training, *Ausbildung*, *Fachausbildung*. The German state, drawing its legitimacy from its pedagogical functions—a new type of legitimacy that obviously inspired the French Third Republic, traumatized by the defeat at Sedan—sought to make ever-broader groups participate in the integrative system of *Bildung*. Social Democratic movements fit perfectly into this dynamics, which led to the notion of *Volksbildung* (popular education) and the multiplication of *Volksbildungsvereine* (popular education associations).

By becoming institutionalized and transforming itself into social glue, *Bildung* lost its individualistic dimension and espoused social strategies. It no longer provided the unity of a culture. In the second of his *Unzeitgemässe Betrachtungen* (*Untimely Meditations*), Nietzsche deplores the fact that historicism has substituted *Gebildetheit* (erudite culture), the prerogative of the philistine (*Bildungsphilister*, a term that appears around 1860), for *Bildung*. According to Nietzsche, Germans, in the grip of historical studies, were losing their human dimension and becoming "creations of historical culture, wholly structure, image, form without demonstrable content and, unhappily, ill-designed form and, what is more, uniform." In fact, for Nietzsche there is no longer any true *Bildung* but only a historical knowledge of its components. People limit themselves to ideas of *Bildung* (*Bildungsgedanken*) or to the feeling of *Bildung* (*Bildungsgefühl*) in order to avoid making a decision about *Bildung* (*Bildungsentschluss*). Far from recognizing culture in contemporary Germany, Nietzsche was persuaded that the Greeks (whom, like Humboldt, he regarded as the criterion in this area) would call Germans "walking encyclopedias." To designate authentic *Bildung*, the *Bildung* that has disappeared, and in particular that of Greece, Nietzsche liked to use the term *Kultur*, emphasizing a living unity, the "unity of artistic style in all the expressions of the life of a people."

B. Culture and organicism

Starting in the middle of the nineteenth century, the term "culture" ceased to designate a future and expressed instead an entity, a state of national communities. Jakob Burckhardt understood *Kultur* as referring to "the totality of the intellectual developments that take place spontaneously and without aspiring to universality or monopoly" (*Die Cultur der Renaissance in Italien*). Processuality is not completely lacking, but it is a process that takes place within the unity of an organism. In relation to the simply totalizing tendencies of holism, organicism implies a quasi-biological functionality. Culture is thus "the process of millions of persons through whom the naïve action determined by their race is transformed into a conscious aptitude." Cultures are born, flourish, and die, and this organic life of cultures is governed by "superior, inaccessible laws of life." For Burckhardt, culture represents the critical authority of civil society as opposed to the state and religion. It includes the fine arts, to be sure, but also livestock-raising, agriculture, maritime shipping, commerce, and crafts; all these elements enter into various combinations in the notion of culture. The diversity of the internal programming of culture allows us to distinguish major historical periods and to speak of cultures in the plural. The sense of the term in Burckhardt is very close to that used by ethnologists. While Burckhardt thinks that "the miracle of language" is at the origin of culture as a federating bond, we must remember that language is also what Franz Boas—who was trained in Germany before leaving for the United States—made central to ethnological investigations and methods.

In Oswald Spengler's *Decline of the West* (*Der Untergang des Abendlandes*, 1923), the concept of culture becomes an operative concept for the historian. To understand Western culture, he wrote, "we must first know what culture is, how it is related to visible history, to life, to the mind, to nature, to the spirit, in what forms it manifests itself and to what extent these forms—peoples, languages, and periods, battles and ideas, the arts and works of art, the sciences, the law, great men and great events—are symbols and can be interpreted as such." Culture corresponds to a network of symbolic forms, to their concentration around a people and even a race—a term that in Spengler's terminology is not too far from that of "culture." Peoples are spiritual entities (*Seelische Einheiten*) based on symbols, but Spengler draws a distinction between primitive peoples, such as the sea people during the Mycenaean period, who do not have a strong coherence, and peoples of culture (*Kulturvölker*), who are much more precisely determined. After the moment of culture, peoples sank into the era of fellahs, the condition of Egypt during the Roman period. Moreover, to primitive cultures Spengler opposes great cultures in a hierarchy of values that is also applied to languages. Whereas *Bildung* is considered only in the singular, cultures are plural and hierarchized.

The symbolism that guarantees a culture's organic unity may be religious in nature. Within a cultural community (*Kulturgemeinschaft*) like Judaism, culture's function is to regulate morals (*sittliche Kultur*). In his *Religion der Vernunft* (*Religion of Reason*), Hermann Cohen further notes that culture, the glue that holds a people together, is based on an unwritten religious law regarding "this eternal, this unwritten that precedes, must precede, all writing and so to speak all culture, because it creates the foundation for all culture." In his *Philosophie der symbolischen Formen* (*Philosophy of Symbolic Forms*), Ernst Cassirer speaks of the "cultural myths (*Kulturmythen*) that differ from natural myths in that their function is not to explain the origin of the world and to legitimate a cosmology, but to explain the genesis of 'cultural goods' (*Kulturgüter*)." Through the intermediary of myths, notably salvation myths, "culture becomes conscious of itself."

C. Culture or civilization

Did Freud write on "Civilization and Its Discontents" or on "Culture and Its Discontents" (*Unbehagen in der Kultur*)? The question that divides translators reveals a semantic dichotomy in which French privileged the term *civilisation* before gradually importing the stakes involved in the German dichotomy. It is certain that for Freud, *Kultur* corresponded to

a constraint exercised on drives: "This replacement of the power of the individual by the power of a community constitutes the decisive step of civilization [*der entscheidende kulturelle Schritt*]. . . . The liberty of the individual is no gift of civilization [*Kulturgut*]." Cosmopolitan, universalist, marked by the spirit of the Enlightenment, democratic in its essence, *Zivilisation* includes on the other hand a threat of decomposition for the national entities that it transcends or federates. The notion of *Kulturkampf* (culture war), which designated the politics of the Prussian Protestant Bismarck with regard to Catholic groups, well expresses the menace that weighs on culture and obliges us to defend it. This defense does not shrink from using radical means, and in the belligerent language used during the First World War, Thomas Mann himself did not hesitate to champion a defense of the idea of culture, including the brutal forms its affirmation might take. In any case Germany, better rooted in nature, was supposed to be resistant to civilization conceived as primarily intellectual. In its exacerbated form, the opposition between culture and civilization reflects the ancient German mistrust with regard to a universality inherited from the Enlightenment that was supposed to conceal a French desire for hegemony. We can understand why the French political vocabulary at the beginning of the twentieth century appealed to the notion of civilization in reaction to the German instrumentalization of the dichotomy. This semantic opposition, which arose from Franco-German distrust, became a structuring factor in ethnological studies that could be scientific only by studying concrete societies rooted in their particularity, and thus cultures, but without seeking to see to what extent these cultures drew on the universal reservoir of possible human behaviors, and thus on a human civilization. When Freud uses the term *Kultur*, he does not do so to appeal to its radically organicist and nationalist dimension, but rather to challenge the pertinence of the opposition itself.

Norbert Elias seeks to outline the sociogenesis of this opposition. While he does not hesitate to use the term "civilization," he does so on the one hand to account for an investigation that is international or at least extends to the whole of the West—he even discusses a national feeling on the part of the West. On the other hand, civilization, which he connects with the "civilities" of court society, includes forms of concrete life that the history of mentalities has taken as its favorite object of study:

> The French and English concept of civilization can refer to political or economic, religious or technical, moral or social facts. The German concept of *Kultur* refers essentially to intellectual, artistic, and religious facts, and has a tendency to draw a sharp dividing line between facts of this sort, on the one side, and political, economic, and social facts, on the other. The French and English concept of civilization can refer to accomplishments, but it refers equally to the attitudes or "behavior" of people, irrespective of whether or not they have accomplished anything. In the German concept of *Kultur*, by contrast, the reference to "behavior," to the value which a person has by virtue of his mere existence and conduct, without any accomplishment at all, is very minor.

> Elias, *Über den Prozess der Zivilisation*

These definitions show the spiraling overdeterminations to which these terms have been subjected. Taken over by the social sciences long ago, the term "culture" can have in German the sense that Elias gives to the term *Zivilisation*. But the national closure of culture in 1936 made the word unusable in German for a discourse that intends to be international. The term *Zivilisation*, against which Thomas Mann railed during the First World War, was invested with the most positive semantic core of the term "culture," culture becoming in turn the refuge of *Geist*, with which the sociologist was incapable of coping. *Kultur* and *Zivilisation* are in fact semantic variables that can draw, depending on the intellectual context, on an interpretive tradition based on the postulate of a Franco-German opposition.

▪ See Boxes 2 and 3.

Michel Espagne

BIBLIOGRAPHY

Assmann, Aleida. *Construction de la mémoire nationale. Une brève histoire de l'idée allemande de Bildung*. Paris: Maison des Sciences de l'Homme, 1994.

Benveniste, Émile. *Civilisation: contribution à l'histoire d'un mot*. In *Eventail de l'histoire vivante*, Mélanges Lucien Febvre, edited by F. Braudel, vol. 1, 47–54. Paris: Armand Colin; repr. in *Problèmes de Linguistique générale*. Paris: Gallimard / La Pléiade, 1966, 336–45. Translation by M. E. Meek: *Problems in General Linguistics*. Coral Gables, FL: University of Miami Press, 1971.

Berg, Christa, ed. *Handbuch der deutschen Bildungsgeschichte*, vol. 4, 1870–1918. *Von der Reichsgründung bis zum Ende des Ersten Weltkrieges*. Munich: Beck, 1991.

Brunner, Otto, Werner Conze, and Reinhart Koselleck, eds. *Geschichtliche Grundbegriffe*. 8 vols. Stuttgart: Klett, 1972–. Art. "Bildung" by R. Vierhaus, vol. 1 (1972) and art. "Civilization, Kultur" by J. Fisch, vol. 7 (1992).

Burckhardt, Jakob. *Die Cultur der Renaissance in Italien*. Stuttgart: Kröner, 1976.

Cassirer, Ernst. *Philosophie der symbolischen Formen*. Vol. 2. Darmstadt, 1964.

Cohen, Hermann. *Religion der Vernunft*. Wiesbaden: Fourier, 1988.

Dumont, Louis. *L'idéologie allemande. France-Allemagne et retour*. Paris: Gallimard / La Pléiade, 1991.

Eisler, Rudolf. *Kant-Lexicon*. Edited by A.-D. Balmès and P. Osmo. Paris: Gallimard / La Pléiade, 1994.

Elias, Norbert. *Über den Prozess der Zivilisation*. Vol. 1. Frankfurt: Suhrkamp, 1981. Translation by Edmund Jephcott: *The History of Manners*. Vol. 1. New York: Pantheon, 1978.

Fichte, Johann Gottlieb. *Addresses to the German Nation*. Edited and translated by Gregory Moore. Cambridge: Cambridge University Press, 2008.

Freud, Sigmund. *Das Unbehagen in der Kultur*. Frankfurt: Fischer, 1953. Translation by James Strachey: *Civilization and Its Discontents*. New York: Norton, 1961.

Goethe. *Wilhelm Meisters Lehrjahre*. In *Werke*. Vols. 7–8. Edited by E. Trunz. Munich: Beck, 1973.

Hegel, Georg Wilhelm Friedrich. *The Phenomenology of Mind*. Translated by J. B. Baillie. New York: Humanities Press, 1977.

Herder, J. G. *Auch eine Philosophie der Geschichte zur Bildung der Menschheit*. In *Werke*. Vol. 1. Edited by W. Pross. Darmstadt: WBG, 1984.

Humboldt, Wilhelm von. *Briefe an Fr. A. Wolf 1792–1823*. Berlin: De Gruyter, 1990.

———. *Über das Studium des Altertums*. In *Werke*. Vol. 2. Darmstadt: WBG, 1986.

Jaeger, Werner. *Humanistische Reden und Vorträge*. Berlin: De Gruyter, 1960.

Jeismann, Karl-Ernst, and Peter Lundgreen, eds. *Handbuch der deutschen Bildungsgeschichte*, vol. 3, *Von der Neuordnung Deutschlands bis zur Gründung des deutschen Reiches 1800–70*. Munich: Beck, 1987.

Kant, Immanuel. *Über Pädagogik*. In *Gesammelte Schriften*. Vol. 9. Berlin: De Gruyter, 1923. First published in 1803.

Le Rider, Jacques. "Cultiver le malaise ou civiliser la culture?" In *Autour du malaise dans la culture de Freud*, edited by J. Le Rider et al., 79–118. Paris: Presses Universitaires de France, 1998.

Lessing, Gotthold Ephraim. *Werke*. Vol. 6. Edited by G. Göpfert. Munich: Hanser, 1974. Translation by E. A. McCormick: Baltimore: Johns Hopkins University Press, 1984.

Menze, Clemens. *Die Bildungsreform Wilhelm von Humboldts*. Hanover: Schroedl, 1975.

Natorp, Paul. *Die Seele des Deutschen*. Jena: Diedrichs, 1918.

Nietzsche, Friedrich. *Untimely Meditations*. 2nd ed. Translated by R. J. Hollingdale. Cambridge: Cambridge University Press, 1997.

———. *Werke*. Vol. 1. Edited by K. Schlechta. Munich: Hanser, 1966.

Schelling, Friedrich Wilhelm Joseph. *Of Human Freedom*. Translated by J. Gutmann. Chicago: Open Court, 1936.

———. *On University Studies*. Translated by E. S. Morgan. Athens: Ohio University Press, 1966.

———. *Schellings Werke*. Edited by O. Weiss. Leipzig: Eckhardt, 1907.

Schlegel, Friedrich. *Ausgabe*. Vol. 5. Edited by E. Behler. Munich: Schöningh, 1962.

Spengler, Otto. *Der Untergang des Abendlandes*. Munich: DTV, 1974.

Troeltsch, Ernst. *Der Historismus und seine Probleme*. Tübingen: Mohr, 1922). Translation: *Historicism and its Problems*. Tübingen, 1922.

Weber, Max. *The Sociology of Religion*. Introduction by T. Parsons. Boston: Beacon Press, 1993.

2

Kulturgeschichte

In 1909, the historian Karl Lamprecht founded in Leipzig an Institut für Kultur und Universalgeschichte (Institute of Cultural and Universal History). Its goal was to introduce into the field of historical studies, in opposition to the political mode of historiography that was then dominant, the economy, artistic productions, the history of printing, and all the other phenomena of life that might play a role in defining a historical period. While the notion of *Kultur* designates an effort to apprehend concrete life in all its aspects, an effort facilitated by the regionalist orientation of Lamprecht's first works, the epithet "universal" immediately corrects

that limitation. Cultural history seeks to be universal, and Lamprecht's institute was characterized by a concern to see to it that the cultural histories of the diverse nations were taught, and in their own language. It was the whole method of historical studies that was overthrown by cultural history's self-definition, unleashing in the last years of the nineteenth century the methodological quarrel (*Methodenstreit*), but also echoing a tradition discernible among the historians in Göttingen at the end of the eighteenth century. Even though the direct connection is controversial, cultural history precedes and in a way anticipates the kind of investigations

carried out by Marc Bloch and Lucien Febvre under the name of the history of mentalities.

The theoretical basis for Lamprecht's attempt to write a cultural history was located farther back in German psychology's tendency to broaden its domain of application from experimental psychology to the psychology of peoples. The term *Völkerpsychologie*, which is the logical if not lexical antecedent of *Kulturgeschichte* (cultural history), does not designate the psychological characteristics that an empirical science is supposed to have attributed to

(continued)

(continued)

different peoples. For Wilhelm Wundt, it was a matter of attempting a universal history of the psyche after observing that when experimental psychology ignores the social dimension, it ends up in an impasse. This general history of the psyche brings in social practices, the economy, and art. A particularly important element of collective psychology explored by Heymann Steinthal and Wilhelm Wundt, who thus

opened the way to the concept of cultural history, was provided by language. Although Wundt's psychology, like Lamprecht's historiography, rejects Hegelianism, one cannot fail to see a continuity between cultural history and the efforts made by Hegel's disciples and readers to realize the concrete elements of an encyclopedic system that was only sketched out. The history of art played an especially important role in this deconstruction-realization of Hegelianism.

It cannot be denied that in some respects the universalist dimension of *Kulturgeschichte* could serve as a justification for the Wilhelmine Empire's imperialist tendencies, the reference to *Kultur* not being capable, in the context of 1900, of eliminating all ambiguity. It was only through a series of predictable linguistic shifts that the term "cultural history" came more recently to designate the history of intellectual life in these diverse forms, reducing the initial *Kulturgeschichte* to only one of its dimensions.

3
"Humanities" (or "The Unnatural Sciences")

The Anglo-American term "the humanities" overlaps with the French *sciences humaines* and the German *Geisteswissenschaft* but only to a small and questionable degree. Most of the *sciences humaines* would be called social sciences in English, and *Geisteswissenschaft* is usually translated, all too narrowly, as "intellectual history." History itself, understood in its broadest sense, is taken in some (although far from all) American divisions of the territory to be a social science.

"Humanities" is a term much used now in the United Kingdom, the United States, and Latin America, but until recently the applicable word, in the United Kingdom especially, was "arts," as opposed simply to "sciences." This old usage is still visible in the names of faculties in the United States called Arts and Sciences. Confusingly, "the Arts" now refers more and more to the practice of the arts, and "humanities" refers to the informed study of such arts (literature, theater, cinema, painting, sculpture, dance, photography, etc.), along with philosophy and languages, native and foreign.

Nietzsche did not have all of these matters in mind when he wrote of the "unnatural sciences," but his notion of the unnatural in this context evokes almost everything that now seems difficult, bewildering, and necessary about the humanities:

The great certainty of the natural sciences in comparison with psychology and the critique of the elements of consciousness—with the unnatural sciences, one might almost say—rests precisely on the fact that they take the strange as their object, while it is nearly contradictory and absurd even to want

to take the not strange as one's object [*The Gay Science*].

"Psychology and the critique of the elements of consciousness" have turned specifically into (some) psychology, (some) philosophy, and several zones of literary theory and anthropology—and more broadly into the humanities themselves. Again, Nietzsche says, "What is known is what is hardest to know," which we might translate as "The humanities as forms of organized knowledge seek to make intelligible what seems mysterious because it is familiar." Students of literature, for example, manage to make interesting sense of a whole series of magnificent but not-at-all strange objects, from the predictable rage of Achilles to the inevitable fall of Milton's Adam and Eve, and from Candide's unsurprising adventures to Molly Bloom's repetitive infidelities.

In his book *The Humanities and the Dream of America*, Geoffrey Harpham recognizes that the term "humanities" "did not appear for the first time in the United States," and astutely tracks its European history, and its shifting meaning within the United States. In the 1980s the humanities in America were part of what Professor Harpham calls "the milieu," in the 1990s they bore the blame for every instance of disaffection, relativism, and "weakening of our vision and resolve." Harpham lists some of the "many . . . notions associated with the humanities," and the list is impressive:

[they] inculcate, often through attention to works of art, a sense of other minds and cultures; require and reward attention to formal and textural features as well as to literal or manifest

meaning; invite individual interpretation and inference; cultivate the faculty of judgment; awaken a sense of values; engage the emotions as well as the intellect; enlarge our imaginative capacities; challenge, deepen, and enrich our understanding of the world; provide fertile ground for the growth of self-knowledge; and under the right circumstances, open the way to tolerance, restraint, humility, and even wisdom.

This is a lot; but there is also a certain modesty lurking everywhere in the list, except perhaps in its last clause. The humanities will not make bad persons good, they may even help them to justify the way they live; and they will not support one political program rather than another. This is why Harpham's last clause, even with its careful "under the right circumstances" and "open the way," goes too far. People have been known to become tolerant and wise while pursuing humanistic studies, and it may seem as if their studies have made them tolerant and wise. But as long as those same studies are pursued by torturers and camp commandants, without any noticeable effects on their careers, it is fitting to claim less rather than more for the disciplines of the humanities. Indeed, properly understood, less *is* more. It would, in an extreme but not perverse sense, be part of humanistic understanding to allow even torturers and camp commandants to make what they will of their education. Whether they should be allowed to have the jobs they have is another question.

Harpham carefully considers useless knowledge, knowledge that is "useless in the best sense." He also writes of "the usefulness of useless knowledge." There are two crucial ideas lurking in these phrases. One is that much useful knowledge, especially in physics and medicine, started out as useless knowledge, that is, as disinterested inquiry, inquiry for inquiry's sake. If no one risks pursuing knowledge for no reason, there will finally be no knowledge that matters. This is a powerful claim, and a fine argument against eager pragmatists. The other claim is more elusive but also more humanistic. It is that disinterested inquiry is a value in its own right, even if it is never cashed in materially. It is one part of being human, and in this sense string theory is as humanistic as Aristotle, more so in a way because less practical. It is easy to see that these two claims go together: the first denies ultimate or inevitable uselessness, the second helps scholars to keep going in the dark, and redeems uselessness if it needs redeeming. The first claim on its own is a little too pragmatic, and could be accused of selling inquiry short, even in the longest run; the second claim may be a little too pure, and certainly, in hard political times, needs all the reinforcement it can get from the first.

Michael Wood

BIBLIOGRAPHY

Daedalus (Winter 2009) ("Reflecting on the Humanities").
Harpham, Geoffrey. *The Humanities and the Dream of America*. Chicago: University of Chicago Press, 2011.
Nietzsche, Friedrich. *The Gay Science*. Translation by Josefine Nauckhoff. Cambridge: Cambridge University Press, 2001.

BOGOČELOVEČESTVO [богочеловечество] (RUSSIAN)

FRENCH   *divino-humanité, théanthropie, déihumanité, théandrie*
GREEK   *to theandrikos* [τὸ θεανδρικός]
LATIN   *Deus-Homo*

➤ GOD, HUMANITY, and AIÔN, GOOD/EVIL, HISTORIA UNIVERSALIS, MENSCHHEIT, MOMENT, NAROD, RUSSIAN, SOBORNOST', SVET

Bogočlovečestvo [богочеловечество] (divino-humanity), a Russian term that refers to the Greek patristic concept *to theandrikos* [τὸ θεανδρικός], has a central place in nineteenth- and twentieth-century Russian philosophy. It designates two movements directed toward each other: that of the divine moving toward man and that of humanity rising toward the divine. It presents both Christ in the hypostatic union of his two natures, divine and human, and the humanity of men taken in the sense of the accomplishment of their true divine-human relation. In both cases it involves an ontological encounter.

The term *bogočlovečestvo* is marked by the influence of diverse philosophical traditions, mystical par excellence, and Western as well as Eastern. Two aspects are essential for understanding it. An initial interpretation allows us to see in it a "theanthropy" that takes into account a whole previous patristic heritage and appeals solely to debates about the nature of Christ, the Incarnation, and the meaning of salvation and original sin. A second interpretation is authentically Slavophile and Russocentric and refers to questions concerning the destiny of humanity, the Russian people, Slavic unity, Orthodoxy, and the universal church (*vselenskaja tserkov'* [вселенская церковь]).

I. The History of the Word

In the form *obožitisja* [обожитися] (become God), which refers to *theôsis* [θέωσις] (divinization), the idea of the ontological encounter of the human with the divine is already present in 1076 in the *Izbornik* ("Compilation") (RT: *Materialy dlia slovaria drevnerusskogo iazyka*, 2:532). Greek authors (such as John Climacus, Symeon the New Theologian, Gregory of Sinai, and Gregory Palamas) who stressed the idea of the divinization of man were subsequently translated into Slavic languages. There is an uninterrupted tradition, both literary and practical, that leads from the Greek Hesychasts (Gregory Palamas, Gregory of Sinai, Nicholas Cabasilas, Nicephorus) to the Russian Hesychasts (Nil Sorksy, fifteenth century) and ultimately to the *startsy* [старцы] (eremitic fathers) of Optina Pustyn', a monastery in Central Russia that Vladimir Solovyov and Dostoyevsky visited during the summer of 1878, the year in which Solovyov wrote his *Lectures on Godmanhood* (*Bessedy o Bogočlovečestve*).

In the *Lectures* we encounter for the first time the term *bogočlovečestvo* [богочеловечество] with a philosophical meaning, in the context of universal history. In turn, Sergei Bulgakov considerably enriched this notion by attributing to it strictly theological—and particularly Christological and Trinitarian—meanings in his work on divine wisdom and theanthropy (1933–36). The notion was developed in the direction of religious existentialism and Russophile universalism by N. Berdyaev in his *Spirit and Reality* (1932), *The Russian Idea* (1946), and *The Divine and the Human* (1949). It was later given various inflections—cosmic and salvational in the work of G. Fedorov, personalist in L. Chestov and S. Frank, and "mathematicizing" in P. Florensky.

Bogočlovečestvo is the strange product of disparate intellectual influences in the form of a synthesis of the Jewish Kabbalah, the anthropology of the Greek church fathers, the mysticism of Jakob Böhme and Meister Eckhart, and finally of Spinoza and the German philosophy of identity, in particular in Schelling's system. The latter's influence on the work of V. Solovyov is remarkable. Thus *vseedinstvo* [всеединство] (uni-totality), a central notion in Russian universalist philosophy, is nothing other than a Russian version of the German *Alleinheit*; similarly, Solovyov's *vseobščee znanie* [всеобщее знание] echoes Schelling's *Anschauung*. For his part Berdyaev wrote two important studies on Jakob Böhme and his influence on Russian thought (Berdyaev, *Mysterium Magnum*, 1:5–28, 29–45). The influences of German philosophy were exercised on this notion in parallel (Stepoun, 1923) with purely Russophile intentions, creating a conception of the world based on the ecclesiastical consciousness of Russian Orthodoxy (A. Khomiakov, I. Kiryevski, I. Samarin, C. Aksakov).

II. Semantics: Theandry or Divino-Humanity

Bogočelovečestvo is translated in English in different ways: by "theanthropy" or "theandry," or again by "divino-humanity" or "Godmanhood." From the linguistic point of view, the term is composed of two parts: God (*bog* [Бог]) and humanity (*čelovečestvo* [человечество]). Both Berdyayev and Solovyov define divinity (*božestvennoe* [Божественное]) by drawing on Eckhart's *Gottheit* and Böhme's *Ungrund* but also on the mystery of the Trinity so dear to the Greek fathers. For Berdyayev, "divinity . . . is deeper than God the Father, the Son, and the Holy Spirit. It is absolute freedom, the result of everything, including God, freedom in which even the difference between good and evil is not defined. This ineffable, transcendent Divinity has come into the world in the form of the Trinity, in three hypostases," to complete its creation with humanity, whose goal is to become divino-human (Berdyayev, *Meaning of the Creative Act*). This difference between divinity and God implicit in *bogočelovečestvo* refers to the process of a theogony that is pursued in the revelation of the divine through the history of humanity.

Berdyayev draws on the "divine void" (*božestvennoe ničto* [божественное ничто]), in Greek *to meon* [τὸ μέον]), which is the basis for all creation and is located within human nature (particularly within the person (*ličnost'* [личность]). Solovyov emphasizes instead the primordial universalism of human consciousness, which, once restored in Christ, will return universality to all partial existences and restore the unitotality *vseedinstvo* [всеединство] lost by fallen humanity:

> Since the divine principle is the real object of religious consciousness, that is, an object that acts on consciousness and reveals its content in it, religious development is a positive, objective process, a real interaction between God and man, and thus a divino-human process.

(Solovyov, *Lectures on Godmanhood*)

Semyon Frank goes still further in affirming an incomplete creation of the world. He considers knowledge (*znanie* [знание]) the true blossoming of being, the growth of life: thanks to this form of anthropogony, theogony and cosmogony attain their real goal (cf. Berdyayev, *Tipy religioznoj mysli v Rossii* [The variety of Russian religious thought]). The second part of the term *bogočelovečestvo*—that is, *čelovečestvo* (человечество [humanity])—raises fewer problems of translation. While signifying the humanity of Christ, *čelovečestvo* has in Russian religious thought a second, very specific meaning: that of a humanity united in the community of Spirit (*sobornoe čelovečestvo* [соборное человечество]). Vladimir Solovyov writes: "Reunited with its divine principle through the intermediation of Christ, humanity is the church" (Solovyov, *Lectures*); thus it is, according to an idea dear to Gregory of Nyssa and adopted by G. Fedorov, the unity constituted by the living, by the dead, and by those who are yet to be born.

III. The Actualization of the Patristic Heritage

Although it echoes the capital formula of Saint Irenaeus ("The Word of God was made man and the one who is the Son of God was made the son of man, united with the Word of God, so that man might be adopted and become the son of God" (*Adversus haeresis* [Against heresies], III, 19, 1, 939b) and was abundantly taken over by Saint Athanasius, Gregory the Theologian, and Gregory of Nyssa, the notion itself, whose meaning *bogočelovečestvo* rearticulates, goes back to Pseudo-Dionysius the Areopagite. The creation of the word *bogočelovečestvo* is nothing more than a nominalization of the adjective "theandric" [θεανδρικός] used by Pseudo-Dionysius in his fourth letter to express the idea of the humanity of Christ (RT: *PG*, vol. 3, letter 4, col. 1072C). The adjective "theandric" designates a mode of activity peculiar to the God-made-man (*andrôthentos theou* [ἀνδρωθέντος θεοῦ]), which he has carried out in our favor (*kainên tina tên theandrikên hêmin pepoliteumenos* [χαινήν τινα τὴν θεανδρικὴν ἡμῖν πεπολιτευμένος]; ibid.) Pauline anthropology opened the way to the idea of the ontological encounter between the divine and the human in the person of Christ, the second Adam, whose sacrifice paved the way for the renaissance of humanity (Rom 5:12; 1 Cor 15:22, 45; Gn 1:26). The whole later anthropology of the Greek church fathers develops this idea. Orthodox patristics proposed a mystical vision of the world in which the divine work is never finished and goes on in the creation of humanity by humanity itself. In some passages Russian authors literally echo patristic expression. "It is toward the God-man [*bogočelovek* (богочеловек)] that the whole history of humanity tended," Solovyov writes in his *Lectures*.

In the theological register *bogočelovečestvo* is the synthetic notion that expresses in a single concept two symmetrical events in Christian history. The first of these events is the Incarnation of the Word, its *kenôsis* [κένωσις], that is, in Greek *enanthrôpêsis* [ἐνανθρωπήσις] (in Russian, *bogovoploščenie* [боговоплощение] in which *voploščenie* [воплощение] (incarnation) has its origin in *plot'* [плоть] (flesh)). The second event is the divinization of man, *theôsis*, that is, *anakephalaiôsis* [ἀνακεφαλαίωσις] (in Russian, *oboženie čeloveka* [обожение человека]). The term *kenôsis* was formed by the Greek fathers on the basis of the verb *kenoô* [κενόω], that is, "to empty" (with the reflexive pronoun "to empty oneself"). It has its origin in an expression in Paul's Epistle to the Philippians, 2:7. The naming of Jesus as Lord (ibid., 2:9) is preceded by a sequence that describes the humbling of the one who was "in the form of God" (ibid., 2:6). His elevation comes at the end of a descent (in Russian, *sošestvie* [сошествие]) and an annihilation (*heauton ekenôsen* [ἑαυτὸν ἐκένωσεν]) until he reaches the obedience that makes him accept death on the Cross. This theory of *kenôsis* also invaded Russian Orthodoxy. V. Tareev (1866–1934) developed the idea that the creation itself was a kenotic act. But his most original ideas had to do with the temptations over which Christ triumphs by accepting his kenotic state. Bulgakov reinforces this idea of Tareev. For him, there is *kenos* [κενός] in the Incarnation only because there is a *kenôsis* in the Trinity as a whole and a divine *kenôsis* in the Creation. The *kenôsis* in the Trinity consists in the mutual love of the divine persons, which surpasses any individual state. The Creation inserts God into time and includes a certain risk. The *kenôsis* of the Incarnation is located above all in God, in the Word's will to love (Solovyov, *Lectures*), and appeals to the personalization of the Trinity that turns out to be so important for Orthodox theology.

In Greek patristics *kenôsis* and *theôsis* are symmetrical. The notion of *theos anthrôpos* [Θεὸς ᾿Ανθρωπος] was the cornerstone of Greek soteriology, whose meaning is found literally in the idea of the real union of man and God. The Incarnation represents the two sides of a single mystery:

> We say in fact that God and man serve each other as models, and that God humanizes himself for man in his love of man, to the very extent to which man, strengthened by charity, transposes himself for God in God.

> (Maximus the Confessor, *Ambigua*, RT: *PG*, 91:10, 113)

In Christian theosophy the point of contact between these two movements of *kenôsis* and divinization is man, but the way of conceiving the latter's relation to God differs in the Catholic and Orthodox anthropologies.

■ See Box 1.

IV. *Bogočelovečestvo* and the "Russian Idea"

The Russian philosophers of the nineteenth and twentieth centuries often emphasized the elaboration of a new kind of philosophy opposed to the positivism and empiricism prevalent in the West. They considered themselves the inventors of a genuine religious anthropology and of its true language, in which *bogočelovečestvo* is a central term. The originality of this notion consists in the intense attempt to make the subtleties of the dogma of the humanity of Christ work together with the idea of the divinization of man and the historical conception peculiar to Russian Slavophiles of the period, at the center of which was the Russian idea (*russkaja ideja* [русская идея]). The latter's historical source resides in the quasi-nationalistic and statist construct elaborated by the monk Philotheos (end of the fifteenth century), who made Moscow the "third Rome." In the nineteenth century the Russian idea consisted in a critical, messianic vision of European humanity as divided into two opposed worlds: the Catholic West and the Orthodox East. Solovyov, and later Berdyayev, following the Slavophiles, condemned the "decadent West" and asserted the particular role of Russia, which is neither Eastern nor Western, but a great "comprehensive East-West" that, alone on earth, "holds the divine truth and represents God's will" (Solovyov, *Lectures*).

The opposition between East and West has its roots in the history of the Christian church, namely in the schism between a Catholic West (the material part) and an Orthodox East (the spiritual part):

> Thus before the perfect union, there is the division . . . of Christianity into two halves, the East clinging with all its strength to the divine principle and preserving it by maintaining within itself the necessary conservative and ascetic spirit, and the West expending all its energy on developing the human principle, to the detriment of divine truth, which is first deformed and then completely rejected.

> (Ibid.)

1

Orthodox and Catholic soteriologies

Beyond the historical and theological subtleties of the period of ecumenical councils, this is where we find the key to the divergences between the anthropologies of the Greek and Latin fathers. Starting out from the idea that original sin introduced death into human existence and caused man to lose the grace of being "in the image of God," Orthodox anthropology remains very attached to the idea of the spiritual improvement of humans in their history and to the accomplishment of the deifying contemplation at the end of time (*apokatastasis* [ἀποκατάστασις]), the restoration of humanity and things at the Last Judgment, adopted by Origen and Gregory of Nyssa. The Word was made flesh, according to the Greeks, in order to restore to man the resemblance to God that he had lost through Adam's sin and to deify him. This resemblance guaranteed man's immortality, which original sin had caused him to lose. That is why the Incarnation of the Word is defined by the Greek fathers as the necessary condition for accomplishing the promise of eternal life. It is through love for man that God sought, by means of the sacrifice of Christ, to save fallen humanity (Athanasius [295–373], *De incarnatione*, 6, 5) (Méhat, 1966, 82–86). Man "would have been lost had the Son of God, the Lord of the Universe and the Savior, not come to put an end to death" (Athanasius, *De incarnatione*, 9, 2). The metaphor that is important for the whole Orthodox terminology and that remains present in Russian philosophy is that of the "divine thirst," the "lack" manifested by God with regard to humanity, to which he shows his love by creating it pure and wanting to save it.

Confronted by this Orthodox soteriology, Anselm of Canterbury (1033–1109) developed a Latin soteriology in terms of "divine *dominium*," of cosmic order and justice corrupted by human sin. It is especially in accord with the register of property or legitimate possession (*possessio, dominium, dominus*) that Anselm sets forth the relations between the creature and his Creator. The latter is the master (*dominus*), and the creatures endowed with intelligence (angels and men) are this master's slaves, the serfs or servants (*servi*, *conservi*). Man has offended the Creator of justice and order in his will and in his honor (*Dei honori*): original sin consisted in disobeying the *Dominus*. The ideas of *rectitudo*, of *rectus ordo*, which are identified with those of *justitia* or *debitum*, are essential in Saint Anselm's doctrine (Roques). Having fallen, man is not capable of giving God his due. Christ, on the other hand, owes the Father nothing but repays the human debt to him. Finally, humanity is indebted in two ways: for Adam's sin and for the death of Christ.

The Greek (Orthodox) and Latin (Catholic) anthropologies are opposed as being, respectively, that of divinization and that of redemption, of grace and debt, of restoration (re-creation) and reparation (restitution), of divine love and divine honor, of participation in order, of rebirth and buying back, of loss and debt, of economy and speculation, of contemplation and calculation, of sanctification and satisfaction. This difference between the Greek and Latin anthropologies is taken over by Dostoyevsky in the legend of the Grand Inquisitor (*The Brothers Karamazov*).

According to Solovyov, if modern history had been limited to the development of the West, it "would have ended in disintegration and chaos" (ibid.) However, "if history had stopped with Byzantine Christianity, the truth of Christ [divino-humanity, *bogočelovečestvo*] would have remained incomplete for lack of the free and active human principle that is indispensable for its accomplishment" (ibid.) Russia's messianic vocation consists in combining the "divine element of Christianity" preserved in the East and the human principle freed and developed in the West (ibid.) The "catholic character" (*narod* [народ]) of the Russian people, that is, its "conciliarity" (see SOBORNOST') makes it possible to realize this vocation. Solovyov picks up here the idea of the Slavophile A. Khomiakov, according to which it is within the ideal church as a divino-human, theanthropic unity, that *sobornost'* [соборность] (the communion of the Spirit) is developed.

> However, since man can receive the Divinity only in his absolute wholeness, that is, in union with all things, the man-God is necessarily a collective, universal being: it is pan-humanity, or the universal church [*vselenskaja tserkov'*].
>
> (Ibid.)

Solovyov's universal church is the living analogy of the Absolute. Thus, according to the Russian idea, humanity is *bogočelovečestvo*: a human community in the history of which the divine is manifested and gradually reveals itself. In overcoming its division, this community must pass from the stage of history to that of metahistory. The latter is nothing other than the intrusion of eternity into historical time, a sort of accomplishment of time, the *kairos* [καιρός] that manifests itself solely in encountering the *sobornost'* of reunited humanity.

Tatyana Golitchenko

BIBLIOGRAPHY

Anselm, Saint, Archbishop of Canterbury. "Cur Deus Homo: Or Why God Was Made Man." In *Basic Writings*, edited and translated by Thomas Williams. Indianapolis: Hackett, 2007.

Berdyayev, Nicolay. *The Bourgeois Mind and Other Essays*. Freeport, NY: Books for Libraries Press, 1966.

———. *Christian Existentialism: An Anthology*. Translated by D. Lowrie. London: Allen and Unwin, 1965.

———. *The Destiny of Man*. London: G. Bles, Centenary Press, 1937.

———. *The Divine and the Human*. London: G. Bles, 1949.

———. *The Meaning of the Creative Act*. Translated by Donald A. Lowrie. London: Gollancz, 1955.

———. *The Russian Idea*. Translated by R. M. French. Hudson, NY: Lindisfarne Press, 1992.

———. *Spirit and Reality*. London: G. Bles, 1946.

Bulgakov, Sergei. *Sophia, the Wisdom of God: An Outline of Sophiology*. Hudson, NY: Lindisfarne Press, 1993.

Koyré, Alexandre. *La philosophie et le problème national en Russie au début du XIXème siècle*. Paris: Gallimard / La Pléiade, 1929.

Maximus. *St. Maximus the Confessor's Questions and Doubts*. Translated by Despina D. Prassas. DeKalb: Northern Illinois University Press, 2010.

Solovyov, Vladimir. *Lectures on Godmanhood*, introduction by Peter Zouboff. London: D. Dobson, 1948.

C

ÇA

The French demonstrative pronoun *ça*, a contraction of *cela*, is the widely accepted translation of the German *es*, a third-person singular neuter pronoun that Freud uses, in his second topology, to designate the third construct (id) of the psychic apparatus alongside the *Ich* (ego) and the *Über-Ich* (super-ego): see ES, and DRIVE, I/ME/MYSELF, UNCONSCIOUS, WUNSCH; cf. ANXIETY, ENTSTELLUNG, LOVE, PLEASURE, VERNEINUNG.

Es is also used in the German expression *es gibt*, which French renders as *il y a*. See ES GIBT, ESTI, *IL Y A*.

➤ CONSCIOUSNESS, DASEIN, ERLEBEN, *IDENTITY*, SIGNIFIER/SIGNIFIED, *SELF*, SUBJECT

CARE

FRENCH   *souci, soin, sollicitude*
GERMAN   *Sorge, Fürsorge, Besorgen*

➤ *SOUCI* and ANXIETY, *AUTRUI*, DASEIN, GENDER, LAW, LOVE, *MALAISE*, MORALS, SECURITAS, SEX, SORGE, VERGÜENZA

The word "care" has recently been used with increasing frequency in English philosophy, but its translation into other languages raises a problem for two reasons in particular. First, it is used to translate the Heideggerian term *Sorge* (*Sein und Zeit*), and second, it appears in the expression "the ethics of care," which feminists oppose to the impartiality of "masculine justice" (Gilligan, *Different Voice*; Young, *Justice*). In both cases, it is impossible to translate "care" into French.

I. The Translation of *Sorge* by "Care"

We must note first that "care" does not derive from Latin *cura* but rather from Old High German or Gothic *Kara*, which means "care," "lament," "sorrow." The word initially designated a painful mental state such as concern or anxiety, and it was indeed appropriate to use "care" to render the German *Sorge* as it is used by Heidegger. For Heidegger the very Being of *Dasein* is "care" (*Sorge*) (*Sein und Zeit*), so that the latter is in the world in the form of *Besorgen* (concern). Cares, tribulations, and melancholias are distinct states, but they are part of the ontological structure of *Sorge*: "*Dasein* exists as an entity for which, in its Being, that Being is itself an issue" (*Being and Time*, 274).

The word "care" also designates the effort to anticipate a danger or to protect oneself from the uncertainties of the future by acting responsibly. That is the most common meaning of the term in English, and here again we see how well the importance of temporality in "care" corresponds to Heideggerian concerns: "The ontological meaning of care is temporality" (ibid.). But the deficiencies of the English translation of *Sorge* by "care" rapidly make

themselves felt because the element of nothingness is absent in "care": "Death, conscience, and guilt are anchored in the phenomenon of care."

Finally, Heidegger connects *Sorge* with curiosity, which leads him to retranslate Aristotle: "All men by nature desire to see" (*pantes anthropoi tou eidenai oregontai phusei*) (ibid.)—taking *eidenai* in the original sense of "to see" and connecting *oregontai* (lit., "seek") with *Sorge*, "care." And he translates Aristotle in these terms: "The care for seeing is essential to man's Being." Thus he makes an association between "seeing" and "thinking" in Western metaphysics that the English translation as "care" cannot render. There is no possibility of making the connotations specific to the German *Sorge* flow into the English "care," and the current development of the meaning of "care" that is drawing this word in the direction of interpersonal relations and concern about others makes the translation of Heidegger given here in English rather enigmatic.

II. "Care" and "Solicitude"

German distinguishes more clearly than English or French between care for oneself or *Selbstsorge* (which, Heidegger says, is "tautological," *Being and Time*, 366), on the one hand, and on the other *Fürsorge* or "care for the other," which Macquarrie and Robinson translate not by "care" but by "solicitude" and which the French translator renders as *assistance*. Solicitude, which is "an affectionate care for others," has a meaning different from "care" and must be attached to a different register, that of action in matters of help and social aid. "Care" designates the whole set of public arrangements necessary for the welfare of the population in a welfare state. That is a meaning for which there is no French equivalent. For example, the expressions "prenatal care" and "postnatal care" refer particularly to the responsibilities of public health agencies with regard to pregnant women and infants. Caregivers are people who, whether as volunteers or not, take care of the elderly or anyone in need.

Since in many countries the great majority of caregivers are women, feminists have offered a critique of the ethics of justice in the name of the virtues attributed to these disinterested, noncompetitive, nonquantifiable, nonpossessive behaviors that constitute most of women's nonremunerated work: caring for children and the elderly, efforts to keep the family group intact, etc. Thus these militants seek to oppose to the "masculine" ideal of an ethics of impartiality and justice an "ethics of care." Without taking a position regarding the "feminine" character of the values in question, we can say that these feminists' reflections have led to a genuine "deconstruction" of universalist morality and the principle of identity, in accord with a trajectory that merges with the Heideggerian heritage of *Sorge*, though we cannot say that the common use of the word "care" has played a role in this matter.

Catherine Audard

BIBLIOGRAPHY

Gilligan, Carol. *In a Different Voice*. Cambridge, MA: Harvard University Press, 1982.

Heidegger, Martin. *Sein und Zeit*. Tübingen: Max Niemayer Verlag, 1953. First Published in 1927. Translation by J. Macquarrie and E. Robinson: *Being and Time*. Oxford: Blackwell, 1978.

Young, Iris Marion. *Justice and the Politics of Difference*. Princeton, NJ: Princeton University Press, 1990.

CATEGORY

"Category" is derived, via Vulgar Latin, from the Greek *katêgoria* [κατηγορία], (*kata* [κατά], against, on, and *agoreuô* [ἀγορεύω], speak in public), which designates both the prosecution in a trial and the attribution in a logical proposition—that is, the questions that must be asked with regard to a subject and the answers that can be given. From Aristotle to Kant and beyond, logic has therefore determined a list of "categories" that are as well operations of judgment (cf. *JUSTICE*); see ESTI (esp. Box 1) and HOMONYM. On the lexical networks implied by this ontological systematics, see BEGRIFF, MERKMAL, PREDICATION, PROPOSITION, SUBJECT, and cf. ESSENCE, PROPERTY, *TO BE*, TRUTH, UNIVERSALS.

➤ AUFHEBEN, *GENRE*, OBJECT, PRINCIPLE, *WHOLE*

CATHARSIS, KATHARSIS [κάθαρσις] (GREEK)

FRENCH   *purgation, purification*

➤ ART, MELANCOLY, MIMÊSIS, MITMENSCH, BOX 1, NATURE, BOX 1, NEIGHBOR, PATHOS, PLEASURE, PROPERTY, SUBLIME

The word *katharsis* initially was connected with rituals of purification before becoming a Hippocratic term in the theory of humors. Aristotle's *Poetics* inflected its meaning by maintaining, in opposition to Plato, that tragedy and theater can care for the soul by giving it pleasure. In the traditional translation as "purgation," it was part of French classical discourse on tragedy (Corneille, 1660) before reappearing in its Greek form in Lessing's works criticizing Corneille's criticism of Aristotle (the Greek word, which was already present in English, then returned in nineteenth-century discussions of Lessing; see RT: *DHLF*, s.v. "Catharsis"). In psychoanalysis and psychotherapy, the "cathartic method" that Freud gradually disengaged from its association with hypnosis is connected with abreaction, the emotional discharge that makes it possible, through language, to eliminate the affect bound up with a traumatic event. The word's oscillation between the meanings "purification" and "purgation" while remaining constant through various languages has continually provided material for polemics and reinterpretations.

I. From Scapegoat to Tragic Pleasure

The adjective *katharos* [καθαρός] associates material cleanliness, that of the body (Homer calls it an "uncovered place";

it is applied to water, to grain; cf. RT: *Dictionnaire étymologique de la langue grecque*), with the moral or religious purity of the soul—thus Empedocles's *Purifications* contains both a project of perpetual peace, constructed around metempsychosis, and alimentary prohibitions. *Katharsis* [κάθαρσις] is an action noun corresponding to the verb *kathairô* [καθαίρω] (clean, purify, purge). Initially it had the religious sense of "purification," and referred particularly to the ritual of expulsion practiced in Athens on the eve of the Thargelia. During these festivals traditionally dedicated to Artemis and Apollo, a loaf of bread, the *thargêlos* [θάργηλος], made from the first grain harvested that year, was offered; but beforehand the city had to be purified by expelling criminals from it (cf. Harpocration's lexicon: "The Athenians, during the Thargelia, drove two men, as purifying exorcisms, out of the city, one for the men, the other for the women," and then scapegoats, according to the ritual of the *pharmakos* [φαρμακός]). Apollo himself is called *katharsios* [καθάρσιος], "purifier," and moreover is forced to purify himself after killing Python in Delphi. According to Socrates in Plato's *Cratylus*, he is fittingly named *apolouôn* [ἀπολούων], "the washer," insofar as the music, medicine, and divination that characterize him are so many *katharseis* [καθάρσεις] and *katharmoi* [καθαρμοί], practices of purification (405a–c).

According to the *kathairontes* [καθαίροντες], the "purgers," "the body will receive no benefit from taking food until the internal obstacles [*ta empodizonta . . . tis ekbalêi* [τὰ ἐμποδίζοντα . . . τις ἐκβάλῃ] have been removed" (Plato, *Sophist*, 230c). The purgative method that works for the body also works for the soul, which cannot assimilate knowledge before it has been purged of its opinions by *elegchos* [ἔλεγχος], "refutation"; the patient "must be purged of his prejudices and made to think that he knows only what he knows, and no more" (230d). But there is a still more radical purification that Plato transposes from the religious domain, Orphic and Pythagorean, to philosophy (cf. Dodds, *The Greeks and the Irrational*, chaps. 3 and 5): "purification consists in separating the soul as much as possible from the body" (*Phaedo*, 67c); if only the pure, purified thought can take possession of the pure, the unmixed (*to eilikrines* [τὸ εἰλικρινές]) that is truth, mustn't the soul leave the body?

Katharsis connects purification with separation and purging, not only in the religious, but also in the political (Plato, in the *Laws* [5.735b–736a], describes painful purges as the only efficacious ones) and the medical domains. In Hippocratic medicine, *katharsis* was connected with the theory of the humors and names the process of physical purgation through which harmful secretions are expelled, naturally or artificially, through the upper or the lower orifices: the term can designate not only purging as such, but also defecation, diarrhea, vomiting, and menstruation (Hippocrates, *Aphorisms*, 5.36; 5.60; cf. *De mulierum affectibus*). This Hippocratic meaning is valid in Aristotle's whole naturalist corpus (in the *Historia animialium*, 7.10.587b, for example, the term designates the rupture of the amniotic sac, various bodily discharges, etc.; cf. RT: *Index aristotelicus*, s.v.). However, as a remedy—Greek *to pharmakon* [τὸ φάρμακον], the same word, in the neuter gender, as the one designating the scapegoat—*katharsis* implies more precisely the idea of a homeopathic medicine: purgation is a way of curing harm by harm, the same by the same, and it is also why every *pharmakon* is a "poison" as much as a "remedy," the dosage of the harmful thing alone producing a good result (see NATURE, Box 1).

Here we have one of the possible keys to the rhetorical, poetic, and aesthetic meaning of *katharsis*, which Lausberg characterizes as "a homeopathic hygiene for the soul" (RT: *Handbuch der literarischen Rhetorik*, §1222). This kind of cure is connected with the *katharsis* produced by sacred melodies, mentioned in Aristotle's *Politics*. There are enthusiastic, possessed individuals who "fall into a religious frenzy, whom we see as a result of the sacred melodies—when they have used the melodies that excite the soul to mystic frenzy (*tois exorgiazousi . . . melesi* [τοῖς ἐξοργιάζουσι . . . μέλεσι])—restored as though they had found healing and purgation (*iatreias . . . kai katharseôs* [ἰατρείας . . . καὶ καθάρσεως])" (7.1342a 7–11). More generally, for Aristotle (who here goes beyond a Plato, whom he salutes but subverts; cf. *Republic*, 3, starting at 398) *katharsis* is one of the functions of music, along with education and a good way of life, and with leisure and a relaxation of tension: for all those in the grip of passion "are in a manner purged and their souls lightened and delighted (*kouphizesthai meth' hêdonês* [κουφίζεσθαι μεθ ἡδονῆς])." The purgative melodies likewise give humans an innocent pleasure (*charan ablabê* [χαρὰν ἀβλαβῆ]) (*Politics*, 7.1342a 14–16).

This homeopathic meaning is maintained in the *Poetics*: tragedy includes "incidents of pity and fear, wherewith to accomplish its catharsis (*katharsin* [κάθαρσιν]) of such emotions" (6.1449b 27–28). This is a purgation of the same by the same, or rather by the representation of the same. But unlike participants in Corybantic rites that seek to cure the soul of a furious madness, the spectator of tragedy is in full command of his faculties; he has no need to be cured. Whence a second meaning, which is in a way allopathic: the passions are purified by the spectator's seeing them, to the extent to which the poet shows him things that have themselves been purified and transformed by *mimêsis* [μίμησις]: "The Plot in fact should be so framed that, even without seeing the things take place, he who simply hears the account of them shall be filled with horror and pity at the incidents.. . . The tragic pleasure is that of pity and fear, and the poet has to produce it by a work of imitation" (14.1453b 4–13). Purgation, that is, the representation of diagrams by means of a musical or poetic work, substitutes pleasure for pain. Ultimately it is pleasure that purifies the passions, lightens them, relieves them of their excessive, invasive character, and resituates them in a point of equilibrium.

Finally, to radicalize catharsis, we have to follow the skeptical physician Sextus Empiricus in choosing for the soul as for the body a remedy capable of "eliminating itself at the same time that it eliminates the humors" or dogmas: the skeptical modes of expression are thus in their very form, which includes doubt, relativity, relationship, and questioning, self-purging (*Outlines of Pyrrhonism*, 1.206; cf. 2.188; cf. Voelke, "Soigner par le logos").

II. Purgation of the Passions and Purification of Morals in the Classical Theater

This twofold meaning connecting the remedy with pleasure is the basis for the ambiguity and at the same time the richness of later interpretations. The influence exercised by Aristotle's *Poetics* on the French theory of the dramatic poem was accompanied by a reworking of the ancient problematics in relation to new concerns connected with a profoundly different conception of the passions. From a Christian point of view, it is the passions themselves, and not merely their excesses, that are considered bad. It is no longer a matter of purifying the passions but of purifying oneself of passions, that is, of purifying morals. What seventeenth-century authors meant by "purgation of the passions" thus does not have quite the sense that *katharsis* had in Aristotle. The French emphasize the moral and especially the pedagogical aspect attached to the idea of theatrical *katharsis*. "The main goal of poetry is to benefit . . . by purifying morals," Father Rapin wrote (*Réflexions sur la Poétique*, 9). "Poetry is an art that was invented for the instruction of men. . . . The ill are treated, and tragedy is the only remedy from which they are able to benefit, for it is the only amusement in which they can find the pleasant and the useful," Dacier wrote in the preface to his French translation of Aristotle's *Poetics* (1692). Although it appeals to Aristotle's authority on this point, this way of conceiving the purgation of the passions in the theater has little to do with Aristotelian *katharsis*. Corneille makes the same error when he criticizes Aristotle on this point, rejecting the idea that tragedy can purify the spectators' passions: he thinks he is deviating from Aristotle, whereas he is merely opposing the interpretation his contemporaries gave of him. Racine is one of the few writers to remain faithful to Aristotle: "Tragedy," he wrote, "exciting pity and terror, purges and tempers these sorts of passions, that is, by arousing these passions, it deprives them of what is excessive and vicious in them, and returns them to a state that is moderate and in conformity with reason" (*Œuvres complètes*, quoted by J. Tricot in his translation of Aristotle's *Politics*). It is true that unlike Corneille, Racine understood Greek, and translated and annotated whole passages of the *Poetics* and the *Nicomachean Ethics*.

■ See Box 1.

Relying on Corneille's criticism, but at the same time respecting convention and what he thought was Aristotle's thought, Du Bos developed a rather confused reflection on this subject that concludes as follows: "Thus tragedy purges the passions rather as remedies cure, and as defensive weapons protect against offensive ones. It doesn't always happen, but sometimes it does!" (*Réflexions critiques sur la poésie et sur la peinture* [1719], §44, "Que les poèmes dramatiques purgent les passions").

III. The "Carthartic Method" in Psychoanalysis

The "cathartic method" is part of the prehistory of psychoanalysis. It was developed by Josef Breuer and Sigmund Freud on the basis of their research on the etiology of symptoms of hysteria, as they explain in their work *Studien über Hysterie* (*Studies on Hysteria*, 1895). In seeking the causes of the pathological phenomena of hysteria, the two Viennese physicians noticed that their patients' symptoms were causally connected with a traumatic situation that the patient could not consciously remember (cf. "Über den psychischen Mechanismus hysterischer Phänomene" ["On the Psychical Mechanism of Hysterical Phenomena," 1893], in *Studien über Hysterie*). The affect involved in this "psychic trauma [*psychische Trauma*]," "blocked" (*eingeklemmte*) and not discharged through the normal channels, is transformed into a hysterical conversion. "Catharsis" is produced when under treatment the path leading to consciousness and the normal discharge of the affect [*normale Entladung des Affekts*] is opened up ("*Psychoanalyse*" *und* "*Libidotheorie*" [*Psychoanalysis and Theory of the Libido*] [1922]). The "cathartic procedure," as Breuer called it, consists in using hypnosis to treat the patient through catharsis. The narrative of the "psychic trauma" is in fact usually followed by a discharge of affect (abreaction) that constitutes "catharsis" proper (cf. *Selbstdarstellung* [*Self-representation*], 1924).

After the publication of *Studien über Hysterie*, the two collaborators' positions regarding the etiology of hysteria diverged: "Breuer gave priority to what might be called a physiological theory," whereas Freud confirmed the sexual content at the origin of hysterical phenomena, also pointing out the importance of "the differentiation between unconscious and conscious mental acts" (*Selbstdarstellung*). Later on, Freud abandoned hypnosis and suggestion in favor of free association, thus creating "psychoanalysis." However, the effectiveness of catharsis allowed him to confirm two fundamental results, which were subsequently confirmed, as he says himself:

First, hysterical systems have meaning and significance because they are substitutes for normal mental acts; and second, the disclosure of this unknown meaning coincides with the suppression of the symptoms, and thus here scientific research and therapeutic effort coincide.

Studien über Hysterie

Barbara Cassin
Jacqueline Lichtenstein
Elisabete Thamer

BIBLIOGRAPHY

Aristotle. *Poetics*. In *The Complete Works of Aristotle*. Edited by J. Barnes, vol. 2, 2316–3240. Princeton, NJ: Princeton University Press, 1984.
———. *Politics*. Translated by J. Tricot. Paris: Vrin, 1970.

Belfiore, Elizabeth. *Tragic Pleasure: Aristotle on Plot and Emotion*. Princeton, NJ: Princeton University Press, 1992.
Bernays, Jacob. *Zwei Abhandlungen über die aristotelische Theorie des Drama*. Berlin: W. Herz, 1880 ; repr., Darmstadt: Wissenschaftliche Buchgesellschaft, 1968.
Corneille, Pierre. *Œuvres*. Paris: Éditions du Seuil, 1963.
———. *Chief Plays*. Translated by L. Lockert. Princeton, NJ: Princeton University Press, 1957.
Dacier, André. *La poétique d'Aristote*. Barbin, 1692.
———. *The Preface to Aristotle's Art of Poetry*. Los Angeles: William Andrews Clark Memorial Library, University of California, 1959. First published in 1705.
Dodds, Eric Robertson. *The Greeks and the Irrational*. Berkeley: University of California Press, 1959.
Du Bos, Jean-Baptiste. *Réflexions critiques sur la poésie et sur la peinture*. Paris: École nationale supérieure des beaux-arts, 1994. First published in 1719. Translation by T. Nugent: *Critical Reflections on Poetry, Painting and Music: With an Inquiry into the Rise and Progress of the Theatrical Entertainments of the Ancients*. London: Printed for J. Nourse, 1748.
Freud, Sigmund. "*Psychoanalyse*" *und* "*Libidotheorie*." Vol. 13 in *Gesammelte Werke*. Frankfurt: Fischer, 1999. First published in 1922.
———. *Selbstdarstellung*. Vol. 14 in *Gesammelte Werke*. Frankfurt: Fischer, 1999. First published in 1922.
———. *The Standard Edition of the Complete Psychological Works of Sigmund Freud*. Edited by J. Strachey. London: Hogarth Press–Institute of Psychoanalysis, 1953–74.
———. *Studien über Hysterie*. Vol. 1 in *Gesammelte Werke*. Frankfurt: Fischer, 1999. First published in 1895.
Lessing, Gotthold Ephraim. *Hamburgische Dramaturgie*. Edited by K. L. Berghahn. Stuttgart: Reclam, 1981. First published in 1767–68. Translation by V. Lange: *Hamburg Dramaturgy*. New York: Dover Publications, 1962.
Papanoutsos, Evangelios P. *La catharsis des passions d'après Aristote*. Athens: Collection de l'Institut français d'Athènes, 1953.
Plato. *Sophist*. In *Plato: The Collected Dialogues*. Edited by Edith Hamilton and Huntington Cairns. Princeton, NJ: Princeton University Press, 1961.
Racine, Jean. *Complete Plays*. Translated by S. Solomon. New York: Random House, 1967.
———. *Œuvres Complètes*. 2 vols. Paris: Gallimard / La Pléiade, 1952.
Rapin, René. *Réflexions sur la Poétique d'Aristote, et sur les ouvrages des poètes anciens et modernes*. Edited by E. T. Dubois. Geneva: Droz, 1970. First published in 1674. Translation by M. Rymer: *Monsieur Rapin's Reflections on Aristotle's Treatise of Poesie*. London, 1694.
Voelke, André Jean. "Soigner par le logos: la thérapeutique de Sextus Empiricus." In *Le Scepticisme antique. Perspectives historiques et systématiques*. Cahiers de la Revue de Théologie et de Philosophie, 15. Geneva, 1990.

1

From Aristotle to Corneille and back

Corneille's criticism of the idea of theatrical catharsis illustrates the way his contemporaries transformed this problem. The purgation of the passions in the sense in which Corneille thought Aristotle understood it is for him purely "imaginary": tragedy, he wrote, has the particular "utility" that

> by means of pity and fear it purges such passions. These are the terms Aristotle uses in his definition, and they tell us two things: first, that it [catharsis] excites pity and fear, and second, that by means of them, it purges similar passions. He explains the first at some length, but he says not a word about the latter, and of all the

conditions he uses in this definition, this is the only one he does not explain. . . . If the purgation of the passions happens in tragedy, I hold that it must happen in the manner that I say; but I doubt that it ever happens, even in those that meet the conditions set by Aristotle. They are met in *Le Cid* and caused its great success: Rodrigue and Chimène have the probity subject to passions and these passions cause their misfortune because they are as unhappy as they are passionate for one another . . . their misfortune elicits pity, that is certain, and it cost the audience enough tears to make that incontestable. This pity must make us fear that we will fall into a similar

misfortune and purge the excessive love that causes their misfortune and make us feel sorry for them, but I do not know whether pity gives it to us or if it purges it, and I fear that Aristotle's reasoning on this point is just a fine idea that has never actually produced its effect. I leave this up to those who have seen the performances: they can examine it in the secrecy of their hearts and go over what moved them in the theater, in order to see if in this way they arrived at reflective fear, and whether it rectified in them the passion that caused the disgrace that they so lamented.

Discours de la tragédie, 1660

In his *Hamburg Dramaturgy* (1767–68), Lessing reproached Corneille precisely for not having understood the sentence in chapter 6 of the *Poetics* and of having unfairly criticized Aristotle:

> Finally, as for the moral goal that Aristotle assigns to tragedy, and that he thought he had to include in his definition, we know how many debates about it have arisen, particularly recently. I feel sure

that I can show that those who have blamed Aristotle on this point have not understood him. They have lent him their own thoughts before finding out what his were. They are battling chimeras with which they are themselves obsessed, and flatter themselves that they victoriously refute the philosopher when they defeat the phantoms of their own brains.

48th Evening

BIBLIOGRAPHY

Corneille, Pierre. *Discours de la tragédie.* In *Œuvres.* Paris: Éditions du Seuil, 1963.
Lessing, Gotthold Ephraim. *Hamburgische Dramaturgie.* Edited by K. L. Berghahn. Stuttgart: Reclam, 1981. First published by 1767–68. Translation by V. Lange: *Hamburg Dramaturgy.* New York: Dover Publications, 1962.

CERTITUDE

"Certitude," from ecclesiastical medieval Latin *certitudo,* designating in particular "Christian conviction," is heir to two meanings of the adjective *certus,* one "objective" and the other "subjective": "beyond doubt, fixed, positive, real," regarding a thing or knowledge, or "firm in his resolutions, decided, sure, authentic," regarding an individual. Although *certitudo* has no Greek equivalent, the Latin verb *cerno, cernere,* from which *certus* is derived, has the concrete meaning of "pass through a sieve, discern," like the Greek *krinein* [κρίνειν] (select, sieve, judge), which comes from the same root. Thus begins the relationship between certitude, judgment, and truth, which since Descartes has been connected with the problematics of the subject and of self-certainty. The whole terminological system of truth is thus involved, from unveiling and adequation to certitude and obviousness: see TRUTH, and ISTINA, PRAVDA.

I. Certainty, Objectivity, Subjectivity, and Linguistic Systems

1. The objective aspect manifests itself first, *certitudo* translating for example the "determined nature" of objects or known properties (as in Arab commentaries on Aristotle's *Metaphysics* translated into Latin), or the incontestably true nature of principles: see TRUTH, Box 6; cf. RES (and *THING*), PRINCIPLE.

2. With the revolution of the subject inaugurated by Cartesian philosophy, the second aspect comes to the fore: some "reasons," "ideas," or "propositions" are "true and certain," or "true and evident," but the most certain and the most evident of all, and thus in a sense the truest, is the certitude of my own existence, a certainty that the subject attributes to itself: see SUBJECT and I/ME/ MYSELF, SELBST. The thematics of certainty precedes that of consciousness both historically and logically, but it ends up being incorporated and subordinated by it: see CONSCIOUSNESS; cf. ES and UNCONSCIOUS.

3. Certainty thus becomes a quality or disposition of the subject that reproduces, in the field of rational knowledge, the security or assurance that the believer finds in religious faith, and that shields him from the wavering of the soul, see CROYANCE [BELIEF, GLAUBE]; cf. DASEIN, *MALAISE,* and esp. *LIFE/LEBEN,* SEHNSUCHT.

4. It will be noted that French retains the possibility of reversing the perspective by exploiting the Latin etymology, as Descartes does in the *Principles of Philosophy* when

he transforms the *certitudo probabilis* of the Scholastics (Aquinas) into "moral certainty." On the other hand, English tends to objectify certainty to the maximum in opposition to belief (see BELIEF), whereas German hears in the term *Gewissheit* the root *wissen* (to know, to have learned) and situates it in a series with *Bewusstsein* and *Gewissen* (see CONSCIOUSNESS), clearly marking the constitutive relationship to the subject in opposition to *Glaube* on the one hand, and to *Wahrheit* and *Wahrscheinlichkeit* (lit., "appearance of truth," i.e., "probability") on the other (see TRUTH, II.B).

II. Knots of Problems

1. On the relations between certainty and belief, the modalities of subjective experience, see *CROYANCE.*

2. On the relation between individual certainty and the wise man's constancy, see PHRONÊSIS and PIETAS; cf. MORALS, VIRTÙ, *WISDOM.*

3. On the relations between certainty and truth, the confrontation between subjectivity and objectivity in the development of knowledge, see—in addition to TRUTH— ANSCHAULICHKEIT, *EXPERIENCE,* PERCEPTION, REPRÉSENTATION.

4. On the relations between certainty and probability, the modalities of objective knowledge insofar as it is related to a subject's experience, see—in addition to *PROBABILITY*— CHANCE, DUTY, DOXA, *SENS COMMUN* [COMMON SENSE, SENSUS COMMUNIS], MATTER OF FACT.

➤ SOUL, *TO BE,* UNDERSTANDING

CHANCE / PROBABILITY

FRENCH   *chance, probabilité, avantage*

➤ *PROBABILITY,* and *DESTINY,* ENGLISH, HISTORY, UTILITY

The English notions of chance and probability, which were long confused with each other, each took on a specific meaning with their entry into the field of mathematical calculation, which made it necessary to distinguish them as early as the second half of the eighteenth century and to distinguish them even more clearly in the nineteenth century. No doubt there were some cases in the eighteenth century where "chance" had exactly the same meaning as "probability." For example, in his *Essay towards Solving a Problem in the Doctrine of Chances* (1763), Thomas Bayes declares that "[b]y *chance* I mean the same as probability," even though his work brilliantly demonstrated that they are not the same. Chance clearly retains the "subjective" spirit of arbitrary randomness, since we speak of the "chance of being right" (in assigning a degree of probability between two selected degrees); thus it represents, in the tradition of J. Bernoulli's *Ars conjectandi*, a fraction of certainty. On the other hand, probability is clearly "objective" in that it seems to apply more directly to events. In dice, the probability of rolling an ace is one in six; it seems to be a property of the situation. Nonetheless, the preceding proposition can also be interpreted and formulated as follows: the chance of being right when one says that an ace will be rolled is one in six.

I. Probability of Chances and Probability of Causes

Between the 1650s, when Pascal, along with Fermat, invented the "geometry of chance" (*géométrie du hasard*) and tried to enumerate the chances and to calculate odds (*calculer le parti*), and the end of the eighteenth century, "chance" and "probability" had time to change meaning. The last chapter of *La logique de Port-Royal*—of which Pascal was at least the inspiration, if not the author—determines probability by calculating the odds (of winning if a given event occurs). At each step in the complex gaming situation he is analyzing, Pascal calculates the players' odds, that is, the amount each would have to be paid if the game were to stop before chance determined the winner in accord with the rules. Nonetheless, "calculating the odds" is taken as a verb, whereas "probability" is usually taken by Pascal and in the *La logique de Port-Royal* as the equivalent of "chance." In 1739, Hume, in *A Treatise of Human Nature*, grasped the two major axes along which the two notions are divided when they are not considered synonyms. The first opposes the "probability of chances" to the "probability of causes." When in a given situation we can draw up a table of all the possible outcomes and calculate that a given situation will occur rather than another, we speak of the "probability of chances." Thus, in calculating the odds in a game, we tend to speak of the "probability of chances" because the mind can make a concise inventory of all the situation's possible outcomes. The Pascalian term *hasard* is perfectly rendered by the English word "chance" (Maistrov, *Probability Theory*).

We speak of the "probability of causes" in very different circumstances, which Hume clearly distinguishes: if a sequence of similar events $A_1 B_1$, $A_2 B_2$, $A_3 B_3$ . . . $A_n B_n$ has been witnessed by one or more persons and an event of type A occurs, we can use Newton's binomial to calculate the probability that an event B will occur; in this case we will speak of the "probability of causes." Note that on the basis of an event of the type B, we could have calculated in the same way the probability that an event A preceded it. It is clear that, borrowing Hume's image, the probability of causes is assessed not by making a complete count in a system of cases that have to be inventoried in every direction, but more linearly, in the way that one plows a furrow in a single direction. Although the weight of past cases bears on the determination of the probability of a cause or an effect in a present situation, taking into account past situations in the situation of a game (of chance) has nothing at all to do with the probability of chances

and constitutes a genuine epistemological obstacle to its evaluation.

II. Subjective Probability (Chance) and Objective Probability (Probability)

Cutting across this first opposition between the "probability of chances" and the "probability of causes" and contradicting it to some extent, there is another opposition that has been even more influential not only in mathematics, but also in the domains of religion, economics, jurisprudence, and society: the one that distinguishes subjective probability (generally called chance) and objective probability (generally called probability). Price is correct in saying that Bayes (*An Essay*) deviated from common usage on this point. If I roll a mathematician's six-sided die that is well balanced and not loaded and that clearly shows one of its faces when it has finished rolling, the probability of obtaining an ace, or indeed any other face, is one in six. Probability seems here to apply directly to the event, even if that is not the case and if it is a pure fiction connected with the discourse that allows us to make a prediction. But if I am in a situation where I am drawing winning and losing lots from an urn, I calculate the value of the relation between the number of losing lots and the number of winning lots that it contains on the basis of the drawings I have already made, and I attribute a probability to the outcome of the drawing I am about to make with a chance of being right or wrong. Bayes's rule relates the probability that an event will occur to the chance of being mistaken when I calculate it. His rule calculates, as Price puts it, borrowing Bayes's own expression:

> . . . the chance that the probability for the happening of an event perfectly unknown should be between any two named degrees of probability, antecedently to any experiments made about it.

Chance no longer bears directly on the event but, rather, indirectly on my estimate of its probability. In a given initial situation, I can decide as I wish to situate between two degrees the probability that an event will occur; the "chance of being right" changes, of course, as this situation develops, that is, as I collect new information regarding the event in question. The degree of chance is calculated by an understanding that measures the value of a decision in relation to the probability of a given event in a given situation or at various stages of that situation. Curiously, since in this new function it is difficult to use the term "chance" in the plural, an author like Price substitutes the word "odds" for it and speaks of the "odds of chance" or the "odds of probability" (*An Essay*). The point is all the more remarkable because for a long time the English word "odds" was used only in the singular. Although "odds" clearly takes on the meaning of the French word *cote* in a wager that can receive a cardinal number, "odds" initially designated the strangeness of an event, the unexpected characteristic that made it an unusual, even unparalleled, event; but this does not mean that the word has no relation to arithmetic, since we commonly speak of odd numbers. In its singularity, the event is incommensurable, but in a contradictory fashion it thereby acquires the status of a unit constitutive of a number that preserves its character of being imperfect, odd, and difficult to divide.

III. The Importance of the Distinction between Chance and Probability in Religious and Juridical Debates

We can now see why the reversal of a "subjective" interpretation of the arguments of natural religion, which had been previously based on analogies (e.g., God is to the universe as an architect is to a building) turned out to be particularly devastating. The "chance of being right" evaluates various competing hypotheses; it does not limit itself to the examination of a single analogy whose terms are considered without showing any imagination. This technique of argumentation, which does not always adopt Bayes's terminology, is that of Hume's *Dialogues concerning Natural Religion*.

The shift from a perspective that is allegedly *de re* (bearing directly on things) to one that is *de dicto* (by chance) proved to be very efficacious in the juridical domain, especially in criminal law. Jacques Bernoulli, who in his *Ars conjectandi* defined probability as a fraction of certainty, saw very early on the interest of probabilities for economic, juridical, political, and social calculations; but it was the Bayesian perspective, which was to be that of Bentham's utilitarianism down to our own time, and also that of Laplace and Poisson, that gave these calculations their true value. If society, not only as the guardian of the laws, of order, and of security but also of justice, has an interest in such and such a crime or offense being punished, we can calculate our chances of being right in attributing this crime or offense to such and such a person whom we are preparing to punish, and at the same time evaluate, on that basis, whether it is just to proceed with this punishment (see EIDÔLON, Box 1).

IV. Probability, Chance, Expectation

Our difficulty in translating the terms "probability" and "chance" can thus proceed from certain contradictions in the use of "chance": in the first opposition between chances and causes, it has an essentially objective meaning connected with counting up situations, whereas in the second opposition, it has the subjective meaning of a relationship of values; the context will always indicate which type of opposition is concerned.

Nevertheless, the notion of expectation, which is very close to those of probability and chance, adds to the difficulty. Although it is usually appropriate to avoid translating "expectation" by the French word *attente* in contexts where it clearly refers to an evaluation of probability and to prefer the term *espérance*, we have to acknowledge that the latter term lacks clarity. Pascal, whom we have presented as the author par excellence of the "probability of chances," reasons less on probability than on expectation; however, it is a question of calculations that belong precisely to the domain of objective probabilities. Subjective probabilities, on the other hand, were later to be characterized by a fundamental use of expectation on the basis of which probability alone is defined, as we see in Bayes (*An Essay*), who posits the probability of an event as the relation between the expectation attached to this event and the benefit one hopes to realize if it occurs:

> The probability of any event is the ratio between the value at which an expectation depending on the happening of the event ought to be computed, and the value of the thing expected upon its happening.

This is the place to note that the idea of subjective probability arose in a language that allowed this complicated formation by means of gerunds that cannot really be translated into French (see ENGLISH)—even if, a few years later, Continental mathematicians dealt with this idea with the same ease as mathematicians working in English.

Jean-Pierre Cléro

BIBLIOGRAPHY

Arnauld, Antoine, and Pierre Nicole. *La logique de Port-Royal*. 1662. Translation by James Dickoff and Patricia James: *The Art of Thinking: Port-Royal Logic*. Indianapolis, IN: Bobbs-Merrill, 1964.

Bayes, Thomas. *An Essay towards Solving a Problem in the Doctrine of Chances, with Richard Price's Foreword and Discussion*. In *Facsimiles of Two Papers by Bayes*. New York, Hafner: 1963. First published in 1763.

Bernoulli, Jakob. *Ars conjectandi* (opus posthumum). "Pars Quarta (tradens usum & applicationem praecedentis Doctrinae Civilibus, Moralibus Oeconomicus)." Basel: Thurnisiorum fratrum, 1713. Translation by E. Dudley Sylla: *The Art of Conjecturing, Together with Letter to a Friend on Sets in Court Tennis*. Baltimore: Johns Hopkins University Press, 2006.

Hacking, Ian. *The Emergence of Probability. A Philosophical Study of Early Ideas about Probability, Induction and Statistical Inference*. Cambridge: Cambridge University Press, 1975.

Hume, David. *Dialogues concerning Natural Religion and Other Writings*. Edited by D. Coleman. Cambridge: Cambridge University Press, 2007. First published in 1779.

———. *A Treatise of Human Nature*. Edited by L. A. Selby-Bigge. Oxford: Clarendon Press, 1978. First published in 1739–40.

Laplace, Pierre-Simon de. *Mémoire sur la probabilité des causes par les événements*. In vol. 8 of *Œuvres complètes*. Paris: Gauthier-Villars, 1891.

———. *Philosophical Essay on Probabilities*. Translated by A. I. Dale. New York: Springer-Verlag, 1995.

———. *Théorie analytique des probabilités*. Paris: Courcier, 1814.

Maistrov, Leonid E. *Probability Theory. A Historical Sketch*. Translated and edited by S. Kotz. New York: Academic Press, 1974. First published in 1967.

Moivre, Abraham de. *The Doctrine of Chances*. Guilford: Frank Cass, 1967. First published in 1718.

Pascal, Blaise. *Œuvres complètes*. Paris: Éditions du Seuil, 1963.

———. *Pensées and Other Writing*. Translated by H. Levi. Oxford: Oxford University Press, 1995.

Poisson, Siméon-Denis. *Recherches sur la probabilité des jugements en matière criminelle et en matière civile précédées des règles générales du calcul des probabilités*. Paris: Bachelier, 1837.

Todhunter, Isaac. *A History of the Mathematical Theory of Probability from the Time of Pascal to That of Laplace*. New York: Chelsea, 1965. First published in 1865.

CHÔRA [χώρα] (GREEK)

➤ DESCRIPTION, *FORM*, GREEK, *LIEU*, POLIS, *REASON*, TO TRANSLATE, *WORLD*

Inasmuch as *chôra* has no meaning—at least not in this classical sense—it is intrinsically untranslatable. It is such as to disrupt the very operation of translation.
—Sallis, *Chorology*

In general, where it is used in Plato's *Dialogues*, the word *chôra* [χώρα] has, according to the context, the commonplace meaning of "land," "place," "space," or "room" (Algra, *Concepts of Space in Greek Thought*). As Casey points out, its primary connotation is "occupied space," as in "a field full of crops or a room replete with things" (Casey, *The Fate of*

Place). This is the signification of the first appearance of the word in the *Timaeus*, where Socrates is characterizing the country outside the city proper (Cornford, *Plato's Cosmology, Timaeus*, ¶19). Such a sense of extraterritoriality and extension certainly anticipates the way in which it is used later in the dialogue. But in the following creation story, narrated by Timaeus, Plato endows *chôra* with a special significance, and a corresponding ambiguity, which has been debated ever since, from Aristotle to Derrida.

The *Timaeus* as a whole is concerned with foundation of the just city, and with the corresponding idea of beginning, starting with the creation of the cosmos itself. The dialogue purportedly takes place following a conversation the day before concerning the perfect city—a summary of the conversation by Socrates makes a clear reference to the central aspects of the city outlined in the *Republic*; but Socrates professes to be dissatisfied with the static and abstract nature of the picture drawn so far. He demands a livelier image, one that sets the city in motion so to speak, and Critias suggests that the heroic story of the war between ancient Athens and Atlantis would supply the requisite action. But before a narrative of city foundation, Timaeus, with his astronomical knowledge, proposes to establish the story of cosmic becoming. This then is the context for the elaboration of the concept of *chôra*.

The word *chôra* itself first appears in its newly ambiguous, but philosophical, form in paragraph 52b of the *Timaeus*. But its appearance has been prepared for by Plato some paragraphs before. In brief, the argument up to the introduction of *chôra* goes something like this: Timaeus has, in the first part of the dialogue, given an account of how the universe "came into being" (Cornford, *Plato's Cosmology, Timaeus*, ¶27), distinguishing between two states: "that which is always real and has no becoming" and "that which is always becoming but is never real." The former is "apprehensible by the intelligence with the aid of reasoning," the latter is an "object of opinion and irrational sensation, coming to be and ceasing to be, but never fully real" (Cornford, *Plato's Cosmology, Timaeus*, ¶28). Thus separating out the unchanging (rational) reality, from the changing (sensible), lived, reality, Timaeus uses this well-known Platonic distinction between the ideal primary reality and the physical secondary reality to sketch out the steps taken by the demiurge (*dêmiourgos* [δημιουργός], "maker," "father," "constructor") as he "keeps his eye on the eternally unchanging and uses it as his pattern for the form and function of his product." This is so that he can ensure a "good" result, for whenever he looks to "something which has come to be and uses a model that has come to be, the result is not good" (Cornford, *Plato's Cosmology, Timaeus*, ¶28). Timaeus uses the word *kalos* [καλός], which can mean "good," but also "satisfactory," "desirable," and, of course, "beautiful." In this way, as Francis Cornford notes, "the visible world . . . is a changing image or likeness (*eikon*) of an eternal model" (*Plato's Cosmology*). A postulate that raises as many questions as it answers: if something is in a state of becoming, does it begin at any one point? Or, what might be the "cause" of such becoming, as opposed to the state of being, or the same? Or, finally, is the "real," as copy, really real, or simply a dream or shadow of the real? Plato compounds these difficulties by having Timaeus state that what he is describing is no more than a "likely story," for mortals are in the end

"unable to render an account at all points entirely consistent with itself and exact . . . (or) furnish accounts no less likely than any other" (Cornford, *Plato's Cosmology, Timaeus*, ¶29c). And, as Derrida will note, the problem extends not only to reasonable stories, but also to naming. Even the "Heaven," "world," or "cosmos" may take different names: "let us call it," says Timaeus, "by whatsoever name may be most acceptable to it" (Cornford, *Plato's Cosmology, Timaeus*, ¶28b).

This, then, is the procedure of the "demiurge," compared by Plato to a craftsman (*dêmiourgos* [δημιουργός]), who as "intelligence" itself, "framed the universe," fashioning "reason within soul, and soul within body," as a living creature. Not a god, or "God," the demiurge operates like a craftsman on materials he did not himself create, with reason guiding his design. Out of the four primary bodies—fire, air, water, and earth—he fashions a universe bound together by proportion and thereby "visible and tangible" (Cornford, *Plato's Cosmology, Timaeus*, ¶32b). The aesthetics of this work, "a living being whole and complete, of complete parts . . . single, nothing being left over," "a single whole consisting of all these wholes" (Cornford, *Plato's Cosmology, Timaeus*, ¶33a), has had a long history in Neoplatonism and neoclassicism: this "shape rounded and spherical, equidistant every way from center to periphery—a figure the most perfect and uniform of all . . . perfectly smooth" (Cornford, *Plato's Cosmology, Timaeus*, ¶33b) has held a privileged position in the theory of ideal forms. Endowed with a centrally positioned world-soul, itself the embodiment of reason and harmony, and incorporating, like some perfect armillary, the motions of the seven planetary rings, this world incorporates time within its circularity, marked by the differential motions of the planets.

Such was the world constructed as Plato recounts "by the craftsmanship of Reason" (Cornford, *Plato's Cosmology, Timaeus*, ¶47e); but it failed to take note of a second equally powerful cause, that of Necessity (*anankê* [ἀνάνκη]). Here Plato makes it clear that his "demiurge" is by no means the omnipotent creator of everything out of nothing construed by later religions. Rather his craftsman works with materials already at hand—fire, water, air, and earth "before the generation of the Heaven" (Cornford, *Plato's Cosmology, Timaeus*, ¶48b), materials whose prior existence has not been explained by Reason's work, and that demand what Plato terms an "errant cause" as "origin." But this origin is immediately subject to question, for as Plato states, "'first principle or 'principles'—or whatever name men choose to employ" are exceedingly difficult to explain. Indeed, Timaeus affirms that the explanation should not be demanded of him, as it poses too "great a task"; rather he promises to give "the worth of a probable account," one "no less probable than any other, but more so" (Cornford, *Plato's Cosmology, Timaeus*, ¶48d).

In beginning again, then, "once more" and in moving toward "the conclusion that probability dictates," in starting over with his account of creation, Plato acknowledges the impossibility of certainty for the first time. If one can be certain about the forms of Reason, those of Necessity demand a more speculative approach. The need for this fresh beginning, principle, or starting-point arises from this intrusion of the irrational, that which can be controlled by Reason, but that Reason did not bring into being.

Here then is the already uncertain context into which *chôra* is introduced.

For in starting again to describe the universe, Plato now joins to his two principal orders of existence—the unchanging intelligible model and the changing and visible copy—a third, a medium of sorts that supports the two. This medium is of a "form difficult and obscure" (Cornford, *Plato's Cosmology, Timaeus*, ¶49) but its nature can be stated as that of the "receptacle (*hupodochê* [ὑποδοχή])—as it were, the nurse—of all Becoming." Such a "receptacle" unlike its contents—fire, water, air, and earth that are in a perpetual state of change—is unchanging and permanent. Plato, as Cornford notes, somewhat misleadingly, compares it to the gold out of which one makes all kinds of figures. The receptacle "must be called always the same; for it never departs at all from its own character; since it is always receiving all things, and never in any way whatsoever takes on any character that is like any of the things that enter it" (Cornford, *Plato's Cosmology, Timaeus*, ¶50b). It is, Plato explains, a kind of "matrix" for everything, that, although it is changed by the things that enter it, and may appear to have different qualities at different times, is in itself always the same.

In a passage that much later had implications for feminist readings, Plato, always trying to explain that "which is hard to express," seeks another comparison through gender: "the (intelligible) model in whose likeness that which becomes is born," is compared to a father; "that which becomes (the copy)" is like an offspring, and "that in which it becomes" (the receptacle) inevitably takes on the characteristics of a mother (Cornford, *Plato's Cosmology, Timaeus*, ¶50 c–d). This apparently simple simile, one that gives the character of generation to the receptacle, is, however, immediately contradicted in what follows: for Plato insists that the receptacle, whatever else it is, is "invisible and characterless, all receiving," a "nature" that, precisely because it is free of all the characters that come from elsewhere, enter into it, and pass out of it, cannot be endowed with a specific gender. Plato compares this lack of character to the liquid base used by the makers of perfumes that is as odorless as possible: "Thus it is, in the first place, for the perfumes that one prepares artistically, in order to give them a good odor. The perfume makers avoid first of all as much as possible all odor in the liquid base which must receive them" (*Timaeus*, 50e). It should be noted here, as Derrida will observe in his essay "La Pharmacie de Platon," that "the *pharmakon* also means perfume. Perfume without essence, as we said above, drug without substance. It transforms order into ornament, the cosmos into cosmetic." Would this mean that, by the same token, Plato is comparing the "receptacle," not yet named *chôra*, to a *pharmakon* [φάρμακον], a drug that, without smell, receives all smells that pass into, through, and out of it, with the implication that such smells are transformed into dangerous perfumes? At this point we are better taking Plato at his word when, even as he struggles for comparisons and mixes his metaphors, he states baldly that this receptacle partakes "in some very puzzling way of the intelligible" and is "very hard to apprehend" (Cornford, *Plato's Cosmology, Timaeus*, ¶51b).

What is certain is that Plato has determined the need for three things: the unchanging "Form," "ungenerated and indestructible"; that which "bears the same name and . . . is sensible"; and a third, previously called the receptacle, but

which now gains a name: *chôra* (Cornford, *Plato's Cosmology, Timaeus*, ¶52). *Chôra* is now finally "defined" as "everlasting, not admitting destruction," somewhat like the Form, but different in that it can be apprehended. Its apprehension, however, is not by reason or the senses, but by what Plato calls "a sort of bastard reasoning" with a status somewhere between the two; you have to think about it, but nevertheless it is in the visible world, invisibly (Cornford, *Plato's Cosmology, Timaeus*, ¶52b). We apprehend *chôra* then as "in a dream" forcing ourselves to acknowledge that "anything that is must needs be in some place and occupy some room, and that which is not somewhere in earth or heaven is nothing" (Cornford, *Plato's Cosmology, Timaeus*, ¶52b). This very act of recognizing that all objects demand situation, Plato argues, leads to the "hybrid" or "bastard" reasoning that in turn forces recognition of *chôra*.

The ambiguity of *chôra*'s nature is further complicated by Plato's next analogy, advanced to explain the emergence of chaos, a chaos readying itself for the reasoning work of the demiurge. *Chôra* once again becomes the "nurse of becoming," but a nurse immediately transformed into a winnowing basket that is shaken by its contents and in turn shakes them: "just when things are shaken and winnowed by means of winnowing-baskets and other instruments for cleaning corn, the dense and heavy things go one way, while the rare and light are carried to another place" (Cornford, *Plato's Cosmology, Timaeus*, ¶52d). In this way were like and unlike things separated, and made ready for the demiurge.

At this point in his attempt to characterize the invisible *chôra*, Plato has assembled a number of apparently contradictory "images" or what were later to be called "metaphors," drawn from the arts of fabrication (*technê* [τέχνη]) as if to underline the action of the demiurge. Yet the *chôra* anticipates the arrival of this grand artisan—*chôra* is, so to speak, always already there. It is at once all-receiving, a receptacle, and something that harbors, shelters, nurtures, and gives birth. It is infinitely malleable like gold, and it is a matrix for all things. As things shake, it winnows like a basket, separating out the chaff from the grain. What is clear, as Cornford points out, is that the *chôra*, while not a void, is not "matter" in itself, as subsequent interpreters will have it. (Cornford, *Plato's Cosmology*).

When resituated in the context of the city narratives of the *Timaeus* and *Critias*, it becomes clear that Plato's use of the word's ambiguities is consistent with the need to provide a firm and original foundation, one that originally emerged out of the earth and the cosmos, not only for ancient Athens but for a renewed city that could be projected as emerging out of and within a *chôra* that was ever-ready to receive and nurture, and that in all its connotations was connected to a content-filled and cultivated land, with room for the polis.

In subsequent rereadings and reinterpretations, the Platonic *chôra* was subjected to oversimplification (Aristotle) and overinterpretation (Chrysippus, Proclus). In Aristotle, place (*topos* [τόπος]) takes precedence over Plato's semi-mystical creation fables—as Casey remarks, "Chôra yields to Topos, the bountiful to the bounded" (Casey, *The Fate of Space*; and Algra, *Concepts of Space in Greek Thought*). Indeed, Aristotle's reading of the *Timaeus* explicitly (and perhaps deliberately) identifies the receptacle with the *chôra*, and thence the *chôra* with matter, going on to conflate *chôra* with *topos* (Aristotle, *Physics*, 4.209b; cited in Sallis, *Verge of Philosophy*). For Epicurus, however, *chôra* retains a certain Platonic energy; the root verb is *chôrein*, "to go" or "to roam." As Sextus Empiricus explains, Epicurus distinguished among "void" (*kenon* [κενόν]), "place" (*topos*), and "room" (*chôra*), where "room" affords the space for the constant motion of the atoms, the "*spielraum* of atomic bodies*," as Casey calls it. The Stoic Chrysippus goes further, characterizing such a "room" or *chôra* as space for both roaming and also extension, a connotation followed by the Neoplatonist Syrianus (Casey, *The Fate of Space*), and thence by Proclus in his exhaustive commentary on the *Timaeus*.

Since Proclus's commentary, and throughout the myriad subsequent textual analyses that have ranged in their emphasis from Pythagorean geometry, cosmological symbolism, and biological geneticism, to the form of the ideal polis, the search for the lost Atlantis, and the mythologies of ancient Athens, little or nothing indicated *chôra* as a keyword, beyond the indices accompanying the translation of many such terms in Plato. Indeed, John Sallis, in his attempt to describe or found a "chorology" after Plato is hard pressed to find, save by omission and post-Derridean inference, a problematic role for, or even a mention of, the word.

Nevertheless, the word *chôra* gained ground as a keyword in philosophy in the 1970s. Its status as a term to be confronted by and for deconstruction was tagged by Derrida in 1968, adopted within semiotics by Kristeva in 1974, and taken by Irigaray and others as a point of departure for a questioning of gender categories. In 1985 it was presented by Derrida as a problem for (Peter Eisenman's) architecture, thence to become a moment for reflection on architecture's gender in the work of Anne Bergren, on deconstruction and architecture in Jeffrey Kipnis, and on the grounding of architecture itself in Eisenman and Derrida's project for a garden in Bernard Tschumi's La Villette. Taken back into philosophy by Derrida in 1987 and 1993, *chôra* was re-inscribed within Neoplatonic interpretation by John Sallis in 1999.

It was Derrida, who, in a sideways glance at the word in his discussion of "La Pharmacie de Platon" ("Plato's Pharmacy") first opened up a question that has since developed into a critical field of inquiry of its own. The context is significant. The essay is concerned with another word whose meaning is obscured by multiple uses, significations, and (mis) translations, but which nevertheless, when identified as a sign, stands out as a mark of Plato's deep ambiguity toward writing, a *pharmakon* that might be at once a "drug" or "remedy," dangerous or helpful. Speaking of the untranslatability of the word *pharmakon* in the *Phaedo* (but also everywhere that it appears in Plato), Derrida writes of "this regulated polysemy which has allowed, by ineptness, indetermination or over determination, but without contradiction, the translation of the same word by 'remedy,' 'poison,' 'drug,' philter,' etc." Such errancy in definition and translation has indeed undermined "the plastic unity of this concept, its very rule, and the strange logic which links it to its signifier" in such a way that it has "been dispersed, masked, obliterated, struck with a relative unreadability, by the imprudence or empiricism of the translators, certainly, but first and foremost by the redoubtable and irreducible difficulty of translation." But this is the result, Derrida argues, less of the difficulties

of passing from one language to another, or even from one philosophical language to another, and more of a question within the Greek language itself, of that "violent" tradition whereby a non-philosophical language is transferred into a philosophical one. "With this problem of translation," Derrida notes, "we will be dealing with nothing less than the problem of the passage to philosophy." And later he concludes: "La *khôra* est grosse de tout ce qui se dissémine ici" (*chôra* is pregnant with everything that is disseminated here). For Derrida, indeed, *chôra* was "grosse," a word that indicated the difficulty of naming, categorizing, or even writing the "origin," or at least that "origin" posited by Plato, before the entry of the demiurge in order to shape the world.

Derrida was already engaged in writing his essay "Khôra" in homage to Jean-Pierre Vernant. Here he takes on the apparent confusion of "metaphors"—he prefers not to call them metaphors for reasons he will later divulge—used by Plato to describe, characterize, or define *chôra*, or the "receptacle," in order to demonstrate that these turns of phrase are irreducible questions of writing. In a long citation from Albert Rivaud's edition of the *Timaeus*, Derrida demonstrates the confusion surrounding the word and question of "place," or *chôra* (citing Rivaud, *Platon*). Rivaud had noted the proliferation of what he called "metaphors for *chôra*, metaphors for the 'place,' the 'site,' 'this in which' things appear, 'this on which' they manifest themselves, the 'receptacle,' the 'matrix,' the 'mother,' the 'nurse'—it is container and contained at the same time, 'the space that contains the things.'" Rivaud himself translates *chôra* as a "porte-empreinte," literally "carrier of the imprints" (as in *porte-parole*, "carrier of the word"), the "excipient," or, "the entirely de-odorized substance, or the gold with which the jeweller can impress a quantity of different figures." Derrida exposes the ambiguity of Plato's introduction of the "third genre" of being.

Derrida, however, was inevitably dissatisfied with the notion of "metaphor," and "comparison," working rather to identify the aporias in Plato's own discourse. The paradox is clear: what is named "chôra" or "place" cannot itself be situated or "assigned a home"; "it is more situator than situated." Indeed, Derrida resists all attempts to define the word, translate the word, or supply additional metaphors or comparisons for the word. Indeed, the "interminable theory of exegeses" (Derrida, *Khôra*) that surrounds *chôra* "seems to reproduce that which, following the discourse of the *Timaeus*, would happen not with Plato's text, but with *khôra* herself." All translations, he writes, remain "on the level of interpretation" and thereby subject to anachronism. There is, therefore, no question of proposing "le mot juste" for *chôra*; rather than reducing it falsely to a name or essence, it has to be understood as a structure. As Derrida concludes, "one cannot even say of it that it is *neither* this, *nor* that, or that it is *at the same time* this and that." Marking the continuing ambiguity, Derrida and Sallis engaged in a friendly debate as to whether the word should be written without an article (*khôra*) as Derrida insisted, or with an article (the *chôra*) as Sallis preferred. For Derrida the article "presupposes the essence of the thing," which had no such essence in Plato's usage; for Sallis omitting the article "would risk effacing all difference between the word and that of which the word would speak" (Sallis, *Verge of Philosophy*). *Chôra*, indeed, remained elusive to the end and still, as a recent commentator notes, the question remains "multilayered" and "incoherent" (Sayre, "Multilayered Incoherence of Timaeus' Receptacle").

But perhaps the problem of *chôra* would not have surfaced in so poignant a form if, as he recounts, Derrida had not been introduced by the architect Bernard Tschumi to the architect Peter Eisenman in 1985, and suggested that a concept on which he was writing a paper would perhaps serve to open a discussion that would launch their collaboration in the design of a garden for Parc La Villette. The concept was named "chôra"; in common translation, the special nature of this term, taken from Plato's dialogue the *Timaeus*, was rendered "place" or "space." Apparently an innocent enough suggestion, the debates over the "meaning" of the word extended into seven taped discussions, seemingly replicating the Socratic model of the original, and eventually a book of transcriptions, drawings, and the translation of a version of Derrida's own essay on *chôra* appeared. In this way, a word, long-forgotten in the footnotes of Plato translation and exegesis was launched into a veritable, architectural discourse, not perhaps as a solution to any "space of deconstruction," but rather as an insoluble conundrum set by the philosopher for the architect, to test the capacity of architecture to signify its own origins, its groundings in *chôra*.

Anthony Vidler

BIBLIOGRAPHY

Algra, Keimpe. *Concepts of Space in Greek Thought*. Leiden: Brill, 1994.
Bergren, Anne. "Architecture Gender Philosophy." In *Strategies in Architectural Thinking*. Edited by J. Whiteman, J. Kipnis, and R. Burdett. Chicago: The Chicago Institute for Architecture and Urbanism and MIT Press, 1992.
Casey, Edward S. *The Fate of Place*. Berkeley: University of California Press, 2013.
Cornford, Francis. *Plato's Cosmology: The Timaeus of Plato*. London: Routledge, 1935.
Derrida, Jacques. "La Pharmacie de Platon." *Tel Quel* 32–33 (1968); repr. in *La dissémination*. Paris: Éditions du Seuil, 1972.
———. "Khôra." In *Poikilia. Études offertes à Jean-Pierre Vernant*. Paris: Éditions de l'EHESS, 1987.
———. *Khôra*. Paris: Éditions Galilée, 1993. Translation by J. Kipnis and T. Lesser: *Chora L. Works: Jacques Derrida and Peter Eisenman*. New York: Monacelli Press, 1997.
Irigaray, Luce. *Speculum de l'autre femme*. Paris: Éditions du Minuit, 1974.
Kristeva, Julia. *La révolution du langage poétique*. Paris: Éditions du Seuil, 1974.
Plato. *Œuvres completes. Timée, Critias*. Edited by Albert Rivaud. Paris: Les Belles Lettres, 2001.
Sallis, John. *Chorology: On Beginning in Plato's Timaeus*. Bloomington: Indiana University Press, 1999.
———. *The Verge of Philosophy*. Chicago: University of Chicago Press, 2008.
Sayre, Kenneth. "The Multilayered Incoherence of Timaeus' Receptacle." In *Plato's Timaeus as Cultural Icon*, edited by Gretchen J. Reydams-Schils. Notre Dame: University of Notre Dame Press, 2003.

CIVIL RIGHTS

FRENCH   *droits civils, droits civiques*

➤ *DROIT*, and CIVIL SOCIETY, CIVILTÀ, LAW, MENSCHHEIT, POLITICS, RULE OF LAW, STATE

The expression "civil rights" can be rendered in French by both *droits civils* and *droits civiques*. In the first case, the reference is to the customary classifications of rights that distinguish civil rights (such as property) from political rights or social rights. In the second case, the reference is to the meaning acquired by "civil rights" in the context of the American civil rights movement of the 1950s and 1960s, whose main goal was to put an end to racial segregation and, more generally, to the discrimination of which minorities were the victims.

If we want to understand why English speaks of "civil rights" (including the right to vote) and even of "civic rights" (i.e., citizens' rights), where we might think the "rights of man" or "human rights" ought to be in play, we have to refer to American constitutional history. After the Civil War, the United States adopted three amendments to the Constitution that should have put an end to slavery and its aftereffects. The Thirteenth Amendment abolished slavery; the Fourteenth Amendment states that

> [a]ll persons born or naturalized in the United States, and subject to the jurisdiction thereof, are citizens of the United States and of the state wherein they reside. No state shall make or enforce any law which shall abridge the privileges or immunities of citizens of the United States; nor shall any state deprive any person of life, liberty, or property, without due process of law; nor deny to any person within its jurisdiction the equal protection of the laws.

The Fifteenth Amendment protects citizens' right to vote against any restriction based on "race, color, or previous condition of servitude." But the juridical and political development of the United States led to these amendments being deprived of much of their substance by racial segregation and various artifices designed to deprive blacks of their right to vote on various pretexts (e.g., literacy tests); moreover, the Civil Rights Act of 1875, which sought to prohibit racial discrimination in public rights, was declared unconstitutional by the Supreme Court in deciding a set of civil rights cases in 1883. To the extent that the fight against discrimination, relying on the new liberal orientation of the 1960s Supreme Court, sought to restore the full scope to the rights of American citizens, and not simply to guarantee the rights of individuals, it was natural that it would present itself as a movement for civic rights. Its goal was not only to guarantee human rights, but also to see to it that black Americans would be recognized as full-fledged citizens.

Philippe Raynaud

BIBLIOGRAPHY

Balkin, Jack, ed. *What Brown v. Board of Education Should Have Said: The Nation's Top Legal Experts Rewrite America's Landmark Civil Rights Decision*. New York: New York University Press, 2001.
Boxill, Bernard. *Blacks and Social Justice*. Rev. ed. Lanham, MD: Rowman & Littlefield, 1992.
Holmes, Stephen, and Cass Sunstein. *The Cost of Rights*. New York: W. W. Norton, 1999.
Kersch, Kenneth. *Constructing Civil Liberties*. Cambridge: Cambridge University Press, 2004.
Waldron, Jeremy. *Liberal Rights*. Cambridge: Cambridge University Press, 1993.

CIVIL SOCIETY

ENGLISH   civil society, political society
GERMAN   *bürgerliche Gesellschaft*
GREEK   *koinonia politike* [κοινωνία πολιτική]
LATIN   *societas civilis*

➤ BILDUNG, CIVIL RIGHTS, CIVILTÀ, *DROIT*, ECONOMY, HISTORIA UNIVERSALIS, LAW, OIKONOMIA, PEOPLE, POLIS, POLITICS, SECULARIZATION, *STATE*

Far from simply designating a recent notion introduced by Hegel or Marx in the wake of Anglo-Scottish economists, the expression "civil society" (*societas civilis, société civile, bürgerliche Gesellschaft*) belongs to the most classical vocabulary of political philosophy. Originally, it corresponded to the Latin (and then French) translation of Aristotle's *koinonia politike* [κοινωνία πολιτική] (political community). It thus initially designated the form of human existence that prevails when men live under political or civil laws. The same situation persists with modern contractualist theories, in which "civil society" is opposed to the state of nature (Hobbes) and fuses with political society (Locke) or even in authors like Kant, for whom civil society is another name for the state. The distinction between civil society and the state, which seems obvious since Hegel and Marx, should thus be understood as the fruit of a complex and paradoxical history. And the history of these concepts is inseparable from that of their translation.

I. *Koinonia Politike* and *Societas Civilis*

In order to understand the history of the concept of civil society, our first obligation is to avoid confusing the Aristotelian lexicon for political community with that for society, by identifying, for example, man's character as a "political animal" with a simple natural sociability. The political community described in book 1 of the *Politics* is not the simple product of sympathy or of the incapacity of each individual to suffice on its own, since it is distinguished essentially from such other forms of community as the couple, the family, or the village. The domestic community is characterized by an unequal relation of authority in which the head of family commands those who are by nature destined to obey him, whereas in the "political community" (*he polis kai he koinonia he politike* [ἡ πόλις καὶ ἡ κοινωνία ἡ πολιτική]), authority is exercised over free and equal men who, in various ways, participate in public affairs. Understood in such terms, the city is first in nature because *it* is what makes it possible to "live well" and for man to realize fully his nature, but it is encountered only under certain conditions, which are not to be found, for instance, in despotic regimes or empires. Aristotle's thought on political community is thus strictly derived from the political experience of the Greek city-state. And it can be easily understood that the translation of Aristotle's concepts posed some difficulties in the Roman—and subsequently Christian—world. Conventionally, in keeping with a usage to be found in medieval translators of Aristotle, *polis* [πόλις] was translated as *societas civilis* while maintaining as synonyms the city-state, the political community thus become civil society, and the republic (*civitas sive societas civilis sive republica*), but the Latin plainly has different connotations from the Greek. *Societas* designates a juridical link that is not necessarily political and is defined above all by consensus and the pursuit of common ends. Latin authors like Cicero also

evoke the Stoic idea of a society of the human race (*societas generis humani*) that could certainly not consitiute a political community in the Aristotelian sense. *Civis, civilis,* and *civitas* thus acquire a universalist dimension, linked to Rome and Roman law's capacity to spread citizenship quite broadly, in a manner unknown in the classical Greece of the city-states (Moatti, *La Raison de Rome*). The properly French notion of contemporary civil society, which evokes the universality of the juridical bond between individuals more than a shared belonging to a particular civic entity, continues to bear the trace of that transformation.

■ See Box 1.

II. City of God and Civil Society

The fate of civil society derives equally from an intellectual and moral revolution favored by Roman experience, the spread of Christianity, and particularly the theory of two cities defended by Saint Augustine in *The City of God*.

For Saint Augustine, civil society is assuredly a natural reality, participating in the goodness of the created world, but the corruption of human nature that followed the Fall prevents attributing full self-sufficiency to him and renders precarious in advance all efforts to attain happiness on earth, which is nonetheless the object of the earthly city. While awaiting the Last Judgment, the two cities coexist in humanity (like the elect and the reprobate), and their relation cannot be resolved by the pure political abstention of the just. On the one hand, the Christian must indeed obey the civil power and accomplish his civic duties, but on the other, he can and must not forget that the natural *societas* is linked to original sin and that it is grounded in self-love pressed to the point of contempt of God, the heavenly city being alone able to establish true communication between men. Even if the visible church does not coincide with the celestial city (since it contains sinners and reprobates), that complex relation between the two orders of nature and grace manifests itself in the church's ambivalent relation to the state: the church must acknowledge the specific consistency of civil society, but it must also act in the earthly city to help men attain their natural and supernatural ends. The medieval posterity of Saint Augustine would explore the possible solutions to this theologico-political dilemma, which went from pontifical theocracy to Luther's doctrine of the two realms by way of theories favorable to the primacy of the emperor or the king (Quillet, *Les Clefs du pouvoir au Moyen Age*). In the evolution of modern thought, one can schematically distinguish five solutions to the problem of the relations between civil society and the city of God. The first is that of the Catholic Church, which is remarkably stable and consists of positing simultaneously the consistency proper to civil society and its essential incompletion, which implies an acceptance of the civil power, but also the affirmation of a minimal (and eminently variable) political competence of the church. This is why, even today, the expression "civil society" is synonymous, for political theologians, with "political order." That position can be distinguished simultaneously from Luther's (which insisted on the essentially repressive role of the political power while affirming the principle of inner liberty) and from the doctrines of the Catholic Counter-Reformation

1

Gemeinschaft and *Gesellschaft,* community and society

Even if the opposition between *Gemeinschaft* and *Gesellschaft*, which was introduced in sociological theory by Ferdinand Tönnies (*Community and Society*), has no true equivalent in the prior history of political philosophy (Pasquino, "Communauté et société"), it can be compared to certain major themes introduced in Germany by political romanticism and the School of Law: where German jurists distinguished two modes for the formation of law ("natural" and spontaneous or, on the contrary, "artificial" and deliberate), Tönnies opposes two types of human collectivity. Community (*Gemeinschaft*), in which familial economy and agriculture predominate, rests on unanimous and spontaneous adherence to substantial values, whereas society (*Gesellschaft*), which is commercial and industrial, is based on an individualization of interests, a quest for compromise, and voluntary association. *Gemeinschaft* evokes themes out of romanticism, and the model of *Gesellschaft*

is furnished by the anthropology of Hobbes. It is not merely types but also stages of cultural development that follow each other according to a logic that runs the gamut from unconscious to deliberate: "the age of society follows that of community. The latter is characterized by social will as concord, custom, and religion; the former by social will as political convention and public opinion" (Tönnies, *Community and Society*). Tönnies, however, is not a simple nostalgic conservative: he is rather in search of a way of moving beyond the opposition between *Gemeinschaft* and *Gesellschaft*, which explains his interest in modern socialism, which, while expressing the conflicts in society, shows the necessity of reconstructing a lost unity.

The distinction between *Gemeinschaft* and *Gesellschaft* can be connected with other couplings of similar concepts in the sociological tradition, such as the organic and critical epochs in Auguste Comte, the

dual—mechanical and organic—forms of solidarity in Durkheim, or, more recently, the holistic and individualistic societies of Louis Dumont. Max Weber offered a reconstruction of the opposition in individualistic terms, through his distinction between *Vergemeinschaftung* and *Vergesellschaftung*, which puts the accent on the type of activity—affective and traditional or, on the contrary, rational—predominating in social relations (Raynaud, *Dictionnaire de philosophie politique*); but most contemporary representatives of methodological individualism tend to reject Tönnies's conceptions, bringing to the fore the conflictual or calculating dimension of communitarian bonds (see RT: *Dictionnaire critique de la sociologie*, s.v. "Communauté").

BIBLIOGRAPHY

Tönnies, Ferdinand. *Community and Society.* Edited and translated by Charles P. Loomis. East Lansing: Michigan State University Press, 1964.

(Bonald, de Maistre), which led to the negation of any autonomy of civil society, all to the benefit of the church. The millenarian tendencies of the Thomas Münzer sort (violently opposed by Martin Luther) can, for their part, be considered attempts to achieve the city of God on earth, to the detriment of all the institutions of civil society, such as marriage and property. The fascination exercised by Thomas Münzer on Marxist thinkers, from F. Engels to E. Bloch, thus connects them to fanatical currents hostile to civil society (Colas, *Civil Society and Fanaticism*). Finally, the philosophies of history issuing from German idealism are the fruit of an effort to think the continuity between civil society (or the state) and the heavenly city: thus it is that for Hegel the true Christian state is the one that fully ensures the autonomy of the political order—on the condition, to be sure, of its distinctness from civil society.

III. State and Civil Society

If the Roman invention of the *societas* permitted a certain affirmation of the universality of law, it could do so only by insisting on the law's foundational capacity, which, in the case of Rome (whose tradition on this matter was quite different from what prevailed in canon law), was not without a certain artificiality (see, for instance, Thomas, "Fictio legis," on the importance of *fictio* in Roman law). It also had the effect of undoing the bond, affirmed by Aristotle, between the political community and political freedom, following a logic amplified by the Christian transformation of the political order: the universality of humanity is emphatically proclaimed by Christianity, but Christian monarchies (in which power, to be sure, is not exercised over free and equal men) are fully

accomplished forms of civil society. Whatever the case, despite the distance separating the political community of Aristotle from the civil society of the Christians, the two notions share the feature of designating a natural reality which, even if it may entail an internal hierarchy, fully coincides with the human political order; and it was precisely on these two points that the subsequent transformations of the concept of civil society would bear.

Contractualist theories of modern natural law fully maintain the equivalence between civil society and the political condition or the Republic, and that feature would be maintained in the Continental tradition up to and including Kant's *Doctrine of Right*. But the dominant trend in modern political philosophy, embodied by Hobbes, is also clearly artificialist, in that it is opposed to the Aristotelian idea of the naturalness of the political bond, which is not without consequences for the status of civil society. The logic at work here leads, in fact, on the one hand, to making of the preservation of subjective freedom the aim of political association, and thus of affirming the eminent value of what is today called the private sphere, all the while entrusting to political power the protection and even the definition of the rights of the members of the civil association. This is why, on the one hand, thinkers as statist in orientation as Hobbes or Rousseau are also individualists and, on the other, a philosopher like Kant affirms the necessary primacy of public law while considering as rational and irreducible the distinction between private and public law. It thus is possible, on the basis of the distinction between private and public law that guarantees it, to think something like an opposition between civil society and the state, even if, for example, Kant calls natural society the sphere of private relations in order to reserve the title of civil society (*societas civilis*) for public law and the state (Ferry, "L'émergence du couple État/société").

The genesis of the contemporary concept of a civil society essentially distinct from the state thus passes through the invention of new schemata, native to English-language philosophy, on the basis of an idiosyncratic experience and juridical categories quite different from those of the law and philosophy of the Continent. The most familiar aspect of that invention is the formation of political economy accompanying the expansion of mercantile relations: modern economics leads to seeing in society the fruit of an indefinite quantity of political behaviors, which brings one to "a new conception of society, as opposed to the idea of a political nature of man (Aristotle) as it is to a sociality constructed against nature (contractualist theories)" (Collot-Thélène, "État et société civile"). Now that experience is all the more easy to conceptualize in the framework of English thought in that that thought disposes (with "common law") of juridical categories that allow one to distinguish with relative ease between law and statute law (i.e., such law as is advanced by a legislator) and to recognize the necessity of a power of constraint to force respect of the law without for as much according it a pre-eminent role in the formation of law. "Civil society" thus includes institutions that are already political, such as tribunals, because its "other" is less the state than the government, which is not the sole source of law.

Anglo-Scottish reflection on civil society also presents another extremely important aspect, developed by Ferguson (*An Essay on the History of Civil Society*, 1759), by Millar, and by Hume: civil society has a history, which passes through the affirmation of *civility* and leads to a general progress of *civilization*. That history shows how, in modern Europe, the growth of mercantile exchanges permitted the enrichment of human experience while reducing the importance of constraint and military force in the government of societies. It is inseparable from the great modern debate over the respective merits of (modern) "commerce" and (ancient) civic virtue, in which, moreover, Ferguson and even Smith have more nuanced positions than is usually believed (Gauthier, *L'Invention de la société civile*; Pocock, *Virtue, Commerce and History*). Finally, it encounters the thought of Montesquieu, for whom the apology of the British regime was inseparable from the idea that the ancient civic sense belonged to a past long gone. It was by way of this motif that the "English" problematic of civil society was to have an echo in all of European philosophy, including among authors with an investment in the traditional identification between civil society and the state (see, for example, Kant, *Idea of a Universal History from a Cosmopolitical Point of View*, 1784).

The extraordinary power of the reconstruction effected by Hegel is evident in his *Principles of the Philosophy of Law*, in which one finds both the heritage of antiquity and that of Christianity, the contribution of modern natural law and that of the Anglo-Saxon thinkers or Montesquieu (including the opposition virtue/commerce). We have already seen how Hegel's philosophy can be considered as a legitimization of the process of secularization of modern societies, as a truth of the Christian state; in the same manner, the distinction between civil society and the state allows one to surmount the antinomy of ancient virtue and modern commerce, even while making of civil and political existence the guarantor and truth of the "right to subjective freedom" that lies at the core of the modern world. Civil society in the strict sense, which succeeds the family, allows the individual to surpass the immediate naturalness of familial relations and is comprised of three moments: the system of needs (which corresponds to the world of political economy), the protection of freedom and property by the administration of law, and finally the police and corporation (understood as organs of economic regulation and not only of maintenance of political order), which are necessary to correct the spontaneous effects of mercantile economy. Civil society thus itself calls for a superior unity, which will be given in the state, which alone allows man to lead a universal life. Thus, even as it is the point in which the greatest split between the particular and the individual is effected, civil society is also what permits that higher unity of the individual and the whole that endows modernity with its meaning. Significantly, Hegel, moreover, indicates that civil society is the privileged terrain of the development of culture (*Bildung*), which indicates simultaneously its debt to the English problematic of civilization and its will to distinguish itself from it (*Bildung* is said to be more internal than civilization).

Starting with Hegel, the meaning of the notion of civil society appears to be more or less fixed, a circumstance that in no way prevented it from being the object of profound meditations. This is not the place, for instance, to show the extent of Marx's originality, concerning which we will offer but a few brief terminological remarks. The first concerns the perpetual interplay of two notions that Marx distinguishes quite well, but often takes pleasure in fusing: civil society (*bürgerliche Gesellschaft*) cannot be reduced to bourgeois society, even if it is the emancipation of property that allowed the state to acquire "a specific existence alongside civil society and outside it." That interplay shows Marx's ambivalence regarding the notion of civil society: of the original English concept he scarcely retains anything but the economic aspect ("the conditions of material existence") since he makes juridical relations elements of the superstructure. On another front, Marx—from the *Critique of Hegelian Political Right* to *The Civil War in France* (1871)—was always a determined adversary of the state, for whose final reabsorption in a regenerated civil society he called. Historical materialism thus appears to be a radicalization of English political economy, pressed into the service of a radical critique of the divisions of the human city. It remains for the reader to determine whether we are confronted with a fertile reversal of juridical idealism or a radical negation of the juridical and political conditions of civil society.

Philippe Raynaud

BIBLIOGRAPHY

Abramson, Jeffrey. *Minerva's Owl: The Tradition of Western Political Thought.* Cambridge, MA: Harvard University Press, 2009.

Colas, Dominique. *Civil Society and Fanaticism: Conjoined Histories.* Translated by Amy Jacobs. Stanford: Stanford University Press, 1997.

Colliot-Thélène, Catherine. "État et société civile." In *Dictionnaire de philosophie politique.* Edited by P. Raynaud and S. Rials. Paris: Presses Universitaires de France, 1996.

Ferry, Luc. "L'émergence du couple État/société." In *Histoire de la philosophie politique*, edited by Alain Renaut. Vol. 4, *Les Critiques de la modernité politique*. Paris: Calmann-Lévy, 1999.

Gautier, Claude. *L'Invention de la société civile: lectures anglo-écossaises: Mandeville, Smith, Ferguson*. Paris: Presses Universitaires de France, 1993.

Hammond, Scott J. *Political Theory: An Encyclopedia of Contemporary and Classic Terms*. Westport, CT: Greenwood Press, 2009.

Moatti, Claudia. *La Raison de Rome: naissance de l'esprit critique à la fin de la République*. Paris: Éditions du Seuil, 1997.

Pasquino, Pasquale. "Communauté et société." In *Dictionnaire de philosophie politique*. Edited by P. Raynaud and S. Rials. Paris: Presses Universitaires de France, 1996.

Pocock, J.G.A. *Virtue, Commerce, and History: Essays on Political Thought and History, Chiefly in the Eighteenth Century*. Cambridge: Cambridge University Press, 1985.

Quillet, Jeanine. *Les Clefs du pouvoir au Moyen Age*. Paris: Flammarion, 1972.

———. "Augustin. Saint Augustin et l'augustinisme médiéval." In *Dictionnaire de philosophie politique*. Edited by P. Raynaud and S. Rials. Paris: Presses Universitaires de France, 1996.

Raynaud, Philippe. *Max Weber et les dilemmes de la raison moderne*. Paris: Presses Universitaires de France, 1987.

Thomas, Yan. "Fictio legis. L'empire de la fiction romaine et ses limites médiévales." *Droits* 21. *La Fiction*. Paris: Presses Universitaires de France, 1995.

CIVILITY

"Civility" derives from Latin *civilitas*, which means first of all everything that has to do with the city, *civitas*, and the citizen, *civis*; for example, *civilitas* is the term Quintilian chooses (2.15.25) to translate Plato's *hê politikê* [ἡ πολιτική]. But the Latin word also designates a certain kind of relationship, gentle and ennobled, among people (*clementiae civilitatisque*, "his clemency and courtesy," Suetonius says [*Augustus*, 51.1]); see MENSCHHEIT, Box 1; cf. PARDON.

In the eighteenth century, "civility" thus became a synonym of "politeness," with various subtle variations depending on the authors. Here we examine mainly:

1. Italian thought on civility and politeness; see CIVILTÀ, "civility/civilization," and CIVILIZATION, SPREZZATURA.
2. The way in which "civility" continues to spread in "civil society"; see CIVIL SOCIETY.

On the more general relationship to politics and progress, see CIVILIZATION.

➤ BEHAVIOR, *CULTURE*, INGENIUM, *PRUDENCE*, *WITTICISM*

CIVILIZATION

"Civilization" is a word that emerged in the eighteenth century (Mirabeau the elder, *L'Ami des hommes*, 1758) to designate dynamically what civility designated "statically" (see *CIVILITY*): civilization is a process through which humans become "civil" by overcoming primitive barbarity through gentler customs and the establishment of "civic" ties.

I. "CIVILIZATION," *CIVILISATION, CIVILTÀ, ZIVILISATION*

Here we have chosen to give priority to the following:

1. Italian thought about *civiltà*, a single term to designate what French calls *civilité* and *civilisation* (cf. SPREZZATURA and VIRTÙ).

2. The German distinction between *Kultur* and *Zivilisation*, discussed in the entry on BILDUNG (see *CULTURE*).

II. Civilization and Politics

On the relation between politics and "civil/civic," see CIVIL SOCIETY. More particularly, see the following:

- on the Greek notion of political community and its connection with the humanity of man, see POLIS and LOGOS, II.A;
- on "barbarity," see TO TRANSLATE, Box 1;
- on Latin *civitas*, see LEX;
- on civil society, see LIBERAL, and the difference between "politics" and "policy" in POLITICS.

See also *DROIT, JUSTICE,* and LAW.

On the relationship to progress, see CORSO, HISTORIA UNIVERSALIS, HISTORY, PERFECTIBILITY, *PROGRESS,* SECULARIZATION; cf. *DESTINY*, GLÜCK, MENSCHHEIT.

➤ *CULTURE*

CIVILTÀ   (ITALIAN)

ENGLISH	civility, civilization
FRENCH	*civilité, civilisation*
GREEK	*asteiosunē* [ἀστειοσύνη], *paideia* [παιδεία], *politeia* [πολιτεία]
ITALIAN	*cortesia, urbanità, gentilezza, buona creanza*
LATIN	*civilitas, urbanitas*

➤ BILDUNG, *CIVILITY*, and CIVILIZATION, and INGENIUM, POLIS, SPREZZATURA, *STATE, WITTICISM*

In French, two different words, *civilité* and *civilisation*, correspond to two distinct notions, whereas in Italian, a single word, *civiltà*, covers a broad semantic field that includes them both. Here we will seek, if not to explain this divergence from a common origin (Lat. *civis* and its derivatives), at least to show how reflection on this terminological proximity and distance sheds light on the way in which Western societies have conceived their historical destiny.

I. The Connection between Politics and Ethics

The Italian word *civiltà* and the French words *civilité* and *civilisation* have common etymological roots: the Latin *civis* (free member of a city, citizen), its abstract derivative *civitas* (citizenship, citizenry, city), the adjective *civilis* (relating to a citizen, civil; concerning the citizenry as a whole, politics; what is suitable for citizens; popular, affable, benevolent, gentle), the noun *civilitas* (quality of being a citizen, sociability, courtesy), and the adverb *civiliter* (as a citizen, as a good citizen; lawful; with moderation, with gentleness). In all of these uses, we must note the twofold connotation: one political, referring to the particular way of organizing life in common represented by the ancient city-state, and the other moral and psychological, referring to the moderation of manners that life in a city is supposed to produce. The second meaning is also expressed by the term *urbanitas*, which alludes to the *urbs*, the city in its concrete reality, understood as a place where individuals are in permanent contact, thanks to which manners and language lose their "rusticity" (from *rus*, "countryside"), Rome being the City par excellence, the *Urbs*. Moreover, in the semantic field of Greek, we can note the same group of meanings. *Civitas* corresponds to *polis* [πόλις], *civis* to *politês* [πολίτης], *civilis* to *politikos* [πολιτικός] (the latter meaning "what concerns citizens," "what concerns the state," and also "capable of living in society," "sociable"). In addition, *astu* [ἄστυ] designates, like *urbs*, the city as opposed to the countryside, and often, when used without an article, Athens. The adjective *asteios* [ἀστεῖος], "regarding a citizen," qualifies "what is in good taste, cultivated, elegant," and, speaking of language and style, "subtle, witty" (*asteia* are *bons mots*). It is worth pointing out here that the French word *politesse* does not derive, as is often thought, from Greek *polis*, but from Italian *polito* (smooth, clean), which is itself derived from Latin *politus* (made smooth, clean, by polishing). We find the same duality in the Italian, French, and Spanish words derived from the Latin root.

In contemporary Italian, *civiltà* (formerly *civilità*) designates on the one hand "the state of a people that has reached a certain degree of technical and intellectual progress," "all human achievements in the political, social, and cultural domain," "all the manifestations of the economic, social, and moral life of a people at a given point in its history" (RT: *Grande dizionario della lingua italiana*, s.v.). In the first two senses (the third being modern), the word was already used by Torquato Tasso, in his verse play *Aminta* (1573), for example. Giambattista Vico speaks of "laws suitable for domesticating a barbarous people to lead it to *un' umana civiltà*" (*La scienza nuova*, §100), but in general he uses instead the word *umanità*, which in his work does not designate "the human species," but rather both the process through which nations cease to be "barbarian" and become "fully human," and the final result of this process. On the other hand, *civiltà* also designates a behavior characterizing social life, that of "a cultivated, educated person with elevated feelings." In this case, the word is synonymous with *cortesia*, *urbanità*, *gentilezza*, and *buona creanza*.

A comparison with French is instructive. *Civilité* is first attested in the fourteenth century, in Nicole Oresme's translation of Aristotle's *Ethics*, where it is defined as "the manner, ordering, and government of a city or community" (2.1.9). Here the word retains its first Latin meaning, which is political. But as early as the following century, by a shift already found in Latin, as we have seen, the meaning becomes moral and psychological, designating a certain quality of the relations between members of a community. Thus Antoine Furetière, in his *Dictionnaire universel*, defined *civilité* as "a decent, gentle, and polite way of acting or conversing together" (RT: *Dictionnaire universel*, s.v.). A century later, Denis Diderot and Jean Le Rond d'Alembert's *Encyclopédie* noted that "civility and politeness are a certain decorum in manners and words tending to please and to show the respect that we have for each other" (RT: *Encyclopédie ou Dictionnaire*, s.v.). The word continued to have this meaning, though it was used increasingly less frequently. According to the dictionaries (e.g., RT: *Le nouveau petit Robert*, s.v.), *civilité* is an "old-fashioned" word. However, at the present time there seems to be a renewed

interest in the term, which better expresses the "citizen" (*citoyen*) aspect (the word *citoyen* now being used, contrary to its classical use, adjectivally with a view to supplanting *civique*) of the felt need to return to a minimal politeness.

II. When "Civilization" Separates from "Civility"

The question is when and how, if not why, the word *civilisation* appeared in the French language (especially since it is so close in form and etymology to *civilité*, though it has a different meaning), whereas in Italian *civiltà* continues to express a semantic content that is now divided between two different words in French.

The history of the French word *civilisation* is well known. If we grant that this noun appears for the first time in a work by the Marquis de Mirabeau, *L'Ami des hommes ou traité de la population* (1757), it is interesting to note that in this author's writing, the neologism still has a meaning very close to that of *civilité*, since Mirabeau writes elsewhere that "*civilisation* is the moderation of manners, urbanity, politeness, and knowledge disseminated in such a way that decorum is observed and takes the place of detailed laws" (*L'Ami des femmes ou traité de civilisation*, draft for a book, cited in Starobinski, *Blessings in Disguise*, 7). It was only a little later that *civilisation* acquired the meaning that it still has in French, the definition of which we can take from François Guizot, who wrote *Histoire de la civilisation en Europe* (1828). For Guizot, civilization was a "fact," "a fact like others, that can be studied, described, narrated," but also a fact that is not like others, because it is "a fact of progress, of development," so that "the idea of progress, of development" seemed to him "the fundamental idea contained in the word *civilisation*" (trans. Hazlitt, 12, 16).

The French linguist Émile Benveniste, in his article "Civilisation," has shown how *civilité*'s ending in -*té* made it a static term that no longer sufficed to express an idea that was becoming established in the second half of the seventeenth century, the idea of a general progress of human society through time, and how *civilisation*, by its ending in -*isation*, corresponded better, by its very form, to the dynamic aspect of this development. This explains the ease with which people at the end of the century of Enlightenment adopted the Marquis de Mirabeau's neologism. However, we must note the significant resistance of the English writer Samuel Johnson, who, in 1773, as his biographer James Boswell tells us, refused to include the word "civilization" in his famous *Dictionary*, because "civility" sufficed (Boswell, *Life of Samuel Johnson*).

Italian, we might say, agrees with Johnson. As we have seen, it has preserved *civiltà* in the sense of "civility" and "civilization." The less frequently used term *incivilimento* expresses the dynamic movement of which *civiltà* is the result. *Civilizzazione*, modeled on the French *civilisation*, was introduced into Italian in the early nineteenth century, and is found in Alessandro Manzoni and Giacomo Leopardi, but it never became really established, for revealing reasons. Around 1860, for example, Filippo Ugolini wrote: "*Civilizzazione*; let us leave this word to the French, and let us be satisfied with our *incivilimento*, from *costume*, or with *vivere civile*, from *civiltà*. We had these words long before the French had either the word *civilisation* or the state that corresponds to it" (Ugolini, *Vocabulario di parole e modi errati).* This remark, which is obviously polemical, was inspired by Italians' exacerbated nationalism at the time, but it is also connected with an older trend of thought, the equivalent of which is found in Germany. It was France, the country of the Enlightenment and then of the Revolution, that was in question. France is reproached for its political, ideological, and linguistic expansion, and more profoundly, for its dry rationalism, its conception of progress based solely on scientific, technical, and economic values, its loss of the sense of historical values, of tradition, of popular roots. In contrast, Italian *civiltà* refers, if not to ancient Rome, at least to the Renaissance, a period in which Italy was a model for Europe as a whole. It is the bearer of humanistic values and expresses itself in every domain, from politics and morals to aesthetics. Less oriented toward the future than toward a certain past considered as a model, exempt from hubris, it emphasized the improvement of humans as individuals and still more as social beings (whence the very important dimension of "civility," rather than mastery over nature, in the notion of *civiltà*).

Alain Pons

BIBLIOGRAPHY

Benveniste, Émile. "Civilisation: Contribution à l'histoire du mot." In *Problèmes de linguistique générale*, vol. 1. Paris: Gallimard / La Pléiade, 1966. Translation by M. E. Meek: "Civilization: Contribution to the History of the Word." In *Problems in General Linguistics*. Coral Gables, FL: University of Miami Press, 1971.

Boswell, James. *The Life of Samuel Johnson.* Edited by R. W. Chapman and Pat Rogers. Rev. ed. London: Oxford University Press, 1970. First published in 1791.

Febvre, Lucien. "Civilisation: Évolution d'un mot et d'un groupe d'idées." In *Civilisation: Le mot et l'idée*, Première semaine internationale de synthèse, 2nd fasc. Paris: La Renaissance du livre, 1930.

Guizot, François. *Histoire de la civilisation en Europe.* Paris: Hachette, Pluriel, 1985. First published in 1828. Translation by W. Hazlitt: *The History of Civilization in Europe.* Introduction by L. Siedentop. London: Penguin, 1997.

Mirabeau, Victor Riqueti, Marquis de. *L'Ami des hommes ou traité de la population.* Reprint, Charleston, SC: Nabu Press, 2010. First published in 1757.

Oresme, Nicole. *Le livre des Éthiques d'Aristote.* Edited by A. D. Menut. New York: G. E. Stechert, 1940.

Starobinski, Jean. *Blessings in Disguise.* Translated by Arthur Goldhammer. Cambridge, MA: Harvard University Press, 1993.

———. "Le mot civilisation." In *Le temps de la réflexion*, vol. 4. Paris: Gallimard / La Pléiade, 1983.

Ugolini, Filippo. *Vocabulario di parole e modi errati.* Naples, It.: G. de Stefano, 1860.

Vico, Giambattista. *La scienza nuova.* In *Opere*, edited by A. Battistini. Milan: Mondadori, 1990. First published in 1744. Translation by T. G. Bergin and M. H. Fisch: *The New Science of Giambattista Vico.* Ithaca, NY: Cornell University Press, 1984.

CLAIM

| FRENCH | *exigence, revendication* |
| GERMAN | *Anspruch* |

➤ *EXIGENCY*, and *DROIT*, DUTY, ENGLISH, LAW, *POWER*, *VOICE*

Derived from Old French *clamer* (in Latin, *clamare*, from the same semantic field as *clarus*, "clear, strong"), the verb "to claim" initially meant, in its first historically recorded uses, "to call, cry, proclaim" (call loudly). However, the current uses of the English verb "claim" and the noun "claim" lack equivalents in French. Contemporary French translations of "claim", such as *revendication, réclamation*, and *pretention*, all have a tone that is, if not pejorative, in any case negative, as if the demand expressed in "claim" needed to be supplemented by a justification (as in the French expression *revendication légitime*). But in its initial usages, juridical or political, "claim" posits the demand as founded, in nature if not in right, and it could be adequately translated in French by *titre*: thus we have to explore the complex relationship between "claim" and "right" (*droit*), a notion which, as Alasdair MacIntyre has pointed out, emerged later on and of which "claim" (a demand founded on a need) might have constituted an early form, thus raising the problem of rights itself. This juridical use has persisted in contemporary Anglo-Saxon discussions of the philosophy of law, of which it constitutes one of the specific features.

In the nineteenth and twentieth centuries, "claim" moved from the political and juridical fields to that of the theory of knowledge, and then more generally to the philosophy of language. "Claim" becomes a "claim to know" and then a "thesis." The use of the term raises first the problem, which emerged from English empiricism and was then taken up by Kant, of the legitimacy of knowledge, of my claims to know and say. There is an equivalent in German (*Anspruch*), but none in French. Finally, "claim," as in Stanley Cavell (*The Claim of Reason*), becomes a "statement" to be maintained or claimed ("my claim is").

I. "Claim" as a Juridical and Political Demand

A. "Claim about," "claim to": A demand for something that is owed, the demand for a right

The noun "claim" and the verb associated with it designate a demand for something as owed: "Not to beg and accept as a favor but to exact as a due." Then "claim" is rendered in French by *exigence* or *titre*. But this raises the question of the legitimacy of the demand, whereas "claim" acquires a juridical (and philosophical) meaning only with the emergence, apparently relatively late, of the term "right." Its meaning then becomes more specific: "an assertion of a right to something" (RT: *Oxford English Dictionary*). A whole juridical vocabulary develops around "claim," as is shown by a multitude of expressions such as "lay claim," "make a claim," "enter a claim," and so forth.

The development of the uses of "claim" raises essential problems connected with the nature of rights. "Claim" originally designated a fundamental demand, the satisfaction of a physical need, or the recuperation of a vital good that has been taken away (which is the use we find in Shakespeare: in *King John*, a character *claims* his wife when she has been taken away by another). But this raises the question of the naturalness and the possession of rights.

> One reason why claims about goods necessary for rational agency are so different from claims to the possession of rights is that the latter in fact presuppose, as the former do not, the existence of a socially established set of rules. . . . [T]he existence of particular types of social institution or practice is a necessary condition for the notion of a claim to the possession of a right being an intelligible type of human performance. . . . Lacking any such social form, the making of a claim to a right would

be like presenting a check for payment in a social order that lacked the institution of money.

(A. MacIntyre, *After Virtue*, 67)

Thus is raised the problem of the status of property claims or titles, which has become central in Anglo-Saxon juridical and political thought: a claim is a demand and a title to ownership of an object that one already legitimately owns. It is, moreover, noteworthy that the use of the term underwent a concrete extension precisely at the time when pioneers were conquering new territories. In America and in Australia, a claim designated a parcel of land acquired by occupation (and not granted or inherited), for example, by miners. This "local" American sense of the word "claim" underlies a certain conception of the claim to property rights as fundamental, and perhaps also to rights in general as (re)taking possession of one's own territory (a territory later claimed by Native Americans was called an "Indian claim"). This clarifies a meaning of "claim to a right": I demand what is mine and always has been.

It is obvious that a certain conception of claims is based on these earlier senses of the word, and that the latter, far from having been erased or integrated into "right," remains in competition with it. We see the result of this in the numerous recent discussions of W. N. Holfeld's book *Fundamental Legal Conceptions* (1919), in which a claim becomes the right par excellence, defined as a privilege or immunity, a "perimeter of protection" (cf. J. Y. Goffi, *Le philosophe et ses animaux*). A "right-claim" is more than a simple right, for it is not merely the permission to perform a certain act (tolerance), or even a prohibition on preventing someone from performing it (right), but implies society's obligation to see to it that the claim is respected, to make the act possible. The theoretician of the norm, Von Wright, shows in *Norm and Action* (86f.) that deontic logic cannot function in accord with two contradictory terms A/non-A, for example, prohibited/authorized, but it is necessary to posit a third term, a supplementary degree of authorization, or of the right, which is the claim. A claim, far from being absorbed into the idea of right, is thus a radicalization of the latter, which explains the anti-authority and territorial form taken too often by questions of right(s) when they have the status of a claim.

B. "Claim on": Locke, or the possible illegitimacy of the political "claim"

This radical, possessive dimension is found in another use of "claim," in the sense of a "claim on" someone. The political sense of "claim" exists in neither Hume nor Hobbes, though it is widespread in Locke. In Hume, a right (that of property, for instance, or that of a sovereign over his subjects) is connected with a conventional agreement or contract that does not need to be founded on anything other than custom and habit. Conversely, Locke calls a "claim" the ruler's authority over a subject, and differentiates it from paternal authority. "Governments claim no power over the son because of that they had over the father" (*Second Treatise on Civil Government*, §118).

Here we encounter an idea of a claim that applies to the person the originary concept of a claim, but—and this is the specificity of Locke and his heirs—redefines it. The claim to power over a subject must always be explained and justified in terms of natural law: it is because of this justification that it is necessarily a claim, and not a natural authority. Thus in Locke a claim can be illegitimate, made without the people's consent and against its interests, and in fact it is usually in this sense that Locke uses the term.

> If anyone shall *claim* a power to lay and levy taxes on the people by its own authority, and without consent of the people, he thereby invades *the fundamental law* of property, and subverts the end of government [emphasis added].

(Ibid., §140)

The one who holds power is not a lawgiver, but a mere representative of the law (executor), and has a right to be obeyed only in this capacity; he cannot claim it for himself:

> Allegiance being nothing but an obedience according to law, which, when he violates, he has no right to obedience, nor can claim it otherwise than as the public person vested with the power of law.

(Ibid., §150)

Locke's theory can thus be interpreted as an attempt to bring claims into the field of rights, and to subordinate the claim to power to natural law. That is what determines, for him, the possibility of the people rejecting authority. A bad ruler who "claims that power without the direction of the law, as a prerogative belonging to him by right of his office" (ibid., §164), thus gives the people a reason to "claim their right and limit that power." A claim therefore requires a right, and is no longer a foundation or origin but a demand that itself has to be grounded.

Thus in Locke we find for the first time the curious verb "disclaim" (ibid., §191): I can disclaim my membership in the community governed by law and withdraw from it (I will then be outside its jurisdiction, losing the rights inherent in that membership). Whence the later appearance of the expression "to issue a disclaimer" (symmetrical with "enter a claim"), which means to reject a responsibility or to renounce a right and thus one's membership. Thus in and with the notion of a claim, a twofold problem is posed: that of the foundation of authority, of entitlement, and that of the recognition of this authority by its subjects: here we move from the political question to the more general question of the community.

II. "Claim" as a Demand for Knowledge

The problem of authority, of the claim to power, moves from the political field to that of knowledge and argumentation, but the political question still underlies the epistemological problem. In *The Claim of Reason*, Cavell explores this semantic transfer and remarkably develops the relationship of the juridical to the cognitive, and then to the linguistic.

The cognitive concept, like its political ancestor, emerges from discussions of empiricism. What is the question of empiricism, and correlatively, of skepticism? It is the question of legitimacy, of the right to know. What allows us to say that we know? Hume examines our claim to know by reasoning on the basis of experience (note that when in the *Enquiry Concerning Human Understanding* he asks "what is the foundation of all reasoning and conclusions from experience?" he uses, not "claim," but "pretension"). We "claim" to know, but with what right? The question is taken up again by Kant, in whose work we can discern the emergence of an equivalent of "claim": *Anspruch*, which designates the claim of reason to ask questions that are beyond its power but are legitimate and natural. The legal sense of "claim" can thus be found in the Kantian *quid juris*. The problem of reason is the problem of the claim: a demand that is both inevitable and impossible to satisfy, and is thus fated to remain a claim forever.

Cavell develops this tension between the arrogance and the legitimacy of the philosophical pretension indicated by "claim." At the outset, *The Claim of Reason* defines "claims" as "claims to community." Underlying the question of the basis for knowledge is the political and not solely epistemological question of the foundation of our common use of language. For Cavell, my claim to know masks a prior claim: the claim to speak for others, and to accept that others speak in my name.

> The philosophical appeal to "what we say," and the search for our criteria on the basis of which we say what we say, are claims to community. And a claim to community is always a search for the basis on which it can be, or has been, established.
>
> (Cavell, *The Claim of Reason*)

The juridical and gnoseological problems raised by "claim" are transformed into a question about our common criteria, our agreements in language.

> When I remarked that the philosophical search for our criteria is a search for community, I was in effect answering the second question I uncovered in the face of the claim to speak for "the group"—the question, namely, about how I could have been party to the establishing of criteria if I do not recognize that I have and do not know what they are.
>
> (Ibid.)

The question is that of my membership in the community of language, and also that of my representativeness: where do I get the right or claim to speak for others? According to Cavell, this question is the very one that ordinary language philosophers like Austin and Wittgenstein ask. The meaning of "claim" is inseparable from the possibility of losing my representativeness or membership, of being reduced to silence.

> For all Wittgenstein's claims about what we say, he is always at the same time aware that others might not agree, that a given person or group (a "tribe") might not share our criteria.
>
> (Ibid.)

Thus Cavell offers an analysis of Rousseau in terms of claims:

> What he claims to know is his relation to society, and to take as a philosophical datum the fact that men (that he) can speak for society and that society can speak for him.
>
> (Ibid.)

My society must be my expression. That is what the theoreticians of democracy always hope, and it is the illusion that Cavell denounces in the work of John Rawls, for instance: if others silence my voice, claim to speak for me, in what way have I agreed to this?

> To speak for yourself then means risking the rebuff—on some occasions, perhaps once for all—of those for whom you claimed to be speaking; and it means risking having to rebuff—on some occasions, perhaps once for all—those who claimed to be speaking for you.
>
> (Ibid.)

The social contract implies the constant possibility of withdrawing from ("disclaiming," Locke said) the community. Linguistic or political agreement among humans, precisely because it is still a claim, is as fragile as it is profound. This essential fragility of political agreement, which is always threatened by skepticism, constitutes the linguistic sense of "claim."

III. "Claim," The Voice of Ordinary Language

Political agreement is of the same nature as linguistic agreement, which Wittgenstein called *Übereinstimmung* (*Philosophical Investigations*, §241), and which is translated in French as either *concorde* or *accord*, the better to indicate the presence of the voice, the *Stimme* (see STIMMUNG). This agreement exists only insofar as it is claimed, invoked, appealed to. Thus, along with "claim" is defined an agreement that is neither psychological nor intersubjective and is founded on nothing other than the validity of a voice (*Stimme*): my individual voice claims to be, and is, a "universal voice."

With the appeal to the voice, we encounter the first sense of "claim" (*clamare*, "to cry out, to call"). The concept of voice turns out always to underlie the technical concept of "claim." A voice claims when it asserts, on the basis of itself alone, a universal assent—a claim that, no matter how exorbitant it might be, Cavell seeks to formulate in a still more shocking way, without basing it, as in Kant, on something transcendental, or on some rational condition.

To show how the concept of "claim" rethought in this way provides a reply to skepticism, we can point to the universality characteristic of aesthetic judgment in Kant. In his earlier book *Must We Mean What We Say?* Cavell shows how close the approaches of ordinary language philosophers like Wittgenstein and Austin are to Kant's: for them, I always appeal to *myself* to say what *we* say, and this can be rendered only by "claim," or *Anspruch*. To understand this, we have to see what the ordinary language philosophers' approach consists in, on the basis of "what we say when":

> I will suggest that aesthetic judgment models the sort of claim entered by these philosophers, and that the familiar lack of conclusiveness in aesthetic argument, rather than showing up an irrationality, shows the kind of rationality it has, and needs.
>
> (Cavell, *The Claim of Reason*)

It is Kant who offers the deepest thinking about "claim." The idea of a universal agreement based on my individual voice makes its appearance in the famous §8 of the *Third Critique*. In aesthetic judgment, Kant discovers "a property of our cognitive faculty," "a claim [*Anspruch*] to the universal validity [*Allgemeingültigkeit*] of its judgment," so that "satisfaction in the object is imputed to *everyone*" (trans. Bernard, *Critique of Judgment*, §8, 49). We know how Kant distinguishes the pleasing from the beautiful (which claims universal assent) in terms of private versus public judgment. How can a judgment that has all the characteristics of the private claim to be public? That is the problem raised by the notion of a claim. Judgments of taste require and demand universal assent; "in fact it imputes this to everyone for each of its judgments of taste, without the persons that judge disputing as to the possibility of such a claim [*Anspruch*]" (ibid. §8, 49). In such a claim, "nothing is postulated but a . . . universal voice (*allgemeine Stimme*)" (ibid., §8, 50). This is the "voice" that is heard in *übereinstimmen*, the verb Wittgenstein uses with regard to our agreement ("in language," cf. *Philosophical Investigations*, §241).

The proximity of the Kantian universal voice and the theses of ordinary language philosophy appear with this final sense of "claim," simultaneously *Anspruch* and *Stimme*: a claim that is empirically unfounded and thus threatened by and pointed out by skepticism, to speak in the name of everyone. Kant's "universal voice" is what we hear in Cavell's claims about "what we say" (*Must We Mean What We Say?* 94).

By redefining "claim" in this way, Cavell brings together the diverse semantic traditions. My assertions or theses—claims—are always based on an agreement in language, on a claim to my representativeness, which is itself political and legal in nature—hence on my voice as singular and universal. To recognize the close connection between all these senses of the word "claim" is to recognize that language, expression—in the cognitive as well as in the political domain—is always also a voice that wants to make itself heard.

Sandra Laugier

BIBLIOGRAPHY

Cavell, Stanley. *The Claim of Reason*. New York: Oxford University Pres, 1979.
———. *Must We Mean What We Say?* Cambridge: Cambridge University Press, 1969.
———. *A Pitch of Philosophy*. Cambridge, MA: Harvard University Press, 1994.
Goffi, Jean-Yves. *Le philosophe et ses animaux*. Nîmes, Fr.: Jeanine Chambon, 1994.
Holfield, Wesley Newcomb. *Fundamental Legal Conceptions as Applied in Judicial Reasoning*. New Haven, CT: Yale University Press, 1919; reprint, Aldershot, UK: Ashgate, 2008.
Hume, David. *An Enquiry Concerning Human Understanding: A Critical Edition*. Oxford: Clarendon Press, 2000. First published in 1748.
Kant, Immanuel. *Critique of Judgment*. Translated by J. H. Bernard. New York: Hafner-Macmillan, 1951.
Larrère, Catherine. "De l'illicite au licite, prescription et permission," *CREDIMI* 16 (1996): 59–78.
Locke, John. *Second Treatise of Civil Government*. Edited by J. W. Gough. Oxford: Blackwell, 1946. First published in 1690.
MacIntyre, Alasdair. *After Virtue: A Study in Moral Theory*. Notre Dame, IN: University of Notre Dame Press, 1981.
Wittgenstein, Ludwig. *Philosophical Investigations*. Translated by G.E.M. Anscombe. Oxford: Blackwell, 1953.
Wright, Georg Henrik von. *Norm and Action*. London: Macmillan, 1963.

CLASSIC, CLASSICISM NEOCLASSIC, NEOCLASSICISM

FRENCH	*classique, classicisme; néoclassique, néoclassicisme*
GERMAN	*klassik, Klassizismus*
ITALIAN	*classicismo; neoclassico, neoclassicismo*
LATIN	*classicus*

➤ AESTHETICS, BAROQUE, GOÛT, MANIERA, MIMÊSIS, NEUZEIT, ROMANTIC

The ease of translating the term "classic" into all European languages, which is due to a common Latin root (*classicus*), masks differences in content depending on the languages and cultures concerned. The adjective *classicus* (first-class) was used by Aulus Gellius to designate the best authors, from Demosthenes to Virgil, the ones humanist educators used in their classes (whence an amusing false etymology, still given in Furetière's dictionary [RT: *Dictionnaire universel*]). The word is used in this sense in all European languages, each of which has its own "classics." It is also used more specifically to designate the artistic works inspired by antiquity (the classical language of architecture, classical sculptures and ornaments) that the romantics opposed.

But two derived and divergent uses—in France, on the one hand, to qualify the art of the century of Louis XIV, considered as the period of a perfection equal to that of the centuries of Pericles and Augustus, and on the other hand in Germany, to designate the formal system of the Italian High Renaissance in opposition to that of the baroque—eventually created a semantic nexus that was complicated still further by a final difference between the German use of *Klassizmus*, the reaction to Rococo that itself came to be opposed to romanticism, and other Europeans' use of "neoclassicism" (*néoclassicisme*, neoclassicismo) to describe the renewal of taste connected with the discovery of Pompeii, Greece, and Egypt.

I. The Adjective "Classic"

In seventeenth-century France, only the adjective *classique* was used: "it is used almost exclusively to describe the authors read in classes, or who enjoy great authority," Furetière notes in his RT: *Dictionnaire universel* (1690). Following Aulus Gellius, he cites, among these good classical authors, Cicero, Caesar, Sallust, Virgil, and Horace, "who lived in the time of the Republic and toward the end of Augustus, when good Latin was still written, before it began to be corrupted in the time of the Antonines," thus suggesting a threefold link between the idea of the classic and the authority of the ancients, the purity of the language, and teaching.

But in his *Discourse on Theophrastus*, which is situated in the context of the Quarrel of the Ancients and the Moderns, La Bruyère observes, "We who are moderns, will be ancients in a few centuries." As early as the eighteenth century, the word is extended to good French authors, "whose perfect models should be imitated as much as possible"; "you have given me great pleasure," Voltaire writes, "in telling me that the Academy is going to do France and Europe the favor of publishing a collection of our classic authors, with notes that will stabilize language and taste" (see 1761 letter from *Selected Letters of Voltaire*, trans. L. C. Syms, 150). We find again here the role of authority—in this case, of the Academy—and the concern for the preservation of a good state of the language and for the imitation of good models. The lectures given at the Royal Academy of Painting and Sculpture, in which the works in the king's collection (especially those by Poussin, considered the leader of the French School of painting), on the one hand, and on the other the courses given by Jacques François Blondel, who celebrated the works of François Mansart, paved the way for the extension to the fine arts of this notion of "French classics," and particularly the "classics" of the century of Louis XIV.

This development was not limited to France: the preface to the first volume of the *Literary History of France* published by the Benedictines in 1733 emphasizes that "[w]e have seen several foreign nations, far less studious than ours, priding themselves on collecting in a library all the authors they have given to the Republic of Letters."

II. How French Classicism Became Baroque

The French word *classicisme* was created on the basis of the adjective *classique* in the context of the battle with romanticism. In 1873 Émile Littré still considered it a neologism, and defined it as the "system of the exclusive partisans of the writers of antiquity or of the classic authors of the seventeenth century." The word is also used in a related sense in the field of the fine arts: works that "claim to imitate the works of ancient statuary" are called *classique*, and David's "new school" is called the *école classique* because its "compositions are regular and imitate the Greeks."

In Germany, the term *Klassizismus* is still used to designate the international movement at the end of the eighteenth and the beginning of the nineteenth centuries, which in France is called *néoclassicisme*, a more accurate term because the source of classicism, the imitation of the ancients, was renewed at that time by the discovery of Greek architecture and by the rationality of the Enlightenment.

In French culture, on the contrary, the notion of classicism was shifted to the art and literature of the second half of the seventeenth century. In the aftermath of the battle over romanticism, instruction in the universities and schools tried to make French literature of the seventeenth century the expression of the French genius: clearness of expression, sober elegance, nobility, and decorous sentiments. This notion was extended to the fine arts, and it was claimed that the same qualities could be found in the works of Poussin, Le Sueur, and Lebrun. Since this period corresponded to the reign of Louis XIV, it was called the "Classic Age," as the Spanish speak of the "Golden Age."

However, writers on German art history adopted the term *Barock*, which had up to that point been pejorative (see BAROQUE) in referring to the art of the Seicento (H. Wölfflin, *Renaissance und Barok*), and, on the other hand, they constructed a visual analysis on the basis of the contrast between the classical aesthetics of the early Cinquecento and the baroque aesthetics of the Seicento (H. Wölfflin, *Kunstgeschichtliche Grundbegriffe*, 1915). French classicism was thus contemporaneous with Italian baroque.

Certain national specificities (it was forgotten that they were not peculiar to the century) and the existence of lively debates regarding the role of ornament or antique models (it was forgotten that they cut across the two cultures) made it possible for a time to maintain the opposition between (French) classicism and (Italian) baroque. But when the notion of baroque was broadened on cultural (*stile trentino*) or

formal (the "grand style") bases, it was difficult not to see that some aspects of French art in the seventeenth century, from Simon Vouet's decorative lyricism to the grand style of Hardouin-Mansart, belonged to this international model. Describing French classical art as baroque reversed the way it was read, leading to a rediscovery of the theatricality of works that had earlier been admired for their balance and clarity, and of the baroque grandiloquence of Versailles, previously celebrated for its classical moderation—whence the necessity of introducing other notions like that of Atticism (Merot, *Éloge de la clarté*, 1998). Roland Barthes discerned a dark Racine who might have read Sade, and Anthony Blunt found in François Mansart a paranoid anxiety about the perfect form that relates him to Borromini. The internal tensions within the two cultures were rediscovered in their common reference point, which was, however, differentiated from that of antiquity: the tense expression of Pierre Puget's statue of Milo of Croton, conceived in emulation of the ancient Laocoön, is contrasted with the calm gestures of the nymphs in Girardon's sculpture *Les bains d'Apollon*, which is inspired by the Apollo of Belvedere; Bernini takes the same statue as his starting point, giving it life in his "Apollo and Daphne," whereas Poussin, inversely, idealizes the figures or the models that pose for him.

For literature as for the arts, classicism is not a doctrine but a horizon.

Claude Mignot

BIBLIOGRAPHY

Mérot, Alain. *Éloge de la clarté, un courant artistique au temps de Mazarin, 1640–1660*. Dijon-Le Mans, Fr.: Réunion des Musées Nationaux, 1998.

Summerson, John. *The Classical Language of Architecture*. London: British Broadcasting Corporation, 1963.

Voltaire. *Selected Letters of Voltaire*. Translated by L. C. Syms. New York: American Book Company, 1900.

Wölfflin, Heinrich. *Die Klassische Kunst, eine Einführung in die italienische Renaissance*. Munich: Bruckmann, 1899. Translation by P. and L. Murray: *Classic Art: An Introduction to the Italian Renaissance*. London: Phaidon, 1994.

———. *Kunstgeschichtliche Grundbegriffe: Das Problem der Stilentwicklung in der neueren Kunst*. Munich: Bruckmann, 1915. Translation by M. D. Hottinger: *Principles of Art History: The Problem of the Development of Style in Later Art*. New York: Dover, 1950.

———. *Renaissance und Barok*. Bâle, Ger.: Schwabe, 1888. Translation by K. Simon: *Renaissance and Baroque*. Ithaca, NY: Cornell University Press, 1966.

COMBINATION AND CONCEPTUALIZATION

A "Particle Metaphysics" in German

➤ GERMAN, and *DESTINY*, ENGLISH, FRENCH, *TO BE*, TO TRANSLATE

While the use of any linguistic system is based on a double operation of selection (paradigmatic) and combination (syntagmatic), the German language is characterized by the great importance of combination, both at the systemic level and as a process of semantic innovation. This "Lego set" functions both in everyday language and within each code or subsystem. We also find it in philosophical language, where the omnipresence of combinations plays a crucial role in conceptualization. That certainly does not mean that speakers of German spontaneously become "philosophers" or theoreticians merely by virtue of their language, but it remains that in German one can, quite differently from in French, conceptualize on the basis of the language's basic rules and, as it were, "do philosophy with grammar."

But the philosophical use of German grammar is based on a paradox. On the one hand, philosophical language seems to seek to make manifest language's ontological implications, and on the other, it extracts itself from the natural gangue of language by using the flexibility inherent in writing to bring out the difference between the concept and the linguistic given, thus emphasizing the emergence of the concept. Without claiming to offer a historical account or a rigorous study of the properly linguistic aspect of this question, we will first examine briefly the role played by combination at the level of individual words and then bring out, using the extreme example of the language games peculiar to Heidegger, the simultaneously linguistic and philosophical conditions of the translatability and untranslatability of the concept of *Gestell*. Then we will show how, by creating the concept of *Gefährt*, the philosopher Hans-Dieter Bahr rewrites and unwrites the Heideggerian *Gestell* by giving language still another twist.

I. Combinations and Conceptual Resources

A. The double register of combinations

The German language constantly uses a double register of combinations. The first register corresponds to the mechanism that Saussure called, in chapter 6 of his *Course on General Linguistics*, "syntagmatic interdependence," and which is a generalizable phenomenon of the constitution of meaning. The second register is completely specific to German and entails important consequences regarding the nature of philosophical writing.

By "syntagmatic interdependence" Saussure refers to the fact that in any arrangement of signs, the combination of elements functions as a mathematical "product" insofar as combination creates meaning independently of the original meaning of the elements it arranges. He speaks of a "combination of interdependent elements, their value deriving solely from their mutual contributions within a higher unit" (see RT: *Cours de linguistique générale*; English trans. here by Roy Harris) and gives as an example *désireux*, which is not a semantic addition of two elements—*désir* and *eux*, but rather the mathematical "product" of their juxtaposition.

But for word construction German uses a parallel type of construction in which, at the end of the process of combination, each original element retains more or less completely its literal meaning. Whence the impression that German is more "motivated" than French, that is, that the sign is less arbitrary in German because the relation between signifier and signified is more constantly discernible. Thus a railway station or yard is called a *Bahnhof* (*Bahn* = way [cf. *Eisenbahn* (railway)] + *Hof* = court or yard), whereas *Bauernhof* (*Bauer* = farmer + *Hof*), that is, a farm, is verbatim a "peasant's yard," and *Gasthof* (inn) is the combination of *Gast* (guest) and *Hof*, etc. Similarly, a restaurant in a railway station is a *Bahnhofgaststätte*, that is, a railway (*Bahn*) + court (*Hof*) + guest (*Gast*) + place (*Stätte*).

Of course, the rules of combination are governed by numerous constraints, whether within the words or in their arrangement; it remains that the resources of combination in German are particularly rich in comparison with those of other European languages. They are even virtually unlimited, and the result is constant linguistic innovation. Although German has retained a certain number of combinations that eventually join the reservoir of words reflected by a given historical state of the dictionary, creation is incessant. New combinations can be invented at any time, no matter what later happens to them.

We could say that in a certain sense combination is more important than selection, or that it draws selection to it, or that it exercises a pressure on it, with the result that a few elements make it possible to deploy a multiplicity of meanings. For example, it suffices to take verbs as polyvalent as those corresponding to *mettre* and *poser* in French—*setzen*, *legen*, and *stellen*—and to combine them with prepositions such as *an*, *aus*, *ab*, *vor*, etc., or with verbal particles such as *dar*, *ver*, *zu*, *ent*, *um*, etc., in order to deploy, by combining verb and preverb, a considerable number of meanings that in French would require recourse to an equally considerable number of different verbs. If we actuate the combinatorial process that governs the syntagmatic environment of the verbs *legen*, *stellen*, and *sitzen* alone, we obtain the following translations—and here we are limiting ourselves to indicating just a few of their common arrangements—*sich auf etwas einstellen*, "adapt to something" (whereas "to meddle or be involved in something" is expressed by *sich mit etwas abgeben*); *etwas umstellen*, "invert or rearrange something"; *sich umstellen*, "adapt to a new situation"; *seine Uhr umstellen*, "reset one's watch"; *auf ein Pferd setzen*, "bet on a horse"; *Wert auf etwas legen*, "assign value to something"; *zulegen*, "speed up"; *eine Platte auflegen*, "put a record on"; *etwas verstellen*, "mislay something"; *sich verstellen*, "dissimulate"; *sich einsetzen*, "go to bat for something or someone"; *sich durchsetzen*, "assert oneself" or "pay dearly for something"; *etwas jemandem zustellen*, "mail something to someone"; *Vieh umlegen*, "slaughter livestock"; *sich auf etwas hinsetzen*, "sit down on something"; *jemandem etwas hinstellen*, "deposit or put something somewhere for someone," etc.

It has to be emphasized that in German determination by particles and preverbs is very clearly spatial in nature: for example, the preverb *an* is formed on the basis of the preposition *an*, which indicates the idea of contiguity, whereas the particle *um* is formed on the basis of the preposition *um*, which means "around." But *an* also has a temporal, inchoative value, and the preverb *um* can indicate a process of change (*seine Uhr umstellen*, "to reset one's watch"; *sich umstellen*, "to adapt"; *etwas umwerfen*, "overturn something"); the idea of a Freudian *Verschiebung* (displacement) is already in the particle *ver-*, which itself indicates movement or delay, just as *Entstellung* is semantically invoked by the particle *ent-*, itself indicating an idea of deformation, etc. Not only is the concrete and spatial aspect usually more visible than it is in French, whose Latin substrate is not in principle obvious and requires a knowledge of etymology (for example, to discern the Latin preposition *ad* in *apporter*, from *ad* and *portare*, or *inde* in *emporter*, from *inde* and *portare*), but the rise from the empirical to the transcendental is implicit in the play of combination in German, since it allows the passage from the spatial to the temporal, from the concrete to the conceptual, and from the representable to the idea.

B. The resources made available to philosophical language by ordinary combination

These procedures, which are particularly effective at the level of the linguistic system, offer conceptualization and philosophical language unlimited resources.

It suffices, in fact, to repeat this movement of language by reusing its elements and the rules of their combination to promote the word to the status of a concept. But moreover, this reuse of grammar is never limited to a simple repetition. There is repetition and differentiation.

In his book on Freud's language, Georges-Arthur Goldschmidt states, not without forcing things a bit:

> There is nothing simpler or more immediate than the philosophical vocabulary. Chapter 1 of the *Phenomenology of Mind,* "Die sinnliche Gewißheit" ("Sense-certainty"; it is true that German can hardly differentiate between "sensible," "sensorial," and "sensual"), consists from beginning to end of words familiar to a five-year-old child (with perhaps the exception of *Vermittlung,* "mediation," and *Unmittelbarkeit,* "immediacy").

> (G. A. Goldschmidt, *Quand Freud voit la mer*)

There is something profoundly true in this exaggeration, and it is hardly exaggerated to say that the most common, everyday German is very often potentially the German of ontology. For example, when one wants to say that someone is undergoing withdrawal (from drugs, etc.), one says that *er leidet unter* (he suffers under) *Entzugserscheinung. Erscheinung* also means "apparition," "phenomenon" in the philosophical sense, and *Entzug,* which here means "weaning," also means "withdrawal." Suffering is thus expressed by the same words that serve to refer to the withdrawal of Being.

It would, of course, be a kind of fetishization to conclude that German, like Greek, is from the outset and by nature the language of metaphysics (the shame-faced French version) or, worse yet, that one can philosophize only in German (the triumphalist German version).

All the examples just mentioned show that two effects are in fact conjoined: at the lexical level we see the possibility of an immediate passage from ordinary language to philosophical language—as if the latter "mirrored" the everyday, and vice versa; and at the syntactical level, combinatorial procedures that are particularly effective for language proper offer major resources for conceptualization and philosophical language.

Let us emphasize once again that this does not mean that we move immediately from everyday language to the language of philosophy. There is both repetition and differentiation. There is repetition because it suffices to reduplicate processes of linguistic combination, reusing their elements and rules to extract the concept from a preconceptual discourse. But the repetition is marked as both repetition and difference. To give a famous example, the noun *Aufhebung* does exist in language in its normal and normed state, but it does not have the double meaning that Hegel

gives it, whereas the verb *aufheben* can in fact mean "preserve," "raise," or "cancel." The properly dialectical meaning that Hegel gives the noun *Aufhebung* is as distant from the norm in German (because normally *Aufhebung* means simply "abolition," "suspension [of a session]") as it is irremediably untranslatable in French. On the other hand, Hegel himself often uses the verb *aufheben* in the completely customary sense of "cancel." The concept deepens the gap between ordinary language and philosophical language but without there being any need to invent a new terminology (see AUFHEBEN).

It is here that we encounter the problem of the *Fremdwort,* that is, the use of a foreign term, usually of Latin or French origin, in order to express what German can say by means of the procedures we have just isolated. Concepts of foreign origin, precisely because they are outside the ordinary language / philosophical language circuit, are perceived as odd, arbitrary, even incomprehensible. Thus *Willkür,* from *Wille,* "will," and *Kür,* "choice," hence "free will," but the word *Arbitrarität* is "not well-received." It is spontaneously rejected.

C. Untranslatability and the evolution of translations

Taken all together, these phenomena are prodigiously effective for German philosophical writing and constitute one of the main reasons why a large part of its vocabulary cannot be translated word for word. The latitude that German grants combination contrasts very strongly with the situation of French, where the irreducible distance between one word and another requires conceptual creation to take quite a different path: the concept of writing cannot mean the same thing in German and French because the processes of conceptualization do not take place on the same stage.

The result is a strange to-and-fro between German and French, the direction of which can be totally reversed over time. Thus, it is striking to note that in the nineteenth century French translations of German philosophical texts had a strong tendency to Gallicize the text, whereas in the twentieth century, and especially after World War II, the tendency was on the contrary to "Germanize" French philosophical language. Under the pressure of this new *habitus,* we are no longer surprised to read *chosification* (modeled on *Verdinglichung*) or *déterminité* (modeled on *Bestimmtheit*). The effect of contamination is obvious and in no way disconfirms what has just been said. In this case, although the words are French, it is a question of a peculiarly German philosophical idiom that has been acclimated in the philosophical language. Generalized, it would lead to an idiom completely separate from everyday French, whereas for the German philosophical language the same phenomena have their very distant source in the abandonment of Latin as the scholarly language in modern Germany, especially since the eighteenth century.

II. An Extreme and Revealing Example: The Heideggerian *Ge-Stell*

A. The terminological constellation of technology

Let us take, as an extreme illustration, the case of Heidegger. In *Die Technik und die Kehre,* he sets forth his philosophy of technology on the basis of a small group of words whose treatment illustrates perfectly the mechanisms under discussion: the concept is dissociated from ordinary language in accord with principles of combination and re-marking. The word *Kehre*, which was used from the sixteenth to the nineteenth centuries and meant "turn," "return" (like the plow at the end of the furrow) or, in a Pietist context, "(spiritual) conversion," has disappeared from ordinary language, which uses the forms of *kehr-* only in the form of a combinatory element—for example, *Rückkehr*, "return from," *Abkehr*, "the act of turning away from," *Verkehr*, "commerce, traffic," *Wiederkehr*, "return, comeback," etc.—or of *kehrt-* (for example, *kehrtmachen*, "make a U-turn, turn back"). The linguistic "turn" represented by *die Kehre*, the "twist" that Heidegger gives language, thus consists in fabricating a word, *die Kehre*, by analogy with *die Wende*, "the turning point, the reversal," with the strong connotations of temporality that the word implies, especially in the sense of "historical turning point" or "reversal of the sequence of events."

The twist to which Heidegger subjects the language leads him to a deliberate overdetermination: *die Kehre* is a return(ing), a turning like returning. Heidegger designates thereby the return/anamnesis of Being manifested and concealed by technology, or a new way of conceiving technology in its nontechnological essence.

The two other verbs that provide the linguistic core of conceptualization in this text are *bergen* and *stellen*. *Bergen*, *stellen*, *Ge-Stell*, *Kehre*, to which is added *Bestand* (from the verb *bestehen*, "exist"), form a constellation of words on the basis of which Heidegger conceptualizes technology's relation to Being.

B. The re-marking of *Ge-stell*

In the case of *Ge-stell*, a typical example of the untranslatable, Heidegger, who is well aware that the word he is creating is unusual, excuses himself for the challenge that his creation represents and feels obliged to explain it in order not to be incomprehensible. "Wir wagen es, dieses Wort in einem bisher völlig ungewohnten Sinne zu gebrauchen" ("We dare to use this word in a way completely unusual up to now"; *Die Technik und die Kehre*, 1978, p. 19). After reminding us that the Platonic term *eidos* is far more daring than *Ge-Stell*, he concludes by saying that the use he makes of the latter almost demands too much of language and thus might lead to misunderstandings.

- See Box 1.

Ge-Stell, an untranslatable term par excellence, has unfortunately been acclimated in French in the form of the term *arraisonnement*. In André Préau's translation of Heidegger's *Essais et Conférences*, we find the following note (p. 26), which seeks to justify the choice of the term:

> We have seen this root figure in a small group of verbs designating either fundamental operations of reason and science (following the trace, presenting, highlighting, representing, explaining) or measures of technology's authority (questioning, requiring, deciding, committing, setting up, ensuring, etc.). *Stellen* is at the center of this group; here it is "to stop someone in the street to demand an explanation, to force him to *rationem reddere*" (Heid.), that is, to ask for his sufficient reason. The idea is taken up again in *Der Satz vom Grund*

(1957). Technology calls nature to account, boards and inspects it [*l'arraisonne*], requires that everything justify itself before the tribunal of reason and in accord with its norms.

In *Questions IV*, the translator's note on p. 155 is hardly more illuminating, and translators, who rightly challenge the translation given in *Essais et Conférences*, clear themselves of responsibility by concluding that the term is untranslatable:

> And they add: "It seemed to us impossible to find in French a word corresponding to *Stellen* and rendering all the derivations Heidegger attaches to the verb *stellen*: *Gestell*, *Nachstellen*, *nachstellen*, *verstellen*, *Bestellen*.

There is, of course, no single verb that translates the German *stellen* in all cases and in such a way that one could find it in all the combinations of the original. But there are other factors that help make *Ge-stell* untranslatable. To lay out the logic of the concept insofar as it arises in and through writing, we can start from the place in the text where Heidegger explains the reasons for his choice. He writes:

> Wir nennen jetzt jenen herausfordernden Anspruch, der den Menschen dahin versammelt, das Sichentbergende als Bestand zu bestellen—das Ge-Stell . . . . Ge-Stell heißt das Versammelnde jenes Stellens, das den Menschen stellt, d.h. herausfordert, das Wirkliche in der Weise des Bestellens als Bestand zu entbergen. Ge-Stell heißt die Weise des Entbergens, die im Wesen der modernen Technik waltet und selber nichts Technisches ist. Zum Technischen gehört dagegen alles, was wir als Gestänge und Geschiebe und Gerüste kennen und was als Betand-stück dessen ist, was man Montage nennt.

Here is André Préau's French translation of this passage in *Essais et Conférences*:

> Maintenant cet appel pro-voquant qui rassemble l'homme (autour de la tâche) de commettre comme fonds ce qui se dévoile, nous l'appelons—l'Arraisonnement . . . . Ainsi appelons-nous le rassemblant de cette interpellation qui requiert l'homme, c'est-à-dire le pro-voque à dévoiler le réel comme fonds dans le mode du « commettre ». Ainsi appelons-nous le mode de dévoilement qui régit l'essence de la technique moderne et n'est lui-même rien de technique. Fait en revanche partie de ce qui est technique tout ce que nous connaissons en fait de tiges, de pistons, d'échafaudages, tout ce qui est pièce constitutive de ce que l'on appelle un montage. (28–29)

Here we can make three observations:

1. Heidegger clearly distinguishes between the technicity of technology, represented by the terms for which he gives the generic principle of construction, and thus technology as a material procedure functioning by means of machine-like arrangement, from the nontechnical essence of technology, which is the object of his reflection. This distinction itself corresponds to a double use of language: the normal use, which describes technology as machinery, and the term *Ge-Stell*, which reconstructs language by combining two elements against their nature: *Ge*, which refers to the seme of

1

Gestell

➤ VORHANDEN

In German, the word *Gestell* usually means frame(work), mount, setting. As Heidegger remarks, "In ordinary usage, the word *Gestell* refers to some kind of apparatus, for example, a bookrack. *Gestell* is also the name for a skeleton" (*Question concerning Technology*). The word entered the philosophical vocabulary in Heidegger's work—probably in the 1953 lecture "The Question of Technology," where it characterized the essence of modern technology—or technology as such. Although it is not a neologism, the term must nonetheless be understood as a neologism in view of the fact that it is used by Heidegger in a broad, unexpected, unusual sense to designate the whole or the collection (which is indicated by the prefix *Ge-*) of all the modes of setting (Ger. *stellen*) that causes man's way of wanting to impose modern technology on the whole planet ultimately to enslave him as the servant of what he intended to have at his service.

Starting in the 1950s, Heidegger called *Gestell* what in the 1930s he had called *Machenschaft*—not, of course, in the common sense of "machination," but as "the realm of doing" or even "efficiency."

Regarding the choice of the term *Gestell*, Heidegger told the German news magazine *Der Spiegel*:

Das Wesen der Technik sehe ich in dem, was ich das "Ge-Stell" nenne. Der Name, beim ersten Hören leicht mißverständlich, recht bedacht, weist, was er meint, in die innerste Geschichte der Metaphysik zurück, die heute noch unser Dasein bestimmt. Das Walten des Ge-Stells besagt: Der Mensch ist gestellt, beansprucht und herausgefordert von einer Macht, die im Wesen der Technik offenbar wird.

(I see the essence of technology in what I call the *Ge-Stell*. This term, which is easily misunderstood when first heard, when correctly conceived refers what it designates back to the innermost history of metaphysics, which still determines our existence. The reign of the *Ge-stell* means: man is subject to the control, the demands, and the provocation of a power that is manifested in the essence of technology.)

("Martin Heidegger im Gespräch," in *Antwort*; M. Heidegger, *Reden und andere Zeugnisse eines Lebensweges*)

As he remarked as early as a lecture given in 1953, Heidegger proposes to interpret *Gestell* in a "completely unusual" (*völlig ungewohnt*) way, on the model of *Gebirg* (mountain range) or *Gemüt*.

Let us attempt here a brief comparison of two French translations of the term *Gestell*. *Arraisonnement*, a public-health term, means "a careful examination of a ship that is suspect for health reasons" (Littré), and *arraisonner un navire* also means, in a maritime and hygienic context, "to find out where a vessel is coming from and where it is going." But, in addition, *arraisonner* means "to seek to persuade by giving arguments." It is this twofold meaning that A. Préau has in mind when he justifies his translation: "Technology calls nature to account, boards and inspects it [*l'arraisonne*], requires that everything justify itself before the tribunal of reason and in accord with its norms" (translator's note in "La question de la technique," tr. Préau, 26). The translation of *Gestell* by *arraisonnement* is certainly a discovery that stimulates thought by situating the essence—or rather the site of modern technology—in the realm of reason and the principle of reason, *rationem reddere*. But it is also open to criticism because the *Gestell* does not express itself using the vocabulary of reason. "A good translation" and at the same time one that is "eminently interpretive," says F. Fédier, and in addition one that "lets us glimpse what the word *Gestell* means as Heidegger uses it," but only on condition that the word *arraisonnement* be understood "to express a rational, systematic treatment in which everything is already grasped in the framework of arrangements to be made in order to provide a *solution* for *problems*" (*Regarder voir*, pp. 206–8). Fédier himself proposes *dispositif* (apparatus) as a translation for *Gestell* or, in a more developed way, *dispositif unitaire de la consommation*, meaning by that "all the prior measures by means of which everything is made available in advance in the framework of a putting in order." Here all explicit reference to reason has disappeared. On the other hand, the root *stell* of the verb *stellen* (set, set up) has a prominent place in the apparatus. Nonetheless, a circumlocution is necessary to render the meaning of the German collective prefix *Ge-* : *unitaire* and the *cum* in *consommation* indicate it doubly.

Pascal David

BIBLIOGRAPHY

Fédier, François. *Regarder voir*. Les Belles Lettres/ Archimbaud, 1995.

Heidegger, Martin. *Antwort—Martin Heidegger im Gespräch*. Pfullingen, Ger.: Neske, 1988.

———. "The Question concerning Technology," in *Basic Writings*, edited by D. F. Krell. San Francisco, CA: HarperSanFrancisco, 1993.

———. "Only a God Can Save Us: The Spiegel Interview with Martin Heidegger." In *Heidegger, the Man and the Thinker*, edited by T. Sheehan, 45–67. Chicago: Precedent, 1981.

———. *Reden und andere Zeugnisse eines Lebensweges*. In *Gesammtausgabe*, vol. 16. Frankfurt: Klostermann, 2000.

construction (the act of putting together, assembling) and *stell*, torn away from the usual semantics of the word *Gestell*, which can mean, for instance, "scaffolding, rack, skeleton" (these are Heidegger's own examples). There is a layering, and the product thus obtained becomes useless for ordinary use—whence Heidegger's fears of being misunderstood. The word is uprooted, and the usual rules of combination (*Ge* + *stell*) have produced a surplus of meaning well indicated by Heidegger's way of writing the word with the dash characteristic of re-marking.

2. When Heidegger writes: "What originally unfolds mountains in lines and runs all through them in the fold of their cohesion is this collector we call a 'mountain range'" (Was die Berge ursprünglich zu Bergzügen entfaltet und sie in ihrem gefalteten Beisammen durchzieht, ist das Versammelnde, das wir Gebirg nennen) (*Die Technik und die Kehre*), this sentence is difficult to understand if one does not see in it the play of oppositions between traits (*Bergzügen*, translated here as "lines" [*lignes*]), fold (*entfaltet*, "unfolds," and *gefaltet*, "folded," with all the Leibnizian and Goethean connotations of *Vielfalt* and *Mannigfaltigkeit*, "multiplicity" and "diversity"), and cohesion (*Beisammen*). In this semantic constellation the *Ge-* in *Gebirge* (*der Berg*, "mountain," *das Gebirge*, "mountain range") is equivalent to the seme Totality

(a collecting totality). Just as the range is what "runs through" and collects the diverse, the *Ge-* in *Ge-stell* attracts attention to what, beyond the functionality of machine-like construction, is the whole—an ideal, nonpresentable whole that merges with Being and masks it in and through its function and state. That is what all French translators note, following in the footsteps of Heidegger (*Essais et Conférences*, 26n1 and 348n2; *Etre et temps*, 355n1). It is clear that the French term *arraisonnement* in no way reflects these remarks, unlike Fédier's *dispositif unitaire*.

3. The semantic derivation of *Gestell* on the model of *Gebirge* (the idea of collection) and not of *Gestänge* or *Geschiebe* (assembly or collection) thus moves the seme "assembly" toward the seme "collection." But this holds only for the *Ge-* in *Ge-stell*. The second part of the term has to be related to the system of conceptual marks that Heidegger elaborates around *stellen*, and which it is not impossible to describe, despite what the translators of *Questions IV* say. The meaning of *stellen* that André Préau borrows from Heidegger and cites in his note ("to stop someone on the street to demand an explanation, to force him to *rationem reddere*") might provide support for the idea of *arraisonnement*. But in *Der Satz vom Grund*, Heidegger gives a quite different commentary on the relation between *stellen* and *rationem reddere*. As always in his work, the commentary gives rise to new expansions of the conceptual constellation. Everything turns on the meaning of *reddere*. Heidegger emphasizes that *ratio* is *ratio reddenda*, reason is a rendering. After proposing as German translations for *reddere* the words *zurückgeben*, "to render, give back," and *herbeibringen*, "to bring," he adds *zu-stellen*, with the hyphen of the philosophical remark. The postal analogy is explicit: "Wir sprechen von der Zustellung der Post. Die ratio ist ratio reddenda" (We are speaking of delivering the mail. Reason is *ratio reddenda*) (*Der Satz vom Grund*, 47). "Delivering the mail": we are far from the pirate metaphor of boarding and inspecting (*arraisonnement*); instead, we are concerned with the logic of the return to sender. Reason sends the world back to itself and thereby renders account of it. The spatial metaphor (return to sender) can be related systematically to the thematics of Being as "a sending" (*Schickung* or *Geschick*), rendered in French as *envoi*, a word that plays cleverly (let us note in passing that "cleverly" can be translated as *geschickt, mit viel Geschick*) on the semantic ambivalence between destiny (see SCHICKSAL) and sending, which in Heidegger is systematically related—but in a rhizomatic way—with history and historicity (see GESCHICHTLICH). Heidegger never ceases to *zu-stellen*. In the lines following the paragraph quoted above, he says explicitly that he includes in the verb *stellen* the connotations of *her-stellen*, "fabricate, produce," and *dar-stellen*, "represent," both referring to *poiêsis*. If then *Ge-Stell* brings together the whole of the construction, it produces and represents. It is the essence of technological construction as presenting totality. But in order to present Being, technology penetrates it. It opens it up, pierces it, transforms

it, redistributes it, and in that way brings it out, reveals it—that is the concept of *Entbergen*.

The constellation of concepts grouped around the verb *bergen*—which is central for Heidegger, since it is explicitly developed elsewhere to explain the concept of truth as *Unverborgenheit*, on the basis of the Greek *alêtheia*—refers in German to an original ambivalence given by language. Like the famous verb *aufheben* at the origin of Hegelian thinking, the verb *bergen* is ambiguous from the outset, because it means both "conceal" (like *verbergen*) and "bring out" (for example, victims buried under ruins). Heidegger recomposes the Greek *alêtheia* by resorting to the concept of *Unverborgenheit*, constructed on the basis of the verb *verbergen* ("conceal," but also "hide from our sight"). Thus *alêtheia* is the essence of what was hidden from our sight (*verborgen*) and appears as if unburied, un-concealed. That is why the "poïetic" part of *Ge-Stell* refers to the ambivalence of technology, which brings out Being but at the same time veils it, since reason receives back only its own image, which it sends to itself.

However, since each displacement, each condensation of the term, encounters not words belonging to the "natural" state of language but ones that have already been displaced, uprooted from their meaning, things are still more complicated. For example, there is *bestellen*, which is caught up in the rhizomatic links surrounding *-stell* and *Ge-stell*, and in no way corresponds to the normal sense.

Normally, to *bestellen* something means to "order something" (as one orders an article from a catalogue), or to "reserve" (for example, a theater seat), or again "ask someone to come somewhere, summon," not to mention other uses, such as *schlecht bestellt sein um jemanden*, "someone is in a bad way." But in Heidegger, and especially in the context of *Die Technik und die Kehre*, the verb *bestellen* means something else. Its use, which is completely unusual and in reality incorrect in all its occurrences, elicits each time, and always indirectly, the idea of having something at one's disposal, of using an apparatus or being dependent on it. As such, *bestellen* is thus opposed to *Bestand*, "inventory," as *Ge-Stell* is opposed to the idea of construction; the opposition is anchored in part in language, through the opposition between *stehen*, "to stand," and *stellen*, "to set up." *Bestellen* is the act of "putting in" (put in an order, put in place, put in cultivation, etc.). Reason catches nature in a trap and by doing so is caught in its own trap.

The technological availability of the world thus catches Being in a trap, tracks it down; entities are thus sought, observed, invented; nature is pursued in an apparatus of representation until the object (*Gegenstand*: that which is [*steht*] before [*gegen*] the eyes) disappears as an object and, becoming inconsistent (*gegenstandlos*), it reappears as a simple inventory, as consistency (*Bestand*): it is the movement from *Gegenstand* to *Bestand* (see OBJECT). In ordinary language *Bestand* corresponds to being appropriated and possessed (patrimony, inventory, substance, list), to whatever constitutes some existing thing in the mode of belonging. To constitute a *Bestand* is to store up such things, in and through technology.

Ge-Stell is thus the part of Being that we have made available (*bestellbar*, in Heidegger's vocabulary) and which manifests it by disguising it as *Bestand*. That is why, as Heidegger says toward the end of the text, if the fate of being (*das Geschick*), its sending, reigns in the mode of the *Ge-Stell*, then we are "in the greatest danger." But this conclusion differs from the view of the ecology movement because the famous "return/turning point" (*Kehre*), the "conversion" with which Heidegger's reflection ends, is the recognition that the greatest danger is also the greatest good fortune—even the salvation that is evoked by Hölderlin's verses quoted by Heidegger: "Wo aber Gefahr ist, wächst / Das Rettende auch." Salvation consists in turning toward that which—in technology, but beyond its *Ge-Stell* and the narcissistic trap of its apparatus—manifests the sending/destiny of Being.

The *Ge-Stell* is thus not an *arraisonnement*. It might be better to render *Ge-Stell* as "un-hiding" or even "hide and seek."

III. *Gefährt* and *Gestell*:
Hans-Dieter Bahr's reply to Heidegger

Heidegger's language constitutes a limit-state for philosophical writing, and if the contagion of the operation of re-marking is unlimited in his work—the term "rhizome" is clearly not excessive to describe what happens in it—it would be wrong to believe that the contagion is limited to the margins of his work. In philosophy, as in literature, a text never comes along all by itself. From Adorno to Ernst Bloch or Ulrich Sonnemann, to mention only them, there is no lack of examples that would show the permanence of a philosophical writing that contrasts strongly with the pompous waffling of certain contemporary German philosophers, who consider the excess of personal writing style peculiar to Heidegger as inseparable from his political compromises and who have inevitably concluded that precision of thought involves giving up a personal style. The following few lines by Hans Dieter Bahr, one of the young German philosophers who have not given up a personal writing style, shows that the reply is never long in coming. In the essay from which these lines are taken, which appeared in 1985 under the title *Sätze ins Nichts* (Sentences [cast] into Nothingness, or Leaps into Nothingness) and which is devoted to the subject of the city, Bahr replies, in a very beautiful language whose richness makes most of the terms untranslatable into French, to the Heideggerian *Ge-stell*.

Das Gefährt . . . Aus mehreren Gründen scheint mir das Technische genauer als Gefährt denn als "Gestell" verstehbar zu sein. Beschreibt Heidegger auch durchaus Fahrt und Gefahr der Technik, so doch zu sehr an eine enge Dialektik unbeständiger Bestandssicherung gebunden, als verfügten wir bereits über eine neue Schrift, die jene Technik wiedergebe. Über das Technische der Verfügungen, Sicherungen und steuernden Verschickungen hinaus mit all ihren katastrophalen Entgleisungen, ist Technik zudem Trans-Mission, schwappt über sich als Sendung und Nachricht, als Zutragung und Zuständigkeit hinaus, schreibt sich über unser Können und Verstehen hinaus, in Schriften, die man nicht weniger mühevoll dechiffriren wird als jene der Natur, schwerer vielleicht, zumal wenn sich das genealogische Vertrauen vorschiebt und technische Dinge als irgendwie menschliche Kinder, Ausdruck unserer selbst, unserer Triebe und Willen oder als Geburten artungleicher

Befruchtungen zwischen Natur und Menschen begriffen werden sollen.

(The vehicle . . . For many reasons, it seems to me that technology is more precisely understood as *Gefährt* [vehicle] than as *Gestell*. Heidegger does refer to technology as a journey and a danger, but in doing so remains too closely bound to a narrow dialectic of the erratic [*unbeständiger*] preservation of what has been acquired [*Bestandssicherung*: "preservation of the status quo, of a stock of goods"] as if we already had a new writing style that renders this technology. Beyond the technology of controlling, securing, and regulating sendings, with all its catastrophic derailments, technology is also trans-mission, it exceeds its sendings and reports, its deliveries and its jurisdiction, and writes itself beyond our capacities and our understanding, in writings that humans will decipher with no less difficulty than those of nature, perhaps even more, especially if trust in genealogy shoulders its way in and technological things are seen as a kind of human children, an expression of ourselves, our drives and our wills, or as the progeny of unnatural cross-fertilizations between humans and nature.)

(*Sätze ins Nichts*)

Here *Gefährt* is played against *Gestell*. But it is not enough to note the substitution of one term for the other; we also have to look into the use of language that makes the substitution possible. Hans Dieter Bahr, who refuses to continue thinking technology on the basis of the idea of "collection" (*Versammlung*), prepares his operation of destitution by thematizing—using the example of the description of Greek vases based, from Aristotle to Heidegger by way of Simmel, on the concept of collection—their multiple function as "trans-lators." The word "trans-lation" (*Übertragung*) does not mean "transport" in the sense that the distance between two places is abolished. The translation carried out by the recipient is a vehicular movement, in that it accompanies what it moves, and the history of its sending is one of the dangers that lie in wait for both its content and its goal. The vehicle/recipient is not only the bearer of changing contents, but is itself borne, it is the bearer/borne, and its content is as ambivalent as its being since it can both "bring misfortune by transporting the damage, the poison, or even the ashes of the dead or a simple emptiness, after being robbed on the way." Whereas in the *Interpretation of Dreams* Freud uses the two different concepts, *Übertragung* ("translation," and then "transfer") and *Verschiebung* (displacement) to make a distinction between the transportation of one entity into another, Bahr connects them. This connection, and the semantic renewal that it produces, is based on what claims to be a literal interpretation of the verb *übertragen*: *über-tragen* means movement (*über*) and carrying (*tragen*), and thus *Übertragung* is a kind of "passage-support." For Bahr the trans-lation (*Über-tragung*) carried out by the recipient is a vehicular movement insofar as it accompanies what it moves.

Although the content of the text runs counter to Heidegger's philosophy of technology, whose "narrow dialectic" it criticizes, the counter-thesis remains inseparable from a subversion of the writing style, which consists in disengaging the Heideggerian *Gestell* from its semantic interconnections and in displacing it, as it were, in situ. This is precisely the idea of displacement that then proceeds to disturb the play of Heideggerian style and to destabilize its stakes.

Das Gefährt is the vehicle. The word in ordinary language would be *Fahrzeug* or in technical language, *Vehikel*, and the term *Gefährt* is, moreover, old-fashioned. But once it has been torn out of the register to which usage has limited it, it "de-dialecticalizes" that which, in the Heideggerian *Gestell*, referred multiplicity and arbitrariness to the fate of Being. Language, no less inventive and filled, by its very richness, with untranslatables, is open to the world as the thematics it sets forth, namely, a technology that is, like language, a mode of writing, and to which it would be vain to think that we can ever get the key in advance.

Heidegger is no doubt the one who has made the most vertiginous use of the procedures described here, and few German philosophers currently use the resources of German style to as much effect as Hans Dieter Bahr. The question remains open to what point this extreme tendency shown by Heideggerian writing reconnects with a kind of writing whose tracks lead back to the mystics of the Rhineland, and also to what extent it is connected with the affirmation of a specifically German philosophical tradition whose appearance coincided with the need to distinguish itself from both the use of Latin and the literary use of the language. There are many studies on this question, and research is far from complete. The role of Christian Wolff in the eighteenth century and his explicit project of constituting a linguistic artificiality drawing its resources exclusively from German, notably by elaborating adequate artifices, *Künstwörter*, were crucial for the specific development of German philosophical writing. But we also have to take into account the archeology of the German philosophical language and the play of exchange and differentiation between linguistic procedure and conceptual procedure proper that we have described here. No doubt this work remains largely to be done.

Jean-Pierre Dubost

BIBLIOGRAPHY

Bahr, Hans Dieter. *Sätze ins Nichts*. Tübingen: Konkursbuch, 1985.

Belaval, Yvon. *Les philosophes et leur langage*. Paris: Gallimard / La Pléiade, 1952.

Dubost, Jean-Pierre, and Winfried Busse. *Französisches Verblexikon: Die Konstruktion der Verben im Französischen*. Stuttgart: Ernst Klett, 1983.

Goldschmidt, Georges Arthur. *Quand Freud voit la mer: Freud et la langue allemande*. Paris: Buchet-Castel, 1988. Reprinted 2006.

Heidegger, Martin. *Basic Writings*, edited by D. F. Krell. San Francisco, CA: HarperSanFrancisco, 1993.

———. *Essais et conférences*. French translation by A. Préau. Paris: Gallimard / La Pléiade, 1958.

———. *Etre et temps*. Translated by Claude Roëls and Jean Lauxerois. Paris: Gallimard / La Pléiade, 1986.

———. *Questions IV*. French translation by F. Beaufret. Paris: Gallimard / La Pléiade, 1976. Translation by A. Mitchell and F. Raffoul: *Four Seminars*. Bloomington: Indiana University Press, 2003.

———. *Der Satz vom Grund*. Pfullingen: Neske, 1957. French translation by A. Préau. Paris: Gallimard, 1962. Translation by R. Lilly: *The Principle of Reason*. Bloomington: Indiana University Press, 1991.

———. *Die Technik und die Kehre*. Pfullingen: Neske, 1978. Translation by W. Lovitt: "The Turning." In *The Question concerning Technology and Other Essays*, 36–49. New York: HarperPerennial, 1982.

Rousseau, André. "Fonctionnement des préverbes allemands." In *Les préverbes dans les langues d'Europe. Introductions à l'étude de la préverbation*, 127–88. Presses Universitaires du Septentrion, 1995.

COMMON SENSE (ENGLISH)

FRENCH	*sens commun*
LATIN	*sensus communis*

➤ *SENS COMMUN*, and ENGLISH, MORALS, PHRONÊSIS, POLITICS, PRINCIPLE, SENSE, TRUTH

The clearest philosophical uses of the expression "common sense" date from the early eighteenth century and especially the work of Shaftesbury and Thomas Reid. The tradition of commonsense philosophy that begins with eighteenth-century English and Scottish writers starts from the meaning of "common sense" as a shared way of feeling and assessing (*sensorium commune*) to find its origin in an evocation of sociability, a sense of community (*sensus communis*). But English-language philosophy also defends the possibility of common sense as a true judgment or opinion that serves as the foundation for philosophy. Philosophical discourse is thus based on principles that are obvious truths for common sense and are preliminary to any knowledge. Reflection on common sense assumes that ordinary life has truth-value.

I. The Concept of "Common Sense"

Common sense, according to a minimal definition, is not a philosophical term. It designates a form of popular good sense. When one says, "Just use your common sense!" one is referring to the possibility of a practical wisdom, an ordinary apprehension of things. Thus to help people better understand love, marriage, children, and so on, there exist books with titles like *The Common Sense Book of Love and Marriage* and *The Common Sense Book of Baby and Child Care*. "Common sense" can also refer to the register of shared opinion. In David Hume, recourse to the general opinion of humanity, which prevents philosophy from going astray, functions like a common sense: "The general opinion of mankind has some authority in all cases; but in this of morals 'tis perfectly infallible" (*Treatise of Human Nature*, 552). Though the general opinion of mankind defines a common sense necessary for the establishment of a moral philosophy, the resort to common sense is sometimes more ambiguous; thus Hume mentions the truth of the proverb about the pointlessness of arguments about taste: "And thus common sense, which is so often at variance with philosophy, especially with the sceptical kind, is found, in one instance at least, to agree in pronouncing the same decision" (*Essays*, 235). Even if common sense is part of a relationship to the world different from that of philosophy, it sometimes allows us to save philosophy from the dangers of metaphysical uses by bringing it back to the ordinary uses of discourse. In other words, common sense serves as a point of anchorage in the usual, in the ordinary, in order to invoke the position of opinion with regard to a philosophical question: "Are there any irreducibly social goods? . . . Common Sense is divided on the issue, and confused" (Taylor, *Philosophical Arguments*, 127). We might say that this recourse to the *sensus communis* has existed since Greek antiquity and does not constitute something specific to common sense. The originality of the tradition of common sense resides in the concern to move from a simple appeal to common sense to a concept of common sense. That is the goal of Shaftesbury's *Essay on the Freedom of Wit and Humor*. The work begins with an account of an entertaining conversation on morals, politics, and religion. Among the different participants, some occasionally take "the liberty to appeal to common sense" (*Characteristics of Men*). Next, common sense is defined:

> But notwithstanding the different Judgments of Mankind in most Subjects, there were some however in which 'twas suppos'd they all agreed, and had the same Thoughts in common.

However, this definition of common sense is not developed further, because the emphasis is put on the impossibility of finding fundamental principles or common ideas of religion, morals, or politics. How could common sense help construct a practical philosophy?

II. The Sense of the Common Good

Shaftesbury, who was a great reader of the Stoics, took an interest in the use of "common sense" as *sensus communis*. In the works of Marcus Aurelius (*Meditations*, 1.16), *sensus communis*, which translates the Greek *hê koinonoêmosunê* [ἡ κοινονοημοσύνη], designates a sense of community, a sociability. Shaftesbury adopts this heritage and then gives priority to *common* (what is common to a community, the common good) over *sense* (the sensorial or cognitive faculty). "Common sense" refers to critical work performed on our representations to make them conform to the common good. Common sense expresses the "sense of publick weal, and of the common interest, the love for community or society, natural affection, humanity, obligingness, or that sort of civility which rises from a just sense of the common rights of mankind, and the natural equality there is among those of the same species" (*Characteristics of Men*). It is both a moral and a social sense of reason, structured by a virtue that consecrates the profound nature of man, honesty: "Men's first thoughts, in this matter, are generally better than their second; their natural notions better than those refined by study, or consultation with casuists. According to common speech, as well as common sense, Honesty is the best policy" (*Characteristics of Men*). Common sense differs from good sense to the extent that the latter, as the natural faculty of distinguishing the true from the false, is a factor of knowledge rather than of practical philosophy. Common sense is the social and political equivalent of moral sense. The latter designates a disposition or ability to form adequate ideas of the moral good. In contrast, common sense designates a disposition to form adequate ideas of the common interest. It presupposes the idea of a public space or public sphere. It is this meaning of "common sense," which is particularly present in English-language philosophy, that Michael Walzer discusses in *Interpretation and Social Criticism*.

The definition of the apprehension of the social world in the mode of social criticism continues this tradition of the sense of the common interest.

III. The Epistemology of "Common Sense"

It remains that common sense is also a fundamental concept for the theory of knowledge. The thought of Thomas Reid presupposes a rational comprehension of sense as judgment in order to establish an epistemological role for common sense:

> In common language sense always implies judgment. . . . Good sense is good judgment. . . . Common sense is that degree of judgment which is common to men with whom we can converse and transact business.

> (*Essays on the Intellectual Powers of Man*, 426)

In this case, common sense is close to good sense. Common sense as good sense is a judgment: it designates the part of reason that includes the primitive and natural judgments common to all humanity. It is, in a way, a common intelligence that spontaneously bears upon a certain number of objects of knowledge. From this point of view, this activity of the mind or exercise of judgment is more or less developed in each of us, depending on whether we are more or less experienced in making such judgments, more or less gifted:

> Common sense is . . . an exercise of the judgment unaided by any Art or system of rules: such an exercise as we must necessarily employ in numberless cases of daily occurrence. . . . He who is eminently skillful in doing this, is said to possess a superior degree of Common Sense.

> (Whately, *Elements of Logic*, preface)

Not having common sense does not amount here to a lack of wisdom in life's ordinary affairs; according to both Whately and Reid, it is, in a way, to lack intelligence, to deprive oneself of an a priori undetermined mode of judgment. Common sense constitutes the practical precondition for any knowledge, the whole of the pre-knowledge that is taken for granted and that it is harmful to put into doubt. It is embodied in principles that simply affirm the existence of our different ways of knowing. That is the case for the principle of the reality of the phenomena of consciousness: it has to be considered self-evident that people think, remember, and so on (*Essays*). The existence of the knowing subject is a factual truth, a principle of common sense or a natural judgment that is common to humanity and can thus be produced by anyone.

IV. Common Knowledge and Ordinary Life

Common sense is thus part of a philosophy and an epistemology through which, according to G. E. Moore, a commonsense view of the world can be achieved. It is not that common sense does not contain some false propositions, but the massive certainties that it contains, taken all together, constitute the truth of the commonsense view of the world. In a way, in conformity with Thomas Reid's philosophy, the mind can have immediate knowledge of the existence of objects, of matter, of other minds, that defines true beliefs for which it is pointless to provide a justification. Common sense is the mental authority through which we know with certainty that many very ordinary propositions are true. In the register of the definition of a theory of knowledge, the question of common sense suggests a way of approaching a common fund of knowledge, a common knowledge in which anyone with judgment can share. There is a community of judgments that can reconcile us all, despite doctrinal philosophical differences. Common sense suggests the possibility of a philosophical communicability:

There is this advantage in putting questions from the point of view of Common Sense: that it is, in some degree, in the minds of us all, even of the metaphysicians whose conclusions are most opposed to it.

(Sidgwick, *Philosophy*, 42)

The philosophical meaning of "common sense" presupposes a defense of common sense. Reflection on common sense is in part continued by reflection on ordinary life in contemporary American philosophy—for example, in the work of Stanley Cavell (*In Quest of the Ordinary*), who does not limit himself to saying that the formulations of ordinary life are true in their ordinary sense. He tries to determine what their ordinary sense means—just as the philosophy of common sense seeks the meaning of common sense.

Fabienne Brugère

BIBLIOGRAPHY

Cavell, Stanley. *In Quest of the Ordinary*. Chicago: University of Chicago Press, 1988.
Hume, David. *Essays, Moral, Political and Literary*. Indianapolis, IN: Liberty Classics, 1985. First published in 1777.
———. *A Treatise of Human Nature*. Oxford: Clarendon, 1985. First published in 1739–40.
Moore, George Edward. *Philosophical Papers*. London: Allen and Unwin, 1959.
Reid, Thomas. *Essays on the Intellectual Powers of Man*. First published in 1785. In *Thomas Reid: Philosophical Works*, edited by Derek Brookes, 8th ed. Edinburgh, Scot.: Edinburgh University Press, 2002.
Schulthess, Daniel. *Philosophie et sens commun chez Thomas Reid*. Bern: Lang, 1983.
Shaftesbury, Anthony Ashley Cooper. *Characteristics of Men, Manners, Opinions, Times*. Edited by Lawrence Klein. Cambridge: Cambridge University Press, 1999.
Sigdwick, Henry. *Philosophy, Its Scope and Relations*. London: Macmillan, 1902.
Taylor, Charles. *Philosophical Arguments*. Cambridge, MA: Harvard University Press, 1995.
Walzer, Michael. *Interpretation and Social Criticism*. Cambridge, MA: Harvard University Press, 1987.
Whately, Richard. *Elements of Logic*. 9th ed. London: John W. Parker, 1851.

COMMONPLACE

FRENCH	*lieu commun*
GREEK	*topos* [τόπος], *topêgoria* [τοπηγορία], *deinôsis* [δείνωσις]
LATIN	*locus communis, indignatio*

➤ COMPARISON, CONCETTO, *CONSENSUS, DESTINY, DOXA, IMAGE,* INGENIUM, MIMÊSIS, PATHOS, *PROBABILITY,* SUBLIME, TRUTH

The modern expression "commonplace," in the sense of a cliché or banal saying, has a history going back at least three centuries. If it has a pejorative connotation nowadays, for a long time it had a positive meaning, as an essential element of one's intellectual and artistic development. From the sixteenth to the eighteenth centuries, *lieu commun*, or "commonplace," was a technical term in France and across Europe. Broadly speaking, it had two very distinct meanings, which are both in their own way present in the modern sense of the term. On the one hand, "commonplace" was an element of oratorical training; on the other, it referred to the different headings of a catalogue. These two senses in turn go back to the sense of *topos* [τόπος] in ancient rhetoric, defined by Aristotle as "that which groups together a multiplicity of enthymemes" (*Rhetoric*, 2.26.1403a16–17), those syllogisms of probability that characterize rhetoric.

I. *Topos*: The Commonplace as a Reservoir of Premises

The first of the three meanings goes back to Aristotle's *Rhetoric*. The Greek word was simply *topos* [τόπος], "place" (or *lieu* in French, which was how Médéric Dufour translated it in his edition, *Aristote*, introducing in French a distinction between *lieux propres* or *lieux spécifiques* [particular or specific expressions] and *lieux communs* [commonplace or general expressions] in 1.2.1358a13ff., and in 2.22.1396b28). The *topos*, according to Aristotle, is a *stoicheion*, an element of the enthymemes: "It is that which groups together a multiplicity of enthymemes" (*eis ho polla enthumêmata empiptei* [εἰς ὃ πολλὰ ἐνθυμήματα ἐμπίπτει], 2.26.1403a17). This is why, unlike premises, or "protases," which are specific to only one of the oratorical genres—the deliberative, the judicial, and the epideictic; so, for example, the useful or honest instead of the deliberative—a "place" or generality is always "common" (*houtoi hoi koinoi* [οὗτοι οἱ κοινοί], or *koinê* [κοινῇ]: "generalities are the commonplaces of law, of physics, of politics"; 1358a13–14), for example, "the generality of the more or less." As Jacques Brunschwig emphasizes, "the topos is a machine that produces premises from a given conclusion, so that one and the same generality has to be able to deal with a multiplicity of different propositions, and one and the same proposition must be able to be to dealt with by a multiplicity of generalities" (preface to his edition of the *Topics*). In the subsequent history of rhetoric, this first meaning of "commonplace" will obviously not be forgotten. In Latin rhetoric, that of both the ancients and the moderns, *locus communis* is contrasted, in a way that is clearer and more pedagogical than in Aristotle, to the "particular" expressions of each of the three genres. "Commonplace" refers, then, to a list that has almost no variants, which goes from the Definition (then the Etymology, the Enumeratio partium, etc.) to "Adjoining expressions" (Adjuncta), by way of expressions of Opposition and of Comparison. As in Aristotle, these expressions are, by hypothesis, "general invented expressions." Every generality is indeed a reservoir, a "place-to-find" arguments (see COMPARISON). Moreover, Aristotle did not invent the term *topos*, which in all probability goes back to the arts of memory. But his distinctive gesture was to have completely reconceived, as he so often did, a term that the usage of the Greek language gave to him in an unelaborated form. So it is logical that all the subsequent topics should refer *topos* as a concept back to the *Rhetoric*, and even more so to the Aristotelian *Topics*.

■ See Box 1.

1

Rhetorics of the *topos*, rhetorics of the *kairos*

➤ ART, LOGOS, MOMENT

Rhetoric, or *rhêtorikê <technê>* [ῥητορική <τέχνη>], is a term that appeared for the first time in Plato's *Gorgias*. It only appears for its claim to be an art, *technê*, to be discredited, and reduced to the paradoxical status of *alogon pragma* [ἄλογον πρᾶγμα] (a thing deprived of *logos* [λόγος], or if one prefers, a "practice without reason"; 465a). It is thus the eloquence of Gorgias and of the Sophists (their oratorical success and their teaching) that is excluded from philosophical discourse and rationality. A good rhetoric still needs to be invented: the philosophizing rhetoric of *Phaedrus*, that is, the "dialectic," "the art of dividing and gathering together" (266b), whose aim is not to persuade but to elevate the soul (this is what was termed "psychagogy"; 261b).

The subsequent elaboration of rhetoric in Plato, as well as in Aristotle, consisted in devaluing, even prohibiting, a certain type of rhetoric in favor of another type. Deprived of art and of reason, this rhetoric deals with time and speech (a rhetoric of improvisation, *schedioi logoi* [σχέδιοι λόγοι], or "hurried," *ex tempore* speech; a rhetoric of the *kairos* [καιρός], or the "opportune moment," which is able to exploit the paradoxes of speech with these *kataballontes* [καταβαλλόντες]

invented by Protagoras, or catastrophic arguments that are inverted as soon as they are spoken). This rhetoric is valued as authentic and truly technical; it focuses on what is said, and it brings time back to the space being dominated. Described by the philosophers, discourse was an organism that was widespread and finely articulated, and one had to be able to "divide it up" while respecting its overall plan (cf. Plato, *Phaedrus*, 265b). It was made up of a hierarchy of *sun* [σύν], "with," which went from predicative syntax to the syllogisms, and conformed to the norms of *hama* [ἅμα], or "at the same time," as prescribed by the principle of noncontradiction. It thus privileged stability of meaning over the disruptive effects of the signifier, of homonymy, of puns (the entire *organon*, Aristotle's metaphysical and logical apparatus from the *Metaphysics* Γ to the *Sophistical Refutations*); it described "periods" (literally, "complete turns" that could be taken in with a single glance; *Rhetoric*, 3.9.1409b1) and used visual figures of speech ("metaphor," which carries across, and "metonymy," which takes the part for the whole) at the expense of auditory ones (those alliterations that claim to be poetic; 3.1.404a24–29). The importance

accorded to *topos* [τόπος], or "place," was obviously an essential part of this system. It is easy to see how the power of place could fire the imagination of commentators, and they proposed a whole series of rich metaphors relating to space in order to define this term: mold, matrix, seam or vein, circle, sphere, region, well, arsenal, reservoir, seat, store, treasure house, and not forgetting Ross's "pigeon-hole" (Brunschwig, preface to *Topics*).

With *topos*, philosophizing rhetoric spatialized the temporality of speech, and succeeded in turning even invention into a kind of thesaurus.

Barbara Cassin

BIBLIOGRAPHY

Cassin, Barbara. *L'effet sophistique* [Part 3]. Paris: Gallimard / La Pléiade, 1995.

McCoy, Marina. *Plato on the Rhetoric of Philosophers and Sophists*. Cambridge: Cambridge University Press, 2008.

Poulakos, John. *Sophistical Rhetoric in Classical Greece*. Columbia: University of South Carolina Press, 1995.

II. The Latin *Locus Communis*: The Commonplace as a Part of Oratorical Training

This second sense bears the trace of the other great thinker on rhetoric, Cicero, even if this meaning was already present in the *Rhetoric to Herennius*. In the Latin Europe of the sixteenth to eighteenth centuries, it was the predominant meaning, and also paradoxically the one we have lost from sight. On first analysis, it appears not to fit with the Aristotelian *topos*. Even though it is also linked to *doxa* and to the general, its essential difference is that it cannot be defined solely in terms of invention. The *topos* is not a set of propositions (or of sentences, if one prefers), but the means by which propositions are produced. The *locus communis* in Cicero's sense of the term is first of all an often very oratorical embellishment, or quite simply a passage in a speech, or even what is commonly known as a tirade (so in Aristotelian terms, a set of propositions, of arguments, etc.). It is only very distantly and indirectly a "place." Whatever the case may be, it would be best at this point to treat this new concept or object as a simple homonym of its Greek predecessor.

The Ciceronian *locus communis* has three characteristics. The first is the fact that it gathers up received ideas, or *doxa*. The second is that it speaks in general terms, *generaliter*. Finally, this generalization is extensive; it is not limited to a brief statement, or to a proverbial saying. One of the

clearest texts on this is without doubt Cicero's *On Invention*, at the end of book 1, §100–105. In a legal context, the canonical moment for the commonplace expression is the peroration. This is the moment when the prosecution makes its closing speech, and when the accuser speaks no longer against the accused he is facing, but against the crime in general—when our prosecutors inveigh no longer against Mr. so-and-so who has raped or killed, but against rape or murder in general. In ancient treatises, the usual example was parricide, which in Rome was the unforgiveable crime par excellence: in Cicero's *For Milon*, the classic example is the praise of self-defense.

As for the *doxa*, it is immediately apparent how serious the stakes are. Of course *doxa* is a matter of mere opinion, not of truth. But for the rhetorician, the fact that the *doxa* is not true does not mean it has no value. On the contrary, it is heavy with *gravitas*. We thus encounter one of the meanings of the word *doxa* in Greek, the positive meaning of "reputation, fame": the *doxa* is all of the values that are current in a given society, and it is defined most clearly whenever these values are treated with contempt. Parricide aroused particular indignation among the Romans—and *indignatio* is precisely one of the words Cicero uses to refer to the commonplace. This new word has the advantage of being less formal than the expression *locus communis*, which for rhetoricians used to the very idea of "place" is grammatically incorrect. *In-dignatio* allows us to reformulate what is at work, since within the word we find *dignitas* or "dignity", or even the "decency" of *decet* and *non decet*, which are close etymologically, that is, the notion of "decorum" (see MIMÊSIS, Box 6; and the article "Decorum" in RT: *Historisches Wörterbuch der Rhetorik*). Parricide, racism, even rape, shatter the *decorum* or, in the French of the seventeenth century, the *bienséance* (rules of social propriety), that is, they threaten the entire edifice of social relations.

In this legal context, this shift to the general also takes on a particular significance. By generalizing, a lawyer "elevates" the debate, as we still say, quite justifiably. This elevating movement also elevates emotion, raising it to a higher level, since in raising up we appeal to the great and general principles. General principles move the general public, by arousing great feelings. We are at the height of the effects that rhetorical art is capable of producing, what Cicero named *movere*, and which translates the Greek *pathos* [πάθος]. And once the movement of generalization is a movement that raises up, at its highest point we inevitably find the question of the political. In Cicero himself, we go very quickly from parricide trials to properly political trials, whose theme is that one's homeland is in danger. When Verrès crucifies a Roman citizen in Sicily with his eyes turned toward Italy, he is assassinating the very idea of Roman citizenship. As Quintilian notes, with this example we reach not only the highest point, or *summum*, but in a way what is above the highest point, the *supra summum* ("*non modo ad summum, sed quodam modo supra summum*"; *Institutes of Oratory*, 8.4.4). We are at the highest point of emotion and of the intolerable, that is, the height of the sublime.

The third and final trait of the commonplace relates to another term that is no less important for rhetoric, particularly in Latin: length or extent, *copia*. It is not just a matter of long, flowing speech, of quantitative length, since *copia* is above all qualitative. Formed from *opes* (forces, particularly military forces), *copia* is an army of arguments, a Roman army. Depending on which of the images Cicero happens to like, *copia* is either a river that has burst its banks or a devastating fire. In both cases, it is irresistible. It is not for nothing that the canonical moment of indignation is the peroration. The end of the river-speech sweeps one up and finishes one off; the last remaining dikes of resistance collapse. Indignation against the accused and pity for the victims are the two essential *loci communes*, typical of peroration, for which Cicero's *De inventione* gives a list of particular "places," this time in the canonical sense of argument. One could ultimately compare such oratorical arguments with a great aria from an opera rather than with a tirade. What people expect the most is not the least enjoyable and arouses no less applause. Great emotion unites a public, and even more so a community. It can even, as in the case of Verdi, lead to the birth of a nation. So pathos is not vulgar, but worthy of that beautiful name *common*, which has indeed, since Cicero, been one of the connotations of *locus communis*.

It is clear, then, that the Ciceronian *locus communis* is in no way a synonym for the Aristotelian *topos*. The same word refers to two quite distinct realities. Now that these two senses have been identified, one might wonder what the Greek equivalent is for *locus communis* or *indignatio* in Aristotle, and the Greek rhetoricians generally. It would indeed be surprising if Aristotle's *Rhetoric* paid no attention to such an important phenomenon.

For the later Greek rhetoricians, and in particular those who came after Cicero, the answer is easy. As a technical term, the strict equivalent of *indignatio* is *deinôsis* [δείνωσις]. A very full history of this term can be found in the article "Deinotes" in RT: *Historisches Wörterbuch der Rhetorik*, in particular, column 468: "*der früheste rhetorische Terminus, der mit* deinos *verwandt ist, ist* deinôsis (= lat. Indignatio)." The emblematic figure for *deinôsis* was Demosthenes; for example, when Quintilian quotes in Greek the word *deinôsis* and associates it with *indignus* and *indignitas* (6.2.24; see also 8.3.88 and 9.2.104); or in Longinus (12.5 in particular: "Demosthenes is sublime in the *deinôseis* [ἐν ταῖς δείνωσεις]"). Denys of Halicarnassus more than anyone, in his *Demosthenes*, attributed *deinotês* [δεινότης] to his hero as one of his major qualities. The *deinos* was, first and foremost, the terrifying appearance of the sacred, the equivalent of the Latin *terribile*—so Phoebus Apollo's bow that sent down a plague was described as *deinos* (*Iliad*, 1.49). From there the meaning shifts to "powerful" and also "skillful," used for any artisan who is a master of his art, and, in particular, for the rhetorician or the Sophist. The artisan who is *deinos*, as a master of his art, is like a god whose techniques are hidden and whose effects are spectacular. How to become *deinos* is the only thing that Gorgias promises to teach (Plato, *Meno*, 95c). The adjective denotes an entire program: power and skill, mastery of the effects on the public, a "huge" success, all of the truly terrifying and sacred promises of rhetoric are condensed into this one word—the art of making oneself a master and possessor of the hearts of men.

So when Demosthenes is *deinos*, he is no longer an orator, but a god who paralyzes and galvanizes his audience, who does what he wants with them, irresistibly. This is no longer a "tirade," but what one might call a thunderous "exit," a cataclysmic lightning bolt hurled down by Jupiter. So *deinôsis* limits the *locus communis* to its most visible dimension, that of the prosecution, and forgets pity (which in Cicero is also a construction, a commonplace). From this limitation we even move on to a further one. Longinus describes *deinôsis* solely in terms of its brevity, so as to contrast it with the particular form of the Ciceronian sublime, which involves extension or *copia*. On the one hand, the thunderous "exit," on the other the devastating river of the Ciceronian commonplace: these are the two modalities of the same sublime. What is more, when Longinus writes in Greek to a Roman he invents the neologism *topêgoria* [τοπηγορία], which would never actually pass into general usage, to designate Cicero's *locus communis*. The term was formed from *topos*, but with a suffix that referred to public speaking, or *agora* (*agoreuein* [ἀγορεύειν], "to speak in front of the Assembly"); *On the Sublime*, 12.5: Demosthenes is sublime "in the *deinôseis* and the violent passions," Cicero "in the *topêgoriai* and the perorations."

As for Aristotle, his *Rhetoric* only uses *deinôsis* incidentally, four times according to the Belles Lettres edition, which quite rightly translates the term as a "feeling of revolt, indignation, exaggeration." This incidental usage underlines the fact that Aristotle, for once, has not reformulated the term as a concept. He takes the usage as it is given to him and does nothing more with it. The usage he records is rather interesting since on the face of it, it is already codified by rhetoric: either pity or *deinôsis* (*ê oikton ê deinôsin* [ἢ οἶκτον ἢ δείνωσιν]) (3.16.1417a13); "the passions (*pathê* [πάθη]) to be aroused when the facts are established are pity, *deinôsis*, anger (*eleos kai deinôsis kai orgê* [ἔλεος καὶ δείνωσις καὶ ὀργὴ])" (3.19.1419b26). We again find the crucial moment of the peroration, once the facts are established (see also its use in 2.24.1301b3), as well as the fundamental vacillation of the prosecution between pity for the client and indignation for his accuser. This vacillation is already in Plato, who also records the usage of his time: "pity and *deinôsis* [ἐλεινολογίας καὶ δεινώσεως] (*Phaedrus*, 272a). The vacillation recalls, in Aristotle's *Poetics* (6.1449b28), the famous passage on *katharsis* (purification, purging), in which "pity and *phobos* [φόβος]" serve as emblems and as a condensed form of other passions [ἐλέου καὶ φόβου] (see also *Poetics*, 13; and in 19.1456b1: "and the others of this kind"; cf. CATHARSIS).

This detour through the *Poetics* is useful in putting our investigation onto the right track. Four incidental usages do not constitute a theory. But there is one place where the *Rhetoric* systematically discusses *indignatio*, but gives a completely different name than *deinôsis*; this is in 2.9, which is the precise counterpart to 2.8, on pity. We are in the moment of fundamental vacillation, between pity and then sacred terror. The clue that Aristotle is at this point rethinking the trivial notion of *deinôsis* is in the change of vocabulary. In 2.9 he names it *nemesis* [νέμεσις], as the goddess or incarnation of Justice. Most of the Latin translations of Aristotle are quite content to render it as *indignatio*, along with its derived terms, as is the French Belles Lettres translation, which talks of "indignation." The immediate opening of the chapter underlines the fact, as if it were necessary, that the use of such a highly charged term relates to the sacred: "if we attribute indignation to the gods" (*nemesan* [νεμεσᾶν]; 1386b14), it is because the gods feel this sentiment when they see that those who do not deserve to be, who are thus unworthy of it, are happy. Such a divine emotion is clearly distinguished from the more human envy, or *phthonos* [φθόνος], that we feel toward the happiness of our equals and rivals, which in our eyes is undeserved. Indeed, like spectators in a tragedy, we will be like gods if in this respect we have "no personal interest" (1386b15–20). That we are clearly dealing here with a work of conceptualization is again emphasized by the comparison with the *Nichomachean Ethics* (7.1108b1), where it is once again stated that *nemesis* is to envy what true courage is to temerity. *Nemesis* is the "happy medium" of indignation, it is a *just* form of indignation.

By reformulating the concept, Aristotle draws out what is truly at stake. His description is clearly informed by that of *deinôsis*, like Demosthenes' "exit" or Cicero's peroration. But the sacred quality of *deinos* could always be suspect, and anyone who places himself in the divine role of prosecutor could be motivated by personal interests. The fundamental question is: who made you the prosecutor? In order to reach the truly sublime, the one who thunders must by this very fact be inhabited by a god, who for both Demosthenes and Cicero is the god of the homeland in danger. Or to put it another way, he has to have Justice with him, he has to be able to

appear as the very incarnation of Justice. Here as elsewhere, Aristotle's *Rhetoric* shows that it is truly an ethics, much like Quintilian's (who makes a number of remarks along the same lines).

In the seventeenth century, the Christian rereading of this chapter is not entirely self-evident. Is one not, in feeling indignant toward those who are unworthy (*indigne* in French), acting as if one were God himself, and doubting his Providence, which mysteriously rewards those on this earth who do not deserve it? A professor of rhetoric such as Christoph Schrader (at the University of Helmstedt) argues for the rights of Christian indignation in the choices that depend on human free will. One should not, for example, in use and in public office "prefer the unworthy to the worthy (*ne indigni dignis praeferantur*)" (commentary ad loc, 332: this opens up the question of merit or worthiness). But other than this, and from a more metaphysical point of view (*De rhetoricorum Aristotelis sententia et vsv commentarius*), he uses Aristotle's chapter as an incitement to asceticism, for example, toward the goods listed in 1387a12, "riches, power," as well as the gifts one is born with, which is in fact everything that comes from *Fortuna* or Providence. At that point we need to hold back our desire for *indignatio*, and leave this feeling to God alone. We are not Nemesis, and this is a way of emphasizing the extent to which the sublime that is described here, from Aristotle to Longinus, is a manifestly pagan sublime.

III. Commonplaces as Categories of an Index

This is again a homonym. In the sixteenth century, "commonplaces" in the plural was used to designate the categories under which a reader would classify the quotations that for him seemed noteworthy. So it was a sort of filing system, or index, or repertoire. This pedagogical tool had two objectives: to train one's memory, and to develop one's judgment.

One term from this period expressed this dual ambition, the verb "to digest," and the noun "digest" is still used to convey this idea in English. Technically speaking, the verb refers to the idea of classifying a quotation under such and such a category: *digerere* means to distribute elements, each one into the box where it belongs. The usual expression designating this sorting out of commonplaces is thus "*per locos communes digesta*" (each thing in its own category). The word "digest" has to do with the body, but also with the mind. The mind will retain better what it has digested better. This is the meaning of the famous image of the bee that Seneca uses in his letter 84 to Lucilius, the terms of which are endlessly cited and reworked by Erasmus throughout his work—Erasmus himself transforms it into a real cliché that is constantly borrowed and adapted during the sixteenth and seventeenth centuries. The bee gathers pollen from flowers: this is the moment when a pupil notes down in his notebooks or on a slate the "flowers" of literature and history (cf. Hamlet noting down in his "common-place book" that his uncle is a "villain," just after he has seen the ghost!). When the bee is back in the hive, the pollen that has been gathered is redistributed into the different alveoli of the hive: this is the moment of "digestion," of distribution, when the pupil copies out onto the large *in-folio* of blank pages that he keeps at home. It is then that the mind can make its own honey and incorporate knowledge from outside.

It is clear that without any judgment or critical perspective this act could turn into one of pure compilation. This was strongly emphasized by the Reformer Melanchthon (1497–1560), who was rector of the celebrated university at Wittenberg after Luther. The pernicious double of *digerere* was *congerere*: to accumulate for the sake of accumulating. The solution was order at every moment of the process (see the booklet *De locis communibus ratio*). Order reigns, both in reading and in writing: to classify well was to think well, was to write well. One of the aims of commonplaces was to educate oneself in the field of knowledge one decided principally to pursue. As far as reading was concerned, for Melanchthon the category-words had to be organized in analytical order, which he preferred to the jumble of alphabetical order. The model was the encyclopedia, as a tree with branches. Whatever his domain, a student would develop his memory and his critical faculties by organizing his collection of commonplaces according to the big and then small categories of his discipline. As for writing, his discourse would also benefit from this same order, since without a well-conceived plan it could turn into a compilation of arguments. One has only to reread Quintilian's comments on *dispositio* to find the same aversion to what is, precisely, difficult to digest: "a copious abundance of ideas, no matter how large, would merely provide a heap or a kind of congestion [*cumulum atque congestum*], if they were not put into order by this same disposition [*in ordinem digestus*]" (7, prologue 1).

As an essential element of the pedagogy of the Jesuits, this method played a very important role in the organization of study across Europe and in all fields of knowledge. For commonplaces in the sense of categories was by no means confined to literature, or even to the humanities more broadly speaking. The method was an often explicit adaptation of the first tool of Aristotle's *Topics* (1.14.105a ff.), that is, the idea of collecting premises, commonly accepted propositions (*endoxai* [ἔνδοξαι]). Aristotle himself earned the sobriquet of "reader" because of this: read everything, index everything. This was how he wrote *The History of Animals* or *Politics*, beginning by drawing up an inventory and classifying—by "digesting"—all the available information. This was also how Bodin wrote his *République* in the sixteenth century: the vast compilation of all the existing constitutions was a prelude to his induction, which for Bodin would then reveal a new concept of sovereignty.

What is the relationship between oratorical training and an index of categories? We might turn again to Melanchthon for the answer. We should first of all emphasize the context, which was not rhetorical but theological. His *Lieux communs de théologie* (Commonplaces of theology), which appeared in 1521, was conceived as a manual, and we can see it as one of the first comprehensive works of Lutheranism. The main doctrinal questions were addressed systematically and provided a coherent body of doctrine that was contrasted with the previous one. Order here was only necessary because of the context of theological controversy. If one's principles were not good, one could not formulate good discourses, and if Melanchthon drew attention to the term "commonplace," it was because the Reformer had read Cicero very well. He understood that for Cicero the movement toward generality was at the heart of his rhetoric. The movement upward from the particular to the general produced the essential ideas, the framework, and the overall articulation, and these ideas organized the arguments of the speech and aroused the moments of most intense emotion.

IV. The Commonplace in the Modern Era

The commonplace in the modern sense is both a *faux ami*, which looks deceptively like the word in its classical sense, and a true heir. It is a *faux ami* in a text as apparently simple as the following, written by Pierre Bayle in 1686:

> C'est ce que je réponds au lieu commun qui a été si rebattu par les ignorants, que le changement de religion entraîne avec lui le changement de gouvernement, et qu'ainsi il faut soigneusement empêcher que l'on n'innove.
>
> (This is what I reply to the commonplace, which has become so worn out from use by ignorant people, that the change of religion brings with it a change of government, and that therefore we have to be careful to prevent any innovation.)
>
> (*Commentaire philosophique sur ces paroles de Jésus-Christ*)

The proximity of *lieu commun* and *rebattu* gives the impression that we are already dealing with its contemporary meaning. We are already, it is true, in generality, and even political conservatism, the very kind that Flaubert scorns so joyously in his *Dictionary of Received Ideas*. But what the *faux ami* prevents us from seeing is that Bayle is here referring to an entire historical development. Those who are ignorant have for a long time, passionately, discussed the question that concerns, as in Cicero, the homeland in danger. The category-word is something like "Government" or 'Dangerous Innovations," and on this subject arguments and quotations have been collected eagerly since it is known in advance that they can be reused. The author only gives us the substance of these long developments on a question of principle. He is the one who abbreviates it, and who gives us the false impression that the commonplace is reduced to one or two expressions, to what we nowadays understand as "cliché."

And yet the very possibility of such a reduction is not unfaithful. A cliché only needs to be expanded, just as the expansion itself can be abbreviated. This is not the main point, which is rather the excessive visibility that the method *of* commonplaces has given *to* the commonplace. Bayle is not reproaching the commonplace for being overused, but for being worn out through overuse by ignorant people. What we reproach the cliché for, following Flaubert, is to be overused, period, by intelligent as well as by ignorant people. In other words, if the commonplace in the modern sense is truly the distant heir of former meanings of the term, it is that the legacy itself has become too ponderous. Doxa was once near to Wisdom, and we now find it closer to Stupidity.

Francis Goyet

BIBLIOGRAPHY

Amossy, Ruth. *Les idées reçues: Sémiologie du stereotype*. Paris: Nathan, 1991.

———. *Stéréotypes et clichés: Langue, discours, société*. Paris: Nathan, 1997.

———, and Michel Delon, eds. *Critique et legitimité du prejugé (XVIIIe–XXe siècle)*. Brussels: Editions de l'Universite de Bruxelles, 1999.

———, and Elisheva Rosen. *Les discours du cliché*. Paris: Société d'édition d'enseignement supérieur, 1982.

———, and Meir Sternberg. "Doxa and Discourse: How Common Knowledge Works." *Poetics Today* 23 (2002): 369–555.

Aristotle. *Aristote: Rhétorique*. 3 vols. Edited and translated by Médéric Dufour. Paris: Presses Universitaires de France, 1973.

———. *The "Art" of Rhetoric*. Translated by John Henry Freese. Loeb Classical Library. Cambridge, MA: Harvard University Press, 1975.

———. *Rhetoric*. In *The Complete Works of Aristotle*. Bollingen Series, 71. Vol. 2, edited by Jonathan Barnes. Princeton, NJ: Princeton University Press, 1984.

———. *Topiques*. Edited and translated by Jacques Brunschwig. Paris: Les Belles Lettres, 2007. First published in 1967.

Bayle, Pierre. *Commentaire philosophique sur ces paroles de Jesus-Christ: Contrain-les d'entrer* [= sur les conversions forcées]. In *Œuvres diverses*, edited by P. Husson et al., 1727, vol. 2. Repr. E. Labrousse, ed. Hildesheim, Ger.: Olms, 1965.

Blair, Ann. *The Theater of Nature: Jean Bodin and Renaissance Science*. Princeton, NJ: Princeton University Press, 1997.

Bodin, Jean. *Method for the Easy Comprehension of History*. Translated by Beatrice Reynolds. New York: W. W. Norton, 1945.

Cauquelin, Anne. *L'art du lieu commun: Du bon usage de la doxa*. Paris: Éditions du Seuil, 1999.

Cicero. *De inventione. De optimo genera oratorum: Topica*. Translated by H. M. Hubbell. Loeb Classical Library. Cambridge, MA: Harvard University Press, 1968.

———. *The Treatise on Rhetorical Invention*. In *The Orations of Marcus Tullius Cicero*, vol. 4, translated by C. D. Yonge. New York: Dodo Press, 2008.

Copeland, Rita. *Rhetoric, Hermeneutics, and Translation in the Middle Ages: Academic Traditions and Vernacular Texts*. Cambridge: Cambridge University Press, 1991.

Couzinet, Marie-Dominique. *Histoire et méthode à la Renaissance: Une lecture de la* Methodus ad facilem historiarum cognitionem *de Jean Bodin*. Paris: Vrin, 1996.

Dionysius of Halicarnassus. "Demosthenes." In *The Critical Essays*, translated by Stephen Usher. Vol. 1. Loeb Classical Library. Cambridge, MA: Harvard University Press, 1974.

Goyet, Francis. *Le sublime du "lieu commun": l'Invention rhétorique dans l'Antiquité et à la Renaissance*. Paris: Champion, 1996.

———. "Hamlet, étudiant du XVIe siècle." *Poétique* 113 (1998): 3–15.

Hesk, Jon. " 'Despisers of the Commonplace': Meta-Topoi and Para-Topoi in Attic Oratory." *Rhetorica* 25 (2007): 361–84.

Longinus. *On the Sublime*. Translated by James A. Arieti and John M. Crossett. New York: Edwin Mellen Press, 1985.

———. *Poetics*. Edited and translated by W. H. Fyfe. Loeb Classical Library, 199. Cambridge, MA: Harvard University Press, 1995.

Melanchthon, Philipp. *De locis communibus ratio*, fascicle bound with *De formando studio* of Rodolphus Agricola. Bâle: H. Petrus, 1531.

Mortensen, Daniel E. "The Loci of Cicero." *Rhetorica* 26 (2008): 31–56.

Moss, Ann. "Commonplace-Rhetoric and Thought-Patterns in Early Modern Culture." In *The Recovery of Rhetoric: Persuasive Discourse and Disciplinarity in the Human Sciences*, edited by R. H. Roberts and J.M.M. Good, 49–60. Charlottesville: University Press of Virginia, 1993.

———. *Printed Commonplace-Books and the Structuring of Renaissance Thought*. Oxford: Clarendon, 1996.

Murphy, James J. *Rhetoric in the Middle Ages: A History of Rhetorical Theory from Saint Augustine to the Renaissance*. Berkeley: University of California Press, 1974.

Quintilian. *The Orator's Education*. 5 vols. Loeb Classical Library. Cambridge, MA: Harvard University Press, 2001.

Schrader, Christoph. *De rhetoricorum Aristotelis sententia et usu commentaries*. Helmstedt, Ger.: H. D. Müller, 1674.

Summers, David. " 'The Proverb Is Something Musty': The Commonplace and Epistemic Crisis in Hamlet." *Hamlet Studies* 20 (1998): 9–34.

| COMMUNITY

"Common" derives from Latin *communis*, "what belongs to everyone," from *cum*, "with," and *munis*, "what fulfills its task, its duty" (related to *munus*, office, gift); it corresponds to Greek *koinos* [κοινός], "common, public," in which we probably see the same root as in the Latin *cum*, and which contrasts with *idios* [ἴδιος], "peculiar, private." "Community" designates the fact of being in common, what is held in common, and the group or institution that shares what is held in common.

I. Common and Community

1. What is held in common is opposed to what is one's own and to property: see PROPERTY.
2. "Common" can be used in reference to different levels of community. It can refer to humanity as a whole: see LOGOS, *SENS COMMUN*, UNIVERSALS, as well as *AUTRUI, HUMANITY* [MENSCHHEIT], *IDENTITY*, [I/ME/MYSELF, SAMOST', SELBST]. Or it can refer to a particular human community defined as a people (see PEOPLE and NAROD; cf. HEIMAT), or as a culture (see BILDUNG, CIVILTÀ, *CULTURE,* TO TRANSLATE) considered distinctive because of some privileged trait (see *MALAISE*).

II. Political Community and Society

1. The entry CIVIL SOCIETY explores the main systems used to describe the community, as opposed to society and the state. For Greek, in addition to *koinônia politikê* [κοινωνία πολιτική] (CIVIL SOCIETY, I), see the entries for POLIS, OIKEIÔSIS, OIKONOMIA. For Latin, in addition to *societas civilis* (CIVIL SOCIETY, I), see PIETAS, RELIGIO, and cf. LEX. On the distinction between *Gemeinschaft* and *Gesellschaft* in German, see CIVIL SOCIETY, Box 1.
2. In *mir* [мир], Russian has a special constellation that refers simultaneously to peace, the world, and the peasant community; see MIR and SOBORNOST' (conciliarity, communion), and cf. NAROD (people); cf. *CONCILIARITY*.
3. The contemporary avatars of the political promotion of the community are considered in the entry LIBERAL, Box 3.

➤ *ALLIANCE, CONSENSUS, OBLIGATION, STATE*

| COMPARISON

FRENCH	*comparaison*
GREEK	*sugkrisis* [σύγκρισις], *antithesis* [ἀντίθεσις], *parathesis* [παράθεσις]
ITALIAN	*paragone*
LATIN	*comparatio, contrapositum, adpositum*

➤ ANALOGY, COMMONPLACE, CONCETTO, *IMAGE*, INGENIUM, MIMÊSIS, PROPERTY

Comparison or simile has suffered by the recent success of metaphor. It has served as a foil for its brilliant alter ego. To restore its interest, we have only to recall that the apparently canonical *comparatio-metaphora* pair is deceptive. This pair comes from a passage in Quintilian that has been taken out of context. In Latin, *comparatio* designates only in a marginal way a similarity introduced by a word such as "like." It refers to a mental operation: making a parallel between *x* and *y* in order to bring out resemblances and differences. The expression *comparaison n'est pas raison* (comparison is not reason) reminds us both that comparison is an instrument for producing intelligibility and that this instrument works well, almost too well: from here comes the need to be prudent in using the extremely fertile method of *comparatisme* (comparative studies).

I. *Comparatio, Sugkrisis,* "Parallel"

Comparison is an image or figure of speech in a specialized and marginal sense. In the whole of Quintilian's *Institutio oratoria* (*The Orator's Education*), this sense appears only once among the twelve occurrences of the words *comparatio* and *comparativus* listed in the index of the Belles Lettres edition. In a massive, generic way, *comparatio* designates a parallel: the comparison of *x* and *y* in order to discern their resemblances and differences, and often to emphasize the superiority of one over the other. In Greek, the equivalent word is *sugkrisis* [σύγκρισις], which is frequently used with this meaning, but in the late period (from Philodemus to Plutarch). As *sugkrisis* suggests, the point is to exercise one's judgment, to judge one thing in relation to another—*sug-krisis* [σύγ-κρίσις] is put together from *sun* (with) and *krisis* (judgment). The result is not a little formula tossed off in passing, a figure of style, but a long, complete development.

Thus *comparatio* is one of the preliminary exercises given in rhetoric classes (Quintilian, *Institutio oratoria,* 2.4.21). It has the length of an academic "assignment," and as such, it was part of the baggage of every cultivated person from antiquity to the ancien régime. In this culture, to make a comparison was also to provide oneself with the means to construct a whole development. Thus comparison is a "figure of thought," or more literally, a "figure of sentences" (Lat. *figura sententiarium*), that is, one that extended over one or more sentences. Similarly, comparison is related to conception and invention: considering something in a nutshell and then developing what one has seen in all its consequences. A visionary like Victor Hugo was well aware of its virtually endless possibilities. For example, in his novel *Notre-Dame de Paris,* the formula "Ceci tuera cela" (This will kill that, 5.2) launches the extensive *comparatio* between *x,* the book, and *y,* the cathedral.

One example of a class assignment with its possible developments is found in Quintilian's *Institutio oratoria* (8.4.14; cf. 8.4.9–14). Discussing one of Cicero's speeches, Quintilian notes that "here Catiline is compared to Gracchus, the constitution of the state to the whole world, a slight change for the worse to fire and sword and desolation, and a private citizen to the consuls, all comparisons affording ample opportunity for further individual expansion, if anyone should desire to do so." This allows us to understand better the most common specialized sense of *sugkrisis.* The Greek word designated a classic exercise in literary criticism: a parallel between two authors or two works, the better to differentiate them. There again, academic culture long retained the memory of this: we recall the classic assignment on Racine and Corneille, people as they are and as they should be. Longinus's *On the Sublime* includes a number of such exercises, whether the parallel/difference between the *Iliad* and the *Odyssey,* between Plato

and Lysias, or between Demosthenes and Cicero. A pairing like Demosthenes and Cicero, developed at greater length, is the basis for Plutarch's *Parallel Lives.* Plutarch concludes the discussion of almost every pair of men with what he calls literally a *sugkrisis*: a comparison of Theseus and Romulus, Lycurgus and Numa, and so on.

II. *Eikôn* and *Metaphora, Similitudo* and *Tralatio*: The Status of "Like"

With respect to this fundamental meaning, a comparison in the modern sense is called a "simile"; the English renders the Latin *similitudo,* which itself rendered the Greek *eikôn,* "icon" or "image." Moreover, the idea that metaphor is an abbreviated simile comes from Quintilian (*Institutio oratoria,* 8.6.8). Quintilian takes from Aristotle the excessively famous example of "Achilles is like a lion," as opposed to "Achilles is a lion" (Aristotle, *Rhetoric,* 3.4.1406b20–24; Quintilian, *Institutio oratoria,* 8.6.9). Aristotle distinguishes between *eikôn* [εἰκών] and *metaphora* [μεταφορά] (*Rhetoric,* 3.4.1406b20–23), and Quintilian between *similitudo* and *tra[ns]latio,* the latter word being itself the Latin equivalent of the Greek *metaphora,* which Quintilian also uses:

Aristotle		Quintilian
eikôn	=	*similitudo*
metaphora	=	*tra[ns]latio*

■ See Box 1.

Note that the concept of *comparatio* is not part of this table—of this register of concepts. Quintilian imports the noun *comparatio* for explanatory purposes, to show what happens in a simile and thus also in a metaphor. In his work, *comparatio* is hardly more than a deverbal noun derived from the verb *comparare,* which he had initially used. A simile is "like" a parallel/difference, the latter being as familiar to readers of Quintilian—or Aristotle—as it is unfamiliar today:

> In totum autem metaphora brevior et similitudo, eoque distat quod illa comparatur rei quam volumus exprimere, haec pro ipsa re dicitur. Comparatio est cum dico fecisse quid hominem "ut leo," tralatio cum dico de homine "leo est."

> (On the whole *metaphor* is a shortened form of *simile,* while there is this further difference, that in the latter we compare some object to the thing which we wish to describe, whereas in the former this object is actually substituted for the thing. It is a comparison when I say that a man did something like a lion, it is a metaphor when I say of him, "He is a lion.")

> (Quintilian, *Institutio oratoria,* 8.6.8–9, trans. Russell)

From *comparare* to *comparatio,* the verb and noun are there to make it understood that the essential point is not the presence or absence of the word "like." The point is that a parallel between Achilles and a lion would develop at length everything that belongs to the hero and everything that belongs to the animal to discriminate between them by means of a parallel/difference. This very intellectual process is thus the inverse of metaphor. The simile maintains the distance

1

Reminder: Aristotle's definition of "metaphor"

➤ ANALOGY, INGENIUM, LOGOS

The recent success of metaphor draws its title of nobility from Aristotle. Metaphor, unlike comparison or simile, is a trope, a "figure of words," namely, according to its canonical definition in the *Poetics*, "giving a thing a name that belongs to something else" (*onomatos allotriou epiphora* [ὀνόματος ἀλλοτρίου ἐπιφορά], 1457b7–8, trans. Bywater, 1476). This may be done by moving from the genus to the species, from species to species, or, finally and especially, in accord with a relationship of "analogy": a metaphorical expression then abbreviates and summarizes a proportional relationship (to call the evening "day's old age" is to imply that evening is to day as old age is to life). Whereas for Quintilian, metaphors are "abbreviated similes," for Aristotle "comparisons [*eikones* (εἰκόνες)] are metaphors that need

logos [*logou deomenai* (λόγου δεόμεναι)]," that is, as Dufour and Wartelle translate it, that "need to be developed" (*Rhetoric*, 3.4.1407a14–15), but "just because it is longer, it is less attractive" (3.10.1410b18–19). Both metaphor and simile are mental operations. So far as metaphor is concerned, "when the poet calls old age a 'withered stalk,' he conveys a new idea, a new fact [*epoiêsen mathêsin kai gnôsin* (ἐποίησεν μάθησιν καὶ γνῶσιν)]] to us by means of the general notion of 'lost bloom' which is common to both things" (3.10.1410b15–16). And "in philosophy also an acute mind will perceive resemblances [*to homoion theôrein* (τὸ ὅμοιον θεωρεῖν)]] even in things far apart" (3.11.1412a12–13). The success of a metaphor, even in the form of a witticism (*asteion* [ἀστεῖον], 3.11.1411b22–24), has to do with

the brilliance of the connection it makes between philosophy and poetry.

One of our problems with the passage from Aristotle to Quintilian is a problem of translation, namely, a difference in the way the Greek is rendered in Latin and in French: Quintilian translates *eikôn*, the other word Aristotle uses for "metaphor," which is generally translated in French by *comparaison*, as *similitudo* and not *comparatio*.

Barbara Cassin

BIBLIOGRAPHY

Aristotle. *Poetics*. Translated by Ingram Bywater. In *Basic Works of Aristotle*, edited by R. McKeon. New York: Random House, 1941.
———. *Rhetorique*. Edited by M. Dufour and A. Wartelle. Paris: Belles Lettres, 1980.

between Achilles and the lion (see here the verb *distat*, which is typical of *comparatio*), whereas metaphor fuses these two poles in a flash of intuition. Length in one case and brevity in the other merely indicate the difference between these two mental processes. On the whole, the presence of "like," which has so hypnotized criticism, is just the tip of the iceberg. It emblematizes the essential, since the "like" forestalls complete assimilation. But making it the absolute criterion for distinguishing between simile and metaphor is erroneous and leads to many disappointments: this criterion doesn't work.

So let us set aside comparison in the modern sense. In "comparison" in the sense of parallel/difference, the point is to juxtapose two elements that then correspond—without ever being conflated. Let us take an example. In his chapter on the verbal figures, Quintilian deals with an effect of repetition taken from Cicero. Here the repetition involves the first words of the parts of the period, "you" and "him," in a parallel between you the jurist and him the military leader—a famous parallel because, contrary to all expectations, Cicero gives the advantage to the military man:

Vigilas tu de nocte ut tuis consultoribus respondeas, ille ut eo quo intendit mature cum exercitu perveniat; te gallorum, illum bucinarum cantus exsuscitat; tu actionem instituis, ille aciem instruit; tu caves ne tui consultores, ille ne urbes aut castra capiantur

(You pass wakeful nights that you may be able to reply to your clients; he that he and his army may arrive betimes at their destination. You are roused by cockcrow, he by the bugle's reveillé. You draw up your legal pleas, he sets the battle in array. You are on the watch

that your clients be not taken at a disadvantage, he that cities or camps be not so taken.)

(Cicero, *Pro Murena*, 22, quoted in Quintilian, *Institutio oratoria*, 9.3.32, trans. Cousin)

This is a good example of the possible length: the parallel extends over ten paragraphs, from §19 to §28. Moreover, it is accompanied by another that serves as its conclusion, the parallel between the orator and the jurist, the orator being just as superior to the jurist as the military leader is (§29–30). Quintilian quotes this passage and comments: "In antitheses and comparisons [*in contrapositis vel comparativis*], the first words of alternate phrases are frequently repeated to produce correspondence [*solet respondere primorum verborum alterna repetitio*]" (9.3.32).

Contra-positum: this is not far from the Italian word *contrapunto*, "counterpoint," and the French *contraste*, one of the words by which French rhetorical textbooks of the eighteenth century retranslate *comparatio*.

III. *Contrapositio* and *Antithesis*

Contrapositio is the Latin word that Quintilian uses in the same chapter 3 of book 9 to render the Greek *antitheton* [ἀντίθετον] in referring very specifically to the verbal figure called "antithesis." In all of these words, the prefixes *anti-* [ἀντί] or *contra-* largely determine the meaning. The Greek word for "antithesis" can designate any kind of parallel. It refers literally to the act of setting one thing next to another, *-positum* translating *-theton*, and *contra-* translating *anti-*. In this very general sense, antithesis is a special case of parathesis. When two elements are set opposite each other, they correspond either by being similar, symmetrical (*para* [παρά], parallelism, parathesis, *adposita*; cf. Quintilian, *Institutio oratoria*, 5.10.86: "Adposita vel comparativa") or by being dissimilar, opposed (*anti-*, contrast, antithesis, *contraposita*). Furthermore, *anti-* does not necessarily signify the exact contrary: the island of Anticythera is simply the one that is across from Cythera; *x* and *y* face each other. We could say the same about the prefix *para-*; *parallêlos* [παράλληλος] is constructed on the basis of *allêloi* [ἀλλήλοι], "one and the other": to juxtapose. One of the words in the entry on *sugkrisis* in Hesychius of Alexandria's Greek dictionary even combines the two prefixes *anti-* and *para-*. This word is *antiparathesis* [ἀνθιπαράθεσις], which is used, for example, by Dionysius of Halicarnassus to designate, very simply, a parallel/difference—in short, a contrast, in this case between the bad Hegesias and the excellent Homer (*On Literary Composition*, 6.18.24). Elsewhere, Quintilian says again that he translates the Greek *antistasis* [ἀντίστασις] by *comparatio*: this clearly emphasizes that the essential element is the prefix (Quintilian, *Institutio oratoria*, 7.4.12).

IV. Comparison and Comparatism: Double Attention and the Aesthetics of Counterpoint

This terminological complex thus allows us to broaden the brief article "*Comparaison*" in Lalande's *Vocabulary* (RT: *Vocabulaire technique et critique de la philosophie*, s.v.). The latter refers, rightly, to Étienne Bonnet de Condillac and his school. The quotation from Condillac's *Logique* (1.7) is interesting:

As we give our attention to an object, we can give it to two at once. Then, instead of one exclusive sensation, we experience two, and we say that we are comparing them, because we experience them exclusively in order to observe them side by side, without being distracted by other sensations: and this is exactly what the word "compare" means. Comparison is thus only a double attention.

This quotation reminds us in a remarkable way of the following passage in Petrarch, which Condillac probably did not know. Petrarch develops his long and famous parallel, or *comparatio*, between solitude and urban life (*On the Solitary Life*, 1.1.8). He notes:

I think that I shall describe all this better if I do not devote separate developments to everything that it seems to me could be said about these two ways of life; I shall on the contrary mix them, referring by turns to a given aspect of one of them, so that attention [*animus*] is directed now to one side, now to the other, and that it can gauge, looking from the right and from the left as one does with an alternate movement of the eyes, the difference that separates the most dissimilar objects placed next to each other.

This quotation show how reductive it would be to limit oneself to Condillac alone. The philosopher elaborates in his own idiom, explicating a notion that he finds in "ordinary" language—a notion that was elaborated a long time before and that he inherited from the whole rhetorical culture of his time. Before Condillac there was at least Aristotle. In his *Topics*, comparison is involved in two of the four

instruments, or *organa*, that provide an abundant source of propositions. These are the third and fourth instruments: attention directed toward differences and then resemblances (*Topics*, 1.16.107b–17.108a).

▪ See Box 2.

As Aristotle described it, comparison serves first of all to make inductions: to bring out the universal by comparing individual cases (*Topics*, 1.18.108b). By whatever mediation, the idea of *comparatio* is at the origin of all the comparative disciplines that emerged at the beginning of the nineteenth century. Comparative anatomy was inaugurated by Georges Cuvier's *Leçons d'anatomie comparée* (1800–1805), and was soon followed by comparative physiology (1833), comparative embryology, and so on. François Raynouard's *Grammaire comparée des langues de l'Europe latine dans leurs rapports avec la langue des troubadours* (1821) provided the foundation for the discipline of *Romanistik* founded by Friedrich Diez some fifteen years later. Comparative geography was inaugurated by Carl Ritter's *Die Erdkunde im Verhaeltnis zur Natur und zur Geschichte des Menschen oder allgemeine vergleichende Geographie* (1817–59), part of which was translated into French by Eugène Buret and Édouard Desor as *Géographie générale comparée* (1835–36). In his anthology, *Cours de littérature comparée* (1816–24), François Noël limited himself to juxtaposing texts in French, Latin, English, and Italian. In his *Mémoires d'outre-tombe* (1848–50), Chateaubriand went so far as to call his *Essai sur les révolutions*, originally published in 1797, "a comparative work on revolutions [*un ouvrage sur les révolutions comparées*]." The general movement is in fact that of the "double attention" Condillac talked about. More than *comparé* (compared), this should be called *comparant* (comparing), as in German (*vergleichend*), or "comparative," as in English. What counts is not so much the two objects juxtaposed as the intellectual act of bringing them together.

The fact that comparison does not always provide proof in no way deprives the method of interest: because it is inherently plural, comparison elicits thought. To put the point in the old terms, comparison is part of topics, which is a matter of invention and not of criticism, which concerns judgment. First *invenire*, then *iudicare*. First find, produce results, then weigh and reweigh, decide what the results mean. To reject the comparative method because some of its results are unacceptable is to fail to understand its role as an instrument, a tool. This negative judgment generally goes hand-in-hand with an inability to explain one's own topics, one's way of collecting the materials for thought.

Comparison thus understood can be used not only as an intellectual tool but also as an aesthetic means. We have seen this in the quotation from Cicero's *Pro Murena*, in which the alternating repetition of the first words produces a figure, a sort of rhythm, "you . . . him." Here are two further examples.

In musical terms, contrast or contraposition is somewhat like counterpoint. The Greek word *sugkrisis* is attested, in the Septuagint, in the very specialized sense of "musical concert": Ecclesiasticus (Sirach) 32 (35):7. Here we are in a context of harmony: the person presiding over the banquet is asked not to "strike a false note" by inappropriately lecturing people who want to party. Good taste consists, on the contrary, in being like "a carbuncle seal on a ring," like "a

2

The comparison of the arts

The comparison of the arts is a literary genre that began in the Renaissance and continued throughout the classical period. It took several forms. The first and most important was a parallel between the arts of the visible and those of discourse: painting and sculpture on the one hand, poetic arts on the other. On the basis of this comparison, which is in a way generic, more specific forms of comparison emerged—comparisons between painting and sculpture, or between painting and music. The Italian word *paragone*, which means "comparison" in general, was used in all European languages to designate the comparison between painting and sculpture that gave rise to many debates in the sixteenth century. The comparison between painting and music (the analogy between sound and color, reflections on the notion of harmony) was also present in the Renaissance and in the classical age. It was revived in the twentieth century with the birth of abstract art.

The comparison between the arts of the eye and those of the ear is part of a long tradition that, according to Plato, goes back to Simonides, and that was spread during the Renaissance through the reading of Horace. In the *Art of Poetry*, Horace says, "What is heard, not seen, is weaker in the mind than what the eyes record faithfully as it happens" (*Art of Poetry*, trans. Raffel). But it is another remark of Horace that was to play a crucial historical role, the one in which he drew a parallel between painting and poetry: "ut pictura poesis erit," a poem is like a picture (ibid.). Adopted by the theoreticians of the Renaissance, this comparison is at the origin of what has been called the doctrine of *ut pictura poesis*. But this doctrine is based on a misunderstanding, or rather an inversion: whereas Horace compared poetry to painting, relating the arts of language to those of the image, Renaissance authors inverted the direction of the comparison. "A poem is like a picture" became "a picture is like a poem." The phrase *ut pictura poesis*, as it was understood

in the field of discourse on art, always consisted in defining painting, in determining its value, in relation to criteria of the poetic arts. This doctrine was unquestionably fertile for several centuries; it played an essential role in helping painting acquire the dignity of the liberal arts (see ART). Through this comparison, the painter was able to accede to the rank of the poet and the orator. The expressions *pictura loquens* and *muta poesis* are topoi that serve to qualify poetry and painting, the latter being often represented in engravings by a figure wearing a blindfold or holding a finger to its mouth. Painting is a "mute poetry" and poetry is a "speaking picture." Seventeenth-century French writers called them "sisters" (*sœurs*; the English called them the "sister arts") and described them as united in a constant relationship of reciprocal emulation. Thus André Félibien, in his work *Le songe de Philomathe*, stages *ut pictura poesis* by means of a dialogue between two sisters, one blonde, the other brunette, the former expressing herself in verse, the latter in prose (published in 1683, reprinted as an appendix to book 10 of the *Entretiens sur les vies et les ouvrages des plus excellents peintres anciens et modernes*, 1666–88).

Ut pictura poesis did not limit itself to changing the image and status of the painter; it also transformed the definition of the painter by imposing on him the categories of poetics and rhetoric (*inventio*, *dispositio*) and by attributing a narrative goal to him. The doctrine of *ut pictura poesis* also triumphed in history painting, long considered the most noble kind of painting.

But very early on, reservations were expressed with regard to a comparison that subjected painting a little too much to the order of discourse. Thus Leonardo da Vinci preferred to describe poetry as blind painting rather than as speaking painting, to maintain the equality between the two arts: "Painting is a mute poetry and poetry a blind painting; both seek to imitate nature in accord with

their means" (*Traité de la peinture*, trans. Chastel, 90). But Gotthold Lessing, in his *Laocoön* (1766), was the first to provide a systematic critique of the doctrine of *ut pictura poesis*. Disqualifying the very idea of a comparison between the arts, Lessing insists on their differences and the limits that separate them, as is shown explicitly by his book's subtitle: *Laocoön: An Essay on the Limits of Painting and Poetry*. The rejection of the parallel in the name of the argument for specificity was extensively developed in the nineteenth century, following Charles Baudelaire, by all the defenders of "modernity." This argument has played a major role in the contemporary analysis of art. In 1940, Clement Greenberg published in the *Partisan Review* an article, "Towards a New *Laocoön*," that was to become one of the main texts of "modernist" criticism. Appealing specifically to Lessing, Greenberg writes: "The avant-garde arts have in the last fifty years achieved a purity and a radical delimitation of their fields of activity for which there is no previous example in the history of culture. The arts lie safe now, each within its 'legitimate' boundaries, and free trade has been replaced by autarchy" (1:32).

Jacqueline Lichtenstein

BIBLIOGRAPHY

Greenberg, Clement. "Towards a New *Laocoön*." In *Collected Essays and Criticism*, edited by J. O'Brian, 1:23–37. Chicago: University of Chicago Press, 1986.

Horace. *The Art of Poetry*. Translated by B. Raffel. Albany: State University of New York Press, 1974.

Lee, Rensselaer Wright. *Ut pictura poesis: The Humanistic Theory of Painting*. New York: W. W. Norton, 1967.

Leonardo da Vinci. *Traité de la peinture*. Translated by A. Chastel. Paris: Berger-Levrault, 1987.

Lessing, Gotthold Ephraim. *Laocoön: An Essay of the Limits of Painting and Poetry*. Translated by E. A. McCormick. Baltimore: Johns Hopkins University Press, 1984.

musical concert during a banquet"—that is, the ornament that crowns everything. The Vulgate translates this as "et comparatio musicorum in convivio vini." Although very specialized, this meaning is within the logic of the terms *sugkrisis* and *comparatio*. Whether it be music as harmony or social harmony as music, in both cases the idea is that each element should be in its proper place. It is a matter of decorum, that is to say, of appropriateness (see MIMÊSIS, Box 6). The focus of attention is shifted from the parts to the whole. It is no longer a double attention, but, so to speak, a triple

one. If intellectual contrast serves to examine each of the two elements, to illuminate each by the other, contrapuntal harmony seeks to merge them into a whole that simultaneously transcends and respects them. Then the whole is more than the sum of its parts, and the parts in turn are enhanced by the light that their comparison yields. Taken as a whole, the aesthetic dimension is the pleasure of *com-prehending* in the sense of holding the two contrapuntal lines together.

The other example reminds us that this phenomenon is exceedingly classical. This example is poetry. In this case, what does it mean to set two things face to face so that they correspond to each other? The effect of contrasted symmetry is emblematic of the Italian sonnet. First, there are the two quatrains. Not only is each symmetrical in itself, *ab* and then *ba*, but also and especially the two quatrains correspond to each other. The repetition of rhymes is not in itself very important. The essential fact is that this repetition is accompanied by a general schema in which everything tends toward symmetry: to *comparatio*. All of the variations of symmetry are then possible, whether the poet draws the symmetry from resemblance or from difference, from the *adpositum* or from the *contrapositum*. Joachim Du Bellay's *L'Olive* reintroduced the sonnet in France in 1550; the same year, Pierre Ronsard's *Odes* broadened the practice. The imitation of the Pindaric model made it possible to make two segments and not merely two quatrains correspond to each other: *strophe* and *antistrophe*. In Greek poetics, the *antistrophe* corresponded to the *strophe* in having the same metrical scheme; the chorus chanted the *strophe* while dancing in one direction, and the *antistrophe* while dancing in the opposite direction. In the Ronsardian ode, though the rhyme scheme is the same in the *strophe* and the *antistrophe*, the rhymes themselves are not the same, unlike those in the quatrains of the Italian sonnet. This underlines the essential fact. The symmetry has to do not with the repetition of rhymes but with the will to symmetry: with the pure fact of counterpoint, of setting two elements beside one another, of comparing.

Francis Goyet

BIBLIOGRAPHY

Dionysius of Halicarnassus. *Roman Antiquities*. Translated by E. Cary. Cambridge, MA: Harvard University Press, 1937–50.

Hesychius Alexandrinus. *Lexicon*. Edited by M. Schmidt. Halle, Ger.: Dufft, 1861. Reprinted Amsterdam, Neth.: Hakkert, 1965.

Longinus. *On the Sublime*. Translated by W. H. Fyfe. Revised by D. Russell. In *Aristotle: Poetics; Longinus: On the Sublime; Demetrius: On Style*. Loeb Classical Library. Cambridge, MA: Harvard University Press, 1995.

Petrarca, Franscesco. *De vita solitaria: The Life of Solitude*. Translated by J. Zeitlin. Urbana: University of Illinois Press, 1924.

Quintilian. *The Orator's Education*. Edited and translated by Donald A. Russell. Cambridge, MA: Harvard University Press, 2001. French translation by Jean Cousin: *Institution oratoire*. Paris: Belles Lettres, 1975–80.

Ronsard, Pierre. *Odes*. In *Œuvres complètes*, edited by J. Céard, D. Ménager, and M. Simonin. Paris: Gallimard / La Pléiade, 1993–94.

———. *Poems of Pierre de Ronsard*. Translated and edited by N. Kilmer. Berkeley: University of California Press, 1979.

Saussy, Haun, ed. *Comparative Literature in an Age of Globalization*. Baltimore, Johns Hopkins University Press, 2006.

| COMPORTMENT

"Comportment" corresponds to the French *comportement*, which, along with *conduite*, serves as the standard translations of the English "behavior." Adjacent to "behavior," "comportment" particularly emphasizes the objective, observable aspect of ways of acting, as reactions to the world and manifestations of internal dispositions. The article BEHAVIOR studies the differences between behaviorism and the psychology of *comport(e)ment*.

Regarding the relation between an organism and its environment, see AFFORDANCE, *DISPOSITION*.

On modalities of action, see *ACT*, AGENCY, PRAXIS. On the relation between the mind or the mental and the corporeal, see particularly CATHARSIS, CONSCIOUSNESS, DRIVE, *FLESH, MALAISE,* PATHOS, SOUL, UNCONSCIOUS.

On the specificity of the human, see *HUMANITY*; cf. ANIMAL, ERLEBEN.

➤ DASEIN, GEISTESWISSENSCHAFTEN, STRUCTURE

| CONCEPT

"Concept" is borrowed from the Latin *conceptus*, based on *concipere* (*cum-capere*, take entirely, contain). The *conceptus* is what one conceives in two senses of the term, the product of an internal gestation (the concept is mind's fetus) and collection in a unit, generality: CONCEPTUS; cf. INTELLECT, INTELLECTUS, SOUL, UNDERSTANDING. On the difference between "nominalism" and "conceptualism," see TERM.

Only the act of intellectual grasp subsists in *Begriff*, which corresponds to *comprehendere* and *comprehensio*, and belongs to the Stoic idiolect *katalepsis* [κατάληψις] (BEGRIFF, Box 1); see BEGRIFF, where the development of terminologies of understanding is analyzed through German and English; cf. AUFHEBEN, MERKMAL, PERCEPTION.

Finally, Italian *concetto* has a very special status. It is an ingenious invention situated between aesthetic design and witticism; see CONCETTO; cf. ARGUTEZZA, DISEGNO, INGENIUM.

➤ *CATEGORY*, EPISTEMOLOGY, *JUSTICE, REASON*

| CONCEPTUS (LATIN)

ENGLISH	concept
FRENCH	*concept*

➤ BEGRIFF, *CONCEPT*, CONCETTO, and INTELLECT, INTELLECTUS, INTENTION, REPRÉSENTATION, SIGN, SIGNIFIER/SIGNIFIED, SPECIES, TERM, UNDERSTANDING, UNIVERSALS, WORD

The Latin masculine noun *conceptus* (genitive: *conceptus*) came to occupy a distinctive place in Western philosophical terminology only in the second half of the thirteenth century. Meaning literally "fetus," it had been used figuratively since Roman antiquity to designate an intellectual representation developing in the mind (Macrobius, Priscian). But it was with Thomas Aquinas (ca. 1255–74) that the noun *conceptus* became prominent and then spread among epistemologists. This rapid success can be explained by two factors. First is the ambiguity of the term that had previously been dominant, *intellectus*, which designated both the intellectual faculty and the units it represented—and sometimes even the meanings of words. Second and above all is the very semantics of *conceptus*: on the one hand, it denotes, in the literal sense, the product of internal gestation; on the other hand, its etymology (*con-capere*, "take together") alludes to the collection of a plurality of elements in a single perception, that is, nothing less than the notion of generality. The internal production of thought on the one hand, and generality on the other: these are the two key components of *conceptus*. Though the later use of "concept," or *Begriff,* oscillates between reference to an abstract, entirely depsychologized object (as in Frege) and reference to a mental representation (as in the cognitive sciences), the medieval notion surely belongs far more to the second of these two approaches.

I. *Intellectus/Conceptus*

The Latin used in medieval schools had numerous terms for the mental unit of intellectual representation. *Intellectus* designated the understanding itself, of course, but often also the internal objects of understanding. *Species intelligibilis*—paired with *species sensibilis*—put the accent on the representation of the thing in thought, the term *species* initially signifying something like aspect, appearance, or image (see SPECIES). *Verbum mentis* or *verbum cordis*—literally, the mind's or heart's word—related, in the wake of Augustine, to the comparison of human thought with the divine Word. *Intentio* often refers to the unit of thought insofar as it is directed toward some external object (from which comes the famous theme of intentionality). As for *conceptus,* which at the end of the Middle Ages became the key term in this semantic field, it referred first of all to something produced internally.

Literally, *conceptus* designates the fetus conceived in the womb of the mother, but already Macrobius (fifth century) used it in the derivative sense to say that intentions are born from a mental concept (*conceptus mentis,* in *Saturnales,* 1.18.17). But especially the grammarian Priscian (sixth century) wrote, in a passage that was very influential in the Middle Ages, that the spoken word (*vox,* see WORD) indicates a mental concept (*mentis conceptum*), which he also called *cogitatio* (*Institutiones grammaticae,* 11.7). But this use remained metaphorical and marginal. The term was not part of Augustine's usual vocabulary (though he often uses—especially in *De Trinitate*—the corresponding verb *concipere* to designate the mental act giving rise to a "mental verb" within itself). Boethius, translating and commenting on Aristotle's logic in the early sixth century, resorted to *intellectus* to refer to units of intellection (and to render the Greek *noêma* [νόημα]). *Intellectus* is also frequently used in the same sense during the twelfth and thirteenth centuries—especially by Abelard. Bonaventure and Albert the Great, for example, much prefer to use *conceptus* for what we would now call a "concept."

In the first half of the thirteenth century, in fact, *conceptus* used in the abstract sense seems to appear regularly only in direct or indirect relationship with the passage in Priscian mentioned above, according to which the spoken word signifies a "mental concept." In this case, it is opposed to *affectus,* grammarians and logicians (for example, Peter of Spain, *Syncategoreumata,* 2.2, and 8.6) distinguishing between signifying in the mode of the concept ("per modum conceptus") and signifying in the mode of affect ("per modum affectus") (cf. Rosier, *La parole comme acte,* chaps. 2, 3, and 5). But even in this limited context, when one encounters the form *conceptum*—the most frequent, and the one that appears in Priscian—it is not always easy to decide whether it is the accusative of the noun *conceptus* or the past participle of the verb *concipere.* The difference between these two possibilities is large, because taken as a past participle (nominalized or not), *conceptus*—or *conceptum*—normally refers to the thing conceived and not to a mental unit. Roger Bacon in particular proposes to interpret Priscian's work this way, and consequently sees in it the idea that the word signifies the thing itself rather than a mental concept (*Compendium studii theologiae,* 61).

It is with Aquinas, between about 1255 and 1274, that the noun *conceptus* becomes really prominent in the philosophical vocabulary. A half-century later, at the time of William of Ockham, it was in widespread use among epistemologists. In fact, in the middle of the thirteenth century, the ambiguity of *intellectus,* which denoted both the intellectual faculty and its units of representation, and sometimes even the meaning of words, became all the more intolerable because the ambient Aristotelianism distinguished not only various types of intellectual representation ("intellectus simplex" and "intellectus compositus," for example), but also various types of intellect, or in any case, various functions of the intellect ("intellectus agens," "intellectus possibilis," "intellectus adeptus," "intellectus speculativus," "intellectus practicus," etc.; see INTELLECTUS); using a single word obviously risked leading to the most complete imbroglio. *Conceptus,* related to the verb *concipere,* which was already current in the philosophical vocabulary, had a twofold semantic peculiarity that was particularly attractive in this context: on the one hand, it denoted, in the literal sense, the product—or sometimes the process—of internal gestation; on the other hand, its etymology (*con-capere:* "take together") itself suggested the unification of a plurality in a common apprehension. But a major epistemological problem faced by Aquinas and his contemporaries was precisely how to join the Augustinian doctrine of *verbum mentis* (literally, "mental speech") that was so important in theology and that emphasized the mind's engenderment of an internal, prelinguistic thought, with the Aristotelian theory of abstraction that was taught in the faculty of arts on the basis of *De anima,* and that was supposed to account for the formation of general ideas in the mind.

II. Mental Speech and Internal Discourse

For Aquinas, the *conceptus*—which he also calls *conceptio, ratio,* or *verbum mentis*—is a purely ideal object, an internal product existing in the mind in an "intentional" rather than a real way, and representing some external reality in the order of the intelligible. The metaphorical relationship between this *conceptus* and the fetus, often forgotten in modern translations, has to do precisely with the fact that the intellect has to give birth to the *conceptus* within itself, as Aquinas clearly explains: "And when it is in the act of understanding, our intellect forms something intelligible that is, so to speak, its child [*proles*], and that for this reason we call a mental concept [*mentis conceptus*]" (*De rationibus fidei,* chap. 3).

This recourse to *conceptus* understood in this way was very controversial at the end of the thirteenth and the beginning of the fourteenth centuries. Several authors, especially Franciscans such as Pierre de Jean Olivi and William of Ware, complained that Aquinas had introduced between the act of understanding and the external thing that is its true object a useless and harmful intermediary that could act as a screen (cf. Panaccio, *Le discours intérieur,* chap. 6). Gauthier Burley, for example, is very explicit: "There are in the understanding no such concepts that are formed by the act of understanding and are at the same time representations of things [*similitudines rerum*]" (*Quaestiones in librum Perihermeneias,* 3.8).

But for all that, the word *conceptus* was not abandoned, even by Thomism's adversaries. Ultimately, the main debate was about whether *conceptus*, understood as an intellectual representation, had to be seen as a purely ideal object that was the mental correlate of the act of understanding, as Aquinas maintained, or as this act itself. Medieval thinkers were thus very aware of an ambiguity that was long to affect ideas like "concept," "understanding," and "representation," suggesting sometimes a process or an episode (an "act," the Scholastics said) and sometimes its object or result (occasionally seen as a purely intelligible entity).

After a few hesitations, William of Ockham ended up adopting the theory of the act. From this point of view, the *terminus conceptus*—or just *conceptus*—loses its status of intentional object and is identified with a mental quality of the individual subject, a quality endowed with a real existence in the mind (like that of "a white spot on a wall," Ockham explains), and in this school of thought, the original idea of an ideal product of the understanding fades away.

Starting in the fourteenth century, the remaining element common to most schools' use of the widespread term *conceptus* was the idea of a general intellectual representation that could appear as either subject or predicate in true or false mental propositions and play certain precise roles in reasoning. William of Ockham, Jean Buridan, and their followers made abundant use of *conceptus* to designate the simplest unit of mental discourse ("oratio mentalis"), in which they saw a natural sign that could have various semantic properties (*significatio, connotatio, suppositio*). Logical and semiotic functions thus become more important in this vocabulary than the mental dynamics. But the psychological dimension was not eliminated—far from it: contrary to the Fregean *Begriff*, the medieval *conceptus* is always mental; it exists, in one form or another, only in individual minds.

The common English translation of *conceptus* by "concept" remains, of course, the best available choice, but the very obviousness of this simple transposition usually conceals the complexity and diversity of characteristics that were simultaneously or successively associated with this term in the Middle Ages, from the relationship to the vocabulary of childbirth to the crucial insertion of the word into the very heart of the logic called "terminist" and seen as a grammar of thought.

Claude Panaccio

BIBLIOGRAPHY

Augustine. *On the Trinity*. Translated by A. W. Haddan. Revised by W.G.T. Shedd. In *Basic Writings of Saint Augustine*, edited by W. J. Oates, 2:667–878. New York: Random House, 1948.

Bacon, Roger. *Compendium of the Study of Theology*. Edited and translated by T. S. Maloney. Leiden, Neth.: Brill, 1988.

Boethius. *First and Second Commentaries*. In *On Aristotle On Interpretation 9*, edited by David L. Blank, translated by N. Kretzmann and David L. Blank. London: Duckworth, 1998.

———. *In librum Aristotelis Peri Hermenias*. Edited by C. Meiser. 2 vols. Leipzig: Teubner, 1877–80.

Gauthier, Burley. *Quaestiones in librum Perihermeneias*. Edited by S. F. Brown. *Franciscan Studies* 34 (1974): 200–295. First published in 1301.

Macrobius. *The Saturnalia*. Translated by P. V. Davies. New York: Columbia University Press, 1969.

Panaccio, Claude. *Le discours intérieur: De Platon à Guillaume d'Ockham*. Paris: Éditions du Seuil, 1999.

———. *Ockham on Concepts*. London: Ashgate, 2004.

Peter of Spain. *Syncategoreumata*. Edited by L. M. de Rijk. English translation by J. Spruyt. Leiden, Neth.: Brill, 1992.

Priscian. *Institutionum grammaticarum libri XVIII*. Edited by M. Hertz. In *Grammatici latini*, vols. 2–3. Reprint. Hildesheim, Ger.: Olms, 1961.

Rosier, Irène. *La parole comme acte: Sur la grammaire de la sémantique au XIIème siècle*. Paris: Vrin, 1994.

Thomas Aquinas. *An Aquinas Reader*. Edited by M. Clark. 3rd ed. New York: Fordham University Press, 2000.

———. *De rationibus fidei ad Cantorem Antichenum*. In *Opera omnia*, vol. 40. Rome: Leonine, 1969.

———. *Quaestiones disputatae de potentia*. In *Quaestiones disputatae*, edited by P. Bazzi, M. Calcaterra, T. S. Centi, E. Odetto, and P. M. Pession, vol. 2. Turin: Marietti, 1965.

———. *Quaestiones disputatae de veritate*. In *Opera omnia*, vol. 22. Rome: Leonine, 1970.

———. *Summa contra Gentiles*. In *Opera omnia*, vols. 13–15. Rome: Leonine, 1918–30. Translation by A. C. Pegis: *On the Truth of the Catholic Faith: Summa contra Gentiles*. Garden City, NY: Hanover House, 1955–57.

———. *Thomas Aquinas: Selected Writings*. New York: Penguin Classics, 1999.

William of Ockham. *Ockham's Theory of Terms: Part 1 of the* Summa logicae. Translated and with an introduction by M. J. Loux. Notre Dame, IN: University of Notre Dame Press, 1974.

———. *Ockham's Theory of Propositions: Part 2 of the* Summa logicae. Translated by A. J. Freddoso and H. Schuurman, introduction by A. J. Freddoso. South Bend, IN: St. Augustine's Press, 1998.

———. *Summa logicae* (1325). In *Guillelmi de Ockham Opera philosophica*, edited by P. Boehner, G. Gál, and S. Brown, vol. 1. New York: The Franciscan Institute, 1974.

CONCETTO (ITALIAN)

ENGLISH	conceit, concept, idea, thought, representation
FRENCH	concept, *idée, pensée, représentation*
GERMAN	*Begriff*
LATIN	*conceptus*

➤ BEGRIFF, *CONCEPT*, CONCEPTUS, and ARGUTEZZA, COMPARISON, DISEGNO, GENIUS, *IDEA*, *IMAGE*, INGENIUM, MIMÊSIS, REPRÉSENTATION, SPECIES, STRUCTURE

The word *concetto* presents no particular difficulties in contemporary Italian philosophical discourse insofar as, like the word *concept* in French, its meaning is presently strongly determined by the massive contribution of German philosophical texts. Since Immanuel Kant, French and Italian have reelaborated their definitions of *concept* and *concetto* with reference to *Begriff*. But this modern equivalence threatens to obscure the fact that in the Italian tradition from Dante to Benedetto Croce, *concetto*, indissolubly philosophical and rhetorical, refers both to the ingenious invention at work in the image and in the idea, and to the operation of the understanding involved in what we call the "concept." Only since the nineteenth century has the word referred almost exclusively to the operations of generalization and abstraction as we understand them today. In fact, neither Giordano Bruno, nor Tommaso Campanella, nor Giambattista Vico saw in the *concetto* an act having to do with the intellect alone and with its logical and cognitive functions.

I. The Semantic Autonomy of *Concetto* with Respect to *Conceptus*

At a time when Latin (that is, the Latin of the Scholastics) constituted almost the whole of the intellectual language,

Dante's use of the word *concetto* already raised most of the problems we encounter in philosophical language proper. This is all the more remarkable because it was only starting in the fourteenth century that the word was gradually affected by the rhetorical tradition, the aesthetic and artistic thought of the Renaissance, Marsilio Ficino's Neoplatonism, and the Aristotelianism of the Jesuits in the seventeenth century. In Dante, *concetto* shows an amazing autonomy with respect to the Latin *conceptus*, as if there were no interpenetration between Scholastic discourse and poetic discourse. Thus in the *Paradiso* (in the *Divine Comedy*), Dante offers us a number of ways to use the term; for example:

1. "Ne' mirabili aspetti vostri risplende non so che vi trasmuta da' primi concetti" (In your admirable appearance something divine shines forth that transmutes your earlier image).
2. "Queste sustanze . . . non bisogna / rememorer per concetto divisa" (These substances . . . need not / be remembered by separate ideas).
3. "O quanto è corto il dire e come fioco al mio concetto!" (O how inadequate is speech and how dim my thought!).

(*Paradiso*, 3.58–59, 29.79–81, 33.121–22, trans. Sisson)

Idea, concept, thought, image, intention (in the sense of an intellectual and artistic project), an act of the creative imagination, the *concetto* thus tends very early on to designate a number of intellectual activities, in an extension that produces an exceptional polysemy.

■ See Box 1.

II. The Productivity of *Concetto*

In the sixteenth century, the word *concetto* tends to bring out the originality of the production of schemas and representations by showing *in actu*, as it were, the activity of the mind, which can be the *ingegno* or the *intelletto*. From this comes the gradual extension of *concetto*, which, while claiming to be the expression of the idea, shows ostensibly the activity of the imagination, the subtlety of the mind in the metaphorical comprehension of the world that is specific to *conceptismo*. The semantic polyvalence of the word, which is used in extremely heterogeneous fields of application, can proliferate in a single text (the Platonic or pictural, symbolic, or metaphysical meaning, as in Giordano Bruno) and end inevitably in ambiguities. But these semantic ambiguities are not derived from etymological contingencies; on the contrary, they are carefully maintained and favored by authors insofar as the goal is precisely to substitute for the idea the more subtle nuances of the *concetto*. That is why it is ultimately not important to know that *concetto* is derived from *concepire* in the sense of "conceive" or "imagine," since only the multiple goals in the service of which the word is used matter.

The diversity of uses, intentions, and meanings is such that German translators of the word *concetto*, particularly when used in reference to the baroque, usually retain the Italian word, except, of course, in the case of poetic texts. In the case of philosophical texts, French translations of *con-cetto* by *concept*, *idée*, or *pensée* are merely arbitrary solutions and are seldom satisfactory. Thus, to translate a sentence from

Campanella, "Il mondo è il libro dove il sénno eterno scrisse i propri concetti" (*La città del sole* [1623], in Seroni, 326), we can propose, "The world is a book in which eternal reason writes its own thoughts" or ". . . its own ideas." But we will never be able to translate *propri concetti* by "its own concepts," because the divine intellect, which is identified with universal reason, does not really express itself through concepts, but through ideas. Moreover, the topos of the Book of the World refers back to the idea that the totality of the objects in the universe constitutes a system of signs expressing God's thought, which cannot be treated as simple concepts.

The difficulties regarding the possible translation of *concetto* as a specific expression of the modalities of thought culminate in the work of Giordano Bruno. In *De gl'heroici furori* (On heroic furor), Bruno's philosophical and sapiential thought is usually analogic: he sets forth his ideas most precisely in the interpretations of allegories, emblems, and devices around which the dialogues are articulated. The text tends to exemplify all the modalities of the idea insofar as it is based on a symbolic image and is fully intelligible in relation to the latter. Bruno usually calls this idea a *concetto*, as in this passage:

On the doubtful road of uncertain reason and affection to which Pythagoras's letter refers, where on the right appears the difficult path, thornier, rougher, and more deserted, on which the hunter unleashes his hounds and mastiffs to track down wild beasts, which are the intelligible species of ideal concepts [*le specie intelligibili de concetti ideali*].

(*De gl'heroici furori* [1585], 1.4)

Because we cannot use the word "idea" to translate *concetti ideali*, the translator has to content himself with rendering the Italian literally. The difficulty is not that truth and beauty can be adequately designated only in the allegorical mode (in this case, the allegory of the myth of Acteon), but that *concetti ideali* can be attained only through a symbolic image. The notion of an ideal concept, which is already vague, is not capable of making it clear how *concetto* has a connotation that is in a way figurative and closely connected with the activity of the imagination.

Another example, also from Bruno, shows the proximity of the *concetto* and the idea:

High and deep, and always alert, o my thoughts [*pensieri*], ready to leave the maternal lap of the suffering soul, you, archers well-armed to hit the target from which the sublime idea [*alto concetto*] is born, along these rough paths Heaven does not allow you to encounter a cruel beast.

(Ibid.)

This passage describes symbolically how the soul, seeking reconciliation with the heart, must call upon archers whose function is to drive away the seductions of the senses, those of sight, so as to allow access to a superior beauty. These archers must in addition repress their own sight, close their eyes, the better to flush out the *alto concetto*, well rendered by "sublime idea" insofar as it is a matter of a quest for the beautiful and the true in a perspective inspired by Neoplatonism in the wake of Marsilio Ficino.

1

The *concetto*, an aesthetic rival of "idea"

Although they seem far from a philosophical procedure, Michelangelo's two verses cited by Erwin Panofsky in Italian in his book *Idea* perfectly exemplify the difficulties that translators still encounter: "Non ha l'ottimo artista alcun concetto ch'un marmo solo in sè non circonscriva col suo soverchio" (The excellent artist has no *concetto* that a marble alone does not include with its superabundance: *Le rime di Michelangelo Buonarroti*). The Italian text is rendered by the French translator of Panofsky's book this way: "L'artiste excellent n'a aucun concept qu'un marbre seul en soi ne circonscrive de sa masse" (Panofsky, *Idea*, trans. Joly). We could point out to the translator that the word *concept* does not reflect Michelangelo's obvious Neoplatonism, and that the word *idée* would have already been more adequate. But above all, we must explain that *concept* cannot really illuminate the problematics at work in *concetto* as it is encountered in Renaissance theoreticians of art, so that the word *concept* means almost the opposite of what Michelangelo intended. The German translator Karl Frey (*Die Dichtungen des Michelangelo Buonarroti* [1897]) shows that he is better informed and more prudent when he renders "Non ha l'ottimo artista alcun concetto" as "Im *Geiste* kann nicht mal der grösste Meister ein Bild sich machen" (literally, "The greatest master cannot form an image in his mind"). Of course, "ein Bild sich machen" lacks Platonic overtones, suggesting activity that is more properly psychological than aesthetic and metaphysical. In reality, a satisfactory understanding of the ways in which the word is used by Italian theorists would require a more precise knowledge of their own philosophical reference points. Even in Michelangelo, the question of whether he takes *concetto* in a Neoplatonic or an Aristotelian sense is controversial (Panofksy and Götz Pochat are opposed on this point). This divergence in interpretation regarding *concetto* already appears among Michelangelo's contemporaries. Fortunately, we have a text written during the author's lifetime by an academician, Benedetto Varchi, that correctly analyzes Michelangelo's text from a philological point of view. Even if we take into account Varchi's tendency to Platonize the sense of Michelangelo's poem, as a philologist and historian he confirms the correspondence—or even equivalence (which is more debatable)—between *concetto* and *idea*:

As our poet uses it, *concetto* corresponds to what the Greeks called *idea*, the Romans *exemplar*, and what we call *modello*, that is, the form [*forma*] or representation [*imagine*], called by some "intention," that we have in the imagination [*fantasia*], of everything we intend to do or say; which intention is spiritual . . . and serves as an efficient cause for everything we say or do.

(*La lezzione di Benedetto Varchi sopra il sottoscritto sonnetto di Michelangelo Buonarroti*, in Barocchi, *Scritti d'arte*, 2:1330)

Through the tension it maintains between a poorly elucidated Platonism and an Aristotelianism that holds that the artist realizes his *concetto* in matter, Varchi's analysis has the merit of showing the extraordinary plasticity of the word, its fundamental polysemy that proves to be very fertile in the expression of intellectual functions. The definitions Varchi gives are simply possible interpretations of the word as it might have been understood by a Renaissance humanist who was especially concerned to show that the aesthetic thought of the period was in perfect harmony, in Italian, with Neoplatonic ideas.

We see here how *concetto* expresses an allegorical, symbolic, and philosophical procedure that results in an increasingly redoubtable polysemy. Two currents glorify still further the productivity of the *concetto*: on the one hand, the theory of art, whose paradigm, after Alberti's *De pictura*, remained Cicero's *De oratore*, which emphasizes artistic invention; and on the other hand, *conceptismo*, which connects the activity of the mind solely with language as such.

III. *Concetto* in Theories of Art

In Georgio Vasari, the word *concetto* is close to the idea considered as a general representation:

Da questa cognizione nasce un certo concetto e giudizio, che si forma nella mente quella tal cosa che poi espressa con le mani si chiama disegno.

(From this apprehension is formed a concept, a reason engendered in the mind by the object, whose manual expression is called drawing.)

(Vasari, *Le vite* [1568])

In Vasari, *concetto* denotes a particularly active intellectual act, a conception, whose function is to promote the art of drawing as a form of thought. The idea of the beautiful in the sense of "ideal" is the ultimate reference point of the artist's thought, and the *concetto* becomes the mark of the activity of the *intelletto*, which, through its ingenuity and fecundity, makes it possible to construct a priori the system of rules governing the production of artworks. The clear desire to intellectualize the theory of art rapidly eventuates, at the end of the sixteenth century—that is, with the generation that followed Vasari—in a semantic inflation of the word *concetto* that could only produce further ambiguities. From then on, no art was conceivable without the productive activity of the *intelletto*, of the *ingegno* (in the sense of ingenuity or genius), so that the *concetto* tends to slowly eclipse the idea in metaphysical reflection on art. This ascension of the act of conceiving ends up including metaphysics, theology, and thought about art, as is shown, for example, by Federico Zuccaro's theory of *disegno*:

Ben è vero che per questo nome di disegno interno io non intendo solamente il concetto interno formato nella mente del pittore, ma enco quel concetto che forma qual si voglia intelletto.

(It is quite true that by this name of *disegno interno* I mean not only the internal concept formed in the mind of the painter, but also this concept that any intellect can form.)

(*L'idea de' pittori, scultori e architetti* [1607])

Disegno is almost identified with *concetto* in the sense of an original conception of the intellect, since it is a matter of analyzing the faculties that make artistic creation possible.

Thus *concetto* is deliberately distanced from the idea in the Platonic sense and becomes the intellectual act of a creative freedom exercised on signs, forms, representations. But sometimes the *concetto* is so strongly imbued with divine ideas that it is no longer a product of the *intelletto*, but rather a form of the intellect's participation in God, as Zuccaro says explicitly:

> In questo modo essendo l'intelletto e i sensi soggetti al Disegno e al concetto, possiamo dire, che esso Disegno, come Principe, rettore e governatore di essi se ne serva come cosa sua propria.

> (In this way the intellect and the senses being subjected to the *disegno* and to the *concetto*, we can say that this *disegno*, as the Prince, orator, and governor, makes use of them as its own property.)

> (Ibid.)

In this case, we could translate *concetto* as "ideal representation" or even "ideal and ingenious representation." With Zuccaro's generation and the first treatises written by the Jesuit theoreticians of the seventeenth century, the *concetto* acquires the remarkable characteristic of being both very close to the idea as the principle of the production of forms, and very distant from it because it breaks with any reference point, and especially with any possible resemblance, to become only a mental, plastic, figurative, and symbolic expression. From this comes the confusion of translators—for example, those of the seventeenth century—who limited themselves to terms that were frequently too general, such as *conception d'esprit*, *pensée*, or *imagination*, as did Nathanaël Düez in his *Dictionnaire italien-français* (1670). At the opposite pole from the idea, which retained its prestige as a metaphysical authority, the *concetto* gained a field of application extending beyond ingenious inventions (all the symbolic figures: allegories, emblems, devices, graphic enigmas) as far as the language of the angels (*i concetti divini*) and even the coded language of God that transforms the world into a vast system of enigmatic, allegorical, emblematic signs. From that point on, the possible ways of translating *concetto* become steadily more limited and should lead us to resort to the equivalents proposed by French theoreticians of the seventeenth century: *idées ingénieuses*, *représentations savantes*, and even *inventions savantes*.

IV. *Concetto* and *Conceptismo*

From the sixteenth to the seventeenth century, *concettismo* (Italian) or *conceptismo* (Spanish) was an effort to radicalize the rhetorical tradition in the sense of an almost exclusive primacy of metaphorical thought that was developed both in the order of discourse (the art of the witticism) and in that of plastic or symbolic representations. The authors sought to extend all forms of eloquence as far as possible, from discourse to pictorial representation, in order to glorify the resources of the *ingegno*.

The theoreticians of mannerism and the Jesuits tried to reconcile the Ciceronian ideal of eloquence with the philosophical categories of Aristotle and Aquinas. The expression of the idea henceforth demanded a more witty, more *concettoso* discourse, more subtle than really conceptual. The *concettosità* of an ingeniously formulated idea is precision of thought insofar as it succeeds in realizing itself in an analogical and metaphorical mode. *Conceptismo* as it was theorized by Jesuit pedagogy postulates very explicitly that every thought and every language are originally metaphorical, so that the existence of a literal meaning of a proposition or even of an image seems not only prosaic or illusory, improbable or deficient, but also a form of potential symbolism. And that means that every *concetto*, that is, every *concetto ingegnoso*, presupposes a conception of metaphor and figure situated in a kind of general semiotics. To think in a *concettosa* manner is to know how to reconcile the austere rigor of the concept with the inventiveness of metaphor. That is why the word "concept" cannot adequately translate *concetto*. The *concetto della bellezza* cannot be rendered precisely by the "concept of the beautiful," because the English word remains in conformity with the Latin *conceptus*, that is, it is incapable of rendering the productivity of the imagination and the aesthetic inventiveness peculiar to the Italian word. In authors like Matteo Peregrini and Emanuele Tesauro, who were theoreticians of metaphor, symbolic expression, and the witticism, the *concetto* was subjected to the new requirements of *argutezza*, an infinite source of ingenious expression. *Argutezza* became the supreme faculty of inventions and symbolic creations in most of the arts of discourse and plastic arts, so that in his *Cannochiale aristotelico* (1654), Tesauro declared it the "gran madre d'ogni 'ngnoso concetto" (grandmother of every ingenious *concetto*). The word *concetto* refers to what consciousness produces in its metaphorical activity and to any representation that contains wit and subtlety. Here, the problematics of the *concetto* are completely absorbed by the hegemony of the rhetorical and sophistic problematics of the *argutezza*.

Jean-François Groulier

BIBLIOGRAPHY

Barocchi, Paola, ed. *Scritti d'arte del cinquecento*. Milan: Ricciardi, 1971.

Bruno, Giordano. *De gl'heroici furori*. Milan: Mondadori, 2011. First published in 1585.

Dante Alighieri. *The Divine Comedy*. Edited by D. H. Higgins. Translated by C. H. Sisson. Oxford: Oxford University Press, 2008.

Düez, Nathanaël. *Dittionario italiano e francese—Dictionnaire italien-français*. Leiden, Neth.: Jean Elsevier, 1670.

———. *Oxford-Paravia Italian Dictionary*. New York: Oxford University Press, 2007.

Lange, Klaus Peter. *Theoretiker des literarischen Manierismus*. Munich: Fink, 1968.

Michelangelo. *Die Dichtungen des Michelangelo Buonarroti*. Translated by Karl Frey. Berlin: Grote, 1897.

———. *The Poetry of Michelangelo*. Annotated and translated by James M. Saslow. New Haven, CT: Yale University Press, 1991.

Panofsky, Erwin. *Idea, ein Beitrag zur Begriffsgeschichte der älteren Kunsttheorie*. Leipzig: B. G. Teubner, 1924. English translation by J.J.S. Peake: *Idea: A Concept in Art Theory*. Columbia: University of South Carolina Press, 1968. French translation by Henri Joly: *Idea*. Paris: Gallimard / La Pléiade, 1989.

Peregrini, Matteo. *Delle acutezze, che altrimenti spiriti, vivezze e concetti, volgarmente si appellano*. Genoa, It.: Ferroni, 1639.

Pochat, Götz. *Geschichte der Äesthetik und Kunsttheorie*. Cologne, Ger.: Du Mont, 1986.

Seroni, Adriano, ed. *La città del sole e Scelta d'alcune poesie filosofiche*. Milan: Feltrinelli, 1962.

Tesauro, Emanuele. *Il cannocchiale aristotelico*. Turin: Bartolomeo Zauatta, 1654.

Vasari, Georgio. *Le vite de' più eccellenti pittori, scultori e architetti*. Florence: Appresso I Giunti, 1568. Translation by J. Conaway Bondanella and P. Bondanella: *The Lives of the Artists*. Oxford: Oxford University Press, 1998.

Zuccaro, Federico. *L'idea de' pittori, scultori e architetti*. Turin: Disserolio, 1607.

CONCILIARITY

This is the customary translation of the Russian *sobornost'* [соборность], which designates the type of solidarity and community connected with the Russian Orthodox Church; see *OBLIGATION* and SOBORNOST'; see also NAROD (people) and PRAVDA (truth, justice), and cf. BOGOČELOVEČESTVO (theandry), MIR (peace, world, peasant community), SVET (world-light).

Cf. Hebrew BERĪT [בְּרִית], which designates the pact between the people and its god; see BERĪT, *ALLIANCE*; cf. DUTY and EUROPE.

➤ *COMMUNITY, CONSENSUS*, GOD, *HUMANITY*

CONNOTATION

FRENCH	*connotation*
GERMAN	*Konnotation*
LATIN	*connotatio, consignificatio*

➤ ANALOGY, HOMONYM, PARONYM, PRÉDICABLE, PREDICATION, SENSE, SUBJECT, SUPPOSITION

Commonly used in linguistics since L. Bloomfield (1933), theorized by Hjelmslev, abundantly exploited by Roland Barthes and Umberto Eco, and central to semiotics and the theory of the text, the notion of connotation has a number of remarkable ambiguities that can be described, if not completely mastered, by considering the term's slow maturation, opposed to that of "denotation" (Fr. *dénotation*, Ger. *Denotation*), at the heart of the system of notions that articulate, in modern philosophy, the fields of ontology, semantics, philosophy of logic, and philosophy of language.

The first documented uses of the word *connotation* in French designate the confused meaning of a word or a concept, as opposed to a clear meaning (Port-Royal). This French sense of the word corresponds to the stress put on an element that was initially present in the semantic field of the medieval Latin *connotatio*—the derivative or secondary aspect, also marked in the synonymous term *consignificatio*—as if the confused/distinct pair were superimposed on the more general derived/direct pair. The original meaning of the Latin *connotatio*, which is also found in the English expression "associative meaning" (equivalent to "connotative meaning") poses no particular problem. Linguists and theoreticians of literary texts both oppose the "contextual coloring" (*coloration contextuelle*) or "implications" that a term can have in a given context (i.e., its "connotation") to its so-called referential, conceptual, or cognitive meaning indicated by the term "denotation." However, the idea of connotation involves a philosophical difficulty because of the possible interferences between the system of direct (distinct) and secondary (confused) signification on the one hand, and on the other the Fregean system of *Sinn* and *Bedeutung*, whose discordant translations ("sense" vs. "reference," or "sense" vs. "denotation") are a source of troublesome ambiguities.

I. Connotation/Clear or Primary Meaning and Connotation/Denotation

The sense of "confused meaning" was introduced in the *Grammaire de Port-Royal* (1676):

the reason that a noun cannot subsist by itself is that in addition to its distinct meaning, there is another confused meaning that can be called the connotation of something associated with the distinct meaning. Thus the distinct meaning of "red" is redness. But it signifies it by indistinctly marking the subject with this redness, and that is why it does not subsist alone in discourse, because it must be implicit in the word that signifies this subject. Just as this connotation makes the adjective, when it is separated from words that signify accidents, substantives are made from them, as from *coloré, couleur*; from *rouge, rougeur*; from *dur, dureté*; from *prudent, prudence*, etc. And when on the contrary we add to words that signify substances this connotation or confused meaning of something with which these substances are connected, we make adjectives of them: from *homme, humain; genre humain, vertu humaine*, etc. The Greeks and Romans have an infinite number of such words, *ferreus, aureus, bovinus, vitulinus*, etc. But Hebrew, French, and other vulgar languages have fewer of them. French explains it by a *de, d'or, de boeuf*, etc. If these adjectives based on the names of substances are stripped of their connotation, they are made into new substantives, called abstract or separate. Thus *homme* having made *humain*, from *humain* we make *humanité*, etc.

In English, we find the same opposition in John Stuart Mill, where it is colored by an additional trait, the opposition between the comprehension and the extension of a concept or a term, which enables him to define denotation as "the things an expression applies to," connotation being the complementary "information" that any common noun normally "brings to mind" regarding the objects that it "denotes." The problem raised by the use of connotation in philosophy is that its opposite, "denotation," has gradually merged with the German *Bedeutung* taken in its Fregean meaning. As a result, there is a danger of confusing two oppositions that do not necessarily coincide: denotation (*Bedeutung*) and meaning (*Sinn*), on the one hand, and primary meaning (*significatio prima, principalis*) and secondary meaning (*significatio secundaria, ex consequenti, connotatio*) on the other. Even if English tends to use the term "denotation" to explain that two expressions applying to the same thing (i.e., having the same denotation) can differ in meaning, we must avoid identifying, by means of the word "connotation," this meaning with Frege's *Sinn*. A quick examination of the origins of the term "connotation" shows that this tendency or temptation is connected with the polysemy of the Latin *connotatio*, which, from the outset and through the diversity of disciplines in which the notion is used, mingles inextricably the logical, linguistic, and ontological registers.

The Latin term *connotatio* appeared in the twelfth century, and its first use was essentially theological, in the domain of Trinitarian semantics. The verbs used to express the idea of connotation (*notare, connotare, consignificare, innuere*) all refer to the same idea: making something different known with (*cum*) itself—whence the specialization of connotation in the sense of "secondary meaning of a word" and the close connection of the various terms expressing this idea with the idea of consignification (*consignificatio*) or co-intellection (*cointellectio*).

■ See Box 1.

1

Denotatio/connotatio in medieval logic

In medieval logic, the distinction between "connotation" and "denotation" does not exist in the form of an opposition between *connotatio* and *denotatio*. The verb *denotare* emerged along with terminist logic. It is found in Peter of Spain, for instance. Analyzing the sentence "sedentem possibile est ambulare" (it is possible that the person who is seated walks), Peter notes that the participle "refers to" or "includes a simultaneity" (*importat concomitantiam*). This *concomitantia* can be signified either in relation to the verb *ambulare* (in the sense of "dum sedeo, me ambulare est possibile" [while I am sitting, I can walk]), which is false, or denoted relative to the predicate (in the sense of "dum sedet, potentiam

habet ad ambulandeum postea" [while he is sitting, he has the capacity to walk later], which is true. Peter therefore observes, in a more general way, that

Quando denotatur concomitantia respectu hujus verbi *ambulare*, tunc ponitur possibilitas supra totum dictum, et sic est falsa; quando autem denotatur concomitantia respectu praedicati, tunc possibilitas ponitur supra subjectum dicti, et sic est vera.

(When simultaneity is denoted in relation to the verb "to walk," then the possibility bears on the whole of the *dictum*, and the proposition is false; when it is denoted in

relation to the predicate, it concerns the subject of the *dictum*, and the proposition is true.)

Tractatus, 7.70

This example suffices to show that *denotare* was not initially opposed to *connotare*, as "denotation" is opposed to "connotation" in modern linguistics. In Peter of Spain's text the verb *denotare/denotari* is a simple synonym of *significare/significari*.

BIBLIOGRAPHY

Peter of Spain. *Tractatus Called Afterwards "Summulae Logicales."* Edited by L. M. De Rijk. Assen, Neth: Van Gorcum, 1972.

In the late Middle Ages, the analysis of *connotatio* focused on a more specific phenomenon: the meaning of "denominative" terms (*denominativa*; see PARONYM), that is, concrete accidental terms (like "white"), and finally ended up in Ockham's distinction between absolute and connotative terms. This shift explains in part the diversity of the problems the Middle Ages encountered with the notion of connotation: the distinction between signification in itself and accidental signification (*significatio per se* and *significatio per aliud*), primary signification and secondary signification (*principaliter significare* and *secundario significare*), direct signification (*in recto*) and indirect signification (*in obliquo*), signification according to the anterior and the posterior (*secundum prius et posterius*) or analogical (see ANALOGY)—all combined with the problems involved in the semantic distinction between signification (*significatio*) and reference (*suppositio, appellatio*).

II. *Connotatio* and *Consignificatio*

Secondary meaning, as opposed to primary meaning, was at first designated by the term *consignificatio* and the corresponding verb, *consignificare*. These terms were used for different problems:

1. "Secondary signification" is used for tense, which is "consignified" and not signified by the verb, and also for composition, or the predicative function (*prossêmainein* [προσσημαίνειν] in Aristotle)—the questions of contingent future tenses, of divine prescience, and of the unity of the articles of faith could all benefit from this notion of consignification because it made it possible, for example, to posit a unity of the articles of faith independently of the accidental, temporally determined forms in which they were formulated (Christ will be born / is born / was born).

2. It is also said that the denominative term (or paronym) consignifies the subject (e.g., *album* signifies whiteness primarily, and consignifies the subject of the whiteness).

3. In the Platonizing analyses of the early twelfth century, the paronyms "whiteness" (*albedo*), "whitish" (*albet*),

and "white" (*albus*) are said to signify the same quality, or form, or idea, but in different ways, and hence with different consignifications (cf. Bernard of Chartres: "'whiteness' signifies a pure virgin, 'whitish' the same entering a bed chamber or lying on a bed, 'white' again the same, but deflowered").

4. "Consignification" is used for all parts of speech that are neither subject nor predicate, those that are "consignificant" (*consignificantia, consignificativa*) or syncategorematic; then it is said that not everything signifies the universal, but consignifies universally.

We can mention two other less important meanings:

5. *Consignificare* can also be equivalent to "signify the same thing," as when one says that in a proposition the subject and the predicate "consignify."

6. It is also said that the parts of a compound noun "consignify," for example, *equus* (horse) and *ferrus* (savage) in the compound *equiferrus* because they retain something of their meanings, but do not signify strictly speaking because these meanings merge in a single meaning, which is that of the compound.

By extension on the basis of (1), most grammatical accidents will be described, starting in the twelfth century, as consignifications (person, number, etc.) because they are properties that are accidental with regard to the primary grammatical meaning that makes it possible to define the word as belonging to this or that part of speech. The Modists of the thirteenth century maintained that all grammatical properties, both essential (defining the class of words and its species) and accidental, were consignified because they corresponded to different ways of apprehending the thing signified. The modes of signifying (or modes of consignifying) are here opposed to the lexical meaning, whereas earlier *consignificata* were only a part of the latter, the accidents. The term *consignificare* can thus have two distinct meanings, either "signify with" (*significare cum*), as when one says that the verb consignifies the tense (it refers to its signified with a secondary temporal meaning), or "signify in such a way" (*significare sic*), as when one says that the noun *motus* signifies movement in the mode of substance, the verb *movere* signifies it in the mode of movement, etc. It was only in the first sense that *consignificare* was replaced, notably in the logical tradition, by *connotare*; in the fourteenth century, for instance, writers referred to a verb's temporal connotation (cf. Maierù, *Terminologia logica della tarde scolastica*).

The notion of *consignificatio* is a useful tool for distinguishing between terms that are clearly related on the semantic level without being synonyms. This holds for the first three meanings listed above, and for their extensions: the noun *cursus* (race) and the verb *currit* (he runs) have the same meaning, but they differ because only the second consignifies time; the denominative "white" signifies the same thing as the corresponding abstract noun "whiteness," but by connoting the subject of the quality; the noun "suffering," the verb "to suffer," and the interjection "ow!" all mean the same thing, but signify different real properties that are indicated by membership in different grammatical categories.

III. *Connotatio* in Theology

Theologians are confronted by the problem of distinguishing not between terms that are close in form and differ only partly in meaning, but between terms that are "identical" when they are used to speak of created realities and God. Moreover, they have to explain why different attributes can be predicated of God, signified by different words, whereas God himself is simple and indistinct. The notions of *consignificatio* and *connotatio* proved to be useful tools for coping with these two problems.

Starting in the second half of the twelfth century, theologians believed that it did not suffice to oppose a predication regarding God to the same predication regarding a created reality—as in the example of Boethius's *De Trinitate*: "God is just/ man is just," where they said that in the latter case the usage is correct because it is in conformity with the first meaning of the term, whereas in the former case we are dealing with a figurative, transferred, equivocal usage (see TO TRANSLATE). In "God is just" and "God is good," the same divine essence is predicated, but these statements are not identical in meaning because something different is consignified or "compredicated," for example, that God is the cause of justice, on the one hand, and that he is the cause of goodness on the other. Analogously, "God is just," in which "just" consignifies that God is the cause of justice, can be contrasted with "man is just," where the same adjective consignifies that man is the effect of divine justice. Thus it was possible to maintain that every predicate amounts to attributing to God the same divine essence, which is "essentially signified," but that it "signifies secondarily" or consignifies a different effect in the creature. This explains why different attributes are not synonymous when they are attributed to God: even if "just" and "merciful" signify the same thing in God, in the sense that there is no distinction between justice and mercy in God, who is an absolutely simple entity, it is not tautological or redundant to say "God is just and merciful" because the two adjectives have different connotations, since the effects of justice and mercy on human beings are different. From this two rules regarding the functioning of conjunction are drawn: in ordinary

statements (e.g., "Man is just and courageous") conjunction associates the signifieds; in theological statements (e.g., "God is just and merciful") it associates (*copulat*) the "consignifieds" (*consignificata*), namely, the effects that are "compredicated" in this proposition, but not the divine essence, which is identically "predicated" by each of the two adjectives. The problem of co-reference raised by statements such as "Deus est justus et talis est Petrus" (God is just and so is Peter) is resolved in an analogous way: even if divine justice and Peter's justice have nothing in common, they can be compared because the comparison is made solely on the level of consignification. The identity of predicates in God thus becomes compatible with the diversity of names that designate them and the meanings that are conventionally associated with them. This theory of consignification allowed Prévostin to propose the idea that there is a *univocatio et non equivocatio* (see HOMONYM) in the statements "God is just" and "man is just," precisely because the two predications have something in common. Toward the end of the twelfth century, the terms *connotare/connotatio* were used instead of *consignificare/consignificatio*, which nonetheless continued to be used in the logical and grammatical traditions. We note as well the use of *compraedicare* and *coassertare* to distinguish between primary and secondary predication.

However, the ad hoc character of this idea of connotation elicited criticisms. It was appealed to whenever there was a need to distinguish within a single term something identical and something different; it could even be used to demonstrate the doctrinal unity of the "authorities" that are supposed to be strictly speaking contradictory since one had only to say that the controversial pages use the same words with different "connotations." At the turn of the thirteenth century, there were lively debates about how to determine this difference indicated by connotation: should connotation be thought from the point of view of God (the cause) or from that of the creature (the effect) (*connotatio a parte rei/a parte creaturae*)? Should one acknowledge that relational nouns, even when predicated of God (e.g., "Deus est creator"), connote something about creatures, but not about God? Indeed, why not attribute all names to God since he is the cause of all the things they signify? These difficulties eventually undermined the theory of connotation, and first Albert the Great, then Aquinas, found new solutions to the same problems. (Cf. Rosier, "Res significata et modus significandi"; Valente, "Justus et misericors")

∎ See Box 2.

IV. Connotative Terms

For William of Ockham, the classification of categorematic terms into absolute and connotative terms is central, and is based on the same criteria as before. The connotative name "is one that signifies something in a primary way [*primario*] and signifies something else in a secondary way [*secundario*]." The absolute name is one that does not signify something in a secondary way, and is thus such that it signifies everything it signifies primarily and *in recto*. Thus "animal" signifies an ox, an ass, etc.; it signifies and thus constitutes a reference (*suppositio*) to each of the individuals of whom it may be true to say "this is an animal." It corresponds to "natural kind terms." The category of absolute name includes all the

2
Connotatio in the work of Roger Bacon

In *De signis* and then in the *Compendium studii theologicae*, Roger Bacon developed a sophisticated analysis of connotation. For him, the different modes of connotation are based on analogy: connotation is produced when a term signifies, by imposition, one thing, and one or more things are associated with it through a relation of natural signification, so that several things are "made readable" by the same word. The word thus signifies one thing "conventionally," but because of the different natural relations that exist between that thing and other things, it can "naturally" signify these other things. Because of the conventional relation of the word to the thing signified, and because of the natural consequent relation between the thing signified and the thing connoted, we can say that the word naturally implies the latter.

Roger Bacon distinguishes seven modes of connotation:

1. non-being is understood in being by privation;
2. the names relating to God connote the creature (the Latin word *creator* signifies secondarily the creature, which is the result of the relation of creation);
3. the names of creatures imply the creator, because of their dependence on him (whence the valid inference: "there is a creature, therefore there is a creator");
4. the accident connotes the substance, and vice versa;
5. the universal implies the vague particular ("man exists, therefore a man exists") or the particular in disjunction ("man exists, therefore Socrates or Plato or ... exists");
6. an essential part (e.g., a roof) implies another essential part (e.g., a wall)—this example is taken from Avicenna and al-Ghazālī;
7. the name of a relative implies its correlative (e.g., father-son).

In a statement, the word signifies only its primary signified ("double" does not signify "half") and the statement is verified only for this primary signified. However, the speaker can do as he pleases (*ad placitum*) by reimposing the word, changing its meaning, so that the secondary signified becomes the primary signified and that the word then signifies the latter *ad placitum*. It is interesting to note that Bacon does not use the term *connotare* in *De signis*, although in the *Compendium* he uses it with the same examples, calling attention to the theological origin of this term:

> The name given to a single thing outside the soul may signify several things outside the soul at the same time, and these are what philosophers call *cointellecta* and theologians call *connotata*. In fact, all things that follow by natural and necessary implication from the name of another thing are understood with it (*cointellecta*) and connoted by it, for otherwise we could not say that they follow from it necessarily, for example, "creature therefore creator" and "creator therefore God," since only God creates. And every specific accident connotes its subject, thus "capable of laughter, therefore man."

Among the examples we find words that clearly indicate this theological origin of the notion, such as "creator," which was also to be the case in the work of William of Ockham.

BIBLIOGRAPHY

Bacon, Roger. *Compendium studii theologiae*. Edited by T. Maloney. Leiden, Neith.: Brill, 1988.

---

nouns (abstract and concrete) of the category of substance, and the abstract nouns of the category of quality (William of Ockham, *Summa logicae*, I, chap. 10).

Absolute nouns have no nominal definition (*definitio quid nominis*) but only a real definition (*definitio qui rei*); conversely, connotative nouns have no real definition (because they cannot be defined by reference to a particular class of objects) but only a nominal definition that accounts for their hierarchized semantic structure, composed of at least one word in the nominative (*in recto*) and one word in an oblique case (*in obliquo*). They include, first, the concrete categorematic terms of the category of quality, the denominatives (*denominativa/paronyma*). Thus "white" means "something formless informed by whiteness" or "possessing whiteness"; it signifies primarily individual substances that are white, and connotes secondarily their individual whitenesses: what is *in recto* in the definition designates the *significatum* (something), and what is *in obliquo* designates the *connotatum* (whiteness). Relational nouns like "father" are also connotative; in a propositional context, "father" refers to the individuals of whom it is true to say "this is a father," but in addition it connotes something else, namely, the individuals who have a father, and this implies that a relational term cannot receive a complete definition without the intervention of its correlative, and vice versa ("father" = a sensible substance having a child; cf. *Summa logicae*, III–3, chap. 26); the two correlatives do not have the same nominal definition and thus are not synonyms since what intervenes *in recto* in the definition of one is found *in obliquo* in the definition of the other, and vice versa. Also included among the connotatives are categorematic terms belonging to categories other than those of substance and quality, negative expressions (e.g., "immaterial") and philosophical terms such as "true," "good," "intellect," "will," and so on. This notion of connotation also allows Ockham to defend the fundamental idea of an extensionalist conception of reference, according to which all categorematic terms signify and refer to particular substances or qualities. One of the points that has been controversial among Ockham's interpreters is whether there were connotative terms in mental language or whether they could always be eliminated from mental language if a nominal definition that included only absolute terms was substituted for them (Paul Spade). A crucial argument against this claim is based on relational terms (e.g., "father") whose nominal definition necessarily includes their correlative, as we have seen; this shows that it is impossible to totally eliminate connotatives from mental language (Claude Panaccio).

According to Spade, since a connotative term could always be substituted for its nominal definition, which contained only absolute terms (if the first nominal definition contained a connotative term, the latter could in its turn be replaced by its nominal definition until there were no longer any connotative terms), there was no need to postulate connotative terms in mental language. Panaccio has opposed this analysis, on the one hand by pointing to passages clearly indicating that for Ockham there were connotative terms (notably relational terms) in mental language, and on the other hand by showing that this was an essential part of Ockham's theory. The previously mentioned argument based on relational terms is crucial: since the nominal definition of a relational term necessarily contains another connotative term, namely, its correlative, this implies that relational terms, and thus connotative terms, cannot be totally replaced by absolute terms at the level of mental language, and thus that they exist in mental language (cf. Panaccio, "Guillaume d'Ockham").

We find interesting elements in other medieval logicians. Buridan in particular attributes a referential function both to what is signified (the *suppositio*) and to what is connoted (the *appelatio*): the connotative term (e.g., "white") connotes that to which the corresponding abstract term ("whiteness") refers; it "refers to" what it signifies primarily and "calls" what it connotes (see SUPPOSITION). Elsewhere, Buridan explains:

> There is essential predication between two terms when neither of them adds to the signification of the other a connotation extraneous [*extranea*] to that to which the terms refer. There is non-essential or paronymic predication when one of the terms adds to the signification of the other a foreign connotation, like "white," which refers to a man and calls up (that is, connotes) whiteness insofar as it is added to it. Therefore: the proposition "Man is [an] animal" is essential, whereas "Man is white" or "Man is capable of laughter," is paronymic.
>
> *Summulae de dialecta*, III–3, chap. 26;
> cf. Klima, *John Buridan*

Alain de Libera
Irène Rosier-Catach

BIBLIOGRAPHY

Buridan, Jean. *Sophismata*. Critical edition by T. K. Scott. Stuttgart: Frommann-Holzboog, 1977.

Klima, Gyula. *John Buridan*. Oxford: Oxford University Press, 2008.

Maierù, Alfonso. *Terminologia logica della tarde scolastica*. Rome: Edizioni dell'Ateneo, 1972.

Panaccio, Claude. "Guillaume d'Ockham, les connotatifs et le langage mental." *Documenti e studi sulla traditione filosofica medievale* 11 (2000): 297–316.

———. *Le discours intérieur: De Platon à Guillaume d'Ockham*. Paris: Éditions du Seuil, 1999.

———. *Ockham on Concepts*. Aldershot UK: Ashgate, 2004.

Rosier, Irène. "*Res significata* et *modus significandi*. Les enjeux linguistiques et théologiques d'une distinction médiévale." In *Sprachtheorien in Spätantike und Mittelalter*, edited by S. Ebbesen, 135–68. Tübingen: Gunter Narr, 1995.

Spade, Paul V., ed. *The Cambridge Companion to Ockham*. Cambridge: Cambridge University Press, 1999.

———. *Thoughts, Words, and Things: An Introduction to Late Medieval Logic and Semantic Theory*. http://pvspade.com/logic/docs/thoughts1_1a.pdf.

Valente, Luisa. "Justus et misericors: L'usage théologique des notions de *consignificatio* et *connotatio* dans la seconde moitiédu XIIe siècle." In *Vestigia, Imagines, Verba: Semiotics and Logic in Medieval Theological Texts (1150–1450)*, edited by C. Marmo, 38–59. Turnhout, Belg.: Brepols, 1997.

William of Ockham. *Ockham's Theory of Terms, Part I of the Summa logicae*. Translated by M. J. Loux. Notre Dame, IN: University of Notre Dame Press, 1974.

———. *Ockham's Theory of Propositions: Part II of the Summa logicae*. Translated by A. J. Freddoso and H. Schuurman; introduction by A. J. Freddoso. South Bend, IN: St. Augustine's Press, 1998).

CONSCIOUSNESS, CONSCIENCE, AWARENESS

DUTCH	*innerlijke medewetingh, innerlijckste bewustheyt, meêwustigheyt*
FRENCH	*conscience*
GERMAN	*Bewusstheit, Bewusstsein, Gewissen, Gewissheit*
GREEK	*sunaisthêsis* [συναίσθησις], *suneidêsis* [συνείδησις], *sunesis* [σύνεσις], *suntêrêsis* [συντήρησις]
ITALIAN	*consapevolezza, coscienza*
LATIN	*conscientia*

➤ *ACT, CROYANCE* [BELIEF, GLAUBE], *FAITH,* I/ME/MYSELF, PERCEPTION, SENSE, SOUL, SUBJECT, UNCONSCIOUS

Although it was created by philosophers, the concept of consciousness has become absolutely commonplace, denoting the individual's or the group's relation to itself. Thus it refers to what the philosopher and the "common man" have in common, and as a result, like "criticism" or "wisdom," it can designate philosophy itself. The same was not true of the ancient terms (*suneidêsis* or even *conscientia*), which are usually given as its equivalents. Thus modern European philosophy has endowed itself with a common past, though it cannot establish a complete equivalence between essentially untranslatable paradigms. After distinguishing the effects of retroversion associated with the Greco-Roman heritage proper, we will show how, starting in the sixteenth century, three great episodes in the European invention of consciousness followed one another. The mark they left is visible everywhere: the religious and political institution of "freedom of conscience" that led to the identification of the latter with the "citizen subject"; the construction of a theory of consciousness as a general faculty of knowledge by John Locke and his successors (Étienne Bonnot de Condillac, Christian Wolff, Immanuel Kant); the conflict of metaphysics of personal identity and of self-consciousness (*Selbstbewusstsein*).

The circulation of concepts and the relative unification of terminologies obtained by the early nineteenth century, when philosophical modernity sought new foundations for itself, did not erase major differences among Romance languages, German (*Gewissen* and *Gewissheit, Bewusstsein* and *Bewusstheit*), and English ("consciousness" and "awareness"), without which it would be difficult to understand the way in which the heritage of transcendental philosophy and the new field of the "cognitive sciences" or the "philosophy of mind" are developing today. This is what makes it possible to foresee, if not an end of consciousness, at least a change in its referents and in the possibilities of translating it.

In France, the national point of view gives rise to an illusion that the different senses of the French word *conscience* are distributed over two or more corresponding words in other languages or that the French term unifies what other languages divide. But it is not clear that the semantic fields of other languages are divided, or that they are all included in what French calls *conscience*. It may be that taken together they effect a displacement in usage, which is broader than any one of them, but more restrictive than their sum. This illusion goes hand in hand with a question peculiar to French, which is whether the apparent unity of the word *conscience* should be considered a simple homonym or an analogy, the expression of a kernel of signification circulating among particular meanings. Dictionaries do not take a single view on this point, and they are evolving. Obviously, these fluctuations are related to the history, which is itself transnational, of linguistic innovation in the area of "thought about thought." Here we find ourselves confronted by a privileged case for the study of what Renée Balibar calls "European co-lingualism."

I. The Legacy of Antiquity and Scholasticism

In Romance and Germanic languages, the main terms derive from two main roots: on the one hand, *scire, scientia,* whence *conscius* (and its antonyms *nescius* and *inscius*), *conscientia, conscient* and *conscience,* and so on; on the other hand, *wissen,* whence *gewiss, Gewissen* and *Gewissheit, bewusst* (*unbewusst*) and *Bewusstsein, Bewusstheit,* and so on. It has become customary to say that the meanings of the modern French word *conscience* are connected with different uses of the Latin *conscientia* and the Greek *suneidêsis.*

As far as the Greek word is concerned, this clearly involves retroversion on the basis of correspondences established by Romans seeking to create their own moral terminology. From the poets to the philosophers, the Greek terminology for the relationship to oneself in the order of knowledge and ethics is much more complex. Thus it was only in the Hellenistic period that *suneidêsis* came into common use in the schools of ethics to designate the way in which the individual, "[alone] with himself," evaluates the worthiness of his conduct and the value of his person, in this life or in anticipation of death. The question remains whether St. Paul had such a meaning in mind in important passages in his epistles such as this one:

> They show that what the law requires is written on their hearts, while their conscience also bears witness [*summarturousês autôn tês suneidêseôs* (συμμαρτυρούσης αὐτῶν τῆς συνειδήσεως)] and their conflicting thoughts accuse or perhaps excuse them on that day when, according to my gospel, God judges the secrets of men [*ta krupta tôn anthrôpôn* (τὰ κρυπτὰ τῶν ἀνθρώπων)] by Christ Jesus.
>
> (Romans 2:15)

However that may be, it was on the basis of these formulations and metaphors they share with the Stoic tradition (the "inner voice," the "stage" on which each person makes his acts appear, or the court before which he "bears witness" for or against himself, etc.) that the age-old dialectic between the "natural" and "supernatural" character of the moral consciousness was carried out.

■ See Box 1.

Although it still poses problems, the history of the Latin *conscientia* is better known. Before Cicero made it a key term in *humanitas,* the uses of the word developed in the two directions in which *cum* can be interpreted (cf. C. S. Lewis, "Conscience and Conscious"): on the one hand, the direction that connotes appropriation and achievement (know well, be well informed about); on the other hand, the one that connotes a private or secret "sharing." From that point on, there was the idea of a knowledge reserved for a few people, each of whom "confided in himself." This meaning led to the fundamental representation of an internal testimony given to oneself (whence Quintilian's famous formula: "*conscientia mille testes*" [conscience is as good as a thousand witnesses]), and finally to the idea of a "judgment" that is made within us with regard to our acts and thoughts. This is the source of an authority that can be opposed to that of any

institution: at once the "interior master" and a guarantee of autonomy. This union of contraries, to which the Augustinian tradition was to give an ontological weight, has persisted down to our own time.

■ See Box 2.

The Church Fathers identified *conscientia* with the soul that had to confront its creator, and it was thus not only judge but judged. In Augustine, *conscientia* is subordinated to a more fundamental notion, *memoria,* the true name of the self-presence that has always already confessed God's Word: by questioning the "secrets of his conscience" in his "innermost depths" ("*interior intimio meo*," Augustine says in his *Confessions* [book 3]), man does nothing less than discover transcendent truth in himself ("*superior summo meo*," "higher than all my height"). St. Jerome says that the spark of conscience put within us, *scintilla conscientiae,* continues to burn even in criminals and sinners (*Commentary on Ezekiel,* in RT: *PL*).

As for Scholasticism's speculative developments of the term, they also proceed from Jerome, but through a stunning error: copyists, thinking they had found in his text a word *suntêrêsis* [συντήρησις], interpreted it at first as a derivative of *têrêsis* [τήρησις], *conservatio* (preservation), then as a derivative of *hairesis* [αἵρεσις], *electio* (choice). Thus was forged a fictive Greek word, *synderesis,* that performed the essential task of making double use of consciousness as a passive faculty (a trace of divine creation) and an active faculty (operating under conditions of sin, after the Fall). Scholastic theologians then formulated the "practical syllogism" of the process through which Revelation illuminates our actions and guides them: (1) *syntheresis,* (2) *conscientia,* (3) *conclusio* (cf. Chollet, "Conscience"). This is a fundamental intellectualist scheme of thought that continued to be influential after its theological justification evaporated: without referring to it, it would be difficult to understand the place that consciousness occupies in G.W.F. Hegel as the middle term of the spirit's becoming, between universality and singularity.

With the Reformation, however, *syntheresis* (or *sunderesis,* or *synderesis*) fell into disuse, and the immediacy of *conscientia* as the inner testimony of morality and a sign of grace won out: it became in German (Luther) the *Gewissen,* with its own certainty (*Gewissheit*), in French (Calvin) the *conscience* associated with the systematic practice of the *examen de conscience.* Thus we find ourselves at the starting point of the drama in three episodes that led to making "self-consciousness" the privileged expression of the philosophical idea of "subjectivity" in the West: in it we witness the European invention of consciousness.

■ See Box 3.

II. The European Invention of Consciousness

The first episode in the drama corresponds to the debates aroused by the Reformation concerning "freedom of conscience"; the second leads to an identification of the "self" with the mind's reflective activity, to which Locke gave the name "consciousness"; the third, at the turning point of the eighteenth century, led to a reinterpretation of the principles of knowledge and morality as expressions of *Selbstbewusstsein.*

1

The Greek for "consciousness": Retroversions

➤ OIKEIÔSIS, SENSE

It is said that the Greeks did not know about consciousness. In fact, there is no Greek word corresponding to "consciousness," but there is a great variety of terms and expressions onto which "consciousness" is projected, and that sometimes refer to a relationship to the self, sometimes to a moral judgment, and sometimes to a perception, often producing a crossing or derivation among several of these meanings.

From the Homeric poems to the Socratic dialogues by way of tragic dramaturgy, every Greek hero essentially carries on a conversation with himself, and in doing so he thinks his thoughts, feels his emotions, and debates courses of action. The "organs of consciousness" (RT: *Origins of European Thought*, chap. 2) of the Homeric hero are words that we find very difficult to translate because they refer to a physiology loaded with meaning: *kêr* [κῆϱ], or *kradiê/kardia* [κϱαδίη/καϱδία], the "heart" or even the "stomach," as an organ that can be pierced; *êtor* [ἦτοϱ], the "heart" as the seat of emotions and intelligence. But it is especially the *thumos* [θυμός], which is lodged in the *phrên* [φϱήν] or the *phrenes* [φϱένες] (the entrails, the diaphragm, the lungs, but the word belongs to the family of *phronein* [φϱονεῖν], "to be informed, think"), which is also rendered by "heart," that constitutes the privileged interlocutor in the dialogue of the self with itself. The *thumos* is both an impulse (Chantraine connects it with *thuô* [θύω], "to rush forward with fury"; RT: *Dictionnaire étymologique de la langue grecque*) and the breath of life, a vapor or spirit connected with hot and boiling blood (Boisacq [RT: *Dictionnaire étymologique de la langue grecque*] derives it from the Sanskrit *dhûma-*, whence the Greek *thumiaô* [θυμιάω], "make smoke" [Latin *fumus*], which must be clearly distinguished from *psuchê* [ψυχή], the breath of the "soul" that escapes from the mouth of the dead and goes to reside in Hades, whereas the *thumos* is eaten and dissipates) (RT: *Origins of European Thought*, chap. 3). Thus, when he is about to abandon Patroclus's body, Menelaus "speaks to his magnanimous *thumos*" and "launches [these words] through his *phrên* and his *thumos*" (*Iliad* 17.90, 106). The philosophical outcome of this reflexive conversation is the Platonic definition of thought (*dianoia* [διάνοια]) as "the internal dialogue of the soul with itself, without voice [*entos tês psuchês pros hautên dialogos aneu phônês* (ἐντὸς τῆς ψυχῆς πϱὸς αὐτὴν διάλογος ἄνευ φωνῆς)]" (*Sophist* 263e; cf. *Theatetus* 189e), which opens

out, through the Socratic demand for "the agreement of the self with itself [*homologein autos heautôi* (ὁμολογεῖν αὐτὸς ἑαυτῷ)]" (*Protagoras* 339c), onto the moral dimension of self-consciousness. To the individual who never ceases to refute Socrates and to shame him, "his closest relative, who lives in the same place," "centuries to come were to give . . . the name of consciousness" (*Hippias Maior* 304d).

There is no Greek term that brings together all of the values of this dialogue of the self with itself, but we see the concurrence of several words in *sun-* (con-) followed by a verbal action whose meaning varies considerably depending on context, and which is translated by "consciousness." In the domain of perception-apperception, *sunaisthêsis* [συναίσθησις] is, particularly in Plotinus (*Enneads* 3.8.4), translated by "self-consciousness" (RT: LSJ, s.v.): as Bréhier put it, the "intelligence" (*sunêsis* [σύνεσις], another candidate for "consciousness") and "self-knowledge" (*sunaisthêsis*) allow nature to see and produce what is around it. But the term is in competition, even in Plotinus, with the sequence "*to aisthanesthai kai parakolouthein hautôi* [τὸ αἰσθάνεσθαι καὶ παρακολουθεῖν αὑτῷ]" (in Bréhier, *Histoire de la philosophie*: "feeling and self-consciousness"—literally, "the accompanying of oneself") that characterizes wisdom when it refers, no longer to this nature that is to us as a sleeper is to a person who is awake, but rather to the wise man himself, concerning whom the Stoics wondered whether he remained happy when he was sleeping. Furthermore, we should note that in Aristotle in particular, it is *aisthanes-thai* [αἰσθάνεσθαι] (to feel) alone that is most commonly translated as "to be aware of" (Tricot, referring precisely to the apperceptive function of "common sense," translates it this way in the *Nicomachean Ethics* 9.9, where the question is whether the happy man needs friends), whereas *sunaisthanesthai* [συναισθάνεσθαι] means very explicitly "feel with," like "eat with," or "live with," not with oneself, but with other selves that are one's friends (see *Eudemian Ethics* 7.12, 1244b26 and 1245b25).

We move imperceptibly from the epistemic to the ethical with *sunesis* (from *sun-eimi* [σύν-ειμι], says *Cratylus* 412b, "to go with, accompany," or from *sun-iêmi* [συν-ίημι], "to throw together, bring closer," and in both cases, "understand"), whose meaning ranges from sagacity to the awareness of wrong. Thus *sunesis*, translated as "intelligence," is, with *eusunesia* or "perspicacity,"

the critical virtue of those who know how to use "prudence" (*phronêsis* [φϱόνησις]; see PHRONÊSIS), because they learn quickly (Aristotle, *Nicomachean Ethics* 6.11); but Dumont chooses *conscience* in translating in Democritus (B77 DK: "Fame and riches without consciousness are fragile possessions"), and here is how Méridier translates Orestes's reply to Menelaus when the latter asks what illness is killing him: "Ma conscience. Je sens l'horreur de mon forfait" (*hê sunesis* [ἡ σύνεσις]—literally, "the awareness that I know [*sunoida* (σύνοιδα)] I have committed terrible acts," Euripides, *Orestes* 396).

Finally, *suneidêsis* (from *sun-oida*, precisely) is retrospectively the best calque for *consciousness*. Democritus uses it to designate "the awareness of the badness of a life" that arouses fear and encourages the invention of eschatological fictions (B297). The sense of the noun (which is not found in Plato) becomes clearer starting in the Hellenistic period, especially in the Stoic doctrine of *oikeiôsis* [οἰκείωσις]. Thus, regarding the animal's primitive inclination to preserve itself, nature attaching it to itself from the outset, Diogenes Laertius (7.85, trans. Yonge) quotes this comment of Chrysippus, in the first book of his treatise *De finibus*: "The first and dearest object [*oikeion* (οἰκεῖον)] to every animal is its own existence [*tên hautou sustasin* (τὴν αὑτοῦ σύστασιν)], and its consciousness of that existence [*tên tautês suneidêsin* (τὴν ταύτης συνείδησιν)]. For that it is not natural for any animal to be alienated from itself [*allotriôsai* (ἀλλοτϱιῶσαι)]."

Its scope, from the Stoics to the New Testament, ranges from the appropriate relation to oneself to the awareness of good and evil. None of these terms, of course, shows as well as the Homeric descriptions how much the Greek "subject" speaks to himself at the same time that he thinks and acts.

Barbara Cassin

BIBLIOGRAPHY

Aristotle. *Éthique à Nicomaque*. Translated by J. Tricot. Rev. ed. Paris: Vrin. 1994.
Bréhier, Émile. *Histoire de la philosophie*. Vol. 1: *L'antiquité et le Moyen Age*. Paris: Presses Universitaires de France, 1967.
Cancrini, Antonia. *Suneidêsis: Il tema semantico della "con-scienti" nella Grecia antica*. Lessico intellettuale Europeo 6. Rome: Ateneo, 1970.
Diogenes Laertius. *Lives and Opinions of Eminent Philosophers*. Translated by Charles Duke Yonge. Riverside, CA: Ulan, 2012.

2

Conscientia

The language of Latin philosophy, even though it is marked by the spread of Stoicism (see Box 1), was elaborated at the same time that Cicero, Lucretius, and Seneca were helping to write a critical history of philosophy. That is why the uses of *conscientia* in classical Latin present—synchronically—the different historical and literary strata that constituted the experience of and ways of expressing consciousness.

In many of its occurrences, *conscientia* designates the experience of having done something wrong (the latter is often made explicit by a genitive: *conscientia scelerum*) and the remorse that flows from it: these uses have to be related to those we find in juridical contexts, where *conscientia* and *conscius* designate recognized guilt and the sentence handed down.

As a form of remorse, *conscientia* appears in the lists of the passions ("ardentes tum cupiditate, tum metu, tum conscientia," "inflamed by passion, fear, remorse," Cicero, *De legibus* 2.43, trans. Keyes) and is the object of topical descriptions derived from tragedy: "conscius ipse animus se forte remordet" (The soul that knows itself to be guilty torments itself: Lucretius, *De rerum natura* 4.1135).

Thus the noun includes both the tragic moment of the self's knowledge of itself through the suffering of the body (gnawing, burning, suffocating) and the interpretation that Hellenistic philosophies gave of this moment: "Mens sibi conscia factis / praemetuens adhibet stimulos torretque flagellis" (The conscience-stricken mind through boding fears applies to itself goads and frightens itself with whips: Lucretius, *De rerum natura* 3.1018, trans. Munro, 134). Lucretius's analysis is also found in Cicero's *De legibus* (1.40): "Non ardentibus taedis sicut in fabulis sed angore conscientiae fraudisque cruciatus" ([The guilty are not pursued] by flaming torches but by the fear to which their fear gives rise and by the crime that tortures them).

More positively, *conscientia* coincides with the experience of self that is not immediately given but is constructed in (re)collection, recapitulation, memory (which is suggested by the formation of the word, *cum-scire*)—that is, what Cicero refers to in *De re publica* (6.8),

"sapientibus conscientia ipsa factorum egregiorum amplissimum virtutis est praemium" (For the wise, the simple awareness of having performed remarkable acts constitutes the highest reward of their virtue), and in *De senectute* (9), "conscientia bene actae vitae multorumque bene factorum recordatio iucundissima est" (Nothing more pleasant than the consciousness of having led one's life well and the memory of many good acts that one has done).

This movement of self-evaluation is also clearly marked in a second series of occurrences in which the term appears especially in expressions that explain the origin of moral evaluation: *conscientia deorum / conscientia hominum* (Cicero, *De finibus* 1.51: "qui satis sibi contra hominum conscientiam saepti esse et muniti videntur, deorum tamen horrent" [Those who think themselves sufficiently protected and sealed off to escape the judgment of men are nonetheless afraid of the gods' judgment]). Taking others' judgment into account in evaluating responsibility gives *conscientia* a meaning close to that of *pudor* (aidôs [αἰδώς]): the internalization of this judgment (which may or may not be emphasized in the syntagma *conscientia animi*) is developed in two divergent directions. Either one appropriates external norms of judgment, in accord with a split point of view that tends to be expressed in metaphors of an internal theater (one judges oneself, one provides a spectacle for oneself), or one opposes one's own criteria of evaluation to those of external authorities: images of barriers and roofs delimit a space of interiority that protects the rectitude of judgment and its inalienable character against *fama* and *opinio*.

The first direction can be seen in the following remarks by Cicero: "nullum theatrum virtuti conscientia maius est" (Virtue has no greater theater than the conscience: *Tusculan Disputations* 2.64, trans. King); and by Seneca: "conscientia aliud agere non patitur ac subinde respondere ad se cogit" (The guilt [that tyrants feel] does not allow them to amuse themselves: it constantly forces them to answer for their acts before its tribunal: *Epistulae* 105.7, trans. Gummere), "bona

conscientia prodire vult et conspici ad se cogit" (Good conscience wants to show itself and subject itself to public view: ibid., 97.12).

The second direction can be seen in these remarks: "dicitur gratus qui bono animo accepit beneficium, bono debet; hic intra conscientiam clusus est" (It is said that a man who gladly receives a favor and gladly returns it is grateful: he is grateful in the innermost chamber of his conscience: Seneca, *De beneficiis* 4.21); "mea mihi conscientia pluris est quam omnium sermo" (In my opinion my conscience is worth more than what everyone else says: Cicero, *Ad Atticum* 12.28.2).

Between these two aspects of internalization, we cannot see the lines of an evolution any more than we can rigorously divide the uses of the genitive or the dative in the phrases *conscientia animi / scelerum / hominum—conscius sibi*. On the contrary, the uses of *conscientia*—and their networks of metaphors—suggest at the same time interiority and exteriority, at the moment when the fundamental question of ethics concerns the validity and the scope of natural norms. Then we grasp, in the unceasing back-and-forth movement, the historical and philosophical moment in which the subject can be constructed.

Clara Auvray-Assayas

BIBLIOGRAPHY

Cicero. *De re publica, De legibus*. Translated by Clinton Walker Keyes. London: Heinemann, 1928.

———. *On Moral Ends*. Translated by Raphael Woolf. Cambridge: Cambridge University Press, 2001.

———. *On Old Age and Friendship*. Translated by W. A. Falconer. Cambridge, MA: Loeb Classical Library, 1923.

———. *Tusculan Disputations*. Translated by J. E. King. Cambridge, MA: Loeb Classical Library, 1927.

Munro, H.A.J. *The Stoic and Epicurean Philosophers*. New York: Modern Library, 1957.

Seneca. *Moral Epistles*. Translated by Richard Gummere. 3 vols. Cambridge, MA: Loeb Classical Library, 1917–25.

A. The metonymy of conscience

The first episode is here named the "metonymy of conscience" because its most striking achievement was the possibility of using the French word *conscience* to designate not only a faculty of the mind, even personified or identified with the internal testimony of a double of the subject, but as the other name of a single individual. This personification is manifested in the possibility of qualifying consciousness-subjects with regard to their actions and experiences: a *conscience noble*, *conscience éclairée*, *conscience*

3

Conscientia and *Gewissen* in Luther

➤ BELIEF, GLAUBE

Luther has been called "the inventor of the *Gewissen*" (Hermann, *Luthers Theologie*), and Lutheranism the "religion of *Gewissen*" (Holl, "Was verstand Luther unter Religion?"). For many people, Luther, the first theoretician of *Gewissen* in the German language, is also the first modern theoretician of the conscience. That is what his famous 1521 reply at the Diet of Worms is supposed to proclaim, in a heroic mode, when he states the reasons that prevented him from retracting when confronted by the Church of Rome:

> Unless I am convinced by the testimonies of the Holy Scriptures or evident reason (for I believe neither in the Pope nor councils alone, since it has been established that they have often erred and contradicted themselves), I am bound by the Scriptures adduced by me, and my conscience [*Gewissen*] has been taken captive by the Word of God, and I am neither able nor willing to recant, since it is neither safe nor right to act against conscience. God help me. Amen.

> (*Verhandlungen mit D. Martin Luther auf dem Reichstage zu Worms* [1521], in *Dr Martin Luthers Werke* 7:838.2–9)

This refusal has often been seen as an appeal to freedom of conscience and thus as the birth certificate of modernity. On reading the text, however, one may be astonished by this view: What is this *conscientia* that Luther invokes as an inalienable good but that he says has been "taken captive by the Word of God"?

1. In the wake of the historical debate regarding the birth of modernity, the debate about Luther's notion of conscience has often concerned the latter's autonomy. Without being explicitly rejected, the distinction between *suntheresis* and *conscientia* henceforth becomes secondary. This is Luther's conceptual innovation in relation to Scholastic theories of conscience: for him there is now only *one* conscience, defined as "the origin or site of the strongest affects" (Hirsch, *Lutherstudien*), that a person can experience. Confronted by the Law, by the Promise, the conscience alternately rejoices, hopes, worries, gets frightened, despairs: Luther's conception of conscience involves first of all descriptions of *states*, feelings, affects. These analyses, which we could call "psychological" if we were sure that they were ultimately based on a concept of the psyche, show that conscience is no longer so much a faculty of the mind tending toward the good as the precise site where the relation between man and God is produced. It is there that man is destroyed or raised before God (cf. *Vorlesung über den Römerbrief* [1515–16], in *Werke*, 56:526.31–32). Thus Luther did not conceive of the conscience as autonomous. If it is defined as "something higher than Heaven and Earth," that is only by virtue of its tendency to be "killed by sin" or, on the contrary, "given life by the Word of Christ," depending on the nature of the relation between man and God (*Vorlesungen über 1. Mose* [1535–45], in *Werke*, 44:546.30–31). At no time is man alone with his conscience. The latter is in no way productive, it is only the reflection or "bearer" (*Träger*: Hirsch, *Lutherstudien*) of a relationship whose establishment does not depend on it. That is why Luther's statements regarding conscience vary so much. He also calls it an "evil beast" (*mala bestia*) that "makes man oppose himself" when it persuades him to put his trust in good works rather than in faith to gain salvation (*Vorlesungen über 1. Mose*, in *Werke*, 44:545.16–17). The conscience may be praised or blamed, depending on whether it is Christ or the Devil who controls it: in both cases, it is not free in the sense that it constitutes an original site of freedom.

2. Beyond these contradictory judgments, according to Luther the conscience is nonetheless unified by a certain number of conceptual decisions and linguistic usages. Luther's other great innovation is in fact to have established conscience in a paradigm that also includes "faith" and "certainty." He breaks with the intellectualism of Scholastic theories by associating conscience with "faith" and the "heart" (cf., e.g., *Invokavitpredigten* [1522], in *Werke*, 10/3:23–24). The principle is this: as faith is, so is conscience, so are the works; or, only faith can give conscience the certainty that the works accomplished are good (cf. *Von den Guten Werken* [1520], in *Werke* 6.205.1–13).

In at least three ways, the relation between conscience and certainty is central to Luther's theory of conscience. Conscience is defined first of all by a *need* for certainty: it is this need that Luther objects to in what he considers to be Erasmus's skepticism (*De servo arbitrio* [1525], in *Werke*, 18:603.23–24).

Second, conscience is the *site* of certainty, on the condition that it has been previously invested with faith (cf. *Das schöne confitemini . . .* [1530], in *Werke*, 31/1:176–77: "Ein hertz, das . . . fur Gott von allem dinge gewis urteilen und recht reden kan . . . ein froelich, sicher, muetig gewissen" [A heart that . . . can judge with certainty and speak correctly of all things . . . a joyous, sure, courageous conscience], once again associating faith with the heart). Finally, the conscience serves as a *refuge* from the uncertainty of faith, and in that very way, as the ultimate certainty: no one is ever certain (*gewis*) of having faith, but everyone has to rely on the *Gewissen* that tells him that faith alone provides salvation (cf. the important text in *Von der Wiedertaufe an zwei Pfarrherrn* [1528], in *Werke*, 26:155.14–28, in the context of the Anabaptist polemic).

It is in this perspective that we must understand the famous theory of "freedom of conscience," which is, according to Luther, synonymous with "Christian or Evangelical freedom." Luther's *conscientia* is in no way a principle of action; it is "not a faculty for performing works, but a faculty of judging these works" (*De votis monasticis* [1521], in *Werke*, 8:606.30–35). Here, internalization is pushed so far that freedom of conscience can coexist with the servile will (see ELEUTHERIA, Box 2). This is because conscience does not draw its freedom from itself: here, we find once again the motif of its heteronomy. However, the most important thing is that in Luther, freedom of conscience merges with its certitude: a conscience is free only if faith has made it sure (cf. *Vom Abendmahl Christi. Bekenntnis* [1528], in *Werke*, 26:505.34 : "frey und sicher ym gewissen").

In Luther's German, the association of conscience with certainty, *gewiss* with *Gewissen*, is immediate: it will be found again, raised to a concept, in Hegel, *Gewissheit* replacing the adverb *gewiss*, to which Luther usually limits himself (cf. Hegel, *Phenomenology of Mind*, 6.C.c). However, we must avoid concluding that it is the proximity of the words that led Luther to associate the ideas, to the point of imbuing certainty with his concept of conscience. It is remarkable that Luther's Latin makes exactly the same connection, this time without an echo effect, between *conscientia* and *certitudo*: from Latin to German, Luther's concept of conscience does not vary (cf., e.g., *De servo arbitrio*, in *Werke*, 18:620.3: "certitudines conscientiae"). From such a convergence, we might conclude that Luther's Latin is "completely imbued with his German" (Bornkamm, *Luther's World of Thought*): in writing *conscientia*, Luther might have been thinking *Gewissen*. Without trying resolve this question of precedence (did Luther think first in German or in Latin?), we can suggest that Luther's theological invention, the establishment of the *Glauben-Gewissen-Gewissheit* paradigm, was taken over by the potentialities of the German language, which were in turn more than exploited, and this time explicitly, by the tradition that the *Wissen-Gewissen-Gewissheit* paradigm followed in philosophy from Kant to Wittgenstein. By reattaching Luther's invention to its antecedents (first of all, the theological debates of the thinkers of the Middle Ages and the Reformation regarding the certainty of salvation), we would gain the means to give a long historical account of conscience that would at the same time be a history of bilingualism (in this case, German/Latin) in European philosophy.

Philippe Büttgen

BIBLIOGRAPHY

Bayer, Oswald. *Martin Luther's Theology: A Contemporary Interpretation*. Translated by T. H. Trapp. Grand Rapids, MI: W. B. Eerdmans, 2008.

Baylor, Michael G. *Action and Person: Conscience in Late Scholasticism and the Young Luther*. Leiden, Neth.: Brill, 1977.

Bornkamm, Heinrich. *Luther's World of Thought*. St. Louis, MO: Concordia, 2005.

Hermann, Rudolf. *Luthers Theologie*. Göttingen, Ger.: Vandenhoeck and Ruprecht, 1967.

Hirsch, Emanuel. *Lutherstudien*. Vol. 1. Gütersloh, Ger.: Bertelsmann, 1954.

Holl, Karl. "Was verstand Luther unter Religion?" In *Gesammelte Aufsätze zur Kirchengeschichte*, vol. 1. Tübingen: Mohr, 1948.

Jacob, Günter. *Der Gewissensbegriff in der Theologie Luthers*. Tübingen: Mohr, 1929.

Lohse, Bernhard. "Gewissen und Autorität bei Luther." In *Evangelium in der Geschichte*. Göttingen, Ger.: Vandenhoeck and Ruprecht, 1988.

———. *Martin Luther's Theology: Its Historical and Systematic Development*. Translated by R. A. Harrisville. Minneapolis, MN: Fortress Press, 1999.

Luther, Martin. *Dr Martin Luthers Werke*. 121 vols. Kritische Gesamtausgabe. Weimar, Ger.: Heidelberger Akademie der Wissenschaften, 1883–2009.

———. *Works of Martin Luther*. Edited by Henry Eyster Jacobs and Rudolph Spaeth. Philadelphia, PA: Muhlenberg Press, 1943.

malheureuse, conscience déchirée, and so on (following a procedure that under other circumstances can also be applied to the soul, the mind, the heart, and the understanding). Such a potentiality is exercised especially in the languages in which the Calvinist Reformation, humanist irenicism, skepticism, and Neostoicism collided in the sixteenth and seventeenth centuries: a period when absolutism was developing and the first demands for citizen's "rights" were being heard.

Everything begins with John Calvin's definition of *conscience*: identified with the Christian's faith, which resides in his "innermost heart" (*for intérieur*), it expresses in itself the mystery of an absolute submission that is at the same time a liberation because it subjects the individual only to grace. The metonymy is already common in Calvin: "I say that these remedies and reliefs are too narrow and frivolous for troubled consciences that are downcast, afflicted, and frightened by the horror of their sin" (*Institution de la religion chrétienne*, 4.41). Nonetheless, it is the experience of political struggle that puts this metonymic play at the heart of the uses of the word *conscience* by making the *for intérieur* also a "fort" and a "force" (whose concept competed throughout the seventeenth century with those of "mind" and "genius" to designate the principle of individuality). Whereas the Anabaptists invented the "objection of conscience," Calvin defended the "adhesion of conscience." The English Puritans of the seventeenth century subjected all their actions to the absolute command of conscience from which conviction proceeds ("convinced in conscience of the righteousness of the Parliament's cause," quoted in Walzer, *Revolution of the Saints*). The corresponding adjective is "conscientious."

The Wars of Religion also produced the idea of a withdrawal into the *for intérieur* when people were called to account by states and churches. The two representatives of the European irenicist trend that played a decisive role here are Sebastian Castellion and Dirck Coornhert. The former, who translated the Rhineland mystics into Latin and French, was the great theoretician of freedom of conscience, understood as an inalienable individual right. He established its originary character by adopting the classical form of the *elegchos* [ἔλεγχος]:

I find that the first and efficient cause of . . . the sedition and war that torments you is necessarily [a matter] of consciences. . . . I am sure that the cause that I am now dealing with would be voided by a single word of evident truth, and that no one would dare to contradict it even a little. For all one has to say to those who compel other people's consciences is: "Would you want yours to be compelled?" And suddenly their own consciences, which are worth more than a thousand witnesses, would convince them so fully that they would all be struck dumb.

(*Conseil à la France désolée*, 1562)

As for Coornhert, in 1582 he published *Synodus van der Conscientien vryheyt* (Synod on freedom of conscience). Arguing against both rigorous Calvinism and the Neostoic reason of state, he naturalized in a very Latinized Dutch the "compulsion of consciences" as "*dwang der conscientien*" and became the master of "Christians without a church" all over northwestern Europe. Traces of his "individualism" or "subjectivism" are still found even in some late seventeenth-century German Socinians—in the sect of the *Gewissene* or "conscientious people," for whom conscience was the sole authority in matters of faith (*Glauben*) or certitude (*Gewissheit*) (Kittsteiner, *Die Entstehung des modernen Gewissens*). The connection between the two may be found in the pages of Louis Meyer's *Philosophia sacrae scripturae interpres* (1666), in which Meyer, who was a friend of Spinoza's, appealed to "clear and distinct perception" to reject both literalist interpretations of the Scriptures and the inspired "enthusiasm" of the Quakers. In the Dutch version of his book, Meyer himself sought equivalents of the Latin *conscientia: innerlijke medewetingh, innerlijckste bewustheyt, meêwustigheyt.*

Finally, we should mention the itinerary followed by the skeptics, of whom the most brilliant is Montaigne, who began from a philosophy inspired by Stoicism to create an unprecedented mode of public confession. Jean Starobinski (*Montaigne in Movement*) showed how personal identity is infinitely sought here in the movement of writing, which in Montaigne becomes the real basis of consciousness:

> Let me excuse here what I often say, that I rarely repent and that my conscience is content with itself—not as the conscience of an angel or a horse, but as the conscience of a man. . . . I speak as an ignorant inquirer, referring the decision purely and simply to the common and authorized beliefs. I do not teach, I tell.
>
> (*Essays of Montaigne*, 3.2, trans. Frame)

In politics, Montaigne was a conservative, an admirer of Justus Lipsius. In his work, *conscience* is related to *inscience* and opposed to "faith" ("an enormous distinction between devoutness and conscience": ibid., 3.12). If we do not keep these facts in mind, we can understand neither the effects of the Cartesian revolution nor Hobbes's attack on the idea of conscience. In his *Leviathan*, Hobbes relates the word "conscious" to its Latin etymology (*con-scire*, "to know together") and identifies "conscience" with "opinion." Such a notion is intermediary between the concept of judgment and what we would now call "ideology." It allows us to understand why the "plea of Conscience" must be absolutely rejected by the state, and dissociated from the *for intérieur*:

> And last of all, men, vehemently in love with their own new opinions . . . gave those their opinions also that reverenced name of Conscience, as if they would have it seem unlawfull, to change or speak against them; and so pretend to know they are true, when they know at most, but that they think so.
>
> (*Leviathan*, 1.7)

Hobbes's citizen constructs his personality not on the basis of consciousness/conscience, but on "will" and "authority" or on representation.

B. Knowledge and ignorance of the "self"

Historians of philosophy tell us that the major moment when consciousness begins to designate the essence of subjectivity coincides with a return to the metaphysical foundation of the faculty of judgment summed up in the Cartesian *cogito*. The reality is more complex, as is shown by a remarkable series of semantic shifts and lexical inventions. René Descartes was not the "inventor of consciousness." The French word *conscience* never appears in his work, either in the texts he wrote himself or in translations of them that he read and revised. And *conscientia* in Latin comes up only once, in a paragraph in the *Principia philosophiae* (1.9) devoted to the definition of "thought" (*cogitatio*). The equivalent of *conscius esse* that Descartes accepted was simply *connaître*, which was here close to *sentir*. The philosophy of the *Meditations* is not

that of consciousness but of "certitude" and its modalities. Descartes nonetheless played a role in the invention of consciousness in the seventeenth century because of his thesis that "the mind always thinks," on which he founded the idea that the soul or mind is "easier to know than the body." As Geneviève Lewis has shown, the term *conscience* was spread by the first Cartesians, who were in reality mainly "Augustino-Cartesians," though they were no more faithful to Augustine's question (How does God make himself felt in the "innermost part" of my soul?) than to Descartes's (Who am I, I who am certain of my thinking existence?). The first of these followers was Louis de La Forge, author of the *Traité de l'esprit de l'homme* (1667). In this work he described the "admirable function" of thought as "the perception, consciousness or internal knowledge that each of us feels immediately by himself when he perceives what he is doing or what is happening in him." Antoine Arnauld identified the Latin *conscius esse* with the "reflection that may be called virtual and that is found in all our perceptions," and that allows us to define thought as "essentially reflecting on itself" (*Des vraies et des fausses idées*, 1683). In this sense, the Cartesians are the true inventors of what Wolff was to call "rational psychology." This first trend in the (re)definition of consciousness is at the origin of the tradition of French *spiritualisme* (cf. Victor Cousin), the influence of which has never really disappeared.

Far more important is the English development manifested in the invention of the neologism "consciousness." The first to use it was Ralph Cudworth, in *The True Intellectual System of the Universe* (1678): this is a refutation of atomism and materialism, to which the leader of the Cambridge Platonists opposed a monism based on Neoplatonism. For Cudworth, nature can be understood as a hierarchy of beings based on the sole principle of the formation of individuals in which vital force and thought are two successive degrees. It is to mark the passage from one to the other that Cudworth forged the word "consciousness" (itself part of the series Con-sense, Consciousness, Animadversion, Attention, Self-Perception), merging Plotinus's terms *sunaisthêsis* and *sunesis*. Consciousness is thus the highest form of the feeling or perception of the self (which is also a "self-enjoyment") that characterizes all life. Of course, it does not belong essentially to human beings, but eminently characterizes the divine spirit. In opposition to Cartesian dualism, Cudworth maintains that the obscure or dormant forms of consciousness begin below humanity, just as its lucid or purely intellectual forms extend beyond the human mind. That is why he also uses the term "inconscious." His influence was to be considerable, especially on Gottfried Leibniz, to whom he transmitted Plotinus's term "monad."

Locke appears to be far more Cartesian. The drafts of the *Essay on Human Understanding* (1690; 2nd enlarged ed., 1694) show that the word "consciousness" was not part of his vocabulary before Cudworth published his work. In the final version, however, he sums up the essence of the gap between the immediacy of *sensation* and the *reflection* by which the mind perceives its own operations, giving the definition that was to become famous: "Consciousness is the perception of what passes in a Man's own mind" (2.1.19). From this proceed all the developments of Locke's philosophy of mind, from the reformulation of the Cartesian idea that the mind cannot think without knowing, to the description of "the experience of consciousness": an uneasy movement in the course of which all knowledge is formed. In a supplementary chapter in the second edition (2.27, "Of Identity and Diversity"), loaded with allusions to the controversies of the time regarding the immortality of the soul and the perspective of the Last Judgment, he makes consciousness the criterion of personal identity and responsibility. In this chapter, Locke deepens his conception of the relations between consciousness and the "inner sense," described as essentially an internal memory, in a kind of secularization of Augustinian theses. Consciousness, which is self-identical in the continual flux of its perceptions, can thus function as the operator of a *self-recognition*: it is through consciousness that an individual can consider "himself as the same," that is, as a *Self*.

The French translation of "consciousness" as *conscience* could not, as is now acknowledged, be taken for granted: it collided with the linguistic habit that reserved this term for a moral faculty, and conflicted with the new uses introduced by the Cartesians and by Malebranche. That is why Locke's first translators (J. Le Clerc, P. Coste) preferred at first to render "to be conscious" by *concevoir* or *être convaincu*, and "consciousness" by *sentiment* or *conviction*. It took a semantic revolution to *re-create* the word *conscience* in French with a new meaning. But this revolution put European philosophy on a new path (because in the eighteenth century, the whole "Republic of Letters" read Locke in Coste's French translation), where the conflict between psychologism and transcendental philosophies would eventually arise.

- See Box 4.

In the end, not until Condillac did *conscience* become a full-fledged metaphysical term. Condillac made no reference to Descartes; he introduced, in addition to the concept of consciousness, that of attention, which is a differential consciousness, an "additional consciousness" accorded to some perceptions and not to others. Following Locke, and so to speak in the margins of his text, Condillac arrived at "the feeling of my being," the recognition of the permanence of a "being that is constantly the same," the identity of the "self of today" with the "self of yesterday." Consciousness then became in French as well a concept designating the perception of an internal unity subsisting through the succession of its own representations, but also capable of splitting into "multiple personalities" (Condillac, *Essai sur l'origine des connaissances humaines*).

C. A conflict in continental philosophy:
Selbstbewusstsein or *sens intime*

Locke himself uses "self-consciousness" just once:

> For as to this point of being the same self, it matters not whether this present self be made up of the same or other Substances, I being as much concern'd, and as justly accountable for any Action that was done a thousand years since, appropriated to me now by this self-consciousness, as I am for what I did the last moment.

> (*Essay Concerning Human Understanding*, 2.27.16)

This formulation, which closely links (self-)consciousness, memory, and responsibility, is in the logic of equivalence that it constructs between the problematics of self and of consciousness. But it is especially significant retrospectively, insofar as it marks for us the starting point of the conflicts in modern philosophy. Coste was not able or willing to translate, but added in a note: "*Self-consciousness*: an expressive word in English that cannot be rendered in French in all its force. I put it here for the benefit of those who understand English."

The difference between the psychological and the transcendental that is latent here could be made explicit only in another language. *Bewusstsein* (a nominalized infinitive, at first written *Bewusst sein* to translate the Latin [*sibi*] *conscium esse*) was invented by Wolff only in 1719, while he was writing works that wrenched the term *Psychologie* away from its first meaning of the theory of specters or spirits to make it a "science of the inner sense" (*Psychologia empirica*, 1732; *Psychologia rationalis*, 1734). In this neologism, introduced alongside the traditional *Gewissen* as the term corresponding to *conscientia*, we can see, more than a transposition of the Cartesian *conscientia-cogito* (as is usually thought), a response to Locke's distinction between "conscience" and "consciousness." From then on, *Bewusstsein* was used in Germany both by the metaphysicians of the *Aufklärung* (Alexander Gottlieb Baumgarten) and by the theorists of a more empirical anthropology (Johannes Niklaus Tetens).

For Kant, *Bewusstsein*, whether empirical or pure, is always a knowledge of our representations of objects, that is, a connection between the elements that constitute them: intuitions and concepts. The underlying link is basically a speculative interpretation of the conjunction of *sunaisthêsis* and *suneidêsis*, which Kant understands negatively, in the famous formula: "Thoughts without content are void; intuitions without conceptions blind" (*Critique of Pure Reason*, trans. Guyer and Wood). To sense-consciousness must be added an intellectual consciousness to produce the mechanism typical of transcendental consciousness, which is capable of grasping its own form (or of "thinking thought" in its conditions of possibility, in accord with the ancient Aristotelian ideal of a *noêsis noêseôs* [νόησις νοήσεως]).

- See Box 5.

The difficulties of "self-consciousness" constitute both a point of contact and a source of permanent misunderstandings between the German and French traditions in the philosophy of the subject. The "same" expressions take on values that are in fact profoundly different.

The *Selbst-* that is part of constructions such as *Selbst-achtung, Selbst-bewegung, Selbst-bestimmung*, and *Selbst-bewusstsein*, is understood sometimes in a subjective sense, sometimes in an objective sense: as spontaneous self-expression or as a capacity for being affected by something that is "oneself." Thus Kant immediately turns around the question from which the concept of transcendental apperception emerged. He asks not only how we can separate the pure form of an "I think" (*Ich denke*) from the empirical consciousness and its contents, but also how our activity of thinking *affects us ourselves*, in the "inner sense." How does the "I think" know itself or perceive itself thinking? This auto-affection is still a *Selbst-bewusstsein*, this time in the sense of a consciousness (of the activity of) the self, that is, of an *experience* (which is sensible in a way, even though

4

Consciousness and *con-science*: The role of Coste's translation

Produced in close collaboration with the author and reprinted several times between 1700 and 1755, the translation of Locke's *An Essay Concerning Human Understanding* by the Protestant Pierre Coste is still the only complete French version available. Two translator's notes concerning new terms necessary to translate "the Self" and "consciousness" indicate the difficulty of finding in French, at the end of the seventeenth century, an equivalent for the neologism created by Cudworth and Locke:

> The English word is "consciousness," which could be expressed in Latin by *conscientia*. . . . In French, we have, in my opinion, only the words *sentiment* and *conviction* that correspond to some extent to this idea. But in several places in this chapter they can express only imperfectly Mr. Locke's thought, which makes *personal identity* depend absolutely on this act of Man *quo sibi est conscius*. . . . After having reflected for some time on ways of remedying this difficulty, I found nothing better than to use the term *conscience* to express this very act. . . . But, it will be said, it is a strange license, to turn a word away from its ordinary meaning and give it one that it has never been given in our language. . . . I see finally that I could have simply used our word *conscience* in the sense that Mr. Locke used it ["consciousness"] in this chapter and elsewhere, since one of our best writers, the famous Father Malebranche, did not scruple to make use of it in this same meaning in several places in *La recherche de la vérité*.

> (*Essai philosophique concernant l'entendement humain*, 2.27.9n)

In her study Conscience *as Consciousness*, Davies shows that here we see not only important evidence for the formation of the modern conception of "consciousness," but also an actual moment of that formation. Why did Coste render the definition in 2.1.19 by "cette conviction n'est autre chose que la perception de ce qui se passe dans l'âme de l'Homme" before suddenly changing in 2.27.9 to render "since consciousness always accompanies thinking, and 'tis that, that makes everyone to be, what he calls self," as "puisque la *conscience* accompagne toujours la pensée, et que c'est là ce qui fait que chacun est ce qu'il nomme *soi-même*"? The only evidence provided by the context is the collocation in the same sentence of the two fundamental theoretical terms that are henceforth correlative: "the self" and "consciousness." Coste thus invents *con-science* at the precise moment when he is forced by the theoretical matter to create not one but *two* neologisms, one lexical, the other semantic.

An enigma arises here, however. If the term *conscience* in the sense of pure self-knowledge already existed, why did Coste allow himself a neologism? In reality, this is one and the same problem. If Locke's translator, obliged to create *con-science*, has to try to differentiate himself from Malebranche at the same time that he appeals to him as a precedent, that is because the meanings of *conscience* as Malebranche uses it and Locke's "consciousness" are in reality in conflict. The notion of *conscience* that Malebranche identifies with the "inner feeling" (*Recherche de la vérité*, 3.7, ed. Lewis) is ultimately anti-Cartesian: it is the imperfect knowledge we have of the soul ("we know of our soul only what we feel happen in us"), thoroughly mixed with the "feeling of what is happening in our body," and liable to all sorts of illusions. Malebranche is well aware that he is thereby destroying the very heart of Cartesianism:

> I have said in several places, and I believe I have sufficiently proved . . . that we have no clear idea of our soul, but only *conscience* or inner feeling; that thus we know it much more imperfectly than we do extension. This seems to me so evident that I did not believe it was necessary to prove it at length. But the authority of M. Descartes, who says positively . . . *that the nature of the mind is better known than anything else*, has so preoccupied some of his disciples that what I have written has served only to make me seem to them a weak person who cannot take a clear position and hold firm to abstract truths.

> (*XIe Éclaircissement*, in *Recherche de la vérité*, 3:98ff.)

Thus Malebranche's *conscience* has to do less with knowledge than with ignorance of oneself, whereas Locke, for his part, is opposed to Descartes not epistemologically but ontologically. His "consciousness" is not ignorance but, on the contrary, the immediate recognition by the mind of its own operations on the inner "stage" of which it is the spectator. What Locke inaugurates is the turning of the Cartesian idea of self-knowledge against the idea of the mind or soul (*mens*) as substance. For all that, the ignorance of the self inherent in consciousness will not disappear: it reemerges, notably in Kant's analysis of the "paralogism of rational psychology" that opens the *critical* phase of transcendental philosophy and bases it on the idea of an originary ambivalence inherent in the subject's relationship to itself.

BIBLIOGRAPHY

Davies, Catherine Glyn. Conscience *as Consciousness: The Idea of Self-Awareness in French Philosophical Writing from Descartes to Diderot*. Oxford: The Voltaire Foundation,1990.
Malebranche, Nicolas de la. *Recherche de la vérité*. Edited by Geneviève Lewis. Paris: Vrin, 1945–.

it refers to any content of consciousness). Kant identifies it with the pure experience of time and is concerned to show that it must never be confused with the concept of transcendental apperception, since it constitutes the *Ich* as a phenomenon. But he also shows that the confusion is constantly induced by the very structure of thought ("Paralogisms of Pure Reason," in *Critique of Pure Reason*, trans. Guyer and Wood). This aporia is the starting point for all of the discussions of German idealism concerning the "experience of consciousness" torn between truth and illusion, infinitude and finitude, interiority and exteriority.

The question raised by Maine de Biran (*Essai sur les fondements de la psychologie* [1811], published in 1859), and after him by a French tradition that extends to Henri Bergson and Maurice Merleau-Ponty, is quite different. For Maine de Biran, self-consciousness (for which he also uses the Latin expressions *conscium sui* and *compos sui*), "an original fact of the inner sense" that founds all philosophy, is an individual feeling (as in Malebranche) and has as its prototype the "immediate apperception" of one's own body. He expresses the irreducibility of the union of mind and body as it is experienced in particular in "effort"; this feeling contains

5

Consciousness, self-consciousness, and "apperception"

In the *Critique of Pure Reason* (1781), Kant makes *Selbstbewusstsein* the supreme principle of knowledge and, at the same time, its own critical judge. Such an act of thought must therefore be considered a "transcendental apperception," that is, a grasping by the understanding itself of the pure form of the unity that it imposes on every representation of an object. This is another translinguistic equivalence that conceals, however, a syntactical and historical difficulty.

This difficulty begins with Leibniz, who, confronted by the Cartesian conception, had taken a position opposite that of Locke: for innate ideas, but against the idea that the mind can know itself through its own thinking. In his correspondence with Arnauld, Leibniz still referred to *conscience* (associated with *expérience intérieure*, *pensée*, and *réminiscence*). But in *Nouveaux essais sur l'entendement humain* (2.27), he retranslates "consciousness" as *consciosité* or *consciensciosité*, rejecting Coste's neologism. This attempt, which was not adopted by others, clearly shows the tension between the two aspects of the notion of "consciousness": "self-presence" and "self-knowledge." For Leibniz, however, the only really adequate notion is that of "apperception" (from the verb *apercevoir*, or rather

from *s'apercevoir*); it makes it possible to hierarchize perceptions: a clear perception is not necessarily distinct, that is, it does not necessarily include a knowledge of its own constitution (*Monadologie*, §14). Leibnizian apperception is the mind's perception of the representations that develop (or unfold) in front of it the world of which it is a part, so that it can situate itself in it. The Kantian *transzendentale Apperzeption*, on the other hand, is only the way the consciousness reflects its own invariant form through the diversity of objective contents. But in exchange, it immediately raises itself to universality; it is the condition of all possible experience, individual or collective.

Must we then render *Selbstbewusstsein* in French by *conscience de soi* or, as translators like Pierre-Jean Labarrière and Gwendolen Jarczyk, who have reflected at length on Hegel's use of the term, prefer, by *auto-conscience*? It seems that in Kant's text (and notably in the "Transcendental Deduction" section of the *Critique of Pure Reason*), we can find a significant difference between the notions of the "Bewusstsein [der Identität] seiner [meiner] selbst," and *Selbstbewusstsein*: the homonymy of the psychological and the transcendental is constitutive. In Hegel, on the

contrary—as Derathé emphasizes (96) in his translation of the *Grundlinien der Philosophie des Rechts* (1821)—the "play" between *Selbstbewusstsein* and *Bewusstsein von sich* occupies an important place, but refers rather to the subtle distinction between *conscience de soi* and *conscience du soi* (or *du moi*) ("self-consciousness" and "consciousness of the self"). Note that this can be translated into Italian without apparent problems by *auto-coscienza*—and by *coscienza di se*—with a clearer connotation of "consciousness of the self," which *consapevole* suffices to express in practice. English, obviously, uses "self-consciousness." These variants are connected with a more general problem in expressing reflexivity on the basis of Greek and Latin models (*auto-*, *sui*).

BIBLIOGRAPHY

Hegel, G.W.F. *Grundlinien der Philosophie des Rechts*. Translated into French by R. Derathé. Paris: Vrin, 1975. English translation by T. M. Knox: *Elements of the Philosophy of Right*. Oxford: Oxford University Press, 1942. English translation by H. B. Bisnet: *Elements of the Philosophy of Right*. Edited by Allen W. Wood. Cambridge: Cambridge University Press, 1991.

---

immediately the positing of an antithesis between the self and the external world to which it is opposed. Thinking about self-consciousness is thus thinking about the two terms of this antithesis, their separation and their complementarity insofar as they are part of the same lived experience. The problem Maine de Biran raises is thus at the origin of French existentialism, and in this sense explains why French philosophy has never ceased to "translate" into existential terms the problems of the relation between psychology, phenomenology, and the transcendental dialectic of consciousness. But correlatively, the detour through *Bewusst-sein* (a way of writing it introduced in the twentieth century in analogy with the Heideggerian *Da-sein*) allows us to understand what is at stake in the post-Kantian aporia of "auto-affection" as well as in the post-Biranian questioning of the duality of the "simple fact": a reflection on the being of the "conscious being."

III. Contemporary Theoretical and Semantic Problems

Since the invention of consciousness, two problems have dominated the expression of the subject in the three great European philosophical languages and maintain permanent gaps among them, bordering on untranslatability, whereas the equivalences are in theory fixed. The first problem concerns the gap between the German paradigm of *Wissen* and

the French paradigm of *science*. The second concerns the difficulties inherent in psychological discourse, as shown in the problem of translating the English words "consciousness" and "awareness." They develop in opposite directions, but in both cases they illustrate the latent competition between the dichotomous oppositions of which philosophy is so fond (the moral point of view versus the psychological point of view) and more complex derivations that better reflect the mutual influence of language and concept.

A. "Conscience" and "certitude": *Gewissen, Gewissheit, and Bewusstsein* from Kant to Wittgenstein

The paradigm of *wissen* (Gr. *oida* [οἶδα], Lat. *scire*) is of fundamental importance for modern philosophy as a whole. In general, it does not have the same structure as that of the French *savoir* (as is shown by the different uses of *science* and *Wissenschaft*). But the correspondence between *conscience* and *Bewusstsein* raises specific problems. This has to do first with the fact that *Bewusstsein*'s etymology implies a more explicit decomposition than the one found in *conscientia* (*cum* + *scire*). Present from the start (in Wolff) in the competition between *Bewusst sein* and *Bewusstsein*, this latent decomposition is still at work in philosophical writing. It is reinforced by the parallelism between the active and the passive forms: *bewusst werden* (become conscious) thus corresponds to *bewusst sein* (to be conscious), which connotes the result or the faculty (consciousness). Whereas rational and later experimental psychology takes the new substantive for an equivalent of the English term "consciousness," Hegel and his followers restored the ontological emphasis on *Sein*. From this comes Karl Marx's formula: "Consciousness [*das Bewusstsein*] can never be anything other than the conscious being [*das bewusste Sein*]" (Marx, *The German Ideology*). Martin Heidegger also played on this, but turned it around, opposing to the *Bewusst-sein* of the critical tradition simply *Da-sein*, "being there," thrown into the world, rather than "being conscious" or being as consciousness. On the contrary, the transcendental tradition from Kant to the Marburg School and Edmund Husserl tried to erase this ontological mark and retain only the idea of faculty or function. In the end, it had to situate this denegation in the terminology itself: it seems that *Bewusstheit*, a substantive of quality that escapes the question of "being" and is basically a German transposition of Leibniz's *consciosité* or *conscienciosité*, was introduced by Paul Gerhard Natorp and at the same time by Wilhelm Wundt (on this point, see Husserl, *Logische Untersuchungen*, vol. 2, "Untersuchungen zur Phänomenologie und Erkenntnislehre," part 2, "Remark on the Translation of Certain Terms"). The *Bewusstheit/Bewusstsein* pair separates in the negative: *die Unbewusstheit* corresponds to "unawareness" (which would be rendered in French by *inconscience*), whereas *das Unbewusste* corresponds to "the unconscious" (which would be rendered in French by *l'inconscient*) (Ellenberger, *Histoire de la découverte de l'inconscient*, 728n).

But the most interesting point lies elsewhere. The paradigm of *wissen* is broader than that of *scire*: it includes not only *Gewissen* and *Bewusstsein*, but also *Gewissheit*, taken as an equivalent of the Latin *certitudo*. Thus here we should abandon the idea that all the relevant meanings are included in the field of the French *conscience*. For German philosophy, it is not from outside that certitude intervenes in consciousness: from the outset, it is part of the same kernel of meanings, which philosophers organize in different ways. Keeping in mind the theological background (*gewiss* and *Gewissheit* are essential signifiers in the Lutheran faith, closely linked to the anti-intellectualism of the Reformation; see Box 3), we will discuss four configurations. In Kant, the fundamental problem concerning *Bewusstsein* resides, as we have seen, in the distinction between an empirical phenomenon and a transcendental condition for the possibility of thought ("It must be possible for the 'I think' to accompany all of my representations," *Critique of Pure Reason*, §16, trans. Guyer and Wood), followed by the return to the empirical in the form of the subject's self-perception. *Selbstbewusstsein* thus connotes simultaneously an auto-affection of the subject, an "internal sensibility," and the pure logical form of self-identity (for which Johann Gottlieb Fichte later created the formula *Ich = Ich*). The possibility of this critical distinction rests not only on the abstract opposition of two heterogeneous modes of representation (transcendental apperception and the inner sense), but also on the actual discovery of forms of consciousness that are concerned solely with pure thought: in the area of theory, the experience of the apodictic certainty of judgments; in the area of practice, the experience of the categorical imperative or the moral consciousness. It is remarkable that these two concepts are

defined by Kant using symmetrical formulas that attach both of them to *Bewusstsein* as the "common name" of transcendental subjectivity. *Gewissheit* is defined as "consciousness of the necessity [*Bewusstsein der Notwendigkeit*] of judgments" (*Logic*, Introduction, 9). *Gewissen* is defined as "consciousness [*Bewusstsein*] of a free submission of the will to the law" (*Critique of Pure Reason*), or else as "the consciousness [*Bewusstsein*] of a tribunal within man" (*Metaphysics of Morals*), and so on. The complete organization of the notions is thus as follows: *Bewusstsein*, insofar as it grasps itself as a pure form, is the transcendental unity of *Apperzeption*; insofar as it is the theoretical consciousness of necessity, it is *Gewissheit* (we might say "pure logical feeling"); insofar as it is the practical consciousness of the law, it is *Gewissen*; finally, in one or another of these modalities, the subject affects itself, "from the inside," as a psychological *Selbstbewusstsein*. This semantic organization is ternary, not binary.

The Hegelian organization is entirely different, particularly as it is set forth in the *Phenomenology of Mind*. There, Hegel offers an account of the genesis of *Bewusstsein* from *Gewissheit*, taking the latter's modalities as a guiding thread. From "sense certainty" to "the mind's certainty of itself," *Gewissheit* is *Bewusstsein*'s active *relationship to itself*, which explains why consciousness can experience itself as truth in each of its experiences, and why it must nonetheless repeatedly divest itself of itself in discovering its error. As a concept, *Bewusstsein* can emerge only with a first negation of *Gewissheit*, of perception; but on the other hand, the problem of *Gewissheit* can be taken beyond *Bewusstsein*, or better yet, it can take consciousness beyond itself, into the concept of absolute Spirit or Knowledge. In this context, the question of the *Gewissen* is treated in a localized way, as a particular figure of consciousness (*Bewusstsein*) and of its own *Gewissheit* (certitude). But this figure is privileged: it is the key moment in which *Bewusstsein* knows (*weiss*) itself as a pure subject (the concept of a pure subject is thus fundamentally a moral concept), and conceives itself essentially as *Selbstbewusstsein*, having only itself as its "object." This subjective figure of truth, which is deeply illusory, is entirely imbued with a self-referential *Gewissheit*.

■ See Box 6.

In *Sein und Zeit* (§§54–55), Heidegger centers his analysis of the *Gewissen* on the common expression "the voice of conscience." Contrary to the "metaphor of the tribunal," it is supposed to refer to an originary characteristic of *Dasein*: interpellation, the "call" (*Ruf, Anruf*) to responsibility (*Schuld*), to "being oneself" (*Selbstsein*). Such a voice by which "*Dasein* calls to itself" is always already of the order of discourse (*Rede*), even though it is essentially quiet or speaks only by keeping silent, that is, it determines no task or duty (*Pflicht*). This description is thus opposed term-for-term to Kant's definitions. Neither *Gewissheit* nor *Bewusstsein* plays any role in it. They are concepts basically foreign to Heidegger's thought, which reserves them for the description of the metaphysical moment of subjectivity that was opened up historically by Cartesianism and culminates in Hegel. It is hard to imagine that this phenomenology did not play a role in the way Jacques Derrida "deconstructed" the Husserlian conception of consciousness, in a chapter entitled

6

Translations of Hegel's *Phenomenology of Mind*

It is remarkable that none of the three French translations of Hegel's *Phenomenology of Mind* has adopted the same equivalent for *Gewissen*. Each has recognized the difficulty and chosen to draw the system in a different direction. J. Hyppolite (1939) translates *Gewissen* as *conscience morale* or *bonne conscience*, in order to "avoid the possible confusion of *Bewusstsein* and *Gewissen*." J.-P. Lefebvre (1991) is the only translator who has noted "the connotation of certainty that is associated with [*Gewissen*]" and translated it as *conviction morale*, "so as to indicate the intimate dimension of *Gewissen*" (in your soul and conscience) by reserving *persuasion* for *Überzeugung*. Finally, G. Jarczyk and P.-J. Labarrière (1993)—who proposed that *Selbstbewusstsein* be rendered as *auto-conscience* (see Box 5)—render *Gewissen* as *certitude-morale*, which fuses the two concepts, but give the tautology "la certitude inflexible de

la certitude-morale" as a translation of "die unwankende Gewissheit des Gewissens"—reserving *conviction* for *Überzeugung*. For his part, in a note to his translation of *Grundlinien der Philosophie des Rechts* (168), Derathé offers this comment on the difficulty:

> The German language distinguishes between *Gewissen* and *Bewusstsein*. It thus has two words to designate what we call in French *la conscience*. For Hegel, the words *Bewusstsein* and *Selbstbewusstsein* (self-consciousness) are related to *Wissen*, to scientific knowledge or to knowledge in general. On the other hand, Hegel regards *Gewissen* as a form of *Gewissheit*, of certainty, or, more exactly, of self-certainty: "This pure self-certainty, Hegel says, pushed to its extreme limit, is manifested in two forms, one of which passes immediately into the other in the

form of conscience and in the form of evil . . ." (*Encyclopaedia*, §511). To avoid confusion, *Gewissen* is often rendered in French by *conscience morale* and *Bewusstsein* by *conscience*. I prefer to follow the example of Bayle and Rousseau and translate *Gewissen* simply by *conscience* without further qualification. However, let us recall that for Rousseau, conscience is "the infallible judge of good and evil, which makes man like God," whereas for Hegel, it is simply a subjective certainty that can deviate from the truth and take evil for good. That is why Hegel raises the question (*Grundlinien der Philosophie des Rechts*, §137) of true or veridical conscience [*Gewissen*], which is the disposition to want that which is good in itself and for oneself and that, for Hegel, appears only at the level of ethical life or *Sittlichkeit*.

"The Voice That Keeps Silence," writing, for example, that "it is this universality that ensures that, structurally and by right, no consciousness is possible without the voice. The voice is the being which is present to itself in the form of universality, as con-sciousness [*con-science*]" (*La voix et le phénomène*, 89). Thus Derrida plays in French on the etymology and connotations of a German concept, but at the same time he diverts them and to some extent can authorize criticism of them. His "con-sciousness" (which he writes as Coste did when translating Locke) is a *Bewusstsein* haunted by the Heideggerian analytic of *Gewissen*, which makes the certainties of phenomenological experience vacillate in a special *Ungewissheit*. We might quote partly similar remarks from Paul Ricœur's *Soi-même comme un autre* (1990).

Our last witness is Ludwig Wittgenstein. Here again, *Bewusstsein* is no longer central, but for reasons different from Heidegger's. The *Tractatus Logico-Philosophicus* replaced this term with *Gefühl*, moving it entirely into the realm of subjectivism and even of "mysticism" (§6.45). And the posthumous collection *Über Gewissheit* reduces *Bewusstsein* completely to the latter term, understood in its subjective meaning. The whole book is constructed around the question of what *Ich weiss* (I know) means, and thus around the relationship between *wissen* and *Gewissheit* in various language games. Something of the battle Wittgenstein's aphorisms wage against tautology is irremediably lost as soon as we pass into French or English:

> And in fact, isn't the use of the word "know" [*wissen*] as a preeminently philosophical word altogether wrong? . . . "I believe I know" [*Ich glaube es zu wissen*] would not need to express a lesser degree of certainty [*Gewissheit*].
>
> (*Über Gewissheit*, trans. Paul and Anscombe)

Against the heritage of "Cartesianism," we need to return here to a very close examination of Descartes's own language.

B. Consciousness or experience

The translation of the terms "awareness" and "consciousness" has the interest of bringing out a theoretical difficulty of which insular philosophers may themselves not be aware. "Aware" is an old English word meaning "to be awake, on one's guard, recognize." On the other hand, "awareness" does not appear before the nineteenth century (RT: *Oxford English Dictionary*, s.v.). Short of a paraphrase, it can, of course, be translated into French by *conscience* when the term is used by itself. The difficulties begin when it is necessary to render "consciousness" and "awareness" in the same context (expressions such as "conscious awareness" even occur). The situation becomes critical when statements in the form of definitions risk turning into tautologies: "Conscious experience names the class of mental states that involve awareness" (Flanagan, *Consciousness Reconsidered*); "This consciousness, in the 20th century, has come to mean a 'full, active awareness' including feeling as well as thought" (Scott, "The Evidence of Experience"). Then translators hesitate between indicating the English term in parentheses (Dennett, *Consciousness Explained*) and the introduction of expressions that particularize usage and suggest philosophical interpretations (*connaissance immédiate* for "awareness": Penrose, *The Emperor's New Mind*)

Thus we can understand why, in his own French adaptation of his famous lecture "Does Consciousness Really Exist?" (1912), William James used the French word *aperception*, which current French translators no longer dare to use. The essence of the problem seems to be the following: The uses of "awareness" and "consciousness" are obviously not distinct, and even less codified. On the other hand, they are dominated by recurrent questions regarding the pertinence of the concept of consciousness inherited from classical philosophy: ontological problems (as James Mark Baldwin put it, "It is the point of division between mind and not mind," *Dictionary of Philosophy and Psychology*), or problems bearing on the ability of the neurosciences to "explain consciousness"—that is, to objectivize the subject—or on the connection between consciousness and personal identity. The contexts show that the term "awareness" sometimes constitutes a nontechnical equivalent of "consciousness," which is supposed to provide access to a common experience and serve as a point of reference for the elaboration of a scientific concept, and sometimes the name of an elementary phenomenon to which the enigma of the specificity of psychic phenomena might be reduced. It is a question of simultaneously showing the circular nature of the definitions of consciousness and trying to break it. Then we see that the argumentative structure of the expositions generally consists (with or without a classification of the forms or degrees of consciousness, as in Ryle [*The Concept of Mind*] or Flanagan [*Consciousness Reconsidered*]) in situating the field of the phenomena of consciousness between the two extreme poles of "awareness" and "the self." For the whole of this field, a metonymic term is necessary, one that transcends the difference between "awareness" and "consciousness," while at the same time expressing their intrinsic relationship: this term is generally "experience," which thus represents, as in Locke, Hegel, or James, the most general name of subjectivity.

This remark leads to another. Since awareness forms the first anchoring point for consciousness within experience, its meaning is obviously not unequivocal: it depends on theoretical positions that are mutually contradictory, oscillating between the idea of the necessary presence of a personal subject and that of the latter's absence. However, what remains constant is the argumentative function of refutation or *elegchos* performed by the reference to awareness. In fact, "aware" is synonymous with "not unconscious": consciousness is that which is not unconscious, thus aware, or present to itself. As always in philosophy, double negation tends to connote the originary. The semantic structure (awareness + consciousness = experience) is not at all limited to cognitive contexts. On the contrary, it appears in the same way in the contexts of moral and political philosophy. Thus it shows the dependency of all these domains in relation to a single implicit phenomenology.

But furthermore, it competes with a second, formally similar structure that seems to be more or less reserved for the adversaries of cognitivism (like Searle [*Minds, Brains and Science*]), and that is based on the interpretation of experience in terms of consciousness + intentionality. This seems to pose no problems of translation. But our desire to resolve the problem (which is basically insoluble) raised by the doublet "consciousness"/"awareness" can thereby only be whetted. The symmetry of these two constructions competing with "experience" corresponds to the fact that from an "objectivist" point of view, the problem is the immediate relation of the subject to himself (designated by "awareness"), whereas from a "subjectivist" point of view, the problem is the immediate relation of the subject to objects (designated by

"intentionality"). On closer inspection, we see that here "intentional" and "intentionality" are based on the same "double negation" as "aware" and "awareness": it is a matter of naming the "not-unconscious." This amounts to saying that in all cases, the "definitions" of "consciousness" that want to avoid self-reference rely on the attempt to find a word to express this limit of thought.

IV. The Borders of *Conscience* and Linguistic Clues

Ever since consciousness was invented, the expression of the problems it has synthesized has constantly been racked by the gaps between linguistic paradigms. The plurality of meaning we have described is clearly not a defect, but the source of a continually renewed dynamics of thought that plays with the possibilities of problematization that are concealed by words in other languages that are more or less equivalent to the French word *conscience*. This process can change reference points, but it cannot stop. Its meaning has been temporarily masked by the way in which the philosophy of the first part of the twentieth century (Léon Brunschvicg, Ernst Cassirer) brought the various "manifestations" or "degrees" of *la conscience* into a figure of a great progress, which was ultimately identical to humanity's march toward the realization of its own essence, conceived on the classical European model. The debates aroused by psychoanalysis (attached by Freud to the expression *das Unbewusste*, "the unconscious," which was forged by the Romantics at the beginning of the nineteenth century), or by the "deconstruction of the subject" in the twentieth century after Heidegger and the various structuralisms, did not alter significantly the feeling that it was unequivocal. The same will not be the case, probably, for the two phenomena that are going to mark the coming years: the intensification of confrontations between the ways of conceiving of individuality, personality, the psychic apparatus, knowledge, and so on in Western and non-Western cultures and systems of thought, and the diffusion and development of the paradigm of the cognitive sciences. These two phenomena (which are perhaps connected) will go hand-in-hand with a new revolution in the economy of linguistic exchanges, both in the sense of a multiplication of translations between European and extra-European idioms, and in the sense of the imposition of a new technical-conceptual *koinê*, basic Anglo-American. The question of what place the words and notions "conscience," "consciousness," and "awareness," *Bewusstsein*, *Gewissheit*, and *Gewissen*, will have at the point where philosophy, the sciences, ethics, and even mysticism intersect, in common language and in scientific languages, now seems wide open.

Étienne Balibar

BIBLIOGRAPHY

Ayers, Michael. *Locke: Epistemology and Ontology*. New York: Routledge, 1991.

Azouvi, François. *Maine de Biran: La science de l'homme*. Paris: Vrin, 1995.

Baldwin, James Mark. *Dictionary of Philosophy and Psychology*. London: Macmillan, 1905. Reprint, 1960.

Balibar, Renée. *Le colinguisme*. Paris: Presses Universitaires de France, 1993.

Bourcier, Elisabeth. *Examen de conscience et conscience de soi dans la première moitié du XVIIe siècle en Angleterre*. In *Genèse de la conscience moderne: Études sur le développement de la conscience de soi dans les littératures du monde occidental*, edited by R. Ellrodt. Paris: Publications de la Sorbonne, Presses Universitaires de France, 1983.

Chollet, A. "Conscience." In *Dictionnaire de théologie Catholique*. Edited by Alfred Vacant, Eugène Mangenot, and Émile Amann. Paris: Letouzey and Ané, 1903.

Condillac, Étienne Bonnot de. *Essai sur l'origine des connaissances humaines*. In *Œuvres philosophiques*, edited by G. Le Roy. Paris: Presses Universitaires de France, 1947. First published in 1746. Translation by H. Aarsleff: *Essay on the Origin of Human Knowledge*. Edited by H. Aarsleff. Cambridge: Cambridge University Press, 2001.

Dennett, Daniel. *Consciousness Explained*. Boston: Little, Brown, 1991. French translation by P. Engel: *La conscience expliquée*. Paris: Odile Jacob, 1993.

Derrida, Jacques. *La voix et le phénomène*. Paris: Presses Universitaires de France, 2009. Translation by Leonard Lawlor: *Voice and Phenomenon*. Chicago, IL: Northwestern University Press, 2010.

Ellenberger, Henri F. *Histoire de la découverte de l'inconscient*. Translated by J. Feisthauer. Paris: Fayard, 1994.

Flanagan, Owen. *Consciousness Reconsidered*. Cambridge, MA: MIT Press, 1992.

James, William. *Essays in Radical Empiricism*. Edited by F. Bowers and I. K. Skrupskelis. Cambridge, MA: Harvard University Press, 1976.

Jung, Gertrud. "Suneidesis, Conscientia, Bewusstsein." In *Archiv für die Gesamte Psychologie*, vol. 89. Leipzig: Akademische Verlagsgesellschaft, 1933.

Kant, Immanuel. *Critique of Pure Reason*. Translated and edited by P. Guyer and A. Wood. Cambridge: Cambridge University Press, 1998.

Kittsteiner, Heinz D. *Die Entstehung des modernen Gewissens*. Darmstadt, Ger.: Wissenschaftliche Buchgesellschaft, 1992.

Koffka, Kurt. "Consciousness." In *Encyclopedia of the Social Sciences*, vol. 4, edited by E.R.A. Seligmann and A. Johnson. New York: Macmillan, 1935.

Kolakowski, Leszek. *Religion: If There Is No God*. London: Fontana, 1993.

———. *Świadomość religijna i więź kościelna: Studia nad chrześcijaństwem bezwyznaniowym XVII wieku*. Warsaw: Wydawn. Nauk, 1997.

Lewis, Clive Staples. "Conscience and Conscious." In *Studies in Words*. Cambridge: Cambridge University Press, 1967.

Lewis, Geneviève. *Le problème de l'inconscient et le Cartésianisme*. Paris: Presses Universitaires de France, 1950.

Locke, John. *An Essay Concerning Human Understanding*. Edited by P. H. Nidditch. Oxford: Oxford University Press, 1975. French translation by Pierre Coste: *Essai philosophique concernant l'entendement humain*. Edited by Emilienne Naert. Paris: Vrin, 1972.

Marx, Karl. *The German Ideology*. New York: Prometheus, 1998.

Merleau-Ponty, Maurice. *L'union de l'âme et du corps chez Malebranche, Biran et Bergson*. Edited by J. Deprun. Paris: Vrin, 1978. Translation by P. B. Milan: *The Incarnate Subject: Malebranche, Biran, and Bergson on the Union of Body and Soul*. Edited by A. G. Bjelland Jr. and P. Burke. Amherst, NY: Humanity Books, 2001.

Meyer, Louis. *La philosophie interprète de l'Écriture sainte*. Edited by J. Lagrée and P. F. Moreau. Paris: Intertextes, 1998.

Montaigne, Michel de. *The Essays of Montaigne*. Translated by Donald Frame. Stanford, CA: Stanford University Press, 1958.

Penrose, Roger. *The Emperor's New Mind: Concerning Computers, Minds, and the Laws of Physics*. Oxford: Oxford University Press, 1990. French translation by F. Balibar and C. Tiercelin: *L'esprit, l'ordinateur et les lois de la physique*. Paris: InterÉditions, 1992.

Ryle, Gilbert. *The Concept of Mind*. London: Hutchinson, 1949.

Schrader, Wolfgang H. *Theorien des Gewissens*. In *Oikeiôsis: Festschrift für Robert Spaemann*, edited by R. Löw. Weinheim, Ger.: Acta Humaniora, 1987.

Scott, Joan W. "The Evidence of Experience." In *Feminists Theorize the Political*, edited by J. Butler and J. W. Scott. New York: Routledge, 1992.

Searle, John. *Minds, Brains and Science*. Cambridge, MA: Harvard University Press, 1984.

Starobinski, Jean. *Montaigne in Movement*. Translated by Arthur Goldhammer. Chicago, IL: University of Chicago Press, 1985.

Stelzenberger, Johannes. *Syneidesis, Conscientia, Gewissen, Studie zum Bedeutungswandel eines moraltheologischen Begriffes*. Paderborn, Ger.: Schöningh, 1963.

Tugendhat, Ernst. *Selbstbewusstsein und Selbstbestimmung: Sprachanalytische Interpretationen*. Frankfurt: Suhrkamp, 1979. Translation by P. Stern: *Self-Consciousness and Self-Determination*. Cambridge, MA: MIT Press, 1989.

Walzer, Michael. *The Revolution of the Saints: A Study in the Origins of Radical Politics*. Cambridge, MA: Harvard University Press, 1965.

Wittgenstein, Ludwig. *Über Gewissheit*. In *Werkausgabe*, vol. 8. Frankfurt: Suhrkamp, 1989. Translation by D. Paul and G.E.M. Anscombe: *On Certainty*. Edited by G.E.M. Anscombe and G. H. von Wright. Oxford: Blackwell, 1969.

CONSENSUS

"Consensus" is a direct borrowing from the Latin, which means "agreement, unanimous judgment" (from *cum*, with, together, and *sentire*, perceive, feel, think, judge), and translates the Greek *sumpatheia* [συμπάθεια] (*sun-* [σύν], with, like the Latin *cum-*, and *paschein* [πάσχειν], to be affected, undergo, suffer). It was used in particular by the Stoics to designate agreement, conspiracy, and a certain number of things between the two, and it was adopted by physiology to designate the interdependence of bodily organs (cf. IMPLICATION, OIKEIÔSIS, PATHOS). But "consensus" is also, at least in English and French, a good translation of Greek terms such as *homonoia* [ὁμόνοια] (literally, identity of thought, whence unanimity, concord), and even *homologia* [ὁμολογία] (identity of discourse, whence agreement), which opens out onto the city and the constitution of politics; see LOGOS, II.A, LOVE, II.B.2, SPEECH ACT (esp. Box 1); cf. POLIS, POLITICS (cf. IMPLICATION, OIKEIÔSIS, PATHOS).

Consensus clearly points toward "common sense," that to which everyone can adhere: see *SENS COMMUN* [SENSUS COMMUNIS, COMMON SENSE] and SENSE, as well as COMMONPLACE and DOXA.

In contemporary usage, "consensus" designates not only agreement but the human community that is based on it beyond its divisions, whether the unifying element is civil or religious: see *ALLIANCE,* CIVIL SOCIETY, PEOPLE, PEOPLE/RACE/NATION (esp. Box 1), SOBORNOST'; cf. *COMMUNITY, DROIT,* WELTANSCHAUUNG.

➤ PRAXIS, SECULARIZATION, *WHOLE*

CONSERVATIVE

The word "conservative" derives from the Latin *conservare* (to preserve, respect, save), which designates the fact of preserving and faithfully observing: see PIETAS, RELIGIO.

Here we will focus, as in the entry for "liberal," on the difference between modern political uses of the term in French and English. The English term "conservative" originally designated one of the great traditional parties in Great Britain, occupying the place that would in France be that of the "right" (*droite*), and later referring to a more general political and even moral position hostile to the most antitraditional aspects of modern society. In any case, the position of the "conservatives" is always understood in a relative way, as is shown by the two series of oppositions analyzed here: see WHIG/TORY, for the birth of the modern British political system, and LIBERAL, for the contemporary usage that divides the main political currents into conservative, liberal, and radical.

➤ CIVIL SOCIETY, LAW, *LIBERTY*, POLITICS

CONTINUITET / CONTINUERLIGHED / CONTINUERLIGT (DANISH)

ENGLISH	continuity, continual
FRENCH	*continuité, continuellement/continûment*
GERMAN	*Kontinuität, Kontinuierlichkeit/kontinuierlich*

➤ CONTINUITY, and AIÔN, DASEIN, LEIB, *PERSON*, PLUDSELIGHED, PRESENT, *TIME*

To render the idea of continuity, the Kierkegaardian lexicon uses two terms: *Continuitet* and *Continuerlighed*, which are denoted in the following by "continuity (A)" and "continuity (B)." In French and English, there is a subtle difference between *continûment*/"continuously" (without interruption) and *continuellement*/"continually" (possibly repeatable). In some cases, either of the two Danish concepts can be used, and yet one can recognize in the use of the second one (*Continuerlighed*) a concern to emphasize the dialectical particularity of the existential continuity, to oppose it to permanence and to the stability of nature.

Continuity (B) designates the fact that an existing individual is continuous in becoming by virtue of a decision that has the value of an origin. For nature or for ordinary existence, time is only "the dialectic that comes from outside." On the other hand, for the individual who lives his existence on the basis of himself, who is "originally dialectical in himself," time operates in such a way as to bring out "the metamorphosis of the most precisely determined continuity as process, succession, continuous transformation through the years."

Continuity (B) characterizes the cohesion of ethical life in harmony with the requirements of social reality, of life that escapes dissolution, diffusion (*dæmrer*) in the humors, and momentary affective tonalities. This concrete continuity, which "masters the humors [*Stemning*]" (see STIMMUNG), is described in contrast to the abstract continuity of the mystic. The ethical choice of oneself involves becoming-oneself as a task of existence in its continuity in accord with duration. That is the origin of "the concrete person in continuity [A]." Ethical triumph has to do with the "fact of being continuous"—continuity (B); it is the fact of being at once hope and memory. In fact, the unhappy relationship to the past and to the future of man deprived of presence is at the opposite pole from the positivity of movement backward (repentance) and forward (desire), which characterizes the purity of heart of the person who desires the One. "Repentance must have its time," which is nothing other than the return to a past marked by the lack of this desire. It works in favor of the cohesion of life animated by movement forward.

Aside from continuity (A) as the permanence of humanity, that is, "descent as continuity in the history of the species," recourse to this notion appears especially when there are figures or situations whose traits are marked by an absence of continuity. That is the case for the aesthetician, the ironist, who has no continuity (A) other than boredom. Kierkegaard was inspired here by the ironic negativity that Hegel dealt with in his *Aesthetics* apropos of romantic art. (It also anticipates Nietzsche's Zarathustra, who is "tired of poets.") The ironist frees himself from continuity (A) with the real

conditions of a temporal existence; he lives an "eternity without content," a felicity without joy, a superficial depth of the being at the same time starved and sated. He lacks continuity; being prey to successive humors "that instantly succeed one another," he is, as it were, confusedly diffused in them. To that is connected, in *Either/Or*, "the poetic infinity" of boredom or of the void characteristic of "demonic pantheism" (ibid.), or again, of the unhappy eternity of the bookkeeper, sketched in counterpoint to the happy eternity of "a voluptuously beautiful woman in a harem, reclining on a sofa in all her allure" (ibid.; see PLUDSELIGHED).

The interruption of continuity also has a gnoseological meaning. For instance, when faced by becoming in its diverse forms, it is not bodies of knowledge in continuity with each other but, rather, "opposed passions" that are established. That is the case of faith and doubt, which are dependent not on conclusions but on a decision. The loss of "continuity with oneself" marks the "new creature" constituted by the believer, who is, as it were, born a second time. The demonic and this believer are thus two antagonistic figures with respect to continuity. Alongside the properly theological development of the continuity of sin and eternity, the Christian theory of the instant is the occasion for a barely veiled critique of Hegelianism. It denounces the reduction to this "simple continuity [A]" that is carried out by thinking that ignores the instant as a "plenitude of time." It consists in believing that the meaning of the past can be brought out, not on the basis of what it really was (incarnation, redemption), but in a relationship of "simple continuity" with the future, namely, progress and history in conformity with the *Weltgeist*. Similarly, to think we can access the future not on the basis of what it will be (resurrection, judgment) but in continuity with the historical present is to underestimate the import of the instant instituted by Christianity.

The most explicit discussions of continuity and discontinuity with respect to the rhythm of thought are found in the great "theoretical" work of 1846, the *Concluding Unscientific Postscript*. When thought believes it can find a foundation in the "solidity of the continuous," it feels sure of itself, and consequently directly communicable *sub specie aeterni*. Like Socrates, the existent aware of "the deceptive life" in which he interacts with the idea finds himself "isolated," having only an "extremely private relationship with it." The possibility of death, which foils infinity's deceptions, casts doubt on any kind of positive assurance. The consciousness of finite time impedes continuous thought and situates man in the time of becoming. Time imposes its law and prevents this "abstract continuity which is not a continuity" from being prolonged. Thought's passion is opposed to the false continuity of abstract thought, because it is the "momentaneous continuity [B] that both slows the movement and is its impetus." Time, which cannot fail to affect thought, imposes on it a discontinuous rhythm, suspends the immanent continuity of conceptual sequences. It is in the staccato temporality of individual existence and not in the great continuity of world history that the relationship to the Absolute is played out, a relationship that consists of suffering and tribulation. Whereas in the ethical order temptations and tests attack temporal existence at its weak points, (religious) tribulations are like "Nemesis bearing on the powerful instant of the absolute relationship." Continuity (B) is broken when "the real resistance of the Absolute" is expressed.

Jacques Colette

BIBLIOGRAPHY

Kierkegaard, Søren. *Kierkegaard's Writings*. Edited by H. V. Hong and E. H. Hong. 25 vol. Princeton, NJ: Princeton University Press.

CONTINUITY

"Continuity" (from *tenere* [to hold, last, persist] and *cum* [with, together]) designates an uninterrupted persistence in time and also in space. Kierkegaard's proposal of original terminological distinctions in Danish is discussed in CONTINUITET; we will complete the Kierkegaardian lexicon concerning time in the articles PLUDSELIGHED (suddenness-without-consequence), MOMENT, Box 3, and NEUZEIT, Box 1.

We have also studied the expression of continuity through the "aspect" of verbs, which denotes the mode in which action develops: see ASPECT.

More broadly, see *TIME* [AIÔN, MEMORY, PRESENT].

➤ EPISTEMOLOGY, FORCE, PERCEPTION

CORSO, RICORSO (ITALIAN)

ENGLISH	*course, return, recurrence*
FRENCH	*cours, retour, récurrence*

➤ *RÉVOLUTION*, *TIME*, and AIÔN, AUFHEBEN, CIVILTÀ, *DESTINY*, HISTORIA UNIVERSALIS, HISTORY, MENSCHHEIT, PEOPLE/RACE/NATION, PERFECTIBILITY

Two words in everyday Italian, *corso* and *ricorso*, have acquired philosophical status because of Giambattista Vico's use of them in his *Scienza nuova* (1744). These words are associated with the idea of a cyclical conception of history that Vico is supposed to have defended at a time when the linear conception of an indefinite progress of humanity was being established. For a long time, Vico's work has been generally known only from this point of view, but an attentive study of his texts shows that it is very questionable whether in his *Scienza nuova* Vico merely adopts the ancient theme of the cyclical nature of time. This superficial and even erroneous interpretation of what he calls the *corso* and *ricorso* of nations prevents us from seeing the depth and originality of his thought.

I. Neither Cycle nor Spiral

The Italian word *corso* derives from Latin *cursus* (from *currere*), which designates a race, the act of running, and figuratively the course or itinerary followed by something (*cursus rerum, cursus vitae*). Vico uses it in the expression *corso che fanno le nazioni* (the course followed by nations), which serves as the title of Book Four of the *Scienza nuova*, designating the development of nations through time (Vico speaks only of "nations," which are concrete realities, and not of "humanity," an abstract term designating the human species). The "scientific" study of this necessary, universal evolution and

unfolding is the *Scienza nuova*'s chief goal: "since these institutions have been established by divine providence, the course of the institutions of the nations had to be, must now be, and will have to be such as our Science demonstrates, even if infinite worlds were born from time to time through eternity, which is certainly not the case" (§348). This is what Vico calls "eternal ideal history" (*storia ideal' eterna*). The actual history of nations is thus governed by a law of succession and can be divided into three "ages," that of the gods, that of heroes, and that of men. In the course of this history human beings, starting from a virtually animal state, develop the seeds of "humanity" that exist in them. The last state is that of "reason completely developed" (*ragion tutta spiegata*), with the appearance and flourishing of abstract thought, of philosophy and science. On the political level, it coincides with the emergence of the popular republic or democracy.

Thus we might think that *corso* so defined is a kind of constant progress leading, as Vico puts it, to an *akmê* (culmination). But history, with the examples of Greece and especially Rome, on which Vico concentrated his analyses almost exclusively, shows that it is difficult if not impossible for nations to maintain themselves in this state of complete perfection of their humanity, and that, as is shown by the paradigmatic fate of Rome, the principle of freedom, which is that of democracy, makes the latter degenerate into anarchy and corruption.

This is where Vico's text has to be examined very closely. For this state of disorder in which cities then find themselves, divine providence has three remedies, according to Vico. The first is the appearance of a monarch who, like Augustus, holds the institutions and the laws in his hands, makes order and equity reign, and makes subject peoples content with their fate. The second is that degenerate populations fall into the hands of better populations and are reduced to the status of provinces. The third and most radical occurs when the first two have proven impossible. When the social disintegration provoked by the "barbarity of reflection" (*barbarie della riflessione*) has reached its extreme, nations return to the primitive state of "barbarity of sensation" (*barbarie del senso*) from which they had long before emerged. A new *corso* begins, which Vico calls a *ricorso*, and it will repeat, not in their events, but in their temporal structure, the three stages of the *corso* defined through the study of the history of Greece and Rome. The fifth and last book of the *Scienza nuova*, which is devoted to the *ricorso delle cose umane* (the *ricorso* of human affairs), thus offers a panorama of the history of Western nations taken as a whole and seen as one and the same nation after the fall of the Roman Empire. The West moves from an "age of the gods," then from an "age of heroes"—which coincides with what we call the Middle Ages and what Vico calls "the barbarous times come again" (*tempi barbari ritornati*)—to an "age of men" (*età degli uomini*), which is the modern world.

As we see, the word *ricorso* does not refer, as is often believed, to a backward movement, to a regression, a process of involution that makes nations retrace their steps and brings them back to their point of departure (understood in that way, the *ricorso* would be the inverse of the *corso*). The return to the starting point comes at the end of a *corso*, and makes it possible for another *corso* (*ri-corso*), identical in its general structure, to begin.

Before inquiring into the view of the history of nations that emerges from these analyses, we must note two important points. On the one hand, Vico does not speak of the "*ricorso* of human affairs" in the first edition of the *Scienza nuova* (1725), in which the principles of his "science" are already laid out, which proves that the question is not essential for him, and that it is merely a confirmation of the general validity of these principles. And on the other hand, he never uses, in the final version of his work, the words *corso* and *ricorso* in the plural, which disconfirms the common interpretation that holds that for Vico history offers the spectacle of a series of *corsi* and *ricorsi* indefinitely succeeding each other—unless, to give this succession the appearance of a progress, these cycles are seen as a spiral; but neither this image nor the idea connected with it is found in Vico's work.

Corso can be translated into French by *cours*, but the translation of *ricorso* is more delicate. *Recours* (recourse, appeal) appears in the juridical vocabulary, and if we can acknowledge that Vico's *ricorso* does indeed have the meaning of an "appeal" that nations might make before the tribunal of history, it does not refer, or no longer refers, to the repetition of a course, of a run (the verb *recourir*, in one of its common meanings, preserves this idea, and a course that has not been properly run has to be rerun). Jules Michelet translates *ricorso* by *retour*, but we might also suggest *récurrence* as a rendering.

II. Is the *Ricorso* Inevitable?

While the common interpretation of *ricorso* in Vico as merely a simple (and regrettable, according to some writers) borrowing of the old theme, naturalistic in origin, of the cycle of life and death, here applied to nations, is not defensible, the *Scienza nuova* nonetheless raises questions that are difficult to answer. However, a careful reading allows us to arrive at some reasonable conclusions. For Vico, the *corso* followed by nations is an "idea" realizing itself in time, an idea inferred from an informed observation of the history of various nations, and whose specifically "scientific" value derives from the fact that it can be deduced, in an axiomatic way, from the study of fallen human nature after original sin. This idea allows us to understand the temporal destiny of all nations, and has at the same time an heuristic value: thus Vico "discovers" the true identity of Homer (Book 3 of the *Scienza nuova* is entitled "Discovery of the True Homer"), and between the first and last editions of his work, he "discovers" that the Middle Ages is simply a repetition of the "divine" and "heroic" ages of Greek and Roman antiquity. An idea cannot be pluralized; it is unique, and this implies, as we have seen, that all nations that have existed, or now exist, or will exist, have had, have, and will have a history whose general movement follows the *corso* outlined by Vico. Ultimately, and in a more concrete way, Vico merely affirms that the emergence and development of all human societies are based on religious, moral, juridical, and political values embodied in institutions whose form changes in accord with an immutable temporal order, as the nature of fallen man changes and transforms itself, "humanizes itself," without the effects of the original Fall ever completely disappearing.

Does that mean that at the end of the *corso* followed by each nation there is necessarily a final decadence and dissolution, and that to save humankind providence must always use its ultimate means, which is to bring nations violently back to their principles, which are also their beginnings, in order to allow them to begin all over again? This is not certain. Vico offers few explanations on this point, but in any case we find nowhere in his work the idea of a mechanical or organic necessity that would condemn nations to an ineluctable death, other nations taking their place in order to follow the same process. In the case of Rome, the final dissolution was the result of the failure, due to humans themselves, of the first remedy that providence provided them, namely the establishment of a rational monarchy. Was this failure inevitable? Are "human" times, those of "completely developed" reason, always condemned to corruption and death? The question remains open, and Vico himself gave no categorical response to it. When at the end of the *Scienza nuova* he speaks of the situation of modern Europe, he appears to think that "today a complete humanity [*umanità*, in the sense of "civilization"] seems to be spread abroad through all nations, for a few great monarchs rule over this world of peoples" (§1089). But this declared optimism is counterbalanced by a severe judgment on modern culture, and in particular on the philosophy of his period, whose dominant trends seem to Vico to adopt the positions of those who, in antiquity, participated in the general corruption by preaching a dissolving individualism (Skeptics, Epicureans, Stoics). But he never predicts the final catastrophe, even if he fears it. The world of nations, he repeats, is not prey to the *casus* (accident) or to the *fatum* (fate). The "new science" he claims to have founded permits him, as he says in a passage in the 1725 edition, only to offer a "diagnosis" of the state of the nations, to call them to the order of freedom and justice, with respect for the founding principles of every society, religion, and the family. So far as the rest is concerned, nations hold their destiny in their own hands, under the watchful eye of the providence that wants to "preserve the human race upon this earth" (§1108).

Alain Pons

BIBLIOGRAPHY

Vico, Giambattista. *The First New Science*. Translated by L. Pompa. Cambridge: Cambridge University Press, 2002. The first edition of *Scienza nuova* was published in 1725, with subsequent editions in 1744 and 1774.

———. *The New Science of Giambattista Vico*. Translation of the third edition (1774) with the addition of "Practice of the New Science." Edited by T. Goddard Bergin and M. H. Fisch. Ithaca, NY: Cornell University Press, 1984.

CROYANCE

The French word *croyance* derives from the Latin *credere*, which means "to confide in," "believe, think," and, in an intransitive sense, "to be confident" or "to believe, have faith." The term is thus capable of combining two heterogeneous notions: a logical and epistemological one of opinion and assent, and another religious or even superstitious one of faith.

I. *Croyance* and *Foi: Der Glaube*

The two registers are not, however, differentiated in the same way in all languages. While French can choose to oppose *croyance* and *foi*, as English opposes "belief" and "faith," the German expression *der Glaube* (belief, faith) cannot by itself indicate the distinction between logical assent and adherence to a religious content. Whence the difficulty encountered by French and English translators in making intelligible both the Kantian adage "I had to limit knowledge [*Wissen*] to make room for belief/faith [*Glauben*]" and the transition to the Hegelian problem of the relations between "faith" and "knowledge" after the Enlightenment: see GLAUBE. See also *FAITH, RELIGION,* SECULARIZATION.

II. *Croyance* and *Assentiment*

1. The English term "belief," which is derived from Germanic *Glaube*, gradually detached itself from "faith" (from Latin *fides* [faith, confidence, sincerity, protection]) to designate, from Hume to Wittgenstein, the whole field of a "grammar of assent" on the basis of the polarity of feeling and judgment. See BELIEF.
2. On the degrees of assent and the relationship to the object or to reality, see DOXA, PERCEPTION, Box 3, REPRÉSENTATION, TRUTH, WILL. See also VERNEINUNG; cf. *CERTITUDE, PROBABILITY, REASON.*
3. On the belief in the external world, the existence of the object, and the "suspension" demanded by skepticism and phenomenology, see EPOCHÉ; cf. BEGRIFF, Box 1, GREEK, OBJECT.

➤ CLAIM, EPISTEMOLOGY, MATTER OF FACT

| CULTURE

The French word *culture*, like its analogues in various European languages, comes from the Latin *cultura*, which designates agriculture and the transformation of nature, implying a relationship to places and to gods (*colere*, the verb from which it derives, also means "inhabit" and "worship"), and, starting with Cicero, the cultivation of the mind and the education of the individual. It denotes a tension between the natural and art or artifice, on the one hand, and between the human universal and particularity or singularity on the other.

I. *Cultura* (Lat.), *Paideia* (Gr.), *Bildung* (Ger.)

The Latin *cultura*, which concerns the harmonious adaptation of nature, proposes a model entirely different from that of the Greek *paideia* [παιδεία], in which we hear the Promethean art of making a little man (*pais* [παῖς]), or rather a little Hellene (see BILDUNG, Box 1, TO TRANSLATE, I, and ART, I). The term, which is exceptionally rich and full of connotations, is connected with *Bild*, "image" (see BILD and *IMAGE*), with *Einbildungskraft*, "imagination" (see *IMAGINATION*), and refers to "formation" (*bilden*) and "plasticity" (see PLASTICITY and ART, Box 2).

II. *Bildung/Kultur/Zivilisation* (Ger.), *Culture/ Civilisation* (Fr.), *Civiltà* (Ital.)

Bildung, which retains the element of particularity in the notion of individual formation, is distinguished from both *Kultur* and *Zivilisation* in an unparalleled triplet. See BILDUNG for the evolution of these three terms from the Enlightenment onward (cf. LIGHT).

See the same entry for the way in which the Franco-German relationship has been determined by the meaning and value of the French word *civilisation* in relation to the German *Kultur*. Finally, Italian *civiltà* refers both to "civilization" and "civility"; see CIVILTÀ.

III. Culture/Cultures

On the tension between universal civilization and particular culture, see MENSCHHEIT, Box 1; TO TRANSLATE, Box 2; cf. EUROPE, LOGOS, NAROD, PEOPLE.

IV. The Great Interactions

1. On the relation between culture and nature, see ART, BILDUNG, *FATHERLAND,* GENIUS, INGENIUM, NATURE.
2. On the relation between culture and history, see HISTORIA UNIVERSALIS, HISTORY, SECULARIZATION.
3. On the relation between culture and art, see ART, KITSCH, MIMÉSIS (and BILDUNG, Box 1, for *mimêsis rhêtorikê* [μίμησις ῥητορική]).

➤ GEISTESWISSENSCHAFTEN, RELIGIO

DAIMÔN [δαίμων] (GREEK)

ENGLISH demon
FRENCH *démon*

➤ *DEMON*, and BOGOČELOVEČESTVO, *DESTINY*, DEVIL, DUENDE, GENIUS, GOD, *HAPPINESS*, MORALS

"Demon" was closely associated with "devil" in early Christianity and thus acquired very negative connotations, but the Greek *daimôn* was initially undetermined axiologically. Neither good nor bad in itself, it was characterized just as much by its ontological ambivalence.

I. *Daimôn* and Distribution (*Daiomai*)

In Homer the word may designate a *theos* [θεός], a god, but in a relatively vague way. More exactly, in its use in Homer, *daimôn* seems to refer sometimes to a divine power that manifests itself in a diffuse way, and sometimes to a particular god who is not precisely identified.

To determine this more closely, we will begin with the etymology of *daimôn*. Plato suggested that the *daimôn* was a *daêmôn* [δαήμων], that is, an intelligent, clever being (*Cratylus*, 398b), but it is in fact a term derived from the family of *daiomai* [δαίομαι], "share (out)" or "distribute," and *dais* [δαίς], "part" or "lot." In accord with this etymology, the *daimôn* can be understood as the being that distributes lots, or as the effect of this distribution: then it is—and this is once again a significant indeterminacy—either the power that distributes lots or the lot itself that falls to someone, whence in both cases a strong connection with the idea of fate (*heimarmenê* [εἱμαρμένη]; *potmos* [πότμος]). And although Homer's use of the word scarcely reflects this etymology, we can clearly see its influence in the compound adjectives *eudaimôn* [εὐ-δαίμων], "happy," literally, "one who has a good *daimôn*," used from Hesiod on, and its antonym *dus-daimôn* [δυσ-δαίμων], which Empedocles created precisely to qualify fate (*potmos*, cf. 31 B 9, 4 DK).

For his part, Hesiod presents daimons as men of the golden age who have become "guardians of mortal men" after their own deaths (*Works and Days*, 122–23). This usage persisted for a long time because taken literally it helped to endow daimons with personal, functional characteristics and situated them as a category of beings intermediary between gods and humans that played a providential role with regard to the latter.

Was this the result of learned reflection on the adjectival use? In any event, Empedocles went still further than Hesiod, and in his poem *Hoi Katharmoi* (The purifications) he created a narrative whose protagonist is a daimon who has been exiled, like others of his kind, from the domain of the gods (31 B 115 DK; in this narrative the daimon, designated as an active, knowing subject, expresses himself

in the first person). The real etymology of *daimôn* plays a major role here: Empedocles's demonogonic narrative shows explicitly that the daimon is the result of a willed separation from the divine world—and that its development, begun by this exile far from the gods and punctuated by the incarnations that necessity imposes on it, involves moving from the misfortune of birth and mortality (a true *dus-daimonia* [δυσ-δαιμονία]) to happiness and apotheosis (31 B 146–47 DK). The result is a mutation: it is no longer a matter of becoming *eudaimôn* but rather *makar* [μάκαρ], the equal of the gods, that is, blissful. By individualizing the daimon in this way, Empedocles inaugurates, although he does not pursue, a profound evolution in the use of the term that makes it signify a kind of personal principle, connected with the individual human without merging with the latter.

II. Plato: Interpreting the Intermediary

It can be said that all the later semantic developments of this term in philosophical thought are determined by the use made of it by Homer, Hesiod, and Empedocles. Plato summed up pretty much all of them, and provided in the *Symposium* the standard philosophical text that was to nourish and guide all later demonological speculations. The daimon, of which Eros is the prototype, is seen as an intermediary (*metaxu* [μεταξύ]) between humans and the gods that allows them to enter into communication (202d). Elsewhere, Plato also refers to daimons that serve as guardians (*Laws*, 713d, for the golden age of the past) or even as upholders of the laws, when he endorses the widespread idea that a personal daimon is attached to each soul and determines its life on earth (*Republic*, 10.617e) and after death (*Phaedo*, 107d–108c). But in the *Timaeus*, it is man's *nous*, his intellect, which is designated as a daimon within him (90a); this metaphorization of the term, this connection between the daimon and humans, reminds us not only of Empedocles, but also of Heraclitus's enigmatic formula, frequently glossed by commentators: "man's character, his daimon" (*ethos anthrôpôi daimôn* [ἦθος ἀνθρώπῳ δαίμων], B 119 DK; see MORALS, Box 1), not to mention Socrates's famous daimon.

■ See Box 1.

Plato's diverse uses of the term show how many interpretive possibilities it provides.

III. Demonologies: From the Principle of Transcendence to the Fallen Angels

The whole later tradition down to the period of the Roman Empire was marked by abundant speculation on the nature of daimons, inspired by the meanings we have just examined, coordinating them or selecting them in order to found a genuine demonology. Thus various medio- and Neoplatonic

1

Socrates's demon

According to the testimony of Plato (more precise than that of Xenophon), Socrates's demon is most often designated by the adjective *to daimonion* [τὸ δαιμόνιον]: this would be, in Socrates's own sayings, "the demonic" that manifests itself to him; but in truth the complete expression is "demonic sign" (*to daimonion semeion* [τὸ δαιμόνιον σημεῖον]; see, particularly, *Republic*, 496c and *Euthydemus*, 272e). These terms suggest that he perceives this internal sign as a direct intervention of which he does not seem to be able to specify the exact nature (except to note that this sign manifests itself to him as a voice; cf. *Apology*, 31d). "Demonic" means no more and no less than that it is a matter of something that is beyond him, related to the divine, to a form of transcendence (for the first time in the *Apology* Socrates evokes "*theion ti kai daimonion*" [θεῖόν τι καὶ δαιμόνιον], "something divine and demonic"; 31c), although (according to Plato at least) this "demonic" is never taken by Socrates to represent a demonic being. "Demonic sign" means therefore for Socrates a sign sent by the god and for this reason of a demonic nature. What is more, this "demonic" manifests itself only in a negative manner, and it only distracts Socrates from doing such and such a thing, without offering any positive incitement (*Apology*, 31d). Socrates's demonic sign would thus be the minimal form of the personal demon of which we see the emergence beginning with Empedocles (or even Heraclitus), and which Plato will constantly refer to; indeed, this sign, which is beyond Socrates, is at the same time what most intimately belongs to him: it addresses itself to him and to him alone; it is a sign sent by the god, through a personal relation to this individual who is Socrates. Is it the mark of a chosen man? Socrates does not contest or confirm that others apart from him could be the beneficiaries of such divine signs, but he compares, without claiming they are identical, this demonic communication to a sort of divination, an art that is itself exceptional and of which he does not in any case deny the reality (cf. *Apology*, 33c). For these reasons, we will not take the Socratic demon as a simple figure for internal consciousness or conscience—this rationalist interpretation is too reductive; the phenomenon of the demonic certainly indicates Socrates's adherence to a divine principle, in the absence of a profound belief in the traditional gods. Truth is, for Socrates, the exclusive possession of the god—the demonic helps him to grasp shreds of it, which are valid for him and comfort him in his divine "mission," as it was announced by the Delphic oracle (cf. *Apology*, 21ab).

texts, as well as Stoic, hermetic, or Gnostic texts, bear the marks of thought about demonic beings classified into types: personal or not, simple or double, guardian or avenging, good or bad, and so on. Questions were raised about their nature and capacities for action, about where they were, and also about their ability to transform themselves, for a certain plasticity was attributed to these gods who were less than gods. A classic view in this regard, reflecting the speculations of the Old Academy (*Epinomis*, Speusippus, Xenocrates), is that of Plutarch, who defines daimons as divine beings subject to passions, even though they have no bodies (cf. *De defectu oraculorum*, 416C), a position that allows him to detach the true gods from mythological narratives that were supposed to represent daimons. At the same time, Plutarch acknowledges that daimons manifest themselves in diverse forms; located on the moon, they have a place in the hierarchy of beings between the gods and the souls of humans and animals. But in the end, for Plutarch daimons represent a superior degree of purification for souls. Up to the third century CE, the meaning of *daimôn* remained unstable, so that we see a proliferation of the types of daimons, encouraged by unbridled interpretation of poetic and philosophical texts and religious traditions (but occasionally condemned by the Epicureans).

It is remarkable that a quite different mode of interpretation was proposed by Plotinus in the third century, although it spiritualized the daemonic principle too much to succeed in permanently affecting the use of the term. Plotinus saw in the daimon nothing other than the name of a principle of transcendence for the being to which it is attached (cf. *Enneads*, 3.4 [15]). Plotinus thereby combines the idea of destiny with that of personal identity, while at the same time overcoming the antinomy between them: we are ourselves our daimons insofar as we are our destiny, and insofar as we are capable of transcendence.

This way of spiritualizing the notion of the *daimôn* was conveyed instead in the notion of genius, that is, through a translation that made the Greek *daimôn* correspond to the Latin *genius* (which evolved much more clearly from the meaning of "daemonic being" to that of a personal principle). To the church fathers writing after the New Testament, the term *daimôn* (taken literally, it was simply transliterated into Latin: *daemon*) was seen as referring to a powerful, evil being. In Christian doctrine, demons are fallen angels who obey the orders of their leader, the Prince of Evil, Satan, the devil (*diabolos* [διάβολος], "slanderer" in classical Greek, taken in a radical sense corresponding to *sāṭān* [שָׂטָן] in Hebrew, of which it is essentially a translation). The anti-pagan polemic led logically to presenting the pagan gods themselves as demons; Plutarch's argument against mythology was thereby amplified and generalized. With Christian doctrine's association of the daimon with the devil Satan, the term underwent a decisive and almost permanent change. Although at first it had referred to a divine manifestation, "daimon" subsequently designated a mediating semi-divine being and a personal principle for humans before it came to be the name of evil beings hostile to God and to humans—through an almost complete semantic reversal.

Jean-François Balaudé

BIBLIOGRAPHY

Balaudé, Jean-François. *Le démon et la communauté des vivants: Étude des interprétations antiques des Catharmes d'Empédocle*. PhD diss., Lille, 1992.

Burkert, Walter. *Greek Religion*. Translated by J. Raffan. Cambridge, MA: Harvard University Press, 1985.

Chantraine, Pierre. "La notion de divin depuis Homère jusqu'à Platon." In *Entretiens sur l'antiquité classique.* Geneva: Fondation Hardt, 1954.

Détienne, Marcel. *De la pensée religieuse à la pensée philosophique: La notion de "daïmon" dans le pythagorisme ancient.* Paris: Les Belles Lettres, 1963.

Doods, E. R. *The Greeks and the Irrational.* Boston: Beacon Press, 1951.

François, Gilbert. *Le polythéisme et l'emploi au singulier des mots* Theos *et* daïmon *dans la littérature grecque d'Homère à Platon.* Paris: Les Belles Lettres, 1957.

Gernet, Louis, and André Boulanger. *Le génie grec dans la religion.* Paris: Albin Michel, 1969; repr., Paris: La Renaissance du livre, 1992.

Hesiod. *Hesiod: The Works and Days.* Translated by R. Lattimore. Ann Arbor: University of Michigan Press, 1959.

Langton, Edward. *Essentials of Demonology.* London: Epworth Press, 1949.

Plato. *Socrates' Apology; Cratylus; The Laws; The Republic; Phaedo; Timaeus.* In *Complete Works,* edited by J. M. Cooper. Indianapolis, IN: Hackett, 1997.

Plotinus. *Ennead III, 4 [15].* In *Plotini opera,* edited by P. Henry and H. S. Schwyzer. Oxford: Oxford University Press, 1964.

———. *The Enneads.* Translated by S. MacKenna. London: Faber and Faber, 1966.

Plutarch. *On the Failure of Oracles.* In *Plutarch's Moralia,* vol. V. Loeb Classical Library, 405. Cambridge, MA: Harvard University Press, 1936.

———. *On the Sign of Socrates.* In *Plutarch's Moralia,* vol. VII, translated by P. H. de Lacy and B. Einarson. Loeb Classical Library, 405. Cambridge, MA: Harvard University Press, 1959.

Soury, Guy. *La démonologie de Plutarque.* Paris: Les Belles Lettres, 1942.

DASEIN / EXISTENZ (GERMAN)

ENGLISH	life
FRENCH	*existence, réalité humaine, être-là/existence, temps, durée d'une existence, présence, vie, être*
GERMAN	*Kampf ums Dasein* (struggle for life)
ITALIAN	*essere-ci, esserci, adessere*
LATIN	*existentia*

➤ ESSENCE, *LIFE/LEBEN*, and ACT, AIÔN, *DESTINY*, EREIGNIS, ERLEBEN, ES GIBT, I/ME/MYSELF, PRESENT, REALITY, SOUL, SUBJECT, *TO BE*, VORHANDEN

Dasein, in its contemporary (Heideggerian) usage, has become a paradigm of the untranslatable. It is a common word that Heidegger transformed into a neologism (as is also the case for his use of terms such as *Bestand, Machenschaft, Gestell, Ereignis*, etc.) to the point of proposing an alternative pronunciation, accenting, against normal usage, the second syllable, *sein* (being). When Heidegger injected a new meaning into *Dasein* to make it signify, in *Sein und Zeit* (*Being and Time*), the being whose own existence is at stake, the term was already charged with history and diverse meanings: time, the duration of an existence, presence, and also life, being, existence, being-there. All these meanings intersect with one another in the course of a tumultuous history, especially from Kant to Schelling, by way of Goethe, Schiller, and Fichte. Nonetheless, they have a common denominator in the complex relationships between *Dasein* and its pseudo-doublet *Existenz*, which emerged directly from Latin *existentia*.

Dasein's resistance to any translation emerged in the twentieth century as an outcome of the Germanization of the Latin *existentia* into *Dasein*, as if *Dasein* had ultimately never recovered from this blow and continued to point toward an entirely different area of meaning from the one to which the metaphysical term *existentia* tried to assign it. It is this history that we need to look into first.

As a substantive, *Dasein* appeared only rather recently in German: not until the seventeenth century was the verb *dasein* (to be present, *vorhanden*) nominalized, and far from being a technical term, it was formidable only in its disarming simplicity, comparable to that of the French expression *ça y est* (that's it; there you have it). We should distinguish the various acceptations with which the term is loaded: modal (Kant), emphatic (Goethe, Schiller, Jacobi, Hamann, Herder), passive (Fichte), ecstatic (Schelling), and finally ontological or existential (Heidegger).

I. *Dasein, Wirklichkeit, Existenz*: Kant

In his 1763 opuscule, *Der einzig mögliche Beweisgrund zu einer Demonstration des Daseins Gottes* (*The Only Possible Argument in Support of a Demonstration of the Existence of God*), Kant renders the Latin *existentia* by the expression *Dasein Gottes*, a translation that Hegel adopted in his 1829 *Vorlesungen über die Beweise vom Dasein Gottes.* In Kant's *Critique of Pure Reason*, this acceptation of *Dasein* is found again, in the table of the categories, under the second category of modality: as a dynamic category, *Dasein* is opposed to *Nichtsein* (nonbeing), and is intercalated between the possible and the necessary. The second of the postulates of empirical thought in general is called *wirklich*, which is in accord with the material conditions of experience. *Dasein* is thus what is (the existent, nature) as *wirklich*. It is the real insofar as it is differently "positioned" than the possible, but without "containing" anything more than the possible: "Sein ist offenbar kein reales Prädikat" (Being is obviously not a real predicate; *Critique of Pure Reason*). Kant seems not to have distinguished between *Dasein* and *Existenz*. The article "Dasein" (RT: *Kant-Lexikon*) refers to *Existenz, Sein, Wirklichkeit, Natur*, etc.

We know that the *ens realissimum* whose *Dasein* the 1763 opuscule sought to prove was in 1781 assigned the status of a simple ideal of pure reason. The paradox inherent in Kant's use of *Dasein* as a Germanic substitute for *existentia* is that the ecstatic dimension of the notion of existence (in the sense of a movement toward an outside) is subverted, turned inside out. The *Dasein Gottes*, or the "there is–ness" of God ("Es ist ein Gott" [There is a God], Kant writes in boldface letters at the beginning of his 1763 opuscule: *Akademia Ausgabe des Kants Schriften* (*AK*), 2:65—cf. Wolff, *Deutsche Metaphysik*, §946: "Das ein Gott ist" [That there is a God]) will in fact be understood in Kant's mature critical philosophy as inherent to ethical-practical reason, "but not as a being outside man." Kant's unpublished work is very explicit on this point (*AK*, 21:144–45): "Gott muss nicht als Substanz ausser mir vorgestellt werden. . . . Gott ist nicht ein Wesen ausser mir sondern bloss ein Gedanke in mir" (God must not be pictured as a substance outside of me. . . . God is not a being outside of me but simply an idea in me). If existing means "having a being or substance outside my thought"—*ex-sistere*—Kant is the one who asserts both that there is a God and that God, strictly speaking, does not ex-sist, or has no being other than that of a simple ideal of pure reason, a rational fiction necessary for the deployment of practical reason. If Descartes could write, "[B]y *essence* we understand the thing insofar as it is objectively in the intellect, by *existence* [*existentia*], this same thing insofar as it is outside the intellect [*rem eandem prout est extra intellectum*]" (*Correspondance*, vol. 4), we can see how aberrant it is to render *existentia* by *Dasein* when the latter term is supposed to express an in-existence, an ideal being *in mir* (in me).

- See Box 1.

Thus the Latin word *existentia* already had a rather turbulent past, without which we cannot really understand it, when Kant took it up and Germanized it as *Dasein*, taking as his guide the Wolffian equation *existentia-actualitas* and identifying *Dasein* with what is *wirklich* (real, actual). In Wolff, the question of the *existentia Dei* was summed up in the demonstration of an independent essence, a being that was "autonomous" or "self-standing," for which the name "God" was appropriate because of the connection between *stare*, *sistere* and *stehen*, and *ständig* (*Deutsche Metaphysik*, §929). Wolff's

---

1

Note on Latin *existentia* and French *existence*

Before we arrive at the problematic rendering of the Latin *existentia* by the German *Dasein*, we encounter a difficulty in (a) the plasticity of *existentia* and (b) the gap between the Latin *existere* (i.e., *exsistere*) and the French *exister*. Even in Latin, during the classical, patristic, and Scholastic periods, their meanings overlap and sometimes blur in instructive ways.

In classical Latin, the verb *exsisto* (a compound of *ex* and *sisto*, from *stare*, "stand") does not mean "exist," but rather "step up, come forth, arise," and by extension, "appear, emerge." Thus in Cicero we read "timeo ne existam crudelior" (I fear *to show myself* too severe; *Letters to Atticus*, 10.11.3) and "existunt in animis varietates" (there *emerges* a certain diversity among minds; *De officiis*, 1.107), or in Lucretius, "existere vermes / stercore" (living worms *spring out* / of stinking dung; *De rerum natura*, 2.870–71). The young Descartes still echoes this classical sense when he mentions, in his *Cogitationes privatae*: "hoc mundi theatrum . . . , in quo hactenus spectator exstiti" (this theater of the world in which I have up to now *appeared* only as a spectator).

Unknown in classical Latin, the noun *existentia* seems to appear only in the fourth century CE, in Marius Victorinus, who, after his conversion to Christianity, translated Plotinus's *Enneads* into Latin, and in Candidus the Arian, who also uses (*De generatione divina* 1; RT: *PL*, 8.1013) the derivatives *existentitas* (existentness) and *existentialitas* (existentality). According to Marius Victorinus (*Adversus Arium* 1.30.1062 c 18ff.), "the sages and the ancients" definitely distinguished between *existencia* and *substantia*, defining *exsistentiam* (existence) and *existentialitatem* (existentiality): "praeexistentem subsistentiam sine accidentibus . . ." (as the initial foundation, preexisting the thing itself, in its accidents . . .), even though, according to the usual meaning of the terms (*in usu accipientes*), *existencia* and *substantia* did not differ, and it was even "permissible to use equivalently existence, substance, or being" (*sive existentiam, sive substantiam, sive quod est esse*). Contrary to all expectations, *existentiality* refers to an existing substance provided with all its accidents.

We can gauge here the violence deliberately and explicitly done to the usual meanings of the terms *exsistencia* and *exsistentialitas* by using them as technical terms in the context of the Trinitarian controversies. This violence is connected with the difficulty of acclimating in Latin, and in Christian dogma, the vocabulary of Greek Platonic and Neoplatonic ontology. From a strictly lexicographic point of view, Candidus the Arian and Marius Victorinus are nonetheless the precursors of the vocabulary of *existentiality* (German, *Existentialität*) in the twentieth century.

In general, "ex-sistere signifies . . . less the fact of being itself than its relationship to some origin" (Gilson, *L'être et l'essence*), and that is why the Scholastics basically understood *existere* as meaning *ex alio sistere*, that is, "accede to being by virtue of another origin," thanks to a detachment with respect to a provenance that was ultimately to be interpreted as *causa* (French, *cause*; German, *Ursache*; cf. Gilson, *L'être et l'essence*). In a classic text (*De Trinitate* 4.12), Richard of St. Victor strongly emphasizes that when we say that something exists (*exsistere*),

> subintelligitur non solum quod habeat esse, sed etiam aliunde, hoc est ex aliquo habeat esse. . . . Quid est enim existere nisi ex aliquo sistere . . . ?

(this implicitly refers, not only to what has being, but to what derives it [i.e., being] from elsewhere, namely, from some other. . . . What is it, in fact, to exist [*ex-sistere*], if not to receive one's being from something else [*ex aliquo sistere*] . . . ?)

The question of *existentia* then undergoes a shift toward that of *causa*, and that is the tradition, via Suárez, Leibniz, and Wolff, of which Kant's *Critique of Pure Reason* is the heir: Kant took up the "privileged" dimension attributed to human existence (as a disposition of the "personality") in freedom, as the *ratio essendi* of the moral law, only under the banner of *causality* (Transcendental Dialectic, third antinomy)—whence also the crucial issue constituted by the question of causality in the debate between Kant and Hume.

For Suárez, in fact, *ex-sistere* is *extra causas sistere*, "to stand outside causes," or even "to be apart from causes," as is established in the *Disputationes metaphysicae*, 31.4.6:

> . . . existentia nihil aliud est quam illudesse, quo formaliter et immediate entitas aliqua constituitur *extra causas suas* . . .

> (. . . existence is nothing other than this being by virtue of which a certain entity is constituted, formally and immediately, *apart from its causes* . . .)

Similarly, for Eustache de Saint-Paul (*Summa philosophiae*, 4.37) what "exists" (*existit*) "is the thing [that] is said to be in actuality or outside its causes" (*res [quae] dicitur esse actu sive extra suas causas*), and this thing "begins to exist only when it advances outside by virtue of its causes" (*[res] incipit existere cum virtute causarum fors prodit*). For something to exist, it has to come out of its hole, and in being driven out, to emancipate itself from its causes, but also thereby confirm their tutelary power. It is under the pressure of actuality that the fate of *existentia* will henceforth be played out, rethought in the light of the two pairs, *causa/effectus* and *potentia/actus*, as is the case in Wolff, where *existentia* is equivalent to *actualitas* (*Philosophia prima sive ontologia*, §174).

We owe to Leibniz the further enrichment of the Latin vocabulary of *existere*, which was already very rich, as we have seen, with the derivatives *existentia*, *existentitas*, and *existentialitas*, by resorting, in his *General Investigations Concerning the Analysis of Concepts and Truths*, and in a Latin worthy of Hermolaus Barbarus (cf. *Theodicy*, art. 87), to the present participle of the factitive of *existere*, *existentificans* (existifying), as well as to the desiderative *exstiturire*. We probably cannot understand "*Omne possibile EXISTITURIRE*" as meaning that "everything possible is a future existent" (cf. M. Fichant's French translation), given that the author of *De libertate* elsewhere asserts that he has considered "those things among the possible that are not, will not be, and have not been." The meaning is rather that every possible is "futurable," admissible, promotable, or susceptible to be promoted to reality, except when it conflicts with other co-possibles. Leibniz does not say that every possible exists by futurition, if not virtually, but rather that the realizable non-real can—and wants to—present itself as something realizable, or "existentiable," namely, "existentifiable." Commenting on this Leibnizian *hapax*, Heidegger (in *Nietzsche*) writes: "Existence itself is of an essence such that it provokes the power of wanting oneself [to be]." We can also compare the way Leibniz uses the word *existere*, in his meditation on the status of the possible, on the formation of the future tense in ancient Greek, as it developed from an earlier desiderative present and includes, unlike Latin, a genuine future infinitive (RT: Meillet, *Aperçu d'une histoire de la langue grecque*).

Thus, by means of an unprecedented radicalization of what remained in a state of incubation during the Middle Ages, Leibniz can be said to have pushed to its ultimate consequences, and at the same time to its last entrenchments, the saturation of the vocabulary of existence by that of efficiency, in conformity with his interpretation of substance as "a Being capable of action" (*Principes de la nature et de la grâce*, art. 1), and faithful to the language of causality and the principle of reason—*ratio seu causa*.

From Candidus the Arian and Marius Victorinus to Suárez and Leibniz, by way in particular of Richard of Saint Victor, Latin philosophy was able to discern a major speculative issue in the lexicon of *ex-sistencia*, to the point that it exhausted the field of its lexical variations. From Suárez's extracausal *existentia* to Leibniz's existentification, or the reinterpretation of existence on the basis of efficiency, to the Kantian inquiry into the *Kausalität der Ur-sache*, the "causality of the cause" (*Critique of Pure Reason*), the history of the problems that critical philosophy took up was played out, in a secret genealogy, and handed on to German idealism.

Whatever may be said about the various acceptations of the Latin *existentia*, we have finally to note the narrow but sensitive and delicate difference between *existentia* and the French *existence*. The difficulty inherent in translating the Latin word by the French one was emphasized by Scipion Dupleix in his *Métaphysique* (1617):

> [W]e are obliged to note that in our French language we have no term that corresponds energetically to the Latin *existentia*, which means the bare entity, the simple and naked being of things, without considering any order or rank that they hold in relation to the others.

BIBLIOGRAPHY

Cicero, Marcus Tullius. *Cicero's Letters to Atticus*. Edited by D. R. Shackleton Bailey. Cambridge: Cambridge University Press, 1965–68.
Descartes, René. *Cogitationes privatae*. In *Oeuvres*, vol. 10. Edited by Charles Adam and Paul Tannery. Paris: Éditions du Cerf, 1897–1913. Reprint, Paris: Librairie Philosophique, J. Vrin, 1983.
Dupleix, Scipion. *Métaphysique*. Paris: Fayard, 1992. First published in 1617.
Éthier, Albert-Marie. *Le "De Trinitate" de Richard de Saint-Victor*. Paris: Vrin; Ottawa: Institut d'Etudes Médiévales, 1939.
Eustache de Saint-Paul. *Summa philosophiae*. Paris, 1609; 2nd ed., 1626.
Gilson, Étienne. *Being and Some Philosophers*. Toronto: Pontifical Institute of Medieval Studies, 1949.
———. "Existentia." In *L'être et l'essence*. 2nd ed. Paris: Vrin, 1972. First published in 1948.
———. *Index scolastico-cartésien*. Paris: Vrin, 1979.
Heidegger, Martin. *Nietzsche*. Translated by D. F. Krell. San Francisco: Harper and Row, 1979–87.
Leibniz, Gottfried Wilhelm. *General Investigations Concerning the Analysis of Concepts and Truths*. Translated by W. H. O'Briant. Athens: University of Georgia Press, 1968.
———. *Philosophical Essays*. Translated and edited by Roger Ariew and Dan Garber. Indianapolis, IN: Hackett, 1989.
———. *Principes de la nature et de la grâce*. Edited by A. Robinet. Paris: Presses Universitaires de France, 1954. Translation by R. S. Woolhouse and R. Francks: *Principles of Nature and Grace*. In *Philosophical Texts*. Oxford: Oxford University Press, 1998.
———. *Theodicy: Essays on the Goodness of God, the Freedom of Man, and the Origin of Evil*. Edited by A. Farrer. Translated by E. M. Huggard. New Haven, CT: Yale University Press, 1952.
Marius Victorinus, Caius. *Adversus Arium*. In *Theological Treatises on the Trinity*. Translated by M. T. Clark. Washington, DC: Catholic University of America Press, 1981.
Suárez, Francisco. *Disputationes metaphysicae*. Hildesheim, Ger.: George Olms Verlag, 1999.
Wolff, Christian von. *Philosophia prima sive ontologia*. Halle, Ger.: In Officina Libreria Rengeriana, 1736.

German work nonetheless remained very Latin in its conceptualization, and it was for the generations that followed Wolff and Kant to rediscover, beneath the outer bark of a borrowed conceptuality, a very vital sap.

II. *Dasein*: The Reconquest of the Verb—From Goethe to Jacobi

From Goethe to Jacobi, and even as late as Nietzsche (cf., for example, *The Gay Science*, bk. 4, §341: "die ewige Sanduhr des Daseins"), *Dasein* was to be revived in a form quite different from that of a technical term. That explains its use in Goethe, which is indissociable from wonderment before the very presence of things, the simple fact of their coming into being. Goethe seems to reconnect with a prephilosophical or at least pretechnical sense of *Dasein* as life, being, existence, the pure miracle of things offered to human perception. It is the good fortune, always unique and singular, of being able to say "I was there!" (*ich war dabei*), as in Goethe's famous declaration after the battle of Valmy. *Dasein* comes to mean *dabei sein*, as if the verbal nature of the verb *dasein* had been wrested away from its conceptual fixation in *Dasein*.

As for Jacobi, he adopts this emphatic sense of *Dasein*, especially in a typical, even emblematic expression of his enterprise: *Dasein enthüllen* (disclose the *Dasein*). The term *Dasein* could thus serve as a banner for an antiphilosophical enthusiasm (according to Schelling) in the context of the pantheism controversy. A passage in Jacobi's *Über die Lehre des Spinoza in Briefen an den Herrn Moses Mendelssohn*, copied out by Hölderlin (*Grosse Stuttgarter Ausgabe*) and by Schelling (cf. the preface to *Vom Ich*), calls the disclosure and revelation of *Dasein* "the greatest merit that a thinker can have." The feeling of existing/*Gefühl des Daseins*, what Rousseau called, in the fifth of his *Rêveries d'un promeneur solitaire*, "the feeling of existence divested of any other affection," seems to have been the rallying cry of a new sensibility that defined an era (Tieck, Moritz, Jean-Paul [Richter], Novalis. On this point, cf. X. Tilliette, *L'intuition intellectuelle de Kant à Hegel*).

III. *Daseyn, Daseyen, Da-sein*: Fichte and Hegel

A frequently overlooked passage in Fichte's *Die Anweisung zum seligen Leben* makes a great deal of the term *Dasein* (using its old spelling):

Inwiefern das göttliche Daseyn unmittelbar sein lebendiges und kräftiges Daseyen ist—Daseyen sage ich, gleichsam einen Akt des Daseins bezeichnend . . .

(Insofar as the divine existent is immediately its living and powerful existentifying—by which I mean an act of the existent, as it were . . .)

Thus Fichte clearly distinguished between *Daseyn* and *Daseyen*, defining the latter as "an act of *Dasein*," a pure acting, an "actness." We can also admire both Fichte's sure sense of the German language in his neologizing concern to reawaken, in conformity with the spirit of his philosophy, the verbal and even thetic character of *Dasein*, and the strange escalation represented by the nominalization (or deverbalization) in the sequence *dasein–Daseyn–Daseyen*. The Fichtean *Daseyen* is not "found there" in the sense of the equivalence between *Seyn* and *Vorhandenseyn* present elsewhere in Fichte; it "sets itself there." Nonetheless, Fichte is probably the first philosopher writing in German to have seen a philosophical stake in the word *Dasein*. If *Dasein* was in Kant a classical philosophical term, but definitely not German, and in Goethe a German term, but definitely not a philosophical one, it is only with Fichte that it becomes a term of "classical German philosophy" (on the problematization of these oppositions, cf. Bourgeois, *La philosophie allemande classique*).

Hegel, for his part, understood in *Dasein* the *da* of *Sein*, a figure of immediacy (cf. his *Wissenschaft der Logik*, bk. 1, §1, chap. 2 A.1). Hegel conceives *Dasein* as the *Sein* that never solely *da*, in a "certainty of perception" that asks only to be allowed to mobilize and defer itself until "absolute knowledge" arrives, at first mesmerized by the immediacy of the *hic et nunc*, then shaken and set in motion by the dialectic that it bore within itself, without knowing it, from the start: the being-there of *Dasein* is where it is only because it has not yet reached the stage where what can be known through it awaits it. Thus the translation of *Dasein* by "being there" is probably more suited to Hegel's language than to Heidegger's. Moreover, Hegel himself did not fail to emphasize, in *Wissenschaft der Logik*: "*Dasein*, etymologisch genommen, Sein an einem gewissen Orte" (*Dasein*, understood etymologically, [is] being in a specific place). In Hegel, unlike in Heidegger, *Dasein* is thus conceived on the basis of its evident etymology. For the very numerous occurrences of the word *Dasein* in the *Phenomenology of Mind*, see the impressive inventory drawn up by Jarczyk and Labarrière as an appendix to their translation.

IV. *Existenz/Dasein*: Schelling

However, it was Schelling who reawakened in modern philosophy the ecstatic dimension of existence that the Kantian equation of *existentia* with *Dasein* had made somewhat dormant, and as a result, radically dissociated *Dasein* and *Existenz*: "in attributing to God . . . *Existenz*, *Daseyn*, you have to recognize a nature in him."

These lines, from the first version (1811) of *Die Weltalter*, deliberately adopt a vocabulary that is more Jacobi's than Schelling's own, to divorce terms that Kant had married, to radically dissociate *Daseyn* and *Existenz* by understanding *Existenz* (returning from Scholastic Latin to classical Latin and from classical Latin to classical Greek) in opposition to

Grund (obscure background). Nothing exists, strictly speaking, except that which is capable of dissociating itself from its own background, wrenching itself away from it in response to a crisis, as analogically, light extracts itself from mass. *Existenz* is not simply *Dasein*, because it detaches itself from *Daseyn* and posits outside itself, at its own peril, something that, unless it resolves to exist, must be content simply to be. All being is an *ex-stans*—cf. Schelling: *das existierende* [ἐξίσταμαι]/*existo*/[ἐξιστάμενον] = "ein außer sich gesetztes . . . Seyendes" (an existent set outside itself). While Kant moved from *existentia* to *Dasein*, Schelling awakens, in the torpor of *Dasein*, the mute and disturbing dimension of the Existent, in its constitutive "eccentricity," of that "existence which is precisely nothing other than ecstasy," as he put it in the 1830 introductory course in philosophy (*Einleitung in die Philosophie*, lecture 27). The term *Existenz* is thus privileged in relation to *Dasein*, which for Schelling is strongly marked by Jacobi's vocabulary, but does not for all that go beyond ordinary usage.

How should we understand Schelling's "extra-logical nature of existence [*Existenz*]"? How can we think of that which exceeds all thought without thereby making it a simple content of consciousness? That was to be the question of positivist philosophy. In Schelling, the Existent (*das Existierende*) takes on a pregnant meaning that was to echo, via Kierkegaard, as far as Heidegger.

V. Heidegger's *Dasein*

The development that began with Kant's little work of 1763 reached its high point in Heidegger's *Sein und Zeit* (1927). From Kant to Heidegger, the movement seems to have been reversed: it is no longer *Dasein* that is conceived on the basis of *existentia/Existenz*, but existence, understood quite differently, that is conceived on the basis of *Dasein*. Except that the existential analytic, which in 1927 is a structure for the acceptance of *Dasein*, presents itself as an implicit theology (cf. Heidegger, *Metaphysische Anfangsgründe der Logik Gesamtausgabe*): the expression even of a *Dasein Gottes* (Kant, Hegel) has become impossible, the term *Dasein* being reserved, in Heidegger's thinking, for *menschliches Dasein*, human *Dasein*. The breadth acquired by the term *Dasein* goes hand in hand with its restriction to the being of the human being, delimiting a finite realm.

The history of *Dasein* thus finds, in *Sein und Zeit*, an unexpected new departure. In this work the term reaches its culmination and its limits: it designates the very being of the being that we are, essentially or inessentially, not in the sense of an identity, but in proportion to a being that we have "to be"—*zu sein*, with movement (cf. *Hier zu haben*), which corresponds etymologically to the English "to be," Russian *do* [цо], Danish *at* (*vaere*)—in a transitive and even factitive sense (whence the hermeneutics of factivity that was the prelude to *Sein und Zeit*). In Heidegger, the *da* in *Dasein* almost means *zu* (toward). *Dasein* is never "localized," but localizing; it must be thought of with movement, in the accusative.

Does that mean that the term *Dasein*, in Heidegger's terminology, has no parallel in Western thought? Heidegger himself seems to have provided a way to explore that question: the being of *Dasein* was assuredly not unknown in antiquity, if only as *praxis* [πρᾶξις] (*Metaphysische Anfangsgründe der Logik*). Consider as well the problem of the connection between *Dasein* and *psuchê* [ψυχή] in *Sein und Zeit*, §4.

In certain respects, the history of the translations of *Dasein* into French reflects that of the (anthropological and existentialist) misunderstandings committed in the course of the reception of Heidegger's thought: from *réalité humaine* (Corbin, Sartre) to *être-là* (Ital., *esserci*), to the point that Heidegger's translators now prefer to translate *Dasein* as . . . *Dasein*.

The untranslatable (*unübersetzbar*) nature of *Dasein* was, moreover, emphasized by Heidegger himself in his letter to Beaufret on November 23, 1945 (published as an appendix to the bilingual French and German edition of the *Lettre sur l'humanisme*):

Da-sein . . . bedeutet für mich nicht so sehr "me voilà!" sondern, wenn ich es in einem vielleicht unmöglichem Französisch sagen darf: être-le-là.

(For me, *Dasein* means not so much "here I am!" as, if I may put it into what may be impossible French: *être-le-là* ["being the there"].)

Similarly, in a 1941 lecture (*Metaphysik des deutschen Idealismus*), he observes that:

Das Wort "Da-sein" ist daher auch in der Bedeutung, nach der es in Sein und Zeit gedacht wird, unübersetzbar. Die gewöhnliche Bedeutung von Dasein = Wirklichkeit = Anwesenheit lässt sich nicht mit présence oder "Realität" übersetzen. (Vgl. z. B. die französische Übersetzung von "Dasein" in "Sein und Zeit" mit "réalité humaine"; sie verbaut alles in jeder Hinsicht.)

(The term *Da-sein* is therefore untranslatable, even in the acceptation in which it is conceived in *Sein und Zeit*. The usual meaning of *Dasein* = *Wirklichkeit* = *Anwesenheit* cannot be translated by "presence" or "reality." (Cf. for instance the French translation of *Dasein* in *Sein und Zeit* by "réalité humaine"; this blocks everything in every regard.)

Hence Heidegger himself tells us that *Dasein* is untranslatable, reversing Kant's assumption that *existentia* can be translated by *Dasein*. The vocabulary established in *Sein und Zeit* allows us, however, to situate *Dasein*, to know this being that we are, and that we have to be, as part of an existential, and no longer categorical, logic that requires the existential analytic to bring out these existentials that are irreducible to properties attributed to things. *Vorhandensein*, or "being at hand," no longer characterizes anything but the mode of things' presence, which "are found there," in contrast to *Dasein* struggling with its "difficulty of being" and with the care that is its essence, its *arkhê*-structure (*Urstruktur*, in *Gesamt-ausgabe* [*GA*], vol. 20). In the francophone world, the debates about the translation of *Vorhandenheit* and *Zuhandenheit* have probably been too marked, or even obsessed, by the presence of the word *Hand* in these two compounds—the comparison made by J. Taminiaux, in *Lectures de l'ontologie fondamentale*, between the *Vorhandenes* in *Sein und Zeit* and the *procheira* [πρόχειρα] mentioned in Aristotle's *Metaphysics* (A2 982b 13) is an example of this.

But *Hand* is no more audible than, for example, *main* in contemporary French (cf. E. Martineau's foreword to the French translation of Heidegger's *Interprétation phénoménologique de la "Critique de la raison pure" de Kant* and the translator's notes; J.-F. Courtine's foreword to the French translation of Heidegger's *Les problèmes fondamentaux de la phénoménologie*).

If Heidegger later abandoned the expression *menschliches Dasein* (human *Dasein*), that is because it seems redundant, or does not sufficiently avoid the risk of being anthropologized: "*Dasein* is not the human being . . ." (*Beiträge zur Philosophie*).

The connection between *Dasein* and *Existenz* is established by §9 in *Sein und Zeit*: "*Das 'Wesen' des Daseins liegt in seiner Existenz*" (The "essence" of *Dasein* resides in its existence; italics in the German text). The quotation marks around the word *Wesen* indicate that this no longer refers to the *essentia* traditionally distinguished, in the metaphysical vocabulary, from *existentia*, but rather of a "realm" that Heidegger's translators have sought to render in French by *déploiement* (F. Fédier), *aître* (G. Guest), or in English by "root-unfolding" (P. Emad and K. Maly).

Existenz designates the mode of being peculiar to *Dasein*, in its irreducible specificity, the dimension within which it is imparted and to whose share it has fallen to deploy its being, as distinguished from existence/*existentia* understood metaphysically in opposition to essence, that is, as *Vorhandenheit*. *Existenz*, in its pregnant sense, characterizes *Dasein*'s mode of being, its *Weise* (*Sein und Zeit*, §9), which should be understood as "guise" or "melody" (*GA*, vol. 29/30: "eine Weise im Sinne einer Melodie"; *GA*, vol. 79: "eine eigene Weise, mehr im Sinne von einer Melodie". The existent is no longer understood as being what is at hand (*Vorhandenes*), but as being in proportion to *Dasein* (*daseinsmäßig*), which the existential analytic envisages purely and simply in its relation to being, to the exclusion of any other kind of consideration (cf. *Sein und Zeit*, §10). That is what underscores the difference between the *existentiel* and the *existential*. The set of the ontological structures of human existence constitutes existentiality as the dimension on the basis of which existence must be understood.

The phrase "Dasein existiert" (*Sein und Zeit*, §12; *GA*, vol. 2) is thus in itself an extraordinary concentrate of the difficulties we have just pointed out. The history of the concept of *Dasein* and its semantic curve show the gradual emergence of a major philosophical issue in the very development of the language. Thus it is hardly surprising that its ins and outs are echoed in a text Heidegger addressed to M. Boss (*Zollikoner Seminare*):

Sofern aber diese [i.e., Existenz] durch das Da-sein ausgezeichnet bleibt, muss auch schon die Benennung "Da-sein" in einem Sinn verstanden werden, der sich von der geläufigen Bedeutung des Wortes "Da-sein" unterscheidet. Die unterschiedliche Schreibweise [i.e., Da-sein] soll dies andeuten. Die gewöhnliche Bedeutung von "Dasein" bedeutet soviel wie Anwesenheit, so zum Beispiel in der Rede von den Beweisen für das Dasein Gottes.

(However, insofar as this [i.e., *Existenz*] remains marked out by *Da-sein*, the term *Da-sein* must be understood in a sense distinct from the usual meaning of the word *Dasein*. That is what the different way of writing it [i.e., *Dasein*, with a hyphen] is supposed to indicate. The usual meaning of *Dasein* is roughly synonymous with existence, as for example when one speaks of proofs of the existence [i.e., *Dasein*] of God.)

From the *Dasein* (*Gottes*) to the *Da-sein* Heidegger speaks of, from the existence of God designating simply his *Daß* (*that he exists*) to his existential (*existential*) dimension at the heart of which the being of the human being is electively deployed, structured by care / Lat. *cura* / Ger. *Sorge*, a movement, a gap has occurred, which a simple hyphen seeks to mark, typographically.

Pascal David

BIBLIOGRAPHY

Beaufret, Jean. *De l'existentialisme à Heidegger*. Paris: Vrin, 1986.
———. *Dialogue with Heidegger: Greek Philosophy*. Translated by M. Sinclair. Bloomington: Indiana University Press, 2006.
Bourgeois, Bernard. *La philosophie allemande classique*. Paris: Presses Universitaires de France, 1995.
Courtine, Jean-François. *Suárez et le système de la métaphysique*. Paris: Presses Universitaires de France, 1990.
Descartes, René. *Correspondance*. Edited by Charles Adam and Paul Tannery. 4 vols. Paris: Vrin, 1976.
———. *Philosophical Essays and Correspondence*. Edited by R. Ariew. Indianapolis, IN: Hackett, 2000.
Fichte, Johann Gottlieb. *Die Anweisung zum seligen Leben, oder auch die Religionslehre*. Vol. 5 in *Fichtes Werke*. Berlin: De Gruyter, 1971. Translation by William Smith: *The Way towards the Blessed Life; or, The Doctrine of Religion*. In *The Popular Works of Johann Gottlieb Fichte*. Bristol, UK: Thoemes Press, 1999. First published in 1806.
Hegel, Georg Wilhelm Friedrich. *Phenomenology of Mind*. Translated by G. Jarczyk and P.-J. Labarrière. Paris: Gallimard, 1993.
———. *Vorlesungen über die Beweise vom Dasein Gottes*. Edited by G. Kasson. Hamburg: Meiner, 1966. Translation by E. B. Speirs and J. B. Saunderson: *Lectures on the Philosophy of Religion: Together with a Work on the Proofs of the Existence of God*. London: Kegan Paul, Trench, Trübner, 1895.
———. *Wissenschaft der Logik*. Edited by Georg Lasson. Hamburg: Meiner, 1923. Translation by W. Wallace: *Hegel's Logic*. Oxford: Clarendon Press, 1975.
Heidegger, Martin. *Beiträge zur Philosophie (Vom Ereignis)*. In *Gesamtausgabe*, vol. 65. Frankfurt: Klostermann, 1989. First published in 1936–38.
———. *Lettre sur l'humanisme*. Translated to French by Roger Munier. Paris: Aubier, 1964. First published in 1946.
———. *Metaphysik des deutschen Idealismus*. In *Gesamtausgabe*, vol. 49. Frankfurt: Klostermann, 1991. First published in 1941.
———. *Metaphysische Anfangsgründe der Logik im Ausgang von Leibniz*. In *Gesamtausgabe*, vol. 26. Frankfurt: Klostermann, 2007. First published in 1928.
———. *Les problèmes fondamentaux de la phénoménologie*. Translated to French by J.-F. Courtine. Paris: Gallimard, 1985.
———. *Sein und Zeit*. In *Gesamtausgabe*, vol. 2. Frankfurt: Klostermann, 1977. Translation by J. Macquarrie and E. Robinson: *Being and Time*. Oxford: Blackwell, 1967. First published in 1927.
———. *Zollikoner Seminare, Protokolle—Gespräche—Briefe, herausgegeben von M. Boss*. Frankfurt: Klostermann, 1987. Translation by Franz Mayr: *The Zollikon Seminars, Protocols—Conversations—Letters*. Edited by M. Boss. Evanston, IL: Northwestern University Press, 1991.
Hölderlin, Friedrich. *Grosse Stuttgarter Ausgabe*. Edited by Friedrich Beissner and Adolf Beck. Stuttgart: Cotta, 1943–85.
Jacobi, Friedrich Heinrich. *The Main Philosophical Writings and the Novel "Allwill."* Edited by G. di Giovanni. Montreal: McGill-Queen's University Press, 1994.
———. *The Spinoza Conversations between Lessing and Jacobi*. Translated by G. Vallée, J. B. Lawson, and C. G. Chapple. Lanham, MD: University Press of America, 1998.
———. *Über die Lehre des Spinoza in Briefen an den Herrn Moses Mendelssohn*. Edited by K. Hammacher, I. M. Piske, and M. Lauschke. Hamburg: Meiner, 2000.
Kant, Immanuel. *Critique of Pure Reason*. Edited and translated by P. Guyer and A. Wood. Cambridge: Cambridge University Press, 1998.
———. *Der einzig mögliche Beweisgrund zu einer Demonstration des Daseins Gottes*. In *Akademia Ausgabe des Kants Schriften*, vol. 2. Berlin, 1902; reprint, 1968. Translation by G. Treash: *The One Possible Basis for a Demonstration of the Existence of God*. Lincoln: University of Nebraska Press, 1994. First published in 1763.
———. *Nachlass*. In vol. 21 of *Gesammelte Schriften*. Berlin: Akademia Ausgabe, 1936. Translation by Curtis Bowman, Paul Guyer, and Frederick Rauscher: *Notes and Fragments*, edited by P. Guyer. New York: Cambridge University Press, 2005.
Leibniz, Gottfried Wilhelm. *De summa rerum: Metaphysical Papers, 1675–1676*. Translated by G.H.R. Parkinson. New Haven, CT: Yale University Press, 1992.
———. *General Investigations Concerning the Analysis of Concepts and Truths*. Translated by W. H. O'Briant. Athens: University of Georgia Press, 1968.
Martineau, Emmanuel. "Avertissement à la traduction française de Heidegger." In *Interprétation phénoménologique de la "Critique de la raison pure" de Kant*. Paris: Gallimard, 1982.
Nietzsche, Friedrich. *The Gay Science*. Edited by B. Williams. Translated by Josephine Nauckhoff and Adrian Del Caro. New York: Cambridge University Press, 2001.
Rousseau, Jean-Jacques. *Les rêveries du promeneur solitaire*. In vol. 1 of *Œuvres complètes*. Paris: Gallimard / La Pléiade, 1959. Translation by Peter France: *Reveries of the Solitary Walker*. New York: Penguin, 1980.
Schelling, Friedrich von. *Einleitung in die Philosophie*. Edited by W. E. Ehrhardt. Schellingiana, no. 11. Stuttgart: Frommann-Holzboog, 1989. First published in 1830.
———. *Vom Ich als Prinzip der Philosophie oder über das Unbedingte im menschlichen Wissen*. In *Werke*, edited by W. G. Jacobs, J. Jantzen, W. Schieche, et al. Stuttgart: Frommann-Holzboog, 1976–. Translation by F. Marti: *The Unconditional in Human Knowledge: Four Early Essays, 1794–96*. Lewisburg, PA: Bucknell University Press, 1980. First published in 1795.
———. *Die Weltalter*. Edited by M. Schröter. Munich: Beck, 1946. Translation by F.d.W. Bolman Jr.: *The Ages of the World*. New York: Columbia University Press, 1942. First published in 1811.
Taminiaux, Jacques. *Lectures de l'ontologie fondamentale*. Grenoble: Jérôme Millon, 1995.
Tilliette, Xavier. *L'intuition intellectuelle de Kant à Hegel*. Paris: Vrin, 1995.
Vezin, François. "Le mot 'Dasein,'" in an appendix to the French translation (*Être et temps*) of Heidegger's *Sein und Zeit*. Paris: Gallimard, 1986.
Wolff, Christian. *Deutsche Metaphysik*. Halle, Ger., 1751. Reprint, Hildesheim, Ger.: Olms, 1997.

| DECEPTION

From the Latin *decipere*, which literally means "to take [*capere*] by causing to fall into a trap, to fool, to deceive," "deception" implies illusion, seduction, and fraud. The term relates in philosophical contexts to the power of speech or discourse to create illusion (*apatê* [ἀπάτη] in Greek), and becomes a theme in the discussion of rhetoric and sophistry. See TRUTH, Box 3; see also *RUSE* [MÊTIS]; cf. *FALSE, FICTION,* LOGOS, *LIE*, SPEECH ACT.

"Deception" relates equally to the notion of *desengaño* characteristic of the golden age of Spanish literature, where the term refers to disillusionment as both "being saved from error" and "disenchantment"; see DESENGAÑO; cf. BAROQUE, *MALAISE, RÉCIT,* SECULARIZATION, SPREZZATURA.

➤ *NEGATION,* VERGÜENZA

DEFORMATION

1. "Deformation," as well as "distortion" and "displacement," are standard translations of the German *Entstellung*, which Freud uses to designate one of the mechanisms of repression. See DRIVE, ENTSTELLUNG, VERNEINUNG, WUNSCH; cf. ES, SUBLIME, Box 3, UNCONSCIOUS.
2. On the distortion of reality implicated in the act of putting into speech, see HISTORY, LOGOS, MIMÊSIS; cf. *FICTION, RÉCIT*.
3. On the form of the word itself, see COMBINATION AND CONCEPTUALIZATION; cf. *NEGATION*.

➤ CONSCIOUSNESS, *FORM*

DEMON

In modern English, *demon* (Lat. *daemon*, Gr. *daimôn* [δαίμων]) is, by way of Church Latin, very close to *devil*; see DEVIL (*diabolos* [διάβολος] in the Greek Bible, Semitic and Arabic *Sāṭān* [שָׂטָן]).

In Greek, a *daimôn* may be either good or bad; see DAIMÔN, and its semantic descendants in German (e.g., Hölderlin's "demonic"); see also the Spanish DUENDE, which contains the same ambiguity. Through *daiomai* [δαίομαι], "to share," *daimôn* is related to destiny; see *DESTINY* [KÊR].

The semantic field also implicates singular aesthetic creation; see notably DICHTUNG, GENIUS, INGENIUM, LEGGIADRIA, MADNESS; as well as satisfaction, moral or otherwise: *HAPPINESS*, GLÜCK, MORALS, PLEASURE, *WISDOM*; cf. ACEDIA.

On the relationship between religion and revelation, see DEVIL and GOD. See also BOGOČELOVEČESTVO, PIETAS, RELIGIO.

➤ AIÔN, EUROPE, PEOPLE

DEMOS [δεμός] / ETHNOS [ἔθνος] / LAOS [λαός] (GREEK)

➤ *GOVERNMENT, STATE*, and LAW, POLIS, POLITICS, RULE OF LAW, STATE/ GOVERNMENT, STATO

Many debates among historians, sociologists, political theorists, and philosophers in the twentieth century were framed in terms of an opposition between "two concepts of the nation": one (closest to the etymology of Lat. *natio*, from *nascere, natum,* which also generates *natura*) associates it with a traditional bond transferred from one generation to another (whence the idea of a common "substance" of the community, be it cultural or racial); the other (often supposed to have triumphed with the great "bourgeois" revolutions of the late eighteenth century: North American, French, Haitian, Venezuelan), would embody the ideals of the Enlightenment and follow the model of a contractual community of "citizens." This ideal dichotomy is often combined with genealogies of nationalism and imperialism as typical "modern" phenomena, whose roots may lie in a bifurcation in the understanding of the notion of a "people." This is nowadays increasingly defined as the opposition of the people qua *demos*, and the people qua *ethnos*, following ancient Greek models. One can argue, however, that this is a truncated genealogy, leading to a mystifying alternative. Debates about "nations" and

"nationalism" require at least a *third concept*, for which there also exists a Greek name: *laos*. The system of oppositions is a more complex one. And so, accordingly, are the applications to contemporary dilemmas.

Recent uses of the "Greek" pair of words *ethnos* versus *demos* seem to have been initiated by the Austrian-born sociologist Emerich K. Francis in 1965. In his presentation, the opposition has a primarily anthropological meaning, contrasting "prenational societies," whose collective identity and integration are secured by the domination of "genealogy" (in the strict sense of kinship, or in a broader sense of inherited traditions and memberships), with "nations" (or "national societies"), where the dominant principle of integration (what he calls the "demotic bond") is territorial and legal, relating each individual citizen to the state and the public administration. The model for the national society is provided by European states, and the opposition clearly matches other evolutionary patterns invented by the sociological tradition: "status" and "contract," *Gemeinschaft* and *Gesellschaft*, and so forth, albeit with a special insistence on the "deconstruction of kinship" carried on in the process of nation building.

Apart from applications in the anthropological field, the main fortunes of the antithesis followed from its subsequent use within debates bearing on what type of collective identity could be provided by European integration. They followed from a seminal 1986 essay by Rainer M. Lepsius, in which he also discussed the latent conflict of two traditions in the history of Central Europe (*Mitteleuropa*): one of "ethnic nationalism" and one of "civic nationalism." The question was now to decide whether this "unnamable political object"—the new European Union—should involve a return to the idea of a shared inherited identity, or a progress toward a purely "constitutional" construction. After being adopted in that sense by Jürgen Habermas in his discussion of *Verfassungspatriotismus* (patriotism of the constitution) and the "postnational constellation," it became standard in political and philosophical debates.

It is indeed interesting to observe the variety of "cases" to which the *ethnos* versus *demos* antithesis, whether explicitly referred to a "Greek" dilemma or not, has now been applied, retrospectively or prospectively. The following are but a few examples, but they bring interesting connotations:

1. When the demonstrations against the regime of the German Democratic Republic began in 1989, in the form of popular marches around the main city-square in Leipzig, the motto was *Wir sind das Volk!* (meaning "we are the citizens," in whose name this regime falsely claims to govern); but toward the end, when the Federal Republic of (Western) Germany had announced that it would integrate the Eastern *Länder* immediately, the motto became *Wir sind ein Volk!* (meaning "we are a single historical people," or nation, ranging from East to West, and divided artificially by history). One could easily argue that the demonstrators had passed from *demos* to *ethnos*, even if the Federal Republic could be perceived—in spite of the name—as more "democratic" than its socialist counterpart.

2. Sometime later (2000), the same (reunited) FRG modified its legal framework for the "normal" access to citizenship (apart from naturalization), both to ease the relationships with its increasing Turkish minority, and to come closer to the French and U.S. model of *ius soli* (as opposed to *ius sanguinis*), or to promote territorial law as opposed to genealogy—the former being perceived to incarnate a less "exclusivist" conception of the nation. This time it was moving from *ethnos* to *demos*.

3. Another interesting example is provided by the debate about the definition of the State of Israel (which originates in the Zionist project called by its founder Theodor Herzl *der Judenstaat*, "the State of the Jews"): it refers to itself officially as "a Jewish democratic state," but the dominant political parties in Israel understand it as "a Jewish state that is also democratic" (therefore essentially deriving its collective identity from the real or mythical Hebrew origins of the majority, relegating the Arab minority to a condition of "internal outsiders"); whereas others understand it as "a democratic state" in which all citizens ought to be fully equal, even if it was founded by Jews fleeing persecutions and genocide in Europe at the expense of an autochthonous population. The situation is rendered even more complicated by the fact that both the Jewish majority in Israel and the dispersed Palestinian communities refer to a "right of return" based on a combination of descent and affiliation to the territory. In this case, *ethnos* and *demos* seem to be undermining each other.

These examples, however partial and quick, show the semantic weight carried by the *ethnos* versus *demos* antithesis. They make it all the more important to explain why the discursive and historical pattern is, in fact, more complicated. This begins with two philological remarks.

The full meaning and intentions of the opposition can hardly become isolated from a web of juridical, sociological, anthropological, and political contexts. One of them is particularly important because—in Foucauldian terms—it illustrates the relationship with the "biopolitics" of the modern (bourgeois) state. *Ethnos* could not be brought into this opposition independent of the fact that a "discipline" describing the customs and social structures of non-European peoples (colonial or virtually colonized) was called "ethnography" (created by German scholars in 1807). And *demos* could not be used independent of the fact that European modern states claimed to be essentially "democratic," at least in this sense that their legitimacy derived from a collective right of "self-determination" and the "popular will." The latent pattern is that of an "ethnographic object" observed by "democratic subjects." But the European states also developed a discipline called "demography," which includes questions of the type raised by ethnographers (social effects of marriage, for instance), albeit applied to nation-states and not to prenational "tribes" or "cultures" (the name was coined in 1855 in French to name statistics of populations, replacing the old "political arithmetic"). It is interesting to ask if the semantic quadrangle can be completed with a term "ethnocracy": this is actually the case since political

theorists (in particular comparing the discriminations in Israel with those of apartheid South Africa—whether rightly or wrongly) have supported the idea that the modern *demos* is haunted by the figure of the *ethnos*, particularly in regimes that grant a legal privilege, or a "leading role," to one of the "nationalities" forming the nation itself. The *ethnos* versus *demos* opposition thus proves capable of generating a complete system of theoretical distinctions.

The reference to a "Greek" model becomes, then, all the more surprising. As it was presented, for example, in Aristotle, a Greek conception of the political distinguishes two great types of "communities" (*koinôniai*) in which human beings can live: some are based on the tribal structures and obey chieftains or kings, and they are called *ethnè*; others, considered more civilized (therefore more perfectly "human"), distinguish the private and the public sphere, they are called *poleis* (which we translate with the Latin name for "city," *civitas*). *Demos* is not directly opposed to *ethnos*: rather, it names the multitude of the citizens, independent of their social status or rank. And insofar as in "cities" all citizens enjoy certain basic rights (such as deliberation in the public assembly), their regime contains, according to Aristotle, a "democratic element."

But there were several other terms in ancient Greek to designate the "popular" element (see PEOPLE). The most important for our purpose is *laos*: central in the Homeric terminology, where it designated the community of the warriors, whose collective power would normally become subjected to the authority of "princes" (*anax*), but could also challenge it (as in famous episodes of the *Iliad*), it had become an archaic notion in classical Greece. Its importance for modern debates about the political function of the nation comes from its having been selected by the translators of the Septuagint who, working in Alexandria between the third and the first century BCE, translated the *Torah* (followed by other parts of the Bible) into *koinè* Greek, to render Hebrew *'am*, the proper name of the "Elect People of God" (or the Hebrew nation). More precisely they used *ethnè* to call the "other nations" (more simply "the nations" [*goy'im*]) and *laos* for the Elect People. In Latin (*Vulgata* or "vulgate") it became the opposition of *populus* (*electus*) and *nationes* or *gentes* ("the Gentiles"). This is a completely different opposition than *ethnos* versus *demos*; but it is from there that many of the emphatic notions of nationhood and its political mission derive in modern times, because it becomes the bearer of the "universalistic" and "messianic" dimension of the nation.

Already in the eschatological perspective of the Old Testament, the universalistic perspective is present because the Hebrew people, which distinguishes itself from all others by the fact that "its God" is unique and is the (only) true God, is also the one that has been "chosen" by God to reveal the truth to humankind and achieve the redemption of the others through its own redemption. In the prophetic books (especially Isaiah, where the messianic perspective becomes explicit), this redemptory function is attributed only to the "remnant" (*She'erit*) who remained obedient to the Law or faithful to God in the Exile, therefore forming a group similar to a "people in the people" (or a "people of the people"). This function in Christian theology is displaced by the church (or the community of the faithful who acknowledge Jesus as the Messiah and await his return) as the "New Israel," and therefore the (mystical) equivalent of the "Chosen People." It is this theological notion (also used to name the Christian or Roman Empire) that modern nationalism would "secularize." Let us note here an important twist: if according to the general perspective, *laos* is the totality of the Christian people forming the church (*ekklèsia*, taken from the name of the "assembly of the citizens" in the Greek political terminology), it is also more precisely the "simple faithful" as opposed to the *klèros* (or the priests, who are the theological equivalent of magistrates). Therefore it retains at the same time a sense of mission or destination, and a "popular" determination—a very powerful way of merging the categories of universality and community.

On this basis it becomes easier to understand how the (secularized) political theology of the modern states as "universal" political communities—both in the *intensive* sense (realizing equality and liberty, or rather, a universalization of rights, among their citizens) and the *extensive* sense (spreading civilization, or democracy, or republicanism, in the world, and easily associated with an "imperial" destiny)—permanently evokes the legacy of the *laos* rather than either *ethnos* or *demos*. Two "lines of descent" are particularly significant.

One belongs to the English-American tradition. As extensively documented by J.G.A. Pocock (critically discussing Michael Walzer's *Revolution of the Saints*), English Republicanism, especially in its "Puritan" form, during the Civil War developed a specific combination of apocalyptic and civic consciousness, which made it possible to represent "God's Englishmen" as an "Elect Nation" constituting its Commonwealth against the tyranny of idolatrous monarchs. Pocock would also argue that an "apocalyptic Whiggism" formed part of the political heritage that Puritans carried over to the American colonies. And perhaps it is not wrong to accept that this combination was still there when, during the American Revolution and with decidedly more imperialist resonance than the Puritans' uprising in England, the United States went on to conceive of itself as the subject of a "manifest destiny," first in the Americas, then with respect to the world.

Another line belongs to the French-German dialogue over the relationship between "nation," "cosmopolitanism," and "emancipation" in the nineteenth century (with twentieth-century sequels). It begins with the proclamation of the "sovereignty of the nation" (as opposed to the king) in the *Déclaration des droits de l'homme et du citoyen* (a "secular" document undoubtedly, but also located at the core of a new "civil religion," and often printed in images imitating the traditional representation of Moses's Tablets of the Ten Commandments. When Republican France turned imperial and presented itself as *La Grande Nation* (not very different from the idea of a "manifest destiny" in American terms), it led German "Jacobins" like the philosopher Johann Gottlieb Fichte to write about the special mission of *Die Deutsche Nation*, whose inflexible resistance to foreign invasion, based on absolute moral values, would restore the possibility of perpetual peace on the European Continent. But it is especially in the antithetic figure of the Marxian proletariat

as "universal class" that an eschatological notion of the "people of the people" became reinvented—at the same time revolutionary and cosmopolitan ("internationalist," or gathering its people among the excluded multitude from all countries). Whereas the French notion of *laïcité* (deriving from *laikos*, the opposite of *klèrikos*: as if the Christian people had liberated itself from its own hierarchy) until today retains the democratic and assimilationist connotations of the *grande nation* (see SECULARIZATION).

Greece, Rome, and Jerusalem are thus more than ever providing symbols for the invention of political modernity. Centuries have passed, but who can say that this is over?

Étienne Balibar

BIBLIOGRAPHY

Agamben, Giorgio. *The Time that Remains: A Commentary on the Letter to the Romans*. Translated by Patricia Dailey. Stanford, CA: Stanford University Press, 2005.

———. "What Is a People?" In *Means Without Ends: Notes on Politics*, translated by Vincenzo Binetti and Cesare Casarino. Minneapolis: University of Minnesota Press, 2000.

Aristotle. *Politics*. Bks. 1 and 3. Edited by H.W.C. Davis. Translated by Benjamin Jowett. New York: Cosimo Classics, 2008.

Balibar, Étienne. "Fichte and the Internal Border: On *Addresses to the German Nation*." In *Masses, Classes, Ideas: Studies on Politics and Philosophy before and after Marx*, translated by James Swenson, 61–84. New York: Routledge, 1994.

———. "Le moment messianique de Marx." In *Citoyen Sujet et autres essais d'anthropologie philosophique*, 243–64. Paris: Presses Universitaires de France, 2011.

Bastian, Adolf. *Die Vorgeschichte der Ethnologie*. Berlin: Dümmler, 1881.

Boyer, Frédéric, trans. "Glossaire." In *La Bible*. Introduction by F. Boyer. Paris: Bayard, 2001: "AM/GÔY," 3103–4; "ETHNOS/LAOS," 3152–54.

Campbell, Richard Charles. "The Church as the New Israel." Wheaton College, 1954.

Cherry, Conrad, ed. *God's New Israel: Religious Interpretations of American Destiny*. Chapel Hill: University of North Carolina Press, 1998.

Cody, Aelred. "When Is the Chosen People Called a Gôy?" *Vetus Testamentum* 14, no. 1 (January 1964): 1–6.

Francis, Emerich K. *Ethnos und Demos: Soziologische Beiträge zur Volkstheorie*. Berlin: Duncker and Humblot, 1965. Translation: *Interethnic Relations. An Essay in Sociological Theory*. New York: Elsevier, 1976.

Godechot, Jacques. *La Grande Nation: L'Expansion révolutionnaire de la France dans le monde de 1789 à 1799*. 2nd rev. ed. Paris: Aubier-Montaigne, 1983.

Habermas, Jürgen. *The Postnational Constellation: Political Essays*. Translated by Max Pensky. Cambridge: Polity Press 2001.

Haubold, Johannes. *Homer's People: Epic Poetry and Social Formation*. Cambridge: Cambridge University Press, 2000.

Jewish Encyclopaedia. "Chosen People." http://www.jewishencyclopedia.com/articles/4355-chosen-people.

Kantorowicz, Ernst H. *The King's Two Bodies: A Study in Medieval Political Theology*. Princeton, NJ: Princeton University Press 1957.

Le Bras, Hervé. "Démographie et démocratie." *Revue européenne des sciences sociales* no. 31 (1993): 59–77.

Lepsius, Rainer M. "*Ethnos* oder *Demos*: Zur Anwendung zweier Kategorien von Emerich Francis auf das nationale Selbstverständnis der Bundesrepublik und auf die Europäische Vereinigung." In *Interessen, Idee und Institutionen: Aufsätze zur Makrosoziologie*. Opladen, Ger.: Westdeutscher Verlag 1990. Essay first published in 1986.

Pocock, J.G.A. *The Machiavellian Moment: Florentine Political Thought and the Atlantic Republican Tradition*. Rev. ed. Princeton, NJ: Princeton University Press, 2003.

Schmid, Bernard.: "L'Allemagne instille du droit du sol." *Plein Droit* [special issue "Quelle Europe pour les étrangers?"] no. 49 (April 2001).

Sériot, Patrick. "Ethnos et Demos: La construction discursive de l'identité collective." In *Langages et Société*, 39–52. Paris: Maison des Sciences de l'Homme, 1997.

Stephanson, Anders. *Manifest Destiny: American Expansion and the Empire of Right.* New York: Hill and Wang, 1996.

Walzer, Michael. *The Revolution of the Saints: A Study in the Origins of Radical Politics.* Cambridge, MA: Harvard University Press, 1965.

Yiftachel, Oren. *Ethnocracy: Land and Identity Politics in Israel/Palestine.* Philadelphia: University of Pennsylvania Press, 2006.

| DÉNÉGATION

Borrowed from the Latin *denegatio* (denial), the word was taken up in psychoanalysis to translate Freud's term *Verneinung*: see VERNEINUNG. The German, word, however, refers both to negation in the logical sense (as opposed to affirmation, *Bejahung*; or assertion, *Behauptung*: see FALSE, NEGATION, NOTHING, PROPOSITION) and to the process Freud describes as a refusal, defensive or not, to admit that one has said something. Negation is thus a form of repression: see DRIVE, ENSTELLUNG, ES, UNCONSCIOUS, WUNSCH; cf. CONSCIOUSNESS, EGO, SUBJECT. The difficulty of translating *Verneinung*, notably into French and English, is thus related to the loss of the term's logical and psychological ambivalence.

➤ BELIEF, *CROYANCE*, REPRÉSENTATION, TRUTH

| DESCRIPTION / DEPICTION

FRENCH	*description, représentation*
GREEK	*ekphrasis* [ἔκφρασις]
LATIN	*descriptio, depiction*

➤ *RÉCIT*, and CONCETTO, DICHTUNG, DISEGNO, ERZÄHLEN, *FICTION*, HISTORY, *IMAGE*, MIMÊSIS, REPRÉSENTATION, SIGN, SPEECH ACT, STRUCTURE

English and French distinguish description and narration in the same way. In English, however, description may also be opposed to depiction, the latter taking on a visual connotation that contrasts with the verbal resonance of "description." This second distinction does not have a French equivalent. While French can distinguish the act of depicting (*dépeindre*) from that of describing (*décrire*) or narrating (*narrer*), of these three verbs *dépeindre* is the only one without a noun form in ordinary usage. Where English has "depiction," French must use *représentation*. Hence the difficulty in translating into French the distinction between depiction and representation, which, like that between depiction and description, plays a very important role in theories of aesthetics in the analytic tradition. This has led to the recent introduction of the term "depiction" into French philosophical language.

I. Different Ways of Making Someone See

The Latin *descriptio* denotes either a drawing or a written or oral description. More rarely, a *descriptio* is a visual sketch, but also a verbal description or a representation in the imagination. There is an image in both cases, but the visualization is not necessarily literal: in both cases, the *de-* prefix indicates that one "de-scribes" or "de-picts" *from* a model or the original.

Until the seventeenth century, the English word "description" could mean a pictorial representation—a portrait. The word is still used by Hogarth ("a description of such lines as compose the features of a face"), but more in the sense of a drawing or delineation, whereas "depiction" contains the root "pict"—that is, paint, color, pigment. Svetlana Alpers continues to use "description" with visual connotation, opposing the description characteristic of Dutch painting and a new visual culture with the narration characteristic of Italian painting and traditional text-based culture. Most often, however, "description" designates a verbal mode of visualization or metaphorical representation that compares poorly with the visual arts. Addison emphasizes its ambiguous or secondary status as "resembling even less" than painting (which itself resembles its objects less than sculpture), though "description" is still closer to what it represents than music.

Sometimes functioning as simple stylistic variations of "describe" and "description," "depict" and "depiction" may denote both representations that are literally visual as well as metaphorical visualization by writing that "makes one see" (also called "picturing" or, in the manner of Ruskin, "word-painting"). Edgar Allan Poe uses "depict" to denote the art of the portraitist ("for her whom he depicted so surpassingly well," in "The Oval Portrait"), but also for the art of the narrator or psychological portraitist ("This depicting of character constituted my design," in "The Mystery of Marie Rogêt"). We find comparable uses in recent criticism. In Williams, "depiction" refers mainly to visual representation by daguerrotype ("depiction of face in portraiture," passim), but also occasionally to painting by means of literary text ("depiction of portrait in sentimental fiction," "depiction of spectatorship in *The House of the Seven Gables*"). Flaxman clarifies "description" as "visually oriented description," while, by contrast, Krieger defines "ekphrasis" as a verbal description without thereby implying that there are nonverbal ones. He defines description as being essentially verbal in a quasi-tautological manner, and in fact uses "verbal depictions" as a variant with exactly the same meaning. Becker, on the other hand, in his detailed commentary on the shield of Achilles, falls back on a clear and explicit distinction between "description" and "depiction." "Visual depiction" denotes what Achilles's (fictional) shield is supposed to represent, while "verbal description" refers to the way in which the poet describes that representation: "In a description of a depiction of the sun (484), the same phrase is used as in a description of the actual sun (239)." According to Becker, Homeric ekphrasis is often a simultaneous description of the shield and what is depicted on the shield, and this Homeric mode of ekphrasis is distinguished from later modes precisely because it continues to direct our attention to the material nature of the fictional object, to the images in metal as well as the story they relate, rather than simply using the fictional imagistic representation as a pretext to introduce the narrative.

■ See Box 1.

II. Modes of Denotation or of Perception?

That this distinction has acquired the status of a conceptual opposition operative in philosophical discourse is essentially due to the work of Nelson Goodman. Goodman distinguishes between "verbal description" (where the adjective denotes, as

1

"Ekphrasis": From word to word

"Ekphrasis" (from *phrazô* [φράζω], "to declare," and *ek* [ἐκ], "completely") is a putting into words that exhausts its object; the term denotes minute and complete descriptions of works of art.

The first, and no doubt the most famous, known ekphrasis is the one Homer gives at the end of book 18 of the *Iliad*, the subject of which is the shield of Achilles, forged by Hephaistos. It was made at the request of Achilles's mother, Thetis, not to allow her son to evade death, but so that "all should marvel"(466ff.) when he did meet his destiny. The work is cosmo-political, representing not only Earth, Sky, and Sea, bordered by the river Ocean, but also two cities in living detail, one at peace and one at war. The blind poet gives the first synthesis of the world of mortals, thus proving for the first time that poetry is more philosophical than history.

Not only is this first ekphrasis a description of a fictional object, but its historical successor is a second ekphrasis whose model is the first ekphrasis, as though the author were doing a remake. Here the subject is the shield of Hercules, and is attributed to Hesiod. This palimpsest therefore does not follow a phenomenon—a real shield—nor does it follow nature itself or human cities, but only a *logos*. Swathed in culture, the object loses both its natural reference and what is called, following Aristotle, the life of the narrative. As Paul Mazon notes, making the value judgments we expect: "Through it all there is not a gesture which is truly 'seen,' which gives the impression of life. Nor is there a word on the lips of the characters which emits a clear and frank tone: everyone speaks a language of pure convention." Ekphrasis is thus at the furthest remove from metaphor, the craft of which consists in placing things *pro ommatôn* [πρὸ ὀμμάτων], "before the eyes," following the doctrine of *ut pictura poesis*—in order to produce a new and original understanding. "When the poet calls old age 'a withered stalk,' he conveys a new idea, a new fact, to us by means of the general notion of 'lost bloom' which is common to both things" (Aristotle, *Rhetoric*, 3.10.1410b 14–16; cf. *Poetics*, 21, 22). Ekphrasis is no longer here imitating painting insofar as it attempts to place the object before our eyes—to present the object as a painting would—but to imitate painting insofar as it is a mimetic art—to paint painting itself. Imitating imitation in order to produce an understanding, not of the object, but of the fiction of an object—of objectification: ekphrasis is literature.

Ekphraseis proliferated in the second Sophistic period, including Philostratus's *Images* and Callistratus's *Descriptions*, to the point of constituting a genre in its own right. With the *xenia*, critiques of still lives that a host would give as presents to his guests, and which depicted the dishes they may have eaten at his house, the object itself is now at three removes, and has become a mere pretext for a literary representation of a pictorial representation. The original is no longer available to perception and can no longer be the object of an adequate description; it is at most presupposed or produced following an act of fiction (see SPEECH ACT, Box 1).

The fate of ekphrasis is linked to that of the novel. Not only do novels abound with ekphrases, but more decisively, novels are often structured by an ekphrasis. In the opening lines of *The Adventures of Leucippe and Clitophon*, for example, the narrator, having just escaped from a storm, looks at the votive offerings and stops at a hanging painting that contains the template of the story of the novel itself—in the course of which we witness the offering of the painting by the protagonist. The paradigm case of ekphrasis, however, comes from Longus's pastoral romance *Daphnis and Chloë*. The entire novel is the ekphrasis of an ekphrasis since the story is modeled on a painting, which is itself, we learn, composed not of lines and colors but words:

When I was hunting in Lesbos, I saw, in a wood sacred to the Nymphs, the most beautiful thing that I have ever seen—a painting that told a love-story. The wood itself was beautiful enough, full of trees and flowers, and watered by a single spring which nourished both the flowers and the trees; but the picture was even more delightful, combining excellent technique with a romantic subject. It had become so famous that crowds of people used to go there even from abroad, partly to pray to the Nymphs, but mainly to see the picture. In it there were women having babies and other women wrapping them in swaddling clothes, babies being exposed, sheep and goats suckling them, shepherds picking them up, young people plighting their troth, pirates making a raid, enemies starting an invasion.

After gazing admiringly at many other scenes, all of a romantic nature, I was seized by a longing to write a verbal equivalent to the painting. So I found someone to explain the picture to me, and composed a work in four volumes as an offering to Love and the Nymphs and Pan, and as a source of pleasure for the human race—something to heal the sick and comfort the afflicted, to refresh the memory of those who have been in love and educate those who have not.

In this story, nature is less beautiful than painting ("painting held more charm"). The painting that the ekphrasis describes is already a story: "a painted image, a love story." This painted story, finally, requires a "response." The Greek expression, "*antigrapsai tei graphei*," is more precise: it is a matter of writing "against" the original and "starting over"—to replicate it and compete with it, playing the roles of both attorney for the defense and recording clerk. This "rewriting" or "response" is the interpretation of the painting over the course of four books. The *ut poesis pictura* of the *graphê*, that is, the painting, is followed by the *ut pictura poesis* of the *antigraphê* [ἀντιγραφή], the pastoral itself. There is thus only an *ut poesis poesis* that moves from word to word.

With ekphrasis, we are at the furthest remove from both nature and the first natural science of philosophy, whose goal is to tell things as they are—and insofar as they are, and by what cause. We are also at the furthest remove from an immediate and ontologically innocent phenomenological description. We find ourselves in the world of art and artifice, ruled by and following the performative, effective power of speech that has been freed from truth and falsehood, as it sets out not to say what it sees, but to make seen what it says.

Barbara Cassin

BIBLIOGRAPHY

Aristotle. *The Complete Works of Aristotle*. Vols. 1–2. Edited by J. Barnes. Princeton, NJ: Princeton University Press, 1984.

Blanchard, Marc Élie. "Problèmes du texte et du tableau: les limites de l'imitation à l'époque hellénistique." In *Le plaisir de parler*, edited by B. Cassin, 131–54. Paris: Éditions de Minuit, 1986.

Cassin, Barbara. *L'effet sophistique*. Paris: Gallimard / La Pléiades, 1995.

Imbert, Claude. *Phénoménologie et langues formulaire*. Paris: Presses Universitaires de France , 1993.

Krieger, Murray. *Ekphrasis: The Illusion of the Natural Sign*. Baltimore: Johns Hopkins University Press, 1992.

Longus. *Daphnis and Chloë*. Translated by Paul Turner. London: Penguin, 1969.

Mazon, Paul. *Hésiode*. Paris: Les Belles Lettres, 1967.

for Krieger, a constant feature of description), and "pictorial representation," or "depiction" (in *Reconceptions in Philosophy*, Goodman professes a definite preference for "depiction" over "representation," which he uses from then on in "a wider, more flexible sense"). Goodman sees in "description" and "depiction" two modes of denotation—two ways of referring to or representing something—but he vigorously opposes the idea that depiction has anything to do with resemblance. According to him, descriptions or predicates (nouns, descriptive phrases . . .) are composed of linguistic symbols that belong to digital systems (formed of discrete units), whereas pictures, in the case of depiction, belong to dense or analog systems. Goodman uses "description" in a wide sense that seems to cover practically any linguistic formulation. Alongside the description/depiction distinction, we find in Goodman distinctions between names and descriptions, on one hand, and pictures on the other, and again between paragraphs and pictures, or predicates and pictures.

The distinction between depiction and representation, developed in particular by Peacocke, introduces a supplementary distinction, internal to the act of perception, between a first level that derives from a pure perception and a second level that requires the mastery of a symbolic system. This distinction, which is reminiscent of Panofsky's distinction between the pre-iconographic and iconographic stages, plays an important role in the analysis of the perception of artworks. When I look at a painting, I can identify an object (a child, an old man, or a lamb) without knowing what it represents (love, time, or Christ). This first identification would correspond to the perceptual experience of the depiction. But the existence of a precognitive and pre-predicative level of perception, which would define what some call a stage of pure perception, is a thesis that is far from generally accepted today.

Jean-Loup Bourget

BIBLIOGRAPHY

Addison, Joseph. *The Spectator* [no. 416, 27 June 1712]. Edited by D. F. Bond. Oxford: Clarendon Press, 1965.
Alpers, Svetlana. *The Art of Describing: Dutch Art in the Seventeenth Century*. Chicago: University of Chicago Press, 1983.
Becker, Andrew Sprague. *The Shield of Achilles and the Poetics of Ekphrasis*. Lanham, MD: Rowman and Littlefield, 1995.
Flaxman, Rhoda L. *Victorian Word-painting and Narrative: Toward the Blending of Genres*. Ann Arbor, MI: UMI Research Press, 1987.
Goodman, Nelson. *Languages of Art: An Approach to a Theory of Symbols*. 2nd ed. Indianapolis: Hackett, 1976.
Goodman, Nelson, and Catherine Z. Elgin. *Reconceptions in Philosophy and Other Arts and Sciences*. Indianapolis: Hackett, 1988.
Hogarth, William. *The Analysis of Beauty*. Edited by R. Paulson. New Haven, CT: Yale University Press, 1988. First published in 1753.
Irwin, Michael. *Picturing: Description and Illusion in the Nineteenth Century Novel*. London: Allen and Unwin, 1979.
Krieger, Murray. *Ekphrasis: The Illusion of the Natural Sign*. Baltimore: Johns Hopkins University Press, 1992.
Panofsky, Erwin. *Studies in Iconology: Humanistic Themes in the Art of the Renaissance*. New York: Harper and Row, 1972.
Peacocke, Christopher. "Depiction." *Philosophical Review* 96, no. 3 (1987): 383–410.
Poe, Edgar Allan. *Collected Works*. Edited by T. O. Mabbott. Cambridge, MA: Belknap Press of Harvard University Press, 1978.
Williams, Susan S. *Photograph and Portraiture in Antebellum American Fiction*. Philadelphia: University of Pennsylvania Press, 1997.

DESENGAÑO (SPANISH)

CATALAN	*desengany*
ENGLISH	disillusionment, disenchantment, disappointment
FRENCH	*désillusion*
GERMAN	*Enttäuschung*
ITALIAN	*disinganno*
PORTUGUESE	*desengano*

➤ DECEPTION, and Baroque, *FALSE, LIE, MALAISE*, PLEASURE, SPREZZATURA, TRUTH, VERGÜENZA

The noun *desengaño* comes from the verb *desengañar* (composed of the negative prefix *des* and the verb *engañar*), which comes, according to RT: Corominas and Pascual, *Diccionario critico etimológico castellano e hispánico*, from the medieval Latin *ingannare* (mock, scoff at, deride), which itself comes from the classical onomatopoeia *gannire* (yap, bark); similarly for the Catalan *desengany*, the Italian *disinganno*, and the Portuguese *desengano*. "Disillusion" in English and *Enttäuschung* in German represent the two senses between which the different significations of *desengaño* oscillate: on one hand, knowledge, overcoming blindness, being disabused, all of which correspond to the fact that one has escaped error and illusion; on the other, disappointment at the fact that a hope has not been realized.

The word *desengaño* achieved its full splendor in the sixteenth and seventeenth centuries. Beginning in 1492, when the Jews were forced to choose between leaving Spain and converting to Catholicism, the theme of *desengaño* in picaresque and mystical writing was a way for "new Christians" (children of converted Jews) to imagine pathways and openings in a hostile society that had closed all its doors to them. Cervantes wrote *Don Quixote* in this spirit. A bit later, toward the middle of the seventeenth century, when the Society of Jesus had consolidated its victory and Spain had become a bastion of the Counter-Reformation, Baltasar Gracián responded to the continuing experience of *desengaño* by dramatizing it and by praising appearance as the only reality.

Today *desengaño* retains traces of its former richness and still has a variety of meanings.

I. The Principal Meanings: Knowledge by Which We Are Disabused, Deception, Deceit

1. The first of the senses of *desengaño* that are currently in use is that of the grasping of a truth that lifts someone out of a state of being deceived or mistaken. In his RT: *Tesoro de las dos lenguas española y francesa*, César Oudin, the first translator of *Don Quixote* into French, translates *desengañar* as "détromper, désabuser quelqu'un, lui ouvrir les yeux." According to Covarrubias (RT: *Tesoro de la lengua castellana o española*), *desengañar* also means "to express oneself with full clarity such that one does not conceive something by taking it for something else" (*hablar claro, porque no conciban una cosa por otra*). The example he chooses confirms the idea that it is the truth itself that disabuses us ("La misma verdad nos desengaña"). *Desengaño* then takes on a two-part character: first, the revelation of a new truth—a veritable illumination; second, thanks to this acquired knowledge, a slower movement that consists in an "escape" from error ("conocimiento de la verdad con que se sale del engaño [deception] en

que se establa"), as in the Latin phrase *ab errore deductus* (RT: *Diccionario de autoridades*). *Desengaño* is thus a form of knowledge with practical effects: it deals not with an abstract truth, but with lived truth, one that provokes a change.

2. This change constitutes the second meaning of the word, which is defined by the RT: *Diccionario de la lengua española* as an "effect of this [new] knowledge on one's state of mind" (*efecto de ese conocimento en el ánimo*). The *Diccionario* suggests a distinction between a neutral meaning and one that is clearly negative and restricted to the plural of *desengaño*, corresponding to "lessons learned at the cost of bitter experiences." Manuel Seco et al. (RT: *Diccionario del español actual*) provide a synthesis of these two strains by characterizing *desengaño* as a negative impression felt by someone who discovers that a person or thing does not meet their expectations. He offers several examples taken from contemporary literature, notably from the work of Diaz Plaja, *El español*: "[S]exual intercourse includes a punishment, that of the violent death of Calisto and Melibea, or simply the *desengaño* that follows climax [*el desengaño que sigue al goce*]"; from Calvo Sotelo, *Resentido*: "Lo normal es que quienes sufren ese desengaño terrible se hagan resentidos" (It is normal for those who suffer this terrible *desengaño* to become full of resentment); from Miguel Delibes, *Emigrante*: "La chavala se ha llevado un desengaño de órdago, por más que ella diga misa" (The girl suffered a terrible *desengaño*, even if she claims otherwise)—literally, "even if she recites the Mass"; in informal Spanish "to recite the Mass" means to say things that no one believes, however solemn they appear. These quotations recall the context in which the different senses of *desengaño* developed from the classical to the contemporary period. When the word is close to disappointment or disillusionment, it deals primarily with disappointment in love, which may entail punishment, especially if there was pleasure (*goce*) involved. The informal common usage cited in the last passage shows how much *desengaño* remains secretly linked with a religious notion of lacking or loss, even today.

3. The third sense of *desengaño* indicates the word or judgment by which one blames someone for something. This meaning is primarily expressed by the familiar and figurative form taken by the adverb and adjective: *desengañadamente* (*malamente, con desaliño y poco acierto* [in a negligent and improper way]) and *desengañado* (*despreciable y malo* [despicable and bad]). The effect of disappointment is here attributed to the unsteady or poor character of the person who has disappointed; he did what he did without believing in it, that is, poorly: "Cuando se pondera que alguno ha ejeccutado mal alguna cosa, se dice bien desengañadamente lo ha hecho." In this sense, *desengañado* translates the Latin *perversus*, "bad" (RT: *Diccionario de autoridades*). The adjective can sometimes pass on to the noun this sense of malignance. The RT: *Diccionario de autoridades* thus attributes to the object of deception a face that has become, in the context of sin, terrible and frightening. *Desengaño*

now indicates the horrible object that gives rise to the feeling: "Vida de San Borja: Vióse en su mismo original la cara del desengaño, tan terrible, que bastaba a introducir susto hasta en los mármoles del templo" (The Life of Saint Borgia: He saw in his own model the face of *desengaño*, so terrible that it alone sufficed to create fear even in the marbles of the temple). In a more satirical vein, but a no less serious one, Francisco Quevedo goes to the point of transforming this *desengaño* into a refusal of all illusion and all seduction; it becomes the truth—that of books, as opposed to the lies of living beings—truth that traversed the inanity of appearances as well as the vanity of pleasure and existence:

> Pareciéndome que los muertos pocas veces se burlan, y que gente sin pretensión y desengañada más atienden a enseñar que a entretener.

> (As it seemed to me that the dead rarely laugh and that, being unpretentious and disillusioned people, they would rather teach than amuse.)

> *Visita de los chistes* (cited in RT: *Diccionario de construcción y regimen de la lengua castellana*)

II. Picaresque Contempt for the Law and Mystic Wisdom

José Luis Alonso Hernández (RT: *Léxico del marginalismo del siglo de oro*) notes that the adjective *desengañado* takes on the sense of "crook, cheat, swindler" when it is turned into a substantive. *Desengañado*: a picaresque character, crook, or thief, in the sense that he is familiar with all possible forms of deception (*engaño*)—"he will return to drinking and invite others as disabused as he is" (tornó a beber y a convidar a otros tan desengañados como él; M. de Obregón).

■ See Box 1.

Unlike in the religious sense, according to which *desengaño* is related to sin and failure, and hence to a sort of surfeit of law, the familiarity with evil in the picaresque novel is identified with contempt for the law bordering on insouciance, either real or fake (it does not matter which); sometimes it even approaches an uncommon degree of anger, as for Mateo Alemán (*Life of Guzman*). His revolt derives, of course, from being used to hunger and poverty, but especially from a keen sensitivity to the respectable arrogance of the affluent—that is, the "old Christians."

However, in the golden age as well as today, the adjective *desengañado* also indicates the opposite of *pícaro* and appears as a synonym for "wise." It is applied to a man who, retired from the bustle and commerce of the world, lives privately and far away, desiring nothing other than to live in peace away from the tribunals of a society that has no room for nonconformists:

> Dichoso el que jamás ni ley ni fuero,
> Ni el alto tribunal de las ciudades;
> Ni conoció del mundo el trato fiero.

> (Happy he who has never known laws or statutes,
> Nor the high court of the cities,
> Nor the harsh treatment of the world.)

> (Luis de León, *En una esperança que salió vaga*)

1

Pícaro

Of uncertain origin, this word means in the first instance "rascal," "rogue," or "beggar"; someone without shame in the sense of modesty (*vergüenza*) or honor (*honra*), the most Christian of values according to the drama of Lope de Vega, the "official" author of the Spanish Golden Age (sixteenth and seventeenth centuries). The *pícaro* is thus first and foremost a mischievous character, malicious (*descarado*) as well, but above all, an outlaw. In the hands of some authors, such as the writer of *Lazarillo de Tormes*, the character is a crafty one, sometimes dishonest, but with a genuine awareness both of himself and the boundaries of the world, in particular those that separate his world from that of his masters and those of his own subjectivity. Despite the apparent paradox of such a genealogy, the *pícaro* may be considered a remote descendant of the mystics. As in Mateo Alemán's work, *pícaros* and mystics share an acute and sometimes tragic awareness of the rules of social power and the "falseness" of all worldly authority, which Teresa of Avila called, with "picaresque" contempt, "authorities of junk" (*autoridades postizas*). But Alemán's *Guzmán de Alfarache* dares to attack God and his creation, which he considers to be an utter failure. The mystic's rejection of the world as it is remains, for the *pícaro*, a rejection of all transcendence.

Luis de Léon, an Augustinian monk with a subtle command of Greek and Hebrew, a professor at the University of Salamanca, and one of the greatest poets of his time, also dared to defy the law (which in his case was an Inquisitorial interdiction against translating the Bible into Castilian), offering a beautiful lyric version of the Song of Songs to a Carmelite nun. And yet his poems retain a clear and sharp aggressivity that is in the same vein as Mateo Alemán's harsh and resounding revolt, despite being in a completely different register. Without actually naming them, the RT: *Diccionario de autoridades* shows that the adjective *desengañado* designates precisely these "new Christians," such as Mateo Alemán, Luis de León, or Teresa of Avila, who endlessly told her charges that true virtue is hidden in works and not in one's birth: "Los desengañados dicen, que la nobleza no se adquiere naciendo, sino obrando" (The *desengañados* say that nobility is not acquired by being born but by acting).

Some words of classical Castilian, like *desengaño*, seem to have been forged through a play of violent and almost exaggerated oppositions in an extreme tension between an internal and external aspect with regard to social and religious laws, and sometimes at the edges of their laws' own fluctuating boundaries. Américo Castro, a historian exiled from Spain after the civil war and a close confidant of Marcel Bataillon, "one of the masters of Cervantism" according to Jean Cassou in his introduction to *Don Quichotte*, offered constant reminders that all of the spiritual and mystic literature of the fifteenth and sixteenth centuries shared a common origin with picaresque novels, with *La Celestina*, and especially with *Don Quixote*. This literature is caught between a Christian optimism colored by Erasmism and a picaresque *desengaño* and was born and developed precisely among the children of the first converted Jews, who became Christians with lives "on the frontier," psychologically speaking. In the picaresque novel, derision, provocation, and constant games with the law, as in *Lazarillo de Tormes*, often hide a distance as well as a brutal acceptance bordering on submission. Having become a respectable husband at the end of the novel, Lázaro accepts with philosophic calm that his wife, the servant of the archpriest, should remain the latter's mistress—Lázaro's world is too narrow, unlike that of Cervantes, to allow for a dream of freely chosen love or even nostalgia for an inner world, which *pícaros* scorn as useless anyway. Sometimes the distance between desire and reality becomes so great, as in *Guzmán de Alfarache*, that it is transformed into an immense revolt. For this antihero, *desengaño* becomes both submission and permanent transgression, which comes up empty, although it has a healthy outlet in writing.

In mystical literature, on the other hand, *desengaño* comes with a flight into the backcountry of subjectivity and inner life in order to recreate another world through prayer and writing, a world that is invisible but truer, that of the *El castillo interior*, secret and indestructible, a castle of the soul "all of diamond and clear crystal," as Teresa of Avila put it. She is, indeed, a great *desengañada*, but one whose desire never steered her wrong: "Déjanla [el alma] no solamente desengañada de lo que la falsa imaginación le ofrecía, sino tan ansiosa del bien, que vuela luego a él con deseo que hierve" (It [the soul] remains not only *desengañada* with what the false imagination offered it, but so avid for the good that it flies toward it boiling with desire; L. de León, dedication of *Obras Sta. Teresa*, quoted in RT: *Diccionario de construcción y regimen de la lengua castellana*).

III. *Desengaño* and Desire to Live in *Don Quixote*

Américo Castro was one of the first to point out the link between the eroticism of mystical texts and that of Renaissance pastoral literature, which is so present in Cervantes's novel. In *Don Quixote* (pt. 1, chap. 14), the praise of *desengaño* belongs first to a woman. The shepherdess Marcela, having chosen, "in order to be able to live free, the solitude of the countryside," refuses all blame for the suicide of her lover. She claims to have always opposed the hope that sharpens desire with the *desengaño* that disabuses. On her lips, *desengaño* becomes knowledge of the absolute freedom of the object of desire; in other words, recognition and acceptance of her independence: "Those whom I have made amorous by my appearance, I have disabused with my words" (A los que he enamorado con la vista he desengañado con las palabras). A tragic knowledge for Marcela's suitors, blinded by her beauty and their own desire; an unacceptable knowledge to which Grisóstomo prefers death; a knowledge that the pretty shepherdess nonetheless defends until the end, refusing to confuse the truth of her desire—the cruel absence of reciprocity between men and women; that is, *desengaño*—with contempt: "Setting someone straight should not be taken for disdain" (Que los desengaños no se han de tomar en cuenta de desdenes).

As with Marcela, the desire for life on the part of the knight errant and his squire is all the greater given the extent of the *desengaño*. Sancho, having been the governor of the imaginary island of Barataria and disappointed to learn that the dream of power was just a lack of freedom, feels a *desengaño* that is not at all bitter. It resembles, rather, a strong reassurance of feeling truly alive; stripped, Sancho feels his existence: "Desnudo nací, desnudo me hallo, ni pierdo ni gano" (I was born naked, and now find myself naked; I neither lose nor win; pt. 2, chap. 57). This book in which "Spain finds itself ceaselessly mirrored" (Cassou, Introduction) is also the work of a descendant of converted Jews, to whom Philip II twice refused the post in the Indies for which Cervantes pleaded. Only those who could prove their "Christian blood" had the right to such posts. Cervantes, like the majority of mystics and picaresque authors, invented points of reference other than the Church and social power to communicate the brutal conflict between dream and reality. Don Quixote dies of it—we do not know whether he dies "of melancholy [*melancolía*], of having been defeated, or of the will of Heaven" (pt. 2, chap. 74)—but Cervantes writes his own *Don Quixote* through to the end, despite the existence of the fake version by Alonso Fernández de Avellaneda. The term *desengaño* appears 357 times in the two parts of the novel. As if *desengaño* had become the bearer of an extraordinary life force, in the dedication of *The Trials of Persiles and Sigismunda*, which was written a few days before his death, Cervantes claims to live only through that desire: "Ayer me dieron la extremaunción y hoy escribo ésta; el tiempo es breve, las ansias crecen, las esperanzas menguan y, con todo esto, llevo la vida sobre el deseo que tengo de vivir" (Yesterday they gave me extreme unction and today I'm writing this. Time is short, my agony waxes while hope wanes, and yet despite all this, my desire to live keeps me alive).

In *Don Quixote*, *desengaño* leads to a new richness, one that lies beyond good and evil, since dogmas and moral categories have disappeared in favor of writing that seeks neither to prove nor to convince but rather prefers to be a pure art of life. Further, the exceptional and fundamental feature of this art is that it is completely lacking in desire for any kind of religious solution. All that remains is fiction, dreams, nostalgia, anxiety, pleasure, and above all, a great need for true, genuine life—"la verdad adelgaza y no quiebra" (truth can be reduced to a thread but does not break; pt. 2, chap. 10).

In the novel, life away from the court and big cities is made up of pleasure in the simplest things—Sancho and Don Quixote, both alone and together, often improvise delicious lunches on the grass by the side of the road, ones that would make the princes of the Earth die of envy. It also contains the most fantastical and unreal elements, like the dream of the cave of Montesinos, which resembles a Platonic myth (pt. 2, chaps. 22 and 23). And then again, life is made up of words as alive as anything: words read in books of chivalry; the words written by the author, Miguel de Cervantes, and by the Arab narrator of the second part, Cide Hamete Benengeli; the words translated by a Christian for the author; and also spoken words, usually reported by a witness of the countless characters who come and go and are transformed over the course of the story—all these words are there to indicate a radical alliance with the elements of life, including the most frightening ones, the most extravagant one, the craziest ones. And so *desengaño*, rather than taking the form of bitterness or escape, becomes a pure complicity with the adventure of living, painful or happy depending on the course of events. It is as though all these words of life and literature existed only for the sake of giving the most beautiful form possible to the experience of *desengaño*, one that is found especially in the gap between desire and reality and from which fiction is born—and for Sancho and Don Quixote, the space in which they can breathe. And it allows desire, if it cannot reach its object, at least to come back to itself after its long travels (pt. 2, chap. 72).

IV. Gracián and the Strategy of *Desengaño*

The cycle of *desengaño* was completed at the end of the baroque era in Spain with a triumphant Catholic form that was practically official: the Jesuit Gracián responded to *desengaño* with a strategy of stagecraft and manipulation, praising appearance as the sole reality. With Gracián, we are practically at the other end of the spectrum from picaresque and mystical *desengaño* and much closer to a kind of disillusionment that comes from perfect courtly duplicity. The bitter lightness of picaresque *desengaño* and the mystical audacity that consists in inventing an internal world to respond to the *desengaño* that comes from the world as it is become in this context the construction of a much weightier kind of staging, where the difference between being and seeming comes only in flashes before disappearing entirely in favor of the idea that being consists in nothing other than seeming—and in obedience to the rules of the court: "Man without illusions, wise Christian. Philosopher courtier: but without appearing so, let alone affecting it." (Varón desengañado, cristiano sabio. Cortesano filósofo: mas no parecerlo; menos afectarlo; *Art of Worldly Wisdom*, §100).

A rebel in his own bizarre way, Gracián spent half of his time in trouble with the Society of Jesus. Ignoring the interdictions, he went so far as to publish his books at his own expense—in particular the last parts of the *Criticón* (1653 and 1657), which he had printed without the slightest authorization and only partially hiding his identity—before later returning to the fold, which he had never completely left. For this "Christian" disciple of Machiavelli, a Hobbesian before his time, a defender of the power that comes with secrecy and dissimulation who was convinced of the need to manipulate in order to survive, and an ambitious connoisseur of the social passions that he dared to expose—for him, *desengaño* became a weapon, a projectile, an explosive destined to trap the naïve and the imprudent. The weapon became invisible, and he practically turned it on himself toward the end of his life by proclaiming his obedience to the law of the double life (which Pascal considered Jesuitical) and by transforming his initial disillusionment into a need for constant calculation, an infinite casuistry, in order to escape the threat of death lurking at all times:

A breast without a secret is an open letter. Where there is a solid foundation secrets can be kept profound: there are spacious cellars where things of moment may be hid. Reticence springs from self-control, and to control oneself in this is true triumph. You must pay ransom to each you tell. The security of wisdom consists in temperance in the inner man. The risk that reticence runs lies in the cross-questioning of others, in the use of contradiction to worm out secrets, in the darts of irony: to avoid these, the prudent become more reticent than before. What must be done need not be said, and what must be said need not be done.

(Gracián, *Art of Worldly Wisdom*)

Desengaño enjoyed a resurgence with Romanticism, this time characterizing the disappointments and sufferings of love, politics, and history, in the spirit of the times. Originally, however, the underground complexity of *desengaño* developed on the side of the very ones who, "disabused" and "disenchanted" because of their banishment by a hostile society, often in highly marginalized situations—whether in prison like Luis de Léon or Cervantes or, like Gracián, in the heart of one of the most powerful institutions of the Spanish Counter-Reformation, in relation to which he remained independent and dissident— invented other worlds and alternative pathways, which are still present in the language of today, to communicate this experience and transform it through writing.

Mercedes Allendesalazar

BIBLIOGRAPHY

Alemán, Mateo. *The Life of Guzman d'Alfarache; or, The Spanish Rogue. To Which Is Added, the Celebrated Tragi-comedy, Celestina.* 2 vol. Reprint, London: Constable, 1924. First published in 1707–8.

Baruzi, Jean. *Luis de León, interprète du livre de Job.* Paris: Presses Universitaires de France, 1966.

Cassou, Jean. Introduction to *L'ingénieux hidalgo Don Quichotte de la Manche*, by Miguel Cervantes. Paris: Gallimard, 1934.

Castro, Américo. *Cervantes y los castisimos españoles.* Madrid: Alianza Editorial, 1974. First published in 1966.

———. *De la edad conflictiva.* Madrid: Taurus, 1976. First published in 1961.

———. *Hacia Cervantes.* Madrid: Taurus, 1967. First published in 1957.

———. *El pensamiento de Cervantes.* Barcelona: Editorial Noguer, 1972. First published in 1925.

———. *Teresa la Santa y otros ensayos.* Madrid: Alianza Editorial, 1971. First published in 1929.

Cervantes, Miguel de. *Don Quixote.* Translated and edited by J. Rutherford. London: Penguin Classics, 2003.

———. *The Trials of Persiles and Sigismunda.* Translated by C. R. Weller and C. A. Colahan. Reprint, Indianapolis, IN: Hackett, 2009.

Criado del Val, Manuel. "Santa Teresa de Jesús en la granpolémica española: Mística frente e picaresca." *Revista de Espiritualidad* 22 (1963): 377–84.

Gracián, Baltasar. *The Art of Worldly Wisdom.* Translated by Christopher Maurer. New York: Doubleday, 1991.

The Life and Adventures of Lazarillo de Tormes. Translated by T. Roscoe. London: J. C. Nimmo and Bain, 1881.

Pelegrín, Benito. *Ethique et esthétique du baroque: L'espace jésuitique de Baltasar Gracián.* Arles, Fr.: Actes Sud, 1985.

Rojas, Fernando de. *The Celestina: A Novel in Dialogue.* Translated by L. B. Simpson. Berkeley: University of California Press, 1955.

Rosales, Luis. *El sentimiento del desengaño en la poesía barroca.* Madrid: Ediciones de cultura hispánica, 1966.

Rosset, Clément. Appendix 2 of *Le choix des mots.* Paris: Minuit, 1995.

Teresa of Avila. *The Complete Works of Saint Teresa of Jesus.* Translated and edited by E. A. Peers. London: Sheed & Ward, 1950.

Wardropper, Bruce W. *Siglos de oro: Barroco.* Historia y crítica de la literatura español, under the direction of Francisco Rico. Barcelona: Editorial Crítica, Grijalbo, 1983.

DÉSINVOLTURE

Désinvolture is one of the possible translations of the Italian *sprezzatura*, introduced by Baldassare Castiglione in *The Book of the Courtier* (1528), where it relates to Italian thinking about civility and politeness.

See SPREZZATURA; see also *CIVILITY, GRACE,* ITALIAN, LEGGIADRIA, *STYLE.*

DESIRE

The etymology of "desire" is highly informative. The word comes from the Latin *desiderare*, composed of the privative *de-* and *sidus, sideris* (star). Thought to be an ancient term from divinatory or maritime language, *desiderare* literally means "to stop seeing the star," "to condemn the absence of, to miss," while *considerare* means "to see the star," "to examine with care or respect."

The term appears here first insofar as it is relevant to the vocabulary of psychoanalysis, and more precisely, as one of the received translations of the Freudian *Wunsch*: see WUNSCH and DRIVE (especially DRIVE, Box 2). Cf. ES, UNCONSCIOUS.

More widely, it is part of a variety of networks:

1. The network of absence and satisfaction, of lack and plenty: see PLEASURE as well as GLÜCK (cf. *HAPPINESS*) and *MALAISE*; cf. *ACT.*
2. The network of love, including sexual love, and passion: see LOVE, PATHOS (cf. *PASSION*), TALENT, and cf. GENDER, GESCHLECHT, SEX.
3. The oppositional network of freedom and the will: see *LIBERTY* [ELEUTHERIA], WILL, WILLKÜR.
4. The network of the powers of the soul: see SOUL, GOGO; cf. I/ME/MYSELF, GEMÜT.

➤ GOÛT, INTENTION, MADNESS

DESSEIN

Dessein is, along with *dessin*, one of the received translations of the Italian *disegno*. Eighteenth-century French broke with Italian tradition and, like German and English, separated the semantic fields of *dessein* and *dessin*. See DISEGNO and *DESSIN*; cf. CONCETTO and LEGGIADRIA.

Nevertheless, *disegno* is to be thought of alongside "design," which not only means "drawing" (*dessin*) but also "the ability to grasp patterns"; see STRUCTURE, IV.

On the importance of *dessein* for aesthetics, see also GENIUS, INGENIUM, MANIERA, MIMÊSIS, TABLEAU.

For the relation between *dessein* and finality, see *DESTINY* and especially KÊR, Box 1; for *boulê* [βουλή], the design of Zeus, see OIKONOMIA and TALAṬṬUF; HISTORIA UNIVERSALIS; cf. PRINCIPLE.

On the relation between design, intelligence, and moral action, see AGENCY, INTENTION, MÊTIS, PHRONÊSIS, POSTUPOK, PRAXIS, *WISDOM,* VIRTÙ, WILL.

➤ *IDEA*, SENSE

DESSIN

Dessin is, along with *dessein*—from which it diverges around 1750—one of the received translations of the Italian *disegno.* See DISEGNO and *DESSEIN.* Cf. CONCETTO and LEGGIADRIA.

The term is similar to "design," which means not only "drawing" (*dessin*) but also the "ability to grasp patterns"; see STRUCTURE, IV.

See also, for the role of *dessin* in aesthetics, MANIERA, MIMÊSIS, TABLEAU.

DESTINY

The use of "destiny," from the Latin *destinare* (to fix, to subject), is in Romance languages one of the ways in which we designate the part of what happens to us that escapes us or is not in our power. The terminological networks of Greek and German are especially well furnished in this regard.

I. The Important Constellations

A. The fortune of Greek representations

The Greek words related to the idea of destiny are numerous, and they carry images and representations along with them that are always present: death, one's lot, thread, linkage, constraint, completion, suspense. See KÊR [MOIRA, AISA, HEIMARMENÊ, ANAGKÊ, PEPRÔMENÊ, TUCHÊ]. While *fortuna* translates the occurrences characteristic of *tuchê* [τύχη] (see KÊR, Box 3, and VIRTÙ, I), the Latin *fatum*, from *fari* (to speak) opens up another paradigm (see KÊR, I.C; see also PORTUGUESE, Box 1). See also DAIMÔN, THEMIS.

B. Calling, destination, historicity

In German, Heidegger brings out the connotations belonging to *Schicksal* in which determinism and history are interwoven. See SCHICKSAL; cf. EREIGNIS, GESCHICHTLICH. The network includes *Verhängnis* (suspense, in the Stoïc sense of *heimarmenê* [εἱμαρμένη]), and *Bestimmung*, which opens up a new swath of terminology related to call and response (see BERUF, STIMMUNG, *VOCATION*) and to determinism. See also ES GIBT, HISTORY, *TO BE*.

II. Destiny, Freedom, and Necessity

1. "Destiny" relates to necessity, whatever its nature may be, reasoning or divine decision, the natural or cosmological course of events that controls human life and therefore expresses determinism, finality, and freedom. See *LIBERTY* [ELEUTHERIA, Box 2; SVOBODA], WILL.
2. For the relationship between God and humans, see especially *ALLIANCE* [BERÎT, PIETAS, RELIGIO, SOBORNOST'], BELIEF, DAIMÔN, DEVIL, GOD, *HUMANITY*.
3. For causality, see EPISTEMOLOGY, FORCE, NATURE, PRINCIPLE, *THING, WORLD*. For probability and chance, see CHANCE and KÊR, Box 2.
4. For human life, see *MALAISE, LIFE* [AIÔN, ANIMAL, DASEIN, ERLEBEN].
5. For the relationship between necessity, freedom, and moral action, see GLÜCK, MORALS, POSTUPOK, PRAXIS, *PRUDENCE,* VIRTÙ.
6. It is also possible to imagine other ways, referring to humans themselves, of theorizing that part of human life that escapes us; see DRIVE, ES, UNCONSCIOUS, VERNEINUNG; cf. GENDER, GESCHLECHT, *MALAISE,* PATHOS, SEX.

➤ LAW, PERFECTIBILITY, *PROGRESS,* SECULARIZATION

DEVIL

FRENCH	*diable*
GERMAN	*Teufel*
GREEK	*diabolos* [διάβολος], *daimôn* [δαίμων]
HEBREW	*sāṭān* [שָׂטָן]
ITALIAN	*diavolo, demonio, demone*
LATIN	*diabolus, daemon*
SPANISH	*diablo*

➤ DAIMÔN, DUENDE, GOD, GOOD/EVIL, *IMAGE* [EIDÔLON], INGENIUM, MADNESS, PLEASURE, *RUSE*

Within the theologies and demonologies of the different religious and philosophical systems of the East and the West, we find questions such as that of whether, if they accord individual existence and power to an agent of Evil, that agent is fully autonomous (as in dualist systems) from the principle of Good or, on the contrary, acts only under the power of the latter, the supreme god who alone is eternal, to whom all evil influence in the world is subordinate. There follow questions concerning the relationship between the Prince of Evil and the lesser demons who function as his instruments. Regardless of the possible answers to these questions, the Evil One is designated in most European languages by reference to the *daimôn* [δαίμων] of Greek or Latin antiquity, as well as to the Semitic (*sāṭān* [שָׂטָן] in Hebrew, *šayṭān* [شيطان] in Arabic, and *satanas* [Σατανᾶς] in Greek), designated by the name of *diabolos* [διάβολος] in the Greek Bible. Thus, in French, Satan may be called Diable or Démon indifferently (with a variety of synonyms). In German, on the other hand, the two semantic paths remain distinct. The second, that of *daimôn* [see DAIMÔN] or "demonic" remains clearly detached from that of *diabolos,* that is, what we understand by the words "diabolical" or "satanic."

I. From Satan to the Devil

The Hebrew name *sāṭān* is given to the Prince of Demons in the Hebrew Bible, as well as the New Testament and the Qu'ran. The Septuagint translates the name by the Greek noun *diabolos* [διάβολος], created from *diaballein* [διαβάλλειν] (*ballein* [βάλλειν], "to throw," "to push"; *dia* [δια], "between," "across," "from one end to the other"; hence "to divide," "to separate," "to accuse," "to slander"). The biblical Satan (from the root *satan*, derived from the Akkadian *sattânu*, which means "to attack," "to urinate on," "to fight") is named as "the adversary" (cf. 2 Sm 19:23; 1 Kgs 5:18; 11:14, 23, 25) or "the accuser [before a tribunal], the slanderer, the denigrator" (cf. Ps 109:6). But in Job 1:6, as well as Zechariah 3:1–2, this name, preceded by an article, is still only a common noun. It does not seem to become a proper noun until the first book of Chronicles, where it is said that "Satan rose" (21:1), behavior arising from pride.

In the Qu'ran, "Satan" is not at first a proper noun. It is used sometimes in the singular, *šayṭān* [شيطان], sometimes in the plural, *šayāṭîn* [شياطين], and usually with an article. *Al Šaytân* thus designates the Demon, while *al šayâṭîn* designates the various demons. *Satan* is the same word in Arabic and Hebrew, related to a verb meaning "to be separated [from the truth or divine mercy]". The Qu'ran also mentions this same Satan by the name of Iblis, which is related to the Greek *diabolos* and designates the rebel angel, head of the revolt against God and of unbelief: "And when we said to the angels 'Prostrate yourselves before Adam,' they all prostrated themselves except Satan, who hid his pride, refused and became an unbeliever" (2:32). The six other passages mentioning the name of Iblis in a similar context also describe him as an angel, cursed and fallen because of his disobedience, like the demon of the Jewish and Christian traditions. In effect, the three great monotheistic religions originally viewed the angels as members of a celestial court, then as messengers from the Most High, some of whom revolted against the divine order.

The spread of the Greek Septuagint among the early Christian communities led the holy writers and the church fathers to adopt the Greek *diabolos* and the Latin *diabolus* to indicate the Satan of the Hebrew texts. The book of Revelation (12:9) designates the evil spirit as "the *Diabolos* or the *Satanas* [Σατανᾶς]": "And the great dragon was cast out, that old serpent, called the Devil, and Satan, which deceiveth the whole world (of the *oikumene* [οἰκουμένη])." In the Gospel of John (8:44), Jesus tells his coreligionists at the height of a quarrel with them: "Ye are of your father the devil (*humeis ek tou patros tou diabolou este* [ὑμεῖς ἐκ τοῦ πατρὸς τοῦ διαβόλου ἐστὲ]; in the Vulgate, *vos ex patre diabolo estis*])." In the same way, Latin Christian literature, for example, Tertullian (*De anima*, 35), adopts the term *diabolus* from the Septuagint to designate Satan, even while giving a number of other names to the principle of evil, such as the Demon, the Adversary, the Tempter, the Father of Lies, the Prince of This World, the Antichrist, the Beast, the Clever One, the Prince of Darkness, Lucifer. In addition, the New Testament, the apocryphal Christian writings, and the church fathers use the term "demon" to designate fallen angels, as well as the pagan gods, which they call "the idols" (*eidôla* [εἴδωλα]: 1 Cor 12:2; cf. Septuagint, 4 Kgs 17:12).

▪ See Box 1.

Rabbinic and Talmudic Judaism could not accept the translation of the Bible by the Alexandrian diaspora without reservation, and remained faithful to the name of Satan (or Sammaël, the Angel of Death), mentioned, however, with the definite article. "The Satan" reigns, then, over a certain number of demons (*šēdîm* [שֵׁדִים]) described as "pernicious" (*mazzīqîm* [מַזִּיקִים]) by the Midrash and the Talmud, such as Beelzebub, Azazel (the personification of the desert into which the scapegoat is sent in the ritual of Yom Kippur), Belial (or Beliar), Asmodeus (the demon who kills in succession the first seven husbands of Sara, the future wife of the young Tobias), Behemoth, and Leviathan. We also find female demons in these writings, such as Lilith, Adam's first wife according to Rabbinic Judaism, or even the consort of Sammaël: according to the Targums and the midrashim, Sammaël was the serpent from Genesis 3 who seduced Eve, fathering Cain, henceforth known as the "son of the Devil." However, it is the Hellenistic tradition of *diabolos* that has been taken up in our current languages to name the Evil Angel, as we see with "devil," *diavolo* (Ital.), *diablo* (Sp.), and even with *Teufel* (Ger.), as well as the *Iblis* of the Qu'ranic tradition.

II. From the Slanderer to the Tempter

In the three monotheistic traditions, the Devil commands a legion of demons as his servants or instruments, so that it is difficult to tell from one text to another whether we are dealing with Satan himself or one of his acolytes. With the exception of the aforementioned passage in Chronicles, the Hebrew Bible generally refers indeterminately to a *satan* (or *diabolos*). It may be the same with the angel who becomes Job's accuser in the midst of his trials, before the tribunal of God. And even in the first part of Goethe's *Faust*, when the hero meets Mephistopheles (a name whose etymology is uncertain but recalls the Low Latin adjective *mephiticus*,

---

1

Lucifer

The name Lucifer (Lat. "bringer of light"), which designated the planet Venus among the ancients, was incidentally attributed in the New Testament to Christ himself, who is there referred to, according to Ecclesiastes (50:6), as *Stella matutina*. The name remains, however, in the early centuries of the church and under the persistent influence of Judaism, one of the names of Satan. Beginning with Saint Jerome and especially in the Middle Ages, the Prince of Demons comes to be assimilated, as in Dante (*Inferno*, 31, 143; 34, 89; etc.), with the figure of the fallen angel. The source is no doubt the biblical passage in Isaiah on the fall of the king of Babylon, either Nebuchadnezzar or Nabonidus, or perhaps another Assyrian tyrant, either Sargon or Sennacherib:

> How art thou fallen from heaven, O Lucifer, son of the morning! [how] art thou cut down to the ground, which didst weaken the nations!
> For thou hast said in thine heart, I will ascend into heaven, I will exalt my throne above the stars of God: I will sit also upon the mount of the congregation, in the sides of the north.... Yet thou shalt be brought down to hell, to the sides of the pit.
>
> Isaiah 14:12–15.

Thus, for Christianity, Lucifer, the angel of light, becomes Satan through his revolt against God. According to some esoteric traditions, this revolt took place in the framework of a cosmic battle.

"exhaling a pestilential and harmful odor"), he only sees him as "the frozen fist of the Devil [*die kalte Teufelsfaust*]," that is, one of the many "negating spirits" constituting an anonymous infernal society. However, the texts of the New Testament and the Jewish and Christian apocrypha, as well as the Mishna and the Talmud, designate the Devil more and more frequently by his proper name, presenting him most of all as the Tempter (Lat., *temptator*; in Gr., *ho peirazôn* [ὁ πειράζων]; in Hebrew, the equivalent would be *massâh* [מַסָּה], which means "test"; cf. Ex 17:7). In this way, according to Matthew 4:1–3, "was Jesus led up of the Spirit into the wilderness to be tempted of the devil [*peirasthênai hupo tou diabolou* (πειρασθῆναι ὑπὸ τοῦ διαβόλου)]. . . . And when the tempter came to him, he said. . . ."

The fact that the Devil goes from being the "accuser" to being the "tempter" or "seducer" may be explained by the emphasis on the notion of envy or jealousy (*phthonos* [φθόνος] in the Septuagint; *invidia* in the Vulgate). That notion is in fact not far from some of the recognized meanings of the Hebraic *sāṭān*, notably that of the denigrator, the malevolent, the divider. It is envy that prompts the Evil One to introduce death into the world (Wis 2:24), and to persuade Eve to disobey and eat the forbidden fruit, as Flavius Joseph (*Antiquities of the Jews*, 1.1–4) and especially Philo of Alexandria (*De opificio mundi*, §151–69; *De agricultura*, §95–110) point out. According to the *De opificio mundi*, it is because he loves pleasure (*philêdonos* [φιλήδονος]), especially pleasures of the senses (*aisthêsis* [αἴσθησις]), that man may be tempted by the serpent, the personification of sensual pleasure and its charms (*hêdonê sumbolon* [ἡδονὴ σύμβολον]): "It is said of old the venomous reptile . . . having one day approached the wife of the first man, reproached her for her slowness of mind . . . since she postponed and delayed gathering the most beautiful fruit to be seen, the most pleasant to taste [*hêdiston* (ἥδιστον), superlative of *hêdus* (ἡδύς), pleasant], and besides the most useful, since, thanks to it, she could know good and evil." For the serpent's part, it is not a matter of persuading (*peirô* [πειρῶ]) his victim, but of tempting, in the sense taken on by the Greek *peirazô* [πειράζω] (derived from *peira* [πεῖρα], "test") in the Bible and the New Testament. Thus, Jesus says in his agony, "Pray, that ye enter not into temptation" (*eis peirasmon* [εἰς πείρασμον]) (Lk 22:40), just as the prayer that he teaches his disciples, the Our Father, ends with the phrase "And lead us not into temptation" (*eis peirasmon* [εἰς πείρασμον]) (Lk 11:4).

Neither Josephus nor Philo identifies the serpent-tempter with the Devil himself. The genre of allegory, however, which, especially in Alexandrian literature, consists of "philosophizing by symbols," provides the basis for a psychotheology that turns the serpent into a symbol, not for just any demon, but for the Tempter himself. Under the aspect of a serpent, portrayed here in his capacity as a seducer of the feminine soul (by the intervention of sensation or *aisthêsis*), the Tempter here represents according to the Jewish and Christian traditions the Devil's role as the "Counselor of Man" with regard to perversity. The role of *sumboulos* alluded to by Philo in his *De agricultura* (§97) may be an allusion, though attenuated and unique to Philo, to the *diabolos* of the Septuagint: "counselor of man [*sumboulos anthrôpou*

(σύμβουλος ἀνθρώπου)] who enjoys ruining what is better than him."

- See Box 2.

III. Devil or Demon?

While "Devil" and "Demon" seem to function as equivalents in Christian theology or ordinary ways of speaking, the same cannot be said for the German *Teufel* and *Dämon*. The latter, which is synonymous with *Unhold* (malevolent or harmful spirit—antonymous with *hold*, "gracious," "charming"), corresponds to the ancient idea of a *daimôn* [δαίμων] in the sense of a divinity or personal spirit, even a goblin, good or bad. The religious sense of "demon," on the other hand, can only be adequately rendered by *Teufel*. Thus, Freud's work entitled "Eine Teufelneurose im Siebzehnten Jahrhundert" was translated into French in 1933 by M. Bonaparte and E. Marty as "Une névrose *démoniaque*," then in 1985, in a new edition by J.-B. Pontalis, as "Une névrose *diabolique*"—the two translations being semantically identical. In the reverse case, however, the expressions *névrose démoniaque* and *névrose diabolique*, when they relate to a pact between a person and the Devil (*Teufelsbund* or *Teufelspakt*), as they do in Freud's work, would both be translated into German as *Teufelsneurose* rather than *Dämonsneurose*—the latter could possibly refer to a case of pathological enthusiasm.

In English, the Devil is also called the "Evil One" or the "Fiend." "Fiend," like "demon," has rather the same sense as *Dämon* in German; in Shakespeare's *The Merchant of Venice*, Lancelot calls Shylock "the fiend who is the devil himself." The different contemporary languages use the terms "devil" and "demon" in derivative senses which seem to downplay or exorcise the malignance retained by these other terms. Thus, in French and English we find various locutions that involve sympathy mixed with indulgence or admiration (*petit diable*, *pauvre diable*, *bon diable*, *un diable d'homme*, little devil, poor devil, the devil of a time, the devil's luck), a nuance of rejection or repulsion (*envoyer au diable*, *aller au diable*, go to the devil), obsessions or volatile situations (*avoir le diable au corps*, *tirer le diable par la queue*, *démon de midi*, *démon de jeu*, face one's demons, needs must when the devil drives). These generally have to do with metaphorical senses whose extreme character is indicative of the personality of the possessed (Ger. *besessen*) or the "energumen" (*energumenos*, formed by the early Christian writers from the passive of *energein* [ἐνέργειν] to indicate someone who is "worked on" by an evil spirit, but also, in the first instance, someone who is struck with a physical disability preventing him from being baptized). Along these lines, we find Dostoyevsky's novel translated into French with the title *Les possédés* (and in English, *The Possessed*), even though the novel deals precisely with demons—the book cites a passage from the Gospel of Luke (8:32–36) in which Jesus drives a multitude of tormenting spirits from the body of a victim, and allows them to enter a herd of pigs, which then throw themselves into a nearby lake and drown.

In fact, while the French *diable*, the Latin *diabolus*, the Italian *diavolo*, the English "devil," and the German *Teufel* may have figurative meanings like those listed above (not to mention interjections like *que diantre* invented in order

2

Satan the Contradictor as "historical being" according to Schelling

➤ OIKONOMIA, SUBLIME

Schelling develops his conception of the figure of Satan, and particularly "of his eminent place and function" in the history of Christianity, in his *Philosophy of Revelation* (especially Lesson XXXIII). He contests the standard representation of the Prince of Shadows common to pagan as well as Jewish mythology, according to which he is an angel, originally good, a spirit created as an individual, who wished to rise above God, and was for this reason cast down, bringing the world and humanity down along the way. Schelling clarifies straightaway that this act of opposition, which is peculiar to him, does not diminish Satan's dignity in any way, but rather ascribes to him a great reality and a more pre-eminent significance, although these are inscribed in determinate moments of the history of salvation.

He notes that in the Hebrew Bible, the name of Satan in the first instance refers only to the notion of "contradictor in general," and then—only with the article—to that of a determinate contradictor, as when, for example, said Satan argues with Yahweh concerning the suffering Job. The Hebrew verb *saṭan* [שָׂטַן] in effect has the very general meaning of contradicting someone or opposing an undertaking. Thus, in the story of Balaam (Num 22:22), "when the Lord's Angel places himself in his path in order to 'resist' him and hold him back, the Hebrew

uses the verb *saṭan*, which consequently means nothing more than 'to hold back,' to thwart or hinder a movement. The Hebrew noun was translated into Greek as *diabolos* [διάβολος], from *diaballein* [διαβάλλειν], which means nothing more than 'interjicere se ad obstinendum,' whence our German word *Teufel*." The same Greek word "is also originally used in a completely general way . . . with regard to any *contrarium*, to anything by which one is led astray" (*Philosophy of Revelation*).

This role of Contradictor, however, is one that Satan exercises most notably with regard to Christ himself. The Scripture informs us that a *kingdom* belongs to this adversary, just as one belongs to Christ, even if the former's is "opposed to and resistant to that of Christ." Thus, Satan "finds himself to a certain extent placed on the same footing as Christ, even if it is as a contradictor, as he whose reign and works Christ has come to destroy." It follows that a certain sublimity (*Erhabenheit*) is attributed to him, just as to Christ, in such a way that this elevation entitles him, according to a large part of the New Testament, to be considered the prime author of evil. In his role as master of such a kingdom he "appears . . . as a principle belonging to the divine economy" and is recognized by God as such. Facing God, Satan places himself at determinate moments as the great

skeptic and contradictor who casts doubt on all belief, notably in the creation, through the seduction he works on the first man and in his debate with God regarding the tests of Job.

As a part of the divine economy, Satan is thus defined, according to Schelling, as a "historical being" who one day sees his work completed. "His mission ends and, with it, his power," which consisted in "maintaining contradiction, malediction, discord and disunity," but which needed to be broken by Christ and by the triumph of the cause of God (*Sache Gottes*). Until that time, "it is a great power, necessary to the final glorification of God, and which for this reason must be neither criticized nor held in contempt." Such a representation of Satan as a principle of the divine economy that is *necessary* at a given time thus breaks with the traditional mythological representations, which persist in seeing in this Contradictor an absolutely bad (although created) principle of self, universal and as eternal as God himself.

BIBLIOGRAPHY

Schelling, Friedrich W. J. von. *Philosophie der Offenbarung*. Frankfurt: Suhrkamp, 1977. Translation by V. C. Hayes: *Schelling's Philosophy of Mythology and Revelation*. Armidale, NSW: Australian Association for the Study of Religions, 1995.

to avoid naming the Unnamable One directly), those terms which, in contemporary languages, are derived from the Greek *daimôn* or the Latin *daemon* are not used to refer to the person of the biblical Satan himself, not even to evil spirits when it is a matter of demons in the extended, religious sense. For example, with regard to those among them who wish, according to Luke the Evangelist, to enter the herd of pigs, Luther invariably translates the Greek plural *daimonia* [δαιμόνια] (or *polla daimonia* [πολλὰ δαιμόνια]) by *Teufee* (or *viel Teufee*). As a result, in Anglo-Saxon languages, the "demonic" (a term known by 1422, and no doubt borrowed from the Greek *daimonikos* [δαιμονικός], an adjective that means "possessed by a god" in Clement of Alexandria) remains distinct from what is called in French the *démoniaque* (demoniacal). This is still the case in German, where *démoniaque* would be translated as *teuflisch* (or *satanisch*), and *démonique* as *dämonisch*.

The fact that Satan is known in French, on the other hand, as either "le Démon" or "le Diable," unlike in other languages (especially Anglo-Saxon ones), seems to be due to the distance these other languages have acquired from ecclesiastical vocabulary. In Jewish and Christian writings, there is no semantic difference between Satan (Hellenized as *Satanas*

[Σατανᾶς]) and *diabolos*. The latter term is more common in the Septuagint, but it is found with equal frequency as *Satanas* in the New Testament. The Alexandrian Bible, however, also gives the name of *daimonia* (neuter plural of the adjective *daimonios* [δαιμόνιος]) to the infernal spirits, such as Asmodeus (Tob 3:8). The same term is used in the New Testament (along with *pneumata* [πνεύματα]) to designate these harmful beings. The Vulgate and Church Latin translate *daimonion* by *daemonium*, but with the unique meaning of malevolent spirit, and with no trace of the ancient sense of divinity, guiding spirit, or inner voice. Considering in addition that the *daimôn* in Matthew 8:16 is a hapax in the New Testament, we can see that Christian demonology creates a turning point with regard to the Greek and Latin meaning of the term. Thus, in French, *demoygne* appears in the thirteenth century, and *démon* in the sixteenth, which corresponds to just such a change, whereas Anglo-Saxon languages, especially German, remain faithful to the primitive meaning of *daimôn*, as though they held back from fully adhering to this semantic transformation. Moreover, French, like Italian and other Romance languages, furnishes itself with the metonymy assimilating the "Démon" to the "Diable" of the Septuagint Bible.

In these languages, the title of Demon (in the singular) simply reinforces the authority of the leader over his agents and accomplices, the innumerable demons or demonesses and she-devils, among which popular, romantic, and religious imagination places a host of infernal spirits of varying degrees of lewdness: werewolves, incubi, succubi, ghouls (from the Arabic *ġūl* [غول], "demon"), vampires, and so on. In the eighteenth century, these satanic fiends were also called *oupires*, from the Russian *upyr'* [упырь]—and perhaps from the Turkish *uber*, "witch"—whence the first occurrence of the term in Europe, as the German *Vampir*. This monarchy of the Devil or the Demon at the head of a kingdom of evil was already present in Iranian dualism, but unknown in the majority of other Eastern cultures; it is explained by the monotheism on which it is based, in the medieval demonology of the religions of the Abrahamic tradition. Satan represents, in effect, the One God's antagonist, and is characterized in the image of his adversary. Nor is this uniqueness compromised when his medieval mask is removed, and he is transformed into the angelic lord of the revolt by the literary Satanism of the nineteenth century.

In reality, the role that Western imagination assigned to the Devil has, according to Freud, the same origin as that which it assigned to God—the antagonism between the two figures both derive from a single source, namely, the figure of the father. In his study of the "diabolical neurosis" of an Austrian painter in the seventeenth century, Freud shows that the Devil of Christian mythology originally constituted, with God, a single figure, that this unitary being was then divided into "two clearly contrasted opposites"—one good, the other bad—and finally, that this antagonism only reflects the ambivalence, in a cultural deployment, which affects the paternal figure himself. Thus the Devil is "the substitute for the father," according to Freud, and the vocabulary of demonology takes up the tyrannical and cruel aspects of the father figure. What made the troubles of Freud's Austrian painter so memorable was that he reinforced these aspects of the figure of the Devil in his nostalgia for his dead father, by way of a pact with Satan.

Charles Baladier

BIBLIOGRAPHY

The Apocryphal New Testament. Edited by J. K. Elliot. New York: Oxford University Press, 1993.

Browning, W.R.F. *A Dictionary of the Bible*. Oxford: Oxford University Press, 2004.

Citati, Pietro. *Goethe*. Translated by R. Rosenthal. New York: Dial Press, 1974.

Freud, Sigmund. "Ein Teufelneurose im Siebzehnten Jarhundert." *Imago* 9, 1.34; *GW*, vol. XIII, 317–53. Translation: "A Seventeenth-Century Demonological Neurosis." In *The Standard Edition of the Complete Psychological Works*, edited by J. Strachey, vol. XIX, 72–105. London: Hogarth Press, 1923.

Kirschschläger, W. "Satan et demons." In *Dictionnaire de la Bible. Supplément*, vol. 12. Paris: Letouzey, 1996.

Praz, Mario. *La carne, la morte e il diavolo nella letteratura romantica*. Firenza: Sansoni, 1966. Translation by A. Davidson: *The Romantic Agony*. London: Oxford University Press, 1933.

The Qur'an. Translated by M.A.S. Abdel Haleem. Oxford: Oxford University Press, 2008.

Russell, Jeffrey Burton. *The Devil: Perceptions of Evil from Antiquity to Primitive Christianity*. Ithaca, NY: Cornell University Press, 1977.

Satan, special issue of *Études carmélitaines*. Paris: Desclée de Brouwer, 1948.

Teyssèdre, Bernard. *Le Diable et l'enfer au temps de Jésus*. Paris: Albin Michel, 1985.

———. *Naissance du Diable: De Babylone aux grottes de la mer morte*. Paris: Albin Michel, 1985.

DIALECTIC

The history of "dialectic," of the understandings and reinterpretations, of the appraisals and reappraisals, of the term beginning with Plato, Aristotle, and the Stoics, and continuing through the modern age, would by itself be a good account of the history of philosophy. The word, however, travels across competing senses while itself remaining the same, starting with the Greek and by way of its Latin transliteration, through different European languages. For this reason, we will give only an indirect presentation of it here.

1. The Greek *dialektikê* [διαλεκτική] (classified as a *technê* [τέχνη], and sometimes as *epistêmê* [ἐπιστήμη], thus, the craft or science of dialectic) derives from *logos* [λόγος]. It refers to the art of discussion (*dia* [διά], from "dialogue") by question and answer, practiced by Socrates, and thus opposed to long discourses and Sophistic *epideixis* [ἐπίδειξις]; see SPEECH ACT, I. Plato invests the term with great significance; in his hands it designates the practice of philosophy itself, reaching up to the "ideas"; see SPECIES, Box 1, and BEAUTY, MIMÊSIS. For Aristotle it refers to a part of logic, related to the rhetoric of what is probable, in contrast with scientific demonstration; see DOXA. The Stoics bestow upon it the status of a science (and make it a virtue), dealing with language and reasoning, the true and the false, the signifier and the signified; see WORD, SIGNIFIER/SIGNIFIED, and BEGRIFF, Box 1. These terminological tensions among Aristotelianism, Stoicism, and Neoplatonism determine the complexity of medieval usage, notably visible in Augustine's *De dialectica*; see also PROPOSITION. On all of this, obviously, see LOGOS.

2. Beginning with a negative interpretation of Scholastic usage, according to which dialectic is a rhetorical exercise making use of subtleties in formal logic (see *SOPHISM*), the moderns, from Descartes to Kant, see in dialectic an appearance of logic or a logic of appearance; on "transcendental dialectic," the logic of transcendental appearance, see ERSCHEINUNG. The positive re-evaluation is related to the Hegelian and Marxist analysis of the processes at work in the history of being and thought; see AUFHEBEN, PLASTICITY, and GERMAN, ATTUALITÀ, COMBINATION AND CONCEPTUALIZATION, PRAXIS, RUSSIAN, II; cf. *IDENTITY*. *Dialectic* is part of cutting-edge philosophical metadiscourse today; see, for example, CONSCIOUSNESS or CONTINUITET.

▶ EPISTEMOLOGY, OIKONOMIA, PRINCIPLE, SUBJECT, TERM, WORK

DICHTUNG (GERMAN)

ENGLISH   literature, poetry, fiction
FRENCH   *littérature, poésie, fiction, invention, affabulation*

▶ *POETRY*, and ERZÄHLEN, *FICTION*, HISTORY, LOGOS, PRAXIS, SPEECH ACT, WORK

The German word *Dichtung* does not, properly speaking, have an equivalent in other European languages, except for those Scandinavian languages that borrowed it. To translate it, English and French must resort to the words "literature" (*littérature*), "poetry" (*poésie*), or more vaguely, "fiction" (*fiction*). These words certainly get close to the meaning of the German noun but do not nearly exhaust the multiple notions of semantic unrealities (invention, confabulation, poetry). The German language also has the terms *Literatur*, *Poesie*, and *Fiktion*—but *Dichtung*, while it participates in all of these, contains and goes beyond them. This German-specificity confers peculiar density upon *Dichtung*, a sort of closure that was well exploited in German discussions on language, from Herder—who played knowingly on the essentially German character of the word—to Heidegger. Further, in 1973 the Germanist K. Hamburger emphasized that the concept of *Dichtung* is "superior to that proposed by the terminology of other languages, and in the first instance, to the very concept of literature [*Literature*]." By *Dichtung*, the German language tends to define for itself a specific operation of thought and language. The proximity of *Dichtung* with *dicht* (dense, sealed) is therefore not the result of purely accidental homophony. *Dichtung* yields such a dense succession of strata of meaning that the word becomes effectively sealed off from other languages.

I. *Dichtung* and *Dichten*: The Natural Language of Humanity, between Literature, Poetry, and Fiction

Dichtung is derived from the verb *dichten*, which even in the Old High German period had two principal meanings. In the broad sense, firstly, *dichten* means to invent, to imagine, to make up—a meaning that may also have negative connotations. Close to *erdichten* in that regard, *dichten* thus means to invent in order to delude, or to imagine in order to deceive. In the narrow sense, on the other hand, the word refers to the action of conceiving a poem or text so that it may then be written down and read. According to this meaning, the word has a particular predilection for the domain of poetic creation and thus means to versify, to compose a poem (even if the application to prose is not ruled out).

From *dichten*, *Dichtung* inherited its semantic substance as well as its difficulties. Like the verb, the noun has at its core the complex relationship between fiction and reality. In a pejorative sense *Dichtung* relates to the idea of fallacious invention or confabulation, of lying. In a positive sense, however, the term designates the creation of a fictional world, invested with a singular truth. *Dichtung* evokes the creation of an imaginary universe, self-contained, produced by the power of invention of a single individual—the elaboration of an unreal space, in sum, but for all that no less veridical than concrete reality. In this sense *Dichtung* is intimately related to the romantic consecration of artworks. This meaning oscillates between the negative and positive kinds of virtuality of *Fiktion*, but a narrower meaning may be added to it. *Dichtung* may simply designate literary creation in the precise sense of the term, especially poetic creation, hence merging the terms *Literatur* and *Poesie*.

Even though *Dichtung* participates in these three meanings of *Literatur*, *Fiktion*, and *Poesie*, it has nonetheless continuously strived to distinguish itself from them by assimilating unique meanings, born of the historical and philosophical circumstances that created it. The term, in fact, is a recent creation. It is certainly attested from 1561 onward, but only in the 1770s does it make its real and imposing entrance into the German language, even though its verbal template, *dichten*, had existed for centuries (see RT: *Deutsches Wörterbuch*, vol. 2, s.v. "*dichte*" and "*Dichtung*"). Sulzer completely ignores the noun

in the *Allgemeine Theorie der schönen Künste* (General theory of the fine arts), and Adelung cites it as a "new term" in the first edition of his dictionary (see RT: *Versuch eines vollständingen grammatisch-kritischen Wörterbuches der hochdeutschen Mundart*, vol. 1, s.v. "*Dichtung*"). Herder gives us what is essentially the introduction of *Dichtung* to the German language—a paternity that also explains the unique aura that surrounds it. In his 1770 essay on the origin of language, Herder resorts to the hitherto unused word to refer to the faculty of poetic invention that presided over the first language of humanity—this original and natural language that preceded prose. *Dichtung* is "the natural language of all creatures [*Natursprache aller Geschöpfe*]," transposed into images according to which, to cite a later variation on the theme, its source lies in nature (*Über den Ursprung der Sprache*, *Sämtliche Werke*, vol. 5:¶ 56, 1772; *Über Bild*, *Dichtung und Fabel*, *Sämtliche Werke*, vol. 15:535ff., 1787). Beginning with its birth, then, the notion of *Dichtung* is invested with a triple meaning. It is poetic, original, and natural, to which qualities an ultimate one is added: it is authentic. An idea, in effect, consistently underlies the Herderian usages of the term: the fictional universe to which *Dichtung* relates is no less real than reality itself. It is not opposed to the sensible world but in fact, rather, is its "distillate"—a principle that is given hidden support by the lucky homophonic proximity of the term to the words *Dichte* and *dicht* (density, dense). The idea will be developed in a philosophical mode a little later by Kant (*Kritik der Urteilskraft*, 1790, §53) and then by Schlegel.

> The limit between science and art [*Wissenschaft und Kunst*], between the true and the beautiful, has at this point become so blurred that the certainty of the fixity of these eternal boundaries has been shaken practically everywhere. Philosophy creates poetry [*poetisiert*] and poetry [*Poesie*] philosophizes [*philosophiert*]: history [*Geschichte*] is treated as fiction [*Dichtung*], and the latter is treated as history.
>
> (Schlegel, *Über das Studium der griechischen Poesie* [1795])

■ See Box 1.

II. *Deutsche Dichtung* and *Französische Literatur*

Over the course of the nineteenth century, however, *Dichtung* quickly became loaded with heavy national associations. In a Germany seeking a national identity, it was easy to see how much could be wrought from this specifically German noun, rich in multiple semantic or homophonic connotations and, for these reasons, difficult to translate into other languages. *Dichtung* allowed the German language to refer to a specific mode of intellectual invention, whose products—literature, language, and poetry—became loaded with singular qualities: unmediated relations with nature, original naïveté, poetic inspiration, brilliance, and so on. The Herderian distinction between *Naturpoesie* and *Kunstpoesie*, partially directed against French classicism, was reinterpreted by posterity in the sense of an opposition between a *deutsche Dichtung* and a *französische Literatur*, with the Germanic *Dichtung* designating literary production blessed with originality and

1

Verum factum and poetic wisdom in Vico

➤ ACT, CIVILTÀ, CORSO, FICTION, GOD, HISTORIA UNIVERSALIS, ITALIAN, RELIGION, TRUTH

In *De antiquissima Italorum sapientia* (On the very ancient wisdom of the peoples of Italy), 1710, one of his first works, Vico affirms that in Latin, "verum et factum convertuntur" (the true and the fact are convertible), and as a consequence *verare* (to tell the truth) and *facere* have the same meaning: "it follows from this that God knows the physical things, and man the mathematical ones" (chap. 1). As early as 1709, in the discourse *De nostri temporis studiorum ratione* (The method of studies of our time), he had written that "the propositions of physics are merely likely," because God alone is able to know Nature, insofar as he created it: "we will demonstrate geometrical things, since we create them; if we could demonstrate physical things, we would create them" (chap. 4).

Vico has a positive use for this metaphysical and epistemological principle, which initially seems to condemn human knowledge to what is merely likely, reserving the title of "science" for mathematicians alone; he uses the principle as the basis of his *Principi di scienza nuova d'intorno alla comune natura delle nazioni* (Principles of the new science concerning the common nature of nations), the first edition of which dates from 1725 and the last, extensively revised, from 1744. In this last text he lays out, in effect, the foundations of the "new science," which he prides himself on having invented, in the following terms:

> But in this night of thick shadows that covers early antiquity, so far away from us, appears the eternal light which is never extinguished of this truth that one can in no way call into question: this civil world was certainly created by men, and as a result we may, because we must, find its principles in the modifications of our human mind itself. Whoever thinks about it can only be surprised to see how all the philosophers have spent their best efforts trying to acquire the science of the natural world, of which God alone, since he created it, possesses the science, and how they have neglected to consider the world of nations, or the civil world, of which men, since they created it, may acquire the science. (*Principles of the new science*, 1744, § 331)

What is the meaning of this famous claim, which has been interpreted in a variety of ways and in which Michelet and many others have wished to discover a "Promethean" proclamation? In fact, Vico's claim is unequivocal: the principles of the world made by man must be sought in the "modifications of [the]

human mind." Classically, these modifications are, according to Vico, the modes of the thinking substance—sensation, imagination, and understanding. Vico's originality consists in placing these modes in order, both chronological and logical, in the evolution of humanity (Vico speaks rather of "nations"), as they are manifested and developed in the individual. This means that the fully human man, whose reason is "fully developed" and whose *umanità* is fully realized, has not always existed. He was preceded, rather, and prepared by a man who was practically entirely animal, "immersed in the body," given only to sensation, only to passion, then by a man dominated by a powerful imagination (*fantasia*), that is, a function that is still largely dependent on the body. Vico is primarily interested in this "imaginative" moment, which Descartes and his successors refused to accept, and does not rest with merely rehabilitating the imagination; he gives it a primary role, "poetic," properly speaking—that is, "creative"—in the genesis of the institutions that characterize the humanity of all nations:

> The first men of the pagan nations, as the children of the nascent human race . . . created things by imagining them, which is why they were called "poets," which in Greek means "creators." (Ibid., § 376)

Vico devotes Book II of the *New Science*, entitled *On Poetic Wisdom*, to this "poetic" creation of things. What does this creation, discussion of which occupies almost half the book, consist in? To analyze what we call the "primitive mentality," he uses tools provided by classical poetics and rhetoric (he was a professor of rhetoric), in particular the theory of metaphor and of tropes in general.

> The most sublime work of poetry is to give sensitivity and passion to things that lack sensitivity, and it is characteristic of children to take inanimate things in their hands and, in play, to speak to them as if they were living persons. This philosophico-philological axiom proves that the men of the world were, in their infancy, sublime poets by nature. (Ibid., § 186–87)

Men are therefore sublime poets by nature by virtue of the fundamental axiom according to which "man, because of the indefinite nature of the human mind, makes himself the measure of the universe when he falls into ignorance" (ibid., § 120). Another axiom makes it clear that "men who are ignorant of the natural causes that produce things give things their own nature, when they cannot explain

them by similar things" (ibid., § 180). It is thus that man, "by himself, made an entire world [di se stesso ha fatto un intiero mondo]":

> In the same way in which the metaphysics born of reason teaches that "homo intelligendo fit omnia," this metaphysics born of the imagination likewise demonstrates that "homo non intelligendo fit omnia"; and this latter claim may be more true than the first, since man, by understanding, spreads his mind and grasps things themselves, while when he does not understand, he makes things from his own self, and by transforming himself into them, he becomes those things. (Ibid. § 405)

This "metaphysics born of the imagination" is at work in fables and in pagan mythology, of which Vico has an extremely original reading: he distances it from purely literary analyses and turns it into the testimony of the way in which people from the "dark times" understood the natural world and constructed their human world. Poetic metaphysics, in effect, is nothing other than a "theology": "Poetry may be considered as a poetic metaphysics, by which the theologian poets imagined that bodies were for the most part divine substances" (ibid., § 400). The "theologian poets" are the first men, not insofar as they speak poetically of the gods, but rather insofar as they "speak gods," as one speaks a language. Their speech is the "fantastic speech of animate substances, imagined for the most part as divine" (ibid., § 401). These gods are what Vico calls "poetic characters," or again "fantastic universals," that is, "marks" or signs, concrete images allowing people without any capacity for abstraction or universalization to escape the infinite diversity of the sensible world, to perceive stabilities, to have a first experience of the world. By creating gods, men began to think in a human way.

However, one cannot simply create gods with impunity. Vico cites the dictum of Tacitus: "*fingunt simul creduntque* [they imagine, and at the same time, they believe]." This is to say that these imagined gods speak to men, give them orders, make themselves feared by them. The lives and actions of men will be determined by these animated substances that were created by their own imagination. This is what is expressed so well by the story in the *Scienza nuova* of the birth of the first divine "character," the "first of all the human thoughts of paganism," of

(continued)

(continued)

the first god, Jupiter, a radical event that will place men on the road to the fulfillment of their destiny. In the "immense forest" that has covered the earth since the flood, barely human beings, *bestioni*, wander about without end. Suddenly the first thunderclap rings out.

> Horrified and astonished by this great effect whose reason they do not know, they raise their eyes and pay attention to the sky. And because in such a case the nature of the human spirit is led to attribute its own nature to the effect, and since the nature of these beings was that of men who were only the robust forces of body and who expressed their violent passions by screaming and roaring, they imagined that the sky was a big animate body, which, under this aspect, they named Jupiter . . . and who wished to tell them something through the whistling of the lightning bolts and the noise of the thunder. (Ibid., § 377)

According to Vico, in effect, Jupiter was first named *Ious* by the Latins, after the noise of thunder, and Ζεύς by the Greeks, after the whistling of lightning (ibid., § 447). And he clarifies:

> The first men, who spoke by signs, believed according to their nature that lightning bolts and thunderclaps were signs made by Jupiter (this is why "divine will" was called *numen*, from *nuo*, "to indicate with the head"), that Jupiter gave commands by signs, and that these signs were real words [that is, having the character of "things"], and that nature was the tongue of Jupiter. (Ibid., § 379)

Thus was imagined "the first divine fable, the greatest of all that were imagined later, that of Jupiter, king and god of men and gods, casting a lightning bolt: a fable that was so popular, so troubling, and so instructive that even those who invented it believed it, and with dreadful religious practices . . . feared him, revered him, and honored him" (ibid., § 379).

The effects of this initial fear are religion, family, property, the law, cities (first aristocratic, then popular, finally monarchical), until such time as "fully developed reason" should rule. Having reached this point, however, nations risk losing the "poetic" force, which Vico also calls "heroic," and which allowed the birth of the civil world. Cynicism, skepticism, materialism, and atheism thus led to the dissolution of social bonds and to "barbarity of thought." Thus begins a new *corso*, a *ricorso*, which will run through the same stages whose succession constitutes the "eternal ideal history" (see CORSO).

Alain Pons

BIBLIOGRAPHY

Vico, Giambattista. *The Autobiography of Giambattista Vico*. Translated by M. H. Fisch and T. G. Bergin. Ithaca, NY: Cornell University Press, 1944.
———. *The New Science of Giambattista Vico*. Translated by T. G. Bergin and M. H. Fisch. Ithaca, NY: Cornell University Press, 1984.
———. *On the Most Ancient Wisdom of the Italians: Unearthed from the Origins of the Latin Language: Including the Disputation with Giornale de' letterati d'Italia*. Translated by L. M. Palmer. Ithaca, NY: Cornell University Press, 1988.
———. *On the Study Methods of Our Time*. Translated and edited by Elio Gianturco, with a translation of "The Academies and the Relation between Philosophy and Eloquence," translated by D. P. Verene. Ithaca, NY: Cornell University Press, 1990.
———. *Opere*, 2 vols. Edited by A. Battistini. Milan: Mondadori, 1990.
———. *Vico: Selected Writings*. Edited by L. Pompa. New York: Cambridge University Press, 1982.

authenticity, while the Latin-derived *Literatur*, on the other hand, evoked artifice and complexity.

These diffuse connotations, implicit in use but rarely mentioned in the dictionaries, are what explain the remarkable ascent of the term in the German lexicon between 1770 and 1850. Still largely dominated by its rivals, *Poesie* and *Literatur*, at the end of the eighteenth century, *Dichtung* appears to have completely supplanted them by the middle of the nineteenth century. The process was tentative at first. Thus, only in the second edition of the essay *Über naive und sentimentalische Dichtung*, in 1800, does Schiller decide to introduce the word *Dichtung* in the title; the term itself, as it happens, is noticeably rare in the actual work. The publication, starting in 1811, of Goethe's autobiography, *Dichtung und Wahrheit* (usually translated into French as *Poésie et Vérité*), marks an important stage in this ascent: the word *Dichtung* is, according to the author's repeated declarations, complementary rather than in opposition to the word *Wahrheit*. "Therein lies all that results from my life, and each of the facts recounted here only serves to support a general observation, *a higher truth [eine höhere Wahrheit]*" (Eckermann, *Gespräche mit Goethe*, 30 March 1831). Already by 1787, in the poem *Zueignung*, Goethe had described himself as receiving "the veil of poetry from the hand of truth [der Dichtung Schleier aus der Hand der Wahrheit empfangen]" (v. 96). The growing success of the term is confirmed by Hegel, who, in his *Lectures on Aesthetics* given between 1818 and 1829, baptizes *Dichtung* as the third "romantic" art (the others being music and painting). In 1853 G. G. Gervinus reedits a history of German literature, originally published in 1835–42 as *Geschichte der poetischen Nationalliteratur der Deutschen*, with the new title of *Geschichte der deutschen Dichtung*. It is under the name of *Dichtung* rather than that of *Literatur* or *Poesie* that German literary production reaches a veritable historical consecration in the nineteenth century.

Very often used between 1900 and 1950, from Dilthey to E. Staiger by way of T. Mann or J. Petersen, the word nonetheless seems to undergo a decline in the second half of the twentieth century. The very connotations that had been the basis of its ascent rendered it suspect in postwar Germany. In 1973 the Germanist Rüdiger pleads on that basis for the proscription of the term from scientific usage and suggests replacing it with the wider, more neutral term *Literatur* ("Was ist Literature?"). Restricted to the henceforth abandoned tradition of belles lettres, *Dichtung* seems moreover to be too tarnished with romantic holiness and nationalist connotations. This abandonment, clear in usage and sanctioned by dictionaries, did not take place without some resistance, as indicated by Hamburger's plea ("Das Wort 'Dichtung'"). It is worth noting that the term, though abandoned by literary types, is given a central role by the philosopher Heidegger, even in his last works.

■ See Box 2.

Although *Dichtung* certainly takes its meaning from a conceptual network peculiar to Heideggerian language, it is

2

Heidegger's *Dichtung*: Poetry and thought

The term *Dichtung* begins to stand out beginning with § 34 of *Sein und Zeit* (*Being and Time*, 1927), in a way that is still discreet, but whose importance should not, according to Hermann ("Poétiser et penser . . .," 2000, p. 78), be overlooked:

> Die Mitteilung der existenzialen Möglichkeiten der Befindlichkeit, das heißt das Erschließen von Existenz, kann eigenes Ziel der "dichtenden" Rede sein. (*Sein und Zeit*)

> La communication des possibilités existentiales de l'affection, autrement dit l'ouvrir de l'existence, peut devenir le but autonome du parler "poétique." (The communication of the existential possibilities of affection, in other words the opening of existing, can become the autonomous goal of "poetic" language.) (*Être et Temps*)

> La communication des possibilités existentiales de la disposibilité, c'est-à-dire la découverte de l'existence, peut être la fin que se fixe la parole qui "parle en poème." (The communication of the existential possibilities of arrangeability, that is the discovery of existence, may be the end that is set for itself by the word that "speaks in poems.") (Fr. trans. F. Vezin)

The quotation marks surrounding the term *dichtend* (poetic, speaking in poetry) are at the least the formal indication of a completely new way of approaching poetry, such that it is no longer subordinate to but coordinate with thought: poem and noema. Such a gesture supposes a return to the revelatory character of *Dichtung* and a distinction between *Dichtung* in the strict sense ("poetry") and in a wider sense.

The return to the revelatory character of *Dichtung* can be accomplished, but in fact it is rather rarely the case, in light of the etymology of the term, which suggests a distinction into four stages, as the following text shows:

> "Dichten"—was meint das Wort eigentlich? Es kommt von ahd. tithôn, und das hängt zusammen mit dem lateinischen *dictare*, welches eine verstärkte Form von *dicere* = sagen ist. *Dictare*: etwas wiederholt sagen, vorsagen, "diktieren," etwas sprachlich aufsetzen, abfassen, sei es einen Aufsatz, einen Bericht, eine Abhandlung, eine Klage—oder Bittschrift, ein Lied oder was immer. All das heißt "dichten", sprachlich abfassen. Erst seit dem 17. Jahrhundert ist das Wort "dichten" eingeschränkt auf die Abfassung sprachlicher Gebilde, die wir "poetische" nennen und seitdem "Dichtungen." Zunächst hat das Dichten zu dem "Poetischen" keinen ausgezeichneten Bezug. . . .

> Trotzdem können wir uns einen Fingerzeig zunutze machen, der in der ursprünglichen Wortbedeutung von tithôn—*dicere* liegt. Dieses Wort ist stammesgleich mit dem griechischen *deiknumi*. Das heißt zeigen, etwas sichtbar, etwas offenbar machen, und zwar nicht überhaupt, sondern auf dem Wege eines eigenen Weisens. (Heidegger, *Hölderlins Hymnen*)

> *Dichten*—what does that word actually mean? It comes from the Old High German *tithôn* and is related to the Latin *dictare*, which is an intensified form of *dicere* = to say. *Dictare*: to say something repeatedly, to say out loud, to "dictate," to set something out in speech, to compose, whether it is an essay, a report, a treatise, a complaint—or a request, a song, or whatever. All of this is called *dichten*, to express linguistically. It is only in the seventeenth century that *dichten* was restricted to the composition of pictures in language, which we call "poetic," and since then *Dichtungen* (poems). Originally *dichten* had no privileged relation to the "Poetic." . . .

> Nevertheless, we can make use of a quick indication contained in the original meaning of the word *tithôn*. This word has the same root as the Greek *deiknumi*. This means: to show, to reveal, to make visible or manifest, and not as a general revelation but as an indication leading up a specific path. (Ibid.)

Whence the necessity of distinguishing wide and strict senses of *Dichtung*. In the strict sense, which thus corresponds to its modern meaning dating from the seventeenth century, *Dichtung* is equivalent to *Poesie* (poetry), that is, one art among others, which Heidegger calls "a mode among others of the project of clarifying the truth" (*Pathmarks*). In the wide sense *Dichtung* is this very "project of clarifying the truth" in all its fullness—what Heidegger also calls *Dichten*, to poetize (ibid.): poetry comes from the Poem, as do architecture, sculpture, or music. Every work of art is thus a Poem, insofar as it is rooted in the deployment or the domain of the word, which is only *Urpoesie* (primordial poetry), in its turn by virtue of being a Poem (ibid., 84).

Pascal David

BIBLIOGRAPHY

Froment-Meurice, Marc. *That Is to Say: Heidegger's Poetics*. Translated by J. Plug. Stanford, CA: Stanford University Press, 1998.
Heidegger, Martin. *Être et Temps*. Translated by E. Martineau. Authentica, 1985.
———. *Être et Temps*. Translated by F. Vezin. Paris: Gallimard / La Pléiade, 1986.
———. *Hölderlins Hymnen "Germanien" und "Der Rhein."* In *Gesamtausgabe*. Frankfurt: Klostermann, 1980.
———. *Holzwege*. Frankfurt: Klostermann, 1980. Translation by J. Young and K. Haynes: *Off the Beaten Track*. Cambridge: Cambridge University Press, 2002.
———. *Pathmarks*. Edited by William McNeill. Cambridge: Cambridge University Press, 1998.
———. *Sein und Zeit*. Tübingen: Neimeyer, 1976.
Hermann, Friedrich-Wilhelm von. *Heideggers Philosophie der Kunst*. Frankfurt: Klostermann, 1980.
Warminski, Andrzej. "Monstrous History: Heidegger Reading Hölderlin." *Yale French Studies*, no. 77, Reading the Archive: On Texts and Institutions, 1990.

nonetheless worth recalling that it is not to be understood solely within the bounds of that philosophy. The word brings with it a semantic history—of which Heidegger is highly conscious—beginning with Herder in the eighteenth century and still resonating with nationalist sentiments about the genius of the German language expressed in the nineteenth century.

Élisabeth Décultot

BIBLIOGRAPHY

Eckermann, Johann Peter. *Gespräche mit Goethe in den letzten Jahren seines Lebens*. Vol. 2: *1828–1832*. Leipzig: Barsdorf, 1895. Translation by J. Oxenford: *Conversations of Goethe*. Edited by J. K. Moorhead. New York: Da Capo, 1998.
Hamburger, Käthe. *Die Logik der Dichtung*. Stuttgart: Ernst Klett Verlag, 1957. Translation by M. J. Rose: *The Logic of Literature*. Bloomington: Indiana University Press, 1973.
———. "Das Wort 'Dichtung.'" In *Literatur und Dichtung. Versuch einer Begriffsbestimmung*. Edited by H. Rüdiger, 33–46. Stuttgart: Kohlhammer, 1973.

Herder, Johann Gottfried von. *Against Pure Reason: Writings on Religion, Language and History*. Edited by M. Bunge. Minneapolis, MN: Fortress Press, 1993.

———. *Sämtliche Werke*. 33 vols. Edited by B. Suphan. Berlin: Weidmann, 1877–1913.

———. *Selected Writings on Aesthetics*. Edited and translated by G. Moore. Princeton, NJ: Princeton University Press, 2006.

Rüdiger, Horst, ed. *Literatur und Dichtung: Versuch einer Begriffsbestimmung*. Stuttgart: W. Kohlhammer, 1973.

Schlegel, Friedrich. *Über das Studium der griechischen Poesie*. In *Kritische Friedrich-Schlegel-Ausgabe*, vol. 1. 35 vols. Edited by E. Behler. Paderbon: Schöningh, 1958–.

Sulzer, Johann Georg. *Allgemeine Theorie der schönen Künste*. 2 vols. Leipzig: Weidemanns Erben und Reich, 1771–74.

DICTUM / ENUNTIABILE (LATIN)

ENGLISH   stateable
FRENCH   *dictum, dit, énoncé; énonçable; exprimable*
GREEK   *lekton* [λεντόν]

➤ PRÉDICABLE, PREDICATION, PROPOSITION, SACHVERHALT, SIGN, SIGNIFIER/SIGNIFIED, TRUTH, WORD

The terms *dictum* and *enuntiabile* are used, beginning in the twelfth century, to indicate of a proposition "what it says" or "what it may state." This begins with a series of questions that are not only semantic in nature (do propositions have a signification, like words, and if so, of what nature—real or in the world or in the mind), but also logical (the problem of truth-bearers), and ontological (the problem of what makes a proposition true). And further, a host of different questions of a theological nature arise as well; when we inquire as to the nature of divine knowledge, which is necessarily eternal (if God knows eternally that *P*, what is *P*?)

I. *Lekton* and *Dictum*

Seneca uses the terms *effatum, enuntiativum, enuntiatum* in a passage from letter 117 (117.13; RT: *Die Fragmente zur Dialektik der Stoiker* 892), to characterize what is in fact only a subgroup of *lekta*, (a) those that are complete, and (b) those that are capable of being true or false, that is, assertions or *axiômata* (see SIGNIFIER/SIGNIFIED, PROPOSITION).

The term *dicibile*, as used by Augustine in the *De dialectica*, cannot be considered a translation of *lekton* for two reasons: first, Augustine focuses his discussion on the basic unit, the word, *dictio*, whence the use of a term formed from the same verb *dicere*, that is, *dicibile*, whereas the Stoic *lekton* is not necessarily simple. Second, the *lekton* is more often than not a thought insofar as it is expressed by words. Augustine, however, defines the *dicibile* as something that exists in thought before being expressed (*ante vocem*), that can be expressed, and that is created in the mind of the hearer by the sign (see WORD, Box 3). *Dicibile* seems rather to translate the Greek *ekphorikon* [ἐκφορικόν], as used by the Stoics (see Nuchelmans, *Theories of the Proposition*). The claims of equivalence between *lekton* and *dictio* or *dictum* are isolated and derive from Isidore of Seville (*Etymologiae*, 2.22.2: "nam *lekton* dictio dicitur"), followed by Alcuin, who explains that dialectic deals with *dicta*, then in the twelfth century, by Jean of Salisbury in the *Metalogicon* (2.4: "*lekton* greco eloqui [sicut ait Isidorus] dictum appellatur"). The latter only appeals to Augustine's *De dialectica* in order to align the Boethian triad of *vox-intellectus-res* with a supposedly Augustinian triad

of *diction-dicibile-res*, and the omission of the fourth term, *verbum*, completely distorts the sense of the original (*Metalogicon*, 3.5: "Est autem res de quo aliquid, dicibile quod de aliquo, dictio quo dicitur hoc de illo").

II. Abelard and *Dictum*

Whereas Abelard gives *dictum* a technical sense in the exposition of his theory of propositions, as we will see, the term *enuntiabile* becomes generalized a bit later, both in logic and in theology. An author from the end of the twelfth century considers it a novelty in his time:

> In reading and rereading Aristotle and Boethius, I have not found a single passage in which it is written that the true and the false were "statable," or inversely, and Aristotle has always taken "statable" for "predicable," saying "statable of something", i.e., "predicable of something," and "to be stated" for "to be predicated," from which it follows that the proposition is the statement of something about something [Aristotle, *De interpretatione*, 5.17a 25–27, *translatio Boethii, Aristoteles latinus* II, 1–2].

Later, both terms were perceived as equivalent (cf. *Ars Burana*). They have distinct histories, however, which are divided into two periods in which different problems are discussed.

We should note, first of all, that the discussions of *dictum* or *enuntiabile* are related to the existence in Latin of infinitive clauses. "Socrates currit" says that Socrates runs; the infinitive "Socratem currere" (or the completitive "quod Socrates currit") is the name (*appellatio*) of what the proposition (*dictum*) says. The statable is "called" by the "appellatio dicti" ("hominem esse animal") (just as the individual Socrates is called by the proper name Socrates), and "signified" by the proposition ("homo est animal"). One may speak of modality *de dicto*, when the modality bears on the *dictum*, in contrast with modality *de re*: "Socrates currit est possibile" according to the *de dicto* interpretation signifies "(that Socrates runs) is possible"; or the *de re* interpretation, "Socrates can run." A single phrase may naturally be capable of different truth values depending on the interpretation given to its modality. Thus, to take a Sophistic example, "possibile est stantem sedere" is false *de dicto*: it is impossible for the proposition "he who is standing is sitting" to be true; on the other hand, the same proposition is true *de re*: the "thing" that is standing can certainly sit. Classical Latin tended to prefer infinitive clauses, with the subject in the accusative, for the *de dicto* interpretation—"Dicitur Homerum caecum fuisse"—and the attribute in the nominative, constructed with the infinitive, for the *de re* interpretation: "Homerus dicitur caecus fuisse." In medieval Latin, logicians considered the first example to be capable of two interpretations. There are various possibilities for translating the infinitive clause: one may use the complement clause ("it is possible that Socrates runs"), but then we lose the distinction with the Latin complement phrase as well as its status as a nominal phrase, or a gerundive phrase ("Socrates-running is possible").

The introduction in the beginning of the twelfth century of the notion of *dictum* is motivated by logico-grammatical questions. Abelard is inquiring as to the nature of the declarative proposition, to demonstrate that what characterizes it cannot be its meaning: in effect, "Socrates currit" means the same thing as "Socratem currere" or "Socratem currens," and we find in each the expression of the inherence of a quality in a subject. All of these expressions involve "complex intellections," though this point was not unanimously agreed upon at the time. What characterizes the first is that it says (*dicit*) or "proposes" (*proponit*) something, that something is the case ("state" in English is a good approximation; see PROPOSITION). These expressions mean the same thing, have the same intellection (*intellectus*), but only the first has a *modus enuntiandi* or *modus proponendi*. A proposition thus signifies a complex intellection, composed of the intellections of its categorematic parts, but beyond this, "says" or "poses" its *dictum*. For Abelard, the statement of a declarative sentence (such as "Socrates est albus") corresponds, in effect, to a threefold action of the intellect, consisting in focusing one's attention on something (Socrates), on a quality (the individual whiteness), and associating the two objects by a further act. For this reason, Abelard maintains that the *dictum* is "not absolutely anything," that it is "not a thing": in effect, if a proposition (understood here as a significant sequence) speaks of things ("agit de rebus") and not intellections of words, what it says is not a thing, but rather corresponds to the way in which the intellect puts things in relation to one another, or in which it posits their existence. Only as a subsequent step, by confronting what the proposition says with the state of things ("eventus rerum" or rei, "esse rei," "status rerum" or rei, "natura rerum"; cf. "natura rerum ex qua veritatem vel falsitatem [propositiones] contrahunt [the nature of things from which propositions take their truth or falsity]; *Glossae super Peri hermeneias*), may the *dictum* be declared true or false ("Et est profecto ita in re, sicut dicit vera propositio, sed non est res aliqua quod dicit [It is indeed thus with things [or with reality] as the true proposition says, but what the proposition says is not a thing]"; *Dialectica*). The *dictum* is thus not the state of things, that is, the truth-maker, but the truth-bearer, which can receive the predicates "true" and "false." It is not itself a "something" since the intellect may liberally "posit" relations between things, or, in other terms, put forward a hypothesis about things, whether things are as it says or not. I may just as easily say "Socrates est homo" (Socrates is a man) as "Socrates est lignum" (Socrates is wooden): each of these propositions says something—has a *dictum*—and the "existence of things" said by the proposition are no more a part of reality in the first case than in the second. The proposition is true when what it posits corresponds to what is ("Omnis enim propositio vera dicitur, qui ita est in re, ut proponit"; *Glossae super Peri hermeneias*). The expression *eventus rerum* contains a remarkable ambiguity, in fact, as Abelard explains in a discussion of future contingents (*Glossae super Peri hermeneias*). In one sense, it relates to reality as it exists, to the things as they come about ("res ipsas quae eveniunt"), independently of the way in which they are conceived or spoken of, to the objective "event" (in the sense of what "happens" or "occurs"; *evenit*), which makes the proposition true or false ("veritas propositionum ex eventu rerum pendet"). In another sense, the expression relates to reality as we speak of it ("id totum quod propositio dicit") and which in that sense has no reality other than that of being said: it is the event as it is posited by the proposition or *eventus propositionis*

(cf. "If someone says, for example, *Socrates will eat* or *will die tomorrow*, he posits an indeterminate event which the nature of things can in no way make certain for us [indeterminatum eventum proponit de quo scilicet nulla natura rei cujusquam nos certificare potest]; "eventus proprie dicimus dicta propositionum"), and it is in this sense that the *dictum* is "nothing at all."

Even if the terms *dictum* and *enuntiabile* are sometimes seen as equivalents, it is often noted that the second has a nuance of potentiality that the first lacks (whence its translation as "stateable," correlative with "statement" for *enuntiatio*, in Lewis, "William of Auvergne's account of the *enuntiabile*"): "The stateables, according to the *Ars Meliduna* (ca. 1170) are what propositions signify; they are thus called in virtue of the fact that they are stated or apt to be stated." The anonymous author can thus claim that the *enuntiabile* remains true even if it is not stated, even if there were no longer any expression for stating it, since it would still be possible to "impose" a new *vox* in order to state it: "the stateable, in effect, is not so-called according to the act, but according to aptitude (non ab actu, sed ab aptitudine)." Thus, whereas Abelard's *dictum* resembled a conception of the proposition as an "act" or "statement," the *enuntiabile* is better placed alongside the objectified and independently existing propositions of the Fregean tradition. That said, the nature of the *enuntiabile* varies greatly from theory to theory, but these differences are related to a problem that is not strictly logical.

III. The Question of Divine Knowledge

The theological implications of the notion of *dictum* become apparent when we inquire, as Robert de Melun does, as to the eternal nature of *dicta*: if *dicta* exist for all eternity, this implies that something other than God himself is eternal. That unfortunate implication was the object of lively debate until the end of the fifteenth century, in the wake of the Parisian condemnations of 1241, when William of Auvergne declared that it was forbidden to teach "quod multae sunt vertates ab aeterno quae non sunt Deus" (that there are a large number of eternal truths distinct from God). In the twelfth century, the notions of *dictum* and *enuntiabile* were used more specifically to discuss the problems related to the immutability of divine knowledge, power, and will. Although he does not use the notion of *dictum* developed in his logic textbooks, Abelard is the first to introduce a thesis often considered characteristic of nominalism, called *semel/semper*: what God knows once, he knows forever, since "what is true once, is true forever [quidquid semel est verum, semper est verum]." The term *dictum* designates the object of knowledge among his contemporary theologians, who are also divided as to the nature of the *dictum* or *enuntiabile*, its truth, and its changeless character. The Nominales think that stateables are the objects of divine knowledge, that, once true, they are always true, and are thus independent of time. A single stateable-type (e.g., "Christ is born") uttered at t1 (before the birth of Christ), t2 (at the moment of Christ's birth), t3 (after Christ's birth), corresponds to three different stateables (a given stateable associates Christ and his birth at a given time, and so if it is true at a given moment, it will always be true). A single stateable ("Christ is born") is expressed at different moments in time by three statements, at t1 by "Christ will be born," at t2 by "Christ is born," and at t3 by "Christ has been born." On the other hand, the Reales think that the objects of divine knowledge are the *res*, and that the stateables vary in their truth conditions. Subsequently, the analysis of propositions expressing divine knowledge (e.g., "Deus praescivit Antichristum esse") is expanded to include propositions containing a belief-verb, and thus return to the domain of logic.

There are multiple opinions as to the nature of an *enuntiabile*: several are mentioned by the *Ars Meliduna* (see De Rijk, *Logica modernorum*; Iwakuma, "*Enuntiabilia*"). The differences turn on (a) the simplicity or complexity of their nature, (b) the nature of what is composite: *terms* (mental, spoken, or written), or the *things signified* by these terms; (c) their eternal or temporally bound character; (d) their mode of existence: some posit that they do not exist (cf. Abelard), others that they do; for the latter, they are therefore things (*res*), but some consider them to be substances, others accidents, and still others consider them "extracategorial" (*extrapredicamentale*) entities, enjoying their own distinct mode of existence, as universals do.

While there is no clear path from the Stoic *lekton* to the medieval *dictum* or *enuntiabile*, the doctrinal relations between these notions are not evident either. We may note, however, that when Seneca associates the *lekton* with *quod nunc loquor* (what I say now), he is close to Abelardian formulations of *dictum* as "what the proposition says." There is nothing mental about Abelard's *dictum*, however: it is precisely by explaining that the predicates "true" and "false" cannot apply to either words or intellections that he is able to show that they apply to *dicta*. These *dicta* are more on the side of things, even if they are not existent things: just as names have a signification in thought (a simple intellection) and a signification in things, propositions have a signification in thought (a complex intellection) and a *dictum*. As for subsequent theories, we have seen that at the ontological level, the *dictum* or *enuntiabile* may be of different natures, real or mental, depending on the theory.

IV. The "Complexly Signifiable"

In the fourthteenth century, *dictum* and *enuntiabile* are replaced by the notion of the "complexly signifiable," *significabile complexe* (Gregory of Rimini) or "signifiable by complex," *significabile per complexum* (Adam Wodeham), that is, what is signifiable only by a linguistic *complexum* (an infinitive clause, or what English-speaking logicians call a "that-clause," in German, *Daß-Satz*). Since Hubert Élie, the "complexly signifiable" has been considered a medieval formulation of the notion of a state of affairs (*Sachverhalt*), interpreted more or less in a realist sense, making it related to Meinong's *Objektiv* (see SACHVERHALT). That is how its medieval adversaries understood it; using the support of the condemnation of 1241, they accused those who accepted the *significabile complexe* of maintaining that *mundum fore* ([the fact] that the world would exist) and *Deum esse* ([the fact] that God exists) have been throughout eternity, "without being God." This interpretation does not take account of all aspects of the theory, however. Gregory of Rimini affirms, as Abelard sometimes does, that the *significabile complexe* is "nothing"—that it does not exist. This claim suggests that the "signifiable by complex" cannot be something in the world that would make true a

truth of any sort (contingent or necessary). But the claim can only be fully understood by noting that Gregory's goal is not, contrary to what is often said, to build a nominalist theory of the proposition (or, a fortiori, a "realist" one), but only to explicate the notion of *notitia judiciaria* (judicial knowledge) of God. The difference between "things" and *Sachverhalte* may be confirmed in Gregory's thought only insofar as it is fundamentally related to the problem of divine knowledge. That being the case, two incompatible semantic theories confront one another over the "signifiable," whose "offspring" are still observable at the end of the nineteenth and beginning of the twentieth centuries. One, standard "reductionist" nominalism, distinguishes *truth-maker*, the individual thing signified by the subject term, and *truth-bearer*, the *token* proposition; the other, that of Gregory of Rimini, ultimately identifies *truth-maker* and *truth-bearer* in the form of the "complexly signifiable," called "true" or "false" by an "intrinsic denomination" on the basis of the uncreated Truth.

Take, for example, Mark 14:40: "Verily I say unto thee, That this day, [even] in this night, before the cock crow twice, thou shalt deny me thrice." Was the corresponding stateable, that is, "Petrum esse paccaturum in A" (that-Peter-would-sin-at-time A) true for all eternity? Gregory sets aside the hypothesis according to which the "created statement," the oral proposition reported in Mark 14:30, would have been true for all eternity: since it did not exist for all eternity, it could not have been true for all eternity. As for the stateable that the proposition states, he distinguishes "being for all eternity" from "being true for all eternity." If the proposition of "created statement" had existed for all eternity (which is not the case), it would be true for all eternity, but contingently so. The complexely signifiable "Petrum esse peccaturum in A" was, on the other hand, true for all eternity, but it was neither eternal nor everlasting. The importance and the meaning of the thesis affirming the non-existence of the *significabile complexe* here clearly appear. The complexly signifiable "is nothing": it is not and never was an "entity by itself." It cannot therefore be or have been for all eternity. On the other hand, the "signified complex" of Mark 14:30 was true for all eternity, not necessarily, but contingently, "by an extrinsic denomination coming from the uncreated Truth and from the eternal judgment of God judging that 'Peter-would-sin-at-time A.'"

The expression "extrinsic denomination" derives from a widely used medieval distinction between two types of denomination, that is, paronymic attribution (see PARONYM): (a) formal denomination in which what gives the name is in what is named "as in a subject"—this is the case with the whiteness that denominates x in "x is white," and (b) causal denomination, in which what gives the name is in the agent or efficient cause, not in the patient—this is the case with the thought or intellection that the thinking mind has of it in "x is [a] thought" or "x is thought." The thought is "as in a subject" with respect to the thinking mind, not what is thought. This second type of denomination is what Gregory calls "extrinsic denomination." The truth of the stateable relative to Peter's sin is thus in the first instance, and causally speaking, in God, who makes the judgment—in his judgment or act of judging; it is only an attribute of the stateable in an external, "paronymic" way. It is insofar as it is judged by the primary Truth that the stateable is called "true" and hence also "true for all eternity." The structure of "extrinsic denomination" expresses a central thesis of Gregory's ontology: the alethic modality "true" is an attribute of the Judge and his eternal act of judging, not of the object of judgment or its content, which are all called true by causal denomination (Gregory of Rimini, *Lectura*, I, d. 38, q. 2). In other words: a stateable is called "true" paronymically by extrinsic denomination on the basis of the primary uncreated Truth and its eternal judgment, and, in turn, this stateable, which is not itself an "entity," is what verifies our own judgment, our own propositions. There are thus two stages of correspondence, or "rightness," for a true stateable according to Gregory: a stateable is true insofar as it corresponds to the act of divine judgment, and it is that to which thought makes itself correspond ("consents," "acquiesces," or "assents") when it judges—what makes judgment and proposition true. The second correspondence brings the Gregorian theory close to the phenomenological theory popularized at the beginning of the twentieth century by Anton Marty, who redefines truth (see TRUTH)—in Latin—as "adaequatio cogitantis et cogitatum" (correspondence of the thinker with the content of thought), instead of "adaequatio rei et intellectus" (correspondence between the thing and the intellect). The "complexly signifiable" is, as we can see, an important element in the genealogy of the theory of *Sachverhalte*.

Alain de Libera
Irène Rosier-Catach

BIBLIOGRAPHY

Abelard, Peter. *Glossae super Peri hermeneias*. Edited by Bernhard Geyer. Munster: Aschendorff, 1927.

Ashworth, Earline Jennifer. "Theories of the Proposition: Some Early Sixteenth Century Discussions." In *Studies in Post-Medieval Semantics*. London: Variorum Reprints, 1985.

De Rijk, L. M. "La signification de la proposition (*dictum propositionis*) chez Abelard." *Studia Mediewistyczne* 16 (1975): 155–61.

———. *Logica modernorum: A Contribution to the History of Early Terminist Logic*. 2 vols. Assen: Van Gorcum, 1962–67.

Élie, Hubert. *Le signifiable par complexe. La proposition et son objet: Grégoire de Rimini, Meinong, Russell*. Paris: Vrin, 2000. First published in 1936.

Gregory of Rimini. *Lectura*. Vol. 3 in *Spätmittelalter und Reformation Texte und Untersuchungen*. Edited by D. Trapp and V. Marcolino. Berlin: De Gruyter, 1978–87.

Iwakuma, Yukio. "*Enuntiabilia* in Twelfth-century Logic and Theology." In *Vestigia, imagines, verba*, edited by C. Marmo, 20–35. Brepols, 1997.

Jacobi, Klaus, Christian Strub, and Peter King. "From *intellectus verus/falsus* to the *dictum propositionis*: The Semantics of Peter Abelard and His Circle." *Vivarium* 34, no. 1 (1996): 15–40.

Jolivet, Jean. *Arts du langage et théologie chez Abélard*. 2nd ed. Études de philosophie médiévale, 57. Paris: Vrin, 1982.

Kneepkens, Cornelius H. "Please don't call me Peter: I am an *enuntiable*, not a thing. A note on the *enuntiable* and the proper noun." In *Vestigia, imagines, verba*, edited by C. Marmo, 82–98. Brepols, 1997.

Lewis, Neil. "William of Auvergne's Account of the *enuntiable*: Its Relations to Nominalism and the Doctrine of the Eternal Truths." *Vivarium* 33 (1995): 113–36.

Libera, Alain de. "Abélard et le dictisme." In *Abélard. Le "Dialogue." La philosophie de la logique*, Cahiers de la revue de théologie et philosophie 6 (1986): 59–97.

———. *La référence vide. Théories de la proposition*. Paris: Presses Universitaires de France, 2002.

Maierù, Alfonso. *Terminologia logica della tarde scolastica*. Rome: Edizione dell'Ateneo, 1972.

Marenbon, John. *The Philosophy of Peter Abelard*. Cambridge: Cambridge University Press, 1997.

Marty, Anton. *Untersuchungen zur Grundlegung der Allgemeinen Grammatik und Sprachphilosophie*. Vol. 1. Halle: Niemeyer, 1908.

Nuchelmans, Gabriel. *Theories of the Proposition: Ancient and Medieval Conceptions of the Bearers of Truth and Falsity*. Amsterdam: North Holland, 1973.

———. *Late-scholastic and Humanist Theories of the Proposition*. Amsterdam: North Holland, 1980.

Rosier-Catach, Irène. "Abelard and the Meaning of Propositions." In *Signification in Language and Culture*, edited by H. S. Gill, 23–48. Shimla: Indian Institute of Advanced Study, 2002.

Smith, Barry. *Austrian Philosophy: The Legacy of Franz Brentano*. Chicago: Open Court, 1994.

DISCOURSE

"Discourse" is a transposition of *discursus*, from the Latin *discurrere* (to run here and there, run through in all directions). *Discursus* acquires the sense of "conversation, dialogue" rather late, following a metaphor that highlights the hazardous nature of verbal exchange (RT: *Dictionnaire Historique de la Langue Française*). Philosophers, however, focus on the order and method with which propositions and thoughts succeed one another: "discursiveness" implies entailment and correct reasoning, and practically becomes a synonym for "rationality."

It is thus that "discourse" is one of the received translations for the Greek *logos* [λόγος], which is just as well translated by "reason," although *logos* refers as well to each of the elements that compose language: see LOGOS.

I. Discursiveness, Rationality, and Humanity

Discursiveness, as a faculty and exercise of language and reason, is conceived (explicitly by Aristotle) as peculiar to man: see, besides LOGOS (under which, notably, the Hebrew *dābār* [דָּבָר] and the German *Sprache, Rede*, are also discussed), CONSCIOUSNESS, *DIALECTIC*, DICHTUNG, HOMONYM, II.B, *HUMANITY, REASON* [CONCEPTUS, INTELLECT, INTELLECTUS, UNDERSTANDING], TRUTH; cf. BILDUNG, GEISTESWISSENSCHAFTEN, PLASTICITY, SUBJECT.

II. Discourse, Language, and Languages

1. On the relation between discourse and multiple languages, see EUROPE, TO TRANSLATE.
2. On the possible divisions (or lack thereof) among what the French language refers to, after Saussure, as *langue, langage*, and *parole*, see LANGUAGE.
3. On the relationship between discursiveness and linguistic performance, see SPEECH ACT; cf. *ÉNONCÉ, PERFORMANCE, PRAXIS, VOICE*.

III. Discourse, Internal and External

1. On the parts of discourse, see PROPOSITION, TERM, *VERB*, WORD; cf. PRÉDICABLE, PREDICATION, SUPPOSITION, UNIVERSALS.
2. On the kinds of discourse, see *GENRE*, I/ME/MYSELF [ERZÄHLEN, HISTORY].
3. On the relationship between discourse and external reality, see *NONSENSE*, OBJECT, REALITY, SENSE, SIGN, SIGNIFIER/SIGNIFIED, *THING*, TRUTH, as well as PRAVDA, ISTINA; see the following more specifically for its logical content: MATTER OF FACT, *PROPOSITIONAL CONTENT*,

REPRÉSENTATION, *STATE OF AFFAIRS*. See also *DECEPTION, DOXA*, and *FALSE*.

4. On the relation between discursiveness and invention, at the intersection of the ontological relationship with things in the world and the literary relationship with genres of discourse, see especially, besides DICHTUNG and *GENRE, I,* CONCETTO, *FICTION, IMAGINATION,* INGENIUM, MIMÊSIS, *WITTICISM.*

DISEGNO (ITALIAN)

ENGLISH	design, drawing
FRENCH	*dessein, dessin*
GERMAN	*Zeichnung*
LATIN	*designo*

➤ *DESSEIN, DESSIN,* and ART, BAROQUE, CONCETTO, *IDEA, IMAGE,* INGENIUM, INTENTION, SIGN

Disegno is one of the major concepts of the Renaissance theory of art. It means both design and project, outline and intention, idea in the speculative sense as well as in the sense of invention. It thus refers to a thoroughly intellectual activity. The French word *dessein,* as used by theorists of art in the seventeenth century, is an adequate translation of the Italian meaning of *disegno* as used in the preceding century, and preserves its double meaning, but the distinction between *dessin* and *dessein* (design and drawing), which comes into use around the 1750s, yields a fundamental break with the Italian tradition. In the eighteenth century, Racine may still write, "le dessein en est pris, je pars cher Théramène" (the plan is made, I am leaving, dear Theramenes), but from that time on at the Académie Royale of Painting and Sculpture, the arts of "dessin" were taught, but not of "dessein." The two semantic fields that were unified in *disegno* are separated from then on in French, as in English and German.

I. From *Disegno* to *Dessein* and *Dessin,* to "Design," to *Zeichnen*

In the seventeenth century, what the French now call *dessin,* that is, the part of painting that is distinct from color, was always written *dessein,* sometimes even *desseing.* It is derived from the Italian *disegno,* and it kept all the richness of the Italian word. Antoine Furetière defines it thus in his RT: *Dictionnaire universel:* "Project, enterprise, intention. . . . Also, the thought one has in the imagination of order, of the distribution and construction of a painting, a poem, a book, a building. . . . Also said in painting of images or paintings that are without color." There is no homonymy here, however. When used about painting, *dessein* means something more but not something different. Though it has a specialized usage, it continues to signify the project or intention. The word expresses here in the most explicit way what the thing is for the artist, an art theorist, or an expert on the seventeenth century. It implies a certain way of thinking about drawing, as the realization of a design—that is, an intellectual project. The word *dessin,* which would be substituted for it a century later has a much narrower meaning, restricted to the last sense given by Furetière. It no longer

evokes a necessary relation between the drawing and the thought. The loss of a letter thus does not simply lead to a loss of meaning. Rather, it corresponds to a genuine semantic mutation that implies a completely different conception of drawing than that which the French took over from the Italians. Since *dessein* became *dessin,* French no longer has an equivalent to *disegno.* Several words are henceforth required to say in French what a single word, faithful to its Italian roots, said in the seventeenth century through several meanings. This is why the modernization of spelling in the publication of French texts on the art of the seventeenth century actually leads to serious confusions of meaning.

The same is true for English and German, which borrow from different lexica in order to say either drawing or intention. English thus distinguishes "drawing," in the sense of an outline, from "design," which corresponds to the French *dessein* and thus retains a part of the semantic field that the Italian *disegno* covered. In fact, it was starting with the Italian word that Anthony Ashley Cooper, Earl of Shaftesbury, constructed the concept of design, which he is the first to have introduced into English (*Letter Concerning the Art, or Science of Design,* 1812). Faithful to the double meaning of the Italian and French words, Shaftesbury constantly plays on the senses of "design" as the unity of a project and as a drawing. In this sense, "design" is a pure translation of *disegno* and *dessein.* As in French, however, the two meanings come apart very quickly in English, and the separation arises from the same transformations in the theory of art. The double meaning of conception and execution nevertheless reappears in the modern and worldwide usage of "design" today, as referring in all languages to a certain kind of industrial art coming out of the Bauhaus tradition. In German, *Zeichnung* (drawing) is not related to the terms for intention or intellectual projects either, terms such as *Abzicht* or *Entwurf.* Like *disegno,* which comes from *signum, Zeichnen* derives from *Zeichen,* which means sign. It can mean a plan or project, but only in a material sense (for example, an architectural plan), not in a purely speculative sense like *disegno* and *dessein.* The fact that *Zeichnen* is derived from *Zeichen* (sign), that it is related to *bezeichen* (designate), indeed to *zeigen* (to show), may justify the strongly logocentric presuppositions of some contemporary research on the nature of pictorial images. Thus, Walter Benjamin, in a text entitled "Über die Malerei oder Zeichen und Mal," builds his definition of painting using *Zeichen* as the source from which *Zeichnen* is a sort of derivative product, akin to a stain or spatter (*das Mal*). This means that all figurability would in the end be predetermined by a *Zeichen,* that is, an act of naming (*Benennung* or *Benennbarkeit*), such that the end of all figuration would be referred implicitly and necessarily to the word as such (*Ästhetische Fragmente,* in *Gesammelte Schriften,* 2:603f.).

The lexical distinctions that exist in English and German thus make a mockery of any attempt to translate *disegno* in the sense intended by the Renaissance writers. Conscious of this difficulty, historians and art theorists tend more and more to keep the Italian word without attempting to translate it into their own language, and speak of Raphael's *disegno* or Vasari's definition of *disegno.*

II. *Disegno* in the Renaissance

Disegno certainly has the sense of "drawing" in the Renaissance, as in Benvenuto Cellini, who distinguishes between several types of *disegni*, each corresponding to a *modo di disegnare* (Barocchi, *Discorso sopra l'arte del disegno*, 8:1929). Like *disegnare* however, which means both to draw and to formulate a plan, *disegno* embeds the notion of drawing in a special configuration, made up of a twofold network of meanings that overlap with one another. *Disegno* is in a way a topical term that refers to the spread of this entanglement. To indicate drawing in the sense of line, outline, or contour, the theorists use other terms, notably *circonscrizione*, which we find, for example, in Leon Battista Alberti's *De pictura* (It., *Della Pittura*; Eng., *On Painting*). In the first version of the treatise, published in Latin, Alberti writes, "Nam est circumscriptio aliud nihil quam fimbriarum notatio" (Circumscription is nothing other than the notation of contours) (trans. C. Grayson, *De pictura / On Painting*). When he adapts his text into the vernacular a short time later, Alberti translates *notatio* as *disegnamento*—"la circonscrizione é non altro che disegnamento dell'orio"—which goes into English as "Circumscription is nothing but the drawing of the outline" (trans. J. R. Spencer, *Della Pittura Della Pittura / On Painting*, 68). *Disegno* is thus not *circonscrizione*, nor *linea*, nor *orlo*, even if it implies all of these. It is not drawing. *Disegno* brings drawing into a completely different semantic field from that to which its properly physical characteristics belong. It means drawing as an expression of a mental representation, of a form present to the mind or imagination of the artist. Giorgio Vasari defines it thus:

This is like the form (*forma*) or idea (*idea*) of all the objects of nature, always original in its proportions. Whether it is a matter of the human body or those of animals, plants or buildings, sculpture or painting, one grasps the relation of the whole to its parts, the parts amongst each other and with the whole. From this grasping (*cognizione*) a concept (*concetto*) is formed, a reason (*giudizio*) engendered in the mind (*mente*) by the object, the manual expression of which is called drawing (*disegno*). The latter is thus the perceptible expression, the explicit formulation of a notion internal to the mind or mentally imagined by others and developed as an idea [si pu conchiudere che esso disegno altro non sia che una apparente espressione e dichiarazione del concetto che si ha nell'animo, e di quello che altri si è nella mente imaginato e fabricato nell'idea].

(trans. L Bondanella and P. Bondanella,
The Lives of the Artists)

By linking *disegno* to *forma*, *concetto*, and especially to *idea*, this text illustrates the way in which the Renaissance used the categories inherited from the rhetorical tradition, and, through it, Aristotle's philosophy, in order to develop a new theory of art. As Panofsky showed, the meaning of "idea" among art theorists results from a transformation of the idea into an ideal, which derives from the passage in Cicero's *De oratore* in which he defines the Platonic Idea as a form, an interior model existing prior to and informing its realization:

As, therefore, in mere bodily shape and figure there is a kind of perfection, to whose ideal appearance every production which falls under the notice of the eye is referred by imitation; so the semblance of what is perfect in Oratory may become visible to the mind, and the ear may labour to catch a likeness. These primary forms of thing are by Plato (the father of science and good language) called Ideas.

(trans. E. W. Sutton and H. Rackham, *De oratore*
[On the orator])

Giovanni Pietro Bellori, indeed, defines "idea" in the following way, just before citing the same passage from Cicero: "The idea of the painter or the sculptor is this perfect and excellent model in the mind which things before our eyes resemble, since they imitate the imagined form" (Idea del Pittore et scultore é quel perfetto ed eccellente esempio della mente, all cui immaginata forma imitando si rassomigliano le cose, che dadono sotto la vista) (trans. A. Sedgwick, "Idea of the Painter," in *The Lives of the Modern Painters*). *Disegno* is not just "idea," however; it is also, as Vasari says, the perceptible expression of the idea. The difficulty we may have in grasping the problem of *disegno* in its full complexity derives from the fact that it is both a pure act of thought as well as its visible result, in which the physical work of the artist participates as well. As the act of the painter's mind, *disegno* corresponds to invention, in the rhetorical sense of the term—that is, to the choice of subject. As the action of the painter's hand, it presupposes a technical skill. "*Disegno*," writes Vasari, "when it has extracted the invention of something from thought, requires the hand, practiced through years of study, to be able to render exactly what nature has created, with the pen or the point, the pencil, the stone, or any other means" (*The Lives of the Artists*). Material *disegno*, which we call drawing, is thus always the realization of a mental *disegno*. This is why *disegno* is, according to its theoreticians, superior to color. Unlike drawing, they say, whose quality demonstrates not only the skill of the painter but also the beauty of the idea that animates and directs the hand, color owes its luster entirely to the materials that compose it.

Several decades later, Federico Zuccaro systematizes his theory of *disegno* by distinguishing *disegno interno* from *disegno esterno*:

Per questo nome di disegno interno io non intendo solamente il concetto interno formato nella mente del pittore, ma anco quel concetto che forma qual si voglia intelletto.

(By the word *disegno interno* I mean not only the internal concept formed in the mind of the painter, but also the concept which any intellect forms.)

(Zuccaro, *Idea de'pittori*, in P. Barocchi, *Scritti d'arte del Cinquecento*, 2065; Eng. trans. based on Fr. trans. by C. Alunni in *La Peinture*, ed. J. Lichtenstein, 147)

The definition of *disegno interno* thus extends well beyond the domain of art: "e il concetto e l'idea che per conoscere et operare forma chi sia" (the concept or the idea formed by anyone in order to know and to work) (ibid.). Zuccaro, in fact, recognizes that he could just as well have used the terms *intenzione*, *essemplare*, or *idea*, but he preferred to leave those to the philosophers and theologians, as he was writing as a painter, addressing artists. Thus, though it comes out of a usage peculiar to the domain of art, the concept of *disegno* has a theological underpinning according to Zuccaro. It allows for an analogy between artistic creation and divine creation: "To work externally, God . . . necessarily looks at and contemplates the internal *disegno* in which he knows all the things that he has accomplished, that he is accomplishing and that he will accomplish, or that he could accomplish at a single glance" (ibid.). In forming his internal *disegno*, the painter thus resembles God. The operation by which he conceives it in his mind is a pure act, a spark of the divine within him, which makes *disegno* a veritable *segno di dio*, Zuccaro writes, playing on the word to get the meaning across. As for *disegno esterno*, "It is nothing other than *disegno* delimited as to its form and denuded of any material substance: pure line, delimitation, proportion and shape of anything imagined or real" (altro non é che quello che appare circonscritto di forma senza sonstanza di corpo. Simplice lineamento, circonscrizzione, misurazione e figura di qual si voglia cosa imaginata e reale) (in Barocchi, 2084; in Lichtenstein, 150).

By defining painting as an *arte del disegno*, Italian theorists thus do not rest with affirming the superiority of drawing over color. They proclaim the intellectual nature of pictorial activity, which they raise up to the nobility and dignity of a liberal art. It is *disegno* that makes painting *una cosa mentale*, to take over Leonardo's expression. This explains why the concept of *disegno* often takes on a polemical function, and why it could be used against all pictorial forms that seemed to endanger the newly acquired status of painting as a liberal art, from the "Gothic" manner of drawing to the practices of the colorists.

III. From *Dessein* to *Dessin*

The French adopt more or less the same use of *dessein*, though they add a slightly more polemical touch. This is, first, in order to defend a certain style of drawing—the grand manner—whose grandeur comes from the fact that it is the expression of a grand design, as Michel Anguier states in the lecture he gave on 2 October 1677, at the Académie Royale of Painting and Sculpture, "Sur le grand goût de dessein": "Great design [*dessein*] is a fire that illuminates the understanding, [inspires] the will, strengthens memory, purifies the mind, in order to penetrate the imagination. One would have to be Prometheus to steal the fire from heaven in order to illuminate this beautiful intelligence for us." A second reason is to respond to Rubenists who, starting in 1670, increased their attacks against the prestige of drawing. Thus, Le Brun praises drawing by adopting Zuccaro's distinction:

> One ought to know that there are two sorts of drawing: one which is intellectual or theoretical, the other practical. That the first depends purely on the imagination. . . . That practical drawing is produced by the intellectual and thus depends on the imagination as well as the hand. The latter, by means of the pencil, gives the form and the

proportion, and imitates all the visible things, going so far as to express the passions.

> (Lecture of 9 January 1672, in A. Mérot,
> *Les Conférences de l'Académie*, 219)

It is precisely this distinction that calls the colorist doctrine, as formulated by its exponent, Roger de Piles, into question. Upending a hierarchy that was believed to be solidly established by tradition, the latter in effect reduces drawing to its purely practical dimension. For him, drawing constitutes the "mechanical" part of painting, though he means this word in a very different sense from that given to it in the Middle Ages, and which bears witness to a new way of understanding technique. Drawing comes from training based on the imitation of ancient work, the study of perspective and anatomy, all indispensible knowledge for the acquisition of "accuracy of the eyes and facility of the hand" (*Cours de peinture par principes*, 194). This part, common to painting and sculpting, is certainly necessary to the work of the painter, but is insufficient to define the particularity of his or her art. Obeying the rules of accuracy of proportion and correction of contours, drawing is no longer the expression of an intellectual design, for Piles, but a manual dexterity that is based on a technical kind of knowledge, in which theory is entirely subordinated to practice. All the characteristics that gave *disegno* its intellectual and metaphysical, even theological, significance—genius, fire, invention, idea, form—are stripped from drawing and attributed to color. There is thus no longer any reason to use *dessein* for *dessin*. With the victory of colorist ideas at the dawn of the eighteenth century, a profound change was thus produced in the theory of art, which its language takes into account several decades later.

Jacqueline Lichtenstein

BIBLIOGRAPHY

Alberti, Leon Battista. *De Pictura / Della Pittura*. Bilingual Latin/Italian edition. Edited by Cecil Grayson. Rome: Laterza, 1975. *De Pictura* was first published in 1435, *Della Pittura* in 1436. Translation by Cecil Grayson: *De Pictura / On Painting*. Bilingual Latin/English edition. Edited by Martin Kemp. London: Penguin, 1991. Translation by J. R. Spencer: *Della Pittura / On Painting*. Bilingual Italian/English edition. New Haven, CT: Yale University Press, 1966.
Barocchi, Paola, ed. *Scritti d'arte del Cinquecento*. 3 vols. Milan: Ricciardi, 1971–77.
———. *Italy in the Baroque: Selected Readings*. Edited by B. Dooley. New York: Garland Publishing, 1995.
Bellori, Giovanni Pietro. "L'Idea del Pittore, della scultore e dell'architetto," introduction to *Le vite de'pittori, scultore e architetti moderni*. Rome, 1672. Translation by S. Sedgwick: *The Lives of the Modern Painters, Sculptors and Architects*. New York: Cambridge University Press, 2005.
Benjamin, Walter. *Ästhetische Fragmente*. In vol. 2 of *Gesammelte Schriften*, edited by R. Tiedemann and H. Schweppenhäuser. Frankfurt-am-Main: Suhrkamp, 1991.
Cellini, Benvenuto. *Discorso sopra l'arte del disegno*. In vol. 2 of P. Barrochi, ed., *Scritti d'arte del Cinquecento*. Discorso was first published in 1568.
Cicero. *De oratore* [On the orator]. 2 vols. Translated by E. W. Sutton and H. Rackham. Loeb Classical Library. Cambridge, MA: Harvard University Press, 1948.
Cooper, Anthony Ashley, Earl of Shaftesbury. *Letter Concerning the Art or Science of Design*. In vol. 3 of *Characteristicks*. London, 1733. Written in 1712.
Mérot, Alain. *Les Conférences de l'Académie royale de peinture et de sculpture au XVIIe siècle*. Paris: Ecole Nationale Supérieure des Beaux-Arts, 1996.
———. *French Painting in the Seventeenth Century*. Translated by C. Beamish. New Haven, CT: Yale University Press, 1995.

Panofsky, Erwin. *Idea: Ein Beitrag zur Begriffsgeschichte der älteren Kunsttheorie*. Berlin: V. Spiess, 1985. Translation by J. S. Peake: *Idea: A Concept in Art Theory*. Columbia: University of South Carolina Press, 1968.

Piles, Roger de. *Cours de peinture par principes*. Paris: Gallimard / La Pléiade, 1989. First published in 1709. Translation: *The Principles of Painting*. London: J. Osborn, 1743.

Vasari, Giorgio. *La vite de' piu eccellenti pittori, scultori e architettori*. Florence, 1568. Translation by Linda Bondella and Peter Bondanella: *The Lives of the Artists*. Oxford World Classics. Oxford: Oxford University Press, 2008.

Zuccaro, Federico. *L'Idea de pittori, scultori et architetti*. In vol. 2 of P. Barrochi, ed., *Scritti d'arte del Cinquecento*. *L'Idea* was first published in 1607 in Turin.

DISPOSITION

"Disposition," from the Latin *disponere*, refers to an arrangement, an organization, in particular in the rhetorical (*dispositio/inventio*, cf. COMMONPLACE and COMPARISON) and religious (*dispositio/dispensatio*, see OIKONOMIA) traditions. But a related group of words in French, such as *disponible* and *dispositif*, is enjoying a resurgence, notably by way of Gilles Deleuze and his translations of Heidegger.

I. "Disposition," *Disponible, Dispositif,* "Utility"

Disponible is not a technical philosophical term, but rather a translators' expedient for rendering Heidegger's distinction between *vorhanden* and *zuhanden* (adj.), or *Vorhandenheit* and *Zuhandenheit* (n.). *Zuhandenheit* is the mode of being of what is manipulable, at hand, or within reach (*procheira* [πρόχειρα]), while *Vorhandenheit* is the more neutral or indifferent mode of being of what is present, what is there (for example, books on the shelves of a library), what is subsistent. See VORHANDEN.

Similarly, *dispositif* is a possible translation of *Gestell* (frame, mount; a shelf, in fact), which for Heidegger characterizes the essence of modern technique. See COMBINATION AND CONCEPTUALIZATION; cf. DASEIN, ES GIBT, *IL Y A*.

This mode of being intersects with the ways of saying and understanding what a *thing* is: see RES, Box 1, on the Greek *chrêma* [χρῆμα], *pragma* [πρᾶγμα], and cf. GEGENSTAND, OBJECT, REALITY.

Finally, English confers a special value on utility, through the neologism "utilitarian" invented by Bentham: see UTILITY, and cf. ECONOMY, FAIR, *VALUE*.

On the arrangement that constitutes a *dispositif*, especially in the Deleuzian sense, cf. STRUCTURE and FRENCH.

II. Subjective Disposition

"Disposition" is one of the possible translations of *Stimmung*, although it lacks the musical resonance emphasized by Heidegger to designate a certain "harmony" of the subject: see STIMMUNG (with the term *Befindlichkeit*, sometimes translated into French as *disposibilité*); cf. ANXIETY, DASEIN, GESCHICHTLICH, HEIMAT, *MALAISE, SERENITY*, SORGE, SUBLIME.

On the disposition of the soul, particularly in ethics (*diathesis* [διάθεσις]), related to one's habitual way of being (*hexis* [ἕξις]), see MORALS, I, PHRONÊSIS, VIRTÙ; for Stoic "diathesis" and the relation between physics, ethics, and grammar, see I/ME/MYSELF, Box 1. On the relation to naturalness implied by "disposition," and its link with aesthetics, see also GENIUS, GOÛT, INGENIUM; cf. GEMÜT.

More generally, for the network of terms that detail the strict relation between agency and passivity, objectivity and subjectivity, with respect to being affected as well as to action, see AGENCY, PATHOS; cf. DRIVE, GEMÜT, LOVE, PLEASURE. The neologism "affordance" picks out in particular the intersection between perception and the possibility of acting; see AFFORDANCE; cf. LEIB, REPRÉSENTATION.

➤ UTILITY

DOMINATION

Etymologically, "domination" suggests the power of the master (*dominus*) over things (*dominium*, "property rights"), and even more, the power of the master over the slave (*potestas dominica*); cf. OIKONOMIA and ECONOMY, PROPERTY.

"Domination" is, according to the RT: *Dictionnaire de la langue française*, an "authority which, accepted or not, exercises itself fully"; the language of law and political theory is faithful to this idea, since it uses "domination" to refer to an asymmetric relation, which may be legitimate, but which exists prior to the consent of which it may be the object; compare the significant hesitation of Max Weber's translators over the German *Herrschaft*, which they render in French not only by *domination* but also by *autorité*; see HERRSCHAFT and MACHT; cf. AUTHORITY, POWER.

➤ *DROIT*, DUTY, LAW, *LIBERTY*, PRINCIPLE, RIGHT

DOR (ROMANIAN)

ENGLISH	melancholy, homesickness, spleen, loneliness
FRENCH	*désir, douloureux, deuil, tristesse, nostalgie*
GERMAN	*Sehnsucht*
ITALIAN	*duolo*
LATIN	*dolus*
PORTUGUESE	*saudade*
SPANISH	*duelo*

➤ *NOSTALGIA*, and ACEDIA, DASEIN, *MALAISE*, MELANCHOLY, PATHOS, PLEASURE, SAUDADE, SEHNSUCHT, WUNSCH

The Romanian word *dor*, like "spleen," *acedia*, *Sehnsucht*, or *saudade*, is related to the notion of malaise, but gives it a particular meaning by turning it toward an object or toward being. It is a lyrical expression of the feeling of finitude, between folk metaphysics and philosophical reflection, and is self-consciously Romanian. It does not have an equivalent in French, where it is related to painful desire, mourning, sadness, melancholy, nostalgia, languor, the feeling of erotic desire, of internal malaise. The word is related to *dol* in Catalan, Provençal, and Old French (from the last of these come the expressions *dolent, faire dol, avoir dol*). The Romanian *dor* comes from *dolus*, a vernacular Latin noun referring to pain, suffering, mourning (from the classical Latin *doleo, dolere*, from which derive *deuil* in French, *duelo* in Spanish, and *duolo* in Italian). Two verbal and semantic branches come into Romanian from the single Latin root *dolus*: *a dori* (noun *dorinţà*), which means "to desire"; and *a durea* (noun *durere*), which means "to be in pain," "to feel a physical pain."

I. The Asymptotic Experience of *Dor*

The word *dor* is at the center of a constellation of meanings related to the experience of a specific pain: that which one feels as a result of missing something or someone (a person or a cherished place), or as a result of an intimate hope (a desire for what one considers to be a deep fulfillment, for example, the return of a lost relative or friend, a return home, and so on). This experience may have physical manifestations and be made apparent by visible signs (expressions or clothing related to mourning, for example), but the origin of the pain and related feelings is not physical in nature. *Dor* is an affect of the soul, but it is not the expression of a vague feeling; it is always directed at an object, even if the latter is not always identified or definable, and it never expresses a state of passivity, of submission, of withdrawal into oneself or acceptance of one's fate (as is the case with the Portuguese *saudade*, where the presumed solitude is also felt). It refers, on the contrary, to a straining after something, a mobilization of being that seeks actively to acquire or recover a missing object. The frustration felt as pain yields to the quest for a return (like the Greek *nostos* [νόστος]), a search that perpetually feeds itself.

The closest term to *dor* is probably the German *Sehnsucht*. For both terms, the pain is a consequence of absence and is expressed as an impulse, impatience, hope, an internal need, a burning desire to overcome this absence or imperfection. Further, even though it refers to a hope or a despondence aimed at a more or less precise and discrete object, *dor* suggests the impossibility of attaining that object in this life. The tension is positive, but the desire remains unsatisfied and fulfillment impossible. The geometrical figure that best illustrates this tension is the asymptote. *Dor* thus feeds a feeling promising only failure, the impression of desire and the painful experience of the impossibility of attaining fullness. As a lyrical expression of the metaphysical sentiment of being, *dor* is the primeval witness in contemporary language of being qua being, that is, of finite being hoping to go beyond its limits.

II. *Dor* in Romanian Philosophy

The notion of *dor* is widespread in popular poetry and arises in many idiomatic expressions, such as *dor de ducà* (the desire to leave without a particular destination—to go wandering) and *în dorul lelii* (to accomplish something without a precise objective, and reluctantly). *Dor* has been lexicalized and has numerous variations and diminutives (*doruleṭ, doruṭ*), but it is, in fact, ahistorical, and is mainly discussed in the field of literary studies. However, because of its frequency, popularity, and connection with a sort of folk metaphysics, practically untranslatable and indefinable given its diversity of nuance, it has inspired philosophical reflection. Thus, in the poet and philosopher Lucian Blaga and the philosopher Constantin Noica, both very close in their thought to Martin Heidegger, we find developments of *dor* as an expression of the constitution of a self-consciousness and as a characterization of a peculiarly Romanian type of metaphysical research.

Blaga, in "Despre *dor*," determines the philosophical content of *dor* starting from the personifications given to the term in popular poetry and Romanian folklore. He calls this sort of personification, both basic and subtle, "hypostasis," a term borrowed from Neoplatonism and the theology of the first Christian councils. This leads him to define *dor* as an impersonal force, almost malevolent and invincible, which comes to take over the soul, to subordinate it and, having joined with it, to become a sort of cosmic illness, a second nature or a material and spiritual alter ego for the individual. *Dor* as a hypostasis would thus be the equivalent of existence as the unrealization of being and would represent a sort of plea that gets lost, a hope to pierce the horizon and to make being dissolve into something unnamable and indefinite.

For Noica, preoccupied with building up a Romanian philosophy beginning with certain terms and certain specific expressions, *dor* practically has the value of a key word, and all philosophical research in Romanian should, according to him, begin with "an introduction to *dor*" (see Noica, "Introducere la *dor*"). The term represents, in effect, the prototype of a fusion of contraries that does not take place through composition; it is a sort of organic fusion, or a whole that does not admit of being distinguished into parts. Thus, in *dor*, pain meets pleasure and pleasure is born without knowledge of pain. The translation of *dor* should therefore be "pleasure of pain," as the translation of the German *Sehnsucht* should be, according to Noica, "the search for the unfindable." If every word has a share of pain—the pain of not being able to say anything without an inexpressible part remaining, the pain at the fact that no word is genuine speech—then *dor*, with its straining after the infinite, belongs to the common and archaic basis from which thought has extracted both its means of expression and its reason for being.

Anca Vasilu

BIBLIOGRAPHY

Blaga, Lucian. "Despre *dor*" [On *dor*]. In *Spaţiul mioritic* ["Mioritic" space], 289–94. Bucarest: Minerva, 1985. First published in 1936.

Bucur, Marin. *Lucian Blaga, dor şi eternitate* [Lucian Blaga, *dor* and eternity]. Bucarest: Albatros, 1971.

Noica, Constantin. "Introducere la *dor*" [Introduction to *dor*]. In *Creaţie şi frumos în rostirea românească* [Creation and beauty in Romanian speech], 13–17. Bucarest: Eminescu, 1973.

DOXA [δόξα] (GREEK)

ENGLISH   appearance, false appearances, reputation, expectation, glory, opinion, esteem, hallucination, received idea, prejudice

➤ *APPEARANCE*, BELIEF, *PHÉNOMÈNE*, and EIDÔLON, EPISTEMOLOGY, BOX 3, ERSCHEINUNG, GLAUBE, LOGOS, PHANTASIA, *TO BE*, TRUTH

Doxa, from *dokeô* [δοκέω], "to appear" (from the same family as *dechomai* [δέχομαι], "to receive, to welcome, to accept"; cf. Lat. *decet*), is one of the most polysemic Greek words.

To understand the breadth of its meaning, we must combine what we call the objective and the subjective with a spectrum of values ranging from the most positive to the most negative: we can thus range, across different times and doctrines, from the opinion of mortals (subjective negative) to the glory of God (objective positive). Since the term has never ceased to be the subject of philosophical working and reworking, the history of the senses of *doxa* is bound up with a good portion of the history of philosophy.

I. Breadth of Meaning

Doxa combines what a distinction between subjective and objective separates: the former being what one expects, what one believes, what one judges to be good (in Homer we find only *apo doxês* [ἀπὸ δόξης], "against expectation"; *Iliad*, 10.324, and *Odyssey*, 11.344), the latter being what appears, what seems to be the case. The range of meanings on each side covers the full range of values as well, from the most negative to the most positive: from hallucination (false opinion, imagination, conjecture) to the normative rightness of the accepted idea (expectation, esteem, conjecture, belief, dogma, reputation), and from deceptive appearance (illusion, false appearances) to appearance in all its splendor (phenomena, glory). The common translation of "opinion" obviously does not get all that across.

II. Philosophical Elaborations

Doxa has been constantly reworked and reappropriated from system to system. It constitutes, in fact, a sort of indicator for the history of philosophy.

A. The *alêtheia/doxa* distinction

Parmenides gets things started (see TRUTH). The goddess of the poem, for one thing, deploys a distinction between *alêtheia* [ἀλήθεια] and *doxa*, truth and opinion, to structure her revelation: "You must be instructed in everything, both of the untrembling heart of the persuasive truth [*hêmen alêtheiês . . . êtor* (ἠμὲν ἀληθείης . . . ἦτορ)], and of what appears to mortals [*hêde brotôn doxas* (ἠδὲ βροτῶν δόξας)], where there is no true belief [*pistis alêthes* (πίστις ἀληθής)]" (1.28–30); this is picked up again in 8.50–52: "I stop there the faithful speech [*piston logon* (πιστὸν λόγον)] for you and the thought about truth [*êde noêma amphis alêtheiês* (ἠδὲ νόημα ἀμφὶς ἀληθείης)]. Learn henceforth the opinions of mortals [*doxas . . . broteias* (δόξας . . . βροτείας)], by listening to the deceptive ordering [*apatêlon* (ἀπατηλὸν); see TRUTH, Box 7] of my words."

Furthermore, she makes all of the ambiguity of *doxa* manifest, both negative and positive: "You will also learn this: how the things which appear [*ta dokounta* (τὰ δοκοῦντα)—neuter plural participle of *dokein* (δοκεῖν)] must be in their appearing [*chrên dokimôs*—adverb derived from *dokein*, "as is fitting, honestly" according to RT: *Dictionnaire grec-français*, "really, genuinely" for the RT: LSJ—*einai* (χρῆν δοκίμως εἶναι)], those which through all it penetrate all things" (1.31–32). We can gauge the adventurous despair of Parmenides's translators by comparing the translations, all accurate and inaccurate at the same time. Thus, in French, Jean Beaufret gives us, "Apprends aussi comment la diversité qui fait montre d'elle-même devait déployer une présence digne d'être reçue" (*Parménide: Le Poème*); and Marcel Conche, "Tu n'en apprendras pas moins encore ceci: comment il était inévitable que les semblances aient semblance d'être" (*Parménide: Le Poème*; cf. Cassin, *Parménide*). German has more of an even match, but no less diverse. RT: DK gives us, "wie das ihnen Scheinende auf eine probehafte, wahrscheinlich Weise sein müsste"; Ernst Heitsch gives us, "wie das Geltende notwendigerwise

gültig sein musste" (*Parmenides*). The problem is that talk with and about *doxa* is always double-sided: from the point of view of Truth and the One Being, it is ontologically contradictory ("they have chosen to name two forms, thinking that one might not be, in which they are mistaken. They have divided the structure into contraries"; 8.53–55); from the point of view of *doxa* and the *kosmos* [κόσμος], it is phenomenologically splendid and physically dominant, a vector of the beauty of the world captured in poems, myths, and forms of wisdom (cf. Cassin, *Parménide*).

B. *Doxa* as *metaxu*, "intermediate"

In developing an ontological and epistemological system in the *Republic*, Plato elaborates the distinction between "science" (*epistêmê* [ἐπιστήμη]), a faculty or capacity (*dunamis* [δύναμις]) that deals with being and knows it as it is ("*to on gnônai hôs echei*" [τὸ ὄν γνῶναι ὡς ἔχει]; 6.478a), and "opinion," an intermediate (*metaxu*) faculty between knowledge and ignorance, which deals "neither with being nor with non-being" (478c), but grasps "what wanders in between" (*to metaxu planêton* [τὸ μεταξὺ πλανητόν]; 479d). *Doxa* thus constitutes a middle way between the way of non-being (that which is not an object at all, neither an object of science nor an object of opinion) and the way of being or the science of "ideas": thus, "philosophers" look at *auto to kalon* [αὐτὸ τὸ καλόν], "the beautiful itself" (479e), while the mass of "philodoxes" (*philodoxous* [φιλοδόξους]) prefers only to look at "beautiful colors" (480a). The distinction is structured as a separation between the intelligible world and the sensible world, with the image of the line on which *epistêmê* and *dianoia* [διάνοια] jointly constitute *noêsis* [νόησις], which deals with *ousia* [οὐσία] (let us allow, in E. Chambry's terms—it is a nest of untranslatables, however—that "science" and "discursive thought," brought under the head of "intelligence," aim at "essence"), while *pistis* [πίστις] and *eikasia* [εἰκασία], brought under the head of *doxa*, deal with *genesis* [γένεσις] ("faith" and "conjecture," forming "opinion," aimed at "becoming"; 7.533e–534b; cf. 6, end). The Platonic phrase *orthê doxa* [ὀρθὴ δόξα], "right opinion," signals this intermediate status: "right opinion is intermediate between intelligence and ignorance" (*metxu phronêseôs kai amathias* [μεταξὺ φρονήσεως καὶ ἀμαθίας]; *Symposium*, 202a); unlike false opinion, it brings together good sensation with good thought ("*en têi sunapsei aisthêseôs pros dianoian*" [ἐν τῇ συνάψει αἰσθήσεως πρὸς διάνοιαν]; *Theaetetus*, 195d), and is enough that it should be *meta logou* [μετὰ λόγου] (201c, accompanied by reason; but see LOGOS, Box 3) to become science. But, as *doxa*, it can only achieve a lesser truth and a lesser being.

C. The endoxic

The Aristotelian reworking of *doxa* proceeds by way of a re-evaluation of this world, the individual, the contingent, the probably, the persuasive, the common. There can be science, with definition and demonstration, only of the universal and necessary, agreed; but that is then to say, more positively, that there is *doxa* of the individual, which is at the level of "each" (*to kath'hekaston* [τὸ καθ' ἕκαστον]). There is *doxa* of what can be other than it is ("*doxa esti tou endechomenou allôs echein*" [δόξα ἐστὶ τοῦ ἐνδεχομένου ἄλλως ἔχειν]; *Metaphysics* Z, 15, 1039b34–1040a1). The object of *doxa* (*to doxaston* [τὸ δοξαστόν]) may be true and existing ("*tina alêthê men kai onta*" [τινὰ ἀληθῆ μὲν καὶ ὄντα]), but it remains contingent (*Posterior Analytics*, 1.33.88b30–33). This is why opinion is defined as a grasping of immediate and nonnecessary premises ("*hupolêpsis tês amesou protaseôs kai mê anagkaias*" [ὑπόληψις τῆς ἀμέσου προτάσεως καὶ μὴ ἀναγκαίας]; 89a3–4). These "premises in accordance with opinion" (*ek ton kata doxan protaseôn* [ἐκ τῶν κατὰ δόξαν προτάσεων]) serve for the construction of "dialectical syllogisms," as opposed to scientific or demonstrative syllogisms (*Prior Analytics*, 1.46a8–10). Aristotle's use of the word *endoxon* [ἔνδοξον] (literally, that which is "in *doxa*") as a term for this type of premise is an innovation: "A syllogism is dialectical if it proceeds from probable premises [in Brunschwig's translation; 'from accepted ideas' in Tricot's translation]" (*dialektikos de sullogismos ho ex endoxôn sullogizomenos* [διαλεκτικὸς δὲ συλλογισμὸς ὁ ἐξ ἐνδόξων συλλογιζόμενος]) *Topics*, 1.100a29–30; and he defines *endoxa* [ἔνδοξα] as distinct from "true and primary" propositions as "that which is accepted [*ta dokounta*] by all or by the greatest number, or by the wise [*sophois* (σοφοῖς)], and among the latter, either by all or the greatest number, or by the best known [*gnôrimois* (γνωρίμοις)] and most respected [*endoxois* (ἐνδόξοις)]" (100b21–23). We see how *ta endoxa*, likely premises and received ideas, imply the *doxa* of the *endoxoi*, the opinions of illustrious thinkers. We may thus understand why Aristotle's treatises should begin by the structured review of these opinions, which make up the history of the different disciplines: physics (*Physics*, 1), metaphysics (*Metaphysics* A), and so on; and how "doxography," literally "the writing of opinions," should become a genre of its own beginning with Theophrastus's *Phusikôn doxai* (the *Placita* in Latin).

D. The rays of divine glory

The semantic high-point for *doxa* is in the biblical tradition, where the "glory" (*kabod* [כָּבוֹד] in Hebrew) of God is pronounced as soon to be manifested by the crushing of the Egyptians once the Hebrews have crossed the Red Sea: "In the morning, you will see the glory of God" (*kai prôi opsesthe tên doxan tou Kuriou* [καὶ πρωῒ ὄψεσθε τὴν δόξαν τοῦ Κυρίου]) (Exod. 16:7). In the same book (33:18), Moses addresses this prayer to God: "Let me see your glory." The New Testament mentions the spreading of God's glory in the great events of the life of Jesus, especially his baptism (Luke 4:21) and his transfiguration (9:28f.). The disciples see in it the advance signs of "the arrival of the Son of Man in his glory" (Matt. 24:30; Mark 8:38). The glory or splendor of God is often mentioned in the passages of the New Testament or the patristics, especially the Eastern ones, which deal with the blessed vision of the divine essence. The Byzantine theologian Gregory Palamas considers this vision to be inaccessible to created beings, however, and substitutes an understanding of the vision of divine glory as a simple radiance of the energies by which God communicates in his works (see SVET, Box 1).

The bursting forth of the "Presence of God" in the world also occupies an important place in Rabbinic literature, where it is called Shekhinah. This Shekhinah, the name of

which corresponds to the Hebrew *kabod* (though it is not found in the Bible), is often the personification of the "Presence of God" and evokes the mysticism of the celestial light.

Barbara Cassin
Charles Baladier (II, D)

BIBLIOGRAPHY

Aristotle. *Topics*. In *The Complete Works of Aristotle*, vol. 1, edited by J. Barnes, 167–277. Bollingen Series, 71. Princeton, NJ: Princeton University Press, 1984.

Beaufret, Jean. *Parménide: Le Poème*. Paris: Presses Universitaires de France, 1995.

Bringhurst, Robert, et al. *Carving the Elements: A Companion to "The Fragments of Parmenides."* Berkeley, CA: Editions Koch, 2004.

Cassin, Barbara. *Parménide, sur la nature ou sur l'étant: La langue de l'être?* Paris: Éditions du Seuil, 1998.

Conche, Marcel. *Parménide: Le Poème: Fragments*. Paris: Presses Universitaires de France, 1996.

Heitsch, Ernst. *Parmenides*. Munich: Heimeran, 1974.

Plato. *The Republic*. In *Complete Works*. Edited by J. M. Cooper. Indianapolis, IN: Hackett, 1997.

Parmenides of Elea. *Fragments: A Text and Translation*. Edited by D. Gallop. Toronto: University of Toronto Press, 1984. Translation by L. Tarán: *Parmenides*. Princeton, NJ: Princeton University Press, 1965.

DRIVE, INSTINCT, IMPULSE

FRENCH	*pulsion*
GERMAN	*Trieb*
LATIN	*pulsio*

➤ ANXIETY, ENTSTELLUNG, ES, FORCE, GENDER, GESCHLECHT, LEIB, LOVE, PATHOS, PLEASURE, SOUL, UNCONSCIOUS, VERNEINUNG, WUNSCH

The translation of the German psychoanalytic concept *Trieb* into French gave new life to the French word *pulsion*, derived from the Latin *pulsus* or *pulsio* and previously reserved for the physical domain, as the equivalent of force or thrust. Drawing on the romantic tradition (the life-force), on psychophysiology (measurable strength), and on biology (where *Trieb* designates instinct), Sigmund Freud's *Trieb* made it possible to understand the physical transcription of the major somatic forces. Though the translation of *Trieb* as *instinct* was long standard in France, that was chiefly because the specificity of the Freudian notion had not been clearly defined: the object of a *Trieb* is not predetermined. The translation as *pulsion* was established in order to indicate that specificity. On the other hand, the various English translations ("instinct," "drive," and "instinctual drive") remain independent of a precise theoretical choice: the choice of "drive," a term that derives from the same proto-Germanic root as *Trieb*, may very well be accompanied by a biological reading of Freudian theory.

I. The Old Use of the French Term *Pulsion*

Despite a period of fluctuations and hesitations arising from the notion's complexity, French adopted the term *pulsion* rather than *instinct* to translate the German word *Trieb* in Freud's work.

Pulsion, a technical term in the Freudian vocabulary, has become part of ordinary language, which may be explained by the popularization of psychoanalysis. Nonetheless, it was not necessary to create a neologism to translate *Trieb* into French, because *pulsion* was already present in the language, although rarely used before the twentieth century. It is not found, for instance, in Jean-François Féraud's *Dictionnaire* in 1788 (RT: *Dictionnaire critique de la langue française*), or in the 1890 RT: *Dictionnaire général de la langue française du commencement du dix-septième siècle jusqu'à nos jours*. On the other hand, it does appear in Jacob Stoer's *Grand dictionnaire français-latin* (1625), in the sense of "action of impelling." We find an occurrence in Voltaire with the same meaning: "La substance du feu, en entrant dans l'intérieur d'un corps quelconque le dilate en poussant en tout sens ses parties; or cette 'pulsion' . . ." (The substance of fire, entering the interior of any body, dilates it by impelling its parts in all directions. Now, this pulsion . . . : Voltaire, *Essai sur la nature du feu*). *Pulsion* was thus used as a scientific doublet of *poussée*, probably because of its proximity to Latin. The term *pulsion* is in fact directly derived from Latin *pulsum*, the supine of *pellere*, which means "to put in motion, to impel, to repel." Note that the substantive of *pellere* is *pulsus*. *Pulsio*, which means precisely "action of repelling," is a late and rare usage (fourth century CE). Moreover, according to W. von Wartburg's *Französisches Etymologisches Wörterbuch* (1959), *pulsion* does not come from *pulsio* but from a "scholarly derivation from the radical of *pulsare*, *pulsare* being an intensive form of *pellere* and meaning strike, impel violently."

II. The Meaning of *Trieb*

We find this sense of "impel" in the meaning of the German *Trieb*, which derives from the verb *treiben*, whose general meaning is "to put in motion." But why did the requirements of translating Freud's works lead to reviving a disused term? As is often the case in German, we are dealing with a Germano-Latin doublet: *Trieb* is a word derived from a Germanic root that forms a doublet with the word of Latin origin, *Instinkt*, whose use began to spread in scientific literature only in the nineteenth century (in 1760, H. S. Reimarus entitled his book on animal instincts *Triebe der Thiere*). But as is also often the case, the two terms are not equivalent. *Trieb* is an old word in common use, whereas *Instinkt* is a learned word that has the precise meaning of "instinct" in biology, namely, "the innate tendency to determinate acts (depending on the species), executed perfectly without previous experience, and subject to the conditions of the environment" (RT: *Le nouveau petit Robert*, s.v.). *Trieb* has more senses that offer variations on a common theme, the action of driving or impelling: (1) a mechanical impulsion; (2) starting in the late eighteenth century, an internal impulse, exercised either on the organism (particularly the force that makes a plant "grow") or on the mind, on the psychic apparatus. According to the 1984 edition of the Grimms' German dictionary (RT: *Deutsches Wörterbuch*), the main meaning given for *Trieb* is "an internal force that impels, that puts in motion [*innere treibende Kraft*]." Very roughly, we can thus already say that German *Instinkt* contains the idea of a determinate object or action, whereas *Trieb* emphasizes the motive force that puts the organism or the psyche in motion.

- See Box 1.

III. *Trieb* in Freud's Work

In his translations of a few texts by Hippolyte Bernheim (1888, 1892), Freud uses *Instinct* (or *Instinkt*) and *Trieb* interchangeably. However, he moves toward his own later concept of *Trieb*, first regarding the great needs of psychic activity, in his *Project for a Scientific Psychology* (*Entwurf einer Wissenschaftlicher Psychologie*), a study dating from 1895 that was published after his death, and then in the *Interpretation of Dreams* (*Traumdeutung*, 1900), where he mentions desire as a "driving force" (*Triebkraft*) necessary to the formation of dreams. Not until 1915 do we find precise definitions of *Trieb* in his work, in the metapsychological article "Instincts and Their Vicissitudes" ("Triebe und Triebschicksale") and in a reworked paragraph of *Three Essays on the Theory of Sexuality* (*Drei Abhandlungen zur Sexualtheorie*), whose first edition goes back to 1905. In this later version he writes:

> By an "instinct" is provisionally to be understood the psychical representative of an endosomatic, continuously flowing source of stimulation, as contrasted with a "stimulus," which is set up by *single* excitations coming from *without*. The concept of instinct is thus one of those lying on the frontier between the mental and the physical. The simplest and likeliest assumption as to the nature of the instincts would seem to be that in itself an instinct is without quality, and, so far as mental life is concerned, is only to be regarded as a measure of the demand made upon the mind for work. What distinguishes the instincts from one another and endows them with specific qualities is their relation to their somatic sources and to their aims. The source of an instinct is a process of excitation occurring in an organ and the immediate aim of the instinct lies in the removal of this organic stimulus.

> (*Drei Abhandlungen zur Sexualtheorie* 1.5, in *Gesammelte Werke*, 5:67–68; trans. Strachey, *Three Essays on the Theory of Sexuality*, 34)

The article "Instincts and Their Vicissitudes" adds two elements to the definition of the *Trieb*, one relating to its source and the other to its end. First, it gives a name to the quantitative element in a drive, to its "motive factor, the sum total of force or the measure of the demand for work that it represents" (in *Gesammelte Werke*, 10:211; trans. Strachey, 14:110): this is *der Drang*, rendered in the first French translations as *poussée*. Here we have the action of impelling in its quantitative form, which Voltaire called *pulsion*. Freud explains, in the French version, that "ce caractère de poussée . . . est l'essence même de la pulsion" (This driving-character is . . . the very essence of the drive: *Les pulsions et leurs destins*, 32–33). The redundant nature of the formula is peculiar to the translation. In German, *Trieb* is an extension of *Drang* to the mind-body as a whole; in French, *pulsion* is initially used as a learned, technical form of *poussée*. Second, the same article indicates that the drive has an object. And the definition of the relation between the drive and its object has strongly influenced the choice of a term other than *instinct* to translate *Trieb*: "The object of the drive is that in which or by which the drive can attain its goal. It is what is most variable in the drive, but is assigned to it only by virtue of its ability to make satisfaction possible" (Freud, *Instincts and Their Vicissitudes*, in *Gesammelte Werke*, vol. 10, trans. Strachey).

1

TRIEB in Kant and Goethe

➤ ANIMAL, BILDUNG

We find a trace of the distinction between *Trieb* and *Instinkt* in Kant's *Critique of Judgment*. In §83, *Trieb* is used to designate animal desire in *man*: ". . . the despotism of desires [*Begierden*]. By these, tied as we are to certain natural things, we are rendered incapable even of choosing, while we allow those impulses [*Triebe*] to serve as fetters which nature has given us as guiding threads, that we should not neglect or injure the destination of our animal nature" (trans. Bernard). In a note to §90, *Instinkt* signifies the determined activity of the animal: "We then try at the same time to show that the ground of the artisan faculty of beasts [*des tierischen Kunstvermögens*], which we call instinct [*Instinkt*], specifically different as it is in fact from reason, has yet a similar relation to its effect (the buildings of the beaver as compared with those of men)" (trans. Bernard).

But the distinction is not actually so sharp: in the nineteenth century, *Trieb* could be used in the precise sense of instinct as "innate tendency to specific acts," and *Instinkt* could have the more general sense of "natural internal force" (Goethe to Schiller: "Last week I fell under the sway of a strange instinct [*Vorige Woche bin ich von einem sonderbaren Instincte befallen worden*]"). But the meanings remain distinct, and *Trieb* is not a simple doublet of *Instinkt*.

In addition to its common meaning, in the eighteenth century, *Trieb* was used to Germanize a Latin expression, *nisus formativus* (the formative impulse), which designates living matter's organizing principle, or, more precisely, the activity of organized matter in its formative operation. In §81 of the *Critique of Judgment*, which is about epigenesis and preformation, Kant cites the work of the epigeneticist Johann Friedrich Blumenbach, *Über den Bildungstrieb* (1781). He notes that Blumenbach distinguishes this "formative impulse" as "faculty of matter [*Vermögen der Materie*]" from the "merely mechanical formative power [*bloß mechanische Bildungskraft*]" (trans. Bernard). *Bildungstrieb* is rendered in A. Philonenko's French translation (1986) as *tendance formatrice* and in A. J.-J. Delamarre's translation (1985) as *pulsion de formation*. In his work on morphology, Goethe adopts this distinction: "The word 'force' [*Kraft*] refers first of all to something purely physical, or even mechanical, and what is to be organized on the basis of this matter remains for us obscure and incomprehensible. It was Blumenbach who invented the definitive and perfect expression by giving an anthropomorphic twist to the solution to the riddle and calling the subject of debate a *nisus formativus*, an impulse [*Trieb*], an intense activity that was supposed to be the actual principle of formation" (Goethe, *Zur Morphologie*).

BIBLIOGRAPHY

Goethe, Johann Wolfgang von. *Zur Morphologie*. In *Sämtliche Werke*, edited by Hans J. Becker, Gerhard H. Müller, John Neubauer, and Peter Schmidt, vol. 12. Munich: Hanser, 1989.

Kant, Immanuel. *A Critique of Judgment*. Translated by John Henry Bernard. London: Macmillan, 1914.

Thus Freud's *Trieb* combines several dimensions:

1. The biological dimension: the reference to the body's major needs, which indicates the biological nature of the drive, is constantly present. This is shown in the opening lines of the first edition of *Three Essays on the Theory of Sexuality*, which were never changed: "The fact of the existence of sexual needs in human beings and animals is expressed in biology by the assumption of a 'sexual instinct,' on the analogy of the instinct of nutrition [*Trieb nach Nahrungsaufnahme*], that is, of hunger" (in *Gesammelte Werke* 5:33; *Three Essays on the Theory of Sexuality*, trans. Strachey). In his preface to the fourth edition, Freud speaks of a "part of the theory which lies on the frontiers of biology" (*Three Essays on the Theory of Sexuality*, trans. Strachey). We can assume that he is alluding to the drive.

2. The romantic dimension: in the late eighteenth century, when *Trieb* acquired its meaning of "natural internal force acting on the mind and the body," this term became a key concept in German romanticism. The relation to a determinate object was less important than the idea of multiple activities. In Goethe, who identifies multiple *Triebe* (*Goethes Werke*, vol. 47), we find *Äußerungstrieb* (drive to externalize), *Lusttrieb* (drive to pleasure), *Nachahmungstrieb* (drive to imitate), and *Bildungstrieb* (drive to education). Henri Vermorel emphasizes the importance of the term in the poets and naturalists (starting with Goethe), the philosophers (e.g., Johann Gottlieb Fichte), and the German romantic psychiatrists (notably J.C.A. Heinroth): "In founding a psychology incorporating the concept of the unconscious, the romantics used the word *Trieb* in the sense of a psychic life force" (Vermorel, "La pulsion de Goethe à Freud").

3. The psychophysical dimension: the *Project for a Scientific Psychology* testifies to the importance of an energetic schema of physical origin applied to psychic functioning. Freud, through his teacher E. W. von Brücke, was connected with the psychophysical trend of the second half of the nineteenth century, and especially with Hermann von Helmholtz, who used the term *Triebkraft* to designate mechanical force (Vermorel). We can note, however, that Helmholtz's school, beneath its apparently strict positivism, remained closely dependent on the *Naturphilosophie* that came out of F.W.J. Schelling in particular: the romantic inspiration thus seems central, and allows us to understand, for instance, Freud's speculations on the death drive and his constant references to Goethe's *Faust*.

It is the precise meaning that *Trieb* acquires in Freud starting in 1915 that will enable us to follow the avatars of the sexual "drive," especially in the form of "partial drives" (*Partialtriebe*). References to biology are not, of course, eliminated, but Freud no longer speaks of the drive's determinate relation to an object. And the connection with biology seems still more problematic when Freud forms the hypothesis of a "death drive" in *Beyond the Pleasure Principle* (1920).

IV. French Translations of Freud's *Trieb*

The complexity of Freud's notion explains the hesitations of French translators. We can say of Freud what Charles Du Bos said of Goethe: "To render all the essential connotations of the word *Trieb* in Goethe, we would need our three words *instinct*, *besoin*, and *propulsion*, not to mention *impulsion*" (cited in Vermorel, "La pulsion de Goethe à Freud"). The task is to render the idea of motive force and tendency without prejudging the question of the innate or acquired nature of the process (for Freud, while partial sexual drives are innate, their vicissitudes are largely connected with the individual's history, but only in part, because *Three Essays on the Theory of Sexuality* emphasizes the hereditary character of the psychic dikes—disgust, shame, and so on—erected against partial pulsions during the so-called latency period). *Besoin* is reserved for *Bedürfnis*, and *impulsion* for *Impuls*. But how has the term *Trieb* itself been translated into French?

Although translations of Freud into French began very late—with one exception, not before 1920—the problems of standardizing their vocabulary were raised quite early. Shortly after the creation of the Société psychanalytique de Paris (1926), a linguistic committee was set up to standardize the French psychoanalytic vocabulary. In the review of the meeting held on 31 May 1927, we read: "At M. Hesnard's suggestion, the term *pulsion* is unanimously adopted to translate *Trieb*" (*Revue Française de Psychanalyse*, no. 1 [1927]). But before the 1967 publication of RT: *Vocabulaire de la psychanalyse*, which established this terminological choice, the committee's decision had little effect. The discussion here will be limited to the translation of two major texts.

The 1934 French edition of *Trois essais sur la théorie de la sexualité*, translated by Blanche Reverchon (1923), ignores the committee's decision to use *pulsion*. *Trieb* is rendered as *instinct* (in the most "biological" expressions) or *tendance* (notably when Freud gives a rigorous definition of the concept); sometimes the word is not translated at all (thus *sexuelle Triebkräfte* is rendered as *forces sexuelles*). In 1936, Marie Bonaparte and Anne Berman translated *Triebe und Triebschicksale* as *Les pulsions et leurs destins*. But the title is misleading. There are some surprising hesitations: "Comment l'instinct se comporte-t-il par rapport à l'excitation? Rien ne nous empêche d'intégrer le concept de la pulsion dans celui de l'excitation, ni de dire que l'instinct est une excitation au sens psychique" (How does instinct behave in relation to excitation? Nothing prevents us from including the concept of drive within that of excitation, nor from saying that instinct is an excitation in the psychic sense: *Les pulsions*, 30). But the term *instinct* was later used almost exclusively.

We can see which interpretation of the notion of *Trieb* prevailed in France by following a theoretical study by Bonaparte that appeared in the *Revue Française de Psychanalyse* in 1934, entitled "Introduction à la théorie des instincts." Although it paraphrases the text of *Three Essays on the Theory of Sexuality*, it interprets it in a clearly biological way:

> People have long said that the two great instincts that motivate living beings are hunger and love. But whereas the term "hunger" itself already implies the dynamic notion of a biological drive [*pulsion*], the drive [*pulsion*] that is the source of amorous tendencies does not have an

equivalent name in ordinary language. However, this kind of drive is to be postulated, and that is why the psychoanalytic science created by Freud has given the generic name of *libido* to the biological force that manifests itself in all the phenomena of sexuality.

Freud's originality seems to come down to having granted a preponderant place to the "sex drive," and not to having given the concept of *Trieb* a meaning that is irreducible to its common biological meaning. We see that with the term *pulsion* being interpreted in a biological sense, *instinct* can be used in the rest of this text, and particularly in the title.

Thus it was the *Vocabulaire de la psychanalyse* that determined the use of *pulsion* to translate *Trieb*, a usage reaffirmed in the *Œuvres complètes de Freud/Psychanalyse*. Laplanche and Pontalis stress the difference between *Trieb* and the Freudian use of *Instinkt*, which designates "a behavior determined by heredity and appearing in an almost identical form in all individuals of a single species" (RT: *Vocabulaire de la psychanalyse*, s.v. *Pulsion*). According to them, translating *Trieb* by *instinct* or *tendance* would be tantamount to "blurring the originality of the Freudian conception, notably the thesis of the relatively indeterminate character of the motivating impulse, the notions of the contingency of the object, and the variability of the goals" (RT: *Vocabulaire de la psychanalyse*, s.v. *Instinct*).

■ See Box 2.

V. English Translations: "Instinct" and "Drive"

Regarding English translations of *Trieb*, we must once again distinguish several questions. From a strictly terminological point of view, "drive" is the equivalent of *Trieb*: the two words come from the Gothic *dreiban*. Although "drive" well expresses the idea of movement ("to drive" retains mainly the first, physical meaning of *treiben*: "to set in motion"), the meaning of "natural internal force," which was established by German romanticism, appears very late in English: it is still absent from the 1933 edition of the *Oxford English Dictionary*. The 1980 edition mentions a psychological meaning that amounts to making "drive" a synonym of "instinct," a word that has long been used to designate an innate tendency of living beings to perform certain acts: "What instinct hadst thou for it?" (Shakespeare, *Henry IV, Part 1*, 2.4.299). "Instinct" is the term adopted by James Strachey, the main translator of the English version of Freud's complete works (1953–66). He explains the reasons for this choice in his "Notes on Some Technical Terms Whose Translation Calls for Comment" (*Standard Edition*, 1:xxiv–xxv). (His justification is itself, once again, an interpretation: "There seems little doubt that, from the standpoint of modern biology, Freud used the word '*Trieb*' to cover a variety of different concepts" [ibid.].) But is this point of view the only pertinent one? Didn't Freud give a precise definition of what he meant by *Trieb*?

We must note that, unlike the French *pulsion*, "drive" is a very common word (especially in American English), but one whose psychobiological use is recent. It is not rigorously distinguished from "instinct." We can observe an odd effect of intersection: Strachey's note is contemporary with the *Vocabulaire de la psychanalyse*, but its meaning and its effect were inverse. The *Vocabulaire* definitively established the

2

The *libido* as the driving force of sex life

Whereas the adjective *libidineux* (from Lat. *libidinosus*, frequent in Cicero and Seneca) appeared in French in the eighteenth century (in the *Roman des sept sages*) and was adopted by the French Academy in 1762, the substantive *libido* appeared in French, as in other European languages, only in the nineteenth century, as a term in the vocabulary of medical psychology and sexology, especially in German. In the early twentieth century, it took its place as one of the untranslatable terms in psychoanalysis, with the sense of "the driving force of sex life" that Freud gave it, for example, in his *New Introductory Lectures on Psychoanalysis* (1933). It was around this notion that Freud developed the stages of his theories of the drives and of the role of sexuality in the psyche. In 1905, in the first of *Three Essays on the Theory of Sexuality*, he explained the choice of this word by analogy with the instinct of nutrition that is called hunger. "Everyday language possesses no counterpart to the word 'hunger,' but science makes use of the word 'libido' for that purpose" (*Gesammelte Werke*, vol. 5, trans. Strachey). In a note added to this study in 1910, Freud remarks: "The only appropriate word in the German language, *Lust*, is unfortunately ambiguous, and is used to denote the experience both of a need and of a gratification" (ibid.; see PLEASURE).

The Latin *libido* (or *lubido*), which derives from the impersonal *libet* (or *lubet*), with the meaning of "it pleases," and which signifies "desire, craving, and particularly sensual and erotic desire" (RT: *Dictionnaire étymologique de la langue latine*, s.v. *lubet*), comes from an "Indo-European root that was probably popular in nature," notably from the Sanskrit *lubh* (*lúbhyati*, "he desires"), and is found in German *Liebe* and English "love." Present particularly in Cicero, who prefers it to *cupiditas* as a translation of the Greek *epithumia* [ἐπιθυμία] (desire), in Ovid the term *libido* seems to suggest the idea that such a form of desire is in some way a prerogative of feminine sexuality. That is an idea that reappears in German *Sexualwissenschaft* when it makes the clitoris the *sedes libidinus* (cf. P. Kaufmann,

in *Encyclopædia Universalis*, s.v. *Libido*), whereas Freud combats it by writing that "there is only one *libido* that is put in the service of both the masculine and the feminine sexual function," and that although the connection conventionally made between virility and activity inclines us to describe it as virile, it is nonetheless not without passive goals (*New Introductory Lectures on Psycho-analysis*, in *Standard Edition*, trans. Strachey, vol. 22).

The *libido* occupies a major place in Christian moral theology, especially in Saint Augustine, that deeply influenced later periods on this point. Of the three terms *cupiditas*, *concupiscentia*, and *libido*, which are not, moreover, univocal, Augustine makes the latter a synonym of *concupiscentia carnis*, that is, of sexual desire, except when it is specified that the *libido* has an object other than a sexual one (such as drink, money, or power). But the principal characteristic of this Augustinian *libido* is that it is a desire morally unbalanced by a vehemence that perverts the will. It becomes a pleasure in evil that proceeds from the first pleasure that humanity experienced in original sin and that arouses the appetite for new sins, the personal sins of every descendent of Adam through which "the obscene areas of the body are excited." Despite his insistence on the moral disorder of the will that the *libido* represents in his view, in connecting it essentially with the sex drive, which has its own dynamism, Augustine nonetheless appears to be closer to Freud than are the sexologists of the late nineteenth century, and especially than Carl Jung. The former—figures such as Albert Moll, Henry Havelock Ellis, and Richard von Krafft-Ebing—used the Latin expression *libido sexualis*, which was considered more "scientific," to designate the subject of a new discipline that sought to describe the characters, classified as either normal or pathological, of an "instinct" connected with biology or with culture in general. As for Jung, whereas Freud's *libido* is the desire for an object whose enjoyment constitutes the goal of the sex drive, in his *Wandlungen und Symbole der Libido* (1912), he makes it a completely

desexualized tendency turned toward the world and not toward an object of erotic satisfaction, open to the future rather than determined by the subject's past, assimilated to a kind of *élan vital*, and reduced to a simple "interest" of an existential nature.

In Freud, the *libido*, which is identified with the energy of the sex drive, is cathected on objects in whose investment it can change at will, just as it can also change its goal, as in sublimation. In reality, it is through this *libido* understood in the sense of an appetite for an object throughout a series whose initial moment goes back to the "first helping presence," that of the nursing mother, that Freud, despite the importance—secondary, in fact—that he accords to the "*libido* of the self," opposes most radically Jung's theory, which is based on "introversion," that is, the withdrawal of the *libido* toward the subject's inner world. And even when he posits a new dualism between the life-force and the death-drive and assimilates the *libido* to the *Eros* of the poets and philosophers, the author of *Beyond the Pleasure Principle* retains all of the life-force's power in its Latin form, which renders the universality of the concept of sexuality and therefore does not require transcription into other languages. In this respect, by retaining the Latin term, Freud subverted the old jargon of the specialists. He made the *libido* the focus of a scandal that began in 1910 with the multiple forms of resistance with which psychoanalysis met in each country, where it was always and everywhere described as a pansexualist doctrine: "Too 'Germanic' in the eyes of the French, . . . too 'Jewish' for Nazism, too 'bourgeois' for communism—that is, as for Jung, always too 'sexual'" (RT: *Dictionnaire de la psychanalyse*, s.v.).

Charles Baladier

BIBLIOGRAPHY

Freud, Sigmund. *Gesammelte Werke*. 18 vols. Frankfurt: Fischer, 1940–52. Translation by James Strachey: *The Standard Edition of the Complete Psychological Works of Sigmund Freud*, edited by James Strachey. 24 vols. London: Hogarth Press, 1953–66.

choice of an unusual word to translate a complex concept, on the borderline between the biological, the psychological, and the physical. All subsequent French translations have adopted this choice. Strachey's choice was immediately criticized. Before the *Standard Edition*, English translations rendered *Trieb* by "drive," "instinct," or "impulse" (E. Jones, A. A. Brill, H. W. Chase, J. Rivière).

If we examine the *Psychoanalytic Quarterly* over an extended period, from the 1940s to the 1980s, we find three terms used to translate (or to refuse to translate) Freud's *Trieb*: "instinct," "instinctual drive," and "drive." We should not conclude from this that Freud's definition and the distinction between *Instinkt* and *Trieb* are not taken into account, as is shown by the following:

Every attempt to apply the idea of instinct to human beings was made difficult by the fact that since Antiquity, it has been thought that animals in particular are guided in their actions by instincts. So that in the nineteenth century instinct was generally conceived not only in its physiological and hereditary dimension, but also as more specifically animal than human. In English, the term was ambiguous. But scientists writing in German, like Freud, were capable of distinguishing *Instinkt*, the instinct of animals, from *Trieb*, the drive in humans, the latter term referring to the idea of impulse and implying, up to a certain point, thought processes: its nature is thus not purely automatic or reflex.

> (Burnham, "Medical Origins," 196–97)

The theoretical recognition of Freud's *Trieb* thus does not necessarily affect language (e.g., a work that appeared in 1970 has the title *Basic Psychoanalytic Concepts of the Theory of Instincts*). The situation is comparable to that in France before Laplanche and Pontalis, under Jacques Lacan's influence, emphasized the specificity of Freud's concept and the necessity of a translation that does it justice. It is striking that in the articles published in the *Psychoanalytic Quarterly*, the terminological variation is accompanied by an interpretation of *Trieb* in the most diverse senses: ego-psychology, behaviorism, and even Pavlovian conditioning.

Alexandre Abensour

BIBLIOGRAPHY

Bonaparte, Marie. "Introduction à la théorie des instincts." *Revue Française de Psychanalyse* 7, no. 3 (1934): 417–52.

Burnham, John C. "The Medical Origins and Cultural Use of Freud's Instinctual Drive Theory." *Psychoanalytic Quarterly* 43, no. 2 (1974): 193–217.

Frank, George. "*Triebe* and Their Vicissitudes: Freud's Theory of Motivation Reconsidered." *Psychoanalytic Psychology* 20 (2003): 691–97.

Freud, Sigmund. *Collected Papers*. Edited by Ernest Jones. Translated by Joan Rivière. 5 vols. London: International Psycho-Analytical Press, 1924–50.

———. *Gesammelte Werke*. 18 vols. Frankfurt: Fischer, 1940–52. Translation by James Strachey: *The Standard Edition of the Complete Psychological Works of Sigmund Freud*. Edited by James Strachey. 24 vols. London: Hogarth Press, 1953–66.

———. *The Interpretation of Dreams*. Translated by A. A. Brill. London: W. H. Allen, 1913.

———. *Œuvres complètes de Freud/Psychanalyse*. Translated by A. Bourguignon, P. Cotet, and J. LaPlanche. Paris: Presses Universitaires de France, 1988.

———. "The Origin and Development of Psychoanalysis." Translated by H. W. Chase. *American Journal of Psychology* 21 (1910): 180–225.

———. *Les pulsions et leurs destins*. Translated by Marie Bonaparte and Anne Berman. *Revue Française de Psychanalyse* 9, no. 1 (1936).

———. *Selected Papers on Hysteria and Other Psychoneuroses*. Translated by A. A. Brill. New York: Journal of Nervous and Mental Disease Publishing Company, 1910.

———. *Three Contributions to the Sexual Theory*. Translated by A. A. Brill. New York: Journal of Nervous and Mental Disease Publishing Company, 1910.

———. *Three Essays on the Theory of Sexuality*. Translated by James Strachey. New York: Basic Books, 2000.

———. *Trois essais sur la théorie de la sexualité*. Translated by B. Reverchon. Paris: Gallimard / La Pléiade, 1934.

Goethe, Johann Wolfgang von. *Goethes Werke*. Stuttgart: J. G. Cotta, 1828–42.

Mijola, Alain de, ed. *International Dictionary of Psychoanalysis*. Detroit, MI: Macmillan Reference USA, 2005.

Mills, Jon. "Clarifications on *Trieb*: Freud's Theory of Motivation Reinstated." *Psychoanalytic Psychology* 21 (2004): 673–77.

Ornston, Darius Gray, Jr. "Freud, 'l'école de Helmholtz' et la médecine romantique." In *Freud: Judéité, lumières et romantismes*, edited by Henri Vermorel, Anne Clancier, and Madeleine Vermorel. Lausanne, Switz.: Delachaux-Niestlé, 1995.

Solms, Mark. "Controversies in Freud Translation." *Psychoanalysis and History* 1 (1999): 28–43.

Steiner, Riccardo. "A World Wide International Trade Mark of Genuineness?—Some Observations on the History of the English Translation of the Work of Sigmund Freud, Focusing Mainly on His Technical Terms." *International Review of Psychoanalysis* 14 (1987): 33–102.

Vermorel, Henri. "Dossier: Freud traduit et traducteur." *Revue Française de Psychanalyse* 50 (July 1986): 1231–96.

———. "La pulsion de Goethe à Freud." *Bulletin du Groupe Lyonnais* 16 (1989): 13–27.

Voltaire. *Essai sur la nature du feu et sur sa propagation*. In *Œuvres complètes de Voltaire*, edited by Louis Moland, vol. 22, *Mélanges* 1. Paris: Garnier, 1879.

Wartburg, Walther von. *Französisches etymologisches Wörterbuch*. Basel, Switz.: Zbindinden, 1959.

| DROIT

Droit comes from *directus*, "in a straight line, without deviation," from *dirigere*, "to trace paths," then "to trace the path," from the root *reg'-, which indicates movement in a straight line, and which is also the source of *règle* (*regula*) and *roi* (*rex*). This metaphor of rectitude is found in most European languages (Eng. "right," Ger. *Recht*). *Droit* today refers to a body of rules considered to be just or legitimate that link the legal domain to the moral domain, as is especially visible in the English "right"; see RIGHT/JUST/GOOD.

I. *Droit* and Law

In Greek, the originally geometrical concept *orthotês* [ὀρθότης], "straightness," is strictly logical or moral in its extension; see TRUTH and THEMIS. Even though *dikê* [δίκη] can be used to refer to the same thing as *jus* (what one applies when rendering a judgment), the network of law, justice, and right is only established later, in Latin—*lex*, *jus*, and *directum*—a crucial component of the Roman Empire, which considers itself to have a proprietary claim over *jus*; see LEX, and LAW, TORAH. See also *AUTHORITY, JUSTICE* [FAIR, RIGHT/JUST/GOOD].

II. *Droit, Droits, État de Droit*

Topics of interest include the relationship between law (*droit naturel*, *droit positif*), rights (*droits de l'homme*, *droit des minorités*), and the rule of law (*l'Etat de droit*, *Rechtsstaat*), as reflected in different histories and national traditions; see, besides LEX, which provides the matrix of principal distinctions, CIVIL RIGHTS, CIVIL SOCIETY, *JUSTICE*, RULE OF LAW; cf. CIVILTÀ, *STATE* [POLIS, STATO].

III. *Droit*, Duty, Fact

1. *Droit* arises in morality as related to permission and promising, in counterpoint to duty and debt; see DUTY, SOLLEN, WILLKÜR; cf. *ALLIANCE, DESTINY, OBLIGATION*, PARDON.
2. The legal question "*Quid facti/quid juris?*" (What is the matter of fact, what is the matter of law?) is echoed in the moral distinction between being and how one ought to be, which cuts across a grasping and an appreciation of the real, and of the requirements that demand satisfaction; see CLAIM, MATTER OF FACT, REALITY, RES, TATSACHE; cf. ES GIBT, *FACT, IL Y A*, SACHVERHALT, *TO BE*.

➤ MORALS, *SOCIETY*

DRUGOJ [другой] (RUSSIAN)

ENGLISH   the other, others

➤ *AUTRUI*, MITMENSCH and I/ME/MYSELF, LOVE, POSTUPOK, RUSSIAN, SAMOST', SOBORNOST', STRADANIE, SVOBODA, TRUTH

In Russian, the numerical distinction between *odin* [один] (the one) and *drugoj* [другой] (the other) implies proximity: *drugoj*, "other, second," is formed from the root *drug*, "friend, comrade." Thus, in philosophy, in Florensky and Bakhtin, *drugoj* has the connotation of "friend, loved one, *philos* [φίλος]."

I. The Semantic Constellation

The Old Slavic root *drug* is still found in most Slavic languages: in the Russian *drug* [друг], the Polish *druh*, "friend," the Serbo-Croatian *drug*, "companion, comrade," the Czech *druh*, "species, kind." It has in addition a number of derived forms that express, in one way or another, the idea of association: Russian *družba* [дружба], "friendship," Serbo-Croation *družba*, "organization, group, coterie," Czech *družice*, "satellite," Polish *družyna*, "team, detachment," Ukranian *družyna* [дружина], "spouse," etc. (see RT: *A Dictionary of Slavic Word Families*, 109–11).

Most etymological dictionaries link the Old Slavic *drug* with the Indo-European root **dhrugh*, "to be firm, solid," and **dhreu*, "firm, faithful" (see, for example, RT: *Etymological Dictionary of the Russian Language*, 198; *Etymologičny*, 2: 134). Among the terms with the same origin, we find the German *trauen*, the English "trust" and "truth," the Greek *drus* [δρῦς], "tree, oak" (cf. "tree," Slavonic *drevo* [древо], "tree," *dryad*, etc.—see RT: *Le Vocabulaire des institutions indo-européennes*, vol. 1). The secondary sense of *drug*, as a numerical pronoun and adjective, was developed by way of the expression "*drug druga*" (one another). This kind of development, from a primary sense of the root, "friend" (*amicus*), toward the sense of "other" (*alius*) and of "second" (*secundus*) by inversion, is a widespread phenomenon in Slavic languages (see RT: *Ètimologičeskij slovar' russkogo jazyka*, 543; *Etymologičny*, vol. 2).

The word *drug* in modern Russian refers to "a person related to another by mutual trust, devotion, friendship" (see RT: *Ètimologičeskij slovar' slavianskykh jazykov*, vol. 5). In fact, the simple numerical distinction between *odin* [один] (the one) and *drugoj* (the other) implies in Russian proximity rather than externality or difference. That is why in philosophy *drugoj* connotes not only difference but also intimacy and friendship.

II. *Drugoj* as a Personalist Term

Philosophy has often taken advantage of this unique linguistic feature. Thus, Paul Florensky, in *The Pillar and the Ground of Truth*, claims that in *družba* (friendship) a person goes beyond his own limits and discovers another (*drugoj*)—a friend, *drug*. Florensky compares the Russian *drug* and the Greek *philos* [φίλος]; he writes that *družba* is based on "the love of friendship" or "friendly love" (*druzeskaja ljubov'* [дружеская любовь]). According to Florensky, the love of friendship is "the love that includes a part of *erôs* [ἔρως], of *philia* [φιλία] and *agapê* [ἀγάπη], which the Ancients attempted to indicate by the compound *philophrosunê*, [φιλοφροσύνη] (ibid.). *Philophrosunê*, translated by "benevolence" or "good mood,"

is formed from *philophroneô* [φιλοφρονέω], "to think, to feel *philia* ("love/friendship"; see LOVE)." A common life of friendship "means that joy (*radost'* [радость]) and suffering (*stradanie* [страдание]; see STRADANIE) are common" (ibid.); the soul (*duša* [душа]) itself is shared between friends. For Florensky, *družba* is the discovery of another I (*drugogo ja* [другого я]) in a friend (*v druge* [в друге]) (ibid.).

Similarly, Bakhtin, in his early work, puts the relationship between *ja* [я] (I) and *drugoj* (another) at the center of his personalist aesthetics. "To contemplate aesthetically means to refer an object to the valuative plane of the *other*" (Bakhtin, "K folosofii postupka"). The task of the author (*avtor* [автор]) consists in finding "an essential approach to life from outside" (*izvne* [извне])" (Bakhtin, "Avtor i geroj"). To do this, he must see in his *drugoj* (in the heroic character of the novel) what the *drugoj* is incapable of seeing in himself. The author must complete and perfect the life of the hero until it forms a totality. He only succeeds, however, if he approves with a love (*ljubov'* [любовь]) that accepts all (*priemlet vsü* [приемлет всё]), the *drugoj* as a living and mortal [смертный] human being. The aesthetic vision of Bakhtin is a sort of creator's love, "loving contemplation," a compound of *philia* and *theôria* [θεωρία]. "Only love is capable of being aesthetically productive; only in correlation with the loved is fullness of the manifold possible." In this way the relationship of *philophrosunê* to *drugoj*, which makes no judgment, can achieve the meaning of a universal aesthetic principle.

Andrij Vasylchenko

BIBLIOGRAPHY

Bakhtin, Mikhail. "Avtor i geroj èstetičeskoj deiatel'nosti." In *Èstetika slovesnogo tvorčestva*. Moscow: Iskusstvo, 1979. Written in the 1920s. Translation by V. Liapunov and K. Brostrom: "Author and Hero in Aesthetic Activity." In *Art and Answerability: Early Philosophical Essays*, edited by M. Holquist and V. Liapunov. Austin: University of Texas Press, 1990.

———. "K folosofii postupka." In *Filosofija i sociologija nauki i texniki* [Philosophy and sociology of science and technology]. Moscow: Nauka, 1986. Written at the beginning of the 1920s. Translation by V. Liapunov: *Towards a Philosophy of the Act*, edited by V. Liapunov and M. Holquist. Austin: University of Texas Press, 1993.

Florensky, Paul. *The Pillar and the Ground of Truth*. Translated by B. Jakim. Princeton, NJ: Princeton University Press, 1997.

DUENDE (SPANISH)

ENGLISH   spirit, wit, charm, spell, cunning

➤ *DEMON* [DAIMÔN], and DEVIL, GOD, *GRACE*, INGENIUM, LEGGIADRIA, MÊTIS, OIKONOMIA, PIETAS, RELIGIO

The Spanish word *duende*, marked by folklore and by its regional origins, does not have a stable definition, although more and more it becomes clearly related to the demonic and to poetic creativity. For approximations, we need to use two different registers, one more archaic, which is related to the will o' the wisp, goblins, and sprites; the other more figurative, which is related to notions of charm, enchantment, and spells but also to grace.

The noun *duende* appears in Leonese in the thirteenth century with the meaning "master [of the house]," from duen (de casa), derived from dueño (master, owner), which itself comes from the Latin dominus (master, lord). In fifteenth-century Castilian, it sometimes has the meaning of "mischievous spirit," but more commonly that of a "spirit which haunts the house." It became widespread in this popular sense, as shown by RT: *Tesoro de la lengua castellana o española* (1611): "*Duende*: one of the spirits who fell with Lucifer . . . , of whom some stayed at the surface of the Earth. They have a habit of frightening people by appearing in houses, mountains, and caves, taking on a fantastical body." A variety of legends appeared concerning these evil spirits: they guard mysteriously buried treasures; they fight greedy men; they have a possibility of becoming all-powerful. It was even claimed, for revenge, for gain, or as a joke, that certain houses were indeed haunted by a *duende*.

An evil spirit of this sort is related to local genii, lemures, larvae, lares, and penates of Roman mythology. In RT: *Tesoro de las dos lenguas española y francesa* (1607), Oudin, the interpreter for King Henry IV of France, defines it thus: "Goblin, sprite, wisp, spirit which travels through houses at night. In jargon, the rounds [that is, the rounds of argousins who burst in without warning]." RT: *Diccionario de autoridades* (1726) gives an unexpected etymology for the word (the Ar. *douar* [دوار], "house," is given as the source) but nonetheless offers a precise report of the meaning that was accepted from then on: "Species of goblin or demon who is so called because it usually infects houses." This meaning is indeed the one that Calderón de la Barca uses, with humor, in his comedy entitled *La dama duende* (1620), in which the heroine plays a dazzling game of amorous hide-and-seek.

In the eighteenth century, with the rise of the press, the word became the title of an eclectic publication by a certain Juan Antonio Mercadal, whose identity is unknown: *El duende especulativo, sobre la vida civil* (The speculative spirit, on civil life; 1761). In the nineteenth century, no doubt inspired by this example, the romantic writer José Mariano de Larra founded the short-lived magazine *Duende satírico del día* (Feb.–Dec. 1828), to which he was in fact the only contributor. RT: *Diccionario nacional ó gran diccionario clásico de la lengua española*, by R. J. Dominguez, notes the following sense, henceforth established: "Spirit that, according to the common people, resides in certain houses, worrying the inhabitants and causing a great amount of noise and destruction at night." He adds two expressions that are still in use today: *tener duende* (to be preoccupied by something), and *parecer un duende, andar como un duende* (to spring up like a devil).

Later, the word acquires a more and more figurative sense. The satirical meaning takes a virulent turn in one of B. Pérez Galdós's historical novels, *Los duendes de la camarilla*, which describes the corruption of the regime and the wild political intrigues under Isabella's reign on the eve of the Revolution of 1868. The 1956 edition of the dictionary of the Real Academia Española takes over the definition of R. J. Domínguez word for word but adds a new meaning, which is fundamental: that of "mysterious and ineffable charm." This last one is a regional meaning, but it became firmly established. The meaning of *duende* had become somewhat frozen in the dictionaries, but it nevertheless flourished in a region of Spain with which it had a deep affinity: Andalusia.

In his famous lecture entitled *Play and Theory of the Duende*, given in Havana in 1933, Federico García Lorca, himself possessed by a *duende*, that is, by the pure genius of speech, song, and music or dance that is expressed in the *cante jondo* or *cante flamenco*, declared: "Throughout Andalusia, . . . people constantly speak of *duende* and detect it as soon as it is manifested with an accurate instinct." And, taking up Goethe's and Eckermann's idea according to which "the demonic is what is insoluble by intelligence and reason," the poet defined *duende* as a "mysterious power which everyone feels and no philosopher can explain." He added:

> The duende, then, is a power, not a work; it is a struggle, not a thought. I have heard an old maestro of the guitar say, "The duende is not in the throat; the duende climbs up inside you, from the soles of the feet." Meaning this: it is not a question of ability, but of true, living style, of blood, of the most ancient culture, of spontaneous creation. . . . The duende I am talking about is the dark, shuddering descendant of the sprightly marble-and-salt demon of Socrates, the one who angrily scratched him on the day he swallowed the hemlock, and of that melancholy demon of Descartes, a demon who was small as a green almond and who sickened of circles and lines and escaped down the canals to listen to the songs of blurry sailors.

After evoking the awakening of the *duende*, under several forms, "in the furthest reaches of blood," and after distinguishing it from the muse or the angel, García Lorca concluded his talk with these words:

> Where is the duende? Through the empty arch comes a wind, a mental wind blowing relentlessly over the heads of the dead, in search of new landscapes and unknown accents; a wind that smells of baby's spittle, crushed grass, and jellyfish veil, announcing the constant baptism of newly created things.

With that, in the *duende*'s going from the home, of which, according to its initial meaning, it is the master, over to the "furthest reaches of blood," which it inhabits in secret, it merely, so to speak, changes location; it remains the master of the domain, always present, always absent—the ungraspable genius of all creation.

Bernard Sesé

BIBLIOGRAPHY

Calderón de la Barca, Pedro. *La dama duende*. Madrid: Maria de Quiñones, 1636. First published in 1629.

———. *The Phantom Lady*. Translated by J. Nelson. Edited by D. Beecher. Ottawa: Dovehouse Editions, 2002.

García Lorca, Federico. *Play and Theory of the Duende*. Translated by Christopher Maurer. In *In Search of Duende*. New York: New Directions, 1998.

Mercadal, Juan Antonio. *El duende especulativ, sobre la vida civil*. Madrid, 1761.

Pérez Galdós, Benito. *Los duendes de la camarilla*. Episodios nacionales 4. Madrid: Alianza Editorial, 2007.

DUTY, DEBT

FRENCH	*devoir, dette*
GERMAN	*Schuld, schuldig sein, fallen, müssen, sollen*
ITALIAN	*debito, dovere*
LATIN	*debitum, debere, fallere*
SPANISH	*deuda, deber*

➤ *DESTINY, DROIT*, ENTSTELLUNG, *JUSTICE, OBLIGATION*, PARDON, SOLLEN, TRUTH, *VALUE*, WILLKÜR

In many European languages, both Romance and Germanic, the verbs or nouns that evoke the idea of duty (for example, *dovere* and *debito* in Italian, *deber* and *deuda* in Spanish, "debt" in English [*det* and *dette* in Middle English]), coming from the Latin verb *debere* and the noun *debitum*, give rise to ambiguity that connects three distinct meanings: debt, that is, the fact of being "indebted" to someone, obligation ("I must [legally or in good conscience]"), and finally evaluation, presupposition, or reckoning ("He ought to have received it by now"). In some languages this equivocity becomes more complicated. In German for example, while *müssen* is an auxiliary verb (related to the English "must") that indicates the fact of being subject to necessity or an unavoidable obligation, a different verb—*sollen*—is used to express moral obligation or eventuality, probability, or approximation. The latter does not, however, directly express the meaning of being in debt, even though it is literally present in the phrase *ein Soll haben*, which means "to have a debt." Additionally, the idea of debt is combined in German with the idea of fault, such that the two notions are both expressed by the same noun, *Schuld*, just as the adjective *schuldig* means both guilty and indebted—even though, among the words derived from *Schuld*, some relate almost exclusively to the notion of debt (like *schulden*, "to be indebted"; *Entschuldung,* "repayment of debts"), and others exclusively to the notion of fault (*Entschuldigung*, "to excuse, demand pardon"; *Schuldhaftigkeit,* guilt; *entschuldbar*, excusable, pardonable), and others like *Schuldigkeit,* to the idea of obligation or duty in the strict sense.

I. The Combined Notions of Obligation, Probability, and Debt

For languages in which the word for duty covers not only obligation or simple possibility but also the notion of debt, it is possible to translate wordplay that turns on these meanings from one to another. Charles Malamoud opens one of his remarkable studies on the notion of debt with a brief exchange between Sancho and Tosillos in *Don Quixote*. Tosillos says to Sancho: "Sin duda, este tu amo, Sancho amigo, *debe* de ser un loco [No doubt, friend Sancho, your master must be crazy]." Sancho replies, "Como debe? No *debe* nada a nadie.... [What do you mean must? He owes nothing to no one....]." Malamoud notes that this ambiguity exists in English as much as in Romance languages (but by playing with the neighboring verbal forms *ought* and *to owe*), as well as in German and even Russian. In most of our languages, this is explained by the semantic evolution of the Latin verb *habeo*, which comes from *de-habeo* and which means "to have [something] that has been received from someone." Whence *debitum* (what is "due"), then *debitor*, which is opposed to *creditor*. And as the *Dictionnaire étymologique de la langue latine* by Ernout and Meillet points out, "in the later period, the sense of obligation had a tendency to weaken such as to form only a sort of future periphrastic ... or introduce a

hypothesis." These different meanings of the Latin verb *debere* thus found their way into French, but appeared in what was in a way a reverse sequence, the stages of which are given by RT: *DHLF*: "[T]he idea of obligation, necessity (842), its weakening into the future (around 1050) indicating probability, wish or intention (1080), as well as the idea of owing something to someone (before 1188)."

We should note, however, that there are some ways of expressing the idea of "must-ness" in the sense of probability that do not relate to *debere*. In Italian, for example, the future tense is used: in "*Sarà felice* [He *must* be happy]." It is in German, however, that the vocabulary related to the notion of "duty" is especially interesting. The fact that different senses of the notion of necessity are expressed by two distinct verbs, *sollen* and *müssen*, can lead to difficulties of translation. There was a question, for example, as to how to translate into French the title of one of Arnold Schönberg's *A capella choruses opus 27* (1926): *Du sollst nicht, du musst....* Illustrating the composer's return to the Jewish faith, the work defines that faith as forbidding all representation in the following way: "You must not [*Du sollst nicht*] make images of the Divinity; it is necessary for you [*du musst*] to cleave to the Spirit." In reality, *ich soll*, which comes from *sollen* ("must" in the sense of "must be"), functions in the mode of giving positive or prohibitive orders, and means "I have an obligation to...." This obligation may itself derive from an understood *Schuld* or from a debt to be repaid, or from a mistake to be rectified. On the other hand, *ich muss* comes from *müssen*, which also means "must," but implies a duty understood as a necessity deriving the idea of requirement, that is, to stay within the same etymological domain, from an idea of a defect to be repaired or a lack to be filled (see WILLKÜR). Further, when Kant asks the second question of his philosophical program ("What must I do?"), he uses the verb *sollen*: *Was soll ich tun?* Similarly, when he gives himself a moral imperative that escapes from the "pathology" of human interests and so derives only from the law of "respect" (and in which Nietzsche will see, like Sade, an "imperative of cruelty"), he takes care to formulate it in the mode of *sollen*: *Du sollst*, and not *Du musst* (which would appeal to a constraint belonging to the order of necessity or need).

In addition, the idea of debt combined with that of obligation presents an interesting peculiarity in German, as Malamoud points out: "[T]here is an echo to the verb *sollen*, '*devoir*' (here expression of the modality of probability), in order to express the notion of 'being in debt,' not from another construction or another form of the same verb, but from the expression *ein Soll haben*, 'to owe, to have a debit'; in accounting, in effect, *Soll* is the amount owed as opposed to the amount possessed" ("Dette [Anthropologie]"). We may also note, to return to Kant, that the idea of obligation may be rendered in German by the abstract noun *Schuldigkeit*, corresponding to *Schuld*, which means both "transgression" and "debt." In effect, while we generally translate Kant's *Verbindlichkeit* (from *binden*, to bind), by "obligation" (from Lat. *ligare*, "to bind," see RELIGIO), some Germanists suggest using "obligation" to translate *Schuldigkeit*, which literally contains the idea of a fundamental guilt, which itself becomes a source of obligation (see Kant, *Critique of Practical Reason*, trans. M. Muller and M. Weigelt; for the relationship between the formulations of debt, transgression, and obligation, see R. B. Onians, *Origins of European Thought*).

The same combination of the three meanings that we have just described is found in English, in which the ideas of obligation and of possibility are expressed by "ought," which is none other than the past tense of "to owe," meaning "to be in debt" or "to have an obligation to someone"—as is the case in *The Merchant of Venice* and the *bound* (or the *bond*) that binds Antonio to Shylock. Nietzsche could have been thinking of this example of a pact and a "conscientization" of debt when he wrote the following:

> The debtor (*Der Schuldner*), in order to inspire confidence that the promise of payment will be honoured (*Um Vertrauen für sein Verspreche der Zurückbezahlung einzuflössen*), in order to give a guarantee of the solemnity and sanctity of his promise, and in order to etch a duty and obligation of repayment into his conscience (*um bei sich die Zurückbezahlung als Pflicht, Verpflichtung seinem Gewissen einzuschärfen*), pawns something to the creditor by means of the contract in case he does not pay, something that he still "possesses" and controls, for example, his body, his wife, or his freedom or his life.

(trans. Carol Diethe, On the Genealogy of Morality)

The allusion to the "pound of flesh" to be taken by Shylock from the body of his debtor Antonio seems even more plausible when Nietzsche, even though he is only mentioning the Egyptians, continues in these terms:

> [T]he creditor (*Der Gläubiger*) could inflict all kinds of dishonour and torture on the body of the debtor, for example, cutting as much flesh off as seemed appropriate for the debt: from this standpoint there were everywhere, early on, estimates which went into horrifyingly minute and fastidious detail, legally drawn up (*zu Recht bestehende*) estimates for individual limbs and parts of the body.

(Ibid.)

II. Error and Falsehood; Failure and Requirement

There is, thus, in most modern European languages a close relationship between on one hand, the senses of "must" as in "I must forgive him" and "That must happen to me" and, on the other, the idea of owing something to someone. But within the notion of debt, that of duty is also combined with that of error, as we see in German, where the same word *Schuld* means both "debt" and "error":

> *Schuld* comes from a Gothic form *skuld* which itself belongs to a verb, *skulan*, "to be obliged," "to be in debt" (it translates the Greek verb *opheilô*, which has both meanings), as well as "to be in error." Further, from the same Germanic root **skal*, but with a different treatment of the first letter, descends the German verb *sollen*, "ought (to do)," and the English *shall*, which, though today restricted to the expression of the future tense, meant "ought" in the full sense of the word at an earlier stage of the language.

(C. Malamoud, "Dette [Anthropologie]")

Referring to Jakob Grimm's *Deutsche Mythologie*, Freud points out in this regard that the name Skuld, that of the third Norn from Scandinavian folklore, "recalls the English words *shall*, *should*, and the German *soll*, *Schuld*, which connote the idea of

duty and some of which express the future." He adds that "we can therefore suppose that the three names [of the Norns] appeal respectively to the past, the present, and the future" ("The Uncanny"). The fact that *Schuld* in German has the double meaning of "debt" and "transgression" means that we must look to the context in order to know which meaning is at issue in a given occurrence. Still, we may note that Nietzsche, attacking the "genealogists of morals" for their ignorance of philology, distinguishes the two meanings while explaining that "the concept of *Schuld* [transgression], for example, the fundamental concept of morality, derives from the very material concept of *Schulden* [debts]," where this plural had at the time a very concrete force (*On the Genealogy of Morality*).

However, this link between the idea of debt and that of transgression leads to another terminological configuration that includes, in French, for example, the verbs *faillir* and *falloir*, the expression *il faut* (one must, it is necessary), and the nouns *faute* (fault) or *défaut* (default, defect). This collection of notions forms a skein that sometimes gets tangled through the evolution of language—to the point where RT: *Dictionnaire étymologique de la langue latine* declares their etymology to be confusing The French "*faute* comes from the vernacular Latin *fallire*, which is a modification of the classical verb *fallere* (from the Gr. *sphallein* [σφάλλειν] and meaning "to deceive, to fail, throw off balance") and which yields *faillir* and *falloir* in French. Within the field of derivation we find the following to be notable, starting with Old French: *faille* (error, lie), *faillement* (fall, annihilation, defect), *faillance* (fault, weakness), *faut* (lack, starting in the sixteenth century), *faute* (in the sense of *faute de* [for lack of]; lack, sin), *defaillir* (to default, to be extinguished), *mesfaillir* (to commit an error, from the sixteenth century). The impersonal *il faut* (which is translated by the Ger. *es muss*, *es ist nötig*, or by *ich soll*, *du sollst*, and so forth, with the infinitive) therefore contains either the idea of obligation or that of necessity.

In German the same etymology yielded the verbs *fehlen* (to fail, to sin) and *fallen* (intransitive, which means "to fall, to sink"), the nouns *der Fehler* and *das Fehlen* (fault, error, lack), the adjectives *fehlerfrei* and *fehlerlos* (perfect, without defect). The verb *fallen* has as a derivative the noun *Einfall*, which may be translated by "fall" but also by "intuition," and even by "eruption." It is for this reason that, as Georges-Arthur Goldschmidt notes, "[T]he entirety of Freud's oeuvre was perhaps a constant modulation on the verb *fallen*. Failed actions, the celebrated *Fehlleistungen*, which have such pride of place in Freud's work, are what we notice, what arises suddenly in speech; they are that which *fällt auf*, *es fällt auf*; it is striking, we notice it, even if it comes about only by chance, by *Zufall*, by "what happens to fall in front of you" (G.-A. Goldschmidt, *Quand Freud voit la mer*).

In English, while "duty" (*dewe* in Middle English) and "due" seem to derive from the Latin *debere*, the configuration that comes from *fallere* includes notably the verbs "to fall" and "to fail," the nouns "fault" and "failure." In Romance, Anglo-Saxon, and Germanic languages, the idea of lacking and defect or failure is joined with that of falsehood, falsification, the fallacious, and so on: "false" in English and *falsch* in German come from *falsus*, the past participle of *fallere*, a verb whose principal meanings of "to deceive" and "to escape" would seem to go back to a single earlier meaning of "to hide, to be hidden," or "to elude" (cf. *Dictionnaire étymologique de la langue latine*, s.v. *fallō*).

III. Vedic Debt: Debt Which Does Not Arise from Fault, and Exists Prior to Responsibility

We can then measure what was lost from the idea of debt in this network centered around the notion of transgression and deriving from the root *faill-*. On this topic, taking up the subject of the institution of loaning money on interest, Malamoud shows in effect that if debt is close to duty, this is because

[D]uty is debt when there is an obligation not to do but to return something. There is debt when the task or expense or sacrifice demanded by duty is presented or thought of as restitution, a return, compensation. "To have to pay a hundred francs" is not the same thing as "to owe a hundred francs." More precisely, "to owe a hundred francs" is a special case of "having to pay a hundred francs." . . . As a model of duty, having-to-return is the guise taken up by other duties . . . . We go astray from duty pure and simple when debt becomes a relation that makes not just the debtor and the creditor present, but the borrower and the lender, when debt becomes a regulated institution, when it deals with material and measurable goods, and especially when interest must be paid.

("Dette [Anthropologie]")

The link between duty, debt, and transgression does not exist in all languages, even if we come across it in many Indo-European languages and others such as Hebrew. Thus, the Sanskrit term corresponding to "debt," *ṛṇa*, "is without any etymological relation of any sort to a verbal root that means *devoir* nor with the nouns that designate the different forms of obligation." In reality, what characterizes Indian thought is the idea that every man, simply in virtue of being born, is from the beginning loaded with debts to such an extent that he is defined as being himself a "debt" by origin and constitution: "Debt to death, on one hand: his very existence is a deposit that the god of death, Yama, will necessarily reclaim; and on the other hand, debt to a fourfold group of creditors: the gods, ancestors, the seers who transmitted the sacred texts of the Veda . . . , and finally other people" (ibid., 297–98). In this way a man who has a son will be freed from this essential debt, or who fulfills the prescribed sacrificial rites, or who leads a life of Brahmanic study. But Vedic theology does not offer an answer to the question of what makes man thus indebted or of the nature of the loan by which he became a debtor. This forces the exegete to come back to problems of vocabulary:

[T]he term *ṛṇa*, debt, has a precise technical sense; it belongs to the vocabulary of economics, and refers to the obligation to return borrowed goods, or their equivalent, and cannot be a synonym for "duty" or "obligation" in general. We are thus in the presence of the following paradox: a debt without prior borrowing, or at least without awareness of the event of the borrowing, a consequence without a cause, a present without a past. The current constraint therefore cannot be perceived as the result of a fault which has been committed; if the congenital debt is a failure (to be overcome by the execution of a program of rites), it is not a defect, even less a sign of sin, the endpoint of a fall; and the restitutive obligations that are demanded of man are not an expiation, are not

dictated by a condemnation, and there is no occasion for the feeling of guilt. Not that the Vedic religion does not contain the notions of sin and stain; on the contrary.

(C. Malamoud, in *L'Apport freudien*, ed. P. Kaufmann)

Nevertheless, even though Vedic theology is unclear as to the origin of the congenital debt affecting every man, it remains open to connotations of the term *ṛṇa* in which "the notions of 'fault' and 'debt' (the two senses of the German word *Schuld*) are conjoined." This explains how individuals may end up questioning themselves in fear of any past mistakes, as though they could allow for an understanding of their current misfortunes and the "unpaid debt that they have down here" toward Yama, the god of death and the controller of all debts.

■ See Box 1.

At the very least, in languages where the equivalent of *devoir* belongs to the same family as the Latin *debere*, and perhaps as well in Vedic India, the "symbolic debt" seems to delimit a lexical field in which the obligation involves a deeper sense than that which comes from the legal or financial context in which one must return a thing or a borrowed sum. The first of these two registers, in effect, "deals with obligation in the sense of reciprocity (one would therefore be in the domain of gifts and counter-gifts)," in a sphere governed by the exchange of gifts—this gift calls for one in return (cf. M. Hénaff, *Le prix de la vérité*, 274). On the other hand, in the pecuniary relationship established between creditor and debtor, the latter is, in virtue of his contractual obligation, exposed to punishment that can be without mercy if the debt is not repaid. It is on this model that Nietzsche seems to base his entire conception of a debt that cannot fail to create in the debtor a state of dependency and humiliation with its train of fear, bad conscience, and the feelings of guilt or worthlessness characteristic of shame (cf. F. Tricaud, *L'Accusation*).

Charles Baladier

BIBLIOGRAPHY

Freud, Sigmund. *The Uncanny*. Translated by David McClintock. London: Penguin, 2003.

Goldschmidt, Georges-Arthur. *Freud et la langue allemande: 1, Quand Freud voit la mer*. Paris: Buchet Chastel, 2006.

Hénaff, Marcel. *Le prix de la verité: Le don, l'argent, la philosophie*. Paris: Éditions du Seuil, 2002.

Kaufmann, Pierre, ed. *L'Apport Freudien: Éléments pour un encyclopédie de la psychanalyse*. Paris: Bordas, 1993.

Malamoud, Charles. "Dette (Anthropologie)." In *Encyclopœdia universalis*, 7:294–300. Paris: Encyclopœdia Universalis, 1990.

Kant, Immanuel. *Critique de la raison pratique*. Translated by L. Ferry and H. Wismann. Paris: Gallimard / La Pléiade, 1985.

——. *Critique of Practical Reason*. Translated by Max Muller and Marcus Weigelt. London: Penguin, 2008. German text first published in 1788.

Nietzsche, Friedrich. *On the Genealogy of Morality and Other Writings*. 2nd ed. Edited by Keith Ansell-Pearson. Translated by Carol Diethe. Cambridge Texts in the History of Political Thought. Cambridge: Cambridge University Press, 2006. First edition published in 1994. German text first published in 1887.

Oninans, Richard Broxton. *The Origins of European Thought about the Body, the Mind, the Soul, the World, Time, and Fate: New Interpretations of Greek, Roman and Kindred Evidence also of Some Basic Jewish and Christian Beliefs*. Cambridge: Cambridge University Press, 1988.

Tricaud, François. *L'Accusation*. Paris: Dalloz, 1977.

1

"Symbolic debt" in Lacan

➤ SIGN

One might wonder whether it is possible to find an echo of this Vedic theology regarding man as an indebted creature in what Jacques Lacan calls "the implacable game of debt," referring to the cosmic metaphor (*Écrits*) that Rabelais puts thus by way of Panurge, in the *Tiers Livre*:

> You ask me when I will be out of debt. Well, to go yet further on, and possibly worse in your conceit, may Saint Bablin, the good saint, snatch me, if I have not all my lifetime held debt to be as a union or conjunction of the heavens with the earth, and the whole cement whereby the race of mankind is kept together; yea, of such virtue and efficacy that, I say, the whole progeny of Adam would very suddenly perish without it. Therefore, perhaps, I do not think amiss, when I repute it to be the great soul of the universe, which, according to the opinion of the Academics, vivifieth all manner of things.

Throughout his *Séminaire*, in fact, Lacan makes this idea of a fundamental debt an important key to his theory of the symbolic:

> The commandment of death is there [in ancient tragedy]. And to be there in a veiled form, it may be formulated and received as coming from this debt which

accumulates without a guilty party and is discharged on a victim without his deserving any punishment.

(Lacan, *Le transfert* [*Transference*])

The Word [of the Gospel] is for us not at all only the law where we insert ourselves in order to carry, each of us, the debt which is our destiny. It opens for us the possibility, the temptation whence it is possible for us to curse ourselves, not only as a particular destiny, as life, but as the very way where the Word engages us and as a meeting with Truth, as the hour of truth. We are no longer simply within range of being made guilty by symbolic debt. It is having the debt on our account for which we can be, as closely as this word can indicate, reproached. In sum, it is the debt itself where we had our place which may be stolen from us, and it is there that we may feel completely alienated from ourselves.

(Ibid., 354)

In reality, before he considered this theme in relation to death and to the law given by the Word, Lacan made debt the pillar of a system that he defined, inspired by Claude Lévi-Strauss, as the "symbolic chain," as opposed to the "chain

of experience" in which nothing is articulated or built up. Lived experience, in effect, is not ordered, does not take on meaning, and cannot be analyzed "except beginning with the moment when the subject enters into an order which is the order of symbols, the legal order, symbolic order, symbolic chain, order of symbolic debt" (*La relation d'objet*). Such an order exists prior to anything which, in experience, happens to the subject, its events, its satisfactions, its disappointments.

BIBLIOGRAPHY

Lacan, Jacques. *Écrits*. Paris: Éditions du Seuil, 1966. Translation by Bruce Fink: *Écrits*. New York: Norton, 2007.
———. *La relation d'object. Le Séminaire, Book IV*. Paris: Éditions du Seuil, 1994.
———. *L'Éthique de la psychanalyse. Le Séminaire, Book VII*. Paris: Éditions du Seuil, 1986. Translation by Dennis Porter: *The Ethics of Psychoanalysis*. New York: Norton, 1997.
———. *Le transfert. Le Séminaire, Book VIII*. Paris: Éditions du Seuil, 1991. Translation by Cormac Gallagher: *Transference*. London: Karmac Books, 2002.
Rabelais, François. *The Works of Rabelais*. Translated by Thomas Urquhart and Peter Motteux. Derby, UK: Moray Press, 1894.

| DYNAMIC

"Dynamic" is formed from the Greek *dunamis* [δύναμις], "force" (cf. *dunasthai* [δύνασθαι], to be capable of, to be able, to have a power; in speaking of a word or currency: to be worth, to signify; in mathematics: the square [i.e., second power]), and it refers to the study of force, from the physical-mathematical perspective as well as the ontological one, notably in Leibniz, who introduced the term. The Greek *dunamis*, like the Latin *potentia*, and "power," contains an essential ambiguity: it is power in the sense of "in potentiality," *potentia*, potential, as opposed to the actualization and the act; but it is also "the power to X," *potestas*, capacity, ability.

I. Dynamics, Potentiality, Actuality

The collection of physical and ontological networks, and the difference between "force" and "energy," are explored in the entry on FORCE. See also MOMENT and STRENGTH (as opposed to "force"). Cf. EPISTEMOLOGY.

For more on the Greek, see FORCE, Box 1, PRAXIS, TO TI ÊN EINAI; cf. ESSENCE.

See also *ACT* and VIRTÙ.

For the logical relation between potentiality and possibility, see *POWER, PROBABILITY*.

II. Dynamics and Power

See *POWER*, and especially for the German distinction *Macht/Gewalt*, which partially reworks the Latin distinction *potestas/potentia*; see MACHT.

III. Dynamics and Movement

1. For the dynamic as a force and movement in history and the course of events in the world, see HISTORIA UNIVERSALIS, HISTORY, PERFECTIBILITY, *TIME*; cf. *RUSE*.
2. On the relation between dynamics and the psyche, especially with respect to the Freudian dynamic, see DRIVE; cf. ES, PLEASURE, SVOBODA, UNCONSCIOUS, WILL, WUNSCH.

➤ SENSE

ECONOMY

FRENCH *économie*
GERMAN *Wirtschaft*

➤ BERUF, CIVIL SOCIETY, OIKONOMIA, PEOPLE, POLIS, POLITICS, PROPERTY, *PRUDENCE*, UTILITY

The word "economy" is a direct import from Greek, used in a number of European languages, although German prefers *Wirtschaft* over *Ökonomie*. It has retained a number of senses related to its original one (the "rules," *nomoi*, of having a well-run "house," *oikos*), which are very similar from one language to the next. Behind this apparent unanimity, however, there are fundamental and far-reaching differences. As a starting point, we have taken the current extension of the meaning in English, according to which "economy" is a synonym for "country." French has not adopted this extension, which encroaches on the domain reserved for political matters. English and French thus fall on either side of the distinction between the economic and the political, which is decisive for the definition of "economy." The German *Wirtschaft* seems to escape from the dilemma since it rests on the metaphor of the innkeeper (*der Wirt*), which allows for the inclusion of both economic and sociopolitical agents in an organic whole. Nevertheless, the claim of economics to be the incarnation of collective rationality must then fall back on the word "people" (*Volk*) in order to be clear (*Volkswirtschaft*).

The aristocratic Homeric domain can no longer be used to describe the modern economy. By way of the link with *oikos*, however, the word "economy" continues to carry the mark of its origins, though confined to material tasks and day-to-day subsistence.

I. *Économie* and Economy

The words *économie* and "economy" come from the Greek *oikonomia*, which means the direction and administration of a "house," that is, in the Homeric era, a manorial estate.

In French, *économie*, like the adjective *économe*, refers to a virtue or quality, a kind of prudence; the result of the exercise of that virtue (*faire des économies*); a social science and its subspecies (*économie appliquée*, *économie monétaire*); the object of those sciences (*économie des pays développés*); finally, the harmony or organization of the parts of a whole (*économie libidinale*) (see OIKONOMIA). Except for this last sense, which can be applied to anything from a literary work to divine creation to the human body, the use of the word delimits the field of the material activities of production, distribution, and consumption of goods. The field has a technical character: a text on economics will most often contain figures and symbols of physical magnitudes. It is, further, defined by the economic/political distinction. In this way the transformation of the European Economic Community into the European Union—i.e., the disappearance of the word "Economic" from the name—represents what is considered to be an important evolution for this group of countries.

The border that separates the economic from the political is a sensitive point in contemporary society. Some say it is odious for multinational corporations to overturn a government; some say it is odious for the state to intervene and micromanage the economy.

The English word "economy" covers all of the French senses except for that of the science, which is designated by "economics." On the other hand, one of the senses has developed so much that it goes beyond the French one. This is the sense that designates a part of social life, but also an autonomous part, and by a metonymy that is less and less perceptible, a whole, which in English can be the whole of society itself. In this case, it is translated into French as *pays* (country).

Thus, Paul Samuelson and William Nordhaus write in their widely read economics textbook, "How can we explain that a country like Japan . . . has become the world's most productive economy?" (*Economics*, 700). Japan is an economy. An economy is a being endowed with a personality, and there can be many of them: "Market economies are many times wealthier than they were at the age of Adam Smith" (ibid., 724). The synonymy appears even more clearly in other cases: "At the end of the 1980s, the walls of the centrally planned economies of Eastern Europe were knocked down and these countries began the swift transition to market economies" (ibid., 375).

The use of "economy" to refer to countries has developed especially in Asia. Two of the Asian "dragons," Hong Kong and Taiwan, are not "countries" in the diplomatic sense. Their presence in the Asia Pacific Economic Co-operation (APEC) forum requires the member countries, including the United States, to refer to themselves as "economies" in this framework. This sense does not exist in French, where we find, on the other hand (see RT: *Le nouveau petit Robert*), that of "activity, economic life; a group of facts related to the production, distribution, and consumption of wealth in a human group. *Ministère de l'Économie nationale*." Thus stated, the economy is a part of the collectivity, as is emphasized by the example chosen.

The Organization for Economic Cooperation and Development (OECD) is an organization whose two official languages are English and French. Since it deals primarily with economies, it has had to face this question. The *Glossary* of the OECD, which was set up to resolve this sort of difficulty, suggests translating "economy" as *pays* (country). For example, "adv*économie de marché*.

II. Economics and Politics

It looks as though French is saturated with the priority of the political. It is not possible, for the moment, to say "*la France est une économie*," whereas "the United States is an economy" is acceptable in English.

Understandably, "policy" poses a reciprocal problem of translation. As the sense of "economy" expands to include a political dimension, that of "policy" diminishes. Thus the sense of "policy" is more restricted than that of *politique* in French, since it only designates the nonpolitical aspects of the actions of the state—questions that are, properly speaking, political are referred to as "politics." Its usage is extremely broad, however, and it does much to encourage the idea that the actions of the state are not necessarily political.

The problem may be resolved when "policy" is used as a noun: one can say "*politique gouvernementale*" or speak of a plurality of *politiques* in French. It is more difficult when "policy" is used as an adjective. Thus, "policy action" would be translated as *action gouvernemental, action publique, mesures gouvernementales*; "policy area" by *domaine / secteur d'action (des pouvoirs publics)*; "policy debate" by *débat sur les mesures à prendre / les politiques à suivre*; "policy context" by *cadre d'action* (*Glossary*, OECD, 1982). None of these translations uses the word *politique* in the singular. There is an obstacle to avoid: the word *politique* has an almost sacred status in French. It casts a wide shadow. To translate "policy debate" by *débat politique* would be a serious mistranslation, whereas the reverse is not true. To know whether a *débat politique* is a "political debate" or a "policy debate," it is necessary to determine whether it deals with goals or with means of application, which may be difficult.

Thus, the difficulty with translating *économie* by "economy" is related to the relationship between economics and politics. The problem lies in knowing whether there is a master of the house (*oikos*) and what his prerogatives are. The watchword of economic liberalism, on which Western societies are based, is that the production and distribution of wealth ("economic" activities) should be left as much as possible to private initiative. If that is the case, and in particular if private initiative is the initiative of all the citizens, the state's scope for intervention—that is, the political—may be reduced to a lesser portion, or even to zero. A system of pricing and markets would be capable of coordinating people and businesses without any central intervention.

In French the economy is a part of the social whole and remains subordinate to a master, the nation-state, which is the only thing representing the whole. English and French have thus each received one of the two halves of liberalism's legacy. These languages remain marked by this historical experiment, and each develops one of the poles of the economic/political distinction.

III. *Wirtschaft*

German seems to evade this dilemma, since it mainly uses *Wirtschaft*, whose primary meaning is "collection of methodical actions combining to satisfy needs" (see RT: *Der Neue Brockhaus*, vol. 5, s.v. "Wirtschaft"). The word comes from *der Wirt*, which means "innkeeper, host," as well as "head of household." There is thus clearly a master of this household. One cannot have an inn without an innkeeper. The existence of politics is thus not threatened by the wide sense of *Wirtschaft*, since it is neither above nor below it; the two are consubstantial. By transposing the Greek estate into the metaphor of the inn, German preserves the link between economics and politics. The inn, however, is a private place, despite being open to the public. The metaphor of the host is powerful in German. Thus, foreign or immigrant workers are called *Gastarbeiter*

(guestworkers). However, it does not suffice for the representation of a national reality.

The problem of the extension of the meaning of *Wirtschaft* to an autonomous social reality, able to exist in the plural (international), is solved in German by the word *Volkswirtschaft*:

> Die Moderne Wirtschaft ist eine gesellschaftlicharbeitsteilige Tauschwirtschaft, die ihrer regionalen Ausdehnung nach über die nationalen Grenzen der einzelnen Volkswirtschaften hinaus sich zu einer die Erde umspannenden Weltwirtschaft entwickelt hat.

> (The modern economy is an economy of exchange based on the form of society and the division of labor, which has gone beyond the regional divisions of the different national economies to become a worldwide economy encompassing the entire earth, beyond national borders.)

> (Ibid., "Volkswirtschaft")

But even in its domestic sense, *Wirtschaft* does not extend to economic rationality. Max Weber feels the need to define the word precisely. It is often the object of "inappropriate usage" that involves speaking of *Wirtschaft* to refer to "any behavior that is rational with regard to its goals," or to refer, on the Leibnizian model of a "principle of economy," to the "universal technique of the optimal, that is, the pursuit of the greatest result with the least expense"—which for Weber is only a technique. According to Weber, one should only speak of *Wirtschaft* "when, in order to satisfy a need, we find ourselves faced with means that seem limited in the eyes of the actors, and when this state of affairs becomes the foundation of a specific behavior that takes that into account" (*Economy and Society*). The economy is the specific activity of agents occupied with the satisfaction of needs, insofar as this satisfaction is in turn specific with respect to the rest of social life. It is, in a way, their profession (*Beruf*).

Weber makes it clear that the action takes two forms:

> Mann kann unter zwei verschiedenen Gesichtpunkten wirtschaften. Einmal zu Deckung der Alltagsbedürfnisse. . . . Gegenüber der Wirtschaft zur Deckung des eigenes Bedarfs ist die zweite Art des Wirtschaftens Wirtschaft zum Erwerb: die Ausnutzung des spezifisch ökonomischen Sachverhalts: Knappheit begehrter Güter, zur Erziehung eigenen Gewinn an Verfügung über diese Güter.

> (There are two ways of behaving economically. The first consists in seeking to satisfy one's daily needs. . . . Besides the economy aiming to satisfy needs, there is a second way of acting economically: the use of the specific state of economic affairs, that is, the poverty of desired goods, to attain the personal goal of a profit in the disposition of these goods.)

> (Weber, *Economy and Society*)

The legitimation of personal profit in Western societies (the Protestant ethic) is a modality of this action.

Once again, the simple rational action of the human being seeking to satisfy his material needs cannot serve to legitimate a social system—when it is not expressed by a Greek word.

Wirtschaft seems closer to "economy" than to *économie*, since it can encompass all the agents of economic action. If each citizen becomes an economic actor, the social class envisaged by Weber comes to apply to the whole of society. But *wirtschaften* is just as distant from French as it is from English, which thus find themselves on the same side of the barrier; in effect, the verbs *économiser* and "to economize," which both have the sense of "to save," prevent the notion from becoming dynamic and prevent the appearance of economic actors and aspects of economic action that have nothing to do with the act of "saving" (for example, investment). These remain hidden in English and in French behind the watchword of prudence in spending, which decorates the economy in the feathers of virtue.

Frédéric Langer

BIBLIOGRAPHY

Samuelson, Paul, and William D. Nordhaus. *Economics*. 11th edition. New York: McGraw-Hill, 1989.
Weber, Max. *Economy and Society: An Outline of Interpretive Sociology*. Edited by G. Roth and C. Wittich. Berkeley: University of California Press, 1978.

EIDÔLON [εἴδωλον] / EIKÔN [εἰκών] / PHANTASMA [φάντασμα] / EMPHASIS [ἔμφασις] / TUPOS [τύπος] (GREEK)

ENGLISH	image, picture
FRENCH	*image*
LATIN	*figura, effigies, forma, imago, pictura, simulacrum, species*

➤ *IMAGE* [BILD], and DOXA, ERSCHEINUNG, *IMAGINATION* [PHANTASIA], INTENTION, LIGHT, MEMORY, MIMÊSIS, OIKONOMIA, PERCEPTION, REALITY, SPECIES, TRUTH

The French *image* is based on the Latin *imago*. The Latin term itself does a poor job of transmitting the multiple echoes that accompany the Greek vocabulary related to images, which includes *eidôlon* [εἴδωλον], *eikôn* [εἰκών], *phantasma* [φάντασμα], *emphasis* [ἔμφασις], *tupos* [τύπος], etc., and is much richer and more evocative than Latin. But none of these terms is an exact equivalent for the French *image*, nor are they equivalents among themselves. Hence, serious difficulties arise for translation, whether it is a matter of what a drawing represents or what is presented in a mirror. For this richness is not a matter of chance: far from being simple, the notion of image itself is something multiple and ambiguous. It is neither one thing, nor one concept, but "a visible thing that yields the vision of another"; a second-order visible that itself may not be the direct result of a sensation, but a product of memory or imagination. In addition, the way in which the image has been conceived has greatly evolved, owing to theories of vision and the successive discoveries of optics. From these, other misunderstandings become possible, since even for a term for which the translation *image* seems natural, any anachronistic interpretation may lead to missing the point of a passage as a result of a specifically cultural misunderstanding.

I. The Greek Terms and the Archaic Features of the Image

The ancient Greeks were prompted to thought by what they saw in a mirror or a painting. The standard terms by which they referred to images had archaic features that left traces in their philosophical reflection.

The most common term for image, *eidôlon* [εἴδωλον], has as its root the verb meaning "to see," through its aorist infinitive *eidon* [εἶδον]. The *eidôlon* is what we see as if it were the thing itself, but which is in fact a double: shadows of the dead in Hades (*Odyssey*, 11.476); Helen's double created by Hera (Euripides, *Helen*, 33); an effigy or portrait, which places someone absent before our eyes; or finally what is displayed in a mirror, which is not really there. In other words, the *eidôlon* is the bearer of visual illusion, as opposed to the *eidos* or *idea* [ἰδέα], from the same root—the true and perfect *form*, which becomes Plato's "idea." Epicurus chose the plural *eidôla* as a technical term to refer to the thin envelopes of atoms emanating from the surfaces of objects, which cause us to see them by penetrating our eyes (*To Herodotus*, 46.9). They are a kind of traveling duplicate, remaining invisible during their journey, and which are the sources of mental images or *phantasiai*, which allow us to validate or invalidate what we see (ibid., 50.2). Because of its illusory and insubstantial aspect, *eidôlon* acquired a sometimes pejorative meaning, which is found in the "idol" of the Septuagint (2 Kings, 17, 12), and the "idolaters" of the iconoclasts.

The second term, also common, is *eikôn* [εἰκών], which comes from **Feikô* (to resemble). The primary sense thus reveals an aspect of images, related to the first, namely, their similarity to the objects. The classical uses are analogous to *eidôlon*, but the sense of statue or portrait is prior to that of a mirror image or a ghost. An effigy always preserves some aspect of its model, even though there are degrees of resemblance. When Plato performs a division of the art of mimesis in the *Sophist*, he defines *eikôn* as a faithful reproduction, which strictly preserves the proportions and the colors of the original (235d–e). *Eikôn* thus tends to evoke the positive aspect of imitation, that which sticks to what exists, and so it is understandable that the term gave us *icon* and its cognates. Plato contrasts *eikôn* with *phantasma* [φάντασμα], a noun derived from the verb *phainesthai* [φαίνεσθαι] (to shine, to show oneself, to appear), by way of *phantazesthai* [φαντάζεσθαι] (to appear, to show oneself). He defines *phantasma* by taking as an example the practice of painters who represent objects not as they are, but as they appear according to their position and the point of view of the observer (236b). It seems imprecise to translate *phantasma* here as *simulacrum*, which has often been used, but which today evokes something in which we do not really believe (as when we speak of a simulacrum of peace), whereas *phantasma* strongly suggests an appearance that we could mistake for reality, bearing all the credibility possessed by a successful trompe l'oeil. Characteristically, with regard to the ontological status of the image, whereas we would attribute error or illusion to a *subjective* mistake, Plato thinks that the art of imitation confers a presence in the world upon the false. To say the least thing about the false, it is necessary to establish that "non-being is," whether we hear it in opinions or speeches that say what is not the case, or see it in images (*eidôla*), reproductions (*eikôna*), imitations (*mimêmata*), or trompe l'oeils (*phantasmata*), which depict what is not (241e).

■ See Box 1.

1

To eikos, or how what is likely is the measure of truth

The terms deriving from **Feikô* (mainly seen in the perfect, *eoika* [ἔοικα]), constitute an instructive semantic family. Besides *eikôn* (image, representation, as well as comparison and indication), we find verbs such as *eiskô* [εἴσκω], "to make similar," "to compare to" (in Homer and Sappho), and *eikazô*, "to represent by an image," "to deduce from a comparison," "to conjecture." The group formed by *eikazô* and its related terms, according to Chantraine (RT: *Dictionnaire étymologique de la langue grecque*, s.v. *eoika*), "illustrates the shift from the sense of 'image, resemblance' to that of 'comparison, conjecture.'" *Eikasia* [εἰκασια], for example, indicates not only the image (Xenophon, *Memorabilia*, 3.10.1) but also conjecture, both that of both soothsayers and of doctors (Plato, *Republic*, 534a; Hippocrates, *On Diseases*, 1; cf. *to eikastikon* [τὸ εἰκαστικόν], Lucian, *Alexander*, 22).

More widely, "a semantic group came out of the notion of image and resemblance, related to the intellectual and moral world" (RT: *Dictionnaire étymologique de la langue grecque*). This is especially clear in cases of the adjective *epieikes* [ἐπιεικής] and the noun *epieikeia* [ἐπιείκεια] (literally, in keeping with what resembles), which refer not only to the "fitting," but in Aristotle, for example, as a technical use, to the "equitable" and "equity." That is, it indicates the indulgence that is a good quality of the virtuous man—the *spoudaios* [σπουδαῖος], whose zeal, nobility, and qualities as a citizen are contrasted with the bad or common, *phaulos* [φαῦλος]; it is the virtue of the judge who is capable of correcting the laws by considering cases, unlike *dikaion* [δίκαιον] and *dikaiosunê* [δικαιοσύνη], "the just" and "justice," which deal with the strict application of the law, which as such is general (*Nicomachean Ethics*, 5.14; see THEMIS).

The most remarkable is no doubt the importance for rhetoric of the nominalization of the neuter perfect participle, *to eikos* [τὸ εἶκος]. *Eikos* is what resembles and seems, that is, in fact, what seems to be true, good, or normal—what is likely, as opposed to what is true and to what is implausible. We must note, however, the distortion introduced by the common translation into French, *vraisemblable*—this imposes truth as a model, unlike the Greek. The primary characteristic of the *eikos* is that it follows the law of the comparative: the "more likely" (*eikoteros* [εἰκότερος]) wins out over the likely, and this is the domain of the debates between the prosecution and the defense. Antiphon's *Tetralogies* provide the model: "Apparently [*eikotôs* (εἰκότως)], he killed the man," says the accuser (1.a.6); the defendant responds, "if it is likely [*eikotôs*] that I appear guilty to you, it is even more likely [*eikoteron* (εἰκότερον)] that I would have foreseen the suspicion of today" (1.b.3). In other words, rhetorical likelihood never justifies a conclusion that something is true, and only persuasion (*peithô* [πείθω]) is able to determine the listener's belief (*pistis* [πίστις]), as well as the strength of the evidence, which is also related to the trust (*pistis* again) accorded to the orator.

The political utility granted by Aristotle to rhetoric, in contrast to Plato's contempt, finds its source here: "the true and the just have a greater natural force [*kreittô têi phusei* (κρείττω τῇ φύσει)] than their contraries." However, the litigators who are telling the truth sometimes lose; thus help is required from the *technê rhêtorikê* [τέχνη ῥητορική], which allows us to discover what is persuasive in each case (*to endechomenon pithanon* [τὸ ἐνδεχόμενον πιθανόν])—for it is even more shameful to be unable to defend

oneself with one's *logos* [λόγος] than with one's body (*Rhetoric*, 1.1.1355a21–b7).

If that is the case, it is because the *eikos*, what is likely, is always capable of being truer than the truth. That is, in fact, the domain of poetry, and therein lies its superiority: "the poet's function is to describe, not the thing that has happened [*ta ginomena* (τὰ γινόμενα)], but a kind of thing that might happen, i.e., what is possible as being probable or necessary [*kata to eikos ê to anagkaion* (κατὰ τὸ εἰκὸς ἢ τὸ ἀναγκαῖον)]" (*Poetics*, 9.1451a36–38). It is indeed because the likely is on the side of the necessary and general (*ta katholou* [τὸ καθόλου]), and not that of the reality of particular facts (*ta kath'hekaston* [τὰ καθ' ἕκαστον]), that poetry is "more philosophical and more virtuous (*philosophôteron kai spoudaioteron* [φιλοσοφώτερον καὶ σπουδαιότερον]" than history (b5–7). This is why "we must prefer the likely but impossible to the unpersuasive but possible [*adunata eikota mallon ê dunata apithana* (ἀδύνατα εἰκότα μᾶλλον ἢ δυνατὰ ἀπίθανα)]" (24.1460a27–28). It is, besides, "likely that even the unlikely should take place" [*eikos kai para to eikos ginetai* (εἰκὸς καὶ παρὰ τὸ εἰκὸς γίνεται)]" (25.1461b15). In rhetoric as in poetics, the likely is the measure of the true, or in other words, resemblance is the measure of the real.

Barbara Cassin

BIBLIOGRAPHY

Antiphon. *Speeches*. Edited by M. Gagarin. Cambridge: Cambridge University Press, 1997.
Aristotle. *Poetics*. Vols. 1 and 2 in *The Complete Works of Aristotle*, edited by J. Barnes, translated by Ingram Bywater. Princeton, NJ: Princeton University Press, 1984.

Another, more technical term, is that of *emphasis* [ἔμφασις], which, like *phantasma*, comes from *phainesthai*. Aristotle uses it to refer to the visual effect of a "break" or reflection (*anaklasis* [ἀνάκλασις]) of vision that meets an obstacle, whether the effect is a clear image or not, since it may be reduced to simple colored patches (*Meteorology*, 372a30–372b8). The term is to be compared with *enoptron* [ἔνοπτρον] or *katoptron* [κάτοπτρον] (mirror), which refers to "that *in which* (or *in the depths of which*) we see." *Emphasis* is "what appears in" water or the bronze of armor: a pure appearance, which may only be appearance, like the rainbow that offers multiple reflections of the sun in the droplets of water of a cloud, but does not exist in its own right. It is appearance in the sense of the apparitions (*phantasmata*) of our dreams, whose mutable character is reminiscent of an image trembling in the water at the slightest breath (*On Divination in Sleep*, 464b8–13). The optical

sense of *emphasis* thus lends itself to anachronism despite its new technical meaning. To take the *visual* effects of reflection into account, the analyses of the *Meteorology* rest on the idea that it is *vision* and not light that bounces off an obstacle, as does all geometrical optics up until the eleventh century. In addition, there is still only one word (*anaklasis*) to refer both to reflection and to refraction. *Emphasis* remains clearly, in the fourth century BCE, that which is seen behind a reflective or refractive surface, an illusion without substance, which is not really where we see it, or how we see it.

Finally, another term is that of *tupos* [τύπος] (imprint), which has led to many misunderstandings. In the first instance, it is the trace of a footstep in the sand, or of a seal on wax. This was one of the models used up until the fourth century BCE to explain the presence of images in mirrors, as though they were imprinted there by the intervening air.

It even explains vision in Democritus, starting with the image-imprint that is seen in the eye of another when we look at it closely (*Sense and Sensibilia*, 437b5–10). René Mugnier here translates *emphasis* by *reflected* image, and thus the meaning of the passage escapes him (*Petits Traités d'histoire naturelle*). It is explained that in the *Timaeus* (71b), Plato compares the smooth surface of the liver to "a mirror where forms (*tupoi*) are imprinted and yield visual images (*eidôla*)" in order to explain how the impressions sent by the intellect can dominate those imprinted there by the visions and phantasms of the desiderative soul. The meaning and the import of the text are missed if we introduce modern concepts of vision by translating, as does Albert Rivaud in Plato's *Timaeus*: "comme un miroir qui reçoit des rayons et laisse apparaître des images" (like a mirror that receives the *rays* and allows the images to appear), or as does Mugler in *Dictionnaire historique de la terminologie optique des Grecs*: "comme un miroir qui reçoit des impressions lumineuses et permet de voir des images" (like a mirror that receives *luminous* impressions and enables us to see images; s.v. *eidôlon*). What is in play is not just the explanation Plato gives of our dreams on the basis of these nocturnal impressions or imprints, and his concomitant justification of dream interpretation. Also at stake is the origin of later conceptions of imagination and memory (see PHANTASIA), the surprising relation between Platonic dream interpretation and Etruscan haruspicy, and finally, the long-standing belief concerning the ability of pregnant women's desires to produce birthmarks on newborns, which we still find in Descartes's *La dioptrique* (discourse 5).

The image is one of those notions whose supposed obviousness is deceptive, and must be resisted. Among the Greeks, it is defined by the brute fact of its visibility, and it is only beginning in the third century BCE, approximately, that it comes to be explained by reflection—and that only in a learned theory of mirrors, and only by the notion of *visual rays*. We misunderstand the famous text of *Republic*, 6.510a, where Plato places mirror images with shadows in the last type of being—the least clear one, which produces illusions and beliefs—if we forget that he has in mind visible fictions imitating real visible objects—insubstantial reproductions that haunt and falsify this world. Any reference to reflection of *luminous* rays confers on this ancient Greek image a physical objectivity that is not there.

II. The Latin *Imago* and the Technical Vocabulary of Medieval Optics

Of all the Latin terms that answer in some way or other to the notion of "image," such as *simulacrum, figura, forma, effigies, pictura*, or even *species* (derived from *specio*, to look at), the term *imago* corresponds best to our term *image*. It is still best to be wary of its apparent obviousness, since the notion was made internal over time, as attested by our derived terms *imaginary* and *imagination*.

Imago suggests in the first instance, because of its origin (its root is *im-*, which is found in *imitor*), a material imitation. It refers in fact to statues or portraits (Cicero, *Epistulae ad familiares*, 5.1.7), and in particular to the wax effigies that nobles would have carried in funeral processions (idem, *In C. Verrem actio secunda*, 2.5.36). Thus, it is something that appears as a double, which may also be the shadow of a dead person (Virgil, *Aeneid*, 4.654), a specter (ibid., 4.773), or a mirror image (Lucretius, *De rerum natura*, 4.156). But although the *imago* may appear in a hallucinatory or virtual way, it most often has the reality of a reproduction. Cicero (*De finibus*, 1.21) translates the Epicurean material *eidôla* by the plural *imagines*; they are what we receive in our eyes and what make us see the things from which they emanate. Lucretius most often uses the term *simulacra*, derived from *simulo* (to copy, to imitate) (*De rerum natura*, 4.159, etc.). The meanings of the two words are very close; in both cases, they refer to image-portraits of the object, an idea that we associate with results of methods of reproduction, variously called *figura, forma, effigies*, or *pictura*. Because of the resemblance between the *imago* and that of which it is an image, the meaning is involved with the two opposing directions of truthful similarity: that of the son who is a *portrait* of the father (Cicero, *Epistulae ad familiares*, 6.6.13), or, in contrast, that of deceptive similarity, such as the usurpation of someone else's appearance (Plautus, *Miles gloriosus*, 151). Further, there are the figurative uses, according to which the face is the *mirror* of the soul (Cicero, *De oratore*, 3.221), or ambition takes on the *mask* of modesty (Tacitus, *Historiae*, 4.86). The internalized notion only appears later, with the *evocation* of sad or pleasant things (Tacitus, *Annales*, 2.53), or again of an absent friend (Pliny the Younger, *Epistulae*, 7.5.1).

No doubt it is along these lines that *imago* led to *imaginari* and *imaginatio* in the Imperial period, which is where "to imagine" and "imagination" come from, with the sense of "to represent to oneself," without the extreme semantic diversity of the Greek term *phantasia*. We may see the difficulty Latin writers had in getting beyond the strict sense of material reproduction toward that of mental representation found in Saint Augustine. In book 10.7–21 of the *Confessions*, he analyzes the contents of what he calls the palace of his memory. A careful reading shows that the metaphor is developed with the idea of a receptacle of images (*imagines*) of sensible impressions, classed as visual, auditory, and so on (like so many portraits?), of which he asks "how they have been made" (10.13). The study develops further with the memory of the sciences, of the affects, of remembering itself, arriving at the limiting case of the memory of forgetting. How can the image of forgetting subsist in memory, if it is itself a forgetting imprinted upon us (10.25)? This is not an issue of paradoxical subtleties, as some have supposed. Rather, we must see this as an attempt to get beyond the idea of a mental image as a strict reproduction of what it represents, an idea that still lies beyond some conceptions of memory and imagination in the nineteenth century. Again, it is not so much a difficulty about choosing a modern equivalent of the term, as about the archaic content that the term carries with it.

The subsequent evolution of optics adds a great deal of complexity to these first personal extensions of the notion of *imago*. Unlike the Epicurean theory, the hypothesis of a visual flux, on which ancient geometrical optics was based, could do completely without the journey of some image through the air and into the eye and body, since in this theory, it was vision itself that supposedly reached out to touch the external object in order to sense it. In the beginning of the eleventh century, however, the Arab scholar Ibn al-Haytham

(Alhazen) conceived an optics based on the entry of light rays into the eyes, which required him to think seriously about the formation of a quasi-image of the object on the lens, which he held to be a sense organ, and about its transmission to the encephalon. The image of an external visible object thus also became an internal object formed in the eye and traveling along the optic nerve to the seat of the visual faculty. His *Optics* was translated into Latin, no doubt at the very end of the twelfth century, and led to a transformation of the vocabulary of vision, based on his Arabic.

One ambiguous term is that of *forma*, whose equivocality leads to its being transposed to *form*. As A. I. Sabra points out (*The Optics of Ibn al-Haytham*), it is translated from the Arabic *ṣūra* [الصورة], which ordinarily relates to all of the notions we have seen connected to that of the image, such as form, figure, effigy, appearance, and so on. The first Arabic translators used it to translate a number of Greek words, including *eidos, idea, eidôlon, morphê, tupos*. In Ibn al-Haytham's optical works, *ṣūra* has at least three meanings. First, the term indicates light, and by extension color, insofar as these exist in luminous or colored objects as *essential or accidental forms*, according to whether the objects are luminous or colored by themselves or in virtue of an external source. It thus refers to a property or quality *of the thing*. In the theory of vision, *ṣūra* also has two meanings, which the author does not always distinguish. The first is what the sense organ (the lens) periodically receives from an external, luminous, and colored point: it is thus the sensory image of a point—the two proper sensibles of sight being light and color. Second, it is the grasping of the object in all of its visual determinations: its outline, of course, as a collection of luminous and colored points, which also corresponds to our notion of an image—but also the twenty other *intentiones visibiles* that characterize it, from its size, its shape, its position or movement, to its smooth or rough character, its continuity or discontinuity, beauty or ugliness. In other words, it is what the final visual faculty transmits to memory for recollection, or to the intellect for judgment.

Related to the notion of *forma*, a second, even more equivocal term thus appears, namely, *intentio*. It translates the Arabic *ma'nā* [المعنى], which an ancient lexicographer, Ibn al-Arabi, defines as "the intention that externalizes itself, and that manifests itself in the thing when it is sought" (see IN-TENTION). The Arabic translators of the ninth century use the word in a rather wide sense, to translate *noêma* [νοήμα], *logos* [λόγος], or *pragma* [πρᾶγμα] in philosophical texts. Isḥāq ibn Ḥunayn uses it in the plural to translate *ta pragmata* in Aristotle's *De interpretatione*, where it refers to the "things" whose affections are signified by the sound of words and the marks of writing. In the translation into Latin of Ibn al-Haytham's *Optics* it takes on a technical sense, in expressions such as *intentiones visibiles, intentiones subtiles*. It refers to the collection of qualities, relations, and properties thanks to which an object is completely manifested to those who look at it. The latter grasp them of course thanks to the luminous and colored image that comes to them, but also because of the interpretation they give it out of habit, judgment, or reasoning. However, unlike Avicenna, for whom *ma'nā* refers to the sighting of what is associated with an object without itself being visible—such as the dangerousness of a wolf—the

term in Ibn al-Haytham lies entirely in the scope of genuine vision. But it lends the vision of form (*forma*) a status that cannot be reduced to our contrast between subjective and objective, between mental image and the thing *stricto sensu*. As a result, the medievals have a theory of knowledge that does not match up with our own.

Further, being by nature luminous, the image that is created in a mirror acquires as such a primary consistency, while according to the theory of visual rays, it would have its being only derivatively from the object against which the visual ray ricochets. Characteristically, it finally receives a technical and univocal designation itself in the Latin texts: "Et forma comprehensa in corpore polito nominatur imago" (And we call image the form apprehended in a polished body; *Opticae thesaurus, Alhazeni arabis libri septem*, 5, proemium). This usage becomes standard in the thirteenth century. Witelo's *Optics*, which was inspired by Ibn al-Haytham and became a classic, also says: "Imago dicitur forma in speculo comprehensa" (We call image the form apprehended in a mirror; *Vitellonis Thuringopoloni opticae libri decem*, 5, def. 13).

III. Optical Images and Mental Images

The notion of image evolves again during the early modern period with the progress of optics. For Kepler, the image *seen* in a mirror or through a refractive surface, which he refers to as *imago*, remains an object of vision that is deceptive in its localization, and sometimes in its proportions and colors. Like the medievals, he believes that it is "almost nothing," "a thing composed of real luminous and colored species, and of intentional quantities" (*Ad Vitellionem paralipomena*, proposition 2, def. 1). He distinguishes it from *pictura*, the painting one can *collect* on a screen in a *camera obscura* (ibid., proposition 5). However, despite his reference to the medieval *imago*, Kepler modifies the situation profoundly. He shows that the lens does not have the function of receiving the sensory form of the object, but of making the rays entering the pupil converge, in order to yield a *pictura*—a real stigmatic image—on the retina. We must then ask how this authentic "painting" can travel along the obscure and tortuous conduits of the optic nerve. The problem of the transmission from eye to brain is posed afresh.

Descartes, in discourse 4 of his *Dioptrique* (1637), responds by noticing that resemblance to the object is not necessary for the mental image, especially because if it were, we would need another set of eyes in the brain in order to apprehend it. It suffices that the soul should be able to distinguish the different properties of things on the basis of differential signs transmitted by the nerves to the brain, as it does for example with the sounds of language. Early modern reflection thus moves decisively in considering mental life from the image-portrait to the image-sign. The model of language begins to compete with that of the effigy or mirror. The psychological description of what is evoked in us by things becomes a major philosophical issue. The old term *idea* changes its use, becoming for Locke (1690) simply a conscious representation (see CONSCIOUSNESS), without further metaphorical reference to the form, or, by way of it, to the visible. And what our ideas correspond to becomes problematic.

In parallel fashion, the image we see in a mirror or through glass ceases to be the evanescent and deceptive wisp of the ancient opticians. Following the discoveries made possible by Galileo's telescope (1610), it acquires a respectable kind of objectivity over the years, thanks to the understanding of its role in enlargements produced by optical instruments. Subsequent progress only amplifies this objectification of the image, which is no longer held to be only a means of creating illusion, but becomes more and more a way of perfecting vision. By the techniques that, beginning with the era of photography, capture and manipulate it, it even becomes a thing among others, rigorously definable, and thus no longer offering any problem of translation from one language to another.

Has it lost its mystery and power then? To retain them, we may first come back to the immediacy of seeing. In *L'œil et l'esprit*, Maurice Merleau-Ponty reintroduces, regarding painting, the "suspect" aspect of the resemblance of mirror images, and the "power of icons," which somehow cannot be pinned down. To give an account of it, he is required in *Le visible et l'invisible* to make a fresh start and reformulate the immersion of the seeing person in the material world, with terms like *chair* (flesh), *entrelacs* (interlacing), *réversibilité* (reversibility), and so on, which do not always have equivalents in other languages, since they fall outside of the classical philosophy of perception (see LEIB). But to recapture the fullness and the value of the image, we may also explore the sources of drives related to our imagination, the direction in which psychoanalysis rapidly turned with the concept of *imago*.

- See Box 2.

As an immediate object of vision, the image has always both been and not been the thing. Even though our sciences and our techniques attempt to reduce it to its objective character of faithful reproduction, it has retained its symbolic equivocality through this existential ambivalence.

Gérard Simon

BIBLIOGRAPHY

Augustine. *Confessions*. Edited by M. Foley. Translated by F. J. Sheed. Indianapolis, IN: Hackett, 2006.

Descartes, René. *La dioptrique*. Vol. 6 in *Œuvres de Descartes*. Edited by Charles Adam and Paul Tannery. Paris: Vrin, 1983. Translation by P. J. Olscamp: *Discourse on Method, Optics and Geometry*. Indianapolis, IN: Bobbs-Merrill, 1965. First published in 1637.

Ibn al-Haytham. *Alhazeni arabis libri septem*. In *Opticae thesaurus*. Basel, Switz., 1572. Reprint, New York: Johnson Reprint Corp., 1972.

———. *The Optics of Ibn al-Haytham*. Translated by A. I. Sabra. London: Warburg Institute, University of London, 1989.

Kepler, Johannes. *Ad Vitellionem paralipomena*. In vol. 2 of *Gesammelte Werke*. Munich: Beck, 1939. Translation by W. H. Donahue: *Optics: Paralipomena to Witelo and Optical Part of Astronomy*. Santa Fe, NM: Green Lion Press, 2000. First published in 1604.

Lacan, Jacques. *Écrits*. Paris: Seuil, 1966. Translation by Bruce Fink: *Écrits*. New York: W. W. Norton, 2007.

Merleau-Ponty, Maurice. *L'œil et l'esprit*. Paris: Gallimard, 1964. Translation: *The Eye and the Mind*. In *Maurice Merleau-Ponty: Basic Writings*, edited by T. Baldwin. New York: Routledge, 2003.

———. *Le visible et l'invisible*. Paris: Gallimard, 1964.

Mugler, Charles. *Dictionnaire historique de la terminologie optique des Grecs*. Paris: Klincksieck, 1958.

Mugnier, René. *Petits traités d'histoire naturelle*. Paris: Les Belles Lettres, 1965.

Rivaud, Albert, trans. *Platon, Timée. Critias*. Paris: Les Belles Lettres, Collection des Universités de France, 1925.

Witelo. *Vitellonis Thuringopoloni opticae libri decem*. In *Opticae thesaurus*. Basel, Switz., 1572. Reprint, New York: Johnson Reprint Corp., 1972.

2

Imago in psychoanalysis

The term *imago*, which is also used in zoology to refer to the definitive state of insects that undergo metamorphosis, was adopted in psychoanalysis around 1910. It remained untranslated in all the languages used, and so kept, like *libido*, its Latin spelling. The Freudian milieu had taken special note of it in 1906, when a novel titled *Imago* was published by a Swiss writer, Carl Spittelberg (1845–1924), who would receive the Nobel Prize in 1919. In it, the author recounts the story of a poet, Victor, who spends his time inventing an imaginary woman who fulfills his deepest desires, instead of with a more prosaic but real lover. The publication in 1903 of Wilhelm Jensen's *Gradiva* had already opened psychoanalysts up to the literary theme of a woman who is as fascinating as she is unreal, and to the art of creating one or cultivating her image. Freud titled the new journal that he created with Otto Rank in 1912 *Imago*, as a reference to Spittelberg's work. The journal was meant to deal with nonmedical applications of psychoanalysis, as a complement to the *Internationale ärtzliche Zeitschrift für Psychoanalyse* (*Standard Edition*, 19:168n2).

In Freud's work itself, it is true, we find only five occurrences of the word *imago*, and terse ones at that. There, it is a question only of "foreign objects chosen according to the model [*imago*] of childhood objects" (*La vie sexuelle*, 57), of the case in which "the libido has revived the childhood *imagos* of the subject" (*Standard Ed.*, 12:102), or, again, of the father-*imago* (ibid., 12:100)—but here with the mention of Jung as the originator of such an "appropriate" notion. Jung, indeed, not long before their rupture, described *imagos* (paternal, maternal, and fraternal), in *Metamorphoses and Symbols of the Libido* (1911), as being primordial representations (*Urbilder*), which he then categorized among the impersonal archetypes of the collective unconscious.

Jacques Lacan makes an appeal to the notion of *imago* in a work considered to be a precursor to his official teaching (his contribution to volume 8 of the *Encyclopédie française* in 1938). He compares this notion to that of a complex. While a complex characterizes the effect on the subject of the interpersonal constellation that is the institution of the family, *imago* refers to an imaginary survival, which may become reshaped, and is often unconscious, of one or another relation of the same subject with a familial experience. Thus we have the *imagos* of the maternal breast, or one's fellow creatures, or of the body itself, this last corresponding to the specular image contemporary with the initial phase, called the mirror stage, in which the infant becomes alienated in his identification with the image of the other.

Charles Baladier

BIBLIOGRAPHY

Freud, Sigmund. *The Standard Edition of the Complete Psychological Works of Sigmund Freud*. Edited and translated by James Strachey in collaboration with Anna Freud. 24 vols. London: Hogarth Press, 1956–74.

———. *La vie sexuelle*. Translated to French by Denise Berger and Jean Laplanche. Paris: Presses Universitaires de France, 1969.

ELEUTHERIA [ἐλευθερια] (GREEK)

ENGLISH	liberty, freedom
FRENCH	*liberté, libre arbitre*
GERMAN	*Freiheit, Willkür*
LATIN	*libertas, liberum arbitrum*

➤ LIBERTY, SVOBODA, and *DESTINY*, DUTY, LAW, LIBERAL, LOVE, MORALS, NATURE, PEOPLE, PHRONÊSIS, POLIS, PRAXIS, WILLKÜR

The vocabulary of freedom is divided along etymological lines: while some languages privilege the idea of a kind of growth that is deployed and then fully flourishes—*eleutheria* [ἐλεύθερια], *libertas*, "liberty"—others determine freedom based on "the belonging to a closed group of those who call each other friends" (Benveniste)—"freedom," *Freiheit*. English even has both terms, "liberty" and "freedom." However, the most basic division for the history of philosophy runs between the Greek meaning of the word *eleutheria*, which, for Plato at least, refers to the regulated development of the natural philosopher, and the medieval and modern sense of *libertas*, related to free will and the invention of the will.

I. Etymology as a Means of Accessing the Greek Philosophical Meaning of Liberty

The striking thing about the Greek vocabulary relating to freedom is its extreme richness. Besides the fundamental notion of *eleutheria*, we also find the adjectives *hekôn* [ἑκών], *hekousios* [ἑκούσιος] (antonym: *akôn* [ἄκων]), "willingly," the first referring primarily to a disposition of the agent, the second to the act performed. The term is fundamental not only in the tragedies of Euripides, in which it refers to the hero's consenting to death, which is contrary to a death imposed from outside (cf. Nestle, *Eleutheria*), but also in the Platonic problem of the so-called involuntary error, according to which "there is not a single man who commits error willingly" (*Protagoras*, 345e), as well as in the theory of decision (*proairesis* [προαίρεσις]) and responsibility in book 3 of the *Nicomachean Ethics*. Later the notion of *ta eph' hemîn* [τὰ ἐφ' ἡμῖν] refers, in Stoic contexts, to what depends on us rather than on fate; it is accompanied by a new word, *to autexousion* [τὸ αὐτεξούσιον], which appears along with *exousia* [ἐξουσία] (authority, mastery), to refer to the mastery of oneself. Finally, there is the whole vocabulary of intention, wish, and hope (*boulêsis* [βούλησις], *boulesthai* [βούλεσθαι], *thelêsis* [θέλησις], *(e)thelein* [(ἐ)θέλειν]), of deliberation (*bouleusis* [βούλευσις], *bouleuesthai* [βουλεύεσθαι]), and of decision (*hairesis* [αἵρεσις], *proairesis* [προαίρεσις]), which comes up in passages that we would tend, in a modern discussion, to interpret uniformly in terms of "freedom." Such a translation, though, not only tends to homogenize the diverse meanings and to flatten the richness of Greek; it also projects onto these different terms an interpretive schema that itself flows entirely from a historical evolution. We thus risk understanding Plato and Aristotle based on a medieval or modern discussion of *libertas* that is entirely foreign to their philosophical perspective.

When we speak about liberty in French, we transpose, rather than translate, a Latin word that is loaded with a philosophically weighty past. *Libertas*, in the Scholastic and then in the modern sense, includes both: (1) the idea of the absence of compulsion or constraint (*libertas a coactione*), the idea of pure spontaneity; and (2) the notion of a will that is not in any way determined to choose one or another of two contraries (*libertas a determinationis, ad utrumlibet*), and which can therefore: (a) act or not act (*libertas quoad exercitium actus*, freedom of action), (b) choose an action or its contrary (*libertas quoad speciem actus*, freedom of specification). The second of these determinations corresponds to the concept of free will, as formulated by Molina (*De concordia*, 14.13.2): "Illud agens liberum dicitur, quod positis omnibus requisitis ad agendum, potest agere et non agere, aut ita agere unum ut contrarium etiam agere posit" (We call an agent free when, all the conditions for his action being posited, he can act and not act, or act in such a way that, if he performs one of the two contrary actions, he could equally well have performed the other). This definition is partially taken up by Descartes (cf. *Meditations*). Liberty as we understand it, then, expresses the notions of absence of constraint, spontaneity, not making any difference, and self-determination.

Some of these senses may well be present in Greek, but none of them seems sufficient, or even necessary, for understanding what is involved in the concept of *eleutheria*.

For a long time, it was common to attempt to understand the primary sense of the word based on the etymology that the Greeks themselves gave it, according to which *eleutheria* had a root, ελυθ-, with ελευθ- expressing the idea of "going where one wants"—"*to elthein hopou erai*" [τὸ ἐλθεῖν ὅπου ἐρᾷ], "going where you like." This etymological explication is often paired with a philosophical interpretation of the term that gives priority to its political meaning: the free man is one who, unlike the slave, could move as he wished and was not restricted in his movements. (cf. Hegel, *Encyclopedia*, §486; Arendt, *Life of the Mind*; Festugière, *Liberté et civilisation chez les Grecs*; Pohlenz, *Griechische Freiheit*). The negative meaning of the term—the free man as opposed to the slave (where "free" is practically synonymous with "citizen" since the free man is the one who participates in power in the city, defined by Aristotle as the "community of free [men]" (*koinônia tôn eleutherôn* [κοινωνία τῶν ἐλευθέρων]) (*Politics*, 3.6.1279a21; see POLIS)—could be considered along these lines to be the only authentic Greek sense of the word. Hannah Arendt sums up this thesis, in its most radical form: "There is no concern with freedom [in a nonpolitical sense] in all of the history of great philosophy from the Presocratics up to Plotinus, the last ancient philosopher" (*Between Past and Future*).

This etymological explication is now outdated. Contemporary research by H. Frisk (RT: *Griechisches etymologisches Wörterbuch*) and Benveniste (*Le vocabulaire des institutions indo-européennes*) (cf. also RT: *Dictionnaire étymologique de la langue grecque*) has revealed that the term was semantically richer than that. In fact, the primary sense of *eleutheria* is not a negative one ("not being prevented from going where one wishes"), related to constraint and restriction, but a positive one. As Benveniste showed, the radical from which *eleutheros* is drawn [ἐλεύθερος], namely, **leudh-*, means "to grow, to develop," and also yielded the terms for "people" in Slavic and German (*Leute*). The word *eleutheria* thus articulated two primary meanings, whose relationship must be understood:

the belonging to an ethnic stock (people), and the idea of growth that leads to a complete form, which ends in its full flourishing. We must therefore conclude that "the primary sense is not, as one might imagine, 'relieved of something'; it is that of belonging to an ethnic stock designated by a metaphor of the growth of plants. This belonging confers a privilege which the foreigner and the slave never enjoy" (*Le vocabulaire des institutions indo-européennes*). To be "free" is thus to belong to a "growth group" that defines "an ethnic subdivision, the collection of which were born and developed together." The primary sense of *eleutheros* might thus be: "belonging to the people," "with one's own," as opposed to *barbaros* [βάϱβαϱος]. This is how Modestus van Straaten interprets the first known occurrence of the term in a controversial passage of the *Iliad* (6.455): Andromache, brought far away from Troy, loses *eleutheron êmar* [ἐλεύθεϱον ἦμαϱ], "the day of liberty." This translation as "liberty," according to van Straaten, does not capture the primary signification of the word in Greek: "belonging to the people, at home" ("What Did the Greeks Mean by Liberty?"). To lose *eleutheria* is first and foremost to lose the day that breaks over the homeland, where Andromache is at home: "it seems to be quite possible that in those ancient times the Greeks felt this *home* as the primary element in the phrase and *free* only as a consequence" (cf. also Muller, "Remarques sur la liberté grecque").

Eleutheria thus does not at first have a political meaning, but a biological (stock, line, people) or physical ("growth," and more precisely completed growth, which concludes with the full flourishing of the form—whence "form, figure, stature") one. Is this, as Benveniste thinks, a matter of a simple "metaphor"? That, in a sense, is the whole question.

- See Box 1.

II. Freedom, Growth, Nature: *Eleutheria* and *Phusis*

The growth that ends in a fully present flourishing, as a movement from oneself and toward oneself, is in effect what the Greek *phusis* [φύσις] refers to. As Heidegger emphasizes in *The Principle of Reason*, *phusis* was not, for the Greeks, a being among others, but rather the original determination of being: "Being is *phusis*, that is, what is manifest of oneself." *Phusis* is the kind of mobility that belongs to moving things *according to their mode of being*, that is, their entry into presence: "Only when such understanding has become possible is *phusis* graspable in its mode of deployment as the original power over the motion of the movable object from itself and in the direction of itself" ("Ce qu'est et comment se détermine la *phusis*," 212). It designates the mode of flourishing of being in presence, as growth, deployment, blooming, flourishing. In that sense, does not *phusis* prescribe its primordial meaning for the Greek notion of *eleutheria*? One could argue this on the basis of a number of texts; we will take only two examples.

A passage from the *Theaetetus* (173a–b) clearly shows that the "free man" is first and foremost the one who has flourished as a man, that is, who has managed to fully express his human form and shape (cf. Muller, "Remarques sur la liberté grecque"). Socrates compares the Sophists, clever in legal arguments, who have spent their time in the courts of law from

a young age, with the philosophers. The former are, compared to the latter, like people raised to serve compared to free men (*eleutherois* [ἐλευθέϱοις]). The litigants have no leisure: for them, the time for their speeches is always counted. Thus, the education they receive makes them clever, but "[causes their souls] to be small and warped" (*smikroi de kai ouk orthoi tas psuchas* [σμικϱοὶ δὲ καὶ οὐκ ὀϱθοὶ τὰς ψυχάς]). And Socrates adds:

His early servitude prevents him from making a free, straight growth; it forces him into doing crooked things by imposing dangers and alarms upon a soul that is still tender. He cannot meet these by just and honest practice, and so resorts to lies and to the policy of repaying one wrong with another; thus he is constantly being bent and distorted.

(*Theaetetus*, 173a–b)

From this Socrates can infer that only the philosopher makes use of freedom (*eleutheria*) in his discourse (*logos* [λόγος]) and in moving from one discourse to the next (173b). This text associates freedom and growth (*auxê* [αὔξη]) in an extremely clear way, leading to straight posture, rectitude in behavior (*to euthu* [τὸ εὐθύ]), whereas the slavery of the litigants and nonphilosophical rhetors is the product of a constraint (*anagkazousa*) by which this growth is seemingly blocked, unable to flourish freely, and yields twisted, stunted, and devious beings (cf. Muller, "Remarques sur la liberté grecque"). To be free, on the other hand, is nothing other than to achieve one's fulfillment as a man (cf. *Laws*, 1.635d: the goal is to raise, by education, brave and free men, that is, complete men), just as a plant comes to its full flourishing in a flower.

By this standard, *eleutheria* is not contrary to *phusis* the way modern liberty is contrary to natural determinism, but rather leads back to it. Indeed, if, as Aristotle maintains, "For what each thing is when fully developed, we call its nature [*phusis*]" (*Politics*, 1.2.1252b32–33), then *eleutheria* completes *phusis*. This is shown, for example, in the passages Aristotle devotes to natural slavery, in which the same "physical" or "plant-like" paradigm appears. We read in the *Politics* that if there are natural slaves, that is because there are men whose stature and shape are distinct from those of free men, because of an incomplete growth: if the natural slave is not entirely a man, it is because "he who can be, and therefore is, another's, and he who participates in reason enough to apprehend, but not to have, is a slave by nature" (*Politics*, 1.5.1254b22). The natural slave stoops, unlike the free man who stands erect (1254b27), where this rectitude is what, along with reason, gives man his divine character (*De partibus animalium*, 4.10.686a28), since, he adds, *phusis* does not always produce what it wishes (*Politics*, 1.5.1255b3–4). These descriptions of the natural slave would remain entirely unintelligible to us if we did not grasp that liberty, understood as the goal of *phusis*, signifies the full completion or flourishing of the man as such—that is, a s being such, having such or such a "nature." Aristotle is not here speaking of real slaves as they existed in fourth-century Athens since he immediately clarifies that "the opposite often happens—that some [slaves] have the souls

1

The two paradigms: "Freedom"/"liberty"

The English language has two words, "freedom" and "liberty," which are both opposed to serfdom or slavery, but whose connotations are very different. "Freedom" is the more general term, which designates the power a person possesses to act according to his or her will, without constraint or, at least, without legitimate constraint; it is therefore used equally in general philosophy to speak of the "freedom of the will," "free will," and so forth, and in political philosophy to designate the state enjoyed by the citizens of a "free" community. "Liberty" has a more specifically juridical and political meaning: it designates the absence of all restrictions other than those that are justly required by the law, and it thus has positive connotations that explain the use made of it by liberal thinkers or republicans attached to political liberty, that is, to the fact of living according to the law.

English thus functions as the moderator between the two paradigms, highlighted by Benveniste (*Le vocabulaire des institutions indo-européennes*, vol. 1, chap. 3), at work in Indo-European languages to construct the idea of liberty. "Liberty" looks back to the Latin *liber* and *libertas*, as well as to the Greek *eleutheros* (ἐλεύθερος), *eleutheria* (ἐλευθερία): Latin and Greek can effectively be superimposed on the linguistic plane and have (via the old Venetian *(e)leudheros*), the same root *leudh-*, "to grow, to develop," from which come seemingly heterogeneous terms like *Liber* (Lat.), the ancient god of the vine, *liberi* (Lat.), "the children" who are well born, legitimate, and *Leute* (Ger.), "people." Hence the insistence on the ethnic stock and on growth.

But there is another genealogy, which first sets in play a set of notions relating to the individual: the English "free" like the German *frei* stems from an Indo-European adjective, *priyos*, which expresses the belonging to oneself, the relation with oneself and others (dear). What is decisive in this instance is belonging to the closed group of those who call each other friends (*Freunde* in German): it is not birth but the affective and institutional mutuality of the group that constitutes freedom. A whole array of words can be mobilized to indicate that one is only "oneself" when one is among other similar "selves": thus we find the Indo-European *swe* to indicate the self, the reflective, the proper (Gr. *idios* [ἴδιος]; see PROPERTY) as well as to signify the ally, the relative (Gr. *etês* [ἔτης]), the companion, the colleague (Gr. *hetairos* [ἑταῖρος], Lat. *sodalis*) (see SVOBODA).

This double linguistic paradigm, which reveals two ways of making freedom/liberty perceptible and of identifying a person, helps to throw light on certain distortions in history and philosophy, including no doubt confusions between terms that arise from the same paradigm.

Barbara Cassin
Philippe Raynaud

BIBLIOGRAPHY

Benveniste, Émile. *Le vocabulaire des institutions indo-européennes*. Paris: Minuit, 1969.

and others have the bodies of freemen" (1254b31). In this ideal portrait of what a slave "ought to be"—and what the slaves existing in fact at Athens are precisely not!—the nature of the slave is thus grasped "by contrast" with the free man (and not the reverse) as a failed man, "the free man [being] the completed, flourishing man, since he is not restricted in his development, and is thus in conformity with his own nature" (Muller, "La logique de la liberté dans *La Politique*"). Thus, "since" the completed man has the capacity to deliberate (*to bouleutikon* [τὸ βουλευτικόν]), prudence (*phronêsis* [φρόνησις]; see PHRONÊSIS), and acts by choice (*proairoumenos* [προαιρούμενος]), the slave must be lacking these three traits (*Politics*, 3.9.1280a34). This is why he can neither command nor participate in the goals of the city: well-being, or happiness (1280a31). A fortiori the "natural" slave cannot participate in the highest activity of man, in which he fully flourishes as himself and completes his own nature, coinciding with his *telos* [τέλος]: contemplation. Aristotle refers to the contemplating man as *eleutheros* (*Politics*, 3.23.1325a19), not only because he is freed from political obligations, but because he fully actualizes his essence as a man, while at the same time rising up to the most divine part of man, by imitating divine self-sufficiency.

III. Greek Free Will?

For both Aristotle and Plato, in this sense, *eleutheria* does not necessarily entail the modern notion of undetermined choice. If we absolutely had to find an ancestor for the modern concept of freedom, we would more likely find it in the Sophists, by virtue of their different understanding of the *phusis/nomos* [φύσις/νόμος] relationship. In the *Gorgias*, Plato uses Callicles, a disciple of the Sophists and a radical defender of the pleasure principle, to incarnate a conception of freedom as a frenzied permissiveness in the search for one's own good, the absence of any external restraint, and, consequently, a pure subjective will (491e–492c). This conception is based on a completely different relationship between law and nature. "Freedom" (*eleutheria*) no longer refers to unrestrained flourishing "in accordance" with *phusis*, such that *phusis* is in fact what regulates development and gives it its own law, and where flourishing consists precisely in this agreement or conformity of the individual with the law of his essence. Rather, the idea behind the Sophistic conception of freedom is that of a development that is its own law unto itself, as long as it meets no obstacles, of a force that follows through completely and is only limited by another force. "Freedom" is not understood by Callicles as the perfect flourishing of a being in accordance with the law of its essence, but as a growth, a development that is not regulated by any law or essence, by any *phusis* in the Platonic sense (which always presupposes a norm or *telos*), and is its own measure. The only *phusis* of man, from that point on, is not to have a *phusis*, to be able to realize one's most extreme possibilities without any opposing restraint or restriction.

Plato's response is that this kind of absolute permission is only a false freedom. First, it rests on a purely negative idea of freedom: independence from any restraint and all obligation does not give *eleutheria* any positive content. This becomes the power to do anything, good or bad, and can be summed up in a single phrase: "do what one wishes" (*poiei ha bouletai* [ποιεῖ ἃ βούλεται]) (*Republic*, 10.577d). Second, this sort of power without restraint may be an illusion. Are we not prisoners of opinion when we act just as we please? And is not the restraining force of opinion the strongest, most unbreakable of bonds? We must counter the maxim "do what seems good" with the true knowledge of the good, which alone yields freedom. Thus, Sophistic *eleutheria* is put down to a tyrannical disposition according to which a man is "pushed towards a general disorder [*pasan paranomian* (πᾶσαν παρανομίαν)], to which the people who do the pushing (the bad educators) give the name of complete freedom [*eleutherian hapasan* (ἐλευθερίαν ἅπασαν)]" (*Republic*, 10.572e). However, "the soul which rules a tyrant will do what he pleases least of all "(*kai hê turannoumenê ara psuchê hêkista poiêsei ha an boulêthê* [καὶ ἡ τυραννουμένη ἄρα ψυχὴ ἥκιστα ποιήσει ἃ ἂν βουληθῇ]) (577e). Plato thus turns the Sophists' concept of freedom against them: doing what one wishes in complete ignorance is the very definition of slavery: "*ho tôi onti turannos tôi onti doulos* [ὁ τῷ ὄντι τύραννος τῷ ὄντι δοῦλος]" (he who in his being is a tyrant is in his being a slave) (579d).

Unlike a tyrannical disposition, the philosopher, the kingly man, does not in the first instance exercise his royalty upon others; rather, he cannot do so except insofar as he first exercises it on himself, that is, insofar as he is free: "This person is the most kingly, and he exercises his royalty upon himself" (*basileuonta hautou* [βασιλεύοντα αὑτοῦ]) (580b–c). This perfect royalty lies in the priority of *nous* [νοῦς], the intellect, over the other two parts of the soul distinguished in the *Republic*, *epithumia* [ἐπιθυμία] (desire) and *thumos* [θυμός] (courage). In effect, *nous* alone is free by itself, as the key text of the *Laws* clarifies: "*Nous* cannot be a servant or a slave of anything without impiety; it must be, on the contrary, the universal master, if it is really true and free as its nature demands" (*Laws* 9.875c–d). *Eleutheria* can thus be defined by Plato as this "symphony internal to the soul" (*tês en tôi psuchei . . . sumphônias* [τῆς ἐν τῇ ψυχῇ . . . συμφωνίας]) (*Republic*, 591d), which cannot be dissociated from the reigning justice among its faculties, or again, for the free man, from the good "constitution of the city which is in him" (*tên en hautôi politeian* [τὴν ἐν αὑτῷ πολιτείαν]) (591e). There is harmony or "symphony" in his internal city—"freedom"—only because *nous* is not commanding by restraint or violence, but by a mild persuasion (cf. *Timaeus*, 47e–48a). Under its authority, all the parts of the soul are in agreement, seek the common good together, and harmonize. The harmony that is put into place, like any harmony, presupposes the agreement of the different parties for the sake of the whole, that is, with an eye toward a goal, the good of the whole soul, which only the intellect knows. Freedom thus understood is at the furthest remove from the capacity to do either a thing or its contrary, as we can see from a fundamental text in the *Laws* (1.645a), where the free man is compared

to a puppet created by the gods, which does not allow itself to be dragged along by the iron thread of the passions (pleasure, pain, hope, and fear), but only by the "golden thread" of *nous* and law. To understand this text in light of the modern notion of freedom would only accord human beings a poor kind of "freedom" since, even worse that the "freedom of the turnspit" that Kant criticizes with regard to Leibniz, this would be a freedom of puppets! But the sense of this passage is completely different: insofar as "the god is the measure of all things" (*Laws*, 4.716c), to be subordinate to the gods is to be free, since it is knowing the good that provides the measure of what is human, and thus what it is to be a man in the full sense of the term. Freedom for man thus means the development of his being, not at all as a disorderly and anarchic growth, but as flourishing in accordance with *phusis*—flourishing that operates thanks to the harmony and the justice that obtains among the faculties, the noblest commanding the other two. As an internal submission to *logos*, freedom is at the same time a knowledge of the good by which the soul becomes, so to speak, similar to the *logos*, that is, good; it is a submission to the gods by which *nous* reveals its "divine" character, such that freedom as the knowledge of the good is justice. Only the just man is free, since justice as *aretê* [ἀρετή] (excellence; see under VIRTÙ) constitutes the highest achievement of human development.

IV. Choice, Decision, Freedom

But do we not find in Aristotle's theory of *proairesis* at least a foreshadowing of the modern concept of "freedom"? This may be doubted, and for several reasons. First, *proairesis*, often translated as *electio* into Latin, does not always indicate a "choice," which would involve an alternative. One of the examples from the *Nicomachean Ethics* will suffice: deliberation is like a kind of "calculation," Aristotle claims, and *proairesis* like a syllogism. Let the desired end be health; health is produced by the balance of the humors, and that by heat, and heat by friction; we are able to create friction; thus, we must create friction (6.2.1139a11). There is no "choice" here since there is no alternative, but rather a "decision" regarding the execution of means with a view to an end that is already given. Second, and this point is crucial, *proairesis*, unlike *electio*, is in no way the act of a "will," as this concept is entirely missing from Aristotle's conceptual scheme. Aquinas completely misunderstands things when he translates *proairesis* by *electio* and *boulêsis* by *voluntas* (cf. *Summa theologica*, I, q. 82, art. 1, obj. 2, where he interprets the passage from *De anima*, 432b5, "*en te tôi logistikôi gar hê boulêsis ginetai* [ἔν τε τῷ λογιστικῷ γὰρ ἡ βούλησις γίνεται]," as saying that "the will is in reason"), and even by *liberum arbitrium*: "*Boulêsis* is the free will. For . . . it is the desire for one thing as compared with another" (*Summa theologica*, I, q. 83, art. 4, obj. 1). Indeed, whereas *proairesis* refers to an act of reason for Aristotle (*nous hairetai* [νοῦς αἱρεῖται]; *Nicomachean Ethics*, 9.9.1169a17), and more precisely, the judgment of practical reason that terminates deliberation and yields actions, *electio* is understood by Aquinas as an act of the will aimed at the goal, which has hitherto been revealed by reason deliberating on its means. Here again, Aquinas thinks he can appeal to a passage from the *Nicomachean Ethics* (6.1139b4–5), where Aristotle defines *proairesis* as "desiring reason [*orektikos nous* (ὀρεκτικὸς νοῦς)] or reasoning desire [*orexis dianoêtike* (ὄρεξις διανοητική)]," to attribute the act to the choice of the faculty that combines desire and reason, to the *appetitus rationalis*, that is, to the *voluntas* (*Summa theologica*, I, q. 82, art. 2, obj. 3). This is obviously a misinterpretation. Nothing in Aristotle's theory of *proairesis* allows it to be the locus of a free will, as Pierre Aubenque makes clear: "To approach the notion of *proairesis* from the point of view of the problem of the 'freedom of the will' is to condemn oneself to expect what is not there from these Aristotelian texts, and to ignore what is" (*La prudence chez Aristote*). It would thus be more appropriate to translate this word that Aristotle introduces into philosophical vocabulary by "decision" rather than by "choice" or "free choice": literally that which, in advance (*pro-*), allows us to examine the means with a view to a good end (*to haireton* [τὸ αἱρετόν], "the good").

The strangeness of the Aristotelian conception of *eleutheria* with regard to any modern conception of freedom comes out in a decisive passage from the *Metaphysics*. Aristotle asks, in this passage, as to the manner in which the good is present with respect to the whole: as something separate, or as the order that reigns throughout the whole itself? He responds that the good is not immanent to the world, but rather transcendent, like the Prime Mover. To establish that, he emphasizes the amount of arbitrariness and contingency that we find in the world and that prevents it from being entirely in conformity with the good:

> But it is as in a house, where the freemen are least at liberty to act as they will [*etuche poiein* (ἔτυχε ποιεῖν)], but all things or most things are already ordained for them [*tetaktai* (τέτανται)], while the slaves and the beasts do little for the common good, and for the most part live at random [*to de polu ho ti etuchen* (τὸ δὲ πολὺ ὅ τι ἔτυχεν)]; for this is the sort of principle that constitutes the nature of each.

(*Metaphysics*, Γ, 10, 1075a19–23)

Eleutheria thus does not consist in an unrestricted will, in the possibility of acting however it may chance (*etuche poiein*); on the contrary, it consists in action in accordance with the rule, that is, subordinate to the good. Only slaves and animals, who are precisely not free in the true sense, are likely to act in an arbitrary way. Free men, on the contrary, are those whose behavior is the most constant, and who thus become closer to the undisturbable regularity of the stars and the immutability of the Prime Mover. The indiscriminate behavior of someone who can choose one thing or another "indifferently" is thus the exact opposite of *eleutheria*.

One may still object that we do find, in other texts of Aristotle, and especially in chapter 9 of *De interpretatione*, a "freedom of choice" that resembles the modern notion of free will. Aristotle claims there, in effect, that if Diodorus's necessitarianism were true, "So there would be no need to deliberate or to take trouble (thinking that if we do this, this will

happen, but if we do not, it will not)" (18b31–32). Is this not an affirmation that choice is somehow undetermined? In fact, what Aristotle is trying to preserve in this passage is the existence of some amount of "objective" chance in the world, of contingency, of some indeterminacy among events in virtue of which it is possible to deliberate and to decide one way or another. He is not affirming indeterminacy of choice itself, but rather of the circumstances in which choices must be made.

This is why it seems necessary to distinguish Aristotle's position clearly from that of a later commentator such as Alexander of Aphrodisias, whose conceptual scheme is steeped in Stoicism, and who reinterprets Aristotelian freedom as a sort of "internal chance" (cf. *De anima, liber alter*): there is non-being, he asserts, which when it is found among the causes that are outside us, yields chance or luck (*tuchê* [τυχή], *automaton* [αὐτόματον]), and which, when found among the causes internal to us, makes it the case that some things are in our power (*ta eph' hêmin* [τὰ ἔφ' ἡμῖν]), and whose opposites are equally possible (cf. Hamelin, *Le système d'Aristote*). That is the origin of our freedom. But the affirmation of freedom as "internal chance and freedom of choice" (*exousia tês haireseôs* [ἐξουσία τῆς αἱρέσεως]; *On Fate*, 11.179.10) is not at all Aristotelian. Alexander of Aphrodisias is here reading Aristotle through the lens of Epictetus, Cicero, and Stoicism.

V. *Eleutheria/To Autexousion*

Before coming to the Latin translations of *eleutheria* (*libertas, liberum arbitrium*), we should pause on a term that appears as a noun in the second century CE, both in a nonphilosophical context (Philo of Alexandria, Flavius Josephus, Clement of Alexandria, Origen) and as a technical term in Imperial Stoicism (Epictetus): this is the substantival adjective *to autexousion*. The primary sense of the adjective *autexousios* [αὐτεξούσιος] is "master of oneself." This is the term, present especially in Christian thought (from Clement of Alexandria to Nemesius of Emesa and John of Damascus), which is later translated into Latin as *liberum arbitrium*.

However, the Stoic notion of *autexousios* is not a liberty of choice or will, but rather independence with respect to the passions. *To autexousion* is practically synonymous with *to eph' hêmin*, "what is up to us." This is attested by a passage from Epictetus's *Discourses*:

> What did [God] give me which is mine and independent [*emoi kai autexousion* (ἐμοὶ καὶ αὐτεξούσιον)]? What did he keep for himself? He gave me things which come from choice [*ta proairetika* (τὰ προαιρετικά)], which he made up to me [*ep' emoi* (ἐπ' ἐμοί)], without my meeting any obstacle or hindrance.

(*Discourses*, 4.1.99)

Authority over oneself (*autexousion*) here has the sense of autonomy (*autonomon* [αὐτόνομον]) with regard to any emotional obstacle, and freedom (*eleutheria*; cf. *Discourses* 4.1.56), for the sage, lies in this apathy. Unlike the meaning that develops bit by bit through the translation of autexousion by *liberum arbitrium*, the Stoic meaning of the term does not, therefore, contain the idea of indifference with regard to opposite actions, precisely insofar as the concept of "will" in the modern sense, as essentially rational appetite, is not relevant. Freedom, for Epictetus and Chrysippus before him, does not have anything to do with "voluntary" action, but rather determines assent (*sugkatathesis* [συγκατάθεσις]), which is given to a representation (*phantasia* [φαντασία]) and assent is a function of reason (*logos*). Freedom thus resides in the correct use of representations, that is, in the assent that is conscious and in accordance with reason, unlike the false judgment that gives rise to passions.

How do we get, then, from *to autexousion* to its Latin translation, *liberum arbitrium*? This question intersects the whole history of the invention of the unified concept of will (see WILL). We may put forward the following hypothesis, however: in order to think of something as a "free will," it was first necessary for the locus of freedom to move from the judgment of the intellect in accordance with *logos* to choice, or to the choosing (*arbitrium*) between two contraries. It is possible that late Stoicism may have in fact played a major role in that evolution (cf. Gauthier, Introduction to *L'Éthique à Nicomaque*). For Antipater of Tarsus, the technical notion of *eklogê* [ἐκλογή], which the Latin writers translated by *electio* or *selectio*, "choice," applies exclusively to the selection of things to which wisdom is "indifferent": health or sickness, richness or poverty, honor or dishonor, and so on. The choice of health, for example, does not derive from right action (*katorthôma* [κατόρθωμα]), but is only a simple function (*kathêkon* [καθῆκον], *officium*) since these things that make no difference in themselves only receive their moral shading from the choice, insofar as it is made in conformity with nature or not.

While right action consists, therefore, in adherence (*hairesthai* [αἱρεῖσθαι]) to the good or in fleeing (*pheugein* [φεύγειν]) evil, function (*kathêkon*) consists only in choosing (*eklegesthai* [ἐκλεγέσθαι]) from among the indifferents the ones that are in conformity with nature: the notion of *eklogê* refers here to a much weaker link than adherence or flight (cf. Pohlenz, *Die Stoa*). In Imperial Stoicism, however—for example, in Cicero—the decline of the ideal of the sage and the emphasis placed on function (*officium*) lead to an increased importance for the notion of choice (*electio*). Thus, even the fundamental concept of *phronêsis*, *prudentia*, wisdom, is reinterpreted as a choice (*electio*) between goods or evils (whereas there was only *eklogê*, for Antipater, and only between indifferents: "*prudentia est enim locata in dilectu bonorum et malorum*" (*De officiis*, 3.17.71). Saint Augustine no doubt owes his definition of wisdom to this misinterpretation of Cicero: "prudence is a love which knows how to choose" (*De moribus ecclesiae catholicae*, 1.15.25, in RT: *CSEL*, 90). If prudence consists in knowing how to choose, however, freedom consists, in the end, in the choice itself. From the originally Stoic notion of a choice of things that make no difference, we thus slide, over the

centuries, to the modern notion of a choice that makes no difference.

VI. *To Autexousion/Liberum Arbitrium*

Thus, it is following this emphasis on the concept of *electio*, which soon comes to translate and to eclipse Aristotle's *proairesis*, that the translation of *to autexousion* by *liberum arbitrium* becomes established in the heart of Christian thought. In Clement of Alexandria, for example, "free will" (*to autexousion*), which is necessary for faith (cf. *Stromates*, 5.1.3.2) and indissociable from grace (5.13.83.1) puts the Christian's faculty of choice (*proairesis*; 5.1.7.1) in play each time.

But the most powerful and radical analysis of free will comes from Saint Augustine. His notion of free will is defined less by the power of choosing between good and evil (otherwise, God himself would be deprived of free will: "if only he who can will two things, that is, good and evil, is free, then God is not free, since he cannot will evil"; *Contra Julianum opus imperfectum*, 1.100) than by the power not to sin: "I say that the first man who was created possessed the freedom of his will [*liberum voluntatis arbitrium*]. He was created in such a state that nothing would have blocked his will had he wished to observe the commandments of God" (*Contra Fortunatem*, §22 [RT: *CSEL*, 25]; cf. Gilson, *Introduction à l'étude de Saint Augustin*). On this account, free will is abandoned in original sin and can only be restored through grace. For, insofar as it is a good given by God, free will must itself reach out toward the good. Sin, which is non-being, is unable to define it. It is thus the correct use of free will confirmed by grace that defines freedom as *determinatio in bonum*; free will is only really free when it is itself liberated by grace, that is, when it adheres to God by love and "delights" in him: "Ecce unde liberi, unde condelectamur legi Dei: libertas enim delectate" (That is what makes us free, that is how we find our delight in the law of God: freedom is, in effect, a cause of joy) (*In Johannis evangelium tractatus*, 41.8.10 [RT: *CCSL*, 36]).

Freedom for Saint Augustine is thus not yet a pure power for opposite actions, a freedom of indifference in the modern French sense. That, among other reasons, is because the concept of *voluntas* still includes, for him, a nontechnical meaning (see WILL), distinct from its medieval sense of *appetitus rationalis*, and remains a synonym for "desire" in general and for "love" in particular (*De Trinitate*, 15.21.41 [RT: *CCSL*, 50]). Only with the rise of the technical concept of the will, in Maximus the Confessor, John of Damascus, Nemesius, and Thomas Aquinas, can free will take on the meaning of a pure power of contrary actions, completely undetermined. Free will, writes Aquinas, is "the will for one thing by comparison with another" (*per comparationem ad alterum*) (*Summa theologica*, I, q. 83, art. 4, obj. 1). In other words, the *liberum arbitrium* is "free choice"; its proper action is *electio*: "We must therefore consider the nature of free will according to choice [*ex electione*]"(I, q. 83, art. 3 reply). Choice, however, connects the will to the intellect. According to this new formulation of the problem, which becomes fundamental for all modern philosophy, the problem of freedom thus becomes that of the relationship that links the will to the understanding: in the case in which the will has primacy in the act of choosing, we speak of "voluntarism"; in the other case, of "intellectualism" (see INTELLECTUS).

Thus the modern problem of free will seems to be the fruit of a long history. Far from being, as Descartes thinks, "that which is known without proof, by the experience we have of it alone" (*Principles*, I, §39), it may well be that "freedom of the will" is one of the most sophisticated and least obvious inventions of the "legacy of Western philosophy."

■ See Box 2.

Claude Romano

2

Enslaved judgment

Alongside the French term *libre arbitre*, "free will" or "free judgment," the concept of the *serf arbitre*, the "enslaved will" or "enslaved judgment," deserves to be noted for its rarity and for what it reveals about the history and the difficulties of its glorious antonym. The Latin expression *servum arbitrium* has its first occurrence with Saint Augustine, in the context of the anti-Pelagian controversy:

> But you, you are in haste, and in your haste you rush to abandon your premise. Here you wish man to be perfect, and if possible by a gift of God and not by the free, or rather the enslaved judgment of your will [*et non libero, vel potius servo proprie voluntatis arbitrio*].

The passage is cited several times by Luther, notably in the great treatise *De servo arbitrio* (1525), to which it gives its title:

> This is why Augustine qualifies the judgment as enslaved rather than free, in the second book of *Against Julian*.

There is an obvious distortion here. What in Augustine is a quickly forgotten phrase becomes in Luther a slogan that is supposed to summarize the Augustinian position on free will.

This explains the difficulty experienced by Luther's translators when faced with the expression *servum arbitrium*. The first German translation, by Justus Jonas, a disciple of Luther, transforms the original title *De servo arbitrio* into a complete proposition: *Daß der freie Wille nichts sei* (That free will is nothing) (Wittenberg, 1525). Later translations do not go so far, but they still avoid literal translation. *Vom unfreien Willen* (Of unfree will) is the most current title; in England there is the paraphrase *The Bondage of the Will*.

Without taking into account the transformation that leads from *arbitrium* to *Wille* and from the paradigm of judgment to that of the will (see WILLKÜR), we see that French is the only language that renders the Latin pairing *liber/servus*. In any case, where does this rejection of literal translation come from, since it does not seem to be grounded in any linguistic need? The first reason for it lies in the difficulty of the text *Contra Julianum*. The expression *servum arbitrium* is used there in an ambiguous manner, in an argument (a "premise") attributed to the "enemies of grace" (2.8.22). Furthermore, this "Pelagian" argument, that is, in favor of free will against grace, is not a direct argument. It applies to texts by Saint Ambrose that Augustine has just used, and seeks to limit their conception of the paths of salvation to an opposition between the gift of God alone and free will alone. For Augustine, who is defending Ambrose against this interpretation, free will left to itself can only be *servus*, unfree, since grace, far from "evacuating" free will, rather permits us to "establish" (*statuere*) it. (cf. *De spiritu et littera* 30.52 [RT: *CSEL*, 60]).

So Luther distorts the Augustinian usage of *servum arbitrium*, and the refusal of literal translation is already related to a discomfort experienced in the face of this undue radicalization of the proposition. But it is more deeply related to the impossibility of thinking to its logical end the notion of the enslaved judgment, as well as the opposition it forms with free judgment. We may doubt that the *servum arbitrium* is an Augustinian notion; at the same time, Augustine's conception does pose the problem, which appears in the pairing *liberum arbitrium captivatum/liberum arbitrium liberatum*, and in the difficult idea that free judgment must previously be liberated by grace in order to be what it is (cf., e.g., *Contra duas epistolas Pelagianorum*, 3.8.24 [RT: *CSEL*, 60]; on the question of whether one can still speak of free judgment, cf. the discussion by Williams, *Grace of God*). Similarly Luther is constrained to recognize the existence of free judgment in temporal affairs (cf. *De servo arbitrio*; with the distinction between affairs that are "higher" and "lower" than man, free judgment is admitted among the latter). What is more, and very significantly, the expression *servum arbitrium* never appears in Luther's treatise except in the title and in the quotation from Augustine; what Luther opposes to *liberum arbitrium* is most frequently *necessitas*.

The refusal to translate *servum arbitrium* literally thus makes apparent a doubtless fundamental impossibility: that of creating a hypostasis of the opposite of free judgment (and one understands that translators have preferred to conceive this opposite as a simply logical possibility, *unfrei*, or like a certain state of the will, "bondage"). More generally, the opposed pairs always appear unbalanced: it is the case even in Augustine, who to the *liberum arbitrium* (*captivatum*) opposes the lost *libertas* of the Christian (cf. *De natura et gratia*, 46.77 [RT: *CSEL*, 60] and Gilson's commentary, *Introduction a l'etude de Saint Augustin*), while Luther allows the *servum arbitrium* to exist alongside *libertas Christiana*, the Latin title of a treatise from 1520, *Von der Freiheit eines Christenmenschen*. It seems that the very idea of judgment (or will) attached to free judgment implies that we must expel its opposite from the argument, into an external "necessity"—and in this respect the *servum arbitrium*, a strange discovery, a possibility scarcely translated and never realized, allows us both to test and to feel the solidity of the historical linkages between subjectivity and interiority.

Philippe Büttgen

BIBLIOGRAPHY

Gilson, Étienne. *Introduction à l'étude de Saint Augustin*. Paris: Vrin, 1929. Translation by L.E.M. Lynch: *The Christian Philosophy of Saint Augustine*. New York: Random House, 1960.

Luther, Martin. *Bondage of the Will*. Vol. 33 in *Luther's Works*. Translated by P. S. Watson and B. Drewery. Philadelphia: Fortress Press, 1972.

———. *De servo arbitrio*. Vol. 18 in *Dr Martin Luthers Werke, kritische Gesamtausgabe*. Weimar, Ger.: Böhlau, 1883–.

———. *Vom unfreien Willen*. Vol. 3 in *Luther deutsch*, edited by K. Aland. Göttingen, Ger.: Vandenhoeck and Ruprecht, 1967.

McGrath, Alister E. *Justitia Dei: A History of the Christian Doctrine of Justification*. Vol. 1. New York: Cambridge University Press, 1989.

Williams, Norman Powell. *The Grace of God*. London: Longman, 1930.

BIBLIOGRAPHY

Alexander of Aphrodisias. *Alexander of Aphrodisias on Fate*. Edited by R. W. Sharples. London: Duckworth, 1983.

Aquinas, Thomas. *Summa theologica*. Translated by L. Shapcote and D. Sullivan. 2 vols. Chicago: Encyclopedia Britannica, 1990.

Arendt, Hannah. *The Life of the Mind*, vol. 2, *Willing*. New York: Harcourt Brace Jovanovich, 1978.

———. "What Is Liberty?" In *Between Past and Future*. New York: Penguin, 2006.

Aristotle. *Nicomachean Ethics; Metaphysics; Politics*. In *The Complete Works of Aristotle*. 2 vols. Edited by Jonathan Barnes. Princeton, NJ: Princeton University Press, 1984.

Aubenque, Pierre. *La prudence chez Aristote*. 3rd ed. Paris: Presses Universitaires de France, 1986.

Augustine. *Sancti Augustini . . . opera omnia*. Edited by the Benedictines of the congregation of St. Maur. In RT: *PL*.

———. *The Works of Saint of Augustine*. Edited by Boniface Ramsey. 50 vols. Hyde Park, New York: New City Press, 1990-. http://www.nlx.com/collections/148.

Barnes, Jonathan. *Aristotle*. Oxford: Oxford University Press, 1982.

Benveniste, Émile. *Le vocabulaire des institutions indo-européennes*. Paris: Minuit, 1969.

Cicero. *De officiis*. Translated by W. Miller. Cambridge, MA: Harvard University Press, 1913.

Clement of Alexandria. *The Stromata or Miscellanies*. 8 vols. Whitefish, MT: Kessinger Publishing, 2004.

Descartes, René. *Œuvres*. Edited by C. Adam and P. Tannery. 11 vols. Repr. Paris: Vrin, 1996.

———. *Philosophical Writings of Descartes*. Edited by J. Cottingham, R. Stoothoff, and D. Murdoch. Cambridge: Cambridge University Press, 1985.

Epictetus. *The Discourses as Reported by Arrian, the Manual, and Fragments*. Translated by W. A. Oldfather. 2 vols. Cambridge, MA: Harvard University Press, 1967.

Festugière, André-Jean. *Liberté et civilisation chez les Grecs*. Paris: Editions de la Revue des Jeunes, 1947. Translation by P. T. Brannan: *Freedom and Civilization among the Greeks*. Allison Park, PA: Pickwick Publications, 1987.

Gauthier, René-Antoine. Introduction. In *L'éthique à Nicomaque*. Louvain, Belg.: Publications Universitaires de Louvain, 1970.

Gilson, Étienne. *Introduction à l'étude de Saint Augustin*. Paris: Vrin, 1929. Translation by L.E.M. Lynch: *The Christian Philosophy of Saint Augustine*. New York: Random House, 1960.

Hamelin, Octave. *Le système d'Aristote*. 4th ed. Paris: Vrin, 1985.

Hegel, G.W.F. *Encyclopedia of the Philosophical Sciences*. Translated by William Wallace. Oxford: Clarendon Press, 1971.

Heidegger, Martin. "Ce qu'est et comment se détermine la *phusis*." In *Questions* II, trans. F. Fédier. Paris: Gallimard, 1968.

———. *Der Satz vom Grund*. In *Gesamtausgabe*, vol. 10. Frankfurt: Klostermann, 1976. First published in 1957. Translation by R. Lilly: *The Principle of Reason*. Bloomington: Indiana University Press, 1991.

———. "Vom Wesen und Begriff der *phusis*." In *Wegmarken* in *Gesamtausgabe*, vol. 9. Frankfurt: Klostermann, 1976. Translation: "On the Essence and Concept of Φύσις in Aristotle's *Physics* B, I." In *Pathmarks*, edited by W. McNeill. New York: Cambridge University Press, 1998.

Kraut, Richard, ed. *The Blackwell Guide to Aristotle's "Nicomachean Ethics"*. Oxford: Blackwell, 2006.

Kretzmann, Norman. *The Metaphysics of Theism: Aquinas's Natural Theology in "Summa Contra Gentiles" I*. Oxford: Clarendon Press, 1997.

Lottin, Odon. "Le libre arbitre chez Thomas d'Aquin." *Revue thomiste* 34 (1929): 400–430.

Molina, Luis de. *Liberi arbitrii cum gratiae donis, divina praescientia, providentia, praedestinatione et reprobatione concordia*. Antwerp, 1595.

Muller, Robert. "La logique de la liberté dans *La Politique*." In *Aristote Politique*, edited by P. Aubenque and A. Tordesillas. Paris: Presses Universitaires de France, 1993.

———. "Remarques sur la liberté grecque." *Dialogue* 25 (1986): 421–47.

Nestle, Dieter. *Eleutheria: Studien zum Wesen der Freiheit bei den Griechen und im Neuen Testament*, vol. 1, *Die Griechen*. Tübingen: Mohr, 1967.

Plato. *Complete Works*. Edited by J. Cooper. Indianapolis, IN: Hackett, 1997.

Pohlenz, Max. *Die Stoa*. 2 vols. Göttingen, Ger.: Vandenhoeck and Ruprecht, 1970–72.

———. *Griechische Freiheit*. Heidelberg: Quelle and Meyer Verlag, 1995. Translation by C. Lofmark: *Freedom in Greek Life and Thought: The History of an Ideal*. Dordrecht, Neth.: D. Reidel, 1966.

Tefler, William. "Autexousia." *Journal of Theological Studies* 8 (1957): 123–29.

van Straaten, Modestus. "What Did the Greeks Mean by Liberty?" *Thêta-Pi* (1979): 105–27.

ENGLISH

The English Language, or The Genius of the Ordinary

➤ AGENCY, ASPECT, CLAIM, COMMON SENSE, FEELING, MATTER OF FACT, SENSE, SPEECH ACT

A refusal to rise above the facts of ordinary life is characteristic of classical English philosophy (from Berkeley to Hume, Reid, and Bentham) and American philosophy, whether in transcendentalism (Emerson, Thoreau) or in pragmatism (from James to Rorty). But this orientation did not become truly explicit until after the linguistic turn carried out by Wittgenstein, Ryle, and especially Austin, when it was radicalized and systematized under the name of "ordinary language philosophy."

This preponderant recourse to the ordinary seems inseparable from certain peculiar characteristics of the English language (such as the gerund) that often make it difficult if not impossible to translate. It is all the more important to emphasize this paradox because English claims to be as simple as it is universal, and it established itself as the dominant philosophical language in the second half of the twentieth century.

English-language philosophy has a specific relationship to ordinary language, as well as to the requirements of everyday life, that is not limited to the theories of the "philosophy of language," in which English philosophers appear as pioneers. It rejects the artificial linguistic constructions of philosophical speculation (that is, metaphysics) and always prefers to return to its "original home," as Wittgenstein puts it: the natural environment of everyday words (*Philosophical Investigations*, §116). Thus we can discern a continuity between the recourse to the ordinary in Hume, Berkeley, Reid, and Bentham and what will become in Moore and Wittgenstein (after he started using English, at least orally) and then Austin ordinary language philosophy.

This continuity can be seen in several areas: first, in the exploitation of all the resources of the English language, which is considered as a source of information and is valid in itself; second, in the attention given to the specificities—and even the "defects"—of English which become so many philosophical characteristics from which one can learn; and finally, in the affirmation of the naturalness of the distinctions made in and by ordinary language, seeking to challenge the superiority of the (technical) language of philosophy—the former being the object, as we will see, of an "agreement" deeper than the latter.

■ See Box 1.

I. The Variety of Modes of Action

A. The passive

In English there are several modes of agency, and these constitute both part of the genius of the language and a main source of its problems in translation. Agency is a strange intersection of points of view that makes it possible to designate the person who is acting while at the same time concealing the actor behind the act—and thus locating agency in the passive subject itself (see AGENCY). A classic difficulty is illustrated by the following sentence from John Stuart Mill's

1

Langage, langue, parole: A virtual distinction

➤ LANGUAGE

Contrary to what is too often believed, the English language does not conflate under the term "language" what French distinguishes (following Saussure) with the terms *langage, langue,* and *parole*. In reality, English also has a series of three terms whose semantic distribution makes possible exactly the same trichotomy as French: "tongue," which serves to designate a specific language by opposition to another; "speech," which refers more specifically to *parole* (but which is often translated in French by *discours*); and "language" (in the sense of *faculté de langage*). Nonetheless, French's set of systematic distinctions can only remain fundamentally virtual in English, notably because the latter refuses to radically detach *langue* from *parole*. Thus in *Chrestomathia*, Bentham uses "tongue" and "language" interchangeably and sometimes uses "language" in the sense of *langue*: "Of all known languages the Greek is assuredly, in its structure, the most plastic and most manageable." He even uses "speech" and "language" as equivalents, since he speaks of "parts of speech." But on the contrary, he sometimes emphasizes differences that he ignores here. And he proceeds exactly like Hume in his essay "Of the Standard of Taste," where we find, for example,

> But it must also be allowed, that some part of the seeming harmony in morals may be accounted for from the very nature of language. The word, *virtue*, with its equivalent in every tongue, implies praise; as that of *vice* does blame.

BIBLIOGRAPHY

Bentham, Jeremy. *Chrestomathia*. Edited by M. J. Smith and W. H. Burston. Oxford: Clarendon Press, 1983.

Hume, David. "Of the Standard of Taste." In *Four Dissertations*. London: Thoemmes Continuum, 1995. First published in 1757.

Saussure, Ferdinand de. *Course in General Linguistics*. Edited by C. Bally and A. Sechehaye. Translated by R. Harris. LaSalle, IL: Open Court, 1986. First published in 1983.

Considerations on Representative Government: "I must not be understood to say that . . ." To translate such a passive construction, French is forced to resort to the impersonal pronoun *on* and to put it in the position of an observer of the "I" (*je*) as if it were considered from the outside: "On ne doit pas comprendre que je dis que . . ." But at the same time, the network of relations internal to the sentence is modified, and the meaning transformed. Necessity is no longer associated with the subject of the sentence and the author; it is made impersonal. Contemporary English philosophical language also makes frequent use of the diverse characteristics of the passive. Here we can mention the crucial turning point in the history of linguistics represented by Chomsky's discovery (*Syntactic Structures*, 1957) of the paradigm of the active/passive relation, which proves the necessity of the transformational component in grammar. A passive utterance is not always a reversal of the active and only rarely describes an "undergoing," as is shown by the example "She was offered a bunch of flowers." In particular, language makes use of the fact that this kind of construction authorizes the ellipsis of the agent (as is shown by the common expression "English spoken"). For philosophers, the passive is thus the privileged form of an action when its agent is unknown, indeterminate, unimportant, or, inversely, too obvious. Thus without making his prose too turgid, in *Sense and Sensibilia* Austin can use five passives in less than a page, and these can be translated in French only by *on*, an indeterminate subject (defined as differentiated from *moi*, I):

> It is clearly implied, that . . . Now this, at least if it is taken to mean . . . The expression is here put forward . . . We are given, as examples, "familiar objects" . . . The expression is not further defined . . .

> (On sous-entend clairement que . . . Quant à cela, du moins si on l'entend au sens de . . . On avance ici l'expression . . . On nous donne, comme exemples, des "objets familiers" . . . On n'approfondit pas la définition de l'expression . . .)

To gauge the naturalness of the passive construction in English, it suffices to examine a couple of newspaper headlines: "Killer's Car Found" (*On a retrouvé la voiture du tueur*), "Kennedy Jr. Feared Dead" (*On craint la mort du fils Kennedy*); or the titles of an American philosophical article and book: "Epistemology Naturalized" (*L'Épistémologie naturalisée*; translated by J. Largeault as "L'Épistémologie devenue naturelle"; a famous article by Quine that was the origin of the naturalistic turn in American philosophy) and *Consciousness Explained* (*La conscience expliquée*) by Daniel Dennett. We might then better understand why this kind of construction—which seems so awkward in French compared with the active voice—is perceived by its English users as a more direct and effective way of speaking.

More generally, the ellipsis of the agent seems to be a tendency of English so profound that one can maintain that the phenomenon Lucien Tesnière called *diathèse récessive* (the loss of the agent) has become a characteristic of the English language itself, and not only of the passive. Thus, for example, a French reader irresistibly gains the impression that a reflexive pronoun is lacking in the following expressions: "This book reads well" (ce livre se lit agréablement); "His poems do not translate well" (ses poèmes se traduisent difficilement); "The door opens" (la porte s'ouvre); "The man will hang" (l'homme sera pendu). In reality, here again, English simply does not need to mark (by means of the reflexive pronoun *se*) the presence of an active agent.

B. "Do," "make," "have"

English has several terms to translate the single French word *faire*, which it can render by "to do," "to make," or "to have," depending on the type of agency required by the context. Because of its attenuation of the meaning of action, its value as emphasis and repetition, the verb "to do" has become omnipresent in English, and it plays a particularly important role in philosophical texts. We can find a couple of examples of translation problems in the work of Austin. In *Sense and*

Sensibilia, he has criticized the claim that we never perceive objects directly and is preparing to criticize its negation as well:

I am not going to maintain that we ought to embrace the doctrine that we do perceive material things.

(Je ne vais pas soutenir que nous devons embrasser la doctrine selon laquelle nous percevons vraiment les choses matérielles.)

Finally, let us recall Austin's first example of the performative, which plays simultaneously on the anaphoric value of "do" and on its sense of action, a duality that seems to be at the origin of the theory of the performative (see SPEECH ACT, IV): "I do (take this woman to be my lawful wedded wife)—as uttered in the course of the marriage ceremony" [Oui (à savoir: je prends cette femme pour épouse)'énoncé lors d'une cérémonie de mariage; *How to Do Things with Words*].

On the other hand, whereas *faire* is colored by a causative sense, English uses "to make" and "to have"—"He made Mary open her bags" (il lui fit ouvrir sa valise); "He had Mary pour him a drink" (il se fit verser un verre)—with this difference: that "make" can indicate, as we see, coercion, whereas "have" presupposes that there is no resistance, a difference that French can only leave implicit or explain by awkward periphrases.

Twentieth-century English philosophers from Austin to Geach and Anscombe have examined these differences and their philosophical implications very closely. Thus, in "A Plea for Excuses," Austin emphasizes the elusive meaning of the expression "doing something," and the correlative difficulty of determining the limits of the concept of action—"Is to sneeze to do an action?"

There is indeed a vague and comforting idea . . . that doing an action must come down to the making of physical movements. . . . Further, we need . . . to ask what is the detail of the complicated internal machinery we use in "acting."

(*Philosophical Papers*)

No matter how partial they may be, these opening remarks show that there is a specific, intimate relation between ordinary language and philosophical language in English-language philosophy. This enables us to better understand why the most prestigious representatives of contemporary English-language philosophy are so comfortable resorting to idiomatic expressions (cf. H. Putnam) and even to clearly popular usage: "Meanings ain't in the head"; "It ain't necessarily so." As for the title of Quine's famous book *From a Logical Point of View*, which at first seems austere, it is taken from a calypso song: "From a logical point of view, / Always marry women uglier than you."

II. The Operator "-ing": Properties and Antimetaphysical Consequences

A. "-ing": A multifunctional operator

Although grammarians think it important to distinguish among the forms of "-ing"—present participles, adjectives, the progressive, and the gerund—what strikes the reader of scientific and philosophical texts is first of all the free

circulation among these forms. This formal continuity promotes a great methodological inventiveness through the interplay among the various grammatical entities that it enables.

1. The gerund: The form of "-ing" that is the most difficult to translate

English is a nominalizing language. Any verb can be nominalized, and this ability gives the English philosophical language great creative power. Nominalization is in fact a substantivization without substantivization: the verb is not substantivized in order to refer to action, to make it an object of discourse (which is possible in any language, notably in philosophical French and German), but rather to nominalize the verb while at the same time preserving its quality as a verb (see SENSE), and even to nominalize whole clauses. French can, of course, nominalize *faire, toucher*, and *sentir* (*le faire, le toucher*, even *le sentir*), and one can do the same, in a still more systematic manner, in German. However, these forms will not have the "naturalness" of the English expressions: "the making," "the doing," "the feeling." Above all, in these languages it is hard to construct expressions parallel to, for example, "the making of," "the making use of," "my doing wrongly," "my meaning this," "his feeling pain," etc., that is, mixtures of noun and verb having—and this is the grammatical characteristic of the gerund—the external distribution of a nominal expression and the internal distribution of a verbal expression.

These forms are so common that they characterize, in addition to a large proportion of book titles (for example, *The Making of the English Working Class*, by E. P. Thomson; or, in philosophy, *The Taming of Chance*, by I. Hacking), the language of classical English philosophy. The gerund functions as a sort of general equivalent or exchanger between grammatical forms. In that way, it not only makes the language dynamic by introducing into it a permanent temporal flux, but also helps create, in the language itself, a kind of indeterminacy in the way it is parsed, which the translator finds awkward when he understands the message without being able to retain its lightness. Thus, in *A Treatise of Human Nature*, Hume speaks, regarding "the idea," of "the manner of its being conceived," which a French translator might render as *sa façon d'être conçue* or perhaps, *la façon dont il lui appartient d'être conçue*, which is not quite the same thing. And we see agency and the gerund connected in a language like that of Bentham, who minimizes the gaps between subject and object, verb and noun: "much regret has been suggested at the thoughts of its never having yet been brought within the reach of the English reader" (*Chrestomathia*).

Translators often feel obliged to render the act expressed by a gerund by the expression *le fait de*, but this has a meaning almost contrary to the English. With its gerund, English avoids the discourse of fact by retaining only the event and arguing only on that basis. The inevitable confusion suggested by French when it translates the English gerund is all the more unfortunate in this case because it becomes impossible to distinguish when English uses "the fact" or "the case" from when it uses the gerund. The importance of the event, along with the distinction between "trial," "case," and "event," on the one hand and "happening" on the other, is crucial in discussions of probability. The very definition of probability with which Bayes operates in *An Essay towards Solving a Problem*, the first great treatise on "subjective probability," is based on this status of the "happening," the event conceived not in terms of its realization or accomplishment but in terms of its expectation:

> The probability of any event is the ratio between the value at which an expectation depending on the happening of the event ought to be computed, and the value of the thing expected upon its happening.

2. The progressive: Tense and aspect

If we now pass from the gerund to the progressive, another construction that uses "-ing," a new kind of problem appears: that of the aspect and temporality of actions. An interesting case of translation difficulty is, for example, the one posed by Austin precisely when he attempts, in his presentation of performatives, to distinguish between the sentence and the act of saying it, between "statement" and "utterance": there are "utterances," such as "the uttering of the sentence is, or is part of, the doing of an action" (*How to Do Things*). The translation difficulty here is caused by the combination in the construction in "-ing" of the syntactical flexibility of the gerund and a progressive meaning. Does the "-ing" construction indicate the act, or the progressiveness of the act? Similarly, it is hard to choose to translate "On Referring" (P. F. Strawson) as "De la référence" rather than as "De l'action de référer." Should one translate "On Denoting" (B. Russell) as "De la dénotation" (the usual translation) or as "Du dénoter"?

The progressive in the strict sense—"be" + verb + "-ing"—indicates an action at a specific moment, when it has already begun but is not yet finished. A little farther on, Austin allows us to gauge the ease of English in the whole of these operations: "To utter the sentence is not to describe my doing of what I should be said in so uttering to be doing." The French translation gives, correctly: "Énoncer la phrase, ce n'est pas décrire ce qu'il faut bien reconnaître que je suis en train de faire en parlant ainsi," but this remains unsatisfying at best, because of the awkwardness of *en train de*. Moreover, in many cases, *en train de* is simply not suitable insofar as the "-ing" does not indicate duration: for example, in "At last I am seeing New York." It is interesting to examine from this point of view the famous category of verbs of perception. It is remarkable that these verbs (see, hear) can be in some cases used with the construction "be" + verb + "-ing," since it is generally said (even in grammar books) that they can be used only in the present or simple past and not in the progressive. This rule probably is thought to be connected with something like the immediacy of perception, and it can be compared with the fact that the verbs "to know" and "to understand" are also (almost) always in the present or the simple past, as if the operations of the understanding could not be presented in the progressive form and were by definition instantaneous; or as if, on the contrary, they transcended the course of time. In reality, there are counterexamples: "I don't know if I'm understanding you correctly"; "You are hearing voices"; and often

in philosophy, "You are seeing something" (Austin, *Sense and Sensibilia*, regarding a stick in water); "I really am perceiving the familiar objects" (Ayer, *Foundations of Empirical Knowledge*). The passage to the form "be" + verb + "-ing" indicates, then, not the progressiveness of the action but rather the transition into the metalanguage peculiar to the philosophical description of phenomena of perception. The sole exception is, curiously, "to know," which is practically never used in the progressive: even if we explore the philosophical and epistemological literature, we do not find "I am knowing" or "he was knowing," as if knowledge could not be conceived as a process.

In English, there is a great variety of what are customarily called "aspects," through which the status of the action is marked and differentiated in a more systematic way than in French or German, once again because of the "-ing" ending: he is working / he works / he worked / he has been working. Unlike what happens in Slavic languages, aspect is marked at the outset not by a duality of verbal forms but instead by the use of the verb "to be" with a verb ending in "-ing" (imperfect or progressive), by opposition to the simple present or past (perfect). Moreover, English mixes several aspects in a single expression: iterativity, progressivity, completion, as in "it cannot fail to have been noticed" (Austin, *How to Do Things*). These are nuances, as Labov and then Pinker recently observed, that are not peculiar to classical or written English but also exist in certain vernaculars that appear to be familiar or allegedly ungrammatical. The American black vernacular seems particularly sophisticated on this point, distinguishing "he be working" from "he working"—that is, between having a regular job and being engaged in working at a particular moment, standard American usage being limited to "he is working" (Pinker, *Language Instinct*). Whether or not the notion of aspect is used, it seems clear that in English there is a particularly subtle distinction between the different degrees of completion, of the iterativity or development of an action, that leads English-speaking philosophers to pay more attention to these questions and even to surprising inventions.

B. The linguistic dissolution of the idea of substance

1. Fictive entities

Thus the verb + "-ing" operation simply gives the verb the temporary status of a noun while at the same time preserving some of its syntactic and semantic properties as a verb, that is, by avoiding substantivization. It is no accident that the substantiality of the "I think" asserted by Descartes was opposed by virtually all the English philosophers of the seventeenth century. If a personal identity can be constituted "by the making our distant perceptions influence each other, and by giving us a present concern for our past or future pains or pleasures" (Hume, *Treatise of Human Nature*), it does not require positing a substance: the substantivization of "making" and "giving" meets the need. We can also consider the way in which Russell (*Analysis of Matter*, chap. 27) makes his reader understand far more easily than does Bachelard, and without having to resort to the category of an "epistemological obstacle," that one can perfectly well posit an atom as a series of events without according it the status of a substance.

This sort of overall preeminence in English of the verbal and the subjective over the nominal and the objective is clear in the difference in the logic that governs the discourse of affectivity in French and in English. How would something that "one is" correspond to something that "one has," as in the case of fear in French (*avoir peur*)? It follows that a Frenchman—who takes it for granted that fear is "something" that one feels or senses—cannot feel at home with the difference that English naturally makes between something that has no objective correlative because it concerns only "feeling" (like fear; see FEELING) and what is available to sensation, implying that what is felt through it has the status of an object. Thus in English something is immediately grasped that in French seems a strange paradox, namely that passion, as Bentham notes in *Deontology*, "is a fictive entity." Thus what sounds in French like a nominalist provocation is implicated in the folds of the English language. A symbolic theory of affectivity is thus more easily undertaken in English than in French, and if an ontological conception of affectivity had to be formulated in English, symmetrical difficulties would be encountered.

2. Reversible derivations

Another particularity of English, which is not without consequences in philosophy, is that its poverty from the point of view of inflectional morphology is compensated for by the freedom and facility it offers for the construction of all sorts of derivatives.

a. Nominal derivatives based on adjectives and using suffixes such as "-ity," "-hood," "-ness," "-y." The resulting compounds are very difficult to differentiate in French and to translate in general, which has led, in contemporary French translations, to various incoherent makeshifts. To list the most common stumbling blocks: privacy (*privé-ité*), innerness (*intériorité*, not in the same sense as "interiority"), vagueness (*caractère vague*), goodness (*bonté*, in the sense of *caractère bon*), rightness (*justesse*), sameness (*similarité*, in the sense of *mêmeté*), ordinariness, appropriateness (*caractère ordinaire, approprié*), unaccountability (*caractère de ce dont il est impossible de rendre compte*).

b. Adjectival derivatives based on nouns, using numerous suffixes: "-ful," "-ous," "-y," "-ic," "-ish," "-al" (e.g., meaningful, realistic, holistic, attitudinal, behavioral).

c. Verbal derivatives based on nouns or adjectives, with the suffixes "-ize," "-ify," "-ate" (naturalize, mentalize, falsify), and even without suffixes when possible (e.g., the title of an article "How Not to Russell Carnap's Aufbau" ([i.e., how not to "Russell" Carnap's Aufbau]).

d. Polycategorial derivatives based on verbs, using suffixes such as "-able," "-er," "-age," "-ism" (refutable, truthmaker).

The reversibility of these nominalizations and verbalizations has the essential result of preventing the reification of qualities or acts. The latter is more difficult to avoid in French and German, where nominalization hardens and freezes notions (compare *intériorité* and "innerness," which designates more a quality, or even, paradoxically, an effect, than an entity or a domain). But this kind of ease in making compounds has its flip side: the proliferation of "-isms" in English-language philosophy, especially in America, which makes their translation particularly indigestible, especially in French, where *-ismes* gives a very Scholastic feel to the classifications translated. In addition to the famous term "realism," which has been the object of so many contradictory definitions and so many debates over past decades that it has been almost emptied of meaning, we may mention some common but particularly obscure (for anyone not familiar with the theoretical context) terms: "cognitivism," "noncognitivism," "coherentism," "eliminativism," "consequentialism," "connectionism," etc. Such terms (in which moral philosophy is particularly fertile) are in general transposed into French without change in a sort of new, international philosophical language that has almost forgone translation.

More generally, in English as in German, words can be composed by joining two other words far more easily than in French—without specifying the logical connections between the terms: "toothbrush," "pickpocket," "lowlife," "knownothing"; or, for more philosophical terms: "aspect-blind," "language-dependent," "rule-following," "meaning-holism," "observer-relative," which are translatable, of course, but not without considerable awkwardness.

3. Toward an international philosophical neo-language?

Contemporary philosophy in English seeks to establish a language that is stylistically neutral and appears to be transparently translatable. Certain specific problems—the translation of compound words and constructions that are more flexible in English and omnipresent in current philosophical discourse, such as "the thesis that" (*la thèse selon laquelle*), "the question whether" (*la question de savoir si*), and "my saying that" (*le fait que je dise que*)—make French translations of contemporary English philosophical texts very awkward, even when the author writes in a neutral, commonplace style. Instead, these difficulties, along with the ease of construction peculiar to English, tend to encourage French analytical philosophers to write directly in English, following the example of many of their European colleagues, or else to make use of a technical "vernacular" (we have noted the "-isms" and compounds) that is frequently heavy going and not very inventive when translating terms which are usually transliterated). This situation is certainly attributable to the paradoxical character of English, and then to American English, which established itself as the dominant philosophical language in the second half of the twentieth century: it is a language that is apparently simple and accessible and that thus claims a kind of universality but that is structured, both linguistically and philosophically, around major stumbling blocks (to do, -ing, etc.) that often make it untranslatable. It is paradoxically this untranslatability, and not its pseudo-transparency, that plays a crucial role in the process of universalization.

■ See Box 2.

III. The Austinian Paradigm: Ordinary Language and Philosophy

The proximity of ordinary language and philosophical language, which is rooted in classical English-language philosophy, was theorized in the twentieth century by Austin and can be summed up in the expression "ordinary language philosophy." Ordinary language philosophy is interested

2

A "defect" in the English language? "Between" according to Bentham

English philosophers are not very inclined toward etymology—no doubt because it is often less traceable than it is in German or even in French and discourages a certain kind of commentary. There are, however, certain exceptions, like Jeremy Bentham's analysis of the words "in," "or," "between," "and," etc., through which English constructs the kinds of space that belong to a very specific topic. Let us take the case of "between," which French can render only by the word *entre*. Both the semantics and the etymology of *entre* imply the number *three* in French, since what is *entre* intervenes as a third term between two others which it separates or brings closer (in Lat., *in-ter*; in Fr., *en tiers*; "as a third"). This is not the case in English, which constructs "between" in accord with the number two (in conformity with the etymology of this word, "by tween," in pairs), to the point that it can imagine an ordering, even when it involves three or more classes, only in the binary mode:

> ... comparison between three? relation between three?—the hue of self-contradictoriness presents itself on the very face of the phrase. By one of the words in it, the number of objects is asserted to be three: by another, it is asserted to be no more than two. . . . To the use thus exclusively made of the word *between*, what could have given rise, but a sort of general, howsoever indistinct, perception, that it is only *one to one* that objects can, in any continued manner, be commodiously and effectually compared. . . . The English language

labours under a defect, which, when it is compared in this particular with other European langues, may perhaps be found peculiar to it. By the derivation, and thence by the *inexcludible* import, of the word *between* (i.e., *by twain*), the number of the objects, to which this operation is represented as capable of being applied, is confined to two. By the Latin *inter*—by its French derivation *entre*—no such limitation seems to be expressed.

(*Chrestomathia*)

BIBLIOGRAPHY

Bentham, Jeremy. *Chrestomathia*. Edited by M. J. Smith and W. H. Burston. Oxford: Clarendon Press, 1983.

in "what we should say when. . . ." It is, in other words, a "philosophy of language," but on the condition that we never forget that "we are looking not *merely* at words (or 'meanings,' whatever they may be) but also at the realities we use the words to talk about," as Austin emphasizes ("A Plea for Excuses," in *Philosophical Papers*).

During the twentieth century (or more precisely, between the 1940s and the 1960s), there was a division of the paradigms of the philosophy of language between the logical clarification of ordinary language, on the one hand, and the immanent examination of ordinary language, on the other.

The question of ordinary language and the type of treatment that it should be given—a normative clarification or an internal examination—is present in and even constitutive of the legacy of logical positivism. Wittgenstein's work testifies to this through the movement that it manifests and performs, from the first task of the philosophy of language (the creation of an ideal or formal language to clarify everyday language) to the second (the concern to examine the multiplicity of ordinary language's uses). The break thus accomplished is such that one can only agree with Rorty's statement in his preface to *The Linguistic Turn* that "the only difference between Ideal Language Philosophers and Ordinary Language Philosophers is a disagreement about which language is ideal." In the renunciation of the idea of an ideal language, or a norm outside language, there is a radical change in perspective that consists in abandoning the idea of something beyond language: an idea that is omnipresent in the whole philosophical tradition, and even in current analytical philosophy.

A. Critique of language and philosophy

More generally, Austin criticizes traditional philosophy for its perverse use of ordinary language. He constantly denounces philosophy's abuse of ordinary language—not so much that it forgets it, but rather that it exploits it by taking liberties with the natural uses of the language. The philosophers ask, for example, how they can know that there is a real object there, but the question "How do I know?" can be asked (in ordinary language) only in certain contexts, that is, where it is always possible, at least in theory, to eliminate doubt.

The doubt or question "But is it a *real* one?" has always (*must* have) a special basis, there must be some "reason for suggesting" that it isn't real, in the sense of some specific way . . . in which it is suggested that this experience or item may be phoney. . . . The wile of the metaphysician consists in asking "Is it a real table?" (a kind of object which has no obvious way of being phoney) and not specifying or limiting what may be wrong with it, so that I feel at a loss "how to prove" it *is* a real one. It is the use of the word "real" in this manner that leads us on to the supposition that "real" has a single meaning ("the real world," "material objects"), and that a highly profound and puzzling one.

(Austin, *Philosophical Papers*)

This analysis of "real" is taken up again in *Sense and Sensibilia*, where Austin criticizes the notion of a "sense datum" and also a certain way of raising problems supposedly "on the basis of" common opinion (for example, the common opinion that we "really" perceive things)—but in reality on the basis of a pure construction. "To state the case in this way," Austin says, "is simply to soften up the plain man's alleged views for the subsequent treatment; it is preparing the way for, by practically attributing to *him*, the so-called philosophers' view." Philosophy's (frequent) recourse to the ordinary is characterized by a certain condescension toward the common man.

The error (or deception) consists in arguing the philosopher's position against the ordinary position, because if the latter exists, it is not on the same level. The philosopher introduces into the opinion of the common man particular entities, in order then to reject, amend, or explain it.

B. The method of ordinary language: "Be your size. Small Men."

Austin's immanent method comes down to examining our ordinary use of ordinary words that have been confiscated by philosophy, such as "true" and "real," in order to raise the question of truth:

> "Fact that" is a phrase designed for use in situations where the distinction between a true statement and the state of affairs about which it is a truth is neglected; as it often is with advantage in ordinary life, though seldom in philosophy. . . . So speaking about "the fact that" is a compendious way of speaking about a situation involving both words and world.

> *(Philosophical Papers)*

We can, of course, maintain (along with a whole trend in analytical philosophy from Frege to Quine) that these are considerations too small and too trivial from which to draw any conclusions at all. But it is this notion of fact that Austin relies on to determine the nature of truth and thus to indicate the pertinence of ordinary language as a relationship to the world. This is the nature of Austin's approach: "the foot of the letter is the foot of the ladder" (ibid.). For Austin, ordinary words are part of the world: we use words, and what makes words useful objects is their complexity, their refinement as tools (ibid.):

> We use words to inform ourselves about the things we talk about when we use these words. Or, if that seems too naïve: we use words as a way of better understanding the situation in which we find ourselves led to make use of words.

What makes this claim possible is the proximity of dimension, of size, between words and ordinary objects. Thus philosophers should, instead of asking whether truth is a substance, a quality, or a relation, "take something more nearly their own size to strain at" (ibid.). (The French translators render "size" by *mesure*, which seems excessively theoretical; the reference is to size in the material, ordinary sense.)

> One cannot know everything, so why not try something else? . . . Advantages of slowness and cooperation. Be your size. Small Men.

> *(Conversation cited by Urmson in "A Symposium")*

Austin emphasizes that this technique of examining words (which he ended up calling linguistic phenomenology) is not new and that it has existed since Socrates, producing its "slow successes." But he is the first to make a systematic application of such a method, which is based, on the one hand, on the manageability and familiarity of the objects concerned and, on the other hand, on the common agreement at which it arrives in each of its stages. The problem is how to agree on a starting point, that is, on a given. This given, for Austin, is language, not as a corpus consisting of utterances or words, but as the site of agreement about "what we should say when." Austin regards language as an empirical datum or experimental data.

To my mind, experience proves amply that we do come to an agreement on "what we should say when" such and such a thing, though I grant you it is often long and difficult. . . . I should add that too often this is what is missing in philosophy: a preliminary *datum* on which one might agree at the outset. . . . We do not claim in this way to discover all the truth that exists regarding everything. We discover simply the facts that those who have been using our language for centuries have taken the trouble to notice.

> *("Performatif-Constatif")*

Austinian agreement is possible for two reasons:

1. Ordinary language cannot claim to have the last word. "Only remember, it is the *first* word" (*Philosophical Papers*). The exploration of language is also an exploration of "the inherited experience and acumen of many generations of men" (ibid.).
2. Ordinary language is a rich treasury of differences and "embodies all the distinctions men have found worth drawing, and the connections they have found worth marking, in the lifetimes of many generations." These are certainly more subtle and solid than "any that you or I are likely to think up in our arm-chairs of an afternoon" (ibid.). It is this ability to indicate differences that makes language a common instrument adequate for speaking things in the world.

C. Who is "we"? Cavell's question

It is clear that analytical philosophy, especially as it has developed in the United States since the 1940s, has moved away from the Austinian paradigm and has at the same time abandoned a certain kind of philosophical writing and linguistic subtlety. But that only makes all the more powerful and surprising the "return to Austin" advocated by Stanley Cavell and the new sense of ordinary language philosophy that is emerging in his work and in contemporary American philosophy. What right do we have to refer to "our uses"? And who is this "we" so crucial for Austin that it constantly recurs in his work? All we have, as we have said, is what we say and our linguistic agreements. We determine the meaning of a (given) word by its uses, and for Austin, it is nonsensical to ask the question of meaning (for instance, in a general way or looking for an entity; see NONSENSE). The quest for agreement is founded on something quite different from signification or the determination of the common meaning. The agreement Austin is talking about has nothing to do with an intersubjective consensus; it is not founded on a convention or on actual agreements. It is an agreement that is as objective as possible and that bears as much on language as on reality.

But what is the precise nature of this agreement? Where does it come from, and why should so much importance be accorded to it? That is the question Cavell asks, first in *Must We Mean What We Say?* and then in *The Claim of Reason*: what is it that allows Austin and Wittgenstein to say what they say about what we say? A claim (see CLAIM) is certainly involved here. That is what Wittgenstein means by our "agreement in judgments," and in language it is based only on itself, "on the we," as Cavell says in a passage that illustrates many of the difficulties of translation we have discussed up to this point:

> We learn and teach words in certain contexts, and then we are expected, and expect others, to be able to project them into further contexts. Nothing ensures that this projection will take place (in particular, not the grasping of universals nor the grasping of books of rules), just as nothing ensures that we will make, and understand, the same projections. That we do, on the whole, is a matter of our sharing routes of interest and feeling, modes of response, senses of humor and -of significance and of fulfillment, of what is outrageous, of what is similar to what else, what a rebuke, what forgiveness, of when an utterance is an assertion, when an appeal, when an explanation—all the whirl of organism Wittgenstein calls "forms of life." Human speech and activity, sanity and community, rest upon nothing more, but nothing less, than this. It is a vision as simple as it is (and because it is) terrifying.

(Must We Mean What We Say?)

The fact that our ordinary language is based only on itself is not only a reason for concern regarding the validity of what we do and say, but also the revelation of a truth about ourselves that we do not always want to recognize: the fact that I am the only possible source of such a validity. That is a new understanding of the fact that language is our form of life, precisely its ordinary form. Cavell's originality lies in his reinvention of the nature of ordinary language in American thought and in the connection he establishes—notably through his reference to Emerson and Thoreau, American thinkers of the ordinary—between this nature of language and human nature, finitude. It is also in this sense that the question of linguistic agreements reformulates that of the ordinary human condition and that the acceptance of the latter goes hand in hand with the recognition of the former.

In Cavell's Americanization of ordinary language philosophy there thus emerges a radical form of the return to the ordinary. But isn't this "ordinary," for example, that of Emerson in his *Essays*, precisely the one that the whole of English philosophy has been trying to find, or rather to feel or taste, since its origins? Thus we can compare the writing of Emerson or James, in texts like "Experience" or *Essays in Radical Empiricism*, with that of the British empiricists when they discuss experience, the given, and the sensible. This is no doubt one of the principal dimensions of philosophical writing in English: always to make the meaning more available to the senses.

Jean-Pierre Cléro
Sandra Laugier

BIBLIOGRAPHY

Austin, J. L. *How to Do Things with Words*. Oxford: Clarendon Press, 1962.
——. "Performatif-Constatif." In *La philosophie analytique*, edited by J. Wahl and L. Beck. Paris: Editions du Minuit, 1962. Translation in "Performative-Constative." In *Philosophy and Ordinary Language*, edited by C. E. Caton. Urbana: University of Illinois Press, 1963.
——. *Philosophical Papers*. Edited by J. O. Urmson and G. J. Warnock. Oxford: Clarendon Press, 1962.
——. *Sense and Sensibilia*. Oxford: Clarendon Press, 1962.
Ayer, A. J. *The Foundations of Empirical Knowledge*. London: Macmillan, 1940.

Bayes, Thomas. *An Essay towards Solving a Problem in the Doctrine of Chances, with Richard Price's Foreword and Discussion*. In *Facsimiles of Two Papers by Bayes*. New York: Hafner, 1963. First published in 1763.
Bentham, Jeremy. *Chrestomathia*. Edited by M. J. Smith and W. H. Burston. Oxford: Clarendon Press, 1983.
——. *Deontology*. Edited by A. Goldworth. Oxford: Clarendon Press, 1983.
——. "Essay on Language." In *The Works of Jeremy Bentham*, edited by J. Bowring. Edinburgh: William Tait, 1838–43.
Berkeley, George. "Of Infinities." In vol. 2 of *The Works*, edited by A. A. Luce and T. E. Jessop, 408–12. London: Nelson, 1948–57. Reprint, New York: Kraus, 1979.
——. *A Treatise concerning the Principles of Human Knowledge*. Edited by J. Dancy. Oxford: Oxford University Press, 1998.
Cavell, Stanley. *The Claim of Reason*. New York: Oxford University Press, 1979.
——. *In Quest of the Ordinary*. Chicago: University of Chicago Press, 1988.
——. *Must We Mean What We Say?* Cambridge: Cambridge University Press, 1969.
——. *This New Yet Unapproachable America*. Albuquerque: Living Batch Press, 1989.
Chomsky, Noam. *Syntactic Structures*. The Hague: Mouton, 1957.
Emerson, Ralph Waldo. *Essays, First and Second Series*. New York: Library of America, 1990.
Hacking, Jan. *Why Does Language Matter to Philosophy?* Cambridge: Cambridge University Press, 1975.
Hume, David. *Dialogues concerning Natural Religion*. Edited by D. Coleman. Cambridge: Cambridge University Press, 2007.
——. *Essays, Moral, Political and Literary* Edited by E. F. Miller. Indianapolis, IN: Liberty Classics, 1987.
——. *A Treatise of Human Nature*. Edited by L. A. Selby-Bigge. Oxford: Oxford University Press, 1978.
Laugier, Sandra. *Du réel à l'ordinaire*. Paris: Vrin, 1999.
——. *Recommencer la philosophie*. Paris: Presses Universitaires de France, 1999.
Locke, John. *An Essay concerning Human Understanding*. Oxford: Oxford University Press, 2008.
Mill, John Stuart. *Considerations on Representative Government*. In *Essays on Politics and Society*, vol. 19 of *Collected Works*, edited by John M. Robson. Toronto: University of Toronto Press, 1977.
——. *Essays on Ethics, Religion and Society*. Vol. 10 of *Collected Works*, edited by John M. Robson. Toronto: University of Toronto Press, 1969.
——. *A System of Logic Ratiocinative and Inductive*. Toronto: University of Toronto Press, 1973.
Nedeljkovic, Maryvonne. *David Hume, approche phénoménologique de l'action et théorie linguistique*. Paris: Presses Universitaires de France, 1977.
Pinker, Steven. *The Language Instinct: The New Science of Language and Mind*. London: Penguin, 1994.
Putnam, Hilary. *Mind, Language and Reality*. Vol. 2 of *Philosophical Papers*. Cambridge: Cambridge University Press, 1975.
——. *Realism with a Human Face*. Edited by J. Conant. Cambridge, MA: Harvard University Press, 1990.
Quine, Willard V. *From a Logical Point of View*. Cambridge, MA: Harvard University Press, 1953.
——. *Word and Object*. Cambridge, MA: MIT Press, 1960.
Ricœur, Paul. *Memory, History, Forgetting*. Translated by K. Blamey and D. Pellauer. Chicago: University of Chicago Press, 2004.
Rorty, Richard, ed. *The Linguistic Turn*. Chicago: University of Chicago Press, 1992. First published 1967.
Russell, Bertrand. *The Analysis of Matter*. London: Allen and Unwin, 1954.
——. *An Inquiry into Meaning and Truth*. New York: Routledge, 1996. First published in 1950.
Tesnière, Lucien. *Éléments de syntaxe structural*. Paris: Klincksieck, 1965.
Urmson, J. O., W.V.O. Quine, and S. Hampshire. "A Symposium on Austin's Method." In *Symposium on J. L. Austin*, edited by K. T. Fann. London: Routledge and Kegan Paul, 1969.
Wittgenstein, Ludwig. *The Blue and the Brown Books*. Edited by R. Rhees. Oxford: Blackwell, 1969. First published in 1958.
——. *Philosophical Investigations*. Translated by G.E.M. Anscombe. Oxford: Blackwell, 1953.

ÉNONCÉ

Énoncé, from the Latin *enuntiare* (to express, divulge; from *ex* [out] and *nuntiare* [to make known]; a *nuntius* is a messenger, a "nuncio"), ranges over the same type of entity as do "proposition" and "phrase": it is a basic unit of syntax, the relevant question being whether or not it is the bearer of truth values. An examination of the differences among these entities, and the networks they constitute in different languages (especially in English: "sentence," "statement," "utterance"), appears under PROPOSITION. See also DICTUM and LOGOS, both of which may be acceptably translated by *énoncé*. Cf. PRINCIPLE, SACHVERHALT, TRUTH, WORD (especially WORD, Box 3).

The essential feature of an *énoncé* is that it is considered to be a singular occurrence and thus is paired with its *énonciation*: see SPEECH ACT; cf. ENGLISH, LANGUAGE, SENSE, SIGN, SIGNIFIER/SIGNIFIED, *WITTICISM*.

➤ *DISCOURSE*

ENTREPRENEUR (FRENCH)

ENGLISH   adventurer, contractor, employer, enterpriser, entrepreneur, manager, projector, undertaker, superintendent

➤ *ACT*, AGENCY, BERUF, ECONOMY, LIBERAL, OIKONOMIA, PRAXIS, UTILITY

At the end of the nineteenth century, a new word appeared in the vocabulary of anglophone economists: "entrepreneur." It was explicitly borrowed from French political economy, and in particular from Jean-Baptiste Say, for whom the *entrepreneur*, the primary agent of production, must be distinguished from the owner of the capital. According to anglophone commentators, the naturalization of this word answered a need, since the English language did not have any term that could express the concept necessary for economists, and especially theoreticians of "free enterprise."

The concept of an entrepreneur, developed over the twentieth century in Anglo-American literature, there acquired its proper substance. The recent adoption of the English "entrepreneurial" (led by a spirit of enterprise) by French economic vocabulary marks in turn the desire to give the French word *entrepreneur* the specific values acquired by its English, and especially its American, usage, in particular to indicate that someone resolutely embraces the dynamics of free enterprise. Thus, at the end of the twentieth century in France, as at the end of the nineteenth century in the United States and England, *entrepreneur* is a concept that arrived from outside and is indeed a transnational linguistic creation.

I. The French History of the Word

When the economic concept of the *entrepreneur* appeared in France at the beginning of the eighteenth century, the word already had a rich history. Its origin lay in the Old French *emprise*, then *entreprise*, which refers to an action insofar as it is an engagement with a project that implies risk. The semantic field of *entrepreneur* extends to the military domain: an *entrepreneur* is someone who leads a campaign or siege; to the political domain: someone who undoes the bonds that form the basis of the kingdom by means of calculated plans; to the legal domain: someone who contravenes the hierarchical order of the professions and subverts their rules; finally, to the economic domain: someone who agrees, on the basis of a prior contract (an established price) to execute a project (collection of taxes, supply of an army, a merchant expedition, construction, production, transaction), assuming the hazards related to exchange and time. This last usage corresponds to practices that became more and more socially prominent starting in the sixteenth century.

Let us focus on the term in economics. The engagement of the entrepreneur in his project may be understood in various ways, and the noun *entrepreneur* translated in various ways into English: by "contractor" if the stress is placed on the engagement with regard to the client to execute the task according to conditions negotiated in advance (a certain time, a fixed price, firm price, tenant farming); by "undertaker" (now rare in this sense) when we focus on the engagement in the activity, taking charge of the project, its practical realization, the setting in motion of the transaction; and by "adventurer," "enterpriser," and "projector," to emphasize the risks related to speculation. At the end of the eighteenth century, the French word *entreprise* acquired the new meaning of an "industrial establishment." *Entrepreneur* accordingly acquired the sense of the head or direction of a business of production (superintendent, employer, manager).

In France, at the beginning of the eighteenth century, the noun *entrepreneur* had strong political connotations, in particular in the abundant pamphlets containing *mazarinades* denouncing the entrepreneurs of tax farming. The economist Pierre de Boisguilbert wrote the *Factum de la France*, "the largest trial ever conducted by pen" against the big financiers, "*entrepreneurs* of the wealth of the kingdom," who take advantage of its good administration (its political economy) in the name of the "entrepreneurs of commerce and industry," who contribute to the increase in its wealth). Boisguilbert failed in his project of reforming the tax farm, or tax business, and it was left to a clever financier, Richard Cantillon, to create the economic concept of the *entrepreneur*.

II. Chance in Business: Risk and Uncertainty

There is no trace of Boisguilbert's moral indignation in Cantillon's *Essai sur la nature du commerce en générale* (Essay on the nature of commerce in general). Having shown that "all the classes and all the men of a State live or acquire wealth at the expense of the owners of the land" (bk. 1, chap. 12), he suggests that "the circulation and barter of goods and merchandise, like their production, are conducted in Europe by entrepreneurs and haphazardly" (bk. 1, of chap. 13). He then describes in detail what composes the "uncertain" aspect of the action of an entrepreneur, in which he acts "according to his ideas" and "without being able to predict," in which he conceives and executes his plans surrounded by the hazard of events. The uncertainty related to business profits turns especially on the fact that it is dependent on the forms of consumption of the owners, the only members of society who are independent—"naturally independent," Cantillon specified. Entrepreneurs are those who are capable of breaking out of their natural dependence by means of their frugality (which is the renunciation of the subsistence provided by their wages) and by their industriousness (which allows them to take on the risks of uncertainty). They thus acquire a relative independence, as much as is allowed by their capacity for acquisition and that is related to their ability to anticipate. Thus, Cantillon manages to reconcile the two values of the term that Boisguilbert could only make mutually exclusive, and he creates the concept of the entrepreneur.

Cantillon, an Irish banker established in France, dabbled in the financial practices of entrepreneurs, to his advantage. But his analysis is markedly English, both in terms of the essay form employed and by the content. He relies on Petty for his calculations and for the "equated pairs"—consumption and production, land and work—which he draws out. He also is indebted to John Locke for the starting point of his theory of the origin of society, the importance given to freely entered contracts in the formation of political ties. However, he sharply criticizes each for their hasty empirical generalizations, whether it is Locke's conventionalism or Petty's inductions on the basis of a few calculations, and for their indifference to concrete conditions, especially sociopolitical ones, that determine the cycles of wealth and contribute to the uncertainty confronted by the entrepreneur. As a result, both the content and the importance of the concept of the entrepreneur seem to be the fruit of a confrontation between French political economy—understood as good administration of the kingdom, which can only be attained if we take the concrete determinations of the circulations of wealth such as currency, merchandise, and credit into account and in detail (*Détail de la France* is the title of a major work by Boisguilbert)—and English political economy, which is more focused on discovering the general laws of the market. Cantillon's theory constitutes a paradoxical episode in relation to the commonplace that the French are theoreticians whereas the English deal with practice.

III. Business and Innovation, "Projector" and "Contractor"

In 1787, a second episode took place with the publication of Jeremy Bentham's *Defence of Usury*. There, Bentham argues against Adam Smith on behalf of the entrepreneur (projector), who, by taking the risks related to invention and innovation, not only contributes to the opening of new avenues for industrial progress, but even by his failures, reduces the field of investigation for his successors and helps them avoid errors. Bentham's attachment to the French intellectual tradition is well known. Less well known is the fact that his defense of the *projector* is part of a debate that was very active at the time in France among administrators and engineers over *hommes à projets* (project men). The same year, in *Panopticon*, he emphasized the importance for business of relying on contract management and on the interest of the entrepreneur, or contractor, rather than on the system of trust management used for putting prisoners to work. This question of the choice between business, where activity is motivated by the quest for profit, and trust management, where the "household"—the running of activities—is led by one's attachment and faithfulness to the service of the king, is the crucible in which the representation of

the entrepreneur was forged in France. It is at the center of the reflections and inquiries conducted by politicians and administrators, beginning with Sully, then Colbert, Vauban, and Turgot. More essentially, the distinction between business and trust management is in fact that of conscience—taking care to fulfill the details of one's obligations as described in the stipulations of the contract—and confidence—the immediate exercise (without the mediation of calculation of reciprocal interests) of faithfulness to the king, where action has no other motive than the attachment to the general interest of the kingdom. The tension between these two modes of realizing the general interest, and thus the search for their appropriate balance, animated the debates belonging to the history of French political economy and allowed the concept of business profits to be discovered.

By taking over the opposition between "contract" and "trust," Bentham introduced the logic belonging to the French debate over business profits into English economic analysis. His attempt was bound to fail, as it was in conflict with the conception of political economy being constructed by Adam Smith and David Ricardo: a science dealing with laws of exchange and the creation of value and prices in which profit can only be that of capital.

IV. The Industrial Entrepreneur

For Jean-Baptiste Say, the social importance of the "industrial entrepreneur," who conducts the organization of his business, that is, the distribution of time, men, materials, and machines, is part of a radical position in the debate over business: an action is moral, he claims, if it is performed with a view to one's own interest. "People complain that everyone only listens to their own interests: I am worried about the opposite! Knowing one's true interests is the beginning of morality," he writes in *Olbie, ou essai sur les moyens de réformer les moeurs d'une nation*, a utopia that is an "essay on the means of reforming the morals of a nation." By formulating this idea in a utopia that allows him to give these principles the force of an absolute beginning, Say turns his back on French debates over business as a subversion or realization of the ties of the State and resolutely takes on a twofold project: to thrust the theoretical approach founded by Smith—whom he "reveres" and recognizes as his master (introduction to his *Traité*)—into French political economy and to give France, which was obsessed with the goal of closing the industrial gap with England, the means of doing so. Political economy can only contribute to this if it is restricted to "the knowledge of the laws which govern the creation, distribution, and consumption of wealth" (Say, *Cours*, vol. 1). It must not be separated from the analysis of the moral and political conditions of its realization, since it is "the economics of society," "social economy," or even more generally, "social science." Say actively spread his analysis in society and, in particular, among heads of industry. As an ideologue—he was one of the founders and editors in chief of the *Decade Philosophique*—Say believed in the virtues of instruction understood as the education of judgment, of the entrepreneurial capacity to invent adequate solutions. His goal remained that of his teachers at the École Normale in the year 3 who wished to transform minds to produce an enlightened opinion capable of influencing governmental decisions.

John Stuart Mill, who was familiar with Bentham's and Say's works and a staunch francophile, takes up Say's criticism of Smith and his disdain for "'this supposed labour of inspection and direction' [*Wealth of Nations*, bk. 1, chap. 6] of the work of the person he calls the undertaker" in his *Principles of Political Economy* (1848). Mill notes that the word *entrepreneur*, in the sense given it by Say, is not familiar to English speakers, which restricts the powers of analysis of English political economy. "French political economists enjoy a great advantage in being able to speak currently of 'les profits de l'entrepreneur'" (bk. 2, chap. 15, §1). We thus owe the introduction of the term into English political economy to Mill.

Francis A. Walker, the first president of the American Economic Association, echoed Mill in 1876 in *The Wages Question* (chap. 14), noting:

It is much to be regretted that we have not a single English word which exactly fits the person who performs this office in modern industry. The word "undertaker," the man who undertakes, at one time had very much this extent; but it has long since been so exclusively devoted to funereal uses as to become an impossible term in political economy. The word "adventurer," the man who makes ventures, also had this sense; but in modern parlance it has acquired a wholly sinister meaning. The French word "entrepreneur" has very nearly the desired significance; and it may be that the exigencies of politico-economical reasoning will yet lead to its being naturalized among us.

However, the economic role of the entrepreneur as a driving force could not find a place in neoclassical economics. Alfred Marshall's *Principles of Economics* (1890) contains remarks that indicate both the impossibility, after Mill and Walker, of entirely ignoring the economic action of the entrepreneur, and the impossibility, in a moral way, of thinking that "exceptional habilities, which are not made by human effort, and are not the result of sacrifices undergone for a future gain" might justify anything other than a surplus income, a "quasi-income." Such action could in no way be considered "the prime mover of the whole economy," as Charles Gide wrote in 1884. The idea of "business profits" and a "spirit of business" here comes into conflict with a moral position analyzed by Max Weber as the "spirit of capitalism" (only effort deserves compensation by profit), as well as with the attempts at mathematical formalizations that characterize neoclassical economics and does not allow for factors that are not reducible to scientific analysis. The word *entrepreneur* nevertheless entered into English economic vocabulary. In 1904, W. A. Veditz, an American professor of economics who translated—or rather adapted for anglophone students—Charles Gide's *Principes d'économie politique*, noted that "The French term *entrepreneur*, literally meaning undertaker (the person at the head of any undertaking), has now acquired current usage in English."

V. Probability and Uncertainty

It was left to Frank H. Knight to produce a theory of the entrepreneur and of business profits for Anglo-American discourse in *Risk, Uncertainty and Profit* (1921). He clarifies in his preface:

The particular technical contribution to the theory of free enterprise which this essay purports to make is a fuller and more careful examination of the role of the *entrepreneur*, or enterpriser, the recognized "central figure" of the system, and of the forces which fix the remuneration of his special function.

Knight is attacking at the strong point of economic theory by trying to look closely at the irreducible aspect of innovative business: he distinguishes "insurable risk" from "non-insurable uncertainty"; this uncertainty, where the judgment of the entrepreneur enters the picture, yields situations that cannot be captured by science and calculation since they are not repeatable: "situations in regard to which business judgment must be exercised do not repeat themselves with sufficient conformity to type, to make possible a computation of probability" (*Economic Organization*). Since then, and in the same spirit, attempts have been made to further reduce the irreducible components of business profits, which has led to an emphasis on the action of the entrepreneur, which has thus become "the phenomenon which is more emphasized yet least understood by economists" (Kanbur, "Of Risk Taking"). Whether it is a matter, as with Schumpeter, of the will to innovate of the rebel entrepreneur; or, as with Keynes, of "animal spirits" (Keynes, *General Theory of Employment*) that animate the drive of undertaking something; or more recently, as with Shackle, of the entrepreneur as *originator*, in the same mold as an artist or great mathematician (Hebert and Link, intro., *Entrepreneur*), the fundamental question of business and the entrepreneur has been psychologized. What in French economic literature was related to the political order, then to the social one, has become in Anglo-Saxon countries that part of human nature which resists or goes beyond the rationality of economic discourse.

VI. A French Word, an American Concept?

Knight's effort is part of a theory of economics that energetically claimed to be a theory of free enterprise. The same project drives French economists, who have adopted the adjective "entrepreneurial" into their vocabulary. Similarly, the recent transformation of the CNPF (Conseil du patronat français) into the MEDEF (Mouvment des entreprises de France) aims to contribute to spreading a different image of the entrepreneur. This change of name was accompanied by a publicity campaign, *En avant l'entreprise* (Forward, Business), whose founders noted their desire to "put business at the center of French society" by "promoting the freedom to undertake (*entreprendre*), entrepreneurial vocations, and their success in the economy" and "by pursuing the spirit of business and its spread throughout all the parts of society" (*Le Monde*, 28 October 1998).

This falls entirely within the tradition of French political economy of the nineteenth and twentieth centuries, as expressed by Say or Gide. Either one could have written those sentences. We may even discern the echoes of the meaning of *entrepreneur* proper to the eighteenth century in France, in the desire expressed in this campaign to lead "a veritable ground war against State interventionism" (ibid.). However, in the booklet aimed at explaining the change of the organization's name, E. A. Sellière explains that "'Entreprises' replaces 'Patronat,' and completely naturally invokes 'entrepreneurs,' a term that has become part of ordinary language." Along with all of current economic literature, this confirms that the Anglo-American liberal economy constitutes the reference point: it created a new concept of an *entrepreneur*, which has since been naturalized into everyday language in France. This elusive concept, once again, smuggles in a word from abroad.

Hélène Vérin

BIBLIOGRAPHY

Bentham, Jeremy. *Defence of Usury*. London: Routledge, 1998. First published in 1787.
Boisguilbert, Pierre de. *Détail de la France* (1695), *Factum de la France* (1707), *Traité du mérite et des lumières de ceux que l'on appelle gens habiles dans la finance ou grands financiers* (1707). In *Pierre de Boisguilbert ou la naissance de l'économie politique*, vol. 2. Paris: Institut National d'Etudes Démographiques, 1966.
Cantillon, Richard. *Essai sur la nature du commerce en générale*. London: Fletcher Giles, 1755. Translation by Chantal Saucier: *An Essay on Economic Theory*. Auburn, AL: Ludwig von Mises Institute, 2010.
Gide, Charles: *Principes d'économie politique*. Larose et Forcel, 1884. Reprint, Paris: Sirey, 1921. Translation by C.W.A. Veditz: *Principles of Political Economy*. London: Heath, 1904.
Hebert, R. F., and A. N. Link. Introduction to *The Entrepreneur*, by G.L.S. Shackle. New York: Praeger, 1982.
Kanbur, S. M. "Of Risk Taking and the Personal Distribution of Income." *Journal of Political Economy* 87 (1979): 767–97.
Keynes, John Maynard. *The General Theory of Employment, Interest and Money*. London: Macmillan, 1936.
Knight, Frank H. *The Economic Organization*. New York: Houghton, Mifflin, 1951.
———. *Risk, Uncertainty and Profit*. Boston: Houghton, Mifflin, 1921.
Locke, John. *Two Treatises of Civil Government*. Cambridge: Cambridge University Press, 1988. First published in 1690.
Marshall, Alfred. *Principle of Economics*. London: Macmillan, 1961. First published in 1890.
Mill, John Stuart. *Principles of Political Economy*. In *Collected Works*, vol. 2. London: Routledge, 1996.
Petty, William. *Several Essays in Political Economy*. London: Clavel, 1699.
Say, Jean-Baptiste. *Cours complet d'économie politique pratique*. Osnabrück, Ger.: Otto Zeller, 1966. First published in 1828.
———. *Olbie, ou Essai sur les moyens de réformer les moeurs d'une nation*. Nancy, Fr.: Presses Universitaires de Nancy, 1985. First published in 1800.
———. *Traité d'économie politique*. Paris: Slatkine, 1982. First published in 1803. Translation by C. R. Prinsep: *A Treatise on Political Economy; or, The Production, Distribution & Consumption of Wealth*. Philadelphia: Clayton, Remsen, and Haffelfinger, 1880. Published in electronic form by Kitchener, ON, Canada: Batoche, 2001.
Schumpeter, Joseph A. *Essays on Entrepreneurs, Innovations, Business Cycles, and the Evolution of Capitalism*. New Brunswick, NJ: Transaction Publishers, 1991.
———. *The Theory of Economic Development*. Cambridge, MA: Harvard University Press, 1968.
Smith, Adam. *An Inquiry into the Nature and the Causes of the Wealth of Nations*. London: Strahan and Cadell, 1776.
———. *The Wealth of Nations*. London: Everyman's Library, 1991.
Vérin, Hélène. *Entrepreneurs, entreprise: Histoire d'une idée*. Paris: Presses Universitaires de France, 1982.
Walker, Francis A. *The Wages Question*. New York: Henry Holt, 1981 First published in 1876.

ENTSTELLUNG (GERMAN)

ENGLISH   deformation, disfiguration, alteration, displacement

► *DEFORMATION* and ANXIETY, COMBINATION AND CONCEPTUALIZATION, CONSCIOUSNESS, DRIVE, *FALSE*, MEMORY, *NEGATION*, SIGNIFIER/SIGNIFIED, TRUTH, VERNEINUNG

Derived from *stellen*, "to place something so that it stands upright," "to put something on its feet" (*Stellung*, position), the noun *Entstellung* has two main meanings in ordinary language: deformation (change in something's form) and falsification (change to the truth of, *verfälschen*). The second meaning clarifies the first one: deformation and disfiguration can extend to falsification (a report, an event, the truth). Freud uses *Entstellung* to refer to a mechanism that is the effect of a process: that of repression (*Verdrängung*), first, and later that of denial (*Verleugnung*). The meaning differs depending on the processes at work.

I. *Entstellung* and Deformation

Repression produces a deformation (*Entstellung*) of the contents of memory or fantasies. Memory, outside of the conscious part where everything is felt but nothing recorded, is made up of several layers of traces that undergo a number of deformations (lacunae, chronological disorder, unintelligibility). These deformations are the result of repression. Repressive psychic forces may be witnessed in the resistance, in therapy, to the reappearance of the memory: "The greater the resistance, the greater the deformation (*Entstellung*)" ("Freud's Psychoanalytic Procedure," in *Standard Edition*, vol. 7). Thus, in order to make the unconscious available to consciousness, the deformed materials must themselves undergo deformation. Similarly, "a piece of forgotten truth is present in the delirious idea, which, in returning, must have undergone deformations (*Entstellungen*)" (Freud, *Moses and Monotheism*). Deformation is the only means of access to this forgotten truth.

II. *Entstellung* and *Verschiebung* (Displacement)

In French, the term *déplacement* is used to render *Entstellung*, instead of *déformation*. It has the linguistic sense of metonymy, no doubt related to the contiguity of *Entstellung* and *Verschiebung* (displacement, slippage) in Freud's *Traumdeutung*. Thus, Lacan speaks of the "displacement of the signifier" (*Écrits*, 11) or of "slippage of the signified under the signifier" (ibid., 511). *Entstellung* is a transposition of the dream in which the signification masks the desire of the dream; it is also a de-position (*Ent-stellung*) of the drives (ibid., 662) in the manner of a cohort of displaced persons. It is a distortion (disfiguring) in the grammatical forms of negation (ibid., 663).

But in reality Freud distinguishes *Entstellung* from *Verschiebung*, displacement being an effect of deformation:

> Thus the fact that the content of dreams includes remnants of trivial experiences is to be explained as a manifestation of dream-distortion (by displacement); and it will be recalled that we came to the conclusion that dream-distortion was the product of a censorship operating in the passage-way between two psychical agencies.
>
> (*Interpretation of Dreams, Standard Edition*, vol. 4)

This displacement is one of the essential procedures of deformation: "The consequence of the displacement (*Verschiebung*) is that the dream-content no longer resembles the core of the dream-thoughts and that the dream gives no more than a distortion (*Entstellung*) of the dream-wish which exists in the unconscious" (ibid.). Deciphering the dream unmasks the unconscious desire underneath its disfigurement, just as the access to a repressed memory or a forgotten truth is nothing less than the revelation of the deformations they have suffered.

III. *Entstellung* and *Verfälschung* (Falsification)

In 1939 *Entstellung* is used by Freud in a sense leaning toward that of falsification:

> The distortion (*Entstellung*) of a text is not unlike a murder. The difficulty lies not in the execution of the deed but in the doing away with the traces. One could wish to give the word "*Entstellung*" the double meaning to which it has a right, although it is no longer used in this sense. It should mean not only "to change the appearance of," but also "to wrench apart," "to put in another place." That is why in so many textual distortions (*Entstellung*) we may count on finding the suppressed and abnegated material hidden away somewhere, though in an altered shape and torn out of its original connection. Only it is not always easy to recognize it.
>
> (Freud, *Moses and Monotheism*)

The notion of *Entstellung* as the trace of a process in the psychic apparatus is still present; however, by being applied here to any text whatsoever, whether metapsychological or biblical, it is no longer a trace of repression but of denial (*Verleugnung*). Thus, the meaning it acquires (*Verfälschung*: falsification, alteration, denaturing, counterfeiting) comes from the denial (*Verleugnung*) of the murder (of the father, of Moses) of which it is the written trace, by displacement of a letter or a date. The falsification of traces gives access, in the recording of its after-effects, to their origins: we read a text with the traces that have deformed it, and the modalities of deformation give access to what has been deformed in the text (true, real). *Entstellung* treats the letter of the text the way it treats the impressions of memory recorded, by displacing it, deforming it—by falsifying it. Even while he pulls *entstellen* closer to *verfälschen*, Freud continues to separate them:

> The text, however, as we find it today tells us enough about its own history. Two distinct forces, diametrically opposed to each other, have left their traces on it. On the one hand, certain transformations got to work on it, have falsified (*verfälscht*) the text in accord with secret tendencies, maiming and extending it until it was turned into its opposite. On the other hand, an indulgent piety (*schonungsvolle Pietät*) reigned over it, anxious to keep everything as it stood, indifferent to whether the details fitted together or nullified one another.
>
> (Ibid.)

Deformation is, of course, an effect of falsification ("all later distortions [*Entstellungen*] . . . serve another aim. . . . An endeavour was made to date back to an early time certain laws and institutions of the present . . . , the picture of past times in this way became falsified [*verfälscht*]," ibid.). But Freud distinguishes them from each other. The first is reserved for tradition: of the religion of Moses, "a kind of memory of it had survived, a tradition perhaps obscured and distorted (*entstellt*)" (ibid., 87). The second applies to written narrative: the compromise at Kadesh was made in writing, but

> a long time was to elapse, however, before historians came to develop an ideal of objective truth. At first they [the people from Egypt] shaped their accounts according to their needs and tendencies of the moment, with an easy conscience, as if they had not yet understood what falsification (*Verfälschung*) signified.
>
> (Ibid.)

In 1970, in *L'envers de la psychanalyse*, Lacan extracted the *falsus* as the fall of the written from the *Verfälschung* of the letter. The equivocity between *falloir* and *faillir* (see DUTY) is reunified in the etymology of *fallere* (in the past participle), the notions of "to miss, to fall" and "to mistake, to be deceived." *Falsus* combines the defect of an error and the failure of duty in written mistakes, when a letter drops out or is displaced.

Solal Rabinovitch

BIBLIOGRAPHY

Freud, Sigmund. *Der Mann Moses und die monotheistiche Religion*. In *Gesammelte Werke*, vol. 16. Frankfurt: Fischer, 1942. First published in 1939. Translation by K. Jones: *Moses and Monotheism*. New York: Vintage Books, 1967.
———. "Freud's Psychoanalytic Procedure" (1904 [1903]). In *The Standard Edition of the Complete Psychological Works of Sigmund Freud*, vol. 7. Translated by J. Strachey, 247–54. London: Hogarth, 1901–1905.
———. *Traumdeutung*. In *Gesammelte Werke*, vols. 2–3. Frankfurt: Fischer, 1942. First published in 1900. Translation by James Strachey: *Interpretation of Dreams*. In *The Standard Edition of the Complete Psychological Works of Sigmund Freud*, vol. 4 (1). London: Hogarth, 1995.
Lacan, Jacques. *Écrits*. Paris: Éditions du Seuil, 1966. Translation by B. Fink with H. Fink and R. Grigg: *Écrits: The First Complete Edition in English*. New York: W. W. Norton, 2006.
———. *L'envers de la psychanalyse*. In *Le Séminaire*. Vol. 17. Paris: Éditions du Seuil, 1991. Translation by R. Grigg: *The Other Side of Psychoanalysis*. New York: Norton, 2006.
Weber, Samuel. *Rückkehr zur Freud: Jacques Lacans Entstellung der Psychoanalyse*. Berlin: Verlag Ullstein, 1978, Vienna: Passagen Verlag, 1990. Translation by M. Levine: *Return to Freud: Jacques Lacan's Dislocation of Psychoanalysis*. New York: Cambridge University Press, 1991.

EPISTEMOLOGY

FRENCH   *épistémologie*
GERMAN   *Erkenntnistheorie*

➤ ANSCHAULICHKEIT, BELIEF, CHANCE, GEISTESWISSENSCHAFTEN, PERCEPTION, REPRÉSENTATION, TRUTH

When the term *épistémologie* enters French, no doubt upon the translation in 1901 of Bertrand Russell's *Essay on the Foundations of Geometry*, it is met above all with the apparent serenity of a consensus. As Louis Couturat writes, "Epistemology is the theory of knowledge (*connaissance*) based on the critical study of the sciences, or, in a word, *Critique,* as Kant defined and founded it." When Émile Meyerson, for his part, writes the introduction to his *Identité et Réalité* in 1907, he clarifies, "The present work belongs, in its method, to the domain of the philosophy of science or epistemology, to use a more or less appropriate term which is becoming widely used." He thereupon places the work under the aegis of Hermann von Helmholtz and his theory of unconscious psychic processes. Kant, Russell, Helmholtz: we are dealing with a study of the general laws of thought with reference to the sciences, and there seems at this point to be no difference of emphasis or usage among the terms "epistemology," *épistémologie / philosophie des sciences,* and *Erkenntnistheorie* (or *Erkenntnislehre/ Wissenschaftslehre*).

Today almost none of that homogeneity, posited or hoped for, remains among the different names given to the various discourses concerning science in German, English, and French. The French term *épistémologie,* as well as the German *Wissenschaftstheorie,* simply absorbs under a somewhat superficial harmony a multiplicity of approaches—general theory of knowledge, technical and logical analysis of scientific theories, historical analysis of their development—which English tends to distinguish (epistemology, philosophy of science, history of science). In reality, however, there remains neither a foundational doctrine nor a unified direction in the domain of the theory of knowledge and science. The experience of translation has correspondingly become that of a proliferation of "untranslatable" terms: German terms without exact correlates in English or in French (*Anschaulichkeit, Zusammenhang*), English or American terms without exact correlates in German or in French ("inference to the best explanation," defeasibility). The work of epistemologists today makes the loss of unity in their vocabulary very clear, and they work as though under the assumption that in order to identify their problems, a map of the words is required first.

I. *Erkenntnistheorie*

A. First occurrences of the term

The term *Erkenntnistheorie* appears rather early in the history of German philosophy in the nineteenth century, at least, well before the standard attribution to E. Zeller, who in fact fixes the academic meaning only in the 1860s (see his *Bedeutung und Aufgabe der Erkenntnistheorie,* 1862). Despite the diversity of its meanings, *Erkenntnistheorie* is used into the 1930s to refer to discourse that analyzes the power of knowing by the different sciences (*Wissenschaften*), whether "of the mind" (*Geisteswissenschaften*) or "of nature" (*Naturwissenschaften*). But the history of the term is also in large part that of the reception of Kant over the course of the nineteenth century, a history that evolves from a polemical embrace to a recognition of the intrinsic limitations of the Kantian approach.

The term *Erkenntnislehre* is mentioned as early as 1827, in W. T. Krug's lexicon, which defines it as "the philosophical theory of human knowledge, also called Metaphysics" (see his *Allgemeines Handwörterbuch,* 447). According to K. Köhnke, following F. Ueberweg, the general meaning of *Erkenntnistheorie* had already appeared in Schleiermacher's lectures on dialectic, given in 1811 and published in 1839, the first post-Kantian attempt to develop a theory of knowledge founded not only on pure thought but on sense perception as well. To find the first precise references to a *Theorie der Erkenntnis,* it is no doubt

necessary to look at E. Reinhold's *Theorie des menschlichen Erkenntnisvermögen* (1832); in 1876, H. Vaihinger attributes the beginnings of *Erkenntnistheorie* to Reinhold.

B. Embracing Kant's legacy

Although we do not know the exact date when the term *Erkenntnistheorie* took its place in the language, its meaning is clearly tied to the embrace of Kant's legacy as against that of Hegel's philosophy of nature and German idealism in general. The aim of *Erkenntnistheorie* is, in the most general sense, the study of the presuppositions of knowledge, both in the exact sciences and in historical ones. According to A. Diemer and C. F. Gethmann, we may thus distinguish the following in nineteenth-century German philosophy: (a) a psychological trend, which begins with J. Fries and later develops as empirical psychology—*Erkenntnistheorie* as an "analysis of sensations" (Beneke, Schopenhauer, Helmholtz, Wundt, Stumpf, Avenarius, Mach); (b) opposed to this, a logico-transcendental trend, placing its emphasis either on the methodology of natural sciences with the Marburg School (H. Cohen, P. Natorp, then E. Cassirer), or on moral and historical knowledge (W. Windelband, H. Rickert, E. Lask); (c) a metaphysical realist trend inaugurated by J. F. Herbart and F. A. Trendelenburg, in which *Erkenntnistheorie* is composed of *philosophia prima* (E. Zeller, F. Überweg, E. von Hartmann, and so forth). The diversity of these references to *Erkenntnistheorie,* though irreducible to a single orientation, nonetheless indicates a single general direction: that of a return to an analysis of the power of knowledge and the process of the objectification of phenomena, in opposition to those successors of Hegel and Schelling who claimed to legislate for the natural sciences. Köhnke suggests, thus, that *Erkenntnistheorie* marks three successive returns to Kant: around 1830 with Reinhold, around 1860 with Helmholtz (*Schriften zur Erkenntnistheorie*), and finally at the beginning of the twentieth century with the Marburg School. In all three cases, the term *Erkenntnistheorie* seems to act as a reference point or a sign of recognition for preoccupations that are, in fact, not really Kantian in the strict sense, and are in any case very different from one another (logic, philosophy of language, psychology, physiology, sociology, history, hermeneutics, and methodology of the natural sciences).

- See Box 1.

C. Generalizations and ambivalence in early twentieth-century usage

Though the term *Erkenntnistheorie* is still in use around 1920–30, more than ever in fact, its usage is almost purely symbolic: it serves to maintain a general requirement of rationality and an interest in the problem of knowledge, but in a context in which it is recognized that Kantianism has reached certain principled limits. We may take four examples of this ambivalence.

a. For Husserl, philosophy is still *Erkenntniskritik,* as distinct from the "ingenious and methodical work of the individual sciences" (*Logical Investigations*), and assigned to the elucidation of the essence of the concepts of thing, event, cause, effect, space, time, and so on (ibid., II.15). However, this *Erkenntniskritik* is understood in the new sense of intentionality. In the first of

1

Epistemology

Louis Couturat, in the *Lexique philosophique*, cited by B. Russell (*An Essay on the Foundations of Geometry*), writes,

ÉPISTÉMOLOGIE (English: *Epistemology*) — This term, which epistemologically signifies "theory of science," corresponds to the German *Erkenntnistheorie* or *Erkenntnislehre* (Theory of Knowledge), and to the French expression *Philosophie des sciences*.

It refers to a fundamental part of philosophy, which is wrongly confused in France either with Psychology or with Logic. It is distinguished from Psychology insofar as it is, like Logic, a normative (Wundt) science, that is, its object is not the empirical laws of thought as it is in fact, a mixture of truth and error, but the ideal laws (rules or *norms*) to which thought must conform in order to be correct and true. It is distinguished from Logic insofar as the latter studies the *formal* rules or the *directive* principles that thought must obey in order for its conclusions to follow and to be internally consistent, whereas Epistemology seeks *constitutive* principles of thought, which provide it with a starting point and assure it an objective value. Finally, it is distinguished from applied Logic or Methodology insofar as the latter studies the methods proper to the different sciences (axioms, hypotheses, or postulates) which serve as their bases, and discusses their value and origin (empirical or *a priori*). In sum, Epistemology is the theory of knowledge based on the critical study of knowledge, or, in a word, *Critique* as Kant defined and founded it.

the *Logical Investigations*, we find *Erkenntnislehre*, *Erkenntnistheorie*, and *Erkenntniskritik* used to refer to any approach distinct from empirical psychology, biologism, and skepticism. Phenomenology, for its part, bases its critique of knowledge in a completely different way, relying on a pure ontology of experience. Although the continuing use of the term *Erkenntnistheorie* reveals Husserl's retention of a large part of Kant's approach to the constitution of objectivity, it is in this new perspective of the phenomenological method that he uses the word.

b. According to Moritz Schlick, in the *Allgemeine Erkenntnislehre* [*General Theory of Knowledge*] (1918), philosophy is identified in a very classical way as the "theory of knowledge," with the latter being rigorously distinguished from psychology. The theory of knowledge is defined as the search for the universal foundations of the possibility of valid knowledge in general, which must make possible the clarification of the fundamental concepts of the sciences (that of consciousness in psychology, that of axiom and number in mathematics, those of space and time in physics, and so on). However, Schlick claims to continue the thought of Helmholtz, Kirschhoff, and Hilbert. He understands knowledge as a process of "designating objects" that is radically different both from "intuitive penetration" and from the search for "subject-object correspondence"; he relates this process of designation to a "recognition of the like," which must lead to a reduction of the number of explanatory principles, and claims that the only rigorous method is that of mathematics. Schlick's *Erkenntnistheorie*, though based on an analysis of the power of knowing, thus already represents a clear departure from Kant, and opens the way for the principled kind of anti-Kantianism that characterizes the first writings to come out of the Vienna Circle.

c. The term *Erkenntnistheorie* is just as ubiquitous for Cassirer. Besides the four volumes of *Das Erkenntnisproblem* (1906, 1907, 1920, 1957), his 1920 book on the theory of relativity is entitled *Zur Einsteinchen Relativitätstheorie, erkenntnistheoretische Betrachtungen*, and the aim of his 1936 book on quantum mechanics, *Determinismus und Indeterminismus in der modernen Physik*, is to measure the displacement of the center of gravity of theoretical physics from the point of view of knowledge (*erkenntnistheoretisch*), that is, from the point of view of the determination of the concepts of object and reality, of thing and attribute, of substance and accident. As early as *Substanzbegriff und Funktionsbegriff* (1910), however, the term *Erkenntnistheorie* is released by Cassirer from its strict affiliation with neo-Kantianism, since his aim is to widen the *erkenntnistheoretisch* project at its very base. The *Philosophie der symbolischen Formen* (1923, 1925, 1929) suggests a "critique of culture" and a morphology of the human mind in all its manifestations—sciences, myths, languages, religions—unified by the notion of symbolic form, seen as a rule governing cognitive functions in their concrete diversity. The 1936 book on quantum physics, then, describes the definitive limitation of simplification and profound changes in the forms of thought. Here again, as a result, the Kantian aspect of the term *Erkenntnistheorie* is weakened to the point of almost disappearing entirely.

d. As a last example, the term *Erkenntnistheorie* is spontaneously used by the founders of quantum mechanics: it is common in the titles of N. Bohr's articles (thus, in 1939, "Erkenntnistheoretische Fragen in der Physik und die menschlichen Kulturen," or in 1949, "Diskussion mit Einstein über erkenntnistheoretische Probleme in der Atomphysik"), as well as in publications by W. Heisenberg, W. Pauli, M. Born, and so on. The use of the term in these cases no longer has any association with Kantianism, which is explicitly rejected by Bohr, Heisenberg, and Pauli at the end of the 1920s. The term is used, rather, to indicate a series of philosophical questions concerning the "new situation of knowledge," which requires us to "make a fresh start": the foundations of the description of nature; the widening of the concept of *Anschauung* and of the criteria of *Anschaulichkeit* of a physical theory; the transformation of the conditions of objectivication through the renunciation of simultaneously spatial and causal determinations of phenomena; the necessary redefinition of objectivity with reference to the possibility of unambiguous communication; the critique of the traditional concept of the subject as pure and isolated understanding, placed at the first level of language; the transformation of the concept of reality; the displacement of the opposition between *Wissen* and *Glauben*; and so on. Here then, on the scientific side, the internal difficulties among the questions peculiar to *Erkenntnistheorie* come to a head.

II. "Epistemology"

A. From the problem of objectification to that of "justified belief"

Can we translate *Erkenntnistheorie* by "epistemology"? *Erkenntnistheorie*, however generally we construe it, remains essentially related to the problem of knowing how a subject turns a phenomenon into an object of knowledge, to a certain relationship between an intuition (that is, to the representation of a phenomenon in space and time) and a concept. No doubt "epistemology"—the term appears in English in 1856 in the works of the Scottish philosopher James F. Ferrier—is still defined in dictionaries today as the study of the sources, nature, and limits of human knowledge. However, it is immediately clarified that the central occupations of epistemology, determined by the Fregean starting point and by the "linguistic turn," concern logic and formal systems, language and the concept of truth, mind and mental states, and that one of its major projects is to understand what a "justified belief" is (where "belief" refers to the act of holding a statement to be true), as well as a "justified true belief." Several types of responses are offered to this question and to the questions associated with it (the concept of truth, the notions of truth and demonstration, the theory of valid inference, and so on): there are "normative" responses, "naturalistic" responses, or "skeptical" responses; understanding these responses requires in turn that one master a specific tradition and its vocabulary. The paradoxes are no longer the same: we move from L. Nelson's argument for the impossibility of the theory of knowledge (*Die Unmöglichkeit der Erkenntnistheorie*, 1912; cf. *Gesammelte Schriften*, ed. P. Bernays et al.) to Gettier's problems (E. Gettier, "Is Justified True Belief Knowledge?" 1963). Nor do the divisions occur in the same places: foundationalism unifies classical empiricism and rationalism in the idea that there is a foundational structure comprising fundamental beliefs, by contrast with "coherentism," which claims that each belief receives its justification from other beliefs. But both are in conflict with naturalized epistemology, which considers that human understanding is a natural entity, interacting with others, and that the results of its scientific study are crucial for the epistemological enterprise. Concepts or topics that are universally known in current English-language literature sometimes provoke no particular reaction in other languages. To take some particularly gross examples: though distinctions such as that between sense and reference or examples like "the present King of France is bald" are now classic, it remains difficult in French to discuss the import of Bayesianism or different interpretations of the notion of probability, or problems related to the underdetermination of theories by experience, the private language argument, the notion of projectible predicates, or the notion of

a degree of evidential support, and so on. Even proper names do not have the same meaning. Aristotle, Descartes, Anselm, and Thomas Aquinas are terms that function as "definite descriptions," which differ from one language to the next. It is clear that "epistemology" refers to different preoccupations from *Erkenntnistheorie*, and that it makes sense only within the network of specific concepts associated with it.

B. The evolution of "epistemology"

How was this difference between two worlds of thought in the philosophy of knowledge established? To understand it, it would be necessary to delve into the history of English-language philosophy in detail. Here, we will only briefly recapitulate four moments in this history.

a. The first, usually considered to be the birth of analytic philosophy, is the revolt of Russell and Moore against the Hegelian idealism that had become fashionable in English philosophy at the end of the nineteenth century. According to Russell, a "new philosophy" began with Moore's article, "The Nature of Judgment," published in *Mind* in 1899, in which he rejects both the Kantian problem of the possibility of knowledge and the Hegelian one of the Absolute Spirit. This beginning is more sensational than subtle, but we must grasp its polemical necessity: "With a sense of escaping from prison, we allowed ourselves to think that grass is green, that the sun and stars would exist if no one was aware of them, and also that there is a pluralistic timeless world of Platonic ideas" (B. Russell, "My Mental Development," 12).

b. Established from the beginning in opposition to Kantianism and to German idealism, the English tradition of epistemology subsequently acquires its distinctive character with the creation of a new link between empiricism and symbolic logic. Russell's theory of definite descriptions ("On Denoting," in *Mind* [1905]) thus gives a model for the resolution of a philosophical problem by means of logic. Philosophy is thus grouped with mathematics and logic, as a deductive and a priori approach whose function is clarification and analysis—while the natural sciences are seen as the essential route to any new knowledge about the world. The ideas, common to Russell and Wittgenstein, that logical analysis makes it possible to break language up into a collection of atomic propositions and that the structure of propositions and the structure of reality mirror one another, persist throughout all the subsequent developments of epistemology. The hypothesis that there is a logical form hidden in ordinary language continues to divide the two branches of Wittgenstein's legacy today: the one being that of his *Tractatus* and the other that of his *Philosophical Investigations*.

c. A third essential moment is that of the appearance of "logical positivism" and "logical empiricism." The movement of the Vienna Circle, born informally in 1924 and endowed in 1929 with a manifesto entitled "The Scientific World-Conception" (see English translation in *The Emergence of Logical Empiricism*), takes up the opposition to idealism and metaphysics and amplifies it further, as well as the faith in the power of logic and the idea that the function of philosophy is to clarify the meaning of scientific statements and concepts. Associated with an analytic-synthetic distinction that is rejected by W. V. Quine in 1951, the different versions of the criterion of empirical verifiability (verifiability criterion of factual meaningfulness), whose first formulation by M. Schlick simply stated that the meaning of a statement was its means of verification, were tirelessly discussed between 1930 and around 1960—first in the context of the theory of protocol sentences and physicalism, then in that of the different conceptions of "testability," of confirmation, falsifiability, of the structure of the theories, and of reductionism.

d. Finally, a fourth moment that characterizes the tradition of epistemology is that which marks, at the end of the 1960s, the recognition of the failure of logical empiricism and the rather chaotic search for new directions. Leaving to one side the philosophy of mind and its debates about the new materialism, as well as the sociology of science, we may say that in the domain of the philosophy of science, the epistemology of the past twenty years has attempted in several ways to move beyond the opposition between a normative theory of knowledge and a skeptical or historicist conception. It is in this perspective that we must situate the debate over "scientific realism" and its alternatives—"antirealism," "constructive empiricism," "fictionalism"—or more technically, over conceptions of physical theories that are, respectively, syntactic, semantic, or structuralist.

▪ See Box 2.

C. "Untranslatability"

Given all this, is it still possible to translate *Erkenntnistheorie* by "epistemology," even though the latter is based on an open opposition to the German tradition of the analysis of the conditions of the possibility of knowledge, as well as on a collection of new theses in logic and the philosophy of language? No doubt the term *Erkenntnistheorie* was sufficiently broad to include numerous alternatives to Kantianism, from Helmoltz's theory of signs to the positivism of Schlick and the Vienna Circle, as well as to Cassirer's critique of culture. There is, however, a profound difference between the ways of posing the question of knowledge that respectively characterize *Erkenntnistheorie* and epistemology: the former beginning with a relationship between intuitions and concepts, and reflections concerning the mode of presentation of phenomena; the latter beginning with the analysis of language and the logical form of theories. This difference does not derive from anything essential to either language, nor to any grammatical characteristic of their structure. Some aspects of epistemology, indeed, were developed thanks to works (those of Frege, Wittgenstein, and Carnap) that are rooted in the German language. We might thus think that the existence of an "untranslatability" is primarily a sign of an evolution within philosophy itself, because of a recognition of the limits of the approaches of *Erkenntnistheorie* and the search for fundamental reformulations of the problem of knowledge.

III. Conclusion

What does the foregoing sketch of a map of words show? That if we allow that the alleged current loss of homogeneity in the vocabulary proper to philosophical discussions of science comes from a precise and datable break in the history of philosophy, then the most plausible hypothesis is one that locates this break at the beginning of the twentieth century, in the divisions made then between German *Erkenntnistheorie* and English "epistemology." The term *Erkenntnistheorie*, regardless of the diversity of its meanings, referred in German philosophical language to an approach whose aim was a determination of acts of objectification—that is, that would allow for an understanding of how the knowing subject transforms given phenomena into objects of knowledge. Opposed to this approach of objectification or constitution inherited from Kant, and providing a common language to the natural sciences up until the 1930s, the utterly different approach of epistemology is defined first by B. Russell and G. E. Moore by a polemical affirmation of "the independence of facts with regard to experience," and then develops in the direction of the logical analysis of language and the structure of physical theories. The untranslatability between the two traditions is, as it turns out, so large that the epistemology of German scholars between 1850 and 1930 was long suspected of being unintelligible in English-language words of philosophers of science after 1945, or it was simply ignored.

This division of the field by *Erkenntnistheorie* and epistemology is what this article has so far attempted to analyze. It remains to retrace more precisely the development of the numerous differences that have since deepened within languages, especially in French, where epistemology takes on a distinctive character with the introduction of theories of the nature of concepts supported by the history of science and a reflection on the notions of value and power (G. Bachelard, G. Canguilhem, M. Foucault). But it bears repeating that the break between *Erkenntnistheorie* and epistemology, if it marks a turning point, should not be viewed as the effect of an irreducible divergence between the philosophical thought of the two languages, or between traditions of thought that do not communicate with one another. In the 1930s, the term *Erkenntnistheorie* ended up referring to such a variety of positions that it could no longer strictly be associated with the Kantian approach in which it originally appeared. Similarly, in the 1970s, the term "epistemology" comes to refer to a variety of positions that are just as distant from Russell's original claims. The linguistic difference thus clearly expresses only a difference of perspective regarding the problems posed by discourse on science and the philosophy of knowledge since the first third of the twentieth century, under the influence of the crisis in logic, mathematics, and physics. These problems, in turn, are driving the search for very different avenues in philosophy even today, and it is natural that the untranslatability of these conceptual networks is revealed more strongly where the avenues have diverged the most.

▪ See Box 3.

Catherine Chevalley

2

Major trends in contemporary epistemology

Just as the term "knowledge" refers both to ordinary knowledge and to scientific knowledge, the word "epistemology"—from the Greek *epistêmê* [ἐπιστήμη], knowledge—refers to the theory of knowledge understood either in the narrow sense of a theory of scientific knowledge, or in the wider sense of a theory of knowledge without any distinction as to its objects. This latter sense is the more prevalent for the English term "epistemology," relating to the study of knowledge and the justification of belief, that is, what may be called the "theory of knowledge" and, in French, *gnoséologie*. In this sense of the term, science is neither the only nor even the primary domain of inquiry for epistemology, since the question of the justification of beliefs and knowledge is also raised in the ordinary case of judgment from perception, memory, or beliefs formed on the basis of testimony from others. Epistemology understood in this sense is not called upon to describe or to evaluate particular systems of argument or proof, but rather to make explicit what, exactly, constitutes justification for true beliefs, such that they achieve the status of knowledge. The concept of justification may itself be understood either as an "internalist" requirement, dealing with the characteristics of the knowing subject and the reasons he or she has for holding a given proposition true, or as an "externalist" demand that there be an appropriate link—causal, or more generally, nomological—between the knowing subject and the known object.

There are two ways of approaching epistemological problems: one is "normative" and seeks to clarify the principles that justify the rational acceptance of a belief; the other is "naturalist" and derives the status of a belief from the conditions in which it is acquired.

The normative sense of epistemology is subdivided into two trends. "Foundationalism" starts with the empiricist thesis according to which all knowledge derives from experience. In its strongest version, it maintains that all of our beliefs are built up from basic beliefs whose content is immediately given in sensory experience, and that beliefs about these contents of experience are infallible (R. Chisholm, *Theory of Knowledge*). The main

objection to foundationalism is that no belief is infallible. By believing that things seem to be thus, the subject is not infallible, since he or she may use the wrong term to qualify the experience. A weaker version of foundationalism posits that certain beliefs have prima facie justification, that is, they may be contradicted by other, subsequently acquired true beliefs (they are "defeasible").

"Coherentism" maintains, for its part, that the system of beliefs is not deployed in an asymmetrical way from basic beliefs obtained through perception up to inferred beliefs, but rather constitutes a coherent totality of mutually explanatory beliefs: no belief is in principle "immune to revision" (K. Lehrer, *Knowledge*). From the coherentist point of view, justification is a question of degree, which depends on the support given to each belief by the others. The rules of inference, equally, find their justification in the increase in coherence resulting from their adoptions. Fallibilism does not constitute a defect, as it does in foundationalism, but is rather an integral part of the work of revising beliefs in order to achieve greater coherence. Coherentism, unlike foundationalism, considers the acquisition of knowledge to be a social phenomenon: the testimony of others can increase the coherence of a system of beliefs and its degree of justification.

These two normative currents were endangered in spectacular fashion by E. Gettier ("Is Justified True Belief Knowledge?). In a three-page article, the author shows that a true belief may be derived from a proposition that is "justified" but false. Gettier thus shows that the truth of the belief in question, which is justified from the foundationalist and from the coherentist points of view, is a matter of coincidence—and we cannot call such a belief "knowledge." The normative tradition has responded to Gettier by offering a theory of defeasibility (according to which knowledge is a justified true belief that is not defeasible by other truths).

Naturalist epistemology has, for its part, adopted a different strategy, consisting in the search for the properties of a process that leads to the formation of knowledge. We may again discern several meanings covered by the term "naturalist epistemology," depending on the

part played, respectively, by rational evaluation and the pursuit of truth or the description of psychological and social processes of knowledge formation. The naturalist/evaluative trend explores the notion of a "reliable" method of belief acquisition by examining the cognitive properties that allow the subject to deal with information and to reason (A. Goldman, *Epistemology and Cognition*). "Social epistemology" pursues this "reliabilist" approach, while extending the role of social factors in the formation and justification of beliefs.

"Evolutionary epistemology" (the term comes from Donald T. Campbell) places epistemic norms in the context of the history of approaches and the choice of theories. Karl Popper, one of the philosophers who reinvigorated this Darwinian-inspired trend, developed all the consequences according to a strictly "falsificationist" point of view, according to which knowledge (scientific or ordinary) consists in hypotheses that have survived competition.

The most descriptive sense of naturalist epistemology attaches to the attempt to retrace the stages of development of operational and conceptual capacities at work in knowledge, which inspired the genetic epistemologist Jean Piaget. It is often objected that the neutralization of the critical and reflective dimension of epistemological inquiry forces the term "epistemology" to undergo a semantic mutation that goes beyond what doctrinal flexibility may authorize.

Joëlle Proust

BIBLIOGRAPHY

Chisholm, Roderick. *Theory of Knowledge.* Englewood Cliffs, NJ: Prentice Hall, 1966.
Goldmann, Alvin. *Epistemology and Cognition.* Cambridge, MA: Harvard University Press, 1986.
———. *Knowledge in the Social World.* Oxford: Oxford University Press, 1999.
Lehrer, Keith. *Knowledge.* Oxford: Oxford University Press, 1972.
Piaget, Jean, ed. *Logique et connaissance scientifique.* Paris: Gallimard, 1967.
Popper, Karl. *Objective Knowledge, an Evolutionary Approach.* Rev. ed. Oxford: Oxford University Press. 1979.

3

"Knowledge," *savoir*, and *epistêmê*

➤ DOXA

Though the works of Michel Foucault have received a great deal of attention in English-speaking countries, it has largely focused on

his questioning of the established order of dominant morality, and only to a lesser degree on the critical aim of his approach to the

sciences. The specifically epistemological import of his work has not excited much interest, and remains largely ignored (or a subject of irony) by specialists in the history of science. On the continent, on the other hand, and especially in France, it has had lasting influence. No doubt the works of Bachelard and Canguilhem prepared the way: they drew attention to the notion of epistemological rupture, and the latter taught that we should use caution when handling the notions of a precursor or a source, if we wish to avoid the retrospective illusion that consists in retaining from the past only what might foreshadow a future that leads to our present. However, is this only a matter of opposing schools of thought and context? It may also be that what can seem imprecise or even confused in Foucault's work is accentuated by the necessity of translating it, because of subtle differences in the senses of certain key terms.

The first of them is *savoir*. The most natural and most legitimate term to render it is "knowledge." But is this an exact equivalent? *Knowledge* is dominated by the notions of acquaintance and understanding (*connaissance*). There is, first, a subjective sense: that of which we have experience, of which we are informed, or which we have learned; second, an objective sense: that which is the material of experience, information, or learning. In both cases, it is a matter of positive cognition, whether empirical, factual, theoretical, or scientific. There are various meanings for *savoir*. However, where English uses a single term, *to know*, French has two, *savoir* and *connaître*, which are not always interchangeable. To say that one knows Pierre, *connaît* may be used, *sait* may not (except in a nuanced way of indicating that one knows which Pierre is "ours"). On the other hand, to say that we know Pierre has arrived, *sait* is used, not *connaît*. From this difference, there arise semantic distinctions that are difficult to translate.

Savoir indicates a more performative state than *connaître*, which implies the intellectual grasping of an objective given. To know-*savoir* a language is to be able to understand it, to speak it, to read it, and write it a little; to know-*connaître* a language is to have a grasp of its vocabulary and grammar such as may lead to an inspired vision of it—it is to have a more or less reflective consciousness of what it is. It is not for nothing that we translate *know-how* by *savoir-faire* and not by *connaissance du comment*. *Savoir* relates to a technical and cultural domain that one has mastered; *connaissance* relates to reasons one has to think that one's beliefs are true. The distinction is present starting with classical French: "And anyway, as for bad doctrines, I considered myself already to know [*connaître*] well enough what they were worth, so that I would no longer be deceived, not by the promises of an alchemist, nor by the predictions of an astrologer, nor by the magician's fraud, nor by the artifices or puffery

of any of those who claim to know [*savoir*] more than they know [*plus qu'ils savent*]" (R. Descartes, *Discours de la méthode*).

It is not a recent development that *savoir* refers to a cultural achievement conferring prestige and power on its possessor, which may or may not derive from objective understanding (*connaissance*).

Foucault deepened this distinction between *savoir* and *connaissance* by contrasting the depersonalized anonymity of knowledge-*savoir* in which one moves after having found it already built up (it is a historical a priori that we all appropriate for ourselves) with the subject of knowledge-*connaissance* in classical theories (empiricism, critical philosophy, and so on), going by degrees from perceptual awareness to conceptualization and science.

Rather than running along the consciousness-knowledge (*connaissance*)-science axis (which cannot be freed from the index of subjectivity), archaeology runs along the practical axis of discourse-knowledge (*savoir*)-science. And, while the history of ideas finds the equilibrium of its analysis in the element of knowledge-*connaissance* (finding itself thus forced, even against its will, to meet with transcendental interrogation), archaeology finds its equilibrium point in knowledge-*savoir*—that is, in a domain where the subject is necessarily situated and dependent, without ever being able to be the owner (either through transcendental activity, or empirical consciousness).

(M. Foucault, *L'Archéologie du savoir*; trans. A. M. Sheridan Smith, *Archeology of Knowledge*)

Of course, Foucault includes under knowledge-*savoir* everything left unsaid concerning the order in which things are classified in a given culture, changes that lead to decisive transformations.

What we would like to uncover is the epistemological field, the *epistémê* where understandings (*connaissances*), seen outside of any criteria referring to their rational value or their objective forms, bury their positivity and thus manifest a history which is not that of their increasing perfection but rather that of their conditions of possibility. . . . Rather than a history in the traditional sense of the word, it is an "archaeology."

(Ibid.)

However, the choice of the term *epistémê* to refer to an *epistemological field* that makes knowledge of a certain type possible, to the exclusion of others (the analysis of wealth and not political economy, natural history

and not biology, and so forth) was an unhappy one: in Greek, *epistémê* usually refers to knowledge and science, whereas the term here refers, by contrast, to the historical a priori without which they cannot be built up. Besides, as Foucault indicated himself (*L'Archéologie du savoir*, 27), "the absence of methodological markers may have created the belief in analyses in terms of cultural totalities," further blurring the initial intention.

Foucault's analysis of knowledge-*savoir* remains, in addition, nourished by the continental conception of philosophy and the theory of knowledge. No doubt he repeats often enough his rejection of anything that might recall the primacy of the subject, and in his critique of a history of ideas he places the transcendental point of view of an underlying subject on the same level as the empiricist point of view of a genesis of the known entity from a sensation that is supposedly its origin. But this double rejection in fact masks a false symmetry. For, with the notion of an a priori, he takes up in terms of cultural historicity what was dealt with in the Kantian tradition in terms of human nature, and thus goes further than Kant in affirming the idea of a preconstituted rationality that organizes experience, in opposition to the Lockean *tabula rasa*. A given epistemological field, even if it characterizes a culture and is transitory, even if it is a question of things left implicit that must be discerned by the analysis of the archaeologist, is the directing element of interpretation of the data for the people of that time, and what determines the distribution and the norms of their statements. This presence of a *tertium quid* between the said and the perceived puts Foucault at the furthest remove from logical positivism and analytic philosophy.

Thus, between Foucault's *savoir* and the term "knowledge," there is a deep divide, for reasons that are both semantic and philosophical, which may have produced reactions of incomprehension and rejection—especially in the domain of epistemology, where his contribution remains largely unknown in English-speaking countries.

Gérard Simon

BIBLIOGRAPHY

Descartes, René. *Discours de la méthode*. Vol. 6, Part I. Edited by C. Adam and P. Tannery. Paris: Vrin, 1973. First published 1637.
Foucault, Michel. *Les mots et les choses*. Paris : Gallimard, 1966. English translation: *The Order of Things: An Archaeology of the Human Science*. Reprint. London: Routledge, 2002.
———. *L'archéologie du savoir*. Paris: Gallimard, 1969. Translation by A. M. Sheridan Smith: *Archeology of Knowledge*. New York: Pantheon Books, 1972.

BIBLIOGRAPHY

Bohr, Niels. *Atomic Physics and Human Knowledge*. New York: Wiley, 1958.

Cassirer, Ernst. *Das Erkenntnisproblem in der Philosophie und Wissenschaft der neueren Zeit*. Berlin: B. Cassirer, 1906–7. Translation by W. H. Woglom and C. W. Hendel: *The Problem of Knowledge: Philosophy, Science, and History since Hegel*. New Haven, CT: Yale University Press, 1950.

Chevalley, Catherine. "Hermann von Helmholtz." In *Routledge Encyclopedia of Philosophy*. Edited by Edward Craig. London: Routledge and Kegan Paul, 1998.

Diemer, Alwin, and Carl Friedrich Gethmann. "Erkenntnistheorie, Erkenntnislehre, Erkenntniskritik." Vol. 2 of *Historisches Wörterbuch der Philosophie*, edited by J. Ritter. Basel: Schwabe, 1972.

Fichant, Michel. "L'épistémologie en France." Pp. 135–78 in *Histoire de la philosophie. Le XXème siècle*, edited by F. Châtelet. Paris: Hachette, 1973.

Gettier, Edmund. "Is Justified Belief Knowledge?" *Analysis* 23 (1963): 121–23.

Husserl, Edmund. *Logical Investigations*. Translated by Dermot Moran. London: Routledge, 2001.

Köhnke, Klaus. *Entstehung und Aufstieg des Neukantianismus*. Frankfurt: Suhrkamp, 1986. Translation by R. J. Hollingdale: *The Rise of Neo-Kantianism*. Cambridge: Cambridge University Press, 1991.

Krug, W. T. *Allgemeines Handwörterbuch der philosophischen Wissenschaften*. 2nd ed. Leipzig: Brockhaus, 1832. First published in 1827.

Nelson, Leonard. *Die Unmöglichkeit der Erkenntnistheorie*. In *Gesammelte Schriften*, edited by P. Bernays et al. Hamburg: Meiner, 1970–77. *Die Unmöglichkeit der Erkenntnistheorie* first published in 1911.

Orth, Ernst Wolfgang. *Von der Erkenntnistheorie zur Kulturphilosophie*. Würzburg, Ger.: Königshauen und Neumann, 1996.

Papineau, David, ed. *The Philosophy of Science*. Oxford Readings in Philosophy. Oxford: Oxford University Press, 1996.

Russell, B. Russell, Bertrand. *An Essay on the Foundations of Geometry*. London: Routledge, 1996.

———. "My Mental Development." In *The Philosophy of Bertrand Russell*, edited by P. A. Schilpp. Evanston, IL: Northwestern University Press, 1944.

Sarkar, Sahotra, ed. *The Emergence of Logical Empiricism: From 1900 to the Vienna Circle*. New York: Garland Publishing, 1996.

Schlick, Moritz. *General Theory of Knowledge*. Translated by Albert E. Blumberg. Peru, IL: Open Court Books, 1985. First published in Germany in 1918.

Suppe, Frederick, ed. Introduction to *The Structure of Scientific Theories*. Chicago: Illinois University Press, 1977. First published in 1973.

Van Fraassen, Bas C. *Laws and Symmetry*. Oxford: Oxford University Press, 1989.

EPOCHÊ [ἐποχή] (GREEK)

ENGLISH	epochê
FRENCH	epokhê
GERMAN	epochè

➤ CONSCIOUSNESS and BELIEF, EPISTEMOLOGY, ERLEBEN, GREEK, OBJECT, PERCEPTION, PHANTASIA, *PHÉNOMÈNE*, REPRÉSENTATION, TRUTH

This Greek term, which originates in ancient skepticism and is taken up with slight modifications by Stoicism, literally means "stop, interruption, rupture" and has endured through the centuries in its original linguistic form. It is used frequently by Montaigne as early as the sixteenth century but especially by Husserl in the twentieth, without either substituting a standard French or German term. The question is thus: why choose this Greek term? Why was it preserved in its initial form, without ever being translated?

I. The Two Greek Sources for *Epochê*: A Double Inflexion

A. From Skeptical suspension to Stoic assent

Epochê [ἐποχή] is a central term for ancient Skepticism. Introduced into philosophy by the Pyrrhonian school, it refers to the stopping of all search for truth, which corresponds to a decisive step in attaining happiness. In effect, the Pyrrhonist finds himself initially destabilized by the variety of philosophical systems, which contradict one another. Trying in vain to discover which one is true, he resolves to cease (*epeschen* [ἐπέσχεν]) looking—makes a stop (*epochê*)—and in doing so discovers ataraxia, the peace of the soul (Sextus Empiricus, *Outlines of Skepticism*, I: 49): "Suspension of judgment gets its name from the fact that the intellect is suspended (*epechesthai* [ἐπέχεσθαι])."

In its Skeptical meaning *epechein* [ἐπέχειν] is used in the intransitive sense of "to stop" or "to cease," but it may also be used in the transitive sense of "to stop judging" or "to withhold one's judgment." It is this transitive sense that is later taken up by the Stoic academician Archesilas: "I suspend my judgment" here means "I abandon any claim to truth" or again, "I consent to not knowing as long as I do not have complete certainty." In effect, in the Stoic doctrine as Cicero presents it (*Academica priora*, II: 59; *Letters to Atticus*, XIII: 21), the freedom of the sage comes from his capacity not to make rushed (*propetôs* [προπετῶς]) judgments, that is, to restrain himself from giving his assent (*assensus*) as long as he is not entirely certain of his possession of the truth.

B. Assent and suspension: The later Pyrrhonism

In Sextus Empiricus (Hossenfelder, *Einleitung*, 54ff.), we find the two semantic inflections of *epochê* mixed together. There is the initial Skeptical sense, that is, the stopping of all search for truth because of the contradictions among different philosophical systems, and the later Stoic sense, that is, the ethical requirement not to affirm anything, not to assent to anything as long as absolute certainty concerning truth is not established, which can, in fact, lead to the same result: suspension extended to all judgment.

Such is the syncretic position of the late Pyrrhonist Aenesidemus, who combines Stoic suspension of judgment with the skeptical arrest in the face of contradiction among different positions, while at the same time eliminating the ethical dimension peculiar to Stoicism. By doing so, he comes very close to the initial Skeptical position (Sextus Empiricus, *Outlines of Skepticism*).

II. From Antiquity to the Present Day: Montaigne

> Their sacramental word is *epechô*, that is, I stay still, I do not move. That is their refrain, and others of similar substance. Their effect is that of a pure, complete, and perfect surcease and suspension of judgment.
>
> (Montaigne, "Apologie de Raimond Sebond," *Essais*, Bk. 2, chap. 12, ed. Strowski, 2: 229–30)

The "epechists," as he calls them, are characterized by their immobilism ("I do not move"), and consequently by the fact that they abstain from making any judgment whatsoever ("a perfect surcease"). In this sense Montaigne inherits immobilism from Skepticism, and from the Stoics the suspension of judgment made in full freedom. In any case he paraphrases *epechô*, rather than translating it.

III. The Central Methodological Role of *Epochê* in Husserl's Phenomenology: What Legacy, What Continuity?

The importance accorded by Husserl to *epochê* in its ancient Greek origin may be seen through his abundant use of the Greek term, accompanied, depending on context, by "phenomenological," "transcendental," or even "ethical" adjectives (no fewer than thirty occurrences in the Lectures of 1923–1924 of *First Philosophy* alone): a recent work is devoted to the Skeptical theme of suspension in phenomenology, including its meaning of suspicion (March). Further, the forty-third lesson, which contains the first occurrence of *epochê* in the lectures, analyzes the activity of the spectator who abstains from acting and from manifesting an interest in the objects of the world, who thereby suspends all belief in the world. However, the Stoic origin of phenomenological *epochê* is equally attested (Migniosi); finally, it has been clearly shown how Husserl both based his model directly on the Cartesian method of doubt as a source and radically modified its import without, nevertheless, returning to Skeptical *epochê* (Lowit). Phenomenological *epochê* is a complex act that retains characteristics at least of its three sources, while also freeing itself from them in order to present its own originality. This is probably one of the reasons for which Husserl retains the Greek term.

A. *Ausschaltung*: Placing the object's existence out of bounds

Husserl retains from Skeptical *epochê* the move of halting, interrupting the flow of our natural attitude by an act that removes our contradictory beliefs and prejudices from the field (March), what Merleau-Ponty calls in the *Phenomenology of Perception* the "faith of the world" (371). It is, in fact, a question of placing objects out of bounds, of excluding them, with respect to the validity of their contingent existence. However, though Skeptical *epochê* throws radical doubt on the truth of any given object, phenomenological *epochê* consists simply in abstaining from positing the existence of the object.

B. *In Klammer Setzung*: Bracketing the character of being of the object

What remains is only the object's meaning for me. There is also a methodical dimension that comes back to Cartesian doubt; the latter, however, is provisional (I doubt in order to leave doubt behind), whereas phenomenological *epochê*, like skeptical *epochê*, is definitive: the suspension is an attitude that I adopt in a lasting way (Lowit).

Though it involves putting aside the contingent existence of the object, this is in order to better include the sense of its being for me. The object is literally bracketed insofar as it is for me an appearance in flesh and bone.

C. *Beschränkung*, not *Einschränkung*: Liberation, not delimitation, of the immanent sphere of pure consciousness

Such is the deep meaning of *epochê*: the liberation of a pure field of consciousness whose objects are invested with meaning and are not realities that remain external to it. Such a liberation with regard to objectivism allows the ethical import of *epochê* to shine through, which takes place, in fact, in complete freedom. This is a feature that recalls the early Stoic meaning (Migniosi), which presupposes the reflective activity of a subject put to the test of a decision that has matured over a long period of time: that of not assenting until the evidence of truth is truly undeniable.

Natalie Depraz

BIBLIOGRAPHY

Claesges, Ulrich. "Epochè." In J. Ritter and K. Gründer, *Historisches Wörterbuch der Philosophie*, 595–96. Vol. 2, Basel, Switz.: Schwabe, 1972; Vol. 4, Darmstadt, Ger.: Wissenschaftliche Buchgesellschaft, 1976.

Couissin, Paul. "L'origine et l'évolution de l'épochè." *Revue des Études Grecques* 42 (1929): 373–97.

Hossenfelder, Malte. *Einleitung zu Sextus Empiricus, Grundriß der pyrrhonischen Skepsis*. Frankfurt: Surhkamp, 1968.

———. "Epochè." In J. Ritter and K. Gründer, *Historisches Wörterbuch der Philosophie*, 594–95. Vol. 2, Basel, Switz.: Schwabe, 1972; Vol. 4, Darmstadt, Ger.: Wissenschaftliche Buchgesellschaft, 1976.

Husserl, Edmund. *Husserliana*, Vols. 1, 2, 3, 6, 8, 9, 10. Dordrecht, Neth.: Kluwer, 1950–1968.

Lowit, Alexandre. "L'épochè de Husserl et le doute de Descartes." *Revue de Métaphysique et de Morale* 4 (1957): 2–17.

March, J. L. "Dialectical Phenomenology: From Suspension to Suspicion." *Man and World* 17, no. 2 (1984): 121–42.

Merleau-Ponty, Maurice. *Phénoménologie de la perception*. Paris: Gallimard, 1945. Translation by C. Smith: *Phenomenology of Perception*. New York: Humanities Press, 1962.

Migniosi. "Reawakening and Resistance: The Stoic Source of Husserlian Épochè." *Analect Husserliana* 11 (1981): 311–19.

Montaigne, Michel Eyquem de. *Essais* 2, edited by Fortunat Strowski. Bordeaux, Fr.: F. Pech, 1906. Translation by J. M. Cohen: *Essays* 2. New York: Penguin Books, 1993.

Sextus Empiricus. *Outlines of Skepticism*. Translated by J. Annas and J. Barnes. Cambridge: Cambridge University Press, 1994.

Ströker, Elizabeth. *Das Problem der Epochè in der Philosophie Edmund Husserls*. Dordrecht, Neth.: Kluwer, 1970.

EREIGNIS (GERMAN)

| ENGLISH | event, appropriation, surprise |
| FRENCH | *événement, appropriation, appropriement, sidération, amêmement* |

➤ *APPROPRIATION*, *EVENT*, and *DESTINY*, ES GIBT, OIKEIÔSIS, PROPERTY, TRUTH, VORHANDEN

Ereignis, the key word in Heidegger's thought from 1936 onward, is an equivocal term, which makes it difficult to translate into other languages. "Event," the standard sense of *Ereignis*, does not capture the other dimensions that Heidegger associates with the word, those of an appropriation (*Ereignung*) and of a demonstration (*Eräugnis*, from *das Auge* ["eye"]). It is a case in which the standard sense of a word hides the depth of its philosophical import.

I. Semantic Arc: To Display, to Show, to Show Oneself, to Occur

"*Ereignis* since 1936, the leading term of my thought": this comment by Heidegger (*Gesamtausgabe*, vol. 9, 1976) raises questions concerning the meaning of this *Leitwort* (leading term) from the middle of the 1930s, with the *Beiträge zur Philosophie* of 1936–1938 (*Gesamtausgabe*, vol. 65), which were published only in 1989. The subtitle, *Vom Ereignis*, in fact, announces "the real title of the 'work,' which only finds its start here." *Ereignis* is not the object of the *Beiträge* at all but rather the origin (*von*). Heidegger is not using the term here in its standard sense of "event" (Ger. *Bege-benheit, Vorkommnis*, or *Geschehnis*, "that which has happened," "what took place") but rather in terms of *eigen*, "one's own," or even *Er-äug-nis*, "what is placed before one's eyes."

"*Er-eignis* (as long as we understand *eignis* from *eigen*: what is one's own, proper to one) means the movement that leads to being properly one-self" (Fédier, *Regarder voir*). In this sense *Ereignis* means an "appropriation," which presupposes the contrary possibility of a dis-appropriation (*Ent-eignis*). This term retrospectively clarifies the pair *Eigentlichkeit/Uneigentlichkeit*, laid out in paragraph 9 of *Sein und Zeit*: "propriety/impropriety," rather than "authenticity/inauthenticity," since Heidegger has already distinguished an *unechte Eigentlichkeit* (inauthentic proper-being) and an *echte Uneigentlichkeit* (improperly being in an authentic way) (*Gesamtausgabe*, vol. 21, 1976). The *Eigentlichkeit* of 1927 is itself not possible except through *Er-eignis* (*Gesamtausgabe*, vol. 66, 1997), in "the captious figure, in fact already ap-propiated [*er-eignete*] from 'fundamental ontology'" (ibid.).

Nevertheless, as Wolfgang Brokmeier emphasized, *Ereignis* recalls, even more properly speaking, *Eräugnis*, from the verb *eräugen*, which the *Deutsches Wörterbuch* by the Grimm brothers paraphrases using *vor Augen stellen* (to place before the eyes) or in Latin *ostendere, manifestare*.

> The matrix of the meaning is indeed the verb *äugen*, which also used to be written *eugen* or *eigen*. There are thus two homonyms whose meaning must not be confused: one is (like the English *own*) the indication of what is proper to one, whereas the other indicates the fact of *placing something before one's eyes*. To use *Ereignis* in a sense faithful to its etymology requires above all retaining the ostensive aspect that is manifested in it.
>
> (Fédier, *Regarder voir*, 116)

Though the translation of this leading term of Heidegger's late thought seems certainly to be thoroughly insufficient, the one that is most commonly offered in its place, "appropriation," which emphasizes the root *eigen*, proper, is just as insufficient.

> (Romano, *L'événement et le monde*)

Ereignis (event, appropriation—Kahn: "propriation") comes from *eräugen*—thus, *Auge* ["eye"]—to look at fixedly, "to astonish [*sidérer*]," and from *eigen*: "properly." That which is grasped by *Ereignis* is not alienated but transformed into what it has most properly.... *Ereignis* is thus event, arrival, "appropriating astonishment [*sidération*], the fact of being looked at, concerned by, deeply touched. It is the permanence of a look. Cf. in Greek: Μοῖρα [*Moira*].

> (Beaufret, *Leçons de Philosophie*, 1:27)

II. Import of the Term

Ereignis pertains to us and takes hold of us before we can exercise or influence anything at all, just like that which constitutes "in a way the photographic negative" (*Gesamtausgabe*, 15: 366, 1986) of the essence of modern technique, interpreted by Heidegger as *Ge-stell*.

But what pertains to us is not necessarily what we are looking at. It is not even rare that we lack a view of what pertains to us properly speaking. It is not a chance happening nor a regrettable failure, but a structure, and Heidegger's thought reserves the term *Ereignis* for that structure. What pertains to us is never reducible to what we look at, but inversely, we would be unable to look at anything if there were not something that pertained to us which we were not looking at.

> (David, "Heidegger," 104–5)

The thought about *Ereignis* takes us back to the foundation of modern philosophy, considered as a "metaphysics of subjectivity." In this sense it consists in "restoring to being what makes it into something other than an object. That which makes it the case that water is not a simple liquid, for example, or light a simple lighting; that nothing, in a word, is trapped in functionality. The manifestation of the independence and of the gratuitousness of everything which is—that is precisely what Heidegger successively called *being* and later *event* (Crétella, *Heidegger Studies*, 9:70).

As for translation, however, the event-related or eventual dimension that comes into the foreground in the standard sense of *Ereignis* in German does not authorize us to translate it in Heidegger by "event," rather the contrary. We would have to be able to indicate both the appropriating (*Er-eignung*) and the ostensive (*Eräugnis*) dimensions at the same time. We should note, finally, that if the leading term of *Ereignis* becomes such from the middle of the 1930s in Heidegger's thought, this coincides with that thought's becoming open to poetry, in an elective relationship with Hölderlin's poetry, whose *Mnémosyne* made emphatic use of *Ereignis* and *sich ereignen*.

The difficulty of the thinking concerning *Ereignis* comes no doubt in part from the fact that it resists any thoughts about causality, even divine causality, as is emphasized by a passage from Heidegger's *On the Way to Language*:

> What Appropriation [*Ereignis*] yields through Saying is never the effect of a cause, nor the consequences of an antecedent.... What is yielding is Appropriation itself— and nothing else [*Das Ereignende ist das Ereignis selbst—und nichts außerdem*].... There is nothing else from which the Appropriation itself could be derived, even less in whose terms it could be explained. The appropriating event is not the outcome (result [*Ergebnis*]) of something else, but the giving yield [*die Er-gebnis*], whose giving reach alone is what gives us such things as an "es gibt."

Reflection from and of *Ereignis*, which must not be confused with reflection that has *Ereignis* as its object, tilts toward the dimension of the *Es gibt*, "there is," as irreducible to a disguised form of exchange and even to a gesture whose initiative comes only from the human being. The resistance of the term to translation does not come from complexity but rather from a strange simplicity, from its singular equivocity. As Heidegger says in *Identity and Difference*, "As such, it is just as untranslatable as the Greek *Logos* or the Chinese *Tao*."

Pascal David

BIBLIOGRAPHY

Beaufret, Jean. *Leçons de Philosophie*. Paris: Éditions du Seuil, 1998.

Brokmeier, Wolfgang. "Heidegger und wir." *Genos* (Lausanne, 1992): 61–95.

Crétella, H. *Heidegger Studies* 9:63–75. Berlin: Duncker und Humblot, 1993.

David, Pascal. "Heidegger, la vérité en question." In *La Vérité*, edited by R. Quilliot. Paris: Ellipses, 1997.

Dreyfus, Hubert L. *Being-in-the-World*. Cambridge, MA: MIT Press, 1991.

Fédier, François. *Regarder voir*. Paris: Les Belles Lettres-Archimbaud, 1995.

Guignon, Charles B., ed. *The Cambridge Companion to Heidegger*. Cambridge: Cambridge University Press, 1993.

Heidegger, Martin. *Beiträge zur Philosophie; vom Ereignis*. In *Gesamtausgabe*, vol. 65. Frankfurt: Klostermann, 1989.

———. *Gesamtausgabe*. Frankfurt am Main: Vittorio Klostermann, 1976–2011.

———. *Unterwegs zur Sprache*. Translation by P. Hertz: *On the Way to Language*. New York: Harper and Row, 1971.

Padrutt, Hanspeter. *Und sie bewegt sich doch nicht*. Zurich: Diogenes, 1991.

Romano, Claude. *L'événement et le monde*. Paris: Presses Universitaires de France, 1998. Translation by S. Mackinley: *Event and World*. New York: Fordham University Press, 2009.

ERLEBEN / ERLEBNIS (GERMAN)

ENGLISH	to live, to experience, lived experience
FRENCH	*vivre, faire l'experience, faire l'épreuve, le vécu*
GREEK	*biônai* [βιῶναι], *zôê* [ζωή], *bios* [βίος]
SPANISH	*vivir, experimentar, vivencia*

➤ *EXPERIENCE, LIFE/LEBEN,* and ANIMAL, CONSCIOUSNESS, DASEIN, EPOCHÊ, INTENTION, LEIB, PATHOS, POLIS

Does life reside in the simple fact of living? Is it natural life as given and nothing more, an experience of the immediate? How did the various languages fashion this simple and self-blind fact of living? They attempted to grasp its modes of deployment, whether in communities (as inscribed in the Greek *polis* [πολις] or the practical sociability of the *Lebenswelt*) or as individuals (its reflexive interiorization or its "meaning for me," which the terms "experience" and "existence" also state in their own ways). From *Leben* to *Erleben* and *Erfahrung*, from life to experience, from *zôê* [ζωή] to *bios* [βίος], such a mediation can be seen. Romance languages, which have only one word for life (e.g., *vie*), seem to have folded an excess of life into itself, which seems constitutive of it by means of the term "experience." Does the latter suffice to cover this spectrum?

I. The First Sense of *Erleben*: A Manifestation of the Given

In both its current meaning as well as its classical definitions, whether in the scholarly philosophy of the eighteenth century—in romantic thought or in German idealism (from Kant to Hegel)—or in nineteenth-century psychology, *erleben* is practically indistinct from *leben*, "to live." *Erleben* is characterized by immediacy, immanence, and passivity, which equally define the simple fact of living, as opposed to the abstract meditation represented by reflection and speculation (RT: *Historisches Wörterbuch der Philosophie*). This is the case of the proverb: *wir werden es ja erleben* (lit., we shall live to see it). More often, nevertheless, the word is translated into French by appealing to the paradigm of experience rather than to that of life. Thus, *ich habe etwas erlebt* becomes, in addition to *j'ai vécu ceci ou cela, j'ai fait telle experience, j'ai connu tel événement*. Similarly, *das war ein Erlebnis: c'était une expérience*

(*marquante*), whereas German makes immediate reference to a cognitive, though elementary, process (*etwas erfahren*: to learn something, even by hearsay). In fact, in all these contexts, an intimate experience whose meaning escapes us is privileged (RT: *Deutsches Wörterbuch*, vol. 12, "Leben"). Having a given of this sort within us pushes us beyond ourselves. We thus live every day without reflecting upon what is lived or appreciating the intertwining of these individual experiences with the social and political context, which is always present, if sometimes unperceived.

Only toward the middle of the nineteenth century did *Erlebnis* acquire conceptual significance and find itself bound up with the fundamental notions of the theory of knowledge. In this respect, Fichte is the precursor, who noted the implicit transitional moment where the subject forgets himself in a state of unreflective fullness, by the conjunctive expression *leben und erleben* (*Sonnenklarer Berich*). The first, remarkably precocious, definition of *Erlebnis* is found in the third edition of Krug's *Enzyklopädisches Lexikon* of 1838: "*Erlebnis* means everything one has oneself lived [*erlebt*]: felt, seen, thought, wanted, done, or allowed to happen. Such experiences are by consequence the foundation of internal experience [*eigene Erfahrung*]." Following him, Lotze tends to use *Erlebnis* in his 1841 work *Metaphysik* as a synonym for "interiority," whereas Dilthey, in the framework of a veritable "theory of *Erlebnis*" makes it equivalent to "psychic" (*Einleitung*).

Phenomenology makes this psychic and internal life its central theme: *Erlebnis* is understood as a subjective immanent experience that nevertheless, in order to be known and thus communicated, must be linked to the world through the axis of intentionality, which gives sense and reference to objects. An *Erlebnis* without intentional reference cannot be treated as an object, that is, it cannot be known. Nor is *Erleben* an isolated experience of the subject, but rather is part of the intentional and temporal dynamics of consciousness, which links one *Erlebnis* to the next.

■ See Box 1.

Under the subsidiary expressions of "natural attitude," of "flux of experiences" (*Erlebnisstrom* [Husserl]; cf. RT: *Historisches Wörterbuch der Philosophie*, "Erlebnisstrom"), of "perceptual faith," of Merleau-Ponty's "recomprehension" (*Le visible et l'invisible*), and of Husserlian *Erlebnis*, phenomenologists attempted to capture this highly peculiar quality of our presence in the world as subjects. We are, in effect, living beings who are always behind in our capacity to make what we live from day to day explicit.

II. The Reflexive Mediation of *Erleben*

However, to live is only the simple fact of living for a living thing without self-consciousness, that is, reflexivity. In this respect, German has a term that captures this pure life without self-consciousness: *dahinleben*, which is judiciously translated into French as *végéter*. Though plants are living things without self-consciousness, we cannot say the same for animals, which do indeed have an immanent consciousness of themselves that is visible in the way they displace themselves and nourish themselves and in the different forms of social life they manifest.

Phenomenology gave itself the task of describing this folding-over that life does upon itself, in which I consciously

---

1

The Spanish translation of *erleben* by *vivencia*

It was started by Ortega y Gasset. Translating the first volume of the *Ideas Pertaining to a Pure Phenomenology and to a Phenomenological Philosophy*, he renders *Erlebnis* by *vivencia*, thus choosing an immanentist interpretation of experience, as opposed to a reflexive one. In this regard, if we were translating *vivencia* back into French, we would do so by way of *vivacité* rather than *vécu* (experience).

Javier San Martin, an active Spanish phenomenologist, perpetuates this choice of translation in *La estructura del metodo fenomenologico*. Jorge Semprun, a contemporary writer, has the following judicious note regarding the different translations of *Erlebnis* in French and Spanish (*L'écriture ou la vie*):

In German, there is *Erlebnis*. In Spanish, *vivencia*. However, there is no French word to grasp at one blow the notion of life as experience itself. They must resort to periphrasis, or use the word "*vécu*," which is approximative. And disputable. It is a weak and soft word. First and foremost, it is passive. And in the past tense. The experience of life, however, which life has by itself, of itself while living, is active. And in the present, necessarily. This is to say that it is nourished by the past in order to project itself into the future.

In sum, Spanish grasped what French missed in *Erlebnis*, namely, pure living, whereas French, when translating the German, stops with a simple nonprocessive *vécu*.

BIBLIOGRAPHY

Ortega y Gasset, José. *Investigaciones psicologicas*. Madrid: Revista de Occidente en Alianza Editorial, 1979. Translation by J. Garcia-Gomez: *Psychological Investigations*. New York: W. W. Norton, 1987.
San Martin, Javier. *La estructura del metodo fenomenologico*. Madrid: Universidad de Educacion a Distancia, 1986.
Semprun, Jorge. *L'écriture ou la vie*. Paris: Gallimard, 1994. Translation by L. Coverdale: *Literature or Life*. New York: Viking, 1997.

---

perceive myself living a given moment of my life. Thus the German term *Erlebnis*, in addition, expresses a state rather than an action. Its translation by the past participle *vécu* captures this moment of arrest, practically in the past, in which I perceive that "I have lived." There is discontinuity between the blind push of life, which generates itself, emerges from itself, and the consciousness we have of it (Henry, *C'est moi*; Varela, *Principles*) in a temporality of the moment after, however immediate. Reflexivity (in its dynamic *in statu nascendi*) is constitutive of the apprehension of life, as is the case for Lipps with the notion of natural epoch (*Psychologie des Schönen*). For Husserl, who takes up this notion of immanent life from Lipps (*Erleben/Ausleben*), life appears constantly in his writing, whether it is to characterize consciousness (*Bewußtseinsleben*), its experiences (*Erlebnisse*) modalized as "transcendental," constituting and phenomenologizing life (Fink, *Sixth Cartesian Meditation*), or to refer to the world as the world of life (*Lebenswelt*), weaving together the universal correlation of consciousness and the world (Depraz, "La vie").

If we stay for a moment with the mediation of reflexive consciousness, experience refers to this very intimate quality that consciousness has at the moment it perceives itself in the past. It is thus the upwelling of reflexivity itself from the unreflected given, the reflecting activity that is in play with *Erlebnis*. In this regard, one may also speak of *Erfahrungsleben* (life as experience), as if to separate (the prefix "ex") life that is immanent through experience from its explicit rendering: in phenomenology, "living" is interiorized straightaway, even reflexive. Beside, to speak of a "natural attitude" (*natürliche Einstellung*) to refer to "natural life" is the indication of a phenomenological life that already contains, in virtue of the position occupied by the observing self, a reflexive distance with respect to itself.

III. The Social Mediation of *Erleben*:
From the Greek *Polis* to Husserlian *Lebenswelt*

Erleben's reflexive distance in its phenomenological sense with regard to immediate and natural life is captured precisely in Greek with the distinct usage of the terms *zôê* [ζωή] and *bios* [βίος].

- See Box 2.

In this respect, the Husserlian "lifeworld" (*Lebenswelt*) lies in between the two forms of community distinguished by Aristotle. It is both a natural world of living beings—perceptible, immanent, and practical, situated in close proximity to the natural, prereflective attitude—and also a social, lived world, already penetrated with the common reflexivity proper to the intersubjective experience of the collective being. *The Crisis of European Sciences* brings out this ambivalence in section 38, which the translation "lifeworld" awkwardly renders, refusing to choose between the world of the living and that of experience (Biemel, "Réflexions").

The world of life is this social a priori, the correlative of the a priori of transcendental subjectivity, which aims to hold together the immanent possibility of a self-organization in the natural world of living beings and its irreducibility to the lived social consciousness that emanates from it. In this respect, the most antireductionist contemporary cognitive approach uses the term "emergence," and, more specifically, the expression *couplage structurel autopoiétique* between consciousness and the world (Varela, *Principles*) to refer to that dynamic of collective life.

Natalie Depraz

BIBLIOGRAPHY

Arendt, Hannah. *The Human Condition*. Chicago: University of Chicago Press, 1998.
Biemel, Walter. "Réflexions à propos des recherches husserliennes de la Lebenswelt." *Tijdschrift voor Filosofie* 33, no. 4 (1971): 659–83.
Depraz, Nathalie. "La vie m'est-elle donnée?" *Etudes Philosophiques* 4 (1991): 359–73.
Dilthey, Wilhelm. *Einleitung in die Geisteswissenschaften*. Vol. 1 of *Gesammelte Schriften*. Göttingen: Vandenhoeck and Ruprecht, 1914–. First published in 1883. Translation by R. A. Makkreel and F. Rodi: *Introduction to the Human Sciences*. *Wilhem Dilthey: Selected Works*, vol. 1, edited by R. A. Makkreel and F. Rodi. Princeton, NJ: Princeton University Press, 1989.
Fichte, Johann Gottlieb. *Sonnenklarer Bericht an das grössere Publikum über das eigentliche wesen der neuesten Philosophie*. In *Fichtes Werke*, vol. 3, edited by

Fritz Medicus. Leipzig: Fritz Eckardt, 1911–12. First published in 1801.Translation by John Botterman and William Rasch: *A Crystal Clear Report to the General Public Concerning the Actual Essence of the Newest Philosophy: An Attempt to Force the Reader to Understand*. In *Fichte, Jacobi, and Schelling: Philosophy of German Idealism*, edited by Ernst Behler, 39–118. New York: Continuum, 1987.

Fink, Eugen. *Sixth Cartesian Meditation: The Idea of a Transcendental Theory of Method*. Translated by R. Bruzina. Bloomington: Indiana University Press, 1994.

Henry, Michel. *C'est moi, la vérité. Pour une philosophie du christianisme*. Paris: Éditions du Seuil, 1997. Translation by S. Emmanuel: *I Am the Truth: Toward a Philosophy of Christianity*. Stanford, CA: Stanford University Press, 2003.

Husserl, Edmund. *The Crisis of European Sciences and Transcendental Phenomenology: An Introduction to Phenomenological Philosophy*. Translated by D. Carr. Evanston, IL: Northwestern University Press, 1970.

———. *Ideas: General Introduction to Pure Phenomenology*. Translated by W. R. Boyce Gibson. New York: Macmillan, 1931.

Krug, Wilhelm Traugott. *Encyklopädisches Lexikon in Bezug auf die neueste Literatur und Geschichte der Philosophie*. 2nd ed. 6 vol. Leipzig: Brockaus, 1970. First published in 1838.

Lipps, Theodor. *Psychologie des Schönen und der Kunst*. Vol. 1 of *Grundzüge der Ästhetik*. Hamburg: Voss, 1903.

Lotze, Hermann. *Metaphysik*. Edited by G. Misch. Leipzig: Meiner, 1912. First published in 1841. Translation by B. Bosanquet: *Metaphysic, in Three Books, Ontology, Cosmology, and Psychology*. Oxford: Clarendon Press, 1887.

Merleau-Ponty, Maurice. *La nature. Notes. Cours du Collège de France*. Paris: Gallimard, 1995. Translation by R. Vallier: *Nature: Course Notes from the Collège de France*. Evanston, IL: Northwestern University Press, 2003.

———. *Le visible et l'invisible*. Paris: Gallimard, 1964. Translation by A. Lingis: *The Visible and the Invisible: Followed by Working Notes*, edited by C. Lefort. Evanston, IL: Northwestern University Press, 1968.

Varela, Francisco. *The Embodied Mind: Cognitive Science and Human Experience*. With E. Thompson and E. Rosch. Cambridge, MA: MIT Press, 1991.

———. *Principles of Biological Autonomy*. New York: North Holland, 1979.

2
G. Agamben: The pertinent distinction between *zôê* and *bios*

➤ AIÔN, OIKONOMIA

Like *Leben*, *zôê* captures the simple fact of living and characterizes living beings—animals, men, or gods—at the biological level. *Bios* further indicates a mode or a kind of qualified life: *bios theorêtikos* [βίος θεωρητικός] (contemplative life), *bios apolaustikos* [βίος ἀπολαυστικός] (life of pleasure), *bios politikos* [βίος πολιτικός] (political life). These are attitudes or behaviors that when confronted with life place it straightaway in an ethical or social framework (Plato, *Philebus*; Aristotle, *Nicomachean Ethics*). The dividing line is thus drawn between natural, biological life (*zôê*) and the life of the *polis* [πόλις] (*bios*) to the point where the former is confined to the private life of the family and reproduction (*oikos* [οἶκος]) and is excluded from the *polis* (Aristotle, *Politics*, 1252a26–35).

Even if natural life is a good in itself (ibid., 1278b23–31), and even if God is apprehended as being the bearer of a *zôê aristê kai aidios* [ζωὴ ἀρίστη καὶ ἀίδιος] (a most noble and eternal life; *Metaphysics*, 12.1072b28), political life nevertheless does not refer to an attribute of the living being but rather to a specific difference of the genus *zôion*. Further, although Aristotle refers to the *political man* as a *politikon zôion* [πολιτικὸν ζῷον] (*Politics*, 1253a4), one may equally maintain that this is due to the fact that the use of the verb *bionai* in Attic prose is practically nonexistent.

There is thus a discontinuity between the natural community of living beings, whose primary figure is that of the family, and the political community, which introduces a specific kind of life that includes language and the awareness of justice and injustice.

BIBLIOGRAPHY

Agamben, Giorgio. *Homo Sacer: Sovereign Power and Bare Life*. Translated by Daniel Heller-Roazen. Stanford, CA: Stanford University Press, 1998.

ERSCHEINUNG / SCHEIN / PHÄNOMEN / MANIFESTATION / OFFENBARUNG (GERMAN)

ENGLISH   appearance / illusion / phenomenon / manifestation / revelation

FRENCH   *phénomène, apparition, apparence / apparence, illusion, simulacra / phénomène / manifestation / révélation*

➤ *APPEARANCE*, DOXA, EPOCHÉ, ERLEBEN, GERMAN, *IMAGE*, INTENTION, OBJECT, PERCEPTION, *PHÉNOMÈNE*, REALITY, *THING*, TRUTH

The vocabulary of phenomenality is distributed in German over several linguistic registers: alongside terms of Germanic origin based on the verb *scheinen* (to shine, to appear, to seem) and on the adjective *offenbar* (manifest, clear, obvious)—terms such as *Erscheinung* (phenomenon, appearance) and *Offenbarung* (revelation)—we find terms from foreign languages that constitute the technical vocabulary of modern philosophy, such as *Phänomen*, borrowed from the Greek, or *Manifestation*, taken from Latin.

It is Kant who, with his rigid distinction between *Erscheinung* and *Phänomen* on one hand and *Schein* on the other, gives "phenomenon" its modern definition, whereas Lambert, who was probably the first to use the term "phenomenology," continues to operate under the traditional distinction between truth and appearance. In Hegel, the vocabulary of manifestation appears alongside the Kantian distinction between *Schein* and *Erscheinung*, which he renews; and Schelling, following Fichte, gives the concept of *Offenbarung* (revelation) its fullest range. However, it is in the framework of phenomenology that the concepts of *Phänomen*, *Erscheinung*, and *Schein*, in a new distribution, will return to the center of philosophical debate with Husserl, who emphasizes their "equivocations" and Heidegger, who assigns himself the task in 1927 of providing a fundamental clarification of their meaning.

I. *Schein* and *Erscheinung*: The Kantian Distinction between Phenomenon and Appearance

The work written in Latin and known as the *Dissertation of 1770* that earned Kant the rank of ordinary professor at the University of Königsberg contains the first properly Kantian definition of the *phänomenon* as an object of perception (*objectum sensualitatis*), as opposed to the *noumenon* or intelligible object, which is only knowable through intelligence (*per intelligentiam cognoscendum*):

> The object of sensibility is the sensible; that which contains nothing save what must be known through intelligence is the intelligible. The former was called, in the ancient schools, *phenomenon*; the latter, *noumenon*.

> (Kant, *Dissertation of 1770*, II, § 3, p. 54)

Kant thus breaks with the sense that Descartes and Leibnitz gave to the term *phaenomenon*, a transposition into modern Latin of the Greek *phainomenon* [φαινόμενον], itself a substantive use of a participle of the verb *phainesthai* [φαίνεσθαι], which means "to be visible, to appear," itself derived from *phôs* [φῶς], "light." *Phaenomena* in the Kantian sense no longer refer to known empirical facts, to *apparitiones*, to what appears to consciousness, but simply to perceptible objects, and it is as such that they are opposed not only to *noumena* but also to simple appearances (*apparentiae*):

> In things of sense and in phenomena (*Phaenomenis*), that which precedes the logical use of intellect is called *appearance (Apparentia)*, and the reflective cognition that arises from the intellectual comparison of a number of appearances is called *experience*.

> (Ibid., II, §5)

A complex game of differentiations is thus presupposed here. We move from the distinction between *phänomenon* and *apparitio* to a double distinction between *phänomenon* and *noumenon* at the highest level, but also between *phänomenon* and *apparentia*.

These distinctions are taken up again in the *Critique of Pure Reason* of 1781, in which, alongside *Phänomenon*, borrowed from Latin, appear the terms *Erscheinung* and *Schein*. *Erscheinung* is usually translated into French as *phénomène* (whereas in English it is translated as "appearance") in order to distinguish it from *Schein*, which is translated as *apparence* (and by "illusion" in English), which of course creates some confusion. The difficulty of *Erscheinung* is marked by the fact that *apparence* and "appearance," despite being related, are aligned with the most widely opposed terms, with "appearance" seeming, further, to retain only one aspect of Kantian *Erscheinung* (the first aspect of *phänomenon* of 1770, distinguished from *experientia*); as for the English "illusion," it does capture the aspect of deception contained in *Schein*, but the latter must be immediately corrected by the doctrine of transcendental—that is, necessary—illusion (see infra).

The term *Phänomenologie* itself, probably invented by Johann Heinrich Lambert (1728–77), first appears in his work of 1764, *Neues Organon*, the fourth part of which is entitled "Phenomenology as a Doctrine of Appearance (*Schein*)." In his letter to Lambert on 2 September 1770, Kant takes up this terminology and seems at this time to wish to consider the science of the perceptible only as a simple propaedeutic to metaphysics:

> A quite special, though purely negative science, general phenomenology (*phaenomologia* [sic] *generalis*), seems to me to be presupposed by metaphysics. In it the principles of sensibility, their validity and their limitations, would be determined, so that these principles could not be confusedly applied to objects of pure reason, as has heretofore almost always happened.

> (Kant, *Correspondence*, 108)

At this time, Kant, like Lambert, is still working with the traditional distinction between being and appearing, the intelligible and the perceptible: "It is clear, therefore, that representations of things *as they appear* are sensitively thought, while intellectual concepts are representations of things *as they are*" (Kant, *Dissertation of 1770*, § 4, p. 54).

Later, the *Critique of Pure Reason* offers the "transcendental aesthetic" as an elucidation of *Erscheinung*, in opposition to Lambertian "phenomenology." What Kant refers to with the term is defined as the "undetermined object of an empirical intuition." This definition presupposes that we distinguish between its matter and form: "I call that in the appearance which corresponds to sensation its *matter*, but that which allows the manifold of appearance to be intuited as ordered in certain relations I call the *form* of appearance" (Kant, *Critique of Pure Reason*, B 34, 155–56). This form, which structures perception, cannot be given a posteriori as the matter is and must therefore be found in the mind a priori. With the distinction between matter and form, Kant thus showed that "appearances" are characterized by an intrinsic order. However, they may be further subordinate to a superior order, which is that of the understanding and which alone distinguishes the objectivity of genuine phenomena:

> Appearances, to the extent that as objects they are thought in accordance with the unity of the categories, are called phaenomena.

> (Erscheinungen, sofern sie als Gegenstände nach der Einheit der Kategorien gedacht werden, heissen Phänomena.)

> (Ibid., A 249)

A new distinction is drawn here between *Erscheinung* and *Phänomen*, with the *Fremdwort* being given a special nuance. It is by moving from apparitions to phenomena that Kant is able to break out of the traditional division between truth and appearance. We can only know what appears to us, of course, but our knowledge is not exclusively drawn from the appearances themselves, since it deploys the a priori forms of our understanding, which, though they can only apply to appearances, nonetheless do not originate in them but rather in the human mind.

The "apparition" (*Erscheinung*) is therefore not a simple, fallacious "appearance" (*Schein*) and must be considered as something real and objective, even though we must distinguish between the object as *Erscheinung* and the object in itself (B 69). Kant defines *Erscheinung* very precisely in a note added to this passage in the *Critique of Pure Reason*: "What is not to be encountered in the object in itself at all, but is always to be encountered in its relation to the subject and is inseparable from the representation of the object, is appearance [*Erscheinung*]" (ibid. B 70, note).

This object in itself, which is the nonperceptible cause of our representations and which remains entirely unknown to us, is what Kant called the transcendental "object" (B 522), and which he notes in the first edition is simply "=X" (A 109). This distinction between appearance and the thing in itself is nevertheless not simply a reiteration of the classical distinction between appearance and truth but on the contrary the logical consequence of the definition of *Erscheinung* as *apparition*. For, as Kant explains in the preface to the second edition of the *Critique of Pure Reason*:

Yet the reservation must also be well noted, that even if we cannot *cognize* these same objects as things in themselves, we at least must be able to *think* them as things in themselves. For otherwise there would follow the absurd proposition that there is an appearance [*Erscheinung*] without anything that appears [*ohne etwas . . . was da erscheint*].

(Ibid., B 26)

The concepts of *Ding an sich*, "thing-in-itself," and of *Erscheinung*, "appearance," are thus correlatives and do not refer to two different objects. This is what Kant emphasizes most clearly in the *Opus postumum*:

What is an object in appearance, however, in contrast to the same object but as *thing in itself*? . . . The [*aspectabile* of Space and Time is], a priori, as unconditional unity, the formal element of *appearance*, in contrast with the *thing in itself* [*ens per se*] = x, which is not itself a separate [*absonderliches*] object, but is only a particular *relation* (*respectus*) in order to constitute oneself as object."

(Kant, *Opus postumum*, 22:43, p. 179)

As for fallacious illusions (*Schein*), they arise precisely when we take appearances for things in themselves (B 70, note). For illusion does not arise from perception at all but from judgment:

Still less may we take *appearance* [*Erscheinung*] and *illusion* for one and the same. For truth and illusion are not in the object, insofar as it is intuited, but in the judgment about it insofar as it is thought. Thus it is correctly said that the senses do not err; yet not because they always judge correctly, but because they do not judge at all. Hence truth, as much as error, and thus also illusion as leading to the latter, are to be found only in judgments, i.e., only in the relation [*Verhältnis*] of the object to our understanding.

(Kant, *Critique of Pure Reason*, A 293/B 350)

The transcendental dialectic, as a "logic of illusion," does not deal with either empirical appearances, which come, like optical illusions, from judgments that are led astray by imagination, nor with logical illusions, which come from a failure to attend to the logical rule. Rather, it deals with what Kant calls "transcendental illusion," which is a "natural and unavoidable *illusion* (*Illusion*)," and which derives from the substitution of objective principles for merely subjective ones (A 298).

The *Critique of Pure Reason* thus teaches us not only "that the object should be taken in a *twofold meaning,* namely as appearance [*Erscheinung*] or as thing in itself [*Ding an sich*] (B 27)," but also to distinguish all objects in general into phenomena (*Phänomena*) and noumena (*Noumena*), which Kant attempts to explicate in the last chapter of the "Transcendental Analytic." For if the objects of the senses, the *Erscheinungen*, may be named *Phänomena* insofar as they are subordinated to the categories of the understanding, it remains possible to allow for things, which, as simple objects of the understanding, may be given to nonperceptual intuition: these are what Kant called *Noumena* (A 249). As objects of nonperceptual intuition, *Noumena* have only negative signification (B 342) and do not serve any purpose other than to mark the limits of our perceptual knowledge (B 345). The distinction between *Phänomena* as objects of the senses and *Noumena* as intelligible objects (B 306) is thus superimposed on that between *Erscheinung* and *Ding an Sich*.

II. From *Erscheinung* to *Offenbarung*: Phenomenon, Manifestation, and Revelation in Post-Kantian Idealism

To the extent that what unifies the post-Kantians is the desire to complete what Kant began by attempting to place metaphysics on the safe ground of science, it is not surprising to see them attack what Kantianism retains as unrepresentable for human reason, that is, the "thing-in-itself" and the "noumenon." The stress is thus placed in post-Kantianism on the dimension of appearance, of *Erscheinen*, as a dimension that is internal to the absolute itself, which would be completely ineffective without it. This leads Hegel to claim, in the preface to the *Phenomenology of Spirit*, that

Appearance (*Erscheinung*) is the arising and passing away that does not itself arise and pass away, but is "in itself" [i.e., subsists intrinsically], and constitutes the actuality and the movement of the life of truth.

(Hegel, *Phenomenology of Spirit*, § 46, 27)

Hegel nonetheless retains the distinction between *Erscheinung* and *Schein*, between appearance and illusion, as he explains in the third chapter of *Phenomenology of Spirit*, which deals precisely with *Erscheinung*, where illusion is defined as "*being* that is directly and in its own self a *non-being*," whereas phenomenon or appearance is "a *totality* of show" ("ein Ganzes des Scheins," ibid., 87), insofar as it refers not only to the moment of disappearance, to non-being, but to the whole movement of coming into being and passing away.

Insofar as an *Erscheinung* no longer reveals anything other than itself, since, as Hegel says, "it is manifest that behind the so-called curtain which is supposed to conceal the inner world, there is nothing to be seen unless *we* go behind it ourselves" (ibid., 103), it may be understood as the dimension itself of manifestation. That is, in fact, the term by which Jean Hyppolite, the first French translator of *Phenomenology of Spirit*, often translated *Erscheinung*, though the translations *apparition* or *apparition phénoménale*, used by another translator (Jean-Pierre Lefebvre), are perhaps preferable. We may thus construct the following table, in which the various translations make the difficulty of *Erscheinung* clear:

	Erscheinung	*Schein*	*Phänomen*
Kant	*manifestation sensible* (Barni), *image sensible* (TP), appearance (English)	*apparence* *illusion*	*Phénomene* *Phainomenon*
Hegel	*manifestation* (Hyppolite) *apparition* (Lefebvre) *phénomène* (Labarrière-Jarczyk)		

For Hegel, however, the term *Manifestation* itself, as well as *Offenbarung*, "revelation," which he uses as a synonym, only truly acquire their technical senses in the *Science of Logic*.

In effect, *Erscheinung* is again in question in the "Doctrine of Essence," the second book in the first volume of Hegel's *Science of Logic*, where "Die Erscheinung" is the title of the entire second section of the "Doctrine." The general movement of *Erscheinung* is summed up at the end of the introduction to the second book as follows: "At first, essence *shines* (*scheint*) or *shows within itself*, or is reflection; secondly, it *appears* (*erscheint*); thirdly, it *manifests* itself (*offenbart sich*)" (*Science of Logic*, vol. 1, bk. 2, p. 391).

These three verbs characterize the stages of the process of externalization of essence, as it unfolds in the first two sections of the logic of essence and as it culminates in the third, which deals with actuality (*Wirklichkeit*). The vocabulary of revelation (*Offenbarung*) and manifestation (*Manifestation*) appears in this last section, in order to express the "identity" at this level between form and content, internal and external, whereas their difference is what is made evident in the language of illusion (*scheinen*) and appearance (*erscheinen*). As Hegel emphasizes: "As this movement of exposition, a movement which carries itself along with it, as a way and manner which is its absolute identity-with-self, the absolute is manifestation not of an inner, nor over against an other, but it *is* only as the absolute manifestation of itself for itself (*sich für sich selbst Manifestieren*). As such it is *actuality*" (ibid., 536). It appears clearly here that the terms *Manifestation* and *Offenbarung* refer to the absolutely non-Kantian idea of an externalization without anything left over. The German term *offenbar*, which derives etymologically from the idea of openness or obviousness, is in fact most often translated by the adjective "manifest." Finally, we must add that in German *Manifestation* and *Offenbarung* are terms that belong to theological vocabulary.

In effect, *Offenbarung* is most often translated by "revelation," making use of another Latin term, in which we find an idea that is absent from the term *manifestatio*, namely that of an action consisting in removing a veil (*velum*) and thus uncovering something that was previously hidden. As a term belonging to religious vocabulary, *Offenbarung* is a concept that acquires great importance in post-Kantian philosophy. Here we must mention Fichte's first work, *Attempt at a Critique of All Revelation*, published in 1792, in which

we find an analysis of the concept of *Offenbarung* characterized from the formal point of view as a kind of "making known (*Bekanntmachung*)" (Fichte, *Attempt at a Critique*, 51), and a rational deduction of the concept that allows it to be defined as "a special appearance [by God] in the world of sense, determined expressly for this purpose" and by which he "would therefore have to proclaim himself as moral lawgiver" (ibid., 65). Fichte's goal in this essay, which made him famous since, though published anonymously, it was taken to be Kant's fourth *Critique*, is in effect to reduce religion to morality, as is made clear by one of the conclusions that this critique of the concept of revelation arrives at: "The universal criterion of the divinity of a religion with respect to its moral content is, therefore, the following: *only that revelation can be from God which establishes a principle of morality that agrees with the principle of practical reason and only such moral maxims as can be derived therefrom*" (ibid., 103).

We should place Schelling's posthumous work, the *Philosophy of Revelation* (*Philosophie der Offenbarung*), in the same philosophical rather than strictly religious perspective. The project of these lectures given in Munich and Berlin between 1827 and 1846 was not to lay out a Christian philosophy but only to understand the specificity of Christianity. Schelling explains this point very clearly at the end of the first book, by contrasting his *Philosophie der Offenbarung* with an *Offenbarungsphilosophie*, a revealed philosophy, and he clarifies that he takes the Revelation "as an object, not as a source or authority" (Schelling, *Philosophie der Offenbarung*, 165). The concept of Revelation in effect undergoes an extension with Schelling beyond what Fichte understood by it. The word does not here indicate only "the act by which the divinity would become the cause or author of representations in a given individual human consciousness," but in fact relates to "the *universal* of Revelation" (ibid., 166–67)—to its content, which, though revealing itself factually in history, relates nevertheless to "a more elevated historical sequence, that is to a sequence which goes beyond history itself and Christianity taken as a particular phenomenon" (ibid., 169). What is thus in question in the *Philosophy of Revelation* is not the historical phenomenon of Christianity but the very object of philosophy for the post-Kantians, namely the effectivity of the absolute. The young Schelling, still very Fichtean, affirms this in one of his very first texts, *On the Self* (*Vom Ich*): the ultimate end of philosophy is "absolute pure being" and its duty is "to unveil and to reveal that which can never be reduced to concepts." His *Philosophy of Revelation*, which, from the fact that it gives itself the task of thinking that which goes beyond reason, constitutes the ultimate goal of speculative idealism, continues with the same goal: "It will understand even more and something other than the Revelation alone; what is more, it will only understand the latter because it has earlier understood something else, namely the actually real God" (ibid., 166).

III. *Erscheinung* and *Phänomen*: The Phenomenological Concept of Phenomena (Husserl and Heidegger)

In 1901 the term "phenomenology" reappears in the title of Husserl's work, *Studies in Phenomenology and the Theory of Knowledge*, which is the second part of the *Logical Investigations*, whose first volume had appeared the year before under the title *Prolegomena to Pure Logic*. At this time, still under the influence of Brentano and his *Psychology from an Empirical Standpoint*, Husserl gives the term the sense of a "descriptive analysis," which restricts itself to the pure phenomenal given without presupposing the existence of what it describes. This analysis allows it in effect to distinguish what belongs to the object itself from what belongs to the experience or, in Husserlian vocabulary, the immanent from the transcendent. Take the example of color used by Husserl in the fifth Investigation: we often confuse the colored sensation (immanent) with objective coloration (transcendent). However, the object as such is neither perceived nor conscious, any more than the color that is perceived as belonging to it. It is "outside," not "in" consciousness; however, "in" consciousness there is a corresponding colored perceptual experience. This is not a simple difference of perspective according to which the same phenomenon is considered either objectively or subjectively. The confusion in question comes from the ambiguity in the term "phenomenon" (*Erscheinung*):

We cannot too sharply stress the equivocation (*Äquivokation*) that allows us to use the word "*appearance*" (*Erscheinung*) both *of the experience in which the object's appearing consists* (*Erscheinen*) (the concrete perceptual experience, in which the object itself seems present to us) and of *the object which appears as such*. The deceptive spell (*Trug*) of this equivocation vanishes as soon as one takes phenomenological accounts as to how little of the object which appears is as such to be found in the experience of its appearing. The appearing of the thing (the experience) is not the thing which appears (Die Dingerscheinung [das Erlebnis] ist nicht das erscheinende Ding) (that seems to stand before us *in propria persona* [*in leibhaftiger Selbstheit*]). As belonging in a conscious connection, the appearing of things is experienced by us, as belonging in the phenomenal world (als der phänomenalen Welt zugehörig erscheinen uns die Dinge), things appear before us. The appearing of the things does not itself appear to us, we live through it (die Erscheinungen selbst erscheinen nicht, sie werden erlebt).

(Husserl, *Logical Investigations*, Investigation
V, 1, §2, 2:83)

In the final appendix to the *Investigations*, Husserl comes back to the "ambiguities" of the term *Erscheinung* that make it possible to refer to both objects and experiences in which they figure as "phenomena." In this regard he distinguishes three different meanings given to the word: the concrete experience of an object, the appearing object itself, and, wrongly, the real components of the experience of the object, for example, sensations, which may prompt us erroneously to see phenomenal objects as simple compounds of perceptual contents. Husserl's concern is the strict distinction between the transcendent and the immanent: he aims to distinguish himself from his teacher, Brentano, who considers the intentional object to be immanent in consciousness, whereas for Husserl, on the contrary, consciousness is not a container, nor is the object a real part of the experience. In a passage added to the second edition of 1913, Husserl emphasizes that of the three meanings attributed to the term *Erscheinung*, the second is the one that constitutes "the

original concept of *Erscheinung*," that is, "the concept of what appears or what can appear, of the intuitive as such." Insofar as all experiences, whether they derive from an internal intuition or an external one, may be objectified in reflection, it is possible to call all of these experiences *Phänomene*, which thus become the object of phenomenology defined as the "theory of experiences in general" (*Logical Investigations*).

For what was not clear in 1901 was the status of what Husserl called, in his 1907 lectures on *The Idea of Phenomenology*, the "*pure phenomenon* (*Phänomen*) in the sense of phenomenology," which is to be distinguished from the "*psychological phenomenon*," the object of psychology as a science of nature (ibid., 68). Such a *Phänomen*, insofar as it is an absolute given, is the result of what Husserl here calls, for the first time, "phenomenological reduction," which consists in bracketing—submitting to an *epochê*—the entirety of the transcendent. The pure phenomenon, the object of a pure phenomenology, is thus the "reduced" phenomenon, that is, the appearing object as such, independent of its existence outside of consciousness. Husserl has thus managed to account for the two sides of the phenomenon—subjective and objective:

The word "phenomenon" (*Phänomen*) is ambiguous in virtue of the essential correlation between *appearance* (*Erscheinen*) and *that which appears* (*Erscheinenden*). *Phainomenon* in its proper sense means that which appears, and yet it is by preference used for the appearing itself, for the subjective phenomenon (*Phänomen*) (if one may use this expression which is apt to be misunderstood in the vulgar psychological sense).

(Husserl, *The Idea of Phenomenology*, 11)

The phenomenon in the sense of phenomenology is thus radically distinguished from Kantian *Erscheinung*, which derives from the unknown thing-in-itself or that X that is the transcendental object. In his 1913 work, *Ideas Pertaining to a Pure Phenomenology and to a Phenomenological Philosophy*, Husserl insists on the contrary that it is an "error of principle" to imagine that God "should possess the perception of the thing in itself which is refused to us, finite beings," for that implies the reduction of the perceived thing to an image or a simple sign (ibid., § 43). In effect, according to Husserl it is "absurd" to consider what appears as deriving from anything else that is separate and that would be considered its "hidden cause" (ibid., § 52). For it is of the very essence of the spatial thing to present itself by way of the mediation of *Erscheinung* (which Ricoeur, the French translator of the *Ideas*, always translates by *apparence*) which, precisely because they are not a simple appearance (*blosser Schein*, *pur simulacre* in Ricoeur's translation), do not derive from some "in itself," since everything must *in principle* be able to become a phenomenon. Husserl's break with the Kantian limitation of the phenomenon by the noumenon is here manifest.

Nonetheless, for Husserl as for Kant, *Phänomen* and *Erscheinung* are not clearly distinguished. Heidegger, by contrast, insists on precisely this distinction when he attempts to clarify the sense of the word *phenomenology* on the basis of its two components, *phainomenon* and *logos* [λόγος], first in his lectures of 1925, devoted to the "Prolegomena to the history of the concept of time," then later in the introduction to his 1927 treatise, *Being and Time* (*Sein und Zeit*). Returning to the primitive meaning of the Greek work *phainomenon*, Heidegger defines *Phänomen* as "*that which shows itself in itself*," "the manifest" (*das Offenbare*), and sees in appearance (*Schein*) a privative modification of *Phänomen* by which a thing shows itself precisely as it is not:

> Only when the meaning of something is such that it makes a pretension of showing itself—that is, of being a phenomenon (*Phänomen*)—can it show itself *as* something which it is *not*; only then *can* it "merely look like so-and-so" (*nur so aussehen wie*).

(Heidegger, *Being and Time*, § 7, 51)

Heidegger insists on the fact that the term *Phänomen*, like *Schein*, has nothing to do with that of *Erscheinung*, which he claims in his lectures from 1925 has caused more ravages and confusion than any other (*Prolegomena zur Geschichte des Zeitbegriffs*, 112). *Erscheinen* has, in effect, as Kant himself had emphasized, the sense of an indication by one thing of another, which latter precisely does not appear. *Erscheinen* (to appear) is thus paradoxically a "not-showing-itself," which implies that "phenomena (*Phänomene*) are *never* appearances (*Erscheinungen*)," and that one therefore cannot explain the first term by means of the second, since on the contrary *Erscheinung*, insofar as it is an indication of something that is not shown by means of something that is shown, presupposes the notion of *Phänomen* (*Sein und Zeit*, 52).

It is thus of the utmost importance for Heidegger not to place *Schein* and *Erscheinung* on the same level: the former, as a privative modification of *Phänomen*, includes the dimension of the manifest, while the latter, like all indications, representations, symptoms, and symbols, already presupposes in itself the dimension of the self-display of something, that is, the *Phänomen*: "In spite of the fact that 'appearing' (*Erscheinen*) is never a showing-itself (*Sichzeigen*) in the sense of 'phenomenon' (*Phänomen*), appearing is possible only *by reason of a showing-itself* of something" (*Sein und Zeit*, 53).

Sometimes, however, without regard for the difference in meaning of the two terms, *Phänomen* is defined as the *Erscheinung* of something that does not reveal itself, which leads on the one hand to an opposition between the realm of appearance and that of being in itself, and on the other, insofar as we tend to give ontological priority to the "thing in itself," to devalue *Erscheinung* as "*blosse Erscheinung*"—mere appearance—which is itself identified with *Schein*, illusion. As Heidegger emphasizes in his Lectures of 1925, "Confusion is then carried to extremes. But traditional epistemology and metaphysics live off this confusion" (*Prolegomena*, 114; *History of the Concept of Time*, 83).

Kant himself fell into this confusion, since by defining *Erscheinung* as the object of sense, he understands the latter both as *Phänomen*, that is, what shows itself by itself and is opposed to *Schein*, "illusion," and as *Erscheinung*—the appearance of what never shows itself, the thing in itself. So, in the end, what is a phenomenon in the sense of phenomenology? For Kant himself, it is not what he calls *Erscheinung*, "apparition," that is, the object of perceptual intuition, but what shows itself in the appearances themselves in a nonthematic way, namely time and space as forms of intuition that must be able to become phenomena, that is, to show themselves by themselves in philosophical analysis. For the phenomenon of phenomenology is not "given." It must have, on the contrary, an "explicit exhibition" in order to be perceived. A phenomenon properly speaking is thus what is "hidden" in what is shown at first glance and most often, but nonetheless constitutes the essence and basis of what is manifested, namely the *existence* of being. Between phenomenon and appearance there is thus the same difference as between existence and being. Phenomenology and ontology are thenceforth one: "*Only as phenomenology, is ontology possible*" (*Sein und Zeit*, 60). Heidegger has thus managed to show, like Husserl, that "behind the phenomena of phenomenology, there is essentially nothing else" and that nonetheless what becomes a phenomenon may well be hidden. For "just because the phenomena are proximally and for the most part *not* given, there is need for phenomenology" (ibid.).

Françoise Dastur

BIBLIOGRAPHY

Fichte, Johann Gottlieb. *Versuch einer Kritik der Offenbarung*. Hamburg: Meiner, 1983. Translation by Garrett Green: *Attempt at a Critique of All Revelation*. New York: Cambridge University Press, 1978.

Hegel, Georg Wilhelm Friedrich. *Phänomenologie des Geistes*. Hamburg: Meiner, 1952. Translation by A. V. Miller and J. N. Findlay: *The Phenomenology of Spirit*. Oxford: Oxford University Press, 1977.

———. *Wissenschaft der Logik*, vol. 1, *Die objective Logik*. Hamburg: Meiner, 1978. Translation by A. V. Miller and J. N. Findlay: *Hegel's Science of Logic*. New York: Humanity Books, 1999.

Heidegger, Martin. *Prolegomena zur Geschichte des Zeitbegriffs*. In *Gesamtausgabe*, vol. 20. Frankfurt: Klostermann, 1979. Translation by T. Kisiel: *History of the Concept of Time: Prolegomena*. Bloomington: Indiana University Press, 1992.

———. *Sein und Zeit*. In *Gesamtausgabe*, vol. 2. Frankfurt : Klostermann, 1977. Translation by J. Macquarrie and E. Robinson: *Being and Time*. Oxford: Blackwell, 1967.

Husserl, Edmund. *Die Idee der Phänomenologie*. The Hague: Nijhoff, 1973. Translation by W. P. Alston and G. Nakhnikian: *The Idea of Phenomenology*. The Hague: Nijhoff, 1964.

———. *Ideen zu einer reinen Phänomenologie und phänomenologische Philosophie*, Bk. 1. The Hague: Nijhoff, 1950. Translation by F. Kersten: *Ideas Pertaining to a Pure Phenomenology and to a Phenomenological Philosophy*, Bk. 1. 3 vols. The Hague: Nijhoff, 1980–89.

———. *Logische Untersuchungen*. Tübingen: Niemeyer, 1900. Translation by J. N. Findlay: *Logical Investigations*. New York: Routledge, 2001.

Kant, Immanuel. *Correspondence*. Edited by A. Zweig. New York: Cambridge University Press, 1999.

———. *Inaugural Dissertation of 1770*. Translated by William J. Eckhoff. New York: Columbia College, 1894.

———. *Kritik der reinen Vernunft*. Hamburg: Meiner, 1990. Translation by P. Guyer and A. Wood: *Critique of Pure Reason*, edited by P. Guyer and A. Wood. Cambridge: Cambridge University Press, 1998.

———. "On the Form and Principles of the Sensible and the Intelligible World [Inaugural Dissertation]." In *Kant Selections*, edited by L. W. Beck. Englewood Cliffs, NJ: Prentice Hall, 1998.

———. *Opus postumum*. Translated by Eckart Förster and Michael Rosen. Cambridge: Cambridge University Press, 1995.

Lambert, Johann Heinrich. *Neues Organon, oder Gedanken über die Erforschung und Bezeichnung des Wahren und dessen Unterscheidung von Irrtum und Schein*. Leipzig, 1764; Berlin: Akademie-Verlag, 1990.

Schelling, Friedrich Wilhelm Joseph von. *Sämtliche Werke*, vol. 1: *Philosophische Schriften* (*Vom Ich*) and vol. 13: *Philosophie der Offenbarung* (Bk. 1). Stuttgart: J. C. Cotta. Translation by F. Marti: *The Unconditional in Human Knowledge: Four Early Essays, 1794–1796*. Lewisburg, PA: Bucknell University Press, 1980. Translation by V. C. Hayes: *Schelling's Philosophy of Mythology and Revelation*. Australian Association for the Study of Religions, 1995.

ERZÄHLEN / BESCHREIBEN (GERMAN)

FRENCH   *raconter/décrire*

➤ *RÉCIT*, and ART, BILD, DESCRIPTION, DICHTUNG, EREIGNIS, *FACT, FICTION,* HISTORY, *IMAGE*, LOGOS, MIMÊSIS, ROMANTIC, STRUCTURE, TRUTH

The very different styles of literary studies and the textbooks on which they rely in France and in Germany provide interesting perspectives on the notion of a story and the way in which it is determined by different linguistic and national traditions. The language of the story (and its cognate notions: event, history, description) is marked in German both by the weight of the tradition and by the character of terminological adjustments coming in large part from French literary theory. On the basis of a few key terms—*Erzählung, Bericht, Geschehen, Geschichte, Begebenheit, Beschreibung, Schilderung*—it is possible to see how the untranslatable coming from the tradition is combined with the difficulties entailed by the recent acclimations of vocabulary in this domain.

I. The Collapse of the Romantic Terminology

By including the terms *narrativ/Narrativität* in the sixth volume, Joachim Ritter's *Historisches Wörterbuch der Philosophie* celebrated the entry into philosophical language of terms that until the late 1960s were welcome neither in German-language philosophy nor in the language of poetics and literary critique. From the eighteenth century through the 1950s, not only was there no real textual analysis that required its own vocabulary (even today, terminological questions are neglected in the reedited versions of Gero von Wilpert and Wolfgang Kayser's reference works), but in addition the terminology of *Literaturwissenschaft* ("the science of literature," where French would say "*théorie littéraire* [literary theory]") was still entirely subordinate to the romantic perspective of a literary absolute. The language in which the analysis of texts and questions of poetic narrative were expressed in German, up through the great canonical texts that maintained their influence through the postwar period (Emil Staiger, Günther Müller, Karl Vietör), thus remained that of Goethe, Hegel, or the Schlegel brothers. A literary work was a *literarisches Kunstwerk* (work of literary *art*), literature was a *Dichtkunst* (see DICHTUNG), and the concepts upon which the analysis of narrative texts was based were those of *Gebilde, Gestalt, Gefüge, Fügung, Gliederung, Aufbau, Dichtwerk*, all untranslatables, composite words that are equivalent—but only equivalent—to the ideas of structure, composition, or organization, for the first six. As for the term *Dichtwerk*, made up of *Werk* (work), and *Dicht* for *Dichtung*, we might be able to translate it by the term "work of literary art." There is not a single *Fremdwort* in the 590 pages of Günther Müller's *Morphologische Poetik* (1968), which collects studies from the years 1923 to 1954. Müller himself, in fact, in the article "Über das Zeitgerüst des Erzählens," published in 1950 (*Gerüst* meaning "scaffolding," so that *Zeit gerüst* might be translated as "temporal structure"), writes that

> It is a well-known fact that the study of literature in Germany (*die deutsche Literaturwissenschaft*), in conformity with its Herderian, Schlegelian, and Hegelian origin, is essentially based on the perspective of a historical consideration of facts and that it barely has a tradition

of literary critique behind it, or even a vocabulary appropriate to what would be called *art* in France and *craft* in English. The result is a knowledge and consciousness that are not secure in the specificity of literary works (*literarische Kunstwerke*) and a sort of inhibition in speaking, in discussions of literature (*Dichtung*), about that for which we only have the deceptive term "technique."

(Müller, "Zeitgerüst," 389–90)

Everything changes in the 1950s. Important works such as Lämmert's *Bauformen des Erzählens*, Stanzel's *Typische Formen des Romans*, or Käte Hamburger's *Die Logik der Dichtung* mark the transition to a rigorous analysis of fiction with its own language. Their terminology is both new, suited to their breakthrough in terms of analysis (*Erzählakt* [act of narration], *Erzählstimme* [narrative voice], *Ich-Origo*: new words for new problems), and respectful of the classical and romantic tradition. However, if we compare the language of poetics and the analysis of narratives as generally practiced in German-language *Literaturwissenschaft* through the end of the 1960s with the language in which those same questions are currently treated, we see that the old romantic vocabulary was replaced by a language introduced in the 1970s by importing semiotic and structuralist research, especially from France (though also from English-speaking and Soviet countries, as Germany had to catch up in the space of a few years after lagging behind in the theory of texts, from Russian formalism to French structuralism). Thus, *Struktur* replaced *Aufbauform*, *Form* replaced *Gebilde*, *Figur* replaced *Gestalt*, *Konfiguration* replaced *Gefüge*, *Artikulation* replaced *Verknüpfung*, and so on. Nothing makes the naturalization of this radical change clearer than the language in which Rainer Rochlitz translated the three volumes of Paul Ricoeur's *Temps et Récit*: *Kompositionsregeln, Konfiguration, Refiguration, Konfigurationsvorgang, Rekonstruktion, relogifizieren, entchronologisieren, Modalitäten der Fabelkomposition*, etc. (*règles de composition, configuration, refiguration, . . . reconstruction, relogification, déchronologization, modalités de la mise en intrigue*). All of that would have been unthinkable thirty years earlier.

In some cases it would not have been possible to import the concept except through familiarization with the *Fremdwort*, without which the box for its idea would have remained empty. This is the case, for example, with *Semiotik, Aktant*, and *Funktion*, three concepts that did not exist under the old vocabulary: the first two because they could not have been transformed without compromising the rigor of the Greimasian theory (just as for *Diegese*, a calque of Genette's *diégèse*), the third because, before the terminological upheaval of the 1970s, the idea of function had no place in the vocabulary, which had remained resistant to a logico-semantic treatment of the art of language. Nevertheless, it would be false to speak of a radical change in the environment. In general, rather, we have a cohabitation of two vocabularies: German, to which analytic terminology is now turning for revitalization after having purged the language of its "old-language" obstacles to rigorous analysis, and words of French or English origin (*mise en abyme*, "stream of consciousness," *intradiegetisch, implotment*), when it seems that clarity is gained by using the foreign word.

II. *Erzählung / Bericht: Récit* and Its Untranslatables

How can we translate the French *récit: Bericht, Geschichte, Erzählung*? Germany never had anything like Gérard Genette's attempt in this domain, which led to the trio of *narration, diégèse,* and *histoire,* and the language must either make use of its own resources or fall back entirely on Genette's analysis and look for correlates term by term. Before this terminological cleaning, it was necessary to proceed in a different manner. Thus, for the *récit* as a process, we could use the term *das Erzählen,* literally "the telling" (that is how Käte Hamburger, for example, refers to the narrative process), as opposed to *die Erzählung,* the product of the narrative process. If we wish to avoid all ambiguity, we may appeal to a second distinction, as Käte Hamburger also does, between *das Erzählte* (what is narrated) and *das Erzählende* (the narration), so as to avoid any collision between the intratextual product of the narrative process and the product of the narration as a formal category of the narrative genre (where *Erzählung* corresponds to what we would call "stories": Kafka's *Erzählungen* are Kafka's "stories." This is the only dimension taken into account by Wilpert, for example).

■ See Box 1.

Though there is no fundamental ambiguity in the distinction between *Erzählen/Erzählung*—as long as we are as clear as Käte Hamburger was in the usage of the traditional vocabulary—there is nevertheless much that is untranslatable about the relations between *Erzählung* and *Bericht.*

The Latin equivalents that Grimms' dictionary gives for the term *Bericht* are *relatio, expositio, nuntiatio [Kunde, Nachricht,* and *Unterricht],* which cover a wide field, both rhetorical and narrative, and do not distinguish between an act of discourse, an artifact of discourse, and the transmission of a piece of information or knowledge. *Bericht*'s origin is the same as that of *richtig* (right), and in the sixteenth century *berichten* meant either "to correct mistaken information" (today *berichtigen* is used) or, in its pastoral meaning, "to administer a sacrament." Luther explicitly gives the Greek and Latin equivalents of *synaxis* and *communio (synaxis griechisch, cummunio lateinisch, und Berichten auf Deutsch,* cited by Grimms, "*Bericht*"). In both cases, whether it is a matter of transmitting information or of administering a sacrament, the issue is one of truth: *berichtet werden / sein* (today

unterrichtet werden / sein would be used) is to be in possession of the true version of things and of just wisdom (today, *einer Sache kundig sein*). A *Bericht* is thus a true message (*Kunde*). It is only later that a schism arises in the language between the transmission of truth (or of the sacrament of the Truth) and the narrative and that *Bericht* evolves toward the protocol-based semantics that it essentially has today (*ein Bericht*: a report, as in Kafka, *Bericht an eine Akademie* [Report addressed to an academy]). However, even though this shift has been attested by Adelung and Heyse (Heyse defines *Bericht* as "pflichtgemäße, meist schriftliche Meldung oder Darstellung eines Herganges oder Sachbestandes [official communication, usually written, or representation of an event or state of affairs]"), the *Bericht* of literary theory could not affirm it and take on its dominant contemporary meaning of an objective report as long as the vocabulary for describing narratives did not have a word to refer to the articulation of the narrative language. This is still the case, for example, with Emil Staiger: in his *Grundbegriffe der Poetik* (Basic concepts of poetics), which was an authority for a long time and continues to be one in German studies, he placed the words *Erzähler* and *Bericht* as a pair to express the relation of narrator/story, and this with regard to Homer:

> Er redet die Musen an. Er unterbricht nicht selten einen Bericht, um eine Bermerkung, eine Bitte an die Himmlischen einzuschalten.
>
> (He [Homer] speaks to the Muses. It is not rare for him to interrupt a *Bericht,* in order to insert a remark or prayer addressed to the gods.)
>
> (Staiger, *Grundbegriffe der Poetik*)

How should we understand *Bericht* here? The term opposes the intrusion of the narrator to what we can only translate as "narrative," but a narrative where the narration and what is narrated form a single continuum: such is the classical use of the term in German literary theory.

We ought to be astonished to find the use of the same term in Käte Hamburger's *Logik der Dichtung,* that is, in the fundamental work that creates a break with the very tradition represented by Staiger, who had only contempt for any technical treatment of the untouchable *Dichtung.* Yet, in a passage where she demonstrates that in certain cases

---

1

Narration, "diegesis," "story"

If diegesis is the *recounted world* as it appears in a fiction, narration is the *universe in which one recounts,* that is, the set of acts and narrative procedures that give rise to and govern this fictive universe. This distinction, analytic in nature, requires that we do not confuse the different instances and levels of a narrative fiction and that we maintain the distinction between these two universes. We must, for example, distinguish in principle between a character and a narrator, or a narrator included in a story and a narrative voice at the source of a "recounted world" into which other elements of fiction (words, acts, and events) may be inserted. As for the *story* as a sequence of actions and events, it does not necessarily correspond to the *diegesis,* or "recounted world," which implies other fictive elements like descriptions, for example. Gérard Genette, who has developed these definitions (borrowing from Souriau the use of the term "diegesis" in this sense) and has shown their application through the example of an analysis of *À la recherche du temps perdu* by Marcel Proust (*Figures* III, Seuil), returned to these distinctions in an attempt to clear up certain misunderstandings in his *Nouveau discours du récit,* 5–10.

it becomes impossible to find a criterion of distinction between the narration and what is narrated because the narrative voices become one, Hamburger does say that in such cases "Bericht und Rede fließt uns zusammen in der gestalteten Welt der betreffenden Dichtung [The *Bericht* and the discourse only reach us as a single flux, in the world created in the *Dichtung*]." The *Bericht* here is not a protocol, or the communication of a truth, but the continuum of what is narrated, where the narrative structure dissolves in the flow of the fiction. For Staiger, there was *Bericht* because there was still no conceptual distinction between "narration" and *diégèse* (the fictional world was the work of Homeric diction). For Hamburger, by contrast, insofar as it yields the disappearance of the procedure in the fictional image, the narrative as *Bericht* is the undifferentiated *product* of the word of differentiation. *Bericht* is the mixture of the narrative sequence, the *naturalization* of the narration in the language of fiction, as Barthes would have said. In a sense closer to rhetoric than to narratology, *Bericht* may mean narration without ornament (*sachlichnüchtern*), as opposed to description (*Beschreibung*) or the presence of reflections and commentary (*Erörterungen*) in the narrative. This, for example, is the definition given by Wilpert. However, the question of *Bericht* comes for him from *Stilkunst* (that is, from the stylistics of literary forms). If narrative fiction is not simply an art of discourse on paper but a language in itself, *Bericht* is therefore both what seems not to be a part of the narrative and the mark of the power of narrative language (of its "magic," as Borges would say).

Thus, *Bericht* turns its back on contemporary usage, just as *Erzählen* moves beyond its origins, since *erzellen*, in Middle High German, meant "to count" (the number of facts). The Grimms give two groups of synonyms for *erzählen*: *narrare, enarrare, recitare*, on one hand, *enumerare, recensere, aufzählen* (to count), *vortragen* (to report, to present) on the other. Between *berichten* and *erzählen* we therefore have a chiasmus: whereas *berichten* means initially "to transmit truth" and then "to transpose the given in the continuum of the narrative artifact," *erzählen* is "to make actions and events follow one another in the proper order of the narrative presentation, to order the sequence." From one to the other, the issue is that of an antagonism between Aristotelian poetics, where the account gives order, and a Platonic poetics, where the given is re-given—between recitation and citation.

III. The Narrative of the Event: *Geschichte / Geschehen / Begebenheit*

Suppose we follow Genette and give the name of *histoire* (story) to the sequence of actions and events organized by a certain narrative mode. German has an equivalent term—*Geschichte*—and Genette's German translators did indeed translate *histoire* by *Geschichte* and *diégèse* by *Diegese*. It remains the case that, if we define "story" as a sequence of recounted events, the German words at the disposal of translators are problematic. We may translate "recounted event" by *Ereignis*, but we could also use *Geschehen* (or *Geschehnis*). The two terms come from the same root as *Geschichte* (Old High German *giscïht*, Middle High German *gescïht, sïcht*, or *schïht*, coming from the Old High German *scehan*, from which *Geschehen* comes as well). When the Grimms define *Geschichte* (narrative? story?) as "der zusammenhängende bericht über diese

begebenheiten, das geschichtswerk," we might translate it as "the narrative cohesion of events, the story as a work." However, there is not a single word here that does not pose problems: neither *bericht, begebenheit*, nor *geschichtswerk*, nor even the sense of *zusammenhängend*. Of course, Aristotle's *Poetics* is indeed about the "*sustasis tôn pragmatôn*" [σύστασις τῶν πραγμάτων] of the "presentation of facts," but *Begebenheit* does not translate *pragmata*, and the distinction we should respect between *Bericht* and *zusammenhängend* (the narrative continuum that a narrative holds together as a whole) is not found in Greek. What, then, is the relation between *Geschichte* and *Geschehen, Geschehen* and *Ereignis, Ereignis* and *Begebenheit*?

A. *Begebenheit, casus narrativus*

Let us consult the Grimms again, for *Begebenheit*. They give *eventus, vorfall, ereignis, geschichte* as synonyms. *Begebenheit* is "what happens," derived from the verb *sich (hin) begeben*, "to go somewhere." In the eighteenth century many novels were titled as *Begebenheiten*—the equivalent of the French *histoire* (*Histoire du chevalier des Grieux et de Manon Lescaut*). Goethe greatly contributed to establishing its meaning. First, he used it, contrary to the norm, in the singular: *die Begebenheit* is thus "what happens to us," the force of accident—"Stürzen wir uns in das Rauschen der Zeit, ins Rollen der Begebenheit [Let us throw ourselves into the roar of Time, in what happens to us like the roll of a wave which carries us]" (*Faust I*, around 1775). Second, he distinguishes it from *Tat* (action), so that *Begebenheit* takes the meaning of *gesta, Taten* of *pragmata*: "Im Roman sollen vorzüglich Gesinnungen und Begebenheiten vorgestellt werden, im Drama Charaktere und Taten [In the novel opinions and *Begebenheiten* are what should mainly be presented, whereas in drama, characters and *Taten*]" (*Wilhelm Meisters Lehrjahre*, bk. 5, chap. 7, Weimar ed., 22:178).

In this sense, *Begebenheit* would be the *casus narrativus*, an important occurrence of life or history worthy of being taken into account by the narrative, since it contains both chance and meaning at the same time. It would be a "prenarrativity" in Ricoeur's sense. According to Goethe in *Literarischer Sanculotism* (Weimar ed. 40:148), a *Nationalautor*, a classical national author, is someone who "in der Geschichte seiner Nation große Begebenheiten und ihre Folgen in einer glucklichen und bedeutenden Einheit vorfindet [finds in the history of his nation great *Begebenheiten* and their consequences (gathered) into a significant unity]." Deliberately mixing the "pre-narrative" given and the narrative organization, Goethe says, with regard to a subject that he seeks to exploit in narrative and whose content is suicide:

> Es wollte sich nichts gestalten; es fehlte eine Begebenheit, eine Fabel, in der sie sich verkörpern konnten.

> (Nothing wanted to take form (*sich gestalten*); there was lacking a *Begebenheit*, a Fable, in which they [i.e., his thoughts on suicide] could have been embodied.)

> (Goethe, *Dichtung und Wahrheit*, Weimar ed., 28:200)

Though the structure of the narrative is the *body*, its object here is not an idea but a "Fable." "Fable" (*Fabel*), however, is the word that, from the Middle Ages to Brecht, translates the Aristotelian *muthos* [μῦθος], the *sustasis*—not just *Ereignis*, but also *Begebenheit*—a prearticulated given.

It is on the basis of this conception that Goethe was able to give one of the most pertinent formulations of the genre of the story (*nouvelle*): "Was ist eine Novelle anders als eine sich ereignende unerhörte Begebenheit?": "What is a story other than an incredible <sensational and catastrophic value of the content of the (bad) news> Begebenheit <important narrative given> that takes place (*sich ereignend*)?" The event (*Ereignis*), the *casus*, is here explicitly distinguished from the *casus narrativus*. As for the rest, Goethe adds, call it what you wish: *Erzählung* or otherwise.

B. The (re)appearance of a collective-singular: *das Geschehen*

If *Begebenheit* is a prearticulated given, what is the situation with regard to the relations between *Geschichte* (history) and *Geschehen*—or *Geschehnis* (recounted event)? In everyday language *Geschehen* may be a synonym of *Ereignis*, and it is often used as such by the traditional language of *Literaturwissenschaft*. Gero von Wilpert moves quite simply from *Geschichte* to *Erzählung*, which he defines as "Darstellung des Verlaufs von wirklichen oder gedachten Geschehnissen [representation of the unfolding of true or imagined events]." Here again, it is only by importing the terminology of theories of narrativity that the term finds a new precision and becomes reserved, not for the *how*, but for the *what* of narration. In the most current state of play (M. Martinez and M. Scheffel, *Einführung in die Erzähltheorie*), *Geschehen* and *Geschichte* are the objects of a strict differentiation: a series of events (*Ereignisse*) when related for a *Geschehen*—corresponding to the English "story" or *histoire* in Genette's sense. The term *Geschichte* is reserved, however, to indicate that we are no longer considering the whole of a sequence of actions and events but their unfolding insofar as it reveals a logic of causality and responds to a motivation in the sense of the Russian formalists (thus to a presentation of this plausible series according to the causality inferred by the narration). In this case *Geschichte* corresponds to the English "plot." As for *Geschehen*, it would be, according to this definition, the Whole of the narrative at the level of the *story*—*histoire* in Genette's sense, that is, insofar as it is a sequence of recounted events. However, if we no longer envisage the difference between the unfolding that is recounted in the continuum of history and the unfolding that is motivated by the structures involved in placing it in a narrative, and we consider the fact that this Whole is also the continuum of the fictional, then we may say that *Geschehen* is also the Whole of what is recounted. This is how Käte Hamburger saw it: "Das Erzählen ist das Geschehen, das Geschehen ist das Erzählen [the telling is the story, the story is the telling]."

It is interesting to note that this promotion of *Geschehen* from the status of event (*Ereignis*) to that of the Whole of a series of events or of the Whole of the telling only repeats, some 200 years later, the move from *Geschichten* (narratives) to the collective-singular *die Geschichte*, whose appearance—which does not take place without resistance (we still find *die Geschichten* [here still in the plural] in Herder for stories in the sense of *res gestae*)—accompanied the emergence of a philosophy of history starting in the second half of the eighteenth century (cf. R. Koselleck; see HISTORY, II).

IV. *Beschreibung / Schilderung*: From Images to Writing

The vocabulary of description also has its untranslatables, since the idea of description is distributed over two words, *Beschreibung* and *Schilderung*. Far from being simple equivalents, the words come from two different worlds: that of writing and that of painting. Gero von Wilpert's definition of *Beschreibung* in his *Sachwörterbuch der Literatur* explains them in terms of one another, and both of them through a third, *ausmalen* (to paint). BESCHREIBUNG: "Schilderung und ausmalende Wiedergabe eines Sachverhalts, Gegenstandes (Landschaft, Haus, Raum) oder einer Person durch sprachliche Mittel."

Beschreibung is the *Schilderung*, i.e., the "reproduction" (*ausmalend*, literally "what paints") of a state of affairs, an object (landscape, house, room), or a person by means of language.

A. Painting and writing

To tease the members of this group apart, we should begin by pointing out that *beschreiben* does not originally mean *describe* in the sense of "to make a description," but *inscribe*, "to put down on paper." We still find this meaning today in everyday language when we say, for example, *ein Blatt beschreiben* to mean "cover a page with writing" (the Grimms give *vollschreiben* and *implere paginam* as equivalents for this meaning). On that basis *beschreiben* in geometry means "to draw geometrical figures." The same usage exists in English—no untranslatable here: descriptive geometry is called *beschreibende Geometrie*. In its adjectival use *beschreibend*, "descriptive," corresponds in poetics to the usage of the epithet *descriptif*: *beschreibende Poesie* = "descriptive poetry." Let us also note that although the term *Beschreiber*, the German calque of the Latin *scriptor*, has survived up to the present day in the sense of someone who describes an object or event by a narrative (someone who recounts a journey is a *Reisebeschreiber*, someone who recounts a life is a *Lebensbeschreiber*), the *scriptor* has not been *der Beschreiber* in German since the sixteenth century (Luther uses it in this sense), but rather *der Schriftsteller*. The word was invented by analogy with *Briefsteller* (hence the public writer, who composes [*stellt*] letters [*Briefe*] for others).

If *Beschreibung* is *mimêsis* [μίμησις] by (in)scription, *Schilderung* "thinks" of it as painting. In the seventeenth and eighteenth centuries, the word *Schilderei*, imported from the Dutch, was the equivalent of *Gemälde* and indicated a painting. In his *Geschichten* (Strasbourg, 1677) Philander von Sittewald (Johannes Michael Moscherosch) writes: "Also hat Horatius die picturam der poesi, die Schilderei der Poeterey vorziehen wollen (Horace thus wished to give preference to *pictura* over poetry, to painting over *Poeterey* [which could be translated by 'literature'])." As equivalents for *Schilderei*, the Grimms give *bildliche Darstellung* (imagistic representation), *Gemälde* (painting), *tabula picta*, *imago*, *simulacrum*, *effigies*. *Schilderei* is the *ut pictura poiesis*. In the eighteenth century the word cedes its place to *Schilderung*, which has kept it to the present day. The Grimms note in the nineteenth century that the proper sense of *peinture*, a painting, was forgotten and that the image of description as image-painting had actually been lost "lately." But this was only partly true. Adelung still noted that *Schilderung* was "lebhafte Beschreibung eines Dinges nach allen seinen Teilen, ein rednerisches oder poetisches Bild [living description (*Beschreibung*) of an object according to all its parts, the image of the orator or the poet]," simply transposing the rhetorical imperative of *hypotypose* and *ekphrasis* (*ut ante oculos videatur*) into the domain of literature. And although the meaning of *tableau* in the proper sense disappeared with the arrival of *Schilderung* in the eighteenth century, it remains the case that *Schilderung*, unlike *Beschreibung*, always retained the trace of this lost origin. It is remarkable, for example, that toward the end of the nineteenth century, that is, when German social democracy began to become aware of its power, a large number of titles appeared such as *Schilderung des sozialen Elends* (Painting of social poverty), *Schilderung des Aufstandes der Arbeiter von Paris vom 23. bis zum 26. Juni 1848* (*Schilderung* of the uprising of Parisian workers . . .), *Schilderung des vom preußischen Parlament und vom Zentrum gegen die Bergarbeiter ausgeübten Verrats* (*Schilderung* of Prussian parliament's betrayal of the workers . . .), etc. just as, in the middle of the nineteenth century, we find titles like *Schilderung der in Berns Umgebung sichtbaren Gebirge* (Description of mountains around Bern, 1852). From creating an image of the picturesque Alps to giving a true recounting of the class struggle, *Schilderung* could not mean "description," but rather, in the case of the Alps, "picturesque tableau" and, in the case of political conflicts or poverty, "lively and truthful reconstruction." Whether it is a matter of romantic picturesqueness or political enthusiasm, *Schilderung* is the heir to the figures of *ekphrasis* [ἔκφρασις] and hypotypose (see DESCRIPTION, Box 1). In the vocabulary of narrative technique, it is thus not a simple technical term related to the structuring of the plot or the paradoxes of the relation between narration and description, but the survivor of the power of the imagination in fiction.

But if that is the case, why does Gero von Wilpert need, in his definition of *Beschreibung*, to add to the equivalent *Schilderung* the criterion of *ausmalen*—which comes, like *Schilderung*, from painting rather than writing? *Ausmalen* is not only *depingere*, but to do so in detail. Whence the assimilation of the term to the rhetorical figures of *amplificatio* and *ornatus* and its extension toward two poles. For *ausmalen* is either to lift up by means of more color (in the most concrete sense, of repainting a facade with more lively colors) or to intensify the vivacity of the fictional image by adding details to the narration.

B. From the painting to the image: *Schilderung* and *Bild*

What relationship is there between the fictional tableau and the philosophical status of the word *Bild*? A fictional tableau is not a *Bild* but rather *Abbild*. It is not the schematization of the world but its living tableau. And when romanticism led its crusade against classical imitation, it was by extending the Fichtean view of the imagination as a limitless expansion of the "I"'s powers of self-invention (cf. Walter Benjamin's analyses in his study of German romanticism)—moving from reflection (*Nachahmung, Wiedergabe*) to the absolute reflection of the imagination in its images, both speculative and in competition with the theoretical. It was thus possible to conceive of the imagination, *Einbildungskraft*, as an originating power, and of the work as its product and its origin at the same time. However, the *Schilderei* of the descriptive artifact does not derive from a notion of an originative absolute. It remains,

in the Aristotelian tradition, the procedure of *inscription-image*, whose goal is not to rival the universality of the idea but rather to return to the living of the real its "truth"—after a mimetic detour. This is indeed what Aristotle says about *mimêsis* and its power: "the reason of the delight in seeing the picture is that one is at the same time learning—gathering the meaning of things, e.g., that the man there is so-and-so" (*Poetics*, 4, 1448 b 15). This faculty of giving the truth back its images, the Aristotelian *apeikazein* [ἀπεικάζειν], is not the production of an ideal object as with Plato. Transcendental idealism, which in Germany exerted such pressure on poetic discourse, continues to cast its shadow—that of an inverted Platonic *mimêsis*, one that perdures through the romantic collusion between the Subject and the *Bild*. For Heidegger the *Bild* (*Kant-Buch*, §20) still remains "*Versinnlichung von Begriffen* (a making perceptible of concepts)": from the schema of Kantian representation to the *Anblick*, in viewing the world, the image remains a power of the mind, even though in the end it is kept in its Otherness, like the existence of a painting of the world, in front of the eyes of the mind.

If the vocabularies of narratological instances and mimetic structure still have so much difficulty in freeing themselves from their metaphysical cast, it is precisely because romanticism countered transcendental Idealism with a literary absolute for which the infinite freedom of the mind remains that of the writing or imagining *subject*. As long as the schematization of language remains short-circuited by the absolute of the "I," *poiêsis* [ποίησις] can only be conceived as an infinite power of image production, one that is all the more free as the figures of its infinity are freed from any linguistic categorization (Frederick Schlegel baptizes them *unendliche Fülle* [infinite plenitude] or *Arabeske*). Diametrically opposed, if the infinite will is all that remains for "overthrowing Platonism," as for Nietzsche, the "*Schematisierung der Welt* (schematization of the world)" is indeed the imposition on the world of a *Kunstwerk* that is only the form of the will transformed into a possible world—and real at the same time—beyond the Platonic cleavage between image and truth, and whose infinite Wagnerian melody was for Nietzsche at one time the proof, confirming that the schema and the anti-schema of form are only one single thing as long as the form is not structured "like a language," but free as the song of the Kantian nightingale.

The overthrow of Platonism in the vocabulary of the literary imagination is barely underway in Germany, and the need for it is still far from being perceived in all its domains.

Jean-Pierre Dubost

BIBLIOGRAPHY

Bal, Mieke. *Narratology: Introduction to the Theory of Narrative*. Translated by C. von Boheemen. Toronto: Toronto University Press, 1985.

Benjamin, Walter. *Der Begriff der Kunstkritik in der deutschen Frühromantik*. In *Gesammelte Schriften*, I/1. Frankfurt: Suhrkamp, 1974. Translation: *The Concept of Criticism in German Romanticism*. In *Selected Writings*, vol. 1, 1913–26, edited by Marcus Bullock and Michael W. Jennings. Cambridge, MA: Harvard University Press, 2000.

Booth, Wayne C. *The Rhetoric of Fiction*. Chicago: University of Chicago Press, 1983.

Cohn, Dorrit. *The Distinction of Fiction*. Baltimore, MD: Johns Hopkins University Press, 1999.

Genette, Gérard. *Figures* III. Paris: Éditions du Seuil, 1972. Translation by Jane E. Lewin: *Narrative Discourse*. Ithaca, NY: Cornell University Press, 1980.

———. *Introduction à l'architexte*. Paris: Éditions du Seuil, 1979. Translation by Jane E. Lewin: *The Architext: An Introduction*. Berkeley: University of California Press, 1992.

———. *Nouveau Discours du récit*. Paris: Éditions du Seuil, 1983. Translation by Jane E. Lewin: *Narrative Discourse Revisited*. Ithaca, NY: Cornell University Press, 1988.

Hamburger, Käte. *Die Logik der Dichtung*. Stuttgart: Ernst Klett Verlag, 1957. Translation by M. J. Rose: *The Logic of Literature*. Bloomington: Indiana University Press, 1973.

Kayser, Wolfgang. *Das sprachliche Kunstwerk*. Berne: Francke, 1948.

Lämmert, Eberhard. *Bauformen des Erzählens*. Stuttgart: Metzler, 1955.

Müller, Günther. *Morphologische Poetik*. Tübingen: Niemeyer, 1968.

Staiger, Emil. *Grundbegriffe der Poetik*. Zurich: Atlantis, 1946. Translation by Janette C. Hudson and Luanne T. Frank: *Basic Concepts of Poetics*, edited by Marianne Burkhard and Luanne T. Frank. University Park: Pennsylvania State University Press, 1991.

Stanzel, Franz K. *Typische Formen des Romans*. Göttingen: Vandenhoeck and Ruprecht, 1964. Translation by J. P. Pusack: *Narrative Situations in the Novel*. Bloomington: Indiana University Press, 1971.

ES, ICH, ÜBER-ICH

ENGLISH	id; I, me, self; super-ego
FRENCH	*id; ça; je, moi; surmoi*
GREEK	*egó* [ἐγώ]
LATIN	*id; ego*

➤ CONSCIOUSNESS, DRIVE, ES GIBT, I/ME/MYSELF, *IL Y A, PERSON*, ROMANTIC, SELBST, SUBJECT, UNCONSCIOUS

The first topography developed by Freud starting with *The Interpretation of Dreams* (1900) and that includes the conscious, the preconscious, and the unconscious is based on the classical vocabulary of philosophy and psychology. The only innovation here from the linguistic point of view is the introduction of the preconscious (*das Vorbewusste*). That model thus does not pose any particular problem of translation. It is entirely otherwise with the second topography, which, beginning with the publication in 1923 of the essay "Das Ich und das Es" (The Ego and the Id), uses a vocabulary that is entirely specific to the German language, in order to define the psychological as a complex system in which are confronted, balanced, and dissolved what we might call psychic "figures," bearers of "personality" (the Ego and the Superego), with the latter two deriving their energy from the reservoir of drives that is the Id. Thus, we may say that the Ego is the "center" of the personality and that it tries to find a balance among the threefold demands of reality, of the Superego (which bears the ideal and prohibitions), and of the Id, that is, archaic desires. However, far from being an autonomous being supporting the transparent identity of a subject, the Ego itself is the product of a series of identifications. To give a lively representation of what he calls the "decomposition of the psychic personality," Freud chooses to use substantival pronouns (*Ich*, the personal pronoun of the first-person singular; *Id*, the neuter pronoun of the third-person singular), which he finds in the philosophical and psychological traditions (*das Ich*), among recent authors (*das Es*), or which he invents (*das Über-Ich*).

The difficulty of translating these terms into English or French thus rests both on the difference between the systems of pronouns in the two languages and on the "classical" translations of the substantival *Ich*. Finally, the interpretations themselves of this new topic, and especially of the meaning of *Ich*, help orient the translations, and lead Lacan to reintroduce, following Edouard Pichon, a distinction between *moi* (me) and *je* (I).

I. The Pronoun *Ich*

Ich, the personal pronoun in the first-person singular, corresponds to the Greek *ego* [ἐγώ], the Latin *ego*, the French *je*, and the English "I." German does not have an equivalent of the French *moi*, that is, to a "tonic form" of "I," or as Littré defines it, a "pronoun . . . whose primary role is to serve as an object, but which is also used as a subject when a non-enclitic form, such as *je* and *me*, is required" (RT: *Dictionnaire de la langue française*). In the sixteenth century *je* was felt to be enclitic (we still find in Scarron, *Le Virgile travesti*, "je qui chantai jadis Typhon d'un style que l'on trouvera bouffon"). In German, *Ich* is both the strong and the weak form: *Ich, Ich = moi, je*; *Ich, der = moi qui*, and so on. Thus the famous phrase "Et in Arcadia ego" is translated into French as "Moi aussi, j'ai vécu en Arcadie," and in German (by Schiller, *Thalia*) as "Auch Ich war in Arcadia geboren."

This reinforced form was, reasonably, nominalized in French. It thus represents the I that is the object of psychology:

> Moi, en tant que pensant (*Ich, als denkend*), je suis un object du sense interne et je m'appelle une âme (*und heisse Seele*). Si bien que l'expression: moi (*der Ausdruck: Ich*), en tant qu'être pensant, désigne déja l'objet de la psychologie.

(Kant, *Kritik der reinen Vernunft*)

The Fichtean distinction between *Ich* and *Nicht-Ich* thus becomes that of the I and the not-I, and *moi transcendental* naturally translates Husserl's *tranzendentale Ich*:

> Par l'ἐποχή phénoménologique, je réduis mon moi humain naturel (*mein naturalisches menschliches Ich*) et ma vie psychique—domaine de l'expérience de soi psychologique (*meiner psychologischen Selbsterfahrung*)—à mon moi (*Ich*) transcendental et phénoménologique, domaine de l'expérience de soi (*Selbsterfahrung*) transcendentale et phénoménologique.

(Husserl, *Cartesianische Meditationen*)

We may therefore put the question thus: is the Freudian *Ich* a strong or weak subject? This question seems abruptly to reduce a theoretical question to a grammatical one: however, grammatical considerations are essential for understanding the debates that have animated French psychoanalysis.

■ See Box 1.

II. The Neuter Pronoun *Es*

The translation of *Es* by *ça* in French was not established without difficulty. The group that gathered on 31 May 1927 did indeed adopt *ça* as proposed by Édouard Pichon, against the opinion of Angelo Hesnard, but when Freud apparently voiced disapproval, *soi* was chosen in the end on 20 July 1928. We find a remarkable trace of these difficulties of translation in a note by Hesnard, added to the translation of Freud's *Le moi et le ça* by S. Jankélévitch:

> The Freudian *Es*, neuter pronoun in German, is untranslatable into French. It was suggested that we translate

1

Je and *moi*, from Pichon to Lacan

Founded in 1926, the Société psychanalytique de Paris (SPP) counted among its members the grammarian Édouard Pichon, co-author with Jacques Damourette of the *Essai de grammaire de la langue française*. He started a linguistic commission for the unification of French psychoanalytic vocabulary. At its meeting of 29 May 1927, Pichon was the only one opposed to the translation of *Ich* by *moi*:

> M. Pichon explains why the translation of *Ich* by "moi" seems wrong to him. "Moi" is opposed to not-"Moi"; it contains everything in the subject's psyche; it answers just as well to *das Es* as to *das Ich*: what is proper to *Ich* in his view is the ability to be the subject of conscious thought: this is why he suggests *ego* as a translation, or *je*, terms which are as it happens the least inexact correlates for *Ich*.
>
> (*Revue française de psychanalyse* 2 (1927): 404–5)

Moi won by four votes to one.

Despite his curious assimilation of *Ich* with consciousness, did Pichon anticipate, on the basis of purely grammatical considerations, Lacan's splitting of *Ich* into *je* and *moi*? One might think so on the basis of an article entitled "La personne et la personnalité vues à la lumière de la pensée idiomatique française," dedicated precisely to distinguishing *je* and *moi*, but in a sense rather far away from Lacan's (which Roudinesco does not seem to make clear in *Histoire de la psychanalyse en France*). For Lacan, the distinction between *je* and *moi* corresponds to two fundamentally different psychic functions. The *je* is the subject of the unconscious, the subject of the signifier; yet, the subject, in the "circle of the signifier," cannot "count itself and only act as an absence." Where, then, does the *moi* come from? From the need to overcome this absence, or "the invisible mark that the subject has from the signifier," which "alienates him … in the primary identification which forms the ideal of the *moi*" ("Subversion du sujet et dialectique du désir"). In any case, we will see below whether the Lacanian distinction between *je* and *moi* is necessarily located "inside" the *Ich*.

In the above-cited article, however, Pichon, on the basis of grammar, distinguishes the *je-me* as "thin personality" with the *moi* as "thick personality." It is true that the *je*, however thin, represents the unchangeable part, and the *moi* the changeable, notably by means of the cure: one thus helps a patient "by explaining to him that destroying one part of his *moi* may temporarily cause suffering to his *je-me*, but not mutilate it. . . . And the patient will feel that his new *moi*, that is, the new thickness of his person, fits better than the old one with his *je-me*." Pichon does not show how the *moi* is produced from the *je*. Further, nothing is more foreign to Lacan than this doctrine of thicknesses: how can we be sure of not being taken in by a new narcissistic mirage, by identifying with the analyst? The Lacanian cure is more of a procedure of paring down the *moi*, and grammar should not mask the meaning of psychic functions:

> analyzing whether and how the *je* and the *moi* are distinct and how they overlap in each particular subject is not a matter of the grammatical conception of the functions in which they appear.
>
> (Lacan, "La chose freudienne")

BIBLIOGRAPHY

Lacan, Jacques. "La chose freudienne." In *Écrits*. Paris: Éditions du Seuil, 1966.
———. "La personne et la personnalité vues à la lumière de la pensée idiomatique française." *Revue française de psychanalyse* 3 (1938): 447–59.
———. "Subversion du sujet et dialectique du désir." In *Écrits*. Paris: Éditions du Seuil, 1966.
Pichon, Édouard, and Jacques Damourette. *Essai de grammaire de la langue française (1911–40)*. Repr., Geneva: Slatkine, 1983.
Roudinesco, Élisabeth. *Histoire de la psychanalyse en France*. Vol. 2. Paris: Fayard, 1994.

it by the Latin *Id*. Usage favored the term *Ça* (or *cela*). Many psychoanalysts keep the German term *Es*, contrasted with *Ich* (Moi) and *Über-Ich* (Sur-Moi).

In German, *Es* is a neuter pronoun that is used in a large number of expressions translated in French by *ça* or *il* (e.g., *es regnet*, *il pleut*; *es geht*, *ça va*; see ES GIBT). Its nominalization in Freud's writing is the consequence in German of a whole train of thought (philosophy of nature, Romantic medicine, vitalism), which, over the course of the nineteenth century, used the impersonal *Es* to refer to activities that cannot be controlled by the will or consciousness (cf. Staewen-Haas, "Le terme 'es' ['ça']"; "Zur Genealogie des 'Es' ").

In what is called in French *Le moi et le ça*, Freud claims to be borrowing the term, in its nominalized form, from Groddeck, and further back, from Nietzsche:

> I propose to take it into account, by proposing to call *das Ich* that which comes from the system of *perception* and which is at first *preconscious*, and to call the other psychic element, into which the *Ich* extends and which behaves like the *unconscious*, the *Es*, following Groddeck's usage.

Freud clarifies in a note: "Groddeck probably followed Nietzsche, who frequently uses this grammatical expression to refer to that part of our being which is impersonal and thus subject to natural necessity [*Naturnotwendig*]."

It remains the case that neither Nietzsche nor any of his predecessors (e.g., Georg Lichtenberg and Eduard von Hartmann) construct a real concept of the *Es*. The claim of paragraph 17 of *Jenseits von Gut und Böse* (*Beyond Good and Evil*) is certainly not to replace the Cartesian "I think" with "it thinks," but to show that, in both cases, what remains is the belief in a subject of thought, even if it is impersonal:

> It thinks (*Es denkt*): but that with this "it" (*dies "es"*) we should in fact be dealing with the ancient and celebrated "I" ("*Ich*") is only, to speak politely, an assumption. . . . . . But we still do too much with this "it thinks" ("*es denkt*"): this "it" (*dies "es"*) already contains an interpretation of the process, and does not belong to the process itself.

Nietzsche is thus critiquing Romantic and especially Neo-Romantic usage (note that he preserves the lowercase: he is interested in a grammatical function). This usage is precisely the same as Groddeck's, who gives the expression its nominalizing turn. Freud is able to take over the phrase and to give it a role and a rigorous definition, while still recognizing its fundamentally irrational nature. While not everything dissolves into the *Es*, everything does come out of it.

III. The English Translation: "Ego and Id"

As with other Freudian terms, the English translation took a scholarly direction early on (beginning in 1927 with the translation of *The Ego and the Id* by Joan Riviere): the use of Latin terms, even though English of course possesses an array of pronouns ("I" and "it"), as well as "me," an equivalent of the French *moi* (*c'est moi*, "it's me"—in German, *Ich bin es*). Unlike in France, the choice did not occasion much discussion. It corresponds fully with the medical orientation of psychoanalysis in the Anglo-Saxon world. It must be noted, however, that "ego" was used from the middle of the nineteenth century in psychology to refer to the psychic function corresponding to the pronoun "I": nominalizing this pronoun for psychoanalytic usage would have been a genuine terminological invention. Bruno Bettelheim, in *Freud and Man's Soul*, shows just how much the English translation introduces abstractions where Freud attempts to anchor his second topic in the most everyday language.

English can also, however, use its own resources for creating terms: this is the case, for example, with Winnicott, who creates, alongside the ego, a distinct notion: the "self." Here is how he defines it, in a letter addressed to the translator of one of his articles, who is having difficulty with the translation of "self": "For me the self, which is not the ego, is the person who is me, who is only me, who has a totality based on the operation of the maturational process" (letter of 19 January 1971). However, the French tradition of translating German terms also leads to the rejection of the solutions offered by the French language. In translating "self" by *moi*, the translator of the article in question fears no longer having this term available to translate "ego": whence the preservation, in the translation, of the term "self," declared untranslatable. As we see, the problem does not reside at all in the absence of resources of the target language. But, with the "self" having been declared untranslatable by Winnicott's translators, and without *je* being brought into play, here is the authorized translation: "Pour moi, le *self*, qui n'est pas le moi, est la personne qui est moi."

- See Box 2.

In conclusion, we may see that the choices of translation are not unrelated to the question of the scientific status of psychoanalysis. The second topic represents Freud's desire to break with abstract character of the first (unconscious, preconscious, conscious) and its roots in the vocabulary of psychology and philosophy. Whatever Freud's declarations about the scientific character of his invention, the second topic is more in line with Freud's place in German Romantic literature. Though both French and English translators are aware of this aspect of Freud, the latter did everything possible to hide it and thus give themselves a way of preserving continuity in Freud's work. The former are more hesitant, which is partly due to the absence of a theoretical unity in the French psychoanalytic movement (logic would have required the *moi* and the *soi* or the *je* and the *ça*). Lacan did try to exemplify this unity, but his *je* was not adopted. This was not only because of linguistic inertia: rather, it is because, by splitting Freud's *Ich* into *moi* and *je*, he seems to clarify some aspects of Freud's text at the cost of a formalism that seems excessive. As a Romantic, Freud was no doubt attached to the ambiguity of his notions, which thus reinforces their power of metamorphosis.

Alexandre Abensour

BIBLIOGRAPHY

Bettelheim, Bruno. *Freud and Man's Soul*. London: Hogarth Press, 1983.
Freud, Sigmund. *The Ego and the Id*. Translated by J. Riviere. London: Hogarth Press, 1927.
———. *Le moi et le ça*. Translated by S. Jankélévitch. Paris: Payot, 1971.
———. *The Standard Edition of the Complete Psychological Works of Sigmund Freud*. Edited by J. Strachey. 24 vols. London: Hogarth Press–Institute of Psycho-Analysis, 1953–74.
Groddeck, Georg. *The Book of the It*. Translated by V.M.E. Collins. New York: Funk and Wagnalls, 1950.
Husserl, Edmund. *Cartesianische Meditationen*. In *Husserliana*, vol. 1. La Haye: Nijhoff, 1950.
Hayman, A. "What Do We Mean by Id?" *Journal of the American Psychoanalytic Association* 17, no. 2 (1969).
Kant, Immanuel. *Kritik der reinen Vernunft*. Hamburg: Meiner, 1990.
Lacan, Jacques. *Écrits*. Paris: Éditions du Seuil, 1966. Translation by Bruce Fink: *Écrits*. New York: W. W. Norton, 2007.
Nietzsche, Friedrich. *Jenseits von Gut und Böse*. Edited by G. Colli and M. Montinari. Berlin: De Gruyter, 1988.
Nitzscke, Bernt. "Zur Herkunft des Es. Freud, Groddeck, Nietzsche-Schopenhauer und E. von Hartmann." *Psyche* 9 (1983).
Scarron, Paul. *Le Virgile travesti*. Paris: Delahays, 1858.
Schiller, Friedrich. *Thalia*. In *Resignation, Eine Phantasie*, in *Schillers Werke*, Nationalausgabe, vol. 1, *Geschichte*, 1776–99. First published in 1786.
Staewen-Haas, Renate. "Le terme 'es' ['ça'], histoire de ses vicissitudes tant en allemand qu'en Français." *Revue française de psychanalyse* 4 (1986).
———. "Zur Genealogie des 'Es.'" *Psyche* 2 (1985).
Winnicott, Donald Woods. "Le corps et le self." *Nouvelle revue de psychanalyse* 3 (Spring 1971).

2

The Phrase: "Wo Es war, soll Ich werden"

What is perhaps Freud's most famous phrase, used at the end of his lecture on "The Dissection of the Psychical Personality" (included in the *New Introductory Lectures on Psycho-Analysis*, vol. 22 of the *Standard Edition*), presents a particular translation difficulty that results from the use of nominalized pronouns. The difficulty is compounded by the fact that Freud seems to re-establish the pronominal use (without the articles) while maintaining the nominalized dimension (by writing the pronouns with capitals): "Wo Es war, soll Ich werden" (*Neue Folge der Vorlesungen zur Einführung in die Psychoanalyse*). Word for word, this yields: "Where That was, I should be," or "Where It was, I should be" (Strachey translates it: "Where id was, there ego shall be," thus eliminating the capitalized pronouns).

No translation can preserve the extreme subtlety with which Freud keeps the nouns in writing, even while eliminating them in speech. There are thus two directions:

1. That of the published translations, which do not worry about these subtleties and simply choose to treat *Es* and *Ich* as nouns. The first French translation, by Anne Berman in 1936 (which was the only one available until 1984), even adds a verb that was not in the text: "Le moi doit déloger le ça." The two recent translations, published by Gallimard (1984) and by Presses Universitaires de France (1993), are very close: "Là où était le ça, doit advenir du moi" (Gallimard), and "Là où était du ça, du moi doit advenir" (Presses Universitaires de France). The choice of treating *Es* and *Ich* as partitive is based on the grammatical logic of German: we might miss the pronominal resonance, but the partitive corresponds equally well to the context. Freud, in the immediately preceding sentence, claims in effect that the goal of psychoanalysis is "to strengthen the ego, to make it more independent of the super-ego, to widen its field of perception and enlarge its organization, so that it can appropriate fresh portions of the id" ("The Dissection of the Psychical Personality," *New Introductory Lectures*, vol. 22, *Standard Edition*, and *Gesammelte Werke*, vol. 15).

2. The other direction, one taken by Lacan, grandly ignores this context. Of the several translations that he gives of this Freudian passage, the simplest is no doubt from "La science et la vérité": "Là où c'était, là comme sujet dois-je advenir." This translation, both literal and interpretive at the same time, adds some precision ("comme sujet"), which is completely absent from Freud's text. But the Lacanian interpretation of the second topic is what is at issue here. For Freud, it is clear that the *moi* must conquer territory belonging to the *je*, which is precisely what he calls "cultural work" (*Kulturarbeit*): it is, in fact, the contribution of psychoanalysis to culture at large. Lacan interprets the *Es* in the phrase not as an "uncultivated" part, but as the very location of the subject of the unconscious: in other words, the *moi* must, by entering the location of the subject, become the subject, hence *je*. And the lack of an article does not, for Lacan, make the pronouns into partitives, but rather allows him to leave substantialism behind in order finally to speak the language of ontology:

it appears here that it is into a place: *Wo*, where *Es*, a subject without any *das* or other objectival article, *war*, was, it is a matter of the place of a being, and that in this place: *soll . . .*, *Ich*, I, there must I (as we said: this I-am [*suis-je*], before it is said, is me [*moi*]), *werden*, to become, that is, . . . to come to light from this very place insofar as it is a place of being.

The distinction between *je* and *moi* thus only enters into the *Ich* with regard to the place of the *Es*, that is, for Lacan, of the S: but is Lacan's homophonic trick for moving from one language to another comparable to the game that allows Freud to write one sentence and mean another?

BIBLIOGRAPHY

Freud, Sigmund. *Neue Folge der Vorlesungen zur Einführung in die Psychoanalyse*. In *Gesammelte Werke*, vol. 15. London: Imago, 1915.
———. *The Standard Edition of the Complete Psychological Works of Sigmund Freud*. Edited by J. Strachey. Vol. 22 (1932–36). London: Hogarth Press–Institute of Psycho-Analysis, 1953–74.
Lacan, Jacques. "La chose freudienne." In *Écrits*. Paris: Éditions du Seuil, 1966.
———. "La science et la vérité." In *Écrits*. Paris: Éditions du Seuil, 1966.

ES GIBT (GERMAN)

DANISH	*der er*
ENGLISH	there is
FRENCH	*il y a*

➤ ESTI, *IL Y A*, HÁ, and COMBINATION AND CONCEPTUALIZATION, DASEIN, EREIGNIS, ES, FICAR, LIGHT, LOGOS, OBJECT, SEIN, SUBJECT, *TO BE*, VORHANDEN

Unlike other Germanic languages (Eng. "there is"; Dan. *der er*), German expresses the Gallicism *il y a* by the phrase *es gibt*—literally "he/it gives" (+ accusative), by combining the impersonal pronoun *es* with the verb *geben*, "to give." There thus seems to be a predisposition in the German language to think of what exists under the aspect of being given and to think of its origins as impersonal. This entry investigates that predisposition by following the ways in which German thought exploits and orchestrates the two components of the phrase *es gibt*.

I. From *Datur* to *Es Gibt*

No doubt we should not exaggerate the idiomatic, even specifically Germanic aspect of the phrase *es gibt*, whose strange (*seltsam*) character was noted by the Grimms themselves, while nonetheless underlining its relationship, at least in scholarly language, to the use of the Latin *dare* ("to give") in the passive, hence, *dari*. The Grimms refer to Spinoza (*Ethics*, II, 49): in mente nulla datur absoluta facultas volendi et nolendi ("There is in the mind

no absolute faculty of positive or negative volition"). They comment: *datur* gleich *es gibt*, "*datur* being here equivalent to *es gibt*." We still speak in this sense of the "givens in a problem," the "immediate givens of consciousness" (Bergson), of *sense data* (Wittgenstein).

What exists, what presents itself to our thought (intuition, etc.), without the latter's doing anything is a *datum*, a *Gegebenes*. German philosophy, from Kant to Husserl, explores this route, following the vocabulary of giving (and hence receiving), in the expression *es gibt*. Another route, carved out by Heidegger, instead underlines the strangeness of the impersonal *es* in *es gibt*. The numerous variations in German philosophy that derive from the simple phrase *es gibt* oscillate between the appearance created by the giving itself and that of which or by which the giving takes place (though it is fair to ask: the giving of what, exactly?).

■ See Box 1.

II. From *Es Gibt* to *Gegebenheit*: Kant and Husserl

Intuition takes place only insofar as the object is given to us (*gegeben wird*); "by the intermediary of sensation, objects are given to us (*gegeben*), and it alone brings us intuitions": the whole beginning of the "Transcendental Aesthetic" of Kant's *Critique of Pure Reason* is directed by the distinction between what is given and what is thought (*gegeben/gedacht*), where the priority of the former is recognized. In shifting from a

1

A personal construction of the impersonal

In certain dialects of Thuringia and Hesse, etc., we find this same turn of phrase (*es gibt*) governed by the nominative, as in the example given by the Grimms: "es gibt ein tüchtiger Regen heute" ("there's going to be a lot of rain today," "that's quite some rain we're going to have today"), the meaning of "give" being erased and the object becoming the subject (grammatically: in the nominative), where *es gibt = es ist, es kommt* ("it is," "there is going to be"). The documented passage from the accusative to the nominative indicates that the very idea of giving may no longer have been felt in the very turn of phrase *es gibt*. We also find (notably in Luther), as a variant of *es gibt*: *es ist gegeben* ("it is given").

Latin to a German terminology, Kant is the witness and the privileged agent in the transposition from the Latin *dari* in the vocabulary of receptivity. In effect, the *Dissertation of 1770* can claim (II, §10): "Intellectualium non datur (homini) Intuitus [There is no *intuition* of intelligibles (for man)]" or again (II, §5): "dantur conceptus [concepts are given]"! The Latin *dari*, which, in Spinoza and up until the pre-Critical Kant, kept the thoroughly geometrical aspect of the given in a problem, will find itself explicitly thematized and transformed.

The modality of what is given to us (= what is presented to intuition) is fixed by Husserl in the term *Gegebenheit* (which Kant had not yet ventured), thus nominalizing the past participle of the verb *geben* (to give) in favor of an extension of the sphere of intuition and of the shift from a receptive intuition to a "giving" intuition (*gebende Anschauung*, in *Idées directrices pour une phénoménologie Husserliana*, vol. 2).

Would these variations, Kantian or Husserlian, have seen the light of day if they had not been stimulated by the familiar *es gibt* of everyday conversation? An emphatic use of *es gibt*, in fact, begins to appear in Husserl: "es gibt also ... Bedeutungen [There are meanings]" (*Recherches logiques*, II, §36).

III. *Es Gibt, Es Gilt, Es Gibt Nicht*: Meinong

The exploration of *Gegebenheit* is not, however, restricted to Husserlian phenomenological research. Natorp, Lask, and Meinong all made use of the concept at more or less the same time. In section 3 of his *Gegenstandstheorie*, Meinong writes:

Es gibt Gegenstände, von denen gilt, daß es dergleichen Gegenstände nicht gibt.

(*There are* objects about which it is valid to say *that they do not exist* [about which the proposition according to which they do not exist is valid].)

This is not a crude contradiction, but we should point out that there is some subtle play within *es gibt*: for certain objects we must say that they can only be envisaged as not existing and incapable of existing. This play is redoubled with the assonance between *es gibt* and *es gilt* ("it is valid"). The *es gibt*, for Meinong, applies no less for the unreal. *Es gibt* here is practically equivalent to an "it so happens": it so happens that some objects are nowhere. "What, then, does 'es gibt' mean?"

IV. From Being to Words, Heidegger's *Es Gibt*

This is the question asked by Heidegger in the 1919 lecture at Freiburg titled *Zur Bestimmung der Philosophie*. Three stages may be distinguished in the Heideggerian meditation on *es gibt*:

1. the discussions prior to *Sein und Zeit*,
2. the 1927 treatise, *Sein und Zeit*,
3. the reappraisal of this question in the "Letter on Humanism" (1946), then in *Zeit und Sein* (1962).

1. What, then, does *es gibt* mean?

Es gibt Zahlen, es gibt Dreiecke, es gibt Bilder von Rembrandt, es gibt U-Boote; ich sage: Es gibt heute noch Regen, es gibt morgen Kalbsbraten. Mannigfache "es gibt," und jeweils hat es einen anderen Sinn und doch auch jedes wieder ein in jedem antreffbares identisches Bedeutungsmoment. Auch dieses ganz abgeblaßte, bestimmter Bedeutungen gleichsam entleerte bloße "es gibt" hat gerade wegen seiner Einfachheit seine mannigfachen Rätsel. Wo liegt das sinnhafte Motiv für den Sinn des "es gibt"?

(There are numbers, there are triangles, there are paintings by Rembrandt, and there are submarines; I say: there will be more rain today, there will be roast veal tomorrow [cf. RT: Deutsches Wörterbuch, sense II, 17, e, b, s.v. *geben*]. So many *es gibts*, each one having a different sense, even though each one of these senses contains an identical moment of meaning. And yet this simple *es gibt*, so dull, emptied of precise meanings in a way, contains, in virtue of its very simplicity, numerous riddles. Where does the sense-bearing pattern (*Motiv*) lie for the sense of *es gibt*?)

(Heidegger, *Zur Bestimmung*)

Heidegger thus underlines the multivocity of *es gibt*, its unsuspected richness, and the unity of the generative sense of such a plurality.

2. The occurrences of *es gibt* that we find in *Being and Time*, beginning with section 2, deal either with the world (*Sein und Zeit*), with truth, or with being. The phrase *es gibt* generally occurs in quotation marks, indicating a problematization of the everyday expression, which is thus picked out and questioned. Leibniz asked, "Why *there is* something rather than nothing?" (*Principes de la nature et de la grâce fondés en raison*, §7). For Heidegger, who often came back to Leibniz's declaration, what there is is only something inasmuch as it is not anything, as this something is not equivalent to anything in existence. *There is the there is* (D. Panis).

3. However, it is before *Time and Being*, in the "Letter on Humanism" that *es gibt* is directly addressed, notably with the phrase "*Es gibt Sein* [There is Being]":

In "S. u. Z." (S. 212) ist mit Absicht und Vorsicht gesagt: il y a l'Être: "es gibt" das Sein. Das il y a übersetzt das "es gibt" ungenau. Denn das "es," was hier "gibt," ist das Sein selbst.

(In *Being and Time* (p. 212), *il y a* [*es gibt*] Being is said with design and caution. The *il y a* only approximately translates *es gibt*. For the *cela* [*es*] that *donne* [*gibt*] is Being itself.)

(Heidegger, "Letter on Humanism")

Heidegger interprets the "giving" of *es gibt* immediately afterward as a *gewähren*, "to accord," "to grant." More disturbing is the remark that follows: "Doch über dieses *il y a* kann man nicht geradezu und ohne Anhalt spekulieren [But one cannot speculate straightaway and without reserve on this *il y a*]."

No doubt we should see this as refusing to dissociate *il y a* from Being, since this *il y a* is above all aiming, in this context, to say that Being is not in the same manner in which entities are. This does not prevent Heidegger from coming back to this point in *Time and Being*: "Das in der Rede 'Es gibt Sein,' 'Es gibt Zeit' gesagte 'Es' nennt vermutlich etwas Ausgezeichnetes [There is reason to presume that the 'It' said in 'There is being,' 'There is time' names something typical and exceptional]" (*Time and Being*).

Heidegger clarifies the *es* of *es gibt* in the direction of *Ereignis* (see EREIGNIS). In the *Summary of a Seminar on the Lecture "Time and Being,"* finally, Heidegger declares after citing a passage from Rimbaud's *Illuminations* ("*Enfances*," III"): "The French *il y a* (cf. the idiomatic phrase particular to southern Germany, *es hat*) corresponds to the German *es gibt* but has a greater extension. The exactly parallel translation of Rimbaud's *Il y a* would, in German, be *es ist* (*il est*)" (*Questions IV*).

There remains the question of what separates *il y a* from *es gibt*. The phrase's firm accent on giving—certainly literally indicated, but usually inaudible—may have led J.-L. Marion to overtranslate it by the rendering *cela donne* ("that gives"):

The standard translation of *il y a*, certainly admissible in everyday language, is no longer justified if we desire conceptual precision. It effectively masks the entire semantics of giving that nevertheless structures *es gibt*. We really do not understand F. Fédier's reverse argument: "Every time, then, in translation, *es gibt* is developed in the direction of a *giving*, the translation goes a little too far" (note in *Questions IV*, Paris, 1976, p. 49). Why? Can such a brutal denial be accepted without the slightest justification?

(Marion, Étant donné)

"Conceptual precision" is certainly not the aim of the Heideggerian understanding of the everyday expression *es gibt*: rather than setting up an operational conceptual tool, the point is to listen to the language and its unsuspected resources. F. Fédier's resistance to developing *es gibt* "in the direction of a giving" is nevertheless far from lacking "the slightest justification" if we look carefully at the cited passage:

We should remember that *geben* is the Germanic development of the Indo-European root *ghabh—*, which yielded the Latin *habere*. . . . It is necessary to try to hear the Latin *habere* in accord with *geben* to perceive what *avoir* means in *il y a*—and which is no doubt closer to *tenir* [to hold] than to *posséder* [to possess].

Etymologically, *es gibt* is thus closer to *il y a* than it seems at first blush: it derives from an *avoir* whose meaning, in *il y a*, is surely still worth thinking about. At the same time, this indicates the direction in which *es gibt* must still be examined, both in its proximity to and its difference from *il y a*: in its relationship with the deployment of the word, as Heidegger indicates in *Unterwegs zur Sprache*:

We are familiar with the expression *es gibt* in many usages, such as *es gibt an der sonnigen Halde Erdbeeren* (there are strawberries on the sunny hillside); *il y a, es gibt*, there are, strawberries; we can find them as something that is there on the slope. In our present reflection *es gibt* is used differently. We do not mean "there is the word"—we mean "by virtue of the gift of the word there is, the word gives." The whole spook about the "givenness" of things, which many people justly fear, is blown away.

(Heidegger, On the Way to Language)

When made to refer to words being used, the phrase *es gibt* thus no longer means that there is a word (or words), but that it, the word, gives (*es gibt das Wort = es, das Wort, gibt*). Speech is the domain in which "there is that which gives," as always giving, never given. A final transformation of *es gibt* in Heidegger's thought: the word (*das Wort*) gibt (*das Sein*), the word gives being in the domain in which "there is that which gives."

Pascal David

BIBLIOGRAPHY

Heidegger, Martin. *Brief über den Humanismus*. In *Gesamtausgabe*, vol. 9. Frankfurt: Klostermann, 1976. Translation by Frank A. Capuzzi: "Letter on Humanism." In *Pathmarks*, edited by W. McNeill. Cambridge: Cambridge University Press, 1998.

———. *Sein und Zeit*. In *Gesamtausgabe*, vol. 2. Frankfurt: Klostermann, 1986. Translation by J. Macquarrie and E. Robinson: *Being and Time*. Oxford: Blackwell, 1967.

———. *Unterwegs zur Sprache*. In *Gesamtausgabe*, vol. 12. Frankfurt: Klostermann, 1985. Translation by P. D. Hertz: *On the Way to Language*. New York: Harper and Row, 1971.

———. *Zur Bestimmung der Philosophie*. In *Gesamtausgabe*, vols. 56/57. Frankfurt: Klostermann, 1987. Translation: *Towards the Definition of Philosophy*. New Brunswick: Athlone, 2000.

Husserl, Edmund. *Ideas Pertaining to a Pure Phenomenology and to a Phenomenological Philosophy*, Bk. 1. 3 vols. Translated by F. Kersten. The Hague: Nijhoff, 1980–89.

———. *Ideas Pertaining to a Pure Phenomenology and to a Phenomenological Philosophy: Bk. 2: Studies in the Phenomenology of Constitution*. Translated by R. Rojcewicz and A. Schuwer. Dordrecht: Kluwer, 1989.

———. *Die Idee der Phänomenologie (Husserliana II)*. Lahaye: Nijhoff, 1950. 2nd ed., 1973. Translation by W. P. Alston and G. Nakhnikian: *The Idea of Phenomenology*. The Hague: Nijhoff, 1964.

———. *Ideen zu einer reinen Phänomenologie und phänomenologischen Philosophie*. The Hague: Nijhoff, 1913.

———. *Logische Untersuchungen*. Tübingen: Niemeyer, 1900. Translation by J. N. Findlay: *Logical Investigations*. New York: Routledge, 2001.

Kant, Immanuel. *De mundus sensibilis atque intelligibilis forma et principiis*. Königsberg, 1770. Translation: "On the Form and Principles of the Sensible and the Intelligible World [Inaugural Dissertation]." In *Theoretical Philosophy 1755–1770*, edited by David Walford and Ralf Meerbote. New York: Cambridge University Press, 1992.

————. *Kritik der reinen Vernunft*. Riga: Kartknoch, 1781. Translation by P. Guyer and A. Wood: *Critique of Pure Reason*, edited by P. Guyer and A. Wood. Cambridge: Cambridge University Press, 1998.

Leibniz, Gottfried Wilhelm. *Principles of Nature and Grace*. In *Philosophical Texts*, translated by R. S. Woolhouse and R. Francks, introduction by R. S. Woolhouse. Oxford: Oxford University Press, 1998.

Marion, Jean-Luc. *Etant donné*. Paris: Presses Universitaires de France, 1997. Translation by J. L. Kosky: *Being Given: Toward a Phenomenology of Givenness*. Stanford, CA: Stanford University Press, 2002.

Meinong, Alexius. *Über Gegenstandstheorie*. Hamburg: Meiner, 1988. Translation by I. Levi, D. B. Terrell, and R. M. Chisholm: "On the Theory of Objects." In *Realism and the Background of Phenomenology*, edited by R. M. Chisholm. Glencoe, IL: Free Press, 1960.

Panis, Daniel. *Il y a le il y a*. Brussels: Ousia, 1993.

Spinoza. *Ethics*. Translated by G.H.R. Parkinson. Oxford: Oxford University Press, 2000.

ESSENCE, SUBSTANCE, SUBSISTANCE, EXISTENCE

GREEK	*ousia* [οὐσία], *hupostasis* [ὑπόστασις], *ousiôsis* [οὐσίωσις], *huparxis* [ὕπαρξις]
LATIN	*essentia, substantia, subsistentia, existentia; esse essentiae, esse existentiae*

➤ *ACT, CATEGORY*, ESTI, EUROPE, *IL Y A, PERSON*, RES, SPECIES, SUBJECT, Box 4, *TO BE*, TO TI ÊN EINAI, TO TRANSLATE

The most scholarly and most technical vocabulary with regard to being, now as in the past, does not usually give rise to problems of translation since it often consists in artificial forms that may easily be transposed, with equal violence to the language. It is thus that the Greek *ontotês* [ὀντότης] is immediately translated as *essentitas* (Marius Victorinus), and that from it is derived the series entity, *Seiendheit*, even *étantité*, without difficulty. However, things are not the same when what we take to be the fundamental ontological vocabulary derives in reality from multiple sedimentations, reappropriations, and reinterpretations of the most common words of the language. Plato did not "invent" *ousia* [οὐσία] any more than Seneca or Quintilian did *substantia*. Encroachment from other domains is added to this depth of certain key terms of ontology, related to their prephilosophical history—which justifies reappropriations, reversals, new hierarchies: as, notably, when the translation of the Septuagint, or Jerome's translation, the Vulgate, reintroduces terms that are already philosophically charged (this is notably the case with *hupostasis* [ὑπόστασις] in the Scripture, which progressively imposes its own exegetical methods, or in conciliar dogma). The model of transposing *verbum e verbo* or the use of a calque, even if it initially seems obvious (*hupo-stasis, sub-stantia*), immediately shows itself to be inadequate.

To pursue the geological metaphor for a moment: the sedimentation of layers, which we must attempt to analyze stratigraphically (on a prephilosophical base level, we discover successively Platonic, Aristotelian, Stoic, Philonian, Plotinian, and Neoplatonist usages), is itself profoundly altered by a series of landslides or powerful geographic constraints, especially when we move from an Aristotelian or Stoic ontology to Neoplatonic theology or that of the church fathers, when the laborious formulations of Trinitarian dogma are superimposed on philosophical distinctions.

The twofold hypothesis that we will illustrate below concerns (1) the anchoring of fundamental ontological concepts in language, and the additional translational constraint that demands that we recognize the semantically rich prephilosophical features of language (like the Lat. *substantiam habere, substantiam capere*); and (2) the new doctrinal framework that makes it possible to create new terms (*essentia* is no doubt the most apposite example), or to reappropriate old ones (such as *existentia*) and give them a new career.

At the level of fundamental ontological concepts, the plays made are all the more complicated because the end result is very limited: more or less the same cards are redistributed, but at each round new rules and constraints are imposed. By this we mean that the very idea of "retroversion" can only have a limited application, and that we do not return from *existentia* to *huparxis* [ὕπαρξις] or to the Aristotelian question "*ei esti?* [εἰ ἔστι ;]" without disturbing the conceptual and dialectical context.

I. The Multiple Meanings of "Is" in Most Languages

A. Predication or existence

In his *System of Logic* (1843), John Stuart Mill warned of the "double meaning" of the verb "to be" ("is"), which is used both as a "sign of predication" (see PREDICATION, V) and as a "sign of existence":

> Many volumes might be filled with the frivolous speculations concerning the nature of Being (τὸ ὄν, οὐσία, Ens, Entitas, Essentia, and the like) which have arisen from overlooking this double meaning of the word *to be*; from supposing that when it signifies *to exist*, and when it signifies to *be* some specified thing, as to *be* a man, to *be* Socrates, to *be* seen or spoken of, to *be* a phantom, even to *be* a nonentity, it must still, at bottom, answer to the same idea; and that a meaning must be found for it which shall suit all these cases. The fog which rose from this narrow spot diffused itself at an early period over the whole surface of metaphysics. Yet it becomes us not to triumph over the great intellects of Plato and Aristotle because we are now able to preserve ourselves from many errors into which they, perhaps inevitably, fell. . . . The Greeks seldom knew any language but their own. This rendered it far more difficult for them than it is for us to acquire a readiness in detecting ambiguities. One of the advantages of having accurately studied a plurality of languages, especially of those languages which eminent thinkers have used as the vehicle of their thoughts, is the practical lesson we learn respecting the ambiguities of words, by finding that the same word in one language corresponds, on different occasions, to different words in another. Without this exercise, even the strongest minds will find it hard to believe that things that have the same name do not have the same nature. Yet it becomes us not to expend much labour very unprofitably (as was frequently done by the two philosophers just mentioned) in vain attempts to discover in what this common nature consists.

B. A terrible ambiguity

In *The Principles of Mathematics*, Bertrand Russell laid out the ambiguity of the verb "to be" much more precisely:

> The word *is* is terribly ambiguous, and great care is necessary in order not to confound its various meanings. We have (1) the sense in which it asserts Being, as in

"A is"; (2) the sense of identity; (3) the sense of predication, in "A is human"; (4) the sense of "A is a man" . . . which is very like identity. In addition to these there are less common uses, as "to be good is to be happy," where a relation of assertions is meant, that relation, in fact, which, where it exists, gives rise to formal implication.

No one would deny this "terrible" ambiguity of being or "is" in European philosophical languages; however, we may:

1. with Charles Kahn, ask whether this ambiguity, through the various conceptual analyses, assisted by attempts at translation, did not in fact constitute one of the driving forces of the logical, ontological, and theological development of Western philosophy:

   I do not intend to do battle here against a general thesis of linguistic relativism, and I shall certainly not deny that the union of predicative, locative, existential and veridical functions in a single verb is a striking peculiarity of Indo-European. . . . On the contrary, I want to suggest that the absence of a separate verb "to exist" and the expression of existence and truth (plus reality) by a verb whose primary function is predicative will have provided an unusually favorable and fruitful starting-point for philosophical reflection on the concept of truth and the nature of reality as an object for knowledge.

   ("Retrospect on the Verb 'To Be' ")

2. with Jaakko Hintikka, question the dominance of the Fregean and Russellian distinctions, and denounce not only the anachronistic character of the retrospective application of them to classical authors (starting with Plato and Aristotle), but again, more seriously, the vagueness it introduces into both the analyses of those notions and their summaries and translations, whether intra- or interlinguistic. Hintikka goes so far as to denounce "the modern myth that there is a distinction between the *is* of identity, the *is* of predication, the *is* of existence, and the *is* of generic implication" (*Logic of Being*).

We may also note that, if it is a matter of uncovering and clarifying the grammars (philosophical, logical, theological) of the word "to be," etymology is of no help, for the simple reason that no philosophical European language contains a single, unitary, homogeneous verb "to be." And what goes for being, taken grammatically as a "verb," also goes for the rest of the ontological vocabulary, which—as we can see with terms like "essence," "substance," "existence," "subsistence," and so on—are not developed in the first instance on the basis of some "etymon" (*es, *bhû, *wes), but rather on the basis of the resources of the language, in its multiple uses (see ESTI).

C. Being-essence and act of being—*actus essendi*

Jacques Maritain, in his *Preface to Metaphysics*, calls attention to a different "ambiguity":

Observe that being presents two aspects. One of these is its aspect as *essence* which corresponds particularly to the first operation of the mind. For we form concepts primarily in order to apprehend, though in many cases blindly, essences—which are positive capacities of existence. The other is the aspect existence, the *esse* in the strict sense, which is the end in which things attain their achievement, their act, their "energy" par excellence, the supreme actuality of whatever is.

Étienne Gilson echoes this in *L'être et l'essence*, also emphasizing this "existence aspect" of being that Thomas Aquinas clarified for the first time and without ambiguity:

Whether we say *it is, it exists,* or *there is,* the meaning remains the same. All of these phrases signify the primary action that a subject can exercise. It is primary, in effect, because without it there would be no subject.

It is there as a fact of language (Gilson refers here to Brunot, *La pensée et le langage*), from which he cleverly extracts the logical and metaphysical grammar: the verb *est* is not a copula, but signifies "the primary act in virtue of which a being exists, and the principal function of verbs is thus to signify, not attributes, but actions." By this, Gilson recovers Priscian's canonical definition:

Verbum est pars orationis cum temporibus et modis, sine casu, agendi vel patiendi significativum.

(The verb is that part of speech which signifies, with times and modes, but without cases of declension, action or passion.)

(*Institutiones grammaticae*, 8.1.1)

However, Gilson also recovers an old piece of Scholastic terminology, which perhaps secretly served as a guide for him from the beginning. Being understood as an "action verb," of "this primary action that a subject can exercise," signifies existence as an "act"—*actus exercitus*: "we must admit," he notes, "the presence, at the very heart of the real, of what were once called 'primary acts,' that is, these acts of existing in virtue of which each being is, and from which each one unfurls in a more or less rich multiplicity of 'secondary acts,' which are its operations" (*L'être et l'essence*) (see ACT, and energeia [ἐνέργεια], under FORCE, Box 1, and under PRAXIS, Box 1). Thus existence, in the full sense, is always existence "*ut exercita*, that is, as actualized by a subject" (Maritain, *Preface to Metaphysics*; cf. also: "To exist is to *maintain oneself and to be maintained* outside nothingness; *esse* is an act, a perfection, indeed the final perfection, a splendid flower in which objects affirm themselves").

Thus understood as an "act," or better, as an "exercised act," being is *actus essendi* (act of being): the deepest and most intimate aspect of anything (Thomas Aquinas, *Summa theologica*, Ia, qu. 8, a. 1, ad 4m: "esse autem est illud quod est magis intimum, et quod profundius omnibus est, cum sit formale respectu omnium quae in re sunt" (being is what is the most intimate and profound thing in every thing, since it is the formal element in relation to all things which really are).

On the other hand, what neither Maritain nor Gilson grasped in the least was that this "existentialist" interpretation of being for which they generously credited Thomism derives from a long history, woven from translations, transpositions, and reversals, in which Neoplatonism played a decisive role.

II. "To Be," "To Exist," *Existo*

Existo is one of several compounds of *sisto*, "to stop, to arrest; to present oneself, to appear, to subpoena (before a court)," such as *absisto*, "to distance oneself," *desisto*, "to abandon, to cease," *obsisto*, "to stop in front of, to oppose," *insisto*, "to lean on, to press." *Exsisto* (*existo*), in its classic meaning, thus signifies "to stand up out of, to rise up, come out of the earth, to spring up."

Cicero uses it in this sense in *On Duties* (1.30.107): "Ut in corporibus magnae dissimilitudines sunt, sic in animis existunt majores etiam varietates" (even greater differences are found [are met with] in minds). Or again Lucretius, in *De rerum natura* (2.871): "Quippe videre licet vivos existere vermes/stercore de taetro" (Why, you may see worms arise all alive from stinking dung).

A. *Existentia* as *ex-sistere*

In the twelfth century, in Richard of Saint-Victor's canonical distinction (*De Trinitate* [1148], 4.12.937C–983) we find the echo, amplified and transposed onto a metaphysical and theological level, of this first concrete meaning of the Latin verb *exsisto*:

> Possumus autem sub nomine exsistentiae utramque considerationem subintelligere, tam illam scilicet quae pertinet ad rationem essentiae, quam scilicet illam quae pertinet ad rationem obtinentiae. Tam illam, inquam, in qua quaeritur quale sit de quolibet exsistenti, quam illam in qua quaeritur unde habeat esse. Nomen exsistentiae trahitur verbo quod est exsistere. In verbo sistere notari potest quod pertinent ad considerationem unam; similiter per adjunctam praepositionem ex notari potest quod pertinet ad aliam. Per id quod dicitur aliquid sistere, primum removentur ea quae non tam habent in se esse quam alicui inesse, non tam sistere, ut sic dicam, quam insistere, hoc est alicui subjecto inhaerere. Quod autem sistere dicitur, ad utrumque se habere videtur et ad id quod aliquo modo et ad id quod nullo modo habet subsistere; tam ad id videlicet quod oportet quam ad id quod omnino non oportet subjectum esse. Unum enim est creatae, alterum increatae naturae. Nam quod increatum est sic consistit in seipso ut nihil ei insit velut in subjecto. Quod igitur dicitur sistere tam se habet ad rationem creatae quam increatae essentiae. Quod autem dicitur exsistere, subintelligitur non solum quod habeat esse, sed etiam aliunde, hoc est ex aliquo habet esse. Hoc enim intelligi datur in verbo composito ex adjuncta sibi praepositione. Quid est enim exsistere nisi ex aliquo sistere, hoc est substantialiter ex aliquo esse. In uno itaque hoc verbo exsistere, vel sub uno nomine exsistentiae, datur subintelligi posse et illam considerationem, quae pertinet ad rei qualitatem et illam quae pertinent ad rei originem.

(Now, with the term "existence" we can refer to both [of these] considerations: one concerning the essence's nature and another concerning the nature of obtaining [it]. I mean, [we can refer to] both [the consideration] in which [every being] seeks that which it is in itself and [the consideration] in which every being tries to know from where it derives its being. The word "existence" comes from the [Latin] verb *existere*. We observe that the term *sistere* refers to the first consideration. Equally, we can notice that by adding the preposition *ex* [the word] refers [in meaning] to the second consideration. When we say that something exists—(in the meaning of *sistere*)—those realities, which do not derive their being from themselves but have it from someone [else], are immediately excluded. [These realities] do not really "*ex*-ist"—so to speak—but they rather "*in*-sist," that is, they are joined to some [other] subject. The term *sistere*, however, seems to be appropriate to both of them: both to that which subsists in some way, [and] to that which cannot subsist in any way; both to that which is necessarily subordinated and to that which cannot be [subordinated] in any way. In effect, the first condition is proper to the created nature, the second to the uncreated nature, since that which is not created subsists in itself in such a way that nothing in it can be found, as [if it were its own operating] subject. For this reason, the word *sistere* can refer to both the created and uncreated nature. The term *ex-sistere*, on its part, not only expresses the possession of being, but also the [being's] coming from outside. [It expresses] the fact that one possesses its being because of someone [else]. Indeed, this is shown in the compounded verb, by the preposition that is added to it. What does *existere* mean, in fact, if not *sistere* "from" (= *ex*) someone? That is, [what does it mean if not] receiving one's own substantial being from someone [else]? Consequently, with this single verb *existere*—or with the single noun "existence"—we can intend both that which has to do with the object's nature and that which refers to its own origin.)

B. *Existentia, existentialitas*

We must obviously wait for Candidus the Arian (known by Marius Victorinus, ca. 281/291–361) for the appearance of the feminine singular *existentia*, along with the abstract *existentialitas*, whereas in Chalcidius, in his translation and commentary of the *Timaeus*, *existentia* is still a neuter plural that refers to *onta* [ὄντα]: "*tria . . . auta onta* [τρία . . . αὐτὰ ὄντα]."

It is thus only rather late (the second half of the fourth century), and after a series of translations, that the term acquires its status of philosophical nobility, in the Latin context of Trinitarian theology: in Marius Victorinus, the term is used in effect as a translation of *huparxis* [ὕπαρξις], unlike *substantia*, which translates *ousia* [οὐσία], while *subsistentia* is reserved for the translation of *hupostasis* [ὑπόστασις].

The fundamental difference in the meanings for being is thus that which is drawn, echoing the Greek *huparxis-ousia*, between *existentia* and *substantia*:

> Multo magis autem differt existentia a substantia, quoniam existentia ipsum esse est, et solum est, et non in alio non esse, sed ipsum unum et solum esse; substantia vero non solum habet esse, sed et quale et aliquid esse.

(Much more, however, does existence differ from substance, since existence is "to be" itself, "to be" which is neither in another nor subject of another but solely "to be" itself, whereas substance has not only "to be" but also has a "to be" something qualified.)

(Marius Victorinus, *Candidi epistola*, 1.2.18–22, in *Theological Treatises on the Trinity*, trans. Clark)

C. *Quid—Quod (was—daß)*

We would be wrong to see this as a simple translation, capable of opening a possibility of "retroversion," such as the "well-known" distinction between essence and existence, and we must refrain, pace Suzanne Mansion ("Le rôle de la connaissance de l'existence dans la science aristotélicienne"), from unreflectively projecting the "well-known distinction" onto the Aristotelian questions "ti esti? ei esti?" [τί ἐστι ? εἰ ἐστι ?].

In effect, it is one thing to know of something "to ti esti" [τὸ τί ἐστι], the "what it is," or better, "to ti ên einai" [τὸ τί ἦν εἶναι], the "what it is to be for *x*," the "quiddity" (see TO TI ÉN EINAI), but it is something else to know that it is ("hoti estin" [ὅτι ἔστιν]), that it is the case (*daß*), the "quoddity":

Ἀνάγκη γὰρ τὸ εἰδότα τὸ τί ἐστιν ἄνθρωπος ἢ ἄλλο ὁτιοῦν, εἰδέναι καὶ ὅτι ἔστι (τὸ γὰρ μὴ ὂν οὐδεὶς οἶδεν ὅ τι ἐστίν, ἀλλὰ τί μὲν σημαίνει ἀ; λόγος ἢ τὸ ὄνομα, ὅταν εἴπω τραγέλαφος, τί δ' ἐστὶ τραγέλαφος ἀδύνατον εἰδέναι) . . . τὸ δὲ τί ἐστιν ἄνθρωπος καὶ τὸ εἶναι ἄνθρωπον ἄλλο.

(It is necessary for someone who is to know, whether it is of a man or something else, what it is, which he knows in addition to knowing that it is (in effect, of what is not, no one can know that it is—at most we may know what the definition or the word means, when I say "goat-stag," but what a goat-stag is, is impossible to know) . . . the "what it is, a man," and the human being are different.)

(*Posterior Analytics*, 2.7.92b4–11)

D. *Huparxis-ousia*

The first author, it seems, to use the noun *huparxis*, attested in the Septuagint, is Philo of Alexandria (ca. 20 BCE–41 CE): after having noted in *De opificio mundi* (§170–71) that Moses, by his account of the creation, taught us "that the divinity is and exists" (*hoti esti to theion kai huparchei* [ὅτι ἔστι τὸ θεῖον καὶ ὑπάρχει]), Philo clarifies the importance of this teaching, which was transmitted to us "on account of the godless, some of whom are in doubt and incline in two directions concerning his existence."

As John Glucker rightly points out ("Origin of ὑπάρχω and ὕπαρξις"), Philo's invention presupposes a firm distinction between *ousia*, the essence of something, what it is—or better, "what it is to be *x*"—and *huparxis*. In terms of God or the divine, it is clear that his "essence" is inaccessible to man (*akatalêptos anthrôpôi* [ἀκατάληπτος ἀνθρώπῳ]): the latter can only, at best, recognize his might or his "powers" (*dunameis* [δυνάμεις]), which reveal his providence and his "existence" (*huparxis*).

Leaving aside the dense discussions that concern the interpretations of the terms *huparxis-huparchein* [ὑπάρχειν], or better, the distinction between the two modes of being defined respectively by *huparchein* and *huphestêkenai* [ὑφεστηκέναι] (cf. Hadot, "Zur Vorgeschichte des Begriffs 'Existenz' "), we will restrict ourselves to the well-established

Neoplatonist distinction since, in addition, that is the one that directs the principal translational decisions at issue here: the distinction between *huparxis*, "existence," associated with being purely and simply (*to einai monon* [τὸ εἶναι μόνον]), on one hand, and *ousia-substantia* (*to on* [τὸ ὄν]) on the other.

E. Existence as *"ipsum et solum esse"*

It is in this context that, for Marius Victorinus, *existencia* as a translation of *huparxis* designates being without determination, which is still neither subject nor predicate, unlike determined being (*Adversus Arium*, 1.30.21–26; *Candidi Epistola I*, 2.19–24).

As Pierre Hadot rightly notes (*Porphyre et Victorinus*): "For Victorinus and in the letter of Candidus, existence is the still undetermined being, pure being, taken without qualification, without a subject and without a predicate; substance, on the contrary, is qualified and determined being, the being of something and which is something."

Exsistentiam quidem et exsistentialitatem, praeexsistentem subsistentiam sine accidentibus, puris et solis ipsis quae sunt in eo quod est solum esse, quod subsistunt; substantiam autem, subjectum cum his omnibus quae sunt accidentia in ipsa inseparabiliter existentibus.

([The sages and ancients] define existence and existentiality as preexisting subsistence without accidents because they subsist purely and only in that which is only "to be"; but they define substance as a subject with all its accidents inseparably existing within it.)

(Marius Victorinus, *Adversus Arium*, 1A.30.21, in *Theological Treatises on the Trinity*, trans. Clark)

Exsistentia ipsum esse est et solum esse, et non in alio esse aut subjectum alterius, sed unum et solum ipsum esse, substantia autem non esse solum habet, sed et quale aliquid esse. Subjacet enim in se positis qualitatibus et idcirco dicitur subjectum.

(Existence differ[s] from substance, since existence is "to be" itself, "to be" which is neither in another nor subject of another but solely "to be" itself, whereas substance has not only "to be" but also has a "to be" something qualified. For it is subject to the qualities within it and on that account is called subject.)

(Marius Victorinus, *Candidi epistola*, 1.2.19–23, in *Theological Treatises on the Trinity*, trans. Clark)

F. The *"bare entity"*

It should be noted that the author (Scipio Dupleix [1569–1661]) who apparently first introduced the word *existence* in its technical usage into French also referred, if not to *esse solum* (*to einai monon*), at least to "naked entity":

It is thus certain that there is a notable difference between the existence and the essence of things. But in order to hear it best we must observe that in our French language we do not have a term which responds energetically to the Latin *existentia*, which signifies the bare entity, the simple and bare being of things, without considering any order or rank which they hold among others. But the word *essentia*, for which we might well use *essence*, marks the nature of the thing, and by it the order or rank it must hold among the other things. For example, when I say that man is, this is as much to say that he has his act, that he is, I say, actually: and in this I do not mark anything other than his bare entity and simple existence. But when I say that man is a rational animal, I deploy and manifest his whole essence and nature, and attributing to him his whole kind and his difference it is easy to see that his is in the order of the category of substance under the genus animal.

(Scipio Dupleix, *La métaphysique*)

■ See Box 1.

G. "To exist": To be outside one's causes and from nothing—to be created

Rigorously speaking, existence is never referred back to God—even if Anselm (1033–1109) has the idea of concluding chapter 2 of his *Proslogion* this way: "Existit ergo procul dubio aliquid quo magis cogitari non valet, et in intellectu et in re" (Therefore there is absolutely no doubt that something-than-which-a-greater-cannot-be-thought exists both in the mind and in reality)—but rather to the creature, of which it is more or less redundant to affirm that it exists. Before existing, it only has an essential being (*esse essentiae*), which derives from the possible and betrays, more or less, an *aptitudo ad existendum*, a "demand for existence." The latter is thus clearly, as Giles of Rome (1247–1316) pointed out well before Christian Wolff (1679–1754), the very same thing that, after Aquinas, introduces for the first time the deliberate distinction between essence and existence—a "complement" of essence (cf. on this point the "dossier" by Alain de Libera and Cyrille Michon in *L'être et l'essence: Le vocabulaire médiéval de l'ontologie*).

Quaelibet res est ens per essentiam suam; tamen quia essentia rei creatae non dicit actum completum sed est in potentia ad esse, ideo non sufficit essentia ad hoc quod res actu existat nisi ei superaddatur aliquod esse quod est essentiae actus et complementum. Existunt ergo res per esse superadditum essentiae vel naturae. Patet itaque quomodo differat ens per se acceptum et existens.

(Every thing is being by reason of its essence, nevertheless, because a created essence is not a completed act but is in potency to existence, it is, therefore, not enough that a thing has essence to be actually existing, but existence, which is the act and the completion of an essence, must be added to it. Therefore, things exist by reason of an existence which is added to the essence or nature. From this it is clear how being and existence differ.)

(*Theoremata de esse et essentia*, 13)

What exists therefore ex-sists, referred back to an origin as indicated by Richard of Saint-Victor, to an *ex. . . .* What exists, as Thomas of Vio (Cajetan) (1469–1534) and Suárez

(1548–1617) will repeat at every opportunity, exists "*extra suas causas et extra nihilum* [beyond its causes and beyond nothingness]" ("*id quod realiter existit extra causas suas est ens reale* [what exists really beyond its causes is a real being]"; Cajetan, *De ente et essentia*; Suárez, *Disputationes metaphysicae*). This is why we may also say with Leibniz, who invents the term, that God is *existentificans*, and of the possible essences, we will say that they comprise an *existurire*, an existence that is to come and will be confirmed. The possible contains its own futurity:

Est ergo causa cur Existentia praevalet Non-Existentiae, seu Ens necessarium est EXISTENTIFICANS. — Sed quae causa facit ut aliquid existat, seu ut possibilitas exigat existentiam, facit etiam ut omne possibile habeat conatum ad Existentiam, cum ratio restrictionis ad certa possibilia in universali reperiri non possit. — Itaque dici potest Omne possibile EXISTITURIRE, prout scilicet fundatur in Ente necessario actu existente, sine quo nulla est via qua possibile perveniret ad actum.

(There is, therefore, a cause for which existence prevails over non-existence; in other words, God [the necessary Being] is *existencing*. — But this cause which brings about the existence of things, or in whose possibility existence is demanded, is also such that everything possible has a tendency towards existence, since we cannot find, generally speaking, a reason to restrain this tendency to only certain possibles. — This is why we can say that each and every possible is a future "*existing*," naturally insofar as all *existings* are founded within God [the necessary Being] existing indeed, without which there would be no means of realizing any possibles.)

(Leibniz, *Vingt-quatre thèses métaphysiques*, in *Recherches générales sur l'analyse des notions et des verites*)

III. *Essentia, Ousia-Essentia-Substantiva:* "Essence," "Entity," *Entitas, Entité, Seiendheit, Étance, E(s)tance, Étantité*

A. An *ousia-essentia* calque?

Charles Kahn has established, from rich documentary sources, that the term *ousia*, attested from the time of Herodotus, always refers to *parousia-apousia* [παρουσία-ἀπουσία]—"presence-absence"—compounds. We may add that it is this fundamentally temporal meaning that constitutes the unity of the term, to designate, in its standard meaning, "goods," "property," "wealth" (cf. Ger. *Anwesen*), and, in its philosophical meaning, the "essence" of something, that is, "what-the-thing-is" and "the-thing-which-is." Compare this with *Phaedo*, 78c–d, where *ousia* is clearly that of which there is a *logos*, that of which we must give an account as such, but also being (*to on*), or even the class of beings (*pasê ousia*; *Republic*, 486a), and that which is a thing really is (*auto hekaston ho esti* [αὐτὸ ἕναστον ὅ ἐστι]), each thing that is, in itself, beyond its multiple aspects and appearances—beyond the different affections (*pathê* [πάθη]) that it may undergo, as from outside.

1. Aristotle distinguishes, as is well known, at the beginning of the *Categories*, two meanings of *ousia*: primary

1

Porphyry's "metaphysics": Being-acting without a subject

➤ PRINCIPLE

This same *huparxis-ousia* distinction also corresponds to Damascius's (462–538) usage. Damascius understands *huparxis* [ὕπαρξις], playing on the etymology, as "first beginning, presupposition, foundation of substance":

ἡ ὕπαρξις, ὡς δηλοῖ τὸ ὄνομα, τὴν πρώτην ἀρχὴν δηλοῖ τῆς ὑποστάσεως ἑκάστης, οἷόν τινα θεμέλιον ἢ οἷον ἔδαφος προϋποτιθέμενον τῆς ὅλης καὶ πάσης οἰκοδομήσεως.

(*Huparxis*, as its name indicates, refers to the first principle of each *hupostasis*; it is like a seat or foundation laid down beforehand under the whole of the superstructure and under any superstructure.)

(*Dubitationes et solutiones*, §121)

As clearly noted by Pierre Hadot, we should speak here of "pre-existence" rather than *huparxis* or "existence." *Huparxis*, in its simplicity, refers to the One, prior to the composition of the "substance."

Such is the claim indeed that clarifies the definition of existence given by Victorinus: *praeexistens subsistentia* (*Adversus Arium*, 1.30.22)—what Pierre Hadot translates by "*fondement initial préexistant à la chose elle-même*" (initial foundation existing before the thing itself). Retroversion is called for here: *prouparchousa hupostasis* [προϋπάρχουσα ὑπόσασις] (*Dubitationes et solutiones*, §34). Hadot comments: "It is the 'one' of each thing, its existence, the state according to which substance is still pure being, undetermined and undeployed" (*Porphyre et Victorinus*). "We may say that substance pre-exists itself in existence, which is its state of unity and transcendental simplicity." To understand the emergence and the success of the translations that have become standard—existence/essence-substance—we must thus hypothesize a complete reversal, brought about by Neoplatonism in general, and more particularly by Porphyry's "metaphysics," of the Stoic distinction and hierarchy: for the Stoics, being, *to on* [τὸ ὄν], *to einai* [τὸ εἶναι] (conventionally translated "existence," "to exist"), refers to the ontological plenitude of what is really present, like a body, while *huparxis*, *huphistanai* [ὑφιστάναι] (conventionally translated "subsistence," "to subsist") only designates a secondary reality, which comes from the incorporeal, characteristic of predicates, of temporality, of events (cf. Hadot, *Porphyre et Victorinus*).

Thus Porphyry's originality, not so much with respect to Plotinus as with respect to

Stoicism, consists on the ontological level of eliminating the distinction between *einai* and *huphistanai*, and of identifying *huparxis* with "being pure and simple [εἶναι μόνον]"; which also comes, against Aristotle this time, to treating the verb "to be" as a fully signifying verb—not just "co-signifying," in its function as a copula but as an essentially active verb, which purely and properly expresses the activity of "being," *ousia-energeia* [ἐνέργεια], that of pure essence, taken at its most indeterminate. The reversal is complete with regard to the Aristotelian claim from *De interpretatione*:

οὐ γὰρ τὸ εἶναι ἢ μὴ εἶναι σημεῖόν ἐστι τοῦ πράγματος, οὐδ' ἐὰν τὸ ὂν εἴπῃς ψιλόν. αὐτὸ μὲν γὰρ οὐδέν ἐστιν, προσσημαίνει σύνθεσίν τινα.

(Indeed "to be" and "not to be" are not signs of anything, and no more so when one utters the term "being" by itself; for in itself, it is nothing, but it co-signifies a certain synthesis.)

(16b22–24)

Compare also *Posterior Analytics*, B 7.92b13–14: "τὸ δ' εἶναι οὐκ οὐσία οὐδενί" (being is not the property, the essence, of anything; our translation). Notice—and this point is instructive concerning the changes of meaning in Greek terms—that Michael Psellos (eleventh century) paraphrases the first passage cited thus: "οὐδὲ γὰρ σημεῖά ἐστι τοῦ πράγματος τὰ ῥήματα τοῦ ὑπάρχειν, ἢ μὴ ὑπάρχειν" (indeed, the verbs "to be/to exist," "not-to-be/ not-to-exist" are not signs for a thing) (*Paraphrasis*, fol. M. II^v, 13, cited in Aristotle, *Peri hermeneias*).

This is why Hadot can still note by way of synthesis: "There is not, in the Porphyrian ontology, a distinction between existence and essence. Being is indissolubly action and idea. The fundamental contrast is here that which is established between being, to act without a subject, and existence, which is the primary subject, the primary form resulting from being" (*Porphyre et Victorinus*).

If we accept, as here, the attribution to Porphyry (232–301) of the "Turin fragment" edited for the first time by Kroll in 1892 and considered by Hadot to be a commentary on the *Parmenides* (cf. "Fragments d'un commentaire de Porphyre sur le *Parmé-nide*," in Hadot, *Plotin, Porphyre: Études néo-platoniciennes*), we must indeed emphasize the boldness of the author, who clearly takes a non-Plotinian position in identifying

the One purely One with being. This identification is surely inadmissible for Plotinus (204–70), but also entails a profound redefinition of being (*to einai* [τὸ εἶναι] = *to energein* [τὸ ἐνεργεῖν]), taken in an active sense, and rigorously distinguished from what exists. Recall the key passage of the fragment:

Ὅρα δὲ μὴ καὶ αἰνισσομένῳ ἔοικεν ὁ Πλάτων, ὅτι τὸ ἓν τὸ ἐπέκεινα οὐσίας καὶ ὄντος ὂν μὲν οὐκ ἔστιν οὐδὲ οὐσία οὐδὲ ἐνέργεια, ἐνεργεῖ δὲ μᾶλλον καὶ αὐτὸ τὸ ἐνεργεῖν καθαρόν, ὥστε καὶ αὐτὸ τὸ εἶναι τὸ πρὸ τοῦ ὄντος· οὗ μετασχὸν τὸ ἓν ἄλλο ἐξ αὐτοῦ ἔχει ἐκκλινόμενον τὸ εἶναι, ὅπερ ἐστὶ μετέχειν ὄντος. Ὥστε διττὸν τὸ εἶναι, τὸ μὲν προϋπάρχει τοῦ ὄντος, τὸ δὲ ὃ ἐπάγεται ἐκ τοῦ ὄντος τοῦ ἐπέκεινα ἑνὸς τοῦ εἶναι ὄντος τὸ ἀπόλυτον καὶ ὥσπερ ἰδέα τοῦ ὄντος, οὗ μετασχὸν ἄλλο τι ἓν γέγονεν, ᾧ σύζυγον τὸ ἀπ' αὐτοῦ ἐπιφερόμενον εἶναι· ὡς εἰ νοήσειας λευκὸν εἶναι.

(Look then whether Plato does not also seem like someone who intimates a hidden teaching: for the One, which is beyond substance and Existence, is neither Existence, nor substance, nor act, but rather it acts and is itself pure action, such that he is himself Being who is before Existence. It is in participating in this Being that the second One receives a derived being from this Being: that is "participating in Existence." Thus being is twofold: the first pre-exists existence, the second is that which is produced by the One, who is beyond Existence, and who is himself Being, in the absolute sense, and in a way the idea of Existence. It is by participating in this Being that another One was engendered to which the being produced by this Being is paired. It is as though one were thinking "being-white.")

(Hadot, *Porphyre et Victorinus*)

BIBLIOGRAPHY

Aristotle. *Peri hermeneias*. Translated by H. Weidemann. Berlin: Weingartner, 1978.
Hadot, Pierre. "Fragments d'un commentaire de Porphyre sur le *Parménide*." In *Plotin, Porphyre: Études néoplatoniciennes*. Paris: Les Belles Lettres, 1999.
———. *Porphyre et Victorinus*. 2 vols. Paris: Études Augustiniennes, 1999.

essence as "individual" (*tode ti* [τόδε τι]) ("essence said in the most fundamental, primary, and principal sense, is what is neither said of nor in a subject, for example, a certain man or a certain horse") and secondary essence such as "species" or "genera" ("we call secondary essences the species to which the essences said in the primary sense belong, these species as well as the genera of these species"; on the definition of *ousia prôte*, see SUBJECT, Box 1). One of the classic difficulties of Aristotelian exegesis, which will not delay us here, comes from the fact that in the other parts of the *corpus*, and in particular in book Z of the *Metaphysics*, chapter 3, Aristotle eliminates as "insufficient" the identification of *ousia* with the substrate (*hupokeimenon*: "that of which all the other [determinations] are said"), and that he defines primary essence in terms of form (*morphê* [μορφή], *eidos* [εἶδος]): "εἶδος δὲ λέγω τὸ τί ἦν εἶναι καὶ τὴν πρώτην οὐσίαν" (I call *eidos* [species, form] the "quiddity," that is, the primary essence)" (see QUIDDITY, SPECIES).

2. If the Romans were to look for a scholarly calque to render the Greek *ousia*, one would think that *essentia* or *entia* (not attested) would have spontaneously come to mind. This hypothesis is confirmed in fact by a letter of Seneca's (2–66 CE) (*Letters*, 58.6), crediting Cicero (106–43 BCE) as the source of the term. This attribution creates problems, however, not only because the term is nowhere to be found in extant texts by Cicero—not even in the fragments of his translation of the *Timaeus*, where the Platonic *ousia* is rendered in multiple ways, but never by *essentia*—but especially because it is contradicted by two other important sources, Quintilian (35–100 CE) and Augustine (354–430).

a. Quintilian in effect attributes the creation of the term to Sergius Plautus, a relatively unknown author from the Stoic school, around the first century CE (*De institutione oratoria*, 2.14.1–2). Quintilian refers in this passage to the different translations that were suggested for the Greek *rhêtorikê* [ῥητορική] (*oratoria, oratrix*), then follows up with a more general remark:

> Quos equidem non fraudaverim debita laude quod copiam Romani sermonis augere temptarint. Sed non omina nos ducentes ex Graeco secuntur, sicut ne illos quidem quotiens utique suis verbis signare nostra voluerunt. Et haec interpretatio non minus dura est quam illa Plauti essentia et queentia, sed ne propria quidem.

> (I would not for the world deprive the translators of the praise which is their due for attempting to increase the vocabulary of our native tongue; but translations from Greek into Latin are not always satisfactory, just as the attempt to represent Latin words in a Greek dress is sometimes equally unsuccessful. And the translations in question are fully as harsh as the essentia and queentia of Plautus, and have not even the merit of being exact.)

With regard to this last term, the relatively obscure *queentia*, we note that one may be tempted

to follow the correction given in one manuscript: *atque entia*. Compare also *De institutione oratoria* (3.6.23): "Ac primum Aristoteles elementa decem constituit . . . οὐσίαν quam Plautus 'essentiam' vocat" (Aristotle lays down that there are ten categories. . . . First there is *ousia*, which Plautus calls *essentia*).

b. Saint Augustine, who definitively introduces the term *essentia* into Latin usage at the end of the fourth century, never fails to remind us that it is a new term (*novo quidem nomine*), still unknown in older authors (cf. *De moribus Manichaeorum*, 2.2.2; *De civitate Dei*, 12.2). We may certainly find a few occurrences in the texts that have been preserved between Quintilian and Saint Augustine. In any case, however, the meaning of the term remains largely indeterminate in them, which is shown by the more or less constant shifting between *substantia* and *essentia*, though sometimes indicating more or less clearly a tendency toward the specifically Augustinian sense of the term, to which we will return.

B. *Essentia* and/or *substantia*? The body of substance

1. A complex vocabulary (Apuleius)

The word *essentia* appears notably with Apuleius (second half of the second century), in whom we find *essentia* and *substantia* used, interchangeably it seems, to translate the Platonic *ousia*. In reality, however, things are more complex: in his *De Platone*, for example, Apuleius explicitly asks the question of the equivalence between *ousia* and *essentia*: "οὐσίας, quas essentias dicimus"; but this is in order to substitute *substantia* for it beginning with the following paragraph. Apuleius proposes his translation of *ousiai* [οὐσίαι] by *essentiae* in a development where, following the most classic Platonist distinction, he contrasts two types of different reality and two corresponding modes of being: "two aspects of beings" (*duo eidê tôn ontôn* [δύο εἴδη τῶν ὄντων]) (*Phaedo*, 79a6)—essence strictly speaking, as it presents itself to the pure vision of the mind and may be conceived by *cogitatio* alone, and the sensible reality that is only its shadow and image (*umbra et imago*).

> Οὐσίας, quas essentias dicimus, duas esse ait, per quas cuncta gignantur mundusque ipse; quarum una cogitatione sola concipitur, altera sensibus subjici potest. Sed illa, quae mentis oculis conprehenditur, semper et eodem modo et sui par ac similis invenitur, ut quae vere sit; at enim altera opinione sensibili et irrationabili aestimanda est, quam nasci et interire ait. Et sicut superior vere esse memoratur, hanc non esse vere possumus dicere.

> (According to Plato there are two *ousiai*—we call them essences—which create all things and the world itself. One is conceived by thought alone; the other may be grasped by the senses. The first, however, which is only grasped by the eyes of the mind, is always and in the same way equal to itself, as what truly is; the other, on the contrary, of which he says that it is generated and destroyed, must be evaluated by sensible and irrational opinions. And just as he reminds us that the first is truly, we may also affirm that the second is not truly.)

> (*De Platone et ejus dogmate*)

The central contrast is here that between a *vere esse* and a *non esse vere*, and only intelligible "essence" fully deserves the title *essentia* because of its identity and its permanence: "*semper et eodem modo et sui par ac similis . . . ut quae vere sit*" (like what is properly speaking).

In such a context, the translation of *ousia* by *essentia* was obvious and practically necessary. Translating by *substantia* would require saying in effect that what cannot offer itself to the senses as a subject (*sensibue subjici potest*) is not properly or truly a substance, which would manifestly go against the very spirit of the language. Apuleius, however, does not hesitate to fall back on the vocabulary of substantiality once he attempts to clarify exactly what the "essentiality" of this intelligible essence *really is*. The slide takes place first in the examination of the second type of *ousia*. When Apuleius approaches this "essence" that is not really—the reality that may be offered to the senses—the term of *substantia* in effect comes to complete *essentia*, and then to replace it:

Et primae substantiae vel essentiae primum deum esse et mentem formasque rerum et animam; secundas substantias, omnia quae ab substantiae superioris exemplo originem ducunt, quae mutari et converti possunt, labentia et ad instar fluminum profuga.

(Of the primary essence or substance, is the primary God, the mind, the "forms" of things, and the soul; of the second, whatever is enformed, whatever is born and has its origin in the model of the superior substance, whatever may change and be transformed, slipping and flowing like running water.)

(Ibid.)

Several paragraphs earlier, Apuleius had summarized the teaching of the *Timaeus* concerning matter: it is what precedes the first principles and the simplest elements (water, fire, etc.) for the title of prime matter:

Materiam vero inprocreabilem incorruptamque commemorat, non ignem neque aquam nec aliud de principiis et absolutis elementis esse, sed ex omnibus primam, figurarum capacem, fictionique subjectam.

(For matter, he points out that it can be neither created nor destroyed, that it is neither fire nor water, nor any of the other principles or simple elements; but the first of all the realities capable of receiving forms, and able to be fashioned as a subject.)

(Ibid.)

Matter precedes all the rest, insofar as it is capable, paradigmatically, of receiving shapes. It is practically nothing, not even a body, but nor is it incorporeal: "*sine corpore vero esse non potest dicere, quod nihil incorporale corpus exhibeat*" (nor does [Plato] wish to say that it is without body, since nothing of what is incorporeal exhibits a body [= can make a body manifest]). The status of matter is thus essentially ambiguous since, while it does not have the identifying evidence of the body and is not at all evident, nor is it among the number of things that are only grasped by thought (*ea cogitationibus videri*), that is, among the things that do not have the subsistence, solidity, or stability proper to bodies (*quae*

substantiam non habent corporum*). The connection between *substantia* and *corpus* is of capital importance here.

Thus, when Apuleius wishes to emphasize the relations between *ousia* and *einai*, he speaks of *essentia*—what really is—but when he understands the Greek term as referring to the mode of being (privileged in a different sense) of what is corporeal or sensible, the concept of substance naturally comes into play. To be, in this case, can only be understood univocally as *substantiam habere*, "to have substance," that is, to have a body, to be solid and stable. It is in this same perspective that Apuleius can suggest the thesis that remains in place as guiding the rest: "*Quod nullam substantiam habet, non est*" (What is lacking in all substance is not) (*De philosophia liber*).

We can compare this passage from the *De Platone*, dedicated to matter, with the distinction established by Cicero in his *Topics* between the things that are and those that are only cognized ("*earum rerum quae sunt . . . earum quae intelliguntur*"):

Esse ea dico quae cerni tangive possunt, ut fundum, aedes, parietem, stillicidium, mancipium, pecudem, suppellectilem, penus et cetera. . . . Non esse rursus ea dico quae tangi demonstrarive non possunt, cerni tamen animo atque intelligi possunt, ut si ususcapionem, si tutelam, si gentem, si agnationem definias, quarum rerum nullum subest corpus, est tamen quaedam conformatio insita et impressa intelligentia, quam notionem voco.

(The things which I call existing are those which can be seen or touched; as a farm, a house, a wall, a gutter, a slave, an ox, furniture, provisions, and so on; of which kind of things some require at times to be defined by us. Those things, again, I say have no existence, which are incapable of being touched or proved, but which can be perceived by the mind and understood; as if you were to define usucaption, guardianship, nationality, or relationship; all, things which have no body, but which nevertheless have a certain conformation plainly marked out and impressed upon the mind, which I call the notion of them.)

(*Topics*, 5.27)

"Real" being is clearly defined here as "substantial" being, in the manner of one's land, property or "residence," "means of subsistence"—in contrast with what lacks such a corporeal substrate, that is, a *subesse* proper to the body, in contrast therefore with those things "*quae substantiam non habent corporum*" (which do not have the substance of bodies), as Apuleius puts it, fully developing the logic of the expression.

2. "Substantia a substare" (Seneca)

The Latin *substantia*, created from *substare* (a well-attested verb), appears for the first time in the writings of Seneca. This relatively late appearance is in itself surprising, if we think, for example, about the plurality of compounds using -*antia* created from *stare* (*circumstantia, constantia, distantia, instantia, praestantia*, etc.). We cannot, however, argue on the basis of this silence that it is a creation of Seneca, and in fact, when he uses the word, unlike *essentia*, it never requires explications or particular justifications. The term is clearly part of everyday usage, even if it appears in very determinate contexts in Seneca, where it is generally easy to uncover an underlying

Stoic conception. We read, for example, in the *Quaestiones naturales*, regarding the rainbow:

> Non est propria in ista nube substantia nec corpus est, sed mendacium sine re similitudo.

> (There is neither proper substance nor body in this cloud, but illusion and appearance lacking reality.)

> *(Quaestiones naturales, 1.6.4)*

We can easily recognize, through the contrast initiated by Seneca between *propria substantia* and *mendacium*, or again between *res* and *similituo*, the two terms of *hupostasis* and *emphasis* [ἔμφασις] (reality/appearance), which we find in an exactly parallel context in the pseudo-Aristotelian treatise *De mundo*, for example, and which become standard in this opposition beginning especially with Posidonius. There we read:

> [Τῶν ἐν ἀέρι φαντασμάτων τὰ μὲν ἐστι κατ' ἔμφασιν, τὰ δὲ καθ' ὑπόστασιν.]

> (Among celestial phenomena, some are only apparent, others real.)

> *(De mundo, 395a28)*

We must, however, put aside the question of whether the contrast established by Seneca takes up the underlying Stoic distinction in an exact way, or whether the word *substantia* by itself bears a more specifically Latin meaning, allowing it to correspond in the present case to the Stoic construction. Let us examine in this vein another passage from Seneca, where we again seem to find the contrast "simple" and "received": *substantia/imago*. This is the famous letter 58 to Lucilius, already cited, since it is in the same text that Seneca suggested, relying on Cicero's authority, the neologism *essentia* to translate *ousia*, with the latter term in addition being, unusually, clarified as follows:

> Quomodo dicetur οὐσία—res necessaria, natura continens fundamentum omnium?

> (How shall we render the concept of *ousia*, necessary reality, substance where the foundation of all things resides?)

> *(Letters, 58.6, in Sénèque, entretiens, lettres à Lucilius, translated by H. Noblot)*

(N.B.: we cannot resist this translation, which reintroduces at its core the term "substance" which Seneca avoids!)

After this first attempt at translation, to which in fact Seneca does not feel tied down, he attempts an exposition that is in fact rather muddled since he mixes Platonic *diairesis* [διαίρεσις], Aristotle's categorial analysis, and the scrutiny of the Stoic categories. His goal in any case is to go in search of the primary, of the supreme genus under which lie all the other species:

> Nunc autem primum illud genus quaerimus, ex quo ceterae species suspensae sunt, a quo nascitur omnis divisio, quo universa conprensa sunt.

> (For the moment, we are seeking this primary genus to which all the species are subordinate, from which all divisions emanate, which contains the universality of things.)

> *(Ibid., 58.8)*

This primary genus ("*genus primum et antiquissimum*"; 58.12) is first defined as "being" (*to on* = *quod est*—that which is). "Being" thus construed lies beyond the body ("*aliquid superius quam corpus*"); the *quod est*—that which is—is thus able to appear as either corporeal or incorporeal. This is why, Seneca adds, the Stoics wished to apply another supreme genus to the *quod est* (RT: *SVF*, III, s.v. *genikôtaton genos* [γενικώτατον γένος]; cf. also Alexander of Aphrodisias, *In Topica*, 4), one that is prior or more of a principle ("*aliud genus magis principale*"), the *quid* (= *ti* [τι]). Then Seneca clarifies the ultimate reasons for the Stoic decision thus:

> In rerum, inquiunt, natura quaedam sunt, quaedam non sunt, et haec autem, quae non sunt, rerum natura complectitur, quae animo succurrunt, tanquam Centauri, Gigantes, et quicquid aliud falsa cogitatione formatum habere aliquid imaginem coepit, quamvis non habet substantiam.

> (In nature, they say, there are the things which are, and things which are not. Yet nature embraces the very things which are not and come to mind, like centaurs, giants; products of false concepts, already feigning an image, and yet lacking substance.)

> *(Ibid., 58.15)*

We may conclude from this brief passage that the "things which are" (*to on* vs. *to huphestos* [τὸ ὑφεστός]) are precisely because they "have substance." "To have substance" (*substantiam habere*) may and without any doubt must be understood here as a translation or explication of what is meant by "to be" (*esse*). To be implies truth, not only of being a substance, of being substantially or in the manner of substance, but in fact "to have substance" or "to take substance" ("*substantiam capere*"; Boethius), that is, to be able to be based in a corporal reality defined by its stability and solidity.

3. *Substantiam habere—substantiam capere* ("to have," "to take substance")

We may remark straightaway, taking account of the stereotypical character of the unitary Latin expression *substantiam habere*, that it refers, at least in the passage cited, more probably to the Greek verb *huphistanai* than to the strict concept of *hupostasis*. Nonetheless, it is clear that Seneca means substantiality, proper to what exists in the full sense, as the fact of having a support, a substrate, or a basis guaranteeing consistency and stability.

In this way, "having-substance" always requires or presupposes a body; the body here refers in general to the foundation on which everything must rest in order to be. If being implies having-substance, it is because the fact of having-substance implies the possession of a solid substrate, whose property is precisely the guarantee of consistency and permanence.

After having taken up, as we have seen, the classical contrast between *hupostasis* and *emphasis* in the passage cited above, taken from the *Quaestiones naturales*, Seneca adds:

> Nobis non placet in arcu aut corona subesse aliquid corporis certi.

(We are not of the opinion that there is at bottom, in the rainbow or luminous halo, anything corporeal.)

(*Quaestiones naturales, 1.6.4*)

4. *Substantia—corpus*

One might think that an expression like *subesse corpus* (a body that is at the basis, at the foundation) must have played a determining role in the appearance of the term *substantia* in philosophical contexts. To clarify this convergence, we must quickly go back: we have seen how Cicero, in *De oratore* (5.27), distinguished two types of "things" (*res*) in his analysis of definition: things that are, things that are cognized (*res quae sunt, res quae intelliguntur*). Only concrete beings really are, Cicero affirms, unlike abstract entities that lack material reality: "*quibus nullum subest corpus.*" In the same way, in the *De natura deorum* (1.38), concerning the thesis according to which the "form of god" can only be grasped in thought and not in sensation, and is lacking in all consistency ("*speciem dei percipi coginatione non sensu, nec esse in ea ullam soliditatem*"), Cicero asks:

> Nam si tantum modo ad cogitationem valent nec habent ullam soliditatem nec eminentiam, quid interest utrum de hippocentauro an de deo cogitemus?

(For if [deities] exist only in thought, and have no solidity nor substance, what difference can there be between thinking of a hippocentaur, and thinking of a deity?)

Not having solidity, not having body (we naturally expect a *substantiam habere* here), means not being, in the sense in which the hippocentaur is the very example of inexistence or irreality (*anuparxias paradeigma* [ἀνυπαρξίας παράδειγμα]) (Sextus Empiricus, *Outlines of Scepticism*, 1.162).

It thus looks as though the term *substantia*, whose meaning comes out most fully in composite expressions like *substantiam habere*, was designed to express an immediate understanding of being as corporeity, solidity, ground(s). *Substantia* is thus properly speaking what is at the foundation—*id quod substat*—the reality that stands beneath and that one may use as a foundation, the basis that guarantees being with its subsistence by giving it ontological support. Seneca repeats, clarifying substantiality in the sense of "having substance," which still implies the having of a proper and determinate body (*proprium, certum*):

> Aliquid per se numerabitur cum per se stabit.

(Only what stands by itself is counted by itself.)

(*Letters, 113.5*)

From its first "philosophical" uses, the Latin term thus seems to have a specific understanding, its own coloring, which by itself is sufficient to cast doubt on the hypothesis of a pure and simple scholarly calque from *hupostasis*. The pretheoretical notions implied by *substantia* appear even more clearly if we examine the nontechnical uses of the

word. We must note again, against the "calque" hypothesis, the numerous uses of *substantia* in very modest, concrete, and material senses among jurists of the second and third centuries, where the term retains its ancient meaning of owned property, inheritance, resources, means of subsistence.

In the *De institutione oratoria*, Quintilian suggests for the first time, in a thematic way, that *ousia* be translated by *substantia*. The subject is the figures and the ornaments that they provide for speeches, as well as the dangers of their overuse; he writes:

> There are some who pay no consideration to the weight of their matter or the force of their thoughts and think themselves supreme artists, if only they succeed in forcing even the emptiest of words into *figurative* form, with the result that they are never tired of stringing *figures* together, despite the fact that it is as ridiculous to hunt for *figures* without reference to the matter as it is to discuss dress and gesture without reference to the body.

(*De institutione oratoria, 9.3.100*)

Quintilian mentions elsewhere the questions that can arise in certain trials, not as to the reality of an alleged fact at all, but as to the actual identity of an individual, otherwise well-known:

> ut est quaesitum contra Urbiniae heredes, is quis tanquam filius petebat bona, Figulus esset an Sosipater. Nam et substantiaeius sub oculos venit, ut non possit quaeri, an sit . . . nec quid sit nec quale sit.

([It] may be illustrated by the action brought against the heirs of Urbinia, where the question was whether the man who claimed the property as being the son of the deceased, was Figulus or Sosipater. In this case the actual person was before the eyes of the court [*nam et substantia ejus sub oculos venit*], so that there could be no question whether he existed [*ut non possit quaeri an sit*] . . . nor what he was nor of what kind.)

(Ibid., 7.2.5)

To be manifest (*sub oculos venire*) is precisely what is proper to "substance," proper to that to which a body underlies, proper to that which "has substance" (*substantiam habere*).

We may then demand whether *substantia* would have ever "translated" the Greek *ousia, hupostasis*, or rather if, thanks to some overdetermined translations, it laid the groundwork for new ontological determinations—the very ones that would be inherited by all of *Romania*, without quite knowing it.

5. The notion of substance in Marius Victorinus

In his *Liber de definitionibus*, Marius Victorinus presents a critical summary of the Ciceronian doctrine of the two kinds of definition. Cicero's distinction rests on the Stoic contrast between corporeals and incorporeals (*Topics*, 5.26–27), and it tends to declare unreal anything that does not derive ultimately from a corporeal foundation ("*subesse corpus—ta ontôs huphestôta*" [τὰ ὄντως ὑφεστῶτα], according to Stoic terminology). To overturn—and to confirm—Cicero's account, Victorinus need only introduce the term *substantia*, foreign to Cicero's text, and to expand relation that grounds substantiality beyond pure and simple corporeity. From that point on, the body is only a special case, even if it is empirically privileged, of what can provide a foundation in the manner of a subject or substrate:

> Quamquam Tullius aliter in eodem libro Topicorum ait esse duo genera definitionum: primum, cum enim id quod est definitur; secundo, cum id quod sui substantiam non habet, hoc est quod non est; et hoc partitionis genus in his quae supra dixi clausit et extenuavit. Sed alia esse voluit quae esse dicebat, alia quae non esse. Esse enim dicit ea quorum subest corpus, ut cum definimus quid sit aqua, quid ignis; non autem esse illa intelligi voluit quibus nulla corporalis videtur esse substantia, ut sunt pietas, virtus, libertas. Sed non omnia ista, vel quae sunt cum corpore vel quae sunt sine corpore, si in eo accipiuntur ut aut per se esse aut in alio esse videantur in uno genere numeranda dicimus: ut ista omnia esse intelligantur quibus omnibus sua potest esse substantia, sive illae corporales sive, ut certissimum est et recto nomine appellari possunt, qualitates.

> (In book V of the *Topics* Cicero suggests that there are two kinds of definition: the first in which one defines what is; the second when one defines what does not have proper substance, in other words what is not; and he attempts to circumscribe this kind of definition *a partibus*, and to limit its extension. . . . He wishes to distinguish between the things which he says exist, and those which he says do not exist. He posits that the things to which a body is subjacent are; when we define for example what water is or fire; on the other hand, he wishes us to consider as not being the things which seem to have no bodily substance, like piety, virtue, liberty. We say on the contrary that all these things, whether with or without body, should be classed under the single generic head [that of being, i.e., substantiality], as long as we grasp them insofar as they appear to be by themselves or in another. We must therefore understand that all these things which may always have a proper substance are, either because they are body, or because they are qualities, since that is certainly determined, fully authorizing that determination.)

> (Marius Victorinus, *Liber de definitionibus*)

After having introduced the term *substantia* as needing no further explanation in his account of the Ciceronian analysis, Victorinus's efforts focus entirely on dissociating corporeity and substantiality. For us, he states, as we consider all things "insofar as they appear to be by themselves or to be in another," we must place them under a single head, namely, substance. These are properly speaking all the things for which there may be substance, or better, "proper substance." It does not matter that substance relates from the start to *substare* and the *subesse* of the body, or secondarily the substrate on which a "quality" always comes to belong. "Being-by-itself" is being substance, "being-in-another" is being quality in a substance, which then becomes for the quality in question like its body, its proper substance. This is the usage of *substare* that we find in Boethius (480–524), in *Contra Eutychen et Nestorium*, chapter 3, which we

may gloss in the sense of "to procure a subject for everything else considered as accidents, so that they may be," to "support" their "being in a subject" (cf. Libera, *L'art des généralités*):

> "Substance" [*substat*] is that which gathers as underpinning [*subministrat*] for other accidents [*i.e.* to all the rest considered as accidents] some subject [*subjectum*], so that they may exist [*ut esse valeant*]; indeed it supports them [*sub illis enim stat*], since it is subjected to accidents [*subjectum est accidentibus*].

Suárez doubtless remembers these formulations when he notes, referring to the "etymology" of *substantia*: "Substare enim idem est quod aliis subesse tanquam eorum sustentaculum et fundamentum, vel subjectum" (to be substance is in effect the same thing as to underlie other things as a support, foundation, or subject) (*Disputationes metaphysicae* 33, §1).

■ See Box 2.

C. *Essentia ab esse*: Essence

The term *essentia* only becomes established with Augustine, even though we may find some occurrences, beginning with Apuleius, in other authors influenced by Neoplatonism, like Macrobius or Chalcidius. As we have seen, in its first occurrences, the sense of the word remains unstable and almost inevitably slips onto the side of "substance." The term is, we might say, so unclear that it constantly requires explication in terms of *substantia*. Augustine's work marks a signal reversal in this regard. In his eyes, as we have already noted, *essentia* appears as a recently created term, still rarely used but destined to replace *substantia*, at least in some of the latter's previous senses. Augustine writes, for example, in this early text, the *De moribus manichaeorum*:

> Nam et ipsa natura nihil est aliud quam id quod intelligitur in suo genere aliquid esse. Itaque, ut nos jam novo nomine ab eo quod est esse vocamus essentiam, quam plerumque substantiam etiam nominamus, ita veteres qui haec nomina non habebant pro essentia et substantia naturam vocabant.

> (Indeed nature itself is nothing other than what one cognizes that it is something of this kind. This is why, just as we name it "essence," using a neologism based on "to be," so the ancients, lacking these terms, used "nature" for "essence" and "substance.")

> (*De moribus manichaeorum*, 2.2)

Or again:

> Essentiam dico quae οὐσία graece dicitur, quam usitatius substantiam vocamus.

> (I call *essentia* what is called *ousia* in Greek, and what we more commonly call *substantia*.)

> (*De Trinitate*, 5.8.9–10)

We might even go so far as to suppose that over the course of Augustine's life, and certainly thanks to him, the term must have spread so as to become standard, since in a late work like *City of God* he can write:

2

"Existence" and "subsistence": The Stoic strategy

➤ HOMONYM, SEIN, SENSE, SIGNIFIER/SIGNIFIED, WORD

Following the Stoics, Cicero contrasts in his *Topics* the true (substantial) being of bodies with the "fictive" being ("*to huphestos, kat' epinoian psilên huphistasthai*" [τὸ ὑφεστός, κατ' ἐπίνοιαν ψιλὴν ὑφίστασθαι]) of notions (*ennoêmata* [ἐννοήματα]): "ἐννόημα δέ ἐστι φάντασμα διανοίας, οὔτε τι ὄν οὔτε ποιόν, ὡσανεὶ δέ τι καὶ ὡσανεὶ ποιόν (a concept is a phantasm of thought, which is neither something, nor something qualified, but quasi-something and quasi-something qualified) (Diogenes Laertius, *Lives of Eminent Philosophers*, 7.61; RT: *SVF*, vol. 1, n. 65, p. 19;

Long and Sedley, *Hellenistic Philosophers*; and equally the specification by Libera in Porphyre, *Isagoge*).

Against this doctrine, Marius Victorinus thinks it necessary to appeal to Aristotle, but on the basis of an interpretation of the *ousia* of the *Categories*, and of the distinction between *ousia prôtê* [οὐσία πρώτη] and *ousia deutera* [οὐσία δεύτερα], which has already conceded the only decisive point: the substantial implications of *ousia*. Even when *ousia* is not present strictly speaking, as is paradigmatically the case in corporeal

beings, it may at least be apprehended as a subject of accidents or qualities, which thus find their *substantia propria*.

BIBLIOGRAPHY

Diogenes Laertes. *Lives of Eminent Philosophers*. Cambridge, MA: Harvard University Press, 1999.

Long, Anthony A., and David N. Sedley. *The Hellenistic Philosophers*. 3 vols. Cambridge: Cambridge University Press, 1987.

Porphyry. *Isagoge*. Translated by A. de Libera and A. P. Segonds, introduction and notes by A. de Libera. Paris: Vrin, 1998.

---

ab eo quod est esse vocatur essentia, novo quidem nomine quo usi veteres non sunt latini sermonis auctores, sed jam nostris temporibus usitato, ne deesset etiam linguae nostrae, quod Graeci appellant οὐσίαν.

(so from "to be" [*esse*] comes "being" [*essentia*]: a new word, indeed, which was not used in the Latin speech of old, but which has come into use in our own day so that our language should not lack a word for what the Greeks call *ousia*; for this is expressed very exactly by *essentia*.)

(*De civitate Dei*, 12.2)

The term would thus be recently created in order to respond literally ("*hoc enim verbum e verbo expressum est, ut diceretur essential*") to the Greek *ousia*. Clearly, the term *essentia* is designed, by its very formation, to "translate" *ousia*, but can only appear as such with a new comprehension of being different from that which guided it (*esse* in the sense of "having body," "having substance"). In other words, again, *essentia* can only establish itself as a "translation" of *ousia* when the latter is resolutely interpreted on the basis of the verb *einai*, reinterpreted in the perspective of Porphyrean Neoplatonism. Saint Augustine is perfectly explicit as to the meaning of this derivation, to which he returns again and again:

Sicut enim ab eo quod est sapere dicta est sapientia et ab eo quod est scire dicta est scientia, sic ab eo quod est esse vocatur essential.

(For just as wisdom is so called from being wise, and knowledge is so called from knowing, so essence is so called from being [*esse*].)

(*De Trinitate*, 5.2.3)

Essence must first be understood *ab esse*, or better *ab eo quod est esse*—on the basis of what the verb "to be" expresses, or the act of being.

We can follow rather precisely the upheavals wrought by this new "translation" in a remarkable passage of *De immortalitate animae*: it provides, it seems, the first occurrence of the

term *essentia* in Augustine's writing, but he also proposes a Platonizing reinterpretation of Aristotle. The central Augustinian thesis is formulated thus:

Illa omnia quae quoquo modo sunt ab ea Essentia sunt, quae summe maximeque est.

(Everything which exists in any way derives from that being which is the highest and greatest.)

(*De immortalitate animae*, 11.18)

We must surely read here, we believe, *Essentia* (capitalized). Essence as such, Essence pure and simple, must be understood as a Divine Name. It even names God properly speaking, as the Essence par excellence, that is, as *causa essendi* (*De diversis quaestionibus*, 83, q. 21): the being in virtue of which exist all things that are in one manner or another. The Aristotelian "definition" of *ousia prôtê* is clearly indicated, but in order to be entirely theologized. "*Ousia* in the fundamental, primary, and principal sense" (*hê kuriôtata te kai prôtôs kai malista legomenê* [ἡ κυριώτατά τε καὶ πρώτως καὶ μάλιστα λεγομένη]) is henceforth understood as *Essentia . . . quae summe maxime que est,* that is, God. Nothing is, nothing is existent except through being in him, by his *essentia* ("*omnis essentia . . . non ob aliud essentia est, nisi quia est*").

■ See Box 3.

The term "essence," we believe, can thus only be established in Latin if it contains the echo of what *esse* (*to einai*) expresses verbally. Thus, *essentia* does not simply replace *substantia*, but rather opens up a new understanding of being. It is thus no accident that the term is only fully deployed when it comes to refer primarily to the one who *summe est*, he who, Augustine goes so far as to say, *est est*: "*Est enim est sicut bonorum bonum est*" (he is indeed "is," as [he] is the good of goods) (*Enarrationes en Psalmos*, 134, RT: *PL*, vol. 37, col. 1741; cf. also *In evangelium Johannis tractatus*, 39.8.9: *Est quod est* [he is what is]; *Confessions*, 12.31.46: "*quidquid aliquo modo est, sed est est*" [everything which is in some way anything is in virtue of he who is not in just any way but is is]).

3

The Augustinian reinterpretation of Aristotle

➤ I/ME/MYSELF

It is this fundamental thesis that leads Augustine to adopt the Aristotelian doctrine according to which *ousiai* do not have contraries—at the cost of a complete reversal of the hierarchy of *ousia prôtê–ousia deutera* since "primary essence" is no longer the singular thing as here (*tode ti*), but rather God. The Augustinian transposition of this doctrine singularly clarifies the new understanding of being that is expressed through the translation of *essentia*. Here is the canonical passage from Aristotle:

Ὑπάρχει δὲ ταῖς οὐσίαις καὶ τὸ μηδὲν αὐταῖς ἐναντίον εἶναι. Τῇ γὰρ πρώτῃ οὐσίᾳ τί ἂν εἴη ἐναντίον ; οἷον τῷ τινι ἀνθρώπῳ οὐδέν ἐστι ἐναντίον, οὐδέ γε τῷ ἀνθρώπῳ ἤ τῷ ζῴῳ οὐδέν ἐστι ἐναντίον.

(Another characteristic of substances is that there is nothing contrary to them. For what would be contrary to a primary substance? For example, there is nothing contrary to an individual man, nor yet is there anything contrary to man or to animal.)

(Categories, 5.3b24f.)

Aristotle's aim is not here to contrast being and non-being as principles. Rather, it is simply to show, taking account of the determined "essence" as such or such, that it is *dektikê tôn enantiôn* [δεκτικὴ τῶν ἐναντίων] (such as to receive contraries), making room that contraries can occupy and respond to one another, developing in this way a single configuration ("*kai gar tôn enantiôn tropon tina to auto eidos*" [καὶ γὰρ τῶν ἐναντίων τρόπον τινα τὸ αὐτὸ εἶδος]; *Metaphysics* Z7, 1032b2–3).

In the rather different framework of a demonstration of the immortality of the soul Augustine is led to rely on this passage from Aristotle, attributing to it a new ontological meaning. In the course of his demonstration, and on the basis of an identification of being and truth, Augustine must respond to the objection according to which the soul, turning away from truth, would accordingly lose its very being. The Augustinian response rests on the distinction between the *conversio* and the *aversio*, and especially—and this is the point that interests us—on the claim that the soul, having its being from the very thing that has no contrary, and which *is* paradigmatically—*Essentia*—could not lose it.

The Aristotelian doctrine according to which *ousia* does not have a contrary thus acquires a peculiar illustration, when it becomes a matter of the *Essentia* by which all things exist that are of such or such a sort ("*illa omnia quae quodmodo sunt*"):

Nam si nulla essentia in quantum essentia est, aliquid habet contrarium, multo minus habet contrarium prima illa essentia, quae dicitur veritas, in quantum essentia est.

(If no independent reality has a contrary, insofar as it is an independent reality, much less does that first reality which is called truth have a contrary insofar as it is an independent reality.)

(De immortalitate animae, 12.19)

Essence as such ("*essentia in quantum essentia est*") does not have a contrary because it is said *ab eo quod est esse*: from that which is being. But being (*esse*) has no contrary, except precisely non-being, or nothing. Being has nothing as a contrary; being does not have anything as a contrary: "Esse autem non habet contrarium, nisi non esse; unde nihil est essentiae contrarium" (*De immortalitate animae*, 12.19; cf. also *De moribus manichaeorum*, 2.1.1). Thus the Aristotelian doctrine comes paradoxically to the aid of the thesis of the primacy of the "Essentia quae summe maximeque est," and the treatise of the *Categories* is henceforth pressed into the service of a Porphyrean metaphysics of *einai*. And Augustine can even go so far as to conclude the movement of thought we are examining in this way:

Nullo modo igitur res ulla potest esse contrario illi substantiae, quae maxime ac primitus est.

(In no way, then, can anything be contrary to that reality which exists in the greatest and most fundamental way.)

(De immortalitate animae, 12.19; Fr. transl. mod.)

Augustine can reintroduce the term "substance" here (to accentuate the reference to *Categories*, 5): we can see clearly that the word no longer has a guiding role, and it is to be understood only on the basis of the prior determination of essentiality. It is a diametrically opposed gesture to that of Apuleius in his *De Platone*.

No doubt the Neoplatonic reference does not suffice on its own to clarify this new Augustinian understanding of being (which is precisely not "essentialist"), establishing a career for *essentia*. Without engaging in questions raised by the so-called metaphysics of the Exodus, we must nevertheless note that the interpretation of the mystical Name of God revealed to Moses on Mount Sinai constitutes the focal point of Augustinian meditation. *Essentia* can be understood as a Divine Name, since it expresses that which brings into existence everything that *is*. Essence can even be properly predicated of God: "Quis magis est [essentia] quam ille qui dixit famulo suo Moysi: ego sum qui sum, et: dices filiis Israel: Qui est misit me ad vos?" (And who possesses being in a higher degree than he, who said to his servant Moses: "I am who am," and to the sons of Israel, "He who is, has sent me to you"?) (*De Trinitate*, 5.2.3). God is properly called essence, he has the Name *Essentia*, since only he is *ipsum esse* ("cui profecto ipsum esse . . . maxime ac verissime competit").

BIBLIOGRAPHY

Aristotle. *Categories*. In *The Complete Works*, edited by J. Barnes. 2 vols. Princeton, NJ: Princeton University Press, 1984.

In other words, again, it is first as a Divine Name that *essentia* can be established to express properly the being of he who says of himself: "*sic sum quod sum, sic sum epsum esse*" (as I am what is, so I am Being itself) (*Sermones*, 7.7). It is because he is apprehended as the one who "primarily and pre-eminently" is that God become *ousia prôtê*, that is, now and necessarily: *Essentia*. God does not have attributes, but above all he could not be the subject of attributes: "But it is wrong to assert that God subsists and is the subject of His own goodness [*ut sub-sistat et sub-sit Deus bonitati suae*], and that goodness is not a substance, or rather not an essence, that God Himself is not His own goodness, and that it inheres in Him as in its subject" (*De Trinitate*, 7.5.10).

Jean-François Courtine

BIBLIOGRAPHY

Alexander of Aphrodisias. *In Topica*. RT: *CAG*, vol. 2. Translation by J. M. Van Ophuijsen: *On Aristotle's "Topics 1"*. London: Duckworth, 2001.

Anselm of Canterbury. *Proslogion*. In *The Major Works*. Edited by B. Davies and G. R. Evans. Oxford: Oxford University Press, 2008.

Apuleius. *The Works of Apuleius*. London: G. Bell and Sons, 1881.

Apuleius (Pseudo-). *Peri hermeneias: De philosophia liber*. Edited by P. Thomas. Leipzig: Teubner, 1908.

Aristotle. *Analytica priora et posteriora*. Edited by W. D. Ross. Oxford: Oxford University Press, 1964.

———. *Aristotle's "Posterior Analytics."* Translated by J. Barnes. Oxford: Clarendon Press, 1975.

———. *Categoriae et liber de interpretatione*. Edited by L. Minio-Paluello. Oxford: Oxford University Press, 1964.

———. *Categories and De interpretatione*. Translated by J. L. Ackrill. New York: Oxford University Press, 1975.

———. *Peri hermeneias*. Translated by H. Weidemann. Berlin: Weingartner, 1978.

———. *Prior Analytics*. Translated by R. Smith. Indianapolis, IN: Hackett, 1989.

Augustine. *The City of God against the Pagans*. Edited by R. W. Dyson. Cambridge: Cambridge University Press, 1998.

———. *The Confessions*. Translated by E. B. Pusey. New York: Modern Library, 1999.

———. *Immortality of the Soul*. In *Soliloquies* and *Immortality of the Soul*. Translated by G. Watson. Eastbourne: Oxbow Books, 2008.

———. *The Trinity*. Translated by Stephen McKenna. Washington, DC: Catholic University of America Press, 1963.

Boethius. *The Theological Tractates*. Translated by H. F. Stewart, E. K. Rand, and S. J. Tester. Cambridge, MA: Harvard University Press, 1973.

Brunot, Ferdinand. *La pensée et le langage: Méthode, principes et plan d'une théorie nouvelle du langage appliquée au français*. Paris: Masson, 1922.

Cajetan, Thommaso de Vio. *De ente et essentia D. Thomae Aquinatis Commentaria*. Edited by M. H. Laurent. Turin: Marietti, 1949. Translation by L. H. Kendzierski and F. C. Wade: *Commentary on Being and Essence* (In *De Ente et Essentia d. Thomas Aquinatis*). Milwaukee, WI: Marquette University Press, 1964.

Cicero. *De natura deorum*. Translation by C. D. Yonge. Amherst, NY: Prometheus Books, 1997.

———. *On Duties*. Edited by M. T. Griffin and E. M. Atkins. Cambridge: Cambridge University Press, 1991.

———. *On the Divisions of Oratory*. In *On the Orator: Book 3. On Fate. Stoic Paradoxes. On the Divisions of Oratory*. Translated by H. Rackham. Loeb Classical Library, 349. Princeton, NJ: Princeton University Press, 1942.

———. *Stoic Paradoxes*. In *On the Orator: Book 3. On Fate. Stoic Paradoxes. On the Divisions of Oratory*. Translated by H. Rackham. Loeb Classical Library, 349. Princeton, NJ: Princeton University Press, 1942.

———. *Topics*. In *The Orations of Marcus Tullius Cicero*. Translated by C. D. Yonge. London: G. Bell and Sons, 1913–21.

Damascius. *Dubitationes et solutiones de primis principiis in Parmenidem*. 2 vols. Edited by C. E. Ruelle. Imprimerie nationale, 1889; repr. Brussels: Culture et civilisation, 1964; Amsterdam: A.M. Hakkert, 1966.

Diogenes Laertius. *Lives of Eminent Philosophers*. Cambridge, MA: Harvard University Press, 1991.

Gilles of Rome. *Theoremata de esse et essentia*. Edited by E. Hocedez. Louvain, Belg.: Museum Lessianu, 1930.

Gilson, Étienne. *Being and Some Philosophers*. 2nd ed. Toronto: Pontifical Institute of Mediaeval Studies, 1952.

———. *L'être et l'essence*. 2nd rev. ed. Paris: Vrin, 1979

Glucker, John. "The Origin of ὑπάρχω and ὕπαρξις as Philosophical Terms." In *Hyparxis e hupostasis nel neoplatonismo*, edited by Francesco Romano and Taormina Daniela Patrizia. Florence: Leo S. Olschki, 1994.

Hadot, Pierre. "Existenz, existentia." In *Historisches Wörterbuch der Philosophie*, edited by J. Ritter, vol. 2, cols. 853–56. Basel, Swiz.: Schwabe and Co., 1972.

———. *Marius Victorinus: Recherches sur sa vie et son oeuvre*. Paris: Études Augustiniennes, 1971.

———. *Plotinus or the Simplicity of Vision*. Translated by M. Chase and A. I. Davidson. Chicago: University of Chicago Press, 1993.

———. *Porphyre et Victorinus*. 2 vols. Paris: Études Augustiniennes, 1999.

———. "Zur Vorgeschichte des Begriffs "Existenz," ΥΠΑΡΧΕΙΝ bei den Stoikern." *Archiv für Begriffgeschichte* 13 (1969): 115–27.

Hintikka, Jaako. "The Varieties of Being in Aristotle." In *The Logic of Being*, edited by S. Knuuttila and J. Hintikka, 81–114. Dordrecht, Neth.: Reidel, 1986.

Kahn, Charles. "Retrospect on the Verb 'To Be' and the Concept of Being." In *The Logic of Being*, edited by S. Knuuttila and J. Hintikka, 1–28. Dordrecht, Neth.: Reidel, 1986.

———. *The Verb "Be" in Ancient Greek*. The Verb "Be" and its Synonyms, Philosophical and Grammatical Studies series. Dordrecht, Neth.: Reidel, 1973.

Leibniz, Gottfried Wilhelm. *Recherches générales sur l'analyse des notions et des verities*. Paris: Presses Universitaires de France, 1998.

Libera, Alain de. *L'art des généralités: Théories de l'abstraction*. Paris: Aubier, 1999.

Libera, Alain de, and Cyrille Michon. *L'être et l'essence: Le vocabulaire médiéval de l'ontologie*. Paris: Éditions du Seuil, 1996.

Long, Anthony A., and David N. Sedley. *The Hellenistic Philosophers*. 3 vols. Cambridge: Cambridge University Press, 1987.

Lucretius. *De rerum natura*. 2nd ed. Translated by W.H.D. Rouse, revised by M. F. Smith. Cambridge, MA: Harvard University Press, 1982.

———. *On the Nature of Things* (*De Rerum Natura*). Translated by A. M. Esolen. Baltimore: Johns Hopkins University Press, 1995.

Mansion, Suzanne. "Le rôle de la connaissance de l'existence dans la science aristotélicienne." In *Etudes aristotéliciennes: Recueil d'articles*, edited by J. Follon, 183–203. Louvain, Belg.: Ed. de l'Institut supérieure de philosophie, 1984.

Maritain, Jacques. *A Preface to Metaphysics: Seven Lectures on Being*. New York: Sheed and Ward, 1948.

Marius Victorinus. *Theological Treatises on the Trinity*. Translated by M. T. Clark. Washington, DC: Catholic University of America Press, 1981.

Mill, John Stuart. *A System of Logic*. Edited by T. M. Robson. Toronto: University of Toronto Press, 1973–74.

Philo of Alexandria. *On the Creation of the Cosmos According to Moses* (*De opificio mundi*). Translated by David T. Runia. Leiden, Neth.: Brill, 2001.

Porphyry. *Isagoge*. Translated by A. de Libera and A. P. Segonds, introduction and notes by A. de Libera. Paris: Vrin, 1998.

Priscian. *Institutiones grammaticae*. Vol. 1. Edited by M. Herz. Leipzig: Teubner, 1865.

Quintilian. *De institutione oratoria*. Translated by H. E. Butler. Cambridge, MA: Harvard University Press, 1985.

———. *Quintilian: The Orator's Education*. Vol. 2. Cambridge, MA: Harvard University Press, 2001.

Richard of Saint-Victor. *La Trinité*. Latin text and French translation by G. Salet. Sources chrétiennes, 63. Paris: Éditions du Cerf, 1959.

———. *On the Trinity*. Translated by R. Agelici. Cambridge: James Clarke, 2012.

———. *Selected Writings on Contemplation*. Translated by C. Kirchberger. London: Faber and Faber, 1957.

Romano, Francesco, and Taormina Daniela Patrizia, eds. *Hyparxis e hupostasis nel neoplatonismo*. Florence: Leo S. Olschki, 1994.

Russell, Bertrand. *The Principles of Mathematics*. London: Cambridge University Press, 1903.

Scipio Dupleix. *La métaphysique*. Paris: Gallimard / La Pléiade, 1992.

Seneca. *Letters from a Stoic*. Translated by R. Campbell. Baltimore: Penguin, 1969.

———. *Natural Questions*. In *Dialogues and Letters*. Translated by C.D.N. Costa. Baltimore: Penguin Classics, 1997.

———. *Sénèque, entretiens, lettres à Lucilius*. Translated by H. Noblot; edited by P. Veyne. Paris: Bouquins-Laffont, 1993.

Sextus Empiricus. *Outlines of Pyrrhonism*. Edited and translated by R. G. Bury. Loeb Classical Library. Cambridge, MA: Harvard University Press, 1933.

———. *Outlines of Scepticism*. Edited and translated by R. G. Bury. Loeb Classical Library. Cambridge, MA: Harvard University Press, 1933.

Suárez, Francisco. *Disputationes metaphysicae*. In *Opera omnia*. Vols. 25–26. Edited by C. Berton. Vivès, 1866; repr. Hildesheim, Ger.: Olms, 1965. Translation by J. Kronen and J. Reedy: *On the Formal Cause of Substance: Metaphysical Disputation XV*. Milwaukee, WI: Marquette University Press, 2000.

ESTI [ἐστι], EINAI [εῖναι]

ENGLISH   there is, there exists, it is possible that, it is the case that, it is, exists, is; to be, to exist, to be identical to, to be the case

➤ IL Y A [ES GIBT, HÁ, SEIN, *TO BE*], and ANALOGY, *CATEGORY*, DASEIN, ESSENCE, HOMONYM, NATURE, *NEGATION, NOTHING*, OBJECT, PRÉDICABLE, PREDICATION, REALITY, SPECIES, SUBJECT, *THING* [RES], TO TI ÊN EINAI, TRUTH

Even the verb "to be," which Schleiermacher calls "the original verb," is "illuminated and colored by language" ("Über die verschiedenen Methoden des Übersetzens"). The Greek *einai* [εῖναι] has or may have a number of semantic and and syntactic characteristics capable of giving rise to philosophy as the thought of being, in particular, the collusion among the function of the copula, the existential meaning, and the veridical meaning. It is thus, Heidegger emphasizes, that the Greek language "is philosophical, i.e. not that Greek is loaded with philosophical terminology, but that it philosophizes in its basic structure and formation (*Sprachgestaltung*)" (*Essence of Human Freedom*, §7). Yet, this dictionary's project is in part to attempt to make distinctions among linguistic realities, the idiomatic impact of fundamental philosophical works, and what Jean-Pierre Lefebvre calls "ontological nationalism"—in this case, the projection of a sort of Germany onto a sort of Greece.

Parmenides's *Poem* is fundamental both for Greek thought and for the Greek language. The form *esti* [ἐστι], "is," third-person singular indicative present, which is the name of the route of investigation of the *Poem*, is even more remarkable since at the beginning of a sentence it can mean not only "there is" (see ES GIBT, HÁ), but also "it is possible." Finally, a series of key words and expressions for ontology arise over the course of the works of Parmenides, Plato, and Aristotle simply as derivatives of *einai*: *to on* [τὸ ὄν], "what is"; *to ontôs on* [τὸ ὄντως ὄν], "what really is, that is, true, authentic being"; *ousia* [οὐσία], "being-hood," "essence," "substance"; *to on hêi on* [τὸ ὄν ᾗ ὄν], "being insofar as it is being"; *to ti ên einai* [τὸ τί ἦν εῖναι], the "what it was to be," "quiddity," the "essential of the essence."

Finally, the question of the "is not" and of "what" is not is related to the question of being from Parmenides on. It requires taking account of two possible expressions of negation, prohibitive and subjective (particle *mê*), or factual and objective (particle *ou*), mirroring the difference between "negation" in the strict sense (Gr. *mê*; *to mê on*, "what cannot be," "nothingness") and "privation" (Gr. *ou*; *to ouk on*, "that which as it happens is not [such]"), as well as the various combinations of the negations, which can complement or reinforce each other. These peculiarities of Greek, which Sophists and philosophers take advantage of, in turn shed light on the specific features of the vernaculars that are used to translate them.

I. Greek, the Language of Being?

"Tout ce qu'on veut montrer ici est que la structure linguistique du Grec prédisposait la notion 'd'être' à une vocation philosophique" (all we wish to show here is that the linguistic structure of Greek predisposed the notion of "being" to a philosophic vocation) (Benveniste, *Problems in General Linguistics*). "The fact that the development of Western grammar began with Greek meditation on the *Greek* language gives this process its whole meaning. For along with the German language, Greek (in regard to the possibilities of thinking) is at once the most powerful and the

most spiritual of languages" (Heidegger, *Introduction to Metaphysics*, ¶43). The normally contrary views of Heidegger the philosopher and Benveniste the linguist are in agreement for once, in describing the privilege of *einai* [εῖναι], "to be," in Greek, which is otherwise reckoned to be the source of meaning (Heidegger) or of confusions and mistakes (Benveniste), whether inevitable or accidental. Like any verb, "to be" has a "syntactic function" (Benveniste) related to its "grammar" (Heidegger) and a "lexical sense" (Benveniste) related to its "etymology" (Heidegger). Jacques Derrida analyzes this peculiarity of Greek in terms of the function between the grammatical and lexical functions of the verb "to be": "Although always uneasy and worked upon from within, the fusion of the grammatical and the lexical functions of 'to be' surely has an essential link with the history of metaphysics and everything that is coordinated with it in the West" ("The Supplement of Copula").

A. Lexical function: The semantics of *einai*

Benveniste, in order to measure the semantic peculiarity of the verb "to be" in Greek and in our "philosophical" languages, takes as the counter-example the Ewe language, where, except for the strict identity of subject and predicate marked by *nye*, which is "curiously" transitive, what we indicate by "to be" is expressed on the one hand by *le* (God exists, he is here) or *no* (he remains there), on the other hand by *wo* (it is sandy), *du* (he is king), or *di* (he is thin), with verbs whose only relations to one another are the ones that we, starting from our own mother tongues, project onto them (Benveniste, *Problems in General Linguistics*). Heidegger suggests something analogous in an etymological mode, when he brings up the three Indo-European and Germanic roots at work in the uses of the verb "to be": *es*, in Sanskrit *asus*, "life, the living" (which yields the Gr. *esti* [ἐστι], Fr. *est*, Ger. *ist*, Eng. "is"); *bhû, bheu*, "to grow, to flourish," perhaps "to appear" like *phusis* [φύσις], "nature," in Greek, and perhaps the Gr. *phaineshtai* [φαίνεσθαι], "to seem," which yields the Lat. *fui*, Fr. *il fut*, Ger. *bin*); finally *wes*, Sanskrit *wasami*, "to live, to reside, to remain" (like the Gr. *astu* [ἄστυ], "the city," and *Vesta*, *vestibule*, which yields the Ger. *war, wesen*, or Eng. "was" and "were"). "From the three stems we derive three initial and vividly definite meanings: living, emerging, abiding," meanings that we place at the level of the "existential" sense of "to be" (Heidegger, *Introduction to Metaphysics*; Benveniste, *Problems in General Linguistics*) (see NATURE, Box 1 for *phusis*; LIGHT, Box 1 for *phainesthei*).

B. Grammatical function: The syntax of *einai*

Alongside this exceptionally syncretic semantics, the verb *einai* possesses a grammatical function that is no less peculiar.

1. Cohesive function and copula

Every verb has a cohesive function, allowing it to structure the relation between members of a proposition ("Socrates drinks the hemlock"). But "to be" has this function pre-eminently. It has it first as the copula, guaranteeing the link between subject and predicate, whether as a matter of identity ("Socrates is Socrates") or inclusion ("Socrates is mortal"). It has it a second time—whence its pre-eminence—since this copulative liaison may be substituted for any other one: the copula, as long as we use an appropriate predicate, can replace any verb ("Socrates is drinking-the-hemlock" is equivalent to "Socrates drinks the hemlock"). From Aristotle to Port-Royal, this analysis structures predicate logic (see PREDICATION, WORD):

> [The verb, including even *to be* and *not to be*] is nothing by itself (*ouden esti* [οὐδὲν ἐστι]), but signifies in an additional way a putting into relation (*prossêmainei*, which the medievals translate by "co-signify," *sunthesin tina* [προσσημαίνει σύνθεσίν τινα]), which cannot be conceived without its components.
>
> (*De interpretatione*, 4.16b23–25)

> The verb itself should not have uses other than to mark the link which we make in our minds between the two terms of a proposition; but only the verb *to be*, which we call a substantive, kept this simplicity.
>
> (*Grammar*)

2. Assertive function and veridical sense

"A la relation grammaticale qui unit les membres de l'énoncé s'ajoute implicitement un 'cela est' qui relie l'agencement linguistique au système de la réalité" (to the grammatical relation that links the members of the utterance an implicit "that is" is added that connects the linguistic arrangement to the system of reality) (*Problems in General Linguistics*). A "that is" would accompany all of our sentences, at least the declarative ones, just as a Kantian "I think" would accompany all of our representations. Once again, "to be" has this function pre-eminently. For on the one hand, "Socrates is mortal" asserts that Socrates is mortal, just as "Socrates drinks" asserts that Socrates drinks. But on the other hand, "is," as attested by the "that is" written by Benveniste, or the English "isn't it?"—the French *n'est-ce pas?* but the German *nicht wahr?*—is equivalent to a declaration of this declarative force, a doubling-up or a second degree, while it also functions as a substitute for any affirmation, hence a general equivalent that is as universal with regard to assertion as the copula is with regard to cohesion.

This second function, called the "veridical usage," was recently foregrounded by Charles Kahn as characteristic par excellence of the Greek *einai*: thus, *legein ta onta* [λέγειν τὰ ὄντα] standardly means "to call things as they are," "to say the truth" (cf. Thucydides, 7.8.2, cited by Kahn, *Logic of Being*). As such, it was able to provide the groundwork for the Parmenidean starting point all by itself. Thus, for Pierre Aubenque, Parmenides "confuses" the veridical, universal function ("to be" means "it is the case, it is true," and is contrasted with opinion) and the lexical, particular meaning ("to be" means "to be permanent" and is contrasted with becoming). With the "paralogism" that consists in universalizing the lexical particular meaning in the name of the universality of the syntactic function, thus making the two opposites, "becoming" and "seeming," coincide, we arrive at the *prôton pseudos* (first lie/first error), "foundational to metaphysics" ("Syntaxe et sémantique de l'être"; cf. "Onto-logique").

This assertoric function, which leads to the veridical meaning, is surely intertwined with the existential meaning

(to name *ta onta* is to name existent reality, *Wirklichkeit*), as well as the copulative function ("Socrates is mortal" claims that Socrates is indeed mortal). It is in fact nothing other than a symptom of the "pretension of being outside of language" (the expression is Derrida's, "Le supplément de copule"), or, in other terms, the specifically ontological transference of *logos*. The grammatical characteristic of *einai*, so rightly called a substantive, is thus to be able to take the place of all the others to link them and to declare, in language, in the world or toward the world, and in our thought. "To be" is, alone, the matrix or grammatical projection of this "trinary unity" be-think-speak of which Parmenides's *Poem* is the first manifestation (Hoffmann, *Die Sprache und die archaische Logik*).

To evaluate this fusion or confusion between the function and characteristic meaning of *einai*, we of course have two possibilities: we may declare it an accidental homonymy and a linguistic obstacle to rational intelligibility, or a historic feat and a mark of "the Greek conception of the essence of being [*Wesen des Seins*, the being-hood of being]" (Heidegger, *Introduction to Metaphysics*, trans. ¶70) as opening. Either way, no one denies that it is a fact of language. (See ESSENCE, I, where Mill's comparatist position may be, *mutatis mutandis*, placed alongside Benveniste's, and Hintikka's historicizing, or even "historializing," position alongside that of Heidegger.)

- See Box 1.

II. *Esti*: The Third-Person Singular

A. The route "que esti"

Parmenides's *Poem*, *On Nature or on Being*, is always referred to as a foundational text of ontology. "These few words stand there like archaic Greek statues. What we still possess of Parmenides' didactic poem fits into one slim volume, one that discredits the presumed necessity of entire libraries of philosophical literature. Anyone today who is acquainted with the standards of such a thinking discourse must lose all desire to write books" (Heidegger, *Introduction to Metaphysics*, ¶74). It is the paradigmatic text where this fusion may be deciphered.

This is what the divinity says to the young man:

Εἰ δ' ἄγ' ἐγὼν ἐρέω, κόμισαι δὲ σὺ μῦθον ἀκούσας, αἵπερ ὁδοὶ μοῦναι διζήσιός εἰσι νοῆσαι· ἡ μὲν ὅπως ἔστιν τε καὶ ὡς οὐκ ἔστι μὴ εἶναι, πειθοῦς ἐστι κέλευθος, ἀληθείη γὰρ ὀπηδεῖ, [5] ἡ δ' ὡς οὐκ ἔστιν τε καὶ ὡς χρεών ἐστι μὴ εἶναι, τὴν δή τοι φράζω παναπευθέα ἔμμεν ἀταρπόν· οὔτε γὰρ ἂν γνοίης τό γε μὴ ἐόν, οὐ γὰρ ἀνυστόν, οὔτε φράσαις.

(Come now, and I will tell you (and you must carry my account away with you when you have heard it) the only ways of enquiry that are to be thought of. The one, that [it] is and that it is impossible for [it] not to be, is the path of Persuasion (for she attends upon Truth); [5] the other, that [it] is not and that it is needful that [it] not be, that I declare to you is an altogether indiscernible track: for you could not know what is not—that cannot be done—nor indicate it.)

(II.1–8; *Presocratic Philosophers*, §291)

1

The status of the Aristotelian distinctions

➤ ANALOGY, *CATEGORY*, HOMONYM, *SOPHISM*

Aristotle uses, like any Greek speaker, the verb *einai* in the full range of its meanings. As a philosopher, however, in the *Metaphysics*, he discusses the variety of senses of being and stigmatizes, in the *Sophistical Refutations*, for example, the errors of reasoning and the sophisms that can be attributed to confusion with regard to them. Whether or not he is aware, as Benveniste is, of the relations between categories of thought and of language (*Problems in General Linguistics*), Aristotle proposes ontologically foundational distinctions and constantly makes use of modern distinctions, sometimes "unconsciously," including those that constitute, by way of the "ontologies" of computer science, the structure of the semantic web.

Being (*to einai*), or reality (*to on* [τό ὄν]), is *pollachôs legomenon* [πολλαχῶς λεγόμενον]: it is said in many ways, very precisely differentiated from homonymy (the multiplicity of senses is stated several times in the *Metaphysics*, Δ 7; E2; Θ 10). In one sense, which covers and even defines the copulative function, it is said "according to accident" (*to kata sumbebêkos* [τὸ κατὰ συμβεβηκός]): "when one says 'this is that,' it means that 'that is an accident of this'" (Δ 7.1017a12–13). In a second sense, which covers the veridical sense, being is said "as true (*hôs alêthes* [ὡς ἀληθές]), and non-being as false" (E2.1026a34–35). Further, there are the "figures of the categories" or "heads of predication" (*schêmata tês katêgorias* [σχήματα τῆς κατηγορίας], 36; see WORD, Box 2), a finite and practically invariant list of angles of attack, of imputations (what is may be: "essence, quantity, quality, relative, in a place, at a time"; it may "be in a position, having, acting, suffering," to take the canonical list of chap. 4 of the *Categories*). The first category, however, *ousia* [οὐσία], a noun derived from the participle *on* and translated by "essence" or "substance" (see ESSENCE and SUBJECT, I), is the one that determines the consistency and the subsistence of the subject of predication: it thus picks out the existential sense of *einai*, and unifies the other categories that are only said with regard to the "unique principle" that it constitutes (Γ 2.1003b5–10; see HOMONYM, II). There remains a final sense: that of "in potentiality and in actuality" (*dunamei kai energeiai* [δυνάμει καὶ ἐνεργείᾳ]) (E 2.1026b1–2), which modern linguistics has not taken advantage of (see ASPECT), unlike modern ontology (see *ACT*). This is the most enigmatic one for us, as we do not really distinguish physics (see FORCE, Box 1), praxis (see PRAXIS), and semantics.

Between the two routes of inquiry capable of being conceived, the only one that we may know and express, that of the persuasion that accompanies truth, is called: *esti*, "it is," third-person singular of the present of the verb "to be" (*hê men [hodos] hopôs estin*, the first [route], that it is, 2.3, repeated in 8.1, *muthos odoio . . . hôs estin* [μῦθος ὁδοῖο . . . ὡς ἔστιν], "the word of the path/the account of the route, that it is").

If *einai* is not just any verb, *esti* is not just any form of it. "The definite and particular verb form 'is,' the *third person singular of the present indicative*, has a priority here. We do not understand 'Being' with regard to the 'thou art,' 'you are,' 'I am,' or 'they would be'" (Heidegger, *Introduction to Metaphysics*). *Esti* implies its own mode (the "indicative": it is there, it is the case, it is true—or always already there), a time (the "present": it is now, simultaneous with the utterance—or outside of time), a number (a "singular": it is one, unique—or without number), and a person (the "third": it is the other, exteriority—or impersonal, open).

Of course, as in Latin and unlike in French or English, the indication of a person (third-person singular) is sufficient in Greek for the expression of the subject: "is" just means "is," but *esti*, without a pronoun, may be "is," but also "he (or "she" in the feminine, or "it" in the neuter) is." Normally, of course, when the subject is not expressed, this is because it just was or it is easy to deduce ("Socrates arrives; [he, not expressed in Greek] is ugly").

There are thus two types of translation for *esti*:

a. Those that presuppose a subject ("to suppose" and "subject" would be expressed by the same word if we took up that theme, *hupokeisthai* [ὑποκεῖσθαι], *hupokeimenon* [ὑποκείμενον]; see SUBJECT). The subjects envisioned have been either the closest noun, namely, the route itself, or a name or pronoun contained in the Greek ("being," "reality," "something," "he," "it"), which was then loaded with a more or less heavy metaphysical, physical, or epistemological sense (reality, the true, the object of knowledge). Thus, J. Barnes translates lines 3 and 5 by both "that it is" and "that it is not"—"it" being the object of inquiry (*Presocratic Philosophers*; "Let us take a student, *a*, and an object of study, O; and suppose that *a* is studying O"). G. S. Kirk, J. E. Raven, and M. Schofield do the same, and comment: "What is the '[it]' which our translation has supplied as grammatical subject to Parmenides' verb *estin*? Presumably, any subject of enquiry whatever—in any enquiry you must assume either that your subject is or that it is not" (*Presocratic Philosophers*).

b. Those that understand in the verb only the verb. It is here that the possibility of *esti*'s being an "impersonal" arises (see on this point the different classifications in RT: *Dictionnaire grec française* and LSJ). In Greek, the relation between so-called personal and impersonal forms is all the more noticeable since *esti* (or the pl. *eisi* [εἰσί]) at the beginning of a sentence commonly means "there is." It can even take a modal sense when followed by an infinitive, "it is possible that": thus, in verse 3 of fragment 2, "*kai hôs ouk esti mê einai*" may be translated "and that it is not possible not to be" (cf. 6.1, *esti gar einai* [ἔστι γὰρ εἶναι], "it is possible to be"). We must note that all of our languages, unlike Greek, require an apparent or grammatical subject, whereas *esti* in Greek, or the plural *eisi*, at the beginning of a sentence, is often followed by the "real" subject (not, as in the poem by Rimbaud, which Heidegger liked to cite to explicate the giving of *es gibt*: "au bois, *il y a un nid de bêtes blanches* [in the woods, there is a nest of white animals], but "*esti* un nid de bêtes blanches"). Further, neither French nor German is as fortunate as English in this matter since they ("il y a," "es gibt") cannot reproduce the same as the same ("there is" in English) (see ES GIBT, HÁ).

To understand and translate the *esti* of this route, we must start with the characteristic fusion in Greek of assertion, copula, existence, givenness, and not restrict it to one part or dimension of itself, and hence reject any partial translations, especially those that presuppose or invent a subject, thus blocking a whole series of possible meanings. They have all, however, been proposed or embraced, their proponents sometimes venturing that their choice contains all the others: besides "it is" (Barnes; Kirk, Raven, and

Schofield), we find "it is the case" (Kahn's veridical use), — is— (A. Mourelatos's provisional copula), il y a (M. Conche's givenness). But no one offers the complete freedom of translation by *est* (is), which would allow the poem to take advantage of the combined "is," and to thus establish philosophy as a fact of language.

■ See Box 2.

B. From *esti* (is) to *to eon* (reality)

The reason we should not assume a subject for this first *esti* is that, in a way, the whole poem consists in an effort to construct it. And the reason it is essential to translate *esti* by "is" is that we must be able to perform the nominal development

---

2

The accentuation of *esti*

The Greek texts are initially given to us in the form of *scriptio continua*, in uncial script (letters resembling uppercase), without separations between words, without punctuation, without accents. Their progression to the form in which we publish them, which requires among other things expanding a variety of abbreviations and knowing different forms of ligatures between letters, is obviously a source of mistakes. To "emend" a text, to judge the plausibility of a confusion and hence a correction, we must always pay attention to the conditions of the transmission of manuscripts.

Accentuation was codified not only late, but according to different criteria. As regards *esti*, accents distinguish the type of use being made of the verb: most modern authors write enclitic *esti* as (ἐστι) to indicate the copulative, predicative, or identity uses, and orthotonic *esti* (ἔστι) to indicate existential and potential uses. This rule completes the oldest rule of simple position, with *esti* (ἔστι) accentuated when it is at the beginning (or after words like *alla, ei, kai, hopôs, ouk, hôs*)— actually the two rules overlap each other since an *esti* at the beginning of the sentence or verse is likely to be a strong, "accentuated" *esti*, with the sense of "there is," "there exists," "it is possible."

This late codification, which governs the distinction between the existential and copulative senses, nevertheless is in danger of impeding the free play of the breadth of *esti*, irreducibly semantic and functional, a complete fact of language, and of requiring overdetermined choices with regard to a state of the language, and the work on the language that is being done. This is the case especially in

Parmenides's *Poem* and Gorgias's *Treatise on Non-being*. In any case, it marks choices in the Greek of the interpreters. Thus, in Parmenides, 7.34, with the same accentuation, we may understand *esti* as a verb of existence (Simplicius, Beaufret), or as autonymous (Aubenque, O'Brien, Conche, or Cassin; see Aubenque, "Syntaxe et sémantique de l'être"). But depending on how we accent verse 35, we will understand it as autonymous or as a simple copula. There are thus two possible accentuations, and three types of translation:

ταὐτὸν δ' ἐστὶ νοεῖν τε καὶ
οὕνεκεν ἔστι νόημα
οὐ γὰρ ἄνευ τοῦ ἐόντος, ἐν ᾧ
πεφατισμένον ἐστίν
εὑρήσεις τὸ νοεῖν·

(Or c'est le même, penser et ce à dessein de quoi il y a pensée [Yet thinking and that about which there is thought are the same].)
(Car sans l'être où il est devenu parole, tu ne trouveras le penser [For without the being in which it has become word, you will not find the thought].)

(Beaufret, Parménide)

ταὐτὸν δ' ἐστὶ νοεῖν τε καὶ
οὕνεκεν ἔστι νόημα
οὐ γὰρ ἄνευ τοῦ ἐόντος, ἐν ᾧ
πεφατισμένον ἐστίν
εὑρήσεις τὸ νοεῖν·

(C'est une même chose que penser et la pensée < affirmant > : « est », car

tu ne trouveras pas le penser sans l'être, dans lequel < le penser > est exprimé [Thinking and the <affirming> thought are the same thing: "is," for you will not find the thinking without the being, in which <the thinking> is expressed].)

(O'Brien, Le Poème de Parménide)

ταὐτὸν δ' ἐστὶ νοεῖν τε καὶ
οὕνεκεν ἔστι νόημα
οὐ γὰρ ἄνευ τοῦ ἐόντος, ἐν ᾧ
πεφατισμένον ἐστίν,
εὑρήσεις τὸ νοεῖν·

(C'est la même chose penser et la pensée que « est » [Thinking and the thought that "is" are the same thing] car sans l'étant dans lequel « est » se trouve formulé, tu ne trouveras pas le penser [for without the being in which "is" is formulated, you will not find the thinking].)

(Cassin, Parménide)

BIBLIOGRAPHY

Aubenque, Pierre. "Syntaxe et sémantique de l'être." In *Etudes sur Parménide*. Vol. 2. Paris: Vrin, 1987.

Beaufret, Jean. *Parménide. Le Poème*. Paris: Presses Universitaires de France, 1955.

Cassin, Barbara. *Parménide. Sur la nature ou sur l'étant. La langue de l'être?* Paris: Éditions du Seuil, 1998.

O'Brien, D., and J. Frère. *Le Poème de Parménide*. Paris: Vrin, 1987.

of *to eon* [τὸ ἔον], "being," from or on the basis of this "is"—to create the first subject from the first verb.

The different stages all correspond to grammatical forms: from *esti*, "is," comes the participle *eon*, "being," in its verbal form, that is, without an article. This is made possible by a prior transformation, whose priority is indicated by an "indeed": from "is," we first see the infinitive "to be" come to the fore:

Χρὴ τὸ λέγειν τε νοεῖν τ' ἐὸν ἔμμεναι· ἔστι γὰρ εἶναι (*Chrê to legein te noein t' eon emmenai; esti gar einai*).>

(It is necessary to say this and think this: [it is] in being [that] is; is in effect to be.)

(6.1)

(Regarding the variety of constructions and possible translations of this sentence, see Cassin, *Parménides*; to get an idea of the breadth of the variations, consider: "What is for saying and for thinking of must be; for it is for being" [Barnes, *Presocratic Philosophers*]; "What is there to be said and thought must needs be: for it is there for being"[Kirk, Raven, and Schofield, *Presocratic Philosophers*].)

Finally, in 8.32, the nominalization of the participle yields its definitive fullness of a subject: *to eon*, "being." We must emphasize the role of the article, *ho, hê, to*, descended from the Homeric demonstrative, which confers the consistency of a proper noun (in Greek: *ho Sôkratês* [ὁ Σωκράτης], "the Socrates"; see WORD, II.A), of a subject-substance (the difference between subject and predicate is marked in Greek not by the order of the words but by the presence or absence of the article). The deictic article enters thus into the formation of the third-person personal pronoun, *autos* [αὐτός], "himself," *ipse*, which becomes Platonic terminology for the status of the idea *kath' auto* [καθ' αὐτό], "in itself." Preceded by the article, *ho autos*, it means *idem* and marks in the *Poem* the expression of the self-identity of being (see I/ME/MYSELF, Box 2):

Ταὐτόν τ' ἐν ταὐτῷ τε μένον καθ' ἑαυτό τε κεῖται χοὔτως ἔμπεον αὖθι μένει·κρατερὴ γὰρ' Ἀνάγκη πείρατος ἐν δεσμοῖσιν ἔχει, τό μιν ἀμφὶς ἐέργει, οὕνεκεν οὐκ ἀτελεύτητον τὸ ἐὸν θέμις εἶναι.

(Remaining the same and in the same place it lies on its own and thus fixed it will remain. For strong Necessity holds it within the bonds of a limit, which keeps it in on every side. Therefore it is right that what is should not be imperfect.)

(8.29–32)

Thus, at the end of the route of *esti* lies the sphere of *to eon*, with the very words used to name Ulysses in his heroic identity when he is sung to by the Sirens (Homer, *Odyssey*, 12.158–64; see Cassin, *Parménide*).

III. Greek Ontological Terminology:
to ontôs on, ousia, to on hê on, to ti ên einai

"We may remark that it is one thing to give a report in which we tell about *entities*, but another to grasp entities in their *Being*. For the latter task we lack not only most of the words but, above all, the 'grammar.' If we may allude to some earlier researches on the analysis of Being, incomparable on

their own level, we may compare the ontological sections of Plato's *Parmenides* or the fourth chapter of the seventh book of Aristotle's *Metaphysics* with a narrative section from Thucydides; we can then see the altogether unprecedented character of those formulations that were imposed upon the Greeks by their philosophers" (Heidegger, *Being and Time*, §7). As it happens, philosophers have never stopped creating technical terms, ever more expressions to express more and more intimately the par excellence nature of *to on* as it arises here, exploiting the semantic resources offered by the most common Greek, thus revealing the play of these resources as a possibility for thought.

Thus, the adverb *ontôs* [ὄντως] (made from the participle *on*), which means "really, truly, authentically," confirming the link between the existential and veridical senses. It is used in this sense by Euripides (*Héraclès*, 610: "Did you truly [*ontôs*] go to Hades?" and Aristophanes (*The Clouds*, 86: "If you really [*ontôs*] love me"). Plato uses it in turn like everyone else, correlated with *alêthos* [ἀληθῶς], for example, despite emphasizing its literalness in context ("then it definitely seems that false speech really and truly arises from that kind of putting together of verbs and names"; *ontôs te kai alêthos gignesthai logos pseudês* [ὄντως τε καὶ ἀληθῶς γίγνεσθαι λόγος ψευδής]; *Sophist*, 263d). The Stranger can then play with Sophistical panache on the fact that non-being, as an image or seeming (*eidôlon* [εἴδωλον]), is not "really/authentically" (see REALITY) non-being.

STRANGER: Meaning by *true, really being* (*ontôs on* [ὄντως ὄν]) ?
THEAETETUS: —Yes. . . .
S.: So you're saying that *that which is like* is not really *that which is*, if you speak of it as *not true* (*ouk ontôs ouk on* [οὐκ ὄντως οὐκ ὄν]).
T.: But it *is*, in a way (*esti pôs* [ἔστι πως]).
S.: But not truly (*oukoun alêthôs* [οὔκουν ἀληθῶς]), you say.
T.: No, except that it really is a likeness (*eikôn ontôs* [εἰκὼν ὄντως]).
S.: So it's not really *what is*, but it really is what we call a likeness (*ouk on ara ouk ontôs estin ontôs hên legomen eikona* [οὐκ ὄν ἄρα οὐκ ὄντως ἐστὶν ὄντως ἣν λέγομεν εἰκόνα])?

(*Sophist*, 240b3–13; see MIMÊSIS, I)

Simply put, an image is not really non-being, but the reader is supposed to lose his footing in these matters, and cannot count on the translator (thus Cordero: "That which we say is really a copy does not really exist").

In any case, it is clear that Plato makes the adverb *ontôs* into a technical term by nominalizing the phrase *to ontôs on* [τὸ ὄντως ὄν], which is often translated as "authentic being." For the "friends of the forms" (*tous tôn eidôn philous* [44]), *ontôs on* and *ontôs ousia* [ὄντως οὐσία] refer to real being and real, unchanging, existence, which is the province of reasoning and the soul, in contrast with becoming, which is the province of perception and the body: it refers to the *eidê* themselves (*Sophist*, 248a11; cf. *Phaedrus*, 247c7, e3; cf. also *Republic*, 10.597d1–2, where the god, unlike the carpenter and the painter, wishes "to be really the creator of the bed which really is"; *einai ontôn klinês poiêtês ontôs ousês* [εἶναι ὄντως κλίνης ποιητῆς ὄντως οὔσης]," that is, the idea, *to eidos* [τὸ εἶδος], of "what bed is"; *ho esti klinê* [ὃ ἔστι κλίνη] [597a1]).

These constructions become even more and differently complex, with Neoplatonism, which intermingles the expressions of the *Sophist* and *Parmenides* with Aristotelian and especially Stoic distinctions to yield, by way of *ontôs onta* and *mê ontôs mê onta*, "truly/really existents" and "not-truly/not-really non-existents" a *mê on huper to on* [μὴ ὂν ὑπὲρ τὸ ὄν], a "non-being above being," which contrasts with an "absolute non-being," "pure and simple," *haplôs mê on* [ἁπλῶς μὴ ὄν], and allows us to solve the problem of the definition of God (Hadot, *Porphyre et Victorinus*).

The same philosophical investment of common language is found at the purely semantic level. We know that *ousia* has its standard meaning, coming from the law, of "property, fortune," which implies belonging and possession as well as actual and visible presence (we thus read in Euripides's *Helen* the following dialogue: "Theoclymenus: Tell me, how do you bury those who have been drowned at sea? —Menelaus: As lavishly as a man's substance lets him do (*hôs an parousês ousias* [ὡς ἂν παρούσης οὐσίας]]," ll. 1252–53, Eng. trans. R. Lattimore; see ESSENCE, III). This is the word, however, that Aristotle subsequently uses to refer "chiefly and primarily and almost exclusively" to his object of inquiry: "And indeed the question which, both now and of old, has always been raised, and always been the subject of doubt, viz. what being is, is just the question, what is substance?" (*ti to on, touto esti tis hê ousia* [τί τὸ ὄν, τοῦτο ἐστὶ τίς ἡ οὐσία]) (*Metaphysics* Z.1.1028b1–7). Later, with Epicurus and Plotinus, we find *ousiotês* [οὐσιότης] to mean "substantiality" (*Corpus hermeticum*, 12.1), and the adjective *ousiôdes* [οὐσιώδης] to indicate an aggregate (Epicurus, *De rerum natura*, 14.1).

The nominalization linked to repetition remains the key for philosophical technique. It is thus with *to on hêi on* [τὸ ὂν ᾗ ὄν], "being insofar as it is being," or "being qua being," "and not qua numbers, lines or fire," of which the beginning of book *Gamma* of the *Metaphysics* claims there is a science, the inquiry into which is the work of the philosopher (1.1003a21; 2.1003b15–19 and 1004b5–6). Similarly for the enigmatic *to ti ên einai* [τὸ τί ἦν εἶναι], which duplicates the question, also nominalized, of *to ti esti* [τὸ τί ἔστι] (the "what it is," the "essence," as it is translated), to refer to something like the heart of the heart of being—"the essential of the essence" (see TO TI ÊN EINAI).

IV. *Ouk Esti*: Non-Being, Void, Nothing

A. The two kinds of negation, *ou* and *mê*

1. *Esti, ouk esti* and *to on, to ouk on, to mê on*

Parmenides's *Poem* offers two routes of inquiry, which, since they are contradictory, are apparently symmetrical: *esti* and *ouk esti*, "is" and "is not" (2.3 and 5). The complexity of the meaning of *esti* indeed goes both for its use in affirmation as well as negation: "is," "it is," "there exists," "it is possible that," "it is the case"/"is not," "it is not," "there is no," "it is not possible that, it is not the case" (see above, I and II.A).

But the expression of negation adds another kind of problem since Greek has two ways of negating. One is by *ou* (*ouk, ouch*) [οὐ]: it is a factual, "objective" negation, which is applied to a real fact or one that is presented as such. The other is by *mê* [μή]: this covers both "subjective" and "prohibitive" negation, which implies a will and a supposition of the mind (see, e.g., Meillet and Mendryes, *Traité de grammaire comparé des langues classiques*, §882–83). We find the latter mainly in modes other than the indicative, related in fact to "modality" (subjunctive, optative), to express all the nuances of prohibition, deliberation, wish and regret, eventuality, or virtuality. Similarly, one may distinguish *ouk on* [οὐκ ὄν] and *mê on* [μὴ ὄν], "not being," distributing all the nuances that can come with a participle, whether more factual and causal ones (*ouk on* [x], "insofar as, because, it is not [x]") or more adversative, concessive, hypothetical (*mê on* [y], "although, given that, even though it is not [y]").

The contrast is maintained, of course, when the participle is nominalized. Thus, *ho ouk on, hoi ouk ontes*, in the masculine, is Thucydides's way of referring to the dead (2.44 and 45). Similarly, *to ouk on* is used to refer to a possible passage between being and non-being; for example, Melissus, a student of Parmenides, denies becoming in these terms: "for it would be in pain in virtue of something's passing from it or being added to it, and it would no longer be alike. Nor could what is healthy be in pain, for then what is (*to eon*) would perish and what is not (*to de ouk eon*) would come into being" (30 B 7, §533). In contrast, *to mê on* is what is not, not because it is not, but because it cannot or must not be. *To ouk on* and *to mê on* are thus two distinctive ways of signifying "non-being," contrasting with the unitary *to on*.

In the *Poem*, however, once we advance along the route of "is not," *ouk esti*, we come upon the *mê* rather than the *ouk*, so much so that on this route, unlike that of "is," the verb does not give rise to any subject. *To mê on*, a nominalized participle, refers to non-being insofar as it is not simply non-existent, but prohibited, impossible (2.6–7: "for you could not know what is not—that cannot be done [*to ge mê on*, literally, "the in any case non-being"]—nor indicate it"). The choice of this negation implies that there is neither passage nor commensurability between being and non-being, and that the route of "is not" is a dead end.

However, if we stick to the logic of prohibitive negation, as the Stranger emphasizes in Plato's *Sophist*, there can be no "right speaking about non-being" (239b): to utter *to mê on* is already, from the fact of uttering it, to confer a kind of existence on non-being (the non-*being*); in addition, it grants it, by way of the form of the utterance, a kind of unity (*the* non-being)—two ways of going against the proper meaning of the prohibitive expression whether we like it or not (237a–239b). Whence the philosophical choice of reinterpreting this negation and making it only the mark of otherness, a distinction, a difference, rather than of a contradiction or a prohibition. "Each time we say *to mê on*, it seems, we say not the opposite of *on*, but simply another" (*ouk enantion ti . . . all' heteron monon*, 257b). In this case, against the background of the participation of Ideas in each other, the negation *mê* is brought back to the negation *ou*, and both are brought back to affirmation—not that every determination is negation, as Spinoza would say, but every negation is determination:

So we won't agree with somebody who says that denial signifies a contrary. We'll only admit this much: when "not" (*mê*) and "non-" (*ou*) are prefixed to names that follow them, they indicate something *other* than the names, or rather, other than the things to which the names following the negation are applied.

(*Sophist*, 257b–c)

Plato, following Gorgias, can catch Parmenides in his own trap by stating that to utter non-being is already to make it be. The Parmenidean orthodoxy, on the other hand, would be justified in reducing the move in the *Sophist*, assimilating non-being and otherness, to a pure and simple engagement in the way of *doxa*, this too human way of mortals who do not know how to distinguish "is" and "is not" ("race which does not distinguish, for which to exist and not to be (*to pelein*—archaic form of *einai*—*te kai ouk einai* [τὸ πέλειν τε καὶ οὐκ εἶναι]) are reckoned same and not-same"; 6.9–10; see DOXA).

■ See Box 3.

2. Negation and privation

The difference between "these two particles of negation which the Greek language likely understood before all the others" (Schelling, *Historical-Critical Introduction*) subtly realigns the difference between negation and privation.

Aristotle discusses this difference between "negation" and "privation." They are two of the four ways of "being opposite" (*antikeisthai* [ἀντικεῖσθαι]):

Things are said to be opposed to one another in four ways: as relatives [*ta pros ti*] or as contraries [*ta enantia*] or as privation and possession [*sterêsis kai hexis*] or as affirmation and negation [*kataphasis kai apophasis*]. Examples of things thus opposed (to give a rough idea) are: as relatives, the double and the half; as contraries, the good and the bad; as privation and possession, blindness and sight [*tuphlotês kai opsis*]; as affirmation and negation, he is sitting—he is not sitting [*kathêtai-ou kathêtai*].

(*Categories*, 10.11b17–23; trans. Barnes)

Two kinds of phenomenon, often badly distinguished, arise here. Negation (*apophasis* [ἀπόφασις], from *apo-*, "far from," and *phainô*, "to show"), like affirmation (*kataphasis* [κατάφασις], where *kata*, "on," "about," refers to "saying," i.e., predication), is in the first instance a fact of syntax (see SUBJECT, I). Affirmation and negation are contradictory

---

3

The "Treatises on non-being," or how non-being is non-being

There is no correct expression of non-being. That means that to utter non-being, *to mê on*, contradicts its existence, once we suppose with Parmenides that being, thinking, and saying all belong to one another. The statement contradicts the proposition (see SPEECH ACT).

This also implies that any proposition about it, first and foremost the one asserting its identity, "non-being is non-being," is self-contradictory. As for "to be," semantics is inseparable from syntax. This is Gorgias's position in any case, and it initiates a long series—*Peri tou mê ontos* [Περὶ τοῦ μὴ ὄντος], *De nihilo*, *Elogio del nulla*, and *Glorie del niente* (see Ossola, *Le antiche Memorie del Nulla*), showing for the first time how non-being in a language, Greek in this case, is an exception analogous to that of being—but much more interesting as only it can reveal the exceptional surreptitiousness of being and the proposition asserting the identity of being, without which there would be no ontology.

Εἰ μὲν γὰρ τὸ μὴ εἶναι ἔστι μὴ εἶναι, οὐδὲν ἂν ἧττον τὸ μὴ ὂν τοῦ ὄντος εἴη. Τό τε γὰρ μὴ ὄν ἐστι μὴ ὄν, καὶ τὸ ὂν ὄν, ὥστε οὐδὲν μᾶλλον ἢ εἶναι ἢ οὐκ εἶναι τὰ πράγματα. Εἰ δ' ὅμως τὸ μὴ εἶναι ἔστι, τὸ εἶναι, φησίν, οὐκ ἔστι, τὸ ἀντικείμενον. Εἰ γὰρ τὸ μὴ εἶναί ἐστι,

τὸ εἶναι μὴ εἶναι προσήκει. Ὥστε οὐκ ἂν οὕτως . . . οὐδὲν ἂν εἴη, εἰ μὴ ταὐτόν ἐστιν εἶναί τε καὶ μὴ εἶναι. Εἰ δὲ ταὐτό, καὶ οὕτως οὐκ ἂν εἴη οὐδέν· τό τε γὰρ μὴ ὂν οὐκ ἔστι καὶ τὸ ὄν, ἐπείπερ γε ταὐτὸ τῷ μὴ ὄντι.

(For if not to be is not to be, non-being would be no less than being: indeed, non-being is non-being just as being is being; such that these things are no less than they are not. But if, however, not to be is, it follows that to be is not. Such that in this case . . . nothing would be, as long as to be and not to be are not the same thing. But if they are the same thing, in this case nothing would be: indeed non-being is not, just as being, if indeed it is the same thing as non-being.)

(Gorgias, *On Melissus, Xenophanes, and Gorgias*, 979a25–34)

If we follow the argument, what is genuinely impossible is to make a distinction (the *krisis* of Parmenides's *Poem*) between the series "not to be, non-being, non-existence" (*to mê einai, mê einai, to mê on, mê on*) and "to be, being, existence" (*to einai, einai, to on, on*). As Hegel notes at the beginning of the *Theorie Werkausgabe*, "Those who insist on the difference between being and nothingness must *say* what that difference consists

in." Indeed, in order to make a distinction we must be able to identify, and that is precisely what does not work with non-being. In the identity statement "non-being is non-being" (*to mê einai esti mê einai*), non-being is not self-identical since everything has changed from one occurrence to the next ("it is as though there were two beings"; Gorgias, *On Melissus, Xenophanes, and Gorgias*, 979a39). This is especially true in Greek: since the order of the words is not rule-bound, the predicate is only known by the absence of an article. The required article before the subject is the mark of its consistency or substantiality. It indicates that any assertion of a subject in an identity statement presupposes existence, or again that to say that "non-being is non-being" we must already have admitted that "non-being is" (see I and Box 2, and cf. WORD ORDER).

Far from refusing to distinguish between the different meanings of the *pollachôs legomenon* "to be," as Aristotle asserts, Gorgias in fact makes it clear that the problem, the equivocity, in a word the sophism are the philosopher's fault, since they cleave to "is" and its ontological understanding. With "being is being" the difference between subject and predicate remains imperceptible since the two sequences "being is" and "being is being" confirm one another and even become intertwined, just like the existential and copulative meanings of "is." The traditional identity statement exploits and hides the equivocity of "is" and turns it into a rule. Only the case of non-being makes it possible to become aware of the difference usually written into the statement of identity: the "is not" must become the rule of "is." And it is speech all by itself that, in its constitutive linearity related to its temporality, cannot help producing this catastrophe, which the Sophist aims to make heard.

These statements about the identity of non-being are of course difficult to translate and sources of error. In every treatise on non-being, whether Sophistical and/or apologetic in its aims, pure and simple non-being or non-being beyond being, the difficulties are idiomatic and inventive, related to the syntax of negation, to the grammatical possibilities of moving from a verb to a noun and the other way around (*Il niente annientato* is, for example, the name of a treatise by Raimondo Vidal [1634]) and to the names of non-being. A good example is Charles de Bovelles's *De nihilo* (1509), which attempts to deal with the problems of the Creator, the creature, and creation. It begins with the statement of identity "Nihil nihil est," "Le Néant n'est rien" (Nothingness is nothing), and then extracts two lessons from it:

> hujusque orationis que insit nichil esse nichil, gemina sit intelligentia, negativa una, altera assertiva et positiva.

> (from this proposition "Nothingness is nothing" there are two readings,

one negative and one affirmative and positive.)

> (*Le livre du néant*)

One cannot help but notice the distance between the *incipit* "Nihil nihil est" and its translation "Le néant n'est rien," which, besides the inevitable word order, makes the statement of identity invisible. Perhaps French requires something like a "portmanteau translation" to retain the affirmative character of the sentence: "le néant est néant" and the negative extenuation "le rien n'est rien"—each an equally acceptable translation of the attempted identification.

The most recent treatise on non-being is no doubt the one written by Heidegger in German, over the course of his work, from *Was ist Metaphysik?* and *Vom Wesen des Grundes* (1929) where Nothingness appears as the origin of negation, and not the reverse. No doubt this is the inheritance passed down along a "me-ontological" tradition, which mixes with mysticism and deploys the "annihilating" activity of nothingness, the "nichtende Nicht des Nichts" in which we hear under the aegis of the verb, first the adverb *nicht*, then its nominalization *Nicht*, then the noun *das Nichts*; see Taubes, "Von Adverb 'Nichts'"). Non-being thus becomes, as Gorgias wished, though against his critical intentions, the measure of being—that is, the being of existence:

> Jenes nichtende Nicht des Nichts und dieses nichtende Nicht der Differenz sind

zwar nicht einerlei, aber das Selbe im Sinne dessen, was im Wesenden des Seins des Seienden zusammen gehört.

> (That nihilative "not" of the nothing and this nihilative "not" of the difference are indeed not identical, yet they are the Same in the sense of belonging together in the essential prevailing of the being of beings.)

> (Preface to the 3rd ed. of *Vom Wesen des Grundes*)

BIBLIOGRAPHY

Bovelles, Charles de. *Le livre du néant*. Translated by P. Magnard. Paris: Vrin, 1983.

Breton, Stanislas. *La pensée du rien*. Kampen: Pharos, 1992.

Cassin, Barbara. *Si Parménide. Le traité anonyme De Melisso, Xenophane et Gorgia*. Presses Universitaires de Lille, Éditions de la Maison des Sciences de l'homme, 1980.

Hegel, G.W.F. *Theorie Werkausgabe*. Vol. 1. Frankfurt: V. Klostermann, 1965.

Ossola, Carlo. *Le antiche memorie del nulla*. Rome: Edizioni di Storia et letteratura, 1997.

Taubes, Jacob. "Vom Adverb 'Nichts' zum Substantiv 'das Nichts.' Überlegungen zu Heideggers Frage nach dem Nichts." In *Vom Kult zur Kultur*. Fink Verlag, 1996. Translation in: *From Cult to Culture: Fragments Toward a Critique of Historical Reason (Cultural Memory in the Present)*. Edited by C. E. Fonrobert and A. J. Assmann. Stanford: Stanford University Press, 2009.

propositions that cannot be simultaneously true (see PRINCIPLE, I.B). From this point of view, *ou* and *mê* are on the same level: they are both adverbs of negation that may affect the whole proposition, most often by way of the verb (*ouk esti leukon* could be translated "it is not white," or "it is not true that"—in contemporary jargon, "it is not the case that—it is white"), even though the choice of one negation or the other, as we have seen, is not insignificant. On the other hand, privation (*sterêsis* [στέρησις], from *steromai*, "to lack, to lose," from the same family as the German *stehlen*, "to steal"), which is often expressed by the aptly named alpha privative, affects only the predicate, and is thus entirely different grammatically. However, insofar as it "deprives" something of a predicate, it implies that the subject is concerned with this predicate at least as a possibility, and thus contains a certain sort of affirmation: *akinêton esti* means that something is immobile, but capable of movement—this is why it is strictly speaking said of man, but not plants (which by definition grow but do not move). Here, then, the alpha privative and factual negation by *ou* are on the same side with regard to negation in terms of impossibility or prohibition as *mê*: what is *akinêton*, im-mobile, can move (even though it is not moving actually, *ou kineitai*), and it is not true to say of it the *mê kinêton einai*, that it is "non-mobile."

The difference between negation and privation is, in any case, a question of perspective. A stone, which has no eyes, is obviously "lacking sight," "not seeing" (*mê* negation, as it lies outside the sphere of the predicate). But for a mole, it depends: if we consider it as an animal with eyes, thus by its kind, it is "deprived of sight," "badly seeing" (*tuphlos*: Greek here says affirmatively what French says privatively: *a-veugle*, *ou* negation), since in general animals see. On the other hand, if we consider a mole with regard to the mole species, it is "non-seeing" just like the stone, since no moles see (*Metaphysics*, 4.2.1004a10–16 and 5.22; cf. Cassin and Narcy's commentary in *La décision du sens*).

In any case, the characteristic of privation is to be, according to the phrase of the *Physics* (2.1.193b19–20), *eidos pôs* [εἶδος πώς]: "in a way form." And Heidegger comments in the following way on this "negation," this privation (*sterêsis zur Anwesung*, absencing for presencing), which may be linked with the great privation that is *alêtheia* (see TRUTH, I.B):

> *Sterêsis* as absencing is not simply absentness; rather, it is a *presencing*, namely, that kind in which the *absencing* but not the absent thing) is present.

> (Heidegger, "On the Essence and Concept of *Physis* in Aristotle's *Physics* B, 1)

"Remarks like this may seem subtle," notes Schelling with regard to negation and privation, "but since they relate to effective nuances of thought, they cannot be dispensed with." Different languages, of course, use different marks for them:

The German language has difficulty distinguishing them and can only rely on the accent—if it refuses to make do with Latin expressions. Indeed, it is impossible to be confused as to the difference between *est indoctus*, *est non-doctus*, and *non est doctus*. We can say of a newborn neither the first, *indoctus*, since he has not yet had the possibility, nor the second, *est non-doctus*, since he does not find himself in an altogether impossible condition, but we will concede the third, *non est doctus*, indeed, since it only denies the actuality, but poses the possibility.

(*Historical-Critical Introduction*)

B. The names of non-being:
from *mêden*, "nothing," to *den*, "less than nothing"

What does not exist has several names (see *NOTHING*). We find, starting with Parmenides's *Poem*, two ways of referring to it: *to mê on*, negative symmetric of *on*, "being" (for you will not be able to know *to ge mê on*, the [in any case and certainly] non-being [2.7]), and *mêden*, which is usually translated by "nothing," *rien*, *nichts*, *nada* (*mêden d'ouk esti* [6.2]: nothing is not; see Cassin, *Parménide*). This second designation, and its translations, deserve some attention.

Mêden [μηδέν] is in the first instance a negative term, constituted like *mê on*: a *mê* negation (*mêde* [μηδέ], in this case, "not at all") followed by a positive term, *hen* [ἕν], "one" (which would not surprise a Parmenidean, for whom being and one are one, *convertuntur*). The etymology is obvious: the Plato of the *Sophist*, for example, makes it clear to drive home the point about performative self-contradiction; when one says *mêden*, "nothing," one says *mê ti* [μή τι], "not something," that is, *hen ge ti* [ἕν γε τι], "something one" (237e1–2 and 237d7); *mêden* thus means *mêd'hen*, "not even one." However, unlike *to mê on*, here we have a single word, and not a composite expression: *mêden*, like *ouden*, in a single word, is the neuter pronoun we find even in Homer. With *mêden*, negation becomes an affirmed, even a positive entity, like "nothing" or "no one."

In this regard, the difference between Greek and French is enlightening: in French, *rien*, like *personne*, is positive from the start. *Rien* comes indeed from the Latin accusative *rem*, "thing," and Littré explains that: "1) The etymological and proper meaning of *rien* is thing. 2) With the negation *ne*, *rien* by negating any thing is equivalent to the Latin *nihil*." From the twelfth century on, as shown by expressions such as "pour rien," "de rien," "mieux que rien," or "moins que rien" (RT: *DHLF*), the indefinite pronoun is used in the negative sense with the *ne* dropped out. We may then attempt to taxonomize the names of what does not exist according to whether they are in the first instance negations (*mêden, nihil, néant, niente*, "nothing," *Nichts*) or affirmations: the French *rien*, but also the Spanish *nada* (from the Lat. [*res*] *nata*, "[thing] born"). Above all, we may excuse the wavering mind of a French translator or reader faced with a basic sentence of Greek physics such as *mêden ek mêdenos* [μηδὲν ἐκ μηδενός], source of the Latin adage *nihil ex nihilo*, since the evolution of his language allows him to hear something like "rien (ne) provient de rien," that is, "everything comes from something/nothingness comes from nothingness" (see Boxes 3 and 4). As a side note, we should also forgive translators of Jean-Paul Sartre for not finding the words, in German, for example—even though Sartre does work "like" Heidegger and reformulates his German—to render the difference between *rien*, or *le rien*, and *néant*, or *le néant* (Hans Schöneberg and Traugott König are reduced to distinguishing them by lowercase *nichts* and uppercase *Nichts* [*Das Sein und das Nichts*]; cf. *NOTHING*).

■ See Box 4.

Let us take up again the difference between *mê on/mêden*. Two consequences of very different kinds follow.

1. A syntactic blurring:
Mêden is a composite negation, unlike simple negations such as *mê* (similarly, *ouden* differs from *ou*). We then face the question of the meaning of the successive negations. We cannot say that in Greek two negations are simply worth one affirmation. Indeed, everything changes depending on whether we are dealing with simple or composite negations, and according to their order in the sentence. The grammatical rule is all the more tentative as it must take account of the subject of the negation, whether it is a whole phrase or a word, which cannot be precisely determined by applying a rule. Here is how a well-known grammar book treats the question:

Greek had at its disposal, besides simple negations (*ou* and *mê*), composite forms (*oute/mête, oude/mêde, oudeis/mêdeis*, etc.): following the order according to which they are placed, the negative value of the phrase is either reinforced or destroyed. We gladly teach that a **simple** negation, followed by one or more **composite** negations, yields a *negative reinforcement*, whereas a composite negation, followed by a **simple** negation yields the *unreserved destruction of the negation*, that is, *a total affirmation*. This rule works only very broadly: in particular, it takes no account of the following consideration: is the *first negation*, whether simple or composite, applied really to the *whole sentence*, or only to a *word*?

(Humbert, *Syntaxe grecque*; the bold and italics are in the text)

We may understand the Greek vacillation with regard to such simple successions as: *mêden ouk esti* (composite + simple) and *ouk esti mêden* (simple + composite), which would mean things as different as "there is certainly being" and "certainly, there is absolutely nothing at all." On its own authority, it would rather mean in both cases: "nothing is," "no, nothing is," that is, something analogous to the simple propositions *mêden esti* and *ouk esti*, "nothing is," which only a Gorgias, coming after Parmenides, could varyingly decipher as "no subject for *is*" and "not even the verb *is*."

2. A new semantic adventure:
Mêden is, we have seen, a negative characterization by design. But it becomes a positive entity capable of

4

The French *ne expletive*, a vestige of *mê*

➤ MÊTIS, Box 1, VERNEINUNG

Unlike Old French, which used simple negation with *ne*, modern French uses compound negation. With few exceptions, (je *ne* puis . . ., je *ne* samurais . . .), the absence of "forclusifs" (*pas, mie, goutte, point, plus, rien*, which originally denoted positive entities—including *rien*, from the Latin accusative *rem*, something) gives the sentence a positive value. Thus, in the statement "Je crains que Pierre ne vienne," the omission of *ne* does not change the meaning of the sentence, which expresses fear at the idea that Pierre should come. This statement is distinguished from the statement "Je crains que Pierre ne vienne pas," which expresses the idea that Pierre might not come. In the first, the *ne* has no negating force. Whence the use of the term "expletive," which, according to Littré (RT:

Dictionnaire de la langue française), describes a word "which does not contribute to the meaning of the sentence and is not required by syntax." The expletive *ne* would thus be an empty sign. Grévisse (RT: *Le bon usage. Grammaire française*) looks forward to the imminent disappearance of this "parasitic particle" (ed. 1969, §877b), also called "redundant" or "abusive" (ed. 1993, §983).

However, the use of the expletive *ne* is governed by strict grammatical rules. In subordinate phrases, it appears after verbs of fearing, prevention, or doubt, or after conjunctions like *à moins que* (unless), *avant que* (before), and *sans que* (without) and in comparisons of inequality. French usage is thus continuous with the Latin usage "timeo ne, timeo ne non," and the Greek "dedoika mê, dedoika mê

ouk" "je crains que . . . ne," "je crains que . . . ne . . . pas," where, to borrow an expression from Humbert, "there is an obstacle in the principal phrase which so to speak sends out its negative reflection" onto the subordinate phrase (RT: *Syntaxe grecque*, §654). In other words, the expletive *ne* in the completive retains or accentuates the negative idea expressed by the main verb (*je crains* qu'il ne vienne) and the positive content of the subordinate phrase (je pense *qu'il viendra*); this is precisely what the inventive Damourette and Pichon, later taken up by Jacques Lacan, call the "discordantiel" (RT: *Des mots à la pensée*, vol. VI, chap. 4), a nuance that only French can still express.

Marco Basachera
Barbara Cassin

---

nominalization, "the *mêden*, the nothing." *Mêden* as a positive term (and no doubt also as a word or signifier) is involved in a different history than *mê on*. Democritus indeed creates on its basis a word that does not exist, *den* [δέν] and which the RT: LSJ describes as "*abstracted from oudeis*" (we find it once in Alcaeus, 320 L. P "in a doubtful and obscure text," Chantraine clarifies, "where we translate *denos* by 'nothing' or rather by 'something' (*sic*), and there is "no relationship to the modern Greek *den*, 'nothing'"; RT: *Dictionnaire étymologique de la langue grecque*). Democritus affirms, according to Plutarch, that:

μὴ ἄλλον τὸ δὲν ἤ τὸ μῆδεν εἶναι.

(*den* is nothing other than *mêden*.)

(Fragment 68 B 156 DK)

The doxographers who transmitted the phrase all offer an intra-linguistic translation. For Plutarch, the source of the fragment, *den* names the "body" (Galen says specifically the "atoms"; A 49 DK; see also Simplicius, A 37 DK, tangled up with the Aristotelian translations), and *mêden*, the "void." We can understand the intent: Democritus needs something that is not an *on*, a "being," which is not even a *ti*, a "something" (a term the Stoics fall back on to avoid Platonic-Aristotelian *ousia*): a "less than nothing," therefore, to define this body conceived of as not resembling any body in nature, conceived even to escape the physical, that is, atoms, indivisible. *Den* is a pure signifier, created from a mistaken cut (a manifestation of indivisibility?) on *mêden* or *ouden*, mistaken since the etymology, which can still be heard (*med'hen* or *oud'hen*, not even one), implies that we cut at *hen*, "one." *Den* suits the atoms since like them it is a pure artifact. It is not even a word in the language, it is an *ad hoc* invention, a meaningful play. Lacan sees this very clearly, and returns several times to this joke by Democritus, "who somehow required a clinamen," and who thus

invented the word *den* to say neither *mêden* (against a "pure function of negativity"), nor *hen* ("to avoid speaking of the *one*" [*Le séminaire*]). "Given which, *den* was indeed the clandestine passenger whose silence is now our destiny. In this he is no more materialist than any reasonable person" ("L'Étourdit").

Nothing is harder than to translate a witticism. Dumont (RT: *Les Présocratiques*) suggests: "*Den* [being] is nothing more than *Mêden* [the void]," and the meaning of the invention is immediately lost. Diels and Kranz are lucky enough to be able to rely on a similar invention, a mis-cut on *Nichts* made by Meister Eckhart, where we hear the *iht*, invented to be opposed to *niht* (sermons 57 and 58), and thus translate: "Das Nichts existiert ebenso sehr wie das Ichts."

It is not unfitting that the paths of "Is" and "Is not" leave us with this kind of impasse, alternative, and invention.

Barbara Cassin

BIBLIOGRAPHY

Arnauld, Antoine, and Claude Lancelot, with Christian Duclos. *Grammaire générale et raisonnée*. Introduction by M. Foucault. Republications Paulet, 1969. First published in 1660. Translation: *A General and Rational Grammar*. Menston: Scolar Press, 1968. First published in 1753.

Aubenque, Pierre. "Onto-logique." In *Encyclopédie philosophique universelle*, vol. 1, *L'Univers philosophique*, edited by André Jacob, 5–16. Paris: Presses Universitaires de France, 2000.

———. "Syntaxe et sémantique de l'être." In *Etudes sur Parménide*. Vol. 2. Paris: Vrin, 1987.

Barnes, Jonathan. *The Presocratic Philosophers*. 2nd rev. ed. London: Routledge 1982.

Beaufret, Jean. *Parménide. Le Poème*. Paris: Presses Universitaires de France, 1955.

Benveniste, Émile. "Catégorie de pensée et catégorie de langue," "'Être' et 'Avoir,' dans leurs fonctions linguistiques," and "La phrase nominale." In *Problèmes de linguistique générale*, 63–74, 187–207, and 151–57. Paris: Gallimard / La Pléiade, 1966. Translation by M. E. Meek: *Problems in General Linguistics*. Coral Gables, FL: University of Miami Press, 1971.

Cassin, Barbara. *Parménide. Sur la nature ou sur l'étant. La langue de l'être?* Paris: Éditions du Seuil, 1998.

Cassin, B., and M. Narcy. *La décision du sens*. Paris: Vrin, 1989.

Conche, Marcel. *Parménide. Le Poème: Fragments*. Paris: Presses Universitaires de France, 1996.

Derrida, Jacques. "Le supplément de copule." In *Marges de la philosophie*. Paris: Éditions de Minuit, 1972. Translation by A. Bass: "The Supplement of Copula." In *Margins of Philosophy*, 175–206. Chicago: University of Chicago Press, 1985.

Eckhart, Meister. *Die deutschen Werke*. Edited by J. Quint. Stuttgart: Kohlhammer, 1963.

———. *Meister Eckhart, Sermons and Treatises*. Edited and translated by M. O'C. Walshe. Shaftesbury: Element Books, 1987.

———. *Meister Eckhart, the Essential Sermons, Commentaries, Treatises, and Defense*. Translated and introduced by E. Colledge and B. McGinn. New York: Paulist Press, 1981.

Euripides. *Helen*. In *The Complete Greek Tragedies*, vol. 3, *Euripides*, translated by R. Lattimore. Chicago: University of Chicago Press, 1956.

Hadot, Pierre. *Porphyre et Victorinus*. Vol. 1. Paris: Etudes augustiniennes, 1968.

Heidegger, Martin. *Die Physis bei Aristoteles*. Frankfurt: Klostermann, 1967. First published in 1958.

———. *Einführung in die Metaphysik*. Tübingen: Niemeyer, 1952. Translation by G. Fried and R. Polt: *Introduction to Metaphysics*. New Haven, CT: Yale University Press, 2000.

———. *The Essence of Human Freedom*. Translated by Ted Sadler. London: Continuum, 2002.

———. "On the Essence and Concept of *Physis* in Aristotle's *Physics* B, 1. In *Pathmarks*, edited by William McNeill, 226–27. Cambridge: Cambridge University Press, 1998.

———. *Sein und Zeit*. In *GA*, vol. 2. Frankfurt: Klostermann, 1977. First published in 1927. Translation by J. Macquarrie and E. Robinson: *Being and Time*. New York: Harper, 1962.

———. "Vom Wesen und Begriff der Phusis." In *GA*, vol. 1. Frankfurt: Klostermann, 1982. Translation: "On the Essence and Concept of Φύσις in Aristotle's *Physics* B, I." In *Pathmarks*, edited by W. McNeill. New York: Cambridge University Press, 1998.

———. "Vom Wesen der menschlichen Freiheit; Einleitung in die Philosophie." In *GA*, vol. 31. Frankfurt: Klostermann, 1982. Translation: *The Essence of Truth. On Plato's Cave Allegory and Theatetus*. New York: Continuum, 2002.

Hoffmann, Ernst. *Die Sprache und die archaische Logik*. Tübingen: Mohr, 1925.

Humbert, J. *Syntaxe grecque*. 3rd rev. ed. Klincksieck, 1997.

Kahn, Charles. "Retrospect on the Verb 'To Be' and the Concept of Being." In *The Logic of Being*, edited by S. Knuuttila and J. Hintikka, 1–28. Dordrecht: Reidel, 1986.

———. *The Verb "Be" in Ancient Greek*. Edited by J.W.M. Verhaar. Dordrecht: Reidel, 1973.

Kirk, Geoffrey Stephen, John Earle Raven, and Malcolm Schofield. *The Presocratic Philosopher, a Critical History with a Selection of Texts*. 2nd ed. Cambridge: Cambridge University Press, 1983.

Lacan, Jacques. "L'Étourdit." *Scilicet* 4 (1973): 51.

———. *Le séminaire*, Livre XI, *Les quatre concepts fondamentaux de la psychanalyse*. Paris: Éditions du Seuil, 1973.

Lefebvre, Jean-Pierre. "Philosophie et philologie: Les traductions des philosophes allemands." In *Encyclopaedia Universalis*. Symposium, Les Enjeux, 1, 1990.

Meillet, A., and J. Mendryes. *Traité de grammaire comparé des langues classiques*. 4th rev. ed. Paris: Champion, 1953.

Mourelatos, Alexander P. D. *The Route to Parmenides*. New Haven, CT: Yale University Press, 1970.

Parmenides, of Elea. *Fragments: A Text and Translation*. Edited by D. Gallop. Toronto: University of Toronto Press, 1984.

———. *Parmenides*. Edited by L. Tarán. Princeton, NJ: Princeton University Press, 1965.

Plato. *Platon Le Sophiste*. Translated by N. L. Cordero. Paris: Flammarion, 1993.

———. *Sophist*. Translated by N. White. Indianapolis: Hackett, 1993.

Schleiermacher, Friedrich D. E. "Über die verschiedenen Methoden des Übersetzens" (On the Different Methods of Translation). In *F. Schleiermachers sämtliche Werke*, vol. 3, *Zur Philosophie*. Berlin: Reimer, 1838.

Schelling, Friedrich Wilhelm. *Historical-Critical Introduction to the Philosophy of Mythology*. Translated by M. Richey and M. Zisselsberger. Albany: State University of New York Press, 2007. First published in 1856 as *Einleitung in die Philosophie der Mythologie*.

Schöneberg, Hans, and Traugott König. *Das Sein und das Nichts*. Edited by T. König. Rowohlt Verlag: Reinbek, 1993.

| ETERNITY

Eternity is generally defined as what escapes becoming and time, whether it is a matter of indefinite duration or of being entirely outside of time. However, the very word "eternity" indicates that it is first a question of the duration of a life (Lat. *aevum*, Gr. *aiôn* [αἰών]). Between these two poles, across languages and doctrines, the modulations can be considerable.

I. Eternity: Duration/Time

"Eternity" comes from the Latin *aeternitas*, and was perhaps created by Cicero to refer to a duration with neither beginning nor end. The term goes back to *aevum*, *aiôn* in Greek, which refers, like *aetas* (cf. age), to the duration of a life, and implies an "animated" conception of duration (RT: Ernout and Meillet, *Dictionnaire étymologique de la langue latine*).

This grouping is distinct from another way of thinking and speaking about time, *tempus* in Latin, *chronos* [χρόνος] in Greek, that considers it as determined (a cut, a fraction, a period—the Latin *tempus* has been compared to the Greek *temnô* [τέμνω], "to cut"), and thus capable of being quantified, in particular, as "the number of motion according to before and after" (Aquinas).

See AIÔN for the main difficulties derived from this distinction, the history of which notably intersects with that of the translations of the Bible (*saeculum*, not *aevum*, is used to render *aiôn*, which yields very subtle distinctions and terminological inventions).

On the relationship between time and lifetime, cf. DASEIN, ERLEBEN, *LIFE*. For the relation between time and movement, see FORCE; cf. FORCE, Box 1, on the Aristotelian definition of movement, and NATURE, *WORLD*.

The linguistic and grammatical expression of duration, in its relation to the aspect of verbs and their tenses, is examined under ASPECT.

More generally, see PRESENT and *TIME*.

II. Eternity and Instant

Eternity outside of time is related to the instant (from the Latin *instans*, "present," and "pressing, menacing"), conceived not as a unit of time but, on the contrary, as an exception to the counting, something impossible to measure. The Greeks termed it *kairos* [καιρός], the possibility of an occasion distinct from duration and time: see MOMENT (esp. II), as well as AIÔN. Christian theology uses the instant as *tota simul*, "everything at once," to conceive of divine eternity: see AIÔN II and GOD.

For the relationship between divine eternity and ethical subjectivity, and its expression in Kierkegaard's Danish, see EVIGHED; cf. CONTINUITET, PLUDSELIGHED.

More generally, see *INSTANT*.

III. Procedures of Eternity

Regarding the way in which people attempt to escape from the order of time and enter that of eternity, see BOGOČELOVEČESTVO, HISTORY, JETZTZEIT, MEMORY; cf. LOGOS, LIGHT, Box 1, SVET, *WISDOM*.

➤ *DESTINY, GLÜCK, NOSTALGIA, PROGRESS*

EUROPE

The Languages and Traditions That Constitute Philosophy

➤ ESSENCE, GERMAN, GREEK, LOGOS, SIGNIFIER/SIGNIFIED, TO TRANSLATE, WISDOM

Philosophy came from Greece, as both its partisans and detractors remind us. Among the former, the Muslim philosopher al-Fārābī reminds us that true philosophy came from Plato and Aristotle (*Attainment of Happiness*). And the rabbi, who is one of the characters in the *Kuzari* by Judah ha-Levi, explains that since the philosophers were Greeks, they were not able to benefit from any divine illumination: "There is an excuse for the Philosophers. Being Grecians, science and religion did not come to them as inheritances. They belong to the descendants of Japheth, who inhabited the north, whilst that knowledge coming from Adam, and supported by the divine influence, is only to be found among the progeny of Shem, who represented the successors of Noah and constituted, as it were, his essence. This knowledge has always been connected with this essence, and will always remain so. The Greeks only received it when they became powerful, from Persia. The Persians had it from the Chaldaeans. It was only then that the famous [Greek] Philosophers arose, but as soon as Rome assumed political leadership they produced no philosopher worthy of the name" (*Kuzari,* pt. 1, question/ response 63).

I. Translations

Everyone inherited something from the Greeks, but not everyone inherited the same thing, and not everyone inherited it in the same way. The legacy was transmitted differently according to the geographical region of inheritance: the Arab world embraced almost all of the "philosophy" (including science), but not the "literature." The Byzantine Christians of Syria did not translate Greek literature either. In Arabic, Homer is to be found in only a few anthologies of moral sayings. The Greek tragedies were unknown, which helps explain the absence of the drama in classical Arabic literature.

Europe alone inherited works in Latin, and in particular its poetry (Virgil, Ovid, etc.). Nothing was translated from Latin into Arabic, with the exception of Paulus Orosius's history. Roman law continued to be studied in Latin for a long time in the Christian Middle East, before giving way to the legal traditions of the "barbarians," and then it resurfaced in the eleventh century, notably in Bologna. It was long believed that some part of Roman law passed into Muslim law (*fiqh*); in fact, it now seems that this was only a provincial (foreign) version of Muslim law.

Medieval Europe, on the other hand, was acquainted with only a few texts of Greek philosophy: for example, the start of Plato's *Timaeus*, translated by Cicero, and the start of Aristotle's *Organon*, translated by Boethius. The Arab world knew almost all of Aristotle's work by the ninth century, and knew Plato through summaries, but Europe had to wait until the thirteenth century to have the complete works of Aristotle available. Plato's *Meno* and *Phaedo* were translated into Latin in the thirteenth century but not widely disseminated. Europe had to wait for the other dialogues until Marsilio Ficino in the fifteenth century.

The transmission of knowledge was often understood as a *translatio studiorum*, a purely local displacement, rather like moving house. In reality it never happened that way. Figuratively speaking, as if in accordance with a sort of hydraulic law of connecting vessels, culture tended to level itself out through the transmission of the most advanced civilization toward others that were less well-off culturally. Translations presume a potential public, and that public demand precedes its satisfaction. In Europe, the movement of translations responded to a growing need for a set of intellectual tools set in train by the Papal Revolution at the end of the eleventh century, following the Investiture Controversy, and the revival of juridical studies that accompanied it.

However, works that could not really be used were either not translated at all or were translated but not widely disseminated. So the Arab world knew all of Aristotle, except the *Politics*, which indeed seemed like a set of instructions for an elite political machine. Likewise, Aristotle's *Poetics* was translated but remained almost incomprehensible during the Arab Middle Ages, just as it did during the Latin Middle Ages.

The problem posed by the different linguistic levels was not formulated in the same way in the northern and in the southern Mediterranean. The Arab world did not have the problem of the transition from a scholarly language to a vulgar tongue, as was the case in Europe. This transition simply did not happen, or if it did, it was unconscious: classical Arabic, supposedly the language of the Book of God, was set in an immutable form. In practice, Christians and Jews wrote a form of Arabic freed from its Qur'ānic constraints, known as Middle Arabic, which contained certain simplifications of morphology of syntax. In Europe, Latin was the language of the Roman Empire and of the Vulgate. In the Middle Ages, it remained the language of liturgy and the means of communication between intellectuals, but it was not a holy language, a "language of God."

II. Europe

Europe was conscious of having received its share of the inheritance from people who spoke in other languages. So the Franciscan Roger Bacon appealed to the pope in 1265 to support his plan to set up schools of Greek and Oriental language: "[T]he wisdom of the Latins is drawn from foreign languages: in fact, the entire sacred text and all of philosophy come from outside languages" (*Letter to Clement IV*). The Bible is really itself only in Hebrew (the *hebraica veritas* of Saint Jerome, and before him, Origen): Aristotle's philosophy is really itself only in Greek. Translation involves the sense of a loss with respect to the original. Bacon lamented this situation and compared a text read through several levels of translation to a wine decanted several times losing its flavor (*Moralis philosophia*, 6.4). Translation is necessary, and there is a lot of it. But it is only a last resort in relation to reading the original.

So this is how the problem of translation is posed. In the West it was made necessary by the almost total eradication of knowledge of Greek after Boethius. Greek was forgotten fairly quickly, except in Ireland, whose geographical distance had protected it from barbarian invasions. Among the exceptions, it is worth noting Hilduin, a noble from Lorraine who became a Benedictine monk and abbot of Saint-Denis. He knew enough Greek to be entrusted with the translation of the corpus of works by Pseudo-Dionysius presented to Louis the Pious by Michael III, the Amorian. John Scotus Erigena was able to translate Gregory of Nyssa, Nemesius, and Pseudo-Dionysius.

Yet not many philosophers took the trouble of learning languages other than the language of the dominant culture. In the medieval West, Erigena and the Englishman Robert Grosseteste, the translator of the *Nicomachean Ethics*, are the exceptions rather than the rule. Roger Bacon himself had only a superficial knowledge of Greek and Hebrew. Ramon Llull learned Arabic mainly in order to write and preach in the language rather than to read the works of Muslim philosophers.

In Islamic lands, those who learned the language of a non-Muslim people were extremely rare. Al-Bīrūnī, who learned Sanskrit to undertake an impartial study of Indian religions, was the one brilliant exception. No Muslim seems to have learned Greek and, even less so, Latin. Translators were Christians whose mother tongue or culture was Syriac and for whom Greek was sometimes a family tradition.

III. The Central Untranslated Term: *Philosophia*

In this history of translations, one paradox awaits us at the outset: the word itself that designates philosophy was never translated, literally speaking, into European languages. It is the untranslatable par excellence, or at any rate, an untranslated term. "Philosophy" remained transcribed rather than translated into languages other than Greek. Only the Dutch language coined a word, *Wijsbegeerde*, which was a calque of the etymology of *philosophia* [φιλοσοφία]. In the eighteenth century, the German language had ventured *Weltweisheit*, "wisdom of the world," in the sense of profane wisdom. The word had the honor of being used by Kant in his 1763 text on negative greatness, but it was unable to establish itself in current usage. Fichte remarked on the word *Philosophie* in a text that admittedly was intended to arouse nationalist sentiments (1805): "We have to refer to it by its foreign name, since Germans have not accepted the German name that was proposed a long time ago" (*Address to the German Nation*).

In Islam, *falsafa* [الفلسفة] was perceived as a Greek word from the beginning and has continued to be. The word was broken down and explicated by al-Fārābī, correctly as it turns out, in a fragment devoted to the origin of philosophy, which was cited by the medical biographer Ibn Abī Uṣeybīa in his note on al-Fārābī. This was still true of the historian Ibn Khaldūn in the fifteenth century. The choice of the most authentically Semitic word, *ḥikma* [الحكمة] (wisdom), bears witness to a desire to assume a certain distance with respect to foreign sciences. It was preferred whenever there was a concern to ensure continuity between the disciplines native to Islam and their intellectual elaboration in a synthesis in which Aristotelian elements were juxtaposed with apologetics (*Kalām*) [الكلام] and/or mysticism. We can find the same sense of strangeness in Jewish authors who wrote in Arabic. So in the glossary of difficult terms that he added as an appendix around 1213 to his translation of Maimonides's *Guide for the Perplexed*, which was finished in 1204, Judah Ibn Tibbon still wrote: "*pilosofia*, Greek word."

The continuity of the word did not, however, prevent a semantic evolution that took it far away from its original meaning. This was true even within the Greek language. Since late antiquity, *philosophia* had referred to a way of living as much as to a way of knowing. This fact, which Nietzsche had already discerned, was extensively documented by Pierre Hadot. In Christianity, *philosophia* usually referred to the monastic life, and in Byzantium, as well as in the meaning it normally has for us, the word "philosopher" also referred to a monk. In the eleventh century, in an extraordinary text, Michael Constantine Psellus defined philosophy in a way that was the exact opposite of its "pagan" self-definition: "I call 'philosophers' not those who contemplate the nature of beings, nor those who, seeking the principles of the world, neglect the principles of their own salvation, but rather those whose who scorn the world, and live with supra-worldly 'beings'" (*Chronographia*, bk. 4 ["Michael IV"], chap. 34). The word came to refer to a cultivated man, with a social connotation of belonging to the dominant class, which was not well looked upon by ordinary people. Thus, in animal epics, in the style of the "Roman de Renart," it was the fox who was described as *philosophos*.

The content of European philosophical vocabulary was marked most decisively by Latin, either directly for the Romance languages that emerged out of it, or indirectly for the other languages that had to translate from Latin; so the fact of Latin is fairly pervasive. But Latin itself went through a process that would enable it to translate Greek, which is the native language of philosophy. If we use a Greek word to refer to it, it is because the thing itself was invented by the Greeks.

IV. Greek

The Greek language thus presents us with a unique case: it was in Greek, and only in Greek, that the language had to work on itself, and solely within itself, in order to produce the necessary technical terms. Most of the time these were obtained by modifying the meaning of words already present within the lexicon. So, for example, *ousia* [οὐσία], "fundamental property," took on the meaning of "substance"; *dunamis* [δύναμις], "force," took on the meaning of "potentiality"; *eidos* [εἶδος], "aspect," referred to the Platonic "idea"; *katêgoria* [κατηγορία], "accusation," was used by Aristotle for his "categories," or families of predicates; *aretê* [ἀρετή], the "excellence" of a thing or an animal, denoted moral or intellectual virtue. Other words made a noun from an idiomatic usage of a verb. So, from the verb *echein* [ἔχειν] + adverb, "to be in a determinate state," the noun *hexis* [ἕξις], "habitus," was formed. We might also note a small number of words that were simply invented, such as the two terms Aristotle had to coin to express the full development of a reality: *energeia* [ἐνέργεια] and *entelecheia* [ἐντελέχεια]. This created a certain amount of unease for the man in the street and led Aristophanes, for example, to make fun of all the technical terms ending in *-ikos* (*The Knights*, 1375–81).

It was indispensable for the Greek language to work on itself. It was not enough simply to go with what was already in the language. One might have thought that metaphysics was almost preformed within the structure of the Greek language. Some of its particularities indeed lend themselves to the expression of abstract thought, such as the ease with which it can substantivize whatever it likes with the help of an article. Adolf Trendelenburg argued that the doctrine of the categories was modeled on the grammatical structure of Greek, as did Émile Benveniste. We of course need to nuance this: the impeccable form of the question *ti to kalon* [τί τὸ καλόν], for example, did not stop Hippias from not understanding it (Plato, *Hippias Major*, 287d).

Greek has evolved from Linear B to the present day. In the Byzantine world, there was no recognized continuity between the Greek of the Neoplatonic commentators and that of the Byzantines, which, moreover, was artificial. The Greek of Plethon (fifteenth century), for example, was largely the same as that of the great philosophers of the fourth century BCE, but we might well ask who understood him. Written Greek grew further and further apart from spoken Greek, which corresponds to the increasing isolation of a small layer of intellectuals from the people. It is worth noting, in this respect, the paradox of the translations that were intended explicitly not to be disseminated, such as those of Simeon Metaphrastes (ninth century), who rewrote the popular lives of saints in a more elevated language. The problem is still very much alive in modern-day Greece in the split between popular language (*dhimotiki*) and refined language (*katharevousa*), with their social and political overdeterminations. Byzantine philosophers invented several technical words by using the suffixes -*ikos* or -*otès*, such as *ontotês*, "beingness." In the main, though, the vocabulary has remained the same.

V. Latin

The first attempts to write in Latin about philosophy go back to the first centuries BCE and CE, with Lucretius, Cicero, then Seneca. All lament the poverty of Latin (Lucretius, *De natura rerum*, 1.139 and 1.832; Cicero, *De finibus*, 3.2.5; Seneca, *Ad Lucilium*, 58.1; Pliny the Younger, *Epistulae*, 4.18). Cicero, being the lawyer he was, says in the same place that Latin has no reason to be envious of Greek, but did he believe it for a moment? In any event, when he adapted Stoic treatises, Cicero proposed Latin equivalents for Greek technical terms. Most often, a single Latin word translates a single Greek word, but sometimes they have to be broken down: *euthumia* [εὐθυμία] is translated as *animi tranquillitas* (*De finibus*, 5.5.23). The words thereby coined very often remain our own.

One can see certain inflections in these translations. First of all, a shift from the objective to the subjective. Thus *telos* [τέλος], "the end point of a reality," becomes *ultimum*, "the furthest point (that one can reach)" (ibid., 1.12.42 and 2.7.26). An emblematic translation is that of *axian echon* [ἀξίαν ἔχον], "that which has weight," by *aestimabilis*, "worthy of being valued as expensive" (ibid., 2.6.20); *paradoxos* [παράδοξος], "contrary to expectation," becomes *admirabilis*, "worthy of contemplation" (ibid., 4.27.74). One notices a certain psychologization of tendencies: *hormê* [ὁρμή], "impulse," becomes *appetitus*, "effort to look for" (ibid., 2.7.23, for example). Elsewhere, one can observe a shift from the inner to the outer: *êthikos* [ἠθικός], "having to do with character," becomes *moralis*, "having to do with behavior" (Cicero, *On fate*, 1.1, followed by Seneca, *Ad Lucilium*, 14.89.9, and Quintilian, *Instituto oratoria*, 12.2.15).

The attempt to make philosophy speak Latin was at first not a success, and even Greek philosophers who were settled in Rome, like Epictetus or Plotinus, wrote in their mother tongue. The first of the Romans, the emperor Marcus Aurelius, wrote a very intimate work, his spiritual exercises, in Greek. On the other hand, Apuleius and Aulus Gellius wrote in Latin. A second attempt was more successful, both with Christian writers likes Tertullian and Saint Augustine, who seems to have only known a few words of Greek. Thereafter, for negative rather than positive reasons—the retreat of Greek in the West—Latin was used almost exclusively. This was true of the pagans Macrobius and Martianus Capella (early fifth century) as well as of the Christian Chalcidius.

The Latins did not so much translate, strictly speaking, as adapt. The first true translations are those of Gaius Marius Victorinus, who rendered passages by Plotinus into Latin. Saint Augustine may possibly have read some of these. Boethius, who was from a cultured family of patricians, had planned to translate all of Plato and Aristotle into Latin but was prevented from doing so because of his execution in 524 CE. He was nonetheless able to translate into Latin the start of the *Organon*, Porphyry's *Isagoge*, the *Categories*, and *On interpretation*. We are indebted to him for the equivalents of the fundamental concepts of Aristotelian logic: *genus, species, differentia, proprium, individuum*. He was also the one who took the profoundly influential decision to translate *ousia* by *substantia*, thereby reducing it to one of its dimensions, that of the subjacent (*hupokeimenon* [ὑποκείμενον]), which Aristotle, however, said was insufficient (*Metaphysics*, 7.3).

The Latin of the church fathers needed to be able to express the subtle nuances of the terminology that had been developed by the Greeks in relation to the doctrines of the Trinity or of Christology. Latin often lagged behind Greek. To the question, in the Trinity there are three what? Greek replies with *hupostasis* [ὑπόστασις] and Latin with *persona* (Tertullian, *Against Praxeas*, 11).

Medieval Latin was enriched by the addition of technical terms made necessary by the constant refinement of different problematics. In order to do this, it borrowed words from Greek, such as *categorematicus*, or produced others by working upon the language, such as *compossibilitas, actuositas, immutatio, suppositio, conceptus*.

Certain Greek texts were retranslated into Latin after the Scholastic period and often in reaction to its language, which was judged to be grating to a Ciceronian ear. So, Leonardo Bruni, for example, retranslated the *Nicomachean Ethics*, and Bessarion retranslated the remainder of Aristotle. Latin stayed creative right to the end. The Italian humanist Ermolao Barbaro proposed *perfectihabia* to translate, for better or for worse, Aristotle's *enthelecheia*. Leibniz had no hesitation in fabricating *existentificans* and *existiturire*.

Latin often creates words composed of Greek roots, rendering terms that appear to hark to Greek usages but are, in fact, modern. This is the true of *cosmologia*, adopted as a title by Christian Wolff (1731), and then in French by Maupertuis (1750); of *ontologia*, catalogued in the philosophical dictionary of Rudolph Goclenius (1613); and of *psychologia* (Johannes Thomas Freigius, 1579).

It is amusing that certain technical terms of the Scholastics have unwittingly entered into everyday language. So, for example, the common English word "contraption" comes directly from the noun for the logical operation of *contraposito*.

VI. Arabic

The Greek scientific legacy was translated into Arabic beginning in the ninth century. This was the work of generations of Christian translators, who had to create a language designed to translate philosophical concepts. Unlike the translations into Syriac, words are truly translated; there are very few transliterations. One might cite *usṭuqus* [الأسطقس] for *stoicheion* [στοιχεῖον], "element," and *hayūlā* [الهيولى] for *hulê* [ὕλη], "matter." Even then, these words are in competition with terms that are more in keeping with the genius of the language, like *'unṣur* [العنصر] or *mādda* [مادّة], the substantivized feminine participle of the verb "to extend," which corresponds quite well to Descartes's "extended substance." Translators often feel their way before finding an equivalent that becomes established, which is why there are several terms for translating the same original. When two terms coexist, they each tend to take on a specialized meaning. So *hayūlā* tends to refer rather to primary matter, and *mādda* to the matter of a concrete compound. Or, in the register of causality, *sabab* [السبب], which originally meant the circumstances of an event, refers, rather, to the immediate cause; *'illa* [العلة], which originally meant an illness that excused one's absence in combat (analogous to the Lat. *causa*), refers instead to a distant cause. Arabic sometimes has had recourse to Persian. So the word for "substance" is the Persian *ǧawhar* [الجوهر], which originally meant "jewel": the most precious aspect of a thing is its "substance," in the same way that in French the word *essence* is used to designate the refined state of a chemical body, for both perfumes and gasoline.

Vocabulary choices slightly inflect the meaning of a concept. So the Arabic-Persian translation *jawhar* loses the association with the verb "to be," which is immediately apparent in the Greek *ousia*. The Greek verb *einai* [εἶναι], both in its existential sense and as a copula, has no equivalent in Arabic. For the existential meaning, translators have chosen the verb "find" in the passive: what exists is indeed what "is found" (*mawǧūd* [موجود]). This choice was reflected by al-Fārābī (*Book of Letters*, vol. 1, letter 80). Curiously, the same form is sometimes used as a substitute for the copula in examples of syllogisms. For "nature," *ṭab'* [طبع] or *ṭabīa* [طبيع] removes the idea of plant growth that the Greeks perceived (no doubt wrongly) in the word *phusis* [φύσις], replacing it with that of "imprint," "mark left by a seal."

The language of philosophy seemed "barbaric" in the eyes of grammarians. This can be seen in the celebrated controversy between the Christian philosopher and translator Abū Bishr Mattā ibn Yunūs and the Muslim grammarian Abū Sa'īd al-Sirāfī, which took place in 932 and was reported by Abū Hayyān al-Tawḥīdī in the eighth night of his *al-Imtā' wa 'l-mu'ānasa* [الإمتاع و المؤانسة]. There is still an echo of this in al-Fārābī (*Book of Letters*, vol. 2, pt. 25, letter 156), where he reminds us that some people would rather that philosophy be expressed in purely Arabic terms. For grammarians, logic was nothing more than the grammar of a particular language, the Greek language. There is no longer any need to be reminded of the importance of Arabic in the development of the scientific vocabulary of Latin or vernacular-speaking

medieval and modern Europe: in mathematics (*algebra*), astronomy (*azimuth*), chemistry (*ammonia*). The title of Ptolemy's works on astronomy kept the Greek preceded by the Arabic article: *Almagest*, from *al-Megistè*. Terms that came from philosophy, however, in the narrow sense this word has assumed in modern times, are for the most part Latin or Greek in origin. At best we can cite the famous *helyatin*, which gave commentators of the *Liber de causis* (chap. 9) such a hard time and which is the Arabic *kulliyya* [كلية], translating *holotês* [ὁλότης] from the Greek of Proclus. A problematic that was developed in the *falsafa*, such as that of the possible "conjunction" of the human intellect and the agent intellect, imported the word *conjunctio* itself, a calque of the Arabic *ittiṣāl* [الاتصال], into Latin Scholastics, something Schelling was still aware of (*Introduction to the Philosophy of Mythology*, 20th lesson). One might also note that the Latin *intentio* was influenced by the Arabic *ma'nā* [المعنى], "meaning" (see INTENTION).

VII. Hebrew

In the Middle Ages, Jews living in Islamic lands used Hebrew for religious purposes. This included the liturgy, but also religious "law," such as the literature of the *responsa*. For everyday life and also for philosophy, they used Arabic. So Maimonides wrote the *Mishneh Torah* in Hebrew but the *Guide for the Perplexed* in Arabic. The first to write philosophy in Hebrew was Abraham bar Hiyya Savasorda, a Spanish philosopher and astronomer, with the *Hégyon ha-Nefesh* (the full title of which is "Contemplation of the saddened soul which knocks at the door of repentance"). He invented a whole vocabulary, of which certain elements have survived. In the first book of the *Mishneh Torah*, the *Book of Knowledge*, written around 1180, Maimonides presented a summary of the vision of the world of Arabic Aristotelian philosophy for which he needed new words. He gave to the word *dë'āh* [דֵּעָה], "thought," the new meaning of "intellect," including the intellect of the soul of the spheres.

Philosophical Hebrew, however, developed only to the point where it attained its classical form after the translations from the Arabic by the Ibn Tibbon family. Three generations of this family, driven out of Spain by the Almohads (1148), successively translated texts of Jewish spirituality, then Jewish philosophy, then simply philosophy (Aristotle, Averroës). They modeled Hebrew sentences on the syntax of Arabic to such an extent that they appeared quite strange, even barbaric, so it is hardly surprising that these translations were not immediately accepted. The poet Judah ben Solomon Harizi therefore undertook to write a countertranslation of the *Guide for the Perplexed* in order to give the second Ibn Tibbon a lesson in "beautiful language." But Harizi's philosophical competence was rather limited, and he mistranslated a number of terms, which Ibn Tibbon took satisfaction in enumerating in the preface that he added to the reedition of his own translation. We still have Harizi's translation, but only a single manuscript, whereas Ibn Tibbon's has been very widely disseminated.

Medieval Jewish thinkers had no direct access to Greek and knew only Aristotle and his commentators through Arabic translations. The new words they coined were often borrowed directly from Arabic. Thus Abraham bar Hiyya

Savasorda hebraicizes the Arabic *markaz* [مركز] as *mèrkāz* [מֶרְכָּז], "center," and borrows *ṣūrā* [צוּרָה], from *ṣūra* [صورة)], "form." Other words are modeled on Arabic, such as when *mawǧūd* is translated as *nimṣā* [נִמְצָה]. But other words are obtained by working on the Hebrew itself. So for "substance," Hebrew reuses the biblical word *'èṣèm* [עֶצֶם], which usually means "bone." For "accident" in the philosophical sense of *sumbebêkos* [συμβεβηκός], he uses *miqrèh* [מִקְרֶה], which has the meaning, as does the Latin *accidens*, of "what happens," "incident."

VIII. Modern Languages

It is only fairly recently that the vernacular languages of modern Europe have been used as a medium for philosophy. Latin was still the language of Descartes and Leibniz. Kant often explained his still hesitant German terminology with a Latin word in parentheses, and his *Critique of Pure Reason* was also translated into Latin. Hegel and Schilling wrote their theses, and Bergson his complementary thesis (1888), in Latin. Several scattered philosophical concepts began to appear in the second part of the *Roman de la rose* (Jean de Meun), where there is a translated passage from the *Timaeus* (vs. 19083–19110 = 41a 7b 6), and in Chaucer.

But the first philosophical works in the vernacular date from the thirteenth century. The first "modern" language used in philosophy was Catalan, by Ramon Llull, which was because of Llull's personal history. Originally secular, he was torn from his worldly life in 1263 following an illumination. He became a Franciscan monk, received his university training much later than normal, and thus never knew Latin very well. The *Libre de contemplació en Déu* (1273–74?) was perhaps the first philosophical work in the vernacular in Europe.

German followed soon after. When the Dominican Meister Eckhart preached to nuns who did not know Latin but who were learned enough to be able to write down sermons, he had to transpose Latin concepts into the dialect of the time. He had to translate Scholastic terms quite literally, and the other mystics from the Rhineland did likewise. So *Wesen* for *essentia*, *Zufall* for *accidens*, and so on, explained terms that functioned, in Latin (or English), as ideograms. This practice continued in the seventeenth and eighteenth centuries, when the word *Einbildungskraft* (*vis imaginationis*) was created for "imagination," *Gegenstand* (*objectum*) for "object," *Vorurteil* (*praejudicium*) (seventeenth century) for "prejudice," and *Begriff* (*conceptus*) for "concept" (Christian Wolff).

These transpositions give philosophical German a particular style. The words do not sound strange and even have popular meanings that their equivalents in other languages rarely have. After having said the name of the street he is looking for, a German will ask, "Ist das für Sie ein Begriff?"—literally, "Is that a concept for you?"—where English would say, "Does that mean anything to you?" and the French would ask, "Ça vous dit quelque chose?" The convoluted French expressions *en soi* (in itself) and *pour soi* (for itself), considered rather pedantic, come from a single German expression *an und für sich*, meaning "basically." Before the 1930s, Heidegger liked to use as conceptual terms expressions that were very idiomatic, even commonplace (*Ein Bewandtnis haben, bewenden lassen, vorhanden sein*, etc.), which translators are forced to turn into gibberish. So *Zeug*, "thing for . . ." or "thing

against . . ." (*Regenzeug*, for example, is "something to use in case it rains," an umbrella, a raincoat, etc.), becomes in French, *outil*, "tool" (Emmanuel Martineau), and even *util* (François Vezin).

What is more, the Germanic languages (German, and especially English) often have two parallel terms for one single idea, a learned word borrowed from Latin or from a Romance language, and a native word. The originally synonymous terms tend to diverge in meaning and to support two nuances that can become mutually exclusive. In German, words of Latin origin often have a pejorative nuance, such as *räsonnieren*, and they are rejected by purists. Such purists are often accused of associating the pursuit of linguistic purity with the xenophobic pursuit of racial purity. Conversely, authors such as Adorno take a malicious pleasure in replacing worn-out German words with forced germanizations of non-German words, and for saying, for example, *camouflieren* where the German has *tarnen* or *vertuschen*.

It is only recently that fundamental German terms have appeared that are not translations or transpositions of Latin or Greek terms. Heidegger remarked that it was only with the central word of the late period of his thinking, *Ereignis*, that philosophy truly stopped speaking Greek: "It would be impossible to think *Ereignis* . . . with the help of Greek (which we are concerned precisely to 'go beyond'). . . . *Ereignis* is no longer Greek at all; and the most fantastic thing here is that Greek continues to retain its essential meaning and at the same time can no longer manage to speak as a language at all" (*Four Seminars*; see EREIGNIS).

The other Romance languages have found it harder to disengage from Latin because of their very proximity to it. Italian became a medium for philosophy with Dante. His *Convivio*, written around 1304–7, contains a summary of Scholastic philosophy. After this, the two languages continued to intertwine, combine, and be apportioned differently depending not only on the works of the writers concerned, but also on the milieu in which they were originally written. Dante justified the poetic use of the vernacular, but he did this in Latin, in *De vulgari eloquentia* (ca. 1305). Leonardo da Vinci used Italian because he did not know Latin. Machiavelli wrote only in Italian but gave Latin titles to the chapter of *The Prince*. Petrarch and Vico wrote in both languages. Giacomo Leopardi, whose training was philological, wrote in an archaic Italian that was close to Latin. French was used by Nicole Oresme in his translations of Aristotle and by Christine de Pizan in passages of the *Livre des fais et bonnes meurs du sage roy Charles V*.

The vernacular languages have constantly interacted with each other, and still do. Translations from one to the other constrain the target languages to give completely new meanings to certain words. The dominance of French in Europe during the classical age led to other languages borrowing terms from it. German, for example, transposed *progrès* (progress) as *Fortschritt*, and *point de vue* (point of view) as *Gesichtspunkt*. The present dominance of American English, when it does not involve pure and simple loan words, produces new meanings in other languages. Thus in French, the term *équité*, selected—for want of a better term—to translate the untranslatable "fairness" of John Rawls, has added this meaning to that of *epieikeia* (see FAIR; THEMIS, IV). Certain ideas make a full circle, enriching themselves with new connotations along the way. So, for example, the English "moral sciences," chosen by John Stuart Mill to translate the French *sciences morales*, produced *Geisteswissenschaften* in the German translation, which was retranslated into French as *sciences humaines* (see GEISTESWISSENSCHAFTEN).

The Arabic for "dictionary" is *qāmūs* [قاموس], which comes from the Greek *Ôkeanos* ['Ωκεανός], in the original sense of the liquid expanse covering all of the lands that have emerged, enabling their circumnavigation. Languages are in the same way the locus of a constant movement of exchange in time and place. But words only rarely retain the exotic flavor of their origin. Most of the time they are so well accommodated that we forget the work that was needed to bring them into a new language, to create them, or to adapt them to their new context. So we need a second context in order to restore the murmured sounds of the distances crossed.

Rémi Brague

BIBLIOGRAPHY

Fichte, Johann. *Address to the German Nation*. Translated by R. F. Jones and G. H. Turnbull. Chicago: University of Chicago Press, 1922.

Heidegger, Martin. *Four Seminars*. Translated by A. Mitchell and F. Raffoul. Bloomington: Indiana University Press, 2003.

Schelling, Friedrich. *Historical-Critical Introduction to the Philosophy of Mythology*. Translated by Mason Richey and Markus Zisselsberger. Albany: State University of New York Press, 2008.

EVENT

The word "event," from the Latin *evenire* (to come out of, to have a result, to arrive, to come due, to happen; whence *eventus* [issue, success] and *eventum*, especially in the plural *eventa* [events, accidents]), refers to a fact or phenomenon insofar as it corresponds to a change or makes a mark.

I. Event and Being

"Event" is the most frequently used word for translating the German *Ereignis*, which Heidegger relates to appropriation (*Ereignung*, see PROPERTY) and revelation (*Eräugnis*): see EREIGNIS and cf. *APPROPRIATION*. See also ES GIBT, COMBINATION AND CONCEPTUALIZATION, Box 1, GESCHICHTLICH, and TATSACHE, Box 1; cf. VORHANDEN.

More generally, on the ontology of events, the relationship between event and accident, and the difference with being, see CHANCE, *DESTINY*, ESSENCE, SUBJECT, *TO BE*.

On the "event" of the Incarnation, see BOGOČELOVEČESTVO, LOGOS, III.B, OIKONOMIA.

II. Event, Temporality, and Works of Art

On the temporality of events, see ASPECT, HISTORY, *INSTANT*, JETZTZEIT, MOMENT (esp. MOMENT, II).

On putting events into words, see ERZÄHLEN, HISTORY; cf. *RÉCIT*.

More precisely, for the relation of "event" to works of art, see IN SITU.

EVIGHED (DANISH)

ENGLISH   eternity
GERMAN   *Ewigkeit*

➤ *ETERNITY* and AIÔN, CONSCIOUSNESS, CONTINUITET, I/ME/MYSELF, MOMENT, *PERSON*, PLUDSELIGHED, PRESENT, *TIME*, TRUTH

The majestic eternal moment freezes movement, in contrast with the eternality of the ethical Self. The abstract eternity of the idea, the object of recollection, contrasts with the concrete eternity passionately lived by the existing being stretched toward the eternal as if to the future. The central concept of Christianity, what St. Paul in Galatians 4.4 calls "the fulness of time," /AA requires the idea of an eternity that continuously penetrates into time and of a time that constantly reaches out to grasp eternity for itself. In this ever-present tension—equivalent to that which, without *Aufhebung*, joins the finite and the infinite—the eternal operates in the present both as past and as future (see MOMENT, Box 4).

The multiple senses that Kierkegaard attributes to the concept of *Evighed* correspond to the variations of those of *Continuitet-Continuerlighed*.

1. In the immediacy of the moment of pleasure, the person (the aesthetic self) is as though diffused in affective tonality (*Personligheden doemrer i Stemningen*, vol. 4). The power of the soul to dive completely into "such an instant" allows it to suspend time in a way, to be rescued from the essential fleetingness of the ephemeral, thus to ascend to a kind of eternity.

2. At the other extreme, the choice of self gives the person "his eternal value." Echoing Fichte's formulation (*The Vocation of Man*, in *Popular Works*, ed. William Smith, Nabu Press, 2010, 172), Kierkegaard has the ethical self say: "I cannot become conscious of myself in an ethical way without becoming conscious of my eternal I" (4: 242). This "eternity" is becoming oneself in one's permanence, which comes from progress. By means of ethics, man "becomes what he becomes" (4: 162; see a similar phrase in Fichte, *op. cit.*, 209).

3. "Eternity is the continuity of consciousness, which makes for the depth and the thinking of the Socratic" (7: 91). "For thought, the eternal is the present" (7: 186). The function of reminiscence is "to maintain eternal continuity in the life of man" (9: 10). Despite what separates Socrates from Plato, this thesis (and thus the appeal to abstract eternity) "belongs to both" (10: 192).

Kierkegaard situates Christianity with regard to these three types of eternity. Because of its historical beginning, it is an event that is thus different from Socratism. It posits the instant of access to truth as absolutely decisive. This *punctum* concerns neither pure thought, nor mythology, nor history alone. It essentially affects the existent and thus the existing subjective thinker. If the eternal arises in any ethical decision, continuity is nevertheless always interrupted by new decisions (see PLUDSELIGHED). "For the existent, decision and repetition are the goal of movement. The eternal is the continuity of movement, but an abstract eternity is outside of movement, and a concrete eternity in the existent is the height of passion" (11: 12). "The passionate anticipation of the eternal is nevertheless not, for an existent, an absolute continuity, [it is] the possibility of approaching the unique truth which there may be for an existent" (11: 12–13). Eternity, as the *telos* given in every instant, is only able to be infinitely approximated. Concrete eternity thus has the form of a future. "The future is this incognito where the eternal, insofar as it is incommensurable with time, nevertheless wishes to preserve its commerce with it" (7: 189).

Every existent has its time, receives it rather, for "the eternal wishes to make time its own" (13: 15). Dissolving into abstract existence is the person for whom "existential decisions are only a shadow play floating on the background of what is eternally decided" (10: 210).

Jacques Colette

BIBLIOGRAPHY

Kierkegaard, Søren. *Writings*. Edited by H. V. Hong and E. H. Hong. 25 vols. Princeton, NJ: Princeton University Press, 1983.

EXIGENCY

"Exigency" comes from the Latin *exigere*, literally "to push (*agere*) outside (*ex*)," which means "lead to its end," and "to claim, demand." The term is given here such as one of the possible translations of the English "claim": it does not have a pejorative tone (unlike *prétention*), but, unlike the German *Anspruch*, it struggles to express a demand (with its linguistic and spoken dimension of expression) with its (moral or legal) justification, such that the demand itself constitutes the justification. See CLAIM, and cf. *VOICE*.

The English notion of "claim" is inseparable from the distinction, also a difficult one for translators, between *droit*-law and *droit*-right, which relates to the legitimacy of the demand: see LAW, RIGHT/JUST/GOOD, and more generally *DROIT*, DUTY, SOLLEN; cf. *OBLIGATION*.

On the relation between this "exigency," which is more specifically a claim of knowledge, and Anglo-Saxon ordinary language philosophy, see ENGLISH, cf. COMMON SENSE, LANGUAGE, MATTER OF FACT, SENSE, SPEECH ACT.

➤ EPISTEMOLOGY, *REASON*

EXPERIENCE

"Experience" comes from the Latin *experientia*, "attempt, test, practice, experiment," the same family as *periculum*, "test, risk," or *peritus*, "clever, expert," and from the same vast root **per-* (which means something like "go forward, penetrate") as the Greek *empeiria* [ἐμπειρία], "experience," *peira* [πεῖρα], "attempt, experience," or *peras* [πέρας], "limit" (cf. in French *pore, port*, and *porte*). The word thus connotes both a breakingthrough and an advancement into the world, a gain of knowledge and acquired expertise. The semantic complex yields terminological distinctions peculiar to various languages.

I. Internal Experience

1. The German term *Erleben* refers precisely to the experience and the ordeal of life. See ERLEBEN, and cf. DASEIN, LEIB, *LIFE*.

2. More generally, on the experience of self, see CONSCIOUSNESS, I/ME/MYSELF, SUBJECT; on the difficulties between affect and history or the history of being, see ANXIETY, *MALAISE*, PATHOS (cf. *PASSION*).

3. On the relation between this experience and wisdom or morality, see PHRONÊSIS, *WISDOM*; cf. GLÜCK, OIKEIÔSIS; more generally, for moral experience, including that of moral law, see MORALS, WILLKÜR.

II. Experience and Objective Knowledge

The recurrent philosophical problem is that of the impact of a subject on the object or the phenomenon observed in experience, through the conditions of experience in experimentation as well as the a priori forms of experience in Kantian *Erfahrung*.

1. We have followed the pair *experiment/experience*, in play in Anglo-Saxon empiricism, which does not precisely track the difference between the French *expérience/expérimentation*: see EXPERIMENT; cf. ENGLISH and UTILITY.

2. More generally, on experience as knowledge, and the procedures of constructing its objects, see ABSTRACTION, EPISTEMOLOGY, EPOCHÊ, *INTUITION*, PERCEPTION, REPRÉSENTATION; cf. AFFORDANCE. On the object itself, see GEGENSTAND, ERSCHEINUNG, OBJECT, and cf. PHÉNOMÈNE.

III. Experience and Practice

1. On the manner in which *empeiria* is related to *technê* [τέχνη], to craft, which is defined as being between experience and science, see AESTHETICS, ART, MIMÊSIS.

2. On the relation between practice and conduct, see AGENCY, BEHAVIOR, MORALS, PLEASURE, PRAXIS, WORK; cf. above, I.3.

➤ NATURE, *REASON*, SECULARIZATION, TATSACHE, *WORLD*

EXPERIMENT / EXPERIENCE

➤ CHANCE, ERLEBEN, PATHOS, PERCEPTION

The French translator is tempted to render automatically the English words "experience" and "experiment" as *expérience* and *expérimentation*, conferring a larger share of passivity on "experience" and of activity on "experiment." However, things do not allow such a simplification, especially not in eighteenth-century English. Furthermore, English preserves at the level of the verbs the same distinction as at the level of the nouns (even when completing the words with the ending "-ing": "experiencing," "experimenting"), whereas French has only *expérimenter*, and the verb unites what the nouns keep separate; if one decides therefore to render "to experiment" as *expérimenter* and "to experience" as *éprouver* (to experience in the sense of "feel" or "perceive"), *éprouver* connotes a difficulty that does not exist in "to experience" (cf. the French noun *épreuve*, "proof" or "test"). This asymmetry between French and English makes impossible a shared approach to the distinction, one more notional than real, between empiricism and rationalism. In French, which has only *expérimenter*, empiricism can only be rationalism in hiding, because, after all, there is no experience except that which is active. The English "experiencing" is from the start less framed by rational activity;

one can use the verb "to experience" when this framing is difficult or even impossible.

Furthermore, these nouns are used in close proximity to the terms "case" and "instance," which we must be careful not to render as *cas* and *exemple*. An "instance" is very often the singular fact, the particular occurrence, to which one accedes only by an *expérience* in the French sense; the "instance" becomes a "case" only when the idea of "experiment" is "transferred" to it (Hume, *A Treatise of Human Nature*). The English "case" supposes that a common ground, "a common footing," allows us to refer a registered event to other events judged to be similar or differing only by a decisive element in similar circumstances, so that one can say that it has appeared or has not appeared when one makes a "trial" of it, when one tries it out.

I. The Classical "Experiment": A Phantasm of Activity

One may have the impression that the word "experiment" implies an intervention on the part of the person who observes the phenomena and who works with them to understand or modify the mechanisms: "we make experiments" (Hume, *A Treatise of Human Nature*); while "experience" would be more passive and would concern objects or events that it would be difficult, even impossible, to change directly: "Relation is frequently experienced to have no effect" (ibid.). However, this impression—which is well founded when one reads *The Logic of Scientific Discovery* by Karl Popper, where "experiment" is synonymous with theory testing or falsifying—is much less reliable when one consults eighteenth-century authors.

As an instrument of analysis, the experiment gives rise to phantasms of activity not realizable within the realm of facts. When Hume reread the second book of Aristotle's *Rhetoric* in order, through a play on the constitutive parameters of passional structures, to review the limits of the passions in relation to each other and to their functions, his mode of action was purely linguistic: we could not make or complete the experiments that he prescribes, and that have the air of descriptions, in any other way than by working, by means of writing, on the imagination of the reader. It is on the basis of this symbolic game and its imaginary practices that the experiment can give rise to an inventory of contrary cases and of balanced cases (*A Treatise of Human Nature*). The experiment is real only when, and because, it is first of all symbolically devised.

Whether or not it gives rise to a feeling, it remains deprived of sense unless it is read, written, or made "singular" in a way that allows it to enter a calculation as a unit. Thus the question of knowing whether we can make experiments in the domain of passions, economics, and history is settled: it is obvious that we can (even though it is no easier to modify feelings than movements in the heavens), because the experiment is essentially symbolic, even when it allows for, as is often the case in physics, material manipulation. Price, reflecting on Bayes's rule and taking his examples equally from physics or the study of human nature, speaks of our possibility of determining "what conclusion to draw from a given number of *experiments* that are not countered by *contrary experiments*" (Bayes, *An Essay*). The experiment has the currency of chance: "chance or experiment," Hume says (*A Treatise of Human Nature*).

II. The Ambiguity of "Experience"

"Experience" presents an impressive range of meanings. One of them is very close to "experiment," when a more or less regular set of experiments may give rise to a more or less perfect experience (*A Treatise of Human Nature*), or conversely when "experience" becomes essentialized and autonomous in order to form a past experience or an element of past experience likely to enter into an experiment. Another meaning, in contrast, is very far removed from "experiment," even opposed to it: "experience" can in effect designate that which irreducibly resists explication; discussing the complications of sympathy Hume writes, just before the conclusion of the *Treatise of Human Nature*: "There is something very inexplicable in this variation of our impressions; but it is what we have the experience of with regard to all our passions and sentiments."

Generally, "experience" for Hume is rather that which one finds, which one encounters as a limit, which permits a discovery, which teaches, which permits an inference or a derivation, which proves, which returns, which is repeated (Price speaks of the "returns of an event" or of the "recurrency of events" [Bayes, *An Essay*]), or which can be stored or accumulated, either in the habits of life or by particular observation, in order to lead us to draw conclusions (*A Treatise of Human Nature*).

But if it may be false (ibid.), if it may regulate our judgment (ibid.), it is not possible for it to think in our place or to substitute for an explanation, which can be obtained only by, from, on experience. Whether we create experience through repetition or leave it to itself, whether we consult experience, infer existence through it, or put pressure on it, one way or another it is linked to the making of decisions: the decision to validate ideas, for example, only insofar as they are connected to experience, or the decision not to go beyond the limits of experience (as when Hume recommends that we should not extend the influence of relation beyond experience). It is up to us to render experience "undoubted" (ibid.), so that experience is always invoked in an unavoidable ambiguity: it is convincing on condition that it is not forced, yet it has meaning only when it is provoked and tends toward experiment: "We have happily attained experiments in the artificial virtues," Hume says in conclusion to the second part of the third book on morals of the *Treatise*.

However interwoven it may be with experience, the basic idea of the experiment rests on an artificial simplification of the phenomenon or sequence of events that one seeks to isolate, at least symbolically, in order to maintain greater control of its articulation with other phenomena or its combination with other sequences. Thus, experience is the taking into account of phenomena that cannot be grasped in the simplifying play of the experiment and of events in skeins of sequences or caught up in open systems subject to indefinite complication.

The traditional opposition between rationalism and empiricism no longer appears so clear-cut once one examines in detail the linguistic operations that constitute the dialectical play of experience, experiment, and their authority (ibid). That ideas derive from experience is a principle only if it is understood solely as a methodological rule. Empiricism, in the end, is a philosophy of decision-making, even if it always presents the will as a sentiment or denounces it as a fiction: one has to decide to accept as valid only a proposition that has, in one form or another, the guarantee of experience, and this decision is no less a priori than the categories and principles of rationalism. One passes therefore from empiricism to rationalism by a simple displacement, and the confrontation of these two doctrines is merely imaginary.

Jean-Pierre Cléro

BIBLIOGRAPHY

Bayes, Thomas. *An Essay towards Solving a Problem in the Doctrine of Chances, with Richard Price's Forword and Discussion*. In *Facsimiles of Two Papers by Bayes*. New York: Hafner, 1963. First published in 1763.

Bentham, Jeremy. *Chrestomathia*. Edited by M. J. Smith and W. H. Burston. Oxford: Clarendon Press, 1983. First published in 1816.

Hume, David. *A Treatise of Human Nature*. Edited by L. A. Selby-Bigge. Oxford: Clarendon Press, 1978. First published in 1739–40.

Popper, Karl R. *The Logic of Scientific Discovery*. London: Hutchinson, 1980. First published 1935.

FACT

"Fact" derives from the Latin *factum*, the neuter nominalized participle of *facere*, "to make, to do" (from the same root as the Greek *tithêmi* [τίθημι], "to put, to place"). Facts are distinguished by their positive character, independent of fiction or norms.

I. Fact/Fiction

The term "fact" refers first to what is given, especially in experience as a phenomenon, or in history as an event, and is thus distinguished from the illusory or fictional. We have chosen to study and compare two particular networks: the English network, which we look at on the basis of its idiomatic expressions—see MATTER OF FACT, cf. ENGLISH; and German terminology, which is built up in translation of and in counterpoint to English empiricism: see TATSACHE. TATSACHE, Box 1, examines the study of existential reinvestment of the Kantian *Faktum*, by way of Kierkegaard's Danish.

More generally, on the objective status of facts, see APPEARANCE, *PHÉNOMÈNE*, [ERSCHEINUNG, GEGENSTAND, OBJECT, REALITY, RES], *THING*.

On the language to which it gives rise, see *FALSE, FICTION* [ERZÄHLEN, HISTORY], TRUTH. On facts as statements of a present (*infectum*) by contrast with a "perfect" (*perfectum*), see ASPECT; cf. PRESENT.

II. Fact/Law

The order of facts is contrasted with the order of law. Facts deal with the empirical and the contingent, in accordance with nature or culture, in contrast with logico-mathematical necessity and the norms of practice and law. The intricate relations between the truth of facts and practical and legal norms is especially salient in Russian: see PRAVDA. The relations between truth value (validity) and moral value (value) are especially visible in German: see WERT.

On the relationship to knowledge, see, besides ISTINA and TRUTH, EPISTEMOLOGY, GEISTESWISSENSCHAFTEN.

On the notion of experience, and experience of self, see CONSCIOUSNESS, EPOCHÊ, EXPERIMENT, and cf. *CULTURE, EXPERIENCE.*

On the relation to ethics, see DUTY, MORALS, SOLLEN.

On the question *quid facti / quid iuris?* see DROIT, *LAW* [*RIGHT*, LEX, TORAH, THEMIS], cf. *DESTINY*, FAIR.

➤ *ACT, DISPOSITION, EVENT*

FACTURE

From the Latin *factura* (fabrication), derived from *facere* (to make), the word refers to the way in which a work of art is made, and the French word *facteur* refers to, among other things, a maker of musical instruments. We have focused on the Russian term *faktura* [фактура], which acquires remarkable importance in the early twentieth century (see FAKTURA).

On its relations to material, see ART (esp. Box 2), DISEGNO, *FORM*, PLASTICITY.

On artistic style, see MANIERA, MIMÊSIS, *STYLE.*

➤ AESTHETICS, *DESSEIN, DESSIN*, DICHTUNG

FAIR / FAIRNESS / EQUITY

➤ *JUSTICE*, LAW [LEX], PHRONÊSIS, PRUDENTIAL, RIGHT/JUST/GOOD, UTILITY, VERGÜENZA

The untranslatable "fairness" is of renewed contemporary interest thanks to the original use made of it by the American philosopher John Rawls. In the French translation of his work *A Theory of Justice*, "fairness" was translated as *équité*. Rawls seeks to establish a contrast between a moral "deontological" conception, like his own, in which respect for individual rights and fair treatment are of primary importance, and a teleological conception, in which rights and justice may be sacrificed for the realization of the supreme Good, the ultimate *telos*, as in utilitarian philosophy. Above all, he makes justice the result of an agreement between the parties to a social contract on the model of Hobbes, Locke, and Rousseau. He completely rejects the idea that justice may be the object of an intellectual intuition as held by intuitionist doctrines. This is why the expression "procedural justice" is often associated with this representation of justice as fairness. But the English term "fairness" combines several semantic fields in such a peculiar way that some languages, like German, have opted to take over the term as such without translating it. French, indeed, has adopted the expression "fair play" but must otherwise be content with near equivalents, none of which articulates the central ideas of honesty, impartiality, justice, and equity in the same way as "fairness."

I. Common Uses

In nonphilosophical language, "fair" intersects with several distinct fields. The oldest is that of color, in which "fair" refers to whatever is light, agreeable, or bodes well, as opposed to "foul," which refers to the dark, ugly, and what bodes ill. Thus, in Shakespeare, the "fair maiden" is a pretty girl with blond hair and a light complexion. Similarly, today, "fair weather" is pleasant. In a second semantic field, "fair" refers to what is morally untarnished, honest and without stain, and irreproachable, as when we speak of a clear conscience. Third, a more recent sense, which goes beyond the individual, his character, or his consciousness, characterizes action, conduct, and the general rules of action; "fair" thus lays the emphasis on the absence of fraud and dishonesty, whence the expression "fair play," which refers to a respect for the rules of the game. It is at this level that the notions of honesty and impartiality meet. An action, a method, or a kind of reasoning is fair if it rejects arbitrary preferences, undue favor, or partiality and if it does not aim to win out by dishonest means or by force. Thus, in a fourth sense, the term "fairness" becomes an essential component of the idea of justice: the result of its procedures, methods, reasoning, or decisions is itself fair, that is, justified and deserved, when we take its conditions into account. It is just in the sense that it satisfies the formula "to each his due." The final sense of "fairness" is one according to which, alongside the impartiality of a procedure, a treatment, a decision, and the conformity of their results with justice, we find the idea of measure, of a quantity that is moderate but sufficient.

II. "Fairness" and "Equity"

In philosophical language, the translation of "fairness" by a cognate of "equity" is problematic since in English the term "equity" already exists, coming from the Latin *aequitas* as a translation for Aristotelian "equity," and has been preserved in technical language, kept relatively apart from the semantic field of fairness. Indeed, the term used by Aristotle refers to a different idea—that of a conflict between the letter and the spirit of the law: "the equitable is just but not the legally just but a correction of legal justice" (Aristotle, *Nicomachean Ethics*, 5.10.1137b; see THEMIS, IV). There is thus a jurisdiction in English law (the equity jurisdiction) whose task is to justify exceptions where the law is faulty or too rigid—what legal vocabulary calls "cases of equity" (cf. Rawls, *Theory of Justice*, §38). This worry about equity in the Aristotelian sense lies behind the tradition of common law and the latitude it gives to judges in their interpretation of laws. We thus see how Aristotelian "equity" and Rawlsian "fairness" could come to be opposed to one another.

III. "Fairness" and Impartiality: The Duty of Fair Play

While equity may correct justice, fairness is at the heart of it insofar as it requires impartial treatment of people. This contemporary philosophical meaning goes back to Henry Sidgwick and his attempt to synthesize Kant and utilitarianism, and it stipulates that

> it cannot be right for A to treat B in a manner in which it would be wrong for B to treat A, merely on the ground that they are two different individuals, and without there being any differences between the natures or the circumstances of the two which can be stated as a reasonable ground for difference of treatment.... The principle just discussed, which seems to be more or less clearly implied in the common notion of "fairness" or "equity," is obtained by considering the similarity of the individuals that make up a Logical Whole or Genus.

(Sidgwick, *Methods of Ethics*, bk. 3, chap. 13, §3)

What is original is Sidgwick's extension of the term, which prefigures Rawls's account of fairness. He interprets it in an intersubjective sense as the principle that consists in treating equally "all parts of our conscious life": "I ought not prefer a present lesser good to a future greater good"

(ibid.). By the same reasoning, he extends it intersubjectively to the principle of universal benevolence (ibid.), the utilitarian principle that demands that we maximize the general happiness

> by considering the relation of the integrant parts to the whole and to each other, I obtain the self-evident principle that the good of any one individual is of no more importance, from the point of view (if I may say so) of the Universe, than the good of any other; unless, that is, there are special grounds for believing that more good is likely to be realised in the one case than in the other. And it is evident to me that as a rational being I am bound to aim at good generally,—so far as it is attainable by my efforts.

IV. "Fairness" and Justice

For Sidgwick, the term "fairness" comes to encapsulate a general theory not only of justice but also of rightness, of moral duty. This development reaches maturity in Rawls's account, in which "justice" is defined as fairness in the sense of an equal respect to which all rational beings have a right, that is, in the sense of the Kantian categorical imperative: "the principles of justice are . . . analogous to the categorical imperative" (Rawls, *Theory of Justice*, §40). As with Kant, but for other reasons, this conception of justice is procedural—it applies first to processes, not to an atemporal order. First, it characterizes a certain way of acting toward other humans and living beings in general. Second, it is itself a result of procedures; it does not exist "in itself" or by conformity with an external criterion:

> One must give up the conception of justice as an executive decision altogether and refer to the notion of justice as fairness: that participants in a common practice be regarded as having an original and equal liberty and that their common practices be considered unjust unless they accord with principles which persons so circumscribed and related could freely acknowledge before one another, and so could accept as fair. Once the emphasis is put upon the concept of the mutual recognition of principles by participants in a common practice the rules of which are to define their several relations and give form to their claims on one another, then it is clear that the granting of a claim the principle of which could not be acknowledged by each in the general position (that is, in the position in which the parties propose and acknowledge principles before one another) is not a reason for adopting a practice.

(Rawls, "Justice as Fairness")

Thus, when we examine distributive justice or social justice in the economic domain of exchanges, contracts, salaries, and prices of the market, the term "fairness" takes its meaning as justice in distribution, in pricing, in salaries; these are not just "in themselves" as Aristotle says, but the most just in relation to the special conditions of competition:

> [I]ncome and wages will be just once a (workably) competitive price system is properly organized and embedded in a just basic structure.... The distribution that

results is a case of background justice on the analogy with the outcome of a fair game.

(Rawls, *Theory of Justice*, §47)

Thus, when philosophers wish to think about justice, they have two registers in which they may work: the first is that of fairness and procedural justice, that is, impartiality and honesty, as well as equity in decisions, procedures, exchanges, distributions, contracts, and so on, without independent criteria for evaluating the results. The other is that of just and right, which imply conformity with an external and independent criterion, obligation, and moral and legal duty, with reference to an ideal of objectivity and truth. In philosophical usage, "justice" tends to be applied more to the results of procedural fairness (Barry, *Theories of Justice*). But the differences are often simply a question of use.

We can thus understand why, if we wish to construct an entirely conventional account of justice, as in Hume, which would nevertheless not be arbitrary, the term "fairness" and its anthropocentric aspects may be a legitimate choice. By way of the associated theory, the philosophical meaning retains the reference to human situations in which rational partners attempt to resolve their differences, as in the signature of a contract, without appealing to independent criteria. Rawls's theory is especially interesting from this point of view, since it attempts to achieve equality and social justice on the basis of a procedure rather than imposing them as independent criteria, as is almost always the case. Rawls often uses the terms "just" and "fair" interchangeably, which we may see as resulting from a desire to dispense with all moral realism and to discover principles of justice in the dialectic of interests and passions alone. Indeed, Rawls compares the theory of justice with the pure theory of prices or market equilibrium in such a way that his conception of the first is fully contractualist, in the same sense as for Rousseau—namely, that the just is a result of universal suffrage, that is, from the contract each person has with everyone else. The equitable and the just do not exist in themselves; they result, rather, from an agreement on the conditions of liberty, equality, and impartiality collected under the metaphor of the "veil of ignorance." Any intervention inspired by an external criterion, whether from the threat of force or from an ideology such as equality, would make the decision come out wrong.

V. "Fairness" and Equality

We see, then, that unlike in the second register of just and right, "fairness" does refer to justice, but without the idea of equality playing a role as an independent criterion. In a theory of justice that is itself egalitarian, inequalities may be justified or fair if and only if they are the result of conditions or principles which are themselves fair (Rawls's second principle). Equality is thus indeed a component of justice, but as a result of the procedure rather than as a condition imposed a priori. In his use of "fairness," Rawls announces that it is no longer possible to speak of justice independently of human judgment and procedure. "Fairness" combines impartiality of the conditions of choice, honesty of procedure, and equity with regard to those entering contracts and

thus makes it possible to construct a theory of justice that is purely procedural.

Catherine Audard

BIBLIOGRAPHY

Aristole. *Nicomachean Ethics*. In *The Complete Works of Aristotle*, vol. 2, edited by J. Barnes. Princeton, NJ: Princeton University Press / Bollingen, 1984.
Barry, Brian. *Theories of Justice*. London: Harvester, 1989.
Hume, David. *A Treatise on Human Nature*. Edited by L. A. Selby-Bigge. Oxford: Clarendon Press, 1978. First published 1739–40.
Rawls, John. "Justice as Fairness." *Philosophical Review* 67 (1958): 164–94.
———. *A Theory of Justice*. Cambridge, MA: Harvard University Press, 1971.
Sidgwick, Henry. *The Methods of Ethics*. 6th ed. London: MacMillan, 1901; 7th ed., preface, J. Rawls. London: Hackett Publishing, 1981. First published in 1874.

FAITH

Faith comes from the Latin *fides*, which refers to the confidence one inspires (the "credit" or "credibility" of a speech) and that which one grants, taking its entire extension from the language of law: "solemn engagement, guarantee, oath" (cf. *foedus*, "treaty"), "good faith, fidelity." The same Indo-European root **bheidh-*, "to rely upon, persuade," is found in the Greek *peithomai* [πείθομαι], "to obey," and in the active *peithô* [πείθω], "to persuade." Christian Latin makes the term more specialized, using it as a noun for *credo*, "to believe," in the sense of trust in God.

Different modern languages do not all separate in the same way the legal, rhetorical, and logical network on the one hand—credit and credibility, confidence and belief—and the religious network of "faith," properly speaking, on the other. German, in particular, with *der Glaube*, translated by "faith" or "belief," does not offer this distinction: see BELIEF, GLAUBE, *CROYANCE*.

More generally, for the relationships to the logical network, see ISTINA and TRUTH, PRAVDA, but also *CERTITUDE*, DUTY, EIDÔLON, Box 1, *FICTION*, INTENTION, *PROBABILITY*.

For the religious network, see especially PIETAS, *RELIGION*; cf. *ALLIANCE*, DESTINY, LEX.

➤ SECULARIZATION

FAKTURA [факτура] (RUSSIAN)

ENGLISH	workmanship, texture
LATIN	*factura*

➤ *FACTURE*, and ART, MANIERA, PLASTICITY, *STYLE*

In the traditional sense of the term—which is derived from the Latin *factura* (manufacture)—*faktura* is the combination of characteristics of paintings or sculptures that relate to the ways in which the material has been worked by the artist and that constitutes the concrete element of style. It is thus a nonnegligible result, but one whose value remains secondary. Nevertheless, in the 1910s and 1920s in Russia, the term *faktura* [факτура], which is normally translated as "facture" or "texture," acquired unprecedented conceptual and ideological importance.

Zaoum (Russ. *zaum* [заум])—a poetic form that refuses submission to meaning in order to give priority to the qualities of the verbal material itself—and the possibilities opened up by pictorial abstraction prompted intense reflection on the role of the components of a work. Thus, different typologies of the "plastic elements" appeared. In the Russian context, especially among the constructivists, adepts of a substantial materialism, the "culture of materials" took on a decisive importance. Vladimir Markov was one of the pioneers of this new attention being given to workmanship (*faktura* [фактура]) with reference to the material: "The love of material is an incitement for man. To ornament it and work it yields the possibility of obtaining all the forms that belong to it, the 'resonances' that we call *faktura*" ("Principes de la création").

Several years later, Nicolas Tarabukin made *faktura* autonomous, and hence a plastic element in its own right:

All of the originality of the textural aspect of contemporary painting comes from what has been detached from the ensemble of pictorial problems and transformed into a particular problem, thus creating a whole school of texturalists.

("Pour une théorie de la peinture")

Plastic experimentation with various materials in effect led Tatlin and some other Russian artists to create pictorial reliefs or three-dimensional constructions, such as counter-reliefs, which prompt the viewer to dissociate the "texture" (*faktura*) from the other elements with which it is presented, especially, in the case of painting, color. If, as Tarabukin claims, "it is the material that dictates the form to the artist and not the reverse" (ibid.), the study of the material being put to work—that is, the study of texture—opens up new possibilities: when the material and the form remain fixed entities, the texture creates a dynamic link between them. Coming from the flow, it displays and records the enlivening energy of a dialectic in action.

Denys Riout

BIBLIOGRAPHY

Gan, Aleksei. *Konstruktivizm.* Tverï: Tverskoe izd-vo, 1922.
Lodder, Christina. *Russian Constructivism.* Reprint, New Haven, CT: Yale University Press, 1985.
Markov, Vladimir. "Principes de la création dans les arts plastiques. La Facture." 1914. In *Le constructivisme dans les arts plastiques.* Vol. 1 of *Le constructivisme Russe,* edited by G. Conio. Lausanne, Switz.: L'Âge d'Homme, 1987.
Tarabukin, Nicolas. "Pour une théorie de la peinture." 1923. In *Le constructivisme dans les arts plastiques.* Vol. 1 of *Le constructivisme Russe,* edited by G. Conio. Lausanne, Switz.: L'Âge d'Homme, 1987.

FALSE

"False," like "fault," comes from the Latin *fallo,* which means "to deceive" and, in the passive, "to be deceived" (*falsus* [false, deceptive, someone deceived], probably from the same etymology as the Greek *sphallô* [σφάλλω], meaning "I cause to fall"; see PARDON, II). The false, like the true, involves two registers, linguistic and ontological, and the distinction between

the two leads into ethics. The reader will find under TRUTH, IV a note on the evolution of the antonyms of "true," by way of Greek (*pseudês* [ψευδής], "false" and "deceptive") to Latin (*fallax,* "false"/*mendax,* "lying"). In a general way, each characterization of the truth comprises a characterization of its antonym: see ISTINA, PRAVDA.

I. Logic: False, Proposition, Speech

1. To speak falsely is to say things as they are not. From the point of view of traditional logic, an isolated word cannot be true or false as such, but rather requires "composition": see under PROPOSITION the exploration of the terminology for what is capable of being true and false. See also DICTUM, PRÉDICABLE, PREDICATION, and SUBJECT. For a comparison with the minimal unit, which is the correlate of meaning but not of the true or the false, see SIGN, WORD, and cf. SIGNIFIER/SIGNIFIED. And with the all-encompassing unit of speech, see LANGUAGE, LOGOS.

2. On the content of propositions, their "import" and the object of judgment, see SACHVERHALT; cf. TATSACHE; on what makes a proposition true or false, see SPEECH ACT.

3. The difference between what is false and what lacks meaning altogether is discussed in the context of the English word NONSENSE; see also SENSE.

4. On the logical principles, especially the principle of noncontradiction, which govern truth and error, see PRINCIPLE; cf. HOMONYM.

5. On the validity of demonstrations and their value, see IMPLICATION.

II. Ontology: The False and the Real

1. To speak falsely is also, more radically, to say things that are not. The false is not just a logical issue, but an ontological one as well. The problem of the false thus cuts across that of appearances, as opposed to reality and its objects: see *APPEARANCE* [DOXA, ERSCHEINUNG], *PHÉNOMÈNE, NOTHING.* Some languages combine the veridical with the perceptual, thus the German *Wahrnehmung* (PERCEPTION, Box 3); cf. REPRÉSENTATION.

2. We are thus referred to the objectivity of the object, to the reality of the real; see especially ESSENCE, GEGENSTAND, *IL Y A,* OBJECT, REALITY, *THING, TO BE.*

3. We are also led to the problems of images and imagination, and the ambiguous value of aesthetic illusion: see *IMAGE* [BILD, EIDÔLON], *IMAGINATION* [FANCY, PHANTASIA], MIMÊSIS.

III. Ethics: The False and Fault

1. The direct relationship in some languages between the "false" and "fault" is studied under DUTY, III.

2. The difference between "being deceived" and "deceiving" comes, not in what is said, but in the use made of what is said and the intentions behind it. The Greek *pseudês* does not distinguish them, unlike the nonfixed Latin pair *fallax/mendax* (see TRUTH, IV). On the complexity of intention, see INTENTION, and WILL, WILLKÜR; cf. *DESTINY, LIBERTY,* MORALS. See also *LIE.*

3. Further, we may speak of things that do not exist without the intention of deceiving, see SENSE; cf. HOMONYM.

We then find the problem for speech of aesthetic illusion (see section II.3 above), which deals with the network of fiction: see *DECEPTION*, TRUTH, Box 3, and DESENGAÑO, *FICTION*, HISTORY, SPEECH ACT.

4. Finally, it is possible not to speak while speaking; see in particular VERNEINUNG, cf. *NEGATION*; and, for German words that indicate privation or failure, see COMBINATION AND CONCEPTUALIZATION.

FANCY / IMAGINATION

➤ *IMAGINATION*[PHANTASIA], and BILDUNG, ERSCHEINUNG, FEELING, GENIUS, *IMAGE*[BILD], MADNESS, MIMĒSIS, SUBLIME

At the beginning of chapter 4 of the *Salon of 1859*, "Le gouvernement de l'imagination," Baudelaire cites in English and immediately translates into French a text by Catherine Crow that he sees as confirming one of his own ideas but in which it is also possible to discern a distinction already long at work in English theoretical texts: "By imagination, I do not simply mean to convey the common notion implied by that much abused word, which is only fancy, but the constructive imagination, which is a much higher function, and which, in as much as man is made in the likeness of God, bears a distant relation to that sublime power by which the Creator projects, creates and upholds his universe" (*Œuvres complètes*, 2:623–24). Though he does not specify which edition he looked at—it may be that of 1848 or 1853—Baudelaire explicitly refers to *The Night Side of Nature*, which was first published in London.

This distinction appealed to by Baudelaire goes back to the middle of the fifteenth century, when "fancy" was formed as a contraction of "fantasy" (see RT: *Dictionarium Britanicum*, 1730). It was thus in use for a long time among those English-speaking authors who were sensitive to their language and careful about thinking. It corresponds to two etymologies, one Greek and one Latin "fancy," from *phantasia* [φαντασία] and "imagination" (*imaginatio*), the former referring to the creative force of appearance and the latter to reproduction and images. We thus find in English the same kind of pair as in German (see BILD). The words "imagination" and "fancy" thus only appear to cover the same idea, and we can see their difference by looking at some important texts of the eighteenth century. Nevertheless, this awareness of an imperfect synonymy, which may go as far as complete opposition, does not at all help us to resolve problems of translation.

■ See Box 1.

The distinction between "fancy" and "imagination" is often rendered in French by the contrast between *fantaisie* and *imagination*. It is not always wrong to translate "fancy" as *fantaisie*. We find in Bentham, for example, the expression "principle of caprice or groundless fancy" (*principe du caprice ou de la chimère sans fondement*; this translation by *chimère* could equally well be given by *fantaisie*; *Deontology*, §304). However, even if we wish to relate *fantaisie* with its Greek sense and set aside the more peculiar sense of "more or less unhinged improvisation," which it has acquired, we must note that this distinction almost never captures the sense of the English pair.

I. Imagination and Fancy: The Commonalities

Whether we call the process "imagination" or "fancy," the commonalities are clear once we understand imagination not so much as a faculty but instead as the ideological resolution of conflicts that are naturally or socially impossible to live with or feel. "Imagination," like "fancy," seems to suggest a solution, but this suggestion is already, in a way, a solution. Thus Hume often sprinkles his remarks about the origins of an institution or power with a phrase like "This is founded on a very singular quality of our thought and imagination" (*A Treatise of Human Nature*). Imagination is thus indeed a "mistress of error"—as long as we note, as Pascal did with great subtlety, that this is "all the more deceitful as it is not always so." Imagination is accused of "error" (ibid.) as often as fancy. When Hume writes: "'Tis natural for one, that does not examine objects with a strict philosophical eye, to imagine that those objects of the mind are entirely the same, which produce not a different sensation, and are not immediately distinguishable to the feeling and perception" (*A Treatise of Human Nature*); "to imagine" has the clear sense of "conceive falsely." The same is the case when he writes, concerning the symbolic import of a key, a stone, a handful of earth or wheat, that "the suppos'd resemblance of the actions, and the presence of this sensible delivery, deceive the mind and make it fancy that it conceives the mysterious transition of the property" (ibid.). On both sides, the relation with the passions is treated symmetrically. Something may "satisfy the fancy," just—and just as often—as it may be "agreeable to the imagination" (ibid.).

If imagination and fancy conceive wrongly, however, this implies that they are both capable of conceiving: Hume speaks of the conception of fancy and offers as equivalent "imagination or understanding, call it which you please" (ibid.).

II. The Game of Alliances:
The Topics of "Imagination" and the Dynamics of "Fancy"

Where, then, are the differences, when they exist? The words "and" and "or" have the philosophical function of weaving alliances between notions into a shifting whole, since an alliance at one point and from one perspective will not necessarily be the same at another point and perspective. The game of alliances is the following.

Statistically—although the argument cannot be ignored in a philosophy whose method consists more in enumerating and weighing cases than in the use of the critical scalpel—"fancy" tends to involve the more fantastical aspects of the imagination. *Je me figure telle chose* would be rendered by "I fancy" rather than by "I imagine." The chimerical and system-building philosophers are the ones who, attacking the feminine virtues of modesty and chastity with great vehemence, "fancy that they have gone very far in detecting popular errors" (*A Treatise of Human Nature*). Alexander, wherever he saw men "fancied he had found subjects" (ibid.). This should not lead us to underestimate the "frivolous" dimension of the imagination: "imagination of the more frivolous properties of our thought" (ibid.). However, we would certainly have more difficulty in assimilating "fancy" to "judgment" than to "imagination," as Hume does. The less intellectual connotation of "fancy" relative to "imagination"

1

Fancy

Before Samuel Taylor Coleridge intervened, aesthetic theory tended to synonymize "fancy" and "imagination" to denote either a residual image from the decay of sense (Hobbes, *Leviathan*, chap. 2) or, more positively, the mind's inventive play. Appealing to the Greek *phantasia*, in distinction to the Latin *imaginatio*, Coleridge delimited "fancy" to productions shaped by accidents and contingencies of sense data. In *Biographia Literaria* (1817, chap. 4), he cites Lear's exclamation to a bedraggled beggar on the stormy heath as "Imagination": "What! have his daughters brought him to this pass?" (*King Lear*, 3.4). This is a totalized traumatic psychology—misery can have no other cause for Lear. What may be "contra-distinguished as *fancy*" (Coleridge, *Biographia Literaria*) is a delirium from Thomas Otway's *Venice Preserved*: "[l]utes, lobsters, seas of milk, and ships of amber"—a disarray of sense-data and normal referents. Coleridge returns to his distinction at the end of chapter 13. Where Imagination "dissolves, diffuses, dissipates, in order to re-create, . . . to idealize and unify," fancy plays with the ready-made "fixities and definites" of memory "emancipated from the order of time and space."

Coleridge focuses on the process; Wordsworth ponders the affective impression. If imagination is "the faculty which produces impressive effects out of simple elements," fancy is "the power by which pleasure and surprize are excited by sudden varieties of situation and by accumulated imagery" (note in *Lyrical Ballads*, 1800). Leigh Hunt's *Imagination and Fancy* (1845) preferred an affective scale: fancy is "a lighter play of imagination, or the feeling of analogy coming short of seriousness, in order that it may laugh with what it loves, and show how it can decorate it with fairy ornament." With his painter's eye, John Ruskin distinguished in terms of detail: fancy renders "a portrait of the outside, clear, brilliant, and full of detail. The imagination sees the heart and inner nature, and makes them felt, but is often obscure, mysterious, and interrupted, in . . . outer detail" (*Modern Painters*, vol. 2, 1851).

John Keats's last lifetime volume (*Poems*) joins the traditions of fancy as superficial play to charged feminine personifications: Fancy, the charming cheat. While his iconic poem *Fancy* exhorts, "Ever let the Fancy roam, / Pleasure never is at home" (1–2), the poet of *Lamia* speaks of unlocking "Fancy's casket" for "rich gifts" (1.19–20)—a store with a hint of Pandoran peril. In *The Eve of St. Agnes*, superstitious Madeline is "hoodwink'd with faery fancy; all amort" to the dangerous world around her (8). In *Ode to a Nightingale*, Keats bid a determined, if wistful, adieu to the charm: "the fancy cannot cheat so well / As she is fam'd to do, deceiving elf" (8). In his copy of *Paradise Lost*, he underscored the verse in which Adam explains this she-trickery to a dream-disturbed Eve. While in daylight, "Fansie" may serve "Reason" by forming "Imaginations Aerie shapes" into "knowledge or opinion," in dream-retreat from nature, she merely mimics, while subverting, Reason: "misjoyning shapes, / Wilde work produces . . . / Ill matching words and deeds" (5.102–13).

Susan J. Wolfson

BIBLIOGRAPHY

Coleridge, Samuel Taylor. *Biographia Literaria*. Edited by J. Shawcross. Oxford: Oxford University Press, 1949.
Hunt, Leigh. *Imagination and Fancy*. London: Routledge, 1995.
Keats, John. *Poems Published in 1820*. Oxford: Clarendon Press, 1909.
Ruskin, John. *Modern Painters*. London: Smith, Elder, 1851.
Wordsworth, William. *Lyrical Ballads*. London: Longman, 1992.

---

is also seen in the comparison of "fancy" with "taste," which we often find in the *Treatise*.

Finally, there is a second statistical means of distinguishing the two terms, which becomes fixed in philosophical English in the eighteenth and nineteenth centuries through the joint effects of the development of probability theory and dynamic conceptions of mind. "Imagination" refers to the act by which, from a present situation that we are to consider either with respect to its eventual effects or as the result of concurrent causes, we make a list of situations, in the direction of either the past or the future. Imagination performs a sort of abstraction of the dimensions of time, considered as objective points of reference. Imagination thus takes on a topical sense and refers to the ability of our mind to recognize its current situation among others of a greater or lesser number. Imagination implies a kind of tracking that is often as systematic as that of the understanding, even though it may be cursory, less reliable, and less rapid: imagination "conceives" (ibid.).

"Fancy" is less systematic and refers rather to the particular act of referring to a situation in which one does not actually find oneself. This is why we speak of laws or of "principles of the imagination" (ibid.), which may be said almost without irony to govern men rather than the "laws of fancy," an expression whose unbearable contradiction is immediately obvious. No doubt it is often a question,

for Hume, of the "force" of the imagination, of the effect of events on it, of the flow that carries imagination and fancy both; no doubt "imagination moves" (ibid.). However, "imagination" is more phoronomic than dynamic. By contrast, "fancy" more readily and more consciously calls psychic forces to mind; it implies that a furrow has been dug in a given direction: " 'Tis certain that the tendency of bodies, continually operating upon our senses, must produce, from custom, a like tendency in the fancy" (ibid.). Further, the contrast between "imagination" and "fancy" is clear and distinct when Hume writes in the *Treatise*:

> [E]very thing, which invigorates and inlivens the soul, whether by touching the passions or imagination, naturally conveys to the fancy this inclination for ascent, and determines it to run against the natural stream of its thoughts and conceptions.

In conformity with their etymologies, we may thus prefer to speak of imagination when we are concerned with images and their reciprocal relations in space and time, and of fancy with regard to dynamic imagination, which is the springing up of images rather than the images themselves. Fancy does not stop at any particular image; that is precisely where we find its whimsical and "fantastical" aspect, which misleads us if we use it as a starting point. However, it borrows from belief and reality a sort of vividness that imagination does not have. Curiously, imagination, supposedly less fantastical than fancy, is the less credible of the two, precisely because, being closer to understanding, it is also more easily scrutinized in relation to the true and hence appears more false than fancy, which deals with a logic of fiction escaping the domain of both truth and falsity.

Jean-Pierre Cléro

BIBLIOGRAPHY

Baudelaire, Charles-Pierre. *Œuvres complètes*. Paris: Gallimard / La Pléiade, 1976.

Bentham, Jeremy. *Deontology, Together with a Table of the Springs of Action, and an Article on Utilitarianism*. Edited by A. Goldworth. Oxford: Clarendon Press, 1984.

Crowe, Catherine. *The Night Side of Nature, or, Ghosts and Ghost Seers*. London: T. C. Newby, 1848; New York: Redfield, 1853.

Hume, David. *A Treatise of Human Nature*. Edited by L. A. Selby-Bigge. Oxford: Clarendon Press, 1978. First published in 1739–40.

Pascal, Blaise. *Œuvres complètes*. Paris: Gallimard / La Pléiade, 1954.

———. *Pensées and Other Writings*. Translated by H. Levi. Introduction by A. Levi. Oxford: Oxford University Press, 1995.

FATHERLAND

The Latin *patria*, like the Greek *hê patris* [ἡ πατρίς], means "the land of the father"; cf. PIETAS and RELIGIO. More broadly, see PEOPLE, with the terminological networks that imply soil and blood in contradistinction to those that imply language, culture, politics, and cf. COMMUNITY, STATE.

The German doublet of *Vaterland*, *Heimat*, has other connotations, particularly as used by Heidegger; see HEIMAT. On the way the political community in ancient Greece is designated, see POLIS. On the relationship to *oikos* [οἶκος], the "specific," the "familiar," see, on the one hand, ECONOMY, OIKONOMIA, and on the other, OIKEIÔSIS, a moral conception characteristic of Stoicism, which is rendered by "appropriation" (cf. *APPROPRIATION*).

➤ ANXIETY, GENDER, *LIBERTY*, LOVE, PROPERTY

FEELING / PASSION / EMOTION / SENTIMENT / SENSATION / AFFECTION / SENSE

FRENCH   *sentir, passion, émotion, sentiment, sensation, impression, affection, sens*

➤ COMMON SENSE, CONSCIOUSNESS, ENGLISH, GEFÜHL, *IMAGINATION* [FANCY, PHANTASIA], MORAL SENSE, PATHOS, PERCEPTION, SENSE, STIMMUNG

There is a very complex relationship between the English term "feeling," a word of Saxon origin, and its counterparts in Romance languages. In French, the substantival infinitive *le sentir* is sometimes used, but with little conviction that it can be a consistently used equivalent. For French translators, moreover, the whole cluster of terms around feeling—"passion," "emotion," "sentiment," "sensation," "affection," "sense"—has posed such serious challenges that they sometimes prefer either to leave the English words in parentheses or to create verbal overlays like *passion, émotion, sentiment,*

sensation, impression, affection, or *sens*. The untranslatability of "feeling" in French reveals the peculiarities of a philosophy of affectivity or, at the least, a way of philosophizing, in English.

I. The Distribution of the English Terms

The definitions that seem to fix the meanings of terms do not refer to stable objects. Thus, Hume contrasts "impressions of sensation" with "impressions of reflection." The former, or original impressions "are such as without any antecedent perception arise in the soul, from the constitution of the body, from the animal spirits, or from the application of objects to the external organs." The latter, or secondary impressions, "are such as proceed from some of these original ones, either immediately or by the interposition of an idea" (*A Treatise of Human Nature*). But no sooner has Hume made these distinctions than he calls, without compunction, "sensation" what he has just picked out as "reflexion" and seems to enter into a relativist spiral that gives no term a chance to stand still. In addition, the connotation of the English terms does not coincide at all in this domain with the French terms. The situation thus contains a twofold discrepancy, one between the signs and their referents, and the other between the system of signs in French and that in English.

The place of "feeling" in the company of "sensation," "sentiment," "passion," "emotion," "affection," and "sense" causes problems precisely because French has no analogue for it and thus requires a different delimitation of the homologous terms. The gap that separates "feeling" from the other words clearly derives from its etymology, which owes nothing to Latin but is derived from the Old Saxon *folian* and Old High German, which gives us *fühlen*. The Old English *felan* initially meant "to perceive," "to touch," "to grasp." It is clear that its meaning derived much from "touch" by way of the affective domain. However, we would be wrong to believe that "feeling" took its place among the other terms of affect by filling in an empty space alongside them. We would be equally wrong to expect, moving from English to French, a simply different distribution of the territory of affect, as though affect could be considered a homogenous object with sensations on one side and sentiments on the other, as well as emotions, passions, and sense, the last of which is more normative than any of the others. The words display different attitudes in the understanding of affect rather than different territories. Hence, nothing in itself is referred to by "sensation," any more than by "sentiment," "feeling," or "sense."

The main divisions in English-language philosophies of the passions that make use of them as of a code are along the following lines: structural meanings versus those that come from an instantaneous and event-related affect; normative meanings versus factual ones; finally, meanings that imply a cognitive grasping versus those that do not.

II. Structure and Event

A. "Sensation" and "feeling" / "passion" and "sentiment"

We may speak, in English or in French, with regard to the sense organs, of sensation (*sensation*) of red or green, of heat or dryness, of hunger or sexual desire. However, English also allows for speaking, especially in Hume's idiom, of the "sensation" of one or another passion, to refer to the latter not by its structure but as a felt event, by its own particular experienced quality of pleasure and/or pain. The sensation of a passion is distinguished from sentiment, which is the systematic framework of passion, composed of an object, a subject, qualities, causes, a context, of a trajectory of development and a sort of destiny. This structural or structuring character is clearly seen in phrases like: "These are the sentiments of my spleen and indolence" (*A Treatise of Human Nature*), where we understand that "spleen" and "indolence" are less sentiments than something under which sentiments lie (the sentence should probably be translated: "Tels sont les sentiments qui sous-tendent ma mélancolie et mon indolence"). We may conceive and even establish, according to Hume's turn of phrase, a system of sentiment or of passion ("constant and established passion"; ibid.); there could not be one for sensation or feeling. One sentiment can oppose another, be contrary to another, but a sensation is only indirectly contrary to another sensation, by the contrariety of the sentiment of which it is the momentary and intermittent experience. So much so that sentiment may well remain unconscious, insensate, and only become experienced at certain phases which make its presence known. Hume notes, for example, that "the passage from one moment to another is scarce felt" (ibid.).

Similarly, while passion is structured by the twofold association of impressions and ideas, it is not always obvious that we are "sensible of it" (ibid.), even if the passion is violent. In this sense, the noun "sensation" remains close in English to the adjective "sensible," which is often correctly rendered into French as *conscient*.

While the terms "sentiment," "affection," and "passion" clearly have a structural connotation, the word "feeling" on the other hand is, along with "sensation," no less clearly on the side of lived experience ("feeling or experience" and "feeling and experience"; ibid.). Thus Hume can speak in his essay *Of the Standard of Taste*, without any redundancy, though to the despair of translators, of "feelings of sentiment." M. Malherbe speaks of "ce qui s'éprouve par sentiment"; R. Bouveresse, of "impressions du sentiment"; G. Robel of "émotions du sentiment." None of these solutions is convincing, but is there any way to solve the problem?

B. "Sensation" and "feeling" distinguished by the status of their object

"Sensation" and "feeling" cannot however be substituted for one another indifferently. Unlike Latin or French, English has no verb that, like *sentir*, corresponds to "sensation." Thus the word effects a sort of transcendence of lived experience much more fully than does "feeling," whose proximity to "feel" gives us a simple verbal mode. "Sensation" detaches its object, like a conclusion is detached from its reasoning— which allows Hume to treat "probable reasoning" as "a species of sensation" (*A Treatise of Human Nature*). "Feeling" does not posit its object the way "sensation" does. We can even "feel a reverse sensation from the happiness and misery of others" (ibid.). "Feeling" barely has any consistency independent of what it feels, since it has no means of conceiving, imagining, or representing. "To feel" marks a collaboration in a process; it plays along either in an immanent or an adherent way, unlike sensation, which is more instantaneous

and event-like—so much so that "to feel" is often expressed in the passive, without indicating what is doing the feeling. "Something felt" is said in English, instead of *quelque chose de senti*, as it must be said in French. Hume goes so far as to say that "[a]n idea assented to feels different from a fictitious idea" (ibid.).

The impossibility for "feeling" to have an object in the same way that "sensation" has is not without consequences. "Feeling" cannot have truth like "sensation," if only because sensations can still be *felt*. If it has truth, it cannot be a truth in conformity with an object, but rather the rightness of an internal relation, which Hume calls "reflexion." The objects of "feeling" do not necessarily have reality and are usually fictions such as what we call our self, a force, a passage, an inclination, a propensity, a virtuality ("I feel I should be a loser in point of pleasure"; ibid.), a probability, a difference (of social condition), and so on, and one must learn to be on guard against their apparent reality. I feel an inclination in the way I say I feel my mind ("I feel my mind . . . and am naturally inclin'd"; ibid.); that is, as I feel something happening inside it, where the expression "in it" does not have a direct representational value.

III. The Normative Aspect: "Sense"

However, when it does not mean a sense organ, it is the word "sense" that attracts the collection of normative characteristics of an internal impression (*A Treatise of Human Nature*). One speaks of a sense of beauty, a sense of sympathy, or a moral sense, even at the cost of showing at the same time that there is no moral sense (see MORAL SENSE). We even sometimes use "sense" with the meaning of "good sense" or "reason" (see COMMON SENSE). The term "sense" implies a dimension of appreciation that does not necessarily fit with feeling or sensation. When Hume, in *Of the Standard of Taste*, gives the floor to the skeptic, the latter's argument maintains that sentiment, sensation, or feeling are always true as long as they are really felt; Hume's response consists in distinguishing truth from reality and emphasizing that "sense" implies an internal normativity: "Though this axiom [there is no arguing with taste], by passing into a proverb, seems to have attained the sanction of common sense; there is certainly a species of common sense which opposes it, at least serves to modify and restrain it."

IV. The Cognitive Aspect: "Sentiment," "Sense"/"Feeling," "Sensation"

There remains a final semantic gap with regard to affect in English. In relation to cognition, "sentiment" is clearly close to "sense," unlike "feeling," and certainly unlike "sensation."

Sensations are what they are; they are real but not necessarily true for all that: "All sensations are felt by the mind, such as they really are" (*A Treatise of Human Nature*). To attribute truth to them solely by virtue of their existence is to commit an error, confusing truth with reality.

On the other hand, "sentiment" is often equivalent to "opinion" and "judgment" (ibid.). At least, in the combination of the two concepts that Hume advances so often in his philosophy, "sentiment" frequently shows up near words that impute cognitive character to it. And while "sentiment" is not always equivalent to "opinion," it is in any case an intellectual posture or attitude, an inclination to opine. The essay *Of the Standard of Taste*, which distinguishes sentiment from opinion, nevertheless points out that sentiment is capable of being right, while distinguishing, as against "a species of philosophy, which . . . represents the impossibility of ever attaining any standard of taste," its *rightness* from its reality, as though it were enough for it to be right (see GOÛT and RIGHT/JUST/GOOD).

Some notions that strongly resemble one another when looked at in one perspective can differ dramatically when looked at from another, no less pertinent one with regard to affect. Hume, who gladly joins notions together, comes up with every possible grouping ("feeling or sentiment" [*A Treatise of Human Nature*]; "impression or feeling" [ibid.]), not to mark their equivalence, but rather to show in each case what they contrast with as a pair.

Such a system could never be ontologically stable. Notions are distributed differently depending on the perspective adopted. Thus Hume can write "imagination feels that . . . ," or "fancy feels that . . . ," "judgement feels that . . . ," or "the spirit feels that . . ." (*A Treatise of Human Nature*). He thinks he can express laws with ontological weight concerning affect by emphasizing, like Bowlby in *Attachment and Loss*, that "*being felt . . . is a phase of the process itself*" (S. Langer, quoted by Bowlby; italics in original), whereas in fact he only manages to make the semantic tricks of his language work properly, or, at most, to explain them.

Jean-Pierre Cléro

BIBLIOGRAPHY

Bowlby, John. *Attachment and Loss*. Vol. 1, *Attachment*. London: Hogarth, 1969.
Hume, David. *Dialogues concerning Natural Religion*. Edited by D. Coleman. Cambridge: Cambridge University Press, 2007. First published in 1779.
———. *Essays, Moral, Political and Literary*. Vol. 3 of *The Philosophical Works of David Hume*, edited by Eugene F. Miller. Indianapolis, IN: Liberty Classics, 1985. First published in 1777.
———. *Of the Standard of Taste*. Vol. 3 of *Philosophical Works of David Hume*, edited by T. H. Green and T. H. Grose. London: Longmans, 1874–75. Translation by M. Malherbe: *De la règle du goût*, in *Essais et traités sur plusieurs sujets: Essais moraux, politiques et littéraires*. Paris: Vrin, 1999. Translation by R. Bouveresse: *Les essais esthétiques*. Paris: Vrin, 1974. Translation by G. Robel: *Essais moraux, politiques et littéraires et autres essais*. Paris: Presses Universitaires de France.
———. *A Treatise of Human Nature*. Edited by L. A. Selby-Bigge. Oxford: Clarendon Press, 1978.

FICAR

ENGLISH   to stay, to be, to become

The Iberian verbs *ser* and *estar* have important nuances in their copulative use with respect to the condition of the relation between subject and attribute, whether permanent or transitory, essential or accidental, abstract or concrete, etc. Portuguese adds yet another difference since it has an additional verb for expressing the relation of subject and attribute: the verb *ficar*, which implants and fixes the attributes onto the subject.

I. The Concrete Origin of the Copula in *Ficar*

We rarely feel the concrete verbal meaning of a copulative verb, no doubt because of the semantic force of the attributes that tend to hide it or place it in the role of a simple articulation, even though the metaphysical consequences may be considerable. For the Portuguese verb *ficar* this concrete sense is easier to see. This is in part because of its rather clear etymology and the coexistence alongside it of a non-copulative meaning.

Ficar comes from the Latin *figicare* or *fixicare*, frequentative of *figere*, "to drive down," "to implant," "to fix," as in this expression of the irrevocability of speech: "Fixum et statutum est" (It is fixed and stabilized) (Cicero, *Pro L. Murena*, 62). In this sense it appears as a suffix in some French or English words, such as "crucifix," *crucifier*, "crucify." The use of *ficar*, which is translated as "to remain," more or less retains this sense of a verb of state: "There, well beyond the mouth of the river, . . . she remained (*ficou*), full of fear" (Guimarães Rosa, *Magma*). When the sense of remaining or fixing is transposed from the subject to the relation between the subject and its qualities, we have an attributive phrase. In the preceding example, we may simply remove the comma between the verb "remained" (*ficou*) and the complement "full of fear" to perform the transformation. The referent changes, obviously, since the attribute becomes the more important element of the predication: "*ela ficou cheia de medo* [*elle était remplie de crainte*]" (she remained full of fear). It is as though the attributes were affixed to the subject in a very concrete movement of being hooked onto it. Or rather, as though the subject froze momentarily in certain conditions, qualities, etc. We thus can understand the perfective aspect of the attribution, which results from this fixing.

II. The Aspectual Differences between *Ser*, *Estar*, and *Ficar*

H. Santos Dias da Silva speaks of the "concretizing necessity possessed by the Portuguese mind" (*Expressão linguística da realidade e da potencialidade*; cited in Quadros, "Da língua portuguesa"):

Deus é bom [God is good]: this is the only admissible phrase since God is an eternal subject independent of space and time, that is, non-limited; if we change the subject, and pick a limitable one or one in space or time, with a conditioned existence, the copula may be expressed by verbs other than *ser* [to be]: a) *o homem é bom*; b) *o homem está bom*; c) *o homem fica bom*.

By comparing the different ways of attributing the adjective "good" to the subject "man," we may see how the different verbs used for the copula transform the meaning of the sentence by their aspectual modulation:

A. *Ser*: "O homem é bom"

There is no problem translating it as "the man is good." This means that he is morally good, that he acts honestly, or that his flesh is tasty. His essence, his soul, or his consistency, his flesh—whatever pertains to him specifically, or universally if we speak of man as such—that is good. The verb *ser* in Portuguese expresses this idea of essential attribution.

B. *Estar*: "O homem está bom"

The verb *estar*, by contrast, denotes an instantaneous and momentary aspect, or an imperfect (*infectum*) one, especially if we add gerundives to make verbal phrases that are common and very concrete, such as *estar sendo*, "to be in the course of being." Translation requires a context in order to reconstruct the aspectual information. If the man in question was sick or convalescent, for example, we would translate *está bom* by "he is well." If we used "the man is good" for "o homem está bom" or "o homem está sendo bom," this would be because he is doing an action well, such as his work. If we wish to specify that he is good now, but that no one knows how he will be tomorrow, we may translate "he is keeping well" or "he is holding up." But this translation is not always accurate, as in the famous case of the minister and philosopher E. Portela, who, asked about his selection as the Brazilian minister of culture, declared: "*Eu nâu sou ministro, estou ministro*." The concision of the reply is untranslatable since to specify the aspect we would have to add two adverbial phrases: "I am not a minister eternally, I am only the minister at the moment," where this expression does not connote any political weakness.

With *estar*, it is rare to have a universal attribute. The verb *estar* can only speak of universals if it is a matter of conditions, with circumstantial complements, or adjectives determining dispositions, as if they were the circumstances of mind: "*O homem é um vivente que está sempre atento à própria morte*" (Man is a living being whose condition is to be constantly attentive to his own death). This does not prevent the verb, then, from paradoxically expressing the universal condition of the completion of each particularity, the existential condition of a being that is never completed as long as it is there—*está*—of a being at the moment of circumstance. Whence the importance of the verb *estar* in discussing the problems of existence in Iberian languages.

C. *Ficar*: "O homem fica bom"

Here the attribution has a perfective aspect. If the verb were in the perfect, *ficou bom* (he has been good), we would be back at the previous case: the verb *ficar* replaces the verb *estar* in the perfect without a problem. There would in addition be an idea of completed transformation, of becoming, which in French would either require a non-copulative verb: "*O homem ficou bom*," "*L'homme a recouvré la santé*" (The man regained his health); or a present perfect: "*Et moi, de penser à tout cela, j'ai été* [fiquei] *encore une fois moins heureux. . . . J'ai été* [fiquei] *sombre et malade et saturnien comme un jour où toute la journée le tonnerre se prépare mais n'arrive même pas le soir*" (And I, thinking about all that, I have been [*fiquei*] again less happy. . . . I have been [*fiquei*] somber and sick and saturnine like a day where thunder is being readied all day but never arrives even at night" (Pessoa, *Poemas*). But in Portuguese, if the sentence with *ficar* is in the present, it still seems incomplete—it requires circumstantial complements as mentioned above: Portuguese requires that the circumstances be precise since *ficar* can only perform its copulative task in a precise, definite, and concrete environment. Where, when, how? The categories of time, place, cause, manner, and so on must structure the circumstance of the attribution: "*O homem fica bom*" (the man is good) . . . "*quando educado*" (when he is well brought-up), . . . "*se está só*" (if he is alone) . . .

"*durante o verão*" (in the summer). We may see even more clearly the circumstantial and perfective aspect in the common expression "*ficar com alguém*," literally, "to have been with someone," which indicates a quick sexual affair, usually consisting of a single meeting.

Fernando Santoro

BIBLIOGRAPHY

Cicero. *Selected Political Speeches*. Penguin Classics, 1977.
Guimarães Rosa, João. *Magma*. Rio de Janeiro: Nova Fronteira, 1997.
Pessoa, Fernando. *Poemas de Alberto Caeiro*. 10th ed. Lisbon: Ática, 1993.
Quadros, António. *O espírito da cultura portuguesa*. Lisbon: Soc. De Expansão Cultural, 1967.
———. "Da lingua portuguesa para a filosofia portuguesa." In *Seminário de literatura e filosofia portuguesa (actas)*. Lisbon: Fundação Lusíada, 2001.
Santos Dias da Silva, Hernani. *Expressão linguística da realidade e da potencialidade*. Braga: Ed. Fac de Filosofia, 1955.

| FICTION

"Fiction" comes from *fingo* (in the supine, *fictum*), whose proper meaning is "to model in clay," like the Greek *plassô* [πλάσσω], which also refers to the activity of inventing fiction, as opposed to writing history. Fiction and plasticity are thus semantically linked: see ART, Box 2, HISTORY, Box 3, and PLASTICITY.

In addition, the proximity of *factum*, "fact" (from the Latin *facere*, "to make," Indo-European root **dhē-*, like the Greek *tithêmi* [τίθημι], "to place," which yields, for example, *faktura* [φακτυρα]; see FAKTURA), and *fictum* (from the Latin *fingo*, Indo-European root **dheig'h-*, which yields, for example, *figura*), consistently evokes the relation between fact and fiction, human fabrication (on the relation to Vico, see DICHTUNG, Box 1; Lacan, for example, in *L'étourdit* [in *Autres écrits* (Paris: Éditions du Seuil, 2001)], suggests the portmanteau spelling *fixion*). See also the Portuguese FICAR, which fixes predicates onto subjects.

I. Fiction, Language, and Truth

On the discursive status of fiction, see *DECEPTION*, DESCRIPTION, DICHTUNG (and as a complement, PRAXIS, on the singularity of Greek *poiêsis* [ποίησις] as the poet's "fabrication"; see POETRY), ERZÄHLEN, HISTORY. See also *RÉCIT* and *STYLE*.

More generally, for the relation to human practice, see *ACT*, PRAXIS, SPEECH ACT.

For the relation to truth and the real, see DOXA, ERSCHEINUNG, REALITY, RES, TRUTH; cf. *FALSE*, INTENTION, *LIE*, *THING*.

II. Fiction, Image, and Art

Fiction is related to images and the faculty of imagination; see IMAGE [BILD, BILDUNG, EIDÔLON], *IMAGINATION* [FANCY, PHANTASIA], MIMÊSIS.

For its relationships to artistic activity, see ART, BEAUTY; and regarding its invention, see ARGUTEZZA, CONCETTO, GENIUS, INGENIUM.

➤ GENDER, PEOPLE, SEX

FLESH

"Flesh" translates the French word *chair*, which comes from the Latin *caro, carnis*, which is connected with the Indo-European root **(s)ker-*, "to cut or share" (cf. Gr. *sarx* [σάρξ], "flesh," and *keirô* [κείρω], "I cut") and originally meant "piece of meat."

"Flesh" is one of the possible translations of German *Leib*, insofar as it is coupled not only with *Seele* (soul) but also with *Körper* (inert body). But unlike *Fleisch*, whose literal meaning is "flesh" in the sense of "meat," *Leib* is connected with *Leben*, "life." In the entry LEIB is found a study of the Latin, Greek, and Hebrew systems that constitute the matrices of this set and the meaning of their phenomenological reinvestment. To complete the German system, see ERLEBEN and GESCHLECHT. For the phenomenological and existentialist side, see DASEIN, EPOCHÊ, INTENTION. See also, on incarnation, BILD, BOGOČELOVEČESTVO, and OIKONOMIA.

➤ ANIMAL, GOD, *HUMANITY*, *LIFE*, SOUL

FORCE / ENERGY

FRENCH	*force, énergie*
GERMAN	*Kraft, Energie, Wirkung*
GREEK	*dunamis* [δύναμις], *energeia* [ἐνέργεια], *entelecheia* [ἐντελέχεια]
LATIN	*vis, virtus*

➤ *ACT*, EPISTEMOLOGY, MACHT, MOMENT, *POWER*, REALITY, STRENGTH, *VIRTUE*

In every European language, the word "force" (English) / *force* (French) / *Kraft* (German) underwent an abrupt transformation with the publication in 1847 of the dissertation "Über die Erhaltung der Kraft" [On the conservation of force] by Hermann von Helmholtz. More precisely, whereas in its vernacular usage, the word remained synonymous with power in the vague sense of the term (as in the expressions "having the force of law," "la forza del destino"), its conceptual usage, which until then had been just as vague, was suddenly, "by the force of mathematics," radicalized. After 1847 the word may have two translations: "force"/*force*/*Kraft* (directed action producing or tending to produce movement, in conformity with the laws of Newtonian dynamics), and "energy"/*énergie*/*Energie* (scalar, that is, nondirected, magnitude obeying a metaphysical principle of conservation, just like "matter"). The different manners of referring in German to the conservation of energy ("die Erhaltung der Kraft" / "die Konstanz der Energie" / "Energiesatz") are traces left by the difficult development of this notion.

I. "Force," "Energy," and "Conservation" in German-Language Physics

The word "energy" followed an evolution that was the reverse of the evolution of "force." It is derived from the Greek *energeia* [ἐνέργεια]; we know that Aristotle, in his study of movement, contrasts energy with potentiality and that this duality deeply marked the development of European philosophy and science until the beginning of the eighteenth century, when the word "energy" came to be used only in literature, "force" having supplanted it in discussions of the natural world.

■ See Box 1.

Nevertheless, this eclipse was of short duration: a century later, "energy" makes a noticeable comeback, in the precise physico-mathematical context of rational mechanics. In 1807, Thomas Young writes: "The term energy may be applied, with great propriety, to the product of the mass or weight of a body, into the square of the numbers expressing its velocity" (*A Course of Lectures*,1:59). The word acquires its definitive theoretical status with Helmholtz's 1847 essay "Über die Erhaltung der Kraft," in which it did not appear, but which nevertheless established its current definition. For an isolated system, it is the quantity that maintains a constant value throughout the physical processes taking place within. The meaning of the word in vernacular speech then expands, and it acquires a vague technical sense—even, in the last thirty years, a technocratic one. It is amusing to note that in this register of language that claims scientific exactitude, the sense of the word is completely denatured—as in the expression "energy economizing," which, strictly speaking, is a contradiction, since a quantity that by definition is "conserved" cannot be "economized."

This failure to abide by the basic rules of logic has the virtue of revealing a theoretical difficulty: the idea of conservation is one that is just as erudite as, if not more than, that of energy, and as such, it is inevitably misused by common language. The idea that energy might (and indeed must) be economized in the same way as water, money, or food, as though there were a risk of one day running out of it, is much more natural (and in agreement with the economic morality of the day) than that of a magnitude that is conserved, come what may. The comparison with commonly used French expressions such as "être à bout de force" (to have run out of strength) or "économiser ses forces" (to save up one's strength) shows that the interplay between *force* and *énergie* is actually a three-word game, the rules of which are set by *conservation*. It would not be possible to study the pair of *force*/*énergie* (or *Kraft*/*Energie*) independent of each word's constitutive relation to the word *conservation* (*Erhaltung*). Once this is established, a significant difference immediately appears between English and French on the one hand (along with the other Latin-based languages), and German on the other: although the word *conservation* was not affected by Helmholtz's 1847 article, the word *Erhaltung*, usually translated in French and English as "conservation," fell out of use (as a scientific term), replaced by *Konstanz* by Helmholtz himself in 1881, in the edition of his *Wissenschaftliche Abhandlungen*. The completely German expression "die Erhaltung der Kraft" was changed by its own author into one that he judged to be better upon reflection. We may assess the difficulty presented by the idea of conservation/constancy in German by the fact that today, what the other languages call "conservation of energy" is simply called *Energiesatz* or *Energieprinzip* (law or principle of energy), a surgical way of resolving the question.

We may hypothesize, then, that the difficulties faced by the German language in speaking of "conservation of energy" come from the fact that the historical development of this notion was effected by German-speaking physicists: basically Gottfried Leibniz, who laid the foundation, and Helmholtz, who brought it to a conclusion that today seems as though it must be definitive. Because the conceptual difficulties posed by this notion were first expressed by Germans in their own

1

Dunamis, energeia, entelecheia, and the Aristotelian definition of motion

➤ ART, GOD, NATURE, PRAXIS, PRINCIPLE, TO TI ÊN EINAI, VIRTÙ

We find a common translation in dictionaries for *dunamis* [δύναμις] and *energeia* [ἐνέργεια], namely, "force": *dunamis* is rendered by "power, force" and *energeia* by "force in action, action, act" (both may be said, for example, of the force of a speech; cf. RT: Bailly, *Dictionnaire grec français,* s.v. *dunamis,* III, and s.v. *energeia,* II.2). The difference between these two "forces" is nevertheless a cornerstone of Aristotle's physical (*Physics,* esp. book 3) and metaphysical (*Metaphysics* Θ) terminology:

> The object of his inquiry is *dynamis* and *energeia, potentia* and *actus* in the Latin translation, *Vermögen* and *Verwirklichung* (power and realization) in the German, or also *Möglichkeit* and *Wirklichkeit* (possibility and reality).
>
> (Heidegger, *Aristotle's* Metaphysics Θ *1–3,* trans. Brogan and Warnek, 13)

Aristotle bases the study of physics as a science (*epistêmê theôrêtikê* [ἐπιστήμη θεωρητική], "theoretical science," *Metaphysics* E.1, 1025b18–28) on a few fundamental principles and definitions. Strangely, some remain obvious for us, whereas others, even canonical ones such as that of movement, have become literally unintelligible.

Nature, *phusis* [φύσις], with which the *Physics* is concerned, is defined by movement. All natural beings (*ta phusei onta panta* [τὰ φύσει ὄντα πάντα]), says Aristotle, have in themselves immediately and essentially a principle of movement and fixity (*archên kinêseôs kai staseôs* [ἀρχὴν κινήσεως καὶ στάσεως], *Physics* 2.1, 192b13–14): a tree grows, unlike the products of crafts like a bed or a coat (see ART)—it is a "self-mover." Self-motion in the Aristotelian sense does not necessarily imply, as it does for us, locomotion: *kinêsis,* namely, *kata topon* [κατὰ τόπον], according to the *pou* [ποῦ], the "where," is only for Aristotle a species of the genus *kinêsis* [κίνησις], movement in the wide sense (a genus that, in a very Aristotelian way, is named after the most important species). This movement (*kinêsis*) he also calls change, *metabolê* [μεταβολή], formed from *ballô* [βάλλω], "to throw," and *meta,* indicating a further place or time. Thus, as Heidegger says, "Umschlag von etwas zu etwas" (a change from something into something, in "On the Essence and Concept of Φύσις," trans. Sheehan, 191), movement or change includes, besides displacement:

—generation and destruction, *genesis kai phthora* [γένεσις καὶ φθορά], or

movement according to *ousia* [οὐσία], the "essence";
—alteration, *alloiôsis* [ἀλλοίωσις], movement according to *poion* [ποῖον], the "what";
—growth or diminution, *auxêsis kai phthisis* [αὔξησις καὶ φθίσις], movement according to *poson* [ποσόν], the "how much" (*Physics* 2, 192b14–16; 7.7, 261a27–36).

It is with the general definition of movement, given at the beginning of book 3, that we come across energy and potentiality, or, more literally, entelechy, *entelecheia* [ἐντελέχεια], and power, *dunamis.* Here is the celebrated definition, subject to so many glosses and such close scrutiny:

> hê tou dunamei ontos entelecheia hêi toiouton kinêsis estin [ἡ τοῦ δυνάμει ὄντος ἐντελέχεια ᾗ τοιοῦτον κίνησίς ἐστιν].

> We have distinguished in respect of each class between what is in fulfillment and what is potentially; thus the fulfillment of what is potentially, as such, is motion.
>
> (*Physics* 3.1, 201a10–11, ed. Barnes, 1:343)

We must weigh the ontological freight of this pair, potency and act. It constitutes in effect one of the four senses of being:

> "Being" has several meanings, of which one was seen to be the accidental, and another the true ("nonbeing" being the false), while besides these there are the figures of predication (e.g., the "what," quality, quantity, place, time, and any similar meanings which "being" may have), and again besides all these there is that which "is" potentially or actually.
>
> (*Metaphysics* E.2, 1026a32–b2, trans. Barnes)

Aristotle's physics is thus from the start metaphysical through and through. The first example of movement makes it possible to measure the distance with our kinetics:

> When what is buildable, insofar as we call it such, is in fulfillment, it is being built, and that is building.
>
> (*Physics* 3.1, 201a16–18)

It is the transition from power to act, the energy of the potency that deploys itself throughout the time of the actualization ("neither before nor after," 201b7), that constitutes motion, thus neither pure and inactive potentiality, nor the uncompleted result ("When there is a house [οἰκία], there is no

longer the buildable [οὐκέτ᾽ οἰκοδομητόν]," 201b11).

Movement is thus *energeia atelês* [ἐνέργεια ἀτελής], a putting to work that has not achieved its goal ("an act, but incomplete" or "imperfect," *Physics* 3.2, 201b32; cf. *Metaphysics* Θ.6, 1048b29) or *entelecheia atelês* [ἐντελέχεια ἀτελής], an incomplete fulfillment (*Physics* 8.5, 257b8–9). Aristotle thus uses the terms *energeia* (from *ergon* [ἔργον], "work," and its product, a faculty and its exercise; see PRAXIS) and *entelecheia* (from *telos* [τέλος], the "end" and goal; see PRINCIPLE) to refer to this progressive attainment of the end, the realization of self, which leads to rest. As noted at *Metaphysics* Θ.8, 1050a21–23:

> The *ergon* is the *telos,* and the *energeia* is the *ergon;* this is why the word *energeia* is made from *ergon* and tends to mean *entelecheia.*

J. Tricot translates:

> L'œuvre est la fin, et l'acte est l'œuvre; de ce fait aussi le mot *acte,* qui est dérivé d'*œuvre,* tend vers le sens d'*entéléchie.*

And Bonitz comments (RT: *Index aristotelicus,* s.v. *entelecheia*):

> Whereas *energeia* is the action by which something is led from possibility to the full and perfect essence, *entelecheia* refers to this perfection itself.

By contrast with physical substances (*hai phusikai ousiai* [αἱ φυσικαὶ οὐσίαι]), God, whose substance is only act or energy (*hê ousia energeia* [ἡ οὐσία ἐνέργεια]) (*Metaphysics* Λ.6, 1071b20)—more precisely, "energy of mind (*hê nou energeia* [ἡ νοῦ ἐνέργεια])" and hence "the best and eternal life" (b26–28; see UNDERSTANDING, Box 1)—is necessarily immobile: as the prime mover, he is "that which moves without being moved [*ho ou kinoumenon kinei* (ὃ οὐ κινούμενον κινεῖ)]" (1072a25).

For the same reason, in our sublunary world, *dunamis* is a sovereign and complex notion. It refers first, as early as Homer, to *potestas,* physical or moral force, the power of men or gods, political power. The term can also apply to the value of a word, the power of a number that is squared, armed forces, and then refers to what we could call an effective reality. But *dunamis* also means *potentia,* that is, a "not yet," a pure virtuality, this "potential Hermes that the sculptor perceives in the wood" (*Metaphysics* Θ.6, 1048a32–33), and *virtus*, a faculty ("when we call scientific even one who does not speculate if he has the faculty of speculation [*kai ton mê theôrêsai* (καὶ τὸν μὴ θεωροῦντα ἄν δυνατὸς ἦ θεωρῆσαι)]," 1048a34–35), which Aristotle discusses by way of its pairing with activity. *Potentia* thus touches *possibilitas*, the logical concept opposed to *adunaton* [ἀδύνατον], to impossibility in the sense of contradictory.

> That which is in actuality capable, however, is that for which nothing more is unattainable once it sets itself to work as that for which it is claimed to be well equipped.
>
> (*Metaphysics* Θ.3, 1047a24–26; see also, for analysis of the senses of *dunamis*, *Metaphysics* Δ.12)

The connection between physics, metaphysics, and logic at work in all aspects of human life, from politics to art, rests on this dynamic. But this dynamic is only itself dynamic, in motion, because *energeia* or *entelecheia* is *proteron* [πρότερον], "prior" to potentiality, or "first" with respect to it (*Metaphysics* Θ.8, 1049b5): in Aristotle, as Heidegger points out, we do not move from *potentia* to *actualitas*; according to the proposition that becomes possible with Latinization, "in order for something to be *real* . . . it must first be *possible*" (*Die Physis bei Aristoteles*).

On the contrary, the energy or the act must be already present to attract the power or the force; energy is more *ousia* than potentiality, just as God is with regard to the other beings—or the *morphê* [μορφή], "form," with regard to *hulê* [ὕλη], "matter," within the composite substance (*Physics* 2.1, 193b7–9).

This complex terminology, so subtly developed, related to a cosmology destroyed by modernity, nevertheless continues to evolve, notably through Leibnizian dynamics, coming to encode our new universe as well.

Barbara Cassin

BIBLIOGRAPHY

Aristotle. *The Complete Works of Aristotle*. Vols. 1–2. Edited by J. Barnes. Princeton, NJ: Princeton University Press, 1984.

Heidegger, Martin. *Aristoteles Metaphysik Θ 1–3: Vom Wesen und Wirklichkeit der Kraft*, Gesamtausgabe. Vol. 33: 1931 lecture course. Frankfurt: Klostermann, 1981. Translation by Walter Brogan and Peter Warnek: *Aristotle's Metaphysics Theta 1–3: On the Essence and Actuality of Force*. Bloomington: Indiana University Press, 1995.

———. *Die Physis bei Aristoteles*. Frankfurt: Klostermann, 1967.

———. "On the Essence and Concept of Φύσις in Aristotle's *Physics* B, I." In *Pathmarks*, edited by W. McNeill. New York: Cambridge University Press, 1998.

language, in words that necessarily were not scientific in origin, but borrowed from everyday language, they only remained truly meaningful in that language. The other European languages had to be satisfied with conventional translations—to which they were all the more entitled, as the mathematical formulation of the law of "conservation of energy" is itself utterly unambiguous. We may try to verify this hypothesis by showing that the focus on *Kraft* and *Erhaltung* gives rise, from the words' very usage in ordinary German, to peculiarities that the confrontation between "force" and "conservation" cannot suggest in English, let alone French. Thus, the ambiguities of the word *Kraft* are not, and never will be, rigorously the same as those pertaining to the French and English word "force."

II. The Indeterminacies of Physical Definitions of Force in the Mechanistic Tradition: Internal/External Conservation/Change

In the mechanistic tradition of the eighteenth and early nineteenth centuries, the meaning of the word "force" was subject to an indeterminacy of which physicists before 1847 were fully aware without being able to specify its exact nature (unlike us who were brought up under a strict distinction between the concepts of force and energy). It is particularly flagrant in the 1760 *Letters to a German Princess*, which Leonhard Euler devotes to the question of force (note that the author is a German writing in French, the language of scientific communication at the time):

> The sun and all the planets *are endowed with a* similar *virtue* of attraction by which all bodies are attracted. . . . If the body of the Earth were larger or smaller, the gravity or weight of bodies would also be greater or smaller. From which we understand that all the other large bodies in the Universe, like the sun, the planets, and the moon, *are endowed with a* similar attractive *force*, but one

which is greater or lesser depending on whether they are themselves larger or smaller.

> Le soleil et toutes les planètes *sont doués d'une* semblable *vertu* d'attraction par laquelle tous les corps sont attirés. . . . Si le corps de la terre était plus grand ou plus petit, la gravité ou la pesanteur des corps serait aussi plus grande ou plus petite. D'où l'on comprend que tous les autres grands corps de l'univers, comme le soleil, les planètes et la lune, *sont doués d'une force* attractive semblable, mais plus ou moins grande suivant qu'ils sont eux-mêmes plus ou moins grands.

> (Letters 53 and 55, trans. Hunter [emphasis added])

Force is thus a virtue, a property of bodies, a power that they possess because of their bodily nature itself. Force is thus a property of matter.

The question therefore arises of what the nature of this power possessed by matter is, how it is exercised, how it is manifested, what its effect is, how it is expressed. Note first of all the confusion of the French language, which stutters and is at a loss for words on this point. It would not be the same in German, where the word *Kraft* is unmistakably associated with *wirken*, *Wirkung* (simply look at the corresponding entries in any German dictionary: *Kraft* defines *Wirkung* and *Wirkung* defines *Kraft*). In other words, the German language has a word for referring to the actualization of a power, a force, and this word is lacking in Latin-based languages. The response given by Euler to the question of the determination of the power that must be associated with the word "force" ("a term in common use, although many by whom it is employed have but a very imperfect idea of it") is simple (Letter 76, trans. Hunter): "We understand by the word force whatever is capable of changing the state of a body." (Euler is not clear in this passage, but the state at issue is that of motion, in conformity with the Newtonian doctrine he is promulgating.) We need not seek far: the important word here is "change." "Change," which is the opposite of . . . conservation.

However, to conserve, "conserve itself in the same state, whether rest or motion," is another quality of bodies (unless it is the same one, a question that is only dealt with in 1916 with the theory of general relativity), also related to their bodily natures, which is called "inertia," but which, for Euler, cannot be identified with force without violating language, since it is "rather the contrary," by virtue of the earlier definition of force. Moreover, inertia exists in the body itself (it is *insita*, according to Isaac Newton's adjective), whereas force, as Euler understands it (what Newton calls *vis impressa*), is necessarily external to the body whose state it changes:

> Each time a state of a body is changed, we must never seek the cause in the body itself; it always exists outside the body, and that is the correct idea we must have of a force.

> Toutes les fois que l'état d'un corps est changé, il n'en faut jamais chercher la cause dans le corps même; elle existe toujours hors du corps, et c'est la juste idée qu'on doit se former d'une force.

> (Letter 74, trans. Hunter)

It is plain that the concept of force described by Euler, a defender of Newtonian ideas, is much more complex than what the simplified teaching of Newtonian mechanics suggests: it is first and foremost a power of bodies, which they exercise on other bodies. It is certainly important that this power is directional, and thus that force in this case is mathematically represented by a vector, but this is secondary, in the sense that this is not part of the definition—it results from Newton's second law, which establishes that the power in question has the effect of modifying the quantity of movement, a directed magnitude.

Let us return to Euler and the "correct idea" that must be formed of a force, in virtue of which he is against Leibniz and the system of monads:

> It is false that the elements of matter, or monads, if there are any, are endowed with a force for changing *their* state. It is rather the opposite which is true, that they have the quality of conserving themselves in the same state.

> Il est faux que les éléments de matière, ou les monades, s'il y en a, soient pourvues d'une force de changer *leur* état. Le contraire est plutôt vrai, qu'elles ont la qualité de se conserver dans le même état.

> (Letter 76, trans. Hunter)

The controversy between Newtonians and Leibnizians is thus over the effect of "force," not its existence as a power of bodies. The question is whether a force is capable of changing the state of the body possessing it, or only that of other bodies to which it is external.

> I say therefore something which will seem strange, that the same faculty of bodies by which they attempt to conserve themselves in the same state is capable of providing forces which change the states of others.

> Je dis donc ce qui paraîtra bien étrange, que la même faculté des corps par laquelle ils s'efforcent de se conserver dans le même état est capable de fournir des forces qui changent l'état des autres.

> (Letter 76, trans. Hunter)

The question is thus twofold, or repeated, dealing with two pairs of opposites: internal/external and conservation/change.

Should we, then, like Euler, suppose that the causes of changes of states in bodies are external to them, and thus consider only forces that are necessarily external? (Newton also does so to some extent; though he does not hesitate to speak of *vis insita* with regard to inertia, he nevertheless specifies that a body only exercises this internal force if another external force, *vis impressa*, attempts to make it change its state of motion.) This conception held sway for two centuries, despite the logical difficulties that Euler modestly characterizes as strange, and that are the source of its demise. We know that the strangeness in question disappears once we admit that, as in general relativity, inertia and gravitation are two aspects of a single phenomenon: the interaction of bodies in a space that is itself considered a physical entity. For a modern physicist, after 1916, "force" is synonymous with "correlation." As Hermann Weyl writes, "Force is the expression of an independent power that connects the bodies according to their inner nature and their relative position and motion" (*Philosophy of Mathematics and Natural Science*, trans. Helmer, 149).

Or, should we think with Leibniz that bodies can change their state as the effect of an internal cause, to which it would also be fitting to apply the concept of "force"? The fact that this conception, that of monads, is closer to the modern notion of force—insofar as it implies that a body only exists to the extent that it is related to others, and that it does not exempt itself from space—does not make it superior with regard to what concerns us here, namely the evolution of the word "force"/*force*/*Kraft*. It is interesting rather because it leads naturally to the question of conservation, which we said earlier was intrinsically related to that of force. Indeed, in a conception where the change by which the effect of force is measured affects the state of all bodies, it becomes crucial to look for what remains constant in all this change. Before going further into the examination of what meaning must be given to the word "conservation," we should note that it does not appear explicitly in Newton. The question of whether the idea is there implicitly, hidden in the consequences of the "third law of motion," which states that to every action there corresponds an opposite reaction, is still debated today. We shall stick here, for once, to the "facts": the word does not appear in Newton. We shall restrict ourselves then to examining its meaning where it does appear, namely in the Leibnizian tradition.

III. The Leibnizian Metaphysics of Force: Force and Substance

A. *Vis* or *virtus* and act

"Force" is not subject in Leibniz to the same type of definition as that given by Newton or Euler. The word does not refer to a physical phenomenon characterizing "bodies," but to a metaphysical concept, aimed at clarifying the metaphysical notion of "substance":

> I will say for the present that the concept of forces or powers [*vis* or *virtus*], which the Germans call *Kraft* and the French *la force*, and for whose explanation I have set up a distinct science of *Dynamics*, brings the strongest light to bear upon our understanding of the true concept of substance.
>
> Je dirai que la notion de *vis* ou *virtus* (que les Allemands appellent *Kraft*, les Français *la force*), à laquelle je destine pour l'expliquer la science particulière de la *Dynamique*, apporte beaucoup de lumière à la vraie notion de substance.
>
> ("De la réforme de la philosophie première et de la notion de substance" [1694], trans. Loemker)

Because it is so intimately related to "substance" (etymologically, what lies beneath, what is preserved), force is related to the notion of conservation from the start. However, nothing proves that this conservation is of the same sort as that which, according to Newton, characterizes the state of motion of a body in which no external force is being exercised. In any case, this conservation is not static at all; it is not an inertia, a passive resistance (which is only active if a *vis impressa* is opposed to it). Force, for Leibniz, is above all and essentially active: "It contains a certain act or entelechy and is intermediate between the faculty of acting and action itself." It is a "power of acting," inherent to any substance, such that "some act is always coming from it." This is where, as already noted, an essential difference with force in the Newtonian sense lies (besides the fact that force is related to "bodies" for Newton, but to "substances" for Leibniz).

B. Force and action, *Wirkung*

The word "act" appears in Leibniz as indissociable from the notion of force. It is clearly borrowed from the scholastic tradition. However, it is noticeable that, in this text as in others, Leibniz makes a free use of it, playing with its cognates: *action*, *agir*, terms borrowed from ordinary language. It is thus not surprising to see a notion (destined for great things in mathematical physics) appear under the name of *action* over the course of the development of Leibnizian dynamics—as, for example, in the title of an opuscule in 1692: "Essai de dynamique sur les lois du mouvement, où il est montré qu'il ne se conserve pas la même quantité du mouvement, mais la même force absolue, ou bien la même quantité de l'action motrice" [Essay in dynamics on the laws of motion, in which it is shown that the same quantity of motion is not conserved, but rather the same absolute force, or the same quantity of moving action]. *Action*, however, is the translation of *Wirkung*. The translation is necessarily imperfect, since there is no strict equivalent of *Wirkung* in French, but it does have the merit, for a German-speaking philosopher writing in French, of introducing the concept of action as "naturally" related to that of force. It goes without saying that this link between the words *Kraft* and *Wirkung*, insofar as it rests on an implication, a translation of undertones, is not in the least obvious for a French-speaking reader. Subsequent generations of French-speaking mathematical physicists wondered why *action* (appearing in technical expressions such as the principle of least action, quantum of action, and so on) bears this name, and accepted it as a convention. This lack of obviousness of the link between *action* and *force* (being strong, *fort*, is neither necessary nor sufficient for acting) is probably due to the fact that French has only one word, *force*, where German—and English, thanks to its joint Latin and Saxon origins—has *Kraft* and *Stärke* ("force" and "strength"), which allows it to distinguish between power and vigor (see STRENGTH).

Nevertheless, action (or moving action) is defined by Leibniz as a double product: product of the "formal [or essential] effect" of movement—which itself "consists in what is changed . . . that is, in the quantity of mass that has been displaced and in the space, or the length by which this mass was transferred"—and the speed with which the change takes place. Leibniz has no trouble justifying the fact that the formal effect is not by itself sufficient for characterizing the action (in the sense of *Wirkung*) of the absolute force on the basis of everyday language (French this time, however): "It is clear that that which produces the same formal effect in less time acts more." As to why the action is what gives the measure of absolute force, bringing in speed and even dynamics, rather than the formal effect, which is outside of time, purely static, Leibniz, appealing to the argument he has used countless times according to which matter is not reducible to its extension, explains it thus: "The formal effect consists in the body in motion, taken by itself, and does not consume the force at all." Without entering into the details of this argument, which would require saying more about Leibnizian dynamics, let us simply note the verb used here: *consumer*, to consume—the force is consumed. And Leibniz continues: the action, unlike the formal effect, consumes force—in perfect conformity with the association suggested in German between *Kraft* and *Wirkung*.

C. Maintaining force

Here is where an "axiom of higher philosophy" comes in, which "cannot be geometrically demonstrated," and which, for this reason, would today naturally be described as "metaphysical": "The effect is always equal in force to its cause, or, what is the same thing, the same force is always conserved" (Leibniz, *Theodicy* [1710], 3.346). This is an expression of the principle of congruity, "that is, the choice of wisdom." Let us make this choice, and remember that force is consumed. In order for it to be preserved, it must, like a flame, be maintained. It must be watched over (as in the ritual expression "Gott erhält die Welt"), as an obligation ("Die Selbsterhaltung als Pflicht" [Schiller]), and we must contribute to its maintenance, as we would a dancer or a gigolo; we must conserve it in the same sense as museum curators; in sum, we must act, be active, inject enough action into it. In order for force to be conserved, there must, as Leibniz says, "be during this hour as much motive action in the universe or in given bodies, acting only on each other, as there would be during any other hour we might choose."

Passing by way of action thus makes it possible to specify what we must understand by *conservation* in Leibniz; it is simply the translation of *Erhaltung* in French; *entretien* (maintenance) would probably have been better.

IV. *Die Erhaltung der Kraft*: From Conservation to Constancy and from Force to Energy

When the young Helmholtz (he was 26, not long finished with his studies) uses the word *Erhaltung* in 1847, he places himself, knowingly or not, willingly or not, directly in line with the Leibnizian tradition. Not that he was Leibnizian: like all of his contemporaries, he was firmly convinced of the validity of the Newtonian conception of movement and the operational character of Newton's laws. However, according to Max Planck (*Das Prinzip der Erhaltung der Energie*), the idea—Cartesian in origin but amply used and illustrated by Leibniz—that there is a fundamental entity preserved in all physical processes, from which all movement may be derived, was a commonplace in the German mechanistic tradition:

> As long as there was no clear notion connected with the word "Kraft" any dispute over the quantity of this "Kraft" was without a proper theme. Yet it must be admitted that this dispute had a much deeper content at its foundation; for, the parties to the dispute were to some extent united, even if they did not express this very clearly and often, as to what they wanted to understand under the word "Kraft." Descartes as well as Leibniz, had certainly some, even if not very precise, notion about a principle, which expresses the unchangeability and indestructibility of that from which all motion and action in the world emanates.

> (Cited by Elkana, *Discovery of the Conservation of Energy*, 98)

In sum, the idea of conservation (in the sense of *Erhaltung*) was tucked away in everyone's minds, even when the reference to Leibniz (or René Descartes) had been forgotten. In these conditions, it is not surprising that Helmholtz titled his dissertation "Über die Erhaltung der Kraft"—especially since, despite his young age, Helmholtz had already worked for seven years in the domain of physiology, where the idea of an entity from which the mechanical powers of a living organism are derived, as well as what we may call its vital heat, was defended, among others, by Justus von Liebig. The even vaster idea that the phenomena of nature could all be reduced to a single "force," an idea developed by Kant in the *Metaphysical Foundations of Natural Science*, though not rigorously synonymous with that of conservation, is nevertheless close to it, insofar as both presuppose a unity of the physical world that would be confirmed by the existence of a conserved quantity.

Helmholtz, whose ambition was thus to show that the phenomena known at his time could be unified under the aegis of a conserved entity, proceeds in order from the simplest to the most complex. It is therefore utterly natural that he titles the first section (of six) of his essay "Conservation of Living Force [*lebendige Kraft*]." This magnitude, as everyone knew indeed since Leibniz, is conserved in elastic collisions between bodies, which may be considered the simplest case of a physical phenomenon. Helmholtz then proceeds, in section 2, to a generalization of the first section and shows that, in the more complicated case of a body that moves from one position to another in the course of its movement, it is possible to establish an equivalence between the variation of what we call today its kinetic energy (product of the mass by the square of the velocity) and another magnitude Helmholtz calls "the sum of the forces of tension [*Spannkräfte*] between these two positions." More precisely, the variation of kinetic energy is equal to the *opposite* of the sum of the forces of tension, where that "sum" (today we would say "the definite integral") can itself be expressed differentially, and hence as a change in a certain magnitude. It goes without saying that this "force" of tension does not have the dimension of a Newtonian force, since it has the status of what we would now call "work," which is itself the product of a Newtonian force by a displacement. This hardly bothers Helmholtz, as, like his contemporaries, he is used to giving the word *Kraft*, in a general context, the sense of power, a quantity that is poorly defined but scalar in nature, and in a Newtonian context, the sense of a directed action, hence vectorial in nature.

The important point here is that the equation derived does not deal with two magnitudes but with their variations between a certain initial state and a certain final state; and these variations have opposite signs. Yet, if two magnitudes undergo in a certain process equal changes of opposite sign, this is because their sum does not vary; it remains constant. Helmholtz gives this sum the name *Kraft*, which is fully justified by the procedure of generalization from *lebendige Kraft*, to which he has just appealed. However, can we call this second section *Erhaltung der Kraft*, as he does, without twisting the meaning of *Erhaltung*? The entity that he has just identified as *Kraft* is not conserved, in the sense of being maintained; it is or remains constant, in the sense that it undergoes no variation, which is not the same. Helmholtz's force, from this point of view, is closer to matter, which remains self-identical even when it undergoes transformations, than it is to Leibnizian living force, for which the word *Erhaltung* was perfectly adequate. This comparison with matter that takes various forms (solid, liquid, gas) while remaining basically constant is in fact pursued by Helmholtz in the last four sections of his essay, where he studies in succession the "force-equivalent" of heat, electrical processes, magnetism, and electromagnetism, before concluding with a few words concerning physiological processes. Throughout this part of the 1847 essay, the governing idea is that of conversion—conversion of one form of energy into another—which the word *Erhaltung* does not convey at all. It is thus appropriate that in 1881, Helmholtz replaces it with *Konstanz*, doubtless more exact.

We might think that, on the other hand, the simultaneous transformation of *Kraft* into *Energie* does not correspond to any correction of meaning, and that it is purely conventional. After all, Helmholtz is only giving a different name to the magnitude whose conservation he had demonstrated in 1847 in order to avoid the confusion of two different magnitudes: the scalar magnitude updated by Helmholtz, and Newtonian force, a vectorial magnitude. It is not certain that this name change only follows considerations of convenience. Perhaps we might think that the peculiar construction of the German language in fact plays an essential role. This construction is indeed such that in *Erhaltung* we clearly hear *halten*, which is why Helmholtz could not keep it to refer to the process by which a certain magnitude keeps the same value. However, it is just as impossible, given the almost cliché expression of *Erhaltung der Kraft*, to reserve *Kraft* to refer to this new magnitude that remains constant. *Kraft* is inevitably associated in Helmholtz's mind, and in those of his contemporaries, with *Erhaltung*, and it was impossible for him to speak of the constancy of force (*Konstanz der Kraft*). *Kraft* had to disappear along with *Erhaltung*.

Françoise Balibar

BIBLIOGRAPHY

Elkana, Y. *The Discovery of the Conservation of Energy*. Cambridge, MA: Harvard University Press, 1974.

Euler, Leonhard. *Letters of Euler to a German Princess, on Different Subjects in Physics and Philosophy*. Translated by H. Hunter. 2nd ed. London: Murray and Highley, 1802.

Helmholtz, Hermann von. *Epistemological Writings: The Paul Hertz / Moritz Schlick Centenary Edition of 1921, with Notes and Commentary by the Editors*. Translated by M. F. Lowe. Dordrecht, Neth.: D. Reidel, 1977.

———. "Über die Erhaltung der Kraft." In *Wissenschaftliche Abhandlungen*, 1:12–85. Leipzig: J. A. Barth, 1895. First published in 1847.

Leibniz, Gottfried Wilhelm. "De la réforme de la philosophie première et de la notion de la substance." First published in 1694. In *Œuvres choisies*, edited by L. Prenant. Paris: Garnier Frères, 1939. Translation by Leroy Loemker: "On the Correction of Metaphysics and the Concept of Substance." In *Philosophical Papers and Letters*. Dordrecht, Neth.: D. Reidel, 1970.

———. *Essay on Dynamics*. In *Leibniz and Dynamics: The Texts of 1692*. Edited by P. Costabel. Translated by R.E.W. Maddison. Ithaca, NY: Cornell University Press, 1973.

———. *Theodicy: Essays on the Goodness of God, the Freedom of Man, and the Origin of Evil*. Edited with an introduction by Austin Farrer. Translated by E. M. Huggard. New Haven, CT: Yale University Press, 1952.

Planck, Max. *Das Prinzip der Erhaltung der Energie*. Leipzig: J. A. Barth, 1913.

Weyl, Hermann. *Philosophie der Mathematik und Naturwissenschaft*. 4th ed. Munich: R. Oldenbourg, 1976. First published in 1927. Translation by O. Helmer: *Philosophy of Mathematics and Natural Science*. Princeton, NJ: Princeton University Press, 1949.

Young, Thomas. *A Course of Lectures on Natural Philosophy and the Mechanical Arts*. 2 vols. London: Taylor and Walton, 1845.

FORM

"Form" comes from the Latin *forma*, itself possibly borrowed, by way of Etruscan, from the Greek *morphê* [μορφή], which means "form, beautiful form" and concretely refers both to the mold and to the shape of the resulting object, whether the word concerns arts and techniques (the form of a shoe, the plan of a house, the frame of a painting), norms (a legal formula, the imprint on a coin), or speech (a grammatical form, a stylistic device). The term is especially plastic in French, as in Latin, since it was able to serve to translate the Greek words *eidos* [εἶδος], "idea" (in contrast to *eidôlon* [εἴδωλον], "image") or "form" (in contrast to *hulê* [ὕλη], "matter"); *morphê* [μορφή], "aspect, contour"; *schêma* [σχῆμα], "shape, manner of being"; *ousia* [οὐσία], "essence"; *to ti esti* [τὸ τί ἔστι] and even *to ti ên einai* [τὸ τί ἦν εἶναι], "quiddity"; *paradeigma* [παράδειγμα], "model"; or *charaktêr* [χαρακτήρ], "mark, distinctive sign."

I. Physical and Metaphysical Aspects

The article SPECIES compares the collection of Latin and Greek networks related to "form." Complementary consideration

appears under ESTI and TO TI ÊN EINAI, regarding the more Aristotelian terminology of ontology (see also FORCE, Box 1).

On the relation between form, substance, and subject, see SUBJECT.

On "formal ontology," see INTENTION, REALITY, RES, and SACHVERHALT; cf. MERKMAL.

On the relation between form and phenomenon, see ERSCHEINUNG, cf. AESTHETICS, PERCEPTION, REPRÉSENTATION, SUBLIME.

II. Aesthetic Aspects

For the relation, essential to Platonic ontology, between form-model and image-copy, see EIDÔLON (see *IMAGE*) and MIMÊSIS.

Besides SPECIES, see also CONCETTO, Box 1, DISEGNO, PLASTICITY; cf. ART.

III. Forms and Formalism

For the notion of "form" in grammar, see WORD, II.B and Box 2); for "form" in rhetoric, see *STYLE, I.*

On logical formalism, see especially IMPLICATION.

On legal formalism, see especially LAW and RULE OF LAW.

On moral formalism, see SOLLEN; cf. MORALS, WILLKÜR.

IV. Form and Gestalt Theory

For the study of psychological theory centered on the notion of "form," see STRUCTURE.

➤ *DEFORMATION*

FRENCH
Language Stripped Bare by Its Philosophers

➤ CIVIL SOCIETY, COMBINATION AND CONCEPTUALIZATION, COMMON SENSE, ENGLISH, ERZÄHLEN, EUROPE, GERMAN, GREEK, ITALIAN, LOGOS, PEOPLE, POLITICS, PORTUGUESE, *REASON*, RUSSIAN, SEX, *TO BE*, WORD ORDER

The establishment of thought in the French language took on a political meaning from the start: the privilege given to French does not derive from any intrinsic character of the language, but instead from the possibility of a universal and democratic philosophical communication. A language of women and the working class rather than of scientists, philosophical French relies on the belief that the act of thinking is open to everyone; its intimate relation with literary writing has no other reason behind it. Against a fascination with words and etymology, that is, with origin and substance, French sets the primacy of syntax, that is, of relation and assertion. This is why, once again, philosophy in French is political: between axioms and sentences, against consensus and ambiguity, French plants its certainty and its authority, which are also the source of its persuasive beauty.

In 1637 Descartes published *Discours de la méthode* in French anonymously. This was four years earlier than the publication of *Meditationes de prima philosophia* (*Meditations*), which was in Latin. Descartes never translated the *Discours* into Latin (that was done by Étienne de Courcelles in 1644), but neither did he persist in defending the Latin of the *Meditations*. He consistently said that the French translation by the Duke of Luynes, followed by that of the *Objections and*

Responses by Clerselier, which he thoroughly reviewed, could serve as a reference, or as Baillet said later, that it gave *un grand relief* of his thought (made it stand out clearly) and that it was extremely important to support reading by those who, "lacking the use of scientific language, would not fail to have a love and a disposition for philosophy" (*Vie de Monsieur Descartes*).

Descartes' linguistic strategy is unambiguous. It gives primacy to French, while nonetheless demonstrating to "Messieurs the deans and doctors of the sacred faculty of theology of Paris," the addressees of the prudent and defensive preface of the *Meditations*, that he knows his way around the official scientific language and that he can, like everyone else, praise the authority of the "name of Sorbonne" in decadent Latin.

Similarly, in the twentieth century, the major creative figures in philosophy in French—Bergson, Sartre, Deleuze, Lacan—all claimed the right to write in their native language, in sum the right to *freedom* of language, despite seeking at the same time to show the academy their technical competence. It says much about the strength of this initial intention, which established philosophy in accordance with an undisguised desire to write freely in the mother tongue without seeking an anarchistic break with scholarly institutions.

The problem is understanding what, for Descartes and his successors, the properly philosophical stake of this initiation of thought in the French language was, which was also the beginning of an openly declared equivocation, at the risk of being cursed and cast out by the learned, between the status of philosopher and that of a writer.

I. The Politics of French: The Democratic Communication of Philosophy

The whole point, however, whose consequences are still with us today, is that *the privilege given to French had nothing to do with the language as such.* Unlike what happened little by little—much later—with German and what had taken place in antiquity with Greek, the connection between philosophical technicality and the French language was not accompanied by any speculation about the philosophical characteristics of French. Even better: Descartes was profoundly convinced that the force of thought has nothing to do either with language or with rhetoric:

> Those with the strongest reasoning and the most skill at ordering their thoughts so as to make them clear and intelligible are always the most persuasive, even if they speak only low Breton.
>
> (*Discourse on Method*, part 1, in *Philosophical Writings*, vol. 1)

In other words, the transmission of thought is indifferent to language. It had, for Descartes, three extralinguistic criteria:

1. Reasoning—the ability to string together thoughts on the basis of indubitable axioms, the paradigm of which is geometrical writing, travels across languages universally.
2. The internalization (the "digestion") of ideas, which is their intimate clarification (Boileau's "that which is well-conceived") and whose utterance is only a consequence. But internal thinking, which is the intuition of immanent ideas, is nonlinguistic.
3. Clear and intelligible transcription, which, if criteria 1 and 2 are satisfied, may proceed in any dialect (Low Breton, for example) and persuade any mind.

This last item is of great importance. One of the reasons why, in Descartes's eyes, it would be disastrous to have to scrutinize the singularities of language reflects a principled universalism. No linguistic condition may be attached to the formation of true thoughts, nor to their transmission, nor to their reception. This is one of the meanings of the famous axiom about good sense, that it is "the most equitably shared thing in the world." This is in effect a universalist egalitarian axiom, as Descartes was careful to make clear: "[T]he power of judging well and distinguishing the true from the false . . . is naturally equal in all men," and as for reason, it is "whole in each person" (*Discourse on Method*).

The desire to express philosophy in French is thus related not to a consideration of an appropriation by French of the adequate expression of thoughts, let alone a speculative national doctrine concerning the coincidence of Being and language (German, Greek), but rather to a conclusion that is democratic in origin and concerns the formation and destination of thought. It is a matter of speaking the same language as "everyone"—in France, French—not that it will have special benefits either for concepts (which are themselves indifferent to language) or for the language itself (since French would not acquire any special privileges).

What is more, a point that seems empirical, though we have reasons to believe that it is not at all so, beginning with Descartes and linked to the choice of French, the conviction arose that philosophical discourse must be addressed to women, that the conversation of intelligent women is a means of approval or validation that is much more important that all the decrees of the learned. As Descartes marveled, "Such a varied and complete knowledge of all is to be found not in some aged pedant who has spent many years in contemplation but in a young princess whose beauty and youth call to mind one of the Graces rather than gray-eyed Minerva or any of the Muses" (Dedication to *Principles of Philosophy*, in *Philosophical Writings*, vol. 1). This moment of princesses is in reality a basic democratic intention that turns philosophical discourse toward discussion and seduction, toward Venus rather than Minerva, moving it as far away as possible from academic or scientific entrenchment. This intention will be repeated by all the notable French philosophers, who comprise a significant anthology: Rousseau, and also in his own way Auguste Comte, and then Sartre, as well as Lacan. All of them wished to be heard and admired by women and knew that they must be courted neither in Latin nor in the language of pedants.

We may say that, once philosophy in France became linguistically "nationalized," it followed the path of sociability, ease, and immediate universalism, rather than considering the materiality or the history of languages. It was neither a matter of their being rooted in some mode of original speech that had more or less been forgotten (traditional logic), nor of what rhetoric had imposed in terms of cadence or forms necessary for the deployment of thought (sophistic logic).

The thesis may be put simply: the reason philosophers, starting with Descartes, began writing in French is one that was in their eyes *political in nature*. It is only a matter of answering two questions: Where does philosophy come from? and Who is it for? The answer to the first is that philosophy has no particular single source and may come from anywhere by a free act of which any mind is capable; and to the second, that philosophy is aimed at everyone, which in the end means, as Comte says "systematically" (faithful here to Descartes and Rousseau and anticipating Sartre and Deleuze), at women and the working class.

To whom, further, is philosophy *not* addressed? To the learned, to the Sorbonne. Just writing in French is not enough to prove this. One must write this "modern" French, this writer's French, this literary French, which is distinguished from the "academized," or "correct," French transmitted in universities. Even a philosopher as calm as Bergson established himself with a style that, while certainly fluid and relaxed, was also loaded with comparisons, caught up in an imperious movement, and in the end resonant with the "artistic" language of the end of the nineteenth century. Nor did the learned fail to make fun of the beautiful ladies in furs hurrying to hear his lectures at the Collège de France. Compare more modern work: Lacan's Mallarméan prose, Sartre's novels, Deleuze's scintillation. And earlier, Diderot's dynamic force and Rousseau's invention of the Romantic sentence. And even earlier, Pascal's aphorisms. This is proof that fulfilling the democratic calling of philosophy requires placing thought into literary French, even into the written language "of the day." This carries a risk as well: that by a dialectical reversal familiar to French democracy, philosophy could become an especially aristocratic discipline, or at least snobbish. This is a risk to which the learned have always said that French philosophy would absolutely succumb, even if it meant, in order to excommunicate the "jargon" of a Derrida or a Lacan, claiming for oneself a Cartesian clarity—which is in reality only the foundation of a national link between philosophical exposition and literary writing, one to which Lacan and Derrida are attempting to be faithful as well.

II. Syntax versus Substance: French as a Thin Language

The real question concerns the consequences for philosophy of its being placed in the language of writers, which is itself a paradoxical effect of a choice that was democratic in spirit.

We have already said that a result of this choice was a sort of royal indifference to the philosophical particularities of the national dialect. Despite the most vehement importunities, nothing managed to impel philosophy in France toward the hard German labor of opening words up, deriving their Indo-European roots, entreating them to mean "being" or "community." Nothing ever *destined* the language to anything other than its immediate savor on the tongue and finally, to the bewitching ease, even when sophisticated, of its style. The principal rule, as Corneille said of the theater, is to please and not to ensure, with a slightly priestly gravity, that one's language is indeed the transcendent of thought's promise or the chosen medium of a shattering truth. France always laughed at what Paulhan called "proof by etymology."

Its pride does not take it in the direction of believing that French is philosophically evoked by its origins, but rather toward the idea, also in a way a national one though very different, that a language in the hands of a writer can say exactly what it wishes and, in addition, by its charm seduce and rally those to whom it is addressed. It is true—and even the most tortured French prose (Mallarmé, Lacan, the drugged Sartre of the *Critique de la raison dialectique*) is no exception (on the contrary)—that what is at stake is a transparency to the Idea, and not depth, or a complicity between the thickness of the language and its content.

This is because the latent universalism of any use of French, from Descartes to the present, rests entirely on the belief that the *essence of language is syntax*. Classical French, as it developed after Montaigne or Rabelais and was smoothed out and "compacted" by the joint efforts of policing by the precious salons and the centralized state, is a language that leaves little room for semantic ambiguity, since it subordinates everything to the most energetic, shortest, and most cadenced syntactic placement. This language—whose heart is in La Rochefoucauld's or Pascal's aphorisms, on one hand, and Racine's alexandrines on the other—presents itself to the philosopher as incredibly concentrated around verbs and liaisons, or successions. Unlike English, it is not a language of the phenomenon, of nuance, of descriptive subtlety. Its semantic field is narrow; abstraction is natural to it. Accordingly, neither empiricism nor even phenomenology suit it. It is a language of decision, of principle and consequence. Neither is it a language of hesitation, repentance, of the slow questioning ascent toward the dark and saturated point of origins. In truth, it is a language made impatient by questions that hastens toward affirmation, solution, the end of the analysis.

The perfect order that the (French) adherents of intuition, the perceptual life of creative disorder, imposed on their writings is notable. When Bergson rails against the discontinuous and abstract side of linguistic or scientific intelligence (but accurately; in fact, he is speaking about characteristics of French—its discretion, its abstraction), when he praises immediate data, the continuous élan, or unseparated intuition, he does so in a language exemplary in its transparency and order, where well-defined phrases abound and where all the distinctions, all the binary oppositions, are displayed with unique clarity. And conversely, when Lacan or Mallarmé seem to bring logical rationalism toward a staccato language that is violently discontinuous and whose meaning must be reconstructed, it is decisively the spirit of the maxim that wins out when it concentrates ("la Femme n'existe pas" [Woman does not exist; Lacan] or "toute pensée émet un coup de dés" [every thought sends out a throw of the dice; Mallarmé]) what was first submitted to the test of allusive syntax.

In the end, whether one accepts the vital continuum or semantic discretion, French imposes the syntactic primacy of relations over substances, of composite phrases over terms. No one escapes the order of reasons, since language itself conforms to it. Or at least that is the natural tendency, such that one who wishes to descend into vital intuition must persuade us in the opposite element of symmetrical constructions and grammatical subordinations.

French leads to the hollowing out of all substantiality. For, even if it pauses over the density of a noun (as may be the case for *morceau de cire* [piece of wax], or *racine de marronnier* [root of a chestnut tree], or *prolétaire* [proletarian]), it is in each case only to reduce, bit by bit, its visible singularity in a predicational and relational network so invasive that in the end the initial noun is only an example, easily replaceable, of a conceptual place. Thus Descartes reduces the piece of wax to geometrical extension; Sartre turns the root of the chestnut into the pure surging of a being-in-itself without qualities; and Comte's proletarian may just as well, if accompanied by the epithet "systematic," refer to any philosopher. Even for a thinker oriented toward singularity as much as Deleuze is, the pack of hounds is only a rhizome in motion, and the rhizome is a conceptual placeholder for any multiple, "horizontal" agency removed from the form of binary arborescence.

The rule of syntax in French does not really authorize descriptive delectation or the unsoundable becoming of the Absolute. It is a thin language whose saturation requires a long range of phrases supported by powerful propositional connections.

None perceived and practiced this better than Auguste Comte, no doubt because he wrote an extremely articulated and somewhat pompous language that schoolteachers later imposed on country folk for decades: a precise language no doubt, but one so brutishly declarative that it is always, like an acceptance speech for an awards ceremony, at the edges of ridicule. It is moving, as well, since it attempts (as is already Descartes's goal) to do literary justice to the speaker as well as to what is said. It is a language, in sum, that juxtaposes in philosophemes the speech of the flesh and that of the confession, an improbable bastard of Bossuet and Fénelon; for example, Comte writes:

Il serait certes superflu d'indiquer ici expressément que je ne devrai jamais attendre que d'actives persécutions, d'ailleurs patentes ou secrètes, de la part du parti théologique, avec lequel, quelque complète justice que j'aie sincèrement rendu à son antique prépondérance, ma philosophie ne comporte réellement aucune conciliation essentielle, à moins d'une entière transformation sacerdotale, sur laquelle il ne faut pas compter.

(It would no doubt be superfluous to indicate expressly here that I should never expect anything but active persecutions, obvious or secret, from the theological party, with which, despite my sincerely doing however complete a justice to its ancient predominance as I have, my philosophy in reality contains no essential conciliation, unless there should be a complete transformation of the priesthood, which we must not count on.)

(*Positive Philosophy*, preface)

It is essential for a philosopher writing in French to persuade the reader that he is coming face-to-face with a certainty of such compactness that it would be impossible to doubt what is being said without harming the subject, except (but then we would know that we are dealing with a *political* opposition) by rejecting the whole without examination. Philosophical French is a language of ideological conflict much more than of attentive descriptions, sophistical refutations, or infinite speculations. This is why Comte flanks every noun with an adjective that consolidates it, which is like its subjective bodyguard, just as he rigs out the sentence with robust adverbial padding (*expressément, sincèrement, réellement*), which is to the verbal edifice what the Doric columns are to a temple.

We would be wrong to believe that these are singularities exclusive to the half-mad Comte. When Sartre attempts, in the *Critique de la raison dialectique*, to explore the category of dynamic totality, and thus the apprehension of the movement of totalization and detotalization—when he must, in sum, return to the language what he calls "detotalized totality"—he spontaneously picks up the long, didactic, many-jointed sentences of positivism, given his need, he says, to express the dialectical components of the process all at once. Syntactic heaviness comes to unify semantic contraries at the risk of losing sight of the substantial or empirical singularity and of imposing a uniform rhythm on dialectic that bit by bit drains the historicity of the examples of their color and prosodic amplitude, leaving only, at a distance, the recognizable stamp of verbs and their sequences. To take a phrase from among a thousand (one concerning the workers' riots against Réveillon in April 1789):

Even if, from the depths of the initial and contagional march, negative unity as a future totality was already occasioning *being-together* [*être-ensemble*] (that is to say, everyone's non-serial relation to the group as a *milieu of freedom*) as a possibility which was perceived in seriality and which presented itself as the negation of seriality, the *objective* of the march was still indeterminate: it appeared both as seriality itself as a reaction to the situation, and as an equally serial attempt at *display*.

(*Critique of Dialectical Reason*, vol. 1)

There is in the language an almost heroic effort to make the trumpet of history sound again in the very midst of the conceptual tangle. And the pathos Comte gives for this purpose to adverbs and adjectives, as much as to the syntactic riveting, is here clearly accomplished by a vertiginous stretching of the verbal "dough," in the midst of which we hope that the reader will notice the illicit punctuation provided in the form of the italicized words. However, it is not true that this phrasing—bizarrely similar to continuous Wagnerian melody—pursues different goals from those to which Descartes assigned the philosophical use of French at the beginning. The point here is, again, an instrumental (and not a thematic) use of the language, whose unique purpose is to extract agreement from the readers as a result of their having seen the thought create and expose itself completely, according to its proper declarative force. What is more contrary in appearance to Sartrian totalization than Althusser's grand style, the militant chivalry of the pure concept placed under the ideal of science? And yet:

To speak plainly, it was only possible to pose to the practical political analyses Lenin gives us of the conditions for the revolutionary explosion of 1917 the question of the *specificity* of the Marxist dialectic on the basis of an *answer* which lacked the proximity of its *question*, an answer situated *at another place* in the Marxist works at our disposal, precisely the *answer* in which Marx declared that he had "*inverted*" the Hegelian dialectic.

(Althusser and Balabar, *Reading Capital*)

How we recognize the lengthening of the sentence, ordered to gather up the components of belief all at once, and the italics, blinking beacons for a navigation-reading that is utterly prescribed! How Althusser's clarity carries with it the same insistence as the Sartrian dialectic!

III. The Politics of French, Again: The Authority of the Language

Is this "Marxist" style, then? Political totalization? Let us say, rather, that in French *syntax politicizes every philosophical statement*, including ones that are at the furthest remove from any explicit politicization, including those that (Lacan) locate their crafty charm between puns (an important national tradition, aimed at mocking and discrediting semantic equivocation, which the French loathe) and Mallarméan formulas. Witness how the authority of speech, its foundational political desire, runs through this type of broken melody, even into the usage of one of the most unique resources of French, the imperious interrogative—the question that strikes down its opponent, after which, so far has the subject gone in the earthquake of his speech, there is nothing more to say. And it is not for nothing that this French is appealed to straightaway and as such in the sentence (in order to "translate" Freud's dictum: "Wo Es war, soll Ich werden" [Where the id was, the ego shall be]):

But the French translation says: "*là où c'était....*" Let us take advantage of the distinct imperfect it provides. Where it was just now, where it was for a short while, between an extinction that is still glowing and an opening up that stumbles, the I can [*peut*] come into being by disappearing from my statement [*dit*].

An enunciation that denounces itself, a statement that renounces itself, an ignorance that sweeps itself away, an opportunity that self-destructs—what remains here if not the trace of what really must be in order to fall away from being?

(Lacan, *Écrits*)

How beautiful that all is! It is persuasive beauty, which is more important for any French writer-philosopher than exactitude. Or rather, it is a secondary exactitude, which must be reconstructed inside the beauty and guided by it yet leave it behind, as one must comply with syntactic constraint in order to achieve, just at the end, the release of the Idea. Stylistic commonality often wins out over doctrinal or personal antipathy, as we see in the way Deleuze's vitalism is accentuated in the same way as its psychoanalytic adversary and in the way the same effervescent language is used to say that desire is a lack (Lacan) and that desire lacks nothing (the anti-Oedipal Deleuze–Guattari), since the aim is still, as with Sartre before, to hold opposite predications together in a grammatical formula, to make one fade into the next:

... objets partiels qui entrent dans des synthèses ou interactions indirectes, puisqu'ils ne sont pas partiels au sens de parties extensives, mais plutôt "partiaux" comme les intensités sous lesquelles une matière remplit toujours l'espace à des degrés divers (l'œil, la bouche, l'anus comme degrés de matière); pures multiplicités positives où tout est possible, sans exclusive ni négation, synthèses opérant sans plan, où les connexions sont transversales, les disjonctions incluses, les conjonctions polyvoques, indifférentes à leur support, puisque cette matière qui leur sert précisément de support n'est spécifiée sous aucune unité structurale ni personnelle, mais apparaît comme le corps sans organe qui remplit l'espace chaque fois qu'une intensité le remplit....

(... partial objects that enter into indirect syntheses or interactions, since they are not partial [*partiels*] in the sense of extensive parts, but rather partial ["*partiaux*"] like the intensities under which a unit of matter always fills space in varying degrees (the eye, the mouth, the anus as degrees of matter); pure positive multiplicities where everything is possible, without exclusiveness or negation, syntheses operating without a plan, where the connections are transverse, the disjunctions included, the conjunctions polyvocal, indifferent to their underlying support, since this matter that serves them precisely as a support receives no specificity from any structural or personal unity, but appears as the body without organs that fills the space each time an intensity fills it....)

(Deleuze and Guattari, *L'anti-Œdipe*)

There is an obvious consonance between the *énonciation qui se renonce* (the enuciation that is a renunciation) and the *disjonction incluse* (an inclusive disjunction), between the *conjonction polyvoque* (the polyvocal conjunction) and the *l'extinction qui luit encore* (the extinction that still gleams), as though the slope of language upon hitting an oxymoron to make the thought pivot won out over the taking up of a position. It is as though, lying in ambush behind the concept, an invariable La Rochefoucauld had the idea to fuse the aphorism and to *stretch* the electric arc of the thought between poles distributed ahead of time by syntactic precision in the recognizable symmetry of French-style gardens.

And it is not as though the French all think the same. Philosophy in French is the most violently polemical of all, ignoring consensus and even making little fuss over rational discussion, for, still opposed to the academy, it speaks (politically) to the public and not to colleagues. But this is because the French *really* speak the same language, which means that we appeal to the same artifices to give (public) power to our claims. And this identity is even stronger given that classical French, the only one that philosophy manages to speak despite the consistently abortive efforts to make it flow more wildly, only offers a restricted assortment of effects, all held in the primacy of syntax and univocity over semantics and polysemy.

Someone philosophizing in French is forced to place the concept and its heirs onto the procrustean bed of a sort of sub-Latin. One thing will be said after another, and there will be no verbal exchanges except those authorized by the grammar of sequences and the regulation of univocities.

We know of course (and this is a primary theme of this dictionary) that nothing peremptory can be said about languages that will not be disproven by some writer or poem or other. It is thus that rightly or wrongly we sometimes envy the power of German to lay out in an idolatrous semantics the depths offered by infinite exegesis. We also sometimes wish for the descriptive and ironic resources of English—this marvelous texture of the surface, the argumentation always circumscribed—which does not totalize anything since the grammar is never that of the here and now. And even the branching of Italian—when we stop thinking that it muddles everything at will and is running thirty different conversations at once, all erudite and mimetic, we admire its velocity and that when it affirms something, it keeps a clear eye on the other possible affirmation that a simple repentance over the sentence may bring to mind.

But this is not the style of French. We could show how Heidegger, despite the sometimes pious style of his interpreters and translators, becomes, in French, invincibly clear and almost monotonous; how the empirical sensitivity of English turns inevitably flat if the translator is not creative; and how the quicksilver web of Italian prose becomes nothing more than a discouraging chatter.

What French offers philosophy that is universal in character is always in the form of somewhat stiff maxims or badly nuanced derivations. Again, the latent style is that of a speech that aims to make an assembly, seduced, vote for someone without examining the details too much. One must accept this strength, or weakness. It enters into the composition of eternal philosophy, like that which, from the Greek source, retains mathematics rather than mythology, litigation rather than elegy, sophistical argumentation rather than prophetic utterance, democratic politics rather than tragic caesura.

It will always be said in French that "l'homme est une passion inutile" (man is a useless passion; Sartre), that "l'inconscient est structuré comme un langage" (the unconscious is structured like a language; Lacan), that "la schize ne vient à l'existence que par un désir sans but et sans cause qui la trace et l'épouse" (the *schize* only comes into existence through desire without a goal or cause which traces and espouses it; Deleuze and Guattari), or that "la philosophie est ce lieu étrange où il ne se passe rien, rien que cette *répétition* du rien" (philosophy is that strange place where nothing happens, nothing but this *repetition* of nothing; Althusser). And there will be no end to the examination of the consequences of these maxims, or to the presentation, before captive audiences, of other axioms and other syntactic networks.

Axiomatizing, deriving, and thereby even emptying speech of any individuality that sparkles too much, of any predication that is too colorful; purifying this speech, these excessive turns of phrase like repentances and uncertainties—these are the very acts of philosophy itself, once it orders its Idea in this material *place* that grasps it, runs through it: a language, *this* language, French.

Alain Badiou

BIBLIOGRAPHY

Althusser, Louis, and Étienne Balabar. *Reading Capital*. Translated by B. Brewster. London: Verso, 1998.

Althusser, Louis, Étienne Balabar, Roger Establet, Pierre Macherey, and Jacques Rancière. *Lire le Capital*. Paris: Maspero, 1965.

Baillet, Adrien. *Le vie de Monsieur Descartes*. Paris: Malassis, 2012. First published in 1691.

Comte, Auguste. *Cours de philosophie positive*. Paris: Hermann, 1975. Translation by Harriet Martineau: *The Positive Philosophy of Auguste Comte*, Ithaca, NY: Cornell University Library, 1896.

Deleuze, Gilles, and Félix Guattari. *L'anti-Œdipe*. Vol. 1 of *Capitalisme et schizophrénie*. Paris: Minuit, 1972. Translation by R. Hurley, M. Seem, and H. Lane: *Anti-Oedipus: Capitalism and Schizophrenia*. New York: Penguin Classics, 2009.

Descartes, Rene. *Œuvres complètes*. Edited by C. Adam and P. Tannery. Paris: Vrin, 1997. Translation by J. Cottingham, R. Stoothoff, and D. Murdoch: *Philosophical Writings of Descartes*. 2 vols. Cambridge: Cambridge University Press, 1985.

Lacan, Jacques. *Écrits*. Paris: Éditions du Seuil, 1966. Translation by Bruce Fink: *Écrits*. New York: W. W. Norton, 2007.

Sartre, Jean-Paul. *Critique de la raison dialectique*. Paris: Gallimard, 1960. Vol. 1 translation by A. Sheridan-Smith: *Critique of Dialectical Reason*. London: Verso, 2004; Vol. 2 translation by Q. Hore: *Critique of Dialectical Reason*. London: Verso, 2006.

GEFÜHL (GERMAN)

ENGLISH   feeling, sensation, sentiment, opinion
FRENCH   *sentiment*, *sensation*

➤ SENSE [FEELING], and AESTHETICS, BEGRIFF, COMMON SENSE,
CONSCIOUSNESS, GOÛT, *INTUITION*, MORAL SENSE, *PASSION* [PATHOS],
PERCEPTION

The German pair *Gefühl/Empfindung* is not parallel to the traditional distinction between *sentiment* and *sensation*. Today the use of *Gefühl* is mostly reserved for the sphere of feelings and emotions, more or less corresponding to the use of the English "feeling," whereas its companion, *Empfindung*, refers to both physiological sensation and feeling. This instability is no longer the source of any major philosophical difficulty. By contrast, analyzing the way in which the two terms were placed front and center, contrasted and debated in the eighteenth century, gives us a sort of X-ray of the vocabulary of the subject and of consciousness, from Wolff and Kant and his heirs through the writings of Johann Nicolaus Tetens. The philosophical stakes were at that time far greater than those pertaining to their English and French equivalents. From the theory of perception to that of moral sentiment, by way of the doctrines of consciousness as a feeling of self, the terms *Gefühl* and *Empfindung*, placed at the junction of the various anthropological, aesthetic, and psychological discourses, affect the whole of philosophical study.

I. *Gefühl/Empfindung, Sensation/Sentiment*, "Opinion," "Feeling"/"Sensation"/"Sentiment": The Specificity of the German Pair

Certain terms in French, English, and German, both common and philosophical, that express the difference between feeling and sensation, have, based on the variety of their uses, been highly unstable since the beginning of the modern period. In the case of contemporary French, the terms *sensation* and *sentiment* no longer overlap in meaning, as was the case in the classical period, when *sentiment* meant sensation, feeling, and opinion. Alongside this threefold division in meaning, there was also a properly philosophical usage of the term, both in Malebranche (in the sense of "internal sentiment") and in Pascal, in the sense of intuitive synthetic vision (to prophesize is to speak of God, not by external proof, but by internal and immediate *sentiment*, cf. *Pensées*, Lafuma 328). This usage is clearly laid out in the eighteenth century in the *Encyclopédie*'s article "*Sentiment*": it is the "intimate sentiment that each of us has of his own existence, and of what he feels in himself." *Sentiment* is "the first source and first principle of truth available to us," nor is it "in any way more immediate for us to say that the object of our thought exists with as much reality as our thought itself, since this object and this thought, and the intimate sentiment we have in ourselves, are really only ourselves thinking, existing, and having the feeling."

As for English, we find the same threefold division with "sentiment." Found in English since Chaucer, the word was also used as synonymous with "feeling," "sensation," and "opinion." On the other hand, the term's untranslatability in English comes mainly from the overdetermination of the word "sense," which runs from perception to feeling, reason, reasonableness, and meaning, and from which the concepts, through Hutcheson, Shaftesbury, and Hume through Bentham, of "inner sense," "internal sense," "inward sense," "common sense," and "moral sense" are derived. Coste, the translator into French of Locke's *Essay on Human Understanding*, did not run into any particular trouble over the translation of the English terms "sensation" and "sentiment." In the first case the term is identical in the two languages, and in the second we can go easily from the English "sentiment" in the sense of "mental feeling" to the French *sentiment*. Coste thus translates "due sentiments of Wisdom and Goodness" (bk. I, chap. 7, § 6) by "justes *sentiments* de la sagesse et de la bonté," and in bk. IV, chap. 1, § 4, "the first act of the Mind, when it has any sentiments of Ideas at all" by "le premier acte de l'esprit, lorsqu'il a quelque *sentiment* ou quelque idée." Similarly, Coste finds a parallel usage in English to the specialized philosophical (or metaphysical) usage in French. When Locke writes, for example, "I do not say there is no Soul in a Man because he is *not sensible of it* in his sleep" (bk. II, chap. 1, § 10), Coste translates this as "Je ne dis pas qu'il n'y ait point d'âme dans l'homme parce que durant le sommeil l'homme *n'en a aucun sentiment*."

In philosophical German the essence of these issues was concentrated on the pair *Gefühl/Empfindung*, whose differentiation was the object of a long conceptual inquiry set against a background of ambivalence. The two terms cannot be translated except on a case-by-case basis and respecting what is untranslatable about them, that is, taking account of the redistribution of their relations, which itself depends on the way in which the different German philosophical discourses used them, strategically, to mark out differences with regard to the common uses of words.

Indeed, as shown by Adelung's dictionary or Eberhard's *Versuch einer allgemeinen deutschen Synonymik* (Essay of general German synonymy), 1795, in the eighteenth century *Gefühl* and *Empfindung* were commonly considered synonyms and used more to refer to the perceptual immediacy of a representation. The two words were defined as "intuitive (*anschauend*) representations that participate in our sensibility (*Sinnlichkeit*) to a certain degree" (Eberhard, *Synonymik*, 1:119). And Johann Nicolaus Tetens notes in 1777 in his *Philosophische Versuche über die menschliche Natur und ihre Entwicklung* that "the words *Gefühl* and *fühlen* henceforth have a range of meaning almost as wide as that of the words *Empfindung* and *empfinden*" (1:167ff.). In doing so, he places emphasis simultaneously on the omnipresence of the two pairs of terms, on the difficulty of distinguishing them, and on the confusion reigning in their use.

Similarly, in his *Allgemeine Theorie der schönen Künste* (General theory of the fine arts), J. A. Sulzer begins the article "*Sinnlich*" in these terms:

> In fact, we call sensory (*sinnlich*) what we feel (*empfinden*) by the intervention of the senses external to the body; *but we have extended the meaning of the term* to what we feel (*empfinden*) in our bare interiority (*bloß innerlich*) without the action of the bodily senses, as for example in the case of desire, love, etc.

(Sulzer, *Allgemeine Theorie*, 408)

This admission of instability continuously accompanied the philosophical division of the two notions. Even in the most decisive works we still find many inconsistencies. It seems, for example, that from the start the terms *Gefühl* and *Empfindung* originate, philosophically speaking, in the field of *sensus*, whereas the related term *Rührung* (feeling, emotion), which in the eighteenth century was used commonly in both everyday and philosophical language, comes from the field of *tactus*, since *anrühren* and *berühen* both mean "to touch." Yet Baumgarten, for example, suggests translating *tactus* by *Gefühl* (*Metaphysica*, § 536) and not by its literal (and standard) translation of *Tastsinn*—sense of touch—whereas he himself uses *Tastsinn* and *Gefühl* indifferently for *tactus*. In any case, it is clear that the internalization of *Gefühl*, or its derivation from the intimate sphere of subjectivity, only comes later, thanks to a need for terminological clarification.

II. *Gefühl* and *Empfindung*: The Near Side of the Division between Receptivity and Reflexivity

A. The twofold meaning of *Empfindung* in the Wolffian system

In Christian Wolff's philosophical system the notions of experience and knowledge interact and complement each other against a Leibnizian background of preestablished harmony, insofar as Wolff does not distinguish between a logical system of knowledge based on the a priori metaphysics of scholastic origin and the principles of an empiricist reading of the world. In this framework *Empfindung* is the very source of experience and hence of knowledge; in order to have access to the true being of things, it is therefore enough simply to be attentive. The thesis of *Deutsche Logik* (chap. 5, § 1), according to which "it is by paying attention to our *Empfindungen* that we have experience of everything that we know [Wir erfahren alles dasjenige, was wir erkennen, wenn wir auf unsere empfindungen acht haben]," is mirrored in the *Deutsche Metaphysik* (§ 325): "The knowledge we achieve when we pay attention to our *Empfindungen* and to the modifications of the soul, we customarily call experience." If *Empfindung* is really untranslatable here, it is not because Wolff does not give equivalents; rather, it is because it refers to two philosophically sacred pairs: sentiment/sensation on one hand and sensation/perception on the other. Wolff thus writes in his *Anmerkungen zu den vernünftigen Gedanken von Gott, der Welt und der Seele des Menschen, auch allen Dingen überhaupt*:

> I have explained here [§ 220] what I mean by the word *Empfindung*, namely the kind of *perceptionum* [sic] that is called *sensationes* in Latin. And insofar as we consider these *sensationes* as modifications of the soul by which we are conscious of things that act on our *organa sensoria* [sic], we can call them in Latin *ideas rerum materialium praesentium*.

(Wolff, *Anmerkungen*, § 65)

The equivalence between idea and sensation becomes explicit here by way of Latin. The sensation caused by things comes to be confused with the act of consciousness; sensation is simply a thought:

> Thoughts that have their causes in the modifications of the organs of our body and that are excited by bodily things outside of us, we call *Empfindungen*.

(Wolff, *Deutsche Metaphysik*, § 220)

Wolff does not hesitate to establish the following inferences: having a thought is the becoming aware of a modification of the soul. Thus, becoming conscious of an effect of things external to the soul is a thought; thus sensations are thoughts. And he adds: thoughts of objects insofar as they are present to our soul. There is thus no difference between feeling and knowing, between *empfinden* in the sense of feeling and *erkennen* in the sense of knowing, and it is on this basis that Baumgarten is able to develop his aesthetics, conceived as a science of knowledge (*cognitio sensitiva*, see AESTHETICS). Wolff insists especially on the coincidence between modifications of things and those of the soul, on which point he considers himself in agreement with Aristotle, Descartes, and Leibniz, defending himself again and again against the accusations of Spinozism leveled at him. The syncretism between a form of empiricism and an abstract system assured of the absolute pertinence of logically derived truths leads him to give the name *Empfindung* to the widest philosophical extension: the same term can thus mean the natural irreducibility of sensation (our hearing cannot be affected by the noise of thunder, etc.: cf. *Anmerkungen*, § 69), a modification of the soul, and the fact that it is perceptible to us, thus conscious. *Empfindung* is thus the hinge between soul and world, and makes possible the distinction between *innerliche Empfindung* (internal *Empfindung*), when we consider *Empfindung* as it occurs in the soul, and *äußere Empfindung* (external *Empfindung*), when we consider *Empfindung* as caused by external objects (cf. Johann Friedrich Stiebritz, *Erläuterungen der Wolffischen vernünftigen Gedancken von den Kräften des Menschenverstandes* [Explanation of Wolff's "Reasonable Thoughts" on the forces of human understanding], § 101).

B. The truth of feeling

For Sulzer, who aims to reconcile theoretical and aesthetic thought, the division is no longer, as it is for Wolff, between internal and external *Empfindung*, but between *empfinden* and *erkennen*. Baumgarten's premise in favor of equal dignity for aesthetic or "sensible" knowledge and intellectual knowledge is radicalized in the form of a distinction between *empfinden* and *erkennen*, which is no longer a hierarchy but rather a division of labor. Whereas for Wolff *Empfindung* is a hinge between the I and the world, for Sulzer *empfinden* refers to the capacity to be affected by agreeable or disagreeable feelings and hence comes closer to emotion (*Rührung*). *Empfinden* thus falls unambiguously on the side of subjective knowledge and is contrasted with the objective pole of knowledge (*erkennen*). The article "*Sinnlich (Schöne Künste)*" of the *Allgemeine Theorie der schönen Künste* (1786) presents this topic well:

> We say that we know (*erkennen*), that we grasp (*fassen*), or that we understand (*begreifen*) something when we have the clear perception (*Wahrnehmung*) of its nature (*Beschaffenheit*), and we have a clear knowledge of the things we are capable of explaining, or whose natures we can describe to others. In the state of knowledge, there is something that comes to place itself before our minds (*Beym Erkennen schwebt also unserem Geist etwas vor*), or we are conscious of something that we consider different from ourselves, that is, from our power of acting, and we call this thing an object of knowledge. Conversely, we say that we feel (*empfinden*) something when we are aware of a modification within our power itself.

> (Sulzer, *Allgemeine Theorie*)

The goal of the argument is in fact to show by and with the terminology of knowledge that there is thought in feeling. In order to affirm the dignity of aesthetic thought established by Baumgarten, then, *Empfindung* must be distinguished, as feeling of oneself by oneself, from the constitution of an object of knowledge, which can only take place if we are "spectators of what takes place" (*Zuschauer dessen, was vorgeht*), whereas "in feeling we are ourselves the object in which the change takes place [*beym Empfinden sind wir selbst das Ding, mit dem etwas veränderliches vorgeht*]" (ibid.). This feeling of oneself by oneself will enter not only into the vocabulary of perception but into that of consciousness as well: "Every time we feel something, we are conscious of a change in ourselves [*bey jeder neuen Empfindung sind wir uns einer Veränderung in uns selbst bewußt*]" (ibid.). The radical difference established by Sulzer between feeling (*empfinden*), as a resonance of oneself in oneself, and knowledge (*erkennen*), as separation of the observing consciousness from the objects of knowledge, leads then to the construction of two spheres of equal dignity. In feeling perception "thinks." There is thus a "perceptual thought," a "thought of the senses" (*sinnliches Denken*, ibid.), contrasting with "speculative thought" (*das spekulative Denken*, ibid.). From the point of view of the distinction between *Gefühl* and *empfinden*, the novelty introduced by the problem of perceptual consciousness is that "sensible" thought (which Sulzer is careful to distinguish from that which, in feeling, is only the feeling of feeling) becomes in his terminology the "full feeling" (*das volle Gefühl*) of feeling (*Empfindung*). There is, therefore, at the same time, on the basis of the newly constituted aesthetics, a promotion of feeling to the dignity of knowledge and the persistence of a "mirror" conception of reflection and perception. Thought is found in the folds of feeling.

We may go further and elevate the dignity of this thought-in-feeling, to the point of affirming that it is a cogito. This is indeed what G. E. Schulze does when he speaks in his *Grundriss der philosophischen Wissenschaft* of a *Gefühl der Existenz*, which he numbers among the "*Gefühle des inneren Sinnes*" (feelings of an internal sense), and which he conceives of as an equivalent to the cogito (*Grundriss*, vol. 1).

This equivalence between feeling and knowledge is found again in Herder, who appeals to Wolff in his *Kritische Wälder* to define aesthetics as a "science of the feeling of beauty, that is, of sensible knowledge [*eine Wissenschaft des Gefühls des Schönen, oder nach der Wolffischen Sprache, der sinnlichen Erkenntnis*]." Radicalizing the Wolffian claim in a new way, Herder does not balk at the notion of a "feeling of mind" (*geistige Empfindung*) or at erasing any distinction between *Empfindung* and knowledge, as well as between *Empfindung* and *Gefühl*:

> No knowledge is possible without *Empfindung*, that is without a feeling (*Gefühl*) of good and evil. . . . The knowledge of the soul is thus unthinkable without the feeling of well-being or doing badly, without the deeply intimate and intellectual sensation of the truth and of goodness.

> (Herder, "Vom Erkennen," 236ff.)

III. From Tetens to Kant: The Filtering of the Differences between *Gefühl* and *Empfindung* through the Theory of Faculties

In the philosophy of Johann Nikolaus Tetens and in Kantian critical philosophy, the link between empiricism and abstraction is called into question, making possible a reflection on the difference between *Gefühl* and *Empfindung*. Tetens, relying, it seems, on sensualist principles of Lockean origin, filters *Gefühl* and *Empfindung* by emphasizing that the impingement of the external world on sensation is only ever a starting point and that we must therefore draw a distinction between the primary matter of sensation and its becoming-representation. To say that our ideas come from sensations for him means only that "sensations (*Empfindungen*) are the primary matter (*Grundstoff*) that is available to reason for representation, thinking, and ideas, the matter from which the activity of thought makes them come forward" (*Über die allgemeine spekulativische Philosophie*, 49). Similarly, Kant says in the *Critique of Pure Reason* that sensations are the "matter of our senses" (B 286/A 233–34), the effect of the object on the representational capacity (ibid., "Transcendental aesthetic"), and as such, "the matter of the phenomenon" (ibid., § 8; B 60/A 42–43). What distinguishes waking and dreaming despite their common source in sensations, Tetens argues, is that in the waking state "the capacity for thinking (*Denkkraft*) develops representations from sensations (*Empfindungen*)" (*Über die allgemeine spekulativische Philosophie*). He adds, however, that even in the state of receptivity, the soul is never truly passive and that attention is already itself an activity of the soul. The contradiction between subject and object is thus resolved, insofar as the modifications of the soul that define *Empfindung* for Wolff or Sulzer presuppose a faculty (*Vermögen*) of the soul to be modified. If *Empfindung* is an effect (*Wirkung*) on the soul, "the capacities [of the soul] to be modified are, insofar as they are seated in the soul, participative faculties (*mitwirkende Vermögen*), and they have their source in those which are active" (*Philosophische Versuche*, vol. 1). It is the capacity of soul to animate itself that makes reality accessible. But insofar as knowledge develops or works upon the material of sensation, it "expels it from the soul" and "places it in front of it" (ibid., vol. 1).

Against this background Tetens seeks to remedy the linguistic confusion he perceives in the usage of *Empfindung* and *Gefühl*, reserving the active meaning for the latter (*Gefühl* is the act of feeling) and the connotation of a signal for the former: perception has indicative value with regard to its source. Thus:

> The words *Gefühl* and *fühlen* have a range of meaning almost as large as that of the words *Empfindung* and *empfinden*. And yet, it seems that we must admit a clear difference between them. Feeling (*Fühlen*) relates rather to the act of feeling (*Aktus des Empfindens*) than to the object itself; and insofar as we distinguish them from sensations (*Empfindungen*), there are feelings (*Gefühle*) when we feel a change in ourselves or exerted on us, without this impression permitting us to have knowledge of the object that caused it. To feel (*empfinden*) makes a sign toward an object (*zeiget auf einen Gegenstand hin*) that we feel (*fühlen*) in ourselves by the medium of the sensible impression and that we discover so to speak as a given.
>
> (Ibid., 1:167ff.)

Like Tetens, Kant distinguishes *Empfindung* and *Gefühl* by submitting the relation between feeling and sensation to a rigorous analysis. In section 3 of part 1 of the *Critique of Judgment*, Kant, like Tetens, suggests bringing order to the vocabulary. The passage begins thus: "This at once affords a convenient opportunity for condemning and directing particular attention to a prevalent confusion of the double meaning of which the word 'sensation' is capable." Of course, the context is no longer the same one as for Tetens, since here Kant wishes to contrast aesthetic pleasure that is free of all interest with the interested relation of hedonism toward the object of pleasure. However, the implications intersect:

> When a modification of the feeling (*Gefühl*) of pleasure or displeasure is termed sensation (*Empfindung*), this expression is given quite a different meaning to that which it bears when I call the representation (*Vorstellung*) of a thing (through sense as a receptivity pertaining to the faculty of knowledge) sensation. For in the latter case the representation is referred to the Object, but in the former it is referred solely to the Subject and is not available for any cognition, not even for that by which the Subject *cognizes* itself. Now, in the above definition the word sensation (*Empfindung*) is used to denote an objective representation of sense (*eine objektive Vorstellung der Sinne*); and, to avoid continually running the risk of misinterpretation, we shall call that which must always remain purely subjective, and is absolutely incapable of forming a representation of an object, by the familiar name of feeling (*Gefühl*). The green color of the meadows belongs to *objective* sensation (*gehört zur objektiven Empfindung*), as the perception of an object of sense (*Wahrnehmung eines Gegenstandes des Sinnes*); but its agreeableness to *subjective* sensation, by which no object is represented.
>
> (Kant, *Critique of Judgment*, § 3)

The contrast established here relies on the general notion of "representation" (*Vorstellung*), which acts as a middle term between *Gefühl* and *Empfindung* and presupposes among other things an equivalence between "objective sensation" (*Empfindung*) and what is usually translated as "perception," *Wahrnehmung* (see PERCEPTION). *Gefühl*, understood as simply subjective feeling without a representation of the object (Kant's theme in this part of the *Critique of Judgment*), corresponds nicely with the understanding of *Gefühl* as feeling a change in the soul without knowing its cause, as Tetens defines it in the passage from the *Philosophische Versuche* cited earlier, and which he sometimes calls *Empfindnis* precisely to distinguish it from *Empfindung*. But to say, as Kant does, that the color of a prairie is an "objective sensation" does not amount to saying that the materiality of a color is ignored, as objective reality, by any subjective determination, nor that sensation, insofar as it takes place in the subject, is only relative and arbitrary. The term "objective" here is the product of a break, that of the transcendental aesthetic, which Tetens had not made. For Kant, colors are not physical realities but modifications of our senses. They are "subjective" for this reason. But what affects the subject does not for all that belong to him, any more than space and time belong to him as a priori conditions of sensation—and in this respect they are, like *Empfindung*, "objective." Thus, if it is permissible to split the term for sensation along the two axes of subject and object, it is just as necessary to distinguish clearly *Empfindung*, as what provides the hinge between the world and the individual, from *Gefühl*, as an internal subjective resonance and a signal from the subject to himself. If Tetens does not go so far in defining the principles of sensation (*Sinnlichkeit*) as Kant does in his *Transcendental Aesthetic*, where he designates them as formal a priori conditions of time and space, it is because for Tetens the philosophy of representation still falls under psychological analysis.

IV. The Avatars of Moral Sentiment: *Gefühl, Empfindsamkeit*

It is precisely this break that allows Kant to bring the term *Gefühl* into the moral domain, thus to transcend feeling, but without running the risk of erasing the difference between ethics and aesthetics: respect then becomes the unique "sentiment" (*Gefühl*) of practical reason. This usage of the term *Gefühl* is not in contradiction with the habit of the time. Almost all of the examples that Adelung's dictionary provides for the use of the term *Gefühl* suggest ethical values (love of country, creator, feeling of happiness felt in the presence of a good friend), and they culminate in the following equivalence: "*das moralische Gefühl, die Empfindung dessen, was gut und böse ist* [moral sentiment (*Gefühl*), the feeling (*Empfindung*) of what is good and bad]."

We may contrast with this sense of *empfindend* as "capable of moral sentiment" the term *empfindsam* and the question of *Empfindsamkeit*, whose history comes entirely from the domain of literature and which was institutionalized in German starting from some of Lessing's remarks about the translation of Sterne's *Sentimental Journey* by J. J. Boder (*Empfindsame Reise*, 1768). This sense of *empfindsam* in the eighteenth century meant "capable of emotion" (*Rührung*). Adelung defines it as "*fähig, leicht gerührt zu werden*" ("ability to be easily moved"), whereas Campe speaks of the ability to feel pleasure in emotive participation. For Kant and others *Empfindsamkeit* is denounced as whininess (*Empfindelei, Empfindsamelei*). But the term remains entirely bound to this period, and starting with the nineteenth century only *Sentimentalität* is spoken of.

By thus mixing moral sentiment and the effusion of participation, we get the conceptual hybrid of the *Mit-Gefühl*, that is, a moral feeling of participation in a community, whose uses may be pedagogical (as in Herder, *Ideen zur Philosophischen Geschichte der Menschheit*, 1784–95: the foundation of the community is familial *Mit-Gefühl*), or political—especially with the concept of *Freiheitsgefühl* in Schubart (*Deutsche Chronik*, 1775) or in Schiller's *Fiesko* (1783). Friedrich von Schlegel gave the term an emphatic and conservative tone, attributing to the German character an innate feeling of freedom related to an intuitive feeling of legal justice (*Rechtlichkeit*), based on respect for morality and religion (F. von Schlegel, *Europa*), to which Heinrich Heine soon responded in the preface to the second edition of the *Reisebilder* (1831), contrasting a more French and Jacobin vision of politics with this communitarian conservatism of a "*katholische Harmonie des Gefühls* (Catholic harmony of feeling)."

As for the philosopher of feeling par excellence in the so-called dispute over pantheism, Friedrich Heinrich Jacobi, for him an objective and pure *Gefühl* is the basis of a philosophy conceived of as transcendental. This pure totality indissociable from *Gefühl* obliterates the boundaries between imagination and speech, literature and philosophy. Herder, Bouterwek, Goethe, and Jacobi—all are in agreement as regards the absoluteness of feeling. For Goethe in particular, *Gefühl* is at the source of any discovery and any truth. It is similar, then, to the immediacy of *Anschauung*, of "intuition"—which is, even more, the dimension of genius. The absoluteness of *Gefühl* similarly to be found in Schleiermacher, for whom the essence of religion is neither thought nor action, but "*Anschauung und Gefühl*" (*Über die Religion*, 120ff.). The literary absolute of the Romantics and of Hölderlin makes it the source of all *poiêsis*, all invention, and in the end all culture. Greek poetry, founded on the simplicity and purity of an originating *Gefühl*, becomes the mind's holy site, against which the Hegelian dialectic eventually leads its antiparticularist crusade in the name of *Vernünftigkeit*—rationality.

Jean-Pierre Dubost

BIBLIOGRAPHY

Allison, Henry. *Kant's Theory of Taste*. Cambridge: Cambridge University Press, 2001.

Baumgarten, Alexander Gottlieb. *Metaphysica*. 7th ed. Hildesheim, Ger.: Olms, 1963. First published in 1779.

Cohen, Ted, and Paul Guyer. *Essays in Kant's Aesthetics*. Chicago: University of Chicago Press, 1982.

Corr, Charles Anthony. "The *Deutsche Metaphysik* of Christian Wolff: Text and Transitions." In *History of Philosophy in the Making*, edited by Linus J. Thro, 113–20. Washington, DC: University Press of America, 1982.

Guyer, Paul, ed. *Kant's Critique of the Power of Judgment: Critical Essays*. Lanham, MD: Rowman & Littlefield, 2003.

Heine, Heinrich. *Reisebilder I*. 1824–28. Vol. 5, *Säkularausgabe*. Berlin: Akademie Verlag / CNRS, 1970. Translation by Peter Wortsman: *Travel Pictures*. Brooklyn, NY: Archipelago, 2008.

Herder, Johann Friedrich. "Kritische Wälder oder Betrachtungen, die Wissenschaft und Kunst des Schönen betreffend, nach Maasgaben neuerer Schriften." 33 vols. Vols. 3 and 4 edited by Bernhard Suphan, 1877–1912. Hildesheim, Ger.: Olms, 1967–68. First published in 1769. Translation by Gregory Moore: "Critical Forests (First & Fourth Groves)." In *Selected Writings on Aesthetics*, edited by Gregory Moore. Princeton, NJ: Princeton University Press, 2006.

———. "Vom Erkennen und Empfinden in der menschlichen Seele." In *Sämmtliche Werke*, 33 vols. Vol. 8, edited by Bernhard Suphan, 1877–1913. Hildesheim, Ger.: Olms, 1967–68. First published in 1778. Translation by M. N. Forster: "On the Cognition and Sensation of the Human Soul." In *J.G. Herder: Philosophical Writings*, edited by M. N. Forster. Cambridge: Cambridge University Press, 2002.

Kant, Immanuel. *Kritik der reinen Vernunft*, edited by Königlich Preussischen Akademie der Wissenschaften. In *Kants Gesammelte Schriften*, vols. 3 and 4. Berlin: De Gruyter, 1902–. Translation by Paul Guyer and A. Wood: *Critique of Pure Reason*, edited by Paul Guyer and A. Wood. Cambridge: Cambridge University Press, 1997.

———. *Kritik der Urteilskraft*, edited by Königlich Preussischen Akademie der Wissenschaften. In *Kants Gesammelte Schriften*, vol. 5. Berlin: De Gruyter, 1902–. Translation by James Creed Meredith: *The Critique of Judgment*, edited by James Creed Meredith. Oxford: Clarendon Press, 1952.

Kuehn, Manfred. *Scottish Common Sense in Germany, 1768–1800: A Contribution to the History of Critical Philosophy*. Kingston: McGill-Queen's University Press, 1987.

Kukla, Rebecca, ed. *Aesthetics and Cognition in Kant's Critical Philosophy*. Cambridge: Cambridge University Press, 2006.

Locke, John. *An Essay Concerning Human Understanding*. Edited by Peter H. Nidditsch. Oxford: Clarendon Press, 1975. First published in 1690.

Matthews, Patricia M. *The Significance of Beauty: Kant on Feeling and the System of the Mind*. Dordrecht: Kluwer, 1997.

Schiller, Friedrich von. "Die Verschwörung des Fiesko zu Genua." In *Nationalausgabe*, vol. 4. 50 vols. Weimar: Hermann Böhlaus Nachfolger, 1967. First published in 1783. Translation by G. H. Noehden and J. Stoddart: *Fiesco; or the Genoese conspiracy: a tragedy*. London: Johnson, Edwards, Cadell and Davies, 1796.

———. "Über den Zusammenhang der thierischen Natur des Menschen mit seiner geistigen." In *Nationalausgabe*, vol. 20. Weimar: Hermann Böhlaus Nachfolger, 1962. First published in 1780. Translation with an introduction by J. Weiss: "Connection between Animal and Spiritual Nature in Man." In *The Philosophical and Aesthetic Letters and Essays*. London: Chapman, 1845.

———. "Über die ästhetische Erziehung des Menschen in einer Reihe von Briefen." In *Nationalausgabe*, vol. 20. Weimar: Hermann Böhlaus Nachfolger, 1962. First published in 1795. Translation by Elizabeth M. Wilkinson and L. A. Willoughby: *On the Aesthetic Education of Man: In a Series of Letters*, edited by Elizabeth M. Wilkinson and L. A. Willoughby. Oxford: Clarendon, 1982.

Schlegel, Friedrich von. *Europa*. 2 vols. Stuttgart: J. G. Cotta, 1963. First published in 1803–5.

Schleiermacher, Friedrich. *Über die Religion. Reden an die Gebildeten unter ihren Verächtern*. Stuttgart: Reklam, 1997. First published in 1799. Translation by Richard Crouter: *On Religion: Speeches to Its Cultured Despisers*, edited by Richard Crouter. 2nd ed. Cambridge: Cambridge University Press, 1996.

Schubart, Christian Friedrich Daniel, ed. *Deutsche Chronik: 1774–1777*. 4 vols. Heidelberg: Schneider, 1975.

Schulze, Gottlob Ernst. *Grundriss des philosophischen Wissenschaft*. 2 vols. Hildesheim, Ger.: Olms, 1970. First published in 1788–90.

Sterne, Laurence. *A Sentimental Journey through France and Italy, and, Continuation of Bramine's Journal: The Text and Notes*. Edited by Melvyn New and W. G. Day. Gainesville: Florida University Press, 2002.

Stiebritz, Johann Friedrich. *Erläuterungen der Vernünftigen Gedancken von den Kräfften des Menschlichen Verstandes Wolffs*. Hildesheim, Ger.: Olms, 1977. First published in 1741.

Sulzer, Johann Georg. *Allgemeine Theorie der schönen Künste: in einzeln nach alphabetischer Ordnung der Kunstwörter aufeinanderfolgenden, Artikeln abgehandelt*. 5 vols. 2nd ed. Hildesheim, Ger.: Olms, 1994. First published in 1792–99.

———. "General Theory of the Fine Arts (1771–1774): Selected Articles." Edited and translated by Thomas Christensen. In *Aesthetics and the Art of Musical Composition in the German Enlightenment: Selected Writings of Johann Georg Sulzer and Heinrich Cristoph Koch*, edited by Nancy Baker and Thomas Christensen. Cambridge: Cambridge University Press, 1995.

Tetens, Johann Nikolaus. *Philosophische Versuche über die menschliche Natur und ihre Entwicklung*. 2 vols. Hildesheim, Ger.: Olms, 1979. First published in 1777.

———. *Über die allgemeine spekulative Philosophie*, edited by W. Uebele. In *Neudrucke seltner philosophischer Werke*, vol. 4. Berlin: Reuther & Reichard, 1913. First published in 1775.

Wolff, Christian, Freiherr von. *Deutsche Logik*. In *Gesammelte Werke*, vol. 1. Hildesheim, Ger.: Olms, 1977. Translated as: *Logic, or Rational Thoughts on the Powers of the Human Understanding with Their Use and Application in the Knowledge and Search of Truth*. London, 1770.

———. *Deutsche Metaphysik: Vernünftige Gedanken von Gott, der Welt und der Seele des Menschen, auch allen Dingen überhaupt*. In *Gesammelte Werke*, vol. 10. Hildesheim, Ger.: Olms, 1983.

GEGENSTAND (GERMAN)

➤ OBJECT, and EPOCHÉ, ERSCHEINUNG, ESSENCE, GEFÜHL, INTENTION, PERCEPTION, REALITY, REPRÉSENTATION, RES, SACHVERHALT, SENSE, SUBJECT, *THING*, TRUTH, WERT

Difficulties of translation with regard to objectivity arise most of all in so-called transcendental philosophies, which treat objective sense or objects as acts of the subject. They insist for the most part on the distinction of levels of objectification, that is, on the distinction of stages in the production of objective meaning, which leads to a veritable lexical proliferation, difficult to translate into any language. We may nonetheless note two distinctions within this approach: on one hand, Kant's splitting of the object into "phenomenon" (*Erscheinung*) and "thing in itself" (*Ding an sich*) divides the vocabulary of objectivity in two, whereas Husserl's rejection of the notion of a thing in itself makes this duality disappear. On the other hand, the levels of objectification are, for Kant, relative to the doctrine of faculties and of synthetic functions (the table of categories), hence to the structure of the subject, whereas Husserl, rejecting the Copernican revolution and the doctrine of faculties, makes them relative only to the stratification of objective sense revealed by the intuition of essence (*Wesenschau*).

I. Kant: *Objekt* and *Gegenstand*, between Phenomenon (*Erscheinung*) and Thing in Itself (*Ding an Sich*)

The shift to Critical idealism, with regard to the theme of objectivity, was an etymological awakening. *Gegenstand* and *Objekt* were introduced to translate the Latin *objectum*, which comes from *objicio*, "to throw forward," "to expose." The German *gegen* adds to this idea of manifestation that of direction-toward and that of resistance (*entgegenstehen*, the noun corresponding to which is *Gegenstand*, which initially meant *oppositum esse*, and in Old High German *gaganstentida* had the sense of *obstacula*), and *Stand* (=*stans*), "that which stands," then "that which persists, lasts." The philosophical term *Gegenstand* is thus the product of three registers: *das Gegenüberstehende*, "that which stands in front of me," "that which is op-posed to me"; the *terminus ad quem* of a faculty ("*Gegenstand der Empfindung, der Wahrnehmung*": object of perception); and subsistence or substantiality. In the pre-Critical period, Kant, in the wake of classical thought, covers the register of op-position (phenomenality) by that of subsistence (reality in itself). The turn to transcendental idealism consists in bringing the first two senses of the term *Gegenstand* on this side of the sense of "object subsisting in itself" and to think of them within the bounds of a unified system: the object is the "vis-à-vis" constituted by acts of

objectification originating in the faculties (perception, imagination, understanding) and their functions, but the thing in itself remains its unknowable ontological foundation.

A. The split between phenomenon and thing in itself

In the Latin of Kant's *Dissertatio* of 1770, we find two series of opposed ontological equations: *objectivum=reale=intelligibile=subjecto irrelativum, subjectivum=ideale=sensibile=subjecto relativum*. *Objectivum* is contrasted with *subjectivum*, what resides in or is relative to the subject, and is thus identified with the intelligible (which by contrast with the perceptual does not vary depending on the subject) and with *realitas* (contrasted with *idealitas*, which describes ideas or subjective representations but not existing objects). Thus Kant contrasts *lex subjective, lex quaedam menti insita*, or again the *conditiones subjecto propriae* ("subjective law," "situated in the mind," "conditions proper to the subject": space and time, § 29), to *conditio objectiva*, for example, the "*forma objectiva sive substantiarum coordinatio* [the objective condition or objective form as coordination of substances]." Similarly, he refuses to grant space and time the status of "*objectivum aliquid et reale* [something objective, i.e., real]" (§ 14–15) but rather treats them as "*coordinatio idealis et subjecti* [an ideal, i.e., subjective, coordination]." Whence there results the double meaning of *objectum*, corresponding to the two etymological registers: on one side *res*, "*existens in se*," "*objectum intellectus*," thing in itself and intelligible cause of perceptual affections; on the other side the *phaenomenon*, "*objectum sensuum*":

> Phaenomena ceu causata testantur de praesentia objecti, quod contra Idealismum.
>
> (In so far as [Phenomena] are sensory concepts or apprehensions, they are, as things caused, witnesses to the presence of an object, and this is opposed to idealism. [NB: *praesentia* has, in this refutation of idealism, the meaning of *existentia* and not that of manifestation.])
>
> (Kant, *De mundi sensibilis atque intelligibilis forma et principiis*, § 11; *Form and Principles*, 389)

> Quaecunque ad sensus nostros referuntur ut objecta, sunt Phaenomena.
>
> (Whatever, as object, relates to our senses is a phenomenon.)
>
> (Kant, *De mundi*, § 12; *Form and Principles*, 390)

Despite this amphibology the term *objectum* already tends to be reserved for the appearing object and to be separate from the register of existence in itself: thus section 4, which deals with the formal principle of the intelligible world (with objects in themselves, in consequence), substitutes the terms *res, substantia, aliquid, omnia* for *objectum*. This is why, in the last cited passage, it is best to avoid translating *quaecunque* by "everything which" ("toutes les choses qui," Fr. trans. P. Mouy, Vrin), which implies a reification of the phenomenon, and to reserve "thing" (*chose*) for *res intelligibilis*.

This amphibology is reaffirmed in the Critical period, but with a decisive shift. The object of course retains its twofold meaning, that of thing in itself (referred to as *Ding an sich, Objekt an sich, Gegenstand an sich, Noumenon, das Erscheinende*, that is, "thing in itself," "object in itself," "noumenon," "the appearing thing") and of phenomenon (referred to as *Objekt, Gegenstand, Erscheinung*). But the shift to transcendental idealism gives rise to a crucial displacement: things in themselves are unknowable for the finite subject, even for his understanding. The object in itself thus no longer indicates purely intellectual reality in contrast with sensible reality; rather, it refers now to what is relative neither to perception nor to understanding. In Critical idealism, the phenomenon confiscates the meaning of objectivity for any finite subject, and sensible intuition, by becoming the minimal condition of possibility of experience, becomes as well the minimal condition of possibility of all objective validity and all denotation:

> Also beziehen sich alle Begriffe und mit ihnen alle Grundsätze . . . auf empirische Anschauungen, d. i. auf Data zur möglichen Erfahrung. Ohne dieses haben sie gar keine objektive Gültigkeit.

> (Thus all concepts and with them all principles . . . are nevertheless related to empirical intuitions, i.e., to *data* for possible experience. Without this they have no objective validity at all. [Objective validity is here the equivalent to meaning, signification, or relation to the object; that is, in Fregean language, to denotation (see SENSE)].)

> (Kant, *Kritik der reinen Vernunft*, A 239, B 298)

Objectivity thus recovers the etymological sense of "a manifestation to," as the appearance to perception by way of the affections: *Objectum=Gegen-stand=phaenomenon= ob-jectum=Dawider=*vis-à-vis for the "*intuitus derivatus*."

■ See Box 1.

B. The different concepts of objectivity in itself

Is this to say that the phenomenon seizes all senses of objectivity for itself? No, since the concept of the thing in itself, even though it does not refer to any knowable object, retains several essential functions in transcendental idealism. The concept is in fact a deceptive one, since the "in itself" of "concept of the thing in itself" suggests the exclusion of all relation, whereas Kant, far from thinking of it only as ontological subsistence, defines "thing in itself" as a "*terminus ad quem*" of faculties (infinite intuition, understanding, pure reason, practical reason) whose eventual "correlation" is made possible by the Copernican revolution that Kant envisions for philosophy—and this definition as a result multiplies the concept's meanings.

— The first concept of an object in itself corresponds to the positive sense of noumenon, understood as a pure object of understanding, given to an intellectual intuition or an *intuitus originarius* that creates its object:

> Wenn ich aber Dinge annehme, die bloß Gegenstände des Verstandes sind, und gleichwohl, als solche, einer

---

1

Translating *Gegenstand/Objekt* in Kant

A famous difficulty encountered by Kant's translators concerns his use of the terminological couple *Gegenstand/Objekt*. Existing translations fold the two terms onto each other by translating them both uniformly as "object." Would it be preferable—even necessary—to underscore terminologically the distinction between the apparent object and the thing in itself? And does this distinction line up with the distinction between *Gegenstand* and *Objekt* in Kant's text? Martineau brings the problem to the fore in his preface to the French translation of Heidegger's course on the *Critique of Pure Reason*. Here Martineau suggests adopting *ob-jet* as a translation for the phenomenon (the embedded dash rendering the hint of a separation from intuition by separating the prefix *ob-*), and *objet* as a translation for the thing in itself. The difficulty, noted by the French translators of Eisler's *Kant-Lexikon* (under *objet*), is that Kant frequently uses the two terms interchangeably, making both of them designate either the phenomenon or the thing in itself. One thus finds, manifestly employed synonymously, the expressions *tranzendentaler*

Gegenstand and *tranzendentales Objekt*, *Gegenstand in sich* and *Objekt in sich*, and so on. And yet Kant also commonly employs the two terms simultaneously to produce a contrast—as when, in section 19 of the *Prolegomena to any Future Metaphysics*, he writes: "*Das Objekt bleibt an sich selbst immer unbekannt* [The object in itself remains forever unknown]," but when the relation of sensible representations is determined by the categories, "*so wird der Gegenstand durch dieses Verhältnis bestimmt* [then the ob-ject is determined by this relation]." The pair ob-ject/object would then have to be used without forcing it into a strict correspondence with the pair *Gegenstand/Objekt*, but rather according to the context. In general, the difficulty posed by the pair derives from the fact that Kant at times uses *Gegenstand* to designate the genus covering the two species "phenomenon" and "thing in itself," as signally in the passage that Martineau uses to exemplify the distinction between *Gegenstand* and *Objekt*:

> Die Transzendentalphilosophie betrachtet nur den Verstand, und Vernunft

selbst in einem System aller Begriffe und Grundsätze, die sich auf Gegenstände überhaupt beziehen, ohne Objekte anzunehmen, die gegeben wären (Ontologia); die Physiologie der reinen Vernunft betrachtet die Natur, d. i. den Inbegriff gegebener Gegenstände (sie mögen nun den Sinnen, oder, wenn man will, einer anderen Art von Anschauung gegeben sein).

> (Metaphysics in this narrower meaning of the term consists of *transcendental philosophy* and the *physiology* of pure reason. Transcendental philosophy (*ontologia*) contemplates only our *understanding* and reason themselves in a system of all concepts and principles referring to objects as such, without assuming objects that are *given*. The physiology of pure reason contemplates *nature*, i.e., the sum of given objects (whether given to the senses or, for that matter, to some other kind of intuition).

> (Kant, *Critique of Pure Reason*, A 845, B 873)

Anschauung, obgleich nicht der sinnlichen (als *coram intuitu intellectuali*), gegeben werden können; so würden dergleichen Dinge Noumena (*Intelligibilia*) heißen.

(If, however, I suppose there to be things that are merely objects of the understanding and that, nevertheless, can be given to an intuition, although not to sensible intuition (as *coram intuitu intellectuali*), then such things would be called *noumena* (*Intelligibilia*).)

(Ibid., A 249)

Noumenon and phenomenon are thus defined according to each concept's relation to intuition, inasmuch as this intuition is infinite (noumenon) rather than finite (phenomenon), creative (again, noumenon) rather than receptive (phenomenon), primitive rather than derived. Heidegger, playing on the opposition between the particles *ent-* and *gegen-*, characterizes the two terms as *Entstand* (existent-arising-from-originary-intuition) and *Gegen-stand* or *Dawider* (existent opposed to derived intuition) (cf. Heidegger, *Kant and the Problem of Metaphysics*, § 16). As we have only sensible intuition and cannot show the possibility of an intellectual intuition, such a concept has no objective reality, that is, neither denotation nor content.

— The second is the negative conception of the noumenon, to which the terms "transcendental object (*tranzendentales Objekt*)," "object in general" (*Gegenstand überhaupt*), and "something in general" (*Etwas überhaupt*) correspond. We cannot know the noumenon in any way; but if we wish to avoid Berkleyan idealism, we must attribute to phenomena, as simple representations, the relation to something that is not representation but an ontological cause of intuitions. This "object" has the twofold function of limiting the claims of perception to give us objects in themselves (thus to ensure the transcendental ideality of phenomena) and to guarantee the denotation or empirical reality of the latter:

Da Erscheinungen nichts als Vorstellungen sind, so bezieht sie der Verstand auf ein Etwas, als den Gegenstand der sinnlichen Anschauung: aber dieses Etwas ist insofern nur das transzendentale Objekt. Dieses bedeutet aber ein Etwas = x, wovon wir gar nichts wissen.

(Since appearances are nothing but representations, the understanding relates them to a something, as the object of sensible intuition; but this something is to that extent only the transcendental object. This signifies, however, a something = X, of which we know nothing at all.)

(Kant, *Kritik der reinen Vernunft*, A 250)

This object is defined elsewhere as "*die bloß intelligible Ursache der Erscheinungen überhaupt* [the merely intelligible cause of appearances in general]" (ibid., A 494, B 522), and "*das, was in allen unseren empirischen Begriffen überhaupt Beziehung auf einen Gegenstand, d. i. objektive Realität verschaffen kann* [that which in all our empirical concepts in general can provide relations to an object, i.e., objective reality]."

Insofar as no category can be applied to it in order to determine it, this transcendental object is precisely not a defined "object." It is a pure X, "the concept of an object in general

[*der Begriff eines Gegenstandes überhaupt*]" (ibid., A 251), "the completely undetermined thought of something in general [*der gänzlich unbestimmte Gedanke von Etwas überhaupt*]" (ibid., A 253). It is the *ob-* in the object that guarantees the unitary denotation of our representations, which is correlative to transcendental apperception as the formal unity of self-consciousness.

— The third concept is that of the idea of reason: the "purely intelligible object" or "object of pure thought" ("*bloß intelligibler Gegenstand*," "*Gegenstand des reinen Denkens*," ibid., A 286–87f., B 342–43), that is, the suprasensible object of "*metaphysica specialis*" (the soul, the world, God) as reason claims to determine it using the categories alone, in the absence of any sensible data. As sensibility is the condition of the relation to an object, the categories as pure forms of thought therefore define only "*entia rationis*," "*leere Begriffe ohne Gegenstand*" ("empty concepts without objects," ibid., A 292, B 348), "*hyperbolische Objekte*," "*reine Verstandeswesen (besser: Gedankenwesen)*)" ("hyperbolic objects," "pure beings of understanding (or better, thought)," *Prolegomena* § 45), that is, suprasensible objects without objective reality, without denotation.

— The last concept of the object in itself is correlative to practical reason. Suprasensible ideas have no denotation for speculative reason but do for practical reason, as necessary conditions for following the moral law. The immortality of the soul, freedom, and the existence of God are thus an "objective reality"; they are "objects" in the sense of necessary correlates of rational faith, even though no intuition ensures this objective reality:

Nun bekommen sie durch ein apodiktisches praktisches Gesetz als notwendige Bedingungen der Möglichkeit dessen, was dieses sich zum Objekte zu machen gebietet, objektive Realität, d. i. wir werden durch jenes angewiesen, daß sie Objekte haben, ohne doch, wie sich ihr Begriff auf ein Objekt bezieht, anzeigen zu können.

(Now, through an apodeictic practical law, as necessary conditions of the possibility of what this law commands one *to make one's object*, they acquire objective reality; i.e., we are instructed by this law that *they have objects*, yet without being able to indicate how their concept refers to an object.)

(Kant, *Kritik der praktischen Vernunft*, 135; *Critique of Practical Reason*, 171)

"Objectivity" and "objective reality" signify, of course, the independent subsistence of our knowledge but as necessary correlates of practical reason, which postulates them.

C. The degrees of phenomenal objectivity

The object as phenomenon is thought of as a correlate of the objectivizing functions of thought. In a general way the central problem of critical philosophy is that of the objective validity of our knowledge, that is, the movement from simple subjective representations, valid only for me (*bloß subjektive*), to a representation having both a relation to an object (*Gegenständlichkeit, Beziehung auf ein Objekt*) and objective validity for everyone (*Objektivität*). The uniform translation of all three stages by "objectivity" masks this distinction, as well as the Kantian solution, which is to assimilate *Gegenständlichkeit* (which we might translate as "objectuality") with *Objektivität* (for which we would reserve "objectivity"), understood as necessary (*notwendige Gültigkeit*) and universal validity (*Allgemeingültigkeit*):

> Es sind daher objektive Gültigkeit und notwendige Allgemeingültigkeit (für jedermann) Wechselbegriffe, und ob wir gleich das Objekt an sich nicht kennen, so ist doch, wenn wir ein Urteil als gemeingültig und mithin notwendig ansehen, eben darunter die objektive Gültigkeit verstanden.

> (Objective validity and necessary universal validity (for everyone) are therefore interchangeable concepts, and although we do not know the object in itself, nonetheless, if we regard a judgment as universally valid and hence necessary, objective validity is understood to be included.)

> (Kant, *Prolegomena*, § 19)

Objectivity thus no longer contrasts with subjectivity but only with the "simple subjectivity" (*bloße Subjektivität*), the "purely subjective validity" (*bloß subjektive Gültigkeit*) of sensible modifications of the subject. It is identified with that which is a priori in the subject, namely pure intuitions and categories, which provide the relationship to the ob-ject:

> Daß es a priori erkannt werden kann, bedeutet: daß es ein Objekt habe und nicht bloß subjektive Modifikation sei.

> (That it can be cognized a priori means: that it has an objectand is not merely a subjective modification.)

> (Kant, *Reflexionen*, 5216, trans. Guyer, 111)

However, the concept of object is a generic one whose meaning multiplies as a function of the levels of objectivization that ensure the denotation, universality, and necessity of the phenomenon. It follows that the concept of "objective reality" (*objektive Realität*) is multivocal, and may be divided into levels related to the transcendental conditions (formal, material, general) defining the modalities (possible, actual, necessary) and corresponding to the different scholastic-Cartesian concepts of "reality" (*quidditas* or *realitas objectiva*, *quodditas* or *realitas actualis*, *necessitas* or *ens causatum*). Each level achieves a successive elimination of that which is simply subjective (*bloß subjektiv*): the quality of pertaining to the senses; *ens imaginarium*; and contingency.

— *Realitas objectiva* (*essentia*, *possibilitas*) at the mathematical level is not, however, the possible object, that is, the object simply present in front of us (*da-seiendes*), stripped of its secondary qualities and constituted by primary qualities alone (magnitudes), the conditions of construction in space and time. Rather, *realitas objectiva* is the sense of the object (*gegenständlicher Sinn*), which is contrasted with the *nihil negativum*, the empty object without a concept (*leerer Gegenstand ohne Begriff*) (Kant, *Kritik der reinen Vernunft*, A 292, B 348):

> [Die] Bedingungen des Raumes und der Bestimmung desselben . . . haben ihre objektive Realität, d. i. sie

gehen auf mögliche Dinge, weil sie die Form der Erfahrung überhaupt a priori enthalten.

> ([The] conditions of space and of its determinations . . . have their objective reality, i.e., they pertain to possible things, because they contain in themselves a priori the form of experience in general.)

> (Ibid., A 221, B 268)

Realitas actualis existentia, at the dynamic level, is actuality (*Wirklichkeit*), the perceptually given object with a perceptible matter that guarantees its empirical reality or denotation (*Gegenständlichkeit*, *Beziehung auf einen Gegenstand*), which is contrasted with *ens rationis* and *ens imaginarium*, intuitions or concepts empty without objects (ibid., A 292):

> [Wir müssen] immer eine Anschauung bei der Hand haben, um . . . die objektive Realität des reinen Verstandesbegriff darzulegen.

> ([We must] always have available an intuition for it to display the objective reality of the pure concept of the understanding.)

> (Ibid., B 288)

Finally the *ens creatum sive causatum*, purged of all theological content, corresponds to the "material necessity in existence" (*materiale Notwendigkeit im Dasein*), that is, submission to the principle of causality and to the rule of understanding necessary in the apprehension of phenomena:

> Dasjenige an der Erscheinung, was die Bedingung dieser notwendigen Regel der Apprehension enthält, ist das Objekt.

> (That in the appearance which contains the condition of this necessary rule of apprehension is the object.)

> (Ibid., A 191, B 236)

The idea of a causal order of time prescribes a rule to the subjective succession of apprehension and makes it possible to move from the subjective succession of representations to the representation of an objective succession, from *Erscheinung* to *Objekt*. The object in this sense does not simply denote the existing object but that which has universal and necessary validity. Objectivity as objective validity is thus not completely identical with denotation but adds a further requirement to it, that of the principle of reason or causality, which inserts every object in the necessary order of causation of phenomena and makes it possible for the natural sciences to construct reality, nature being identical for every subject (*allgemeingültig*). We should not confuse this intersubjective validity with the simple claim to subjective universality that characterizes the judgment of taste (Kant, *Kritik der Urteilskraft*, § 8, 5:213–16), since that is only the idea of a universal assent lacking a concept, and hence also lacking objectivity.

— A final concept of objectivity appears on the practical level, where the critical question concerning the objectivity of our principles of action is posed. There are indeed phenomenal objects of practice, namely objects of desire constituted as realizations of the will. But if the principle of determination of an action is an empirical object, namely the feeling of pleasure or pain or the distinction between good and bad, then the action is deprived of its objective validity since its object is an a posteriori matter (Kant, *Kritik der praktischen Vernunft*, 5:21, *Object=Materie*), and thus simply subjective. For it to have objective validity, the practical object must be a *necessary* object of the faculty of desire, whose intersubjective validity is ensured by its formal, a priori character, namely the form of the law, the principle of distinction between good and evil (*Gut* and *Böse*). As in the case of pure reason, we must therefore distinguish between *Gegenständlichkeit* and *Objektivität*, objectuality and objectivity, the latter being guaranteed by its a prioricity, that is, its necessity and universality:

> Unter einem Begriffe eines Gegenstandes der praktischen Vernunft verstehe ich die Vorstellung eines Objekts als einer möglichen Wirkung durch Freiheit.
>
> (By a concept of an object of practical reason, I mean the presentation of an object as an effect possible through freedom.)

> (Kant, *Critique of Practical Reason*, 77)

> Die alleinigen Objekte einer praktischen Vernunft sind also die vom Guten und Bösen. Denn durch das erstere versteht man einen notwendigen Gegenstand des Begehrungs, durch das zweite des Verabscheuungsvermögens, beides aber nach einem Prinzip der Vernunft.
>
> (The sole objects of a practical reason are, therefore, those of the *good* and the *evil*. For by the first one means a necessary object of our power of desire, by the second, of our power of loathing, but both according to a principle of reason.)

> (Ibid., 78)

II. Husserl: From the Object to *Gegeständlichkeit*

The terminology of objectivity in Husserl presents the same kind of difficulties that we find in Kant, insofar as it is technically extended and complicated by the distinction of types of object and objectification. However, Husserl's deployment of the concept of *epochê* [ἐποχή] also serves to simplify the treatment of objectivity (in comparison to Kant's treatment), for *epochê* serves to remove the dissociation of the object into phenomenon and thing in itself, and brings the object back to the phenomenon alone.

A. Multiplying the kinds of object

The key phrase for Husserl is the "*Rückgang auf die Sache selbst*," translated as "return to things themselves." However, "*Sachen sind nicht ohne weiteres Natursachen*" [things are not simply mere things belonging to Nature] (*Ideen* I, § 19, Hua III/1, p. 42; *Ideas pertaining to a Pure Phenomenology*, Eng. trans. F. Kersten, 36); they are, rather, everything that may be ascribed to intuitive self-givenness (*Selbstgegebenheit*) in contrast with what is simply indicated (*bloß vermeint*). There is, as a consequence, a proliferation of types of thematic objects. These Husserl designates by the term *Gegenständlichkeit*, which is better translated into French as "objectity"

(S. Bachelard, Élie-Kelkek-Schérer) than as "objectivity" (Ricoeur), to avoid confusion with the character of what has objective validity (*Objektivität*, see below):

> Ich wähle öfters den unbestimmteren Ausdruck Gegenständlichkeit, weil es sich hier überall nicht bloß um Gegenstände im engeren Sinn, sondern auch um Sachverhalte, Merkmale, um unselbständige reale oder kategoriale Formen u. dgl. handelt.
>
> (I often make use of the vaguer expression "objective correlate" [*Gegenständlichkeit*] since we are here never limited to objects in the narrower sense but have also to do with states of affairs, properties, and nonindependent forms, etc., whether real or categorial.)

> (Husserl, *Logical Investigations*, First Investigation, § 9, 1:281)

Thus, a number, a value, a nation are "objectities" in the same way a tree is. Let us analyze these complexities in the vocabulary of objects.

1. Things of nature and grounded "objectities"

Objectities may be forms of object that are grounded on the infrastructure of material nature and possess layers of superstructural meaning. They are "new types of objectity of a higher order [*neuartige Gegenständlichkeiten höherer Ordnung*]" (*Ideen*, I, § 152, Hua III/1, p. 354), which Husserl refers to by the terms *Gegenstand, Objekt, Gegenständlichkeit, Objektität* (ibid., § 95, Hua III/1, p. 221): animate beings (*Animalien*), objects of value (*Wertobjekte* or *Wertobjektitäten*, see WERT), objects of use (*praktische Objekte* or *Gebrauchsobjekte*), cultural formations (*konkrete Kulturgebilde*: state, law, morality, etc.). The difficulty derives from the distinction between natural infrastructure (that which has value, *werter Gegenstand*), the abstract layer grounded in it (*das Wert*, value as the correlate of an evaluation, *objectified value*), and the concrete objectity resulting from their fusion (*Wertgegenstand*, where the *Naturobjekt* and *Wert* are combined, the *object with value*):

> Wir sprechen von der bloßen "Sache," die werte ist, die Wertcharakter, Wertheit hat; demgegenüber vom konkreten Werte selbst oder der Wertobjektität.
>
> (We shall speak of the mere "thing" that is valuable, that has a value-characteristic, that has *value-quality*; in contradistinction, we speak of *concrete value* itself or the *value-Objectiveness*.)

> (Husserl, *Ideen*, Volume I, § 95, Hua III/1, 221; *Ideas pertaining to a Pure Phenomenology*, Eng. trans. F. Kersten, 232)

Let us take an example. In a museum, I perceive a primitive object first as simply a thing; then, understanding its practical value (*Gebrauchssinn*), I incorporate that to it and perceive the object as an object of use (*Gebrauchsobjekt*). French does not have the ease of German, with its compound words, of rendering the nature of this fusion: "objet-valeur" risks introducing a confusion with objectified (that is, abstract) value, "object having value" (Ricoeur), and thus of suggesting a split between object and value; the expression "chose-évaluée" better suggests the sort of fusion Husserl describes.

Generally speaking, the different levels of objectification and the distinction between abstract and concrete objectities create problems for French.

2. Singular objects and essence

Husserl also widens the domain of objectities by admitting, alongside singular objects, essences as objects of specific intuition:

Das Wesen (Eidos) ist ein neuartiger Gegenstand. . . . Auch Wesenerschauung ist eben Anschauung, *wie eidetischer Gegenstand eben Gegenstand ist.*

(The essence [Eidos] is a new sort of object. . . . Seeing an essence is also precisely intuition, *just as an eidetic object is precisely an object.*)

(Ibid., § 3, Hua III/1, 14; *Ideas pertaining to a Pure Phenomenology*, Eng. trans. F. Kersten, 9)

The difficulty here is not one of translation but of understanding the term *Gegenstand*. If we render it by "object," we must keep in mind "the generalization of the concepts of intuition and of object" ("*Verallgemeinerung der Begriffe 'Anschauung' und 'Gegenstand'*"). In Husserl this "generalization" is not an analogy taking essences on the model of perceptual objects but the understanding of singular objects and essences as species of the genus "any object whatever," of the "universal concept of object, of object as any *something whatever* [*des allgemeinen Gegenstandsbegriffs, des Gegenstands als irgend etwas*]" (*Ideen* . . . I, § 22, Hua III/1, p. 47). Husserl generalizes the fact of being an object (*Objektheit*) to fields other than singularities, even while denouncing any confusion between real and ideal objectities:

Besagt *Gegenstand* und *Reales, Wirklichkeit* und *reale Wirklichkeit* ein und dasselbe, dann ist die Auffassung von Ideen als Gegenständen und Wirklichkeiten allerdings verkehrte "platonische Hypostasierung."

(If *object* and *something real*, actuality and real actuality, have one and the same sense, then the conception of ideas as objects and actualities is indeed a perverse "Platonic hypostatization.")

(Ibid., § 22, Hua III/1, 47; *Ideas pertaining to a Pure Phenomenology*, Eng. trans. F. Kersten, 41)

The term *Wirklichkeiten*, corresponding to the generalized concept of object, does not refer to "realities" (as Ricoeur argues) in the sense of "natural realities" but to anything that has the characteristic of actuality (*Wirklichsein*) and contains different types of ideality (*vielerlei Ideales*: the spectrum of sounds, the number 2, the circle, a proposition, etc.).

3. Syntactic objectities

In the domain of essences, the idea of formal ontology extends the notion of objectivity to the syntactic domain. Material ontologies consider the genera of concrete objects (thing, animal, man, etc.); formal ontology considers the "formal region" (*formale Region*) of any object whatever, "the empty form of region in general" ("*die leere Form von Region überhaupt*," ibid., I, § 10, Hua III/1, 26). Taken in the logical sense, as designating any possible subject of predication, "objects" are not restricted to concrete individuals

like proto-objecticities (*Urgegenständlichkeiten*) or ultimate substrates ("*letzte Substrate*"), but contain "syntactic or categorial objectities [*syntaktische oder kategoriale Gegenständlichkeiten*]" (ibid., I, § 11, Hua III/1, 28–29) derived from these by syntactic construction:

"Gegenstand" ist ein Titel für mancherlei, aber zusammengehörige Gestaltungen, z. B. "Ding," "Eigenschaft," "Relation," "Sachverhalt," "Menge," "Ordnung" usw., die . . . auf eine Art Gegenständlichkeit, die sozusagen den Vorzug der Urgegenständlichkeit hat, zurückweisen.

("Object" is a name for various formations which nonetheless belong together—for example, "physical thing," "property," "relationship," "predicatively formed affair-complex," "aggregate," "ordered set." Obviously they are not on a par with one another but rather in every case point back to one kind of objectivity that, so to speak, takes precedence as the *primal objectivity*.)

(Ibid., I, § 10, Hua III/1, 25; *Ideas pertaining to a Pure Phenomenology*, Eng. trans. F. Kersten, 20)

"Objects" of this sort are purely logical, fundamental concepts; the formal determination of the object as a "something in general" ("*ein irgend Etwas*") taken as the substrate of a statement; objects of a higher order inasmuch as they are derived from the ultimate substrates, the perceptual objects. Thus the state-of-affairs or state-of-things, the *Sachverhalt* "the snow is white," is an object just as much as the snow is, but of a higher order, since it implies the consciousness of the substrate, of the property, and of their combination all at once: it is a compound object of polythetic consciousness ("*Gesamt-Gegenstand polythetischer Bewußtseins*"). The French translation of *Sachverhalt* (see SACHVERHALT) by *état-des-choses* is inaccurate, since the thing is not a thing of nature (*Naturding*) but rather any logical subject of any level; the English "predicatively formed affair-complex," even better than the more common "state of affairs," renders its predicative origin and its much broader reach and common character.

B. Elimination of the object in itself and layers of meaning of the intentional object

The Kantian amphibology of the object (*Erscheinung* and "*Ding an sich*") is eliminated by *epochê*, since placing the natural thesis on the sidelines (*ausschalten*) means bracketing (*einklammern*) any object posited by it, hence any existent in itself, and making the object appear as "intentional object" or *Noema*, terms that refer to the objectival sense sought and constituted by consciousness:

Ähnlich wie die Wahrnehmung hat jedes intentionale Erlebnis . . . sein "intentionales Objekt," d. i. seinen gegenständlichen Sinn.

(Like perception, *every* intentive mental process . . . has its "intentional Object," i.e., its objective sense.)

(Ibid., I, § 90, Hua III/1, 206; *Ideas pertaining to a Pure Phenomenology*, Eng. trans. F. Kersten, 217)

The intentional object is an object not in the sense of being self-subsistent but in the sense in which one speaks of an object of attention, that is, as a correlate or "*terminus ad quem*" (*Worauf*, toward-which, Heidegger will say) of an activity. Not the existing thing ("*das wirkliche Ding*"), but the being-sense (*Seinsinn*) constituted by the giving of meaning by consciousness—noematic trees do not burn! The term *gegenständlich* refers to the relationship to an object and is translated by "objectival" or "objectual" to distinguish it from the term *objektiv*, which refers to what has intersubjective validity. In this way any object being reducible to a being-sense correlative to a target of consciousness, a noema correlative to a noesis, we can—in the same way that a noema may be decomposed into a series of partial goals or intentions—distinguish in the noema different layers of objectival sense corresponding to different degrees of objectification. Thus we come, as in Kant, to a stratification of meanings of the object and objectivity that return us to the constitutive operations of the transcendental subject.

1. The twofold sense of the concept of reality: "reell" and "real"

This reduction of objectivity to the intentional object should not hide the division of the concept of "reality" into two senses: the "reality" of being is referred to by the adjectives *reelle* and *real*, or *immanent* and *transzendent*. What is *reell* refers to what has the mode of being of consciousness and is absolutely given, while what is *real* is what has a material nature (*Naturding*) given by its outlines. The perceived tree is *real*, but my perception of the tree is *reell*, not included in material nature but included in consciousness and in this way *ir-real*. Indifferently translating *real* and *reell* by "real" would gloss over this essential distinction of the modes of being and consciousness of the object, of experience (*Erlebnis*) and the thing (*Ding*), "*des reellen Bestands der Wahrnehmung*" ("the concrete, really inherent composition of perception itself") and "*des transzendenten Objekts*" ("utterly transcendent object") (ibid., I, § 41, Hua III/1, p. 83; *Ideas pertaining to a Pure Phenomenology*, Eng. trans. Kersten, 86). The translation of *irreal* by "unreal" would be inaccurate as well, suggesting that experiences are fictions when in fact they are the absolute given; *ir-real* refers to whatever does not have the mode of being of a worldly thing. Husserl thus takes up terminology inherited from German idealism, in which *Realphilosophie* referred to the philosophy of work, nature, and family (cf. Hegel, *Realphilosophie* of Jena), and in which *real* contrasts with whatever is metaphysical and deals with the philosophy of mind. He extends the concept of *real* to whatever belongs to the world, contrasting it only with ideal and syntactic objectities (see TRUTH).

2. Immanent objectities

While terminology for objects becomes complicated at the top end by the admission of objects of a higher order, it is also complicated at the bottom, when we examine the abstract component of concrete objects. These are "immanent objectities," that is, units identified by consciousness and not objects situated in the world. The time of consciousness is not, therefore, unformed or Heraclitean, but already shaped by permanent units:

> Das Erlebnis, die wir jetzt erleben, wird uns in der unmittelbaren Reflexion gegenständlich, und es stellt sich in ihm immerfort dasselbe Gegenständliche dar: derselbe Ton.

> (The mental process which we are now undergoing becomes objective to us in immediate reflection, and thenceforth it displays in reflection the same objectivity: the self-same tone which has just existed as an actual "now" remains henceforth the same tone.)

> (Husserl, *Die Idee der Phänomenologie*, Hua II, 67; *Idea of Phenomenology*, Eng. trans. Alston and Nakhnikian, 52)

This sound is, of course, an "object" in the sense of a unit apprehended by consciousness, but not an object of nature (*Reales, Naturgegenstand*). Whence the difficulty we encounter in translating the expressions for these immanent "objects," like *Zeitobjekt*:

> In der Wahrnehmung mit ihrer Retention konstituiert sich das ursprüngliche Zeitobjekt.

> (The *primary temporal object* is constituted in perception, along with the retention of consciousness of what is perceived.)

> (Ibid., Hua II, 71; *Idea of Phenomenology*, Lecture 5, Eng. trans. Alston and Nakhnikian, 56)

In French *Zeitobjekt* must therefore be translated by "tempo-object" (Granel) or *objet de temps*, "object of time," and not *objet temporel* or "temporal object" (as Dussort and Lowit do) since, although any object of nature is "temporal" insofar as it is situated in objective time, a melody as an immanent given of consciousness is a "tempo-object," a pure thing-of-duration without spatial or causal character. The same holds for the abstract layer of spatiality, which defines "objects" that are concrete relative to itself but abstract relative to the natural thing: *res extensae*. Here again, we must translate *res extensa* by spatio-object or spatial-thing (with a hyphen) rather than by "extended thing" or "spatial thing," since while every *Naturding* is extended, *res extensa* is only extension, its materiality having been abstracted away, as well as its placement in the causal order of nature: a ghost, a rainbow as pure apparitions. These layers separate out again into new, more abstract layers, such as the *res extensa* in "things" relative to each sense modality (*Sinnendinge: Sehdinge, Tastdinge*, etc.), which are not *choses sensibles* or *choses sensorielles* (Ricoeur), "sensory things" or "things of sense" (Boyce Gibson, Eng. tr. of *Ideen* I)—since every *Naturding* is sensible—but "things pertaining to the senses" (Cairns), things-of-the-senses or things relating to each sense (*choses-des-sens* in French), which we might translate by the Latin *sensualia* (Escoubas, Fr. tr. of *Ideen* II). Thus *Sehding* could be rendered with the help of Latin as *visuale* (Escoubas), or again "visual-thing" or "thing-of-sight," but not by "visual thing" or "visible thing" (Ricoeur), since every *Naturding* is visible (but also tangible, audible, and so on), whereas a *Sehding* is a pure thing-of-sight having only visual properties (e.g., a patch of red color that I see when closing my eyes).

3. Object "pure and simple" and complete object

The analysis of intentional objects and the ways in which they are given allows us to distinguish between a narrow and a wide sense of noema: the central core or pure objectival sense, or the central noematic moment ("*zentraler Kern*," "*purer gegeständlicher Sinn*," "*zentrales noematisches Moment*") is contrasted with the complete intentional object in the manner of its modes of being given ("*volles intentionales Objekt*," "*Gegenstand im Wie seiner Gegebenheitsweisen*"). The same tree may be perceived from different angles, at different seasons, and change predicates (color, shape) while remaining identical; it may be perceived, remembered, imagined, named: this "same" is the minimal objectival sense ("*gegenständlicher Sinn*"). From this "same" of the tree have been eliminated, by abstraction, the acts of apprehension (perception, memory, etc.) that give the tree its *Aktcharaktere* (characters of act) of "perceived," "remembered," etc.; this minimal objectival sense is contrasted with the "*Objekt im Wie*," which is the perceived-tree, the remembered-tree, and so on:

Daß verschiedene Begriffe von *unmodifizierten Objektivitäten* unterscheidbar sein müssen, von denen der "Gegenstand schlechthin," nämlich das Identische, das einmal wahrgenommen, das andere Mal direkt vergegenwärtigt, das dritte Mal in einem Gemälde bildlich dargestellt ist u. dgl., nur einen zentralen Begriff andeutet.

(We must distinguish different concepts of *unmodified objectivities*, of which the "object simpliciter," namely the something identical which is perceived at one time, another time directly presentiated, a third time presented pictorially in a painting, and the like, only indicates *one* central concept.)

(Ibid., I, § 91, Hua III/1, 211; *Ideas pertaining to a Pure Phenomenology*, Eng. trans. F. Kersten, 222)

The expressions "pure objectival sense" ("*purer gegenständlicher Sinn*"), "noematic core" ("*noematischer Kern*"), and "of central core" ("*zentraler Kern*") thus refer to a layer of meaning of the complete object, namely that which we obtain by abstraction of the determinations inherent to the "how" of subjective directedness. The concept of "objectivity" thus has here the sense of the absence of subjective modification, and that of "pure object," the sense of a correlate prior to any changes of meaning related to the character of acts.

4. The distinction between noematic sense and determinable "object"

We said earlier that the Husserlian sense of objectivity reduces to the intentional or noematic sense, at the expense of the thing in itself, and that in this noematic sense the specifically "objective" moment was the core, obtained by eliminating the characters that inhere in the how of subjective directedness (remembered, imagined, and so on). However, the truly foundational sense of object in Husserl does not reduce either to the noematic sense or the noematic core, but to a final noematic layer, that of the "object" as a pure X, a pure "something," pure identical substrate of variable determinations:

Es scheidet sich als zentrales noematisches Moment aus: der "Gegenstand," das "Objekt," das "Identische," das "bestimmbare Subjekt seiner möglichen Prädikate"— das pure X in Abstraktion von allen Prädikaten—und es scheidet sich . . . von den Prädiktnoemen. . . . derart,

daß der charakterisierte Kern ein wandelbarer und der "Gegenstand," das pure Subjekt der Prädikate, eben ein identisches ist. . . . Kein "Sinn" ohne das "etwas" und wieder ohne "bestimmenden Inhalt."

(The identical intentional "object" becomes evidently distinguished from the changing and alterable "predicates." It becomes separated as central noematic moment: the "object," the "Object," the "*Identical*," the "determinable subject of its possible predicates"—*the pure X in abstraction from all predicates*—and it becomes separated *from* these predicates or, more precisely, from the predicate-noemas . . . such that the characterized core is a changeable one and the "object," the pure subject of the predicating, is precisely an identical one. . . . No "sense" without the "*something*" and, again, without "*determining content*.")

(Ibid., I, § 131, Hua III/1, 302-3; *Ideas pertaining to a Pure Phenomenology*, Eng. trans. F. Kersten, 313–15)

What may we say about this sense of the concept of object, manifested in general by the quotation marks? How is it different from the standard concept of intentional object, as well as the concepts of object "pure and simple" and of the noematic core? The noetico-noematic parallelism allows us to understand it: just as at the analytic level any grasp of an object may be decomposed into partial intentions, the noematic sense is broken down into layers of partial senses, the fundamental one being the sense of the noematic core (e.g., a church, abstracted away from knowing whether it is perceived, remembered, etc.) and, more profoundly, the object "pure and simple" (the same church as a material thing, abstracted away from its spiritual predicates). Inversely, however, any directed act, at the synthetic level, no matter what changes affect the object, is not limited to aiming at such or such a state of the object but remains directed at the *same* object (if the church is destroyed or the tree burns, the rubble or ash are indeed the remains of that very object, even though it is unrecognizable). As a result, any grasping of a concrete object involves, at its foundation, the minimal grasp of a pure permanent substrate, the guarantor of the identity of the object. This is the concept of "object": pure *hupokeimenon* [ὑποκείμενον], pure "that-there" or "something," prior to any determination, defined only by permanence and determinability. We find here the function of the Kantian concepts of a transcendental object or *Objekt überhaupt*, or of the category of substance: in the absence of the transcendent existence of the object, grounding the identity of the objective correlate in the permanence of an empty grasping. That there is no sense without the "something" means that the indeterminate relation to the object X (indeed that is the title of the first chapter of the fourth section of the *Ideen* I: "The noematic sense and the relation to the object") precedes any relationship to a determined object, and hence that formal ontology, the theory of the pure "something," has a foundational status for material ontologies. Thus one should, strictly speaking, as in Kant, translate this occurrence of the concept of "object" by "ob-ject," to distinguish it from the object provided with a determined noematic sense, meaning by this the permanence of a correlate for consciousness.

5. The twofold sense of "objectivity":
Objektivität and *Gegenständlichkeit*

Finally the concept of *Objektivität*, which we translate by "objectivity," does not refer like *Gegenständlichkeit* to the relation to an objectity, but to the highest level of objectification, namely intersubjective validity. The objective thing ("*objectives Ding*") is the "intersubjectively identical physical thing" ("*das intersubjektiv identische Ding*," *Ideen* I §151, Hua III/1, 352; *Ideas pertaining to a Pure Phenomenology*, Eng. trans. Kersten, 363), which is a unit constitutive of a higher order ("*eine konstitutive Einheit höherer Ordnung*") insofar as it derives from an intersubjective constitution, related to an indefinite plurality of subjects linked by a reciprocal comprehension "for which *one* physical thing is to be intersubjectively given and identified as the same objective actuality [*für welche ein Ding als dasselbe objektiv Wirkliche intersubjektiv zu geben und zu identifizieren ist*]" (ibid., § 135, Hua III/1, 310–11; Eng. trans. Kersten, 323). In this regard the highest-level objectivity, related to an indefinitely open community, is the "true thing" (*das wahre Ding*), which Husserl calls *das physikalische Ding*, and which is not simply the "*chose physique*" (ibid., § 41, Hua III/1, 83—Ricoeur, or "physical thing," Boyce Gibson), but the thing-of-physical-thought (i.e., as conceived in physics), just as *das physikalische Wahre* refers not to "physical truth" but to the truth sought by physical science, which strips nature of its subjective-relative qualities. The "true thing" is not the thing in itself as intelligible cause of all apprehension but the superstructure built up by mathematical thought on the world of appearing objects.

Dominique Pradelle

BIBLIOGRAPHY

Guyer, Paul. *Kant and the Claims of Knowledge*. Cambridge: Cambridge University Press, 1987.

Heidegger, Martin. *Die Grundprobleme der Phänomenologie*. Edited by Friedrich-Wilhelm von Herrmann. In *Gesamtausgabe*, vol. 24. Frankfurt am Main: Klostermann, 1975. Translation by Albert Hofstadter: *The Basic Problems of Phenomenology*. Bloomington: Indiana University Press, 1981.

———. *Kant und das Problem der Metaphysik*. In *Gesamtausgabe*, vol. 3. Frankfurt am Main: Klostermann, 1991. Translation by Richard Taft: *Kant and the Problem of Metaphysics*. 5th ed. Bloomington: Indiana University Press, 1997.

———. *Phänomenologische Interpretation von Kants Kritik der reinen Vernunft*. Edited by Ingtraud Görland. In *Gesamtausgabe*, vol. 25. Frankfurt am Main: Klostermann, 1977. Translation by Parvis Emad and Kenneth Maly: *Phenomenological Interpretation of Kant's Critique of Pure Reason*. Bloomington: Indiana University Press, 1997.

Husserl, Edmund. *Formal und transzendentale Logik: Versuch einer Kritik der logischen Vernunft*. Edited by Paul Janssen. Husserliana 27. The Hague: Nijhoff, 1974.

———. *Die Idee der Phänomenologie: Fünf Vorlesungen*. Edited by Walter Biemel. Husserliana 2. The Hague: Nijhoff, 1973. Translation by W. Alston and G. Nakhnikian: *The Idea of Phenomenology*. Dordrecht: Kluwer, 1990.

———. *Ideen zu einer reinen Phänomenologie und phänomenologischen Philosophie*. 2 vols. Vol. 1 edited by Karl Schuhmann; vol. 2 edited by Marly Biemel. Husserliana 3.1 and 4. (HUA) The Hague: Nijhoff, 1976, 1952. Translation by F. Kersten: *Ideas pertaining to a Pure Phenomenology and to a Phenomenological Philosophy*. First Book. The Hague: Nijhoff, 1989.

———. *Logische Untersuchungen*. Part 2. Edited by Ursula Panzer. Husserliana 19. The Hague: Nijhoff, 1984. Translation by J. N. Findlay: *Logical Investigations*. 2 vols. London: Routledge & Kegan Paul, 1970.

Kant, Immanuel. *Dissertatio de 1770*. In *Kants Gesammelte Schriften*, vol. 2. Edited by Königlich Preussische Akademie der Wissenschaften. Berlin: De Gruyter, 1902–. Translation by David Walford and Ralf Meerbote: "On the Form and Principles of the Sensible and the Intelligible World." In Immanuel Kant, *Theoretical Philosophy, 1755–1770*, edited by David Walford. Cambridge: Cambridge University Press, 1992.

———. *Kants Gesammelte Schriften*. Edited by Königlich Preussische Akademie der Wissenschaften. Berlin: De Gruyter, 1902–.

———. *Kritik der praktischen Vernunft*. In *Kants Gesammelte Schriften*, vol. 5. Edited by Königlich Preussische Akademie der Wissenschaften. Berlin: De Gruyter, 1902–. First published in 1788. Translation by Werner S. Pluhar: *Critique of Practical Reason*, edited by Werner S. Pluhar. Indianapolis: Hackett, 2002.

———. *Kritik der reinen Vernunft*. In *Kants Gesammelte Schriften*, vols. 4 and 3. Edited by Königlich Preussische Akademie der Wissenschaften. Berlin: De Gruyter, 1902–. First published in 1781, 1787. Translation by Paul Guyer and A. Wood: *Critique of Pure Reason*, edited by Paul Guyer and A. Wood. Cambridge: Cambridge University Press, 1997.

———. *Kritik der Urteilskraft*. In *Kants Gesammelte Schriften*, vol. 5. Edited by Königlich Preussische Akademie der Wissenschaften. Berlin: De Gruyter, 1902–. First published in 1792. Translation by Paul Guyer and Eric Matthews: *Critique of the Power of Judgment*, edited by Paul Guyer and Eric Matthews. Cambridge: Cambridge University Press, 2000.

———. *Prolegomena zu einer jeden künftigen Metaphysik, die als Wissenschaft wird auftreten können*. In *Kants Gesammelte Schriften*, vol. 4. Edited by Königlich Preussische Akademie der Wissenschaften. Berlin: De Gruyter, 1902–. First published in 1783. Translation by Gary Hatfield: *Prolegomena to any Future Metaphysics That Will Be Able to Come Forward as Science; Selections from the Critique of Pure Reason*, edited by Gary Hatfield. Rev. ed. Cambridge: Cambridge University Press, 2004.

GEISTESWISSENSCHAFTEN (GERMAN)

ENGLISH	human sciences, moral sciences, social sciences, humanities, human studies
FRENCH	*sciences humaines, sciences de l'esprit*
ITALIAN	*scienze umane, scienze morali, scienze dello spirito*
POLISH	*nauki humanistyczne*

➤ BILDUNG, EPISTEMOLOGY, HISTORIA UNIVERSALIS, *HUMANITY*, LIGHT, MORALS, SOUL

The expression *Geisteswissenschaften* refers to an object or constellation of objects of experience: man and his actions in the world, by contrast with *Naturwissenschaften*, sciences of nature. This distinction is accompanied by a difference in method summed up by Wilhelm Dilthey in the distinction between "to explain" (*erklären*) and "to understand" (*verstehen*). The translation of *Geisteswissenschaft* gave rise to the formulation of a number of terms that intersect one or the other German meanings, without, however, completely exhausting its sense. Thus one is confronted each time with at least a pair of terms: in English, humanities / moral (social) sciences; in French *sciences de l'esprit / sciences humaines*; in Italian *scienze umane / scienze morali*. As a result, the choice of translation must come from a more or less clearly embraced decision as to what is understood by the very idea of science.

I. Dividing Science: *Geisteswissenschaften* and Its Translations

A. Emergence: Germany-England

Geisteswissenschaft, in the singular, appears toward the end of the eighteenth century in relation to a *Pneumatologie oder*

Geisteslehre (doctrine of the mind), a study of the intellectual and moral faculties of man. The plural *Geisteswissenschaften*, today firmly established, is used by Johann Gustav Droysen in his *Geschichte des Hellenismus* (1843, vol. 2, preface). The irony, however, is that the term starts spreading only in 1849—as a translation of the English "moral sciences." Dilthey is the one who, in 1883 (*Einleitung in die Geisteswissenschaften*), gives it its canonical usage and its conceptual dimension to refer to hermeneutic knowledge of cultural works and of mental objects throughout history.

- See Box 1.

B. "Moral sciences," "social sciences," "humanities"—France-Germany-England

The original expression "moral sciences" is used by John Stuart Mill in the sixth and last book of his *System of Logic, Ratiocinative and Inductive* (1843). But the new sense given to the word by Dilthey to its German translation, *Geisteswissenschaften*, explains, in reverse, the problems faced by the English translators of the *Einleitung in die Geisteswissenschaften*. Yet these latter difficulties are especially significant when one sets about defining and translating *Geisteswissenschaften*. The translation of *Geist* by "mind" does not seem wholly right, inasmuch as "mind" appears to refer primarily to the mental life of the individual; but "mind" may nonetheless also refer to a collection: thus the title of Dilthey's *Geschichte des deutschen Geistes* was translated as *Studies concerning the History of the German Mind*, such that R. G. Collingwood translated *Geisteswissenschaften* as *Sciences of Mind*. However, even though Dilthey refers explicitly to the Hegelian concept of *Geist*, neither "mind" nor "spirit," the two most likely candidates as translations for *Geisteswissenschaften*, prevailed when Hegel's *Phänomenologie des Geistes* was rendered into English. Two other terms were used instead: "moral sciences" and "social sciences."

1. "Moral sciences" and *Geisteswissenschaften*

In French and English, the expressions "moral sciences" and "moral and political sciences," which for a long time were used to translate *Geisteswissenschaften* (see B. Groethuysen, "Dilthey and His School" of 1912, as well as André Lalande's RT: *Vocabulaire technique et critique de la philosophie* of 1938 and its entry for "science," or Raymond Aron's use of these expressions interchangeably with *sciences de l'esprit* in 1935), fell out of use, and were progressively replaced by "human sciences," *scienze umane*, and *sciences humaines* (see the English and French translations of Dilthey's *Einleitung*, in 1988 and 1942 respectively). With their indeterminate connotations, these more recent expressions blur the line between two conceptions of science—the first inductive or mathematized, like economics and some sectors of sociology, the second comprehensive, such as history. This is clearly seen by looking, in contrast, at what Mill means by "moral sciences," namely, essentially political science, sociology, and political economy, underwritten by a science of the laws of mental life.

2. *Geisteswissenschaften* and "social sciences"

In fact, the phrase "social sciences" has an equally valid claim as does "moral sciences" to serve as the description for these pursuits. At first glance, it does not seem illegitimate to defend this claim even as a translation of Dilthey, who, after all, judges it necessary to give as the subtitle of his *Introduction*, "Versuch einer Grundlegung der Gesellschaft und der Geschichte"—"An Attempt to Lay a Foundation for the Study of Society and History," in Betanzos's translation. Nevertheless, the concept of *Geisteswissenschaften* remains irreducible to Mill's project, for, far from wishing to establish the autonomy of the sciences of mind, Mill wishes on the contrary to widen the field of application of the inductive method to the "sciences of Ethics and Politics" or "moral and social sciences," or again to the "sciences of human nature and society." Book VI of Mill's *System of Logic, Ratiocinative and Inductive*, devoted to the moral sciences, is thus only a "kind of supplement or appendix" (2:478) to the rest of the system.

It is thus significant that the epigraph of Mill's book is a quotation from Condorcet's *Esquisse d'un tableau historique des progrès de l'esprit humain* (1793). Why Condorcet, rather than someone like Hume?

The goal of Hume's *Treatise of Human Nature; being an attempt to introduce the experimental method of reasoning into moral subjects* (1793) is in fact literally identical with Mill's, especially since this "science of man" must be completed by the "examination of morals, politics, and criticism." However, Condorcet, though using the expressions *sciences humaines*, *sciences morales et politiques*, and *sciences métaphysiques et sociales* indifferently, deploys social mathematics in an explicit and systematic way, of which Fourierist calculus is a kind of caricature and in relation to which Auguste Comte remains far in the background.

Despite the idea of a science of human "nature" and the ambiguity of the normative connotation of "moral sciences," the way in which Mill conceives of these sciences, whose certainty is uncontestable insofar as they concern "the character and collective conduct of masses" (*System of Logic*, 2:495), explains in advance the future decline of this expression in favor of "social sciences," that is, of "behavioral sciences" (see BEHAVIOR). Whereas the political, cultural, and national sense of Dilthey's project is to restore the "unity of the German vision of the world," the social aim of these sciences is to rationalize society, and, for Condorcet, to reduce inequalities by conceiving of, for example, a system of retirement and life insurance.

To compensate, the subjects that are most resistant to such a treatment—for example, art history as compared to economics—seem doomed to subsist under the name "humanities," with the term "moral" withdrawing of its own accord in deference to the new division between the *natural* and *social* sciences. In this context, "humanities" hardly corresponds to what social sciences covers, in particular because of the connotation of the word "science," whose extension is much narrower than that of *Wissenschaft*. Its choice in 1961 as the translation of Ernst Cassirer's *Logik der Kulturwissenschaft* (cf. also Rudolf Makkreel, who devotes a work to Dilthey in 1975: *Dilthey: Philosopher of the Human Studies*), is in fact much closer in spirit to what Dilthey means. Unlike "humanities" and like the Polish *nauki haumanistyczne*, in which the term means both human and humanist,

1

The structuring of a term: Dilthey's antitheses

With Dilthey, the science of *Geist* (mind) is no longer the knowledge of man in general, his faculties, his critical or moral reason, but rather a bundle of disciplines and empirical sciences whose objects are determined by the different historical manifestations of *Geist*. At the same time, the differences in method within the sciences of nature are no longer limited to a simple partition between two groups of disciplines within the universe of science.

The same year (1883) in which Dilthey published his essay on *Geisteswissenschaften*, Wilhelm Windelband introduced a distinction between what he termed monothetic (*monothetisch*) and idiographic (*idiographisch*) sciences, and applied the distinction to the domains that Dilthey had sought to characterize. The first, monothetic sciences, are those, like the natural sciences, that aim to give order to diverse phenomena by building a system of concepts or laws having the most general possible validity. The second, idiographic sciences, are those that, like the historical sciences, deal with events in their concrete singularity and their individual becoming. In reality, as concerns Dilthey, this distinction is relative not to the object of study but to the method. If the object itself were at issue, it would not be *Geist* but *Kultur*, in the sense understood by Heinrich Rickert, who, in the wake of Windelband, criticizes the concept of *Geist*.

This situation yields two major consequences:

1. On the one hand, *Geisteswissenschaften* become, with their plurality, empirical disciplines, which leads to the translation into French not as *sciences morales* but as *sciences humaines*. By this transformation, the term *Geisteswissenschaften* no longer covers the rigorously scientific sense of a moral or philosophical reflection; rather, it leads to a separation with philosophy, which is thenceforth placed on a higher level of abstraction.
2. On the other hand, and in consequence, this situation yields a definitive fusion of the determinations of method and content in a single term, *Geisteswissenschaften*, which does not take place in other languages. To the contrary: in other languages this situation provokes a proliferation of terminology that the synthetic character of the German term prevents.

These phenomena are perfectly summed up by Dilthey in the following lines:

Besides the natural sciences, a group of conceptual cognitive results emerged naturally from the tasks of life itself.

These results are linked to one another by their common object. [Neben den Naturwissenschaften hat sich eine Gruppe von Erkenntnissen entwickelt, naturwüchsig, aus den Aufgaben des Lebens selbst, welche durch die Gemeinsamkeit des Gegenstandes miteinander verbunden sind.] History, political economy, the sciences of law and of the state, the study of religion, literature, poetry, architecture, music, of philosophical world-views and systems, and finally, psychology are such sciences. All these sciences refer to the same grand fact: the human race [Alle diese Wissenschaften beziehen sich auf dieselbe große Tatsache : das Menschengeschlecht] which they describe, narrate, and judge, and about which they form concepts and theories.

What one customarily separates as physical and psychical is undivided in this fact of the human sciences. It contains the living nexus of both. We ourselves belong to nature, and nature is at work in us, unconsciously, in dark drives. States of consciousness are constantly expressed in gestures, looks, and words; and they have their objectivity in institutions, states, churches, and scientific institutes. History operates in these very contexts.

Of course, this does not exclude the possibility that the human sciences employ the distinction between the physical and the psychical whenever their purposes require it. But then they must remain conscious that they are working with abstractions, not with entities, and that these abstractions are valid only within the limits of the point of view within which they are projected. . . .

For it is clear that the human sciences and natural sciences cannot be logically divided into two classes by means of two spheres of facts formed by them. Physiology also deals with an aspect of man, and it is a natural science. Consequently, the basis for distinguishing the two classes cannot be found in the facts taken on their own. The human sciences must be related differently to the physical and to the psychical aspects of man. And that is in fact the case [Denn es ist klar, daß die Geisteswissenschaften und die Naturwissenschaften nicht logisch korrekt als zwei Klassen gesondert werden können durch zwei Tatsachenkreise, die sie bilden. . . . Die Geisteswissenschaften müssen sich zu der physischen Seite der Menschen

anders verhalten als zur psychischen. Und so ist es in der Tat].

(*The Formation of the Historical World in the Human Sciences*, 101–2; *Die Aufbau der geschichtlichen Welt in den Geisteswissenschaften*, in *Gesammelte Schriften*, 7:91–92)

There is a measurable difference between these later theses and Dilthey's earlier suggestions, in the *Einleitung* of 1883, which still attached the *Geisteswissenschaften* to the domain of particular objects:

All the disciplines that have sociohistorical reality as their subject matter [*welche die geschichtlich-gesellschaftliche Wirklichkeit zu ihren Gegenstände haben*] are encompassed in this work under the name "human sciences" [*Geisteswissenschaften*].

(*Introduction to the Human Sciences*, 1:56; *Einleitung in die Geisteswissenschaften*, in *Gesammelte Schriften*, 1:4)

Nonetheless, the plurality of sciences referred to as *Geisteswissenschaften* seem capable of being brought under a certain unity, that of *Geist*. While the nature of this unity is made increasingly difficult to grasp by Dilthey's evolution, its effects make themselves felt nonetheless. The plasticity of the notion of *Geist*, its semantic richness, meant that German did not feel the need to vary its expressions and add to its lexicon in this regard. Thus, a plurality of terms in other languages is required to correspond to the multivocal German word.

Luca M. Scarantino

BIBLIOGRAPHY

Dilthey, Wilhelm. *Die Aufbau der geschichtlichen Welt in den Geisteswissenschaften, Abgrenzung der Geisteswissenschaften*. Vol. 7 of *Gesammelte Schriften*. Leipzig: Teubner, 1927. Translation by Rudolf A. Makkreel and William H. Oman: "Plan for the Continuation of the Formation of the Historical World in the Human Sciences," in *The Formation of the Historical World in the Human Sciences*. Vol. 3 of *Wilhelm Dilthey: Selected Works*, edited by Rudolf A. Makkreel and Frithjof Rodi. Princeton, NJ: Princeton University Press, 2002.
———. *Einleitung in die Geisteswissenschaften*. Vol. 1 of *Gesammelte Schriften*. Leipzig: Teubner, 1923. Translation by Michael Neville et al.: *Introduction to the Human Sciences*. Vol. 1 of *Wilhelm Dilthey: Selected Works*, edited by Rudolf A. Makkreel and Frithjof Rodi. Princeton, NJ: Princeton University Press, 1989.

"human studies," used from the nineteenth century on, has the particularity of incorporating the social sciences.

■ See Box 2.

II. Conceiving the Science of Man: The Philological and Historical Model

At bottom what determines the gap between *Geisteswissenschaften* and the social sciences is the way in which each conceives of history and the knowledge it is possible to have of it. Already in 1876, Dilthey considered the isolation in which the science of history was confined as responsible for the inability of *Geisteswissenschaften* to constitute themselves as autonomous, and he countered Comte and Mill with the

"German spirit of historiography." The "sciences of mind" are, he argues, the result of the process by which philology and the literary humanities of the Renaissance humanists transform themselves into a comparative study of the productions of the mind. In still other words, two factors are decisive for the birth or acceptance of the idea of *Geisteswissenschaften*: a philological tradition and the appearance of historical consciousness.

In this respect, Dilthey is partially anticipated in both the theses and the terminology of Ernest Renan's *L'Avenir de la science* (chap. 8, written in 1848–49, published in 1890). Educated in the German tradition, Renan contrasts the sciences of nature with the "sciences of humanity," that is, the philological and historical sciences, even while anticipating

---

2

Geisteswissenschaften: French and Italian solutions

When the expression *sciences de l'esprit* is adopted in France after the publication in 1883 of Dilthey's *Einleitung in die Geisteswissenschaften*, it does not appear to take root except in this technical sense, and its use remains limited to it. And even though Renan speaks of *sciences des faits de l'esprit* (sciences of the activities of mind), founded essentially on philology, the French philosophical tradition remains faithful to the expression *sciences morales*, used in the wide sense of the study of human intellectual faculties. This meaning was already to be found in the names of pedagogical institutions, and, since 1795, in that of the Académie des Sciences Morales et Politiques.

The integration into French usage of the constellation of disciplines that Dilthey addresses takes place by way of the notion of *sciences humaines*. These disciplines are distinguished, especially in ordinary usage, from the *sciences sociales*, which often rely on formal methods. In addition, the twofold character of sociological studies, which deal with human problems but in a quantified form, often resisted various attempts to classify this discipline with the human sciences. In order to truly encompass all the disciplines corresponding to Dilthey's *Geisteswissenschaften*, whose work was translated only in 1942 under the title *Introduction à l'étude des sciences humaines* (before the Faculties of Letters became, in 1958, the *facultés des lettres et sciences humaines*), French today tends to use the expression *sciences de l'homme*, which covers the range of studies concerning the human condition, as well as our individual and collective actions, but thoroughly independently of the methods of investigation used. Thus, before taking up his post at the Collège de France, in 1952, Maurice Merleau-Ponty devoted his course at the Sorbonne to

the "Sciences de l'homme dans leur rapport à la phénoménologie," grouping together psychology, sociology, and history. Regarding this question of the field's name and its content, Fernand Braudel points out in *Les Ambitions de l'histoire* that the commonalities and the differences between a human science, history, and the *sciences du social*. These, he writes, are

> more scientific than history, more articulated than it with regard to the mass of social facts. . . . [T]hey are—another difference—deliberately focused on the actual, that is, on life, and they all work on what can be seen, measured, touched . . . . Our methods are not the same as theirs, but our problems [certainly] are . . . . And though there is dependency, and enriching dependency, of the historian with regard to the social sciences, he maintains a position outside them.

> (*On History* [translation modified])

We may note, finally, that a new edition of the French translation of Dilthey's *Einleitung* was published in 1992 under the title *Introduction aux sciences de l'esprit*, as though it was judged preferable to return to a literal translation rather than use the various equivalents that had previously been offered.

Parallel to the moral sciences, which betrays an aspiration of submitting the study of the human mind (moral philosophy) to rules of analysis as precise as those governing the study of nature, we must also mention the notion of *Moralwissenschaft* introduced by Georg Simmel (*Einleitung in die Moralwissenschaft*, 1892) to distinguish it from *Geisteswissenschaften* understood in Dilthey's sense, which Italian rationalism

develops under the name of *scienza della morale*, a variation on *filosofia della morale*, whose meaning is different from *filosofia morale* (cf. Banfi, "Rendiconti del Regio Istituto Lombardo di Scienze e Lettere") The distinction becomes less trivial once Italian begins widely using the notion of *scienze morali* in the same sense as the French *sciences morales*, and the expression *scienze dello spirito* to translate the idealist connotation of *Geisteswissenschaften*. Italian thus appeals to a lexical plurality very much like that of French to satisfy the different connotations of the German expression. Though we may gather together under the notion of *scienze umane* the collection of disciplines defined by Dilthey, they are not all included in *scienze morali*. Antonio Banfi thus points out in his polemic against Benedetto Croce that, "for the rest, . . . in Germany they continue to speak of *Geisteswissenschaft* and *Geisteswissenschaften* in a sense that is comparable to, but wider than, that which the *scienze morali* had for us, and they remember that the position and function of philosophy with regard to these disciplines are still of some interest" ("Discussioni").

Luca M. Scarantino

BIBLIOGRAPHY

Banfi, Antonio. "Discussioni." *Studi filosofici* 2 (1941).
———. "Rendiconti del Regio Istituto lombardo di scienze e lettere." *Sui principi di una filosofia della morale*. 67 (1933–34).
Braudel, Fernand. *Les Ambitions de l'histoire*. Edited by Roselyne de Ayala and Paule Braudel. Vol. 2 of *Les Écrits de Fernand Braudel*. Paris: Éditions de Fallois, 1997. Translation by Sarah Matthews: *On History*. Part 2 of *History and the Other Human Sciences*. Chicago: Chicago University Press, 1980.

the reasons for the limited character of his own reception. Clearly inspired by the use of the term "philology" in Germany, at a time when it was used to describe German studies and the studies of literature, art, and religion, which are structured on the model of studies of antiquity, Renan emphasizes philology as an "*exact science* of the things of the mind" or "science of the products of the human mind," and thus defines the general orientation of the sciences of humanity, rather closely in line with the future Diltheyan conception of *Geisteswissenschaften* (chap. 8).

If we inquire, not what is particularly German about *Geisteswissenschaften*, but rather what in French resists the literal translation of "sciences of the mind," Renan indicates first the absence of philology, which would explain the simplicity and the violence of Auguste Comte's apprehension of history. Renan thinks that the latter's conception of it is "the narrowest" and his method "the coarsest." The model is no longer Comte's ("Comte understands nothing of the sciences of humanity, since he is not a philologist," Renan writes to Mill, 21 October 1844), but rather that of Vico: the history of humanity is deciphered in the history of language. And Condorcet's project of setting up "a universal language" is just as much at the opposite extreme from the philologist's love of language. Deploring the "withering of the scientific spirit" due to the system "of public instruction which makes science a simple means of education and not an end in itself," Renan is in the end targeting what he calls a typical characteristic of the French mind: "a whole petty manner of saying 'bah' to the qualities of the scientist in order to raise oneself up by those of the man of sense and the man of wit . . . and which Mme de Staël so rightly called the 'pedantry of trifling [*pédantisme de la légèreté*]' " (1995, chap. 6).

The Italian reception of Dilthey's project and the acceptance of *scienze dello spirito* is by contrast much easier, given that Benedetto Croce contributes to a revival of interest in Vico, in whom he saw a precursor of Hegel. This reception also, however, has as a background the philological tradition of the Renaissance humanists. The expression of "human sciences," a clear calque of *studia humanitatis*, which the Florentine chancellor Coluccio Salutati, a disciple of Petrarch, distinguished from *studia divinitatis*, appears in French in the seventeenth century with the same meaning (Wartburg, *Französisches etymologisches Wörterbuch*, 11:308), that is, before acquiring its modern meaning. But the idea of the thing had in fact existed before the imposition of the current nomenclature: Vico studies institutions, myths, and language relying on the philology of Lorenzo Valla, and defends the specificity of the philological method and the certainty of its sorts of knowledge relative to the *mondo civile*. We can understand why Renan and Dilthey refer to him, as their respective projects of an "embryogeny" of the human mind and of comparative psychology are inscribed in the tradition of *La Scienza nuova* (1744).

The translations of *Geisteswissenschaften* thus fall on one side or the other of a fault line between two conceptions of the "human sciences," which correspond more or less to the division separating Anglo-Saxon and Continental philosophies. The expression "social sciences," replacing *sciences morales*, refers to a rationality that implies quantification and prediction: the "humanities" are then merely what remains after the social sciences have gone about the tasks of quantification and prediction. By contrast, expressions like *sciences de l'esprit*, "human studies," and *Geisteswissenschaften* have as their background the philological and historical, that is, the interpretive conception of the human sciences.

■ See Box 3.

Jean-Claude Gens

BIBLIOGRAPHY

Baker, Keith Michael. *Condorcet: From Natural Philosophy to Social Mathematics.* Chicago: Chicago University Press, 1975.

Banfi, Antonio. *Principi di una teoria della ragione.* Vol. 1 of *Opere.* Milan: Parenti, 1960. First published in 1926.

3

Between *Sciences Humaines* and the "Human Sciences"

➤ BEHAVIOR, EPISTEMOLOGY, LIGHT, MORALS, PRAXIS, STRUCTURE

The expression *sciences humaines* (human sciences) is specific to French culture, situated in a philosophical discourse (which claims to engage in an "epistemology of the human sciences") and in institutional arrangements (the Département des Sciences de l'Homme et de la Société at the CNRS, the Maison des Sciences de l'Homme). It originated in the reversal of a theological opposition: after contrasting "science of man" with "science of God" (which means that human capacity for knowledge of the world is finite compared with an infinite divine capacity), "science of man" was contrasted with "science of nature." The origins of this reversal can be found particularly in Malebranche (préface to *La Recherche de la Vérité*, 1674). What is fundamentally involved is the articulation of the biological, psychological, and sociological dimensions of the "human phenomenon." The term "anthropology" (until recently always accompanied in French by an adjective: *anthropologie physique, culturelle, sociale, philosophique*, and so on) thus acquired an architectonic function only in the titles of individual works, as a doctrinal position taken and not as an institutional norm. See HISTORIA UNIVERSALIS; cf. CULTURE, HUMANITY.

Things are indeed different in German, where the term *Geisteswissenschaften* bears the stamp of a philosophical conception of the "objective spirit," with or without the methodological opposition between "understanding" (*Verstehen*) and "explanation" (*Erklären*). They also differ in British and American usage, where "anthropology" is common and universal, "social science" is oriented toward practical applications of sociological and economic knowledge, and "human sciences" (by contrast with the humanities, a set of "literary" disciplines) is clearly oriented toward the study of living human beings in their medical and environmental aspects; or in Italian, where *scienze umanese* are distinguished from the *scienze morali*. See also SECULARIZATION.

Condorcet, Jean-Antoine-Nicolas de Caritat, marquis de. "Discours de réception à l'Académie française." Vol. 1 of Œuvres, edited by Arthur O'Connor and François Arago. Paris: Firmin Didot frères, 1847–49. First published in 1782. Translation: "Reception Speech at the French Academy." In Selected Writings, edited by Keith Michael Baker. Indianapolis: Bobbs-Merrill, 1976.

———. Esquisse d'un tableau historique des progress de l'esprit humain. Vol. 6 of Œuvres, edited by Arthur O'Connor and François Arago. Paris: Firmin Didot frères, 1847–49. Translation by June Barraclough: Sketch for a Historical Picture of the Progress of the Human Mind. Westport, CT: Hyperion Press, 1979.

Dewey, John. Reconstruction in Philosophy. 2nd ed. Boston: Beacon Press, 1948.

Dilthey, Wilhelm. Einleitung in die Geisteswissenschaften: Versuch einer Grundlegung für das Studium der Gesellschaft und der Geschichte. Vol. 1 of Gesammelte Schriften. Leipzig: Teubner, 1923. First published in 1883. Translation, with an introductory essay, by Ramon J. Batanzos: Introduction to the Human Sciences: An Attempt to Lay a Foundation for the Study of Society and History. Detroit, MI.: Wayne State University Press, 1988. Translation by Michael Neville, Jeffrey Barnouw, Franz Schreiner, and Rudolf A. Makkreel: Introduction to the Human Sciences. Vol. 1 of Wilhelm Dilthey: Selected Works, edited by Rudolf A. Makkreel and Frithjof Rodi. Princeton, NJ: Princeton University Press, 1989. French translation by L. Sauzin: Introduction à l'étude des sciences humaines. Paris: Presses Universitaires de France, 1942.

Goldmann, Lucien. The Human Sciences and Philosophy. Translated by Hayden V. White and Robert Anchor. London: Jonathan Cape, 1969.

Granger, Gilles-Gaston. Formal Thought and the Sciences of Man. Translated by Alexander Rosenberg. Dordrecht, Neth.: Reidel, 1983.

Hume, David. A Treatise of Human Nature. Edited by P. H. Nidditch. Oxford: Clarendon Press, 1978. First published in 1739.

Lécuyer, Bernard-Pierre. "Sciences sociales (Préhistoire des)." In Encyclopaedia Universalis. Paris: Encylopaedia Universalis, 1984.

Mill, John Stuart. A System of Logic, Ratiocinative and Inductive: Being a Connected View of the Principles of Evidence, and the Methods of Scientific Investigation. Edited by J. M. Robson. Vols. 7–8 in Collected Works. Toronto: Toronto University Press, 1973–74.

Renan, Ernest. L'Avenir de la science. Paris: Flammarion, 1995. First published in 1890. Translation by Albert D. Vandam and C. B. Pitman: The Future of Science: Ideas of 1848. London: Chapman and Hall, 1891.

Vico, Giambattista. La Scienza Nuova. 2 vols. Edited by Fausto Nicolini. Rome: Laterza, 1974. First published in 1744. Translation by Thomas Goddard Bergin and Max Harold Fisch: The New Science of Giambattista Vico. Ithaca, NY: Cornell University Press, 1968.

Wartburg, Walther von. Französisches etymologisches Wörterbuch. Leipzig: Verlag B. G. Teubner, 1934–98.

GEMÜT (GERMAN)

ENGLISH	mind, mood
FRENCH	âme, cœur, sentiments, affectivité, esprit
GREEK	thumos [θυμός]
LATIN	mens, animus

➤ HEART, SOUL, TO SENSE, and CONSCIOUSNESS, FEELING, GEFÜHL, GENIUS, GOGO, INGENIUM, PATHOS

Gemüth (today written Gemüt) is one of those terms that has no substitute, that refers to the register of the soul/mind without any of these equivalents being satisfactory. At the same time, it is one of the oldest philosophical terms in the German language, present from Eckhart to phenomenology. In Gemüth, the prefix ge- indicates a gathering, a unity. The word is formed from Muth, the mind of the man, the state of the soul, courage, humor—its meanings cover the range from the Greek thumos [θυμός] to the English "mood," but it also acquires some highly specific senses, such as Anmuth (grace) and Demuth (humility). Because of its difference from the soul, Seele, it is perceived as the equivalent of the Latin animus in relation to

anima. But W. T. Krug notes precisely that "since the French do not have a special word for Gemüth, they translate it by âme [Seele]," which in turn has repercussions for Gemüt (RT: Allgemeines Handwörterbuch, 2:185–87).

In the strict sense, Gemüt is most often an internal principle that animates the mind and its affections. Its purview is sometimes limited to the affective part when it is in competition with Geist, but not always—especially in its Kantian use. From the heights of mysticism, the word moves progressively, starting in the nineteenth century, into the bourgeois register of comfort and well-being through its adjectivization into gemütlich, which, in common language, took on the sense of "nice"—the French colloquial sympa is in the end a rather faithful translation. But this banalization cannot completely hide the exploitation of Gemüt and of the associated register of terms referring to irrational powers in the pre-Nazi and Nazi years, the 1920s and 1930s, going hand in hand with the exploitation of a tradition of "Germanic" profundity that invoked Eckhart, Cusanus, and Paracelsus: the term Gemüt itself was sufficient to call up the superiority of the German language, rooted in archaic depths.

I. The Mystic Soul

The first conceptual determination of Gemüt comes from German mysticism, where it refers to the whole of a man's internal world, the interior of representations and ideas: "There is a force in the soul which is called gemüete" (Ein kraft ist in der sêle, diu heizet daz gemüete). A "free spirit" is "ein ledic gemüete" (Die rede der unterscheidunge, in Eckhart, Die deutschen Werke, 5:190.9), but gemüete refers to something deeper than the mind, as suggested by the expression "your depth and your mind" (dînen grunt und dîn gemüete, ibid., 5:255.8). Sermon 83 (ibid., 3:437.4–8) establishes the coherence between geiste, mens, and gemüete, referring both to Saint Paul (Eph. 4:34) and to Augustine, which makes it possible to specify that mens or gemüete refers to the superior part of the soul, selen ("caput animae": Enarratio in Psalmum, 3.3; RT: PL 36:73). In the sixteenth century, Grund and Gemüth are still narrowly associated with Paracelsus, where Gemüth refers to the "very depths of ourselves," the place "where we find ourselves entirely reunited" (Braun, Paracelse, 187):

> The Gemüth of men is something so considerable that no one can express it. And like God himself, Prima Materia, and heaven, which are all three eternal and immovable, such is the Gemüth of man. It is thus that man is happy by and with his Gemüth, that is, he lives eternally and no longer dies.
>
> (Paracelsus, Liber de imaginibus)

It goes without saying that the investment of the notion of Gemüth in this tradition is significant, and also includes Jakob Böhme (Of the Three Principles, 10.37), who leaves his own mark on the nascent philosophical vocabulary, as we can see in Gottfried Leibniz.

This determination is massively reaffirmed in German romanticism, in particular in Friedrich Schleiermacher's Discourses on Religion (twenty-four occurrences), where he defends the idea that the seat of religiosity is "a province in the soul [eine Provinz im Gemüt]" (from the "Apologie," Reden), and in Novalis, in particular Heinrich von Ofterdingen (1.6).

II. The Transcendental Faculty

One of the most spectacular deletions in the translation of Kant's works into other languages is the systematic disappearance of the term *Gemüt* in favor of "spirit" or "mind." Yet Kant, unlike the idealist philosophers who follow him, does not, in the *Critique of Pure Reason*, use *Geist*, and he uses it in alternation with *Gemüt* in the *Critique of Judgment*. Vittorio Mathieu, the Italian "reviser" (1974) of Giovanni Gentile's translation (1909) of the *Critique of Pure Reason*, sees Gentile's use of *spirito* for *Gemüth* as a "traduzione tipicamente gentiliana"—in other words, an idealist corruption of Kant's sense, which he corrects by substituting for it the word *animo*.

■ See Box 1.

For Kant, *Gemüt* is presented from the start as a collection of transcendental powers, their foundation and their source at the same time. The *Transcendental Logic* invokes it at the beginning:

> Our cognition arises from two fundamental sources in the mind, the first of which is the reception of representations (the receptivity of impressions), the second the faculty for cognizing an object by means of these representations (spontaneity of concepts).
>
> (*Critique of Pure Reason*, A50/B74, trans. Guyer and Wood)

In the *Critique of Judgment*, *Gemüt* functions as the framework within which the faculties work reciprocally, without being at any moment positively determined, transcendentally or anthropologically. In §49, Kant even defines the *Geist* (mind) at the heart of *Gemüt* as "its vivifying power." This does not make him a mystic, but rather inscribes him in a search for the formulation of a vocabulary of feeling, one of the decisive issues of moral and aesthetic thought in the eighteenth century. In the continuity of the neutral space between passivity and activity linked by sentiment, Kant dissociates *Gemüt* from the practical meaning that the term commonly held before him, in the tradition of Leibnizianism, in works by Christian Wolff, Friedrich Meier, and Moses Mendelssohn. In his 1808 dictionary, Adelung gives a standard account of the word's eighteenth-century meaning, as expressing "the soul" (*Seele*) related to desires and will, by contrast with the theorizing "mind" (*Geist*) (RT: *Versuch eines vollständingen*, s.v.). The term, which thus means for Kant "the set of the transcendental faculties," drifts progressively into the domains of psychology and ordinary language, whereas German Idealism, in its theological inspiration, gives primacy to the term *Geist*. The *Geistesgeschichte* of the beginning of the twentieth century, a sort of history of ideas in a metaphysical mode, reintroduces *Gemüt* forcefully among the irreducibly "Germanic" notions of the mind, opening the way for Nazi exploitation of the term. A characteristic of a certain literary romanticism, *Gemüt* retains, even in its ambiguity, a

---

1

Gemüt in the *Critique of Pure Reason*

The term *Gemüt* is especially frequent in *Transcendental Aesthetic*. In section 1.A.19, intuition is only possible if the object is given to us. That, in turn, necessarily presupposes "dadurch . . . daß er das Gemüt auf gewisse Weise affiziere": in various translations, "if it affects the mind [*das Gemüth*] in a certain way" (Guyer and Wood); "à la condition que si l'objet affecte d'une certaine manière notre esprit [*das Gemüth*]" (Kant, *Critique of Pure Reason*, French translation by Tremesaygues and Pacaud); "si l'objet affecte d'une certaine manière notre esprit" (Barni and Marty); "parce que l'objet affecte l'esprit sur un certain mode" (Renaut, with a note); "in quanto modifichi, in certo modo, lo spirito" (Gentile and Mathieu). The translation of *Gemüth* by *esprit* and *spirito* continues with the word's second occurrence in A.20: "la forme pure des intuitions sensibles en général se trouvera a priori dans l'esprit" (Tremesaygues and Pacaud); "la forme pure des intuitions sensibles en général . . . se trouvera a priori dans l'esprit" (Barni and Marty); "laquelle réside a priori dans l'esprit" (Renaut); "la forma pura delle intuizioni sensibili in generale . . . si troverà a priori nello spirito [*Gemüth*]" (Gentile and Mathieu).

Section 2 of the *Critique of Pure Reason* makes manifest the implications of translating the term when these difficulties are *not* taken into account. Thus we read A.22/B.37, "Der innere Sinn, vermittelst dessen das Gemüt sich selbst, oder seinen inneren Zustand anschauet, gibt zwar keine Anschauung von der Seele selbst, als einem Objekt." For "vermittelst dessen das Gemüt sich selbst," Guyer and Wood translate "the mind intuits itself." Barni and Marty render Kant's phrase as, "Le sens interne, par le moyen duquel l'esprit s'intuitionne lui-même, ou intuitionne son état intérieur, ne nous donne aucune intuition de l'âme elle-même comme d'un objet." In Renaut, we find, "Le sens interne, par l'intermédiaire duquel l'esprit s'intuitionne lui-même, intuitionne son état intérieur, ne fournit certes pas d'intuition de l'âme elle-même comme objet." Gentile and Mathieu give, "Il senso interno, mediante il quale lo spirito intuisce se stesso, o un suo stato interno, non ci dà invero nessuna intuizione dell'anima stessa, come di oggetto." Only Tremesaygues and Pacaud even call our attention to the specificity of Kant's use of *Gemüt*, thus: "Le sens interne, au moyen

duquel l'esprit [*das Gemüth*] s'intuitionne lui-même ou intuitionne aussi son état interne, ne donne pas, sans doute, d'intuition de l'âme elle-même comme d'un objet [*Objekt*]."

All of these translations, even the one by Tremesaygues and Pacaud, have the defect of collapsing *Gemüt* into "mind," losing the contrast between *mens*, *spiritus*, and *animus*, and leading to a backward projection of the German-idealist *Geist* or the spiritualist mind into the Kantian text. Even when it is a matter of translating a passage in which Kant explicitly distinguishes *Gemüt* from *Seele* as *animus* and *anima* (see again A.22/B.37, "Der innere Sinn, vermittelst dessen das Gemüt sich selbst, oder seinen inneren Zustand anschauet, gibt zwar keine Anschauung von der Seele selbst, als einem Objekt," where a distinction is drawn in Kant's German between *Gemüt* and *Seele*; or the note to "Concerning Sömmering's Work on the Soul," AA.13.33), the French translator of the Pléiade edition, Luc Ferry, renders *Gemüt* by *esprit*. Such translations thus integrate Kant into German Idealism, separating him by the same stroke from the tradition of empirical psychology.

descriptive virtue that Husserl's and above all Scheler's phenomenology would turn to advantage.

Denis Thouard

BIBLIOGRAPHY

Ball, Philip. *The Devil's Doctor: Paracelsus and the World of Renaissance Magic and Science*. New York: Farrar, Straus and Giroux, 2006.

Böhme, Jakob. *De Tribus Principiis oder Beschreibung der Drey Principien Göttlichen Wesens*. Originally published in 1619. In *Sämmtliche Werke*, edited by K. W. Schiebler, vol. 3. Leipzig: Barth, 1841. Translation by John Sparrow: *Concerning the Three Principles of the Divine Essence*. London: Watkins, 1910.

Braun, Lucien. *Paracelse*. Geneva: Slatkine, 1995.

Eckhart, Meister. *Die deutschen Werke*. Edited and translated by Josef Quint. 5 vols. Stuttgart: Kohlhammer, 1958–. Translation by M. O'C. Walshe: *German Sermons and Treatises*. 3 vols. London: Watkins, 1979–87.

Kant, Immanuel. *Kritik der reinen Vernunft*. In RT: Ak., vols. 3–4. English translation by Paul Guyer and A. Wood: *Critique of Pure Reason*. Edited by Paul Guyer and A. Wood. Cambridge: Cambridge University Press, 1997. French translation by Luc Ferry: *Critique de la raison pure*. Paris: Éditions de la Pléiade, 1980. French translation by Alexandre J.-L. Delamarre and François Marty, from the translation by Jules Barni: *Critique de la raison pure*. Edited by Ferdinand Alquié. Paris: Gallimard / La Pléiade, 1990. French translation by André Tremesaygues and Bernard Pacaud: *Critique de la raison pure*. Paris: Presses Universitaires de France, 2001. French translation by Alain Renaut: *Critique de la raison pure*. Paris: Flammarion, 2006. Italian translation by G. Gentile (1909) and V. Mathieu (1974): *Critica della ragion pura*. Bari, It.: Laterza, 1987.

Novalis [Friedrich von Hardenberg]. "Heinrich von Ofterdingen." In *Novalis Schriften: Die Werke Friedrich von Hardenbergs*, edited by Paul Kluckhohn and Richard Samuel, 1:181–358. Darmstadt, Ger.: Wissenschaftliche Buchgesellschaft, 1960–. Translation by Palmer Hilty: *Henry von Ofterdingen: A Novel*. New York: F. Ungar, 1964.

Paracelsus. *Essential Theoretical Writings*. Edited and translated by Andrew Weeks. Leiden, Neth.: Brill, 2008.

———. *Liber de imaginibus*. In *Sämtliche Werke I. Abteilung: Medizinische, naturwissenschaftliche und philosophische Schriften*, vol. 4. Edited by Karl Sudhoff. 14 vols. Munich and Berlin: R. Oldenbourg, 1922–33.

Scheler, Max. *Wesen und Form der Sympathie*. Originally published in 1923. In *Gesammelte Werke*, edited by Manfred S. Frings, vol. 7. 6th ed. Bern: Francke, 1973. Translation by Peter Heath: *The Nature of Sympathy*. Introduction by Graham McAleer. New Brunswick, NJ: Transaction, 2008. Originally published in 1954.

Schleiermacher, Friedrich. *Über die Religion* [Discourses on religion]. Stuttgart: Reclam, 1997. Originally published in 1799. Edited and translation by Richard Crouter: *On Religion: Speeches to Its Cultured Despisers*. 2nd ed. Cambridge: Cambridge University Press, 1996.

GENDER

FRENCH	*différence des sexes, identité sexuelle, genre*
GERMAN	*Geschlecht*
ITALIAN	*genere*
SPANISH	*género*

➤ *GENRE*, GESCHLECHT, SEX, and BEHAVIOR, DRIVE, NATURE, PEOPLE, PLEASURE

After the end of the 1960s, when biologists, sociologists, psychoanalysts, and philosophers studying sexuality began to take into account what Anglo-Saxon authors refer to as "gender," the debate reached the fields of other European languages, without there being a decision to use, for example, *genre* in French, *genere* in Italian, *género* in Spanish, or *Geschlecht* in German, as translations of gender. This sort of dodge is explained by the meaning Anglo-Saxon authors, in particular American feminists, gave to "gender" with regard to what goes by the name "sex" in English and *sexualité* in French.

The debate on the differences of the sexes (male and female) began with Robert Stoller's book *Sex and Gender* (1968). In the preface to the 1978 French edition, Stoller defines "the aspects of sexuality which we call gender" as being "essentially determined by culture, that is, learned after birth," whereas what is properly called "sexual" is characterized by anatomical and physiological factors, insofar as they determine "whether one is male or female." If "gender" is a term considered untranslatable, this is because it does not have the same extension as sexuality, *sexualité*. Indeed, sexuality, as understood by psychoanalysis, disappears in the distinction established by these American authors between biological sex and the social construction of masculine and feminine identities. This is a distinction that many adherents are beginning to reinterpret, and that contemporary psychoanalysis can only, and more radically, call into question.

I. The Distinction between "Sex" and "Gender" and Its Reinterpretations

The English term "sex" can reasonably be translated by *sexe* in French, as both languages define sexuality as "the collection of psychological and physiological notions" that characterize it. However, it is sometimes inaccurate to translate "sex" by *sexe*, given that in English "sex" is in many circumstances contrasted with "gender," which is not the case in French. The distinction between "sex" and "gender," which was laid out by Stoller in 1968 and adopted by feminist thought in the early 1970s (see, in particular, Ann Oakley's *Sex, Gender, and Society*), represents for this movement a political and sociological argument in the name of which we must distinguish the physiological and the psychological aspects of sex, without which we would land in a biological essentialism with normative import regarding sexual identity.

The specific attempts to separate the respective contributions of nature and culture in this regard proliferated in the last third of the twentieth century. However, the reliance on a distinction between sex and gender remained unique to English terminology. The *Oxford English Dictionary* mentions, regarding "gender," Oakley's usage ("Sex differences may be 'natural,' but gender differences have their source in culture"). It also refers to feminist usage of the term as representing one of its major uses. The *OED* second edition (1989) defines the term in this way: "[i]n mod. (esp. feminist) use, a euphemism for the sex of a human being, often intended to emphasize the social and cultural, as opposed to the biological, distinctions between the sexes." The most recent online version (June 2011), however, updates the entry to read:

> The state of being male or female as expressed by social or cultural distinctions and differences, rather than biological ones; the collective attributes or traits associated with a particular sex, or determined as a result of one's sex. Also: a (male or female) group characterized in this way.

In this context, psychoanalysis, and the meaning it gives to the difference between the sexes, did not have as decisive an influence in the English-speaking world as it did in France. In the Anglo-Saxon world, behaviorism was dominant during the period in which the distinction between sex and gender was established, a dominance that was especially maintained by British psychology and philosophy. This distinction was thus in line with a climate of confidence regarding the possibilities of modifying behavior relative to the sexual roles previously subordinate to normative criteria. Suddenly, it appeared unnecessary that female behavior should be in step with female sex, biologically understood.

After the 1990s, the term "gender" became more and more common, and passed into general use where "sex" had been used previously. It follows that the psychologists or feminists who currently refer to gender are not assumed to be following strictly the distinction between sex and gender. In addition, feminist theory has in large part rejected the distinction for the following reasons:

1. It is difficult to distinguish what derives from "sex" and what from "gender."

2. The idea that "'gender' as a cultural construct which is imposed upon the surface of matter, understood either as 'the body' or its given sex" has been rejected (Butler, *Bodies That Matter*). This rejection is based on the argument that sex cannot be considered a neutral tabula rasa (see Gatens, "A Critic of the Sex/Gender Distinction").

3. The American feminist Judith Butler often maintains that sex is retrospectively materialized as "primary," as a result of the fact that our approach to gender sees culture as "secondary." She describes "the ritualized repetition by which [gender] norms produce and stabilize not only the effects of gender but the materiality of sex." Her work presupposes that "the construal of 'sex' [is framed] no longer as a bodily given on which the construct of gender is artificially imposed, but as a cultural norm which governs the materialization of bodies" (Butler, *Bodies That Matter*).

4. Some theorists interpret sex itself as a cultural construction. This is the perspective adopted by Thomas Laqueur in *Making Sex*, when he declares:

   It seems perfectly obvious that biology defines the sexes: what else could sex mean? . . . [N]o particular understanding of sexual difference historically follows from undisputed facts about bodies. . . . Organs that had been seen as interior versions of what the male had outside—the vagina as penis, the uterus as scrotum—were by the eighteenth century construed as of an entirely different nature.

   The author explains that he is attempting, in this work, to retrace "a history of the way in which sex, as well as gender, is created."

5. Feminists and other theorists who rely on the term "gender" today do not necessarily adhere to the primitive distinction between sex and gender, especially since the term "gender" has become a euphemism for "sex." Similarly, when a theorist uses "sex," the word is not understood as referring to a notion that, unlike "gender," is universal, abstracted away from history and culture.

Thomas Laqueur's argument has had a profound effect in this regard.

■ See Box 1.

II. The Notion of "Gender" through the Lens of Psychoanalysis

If "gender" is untranslatable in many languages, it is because the term is related to a history of two different problems that were developed in parallel, encroaching on one another without ever meeting. Yet, with regard to Stoller's distinction between biological sex and the social construction of male and female identities, psychoanalysis sees in sexuality a combination of psychological and physiological factors. However, when the problems raised by Stoller and the American feminists reached France, the reevaluation there of the fundamental concepts of psychoanalysis showed that it was necessary to give up the dualism of psychology and physiology to arrive at an understanding of drives and fantasies, as the terrain on which sexual identity is formed. When Freud defines the erogenous body in 1905 (in the *Three Essays on the Theory of Sexuality*) and in 1915 (in *Instincts and Their Vicissitudes*) clarifies out of which heterogeneous elements the drives are constituted—impetus, aim, source, and object—he introduces the idea that these drives have a destiny, which makes them rather different from psychological or physiological givens. The terrain on which it is decided whether a given person identifies as male or female concerns the destinies of these drives, the links they have with scenarios of sexual climax in which the subject is in relation to figures of otherness, taken in part from the details of early interaction with adults. Sexuation thus takes place in the domain of the formation of pleasure, displeasure, and anxiety, from which are woven the experiences and thoughts of infants immersed in an adult world that supports them, threatens them, carries them, even while also being intrusive and alien.

From the point of view of psychoanalysis, the social determinations of gender are one of the materials by which fantasies and drives are created. The physiological givens of sex are one of the other materials in this affair, but they are not on the same level as the others: societies always give a content to the difference of the sexes. This difference, as anthropologists have shown, structures all the activities of exchange, rituals, divisions of space, subsistence, circuits of permitted and forbidden marriages, and so on. Since gender is nothing but the system of the division of social activities, it acquires, depending on the society, different contents. The common point among anthropologists, psychoanalysts, and some theorists of gender is that human sexuation is anything but natural, that it has no content that is commanded by an essence or by nature, even if that nature is determined by the different roles of men and women in procreation. But the agreement between these different approaches stops at this negative point.

To give an account of sexuation, psychoanalysis uses other notions besides the physiological and the psychological. This is why Robert Stoller, like many other psychoanalysts, contributed to a confusion regarding the sexual in the psychoanalytic sense. And gender theories have inherited this confusion. Sexuality is neither physiological

1

Gender and gender trouble

➤ GESCHLECHT, SEX

The term "gender" first assumed its meaning as part of a narrative sequence in feminist theory. First there was "sex" understood as a biological given, and then came "gender," which interpreted or constructed that biological given into a social category. This story was, at least, the one that held sway as feminist anthropologists (Ortner, Rubin) sought to distinguish between an order of nature and an order of culture. Nature was understood to come first, even though no one thought one could identify the scene of nature apart from its cultural articulation. Its "firstness" was then ambiguously temporal and logical. The formulation helped to make sense of important feminist propositions such as the one made by Beauvoir in *The Second Sex*: "One is not born, but rather becomes a woman." If one is not born a woman, then one is born something else, and "sex" is the name for that something else we are prior to what we become. For "gender" to name a mode of becoming had theoretical consequences, since it meant that regardless of what gender is assigned at birth, gender still has to be culturally assumed, embodied, articulated, and made. Moreover, if sex names what is biologically given, and if gender belongs to another order, then there is nothing in one's sex that destines one for any particular kind of position in life; there are no social tasks or cultural meanings that can be derived exclusively or causally from one's sex. One can, for instance, be born with reproductive organs but never give birth. And even if certain forms of heterosexual intercourse are physically possible, that does not mean that it is psychically possible or desirable. In other words, sex does not operate a causal effect on behavior, social role, or task, and so, with the sex/gender distinction in place, feminists actively argued against the formulation that "biology is destiny."

It became clear, though, that if one only understood gender as the cultural meanings that sex acquires in any given social context, then gender was still linked with sex, and could not be conceptualized without it. Some feminists such as Elizabeth Grosz argued that if gender is the cultural interpretation of sex, then sex is treated as a given, and there is no way then to ask how "sex" is made or what various cultural forms "sex" may assume in different contexts. Indeed, if one started to talk about the cultural meanings of "sex," it appeared that one was talking rather about gender. This position became even more difficult to maintain as feminist scholars of science insisted not only that

nature has a history (Haraway), but that even the definition of "sex" is a contested zone in the history of science (Laqueur, Longino). If "sex" has a history, and a conflicted one at that, then how do we understand "gender"? Is it then necessary to take gender out of the narrative sequence in which first there is "sex," which belongs to a putatively ahistorical nature, and only after there is "gender," understood as endowing that natural fact with meaning?

Upending the sex/gender distinction involved taking distance from both structural linguistics and cultural anthropology. But it became all the more important once it was conceded that both sex and gender have histories, and that these histories differ, depending on the linguistic contexts in which they operate. So, for example, the very term "gender" was throughout the 1980s and 1990s nearly impossible to translate into any romance language. There was *le genre* in French and *el género* in Spanish, but these were considered to be grammatical categories and to have no bearing on the concrete bodily existence of those who were alternately referred to as "he" or "she." But experimental writers such as Monique Wittig and Jeannette Winterson contested the idea that grammar was actually separable from bodily experience. Wittig's *Les guérillères* and Winterson's *Written on the Body* became provocative texts that never allowed their readers to settle on the gender of the figures and characters being described. Moreover, they suggested that the way we see and feel gender is directly related to the kinds of grammatical constructions that pose as ordinary or inevitable. By either combining, confusing, or erasing grammatical gender, they sought to loosen the hold that binary gender systems have on how we read, feel, think, and know ourselves and others. Their grammatical idealism proved to be exciting as experimental fiction. And yet, the institutions of gender seemed to march along, even when brave souls refused to give their infants genders at birth, with the idea that such acts might bring to a halt the institution of gender difference.

The translation of "gender" into German was more difficult, since the word *Geschlecht* operates as both biological sex and social gender. This term enforced a strong cultural presumption that the various cultural expressions of gender not only followed causally and necessarily from an original sex, but that gender was in some ways mired in sex, indissociable from it, bound up with it as a single unity. The term for gender in Chinese

carries many of these meanings that are variously expressed by the conjunction of phonemes and numbers: "gender" is *xing(4) bie(2)*. The numbers denote "tones," and there are four of them for each of the two terms. Thus, *xing(2)* means something different from *xing(4)*. Indeed, this roman system is already a translation of Chinese characters, so makes something of a grid out of a graphic sign. *Xing(4)* is a term meaning "category or kind," but it also means "sex" and so sustains a relation with those languages that link sex to species. Only at the beginning of the twentieth century did the term begin to mean "gender," so in order to distinguish gender from sex, some feminist scholars in China put the expression meaning "social"—*she(4) hui(4)*—before the term *xing(4)bie(2)*. *Bie(2)* means "difference," and thus links with those formulations of gender as sexual difference.

Like *genus* in Swedish, which implies species-being, so *Geschlecht* in German implied not only a natural kind, but a mode of natural ordering that served the purposes of the reproduction of the species. That the first German translators of *Gender Trouble* chose to translate "gender" as *Geschlechtsidentität* (sexual identity) may have been an effort to move away from species discourse, or perhaps it was a way of responding to those emerging queer arguments that claimed that binary sex was understood to serve the purposes of reproducing compulsory heterosexuality (Rubin, Butler). The problem with that choice, however, was that it confused gender with sexual orientation or disposition. And part of the analytic work of understanding gender apart from biological causality and functionalism was precisely to hold open for the possibility that gender appearance may not correspond to sexual disposition or orientation in predictable ways. Thus, if the biologically mired conception of sex implies that women and men desire only one another, and that the end result of that attraction is biological reproduction, the queer critique relied on analytic distinctions between morphology, biology, psychology, cultural assignment and interpretation, social function, and possibility. If "gender" named this very constellation of problems, then it sought, in Foucault's language, to undo the "fictitious unity of sex" (*History of Sexuality*, vol. 1) in which drive, desire, and expression formed a single object that became the condition and object for sexual regulation.

(continued)

(continued)

For the French, the term "gender" was at first incomprehensible, since *genre* clearly referred exclusively to grammar and literary form. When *Gender Trouble* was first proposed to a French press, the publisher proclaimed that it was *inassimilable*, suggesting that it was a kind of foreign substance or unwanted immigrant that must be kept outside the French borders. Clearly, it was considered an American term, possibly the intellectual equivalent of McDonald's. Although the term did enter the language through conferences, seminars, the titles of books, and even a newly established field (*études de genre*), its culturalism was somehow associated with its Americanism, and some French intellectuals feared that it was a term meant to deny sexual difference, the body, seduction, and Frenchness itself.

For some feminist historians who worked between French and Anglo-American frameworks, gender became importantly bound up with the question of sexual difference. Joan Scott argued that one should not only consider gender as an attribute of a body, or as a way of endowing biological bodies with cultural meaning. In her view, gender is a "category of analysis" which helps us understand how the basic terms by which we describe social life are themselves internally differentiated. For instance, Scott can analyze terms such as "labor," "equality," or even "universality" using gender as a critical category. As a result, we can criticize how the public sphere and labor are often conceptualized as masculine spheres. The very way in which the sphere is delimited not only valorizes certain modes of labor, and laborers of the masculine gender, but it also reproduces the categories of gender. In Scott's work, those categories do not always adhere to a set of bodies, though sometimes they do. They also provide the implicit scheme by which valuable and nonvaluable work is described, forms of political participation are differentially valorized, and versions of universality are articulated with a masculine presumption and bias.

Scott is one of many feminist theorists who would dispute the absolute difference between sexual difference and gender (cf. Braidotti, Irigaray, and Schor and Weed). "Sexual difference" is not a term that marks an exclusively biological beginning and then becomes transformed in the course of a subsequent and separable cultural and historical articulation. Rather, sexual difference is precisely that which, whether in the biological or the cultural sciences, occasions a set of shifting articulations. Following Lacan, one might say that sexual difference is precisely the site where biology and culture converge,

although not in any causal way (thus, eluding from another direction the "biology is destiny" formulation). For Scott, no one cultural articulation of sexual difference exhausts its meaning, because even though we never find this difference outside of a specific articulation, it eludes any capture or seizure that would fix its meaning for all time. Moreover, sexual difference is as much articulated by forms of power as it is a matrix for actively articulating such modes of power. We are not only talking about sexual difference as a "constructed" difference (though some do that), but in Scott's work, sexual difference is a matrix through which and by which certain kinds of articulation take place. If that seems like a conundrum, it probably is; it is what Scott refers to as one of the paradoxes she has to offer.

Although some feminists sharply contrasted the discourse on "gender" with that of "sexual difference," they usually associated gender with a theory of cultural construction, though that no longer seems to be the case. "Gender" is now the name for a set of debates on how to think about the biological, chromosomal, psychological, cultural, and socioeconomic dimensions of a lived bodily reality. Consider, for instance, the international athletic debate about Caster Semenya, an athlete who was suspected of being more male than female, but who ran as a qualified woman in international athletic competitions. The International Association of Athletics Federations finally adjudicated the case and confirmed that she qualified to run as a woman, without saying whether she "really" was one. For this organization, gender was established by a set of measures and norms that required the expertise of lawyers, biologists, psychologists, geneticists, and endocrinologists. In other words, Semenya's "gender qualifications" were decided by an interdisciplinary committee, and not by a single standard imposed by a single science. Those experts not only had to learn each other's languages, but they had to translate each field into their own to come to an understanding of how best to name gender in this instance. Her gender qualifications were the result of a negotiated conclusion.

Those who debate matters of sexual difference and gender tend to conjecture what happens at the very beginning of life, how infants are perceived and named, and how sexual difference is discovered or installed. The psychoanalyst Jean Laplanche argued that it was not possible to reduce the question of gender to an expression of biological drives, understood as separable from cultural content. To understand gender, we must first understand drives (see Freud, "Triebe und Triebschicksale"). For Laplanche, gender assignment happens at the very beginning of life, but like all powerful

words of interpellation, it is first encountered as so much "noise" to an infant who does not yet have linguistic competence to discern what is being said. In this way, gender assignment arrives on the scene of infantile helplessness. To be called a gender is to be given an enigmatic and overwhelming signifier; it is also to be incited in ways that remain in part fully unconscious. To be called a gender is to be subject to a certain demand, a certain impingement and seduction, and not to know fully what the terms of that demand might be. Indeed, in being gendered, the infant is put in a situation *of having to make a translation*.

Laplanche's first point follows from a correction of a translation error. The "instinct" (a term that Strachey uses too often to translate *Trieb*) makes the drive possible, but the drive institutes a life of fantasy that is qualitatively new, and that is not constrained by the teleologies of biological life. What is endogenous and exogenous converge at the drive, but when something new emerges, it is a sign that the drive has veered away from its instinctual basis. This only happens once biological processes have been intervened upon by the adult world, by forms of address, words, and forms of physical proximity and dependency. Something enigmatic is communicated from that adult world, and it enters into the life of the drive. It is precisely because of this interruption that the infant's emerging sense of his or her body (or a body outside of clear gender categories) is not the result of a biological teleology or necessity.

The literary critic John Fletcher asks, in "The Letter in the Unconscious," how are we to rethink "the psychic constitution and inscription of a sexually and genitally differentiated body image (the repression and symbolization of what enigmatic signifiers?) [as] the ground or, at least, terrain for the formation of gendered identities." In other words, Fletcher, drawing on Laplanche, asks whether the most fundamental sense of our bodies, what Merleau-Ponty would call a "body-image" is in some ways the result of having to translate and negotiate enigmatic and overwhelming adult "signifiers"—terms that relay the psychic demands of the adult to the child.

As we have seen, the term "gender" in English-language contexts usually refers to a cultural meaning assumed by a body in the context of its socialization or acculturation, and so it often makes use of a distinction between a natural and cultural body in order to secure a definition for gender as an emphatically cultural production. But these last positions lead us to ask another question: what is the mechanism of that production? If we start with the naming of the infant, we start to understand gender as a social assignment, but how precisely does that assignment work?

To answer this question, we have to move away from the notion that gender is simply an attribute of a person (Scott has already shown us that). Or, rather, if it is an attribute, we have to consider that it is attributed, and we have yet to understand the means and mechanism of that attribution or more generalized assignment. For Laplanche, gender is resituated as part of the terrain of the enigmatic signifier itself. In other words, gender is not so much a singular message, but a surrounding and impinging discourse, already circulating, and mobilized for the purposes of address prior to the formation of any speaking and desiring subject. In this sense, gender is a problem of translating the drive of the other into one's own bodily schema.

In other words, one is not born into the world only then to happen upon a set of gender options; rather, gender operates as part of the generalized discursive conditions that are "addressed" enigmatically and overwhelmingly to an infant and child and that continue to be addressed throughout the embodied life of the person. Laplanche argues that gender *precedes* sex and so suggests that gender—understood as that bundle of enigmatic meanings that is addressed to the infant and so imposed as part of a discursive intervention in the life of the infant—precedes the emergence of the "sexually and genitally differentiated body image."

This last view is counterintuitive to the extent that we might want to argue that sexual differentiation is, for the most part, there from the start (although recent research on intersex has called this presumption into question throughout the biological and social sciences). But are there conditions under which "sex," understood as sexually differentiated morphology, comes to appear as a "given" of experience, something we might take for granted, a material point of departure for any further investigation and for any further understanding of gender acquisition? Consider that the sequence that we use to describe how gender emerges only after sex, or gender is something superadded to sex, fails to see that gender is, as it were, already operating, seizing upon, and infiltrating somatic life prior to any conscious or reflexive determination of gender. And if gender is relayed, traumatically, through the generalized scene of seduction, then gender is part of the very assignment that forms and incites the life of the drive, sexuality itself, that makes us scramble for words to translate a set of effects that emerge from one domain only to be relayed into another. We might ask, which gender? Or gender in what

sense? But that is already to move ahead too quickly. If gender is relayed through the overwhelming language and gestures of the adult, then it arrives first as a kind of noise, indecipherable, and in demand of translation. For now, it is most important to note that the assignment of gender arrives through the enigmatic desire of the other, a desire by which somatic life is infiltrated and that, in turn, or simultaneously, incites a set of displacements and translations that constitute the specific life of the drive or, sexual desire. Is somatic life determinable outside this scene of assignment? To the extent that bodily "sex" appears as primary, this very primariness is achieved as a consequence of a repression (*refoulement*) of gender itself. Indeed, gender is in part constituted by unconscious wishes conveyed through the enigmatic assignment of gender, so that one might say that gender emerges, from early on, as an enigma for the child. And the question may well not be, "what gender am I?" but rather, "what does gender want of me?" or even, "whose desire is being carried through the assignment of gender that I have received and how can I possibly respond? Quick—give me a way to translate!"

Judith Butler

BIBLIOGRAPHY

Beauvoir, Simone de. *The Second Sex*. Translated by Constance Borde and Sheila Malovany-Chevallier. New York: Vintage Books, 2011.

Braidotti, Rosi. *Nomadic Subjects: Embodiment and Sexual Difference in Contemporary Feminist Theory*. New York: Columbia University Press, 1994.

Butler, Judith. *Bodies That Matter: On the Discursive Limits of Sex*. New York: Routledge, 1993.

———. *Gender Trouble: Feminism and the Subversion of Identity*. New York: Routledge, 1990.

Clarey, Christopher. "Gender Test after a Gold-Medal Finish." *New York Times*, 19 August 2009. http://www.nytimes.com/2009/08/20/sports/20runner.html.

Fletcher, John. "The Letter in the Unconscious: The Enigmatic Signifier in Jean Laplanche." In *Jean Laplanche: Seduction, Translation and the Drives*, edited by John Fletcher and Martin Stanton. ICA Documents, no. 11. London: Institute of Contemporary Arts, 1992.

Foucault, Michel. *History of Sexuality*. Vol. 1. New York: Vintage Books, 1990.

Freud, Sigmund. "Instincts and Their Vicissitudes." In vol. 14 of *The Standard Edition of the Complete Works of Sigmund Freud*, edited by James Strachey, 111–40. London: Hogarth Press, 1957.

———. "Triebe und Triebschicksale." In vol. 10 of *Gesammelte Werke, Chronologish Geordnet*,

edited by Anna Freud et al., 210–32. London: Imago Publishing Co., 1913–17.

Grosz, Elizabeth. *Volatile Bodies: Toward a Corporeal Feminism*. Bloomington: Indiana University Press, 1994.

Haraway, Donna. *Simians, Cyborgs, and Women: The Reinvention of Nature*. New York: Routledge, 1991.

Irigaray, Luce. *An Ethics of Sexual Difference*. Translated by Carolyn Burke and Gillian C. Gill. Ithaca, NY: Cornell University Press, 1993.

Lacan, Jacques. *Écrits: The First Complete Edition in English*. Translated by Bruce Fink. New York: W. W. Norton, 2002.

———. "The Four Fundamental Concepts of Psychoanalysis, 1964." In vol. 11 of *The Seminar*, edited by Alan Sheridan. London: Hogarth Press and Institute of Psychoanalysis, 1977.

Laplanche, Jean. "The Drive and the Object-Source: Its Fate in the Transference." In *Jean Laplanche: Seduction, Translation, and the Drives*, edited by John Fletcher and Martin Stanton. ICA Documents, no. 11. London: Institute of Contemporary Arts, 1992.

Laplanche, Jean, and Susan Fairfield. "Gender, Sex and the Sexual." *Studies in Gender and Sexuality* 8, no. 2 (2007): 201–19.

Laqueur, Thomas. *Making Sex: Body and Gender from the Greeks to Freud*. Cambridge, MA: Harvard University Press, 1990.

Longino, Helen E. *Science as Social Knowledge: Values and Objectivity in Scientific Inquiry*. Princeton, NJ: Princeton University Press, 1990.

Merleau-Ponty, Maurice. *Phenomenology of Perception*. Translated by Colin Smith. New York: Routledge, 2002.

Ortner, Sherry B. "Is Female to Male as Nature Is to Culture?" In *Woman, Culture and Society*, edited by Michelle Zimbalist Rosaldo and Louise Lamphere, 67–87. Stanford, CA: Stanford University Press, 1974.

Rubin, Gayle S. "The Traffic in Women: Notes on the 'Political Economy' of Sex." In *Toward an Anthropology of Women*, edited by Rayna R. Reiter, 157–210. New York: Monthly Review Press, 1975.

Schor, Naomi, and Elizabeth Weed, eds. *The Essential Difference*. Bloomington: Indiana University Press, 1994.

Scott, Joan W. "Gender: A Useful Category of Historical Analysis." In *Gender and the Politics of History*, edited by Carolyn G. Heilbrun and Nancy K. Miller, 28–50. New York: Columbia University Press, 1988.

———. *Only Paradoxes to Offer: French Feminists and the Rights of Man*. Cambridge, MA: Harvard University Press, 1996.

Shepherdson, Charles. *Vital Signs: Nature, Culture, Psychoanalysis*. New York: Routledge, 2000.

Winterson, Jeanette. *Written on the Body*. London: Jonathan Cape, 1992.

Wittig, Monique. *Les guérillères*. Paris: Éditions de Minuit, 1969.

nor psychological. It is related to drives and fantasies. The biological and social givens are only taken into account by fantasies and drives, with their specific organization. Given this conceptual modification, the question of knowing whether Freud was wrong to affirm that there is, during the "phallic phase," a single libido and that it is male in nature may be asked against a different background.

Monique David-Ménard
Penelope Deutscher

BIBLIOGRAPHY

Browne, June, ed. *The Future of Gender*. Cambridge: Cambridge University Press, 2007.

Butler, Judith. *Bodies That Matter: On the Discursive Limits of "Sex."* New York: Routledge, 1993.

———. *Gender Trouble: Feminism and the Subversion of the Identity*. New York: Routledge, 1990.

David-Ménard, Monique. *Hysteria from Freud to Lacan: Body and Language in Psychoanalysis*. Translated by Catherine Porter. Ithaca, NY: Cornell University Press, 1989.

———. "Sexual Alterity and the Alterity of the Real for Thought." Translated by Diane Morgan. *Angelaki* 8, no. 2 (2003): 137–50.

Deutscher, Penelope. *Yielding Gender: Feminism, Deconstruction and the History of Philosophy*. London: Routledge, 1997.

Fraisse, Geneviève. *Reason's Muse: Sexual Difference and the Birth of Democracy*. Translated by Jane Marie Todd. Chicago: University of Chicago Press, 1994.

Gatens, Moira. "A Critic of the Sex/Gender Distinction." In *Imaginary Bodies: Ethics, Power and Corporeality*. New York: Routledge, 1995.

Laqueur, Thomas. *Making Sex: Body and Gender from the Greeks to Freud*. Cambridge, MA: Harvard University Press, 1990.

Oakley, Ann. *Sex, Gender, and Society*. London: Temple Smith, 1972.

Stoller, Robert. *Sex and Gender: On the Development of Masculinity and Femininity*. New York: Science House, 1968.

GENIUS

FRENCH	*génie*
GERMAN	Genie, Geist, Naturell, natürlich Fähigkeit, Witz
LATIN	*genus, genius*

➤ AESTHETICS, ART, CONCETTO, DAIMÔN, DUENDE, GEMÜT, GOÛT, *IMAGINATION*, INGENIUM, MADNESS, MANIERA, MIMÊSIS, PLASTICITY, SOUL, SUBLIME, TALENT

Toward the end of the eighteenth century, La Harpe writes in the introduction to his work *Lycée ou cours de littérature ancienne et moderne*: "But what may be surprising is that these two words, genius and taste, taken abstractly, are never found in Boileau's verses, nor in Racine's prose, nor in Corneille's dissertations, nor in Molière's plays. This manner of speaking . . . is from our century." How did an old word, as rich in diverse and vague meanings as the word "genius" is, come to occupy the center of aesthetic and philosophical discussion in the Enlightenment, in England, France, and Germany? What remains of these debates today?

I. Confusion or Semantic Richness

Concerning the word *genius*, Ernst Cassirer warns in his *Philosophy of the Enlightenment*, in the chapter concerning "the fundamental problem of aesthetics," against "attempting to interpret the developments of thoughts and ideas simply on the basis of the history of a word." Thus, he adds, Shaftesbury "did not coin the word 'genius'; he adopted it

from common aesthetic terminology. He is the first to rescue the term from the confusion and ambiguity that had previously attached to it and to give it a fruitful and specifically philosophical meaning."

Although this analysis is correct, and Shaftesbury was indeed the author of this philosophical "stroke of genius," it remains the case that the history of the word "genius," like that of any word (but in this case especially), will help us clarify what Cassirer calls "confusion" and "ambiguity," which may only be inexhaustible semantic richness.

The word "genius," in its various romance forms, is related to Latin, and hence shares an Indo-European origin common to several languages (**gn*, "to be born," "to engender"). *Gigno, gignere*, thus means "to engender," "to produce," "to cause." Several nouns are derived from it. *Genus* is birth, race, and, in an abstract way, class (see PEOPLE). *Genius* is initially the divinity presiding over an individual's birth, and then each person's guardian divinity, with which the first becomes confused, so much so that *genius* comes to mean one's natural inclinations, appetites, the intellectual and moral qualities peculiar to each individual. In this last sense, the word duplicates the compound word *ingenium*, another derivative of *gigno* (see INGENIUM).

II. From *Ingenium* to *Génie*

When the word *génie*, a calque of *genius*, appears in French in the sixteenth century (François Rabelais, 1532), it manifests the richness of meaning derived from its Latin origins. It refers in general to natural tendencies, character, an innate disposition for an activity or art. It becomes more specific later, referring to a superior mental aptitude (before 1674), and finally, by metonymy, to a superior individual, a *génie* (1686).

Concurrently, however, in the sixteenth century, *génie* takes up the Latin sense of "divinity" and thus comes to mean a "spirit," good or bad, which influences our destiny (hence, eventually, René Descartes's "evil genius," the *malin génie* we find in his *Meditations* of 1641), then, by extension, an allegorical being personifying an abstract idea and its representation, and finally, in fantastical writings, a supernatural being endowed with magical powers (definitions taken from RT: *DHLF*).

These two series of meanings, seemingly very distinct, are in fact intimately related. To be a genius is to have a part of the creative faculty of a god, thus to participate in something external and superior to oneself. To be a genius is to be considered, or to consider oneself to be, a creative source like a god. A certain hubris thus underlies this notion, which is clearly confirmed in the romantic conception of genius (on hubris, cf. VERGÜENZA, II).

It is a peculiarity of French that it did not create a word directly calqued on *ingenium* (except *ingénieur*, "engineer"). However, this Latin word, which we find in the Italian *ingegno* and the Spanish *ingenio*, and which is commonly used in philosophical terminology in the classical period (cf. Descartes's *Rules for the Direction of the Mind* of ca. 1622), refers both to a certain penetration of the mind and to a synthetic faculty for comparing ideas that are distant from one another, and thus to "find" in the sense of "invent." In this sense we may contrast, as Giambattista Vico does in particular, the creativity and inventiveness of "ingenious" thought with the sterility of analytic thought, which remains content with mechanically deriving consequences from premises given at the start. It is admitted, however, in the sixteenth and seventeenth centuries, that *ingenium*, translated into French as *génie*, is at work (to different degrees, to be sure) in all individuals and in all spheres of activity, although the manifestations are especially visible in the cases of poets and artists.

It is in the eighteenth century that the notion of genius takes on a new meaning and becomes throughout Europe an object of reflection in the domain of aesthetics and, more widely, of philosophy (hence claims for the "birth of genius" in the eighteenth century). In earlier centuries it was admitted that a work of art was born on the one hand from the conjunction of knowledge and craft proper to a given art and capable of being acquired, and on the other hand from a quality peculiar to the individual, a natural gift called "genius." During and after the eighteenth century, however, the latter quality acquires a greater importance, even an overblown one, almost to the point of causing the other factors to be forgotten. Genius becomes a power of creation ex nihilo, irreducible to any rule and impossible to analyze rationally. At the same time, whereas classical aesthetics rested on the notion of imitation, genius would come to be characterized by the absolute originality of its productions, by their inimitable character.

Although this new meaning given to the notion of genius is a European phenomenon, it is interesting to note that it is not uniform—there are national differences in the definition of what is given by "genius," in the importance accorded to it, in the interpretation to which it is subject. In this sense, we may speak of an "untranslatability" between the notions of genius that appeared in the literature devoted to it in England, Germany, and France.

III. English "Enthusiasm" and French "Rationalism"

It is generally agreed that Shaftesbury had a decisive influence on the way in which the question of genius was posed in the eighteenth century, by popularizing the notion of "enthusiasm" (*Letter concerning Enthusiasm* [1708]). Enthusiasm comes from the artist's agreement with nature, where the latter is considered the "sovereign artist," "universal plastic nature." The enthusiasm of the artist is a "disinterested pleasure," provoked by the presence within him of a divine inspiration, "genius," which makes him the near kin to, and the equal of, the genius of the world. The artist feels living within him his consubstantiality with the creative act, and Shaftesbury writes that "such a poet is indeed a second *Maker*; a just Prometheus under Jove" ("Soliloquy, or Advice to an Author" [1710], in *Characteristics of Men*, 111). The artist is not content with imitating the products of nature, but rather participates in the act of production itself. His work, which is the giving of form, creation from an internal model, only makes manifest the presence of the infinite in the finite.

Shaftesbury's "enthusiastic" conception of genius was not taken up immediately or without hesitation in France. In fact, most French authors who discuss genius in the first half of the eighteenth century do so in a much more traditional, "rationalist" manner. Their approach to genius is less metaphysical, and more a search for its "natural" and "moral" causes. Thus for Jean-Baptiste Dubos, in his *Réflexions critiques*

sur la poésie et la peinture (1719) (Critical Reflections on Poetry and Painting):

> On appelle génie l'aptitude qu'un homme a reçue de la nature pour faire bien et facilement certaines choses que les autres ne sauraient faire que très mal, même en prenant beaucoup de peine.

> (We call genius the aptitude that a man receives from nature to do certain things well and easily, that others can only do badly, even with great effort.)

In this sense, genius, which concerns all human activity, does not differ much from talent, and Dubos seeks its natural causes in "a happy arrangement of the organs of the brain," the influence of the land and climate, education, and the frequent company of artists and philosophers. No matter what, the natural gift must be developed by training and work: "The happiest genius can only be perfected by long study."

Charles Batteux, in the first part of his highly influential treatise *Les Beaux-Arts réduits à un même principe* (The Beaux-Arts reduced to a single principle [1746]), himself defines genius as

> une raison active qui s'exerce avec art, qui en recherche industrieusement toutes les faces réelles, tous les possibles, qui en dissèque minutieusement les parties les plus fines, en mesure les rapports les plus éloignés; c'est un instrument éclairé qui fouille, qui creuse, qui perce sourdement.

> (an active reason that is exercised with art, that industriously seeks out all its real aspects, all the possible ones, that meticulously dissects its smallest parts, measuring its most distant relations; it is an enlightened instrument that digs, delves, and dully penetrates.)

Genius is thus assimilated into a higher reason, and not into a mysterious power granted to certain men. The imitation of nature remains the supreme law of all arts, but the artist may discover things that have escaped others. Poetic enthusiasm is explained by Batteux in purely psychological terms:

> Ils [les poètes] excitent eux-mêmes leur imagination jusqu'à ce qu'ils se sentent émus, saisis, effrayés; alors *Deus ecce Deus*, qu'ils chantent, qu'ils peignent, c'est un Dieu qui les inspire.

> (They [the poets] excite their imaginations themselves until they feel moved, seized, frightened; then *Deus ecce Deus*, they sing, they paint, it is a God that inspires them.)

It may be Helvetius, in book 5 of his *De l'esprit*, who does the most to reduce the share of mystery and originality of genius. According to him, genius in artists, but also in philosophers and scientists, consists in "inventing," but invention is only possible thanks to favorable conditions, and is facilitated by the environment, the tendencies of the period, and sometimes luck. There is a diffuse mass of genius in the world that only a few lucky people manage to express.

We thus see a typically French resistance (the origin of which we might find in Cartesian mistrust of imagination) to an exaltation of the creative genius that would make the artist a rival of God. Voltaire, in the article "Génie" in *Questions* sur l'Encyclopédie (1772), asks: "But fundamentally is genius anything other than talent? What is talent, except the disposition to succeed at an art?" And for Buffon, genius, if it must imitate nature, must follow its slow, laborious, and obstinate step. It must exhibit more reason than heat, since for Buffon, genius is essentially, according to the remark loaned to him by Hérault de Séchelles, "nothing but a greater aptitude for patience" ("*qu'une plus grande aptitude à la patience*," Séchelles, *Voyages*, 11).

It is this mistrust, this critical and reductive will that aims to submit genius to the laws of reason, even if they are the laws of "sublime reason," that those influenced by Shaftesbury oppose. For them, the presence of genius in a work of art is manifested with brutal clarity; it can only be felt, not analyzed, since indeed it deprives the witness of his critical faculties. This is what Jean-Jacques Rousseau expresses, in his *Dictionnaire de musique* (1768), in the article "Génie":

> Ne cherche point, jeune artiste, ce que c'est que le génie. En as-tu: tu le sens en toi-même. N'en as-tu pas: tu ne le connaîtras jamais. . . . Veux-tu savoir si quelque étincelle de ce feu dévorant t'anime ? Cours, vole à Naples écouter les chefs-d'œuvre de Leo, de Durante, de Jommelli, de Pergolèse. Si tes yeux s'emplissent de larmes, si tu sens ton cœur palpiter, si des tressaillements t'agitent, si l'oppression te suffoque dans tes transports, prend le Métastase et travaille. . . . Mais si les charmes de ce grand art te laissent tranquille, si tu n'as ni délire, ni ravissement, si tu ne trouves que beau ce qui transporte, oses-tu demander ce qu'est le génie ? Homme vulgaire, ne profane point ce nom sublime.

> (Young artist, do not seek out what genius is. If you have it: you feel it in yourself. If you do not have it: you will never know it. . . . Do you wish to know whether some spark of this consuming fire animates you? Run, fly to Naples and listen to the masterpieces of Leo, Durante, Jommelli, Pergolese. If your eyes fill with tears, if you feel your heart palpitate, if you are overcome with trembling, if you feel suffocated in your raptures, take hold of your collected Metastasio, and get to work. . . . But if the charms of this grand art leave you peaceful, if you have neither delirium nor ravishment, if you find merely beautiful that which is transporting, do you dare to ask what genius is? Vulgar man, do not profane this sublime name.)

> (Rousseau, *Œuvres complètes*, 5:837–38)

IV. Diderot and Genius as "Release of Nature"

Denis Diderot, Shaftesbury's translator, goes the farthest in France in deepening the analysis of genius in Shaftesbury's direction. He takes up the idea that the mystery of genius is that of creation, but he makes the source of creative genius not God or gods, but rather nature as a general power. For him, genius is a release or expression of nature ("*ressort de la nature*"), and thus has a biological foundation. As such, it is infallible, like the instincts of animals. This is why, in poetry, it tends to be manifested among those who remain close to nature, like children, women, or primitives ("Poetry wants something enormous, barbarian and savage," *Discourse on Dramatic Poetry* [1758], in Diderot, *Œuvres complètes*, 3:483). The manifestions of the creative power of nature in the artist of genius can only be on the order of the bodily, the perceptual, the affective, the imaginative, and the words *fureur, ivresse, mouvements du cœur* ("furor," "intoxication," "movements of the heart") are used again and again by Diderot and those who follow him, especially in the *Encyclopédie* (RT: *Encyclopédie ou Dictionnaire*).

Thus, in the article "Génie" in the *Encyclopédie* (RT: *Encyclopédie ou Dictionnaire*), written by Jean-François de Saint-Lambert, but to which Diderot seems to have contributed (as suggested by Voltaire in his own article "Génie" in the *Questions sur l'Encyclopédie*), the natural state of genius is *movement*: "More often than not, this movement produces storms," and genius is "carried away by a torrent of ideas." Thus understood, genius is not the special province of artists; philosophy, too, has its geniuses, "whose systems we admire as we would poems, and who construct daring edifices that reason alone does not know how to inhabit." In philosophy, as in art, "the true and the false are not at all the distinctive features of genius," and thus "there are very few errors in Locke and too few truths in Lord Shaftesbury: the former, however, is nothing but an extended mind, penetrating and accurate, and the latter is a genius of the first rank."

Like Diderot in his "*Encyclopédie*" and his *Discourse on Dramatic Poetry*, Saint-Lambert in "Génie" insists on the contrast between taste (*goût*) and genius (*génie*), a question that remains at the center of the problem of genius through Immanuel Kant and even later. "Taste is often distinguished from genius. Genius is a pure gift of nature; what it produces is the work of a moment; taste is the work of study and time. . . . Genius and the sublime shine in Shakespeare like lightning in a long night." (Throughout the eighteenth century, Shakespeare is the paradigm of genius, insofar as he is irreducible to reason, rules, or taste.) Saint-Lambert adds that the rules of taste are constantly transgressed in works of genius, since "strength, abundance, a certain rudeness, irregularity, sublimity, pathos—these are the characteristics of genius in art."

Though the nature of genius remains impenetrable in the final analysis, it is nonetheless possible to study the conditions that favor or disfavor its manifestation. In this regard, what Diderot says about poetic genius in *Discourse on Dramatic Poetry* is of general value. There are times, mores, circumstances that are more poetic, more appropriate for creation than others: "In general, the more civilized and polite a people is, the less their habits are poetic: everything is weakened by becoming gentler." (Vico had already said the same thing in his *Scienza nuova* [1725–44], while giving the notion of poetry a much wider sense, since for him primitive peoples "create" their own world by means of poetry.) Diderot also calls into question the particular conditions—social, political, economic—that may prevent the genius of an individual from manifesting itself, and he shows in the article "Éclectism" in the *Encyclopédie* how men can frustrate the designs of nature. This marks the appearance of the romantic theme of the misunderstood genius, the exceptional man condemned to die of hunger, with the concomitant call that the government should subsidize unknown artists. At the same time, interest begins to shift from the abstract notion of genius to the concrete one, obtained by metonymy, of the "man of genius," who takes up a place in ideal human typology, alongside the saint and the hero.

V. How Germany Takes over the French Word, in Order to Make Genius Its Own

The word *Genie*, borrowed from French, appears in the German vocabulary with Johann Adolf Schlegel's translation in 1751 of Batteux's treatise on the Beaux-Arts. (Batteux's other translators had translated *génie* by *Geist, Naturell, natürliche Fähigkeit,* and above all *Witz*.) Beginning in the eighteenth century, the notion of genius acquires more and more importance in Germany in discussions of art, language, and the history of peoples, especially when the Sturm und Drang literary movement (with political overtones) appears in the 1770s. These discussions obviously reach their full significance in the period in which Germany begins vigorously to affirm itself in literature, philosophy, and politics.

The first German authors of treatises on genius recognized that "the French prompted [them] to think about this concept with care," but very early on their reflection distances itself from its French sources (except Diderot and Rousseau), leading them in new directions. This process happens in stages. Johann Georg Sulzer, with his idea of the "reasonable genius," Moses Mendelssohn, and even Gotthold Ephraim Lessing, so opposed to French influence, attempt to preserve what they can of the "rationalist" critique, notably in the demands of rules and taste, while recognizing that genius, as an expression of nature and creative originality, had its own inalienable rights. With Johann Georg Hamann, the break becomes radical and violent, and the superior rights of genius in art and life are imperiously demanded. Influenced by Rousseau, but especially by the English poet Edward Young—author of the celebrated *Night Thoughts* (1742–45), in which he insists on the absolutely "original" and inimitable character of works of genius, which cannot be discussed but only admired—Hamann adds mystical overtones to these thoughts on genius. Faith has nothing to do with reason, and what faith is in life, genius is in art. His *Socratic Memorabilia* (1760) applies the Socratic method to the notion of genius, which we may see or feel, but never understand. Genius embraces the past and future, and only poetry is capable of capturing its visions.

For Hamann, who goes farther in this sense than Diderot, genius cannot be known by contemporaries. The man who has it is above the crowd, misunderstood and mocked by it, since he is often close to madness, and sometimes there are "incidents at the border between genius and madness." It is not Apollo but Bacchus who governs the arts. Genius has two faces: one denies and holds reason in contempt, the other affirms, creates, and produces: "My crude imagination has always forbade me from imagining a creative genius deprived of *genitalia*" (letter to Herder, 1760).

Johann Gottfried Herder extends Hamann's ideas in the direction of literary nationalism, a notion that flourishes in Germany, and then in the whole of Europe. In many writings, he comes back to the theme of genius, which, for him as well, is indefinable:

It is with genius as with other delicate and complex concepts: we may, in individual cases, grasp them by intuition, but they are nowhere exactly delimited and without mixture. They give as much trouble to philosophers seeking a general, clear and precise idea, as Proteus gave Ulysses when he tried to pin him.

(Cited by Grappin, *La théorie du génie*, 224–25)

However, Herder insists above all on the idea that the genius of an artist is not a purely individual phenomenon, but only expresses the "mind" or, if you like, the "genius" of a people, and is only manifested when the time is right to receive it. Its forms also vary with the times; from this comes the interest in the study of chants and popular traditions that modern poets must nevertheless not simply parrot, pretending to be "Germanic bards," but whose authentic inspiration they must recover, as Friedrich Gottlieb Klopstock and Johann Wolfgang von Goethe did.

VI. Genius According to Kant

We cannot understand the famous pages Kant devotes to the subject of genius in the *Critique of Judgment* (1790) without taking into account the discussions in Germany since the middle of the eighteenth century, of which we have just seen a few examples. Kant effects a balanced synthesis of these writings and gives them in addition the proper philosophical foundation that was lacking. He thus escapes the reductive rationalism of the French tradition and the mysticism of the *Schwärmerei*.

This balance is shown in the definition Kant gives of genius (§46):

Genius is the talent (natural endowment) which gives the rule to art. Since talent, as an innate productive faculty of the artist, belongs itself to Nature, we may put it this way: *Genius* is the innate mental aptitude [*ingenium*] *through which* Nature gives the rule to Art.

(*Critique of Judgment*, trans. Meredith, 168)

Kant thus does not fear using two terms repudiated by the apologists of genius, but for him, nevertheless, the rules ("the beautiful pleases without concepts") are given in works of art not by reason but by nature. We find here the idea that dominates the thought of the eighteenth century since Shaftesbury. For Shaftesbury, nature "gives the rule to art in the subject" by the "agreement of the faculties." Imagination and understanding constitute, by their union, genius, which consists in a "happy relation, which science cannot teach nor industry learn, enabling one to find out ideas for a given concept, and, besides, to hit upon the *expression* for them—the expression by means of which the subjective mental condition induced by the ideas as the concomitant of a concept may be to others" (*Critique of Judgment*, §49, trans. Meredith, 179–80). The proportion and the disposition of these faculties cannot be produced by the rules of science or imitation; those who have the natural gift by which they manage to do so are "favored by nature," and their works have an absolutely original character.

One of the most important characteristics of this definition is Kant's limitation of the notion of genius to artistic creation:

Nature prescribes the rule through genius not to science but to art, and this also only in so far as it is to be fine art.

(*Critique of Judgment*, §46, trans. Meredith, 168)

We must not confuse genius with "powerful brain": Newton can clarify and teach his methods; Homer or Wieland cannot.

In his *Anthropology* (1798), Kant returns to the question of genius, "this mystical name," and seems to widen the term to spheres other than the fine arts, identifying it as the "exemplary originality of talent [*Talent*]": thus Leonardo da Vinci is "a vast genius [*Genie*] in many domains," but we may consider that these "many domains" relate to the "arts" in general, not science, so that there is no real contradiction with what is said in the *Critique of Judgment*. We also find, in *Anthropology*, a remark at the linguistic level whose "nationalist" character is revealing about German sensibilities of the time regarding genius: "We Germans let ourselves be persuaded that the French have a word for this in their own language, while we have no word in ours but must borrow one from the French. But the French have themselves borrowed it from Latin (*genius*), where it means nothing other than an 'individual spirit' [*eigentümlicher Geist*]" (Kant, *Anthropology*, §57, trans. Gregor, 93–94).

Finally, Kant asks whether the world profits from great geniuses because they often cut new paths and open up new perspectives, or whether "mechanical minds" that lean on "canes and crutches to the understanding" have not contributed more to the growth of sciences and the arts. He does not answer the question, saying only that we must be careful of "men called geniuses," who are often only charlatans.

VII. The Twilight of Genius

With romanticism, we witness an apotheosis of genius, corresponding to a veritable "sacralization of art in bourgeois society," as Hans-Georg Gadamer writes in *Truth and Method*. Today, we still speak of the "genius" of an artist, but the notion is hardly an object of theoretical reflection, and we may say, again with Gadamer, that we are witnessing the "twilight of genius." Paul Valéry, in *Introduction à la méthode de Léonard de Vinci*, reacts against the idea that a sleepwalking unconsciousness, quasi divine, mysteriously inspiring, presides over artistic creation. That is, in effect, the "observer's" point of view. If we ask the artist, he is much more down-to-earth about it; he speaks of his technique, not his genius.

Alain Pons

BIBLIOGRAPHY

Batteux, Charles. *Les Beaux-Arts réduits à un même principe.* Critical ed. by J. R. Mantion. Paris: Aux amateurs de livres, 1989.

Bruno, Paul William. "The Concept of Genius: Its Origin and Function in Kant's Third Critique." Ph.D. diss., Boston College, 1999.

Cassirer, Ernst. *The Philosophy of the Enlightenment.* Translated by Fritz C. A. Koelln and James P. Pettegrove. Princeton, NJ: Princeton University Press, 1979.

Diderot, Denis. *Œuvres complètes.* Edited by Roger Lewinter. Paris: Club français du livre, 1969–73.

Dieckmann, Herbert. "Diderot's Conception of Genius." *Journal of the History of Ideas* 2, no. 2 (1941): 151–82.

Dubos, Jean-Baptiste. *Réflexions critiques sur la poésie et la peinture.* Edited by Pierre Jean Mariette. 2 vols. First published 1719. New ed., Geneva: Slatkine Reprints, 1967.

Engell, James. *The Creative Imagination: Enlightenment to Romanticism.* Cambridge, MA: Harvard University Press, 1981.

Fleck, Christina Juliane. *Genie und Wahrheit: Der Geniegedanke im Sturm und Drang.* Marburg, Ger.: Tectum, 2006.

Gadamer, Hans Georg. *Wahrheit und Methode: Grundzüge einer philosophischen Hermeneutik.* Tübingen, Ger.: J.C.B. Mohr, 1960. Translation by Joel Weinsheimer and Donald G. Marshall: *Truth and Method.* 2nd rev. ed. London: Continuum, 2004.

Grappin, Pierre. *La théorie du génie dans le préclassicisme allemand.* Paris: Presses Universitaires de France, 1952.

Kant, Immanuel. *Anthropology from a Pragmatic Point of View.* Translated by M. J. Gregor. The Hague: Martinus Nihjoff, 1974.

———. *The Critique of Judgment.* Edited by Nicholas Walker. Translated by James Creed Meredith. Oxford: Oxford University Press, 2009. First published in 1790.

Klein, Jürgen. "Genius, Ingenium, Imagination: Aesthetic Theories of Production from the Renaissance to Romanticism." In *The Romantic Imagination: Literature and Art in England and Germany,* edited by Frederick Burwick and Jürgen Klein, 19–62. Amsterdam, Neth.: Rodopi, 1996.

La Harpe, Jean-François de. *Lycée ou cours de littérature ancienne et moderne.* Paris: Didier, 1834.

Mathore, Georges, and Algirdas Julien Greimas. "La naissance du génie au XVIIIe siècle: Étude lexicologique." *Le Français Moderne* 25 (1957): 256–72.

Murray, Bradley. "Kant on Genius and Art." *British Journal of Aesthetics* 47, no. 2 (2007): 199–214.

Rousseau, Jean-Jacques. *Dictionnaire de musique.* First published in 1768. In *Œuvres complètes,* vol. 5. Paris: Gallimard-Pléiade, 1995. Translation by William Waring: *A Dictionary of Music.* London, 1779.

Séchelles, Hérault de. *Voyages à Montbard.* Paris: Librairie des bibliophiles, 1890.

Shaftesbury, Anthony Ashley Cooper. *Characteristics of Men, Manners, Opinions, Times.* Oxford: Oxford University Press, 1999.

Wang, Orrin N. C. "Kant's Strange Light: Romanticism, Periodicity, and the Catachresis of Genius." *Diacritics* 30, no. 4 (2000): 15–37.

GENRE

"Genre" is caught up in several different networks, all derived from the Greek *genos* [γένος] (from *gignesthai* [γίγνεσθαι], "to be born, become") and its Latin calque *genus.* These networks are constantly interfering with one another.

I. Biology and Classification

The biological network is the starting point, as witnessed by the Homeric sense of *genos*: "race, line." It is discussed by Aristotle, in particular in his zoological classifications, in contraposition to *eidos* [εἶδος], "genus/species." See PEOPLE.

This network of classifications, in which "genre" takes the meaning of "category, type, species," is notably used in the theory of literature, with the question of "literary genres" (Ger. *Gattung*). See ERZÄHLEN and HISTORY. Cf. *FICTION, RÉCIT, STYLE.*

II. Ontological and Logical Networks

The more philosophically pertinent network is nonetheless that of ontology, as in the case of *eidos*: see *IDEA* and, in particular, SPECIES. *Genos* may thus designate kinds, that is to say also the senses, of being. See PEOPLE / RACE / NATION, Box 5; see also ANALOGY, HOMONYM, *TO BE,* and the explanation of the notion of "category" in ESTI, Box 1.

The ontological network is thus related to the logical network, as we may see in the terms "generic" and "general," as opposed to the singular and the universal: see PROPERTY, UNIVERSALS.

III. The Contemporary Debate over "Gender" and "Sex"

The biological sense of "engenderment" cuts across debates on sexual identity (male or female), which take up the grammatical debates about the "gender" of nouns (masculine, feminine, neuter): see SEX, Box 1. The English "gender" is an example; its translation into French as *genre* understood in the sense of sexuation is clumsy, whereas the German *Geschlecht* easily refers not only to line, generation, people, nation, race, but also to sexual difference: see, besides GENDER and GESCHLECHT, SEX, and *HUMANITY* (esp. MENSCHHEIT).

GERMAN

Syntax and Semantics in Modern Philosophical German: Hegel and Kant

➤ AUFHEBEN, COMBINATION AND CONCEPTUALIZATION, DASEIN, ERSCHEINUNG, LOGOS, SEIN, WORD ORDER

Philosophical German appears comparatively late, alongside a persistent and influential Latin idiom. This double circumstance informs the history of efforts to translate into and from philosophy written in German, and in particular it explains the fetishism that attaches to substantives that are supposed to be "untranslatable" (and are in fact largely left untranslated: *Dasein*, *Aufhebung*, etc.), to the detriment of syntax and context. Hegel's German, which was very early criticized for being unreadable, illustrates the problem in a concentrated form. Confronted by the regular architectonics of Kant's prose, Hegel advocates a different syntax characterized by its economy, by its expansion of the philosophical lexicon, and by transitions and entailments wrought through by negations—and disconcerting for this reason to the translator. However, a detailed study of Hegel's texts, in which a return to ordinary languages is associated with a rigorous effort of conceptualization, shows that these features provide a major point of entry into the Hegelian universe. At the same time the peculiarity and flexibility of Hegelian syntax influence a philosophical terminology that forces the translator to engage in a difficult process of arbitration in order to follow its movement.

I. Semantic Phantoms and Syntactical Energy: What Kind of Esotericism?

Until the end of the eighteenth century, there was little German philosophy in the German language. With a few exceptions—which are not, moreover, particularly noteworthy (Plouquet, Knutzen, Thomasins)—German philosophers wrote in Latin or in French: thus, up to 1770, Althusius, Weigel, Kepler, Agrippa, Sebastian Franck, Paracelsus, Leibniz, and Kant. At the same time, since the beginning of the sixteenth century, religious discourse had been establishing itself in the language of the people (that is the meaning of the adjective *deutsch*), and from the twelfth century forward there had been a literature in German that had assimilated foreign traditions—Latin,

French, Italian, Spanish, etc. This late attempt at devising a properly philosophical discourse from within the language of others bore fruit massively and quickly. Philosophical German takes shape over the course of about three decades, with an explosive force that was to last more than a century, and is in certain respects still not finished: many concepts of today's universal philosophical discourse are rooted in (and sometimes even make direct use of) the philosophical German of the nineteenth and twentieth centuries.

This historical peculiarity was also manifested in philosophical literature in German. There are, for instance, only a few incursions of German into Leibniz's French (his use of the comma, for instance), but traces of Latin abound in the German of philosophers: not only a general rhetoric and a syntax dominated by centuries of scholastic training, but also a lexicon that is often directly transposed—though sometimes varying from author to author—into the new theoretical idiom. Latin phantoms often continue to haunt new German semantic developments, in parentheses, in italics, etc. A tenacious habit is formed, an embarrassing academic tic that is no longer mocked by the laughter of great comedians: a mania for the concept cited in a foreign language, first in Latin, notably in German texts, and now in German, quoted, for example, in French texts.

Thus the reception of German philosophers, in France preponderantly but elsewhere as well, has been marked by a pathology (in the Kantian sense of the term) that goes hand in hand with defeatism and renunciations in the work of translation: a typical (often magical) response to alterity, which we see less among the English, Italians, and others than among the French translators of German philosophy, and still less in French translations of texts in English, Italian, and so on. The respectful, even timid approach to which this has led ends up constructing jetties or breakwaters concentrating difficulties in interpretation around specific notions, usually in the substantival form, and the constant practice in German of nominalization has encouraged this fetishism. We owe to this attitude particular linguistic gestures: a contrite resort to neologisms, a mortified preservation of the German term in French, and to an extent in other languages as well (e.g., *Dasein*). These fixations on the paradigm revive in philosophy the Byzantine debates about words conceived as markers composed of piled-up stones to which everything can be attached: ex-votos, scrolls full of glosses, tresses of exegeses.

These fixed points, veritable intersections of glosses, are so many occasions to depart from the continuous flow of another's discourse to sing the praises of one's own text. But this almost structural reflex long remained blind to the risks it involved: the notions in question are semantic tumuli in which political, ideological, and in general conflictual stakes are constantly appearing and overlapping, thus dividing readers in their own country.

One philosopher concentrates several dimensions of this spreading syndrome: Hegel. On the one hand, he seems to have a vague awareness of it and to try to escape it by practicing an autonomous, relatively new, and innovative language, at the risk of being accused of obscurity. But on the other hand, the very success of his attempt, along with the difficulty of translating and commenting on his discourse, has encouraged the reproduction and return of the very behavior he was opposing. This was also a way of confining his philosophy to his own field and protecting his successors against it: the most Hegelian of these successors, Marx, also played the card of criticizing Hegelian discourse qua discourse. Today, this philosophical language seems to have had its day. Only Heidegger followed its tradition of adopting the linguistic backdrop and foundation of human experience, with consequences that are at once related and very different. Philosophical German seems to have fallen back on an ordinary, translatable, clear discourse that can be put into English. But the subterranean influence of Hegel's philosophical language on modern theoretical discourses in history, psychoanalysis, and anthropology in the broad sense remains considerable and deserves close examination insofar as it has created a new relationship between the totality of the elements of discourse and thought about what is. It exhibits a kind of general relativity that disturbs the previously accepted space-time of speech: the relationship between void and plenitude in discourse is inverted, and syntactical energy alone deploys the conceptual formations that are inconceivable outside this movement of positing and negating. The ordinary, iconic base-10 numeral system collapses and along with it the pantheon of neo-theological concepts: accounting is carried out on the binary basis of what is and what is not; language tends toward the base 2 of identity and difference or, to put it another way, toward the logic (the speech) of being.

This inversion has cast Hegel's writings into a kind of dark night. Hegel is one of the philosophers about whom the question of readability is almost immediately raised: and since this question is practically never posed in connection with other German philosophers of the period, including Fichte and Schelling, who can also sometimes be "hard to follow," it seems that this difficulty constitutes the peculiarity of Hegel without necessarily being conceived as an effect of the singularity of his thought. To it we can oppose (and this opposition also has to do with him and constitutes the essence of his problem) the great clarity of Jacobi, Reinhold, Schopenhauer, Feuerbach, Marx, and other writers and pose the question the other way around: Is it not, according to Hegel, precisely the clarity of a philosopher's writing that reveals that the truth is not displayed, but simulated, play-acted—or even outmoded, old, familiar?

Not only are Hegel's works—if we set aside the notes on his lectures made by students and posthumous publishers—all difficult to read, but they seem to say that it cannot be otherwise. The difficulty of reading them is part of the experience of the truth, of the pain and effort of work. The dressing gown of the do-nothing philosopher mentioned at the end of Hegel's preface to the *Phenomenology of Mind* includes, a contrario, an allusion to the "clarity and distinctness" of Dutch windows and the comfort of the familiarity of the Cartesian "stove-heated room." Finally, the very form of some of his texts shows them to be based on the necessity of an initial obscurity: the *paragraphs* dictated in their rigorous form are then commented upon in the author's explanatory *Remarks*, and then re-commented upon and elucidated in clearer language by the editors, in the form of *additions*.

Today, we can adopt this scheme for reading Hegel at the outset (moreover, in the *Phenomenology of Mind* Hegel analyzes this "advantage" enjoyed by the later reader), but Hegel's contemporaries and first readers did not see things that way. Schelling complained explicitly about the headaches that reading the *Phenomenology* gave him (though these might also have been caused by the book's anti-Schelling polemics). Goethe and Schiller concocted a pedagogical plan that was supposed to allow Hegel, by assiduously consulting a mentor in clarity, to achieve transparency in his discourse (this did not work). As for contemporary reviews, they all deplore "the repetition of formulas and the monotone aspect." In other words everyone at least acted as if the difficulty of Hegel's work had to do with his manner (people fell back on his Swabian origins, his religious training, and the influence of the esotericism of the mystics) and not with the very essence of his philosophy, even though in several places Hegel himself takes up the question of legibility and denounces the esotericism of philosophies of the intuition of the absolute, their obscurity and their elitism. This paradox frames the whole question of Hegel's language. Heine, followed in this by the left-wing Hegelians, proposed a practico-rational response to this paradox: Hegel did not want to be understood "immediately"; he was working for the long term and had first to overcome the barrier of censorship. That, Heine says, is why Hegel's language is *verklausuliert,* hard to understand, en-claused or perhaps "claused-off"—it is not a pathological "manner" from which his prose suffers, imposed and ultimately external, but the objective, strategic effect of a political decision: a mode of the freedom of thought.

The question seems not to have been treated in itself. For instance, Koyré's study, which in theory deals with it, drifts into fragmentary expositions of the system and ultimately proves disappointing. Inversely, Hegel's language is often discussed in more general books, notably in connection with a gloss on this or that term—which is a way of not entering into Hegel's way of expressing himself. However, we can mention a work in recent French philosophical literature that is very interesting from this point of view: Cathérine Malabou's *L'Avenir de Hegel*, which investigates the notion of plasticity in connection with Hegel's way of expressing himself and studies in depth the relationship between the predicative proposition and the speculative proposition.

II. Modern Philosophical Language: The Kantian Model and Its Hegelian Critique

We must first return briefly to the origin of this difficult language and look into Hegel's linguistic culture. The allusion to Hegel's "Swabian speech" (in contrast to that of Berlin, the Rhineland, etc.) connotes a general practice of discourse oriented toward the inner and a weakness of dialogic effort (which Swabian poets compensated by the power of an affective movement toward the other), in short, a kind of regional psychology that is redolent of the Pietist stable and that is supposed to manifest itself also in Hölderlin, Hegel's friend and interlocutor. Robert Minder's study of the Swabian Fathers goes in this direction by emphasizing the influence of religious training and the practice of using a secret code. But there is no lack of counterexamples, beginning with other Swabians like Schelling and Schiller.

Nonetheless, this idiosyncrasy plays a role in a general philosophical language that had been created not long before and had already imposed itself: that of Wolff, Kant, and Fichte, revised by Bardili and Reinhold. But if Kant was quite early on considered the creator of the German (indeed, European) philosophical language, it was especially as the founder of a technical vocabulary that some contemporary commentators already judged to be unfamiliar, esoteric, and obscure.

What characterizes this modern philosophical language?

In the first place the abundance of vocabulary and its specialization, running counter to its ordinary meanings and its ordinary forms: in their great dictionary, the Grimm brothers expressed their astonishment at the philosophical meaning that Kant gave to the word *Anschauung*, which goes back to the traditional *intuitio* with all its ambiguities. Then the extreme length of the sentences and the production of heavily loaded phrases, to which, however, the reader quickly grows accustomed and which are explained in a way by the recourse to an unproblematic syntax, persistent rhetorical procedures, and regular reference points, which are themselves situated in the ground plan of an architecture that is already self-explanatory. Kant's language can thus be approached in an "optical" manner, through geographical intuition: the massiveness of the load implies the simplicity of the articulations. The critical continents each have their own vocabulary, their axes. Only a little practice is required to get one's bearings, and in the end one also discovers many of the characteristics of Latin style.

It is thus a kind of writing that translates well, provided that an effort is made not to forget anything, that one places the commas correctly, and that one has correctly understood the order of modifiers in the German sentence—in order to avoid, for example, making the traditional and in fact rather stupefying error made by French translators who render *reine praktische Vernunft* as *raison pure pratique* (practical pure reason), which is a kind of contradiction, whereas the German phrase means "pure practical reason," as opposed to impure practical reason, that is, to technical reason. This constitutes a double, ongoing offense against the German language and against Kant's thought. If there is somewhere in his work the hypothesis of a practical pure reason (as opposed to what? Certainly not to a *pure* pure reason!), it could be called, hypothetically, nothing other than *praktische reine Vernunft*. The reason for this error has to do with the conditions under which the first translators were working: they were not true speakers of the original language; they translated German as if it were Latin and thus reproduced the modifiers in the order in which they occur in the German phrase.

In addition, this writing justifies the recourse to *lexicons*: even during Kant's lifetime, as early as 1786, lexicalization had begun. Carl Christian Ehrhart Schmid had undertaken to redistribute the Kantian system alphabetically by listing in order the meanings of technical expressions. Kant himself, moreover, did not hesitate to engage in operations of self-lexicalization and definition for which he often provided the Latin equivalent, an attitude virtually nonexistent in Hegel, who was fundamentally hostile to specialized onomastics.

Not only did Kantian discourse translate rather well, but it was good for certain philosophical temperaments: Kant's general ground plan, the reliability of his definitions, the modesty of the critical ambition, all exhibit a set of reassuring reference points. This quality strongly contributed, for example, to the consolidation of the Kantian moment in the pair of thinkers that provided the foundation for teaching philosophy in French schools: Descartes and Kant. At the beginning of the nineteenth century, Kant's language established itself: everyone spoke it, reworked it, adapted it. Everyone except Hegel, who was very familiar with it, but rejected most of it, while at the same time benefiting from the reworking that Fichte was the first to subject it to.

Confronted by this language, Hegel developed, mainly during his stay in Jena, an apparently obscure, even oneiric idiom whose functioning is completely different and presents, among other characteristics, two symptoms. The first of these is the nonexistence, indeed the impossibility, of a *Hegel-Lexikon* comparable to the *Kant-Lexikon*. In this case there are only lists of the occurrences of terms, heavily overloaded by the proliferation of the latter, detailed in the order of the volumes of Hegel's complete works. The notions and concepts of Hegel's philosophy cannot be detailed. They exist meaningfully only in the totality of the text; dictionary classifications break down precisely the moment they are found. Or again: Hegel's notions and concepts exist practically only in syntagmatic expressions. The philosophical reader used to rigorous codes is frustrated: the lack of this tool elicits a malaise that was sufficiently foreseeable for Hegel to warn the reader about it in his preface to the *Phenomenology of Mind*, for instance.

The second symptom—which is no doubt connected with the first, but not for practical reasons—is the Hegelian corpus's resistance to translation. Historically (so far as French is concerned), translation began with a work that was not written by Hegel, the *Aesthetics*, translated by Charles Bénard in the early 1840s, and finished with what was the most "completely his," the *Phenomenology of Mind* and the *Principles of the Philosophy of Right*, with translations appearing almost into the second half of the twentieth century. The *Encyclopedia*, translated by Vera in the second half of the nineteenth century, represents an intermediate linguistic state insofar as it was published with Hegel's explanatory remarks and additions written by the editor after Hegel's death.

We might add to these symptoms a comparative analysis of the different "Hegelian idioms" constructed in French to translate Hegel. While Hegel did not have an opportunity to really consider these symptoms (even though he was the first philosopher to practice what Althusser would call a "symptomatic reading," or *lecture symptomale*, to psychoanalyze his time and to conceive moments and figures as situations), he did think about his difference from other philosophical languages. His is a language that knows it is different, that wishes to be different, that shapes and elaborates its difference, and if necessary exhibits it brutally: Hegel writes against Kant, against Kant's "barbarous" lingo and his dogmatism of subjectivity, which overthrew, to be sure, the dogmatism of objectivity (roughly speaking, eighteenth-century rationalism) but which in a way still speaks the latter's language, insofar as it dogmatically mimes—even in the arrangement of the table of contents—objectivity.

In the same way but more politically, Hegel repeatedly declares his opposition to special languages like "the language spoken by Molière's physicians": that of German jurists and Kantian philosophers. To explain, he uses a democratic argument that may now seem comic when we realize how narrow his own informed readership is. But his criticism of the esotericism of Schelling's absolute knowledge is not based on a criticism of Schelling's discourse (which he long spoke—and created—*with* Schelling, to the point that we cannot always tell who wrote some of the articles in their *Kritisches Journal der Philosophie*).

Hegel's hostility to Kantian discourse ends up taking an extremely aggressive form. A good illustration of this is found in the chapter on Kant in *Lectures on the History of Philosophy* (*Werke*, 20:330ff.). At the beginning of the paragraph devoted to the term "transcendental," Hegel calls such expressions "barbarous." A little later, commenting on the expression "transcendental aesthetics," he almost criticizes Kant's recourse to the etymological meaning of "aesthetic" by contrasting it with the modern sense: "Nowadays aesthetics means the knowledge of the beautiful." A few lines further on, he quotes Kant's statement regarding space: "Space is no empirical Notion which has been derived from outward experiences," and he comments, "But the Notion is never really anything empiric: it is in barbarous forms like this that Kant, however, always expresses himself."

A whole series of such annoyed asides might be collected in Hegel's works. Here is one more, which occurs not long after the ones already cited: "The ego is therefore the empty, transcendental subject of our thoughts, that moreover becomes known only through its thoughts; but of what it is in itself we cannot gather the least idea. (A horrible distinction! For thought is nothing more or less than the 'in-itself.')"

This criticism does not bear solely on Kant's language. Basically, it is aimed at Kant's way of doing philosophy, presenting it as a simple translation of the metaphysics of the Understanding (the Enlightenment) into subjective dogmatism. Kant describes Reason, all right, but in an unreflected, empirical way. His philosophy lacks concept (*Begriff*), and he uses only "thoughts of the Understanding" (*Gedanken*). As a result, and contrary to appearances, Kantianism lacks philosophical abstraction, it "threshes out" ordinary logic: its abstraction is no more than the dead abstraction of already existing concepts; it is not work, effectiveness, creation. Which explains why in other circumstances Hegel is capable, paradoxically, of reproaching Kant for his abstract discourse.

III. Hegel's Language: A Mutation of the Economy of the Syntagma and the Paradigm

Confronted by this situation, Hegel writes a philosophical prose that he considers nondogmatic (neither formal nor mythical), nonabstract, substantial, and well expressed, but which we, on the other hand, often find very abstract, confusing, cryptic, coded, and poorly expressed.

How should we describe this language? Before characterizing it in any way, we must repeat that the specifically Hegelian language is not uniformly distributed. Not only have we seen that his work has several strata, but also we find

in a single work of his whole pages that are not *stricto sensu* "Hegelian," particularly in the prefaces and introductions. But precisely these "protected" pages are also the site of a struggle between discourses: even in the phases of presentation, ordinary language is rapidly enveloped and invested by phenomenological or speculative discourse, and this is shown by the ruptures, anacolutha, and other anomalies that rapidly increase, to the confusion of the reader.

In sum, what characterizes Hegel's language is superficially a certain vocabulary but more profoundly a mutation of the economy of the syntagma and the paradigm in three major aspects.

1. The invasion of the lexical by the syntagmatic: early on, and in a massive way, Hegelian discourse reassembles, from the array of syntactic material before him, what we may call "empty words." By "empty words" we mean those that are now excluded by computer applications, such as articles, personal pronouns, prepositions, conjunctions, common verbal forms—auxiliaries: not only does their mass threaten to saturate research procedures, but the very interest of these words is considered to be nil. In Hegel this procedure of gathering "empty words" has the effect of producing notions that are not fixed in an iconic representation or a traditional semantic content but instead express moments of process or pure relationships. For example, *Sein für anderes, Anderssein, An sich* and *Ansich, Für sich* and *Fürsich, an und für sich, das an und fürsich seiende, bei sich sein, in sich sein*, etc. It is very difficult to make isolated iconic uses of these terms, which can exist only in the movement of sentences in which they slip one into another and divide. In Hegel there are even phases of explicit interest in less common empty words, which he uses in major ways, even as concepts: *also, auch, daher, dieses, eins, etwas, hier, ist, insofern*, etc.

   The bulk of these terms easily absorbs the few elements of ordinary philosophical discourse that were already constituted in the same way and which we encounter in other philosophers writing in German: *das Ich, das Sein, das Wesen*. In the same way this mass absorbs substantivized infinitives (*das Erkennen, das Denken*, etc.), that is, it inserts process, the in-finite, the active verbal element into frameworks usually reserved for nominal substance. We might say the same about the numerous substantivized adjectives: *das Wahre* takes precedence over *die Wahrheit*. In the works' first printed editions, where the first letter of a substantivized adjective is not systematically capitalized, this slippage leads to another difficulty in reading, forcing the reader to choose between this form (e.g., "the True") and the other possibility, namely the elision of a substantive later picked up again, and which must then be found correctly in everything that precedes (e.g., "true knowledge"). Finally, as a result of a sort of "general syntactical preference," Hegel often does not repeat, when he recalls it, a substantive that has been elided but instead substitutes for it a pronoun that is identifiable only by its gender, whereas the reflex of the reader (for instance, the translator) is to repeat this substantive, adding a deictic. The effect of this procedure is to force the reader to memorize, a historicization of the act of reading at the expense of habits of spatial orientation on the material surface of words, the presence of a capital letter on substantives, etc.

The result is a great frequency of identical or quasi-identical forms, which creates an impression of rhapsodic repetition and monotony, sometimes elevated by flights of rhetoric that are polemical or almost lyrical and that break all the more strongly with the whole: suddenly there is a whiff of cultural substance, images or concrete references, a proverb, a quotation of another author that plunges the reader into a second state. In the *Phenomenology* this often happens at the end of chapters, and in the last chapter, but in general Hegel does not use quotation marks to set off quotations, nor does he use proper names, references, and footnotes, just as he avoids examples, metaphors, and comparisons—the substantial baggage that cannot be unpacked without leaving the movement of the dialectical development.

2. This effect of monotony is made stronger by the simplification of the specifically syntactical material. For example, we find in Hegel a near monopoly of the present tense. Heidegger calls that his "vulgarity" and reproaches him for it. Similarly, connectives and modals are reduced to a few that assume identical logical-rhetorical functions: *wenn, dann* (inverted clause), *so, hiermit, somit, indem, erst, nur, oder, überhaupt, bloß, rein, allein, nun.* This relative sobriety seems to be induced by the phenomenon we have just described, the invasion of the lexical by the syntagmatic in Hegel's prose: from a strictly stylistic point of view, by combining with the richness of Schelling's syntactical vocabulary, for example, or by practicing through variation a pseudo-semanticization of syntactical words, the Hegelian text seems to have arrived at a complete disequilibrium, a sort of monster. Nevertheless, the deepest reason for the extreme syntactical austerity in Hegel's prose goes to the heart of his project: what applies to the conceptual lexicon applies also to the syntactical one.

3. The result (and partly the cause) of all this is a prose that makes connections and transitions into so many "decisive" moments. Much is at stake in the emergence and abolition of correlations, which constitutes a major difficulty for French translations that seek to depart from the spatial successiveness of the movement (by reorganizing the order of words in the French manner: that is more or less the tendency of Jean Hyppolite, and we can say that it is encouraged by the tradition of Kant translations that have no difficulty with transitions and displacements within vast wholes whose interior is in some sense open), or to escape the linguistic continuum of semantic networks by recourse to neologisms (or quasi-neologisms: *Anschauung, anschauen: intuitionner; Einsicht: intellection; Gleichheit, gleich,* systematically rendered as *égalité* or *égal* to the detriment of the much more frequent meaning of qualitative identity, or even resemblance), or by setting up new networks; for example, by translating *Selbst* as *soi,* one establishes a false network with the reflexive pronominal *soi* of *en soi, pour soi,* etc. but loses the strong correlation with the paradigm of identity (*dasselbe, selber,* etc.).

In comparison with the Kantian sentence, the Hegelian procedure of arranging-and-loading is completely original. We can intuitively perceive the content of the great, relatively symmetrical Kantian sentences, but in Hegel symmetrical periods are immediately destroyed, bent, and rendered unilateral, or else they twist themselves into ropes because the reversals of symmetries are not rhetorical aspects (specular reminders) of the external exposition but always the movement of the thing itself. Negativity is constantly at work and requires a strong and persistent effort on the part of anyone who wants to recollect the whole. This aspect is connected with Hegel's hostility to "pictures," whose apprehension through reading is never truly free of representation (the concept's being outside itself) and finally emerges in a consciousness that is more religious than philosophical. In Hegel, "picture-like" is clearly pejorative and connotes an address to a weak sort of thought. The necessity of attentive memory, of reading step by step, and of rereading constitutes the difficulty of philosophical work, as opposed to approaches to the true that do not plunge into the thing itself.

IV. The Beginning of the *Phenomenology of Mind*

This verbal strategy excludes direct dialogue with the discourse of others at the same time that Hegel's philosophy presents itself as a pure and simple dialectical collection of what is already there in contemporary philosophical discourse.

Thus the question of the beginning is raised. How can one begin without proceeding like traditional authors, for example, by referring to differences with others, or by definitions? It might be interesting to examine the beginning of the beginning: for example, the first sentences of the first paragraph of the introduction to the *Phenomenology,* which is itself a kind of prolegomenon, an initiation.

The introduction is formally distinct from the content of the experience of consciousness, of which phenomenology is the science, the knowledge, and in a way already the system.

It corresponds to the chapter on Absolute Knowledge, in which all the moments intersect and overlap, and therefore in which there are no longer any moments, where knowledge is complete (and can begin to be set forth as the true). It is thus not a moment but the empty concept of knowledge whose possibility is postulated as knowledge of what is, of the in-itself, of the Absolute, and as a knowledge that cannot be immediate and can attain truth (science as system, the pure logos of being) only by fulfilling and abolishing this difference in a history that is at the same time a demonstration, a succession of verifications in the thing itself.

The person who begins this history is also the one who rejects the last philosopher to have conceived this difference between knowledge and being in itself, that is, Kant. And thus, the first moment in the *Phenomenology* is devoted to Kant. But it is also devoted to another negation, another difference: the one that the philosophy of identity situates between absolute knowledge and natural consciousness. And Hegel's point of departure consists in thinking simultaneously of the unity of the Kantian procedure and the philosophy of identity. To that end Hegel explains that Kant merely reflects common sense, that he simply follows Locke's thought to its logical outcomes. Kant cannot, in fact, know, because he does not move beyond the understanding and does not subject the critique to a dialectical verification. Critical thought is a delusion. Idealism, on the other hand, remains contingent and arbitrary: it does not demonstrate the indifference of the subject and the object but studies each of them in itself, compares and identifies them: identity is constructed, it is not an autogenous result. The *Phenomenology* continues: Kant's philosophy and the philosophy of identity are abstract and based on presuppositions. Kant simply conceives and posits the abstract difference between Being and Knowledge, whereas Fichte and Schelling conceive the abstract identity of being and knowledge. But all of them, under this identity, developed all the forms of the totality, which can now be recuperated: this is the Hegelian windfall. This recuperation is that of the modern, atomized subject whom it is also a question of reconciling with himself, with his culture, with the organic, with religion, the state, ethics, etc., in an adequate language.

It is in this context that the beginning of the *Phenomenology of Mind* should be read. The first sentence is both a stasis in the discourse of common sense and a switching-on of Hegelian discourse:

Es ist eine natürliche Vorstellung, daß, eh in der Philosophie an die Sache selbst, nemlich an das wirkliche Erkennen dessen, was in Wahrheit ist, gegangen wird, es nothwendig sey, vorher über das Erkennen sich zu verständigen, als das Werkzeug, wodurch man des Absoluten sich bemächtige, oder als das Mittel, durch welches hindurch man es erblicke, betrachtet wird.

(C'est une représentation tout à fait naturelle de penser qu'en philosophie, avant d'aborder la chose elle-même, savoir, la connaissance effective de ce qui est en vérité, il est nécessaire de s'accorder préalablement sur la connaissance que l'on considère comme l'outil qui permettra de s'emparer de l'absolu, ou comme le moyen au travers duquel on l'aperçoit.)

(Trans. J.-P. Lefebvre, Paris: Aubier, 1991, 79)

(It is natural to suppose that, before philosophy enters upon its subject proper—namely, the actual knowledge of what truly is—it is necessary to come first to an understanding concerning knowledge, which is looked upon as the instrument by which to take possession of the Absolute, or as the means through which to get a sight of it.)

(Trans. J. B. Baillie, 1910; New York, Harper, 1967, 131)

(It is a natural assumption that in philosophy, before we start to deal with its proper subject-matter, viz. the actual cognition of what truly is, one must first of all come to an understanding about cognition, which is regarded either as the instrument to get hold of the Absolute, or as the medium through which one discovers it.)

(Trans. A. V. Miller, 1977; Oxford, Oxford University Press, 46)

The expression "es ist eine natürliche Vorstellung, daß" has a quasi-trivial status (which the French translator assumes by adding "*tout à fait*" ("entirely"), as one might say "*mais naturellement*" (of course). Similarly, the expressions "die Sache selbst," "das wirkliche Erkennen," "was in Wahrheit ist," "das Absolute," "sich zu verständigen," are all in the ordinary register: the thing itself with which we are concerned, true knowledge, the true, the absolute, coming to agreement, etc. And at the same time Hegel delivers a first packet of rigorous conceptualization, made more precise and stabilized by more than a year of labor on the text of the whole of the *Phenomenology of Mind*: the *Vorstellung, représentation* in the French translation, "supposition" and "assumption" in the English, also has the precise sense that Hegel assigns to it in the *Phenomenology* as a whole, in its definitive hierarchy. The statement is already virtually turned around: to say what follows the word *daß* is nothing but, is only, *Vorstellung*, representation, and furthermore merely *natural* representation, because representation is the concept's being outside itself. *Sache selbst* (the thing itself) will be the principal marching order for the whole dialectical procedure (insofar as it is not external); *wirklich* already connotes the effectiveness that is not a pure and simple thingly or abstract "reality"; *was in Wahrheit ist* can also be read in an ontological sense as what, in truth, is; and *verständigen*, which designates agreement, also connotes the universality of the understanding, *Verstand*.

But it is not solely a matter of intertextual echoes. The words *natürliche Vorstellung*, with which the *Phenomenology* begins, also refer to the current state of philosophical reflection. This moment in the history of philosophy, Hegel's text proposes, has become a "nature," an immediate given whose aporias (here, the richest knowledge is at the same time the poorest: aiming at the truth, one ends up in the clouds of error) necessarily imply that the way of dialectical doubt that the opening of the preface describes is indeed commencing.

If Kant is in fact the subject here, then it is Kant insofar as he was the last to pose the question of knowledge and thus to walk off with the philosophical jackpot. Thus it is a strange Kant, fairly "Lockified" and revised by Fichte. And still, the critique of the *organon* "with which one grasps oneself" and of the milieu "through which one perceives" also refers to the very beginnings of philosophy. And thus we are already in the thing itself in the Hegelian sense, apparently devoting ourselves to avoiding a particular way of missing it. This will be the schema for the writing of the whole *Phenomenology of Mind*; Hegel's opening sentences describe, capture, and instantiate the effect on his writing of a procedure that consists in designating moments that already contain other moments and are already no longer themselves. Or, to put it another way, Hegel's language cannot not be a mere figure, simply a figure, of common language, of the language common to the greatest number of philosophers, and finally of common language as such, insofar as this common language always tends to test once again its "economic" essence, its aptitude for elementary reduction, that is, it tends to reinvest always once again in the word's pure time, leaving it to mute indices to designate images with a gesture, even if these images are complicated concepts that are supposed to be heavy with history.

V. The Dynamicization of Semantemes

What is at issue should not, however, be understood under cover of a cluster of cliches regarding the contradictory meaning of certain terms that can designate a thing and its contrary: Hegelian concepts themselves, considered in their apparent semantic autonomy, are part of these mutations and redistributions. Here we think, of course, of the famous *Aufhebung*, which has become a test of strength for heavy lifters since Hegel himself pointed out that the term could signify both "abolish" and "preserve." He mentioned this precisely because this curiosity did not appear in his statements, because of the elementary law that holds that a term is never alone but is caught up in a general context and a particular syntagma, which guide the term's meaning without there being any need for long additional glosses. And thus, when Hegel says nothing, the term has the sense dominant in the language ("abolish"), which itself explains, by an explicit context, the cases (which are statistically in the minority) in which the term means, on the basis of a primary negative sense, to withdraw something from circulation, from presence *hic et nunc*, and to put this thing aside, to protect it, and to intend it for later. It is precisely because there is no possible iconic use of his concepts but only contextualized uses that this word has the meaning that Hyppolite very calmly translated by *supprimer* (abolish, cancel). Apart from this negative meaning, what does the expression *Aufhebung der Aufhebung* mean in Hegel's work? Only a pure knickknack of semantic inanity would remain.

Another consequence of the dynamics of Hegelian language is the necessity the French translator encounters of sometimes varying, more or less lightly, the translation of terms identical in the German text: thus *gleich* occupies a spectrum ranging from "identical" (dominant) to "equal" (much rarer), by way of "similar" or even "same"; *Anschauung* ranges from "contemplation" to "intuition," by way of "vision" pure and simple, or even "spectacle." These variations cannot but collide with the fetishistic relationship to isolated words. But that relation is precisely what is unfaithful because it obscures the effects of context, which are always semantically decisive. Conversely, certain terms, which are different in German, will be found in context always translated by the same French terms: the French word *intelligence* can translate *Klugheit, Verstand, Einsicht, Intelligenz*. Recourse to translator's notes makes it possible to respect the desire for verification that the reader may feel. Finally, the reading contract between the translator and his reader also commits the former not to play in an arbitrary manner with these necessary variations and to give the reader the benefit of his knowledge of the contexts: on this contractual basis we see that the same expressions are usually translated in the same way, when the author of the original text supervises the play of meaning in these expressions. We might list such cases: *allgemein* (general, universal), *erscheinen* (appear, in the trivial sense; be manifested phenomenally), *bestimmen* (determine, intend), *darstellen* (exhibit, represent), *dasein* (be there, exist), etc. What would one say about a translation that always translated Hegel's different

prepositions (*an, ab, aus, auf, durch,* etc.) each by the same French preposition? The statements would be jammed. In Hegel, no doubt more than in other philosophers, semantic units, semantemes, are themselves subject to movement. If iconic immobility eventually seizes them, it will be because Hegel has lost the game. It is not impossible that he himself may have sometimes contributed to this sclerosis.

Jean-Pierre Lefebvre

BIBLIOGRAPHY

Glockner, Hermann, ed. *Hegel-Lexikon*. Stuttgart: F. Frommann, 1957.

Hegel, Georg Wilhelm Friedrich. *Werke*. Frankfurt am Main: Suhrkamp, 1986.

Koyré, Alexandre. *Etudes d'histoire de la pensée philosophique*. Paris: Gallimard / La Pléiade, 1971.

Malabou, Catherine. *The Future of Hegel: Plasticity, Temporality and Dialectic*. Translated by L. During. New York: Routledge, 2005.

Minder, Robert. "Herrlichkeit chez Hegel, ou le Monde des Pères Souabes." *Etudes germaniques* (1951): 275–302.

O'Neill Surber, Jere. *Hegel and Language*. Albany: State University of New York, 2006.

Warminski, Andrzej. *Readings in Interpretation: Hölderlin, Hegel, Heidegger*. Minneapolis: University of Minnesota Press, 1987.

Züfle, Manfred. *Prosa der Welt*. Einsiedeln, Switz.: Johannes, 1992.

| GESCHICHTLICH (GERMAN)

FRENCH   *historique/historial, historicité/historialité*

➤ *DESTINY*, HISTORIA UNIVERSALIS, HISTORY, and AUFHEBEN, DASEIN, EREIGNIS, ES GIBT, PRESENT, TATSACHE, *TIME, TO BE*

The German term *geschichtlich* is translated into English as "historical" but into French as *historique* when it appears in Hegel and as *historial* in Heidegger (the distinction is not drawn in English translations), and similarly for the noun *Geschichtlichkeit, historicité* or *historialité*. This is not a matter of secondary variation or translator's caprice. What the shift from the *historique* to the *historial* shows in French is the profound debate that took place in German philosophy, from Hegel to Heidegger, on the nature of what is truly *historical*, in other words, what makes a sequence of events history. The resources of the language are here invoked in a complex network that superimposes a famous pair of contraries (*Geschichte/Historie, geschichtlich/historisch*) and a strange etymology, *das Geschehen*, in English "happening, event, becoming," a sort of lexical matrix in which the relation between history and what happens is put into general question.

I. *Geschichte, Historie, Geschehen*

The examination of *Geschichte, geschichtlich* in Heideggerian terminology may begin with this remark of Heidegger in *Gesamtausgabe*:

> The country that can claim R. Descartes among its great thinkers, the founder of the doctrine of humanity understood as subjectivity, does not have a word for *Geschichte* in its language, by which it could distinguish the term from *Historie*.

(Heidegger, *Gesamtausgabe*, vol. 79)

The first difficulty is thus to gain access to what the term *Geschichte* covers. The term is always understood by Heidegger to contrast with *Historie*, in the sense of historical science, historical studies, historiography.

Hegel had noted it:

> In our language, the term History [*Geschichte*] unites the objective with the subjective side, and denotes quite as much the *historia rerum gestarum*, as the *res gestae* themselves; on the other hand it comprehends not less what has *happened* [*das Geschehene*], than the *narration* of what has happened [*Geschichtserzählung*].

(Hegel, *Vorlesungen*, 83; *Philosophy of History*, 60)

Raymond Aron comments:

> The same word in French, English, and German applies to historical reality and the knowledge we have of it. *Histoire*, history, *Geschichte* refer at the same time to the becoming of humanity and to the science that men attempt to build to understand their becoming (even if the equivocation is attenuated, in German, by the existence of words, *Geschehen*, *Historie*, which only have one of the two senses).

(Aron, *Dimensions de la conscience historique*)

The decisive difference does not rest on the fact that German has two words where French has only one: the twofold meaning of *histoire* is also found in *Geschichte*. The important point is that German has, for *Geschichte*, a properly etymological resource in the verb *geschehen*, "to happen, to occur," which yields the noun *das Geschehen*, "becoming," and the substantivized adjective *Geschehene*, "what has become."

It is this resource that is continuously exploited by the philosophers of German Idealism. For Schelling, *das Geschehene*, that which has happened or has become (according to Ranke's expression: *was geschehen ist*)—for instance, Caesar having crossed the Rubicon, the Battle of Marignano in 1515, that is, so-called "factual" history (or "treaties and battles" history, in contrast with the problem-history dear to the Annales school)—is still not at the level of "history properly speaking" (*die eigentliche Geschichte*) or the level of what is "properly historical" (*eigentlich geschichtlich*), as Hegel says (*Vorlesungen*, 83). Schelling writes:

> Was wäre alle *Historie*, wenn ihr nicht ein innrer Sinn zu Hilfe käme? Was sie bei so vielen ist, die zwar das meiste von allem *Geschehenen* wissen, aber von *eigentlicher Geschichte* nicht das geringste verstehen.

> (What would all history be if an inner sense did not come to assist it? It would be what it is for so many who indeed know most all that has happened, but who know not the least thing about actual history.)

(Schelling, *Weltalter*, Einleitung; *The Ages of the World*, Eng. tr. Bolman)

The distinction is twofold: between *Historie* (science of history, historical studies) and *Geschichte* (history, *res gestae*), but also between "everything that has happened" (*das Geschehene*) and "history properly speaking" (*die eigentliche Geschichte*). History properly speaking is irreducible to what

has happened. It gets its meaning only from reappropriation or interiorization, from a way of knowing things not by rote (*auswendig*), but by the heart (*inwendig*), as Hegel says (*Phänomenologie des Geistes*, 35; *Phenomenology of Spirit*, 23–24). Speculatively, the lexical relation between *Geschehenes* and *Geschichte* is thus an index less of the proximity of two concepts or fields, than of the distance, even the abyss, that separates them.

II. *Geschichtlich* and *Historisch*: Heidegger, the Historial, and the Historic

If we move from the lines by Aron cited above to Heideggerian thought, it appears that the attenuation of the ambiguity that obtains between the nouns *Geschichte* and *Historie* becomes a radical differentiation at the level of the corresponding adjectives, *geschichtlich* versus *historisch*. *Historie* having been rejected as the mere chronological listing of events, and thus as the expression of a "calculating thought," *Geschichte* endows itself with a completely different relationship to temporality, proper to a "meditative thought."

We must nevertheless begin by recalling, in François Fédier's words, that "in the first period of his teaching at Freiburg, before 1923, Heidegger means by *historisch* what he will later call *geschichtlich*, that is, what is fully historical—in that any human being can only *live* in view of a dimension of being in the midst of which, having one day transmitted something which will be historical, he becomes fully in his turn the inheritor of a history" (Fédier, "Phénoménologie").

In French, then, Heidegger's adjective *geschichtlich* has been rendered *historial*, and the term *historique* has been used for *historisch*. *Historial* in French is not a neologism but an archaicism. We find it in Vincent de Beauvais, *Le Miroir historial du monde*, French translation of the *Speculum historiale* printed in Paris in 1495, but also in Montaigne. Henry Corbin, one of Heidegger's French translators, declared that "I coined the term *historialité*, and I think the term is worth keeping. There is the same relationship between *historialité* and *historicité* as between *existential* and *existentiel*" (see DASEIN and ESSENCE). This translation was nevertheless contested by J. A. Barash, who maintains *historique* and *historicité*, notably on the grounds that the terms *geschichtlich* and *Geschichtlichkeit* are not neologisms for Heidegger, and the aforementioned translation would amount to distancing him from the debates of his immediate predecessors and his contemporaries "in his age." Without having to settle this debate here, we can restrict ourselves to the following two remarks: (1) Corbin's initiative, which we think a happy one, is also related to his vision of "hiero-history," notably in Iranian Islamic spirituality; (2) the reliance on a single term, from Hegel to Heidegger in this case, does respect an existing lexicographical continuity, but the same term may take on entirely different overtones and thereby be newer than a neologism: thus *divertissement* is not a neologism in Pascal, nor is *Dasein* in Heidegger. In short, translation also takes place within a single language.

Does Corbin's translation of *geschichtlich* (in Heidegger) by *historial* stand up to Barash's criticism? Yes, and we should even be grateful to Corbin, who simply ran into these problems about the meaning of *geschichtlich* in Heidegger first, and brought them to our attention, and in addition found resources in French to solve them. To study this question is to ask: how does *Geschichtlichkeit*—a word that seems to have been created by Hegel, taken over by Schelling and then Heine—take on a different meaning in Heidegger that radically differs from that which it had in Hegel?

III. *Geschichte* and *Geschichtlichkeit*: From Hegel and Schelling to Heidegger

The historicity (*Geschichtlichkeit*) described by German Idealists comes from a metaphysical conception—indeed this is the first time that history is conceived metaphysically—in which it refers to the dimension proper to the Spirit in its path toward itself, the concept of historicity being at bottom only the conceptualization of the necessity of this "toward." This path or ordeal (which is no doubt indissociable from a Christology) is thought of by Hegel as "negativity," with all that entails in terms of seriousness, pain, and patience; it is "the enormous labour of world-history" (*Phenomenology of Spirit*, preface, Fr. trans. J.-P. Lefebvre mod., 38, 46; Eng. trans. Miller, 8, 17). History is a way for Spirit to come to itself, the work of its coming to itself; history accomplishes and reveals (ironically, Schelling would add) what is proper to the Spirit, in a mobility that is essential to it, as Marcuse emphasized in 1932: "Historicity (*Geschichtlichkeit*) indicates the sense of what we aim at when we say of something: it is historical (*geschichtlich*).... What is historical becomes in a certain way (*geschieht*). History as becoming (*Geschehen*), as mobility, that is the problem posed" (*Hegel's Ontology*). The problem Marcuse identifies is also, in a way, the start of German Idealism. There is indeed a "history of self-consciousness," a decidedly transcendental history, as established by Schelling in the *System of Transcendental Idealism* of 1800, translating in his own way the *genetic* preoccupation of Fichte's philosophy. This history becomes legible in mythology understood as theogony, that is, as history rather than as a doctrine of the gods, *Göttergeschichte* rather than *Götterlehre*: it is the theogonic process of human consciousness.

For Heidegger, on the other hand, historicity is not anchored in the Spirit (the very term "spirit," *Geist*, is "avoided" in *Being and Time*, as made explicit in his § 10), but "in" *Dasein* (if we can say that, since *Dasein* has no inside) and its facticity, the investigation of which is the purview of the existential analytic. Remarkably, it is in Heidegger's critical encounter with Aristotle (following the so-called "Natorp report," translated into French as *Interprétation phénoménologique d'Aristote* of 1922) rather than Hegel that historiality (as distinct from historicity) comes to be conceived as mobility inherent to any human life. In the compressed study of the links between Aristotelian ethics and physics, the ethical aspect of the ontological mobility of human life is made apparent. The clarification of the ethics foreshadowed in 1922 is reserved for the existential analytic of *Being and Time*, in the perspective of a "hermeneutics of facticity." *Faktizität* (facticity) constitutes, as Gadamer points out (in "Heidegger und die Griechen"), a sort of counterproof of everything that, in German Idealism, bears the mark of the Absolute (Spirit, self-consciousness, etc.), and as such indicates the difference of the appeal to historicity in absolute idealism and in the existential analytic: whence the abyss that separates *Geschichtlichkeit*-as-historicity from *Geschichtlichkeit*-as-historiality, the world of the Spirit and the "self-world" (*Selbstwelt*).

Heidegger seems indeed to have established a link between the "metaphysics of subjectivity," which Descartes supposedly founded, and the fact that the French language does not have access to this dimension of history referred to by the German term *Geschichte*, or, even worse, collapses the *historial* and the *historique*. No doubt we must understand that *Geschichte* indicates a dimension of history that is not captured by a subjectivity, the action of a subject (even a collective one), understood such that it would be capable of "making history" (cf. Pasternak: "No one makes history"). *Geschichte* indicates a dimension of history that is all the more essential for being incapable of being "made" by man as an actor or agent and does not derive from what Heidegger called *Machenschaft* in the 1930s. *Machenschaft* is, in the common sense of the term, a warped machination, a tissue of dark actings. For Heidegger the term has a stronger sense: *Machenschaft* is what comes out of a doing/*machen*, from the effectivity of an efficient cause, for example, of an "operational" subject and thus derives from an implicit ontology of beings as "doable" or "makeable," that is, an implicit ontology that falls already within the rule or the spirit of modern technique conceived as a *Gestell*, whose counterpoints are *Gelassenheit* and *Ereignis* (cf. F. W. von Herrmann, *Wege ins Ereignis*; see COMBINATION AND CONCEPTUALIZATION, II). "What hells must the human being still cross, before he learns that he does not make himself?" Heidegger asks in a letter of 12 April 1968, to Hannah Arendt. The aspect of "history" designated by the German term *Geschichte* is one that man cannot, then, "make," but which he is able to allow to *geschehen* (become), or not. *Geschichte* thus indicates what comes *to* man, but not *from* man.

IV. *Geschichte, Geschehen, Geschick*: From the Historial to the History of Being

Hegel and Schelling, as we have seen, attempted in a way to separate *Geschichte*, history, from *Geschehen*, what happens or becomes in itself. Heidegger seems, on the contrary, to link them back together. *Geschichte* indicates a *Geschehen*, "becoming" or "happening," whose original meaning Heidegger sometimes traces back to Luther, in whom we find the word in the feminine as *die Geschichte* or *die Geschicht*, but much more frequently in the neuter, *das Geschicht*. In this sense *Geschicht* is *göttliche Schickung*, divine dispensation; Heidegger hears *Geschicht* as Luther does: as if deriving, if not from God, at least from a *Geschick*, a "dispatch" of which man is at best the recipient, and of which he must acknowledge receipt—of which he is even a *Schicksal*, a fate or a destination. What is truly *geschichtlich*, historial, is by that fact *geschicklich*, "destinal" or "epochal."

In sum, *Geschichte* should be understood:

1. on the basis of *Geschehen*, "des *Geschehens* dessen, was wir Geschichte nennen, d. h. des *Seins* dieses Seienden [the happening-occurring of what we call *Geschichte*, that is, of the Being of this being]" (*Gesamtausgabe*, 34: 82), as arrival or advent, and future, to come (Ger. *Zu-kunft*, irreducible to the future; cf. Péguy's French neologism: *évenir*; see PRESENT). *Geschichte* is only accessible as

such to a meditating, noncalculating thought, whence Heidegger's frequent homages to Jacob Burckhardt;

2. in the direction of a *Geschichtlichkeit* (according to the term that first appears in Hegel, Schelling, and Heine), *historicité* or *historialité*, in English "non-historiographical historicality," itself rooted in the temporality of *Dasein*. The specific mobility of *Dasein*, whose time is given on the basis of the future, throws it on an adventure (*Geschehen*) in which its historiality is rooted, related to the finitude of temporality in the being-toward-death taken on as such. Heidegger expresses this way of understanding *Geschichtlichkeit* in this manner: "Die Zeit nicht haben, sondern sich von ihr haben lassen, ist das Geschichtliche (Not having time in our possession, but being such that it takes possession of us, that is the historial)."

The possibility of a *Geschichte* contains the possibility of an *Ungeschichte* (non-history), of a *Geschichtsverlust* (loss of history) or a *Geschichtslosigkeit* (absence of history), when the historial dimension comes to be lacking.

In 1927 historiality is the epic of *Dasein*. But *Geschichte* becomes important to the thinking about fundamental ontology when the latter comes to be inscribed in the perspective of a *Seinsgeschichte* (*histoire de l'être*), or even a *Seynsgeschichte* (*histoire de l'estre*). "Historial" indicates that what concerns us may come to us without coming from us, unlike the "historical," even though the latter term refers both to a chronological account based on a *vulgäres Zeitverständnis* (a "vulgar conception" or "common understanding" of time) and to the idea that history, since it is capable of being made by man, would fall within the domain of the "doable," becoming thus a non-history in which nothing more can happen to us.

Pascal David

BIBLIOGRAPHY

Arendt, Hannah, and Martin Heidegger. *Briefe 1925–1975*. Frankfurt: Klostermann, 1998. Translation by Andrew Shields: *Letters, 1925–1975*, edited by Ursula Ludz. Orlando, FL: Harcourt, 2004.

Aron, Raymond. *Dimensions de la conscience historique*. Paris: Plon, 1985. First published in 1961.

———. *Politics and History: Selected Essays*. Edited and translated by Miriam Bernheim Conant. New York: Free Press, 1978.

Barash, Jeffrey Andrew. *Martin Heidegger and the Problem of Historical Meaning*. Rev. and expanded ed. New York: Fordham University Press, 2003.

Fédier, François. "Phénoménologie de la vie religieuse." *Heidegger Studies* 13 (1997): 145–61.

Gadamer, Hans Georg. "Heidegger und die Griechen." Vol. 3. In *Gesammelte Werke*. 10 vols. Tübingen: Mohr, 1985–95.

Hegel, Georg Wilhelm Friedrich. *Phänomenologie des Geistes*. Vol. 3. Edited by Eva Moldenhauer and Karl Markus Michel. In *Werke*. Frankfurt: Suhrkamp, 1970. Translation by A. V. Miller: *Phenomenology of Spirit*. Oxford: Oxford University Press, 1977.

———. *Vorlesungen über die Philosophie der Geschichte*. Vol. 12. Edited by Eva Moldenhauer and Karl Markus Michel. In *Werke*. Frankfurt: Suhrkamp, 1970. Translation by John Sibree: *The Philosophy of History*. Rev. ed. New York: Wiley, 1944.

Heidegger, Martin. *Beiträge zur Philosophie (vom Ereignis)*. Vol. 65. Edited by Friedrich-Wilhelm von Herrmann. In *Gesamtausgabe*. Frankfurt am Main: Klostermann, 1989. Translation by Parvis Emad and Kenneth Maly: *Contributions to Philosophy: From Enowning*. Bloomington: Indiana University Press, 1999.

———. *Identität und Differenz*. Vol. 11. Edited by Friedrich-Wilhelm von Herrmann. In *Gesamtausgabe*. Frankfurt am Main: Klostermann, 2006. Translation by Joan Stambaugh: *Identity and Difference*. New York: Harper & Row, 1969.

———. *Phänomenologische Interpretationen zu Aristoteles: Einführung in die phänomenologische Forschung*. Vol. 61. Edited by Walter Bröcker and Käte Bröcker-Oltmanns. In *Gesamtausgabe*. Frankfurt am Main: Klostermann, 1985. Translation by Richard Rojcewicz: *Phenomenological Interpretations of Aristotle: Initiation into Phenomenological Research*. Bloomington: Indiana University Press, 2001.

———. "Was ist Metaphysik?"; "Vom Wesen des Grundes"; "Vom Wesen der Wahrheit"; "Zur Seinsfrage." In *Wegmarken*. Vol. 9. Edited by Friedrich-Wilhelm von Herrmann. In *Gesamtausgabe*. Frankfurt am Main: Klostermann, 1976. Translation by David Farrell Krell, William McNeill, et al.: "What is Metaphysics?"; "On the Essence of Ground"; "On the Essence of Truth"; "On the Question of Being." In *Pathmarks*. Edited by William McNeill. Cambridge: Cambridge University Press, 1998.

Kisiel, Theodore, and Thomas Sheehan, eds. *Becoming Heidegger: On the Trail of His Early Occasional Writings, 1910–1927*. Evanston, IL: Northwestern University Press, 2007.

Le Goff, Jacques. *Saint Louis*. Translated by Gareth Evan Gollrad. Notre Dame, IN: University of Notre Dame Press, 2009.

Marcuse, Herbert. *Hegel's Ontology and the Theory of Historicity*. Translated by Seyla Benhabib. Cambridge, MA: MIT Press, 1987.

Parvis, Emad. *On the Way to Heidegger's Contributions to Philosophy*. Madison: University of Wisconsin Press, 2007.

Péguy, Charles. *Œuvres Complètes en prose*. Vol. 2. Paris: Gallimard / La Pléiade, 1988.

Polt, Richard. *The Emergency of Being: On Heidegger's Contributions to Philosophy*. Ithaca, NY: Cornell University Press, 2006.

Renthe-Fink, L. von. *Geschichtlichkeit: Ihr terminologischer und begrifflicher Ursprung bei Hegel, Haym, Dilthey und Yorck*. Göttingen: Vandenhoeck and Ruprecht, 1964.

Schelling, Friedrich von. *Weltalter-Fragmente*. Edited by Klaus Grotsch. Vol. 13. In *Schellingiana*. Stuttgart: Frommann-Holzboog, 2002. Translation by Jason M. Wirth: *The Ages of the World*. Albany: State University of New York Press, 2000.

GESCHLECHT (GERMAN)

ENGLISH   race, kinship, lineage, community, generation, gender, sex

➤ *AUTRUI*, DASEIN, GENDER, *GENRE*, HUMANITY, LEIB, MENSCHHEIT, PEOPLE, SEX

As Heidegger reminds us, in a text that Derrida has commented upon at length, *Geschlecht* is impressively multivocal. It refers to race but also to kinship, generation, and gender, as well as the notion of sex, which divides all of the former: "The word equally means the human species [*das Menschengeschlecht*], in the sense of humanity [*Menschheit*], and species in the sense of tribe, stock, or family [*Stamme, Sippen, und Familien*], all of which is further intersected by the generic duality of the sexes [*das Zeifache der Geschlechter*]." This is why *Geschlecht* lends itself to a serious task of intralinguistic translation, which consists in finding equivalents for its various significations, in order to better circumscribe its meaning. The stakes of such a task are twofold: it must remove confusion about the different orders of belonging but also question the constitution and destination of human diversity.

I. The Multivocity of *Geschlect*

Four meanings of *Geschlecht* must be distinguished:

1. Paternal or maternal lineage (*Geschlecht vom Vater / von der Mutter*). It serves in this sense to assign identity. Thus, in Gotthold E. Lessing's play *Nathan the Wise* [*Nathan der Weise*], Nathan reveals that of his adopted daughter: "Do you not even know of what lineage the mother was [was für Geschlechts die Mutter war]?" (IV, 7). But once this

identity is specified in the sense of belonging to a lineage, it may become a sign of distinction. This is why *Geschlecht* also refers, in a more restrictive way, to nobility. To belong to a *Geschlecht* also refers, more narrowly, to nobility, as is shown in the same play (ibid., II, 6) by the exchange between Nathan and the Templar regarding von Stauffen's family: "NATHAN: Von Stauffen, there must be more members of this noble family [*des Geschlechts*]. TEMPLAR: Oh, yes, they were, there are yet many members of this noble family [*des Geschlechts*] rotting here."

2. *Geschlecht* also refers to a larger community, whose extension varies from tribe to humanity in general, by way of a people or a race. Humanity as a whole is thus referred to as *das Menschengeschlecht, das sterbliche Geschlecht,* or *das Geschlecht der Sterblichen* (the race of mortals). In a significant displacement of meaning from vertical to horizontal solidarity, *Geschlecht* may also mean a collection of individuals born at the same time: a generation.

3. In a different register *Geschlecht* refers to sexual difference (*der Geschlechtsunterschied*). *Geschlecht* is both sex in general and each sex in particular, male (*das männliche Geschlecht*) and female (*das weibliche Geschlecht*).

4. Finally, in a more abstract register, *Geschlecht* refers to the genus, in the sense of logical category, in the widest sense. It thus refers to the different genera of natural history as well as all sorts of objects and abstractions.

This multivocity, which owes much to the Greek *genos* (see PEOPLE), is problematic when we must translate *Geschlecht* into other languages. While the last two senses are easily identifiable and do not lead to confusion as long as context reveals when we must think of a sex or genus in a logical sense, translation becomes infinitely more complex once the term refers to a lineage, a generation, or a community or when it intersects with terms referring to people, nation, or race. In such cases the polysemy of *Geschlecht* is compounded by the polysemy of terms like "people," "race," and "nation" that must nonetheless be kept distinct from one another and from *Geschlecht*. What is more, this polysemy turns out to be problematical even in German itself, where *Geschlecht* competes with terms that share aspects of its sense, and which, whenever they are introduced or used, raises a theoretical difficulty and entails a polemic.

II. The Disambiguation of *Geschlect* and Its Difficulties

Between Kant and Herder a whole enterprise of terminological distinction may be said to be undertaken that aims at restricting the uncontrollable breadth of meanings of *Geschlecht* and substituting for it new, univocal concepts: *Stamm* and *Rasse*. In the essay *Determination of the Concept of Human Race* [*Bestimmung des Begriffs einer Menschenrasse*, 1785], Kant attempts to give *Rasse* a restrictive sense that preserves the unity of human kind, removing all equivocal use of the term. The goal is to avoid all confusion between species or kind and the races and to block attempts to think of the diversity of the "races" as grounded in an original diversity of distinct generations:

Thus the concept of a race [*der Begriff einer Rasse*] contains first the concept of a common phylum [*der Begriff eines gemeinschaftlichen Stammes*], second *necessarily hereditary* characters of the classificatory difference among the latter's descendants. Through the latter, reliable grounds of distinction are established according to which we can divide the species [*die Gattung*] into classes [*in Klassen*], which then, because of the first point, namely the unity of the phylum [*die Einheit des Stammes*], may only be called *races* [*Rassen*] and by no means *kinds* [*Arten*].

(Kant, *Bestimmung des Begriffs*)

Races (*Rassen*) are thus different classes of a genus whose unity of origin remains intact. This implies, however, that peoples and nations are no longer the primary natural divisions of humankind. *Rasse* intervenes between *Volk* and *Geschlecht*. This is why, in the same year in which Kant's essay is published, Herder argues in the second part of *Reflections on the Philosophy of History of Mankind* (1785) against the idea that we might use *Rasse* (for which he writes "Race") as an operative concept to determine such a primary division:

Some for instance have thought fit, to employ the term of *races* for four or five divisions, originally made in consequence of country or complexion: but I see no reason for this appellation. Race refers to a difference of origin, which in this case either does not exist, or in each of these countries, and under each of these complexions, comprises the most different races. For every nation is one people.

(Herder, *Reflections*)

However, it is above all in *Anthropology from a Pragmatic Point of View* (1797) that Kant attempts to fix the meanings of the term, by way of the characteristics that differentiate four types: those of the person (*der Person*), the people (*des Volks*), race (*der Rasse*), and the human species (*der Menschengattung*). *Geschlecht* and *Rasse* are essentially distinguished, then, by their finality. The first term, *Geschlecht*, is reserved for sexual difference, which has a twofold end in nature—the preservation of the species and, thanks to femininity, the culture and refinement of society. The second, *Rasse*, applies to a difference whose only end is assimilation, the mixing that gives the human its unity (*die Zusammenschmelzung verschiedener Rassen*). *Geschlecht, Stamm, Rasse*: the issue of the choice of terms is thus twofold. It relates both to considerations of the unity of humankind and of its finality.

Another sign of difficulty raised by *Geschlecht* comes from the possibility of using the word to refer to both horizontal solidarity (a generation) and vertical solidarity (the succession of generations). Such is, in effect, the reorientation of meaning that Luther declares, in a text that illustrates the difficulties of the word:

And his mercy extends from one generation [*Geschlecht*] to another. We must become accustomed to the usage in the Scripture which calls the succession of begettings and natural births *Geschlechter*. This is why the German word *Geschlecht* is not sufficient, but I do not know of a better. We call *Geschlechter* the stocks and the union of blood brotherhoods [*geblüter Freundschaften*], but the word here must mean the natural succession between father and the child of his children, such that each of the members of this succession has the name *Geschlecht*.

(Grimm, art. "Geschlecht," 1984)

This confusion is found in the translation of the Hebrew term *tōledōt* [תּוֹלְדֹת], in Genesis 10, where, describing Noah's descendants, a shared humanity that Luther describes as "the table of peoples [*die Völkertafel*]" is laid out:

These *are* the families [*die Nachkommen*] of the sons of Noah, after their generations, in their nations [*in ihren Geschlechtern und Leuten*]: and by these were the nations divided in the earth after the flood.

(Gn 10:32, Luther's terms in brackets)

The retranslation of the same passage by Martin Buber and Franz Rosenzweig is thus significant (*Die fünf Bücher der Weisung*). They use *Sippe* (kinship) rather than *Nachkommen*, and the phrase *nach ihren Zeugungen, in ihren Stämmen* (according to their generations, in their tribes) instead of *in ihren Geschlechtern und Leuten*, thus distinguishing between vertical begetting (*Zeugungen*) and differentiated horizontal division (*Stämmen*). *Geschlecht* disappears, as though it were loaded with too much ambiguity to still refer to generation in the strict sense of begetting.

Geschlecht thus concentrates, even more than "people," "nation," or "race," the risks involved with any designation of community: that of being led back to an order of belonging deriving primarily from generation and ascendancy (thus from sexuality as well)—that is, the risk of a contamination of politics by genealogy.

Marc Crépon

BIBLIOGRAPHY

Derrida, Jacques. "Geschlecht I and II." In *Psyché: Inventions de l'autre*, 395–453. Paris: Galilée, 1987. Translation by Ruben Berezdivin and Elizabeth Rottenberg: "Geschlecht I: Sexual Difference, Ontological Difference." Translation by John P. Leavey, Jr.: "Heidegger's Hand (Geschlecht II)." In *Psyche: Inventions of the Other*. 2 vols. Edited by Peggy Kamuf and Elizabeth Rottenberg, 2:7–62. Stanford: Stanford University Press, 2007–8.

Heidegger, Martin. *Unterwegs zur Sprache*. Edited by Friedrich-Wilhelm von Herrmann. In *Gesamtausgabe*. Vol. 12. Frankfurt am Main: Klostermann, 1985. Translation by Peter D. Hertz: *On the Way to Language*. New York: Harper and Row, 1971.

Herder, Johann Gottfried. *Ideen zur Philosophie der Geschichte der Menschheit*. Vol. 13. In *Sämmtliche Werke*, edited by B. Suphan. 33 vols. Berlin: Weidmann, 1877–1913. Translation by Frank E. Manuel: *Reflections on the Philosophy of the History of Mankind*. Chicago: University of Chicago Press, 1968.

Kant, Immanuel. *Anthropologie in pragmatischer Hinsicht*. Edited by Königlich Preussischen Akademie der Wissenschaften. In *Kants Gesammelte Schriften*. Vol. 7. Berlin: De Gruyter, 1902–. Translation by Robert B. Louden: *Anthropology from a Pragmatic Point of View*. Edited by Robert B. Louden. Cambridge: Cambridge University Press, 2006.

———. *Bestimmung des Begriffs einer Menschen Rasse*. In *Gesamtausgabe*. Vol. 8. *Determination of the Concept of a Human Race*. §6 in *Anthropology, History, and Education*, edited by R. Louden and G. Zöller. Cambridge: Cambridge University Press, 2011.

Krell, David Farrell. "One, Two, Four—Yet Where Is the Third? A Note on Derrida's Series." *Epoché* 10 (2006): 341–57.

GLAUBE (GERMAN)

ENGLISH	faith, belief
FRENCH	*foi, croyance*

➤ BELIEF, *CROYANCE*, and *FAITH*, FEELING, GEISTESWISSENSCHAFTEN, TRUTH

German vocabulary does not mark the distinction between faith and belief. It has a single word, *Glaube*, where English, French, and most Romance languages have two, which refer respectively to the (more or less deeply held) adherence to the dogmas of a religion and the (more or less perceptible) assent to all manner of representation or propositional content. This does not mean that German speakers do not have an idea of the distinction, but they nonetheless have difficulties giving it an expression in language.

I. The Difficulty of Translating Hume into German

A good example of these difficulties is found in German translations of English-language philosophical works that rely particularly on the notion of belief. Hume's *Enquiry Concerning Human Understanding* may be seen as a test case. The second part of section 5 aims to give, on the basis of the notion of *belief*, a "solution" to the "sceptical doubts concerning the operations of the understanding" raised in section 4. The conclusions we derive from experience rest on a *belief* that derives from *sentiment* or *feeling*, or even *some instinct* or *mechanical tendency*, and that may be described as a union of perception (direct or indirect, by way of memory) of an object and a certain link discerned between this object and another by habit. The German translations of this text—whether modern ones such as Richter's or older ones such as that by W. G. Tennemann, which contains Reinhold's essay *On Philosophical Scepticism* and in which German Idealism read Hume—systematically rendered "belief" by *Glaube*. However, for the same reason, as remarked by Richter in the English-German glossary accompanying his edition, these translations cannot capture the difference with "faith" as discussed in section 10, on miracles; for "faith" "in the religious sense," they still rely on *Glaube*.

II. Luther's Work on Language: *Glauben / Der Glaube*

The difficulty is also felt within German texts themselves, as the example of Luther shows. It is no doubt in his work, as the theologian of salvation by "faith alone [*sola fide*]" (as opposed to works) that *Glaube* takes on the status of a concept: his emphatic use of the word leaves a lasting mark on philosophy, most of all German Idealism. What is more, we find in Luther linguistically oriented remarks regarding the construction of the verb *glauben* (for instance, whether it should take the preposition *an*, rather than *in*). In a sermon from 1544 transcribed by Veit Dietrich, Luther draws the distinction between faith and belief:

A rich man, possessing great wealth and money, if he believes [*glaubt*] that he will not die of hunger this year, this is not faith [*Glaube*]. He who, by contrast, is destitute and yet still holds to the Word of God, according to which God will as his father procure him subsistence . . . , he does believe [*glaubt*] correctly.

(Luther, *Hauspostille*, WA, vol. 52)

As in French and other Romance languages, the verb *glauben* may refer both to what we call "faith" and to "belief," depending on their objects (in this case, believing in one's fortune and in the generosity of God). But in the first phase, the verb is in a strange way opposed to the noun of the same family, *Glaube*: there are ways of believing, *glauben*, that do not manifest *Glaube*. The problem is that Luther has a single family of words, *glauben/Glaube*, to describe the terms he is contrasting. This is not strictly speaking a problem of translation: French and other Romance languages have always drawn the distinction in this in advance. But the distinction that these languages have at their disposal does not make it possible to render Luther's work on his own language, except by violating its usage.

III. *Glaubensphilosophie*

A problem of translation does arise later, with the controversy started by Jacobi and what was called *Glaubensphilosophie*. Its origin lies in Kant's expression: "I was obliged therefore to abolish knowledge [*Wissen*] to make room for belief [*Glauben*]" (*Kritik der reinen Vernunft*). The translation of *Glauben* here is difficult. The objects that Kant attributes to it—God, liberty, immortality—are suggestive of faith, but the jurisdiction to which it belongs, practical reason, blocks any translation that would refer too directly to a religious reality. *Croyance* (belief) is in fact the translation adopted by all the French translators of the *Critique of Pure Reason*, from J. Barni, revised by P. Archambault, to A. Renault; in English, Kemp-Smith gives "to make room for *faith*," as do Paton and (more recently) Guyer and Wood.

Glauben here has a suppleness that French and English, always forced to choose between *foi* and *croyance* or "faith" and "belief," between religious and epistemological usages, do not. A grammatical phenomenon arises in addition. In the problem raised by Kant, it is a question not of a *Glaube*, but of a *Glauben*, that is, of a nominal infinitive, the "to believe," against which another nominal infinitive is contrasted, the "to know." In addition, the difference of form between *der Glaube* and *das Glauben* is tenuous: *Glaube*, a weak masculine, becomes *Glauben* in the accusative and the dative.

The title of Hegel's response to Kant, Fichte, and Jacobi in 1802, *Glauben und Wissen*, should thus be translated as *To Believe and To Know*, except that this is also misleading: the work's concern is not just with an investigation, à la Hume, of the degrees of certainty and of assent in human understanding. When Jacobi claims that all *Wissen* must "rise up" to a *Glauben*, he has God in mind above all, which—here Jacobi follows Kant—cannot be known, only believed. Kant, Fichte, Schelling, Jacobi, and Hegel all have the same object in view in the controversy: God, or the absolute. The title *Faith and Knowledge—Foi et savoir* in French—as a translation of Hegel's work would thus allow us to get around the difficulty, but it immediately gives rise to another one. A francophone reader may in effect be tempted unilaterally to lay down a familiar distinction between faith and reason, whereas for Kant, whom Hegel is discussing, *Glauben* is not distinguished from reason but rather results from the transfer of competencies of theoretical reason to practical reason. In fact, the question of *Glauben und Wissen*, which is prevalent throughout the beginning of German Idealism, brings together two questions that French habits tend to separate: that of the relationship between faith and reason on one hand, and that of the certainty to which

human knowledge may lay claim on the other (and we may see in this a continuation of the debate between Kant and Hume: cf. Jacobi, "David Hume"). The characteristic use of *Glaube* in German makes it possible to intertwine these questions so as to make them inseparable, whereas the separation of faith and belief encourages the French- and Romance-language reader to distinguish two different orders of problems.

Philippe Büttgen

BIBLIOGRAPHY

Di Giovanni, George. *Freedom and Religion in Kant and His Immediate Successors: The Vocation of Humankind, 1774–1800*. Cambridge: Cambridge University Press, 2005.
———. "Hume, Jacobi, and Common Sense: An Episode in the Reception of Hume in Germany at the Time of Kant." *Kant-Studien* 88 (1997): 44–58.
Fries, Jakob Friedrich. *Wissen, Glauben und Ahndung*. Edited by L. Nelson. Göttingen: Vandenhoeck and Ruprecht, 1905. First published in 1805. Translation by Kent Richter: *Knowledge, Belief and Aesthetic Sense*. Edited by Frederick Gregory. Köln: J. Dinter, 1989.
Hegel, Georg Wilhelm Friedrich. *Glauben und Wissen*. Edited by H. Glockner. In *Jubiläumsausgabe*. Vol. 1. 4th ed. Stuttgart-Bad Cannstatt: Frommann-Holzboog. Translation by Walter Cerf and H. S. Harris: *Faith and Knowledge*. Albany: State University of New York Press, 1977.
Hume, David. *An Enquiry Concerning Human Understanding and Other Writings*. Edited by Stephen Buckle. Cambridge: Cambridge University Press, 2007. Translation by Raoul Richter: *Eine Untersuchung über den menschlichen Verstand*. Edited by Raoul Richter. 12th ed. Hamburg: Meiner, 1993. Translation by M.W.G. Tennemann: *Untersuchung über den menschlichen Verstand*. Jena: Akademische Buchhandlung, 1793.
Jacobi, Friedrich Heinrich. "David Hume über den Glauben, oder Idealismus und Realismus: Ein Gespräch." 1787. In *Werke*. Vol. 2. Leipzig: Fleischer and Jüng, 1815. Translation by George di Giovanni: "David Hume on Faith, or Idealism and Realism: A Dialogue." In *The Main Philosophical Writings and the Novel Allwill*, edited by George di Giovanni, 253–338. Montreal: McGill-Queen's University Press, 1994.
———. "Von den göttlichen Dingen und ihrer Offenbarung." In *Werke*. Vol. 3. Leipzig: Fleischer and Jüng, 1816.
Kant, Immanuel. "Vorrede zur zweiten Ausgabe." In *Kritik der reinen Vernunft*, edited by Königlich Preussischen Akademie der Wissenschaften. In *Kants Gesammelte Schriften*, 4:7–26. Berlin: De Gruyter, 1902–. Translation by Paul Guyer and A. Wood: "Preface to the Second Edition." In *Critique of Pure Reason*, edited by Paul Guyer and A. Wood, 106–24. Cambridge: Cambridge University Press, 1997.
Luther, Martin. *D. Martin Luthers Werke, Weimar 1883–1929* (Weimarer Ausgabe—WA). Online at http://www.lutherdansk.dk/WA/D.%20Martin%20Luthers%20Werke,%20Weimarer%20Ausgabe%20-%20WA.htm.
———. *Luther's Works*. Edited by Helmut T. Lehmann and Jaroslav Pelikan. 55 vols. St. Louis, MO: Concordia, 1955.
———. *Werke: Kritische Gesamtausgabe*. Weimar: Böhlar, 1883–.
Tavoillot, Pierre-Henri. *Le Crépuscule des Lumières: Les documents de la "querelle du panthéisme" (1780–1789)*. Paris: Éditions du Cerf, 1995.

GLÜCK, GLÜCKSELIGKEIT, SELIGKEIT, WOHLFAHRT (GERMAN)

ENGLISH	happiness, luck, welfare
FRENCH	*bonheur, félicité, béatitude, chance, fortune, prospérité*
GREEK	*eudaimonia* [εὐδαιμονία], *eutuchia* [εὐτυχία], *makariotês* [μακαριότης]
LATIN	*felicitas, beatitudo*

➤ *HAPPINESS*, and DAIMÔN, *DESTINY, LIBERTY*, MORAL SENSE, MORALS, PLEASURE, PRAXIS, *VIRTUE*

The difficulty of the German *Glück* comes from its double meaning of "happiness" and "luck." Among German-speakers themselves, the criticisms of eudaimonism, beginning with Kant, focus on an unhealthy closeness between merit and chance. This explains in particular the addition of the compound *Glückseligkeit* (from *selig*, "blessed"), awkwardly translated into French as *félicité*, whereas the term usually only aims to express—with varying degrees of success—the conception of happiness dissociated from the accidents of chance. However, the difficulties of the users of *Glück* also relate to the power of the Aristotelian tradition in the moral thought of the German Enlightenment, and leads to the European or supranational dimension of the problem. The pair *Glück-Glückseligkeit* is consciously related to the distinction drawn in Aristotle's *Nicomachean Ethics* between *eutuchia* [εὐτυχία] (good fortune) and *eudaimonia* [εὐδαιμονία] (happiness), to which the difficulties of the third term *makariotês* [μακαριότης], which refers to the happiness of the gods, must also be added. The translation of the last term by *Seligkeit* and the intensive use of the word in religious contexts is reflected in *Glückseligkeit*, whose spiritual dimension resists attempts at translation. In English, at the same time, it is on the contrary the absence of this internalized dimension that explains how "happiness" could have opened the way to a philosophy of the common good and political happiness, for which other European countries do not have an equivalent.

I. The Greek Roots of the Debate

A. *Eudaimonia* and *eutuchia*

The question of happiness is a central problem of Greek thought. In the first pages of the *Nicomachean Ethics*, Aristotle summarizes the tradition:

> Let us resume our inquiry and state, in view of the fact that all knowledge and choice aims at some good, what it is that we say political science aims at and what is the highest of all goods achievable by action (*tôn praktôn agathôn* [τῶν πρακτῶν ἀγαθῶν]). Verbally there is very general agreement; for both the general run of men and people of superior refinement say that it is happiness, (*tên eudaimonian* [τὴν εὐδαιμονίαν]) and identify living well and faring well with being happy (*to d'eu zên kai to eu prattein* [τὸ δ' εὖ ζῆν καὶ τὸ εὖ πράττειν]) σοντ λα μᾶμε ψησσε Θυῷᾶτρε ηευρευχ (*tâeudaimonein* [τῷ εὐδαιμονεῖν]).

(1.4, 1095a ll. 14–20; Barnes trans.)

The term *eudaimonia* [εὐδαιμονία] used by Aristotle is not found in archaic texts; it does not appear in Homer, and is rare in Pindar. *Olbos* [ὄλβος], the Homeric term usually translated as "happiness," designates prosperity given by the gods to men, the enjoyment of that material happiness (and not just wealth, *ploutos* [πλοῦτος]) which, in a well-ordered cosmos, is the sign of a good life. *Olbos* is progressively replaced by *eudaimonia*, a term coming from the family of *daiomai* [δαίομαι], "to share": *eu-daimôn* [εὐ-δαίμων] is literally he "who has a good *daimôn*," a good distributive divinity (a good spirit), and hence "a good share." *Eudaimonia*, like *olbos*, refers in the first instance to the prosperity and happiness of the man favored by the gods (thus, Hesiod, *Works*, 824: *eudaimôn te kai olbios* [εὐδαίμων τε καὶ ὄλβιος]). It would be difficult to speak, regarding *eudaimonia*, of an internalization of the idea of happiness; someone is *eudaimôn* who knows how to take advantage of the external conditions of existence.

However, through the Aristotelian conception, the term acquires a practical and ethical specificity: *eudaimonia* is decidedly distinguished from good luck (*eutuchia* [εὐτυχία], from *tuchê* [τύχη], "fate, fortune"): "For many declare happiness (*eudaimonia*) to be identical with good luck (*eutuchia*)," Aristotle writes in the *Eudemian Ethics* (1.1.1214a25f; Barnes trans.). Euripides, however, is able to play with the three terms: "No man can count on his happiness (*eudaimôn anêr* [εὐδαίμων ἀνήρ]). Some have luck (*eutuchesteros* [εὐτυχέστερος]) and fortune (*olbou epirruentos* [ὄλβου ἐπιρρυέντος]) on their side but never happiness (*eudaimôn d'an ou* [εὐδαίμων δ' ἂν οὔ])" (*Medea*, 1228–30; Collier and Machemer trans.). The question of the permanence of the elements that compose happiness, hence the problem of time, plays an essential role here. Contrary to the extreme volatility of fortune and external goods, virtuous activities guarantee happiness by their stability (*bebaiotês* [βεβαιότης]; *Nicomachean Ethics*, 1.10.1100b12):

> Success or failure in life (*en tautais sc. tais tuchais* [ἐν ταύταις sc. ταῖς τύχαις]) does not depend on these, but human life, as we said, needs these as well (*prosdeitai* [προσδεῖται]), while excellent activities or their opposites are what determine happiness or the reverse (*kuriai d' eisin hai kat' aretên energeiai tês eudaimonias* [κύριαι δ' εἰσὶν αἱ κατ' ἀρετὴν ἐνέργειαι τῆς εὐδαιμονίας]).

(1100b ll. 8–11; Barnes trans.)

The Aristotelian definition of happiness may seem like a moral one in the modern sense, insofar as it refers to the virtuous activity of the subject (to the point where Tricot, for example, consistently translates *to ariston* [τὸ ἄριστον], the best, the most excellent, by the French *Souverain Bien* [Sovereign Good], 1.8.1098b32, for example). However, the supplement *eutuchia* once again relates this definition of the happiness of a man to the share granted to him by the gods.

B. *Eudaimonia* and *makariotês*

The temporal perspective that plays an important role in determining the difference between *eutuchia* and *eudaimonia* also comes into play for the term *makariotês* [μακαριότης]. *Hoi makares* [οἱ μάκαρες], the blessed ones, is the expression that designates the gods (*Iliad*, 1.329). This happiness proper to the gods can only be tasted by mortals after death. This is why *makarios* [μακάριος] often refers to the deceased (the Ger. *selig*, "blessed," has the same use: *die Seligen*)—unless the vocative in familiar speech is just equivalent to "my good man" (Plato, *Protagoras*, 309c). Thus when Aristotle, putting the final touches on his definition of *eudaimonia*, adds to virtuous activity the fact of being sufficiently provided with external goods, and not simply living but also dying in this state, he also expresses the maximum and the limit of this conception:

> We shall call blessed (*makarious* [μακαρίους]) those among living men in whom these conditions are, and are to be, fulfilled—but blessed *men* (*makarious d'anthropous* [μακαρίους δ' ἀνθρώπους]).

(*Nicomachean Ethics*, 1.10.1101a ll. 20–21)

The divide between happiness and blessedness is that between profane and sacred, immanence and transcendence.

It is of course made much of in religious texts, and is found discussed in almost all languages. In Saint Thomas Aquinas, this important Aristotelian concession is immediately emphasized: "[Aristotle] maintained that man does not achieve perfect felicity, but only a limited kind" (Posuit hominem non consequi felicitatem perfectam, sed suo modo) (*Summa contra gentiles*, III, 48). Aquinas reaffirms this distinction in the *Summa theologica* in a systematic way, contrasting *imperfecta beatitudo* (accessible to men on earth) to celestial *beatitudo perfecta* (which is inaccessible to them):

> Final perfection for men in their present life is their cleaving to God by activity which, however, cannot be continuous or consequently single, for activity becomes multiple when interrupted. That is why we cannot possess perfect happiness now, as Aristotle admits.
>
> Aquinas, *Summa theologica*, *prima secundae*, q. 3, a. 2, reply 4; T. Gilby trans.

In Latin, the original distinction between a profane *felicitas* (= *eudaimonia*) and a sacred *beatitudo* (= *makariotês*) is lost. Seneca's *vita beata* is not peculiar to the gods. The Latin words *felicitas* and *beatitudo* are practically synonymous; for Aquinas, it is thus the adjective that introduces the necessary distinctions.

- See Box 1.

II. *Glückseligkeit*: Internal Happiness

In German, the distinction between blessedness and happiness does not pose a problem. The adjective *selig* and the corresponding noun *Seligkeit* clearly contrast with *Glück* and *glücklich*. The division, however, is not always so strict: we must emphasize the importance, in the eighteenth century, of the movement that leads the German language to use sacred vocabulary in profane contexts, under the influence especially of the sacralization of the world in Pietist language. Thus, without being celestial, the extreme happiness of a heart fully absorbed by love, that of the sage or monk, may demand the use of the term *Seligkeit*. However, despite its relative desacralization, *Seligkeit* still designates a happiness that can do without the external world, a religious happiness, or at least, a highly spiritualized one.

By contrast, the most commonly used word in German for expressing immanent or profane happiness does raise some difficulties. *Glück* reunites what the Greek disjunction between *eutuchia* and *eudaimonia* tried to separate. On one side, *Glück* refers to chance. It lies on the side of luck, or "favorable accident." In ancient texts, the word *Glück* is often used in a neutral way, without any positive connotation. We find some examples in Goethe:

> Das Glück ist eigensinnig, oft das Gemeine, das Nichtswürdige zu adeln und wohlüberlegte Taten mit einem gemeinen Ausgang zu entehren.
>
> (Fortune is capricious; she often ennobles the common, the worthless, while she dishonors well considered actions with an ignoble outcome.)
>
> (*Egmont*, act IV, scene 2)

Here, the French and English equivalents of the word *Glück* would be "fortune." In this sense, *Glück* seems like an inappropriate word for philosophers: it is too inconstant, independent of the will of men, and associated with the unpredictable wheel of fortune (*das Glücksrad*). In French, the word for "happiness," *bonheur*, also, originally, has the sense of good fortune (the word comes from *bon* and *heur*). But today it only seems to have this meaning in a secondary way, and in rare fixed expressions (*porter bonheur à quelqu'un, au petit bonheur, par bonheur,* etc.). Voltaire's article on "Félicité" in the RT: *Dictionnaire philosophique* clarifies the difference between *un bonheur* and *le bonheur*: "*Un bonheur* is a happy event. *Le bonheur*, taken indefinitely, means a *succession* of such events."

1

From happiness to apathy and *ataraxia*

The independence of *eudaimonia* [εὐδαιμονία] with regard to external goods is already invoked by Democritus (B 40, 170, 171 DK), who, like Heraclitus (B 119 DK), reinterprets the *daimôn* [δαίμων] psychologically and ethically, and is solidly established with Plato (*Laws*, 664c). However, it remains a paradoxical idea; when Xenophon relates the dialogue between Euthydemus and Socrates, this paradox is clearly still fresh:

> "But, granting this to be as you say," added Euthydemus, "you will certainly allow good fortune to be a good?" "I will," said Socrates, "provided this good fortune consists in things that are undoubtedly good." —"And how can it be that the things which compose good fortune should not be infallibly good?" —"They

are," answered Socrates, "unless you reckon among them beauty and strength of body, riches, honours, and other things of that nature." —"And how can a man be happy without them?" —"Rather," said Socrates, "how can a man be happy with things that are the causes of so many misfortunes?"

> (*The Memorable Things of Socrates*, Bysshe trans.)

Aristotle, in turn, conceptualizes *eudaimonia* contrary to what the word says: minimizing the share of chance and external goods (*eutuchia* [εὐτυχία]), he makes happiness depend on the highest excellence, that is, not on politics but on *theôria* [θεωρία], which makes man similar to god (*Nicomachean Ethics*, 10.7; see PRAXIS). But

the Stoics and Epicureans, who push the self-sufficiency of the sage to the extreme in different ways, are in the end forced to make real terminological inventions. For the two schools, happiness, far from being the good share that we enjoy until the end, is essentially characterized by its privative aspect, a point on which Stoic *a-patheia* [ἀ-πάθεια] (absence of passion, passivity; Plutarch, *Dion*, 32) and Epicurean *a-ponia* [ἀ-πόνια] and *a-taraxia* [ἀ-ταραξία] (absence of bodily suffering and absence of disturbance in the soul; Diogenes Laertius, 10.96; see PLEASURE) converge.

BIBLIOGRAPHY

Xenophon. *The Memorable Things of Socrates*. Bk. 4, chap. 2. Translated by E. Bysshe. London: Cassell, 1888.

The second meaning of *Glück* is indeed that of happiness strictly speaking: the fully satisfied consciousness, as the RT: *Le nouveau petit Robert* French dictionary has it. Standard German uses the two senses of *Glück* and its antonym *Unglück* (bad luck or unhappiness). The union within a single German word of the idea of a happy accident, luck, and that of happiness strictly speaking, is to some extent inconvenient for philosophers. For it is impossible to speak of happiness in the absence of a certain duration or stability: "For one swallow does not make a summer, nor does one day; and so too one day, or a short time, does not make a man blessed and happy" (*Nicomachean Ethics*, 1.7.1098a 18–20; Barnes trans.).

The extremely strong influence of Aristotelian reflection on happiness, beginning with the Renaissance, clearly explains the efforts at lexical differentiation, and especially the introduction of the compound *Glückseligkeit*, related to the attempts at definition made throughout the eighteenth century by Christian Wolff and his successors. In Wolff's *German Ethics*, joy (*Freude*) is defined as a sort of permanent pleasure (*Vergnügen*), and happiness (*Glückseligkeit*) as a "state of permanent joy." The stability of *Glückseligkeit* is thus vigorously championed. Lexically, happiness-*Glückseligkeit* seems to escape the instability characterizing *Glück*. The adjective *glückselig*, formed from *Glück* and *selig*, initially means "marked by happiness, rich in happiness." Happiness-*Glückseligkeit* is not an accident. While the word is not a neologism, it acquires an important role in philosophical and theological texts in the seventeenth and eighteenth centuries. In a certain way, behind *Glückseligkeit*, it is usually appropriate to read *eudaimonia*. This is also what is suggested by the philosophical dictionary of synonyms published at the end of the Enlightenment by Johann August Eberhard, RT: *Versuch einer allgemeinen deutschen Synonymik*:

> *Glückseligkeit* includes physical and moral good. The Greek word *eudaimonia*, which in the most widespread philosophical schools refers to the quintessence of all sorts of good, has thus been translated by it.

For the texts of the eighteenth century in Germany, the translation of *Glückseligkeit* by "happiness" or *bonheur* seems in this sense more appropriate than "felicity," which in French (*félicité*) is of a more limited usage.

Philosophical German appeared to have recovered the Greek triad *eutuchia/eudaimonia/makariotês* in the form of *Glück/Glückseligkeit/Seligkeit*. In fact, however, the philosophical and lexical status of *Glückseligkeit* remains rather precarious. On one hand, the influence of *Seligkeit* confers a passive connotation onto *Glückseligkeit*, which becomes as a result "apathetic" or "quietist," and in this way clearly different from the *eudaimonia* that Aristotle had defined as a kind of "activity." Aristotle had compared happiness-*eudaimonia* with "living well and faring well" (to eu zên kai to eu prattein [τὸ εὖ ζῆν καὶ τὸ εὖ πράττειν]), but *eu prattein* also means "to succeed" (*Nicomachean Ethics*, 1.2.1095a19). The modern era did not really take over this dynamic conception of happiness inherent to Aristotle's position; whether defined as freedom from worry, in the Epicurean manner, or as a moment of satisfaction, modern happiness remains relatively static. A notable exception is the distinction established by Diderot between what he calls "circumscribed happiness" and "expansive happiness":

> There is a circumscribed happiness which remains in me and which does not extend beyond. There is an expansive happiness which propagates itself, which throws itself on the present, which embraces the future and which revels in moral and physical enjoyments, in reality and fantasy, hoarding money, honors, paintings and kisses pell-mell.
>
> ("*Man*")

By contrast, the definition proposed by Christian Wolff places happiness decidedly on the side of the sentiments; *Glückseligkeit* is both more internal and more spiritualized than the Greek word. This tendency is again emphasized by the erroneous but widespread etymology of the eighteenth century, according to which *selig* and *glückselig* (indeed often written *seelig*, *glückseelig*) are descended from *Seele*, soul. Beginning in the early nineteenth century, *glückselig/Glückseligkeit* undergo a certain evolution. Today, they refer to little more than a very spiritualized happiness. The severe critique of eudaimonism by Kant and his successors seems thus to be accompanied by certain lexical modifications. *Glückseligkeit*, though it has not entirely disappeared, has fallen into disuse. In contemporary texts, we find *Glück* (or *glücklich*) where an eighteenth-century author would have used *Glückseligkeit* (or *glückselig*) without fail. Thus, if the eighteenth century in Europe is the one in which happiness is most discussed, it is one in which happiness is not discussed with the same terms as those in common use today. Kant had already shown the way by using the adjective *glücklich* rather than *glückselig* with *Glückseligkeit*, most of the time. For in everyday language, *Glück* was always the more frequently used word for referring to happiness.

III. The Inconstancy of Fortune: *Glückseligkeit*, Nature, and Freedom in Kant

Whereas contemporary usage draws a rather clear line between *Glück* and *Glückseligkeit* and places the latter term on the side of a notion of felicity that seems to be definitively outmoded, the Kantian critique tends, in contrast, to devalue happiness-*Glückseligkeit* because of its compromising association with *Glück*. It is impossible, first, to give an objective definition of happiness:

> It is unfortunate that the concept of happiness is one which is so vague [Es ist ein Unglück, daß der Begriff der Glückseligkeit ein so unbestimmter Begriff ist], such that even though all men wish to achieve happiness, they are never able to say in a clear and univocal fashion what they truly wish for and desire.
>
> ("Grundlegung zur Metaphysik der Sitten," in *Kants Gesammelte Schriften*)

By playing on the German words *Unglück* and *Glückseligkeit*, Kant shows that the philosophical question of happiness and eudaimonism is also a problem of vocabulary. *Glückseligkeit* is a feeling; the search for happiness is a desire. Yet, a feeling, wherever it may come from, is always physical (cf. *Groundwork of the Metaphysics of Morals*). It is this point that explains the Kantian refusal to make happiness the final end of human activity. To construct a practical philosophy on the idea of happiness would be, for Kant, to accept the contamination of morality by the pleasure principle. Moreover (and this would be the second moment of Kant's critique of the misuse of *Glückseligkeit*), the concept of *Glückseligkeit* is related to external circumstances and thus to the happy accidents referred to by *Glück*. The subject is incapable of determining the conditions that make it possible for him to achieve happiness:

> The problem of determining reliably and universally which action would advance the happiness of a rational being is completely insoluble, and hence. . . there can be no imperative with regard to it that would in the strict sense command to do what makes us happy because happiness is not an ideal of reason, but of the imagination.

> (*Groundwork of the Metaphysics of Morals*)

Kant emphasizes the fundamentally empirical element of the definition of happiness:

> To be happy (*glücklich zu sein*) is necessarily the demand of every rational but finite being and therefore an unavoidable determining ground of its faculty of desire. For satisfaction (*die Zufriedenheit*) with one's whole existence is not, as it were, an original possession and a beatitude (*Seligkeit*), which would presuppose a consciousness of one's independent self-sufficiency, but is instead a problem imposed upon him by his finite nature itself, because he is needy and this need is directed to the matter of his faculty of desire, that is, something related to a subjective feeling of pleasure or displeasure underlying it by which is determined what he needs in order to be satisfied with his condition.

> (*Critique of Practical Reason*, §3)

Kant thus destroys the efforts made in Germany to differentiate *Glückseligkeit* and *Glück*. Happiness-*Glückseligkeit* suffers from the inconstancy of fortune (*Glück*). For Kant, happiness remains fundamentally within the sphere of nature. Human freedom has no part of it.

- See Box 2.

IV. Political Happiness: The Anglo-American Path

The English translation of *eudaimonia*, "happiness," does not have the spiritualist aura and connotation of *Glückseligkeit*. The dividing line between "happiness" and "bliss," "happy" and "blessed" or "blissful" is clearly marked. "Happiness" has a much more immanent ring than the German *Glückseligkeit*; its etymological connection to chance and "happening" (happenstance, happily) remains strong. This no doubt explains why the English word is able, in the eighteenth century, to raise the political possibilites implicit in the Aristotelian understanding of happiness, notably in the

---

2

Glückseligkeit in Hegel

Hegel takes up the Kantian criticism of eudaimonism:

> To estimate rightly what we owe to Kant in the matter, we ought to set before our minds the form of practical philosophy and in particular of "moral philosophy" which prevailed in his time. It may be generally described as a system of Eudaemonism, which, when asked what man's chief end ought to be, replied Happiness (*Glückseligkeit*). And by happiness Eudaemonism understood the satisfaction of the private appetites, wishes, and wants of the man: thus raising the contingent and particular into a principle for the will and its actualization. To this Eudaemonism, which was destitute of stability and consistency, and which left the "door and gate" wide open for every whim and caprice, Kant opposed the practical reason, and thus emphasized the need for a principle of will which should be universal and lay the same obligation on all.

> (*Encyclopedia of the Philosophical Sciences I*, addition to §54)

In the *Philosophical Propaedeutic* from the years 1808 to 1811, Hegel had strongly emphasized the necessary terminological distinctions:

> Well-being (*Wohlsein*), as the adaptation of the external to our internal being, we call Pleasure (*Vergnügen*). Happiness (*Glückseligkeit*) is not a mere individual pleasure but an enduring condition [which is] in part the actual Pleasure itself [and], in part also, the circumstances and means through which one always has, at will, the ability to create a state of comfort and pleasure for himself. The latter form is the pleasure of the mind. In Happiness, however, as in Pleasure, there lies the idea of good fortune [good luck] (*Glück*): that it is an accidental matter (*zufällig*) whether or not the external circumstances agree with the internal determinations of the desires. Blessedness (*Seligkeit*), on the contrary, consists in this: that no fortune [luck] pertains to it: that is, that in it the agreement of the external existence with the internal desire is not accidental. Blessedness can be predicated only of God.

The opposition to the principles of eudaimonism is especially virulent in Hegel's early works. Thus, in the article "Faith and Knowledge" of 1802, Hegel even accuses Kant, Jacobi, and Fichte of unconscious eudaimonism:

> What is the relation of this basic character to the philosophies of Kant, Jacobi, and Fichte? So little do these philosophies step out of this basic character that, on the contrary, they have merely perfected it to the highest degree. Their conscious direction is flatly opposed to the principle of Eudaemonism. However, because they are nothing but this direction, their positive character is just this principle itself.

Nevertheless, one has the impression that, without rejecting the fundamental criticism of eudaimonism, Hegel later seeks to attenuate Kant's critiques of the concept of happiness. In the *Phenomenology of Spirit* (§602), he notes:

> The moral consciousness cannot renounce happiness and drop this element out of its absolute purpose. . . . The harmony of morality and nature, or—seeing that nature is taken account of merely so far as consciousness finds out nature's unity with it—the harmony of morality

(*continued*)

(continued)

and happiness, is thought of as necessarily existing; it is *postulated*.

Hegel confers a certain dignity upon happiness-*Glückseligkeit* in this manner. The first version of the *Encyclopedia of the Philosophical Sciences* explained that the idea of happiness conditioned a choice that must be made from among one's various present desires: Happiness is the confused representation of the satisfaction of all drives, which, however, are either entirely or partly sacrificed to each other, preferred and presupposed. Hegel no longer rejects the superior form of the concept of happiness (*Glückseligkeit*) on the side of nature, as Kant had done. Similarly, in the additions to the *Elements of the Philosophy of Right* due to his student Gans, we read:

> In happiness, thought already has some power over the natural force, of the drives, for it is not content with the instantaneous force of the drives, for it is not content with the instantaneous,

but requires a whole of happiness (*eni Ganzes von Glück*).

In this passage, the coexistence of the terms *Glückseligkeit* and *Glück* nevertheless poses problems for the translator. In his translation of the *Principles of the Philosophy of Right*, Robert Derathé translates the two terms respectively as *félicité* and *bonheur*. Here, *Glückseligkeit* does indeed refer to a superior form of happiness, a stable and spiritualized happiness, and *Glück* a temporally more limited happiness—good fortune. However, the Hegelian passage also refers to the whole of pre-Kantian thinking on *Glückseligkeit*, very visible especially in popular philosophy of the eighteenth century, and Aristotelian and Leibniz-Wolffian in inspiration (see, for example, the translation of the *Nicomachean Ethics* by Christian Garve, one of the protagonists of popular philosophy). The translation of *Glückseligkeit* by "happiness" in the Hegelian text would enable us to emphasize this intertextual link, but would to some extent smooth over the distinction between *Glückseligkeit* and *Glück*.

BIBLIOGRAPHY

Hegel, G.W.F. *G.W.F. Hegel: Faith and Knowledge.* Translated and edited by W. Cerf and H. S. Harris. Albany: State University of New York Press, 1977.
———. *Hegel: Elements of the Philosophy of Right.* Edited by Allen W. Wood, translated by H. B. Nisbet. Cambridge: Cambridge University Press, 1991.
———. *Hegel's Logic, Being Part One of the Encyclopaedia of the Philosophical Sciences.* Translated by William Wallace with a foreword by Andy Blunden. Marxists Internet Archive, 2009. First published in 1830.
———. *Hegel's Phenomenology of Spirit.* Translated by A. V. Miller. Oxford: Oxford University Press, 1977.
———. *Philosophical Propaedeutic, by GWF Hegel.* Edited by Michael George and Andrew Vincent. Oxford: Basil Blackwell, 1986. First published in 1860.

Scottish school of the philosophy of *moral sense*. Thus, in his *Inquiry into the Original of Our Ideas of Beauty and Virtue* (1725), Francis Hutcheson finds the touchstone of the morality of our actions in the statement "*that Action is best*, which accomplishes the *greatest Happiness* for the *greatest Numbers*" (cf. also the expression of "happiness of mankind"). This possibility is expressed especially clearly in the American Declaration of Independence: "We hold these truths to be self-evident, that all men are created equal, that they are endowed by their Creator with certain unalienable Rights, that among these are Life, Liberty and the pursuit of Happiness." In this text, happiness does not refer only to an individual good, but to a collective one as well, that is, in the proper sense of the term, a civil or *political* good. It concerns, for example, the right to determine the type of government suited to the city (cf., on this point, D. Sternberger's article "Das Menschenrecht, nach Glück zu streben").

In this sense, the term "happiness" approaches the idea of welfare (in Ger. *Wohlfahrt*, "salvation," "prosperity") of which the French Revolutionaries will give a rather exact translation when they speak of the *salut public*. "Welfare" (and *Wohlfahrt*) refers to the image of the traveler who, having escaped the obstacles and dangers of the journey, arrives in a safe harbor. Where "happiness" (or *Glück*) refers only to the sphere of immanence, "welfare" or *Wohlfahrt* often have a religious connotation, though it is barely perceptible today. We may note, in this regard, that the French translation of "welfare state" or *Wohlfahrtstaat* by *État providence* accentuates this aspect that has become attenuated in English and German; the Spanish for welfare state, *Estado de bienestar*, embeds the immanent aspect of the term by compounding *bien*, "well" or "good," with the stative *estar* rather than existential *ser* (see SPANISH). Alongside *Wohlfahrt*, which refers to a public or private salvation, German also has a word reserved for the public sphere: *das Gemeinwohl*, the common good.

Christian Helmreich

BIBLIOGRAPHY

Aquinas, Thomas. *Summa contra gentiles.* Edited by V. Bourke. Notre Dame, IN: University of Notre Dame Press, 1975.
———. *Summa theologica.* Vol. 16. Translated by T. Gilby. London: Blackfriars, 1969.
Bien, Günther, ed. *Die Frage nach dem Glück.* Stuttgart: Frommann-Holzboog, 1978.
Blumenberg, Hans. "Ist eine philosophische Ethik gegenwärtig möglich?" *Studium Generale* 6 (1953): 174–84.
Diderot, Denis. *"Man."* In vol. 2 of *Œuvres completes.* Edited by J. Assézat. Paris: Garnier, 1875. First published in 1773–74.
Goethe, Johann Wolfgang von. *Egmont.* Edited by Frank G. Ryder. New York: Continuum, 1992.
Guyer, Paul. *Kant on Freedom, Law, and Happiness.* Cambridge: Cambridge University Press, 2000.
Kant, Immanuel. *Grundlegung zur Metaphysik der Sitten.* In *Kants Gesammelte Schriften (Akademie Ausgabe),* 4:387–463. Edited by Paul Menzer. Berlin: De Gruyter, 1968. First published in 1785. Translation by Leo Rauch and Lieselotte Anderson: *Fundamental Principles of the Metaphysics of Morals, in Kant's Foundations of Ethic.* Baltimore: Agora, 2007.
———. *Kritik der praktischen Vernunft.* Edited by O. Höffe. Berlin: Akademie Verlag, 2002. Translation and edited by Mary Gregory: *Critique of Practical Reason.* Cambridge: Cambridge University Press, 1997.
Kraut, Richard. "Two Conceptions of Happiness." *Philosophical Review* 88 (1979): 167–97.
Lännström, Anna. *Loving the Fine: Virtue and Happiness in Aristotle's Ethics.* Notre Dame, IN: University of Notre Dame Press, 2006.
Spaemann, Robert. *Happiness and Benevolence.* Translated by Jeremiah Alberg. Notre Dame, IN: University of Notre Dame Press, 2000.
Sternberger, D. D. "Das Menschenrecht, nach Glück zu streben." In *Gesammelte Schriften,* 4:93–114. Frankfurt: Insel, 1990.
Warner, Richard. *Freedom, Enjoyment and Happiness: An Essay on Moral Psychology.* Ithaca, NY: Cornell University Press, 1987.
White, Stephen A. *Sovereign Virtue: Aristotle on the Relation Between Happiness and Prosperity.* Stanford, CA: Stanford University Press, 1992.

GOD

ARABIC	*Allah* [الله]
BASQUE	*jainko / jinko, Jaungoikoa*
FINNISH	*jumala*
FRENCH	*dieu*
GERMAN	*Gott*
GREEK	*theos* [θεός]
HEBREW	*Ēl* [אֵל], *Ēloah* [אֱלוֹהַ], *Ēlohīm* [אֱלֹהִים]
HUNGARIAN	*isten*
ITALIAN	*dio*
LATIN	*deus*
PORTUGUESE	*deus*
RUSSIAN	*bog* [бог]
SPANISH	*dios*

➤ ANALOGY, BOGOČELOVEČESTVO, DAIMÔN, *DESTINY*, DEVIL, DUENDE, OIKONOMIA, OMNITUDO REALITATIS, *RELIGION*, SVET, THEMIS, *TO BE*, WELT

All European languages contain words for designating the divine. This comes from the Judeo-Christian beliefs of the populations that speak them and also from the prebiblical foundations of the European region.

The presence of this vocabulary is not a trivial matter, since Christian missionaries did meet certain peoples for whom it was necessary to borrow a word—the Latin *deus*, for example, used as a proper name—for lack of a native equivalent.

I. European Languages Today

The French *dieu* comes from the Latin *deus*, as does the Spanish *dios*, the Portuguese *deus*, and the Italian *dio*.

Germanic languages use words like the German *Gott* and the English "god." The etymology of these terms is unclear. Two Indo-European roots have been suggested. One means "to invoke," the other "to pour, to offer a libation" (see Gr. *cheô* [χέω]). God would thus be whatever is invoked or that to which a libation is offered. There is a temptation to hear a link, etymologically unfounded however, between "god" and "good." Whence certain euphemisms such as the exclamation "My goodness!" The vernacular French *le bon Dieu* thus sounds mildly pleonastic to the Germanic ear.

The word *bog* [бог], common to Slavic languages with slight variations, may be related to the Sanskrit *bhaga*, "lord." The latter term may come from a root meaning "to distribute," evoking the Greek *daimôn* [δαίμων] (demon) from *daiomai* (δαίομαι) (see DAIMÔN).

The Hungarian *isten* is borrowed from the Persia *ištán*, identical to the Pehlevi *yazdan* (cf. Rédei, "Über die Herkunft").

Jumala in Finnish may originally be a proper name, that of the supreme God, lord of the sky.

The Basque *jainko/jinko* designates both a god in general and the Christian God, also called *Jaungoikoa*, "the Lord on high."

II. Classical Languages and Holy Writings

The Greek *theos* [θεός] exists already in Mycenean as *teo*. Its true etymology remains obscure (see RT: Chantraine, *Dictionnaire étymologique de la langue grecque*). It may be from **thesos* [*θεσος], from *tithêmi* [τίθημι] (cf. also RT: Benveniste, *Le vocabulaire des institutions indo-européenes*; see THEMIS). The Greeks offered various fictional etymologies related to different ways of representing the divine. The first of these etymologies derived *theos* from the verb *tithêmi*, "to place" (Herodotus, II, 52, 1: "they placed [*thentes* (θέντες)] all things"), which suggests the idea of a setting-up of the world, rather than a creation *ex nihilo*. The verb *theô* [θέω], "to run," was also suggested (Plato, *Cratylus*, 397c; Cornutus, *De die natali*, 1). This is based on the identification of the gods with the celestial bodies, found in late Plato (*Timaeus*, 40a–d) and his school (*Epinomis*, 984d), and it plays with the fact that ether (*aithêr* [αἰθήρ], the clarity of the sky in which the gods reside, is itself interpreted as that which "is always running" (*aei-thein* [ἀεὶ-θεῖν]).

The Church Fathers (cf. Prestige, *God in Patristic Thought*) took up both hypotheses and added a third by way of the noun *thea* [θέα], "spectacle"—the gods having made the world visible (Eusebius of Caesaria, *Preparatio Evangelica*, V, 3, 182D).

The ancient form of the Latin *deus* is *deiuos*. The word, paradoxically, has nothing to do with the Greek *theos* but is in fact related to the Sanskrit *devas*. *Ju-*, in *Ju-piter*, designates the clarity of the sky, related to *dies*, "the day"; the sense survives in the expression *sub Dio*, "under the open sky."

The association of the sky with divinity is old and widespread. If we believe Suetonius (*Life of Augustus*, 97, 2), the Etruscan word for "god" was *aesar*, perhaps related to the Germanic word for iron (Ger. *Eisen*), the metal that falls to earth in meteorites (cf. Lat. *sidus* and Gr. *sidêros* [σίδηρος]). There is a late echo of this "celestial" etymology when Hölderlin claims to believe that God is "manifest like the sky [*offenbar wie der Himmel*]" ("In lieblicher Bläue," *Sämmtliche Werke*).

The sacred books of Judaism, and then of Christianity, of course, speak often of God. In them the Greek translates Hebrew terms. Thus the word present in all Semitic languages, *Ēl* [אֵל], which no doubt expressed the idea of power. There is also an elongated form, *Ēloah* [אֱלוֹהַ]. As for *Ēlohim* [אֱלֹהִים], more frequent in Hebrew, the plural ending (-*īm*) probably indicates majesty.

Arabs, both Muslim and Christian, give God the name of Allah [الله]. He is already known as the supreme God and creator of everything before the advent of Islam (Qur'an, XXIX, 61; XXXI, 25; XLIII, 87). The word is the contraction of *al-ilā* [الإلٰه] which pairs a form of the common noun *El* with the article. The word thus oscillates between its linguistic status as a common noun and its usage, which makes it a proper name.

III. Modern Forms

The scholarly register of European languages has kept the Greek root *theo-* and uses it in several dozen technical terms, some more common than others.

Some of them are old, such as "theology." Plato coins *theologia* [θεολογία] to refer to the way in which the gods should be spoken of, one more dignified than what is later called "mythology" (*Republic* II, 379a). The word "theology" keeps that meaning for a long time, as found in Pascal: "The poets made a hundred different theologies" (*Pensées*, Br. 613). In Latin Augustine uses the word in his polemic with Varro to mean a philosophical doctrine concerning the divine, and he explains it as *ratio sive sermo de divinitate*, "reasoning or discourse concerning divinity" (*City of God*, VIII, 1).

For Pseudo-Dionysius the Areopagite, the word also refers to the essence of God in himself, in his tripartite nature, as opposed to the benevolent action of God in human history (*oikonomia* [οἰκονομία], see OIKONOMIA). John Scotus Erigena translates Dionysius's Greek into Latin in *Divine names*, I, 15 (PL, v. 122, col. 463 b): *theologia* becomes *divinae essentiae investigatio*; II, 30 (col. 599b): *divinae naturae speculatio*; then III, 29 (col. 705b): "[investigat] quid de una omnium causa, quae Deus est, pie debeat aestimari [it seeks what should piously be conjectured of the unique cause of everything, which is God]." The word appears in its modern sense in Abelard around 1120, as the title of his *Theology*, named after its opening words, *Summi boni*. It finally becomes established in Thomas Aquinas, as referring to a science.

"Theocracy," most often understood today in the sense of a "clerical regime," did not originally refer to the power of the human administrators of the sacred but rather the opposite: Flavius Josephus coined *theokratia* [θεοκρατία] in a defense of Judaism. He indicates by it the fact that the divine Law is what has power in Judaism, rather than any particular person.

Other technical uses of the root *theo-* are found in the sort of words whose construction gives them an air of antiquity but that are in fact the result of the modern thirst to come up with ancient titles. The most well-known case is that of "theodicy," coined by Leibniz as the title of his book published in 1710, in which he aims to show the justice (*dikê* [δίκη]) of God (see THEMIS).

Rémi Brague

BIBLIOGRAPHY

Hölderlin, Friedrich. *Essays and Letters.* Edited by J. Adler and C. Louth. London: Penguin, 2009.
———. *Essays and Letters on Theory.* Translated and edited by T. Pfau. Albany: State University of New York, 1988.
———. *Poems and Fragments.* Translated by M. Hamburger. Ann Arbor: University of Michigan, 1967.
———. *Sämtliche Werke*, vol. 6. Edited by F. Beissner. Stuttgart: Cotta, "Kleiner Stuttgarter Ausgabe," 1946–1962.
Prestige, George Leonard. *God in Patristic Thought.* London: Heinemann, 1936.
Rédei, Karoly. "Über die Herkunft des ungarischen Wortes *isten*, 'Gott.'" *Linguistica uraclica* [Tallinn] 32 (1996): 238–88.

GOGO (BASQUE)

ENGLISH	power of the soul, mind, spirit
FRENCH	*puissance de l'âme, esprit*
LATIN	*anima, spiritus, mens*

In Basque, *gogo* expresses all the processes of interiority and subjectivity. Despite the efforts of some writers to use the term to replace the neologisms *arima* and *espiritu* from the Latin tradition (transpositions of the Latin *anima* and *spiritus*) in the translations of Christian texts, *gogo* never takes on the sense of "soul" or "spirit." It refers without exception to the power of the soul (memory or will) or to the psychological experience of the subject (desire, wish, thought, consciousness) rather than to the soul as such. While there are terms in Basque for "will" (*nahi*), "desire" (*gura*), "thought" (*asmo*) or "memory"

(or[h]oi), they are in reality often associated and juxtaposed with *gogo* as a generic term. By way of several derivative terms belonging to its semantic field (the RT: *Diccionario retana de autoridades de la lengua vasca* lists about 180), we may thus even express "sympathy," "ennui," and "disgust," among other feelings.

I. *Gogo* as a Principle

Arima has always been the translation of the Christian concept of the soul (*anima*), notably when the latter has a theological sense. In Dechepare, for example, *arima* is understood in relation to the themes of the resurrection: "arima et gorpucetan or vertan pizturic" (souls and bodies, all will be immediately resuscitated; RT: *Linguae vasconum primitiae*, 1.323); of creation: "arima creatu" (ibid., 1.3); of salvation: "arimaren saluacera" (ibid., 1.52: "to save the soul"); or of the soul in pain: "arima gaixoa" (ibid., 1.95: "poor soul"). However, in the first half of the twentieth century, we find several attempts, part of a purist linguistic movement, to replace the term *arima* by *gogo*. We thus read in a dictionary from 1916: "Arima (anima), alma, voz erdérica sustituible por 'gogo'" (*Arima* [*anima*], "soul," foreign term replaceable by *gogo*; López Mendizábal, *Diccionario Castellano-Euskera*).

Altube argues against this tendency (*Erderismos*). The basis of his argument was the fear of a "lexicographical poverty," since the substitution represented a linguistic step backward. In addition, *gogo* never expresses the concept of the soul in the theological sense, namely, the created soul, which may be resuscitated or saved, since it refers rather to soul understood as a *power*.

We might therefore think that *gogo* would be an equivalent for the Latin *anima* conceived in a more philosophical sense, like the collection of powers of memory, will, or understanding in Augustine, or again as an equivalent to Aquinas's *mens*, which groups together intelligence, memory, and will. Pierre de Axular, however, along with all the other authors or translators of Christian texts in the sixteenth to nineteenth centuries, translates this division of faculties of the soul by using *arima*: "Arimac bere penac beçala, arimaren potenciec eta botheréc ere, cein baitira adimendua, vorondatea, eta memoria, içanen dituzte bere pena *moldeac*" (Just as the soul has its pains, the powers and capacities of the soul, which are understanding, will, and memory, also have their own pains; *Gero*, 57:586).

Nor is *gogo* generally used to express this division of the soul, since we only find one occurrence of this use in Perez de Betolaça (sixteenth century): "Arimako potenziak dira iru: lelengoa, zenzuna. Bigarrena, gogoa. Irugarrena, borondatea" (The powers of the soul are three: the first, understanding. The second, *gogo*. The third, will; *Doctrina christiana en romance y basquenze*).

The same impossibility of replacing the calque of the Latin word with *gogo* is confronted by the term *espiritu* (or *izpiritu*), even though we may find a few texts from the seventeenth century in which *gogo* is substituted for *espiritu* in a remarkable way (thus, in Oihenart: "Glori' Aitari, Semeari / Eta Gogo Sainduari" [Glory to the Father, to the Son / and to the Holy *Gogo*]). When Axular, for example, attempts to find equivalents for the Latin *spiritus*, he chooses, in his translation of Augustine, the term *hats* (breath): "in ultimo vitae spiritu . . . axquen *hatsaren* aurthiquitcean" (in giving the last breath; *Gero*, chap. 15). The only context in which *gogo* seems truly close to what we mean by "spirit" or "mind" is that of the subjective sphere of affectivity and thought, of the "mental": "orazione mentala, edo izpirituaz eta gogoz egiten dena" (mental prayer, or that which is done by the spirit and by *gogo*; St. Francis of Sales, *Philotea*). Similarly, Joanes Leizarraga used *gogo* to render what is meant in French by the term *esprit*: "*perplexités d'esprit . . . gogo-arràguretaric*" [perplexities of the spirit] (*Testamentu berria*).

Gogo is thus always relative to the *subject*, and its use cannot extend to something else. In this regard, it is not synonymous with the Greek *nous*, which, according to some, governed the processes of the universe. But we might then think that it is very close to the Latin *animus*, which evokes will, memory, thought, desire, intention, and mood (RT: *Thesaurus linguae latinae*). We should recall in this context what Leizarraga says of the term *arima* in the lexicon that follows his translation of the New Testament (the first ever in Basque): even though he uses *arima* several times in the theological sense, there is nonetheless a meaning of the term that is translatable for him by *gogo*, when the latter is synonymous with "affection": "*Arimá*, hartzen da . . . Batzutan, *gogoagatic* edo affectioneagatic" (*Arimá* is taken . . . sometimes for *gogo* or for affection; *Testamentu berria*, 1202). And indeed, the frequent association of *gogo* with another term referring to a precise feeling or a better defined faculty shows the entirely subjective character of *gogo*.

II. *Gogo*: Different Faculties

Although the powers of the soul are most often referred to by their Latin calques (*zenzuna, memoria, borondate* [sense or understanding, memory, will]), we have seen that Betolaça used *gogo* to translate "memory." Axular, for his part, made *gogo* an equivalent for *borondate*, or "will."

> Hartcen dugu *gogo*, hartcen dugu vorondate, obra onac eguin behar ditugula . . . ordea han . . . beharrenean faltatcen dugu. Ceren hartcen dugun *gogo* eta *vorondate* hura, ezpaita fina, ezpaita cinezcoa eta ez deliberatuqui deliberatua; *nahicundea* baita eta ez *nahia*.

> (We take from *gogo*, we take from will [*borondate*], that from which we do good works . . . and yet . . . we miss the most necessary. Because *gogo* and this will [*borondate*] which we have taken is not authentic, it is not likely and it is not deliberately deliberated; because it concerns bad will ["weak will," *nahikunde*] and not will [*nahi*].)

> (*Gero*, chap. 3)

In this text the three terms Axular used to refer to the will all appear: *gogo, borondate* (or *vorondate*), and *nahi*. Although *borondate* is almost always associated in Axular's work with *gogo*, there are other places where *borondate* is equivalent to *nahi*: "gure nahia, eta vorondatea" (*Gero*, chap. 15). *Nahi* in Basque means either "will" or "desire," and the intertwining of these terms allows this author to associate *gogo* with desire: "Eta *desira* hautan, gueroco *gogoan* eta vorondatean, dembora guztia iragaiten çaicu" (And in these desires, in *gogo* and the *will* of the future, all of our time passes; *Gero*, chap. 3).

A collection of Basque proverbs from 1596 provides us with another example of the usage of these terms. The author translates *nay* into Castilian by *voluntad* (will) or by *deseo* (desire): "Galdu çe eguic aldia, / ta idoro dayc *naya*. No pierdas la sazon/ y hallaras el *desseo*" (Do not miss the opportunity, / and you will find the *desire*; Urquijo, *Refranero vasco*).

However, even though *gogo* may be substituted for *borondate*, for *nahi*, for *desir*, or even for *gura* (another Basque term closer to "desire"), these terms are not entirely equivalent to it. This is why Dechepare could write: "gogo honez nahi dicit çure eguina laudatu" (I want [*nahi*] to praise what you do in good *gogo*; RT: *Linguae vasconum primitiae*, 13). The equivalence between *gogo* and the other terms is not reciprocal: *gogo* may no doubt replace any other term in its vast conceptual field, but the reverse is not true. *Gogo* acts in effect as a power that collects together the semantic fields of the will, desire, and memory ("[cócientcia(k)] orhoitcen çaitu, guztiac [falta] gogora eccartcen derauzquitçu" [(it, conscience) reminds you of them (your faults), it brings them all to *gogo*; Axular, *Gero*, 45]) and of thought ("eguin çuen, Piramide batcuen eguiteco gogoeta, asmua eta pensua" [He had the *gogoeta*, the *asmo* and the thought of making several Pyramids; *Gero*, 1:26]). *Gogoeta*, formed by adding the suffix *-eta*, means the action that *gogo* produces and can thus serve to translate the Latin *cogitatio*. Axular thus writes (*Gero*, 36): "Gure *gogoa* ecin dagoque *gogoeta* gabe; ecin gauteque, cerbaitetan pensatu gabe" (Our *gogo* cannot be without *gogoeta*; we cannot be without thinking about something). Axular here nevertheless remains ambiguous: by preserving the multivocity of *gogoeta*, he keeps within the orbit of the Latin *cogitatio*, but by relating the term to thought alone, he comes close to the reduction that has just been made by Descartes.

Isabel Balza

BIBLIOGRAPHY

Altube, Seber. *Erderismos*. *Euskera* 10, no. 1–4 (1929).

Axular [Pedro Agerre]. *Gero*. Bilbao: Euskaltzaindia (Royal Academy of the Basque Language), 1988. First published in 1643. Translation into Spanish by Luis Villasante: *Gero*. Barcelona: Flors, 1964.

Betolaça, Juan Pérez de. *Doctrina Christiana y Basquence, hecha por mandado de D. Pedro Manso, obispo de Calahorra*. Bilbao: 1596. Republished by J. A. Arana Martija as "Betolazaren 'Doctrina Christiana'." *Euskara* 31, no. 1 (1986): 505–26.

Francis of Sales, Saint. *Philotea*. Translated into Basque by Joanes Haraneder. Tolosa: 1749. Originally published as *Introduction à la vie dévoté*. Lyon: Pierre Rigaud, 1609. Translation: *Introduction to the Devout Life*. New York: Vintage Spiritual Classics, 2002.

Leizarraga, Joanes. *Testamentu berria*. In *Baskische Bücher von 1571 (Neues Testament, Kalender und ABC)*, edited by T. Linschmann and H. Schuchardt. Strassburg: K. J. Trübner, 1900.

López Mendizábal, Isaac. *Diccionario Castellano-Euskera*. Tolosa: 1916.

Oihenart, Arnauld de. *Atsotizac Refravac* [Proverbs]. In *Gastroa Nevrthizetan*. Paris: 1657.

Urquijo e Ibarra, Julio de, ed. *Refranero vasco: Los refranes y sentencias de 1596*. San Sebastián, Sp.: Auñamendi, 1967.

GOOD / EVIL

This dichotomy, fundamental in the fields of ethics and moral inquiry, flows from the Latin: *bonum* and *malum* are the neuter nominalization of the adjectives *bonus* (good, well behaved) and *malus* (bad, evil). The etymology of both Latin adjectives, which combine a physical and an ethical sense, is uncertain.

1. On the relationship between diverse kinds of excellence, nobility, courage, and moral quality, see VIRTÙ, Box 1); cf. *VIRTUE*. On the particularly sensitive relationship in Greek between the good or inner kindness and outward beauty, see BEAUTY, Box 1; cf. DOXA, ERSCHEINUNG, *PHÉNOMÈNE*. On the relationship between the true and the good—or more precisely, the "better," which is fundamental to relativism, see TRUTH, Box 2.

2. The Latinate "good/evil" dichotomy quickly proves unable to render all the nuances of the corresponding Germanic terminological complex, with which it does not coincide. In French, juxtaposing *bien/mal* and *bon/mauvais* or *bon/méchant*, as is commonly done in translating Nietzsche's *Genealogy of Morals*, will not suffice to exhaust the more complex play of oppositions in German: *Gut/Böse, Wohl/Übel, (Weh)-Gut/Schlecht*.

3. Another constellation that is difficult to translate appears in English in the opposition between "right" and "just," which is almost impossible to render in French, and in the relationship between each of these two terms and "good": see RIGHT/JUST/GOOD; cf. FAIR.

4. On the Russian diglossia *dobro/blago*, see RUSSIAN.

▶ DUTY, *HAPPINESS*, MORALS, *VALUE*

GOÛT

ENGLISH	taste
GERMAN	*Geschmack*
ITALIAN	*gusto*
LATIN	*gustus*
SPANISH	*gusto*

▶ AESTHETICS, ARGUTEZZA, BEAUTY, CLASSIC, GENIUS, INGENIUM, MANIERA, SENSE, STANDARD, *VALUE*

Gusto in Italian and Spanish, *goût* in French, *Geschmack* in German, and "taste" in English all have a twofold sense, one gustatory and one aesthetic. European languages borrowed the word for referring to what we now call aesthetic judgment from the vocabulary of the five senses. Though it is important, this semantic ambiguity is not the real source of the constant difficulties presented by the concept of taste in the field of aesthetics. These come rather from specific misunderstandings arising out of the division between aesthetics as a philosophical discipline and ancient theories of art. Related to *giudizio*, the word *gusto* as used by Italians in the Renaissance refers to sharpness of judgment, the capacity for discernment, the specific disposition of an artist. It may have an ethical, psychological, even a political meaning. In the sixteenth and seventeenth centuries, *gusto* in Spanish and *goût* in French retain the senses of sharpness and discernment. Though they are increasingly used in the sense of aesthetic judgment over the course of the seventeenth century, especially in France, their usage does not display a normative character at the start. It is only in the eighteenth century that *goût* is assimilated to *bon goût*, at the same time as it takes on a more and more subjective sense, notably under the influence of new philosophical trends. The conceptual development of taste in English-language philosophies of aesthetic experience gives a new direction to thinking about taste, while still preserving for the term the range of meanings attached to *gusto* and *goût*.

The real break with the tradition of the theory of art takes place with the Kantian definition of taste, which leads to denying judgments concerning taste any possible objectivity. The loss of this minimal objectivity of judgments of taste, proper to aesthetic intersubjectivity as conceived in the classical period, paved the way for a henceforth dominant conception of taste according to which there is no possible correlation between taste as a faculty of evaluation and the aesthetic properties of the work of art (this last understood in the philosophically realist sense given to the term "property," that is, a given that exists independently of consciousness). Still, the question raised by the multivocity of the concept as the tradition transmits it to us, that of the plurality of its functions and its finalities, remains untouched. The same goes for the question of the translatability of what was really thought in these conceptions, which amply exceed the relation to art.

I. The Continent of Taste before the Age of Aesthetics

Gusto in Italian and in Spanish, like *goût* in French, derives from the Latin *gustus*, which means the fact of tasting, the taste of a thing, and the tasting sample (the Indo-European root, which we find in the Greek *geuomai* [γεύομαι], means "to feel," "to taste," "to appreciate, to like" [RT: *Dictionnaire étymologique de la langue latine*]). *Gustus* is in competition with *sapor*, "savor, taste," and "sense of taste," physical and moral; *sapere*, which means "to have taste," with regard to savory things, is also said of people of taste, discernment, relating the qualities of the palate to those of the mind, whence *sapientia*, "wisdom" (Cicero, *De finibus*, 2.24: "non sequitur ut cui cor sapiat, ei non sapiat palatus" [having taste with the mind does not entail lacking taste with the palate]; similarly, and more generally, *sentio* and *sensus* link the senses and judgment; see SENSE).

Though the Italian definition of *gusto* in terms of judgment does not really retain the idea of savor, the French and Spanish definitions do. In his RT: *Thresor de la langue française tant ancienne que moderne*, published in 1606, Jean Nicod, who always explains the meaning of each French word by its corresponding Latin, thus defines taste as *intellectus saporum*, which he himself translates by "judgment of flavors." We also find this sense of flavor present in the definition Baltasar Gracián gives of good taste: "un buen gusto sazona toda la vida" (a good taste adds spice to life).

A. *Gusto* as *habitus*, disposition and judgment in Italian theories

The word *gusto* early on acquired a metaphorical sense very distant from its gustatory origins: it indicates moods, desires, and drives. It may express, as in Dante, a "bold desire" (*ardito gusto*) (*Paradise*, 32.v.122) or a "disdainful indignation" (*disdegnoso gusto*) (*Inferno*, 13.v.70). However, the importance of *gusto*, its influence and its diffusion in European languages, appear in regard to problems about the experience of art in the sixteenth and seventeenth centuries. Thus, when Vasari says that Michelangelo had judgment and taste in everything: *giudizio e gusto in tutte cose* (*Le Vite*,* VII), the word *gusto* does not refer to a perceptual receptivity; it indicates, of course, an ability to discern properly artistic qualities, the acuity of the "judgment of the eyes," as in Leonardo da Vinci, but equally and sometimes exclusively it means the dispositions proper, the idiosyncrasy inherent to an individual (an artist or an art-lover).

This idiosyncracy is often less the mark of artistic sensibility than an expression of temperament, as understood by the then very widespread theory of temperaments, of the specific *complezione* of the personality of an artist. In the relations between masters and students, the first problem is thus to find affinities, a harmony between each person's taste and temperament, so that the teaching may be as productive as possible. This is why Antonio Francesco Doni insists in his treatise, regarding the art of drapery, that the disciple should take care in choosing his master:

Questi panni sono tutta gratia e maniera che s'acquista per studiare una materia fatta d'altro maestro che piu t'é ito a gusto che alcuno altro.

(These draperies are all grace and style [*maniera*], which one acquires by studying a matter created by a master who is better suited to your taste than any other.)

(*Il Disegno*)

What is decisive here is not *gusto* as a capacity of judgment, but rather the disposition or temperament as the expression of a unique individuality, insofar as these determine the artist's *maniera*, or his style. Taste is not just the principle of identity of a *maniera* or an artist: it can also refer to a group, an artistic school, even a nation (for Vasari, for example, the Germans have a *gusto gotico*, which is essentially suited to their dispositions and temperament).

Gusto also takes the meaning of a certain faculty of judging and evaluating aesthetic or artistic qualities and tends progressively to replace *giudizio*, which is often reduced to an act of perception, a way of discerning and distinguishing that calls upon both sensibility and intellect. In the sixteenth century, a text by Paolo Pino shows the orientation of *gusto* in relation to *giudizio*, despite their obvious multivocity:

Sono varii li giudicii umani, diverse le complessioni, abbiamo medesmamente l'uno dall'altro estratto l'intelletto nel gusto, la qual differenzia causa che non a tutti aggradano equalmente le cose.

(The judgments of men are varied and their temperaments different, we have in the same way extracted one from the other the intellect from taste, and this difference is why things do not please everyone in the same way.)

(*Dialogo di pittura*; trans. M. Pardo)

In the seventeenth century, a theorist as careful as Bellori in fixing the clarity and precision of artistic concepts cites Nicolas Poussin's definition of painting (written in Italian) with deference. Yet Poussin considers *gusto* to be a synonym for *maniera* and *stile* (a relatively new word at the time):

Lo stile è una maniera particolare ed industria di dipingere e disegnare nata dal particolare genio di ciascuno nell'applicazione e nell'uso dell'idea, il quale stile, maniera o gusto si tienne dalla parte della natura e dell'ingegno.

(Style is an individual manner and ingenuity in painting and drawing born of a genius which is the individual's alone, in the application and the use of the idea;

this style, manner, or taste, comes from nature and the mind.)

("Osservazioni di Nicolo Pussino," in Bellori, *Le Vite*; trans. A. Sedgwick Wohl)

A different definition by Filippo Baldinucci can in a sense be said to complete this one, by making a fundamental determination, one that in fact dominates artistic activity until the beginning of the nineteenth century: *gusto* is the exercise of judgment in the adequate application of the rules of art:

Gusto e Buon gusto, si applicano anche alle opere d'arte, nelle quali l'autore abbia seguite le regole del bello, ed abbiano grazia, eleganza, garbo, e simile.

(Taste and good taste also apply to works of art, those in which the author has followed the rules of the beautiful and which possess grace, elegance, delicacy, and other similar things.)

(*Vocabolario Toscano dell'arte del disegno*)

In this alliance with systems of rules for the arts, *gusto* can resolve the tension that existed between its original, idiosyncratic, and individual sense, and the demand for universality proper to art and the classical theory of art.

B. Predominance and exemplarity of *gusto*: Baltasar Gracián

In Spanish in the late sixteenth and seventeenth centuries, *gusto* rarely implies a judgment of taste in the properly aesthetic or artistic sense. Indeed, it appears rather more like a mode of implicit evaluation, a value judgment that is exercised in well-determined circumstances, namely in the world of the court and the political sphere. It refers to the idea of skill, the faculty of adapting oneself with ingenuity to the behavior of others, and knowing how to extract the greatest profit from it. In Baltasar Gracián, who develops the most precise theory of taste, *gusto* does not have the creative fertility of *ingenio* (spirit) or *genio* (genius), both of which, however, imply *el ejercicio y cultura del gusto* (the exercise and cultivation of taste) (*Agudeza y Arte de Ingenio*). When it is exclusively a capacity and a mode of judgment, *gusto* is not distinct from *genio*. However, it is distinguished from it insofar as *gusto* is exercised over a period of long maturation; it is the fruit of the study of books, works, and men, even though it reveals itself in an immediate mode. Like *ingenio*, *gusto* is an act that can take place only at the right moment, when the mind is truly absorbed and when matters have arrived at their highest degree of perfection. Whence the difficulty in clearly defining *gusto*, which, like the subtlety of *agudeza* and the dazzling inventiveness of *ingenio*, can capture the characteristic feature within a plurality of relations and sensible qualities, thus attesting to the superiority of someone who is capable of such just and perspicacious judgment. If *ingenio* is the art of spiritual invention, *gusto* is the most perfect acuity in the art of discernment. In this sense, true *gusto* obeys a teleology of perfecting itself as *buen gusto*, as correct evaluation. *Ingenio*, *agudeza*, and *gusto* have a common trait: they occur in a unique, privileged mind, one in which the *genio* reaches its peak of excellence and ephemeral glory, in conformity, in this aspect, with the vision of the world of many Jesuit theorists. Insofar as it is manifest in rare moments of the life of the mind, *gusto* is inaccessible to youth (too un-educated) and impossible in old age (too feeble). It is a form of knowledge (*gustar* implies *saber*, to know). As to its origins, Gracián writes, "Si la admiracion es hija de la ignorancia, también es madre del gusto" (If admiration is the daughter of ignorance, it is also the mother of taste) (*El Criticón*). This admiration, however, which also applies to the circumstances of life, to the most exceptional qualities of things, and to art, requires a superior form of discernment, necessary for the wise man to carry out his task, such that taste in the end encompasses the whole of life, whether practical or contemplative.

With Gracián, the denial of any possible universality to taste appears for the first time with striking clarity, couched in multiple repetitions of the claim that it is a rare capacity. Thus in the *Oráculo manual* (Pocket Oracle), maxim 28: "How truly wise the man who was unhappy at the thought he might please the masses! An excess of applause from the vulgar never satisfies the discreet"; or maxim 39: "Recognize things at their peak, at their best, and know how to take advantage of them. . . . Not everyone can, and not all those who can know how to" (trans. J. Robbins). This power of selection (*elección*), this faculty of judging in both moral and aesthetic matters, goes hand in hand with *ingenio*, since mind and taste are "twin brothers." Only *buen gusto* is able to grasp the imperceptible grace of something, a being or a work, all the nuances of this *despejo*, which Amelot de la Houssaie translates into French as the *je ne sais quoi*, and which represents the *vida de toda perfección* (the life of all perfection). Only *buen gusto* can discern in the *despejo* the superior quality that is the perfection of perfection without which all beauty is dead. Thus,

> Es eminencia de buen gusto gozar de cada cosa en su complemento.
>
> (It's the height of good taste to enjoy things at their most perfect.)
>
> (*Oráculo manual*, §39; trans. J. Robbins)

The idea that taste as specific judgment is known by its extreme rarity, that is to say, by a faculty that only a few can exercise adequately, is thus radicalized. It appears in the seventeenth and nineteenth centuries in France, in Germany with Schopenhauer, who is inspired by de Houssaie's translation for his own translation of Gracián into German, and, more indirectly, in Nietzsche.

C. Taste and rules

The French meaning of *goût* borrows relatively little from the dominant Italian or Spanish models. One of the characteristics of the word and its uses in the seventeenth and eighteenth centuries is to imply, openly or tacitly, a denial of the logical categories inherited by Scholasticism, and to oppose what was then called "the language of pedants." We do not find this desire for autonomy, and sometimes provocation, in Italian or Spanish texts. Narrowly related to tact, fine discernment, the spirit of opportunity, French *goût* is considered more in terms of relations, cleverly mastered situations, or the act of judgment than in terms of judgment of idiosyncratic properties or dispositions as in Italy. The ancient sense of enjoyment and fine discernment takes on a new value in Bossuet, especially when he cites the phrase of the dying Grand Condé: "'Yes,' he said, 'we shall see God as he is, face to face.' He repeated in Latin, with marvelous taste, these great words" (*Oraison funèbre du Grand Condé*, 1687). The word expresses the idea of an extraordinary pleasure, an exceptional acuity of mind, that is a mixture of sympathy in the most affective sense and clairvoyant intelligence.

- ■ See Box 1.

It is precisely this conception of an adjudicating activity whose basis seems to lack any justification that will later become the object of all the misunderstandings and ambiguities surrounding the use of the term "taste." This remark holds true as well for the notion of a rule (the taste that cleaves to the rules described by La Rochefoucauld), indissociable from the power of "good judgment." The rule was never, for the theorists of the seventeenth century, a rigid

---

1

La Rochefoucauld's definition of taste

For La Rochefoucauld, taste refers to a faculty of "judging soundly," which comes close to wit without really being assimilated to it. Like Dominique Bouhours, Antoine Gombauld Chevalier de Méré, and many others among his contemporaries, La Rochefoucauld makes taste a specific form of judgment that does not consist in a purely intellectual act, but that is not reducible to affects either, nor, most importantly, to a feeling like aesthetic pleasure, in the sense used in the eighteenth century. More precise than Pascal's *esprit de finesse*, it is central in the relations to others or toward artworks, even though the logic constituting this mode

of evaluation cannot be analyzed except by a description.

La Rochefoucauld's definition of taste is in a way paradigmatic:

This term "taste" has many meanings, and it is easy to make mistakes with it. There is a difference between the taste which carries us towards things and the taste which makes us know and discern their qualities by applying rules to them: one may like comedy without having taste which is fine and delicate enough to judge it well, and one may have taste which is good

enough to judge comedy well without liking it.

("Du goût," in *Maximes et Réflexions diverses*, §10; trans. E. H. and A. M. Blackmore and Francine Giguère)

If it is possible to "judge comedy well without liking it," this is because there is a faculty of evaluation that can distinguish the artistic or aesthetic qualities of a work with greater clarity than that of most people. That presupposes then that there are unique and exceptional qualities inherent in works and an especially clear-sighted power of evaluation that we call taste.

and more or less arbitrary norm imposed by groups of dominant art-lovers, but rather an essential mediation in relation to a work of art. It is the exemplification of the exceptional achievement of a work (that of a Raphael or a Carracci), to which it is not appropriate to conform, strictly speaking, but which is to be imitated in an act that is itself freely creative. If the translation of the notions of taste and rules rested on so many misunderstandings, it is because aesthetic criticism, especially since Lessing, deliberately referred to the more normative sense that was given to the terms "taste" and "rules" in the eighteenth century by Charles Batteux and, above all, Voltaire.

Taste in the eighteenth century in France takes two different shapes. One tends to affirm the rarity of a faculty that is truly able to discern the unique properties of a work of art. The other is part of the birth of aesthetics, and aims to respond to specifically philosophical demands. In cultivated circles, to write about, interpret, and evaluate a painting or a sculpture requires something other than the general faculty of judgment: above all, "an exquisite taste" is required, that is an aptitude for grasping the rarest nuances and the most delicate aesthetic properties that escape the perception of most viewers.

> There are a thousand men of good sense for one man of taste, and a thousand people of taste for one of exquisite taste.
>
> (Diderot, "Letter on the Deaf and Dumb," trans. Margaret Jourdain)

This belief, though foreign to any elitism in the nineteenth-century sense, certainly runs the risk of being inconsistent with a line of thought primarily concerned with determining the conditions of a universal judgment. The question of the universality of aesthetic judgment tends indeed to arise with the influence of English theorists. Voltaire attempted to resolve this inconsistency in a way that, while not always original, was considerably influential. The importance of his writings on the subject is that they take advantage of the multivocity of *goût*, appealing sometimes to the meaning inherited from the seventeenth century, and sometimes giving the concept an explicitly normative inflection. What distinguishes him from the authors of the previous century is that he defines taste as a necessary reference to the rules of classicism. The rule, which was productive insofar as it had the value of an example, becomes a norm, which is a rule that is henceforth fixed, unchangeable and more or less incontestable. Thus, he writes, "[T]here was no longer any taste in Italy" (*The Age of Louis XIV*). The phrase means that Italian artists no longer conformed to the system of rules proper to the classical ideal, and that they produced extravagant works like those of Bernini and Borromini. Taste is based less on an aesthetic subjectivity than a sort of legislation that is immanent to the works produced, as in this phrase: "The real reason is that, among people who cultivate the fine arts, many years are required to purify language and taste" (ibid.). "Taste" here refers to a sort of ideality in the union of the rules applied correctly and the genius of the artist. Hence, for example, regarding Addison, "Addison's words breathe taste" (ibid.), that is, they are works in which we see the alliance of good sense, imagination, and respect for the rules. This is why Voltaire considers Addison to be a "perfected Rabelais," that is, like a Rabelais who had shown taste. His conception of taste, unlike that of Jean-Baptiste Du Bos or Diderot, constitutes a final movement of resistance against English influence insofar as, for him, the power of aesthetic judgment precisely does *not* derive from sentiment or the intellect: what is most important is the correct fit between the creative act and the system of rules of the theory of classical art. And it is, above all, this somewhat dogmatic position that was widely spread throughout Europe, much more so than the writings of Charles Batteux or Rousseau, to the point where French taste became synonymous with normativity and arbitrary objectivism about aesthetic criteria. This usage and meaning of the word have survived down to the present as a counterexample and a concept to be avoided in any aesthetic theory. They are not, however, especially representative of the thought of the eighteenth century, since we find very different conceptions in Du Bos, the abbé Trublet, Montesquieu, and Batteux. Thus, the abbé Trublet gives an active role to the sentiment of beauty only to those who are genuinely cultivated:

> Since arguments require instruction, it appears that the appreciation of the beautiful belongs in the first instance to people of cultivated taste; the dilemma is resolved in their favor.
>
> (*Essays upon Several Subjects of Literature and Morality*)

However, the original claim in his book is that the more taste, that is, cultivated taste, is developed, the more feeling and reason are destined to blend with one another.

This is the final attempt to surmount the growing antinomy between aesthetic feeling and rational thought in the Enlightenment. But Rousseau prevents this possible synthesis for a long time, by effecting a decisive reversal. The word "taste" now becomes an indefinable notion:

> Of all the natural gifts Taste is the one which is felt the most and explained the least; it would not be what it is, if we could define it: for it judges objects on which judgment has no purchase, and serves, so to speak, as glasses for reason.
>
> ("Goût" in *Dictionnaire de musique*)

In reality, *goût* is an instinct for Rousseau (as it is for Leibniz), and the feeling of the beautiful cannot be a judgment in the sense of an expression relating concepts and empirical data. The judgment of taste is thus not truly a judgment, as understood in logical thought—that is, a statement that may lead to an objective proposition—just as an evaluative proposition for Frege, Wittenstein, and logicians cannot be a true proposition, since its truth-value cannot be determined. Inexpressible sentiment and mental activity irreducible to any objectification—this is how taste, as conceived by Rousseau, appears in the Kantian problem of reflective judgment and in contemporary aesthetics.

II. The Properly Aesthetic Genesis of "Taste"

The aesthetic construction of the English "taste" plays a central role in the eighteenth century, as we are reminded by the author of the entry "Taste" in *A Companion to Aesthetics* (Cooper 1992). The English term inherits a considerable history that began, as we have seen, in the Renaissance. According to the painter Sir Joshua Reynolds, in conformity with Italian and French traditions, "taste" is the instrument of a reflection on the perfection of art in England:

> Every language has adopted terms expressive of this excellence. The *gusto grande* of the Italians, the *beau idéal* of the French, and the *great style, genius,* and *taste* among the English, are but different appellations of the same thing.
>
> ("The Great Leading Principles of the Grand Style . . . ," Third Discourse in *Discourses*)

"Taste" is thus part of the European history of the concept. But it is in England that this history is reworked by philosophers and thenceforth is part of a context that is proper to the Anglo-Saxon tradition.

The usage of "taste" makes it at first a term that rationalizes social distinctions. The word refers to a rule and justification for developing a discourse on civilization, the mores whose danger is always a division between civilized and barbarous tastes. When good taste is exercised, pleasure develops in society. "Taste" is here very close to "relish," or "delectation." But the meaning of the term shifts, coming to refer also to an operation of the subject that begins in feeling. The word thus means aesthetic experience as, and the experience of, contemplation, which presumes both a theory of perception and of evaluation. The fragility and the ambiguities of this concept must then be emphasized, as it attempts to delineate a unique mode of judgment while at the same time recognizing that which is immanent in the emotions.

"Taste" thus appears in the first instance as a prescriptive concept in which art and society are intertwined. The rules of taste do not have an absolute value, but are rather aimed at raising individuals up to a state of being civilized. Taste becomes noticed as part of polite society with Addison and Steele's *Spectator*, which, from 1711 to 1714, offers chronicles of customs, arts, and social behaviors in order to observe and spread the rules of life and British politeness of *gentlemen* and their culture. The intent is "[t]o discover, how we may, to best Advantage, form within our-selves what in the polite World is call'd a *Relish*, or Good TASTE," writes Shaftesbury in *Characteristics of Men, Manners, Opinions, Times.* Making oneself a subject of taste has as a necessary correlate the correction and daily adjustments that politeness requires as a set of collective rules of propriety that yield the improvement of society.

Beyond its application to the production of pleasure in society, the word "taste" is associated with the presence in humans of a natural sense that functions as an immediate possible evaluation. Taste can thus be compared with having a gift or a talent whose innate or acquired nature is debated. Etymologically, "taste" comes from the Latin *tangere*; it is initially a matter of touching, tact, in the proper and the figurative senses. It evokes a delicate and spontaneous appreciation. The use of "taste" presupposes reflection about the notion of sense, understood as sensory device. In 1759 Alexander Gerard published "An Essay on Taste," which

received the prize given by the Edinburgh Society for the Encouragement of Arts for the best essay on the subject. According to the essay, which consists of a summary of different theses on taste being discussed in Scotland at the time, taste structures the perception of "works of art and genius" and may be related to the principles by which the mind receives pleasure or pain. These principles are the *internal senses*: those of novelty, grandeur or sublimity, beauty, imitation, harmony, ridicule, and virtue. The union of the internal senses shapes and perfects taste insofar as it makes it possible to excite the most exquisite pleasures. To discover the deepest qualities of taste, the internal senses are aided by judgment, the faculty that distinguishes different things, separates truth and falsehood, compares objects and their qualities. Judgment introduces the possibility of not only perceiving but also of assessing the meaning of a work. It operates *after* the powerful exercise of feelings by the internal senses, which allow one to experience pleasure or displeasure; judgment *then* brings to taste the depth of penetration. "Taste" now refers to a compound operation, both perceptual and intellectual, immediate and mediated, perceptive and evaluative. Hume, in *Of the Standard of Taste*, also takes account of the composite character of taste. "Taste" cannot be defined only by the internal correctness of sentiments, even if the philosopher must accept the variety of tastes, proof of the vital and ordinary attraction that all individuals have for their own sentiments. At the same time, taste presumes agreement, a process of evaluation that assesses the relations of works to beauty. The delicacy of taste by which the mind refines emotions makes correct expressions of artistic judgment possible. This aesthetic capacity requires an exercise by which the real qualities of a work are identified. Adam Smith, in *The Theory of Moral Sentiments*, offers a similar figure of the "man of taste" who distinguishes slight, often imperceptible differences of beauty or ugliness.

The tension expressed by "taste" between perception and evaluation continues to enrich aesthetic reflection. The work of the English art critic Clive Bell, *Art* (1914), for instance, interestingly extends the construction of aesthetic emotion in terms of "sense" and "taste" by suggesting a return to personal experience in art on the basis of an "aesthetic emotion" that is not reducible to a simple subjective representation of the contemplated object. On the side of the value of art, Malcolm Budd in *Values of Art* (1995), focusing on the determination of the artistic value of a work, posits the experience of the work of art as an act of intelligence and discusses Hume's standard of taste.

III. Taste Put to the Test of Philosophical Reflection: From Transcendental Subjectivity to Taste as a Method of Determining Value

A. The transcendental revolution: *Geschmack* as reflective judgment

Though English philosophers draw attention to the productivity and autonomy of aesthetic subjectivity, they nevertheless remain faithful to traditional conceptions of taste as a faculty of discernment of a certain type. The real break with all previous theories of taste comes with Kant's critical philosophy, which attempts to destroy the idea dear to

Baumgarten of a cognitive aesthetics, founded on rational and normative principles.

It is in Baumgarten's *Metaphysica* and *Aesthetica* that we find one of the first properly philosophical definitions of taste, insofar as it attempts to renew the problem of relations between the sensible and the intelligible. This means that the concept does indeed now fall within the specific domain of philosophy. Baumgarten, however, who writes and thinks in Latin, is keen to preserve the rhetorical and humanist heritage by reconciling it with the demands of Leibnizian metaphysics, here represented especially by Wolff's school. For Baumgarten, *gustus* is, like the other faculties, a form of knowledge (*cognitio inferior*), a sensible experience of reality:

> Gustus significatu latiori de sensualibus, i.e. quae sentiuntur, est judicium sensuum.
>
> (In the widest sense, taste in the domain of the sensible, that is, what is felt, is the judgment of the senses.)

> (*Metaphysica*, §608)

It is thanks to this sensory organ that the object of judgment is felt. *Gustus* is thus determined as a sensible faculty of judgment, but one that presupposes some training to reach full maturity (*maturitas*), a bit as in Gracián: "Talis gustus est sapor non publicus (purior, eruditus)" (The taste that corresponds is an uncommon flavor [purer and more cultivated]) (ibid.). Insofar as this faculty is effectively cognitive, since it accounts for certain experiences of reality, it may commit errors of judgment, as in the case of perceptual illusions. It is thus central as a *facultas diiudicandi*, as a faculty of judging aesthetically.

Kant's aesthetic thought rests in part on the rejection of this perspective, which still makes it possible to intellectualize the forms of sensory judgments, or rather, of judgments, which would imply both a sort of virtual intelligibility and a minimal objectivity. The original meaning of *Geschmack*, as the word is used beginning with the *Critique of Pure Reason*, in the famous note (to §1) on the "Transcendental Aesthetic," is based on a radical rejection of *gustus* as conceived by Baumgarten:

> The Germans are the only ones who now employ the word "aesthetics" to designate that which others call the critique of taste. The ground for this is a failed hope, held by the excellent analyst Baumgarten, of bringing the critical estimation of the beautiful under principles of reason, and elevating its rules to a science. But this effort is futile. For the putative rules or criteria are merely empirical as far as their most prominent sources are concerned, and can therefore never serve as determinate *a priori* rules according to which our judgment of taste must be directed; rather the latter constitutes the genuine touchstone of the correctness of the former.

> (trans. Guyer and Wood, 173)

This note explicitly condemns the project of the *Aesthetica*, and no further allusion is made to it, even in the third Critique, where its claims are indirectly refuted. Indeed, in the *Critique of Judgement* (1.1), the first definition of taste makes it a faculty of judgment that deals less with an object than with a mode of representation:

> Geschmack ist das Beurteilungsvermögen eines Gegenstandes oder einer Vorstellungsart durch ein Wohlgefallen oder Missgefallen ohne alles Interesse. Der Gegenstand eines solchen Wohlgefallens heisst schön.

> (*Taste* is the faculty of estimating an object or a mode of representation by means of a delight or aversion *apart from any interest*. The object of such a delight is called *beautiful*.)

> ("Analytic of the Beautiful," §5; trans. J. C. Meredith)

Kant's desire to conform above all to his project of a transcendental philosophy is clear from this first definition on. For his judgment of taste does not deal with the object as such, nor with its properties, nor with a rule of art, nor even with the aesthetic sensation that the object incites, but with the mode of representation born from the sensation. And this mode of representation in its turn causes a specific sentiment that is none other than the sentiment of pleasure conceived of as the *Bestimmungsgrund* (basis) of the aesthetic experience. Insofar as it is manifested by a sentiment, taste is a form of reflective judgment referring to the structures of aesthetic subjectivity as it is understood from within the project of a transcendental philosophy. This is why the only predicate Kant allows definitively for the beautiful is the feeling of pleasure. One of the great difficulties encountered in making judgments of taste as described in the "Analytic of the Beautiful" is to want to reconcile the self-referential character of taste with the requirement of universal communicability, subjectively grounded—that is, with the claim to subjective universality.

B. *Geschmack* on trial

If Hegel gives a relatively restricted role to the problem of taste in his *Lectures on Aesthetics*, it is because he disqualifies the latter as a criterion for the understanding of a work of art. As a manifestation of aesthetic subjectivity, taste is for him an essential obstacle to the genuinely philosophical analysis of art. A large swathe of aesthetic thought in the twentieth century (especially that of Lukács and Adorno) is influenced by this condemnation, and actively embraces its theoretical consequences. Taste henceforth ceased to be a constitutive element of interpretation; it is no longer anything more than a parasitic form of subjectivism.

In Hegel, *Geschmack* is used without any reference to the problem of reflective judgment that exercised Kant. When he analyzes it, it is exclusively in a polemical way, to attack eighteenth-century theories of art:

> Another kind of interest consisted not in the express aim of producing genuine works of art directly but in the intention of developing through such theories a judgement on works of art, in short, of developing *taste*. As examples, Home's *Elements of Criticism*, the works of Batteux, and Ramler's *Einleitung in die schönen Wissenschaften* were books much read in their day. Taste in this sense concerns the arrangement and treatment, the aptness and perfection of what belongs to the external

appearance of a work of art (*Geschmack in diesem Sinne betrifft die Anordnung und Behandlung, das Schickliche und Ausgebildete dessen, was zur äusseren Erscheinung eines Kunstwerks gehört*). Moreover they drew into the principles of taste views which were taken from the old psychology and had been derived from empirical observations of mental capacities and activities, passions and their probable intensification, sequence, etc. But it remains ever the case that every man apprehends works of art or characters, actions, and events according to the measure of his insight and his feelings; and since the development of taste only touched on what was external and meagre, and besides took its prescriptions likewise from only a narrow range of works of art and a limited training of the intellect and the feelings, its scope was unsatisfactory and incapable of grasping the inner [meaning] and truth [of art] and sharpening the eye for detecting these things.

(Introduction to *Aesthetics: Lectures on Fine Art*, trans. T. M. Knox, 1:27)

The concept of taste thus no longer has anything but a negative meaning, for the purpose of showing the weakness of earlier theories; it refers more to frankly erroneous conceptions than to a precise function. Art lovers and connoisseurs have, according to Hegel, been focusing on technical details, secondary and contingent understandings. This excessive attention to the "external manifestation" of a work of art is the sign, according to Hegel, of an aesthetics that gives a dominant role to sensation, sensory perception, and even sentiment. Taste thus becomes synonymous with immediate sensation, subjectivity that is exclusively attached to the least essential aspects of a work of art. It has not only lost all critical fertility but also turns out to be a secondary activity, screening off the deeper meaning of art, since it refers to the perceptible as such, that is, to what is inadequate for spirit. This contrast between "taste" as sensible knowledge relying on rules external to its object, and "spirit" as true knowledge of art may be surprising, precisely because it remains a pure opposition, ending in a condemnation and a radical rejection of taste. It is thus not as a "moment" that taste is eliminated, but as a false path, noxious and contrary to spirit as interiority. The difficulty of determining a precise meaning, some kind of use for taste comes from the fact that Hegel has subjected it to a trial that is strongly conditioned by an opposition to any form of sensualism or subjectivism. Through this concept, Hegel takes aim above all at the primacy of sensation, at feeling as a positing of subjectivity, at the recognition of appearance as such—in other words, at the eighteenth century.

C. The positivity of *Geschmack* as a fundamental mode of evaluation

Nineteenth-century thought inquires increasingly into the nature and functions of value judgments. This reactivation of value judgments, however—implicit in Schopenhauer, central in Nietzsche, and then problematic in Max Weber and Rickert—brings with it a rehabilitation of taste as a mode of evaluation.

With Schopenhauer, taste regains its philosophical dignity, since it is an expression of the will to live (*Wille zum Leben*). This metaphysical notion of the will to live is based, according to Schopenhauer, on the life sciences. Thenceforth, it is possible to form a physiology of taste, of theories of the specific activity of the sense organs having a positive cognitive value. The *aisthêsis* [αἴσθησις] of taste thus conceived, determined by physiology, optics, and the medical sciences, necessarily escapes transcendental subjectivity and Hegelian critique, becoming itself a major interpretive form, not only of art but also of reality and culture. The meaning of the word is still implicit in Schopenhauer's demonstrations (for example, those regarding the important question of style, and especially philosophical style) and it is never conceptualized as such: *Geschmack* refers most often to taste in the Spanish sense (remember that Schopenhauer translated Gracián), and especially the French sense as transmitted by the eighteenth century. If he thinks of *Geschmack* in the sense of *gusto* and *goût*, it is in order to produce new criteria of a mode of philosophical reasoning of which Nietzsche is the main beneficiary.

When Nietzsche uses *Geschmack*, it is most often as a constitutive element of evaluation and to make it central to a determination of any possible value.

Und ihr sagt mir, Freunde, dass nicht zu streiten sei über Geschmack und Schmecken? Aber alles Leben ist Streit um Geschmack und Schmecken! Geschmack: das ist Gewicht zugleich und Wagschale und Wägender; und wehe allem Lebendigen, das ohne Streit um Gewicht und Wagschale und Wägende leben wollte!

(And you say to me, friends, there is no disputing over taste and tasting? But all of life is a dispute over taste and tasting! Taste: that is weight and at the same time scales and weigher; and woe to anything living that would live without disputes over weight and scales and weighers!)

("Von den Erhabenen," in *Also sprach Zarathoustra*, of *Werke*, 2:373; "On Those Who Are Sublime," in *Thus Spoke Zarathustra*, of *Complete Works*, trans. G. Parkes)

We note that in the translation of the Latin adage "de gustibus coloribusque non disputandum" the German retains only the gustatory part: *Geschmack* and *Schmecken*, taste and what has flavor.

Among the many uses Nietzsche makes of the concept of taste, these lines from *Zarathustra* have the particular interest relying on the three emblematic figures of the scale, weight, and the weigher. The triple relation clearly shows an effort to overcome the purely subjective dimension of the evaluation by positing correlates and constitutive criteria of axiological experience. Balance and weight do not refer to the principle of subjectivity of evaluation, any more than they would be mere metaphors intended to communicate that taste is a value judgment. In reality, the emblematic definition of "taste" is already axiological: it presupposes that any thought is an interpretation, evaluation, and conflict at the same time. This does not mean exactly that taste is a sufficient condition for deciding the value or nonvalue of something, but that it must be rehabilitated insofar as it is constitutive of any evaluation, thus as one of the means of resolving certain ethical and aesthetic questions. "What decides against Christianity now is our taste, not our reasons" (*The Gay Science*, trans. J. Nauckhoff and A. del Caro, §132), or "It is we thinkers who first have to determine the *palatableness* of things and, if necessary, decree it" (*Daybreak*, §505; trans. M. Clark et al.). If any sensation or perception already contains an evaluation, taste must be constitutive of value judgment and evaluation.

■ See Box 2.

IV. Crisis and Reevaluation of the Functions of Taste in Contemporary Aesthetics

The refusal to grant cognitive content to judgments of taste and evaluation is characteristic of a philosophical attitude that is widely shared today. The question of the meaning and the function of "taste" is thus endlessly deferred, or even ruled out a priori, including in the domain of aesthetics. The rather general argument that disqualifies aesthetic judgment founded on taste is that one can never, on the basis of a perception of the artistic and aesthetic properties of a work of art, derive or infer a judgment, or rather a proposition with any sort of objectivity or validity. Taste thus seems fated to refer almost always to the structures of subjectivity, thus to the Kantian problem of reflective judgment. The growing disqualification of value judgment in aesthetic reflection since the nineteenth century only confirmed the discredit cast upon taste.

In contemporary aesthetics, taste is a concept that most often has only a negative meaning, or presents an evident lack of content. Deprived of any possibility of reference (for example, to the work of art as such or to the activity of the subject of aesthetic experience), its definitions are for the most part purely negative. Thus, Reinhard Knodt claims, "Das Zeitalter des guten Geschmacks ist vorbei" (The time

of good taste has passed) (*Aesthetische Korrespondenzen*). This type of claim, returned to over and over again in aesthetic criticism, tends to eliminate the notion of taste as a capacity of discerning aesthetic and artistic properties at one blow, without ever analyzing what it implies. For this critique is directed at a semantic content that was never the one transmitted by the tradition; it relies on the erroneous and anachronistic idea of taste as conformity to a system of more or less arbitrary norms. With few exceptions, defining this concept no longer consists in determining a precise sense for it, but rather in producing ideologically based arguments that are hostile to any idea of any aptitude for discerning aesthetic qualities in a work of art and determining them according to a hierarchy.

In the twentieth century, the aesthetic thought that develops in the field of analytic philosophy is the only one that attempts to restore a precise semantic content to the notion of taste. Taste is not simply assimilated to an arbitrary form of value judgment or an idiosyncratic fact. It is with regard to the question of the definition of aesthetic concepts and the determination of aesthetic properties of a work—hence of acts of predication—that the notion has been rehabilitated, in particular by Frank Sibley. His article "Aesthetic Concepts" (*Philosophical Review*) provoked a number of reactions and polemics, precisely because it claims to affirm the positivity of taste, its productive and effective activity in the determination of an aesthetic property of an object. For Sibley, a statement about specifically aesthetic qualities cannot be distinguished from one about sensible qualities unless we appeal to a type of activity that is different from that of simple perception, namely the exercise of taste: "Therefore, when a word or expression is such that its application requires taste or perceptivity, I will call it an *aesthetic* term or expression, and similarly, I will speak of aesthetic concepts or concepts of taste." Sibley's whole problem, and especially that of his

---

2

"The Yes and No of the palate"

It is precisely this primacy of the evaluative that is most often the object of misinterpretation, incomprehension, and principled opposition by commentators.

The way in which Habermas cites the phrase "the Yes and No of the palate," which Nietzsche uses in §224 of *Beyond Good and Evil*, is in this regard especially significant.

In this paragraph, Nietzsche contrasts the "historical sense" (*der historische Sinn*) that "we other Europeans claim as our peculiarity," this faculty that "the moderns" have for understanding all the forms of evaluation and of tasting all things, with the capacity for rejecting and excluding that "the men of an aristocratic civilization"

had toward anything that did not agree with their own value system. It is thus that the French of the seventeenth century, he says, were incapable of appreciating Homer:

The very definite Yes and No of their palate, their easy nausea, their hesitant reserve toward everything foreign, their horror of the poor taste even of a lively curiosity, and altogether the reluctance of every noble and self-sufficient culture to own a new desire, a dissatisfaction with what is one's own, and admiration for what is foreign—all this inclines and disposes them unfavorably even against the best things in the world which are

not theirs or *could* not become their prey.

(*Beyond Good and Evil*,
trans. W. Kaufmann)

Habermas thus interprets Nietzsche's way of proceeding: "Nietzsche enthrones taste, 'the Yes and No of the palate,' as the organ of a 'knowledge' beyond true and the false, beyond good and evil" ("The Entwinement of Myth and Enlightenment," in *The Philosophical Discourse of Modernity*, 96). To invalidate Nietzsche's thought, Habermas does not even bother with an argument: it suffices for him to emphasize what is in his eyes the exorbitant role of taste as a mode of knowledge, in order to make it a sort of model of irrationality.

successors, is to break out of this somewhat circular reasoning contained in the definition: taste is a necessary condition for the production of aesthetic concepts, and these concepts presuppose the exercise of taste as a specific capacity for discerning the qualities or properties proper to art. Without going further here into this problem, which has the merit of raising again the question of the logic of aesthetic predicates and aesthetic criteria, we may see here a rehabilitation of taste, not as a transcendental faculty but as a necessary condition of the validation of aesthetic concepts.

The appeal to ordinary language, or rather the desire to accept it as such, or as the possibility of resolving certain logico-semantic aporias, are proper to analytic philosophy. Wittgenstein, considering the semantic content of aesthetic concepts just as problematic as that of other philosophical notions, uses the term *Geschmack* several times. In the *Vermischte Bemerkungen*, he writes, "Feilen ist *manchmal* Tätigkeit des Geschmacks, manchmal nicht. *Ich* habe Geschmack" (Sometimes polishing is a function of taste, but sometimes not. *I* have taste)" (*Culture and Value*, trans. P. Winch). In every case, the word *Geschmack* is curiously used in a noncritical, that is, nonphilosophical way. Even though the *Bemerkungen* belong to Wittgenstein's philosophical thought, *Geschmack* here preserves all the density and the clarity of words of ordinary language. This leaves intact the possibility of using the word without losing the useful irresponsibility that allows one to say that, after all, taste is taste.

Jean-François Groulier
Fabienne Brugère

BIBLIOGRAPHY

Alighieri, Dante. *The Divine Comedy*. Translated, with commentary, by Charles S. Singleton. 6 vols. 2nd. ed. Princeton, NJ: Princeton University Press, 1977.

Baldinucci, Filippo. *Vocabolario Toscano dell'arte del disegno*. Vols. 2–3 of *Opere*. Milan, 1809. First published in 1681, in Florence.

Batteux, Charles. *Les Beaux-Arts réduits à un seul principe*. In vol. 1 of *Principes de la littérature*. Lyon, 1802. *Les Beaux-Arts* was first published in 1746. Translation by John Miller: *A Course of the Belles Lettres, or the Principles of Literature*. London, 1761.

Baumgarten, Alexander Gottlieb. *Metaphysica*. 7th ed. Hildesheim, Ger.: G. Olms, 1963. First published in 1779.

———. *Aesthetica*. 2 vols. Hildesheim, Ger.: G. Olms, 1970. First published in 1750–58.

Bell, Clive. *Art*. Edited by J. B. Bullen. Oxford: Oxford University Press, 1987. First published in 1914.

Bellori, Giovan Pietro. *Le Vite de pittori scultori e architettori moderni*. Rome, 1672. Translation by Alice Sedgwick Wohl: *The Lives of the Modern Painters, Sculptors, and Architects*. New York: Cambridge University Press, 2005.

Bouhours, Dominique. *La Manière de bien penser dans les ouvrages de l'esprit*. Paris, 1687. Translated anonymously: *The Art of Criticism: or, the Method of Making a Right Judgment upon Subjects of Wit and Learning*. Introduction by Philip Smallwood. Delmar: Scholars' Facsimiles and Reprints, 1981. English translation first published in 1705.

Budd, Malcolm. *Values of Art*. London: Penguin, 1995.

Cooper, David, ed. *A Companion to Aesthetics*. Oxford: Blackwell, 1992.

Dickie, George. *The Century of Taste: The Philosophical Odyssey of Taste in the Eighteenth Century*. New York: Oxford University Press, 1996.

Diderot, Denis. "Lettre sur les sourds-muets à l'usage de ceux qui entendent et qui parlent." 1751. Translation by Margaret Jourdain: "Letter on the Deaf and Dumb for the Use of Those Who Hear and Speak." Pp. 158–218 in *Diderot's Early Philosophical Works*. Edited by M. Jourdain. Chicago: Open Court, 1916.

Doni, Anton Francesco. *Il Disegno*. Venice, 1549.

Du Bos, Jean-Baptiste. *Réflexions critiques sur la poésie et sur la peinture*. With preface by Dominique Désirat. Paris: École Nationale Supérieure des Beaux-Arts, 1993.

First published in 1719. Translation by Thomas Nugent: *Critical Reflections on Poetry, Painting and Music: With an Inquiry into the Rise and Progress of the Theatrical Entertainments of the Ancients*. 3 vols. London, 1748.

Gerard, Alexander. *An Essay on Taste: With Three Dissertations on the Same Subject by Mr. De Voltaire, Mr. D'Alembert, Mr. De Montesquieu*. London, 1759.

Gracián, Baltasar. *Agudeza y arte de ingenio*. 2 vols. Edited, with notes, by Ceferino Peralta, Jorge M. Ayala, and José Ma. Andreu. Zaragoza, Sp.: Prensas Universitarias de Zaragoza, 2004. First published in 1648.

———. *El Criticón*. Edited, with commentary, by Miguel Romera-Navarro. Philadelphia: University of Pennsylvania Press, 1938–40. First published in 1651. Translation by Paul Rycaut: *The Critick*. London, 1681.

———. *Oráculo manual y Arte de prudencia*. Edited by Benito Pelegrín. Zaragoza, Sp.: Guara, 1983. First published in 1647. Translation by Jeremy Robbins: *The Pocket Oracle and Art of Prudence*. Edited by J. Robbins. New York: Penguin, 2011.

Habermas, Jürgen. *The Philosophical Discourse of Modernity: Twelve Studies*. Translated by Frederick G. Lawrence. Cambridge, MA: MIT Press, 1990. First German edition published in 1985.

Hammermeister, Kai. *The German Aesthetic Tradition*. Cambridge: Cambridge University Press, 2002.

Harrison, Charles, Paul Wood, and Jason Gaiger, eds. *Art in Theory 1648–1815: An Anthology of Changing Ideas*. Oxford: Blackwell, 2001.

Hegel, Georg Wilhelm Friedrich. *Vorlesungen über die Aesthetik*. Vols. 12–14. Edited by Hermann Glockner. Stuttgart: Frommann, 1937. Translation by T. M. Knox: *Aesthetics: Lectures on Fine Art*. 2 vols. Oxford: Clarendon Press, 1975.

Hume, David. "Essay of the Standard of Taste." Pp. 133–53 in *Selected Essays*, edited by Stephen Copley and Andrew Edgar. Oxford: Oxford University Press, 1993. First published in 1757.

Kant, Immanuel. *Kritik der reinen Vernunft*. Vol. 3–4 of *Kants Gesammelte Schriften*. Akademieausgabe: Königlich Preussische Akademie der Wissenschaften. Berlin: De Gruyter, 1902–22. Translation by Paul Guyer and A. Wood: *Critique of Pure Reason*. Edited by P. Guyer and A. Wood. Cambridge: Cambridge University Press, 1997.

———. *Kritik der Urteilskraft*. Vol. 5 of *Kants Gesammelte Schriften*. Akademieausgabe: Königlich Preussische Akademie der Wissenschaften. Berlin: De Gruyter, 1902–22. Translation by J. C. Meredith: *Critique of Judgement*. Edited by J. C. Meredith. Oxford: Oxford University Press, 1952.

Lamarque, Peter, and Stein Haugom Olsen, eds. *Aesthetics and the Philosophy of Art: The Analytic Tradition. An Anthology*. Oxford: Blackwell, 2004.

La Rochefoucauld, François de. *Maximes et Réflexions diverses*. Paris: Gallimard / La Pléiade, 1957. First published in 1678. Translation, with introduction and notes, by E. H. and A. M. Blackmore and Francine Giguère: *Collected Maxims and Other Reflections*. Oxford: Oxford University Press, 2007.

Lessing, Gotthold Ephraim. *Laokoon oder über die Grenzen der Malerei und Poesie*. Stuttgart: Reclam, 1967. Translation, with introduction and notes, by Edward Allen McCormick: *Laocoön: An Essay on the Limits of Painting and Poetry*. Baltimore: Johns Hopkins University Press, 1984.

Méré, Antoine Gombauld, Chevalier de. *Œuvres*. 3 vols. Edited by Charles Henri Boudhors. Paris: Roches, 1930.

———. *Conversations of the Mareschal of Clerambault and the Chevalier de Meré: A Treatise of Great Esteem Amongst the Principal Wits of France*. Translated by Archibald. Lovell. London, 1677.

Montesquieu, Charles de Secondat, baron de La Brède. *Essai sur le goût*. Introduction and notes by Charles-Jacques Beyer. Geneva: Droz, 1967. First published in 1757. Anonymous translation: "Essay on Taste." Pp. 257–314 in *An Essay on Taste: With Three Dissertations on the Same Subject by Mr. De Voltaire, Mr. D'Alembert, Mr. De Montesquieu*, edited by Alexander Gerard. London, 1759.

Moriarty, Michael. *Taste and Ideology in Seventeenth-Century France*. Cambridge: Cambridge University Press, 1988.

Nietzsche, Friedrich. *Beyond Good and Evil*. Translated by Walter Kaufmann. New York: Knopf Doubleday, 1989.

———. *Complete Works*. 18 vols. Edited by Oscar Levy. New York: Russell and Russell, 1964.

———. *Daybreak: Thoughts on the Prejudices of Morality*. Edited and translated by Maudemarie Clark et al. Cambridge: Cambridge University Press, 1997.

———. *The Gay Science: With a Prelude in German Rhymes and an Appendix of Songs*. Edited by Bernard Williams et al. Translated by Josefine Nauckhoff and Adrian del Caro. Cambridge: Cambridge University Press, 2001.

———. *Werke*. 3 vols. Edited by K. Schlechta. Darmstadt, Ger.: Wissenschaftliche Buchgesellschaft, 1997.

Pino, Paolo. *Dialogo di pittura*. Critical edition. Introduction and notes by Rodolfo and Anna Pallicchini. Venice: Daria Guarnati, 1946. First published in 1548. Translation by Mary Pardo: "Paolo Pino's *Dialogo di pittura*: A Translation with Commentary." Ph.D. diss. University of Pittsburgh, 1984.

Reynolds, Joshua. *Discourses on Art*. Edited by Robert R. Wark. New Haven, CT: Yale University Press, 1975. First published in 1790.

Saisselin, Rémy G. *Taste in Eighteenth-Century France: Critical Reflections of the Origins of Aesthetics; or, An Apology for Amateurs*. Syracuse, NY: Syracuse University Press, 1965.

Schaeffer, Jean-Marie. *Art of the Modern Age: Philosophy of Art from Kant to Heidegger*. Translated by Steven Randall. Foreword by Arthur C. Danto. Princeton, NJ: Princeton University Press, 2000.

Schopenhauer, Arthur. *Die Welt als Wille und Vorstellung*. 2 vols. Stuttgart: Reclam, 1987. Translation by Richard E. Aquila and David Carus: *The World as Will and Presentation*. 2 vols. Longman Library. New York: Pearson Longman, 2008–10.

Shaftesbury, Anthony Ashley Cooper. *Characteristics of Men, Manners, Opinions, Times*. Hildesheim, Ger.: G. Olms, 1978. First published in 1711.

Sibley, Frank. "Aesthetic Concepts." *Philosophical Review* 68 (1959).

———. *Approach to Aesthetics: Collected Papers on Philosophical Aesthetics*. Edited by John Benson, Betty Redfern, and Jeremy Roxbee Cox. Oxford: Clarendon Press, 2001.

Smith, Adam. *The Theory of Moral Sentiments*. Edited by D. D. Raphael and A. L. Macfie. Oxford: Clarendon Press, 1976. First published in 1759.

Trublet, Nicolas-Charles-Joseph. *Essais sur divers sujets de littérature et de morale*. Geneva: Slatkine, 1968. First published in 1735. Anonymous translation: *Essays upon Several Subjects of Literature and Morality . . . Translated from the French of the Abbot Trublet*. London: Printed for J. Osborn, 1744.

Vasari, Giorgio. *Le vite de' più eccelenti architettori, pittori et scultori italiani*. 9 vols. Edited by Gaetano Milanesi. Florence: Sansoni: 1878–85. First published in 1568. Translation by Gaston du C. de Vere: *Lives of the Most Eminent Painters, Sculptors and Architects*. 10 vols. New York: AMS, 1976.

Voltaire (François-Marie Arouet). *Le Siècle de Louis XIV*. 2 vols. Paris: Garnier, 1929–30. Translation by Martyn P. Pollack: *The Age of Louis XIV*. Everyman's Library no. 780. London: Dent, 1961.

Wittgenstein, Ludwig. *Culture and Value: A Selection from the Posthumous Remains*. 2nd rev. ed. Edited by Alois Pichler. Translated by Peter Winch. Chicago: University of Chicago Press, 1980.

GOVERNMENT

"Government" comes from the Latin *gubernare*, which, like the Greek *kubernaô* [κυβερνάω], refers to being at the helm of a ship, hence to direct, to command. The term initially refers to governing or directing a collectivity or any kind of institution, before coming to be applied more specifically to political communities. It is applied at once to the way in which a collectivity is directed (good or bad government, or what is today called "governance"), to the regime by which this mode of directing is instantiated (the types of government), and finally to the actual authority exercising "executive" power, which has the power of constraint distinct from "legislative" and "judiciary" powers. We may focus here on the difference between the English and French networks, with English often speaking of "government" where continental traditions speak of the powers of the "State" instead. See STATE/GOVERNMENT, and LAW. See also HERRSCHAFT, POLIS, POLITICS, *STATE*.

➤ *AUTHORITY, DOMINATION, DROIT*, LEX, MIR, *POWER*

GRACE

The Latin *gratia* (from *gratus*, "pleasant, charming, dear, grateful") refers to a way of being agreeable to others or vice versa. It suggests "favor, gratitude, good relations," including at the physical level: "charm, attractiveness." Church language has made special use of it to render the Greek *charis* [χάρις] (e.g., *gratificus*, benevolent = *charistêrios* [χαριστήριος])—when, for example, the Virgin Mary is addressed as "full of grace," we hear that she is dear, benevolent, and charming. The term thus hovers at the boundaries of the aesthetic and the religious.

I. Aesthetics of Grace

1. For the Greek *charis*, and the way in which *chairein* [χαίρειν] refers to the pleasure of being, the joy of existing in the beauty of the world, see PLEASURE, I.A. Cf., for an entirely different connotation, the German *Gelassenheit* (see *SERENITY*).

   See also WELT, Box 1, on *kosmos* [κόσμος]; and BEAUTY, Box 1, on the study of the syntagma *kalos kagathos* [καλὸς κἀγαθός].

2. On the terminological network put in place in the Italian aesthetic of the Renaissance, see LEGGIADRIA, "grace, lightness." See also SPREZZATURA; cf. ARGUTEZZA, CONCETTO, DISEGNO.

3. On the relation between grace and beauty, and the *je ne sais quoi*, see BEAUTY, Box 4, GOÛT; cf. BAROQUE, INGENIUM, STILL.

II. Grace and the Divine

On divine grace as related to the organization of the world, besides *charis* and WELT, Box 1 (see above, I.1), see the Russian SVET, "light, world"; see also BOGOČELOVEČESTVO, "divine-humanity." For the relation between grace and cunning, or divine machination, see OIKONOMIA, TALAṬṬUF; cf. *RUSE*; between grace and pardon, see PARDON.

For *Anmut* and the German terminological network, see GEMÜT.

See also, related to grace as a calling, BERUF; cf. PIETAS, SECULARIZATION.

➤ *DESTINY*, GOD, LOVE, RELIGIO

GREEK

Constancy and Change in the Greek Language

➤ AIÔN, EPOCHÊ, ESSENCE, ESTI, EUROPE, LOGOS, RUSSIAN, SUBJECT, TO TRANSLATE, UNDERSTANDING

We know that it is difficult to translate ancient Greek, the "mother tongue" of philosophy, into any vernacular language, and that it has been thus since it was first translated into Latin. Less well known is the difficulty of translating it into modern Greek, which can be attributed in particular—despite the exceptional longevity of the language—to the vagaries of the diglossia that constitutes its historical evolution.

Theophilos Voreas, professor of philosophy at the University of Athens toward the end of the nineteenth century, is generally recognized as the father of a rigorous policy in the creation of philosophical terminology in modern Greek. Despite his attempt, there is still major variation in the translations into modern from ancient Greek. The teaching of the latter in schools and the domination into the 1970s of an archaist language, Katharevousa, which literally means "purified," hid these difficulties for a long time. Despite the upheaval of syntax between ancient and modern Greek, it seemed that it was enough to use the ancient terms to believe one had a clear idea of what was in question. Intuition and translation are not the same thing, however; the increasing use of the demotic language, beginning in the middle of the twentieth century, made manifest the imprecision in modern uses of ancient philosophical terms and the modifications these had suffered owing to successive translations, as well as to the mediation of other European languages. While it is true that a translator can always resolve difficulties by simply going back to the ancient terms (which is often done), this practice only defers the problem of meaning. The proliferation of translations into modern Greek of the ancient texts written in Greek or Latin, as well as that of modern texts written in other languages, makes it possible to gain a better understanding of the scope of the shifts and the misunderstandings they may cause.

NOTE: For convenience, I have chosen the Erasmian pronunciation for ancient Greek (including for *koinê*), and I have opted for iotacism (generally, the use of "i" for ι, η, ει, οι, υι) for modern Greek—though I have relied on "y" for υ and on "o" for o and ω. For the accents, I have adopted the varied usage of the authors themselves, some adopting ancient accentuation, others simplifying, and still others suppressing the breathings and accents on the monosyllables, but accepting a tonic accent for the rest. Finally, the simplification of current grammar replaces the ancient third declension with the first, which is accepted in Katharevousa; thus, for σκέψις, we write σκέψη. Furthermore, even though current grammar has suppressed the ancient infinitive, it is nevertheless preserved in an idiomatic fashion: we speak of becoming (*to gignesthai* [το γίγνεσθαι]), thinking (*to noein, to phronein, to skepsasthai* [το νοείν, το φρονείν, το σκέπτεσθαι]), and so on. Finally, I have constantly relied on Babiniotis's RT: *Lexiko tês neas Hellênikês glôssas* (Dictionary of the modern Greek language) as a guide.

I. The Historical Context

A. The evolution of Greek

The unity of Greek, since the archaic world, is a phenomenon that never ceases to amaze those who examine it. Recent studies show that this unity goes back to the Mycenean period and has adapted to the specific changes of the evolution of any language. However, Greek has undergone serious crises, especially when attempts have been made to restore an older language or establish a nobler one, with claims that the current language, produced by an evolution marked by cultural integration, has become impoverished.

We find this phenomenon in Russian, for example—where Ferguson distinguishes "diglossia" (the same language containing a vulgar and a noble language) from "bilingualism" or "multilingualism" (the copresence of two or more national languages in the same country). "Diglossia" in modern Greece is considerable, to the point of making it difficult, or even impossible, to translate certain terms from ancient and medieval Greek.

The unity of Greek was acquired piecemeal: first, through the shift from a syllabic linguistic system (the writing called Linear B) to an alphabetical system (inherited from the Phoenicians, who may themselves have gotten it from the Greeks); then, in agreement with a variety of related dialects that clearly did not impede communication; and finally, thanks to the political evolution of archaic Greece, which contributed to the arrival of Hellenic wisdom. From the philosophical point of view, it is this last stage that is essential, since a terminology was built on it that made the progressive creation of a philosophical language possible.

The distribution of cities around cultural and ritual centers such as Delphi and Delos may explain why this first unitary structure of the language had such historical dynamism. These centers radiated in a sphere that was delimited by the colonial extension of the different cities, promoting the constitution of a common world. This type of topology guaranteed Greek a kind of unity, contrasting with the dispersion described in the biblical episode of Babel. In the Hellenic space, even when political actions involve mobility (as in the Trojan War or Ulysses's adventures), the center of reference remains circumscribed by the contours of a fixed territoriality. The Homeric epics and the Hesiodic genealogies constitute a mythical testimony of the formation of a topological unity that assigns Greek its historical rootedness, and attest as well to Greek's status as a lasting reference point for education and culture (see BILDUNG, Box 1), as factors unifying a common world.

These breaks become more pronounced in the classical period. The Attic language, symbol of the Athenian city, animated by democratic structures and a dominant politicoeconomic will, is the product of a break with dialectal practice. The expansion of philosophy owes much to Attic, which consolidated philosophical terminology according to the norms imposed by Athenian philosophy—the Academy, the Lyceum, the Garden, and so on. The adoption of Attic by the Macedonian court, when it concludes the political unification of Greece, is not unrelated to the rapid evolution of Greek into a "common" (*koinê*) language. This language spread throughout Alexander's empire, beyond the Hellenic space. Cosmopolitanism thus favors the banalization of *koinê*, which contributes to the persistence of Greek in the Roman Empire before the domination of Latin (starting in the second century BCE in administration and after the fourth century CE in the cultural sphere). Having become a *lingua franca*, Greek achieved a communicational proximity and produced a civilizing impact without precedence in Europe, imposing Hellenic culture on the whole Mediterranean region.

■ See Box 1.

B. The vagaries of diglossia

The synchronic unity of diverse dialects, to which were added, first, the diachronic unity of Attic, then the more active unity of *koinê*, did not prevent linguistic crises. These concern the deliberate choice of the type of language that could best express Greek in its historical authenticity. It is in

1

Athens, or the homophony of the world

Aelius Aristides (117–189 CE), a Greek from Mysia and a Roman citizen living in the empire, wrote a praise of Rome (*Roman Oration*) and a praise of Athens (*Panathenaicos*), which together are the most extreme praise of the Greek language and a testament to its role in the empire.

For Rome, the world is no longer divided into "Greeks" and "barbarians," since "Roman" became "the name of a sort of common race" (*Roman Oration*, paragraph 63), and the whole ecumene is spatially accessible and "tamed" (101). But while Rome is all-powerful, it is monodic. "Like a well-cleaned enclosure, the inhabited world pronounces a single sound, more precise than that of a chorus" (30); we should even say that it is mute: on the model of the army, an "eternal

chorus" (87), "everything obeys in silence" (31).

Athens presents the reverse model: rather than extending, it is the "center of the center" (*Panathenaicos*, paragraph 15), which offers "an unmixed, pure language [*elikrinê de kai katharan . . . phônên,* as the Katharevousa aims to be], without anything disturbing it, a paradigm of any Greek conversation" (14). Here, the universality is no longer territorial but logical; in Attic, idiom, language, and speech all merge: "All without exception speak the single common language of the race [*tou genous*; see PEOPLE], and through you [i.e., the Athenians] the whole universe has become homophone" (226). Greek, the "definition and criterion of education and culture [*horos tina*

paideias; see BILDUNG]" (227), is the language of sharing, appropriate for public life—to the extent that there can still be one, under Rome.

Barbara Cassin

BIBLIOGRAPHY

Aristides, Aelius. *Panathenaicos* and *Roman Oration*. In *Aristides in Four Volumes*, translated by Charles Allison Behr. Cambridge, MA: Harvard University Press, 1973.
Oliver, James H. "The Civilizing Power." *Transactions of the American Philosophical Society*, n.s., 58, no. 1 (1968).
———. "The Ruling Power." *Transactions of the American Philosophical Society*, n.s., 43, no. 4 (1953).

this context that we may speak of linguistic conflicts peculiar to diglossia.

The first conflict took place, in antiquity, in the name of the defense of Attic against the universalization of Greek, which was interpreted as implying the language's banalization and its integration into different cultural contexts. In this turbulent history, the most significant event is the translation of the Hebrew Bible into Greek, in Alexandria around the third century BCE. By adapting to the "common" language, the Judaic message was spread more easily.

- See Box 2.

Inversely, the reactions in response to the hegemony of *koinê* Greek based their arguments on history itself, endowing the language with an ideological background. In the Hellenistic period, resistance animated by nostalgia gave rise to "Atticism"—a purified and quasi-artificial language, practiced by erudite people and philosophers. Atticism was imposed at the expense of the natural evolution of the language and its dialects, thenceforth establishing two languages, one for intellectuals and one for the people. Thus the problem of diglossia was born in antiquity, and its ideological background has been at work unceasingly within Greek culture ever since.

Much later, in the ninth century, a second major conflict arose over the status of modern Greek. It is likely that the substitution of Latin for Greek in the West and the pressure of the multilingualism of the empire, arising from Roman conquests, led to the fragmentation of *koinê* into several dialects. The Hellenization of the Eastern Empire, which preserves Atticism with few modifications until the Byzantine Renaissance of the eleventh and twelfth centuries, undoubtedly served to slow down the pace of this fragmentation, but it never managed to weaken Greek's diglossia, which was encouraged by the increasingly hierarchical shape the state and the church acquired beginning in the fourth century. Written and administrative language reveals a difference

both of class and culture. During Ottoman domination, new transformations came up against the need to preserve the ecclesiastical language, since the only organized institution was that of the church. During this period, then, not only Atticism but also *koinê* became incomprehensible to people under the pressure of the evolution of the spoken language in a more popular direction, slowly forming what was called the "demotic" language. Knowing all of these languages at once was considered a feat and indicated a higher level of culture.

However, it is not in the regions occupied by the Ottomans, covering the multiethnic collection of the Balkans, that Greek's diglossia displayed its perverse effects, since the clergy spreading the language and the faith was generally little educated and sided with spoken and popular speech. It is rather in the Hellenic schools of Italy, where an archaist language was being taught, that we see the source of the purified language (Katharevousa). By disturbing the natural evolution of the language, the purists initiated a proliferation of debates that were only solved in the second half of the twentieth century (1976), when the Greek government, faced with the excesses of the purified language imposed by the regime of the colonels (1967), decided to install the spoken language as the only official one by a unanimous vote in the parliament.

- See Box 3.

C. The philosophical context of Hellenic modernity

Philosophy was born speaking Greek, which for at least a millennium was its only language. We may add to this another millennium, for while in the West, the hegemony of Greek disappeared in the Roman period, Latin-speaking philosophers continued to use it until the beginning of the Middle Ages. This is a unique phenomenon, implying that there is a "historical" link between a particular language, Greek, and the birth and development of philosophy. Indeed, it is said,

2

Greek, the sacred language

➤ TO TRANSLATE

The Jews of Alexandria, organized in a *politeuma*, spoke Greek and undertook the translation of the Hebrew Bible into Greek beginning in the third century BCE. It is by way of a piece of propaganda coming out of this milieu of Hellenized Jews in Alexandria, the *Letter of Aristeas*, that the legend of the so-called Septuagint translation was disseminated. According to the letter, King Ptolemy II Philadelphus (285–247 BCE) commissioned seventy-two (or seventy) Jewish scholars, sent to Alexandria for the purpose by the high priest of Jerusalem, to translate the Pentateuch into Greek, for the needs of Greek-speaking Jews in Egypt. Each of the translators supposedly worked separately, and they all produced miraculously identical versions. This was the first translation of the sacred Hebrew texts into a Western language and in all likelihood the first collective translation known. The legend of these uniform translations, attributed to divine inspiration, leads paradoxically to the negation of the Septuagint as a product of translation and to the authentication of the translated text as completely homologous to the original. The audience for the translation, encouraged by the legend, came to obscure the Hebrew origins of the translated books and played a decisive role in the process of Hellenization of Jewish monotheism. Further, while rabbinical Judaism, especially beginning with the destruction of the second temple in 70 CE, was hostile to the translation, it was adopted by the authors of the Christian scriptures, and until Saint Jerome, by almost all Christian communities. Thus the Greek version of the Septuagint became the Mediterranean Bible for the more and more Hellenized Jews, and then of the early church, which made it its Old Testament in all the regions of the empire where it spread, until Western Europe opted for Latin.

Cécile Margellos

3

Demotiki and Katharevousa

To understand the contrast between *demotiki* and Katharevousa, we must give some of the cultural context that laid the foundations for the 1821 Greek war of independence against the Ottoman Empire. Several intellectuals, including Adamantios Koraïs, who lived in France, promoted the idea of a return to the past and felt the need for a new language that was adapted to teaching and more authentic than the vulgar language. Was it necessary to return to ancient Greek, or create a purified language, called, for this reason, Katharevousa? The first option was received unenthusiastically, so that although classical antiquity was still idealized, the second option was the one adopted. Koraïs had insisted on the role of language in the formation of a new Greece, affirming that the character of a nation is recognized by its language. For him, ancient Greece had joined liberty and pure language, whereas Ottoman domination favored an impure language. Henceforth, only the knowledge of ancestral texts would be capable of purifying the language of foreign elements. Paradoxically, this partisan of the Enlightenment initiated an ideology of pure language that would have negative effects on philosophy in Greece, thenceforth tributary to the discourse of others, whether modern or European, creators of new thoughts at the time when the Greeks remained under the Ottomans. Once officially recognized, this language was adopted in the universities, especially for the teaching of philosophy.

The defense of a demotic language in science came rather late. It can be attributed to Greeks living in the diaspora in the nineteenth century—in Paris (Psicharis), in England and the Indies (Pallis, Emphaliotis), as well as in Istanbul (Vlastos) and Bucharest (Photiadis). The result of this struggle was the formation of an educational association, in 1910, that fought for the adoption of the demotic as the official language. Meanwhile, however, the translation of the Bible and some ancient tragedies into demotic provoked an outcry and a political debate. The project failed under the pressure of partisans of Katharevousa, led by G. Mistriotis, professor at the University of Athens, who spoke of the need to save the "national language." A vote in the parliament in 1911 provisionally closed debate, despite a liberal government directed by E. Vénizelos, who was sympathetic to the innovators. An article of the Greek constitution forbade the official use of the demotic language, ignoring its place in daily life.

But when, in 1945, Charálampos Theodoridis wrote his *Introduction to Philosophy* in demotic, the book was highly successful. Philosophers continued to hesitate about the choice of language, until the government established demotic as the only official language of the Greek republic in 1976. Six years later, an association for the Greek language published a manifesto signed by seven well-known personalities—including Odysseas Elytis, winner of the Nobel Prize in literature, and Georgios Babiniotis, the most gifted linguist of the time—criticizing the legal establishment of the language, seeing in it a linguistic and expressive constraint likely to destroy "the foundations of the freedom of thought" in the name of an "artificial" demotic established by self-described "modernists." Reactions followed, reopening a debate that was believed closed, and whose tangible result was the retention by some writers of "breathing marks" and accents suppressed by the most recent version of demotic, and the use of a language that avoids what some consider the "mistakes" of modern Greek.

BIBLIOGRAPHY

Browning, Robert. *Medieval and Modern Greek*. 2nd ed. Cambridge: Cambridge University Press, 1983.

Christidis, A. F. [Anastasios Phoebus], ed. *"Strong" and "Weak" Languages in the European Union: Aspects of Linguistic Hegemonism*. 2 vols. Thessaloniki: Center for the Greek Language, 1999.

Ferguson, Charles A. "Diglossia." *Word* 15 (1959): 325–40.

Fishman, Joshua. "Bilingualism with and without Diglossia; Diglossia with and without Bilingualism." *Journal of Social Issues* 32 (1976): 29–38.

Georgakopoulou, Alexandra, and Michael Silk, eds. *Standard Languages and Language Standards: Greek, Past and Present*. Farnham, UK: Ashgate, 2009.

Kopidakês, M. Z. *Historia tês hellênikês glôssas* [History of the Greek language]. Athens: Greek Literature and History Archive, 1999.

Lamprakê-Paganou, Alexandra, and Giôrgos D. Paganos. *O ekpaideutikos demotikismos kai o Kostis Palamas*. [*Teaching the demotic language and Kostis Palamas*]. Athens: Pataki, 1994.

Mackridge, Peter. *Language and National Identity in Greece, 1766–1976*. Oxford: Oxford University Press, 2009.

Moleas, Wendy. *The Development of the Greek Language*. 2nd ed. Bristol, UK: Bristol Classical Press, 2004.

Theodoridis, Charálampos. *Introduction to Philosophy* (in Greek). Athens: Éditions du Jardin, 1945.

under Heidegger's influence, that Greek (with which German is associated) is the philosophical language par excellence.

- See Box 4.

Without rejecting this rather dated view, now shaken up by the worldwide expansion of Anglo-American philosophy, we must admit that Greek, though it has persevered, has not managed to preserve the fertility of the philosophical past that it helped shape, even in the space it rules. The program begun several decades ago in Greece of promoting modern and contemporary Greek philosophers is revealing: their fame can rarely, in current conditions, extend beyond the boundaries of Hellenism.

To explain this shortcoming, it is common to invoke the fall of Byzantium and the rule of Greek-speaking lands by the Ottoman Empire. According to this explanation, the Ottoman Empire comprised four hundred years during which, in the extensive territory populated by people of Greek origin (stretching from Moldova to current Greece and from Asia Minor to the coast of the Black Sea), a complete intellectual desert supposedly lay. The local populations, thanks to the Church and some teachers attempting to preserve Greek, were most often reduced to speaking the popular language. On the other hand, the intellectuals who sought refuge on the Ionian islands that had escaped the Ottomans, or in Italy, were perceived as a source of hope for the future of an independent Greece.

During this period, philosophical texts were sometimes written in Latin and often in an archaist form of Greek, more rarely in simple Greek. They are mostly commentaries on ancient thought, especially Aristotle, who was in fashion in Padua and Venice. Theophilos Korydaleus (d. 1646), who reorganized the patriarchal School of Constantinople, may be considered with Gerasimos Vlachos (d. 1685) to be the pioneer of modern Greek commentary on the works of Aristotle.

Aristotle's presence in the Balkans became a major element of the renewal of ancient philosophy in Greek-speaking space, linking up with the beginning of the Ottoman period when Gennadius II Scholarios, the first patriarch after the fall of Constantinople, established Aristotelianism over against Gemistus Plethon's Platonism.

In the following period, Neohellenic philosophy—essentially that practiced in universities—spoke Katharevousa: a language that brought it closer to its prestigious past, even though that past was read in the light of the European philosophies in fashion at the time. A friend of Adamantios Koraïs, Neophytos Vamvas (d. 1855), took up both the "ideology" of Destutt de Tracy and of F. Thurot, and the rhetoric of H. Blair, which dominated the British landscape of the eighteenth century. He was the first to occupy the chair of philosophy at the University of Athens (1837). T. Reid and D. Steward, through their translations, also had their hour of glory among French-speaking Greek philosophers, alongside the spiritualists V. Cousin and T. Jouffroy, who were ascendant for a time. In another domain of thought, C. Koumas (d. 1836) defended critical philosophy, initiating the more and more active presence of German philosophy in Greece, which in turn intensified the introduction of ancient philosophy in teaching. Thus, the cult of antiquity, illuminated by the lights of European philosophy, became the motive element of the intellectual renewal of modern Greece. In contrast, Greek-Christian ideology remained the permanent point of reference for conservative philosophers in Greece.

At the same time, the social crises opened the way for socialist thought, with Platon Drakoulis and Georgios Skliros (d. 1919). The latter's claims were taken up in turn by J. Kordatos and Dimitrios Glenos, another philosopher trained in Germany, where he participated in debates in favor of the demotic language. On the philosophical level, Glenos opposed to the dynamic idealism of the Hegelian school what he called "dynamic

---

4

Heidegger: "The prephilosophical language of the Greeks was already philosophical"

Let us agree with Jean-Pierre Lefebvre: the way in which Heidegger thinks about the complex historical relationship between Greek, German, and philosophy constitutes "ontological nationalism."

Ousia tou ontos means in translation: The beingness of beings [*Seiendheit des Seienden*]. We say, on the other hand: The being of beings [*Sein des Seienden*]. "Beingness" is a very unusual and *artificial* linguistic form that occurs only in the sphere of philosophical reflection. We cannot say this, however, of the corresponding Greek word. *Ousia* is not an artificial expression which first occurs in philosophy, but belongs to the everyday language and speech of the Greeks.

Philosophy took up the word from its pre-philosophical usage. If this could happen so easily, and with no artificiality, then we must conclude that the *pre-philosophical* language of the Greeks was already *philosophical*. This is actually the case. The history of the basic word of Greek philosophy is an exemplary demonstration of the fact that the *Greek language is philosophical*, i.e., not that Greek is loaded with philosophical terminology, but that it philosophizes in its basic structure and formation. The same applies to every genuine language, in different degrees to be sure. The extent to which this is so depends on the depth and power of the people who speak the language and exist

within it. Only our German language has a deep and creative philosophical character to compare with the Greek.

(Heidegger, *The Essence of Human Freedom*)

Barbara Cassin

BIBLIOGRAPHY

Heidegger, Martin. *The Essence of Human Freedom: An Introduction to Philosophy*. Translated by Ted Sadler. New York: Continuum, 2002.

Lefebvre, Jean-Pierre. "Philosophie et philologie: Les traductions des philosophes allemands." In *Encyclopædia universalis*. Vol. 1, *Symposium: Les enjeux*. Paris: Encyclopaedia universalis France, 1990.

realism," that is, dialectical materialism interpreted by means of a synthesis between Democritus and Heraclitus. For him, any reference to the Greek philosophical past entailed a creative historicity that is able to appropriate it in the context of the concrete givens of contemporary life. Glenos was a subtle analyst of social divisions, which he interprets as the result of diglossia. After him, we must wait until the reform that was urged, between 1950 and 1960, by another German-trained philosopher, E. P. Papanoutsos, to witness the modernization of philosophy in education.

Finally, philosophy is expressed above all in literature, where several authors had already written in demotic. The great poet Kostis Palamas (1859–1943) brought literature and philosophy together in the light of Nietzsche. In his wake, but also in those of Bergson (whose student he was) and Marx, Nikos Kazantzakis (1883–1957) was a fervent defender of *demotiki*, which he enriched with powerful and original work. The real philosophical revolution in modern Greece is thus found, not in pure philosophy, but in literature. Greek literature, a generator of thought, uses new forms to rehearse the origins of Greek thought, when, with Parmenides, Empedocles, and Plato, literature and philosophy were not distinguished from one another. Writers are thus the ones who defended the demotic language against the Katharevousa of academic philosophers.

II. Translating Greek into Greek?

A. *Logos* and *orthologiko*

Since ancient times, the multivocity of the term *logos* is the most spectacular sign of the permanence of the Greek language. Its ambivalence, which mainly conjoins the senses of "speech" and "reason," requires a constant reliance on context, which is sometimes still insufficient to clarify the word's meaning. Yet, while the understanding of *logos* as "word" or "speech" remains intact in modern Greek, it is not so with the senses of "gathering together" and "reason." (We will not pause to consider the first of these, since, occluded in most dictionaries though used by some philosophers inspired by Heidegger, it would require a lengthy study in its own right.)

To say "reason," modern Greek relies, much more than on *logos*, on the semantics of thought (*noisi* [νόηση], *skepsi* [σκέψη]). There are nevertheless vestiges of what may have been the term's ancient semantic core: "what is the reason for your position . . . " (ποιος ο λόγος . . .), "I have no reason to . . . " (δεν έχω λόγο να . . .). However, instead of using *logos* to say "reason" in the sense of *ratio*, modern Greek speaks rather, by inflection, of "what is rational" or of "the logical" (*logiko* [λογικό]). It is from the expression *orthos logos* [ορθός λόγος], "right or straight reason," that we take "rational" and "rationalism," forming the portmanteau words *orthologiko* [ορθολογικό] and *orthologismos* [ορθολογισμός], respectively. We can understand why, given this situation of deficiency and complementation, philosophers prefer to keep the old word, even if the dictionary avoids it. In his translation into modern Greek of Jacques Derrida's essay "Plato's Pharmacy," Lazos writes that "Derrida mainly uses the words *discours*, *parole*, *raison*, or *logos* to translate λόγος. In Greek, *logos* has all these meanings. Thus I translate all these words with the word *logos* and place the corresponding French term in parentheses." In sum, even when he preserves the term *logos*, a Greek today must clarify in parentheses which sense he is using. Moreover, the sense of "reason" is exceptional and is identified with "cause," or, when referring to something "rational," paired with *orthos*: *orthos logos*. This transgression of the modern dictionary is found in other translators, who use *logos* to refer to the Stoic divine (Reason), to the second person of the Christian Trinity (Word), to seminal reason—these are therefore calques rather than translations—as well as to Kant's pure reason. The confusion of these translators is such that they sometimes use *logos* while adding, in parentheses, *logikos* [λογικός] (rational), or, inversely, that they use *logos* for all contentious cases that concern thought (cf. Y. Tzavaras in Plotinus, *Enneads*, 30–33). As a result: either we keep *logos* without translating it, or we translate it by "reasoning," "constitutive power," "logical capacity," "notion," "rationality," "discussion," and so forth, but leaving a fringe of untranslatability.

To get a grip on this situation, Babiniotis draws up, in his *Dictionary*, a table for the word *logikos* [λογικός] (rational, logical), considering how best to express *logos* in the sense of "reason." He explains that "the λογικός (rational) refers to what is related to λόγος, in the sense of the functioning of the intellect (νου), the discursive thought (διάνοιας), the logical thought (λογικής νόησης) of man." Then, having articulated the word's sense by means of contrasts with the irrational, the insane, and so on, Babiniotis appeals to the semantic range attached to the faculty of thinking in the sense of *phrenes* [φρένες], to place in relief the proper character of someone who acts rationally (*emphron*) [έμφρων] or irrationally (*aphron* [άφρων], *paraphron* [παράφρων]). These clarifications confirm that the notion of *logos* [λόγος], "reason," is manifested above all by a derived form, *logikos*, itself clarified by the varied semantics of thinking and thought.

In the face of the texts of ancient philosophy, a Greek-speaker is just as helpless as a French- or English-speaker. Even more so, perhaps, since he or she is tempted to set aside the difficulty by not translating at all, rather than to admit the limits of his or her language.

B. *Skepsis* and the field of thought

To translate "think" and "thought" in ancient Greek, we use, on the one hand, the semantics of the "intellect" (*noos* [νόος], *noys* [νοῦς], *nous*)—to apprehend (*noein* [νοεῖν]), intellection (*noisis* [νόησις]), to think discursively (διανοεῖσθαι), discursive thought (*dianoia* [διάνοια])—and, on the other, that of the "mind" (*phrin* [φρήν])—to think sensibly, in conformity with good sense (*phrono* [φρονῶ]), practical intelligence (*phronisis* [φρόνησις]), and so forth. Later, the notion of "spirit" (*pneuma* [πνεῦμα]) is added, introduced by Stoicism in the sense of "breath" (wind and breath of life); Christianity dematerializes *pneuma* and thus ensures for the term an impressive promotion into more transcendental realms. Although this evolution complicates the project of translation, current confusions are due less to language than to choices that, rather than retaining the usual sense of "intellect," confuse *nous* with "spirit," "wit," "intelligence," as Pierre Hadot does in his translations of Plotinus (cf. his justification in *Enneads*, 38). Such hesitations are also found among

Greeks, when they refer to Le Seene and Lavelle's philosophy of mind by the expression "philosophy of νοῦς" and not *pneuma* [πνεῦμα] (cf. Charálampos Theodoridis, *Introduction to Philosophy*).

But the fact that in modern Greek the ancient terminologies of thought (*noêsis* [νόησις]) and reflection (*skepsis* [σκέψις]) have been fused together leads to more palpable difficulties. *Skepsis*, a concept discussed by the Skeptical school, leads to paradoxes in modern texts, when we speak, for example, of "the thought of the Skeptics"(η σκέψη των σκεπτικών) or the "thinkers of reflection" (ή των στοχαστών της σκέψης). An analogous fusion took place with the semantics of the activity of contemplating (*stochazomai* [στοχάζομαι]). Whereas in antiquity, *stochazomai* means "to aim," "tend toward," or even "to seek" and "to conjecture," in modern Greek it means both the common activity of reflecting as well as the more elevating one of thinking, "meditation" (*stochasmos* [στοχασμός]). In the literature of the nineteenth and twentieth centuries (Solomos [1798–1857] to Palamas [1859–1943]), *stochazomai* is used to indicate thought—whence the use of *stochastis* [στοχαστής] to mean "thinker." In addition, the activity of reasoning and calculating (*logizomai* [λογίζομαι], *ypologizo* [υπολογίζω], *logariazo* [λογαριάζω]) is often confused with the activity of thinking (*skeptomai* [σκέπτομαι]) as well.

Although contemporary Greek translators and philosophers are trammeled by these different inflections of key philosophical terms, they do not confront them as problems. To avoid semantic confusion, they often prefer to keep the ancient terms, although, in common language, the semantics of *skeptesthai* and *skepsis* (for instance) have dominated since the middle of the twentieth century. The junction between ancient and modern Greek occurs at *nous* [νοῦς] (or νους), which expresses the seat of thought, while giving the impression of preserving the ancient sense of "intellect." Although the term was most often used in compound expressions meaning "to have in mind," "to keep one's head," "to be sensible," and so on, it has a general and encompassing sense that goes beyond the archaic one of the noun "project" and the classical one of the highest faculty of thinking, "intuition." Babiniotis speaks of the "collection of spiritual faculties [πνευματικών δυνάμεων] of man, allowing him to apprehend reality and articulate its data." This generalization reveals that we may associate *nous* [νους] with other activities, such as judging (*krino* [κρίνω]), imagining (*phantazomai* [φαντάζομαι]), reasoning (*sullogizomai* [συλλογίζομαι]), reflecting (*skeptomai* [σκέπτομαι]), or meditating (*stochazomai* [στοχάζομαι]). In the latter case, Solomos writes in his dialogue on language: "Come to your [faculty] of thought [τὸνοῦ], contemplate [στοχάσου] the evil produced by written language."

Matters become complicated once we get to the semantics of the word *skepsis*, which is used to clarify the senses of the other terms meaning "to think" and "thought." For *stochazomai* [στοχάζομαι], the *Dictionary* mentions: (1) "I think deeply" (*skeptomai vathia* [σκέπτομαι βαθιά]), "I think discursively" (*dianooumai* [διανοούμαι]); (2) "I think well" (*skeptomai kala* [σκέπτομαι καλά]), with as synonyms "I calculate" (*ypologizo* [υπολογίζω], *logariazo* [λογαριάζω]). The same goes for the other sense of νους: "capacity for someone to think (να σκέπτεται), to produce logical thoughts (σκέψεις), to create in a spiritual way; . . . to judge according to the circumstances," and so forth. This predominance of the semantics of *skeptomai* [σκέπτομαι] and *skepsis/skepsi* [σκέψις/ σκέψη] is the more troubling in not always having been the case: thus, in his *Philosophy of the Renaissance*, Logothetis, a defender of Katharevousa in philosophy, limits the semantics of *skepsis* to specifically Skeptical schools of thought (Montaigne, Charron), associated with *skepsis* and *amphivolia* (doubt), and uses the semantics of *nous* to refer to "thought" and that of *logos* to mean "reason."

With regard to σκέψη, Babiniotis speaks of the "collection of points of view and positions someone holds regarding a social phenomenon, a way of analyzing it and interpreting it; theory," preceding this sense by others such as "process during which we manipulate certain data in our brains, to end up with a result"; or again, "what someone thinks (σκέπτεται) of an affair; idea, reasoning." The duality of the general sense, which brings in both social action and theory (understood as "vision of the world"), widens the domain of action of *skepsis*. If we add to *skeptomai* the sense of reasoning and meditating, we realize that the term has become untranslatable.

We should observe that the semantics of *nous* [νοῦς] has never, since Parmenides's time, replaced fully the semantics of *skepsis*, used since Homer—well before the Skeptics gave the term its philosophical destiny and well before it conquered modern Greek in claiming for itself the sense of "thought." In Homer, *skeptomai* means to look in all directions in order to observe. Ulysses says: "I happened to glance aft (*skepsamenos* [σκεψάμενος]) at ship and oarsmen and caught sight of their arms and legs, dangling high overhead. Voices came down to me in anguish, calling my name for the last time" (*Odyssey*, 12.244–49). This sense of looking attentively in several directions leads to a sense of what one might call "looking at by means of thought," of thinking on the basis of at least two possibilities. For example, in Sophocles, the verb sometimes means "to look at" or "to see" (*Ajax*, 1028) and sometimes "to reflect" or "to think through" (*Oedipus Rex*, 584). In the second case, Creon responds to Oedipus's accusations: "Think [*skepsai* (σκέψαι)] first about this: other things being equal, do you find the cares of power preferable to a rest which nothing disturbs?" We find the same ambivalence in Plato's texts. In the *Protagoras*, Socrates says that the examination of health requires observation of the parts of the body and adds that he desires, in the interest of reflection [*pros tên skepsin* (πρὸς τὴν σκέψιν)], to do the same thing for the pleasant and the good, in order to reveal the thought [*tês dianoias* (τῆς διανοίας)] of his interlocutor and see if his conception is similar to or different from that of most men (352a–b). This last specification isolates the pre-Skeptical sense of *skepsis*: it is a reflection that presents a choice between two or more positions.

The Skeptics reject this choice, giving the same weight to each position and suspending all judgment as a result (see EPOCHÊ). *Skepsis* differs from *dianoia* [διάνοια] (discursive thought), analyzed as identical to "intention." In modern Greek, when we clarify the sense of *dianoia*—which is used most often to mean inventiveness or genius, however—we speak of the "functioning of thought (σκέψης) which codifies sense data in concepts and representations" (Babiniotis).

Everything works as though in modern Greek, *skepsis* and *skeptomai* were the genus of which noetic and discursive thought were the species. This extensive character of *skepsis* is explained by the fact that the process of reflection may intervene in action, alongside "deliberation." The Skeptics exploited this perspective, whereas Plato avoided combining these elements.

To the question "what is scepticism (*skepsis*)?," Sextus Empiricus responds: it is "an ability to set out oppositions among things which appear and are thought of (*ta nooumena*) in any way at all, an ability by which, because of the equipollence in the opposed objects and accounts, we come first to suspension of judgment and afterwards to tranquility" (*Outlines of Scepticism*, 1.8). If the Skeptic supposes that, as a result of the equality of the two sides of an argument, no reasoning may be more persuasive than its opposite or any other, he envisages, thanks to the suspension of judgment, the arrest of discursive thought (*dianoia*), thus also of seeking and deliberation. This approach entangles theory with action, inasmuch as it must take account of all possible directions—with a consequent modification of the semantic landscape of the ancient language. As a result, another path is opened, from which modern Greek derives its own concepts, requiring us to negotiate an intralinguistic translation for a whole collection of past philosophical notions.

The semantic modifications of modern Greek also concern other uses, for example, the use of "brain" or "brains" to refer to the collection of mental faculties, as a synonym of "spirit" (*pneuma*) and "thought." Even more than in French, the metaphor of the brain expresses "human thought" (*anthroponi skepsi* [ανθρώπινη σκέψη]) in Greek—so much so that E. Roussos, translator of the fragments of Heraclitus (*Peri physeos*), renders *tis autôn noos* [τίς αὐτῶν νόος] (fr. 104 DK) first by "what is their brain/thought [το μυαλό]?" and then by "thought" [ὁ νοῦς], whereas K. P. Mihailidis (*Philosophes archaïques*), more prudently, translates *noos* by *nous*. In agreement with other translators, the latter acts with the same prudence when he translates *nous* [νοῦς] and *noein* [νοεῖν] in Parmenides, whereas Roussos once again innovates by translating *noein* by *to na to ennois* [τό νά τό ἐννοεῖς], that is, "I apprehend the meaning" [ἔχω στο νου μον, or again, συλλ αμβάνω στη σκέψη μου]. Further, in his philosophy manual for students, P. Roulia observes that Parmenides "found in thought (σκέψη) the stability necessary for knowledge. However, he was led to identify thought (σκέψη) and reality." And his celebrated statement (fr. 3 DK, τὸ γὰρ αὐτὸ νοεῖν τεκαὶ εἶναι) means: "When we think (σκεφτόμαστε), we determine things (νου) with our intellect. Our thought (νόηση) thus is identified with reality. Reality is as a consequence intelligible (νοητή)." Roulia worries at this point whether students will clearly understand what is at issue here, where three processes may be confused: reflecting, thinking, and apprehending—but many philosophers are in the same position.

Tzavaras, who is currently the most inventive translator working in the field of ancient Greek philosophy, often reserves the ancient Greek for the pre-Socratics, but he takes more chances when translating Plotinus and the German thinkers. As to the first, in his anthology of several texts of the *Enneads* (30–33), he opts in favor of *skeptomai* to translate *phronô*, *noô*, and *dianooûmai*. For example, "They are as good as gods, insofar as they do not think (δενσνέπτονται) sometimes correctly and sometimes wrongly, but think (σνέπτονται) always what is correct in their intellect (μέσα στο νου τους)" (5.8.3.23–25: καλοὶ δὲ ἤθεοί. οὐ γὰρ δὴ ποτὲ μὲν φρονοῦσι, ποτὲ δὲ ἀφραίνουσιν, ἀλλ' ἀεὶ φρονοῦσιν ἐν ἀπαθεῖ τῷ νῷ). Further, even though he has a tendency to preserve the terms *dianoia* and *noêsis*, he sometimes translates "the thoughts" (*hai noêseis* [αἱ νοήσεις]) by "the thoughts of the intellect" (*skepsis tou nou* [σκέψεις του νου]) (5.5.1.24). Additionally, although he translates *voûs voôn* by νοώνν ους, he suddenly changes direction and translates: "however, when you think it (ὅταν ὅμως τον σκέπ τεσαι) . . . , think (σκέψου) that it is a matter of the good, for as the productive cause of the reasonable (ἔλλογης) and intellective (νοητικής) life, it is a power of life and the intellect (νου)" (5.5.10.9–12: ὅταν δὲ νοῇς . . . , νόει τἀγαθόν—ζωῆς γὰρ ἔμφρονος καὶ νοερᾶς αἴτιος δύναμις ὢν [ἀφ' οὗ] ζωῆς καὶ νοῦ).

Given this situation, would not a reverse attitude, reducing all the semantics expressing "to think" and "thought" to that of *skepsis* and *skeptesthai*, have a better chance of expressing what is at issue? This option was taken up by Vayenas to translate some of Heidegger's texts from the *Wegmarken*, using *skepsis* for "thought" most of the time, regardless of the philosopher in question (Parmenides, Descartes, Kant, and Hegel). Parmenides's fragment 3, where it is said that "thinking and being are the same," now becomes: τὸ ἴδιο εἶναι σκέψη καὶ εἶναι. Regarding Kant, he specifies that "I think" (*skephtomai* [σκέφτομαι]) means: "I link up a given variety of representations" (which corresponds to "judge"). Further, he translates *tranzendentale Überlegung* or *Reflexion* by "reflection/transcendental thought" (*huperbatiki skepsi* [ὑπερβατικὴ σκέψη]), *Reflexion-begriffe* by "apprehensions of thought/reflection" (*antilipsis tis skepsis* [αντιλήψεις τῆς σκέψης]), and *Sein und Denken* by "to be and to think" or "Being and thinking" or "Being and Thought" (εἶναι καὶ σκέψη). The Hegelian usage of the Cartesian *ego cogito sum* is rendered as "I think, I am" (σνέπτομαι, εἶμαι)—which we also find in many other works, including high school philosophy manuals. Finally, the Heideggerian formula of "Western thought" is rendered by *dytiki skepsi* [δυτικὴ σκέψη], which resembles common expressions like "modern Greek thought," "socialist thought," whereas one could use *dianoisi* [διανόηση] and *stochasmos* [στοχασμός]. The massive presence in Vayenas's work of the semantics of *skepsis*, no doubt owing to his desire to conform to contemporary linguistic usage, accentuates the confusion and justifies the position of those who wish to return to a pre-Skeptical semantics. These vagaries show how difficult "thought" and its cognates are to translate into modern Greek, if only because the dominant translation by *skepsis* at bottom tends to mean "reflection" rather than "thought."

C. *Ousia, huparxis, hupostasis*: Essence and existence

At first sight, *ousia* [οὐσία] should not pose a problem in modern Greek, since it is commonly used today to indicate the essence and nature of something. However, the evolution of the sense of the term, beginning in antiquity, has greatly complicated the task of modern Greek philosophers. The meaning already shifted importantly between Plato and Aristotle, as the first conceives *ousia* in the common sense of "property" (material goods) and in the philosophical sense as the essence of something, whereas the latter adds other meanings, available and obligatory as a result of identifying *ousia* and *hupokeimenon* [ὑποκείμενον] (this identification requires him to designate by *ousia* sometimes the *eidos* [εἶδος], "form, species, or specificity"; sometimes the composite of matter and *eidos*; and sometimes matter itself). The Stoics in turn envisage *ousia* as an indeterminate substrate, whereas Medioplatonist and Neoplatonist thinkers return to the sense of "essence," and Christology assimilates *ousia* and *hupostasis* [ὑπόστασις], enriching *ousia* with other values, which modern Greek no longer commands.

In addition, the Latin translation of *ousia* by *substantia* creates problems for Greek translators, thenceforth confronted with new philosophies, coming from the Renaissance and modernity, where the notion of substance becomes central. Although they take this mediation more and more seriously, and translate "substance" not by *ousia* but by *hupostasi*, they are usually satisfied with standardizing *ousia* for antiquity and the Byzantine Middle Ages—by not translating it.

The problem arising from the pair "essence"/"existence" is thenceforth rendered very complex. Let us take Vikentios Damodos (d. 1752) as a guide. Trained in Aristotelianism in the Flaginian school in Venice and Padua, he was an adept of nominalism and was influenced by Descartes and Gassendi. He associates *ousia* and *huparxis* [ὕπαρξις] (existence), starting with the Thomist notion of "composite substance" constituted by essence (*essentia*) and being as existence (*esse*)—even though this is for him a conceptual and not, as it was for Aquinas, a real distinction. Damodos knows that in Thomism, the individual substance is not to be confused with the essence, since the latter must combine with being or existence to form substance. However, this distinction was constantly obscured by modern translators when they dealt with philosophies that give accounts of substance, from the Middle Ages to the Renaissance and the modern era. Logothetis, for example, translates *substantia* and *essentia* by *ousia*. He even magnifies the confusion by specifying that Nizzoli considers that *ousia* signifies particular things (*ta kath' hekaston* [τὰ καθ' ἕκαστον]). Tzavaras, aware of the difficulties, is the only one to have taken a different path, choosing in his anthology of texts of Plotinus to translate *ousia* by "to be" (*einai* [εἶναι]). These confusions in the use of a term as important as *ousia* reveal that the word is not only untranslatable in French or English (where it is rendered by "essence," "substance," "reality," "being"), but is equally so in Greek. Moreover, once medieval and modern mediation comes in, associating with *ousia* the notion of "substance" conceived by Thomism according to the unity of *essentia* and *esse* (and *existentia*), things get out of hand entirely.

Let us then start over, beginning this time from the verb *huparchein* [ὑπάρχειν]. It initially meant "to begin," "to be at the origin of," "to take the initiative"; then, "to exist prior to"; and then, "to be at the disposal of"; and finally, "to belong to." The latter sense is used in logic to express "attribution." Aristotle writes, for example, "If A is not attributed to any B, B will not be attributed to any A," or "If A is not an attribute of any B, then B will not be an attribute of any A" (εἰ . . . μηδενὶ τῷ Β τὸ Α ὑπάρχειν, οὐδὲ τῷ Α οὐδενὶ ὑπάρξει τὸ Β; *Prior Analytics* 1.2). The sense of "attribute" conceived

as a mode of belonging may be understood as "that which contributes to something," near the common usage "to be at the disposal of something or someone." It is in this sense that we use the expression *ta huparchonta* [τὰ ὑπάρχοντα]: *ta huparchonta* designates the present situation, existing things. This sense of the expression thus opens onto the question of existence. While in antiquity, the expression's ambivalence is the order of the day, the evolution of the language went in favor of simplification, to the advantage of the sense of "to exist."

This modern usage of *huparchein*, to mean the existence of something or other, had to confront in our own time the problem of translating *existence* as used in existentialism, which assigns existence only to humans. The very name of this school of thought already sets in contrast two terminologies: *huparxismos* [ὑπαρξισμός] and *existentialismos* [ἐξιστενσιαλισμός]. Today, the first expression is generally preferred to the calque. The name of a philosophical school is of course no more than a matter of convention, but the translation of the concept of existence itself reveals more tenacious difficulties. Thus, when Malevitsis translates, in 1970, Jean Wahl's book *Les philosophes de l'existence*, he chooses *hupostasis* [ὑπόστασις], and not *huparxis* [ὕπαρξις], to render *existence*. Malevitsis bases his decision on Heidegger's and Jasper's refusal to be identified as existentialists, and seeks to avoid the confusion between the ontic existence of beings and the existence proper to humankind. This is why he avoids the traditional translation by *huparxis*. The idea is important, for since antiquity, the semantics of *huparchein* has lost its secret complicity with the subtleties of the semantics of *archê/archô/archomai* (principle and beginning, foundation/I command/I begin). The term *hupostasis*, however, also has a long history, which is rooted in Neoplatonism and in Christology, reaching its culmination with the formation of the term *substantia* (substance). The interference with the question of "being" increased the opacity of its meaning to such an extent that even Malevitsis is forced to add the term *huparxis* in brackets to avoid confusion.

Thus, the analysis of the most important words in ancient philosophy can give no comfort to translators who believe in the transparency of meaning, even though they are Greek-speakers.

Lambros Couloubaritsis

BIBLIOGRAPHY

Alexiou, Margaret. *After Antiquity: Greek Language, Myth, and Metaphor*. Ithaca, NY: Cornell University Press, 2002.

Andriopoulos, Dêmêtrios Z. *Neo-Hellenic Aesthetic Theories*. Athens: Kabanas, 1975.

Apostolopoulos, Ntimês. *Syntomê historia tês neoellênikês philosophias* [Concise history of Neohellenic philosophy]. Athens: Hellêno-Gallike Enôsis Neôn, 1949.

Argyropoulou, Rôxanê, Athanasia Glykophrydi-Leontsini, Anna Kelesidou, and George Vlachos. *Hê ennoia tês eleutherias ston neoellêniko stochasmo* [The notion of liberty in Neohellenic thought]. Athens: Academy of Athens, 1996.

Beaton, Roderick, and David Ricks, eds. *The Making of Modern Greece: Nationalism, Romanticism, and the Uses of the Past (1797–1896)*. Farnham, UK: Ashgate, 2009.

Boudouris, Konstantine, ed. *Conceptions of Philosophy: Ancient and Modern*. Athens: Ionia, 2004.

Cassin, Barbara. "Le statut théorique de l'intraduisible." In *Encyclopédie philosophique universelle: Le discours philosophique*, edited by J.-F. Mattéi, 998–1013. Paris: Presses Universitaires de France, 1998.

Couloubaritsis, Lambros. *Aux origines de la philosophie européenne: De la pensée archaïque au néoplatonisme*. 3rd ed. Brussels: De Boeck University, 2000.

———. "Problématique sceptique d'un impensé: *Hè skepsis*." In *Le scepticisme antique: Perspectives historiques et systématiques*. Lausanne, Switz.: Revue de Théologie et de Philosophie, 1990.

Demos, Raphael. "The Neo-Hellenic Enlightenment (1750–1821): A General Survey." *Journal of the History of Ideas* 19 (1958): 523–41.

Derrida, Jacques. *Platōnos pharmakeia / Jacques Derrida: Eisagōgē, metaphrasē, sēmeiōseis* [Plato's pharmacy / Jacques Derrida: Introduction, translation, notes]. Translated to Greek by Ch. G. Lazos. Athens: Agra, 1990.

Ferguson, Charles A. "Diglossia." *Word* 15 (1959): 325–40.

Glykophrydi-Leontsini, Athanasia. *Neoellēnikē aisthētikē kai eurōpaikos diaphōtismos* [Neohellenic aesthetics and the European Enlightenment]. Athens: International Center of Philosophy and Interdisciplinary Research, 1989.

Heidegger, Martin. *Wegmarken*. Translated to Greek by A. A. Vayenas. Athens: Anagnostidi, n.d.

Henderson, G. P. *The Revival of Greek Thought, 1620–1830*. Albany: State University of New York Press, 1970.

Heraclitus. *Peri physeos*. Translated to modern Greek by E. Roussos. Athens: Ekdoseis D. N. Papadêma, 1987.

Homer. *The Odyssey*. Translated by Robert Fitzgerald. New York: Farrar, Straus and Giroux, 1998.

Lexicon of Presocratic Philosophy. 2 vols. Athens: Academy of Athens, 1994.

Logothetis, Constantine I. *Hē philosophia tēs anagennēseōs kai hē themeliōsis tēs neōteras physikēs* [The philosophy of the Renaissance and the foundation of modern physics]. Athens: Organization for the Publication of Textbooks, 1955.

Mihailidis, K. P. *Archaic Philosophers: Introduction, Text, Translation and Commentary* (in Greek). Nicosia, 1971.

Noutsos, Panagiôtês, ed. *Hē sosialistikē skepsē stēn Hellada: Apo to 1875 hôs to 1974* [Socialist thought in Greece: From 1875 to 1974]. 5 vols. Athens: Gnosis, 1990–.

———. *The Origins of Greek Marxism: An Introduction*. Ioannina: University of Ioannina, 1987.

Papanoutsos, Evangelos P. *Neoellēnikē philosophia* [Neohellenic philosophy]. 2 vols. Athens: Vasiki Vivliothiki, 1954–56.

Plotinus. *Enneads*. Translated by Pierre Hadot. Paris: Éditons du Cerf, 1988.

———. *Enneadōn biblia 30–33*. [Enneads]. Translated to modern Greek by Yannis Tzavaras. Athens: Editions Dodoni, 1995.

Psēmmenos, Nikos, ed. *Hē hellēnikē philosophia, 1453–1821* [Greek philosophy, 1453–1821]. 2 vols. Athens: Gnosis, 1988–89.

Roulia, P. Ch. *Principles of Philosophy* (in Greek). Athens: Metaichmio, 1999.

Sextus Empiricus. *Outlines of Scepticism*. Edited by Julia Annas and Jonathan Barnes. Cambridge: Cambridge University Press, 2000.

Solomos, Dhionísios. *I gynaika tis Zakynthos, Dialogos* [The Woman of Zakynthos: Dialogue]. Athens: Editions Patakis, 1997.

Spanos, William V. "Heidegger's Parmenides: Greek Modernity and the Classical Legacy." *Journal of Modern Greek Studies* 19 (2001): 89–115.

Stavropoulos, D. N., ed. *Oxford Greek-English Learner's Dictionary*. Oxford: Oxford University Press, 1988.

Theodoridis, Charálampos. *Introduction to Philosophy* (in Greek). Athens: Éditions du Jardin, 1945.

Wahl, Jean. *Les philosophes de l'existence*. Paris: Éditions Armand Colin, 1954. Translated to Greek by Christos Malevitsis. Athens: Dodoni, 1970.

GUT / BÖSE, WOHL / ÜBEL (WEH), GUT / SCHLECHT (GERMAN)

ENGLISH good/evil, good/bad
FRENCH *bien/mal, bon/méchant, bon/mauvais*
LATIN *bonum, malum*

➤ *GOOD/EVIL*, and BEAUTY, FAIR, GLÜCK, MORALS, PLEASURE, RIGHT/JUST/GOOD, WERT, WILL

Two examples, Immanuel Kant and Friedrich Nietzsche, reveal the link formed in Germany between reflection about good and evil and reflection on the powers of language. Formally, the two philosophers have in common the splitting up of the objects of reflection, adding to the initial pair of "good" (*gut*) and "evil" (*böse*) a second pair, *wohl/übel* or *gut/schlecht*. This in turn requires studying not only the contrast each pair presents, but also the contrast between the pairs.

I. The Kantian Split: Sensibility and Pure Reason

The second section of the Analytic of Pure Practical Reason of the *Critique of Practical Reason* is distinguished by unusual attention on Kant's part to the singularity and power of languages. Good and evil are studied there as "the sole objects of a practical reason" (Kant, *Gesammelte Schriften*, 5:57, trans. Pluhar, 78)—the only two objects possible, according to Kant, since any other object "taken as a principle determining the faculty of desire" makes the will lose its autonomy. Further, these two objects themselves, good and evil, must have a secondary status: they are determined by the moral law, which precedes them as it precedes all content in pure practical reason. This is what Kant calls the "paradox of method in a Critique of practical reason" (218). The demonstration begins by appealing to the "use of language [*Sprachgebrauch*]," which distinguishes the good (*das Gute*) from the pleasant (*das Angenehme*) and excludes the grounding of good and evil on objects of experience, that is, on the feeling of pleasure and pain. Kant can then deplore the "limitation of the language" (80), visible, according to him, in the Scholastic uses of the notions of *bonum* and *malum*, which do not permit a distinction on this point. Latin's ambiguity is best seen in its contrast to German, which, Kant notes, does not countenance it—for which, Kant says, praise is due to the language:

> The German language is fortunate to possess the expressions that keep this difference from being overlooked. It has two very different concepts and also equally different expressions for what the Latins designate by a single word, *bonum* [or *malum*]: for *bonum* it has *das Gute* and *das Wohl*; it has *das Böse* and *das Übel* (or *Weh*), so that there are two quite different judgments according to whether in an action we take into consideration its good and evil or our well-being and woe (bad).

> (Kant, *Gesammelte Schriften*, 5:59–60, trans. Pluhar, 80–81)

German thus divides in two the single opposition *bonum/malum*: into *wohl/übel*, which relates to the agreeable or disagreeable state in which the subject finds himself; and *gut/böse*, which always "signifies a reference to the *will* insofar as the will is determined by the *law of reason* to make something its object" (*Gesammelte Schriften*, 5:60, trans. Pluhar, 81).

Here, the French translator, Francis Picavet, can do nothing but preserve the original terms in italics. This is Picavet's version of Kant's comment:

> La langue allemande a le bonheur de posséder des expressions qui ne laissent pas échapper cette difference. Pour designer ce que les Latins appellent d'un mot unique *bonum*, elle a deux concepts très distincts et deux expressions moins distinctes. Pour *bonum*, elle a les deux mots *Gute* et *Wohl*, pour *malum*, *Böse* et *Übel* (ou *Weh*), de sorte que nous exprimons deux jugements tout à fait différents lorsque nous considerons dans une action [ce]

qui en constitue ou ce qu'on appelle *Gute* et *Böse* ou ce qu'on appelle *Wohl* et *Weh* (*Übel*).

Picavet's discomfort is well expressed by his note to this passage: "By replacing the German words that Kant is attempting to *define* with French words, we could only give a false expression of the thought: their meaning is made clear by their context" (61 n. 2).

The context here is a doubled contrast that French cannot denote: although French does have the pairs of synonyms that Kant adds to clarify what he means by *wohl* and *übel* (*Annehmlichkeit* and *Unannehmlichkeit*; *agrément* and *désagrément*, namely "agreement" in the sense of "agreeableness," and "disagreement" in the sense of "what disagrees with one"; *Vergnügen* and *Schmerze*; *contentement* and *douleur*; "pleasure" and "pain" [*Gesammelte Schriften*, 5:58–59; trans. Picavet, 60]), it has no words other than *bien* and *mal* to render *Gut* and *Bóse*, notions of good and evil that, according to Kant, do not belong to morality.

Kant's praise of German is a delicate interpretive matter. The first French translator of the *Critique of Practical Reason*, Jules Barni (1848), applies the criticism addressed to Latin to French as well, but for Kant it is no doubt less a matter of exalting his mother tongue than, in the spirit of the Enlightenment, of criticizing Scholasticism and its language.

II. Psychological Qualifications or Moral Values?

French is not, in fact, limited to the pair *bien*/*mal*; it also has the pair *bon*/*mauvais*, "good"/"bad," on which Picavet sometimes relies for translating matters related to sensation (cf. 60: "le concept de ce qui est tout simplement *mauvais*," "the concept of what is simply *bad*," for "schlechthin Böse," *Gesammelte Schriften*, 5:58). There is nevertheless a reason why this new pair does not allow us to resolve the difficulty. The two pairs *bien* and *mal* and *bon* and *mauvais* are not of the same grammatical nature. German, however, is able to retain the pairs' grammatical parallelism, since the (somewhat antiquated) pair of adverbs *wohl*/*übel* may be replaced by *gut*/*schlecht*; both are adverbial and adjectival, and thus grammatically parallel to *gut*/*böse*. New difficulties then appear, however, as witnessed by the translation of the first essay of Nietzsche's *On the Genealogy of Morality*.

The title given to this essay, "Gut und Böse, Gut und Schlecht," was translated into French as "Bon et méchant, bon et mauvais." A new split takes place: this time that of two "evaluations" (cf., e.g., §2 and §7, in *Werke*, 6.2:273 and 280; trans. Hildenbrand and Gratien, 21 and 30; trans. Diethe, 12 and 21), of two ways to impose value judgments on reality, namely that of slaves and that of the noble or powerful. Their relations have two main characteristics. First, the splitting of these evaluations reveals that there is a more fundamental division than that of good and evil, that which contrasts the high and the "low" (*einem "Unten"*), the superior and the inferior (§2). Second, and above all, the conflict does not just run through both pairs, but rather opposes them to one another, the bad according to the slaves being "*precisely* the 'good' of the other morality" (§11, in *Werke*, 6.2:288, trans. Diethe, 24). According to Nietzsche, the two oppositions form a system, and this system has a history—the age-old

and "frightful combat" between "two *opposite* values 'good and bad,' 'good and evil' " ("*die beiden entgegengesetzten Werte 'gut und schlecht,' 'gut und böse,' *" §16, in *Werke*, 6.2:299, trans. Diethe, 52)—insofar as it does not (as in Kant) contrast two human faculties (sensibility and pure reason), but rather different and unequal *men*.

It is precisely on reaching the work's conclusion that the French translation reveals its limits:

> Grund genug für mich, selbst zu Ende zu kommen, vorausgesetzt, daß es längst zur Genüge klar geworden ist, was ich *will*, was ich gerade mit jener gefährlichen Losung will, welche meinem letzten Buche auf den Leib geschrieben ist: "*Jenseits von Gut und Böse*." ... Dies heißt zum mindesten *nicht* "Jenseits von Gut und Schlecht."

> Car on aura compris depuis longtemps ce que c'est que je *veux*, ce que je veux justement avec ce mot d'ordre dangereux qui donne son titre à mon dernier livre: *Par-delà bien et mal* (*Jenseits von Gut und Böse*). ... Ce qui du moins *ne veut pas* dire: "Par-delà bon et mauvais" (*Dies heisst zum mindesten nicht: "Jenseits von Gut und Schlecht"*).

> Assuming that it has been sufficiently clear for some time what I *want*, what I actually want with that dangerous slogan which is written on the spine of my last book, *Beyond Good and Evil*. ... At least this does *not* mean "Beyond Good and Bad."

> (§16, in *Werke*, 6.2:302, trans. Diethe, 36)

Here, suddenly, the translation of "Gut und Böse" by "bon et méchant" disappears, pushed off the page by the pair "bien et mal." This is not a small detail, since *On the Genealogy of Morality* is intended, as its subtitle reminds its readers, "to complete and clarify the recently published *Beyond Good and Evil*." The translation "bon et méchant," "good and bad," is not at all imprecise, and it works for everything that has gone thus far; the problem is simply that "Gut und Böse" is both adjectival and adverbial, and means *both* "bon et méchant" and "bien et mal," that is, both the psychological qualifications associated with the adjectives and the more strictly moral qualifications associated with the adverbs. With the adjective *bon*, French can render the indeterminacy of Nietzsche's *Gut*, which appears in both pairs of words, and whose meaning varies precisely depending on whether it is inserted in one or the other; on the other hand, for *Gut* and its antonym, French finds itself required to choose between an adjective ("bon et méchant") and an adverb ("bien et mal"), that is, between a psychological style and a moral style, which Nietzsche's method distinctively refuses to separate. With respect to what we saw in Kant, the problem is thus reversed. It is not that French does not have enough distinctions, but that it has too many: *bien* and *mal* crowd onto *bon* and *méchant* and *bon* and *mauvais*.

We should note that Nietzsche's method aims from the start to be linguistic as well, from its reflections on "the right of the masters to give names" (§2, in *Werke*, 6.2:273, trans. Diethe, 13), through to the final question on the contribution of "linguistics, and especially the science of etymology," to "the history of the evolution of moral sentiments" (§16, in *Werke*, 6.2:303, trans. Diethe, 37). It is furthermore tempting to search out the Greek in Nietzsche's German, especially in the pair *gut/schlecht*, which is, so to speak, retranslated from the pair *agathos/kakos* [ἀγαθός/κακός] (§5). Nietzsche's "good" thus makes us hear the Greek untranslatables *kalos kagathos* [καλὸς κἀγαθός] (see BEAUTY) and *eu prattein* [εὖ πράττειν] (see PRAXIS) (§10), which make his *gut* appear in its two primary dimensions, distinction and activity.

Despite the link of German with Greek, affirmed several times in *On the Genealogy of Morality*, Nietzsche, unlike Kant, does not grant any privilege to the German language. German, for him, does certainly provide exemplary confirmation of the genealogy of evaluations, deriving *schlecht* (bad) from *schlicht* (the senses of "simple," then "base," "of low birth," are listed in the Grimms' dictionary [RT: *Deutsches Wörterbuch, s.v.*], flowing from the senses of "right," "flat or straight"), but it remains the case that "the expressions of the 'good' in the different languages . . . all refer to *the same transformation of the concepts*" (§4, in *Werke*, 6.2:275, trans. Diethe, 14). Here again, the interpretation will differ, depending on whether we stress the progress of the sciences of language or the alleged origin of the "beautiful *blond beast*"—which Nietzsche says, however, might be "Roman, Arabic, Germanic, or Japanese" (§11).

Philippe Büttgen

BIBLIOGRAPHY

Kant, Immanuel. *Kritik der praktischen Vernunft*. Edited by Königlich Preussischen Akademie der Wissenschaften. In *Kants Gesammelte Schriften*, vol. 5. Berlin: De Gruyter, 1908. First published in 1788. Translation by Werner S. Pluhar: *Critique of Practical Reason*. Indianapolis, IN: Hackett, 2002. French translation by F. Picavet: *Critique de la raison pratique*. 9th ed. Paris: Presses Universitaires de France, 1985. First published in 1943.

Nietzsche, Friedrich. *Jenseits von Gut und Böse*. Edited by Giorgio Colli and Mazzino Montinari. In *Werke: Kritische Gesamtausgabe*, vol. 6.2. Berlin: De Gruyter, 1968. Translation by Marion Faber: *Beyond Good and Evil: Prelude to a Philosophy of the Future*. Edited by Marion Faber. Introduction by Robert C. Holub. Oxford: Oxford University Press, 1998.

———. *Zur Genealogie der Moral*. Edited by Giorgio Colli and Mazzino Montinari. In *Werke: Kritische Gesamtausgabe*, vol. 6.2. Berlin: De Gruyter, 1968. Translation by Carol Diethe: *On the Genealogy of Morality*, edited by Keith Ansell-Pearson. Rev. student ed. Cambridge: Cambridge University Press, 2007. French translation by I. Hildenbrand and J. Gratien: *La généalogie de la morale*. Edited by G. Colli and M. Montinari. Paris: Gallimard, 1971.

HÁ / HAVER (PORTUGUESE)

ENGLISH	there is, to have
FRENCH	*il y a, avoir*
GERMAN	*es gibt*
GREEK	*esti* [ἔστι]
SPANISH	*hay, haber*

➤ *IL Y A* [ES GIBT, ESTI], and ASPECT, FICAR, PRESENT, REALITY, SPANISH, *TO BE*

The French *il y a* and the German *es gibt* may be translated into Portuguese (and analogously into Castilian Spanish) by three distinct impersonal verbs: (1) *há*, from the verb *haver* (derived from the Latin *habere*), constructed with neither subject nor adverb but taking an object; (2) *tem*, from the verb *ter* (from the Latin *tenere*), which absorbed all the possessive meaning of *haver*; and finally, in a more elevated, literary, and philosophical register, (3) the pronominal form *dá-se*, analogous to *es gibt*, whose origin is the passive form of the Latin, *datur*. Their usage is not always interchangeable, which emphasizes the semantic differences of the three verbs (in addition to the etymological ones) and may help us see the difference between *il y a* and *es gibt*.

I. The Meaning of *Há*, without a Subject

The Portuguese verb *haver* (*haber* in Spanish) has the same origin as the verb *avoir* (French) "to have": the Latin *habere*. However, it is the Portuguese verb *ter*, much more often than *haver*, that is most often translated into French by *avoir*. *Haver* lost its possessive sense and was replaced by *ter* for such purposes. It has retained auxiliary functions, both aspectual and modal; some rare uses as a main verb with very specific meanings; and above all, the impersonal existential function. This limitation created its meaning and makes it one of the most important verbs in Portuguese, alongside the verb *ser*, "to be," for any fundamental ontological questioning. In a note to her translation of Heidegger's *Being and Time*, for example, Marcia Cavalcante appeals to the sense of the verb *haver* to explain the specific usage of the German verb *geben* in the expression *es gibt*, even though she chooses to translate it by the Portuguese form equivalent to the German, *dá-se*:

> To distinguish the ontological level of the establishment of structures from the ontic level of derivations, *Being and Time* reserves the verb *to give* [*dar-se*] (*geben*), and thus inserts [*incutindo*] the active and transitive meaning in the process referred to by the verb *haver*. As a consequence, to give [*dar-se*] always refers to the movements of being and to its truth in presence, in existence, in temporality, in history.
>
> (*Ser e tempo*)

In its standard meaning, *há* requires neither a subject, real or apparent, nor an adverb of place. The lack of a subject does not pose any grammatical problems in Portuguese; for personal verbs, it is even stylistically desirable insofar as the personal endings are, as in Latin, clearly distinct (*amo, amas, ama, amamos, amais, amam*), unlike in English or French, where they cannot be distinguished phonetically without a subject pronoun ([I] love; [you] love; [he] loves; [they] love). The word once functioned as an adverb of place, as in this sentence by a sixteenth-century grammarian: "E por não ficar confusão em este nome próprio, pois i há muitos homens que têm um mesmo nome" (And so there should be no confusion in this proper name, for there are many men who have the same name; J. de Barros, *Gramática da língua portuguesa*), but that usage gradually disappeared from the verbal expression. There remains only the direct object of the verb: what is projected toward existence. The direct object of *há* cannot be confused with a subject; *há*, like any impersonal verb, is invariant and of course never agrees with its complement in gender or number: *há flores no prado* (there are flowers in the prairie). Indeed, if we needed to find a "real subject," we would rather have to look to the now-vanished adverb of place, which had the logical role of a whole containing the objects, as explained by Mattoso Câmara:

> We may understand it from the usage of *habere* in existential phrases of vulgar Latin, when a noun of place stood first as a subject, for example ... "Africa has lions." The shift towards an impersonal construction took place when we perceived the place as a "décor" rather than as a "possessor." This yields its presentation with the preposition *in* or its expression by the adverb *ibi* (Arch. Port. *hi*, Fr. *y*, etc.): "*in arca Noe habuit homines I*" (Bourciez, 1930). Everyday Brazilian shows that this is a natural inclination of the mind, as it reproduces the change, this time with the verb *ter* [to have, to possess], in the same conditions: "in Africa [there are] lions (*na Africa tem leões*)." We may say that the place name, which was first a subject, was integrated into the fact or the predicate considered in itself, without reference to a possessor external to it.
>
> (*Princípios de ligüística geral*)

Haver and *ter*, in their existential usage, are constructed in exactly the same way, even though there is always a difference of nuance. *Ter*, even as an auxiliary or existential, retains the reassuring and solid aspect of possession. The poet Carlos Drummond de Andrade uses *ter* to refer to a stone encountered on the road: "Tinha uma pedra no meio do caminho" (very roughly, "was a stone in the middle of the road" or "had a stone in the middle of the road" [*Reunião*]; note the absence of "there" or a pronoun, personal or impersonal, such as "one," "he," or "we" in the translations). The verb *haver* could replace *ter*, but the verse would lose

427

its gravity. In contrast, the idea of flourishing, escape, and suppleness of this other verse would completely disappear without *haver*: "Minha alma é uma lembrana que há em mim" (My soul is a memory which is in me; Pessoa, *Poemas inéditos*). In this case, more than being an object which I solidly own, the soul, Pessoa tells his readers, is the eruption of an object, "a memory" in the region of the "I."

The absence of the subject and the adverb of place in Portuguese yields an idea of presence in the world, instantaneous, without any other support than its arrival itself, a starting point neither substantial nor subjective, for anything that exists—like a *satori*, the zen event, which Barthes defines as "a more or less powerful (though in no way formal) seism that causes knowledge, or the subject, to vacillate: it creates an emptiness of language [un *vide de parole*]" (*L'empire des signes*). We may almost always translate *haver* by way of a phrase based on the verb "to have," but we cannot translate this lack of subject, which marks its existential meaning. We cannot render the effect of suspension that it produces in its object by projecting it from nowhere into presence: "Há um azul em abuso de beleza" (There is some blue as the height [or trespass or misuse] of beauty; M. Barros, *O livro das ignorãcas*).

II. *Haver*, the Future, and the Expression of the Future

Neither can we render *haver*'s projective aspect, which anticipates and both outstrips and shoots forth existing objects and the pure event of the future. According to the syntax of the verb *haver*, everything that is posited as real (*isto que há*, lit., what [there] is) gets its existence in an élan that is open in the present. Presence becomes the opening of the future, which, reigning in the power of the possible, anticipates and supports what exists. Thus, "the future" is called *o que haverá* (lit., what will have) by António Quadros, where determination is disclosed by a difference from, and even a surpassing of, the possessive sense of *ter* (to have / to possess):

The future [*o que haverá*] is not yet what is eternally [*não é ainda o que é*] but nor is it already what one is in space time [*não é já o que se é*], it is rather the open and endless horizon of freedom. The future [*o que haverá*] is not what one will have [*o que se terá*] either, but precisely what will transcend having and being had [*o ter e o sermos tidos*—*sermos tidos* is the past personal infinitive of the verb *ter*, to have, in the first person plural; see PORTUGUESE, Box 2], a participation in movement, which never is fulfilled in possession.

(*O espírito da cultura portuguesa*)

It is significant that the idea of a "future" should be framed by a Portuguese philosopher based on the meaning of the verb *haver*. The verb *haver* keeps alive expressions in Portuguese from which flow the future forms in neo-Latin tongues. Benveniste notes a similar phenomenon regarding the origin of the future in Romance languages, coming from a progressive extension of predictions and prophecies, a shift that is "born among Christian writers and theologians beginning with Tertullian (at the beginning of the third century BCE)" (*Problèmes de linguistique générale*, 2:131). This event in the

history of languages is comparable to what happened synchronically in contemporary Portuguese (2:132):

The syntagm *habere* + infinitive coexisted for a long time with the old future, without crossing it, since it conveyed a distinct notion. There were thus two expressions for the future: one as intention (this is the simple form with -*bo*, -*am*), the other has predestination (this is the syntagm: "what is to happen" > "what will happen."

In Portuguese, this ancient verbal syntagm, *haver*, followed by the infinitive of the main verb, no longer coexists with the earlier Latin future but rather with the future from Romance languages in which the verb *habeo*, reduced to a suffix, becomes a simple verbal ending. This recent simple future takes over the intentional meaning of the old Latin future. Thus the two expressions for the future coexist in this sentence from a contemporary writer:

. . . os ímanes que, na sua aldeia, hão-de fazer voar a passarola, cujos, ainda por cima, terão de vir do estrangeiro . . .

(. . . the magnets which in his village *must make* the aerostat fly, which furthermore must come from abroad . . .)

(Saramago, *Memorial do convento*)

The mesoclitic pronoun (the unstressed pronoun object, *lhes* in the example below, is inserted between the radical—the infinitive of the verb—and the ending of the conjugated verb in the simple future of the pronominal voice) highlights this formation of the future in Portuguese:

Aos que têm seara em casa, pagar-lhes-ão a semeadura; aos que vão buscar a seara tão longe, hão-lhes de medir a semeadura e hão-lhes de contar os passos.

(To those who have fields at home, we will pay for the seeds; to those who go far to find fields, we will measure the seeds and count the steps.)

(Vieira, *Sermão da sexagésima*)

This notion of projection, of blooming forth, cuts across most contemporary uses of *haver*, as a future auxiliary as well as an impersonal verb referring to existence. Thus, inasmuch as it refers to this bursting forth into presence, *há* is similar to the Greek *esti* [ἔστι], or in the plural *eisi* [εἰσί], put at the head of a sentence, which is usually followed by a subject with which it agrees. The difference is that in Portuguese what would be the "real" subject is not at all understood nor analyzed as a subject, but really as an object, thrown in front. The future projects itself as an object, and the real anticipates itself—since, from the very start, *há* what is.

Fernando Santoro

BIBLIOGRAPHY

Barros, João de. *Gramática da língua portuguesa*. 3rd ed. Edited by José Pedro Machado. Lisbon: Sociedade Astória, 1957. First published in 1540.

Barros, Manoel de. *O livro das ignorãças*. 2nd ed. Rio de Janeiro: Civilização Brasileira, 1994.

Barthes, Roland. *L'empire des signs*. Paris: Flammarion, 1970. Translation by Richard Howard: *The Empire of Signs*. New York: Hill and Wang, 1982.

Benveniste, Émile. *Problèmes de linguistique générale*. 2 vols. Paris: Gallimard, 1974. Translation by Mary Elizabeth Meek: *Problems in General Linguistics*. Coral Gables, FL: University of Miami Press, 1971.

Câmara, Joaquim Mattoso, Jr. *Princípios de lingüística geral, como introdução aos estudos superiores da língua portuguêsa*. 4th and expanded ed. Rio de Janeiro: Livraria Acadêmica, 1967. Translation by Anthony J. Naro: *The Portuguese Language*. Chicago: University of Chicago Press, 1972.

Drummond de Andrade, Carlos. *Reunião*. Rio de Janeiro: Olympio, 1969.

———. *The Minus Sign: A Selection from the Poetic Anthology*. Translated by Virginia de Araujo. Manchester, UK: Carcanet, 1981.

———. *Travelling in the Family: Selected Poems of Carlos Drummond de Andrade*. Edited by Thomas Colchie and Mark Strand, with additional translations by Elizabeth Bishop and Gregory Rabassa. New York: Random House, 1986.

Heidegger, Martin. *Sein und Zeit*. 13th ed. Tübingen: Niemeyer, 1976. Translation by John Macquarrie and Edward Robinson: *Being and Time*. New York: Harper & Row, 1962. Translation by Marcia Sá Cavalcante: *Ser e tempo*. Vol. 1. Petropolis: Vozes, 1988.

Pessoa, Fernando. *Poemas inéditos 1919–1930*. Lisbon: Ática, 1990.

Quadros, António. *O espirito da cultura portuguesa*. Lisbon: Soc. Expansão Cultural, 1967.

Saramago, José. *Baltasar and Blimunda*. Translated by Giovanni Pontiero. San Diego: Harcourt Brace Jovanovich, 1987.

———. *Memorial do convento*. 2nd ed. Lisbon: Caminho, 1995.

Vieira, Antônio. *Sermão da sexagésima*. Edited, introduction, and commentary by Gladstone Chaves de Melo. Niterói-RJ: Núcleo Editora da Universidade Federal Fluminense, 1985.

———. *Sermões*. Edited by Alcir Pécora. 2 vols. São Paulo: Hedra, 2000.

HAPPINESS

The difficulty of the notion of happiness (luck, good fortune, prosperity, joy, felicity) has to do with the fact that it is located in a double register: the moral and even religious horizon of the goals of life (see *VIRTUE*, and in particular *VIRTÙ*), but also the entirely contingent register of the chance aspects of life (see *DAIMÔN*, *DESTINY*, and particularly *KÊR*). The English term "happiness" thus preserves an etymological connection to a sense of "coming or happening by chance; fortuitous; chance" (RT: *Oxford English Dictionary*, s.v.). In the French term *bonheur*, these different perspectives are now collected in the problematics of satisfaction: see *PLEASURE*.

The group of terms created in German on the basis of *Glück* and *Seligkeit* has the advantage of reflecting the initial complexity of the Greek words that it seeks to translate (*eutuchia* [εὐτυχία], *eudaimonia* [εὐδαιμονία], *olbos* [ὄλβος], *makariotês* [μακαριότης]), as well as that of the Latin (*felicitas*, *beatitudo*), of which French retains only the religious connotations. Compare the English, however—as in Hamlet's dying words to Horatio: "If thou didst ever hold me in thy heart, / *Absent thee from felicity* awhile, / And in this harsh world draw thy breath in pain" (Shakespeare, *Hamlet*, 5.2). In addition, German has created the term *Wohlfahrt*, from the adjective *wohl* (good), borrowed by the English "welfare" to designate material prosperity; it is remarkable that French persists in the religious lexicon by translating "welfare state" as *État-providence*; cf. *BIEN-ÊTRE*.

In almost all European languages, then, happiness is synonymous with luck or good fortune, the advantages we receive by chance. German, however, with the difference between *Glück* and *Glückseligkeit*, seeks to strengthen (in the tradition of Aristotle's distinction between *eutuchia* and *eudaimonia*) an opposition between the moral goal ("happiness") that pertains to the innermost spiritual life) and favorable contingency.

The problems raised by these different terms are discussed in the entry *GLÜCK*.

➤ DUTY, *GOOD / EVIL*, MORALS, *VALUE*

HEART

I. An Essential Organ

The French word *cœur* (like the Eng. "cardiac") derives from the Latin *cor*, *cordis*, which itself derives from the Greek *kardia* [καρδία], a word that is connected with the Indo-European root [*k̑erd-] (whence the Ger. *Herz*, the Russ. *serdtse* [сердце]), which designates an essential organ. But when we compare Greek, Latin, or the Semitic languages, we see that the organs and their functions are far from coinciding in all these languages or at different historical stages so that the word "heart" can serve to translate more than one organ (in Greek, for example, *kêr* [κῆρ], *kardia* or *thumos* [θυμός]), and yet each time "heart" is only one of the possible translations: see in particular CONSCIOUSNESS (esp. Box 1), GEMÜT, GOGO, LËV, SAMOST', SOUL (esp. Boxes 3 and 4).

II. Metaphors and Oppositions

"Heart," which names the central organ in the circulation of the blood and is used by extension for the chest or stomach, comes to designate the seat of the humors and feelings, for example, love but also courage (derived from *cor*). This latter can be located in other cultures and especially in antiquity in the liver, the lungs, or breath (Gr. *thumos*, Lat. *animus*). See, in addition to SOUL and CONSCIOUSNESS, the Italian VIRTÙ; see also ACEDIA, LOVE, MELANCHOLY, PATHOS, and, more generally, *MALAISE*.

As the seat of the feelings and affections, the heart can represent either another source of knowledge—for example, when Pascal declares that "in reality, we know truth not only through reason, but also through the heart" (*Pensées*, 110)—or even the antonym of reason, as when Pascal writes, "The heart has its reasons that reason does not know" (ibid., 423): see LOGOS, MADNESS, *REASON* [INTELLECT, INTELLECTUS, UNDERSTANDING], *TO SENSE*.

In certain spiritual traditions the heart is considered to be the innermost core of the personality. Thus the Bible, also taking into account other internal organs, declares that God is a "searcher of heart and soul" (literally, kidneys and hearts) (Ps. 7:10). Many other passages in the Hebrew text, which are taken over and completed by the Christian scriptures, accord this metaphor a major role: "I will give them one heart, and put a new spirit within them; I will take the stony heart out of their flesh and give them a heart of flesh" (Ezek. 11:19); see LEIB and LËV.

Thus the heart designates what is essential in each thing, its essence. See LËV and cf. ESSENCE, *TO BE*, TO TI ÊN EINAI.

➤ GENIUS, INGENIUM, WILL

HEIMAT (GERMAN)

ENGLISH   homeland
FRENCH   terre natale

➤ FATHERLAND and CIVIL SOCIETY, DESTINY, OIKEIŌSIS, PEOPLE, PROPERTY,
WORLD

Heimat, which is often translated as "homeland," refers, like *Vaterland* (fatherland), if not to one's explicit place of birth, at least to one's place of origin. However, whereas the latter refers explicitly to a genealogy (the *Vaterland* is the *Land des Väters*, the country of one's father), the belonging that is implied by *Heimat* is more complex. *Heimat*, which comes from *Heim* (home, domicile), is in effect the land where one stays and is settled and where the dimensions of the homeland and the home become mixed. It is the place that is ours (or the one that has become it) since it is either destined for or appropriated by us. Unlike *Vaterland*, it thus refers to the proper place, in a sense that is more ontological than genealogical. Different uses, including political ones, result for both terms.

I. *Vaterland*: Belonging through Birth and Political Community

In addition to its first meaning, *Vaterland* acquires a political meaning starting in the eighteenth century. To have a *Vaterland*, a fatherland, is to belong to a public community, which gives (or at least ought to give) a right to citizenship. It is public, insofar as it is clearly identifiable, for everyone, by birth. Thus, Kant writes in his *Rechtslehre* (*Doctrine of Right*) in §50:

> A *country* (*territorium*) [*das Land*] whose inhabitants [*Einsassen*] are citizens [*Mitbürger*] of it [*gemeinen Wesens*] simply by its constitution, without their having to perform any special act to establish the right (and so are citizens by birth [*mithin durch die Geburt*]), is called their native land [*Vaterland*].

> (Kant, *Doctrine of Right, Metaphysics of Morals*, 110)

The *Vaterland* is thus a community to which one belongs de facto. It does not require any particular appropriation. At the same time it is that which naturally gives the right to citizenship. It constitutes a sort of precitizenship. This is shown by the fact that citizenship requires, in return, an attachment to the *Vaterland*, a debt that is manifested notably in an obligation with regard to defense, or even sacrifice. The whole problem of politics is thus to know how to acquire citizenship without having a prior identification of this public community, how to become a citizen of a country when the latter is not one's *Vaterland* by birth, the *Land* (country) of one's fathers.

II. *Heimat*: Ontological Rootedness

Heimat directs the question of belonging in an entirely different way. In general, *Heimat* may refer simply to the place where something has occurred—an invention or a work—the place of birth attributed to it. However, this very generality lends itself to an ontological inflection. *Heimat* is less the place that someone or other recognizes as his own, like a place of birth, than the place where one is and becomes what one was destined to be and become, one's proper place. As a

place of destination (or even mission), *Heimat* then becomes what allows a being to manifest itself and develop, to reveal its essence. That kind of inflection is already noticeable in Hegel's philosophy of history, including that which undergirds his own history of philosophy. Thus, he may write, regarding the Greeks,

> But what makes us specially at home [*bei ihnen ist es uns heimatlich zu Mute*] with the Greeks is that they made their world their home [*sich selbst ihre Welt zur Heimat gemacht haben*]; the common spirit of homeliness unites us both.

> (Hegel, *History of Philosophy*, 150)

However, making one's world a *Heimat* means nothing other than welcoming the *Weltgeist*. *Heimat* is thus the place where the *Weltgeist* (the spirit or mind of the world) is manifested:

> This region, which was long the theatre of world history, does not have a clearly defined nucleus of its own, but is oriented outwards, looking towards the Mediterranean. While the middle and north of Europe were still uncultivated, the world spirit [*Weltgeist*] had its residence [*Heimat*] there.

> (Hegel, *Philosophy of World History*, 195)

It is in Heidegger's work above all that this ontologicization of *Heimat* is most fully developed. For it is defined first with regard to its loss and absence (*Heimatlosigkeit*). *Heimat* is in effect the birthplace in which a man finds himself rooted, the closest place. And this rootedness means first of all that he may develop there, in conformity with his being. In the proximity and familiarity of this place, understood as a gift, he finds the source of a meditative thought and a work. Thus the address *Gelassenheit* ("Serenity") begins in these terms:

> I thank my homeland [*Heimat*] for all that it has given me along the path of my life.

> (Heidegger, *Discourse on Thinking: Translation of* Gelassenheit)

From this flows the three-fold questioning that governs Heidegger's thought with respect to *Heimat*:

1. Is the rootedness of the work (beginning with the work of thinking) not necessary to its production?

   > We grow thoughtful and ask: does not the flourishing of any genuine work depend upon its roots in a native soil [*die verwurzelung im Boden einer Heimat*]?

   > (Ibid.)

   What *Heimat* connotes is thus the idea of a proper basis (*Grund*) understood as a ground (*Boden*) or a land, "the depth of the native soil [*die Tiefe des heimatlichen Boden*]" (ibid.).

2. The appropriation of *Heimat* is thus the object of a summons that, if it is not directly political in itself, leads all politics to this demand for rootedness in a land (*die Bodenständigkeit*). In this way, after the war Heidegger considers the problem of Germans who have become

estranged from their country more troubling than that of refugees:

> Many Germans have lost their homeland [*haben ihre Heimat verloren*]. . . . They are strangers now to their former homeland [*sie sind der alten Heimat entfremdet*]. And those who *have* stayed on in their homeland [*die in der Heimat Gebliebenen*]? Often they are still more homeless [*heimatloser*] than those who have been driven from their homeland [*die Heimatvertriebenen*].
>
> (Ibid., 48)

The first effect of the ontologicization of *Heimat* is thus to make the question of citizenship (that which concerns the *Vaterland*, in the Kantian sense of the term) a secondary problem in relation to the generalized character of this rootlessness that threatens man "in his most intimate being" (ibid.).

3. As a further result, there is a new task for thought, in which its political responsibility would be exhausted: to think and find a new *Heimat* in which human works can again take root:

> Thus we ask now: even if the old rootedness [*die alte Bodenständigkeit*] is being lost in this age, may not a new ground and foundation [*ein neuer Grund und Boden*] be granted again to man, a foundation and ground out of which man's nature and all his works can flourish in a new way even in the atomic age? What could the ground and foundation be for the new rootedness [*welches wäre der Grund und Boden für eine künftige Bodenständigkeit*]?
>
> (Ibid.)

▪ See Box 1.

III. Can There Be *Heimat* without *Vaterland*?

Nevertheless, the term *Heimat* does not lose all political significance. Can there be *Heimat* without *Vaterland*? Can someone who is deprived of rights in a given place make it his own place and home? Is not a depoliticized notion of *Heimat* in reality highly political? This is the question raised by Jean Améry in *Jenseits von Schuld und Sühne*, which raises the question of the status of Jews in Nazi Germany. It is, he explains, because Jews were forbidden to recognize Germany as their *Heimat* that they were able to be deprived of their rights—and thus find themselves without a *Vaterland*. However, it is also because they were deprived of rights that no *Heimat* was possible for them. *Heimat* is therefore not only a proper place but also one that furnishes at least a minimum of security. What the depoliticization of *Heimat* forgets, in falling back on a traditional familiarity, is that for an individual deprived of rights, someone without a country, no *Heimat* is possible:

> [F]irst, with all due brevity, the relationship between homeland [*Heimat*] and fatherland [*Vaterland*] must be clarified, because a widespread attitude claims to accept the idea of homeland in its regional, folkloristic limits at least as something of picturesque value, while fatherland is extremely suspicious to it as a demagogic catch-word and a characteristic of reactionary obstinacy. . . . [S]ince I am a qualified homeless person [*Heimatlos*] I dare to stand up for the value that homeland signifies, and I also reject the sharp-witted differentiation between homeland and fatherland, and in the end believe that a person of my generation can get along only poorly without both, which are one and the same. Whoever has no fatherland—that is to say, no shelter in an autonomous social body representing an independent governmental entity—has, so I believe, no homeland either.
>
> (Améry, *Mind's Limits*)

It is thus when one is deprived that the difference between *Vaterland* and *Heimat* is best discussed, but it is also then that it becomes obscured. The loss of *Vaterland* refers to a very precise political situation. It is the fact of stateless people, and it refers to the difficulty (even impossibility) of acquiring

---

1

The *Heimatlosen* of the "Gay Science"

Being rooted in a *Heimat* may also suggest diametrically opposed demands in philosophy. For Nietzsche, in the voice of Zarathustra, it refers to the collection of attachments (to a land, a countryside, a family) from which one must extricate oneself in order for a new thought or writing to be possible. *Heimat* is not the proper place in which a work is rooted but a place that one must know how to leave, on pain of repeating what was already thought and said. It is both a *Vater-land* and a *Mutterland*, not in the sense of a political community, but a collection of dependencies (a tradition, an authority, insofar as they presuppose and even demand affective links):

> But nowhere did I find home [*Heimat*]; I am unsettled [*unstätt bin ich*] in every settlement, and a departure at every gate. Foreign [*fremd*] to me and a mockery are these people of the present to whom my heart recently drove me; and I am driven out of father- and motherlands [*vertrieben bin ich aus Vater- und Mutterländern*].
>
> (Nietzsche, *Thus Spoke Zarathustra*, "On the Land of Education")

In *The Gay Science*, Nietzsche refers to "the children of the future," to whom his *gaya scienza* is addressed, as "stateless" (*Heimatlosen*).

BIBLIOGRAPHY

Nietzsche, Friedrich. *Also Sprach Zarathustra*. Edited by Giorgio Colli and Mazzino Montinari. In *Kritische Studienausgabe*. Vol. 4. Berlin: De Gruyter, 1988. Translation by Adrian Del Caro: *Thus Spoke Zarathustra: A Book for All and None*, edited by Adrian Del Caro and Robert B. Pippin. Cambridge: Cambridge University Press, 2006.

rights without an identification and a prior belonging to the type of community that the term designates. It affects those who were forced or chose to leave their country. In contrast, the lack of *Heimat* does not necessarily imply displacement or exile. It refers rather to being uprooted, the loss of a place where one can be fully oneself. Except when one or the other is exploited and the two become confused—when belonging to a *Heimat* is what gives one the right to a *Vaterland*—the uprootedness is no longer ontological but rather refers to the lack of a familiar and safe home, a permanent threat to one's own security.

■ See Box 2.

Marc Crépon

2

Das Unheimliche

➤ ANXIETY, ENTSTELLUNG, MALAISE, SUBJECT, THEMIS, UNCONSCIOUS, VERNEINUNG

The substantivized antonym of *heimlich*, *das Unheimliche*, refers to anxiety, which has belonged to the vocabulary of psychoanalysis since Freud. "Worrying strangeness": the German term is "untranslatable," notes Bertrand Féron, who retains Marie Bonaparte's translation but allows that the French glosses it, eliminating the *Heim* of the home, suppressing the *un* of disapproval (*L'Inquietante Étrangeté et autres essais*). James Strachey chooses "uncanny": unable to mobilize an equivalent formed from *home*, he relies on the privative of "canny," from *can*, "to be able, to be capable," from the same family as *to know*.

Freud, in his eponymous essay (1919) is more attentive than ever to his language and to other languages: "The German word *unheimlich* is obviously the opposite of *heimlich* (homely), *heimisch* (native)—the opposite of what is familiar; and we are tempted to conclude that what is 'uncanny' is frightening precisely because it is *not* known and familiar" ("The Uncanny," 17:220). Yet this is false: "the uncanny is that class of the frightening which leads back to what is known of old and long familiar" (ibid.). And Freud, dictionaries in hand, states that "this particular shade of what is frightening" is lacking "in many languages"—perhaps precisely because they are "foreign" to us (ibid., 17:221). What is remarkable is that in a nuance of German, *heimlich* can coincide with its opposite and mean not only "familiar, comfortable" but also "hidden," the "secret [*geheim*]," even though we can understand that, as the brothers Grimm say, from "domestic" comes the concept of what is "withdrawn from the eyes of strangers" (ibid., 17: 225). Freud's attention is drawn there by a remark of Schelling: "We notice that Schelling says something which throws quite a new light on the concept of the *Unheimlich*, for which we were certainly not prepared. According to him, everything is *unheimlich* that ought to have remained secret and hidden but has come to light" (ibid.—Freud cites Schelling via Daniel Sanders [see RT: Sanders, *Wörterbuch der deutschen Sprache*, 1860]; here is Schelling's text, *Philosophie der Mythologie*, 2.2:649: *unheimlich nennet man alles, was in Geheimnis, im Verborgennen, in der Latenz bleiben sollte und hervorgetreten ist*, with the difference that, as David Stimilli notes, Sanders omits *in der Latenz!*).

The context of Schelling's definition, which Freud perhaps did not know, is the status of Nemesis: this "strangely worrying" principle above the law (*nomos* [νόμος]), which the Olympian religion tries to hide (*die Gewalt jenes unheimlichen Princips, das in der früheren Religionen herrschte* [the power of the strangely worrying principle that dominated in earlier religions] [Einleitung in *Philosophie der Mythologie*, 649]). Nemesis is in effect nothing other than "the very power of this supreme law of the world which throws everything into motion, which allows nothing to remain hidden, which requires everything hidden to appear, and forces it, in a way, morally to show itself [*das alles Verborgen zum Hervortreten antreibt und gleichsam moralisch zwingt sich zu zeigen*]" (*Historical-Critical Introduction*, 146–47). Nemesis, the hidden power, by definition brings what is hidden out into the light; Pindar calls her "more just than justice," *huperdikon* [ὑπέρδικον] (*Pythiques*, 10:45; *Olympian Odes*, 8:86).

The *Unheimlich* thus refers to the hidden that is suddenly forced to show itself; in Freudian language, "something repressed which *recurs* [*etwas wiedekehrendes Verdrängtes*]" ("The Uncanny," 17:241). We may understand, Freud says, why "linguistic usage has extended *das Heimliche* (homely) into its opposite, *das Unheimliche*; for this uncanny is in reality nothing new or alien, but something which is familiar and old-established in the mind and which has become alienated from it only through the process of repression [*nur durch den Prozess der Verdrängung entfremdet worden ist*]" (ibid.). It thus constitutes a special kind of anxiety, "when infantile complexes which have been repressed [*verdrängte infantile Komplexe*] are once more revived by some impression," as in Hoffman's "Sandman," or when "something *actually happens* in our lives which seems to confirm the old, discarded beliefs [*überwundene primitive Überzeugungen*]" (ibid., 247–49), as in the unintentional repetition that mimics fatality so well.

Realizing that one is not even at home in oneself is the anxiety of the modern subject in the face of the *Unheimliches*.

Barbara Cassin

BIBLIOGRAPHY

Beach, Edward A. *The Potencies of the God(s): Schelling's Philosophy of Mythology*. Albany: State University of New York Press, 1994.
Freud, Sigmund. "Das Unheimliche." *Freud-Studienausgabe 4: Psychologische Schriften*. 9th ed. Edited by Alexander Mitscherlich, Angela Richards, and James Strachey, 241–74. Frankfurt: S. Fischer, 1997. Translation by James Strachey et al.: "The Uncanny." In *The Standard Edition of the Complete Psychological Works of Sigmund Freud*, Vol. 17 (1917–1919): *An Infantile Neurosis and Other Works*, 217–56. London: Hogarth Press, 1955.
Schelling, Friedrich Wilhelm Joseph. *Philosophie der Mythologie*. Edited by Karl Friedrich August von Schelling. In *Sämmtliche Werke*. Vol. 2.2. Stuttgart: Cotta, 1857.
———. *Philosophische Einleitung in die Philosophie der Mythologie*. Edited by Karl Friedrich August von Schelling. In *Sämmtliche Werke*. Vol. 2.1. Stuttgart: Cotta, 1856. Translation by Mason Richey and Markus Zisselsberger: *Historical-Critical Introduction to the Philosophy of Mythology*. Foreword by Jason M. Wirth. Albany: State University of New York Press, 2007.
Stimilli, Davide. *The Face of Immortality: Physiognomy and Criticism*. Albany: State University of New York Press, 2005.

BIBLIOGRAPHY

Améry, Jean. *Jenseits von Schuld und Sühne: Bewältigungsversuche eines Überwältigen*. Stuttgart: Klette Kotta, 1977. Translation by Sidney Rosenfeld and Stella P. Rosenfeld: *At the Mind's Limits: Contemplations by a Survivor on Auschwitz and Its Realities*. London: Granta, 1999.

Hegel, Georg Wilhelm Friedrich. *Vorlesungen über die Geschichte der Philosophie*. Edited by Pierre Garniron and Walter Jaeschke. 4 vols. In *Vorlesungen*. Vols. 6–9. Hamburg: Meiner, 1986–1996. Translation by E. S. Haldane and Frances H. Simson: *Lectures on the History of Philosophy*. 3 vols. London: Routledge and Kegan Paul, 1974.

———. *Vorlesungen über die Philosophie der Weltgeschichte: Berlin 1822/1823*. Edited by Karl Heinz Ilting, Karl Brehmer, and Hoo Nam Seelmann. In *Vorlesungen*. Vol. 12. Hamburg: Felix Meiner, 1996. Translation by H. B. Nisbet: *Lectures on the Philosophy of World History: Introduction, Reason in History*, edited by Johannes Hoffmeister. Introduction by Duncan Forbes. Cambridge: Cambridge University Press, 1975. Translation by John Sibree: *The Philosophy of History*. Introduction by C. J. Friedrich; prefaces by Karl Hegel and John Sibree. New York: Dover, 1956.

Heidegger, Martin. *Gelassenheit*. Pfüllingen, Ger.: Neske, 1959. Translation by John M. Anderson and E. Hans Freund: *Discourse on Thinking: A Translation of Gelassenheit*. Introduction by John M. Anderson. New York: Harper and Row, 1966.

Kant, Immanuel. *Die Metaphysik der Sitten*. Edited by Königlich Preussischen Akademie der Wissenschaften. In *Kants Gesammelte Schriften*. Vol. 6. Berlin: De Gruyter, 1907. First published 1797. Translation by Mary Gregor: *The Metaphysics of Morals*, edited by Mary Gregor. Introduction by Roger J. Sullivan. Cambridge: Cambridge University Press, 1996.

Klemperer, Victor. *LTI—Notizbuch eines Philologen: An Annotated Edition*. Englishnotes and commentary by Roderick H. Watt. Lewiston, ME: Mellen, 1997. Translation by Martin Brady: *The Language of the Third Reich: LTI—Lingua Tertii Imperii: A Philologist's Notebook*. London: Continuum, 2006.

Nietzsche, Friedrich. *Also Sprach Zarathustra*. Edited by Giorgio Colli and Mazzino Montinari. In *Kritische Studienausgabe*. Vol. 4. Berlin: De Gruyter, 1988. Translation by Adrian Del Caro: *Thus Spoke Zarathustra: A Book for All and None*, edited by Adrian Del Caro and Robert B. Pippin. Cambridge: Cambridge University Press, 2006.

HERRSCHAFT (GERMAN)

ENGLISH   domination

➤ *AUTHORITY, DOMINATION, LIBERTY, POWER* and ECONOMY, MACHT, OIKONOMIA, PRAXIS, PROPERTY, SECULARIZATION, STATE

The term, which is omnipresent in the German medieval tradition and in both legal and political reflection, never really became defined as a concept. It was used from the beginning to refer not only to the dignity of someone who is assumed to be venerable and wise because old but also to the authority exercised by the father of a family considered the head of a clan and to the relation of property exercised by the head of a clan over territory. However, it was never established as a stable equivalent in German for translating Latin notions such as *dominium, dominatio, potestas*, etc. For Kant, and then Marx, the use of the term does not always lead to its conceptualization. In contemporary thought the term still has a wide extension at the cost of definitional rigor; this is the case with the use made by the Frankfurt school, and only Max Weber attempted to make it precise, though more from a functional than thematic perspective.

I. Semantic Evolution

The term *herscaft* or *hertoum*, in Old High German, doubtless comes from the adjective *her*, which means "gray-haired," "dignified." The comparative *heriro*, which translated the Latin *senior* and the Greek *presbuteros* [πρεσβύτερος], was used to make the noun *herre*, in the seventh century, which was more or less equivalent to *dominus* (cf. RT: Grimm, *Deutsches Wörterbuch*, 4.2:1124f.; G. Ehrismann, "Die Wörter für 'Herr' im Althochdeutschen"). Whereas in the Middle Ages the distinction between *potestas* (royal power) and *auctoritas* (papal authority) was constantly being refined, leading to a clear opposition (cf. W. Ensslin, "Auctorita und Potestas"; Habermas, *Structural Transformation*, chap. I, §2)—whose extreme consequences were the establishment of an independent legal system in France (Cujas's reform under Philippe Auguste) and the Anglican schism—the term *Herrschaft* remained, in the Germanic era, relatively indeterminate and referred to the power of the father over a family and servants, in the same way as the relationship to property and serfs. However, it also had the sense of dignity and (moral) superiority, and beginning in the thirteenth century it referred to an official function. The contrast between *Herr/Knecht* is already present in the form of the difference of status between the landowner and someone who only has tenure of it, but this contrast remains, from a terminological point of view, indistinct from that between lord and vassal and that between a king and the royal domain. These two meanings rest on a single translation of the term *dominus*, which is still in the background as the means of expressing the specific power of the emperor—*dominus mundi*. The power of the pope, the king, and the princes is expressed by *Gewalt* or *Macht*, translating *potestas, imperium, regnum*, or *regimen*, whereas *Herrschaft* remains, it seems, linked to a relation that is fundamentally based in the register of property (over the members of the extended family as well as material goods and land). However, at the turn of the thirteenth and fourteenth centuries, when Louis IV of Bavaria openly opposed Pope John XXII, Marsilius of Padua in his *Defensor pacis* (ca. 1324) and William of Ockham in his *Breviloquium de potestate papae* (ca. 1341) distinguish between property and power, with the goal of contesting papal pretensions to temporal power and property, denying that *Herrschaft* can subsume the two aspects or combine them. The *Constitutio in favorem principium* of 1232 establishes the notion of *dominus terrae*, translated as *lantherr*, but we must wait until the fourteenth century for the power of the *Herr im Land* to be associated with the term *Herrschaft*, even though the word's meaning can refer to a function as well as a property (cf. RT: Grimm, *Deutsches Wörterbuch*, s.v. "Landesherrschaft") on which, most often, the exercise of power rests.

Between "property" and "power" (*Gewalt*, power exercised over persons), *Herrschaft* remains both multivalent and abstract. It is difficult to specify it by way of other notions, whether through its French equivalents—*autorité, domination, pouvoir, seigneurie*; its German ones—*Herrschung, Regiment, Obrigkeit, Oberherrschaft*; or English ones—"command," "dominion," "lordship," "reign," "rule." Adelung's dictionary (1775, 2:1133f.) defines *Herrschaft* as a concrete term—unlike *Gewalt*—that refers either to persons exercising authority over land, a place, or a family, or to the domain (abstract or concrete) over which they exercise it.

Nicolas of Cusa is one of the first to contrast, on the basis of natural law, the sovereignty of the people with a domination that does not have the power it exercises (*De concordantia catholica* [1433], p. 152f.), according to Pliny's adage (*Panegyric to Trajan*, 55, 7): *Principis sedem obtines, non sit domino locus* (you have a prince so as not to have a master). It is only then that domination relates to an abusive use of power understood as an exercise overseen by the law and subordinate in one way or another to a relatively independent control. Similarly, Erasmus goes so far as to deny that the term *Herrschaft* (translating *dominium*) is a "Christian term," and contrasts this pagan term with *administratio* (*Institutio principis christiani* [1517], in *Ein nützliche underwisung eines Christlichen fürstur wol zu regieren*, Zurich, 1521, p. 23). These two thinkers thus lay the basis for a semantic tradition whose effects are visible throughout the eighteenth century, where some encyclopedias and dictionaries (RT: Scheidemantel, *Repertorium reale pragmaticum juris publici et feudalis imperii romano-germanici*, vol. 2, 1793, and the *Deutsche Encyclopädie oder allgemeines Real Wörterbuch aller Kunste und Wissenschaften von einer Gesellschaft Gelehrten*, 1790, 15:285f.) register the evolution of the term: the antonyms we find then—*Freiheit, Knechtschaft*—are the focus of a critique of domination understood in this way. Luther offers a more ambiguous account of the situation, since he oscillates between a more critical conception of domination, contrasting *Herrschaft* with *Obrigkeit* and *Regiment*—"Now, whoever wants to be a Christian prince must abandon any intention of lording it over people and using force" (*Von weltlicher Obrigkeit* 11:271f.; *On Secular Authority*, 34)—but also yields to the temptation of justifying power in general:

> Since God gave temporal domination to the pagans and the understanding, he certainly must have created people who, with wisdom and courage, had the desire to dedicate themselves to, who were destined to it, and who knew how to maintain it.

> (Luther, Interpretation of Psalm 101,
> in *Werke*, 51:243)

On one hand he radicalizes the Augustinian doctrine of the two reigns—sometimes considering power to be purely profane (cf. "Wochenpredigten über Matthias" [Weekly sermons on Matthew 5–7] [1530–32], in *Werke*, 32:440)—but he also tries, on the other hand, to legitimate his biases by all theological means available, of which Thomas Münzer accuses him during the peasant uprisings, since Luther was on the side of the nobility. Similarly, he ignores all the contemporary legal constructions, which tended to limit or control power in general. This is what distinguishes him from Calvin, who not only took account of these legal and constitutional innovations but is careful not to give domination any kind of divine origin.

II. *Herrschaft/Knechtschaft*

Hegel first introduced this distinction, the inspiration of which is Pauline, in a theological context (*The Spirit of Christianity* [1798–99], 1907, p. 374): it concerns a split that prevents any free union between individuals, but this distinction is overturned, outmoded by the Christian vision. In the *Phenomenology of Spirit*, the distinction describes a stage of self-consciousness. However, we can neither rigorously determine it from the point of view of a dated historical

development nor reduce it to a psychological interpretation. Vico did attempt to give a pseudo-historical date to this process by referring it to the "domination of the Cyclops" (*La Scienza nuova* 1:324). The difficulty comes, here again, from the indeterminacy that affects the possibility of filling out these two notions: the master is at bottom not defined except by the fact that he is ready to sacrifice his life, whereas the slave prefers submission to death. It is rather the definition of work, refused by the master and accepted by the slave, that is at issue in this distinction, as well as the introduction of negativity as a source of historical evolution. It is clearly difficult to understand the transformation of this distinction into the consciousness of liberty as either an attested fact or a utopia—we would be tempted rather to conceive it as an anticipation by Hegel of the general flow of history after the French Revolution, and more generally as the confirmation that the modern era is crossed by the critique of the established order, a criticism that is justified by the fact that negativity cannot be removed from any social position or any instance of power.

At the strictly lexicographical level, the distinction between *Herrschaft/Knechtschaft* refers first exclusively to a legal semantic domain. In the second half of the eighteenth century, the Aristotelian-Christian tradition, which justified the relation of domination by one man of another, is questioned bit by bit, and the emergent semantic tendency, which seems to reinforce itself in the nineteenth century, gradually removes the legal content from the terms in favor of a wider meaning, of a politico-philosophical order, where what is more and more in dispute is the legal foundation of the nonnatural relation of domination. The influence of the French Revolution was felt across the Rhine, though this did not really lead to a more rigorous, conceptual definition of *Herrschaft*.

III. A Kantian Pause: The Notion of *Hausherrschaft*

It is significant that Kant in his treatise "Towards Perpetual Peace," in which he examines and contrasts different forms of government, does not use the term *Herrschaft*, not even when referring to despotism, the regime he opposes with republicanism, which in Kant's view is the only form of government that seems capable of allowing an evolution toward a constitution founded on law. The term appears, however, in the domain of private law, in Kant's *Metaphysics of Morals* (6:283, §30), where it refers to the power of the master of the house (*Hausherrschaft*), recalling the ancient notion of the *oikodespotês* [οἰκοδεσπότης]. This is indeed a kind of power related to the person (ibid., §30, Gregor, tr., *Metaphysics of Morals*, 66) from within a "society of unequals (one party *being in command* or being its head [*Herrschaft*], the other *obeying*, i.e., serving) (*imperantis et subiecti domestici*)." Kant shows himself to be thoroughly attuned to the erosion of this domestic power, undermined in the eighteenth century by the emergence of the notion of contracts, which in its weakened, contractual form now both justifies the dependence and recognizes the personhood of the one who obeys: this is why the relation of inequality thus described has its limits (ibid.). It nevertheless remains difficult, both in the letter and in the spirit of the categorical imperative, to grant—as Kant *also* does—the possibility to make "direct use of a person *as of* a thing, as a means to my end," even if this use is limited to the "usufruct" of the other's person and consequently does not genuinely attack his status as a person nor "[infringe] upon his personality" (ibid., 126–27, §2 and §3, explanatory remarks on *Metaphysical First Principles of the Doctrine of Right*). The *Critique of Practical Reason* leaves no doubt on that score:

In all of creation everything one wants and over which one has any power can also be used *merely as a means*; only the human being, and with him every rational creature, is a *purpose in itself.*

(Kant, *Kritik der praktischen Vernunft*, 5:87;
Critique of Practical Reason, 112)

The gap signaled by Kant's contradictory treatment of *Herrschaft* is foundational to the subsequent critique of domination, especially in Marx. On one hand the exploitation of the person is condemned—and the arguments appeal to this condemnation, which is morally based on the absolute value of the person—while on the other hand the emancipation of the human race in conformity with the spirit of the categorical imperative has not yet been realized in nature (the only solution seems to be revolution, which must be a "radical revolution which can only be that of radical needs," *Zur Kritik der Hegelschen Rechtsphilosophie* [Critique of the Hegelian Philosophy of Right], introduction, in *Marx-Engels Werke*, 387). The contemporary critique of domination, of whatever nature (racial, sexual, etc.) is also based in the same source: the impossibility of reducing domination, even by a proliferation of regulations and jurisprudence, whether in the private domain or the public one.

IV. Anonymous Domination

Marx effects a remarkable shift in the sense of *Herrschaft* by depersonalizing its content, without, nevertheless, giving it a properly conceptual definition:

The proletariat will use its political supremacy [*politische Herrschaft*] to wrest, by degrees, all capital from the bourgeoisie, to centralise all instruments of production in the hands of the State, i.e., of the proletariat organised as the ruling class; and to increase the total of productive forces as rapidly as possible.

(Marx, *Manifest der Kommunistischen Partei*
[The Communist Manifesto], in *Marx-Engels Werke*,
4:481; *Marx-Engels Reader*)

This depersonalization takes place, however, essentially in the domain that determines all other political and social conflicts, namely the economic one: "Capital is, therefore, not a personal, it is a social power (ibid., 476; *Marx-Engels Reader*, 485)." The main difference between the archaic, "natural" forms of production and those that develop in the framework of a civilization is revealed in the personal or anonymous form of the relation between owner and producer:

In the first case, the domination [*Herrschaft*] of the proprietor over the propertyless may be based on a personal relationship, on a kind of community; in the

second, it must have taken on a material shape in a third party—money.

(Marx, *Die deutsche Ideologie* [The German Ideology],
in *Marx-Engels Werke*, 3:65; *Marx-Engels Reader*)

Nevertheless, and even in developed societies where the most advanced form of modern capitalism reigns—hence, the most anonymous form of domination—we may still interpret "the hidden basis of the entire social structure and with it the political form of the relation of sovereignty and dependence, in short, the corresponding specific form of the state" as a "master-slave" relation: "the direct relationship of the owners of the conditions of production to the direct producers" (*Capital*, 3:555, which is nothing less than the appropriation of extra unpaid work (the presupposition of surplus value). However depersonalized, the relation between the dominant and the dominated retains a "personal" dimension, that of the concrete and immediate experience of domination. Marx does not further clarify the nature of this "personal" dimension—though he does claim that it is essential and that all the rest of the social edifice flows from it. Marxist reflection on the progressive depersonalization of the relations of production, which goes as far as their reification, nevertheless remains silent on what the initial and historical "success" of domination is. In the 1960s–1970s this anonymity of domination becomes caricatured, and a radicalized version is at times set to use in denunciations of a mysterious "system":

If man eats, drinks, is housed, reproduces, it is because the system needs him to reproduce to reproduce itself: it needs men. If it could function with slaves, there would be no "free" workers. If it could function with asexual mechanical slaves, there would be no sexual reproduction. . . . The system can only produce and reproduce individuals as elements of the system. There can be no exception.

(Baudrillard, *Pour une critique de l'économie
politique du signe*)

What the state was for Hegel, the "effective reality of the moral idea," as well as the "effective reality of concrete freedom" (*Philosophy of Right*, §§257, 260), is, for Marx, society without class, emancipation realized, the negation of the liberal distinction between state and society and the identity between economic content and political form. It is, in short, the identity between the material and the formal principles: concrete isonomia, history beyond what was hitherto recognized as the sole engine, beyond the class struggle, humanity freed from domination—from any form of domination. The Communist Revolution "abolishes the rule of all classes with the classes themselves, because it is carried through by the class which no longer counts as a class in society, is not recognized as a class, and is in itself the expression of the dissolution of all classes, nationalities, etc. within present society" (Marx, *Die deutsche Ideologie*). Yet Marx was just as discreet about this radiant future as he was about the "dictatorship of the proletariat" and refrained in both cases from prophecy. Nor did he see that any critique of this order had a precisely Kantian basis, in the fact that idea and reality rarely coincide, and in morality, politics, and social matters, never. Or that the critique cannot work against the material state of affairs without constantly appealing, even if only implicitly, to the formal level. And it is no accident that the reduction of politics to economics, a recurrent theme of Marxism (more than in Marx, in fact), goes hand in hand with a fundamental neglect of law and right (*droit*).

In the *Critique of the Hegelian Philosophy of Right* and *The German Ideology*, then, Marx describes functions that, in the prospective society that has been freed from all form of domination, are related to that very domination in earlier societies, by turning to a vocabulary that allows him to avoid the contemptible term *Herrschaft*—without, however, giving a conceptual solution to the problem that *Herrschaft* presents: *Oberaufsicht* (superior control), *Leitung* (direction), *kommandierender Wille* (directing will), etc.

Related to this situation is the fact that, less than forty years after Marx's death, Georg Simmel also tried to avoid the notion in his *Soziologie*: "Man wants to be dominated [*beherrscht*], the majority of men cannot exist without being guided [*Führung*]" (109). And we know the result of substituting *Führung* or *Führerschaft* for *Herrschaft* in sociological and political terminology.

V. Attempt at Clarification: Max Weber

Max Weber distinguishes three types of domination: rational domination (whose purest form is the domination exercised by means of an administration obeying rigorous criteria, like arithmetical accounting), traditional domination, and charismatic domination (*Economy and Society*, 215). Domination is thus a phenomenon that is common to all the historical forms it takes on—whether it is close to one of the types described or strays from it, following all the possible gradations resulting from mixture and compromise among all three types—and we may see in this a sort of psycho-social anthropological constant. Despite Marianne Weber's efforts to hide the importance of Nietzschean sources in her husband's thought, it must be recognized—in this case as a barely veiled reemergence of the notion of the will to power. Whereas power (*Macht*) means "the probability that one actor within a social relationship will be in a position to carry out his own will despite resistance, regardless of the basis on which this probability rests" (ibid., chap. 1), domination (*Herrschaft*) refers to "the probability that a command with a given specific content will be obeyed by a given group of persons" (ibid.). To impose one's will or to obey an order seem to be the two necessarily complementary components that describe a relation of forces in the framework of power relations. However, we immediately see that this definition clearly ignores the reasons that make it the case that an order is followed: "But a certain minimum of assured power to issue commands, thus of domination, must be provided for in nearly every conceivable case" (ibid.). While he invokes discipline in this context, Weber does not indicate what makes it the case that this discipline is consented to. Insofar, however, as he recognizes that obedience may equally be based on loyalty or fidelity, and that it therefore no longer functions according to a formal relationship between the one who gives an order and the one who takes it (ibid.), it is no longer possible to think that the notion of domination he offers could remain neutral from an axiological point of view, since we would be logically required to include in its definition an impulse or motive resulting from a value judgment. The result is the reappearance of the technical difficulty proper to any critique of domination that aims to proceed by generalized induction. For Weber, the demand of axiological neutrality can only also neutralize the notion of domination: the result is the weakening of the conceptual possibilities of the effective critique of domination. This demand in a way blocks, in equal measure, both the *apologia* of domination (A. Gehlen, 1993) and the general *critique* of domination which, as developed by the Frankfurt School (T. W. Adorno et al., 1950, and especially, with M. Horkheimer, *The Dialectic of Enlightenment* [1944]), leads (without lifting the veil that seems to enshroud domination) to this desperate admission: "In the enigmatic readiness of the technologically educated masses to fall under the sway of any despotism, in its self-destructive affinity to popular paranoia, and in all uncomprehended absurdity, the weakness of the modern theoretical faculty is apparent" (*Dialectic of Enlightenment*, Eng. trans. J. Cumming (Continuum), xiii). These are the same notes resounding in the famous pamphlet by La Boétie:

> The weakness among us men is such: we must often obey force. . . . It is an extreme misfortune to be subjected to a master of whom one can never be certain if he is good, since it is always in his power to be bad when he wishes.

(De la servitude volontaire ou Contr'un [1574])

Marc de Launay

BIBLIOGRAPHY

Adorno, Theodor W., et al. *The Authoritarian Personality*. New York: Harper, 1950.

Baudrillard, Jean. *Pour une critique de l'économie du signe*. Paris: Gallimard, 1972.

Cusanus, Nicolaus [Nicolas of Cusa]. *De concordantia catholica*. Edited by Gerhard Kallen. In *Opera Omnia*. Vol. 14.1. Hamburg: Meiner, 1968. First published in 1433. Translation by Paul E. Sigmung: *The Catholic Concordance*, edited by Paul E. Sigmund. Cambridge: Cambridge University Press, 1991.

Ehrismann, Gustav. "Die Wörter für 'Herr' im Althochdeutschen." *Zeitschrift für neuenglische Wortforschung* 1 (1905–6): 173 ff.

Ensslin, Wilhelm. "Auctoritas und Potestas." *Historisches Jahrbuch* 74 (1995): 661 ff.

Gehlen, Arnold. *Der Mensch, seine Natur und seine Stellung in der Welt*. Edited by Lothar Samson. In *Gesamtausgabe*. Vol. 3. Frankfurt: Klostermann, 1993. First published in 1940. Translation by Clare McMillan and Karl Pillemer: *Man, His Nature and Place in the World*. Introduction by Karl-Siegbert Rehberg. New York: Columbia University Press, 1988.

Habermas, Jürgen. *Strukturwandel der Öffentlichkeit: Untersuchungen zu einer Kategorie der bürgerlichen Gesellschaft*. Darmstadt, Ger.: Luchterhand, 1962. Translation by Thomas Burger with Frederick Lawrence: *The Structural Transformation of the Public Sphere: An Inquiry into a Category of Bourgeois Society*. Cambridge, MA: MIT Press, 1989.

Hegel, Georg Wilhelm Friedrich. "Der Geist des Christentums und sein Schicksal." In *Hegels Theologische Jugendschriften*, edited by Herman Nohl, 241–342. Tübingen: Mohr, 1907. First published in 1798–1799. Translation by T. M. Knox with Richard Kroner: "The Spirit of Christianity and Its Fate." In *On Christianity: Early Theological Writings*, 182–301. Introduction by Richard Kroner. Chicago: Chicago University Press, 1948. Reprinted 2011, Philadelphia: University of Pennsylvania Press.

Kant, Immanuel. *Die Metaphysik der Sitten*. Vol. 6 in *Kants Gesammelte Schriften*, edited by Königlich Preussischen Akademie der Wissenschaften. Berlin: De Gruyter, 1902. First published in 1797. Translation by Mary Gregor: *The Metaphysics of Morals*, edited by Mary Gregor. Introduction by Roger J. Sullivan. Cambridge: Cambridge University Press, 1996.

———. *Grundlegung zur Metaphysik der Sitten*. Vol. 6 in *Kants Gesammelte Schriften*, edited by Königlich Preussischen Akademie der Wissenschaften. Berlin: De Gruyter, 1902. First published in 1785. Translation by Mary Gregor: *Groundwork of the Metaphysics of Morals*, edited by Mary Gregor. Introduction by Christine M. Korsgaard. Cambridge: Cambridge University Press, 1997.

————. *Kritik der praktischen Vernunft*. Vol. 5 in *Kants Gesammelte Schriften*, edited by Königlich Preussischen Akademie der Wissenschaften. Berlin: De Gruyter, 1902. First published in 1788. Translation by Mary Gregor: *Critique of Practical Reason*, edited by Mary Gregor. Cambridge: Cambridge University Press, 1997.

————. "Zum ewigen Frieden." In *Kants Gesammelte Schriften*, edited by Königlich Preussischen Akademie der Wissenschaften, 8: 341–86. Berlin: De Gruyter, 1902. First published in 1795. Translation, introduction, commentary, and postscript by Wolfgang Schwarz: *Principles of Lawful Politics: Immanuel Kant's Philosophic Draft toward Eternal Peace: A New Faithful Translation*. Aalen: Scientia, 1988.

Luther, Martin. "Von weltlicher Obrigkeit." In *Werke: Kritische Gesamtausgabe*, 11: 229–81. 73 vols. Weimar, Ger.: Böhlaus, 1900. First published in 1523. Translation by Harro Höpfl: "On Secular Authority." In *Luther and Calvin on Secular Authority*, edited by Harro Höpfl. Cambridge: Cambridge University Press, 1991. See also "Temporal Authority." In *Martin Luther's Basic Theological Writings*, edited by Timothy F. Lull, 429–59. Foreword by Jaroslav Pelikan. 2nd ed. Minneapolis: Fortress, 2005.

Marx, Karl. *Karl Marx–Frederick Engels: Collected Works*. Translated by Richard Dixon et al. 50 vols. London: Lawrence and Wishart, 1975–2004.

————. *Marx-Engels Reader*. Edited by Robert C. Tucker. New York: W. W. Norton, 1989.

————. *Marx-Engels Werke*. 43 vols. Berlin: Dietz, 1957–1968.

————. *Capital: A Critique of Political Economy*. Vol. 3: *The Process of Capitalist Production as a Whole*. Edited by Friedrich Engels. New York: International Publishers, [n.d.].

Simmel, Georg. *Soziologie: Untersuchungen über die Formen der Vergesellschaftung*. In *Gesammelte Werke*. Vol. 2. 4th ed. Berlin: Duncker and Humblot, 1958. Translation by Anthony J. Blasi, Anton K. Jacobs, and Mathew Kanjirathinkal: *Sociology: Inquiries into the Construction of Social Forms*, edited by A. J. Blasi, A. K. Jacobs, and M. Kanjirathinkal. Introduction by Horst J. Helle. 2 vols. Leiden: Brill, 2009.

Vico, Giambattista. *La Scienza Nuova*. Edited by Fausto Nicolini. 2 vols. Vol. 1. Rome: Laterza, 1974. First published in 1744. Translation by Thomas Goddard Bergin and Max Harold Fisch: *The New Science of Giambattista Vico*. Ithaca, NY: Cornell University Press, 1968.

Weber, Max. *Wirtschaft und Gesellschaft*. Tübingen: Siebeck, 1922. Translation by Ephraim Fischoff et al.: *Economy and Society: An Outline of Interpretive Sociology*, edited by Guenther Roth and Claus Wittich. 2 vols. Berkeley: University of California Press, 1978.

HISTORIA UNIVERSALIS (LATIN)

ENGLISH   world history, general history, universal history
FRENCH   *histoire universelle, histoire générale, histoire mondiale*
GERMAN   *Universalhistorie, Weltgeschichte, Welthistorie, allgemeine (Welt)Geschichte*

➤ CORSO, GEISTESWISSENSCHAFTEN, GESCHICHTLICH, HISTORY, PEOPLE, SECULARIZATION, WELT

The concept is of Latin origin—the first *historia universalis* appears in 1304—and in fact covers two distinct practices: the exhaustive juxtaposition of political histories on one hand, and the link between profane history (restricted to a few choice peoples) with Catholic history on the other. In the second half of the eighteenth century, having collectively rejected both of these methods, French, German, and British thinkers attempted to develop new historical universalities, which make use of terminological choices that do not strictly align. It is not surprising, then, that they all more or less simultaneously, though in different ways, rediscover Vico, whose project had no doubt "anticipated" their own.

I. Catholic Universality, Empirical Universality, Universality of Progress

In 1783 Gabriel Bonnot de Mably distinguishes two concepts of "universal history": the first covers the empirical exhaustiveness of simple "collections of individual histories," the second describes Catholic universality as practiced by Bossuet in his *Discours* of 1681, in which he traced "everything back to a few famous people"(Mably, *De la manière d'écrire l'histoire*). The distinction clearly shows a real equivocity. We could illustrate the first sense by the *Introduction à l'histoire, générale et politique, de l'univers; où l'on voit l'origine, les révolutions et la situation présente des différents États de l'Europe, de l'Asie, de l'Afrique et de l'Amérique* (Introduction to the general and political history of the universe; in which we see the origin, the revolutions, and the present situation of the various States of Europe, Asia, Africa, and America) (Amsterdam, 1721), by which A.-A Bruzen de La Martinière "completed" the work of Samuel von Pufendorf, *Einleitung zur Geschichte der europäischen Staaten* (Frankfurt, 1682), translated by C. Rouxel in 1710. La Martinière's concern is to juxtapose dynastic and military histories, thus above all political ones, from all known nations to the extent that this is possible. In cases such as for the "Negroes of Africa," says La Martinière, their "common customs" will have to do."

In 1756, Voltaire rejects both empirical historiography and the sorts of universal history found in Boussuet and La Martinière. His work of 1756, *Essai sur l'histoire générale et sur les mœurs et l'esprit des nations depuis Charlemagne jusqu'à nos jours* (Essay on general history and on the morals and spirits of nations from Charlemagne to the present), rejects any Augustinianism by offering a history that claimed to be truly universal inasmuch as it was exclusively profane, and thus extended to all peoples of the earth (with the disappearance of the Catholic *telos* all retroactive selection disappears as well). It was also a rejection of political history, a history of princes and battles, in favor of a truly universal history as extended to the "morals and spirits of nations," that is, to anything by which nations had their own substance, independently of those who governed them and their conflicts. The result for Voltaire is "a chaos of events, factions, revolutions, and crimes" but the consequence of this "chaos" is the universalization of the task of thinking of universal history as an essentially worldly and pan-institutional process (it henceforth wins out over all human moral and legal institutions). In France, this new way of thinking about "universal history" leads to the abandonment of the phrase "histoire universelle," and when Condorcet abstains from following Voltaire and writing "the history of governments, laws, morals, manners, opinions, among the different peoples who have successively occupied the globe," he replaces it with a "historical tableau of the progress of the human spirit." The following century will bring a desire to reconcile Catholic universality with "Progress," and in this context it becomes possible to write works such as J. F. A. Boulland's *Essai d'histoire universelle ou exposé comparatif des traditions de tous les peuples depuis les temps primitifs jusqu'à nos jours* (Essay in universal history or comparative presentation of the traditions of all peoples from primitive times to the present day) (Paris, 1836).

II. The "Natural History of Mankind" as *Histoire Raisonnée*

In 1767, Adam Ferguson carefully avoids using the expression "history of the world," which had been the title of a work by Sir Walter Raleigh in 1614, or the expression "universal history," which he might have come across in Henry Boling-broke (*Letters on the Study and Use of History*). He prefers to refer to his undertaking as "the general history of nations" (*An Essay on the History of Civil Society*, I, 10), by which he clearly means "*of all nations*"(II, 1; III, 6; II, 8). It is surprising to see Ferguson translate the plural from the preface of Montesquieu's *De l'esprit des lois*—"les histoires de toutes les nations"—by a collective singular ("the general history"), but it provides evidence for a new universality under construction—a bit in the way that in Vico, "le storie di tutto le nazioni" could be subsumed under "una storia ideal eterna" (*Scienza nuova*, 1744, §145). Indeed, while Ferguson's phrase echoes Voltaire's—Claude-François Bergier translates it correctly into French as "l'histoire générale des nations" (*Essai sur l'histoire de la société civile*)—and while this echo of Voltaire is significant (as Ferguson's work concerns a process that is essentially worldly, worldwide, and civil)—it remains the case that its "generality" is nevertheless different from the sort one finds in Voltaire. Ferguson's results from the empiricist overlay of the trajectories followed by the observable nations; or rather, his "generality" is the abstract process that any nation must follow to the extent that circumstances permit. In this sense, what is abstract is also "natural," and John Millar suggests the expression "natural history of mankind" to describe this way of proceeding (*The Origin of the Distinction of Ranks*). Matters soon get more complicated. When Dugald Stewart suggests in 1793 a French translation of "natural history" thus understood, he does not propose *histoire naturelle* or *histoire générale*, but rather *histoire raisonée* (Smith, *Works and Correspondence*); he has in mind d'Alembert, who in the *Essai sur les éléments de philosophie* in 1759 had invoked "l'histoire générale et raisonnée des sciences et des arts"(chap. 2). The translation is surprising, but not absurd at all: Stewart could evoke, for his English-speaking reader, David Hume's *Natural History of Religion* (1757), but he had to avoid the French phrase "histoire naturelle de l'humanité," which would have necessarily called Buffon to mind for a French readership and entailed an entirely different sort of inquiry. Moreover, the word *raisonnée* contrasted with *révélée* (revealed), as "natural" with "supernatural," which allowed Stewart to preserve what was essential in the original title.

III. *Weltgeschichte* vs. *Universalhistorie*

The German translation of Voltaire's *Essai sur l'histoire générale*, published in 1762, suggests the compound *allgemeine Weltgeschichte* (a "general history of the world"). The expression is Kant's, but the use has changed. Kant uses the compound term in 1784 in stating the ninth proposition of the *Idee zu einer allgemeinen Geschichte*, in which he is concerned, contrary to the later translation of Voltaire's essay, to justify a historical teleology that Voltaire would have rejected. What is this teleology (it is a novel—but we should excuse it for that), if not the realization of what Leibniz had reserved for God, namely, "this novel of human life which tells the universal history of humankind" (*Essai de Théodicée*, II), and which Leibniz contrasts with the "sort of universal history" assigned to man, aimed simply at gathering all the "useful" facts (*Nouveaux essais*, IV)? *Allgemeine Weltgeschichte* is no doubt something like a theodicy of history, and we can just as well say, here in the 1700s, *allgemeine Geschichte, Universalgeschichte*, or *Weltgeschichte*, as Schiller's inaugural lecture at

Jena in 1789 demonstrates ("Was heisst und zu welchem Ende studiert man Universalgeschichte?"). At a pinch, a translator could get by with "general history," "universal history," or "world history" (but "history of the world" would be less anachronistic).

However, the translator would then be at a loss when she comes up against *Welthistorie*, for example, in Ernesti's preface to the German translation of *A General History of the World, from the Creation to the Present Time* (London, 1764–67), under the direction of W. Guthrie and J. Gray, also published under the title *Allgemeine Weltgeschichte von der Schöpfung an bis auf gegenwärtige Zeit* (Leipzig, 1765–1808). She will also be troubled, and much more frequently, by *Universalhistorie*, still commonly used in the 1770s: J. C. Gatterer publishes an *Einleitung in die synchronistische Universalhistorie* in 1771, but in 1785 a *Weltgeschichte in ihren ganzen Umfange*. Similarly, A. L. Schlözer publishes a *Vorstellung einer Universalhistorie* in 1772, and in 1779, a *Vorbereitung zur Weltgeschichte für Kinder*. It is essentially during these years that *Weltgeschichte* wins out over *Universalhistorie*, which is why Kant spontaneously adopts it for rethinking Leibniz's "universal history." Why the substitution, however? The answer lies in Kant, in the last paragraph of the *Idee zu einer allgemeinen Geschichte*, but also in Schlözer, writing a year later:

§1: Universalhistorie war weiland nichts als ein "Gemengsel von einigen historischen Datis, die der Theolog zum Verständnis der Bibel, und der Philolog zur Erklärung der alten griechischen und römischen Schriftsteller und Denkmäler, nötig hatte": war nichts als eine Hilfswissenschaft der biblischen und Profanphilologie. . . .

§2: Weltgeschichte ist eine systematische Sammlung von Tatsätzen, vermittelst deren der gegenwärtige Zustand der Erde und des Menschengeschlechts, aus Gründen verstehen lässt.

(§1: *Universalhistorie* was at the time only a "mix of some historical *data* which were needed by the theologian for the understanding of the Bible and the philologist for the explication of ancient writers and Greek and Roman artists": it was nothing but an auxiliary science for biblical and profane philology.

§2: *Weltgeschichte* is a systematic collection of facts by means of which the current state of the Earth and the human race become comprehensible on the basis of its principles.)

At bottom, choosing *Weltgeschichte* was choosing *Welt* and *Geschichte*. *Welt* to refer to what is *weltlich* (worldly), and not just to *Welt* as universality. *Geschichte* to refer to what is "systematic," in contrast with Greek *historia*, and to distinguish a process from a simple scholarly inventory. *Weltgeschichte* is the evolution of the human race considered in its past, present, even future totality—but always in earthly terms—and it pushes the aggregate of *Universalhistorie* back into the pre-history of history, as a metaphysical substrate. We can thus understand how the precise nature of this systematicity, understood as *Zusammenhang* (teleological connection? a priori? etc.) was what defined the stakes in the debates among German philosophers of history.

Bertrand Binoche

BIBLIOGRAPHY

Alonso-Nuñez, José Miguel. *The Idea of Universal History in Greece: From Herodotus to the Age of Augustus.* Amsterdam: Gieben, 2002.

Bergier, Claude-François. *Essai sur l'histoire de la société civile.* Desaint, 1783.

Bolingbroke, Henry. *An Essay on the History of Civil Society.* Edinburgh: Edinburgh University Press, 1966.

———. *Letters on the Study and Use of History.* Basil, 1788. First published in 1735.

Borst, Arno. "Weltgeschichten im Mittelalter?" In *Geschichte, Ereignis und Erzählung,* edited by Reinhart Koselleck and Wolf-Dieter Stempel, 452–55. Munich: Fink, 1973.

Condorcet. *Œuvres completes.* Firmin-Didot, 1847–49.

Hopfl, Harro M. "From Savage to Scotsman: Conjectural History in the Scottish Enlightenment." *Journal of British Studies* 17 (1978): 19–40.

Koselleck, Reinhart. "Von der 'historia universalis' zur 'Weltgeschichte.'" In vol. 2 of *Geschichtliche Grundbegriffe: Historisches Lexikon zur politisch-sozialen Sprache in Deutschland,* edited by Otto Brunner, Werner Conze, and Reinhart Koselleck, 685ff. 8 vols. Stuttgart: Klett, 1975.

Laudin, Gérard. "Changements de paradigme dans l'historiographie allemande: Les origines de l'humanité dans les 'Histoires universelles' des années 1760–1829." *Pratiques et concepts de l'histoire en Europe, XVI–XVIII siècles,* edited by C. Grell and J. M. Dufays. Paris: Presses de l'université Paris-Sorbonne, 1990.

———. "La cohérence de l'histoire: aspects de la reception de Voltaire dans l'Allemagne des années 1760–1770." In *Voltaire et ses combats,* edited by Ulla Kölving and Christiane Mervaud, 1435–47. 2 vols. Oxford: Voltaire Foundation, 1997.

Link, Anne-Marie. "Engraved Images, the Visualization of the Past, and Eighteenth-Century Universal History." In *Lumen,* edited by Servanne Woodward, 175–95. Kelowna: Academic, for the Canadian Society for Eighteenth-Century Studies, 2006.

Mably, Gabriel de. *De la manière d'écrire l'histoire.* Edited and revised by B. de Negroni. Fayard, 1988.

Mazzotta, Giuseppe. "Universal History: Vico's New Science between Antiquarians and Ethnographers." In *Reason and Its Others: Italy, Spain and the New World,* edited by David R. Castillo and Massimo Lollini, 316–30. Nashville: Vanderbilt University Press, 2006.

Millar, John. *The Origin of the Distinction of Ranks.* Basil: Tourneisen, 1793. First published in 1771.

Pons, Alain. "Vico et la 'barbarie de la réflexion.'" *La Pensée politique* 2 (1994). Translation by Daniel H. Fernald: "Vico and the 'Barbarism of Reflection.'" *New Vico Studies* 16 (1998): 1–24.

Schiller, Friedrich. "Was heisst und zu welchem Ende studiert man Universalgeschichte?" In *Werke, Nationalausgabe.* Weimar: Böhlau, 1970.

Schlozer, August Ludwig. *Weltgeschichte nach ihren Haupteilen im Auszug und Zusammenhange.* Göttingen: Vandenhoek, 1785.

Smith, Adam. *Works and Correspondence.* Oxford: Clarendon Press, 1980.

Söder, Hans-Peter. "From Universal History to Globalism: What Are and for What Purposes Do We Study European Ideas?" *History of European Ideas* 33 (2007): 72–86.

Truyol y Serra, Antonio. "The Idea of Man and World History from Seneca to Orosius and Saint Isidore de Seville." *Cahiers d'histoire mondiale* 6 (1960).

HISTORY / STORY

DUTCH	*Geschiedenis*
GERMAN	*Historie, Historik, Geschichten, Geschichte*
GREEK	*historia* [ἱστορία], *historiê* [ἱστορίη]
ITALIAN	*storia, storiografia*
LATIN	*historia, gesta, res gestae*

➤ DICHTUNG, ERLEBEN, ERZÄHLEN, *FICTION*, GEISTESWISSENSCHAFTEN, GESCHICHTLICH, HISTORIA UNIVERSALIS, LOGOS, MEMORY, MIMÊSIS, MOMENT, PRESENT

The path from the Greek *historia* to the Latin *historia* to the French *histoire* (It. *storia,* Sp. *historia,* Eng. "history," Ger. *Historie*) seems simple and direct. History was always history! One clue, however,

should put us on guard: why did German end up distinguishing *Historie* (a clear translation of the Latin *historia*) from *Geschichte* (referring to what has happened but also the recounting we give of it, the study of the past—"History" with a capital *H*)?

What, then, was the ancient path? From *historiê* [ἱστορίη] (the Ionian form of *historia* [ἱστορία]), from the Herodotean inquiry to Roman *historia,* and from the universal history of the Greek Polybius, a hostage in Rome for seventeen years, to the ecclesiastical history of Eusebius, bishop of Caesarea, and to the sacred history of Augustine, the word has not covered the same field—far from it. We seem to have moved from *historia* by itself, claimed to be a new practice, to *historia* furnished with all sorts of qualifications (universal, ecclesiastical, and so on).

Definitions of history during the Middle Ages were largely inspired by those inherited from antiquity. In the modern era, we have witnessed a progressive differentiation, both semantic and linguistic. The first consequence is a clearer distinction between facts and their narrative. The second is the progressive construction of a reflective dimension. In parallel, while the derivatives from the Latin *historia* were taken up by most languages, German (followed by Dutch) substituted in the place of *Historie* the notion of *Geschichte,* which reunites what has taken place with the narrative report of it. At the same time, German moved from the plural *Geschichten* to the collective singular *Geschichte.* This transformation illustrates in turn the introduction of a totalizing perspective that brings a reflective eye to bear upon the collection of individual histories. Languages that remained in the tradition of the term *historia* effected the same change in perspective, although without giving it formal expression.

The development of a historical science, one echoing the elaboration of a philosophy of history that attempts to reconfigure the relation between past, present, and future, took place within scholarly traditions that became progressively marked by national concerns. Despite the often intense contacts between the respective communities, these evolutions helped fix specific semantic usages. However, the questions that animate the debates among historians are largely held in common: the historicicization of the field of knowledge (associated in German with the term *Historismus*), the relation between relativism and universalism, the relation between the historical object and its exposition by the historian, and the emergence of a history of history (*storia della storiografia,* as it is known in its most prominent, Italian form) gave rise to further developments that inflect and renew the uses of the notion of history and its equivalents.

I. *Historia:* From Greek Inquiry to Latin Histories

A. The *histôr* and the bard

The epic features a character known as the *histôr.* Is he a witness or a judge? For Émile Benveniste, *histôr* refers to the witness. Etymologically, *histôr* [ἵστωρ] (like *historein* [ἱστορεῖν] and *historia* [ἱστορία]) goes back to *idein* [ἰδεῖν], "to see," and to (*w*)*oida* [οἶδα], "I know." "I see," "I know": already the intertwining of seeing and knowing is laid down. The *histôr* would thus be a witness "insofar as he knows, but in the first instance because he has seen" (RT: Benveniste, *Le vocabulaire des institutions indo-européennes*). However, in the two scenes of the *Iliad* where a *histôr* is required, it is clear that we are not in the presence of a witness in the sense of one who knows from having seen. During Patroclus's funeral, Ajax and Idomeneus are in disagreement with regard to knowing who is in front after passing the marker in the chariot race organized by Achilles; Ajax suggests taking Agamemnon as *histôr* (*Iliad*, 23.482–87). Whatever Agamemnon's exact role may be, it is certain that he has not seen the scene at all. Similarly, the extraordinary shield forged by Hephaistos for Achilles contains a representation of a scene in which two men with a serious disagreement (reparations for a murder) decide to call a *histôr* (*Iliad*, 18.497–502). The *histôr* is clearly not a witness to the murder. In both cases, stepping into a dispute (*neikos* [νεῖκος]), the *histôr* is not one who, by his intervention alone, can put an end to the differences by adjudicating between conflicting versions, but is, rather, the guarantor (for the present or indeed for the future) of what will have been agreed upon by the two parties (cf. Scheid-Tissinier, "À propos du rôler").

This first entry into the lexical field of *historia* reveals a broader view of the epic as a sort of prehistory of history. What, in fact, is the mechanism of epic speech, and what is the configuration of knowledge that bears it? The bard, inspired by the muses, daughters of Zeus and Memory (*Mnêmosunê*), is a seer, whereas the omniscience of the muses is based on the fact that they are always there: they see everything. "You are at hand, and you know all things," says the poet in the *Iliad* (2.485). When Odysseus addresses the bard of the Phaeacians, he praises him thus:

> I respect you, Demodocus, more than any man alive— / surely the muse has taught you, Zeus's daughter, / or god Apollo himself. How true to life, / all too true . . . you sing the Achaeans' fate, / all they did and suffered, all they soldiered through, / as if you were there yourself [*autos pareôn* (αὐτὸς παρεών)] or heard from one who was [*akousas* (ἀκούσας)].

> (*Odyssey*, 8.546–51)

This scene has symbolic value. For what will the bard sing at the request of Odysseus? Of the sacking of Troy. It is the first narration of the event, even while the presence of Odysseus certifies that *that* really did happen.

Demodocus, in sum, would be the first historian, and his narrative, the birth of history—although with the following difference, which in fact changes everything: Demodocus was not there and did not see anything (he is blind), whereas Odysseus is both an actor and a witness. Whence the astonishing (false) question of Odysseus: is your account not too precise *not* to come from direct observation? Human vision (a historian before its time, in the sense of seeing with one's own eyes or learning from someone who has seen) becomes, with these two verses, the benchmark of divine vision. It is precisely as if there were a strange and brief juxtaposition of two Demodocuses: one (still) a bard and the other (already) a historian. What happens there is like a lightning bolt cast over a different possible configuration of knowledge: precisely the one that the first historiography will come to occupy, the one to which, it turns out, Herodotus will give both form and name two or three centuries later: *historiê*. Of course, this juxtaposition in the Homeric work neither makes such *historiê* necessary nor even likely—simply possible.

B. *Historiê* and *historein*: Inquiry and inquirer

"Inquiry" in all senses of the term, *historiê* refers more to a state of mind (the fact of one who *historei* [ἱστορεῖ], "inquires into") and a way of proceeding than to a particular domain in which it is specifically exercised. It is a word belonging to intellectual history at this time (the first half of the fifth century BCE), possibly a fashionable word: it means what it means, and each writer bends it to his needs. Without entirely forgetting the *histôr* / judge or guarantor of epic poetry, the word has several layers of meaning and must have functioned as a lexical crossroads.

We can use it to describe the activity of a "traveling-inquirer" like Democritus, a judicial inquiry (seeking to know something, inquiring, certifying something). The tragic poets were aware of it—Oedipus, addressing his daughters, says of himself: "Seeing [*horôn* (ὁρῶν)] nothing, children, knowing [*historôn* (ἱστορῶν)] nothing, I became your father, I fathered you in the soil that gave me life" (Sophocles, *Oedipus Rex*, 1624–6). And the medical writers used it as well.

■ See Box 1.

Borrowing it or otherwise making it his own, Herodotus gives it as the key word for his whole enterprise: "From [of, pertaining to, belonging to] Herodotus of Halicarnassus, here is the account of his *historiê* . . ." (1.1). Given in the genitive, these first words are like an inaugural signature of someone who comes to present, in public and in his own name, the fruits of his research. He is someone who *historei* (he never calls himself a "historian"), coming to claim a position of knowledge that is as yet entirely unconstructed. Beyond the opening sentence, Herodotus uses the verb *historein* to refer to the type of work he has done. Thus, when he attempts to resolve the difficult question of the sources of the Nile, he clarifies:

> I myself travelled as far as Elephantine and saw things with my very own eyes [*autoptês* (αὐτόπτης)], and subsequently made enquiries of others [*akoêi historeôn* (ἀκοῇ ἱστορέων)].

> (Herodotus, *Histories*, 2.29)

Several times (2.19, 34, 118), *historein* is used in a context of oral inquiry, but the traveler has nonetheless first gone to the location in question. In 2.44, seeking to understand who Heracles is, Herodotus specifies that he went as far as Tyre in Phoenicia. There, he saw the sanctuaries that were devoted to the demigod, and he questioned the priests. An "inquiry" (*ta historêmata* [τὰ ἱστορήματα]) is thus the combination of these procedures, the eye and the ear, eyewitness and hearsay: "These enquiries of mine, then, clearly show that . . ." (2.113). To see henceforth, he must make sacrifices (go and see) and learn to see (gather testimony, collect different versions, report them, classify them according to what he knows from elsewhere and according to their degree of likelihood).

From an epistemological point of view, *historiê* functions as a substitute (a sort of ersatz) for original, divine vision, although providing only a limited and never-complete vision. The concern now is only with men and their great accomplishments (the bard, in contrast, sang of both men and gods), in a time that is also that of men alone.

1

The history of doctors

The Hippocratic corpus presents several very interesting examples, beginning with the oath itself, which calls upon the gods as witnesses, that is, as guarantors:

> I swear by Apollo the healer, by Aesculapius, by Health and all the powers of healing, and call to witness [*historas poieumenos* (ἵστορας ποιεύμενος)] all the gods and goddesses that I may keep this Oath and Promise to the best of my ability and judgment.
>
> (Hippocrates, *Ancient Medicine*)

The gods are called upon to hear (not to see) and to be guarantors of the oath made by the applicant. We are again in the presence of the epic *histôr*.

Historion as proof. In *Diseases, IV*, the author lists "proofs" (he has seven of them) that drink does not go into the lungs, before concluding:

> Indeed I would not have advanced any of these proofs in support of my argument, were it not for the fact that it is a very generally held opinion [*dokeousi* (δοκέουσι)] that drink goes into the lung, and against an opinion strongly held one is obliged to advance many proofs [*polla historia* (πολλὰ ἰστόρια)], if one is going to turn the hearer from his former opinion and persuade him by what one says.
>
> (*Diseases IV*, 56.7, in *Hippocratic Treatises*)

Historein

A physician does not violate etiquette even if, being in difficulties on occasion over a patient and in the dark through inexperience, he should urge the calling in of others, in order to learn by consultation the truth about the case, and in order that there may be fellow-workers to afford abundant help.

> (Hippocrates, *Hippocratic Treatises*)

The investigation of what is related to the sick person and his disease proceeds from the common basis established by group consultations.

Historiê as inquiry or the knowledge resulting. The treatise *Ancient Medicine* (or, *Tradition in Medicine*; chap. 20), claiming that only medicine can give us precise knowledge of the nature of man, invokes an inquiry (*historiê*) into "what man is and how he exists because it seems to me indispensable for a doctor to have made such studies and to be fully acquainted with Nature."

We may follow the relationship between *historia* and autopsy or eyewitnessing (the fact that the doctor has seen with his own eyes and has direct knowledge) into the second century CE: *historia* presenting itself as a narrative of autopsy. Thus, in "An Outline of Empiricism," Galen presents and critiques the position of doctors of the empiricist school:

The first and foremost criterion of true history, the empiricists have said, is what the person who makes the judgment has perceived for himself. For, if we find one of those things written down in a book by somebody which we have perceived for ourselves, we will say that the history is true. But this criterion is of no use if we want to learn something new. For we do not need to learn from a book any of those things which we already know on the basis of our own perception. Most useful and at the same time more truly a criterion of history is agreement [*sumphônia* (συμφωνία)].

Galen then presents an example: imagine a medication that one does not know. Everyone writing about it says that it has a certain effect. Should one believe them? Yes, says Galen, from the very fact of the *sumphônia*.

BIBLIOGRAPHY

Galen. "An Outline of Empiricism" [Subfiguratio empirica]. In *Three Treatises on the Nature of Science*. Translated by Richard Walzer and Michael Frede. Indianapolis, IN: Hackett, 1985.

Hippocrates. *Ancient Medicine*. In Vol. 1 of *Hippocrates*, translated by W.H.S. Jones. Loeb Classical Library. Cambridge, MA: Harvard University Press, 1923.

———. *The Hippocratic Treatises "On Generation," "On the Nature of the Child," "Diseases IV."* Translated by Iain M. Lonie. New York: de Gruyter, 1981.

Against time, which erases everything, the historian creates a work of memory, and since instability is the rule, he must give a parallel, balanced account, like a fair judge, of the great and small cities: he will be their guarantor.

The muse as unique announcer having gone silent, a narrative with a twofold structure is put in place: on one hand, the *I*, the inquirer and narrator, who comes and goes, gauging and judging; on the other, the profusion of *logoi* [λόγοι], accounts, maintained by all and sundry (including the anonymous *legetai* [λέγεται], "it is said that"), which he inventories and reports. Between these two, in the movement from one side to the other, is established a process of "interlocution," which is always being renegotiated, that forms the deep texture and that is the purpose of the historical narrative.

C. *Suggraphein*: Transcribing what the eye witnesses

With Thucydides, who is commonly held to be the other, if not the true, founder of history, what is initially striking is the intention to break from Herodotus. *The Peloponnesian War* is at no point put under the heading of *historia*: the noun never appears, nor does the verb *historein*. It is not that Thucydides declined to inquire—quite the contrary; but he put his work in the category of "setting in writing" (*suggraphein* [συγγράφειν]): "Thucydides, an Athenian, recorded the war between the Peloponnesians and the Athenians, writing how they waged it against each other . . ." (1.1). The verb means "to take note," "put into writing," or in a more technical sense, "to write out a legal document, a contract." Later, when history will be a genre, *suggraphein* and *suggrapheus* [συγγραφεύς] (*scriptor* in Latin) will come to mean historical writing and the historian. However, neither *suggrapheus* nor *scriptor* ever refers to historians alone (that is to say, as a distinct vocation): the historian is, rather, a writer practicing a certain kind of writing. But for Thucydides, a historian of the present, to say that he *suggraphei* is to say that he reports what has just happened from up close, what is in fact still going on. He does not write the history of the war but rather puts the war into writing, baptizing forever these thirty years of hostilities as the Peloponnesian War.

To do so, he decisively gives priority to the first of the two means of knowledge available to the historian, the eye (*opsis* [ὄψις]) and the ear (*akoê* [ἀκοή]): the eye is the only one of the two allowing for a clear and distinct vision (*saphôs eidenai* [σαφῶς εἰδέναι]). *Historiê* and *historein*, too closely related to oral forms of inquiry, no longer have their place in his epistemology. The ear is never trustworthy: what is *said* is trafficked, spread, transmitted—everything that comes from memory is subject to deformation and yields, deliberately or insidiously, to the law of pleasure that rules word of mouth. This is why there is no other scientific history but that of the present. And there still remains a need for the eye and the fact of seeing oneself to be sifted through a critique of testimony. Writing history is the transcription of an eyewitnessing, or better, of an autopsy. The goal being sought must be what is useful.

D. History as a genre: A *historia* without *historein*

Neither *historia* nor *historein* reappear immediately. Xenophon made no use of them either. Accounts of so-called Greek matters, *Hellenika*, were written by now-lost chroniclers, and Xenophon wrote his own *Hellenika*, picking up exactly where Thucydides left off. In the fourth century BCE, Ephorus, whom Polybius recognized as his only predecessor in the project of composing universal history (see HISTORIA UNIVERSALIS), did publish *Historiai*, which were a way of linking up with the Herodotean project; however, it is only in the preface to Polybius's *Histories* that we gain a clear confirmation that *historia* has become a genre on its own: "Had previous chroniclers neglected to speak in praise of History in general . . ." (1.1); "if this had been the case," Polybius seems to argue, "then I would have to make the sacrifice, but since this is not the case, I can spare myself." There follows immediately a series of variations on the theme of history as *paideia* [παιδεία] (education), *gumnasia* [γυμνασία] (training), and *didaskalos* [διδάσκαλος] (teacher) in order to face the vicissitudes of life. A century later, Cicero's expression of *historia* as *magistra vitae* (mistress or directress of life; *De oratore*, 2.9, 36) will simply take up this program again and resume the project—and so too will Dionysius of Halicarnassus (a contemporary of Augustus) who defined, or is said to have defined, history as "philosophy on the basis of examples" (*Ars rhetorica*, 11.2): moral philosophy, of course. However, we are now in Rome, or somewhere between Greece and Rome. Henceforth, we have a *historia* without *historein*.

What happened between the fourth and second centuries BCE, when indeed many histories were being written (almost all lost)? What happened to the curious inquirer, emulator, and rival to the bard of the past? Or to the one who, with a different ambition, wished to make his history *the* political science, giving the men of the future a way of understanding their own present? They disappeared, whereas *historia* settled in. However—or so the moderns tell us—in the process, *historia* was caught by rhetoric: it became (as in Isocrates) a branch of eulogy. Aristotle, for his part, relegated it to the domain of particulars. As for Athens, the experience of defeat at the hands of Sparta and its consequences led to a lasting reversal of the situation: to face (or indeed, to avoid) the difficulties of the present, they turned wholeheartedly toward the past with the idea of imitating it. Here is where the theme of history as a provider of examples (*paradeigmata* [παραδείγματα], *exempla*) arises, becoming rapidly and for a long time a topos of the historical genre: history as a

"mistress of life." Faced with a crisis of the present, one may become more concerned with establishing continuities: with recounting the events of the history of the city or the history of the world from the beginning to the present day. The historian, in these circumstances, acquired a greater need for books and headed down the path of libraries. The role of inquiry (*historiê*) diminished, and that of compilation increased: the historian became a reader. Everyone agrees in reckoning that the facts are given, that the facts are there; the important part is to put them together—not what to say, but how to say it.

■ See Box 2.

E. Narrative history: *Narratio*

As Lucian of Samosata reminded us in the second century CE, the historian's "business" is "to superinduce upon events the charm of order, and set them forth in the most lucid fashion he can manage" (*How to Write History*, 51). The historian is like the sculptors Phidias and Praxiteles: we put the primary material at his disposal, and he comes afterward to fashion it and give it form.

There are stylistic models from this point on: they are catalogued and studied; students in schools of rhetoric learn to imitate them. *Historia* has become a literary genre, and when Cicero asks about the beginnings of history, he gives a literary history of history, running from the annals of ancient Rome (organized by year) to a *narratio* that is more and more elaborate and self-conscious. History, to say it in Latin, will be henceforth—maybe even only—*narratio*.

History is useful for the training of orators; as Quintilian emphasizes, however, its goal and expression are different from those that pertain to the eloquence of the forum.

> History [*historia*], also, may provide the orator with a nutriment which we may compare to some rich and pleasant juice. But when we read it, we must remember that many of the excellences of the historian require to be shunned by the orator. For history has a certain affinity to poetry and may be regarded as a kind of prose poem [*carmen solutum*], while it is written for the purposes of narrative [*ad narrandum*], not of proof [*ad probandum*], and designed from beginning to end not for immediate effect or the instant necessities of forensic strife, but to record events for the benefit of posterity and to win glory for its author [*ad memoriam posteritatis et ingenii famam*].
>
> (*Institutio oratoria*, 10.1.31–34)

Historia is a narration of *res gestae*, of what has been accomplished, and especially of the grand deeds of the Roman people: recalling the "high deeds of the greatest people of the world" (1.3): this is Livy's project. *Historia romana* henceforth becomes the past of the city, which "Augustus watches over" (Probus, *Life of Virgil*, 28)—Augustus was himself the author of a monument testament, rightly entitled *Res gestae*, in which he recounted both his actions and those of the Roman Empire.

■ See Box 3.

Whatever debates this genre of *narratio* might have entailed did not have a great influence on historical productions in Rome at the time. (Lucian, for instance, is clearly

2

History between rhetoric and philosophy

Rhetoric and history: Isocrates

Defining philosophy as what is useful "to words and to action," Isocrates never directly dealt with history and never legislated as to what a historical narrative should look like. However, he is taken for a master (a harmful one), whose influence shattered the development of history. Thus, in the nineteenth century, the German historian Johann Gustav Droysen reckoned that Isocrates "drew history into paths from which Polybius vainly exerted himself to bring it back" (*Outline of the Principles of History*). In our day, Arnaldo Momigliano ("History in an Age of Ideologies") compared the position of the American historian Hayden White and that of Isocrates:

> Nor are we entirely on new ground when we hear from Hayden White that history is a form of rhetoric to be treated according to methods of rhetorical research. As I have already implied, some of us still remember that a problematic relationship between history and rhetoric already existed in the school of Isocrates in the fourth century B.C.: then, as now, the problem for history was to avoid being absorbed by rhetoric, whatever the contacts between the two.

While Isocrates does not speak about history, he is clear that he puts the burden of presentation and the deployment of past facts on the *logos*:

> But since discourses [*logoi* (λόγοι)] can naturally be set out in many ways about the same matters, and one can make great things small and give greatness to small things, or set out old issues in a new way and speak in a traditional way about things that have happened recently, we must not avoid issues about which others have spoken before, but rather, we must

try to speak better than they have. What happened in the past is available to all of us [*koinai* (κοιναὶ)], but it is the mark of a wise person to use these events at an appropriate time [*en kairôi* (ἐν καιρῷ)], conceive fitting arguments about each of them, and set them out in good style.

> (*Panegyricus*, 8–9)

Aristotle and *historia*

Aristotle was in part a determined practitioner of empirical inquiries (*historiai*)—the *History of Animals* (*Hai peri tôn zôôn historiai*) is the most well-known example—but he never uses the verb *historein*. On the other hand, he assigns history—this time as the narration of past events—only to the domain of the particular, not granting it access to the universal and hence science (*epistêmê* [ἐπιστήμη]):

> From what we have said it will be seen that the poet's function is to describe, not the thing that has happened, but a kind of thing that might happen, i.e., what is possible as being probable or necessary. The distinction between historian and poet is not in the one writing prose and the other verse—you might put the work of Herodotus into verse, and it would still be a species of history; it consists really in this, that the one describes the thing that has been [τὰ γενόμενα λέγειν], and the other a kind of thing that might be [οἷα ἂν γένοιτο]. Hence poetry is something more philosophic and of graver import than history, since its statements are of the nature rather of universals [μᾶλλον τὰ καθόλου], whereas those of history (*historia*) are singulars [τὰ καθ' ἕκαστον]. By a universal statement I mean one as

to what such or such a kind of man will probably or necessarily say or do—which is the aim of poetry, though it affixes proper names to the characters; by a singular statement, one as to what, say, Alcibiades did or had done to him.

> (*Poetics*, 9.1451a36–b11)

Thus, caught between the orator and the philosopher, the historian does not have his own land and has no choice but to borrow from both while claiming that he can satisfy everyone, as Polybius does, at the risk of pleasing no one but the lovers of stories—with pleasure having replaced both usefulness and truth, which are nevertheless still claimed as the true goals of history.

BIBLIOGRAPHY

Aristotle. *Poetics*. In vol. 2 of *The Complete Works of Aristotle*, edited by Jonathan Barnes, 2322–23. Princeton, NJ: Princeton University Press, 1984.

Droysen, Johann Gustav. *Outline of the Principles of History* (*Grundriss der Historik*). Translated by E. Benjamin Andrews. Boston: Ginn, 1893. First published in 1858.

Isocrates. *Panegyricus*. In *Isocrates II*, translated by Terry L. Papillon. Austin: University of Texas Press, 2004.

Louis, Pierre. "Le mot *historia* chez Aristote." *Revue de Philologie* 21 (1955): 39–44.

Momigliano, Arnaldo. "History between Medicine and Rhetoric." In vol. 8 of *Contributo alla storia degli studi classic e del mondo antico*, Arnaldo Momigliano, 13–25. Rome: Storia e Letteratura, 1987.

———. "History in an Age of Ideologies." *American Scholar* 51 (1982): 495–507.

Ste. Croix, Geoffrey Ernest Maurice de. "Aristotle on History and Poetry (*Poetics*, 9, 1451a36–b11)." In *Essays on Aristotle's Poetics*, edited by Amélie Rorty, 23–32. Princeton, NJ: Princeton University Press, 1992.

playing with these traditional classifications of *historia* in his *True History*.) Eloquence and the orator lost their importance, and *historia* continued to claim, with varying degrees of looseness, to be *historia magistra*—history as educator. Christians took it over. However, the primary shift was when the Bible became *historia* (as reporting true facts that really happened), since it is certain that whatever contradicts it is false. As a result, with Augustine, there is henceforth a *historia divina* and a *historia gentium*. The former, which is found in the Holy Scripture must be decoded, since it is a bearer of hidden meaning.

II. From Particular Histories to History— *Geschichte*—and to the Science of History

A. *Historia* and *gesta*

Throughout the Middle Ages, the meanings of the term "history" were marked by Latin references and hence evolved little. Isidore of Seville refered to the three essential characteristics laid out by Cicero: "history is first a narrative of past facts, through which these events are known" (historia est narratio rei gestae . . . , per quam ea, quae in praeterito facta sunt, dignoscuntur; *Etymologiae*, 1.41). Though it rests first on

3
Historia [ἱστορία], muthos [μῦθος] / fabula, plasma [πλάσμα] / argumentum

If history does belong to the narrative genre, what precisely is its place? How should we locate it in such a vast field—vast inasmuch as a narrative element may be found in every literary work? Once the distinction between a narrative of the facts (*ergon* [ἔργον]) and speech (*logos* [λόγος]) was first established, as in Thucydides, history as a whole was henceforth implicated in narration. It was at this point that both Greek and Latin rhetoricians and grammarians began to suggest different classifications. It is not a question of epistemology, but rather of characterization based on content.

The *Rhetoric to Herennius* (86–83 BCE; anonymous) distinguishes three types of narrative. The third is divided in two—one concerning persons, the other actions:

> That which consists in describing actions has three forms: fable [*fabula*], history [*historia*], fiction [*argumentum*]. Fable contains elements which are neither true nor likely, like those found in the tragedies. History contains events which have taken place, but at a time distant from ours. Fiction is an invented narrative which could have taken place, like the subjects of comedy.
>
> (*Rhetoric to Herennius*, 1.12)

The grammarian Asclepiades of Myrleia (second to first centuries BCE), also a historian of Bithynia, distinguished three parts part of the latter. In general, history is an *amethodos hulê* [ἀμέθοδος ὕλη], an unformed matter, coming from no particular technical skill (ibid., 1.266). We may, in any case, retain here his adoption of the threefold categorization:

> "One of the subjects of history is history [*historia*], another is myth [*muthos*], and the third is fiction [*plasma*]." History, in the restricted sense, "is an exposition of true things which actually happened, such as that Alexander died in Babylon poisoned by plotters, and fiction is when things which did not happen are told like those that did, such as comic plots and mimes, while a myth is an exposition of things which have not happened and are false, such as when 'they sing that' the race of venomous spiders and snakes was born 'from the blood of the Titans' [Nicander, *Poisonous Creatures* 8–10]" (ibid., 1.263–64).

History is not technique. There is no method for distinguishing what is historical (in the restricted sense) from what is not. On Sextus's description, history can escape Aristotelian particulars (*kat'hekaston* [κατ' ἕκαστον]) less than ever. As for historian-grammarians, their judgment (*krisis* [κρίσις]) does not allow them to distinguish between true and false narrative.

BIBLIOGRAPHY

Anonymous. *Rhetorica ad Herennium*. Translated by Harry Caplan. Loeb Classical Library. Cambridge, MA: Harvard University Press, 1954.

Braet, Antoine. "The Oldest Extant Rhetorical Contribution to the Study of Fallacies (Cicero *On Invention*, 1.78–96, and *Rhetoric to Herennius*, 2.31–46: Reducible to Hermagoras?)." *Philosophy and Rhetoric* 40 (2007): 416–33.

Cassin, Barbara. "L'histoire chez Sextus Empiricus." *Le scepticisme antique: Perspectives historiques et systématiques. Cahiers de la Revue de Théologie et de Philosophie* 15 (1990): 123–38.

Sextus, Empiricus. *Against the Grammarians* [*Adversus Mathematicos I*]. Translated by D. L. Blank. Oxford: Clarendon Press, 1998.

direct testimony, it also includes earlier times. On that basis, it thus covers, second, the testimonies of the past to the extent they are thought to be a reliable source of knowledge. Third, the term "history" also refers to the object of historical knowledge, whether it is a single event or a collection of them. Subsequently, the term *gesta*, the neuter plural of *gestum*, referring to facts that have occurred, is grammatically transformed into a feminine singular and becomes synonymous with *historia* (the narration of facts that have occurred; cf. *geste* in Old French) and then comes to refer to one of the four historiographical subgenres: chronicles, which relate to a historical theme, usually developed from its origins down to the present time; annals, which record facts year by year; the *vita*, biography, especially of the hagiographical sort; and the *gesta*, which relates the actions of a series of dignitaries, and through them, the history of an institution (the papacy, the empire, etc.). In addition, derived from the chronicle, we find histories of particular peoples, such as Cassiodorus's history of the Goths. It is only around the twelfth century that the boundary between *res gestae* and *historia* is reclarified: the latter is more reserved for the veridical recounting of the past, whereas the other terms have looser meanings, loosely covering the senses of "actions" or "events."

In the system of *artes liberales*, *historia* was attached, within the *trivium*, to grammar and rhetoric. As *magistra vitae*, in Cicero's phrase, it provides examples that may be used in argument to win the assent of the interlocutor or the reader.

While the humanists rediscovered antiquity and posited at the same time a special relationship between their own time and that of the ancients, they did not, for all that, develop a new concept of history. Lorenzo Valla (*Historia Ferdinandii regis Aragoniae*, 1528) praised history in relation to poetry but insisted above all, like Politian and Budé, on the methodological objective of precision, of *fides historica*. To reach this objective, the humanists added to the knowledge of antiquity, cultivating the technical subtleties of auxiliary sciences, of philology, geography, chronology, genealogy, and numismatics and maximized the methodological gains, but they did not discuss the field of history insofar as it is related to knowledge.

Machiavelli stayed with the idea of *exempla* taken from *istorie*, the works of history, which must serve the actor in the present. It is the immutable character of human nature that guarantees, in a way, the comparability of situations and allows us to jump between antiquity and the present. If we can imitate the examples of the past, this is because fundamentally neither the times nor people have changed. Francesco Guicciardini, for his part, attempted to describe the limits of rational political action. However, neither he nor Machiavelli suggested a new definition of history. They remained entirely oriented toward objects and events whose causal connections they attempted, each in his own way, to discern.

The concept of history became inflected in the sixteenth century by two French authors. In his work dealing with the link between universal history and a jurisprudence directed at the problems of action (*De institutione historiae universae et ejus cum jurisprudentia conjuntione*, 1561), François Baudouin called into action a comparative vision, encompassing ancient and biblical history, sacred and profane history, Eastern and Western history—a history whose underlying unity is the question of the agreement (or disagreement) between human action and the law. He established in this way a fundamental distinction between natural history and the history of man while also bringing into play the stock of new knowledge acquired by the modern era. Some years later, Jean Bodin, formulated the principles of historical knowledge and pushed the degree of methodological rigor further than ever before. He thus took an important step toward the foundation of an empirical science of history (*Methodus ad facilem historiarum cognitionem*, 1566). Finally, the new turning point for history was announced at the same time by a learned Italian, Francesco Patrizi. He proclaimed that "la historia è memoria delle cose humane" (history is the record of human affairs) and thus indicated that historians should move away from the direct observation of things to open up a new, distinct, and proper space of experience (*Della historia: Dieci dialoghi*).

■ See Box 4.

B. The descendants of *historia* versus *Geschichte*

The new turning point in the history of *historia* can be observed in great detail starting in the second half of the eighteenth century with Vico, who constructed a general vision of human history. While distinguishing its stages, he drew attention to the diversity of legal structures, languages, and cultures. In Germany especially, a semantic shift took place: the progressive substitution of the term *Geschichte* for that of *Historie*. Reinhart Koselleck has shown that this change came in two parts. The first of these is the shift from a plurality of individual histories (*Geschichte* as a feminine plural, another form of *Geschichten*) to the collective singular *Geschichte*. The term *Geschichte* refers, from the Middle Ages onward, both to the event and to its recounting. Until the end of the

eighteenth century, however, it was mostly used with regard to singular facts, relating to the multiple forms of a *Geschehen*, a chain of events in the past. The plural usage emphasizes precisely the multitude of particular facts. The singular, which was progressively adopted, not only captures the totality of these individual histories but also their abstraction, their generality. As a result, some authors introduced a reflective dimension, and history entered the field of consciousness. Adelung's dictionary (RT: *Versuch eines vollständingen grammatisch-kritischen Wörterbuches*) of 1775 marks the shift while maintaining the two meanings side by side. According to Adelung, *Geschichte* means

> [w]hat has happened, a thing which has occurred, as well as, in another meaning, any modification either active or passive which happens to something. In a more narrow and customary sense, the word picks out various modifications related to one another which, taken together, constitute a certain whole. . . . In this meaning we often use it as a collective and without a plural form, for several past events of a single species.

It is true that the shift took place slowly. In 1857, for instance, Droysen still contrasted the singular and the plural forms of *historia*, specifying: "Above histories lies History (*Historik*)." By this time, however, the hierarchy was clearly established.

We may also describe this change—this is the second part of the shift discussed by Koselleck—as the progressive absorption of the term *Historie*, taken from the Latin (and Greek), by *Geschichte*. Winckelmann provided a striking example in 1764. In the title of his work *Geschichte der Kunst des Altertums*, we can no longer distinguish whether the stress is placed on artistic objects or on the tableau of the whole that comes from the narrative. In his preface, Winckelmann clarifies:

4

Historia, history, *Geschichte*

At the linguistic level, the use of terms began to stabilize in the major European languages in the sixteenth century. On one hand, the Romance languages more or less took over the meanings created on the basis of Latin and Greek that focus on the narrative presentation of events, as opposed to the events themselves. *Histoire*, *istoria* (which became *storia*), *historia*, etc., are direct translations. English introduced a distinction between "history" and "story," the first being reserved for scholarly use, whereas the second singularizes particular histories and, if necessary, their literary presentation. In German, *Historie* replaced the Latin term but from the beginning of the eighteenth century onward was rivaled by the originally Germanic word *Geschichte*. The Dutch *Geschiedenis* followed the evolution of *Geschichte*, whereas

Scandinavian languages stayed with the semantic group of *historia*. The peculiarity of the semantic family *Geschichte* is that the word means both the narrative of the event and the event itself. The spread of the term *Geschichte* marked a deep transformation in the very conception of history, including in historiographical traditions that remain in the family of *history / histoire*. In *Zur Philosophie der Geschichte*, Hegel himself tried to generalize on the basis of the peculiarities of the semantic evolution of German:

> In our language, the term *History* [*Geschichte*] unites the objective with the subjective side, and denotes quite as much the *historia rerum gestarum*, as the *res gestae* themselves. . . . This union of the two meanings we must regard

as of a higher order than mere outward accident.

The association of the individual and the state is what, according to him, constitutes the very condition of history. It produces history at the same time as the vision that is turned toward it. Hegel leaves aside, however, the fact that his demonstration is based on a linguistic peculiarity restricted to German.

BIBLIOGRAPHY

Evans, Richard J. *In Defence of History*. London: Granta Books, 1997.

Hegel, Georg Wilhelm Friedrich. *Zur Philosophie der Geschichte*. Edited by Hermann Glöckner. Stuttgart: Frommann, 1928. Translation by John Sibree: *The Philosophy of History*. Mineola, NY: Dover, 2004.

[T]he history [*Geschichte*] of the art of Antiquity which I have undertaken to write is not a simple narration of its sequence and its transformations; rather I take the word history [*Geschichte*] in another sense, that which it has in the Greek language, and my intention is to deliver an attempt at a system which is capable of being taught.

By referring to *historia*, Winckelmann formally took over the definitions transmitted from antiquity. These definitions, beginning with Cicero's, had from the beginning allowed individual histories to coexist with a "generic" history that did not require particular objects. At the same time, however, Cicero opened up a new, abstract dimension, which permits the intellectual construction of a totality, a system. Writing just after Vico, Johann Christoph Gatterer used the phrase "system of events" (*System von Begebenheiten*), to which he attributed a temporality different from that which normally regulates the citizen's daily perception of time (*Vom historischen Plan und der darauf sich gründenden Zusammenfügung der Erzählungen*, 1767). For his part, Kant reserved the term *Historie* for empirical history, which simply lines up the facts, whereas *Geschichte*, especially in reference to the conception of an a priori *Geschichte*, that is, as a construction of reason, opens up the possibility of presenting an "aggregation" of human actions in the form of a system, organized according to a logic of the whole. Hegel, by drawing a distinction between a primitive history (*ursprüngliche Geschichte*, history written by witnesses), reflective history (*reflektierende Geschichte*, the history of historians, who construct a special relationship to their object), and a philosophical history (*philosophische Geschichte*), pushed the concept of a systematic history further, which in its most abstract variation takes the form of a *Welt-Geschichte*, a world history. As such, philosophical history deals with the evolution of logical substance, the activity and the work of the spirit as it makes itself the object of its own consciousness and makes effective, by the same stroke, the principle of freedom. All of these reformulations are the indication of a profound change that paved the way for the "historical science" of the nineteenth century. However, they coincided, in particular, with changes in the perception of time that preceded and accompanied the experience of revolution.

C. Change of experience and the mutation of history: *Historisierung*, historicization of the field of knowledge

The simultaneity of the experience of revolution (in the wide sense) with the changes that occurred in the conception of history suggests a clear break—or at least novelty. It indicates, in effect, a twofold link that was decisive in what followed: first, between the experience of the present and the definition of history, and second, between models of temporality and representations of historicity. On both levels, the violent and massive intrusion of manifestations of the revolutionary break produced chain reactions that modified the self-perception of contemporary European cultures. From this point of view, the changes to the notion of *history / Geschichte* led to the heart of the problem of the link between experience and the attempts to rationalize it as a collective phenomenon.

We may observe that a similar internal reform movement arose in France and in England, but in the two historiographical traditions at issue, it rests on different bases. In France the foundational role is often assigned to Voltaire, who, on the theoretical level (*Essai sur l'histoire générale et sur les moeurs et l'esprit des nations depuis Charlemagne jusqu'à nos jours*, 1756) as well as the practical historical one (*Le siècle de Louis XIV*, 1751), introduced a general vision of the historical process. In place of a universal Christian history in the style of Bossuet, Voltaire substituted a history of another type, just as universal, that describes the history of humanity as a long process of civilization leading up to the victory of the human spirit over the forces of obscurantism. In so doing, he put man at the center of history. Although Voltaire was later reproached for the overly "philosophical" character of his approach, it remains the case that he became the model, in his turn, both intellectual and stylistic for at least two generations of French historians. François Guizot, though attempting to establish a new type of history at the methodological level, remains tributary in his *Histoire de la civilisation en Europe* (1828–30) to the conception of a "macro" intellectual history that places the process of civilization center stage, following a teleological schema (see HISTORIA UNIVERSALIS).

In Great Britain, a comparable role was played by William Robertson, with *History of Scotland* (1759), and by David Hume, with *History of Great Britain* (1754–62). The two works became reference points for the new historiography, presenting the high subjects of a nascent national history in a newly revitalized style. Edward Gibbon's *Decline and Fall of the Roman Empire* (1776–88), which follows the same theoretical principles and deploys comparable literary qualities, had considerable influence throughout Europe.

The nineteenth century saw the consolidation of the central role that in the new order fell to history. Here again we may discern two levels: first, the progressive penetration of the whole field of knowledge by a historical vision. This movement affected all disciplines, from philology to linguistics and economics to the new life sciences and the social sciences, even theology. In large part, the scientization of these domains is equivalent to the historicization of their objects. Scientific progress could be measured according to the degree of pertinence of historical schemas of explanation. At a second level, however, the set of histories proper to a specific domain had to become something more than a simple aggregate or accumulation. Rather, they now constituted a specific means of production of knowledge, which lay down as a principle that the intelligibility of human action is always a function of examining it within the dimension of time. The historian's eye is supposed to penetrate the dimension of time and holds the key to it. As a result, history became, in a way, the queen of disciplines in the nineteenth century. It incarnated, more specifically, the idea of progress, in the sense that it alone is able to integrate the sum of knowledge produced by these diverse disciplines. As a science of evolution, it is at the root of any vision of becoming in the world; as a science of explanation, it looks at human action in all its aspects. On the two levels, it was from then on supposed to give accounts of both continuities and discontinuities.

D. The work of history: Poetry, novel, *Anschaulichkeit*

This all-encompassing aspiration gives history a role comparable to that of philosophy on one hand and religion on the other: it becomes in its turn a sort of secular religion. That said, the relations it has with religion remain ambiguous. On one hand, it substitutes its own capacity for explanation for divine providence, which earlier had been the basis for the unfolding of things. In this sense, Gatterer could posit that the goal of history is to restore the *nexus rerum universalis* (a universal connection of things in the world), a term that anticipates Humboldt and Ranke's *Zusammenhang* (interrelation). On the other hand, it does not eliminate references to providence either. For Ranke, it is in fact its relationship to the divine that gives history its unity. The historian must reconstruct the past while recognizing that insofar as each period is directly related to God (*unmittelbar zu Gott*), a part of history always remains hidden, inaccessible to rationality and historical reconstruction. Unity is thus a quality both internal and external to history. We may add Hegel's version, also an all-encompassing one, which emphasizes the work that spirit performs in history, work that gives spirit its progressive knowledge of what it is:

Dieser Prozeß, dem Geiste zu seinem Selbst, zu seinem Begriffe zu verhelfen, ist die Geschichte.

(History is the process whereby the spirit discovers itself and its own concept.)

(*Die Vernunft in der Geschichte*)

These three variations have in common the fact that they all aim at a global level, beyond events and particulars, and thus give comfort to the universalizing aspirations of history.

At the practical level of historiography, we can observe the same universalizing movement. In his article on the task of the historian, Humboldt established a clear distinction between the materials of history ("events," *Begebenheiten*) and history itself (*Geschichte selbst*) that cannot be obtained according to the precepts of the critique of sources. Rather, history itself is revealed to the historian only insofar as he manages to uncover the "internal connection" (*innerer Zusammenhang*) of the facts, the general idea that structures the whole ("Über die Aufgabe des Geschichtschreibers"). In the search for this structure, he must exhibit gifts analogous to those of the poet, and more generally, of the artist. In a letter of 7 May 1821 (*Briefwechsel*) to the jurist F. G. Welcker, Humboldt commented on his text:

There I compared history to art, which does not so much consist in imitating forms as in rendering perceptible the idea which lies in these forms.

(Ich habe darin die Geschichte mit der Kunst verglichen, die auch nicht sowohl Nachahmung der Gestalt, als Versinnlichung der in der Gestalt ruhenden Idee ist.)

Humboldt thus reopened the great debate, which cuts across a wide swath of historiography, on the relationship between history and poetry, history and novels. Diderot had already, with regard to Richardson, contrasted a history that would be a "bad novel" with the novel that would be a "good story [*histoire*]" (*Éloge de Richardson*). In trying to

paint "local color," so-called romantic French historians attempted to include the virtues of the novel, especially those of Walter Scott, in their historical tableaus. Augustin Thierry praised the "prodigious intelligence of the past" deployed by the novelist, at the expense of the simple, blinkered erudition of the traditional historian (preface to *Dix ans d'études historiques*, 1835). According to him, this is because novels, by putting forward clear and coherent principles of intelligibility, come closer to the truth than dusty history, which just gathers facts. In England, Macaulay's *History of England* was strongly inspired by Walter Scott. Ranke, for his part, opposed the novel, establishing a strict distinction between science and fiction. According to him, Walter Scott sins by deforming the facts. The only criteria of historical science must be the historical truth, which can be uncovered by the detailed critique of sources. Ranke constructed his whole historical science both against earlier historiography and against the pretensions of fiction; however, it is easy to see that at the level of the narrative, he nevertheless deployed the formal principles of the novel, aiming for both *Anschaulichkeit* (which relates at the same time to perceptible character, accessible to the senses, and to demonstration by example; see ANSCHAULICHKEIT) and the effect of a whole produced by narration. By insisting on irreducible individuality, by describing even the life of institutions and collectivities as individual evolutions, and by deploying varied stylistic registers, he placed many of the essential ingredients of fiction at the service of history. In doing so, he integrated the two elements of narration and argumentation, whose mixture characterizes historical discourse. In the German historiographical tradition, which emphasizes the scientization of the domain of history, the role of literary techniques has often been underestimated, whereas Michelet in France is widely appreciated for having managed a synthesis of literature and history. Such national distinctions prove misleading if they are too absolutely applied: we may recall that Theodor Mommsen himself saw the imagination not only as "the mother of all poetry, but also of all history" (Die Phantasie ist, wie aller Poesie so auch aller Historie Mutter; *Römische Geschichte*).

■ See Box 5.

E. Historical knowledge, the crisis of history, and historicism

By the middle of the nineteenth century, the meanings of the terms "history," *histoire, storia, historia* on one hand and *Geschichte* (to which the Dutch *Geschiedenes* corresponds) on the other had more or less stabilized. They follow, of course, the small evolutions of historiography and the movements of the philosophy of history, but they remain in the framework of the semantic fields we have been sketching. While some particular kinds of history emerge from it (social history, cultural history, history of mentalities, intellectual history, microhistory, world history, and so on), these can generally be attributed to small rearrangements of the relations between these semantic fields and to the discovery of new approaches or new objects. Even though they most often form within national historiographical traditions, the trends they refer to in general go beyond the frameworks of these traditions, and their terms enter into the process of translation of the international scientific community.

5

Historiography, history of history, *Historik*

The term *historiographie* refers in French to the history of history, historical work that takes historical discourse as its object, the ways of writing history from its beginnings. In German, *Historiographie* retains only a weakened sense and is often taken to be synonymous with "history" (*Geschichte*): "historiography" in the French sense is rendered by *Historiographie-geschichte*, whereas *histoire de l'historiographie* would seem tautologous in French. In Italian, on the other hand, *storiografia* is similar to the German *Historiographie*, as indicated, for example, by the title of the journal *Storia della storiografia*. In English, "historiography" is used in the sense of "history writing," which more or less intersects with the Italian and German meanings. These examples show that we in fact have a continuum, where at one end history is assimilated to any investigation of facts of the past, and at the other, we insist on the reflexive character of any historical operation. To refer to the theory and methodology of history, German uses the term *Historik*, which does not have an equivalent in the other languages. It gives this reflexion a special status, which German historians, in particular Droysen, wished to keep out of the hands of philosophy, especially the philosophy of history. *Historik* refers both to reflection and presentation, especially to the goals of teaching.

In contrast, controversies occasionally arise about the role of history in human experience as well as the different ways of thinking about this experience. Beginning in 1874, Nietzsche led the first attack against the all-encompassing ambitions of history by contrasting the imperatives of life (*Leben*) with a relativist logic of historical method, which pushes the knowledge of detail so far as to lose sight of the whole. According to him, generalized historicism ("das überschwemmende, betäubende und gewaltsame Historisieren") threatened the foundations of culture: "To be so overwhelmed and bewildered by history is, as the ancients demonstrate, not at all necessary for youth" (*Vom Nutzen und Nachtheil*). Against what he considered to be the harmful grip of the past, Nietzsche advanced the logic and the necessities of the present, as well as the action that life calls for. In so doing, he set off the crisis of historicism. Taking Ranke's principle to the extreme, which would prevent the historian from taking on the double role of judge of the past and master of the present, the historical school is alleged to have lost sight of the values that must guide political action. The neo-Kantians of the school of Baden, problematizing the production of sociohistorical knowledge, attempted to get out of this historicist dilemma. They insisted, on one hand, on the difference between the knowledge produced by the sciences of nature, which is organized into rules and laws, and that belonging to the "ideographical" sciences, like history, which describe perceptible (*anschaulich*) configurations. On the other hand, they distinguished between the sciences of nature (*Naturwissenschaften*) and those of culture (*Kulturwissenschaften*), the latter being defined as those that bring historical material into the sphere of values recognized within groups. The neo-Kantians gave Max Weber the tools for a theory of values thanks to which he hoped to reconstruct a form of objectivity required for giving a scientific grounding to the social sciences. Ernst Troeltsch, who was one of the most accomplished thinkers about the crisis of history, used the same theoretical premises to compare the social sciences (*Geisteswissenschaften*) with the problems of action. In parallel with the neo-Kantians, Dilthey, in *The Formation of the Historical World in the Human Sciences* (*Der Aufbau der geschichtlichen Welt in den Geisteswissenschaften*), which sketches the project of a "critique of historical reason," attempted to move beyond Kantian critical philosophy by positing that man as a producer of historical knowledge was himself a historical being ("The primary condition for the possibility of historical science is contained in the fact that I am myself a historical being and that the one who investigates history is the same as the one who makes history [*daß der, welcher Geschichte erforscht, derselbe ist, der die Geschichte macht*]", "Plan for Continuation"). It is not thanks to reason that man manages to understand the past, but to *Erlebnis*, of his capacity as a living being to live and understand situations from the inside.

Furthermore, theorists of history such as Croce claimed to represent the Hegelian school of thought by insisting on the constructed character of historical knowledge. The truth is not in the facts but instead is the result of a fusion between a philological critique and a philosophical attempt at systematization. As a result, Croce emphasized the fact that through the historian's act of thinking, history is anchored in the present: the spirit is both a productive factor in history and the result of the past that precedes it. As a consequence, Croce said, "all history is contemporary history" (*Theory and History of Historiography*). Collingwood (*The Idea of History*, 1946) emphasized in turn the specificity of historical knowledge, which always deals with intellectual materials and never with facts of nature. If Toynbee (*A Study of History*, 1934–61) explored the limits between natural and historical sciences, constructing a world history of societies and cultures, existentialist philosophy placed emphasis back onto the individual. It reconstrues the historicity of being, of *Dasein*, as a fundamental given of existence. Neither Husserl nor Heidegger, however, had much of an impact on historiography or on the conception of history used by historians themselves.

In France, the positivist tradition played a decisive role both before and after Raymond Aron considered the theoretical problem of history by discussing the developments of German philosophy of history and Henri Marrou suggested integrating the question of the varied relationships between historians and their subjects into the discussion of historical knowledge. Even while criticizing it, historians inspired directly by Durkheim's sociology, as well as the historians of politics or, again, the specialists of economic and social history, cleaved to the objectivist ideal of history. That goes for the first Annales school as well, to a certain extent. Through his critique of the "historicizing" history or the "positivist history" of someone like Charles Seignobos, Lucien Febvre sketched a science of history whose all-encompassing ambition, taking in all of the human sciences, is analogous to that of the exact sciences (*Combats pour l'histoire*). It is true that the problem of the form in which the results of research were to be presented was always considered to be a domain separate from that of historiographical activity proper (this distinction is driven perhaps by French literary and rhetorical culture). However, for the majority of historians, this was precisely and *merely* a question of presentation, one without any direct theoretical implications. It is only in the wake of the "linguistic turn" that, for the last twenty or so years, earlier debates about the twofold quality of *Geschichte* as *historia rerum gestarum* and *res gestae* were to some extent realized. Begun in the United States, this debate is now international, although with "national" variations. Countries with a hermeneutical tradition, like Germany or Italy, were initially more receptive than England or France, where empiricist and positivist trends have maintained strong positions. However, it would be misguided to make a simple parallel between, on one hand, the hermeneutical point of view and postmodern relativism, which attempt to reduce history to the creation of a story, and analytical, or objectivist, traditions on the other. The interpenetration of these two dimensions—the abstract construction of the "fact" from a collection of data that are analytic as well as hermeneutic and its presentation in the form of a more or less sophisticated narrative, producing meaning by its organization—is what has always been one of the most essential features of historical activity.

■ See Box 6.

François Hartog
Michael Werner

6

Rhetoric of history and "metahistory"

The debates unleashed by Hayden White's book *Metahistory* pick up a discussion of the questions of historical presentation that had busied historians in France, Germany, and England in the nineteenth century. Although Ranke had attempted to establish the greatest distance possible between fiction and historical science, he nevertheless used a great variety of narrative artifices to present the results of his investigations. Relying on the ideal of a world history whose unity is based on its divine inspiration, he aimed to achieve objectivity thanks to historiographical procedures that precede the writing and hence are independent of it. Droysen, for his part, was aware of the interactions between the construction of historical knowledge and the mode of presentation. For him, presentation is directly related to the other operations constituting history. The historian must choose, from among a variety of possible modes, that which corresponds to the question he wishes to ask of his documents. In his "Topik," Droysen, abandoning the idea that past reality only corresponds to a single presentation, attempted to think of a plurality of forms of presentation that relate to different ways of constructing a relationship between the past and the present. Analytic presentation (*untersuchende Darstellung*), narrative presentation (*erzählende Darstellung*), didactic presentation (*didaktische Darstellung*), and discussive presentation (*diskussive* or *erörternde Darstellung*) are all genres that link the object of empirical research with the present of the historian and that are all aimed at specific audiences.

The discussion provoked by White's book links up with the positions defended by his predecessors and radicalizes them. Reversing the position of objectivist history, White saw in historical discourse only one form among others of producing statements about the past. As a production of knowledge about it, nothing distinguishes history from novels or myths. The historian is caught between discursive constraints and implicit structures analogous to those of the novelist. His freedom is limited to being able to choose between different modes of exposition, but he remains a prisoner of the structural presuppositions of each. By calling into question the notion of a "historical fact" and insisting on the implications proper to the "metahistorical" level, White wished to reunite *history* and *story*, bringing the historiographical operation and the invention of a story closer together. Far from contrasting rhetoric and truth, the *linguistic turn*, by stipulating that every historical discourse produces its own truth, confuses the two elements. The responses to White hardly go beyond the positions advanced by Droysen. Between the objectivism of the partisans of facts and the relativism of the protagonists of postmodern fiction, Droysen, and later Max Weber, posited that historical knowledge does remain possible, as long as we accept its provisional status, due to the fundamental historicity of the categories of perception and analysis used by the historian. It is precisely this account of the perspectivism of knowledge and its anchor in an ever-moving present that gives specificity to the knowledge of a historian. The result is a plurality of forms of presentation that correspond to the variability of the questions posed and the transformations of the historical gaze.

BIBLIOGRAPHY

Droysen, Johann Gustav. "Topik." In *Grundriss der Historik*. Leipzig: Verlag Von Veit, 1868. First published in 1858.
Weber, Max. *Critique of Stammler*. Translated by Guy Oakes. New York: New Press, 1977.
———. *Economy and Society: An Outline of Interpretive Sociology*. Edited by Guenther Roth and Claus Wittich. Berkeley: University of California Press, 1978.
———. *Gesammelte Aufsätze zur Wissenschaftslehre*. Tübingen: Mohr, 1951.
———. *Methodology of the Social Sciences*. Translated and edited by Edward A. Shils and Henry A. Finch. Glencoe, IL: Free Press, 1949.
———. *Roscher and Knies: The Logical Problems of Historical Economics*. Translated by Guy Oakes. New York: Free Press, 1975.
———. "Some Categories of Interpretive Sociology." Translated by Edith Graber. *Sociological Quarterly* 22 (1981): 151–80.
White, Hayden. *Metahistory: The Historical Imagination in Nineteenth-Century Europe*. Baltimore: Johns Hopkins University Press, 1973.

BIBLIOGRAPHY

Arendt, Hannah. "The Concept of Ancient and Modern History." In *The Portable Hannah Arendt*, edited by Peter Baehr. New York: Penguin Books, 2000.

Breisach, Ernst. *Historiography: Ancient, Medieval, and Modern*. 3rd ed. Chicago: Chicago University Press, 2007.

Cassin, Barbara. *L'effet sophistique*. Paris: Gallimard, 1995.

Castelli, Enrico Gattinara. *Epistemologia e storia: Un pensiero all'apertura nella Francia fra le due guerre mondiali*. Milano: Angeli, 1996.

Certeau, Michel de. *L'écriture de l'histoire*. Paris: Gallimard, 1975. Translation by Tom Conley: *The Writing of History*. New York: Columbia University Press, 1988.

Chartier, Roger. *Au bord de la falaise: L'histoire entre certitudes et inquiétude*. Paris: Michel, 1998. Translation by Lydia G. Cochrane: *On the Edge of the Cliff: History, Language, and Practices*. Baltimore: Johns Hopkins University Press, 1997.

Cicero, Marcus Tullius. *De oratore*. Translation by J. S. Watson: *On Oratory and Orators*. New York: Harper & Brothers, 1875.

Croce, Benedetto. *Theory and History of Historiography*. Translated by Douglas Ainslie. London: Harrap, 1921.

Deliyannis, Deborah Mauskopf, ed. *Historiography in the Middle Ages*. Leiden: Brill, 2003.

Diderot, Denis. *Éloge de Richardson*. 1761. In vol. 5 of *Œuvres complètes*, edited by J. Assézat. Paris: Garnier Frères, 1876.

Dilthey, Wilhelm. *Gesammelte Schriften*. 26 vols. Leipzig: Teubner, 1914–2006.

———. *Hermeneutics and the Study of History*, edited by Rudolf A. Makkreel and Frithjof Rodi. Vol. 4 of *Wilhelm Dilthey: Selected Works*. Princeton, NJ: Princeton University Press, 1996.

———. "Plan for Continuation of the Formation of the Historical World in the Human Sciences." In *The Formation of the Historical World in the Human Sciences*, edited by Rudolf A. Makkreel and Frithjof Rodi. Vol. 3 of *Wilhelm Dilthey: Selected Works*. Princeton, NJ: Princeton University Press, 2002.

Droysen, Johann Gustav. *Historik*. Edited by P. Leyh. Stuttgart: Frommann-Holzboog, 1977. First published in 1857.

———. *Outline of the Principles of History* [*Grundriss der Historik*]. Translated by E. Benjamin Andrews. New York: Fertig, 1967.

Febvre, Lucien. *Combats pour l'histoire*. 2nd ed. Paris: Armand Colin, 1965.

Fornara, C.W. *The Nature of History in Ancient Greece and Rome*. Berkeley: University of California Press, 1983.

Gentili, Bruno, and Giovanni Cerri. *History and Biography in Ancient Thought*. Amsterdam: Gieben, 1988. Haskell, Francis. *History and Its Images: Art and the Interpretation of the Past*. New Haven, CT: Yale University Press, 1993.

Grafton, Anthony. *What Was History? The Art of History in Early Modern Europe*. Cambridge: Cambridge University Press, 2007.

Hartog, François. *L'histoire d'Homère à Augustin*. With Greek and Latin translations by Michel Casevitz. Paris: Éditions du Seuil / Points Essais, 1999.

Hegel, Georg Wilhelm Friedrich. *Die Vernunft in der Geschichte*. Vol. 1 of *Vorlesungen über die Philosophie der Weltgeschichte*, edited by Johannes Hoffmeister. Hamburg: Felix Meiner, 1955. Translation by H. B. Nisbet: "The Realisation of Spirit in History." In *Lectures on the Philosophy of World History: Introduction: Reason in History*. Cambridge: Cambridge University Press, 1975.

Herodotus. *Herodotus*. Translated by A. D. Godley. 4 vols. Loeb Classical Library. Cambridge, MA: Harvard University Press, 1981–82.

———. *Histories*. Translated by Robin Waterfield and edited by Carolyn Dewald. Oxford: Oxford University Press, 1998.

Hölscher, Lucian. *Die Entdeckung der Zukunft*. Frankfurt: Fischer, 1999.

Homer. *The Iliad*. Translated by A. T. Murray. 2 vols. Loeb Classical Library. Cambridge, MA: Harvard University Press, 1976–78.

———. *The Odyssey*. Translated by Robert Fagles. New York: Penguin, 1997.

Humboldt, Wilhelm von. *Briefwechsel an F. G. Welcker*. Edited by R. Haym. Berlin: Gaertner, 1859.

———. "Über die Aufgabe des Geschichtsschreibers." In vol. 1 of *Werke*, edited by A. Flitner and K. Giel, 585–606. 5th ed. Darmstadt: Wissenschaftliche Buchgesellschaft, 1966. First published in 1821. Translation by Linda DeMichiel: "On the Task of the Historian." In *The Hermeneutics Reader*, edited by Kurt Mueller-Vollmer, 102–119. New York: Continuum, 2000.

Iggers, Georg G. *The German Conception of History: The National Tradition of Historical Thought from Herder to the Present*. Rev. ed. Middletown, CT: Wesleyan University Press, 1983.

———. *Historiography in the Twentieth Century: From Scientific Objectivity to the Postmodern Challenge*. Middletown, CT: Wesleyan University Press, 1997.

Isidore of Seville, Saint. *Etymologiae*. Translation by Stephen A. Barney, J. A. Beach, Oliver Berghof, and W. J. Lewis: *The Etymologies of Isidore of Seville*. Cambridge: Cambridge University Press, 2006.

Isocrates. *Panegyricus*. In vol. 1 of *Isocrates*, translated by George Norlin. Loeb Classical Library. Cambridge, MA: Harvard University Press, 1954.

Koselleck, Reinhart. *Futures Past: On the Semantics of Historical Time*. Translated and introduction by Keith Tribe. New York: Columbia University Press, 2004.

———. *The Practice of Conceptual History: Timing History, Spacing Concepts*. Translated by Todd Samuel Presner, Kerstin Behnke, and Jobst Welge. Foreword by Hayden White. Stanford, CA: Stanford University Press, 2002.

Lucian. "The Way to Write History." In *The Works of Lucian of Samosata*. Translated by H. W. Fowler and F. G. Fowler. Oxford: Clarendon Press, 1905.

Momigliano, Arnaldo. *The Classical Foundations of Modern Historiography*. Foreword by Riccardo Di Donato. Berkeley: University of California Press, 1990.

Mommsen, Theodor. *Römische Geschichte*. Vol. 1. Reprint, Wien: Phaidon-Verlag, 1932. First published in 1852.

Nietzsche, Friedrich. *Vom Nutzen und Nachtheil der Historie für das Leben*. In Vol. 1 of *Sämtliche Schriften*, edited by G. Colli and M. Montinari. Munich: Deutscher Taschenbuch Verlag, 1988. Translation by R. J. Hollingdale: "On the Uses and Disadvantages of History for Life." In *Untimely Meditations*. Cambridge: Cambridge University Press, 1983.

Patrizi, Francesco. *Della historia: Dieci dialoghi*. Venice: Appresso Andrea Arrivabene, 1560.

Polybius. *The Histories*. Book 1. Translated by W. R. Paton. 6 vols. Loeb Classical Library. Cambridge, MA: Harvard University Press, 1954.

Poovey, Mary. *A History of the Modern Fact: Problems of Knowledge in the Sciences of Wealth and Society*. Chicago: University of Chicago Press, 1998.

Press, Gerald Alan. *The Development of the Idea of History in Antiquity*. Kingston, ON: McGill-Queen's University Press, 1982.

Quintilian. *The Institutio Oratoria of Quintilian*. Translated by H. E. Butler. London: Heinemann, 1922.

Ricœur, Paul. *La mémoire, l'histoire, l'oubli*. Paris: Éditions du Seuil, 2000. Translation by Kathleen Blamey and David Pellauer: *Memory, History, Forgetting*. Chicago: University of Chicago Press, 2004.

Scheid-Tissinier, Évelyne. "À propos du rôle et de la fonction de l'*histôr*." *Revue de Philologie* 68 (1994): 187–208.

Sophocles. *Oedipus Rex*. Translated by R. Fagles. New York: Penguin, 1984.

Thierry, Augustin. Preface to *Dix ans d'études historiques*. Paris: Garnier, 1867.

Thucydides. *The Peloponnesian War*. Translated by Steven Lattimore. Indianapolis, IN: Hackett, 1998.

Winckelmann, Johann Joachim. *Geschichte der Kunst des Altertums*. Dresden: Walther, 1764. Translation by Harry F. Mallgrave: *History of the Art of Antiquity*. Los Angeles: Getty Research Institute, 2006.

HOMONYM / SYNONYM

GREEK   *homônuma* [ὁμώνυμα] / *sunônuma* [συνώνυμα]
LATIN   *homonyma, aequivoca/synonyma, univoca*

► ANALOGY, CONNOTATION, INTENTION, LOGOS, MIMĒSIS, PARONYM, SENSE, SIGN, SIGNIFIER/SIGNIFIED, *SOPHISM*, SUPPOSITION, *TO BE*, TO TRANSLATE, WORD

The words "homonymy" and "synonymy," modeled on the Greek in most modern languages, do not in and of themselves present translation difficulties. But the similarity of the words hides a number of shifts in meaning that are all the more complex, and therefore less often thematized, because they are linked to an ontological landscape that changes according to different doctrines and times, and in particular the avatars of the Aristotelian critique of Platonism. This has led to recurrent difficulties in the understanding of ancient texts, manifested through a certain number of mistranslations, that make them unintelligible nowadays. Indeed, why could we not say there is a relationship of pure and simple "homonymy" between what we today commonly call "homonyms," as in the case of homophones like the English "all" and "awl," or the French *vert* (green) and *verre* (glass), as well as the classic example in Aristotle's *Categories*, which describes a man and his portrait as "homonyms"?

More generally, the question regarding homonymy and synonymy is the question of the conditions, or criteria, of identity of meaning: indeed, since Aristotle, the possibility of a noncontradictory discourse and communication between men is founded on the univocality of words and sentences: "For not to have one meaning is to have no meaning" (*Metaphysics*, Γ.4, 1006b7–8, trans. Barnes). Questioning these criteria of identity of meaning led medieval philosophers to redefine the notions of *equivocatio* and *univocatio*, in order to distinguish between different types of semantic variation. Semantic identity is disrupted as soon as an expression "means" or "stands in for" a number of things, or in a proposition, as soon as it is *multiplex*. But it is not necessarily ambiguous, since it is possible for it to signify clearly several different things at the same time. We are thus confronted by a network of terms—*equivocatio*, *univocatio*, *multiplicitas*, *ambiguitas*—that coexist alongside the terms modeled on the Greek: *homônuma* [ὁμώνυμα], *sunônuma* [συνώνυμα], and the corresponding derivations. The search for homonymy, intentional or not, is thus the first prerequisite of logic, or even of a certain ethics of language.

1. Disentangling the Problems

A. Things or words: The referent-name derivation

The commonly accepted contemporary definitions of homonymy are rather vague. Homonymy is most often defined as the symmetrical opposite of synonymy: broadly speaking, homonymy exists whenever one word has several meanings ("eine Name mit mehreren Bedeutungen"), and synonymy whenever several words have a single meaning ("eine Bedeutung mit mehreren Namen," quoted by Ritter in RT: *Historisches Wörterbuch der Philosophie*, s.v.). This definition is inherited from a long tradition that was already well established among Latin grammarians—for example, in the collection of *Differentiae*, which appeared under the name of Fronton: "Hononymia una voca multa significat, synonymia multis vocibus idem testatur" (Homonymy means several things with the help of one word, synonymy shows one thing with the help of several words, RT: *Grammatici Latini*, 7:525). We can, however, already see an indication of an initial problem between these apparently congruent definitions: Is it a matter of the relationship between words and their meanings (Ritter) or of the relationship between words and things (Fronton)?

One answer to the question of whether homonyms and synonyms refer to things or words was the following: "A specific difficulty of the history of composite words ending in -onym comes from the fact that they are applied successively—and also more seriously, simultaneously—to the referent and to the name itself. . . . History subsequently continued to use this derivation" (Lallot, *La grammaire de Denys le Thrace*, 152), one of the key elements of this history being the Aristotelian critique of the doctrine of Ideas.

Nowadays, homonyms and synonyms are words. In antiquity, they could be things or words. Thus the *Iliad* says that the two Ajaxes, the son of Telamon and the son of Oileus, and not their names, are homonyms (*Iliad*, 18.720, trans. Murray, 283), but the *Odyssey* says that the name "Odysseus" is an eponym (literally "named after," *epi* [ἐπί], in order to indicate a particularly significant etymology), well suited to the man Odysseus, who has "wounded" (*odussamenos* [ὀδυσσάμενος]) his grandfather's heart (*Odyssey*, 19.407–10, trans. Murray, 257–59).

Plato uses homonyms (*Phaedo*, 78e; *Timaeus*, 52a) to describe things that are sensible with respect to the intelligible models that confer upon them both being and eponymy (*Parmenides*, 133d, trans. Gill and Ryan, 136); the art of language, insofar as it claims to fabricate everything, according to the Sophist, is a mimetic art like painting that fabricates copies of copies, "images and homonyms of beings (mimêmata kai homônuma tôn ontôn [μιμήματα καὶ ὁμώνυμα τῶν ὄντων]," *Sophist*, 234b, trans. White, 21; see MIMÊSIS): the relationship of homonymy thus connects Ideas, sensible things, and their simulacra, particularly words (*eidôla legomena* [εἴδωλα λεγόμενα], 234c), so things and words.

Aristotle in turn sometimes explicitly considers things (*Categories* 1), sometimes words, as if this were self-evident (*Sophistical Refutations*). The idea according to which homonymy in ancient times had to do with things is a result of the historical preeminence of its definition in the *Categories*, which indeed contains the first definition of homonyms, and to which one always refers. It has become the normative meaning of homonym, even if one disagrees with it. This explains the term's subsequent fortunes, and the glosses that displace its meaning.

If we are to believe Simplicius (*Commentary on Aristotle's Categories*, 38.19–24), it was Speusippe, Plato's nephew and successor at the head of the Academy, who first introduced the terminological pair *homônumos-sunônumos*, in the context of a systematic classification of "words" (*onomata* [ὀνόματα]) alone.

Greek commentators partially adopted this system, but applied it once again to things. They were followed in this respect by Latin commentators, who used a double set of terms, based on a double set of oppositions—name: identical/different, definition: identical/different (cf. Boethius [*In Categorias Aristotelis commentaria*, 163C–164A, in RT: *PL* 64], who uses the Latin terms; see Desbordes, "Homonymie et synonymie," 61, for the other Latin texts).

The apparent symmetry is obviously an illusion: if different things are *univoca*, *aequivoca*, or *diversivoca*, it is the same thing that is *multivoca*. A multivocal thing is one that is literally designated by several expressions, *voces*, these *voces* being what we nowadays term "synonyms." In this respect, we are following the usage that Simplicius was already calling "modern" (36.30), putting his finger on the motif of an oscillation between the ancient and modern meanings of synonymy: when we study types, we call synonyms several "things" represented by the same word with the same meaning (a man and an ox, when they are both represented as having the same meaning "animal," are synonyms)—this is "the most literal meaning," as Aristotle would say in the *Categories*. But when we are interested in the plurality and variety of words, we call synonyms several "words" that represent the same thing, and that for Speusippe would be termed polyonyms (in the same way that, for Aristotle in his *Rhetoric* [3.2, 1404b37–1405a2, trans. Barnes, 2:2240], "to proceed" and "to advance," *poreuesthai* [πορεύεσθαι] and *badizein* [βαδίζειν], are synonyms): this is the modern meaning that prevailed with the Stoics (for example, Alexander and Paris: see Simplicius, 36.7–32).

Generally speaking, Aristotle's commentators, while asserting that homonyms are things, also apply the adjective "homonymous" to words. Simplicius is particularly aware of this shift ("In its literal sense, it is realities and not words that produce homonymy," RT: *CAG* 8:24.20ff. / "It is clear, then, that a noun is homonymous," 25.5). It becomes the locus itself of a distinction between a conceptualist interpretation of homonymy that has a Stoic nuance to it (one single word, with several *ennoiai* [ἔννοιαι], "mental representations"), and a participatory interpretation that is Neoplatonic in nature (74.28–75.5; see Luna's commentary on Simplicius's *Commentaire sur les "Catégories" d'Aristote*, especially part 3, pp. 88–90). More recently—with Luna, for example—"homonymy" is used to describe things, and "equivocality" to describe words (e.g., ibid., 11 n. 26). The definition of the Grammarians, close to the Stoics, opts for words, and within words, their *phônê* [φωνή]: for Denys of Thrace (2–1 BCE), as well as for Oswald Ducrot and Jean-Marie Schaeffer, homonyms are essentially homophones. But this definition is in opposition to that of the philosophers, namely Aristotle and the commentators of the *Categories*. Boethius makes a clear distinction between the adjective *aequivoca*, which describes not things, but the manner in which they are expressed, and the substantive *aequivocatio*, which describes a phenomenon that has to do with words—not only nouns, but also verbs, prepositions, and conjunctions:

AEQUIVOCA, inquit, dicitur res scilicet, quae per se ipsas aequivocae non sunt, nisi uno nomine praedicentur: Quare quoniam ut aequivoca sint, ex communi vocabulo trahunt, recte ait, aequivoca dicuntur. Non enim sunt aequivoca sed dicuntur. Fit autem non solum in nominibus sed etiam in verbis aequivocatio.

(Equivocal, he says [Aristotle, *Categories*, chap. 1], that is to say things, which are not in themselves equivocal, unless a common noun is predicated upon them. This is why, since the fact that they are equivocal is because they share a common term, Aristotle rightly says: "They are equivocal in their expression." Indeed, they are not equivocal, but are expressed equivocally. Equivocation happens not just with nouns, but also with verbs.)

(*In Categorias Aristotelis commentaria*, 164C, in RT: *PL* 64)

B. The symmetry/asymmetry between homonymy and synonymy

A second knot of problems that needs to be disentangled is the symmetrical or asymmetrical relationship between homonymy and synonymy. The RT: *DHLF* gives some indication of this confusion. In it we read that "*homonyme* is a borrowing from the Latin *homonymus*," "the same pronunciation but with a different meaning," which is itself borrowed from the Greek *homônumos*: "bearing the same name, and using the same denomination," made up of *homos* (from which we get *homo-*) and *onoma*, "name." But we also read

that *synonyme* is borrowed from the Latin *synonymus*, which itself is derived from "the Greek *sunônumos*, 'having the same name as,' from *sun* [σύν] 'with, together,' and *onoma*." Paradoxically, the two Greek adjectives *homônumos* and *sunônumos* end up having the same definition: "bearing the same name," "having the same name as." This confusion is all the more troubling since this definition of synonymy is incompatible with the one that follows, but that is nonetheless also related to its Greek etymology: "[Synonymy] refers in the sixteenth century to a word that has an analogous meaning to another word (a common type), but whose meaning has two different values, etymological and Aristotelian." How can we understand this confusion?

The RT: *DHLF* is certainly not wrong: *synonyme* and *homonyme* start out, in the most ancient attestations, as what we would today call "synonyms," since both describe something different bearing the same name. We come across "homonyms" (*homônumoi* [ὁμώνυμοι]) once in Homer, applied to the two Ajaxes (*Iliad,* 17.720). But Euripides uses "synonym" with exactly the same meaning: Menelaus has just learned that a woman with the same name as Helen is living in the palace, and consoles himself in wondering whether "some other land [can] share the name of Lacedaemon or of Troy" (*Helen,* 495, trans. Burian, 93), pointing out that it is not unusual "for many men to have the same name [*onomata taut' echousin* (ὀνόματα ταῦτ' ἔχουσιν)], and for one city to share a name with another city, one woman with another woman" (497–99). This no doubt explains the belated appearance, and the extreme rarity before Aristotle, of the second term, which was merely a doublet of the first. (Plato, who uses *homônumos* sixteen times, never once uses *sunônumos*.) Later on, one of the favorite games of the commentators of the *Categories* will be to show the sense in which homonyms, such as the two Ajaxes, are also synonyms, by virtue of the constant use of "insofar as": even if "insofar as he is Ajax," the son of Telamon and the son of Oileus are homonyms, "insofar as they are men," they are synonyms (see Pophyry, 62.30 and 64.10–20; Dexippe, 19.20 and 22.15; Simplicius, 29–31 and 35.9–36.6).

■ See Box 1.

II. The Definition of the *Categories*

A. The text and its translation

Aristotle proposed the first known definition of homonyms and synonyms (as well as paronyms; see PARONYM) at the beginning of the *Categories*: this text is the matrix of all commentaries and all subsequent transformations. However, its most common understanding is based on a mistranslation, or at least on a shift that is linked to the misplaced fecundity of a more modern conception of homonymy.

■ See Box 2.

B. Ontological causes and consequences of the Aristotelian definition

1. Nature/culture: The Aristotelian classifications

So the species (man, ox) of a same genus (animal)—or, if one prefers, the species and their genus (man, animal; see, for example, *Topics,* 3.123a 28ff., trans. Barnes,1:206–7)—will always be synonyms of one another—this would be the paradigm

1

The modern asymmetry between homonymy and synonymy: Homonyms and homophones (the case of French)

The asymmetry between homonymy and synonymy often surfaces within modern definitions, as testified by Ducrot and Schaeffer's *Nouveau dictionnaire des sciences du langage*. Indeed, according to them, synonymy takes into account two or more "expressions" (words, groups of words, utterances), whereas homonymy takes into account not the word or expression, but the "phonic reality" (RT: *Nouveau dictionnaire des sciences du langage*, 398–99): homonyms are nowadays essentially homophones, such as the French *vair, verre, vert, vers*, and *vert*, to the extent that we would term "homonym" both several distinct words, as well as one word, or at least one unique spelling of a word (*rame* de papier [ream of paper] and *rame* de navire [ship's oar]). This definition, particularly in its emphasis on the *phônê*, is very close to that of the ancient grammarians (Denys le Thrace, *Technê grammatikê*, 12.6 and 7; *Scholies*, 554.31–32; see Lallot, *La grammaire de Denys le Thrace*, 152).

What is more, the criteria we use for homonymy seem particularly difficult to hold on to. In fact, if it is not easy to decide with synonymy whether two meanings are identical (in terms of connotation, expressive value, and so on), how do we determine whether two meanings are "radically different"? Homonymy, unlike synonymy, is caught within a network of phenomena that are "similar, but of a different nature" (RT: *Nouveau dictionnaire des sciences du langage*, 399), such as "contextual determination" ("This shop is open on Monday": only on Monday / even on Monday?), "polysemy" ("le *bureau* Louis XIV" [Louis XIV desk] and "le *bureau* de poste" [post office]), "extension" (to love one's father, and to love jam),

"indetermination" (what speakers of English call "vagueness": "Am I 'rich'?"), "oppositional meaning" (*small* microbes and *small* elephants).

At the level of syntax and semantics, some linguistics researchers, such as Antoine Culioli, have been interested in the phenomenon of paraphrase: this was a matter of considering formal variations, even very minimal ones, within a family of paraphrastic utterances, so as to go back to the enunciative or predicative operations from which they are derived, and to understand the semantic differences they conceal (for example, in French, to say "Peter eats the apple," one could say: "Pierre, la pomme il la mange" / "La pomme, Pierre il la mange" / "C'est la pomme que mange Pierre," etc.).

The criterion Ducrot and Schaeffer adopt to distinguish between what is a homonym and what is not a homonym is the impossibility of finding any point in common between the different meanings of a word: "no common core, nor even any continuity," no explanation nor any derivation. This corresponds exactly to the Aristotelian criterion used for homonyms that are *apo tuchês* [ἀπό τύχης], "coincidental" (the classic example being *kleis* [κλείς], meaning both "key" and "collarbone"). Yet the arbitrary nature of the distinctions proposed still remains: thus Ducrot and Schaeffer choose not to differentiate between "homonymy" and "ambiguity" ("the phenomena of ambiguity or of homonymy," RT: *Nouveau dictionnaire des sciences du langage*, 399). One might object that the term "ambiguous" (and it is certainly not obvious that it should be contrasted with "equivocal") can in no way be applied to homophones, or to a much broader semantic

field than "homonym" (an ambiguous attitude). One might compare this above all to the way Quine or Hintikka ("Aristotle and the Ambiguity of Ambiguity," 138) use the term: they both, by contrast, distinguish between ambiguity and homonymy on the basis of etymology. The criterion of pure coincidence is only truly met in the case of words that have emerged out of different etymologies (the *rame* [oar] of a ship, from the Sanskrit *aritra*, "which moves," as opposed to the Arabic *rizma* [الرزمة], "packet of clothes," for a *rame* [ream] of paper, according to Littré [RT: *Le Littré: Dictionnaire de la langue française en un volume*]), which Aristotle does not talk about, but for which we might reserve the term "homonyms."

All of these categories are part of a long heritage going back to the different, and sometimes contradictory, distinctions first articulated in antiquity, to precise ontological ends. The apparently arbitrary nature of these differences and these criteria is no doubt due to the fact that we no longer question what is at stake nor what is intended by the concept.

Whatever the case may be, the essential characteristic of modern homonymy is that it is applied exclusively to words, and is even reduced to the phenomena of homophony. It is presented consequently as a marginal phenomenon, linked to the signifier, likely to be of interest mainly to psychoanalysis, or to lovers of witticisms and puns, but of secondary importance for the analysis of language (see SIGNIFIER/SIGNIFIED).

BIBLIOGRAPHY

Hintikka, Jaako. "Aristotle and the Ambiguity of Ambiguity." In *Time and Necessity*, 1–26. Oxford: Clarendon, 1973.

itself of synonymy—as would also singular copies, or the "parts" of one and the same species (see *Categories*, 3a33–b9, trans. Barnes, 1:6): one might say that *phusis* [φύσις], nature as a process of engendering, like natural science as a genealogical classification, proceeds by synonymy (see *Of the Generation of Animals*, 2.1.735a2ff.: "Generation happens by synonymy").

On the other hand, all of those phenomena having to do with *technê* [τέχνη], with art, *mimêsis* [μίμησις], imitation, and with resemblance more generally, will be homonyms: for Aristotle, resemblance is the very paradigm of homonymy. We are no doubt here as far as we could be from our modern conception, according to which a good homonymy is a purely accidental homonymy, as is the case, precisely, with

homophones (see, for example, Box 1, with Jaako Hintikka's forceful critique).

2. The critique of Platonism

We would not be able to understand the choice of this paradigm without reference to the critique of the Platonic doctrine of ideas: Aristotle is keen to emphasize that, by Plato's own admission (see above, I.A), the relationship between model and image (*eidos* [εἶδος] and *eidôlon* [εἴδωλον]), intelligible and sensible, is merely a relationship of homonymy. Now homonymy can only appear, in the Aristotelian system, as a contingent artifact that reveals either the malice of the Sophist or the poverty of language. So, in place of the Platonism of participation, we have to substitute the

2

How to translate the definitions of the *Categories*?

When things have only a name in common and the definition of the being which corresponds to the name is different, they are called *homonymous*. Thus, for example, both a man and a picture are animals. These have only a name in common and the definition of being which corresponds to the name is different; for if one is to say what being an animal is for each of them, one will give two distinct definitions.

When things have the name in common and the definition of being which corresponds to the name is the same, they are called *synonymous*. Thus, for example, both a man and an ox are animals. Each of these is called, by a common name, an animal, and the definition of being is also the same; for if one is to give the definition of each—what being an animal is for each of them—one will give the same definition.

(Ὁμώνυμα λέγεται ὧν ὄνομα μόνον κοινόν, ὁ δὲ κατὰ τοὔνομα λόγος τῆς οὐσίας ἕτερος, οἷον ζῷον ὅ τε ἄνθρωπος καὶ τὸ γεγραμμένον· τούτων γὰρ ὄνομα μόνον κοινόν, ὁ δὲ κατὰ τοὔνομα λόγος τῆς οὐσίας ἕτερος· ἐὰν γὰρ ἀποδιδῷ τις τί ἐστιν αὐτῶν ἑκατέρῳ τὸ ζῷω εἶναι, ἴδιον ἑκατέρου λόγον ἀποδώσει. συνώνυμα δὲ λέγεται ὧν τό τε ὄνομα κοινὸν καὶ ὁ κατὰ τοὔνομα λόγος τῆς οὐσίας ὁ αὐτός, οἷον ζῷον ὅ τε ἄνθρωπος καὶ ὁ βοῦς· τούτων γὰρ ἑκάτερον κοινῷ ὀνόματι προσαγορεύεται ζῷον, καὶ ὁ λόγος δὲ τῆς οὐσίας ὁ αὐτός· ἐὰν γὰρ ἀποδιδῷ τις τὸν ἑκατέρου λόγον τί ἐστιν αὐτῶν ἑκατέρῳ τὸ ζῷω εἶναι, τὸν αὐτὸν λόγον ἀποδώσει.)

(Aristotle, *Categories*, 1.1a1–12, trans. Barnes, 1:3)

We will not translate *zôion* [ζῷον]; the Greek word, from *zôê* [ζωή], "life," means "animate, living being" (see ANIMAL). But it also means "character or figure (man or animal) represented in a painting" (the painted image of an animate being, Herodotus, 3.88, or Plato, *Republic*, 7.515a). Lastly, it has this meaning of a "painted image," even when the model being represented is not living (Herodotus, 4.88, "having represented faithfully according to nature [*zôia grapsamenos* (ζῷα γραψάμενος)], the crossing of the Bosphorus," or Plato, *Laws*, 769a). In other words, *zôion*, referring to any work of a *zôgraphos* [ζωγράφος], a painter, can also denote what we would call a "still life."

The difference between languages here comes fully into play: the classic definition of homonymy and synonymy originates in and around a homonym. At play at this juncture in the *Categories*, in fact, is not just the difference between languages, but also Aristotle's characteristic irony, which consists in exploiting the paradoxical economy of the Platonic doctrine, according to which a living being is never anything more than the response to an idea, without having even to acknowledge that this paradox is inscribed within the Greek.

There is an error that we have to avoid in translation. We may think that with *onoma* [ὄνομα] we are dealing not with a word, or a name, that can be attributed to two homonyms (in this case, the word *zôion*), but with a name that would name homonyms themselves (in this case, the word "man"). This is an error that Tricot commits unfailingly in his translations of Aristotle into French, on the one hand by translating *onoma* by "the name," *le nom* (Zanatta does the same: "*il nome*"), on the other hand by translating *to gegrammenon* [τὸ γεγραμμένον] as "the painting of a *man*," which then becomes "man." "We call *homonyms* the things that only have a *name* in common, whereas the notion referred to by this name is varied. For example, *animal* is equally a real man and a painted *man*. These two things indeed only have in common their *name*" (emphasis added). The example in Tricot's footnote adds to this impression: "Things that are homonyms . . . which only share a name . . . for example . . . *kleis* [ιλεὶς] means a key and a collarbone." But this example is particularly ill-chosen for the case of a man and his portrait, since *kleis* (according to Aristotle, for whom a key and a collarbone are completely unlike one another) is a homonymy where "the difference is considerable, because it bears upon the outer form [*kata tên idean* (κατὰ τὴν ἰδέαν)]" (*Nicomachean Ethics*, 5.2, 1129a26–32; commentators, moreover, use this passage to illustrate "coincidental homonymies").

The example of *kleis*, which precisely does not imply any third term like *zôion*, adds to the belief that for Aristotle, as for us nowadays, homonyms always have the same name and a different definition. We come across the same misinterpretation with synonyms. Here again: "When things have the name in common and the definition of being which corresponds to the name is the same, they are called *synonymous*. Thus, for example, both a man and an ox are animals." which Tricot glosses as: "Synonymous things are identical in nature and *in name*" (trans. Tricot, 25 n. 2 , emphasis added).

It is nevertheless important to understand that neither homonyms nor synonyms must have "the" same name in common, in the sense of "their" name: they have "a" name in common (*onoma*, 1a1 and 9), what Ackrill, in contrast to Tricot, translates carefully as "a name in common," "a common name." It is this single common name, *zôion*, that we sometimes use as a homonym, when its definition has to change from one application to another (a man is endowed with life, but his portrait is not), and sometimes use as a synonym, when the same definition can be given for each occurrence (a man and an ox are each one an animal). Happily, the most recent French translations (of Bodéüs, and of Lallot and Ildefonse) have at last corrected Tricot's misinterpretation.

It should be said, in defense of the mistranslations of the *Categories*, that numerous examples of Aristotelian homonyms work without any third term, that is, directly from the names of the homonyms themselves—for example, the "hand" or the "eye" of both a living being and a dead body (*De anima*, 2.1, 412b14ff., 21, trans. Barnes, 1:657). In each of these cases we find that the word in common is indeed their name, which obviously does not have the same essential definition. Whatever the case, these are simply a subset of the homonyms as previously defined, and do not contradict this definition.

It is worth pointing out, finally, that the commentators' lemmata and Tricot's are translated in the same way, even in English (including those commentators who, like Evangeliou, even quote Ackrill's correct translation): "their name in common." However, in the commentary itself, we find, when it is impossible to do otherwise, and as if compelled by the truth, "a name": thus in Ammonius, lemma, 1a1, 18.18: "that have only *their* name in common"; but ibid., 20.3: "[Ajaxes] have *a name* in common." Boethius's Latin translation of Aristotle is as follows:

Aequivoca dicuntur quorum nomen solum commune est, secundum nomen vero substantiae ratio diversa, ut animal homo et quod pingitur. . . . Univoca dicuntur quorum et nomen commune est et secundum nomen eadem substantiae ratio, ut animal homo atque bos.

(Aristotle, *Categories*, 1a1, trans. Boethius)

But his commentary makes apparent the reading we have just described: we can only talk about things being equivocal if we predicate upon them a name, or a word, in common. Latin, however, encounters another problem that Greek did not have: whereas *zôion* in Greek denotes any representation (not necessarily of a subject), this is not the case with the term "animal." Boethius, who considers the composite expressions "living man" and "painted man" (*homo vivus, homo pictus*), maintains nevertheless that one could apply to them not only the word "animal" (animate being: "Indeed, whether it is a matter of a painted man or a living man, the word *animal being* is used equally for one and the other"), but also the word "animal" and the word "man" considered together ("one or the other could both in fact be called *man* or *animate being*"). Later, he only takes into account the name *homo*, which produces a major change: we in fact move from the perspective of a predication genus-species to the semantic perspective of the "transfer of the name" of one reality to another: "ut ex homine vivo ad picturam nomen hominis dictum est" (From living man, we apply the name of man to a painting; see *translatio*, in TO TRANSLATE). We see, thus, that this change of perspective is partially induced by a problem of translation and of language: the fact that *zôion* and "animal" are not superimposed, and the argument about complex expressions sharing a common name, *homo vivus, homo pictus*, which is maintained even when the latter expression is replaced by *pictura*.

BIBLIOGRAPHY

Ammonius Alexandrinus Hermias. *On Aristotle's Categories*. Translated by S. Marc Cohen and Gareth B. Matthews. Ithaca, NY: Cornell University Press, 1991.

Aristotle. *The Categories; On Interpretation; Prior Analytics*. Translated by Harold P. Cooke and Hugh Tredennick. Loeb Classical Library. Cambridge, MA: Harvard University Press, 1973. English translation and notes by J. L. Ackrill: *Categories and De interpretatione*. Oxford: Clarendon, 1963. English translation by Hippocrates G. Apostle: *Aristotle's Categories and Propositions (De interpretatione)*. Commentary by Hippocrates G. Apostle. Grinnell, IA: Peripatetic, 1980. Italian translation and notes by Lorenzo Minio-Paluello: *Aristoteles Categoriae et liber De interpretatione*. Oxford: Clarendon, 1949. Italian translation and notes by Marcello Zanatta, *Le categorie*. Milan: Rizzoli, 1989. French translation and commentary by J. Lallot and F. Ildefonse: *Les catégories*. Paris: Éditions du Seuil, 2002. French translation by R. Bodéüs: *Catégories*. Edited by R. Bodéüs. Paris: Les Belles Lettres, 2001. French translation and notes by J. Tricot : *Aristote: Organon I, Catégories et Sur l'interpretation*. Paris: Vrin, 1989.

———. *The Complete Works of Aristotle: The Revised Oxford Translation*. 2 vols. Edited by Jonathan Barnes. Princeton, NJ: Princeton University Press, 1984.

Boethius, Anicius Manlius Severinus. *Commentaries on Aristotle's De interpretatione*. Edited by Karl Meiser. 2 vols. New York: Garland, 1987.

———. *Liber Aristotelis de decem praedicamentis*. Edited by Lorenzo Minio-Paluello. Bruges, Belg.: Desclée de Brouwer, 1961.

Cassin, Barbara. *L'effet sophistique*. Paris: Gallimard La Pléiade, 1995.

Cassin, Barbara, and Michel Narcy. *La décision du sens*. Paris: Vrin, 1989.

Desbordes, Françoise. "Homonymie et synonymie d'après les texts théoriques latins." In *L'Ambiguïté: Cinq études historiques*, edited by Irène Rosier, 51–102. Lille, Fr.: Presses Universitaires, 1988.

Dexippus. *On Aristotle's Categories*. Edited and translated by John Dillon. Ithaca, NY: Cornell University Press, 1990.

Evangeliou, Christos. *Aristotle's Categories and Porphyry*. Leiden, Neth.: Brill, 1996.

Weigelt, Charlotta. *The Logic of Life: Heidegger's Retrieval of Aristotle's Concept of Logos*. Stockholm: Almqvist and Wiksell, 2002.

Aristotelianism of predication, which the categories established in the *Categories* allow us to found.

- See Box 3.

3. What it means to speak: Looking for homonymy

The entire Aristotelian logic (meaning of words, predicative syntax, syllogism) depends on "the most stable principle of all," the onto-logical principle that establishes a link between the order of being and the order of discourse, which has come down to posterity as the principle of noncontradiction: "The same attribute cannot at the same time belong and not belong to the same subject in the same respect [*to gar auto hama huparchein te kai mê huparchein adunaton tôi autôi kai kata to auto* (τὸ γὰρ αὐτὸ ἅμα ὑπάρχειν τε καὶ μὴ ὑπάρχειν ἀδύνατον τῷ αὐτῷ καὶ κατὰ τὸ αὐτό)]," *Metaphysics*, Γ.3, 1005b19–20, trans. Barnes, 2:1588). In fact, the refutation of his adversaries—which constitutes the only possible demonstration—is based entirely on the demand for univocality. Aristotle indeed proposes the following series of equivalences as if it were self-evident: "to speak" (*legein* [λέγειν], or what is proper to man, who otherwise would be nothing but a plant, Γ.3, 1006a13–15); "to say something" (*legein ti* [λέγειν τι], 1006a13, 22); "to say something that is significant both for himself and for another [*sêmainein ti kai autôi kai allôi* (σημαίνειν τι καὶ αὐτῷ καὶ ἄλλῳ)]"; "to mean something unique," "for not to have one meaning is to have no meaning [*to gar mê hen sêmainein outhen sêmainein estin* (τὸ γὰρ μὴ ἓν σημαίνειν οὐθὲν σημαίνειν ἐστίν)]" (1006b7–8). The principle of noncontradiction is thus proved and actualized only because it is impossible for the same (word) simultaneously to have and not to have the same (meaning). Univocality is well and truly the necessary condition of the entire logic (Cassin and Narcy, *La décision du sens*, 9–40; see SENSE). So Aristotle tracks down homonymy by proposing to distinguish between the different meanings of the same word, so as to be able to put, if need be, a different word alongside each definition ("tetheiê . . . idion onoma kath' hekaston ton logon [τεθείη . . . ἴδιον ὄνομα καθ' ἕκαστον τὸν λόγον]," *Metaphysics*, Γ.3, 1006b5; cf. 18–20), for "the point in question is not this, whether the same thing can at the same time be and not be a man in name, but whether it can in fact [*to auto einai kai mê einai anthrôpon to onoma, alla to pragma* (τὸ αὐτὸ εἶναι καὶ μὴ εἶναι ἄνθρωπον τὸ ὄνομα, ἀλλὰ τὸ πρᾶγμα)]" (1006b20–22, trans. Barnes, 2:1589; and Cassin and Narcy, *La décision du sens*, 195–97).

Whenever Aristotle's interest is focused on language as such, no longer on its ontological basis, but as a discursive technique, as is the case in the *Sophistical Refutations*, then it is words and words alone, and no longer things, that are said to be homonyms. The cause of homonymy, a deep-rooted linguistic disease, is that there are more things than there are words, and we therefore have to use the same words for several things (*Sophistical Refutations*, 1.164a4–19). Aristotle, in order to make up for the linguistic deficit that the adversaries of the principle use to their advantage, attempts therefore to remedy the arguments by diagnosing

3

Aristotle, or, Against the homonymy of ideas

Socrates, or so Aristotle maintains, did not grant that either universals or definitions had a separate existence. Philosophers who came after Socrates, Aristotle says,

gave them separate existence [echôrisan (ἐχώρισαν)], and this was the kind of thing they called Ideas [ἰδέας]. Therefore it followed for them, almost by the same argument, that there must be Ideas of all things that are spoken of universally [πάντων ἰδέας εἶναι τῶν καθόλου λεγομένων], and it was almost as if a man wished to count certain things, and while they were few thought he would not be able to count them, but made them more and then counted them; for the Forms are almost more numerous than the groups of sensible things [τῶν καθ' ἕκαστα αἰσθητῶν], yet it was in seeking the causes of sensible things that they proceeded from these to the Forms. For to each set of substances there answers a Form which has the same name and exists apart from the substances

[καθ' ἕκαστόν τε γὰρ ὁμώνυμόν ἔστι καὶ παρὰ τὰς οὐσίας], and so also in the other categories there is one character common to many individuals, whether these be sensible or eternal.

(*Metaphysics*, M.4, 1078b30–1079a3, trans. Barnes, 2:1705–6)

(Note that we follow Tredennick's reading of this passage, rather than Jaeger's.)

Commentators note that one would expect to find "synonym" where the Greek reads "homonym." (Indeed, H. Tredennick translates "synonym" in place of "homonym.") Did Aristotle mistake the two concepts? Or should we understand there to be a certain fuzziness in the terminology, as Léon Robin did? Neither alternative is satisfactory; rather, Aristotle's use of "homonym" signals the virulence of his critique of Platonic "participation," which does not even acknowledge that items that participate in the same idea may have a common definition. This is clearly expressed in *Metaphysics* A:

And if the Ideas and the particulars that share them [τῶν ἰδεῶν καὶ τῶν μετεχόντων] have the same Form [ταὐτὸ εἶδος], there will be something common to these; for why should [the numeral] 2 be one and the same in the perishable 2s or in those which are many but eternal, and not the same in the 2 itself as in the particular 2 [αὐτῆς καὶ τῆς τινός]? But if they have not the same Form, they must have only the name in common [ὁμώνυμα ἄν εἴη], and it is as if one were to call both Callias and a wooden image a man, without observing any community between them.

(*Metaphysics*, A.9, 991a2–8; cf. Γ.4, 1008a34–b3, trans. Barnes)

The choice then lies between the so-called third man argument (cf. Plato's *Parmenides*) and homonymy.

Barbara Cassin
Frédérique Ildefonse

---

the voluntary confusions that attempt to derive some benefit from the different sorts of homonymy, which he identifies in terms of *lexis*. Here we come closest of all to the modern conception of homonymy as homophony.

4. The case of being, *pollachôs legomenon*

Is being a genus (which is thus linked to synonymy), or is it not? Is being a homonym, or is it not? Aristotle's most consistent answer to these two questions, which have become epochal, is "no." Indeed, he repeats that being is expressed multiply: it is a *pollachôs legemenon* [πολλαχῶς λεγομένον]—neither homonymy nor analogy but, to borrow Gwilym E. L. Owen's expression, which has become an established term, "focal meaning." Aristotle puts being, like the good or the one, as one of the "homonyms deriving from unity, or which have unity as their aim" ("aph' henos, pros hen [ἀφ ' ἑνὸς πρὸς ἕν]"), which he therefore distinguishes from "coincidental" homonyms (or rather, those occurring "by chance," *apo tuchês* [ἀπὸ τύχης]), and from homonyms "by analogy" (to be understood as proportion: as sight is in the body, so reason is in the soul; *Nicomachean Ethics*, 1.4, 1096b25–30, trans. Barnes, 2:1733; *Eudemian Ethics*, 7.2, 1236a17 and b25). But for being, and specifically in book Γ of the *Metaphysics*, this case is very explicitly distinguished from a case of homonymy: "There are many senses in which a thing may be said to 'be,' but they are related to one central point, one definite kind of thing, and are not homonymous [*pros hen kai mian tina phusin kai ouch homônumôs* (πρὸς ἕν καὶ μίαν τινὰ φύσιν καὶ οὐχ ὁμωνύμως)]," *Metaphysics*, Γ.2, 1003a34; cf. 1003b5–6); "So, too, there are many senses in which a thing is said to be, but all refer to one starting-point

[*pollachôs men all' hapan pros mian archên* (πολλαχῶς μὲν ἀλλ' ἅπαν πρὸς μίαν ἀρχήν)]." How can we satisfactorily account for this shifting status, and where can we place "being"? The difficulty leads to a hardening of homonymies themselves; thus Porphyry chooses to place *aph' henos* and *pros hen* in the category of homonymy, which will lead to a reinterpretation of analogy (see ANALOGY and PARONYM).

III. The Taxonomy of Porphyry and Its Posterity

Porphyry systematizes the various scattered references in Aristotle and proposes a taxonomy of homonyms (65.18–68.1). This will be subsequently taken up and modified by commentators (see Ammonius, 21.15–22.2; Simplicius, 31.23–33.21; on the relationship of the commentators to each other, see, for example, Luna's commentaries on Simplicius, *Commentaire sur les "Catégories" d'Aristote*, 128 and 146; and on the classification, see ibid., 46, schemas pp. 98 and 100), and then taken up again by Boethius (*In Categorias Aristotelis*, 166 B–C, in RT: *PL*, 64), thereby passing into the medieval Latin tradition (see Libera, "Les sources gréco-arabes," and see ANALOGY). In the schema below, *P* indicates the terms used by Porphyry, *B* those used by Boethius (trans. Desbordes, 166B–C, in Desbordes, "Homonymie et synonymie"), and *T* those in the *Paraphrasis Themistiana* whenever they differ from *B* (*Anonymi Paraphrasis Themistiana*, ed. Minio-Paluello [*Aristoteles latinus*, 1.15], 136–37).

In Porphyry, we note that:

The *on* [ὄν], and everything that is *pollachôs*, comes under the heading of homonymy, contrary to the indications in book Γ, for example (see Porphyry, *Isagoge*, 2.10: "Let us simply posit, as in the *Categories*,

Homonyms P homônumai B aequivoca				
1. Coincidental P *apo tuchês* B *casu* T *fortuito* Alexander (son of Priam) / Alexander (king of Macedonia)	**2. Intentional, deliberate** P *apo dianoias* B *consilio* T *hominum voluntate*			
	2.1. By resemblance P *kath' homoiotêta* B *secundum similitudinem* ex. *Man* / real portrait, a portrait of a *man*	**2.2. By analogy** P *kat' analogian* [sc. by proportion] B *secundum proportionem* T *pro parte*	**2.3. single source**	**2.4. single goal**
			P. aph' *henos kai pros hen, pollachôs legomenon* [together, 2.3 and 2.4 designate what comes to be called the analogy of attribution, that is, the case of being]	
		ex. A "*principle*" —understood (by analogy) as the origin in a series of numbers, or as the point in a line	*ab uno* ex. "*Medical,*" as in a "*medical scalpel*" or a "*medical* potion"	*ad unum* ex. A *healthy* walk, *healthy* food, because they furnish or give or lead to *health*

the ten first types as playing the role of so many first principles: assuming we call them all beings, he says, we will do this homonymously, and not synonymously").

The only example of coincidental homonyms is associated with proper names: there is more than one man named Alexander. Yet this is not an Aristotelian example, whereas other examples from the corpus are for their part sometimes presented under this heading: in particular, the example of *kleis*, or key/clavichord, which is given as a homonymy that is easy to identify because it brings into play homonymous things that are visibly different (*Nicomachean Ethics,* 5.2, 1129a27–31). Or elsewhere, the examples of *kuôn* [κύων], dog as a barking animal / Dog as a constellation of stars, and of *aetos* [ἀετός], eagle/pediment, given as "literal tropes" of homonymy, insofar as "the word or expression has several meanings" (as distinct from "tropes of usage," "each time habit makes us speaks thus," *Sophistical Refutations,* 4.166a.15–17). This is perhaps one way of indicating the inherent difficulty of Aristotelian examples: even according to most dictionary definitions, *kleis* implies a resemblance (the collarbone locks together the chest, and has the shape of a hook, like a key; cf. RT: LSJ, on this entry), just as the star constellation resembles a dog, and the pediment spreads its wings over the column. In fact, this resemblance reveals the difficulty of finding unmotivated homonymies, which thus conform to Aristotle's definitions. The only choice is therefore between homophones and specimens (see Hintikka,

"Aristotle and the Ambiguity of Ambiguity," and Cassin, *L'Effet sophistique,* 348–53).

All of the other homonyms come from intentional homonyms. And the *Categories* defines one precisely determined kind, and one alone: homonyms by resemblance. This congruent delocalization allows us to ask again the question of the senses of being.

IV. Ambiguity and the Major New Latin Terms

The notion of *equivocatio,* because of the need to harmonize the different sources, whether Aristotelian (the *Categories,* the *Sophistical Refutations,* the *Topics*) or not (the Stoic sources, beginning with Augustine's *De dialectica*), will become clearer and more divided. As far as the notion of *univocatio* is concerned, it takes on a specific meaning that describes any acceptable variant of a term that does not derive from a new "institution," and thus becomes the key notion of the Terminist theory of *suppositio,* or reference (see SUPPOSITION). Terminologically, these conflicts and reconfigurations led to a specialized understanding, and two distinct usages, of the terms *univoca* and *synonyma,* even though the former served originally as a translation of the latter.

A. Homonymy and ambiguity

Besides the terms already mentioned, Boethius talks in *De divisione* of utterances that are *ambigua,* in relation to the syntactical ambiguity caused by the double accusative (for example, "audio Graecos vicisse Troianos" [I hear that the Greeks have conquered the Trojans / that the Trojans have conquered the Greeks]), which corresponds to *amphibolia* or *amphibologia* in the taxonomy of the *Sophistical Refutations.*

Referring to the *Topics* (1.15) and the *Sophistical Refutations*, he makes a distinction between an expression (*vox*) that is *simplex*, which means one thing only, and a *multiplex* expression, which means several things ("multiplex idest multa significans"). An utterance can be *multiplex* or polysemic if only one of its parts is equivocal, or if it is wholly equivocal: it is a matter of an *amphibola oratio*, a phrase with two senses. Boethius is interested in the different ways of disambiguating ("dividing") a polysemic utterance, by adding a determination, for example, or producing a paraphrase (to use the example cited earlier: "audio quod Graeci vicerint Troianos"; RT: *PL*, 64.889–90). It is the word *multiplex*, along with *duplex*, that is used as the generic term in the medieval tradition. Thus the classification of the first six paralogisms of the *Sophistical Refutations*, those which deal with discourse, established by Galen on the basis of the distinction between effective / potential / apparent, is always given as a classification of the types of *multiplicitates*. (On the difficulty of knowing which Greek term the Latin *multiplicitas* refers to, and on the Greek *ditton* [διττόν], see Ebbesen, *Commentators and Commentaries*, 3:174.)

A proposition that is *multiplex* (or *duplex*) means several things, without necessarily being ambiguous. Thus "Socrates calvus philosophus ambulat" is *multiplex* because "from the point of view of baldness, of philosophy, and of walking, there is nothing unique that can be attached [to the subject]." The case is different for "animal rationale mortale homo est," which is a proposition that is unique (*una*, *simplex*, *singular*) because the different elements of the predicate, spoken continuously, "make something that is one," and thus constitute a unique predicate. "Canis animal est" is both *multiplex* and ambiguous: the predicate *canis* is a term that, because it is equivocal, contains multiple things that cannot be reduced to a unique thing, so it cannot be used to make a unique affirmation: "There is one single *vox* but a multiple affirmation" (Boethius, *In Librum Aristotelis Peri hermeneias*, 2nd ed., 352–56; cf. Aristotle, *Peri hermêneias*, 11). This is why, whenever the question is *multiplex* (if its subject or its predicate are not simple), we also need to reply with a *multiplex* answer (Boethius, *In Librum Aristotelis Peri hermeneias*, 358).

Augustine, in the *De dialectica*, is interested in the sign and its value (*vis*; see SENSE), which is in direct proportion to its capacity to "move the listener." The obstacles preventing this value from being realized, and thereby preventing the sign from attaining truth, are obscurity (*obscuritas*) and ambiguity (*ambiguitas*). Augustine accepts the position of the "dialecticians," that every word is ambiguous, rejecting Cicero's mocking remarks ("How, then, can they explain ambiguities with ambiguities?" from a lost fragment of the *Hortensius*), and adding that this affirmation is valid for words considered in isolation: *ambigua* are dispelled within a line of argument whenever they are joined to other *ambigua* (*De dialectica*, 9). Augustine proposes a classification of "ambiguities," and begins by dividing them into those that are spoken and those that are written. Among the first set are two main types, the *univoca* and the *aequivoca*, defined as "things" (*ea*, neutral pronoun) possessing the same name (whether this name is construed as a proper or a common noun) with an identical/different definition. A child, an old man, a fool, a wise man, a big man, a small man, can all be referred to using the name "man," allowing for the same definition "mortal animal having the ability to reason" (which poses a further problem in the case of a fool, or a child), and additionally having a name and a definition that belong to each of these on its own: the multiplicity of species understood as a single genus is considered here as an endless source of ambiguity in the lexicon. The set of *aequivoca* clearly demonstrates that Augustine has now turned his attention to *names*. The first example testifies to this: "*Tullius* is a name, a dactyl foot, and an equivocation." "Equivocations" are divided into three groups, depending on whether the ambiguity is due to technical, especially grammatical, uses (*ab arte*), which include all those that are metalinguistic and autonymous; whether it is due to usage (*ab usu*); or whether it is due to both of these together. Augustine distinguishes in particular *aequivoca* that have the same origin (including where there is a transfer of meaning—for example, *Tullius* applied to the prince of eloquence or to his statue, as well as other transfers of meaning borrowed from rhetoric, from the whole to the part, from the type to the species, and so on) from those that have a different origin (when a same form, such as *nepos*, has two different meanings). Augustine pays a remarkable degree of attention to metalinguistic ambiguity, to the distinction between a word insofar as it is "used," and a word insofar as it is "mentioned," not only in the *De dialectica*, but also in the *De magistro* (on the opposition *verbum-dictio*, see WORD; this ambiguity also appears independently, it seems, in the term *suppositio materialis* from the twelfth century on; see SUPPOSITION).

The terms *amphibolia* and *amphibologia* are reserved for syntactical ambiguity. In Greek, the terms referring to the idea of ambiguity have been formed from the prefix *amphi-* (on two sides), producing the verb *amphiballesthai* [ἀμφιβάλλεσθαι], "to give rise to ambiguity," and the adjective *amphibolos* [ἀμφίβολος], with its opposite *anamphibolos* [ἀναμφίβολος] (Lallot, "Apollonius Dyscole et l'ambiguïté linguistique"). The term has a generic meaning and encompasses different kinds, including homonymy, homophony, and syntactical ambiguity; but it also refers in a more limited way to ambiguity of syntax or of construction, the second type of paralogism in the *Sophistical Refutations*, and distinct from the first type, homonymy, which is confined to the word. The *Sophistical Refutations* distinguish between two types of syntactical ambiguity. *Amphibolia* is to a sentence what equivocation is to a simple noun, that is, following Galen's terminology, an "actual" multiplicity: indeed, a construction with a double accusative, such as "video lupum comedere canem" ("I see the wolf eating the dog" or "I see the dog eating the wolf"), "in actuality" conveys two meanings, so that grammarians since antiquity have justifiably classed it as one of the "flaws" (*vitia*) of discourse. Conversely, composition (and division) is a "potential" multiplicity, in the same way that an incorrect "accent" is for a simple noun: "vidisti baculo hunc percussum" can mean either, in its divided meaning, "with a stick, you saw this person struck" (false: you did not employ the stick to see the person being struck), or, in its composite meaning, "you saw this person struck with a stick" (true). The two possible meanings do not exist simultaneously, but we can have one or the other, and the problem lies in knowing what it is that "conveys ambiguity" (the graphic sequence, without its intonation or punctuation?). Composition/division proves itself to be an extremely powerful logical tool, allowing us to deal especially with problems of the extent of the logical operators: for example, "omnis homo qui currit movetur" (Any man who runs is in motion), in which *omnis* could refer simply to *homo* (divided meaning) or to *homo qui currit* (composite meaning), which leads to unrestricted or restricted interpretations of the relative pronoun. The same opposition is also used to distinguish the modalities *de dicto* and *de res*: for example, "possibile est sedentem ambulare" (It is possible for someone who is sitting down to walk), which is false according to the divided interpretation ("It is possible—that someone who is sitting down is walking," just as it is false that someone who is sitting down is walking), but true according to the composite interpretation (someone who is sitting down may be able to walk).

B. The difference or juxtaposition of synonyms and univocals

The notion of *univocatio* has a complex history. Throughout the Middle Ages, it characterizes any semantic variation of a word that does not derive from a "new imposition." So the fact that in an expression like "homo currit," *homo* can mean "a man" or "man" (generically), is not a case of equivocation in the same way as the use of the noun *canis*, which is a unique signifier "imposed" on three different things: a dog, a dogfish, and the star constellation. The reflection on *univocatio* is linked, at the beginning of the twelfth century, to the passage on contradiction in *Peri hermêneias* (6.17a34–37). There are three distinct historical moments.

1. Boethius, commenting on this passage, and alluding explicitly to the *Sophistical Refutations*, defines the six conditions of a true opposition (contradiction and contrariness): the terms, in both the affirmative and the negative, must be neither (1) equivocal nor (2) univocal, which is the case for "homo ambulat": "Man as a species and man as someone in particular are univocal" (specialis homo et particularis homo univocas sunt); nor must they be (3) considered in terms of different parts (which corresponds to the *fallacia secundum quid* and *simpliciter* of the *Refutations*, with the example "the eye is white" / "is not white," depending on whether one is referring to the white of the eye or the pupil); nor (4) considered in terms of different relations ("ten is double" / "is not double"); nor (5) considered in terms of different times ("Socrates is sitting down" / "is not sitting down"); nor (6) considered in terms of different verbal moods ("Catullus sees" / "does not see," referring on the one hand to the act of seeing, on the other to the power of sight) (*In Librum Aristotelis Peri hermeneias*, 132–34).

2. Abelard compares this passage on contradiction to Boethius's commentary on the first chapter of the *Categories*. Following Porphyry, Boethius distinguishes first of all, as we saw, between coincidental equivocation and deliberate equivocation. Then, in discussing the different transfers of meaning, he distinguishes between those that are produced for reasons of ornamentation, and are not to be considered as equivocation, and those that are produced "because of the lack

of names" (still understood to cover proper as well as common nouns): a name belonging to a thing is therefore transferred to another thing that does not have one, so it becomes the name for two different things, and thus an equivocal name. Abelard groups under the heading *univocatio* all transfers of meaning that do not come about because of a "lack of names," that is, both poetic transfers and those that Boethius mentioned with regard to contradiction (for example, the generic or specific meanings of *homo*). These different cases can be grouped together into the same category because they share two essential characteristics: they are variations of meaning that do not come from a new, imposed meaning, and they only appear in a given context.

3. The rediscovery of the *Sophistical Refutations* around 1130 allows for a comparison of these conditions with those given by Aristotle as the conditions for a true refutation (167a20ff.). The term "synonym," which appears in the Latin translation of the *Sophistical Refutations* (167a20), is preserved in this form ("Elenchus est contradictio eiusdem et unius, non nominis sed rei, et nominis non sinonimi sed eiusdem" [Refutation is a contradiction that is of one and the same thing, according to a oneness that is not only of the name but of the thing, and of a name that is not only a synonym, but that is one and the same name]), illustrated by the example of the "synonyms" (in the modern sense of the term) Marcus/Tullius, Cicero's two names: *sinonimus* is thus not to be confused with Boethius's *univocus*. The framework provided by the *Refutations* proves to be problematic, since *equivocatio* can cover either the entire range of paralogisms in discourse, or the first of these, "equivocation," or the first kind of equivocation itself. Indeed, we know that equivocation, like *amphibolia*, is divided into three kinds: the first kind is produced when a noun is imposed on different things, which it signifies in an equivalent manner, which is the "coincidental" equivocation that Porphyry or Boethius distinguish in the *Categories* (for example, *canis*), or equivocation strictly speaking. The second kind occurs when the different things that the word signifies are ordered according to a hierarchy "secundum prius et posterius" (according to before and after), which happens in cases of metaphorical usage (and here the example found in the *Categories*, of a living man and the painting of a man, reappears): so this is the case with *translatio*, but also with *univocatio* (if one considers that a name refers *per prius* to individuals, and *per posterius*, for example, to one's one name; see *translatio* in TO TRANSLATE). The third kind originates in the particular meaning a word has in a given context: for example, it is only in the expression *monachus albus* (white monk) that "white" has the meaning of "Cistercian." The different phenomena related to *univocatio* are classified first and foremost under the second kind of equivocation ("All the sophisms that Boethius calls univocal sophisms come under this second kind of equivocation. Aristotle discussed equivocation in a broad sense, since he included univocal meaning":

commentary on the *Sophistical Refutations*, in De Rijk, *Logica modernorum*, 1:302), but equally considered along with other types of paralogism. So, for example, the ambiguity of *homo* in "homo est species" / "Socrates est homo" can be thought of as *equivocatio* (if one considers that it is a transfer of meaning), as *figura dictionis* (while it has the same "form," *homo* has several meanings), or as *accidens* (the type of predication is different) (De Rijk, ibid.; Rosier, "Évolution des notions d'*univocatio* et *equivocatio*").

The phenonemon of univocality will be at the heart of Terminist logic and, insofar as it is applied to things, stays with the translation and commentaries on the first chapter of the *Categories* (cf. Petrus Hispanus, *Tractatus*, ed. De Rijk). All of the different meanings of a "same" term, in a given context, will fall under or be derived from this univocality, and these different meanings will be subject to classification according to the kinds of "supposition" proper to the terms (see SUPPOSITION). The notions of equivocation and univocation will find a new use in theology when it comes to analyzing "divine predications": in the expressions "God is just" / "man is just," the predicate will be, depending on the author, considered as the expression of its subject equivocally (it is the same signifier, but it signifies absolutely different things), univocally (there is something common in the two predications, and something different, which are analyzed particularly in terms of different connotation; see CONNOTATION), or analogically (see ANALOGY; cf. particularly Ashworth, "Analogy and Equivocation").

The following points will help us measure the evolution of the meaning of homonymy, and to chart the gap between the ancient concept and the modern one—which is the primary source of misunderstandings today.

1. In antiquity, homonyms and synonyms are not employed primarily with respect to words, but mainly, and in any case also, in relation to things: the two Ajaxes, the *eidos* and the *eidôlon*, a man and the drawing of a man, a man and an ox.

2. In antiquity, homonyms and synonyms are not in a position of reverse symmetry (one word–several meanings / one meaning–several words): if we follow the canonical definitions in the *Categories*, it is a matter in every case of several things, and one word naming or defining them—though this word can itself have one or several meanings.

3. *Univocatio* is introduced in the Middle Ages, in contrast to *equivocatio*, to describe a multiplicity of meanings of a word that does not derive from a new, imposed meaning, whether it is a matter of metaphorical usages, or of contextually determined meanings of a "same" word. "Univocation" is when one and the same word is being considered, whereas "equivocation" (cf. *canis*: "dog," "constellation") is when there are several words. The notion of univocation plays an important role in the genesis of the theory of supposition, which is concerned precisely with identifying the referential variants of a "same" term. Whereas in the Middle Ages, the emphasis falls on the oneness of a word underlying its multiple meanings, univocation will come to describe the oneness of the meaning of a word: in the Middle Ages, a

univocal word was a word that was "one," behind or in spite of its many varieties of usage; today, in contrast, a univocal word is a word that has only one meaning. In both cases, however, a word such as this is not equivocal in the strict sense, initially because its multiplicity did not affect its original and immutable semantic being, which is defined by imposition, and today because it does not have several meanings. But although univocation in the Middle Ages is "polysemic," modern univocation, by contrast, is not.

Barbara Cassin
Irène Rosier-Catach

BIBLIOGRAPHY

Ammonius Alexandrinus Hermias. *On Aristotle's* Categories. Translated by S. Marc Cohen and Gareth B. Matthews. Ithaca, NY: Cornell University Press, 1991.

Aristoteles Latinus. Vol. 2, books 1–5: *Categoriae*. Edited by Lorenzo Minio-Paluello. Bruges, Belg.: Desclée de Brouwer, 1961.

Aristotle. *The Complete Works of Aristotle: The Revised Oxford Translation*. 2 vols. Edited by Jonathan Barnes. Princeton, NJ: Princeton University Press, 1984.

Ashworth, Earline Jennifer. "Analogy and Equivocation in Thirteenth-Century Logic: Aquinas in Context." *Mediaeval Studies* 54 (1992): 94–135.

Atherton, Catherine. "Apollonius Dyscolus and the Ambiguity of Ambiguity." *Classical Quarterly* 45 (1995): 441–73.

———. *The Stoics on Ambiguity*. Cambridge: Cambridge University Press, 1993.

Blank, David L. *Ancient Philosophy and Grammar: The Syntax of Apollonius Dyscolus*. Chico, CA: Scholars Press, 1982.

Bobzien, Susanne. "The Stoics on Fallacies of Equivocation." In *Language and Learning: Philosophy of Language in the Hellenistic Age*, edited by Dorothea Frede and Brad Inwood, 239–73. Cambridge: Cambridge University Press, 2005.

Boethius. *Commentarium in Librum Aristotelis Peri Hermeneias, Pars Posterior*. Edited by C. Meiser. 2nd ed. Leipzig: Teubner, 1880.

Cassin, Barbara. *L'Effet sophistique*. Paris: Gallimard La Pléiade, 1995.

———. "Who's Afraid of the Sophists? Against Ethical Correctness." Translated by Charles T. Wolfe. *Hypatia* 15, no. 4 (2000): 102–20.

Cassin, Barbara, and Michel Narcy, eds. and trans. *La décision du sens: Le livre Gamma de la Métaphysique d'Aristote*. Paris: Vrin, 1989.

De Rijk, Lambertus Marie. *Logica modernorum: A Contribution to the History of Early Terminist Logic*. 2 vols. Assen, Neth.: Van Gorcum, 1962–67.

Desbordes, Françoise. "Homonymie et synonymie d'après les textes théoriques latins." In *L'Ambiguïté: Cinq études historiques*, edited by Irène Rosier, 51–102. Lille, Fr.: Presses Universitaires de Franca, 1988.

Dexippus. *On Aristotle's* Categories. Edited and translated by John Dillon. Ithaca, NY: Cornell University Press, 1990.

Dionysius Thrax. *Technê grammatikê*. Edited by Gustav Uhlig. Grammatici Graeci 1.1. Leipzig: Teubner, 1883. English translation by Thomas Davidson: *The Grammar*. St. Louis, MO: George Knapp, 1874. French translation by Jean Lallot: *La grammaire de Denys le Thrace*. 2nd rev. and expanded ed. Paris: CNRS Editions, 1998.

Ebbesen, Sten. *Commentators and Commentaries on Aristotle's* Sophistici Elenchi: *A Study of Post-Aristotelian Ancient and Medieval Writings on Fallacies*. 3 vols. Leiden, Neth.: Brill, 1981.

Gallet, Bernard. *Recherches sur kairos et l'ambiguïté dans la poésie de Pindare*. [Bordeaux, Fr.]: Presses Universitaires de Bordeaux, 1990.

Heitsch, Ernst. *Die Entdeckung der Homonymie*. Mainz, Ger.: Verlag der Akademie der Wissenschaften und der Literatur, 1972.

Hintikka, Jaako. "Aristotle and the Ambiguity of Ambiguity." In *Time and Necessity*. Oxford: Clarendon, 1973.

Homer. *Iliad*. Translated by A. T. Murray. 2nd ed. Cambridge, MA: Harvard University Press, 1999.

———. *Odyssey*. Translated by A. T. Murray. London: Heinemann, 1969.

Lallot, Jean. "Apollonius Dyscole et l'ambiguïté linguistique." In *L'ambiguïté: Cinq études historiques*, edited by Irène Rosier, 33–49. Lille, Fr.: Presses Universitaires de Franca, 1988.

Law, Vivien, and Ineke Sluiter, eds. *Dionysius Thrax and the* Technê Grammatikê. Münster, Ger.: Nodus, 1995.

Leszl, Walter. *Logic and Metaphysics in Aristotle: Aristotle's Treatment of Types of Equivocity and Its Relevance to His Metaphysical Theories.* Padua: Antenore, 1970.

Libera, Alain de. "Référence et champs: Genèse et structure des theories médiévales de l'ambiguïté (XIIe–XIIIe siècles)." *Medioevo* 10 (1984): 155–208.

———, ed. "Les sources gréco-arabes de la théorie médiévale de l'analogie de l'être." *Les Études Philosophiques* 3/4 (1989): 319–45.

Owen, Gwilym Ellis Lane. "Aristotle on the Snares of Ontology." In *New Essays on Plato and Aristotle*, edited by R. Bambrough, 69–95. London: Routledge and Kegan Paul, 1965. Reprinted in *Logic, Science and Dialectic: Collected Papers in Greek Philosophy*, edited by Martha Nussbaum, 259–78. London: Duckworth, 1986.

———. "Tithenai ta phainomena." In *Aristote et les problèmes de méthode*, edited by S. Mansion, 83–103. Louvain, Belg.: Éditions de l'Institut supérieur de philosophie, 1961. Reprinted in *Articles on Aristotle I: Science*, edited by Jonathan Barnes, Malcolm Schofield, and Richard Sorabji, 113–26. London: Duckworth, 1975.

Peter of Spain (Petrus Hispanus Portugalensis). *Tractatus (Summule Logicales).* Edited by Lambertus Marie De Rijk. Vol. 22. Assen, Neth.: Van Gorcum, 1972.

Plato. *Parmenides.* Translated by Mary Louise Gill and Paul Ryan. Indianapolis, IN: Hackett, 1996.

———. *Sophist.* Translated by Nicholas P. White. Indianapolis, IN: Hackett, 1993.

Rosier, Irène. "Évolution des notions d'*univocatio* et *equivocatio* au XIIe siècle." In *L'ambiguïté: Cinq études historiques*, edited by Irène Rosier, 103–62. Lille, Fr.: Presses Universitaires de Franca, 1988.

Shields, Christopher John. *Order in Multiplicity: Homonymy in the Philosophy of Aristotle.* Oxford: Clarendon, 1999.

Simplicius of Cilicia. *Commentaire sur les "Catégories" d'Aristote: Chapitres 2–4.* Translated by Philippe Hoffmann, with Ilsetraut Hadot and Pierre Hadot. Notes by Concetta Luna. Paris: Les Belles Lettres, 2001.

———. *On Aristotle's* Categories *1–4.* Translated by Michael Chase. Ancient Commentators on Aristotle. Ithaca, NY: Cornell University Press, 2003.

———. *On Aristotle's* Categories *5–6.* Translated by Frans A. J. de Haas and Barrie Fleet. Ancient Commentators on Aristotle. London: Duckworth, 2001.

———. *On Aristotle's* Categories *7–8.* Translated by Barrie Fleet. Ancient Commentators on Aristotle. London: Duckworth, 2002.

———. *On Aristotle's* Categories *9–15.* Translated by Richard Gaskin. Ancient Commentators on Aristotle. London: Duckworth, 2000.

Taràn, Leonardo. "Speusippus and Aristotle on Homonymy and Synonymy." *Hermes* 106 (1978): 73–99.

Ward, Julie K. *Aristotle on Homonymy: Dialectic and Science.* Cambridge: Cambridge University Press, 2008.

| HUMANITY

"Humanity" designates at once the ensemble of humankind, and, as in the classic Latin *humanitas*, the ensemble of characteristics that define human nature as being separate from animal life, particularly the value of philanthropy—benevolence, culture, politeness, savoir-vivre. The German doublet *Menschheit/Humanität* provides a good entry point into this complex network of meaning.

I. *Menschheit/Humanität*

1. German terminology distinguishes between belonging to the human race (*Menschheit*), which relates to nature, and the sentiment of humanity (*Humanität*, directly connected to the Latin *humanitas*), which relates to culture and opens onto the idea of the "humanities" and "humanism": see MENSCHHEIT, and *cf.* BILDUNG, GESCHLECHT.

2. The link between this community of nature and relations with the other is explored in MITMENSCH (*cf. AUTRUI*).

II. Man/Animal/God: Nature and Culture

1. On the nature of man and the distinction man/animal, see ANIMAL, BEHAVIOR, GESCHLECHT; related to language and reason, see LOGOS, REASON; *cf.* HOMONYM; related to politics and the political, see CIVILTÀ, *CIVILITY, CIVILIZATION,* CIVIL SOCIETY, *COMMUNITY,* POLIS; related to art, see AESTHETICS, ART, MIMÊSIS; related to ways of being in the world, see DASEIN, ERLEBEN, LEIB, *MALAISE*; *cf.* NATURE, PATHOS.

    For the Greek definition of "man," one should consult LIGHT, Box 1, and TO TRANSLATE, Box 1, The Latin derivations of "man" are covered in MENSCHHEIT; see also PIETAS and RELIGIO.

2. On culture as a natural property of humankind, see *CULTURE*, and in particular BILDUNG, Boxes 1, 3, and LIGHT (with an explanation of the meaning of the German *Aufklärung* and the Hebrew *haśkālāh* [הַשְׂכָּלָה] in LIGHT, Box 3), PERFECTIBILITY; *cf.* GEISTESWISSENSCHAFTEN, MORALS.

3. On the difference between man and god/the gods, one should consult *GRACE, RELIGION,* and, in particular, BOGOČELOVEČESTVO.

➤ COMMON SENSE, GENDER, SEX

I / ME / MYSELF

FRENCH *je, moi, soi*
GERMAN *Ich; Selbst*
GREEK *egô* [ἐγώ]
ITALIAN *io; se, si, si-mismo*
LATIN *ego; ipse*

➤ ACTOR, AGENCY, *AUTRUI* [DRUGOJ, MITMENSCH], CONSCIOUSNESS, DASEIN, ES, *IDENTITY*, OIKEIÔSIS, REPRÉSENTATION, *SELF* [SAMOST', SELBST], SOUL, STAND, SUBJECT, TATSACHE

It is striking to note that certain dominant traditions in European philosophy (in particular transcendental philosophy, from Immanuel Kant to Edmund Husserl), and a tradition of grammatical analysis with its origins in antiquity that prevailed in structural linguistics (Roman Jakobson, Émile Benveniste), were united in closely associating the possibility of reflexive thought with the use of personal pronouns, taken as indicators of "subjectivity within language." The Cartesian "ego cogito, ego sum" has thus had its philosophical privilege justified and firmly established. We should qualify this representation in two ways: the linguistic forms that it presupposes are not in any sense universal, and other grammatical analyses are possible; and it is just as important to examine closely the shared linguisticism of Europe and to compare the theoretical effects of the expressions of the so-called *sujet de l'énonciation* (the utterer of the speech-event, the "speaking subject") and the *sujet de l'énoncé* (the "spoken-of" subject, the subject of the utterance), in order to understand how language predisposes thought to reflexivity within different speculative problematics.

Within this perspective, what is sketched out here is a description of the cycle of the "first person" in modern philosophy—going from the German dialectics of the *Ich* and the *Selbst* (Johann Gottlieb Fichte and his equation *Ich = Ich*, then his opposition of the *Ich* to the *Nicht-Ich*; Friedrich Hegel and his problematizing of self-consciousness as the reciprocity of *Ich* and *Wir*), to the English invention of "self" and "own" (at the core of John Locke's self-consciousness), and finally to the European recognition of the ontological primacy of the ego and the alter ego (in Husserl's phenomenology)—so as to then introduce within this thinking the limits envisaged by Arthur Rimbaud's paradoxical expression "Je est un autre" (I is another). This could serve as a common epigraph to the ways thinkers have gone beyond "first-person" subjectivity toward transcendence, impersonal corporeality, or transindividual anonymity, for which Michel Foucault invented the term *pensée du dehors* (thinking of the outside).

I. Having an "I"; Being "a Person"

At the beginning of his *Anthropology from a Pragmatic Point of View* (lectures published in 1797), Kant writes:

> The fact that the human being can have the "I" in his representations raises him infinitely above all other living beings on earth [Dass der Mensch in seiner Vorstellung das Ich haben kann, erhebt ihn unendlich über alle alleren auf Erden lebenden Wesen]. Because of this he is a *person* [Dadurch ist er eine Person]; and by virtue of the unity of consciousness through all changes that happen to him, one and the same person—i.e., through rank and dignity and entirely different being from things, such as irrational animals, with which one can do as one likes. This holds even when he cannot yet say "I" [selbst wenn er das Ich nicht sprechen kann], because he still has it in thoughts, just as all languages must think it when they speak in the first person, even if they do not have a special word to express this concept of "I" [ob sie zwar diese Ichheit nicht durch ein besonderes Wort ausdrücken]. For this faculty (namely, to think) is understanding.

> (*Anthropology from a Pragmatic Point of View*, trans. Louden, 15)

The text goes on—150 years before Paul Guillaume—to discuss the age when small children stop talking about themselves in the third person and start saying "I": "durch Ich zu sprechen." The translator of the French edition of this text, Michel Foucault, renders Kant's *das Ich* by *le Je*. He clearly did not want to adopt the French term—*moïté*—often used for the technical neologism of the German word *Ichheit*, invented at the start of the thirteenth century by Meister Eckhart, not only because he considered this a linguistic barbarism, but also because he clearly saw that Kant's object is the *Je* (the possibility of saying "I"), and not the *Moi* ("Me" or "Myself," that is, the possibility of describing or judging the Self). At the same time, following the main thread of the text, Foucault had to simplify the doubleness hidden within its opening sentence: to be "a person" (who is "one") is to be able to use the word *Ich*, but it also means including (the) *Ich*—this "something" that is not a thing—within its representation. In a sense, this is to represent the unrepresentable that the *Ich* names "for itself [*für sich Selbst*]."

This formulation is connected to the decisive developments of the *Critique of Pure Reason*, where the "transcendental subject" is theorized for the first time (see SUBJECT). A thesis is here being put forward that is both extremely debatable and determining for the development of Western philosophy. It is debatable because it is Eurocentric, and consequently idealist, and only apparently attentive to the materiality of language. Let us admit with Jakobson that every language contains a complete system of references of the code to itself, from the code to the message, from the message to itself, and from the message to the code—and notably that there is necessarily a class of specific units of meaning (shifters, or *embrayeurs* in French) whose function is to refer to the singularity of an actual message. Personal pronouns correspond exceptionally well to this definition (as do demonstratives, adverbs of time and place, verb tenses, and so on). We can thus, following Benveniste's famous analyses, characterize the individual act of appropriating language as a problem of subjectivity in language—"Language is so organized that it permits each speaker to *appropriate to himself* an entire language by designating himself as *I*" (*Problems in General Linguistics*, trans. Meek, 226)—thereby creating a short-circuit between the instance of utterance (*énonciation*) and the statement (*énoncé*). But the fact of using the word "subjectivity" is an indication of the circularity of such definitions, since it takes as given (as was the case in Kant's text cited above) that the "normal" or "implicit" form is one in which the agent, the support of any attribution in a statement, and the "instance of discourse" (ibid.) or what carries the word, that is, the generic speaking being ("man"), can all be subsumed under one and the same concept. This situation is only characteristic of some languages, however, or even some of their usages. The "simplicity" of the Indo-European system of personal pronouns is not a "linguistic universal."

In Japanese, for example, we observe two correlative phenomena (Takao Suzuki) that contrast with the usages of modern European languages (or only occupy a place in European languages deemed to be residual, infantile, artificial, or pathological). On the one hand, the terms we would call personal pronouns (above all, the equivalents of "I" and "you") have no etymological stability: historically, they are substituted for one another, following a continual process of devaluation and replacement, linked to the transformation of marks of respect into marks of familiarity or condescension. On the other hand, the normal form by which speakers are designated in a statement consists of marking their respective position or role in the social relationships (which are almost always asymmetrical) within which communication is initiated. Particularly important in this regard are the terms of kinship that, by a characteristic fiction, can be extended to other types of relationship.

It seems that European languages by contrast are made up, over a very long period of time, of a kind of specific universalism, which neutralizes the qualities and the roles of speakers (or, by contrast, allows them to be emphasized: "The king wishes it to be so," "Grandfather is going to get angry!" "Madame is served"), so as to bring out the abstract, and virtually reciprocal, positions of sender and receiver of spoken language: the one who has spoken will then listen, and vice versa. Jakobson is therefore right when he criticizes Husserl's interpretation of this point in his *Logical Investigations*, where he says that "the word 'I' refers to different persons depending on the situation, and for this reason takes on a new meaning each time." To the contrary, the meaning of "I" is the same every time; it is what speakers—subjects—possess in common, that by which they individually appropriate for themselves the instrument of communication. It would of course be important to study the interaction of linguistic usages, of institutional transformations (the emergence of an increasingly broad sphere of formal equality that encroaches on both the public and the private), and finally of various logico-grammatical theorizations, all of which have made possible the recognition of this norm, its standardization in scholarly as much as in popular language, and its interiorization and conceptualization in notions such as "person," "subject," "agency," "individuality," "ecceity," and so on.

Even though it is falsely universal, this thesis has been a determining one for the history of European philosophy. We can return to it, but critically, particularly by situating it within the horizon of the problem of translation. In elaborating a philosophical discourse concerned with subjectivity, we would have to then pay attention to the reciprocal action between concepts and linguistic forms as they differ from one language to another, against a background of shared characteristics. This is indeed one of the keys to the untranslatable "translatability" that characterizes the sharing or colinguisticity (*colinguisme*) of European philosophy, and it is surprising that there have been no major attempts to use the question of personal pronouns as a basis for developing the same kind of philological and philosophical analyses that have been brought to bear on the syntactical and semantic effects of the verb *être* (to be) in the constitution of classical ontology, from Benveniste to Barbara Cassin. There have been a few notable exceptions, such as Jaakko Hintikka's analyses of the performative nature of the Cartesian *cogito*, or, more recently, Marco Baschera's analyses of the Kantian *Ich denke* as a linguistic act, and also to some extent Ernst Tugendhat's analyses of Wittgenstein, Heidegger, and Hegel. The ground had been laid, however, on the one hand by the tradition of the critique of the metaphysics of the subject as a "grammatical convention," which goes from David Hume and Friedrich Nietzsche to the Ludwig Wittgenstein of the *Tractatus logico-philosophicus* and the *Philosophical Investigations*, and on the other hand by Wilhelm von Humboldt's reflections on the originary nature of reference to the subject in different languages, developed by Ernst Cassirer in the *Philosophy of Symbolic Forms* into a summary of the forms of expression of the *Ich-Beziehung* (I-relation).

We will focus our comments on four groups of problems, which will naturally spill over into one another: the naming of the first person, with the possibilities of mention and negation that this allows (in particular in German); the connotations of the first- and third-person reflexives (in English "self"; in French *moi, soi*; in German *Selbst*); the reasons for the recourse to foreign nouns for the subject (above all, the Latin *ego* in modern languages); and finally, the problems posed by the use of the indefinite and the neuter in philosophy ("one" in English, *ça* and *on* in French, for example). But we have to begin by discussing several difficulties concerning the very notions of person and personal pronoun.

▪ See Box 1.

II. *Vom Ich*

The theory of the subject in German Idealism, from Kant to Fichte and Hegel (we could gather all of these *Vom Ich* under the heading of Schelling's first essay, titled, precisely, "Vom Ich . . .") depends on a certain flexibility of the *Ich*, which can be partially transposed to English, but which has no equivalent in French. French does not nominalize the main subject, but instead offers a reflexive form, *le moi*, which produces the effect of objectivation, whereas *Ich* is immediately perceived as an autonym. As a consequence,

1

True and false persons

➤ ACTOR, Box 1; SUBJECT, Box 6

In his article "The Nature of Pronouns," Émile Benveniste explains that only the first and second persons are "real persons," and the corresponding pronouns "real personal pronouns," since they alone refer to interlocutors, that is, they imply the utterance within the statement itself:

> The third person is not a "person": it is really the verbal form whose function is to represent the non-person. . . . One should be fully aware that the "third person" is the only one by which a *thing* is predicated verbally. The "third person" must not, therefore, be imagined as a person suited to depersonalization. There is no apheresis of the person; it is exactly the non-person, which possesses as its sign the absence of that which specifically qualifies the "I" and the "you." Because it does not imply any person, it can take any subject whatsoever or no subject, and this subject, expressed or not, is never posited as a "person." . . . The third person has, with respect to the form itself, the constant characteristic and function of representing a non-personal invariant, and nothing but that. But if "I" and "you" are both characterized by the sign of person, one really feels that in their turn they are opposed to one another within the category they constitute by a feature whose linguistic nature should be defined. . . . A special correlation which we call, for want of a better term, the *correlation of subjectivity*, belongs to the *I-you* pair in its own right. . . . One could thus define "you" as the *non-subjective person*, in contrast to the *subjective person* that "I" represents; and these two "persons" are together opposed to the "non-person" form (= he). It would seem that all the relations established among the three forms of the singular should remain the same when they are transposed to the plural. . . . The ordinary distinction of the singular and plural should be, if not replaced, at least interpreted in the order of persons by a distinction between *strict person* (= "singular") and *amplified person* (= "plural"). Only the "third person," being a non-person, admits of a true plural.

> (Benveniste, *Problems in General Linguistics*, trans. Meek)

This famous analysis is justified both by its recourse to a contemporary formalism of communication that builds reference into language itself, and by a modern metaphysics opposing persons to things. Indeed, it represents their point of fusion. It is thus contrasted to an older tradition, originating with Aristotelianism and perfected by the time of the Renaissance, according to which (and in a manner one could call realist or objective) it was rather the "third person" that properly characterized what was understood by person. The notion of a person (*prosôpon* [πρόσωπον], *persona*) was conceived on the basis of the notion of a name, signifying the *suppositum* (subject) of an attribution that the statement translates, represents, or expresses:

> The person is the mode of signification via which the verb consignifies the property of speaking not insofar as it is something innate, but insofar as the thing of the verb is applicable to the thing of the *suppositum* subsisting by itself according to the properties of speech. The person thereby affects the verb [*inest verbo*] by virtue of its attributive aptitude with regard to the *suppositum*, according to a varied mode of attribution.

> (Thomas d'Erfurt, *Grammatica speculativa*, quoted by Jacques Julien)

The "names" *ipse, ego*, or *tu*, which "consignify" the person speaking, or to whom one is speaking, must then be interpreted both as abstractions and as targeting the individual being within a situation: singular universals of a kind. One might be tempted to think that this tradition still informs certain reductionist attempts of contemporary analytical philosophy, notably those inspired by Russell ("egocentric particulars") and by Strawson ("individual occurrences").

But this tradition is also opposed to the point of view developed by the logic of the Stoics, and transmitted from there to the grammarians of the same school. Instead of being focused on a determinate person (and, in a sense, then being appropriated by this person), the "subjective" link here between *énonciation* and *énoncé* is by contrast generalized and anticipated in a theory of meaning. Persons are defined equivocally, both in relation to the action described in itself (as agent or patient) and in relation to speech (insofar as they can sustain a discourse about themselves, and more generally they can "attest to" their actions or those of another). To quote Apollonius Dyscolus: "Persons who take part in an act are divided up into grammatical persons . . . but the act itself remains external to the person and to the number, and can thus be combined with all persons and numbers . . .; the term person is appropriate in that it demonstrates a corporeal *deixis* and a mental disposition." Frédérique Ildefonse claims that the coincidence "between the agent of the physical world and the grammatical person," inseparably linked to the way in which "the same term *diathesis* [= disposition] within the realm of signifieds is common to a physical diathesis and mood, that is, to a *diathesis* of the soul," is essential to the Stoic notion of a person. In other words, a person is projected onto different individualities not on the basis of an intrinsic relation between thought and language, but on the basis of events in the world where actions meet words, producing meaning-effects. This is the point of departure for Gilles Deleuze when he conceives the "play of persons" on the basis of a "neutral, pre-individual and impersonal field in which it is deployed" (*The Logic of Sense*, trans. Lester). But alternatively, one can find an echo in the syntactical theory of Jean-Claude Milner, who takes up the question of personal pronouns on the basis of "reflexivity" (in French, *me, moi, se, soi*), and of the way in which, in certain languages, this interferes with the expression of reciprocity and collectivity (the general notion of "coreference").

These irreconcilable perspectives create a tension that is constantly present in modern philosophical theories of the "subject" and the "person." But it is not always resolved in the same way, since each language has its own way of quoting, of being reflexive, of denying, and so on, and philosophical thought suffers the effects of this linguistic particularity (or, if one prefers, exploits its possibilities). Hence the untranslatabilities that also foster the renewal of theories of subjectivity.

BIBLIOGRAPHY

Bardzell, Jeffrey. *Speculative Grammar and Stoic Language Theory in Medieval Allegorical Narrative, from Prudentius to Alan of Lille.* New York: Routledge, 2009.

Benveniste, Émile. *Problems in General Linguistics.* Translated by Mary Elizabeth Meek. Miami, FL: University of Miami Press, 1971, 1973.

Deleuze, Gilles. *Logique du sens.* Paris: Minuit, 1969. Translation by Mark Lester with Charles Stivale: *The Logic of Sense.* Edited by Constantin V. Boundas. New York: Columbia University Press, 1990.

Ildefonse, Frédérique. "La théorie stoïcienne de la phrase (énoncé, proposition) et son influence

(continued)

(continued)

chez les grammariens." In *Théories de la phrase et de la proposition de Platon à Averroès*, edited by Philippe Büttgen, Stéphane Diebler, and Marwan Rashed, 151–70. Paris: Rue d'Ulm, 1999.

Julien, Jacques. "Personne grammaticale et sujet parlant dans le *De causis* de J. C. Scaliger." *DRLAV* (*Documentation et Recherche en Linguistique Allemande Contemporaine, Vincennes*), *Revue de Linguistique* (University of Paris 8), no. 30 (1984).

Milner, Jean-Claude. *Ordres et raisons de langue*. Paris: Éditions du Seuil, 1982.

Russell, Bertrand. *An Inquiry into Meaning and Truth*. London: Allen and Unwin, 1940.

Strawson, Peter F. *Individuals*. London: Methuen, 1959.

the Kantian formulation *das Ich* (which is closely associated with *das Ich denke*, often written as *das: Ich denke*, suggesting by homophony with the conjunction *dass*, "that," a near equivalence between nomination and proposition: "*the* I think," "[the fact] *that* I think") works both as a reference to a subjective being and as a reference to the linguistic form, to the act of speech in which it is said. Writing *le Je* (the I) only works in French if a grammarian is making a mention of the subject pronoun, or as a Germanism in a philosophical translation, which even then is of fairly recent usage (Italian, by contrast, uses the *Io* without any problem, as we see, for example, with Giovanni Gentile, and Spanish philosophy uses *Yo*—in José Ortega y Gasset or Xavier Zubiri, for instance). One could not imagine Blaise Pascal writing "Le Je est haïssable" instead of "Le Moi est haïssable" (The self is detestable; we will return later on to the problem of "Je est un autre" [I is another]). Consequently, it is practically impossible for a French ear to hear the nominal form of *Ich* without assuming the reflexive *le moi*. The ambivalence specific to Kant's analysis of "self-consciousness" as a reciprocal folding together of appearance and truth, of recognition and misrecognition (see SUBJECT), falls back onto the psychological or moral doctrine of the illusions everyone entertains about him- or herself (and particularly the way one over- or underestimates oneself).

The absolute "simplicity" of the word *Ich*, with its particular flexibility, accounts in part for the dialectical power that is deployed in the field of the *Ichheit*, whose literal transposition into French always presents insurmountable difficulties. One understands why it is in the German language that the speculative philosophy of modern Europe has developed the antithesis of the paths of "being" and of "the I," an antithesis that seems to repeat very ancient theological alternatives concerning the "name of God" (Cassirer, "Sprache und Mythos," 139: "Der Weg über das Sein und der Weg über das Ich"). Here are three examples:

1. In the *Wissenschaftslehre* of 1794, Fichte gave an interpretation of the Kantian transcendental apperception that is based on the homology between the logical principle of identity (A = A) and a proposition that can also be written algebraically *Ich = Ich* ("Ich gleich Ich"). This proposition, which can be understood to mean "Ich bin Ich," is ontological in the strict sense, since it expresses what is proper to *Ich* as being, its internal reflexivity and its self-identity, and the way in which *Ich* poses itself as self-consciousness (Fichte's expression for *Selbstbewusstsein* is "Das Ich setzt sich schlechthin als sich setzend" [The *Ich* posits itself as a pure self-positing]). It is thus a subjective absolute that brings to philosophy a new foundation in the form of an intellectual intuition (in this sense, it cancels out the effects of Kant's critique). French can do no better than to translate this as *Moi = Moi*, even occasionally risking *Je suis Je*. A sentence that sought to render Fichte's prose into French might offer the following: "Je suis absolument parce que je suis; et je suis absolument ce que je suis; ces deux affirmations étant pour le Moi [*Ich*]. . . . Le Moi [*Ich*] pose originairement son propre être" (I am absolutely because I am; and I am absolutely what I am; these two statements for the Self. . . . The Self originarily posits its own being: *Œuvres choisies de philosophie première*, French trans. Philonenko, 22). Here, however, the French translation is incapable of conveying the symmetry of the German text. It thus fails to translate (unless it glosses it in a commentary) the movement proper to subjective idealism, which goes further back than the logical principle of identity, to the transcendental identity of the *Ich*, perceiving itself and uttering itself in its own immediacy.

2. This failure of translation is even more apparent in the following stage of the Fichtean dialectic, when it is stated that in its movement of self-positing, *Ich* "posits itself immediately both as *Ich* and as *Nicht-Ich*," contradicting this time the form of the principle of identity in its traditional development (A is not non-A). Indeed, *Nicht-Ich*—the negation not of a predicate, but of a singular term, which for this reason Tugendhat considers an absurdity, *ein Unding*, and which literally also means a "non-thing"—is not (*le*) Non-Moi (Non-Self) but it is, in the simplicity of one and the same negation, both "[all] that which I am not" and the "nothingness of the I," even its annihilation, that is, its being deprived of any substantial determination. A formulation such as ". . . in the self [Fr.: *le Moi*] I oppose a divisible not-self to the divisible self," about which Fichte tells us that "the resources of the absolutely and unconditionally certain are now exhausted" (*Science of Knowledge*, trans. Heath and Lachs, 110), does not allow us—in French, by means of the expression *Non-Moi*—to understand that *Nicht-Ich* still contains within it the form of the subject, but modified by a negation (or that *Nicht-Ich* is an *Ich* that negates itself as such). French masks, therefore, the linguistic roots of the elaboration that led Fichte to overcome the interpretation of the opposition between *Ich* and *Nicht-Ich* as an antagonism between subject and object (or between consciousness and the world, or freedom and nature), and to make it the expression of an intersubjectivity or "constituent interpersonality," an originary unity of the "I" and the "You" (or of the person of the subject and the person of others).

3. Hegel, for his part, incessantly criticized what he considered to be the "formalism," the "motionless tautology [*bewegungslose Tautologie*]," of the equation *Ich = Ich*. This is one of the central threads of the *Phenomenology of Spirit*, which begins with the analysis of the emptiness of sense certainty, described as suspended in a purely verbal self-referentiality ("Das Bewusstsein ist *Ich*, weiter nichts, ein reiner *Dieser*; der *Einzelne* weiss reines Dieses, oder das *Einzelne*," an almost untranslatable sentence because of the equivocality of *Ich* and the alternation of masculine and neuter: "Consciousness, for its part, is in this certainty only as a pure 'I'; or I am in it only as a pure 'This,' and the object similarly only as a pure 'This'"; *Phenomenology of Spirit*, trans. Miller, 58). In the same text, however (the chapter "Die Wahrheit der Gewissheit seiner selbst" [The Truth of Self-Certainty]), Hegel introduces in turn an expression based on the syntax of personal pronouns in order to set in motion the dialectics of self-consciousness: "*Ich*, das *Wir*, und *Wir*, das *Ich*, ist" (ed. Hoffmeister, 140). This expression is immediately followed by the famous discussion of "autonomy and non-autonomy of self-consciousness: lordship and bondage." The extant translations—"*I that is We*" and "*We that is I*" (Fr.: "Un Moi qui est un Nous, et un Nous qui est un Moi," or "Un je qui est un Nous, et un Nous qui est un Je")—do not adequately render the movement of identification that passes through the other, which Hegel makes the active force of the progression of Spirit (*Geist*). In order to mark the appropriation of alterity in the interiority of the same subject, through the negation of negation, we would need to translate by forcing the syntax: "*I that We are, We that I am*" (Fr.: "Moi que Nous sommes, Nous que Je suis").

For once, the detour via the French terminology of the *moi* is useful, since this Hegelian formula transposes an idea originally expressed by Rousseau:

À l'instant, au lieu de la personne particulière de chaque contractant, cet acte d'association produit un corps moral et collectif composé d'autant de membres que l'assemblée a de voix, lequel reçoit de ce même acte son unité, son moi commun, sa vie et sa volonté.

(At once, in place of the individual person of each contracting party, this act of association produces a moral and collective body composed of as many members as there are voices in the assembly, which receives from this same act its unity, its common *self*, its life and its will.)

(*Contrat social*, 1.6, trans. Cress, 24)

But where Rousseau described in a naturalistic manner how an individual was formed from individuals, even if he is attributed the interiority of a consciousness after the fact, as a way of interpreting the enigma of an alienation that is at the same time a liberation, Hegel places us from the outset in the immanence of the subject, which he connotes by the use of the first-person singular and plural. He uses what Benveniste calls the difference between a "person in the strict sense" and an "amplified person" (in other words, the fact that "I" is both opposed to "We" and included in it to make a person) as a

means of presenting the tension between the two terms as a sort of conflictual reflection inherent in the constitution of the subject, which is the decisive moment in the transformation of the individual spirit into a universal spirit that knows itself (*Geist* as an absolute form of the *Selbst*).

III. From the *Moi* to the "Self," from the "Self" to the *Soi*

Leaving aside the semantics of the German *Selbst*, which is remarkable by virtue of the possibilities of forming compound words from it (for example, *Selbstbewusstsein*, *Selbstbestimmung*, *Selbstständigkeit*, *Sebsterfahrung*, *Selbstbildung*, *Selbstverständigung*, etc.) (see SELBST), we will now look more closely at the double displacement that occurs between French and English: from *moi* to "self," from "self" to *soi*. What we have is a minor drama of betrayal. Played out initially within a very short space of time, it has continuously informed the conflictual relationship between the psychologies and philosophies of personal identity that are particular to these two languages (from the opposition between Hume and Rousseau in the eighteenth century, to the difference of approach between the American pragmatists such as William James or George Herbert Mead, and the French phenomenology of Jean-Paul Sartre or Paul Ricœur).

In his *An Essay concerning Human Understanding* (2.27, *Of Identity and Diversity*), Locke invented two major concepts of modern philosophy: "consciousness" and "the self" (see CONSCIOUSNESS). His immediate context and background was the invention of the expression *le moi* in French philosophy and literature (Descartes, Pascal, Malebranche). It was Pascal, as we know, who popularized the *moi*: "Je sens que je puis n'avoir point été, car le moi consiste dans ma pensée" (I feel that I might not have been, since the *moi* consists of my thought [*Pensées*, B469/L135]); "Qu'est-ce que le moi? . . . Où est donc ce moi, s'il n'est ni dans le corps ni dans l'âme? Et comment aimer le corps ou l'âme, sinon pour ces qualités, qui ne sont point ce qui fait le moi, puisqu'elles sont périssables?" (What is the *moi*? . . . Where then is this *moi*, if it is neither in the body nor in the soul? And how is one to love the body or the soul if not for those qualities which are not what makes up the *moi*, since they are perishable? [ibid., B323/L688]). But Descartes, in his *Discourse on Method* (fourth part), had already written: "Ce moi, c'est-à-dire mon âme, par laquelle je suis ce que je suis" (This *moi*, that is to say my soul, by which I am what I am). And this striking formulation had already been interpolated by the French translator in the course of the Fourth Meditation (Descartes, *Œuvres*, 9:62). The substantivization of the self-reference (*ce moi*, *Ego ille*) is at the heart of the Cartesian interrogation of identity. It imposes a very strong grammatical constraint on any translations: to go from the expression *le moi* to "the self" is to enact a profound transformation, such that it is no longer possible to go back the other way. This is why Pierre Coste, the French translator of Locke, had to create, in turn, *le soi*, an innovation whose effects are still felt today. (Coste's note to his translation of Locke's *Essay* says: "Pascal's *moi* in a sense authorizes me to use *soi, soimême*, in order to express the feeling, which everyone has within himself, that he is the one and the same [ce sentiment que chacun a en lui-même qu'il est le même]; or, to put it more clearly, I am thus obliged to translate it out of an indispensable necessity; for I could not express in any other way the meaning it has for my Author, who has taken the same liberty with his own Language. The circumlocutions I could use in this instance would get in the way of what he is saying, and would render it perhaps completely unintelligible.") But present-day usages of the English "self" and the French *soi* do not really correspond to one another. One cannot write in French *mon soi* (as in the English "myself" or "My Self"), much less use this noun in the plural (unlike the English "ourselves"). Rather than establishing a universal concept, translation opens out onto a drifting-apart of meaning.

The way in which Locke takes advantage of the particularities of one language to transform the problematics that originated in another is quite remarkable. Indeed, although English has not developed any expression equivalent to the form *das Ich* or *le moi*, it does have at its disposal a great variety of usages for "self," which incline the English-language conceptualization of the subject to imagine it as a disposition or property of oneself. The term "self" (whose etymology remains obscure) encompasses both a pronominal usage (corresponding to the Latin *ipse*) and an adjectival usage (corresponding sometimes to the Latin *ipse*, and sometimes to the Latin *idem*; thus "myself" and "oneself," or "the same," "the selfsame"). There are early nominal uses, both with and without the article ("self," "the self"). Finally, there are different combinations: "self" compounded with pronouns and possessives, written either as a single word to emphasize its pronominal function (itself, himself, myself, oneself), or as two separate words, introducing a noun tending to substitute for the pronoun itself as a form of intensification (itself, himself, myself, oneself); or compounded with nouns or adjectives, to form notions of an action being applied to the subject itself, such as "self-conscious" and "self-consciousness" (as in the Greek terms formed with *auto-* and *heauto-*, where Romance languages would use a genitive construction: *causa sui, compos sui, cause de soi, maîtrise de soi, conscience de soi*).

■ See Box 2.

No less decisive is the reciprocity, bordering on equivalence, that is established between "myself" and "my own" when the subject, addressing himself, is referring to that which belongs most closely or properly to him. "My own, confirm me!" the poet Robert Browning will write ("By the

---

2

To, auto, h(e)auto, to auto: The construction of identity in Greek

➤ *IDENTITY, SELF* [SELBST, SAMOST'], TO TI ÊN EINAI

We have retained a large number of composite terms calqued from the Greek, often via Latin, and constructed using the pronoun *autos, -ê, -o* [αὐτός, -ή, -ό], such as "autograph, autodidact, automaton, autonomous", to refer to the action that the subject carries out personally and most often on himself (written in one's own hand, someone who teaches himself, that which moves by itself, that which establishes its own laws). This formation was virtually as extendable and generalizable in ancient Greek as the compound words in *Selbst-* are in present-day German (see SELBST); in French it has also brought several recent inventions in which the second term is French (for example, *auto-allumage* [self-lighting, 1904], RT: *DHLF*, s.v. *auto*).

Autos is itself made up of the particle *au* [αὖ], which indicates succession (then), repetition (again), or opposition (on the other hand); and of *ho, hê, to* [ὁ, ἡ, τό], a deictic (this one, that one) that in classical Greek becomes the definite article "the" (although *ho men, ho de* [ὁ μέν, ὁ δέ], for example, continue to mean "this one, that one"). The first and literal sense of *autos* is thus something like "on the other hand, and then this one here, in contrast to that other one" (cf. RT: *Dictionnaire grec français*, s.v.). *Autos* grammatically has three essential uses:

1. In cases other than the nominative, it acts as a reminder pronoun in the third person, with an anaphoric usage (*auton horô* [αὐτόν ὁρῶ], "I see him"; *ho patêr autou* [ὁ πατήρ αὐτοῦ], "the father of him," "his father," as in the Latin *eius, eorum*).

2. It is used as an emphatic pronoun or adjective (Lat. *ipse*, Fr. *même*), either on its own (as in the Pythagorean *Autos epha* [Αὐτὸς ἔφα], "The Master says"), or apposed to a personal pronoun (*egô autos* [ἐγώ αὐτός], "it is me in person who," "myself") or to a noun (*auto to pragma* [αὐτὸ τὸ πρᾶγμα], "the thing itself"; *dikaion auto* [δίκαιον αὐτό], "what is just in itself").

It is often used in this way at the same time as the reflexive pronoun, *heautos, -ê, -o* [ἑαυτός, -ή, -ό], which is itself a combination of two pronouns: *he* [ἕ], a third-person personal pronoun, which we find in Homer, followed by *autos*; when the reflexive is contracted into *hautou, -ês, -ou* [αὐτοῦ, -ῆς, -οῦ], the two are only distinguished in terms of breath (rough breathing for the reflexive, transliterated by an aspirate *h*); thus the Delphic formula given in the *Charmides* (165b), "to gignôskein auton heauton

[τὸ γιγνώσκειν αὐτὸν ἑαυτόν], "to know oneself in oneself," and the fact of being "auto kath' auto" [αὐτὸ καθ' αὐτό] indicates the separate ontological status, "in oneself and by oneself," or perhaps "in oneself and for oneself," of the Platonic idea.

3. Finally, when it is immediately preceded by the article *ho autos, hê autê, to auto* [ὁ αὐτός, ἡ αὐτή, τό αὐτό], it has the same meaning as the Latin *idem*, "the same." The Greek makes a very clear distinction by its word order between "ho autos theos [ὁ αὐτὸς θεός]," "the same god," and "hautos ho theos [αὐτὸς ὁ θεός]," "the god himself."

In Greek, then, a constellation of terms tightly binds together the two aspects of identity: ipseity, or the constitution of a self, and "sameness," the construction of an identity-to-oneself or to another-than-oneself. A number of languages have analogous procedures, such that the presence of an article makes the difference in meaning: French (*soi*) *même* / *le même* (*que*), German *Selbst*/*dasselbe*, in contrast to Latin *ipse*/*idem*, and English "self"/"same." But in Greek, the article is primarily a constituent of the term itself, *au-t-os*. There follows from this a quite singular and informative series of linguistic gestures that one could characterize, along with Friedrich Schleiermacher, as constituting a kind of schema of how the Greeks conceived of identity. This series is, de facto, philosophically determining.

Let us start with the article. Greek only has a definite article (unlike Latin, which has none, or French, for example, which distinguishes between *le*, definite, and *un*, indefinite). In archaic Greek, what will become the article, *ho, hê, to*, manifestly has a strong, demonstrative meaning, which is why it functions referentially, or as a liaison, close to a relative pronoun (see RT: *Aperçu d'une histoire de la langue grecque*, 188, 192ff.). When, after Homer, it becomes an article, this little word remains remarkably consistent. Its presence alone next to a noun confers upon it a presumption or a presupposition of existence, so we find it regularly next to proper names (in Greek, one says *ho Sokratês* [ὁ Σωκράτης], "the Socrates," and not "Socrates"). It is used even more clearly to differentiate the subject from the predicate in a sentence in which word order alone is not sufficient: one would not say in Greek "*a* is *a*," but rather "the *a* is *a* (or "*a* the *a* is," or "is the *a a*," etc.). Someone like Gorgias, for example, uses this as an argument against the identity of the subject and the predicate, in the form in which a statement of identity is made. Thus, for instance, with "to mê on esti mê on [τὸ μὴ ὂν ἐστι μὴ ὂν]," "the nonbeing is a nonbeing," one says, whether one likes it or not, that the subject "to mê on [τὸ μὴ ὂν]," "the nonbeing," has another type of consistency and existence than the predicate "mê on [μὴ ὂν]," "a nonbeing" (*De Melisso Xenophane Gorgia*, 978a25b = G.3–4, in Cassin, *Si Parménide*, 636). This is also why the article can be used so easily to "substantivize" not only adjectives (*to kalon* [τὸ καλόν], "the beautiful one" in Plato's *Symposium*), participles, and infinitives (*to on* [τὸ ὂν] and *to einai* [τὸ εἶναι], "the being" and "Being"), but

all sorts of expressions (see, for example, TO TI ÊN EINAI, the "essence of what being was," the "quiddity" of Aristotle in Latin), as well as words or whole sentences, which go from being used to being mentioned, as if put into quotation marks (in Aristotle, for example, cf. *Metaphysics*, Γ.4, 1006b13–15).

The first and strongest testimony to this organization of identity as a function of the constellation *to, auto, to auto* is the way in which Parmenides's *Poem* constructs the identity of being. Following what he calls "the road of [*it is*]" (which, moreover, is referred to as *hê men* [ἡ μὲν], "this one," in opposition to *hê de* [ἡ δὲ], "that one," 2.3 and 5), Parmenides discusses the whole range of forms and possibilities, syntactical as well as semantic, of the verb *esti* [ἔστι], "is" (third-person singular, 2.3; see TO BE), ending with *to eon* [τὸ ἐὸν], "the being" (substantivized participle, 8.32), that is, the subject identified as such only at the end of the road (and a demonstrative article, emphasized with a particle, will thereafter be sufficient to refer to it: *to ge* [τό γε], 8.37, "the/that in any case," or *to gar* [τὸ γὰρ], 8.44, "the/that indeed"). One of the crucial points of the operation occurs in fragment 3, whose meaning has been so controversial, but acclaimed by Heidegger as the guiding principle of Western philosophy: "to gar auto noein estin te kai einai [τὸ γὰρ αὐτὸ νοεῖν ἐστίν τε καὶ εἶναι]," which could be translated literally as "a same indeed is both thinking and being." One might interpret this phrase as meaning that thinking and being are one and the same, and understand it along with Heidegger not as a declaration of subjectivism and idealism *avant la lettre*—being is only ever what we think it is—but as a "belonging together" of being and thinking, and thus as a determination of man himself (*An Introduction to Metaphysics*). But one could also interpret it in terms of how this *to auto* is formed: *to*, "the"/"this"; *au*, "again, once more"; *to*, "the"/"this." The particle joins together the same element two times; "the

same" in Greek is articulated as "the re-the," "this re-this." In other words, the consistency of identity (*to auto*, "the same" in the sense of a same thing, something identifiable as being the same as itself) is nothing other than the conjunction (*te kai*) of thinking and being. Indeed, this is where being itself, properly articulated, will find in *te eon* the name of a subsisting and knowable subject, or ipseity par excellence.

Barbara Cassin

BIBLIOGRAPHY

Cassin, Barbara, ed. *Si Parménide: Le traité anonyme*. Lille, Fr.: Presses Universitaire de Lille, 1980.

Heidegger, Martin. *Einführung in die Metaphysik*. Edited by Petra Jaeger. Gesamtausgabe, vol. 40. Frankfurt: Klostermann, 1983. Translation by Gregory Fried and Richard Polt: *Introduction to Metaphysics*. New Haven, CT: Yale University Press, 2000.

Loveday, T., and E. S. Forster, eds. and trans. *De Melisso, Xenophane, Gorgia*. In *The Works of Aristotle*, vol. 7 of 12. Loeb Classical Library. Oxford: Clarendon, 1913.

Parmenides. *The Fragments of Parmenides: A Critical Text with Introduction, Translation, the Ancient Testimonia and a Commentary*. Edited by A. H. Coxon. Assen, Neth.: Van Gorcum, 1986.

———. *Parménide: Sur la nature ou sur l'Étant. La langue de l'étre*. Edited, translated, and commentary by Barbara Cassin. Paris: Éditions du Seuil, 1998.

Schleiermacher, Friedrich D. E. *Hermeneutik und Kritik*. Edited and introduction by Manfred Frank. 7th ed. Frankfurt: Suhrkamp, 1999. Translation by James Duke and Jack Forstman: *Hermeneutics: The Handwritten Manuscripts*. Edited by Heinz Kimmerle. Missoula, MT: Scholars Press for the American Academy of Religion, 1977. Translation by Andrew Bowie: *Hermeneutics and Criticism*. Edited by Andrew Bowie. Cambridge: Cambridge University Press, 1998.

Fire Side"). This reciprocity enables Locke to fuse a modern problematic of identity and diversity with an ancient problematic of appropriation (*oikeiôsis, convenientia*; see OIKEIÔSIS), terms at either end of a spectrum between which notions concerning recognition, consciousness, memory, imputation, responsibility for oneself and one's own actions, all insinuate themselves. In English, "own" is both an adjective and a verb. As an adjective, it is combined with the possessives "my," "his," and so on, as an intensifier ("my own house," "I am my own master") and separately ("I am on my own"). As a verb ("to own"), it has a wide range of meanings, including "to possess," "to admit," "to confess," "to recognize," "to declare," and "to claim": these all have the sense of saying something is "one's own." Locke draws together all

the different senses of the term, separately or in different combinations (as in: "owns all the actions of that thing, as its own": *An Essay*, 2.27.17). The result of these constructions is an amalgamation of the paradigms of being and having, which is typical of what has been termed, from the point of view of political philosophy, a "possessive individualism." Basically, "me" is ("I am") "mine," and what is "most properly mine" is "myself" (just as what is most properly "yours" is "yourself," "his" is "himself," etc.).

Even though this amalgamation goes as far back as the Greek discourses on *oikeios* and *idios* describing the particularity of the self (cf. Vernant), it is only with Locke that it occupies the center ground of modern philosophy. It finds its way through to us, continually reinforced, up until the liminal thesis of *Sein und Zeit* (§9), in which Martin Heidegger identifies the existential particularity of human *Dasein* with *Jemeinigkeit*, another neologism (this time a German one, literally "being each time mine") that is just as difficult to translate as the English "self." In a sense, then, Heidegger's neologism "self" turns back into its opposite, since the content of the English "own" (in German *das Eigene*) is merely the imminence of death, the only "thing" that "properly" belongs to each one of us. We will see how Heidegger's reversal of the Lockean tradition is accompanied by a new revolution in the naming of the subject.

In the passages in Locke's *Essay* where the doctrine of personal identity is elaborated (above all, 2.27), all of these virtual senses are brought into play through the slippery movement of the writing. In a first stage we go from the idea of identity as simple "sameness" to that of reflexive identity, or "ipseity": the word "self" at that point becomes a noun. From comparative expressions ("the same with itself"), we move easily to "that is self to itself" (equivalent to the idea of consciousness):

> Consider what person stands for. . . . When we see, hear, smell, taste, feel, meditate, or will any thing, we know that we do so . . . and by this every one is to himself, that which he calls *self* . . . it is the same *self* now as it was then; and it is by the same *self* with this present one that now reflects on it, that that action was done.

> (*An Essay*, 2.27.9)

Locke provides two equivalent expressions, which could be exchanged for one another: "to be one (identical) Person" and "to be one self." In a second stage, "self" sometimes serves as a substitute for the first person, and sometimes as its double, entering into dialogue with it, and showing concern for it:

> Had I the same consciousness . . . I could no more doubt that I, that write this now . . . was the same self, place that self in what Substance you please, than that I that write this am the same my self now whilst I write. . . . That with which the consciousness of this present thinking thing can join its self, makes the same person, and is one self with its, and with nothing else; and so attributes to its self, and owns all the actions of that thing.

> (Ibid., §§16–17)

"Self" as a common noun slips to "self" as an almost proper noun (without an article), while retaining the possibility of being understood as a possessive. In equating expressions such as "I am my self," "I am the same self," and "I am the same my self," Locke turns "self" into the representation of oneself for oneself, the term to whom (or to which) I attribute to myself, what I care for when I care for myself. Finally, Locke gives the name "Person" (which he defines not as a grammatical or theological term, but as a "forensic term") to the "self" that had itself been used to clarify the singularity of "personal identity":

> *Person*, as I take it, is the name for this *self*. Wherever a man finds, what he calls himself, there I think another may say is the same person. . . . This personality extends

its *self* beyond present existence . . . whereby it becomes concerned and accountable, own and impute to it*self* past actions.

> (Ibid., §26)

From the perspective of inner judgment (which anticipates the Final Judgment), Locke translates into the language of the "self" the expression of Descartes, substituting "consciousness" for "my soul" in the process of identifying that by which "I am what I am," and playing once again on the possessive: "that consciousness, whereby I am my self to my self."

This idea of being oneself for one's person obviously suggests an element of reflection, or internal distance. There is thus an uncertainty about the question of knowing whether the identical and identity are "myself," or rather are "in me" as an object, an image, or a verbal simulacrum. But the "self" for Locke is nothing more than an "appearing to oneself" or "perceiving oneself" that is identical through time. It could not, therefore, in fact split in two, whether the split is imagined to occur between a real self and an apparent one (as in Leibniz), or between an actor and a spectator (Hume, Smith), or between subject and object, or between I and Me (in the way that G. H. Mead decomposes the Self into an "I" and a "Me," which continuously switch places: it would be interesting to explore what Mead's model perhaps owes to an oblique relation to French). This vanishing distance is ultimately the pure differential of the subject. It corresponds remarkably to the idea that Locke's theorization of consciousness attempts to found, marked by a tension between the representation of a fixed point to which the entire temporal succession of ideas would be connected, and that of the flux of representation, the continuity of which would itself produce identity. It appears to us primarily, though, as the effect of a play on words—an ironic state of affairs, when we consider the extent to which Locke tried to separate a theory of knowledge based on pure associations of ideas, from the linguistic "garments" of these ideas.

■ See Box 3.

IV. Returns of the *Ego*

French, then, has the duality of the *je* and the *moi*, which allows it to problematize identity, and later introspection, from the perspective of both an affirmation of certainty and a passion for existence (but also for disappearance); German has the flexibility of the *Ich*, which encompasses a dialectics of position, of reflection, and of negation; and English has a synthetic expression of moral responsibility and mental appropriation: the "self." We might then assume that the rules of the game are set, so to speak (unless and until we take into account other, different languages, of course), and that it is all a matter, precisely, of translation. A few enigmas remain, however, of which the most striking is the way in which philosophy in the twentieth century has set about reviving the Latin *ego*, like a *Fremdwort* that is nonetheless, by definition, absolutely familiar.

A. "Ego-psychology"

It is by no means certain that this "return of *ego*" poses exactly the same problems in all contexts, first of all because

3
The "self" in psychoanalysis

It was in the English-speaking world, around 1960, and mainly through the influence of Donald W. Winnicott that the term "self" truly began to appear in psychoanalytical literature. Since then, it has become firmly established in psychoanalysis in its English form, even though there have been occasional attempts to translate it as *soi* in French, as *Selbst* in German, or as an equivalent term in other European languages. What seems to hamper these translations is, on the one hand, a cultural particularity implying that the English "self" refers to an aspect of one's personality that is hidden, or liable to be misunderstood or neglected (as suggested, for example, by the expression "Take care of yourself"), and on the other hand, the epistemological difficulty for contemporary psychoanalysts that an unreserved mobilization around this concept has caused. Indeed, when Winnicott defines the "self" as different from the "I," saying that for him, "the self, which is not me, is the person within me" (see ES), some authors see in this new concept a useful complement to the three psychic terms introduced by Freud in his second topology (the *Ich* [Ego], the *Es* [Id], and the *Über-Ich* [Superego]), whereas others consider it as bastardization that would bring us back to a pre-Freudian, personalist, even Bergsonian phenomenology of autonomy and of a unified I.

In fact, as Jean-Bertrand Pontalis has shown in an excellent analysis of the epistemological aspects of the problem ("Naissance et reconnaissance du 'soi'"), the self according to Winnicott and several other English-speaking psychoanalysts should not be interpreted exclusively from a theoretical point of view, in relation to the conceptual apparatus elaborated by Freud. When they introduce the "self," these authors are in fact concerned about "responding to problems posed by the analysis of their patients, and not about demonstrating the inadequacy or the deficiencies of the Freudian metapsychology." What was at stake for them, then, was "more the determination of a domain of experience, than the theoretical critique of the validity of a concept."

The "self" was actually first used in 1950 by the New York psychoanalyst Heinz Hartmann, who was originally from Vienna, in the context of the "Ego-Psychology" movement. Hartmann set out to dissociate an "I" that is defined by its functions (motor control, perception, experience of reality, anticipation, thought, and so on), from a "self" that represented the person as such, as distinct from external objects and other people. This bipartition in effect isolates narcissism, which is exalted in the feeling of plenitude and the self-sufficiency of one's entire being, whereas, as Pontalis puts it, "the constitution of a self [*moi*] is linked to the recognition of the other, for whom it serves as a model."

As for the problematic elaborated by Winnicott in the context of what he calls the "transitional object" and the "potential space," this leads to a distinction between the "true self" and the "false self," which has often been popularized in a trivial and normative sense. The first is formed in a relation that the subject has with its subjective objects, which takes on a solipsistic character corresponding to the "right to not be discovered, if need be, to not communicate, insofar as any such needs, if they are recognized, reveal that the individual feels he is real in the secret communication that he has with that which is most subjective within him" (Pontalis, "Naissance et reconnaissance du 'soi,'" 180). The "false self" corresponds, for its part, to the need the subject has to adapt to external objects as they are presented to him by the environment. According to Pontalis, this would be close to what Helen Deutsch in 1942 called the "as if" personality, in the sense that it is characterized by a developed behavior and psychological ease that is apparently well adapted, but that functions in a void, notwithstanding a constant oscillation between an extreme submission to the external world and exposure to its misfortunes, and a readiness to react to these misfortunes to one's own advantage. But this bipolarity of the "true self" and the "false self" has nothing to do with a dichotomy between two personality types, where one, the "true self," would be the only authentic one, whereas the other, the "false self," would be more or less alienated by environmental constraints. According to Winnicott, these two "selves" in effect form a pair in which the second protects the first, even if it appears to do nothing more than hide or cross-dress it. For it is important that the "true self," in its position of noncommunication, should need to be protected. There would, then, be only a genuine pathology in cases where there was a clear split between these two aspects of the personality. Then again, however, concepts of this kind are only relevant, in Winnicott's eyes, if they prove to be useful at a given moment in a clinical situation, and they do not compromise the Freudian problematic of the self (*moi*).

Charles Baladier

BIBLIOGRAPHY

Pontalis, Jean-Bertrand. "Naissance et reconnaissance du 'soi.'" In *Entre le rêve et la douleur*. Paris: Gallimard / La Pléiade, 1977.

the fact of writing *ego* or "the ego" in the middle of an ordinary sentence does not produce the same effect of strangeness in all languages. We should reserve a special place for the (by now universal) consequences of the generalization of an English psychoanalytic terminology, in which the *Ich* of Freud's second topological theory was translated as "the ego," whereas *Es* was translated as "the id" (see ES). These effects are easier to understand when we explain not only, following Alexandre Abensour, that the term "ego" in English comes out of a psychological and medical vocabulary, but also that it thereby prematurely gave rise to all sorts of composite words referring to the fact of relating ideas and behaviors "to the self," or even of putting them in "the service of the self" ("ego-attitude," "ego-complex," "ego-consciousness" [sic], "ego-satisfaction," and so on, leading to all sorts of astonishing redundancies, such as "ego-identity," all attested by the *Oxford English Dictionary* [RT] of the nineteenth and twentieth centuries). This influence even extends to certain texts by Lacan, who was notoriously hostile to "ego-psychology," whence his lecture to the British Psychoanalytical Society on 2 May 1951, "Quelques réflexions sur l'*Ego*" (Some reflections on the *ego*, quoted in Ogilvie, *Lacan*, 52), a title that was not lacking in irony. But the fact that Lacan had in mind a theorization of "paranoiac knowledge" suggests another direction: that of the usages, scientific or parodic, of the word "ego" (including the expression "my ego") to refer to the narcissistic image that the subject forms of itself ("the *ego* of the Prime Minister is highly developed").

B. *Das transzendentale Ego*

More directly linked to our discussion is the introduction of "egological" terminology in Husserl's phenomenology, and the very profound effects it produces there. Although Husserl had only used classical terminology in the *Logische Untersuchungen* (*Logical Investigations*) of 1900–1901 and in the *Ideen* of 1913—the terminology of transcendental Idealism, posing the usual problems of translation (thus in *Ideen*, 1.57: "Die Frage nach der Ausschaltung des reinen Ich," which Paul Ricœur translated into French as "Le Moi pur est-il mis hors circuit?" [Is the pure self (Husserl: "the pure 'I'") put out of circulation?])—the texts from his late period, starting with the *Cartesianische Meditationen* (the *Cartesian Meditations* were originally delivered as lectures in German at the Sorbonne in 1929, and were translated into French by E. Levinas and G. Peiffer before they were even published in the original German) begin to introduce another terminology, that of the "transcendental ego [*das transzendentale Ego*]." How should we understand this retranslation into Latin, which could seem merely pedantic? We might look for the reason in the context and the intentions of the text, without going into the complexity of the problems raised by the way in which Husserl's conception of subjectivity evolved. These have provided an endless source of debate for contemporary philosophy, from Sartre's major article on "La transcendance de l'ego" (The transcendence of the ego, 1936), in which he problematizes the relationship between consciousness, the *Je*, and the *Moi* (self), to the controversy between Jacques Derrida (*La voix et le phénomène* [Speech and phenomena], 1967) and Michel Henry (*L'essence de la manifestation* [The essence of manifestation], 1963) in the 1960s around the question of the auto-affection of the subject.

The first and simplest reason resides in the fact that Husserl cites Descartes, whose philosophical gesture he hopes to repeat:

> If we examine the content of the *Meditations*, we note that we are effectuating a return [*Rückgang*] to the philosophical *ego* . . . a return to the *ego* of the pure *cogitationes*.

> (*Cartesian Meditations*, trans. Cairns, Introduction, §1)

The text of Descartes that Husserl invokes is the original Latin text, thus at same time continuing a German university tradition, and marking the persistence of a linguistic *universitas* common to spiritual Europe, a teleological horizon in which Husserl situates, precisely, the primacy of transcendental subjectivity. We might say that with Husserl's reprise of Descartes, the *ego* is immediately perceived as absolutely translatable (unlike Heidegger's *Dasein*, for example, which ends up being perceived as untranslatable into other languages). The Latin Descartes, whose thought (re)inaugurates philosophy, symbolically summarized in the use he makes of the noun *ego* and of the expression "ego cogito, ego sum," is not so much French as European, and thus universal in the sense of European universality, whose crisis Husserl then undertakes to interpret. Husserl was no doubt unaware of the fact that the turns of phrase used by Descartes in the *Meditationes de prima philosophia* (Metaphysical meditations) to problematize *ipseity*, in particular the "ille ego, qui iam necessario sum" of the Second Meditation, would not have been possible without a constant back-and-forth movement between ancient Latin and classical French ("Ce moi, c'est-à-dire mon âme, par laquelle je suis ce que je suis" [This self, that is to say my soul, by which I am what I am]). Kant's reading of Descartes, however, in which *Je* and *Je pense*, even *Je me pense* (I think myself), are taken as names for the subject, is tacitly assumed. A circle is thus traced, which we will have to follow back to its origins in order to reinterpret its meaning.

Two themes, respectively opening and closing the arguments developed in the *Cartesian Meditations*, seem to us to be worthy of attention here. We suggest that bringing them together offers a key to Husserl's linguistic artifice.

First of all, Husserl describes what he calls a "transzendentale Selbsterfahrung" (translated into French by Levinas and Peiffer as "expérience interne transcendentale" [transcendental inner experience], and by Marc de Launay as "auto-expérience transcendentale"; compare Dorion Cairns's English "transcendental self-experience"), by virtue of which we can gain access to "a universal and apodictic structure of the experience of the I [*des Ich*] which extends across all of the particular domains of affective and possible self-experience [*Selbsterfahrung* again]" (§12). This *Selbsterfahrung* has a specific kind of manifestation, in which consciousness "is given" in the mode of "itself" ("im Modus Er selbst") or of "oneself" ("Es Selbst") (§24). It is then described as *Selbstkonstitution* ("constitution de soi-même," "auto-constitution"), which is tantamount to saying that the consciousness that is named *ego* also appears to itself as sufficient, as the origin of its own meanings or qualities. This is what Husserl calls a "transcendental solipsism." Unlike Kant, however, Husserl does not offer this experience in which the "I" (*Ich*) perceives itself as the "identical pole of lived experiences," "the substratum of *habitus*," and so on, as an illusion constitutive of subjectivity. Nor does he see within it, like Heidegger (writing at approximately the same moment in *Sein und Zeit*), the risk of "missing the sense of the being of *sum*." But he makes it the point of departure and the horizon of a "self-interpretation" (*Selbstauslegung*) in which the *ego* will discover progressively what gives it its meaning, which had not been immediately noticed, except partially.

Now, the essential content of this "discovering of the transcendental sphere of being [*Enthüllung der transzendentalen Seinssphäre*]" is the constitutive function that intersubjectivity has for the *ego* itself—what Husserl called, in an analysis that has since become well known, a constitution of the ego as an *alter ego*, or an "original pairing" (*Paarung*) of the *ego*:

> In this intentionality a new meaning of being is constituted, which transcends the limits of my monadic ego in my self-specificity [*der neue Seinssinn, der mein monadisches ego in seiner Selbsteigenheit überschreitet*; Levinas and Peiffer translated this as: "un sens existentiel nouveau qui transgresse l'être propre de mon *ego* monadique"], and it constitutes an ego for itself not as *my-self* [*nicht als Ich-selbst*], but insofar as it is reflected in my own I [*in meinem eigenen Ich*], my monad. But the second ego is not purely and simply there, properly given to us itself [*uns eigentlich selbst gegeben*; Levinas and Peiffer: "donné en personne"], it is constituted on the contrary as an alter ego, and I am myself this ego [*Ich selbst in meiner Eigenheit bin*; Levinas and Peiffer: "c'est

moi-même, dans mon être propre"], designated as a moment by the expression *alter ego*.

(*Cartesian Meditations*, Fifth Meditation, §44)

Solipsism is thus reversed from the inside, or, to be more exact, it opens out onto a new transcendental problem that is deeply enigmatic by Husserl's own admission. This relates to the fact that constitutive intersubjectivity (since the *ego* would not be the subject of a thinking of the world of objects, if this world were not in its origin common to a reciprocal multiplicity of subjectivities) has as its condition the representation of "itself as an other," an *alter ego* that is both generic and concrete, irreducible to (the) *ego* and yet indiscernible from it (that is, from the "I") in its constitution. Husserl calls this elsewhere (§56) "eine objektivierende Gleichstellung meines Daseins und des aller Anderen" (an objectifying placing of my being and that of all others on the same level), which is experienced from the inside (Levinas and Peiffer translate this as: "une assimilation objectivante qui place mon être et celui de tous les autres sur le même plan"; de Launay proposes the following: "une équivalence objectivante de mon existence et de celle de tous les autres").

Through this verbal association, Husserl manages to account for the meaning of his initial choices, but he can only do it by going beyond Descartes and returning to an earlier layer of the humanist tradition. The term *alter ego*, which became commonplace and even banal in the different European languages during the nineteenth century, in the sense of a close friend, a personal representative, someone in whom you can confide, and so on (it first appears in French in Honoré de Balzac), is usually traced back to Cicero's *De amicitia* (*Laelius*), where we actually only find the expressions "tamquam alter idem" and "alterum similem sui" to denote a true friend. The fact is, however, that the expression goes much farther back (Pythagoras: *ti esti philos* [τι ἔστι φίλος]; *allos egô* [ἄλλος ἐγώ], according to Hermias, *In Phaedrus*, 199A). It casts over our entire culture the question of the possibility of experiencing intellectually or affectively something beyond the alternative of self and stranger/other (*Fremd*, in Husserl's text). This is the question Michel de Montaigne asked in an ethical register, for example, about his unique friendship with La Boétie ("Because it was he; because it was I"). Husserl also uses it to inform his reshaping of ontology, at the same time illuminating how we should understand that Descartes had indicated to philosophy the way toward a radical questioning, and yet had missed its transcendental meaning. We might perhaps suggest, then, that from the first, the return to the *ego* and the return of the *ego* (as a universal word) had been overdetermined by the possibility of saying the *alter ego* authentically (see MITMENSCH, NEIGHBOR, and LOVE).

V. *Je Est un Autre*: It Thinks (Me)

Let us immediately articulate this dialectic with another ontologico-linguistic problem, the one indicated by Rimbaud's expression: "Je est un autre" (I is an other). This could be just another way of translating *alter (est) ego*, or even *ille ego*. However, the uncertainty in French between the masculine and the neuter, and the way in which Rimbaud forces the syntax, points toward other interpretations. These are, moreover, in part suggested by Rimbaud's letter to Paul Demeny (15 May

1871), where this expression first appears, since there it is a question for the poet of discovering within himself a disproportionate creative power for which he is not responsible:

J'assiste à l'éclosion de ma pensée: je la regarde, je l'écoute. . . . Si les vieux imbéciles n'avaient pas trouvé du Moi que la signification fausse, nous n'aurion pas balayé ces millions de squelettes qui . . . ont accumulé les produits de leur intelligence borgnesse, en s'en proclamant les auteurs!

(I witness the unfolding of my own thought: I watch it, I listen to it. . . . If the old fools had not discovered only the false significance of the Ego, we should not now be having to sweep away those millions of skeletons which . . . have been piling up the fruits of their one-eyed intellects, and claiming to be, themselves, the author of them!)

(Trans. Oliver Bernard, in Kwasny,
Towards the Open Field, 146)

At issue for Rimbaud, too, is how to recover the meaning of an ancient kind of delirium, in which madness communicates with enthusiasm:

En Grèce, ai-je dit, vers et lyres rythment l'Action. . . . L'intelligence universelle a toujours jeté ses idées, naturellement. . . . Le Poète se fait voyant par un long, immense et raisonné dérèglement de tous les sens.

(In Greece, I say, verses and lyres take their rhythm from Action. . . . Universal Mind has always thrown out its ideas naturally. . . . The Poet makes himself a *seer* by a long, prodigious, and rational disordering of *all the senses*.)

(Ibid., 147)

What suddenly bursts forth here (in certain limit-conditions where the "I" escapes from the "Self" [*Moi*]) is the paradox of the equivalence between the personal and the impersonal, or better still, borrowing Benveniste's categories, between a "person" and a "non-person," in all of its different modalities.

There are basically three types of these modalities, which philosophy has always designated as being on the horizon of the "I," as its other side, or its limit, or its truth. "Das Wesen, welches in uns denkt," Kant wrote in the *Kritik der reinen Vernunft* (374), in which he sketched out a surprisingly tripartite personification: "Ich, oder Er, oder Es (das Ding)"— "What thinks in us," then, could be "Him" or "Her" (God, Being, Truth, Nature); it could be "that" (the body, desires or impulses, the unconscious); it could be "one" (the impersonal of a common thought, what circulates as speech between all subjects). Let us conclude by summarizing these three translations.

"Je est un autre" (I is an other) is to say it is God, the only one capable of using absolutely the *Ich-Prädikation* (Cassirer) in order to name himself. We know that the Bible (perhaps inspired by other models, notably Egyptian, but this is not the place to get into the disputes about which came first) was originally theophanic in its formulation ("Éyéh asher éhyéh," that is, "I am who I am," or "I am who I will be," Ex 3:14; see Box 4). It gives rise in the mystical tradition to some surprising reversals, such as in Meister Eckhart, where we find the exclusive appropriation of the "I" and the "I am" by the "base of the base" of the soul (*Urgrund*), itself conceived as a creative nothingness that precedes the existence of God. If we accept that the secularization of the divine name in philosophy truly begins with the "ego sum, ego existo," or "I am, I exist," of Descartes, we see that this statement, modern by definition, serves in its turn as a point of departure for a series of displacements and reversals. This is the case when Spinoza in the *Ethics* sets down the factual axiom "homo cogitat" (since this undefined "man" is very close to an impersonal "one," he simply expresses one of the ways in which substance or nature thinks itself, and thus produces itself). It is the case in an entirely different way when the romantic and theosophist Franz von Baader "inverts" the Cartesian *cogito*: "cogitor [a Deo], ergo Deus est" (God thinks me, therefore he is, cited by Baumgardt, *Franz von Baader*). Without these precedents, Hegel would not have been able to attribute the Self to the Spirit as universal rationality, that is, to overcome the Cartesian formulation asserting the absolute subjectivity of a "thought of thought."

■ See Box 4.

But "Je est un autre" should also be understood as referring to the power of the individual body, or, as Locke said, to its "uneasiness," that is, its perpetual motion and desire, of which it is confusedly perceived to be the seat. Parodying Descartes, Voltaire had written (*Philosophical Letters*, 13): "I am body and I think: I know nothing more than that" (or "That's all I know about that [je n'en sais pas d'advantage]").

Many authors, particularly German-language ones, from Georg Lichtenberg up to Nietzsche and Wittgenstein, have for their part emphasized the idea that the subject's self-reference, and the irreplaceable identity of which it is meant to be sign, are of no use when it comes to imagining the essence of thought: so one should not write *Ich denke*, except as a derivative effect, but rather *es denkt*, "it thinks" or "there is thought," as one says *es regnet*, "it is raining." The most interesting consequences of these two points of view occur when they are fused together in a doctrine of the unconscious, as is the case with Freud. In his second topology, the "reservoir of drives" is named *Es*, which has been translated into French as (the) *ça*, as opposed to the *moi* (*das Ich*) and the *surmoi* (*das Über-Ich*) (which in some ways is the *Il, Ille* that surmount the *ego*, a divine or paternal model of authority). The meaning of these strange grammatical designations for the "instances of the psychic personality" is no doubt to reestablish the ancient idea of the conflict between the different parts of the soul, but in the modern horizon of thought reflecting upon its faculties of expression. This only comes out clearly once they give rise to a reciprocal formulation: the "Wo Es war, soll Ich werden" of the *New Lectures on Psychoanalysis* (1932), where *Es* should indeed be conceived as a subject (or at least "of the subject"), since *Ich* is by definition a subject. Subjectivity only arises in a process in which the personal and the impersonal can switch places, the places occupied by a thought that reflects upon itself in the at least apparent unity of a first person, and by a thought that undoes itself and misrecognizes itself in the conflict of representations attached to the body (life drives, death drives).

4

Exodus 3:14

The only theophany of the divine Name transmitted by the Old Testament is to be found in the book of Exodus. This happens in two stages. Once he has been "given the mission" by Yahweh to "bring the sons of Israel out of Egypt" (Ex 3:11), Moses asks God by what name he should be called by them: "Then Moses said to God, 'If I come to the people of Israel and say to them, 'The God of your fathers has sent me to you,' and they ask me, 'What is his name?' what shall I say to them?'" Exodus 3:14 gives the double answer: "God said to Moses, 'I AM WHO I AM.' And he said, 'Say this to the people of Israel, "I AM has sent me to you."'" So in theory, Exodus 3:14 contains two names: "I AM WHO I AM" (Ex 3:14a), and "I AM" (Ex 3:14b), the first generally considered by ancient and medieval exegesis as a mystical name, revealed to Moses alone in its fullness, and the second as an exoteric name, intended for "the people of Israel." In relation to the other names used to refer to God in various traditions—Yahweh in the "Yahwist" tradition, El

Shaddaï [The Lord] in the "sacerdotal" tradition—the name revealed to Moses in Exodus 3:14 (a passage belonging to the "Elohistic" tradition) has had a particular, even extraordinary, fate. A feature of the original formulation as it is recorded in the holy writ, "Éhyéh asher éhyéh," is that it does not contain any immediate metaphysical connotation. The natural meaning on which exegetes agree is "I am the Living One who lives," "The absolute Living One" (it being understood that the Living One is also a living *being*, and that the name Yahweh, corresponding to *à éhyéh* in the third person, is commonly understood as "he is"). However, if, as Gilson noted, there is no metaphysics *in* Exodus, there is a "metaphysics of Exodus," an apprehension of God as Being or as The Being, based upon a certain understanding of the revealed Name. This understanding relies on a fact of translation—in this case, on the translation of the passage in the Septuagint, the Greek version of the Old Testament written in order to transmit the biblical message to the Jews of

the Hellenic diaspora, which introduced the word *on* [ὄν].

It is with the transposition by the Judeo-Hellenistic translators of the Septuagint that "Éhyéh asher éhyéh" becomes "I am the Being," the *on* [ὄν], an "ontological" transposition that reaches its peak in Jewish thought with Philo of Alexandria (cf. Starobinski-Safran, "Exode 3, 14," 47–56). This transfer was decisively established in the Latin Vulgate, when Exodus 3:14a was translated as "Ego sum qui sum," and Exodus 3:14b as "Qui est (misit me ad vos)," with the French "Je suis celui qui est" (I am the one who is), prevalent in the seventeenth century, being the product of a collage of 14a and 14b that was dictated by the concern for elegance. (Compare the King James version: "And God said unto Moses, I AM THAT I AM: and he said, Thus shalt thou say unto the children of Israel, I AM hath sent me unto you.") It would be pointless—and impossible—to examine here all of the exegeses that have been proposed of the theophany of Exodus. We shall content ourselves with noting the extremes at either end of their spectrum. At one end, there is the refusal to respond, the "true God not able to put himself at the mercy of men by giving them a name that would express his essence"—a refusal translated by the elliptical nature of a formulation understood as "I am who I am," "I am what I am." At the other end, there is the affirmation of God as Being itself—in the sense of "I am: the one who am/is"—or at least the affirmation of his "existence" (as opposed to nothingness or evil). This would be a guarantee of his truthfulness, with Jesus also referring to himself in this sense by using the expression "I am" in John 8:24: "For you will die in your sins unless you believe *I am*," which contains a transparent allusion to the Name of Exodus, but which translators generally prefer (for reasons having to do with the awkwardness of the original expression) to render as: "You will die in your sins unless you believe *what I am*." What interests us here is more limited in scope, and assumes that one accepts the horizon of the "metaphysical" reading: the play between the I and being, between the *ego* and the *sum*. This play reaches its maximum intensity in Eckhart's interpretation of the Name of Exodus, particularly in his rewriting of Exodus 3:14 as "Deus est ipsum suum esse," which gives rise to all sorts of variations, wavering between "God is himself his being" and "God is the being-oneself." The ultimate expression chosen by Eckhart was "Ipse est 'Qui est'" ("Himself is 'Who is,'" understood in the sense of "it is Himself, this *ipse*"—the *Ich* [= *ego*, "I"] of the German *Sermons*—"who is"). It is an *Ipse*, or more exactly a *Solus Ipse* (Him alone), hidden in the words of Moses,

that Meister Eckhart seeks to uncover in his reading: "Deus est ipsum esse et essentia ipsius est ipsum esse. Ipse est id quod est et is qui est, Exodi 3: Sum qui sum, Qui est misit me. Per ipsum et in ipso est omen quod est, ipsa sufficientia, in quo et per quem et a quo sufficit omnibus" (God is being himself and the essence of himself is being himself. Himself is what is and the one who is, Exodus 3: I am who I am, Who is has sent me. By himself and in himself is all that is, sufficiency itself, in whom and for whom and by whom he is sufficient for all [*In Exodum*, no. 158, in *Lateinischen Werke*, 2:140.5–9]). In Eckhart, the "metaphysics of Exodus" thus tends toward a theology of the *Ipse*, and this is why, basing his commentary of Exodus 3:14 mainly on the testimony of Maimonides, Eckhart is principally interested in showing that in the divine statement, the copula (*sum*) and the attribute (*sum*) are identified with the subject, with this Ego that God alone is in reality (*In Exodum*, nos. 14–21, in *Die lateinischen Werke*, 2:20.1–28, 10). The play between I and being is explicitly thematized in the German sermon 77 by comparing two passages in the Bible: "*Ego* mitto angelum meum" (Luke 7:27): "I send my messenger," which contains the word "I" (*Ego*); and "Ecce, mitto angelum meum" (Mal 3:1): "Behold, I send my messenger," which does not. The absence of the word *ego* signifies the ineffable nature of God: the fact that the soul cannot be expressed or put into words, "when it apprehends itself in its own content," and the fact that "God and the soul are one, to the extent that God can have no property by which he would be distinguished from the soul, or would be anything other than it, such that he cannot

say: *Ego mitto angelum meum*." The presence of the word *ego* signifies, by contrast, "the is-ness [*isticheit*] of God," that is, "the fact that God alone is" and the fact that he is "indistinct from all things," "for God is in all things and he is closer to them than they are to themselves."

Alain de Libera

BIBLIOGRAPHY

Albrektson, Beril. "On the Syntax of *ehyeh 'asher 'ehyeh* in Exodus 3:14." In *Words and Meanings: Essays Presented to David Winton Thomas*, edited by Peter R. Ackroyd and Barnabas Lindars, 15–28. Cambridge: Cambridge University Press, 1968.

Centre d'étude des religions du Livre. *Dieu et l'Être: Exégèses d'Exode 3, 14 et de Coran 20, 11–24*. Paris: Études augustiniennes, 1978.

Eckhart, Meister. *German Sermons and Treatises*. Edited and translated by M. O'C. Walshe. 3 vols. London: Watkins, 1979–87.

———. *Die lateinischen Werke*. Edited by Konrad Weiss and Loris Sturlese. Berlin: Kohlhammer/ Deutsche Forschungsgemeinschaft, 1936.

Gilson, Étienne. "L'Être et Dieu." *Revue thomiste* 62, no. 2 (1962): 181–202; 62, no. 3 (1962): 398–416.

Libera, Alain de, and Émilie Zum Brunn, eds. *Celui qui est: Interprétations juives et chrétiennes d'Exode 3, 14*. Paris: Centre d'Études des religions du livre, Cerf, 1986.

McCarthy, D. J. "Exod. 3:14: History, Philology and Theology." *Catholic Biblical Quarterly* 40 (1978): 311–22.

Starobinski-Safran, Esther. "Exode 3, 14 dans l'œuvre de Philon d'Alexandrie." In *Dieu et l'être*. Paris: Études augustiniennes, 1978.

As Abensour notes (see ES), the very simple and yet improbable translation of "Wo Es war soll Ich werden" proposed by Lacan ("Là où c'était, là comme sujet dois-je advenir" [Where it was, I must come into being], *Écrits*, 864, trans. Fink) allows us to speak again the "language of ontology." Should we be surprised that in this respect, Lacan's translation involves, under the name of *grand Autre* (big Other), a kind of short-circuiting of two previous interpretations of "Je est un autre"? If He is not the unconscious, at the very least we should say, with François Regnault, that "God is unconscious."

But with this Lacanian reference, we come to the third possible way of understanding the "non-person" and of transforming the "I" into its other: this other appears, then, as the order of language itself, the symbolic. As we know, Lacan is not alone in proposing such an interpretation, in which "ça pense" (it thinks) is always already preceded by "ça parle" (it speaks). It was also prevalent in Heidegger, for whom the impersonality of language as constitutive was initially presented pejoratively, as a characteristic of improper

(*uneigentlich*) being, the "one," or "any man" (*das Man*), who is essentially the man of public conversation, of the noisy exchange of opinions (as opposed to the silent figure, "absolutely my own," of care). Fleeing the anxiety felt at the possibility of its own death, *Dasein* or the existent can only respond to the question "Who am I?" by assuming a "public identity," expressed in language through common meanings (*Being and Time*, pt. 1, chap. 4). The precise meaning of the French pronoun *on* ([*das*] *man*) is certainly not easy to understand because of the interrelation between the phenomenological analysis and the value judgment, but its translations are instructive. English has recourse to no less than three correlative terms—"anyone," "one," and "they" (a term originally used in discussing Heidegger's text by the philosopher William Richardson, and retained in the standard English translation by John Macquarrie and Edward Robinson)—which thus shift the anonymity of the one to the many, in a way that allegorically invokes the masses. In Italian, they privilege the impersonal turn of phrase: *si dice*, which represents "tutti e nessuno, il *medium* in cui l'esserci o *Dasein*, si dissipa nella chiacchiera" (Everyone and no-one, the *medium* in which *Dasein* dissolves into chatter: Bodei, "Migrazioni di identità," 646). Spanish has *dicen* and *se dice*; gossip and hearsay are *el qué dirán*, the "what-will-they-say."

But such combinations of private identity and public expression (whose counterpart is the tireless quest for the voices of silence, in mystical experience or in poetry, a non-speech where being preferentially expresses itself, and which would in a sense be situated this side of the "I" as well as of the "one") are not strictly necessary. Beyond the alternative of the Lacanian "subject of the unconscious," speaking or signifying like the truth in the "place of the Other," and of Heidegger's anonymous subject-as-multitude of daily chatter, the most persuasive determination has without doubt been proposed by Michel Foucault in his commentary of the neutral in Blanchot. "The other" is thought turning back to its constitutive exteriority, which is essentially the infinite dispersion of the effects of language:

> The "I" who speaks—fragments, disperses, scatters, disappearing in that naked space. If the only site for language is indeed the solitary sovereignty of "I speak" then in principle nothing can limit it—not the one to whom it is addressed, not the truth of what it says, not the values or systems of representation it utilizes. In short, it is no longer discourse and the communications of meaning, but a spreading forth of language in its raw state, an unfolding of pure exteriority. And the subject that speaks is less the responsible agent of a discourse (what holds it, what uses it to assert and judge, what sometimes represents itself in it by means of a grammatical form designed to have that effect) than a non-existence in whose emptiness the unending outpouring of language uninterruptedly continues.

> (Foucault, *Thought from Outside*, trans. Massumi and Mehlman, 11)

We have covered (at the cost of certain simplifications) the cycle of expressions of the subject in the European code of persons. Two hypotheses have emerged, which call for further investigation. The first is that no one language is absolutely sufficient to complete this cycle, but the unveiling of the relationship between language and thought that the subject "consignifies" (as the Scholastics would say) can only occur by transferring the question from one language into another language, that is, by reformulating it within this other language according its own syntax. The second is that this cycle clearly reproduces the cycle of the statements at the origin of the metaphysical principle: tautology or identity, conflict or contradiction, repetition or reflection, difference or alienation. These ontological figures are not engendered; even less are they predetermined by language. But what is certain is that without a linguistic formulation (*disposition*), and without the culture of this formulation, they would not be thinkable, and therefore would not have been thought.

Étienne Balibar

BIBLIOGRAPHY

Balibar, Étienne. "Ego sum, ego existo: Descartes au point d'hérésie." *Bulletin de la Société Française de Philosophie*, no. 3 (1992).

Baschera, Marco. *Das dramatische Denken: Studien zur Beziehung von Theorie und Theater anhand von I. Kants "Kritik der reinen Vernunft" und D. Diderots "Paradoxe sur le comédien."* Heidelberg: Carl Winter,1989.

Baumgardt, David. *Franz von Baader und die philosophische Romantik.* Halle, Ger.: Niemeyer, 1927.

Benveniste, Émile. *Problèmes de linguistique générale.* 2 vols. Paris: Gallimard / La Pléiade, 1966–74. Translation by Mary Elizabeth Meek: *Problems in General Linguistics.* Miami, FL: University of Miami Press, 1997.

Bodei, Remo. "Migrazioni di identità: Transformazioni della coscienza nella filosofia contemporanea." *Iride: Filosofia e Discussione Pubblica* 8, no. 16 (1995).

Cassirer, Ernst. "Sprache und Mythos—Ein Beitrag zum Problem der Götternamen." In *Wesen und Wirkrung des Symbolbegriffs.* Darmstadt, Ger: Wissenschaftliche Buchges, 1956. First published in 1925. French translation by O. Hansen-Love and J. Lacoste: *La philosophie des formes symboliques.* 3 vols. Paris: Éditions du Minuit, 1972. English translation by Ralph Manheim et al.: *The Philosophy of Symbolic Forms.* 4 vols. New Haven, CT: Yale University Press, 1965–98.

Derrida, Jacques. *La voix et le phénomène.* Paris: Presses Universitaires de France, 1967.

Descartes, René. *Œuvres.* Edited by C. Adam and P. Tannery. 11 vols. Rev. ed. Paris: Vrin, 1996.

Fichte, Johann Gottlieb. *Œuvres choisies de philosophie première: Doctrine de la science.* Translated into French by A. Philonenko. Paris: Vrin, 1980. First published in 1794–97.

———. *Science of Knowledge.* Translated by P. Heath and J. Lachs. Cambridge: Cambridge University Press, 1982.

Foucault, Michel. *La pensée du dehors.* Paris: Fata Morgana, 1986. Translation by Brian Massumi and Jeffrey Mehlman: *Maurice Blanchot: The Thought from Outside.* In *Foucault/Blanchot.* New York: Zone Books, 1989.

Gentile, Giovanni. *Teoria generale dello spirito come atto puro.* Florence: Sansoni, 1959. First published in 1916.

Guillaume, Paul. *L'Imitation chez l'enfant.* Paris: Presses Universitaires de France, 1950.

Hegel, Georg Wilhelm Friedrich. *Phänomenologie des Geistes.* Edited by J. Hoffmeister. Berlin: Akademie-Verlag, 1971. Translation by A. V. Miller: *Phenomenology of Spirit.* Oxford: Oxford University Press, 1977.

Henrich, Dieter. "Fichte's Ich." In *Selbstverhältnisse.* Stuttgart: Reclam, 1982.

Henry, Michel. *L'essence de la manifestation.* Paris: Presses Universitaires de France, 1963.

Hintikka, Jaakko. "*Cogito ergo sum:* Inférence ou performance?" *Philosophie*, no. 6 (May 1985). First published in 1962.

Husserl, Edmund. *Cartesianische Meditationen und Pariser Vorträge.* The Hague: Nijhoff, 1950. French translation by Emmanuel Levinas and Gabrielle Peiffer: *Méditations cartésiennes.* Paris: Armand Colin, 1931. French translation by M. de Launay: *Méditations cartésiennes.* Paris: Presses Universitaires de France, 1994. English translation by Dorion Cairns: *Cartesian Meditations: An Introduction to Phenomenology.* The Hague: Martinus Nijhoff, 1969.

———. *Idées directrices pour une phénoménologie.* Translated into French by P. Ricœur. Paris: Gallimard / La Pléiade, 1950. English translation by W. R. Boyce Gibson: *Ideas: General Introduction to Pure Phenomenology.* London: Allen and Unwin, 1931.

Jakobson, Roman. "Les embrayeurs, les catégories verbales et le verbe russe." Chap. 9 in *Essais de linguistique générale*, translated into French by N. Ruwet. Paris: Minuit, 1963.

Kant, Immanuel. *Anthropologie du point de vue pragmatique.* Translated into French by Michel Foucault. Paris: Vrin, 1984. English translation by Robert B. Louden: *Anthropology from a Pragmatic Point of View.* Edited by Robert B. Louden and Manfred Kuehn. Cambridge: Cambridge University Press, 2006.

———. *Kritik der reinen Vernunft.* Hamburg: Meiner, 1976.

Kisiel, Theodore. *The Genesis of Heidegger's Being and Time.* Berkeley: University of California Press, 1993.

Kwasny, Melissa, ed. *Towards the Open Field: Poets on the Art of Poetry.* Middletown, CT: Wesleyan University Press, 2004.

Lacan, Jacques. *Écrits*. Paris: Éditions du Seuil, 1966. Translation by Bruce Fink: *Écrits*. New York: Norton, 2007.

Libera, Alain de. *La mystique rhénane d'Albert le Grand à Maître Eckhart*. Paris: Éditions du Seuil, 1994.

Locke, John. *An Essay concerning Human Understanding*. Oxford: Oxford University Press, 1975.

McDowell, John. "Reductionism and the First Person." In *Mind, Value, and Reality*. Cambridge, MA: Harvard University Press, 1998.

Mead, George H. *Mind, Self, and Society from the Standpoint of a Social Behaviorist*. Edited by C. W. Morris. Chicago: University of Chicago Press, 1962. First published in 1934. French translation by J. Cazeneuve, E. Kaelin, and G. Thibault: *L'Esprit, le soi et la société*. Paris: Presses Universitaires de France, 1963.

Ogilvie, Bertrand. *Lacan, la formation du concept de sujet*. Paris: Presses Universitaires de France, 1987.

Pariente, Jean-Claude. *Le langage et l'individuel*. Paris: Armand Colin, 1973.

———. "La premiere personne et sa fonction dans le *Cogito*." In *Descartes et la question du sujet*, edited by Kim Sang Ong-Van-Cung. Paris: Presses Universitaires de France, 1999.

Regnault, François. *Dieu est inconscient: Études lacaniennes autour de saint Thomas d'Aquin*. Paris: Navarin/Éditions du Seuil, 1985.

Ricœur, Paul. *Soi-même comme un autre*. Paris: Éditions du Seuil, 1990.

Rousseau, Jean-Jacques. *On the Social Contract*. Translated by D. A. Cress. Cambridge: Hackett, 1987.

Sartre, Jean-Paul. *La transcendance de l'ego: Esquisse d'une description phénoménologique*. Paris: Vrin, 1988. First published in 1936.

Schelling, Friedrich W. J. von. *Vom Ich*. In *Sämliche Werke*, vol. 1. Stuttgart: J. G. Cotta, 1856. First published in 1795.

Suzuki, Takao. *Words in Context: A Japanese Perspective on Language and Culture*. Translated by Akira Miura. Tokyo, Japan: Kodansha International, 1978.

Tugendhat, Ernst. *Selbstbewusstsein und Selbstbestimmung: Sprachanalytische Interpretationen*. Frankfurt: Suhrkamp, 1979. French translation by R. Rochlitz: *Conscience de soi et autodétermination*. Paris: Armand Colin, 1995.

Vernant, Jean-Pierre. *L'individu, la mort, l'amour: Soi-même et l'autre en Grèce ancienne*. Paris: Gallimard / La Pléiade, 1989.

Wittgenstein, Ludwig. *Philosophische Untersuchungen*. In *Schriften*, vol. 1. 4th ed. Frankfurt: Suhrkamp, 1980. Translation by G.E.M. Anscombe: *Philosophical Investigations*. Oxford: Blackwell, 1967.

IDEA

I. Idea and Ontology

1. The word "idea" comes from the philosophical Latin *idea* (from *videre*, "to see"), used notably by Seneca (*Letters* 58.18) in translating Plato's Greek *idea* [ἰδέα] (from *idein* [ἰδεῖν], the aorist of *horaô* [ὁράω], "to see"), which—in a running set of exchanges and cross-references with the closely related term *eidos* [εἶδος]—means "visible form, aspect," and later "distinctive form, essence."

    See SPECIES for analysis of the respective networks of the Latin and the Greek (cf. *FORM*).

2. The word has since Plato been one of the key terms of ontology, constantly invested with different meanings in different languages (*idée* in French, *Idee* in German, and so on), and by different philosophies, at the junction between objectivity (the "Idea" in Plato and Hegel) and subjectivity ("Ideas" in Locke and Kant), a crossing point that is expressed, for example, by the notion of the "objective reality of the idea" in Descartes (see REALITY, III).

See ERSCHEINUNG, ESSENCE, ESTI, REALITY, RES, TO TI ÊN EINAI, UNIVERSALS; and CONSCIOUSNESS, SOUL; cf. CONCEPTUS, PERCEPTION, REPRÉSENTATION.

II. Idea and Aesthetics

In Aesthetics, of particular importance is the relationship between the surface or image, and the underlying reality or model.

See BEAUTY, CONCETTO, Box 1, DISEGNO, *IMAGE* [BILD, EIDÔLON], MIMÊSIS; cf. ART, PLASTICITY.

➤ *FORM, TO BE*

IDENTITY

"Identity" is derived from *identitas*, which is from the pronoun *idem*, "the same" (no doubt a composite of the demonstrative and of an emphatic particle), which is one of a cluster of late inventions that are untraceable in classical Latin. Even the English and French terms are polysemic, weaving together the notions of "sameness" and of "ipseity": it thus encompasses two distinct terminologies in Latin, which open up particular sets of problems.

I. Identity, Sameness, Ipseity

1. In accordance with its Latin etymology, "identity" denotes first of all something that is indiscernible, the "same," in the sense of "the same as," or "identical to," *idem*. The Greek expresses this identity-indiscernibility with the term *ho autos* [ὁ αὐτός], *to auto* [τὸ αὐτό], with the article placed in front of the demonstrative.

2. "Identity" also refers to a person, to personal identity: even in the sense of "oneself," ipseity, from the Latin *ipse*, which means "itself," "in person" (*ego ipse*, myself, *moi-même* in French, etc.). The Greek expresses this identity-ipseity using the same demonstrative, *autos* [αὐτός], but without an article, which is sometimes attached to the pronoun: *egô autos* [ἐγὼ αὐτός], like *ego ipse*, "myself in person." This is the meaning of "identity" in "identity card" and "identification procedure."

    See I/ME/MYSELF (for the Greek, see Box 2), *PERSON*, SAMOST', SELBST; cf. ES.

3. On the transition from the ontological register to the transcendental register, in which "reflexive" identity is conceived as the condition of possibility of speaking, see I/ME/MYSELF, SUBJECT, and cf. CONSCIOUSNESS, *PERSON*, SPEECH ACT.

II. The Inextricable Link between the Different Sets of Problems: Essence, Resemblance

Sameness and ipseity are inextricably linked in several essentially philosophical ways:

1. The first way to be oneself is to be verified as being identical to oneself, just as the subject and predicate are in the principle of identity "*a* is *a*," which requires a comparison between two elements that are said ultimately to be one and the same, and indicated either by their

position in the order of the words (see WORD ORDER), or by the presence or absence of an article (see I/ME/MYSELF, Box 2; see also PRINCIPLE, and cf. SUBJECT and PRÉDICABLE, PREDICATION).

2. Ipseity refers to the definition, to the essence, to the idea whereby a thing is what it is. Plato links the question of ipseity and intelligibility together with the question of the resemblance to the model and to the idea: the two senses of identity are thus joined dialectically; see EIDÔLON, MIMÊSIS, SPECIES: cf. BEAUTY. For a broader perspective, see ESSENCE, ESTI, *TO BE*, TO TI ÊN EINAI.

One could compare this to the French, which makes a distinction in word order between "l'homme même" (the very man) and "le même homme" (the same man).

3. In terms of the question of the image, the expression of identity is directly linked to the question of resemblance, and of similitude, sameness, *similis* (Lat.), *homos* [ὁμός] and *homoios* [ὅμοιος] (Gr.), from the Indo-European root **sem*, "one," allowing for attention to be focused on the common points between two entities that remain distinct; in addition to MIMÊSIS and *IMAGE*, see ANALOGY.

The distinction between sameness and ipseity has been particularly rigorous and inventive in English since Locke (sameness/identity): see in particular STAND, where we see the beginning of a new expression of identity in metaphorical terms (the metaphor of "holding oneself up," of "taking a stand," or even the juridical concept of "having standing"), which is shared by English and German, but not French (*se tenir debout*); cf. STANDARD.

4. Finally, we might consider the problematic extension of self-identity as a question of the individual to a question of collective identity, which leads to varying connotations in names of peoples from one language to another; see NAROD and PEOPLE; cf. *FATHERLAND*, HEIMAT.

➤ ACTOR, OBJECT

| ILYA

Il y a expresses the presence of something, or the way in which the world is given. The French turn of phrase is quite idiomatic, especially because of the adverb *y*, which indicates place (but, according to the *Dictionnaire historique de la langue française*, the *y* in the expression *il y a* "has no meaning that can be analyzed"; RT: *DHLF*, s.v.). Other languages use simple or complex expressions that contain either the verb "to have" (*há* in Portuguese, *hay* in Castilian Spanish), "to be" (*esti* [ἔστι] in Greek, *est* in Latin, "there is" in English), "to give" (*es gibt* in German, *dá-se* in Portuguese, *se da* in Castilian), or "to hold" (*tem* in Portuguese, and analogously in Castilian). See ES GIBT, ESTI, HÁ, and SEIN, Box 1. More generally, on the relationship between being and presence, see also *TO BE* [SPANISH], and ERSCHEINUNG, ESSENCE, NATURE, PRESENT, TO TI ÊN EINAI, WELT.

➤ ASPECT, LIGHT, MEMORY.

| IMAGE

The English "image" is a calque of the Latin *imago*, which literally denotes a material imitation, particularly effigies of the dead, and which psychoanalysis invests with its own meaning (see EIDÔLON, Box 2). We begin with the Greek, because of the multiplicity of non-synonymous words denoting the image in the language, and with the German, because of the large number of terms that are derived from *Bild*.

I. *Eidôlon*: The Complexity of the Greek Vocabulary of the Image

The Greek names for image always privilege one of its defining or functional characteristics: *eikôn* [εἰκών], "similitude," *phantasma* [φάντασμα], "appearance in light" (see PHANTASIA, IMAGINATION, from *phôs* [φῶς], "light," and LIGHT), *tupos* [τύπος], "imprint, impression," and so on. The entry EIDÔLON, the most general term derived from the verb meaning "to see," and that denotes the image as something visible by which we can see another thing, discusses at greater length the main difficulties of interpretation and translation that have arisen in ontology and optics, via the Arabic (*ma'nā* [المعنى]; see also INTENTION).

Many other Latin terms than *imago* can be translated as "image" (*simulacrum, figura, forma, effigies, pictura, species*). These respond, but do not correspond, to the Greek terms: "species," for example, is the translation that Cicero favors for the Platonic *eidos* [εἶδος], "idea, essence"; but in other philosophical contexts, the word can denote *eidôlon* [εἴδωλον], "image" and "simulacrum." The Latin entry SPECIES discusses the Latin translations of *eidos*, in its pairing with *eidôlon* (see ESSENCE, IDEA).

II. *Bild*: The Large Number of German Derivations

The entry for the German BILD discusses a network of terms that are systematically connected to each other, and that allow us to articulate the relationship of the image to its model: *Urbild/Abbild* (model/copy), *Gleichbild* (a copy that is a good likeness), *Nachbild* (ectype), which can be considered in light of the Hebrew terms in Genesis (*ṣèlèm* [צֶלֶם], *demūt* [דְּמוּת]). This exceptionally broad constellation includes *Einbildungskraft*, the imagination as the faculty by which one forms images (see *IMAGINATION*), and *Bildung*, education (see BILDUNG, CIVILIZATION, CULTURE).

III. The Complexity of the Problems

1. The aesthetic dimension of the image is discussed in the entry MIMÊSIS, "imitation/representation" (see *IMITATION*); see also DESCRIPTION, TABLEAU.

2. On the literary and rhetorical dimension of the image, see EIDÔLON, Box 1, and COMMONPLACE, COMPARISON; see also ARGUTEZZA, CONCETTO, INGENIUM.

3. On the possibility of a theology and a politics based on the image as the visible trace of the invisible, see OIKONOMIA (and ECONOMY).

4. On the ontology of being and appearing, see *APPEARANCE*, DOXA, ERSCHEINUNG.

5. On the logic of truth as resemblance and similitude, see *FICTION*, TRUTH.

6. On the cognitive dimension of the image, see REPRÉSENTATION; see also PERCEPTION, SENSE.

IMAGINATION

The English "imagination" comes from the relatively obscure imperial Latin word *imaginatio* (itself derived from *imago*, whose principal meaning is "effigy, portrait"; see *IMAGE*), whereas the Greek root, *phantasia* [φαντασία] (from *phôs* [φῶς], "light"), evolved in the sense of "fantasy, phantasm" (see PHANTASIA, Box 3, for the psychoanalytic lexicon).

I. The Tension between Production and Reproduction

The difference between *phantasia* and *imaginatio*, as shown by the difficulties experienced in translating the Greek into Latin, is the difference between the creative force of apparitions (PHANTASIA, see DOXA and ERSCHEINUNG) and the reproductive faculty of images (see EIDÔLON, MIMÊSIS, and REPRÉSENTATION), each of these terms also itself being internally distressed by this tension and the value judgments that come with it.

On the Scholastic tradition, based on Avicenna's translations of Arabic philosophy, see SENSUS COMMUNIS [COMMON SENSE and *SENS COMMUN*]; cf. INTENTION.

The pair *phantasia* and *imaginatio* is put to work in different ways in the German tradition (*Phantasie/Einbildungskraft*, see BILD and BILDUNG; here we must take into account the extraordinary richness of the family of words that places the image and the imagination on the side of education and culture), and in the English tradition, which tends in contrast to differentiate the power to produce fictions depending upon the extent to which it is arbitrary or necessary (FANCY, see also *FICTION*).

II. The Imagination as a Faculty: Aesthetics and Epistemology

This same tension determines the place of the imagination in the play of faculties and the modalities of being in the world. Is the imagination a faculty that is necessary for the exercise of the other faculties, operating somewhere between passivity (see AESTHETICS, FEELING, PATHOS; cf. SENSE) and activity (see *REASON*; cf. INTELLECT, INTELLECTUS, INTENTION, *INTUITION*, MEMORY, SOUL, UNDERSTANDING)? Or is it rather, as Blaise Pascal puts it, a "mistress of error and falsity" (*Pensées*, frag. 41; see TRUTH)?

1. BILD discusses the difference that Immanuel Kant places at the heart of the *Critique of Pure Reason*, between a "reproductive" empirical imagination and a transcendental imagination that "produces" the schemata, and is thus the condition of possibility of our representations.
2. Prior to and beyond the critical distinctions between concept and intuition, image and idea, the Italian tradition insists on the metaphorical capacity of images and of the imagination in art and in thought (see ARGUTEZZA, CONCETTO, DISEGNO; cf. BEAUTY, INGENIUM).

IMITATION

"Imitation" is borrowed from the derived Latin term *imitatio* (imitation, copy, faculty of imitating). It is one of the major possible translations of the Greek *mimêsis* [μίμησις] (see MIMÊSIS), besides representation (see REPRÉSENTATION). *Mimêsis*, which endured as the key term of aesthetic questions

since Plato and Aristotle, is in fact understood sometimes as resemblance, in terms of a pictorial model (and is in that sense associated with image; see *IMAGE* [BILD, EIDÔLON] and *IMAGINATION*), and sometimes as representation, drawing most proximately on theatrical models (see ACTOR).

I. Imitation and Reproduction

See ART, MANIERA, TABLEAU.
   Cf. BEAUTY, DISEGNO, GOÛT.

II. Imitation, Logic, Rhetoric

See ANALOGY, COMPARISON, DESCRIPTION, ERZÄHLEN.
   Cf. *FICTION, POETRY,* TRUTH.

➤ ARGUTEZZA, GENIUS, INGENIUM

IMPLICATION

ENGLISH	entailment, implicature
FRENCH	*implication*
GERMAN	*nachsichziehen, zurfolgehaben, Folge(-rung), Schluß, Konsequenz, Implikation, Implikatur*
GREEK	*sumpeplegmenon* [συμπεπλεγμένον], *sumperasma* [συμπέρασμα], *sunêmmenon* [συνημμένον], *akolouthia* [ἀκολουθία], *antakolouthia* [ἀντακολουθία]
LATIN	*illatio, inferentia, consequentia*

➤ ANALOGY, PROPOSITION, SENSE, SUPPOSITION, TRUTH

Implication denotes, in modern logic, a relation between propositions and statements such that, from the truth-value of the antecedent (true or false), one can derive the truth of the consequent. More broadly, "we can say that one idea implies another if the first idea cannot be thought without the second one" (RT: Lalande, *Vocabulaire technique et critique de la philosophie*). Common usage makes no strict differentiation between "to imply," "to infer," and "to lead to." The verb "to infer," meaning "to draw a consequence, to deduce" (a use dating to 1372), and the noun "inference," meaning "consequence" (from 1606), do not on the face of it seem to be manifestly different from "to imply" and "implication." Indeed, nothing originally distinguished "implication" as Lalande defines it—"a logical relation by which one thing implies another"—from "inference" as it is defined in Diderot and d'Alembert's *Encyclopédie* (1765): "A logical operation by which one accepts a proposition because of its connection to other propositions held to be true." The same phenomenon can be seen in German, in which the terms corresponding to "implication" (*Nachsichziehen, Zurfolgehaben*), "inference" ([*Schluß*]-*Folgerung, Schluß*), "to infer" (*schließen*), "consequence" (*Folge*[-*rung*], *Schluß, Konsequenz*), "reasoning" ([*Schluß-*]*Folgerung*), and "to reason" (*schließen, Schlußfolgerungen ziehen*) intersect or overlap to a large extent.

The history of the French verb *impliquer*, however, reveals several characteristics that the term does not share with "to infer" or "to lead to." First of all, it was originally (1663) connected to the notion of contradiction, as shown in the use of *impliquer* in *impliquer contradiction*, in the sense of "to be contradictory." This connection does not, however, explain how *impliquer* has passed into its most commonly accepted meaning—"implicitly entail"—in the logical sense of "to lead to a consequence." Indeed, these two senses constantly interfere with one another in European philosophical languages, which certainly poses a number of difficult problems for translators. The same phenomenon can be found in the case of the English verb "to import," commonly given as a synonym for "to mean" or "to imply," but often wavering instead, in certain cases, between "to entail" and "to imply." In French, the noun itself is generally left as it is (*import existentiel*, see SENSE, Box 4). The French *importer* (as used by Rabelais, 1536), "to necessitate, to entail," formed via the Italian *importare* (as used by Dante), from the Old French *emporter*, "to entail, to have as a consequence," dropped out of usage, and was brought back through English. The nature of the connection between the two primary meanings of *impliquer* (or of *implicare* in Italian), "to entail implicitly" and "to lead to a consequence," nonetheless remains obscure. Another difficulty is understanding how the transition occurs from *impliquer*, "to lead to a consequence," to "implication," "a logical relation in which one statement necessarily supposes another one," and how we can determine what in this precise case distinguishes "implication" from "presupposition."

We therefore need to be attentive to what is implicit in *impliquer* and "implication," to the dimension of the *pli* (pleat or fold), of the *repli* (folding back), and of the *pliure* (folding), in order to separate out "imply," "infer," "lead to," or "implication," "inference," "consequence"—which requires us to go back to Latin, and especially to medieval Latin. Once we have clarified the relationship between the modern sense of "implication" and the medieval sense of *implicatio*, we will be able to examine certain derivations (*implicature*) or substitutes ("entailment") of terms related to the field of *implicatio*, assuming that it is difficulties with the concept of implication (the paradoxes of material implication) that have given rise to newly coined words corresponding to the original logical attempts. Finally, this whole set of difficulties becomes clearer as we go further upstream, using the same vocabulary of implication, through the conflation of several heterogeneous logical gestures that come from an entirely different systematics in Aristotle and the Stoics.

I. The Vocabulary of Implication and the *Implicatio*

A number of different terms in medieval Latin can express in a more or less equivalent manner the relationship between propositions and statements such that, from the truth-value of the antecedent (true or false), one can derive the truth-value of the consequent: *illatio, inferentia, consequentia*. Peter Abelard makes no distinction in using the terms *consequentia* for the hypothetical "*si est homo est animal*" (*Dialectica*, 473) and *inferentia* for "*si non est iustus homo, est non-iustus homo*" (ibid., 414). It is certainly true that: (1) *illatio* appears above all in the context of the *Topics*, and denotes more specifically a reasoning (*argumentum* in Boethius), allowing for a consequence to be drawn from a given place (for example, "*illatio a causa, illatio a simili, illatio a pari, illatio a partibus*"); (2) *consequentia* sometimes has a very general sense, as in "*consequentia est quaedam habitudo inter antecedens et consequens*" (De Rijk, *Logica modernorum*, 2.1:38), and is in any case present in the expressions *sequitur* and *consequitur* (to follow, to ensue, to result in); (3) *inferentia* frequently appears, by contrast, in the context of the *Peri hermêneias*, whether it is as part of the square of oppositions, in order to explain the "law" of opposite, subcontrary, contradictory, or subalternate propositions (*Logica modernorum*, 2.1:115), or whether it is in order to determine the rules for converting propositions (ibid., 131–39). Nevertheless, it is one of these three terms (or other related terms) that in the Middle Ages expresses the logical relationship of implication, and not the

terms from the *implicatio* family. In short, *implicatio* does not originally refer to implication.

In the twelfth century, a number of treatises were developed on the "implicits" (*tractatus implicitarum*) that studied the logico-semantic properties of propositions said to be *implicationes*, or relative propositions. The term *implicitus*, the past participle of the verb *implico*, was used in classical Latin in the sense of "to be joined, mixed, enveloped," and the verb *implico* adds to these senses the idea of "unforeseen difficulty" (*impedire*) and even of "deceit" (*fallere*). The source of the logical usage of the term is a passage from *De interpretatione* on the contrariety of propositions (14.23b25–27), in which *implicitus* renders the Greek *sumpeplegmenê* [συμπεπλεγμένη], a term formed from *sumplekô* [συμπλέκω], "to bind together," from the same family as *sumplokê* [συμπλοκή], which since Plato (*Politics* 278b; *Sophist* 262c) has referred to the combination of letters that make up a word, and the interrelation of noun and verb that makes up a proposition:

> Aristotle: hê de tou hoti kakon to agathon sumpeplegmenê estin; kai gar hoti ouk agathon anagkê isôs hupolambanein ton auton [ἡ δὲ τοῦ ὅτι κακὸν τὸ ἀγαθὸν συμπεπλεγμένη ἐστίν· καὶ γὰρ ὅτι οὐκ ἀγαθὸν ἀνάγκη ἴσως ὑπολαμβάνειν τὸν αὐτόν].
>
> (*De interpretatione* [*Peri hermêneias*] 23b25–27)

> Boethius: Illa vero quae est "quoniam malum est quod est bonum" implicata est: et enim quoniam non bonum est necesse est idem ipsum opinari.
>
> (*Aristoteles latinus*, 2.1–2, p. 36, 4–6)

> Jules Tricot: Quant au jugement "le bon est mal," ce n'est en réalité qu'une combinaison de jugements, cars sans doute est-il nécessaire de sous-entendre en même temps "le bon n'est pas le bon."
>
> (Trans. Tricot, 141)

> J. L. Ackrill: The belief that the good is bad is complex, for the same person must perhaps suppose also that it is not good.
>
> (Trans. Ackrill, 66; cf. his perplexed commentary, 154–55)

Aristotle wishes here to define the contrariety between two statements or opinions. Starting from the principle that a maximally false proposition set in opposition to a maximally true proposition deserves the name "contrary," Aristotle demonstrates in successive stages that "the good is good" is a maximally true proposition, since it applies to the essence of good, and predicates the same of the same (which the proposition "the good is the not-bad" does not do, since it is only true by accident); and that the maximally false proposition is one that entails the negation of the same attribute, namely, "the good is not good." The question then is one of knowing whether "the good is bad" also deserves to be called contrary. Aristotle replies that this proposition is not the maximally false proposition opposed to the maximally true proposition. Indeed, "the good is bad" is *sumpeplegmenê*. This term condenses all of the moments of the transition from the simple idea of a container, to the "modern" idea of implication or of presupposition. For Boethius, the proposition is *duplex*, or equivocal: it has a double meaning, "because it contains within itself [*continet in se, intra se*]: *bonum non est*"; and Boethius concludes that only two "simple" propositions can be said to be contrary (*Commentarii in librum Aristotelis Peri hermêneais*, 1st ed., 219). This latter thesis is consistent with Aristotle's, for whom only "the good is not good" (simple proposition) is the opposite of "the good is good" (simple proposition). However, the respective analyses of "the good is bad," a proposition that Boethius calls *implicita*, are manifestly not the same: indeed, for Aristotle, the "doxa hoti kakon to agathon [δόξα ὅτι κακὸν τὸ ἀγαθόν]," the opinion according to which the good is bad, is only contrary to "the good is good" to the extent that it "contains" (in Boethius's terms) "the good is not good"; whereas for Boethius, it is to the extent that it contains *bonum non est*—a remarkably ambiguous expression in Latin (it can mean "the good is not," "there is nothing good," and even, in the appropriate context, "the good is not good"). Abelard goes in the same direction as Aristotle: "the good is bad" is "implicit" with respect to "the good is not good." He explains clearly the meaning of the term *implicita*: "That is to say, implying 'the good is not good' within itself, and in a certain sense containing it [*implicans eam in se, et quodammodo continens*]" (*Glossa super Periermeneias*, 99–100). But he adds, as Aristotle did not: "Because whoever thinks that 'the good is bad' also thinks that 'the good is not good,' whereas the reverse does not hold true [*sed non convertitur*]." This explanation is decisive for the history of implication, since one can certainly express in terms of "implication" in the modern sense what Abelard expresses when he notes the nonreciprocity of the two propositions (one can say that "the good is bad" implies or presupposes "the good is not good," whereas "the good is not good" does not imply "the good is bad"). Modern translations of Aristotle inherit these difficulties. Boethius and Abelard bequeath to posterity an interpretation of the passage in Aristotle according to which "the good is bad" can only be considered the opposite of "the good is good" insofar as, an "implicit" proposition, it contains the contradictory meaning of "the good is good," namely, "the good is not good." It is the meaning of "to contain a contradiction" that, in a still rather obscure way, takes up this analysis by specifying the meaning of *impliquer*. In any case, the first attested use in French of the verb is in 1377 in Oresme, in the syntagm *impliquer contradiction* (RT: *DHLF*, 1793).

These same texts give rise to another analysis in the second half of the twelfth century: a *propositio implicita* is a proposition that "implies," that is, that contains two propositions called *explicitae*, and that are its equivalent when paraphrased. Thus, "*homo qui est albus est animal quod currit*" (A man who is white is an animal who runs) contains the two explicits, "*homo est albus*" and "*animal currit*." Only by "exposing" or "resolving" (*expositio, resolutio*) such an *implicita* proposition can one assign it a truth-value:

Omnis implicito habet duas explicitas. . . . Verbi gratia: *Socrates est id quod est homo*, haec implicita aequivalet huic copulativae constanti ex explicitis: *Socrates est aliquid est illud est homo*, haec est vera, quare et implicita vera.

Every "implicit" has two "explicits." . . . For example: "Socrates is that which is a man," this "implicit" is equivalent to the following conjunctive proposition made up of two "explicits": "Socrates is something and that is a man"; this latter proposition is true, so the "implicit" is also true.

(*Tractatus implicitarum*, in Giusberti, "Materials for a Study," 43)

The "contained" propositions are usually relative propositions, which are called *implicationes*, and this term remains, even though the name *propositio implicita* becomes increasingly rare, perhaps because they are subsequently classified within the larger category of "exponible" propositions, which need precisely to be "exposed" or paraphrased for their logical structure to be highlighted. In the treatises of Terminist logic, one chapter is devoted to the phenomenon of *restrictio*, a restriction in the denotation or the *suppositio* of the noun (see SUPPOSITION). Relative expressions (*implicationes*), along with others, have a restrictive function (*vis, officium implicandi*), just like adjectives and participles: in "a man who argues runs," the term "man," because of the relative expression "who runs," is restricted to denoting the present—moreover, according to grammarians, there is an equivalence between the relative expression "qui *currit*" and the participle *currens* (*Summe metenses*, ed. De Rijk, in *Logica modernorum*, 2.1:464). In the case in which a relative expression is restrictive, its function is to "leave something that is constant [*aliquid pro constanti relinquere*]," that is, to produce, in modern terms, a preassertion that conditions the truth of the main assertion without being its primary object. This is expressed very clearly in the following passage from a thirteenth-century logical treatise:

Implicare est pro constanti et involute aliquid significare. Ut cum dicitur homo qui est albus currit. "Pro constanti" dico, quia praeter hoc quod assertitur ibi cursus de homine, aliquid datur intelligi, scilicet hominem album; "involute" dico quia praeter hoc quod ibi proprie et principaliter significatur hominem currere, aliquid intus intelligitur, scilicet hominem esse album. Per hoc patet quod implicare est intus plicare. Id enim quod intus plicamus sive ponimus, pro constanti relinquimus. Unde implicare nil aliud est quam subiectum sub aliqua dispositione pro constanti relinquere et de illo sic disposito aliquid affirmare.

"To imply" is to signify something by stating it as constant, and in a hidden manner. For example, when we say "the man who is white runs." I say "stating it as constant" because, beyond the assertion that predicates the running of the man, we are given to understand something else, namely that the man is white; I say "in a hidden manner" because, beyond what is signified primarily and literally, namely that the man is running, we are given to understand something else within (*intus*), namely that the man is white. It follows from this that *implicare* is nothing other than *intus plicare* ("folded within"). What we fold or state within, we leave as a constant. It follows from this that "to imply" is nothing other than leaving something as a constant in the subject, such that the subject is under a certain disposition, and that it is under this disposition that something about it is affirmed.

(*De implicationibus*, ed. De Rijk, in "Some Notes," 100)

N.B. Giusberti ("Materials for a Study," 31) always reads *pro constanti*, whereas the manuscript edited by De Rijk sometimes has *pro contenti*, and sometimes *precontenti*, this latter term attested nowhere else.

This is truly an example of what the 1662 *Logic* of Port-Royal will describe as an "incidental assertion."

The situation is even more complex, however, insofar as this operation only relates to one usage of a relative proposition, when it is restrictive. A restriction can sometimes be blocked, and the logical reinscriptions are then different for restrictive and nonrestrictive relative propositions. One such case of a blockage is that of "false implications," as in "a [or the] man who is a donkey runs," where there is a conflict (*repugnantia*) between what the determinate term itself denotes (man) and the determination (donkey). The truth-values of the propositions containing relatives thus differ according to whether they are restrictive, and of composite meaning—(a) "*homo qui est albus currit*" (A man who is white runs)—or nonrestrictive, and of divided meaning—(b) "*homo currit qui est albus*" (A man, who is white, is running). When the relative is restrictive, as in (a), the implicit only produces one single assertion, as we saw (since the relative corresponds to a pre-assertion), and is thus the equivalent of a hypothetical. Only in the second case can there be a "resolution" of the implicit into two explicits—(c) "*homo currit*," (d) "*homo est albus*"—and a logical equivalence between the implicit and the conjunction of the two explicits—(e) "*homo currit et ille est albus*"; so it is only in this instance that one can say, in the modern sense, that (b) implies (c) and (d), and therefore (e).

- See Box 1.

II. "Implication"/"Implicature"

The term "implicature" was introduced in 1967 by H. P. Grice in the William James Lectures (Harvard), which he delivered under the title "Logic and Conversation." These lectures set out the basis of a logical approach to communication, that is, logical relations in conversational contexts. The need was felt for a term that is distinct from "implication," insofar as "implication" is a relation between propositions (in the logical sense), whereas "implicature" is a relation between statements, within a given context. "Implication" is a relation bearing on the truth or falsity of propositions, whereas "implicature" brings an extra meaning to the statements it governs. Whenever "implicature" is determined according to its context, it enters the field of pragmatics, and therefore has to be distinguished from presupposition.

Logical implication is a relation between two propositions, one of which is the logical consequence of the other. The English equivalent of "logical implication" is "entailment." This word is derived from "tail" (Old French *taille*; Middle English *entaill* or *entailen* = en + *tail*), and prior to its logical use, the meaning of "entailment" is "restriction," "tail" having the sense of "limitation." An entailment was originally a limitation on the transfer or handing down of a property or an inheritance. The two senses of entailment have two elements in common: (a) the handing down of a property; and (b) the limitation on one of the poles of this transfer. In logical "entailment," a property is transferred from the antecedent to the consequent, and normally in semantics, the limitation on the antecedent is stressed. One might thus advance the hypothesis that the mutation from the juridical sense to the logical sense occurred by analogy on the basis of these common elements.

In logic, one makes a distinction between material implication and formal implication. Material implication ("if . . . then . . . ," symbolized by ⊃), also called Philonian implication (because it was formalized by Philo of Megara), is only false when the antecedent is true and the consequent false. In terms of a formalization of communication, this has the flaw of bringing with it a counterintuitive semantics, since a false proposition implies materially any proposition: "If the moon is made of green cheese, then 2 + 2 = 4!" The "*ex falso quodlibet sequitur*," which is how this fact is expressed, has a long history going back to antiquity (for the Stoics and the Megarian philosophers, it is the difference between Philonian implication and Diodorean implication): it traverses the theory of consequences in the Middle Ages, and is one of the paradoxes of material implication that is perfectly summed up in these two rules of Jean Buridan: (1) if P is false, Q follows from P; (2) if P is true, P follows from Q (Bochenski, *History of Formal Logic*, 208). Formal implication (see Russell, *Principles of Mathematics*, 36–41) is a universal conditional implication: $\{\forall x \, (Ax \supset Bx)\}$ (for any x, if Ax, then Bx).

Different means of resolving the paradoxes of implication have been used. Lewis's "strict implication" (Lewis and Langford, *Symbolic Logic*) is defined as an implication that is reinforced such that it is impossible for the antecedent to be true and the consequent false, yet it has the same flaw as material implication (an impossible—that is, necessarily false—proposition strictly implies any proposition). The relation of entailment introduced by Moore in 1923 is a relation that avoids these paradoxes by requiring a logical derivation of the antecedent from the consequent (in this case, "if 2 + 2 = 5, then 2 + 3 = 5" is false, since the consequent cannot be logically derived from the antecedent). Occasionally, one has to call upon the pair "entailment"/"implication" in order to distinguish between an implication in the sense of material implication and an implication in George Moore's sense, which is also sometimes called "relevant implication" (Anderson and Belnap, *Entailment*), to ensure that the entire network of terms is covered.

Along with this first series of terms in which "entailment" and "implication" alternate with one another, there is a second series of terms that contrasts two kinds of "implicature." The word "implicature" (French *implicature*, German *Implikatur*) is formed from "implication" and the suffix –*ture*, which expresses a resultant aspect (for example, "signature"; cf. Latin *temperatura*, from *temperare*). "Implication" is derived from "to imply" and "implicature" from "to implicate" (from the Latin *in* + *plicare*, from *plex*; cf. the Indo-European *plek*), which has the same meaning.

1

The Greek vocabulary of implication: Disparity and systematicity

The word *implication* in French covers and translates an extremely varied Greek vocabulary that bears the mark of heterogeneous logical and systematic operations, depending on whether one is dealing with Aristotle or the Stoics.

The passage through medieval Latin allows us to understand retrospectively the connection in Aristotelian logic between the *implicatio* of the implicits (*sumpeplegmenê*, as an interweaving or interlacing) and conclusive or consequential implication, *sumperasma* [συμπέρασμα] in Greek (or *sumpeperasmenon* [συμπεπερασμένον], *sumpeperasmenê* [συμπεπερασμένη], from *perainô* [περαίνω], "to limit"), which is the terminology used in the *Organon* to denote the conclusion of a syllogism (*Prior Analytics* 1.15.34a21–24: if one designates as *A* the premise [*tas protaseis* (τὰς προτάσεις)] and as *B* the conclusion [*to sumperasma* (συμπέρασμα)]). When Tricot translates Aristotle's famous definition of the syllogism at *Prior Analytics* 1.1.24b18–21, he chooses to render as the French noun *consequence* Aristotle's verbal form *sumbainei* [συμβαίνει], that which "goes with" the premise and results from it.

> A syllogism is a discourse [*logos* (λόγος)] in which, certain things being stated, something other than what is stated necessarily results simply from the fact of what is stated. *Simply from the fact of what is stated*, I mean that it is because of this that the **consequence** is obtained [*legô de tôi tauta einai to dia tauta sumbainei* (λέγω δὲ τῷ ταῦτα εἶναι τὸ διὰ ταῦτα συμβαίνει)].
>
> (Ibid., 1.1, 24b18–21; italics J. Tricot, bold B. Cassin)

To make the connection with the modern sense of *implication*, though, we also have to take into account, as is most often the case, the Stoics' use of the same terms. What the Stoics call *sumpeplegmenon* [συμπεπλεγμένον] is a "conjunctive" proposition; for example: "And it is daytime, and it is light" (it is true both that *A* and that *B*). The conjunctive is the third type of nonsimple proposition, after the "conditional" (*sunêmmenon* [συνημμένον]; for example: "If it is daytime, then it is light")

and the "subconditional" (*parasunêmmenon* [παρασυνημμένον]; for example: "Since it is daytime, it is light"), and before the "disjunctive" (*diezeugmenon* [διεζευγμένον]; for example: "Either it is daytime, or it is night") (Diogenes Laertius 7.71–72; cf. RT: Long and Sedley, *The Hellenistic Philosophers*, A35, 2:209 and 1:208). One can see that there is no implication in the conjunctive, whereas there is one in the *sunêmmenon* in "if . . . then . . . ," which constitutes the Stoic expression par excellence (and as distinct from the Aristotelian syllogism). Indeed, it is around the conditional that the question and the vocabulary of implication opens out again. The Aristotelian *sumbainein* [συμβαίνειν], which denotes the accidental nature of a result, however clearly it has been demonstrated (and we should not forget that *sumbebêkos* [συμβεβηκός] denotes accident; see SUBJECT, I), is replaced by *akolouthein* [ἀκολουθεῖν] (from the copulative a- and *keleuthos* [κέλευθος], "path" [RT: Chantraine, *Dictionnaire étymologique de la langue grecque*, s.v. ἀκόλουθος]), which denotes instead being accompanied by a consequent conformity: This connector (that is, the "if") indicates that the second proposition ("it is light") follows (*akolouthei* [ἀκολουθεῖ]) from the first ("it is daytime") (Diogenes Laertius, 7.71). Attempts, beginning with Philo or Diodorus Cronus and continuing to the present day, to determine the criteria of a "valid" conditional (*to hugies sunêmmenon* [τὸ ὑγιὲς συνημμένον]) offer, among other possibilities, the notion of *emphasis* [ἔμφασις], which Long and Sedley translate as "entailment" and Brunschwig and Pellegrin as "implication" (Sextus Empiricus, *The Skeptic Way*, in RT: Long and Sedley, *The Hellenistic Philosophers*, 35B, 2:211 and 1:209), a term that is normally used to refer to a reflected image and to the force, including rhetorical force, of an impression. Elsewhere, "emphasis" is explained in terms of *dunamis* [δύναμις], of "virtual" content ("When we have the premise which results in a certain conclusion, we also have this conclusion virtually [*dunamei* (δυνάμει)] in the premise, even if it is not explicitly indicated [*kan kat' ekphoran mê legetai* (κἂν κατ' ἐκφορὰν μὴ λέγεται)]), Sextus Empiricus, *Against*

the Grammarians 8.229ff., trans. D. L. Blank, 49 = RT: Long and Sedley, *The Hellenistic Philosophers*, G36 (4), 2:219 and 1:209)—where connecting the different meanings of "implication" creates new problems.

One has to understand that the type of logical implication represented by the conditional implies, in the double sense of "contains implicitly" and "has as its consequence," the entire logical, physical, and moral Stoic system. It is a matter of *to akolouthon en zôêi* [τὸ ἀκόλουθον ἐν ζωῇ], "consequentiality in life," as Long and Sedley translate it (Stobeus 2.85.13 = RT: Long and Sedley, *The Hellenistic Philosophers*, 59B, 2:356; Cicero prefers *congruere*, *De finibus* 3.17 = RT: Long and Sedley, *The Hellenistic Philosophers*, 59D, 2:356). It is the same word, *akolouthia* [ἀκολουθία], that refers to the conduct consequent upon itself that is the conduct of the wise man, the chain of causes defining will or fate, and finally the relationship that joins the antecedent to the consequent in a true proposition.

Victor Goldschmidt, having cited Émile Bréhier (in *Le système stoïcien*, 53 n. 6), puts the emphasis on *antakolouthia* [ἀντακολουθία], the neologism coined by the Stoics that one could translate as "reciprocal implication," and that refers specifically to the solidarity of virtues (*antakolouthia tôn aretôn* [ἀντακολουθία τῶν ἀρετῶν], Diogenes Laertius 7.125; Goldschmidt, *Le système stoïcien*, 65–66) as a group that would be encompassed by dialectical virtue, immobilizing *akolouthia* in the absolute present of the wise man. "Implication" is, in the final analysis, from then on, the most literal name of the system as such.

Barbara Cassin

BIBLIOGRAPHY

Aristotle. *Prior Analytics*. Translated by H. Tredennick. Vol. 1 in *Organon*. 3 vols. Cambridge, MA: Harvard University Press, 1938.

Goldschmidt, Victor. *Le système stoïcien et l'idée de temps*. Paris: Vrin, 1953.

Sextus Empiricus. *Against the Grammarians*. Translated with a commentary by D. L. Blank. Oxford: Oxford University Press, 1998.

The Gricean concept of "implicature" is an extension and modification of the concept of presupposition, which differs from material implication in that the negation of the antecedent implies the consequent (the question "Have you stopped beating your wife?" presupposes the existence of a wife in both cases). In this sense, implicature escapes the paradoxes of material implication from the outset. Grice distinguishes two kinds of implicature, conventional and conversational. Conventional implicature is practically equivalent to presupposition, since it refers to the presuppositions attached by linguistic convention to lexical items or expressions. For example, "Mary even loves Peter" has a relation of conventional implicature to "Mary loves other entities than Peter." This is equivalent to: "'Mary even loves Peter' presupposes

'Mary loves other entities than Peter.' " With this kind of implicature, we remain within the lexical, and thus the semantic, field. Conventional implicature, however, is different from material implication, since it is relative to a language (in the example, the English for the word "even"). With conversational implicature, we are no longer dependent on a linguistic expression, but move into pragmatics (the theory of the relation between statements and contexts). Grice gives the following example: If, in answer to someone's question about how *X* is getting on in his new job, I reply, "Well, he likes his colleagues, and he's not in prison yet," what is implied pragmatically by this assertion depends on the context (and not on a linguistic expression). It is, for example, compatible with two very different contexts: one in which *X* has been trapped by unscrupulous colleagues in some shady deal, and one in which *X* is dishonest and well known for his irascible nature.

Alain de Libera
Irène Rosier-Catach (I)
Frédéric Nef (II)

BIBLIOGRAPHY

Abelard, Peter. *Dialectica*. Edited by L. M. De Rijk. Assen, Neth.: Van Gorcum, 1956. 2nd rev. ed., 1970.

—————. *Glossae super Periermeneias*. Edited by Lorenzo Minio-Paluello. In *Twelfth-Century Logic: Texts and Studies*, vol. 2, *Abelaerdiana inedita*. Rome: Edizioni di Storia e Letteratura, 1958.

Anderson, Allan Ross, and Nuel Belnap. *Entailment: The Logic of Relevance and Necessity*. Vol. 1. Princeton, NJ: Princeton University Press, 1975.

Aristotle. *De interpretatione*. English translation by J. L. Ackrill: *Aristotle's Categories and* De interpretatione. Notes by J. L. Ackrill. Oxford: Clarendon, 1963. French translation by J. Tricot: *Organon*. Paris: Vrin, 1966.

Auroux, Sylvain, and Irène Rosier. "Les sources historiques de la conception des deux types de relatives." *Langages* 88 (1987): 9–29.

Bochenski, Joseph M. *A History of Formal Logic*. Translated by Ivo Thomas. New York: Chelsea, 1961.

Boethius. *Aristoteles latinus*. Edited by Lorenzo Minio-Paluello. Paris: Descleé de Brouwer, 1965. Translation by Lorenzo Minio-Paluello: *The Latin Aristotle*. Toronto: Hakkert, 1972.

—————. *Commentarii in librum Aristotelis Peri hermêneias*. Edited by K. Meiser. Leipzig: Teubner, 1877. 2nd ed., 1880.

De Rijk, Lambertus Marie. *Logica modernorum: A Contribution to the History of Early Terminist Logic*. 2 vols. Assen, Neth.: Van Gorcum, 1962–67.

—————. "Some Notes on the Mediaeval Tract *De insolubilibus*, with the Edition of a Tract Dating from the End of the Twelfth-Century." *Vivarium* 4 (1966): 100–103.

Giusberti, Franco. *Materials for a Study on Twelfth-Century Scholasticism*. Naples, It.: Bibliopolis, 1982.

Grice, Henry Paul. "Logic and Conversation." In *Syntax and Semantics 3: Speech Acts*, edited by P. Cole and J. Morgan, 41–58. New York: Academic Press, 1975. (Also in *The Logic of Grammar*, edited by D. Davidson and G. Harman, 64–74. Encino, CA: Dickenson, 1975.)

Lewis, Clarence Irving, and Cooper Harold Langford. *Symbolic Logic*. New York: New York Century, 1932.

Meggle, Georg. *Grundbegriffe der Kommunikation*. 2nd ed. Berlin: De Gruyter, 1997.

Meggle, Georg, and Christian Plunze, eds. *Saying, Meaning, Implicating*. Leipzig: Leipziger Universitätsverlag, 2003.

Moore, George Edward. *Philosophical Studies*. London: Kegan Paul, 1923.

Rosier, Irène. "Relatifs et relatives dans les traits terministes des XIIe et XIIIe siècles: (2) Propositions relatives (*implicationes*), distinction entre restrictives et non restrictives." *Vivarium* 24: 1 (1986): 1–21.

Russell, Bertrand. *The Principles of Mathematics*. Cambridge: Cambridge University Press, 1903.

Strawson, Peter Frederick. "On Referring." *Mind* 59 (1950): 320–44.

IN SITU (LATIN)

ENGLISH	site-specific, in place
FRENCH	*sur place, dans son site, in situ*

➤ *LIEU* and ART, CONCETTO, MOMENT, WORK

In common usage in archeology, the Latin phrase *in situ* was adopted at the end of the 1960s and during the 1970s by critics and artists to refer to a basic trait of a large number of works that were not only produced for a particular site but also designed with the physical, institutional, and symbolic characteristics of the place in mind—galleries, museums, public spaces, or even natural spaces, sometimes very remote, as was often the case for the American earthworks (the creators of which also used the expression "site-specific"), or in the work of Christo and Jeanne-Claude. Understood in this sense, *in situ* has since become part of the vocabulary of aesthetics and criticism.

For archeologists, *in situ* applies to two distinct levels of reality: (1) To an object when it is discovered in the supposed site of its original use. If this is the case, its situation, especially the object's physical relation to the other traces of the past that accompany it, is crucial in clarifying its function and its meaning. (2) To the mode of presentation of the vestiges of the past on the very site of their discovery, in other words, a museographical organization that facilitates the visitors' understanding.

In its aesthetic sense, *in situ* combines the two meanings of its use in archeology. The work *in situ*, constructed in function of the place, has to be viewed on site, and it acquires its full significance in the dialectical relation that it enters into with the place where it is installed. Thus the notion of *in situ* is an assault on one of the fundamental principles of traditional aesthetics, the notion of the autonomy of the work of art. This autonomy, once considered as a sign of freedom that allowed the cultural object or the commemorative monument, for example, to acquire a properly aesthetic dignity, legitimated the existence of the museum as a place where a miscellany of objects torn from their original context were gathered together. It is no coincidence, then, that the term *in situ* became more widely used in the 1970s, when many artists developed a range of strategies for contesting the logic of the museum. Ever since Daniel Buren's projects and those of Land Art popularized the term, it has been used by artists of all kinds.

Denys Riout

BIBLIOGRAPHY

Buren, Daniel. *Au sujet de . . . : Entretien avec Jérôme Sans*. Paris: Flammarion, 1998.

—————. *The Eye of the Storm: Works In Situ by Daniel Buren*. 8 vols. New York: Guggenheim Museum-D.A.P., 2005.

Poinsot, Jean-Marc. "L' *in situ* et la circonstance de sa mise en oeuvre." In *Quand l'oeuvre a lieu: L'art exposé et ses récits autorisés*. Geneva: MAMCO, 1999.

Watson, Stephen H. "In Situ: Beyond the Architectonics of the Modern." In *Postmodernism-Philosophy and the Arts*, edited by Hugh J. Silverman, 83–100. New York: Routledge, 1990.

INGENIUM (LATIN)

ARABIC	*ḥads* [الحدس]
ENGLISH	wit, humor
FRENCH	*esprit*
GERMAN	*Witz*
GREEK	*euphuia* [εὐφυΐα]
ITALIAN	*ingegno*
SPANISH	*ingenio*

➤ *REASON*, SOUL, *WITTICISM*, and ARGUTEZZA, BAROQUE, COMPARISON, CONCETTO, GEMÜT, GENIUS, INTELLECT, INTELLECTUS, INTENTION, NONSENSE, SIGNIFIER/SIGNIFIED, *SOPHISM*, TALENT

The word *ingenium*, commonly used in Latin during antiquity and in philosophical Latin up to the early modern period, is rich in meaning. Of the Romance languages, only the words *ingegno* in Italian and *ingenio* in Spanish have preserved the essence of this richness. In French the numerous derivations of *ingenium* have retained only a partial or more or less distant relation to its source word, and the term *esprit*, often used as an equivalent, has very particular connotations. The English "wit," and the German *Witz*, both have different etymologies and reproduce only in a rather restricted way the semantic constellation expressed by the Latin word, which thus presents modern translators with literally insurmountable difficulties.

I. Ingenium, Euphuia

Ingenium (*in-geno*, *gigno*) is associated with a large Indo-European family of words relating to procreation and birth. Its usage in Latin is spread around four distinct but nonetheless clearly interlinked semantic themes, which are enumerated in Egidio Forcellini's *Totius latinitatis lexicon* (1865). *Ingenium* designates first of all the innate qualities of a thing (*vis, natura, indoles, insita facultas*). Secondly, it is applied to human beings and their natural dispositions, their temperament, the way they are (*natura, indoles, mores*). Then it expresses, among man's natural dispositions, intelligence, skill, inventiveness (*vis animi, facultas insita excogitandi, percipiendi, sloertia, inventio*). Finally it designates, metonymically, persons who are particularly endowed with this faculty (*ingenia* is a synonym for *homines ingeniosi*).

In all of these different uses, *ingenium* expresses, whenever it refers to humans, the innate element within human beings of productivity, of creativity, of the capacity of going beyond and transforming the given, whether it is a matter of intellectual speculation, poetic and artistic creation, persuasive speech, technical innovations, or social and political practices. "It calls," writes Cicero, "for great intelligence [*ingenium*] to separate the mind [*mentem*] from the senses [*a sensibus*] and to sever thought [*cogitationem*] from mere habit" (*Tusculan Disputations* 1: XVI, 41). He elsewhere talks about the *divinum ingenium* that allies men with the gods, but it is in the field of rhetoric that he is most careful to show the importance of *ingenium* as a factor in oratorical invention:

> Since, then, in speaking, three things are requisite for finding argument; genius [*acumen*], method, (which, if we please, we may call art,) and diligence, I cannot but assign the chief place to *ingenium*.

> (Cicero, *On Oratory and Orators*, II, 35, 147–48)

One can see that *ingenium* is assimilated here to its primary quality, *acumen*, a word that designates the acute (*acutus*), penetrating, fine character of something (*acutezza* in Italian and *agudeza* in Spanish are derived from *acutus*, the French equivalent of which is *pointe*, see ARGUTEZZA). What does the action of *ingenium* consist of? Of "leaping over what is at our feet" (*ingenii specimen est quodam transilire ente pedes positum*) in order to grasp the relations, the similarities between things that may be very far from one another. One can understand why the ability to form metaphors, that is, to work with transfers of meanings of words to bring them closer together, is for Cicero one of the privileged manifestations of *ingenium* in the field of persuasive oratory and of poetry.

On this point he is only repeating what Aristotle says about *euphuia* [εὐφυΐα], the "good natural disposition," close to the first meaning of *ingenium*, that is, necessary for finding resemblances and making metaphors:

> But the greatest thing by far is to be a master of metaphor. It is the one thing that cannot be learnt from others; and it is also a sign of genius [εὐφυΐα], since a good metaphor implies an intuitive perception of the similarity in dissimilar: for to make good metaphors is to be good at perceiving resemblances.

> (Aristotle, *Poetics*, 22, 1459a 7)

See COMPARISON, Box 1.

■ See Box 1.

II. The Humanistic and Baroque *Ingenio* and *Ingegno*

The technical significance that the term *ingenium* took on in the field of rhetoric and poetics continues on down the centuries, to the detriment of the richness and depth of the philosophical meaning of this word. Renaissance humanism, however, still attributes to *ingenium* a specific faculty an incomparable power in the field of knowledge and action. The Spaniard Juan Luis Vives wrote, in his *Introductio ad sapientiam* (1524), that *ingenium*, a prerogative of humans, is the "force of intelligence by which our mind examines things one by one, knows what is good to do and what is not." It "is cultivated and refined by means of many arts: it is taught through a broad and admirable knowledge of things, by which it grasps more precisely the natures and values of things one by one."

It has been said that *ingenium*, at the end of the sixteenth century and in the first half of the seventeenth century, had become a mannerist or baroque concept par excellence, with specific reference to authors such as Huarte de San Juan, with his *Examen de ingenios, para las sciencias* (1575); Pellegrini, with *Delle acutezza, che altrimenti spirite, vivezze e concetti, volparmente si appellano* (1630) and *I fonti dell'ingegno ridotti ad arte* (1650); Tesauro, with *Il Canocchiale aristotelico, o sia Idea dell'arguta et ingeniosa elocutione, che serve a tutta l'arte oratoria, lapidaria et simbolica* (1648). For a long time these texts were studied from a purely aesthetic point of view, in relation to the literary trends of Gongorism, Marinism, Concettism, or Preciosity. Looking at them more closely, one can see that the *ingegno* of the Italians and the *ingenio* of the Spanish not only have stylistic and ornamental effects, but also have,

1

Intuition, Arabic *ḥads* (ARABIC [الحدس])

➤ TERM (Box 2)

Aristotle, in discussing scientific knowledge, mentions a capacity he calls "readiness of mind" (*agchinoia* [ἀγχίνοια]), to which he also devotes several lines in his discussion of intellectual virtues (*dianoétiques*) (*Nicomachean Ethics*, VI, 10, 1142b 5; ed., Barnes, vol.2). He defines it as "a talent for hitting upon (*eustokia* [εὐστοχία]) the middle term in an imperceptible time" (*Posterior Analytics*, I, 34, 89b 10ff; ed., Barnes, vol 1). The first Latin translation mistakenly reads *eustochia*, which Thomas Aquinas paraphrases as *bona conjecturatio* (*Commentary on the Nicomachean Ethics*, § 1219). Arabic translators of the *Analytics* have translated this term as *ḏakā* [الذكاء] ("finesse, intelligence"), but explain εὐστοχία by "goodness of the *ḥads* [الحدس]" (*Mantiq Aristu* [منطق أرسطو], ed. Badawi, p. 426, 5). The passage in the *Nicomachean Ethics* is translated as "wisdom of the intellect" (*lawḏaʿīya ʾl'aql* [الوذعية العقل] [Aristu, al-Akhlaq, 222, 15]). Avicenna discusses *ḥads* on several occasions (cf. Goichon, *Lexique de la langue philosophique d'Ibn Sina*, § 140, p. 65ff) and gives it a major place in his epistemology (cf. Gutas, *Introduction to Reading Avicenna's Philosophical Works*, 161–66). He

gives a precise definition of the term: all scientific knowledge is acquired by syllogisms, whose pivot is the middle term. This term can be arrived at through teaching or through "the *ḥads*, [which] is an action of the mind by which [the mind] deduces for itself the middle term." Its teaching, moreover, is itself based in the final analysis on intuitions (al-Šifā, *Avicenna's De Anima, Being the Psychological Part of Kitab al-Shifa*, (vol. 1, part 6). The *ḥads* is thus, on the one hand, the intuition of principles, but it is also the capacity of taking in simultaneously all of the stages of a discursive argumentation. Avicenna thus offers the concept of a knowledge that is neither simply intuitive nor simply discursive but like a discursiveness condensed into a single act of intuition, thereby anticipating Descartes's program (*Regulae*, VII: AT, 10: 387ff)—except that what for Descartes is acquired methodically is for Avicenna an innate gift. For him, whoever possesses *ḥads* has no need of a master and can reinvent all the sciences for himself—which, in fact, is what Avicenna in his autobiography boasts that he has done. This allows him among other things to offer a philosophical theory

of prophetic knowledge. The Latin translators render the term *ḥads* on occasion as *subtilitas* but in most cases as *ingenium* (Avicenna Latinus, *Liber sextus de naturalibus*, 152 ff). To describe someone who is very intelligent as a "genius," and to say that a "genius" is like a prophet, is to place oneself within the tradition of Avicenna.

BIBLIOGRAPHY

al-Šifā, *Avicenna's De Anima, Being the Psychological Part of Kitab al-Shifa*. Translated by F. Rohman. London: Oxford University Press, 1959.

Aristotle. *The Complete Works of Aristotle: The Revised Oxford Translation*. Edited by Jonathan Barnes. Bollingen Series 71.2. Princeton, NJ: Princeton University Press, 1984.

Aristu [Aristotle]. *al-Akhlaq*. Edited by A. Badawi. Kuwait City: Wakâlat al-Matbǔ'ât, 1979.

Avicenna Latinus. *Liber sextus de naturalibus*. Edited by S. Van Riet. Louvain, Belg.: Brill, 1968.

Badawi, A. *Man.tiq Aris.tū*, 3 vols. Cairo: 1948–1952.

Golchon, A.-M. *Lexique de la langue philosophique d'Ibn Sina*. Paris: Desclée de Brouwer, 1938.

Gutas, Dimitri. *Introduction to Reading Avicenna's Philosophical Works*. Leiden, Neth.: Brill, 1988.

first and foremost, a richness in terms of the order of knowledge and of moral and social existence. Cervantes's titles are characteristically subtle: in *El ingenioso hidalgo don Quijote de la Mancha* (1605) and *El ingenioso caballero don Quijote de la Mancha* (1615), *ingenio* is attributed ironically, as if it were an absurd characterization, to the mad knight, who is nevertheless revealed to embody many of the most prized characteristics of humanist intelligence. Gracián, in *El discreto* (1646), which paints a portrait of the "man of discernment," emphasizes the fact that *ingenio* belongs to the "domain of understanding," and he defines it precisely as the "courage of understanding," his work being the *concepto* that immediately establishes a correlation between phenomena that are distant from one another. Because it spreads a "divine light," *ingenio* thus permits man to "decipher the world," which would otherwise remain mute and unknown.

The last and no doubt greatest representative of the ancient humanist tradition for whom *ingenium* is the human faculty par excellence is Vico, who in *De nostri temporis studiorum ratione* (1709) and *De antiquissima Italorum sapientia* (1710) revives the Ciceronian theory of *ingenium*, contrasting its "topical" fertility to the sterility of Descartes's analytic and deductive method. Finally, in *Scienza nuova* (1725, 1730, 1744), Vico notes first that *ingegno* as a power of the imagination rich in metaphors is what characterizes youth; he then proceeds to give it a central place in the life of nations, especially in the

first stages of their development, when men are "poetically" creating their world.

III. The French *Esprit*

In *De ratione*, Vico remarks that "the French, when they wish to give a name to the faculty of the mind that allows one to join together quickly, appropriately and felicitously separate things, which we call *ingegno*, use the word *esprit* (*spiritus*), and they turn this power of the mind that is manifest in synthesis into something quite simple, because their excessively subtle intelligence excels in the finer points of reasoning rather than in synthesis." Whatever the value of this explanation may be, the fact is that the French language, however rich its vocabulary is in words derived from *ingenium* (*ingénieux, ingéniosité, engin, ingénieur, s'ingénier, génie*), has no equivalent of the Latin word, unlike Italian and Spanish. The term *esprit*, whose range of meanings is vast, was used quite early on to translate it, at the cost of a great deal of equivocation, given the vagueness of the French word. The chevalier de Méré, in his *Discours de l'esprit* (1677), for example, writes, "It seems to me that *esprit* consists of understanding things, in being able to consider them from all sorts of perspectives, in judging clearly what they are, and their precise value, in discerning what one thing has in common with, and what distinguishes it from, another, and in knowing the right paths to take in order to discover those that are hidden." He adds that "it is a great sign of *esprit* to invent Arts and Sciences." And it is clear that the *esprit de finesse* that Pascal, a friend of Méré, contrasts to the Cartesian *esprit de géométrie* has many points in common with the baroque *ingenium*. In the eighteenth century *ingenium* again crops up in the definition that Voltaire gives of *esprit* in the article "Esprit" of the RT: *Encyclopédie* of Diderot and d'Alembert:

Ce mot, en tant qu'il signifie une qualité de l'âme, est un de ces termes vagues, auxquels tous ceux qui les prononcent attachent presque toujours des sens différents. Il exprime autre chose que jugement, génie, goût, talent, pénétration, étendue, grâce, finesse; et il doit tenir de tous ces mérites: on pourrait le définir, raison ingénieuse.

(This word, insofar as it signifies a quality of the soul, is one of those vague terms to which everyone who uses it almost always attaches different meanings. It expresses something other than judgment, genius, taste, talent, penetration, expanse, grace, finesse; and it has all of these merits: one could define it as ingenious reason.)

IV. "Wit" and *Witz*

In English "wit" is generally considered to be the closest equivalent of the Latin *ingenium* (it is important to remember, however, that "wit," like *Witz* in German, comes from a different root than *ingenium* and refers to the notion of knowledge and not "natural talent"). Shaftesbury, writing in a tradition different from rationalist intellectualism, understands "wit" to preserve something of the power of metaphorical invention that the *ingenium* so dear to humanist rhetoric contains.

■ See Box 2.

In fact, there can be no real equivalence of meaning between "wit" and *ingenium*, as demonstrated by the difficulties experienced by Vico's English translators, who propose

---

2

"Wit and/or humor"

"Wit" generally designates a cognitive power that is different from "mind" and is an activity of thought (*esprit*) in which the imagination allows for the enjoyment of ideas, and for a sense of the beauty of ideas. "Wit" thus incorporates "humor," which permits a pleasurable, even eloquent, relationship to thought. Thus, in his *Essay on the Freedom of Wit and Humor*, Shaftesbury analyses a critical operation of the mind (*esprit*) that manifests itself in good humor and on the occasion of pleasant conversation among friends. The difficulty of translating into other languages the terms "wit" and "humor," and of understanding them, and understanding how they are connected, flows not from an aversion to joining together that which is funny and that which has to do with intelligence, but also from the polysemy of the terms: what do the French, for example, make of "humor" when it becomes for them *humour* and refers to what they customarily call *l'humour anglais* (the English sense of humor).

a. "Wit" and "mind"

"Wit" is not "mind." "Mind" refers to the nature of the mind, or intelligence (*esprit*), whereas "wit" refers to a cognitive activity and experience. In Hobbes (*Leviathan*, 134–35), "wit" has the sense of the mind as a power of understanding similarities between things that might seem very distant from one another. "Natural wit" is close to *ingenium*; it is an ability to see resemblances that are rarely noticed. According to Hobbes, "to have a good wit" is different from "to have a good

judgment," since judgment consists of identifying differences and dissimilarities, of using discernment. In *An Essay Concerning Human Understanding*, Locke makes a distinction quite close to Hobbes's distinction between "mind," "wit," and "judgment" (*Essay*, 156). Whereas judgment has an analytic function whose aim is to separate out different ideas, the mind or intelligence (*esprit*) as "wit" quickly and pleasantly joins ideas together: "that entertainment and pleasantry of Wit, which strikes so lively on the Fancy, and therefore so acceptable to all People" (ibid.).

b. "Wit" and *Witz*

"Wit" thus resembles the German *Witz*. The two terms refer to a kind of knowledge (the common root is *wissen*) that is not an analytic discursiveness but demonstrates a creative mind that creates resemblances while being aware of the possibility of the sociability of thought (Lacoue-Labarthe, Nancy, and Lang, *L'Absolu littéraire*, 2; *The Literary Absolute*, 53). "Wit" denotes an individual burst of brilliance that, in addition to its value as entertainment, can produce puns and jokes, which are the singular forms by which wit is expressed.

c. The pleasure of using language

In Hume the effect produced by wit may be said to be the same as that produced by eloquence; both bring pleasure to the use of language (*Treatise of Human Nature*, 611). But the pleasure one takes in "wit" or in eloquence is not of the same type as the pleasure taken

in "good humor." "Good humor" is only immediately pleasant to the person speaking and is only then communicated to others through sympathy. "Wit," by contrast, has an immediate social value that is deployed especially in the pleasures of conversation: "As wisdom and good sense are valued, because they are *useful* to the person possess'd of them; so *wit* and *eloquence* are valued, because they are *immediately agreeable* to others" (ibid.). Finally, "wit" and "humor" are distinguished from "wisdom" and "good sense," which are only of value to the person who possesses them. In the eighteenth century, "humor" is often associated with "wit" to express a way of relating to others in a mode of gaiety, or even through jokes and puns. But "humour," before being translated into French as *humour*, signifies humor understood as temperament [*humeur* in French]: "Indeed, what is that you call wit or humour?" (Shaftesbury, "Exercises," 99). However, according to Samuel Johnson's RT: *Dictionary of the English Language*, "humor" means a "general turn or temper of mind" but also "jocularity, merriment," and he includes in his understanding repartee, happiness, even hilarity. Humor already contains something of what the French call *l'humour anglais*, that is to say, something more than a simple disposition of the mind: a singular way of laughing that is very English, and the translation of which into French merely refers one back to the English word "humor," which remains quite indeterminate for a French person.

(continued)

(continued)

d. The tradition of "wit and/or humor" is split into two moments

"Humor" originally referred to humor as temperament. Good humor is when humor as temperament is converted into a joyful disposition. In his *Essay on the Freedom of Wit and Humour*, Shaftesbury proposed subjecting the realm of truth to laughter:

> Truth, 'tis suppos'd, may bear all Lights: and one of those principal Lights or natural Mediums, by which Things are to be view'd, in order to a thorow recognition, is Ridicule it-self.

> (Shaftesbury, *Characteristics*, 1: 61)

In this theory of the critical use of laughter, "wit" consists in an operation of the mind (*esprit*) in which the commerce of joyful passions depends on a regulated play between wit and humor, on the model of an exchange of ideas that is at once playful, pleasant, and polite:

> Wit will mend upon our hands, and Humour will refine it-self; if we take care not to tamper with it.

> (Ibid., 1: 64)

A humor that is not "tampered with" is a humor that does not allow itself to be distorted by melancholy or excessive laughter. "Humor," then, becomes synonymous with other terms often used by Shaftesbury ("raillery," "irony," and "ridicule") but only inasmuch as these words are associated with the possibility of measured and benevolent laughter. "Wit" and "humor" could never include the outrageous comedy of buffoonery and of the burlesque (Shaftesbury, *Characteristics*, 72) that are associated with carnival and cabaret in having entertainment as their sole purpose.

"Humor" in its connection to a physiological disposition comes to mean humor in the second, non-humoral sense. From then on, wit and humor come together to emphasize a remarkable activity of the mind. Humor now forms the basis of the permanent disposition of an individual—we might refer to "a man of great humor." Furthermore, humor produces ambiguous and contradictory figures, as if it never had one single meaning. Alice, in *Alice's Adventures in Wonderland* by Lewis Carroll, is constantly growing bigger and smaller, without ever knowing as she goes through her adventures what it is that makes her bigger or smaller. Could we say that English humor, so difficult to translate in all its figures, is in some sense defined by Lewis Carroll's attempts to show the real world in all of its possibilities simultaneously, creating comic effects by superimposing elements that are logically necessary onto elements that are logically incompatible—and for that reason, unmasterable?

BIBLIOGRAPHY

Carroll, Lewis. *Alice's Adventures in Wonderland*. Edited by Selwyn H. Goodacre. Illustrated by Barry Moser. Preface and notes by James R. Kincaid. Berkeley: University of California Press, 1982.

Hobbes, Thomas. *Leviathan*. London: Penguin, 1968. First published in 1651.

Hume, David. *A Treatise of Human Nature*. Oxford: Clarendon, 1978. First published in 1739–1740.

Lacoue-Labarthe, P., J.-L. Nancy, and A. M. Lang, *L'Absolu littéraire*, Seuil, 1978. Translation by Phillip Barnard and Cheryl Lester: *The Literary Absolute*. Albany: SUNY Press, 1988.

Locke, John. *An Essay Concerning Human Understanding*. Oxford: Oxford University Press, 1975.

Shaftesbury, Anthony Ashley Cooper. "Sensus communis: An Essay on the Freedom of Wit and Humour." In *Characteristicks of Men, Manners, Opinions, Times*. 2 vols. Edited by Philip Ayres. 1: 35–81. Oxford: Clarendon, 1999.

the terms "ingenuity," "invention," "inventiveness," "genius," "perception," and "wit" to try to get close to the semantic richness of *ingegno* in Vico's texts.

The situation is identical in German. It is interesting to see how Kant, in two different contexts, gives two different equivalent terms for the same word, *ingenium*. In the *Critique of Judgment* ("Analytic of the Sublime"), he defines genius (*Genie*) as the "talent (natural gift) [of the mind: *Gemüt*, *ingenium*] that gives the rule to art" (*Critique of Judgment*, § 46). In the *Anthropology from a Pragmatic Point of View*, after having said that "the faculty of discovering the particular for the universal (the rule) is the power of judgment," he adds that, in the same way, "the faculty of thinking up the universal for the particular is wit (*Witz* [*ingenium*]). . . . The outstanding talent in both is noticing even the smallest similarity or dissimilarity. The faculty to do this is acumen (*Scharfsinn* [*acumen*])" (§ 44). In order to define what he means by *Witz*, Kant therefore has recourse to the vocabulary of classical rhetoric—*ingenium* and its *acumen*. At the same time, while he acknowledges the "richness" of *Witz*, he limits its scope to the anthropological realm of worldly life and assimilates it to "a sort of intellectual luxury," which he contrasts to "the common and healthy form of understanding." French translations of Kant reflect the difficulty of rendering the word *Witz* in this text. Among the recent editions of the *Anthropology*, Michel Foucault's translation of the passage just cited proposes the classic word *esprit* (Kant, *Anthropologie du point de vue pragmatique*, Fr. trans. by M. Foucault, 1970, 71).

Another translation, in order to mark the relationship to *ingenium* that Kant himself indicates, prefers *ingéniosité* (Kant, *Anthropologie du point de vue pragmatique*, Fr. trans. by A. Renault, 1993, 149), while a third gives *combinaison spirituelle* (*Anthropologie du point de vue pragmatique*, Fr. trans. by P. Jalabert, 1986, 1019).

■ See Box 3.

Ingenium is thus a notion that in itself is clear, in spite of its complexity and richness, but that certain national languages—and not minor ones from a philosophical point of view—do not succeed in translating satisfactorily.

Alain Pons

BIBLIOGRAPHY

Aristotle. *Poetics*. Edited and translated by Ingram Bywater, notes by Gilbert Murray. Oxford: Clarendon Press, 1920.

Cicero. *De Oratore*. In Cicero, *On Oratory and Orators; with His Letters to Quintus and Brutus*. Translated by J. S. Watson. London: Henry G. Bohn, 1855.

———. *De Oratore*. Translated by E. W. Sutton and H. Rackham. 2 vols. Loeb Classical Library. Cambridge, MA: Harvard University Press, 1948.

———. *Tusculan Disputations*. Edited and translated by A. E. Douglas. Warminster, Eng.: Aris and Phillips, 1985.

Gracián, Baltasar. *Agudeza y arte de ingenio*. Edited and with notes by Ceferino Peralta, Jorge M. Ayala, and José Ma. Andreu. 2 vols. Zaragoza, Sp.: Prensas Universitarias de Zaragoza, 2004. First published in 1648.

———. *El Discreto*. Edited by Miguel Romera-Navarro and Jorge M. Furt. Buenos Aires: Academia Argentina de Letras, 1960. Translation by T. Saldkeld: *The Compleat Gentleman*. London, 1730.

3
Witz according to Freud and his translators

The importance that Freud accorded to the psychic mechanisms of *Witz* belongs manifestly to the semantic field of the *ingenium* of antiquity, organized by the ideas of creativity, acuity, and convention. But since the appearance of the work entitled *Der Witz und seine Beziehung zum Unbewussten* (1905)—which Lacan considered, along with the *Interpretation of Dreams* and the *Psychology of Everyday Life*, as one of the three "canonical" texts of Freud—the translation of *Witz* has caused no end of problems for psychoanalysts. The most recent translation into Castilian Spanish renders *Witz* as *chiste*, "joke." The first French translators of Freud's work, Marie Bonaparte and Marcel Nathan, opted for *mot d'esprit* (*Le mot d'esprit et ses rapports avec l'inconscient*, 1930); Italian similarly translates *Witz* as *motto di spirito* (*Il motto di spirito e la sua relazione con l'inconscio*, trans. S. Daniele and E. Sagittario, 1975). Bonaparte and Nathan's choice was retained by Denis Messier in an excellent new edition in 1988 (*Le mot d'esprit et ses rapports avec l'inconscient*, with a prefatory note by Jean-Bernard Pontalis, in which he discusses the term). This gave rise, it seems, to good deal of hesitation, since Lacan for his part proposed translating *Witz* as *trait d'esprit* (*Écrits*, 1966; see also *Le Séminaire*, bk. 5 (1957–1958), *Les Formations de l'inconscient*, 1998), bringing it closer to another German term, *Blitz*, which refers to a flash of lightning. Moreover, in 1989 the editors of the *Oeuvres complètes de Freud* (Presses Universitaires de France) published the translation of the work on *Witz* in their volume 7 under the title *Le Trait d'esprit*, arguing from the premise that there is supposedly a "Freudian language" that different foreign-language versions have to take into account, especially where *Witz* is concerned. The meaning of *Witz*, they claim, is not *mot d'esprit* but "a characteristic trait of the '*esprit freudien*' [Freudian *Witz*]." Confronted by these oppositions and perplexities, certain psychoanalysts have even asked whether it would not be better to give up trying to translate Freud's *Witz* altogether, just as some have become resigned to doing for the typically British term *nonsense* (see J.-B. Pontalis, foreword to Freud, *Le mot d'esprit et ses rapports avec l'inconscient*, 34).

The question of *Witz* also arose among English-language Freudians, occasionally generating a degree of controversy. In 1916 the Austro-Hungarian–born American psychoanalyst Abraham A. Brill published, along with several other projects of this kind, all adjudged to be equally bad, the first translation of Freud's work on *Witz*, a term Brill chose to translate as "wit," without seeing that this would privilege the meaning of "intellectual witticism," as when one says of someone that he is a "man of wit." James Strachey, who set about revising Brill's translations, made clear at the outset his preference for "joke," which by contrast risked extending the intellectual meaning of the Freudian *Witz* to the entire range of comic expressions (plays on words, witticisms, puns, all kinds of jokes, funny stories—particularly Jewish—sallies in the manner of the Italian *scherzo*, etc.). In a preface to his English translation, (*Jokes and Their Relation to the Unconscious*, in *The Standard Edition of the Complete Psychological Works* [1960], 8: 7) Strachey explains as follows why he decided to choose "joke" (and even "jokes," in the plural):

> To translate it "Wit" opens the door to unfortunate misapprehensions. In ordinary English usage "wit" and "witty" have a highly restricted meaning and are applied only to the most refined and intellectual kind of jokes. The briefest inspection of the examples in these pages will show that "*Witz*" and "*witzig*" have a far wider connotation. "Joke," on the other hand seems itself to be too wide and to cover the German "*Scherz*" as well. The only solution in this and similar dilemmas has seemed to be to adopt one English word for some corresponding German one, and to keep to it quite consistently and invariably even if in some particular context it seems the wrong one.

In this debate one needs to understand moreover that "wit" (which has the same etymology as *Witz*, that of knowing—*wissen*) can mean both witticisms (*mots d'esprit*), as well as the faculty of inventing them, in the same way that the German *Phantasie* means both a particular fantasy and the general power of the imagination (see PHANTASIA, Box 3).

The dilemmas surrounding these different ways of translating the Freudian *Witz* are in part due to the fact that it is considered in its relation to the unconscious. Like the "Freudianslip," the failed act, or condensation in a dream, it has the sense of something jutting out, of a sudden idea (*Einfall* in German), that is, an idea that suddenly appears without one's expecting it to, and that can surprise even the person uttering it. According to Freud, the *Witz* is a successful slip that comes unexpectedly from the unconscious, like the term *famillionaire*—a kind of crasis between "familiar" [as an attitude] and "millionaire"—which so interested Lacan (and Freud himself, more than anyone), and by means of which some poor devil accidentally let it be known that he had been treated kindly by the nonetheless very wealthy Baron de Rothschild. Freud explains and glosses as follows the thought contained in this *Witz*, or this "joke" of the mind (*gestreicher Einfall*): "we had to add to the sentence 'Rothschild had treated him quite as his equal—quite "famillionairely"' a supplementary proposition that, abbreviated to its maximum degree, was expressed as: 'as much as a millionaire is capable of treating anyone'" (*Jokes and their Relation to the Unconscious*, trans. Strachey, 12–13). The source of the pleasure deriving from these games of the mind (*jeux de l'esprit*), or more precisely, of the unconscious, is just such a mechanism of condensation.

Kant, Immanuel. *Anthropologie in pragmatischer Hinsicht*. Edited by Königlich Preussischen Akademie der Wissenschaften. In *Kants Gesammelte Schriften*. Vol. 7. Berlin: De Gruyter, 1902–. Translation by Robert B. Louden: *Anthropology from a Pragmatic Point of View*, edited by Robert B. Louden. Cambridge: Cambridge University Press, 2006.

———. *Kritik der Urteilskraft*. Edited by Königlich Preussischen Akademie der Wissenschaften. In *Kants Gesammelte Schriften*. Vol. 5. Berlin: De Gruyter, 1902–. Translation by Paul Guyer and Eric Matthews: *Critique of the Power of Judgment*, edited by Paul Guyer and Eric Matthews. Cambridge: Cambridge University Press, 2000.

Vico, Giambattista. *On the Most Ancient Wisdom of the Italians, Unearthed from the Origins of the Latin Language: Including the Disputation with the Giornale de' letterati d'Italia* [*De antiquissima Italorum sapientia*]. Translated, with introduction and notes by L. M. Palmer. Ithaca, NY: Cornell University Press, 1988.

———. *On the Study Methods of Our Time* [*De nostri temporis studiorum ratione*]. Translated, with introduction and notes, by Elio Gianturco. Preface by Donald Phillip Verene. Ithaca, NY: Cornell University Press, 1990.

———. *Principi di una scienza nuova d'intorno alla commune natura delle nazioni*. 3rd ed. 2 vols. Napoli, 1744. Translation by David Marsh: *New Science: Principles of the New Science Concerning the Common Nature of Nations*. Introduction by Anthony Grafton. London: Penguin, 2001.

INSTANT

"Instant," from the Latin *in-stare*, "to stand on, hold close," is one of the possible designations of the atom of time: it is the commonly accepted translation of the Aristotelian *to nun* [τὸ νῦν], literally, "the now," of which physical time is made up; see AIÔN.

It is also, this time paying attention to the insistence (which one can hear in "instant") of that which is presently going to happen, a way of naming the pressure of the present at the heart of subjective duration; see MOMENT for a discussion of the Greek *kairos* [καιρός] (opportunity), the German *Augenblick* (blink of an eye), and Kierkegaard's Danish *øjeblik* (to be complemented by PLUDSELIGHED, "suddenness," which emphasizes the discontinuity of irruption); JETZTZEIT, which in Benjamin's vocabulary refers to the messianic effectiveness of an "at-present" in history. See, more generally, PRESENT and *TIME*.

On the way in which an instant can bring together or condense time, see *ETERNITY* [AIÔN], *INTUITION* [ANSCHAULICHKEIT, UNDERSTANDING]; cf. *ACT,* GOD, *WISDOM*.

On the way in which instantaneity is expressed verbally, see ASPECT.

➤ *EVENT*, GLÜCK, HISTORY, MEMORY, *PROGRESS*

INSTINCT

Derived from the classical Latin *instinctus*, which means "instigation, impulse, excitation" (from the Indo-European root **stig-*, "to prick"), the French word *instinct* nowadays means "an innate and powerful tendency, common to all living beings and all individuals of the same species," and in the sciences "an innate tendency of actions that are determined according to species, performed perfectly without any prior experience, and subordinated to the conditions of the environment" (RT: *Le nouveau petit Robert,* s.v.). One finds the word in German as *Instinkt*, in English as "instinct," and in Italian as *istinto*. The difference between animal and man traditionally overlaps with the difference between instinct and intelligence: see ANIMAL, and *DISPOSITION,* UNDERSTANDING, Box 1 (on the Greek *nous* [νοῦς], the meaning of which ranges from the inbred tenacity or the "sense of smell" of a dog, to the divine spirit, to divine intuition); cf. LOGOS, *REASON*.

A particular, major problem regarding the translation of *instinct* has taken shape around the use of the German term *Instinkt* in the vocabulary of psychoanalysis, with some authors assimilating it to *Trieb*, a term of German origin that is the biological equivalent of *instinct*, and that one also finds in Freud, but with a very different meaning. Indeed, according to Laplanche and Pontalis, "When Freud does use the word *Instinkt* it is in the classical sense: he speaks of *Instinkt* in animals confronted by danger . . . when Freud asks whether 'inherited mental formations exist in the human being—something analogous to instinct in animals' he does not look for such a counterpart in what he calls *Trieb*, but instead in that 'hereditary, genetically acquired factor in mental life'" (RT: *Vocabulaire de la psychanalyse,* trans. Nicholson-Smith, 214). This is why in France, after a period of

time when *instinct* was more prevalent, *Trieb* is now normally translated as *pulsion* (impulse), in the sense of an instinctual movement toward an object that is not predetermined. English translators render *Trieb* as "instinct," or more judiciously as "drive," a term that does not have the same origin as *Trieb*, but that nonetheless has some of the biological connotations of Freud's theory. See DRIVE, WUNSCH; see also ES, UNCONSCIOUS.

➤ ERLEBEN, INGENIUM, *INTUITION*, NATURE

INTELLECT, INTELLIGER (FRENCH)

| LATIN | *intellectus, intelligere; concipere, comprehendere* |
| ITALIAN | *intelletto* |

➤ INTELLECTUS, UNDERSTANDING, and CONCETTO, CONSCIOUSNESS, GEMÜT, I/ME/MYSELF, *INTUITION*, *REASON*, SOUL

In the seventeenth century, a period of translation of Latin philosophical language into French philosophical language, most notably through the translation of the major works of Descartes (*Meditationes, Principia philosophiae*), the Latin word *intellectus* appears to be almost untranslatable, at least insofar as it is practically never translated into French by the word that corresponds to it, *intellect*, but by a word belonging to an entirely different semantic field, *entendement* (understanding). Yet the word *intellect* has been part of the French language for centuries. In fact, as early as the thirteenth century we can find it in the *Livres dou Trésor*, by Brunetto Latini (1260), even though it seems that it remains a technical term that has not really passed into common use. The French language has lacked an author comparable to Dante, who contributed greatly to popularizing the word *intelletto* in Italian from the fourteenth century onward. The word *entendement*, by contrast, which first appeared in the *Oxford Psalter* (1120), very soon came into common use. We find it especially in the fourteenth century when Nicole Oresme, associating *entendement* with the word *raison*, uses it in his French translation of Aristotle's *Nicomachean Ethics* (to render the Greek *nous* [νοῦς]), and in the sixteenth century the term is used frequently by Montaigne in his *Essays*, but to refer to a quality rather than a faculty—the quality of the *gens d'entendement* (men of understanding). Furthermore, while Montaigne uses the word *intelligence*, he never uses the word *intellect*.

The term *intellect* did not really become widespread in French until the nineteenth century, following Renan, and in the context of the translation of the Averroist lexicon. The influence of Italian on French also perhaps played some role. In any case, it is striking to see that the term that the otherwise very "Cartesian" Valéry most often uses in his *Notebooks* is not *entendement* but *intellect*.

I. *Intellectus* in the Renaissance: The Example of Bovelles

The key question is knowing whether—aside from a few rare occurrences, most notably in Guez de Balzac or in Malebranche—the near-impossibility of translating *intellectus* into French literally as *intellect*, or even of using the word *intellect* in an original text in the Renaissance and into the early eighteenth century, simply reflects the limits of the vocabulary in use at the time, or whether there is not, linked to this semantic displacement toward *entendement*, a philosophical transformation that is every bit as determining. For at the beginning of the Renaissance, to talk about *intellectus* was not simply to study the workings of human *entendement*, but was above all to invoke the mode of existence and of knowledge of a separate *intellectus*, that of the angels. The 1511 *Liber de intellectu* of Charles de Bovelles is a good example: Bovelles treats human *intellectus* entirely by contrasting it to the pure *intellectus* of angels. According to Renaissance philosophy, human thought could be studied only by comparison with the pure *intellectus* of a separate intelligence. There was a vertical hierarchy of modes of thought: *sensus, ratio, intellectus, mens*, which were prefigured in the *De conjecturis* of Nicolas of Cusa (1440). *Sensus* was a mode of apprehension belonging to the body, *ratio* belonging to humans, *intellectus* to a pure intelligence (*intelligentia*), and *mens* to God. A manuscript note written by Beatus Rhenanus, an Alsatian student of Lefèvre d'Étaples and of Bovelles, identifies four distinct modes of philosophizing, according to these four modes of knowing, with intellectual philosophy thus falling halfway between rational philosophy and the philosophy of the mind. How we can or should conceive of the capacity of knowing proper to humans is played out across this spectrum. If humans are distinguished by reason alone, their knowledge is limited to the abstractive mode of knowing on the basis of sensible types, whereas the intuitive mode is reserved for the pure *intellectus* of angels. As far as humans are concerned, however, Bovelles rejects precisely this originally Scotist separation between abstractive knowledge and intuitive knowledge, the former being the only knowledge available to humans in their life. For Bovelles, by contrast, man is not only reason, but also *intellectus*: he is able to reach a state of fulfillment that raises him to the level of the *intellectus* of angels when his knowledge, originally abstractive, is capable of an intuitive force. Bovelles then talks of a *vis intuitiva* for the *intellectus* of man himself. For Bovelles, the spectrum of *ratio, intellectus, mens* is no longer a limiting principle, but a dynamic schema.

II. The Cartesian Distinction of the Different Modes of Thought: *Intelligere, Concipere, Comprehendere*

A radical shift in the world of the mind obviously occurs between Bovelles and Descartes. The vertical gradation of intellectual beings is no longer the measure of the capacity of fulfillment of the human mind. The enumeration in the "Second Meditation" is well known, in which the terms that are carefully differentiated by medieval and Renaissance Noetics are presented by Descartes as equivalent: "res cogitans, id est, mens, sive animus, sive intellectus, sive ratio" (*Meditationes de Prima Philosophia* in *Œuvres* [AT], 7:27). Now, there is a direct, immediate contrast between man's finite *intellectus* and God's infinite one. The distinctions that Descartes's philosophy sets in place no longer operate among nouns—*ratio, intellectus, mens*—designating both distinct faculties and ontologically different beings; rather, they work among verbal forms that signal the different ways of thinking and knowing proper to man: *intelligere, concipere, comprehendere* (the distinction is made particularly clear in Descartes's *Entretien avec Burman*, in *Œuvres* [AT] 5:154). Contemporary translators of Descartes, such as the duc de Luynes, seem curiously unaware of the distinction between *intelligere* and *concipere*,

and they often translate *intelligere* as "'to conceive." Yet, as Jean-Marie Beyssade suggests, following Descartes's detailed analysis, the gap between *intelligere* and *concipere* is the very gap between the idea and the concept. As for the difference between *intelligere* and *comprehendere*, this is a distinction of principle for the entirety of Cartesian metaphysics. The distinction is drawn in relation to our knowledge of the infinite being: we are capable of "knowing" it (*intelligere*)—or of apprehending it with our intellect (*intelliger* in French, even though this word was not yet in current usage at the time)—without for all that "understanding" it (*comprehendere*).

Descartes was not the first to apply this distinction or these terms to our knowledge of God. The distinction between *mente attingere* and *comprehendere* formulated by Descartes in a letter to Mersenne (January 21, 1641, in *Œuvres* [AT], 3:284), referring to a passage in Saint Augustine, turns out to follow precisely this distinction, as presented in Augustine's text:

> Attingere aliquantum mente Deum, magna beatitudo est: comprehendere autem, omnino impossibile.

> (To reach God in some way with our mind is a great happiness, but to understand Him is impossible.)

> (*Sermo* 117, chap. 3, 5, PL, vol. 38, col. 663; *Sermons*, trans. E. Hill)

It is therefore plausible that Descartes knew of this text by Augustine, which is not however, cited by Zbigniew Janowski in his *Index augustino-cartésien* (83–85). On the other hand, and since the focus of this entry is the transition from the Renaissance to the classical age, we should mention Nicholas of Cusa, who, two centuries before Descartes, had written in book 1 of his *Docte ignorance* that God is *intelligé de manière incompréhensible* (*incomprehensibiliter intelligitur*, "apprehended or 'intellected' without comprehension"). Cusanus's near-oxymoron has not been rendered faithfully by the French translators of the twentieth-century: Abel Rey in 1930 translated it the other way around as *compris sans être saisi* (understood without being grasped), while Maurice de Gandillac in 1942 translated the two words using the same term: *compris de façon incompréhensible* (comprehended incomprehensibly), thereby eliding the distinction between *intelligere* and *comprehendere*, possibly with a view to making the effect of the contrast more radical. The differentiated usage of the two terms is equally present in Cusanus's Latin. Does Cartesian metaphysics, then, simply take up Cusanus's distinction? This is certainly not the case. The *Meditations* do not adapt Cusanus's *docte ignorance* (learned ignorance) for the classical age. Book 1 of the *Docte ignorance* ended by stating the primacy of negative theology; Descartes, by contrast, emphasizes the fact that man is naturally capable of a "positive" knowledge or intellection of the infinite being. It is this capacity itself that characterizes the metaphysical way of thinking.

A tradition of interpretation that emerged in France in the second half of the twentieth century, however, has downplayed the importance of the Cartesian distinction between *intelligere* and *comprehendere*. To take an example: when Ferdinand Alquié wanted to justify the absence of the "Conversation with Burman" from his edition of Descartes's *Œuvres philosophiques*, he translated as *nous comprenons* (we understand) the verb *intelligimus* used by the philosopher in relation to our knowledge of God's perfections (see *Œuvres philosophiques*, 3:766). What is more, in his concern to promote the image of a pre-Kantian Descartes, he spoke in 1950 of an "unknowable transcendence" and of a "metaphysics of an inaccessible being" in relation to the God of the *Meditations* (*La Découverte métaphysique de l'homme chez Descartes*, 113 [p. 109 in 1987 ed.]). More recently, Jean-Luc Marion has developed a similar interpretation by invoking the "unknowability" of an "inaccessible" God in Descartes (*Questions cartésiennes* 2:233, 240). Both conclude by referring to the presence of a "negative theology," or *via negativa* in Descartes (Alquié, *La Découverte métaphysique*, 88; Marion, *Questions cartésiennes*, 246).

These interpretations tend toward replacing the Cartesian metaphysics of the positively known infinite with a theology of an incomprehensible omnipotence. Descartes, however, tells us something very different: in the "Third Meditation" (in *Œuvres* [AT], 7:45), the supremely knowing character (*summe intelligentem*) of the divine substance is affirmed *before* its omnipotence. From this one may then conclude that the name of the supremely "intelligent" being is intelligible to us only to the degree that the supreme being is indeed understood (*intelligo*) to be "supremely intelligent": "*Dei nomine intelligo . . . ,*" writes Descartes in the same sentence. One cannot emphasize enough, then, the importance of the Cartesian distinction between *intelligere* and *comprehendere*. At stake here, no doubt, is our perception of modern metaphysics, since we find in the *Meditations* a metaphysical thinking that does not subscribe to the Scholastic thesis (taken up by Kant in the modern age) of the impossibility for man to have any "intellectual intuition." An attentive rereading of Descartes's Latin texts might then contribute to a reevaluation of the intellective capacities of man, which should continue to inform our use of the word "intellect."

Emmanuel Faye

BIBLIOGRAPHY

Alquié, Ferdinand. *La Découverte métaphysique de l'homme chez Descartes*. Paris: Presses Universitaires de France, 1950. 1st reprint, 1987; 2nd reprint, 2000.

Augustine. *Sermo CXVII: De Verbis Evangelii Joannis*. Patrologia Latina. Vol. 38. Col. 661–71. Translation by Edmund Hill: "Sermon 117: On the Words of the Gospel of John." Pp. 209–33 in *Sermons*. Vol. 4. Edited by John E. Rotelle. Brooklyn: New City Press, 1990.

Bovelles, Charles de. *Quae hoc volumine continentur: Liber de intellectu; Liber de sensu; Liber de nihilo; Ars oppositorum; Liber de generatione; Liber de sapiente; Liber de duodecim numeris; Epistolae complures*. Stuttgart-Bad Cannstatt, Ger.: Friedrich Fromann, 1970. First published in 1511.

Cusanus, Nicolas [Nicolas of Cusa]. "De Coniecturis." In *Mutmaßungen*. Edited and translated by Josef Koch and Winfried Happ. Hamburg: Meiner, 1988. English translation by Jasper Hopkins: "On Surmises." Pp. 163–297 in *Metaphysical Speculations*, vol. 2. Minneapolis: Banning, 2000.

———. *De docta ignorantia* [*Die belehrte Unwissenheit*]. 2nd ed. 3 vols. Edited by Hans Gerhard Senger and Paul Wilpert. Translated by Paul Wilpert. Hamburg: Meiner, 1970–77. English translation by Germain Heron: *Of Learned Ignorance*. Introduction by D.J.B. Hawkins. 1954. Westport, CT: Hyperion, 1979. Heron's translation first published in 1954.

Descartes, René. *L'Entretien avec Burman*. Edited by Jean-Marie Beyssade. Paris: Presses Universitaires de France, 1981. Latin version (AT) edited by C. Adam and P. Tannery: pp. 154–79 in *Correspondance*, volume 5 of *Œuvres de Descartes* (AT). Paris: Vrin 1983. Volume 5 first published in 1903. English translation by John Cottingham: *Descartes' Conversation with Burman*. Oxford: Clarendon Press, 1976.

———. *Meditationes de prima philosophia*. Volume 7 of *Œuvres de Descartes* (AT), edited by C. Adam and P. Tannery. Paris: Vrin, 1983. Volume 7 first published in 1904. Translation by John Cottingham: *Meditations on First Philosophy, with Selections from the Objections and Replies*. Edited by J. Cottingham. Rev. ed. New York: Cambridge University Press, 1986.

———. *Œuvres de Descartes*. Edited by C. Adam and P. Tannery. 12 volumes. Paris: Vrin, 1983–. First published 1896–1913.

———. *Œuvres philosophiques*. 3 vols. Edited by Ferdinand Alquié. Paris: Garnier: 1963–73. Translation by John Cottingham, Robert Stoothoff, Dugald Murdoch, and Anthony Kenny: *The Philosophical Writings of Descartes*. Cambridge: Cambridge University Press, 1988.

———. "Responsiones Renati Des Cartes ad quasdam diffultates ex Meditationibus ejus, etc., ab ipso haustae." Pp. 146–79 in volume 5 of *Œuvres de Descartes* (AT), edited by C. Adam and P. Tannery. Paris: Vrin, 1983. Volume 5 first published in 1903.

Faye, Emmanuel. "Beatus Rhenanus lecteur et étudiant de Charles de Bovelles." *Annuaire des Amis de la Bibliothéque humaniste de Sélestat* (1995): 115–36.

Gouhier, Henri Gaston. "Intelligere et comprehendere." Pp. 208–14 in *La Pensée métaphysique de Descartes*. 4th. ed. Paris: Vrin, 2000.

———. *Philosophie et perfection de l'homme: De la Renaissance à Descartes*. Paris: Vrin, 1998.

Janowski, Zbigniew. *Index augustino-cartésien*. Paris: Vrin, 2000.

Marion, Jean-Luc. *Questions cartésiennes*. 2 vols. Paris: Presses Universitaires de France, 1996.

Renan, Ernest. *Averroès et l'averroïsme* [1852]. Edited by Alain de Libera. Paris: Maisonneuve et Laros - Dédale, 1997.

Valéry, Paul. *Cahiers*. 2 vols. Paris: Gallimard-Pléiade, 1973–74. Translation by Paul Gifford et al.: *Notebooks*. 3 vols. Edited by Brian Stimpson et al. New York: Peter Lang, 2000–2007.

INTELLECTUS (LATIN)

ARABIC	*'aql* [العقل]
ENGLISH	mind, intellect, understanding, meaning, thought
FRENCH	*intellect, entendement, sens, signification, pensée*
GERMAN	*Vernunft, Intellekt, Verstand, Sinn*
GREEK	*nous* [νοῦς], *epinoia* [ἐπίνοια], *logistikon* [λογιστικόν]
ITALIAN	*intelletto, significato*

➤ INTELLECT, *INTUITION, REASON*, UNDERSTANDING and CONSCIOUSNESS, GEMÜT, PERCEPTION, REPRÉSENTATION, SENSE, SOUL

Intellectus is one of the most polysemic terms in medieval Latin. It applies as much to "the meaning of" something (we talk about the *intellectus* of a sentence or of a judgment, Ger. *Sinn*, Fr. *sens*, It. *significato*), as to the verb "to mean" (in the sense of *vouloir-dire* in French, that is, a speaker or writer's intention or "meaning-to-say"), or to the "meaning understood" (that is, the "meaning," "intentional" or not, as it is "received" in the mind of the listener), and more broadly to "signification" or "significance," in the sense of "full of meaning," as is the case in the programmatic expression of theology and of exegesis: *intellectus fideli*, the "intellection" or "understanding" of faith. To mean, to understand, to comprehend: these different meanings do not pose a problem for the translator since vernacular language has often separated them out into terms that have evolved in different ways, to the exclusion of other uses. The word *intellectus* covers, in addition to the spheres of meaning and of understanding, almost all of the notions relating to thought, its activity, and its conditions of possibility. This is where the difficulties lie. As a fundamental term of ancient and medieval psychology, *intellectus* and the series of terms that are derived from or related to it (*intelligere, intellectualis, intelligibilis*) pose particular, if not insoluble, problems for the translator.

The most delicate problem comes from the fact that words such as the English "understanding," or the French *entendement*, or the German *Verstand*, which, at various times, have become accepted equivalents of the Latin *intellectus*, do not correspond to the field that it covers in the Peripatetic and Scholastic lexicon. The transformation of *intellectus* into "understanding" (*entendement*) marks a break in the history of theories of the soul. Indeed, the post-Lockean notion of "understanding" used by Leibniz to discuss the Averroist theory of the "unity of the intellect" no more overlaps with that of *intellectus* than the pair of terms *intellectus/ratio* overlaps with the pair *Verstand/Vernunft* that are Kant's legacy to modernity. Neither an empiricist psychology of understanding nor a theory of the transcendental are possible frameworks within which the Aristotelian *nous* [νοῦς] can be accommodated. The medieval *intellectus,* like the *nous* it harbors, is pulled not only between understanding and reason but also between different meanings of a (supposedly) identical faculty named *entendement*, *Verstand*, "understanding," assigned to it by different philosophers of language, theories, and often incommensurable assumptions. It is, then, an example of an untranslatable term, whose untranslatability flows from a certain undertranslation (its original dimension is only apparent in expressions like "intellectual intuition," the *intellektuelle Anschauung* that Kant rejected for understanding), as well as from a certain overtranslation. This latter has no better example than the case of Ernest Renan, who, because he interpreted *intellectus* as "reason" in the Kantian sense of the term, denounced in the noetics of Averroës an obscure and inadequate affirmation of the "universality of the principles of pure reason" and the no less confused affirmation of a "unity of psychological constitution in all of humankind" (Cf. E. Renan, *Averroès et l'averroïsme,* Maisonneuve et Larose, "Dédale," 1997, 109). Similarly, modern interpretations of the medieval theory of the intellect that replace the concepts of poietic intellect (or agent) and material (or possible) intellect with those of productive and of receptive mind bring to bear on the theory of *intellectus* models of reading that are as foreign to it as they are to the Peripatetic theory of *nous*, which is its source. To understand clearly why the *intellectus-nous* is neither Lockean understanding nor Kantian reason (*Vernunft*), one has to be clear about the inaugural distinction between *nous* and *dianoia* [διανοία] and to distinguish between the Peripatetic and non-Peripatetic uses of the term *intellectus*. Before the Latin translations of *De anima*, *intellectus* did not in fact refer to the *nous* of Aristotle and his Greek commentators but usually to the deeply Stoicist notion of color: *epinoia* [ἐπίνοια]. These two oppositions—*nous* vs *dianoia* and *nous* vs *epinoia*—mark two historical periods of *intellectus*: the one pre-Socratic, when it is synonymous with *opinio*, and the other Scholastic, when it refers to the *intellect-nous* of *De anima* 3.4–5, distinguishing it from *ratio*. We will focus in this entry on the Peripatetic usages, which are the most poorly served by modern translations.

I. The *Intellectus* between *Nous* and *Epinoia*

In the Scholastic vocabulary, *intellectus* has at least ten meanings that are more or less interconnected: (1) the Peripatetic *nous*, understood in the sense of "substance"; (2) the same, in the sense of "faculty" (Ger. *Vermögen*) or "faculty of knowledge" (Ger. *Erkenntnisvermögen*); (3) the nonsensible or suprasensible faculty of knowledge, but not distinct from *ratio* (that is, without taking into account the distinction between intuitive knowledge and discursive knowledge); (4) a cognitive activity, an act of knowledge, intellection or intelligence (synonym: *intelligentia*); (5) the nonsensible intuitive faculty of knowledge, which penetrates the intimate essence of things (according to the medieval etymology bringing together *intelligere* and *legere intus*, see Box 1); (6) the "*habitus* of principles," as distinct from *prudentia*, *sapientia*, and *scientia*, but also from *ratio* and *synteresis* (see CONSCIOUSNESS), the Greek *nous tôn archôn* [νοῦς τῶν ἀρχῶν], and the Latin *habitus principiorum* (for example, "intellectus dicitur habitus primum principiorum," Thomas Aquinas, *Summa theologica*, I, q. 58, 3c, "quendam specialem habitum, qui dicitur intellectus principiorum, ibid., q. 799, 12c); (7) intellectual inspection (Ger. *Einsicht*), synonymous with *intellegentia*, and the antonym of which is *ratio*; (8) conception, comprehension, interpretation, understanding, or meaning (Ger. *Verständnis*, *intellektuelle Auffassung*, for example "*verbum illud Philosophi universaliter verum est in omni intellectu* [this sentence of Aristotle's is absolutely true, whichever way one takes it]," Thomas Aquinas, *Summa theologica*, 1, q. 87, 1 *ad 3m*, "*secundum intellectum Augustini* [according to the sense in which St. Augustine understands it]," ibid. q. 58, 7 *ad 1m*); (9) a nonsensible representation (*Vernunftsvorstellung*) or a notion, synomous with *ratio*, in the sense of a definitional formula (for example, "*voces sunt signa intellectuum*," Thomas Aquinas, *Summa theologica*, q. 13, 1c, "*composito intellectum est in intellectu*," ibid., q. 17, 3a); (10) significance or meaning (Ger. *Bedeutung*, *Sinn*), synonymous with *ratio* (in the sense of the definitional formula, *logos*-formula, *sensus*, *significatio*, *virtus*, *vis* ["expressive force or impact"] of a word).

■ See Box 1.

1

On the etymology of *intellectus*

The word *intellectus* is formed by joining together *inter* and *legere*, where *legere* has the meaning of "to bind," "to bring together," "to collect," which is one of the meanings of the Greek *legô* [λέγω], and of the German *lesen* (see LOGOS). In the Middle Ages *intelligere*, sometimes attested as *intellegere*, is sometimes associated with *intra-* or *intus- legere*, *legere* here having the banal sense of "to read," and not to bind. Several good examples of this "etymology" are provided by Thomas Aquinas: "*Nomen intellectus sumitur ex hoc, quod intima rei cognoscit, est enim intelligere quasi intus legere* [The name 'intellect' is derived from the fact that it knows the intimate nature of a thing: indeed, *intelliger* is tantamount to saying 'to read inside']," *Quaestiones disputate De veritate*, q. 1, 12c); "*Dicitur autem intellectus ex eo quo intus legit intuendo essentiam rei; intellectus et ratio differunt quantum ad modum cognoscendi, quia scilicet intellectus cognoscit simplici intuitu, ratio vero discurrendo de uno in aliud* [it is called 'intellect' because it reads inside, that is, has an intuition of the essence of a thing; intellect and reason differ as to the mode of knowledge, since intellect is an act of simple intuition, whereas reason moves discursively from one thing to another]," *Summa theologica*, I, q. 59, a. 1, *ad. 1m*)

As we can see, certain Scholastic usages of *intellectus* refer to the *nôêsis* [νόησις] of Aristotle, understood at times as thought in general, and at other times as so-called "intuitive" thinking (contrasted to *dianoia* [διανοία] or "discursive" thinking). Other usages refer to the *nous* properly speaking, or the intellect, itself understood by some interpreters as "intuitive reason" and contrasted in this sense to *to dianoètikon* [τὸ διανοητικόν] or "discursive reason." Still others, finally, refer to that which is intelligible or thinkable (= *noêton* [νοητόν]), or even to the concept or the notion of something (= *noêma* [νόημα]). This polysemy, which means that the same term refers at once to a faculty, its operation, and its object, is one of the main difficulties in reading medieval texts, as well as Greek texts (see *aisthêsis* under the entry SENSE).

If in the Scholastic and "Arabo-Latin" tradition *intellectus* has the primary meaning of intellect, in the original "Greco-Latin" tradition (that of Boethius) it sometimes has the meaning of *epinoia* [ἐπίνοια] ("that which comes to mind," "reflection," "imagination," "thought," rather than, by extension, "intelligence" in general, or even "common sense"), which is usually translated as *opinio*. This usage is still attested in the thirteenth century, mainly in William of Moerbeke's translations (*De Anima, in the Version of William of Moerbeke: and the Commentary of St. Thomas Aquinas*, translated into English by Kenelm Foster and Silvester Humphries, Boston: Routledge and Kegan Paul, 1959). It is the word *intellectus*, and not *opinio*, that appears in the translation of the mute citation of *Isagoge*, through which Simplicius, in his *Commentary* on the *Categories*, dismisses the problem of universals from the field of logic: "*si enim sunt universalia sive intellectu solo esse habeant, alterius utique erit negotii inquirere* [to know if universals exist or only have their existence in thought, would in fact be an entirely different kind of study]" (cf. Simplicius, *In praedicamenta Aristotelis*, trans. William of Moerbeke, ed. A. Pattin, Louvain: Publications universitaires–Paris; Béatrice Nauwelaerts, *Corpus Latinum Commentariorum in Aristotelem Graecorum*, V/1, 1971, 71, 44–45. The use of *intellectus* to translate *epinoia*, interpreted this time in the sense of a concept that is "posterior in the order of being," is also attested in Moerbeke's translation of Simplicius's *Commentary*:

> aut quia aliqui perimebant universalia et intellectualia et ea quae qualitercumque intelliguntur aut quia etsi haec essent in natura, intellectus ipsorum posterius accepimus

> (either because some reject universals, intelligibles, and everything that is the object of some form of intellection, or because, even though they actually exist [in nature], we only get their concept [thought] afterwards)

> (Ibid., 261, 83–86)

We might also note in this passage the use of the word *intellectualia* in the sense of "intelligibles." We might finally point out that, in its pre-Socratic usage, *intellectus* is often contrasted both to "reason" and to "intelligence." This distinction, probably borrowed from Boethius's *Consolation of Philosophy*, disappears after the reception of Aristotle.

■ See Box 2.

2

Intellectus vs *intellegentia, ratio* vs *rationalitas*

Given the etymology they provide for *intellectus*, the medievals have a tendency to use *intelligentia* and *intellegentia* (where the form *legô*, "to read," is more immediately transparent) as equivalent terms. Authors in the twelfth century generally go along with Boethius in distinguishing between *sensus, imaginatio, ratio, intellectus* and *intelligentia/intellegentia*—*mens* staying, as it does for Saint Augustine, in a generic position, in the sense of "soul." This is the case, for example, with Isaac of Stella, *Epistula de anima*, PL 194, 1884C–1885B; Sermo, 4, PL 194, 1701C–1702C), with Alcher of Clairvaux (*De spiritu et anima*, chap. 4, PL 40, 782 and 7, PL 40, 787) and with Alain de Lille (PL 210, 673D). At that time *ratio, intellectus*, and *intelligentia/intellegentia* form a real triad of terms. For Isaac (a) "reason," *ratio*, is the "faculty of the soul that perceives the incorporeal forms of corporeal things," (b) "intellect," *intellectus*, is the "faculty of the soul that perceives the forms of truly incorporeal things," (c) and *intelligentia/intellegentia*, "intelligence," is the "faculty of the soul that has God as its immediate object." In

his *De anima*, written between 1126 and 1150, Dominique Gondissalvi developed the distinction by contrasting *intellectus* as a purveyor of science (*scientia*), which separates the intelligible from the sensible (by abstraction), with *intelligentia/intellegentia*, which generates wisdom (*sapientia*), "the superior eye" of the soul, devoted exclusively to contemplating pure intelligibles. This type of knowledge, the "intelligence" that surpasses "science," allows the soul to "contemplate itself" and to "reflect while contemplating them, as in a mirror, both God and the eternal intelligibles." It is assimilated to "rapture," the prototype of which is the ascension to the "third heaven" that the apostle Paul speaks of.

The terms *rationalitas* and *ratio* are often used in the Middle Ages in the obvious sense of "rational" or "discursive faculty" (= *dianoia*). In the treatise *De intellectibus* (whose title means "the intellections" and not "the intellects"), Abelard distinguishes rationality, imparted to all "rational" creatures, from the accomplished reason of those who are capable of exercising it fully. *Rationalitas*

and *ratio* are thus more or less distinguished as "reasoning" (capable of reason) and "rational" (as a positive predicate, referring to the fullness of reasoning in action, rationality as it is exercised). Cf. Abelard, *De intellectibus*:

> Rationality is not the same thing as reason: in fact, rationality belongs to all angelic and human minds, which is why one calls them rational; but reason only belongs to a few, as we have said, namely, only to the minds that are distinct. This is why I think that there is as much difference between rationality and reason, as there is between the power to run, and the power to run easily, according to which Aristotle calls runners "those who possess" the ease of movement of supple limbs. Thus, any mind that can discern using its own nature possesses rationality. But the only person to "possess" reason is the one who is in a state of being capable of exercising it easily, without being hindered by any weakness of his age, or by any bodily handicap, which would cause

him some disturbance, and make him mad or stupid.

(Abelard, *De intellectibus*, §8–9)

If we move on to the vernacular, it is Middle High German that offers the most interesting series of terms for considering the complex relations that developed subsequently in modern languages between *Vernunft* and *Verstand*, "understanding" and "reason." It is essentially a question of the pairs *vernünfi-cheit/vernünftecheit; vernunft; verstentenisse/verstantnisse*, attested in German mysticism, particularly but not exclusively in Meister Eckhart. On the face of it, the law of correspondence seems easy enough to establish: *vernunft* is understood as the equivalent of *ratio*; *verstentenisse/verstantnisse* as the equivalent of *intellectus*; and *venünfticheit/vernünftecheit* hovering somewhere between *intellectualitas* and *ratio*. This system of equivalences is, however, too schematic. In fact, the distinction *ratio/intellectus* continues into Scholastic vocabulary with the division of *intellectus* into *intellectus agens* and

intellectus possibilis, inherited from the Greco-Arabic exegesis of *De anima* 3.4–5. This basic distinction is also expressed in German medieval literature. One important witness here is the opuscule known as *Ein schoene ler von der selikeyt* (A beautiful theory of happiness), attributed to a certain Eckhart of Gründig, who expounds and discusses the theses of Meister Eckhart and of Dietrich of Freiburg on the nature of the beatitudes. In this treatise the "agent" intellect and the "possible" intellect clearly have their German equivalents: for the former, *diu würkendiu vernunft*, and for the latter, *diu müglichiu vernunft*. Cf. W. Preger, "*Der altdeutsche Tractat von der wirkenden und möglichen Vernunft*" [*Sitzb. Ak. Wiss. München, philos.-philol. hist Classe*, 1], 1871, 189, 1–16, for the agent intellect, and 188, 14–25, for the possible intellect. It does not appear possible then to consider that the opposition between *rationalitas* and *ratio* is the same as the German *vernünfti-cheit/vernünftecheit* vs. *vernunft*. All of these terms correspond more to *intellectus* than to the modern *Vernunft*. Moreover, in Meister

Eckhart *vernunftekeit* translates equally as *intellectualitas*, *intellegentia*, and *intellectus* [= *nous*].

BIBLIOGRAPHY

Abelard. *Des intellections–Tractatus de intellectibus*. Edited and translated by Patrick Morin. Paris: Vrin, 1994. Translation by Peter King: *Tractatus de intellectibus*, in Peter King, "Peter Abailard and the Problem of Universals in the Twelfth Century." PhD diss., Princeton University, 1982. Vol. 2 contains a complete translation of Abelard's *Tractatus de intellectibus*.

Guilfoy, Kevin. "Abelard on Mind and Cognition." In *The Cambridge Companion to Abelard*, edited by Jeffrey Brower and Kevin Guilfoy, 200–22. Cambridge: Cambridge University Press, 2004.

Libera, Alain de. "Sermo mysticus: La transposition du vocabulaire scolastique dans la mystique allemande du XIVe siècle." *Rue Descartes* 14 (1995): 41–73.

Urbani Ulivi, Lucia. *La psicologia di Abelardo e il Tractatus de intellectibus*. Rome: Edizioni di storia e letteratura, 1976.

II. *Intellectus* and the Vocabulary of the Peripatetic Noetics

The difficulty of the medieval lexicon of intellect derives first and foremost from the difficulty of Aristotle's vocabulary in *De anima*, and because of the continuous superimposition of translations and commentaries, from Greek to Latin, or from Greek to Arabic. As we read in *De anima* 3.5, the distinction between the different sorts of intellect is quite obscure. It merely touches on the ideas of dynamic intellect (through the phrase *touto de ho panta dunamei eikeina* [τοῦτο δὲ ὅ πάντα δυνάμει ἐκεῖνα]), of poietic intellect or intellect as agent (of the kind, τὸ αἴτιον καὶ ποιητικόν), and of passive intellect (*ho de pathêtikos nous* [ὁ δὲ παθητικὸς νοῦς])", without proposing any systematic construction between them. Indeed, it was the commentators of Aristotle, first among them being Alexander of Aphrodisias, who provided in advance the medieval notions of *intellectus*.

A. Agent intellect, hylic (material, possible) intellect

In *De intellectu*, Alexander of Aphrodisias attributes to Aristotle a distinction among three sorts of intellect: material intellect (*nous hulikos* [νοῦς ὑλικός]), the intellect "according to the habitus" (*nous kath'hexin* [νοῦς καθ' ἕξιν]), and the poietic intellect (*nous poiêtikos* [νοῦς ποιητικός]—"*nous esti kata Aristotelê trittos* [νοῦς ἐστι κατὰ 'Αριστοτέλη τριττός]" (the intellect is threefold according to Aristotle) (cf. P. Moraux, *Alexandre exégète de la noétique d'Aristote*, Liège, Faculté de philosophie-Paris, E. Droz, "Bibliothèque de la faculté de philosophie et lettres de l'Université de Liège," Fasc. XCIX, 1942, 185; ed. Bruns, 106, 19). This tripartite distinction was adopted by all of the commentators and became so widely accepted as Aristotelian that the Arabic translation on which

Averroës based his *Long Commenary* of *De anima* incorporated Alexander's division into Aristotle's text itself.

- See Box 3.

In fact, not only does Aristotle not talk of *nous kath' hexin*, but the very distinction between agent intellect and hylic or possible intellect is far from being as clearly formulated in *De anima* as Alexander leads us to think. Besides the few lines in *De anima* 3.4 and 5, devoted to the intellect as "analogous to matter," similar to a "tabula rasa," which also mention the "possible" intellect, and besides the extremely enigmatic passage in 3.5, referring to the intellect that "produces" intelligibles, one would be hard pressed to cite any text by Aristotle that offered an actual "theory of the intellect." We have to turn instead to the noetic works of Alexander that have come down to us, that is, the *Peri psuchês* [Περὶ ψυχῆς] (*De anima*), edited by I. Bruns in 1887 (*Supplementum Aristotelicum*, II, 1, Berlin, 1892, 1–100) and the *De anima liber alter*, also called *Mantissa* (Bruns, ibid., 101–86), which is a collection of twenty-five treatises comprising notably, in number one, a second and short version of *Peri psuchês* (Bruns, 101, 1–106, 17) and in number two (Bruns, ibid., 106, 18–113, 24) the famous *Peri nou* [Περὶ νοῦ] (On the intellect), in order to look for an exposition of the Peripatetic theory of the intellect, which, through its Greek and Arabic commentators, has permeated medieval Scholastics.

B. Speculative intellect, theoretical intellect

Scholastic philosophers often used the expression *intellectus speculativus*, which modern translations often render with a calque ("speculative intellect," Fr. *intellect spéculatif*, It. *intelletto speculativo*, etc.). While this is not wrong, the literal

3

A translation by Alexander incorporated into Aristotle's original text

The *Textus* 17 = *De anima* 3.5, 430a10–14 on which Averroës comments is the following:

> Et quia, quemadmodum in Natura, est aliquid in unoquoque genere quod est materia (et est illud quod est illa omnia in potentia), et aliud quod est causa et agens (et hoc est illud propter quod agit quidlibet, sicut dispositio artificii apud materiam), necesse est ut in anima existant hee differentie.

(And since, just as in Nature, there is in each kind something that is matter [and is that which is potential in all of these things], and another thing that is cause and agent [and is that by virtue of which everything acts, as is the case with art in relation to matter], these differences also necessarily exist in the soul too.)

(Crawford ed., 436, 1–7)

The original in Tricot's French translation, is as follows:

> Mais puisque, dans la nature toute entière, on distingue d'abord quelque chose qui sert de matière à chaque genre (et c'est ce qui est en puissance tous les êtres du genre), et ensuite une autre chose qui est la cause et l'agent parce qu'elle les produit tous, situation dont celle de l'art par rapport à sa matière est un exemple, il est nécessaire que, dans l'âme aussi, on retrouve ces différences.

(Vrin, 1992, p. 181)

(But since, in all of nature, we distinguish first of all something that is matter in each genus [and it is that which is potential in all of the beings of a genus], and then another thing which is that cause and agent because it produces them all, a situation of which the relationship of art to its matter is an example, we also necessarily find these differences in the soul.)

The decisive change (Alexander's incorporation) occurs in the *Textus* 18 = *De anima* 3.5, 430a14–17, where three differences are mentioned, contrary to the binary division maintained in *Textus* 17:

> Oportet igitur ut in ea sit intellectus qui est intellectus secundum quod efficitur omne, et intellectus qui est intellectus secundum quod facit ipsum intelligere omne, et intellectus secundum quod intelligit omne, quasi habitus, qui est quasi lux. Lux enim quoquo modo etiam facit colores qui sunt in potentia colores in actu.

(So within it there is also necessarily [1] an intellect that is intellect to the extent that it becomes all, and [2] an intellect that is an intellect to the extent that it allows it to conceive of all, and [3] an intellect to the extent that it conceives of everything as a habitus does—that is, in a manner resembling the action of light. For in a certain way, light also makes potential colors into actual colors.)

(Crawford ed., 437, 1–7)

To be compared with Tricot's French:

> Et, en fait, on y distingue, d'une part, l'intellect qui est analogue à la matière, par le fait qu'il devient tous les intelligibles, et d'autre part, l'intellect [qui est analogue à la cause efficiente], parce qu'il les produit tous, attendu qu'il est une sorte d'état analogue à la lumière: car, en un certain sens, la lumière, elle aussi, convertit les couleurs en puissance, en couleurs en acte.

(Vrin, 1992, 181–82)

(And indeed, we can distinguish in it, on the one hand, the intellect that is analogous to matter, by the fact that it becomes all of the intelligibles, and on the other hand, the intellect [that is analogous to the efficient cause], because it produces all, considering that it is in a sort of analogous state to light: for, in a certain sense, light too converts potential colors into actual colors.)

---

translation masks its homonymy. The expression derives from the Latin translation of the *Long Commentary* of Averroës on *De anima*; the analysis of different passages of the Aristotelian *De anima* and its adoption by Averroës demonstrate that the "speculative" intellect in fact refers to three sorts of entities: (1) the faculty referred to by Aristotle as "theoretical intellect" in *De anima* 3.6, 429.25ff. (Arabic *'aql naẓarī* [العقل النظري]), as opposed to the "practical intellect" of *De anima* 3.7, 421a1ff. (Arabic *'aql 'amali* [العقل العملي]); (2) the "composite" of the material intellect and the agent intellect, which Averroës calls "produced intellect" (*factus*), in other words, not a faculty, but an act or activity (that is, the "intellection of indivisibles," according to Aristotle, *ta adiaireta* [τὰ ἀδιαίρετα], *ta hapla* [τὰ ἁπλᾶ], and the intellection of the "composites," or objects of judgment); (3) the agent intellect insofar as it is joined to the material intellect and is for man the essential "form." This is a meaning that originated with Themistius and which he extrapolated from a passage in *De anima* 2. 2, 413b24–25 (Tricot, 76-77), where in speaking of the "intellect and of the theoretical faculty," Aristotle indicates that "it seems indeed that this is an entirely different type of soul, and that on its own it can be separated, as the eternal, from the corruptible" (cf. Themistius, in *III De anima, ad* 430a 20–25; Verbeke, 232, 44–46 and 233, 80–82). These three senses obviously cannot work concurrently. The immediate context allows one in theory to determine the meaning. The Latin *res speculativae* generally refers to the objects of the activity of the theoretical intellect in the second sense of the term, that is, first and foremost, the indivisibles invoked in *De anima* 3.6, 430a26–31. It is worth pointing out that this activity in Averroës is called "representation" (*taṣawwur* [التصوّر], Latin *formatio*, "forming," which survives in "to form a plan," in the sense of "to conceive of a plan"), in that it applies to intelligibles envisaged in themselves, outside of any predication, while the consideration of the "noêmes" (*ma'nā* [المعنى], "intention"), the combination of which in predications "contains truth or falsity," is called "consent" (*taṣdīq* [التصديق], Lat. *fides*, "faith"). In the Arabo-Latin translations of Aristotle (as well as in those of Avicenna and of Averroës), the expression corresponding most often to *noein* [νοεῖν] is *formare per intellectum* (the substantive being *formatio per intellectum* = "representation by the intellect," Arabic *al-taṣawwur bi-al-'aql* [التصوّر بالعقل]).

C. Habitual intellect, acquired intellect, common intellect

The expression "*intellect in habitus*" or "habitual intellect" (*intellectus in habitu*) corresponds to the *nous kath' hexin* of Alexander of Aphrodisias. The notion of *habitus* as the power of the intellect to accomplish its own action—intellection—is illustrated in Alexander by the metaphor of the artisan: "The intellect has another degree, namely when it thinks and possesses the *habitus* to conceive, and is able to assume the forms of the intelligibles through its own power, a power one might compare to the power of those who have the *habitus* within them to make things, and who are capable of producing their own works" (cf. Théry, 76). The expression *intellectus in habitu* appears frequently in Avicenna's Latin texts, in the Latin translation of al-Ghazālī, and from there in most of the Scholastics. Generally speaking, what we call "acquired intellect" or "actual intellect" (*in effectu*) is the intellect that "considers, in act, the conclusions drawn from propositions which are self-evident," while "habitual intellect" refers to those same conclusions insofar as the intellect "possesses them without actually thinking of them." The *intellectus in habitu*, however, is often assimilated to the *habitus principiorum* discussed in the *Second Analytics*. It is in this sense that it appears, for example, in Albert the Great, when, in the *Summa de creaturis*, IIa paragraphs, q. 54, he contrasts the "habitual" intellect, in the sense of the "possession of principles that have not been received from a master," which we know "by simply knowing the terms that compose it," with the "acquired" (*acquisitus*) intellect, meaning the possession of "principles that one acquires in contact with a master through teaching and studying." Since the "acquired" intellect can also refer to the intellect "acquired externally" (*adeptus*, Greek *thurathen* [θύραθεν]), in the more or less mystical sense, extrapolated by Alexander (see Box 4) from a passage in the *Parva naturalia* (*De generatione animalium*, 736b20–29), there is a considerable amount of terminological confusion. The main source of confusion comes from the fact that underneath apparently similar Latin expressions we find notions that are sometimes Greek, sometimes Arabic, and sometimes Greco-Arabic in origin, whose meaning varies from the union or "conjunction" (Lat. *conjunctio, copulatio, connexio*, Ar. *ittiṣāl* [الاتصال]) of the human soul and the separate agent intellect, to the simple acquisition, through teaching or through reason, of a stock of intelligibles.

■ See Box 4.

The notions of *intellectus adeptus* (Ar. *al-'aql mustafād* [العقل المستفاد] and of *intellectus adeptus agens* ("acquired intellect agent," Ar. *al-'aql al-mustafād al-fā'il* [العقل المستفاد الفاعل]), expressing the state of *connexio*, are among the most obscure in medieval psychology. While he may not be able to determine the exact meaning of the doctrines he is confronted with (and which vary considerably from one author to the next, from Alexander to al-Fārābī, and from Avicenna to Averroës), the reader of the noetic texts must always, going back to the Greek, and following Alexander, distinguish between at least two incompatible meanings of the "acquired" intellect: (1) the agent intellect acquired "from outside," that is the *nous ho thurathen* [νοῦς ὁ θύραθεν] (Lat. *adeptus*), and (2) scientific knowledge acquired from the first intelligibles, with or without the help of a master, that is *nous epiktêtos* [νοῦς ἐπίκτητος] (Lat. *acquisitus, possessus, possessivus*].

Although the notion of "common intellect" is sometimes seen as identical to that of the "habitual" intellect, it has an original content. Grafted on to the Aristotelian doctrine of the patient (*passivus, passibilis*) intellect, this creation by Themistius in fact carries a clearly Platonic content, bearing no relation to the pair *in habitu* vs *in effectu*.

■ See Box 5.

D. *Intellectus passibilis* vs. *intellectus possibilis*

De anima 3.5, 430a20–25 alludes to a so-called "patient" or "passive" intellect (*nous pathêtikos* [νοῦς παθητικός]), which is often confused with the "hylic" or material intellect (*nous hulikos* [νοῦς ὑλικός]) of Alexander, that is, the "possible" intellect of the Scholastics. Because it was easy to confuse

---

4

The "acquired" intellect: A misinterpretation that became a technical term

Alexander interpreted the Aristotelian notion of intellect "from outside" in a very particular sense: for him, it was a question of the agent intellect, acquired by the soul at each contemplation of the separate intelligible. Cf. Alexander of Aphrodisia, *De anima*:

> When the intelligible is by its own nature exactly as it is thought [= intelligible] ... it remains incorruptible when it ceases to be thought; so the intellect which thought it is also incorruptible: not the material intellect which serves as its

support (for it is corrupted at the same time as the soul is corrupted, since it is a power of the soul, and at the same time as it is corrupted, its habitus, its capacity and its perfection are also corrupted), but the intellect which, when it was thinking it, had become identical to it in its act (for, given that it becomes similar to each content of thought when this content is thought, what it thinks becomes exactly what it is thinking. And this intellect is the one that comes to us from outside and which is incorruptible. ... So all those

who are intent on having something of the divine within themselves will have to endeavor to succeed in thinking something of this kind.

(Bruns ed., 90, 11–91, 7)

It is worth noting that in the fragments of Theophrastus that have survived we find, by contrast, the question of knowing in what sense the intellect that is "from outside" (*exôthen* [ἔξωθεν]) or "added on" (*epithetos* [ἐπίθετος]) can be said to be "congenital" (*sumphuês* [συμφυής]).

5

The common intellect according to Themistius

The expression "common intellect," coined by Themistius and widely adopted in medieval literature under the name *intellectus communis*, was the source of a great deal of confusion. Despite what the Latin suggests, the *intellectus communis* was not a "common" or "general" concept, as opposed to a "singular" or "particular" concept. The "common intellect" (*koinos nous* [κοινὸς νοῦς]) was the name Themistius gave to Aristotle's passible intellect. Cf. Themistius,

In III De anima, ad 430a 25, and Verbeke, 239, 1–241, 34, who discusses the "so-called 'common' intellect in the way that man is composed of a soul and a body in which anger and desire (Latin *concupiscentia*) reside, which Plato considers corruptible." The "common" or "passible" intellect of Themistius illustrates the Platonic thesis according to which "the intellect alone is immortal, whereas the passions, and the 'reason inherent in them,' which Aristotle

calls the *passive intellect*, are corruptible." Themistius also supports the thesis according to which "human passions *are not entirely irrational, since they listen to reason*, and are susceptible to education and instruction."

BIBLIOGRAPHY

Verbeke, Gérard. *Moral Education in Aristotle.* Washington, DC: Catholic University of America Press, 1990.

---

passibilis and *possibilis* in medieval manuscripts, a theory of the corruptibility of the passive (possible) part of the intellective soul was often attributed to Aristotle, when there was nothing to really justify this. Cf. Aristotle, *De anima*:

> Actual knowledge is identical with its object: in the individual, potential knowledge is in time prior to actual knowledge, but absolutely it is not prior even in time. It does not sometimes think and sometimes not think. When separated it is alone just what it is, and this alone is immortal and eternal (we do not remember because, while this is impossible, passive thought is perishable); and without this nothing thinks.
>
> (Aristotle, *De anima*, 3.5, 430a, Barnes, *On the Soul*, 1: 684)

For ancient and medieval interpreters the intellect that Tricot's French translation presents as "patient intellect" is not the possible or material intellect but either (1) the "speculative" or "theoretical" intellect (Ar. *'aql naẓarī* [العقل النظري]), which, as we saw, refers both to an actual theoretical intelligible (what Alexander calls "habitual intellect" or the intellect *in habitus*) and to the very act of "speculating" (Lat. *considerare*), which, like any physical act or act of the mind, can be engendered and corrupted; or (2) the intellect that Themistius calls "common intellect" (see Box 5); or (3) as Averroës maintains, "the forms of the imagination as the cogitative faculty proper to man acts upon them." In none of these three cases is it the material or possible intellect itself. The confusion between possible intellect and passible intellect has determined the modern interpretation of Averroism. This is well testified by Leibniz's summary of the noetics of Averroës, in the course of which the transformation of *intellectus* into "understanding" (*entendement*) takes place, and which attests to the paradigm shift between medieval psychology and modern psychology mentioned earlier (see UNDERSTANDING).

■ See Box 6.

III. "Intellectus" and Its Derived Terms

Several adjectives are formed from *intellectus*. The adjective *intellectivus, -a, -um* (antonym: *sensitivus, sensibilis*) is

the most widespread. It is used in the most diverse contexts: one talks of *cognitio*, of *apprehensio*, of *operatio*, of *potentia*, of *intentio*, and of *visio i.*, but also of *memoria i.*, and of *habitus i.*, as well as of *anima* and of *substantia i.* If the ancient German translations render *intellectivus* by *übersinnlich*, "suprasensible," nowadays one talks more readily of "intellective," or "intellectual," and even "noetic" knowledge. The term "intellectual" is normally reserved for *intellectualis, -e*, the semantic spectrum of which is almost identical to that of *intellectivus*: one talks of *conceptio*, *cognitio*, *apprehensio*, *existimatio*, *operatio*, *intentio*, *visio i.*, but also of *desiderium*, *appetitus*, *amor*, *delectatio i.* and even of *species i.* (synonymous with *intelligibilis*). Understood broadly, *intellectualis, -e*, characterizes the cognitive function of the intellect, whether it is intuitive or discursive (synonym: *intellectivus, rationalis*); strictly speaking, *intellectualis* applies only to the intuitive cognitive function of the intellect, as distinct from reason (antonym: *rationalis*). It is in this sense that Thomas Aquinas describes angels as "intellectual beings":

> Therefore they [angels] are called intellectual beings (*intellectuales*), because even with ourselves the things which are instantly [*statim* = nondiscursive, sudden, in a single act of intuition] apprehended are said to be "intellected" (*intelligi*); hence intellect is defined as the habit of first principles (*habitus primorum principiorum*). But human souls which acquire knowledge of truth by the discursive method are called rational (*animae ver humane, quae veritatis notitiam per quendam discursum adquirunt, dicuntur rationales*).
>
> (*The Summa Theologica of Saint Thomas Aquinas*, trans. Fathers of the English Dominican Province, rev. Daniel J. Sullivan, 2 vol., London: William Benton, 1952. Vol. 1, q. 58, Art. 3, [Thomas Aquinas's *Answer*], 302)

The noun *intellectualitas* (antonym: *sensibilitas*) usually refers to the state of being intelligible—*intellectualitas* thus has the meaning more of intelligibility than of intellectuality (*Summa theologica* III, q. 23, 2c: "*no autem secundum intellectualitatem, quia forma domus in materia non est intelligibilis*," where *intellectualitas* refers to a

6

Leibniz and Averroës: Medieval psychology and modern psychology

By analogy to the theological expression "monophysite," referring to the thesis of the one nature of Christ (and not Christ's double nature, as divine and human), Leibniz coins the word "monopsychite" to refer to the Averroist thesis of the one intellect, which he presents as a return to the pristine nature of the Soul of the Stoic world:

> Plato's soul of the world has been taken in this sense by some, but there is more indication that the Stoics succumbed to the universal soul which swallows all the rest. Those who are of this opinion might be called "Monopsychites," since according to them there is in reality only one soul that subsists.

> (G. W. Leibniz, *Theodicy: Essays on the Goodness of God, the Freedom of Man and the Origin of Evil*, ed. Austin Farrer, trans. E. M. Huggard, LaSalle, IL: Open Court, 1985, 79)

This single *intellectus* is, however, baptized "Mind," and even then not so much "single" as "universal." Leibniz sometimes coordinates "Mind" with *intellectus*, translated as "understanding" (*entendement*), with *intellectus agens* becoming "active understanding," as opposed to "passive understanding," an expression translating an *intellectus patiens* that has no real equivalent in medieval texts, which talk of either *intellectus possibilis* (possible or "material" intellect), or *intellectus passibilis* (imagination), thereby giving rise to much confusion:

> Some discerning people have believed and still believe today, that there is only one single spirit, which is universal and animates the whole universe and all its parts, each according to its structure and the organs which it finds there, just as the same wind current causes different organ pipes to give off different sounds. Thus they also hold that when an animal has sound organs, the spirit produces the effect of a particular soul in it but that when the organs are corrupted, this particular soul reduces to nothing or returns, so to speak, to the ocean of the universal spirit. Aristotle has seemed to some to have had an opinion approaching this, which was later revived by Averroës, a celebrated Arabian philosopher. He believed that there is an *intellectus agens*, or "active understanding," and that the former, coming from without, is eternal and universal for all, while the passive understanding, being particular for each, disappears at man's death. This was the doctrine of certain Peripatetics two or three centuries ago, such as Pomponatius, Contarini, and others, and one recognizes traces of it in the late Mr. Naudé.

> (Leibniz's "Considérations sur la doctrine d'un Espirit universel unique" [1702], in *Système nouveau de la nature et de la communication des substances et autres textes* (1690–1703), Eng. trans. Leroy E. Loemker, "Reflections on the Doctrine of a Single Universal Spirit" [1702], in *Philosophical Papers and Letters*, vol. 2, Dordrecht, Neth.: Kluwer, 1989, 554)

Leibniz's interpretation of *De anima* 3.5, 430a20–25, and his reading of Averroës's interpretation of Aristotle, are without foundation. For Averroës, the *intellectus passibilis* is nothing but the images that are subject to the activity of the *vis cogitativa*, a condition sine qua non of the activity of the material or possible intellect (see INTENTION, Box 2):

> Now [Aristotle] understands here by *passible intellect* the forms of the imagination as the cogitative faculty proper to man acts upon them. Indeed, this faculty has a rational character, and its activity consists either in leaving the "intention" of the imagined form with the individual, in his memory, or in distinguishing it from him in the "formative" faculty [= *al-muṣawwira* (المصوّرة)] and the imagination. Now, it is clear that the intellect we call "material" receives the imagined entities after this distinction. Consequently, the passible intellect is necessary for the conception by the [material] intellect. Aristotle thus said quite rightly: *And we do not remember, for it is not passible, while the passible intellect is corruptible: and without that, it conceives nothing*. That is to say: without the imaginative and cogitative faculty, the intellect we call "material" conceives nothing.

> (Averroës, *In III De anima*, commentary 20)

mode of cognizability, Ger. *Erkennbarkeit*). The word can however also refer to the fact of being endowed with thought (for example "*intellectualitas consequitur immaterialitatem*," *Summa theologica* I, q. 105, 3c). The neuter plural noun *intellectualia* denotes either the universals (intelligibles) or the separate substances, as objects of philosophical theology (intelligent intelligibles). The context generally allows one to determine the meaning. The verb *intelligere/intellegere*, whose meaning is apparent (= Gr. *noein* [νοεῖν]), remains difficult to translate. The main translations suggested range from "conceptualize" or "think (noetically)" in English, to *penser*, *concevoir par l'intellect*, or *intelliger* in French (the latter a neologism enabling the series *intellect, intelligible, intelliger* to be preserved). None of these is entirely satisfactory.

Alain de Libera

BIBLIOGRAPHY

Adamson, Peter, and P. E. Pormann, trans. *The Philosophical Works of al-Kindi*. Karachi: Oxford University Press, forthcoming.

Averroës. *Commentarium magnum in Aristotelis De anima libros*. Edited by F. Stuart Crawford. Cambridge: Medieval Academy of America, 1953. Translation, introduction, and notes by Richard C. Taylor with Thérèse-Anne Druart: *Long Commentary on the De Anima of Aristotle*. New Haven, CT: Yale University Press, 2009. Translation, introduction, and notes by Alain de Libera: *L'intelligence et la pensée: Grand commentaire du De anima: Livre 3 (429 a 10–435 b 25)*. Paris: Flammarion, 1998.

Avicenna. *Liber De anima, seu Sextus De Naturalibus: Édition critique de la traduction latine médiévale*. Edited by S. van Riet. 2 vols. Louvain, Belg.: Éditions orientalistes, 1968. *Avicenna's De anima (Arabic text): Being the Psychological part of Kitāb al-Shifā'*. Edited by F. Rahman. London: Oxford University Press, 1959. Translation by Edward Abbott Van Dyck: *A Compendium on the Soul*. Verona, It.: Paderno, 1906. "Avicenna on Common Nature." In *Medieval Philosophy: Essential Readings with Commentary*, edited by Gyula Klima, with Fritz Allhoff and Anand Jayprakash Vaidya. Malden, MA: Blackwell, 2007.

Bakker, Paul J.J.M, and Johannes M.M.H. Thijssen, eds. *Mind, Cognition and Representation: The Tradition of Commentaries on Aristotle's* De Anima. Aldershot, UK: Ashgate, 2007.

Blumenthal, H. J. *Soul and Intellect: Studies in Plotinus and Later Neoplatonism.* Aldershot, UK: Variorum, 1993.

Davidson, Herbert A. *Alfarabi, Avicenna, and Averroes, on Intellect: Their Cosmologies, Theories of the Active Intellect, and Theories of Human Intellect.* New York: Oxford University Press, 1992.

Endress, Gerhard, and Jan Aertsen, with Klaus Braun, eds. *Averroes and the Aristotelian Tradition: Sources, Constitution, and Reception of the Philosophy of Ibn Rushd (1126–1198): Proceedings of the Fourth Symposium Averroicum, Cologne, 1996.* Leiden, Neth.: Brill, 1999.

al-Fārābī. "De Intellectu et Intellecto." Edited and translated by Étienne Gilson. "Les sources gréco-arabes de l'Augustinisme avicennisant." *Archives d'histoire doctrinale et littéraire du Moyen Age* 4 (1929–1930): 108–41. Rpt. Paris: Vrin, 1981.

———. "On the Intellect." In *Classical Arabic Philosophy: An Anthology of Sources.* Edited and translated by Jon McGinnis and David C. Reisman, 68–78. Indianapolis, IN: Hackett, 2007.

Giele, Maurice, Fernand Van Steenberghen, and Bernard Bazán, eds. *Trois commentaires anonymes sur le Traité de l'âme d'Aristote.* Philosophes médiévaux. Vol. 11. Louvain, Belg.: Publications universitaires, 1971.

Hasse, Dag Nikolaus. *Avicenna's De Anima in the Latin West: The Formation of a Peripatetic Philosophy of the Soul, 1160–1300.* London: Warburg Institute, 2000.

Jolivet, Jean, ed. and trans. *L'intellect selon Kindī.* Leiden, Neth.: Brill, 1971.

Kelly, Brendan R. "On the Nature of the Human Intellect in Aristotle's *De anima*: An Investigation into the Controversy Surrounding Thomas Aquinas' *De unitate intellectus contra Averroistas.*" PhD diss., University of Notre Dame, 1995.

Libera, Alain de. *Albert le Grand et la philosophie.* Paris, Vrin, 1990.

———. "Existe-t-il une noétique avveroïste? Note sur la réception latine d'Averroès au XIIIᵉ siècle." In *Averroismus im Mittelalter und in der Renaissance*, edited by F. Niewöhner and L. Sturlese, 51–80. Zurich: Spur, 1994.

———. *L'unité de l'intellect: Commentaire du De unitate intellectus contra Averroistas de Thomas d'Aquin.* Paris: Vrin, 2004.

Libera, Alain de, Abdelali Elamrani-Jamal, and Alain Galonnier, eds. *Langages et philosophie: Hommage à Jean Jolivet.* Paris: Vrin, 1997.

McCarthy, R., trans. "Al-Kindi's Treatise on the Intellect." *Islamic Studies* 3 (1964): 119–49.

McInerny, Ralph M. *Aquinas against the Averroists: On There Being Only One Intellect.* West Lafayette, IN: Purdue University Press, 1993.

Perler, Dominik, ed. *Ancient and Medieval Theories of Intentionality.* Leiden, Neth.: Brill, 2001.

Schroeder, Frederic M., and Robert B. Todd, eds. and trans. *Two Greek Aristotelian Commentators on the Intellect: The "De intellectu" Attributed to Alexander of Aphrodisias and Themistius' Paraphrase of Aristotle "De Anima" 3.4–8.* Toronto: Pontifical Institute of Mediaeval Studies, 1990.

Siger de Brabant. *Quaestiones in tertium De anima. De anima intellectiva. De aeternitate mundi: Édition critique.* Edited by Bernardo Bazán. Louvain, Belg.: Publications universitaires, 1972. Translation and introduction by Cyril Vollert, Lottie H. Kendzierski, and Paul M. Byrne: *On the Eternity of the World (De aeternitate mundi).* Milwaukee, WI: Marquette University Press, 1964. "Siger of Brabant on the Intellective Soul." In *Medieval philosophy: Essential Readings with Commentary*, edited by Gyula Klima, with Fritz Allhoff and Anand Jayprakash Vaidya. Malden, MA: Blackwell, 1990.

Thomas Aquinas. *The Commentary of St. Thomas Aquinas on Aristotle's* Treatise on the soul. Translated by R. A. Kocourek. St. Paul, MN: College of St. Thomas, 1946.

———. *On the Unity of the Intellect against the Averroists [De unitate intellectus contra Averroistas].* Translated and with introduction by Beatrice H. Zedler. Milwaukee, WI: Marquette University Press, 1968. Translation, introduction, bibliography, and notes by Alain de Libera: *L'unité de l'intellect contre les averroïstes: Suivi des textes contre Averroès antérieurs à 1270.* Paris: Flammarion, 1994.

INTENTION

ARABIC	*ma'nā* [المعنى]
	ma'qūl [معقول]
FRENCH	*intention*
GERMAN	*Intention, übersinnliches Erkenntnisbild, Vorstellung der Vernunft, Begriff*
GREEK	*noêma* [νόημα]
ITALIAN	*intenzione*
LATIN	*intentio*

➤ CONCEPT, CONSCIOUSNESS, DASEIN, EPOCHÉ, ERLEBEN, *FORM, IMAGE,* LOGOS, OBJECT, *PHÉNOMÈNE,* REALITY, REPRÉSENTATION, RES, SACHVERHALT, SENSE, SOUL, UNIVERSALS, WILL

"Intention" is a doubly polysemic term. As well as the equivocation that exists in French or Italian between the accepted meaning of the term—that of intention as in "to intend to" or as in "moral intention"—and the psycho-phenomenological meaning (which does not exist in German, where the first meaning is expressed as *Absicht*), the term presents, in this second, psycho-phenomenological register, a radical ambiguity, and is deeply divided between divergent philosophical paradigms. Indeed, the semantic field of "intention" covers a series of distinct phenomena, whose progressive coordination in the history of philosophy partly explains how saturated the modern notion of intentionality has become, torn as it is between the Husserlian phenomenological model, and that of the philosophy of mind. Thus, as Hilary Putnam has shown, the term "intentionality" has, in actual usage, widely diverse senses, namely, (1) for words, sentences, and other representations to have a meaning; (2) for representations to be able to designate (that is, to be true for) an actually existing thing, or, when there are several things, to designate each one of these; (3) for representations to be able to apply to something that does not exist; and (4) for a "state of mind" to be able to apply to a "state of affairs" (Putnam, *Representation and Reality*, 1). We will attempt to show here how the same word has come to mean, in German and thereafter in the other languages of philosophy, "the intentionality of linguistic expressions [*die Intentionalität von sprachlichen Äußerungen*]," the intentionality of acts of the mind or of thought (*die Intentionalität von Denktaten*), or that of acts of perception (*die Intentionalität von Wahrnehmungen*).

I. Intention and Meaning

The relation between intention and meaning, or sense, is attested in several theses in Edmund Husserl's *Ideen*, especially when he defines the "fundamental element of intentionality" by equating the "intentional object [*Objekt*]" with "objective sense or meaning," and posits that "to have a meaning, to aim at some meaning," is the fundamental character of all consciousness, which as a consequence is not only lived experience, but a lived experience that has a "noetic" meaning ("*Sinn zu haben, bzw. etwas 'im Sinne zu haben' ist der Grundcharakter alles Bewußtseins, das darum nicht nur überhaupt Erlebnis, sondern sinnhabendes, 'noetisches' ist,*" *Ideen* 1, §90, p. 185 [206], trans. Kersten). In fact, the distortions or gaps that Putnam points out are in part due to the fact that the Husserlian intentional lived experience is assigned two aspects, a "noetic" aspect and a "noematic" aspect; the latter includes precisely the sense "separated out from this lived experience, insofar as it casts its look appropriately." The "sense" in question is not, however, "significance" or "meaning" as it is commonly understood, but concerns existence and nonexistence.

The "situation" that, according to Husserl, defines "sense" is the fact that "the non-existence (or the conviction of non-existence) of the objectivated or thought of Object pure and simple pertaining to the objectivation in question (and therefore to any particular intentive mental process whatever) cannot steal its something objectivated as objectivated, that therefore the distinction between both must be made" (*Ideen* 1, §90, p. 185 [206], trans. Kersten). The fact that "sense" is indifferent to the existence or nonexistence of the object is therefore the salient phenomenon indicated by the word "sense" in the analysis of intentionality. Husserl says, in this regard, that "the Scholastic distinction between the mental [*mentalem*], intentional or immanental Object on the one hand, and the actual [*wirklichem*] Object on the other hand," refers to the distinction between the object and the existence of the object. Yet he radically contests the assimilation of the intentional object to an immanental object in the sense of an object "actually present in phenomenological purity" (*Ideen* 1, §90, p. 186 [206], trans. Kersten): sense is not a real component of lived experience, like *hulê* [ὕλη] (that is, for example, the data of sensation, *Empfindungsdaten*, and what is more, "*not every really inherent moment* in the concrete unity of an intentive mental process itself has the *fundamental characteristic, intentionality*," *Ideen* 2, §36, trans. Kersten). Nor is it a psychic reality, or even a portrait or a sign. To attribute a "copy function" to intentional lived experience would lead to an "infinite regress": "A second immanental tree, or even an 'internal image' of the actual tree standing out there before me, is in no way given, and to suppose that hypothetically leads to an absurdity" (ibid.). Husserlian "sense" is thus not to be understood as simply borrowing the notion of "immanent object," but as a "*correlate belonging to the essence of phenomenologically reduced perception [das zum Wesen phänomenologisch reduzierten Wahrnehmungen gehörige Korrelat]*" (*Ideen* 1, §90, p. 187 [209], trans. Kersten). Insofar as it is limited to the vague notion of representation, the connection Putnam makes between intentionality and nonexistence does not fully capture the Husserlian notion of "sense" (nor, a fortiori, that of a "complete noema" distinguished from a "core of meaning"). Nonetheless, the sense of "intention" or "intentionality" is marked by a series of oscillations that Putnam's taxonomy translates very well.

II. Intention and Intentionality

The conception of intentionality that has for a long time been predominant in French-language literature comes principally from Husserl's *Cartesian Meditations*. According to this conception, (a) "without exception, every conscious process is, in itself, consciousness *of* such and such, regardless of what the rightful actuality-status of this objective such-and-such may be, and regardless of the circumstance that I, as standing in the transcendental attitude, abstain from acceptance of this object as well as from all my other natural acceptances" (*Cartesian Meditations*, trans. Cairns); and (b) every state of consciousness "aims at" something, and carries within itself, as that which is "aimed at" (as the object of an intention), its "respective *cogitatum*"—what Husserl summarizes as follows in the famous formula of §14 of the Second Meditation:

> Wobei das Wort Intentionalität dann nichts anderes als diese allgemeine Grundeigenschaft des Bewußtseins, Bewußtsein von etwas zu sein, als *cogito* sein *cogitatum* in sich zu tragen, bedeutet.

> The word intentionality signifies nothing else than this universal fundamental property of consciousness: to be conscious *of* something; as a *cogito*, to bear within itself its *cogitatum*.

(*Cartesian Meditations*, §14, ed. Ströcker, 35; trans. Cairns)

(N.B.: It is worth pointing out how closely this resembles the formulas introducing the *cogito* in §14, ed. Ströcker, 34: "*Der Transzendentale Titel ego cogito muß also um ein Glied erweitert werden: Jedes cogito, jedes Bewußtseinserlebnis . . . meint irgend etwas und trägt in dieser Weise der Gemeinten in sich selbst sein jeweiliges cogitatum, und jedes tut das in seiner Weise.*")

Several francophone and anglophone interpreters tend nowadays to forget, however, the "fundamental property" of consciousness, "to be conscious *of* something," for Husserl refers neither to "a relation between some psychological occurrence—called a mental process—and another real factual existence [*realen Dasein*]—called an object," nor to "a psychological connection taking place in Objective [*objektiven*] actuality between the one and the other," but rather to "mental processes purely with respect to their essence," that is to say, to "pure essences and . . . that which is 'a priori' included in the essences with unconditional necessity" ("*Vielmehr ist von Erlebnissen rein ihrem Wesen nach, bzw. von reinen Wesen die Rede und von dem, was in den Wesen, 'a priori,' in unbedingter Notwendigkeit beschlossen ist*": *Ideen* 1, §34, p. 64 [74], trans. Kersten). Intentionality is not a connection between a physical fact and a psychic fact.

When we are caught in the contemporary, post-Wittgensteinian opposition between "empiricism" and "intentionalism," we tend to forget that we often invoke intentionality over and against a conception of mental acts that states that no mental act can have an extra-mental entity as its content. So "intentionalism" consists in maintaining the "intentionality of the mind," which means that our acts orient us toward things outside ourselves. This is, however, a weak (even trivial) characterization of phenomenological intentionality, which does not greatly value the Husserlian distinction between a "thing pure and simple" (*Sache*) and a "complete intentional object [*Objekt*]" (*Ideen* 1, §34, pp. 66–67, trans. Kersten). Similarly, the discussions generated by the behaviorist proposition according to which we can and must eliminate all intentional entities (the "mentalist expressions" of natural language) gives "intentional" a meaning that is so reduced or so metaphorical that we might wonder whether "intention" here had anything whatsoever to do with phenomenology. Even more complex debates have developed beyond the field of basic Husserlian studies, particularly in anglophone philosophy. One example of this is the discussion between Wilfrid Sellars and Roderick Chisholm on the relationship between thoughts and the semantic properties of language. Sellars states that "thoughts as intentional entities are derived from the semantic properties of language," which means that "intentionality resides in the metalinguistic utterances that express the semantic properties of an object language" (the so-called weak irreducibility thesis), whereas Chisholm maintains, on the contrary, that "the semantic properties of language, and thus the metalinguistic utterances that express them, are derived from the properties of thoughts, which are the fundamental support of intentionality" (the so-called strong irreducibility thesis; cf. Cayla, *Routes et déroutes de l'intentionnalité*).

III. Intention and *Intentio*

As fragmented as it might at first appear, the plurality of meanings of "intention" can be seen as relatively coherent if it is considered as the continuation, or as another version, of the original polysemy of the Latin *intentio*. Indeed, in this term we find not only the effects wrought by successive translations, but also the shadow cast over the modern philosophical lexicon by the different stages of the genesis of the medieval notion. Certain contemporary debates about intentionality might, then, appear to some extent to rearticulate—by simplifying or complicating them—problems that were tackled in the Middle Ages within a more unitary framework.

The Scholastic Latin *intentio* presents an extraordinarily rich array of meanings. The term can in fact be translated as (1) attention (German *Aufmerksamkeit*); (2) aim, objective, purpose (German *Anstrebung*, *Absicht*, *Vorhaben*); (3) relationship, rapport (synonym *habitudo*, German *Beziehung*, cf. Thomas Aquinas, *In Sent. I*, d. 25, qu. 1.3c); (4) meaning, in the sense of a speaker's intention to mean something (*intentio loquentis*, *intentio proferentis*); (5) image, copy, resemblance, similarity (synonym *similitudo*, German *Ähnlichkeit*, *Abbild*); (6) representation, notion, concept (synonyms *conceptio intelligibilis*, *ratio*, *conceptus*, *repraesentatio*, German *übersinnliches Erkenntnisbild*, *Vorstellung der Vernunft*, *Begriff*); (7) intelligible form (synonym *species*); or (8) extra-mental resemblance. The polysemy of *intentio* is mentioned by Duns Scotus (*Reportata Parisiensa* 2, d. 13, art. un., trans. McCarthy, 39; *Ordinatio*, trans. McCarthy, 26), who reduces it to four primary meanings:

> Notandum est quod hoc nomen "intentio" est equivocum. Uno modo dicitur actus voluntatis "intentio." Alio modo: ratio formalis in re, sicut intentio rei a qua accipitir genus differt ab intentione a qua accipitur differentia. Tertio modo dicitur conceptus. Quarto modo, dicitur ratio tendendi in obiectum, sicut similitudo dicitur ratio tendendi in illus cuius est. Et isto modo dicitur lumen "intentio" vel "species" lucis.

> We have to note that the noun "intention" is equivocal. The first meaning of "intention" is an act of will. A second is: a formal reason present in a thing, in the sense that in a thing, the intention from which the generic type is derived is different from the intention from which the (specific) difference is derived. A third meaning of "intention" refers to a concept. And a fourth meaning [of intention] refers to the way in which one reaches out or extends towards an object, in

the sense that a resemblance is one way of extending towards the thing which it resembles. And it is in this sense that the light emitted is the "intention" or the [intentional] "species" of the source of a light.

A. *Intentio* as *actus voluntatis*: Intention and attention

The ethical meaning of *intentio*, the first one that is historically attested, is closely related to the contemporary meaning of voluntary intention. However, since St. Augustine, the dimension of active orientation immanent to the notion of *intentio* has been presented as a characteristic not only of the will, but also, by extension, of any cognitive process. Understood in this sense, *intentio* becomes synonymous with attention. The proximity of intention to attention is well known to phenomenologists. Husserl gives a unified discussion of this (from the noetic and noematic point view) in his analysis of "mutations" or "attentional modifications," when he attempts to describe, for the "complete noema," the variations of the correlative appearance of the noetic modifications (*Ideen* 1, §92, pp. 189–190, trans. Kersten). He stresses, moreover, that

> nicht einmal des Wesenzusammenhang zwischen Aufmerksamkeit und Intentionalität—diese fundamentale Tatsache, daß Aufmerksamkeit überhaupt nichts anderes ist also eine Grundart intentionaler Modifikationen—ist meines Wissens früher je hervorgehoben worden.

> not even the essential connection between attention and intentionality—this fundamental fact: that attention of every sort is nothing else than a fundamental species of *intentive* modifications—has ever, to my knowledge, been emphasized before.

(*Ideen* 1, §92, p. 192 [215] n. 1, trans. Kersten)

The couple "intention"/"attention" (which corresponds also to the English "directedness") was attested, in exemplary fashion, in St. Augustine's analysis of visual sensation:

> Itemque illa animi intentio, quae in ea re quam videmus tenet sensum, atque utrumque coniungit, non tantum ab ea re visibili natura differt: quandoquidem iste animus, illud corpus est: sed ab ipso quoque sensui atque visione: quoniam solius animi est haec intentio.

> Further also, that attention of the mind which keeps the sense in that thing which we see, and connects both, not only differs from that visible thing in its nature; in that the one is mind, and the other body; but also from the sense and the vision itself: since this attention is the act of the mind alone.

(*De Trinitate*, 11.2.2, ed. Haddan and Knight)

Intentio and *attendere*, "to pay attention to," "to intend" (German *Aufmerksamkeit*), are often combined. This is true of Abelard, in his theory of abstraction as selective attention (which prefigures the theories of John Stuart Mill and of William Hamilton):

> Dum in homine hoc solum quod ad humanitatis naturam attinet intelligere nitimur, utpote animal rationale

mortale, circumscriptis scilicet omnibus aliis que ad substantiam humanitatis non attinent, profecto multa se per imaginationem nolenti animo obiiciunt que omnino ab intentione abiecimus. . . . Adeo . . . ut . . ., dum aliquid tamquam incorporeum per intellectum attendo, sensum usu tamquam corporeum imaginari cogor.

While we try only to conceive in man that which concerns the nature of his humanity—that is, as a mortal, rational animal—, after having eliminated everything else that does not concern the substance of humanity, many things that we had completely rejected from our purview become ob-jects of the mind through the imagination. . . . While I attend to a thing as incorporeal in an act of intellection, I am forced through the use of my senses to imagine it as corporeal.

(Abelard, De intellectibus §19)

The ad-tension (the "tension-toward" or "tending-toward") or the attention in the expression "directedness toward" is thus the first meaning of *intentio* in the field of cognition, whether this "tending-toward" is provoked by the thing itself (that is, the ob-ject present), or whether it is spontaneous (that is, as the aim of a distant or absent term). The etymology of *intentio* as *tendere in aliud* suggests a limited distinction between attention, and aim or purpose strictly speaking (lexicalized in German as *Aufmerksamkeit*, and *Absicht*, *Anstrebung*, and *Vorhaben*). It is in the first sense that Thomas Aquinas writes that attention is the "condition required for the activity of any cognitive faculty" ("*ad actum cuiuslibet cognoscitivae potentiae requiritur intentio*," *De veritate*, quarto 13.3c). In the second sense, he stresses that *intentio* refers to the activity of the faculty of thought insofar as it "directs what it apprehends to the knowledge of something else, or to some operation [*id, quod apprehendit, ordinat ad aliquid aliud cognoscendum vel operandum*]" (*Summa theologiae* 1, q. 79, a. 10 ad 3m). As Duns Scotus writes, however, precisely insofar as *intendere* means "*in aliud tendere*," and if it is true that every cognitive power is said to aim or extend toward an object, solely by virtue of the fact that an object is ob-jected with respect to this power: to this degree and under these circumstances, *intendere* is to be understood more precisely as that which is voluntarily oriented toward an object, whether it is absent or present (*Reporta Parisiensa* 2, d. 38, q. 1). Voluntary attention is thus a fundamental and inextricable aspect of *intentio*. This sense is undoubtedly inherited from St. Augustine, for whom it played a central role in his theory of perception and memory. He used this sense of *intentio* almost identically in both his tripartite corporeal vision (that is, [a] the form the body perceived, [b] the image that is formed of it in the intention of the person discerning it, and [c] the attention of the will that joins these two together) and his description of the operation of memory (which also has a tripartite structure: [1] the imaginary vestige that remains in one's memory; [2] the impression of this vestige in the mind's intention, when one recalls it; and [3] the attention of the will that, once again, joins these two together. The original Latin is as follows: "*[a] forma corporis, [b] conformatio que fit in cernentis aspectu, [c] intentio voluntatis utrumque coniungens*" [*De Trinitate*, 14.3.5, pp. 354–56], and

"*1. imaginatio corporis que in memoria est, 2. informatio, cum ad eam convertitur acies cogitantis, 3. intentio voluntatis utrumque coniungens*" [*De Trinitate*, 15.3.5, pp. 430–33]).

B. *Intentio* as form (*ratio formalis in re*)

Intentio can often mean "form." This form has nothing to do with the "form of the body perceived," as described in St. Augustine's theory of vision, but is rather the Aristotelian idea of form. This is to be understood as both the form and the definition (or the definitional form) realized in extra-mental things, according to one of the characteristic ambiguities of the term *logos* [λόγος]. (On the distinction between the two meanings of logos—*logos*-definition and *logos*-form—see Cassin, *Aristote et le logos*, 107–10, as well as 257–93, in particular 260–63.) As *ratio formalis in re* (Scotus, "a formal reason present in a thing"), *intentio* thus refers to what Alexander of Aphrodisias called the *logos koinos* [λόγος κοινός], both a common notion (*logos*-formula) and a common form (*logos*-form), or, if one prefers, the "common definition" and "common nature" fully present in each thing, and equally, which is to say entirely, predicated of all things that are fully what they are by virtue of this common notion and form. The use of the word *intentio* as *ratio formalis in re* continues, then, the idiosyncrasy of Alexander's vocabulary. When, for example, he states that "the definition of man" ("a bipedal terrestrial animal") is common because it applies to "all" men, and is "fully in each one," he substitutes the definition itself for the "common quality named in this definition," thereby combining an expression and what it refers to. This understanding of *intentio* is the one determining what Lloyd calls, with respect to Alexander, the "conventional picture of forms as universals *in re*" (cf. Lloyd, *Form and Universal*, 51), a thesis based on a "confusion of the universal with the form."

C. *Intentio* as *conceptus* (concept)

"Concept" is one of the most frequently attested meanings of *intentio*. It is very clear in the following description by Thomas Aquinas of the process of conceptualization, which includes all of the implied terms:

> Intellectus per speciem rei formatus intellegendo format in seipso quandam intentionem rei intellectae, quae est ratio ipsius, quam significat definitio.

> Formed from a species [form] of a thing, whenever the intellect conceives, it forms within itself an intention of the thing conceived, this intention being the notion of the thing as signified by its definition [or: "by the term 'definition' (when applied to that notion)"].

(*Summa contra Gentiles* 1, q. 53)

Intentio is thus obviously linked to *conceptio*, *conceptus*, and *ratio*, without ever being exactly synonymous with them. In the above passage from the *Summa contra Gentiles*, intention appears as the content of a notion (= *ratio*), expressed/signified by its definition. But not all texts define it so decisively. In many discussions, *intentio* and *conceptus* are considered to be equivalent. In others, *intentiones* replaces the awkward expression *passiones animae*, which constitutes the top of the semiotic triangle of *De interpretatione* (see SIGN). In this case, it is the tripartite nature of the *phônai* [φωναί]—that is, as "vocal sounds," as *noêmata* [νοήματα] (noemata or concepts), and as *onta* [ὄντα] (beings, also called "things," *ta pragmata* [τὰ πράγματα])—inherited from the Neoplatonic commentaries on the *Categories* that, when superimposed on the triangle "vocal sounds, affects or passions of the soul, and things," explains the appearance in this context of *intentio* as noema, or concept. *Intentiones* in the sense of *noêmata* is thus part of a history that goes back a long way, with the earliest attested reference perhaps the distinction mentioned by Clement of Alexandria (*Stromates*, 8.8.23.1, ed. Stählin, 3:94.5–12) between *onomata* [ὀνόματα] (names), *noêmata* (concepts, whose names are symbols), and *hupokeimena* [ὑποκείμενα] ("actual substrata, of which concepts are the impressions made within us"; cf. on this point Pépin, "Clément d'Alexandrie," in particular 271–79).

D. *Intentio* as *ratio tendendi in obiectum*, the angle of the aim or intention

The fourth sense of *intentio*, which at first glance is close to what Franz Brentano calls "*die Richtung auf ein Objekt*" (the orientation toward an object), is in fact the most enigmatic. In some ways, it is bound up with the third sense, if *ratio tendendi* refers to what serves as a formal principle in the act of intention by which a cognitive power is oriented toward its object ("*illud per quod tamquam per principium formale in obiectum tendit sensus*"). In this case, *ratio tendendi* indeed refers to a conceptual *similitudo* that constitutes the angle of the aim or intention. But the analysis becomes complicated when Duns Scotus includes in this fourth sense a resemblance that is both extra-mental and nonconceptual, stating that "*ipso modo dicitur lumen 'intentio' vel 'specio' lucis*" (It is in this sense that the light emitted [or luminosity] is said to be the "intention" or the "species" of the source of the light). There is something quite puzzling about this thesis. First, it assumes that we can treat luminosity (*lumen*) as a *conceptum* produced by an extra-mental thing (*lux*), independent of any activity or act of the intellect. Yet this statement corresponds to a precise theory of intentionality that stipulates that "every concept is [the concept] of a first intention which [the concept] is naturally producible immediately by the thing itself, without any operation or act of the intellect" (Duns Scotus, *Ordinatio* 1.23, ed. Balić, 5:360: "*omnis conceptus est intentionis primae qui natus est fieri immediate a re, sine opere vel actu intellectus negociantis*"). Here, the term *intentio* is used to express an intuition that would be directly opposed to that of modern "intentionalism," insofar as it suggests that objects themselves engender the concepts that represent them to the mind (a thesis that is compatible with the statement by which the *noêmata* are the impressions made within us by the *hupokeimena* [ὑποκείμενα]). This intuition is also in contrast to the theory one assumes to be standard, according to which all intentions, in the sense of concepts, are produced by the intellect, or are the species formed by the intellect, and are existing within the intellect. The example Duns Scotus gives is not, however, a neutral one.

The classical distinction in the medieval theory of light between *lumen*, as the light emitted or radiating in a transparent or diaphanous milieu, and *lux*, as the source of light, assumes that there is an engendering relation between *lux*

and *lumen*, which paradoxically recalls one of the oldest meanings of the concept: the fruit (*proles*) of conception in the literal sense of the term. It is indeed this register that underlies the use of *intentio* when the example of light is discussed: the source of light "engenders" luminosity. "*Lux*," writes Scotus, "*gignat lumen tamquam propriam speciem sensibilem sui*" (*Ordinatio* 2.13, trans. McCarthy, 276). This vocabulary, which one could readily term "Augustinian," is even more pronounced among theorists of optics or *perspectiva*, particularly when they discuss the theme of the "multiplication of species." One of the founding fathers of the theory, Robert Grosseteste, writes literally that the generic term *lux* has to be broken down into light that engenders (*generans*) or gives birth (*gignens*), and light that is engendered (*generata*) or given birth to (*gignata*): "The light that is in the sun engenders from its substance the light that is in the air [*lux quae est in sole gignit ex sua substantia lumen in aere*]" (Grosseteste, *Commentarius in Posteriorum analyticorum libros* 1.17, ed. Rossi, 244–45). This engendering relation, which preserves both the alterity and a certain essential unity between what engenders and what is engendered, undoubtedly explains why one can discuss, on the shoulders of a further play on the word "species," the theme of the propagation of light, and then the theme of the perception of colors, and beyond that of perception itself, by resorting to the language of propagation, and of the multiplication of natural species. Matthieu of Aquasparta explains in these terms that "every corporeal or spiritual form, real or intentional, has an engendering and self-disseminating force, either actually, as in the case of forms subjected to generation and corruption, or intentionally" (*Quaestiones disputate de gratia*, q. 8, ed. Doucet, 214).

As surprising as it might seem, *intentio* is thus both a rival of *conceptus*, coming from another network and another interlinguistic field (Arabo-Latin, as we shall see, and no longer Greco-Latin), and an equivalent of *conceptus*, as far as the semantic aspect of generation and conception is concerned. Duns Scotus, who was among the first to articulate an authentic theory of intentionality as an orientation toward an object, also played a major role in naturalizing intentionality. He was well aware that *intentio* understood as *conceptus* derived from Arabic theories of optics, and that as *similitudo* or *species*, *lumen* that is multiplied according to three different types of ray (*rectus*, *fractus*, *reflexus*) denotes the "sensible species of *lux*, immediately engendered by it." But he consciously used this perspectivisit theory to explain that the formal reason of a given intellection, the *species genita* (engendered form), which is nothing other than that of the *imago gignentis* (the image of what engenders it), requires a "real presence" of the object to the cognitive power, that is, a "sufficient proximity to enable engendering" of the said species by the object itself, an engendering that places the present object "*sub ratione cognoscibilis vel repraesentati*," in short, makes it knowable or representable (*Ordinatio* 1.3.3.1, ed. Balić, 6:232). Briefly, then: the word *intentio* serves here to express the process by means of which objects directly engender their image in the intellect. A movement whose directionality is exactly opposite that of an orientation toward the object troubles any understanding of *intentio* as "*ratio tendendi in obiectum*."

This tension is only relieved once the perspectivist theory of *intentio* is rejected as an epistemological model, and as a framework for a theory of perception based on a direct gnoseological realism—that is, once intentionality no longer functions as a characteristic or a mode of being of *similitudo* or *species* engendered by an object, independent of any perceiving subject. We are now able to trace this decision back to Pierre d'Auriole, who opened up the space for a new reflection on the phenomenality of appearing. Indeed, it was against the idea that once could admit every extra-mental intentional existence that Pierre d'Auriole established his theory, reducing the intentional being of *lumen* to a real being, and reformulating the notion of intentional being in terms of apparent or phenomenal being (*esse apparens*), with intentional being reserved, in the strictest sense, for the mode of being of color in a rainbow. *Esse intentionale* became, on this basis, a synonym of *esse obiectivum* or *fictitium sive apparens* ("objective or fictive or apparent being," that is, phenomenal), and was contrasted to "*esse reale et fixum in rerum naturae absque omni apprehensione*" (real being remaining stable in natural reality outside of any perception). Anything accorded intentional being could not exist outside of perception: it is merely a *conceptus objectivus* (objective concept), or, to put it more accurately, an *apparitio objectiva* (objective phenomenon: *Scriptum*, 1.23, ed. Pinborg, 133–34).

IV. The Geneses of Intentionality

A. In-existence

It was Brentano, consciously borrowing from the Scholastics, who introduced the term "intentionality" (*Intentionalität*) into the vocabulary of psychology. This initiative was directly responsible for the adoption of the term and the concept in intentional psychology and phenomenology. Brentanian intentionality is supposed to define the specificity of mental phenomena, by a kind of relation that is named, rather unfortunately, "intentional in-existence":

> Jedes psychisches Phänomen ist durch das charakterisiert, was die Scholastiker der Mittelalters die intentionale (auch wohl mentale) Inexistenz eines Gegenstandes genannt haben, und was wir, obwohl wir nicht ganz unzweideutigen Ausdrücken, die Beziehung auf einen Inhalt, die Richtung auf ein Objekt (worunter hier nicht eine Realität zu verstehen is), oder die immanente Gegenständlichkeit nennen würden.

> Every mental phenomenon is characterized by what the Scholastics of the Middle Ages called the intentional (or mental) inexistence of an object, and what we might call, though not wholly unambiguously, reference to a content, direction toward an object (which is not to be understood here as meaning a thing), or immanent objectivity.

> (Brentano, *Psychologie- vom empirischen Standpunkt*, 1:124–25 ; trans. Rancurello et al., 88)

One might wonder about the translation of "die immanente Gegenständlichkeit" by "an immanent objectivity." The definite article (*die*) could suggest that it is rather a question of "immanent objective existence," of the opening of the object

as immanent to the psychic. *Gegenständlichkeit* is, however, an expression that is as equivocal as *Intentionalität*. One might also assume that Brentano is using it in the same sense as Bernard Bolzano when, in discussing the influence of "things that make no claim to existence [*Dinge, die keinen Anspruch auf Wirklichkeit machen*]," he wonders about the *Gegenständlichkeit* (objective existence) of the concept "which we quite rightly associate with the word *infinite*." "The next question to be asked," Bolzano writes, "is that concerning its *objective existence*—that is, whether there exist objects to which it can be applied, whether there exist sets which we may judge to be infinite in the sense here" (cf. Bolzano, *Paradoxien des Unendlichen*, §13, p. 13, trans. Prejonsky, 84). "In-existence," which has nothing to do with nonexistence (German *Nicht-Existenz*), denotes a type of presentification that has to do with inherence, in the sense of "being present," "existing in," "residing in" (German *Innewohnen*): in all psychic phenomena, there is an object.

In this sense, intentionality expresses the fact that, as Aristotle writes in *De anima* (8.431b30–432a1), "it is not the stone itself that is in the soul, but the form of the stone" ("*ou gar ho lithos en têi psuchêi, alla to eidos* [οὐ γὰρ ὁ λίθος ἐν τῇ ψυχῇ, ἀλλὰ τὸ εἶδος]"). To speak about intentionality here amounts to saying that the mode of presence of a stone in the soul is intentional and not real, that the extra-mental thing is not "really" but only "intentionally" inherent in the soul. This lexical choice has a history, and its reasons. The notion of "intentional being" must not be confused with that of *esse obiectivum* or "objective." The mention of the "direction toward an object" nonetheless places emphasis on a dimension of mental in-existence—that is, the orientation or direction toward an object—that has caused many problems for readers of Brentano. According to Putnam, Brentano, in contrast to Husserl, did not maintain that "the intentionality of the mental . . . provided a way of understanding how mind and world are related and how it is that in acts of consciousness we come to be directed to an *object*" (cf. Putnam, *Representation and Reality*, 88); rather, he merely wished to indicate that "mental phenomena were characterized by being directed toward contents" (ibid.). Whether or not Putnam's interpretation is well founded, it remains the case that the "tending toward an object" suggested by the currently accepted Latin etymology of the verb *intendere* (*tendere in*) was very early on considered as a characteristic aspect of the kind of mental presentation envisaged by Aristotle in *De anima* (8.431b30–432a1). Radulphus Brito defines intentionality on the basis of this "tending toward": *intentio* is "that by which an intellect tends toward a thing [*tendit in rem*]" (Pinborg, "Radulphus Brito's Sophism," 141 n. 49). In medieval texts, the directionality of *intentio* competes explicitly with the very notion of a mental content. In fact, the same term refers both to the movement by which the intellect is directed toward an object or apprehends a mental content, and to the intrapsychic mode of presentation of this same object and content. This overlap is not without consequences for the status of intentionality in modern philosophy. The nature of this polysemy is fundamentally linked to the history of its translations. Indeed, the word *intentio* only appears in its different usages, at the end of the twelfth century, in the Arabo-Latin translations of Aristotle and of the Peripatetic corpus as a translation of the Arabic ma'na [المعنى]. Its ambiguity is at its origin, the same as that of the term it translates. The word ma'na [المعنى] corresponds to the Greek logos [λόγος], noêma [νόημα], dianoia [διάνοια], ennoia [ἔννοια], theôrêma [θεώρημα], and pragma [πρᾶγμα], among others (Endress, "Du grec au latin à travers l'arabe," 151–57). The Arabo-Latin intentio has just as many meanings, since it is equivalent to at least three kinds of term: (a) a thought, concept, idea, notion; (b) a signification (in which we find the dimension of the English "to mean," or the French vouloir dire); and (c) an entity. That the same term refers at the same time to a mental act, a content, a cognitive state, and an object is clearly apparent in the fact that, from the thirteenth century on, intentio has equally meant either the concept of a thing, or the thing itself as it is conceived, or both at once. So the notion of "relational intention" is thus from the outset, in the Middle Ages, programmatically inscribed within the idea of an originary shared belonging of intentio rei and res intenta. In the same register, there is a further ambiguity in the pair logos-ma'na [المعنى], which progressively colors the term intentio with the double nuances of "form" (as in the expression "the intention of a thing," intentio rei—that is, the "form of a thing") and "formulation" (as in the expression "the intention of

man," intentio hominis—in other words, "the definitional formulation characterizing the concept of man," that is, "rational, mortal, bipedal animal").

■ See Box 1.

B. Intentio as an optical term

If intentio is often a synonym both for a concept and for the thing conceived, the notion itself of presentation / presentification / intentional presence covers several other lexical networks. A first set is linked to the technical vocabulary of optics, and to the dissemination of the theories and the work of Alhazen, for whom intentio was the name of the form affecting the apparatus of sight, and then by extension its mode of being in the physical medium of transmission: one speaks, in this sense, of the esse intentionale of the thing in medio. This is the sense in which the Latin translation of the Averroës Magnum commentarium on Aristotle's De anima discusses the "spiritual being" of the extra-mental things affecting sight: in the medium of transmission, the res has an esse spirituale, not an esse materiale. The equivalence between spirtuale and intentionale is a characteristic of the Latin lexicon of Averroës (cf. Averroës, Magnum commentarium in De anima 2, comm. 97, ed.

1

Intentio and ma'nā [المعنى]

The Arabic ma'nan (with the article: al-ma'nā [المعنى]) means what is on one's mind, what one is referring to, what one means (German meinen—no etymological link to English "mean"; French vouloir dire) by a word, or a notion. The Arabic root 'NY [ع ن ى] indeed means "to aim." Ninth-century translations chose the word to translate several meanings of the Greek logos [λόγος]. So in Aristotle's treatise De anima, we read that sensation is affected by color, or flavor, or sound, not insofar as each of these is said, but to the extent that it is such and such a quality, and "according to logos" (2.12, 424a24, trans. Barnes). Commentators have sought to define more precisely the status of this being which affects sensations in this way. Themistius (Paraphrase of De anima, ed. Heinze, p. 78, 3.10.13) also uses logos [λόγος]. The Arabic translates the term in Themistius's paraphrase of Aristotle as ma'nā [المعنى] (1.7.11, trans. Lyons), as it does for Aristotle's original (Averroës, Magnum commentarium in De anima, §121, ed. Crawford; cf. Bos, Aristotle's De anima Translated into Hebrew, 107.658). Avicenna uses the term in a number of different senses (cf. RT: Goichon, Lexique de la langue philosophique d'Ibn Sînâ, §469, pp. 253–55), including one meaning, very close to our own, that was close to the lekton [λεκτόν] of the Stoics (Avicenna's De anima, 287). In the twelfth century, the word

was translated from the Arabic of Avicenna and Averroës by the Latin word intentio. Likewise, Jewish translators from the Ibn Tibbo (or Ibn Tibbon) family translated it as 'inyan [עִנְיָן]. Latin translations popularized this meaning, which thus has little in common with our "intention," in the sense of "to intend to do something." It is in this sense that we talk of "intentional species" (Roger Marston was the first to use the term) as what our perceptive organs receive, stripping concrete things of their matter to retain only their form. Avicenna defined the object of logic as being "the second intellected concepts [ma'ani (معاني)] which are based on the first intellected concepts, [and which are based on them] from the point of view of [the fact of their having] the quality of [being] that by which we attain the unknown from the known, not from the point of view of the fact of their being intellected: they have an intellectual existence that depends on absolutely no matter, or that depends on noncorporeal matter (Shifa': Métaphysique, 1.2, 10.17–11.2). The Scholastics followed him by distinguishing intentio prima and intentio secunda (starting with Godefroid de Fontaines), and this usage became so common that it enabled François Rabelais to joke: "comedere secunda intentiones" (to eat second intentions: Pantagruel 1.7), that is to say, pure abstractions (see Box 2 below). This mode of existence

in the intellect alone was sometimes called intentionalitas (Pierre d'Auriole, Étienne de Rieti), and the phenomenological usage of "intentionality," borrowed by Husserl from Brentano, is the most recent part of this history.

Rémi Brague

BIBLIOGRAPHY

Aristotle. The Complete Works of Aristotle. Translated by Jonathan Barnes. 2 vols. Bollingen series, 71.1–2. Princeton, NJ: Princeton University Press, 1984.
Averroës. Magnum commentarium in De anima. Edited by F. Stuart Crawford. Cambridge, MA: Mediaeval Academy of America, 1953.
Avicenna. Al-Shifa': La Métaphysique. Edited by G. C. Anawati. Cairo, Egypt: Organisation générale des imprimeries gouvernementales, 1960.
———. Avicenna's De anima. Edited by F. Rahman. Oxford: Oxford University Press, 1959.
Bos, Gerrit. Aristotle's De anima Translated into Hebrew by Zerahyah b. Isaac b. Shealtiel Hen. Leiden, Neth.: Brill, 1994.
Themistius. Paraphrase of De anima. 4th ed. Edited by R. Heinze. In RT: CAG, 5-3. Translation by Robert B. Todd: On Aristotle On the Soul. London: Duckworth, 1996. Arabic translation by M. C. Lyons: An Arabic Translation of Themistius's Commentary on Aristoteles, De anima. Oxford: Cassirer, 1973.

Crawford, 277.28–30): "*Color habet duplex esse, scilicet esse in corpore colorato [et hoc est esse corporale] et esse in diaffono [et hoc est esse spirituale],*" which Albertus Magnus translated as, "In matter, form has material being, in the diaphanous, on the contrary, color does not have a material being, but a spiritual being" (Albertus Magnus, *De intellectu et intelligibili*, 1.3.1).

C. *Intentio* as the form of the inner senses

A second lexical network is provided by the terminology particular to the *Avicenna latinus*, which uses the word *intentio* to refer to a representation whose origin is nonsensible, formed in the inner senses, and associated with a sensible apprehension effected by the outer senses. In this network, *intentio* refers in its literal sense to the *vis aestimationis* or estimative faculty, the role of which is to apprehend "unsensed intentions residing in singular sensibles." Understood in this way, "intentions" are what the inner senses perceive of a sensible reality without the "intermediary of the outer senses." The "unsensed intentions of the sensibles" are thus contrasted with the "forms of the sensibles" that are at first perceived by the outer senses, and only subsequently by the inner senses (and because of them). A characteristic example of an "intention" in this sense is the property or character of "dangerousness" of a wolf, which a sheep perceives in a nonsensible way, and which causes it to run away at the sight of a wolf, that is, when its "form" is presented to its outer senses (see Box 2 here, and SENSUS COMMUNIS). In Averroës, the opposition between intention and image acquires a new, almost "iconic" aspect. Indeed, for him, an image only "depicts" certain external characterisitics of a real object, or certain of its particular or common sensible properties (color, "form" in the sense of "figure," etc.), but it does not "represent" them. *Intentio*, by contrast, represents certain elements of the "individual this" that are not given in an image, and that correspond to what this individual is insofar as it is "this individual." To speak of the iconic aspect of *intentio* thus means that *intentio* alone makes present a given individual as the individual he or she is, whereas an image only presents a set of sensible characteristics. For Averroës, it is a specialized faculty, the cogitative faculty, that is capable of separating out *intentio* (*ma'nā al-khayāl* [معنى الخيال] from the image (*al-khayāl* [الخيال]).

▪ See Box 2.

The distinction Porphyry makes between first imposition (*prôtê thesis* [πρώτη θέσις]) and second imposition (*deutera thesis* [δευτέρα θέσις]) of names is partly what forms the basis for the medieval analysis of *intentiones* as first intentions and second intentions. According to Porphyry, names are first applied ("first imposition") to sensibles, and only subsequently to intelligibles, considered as things that are "anterior in themselves" (that is, naturally), but posterior in the order of perception (Porphyry, *In Categoria Aristotelis*, ed. Busse, 90.20ff. and 91.20–27). Being perceived first (i.e., before the "commons"), sensibles or individuals are the first objects of signification (ibid., 91.6–12). Intelligibles are thereby the object of a "secondary" linguistic imposition. In the Middle Ages, the distinction between the two types of imposition was used as a tool for differentiating between the ways in which thought is oriented toward an object. For Pierre

d'Auvergne, "the intellect has two ways of being oriented towards things [*supra res ipsas intellectus duplicem habet motum*]." A first movement orients it directly or immediately toward things themselves. Through this movement, it obtains knowledge of the nature of the things on which it imposes a name. This "nature" is the quiddity of a thing, and the name imposed is a name of first intention ("man," "animal," "Socrates"), because it signifies "the concept of the intellect that is first oriented toward the thing itself [*in rem ipsam primo intellectus intendentis*]." The second movement is the one whereby the intellect is oriented toward a thing that is "already apprehended," in order to attach to it the "conditions" of consideration upon which depends the attribution of a second-intention name, or "universal name." Starting out from the same premises, the Modists developed an actual theory of intentions.

The *modista* Radulphus Brito (Raoul le Breton) defined *intentio* as "that by which the intellect is oriented towards a thing [*tendit in rem*]." He articulated the contemporary distinctions (those of Simon of Faversham or Pierre d'Auvergne) into an actual combined system where we find both the Aristotelian and Thomist topos of the "three operations of the intellect" (apprehension, judgment, reasoning) and the Modist semantic theory of paronyms. He was thus able to bring into play a single distinction between the abstract and the concrete at the three levels of operation, allowing him to conflate the trivial opposition between the intention and the thing. At the level of the first operation (the apprehension of a reality according to its own particular mode of being), Brito made the distinction between a first abstract intention, or "knowledge of the thing" (*cognitio rei*), and a first concrete intention, or "the thing as it is known" (*res sic cognita*). He thus returned to the theme of paronymy (the abstract/concrete relation), which had provided his predecessors with the general framework for the intelligibility needed to elucidate the status of second intentions. For Brito, however, the correspondence between the paronymic meaning and the semantic status of intentions could be generalized into an actual theory of intentional objectness, since he maintained that every kind of knowledge "names its object" in the same way that "abstract accidents name their subject," which is to say, concretely: "*Et ita semper cognitio denominant suum obiectum, sicut accidentia abstracta denominant suum subiectum*" (cf. Pinborg, "Radulph Brito's Sophism," 141). From this basis, an entire taxonomy was established, encompassing *prima intentio in concreto* (joining together *res intenta*, "the thing intended," and *prima intentio in abstracta*, "first abstract intention"), *intentio secunda in abstracta*, and *intentio secunda in concreto*, these last two assigned once again to the second and then the third operations of the intellect. This ponderous architecture was brutally shaken up by the Nominalists, particularly William of Ockham, who reconfigured the theory of impositions and the theory of intentions into an entirely different doctrine.

Taking into account what was for him a cardinal difference separating words in spoken and written languages from the concepts and terms of the language of the mind, William of Ockham redefined the relationship between "impositions" and "intentions."

▪ See Box 3.

2

"Cogitative" and its Greek, Arabic, and Latin equivalents

In the vocabulary of medieval philosophical psychology, the distinction between *nous* [νοῦς], *to noêtikon* [τὸ νοητικόν], and *to dianoêtikon* [τὸ διανοητικόν] (literally "intellect," "intellective or noetic faculty," and "dianoetic faculty") was usually reduced to an opposition between the Arabic or Latin equivalents of *nous* and *to dianoêtikon*. This reduction corresponds to the fact, noted by Bodéüs (Aristotle, *Catégories*, ed. Bodéüs, 146 n. 6), that *De anima* does not strictly delineate between the faculty called *to dianoêtikon* in 413b13, 414b18, or 431a14, and the faculty is elsewhere referred to as *to noêtikon*. The French translations of the Greek, which range from *faculté discursive* (discursive faculty: Tricot) to *réflexion* (reflection: Bodéüs), show that for them, the basic opposition was between *dianoia* [διάνοια]— so-called discursive thought—and *noêsis* [νόησις]—so-called intuitive thought. This same division commands how the field was organized in medieval times, when it was structured around the pair *vis cogitativa* and *intellectus*.

In the tradition of Arabic Peripateticism, *to dianoêtikon* appears at the center of a three-term system, corresponding to the so-called passible or material "faculties of perception": the imaginative, the cogitative, and the rememorative. These terms need to be clarified, however. In Avicenna, for whom there are five inner senses (see SENSUS COMMUNIS), the cogitative refers to the same faculty as the imaginative. It is the third inner sense, the *vis cogitativa* (*al-quwwat al-mufakkira* [القوة المفكّرة]) in man, or *imaginativa* in animals, whose function is to divide and compose the images retained by the imagination, the second of the inner senses. In Averroës, on the other hand, for whom the division of the inner senses is tripartite, the cogitative assumes part of the functions that Avicenna reserves for the estimative: perceiving intentions (see Box 1). In his commentary on *De sensu et sensato*, Averroës describes as follows the functioning of the three faculties relating to the "inner senses": "The sense perceives the extra-mental thing, then the *formative faculty* [i.e., the imaginative faculty] forms [an image] of it; then the *distinctive faculty* [i.e., the cogitative faculty] distinguishes the intention of this form from its description; then the retensive faculty receives what the distinctive faculty has distinguished" (cf. Black, "Memory, Individuals, and the Past," 168–69). In the Latin translation of Averroës's *Magnum commentarium* on Aristotle's *De anima*, these three faculties are designated using the triad (*virtus*) *imaginativa-cogitativa-rememorativa*—three

faculties whose function is to "make present the form of the thing imagined in the absence of the corresponding sensation."

The five faculties distinguished by Avicenna—(a) common sense (*banṭāsiā* [بنطاسيا]), (b) imagination, (c) imaginative (for animals) or cogitative (for man), (d) estimative, (e) memory—are thus reconfigured by Averroës: (1) *imaginativa* = (a), (b); (2) *cogitativa* = (c), (d); (3) *rememorativa* = (e). In fact, the particular role of the "cogitative" faculty endowed with a "rational character" consists of either (1) depositing or registering in memory the "intention" of the imagined form taken with the individual, which serves as the substrate of that form, or (2) distinguishing memory from this individual substrate in the "imaginative" (*al-mutakhayyila* [المتخيّلة]) or "formative" (*al-muṣawwira* [المصوّرة]) faculty and in the "imagination." The cogitative is thus in a median position relative to these two other faculties: in relation to imagination, because of its abstractive activity, which works with images; and in relation to memory, because of its activity of depositing, which consists of transmitting abstract individual intentions to a receptacle (a faculty of the mind conceived as the "receiving faculty" or instance). It is from this deposit, receptacle, or store that one draws the "imagined intentions" necessary for the noetic process of abstraction: the cooperation among the faculties of the inner sense enables the "presentation of the image of a sensible thing" upon which the activity of the "*virtus rationalis abstracta*" is exerted. This activity, as the agent intellect, "extracts a universal intention" and then, as the material intellect, "receives" it and "apprehends" it (or "comprehends" or "thinks" it). For Averroës, the distinction between "cogitative faculty" and "intellect" (cf. *Magnum commentarium in* De anima 2.29, ed. Crawford, 172.25–173.32, in relation to 414b18: "*Deinde dixit: Et in aliis distinguens et intellectus. Idest, et ponamus etiam pro manifesto quod virtus cogitativa et intellectus existunt in aliis modis animalium que non sunt homines*") is misinterpreted in the Galenic tradition. It is also misinterpreted by all those who attribute to Aristotle a doctrine of the intellect as a "faculty existing in a body." In the Scholastic tradition, "cogitative" generally retains this meaning. Certain authors, however, stress the aspect of "individual abstraction." If the cogitative does not produce universal concepts, it at least presents or delivers the individual form of a thing insofar as it is such-and-such a "thing" (for example, a "man" or a "line"). This individual "form" is not reduced to the collection of particular or common accidents that

characterize each individual as an "individual" (this man, this line).

Ipsa [= virtus cogitativa] cognoscit intentiones, id est formas individuales omnium decem praedicamentorum, ut formam individualem huius hominis, secundum quod hic homo, et hanc lineam . . . et huiusmodi plura ita quod non tantum cognoscit accidentia sensibilia communia et propria, sed intentionem non sensatam, et exspoliat eam ab eis, quae fuerunt ei coniuncta de sensibilibus communibus et propriis.

It is this [*virtus cogitativa*] which knows intentions, that is, the individual forms of what falls into one of the ten categories, like the individual form of this man inasmuch as he is this man, or like this line . . . and many other things of this same kind, such that it does not only know the common and particular sensible accidents, but also the nonsensible intention, which it extracts and separates out from the common and particular sensibles that are connected to it.

(Jean de Jandun, *Super libros Aristotelis De anima*, 214)

BIBLIOGRAPHY

Aristotle. *Catégories*. Edited by R. Bodéüs. Paris: Les Belles Lettres, 2002.

Averroës. *Averroes' Middle Commentary on Aristotle's De Anima: A Critical Edition of the Arabic Text.* Edited, translated, with introduction and notes by Alfred L. Ivry. Provo, UT: Brigham Young University Press, 2002. Translation by F. Stuart Crawford: *Magnum commentarium in* De anima. Cambridge, MA: Mediaeval Academy of America, 1953.

Black, Deborah L. "Memory, Individuals, and the Past in Averroes's Psychology." *Medieval Philosophy and Theology* 5 (1996): 161–87.

Davidson, Herbert A. *Alfarabi, Avicenna, and Averroes, on Intellect: Their Cosmologies, Theories of the Active Intellect, and Theories of Human Intellect.* New York: Oxford University Press, 1992.

Elamrani-Jamal, Abdelali. "Averroès: La doctrine de l'intellect matériel dans le *Commentaire moyen* au De anima d'Aristote. Présentation et traduction, suivie d'un lexique-index du chapitre 3, livre III: *De la faculté rationnelle*." In *Langages et Philosophie, Hommage à Jean Jolivet*, edited by A. de Libera, A. Elamrani-Jamal, and A. Gallonnier. Études de Philosophie Médiévale 84 (1997): 281–307.

Jandun, Jean de. *Super libros Aristotelis De anima.* Venice, 1587. Reprinted Frankfurt: Minerva, 1966.

3

Intentions and imposition according to William of Ockham

William of Ockham calls categorematic signs "first-imposition names," that is, oral or written words that conventionally signify individual extra-mental things. He calls the natural conceptual signs of the individual things to which they are subordinate "first intentions"; the categorematic oral or written words conventionally signifying other conventional signs he refers to as "second-imposition names"; and the mental categorematic conceptual signs that signify naturally other mental signs he calls "second intentions." This general grid proves to be remarkably complex in its concrete applications. The expression "second-imposition name" can be understood, in fact, in two ways. (1a) In the broad sense, any name that signifies conventionally instituted sounds as conventionally instituted sounds is a second-imposition name, that is, insofar as it signifies, whether or not it is applicable to the intentions of the soul (which are natural signs). This is the case for expressions such as "noun," "pronoun," "conjunction," "verb," "case," "number," "mood," "tense," and so on, "understood in the way a grammarian uses them," that is, "to signify the parts of speech *while* they signify" (nouns that are predicable of vocal sounds both *when* they do not signify and *when* they do signify are thus not second-imposition names). (1b) In the strict sense, any name that signifies conventionally instituted signs without being able to be applied to the intentions of the soul (which are natural signs) is a second-imposition name. This is the case for expressions such as "conjugation" or "figure,"

which cannot signify an intention of the soul (and this is the only reason to exclude them from second-imposition names in the strict sense), since there are no distinctions of conjugations or of figures for "mental" verbs.

First-imposition names are all names that are neither names in the sense of (1a) nor names in the sense of (1b). However, the expression "first-imposition name" can be understood in two ways. (2a) In the broad sense, everything that is not a second-imposition name is a first-imposition name: in this sense, syncategorematic terms are first-imposition names. (2b) In the strict sense, only categorematic names that are not second-imposition names are first-imposition names.

First-imposition names in the strict sense of (2b) are themselves of two sorts, that is, certain among them (3a) are second-intention names, others (3b) are first-intention names. Second-intention names are those which are "precisely" imposed in order to signify both intentions of the soul that are natural signs, and other signs that are instituted conventionally (or however such signs are characterized). There is thus (3a1) a broad sense and (3a2) a strict sense of the expression "second-imposition names." In the broad sense (3a1), a second-intention name is a name that signifies intentions of the soul (which are natural signs), and that can also signify or not "conventionally instituted signs, only *when* they are signs," that is, second-imposition names in the sense (1a). In the sense (3a1), a second-intention name can also be at the same time a second-imposition name. This is the case

for names used in relation to what are called "universals." The names "genus," "species," and so on, like the names "universal" and "predicable," are second-intention names because they signify "nothing other" than intentions of the soul (which are natural signs), or arbitrarily instituted signs. In the strict sense (3a2), a second-intention name is a name that only signifies intentions of the soul (which are natural signs). In the sense (3a2), "no second-intention name is a second-imposition name."

First-imposition names are all other names, that is, all those that signify things that are neither signs, nor what characterizes these signs. But here again, we can distinguish between (3b1) names that signify "precisely" things that are not signs intended to substitute for other things, and (3b2) names that simultaneously signify such things and signify signs, such as the names "thing," "being," "something" (*aliquid*), and so on, that is, what the Scholastics termed "transcendentals."

There are thus signs that signify both conventional signs and mental signs: these are second-imposition names in the broad sense (1a), which are either oral words or written words, and second-intention names in the broad sense (3a1), which are concepts. There are also names that are both first imposition and second intention: first imposition, because they do not signify a conventional sign; but second intention, because they signify a mental concept: the case par excellence is the oral word "concept."

This complex classification—which allows us to foreground a metalinguistic aspect by identifying the possibility of a reciprocal application at the two levels of mental language and conventional language (since a second-imposition name can be applied to a mental concept, and a second-intention name can be applied to a conventional sign)—is, if we forget the "particularist" ontological thesis that supports the whole thesis, one of the three pillars of the doctrine of universals.

V. Intentionality as an Anti-Aristotelian Theory

A. Action of things or of the intellect?

The medieval theory of intentionality, even if it is based on a rereading of *De anima* 3.8, 431b30–432a1, is to some extent anti-Aristotelian. To be more exact, it opposes the naturalist dimension of the notion of psychic impression elaborated by commentators on the basis of the opening lines of *De interpretatione*. Indeed, the principal function of the idea of an intentional presence of the thing to the intellect is to break

with a strictly empiricist (or, as one might say, "inscriptionist") reading of the *passio animae*, attributing to Aristotle a reduction of concepts to simple impressions or inscriptions (or resemblances) of things "in" the soul. Because intentionality is here understood as an orientation of the intellect toward the object, the explanation of thought as the impression of a *species* in the soul by the thing itself—a causal model that poses the problem of how one passes from a sensible impression to an intelligible concept, and makes it necessary to distinguish between two types of *species*: a *species* that is "imprinted in the senses" (*species impressa*) and a *species* that is "expressed in thought" (*species expressa*)—gives way to the description of the process by which a cognitive power is actively oriented toward an object, where its act terminates. In Aristotelian terms, there is thus a shift in the problematics of the theory of intentionality. It is no longer a matter of explaining what action exterior things exert on the soul through the intermediary of sensible *species*, but rather of describing the way in which the intellect, understood as a power of apprehension (*potentia apprehensiva*), moves to act (*perficitur*) and ends (*terminatur*) as an apprehension "of something" (see SENSE, Box 1).

Duns Scotus gives the theory its canonical formulation when he posits that "in an apprehensive power, the motor principle does not have to be the proper object of this power from the angle where it is a motor, but the object from the angle where it terminates the given power," that is to say, its endpoint, its pole of actualization, its "ending"—which is tantamount to saying that "cognitive power does not so much have to receive the *species* of an object [*recipere speciem obiecti*], as to be oriented by its activity toward it [*tendere per actum suum in obiectum*]."

B. Intention, representation, and aim

The Brentanian thesis of "intentional in-existence," which defines psychic phenomena by the fact that they "contain an object within them intentionally," goes hand in hand with a second thesis, equally popular, that affirms that every mental act is either a representation (*Vorstellung*) or "based on a representation" (this is the case, for example, with judgments and affections). For the school of thought around Brentano, then, the question of intentionality develops spontaneously out of the notion of representation, which is understood as essentially "oriented" toward an object (*Gegenstand*). The notion of intentional object is therefore explored from the point of view of representation, against the background of a distinction between the ob-ject itself, the *ob-stant* or *Gegenstand* ("the object taken independent of thought" or the object "as it stands before" thought, and is "that toward which representation is directed"; Twardowski, *Zur Lehre von Inhalt und Gegenstand der Vorstellungen*, 4), and the "immanent object" (*immanentes Objekt*) or "content" (*Inhalt*) of representation, which alone deserves the name of "intentional object," literally speaking. Now, however, the case of "representations without objects" (*gegenstandslose Vorstellungen*), following the terminology previously introduced by Bolzano, will stand in need of redefinition. It is not enough to say that every representation has a content, but that each representation does not for all that have its corresponding ob-ject. It is false, from the point of view of terminological rigor, to talk about "inobjective" representations. According to Twardowski, there are no representations "which would not represent something as an object" (ibid., 25), or representations "to which would correspond no object." There are, however, a number of representations "for which an object does not exist" (ibid., 29). Even if these comments fall far short of the "broadening of the sphere of the object even beyond being and non-being" (which only Alexius Meinong's "theory of objects" will provide), the idea of "representations for which an object does not exist" exposes one of the fundamental problematics conveyed by the notion of intentionality (see RES).

The medieval theory of objectual intention (*aspectus*) is, in this sense, part of the proto-history of the *gegenstandslose Vorstellungen* (representations without objects). According to this theory, particularly elaborated by Pierre-Jean Olieu (Olivi) around 1280, every cognitive act (sensible or intelligible) requires an *aspectus* "having as its actual term an object" or, more literally, "ending in actuality on an object [*super obiectum actualiter terminatus*]." This does not mean that the principle of the cognitive act must in all cases be a real object, functioning as a cause of perception: in many cases, on the contrary, it is a substitutive, purely "terminative and representative" object that is the principle of the cognitive act—for example, a memorial *species* (if it is a question of a "thought of absent objects")—and that "presents itself in place of the external thing," when "this thing is not itself the object of an aim or intention" (Olieu, *Quaestiones in secundum librum Sententiarum*, q. 74, ed. Jensen, 3:113). A representation, an image, a *species*, or a "presential object" (*praesentialis*) thus provides a substitutive presence, which "is the object of an aim or intention, and terminates it," whenever there is no object (really) present. The distinction between a terminative object and a causal object gives a more interesting range of meaning to intentionality understood as orientation toward an object.

C. "Intention"/"in-tension"/"pro-tention"

If the triad "in,tention"-"pro,tention"-"re,tention" has enjoyed a particular fortune in the phenomenological analysis of the intimate consciousness of time, the intentional structure of thought itself was presented in the Middle Ages in terms of "pro-tention." The vocabulary of "tending" (*in/pro*) immanent to intentionality was established more permanently in the fourteenth century. During this time, it combined with the vocabulary of "aiming" expressed with and around St. Augustine's and Boethius's notion of the "highest pointing of the mind" (*acies mentis*; see ARGUTEZZA). For medieval philosophers, to say that the "intentional power," the *vis inventiva* of a cognitive faculty (*potentia cognitiva*), "tends toward an object [*in obiectum intendit*]" was to say that it "extends toward it within itself [*intra se protenditur*]" and that, "in this pro-tention" itself, "it points toward that which is ob-jected" (*"et protendendo acuitur quod est acute ad aliquod sibi obiectum intenta"*). "Acuity" does not refer, then, to a circumstantial modality of thought that is subject to variation: it is a constitutive trait of its intentionality. Intention, as an "actual aim" (*aspectus actualis*), is fundamentally pro-tentive. It is a movement of tending toward, of opening out or unfolding, by which a cognitive faculty "is sharpened" and "points" in the direction of the object (Olieu, *Quaestiones in secundum librum Sententiarum*, ed. Jensen, 3:64).

Alain de Libera

BIBLIOGRAPHY

Augustine. *De Trinitate*. Edited by A. W. Haddan and K. Knight. Translated by Arthur West Haddan. In *Nicene and Post-Nicene Fathers*, 1st ser., vol. 3, edited by Philip Schaff. Buffalo, NY: Christian Literature Publishing Co., 1887. Revised and edited for New Advent by Kevin Knight.

Auriole, Pierre d'. *Scriptum*. In "Radulphus Brito on Universals," edited by Jan Pinborg. *Cahiers de l'Institut du Moyen Age Grec et Latin* 35 (1980): 133–37 [edition of part of the *Scriptum*, d. 23, on the basis of MS BAV, Vat. Lat. 329].

Averroës. *Magnum commentarium in De anima*. Edited by F. Stuart Crawford. Cambridge, MA: Mediaeval Academy of America, 1953.

Banchetti-Robino, Marina Paola. "Ibn Sina and Husserl on Intention and Intentionality." *Philosophy East and West* 54 (2004): 71–82.

Biard, Joël. "Intention and Presence: The Notion of *Presentialitas* in the Fourteenth Century." Translated by Oli Sinivaara. In *Consciousness: From Perception to Reflection in the History of Philosophy*, edited by Sara Heinämaa, Vili Lähteenmäki, and Pauliina Remes, 123–40. Dordrecht, Neth.: Springer, 2007.

———. "Intention et signification chez Guillaume d'Ockham: La critique de l'être intentionnel." In *Langages et philosophie: Hommage à Jean Jolivet*, edited by

Alain de Libera, Abdelali Elamrani-Jamal, and Alain Galonnier, 201–20. Paris: Vrin, 1997.

Black, Deborah L. "Mental Existence in Thomas Aquinas and Avicenna." *Medieval Studies* 61 (1999): 45–79.

Bolzano, Bernard. *Paradoxien des Unendlichen*. Edited by B. Van Rootselaar. Hamburg: Felix Meiner Verlag, 1975. Translation by F. R. Prejonsky: *Paradoxes of the Infinite*. London: Routledge and Kegan Paul, 1950.

Boulnois, Olivier. *Être et représentation: Une généalogie de la métaphysique moderne à l'époque de Duns Scot, XIIIe–XIVe siècle*. Paris: Presses Universitaires de France, 1999.

Brentano, Franz Clemens. *Psychologie vom empirischen Standpunkt*. Edited by Oskar Kraus. 2 vols. Hamburg: Meiner, 1974. First published in 1874. Translation by Antos C. Rancurello, D. B. Terrell, and Linda L. McAlister: *Psychology from an Empirical Standpoint*. Edited by Oscar Kraus and Linda L. McAlister. New introduction by Peter Simons. London: Routledge, 1995.

Cassin, Barbara. *Aristote et le logos: Contes de phenomenology ordinaire*. Paris: Presses Universitaires de France, 1997.

Cayla, Fabien. *Routes et déroutes de l'intentionnalité*. Combas, Fr.: Éditions de l'Éclat, 1991.

Chisholm, Roderick M. *Theory of Knowledge*. Englewood Cliffs, NJ: Prentice-Hall, 1977.

Chisholm, Roderick M., and Wilfrid Sellars. "Intentionality and the Mental: Chisholm-Sellars Correspondence on Intentionality." In *Intentionality, Mind and Language*, edited by Ausonio Marras, 214–48. Chicago: University of Illinois Press, 1972.

Clark, Elizabeth A. *Clement's Use of Aristotle: The Aristotelian Contribution to Clement of Alexandria's Refutation of Gnosticism*. New York: Mellen, 1977.

Clement of Alexandria. *Stromates*. Edited by Otto Stählin. Leipzig: J. C. Hinrichs, 1939.

Denery, D. G. "The Appearance of Reality: Peter Aureol and the Experience of Perceptual Error." *Franciscan Studies* 55 (1998): 27–52.

Duns Scotus. *Opera omnia: Ordinatio*. Prologus, vol. 1. Edited by Karl Balić. Rome: Typis Polyglottis Vaticanis, 1950.

Endress, G. "Du grec au latin à travers l'arabe: La langue créatrice d'idées dans la terminologie philosophique." In *Aux origines du lexique philosophique européen*, edited by Jacqueline Hamesse, 151–57. Textes et études du Moyen Âge 8. Louvain, Belg.: Fédération internationale des Instituts d'Études Médiévales, 1997.

Grosseteste, Robert. *Commentarius in Posteriorum analyticorum libros*. Edited by Pietro Rossi. Florence: L. S. Olschki, 1981.

Hamesse, Jacqueline., ed. *Aux origines du lexique philosophique européen: L'influence de la Latinita*. Textes et études du Moyen Âge 8. Louvain, Belg.: Fédération internationale des Instituts d'Études Médiévales, 1997.

Hickerson, Ryan. *The History of Intentionality: Theories of Consciousness from Brentano to Husserl*. London: Continuum, 2007.

Husserl, Edmund. *Cartesianische Meditationen und Pariser Vorträge*. Edited by S. Strasser. The Hague: Nijhoff, 1973. Translation by Dorion Cairns: *Cartesian Meditations: An Introduction to Phenomenology*. The Hague: Nijhoff, 1977.

———. *Ideen*. Edited by Karl Schuhmann. In *Husserliana: Gesammelte werke III:1* and *III:2*. The Hague: Nijhoff, 1976. Translation by F. Kersten: *Ideas Pertaining to a Pure Phenomenology and to a Phenomenological Philosophy, First Book: General Introduction to a Pure Phenomenology*. Dordrecht, Neth.: Kluwer, 1983.

Lambertini, Roberto. "La teoria delle *intentiones* da Gentile da Cingoli a Matteo da Gubbio: Fonti e linee di tendenza." In *L'insegnamento della logica a Bologna nel XIV secolo*, edited by D. Buzzetti, M. Ferriani, and A. Tabarroni, 277–351. Bologna, It.: Istituto per la storia dell'università, 1992.

Lloyd, Antony C. *Form and Universal in Aristotle*. Liverpool, Eng.: Francis Cairns, 1980.

Matthew of Aquasparta. *Quaestiones disputate de gratia*. Edited by Victorin Doucet. Florence: Quaracchi, 1935.

McCarthy, Edward R. "Medieval Light Theory and Optics and Duns Scotus' Treatment of Light in D. 13 of Book II of His Commentary on the *Sentences*." Ph.D. dissertation. City University of New York, 1976.

Münch, Dieter. *Intention und Zeichen: Untersuchungen zu Franz Brentano und zu Edmund Husserls Frühwerk*. Frankfurt: Suhrkamp, 1993.

Normore, Calvin. "Meaning and Objective Being: Descartes and His Sources." In *Essays on Descartes' Meditations*, edited by Amélie Orksenberg Rorty, 223–41. Berkeley: University of California Press, 1986.

Olieu, Pierre-Jean [Peter John Olivi]. *Quaestiones in secundum librum Sententiarum*. 3 vols. Edited by B. Jensen. Florence: Quaracchi, 1922–26.

Panaccio, Claude. *Ockham on Concepts*. Aldershot, Eng.: Ashgate, 2004.

Pasnau, Robert. *Theories of Cognition in the Later Middle Ages*. Cambridge: Cambridge University Press, 1997.

Pépin, Jean. "Clément d'Alexandrie, les *Catégories* d'Aristote et le fragment 60 d'Héraclite." In *Concept et Catégories dans la pensée antique*, edited by P. Aubenque, 271–84. Paris: Vrin, 1980.

Perler, Dominik, ed. *Ancient and Medieval Theories of Intentionality*. Leiden, Neth.: Brill, 2001.

Pinborg, Jan. "Radulphus Brito's Sophism on Second Intentions." *Vivarium* 13 (1975): 119–52.

Pini, Giorgio. *Categories and Logic in Duns Scotus: An Interpretation of Aristotle's Categories in the Late Thirteenth Century*. Leiden, Neth.: Brill, 2002.

Porphyry. *In Categoria Aristotelis*. Edited by Adolf Busse. Berlin: De Gruyter, 1887.

Putnam, Hilary. *Representation and Reality*. New ed. Cambridge, MA: MIT Press, 1992.

Richardson, R. "Brentano on Intentional Inexistence and the Distinction between Mental and Physical Phenomena." *Archiv für Geschichte der Philosophie* 64 (1982): 250–82.

Searle, John R. *Intentionality: An Essay in the Philosophy of Mind*. Cambridge: Cambridge University Press, 1983.

Sorabji, Richard. "From Aristotle to Brentano: The Development of the Concept of Intentionality." *Oxford Studies in Ancient Philosophy* 9, suppl. (1991): 227–59.

Tachau, Katherine. *Vision and Certitude in the Age of Ockham: Optics, Epistemology and the Foundations of Semantics (1250–1345)*. Leiden, Neth.: Brill, 1988.

Twardowski, Kazimierz. *Zur Lehre von Inhalt und Gegenstand der Vorstellungen*. Vienna: Hölder, 1894. Translation by Reinhardt Grossmann: *On the Content and Object of Presentations*. The Hague: M. Nijhoff, 1977.

INTUITION

➤ BEAUTY, BILD, COMPARISON, *IMAGINATION*, *INSTANT*, INTENTION, MEMORY, MERKMAL, SIGN

"Intuition" comes from the Latin *intuitio*, which in Chalcidius's translation of Plato's *Timaeus* refers to an image reflected in a mirror. The term is derived from the verb *intueri*, which means "to see," "to look upon" (*tueri* means "to see" and "to look over," "to protect"), with a connotation of intensity—attentively, fixedly, admiringly, immediately, and all at once—and applies as much to sight in the literal sense, that of the eyes of the body, as to metaphorical sight, through the eyes of the soul. Intuition is thus a direct vision of something given that presents itself immediately as real and true. In modern philosophy, the term brings together a Cartesian source (what is clear and evident) and a Kantian source (the objectivity of the object).

I. Intuition and the Evident

A. Intuition, sensation, intellect

The first network is that of sensible intuition, which is connected to the immediacy of perception and thus to its truth (see PERCEPTION, Box 3; SENSE, I.A and Box 1; cf. *TO SENSE,* TRUTH). The second is connected to intelligible intuition, which has to do with ideas (see *IDEA*). The English and French *intuition* covers a wide range of terms denoting, even before Plato, this kind of instantaneous intellection; it is frequently used to translate the Greek *nous* [νοῦς], "mind," or *noêsis* [νόησις], "thought," and even *noêma* [νόημα], "object of thought," whenever they are being contrasted with more discursive procedures, such as *dianoia* [διάνοια], but it is equally often used to translate *epibolê* [ἐπιβολή] (from *epiballô* [ἐπιβάλλω], "to throw onto," from which we get the standard meanings of "imposition," "apposition," "superimposition," "an imposed tax," "project"), a terminology that, from Epicurus to Plotinus and beyond, refers to the direct application of the mind. The various Latin translations are just as complex: *intellectus* is one of the translations of *nous* (but only one, since *nous* is also translated as *sensus*; see SENSE), and yet it is not translated into French by *intuition*, but rather by *intellect* or *entendement* (understanding); and we find the Latin *intuitus* in the philosophical texts of the European classical age, in Descartes, for example (the Scholastics had coined *notitia* or *cognitio intuitiva*, which were taken up by Spinoza and Leibniz). (On this cluster of terms linked to the names of the faculties, see INTELLECT, INTELLECTUS, UNDERSTANDING; cf. *CONCEPT, REASON*.)

B. Intuition and the relation to the divine

"Intuition," via *nous* and *intellectus*, is one of the ways of characterizing God (see INTELLECTUS, TERM, Box 2; cf. GOD, LOGOS).

The theological importance of intuition relates to the problem of "beatific vision" or "transparency," which was later on transposed in the metaphysics of Malebranche as a question of the "vision in God"; intuition is also both closely connected and opposed to the thematics of truth as "light" or "suddenly seeing clearly" (see LIGHT, SVET, TRUTH; cf. OIKONOMIA).

C. Intuition and subjectivity

Apperception, properly speaking, which is connected to the consciousness that a subject has of itself, constitutes a particular case of intuition (see COMMON SENSE, CONSCIOUSNESS, ERLEBEN, I/ME/MYSELF, PERCEPTION, *SELF*, SENSE, SOUL, SUBJECT, TATSACHE (and below, §III); cf. *ACT, CERTITUDE, DASEIN*).

A constituting relation-to-self opens out on to the singularity of the individual (see GENIUS, INGENIUM, *PERSON*). Intuition is characterized in this context by an intelligent, but always spontaneous or sudden behavior, perhaps even a prephilosophical one, based in a certain analogy of *noêsis* with "flair" (see UNDERSTANDING, Box 1); it can be understood in terms of the connotations of *ḥads* [الحدس] in Avicenna's Arabic (see INGENIUM, Box 1), and it is found in the opposition English speakers make between semantic intuition and pragmatic insight (the "sight" that illuminates or clarifies a difficulty).

More generally, the position of the subject determines a *Weltanschauung*, an "intuition of the world," whose meaning ranges from the cosmological to the romantic, and even ideological (see WELTANSCHAUUNG).

II. Intuition and the Object of Intuition

A. The various usages of *Anschauung*

The Kantian revolution split the history of the different usages of *Anschauung* (and of "intuition") in two, insofar as it set up in opposition to the intellectual intuition (we already find *intuitio intellectualis* in Nicholas of Cusa) inherited from *noêsis*, which is contrasted with the empirical and the sensible world, the paradoxical concept of a sensible intuition (*sinnliche Anschauung*) that is nonetheless susceptible of being "pure" and that constitutes the foundation of the given of phenomena or of the diversity of experience. For Kant, the former is deeply illusory, and the latter forms a system with the concept (*Begriff*) and constitutes the field of representation. (On the singularity of Kant's vocabulary, see BEGRIFF and *CONCEPT*, ERSCHEINUNG, GEGENSTAND, REALITY, REPRÉSENTATION, SEIN: cf. OMNITUDO REALITATIS.) Kant's revolution is correlative with the broadening of the meaning of "aesthetics" to cover the general science of sensibility (see AESTHETICS; cf. GEFÜHL, SENSE).

In French, *comprendre* and *penser* correspond to some extent to the activity of *Begriff*, but the language lacks a technical term for *anschauen* and so has coined the verb *intuitionner* (see BEGRIFF, GEMÜT, Box 1, and GERMAN).

Since Kant, transcendental idealism has explored the possibility of separating out the pure intuition of the sensible, but without reference to a noumenal "thing in itself," so conferring upon it the meaning of a constitutive activity (see TATSACHE). Conversely, the epistemology of quantum physics has explored a problem of visualization that is not connected to a sensible given, but instead to the theoretical possibility of representation (see ANSCHAULICHKEIT and the particularly significant evolution of the meaning of this term).

B. The "given"

Intuition implies a certain mode of access to an object. Its character of being immediately obvious culminates in the problematic of the given and of the "donation without a donor" (see ES GIBT, HÁ, and more generally, *IL Y A*).

Contemporary philosophy has been divided between a devalorization of intuition in favor of praxis in the Marxist tradition (see PRAXIS) and the reconstitution of a doctrine of the intuition of essences on the far side of the Kantian critique of the intelligible world, in Husserl and some of the phenomenological tradition, with the thematics of *Wesenschau* or *Wesenanschauung* (see GEGENSTAND).

III. Intuition and Intuitionism

Intuitionism can be understood in several ways, all of which refer to a valorization of the immediacy of a type of knowledge.

On its usage in moral philosophy, in particular in the Anglo-Saxon world, see FAIR and compare MORAL SENSE, UTILITY, WERT. On its usage in the epistemology of mathematics, and more generally in the field of analytical philosophy, where "intuitionism" (Poincaré, Brouwer) is opposed to "formalism" and "logicism," see EPISTEMOLOGY and PRINCIPLE, and compare ANSCHAULICHKEIT.

ISTINA [истина] (RUSSIAN)

ENGLISH	truth
FRENCH	*vérité*
GREEK	*alêtheia* [ἀλήθεια]
HEBREW	*'emet* [אֱמֶת]
LATIN	*veritas*

► TRUTH, and DASEIN, MIR, POSTUPOK, PRAVDA, REALITY, RUSSIAN, SOBORNOST', SVOBODA, *TO BE, WORLD*

The Russian word *istina* [истина], unlike its French translation *vérité*, has a primarily ontological sense: it means: "what is, what truly exists." The epistemological sense of "a statement conforming to reality, a true judgment," is secondary and derived in relation to this ontological sense. The logical sense of "veracity" is, moreover, translated by a different Russian noun, *istinnost'* [истинность], so that *istina* and *istinnost'* are translated into English using the same word, "truth." In Russian philosophy there is a fundamental opposition between *istina* as true existence and *istina* as true judgment. Considered separately from its epistemological meaning, the term *istina* can then be understood in two contrasting ways. In the philosophy of Vladimir Solovyov, it has an objective and impersonal character: *istina* is the objective self-identity of reality; but for the existentialists, *istina* takes on a dynamic meaning: "what is" is nothing other than the identity of the act and the event.

I. *Istina*: Truth as the Reality and Self-Identity of Being

The modern Russian word *istina* [истина], like the Slavonic *istina*, corresponds to the Greek *alêtheia*. It comes from the Slavonic *ist*, *istov*, "true," "real" (RT: *Ètimologičeskij slovar' russkogo jazyka*, 144; Preobazhenskij, *Ètimologičeskij slovar' russkogo jazyka*, 1:275–76). Dictionaries propose three versions of the etymology of *ist*: according to the oldest thesis this term is derived from the Indo-European *es*- (to be); according to another it is formed from the prefix *iz*- and from the form *sto*- ("that which is upright," "which is upright"), as in the Latin *ex-sistere*, *ex-stare*; finally, according to Vasmer, the most likely version links *ist* and *istina* to the pronominal form *is-to* ("the same"), analogous to the Latin *iste*. *Ist* means "the same" in modern Bugarian, like the Slovenian *îsti*, and the Serbian and Croatian *ìstî* (Vasmer, *Ètimologičeskij slovar'*, 144).

Pavel Florensky, in *The Pillar and Ground of the Truth*, undertakes a comparative study of the notion of truth among the Slavs, the Greeks, the Romans, and the Jews. For him the Greek *alêtheia* [ἀλήθεια] has a gnoseological meaning of "that which resists forgetting," while the Latin *veritas* has a primarily cultural and juridical sense (it is "the real state of the thing judged"), and the Hebrew *'emet* [אֱמֶת] "comes from the history of the holy word, from theocracy" (*'emet* meaning "faithful word," "reliable promise"). Florensky writes the following about the Russian word:

Our Russian word for "truth," *istina*, is linguistically close to the verb "to be": *istina—estina*. *Istina* in Russian has thus come to mean, by itself, the notion of absolute reality: *istina* is what is (*susče* [сущее]), what truly exists (*podlinno suščestvujuščee* [подлинно существующее]), *to ontôs on* or *ho ontôs on*; as opposed to what is illusory, apparent, not real, impermanent. The Russian language marks the ontological aspect of this idea in the word

istina. *Istina* thus means an absolute self-identity, or being equal to oneself, absolute exactness and authenticity (*podlinnost'* [подлинность]).

(Florensky, *Pillar and Ground*)

The term *susče* (in Greek, *to ontôs on* [τὸ ὄντως ὄν]) has been translated into French as *ce qui est* (what is) or *l'être* (being) (Berdyayev, *Khomiakov*, 195), as *existant concret* (concrete existent) (Berdyayev, *Essai de métaphysique eschatologique*, for example, 111), and more rarely, as *étant* (being) (Berdyayev, *Khomiakov*, 196). If in French *étant* is opposed to *existant*, in Russian *suščestvujuščee* (that which exists) and *susče* are considered as synonyms, as are *bytie* [бытие] (being) and *suščestvovanie* [существование] (existence); their opposition normally requires a reference to the French *existence* or the German *Existenz*. So by situating *istina* within this ontological field, Florensky is relating it to the identity of being in itself.

It is this ontological concept of truth that has often led Russian philosophers to stress the fundamental opposition between truth as authentic being (*bytie*) and truth as true judgment. Nicolas Berdyayev acknowledges this:

Russians do not accept that truth (*istina*) can be discovered by purely intellectual means, by reasoning. They do not accept that truth (*istina*) is merely judgment. And no theory of knowledge, no methodology is evidently capable of shaking this pre-rational conviction of the Russians, namely that apprehending what is, can only be given in terms of the complete life of the mind [*esprit*], the fullness of life.

(Berdyayev, *Khomiakov*, 81–82)

Istina, understood then as being and the identity of the real, is not accessible to the purely logical or intellectual subject but is always related to the act of a person, to a choice one makes.

II. *Istina* and the Supra-personal Subject (Solovyov)

There are, however, two ways of conceiving of the relation to *istina*. The first, in Vladimir Solovyov, associates the objectivity of being (*istina* as *ousia*, substance and quiddity) with going beyond subjectivity. In reaction to this, the second one, that of the Russian existentialists, interprets *istina* as *energeia* [ἐνέργεια], an act or exercise rooted in the person. In his *Teoretičeskaja filosofija* (Theoretical philosophy), Solovyov makes a distinction between the truth of an isolated fact, or a formally universal logical truth, and truth properly speaking, that is, truth as *bezuslovno-susče* [безусловно-сущее] (what exists absolutely). *Bezuslovno-susče* is a noun made up of the substantivized participle corresponding to the Greek *to on* [τὸ ὄν] (being), and the adverb *bezuslovo* (unconditionally), analogous to the Greek *anupothetôs* [ἀνυποθέτως]. Truth in this latter sense constitutes the (possibly inaccessible) object of the risky enterprise that is philosophy. Although philosophy is a personal matter, it requires going beyond the limits of a particular existence. Solovyov writes:

True philosophy begins when the empirical subject rises up through supra-personal inspiration to the realm of truth (*istina*). For even if one cannot define in advance what truth (*istina*) is, one must at least say what it is not. It is not in the realm of the separate and isolated self.

(Solovyov, *Teoretičeskaja filosofija*, 213)

In short, truth, namely "what truly exists," is objective. This is why it is only revealed to the "mind" (*esprit*), that is, to the supra-personal or properly philosophical (*dux* [дух], "mind") subject, insofar as it is distinguished from the empirical (*duša* [душа], "soul") and the logical (*um* [ум], "intellect") subject. For Solovyov, a classical thinker of the nineteenth century in the tradition of Hegel and of rationalism, *istina* is thus the self-identify of the supra-personal objective world; it is revealed to the mind that thinks itself.

III. *Istina* and Existentialism

In contrast to Solovyov's objectivism, we find three distinct interpretations of *istina* in Russian existentialism: the term forms part of an individualist problematics with Shestov, a creationist problematics with Berdyayev, and an ethical problematics with Bakhtin.

A. Lev Shestov: *Istina* and the singularity of a person (*ličnost'*)

In the fourth chapter of *Athens and Jerusalem* (1951), Shestov contrasts truth (*istina*) to truths (*istiny* [истины], the plural of truth):

> In searching for the origins of being, metaphysics has not been able to find universal and necessary truth (*istina*), whereas in studying what comes from these origins, the positive sciences have discovered a number of "truths" (*istiny*). Does this not mean that the "truths" (*istiny*) of the positive sciences are false truths (*istiny ložnye* [истины ложные]), or at least fleeting truths, which last no more than an instant?

(Shestov, *Athens and Jerusalem*, 334)

"Universal and necessary truth," like Solovyov's "logical truth," is revealed to the "logical subject," designated by the pronoun *vse* [все] ("all," often in quotation marks), analogous to the German *man* (one). The fact that philosophy has been incapable of reaching this "universal and necessary truth" is far from being an objection against metaphysics. On the contrary, "metaphysics does not want to, and must not, give us truths (*istiny*) that are compulsory for all" (ibid.), since they would then merely lead to "constraining truths," likes those that the positive sciences offer us. In order to discover authentic truth, metaphysics has precisely to give up the "sword of necessity," that is, its claims to a valid universal truth.

However, if the logical subject in Shestov and Solovyov is incapable of discovering authentic truth, from an existential point of view, Solovyov's supra-personal subject does not exist. On the contrary, "the truth (*istina*) is revealed to an empirical person (*ličnost'* [личность]), and only to an empirical person" (ibid., 336). Contrasting the empirical person to the *vse* [все] (all), Shestov compares the empirical/transcendental distinction with that of living/dead: "Someone who is alive, what this school of thought calls an empirical person, was the main obstacle for Solovyov" (ibid.). *Istina* thus acquires an existential character: like, for example, Socrates's

demon or Saint Paul's vision on the road to Damascus, it cannot be recognized by "all." Unlike *istina*, which necessarily applies to "all" (*istina* as judgment), *istina* as "what is" is one particular and personal truth, "what truly exists for an empirical person, when this person is alone with him or herself":

> It is only when we are alone with ourselves, under the impenetrable veil of the mystery of individual being, of an empirical personality (*ličnost'*), that we sometimes decide to renounce these real or illusory rights, these prerogatives that we enjoy by virtue of our participation in a world that is common to all. It is then that the final, or near-final truths (*istiny*) suddenly burn brightly before our eyes.

(Ibid., 335)

Unspeakable, incommunicable, these ultimate truths die by being expressed in the words and structures of language that attempt to transform them into rational, necessary, comprehensible, and obvious judgments "for ever and for all."

B. Nicolas Berdyayev: *Istina*, communion (*soobščenie*), and creative freedom (*svoboda*)

Berdyayev also opposes truth as judgment and truth as existence:

> *I am the way, the truth (istina) and the life.* What does this phrase mean? It means that truth (*istina*) is not intellectual or exclusively gnoseological in character, but that it has to be understood comprehensively: it is existential.

(Berdyayev, *Truth and Revelation*, 21)

However for Berdyayev, unlike Shestov, existential *istina* is a matter not of the individual, but of intersubjectivity: "Truth is communitarian (*istina kommjunotarna* [истина коммюнотарна]); in other words, it assumes contact (*soobščenie* [сообщение] and fraternity between men" (ibid., p. 24). The best translation of *soobščenie* in French is *communion*; indeed, Berdyayev often uses two words, *soobščenie* and the transliteration of the French word "communion," as synonyms (Berdyayev, *Ja i mir objektov*, 165). Communion is the fruit of love (*ljubov'* [любовь]) and of friendship (*družba* [дружба]). The adjective *kommjunotarnyj* [коммюнотарный], often used as a secular equivalent of *sobornyj* [соборный] (catholic, universal), is also borrowed from the French. That which is communitarian, as opposed to collective, is based on the freedom (*svoboda* [свобода]) of each person. The idea of "original freedom" as a source of creation, whether divine or human, is central to Berdyayev's metaphysics, which are developed out of Jakob Böhme's doctrine of *Ungrund*. This freedom, *svoboda*, gives an absolute character to human subjectivity. But human creation always implies a departure from self, an elimination of self, and is only realized in the communion with others.

Reality as an "objective given (*ob'ektivnaja dannost'* [объективная данность]" that is imposed from "outside (*izvne* [извне])" the person (*ličnost'*) is at the opposite extreme of creative human existence. Berdyayev sees it as the source of slavery and of the submission of man: "It is completely wrong to attribute a purely theoretical meaning to truth (*istina*), and to only see it as a kind of intellectual submission of the knowing subject to a reality which is given to it from the outside" (*Truth and Revelation*, 22–23). *Istina*, as "what truly exists," has nothing in common with given reality; but this reality can be transformed or transfigured by the creative energy of the original freedom present in the creative act. It is in this sense, then, that we should understand the following sentence: "Truth (*istina*) is not a reality, nor a corollary of the real: it is the very sense of the real, its *Logos*, its supreme quality and value" (ibid., p. 22). *Istina*, which is thus dynamic in nature, is "what truly exists in reality: subjectivation, the transfiguration of the real." Truth as transfiguration ultimately has a theological and eschatological meaning: it leads, through communion and the creative act of a person, to the "definitive victory" over our "fallen state of objectivation" (Berdyaev, *Essai de métaphysique eschatologique*, p. 63), or in other words, toward the end of being (*bytie*).

C. Mikhail Bakhtin: *Istina* and *pravda*

Bakhtin, for his part, contrasts logical *istina* not to ontological *istina*, but to *pravda* [правда] (truth in justice), a term that translates the Greek *dikaiosunê* [δικαιοσύνη], but understood within an entirely different set of oppositions, such that it is usually translated into French, for want of anything better, as *vérité* (truth). This opposition needs to be read in the context of Bakhtin's critique of the "abstraction" of scientific philosophy, as presented in his theory entitled *Toward a Philosophy of the Act* (written at the start of the 1920s and never completed). For him, the theoretical world with its "abstract truth (*otvlečënnaja istina* [отвлечённая истина])," is incapable of containing *postupok* [поступок] (an ethical act). Contrasting "theoretical abstraction" to what he termed "participating thought," one that considers the being "inside the act (*postupok*)," he proposed an original version of existentialism: ethical existentialism. His "subject" is no longer the knowing subject, but the acting subject.

Pravda does not exclude theoretical *istina*. On the contrary, it assumes and completes it through a personal responsibility: "The entire infinite context of possible human theoretical knowledge—science—must become something *answerably known* [uznanie]. . . . This does not in the least diminish and distort the autonomous truth (*istina*) of theoretical knowledge, but, on the contrary, completes it to the point where it becomes compellingly valid truth-justice (*pravda*)." (*Toward a Philosophy*, 49) The absolute nature of *istina* is preserved, since a responsible action does not imply any relativity:

When considered from our standpoint, the autonomy of truth (*istina*), its purity and self-determination from the standpoint of method are completely preserved. It is precisely on the condition that it is pure that truth can participate answerably in Being-as-event (*bytie-sobytie* [бытие событие]); life-as-event does not need a truth that is relative from within itself (*otnositel'naja istina* [относительная истина]). The validity of truth (*istina*) is sufficient unto itself, absolute, and eternal, and an answerable act or deed of cognition takes into account this peculiarity of it; that is what constitutes its essence.

(Ibid., 9–10)

So *istina* retains its epistemological meaning, "what is, from the objective or scientific point of view," but it is relieved of its ontological meaning: it can no longer refer to "what truly exists," nor to what French translators have sometimes rendered (for example, Berdyaev) as *vérité philosophique* (philosophical truth) (Khomiakov, 7). For Bakhtin metaphysics (for which he uses the expression *prima philosophia*, or doctrine of "being as being") has to go beyond the limits of the theoretical world: "It is only from within the actually performed act (*postupok*), which is once-occurrent, integral, and unitary in its answerability, that we can find an approach to unitary and once-occurrent Being in its concrete actuality. A first philosophy can orient itself only with respect to that actually performed act (*postupok*)" (ibid., 28). "What truly exists" is not *istina*, but *postupok*, an act invested with *pravda*. The world of "what is," within which *postupok* takes place, is the being-event (*bytie-sobytie*). With this term Bakhtin introduces an etymological metaphor: *sobytie* means "event," but literally *so-bytie* signifies "co-being," "co-existence," that is, a shared world. *Bytie-sobytie*, analogous to the German *Mitwelt*, is the antonym of the world of theoretical *istina*: it implies authentic existence and participation.

■ See Box 1.

Since *istina*, like *pravda*, is normally translated as "truth," the precise meaning of these two terms is thereby lost. This is why, in contexts where *istina* is set in opposition to *pravda*, the least incorrect solution is to explain the first term in terms of "philosophical truth," or "theoretical truth," or even "abstract truth," which marks a clear distinction with *pravda*, whose meaning is "truth in justice" (see, for example, Berdyaev, *Khomiakov*, 7). Whereas *istina* expresses the authenticity of "what is," *pravda* emphasizes the fact that the thing has the character of being right or just.

Andriy Vasylchenko

BIBLIOGRAPHY

Bakhtin, Mikhail. "K filosofii postupka." *Filosofija i sociologija nauki i tekniki*. Moscow: Nauka, 1986. Translation and notes by Vadim Liapunov: *Toward a Philosophy of the Act*. Edited by Vadim Liapunov and Michael Holquist. Austin: University of Texas Press, 1993.

Berdyaev, Nicolas. *Aleksei Stepanovich Khomiakov*. Tomsk: Izdatel'stvo Vodolei, 1996. First published in 1912. Translation by V. and J.-C. Marcadé, with E. Sebald: *Khomiakov*. Lausanne, Switz.: L'Âge d'Homme, 1988.

———. *Istina i otkrovenie: prolegomeny k kritike otkroveniia*. St. Petersburg: Izd-vo Russkogo Khristianskogo gumanitarnogo in-ta, 1996. Translation by R. M. French: *Truth and Revelation*. London: Bles, 1953.

———. *Ja i mir objektov*. Paris: YMCA, 1934. Translation by Irène Vildé-Lot: *Cinq méditations sur l'existence: Solitude, société et communauté*. Paris: Aubier, 1936.

———. *Opyt èskhatologicheskoi metafiziki: tvorchestvo i ob'ektivatsiia*. Paris: YMCA, 1947. *Essai de métaphysique eschatologique*. Paris: Aubier, 1946. Translation by R. M. French: *The Beginning and the End*. New York: Harper, 1952.

Florensky, Pavel. *Stolp i utverzhdenie istiny: opyt pravoslavnoi teoditsei v dvenadtsati pis'makh*. Moscow: Lepta, 2002. First published in 1914. Translation and annotation by Boris Jakim: *The Pillar and Ground of the Truth*. Introduction by Richard F. Gustafson. Princeton, NJ: Princeton University Press, 1997.

Shestov, Lev. *Afiny i Ierusalim*. Paris: YMCA, 1951. Translation and introduction by Bernard Martin: *Athens and Jerusalem*. Athens: Ohio University Press, 1966.

Solovyov, Vladimir Sergeyevich. "Foundations of Theoretical Philosophy." Translated by Vlada Tolley and James P. Scanlan. In *Russian Philosophy*, edited by James M. Edie et al., 99–134. Vol. 3. Chicago: University of Chicago Press, 1965.

———. *Sobranie sochinenij*. St. Petersburg: Prosveshchenie, 1911–14.

1

Podnogotnaja, truth, and the practice of the question

There is a synonym of *istina* that is also translated as "truth": this is the term *podnogotnaja* [подноготная], which refers to "a truth hidden by someone, circumstances or details carefully concealed." It is encountered in situations where there is a question of "throwing light on" an affair, of trying to "uncover" the truth, for example, in a trial: it is an adjectival noun formed from the group of words *podnogotnaja istina*. Originally, *podnogot-naja* referred to a sort of torture, or an interrogation, as when pointed objects are thrust "under the fingernails"—*pod nogti* [под ногти], or in the singular *pod nogot'* [под ноготь] (cf. RT: *Ètimologičeskij slovar' russkogo jazyka*, 352). Similarly, the term *podlinnyi* [подлинный] (authentic) is etymologically linked to the ancient practice that consists, in a trial (*pravëz* [правёж]), of beating a suspect with a "long stick (*podlinnik* [подлинник])" to force him to tell the truth (RT: *Etymological Dictionary of the Russian Language*, 2:186).

The Russian term isolates a part of the meaning of the Greek *alêtheia* [ἀλήθεια], which also comes from a judicial trial. *Alêtheia*, which etymologically means "unveiling," "dis-covering," was uncovered quite normally during a trial through the use of torture (*basanizein* [βασανίζειν]) on slaves called to testify, who were freed in this way from allegiance to their masters. But *alêtheia* as "un-veiling" embraces all of the senses of truth, from authenticity to justness; and the Greek system of justice opens out onto judgment and the faculty of discriminating (*krisis* [κρίσις], *krinein* [κρίνειν]). Conceived as *alêtheia,* the truth extends its semantic orbit to the questioning of philosophy itself, as attested by the way in which Plato calls as a witness the verses by Parmenides in order for them to confess under torture that the false presupposes the existence of non-being (*The Sophist*, 237a–237b; Eng. ed. N. White (Hackett), 25): " 'Never shall this force itself on us, that that which is not may be; While you search, keep your thought far away from this path.' So we have his testimony to this. And our own way of speaking itself would make the point especially obvious if we examined it a little (*basanistheis* [βασανισθείς])."

ITALIAN

A Philosophy for Nonphilosophers Too

➤ ART, ATTUALITÀ, BEAUTY, CIVILTÀ, EUROPE, FRENCH, GOÛT, LEGGIADRIA, MÊTIS, PRAXIS, SPREZZATURA, VIRTÙ

The public of nonphilosophers are privileged interlocutors of Italian philosophers, who consider all humans not only as animals endowed with reason, but also as animals who nurture desires and formulate projects. What characterizes Italian philosophy, and what is reflected in its network of concepts, the styles of its research, and its language, is—to quote Machiavelli—the fact that it does not simply search for logical truth, but rather "the effective truth of the thing" in all its complexity. The fundamental terms of the Italian philosophical lexicon are common to the European tradition: where they are distinctive is in the expressive quality each singular author brings to them. The margin of untranslatability of these terms is thus not because of the "spirit of the language" but of the particular poetic or artistic "stamp" of the individual writers who create or reinterpret them. They are born of language that is cultivated but not specialized, clear but not technical, intuitive but not mystical: language in which the greatest mathematical rigor exists alongside the most intense pathos. In this sense, its register is characterized by an interweaving of reason and imagination, of concept and metaphor.

I. A Civil Philosophy

In the West, philosophy is for the most part transnational. If one were, as a hypothetical experiment, to trace contour lines and isobars to connect theories belonging to the same genre, but dispersed across different geographical areas, one would plainly see that these would lead us to draw maps whose borders do not coincide at all with those of existing states or national languages. Despite this, it is undeniable that Italian philosophy—like other philosophies—has acquired and retained a distinctive set of features of its own, and possesses a personal repertory of recurring themes, and of references to a particular expressive and conceptual register.

From a broad historical perspective, and taking into account the limits imposed by its irreducible complexity, the Italian language has been characterized by a constant and predominant civil vocation. By "civil" I mean a philosophy that is not immediately tied to the sphere of the state, nor to that of religion, nor to that of interiority. In fact, ever since its humanist and Renaissance origins, its privileged interlocutors have not been the specialists, clerics, or students attending university, but a wider public, a civil society one has sought to orient, to influence, to mold.

The first circle of interlocutors was made up of compatriots, fallen heirs of a great past, citizens of a community that in the beginning was simply a linguistic community, politically divided into a plurality of fragile religious states and, from a spiritual point of view, conditioned by a Catholic church that was too powerful (Italian philosophy has consequently developed a number of supplementary functions in the face of weak political institutions, and a certain contentiousness in the face of the massive presence of the Catholic church). The second circle—with the emphasis here on "universalist" traits—is made up of all people.

The most representative Italian philosophers, then, have not closed themselves off in narrow local circles, any more than they have devoted themselves to questions having to do with a particular logical, metaphysical, or theological sublime, as was the case in other nations—England, Germany, and Spain—where the weight of Scholastic or academic philosophy was felt for a much longer time, precisely because the caesura that humanism and the Renaissance represented was not so strong in these countries. These Italian philosophers took as their object of investigation questions that implicated virtually all of the population (the "nonphilosophers," as Benedetto Croce called them), knowing full well that they were dealing with animals who not only were endowed with reason but who also nurtured desires and formulated projects, animals whose thoughts, acts, and expectations were not bound by already established forms of argumentation, or even by defined—rigorously, of course—methods and languages, but shaped in an abstract and general way.

II. "The Effective Truth of the Thing"

Italian philosophy has consequently been at its best in its attempts to find solutions to problems where the relations between the universal and the particular are at stake, where logic comes up against empiricism. These problems (and the vocabulary to express them) are born of the overlapping of social relations and the variables that have mixed with them. This has produced an individual conscience divided between an awareness of the limits imposed by reality and the projection of desires, between tradition and innovation, between the opacity of historical experience and its transcription in images and concepts, between the powerlessness of moral laws and the implacable nature of the world, between thought and lived experience. Whence the many—often successful—attempts to carve out spaces of rationality in territories that seem deprived of it, to give meaning to forms of knowledge and practices that often appear to be dominated by the imponderable nature of power, taste, and chance: political philosophy, the theory of history, aesthetics, and the history of philosophy (these all being fields, moreover, where the weight of subjectivity and of individuality prove to be decisive).

It is important to emphasize that in rejecting the predominant philosophical perspectives, it is not a matter of "weakening" claims to the intelligibility of the real, but on the contrary of the effort to highlight spaces that were all too often hastily abandoned (and left to lie fallow) by a reason that had identified itself excessively with the sometimes triumphant paradigms of the physical sciences and of mathematics, to the extent that it modeled itself on them. Italian philosophers are consequently philosophers more of "impure reason," who take into account the conditioning, the imperfections, and the possibilities of the world, than philosophers of pure reason and of abstraction. In other words, they tend toward the concrete, in the etymological sense of the Latin *concretus*, the past participle of the verb *concrescere*, which refers precisely to what grows by aggregation, in a dense and bushy way (corresponding to the English "thick," as opposed to "thin," in the terms first introduced several decades ago by Bernard Williams, in relation to a moral discourse that is irreducible to formulas and precepts).

Although these philosophies are not interested in the knowledge of the absolute, of the immutable, or of norms that have no exception, they certainly do not abandon the search for truth, and are absolutely not given over to skepticism and relativism. On the contrary, the great tradition of Italian philosophy has never given up hope of the existence of a truth, or of the possibility of attaining it. This has been true since the time of Dante, who expresses it as follows:

Io veggio ben che già mai non si sazia	(I now see well : we cannot satisfy
nostro intelletto, se 'l ver non lo illustra	our mind unless it is enlightened by
di fuor dal qual nessun vero si spazia.	the truth beyond whose boundary no truth lies.
Posasi in esso come fera in lustra	Mind, reaching that truth, rests within it a
tosto che giunto l'ha : e giunger pòllo,	a beast within its lair; mind can attain
se non, ciascun disio sarebbe frustra.	that truth—if not, all our desires were vain.)

(*Paradiso*, IV.124–29, in *La divina commedia*, ed. A. Lanza; trans. A. Mandelbaum in *The Divine Comedy of Dante Alighieri*)

What characterizes Italian philosophy, and what is reflected in its network of concepts, the styles of its research, and its language, is—to quote Machiavelli—the fact that it does not simply search for logical truth, but rather the "verità effettuale della cosa" (effective truth of the thing), which often contradicts what appears in the first instance, and proves, without this being its cause, to be lacking an intrinsic rationality *juxta propria principia* (according to its own principles). But this truth is not reached through simple reasoning. That is, Italian philosophy has always maintained the tension between *epistêmê* and *praxis*, between the knowledge of what cannot be other than what it is, and the knowledge of what can be different to what it is, between the a priori and the a posteriori—not in order to stay midstream, but to cross from one bank to the other.

Although this philosophy distinguishes between the two terms, the world of thought seeks never to lose contact completely with the world of life, in the same way that it seeks not to isolate the public sphere from the private sphere. Despite the importance of the Catholic church and widespread religious practices, or perhaps because of these, a philosophy of interiority, of the dramatic or intimate dialogue with oneself, like the one that developed in France, from Pascal to Maine de Biran, or in Denmark with Kierkegaard, has essentially been absent in Italy. This is not only because of the externalizing tendency and the theatricality of the Roman Catholic rite, or the mental blocks caused by the fear of the Inquisition and the "tribunals of conscience" of the Counter-Reformation, but also because of the highly hierarchized institutionalization of the relations between the faithful and God. Unlike Lutheranism or Calvinism, Roman Catholicism is the guardian of a juridical culture, formalized over the centuries, which meticulously and knowingly regulates the behavior of the faithful. In the Italian philosophical tradition, one can consequently see, in opposition to the Protestant belief according to which *sola fides justificat* (faith alone justifies), the traces of the "religion by good works," of the existence in the world, that are proper to Catholicism—in other words, what is not shown to be effective has no value.

The fundamental terms of the Italian philosophical lexicon (which we will see adopted by a constellation of authors such as Machiavelli, Bruno, Galileo, Vico, Leopardi, Croce, and Gramsci) are generally those common to the European tradition, which has its deepest roots in the trinity "Athens,

Rome, Jerusalem." Where these terms are distinctive is in the expressive quality that each singular author brings to them. In other words, the untranslatability of these terms is not the fruit of the "spirit of the language," but derives rather from the particular poetic or artistic "stamp" of the individual writers who create or reinterpret them (and this pertains as much to their lexicon as to their syntax). Conversely, the apparent ease with which they can be translated is not because they have their source, as is the case for English, in everyday language, but rather because they are born of a language that is cultivated, but not specialized; clear, but not technical; intuitive, but not mystical—a language that, to paraphrase the title of a well-known work by Jean Starobinski, tends rather toward transparency than toward obstacles (*Jean-Jacques Rousseau: La transparence et l'obstacle*, 1971). This is why one needs, more than in other cultures, to know the intellectual history of Italy to understand the terms well. The degree of abstraction of concepts, or more precisely their comprehensibility, is typically higher in Italian than in English (which is lexically far richer, with four or five times the number of words—around seven hundred and fifty thousand words, as opposed to one hundred and fifty thousand) and not as high as in German, such that Italian concepts have to "cover" connotations that, in other languages, are distributed among several subconcepts. The syntax, in addition, does not present any particular irregularities or traps: it is generally less complex, and constructed of clauses that are shorter than the German written by Luther from Latin, but more articulated than the short, dry sentences in English. As a result, the turns of phrase and the punctuation sometimes have to be reworked to match the rhythms of the language into which Italian is translated.

The constant reference, whether implicit or explicit, to the universe defined by the idea of an effective reality proves to be fundamental from a conceptual point of view. It is, of course, close to the Aristotelian tradition of *auto to pragma*, of which the *Sache selbst* (the fundamental matter for thought, the thing itself, the matter itself) and the *Wirklichkeit* (reality) are what, in Hegelian terms, we would mark as the goal or the end point. However, the Italian version of this concept implies something concrete which distances it from other philosophical cultures (for that matter, the young Hegel developed the meaning of *Wirklichkeit* from Machiavelli, whom he studied in order to write his uncompleted work, *The German Constitution*).

▪ See Box 1.

III. *Volgare* and Poetic Logic

In its use of the *volgare* (vulgar), Italian philosophical vocabulary does not make a clean break with the scholarly language by definition, with Latin, since the relationship of the latter to the former is seen as a direct one. Latin remains, in its exemplary and "classical" simplicity, the skeleton beneath the flesh of Italian, which is linked to the spoken language

---

1

Machiavelli: *Verità effettuale della cosa* and knowledge of detail

Machiavelli himself might serve as the primary example, in the field of politics: the understanding of the *verità effettuale della cosa* (effective truth of the thing) is implied by the knowledge of particular things in their specificity. This does not exclude, but on the contrary presupposes, a movement of knowledge toward the universal: this also implies the overcoming (and not the abandonment) of the confused and distorting vision of the imagination and of opinion, as much as that (transparent and well articulated depending on the genre) of norms and laws that are governed by reason, without relying on the experience of concrete situations.

In a chapter of the *Discourses on the First Decade of Titus Livius* entitled "That though Men deceive themselves in Generalities, in Particulars they judge truly," Machiavelli analyzes the situation in Florence after the Medici were banished from there in 1494. In the absence of a constituted government, and because of the daily worsening of the political situation, many people tended at that time to attribute responsibility for this to the ambition of the seignory. But as soon as

one of them in turn managed to occupy a position of high public office, his ideas regarding the real situation of the city came closer and closer to the reality, and he abandoned both the opinions that circulated among his friends, as well as the precepts and abstract rules by which he had to begin his apprenticeship of public affairs:

> From time to time it happened that one or another of those who used this language rose to be of the chief magistracy, and so soon as he obtained this advancement, and saw things nearer, became aware whence the disorders I have spoken of really came, the dangers attending them, and the difficulty in dealing with them; and recognizing that they were the growth of the times, and not occasioned by particular men, suddenly altered his views and conduct; and a nearer knowledge of facts freeing him from the false impressions he had been led into on a general view of affairs. But those who had heard him speak as a private citizen, when they saw him remain inactive after he was made a magistrate, believed that

this arose not from his having obtained any better knowledge of things, but from his having been cajoled or corrupted by the great.

> (trans. Ninian Thompson, *Discourses on the First Decade of Titus Livius*, 1:47)

Whence Machiavelli's explicit intention to remain attached to reality, without following the drifting movement of his imagination and his desires:

> But, it being my intention to write a thing which shall be useful to him who apprehends it, it appears to me more appropriate to follow up the real truth of a matter than the imagination of it; for many have pictured republics and principalities which in fact have never been known or seen, because how one lives is so far distant from how one ought to live, that he who neglects what is done for what ought to be done, sooner effects his ruin than his preservation.

> (trans. W. K. Marriott, *The Prince*, chap. 15)

of different regions. The fundamental categories of the classical and medieval philosophical tradition (*res, natura, causa, substantia, ratio, conscientia* [thing, nature, cause, substance, reason, conscience]) are not seen to require any particular interpretive effort. Unlike German (where a philosophical term is added to that of ordinary language—for example, there is *Differenz* and *Unterschied* [difference])—the concepts used in philosophy in Italy are the same as those used in ordinary language. In order to enrich their meaning, or acquire a greater determination, they only have to go through the "thickness" of reasoning and *exempla* [examples], and travel from the convent cells and university classrooms to the public squares and offices of the most cultivated citizens, and in the process, they are retranslated into spoken language. Bilingualism (Latin/Italian) in philosophy was very early on limited to scholars of other nations or, as was the case with Giambattista Vico, to the inaugural theses read out in an academic context (e.g., his *De nostri temporis studiorum ratione* of 1708 and *De antiquissima Italorum sapientia, ex linguae latinae originibus eruenda* of 1710). The widespread practice of using the vulgar language was helped by the fact that Italian, at least from the sixteenth century to the end of the eighteenth century, was recognized as a language of culture (a language, it is true, that was generally carried along more by melodrama, theater, and literature, than by philosophy).

■ See Box 2.

Whereas German philosophers from Hegel to Heidegger considered their eminently speculative language as the most appropriate to express philosophical thought, it never crossed the minds of Italian philosophers to make such a claim for their own language. Neither did they intentionally seek a specific technical vocabulary, relating to the philosophical *koinê* coming out of the European tradition. Italian philosophy aimed instead for the expressive power of concepts and of argumentation: its ideal was closer to that of music, in which the greatest mathematical rigor exists alongside the most intense pathos. As Giacomo Leopardi (1798–1837) observed of Galileo (*Zibaldone*, ed. Solmi, 2:285), he was guided by "the association of precision with

---

2

The "illustrious vulgar tongue": A language for philosophy

Conscious of the fact that many people had not had any philosophical training, and convinced that "all men want to know" and were thus seeking philosophical knowledge, Dante made a plan to organize a philosophical banquet that the greatest possible number of people could attend. Not only was the *Convivio* (around 1304) conceived as a sort of summary of philosophical knowledge for the illiterate (the *non litterati*), but also it contained an explicit reflection on the transmission of knowledge, and consequently, on philosophical language. Although Dante was certainly not the first to write philosophy in the vulgar tongue, he was the person who articulated most clearly the problem of the relation between language and philosophy, and worked out all of its consequences, thereby transforming both the mode of expression and the content of philosophy. The *Divine Comedy* (1307–20) realized fully the ideal of such a philosophico-moral pedagogy addressed to all, and dedicated to a vast reform of the social and political world "for the good of the world which lives badly" (in pro del mondo che mal vive).

Dante's treatise *De vulgari eloquentia* (On vernacular eloquence), written around the same time as the *Convivio*, attempts to lay the theoretical foundation of a new use of the vulgar. Drawing on an analysis of the different modes of expression, the "vulgar tongue" (*locutio vulgaris*) and the "secondary tongue" (*locutio secundaria, grammatica*) (of which the first is natural, common to all, corruptible and variable, and the second artificial, reserved for the literate, eternal and invariable with regard to place and time), and following a historico-biblical itinerary going from the unity of the Adamic idiom to the infinite division of idioms after Babel, Dante postulates the need for an "illustrious vulgar tongue" that would avoid the disadvantages of the two spoken languages, while retaining their essential qualities (see LANGUAGE). This illustrious vulgar tongue, which he says should be common to all Italian city-states without belonging to any of them, is comparable to the first elements of each genre, which become their measure:

The noblest signs which characterize the actions of Italians do not belong to any city state of Italy and are common to all of them; and we can put among them the vulgar tongue we banished earlier, and which breathes its perfume in each city without staying in any of them. Yet it may breathe its perfume more intensely in one city state than in another, just as the simplest of perfumes who is God breathes His perfume in men more than in beasts, in animals more than in plants, in plants more than in minerals, and in minerals more than in fire, in fire more than in the earth.

(trans. S. Botterill, *De vulgari eloquentia*, I, chap. 16)

This vulgar tongue that the poet-philosopher sought—a few examples of which he recognized in several inspired contemporaries—would make it possible for the existing local vulgar tongues to be measured, evaluated, and compared. The aim of Dante's uncompleted work was to establish the rules, as much from a grammatical as poetic or rhetorical point of view, of this vulgar tongue, which could lay claim to the universalism of Latin without having its rigidity, and to the expressiveness of the vulgar without the irregularities of fragmentation. By writing his "sacred poem," Dante simultaneously produced a model and an exemplum. The language and the form of the *Divine Comedy* were the means he gave himself to create a new philosophy for a new audience: the secular public.

Ruedi Imbach
Irène Rosier-Catach

BIBLIOGRAPHY

Alighieri, Dante. *De vulgari eloquentia*. Edited, translated, and with an introduction by Steven Botterill. Cambridge: Cambridge University Press, 1996. The unfinished Latin text was composed ca. 1302–5 and published in Vicenza, Italy, as early as 1529.

elegance." In this sense, its register is characterized by an interweaving of reason and imagination, of concept and metaphor. Or rather, in Vico's terms, by marrying together the logic of reason and what he refers to in the *Scienza Nuova* as "poetic logic."

Because it is a question of understanding the logic of transformations, of finding a meaning to the continual becoming of things, of confronting this *mutazione* (mutation) so often mentioned by Giordano Bruno in the sixteenth century as the essence of things and the source of *delettazione* (delectation) rather than of sadness and melancholy (see his *Spaccio della bestia trionfante*), the language of Italian philosophy tries to be incisive and enlightening in a familiar mode. It works far better in the form of a dialogue (from Alberti to Galileo and Leopardi), or in statements that are rich in figurative expressions created by the imagination, than in the dry form of a systematic treatise or a metaphysical meditation. But as with Bruno, there is always some order in the swirl of mutations, and at their heart any changes take place around a fixed pivot:

> Time takes away everything and gives everything: all things change, nothing is annihilated; one alone is immutable, one alone is eternal and can remain eternally one and the same. . . . With this philosophy, my spirit takes on another dimension, and my intellect is magnified.

> (*Candelaio*, vol. 1; trans. G. Moliterno, *Candlebearer*)

The fact that there is no hierarchy in the infinite universe, and as a consequence there are no absolute center and periphery, is also reflected in the syntax: given that every element of the sentence, even the commas, could become the center of the discourse, Bruno rejected—as Yves Hersant, one of his French translators, has observed—hierarchical constructions based on subordinate clauses, and his reasoning was almost always expressed using coordinated clauses (which are typically a series of relative clauses). In addition, he mixed together, following the whims of his imagination, the three styles (low, middle, high) of the Aristotelian tradition, and introduced trivial language. The vulgar and the sublime, reason and "heroic fury," logic and the imagination, could thus exist alongside one another and fuse together.

And it was precisely this "poetic logic" of the imagination that Vico called for to show the roots of the "pure mind," which humans attain when they are at the highest point of the development of a civilization. Through the idea of a poetic logic, Vico takes myths, religion, passions, and art out of the sterile space of the irrational and shows that they have a specific and fecund legitimacy, a logic to be exact, with rules that, while not coinciding with those of the "mind opened out" (*mente dispiegata*), illuminate the meaning of what we achieve without intending to, or unreflectively:

> So that while rational metaphysics teaches us that *homo intelligendo fit omnia*, this imaginative metaphysics [*metafisica fantastica*] show that *homo non intelligendo fit omnia*; and perhaps there is more truth in the second statement than in the first, for man, when he understands, opens up his mind and apprehends things, but when he does not understand, he does things from

himself and, transforming himself in them, he becomes these very things.

> (trans. L. Pompa, *The First New Science* [translation modified])

We are indebted to Vico for the discovery that the internal logic of events is not only revealed through reason but also through the imagination, which obeys laws that are in fact more constricting and more demanding than the laws of reason. And this involves a legacy from the past that we cannot suppress. In the *ingens sylva* (the great forest), where he locates the primitive relations that humans have between themselves and with nature, promiscuity reigns. Marriages do not exist, because the considered and solemn choice of a woman with whom to have one's own children has not yet happened. Mating between *bestioni* (wild animals) is thus a matter of force and chance; dead bodies putrefy with no tombs; conflicts are resolved by force, or by cunning. The historical period that follows, however, equally obeys poetic logic—though it is now the birth of a civic order that this logic imposes. The monogamous family and religion appear, and with them, humanity leaves behind its state of savagery. The *gentes majores* (those who claim to be able to interpret the visible order in the skies contemplated from the clearings in the forest [see Box 3]) feel the need to impose from on high laws reflecting a similar order onto those who are living in anarchy. The political imagination of the *gentes majores*—which draws upon myths and supernatural powers, on fears and hopes—is thus at the origin of a fictional order, but in which men believe, thanks to the power of the imagination (*fingunt simul creduntque*). It regulates and gives meaning to the moments that mark the solemn emergence of a life that will from that point on be lived together: it establishes tombs for the dead, the celebration of marriage, the worship of gods. If human history has a meaning, it is not because it derives from a rational logical that is internal to events, but because an order has been imposed on these events that has come forth from the imagination, and that is little by little rationalized through myths, rites, juridical concepts, and moral obligations, all of which appear subsequently. In an effort to express the genesis of the reason that is deployed within imagination, the linear language of the Latin works by Vico becomes, in *The New Science*, complex and overloaded; from a syntactical point of view, parenthetical comments and digressions proliferate. But it is always powerfully expressive.

■ See Box 3.

IV. "Ultraphilosophy"

It was Giacomo Leopardi, however, who really attempted to establish a lasting alliance between philosophy and reason, reason and imagination, clarity and distinctness of concepts and indetermination. He challenged their reciprocal isolation to show how they were complementary in their antagonism. For Leopardi, only someone who is at the same time a philosopher and a poet can understand reality. If he does not want to be only "half a philosopher," a thinker in effect has a duty to experience passions and illusions:

> Anyone who does not have, or has never had, any imagination or feelings, anyone who is unaware of the

3

Illuminismo

➤ LIGHT

Illuminismo has nothing in common with what in French is referred to as *illuminisme*, whether one is talking about the doctrine of certain mystics such as Swedenborg or Böhme, or in psychiatry, "a pathological exaltation accompanied by visions of supernatural phenomena" (*Le Petit Robert*). But *illuminismo*, the Italian Enlightenment, is also distinct from the French *Lumières*, the English Enlightenment, and the German *Aufklärung* in its determination not to lose sight of the psychic faculties and the social conditions out of which reason emerges.

Although Vico did not, strictly speaking, belong to the Enlightenment movement, we already find in him, well before Heidegger, the idea that a "clearing" has a philosophical importance, as a place where light and shadow, order and disorder meet, as well as the site of emergence of rationality and poetic fantasy. Indeed, for Vico, the first men contrasted the disorder of their existence in the *ingens sylva*—the great forest of their origins—with the order of the sky, to which their imagination attributes a name:

> So a few giants, who had to be the strongest of them, and who were spread out in the woods at the tops of the mountains, where the fiercest beasts have their lairs, terrified and astonished by the great effect of which they did not know the cause, raised their eyes and noticed the sky. . . . Then they imagined that the sky was an immense living body which, seeing it thus, they called Jupiter, the first god of the so-called gentes majores, who by the flash of lightning, and the rumble of thunder, wanted to tell them something.
>
> (trans. L. Pompa, *The First New Science*, Book 1 [translation modified])

In this way, the "opened mind" has an origin, which it is impossible to abstract, and a consistency that is continually limited by historical givens, which one cannot deduce rationally (the "certain" and the "blind labyrinth of man's heart"). This "opened mind" is threatened by a return to the stages he had gone through previously, by virtue of which it can happen that those who have attained a high level of civilization "turn cities into forests, and forests into men's lairs" (ibid.). A shadow of new barbarism is thus projected onto the cleared space of civilization.

The figures of the Italian Enlightenment—in its two main centers, Naples and Milan—retain a close contact with civil society and practical life. The explicit refusal of metaphysics and of abstraction is exemplified by Antonio Genovesi (1712–69), the first person in Europe to be appointed to a chair in political economy (in 1754), and whose thought focused on the interwoven interests and aspirations of humankind, and on the struggle against privilege. The Enlightenment philosophy of Lombardy was more oriented toward law; it also found expression in the dynamic review *Il caffè* (1764–66), and its major representatives were Pietro Verri (1728–97) and Cesare Beccaria (1738–94). The Enlightenment project for them, on the one hand, developed in the direction of a modernization of society, facilitating the individual search for happiness, and, on the other, aimed at making the correctional system more humane through the abolition of torture, by humanizing punishment, and by making judgments more clear-cut and quicker. The light of a human reason (and no longer that of Providence) that tried hard to become more just, thus struggled to break through the darkness of social life.

---

possibilities of enthusiasm, of heroism, of vivid and great illusions, of strong and varied passions, anyone who does not know the vast system of beauty, who does not read or feel, or has never read or felt, the poets, cannot by any means be a great, true and perfect philosopher . . . it is absolutely indispensable that a man such as this be a sovereign and perfect poet. Not in order to reason like a poet, but to examine like the coldest and most calculating rationalist [*ragionatore*] what *only* the most ardent *poet* can know. . . . Reason needs the imagination and the illusions it destroys; the true needs the false, substance needs appearance, the most perfect insensibility needs the most vivid sensibility, ice needs fire, patience needs impatience, powerlessness needs sovereign power, the smallest needs the largest, geometry and algebra need poetry, etc.

(*Zibaldone* [4 October 1821])

Leopardi is here stating a more general tendency of Italian philosophy, already present most explicitly in Vico: the determination to break down the walls separating reason from imagination, and philosophy from poetry, without, however, being responsible for confusing these roles. Each, in effect, feeds off the other, while remaining firmly in its place:

philosophy occupies the space of the real, and poetry that of the imagination, which is complementary, and each recognizes the demands of the other. Because of this, the philosopher has to take into account not only truth (this is his principal aim) but also illusions, which are essential ingredients of human nature, and which intervene to a great degree in the existence of individuals. And it is not enough to recognize them as such, and then put them aside, since they have "very strong roots" so that even if one cuts them down and understands their vanity, "they grow back again." However, human "noble nature," as we read in Leopardi's poem *La Ginestra* (vv. 111–17), is heroically opposed to illusions and it sacrifices no part of truth, but has, on the contrary, the courage to confront these illusions ("The noble nature is the one / who dares to lift his mortal eyes / to confront our common destiny / and, with honest words / that subtract nothing from the truth, / admits the pain that is our destiny, / and our poor and feeble state" [Leopardi, *Canti*, trans. J. Galassi]).

Since it recognizes the power of illusions, philosophy consequently must, according to Leopardi, be bound to the experience of the senses, and remain close to the effective truth of the thing. This is different from what happens in the context of German culture, which, in fusing together poetry and philosophy, ends up producing hybrid philosophical poems, chimerical constructions that reach their apogee, Leopardi writes, in the self-celebration of Germany:

> Che non provan sistemi et congetture
> E teorie dell'alemanna gente ?
> Per lor, non tanto nelle cose oscure
> L'un dì tutto sappiam, l'altro niente,
> Ma nelle chiare ancor dubbi e paure
> E caligin si crea continuamente:
> Pur manifesto si conosce in tutto.
> Che di seme tedesco il mondo è frutto.
>
> (Is there something that the systems and conjectures
> And theories of the German people do not prove?
> For them, they are not so many obscure things
> So that one day we know everything, the next nothing.
> But they are clear things that are endlessly clouded by fog
> And continual doubts and fears are born;
> All in all, we see manifestly
> That the world is the fruit of a Germanic seed.)

> (*Paralipomeni della Batracomiomachia*, l.17; trans.
> G. Caserta, *The War of the Mice and the Crabs*, 6)

Yet the Germans (whose philosophical culture Leopardi did not know well) have no reason for self-celebration:

> The German men of letters' lack of a social life, and their ceaseless life of study and isolation in their offices not only divorces their thoughts from men (and from the opinions of others), but also from things. This is why their theories, their systems, their philosophies are for the most part *poems of reason*, whatever the genre they examine: politics, literature, metaphysics, morality, and even physics, etc. Indeed, the English (such as Bacon, Newton, Locke), the French (such as Rousseau and Cabanis), and even some Italians (Galileo, Filangieri, etc.) have made great, *true and concrete*, discoveries about nature and the theory of man, of governments, and so on, but the Germans have made none.

> (*Zibaldone* [30 August 1822])

Leopardi attempts to complete and go beyond rationalism and the Enlightenment, which the cultures of his "superb and foolish" century have blocked. He seeks to do this by elaborating an "ultraphilosophy" that is closely linked with poetry, and that is able to offer an exact assessment of the nature of man as a desiring being, but a being also incapable of realizing the infinity of its desire, and of attaining a lasting pleasure. Paraphrasing Carl von Clausewitz, one might say that "ultraphilosophy" is nothing but the continuation of philosophy through other means, namely, those of poetry—means which, once they are known and used, ought nevertheless not trouble or overly excite "very cold reason."

Philosophy should use the indeterminate beauty of poetry to reject any conception of form as pure, fixed, rigid, and innate form (Platonic in its origin, but taken up by Christianity, and identified with God). Since all knowledge comes from the senses, and is fueled by the imagination and by reason, beginning with a ceaseless working on the materials that are transmitted to them, humans affirm that all things are given

and cannot be deduced—which contrasts with any idea of innateness:

> The destruction of innate ideas destroys the principle of goodness, of beauty, of absolute perfection, as well as their opposites, that is, of a perfection which would be founded on reason, a superior form to the existence of the subjects which contain it, and thus eternal, immutable, necessary, primordial, existing before such subjects, and independently of them.

> (*Zibaldone* [17 July 1821])

It thus becomes absurd to speak of good and evil, of beauty and ugliness, of order and disorder, as absolutes. Indeed, once innate ideas have been eliminated,

> There is no other reason possible why things should be absolutely and necessarily such and such a way—some good, others bad—independently of each will, each event, each *fact*. The only reason that is for all, in reality, resides in these facts, and consequently this reason is always and only ever relative. So nothing is good, true, bad, ugly, false, except relatively; and the conventional relationships between things is also relative, and this, if we can put it this way, is absolutely so.

> (*Zibaldone* [17 July 1821])

In the metaphysical tradition, what is bad, false, or ugly has an eminently negative connotation: they are deprived, respectively, of what is good, true, and beautiful. Leopardi roots out the very assumptions of such a conception. Demonstrating that what is bad is not an accidental, voluntary, human disruption of a divine or natural order that would, if it were not for this, be perfect, he dismisses both the substantialist conception of the plenitude of being, and the thesis of the existence of a *kosmos*, that is, a harmonious and divine structure (synonymous with both beauty and order). The pillars of the architectonics of the good, the true, and the beautiful, which have been present almost continuously from Plato through to Leibniz, thus collapse. The principle of an independent (*absolutus*) order at the root of all things, a source—moral, logical, or aesthetic—of justification of the world and of human actions—this principle now ceases to exist:

> For no one thing is absolutely necessary: that is, there is no absolute reason preventing it from not being, or from not being such and such a way, etc. . . . This is tantamount to saying that there is not, or there has never been, a first and universal principle of things, or that if it exists, or has existed, we cannot in any way know it, since we do not and cannot have the slightest evidence to judge things prior to things, and to know them beyond pure, real facts. . . . There is no doubt that if we destroy the pre-existing Platonic forms of things, we destroy God.

> (*Zibaldone*)

The *Summum malum* falls along with the *Summum bonum*, Satan falls along with God. Men and their histories remain consequently alone in a cosmos that knows nothing of them, and that conceals no finality for them.

V. Historicism and the Nonphilosopher

Italian historicism (from Croce to Gramsci) has contested Jacobin abstractions, which Leopardi had already denounced, by highlighting the obstacles, the blocks, and the specificity—or rather the concrete nature—of each historical situation and the consequent necessity of making reality the measure of thought. Leopardi was inspired more by Vincenzo Cuoco's *Saggio sulla rivoluzione napoletana* (Essay on the Neapolitan Revolution of 1799) than by Marx. That is, he reflected more on failed revolutions and the lessons to be drawn from sudden defeats, than on radical innovations and on preparing for new insurrections. Italian historicism is characterized precisely by the encounter between history and utopia: a history energized, structured, innervated by a utopian goal (that of emancipation) and a utopia held in check and weighed down, forced to take into account certain obligations and the limits of what was possible, the obstacles that lay in the way, and how one navigated one's way through them. In the ethical and political, but also aesthetic domains, the attachment to the real, to the effective truth of the thing, the fidelity to the world and the ability to communicate, are once again valued, by Croce, for example, in opposition to empty interiority and its claims. Beauty, consequently, is nothing other than the effective expression in a singular and unique work of art, of an intuition that would otherwise remain indeterminate and without content in our feelings and in our mind, and of which we are fully conscious only because someone was able to express it. Indeed, beauty is, for Croce, when he writes his *Aesthetic*, "a successful expression, or better, simply expression, since when expression is not successful it is not an expression" (trans. Colin Lyas, *The Aesthetic as the Science of Expression and of the Linguistic in General*). The proof afforded by reality, together with its communicability, shatters the prejudice hidden within the belief that the confused interiority of intention is enough to create a work of art:

> One sometimes hears people say they have many great thoughts in their mind, but they cannot manage to express them. In truth, if they had them, they would have transformed them into fine, ringing words, and thus expressed them. If, when they express them, these thoughts seem to evaporate, or appear to be rare and poor, it is because they did not exist, or because they were rare or poor.

(Ibid.)

Like those who nurture illusions about the value of their own wealth, who are then harshly contradicted by mathematics, we usually tend to overestimate the intensity of our intuitive gifts. Expression—that damned-if-you-do, damned-if-you-don't trap-that-is-also-a-bridge that Croce builds for us here—shows us our limits and, at the same time, makes us more aware of the fact that a painter "is a painter because he sees what others only feel, or glimpse, but do not see" (ibid.).

For Croce, the love of the concrete goes as far as a defense of "nonphilosophy," which he declares as philosophy's legitimate son, and which disseminates a culture, and contributes to the layering of philosophical ideas in the unreflective form of good sense:

> I despise philosophy that is nasty, presumptuous and dilettante: presumptuous when it discusses difficult things as if they were not difficult, and dilettante with respect to sacred things. By contrast, I very much like the nonphilosopher, who does not get upset and remains indifferent to philosophical arguments, distinctions, and dialectics, who possesses truth by stating it in a few simple principles, and in clear sentences, which are a reliable guide for his judgment and action: the man of good sense and of wisdom.

("Il non-filosofo," in *Frammenti di etica*)

This man is, precisely, the philosopher's son, because "good sense is in fact nothing other than the legacy of previous philosophies, which have been continually enriched by their capacity to welcome the clear results of the new kind of philosophizing. This is not a gift of nature, but the fruit of history, a product distilled by the historical labor of thought; and since he welcomes the results, and only the results, unconcerned by how they were obtained, he welcomes them without debate or subtle arguments, and without any doctrinal methods" (ibid.).

For Gramsci, this concern—allied to more political intentions—to build this narrow, treacherous bridge between the philosophical high-mindedness of the elite and the spontaneous philosophy of nonphilosophers, between reason and common sense, is almost obsessive:

> It is essential to destroy the widespread prejudice that philosophy is a strange and difficult thing just because it is the specific intellectual activity of a particular category of specialists or of professional and systematic philosophers. It must first be shown that all men are "philosophers," by defining the limits and characteristics of the "spontaneous philosophy" which is proper to everybody. This philosophy is contained in: 1. language itself, which is a totality of determined notions and concepts and not just of words grammatically devoid of content; 2. "common sense" and "good sense"; 3. popular religion and, therefore, also in the entire system of beliefs, superstitions, opinions, ways of seeing things and of acting, which surface collectively under the name of "folklore."

(*Selections from the Prison Notebooks of Antonio Gramsci*, ed. Q. Hoare and G. Nowell-Smith)

The only difference between the philosophy of philosophers and that of nonphilosophers comes from the level of critical awareness and of active conceptual elaboration that each manifests or claims. Whence, the following rhetorical question:

> [I]s it better to "think," without having a critical awareness, in a disjointed and episodic way? In other words, is it better to take part in a conception of the world mechanically imposed by the external environment, i.e. by one of the many social groups in which everyone is automatically involved from the moment of his entry into the conscious world (and this can be one's village or province; it can have its origins in the parish and the "intellectual activity" of the local priest or

ageing patriarch whose wisdom is law, or in the little old woman who has inherited the lore of the witches or the minor intellectual soured by his own stupidity and inability to act)? Or, on the other hand, is it better to work out consciously and critically one's own conception of the world and thus, in connection with the labours of one's own brain, choose one's sphere of activity, take an active part in the creation of the history of the world, be one's own guide, refusing to accept passively and supinely from outside the moulding of one's personality?

(Ibid.)

■ See Box 4.

The almost neorealist value of concrete lived experience, of the link between determinate historical and economic situations, is also central to Italian historicism in general, including after Croce and Gramsci. It is manifest in the recognition of rights and of the implacable nature of time itself, and by the refusal to take refuge in the corrupt shelter of consciousness, in the comforting but sterile isolation of private space, or to seek a way to escape into glorious but illusory utopias that promise immediate regeneration. According to historians, we should accentuate the link between philosophy and the effective history of men, or the "real roots of ideal choices," since philosophy consists of "recovering the humanity of thought, of rekindling the humanity of thought, the *human flesh* without which these thoughts would not be in the world" (E. Garin, *La filosofia come sapere storico*). Each philosophy thus relies on the fact that men change, as do the intellectual tools used to understand reality. The historian of philosophy from now on discovers "in place and instead of philosophy understood as the autonomous development of a self-sufficient knowledge, a plurality of fields of investigation, of positions, of visions, in relation to which the unity of the act of philosophizing is conceived as a certain level of critical awareness, or at the very most, as the need to unify the different fields of research" (V. Verra, *La filosofia dal'45 ad oggi*). Once again, in historicism, philosophy is conceived as being itself directed toward the concrete, and aims ultimately to become the point of liaison between what is experienced and what is thought.

VI. *Mechanê* and Machines

When we again consider, from the point of view of the sciences, the basic characteristics of Italian philosophy, whether translatable or untranslatable, we note the fundamental contribution made by Italy, from Leonardo da Vinci to Galileo, from Volta to Pacinotti, from Marconi to Fermi. Oddly, we might also observe that there has never been any indigenous reflection on the philosophy of science or on logic—if we exclude Galileo himself and the figures (who for a long time remained rather isolated) of Peano, Vailati, and Enriques. As a consequence, no technical or specialized language has been disseminated, and in general it has recently been imported from the Anglo-Saxon world.

However, Galileo is an excellent example of the particular attitude of the Italian tradition that seeks, on the one hand, to position itself from the point of view of nonphilosophers and nonspecialists alike, and on the other, to show that behind general and abstract formulae lie hidden unexpected situations, but ones that have their own logic, which we understand by respecting the specificity of the object. Thus, through his crystalline prose, Galileo constantly puts himself in these dialogues in the position of an interlocutor, Simplicio, designed to represent in exemplary fashion the way of thinking that was dominant at the time in the scientific community, the one that drew on the well-established authority of Aristotle and Ptolemy. Galileo sought to refute this authority by means of "experiments undertaken and demonstrations that were certain," but certainly not to ignore it. On the contrary, he kept it as a constant point of reference, and as an indicator of a common sense that had to be raised patiently to the level of a new scientific knowledge. As a representative of the Accademia dei Lincei, founded in 1604 by Federico Cesi, Galileo's ideal was precisely to have the eye of a lynx in searching for the truth where it was the most difficult to reach, and where appearances could often be deceptive.

In his research, Galileo advocates starting out from simple elements that, when combined together, offer the meaning of what is more complex:

I have a little book, shorter than Aristotle's or Ovid's, which contains every science and does not demand lengthy study: it is the alphabet; anyone able to assemble vowels and consonants in an ordered way will find in it a source of the truest answers to all questions, and will draw from it teachings of all the sciences and all the arts; this is exactly the way in which a painter, with the different plain colors next to one another on his palette, knows how, in mixing a little bit of one to another, and even adding a little bit of a third, to represent men, plants, buildings, birds, fish, in short, to imitate all visible objects; and yet on his palette there are no eyes, feathers, scales, leaves or stones.

(trans. S. Drake, *Dialogue Concerning the Two Chief World Systems*)

This is the route by which abstractions are incarnated in reality, that is, the letters of the alphabet transformed into terms that have meaning, colors into eyes and feathers, numbers and geometrical figures into physical beings. But Galileo also ventured down an opposing path. According to this latter method, he proceeded by excarnation, as Yves Bonnefoy would say, in order to extract the general rules of the living flesh of particular cases, knowing full well that this could then lead to dead ends. This is why he wrote in praise of the progressive discovery of reality, in its specific and distinct traits, a discovery that has to go beyond false analogies in order to privilege the faculty of discrimination and that also has to sometimes conclude with a declaration of provisional ignorance. This is well illustrated by the parable of the "man gifted by nature with a perceptive mind and an extraordinary curiosity" (Galileo, "Il Saggiatore: The Assayer," in *The Controversy on the Comets of 1618*. trans. S. Drake and C. D. O'Malley), who at first confuses the song of a bird with the sound of a bird whistle, and

4

Storicismo

➤ HISTORY

Although Italian historicism owes its origins in part to the German *Historismus* of a Ranke or a Dilthey, it quickly acquired its own set of features and its originality, especially with Croce and Gramsci. It is based on the thesis of the absolute historicity and immanence of every human life and expression. History is the product of the objectification and the determinate incorporation of our actions in this unique and incredible world, or rather of the fact that the actions of everyone are inevitably caught up in the great deluge of collective events. Whence the rejection of all teleological thinking, the respect for the implacable nature of facts, and the emphasis on individual responsibility. This position, however, does not imply the acceptance of the ineluctable necessity of the course of history. On the contrary, individuals question the past and thus bring it alive and make it present, pressured by needs that are endlessly renewed and manifest, spurred on by the desire to eliminate the obscurities and phantasms that interfere with action, and to escape servitude and the weight of the past.

It is thanks to reflection and philosophy—which is a *metodologia della storiografia*, "methodology of historiography" ("historiography" signifying here, as Croce explains, *historia rerum gestarum* or "historical account of the past," that is, not events but their interpretation in history books), the knowledge of this "concrete universal" present in each event—that we succeed in understanding the meaning of what has been. The historical investigations of historians—and those that each of us undertakes to reconstruct the meaning of our behavior and our past—ease the route to freedom, which is understood as an awareness of necessity and a knowledge of the real possibilities of action. Historicism consequently excludes both the passive acceptance of events as well as the desire to go beyond the determining factor and limits of the real without confronting them. By converting the past into knowledge, and by understanding everything that stirs dimly within us and within the world, we are ready to realize who we are, we become creators of history. Only that which is objectified, and which enters into a relation with the activity of others, leaving behind some sign, has any permanent value—and not the feeble attempts, nor the boasts, nor the paralyses of the will that destroy our minds, nor the endless chatter.

The life of the mind consists precisely in this realization of the movement of the whole in the works of the individual, which are merely functions that are subordinate to this totality. For Croce they become immortal, in a secular sense, and only have value if they consciously accept being the construction materials of a history that is unfolding above their heads, beyond their intentions, and in which they nonetheless believe:

> [N]o sooner is each one of our acts completed than it is separated from us and lives an immortal life, and we ourselves (who are merely the process of our acts) are immortals, because we have lived and are still living.

> ("Religione e serenità," *Frammenti di etica*, 23)

In this one, unique world we maybe suffer, but this world alone contains the objects of our desire, of our passion, of our interest, and of our knowledge. We would not, in fact, want any other, for example, the one promised by religions: we are inextricably tied to this immanence (this is the meaning of the expression *storicismo assoluto* [absolute historicism]). We have to immerse ourselves courageously in it, accept the risk, the possibility of suffering, of disappointments, and of sadness:

> [I]s it worth living when we are forced to take our pulse at every moment, and to surround ourselves with useless remedies, avoiding the slightest draft because we are afraid of falling ill? Is it worth loving, when we are constantly thinking about and accommodating love's hygiene, measuring its doses, taking it in moderation, trying from time to time to abstain from it in order to get better at abstinence, out of a fear of the overwhelming shocks and heartbreaks in the future?

> ("Amore per le cose," in *Frammenti di etica*, 19)

What the Gramscian conception of history aims to do, for its part, is to provide an appropriate theoretical framework for confronting a determinate historical situation of struggle and transition, which is marked by numerous imbalances and tensions, and in which bridgeheads and delays coexist alongside one another. Such a history should in Italy, for example, play a mediating role between the industrial North and the agricultural South, between the high culture of bourgeois tradition and the superstitions or the folklore of the subaltern classes, between philosophy and myth, between the development of productive forces—understood even in the context of a Taylorist system—and the obstacles that come from outmoded or archaic relations of production. By the effort brought about to eliminate the divisions between dominant and dominated, history should be transformed on the basis of a project of collective emancipation, and not contemplated and admired like some unfathomable mystery, rendered cruel by its incomprehensible and eternal essence. Historicism is so radical and immanent that what today is true in this precise situation of historical constraint could well become false, and what is false could, at least to some extent, become true:

> We might even go as far as stating that, while the entire system of the philosophy of praxis could become obsolete in a unified world, many idealist conceptions, or at least certain aspects of these, which are utopian during the period of necessity, could become "truths" after this has passed, etc.

> (*Selections from the Prison Notebooks of Antonio Gramsci*, ed. Q. Hoare and G. Nowell-Smith)

then slowly begins to distinguish this latter sound from the music played by a stringed instrument, and from the sound made by rubbing a finger around the edge of a glass, or by the buzzing of the wings of a fly. Finally, when he tries to understand where the shrill sound of a cicada comes from, "having pulled off the front of its chest and seeing below it a few hard but fine cartilages, and thinking that the chirping came from their vibration" (ibid.), he kills it by dissecting it, so that "he removed both its voice and its life . . . he reached from this such a point of mistrust vis-à-vis his own knowledge, that if anyone asked him how sounds are made, he replied honestly that he knew a few ways, but felt certain that there could be a hundred other unknown and undreamed of" (ibid.).

In this sense, the logic of discovery for Galileo was open to what was new, and was not yet reducible to the compact unity of a theory:

I do not want our poem to be restricted to unity to the point where we can no longer give free rein to circumstantial episodes: all they need is to have some link to what we are saying; it is as if we had gathered to tell stories, and I said allow me to say the one that comes to my mind after hearing yours.

(trans. S. Drake, *Dialogue Concerning the Two Chief World Systems*)

The famous statement about the world being written in mathematical characters does not allow us to deduce from these a priori forms any similarly certain knowledge regarding physical space. Let us look at this text again:

Philosophy is written in this immense book which is always open before our eyes, I mean the Universe, but we cannot understand it if we do no apply ourselves to understanding first of all its language, and to knowing the characters with which it is written. It is written in a mathematical language, and its characters are triangles, circles, and other geometrical figures, without which it would be humanly impossible to understand a single word. Without these, we would just be wandering vainly in a dark labyrinth.

("Il Saggiatore: The Assayer," in *The Controversy on the Comets of 1618*, trans. S. Drake and C. D. O'Malley)

Galileo was well aware that there is a clear difference between mathematical models and physical reality, even though this reality could and had to be read, ultimately, using these very instruments. The engineers, artisans, and workers at the arsenal in Venice, when they built their ships, for example, learned that there was no correspondence between scale models and real models, between abstract theory and the practice dictated by lived experience. Indeed when Salviati, at the beginning of the *Discorsi e dimostrazioni matematiche intorno a due nuove scienze*, recommends that philosophers and theoreticians of nature go to visit the world of those who know how to build machines, he is certainly not arguing in favor of practice over theory: "The constant activity which you Venetians display in your famous arsenal suggests to the studious mind a large field for investigation, especially that part of the work which involves mechanics; for in this department all types of instruments and machines are constantly being constructed by many artisans, among whom there must be some who, partly by inherited experience and partly by their own observations, have become highly expert and clever in explanation" (trans. Henry Crew and Alfonso de Salvio, *Dialogue Concerning Two New Sciences*). As the character Sagredo observes, the fact that in the construction of ships, scale models are not equivalent to real models implies that "in speaking of these and other similar machines one cannot argue from the small to the large, because many devices which succeed on a small scale do not work on a large scale" (ibid.). So geometry is not applicable *sic et simpliciter* (purely and simply) to physical reality. When one goes from a small-scale model of a ship to the real ship, the same elements of the wooden structure that at first resisted and bore the weight and the strains of the materials that rested on them, could then break because of the change in scale. Consequently, the unchanging nature of properties belonging to geometrical figures does not always apply in physics: "Now, since mechanics has its foundation in geometry, where mere size cuts no figure, I do not see that the properties of circles, triangles, cylinders, cones and other solid figures will change with their size" (ibid.).

The case of Galileo, who wondered why abstract mathematical reason could not have the effects on reality that we might intuitively assume it would have, did not lead to the surrender of rationality in its confrontations with aconceptual practices, but on the contrary, to the birth of a new form of knowledge, as is the (exemplary) case with modern mechanics. In order to grasp the innovative nature of Galileo's propositions in this domain, we need to measure the distance with respect to the long tradition that began in ancient Greece, and continued up until his time. The term *mekhanê* originally meant "ruse," "deception," "artifice," and it had already appeared in the *Iliad* (VIII.177) in this sense of the term. It was only later that it referred to machines in general (in a sense that is close to the connotations of the "appropriate use of an instrument" and of "theatrical machine," from which the expression *theos epi mekanêi* (deus ex machina) is derived, and in particular to simple machines—levers, pulleys, wedges for cutting, inclined planes, screws, and then to war machines, and to automatons.

Mechanics, the knowledge concerned with machines, was thus born with this distinctive trait: it was assigned to the construction of artificial entities, of traps fabricated against nature in order to capture its energy and to channel it to the advantage of humans, and according to their whims. But why do machines have a semantic legacy having to do with ruse and deception? We do not understand, for example, how a lever can lift enormous weights with the minimum of effort, nor how a cutting wedge manages to split stones or gigantic tree trunks. The *Quaestiones mechanichae*, for a long time attributed to Aristotle, provide a testimony to this astonishment when they state clearly that "many marvelous things, whose cause is unknown, happen according to the order of nature, while others happen against this order, produced by *technê* for men's benefit" (847a). When nature is contrary to our own usefulness, we succeed in mastering it by means of artifice (*mechanê*). In this way, technique allows us to conquer nature in circumstances where it would otherwise conquer us. On this strange (*atopos*) genre, the treatise again adds that "these are things by which the least triumphs over the greatest," as in the case of the lever, precisely, which enables great weights to be lifted with little effort.

The mechanical arts, because they belong to the realm of the ruse and of that which is "against nature," are not part of physics, which concerns what belongs to the order of nature. What is more, for the Greeks only mathematics and astronomy are sciences in the true sense of the term, in that they are not concerned with things that can be other than what they are, and that therefore do not have the character of being necessary—this is the case of those things linked to *praxis* (Aristotle, *Nicomachean Ethics*, VI.5.1140a and VI.6.1140b). These sciences thus enjoy the privileges of necessity and of a priori knowledge, since they are true independently of experience. In the vast debate on the relation between *phusis* and *nomos*, mechanics has been resolutely defined, since its mythical origins with Daedalus and Icarus, as antinature, whereas medicine, which appears, for example, in the treatises *De arte* (On Art) and *De victu* (On Diet) from the Hippocratic corpus, is presented instead as a science that supplements and imitates nature.

With Galileo, we begin to realize that we command nature by obeying it, that it cannot simply be mistreated and that the main responsibility of mechanics is not to astonish us. In order to master nature, we have to serve it, yield to its laws and its injunctions, taking advantage of its knowledge. The concept of ruse, in the sense in which the weakest gets the better of the strongest, and where a man such as Ulysses deceives the obtuse Polyphemus that is nature, loses its pertinence. For Galileo, there is no longer any need to divert nature from its course, to torture it, to put it on the rack so as to force it to reveal its secrets, as Francis Bacon wanted to do, opposing not the ruse to the force of nature, but a counterviolence. Man, "vicar of the Most-High," can and must, according to Bacon, exert violence upon nature, for the surest method when faced with matter, which, like Proteus undergoes continual metamorphoses, is to stop it, to block the process of its changes: "And that method of binding, torturing, or detaining, will prove the most effectual and expeditious, which makes use of manacles and fetters; that is, lays hold and works upon matter in the extremest degrees" (Bacon, *Wisdom of the Ancients*).

For Galileo, this kind of violence disappears, precisely because mechanics ceases to be against nature. The formula PxFxDxV indicates the conquest of rationality by means of product of four "things" that have to be considered in their reciprocal relations: "namely the burden that one wishes to transport from one place to another; the force which has to move it; the distance it has to be moved; and the time of the said movement, because it is used to determine the speed, since it is all the greater if the moving body, or the burden, travels a larger distance in the same time" (trans. S. Drake, *On Mechanics*, 23–24). If we examine the weight necessary to move a body from one place to another, the force necessary for this operation, the distance this body travels, and the time this movement takes (speed), we can clearly see that one parameter gains what another loses. So using a lesser force is compensated by a longer traction time, as in the case of the lever that lifts great weights with little effort.

Galileo showed, by means of true and necessary demonstrations, that mechanics were disappointed when they wanted to use machines in a number of operations that are by nature impossible. We should not give in to the dream of catching nature out (or with its guard down, so to speak), of getting it to bend to our will:

It has seemed well worthwhile to me, before we descend to the theory of mechanical instruments, to consider in general and to place before our eyes, as it were, just what the advantages are that are drawn from those instruments. This I have judged the more necessary to be done, the more I have seen (unless I am much mistaken) the general run of mechanicians deceived in trying to apply machines to many operations impossible by their nature, with the result that they have remained in error while others have likewise been defrauded of the hope conceived from their promises. These deceptions appear to me to have their principal cause in the belief which these craftsmen have, and continue to hold, in being able to raise very great weights with a small force, as if with their machines they could cheat nature, whose instinct—nay, whose most firm constitution—is that no resistance may be overcome by a force that is not more powerful than it. How false such a belief is, I hope to make most evident with true and rigorous demonstrations that we shall have as we go along.

(trans. S. Drake, *On Mechanics*, 147)

From this perspective, it is precisely machines—which will after Galileo be built according to fully rational criteria and calculations, going beyond the "approximate" empirical system, in the sense in which Alexandre Koyré understands it (*From the Closed World to the Infinite Universe*)—that take away from slavery its advantages of efficiency and low cost, and enable it to be virtually abolished. The force of human labor, in the form of a pure expenditure of energy, is no longer indispensable, whereas—and this is one of Galileo's other great intuitions—machines will henceforth substitute for the lack of intelligence of natural forces, and of animals that expend energy. By means of "artifices and inventions," they will be capable of saving people their energy and money, by transferring to inanimate and animate nature the burden of providing the energy that had previously been oriented toward the "desired effect." What is important here, as often in the whole of the Italian tradition, is the idea of a conscious control over partially spontaneous processes (natural or historical). We sometimes intervene in these latter forces by directing them toward the future on the basis of present mutations, following the principle stated in chapter 2 of Machiavelli's *Il Principe*: "sempre una mutazione lascia l'addentellato per la edificazione dell'altra" (for any change always leaves a toothing-stone for further building" [trans. Q. Skinner and R. Price, *The Prince*, 6]).

Remi Bodei

BIBLIOGRAPHY

Alighieri, Dante. *Paradiso*, Book 3 of *La divina commedia*. In *La Commedia: Nuovo testo critico secondo i più antichi manoscritti fiorentini*, edited by A. Lanza. Anzia, It.: De Rubeis, 1995. Translation by Allen Mandelbaum and Barry Moser: *The Divine Comedy of Dante Alighieri : Paradiso, a Verse Translation*. Toronto: Bantam Books, 1986.

Bacon, Francis. *Wisdom of the Ancients*. Introduction by Henry Morley. London: Cassell, 1905. First published ca. 1609 in Latin.

Bruno, Giordano. *Candelaio*. In vol. 1 of *Opere italiane*. 2 vols. Edited by Giovanni Aquilecchia. Torino: UTET, 2002. *Candelaio* was first published in 1582. Translation by Gino Moliterno: *Candlebearer: A Comedy by Bruno of Nola Academician of No Academy*. Edited by G. Moliterno. Carleton Renaissance Plays in Translation. Ottawa: Dovehouse, 1999.

———. *Spaccio della bestia trionfante*. In vol. 2 of *Opere italiane*, edited by Giovanni Aquilecchia. 2 vols. Torino: UTET, 2002. *Spaccio della bestia trionfante* was first published in 1584. Translation by Arthur D. Imerti: *The Expulsion of the Triumphant Beast*. Edited by A. D. Imerti. Lincoln: University of Nebraska Press, 2004.

Croce, Benedetto. *Estetica comme scienza dell'espressione e linguistica generale*. Vol. 1 of *Filosofia dello spirito*. 2 vols. Bari, It.: Laterza, 1909–12. Translation by Colin Lyas: *The Aesthetic as the Science of Expression and of the Linguistic in General*. Cambridge: Cambridge University Press, 1992.

———. "Frammenti di etica." In *Etica e politica*. Bari, It.: Laterza, 1973.

———. *Politics and Morals*. Translated by Salvatore J. Castiglione. London: Allen and Unwin, 1946.

Galileo. *Dialogue Concerning the Two Chief World Systems, Ptolemaic & Copernican*. Translated by Stillman Drake. Foreword by Albert Einstein. 2nd ed. Berkeley: University of California Press, 1967.

———. *Dialogues Concerning Two New Sciences*. Translated by Henry Crew and Alfonso de Salvio. Introduction by Antonio Favaro. Evanston, IL: Northwestern University, 1946. First published by Macmillan in 1914.

———. *On Motion (De motu, 1590), and On Mechanics (Le meccaniche, 1600)*. Translated, with an introduction and notes, by I. E. Drabkin (*De motu*) and Stillman Drake (*Le meccaniche*). Madison: University of Wisconsin Press, 1960.

———. *Opere*. 20 vols. Edited by Antonio Favaro. Florence: Barbera, 1929–39.

———. "Il Saggiatore: The Assayer." In *The Controversy on the Comets of 1618*. Translated by Stillman Drake and C. D. O'Malley. Philadelphia: University of Pennsylvania Press, 1960.

Garin, Eugenio. *La filosofia come sapere storico: Con un saggio autobiografico*. Roma: Laterza, 1990. Translation by Giorgio Pinton: *History of Italian Philosophy*. Introduction by Leon Pompa. Edited by G. Pinton. Amsterdam: Rodopi, 2008.

Gramsci, Antonio. "Appunti per una introduzione e un avviamento allo studio della filosofia e della storia della cultura." In vol. 2 of *Quaderni del carcere*, edited by Valentino Gerratana. 4 vols. Turin: Einaudi, 1975. English translation: "Notes for an Introduction and an Approach to the Study of Philosophy in the History of Culture." in *The Gramsci Reader: Selected Writings, 1916–1935*, edited by David Forgasc, 324–62. Introduction by Eric Hobsbawm. New York: New York University Press, 2000.

———. *Selections from the Prison Notebooks of Antonio Gramsci*. Edited by Quentin Hoare and Geoffrey Nowell-Smith. London: Lawrence and Wishart, 1971.

Hegel, Georg Wilhelm Friedrich. *The German Constitution*. In *G.W.F. Hegel: Political Writings*. Translated by H. B. Nisbet. Cambridge: Cambridge University Press, 1999.

Koyré, Alexandre. *From the Closed World to the Infinite Universe*. Baltimore: Johns Hopkins University Press, 1957.

Leopardi, Giacomo. *Canti*. Edited By N. Gallo and C. Garboli. Turin: Einaudi, 1993. Translation and introduction by J. G. Nichols: *The Canti: With a Selection of His Prose*. Rev. ed. Richmond: Oneworld Classics, 2008. Translation by Jonathan Galassi: *Canti*. New York: Farrar, Straus and Giroux, 2010.

———. *Paralipomeni della Batracomiomachia*. Edited by F. Russo. Milan: Angeli, 1997. First published in 1842. Translation, with introduction and annotations, by Ernesto G. Caserta: *The War of the Mice and the Crabs*. Chapel Hill: University of North Carolina Department of Romance Languages, 1976.

———. *Zibaldone di pensieri*. In vols. 1–2 of *Giacomo Leopardi's Opere*, edited by Sergio Solmi. Milan: R. Ricciardi, 1966.

———. *Zibaldone di pensieri*. 3 vols. Edited by R. Damiani. Milan: Mondadori, 1997. First published in 1898 in 7 volumes. Translation and introduction by Martha King and Daniela Bini: *Zibaldone: A Selection*. New York: Lang, 1992.

Machiavelli, Niccolò. *Discorsi sopra la prima deca di Tito Livio*. Vol. 2 of *Edizione nazionale delle opere di Niccolò Machiavelli*, edited by Francesco Bausi. 2 vols. Rome: Salerno, 2001. Translation by Harvey C. Mansfield and Nathan Tarcov: *Discourses on Livy*. Chicago: University of Chicago Press, 1996. Translation by Ninian Thompson: *Discourses on the First Decade of Titus Livius*. London: K. Paul, Trench and Co., 1883.

———. *Il Principe*. Vol. 1, edited by Mario Martelli and Nicoletta Marcelli, in Edizione nazionale delle opere di Niccolò Machiavelli. 2 vols. Rome: Salerno, 2006. First published in 1513. Translation by W. K. Marriott: *The Prince*. London: J. M. Dent, 1908. Translation by Tim Parks: *The Prince*. London: Penguin, 2009. Translation by Quentin Skinner and Russell Price: *Machiavelli: The Prince*. Cambridge: Cambridge University Press, 1988.

Verra, Valerio. *La filosofia dal' 45 a oggi*. Torino: ERI, 1976.

Vico, Giambattista. *La Scienza Nuova*. 2 vols. Edited by Fausto Nicolini. Rome: Laterza, 1974. First published in 1744. Translation by Thomas Goddard Bergin and Max Harold Fisch: *The New Science of Giambattista Vico*. Ithaca, NY: Cornell University Press, 1968. Translation by Leon Pompa: *The First New Science*. Cambridge University Press, 2002.

J

JETZTZEIT (GERMAN)

ENGLISH at present, present time, the now time
FRENCH *à présent, temps actuel*

➤ *INSTANT*, and HISTORY, MOMENT, STILL, *TIME*

Although the lexical form of this word existed before Walter Benjamin marked it (it is found, notably in the work of the Romantic poet Jean Paul), Benjamin was the writer who made it into both a heuristic and a philosophico-practical concept. It is not easily translatable. Benjamin seemed to have wanted to emphasize the everyday meaning of "the now-time": its nontechnical, nonscholarly use as a common noun modernized by doubling it up as *jetzt* (now, at present) and *Zeit* (time).

Jetztzeit only appears in Walter Benjamin's late writings, at the end of the 1930s: in his theses "On the Philosophy of History" (often simply referred to as the "Theses") from 1940, in the notes relating to this text, and in the "Notebook N" of the *Passagenwerk* [Arcades Project], which was also devoted to "theoretical reflections on knowledge," in particular critical reflections on the "theory of progress." So it was in a situation of extreme personal and collective danger, and confronted by the imperious need to rethink a potential struggle against a triumphant fascism, that Benjamin attempted to formulate a concept that gives the "time of the now" (one possible literal translation of *Jetztzeit*) a decisive weight, instead of treating it as a vanishing instant, a sort of unrepresentable tipping point between the past (which has gone) and the future (which does not yet exist). This perilous situation and this necessary struggle are also two of the main aspects of this concept. Indeed, the *Jetztzeit* has to enable a construction of history opposed to the "homogenous and empty time" of traditional historiography, particularly that of historicism but also that of the "ideology of progress" denounced in the "Theses." This critical construction proceeds by quite intense interruptions, breaks, and overlapping between the present and the past, accompanied by modernizing political actions:

> Die Geschichte ist Gegenstand einer Konstruktion deren Ort nicht die homogene und leere Zeit sondern die von Jetztzeit erfüllte bildet. So war für Robespierre das antike Rom eine mit Jetztzeit geladene Vergangenheit, die er aus dem Kontinuum der Geschichte heraussprengte.

> (History is the object of a construction whose site is not empty, homogenous time, but time filled with "the now." Thus for Robespierre, ancient Rome was a past laden with "the now," which blasted out of the continuum of history.)

(Thesis 14)

The concept thus has two dimensions: a theoretical dimension, the critique of a spatialized, undifferentiated, and indifferent conception of temporal "unfolding," in which history becomes an infinite accumulation; and a practical and political dimension, interrupting this enumeration, blocking this avalanche (Thesis 17, *Stillstellung, stillstellen* [blockage, blocking, halting]) so as to bring about a knowing transformation of the present, which also transforms the image of the past. So even though *Jetztzeit* is close, in its brief and radiant temporality, to *Augenblick* (another frequent term in the "Theses" and which Benjamin translates as "instant"), the word no doubt borrows many of the characteristics of *kairos*: the ideas of a break, of something discontinuous, of a decisive and irreplaceable moment. Benjamin notes in the *Arcades Project* (N, 10, 2): "Definitions of the fundamental concepts of history: catastrophe—to have missed the opportunity." The "time of the now" is precious and unique, and therefore fragile, but also sharp and decisive; it creates a new image of the past and establishes a new configuration between the present and the past. Because it enables one to act, to escape, to block the catastrophe—history as it is and as it continues to be—it is, in Benjamin's theological vocabulary, "a model of messianic time" (Thesis 18), or it even contains "splinters of messianic time" (Er bergründet so einen Begriff der Gegenwart als der "Jetztzeit," in welcher Splitter der messianischen eingesprengt sind) ("Theses," App. A). It is because decisive and just political action, which happens within the time of the now, is urgent, acute, and extremely precarious, since it has to grasp the "right moment" in midflight, that it is comparable to a messianic redemption that no theology of history or any ideology of progress could guarantee.

No temporal determinism can guarantee when *Jetztzeit* will come to pass either. One of the most difficult aspects of this concept is that it emphasizes the subjective dimension of choice and decision, the dimension precisely of being subjects of historical action, and at the same time it cannot be based on any arbitrary resolution because of the risk of thereby losing its radiant effectiveness. It also necessarily depends on a certain temporal objectivity, on a "historic trace," a sign (*index*) that does not refer to a mechanical causality between past and present but to a sort of condensation when a forgotten, lost, perhaps repressed moment from the past can suddenly be deciphered and known by the present and in the present: what Benjamin calls "the Now of knowability [*das Jetzt der Erkenntbarkeit*]" (*Arcades Project*, N, 3, 1). In order to describe more precisely this convergence of subjective decision and the fabric of objective history, Benjamin will have recourse to different models, in particular the Proustian theory of involuntary memory, the Freudian dialectic between dream and unconscious images and the action of the waking consciousness, and the drifting openness to experience of the Surrealists.

Why, then, did Benjamin not adopt, or even modify, the term *kairos* but instead coin the term *Jetztzeit*? Two hypotheses: first, in order to emphasize better the proximity of the concept to Jewish prophetic and messianic traditions (as opposed to Greek or Christian traditions); and second, to insist on the fact, in the very structure of the word, that only in the present can true historical knowledge and the time of just political action be united.

Jeanne-Marie Gagnebin

BIBLIOGRAPHY

Benjamin, Andrew, ed. *Walter Benjamin and History*. London: Continuum, 2005.

Benjamin, Walter. "Anmerkungen" to "Über den Begriff der Geschichte." In *Gesammelte Schriften*. Edited by Rolf Tiedemann and H. Schweppenhäuser. Vol. 1.3: 1222–66. Frankfurt am Main: Suhrkamp, 1972. Translation by Edmund Jephcott and Howard Eiland: "Paralipomena to 'On the Concept of History.'" In *Walter Benjamin: Selected Writings, Vol. 4, 1938–1940*, edited by Howard Eiland and Michael W. Jennings, 401–11. Cambridge, MA: Harvard University Press, 2003.

———. "Das Passagen-Werk: Konvolut N (Erkenntnistheoretisches; Theorie des Fortschritts)." In *Gesammelte Schriften*. Edited by Rolf Tiedemann and H. Schweppenhäuser. Vol. 5.1: 1222–66. Frankfurt am Main: Suhrkamp, 1982. Translation by Howard Eiland and Kevin McLaughlin: "Convolute N (On the Theory of Knowledge, Theory of Progress)." In *The Arcades Project*, 456–88. Cambridge, MA: Belknap, 1999.

———. "Über den Begriff der Geschichte." In *Gesammelte Schriften*. Edited by Rolf Tiedemann and H. Schweppenhäuser. Vol. 1.2: 691–704. Frankfurt am Main: Suhrkamp, 1974. Translation by Harry Zohn: "On the Concept of History." In *Walter Benjamin: Selected Writings, Vol. 4, 1938–1940*, edited by Howard Eiland and Michael W. Jennings, 389–400. Cambridge, MA: Harvard University Press, 2003.

Cadava, Eduardo. *Words of Light: Theses on the Photography of History*. Princeton, NJ: Princeton University Press, 1997.

Gandler, Stefan. *Materialismus und Messianismus: zu Walter Benjamins Thesen Über den Begriff der Geschichte*. Bielefeld: Aisthesis, 2008.

Mosès, Stéphane. *The Angel of History: Rosenzweig, Benjamin, Scholem*. Translated by Barbara Harshav. Stanford, CA: Stanford University Press, 2009.

Piep, Karsten H. "'A Tiger's Leap Into the Past': On the 'Unhistorical,' the 'Historical,' and the 'Suprahistorical' in Walter Benjamin's 'Theses on the Philosophy of History.'" *New German Review* 20 (2004–5): 41–59.

Steinberg, Michael P., ed. *Walter Benjamin and the Demands of History*. Ithaca, NY: Cornell University Press, 1996.

Tiedemann, Rolf. "Historical Materialism or Political Messianism? An Interpretation of the Theses 'On the Concept of History.'" In *Benjamin: Philosophy, History, Aesthetics*, edited by Gary Smith, 175–209. Chicago: University of Chicago Press, 1989.

———. "Jetztzeit." In *Historisches Wörterbuch der Philosophie*. Edited by Joachim Ritter and Karlfried Gründer. 4:648–49. Darmstadt: Wissenschaftliche Buchgesellschaft, 1976.

| JUSTICE, JUDGMENT

I. Justice and Equity

"Justice" comes from the Latin *justitia*, itself derived from *jus*, which dictionaries translate either as "right" or "justice." In French, as in Latin, justice refers both to the conformity to the law (*droit*; cf. Ger. *Gerechtigkeit*); the justice one dispenses (and which constitutes in modern times one of the three branches of state power, alongside the legislative and the executive); and the sense of equity, the spirit of justice, which is bound up with morality. See LEX, RIGHT/JUST/GOOD, THEMIS, and FAIR, PRAVDA; and cf. ISTINA, POSTUPOK. On equity, refer more specifically to THEMIS, IV; cf. PHRONÊSIS, PIETAS.

II. Justice and Judgment

The judgment (Lat. *judicium*, from *judico, judicare*) that justice entails relates to a much broader sphere; it refers as much to the act of judging in the sense of "pronouncing a verdict," as to that of judging in the sense of "forming an opinion of, appreciating, thinking"—and it also designates the "faculty" described by Kant (in the second part of the Analytic of the *Critique of Pure Reason*) as the "power to subsume within rules," which is the source of the latter. The Greek *krinein* [κρίνειν] does not come from the same root (*krinein* comes rather from **krin-ye/o*, which means "to separate out, to sift"; we find **krin* in the Latin *cerno*, and in the French *critique, critère, crise* [crisis] or *discernement*), but still contains the same breadth of meanings, which range between the judgment of a court and a logical, aesthetic, or moral judgment.

On logical judgment, see BEGRIFF, *CATEGORY*, LOGOS, MERKMAL, PROPOSITION, SACHVERHALT, TRUTH; cf. IMPLICATION, INTENTION, PRINCIPLE.

On aesthetic judgment, see AESTHETICS, GOÛT, STANDARD; see also PERCEPTION, REPRÉSENTATION; cf. INGENIUM.

➤ *ALLIANCE*, MORALS, *VIRTUE*

KÊR [κήρ], **MOIRA** [μοῖρα], **AISA** [αἶσα], **HEIMARMENÊ** [εἱμαρμένη], **ANAGKÊ** [ἀνάγκη], **PEPRÔMENÊ** [πεπρωμένη], **TUCHÊ** [τύχη] (GREEK)

ENGLISH	fate, destiny
FRENCH	destin, fatalité, sort, lot, nécessité, fortune
ITALIAN	fortuna, fato, destino
LATIN	fatum, fortuna
SPANISH	destino

➤ DESTINY [SCHICKSAL], and CHANCE, DAIMÔN, DUTY, GOD, EREIGNIS, GLÜCK, LIBERTY [ELEUTHERIA], LAW, MOMENT, OBLIGATION, PRESENT, THEMIS

Greek uses a considerable number of distinct terms to refer to what the Romance languages generally call "destiny" (Fr. destin, Ital. and Sp. destino, from the Latin root destinare, "to determine, to stop") or "fate" (fatalité, fato, derived from the Latin fatum, from fari, "to say"). These Greek terms convey more or less philosophically reinscribed or elaborated representations and images that are still operative today: death (kêr [κήρ]); the portion assigned and the lot one draws (moira [μοῖρα], heimarmenê [εἱμαρμένη], aisa [αἶσα]); the thread and the knot (Klôthô, the Moirai or Fates themselves); the good or bad effects of fortune (tuchê [τύχη]); the bond and constraints of necessity (anagkê [ἀνάγκη]). Each of these expressions attests in its own way to the formation of a relationship between the gods and men, and a relationship of man to himself.

I. The First Paradigms of Destiny

A. Kêr: The destiny of death

In Greece, up until the end of the fifth century, destiny casts its formidable and irrepressible shadow over man. Whenever it manifests itself as kêr [κήρ], it is literally the "destruction" that threatens human beings. The term is rich in content, as Pierre Chantraine points out (RT: Dictionnaire étymologique de la langue grecque, s.v. kêr), since it "involves at the same time notions of destiny, or death, and of personal demons." In a famous scene in the Iliad, Zeus weighs the kêres of Achilles and of Hector (22.209ff.); we do not know whether the two kêres are personified or not. Both are described as the "kêres of painful death," that is, the destiny of death that each of the heroes has as his double, or phantom, or personal demon. What is curious is that they have a weight, and they can be weighed. Zeus places the two kêres on the scales, and Hector's kêr drops and falls into the house of Hades. Apollo abandons the hero, and his fate is sealed.

In a play that has been lost, Psuchostasia, Aeschylus adapted this scene in the Iliad, but he replaced the kêres with the souls of Achilles and Memnon (RT: TGF, 88–89 N. = 374–77 Radt). Aeschylus clearly interpreted the kêres in the Iliad as psuchai, the sort of psychic doubles or phantoms that live on in Hades after the death of the individual (see SOUL, Box 3). In other cases, however, there is nothing personal about the kêr: in Iliad 8.69ff., Zeus weighs two kêres on the scales, those of the Achaeans and those of the Trojans. This relation to death means that the word kêr is also used in the sense of "misfortune"—for example, in tragedy.

B. Moira, Aisa: One's lot and the thread of one's life

The term moira, used more frequently and more traditionally than kêr to indicate destiny, is inscribed within the semantic field of the "part or portion assigned," the "lot" that is attached to a being from birth. Moira [μοῖρα] derives from the verb meiromai [μείρομαι], "to have one's legitimate part," which in the perfect heimartai [εἵμαρται] or the pluperfect heimarto [εἵμαρτο] means "is (was) marked by fate," whence heimarmenê (moira) [εἱμαρμένη (μοῖρα)], "the part that is imparted."

In Iliad, 24.209–10, the mother of Hector weeps for the death of her son: "So almighty Destiny [Moira] spun with her thread [epenêse linôi (ἐπένησε λίνῳ)], from the moment I gave birth to him." Moira is a spinner who spins around the newborn child the portion of life assigned to him. As we can see in this example, moira or Moira and Moirai are associated with death. In Homer, we come across the expression, tirelessly repeated: "Death and almighty moira [thanatos kai moira krataiê (θάνατος καὶ μοῖρα κραταιή)]"; see, for example, Iliad, 5.83; 16.334).

This semantic value of the notion of destiny in Greek is confirmed by the term aisa [αἶσα], which is a name for "destiny" in the sense of the "portion allocated," the "lot" of one's life, and which is related etymologically to a series of words such as aitios [αἴτιος] and aitia [αἰτία], "cause," which imply responsibility (Iliad, 20.127–28: "After that he will suffer what destiny [aisa] / spun with her thread for him at the moment of his birth, / when his mother brought him into the world"). Aisa and Moira are both personified as spinners, and are sometimes used synonymously (Odyssey, 5.113ff.).

These terms emphasize the fact that the fundamental notion of destiny in Greek is linked to the idea that each person's life is a part of a whole, just as moira is part of a land, or of a country, or of the honor due to a class of persons, and so on. It is a legitimate, singular part, connected to a subject. Along the line of destiny, every event produces a closure; the line itself, made up of a succession of closures, does not unfold as a "trace." Above these events that affect the subject, that for that subject are hic et nunc, the dimensions of the ubique and the semper open up, which is to say the dimensions of the divine (Diano, Il concetto della storia, 252ff.). The subject, beneath the vault of this whole, of the divine, feels present there as a gift, offered and taken back by a mysterious force, by the mysterium tremendum et fascinans.

■ See Box 1.

1

The double epic and tragic motivation: Determinism and responsibility

There is a strange contradiction in Homer between two orders of interpretation that are applied to individual fate. On the one hand, Homeric heroes embrace and assume control of their own deaths, thereby creating the conditions of their freedom; on the other hand, the *Iliad* entrusts to the gods the practical achieving of the hero's death, whether his destiny is *moira, aisa,* or *kêr*. The gods, whether protective or antagonistic, intervene in human affairs via a complex mechanism: they act directly, but also through the Parcae, who weigh up and plan for Zeus (*Dios boulê* [Διὸς βουλή]) and thus embody the complicity between a god and a cursed fate (*oloê moira* [ὀλοὴ μοῖρα]). This paradox has created problems of interpretation that are the source of endless debate.

When a character such as Patroclus says, for example, that the gods bear a heavy responsibility for his fate of death, we can always trace his actions back to the moment when he makes a decision. Patroclus blames Zeus, Apollo, accursed fate, Euphorbus, and finally Hector for his death (*Iliad,* 16.844–50). In this hyperdetermination typical of the *epos*, we do not know which one to choose, but for Achilles there is no doubt about the matter: it is Hector he blames for Patroclus's death, and Hector is the one on whom he will take his revenge. Patroclus could have avoided his death if he had followed Achilles's advice (16.87–96) and not led his army against Ilion. The poet remarks on the gravity of this failure, and apostrophizes his hero, calling him "foolish" or "mad" (*nêpios* [νήπιος]). He adds that Zeus excited his heart and his passion (*thumon* [θυμόν]). With this dual human and divine motivation,

the poet expresses what we would now call the compatibility between determinism and responsibility (see, for example, Bok, *Freedom and Responsibility*, or Derrida, *The Gift of Death*) and presents in his own language the mystery of the fatal, fateful decision. Apollo himself, on four occasions, stops Patroclus and, repeating Achilles's warning, tells him that it is not his destiny (*aisa*) to conquer Troy (*Iliad,* 16.698–709). But Patroclus, addressing Hector, who has just dealt him a mortal blow, refuses to acknowledge his own excessiveness, and prefers instead to produce a list of the agents who have caused his death: he places Hector at the end of this list, a minor agent whom he can thereby humiliate by depriving him of any glory.

Homeric man is free and responsible, although he is represented as being in contact with divine forces: in the case of Patroclus, these forces do not deprive him of this freedom, contrary to what he says, but add nuance by underscoring the excessive nature of his decision. This fate is celebrated by the poet, who attributes glory (*kleos* [κλέος]) to the hero who has chosen to die in the name of such glory, and erects a tomb to him in his immortal song.

The questions that Homer treats are the stuff of tragedy: individual freedom despite fate and the will of the gods. But fate becomes more real and more brutal; the destructive will of the gods becomes more urgent, involving forces such as *atê* [ἄτη], "blindness and destruction" (Aeschylus, *Persians,* 1037); *phthonos* [φθόνος], "the jealousy of the gods" (Aeschylus, *Agamemnon,* 904); *anagkê* [ἀνάγκη], which often refers to a misfortune such as slavery (Aeschylus, *Choephoeri,*

75–78); or the Erinyes, avenging goddesses of family crimes (ibid., 283). The curse of the ancestors (*ara* [ἀρά]: Sophocles, *Electra,* 111) is ineluctable. Prophecy is the text of fate. In Sophocles's *Oedipus Rex,* oracular statements are perceived not only as a form of anticipation, but also as divine will: Oedipus declares that he is the very person Apollo has predicted, the person who will kill his father and marry his mother. Yet human action goes beyond the circle of divine foresight: in blinding himself, Oedipus prevails over his misfortune and, in recognizing himself as a divine victim, acquires a heroic awareness of his destiny. What is more, the divine *telos* [τέλος] is manifest in a series of circumstances constantly referred to as "chances" (*tuchê* [τύχη]): if necessity is helped by chance, is it not that bit less necessary? Chance and necessity cease to be opposed: their juxtaposition is one of the most puzzling innovations of Sophoclean drama.

BIBLIOGRAPHY

Bok, Hilary. *Freedom and Responsibility*. Princeton, NJ: Princeton University Press, 1998.

Derrida, Jacques. "Donner la Mort." In *L'Éthique du don: Jacques Derrida et la pensée du don,* edited by Jean-Michel Rabaté. Paris: Métailié Transitions, 1992. Published separately as *Donner la mort*. Paris: Galilée, 1999. Translation by David Wills: *The Gift of Death*. Chicago: University of Chicago Press, 1995.

Dodds, Eric Robertson. *The Greeks and the Irrational*. Berkeley: University of California Press, 1951.

Pucci, Pietro. *Oedipus and the Fabrication of the Father*. Baltimore: The Johns Hopkins University Press, 1992.

C. *Fatum, destinare*: Word and destination

The semantic field of *moira* and *aisa* contrasts distinctly with that of *fatum,* "fate," in Latin. *Fatum,* from the verb *for, faris, fari, fatus sum,* "to speak," implies precisely the "word" pronounced by fate, or by the oracle: "At si ita fatum erit: nascetur Oedipus Laio" (But if it is according to the "word of fate": "Oedipus will be born to Laius": Cicero, *De fato,* 30). The etymology of *fatum* suggests connections to *fabula* (fable), *fateor* (I confess), *fama* (fame), and so on. *Fatum* has entered into several Romance languages (cf. Fr. *fatal,* Ital. *fato,* Eng. *fate,* etc.).

The Romance languages have also drawn upon another, different semantic field to express the notion of destiny: that of the Latin *destinare* (from *de* and a verbal form linked to *stare*), "to determine, to stop, to assign or destine." Latin itself does not form any words meaning "fate" out of *destinare,* but the Romance languages do: French *destin* (1160 CE),

Italian *destino* (c. 1321), Spanish *destino*—and thence the English "destiny."

II. The Spinners

A. From the "part" (*moira*) to "Moira"

In Greek, the "portion" of one's fate is assigned (*peprôtai* [πέπρωται], from *porô* [πόρω], "to give, to offer") or determined by the gods; sometimes, it "comes upon" or "leaps onto" a human being (like a chance event), but more often it becomes the "thread" of each person's fate. Greek therefore has recourse to the verb *klôthein* [κλώθειν], "to spin," and invents the goddess Klôthô [Κλωθώ], the spinner, making her into a plural, Klôthes [Κλῶθες], the Spinners (*Odyssey* 7.197), or into one of the three Moirai, goddesses of fate, the two others being Lachesis (*lachos* [λάχος], from *lagchanô* [λαγχάνω], which means the "lot," as in drawing lots, for example), and Atropos, "the inflexible one," "the one who cannot be turned aside." So the etymological meaning of *moira* as a "part" is lost, since in assigning to the Spinners the role of producing this "part," the "part" symbolically becomes a thread made by a distaff, an image of human impermanence and vulnerability. Then, through a sort of personification or metonymy, this *moira* becomes the name not of the thread, but of the spinners who, while belying any etymological link to *moira*, will be called Moirai. The operation is a genuine poetic discovery (Dietrich, "The Spinning of Fate in Homer," 88). This rhetorico-religious shift from *moira* (part) to *Moira* (Spinner) does not exclude the mythological connection of the Moirai with other figures. The Spinners have been compared to, among others, the *Norns* of the Norwegian epic, the Anglo-Saxon *Metten(a)*, and the medieval German *Gaschepfen*, who are magical spinners who endow human beings with skill and talents at birth, even if they are not true goddesses or figures of fate. It seems that in Greece in ancient times, spinning was associated with magic: Homer perhaps worked syncretically to synthesize these popular beliefs and the image of the Moirai (Dietrich, "The Spinning of Fate in Homer," 93ff.).

Moira and the Moirai often preside over the death of a human being, with Aisa sometimes taking the place of Atropos. They are daughters of Night in Hesiod (*Theogony*, 211–20); they appear in funeral inscriptions; during worship, they are sometimes associated with the underworld deities Gê, Dêmêtêr, and Korê. Tragedy refers to them as "ancient goddesses" (*palaigeneis* [παλαιγενεῖς]: Aeschylus, *Eumenides*, 172; Sophocles, *Antigone*, 987); and the motif of the Moirai as spinners of fate remains popular in the religious imagination up until the time of the Romans (Eitrem, *Paulys Real Encyclopädie*, s.v., cols. 2479–93).

By associating the Moirai with a thread that is spun and cut, with death and underworld deities, fate for the Greeks takes on melancholic nocturnal and funerary connotations. Already in Hesiod (*Theogony*, 900–906), however, an Olympian version is evolving that has the Moirai as daughters of Zeus and Themis (see THEMIS). Here the associations are all positive, since they are born in the same bed as the Horai—Eunomia, Justice, and Peace—and receive "the highest honor" from Zeus (*pleistên timên* [πλείστην τιμήν]). They are mentioned for the first time as a triad with their own names and specific function: bestowing good and evil upon men. This concept relates them to other deities sharing the same task: for example, the Muses (*Odyssey*, 8.63), and Zeus in particular (first in the *Iliad*, 14.527ff.). They spin threads, but they are not the only ones to do so, since Homer sometimes uses "to spin" (*epiklôthô* [ἐπικλώθω]) for the other gods when, either collectively (*Odyssey*, 1.17, 8.579, 11.139, 20.196; *Iliad*, 24.525) or individually (*Odyssey*, 4.208, 16.64), they make a decision or hand out portions of good fortune and misfortune to men. The Moirai seem to be the metaphorical model beings used to represent this action.

Zeus and Apollo are referred to as *Moiragetai* [Μοιραγέται], a cultic title that defines them as "those who guide the Moirai" and thus preside over fate. Considered in this light, fate for the Greeks takes on a more positive complexion than in Homer, and is used in the end to signify the arc of a human life (Euripides, *Bacchae*, 99, etc.), marriage (Aristophanes, *Birds*, 1731–35, etc.), the decisive moments in life, and death.

B. The Parcae

The spinners become the preferred image in classical poetry, and find their way to Rome, where they acquire the name Parcae. The term comes from *Parca* (from the verb *pario*, "to procreate") and referred to a goddess of birth who was identified with Moira (probably by a false etymology) and, in the plural, with the Moirai. The Parcae fulfill the same imaginary functions as in classical Greek poetry: they intervene at important moments in one's life (Horace, *Odes*, 2.6.9: "Should angry Fate [*Parcae*] those wishes foil . . ."), and they control the length of one's life (ibid., 2.3.13–16: You will enjoy your banquet "while life, and fortune, and the loom of the Three Sisters yield you grace [*dum res et aetas et sororum fila trium patiuntur atra*]").

As they move from Greece to Rome, the Moirai learn to sing and to write. Catullus (64.321) says that the Parcae "divino fuderunt carmine fata" (expressed oracular words [words of fate] with a divine song); *fata*, because of its connection to the verb *fari* (to speak), gains in semantic force and richness. Of the many examples, we might mention Ovid, who describes the Parcae spinning and singing an oracle in the *Metamorphoses* (8.452ff.).

C. The book of fate

In figurative representations, we often see the Moirai with a scroll (*volumen*) in one hand and a distaff in the other (cf. RT: *LIMC*, s.v. *Moirai*, 643 n. 33, 35, etc.). Although they do not write in the book of the father of the gods, the Moirai and the Parcae nonetheless do write. We read, for example, in a funerary text (RT: *CLE*, 2:1332.2): "vixi bene ut fata scripsere mihi" (I have lived well, as the *fata* had written for me): the *Parcae*, then, produced something in writing that prescribed one's destiny and the quality of one's life.

In becoming something written, fate is no longer a part of life, even when symbolically represented by a thread, nor is it a ghostly double of man (*kêr*), but it is a stone tablet or a scroll that carries oracular signs. This implies that the whole within which the particular prescription takes shape is a text.

The book of fate has become proverbial in the literature and imagination of Europe: Shakespeare, to cite him alone, mentions "the book of fate" (*Henry IV, Part II*, act 3, scene 1, v. 45). However, this vast imaginary and conceptual apparatus, and the incantatory force of these phantoms, never prevented the Greeks from seeing man as naked, responsible for his acts, fascinated and horrified by his own death (Adkins, *Merit and Responsibility*, 17–29).

Philosophy creates its own mythology for the Moirai: in Plato (*Republic*, 617c), they are the daughters of Anagkê (Necessity), and they sit on thrones at the side of the celestial circles, singing with the Sirens: Lachesis the past, Klôthô the present, and Atropos the future.

III. *Tuchê*, Attaining the Event

The word for "chance, luck, fortune" in Greek is *tuchê* [τύχη]. This word is derived from the verb *tugchanô* [τυγχάνω] (in the aorist, *etuchon* [ἔτυχον]). Because *tugchanô* has two different connotations ("to attain or achieve, touch, succeed" and "to happen, to occur by chance"), the semantic field of *tuchê* swings back and forth between meanings: sometimes success, or good fortune; sometimes the purely accidental nature of things; sometimes unhappy fate. So *tuchê* is the aoristic "event" that happens, *hic et nunc*. In this respect, it is distinct from *moira* and from *heimarmenê* (*moira*) (from the perfect form *heimartai*), both of which imply a notion of continuity and of completion of an action—a predetermination constituted at the moment of the birth of a human being (see ASPECT).

For ancient thought, *moira* as well as *tuchê* come from the gods, that is, from the powers of the polytheistic pantheon. But from the fifth century BCE on, *tuchê* is the name given to an accidental or contingent event. In this way, *tuchê* acquires a clearly secular connotation since, as Euripides says, "If there is *tuchê*, what then are the gods? And if the gods have any power, *tuchê* is nothing" (frag. 154.4–5, in Colinus, *Nova fragmenta Euripidea*). The Stoics will recall this principle, and they will offer instead the notion of *heimarmenê* (see Box 4).

Tuchê, understood as luck and chance, works in philosophical texts from Aristotle to Epicurus as a means of giving man, beyond the necessity that closes off one's life, play enough to be free and to experience pleasure.

■ See Box 2.

2

Tuchê and *automaton* in Aristotle

➤ ART, PRAXIS

It is during his analysis of causes (*aitiai* [αἰτίαι]) in book 2 of his *Physics* that Aristotle elaborates the notion of *tuchê* by distinguishing it from that of *automaton* [αὐτόματον]. "Fortune" and "chance," to use the standard translations, are both motor causes of what happens (*hothen hê archê tês kinêseôs* [ὅθεν ἡ ἀρχὴ τῆς κινήσεως], 7.198a3; cf. *to kinêsan* [τὸ κινῆσαν], as distinct from matter, *hulê* [ὕλη], form, *eidos* [εἶδος], and finality, *to hou heneka* [τὸ οὗ ἕνεκα], 7.198a22–24). However, they are not causes by themselves (*kath' hauto* [καθ' αὐτό]), as is the quality of "being a builder" or "being an architect" that the builder/architect possesses with respect to the house to be built, but rather are causes by accident (*kata sumbebêkôs* [κατὰ συμβεβηκώς]), as is the quality of "being a flute-player" that that builder/architect might well also possess. Their field of action is not the domain of "what always or most often happens" (the necessary and the universal, which are the domain of science), but that of the contingent, the accidental, which is tied to the infinite, indefinite, indeterminate nature (*aoriston* [ἀόριστον]) of an individual (*apeira gar … tôi heni sumbaiê* [ἄπειρα γὰρ … τῷ ἑνὶ συμβαίη], 4.196a38ff., "for what can happen to an individual is limitless"). We can understand this as the way in which an accident can befall, *sumb-baiê*, a subject, or the way in which heterogeneous series, involving distinct unities, can happen to intersect—for example, the comings and goings of a debtor and of a lender (*sunebê* [συνέβη], 196b35). This is why they can count "for nothing" in the face of causes by themselves (5.197a14).

Nevertheless, we do notice them. This is because of a second characteristic that they possess: fortune and chance are applied only to "events that occur in view of something [*ta heneka tou* (τὰ ἕνεκά του)]," or those which manifest some finality and could be fulfilled by thought and by nature (*apo dianoias,* *apo phuseôs* [ἀπὸ διανοίας, ἀπὸ φύσεως], 5.196b18–22). The event occurs, but "it does not originate in a cause that intended this event," it only appears to have been intended (this is how I understand Aristotle's *hotan mê genêtai to heneka allou hekeinou heneka* [ὅταν μὴ γένηται τὸ ἕνεκα ἄλλου ἐκείνου ἕνεκα], 197b24, a difficult text that is often corrected). This is where the extent of the difference in scope between *automaton* and *tuchê* becomes clear. *Automaton* refers to any appearance of finality whatsoever; but we speak of *tuchê* only when the end lets itself be read in terms of a deliberate choice or decision (*proairesis* [προαίρεσις]) that is characteristic of a *praxis*, of a practical agent. The examples speak for themselves: "The tripod fell over *automatos*: it is now upright to be used as a seat, whereas it did not fall over to be used as a seat" (197b16–18). But when the lender who is out for a walk happens upon his debtor "so he can collect his money [*hoion heneka tou apolabein* (οἷον ἕνεκα τοῦ ἀπολαβεῖν)]" (5.196b33), we refer to this as *tuchê*. In both cases, finality seems to be intrinsic, even though it is not in fact, and this is how *automaton* becomes etymologized as *auto-matên* [αὐτὸ-μάτην], literally, "by itself in vain," of which *tuchê* is one kind: "This is what an *automaton* is, and it is so because of its name: each time that it occurs by itself in vain [*hotan auto matên genêtai* (ὅταν αὐτὸ μάτην γένηται)]" (6.197b29ff.).

It is easy to see why the translation of *automaton* as "chance" was not particularly productive (the French word for chance, *hasard*, is borrowed from the Arabic *al-zahar* [الزهر], "throw of the dice," via the Spanish *azar*; the *DHLF* [in RT] even explains that *zahr* [الزهر], "flower," referred to the flower on one of the faces of the die). Pierre Pellegrin chose to translate *automaton* into French as *spontanéité* (spontaneity), and *tuchê* as *hasard* (chance, 4.195b30): "We also say that *le hasard* [*tuchê*] and *la spontanéité* [*automaton*] are among the causes." Henri Carteron has recently translated this into French as: "We also say that *la fortune* [*tuchê*] and *le hasard* [*automaton*] are causes," but this new translation is very problematic. The paradigm of the game of chance is indeed directly opposed to the Aristotelian conception of *tuchê*: a throw of the dice or an accidental fall are certainly neither one nor the other the object of a rational choice. Indeed, the following statement by Aristotle would be incomprehensible if that were the case: "Nothing inanimate, nor even a beast or a small child, does anything that occurs by chance [*ouden poiei apo tuchês* (οὐδὲν ποιεῖ ἀπὸ τύχης)], because they do not have the faculty of rational choice [*hoti ouk echei proairesin* (ὅτι οὐκ ἔχει προαίρεσιν)]; no more than fortune or misfortune can befall them [*oud' eutuchia oud' atuchia* (οὐδ' εὐτυχία οὐδ'ἀτυχία)], unless it is figuratively speaking" (6.197b7–9). It is all the more incomprehensible given that the Greek division of *tuchê* into *eutuchia* [εὐτυχία] and *atuchia* [ἀτυχία] is made inaudible by the difference between chance/fortune and misfortune.

We can also appreciate the difference that is established between this systematic physics (the four causes) and ontology (accidentality and contingency), and the fate of the epic and tragic hero. Fortune becomes an object of *epistêmê* [ἐπιστήμη], not that it is calculated or measured (the mathematics of probability is still a long way off; see CHANCE), but because it is rigorously analyzed in terms of its "as if."

Barbara Cassin

BIBLIOGRAPHY

Aristotle. *The Physics*. Translated by Philip H. Wicksteed and Francis M. Cornford. 2 vols. Loeb Classical Library. Cambridge, MA: Harvard University Press, 1980.

In the fourth century BCE, *tuchê* passed from scholarly texts, where it had become secularized, into more popular forms, and became the goddess Tuchê, with a propensity for benevolence: good Tuchê, good Luck. The goddess Fortuna would be its Latin equivalent.

■ See Box 3.

3

Fortuna in the Renaissance

➤ *VIRTUE*, VIRTÙ

Understood in terms of its Latin root, and the entire Romance language tradition, as well as in terms of its retranslation of the Greek and Hellenist tradition, *fortuna* is an equivocal term that designates good or bad luck, or something opportune or accidental, and can mean at the same time chance, necessity, or fate, and Providence. It is a notion whose ambiguity was figured and personified as a near-deity, particularly during the period of humanism from the Middle Ages to the Renaissance. The term *fortuna* at that time did not signify fortune in the sense of *tuchê* (Aristotle, *Physics*, 5), or that which we cannot control (Cicero, Seneca). In Dante, it is still a fluid unity in which a number of contradictory themes are condensed, and refers analogically to divine providential intelligence as a protective power.

The notion undergoes two important changes during the Renaissance: this was the period of its most powerful polymorphousness and greatest mobility, representing by analogy with the fine arts a "plastic compromise formulation" between the term's different meanings, to borrow one of Ernst Cassirer's expressions. It was also the period of its delegitimation: Fortuna fell from the status of a stellar goddess who was nearly omnipotent, to that of a wild animal full of furor that one had to learn to hunt and tame. The term in the end came close to designating either chance, devoid of all intention, or the necessity of nature, that is to say, essentially that with which human "freedom of action" is concerned.

In Machiavelli, the term was considered in strict correlation to *virtù*, and covered the entire spectrum of its meanings, with the exception of that of Providence. This fluidity, which was close to disrupting its conceptual unity, was all the more necessary given that Fortuna pointed toward that which was outside our grasp, and took on the status—which Giordano Bruno would systematize—of an idea that we can only approach figuratively, precisely because what is at issue escapes all determinate form.

Nevertheless, not to extinguish our free will, I hold it to be true that Fortune is the arbiter of one-half of our actions, but that she still leaves us to direct the other half, or perhaps a little less.

(Machiavelli, *The Prince*, chap. 25, trans. Marriott)

Machiavelli's sentence asserts the equivalence between *fortuna* and *virtù*. It takes away from theoretical judgment the possibility of making a decision by neutralizing all decisive assessment; it forestalls any accusation of excessiveness, and serves as a prescription for action. *Fortuna* is the name of what escapes us at the very moment we need to contain it or hunt it down. In the same way, at the precise moment *virtù* frees itself from Fortune and chooses the path of force (which happens by calling out to fortune as *kairos* [καιρός]; see MOMENT) according to a relation analogous to the masculine-feminine sexual relationship, *fortuna* reminds us of its presence and envelops *virtù*, since *virtù* itself is what *happens* to a subject. The term thereafter comes to name the paradox of the relation between chance, necessity, and freedom in a manner that remains mythical without being a mystification. The term has too often been considered in the sense of a mythological residue (Cassirer), or of a still-representational prefiguration of the conceptual opposition between freedom and the order of the world. If Machiavelli abolished all trace of Providence from the notion, it was not in order to eradicate its necessarily obscure nature, but, in a powerful way, to retain it as a form of intelligibility.

Gérald Sfez

BIBLIOGRAPHY

Alighieri, Dante. *Convivio*. Translated by William Walrond Jackson. Oxford: Clarendon, 1909.
———. *The Divine Comedy*. Translation and commentary by Charles S. Singleton. 2nd ed. 6 vols. Princeton, NJ: Princeton University Press, 1977.
———. *The Latin Works*. Translated by A. G. Ferrers Howell and Phillip H. Wicksteed. London: J. M. Dent, 1904.
———. *Opere minori*. Edited by Domenico De Robertis et al. 3 vols. Milan: Ricciardi, 1855.
———. *Vita nuova*. Translated with introduction by Mark Musa. Oxford: Oxford University Press, 1992.

Cassirer, Ernst. *Individuum und Kosmos in der Philosophie der Renaissance*. 5th ed. Darmstadt, Ger.: Wissenschaftliche Buchgesellschaft, 1977. Translation by Mario Domandi: *The Individual and the Cosmos in Renaissance Philosophy*. Introduction by Mario Domandi. Philadelphia: University of Pennsylvania Press, 1963.
Flanagan, Thomas. "The Concept of *Fortuna* in Machiavelli." In *The Political Calculus: Essays on Machiavelli's Philosophy*, edited by Anthony Parel, 127–56. Toronto: University of Toronto Press, 1972.
Lefort, Claude. "Machiavelli: History, Politics, Discourse." In *The States of "Theory": History, Art, and Critical Discourse*, edited by David Carroll, 113–24. New York: Columbia University Press, 1990.
———. *Le travail de l'œuvre: Machiavel*. Paris: Gallimard / La Pléiade, 1972.
Machiavelli, Niccolò. *The Chief Works and Others*. Translated by Allan Gilbert. 3 vols. Durham, NC: Duke University Press, 1965.
———. *Discorsi sopra la prima deca di Tito Livio*. Edited by Francesco Bausi. 2 vols. Edizione nazionale delle opere di Niccolò Machiavelli, vol. 2.1–2. Rome: Salerno, 2001. Translation by Harvey C. Mansfield and Nathan Tarcov: *Discourses on Livy*. Chicago: University of Chicago Press, 1996.
———. *Il Principe*. Edited by Mario Martelli and Nicoletta Marcelli. Edizione nazionale delle opere di Niccolò Machiavelli, vol. 1. Rome: Salerno, 2006. Translation by Tim Parks: *The Prince*. London: Penguin Classics, 2009. Translation by W. K. Marriott: *Niccolo Machiavelli: The Prince*. New York: Macmillan, 1916.
Mansfield, H. C. *Machiavelli's Virtue*. Chicago: University of Chicago Press, 1996.
Pocock, John Greville Agard. *The Machiavellian Moment*. Princeton, NJ: Princeton University Press, 1975.
Procacci, Giuliano. *Studi sulla fortuna del Machiavelli*. Rome: Instituto storico italiano per l'età moderna e contemporanea, 1965.
Tarlton, Charles D. "*Fortuna* and the Landscape of Action in Machiavelli's *Prince*." *New Literary History* 30 (1999): 737–55.
Wilkins, Burleigh Taylor. "Machiavelli on History and Fortune." *Bucknell Review* 8 (1959): 225–45.

IV. *Anagkê*: The Bonds of Necessity

The etymology of *anagkê* [ἀνάγκη] is disputed, though the term possibly evokes the sense of "embracing" (RT: *Dictionnaire étymologique de la langue grecque*). Since Homer, the word has meant "constraint," from which comes the sense of divine fate (Euripides, *Phoenician Women*, 1000). In *Prometheus Bound* (511–19), the Moirai and the Erinyes govern *Anagkê*; when the chorus asks who governs Necessity, Prometheus replies: "The three Moirai and the Erinyes with their unyielding memory"; he adds that Zeus himself would not be able to avoid their fate (*tên peprômenên* [τὴν πεπρωμένην]). The word plays an important role in the Orphic writings, as attested by Euripides in *Alcestis* (963ff.): "I have found nothing stronger than Necessity [*Anagkê*], nor any remedy [against it] in the Thracian tablets, which the voice of Orpheus has written." Through a Platonic invention, it becomes the mother of the Moirai (*Republic*, 617b–e).

Anagkê plays a role in Parmenides's system. Associated with *moira* and *dikê* [δίκη] (justice, etymologically meaning "indication"; see THEMIS), *anagkê* ties beings in solid bonds. Barbara Cassin has shown how we can find its palimpsest in the immobility of Odysseus tied to the mast in the episode of the Sirens (*Parménide*, 55ff. and 151). Cassin also analyzes (151) the word and the concept of *anagkê*: the least-contested etymology connects the term with the curve of the arm (*agkos* [ἄγκος]), and the word is in fact constantly linked to circularity, to the turning back upon itself of *telos*, to limits, to bonds, to circles, and to the bands that, like the Styx, the Serpent, and the Ocean, encircle everything (see Onians, *Origin of European Thought*, pt. 3, chaps. 2 and 12; and Schreckenberg, *Ananke*).

The constraint of destiny will become a universal theme: Dante speaks of "la forza del destino" (see the opera by Verdi); Shakespeare says: "All unavoided is the doom of destiny" (*Richard III*, act 4, scene 4, v. 218); and Milton has his Almighty say: "What I will is Fate" (*Paradise Lost*, 7.173). In all of these examples, however, the semantic field of destiny is no longer Greek, but Latin, coming from *destinare* or from *fatum*.

■ See Box 4.

Pietro Pucci

BIBLIOGRAPHY

Adkins, Arthur W. H. *Merit and Responsibility: A Study in Greek Values*. Oxford: Clarendon, 1960.

Alvis, John. *Divine Purpose and Heroic Response in Homer and Virgil: The Political Plan of Zeus*. Lanham, MD: Rowman and Littlefield, 1995.

Berner, Franz. "*Tekhne* und *Tukhe*: Die Geschichte einer griechischen Antithese." Diss., University of Vienna, 1954.

Berry, Edmund Grindlay. "The History and Development of the Concept of *Theia Moira* and *Theia Tychē* down to and including Plato." Diss., University of Chicago, 1940.

Bianchi, Ugo. *Dios aisa: Destino, uomini e divinità nell'epos, nelle teogonie e nel culto dei Greci*. Rome: Signorelli, 1953.

Busch, Gerda. "Untersuchungen zum Wesen der Tyche in den Tragödien des Euripides." Diss., Heidelberg University, 1937.

Brutscher, Cordula. "Cäsar und sein Glück." *Museum Helveticum* 15 (1958): 75–83.

Cassin, Barbara. *Parménide: Sur la nature ou sur l'étant*. Paris: Éditions du Seuil, 1998.

Colinus, Austin, ed. *Nova fragmenta Euripidea*. Berlin: De Gruyter, 1968.

Decharme, Paul. *La critique des traditions religieuses chez les Grecs des origines au temps de Plutarque*. Paris: Alphonse Picard, 1904. Reprint, Brussels: Culture et Civilisation, 1966.

Diano, Carlo. *Forma ed evento: Principii per una interpretazione del mondo greco*. Venice, It.: Pozza, 1952.

———. *Il concetto della storia nella filosofia dei Greci*. Milan, It.: Marzorati, 1955.

Dietrich, Bernard Clive. *Death, Fate and the Gods: The Development of a Religious Idea in Greek Popular Belief and in Homer*. London: Athlone, 1965.

———. "The Spinning of Fate in Homer." *Phoenix* 16 (1962): 86–101.

Eitrem, Samson. "Moira." In *Paulys Real-encyclopädie der classischen Altertumswissenschaft*. 24 vols. Stuttgart: Metzler, 1894–1963.

Erkell, Harry. "Augustus, Felicitas, Fortuna: Lateinisches Wortstudien." Diss., University of Göteborg, 1952.

Feeney, Denis C. *The Gods in Epic*. Oxford: Clarendon, 1993.

Giannopoulou, Vasiliki. "Divine Agency and *Tyche* in Euripides' *Ion*: Ambiguity and Shifting Perspectives." *Illinois Classical Studies* 24–25 (2000): 257–71.

Greene, William Chase. *Moira, Fate, Good and Evil in Greek Thought*. Cambridge, MA: Harvard University Press, 1948.

Gundel, Wilhelm. "Heimarmene." In *Paulys Real-encyclopädie der classischen Altertumswissenschaft*. 24 vols. Stuttgart: Metzler, 1894–1963.

Guthrie, W.K.C. *The Greeks and Their Gods*. London: Methuen, 1950. Reprint, Boston: Beacon, 1985.

———. "The Religion and Mythology of the Greeks." In *Cambridge Ancient History*, rev. ed., vol. 2, chap. 40. Cambridge: Cambridge University Press, 1961.

Krikos-Davis, Katerina. "Moira at Birth in Greek Tradition." *Folia Neohellenica* 4 (1982): 106–34.

Lesky, Albin. "Gods and Men." In *A History of Greek Literature*, translated by James Willis and Cornelis de Heer, 65–73. New York: Crowell, 1966.

———. "Göttliche und menschliche Motivierung im homerischen Epos." *Sitzungsberichte der Heidelberger Akademie der Wissenschaften, Philos. Hist. Klasse* 4 (Winter 1961): 1–52.

Marks, Jim. *Zeus in the Odyssey*. Washington, DC: Center for Hellenic Studies, 2008.

Mourelatos, Alexander P. D. "Constraint-Fate-Justice-Persuasion." In *The Route of Parmenides*, 160–63. Rev. and exp. ed. Las Vegas, NV: Parmenides, 2008.

Nilsson, Martin Persson. *A History of Greek Religion*. Translated by F. J. Fielden. 2nd ed. Oxford: Clarendon, 1949.

Nussbaum, Martha C. *The Fragility of Goodness: Luck and Ethics in Greek Tragedy and Philosophy*. Rev. ed. Cambridge: Cambridge University Press, 2001.

Onians, R. B. *The Origin of the European Thought about the Body, the Mind, the Soul, the World, Time and Fate*. Cambridge: Cambridge University Press, 1989.

Plutarch. *Moralia*. Vol. 7. Translated by Lionel Pearson and F. H. Sandbach. Loeb Classical Library. Cambridge, MA: Harvard University Press, 1959.

Pucci, Pietro. *The Song of the Sirens*. New York: Rowman and Littlefield, 1998.

Reydams-Schils, Gretchen. *Demiurge and Providence: Stoic and Platonist Readings of the Timaeus*. Turnhout, Belg.: Brepols, 1999.

Robinson, T. M. "Presocratic Theology." In *The Oxford Handbook of Presocratic Philosophy*, edited by Patricia Curd and Daniel W. Graham, 485–98. Oxford: Oxford University Press, 2008.

Roveri, Alessandro. "*Tukhé* in Polibio." *Convivio* 24 (1956): 275–93.

Schreckenberg, Heinz. *Ananke: Untersuchungen sur Geschichte des Wortgebrauches*. Zetemata, 36. Munich: Beck, 1964.

Solomon, Robert C. "On Fate and Fatalism." *Philosophy East and West* 53 (2003): 435–54.

Strohm, Hans. *Tyche: Zur Schicksalsauffassung bei Pindar und den frühgriechischen Dichtern*. Stuttgart: J. G. Cotta, 1944.

Van der Horst, Pieter Willem. "Fatum Tria Fata, Parca, Tres Parcae." *Mnemosyne* 11 (1942): 217–27.

Wilamowitz-Moellendorff, Ulrich Von. *Der Glaube der Hellenen*. 2 vols. Darmstadt, Ger.: Wissenschaftliche Buchgesellschaft, 1959.

4

The *heimarmenê* of the Stoics, chain and providence

➤ BEGRIFF, Box 1, ELEUTHERIA, Box 2, IMPLICATION, LOGOS

For the Stoics, everything happens according to fate. Fate is the rational organization of events that occur naturally (Diogenes Laertius, 7.149). No event is exempt: nothing happens without a cause.

The Stoics deny that there is such a thing as fortune or luck. They choose necessity, *heimarmenê*, as a principle of the world, reviving at least etymologically the notion of the part of a whole, although the whole is no longer mysterious. Through a series of plays on words, of verbal allusions, and of literary references (particularly to Homer: see Long, "Stoic Readings of Homer"), Chrysippus and the Stoics broaden the scope and extent of the definitions of *heimarmenê*, which becomes *heirmon* [εἱρμόν], "chain," and *logos* [λόγος], "speech" and "reason."

The oneness of a government of destiny is reciprocated with the oneness of the world itself, which is God. "God, Intellect, Destiny and Zeus are but one" (Diogenes Laertius, 7.135); "Common nature and the common reason of this nature are Destiny, Providence, and Zeus" (Plutarch, *Contradictions of the Stoics*, 34.1050b). Our sensations and our representations (*phantasiai* [φαντασίαι]) are our points of access in the whole network of Destiny, God, or Nature, which is an integrated chain of causes and effects, a total present, a code for the universe. Logical articulation is founded on the organization of the world itself, God or Nature, Providence, Destiny, which it reproduces in the order and the import of the utterances it joins together.

Another word for *heimarmenê* in the sense of fate is *peprômenê*, assigning to every thing its limit, *peras* [πέρας], which is its determination, and therefore "finishing and ending" (Plutarch, *Contradictions of the Stoics*, 34.1056b). Cicero (*De divinatione*, 1.55.125) explains the term *fatum* (from *fari*, "to say," *fatum*, "what has been said"—in Arabic, the word is *mektoub*, "what has been written") as the Latin translation of *heimarmenê*:

By "fate," I mean what the Greeks call *heimarmenê*—an ordering and sequence of causes, since it is the connexion of cause to cause which out of itself produces anything.

(fatum autem id appello, quod Graeci εἱμαρμένην, id est ordinem seriemque causarum, cum causae causa nexa rem ex se gignat.)

(Cicero, *On Divination*, 1.125–26 [RT: *SVF* 2.291], trans. in RT: *The Hellenistic Philosophers*, 337)

In the words of Diogenes Laertius:

Fate is defined as an endless chain of causation, whereby things are, or as the reason or formula by which the world goes on.

(*Zeno*, in *Lives of Eminent Philosophers*, 7.149, trans. Hicks, 235)

The Stoics identify the greatest good, virtue and happiness, which they define as the fact of living in accordance with the events that happen naturally. Nonetheless, the Stoic theory of Fate is irreducible to the "argument of laziness" (if I am going to be cured of my illness, I will be cured, whether or not I call the doctor) and eradicates neither my action nor my freedom, which it appears to suppress: in the rational economy of the confatalia, or events linked together by fate, my illness is linked to the fact that I call the doctor. Human freedom does not reside so much in the choice of the content of our acts as in the active manner in which we embrace the events that happen to us naturally, and in which we thereby insert ourselves into the system of the world. Fate is irresistible. "The fates guide a docile will; they sweep away the one that resists [ducunt fata volentem, nolentem trahunt]"—this is how Seneca (letter 107.11 in *Letters to Lucilius*) freely translates the lines by Cleanthus that are cited at the end of Epictetus's *Manual for Living*. Our action can nevertheless become conjoined to fate, provided we know how to distinguish between simple facts and facts that are linked (*simplicia* versus *copulata*), between perfect and principal causes and auxiliary and adjacent causes (*causae perfectae et principales* versus *adiuvantes et proximae*):

"As therefore," he says, "he who pushes a cylinder gives it the beginning of its motion, but does not give it the power of rolling; so a sense impression when it strikes will, it is true, impress and as it were stamp its appearance on the mind, but assenting will be in our power, and, in the same way as was said in the case of the cylinder, it is pushed from outside but for the rest moves by its own force and nature."

(Cicero, *De fato*, 43, trans. Sharples, 87, 89)

By assent (*sugkatathesis* [συγκατάθεσις]), which is in our power and which is not reduced to a passive acceptance, we have the power to participate actively in the network of Providence. The Leibnizian theory of freedom will return to this motif.

Frédérique Ildefonse

BIBLIOGRAPHY

Cicero. *De fato*. In *Cicero, De fato and Boethius, The Consolation of Philosophy*, edited with an introduction, translation, and commentary by R. W. Sharples. Warminster, Eng.: Aris and Philips, 1991.

Diogenes Laertius. *Lives of Eminent Philosophers*. Translated by R. D. Hicks. London: Heinemann, 1925.

Long, Anthony A. "Stoic Readings of Homer." In *Homer's Ancient Readers*, edited by Robert Lamberton and John J. Keaney. Princeton, NJ: Princeton University Press, 1992.

KITSCH (GERMAN)

ENGLISH   junk art, garish art, kitsch

➤ AESTHETICS, ART, BAROQUE, CLASSIC, *CULTURE*, GOÛT, NEUZEIT, PEOPLE, SUBLIME

The word *Kitsch* is German in origin and had previously been translated into French as *art de pacotille* (junk art) or *art tape-à-l'œil* (garish art), but the original term has now become firmly established in all European languages. Used as an adjective, *kitsch* or *kitschy* (dis) qualifies cultural products intended for the masses and appreciated by them. As a noun the term designates a category of taste, certainly linked to an aesthetics, but even more so to an ethics whose political consequences are obvious. The subtitles of two works devoted to kitsch (Moles; Dorfles) indicate why some people find it attractive while others judge it severely: it is both an art of happiness and an expression of bad taste.

I. A Question of the Public or of Artistic Value?

The notion of *Kitsch* first appeared in the nineteenth century. It became the object of keen attention when mass society—helped by increased leisure time—had at its disposal a "culture for the masses" that, by its nature, seemed to threaten the very existence of authentic culture. *Kitsch* covers all different means of expression once they abandon rigor in order to cater to a wider public. The art of the chromos, pleasantly eye-catching photographs, the religious keepsakes collected by pilgrims, the souvenirs designed for tourists, but also the popular literature sold in railway stations, the comic theater of the boulevards, or the music that simply creates an ambiance: these are all examples of *Kitsch*. As a kind of debased popularization, it offers a decadent model that is all the more alluring for being so easily accessible. This is, at least, what its detractors say.

Hermann Broch, one of the first critics to write seriously about *Kitsch*, sees it as a form of "radical evil" that destroys value systems, since its essence "is the confusion of the ethical category with the aesthetic category" ("Evil in the Value-System," 33). In search of the pleasing effect, one that offers the most inexpensive seduction, kitsch art does not aim to be the product of good work but merely to be an attractive end product. This perverse method means that *Kitsch* uses tried and tested techniques and that it turns its back on creation in order to achieve a risk-free success in its effort to seduce. As Albert Kohn explains in an introductory note to his French translation of Broch's 1955 book *Dichtung und Erkennen*:

> The German word *Kitsch* has no equivalent in French. It refers to all genres of objects in bad taste, of artistically pretentious junk, popularizing commonplace forms through their mass-production, but it also applies to literary, artistic or musical works which aim for easy effects (such as melodrama) and pomposity, and cultivate sentimentality or mindless conformity. For want of being able to use the German word, we have translated it depending on the context as "*art de pacotille*" [junk art] or "*art tape-à-l'œil*" [garish art]. In actual fact, these two meanings are often combined.
>
> (Broch, *Création littéraire*, 17)

There are many disadvantages to translating the term in this way. The two attributes that are substituted for the semantic richness of *Kitsch* greatly reduce its complexity. By devaluing it from the outset, they take as a given what needs to be elucidated. So when Broch writes, "The essence of kitsch is the confusion of the ethical category with the aesthetic category. It is not concerned with 'good,' but with 'attractive' work; it is the pleasing effect that is most important," the translation of *Kitsch* as *tape-à-l'œil* [garish art] is wholly inadequate, first of all because not everything that is "garish" has to do with aesthetics, and then because the second sentence would therefore merely state a banal tautology, namely that the only aim of "garish" art is to produce a "pleasing effect." It is an entirely different matter if we retain the term *Kitsch*. What is more, other linguistic traditions had not hesitated to use the notion in its original language.

Clement Greenberg, for example, published an article in 1939 entitled "Avant-garde and Kitsch" in which he returned to Broch's idea that *Kitsch* borrows "tried and tested techniques," uses "prefabricated signs which, in its hands, solidify into clichés" (11). The merit of Greenberg's article is that he connects the appearance of *Kitsch* to that of another controversial phenomenon, the avant-garde, which also permanently destabilized established aesthetic values. Greenberg contrasts *Kitsch* with the avant-garde. The avant-garde alone seems capable of "continuing to change culture in the midst of ideological confusions and violence" (17):

> In the first place it is not a question of a choice between merely the old and merely the new, as London seems to think—but of a choice between the bad, up-to-date old and the genuinely new. The alternative to Picasso is not Michelangelo, but kitsch. . . . If the avant-garde imitates the processes of art, kitsch imitates its effects.
>
> (Ibid., 13–15)

■ See Box 1.

II. Taste, Effect, or Attitude?

After the war Hannah Arendt reflected upon the mass culture that was developing and of which *Kitsch* remained one of the main components. She pointed to the structural links between the world of aesthetic taste and that of political opinions, which both require a certain persuasiveness. In more general terms culture and politics belong together "because it is not knowledge or truth which is at stake, but rather judgment and decision, the judicious exchange of opinion about the sphere of public life and the common world, and the decision what manner of action is to be taken in it, as well as how it is to look henceforth, and what kind of things are to appear in it" (*Between Past and Future*, 223). Understood from this perspective, *Kitsch* becomes all the more disturbing since, as Hermann Broch had noted, "one cannot work in any art without adding to the mixture a drop of effect" (*Création littéraire*, 361), that is, without adding some drop of *Kitsch*. It was no doubt for this very reason that *Kitsch*, an alarming corruption that could be found even in the most uncompromising works of art, was contested so vigorously.

1

Avant-garde and Kitsch

In his article "Avant-garde and Kitsch" (1939) Clement Greenberg writes:

> Where there is an avant-garde, generally we also find a rearguard. True enough—simultaneously with the entrance of the avant-garde, a second new cultural phenomenon appeared in the industrial West: that thing to which the Germans give the wonderful name of *Kitsch*: popular, commercial art and literature with their chromotypes, magazine covers, illustrations, ads, slick and pulp fiction, comics, Tin Pan Alley music, tap dancing, Hollywood movies, etc., etc. For some reason this gigantic apparition has always been taken for granted. It is time we looked into its whys and wherefores.
>
> The precondition for *Kitsch*, a condition without which *Kitsch* would be impossible, is the availability close at hand of a fully matured cultural tradition, whose discoveries, acquisitions, and perfected self-consciousness *Kitsch* can take advantage of for its own ends. It borrows from that tradition devices, tricks, stratagems, rules of thumb, and themes, converts them into a system, and discards the rest. It draws its life blood, so to speak, from the reservoir of accumulated experience. This is what is really meant when it is said that the popular art and literature of today were once the daring, esoteric art and literature of yesterday. Of course, no such thing is true. What is meant is that when enough time has elapsed the new is looted for new "twists," which are then watered down and served up as kitsch.
>
> (Greenberg, *Avant-garde and Kitsch*)

Over the years the definition of *Kitsch* expanded and became more complex. When Broch returned to the subject in 1951, he stated that he was not talking "truly about art, but about a determinate attitude of life" (ibid., 311) deeply rooted within "kitsch-man." Abraham Moles pursued this logic in his work on *Kitsch*:

> It is not a semantically explicit denotative phenomenon, it is an intuitive and subtle connotative phenomenon; it is one of the types of relationships that human beings have with things, a way of being rather than an object, or even a style. Of course, we often talk of "kitsch style," but as one of the objectifiable supports of the kitsch attitude, and we can see this style becoming more formalized into an artistic period.
>
> (Moles, *Le Kitsch*, 7)

Nevertheless, at a time when pop art was blurring the ordering of established values in the avant-garde world, a new form appeared that staked a claim to *Kitsch*, and this was "camp." This American term is used to describe "something so outrageous or in such bad taste as to be considered amusing" (*Webster's New Ideal Dictionary*, 2nd ed., 1989). Since then, artists in Europe as well as in the United States have been exploiting both the first level—their works are crude, and the second level—they are doing this deliberately, joyously combining what is pleasing to the eye and what is revolting (for example, Jeff Koons). We can no longer tell with such works whether *Kitsch* is simply amusing—there is a kitsch-man perhaps ready to be awakened in every lover of art—or whether it is both funny and critically insightful.

Denys Riout

BIBLIOGRAPHY

Arendt, Hannah. "The Crisis in Culture: Its Social and Its Political Significance." In *Eight Exercises in Political Thought*, 197–226. Introduction by Jerome Kohn. New York: Penguin, 2006.

———. *Between Past and Future*. New York: Penguin Books, 1993.

Broch, Hermann. *Dichten und Erkennen: Essays 1*. Edited and with introduction by Hannah Arendt. In *Gesammelte Werke*. Vol. 6. Zürich: Rhein, 1955. French translation by Albert Kohn: *Création littéraire et connaissance, essais*. Paris: Gallimard / La Pléiade, 1985.

———. "Evil in the Value-System of Art." In *Geist and Zeitgeist: The Spirit in an Unspiritual Age: Six Essays*. Edited, translated, and with an introduction by John Hargraves. New York: Counterpoint, 2002.

———. "Kitsch" (1933) and "Notes on the Problem of Kitsch" (1950). In *Kitsch: The World of Bad Taste*, edited by Gillo Dorfles. New York: Universe Books, 1968.

Dorfles, Gillo, with Vivienne Menkes, eds. *Kitsch: The World of Bad Taste*. New York: Universe Books, 1969.

Giesz, Ludwig. "Kitsch-Man as Tourist." In *Kitsch*, edited by Gillo Dorfles with Vivienne Menkes, 156–74. New York: Universe Books, 1969.

———. *Phänomenologie des Kitsches*. 2nd rev. and expanded ed. Munich: Fink, 1971.

Greenberg, Clement. "Avant-garde and Kitsch." In *Art and Culture*, 3–21. Boston: Beacon Press, 1989. First published in 1939.

Gurstein, Rochelle. "Avant-Garde and Kitsch Revisited." *Raritan* 22, no. 3 (2003): 136–58.

Moles, Abraham A. *Le kitsch: L'art du bonheur*. Paris: Mame, 1971.

L

LANGUAGE

CATALAN	*llengua, lenguatge, parla*
ENGLISH	language, tongue, speech
FRENCH	*langue, langage, parole*
GERMAN	*Sprache, Rede*
GREEK	*logos* [λόγος]*, glôssa* [γλῶσσα]*, idiôma* [ἰδίωμα]
ITALIAN	*lingua, linguaggio, favella, parlare*
LATIN	*eloquium, lingua, loquela, idioma, locutio, sermo, oratio*
PORTUGUESE	*língua, linguagem, falar*
ROMANIAN	*limba, limbaj, vorbire*
RUSSIAN	*jazyk* [язык]*, reč'* [речь]
SPANISH	*lengua, lenguaje, favella, habla(r)*

➤ DISCOURSE, LOGOS, MANIERA, SIGN, SIGNIFIER/SIGNIFIED, SPEECH ACT, TERM, TO TRANSLATE, WORD

From the unity of *logos* to the multiplicity of Latin terms, by way of the overt binary (for example, the German *Sprache/Rede*), or ternary oppositions (for example, the French *langue/langage/parole*), history shows us that, when referring to relatively circumscribed realities (the speech organ, the faculty of speech, the means of expression particular to a group, the set of terms, the particularity of style, usage) or precise oppositions (individual/common, etc.), the same terms have sometimes been used with opposite meanings, and these shifts of meaning are clear and identifiable. The different theories of language have opted, within the multiplicity, even profusion, that each language offers, for a set of terms that in each case is quite limited. They have defined them in contrastive fashion in order to posit the oppositions they required, and in order thereby to specify the subject of the discipline. There is nothing, moreover, preventing a later theory that starts out with the same set of terms from giving different definitions of these terms.

I. The Emergence of the Differentiation of *Langue/Langage/Parole*

A. From language to the language sciences

The first attested meaning of *lingua, lingue* (ca. 980) was an "organ situated in the mouth," from the Latin *lingua* (which accounts for the metonymy of the French expression *mauvaise langue*, "malicious gossip," from 1260 on, in the sense of "malicious words," then of "malicious person"). The meaning of a "system of expression particular to a group" is attested at the same period, but more in the sense of "shared language," except when the noun is qualified or determined in some way. The French word *idiome* (idiom), a gallicization of *idiomat*, borrowed from the Low Latin *idioma*, also had the meaning of a "language or way of speaking particular to a region," and then much later of a "particularity of style." *Langage* in French, first noted as *lentguage* (ca. 980), designated the properly human faculty of expressing oneself and communicating. But from the

twelfth century on, the word meant "speaking" or "speech," sometimes with pejorative connotations (*bavardage*, "gossip"), with *parole* later taking on this sense. *Langage* in the sense of a "way of speaking particular to a people" would give way to *langue*, but would subsist as a "way of speaking particular to an individual or a group" (cf. "diplomatic language"). Its definition as an organized system of signs used to communicate would enable it to be extended to nonlinguistic systems ("the language of art, of colors") (RT: *DHLF*). The English term "language" was borrowed from the Old French *lenguage* around 1280, in the sense of a "way of speaking," then, of a "national language."

In 1765, Diderot, in the RT: *Encyclopédie*, criticized the common definition of *langue* as a "succession or accumulation of words and expressions" (cf. RT: *Dictionnaire universel*), saying that it in fact described a "vocabulary" rather than a "language," a term that covered not only words and their meanings, but also all the figurative turns of phrase, the connotations of words, the way the language was constructed, and so on. *Langue* would need to be defined more precisely, as the "totality of the usages of the voice belonging to a nation," insofar as one should consider "the expression and communication of thoughts, according to the most universal views of the mind, and the views most common to all men," and not the particularities specific to a nation and the ways it speaks, for which the term *idiome* would be used, with *parole* referring to language in general ("*La parole* is a sort of painting of which thought is the original"). This division allowed for a distinction to be made between *Grammaire générale* (Standard Grammar) considered as a "science" concerned with the "immutable and general principles of the spoken and written word," and "particular grammars" understood as "arts" that study the ways the practical usages of a language are applied to these general principles of spoken language (see Auroux, *L'encyclopédie: "Grammaire" et "langue" au XVIIIe siècle*).

The distinction between *langue* and *parole* drawn in Ferdinand de Saussure's RT: *Cours de linguistique générale* (*Course in General Linguistics*) allows one to distinguish the code from its use, the social from the individual, the essential from the accidental, and thereby enables the science of language to become a stable object, with *langage* referring to the faculty (see section B, below). The same epistemological necessity would lead Chomsky to distinguish between "competence" and "performance," though we cannot superimpose these two conceptual pairs, especially since, if the Saussurean *langue* is envisaged as a "treasure trove," a passive container full of isolated "signs," Chomskean "competence" is in contrast a set of "rules" allowing one to generate an infinite set of possible combinations of a given language, from a universal and innate linguistic faculty. For other linguists, such as Antoine Culioli, *langage* does not fall outside of the field of linguistics, nor is it the concern of physiology, psychology, or even philosophy (cf. the "philosophy of language"), but it is precisely linguistics' own ultimate object, insofar as it is apprehended on the basis of the diversity of *langues* (whence the plural expression in French, *sciences du langage* "sciences of language," often preferred nowadays to *linguistique*, "linguistics," to describe the discipline).

B. The Saussurean pair *langue/parole* and its translations

1. *Langue/parole*

The terminological pair *langue/parole* has become widely accepted on the basis of the importance Ferdinand de Saussure conferred on it. Indeed, in chapter 3 of the *Course in General Linguistics* we read:

> By distinguishing between the language itself [*la langue*] and speech [*la parole*], we distinguish at the same time: (1) what is social from what is individual, and (2) what is essential from what is ancillary and more or less accidental.
>
> The language itself is not a function of the speaker. It is the product passively registered by the individual. . . .
>
> Speech, on the contrary, is an individual act of will and the intelligence, in which one must distinguish: (1) the combinations through which the speaker uses the code provided by the language in order to express his own thought, and (2) the psycho-physical mechanism which enables him to externalize these combinations.

In fact, Saussure's chapter is marked by a torrent of distinctions. Upstream, we find an initial split being made between *langage* and *langue* (*langage* has to be discarded because this term is too "heterogeneous"). But the presumed "homogeneity" of *langue* requires a new demarcation (or "separation"), one that distances it precisely from *parole*, to the extent that it produces two clearly opposable "linguistics," in the same way the "social" is opposed to the "individual," and even more so, the "essential" to the "accidental." This distinction is reinforced by the term "subordination"—that is, of *parole* to *langue*—such that:

> It would be possible to keep the name linguistics for each of these two disciplines. We would then have a linguistics of speech. But it would be essential not to confuse the linguistics of speech with linguistics properly so called. The latter has linguistic structure as its sole object of study.

It is obvious that we have now left the realm of methodology and are entering that of ontology, which raises a formidable problem. Should the lived experience of a language be the deciding factor here, or should it be the conceptual imposition of the theorist? Is the latter not setting him- or herself up as a supreme judge, who is in danger of forcing the summoned "object" to submit to his decisions as an interpreter and organizer? And a theorist consolidates her authority even more through the power of an undisputed conclusion—indeed, as history will go on to confirm, this distinction between *langue* and *parole* has for a long time now been accepted as an indisputable axiom of any linguistics worthy of the name.

2. Binary or ternary, depending on the language

Saussure's *Course*, however, manifests a certain reticence in this regard:

> [T]he distinctions established are not affected by the fact that certain ambiguous terms have no exact equivalents in other languages. Thus in German the word *Sprache* covers individual languages [*langue*] as well as language in general [*langage*], while *Rede* answers more or less to "speech" [*parole*], but also has the special sense of "discourse." . . . No word corresponds precisely to any of the notions we have tried to specify above. That is why all definitions based on words are vain. It is an error of method to proceed from words in order to give definitions of things.

This is a strange statement for a linguist to make, even more so for one who is an avowed partisan of the "arbitrary nature of the linguistic sign" (unless we hold the editors of the *Course* responsible on this point, and not Saussure himself). Whatever the case may be, if we turn our attention back to words, we have to admit that they do float around without any secure points of anchorage. This is confirmed by Eugen Coseriu who, while stating that this duality works in most languages, is forced to accept that it is displaced and complicated by a second distinction between two varieties of language, that is, those that have only a binary distinction, and those that present a ternary distinction. So we have:

a. Binary type (*langage-langue/parole*)

German	English	Russian	Latin
Sprache	language/tongue	*jazyk* [язык]	*lingua*
Rede	speech	*reč'* [речь]	*sermo/oratio*

b. Ternary type (essentially the Romance languages)

French	Italian	Spanish	Portuguese	Romanian	Catalan
langage	*linguaggio*	*lenguaje*	*linguagem*	*limbaj*	*llenguatge*
langue	*lingua*	*lengua*	*língua*	*limba*	*llengua*
parole	*favella/parlare*	*habla(r)*	*fala(r)*	*vorbire*	*parla*

The elements provided by Tullio de Mauro (critical edition of the *Cours de linguistique générale*), however, give a ternary structure also for Polish (*jezyk / mowa / mowa jednostkowa*) and for Magyar (*nyelvezet/nyelv/beszéd*), which relativizes the exclusive privilege accorded to Romance languages. What is more, he stresses the specific complexities of German, English, and Italian, and we can already see a blurring of terms in the table above (there are sometimes several words on the same line, and one could add *govorenie* [говорение] to the Russian *reč'*). We can assume, therefore, that the premise of an orderly distribution (between languages, and within each language) has to be significantly qualified. So it is reasonable to formulate the hypothesis that if one looks hard enough, one will always find a way to expand or reduce the desired number of categories. The lists of categories thus end up confirming the theory of the "arbitrary nature of the linguistic sign": signifiers (*signifiants*) have no fixed meaning, and attempting to distribute them leads to their dispersion, which is consequently followed by a dispersion of signifieds (*signifiés*). Should the distinction between *langue* and *parole* be described, then, as "factitious," in Descartes's sense (*factae*; in *Meditatio*, 3a)?

3. The dynamics of oppositions

We should begin by challenging the rather casual opposition between "factitious" and "innate" (or between "accidental" and "essential"). The concept presented to us in this terminological pair is precisely duality itself, that is, a dynamic relation with no separation or merging of the terms—or, even more radically, with no "subordination" of one term to the other. Such subordination remains the strongest temptation when the schematization of aspects of language is attempted, with the most perverse of effects (we have to put everything into one of the terms—*langue*—so as not to leave a merely insignificant residue in the other, at the expense of their mutual disqualification). We can find a clue if we go further upstream from Saussure, to Wilhelm von Humboldt, who is perhaps his hidden counterpart. The aspect of language that holds and stimulates his interest most keenly is the fact that it appears as both object and subject, in a paradoxical coincidence of opposites (or of terms judged as such by abstract understanding):

Language is as much an object and independent as it is a subject and dependent. For nowhere does it have . . . any permanent foundation, but it must always be produced anew in one's thought, and consequently come down entirely on the side of the subject: but the characteristic property of the act of this production is to convert it immediately into an object; in so doing it involves at every moment the action of an individual, an action that is already linked in itself by all of its present and past operations.

(Die Sprache ist gerade insofern Object und selbständig, also sie Subject und abhängig ist. Denn sie hat nirgends . . . eine bleibende Stätte, sondern muß immer im Denken aufs neue erzeugt werden; es liegt aber in dem Act dieser Erzeugung sie gerade zum Object zu machen: sie erfährt auf diesem Wege jedesmal die ganze Erwirkung des Individuums, aber dieser Einwirkung ist schon in sich durch das, was sie wirkt und gewirkt hat, gebunder.)

(*Schriften zur Sprachphilosophie*
[*Writings on the Philosophy of Language*])

Humboldt was endlessly fascinated by this interweaving of opposite and complementary poles, and it led him in the end to a famous and obscure pair, which moreover he expressed in Greek: *ergon/energeia*. These, however, could be replaced with other terms, for example, *Macht* (the sheer power of the elements memorized) as opposed to *Gewalt* (the enthusiastic initiative of an individual). Humboldt's investigation of this string of terminological couples led him finally to what is perhaps the most striking and provocative statement in his work:

[I]t is just as correct to say that the human race only speaks one language as it is to say that every man possesses his own language.

([D]aß man ebenso richtig sagen kann, daß das ganze Menschengeschlecht nur Eine Sprahce, als daß jeder Mensch eine besondere besitzt.)

(ibid.)

The power of language does not allow itself to be distributed into moments (increasing or decreasing, widespread or restricted, essential or ancillary). The universal and the singular exist side by side, or to put it more precisely, they only appear in their reciprocal tension, or their productive interaction (a coordination without subordination).

In the tradition that flows from Humboldt, then, coordination inevitably prevails, even at the expense of more or less happy or loose compromises, which accept the agreement of the reconciled dualities. This is true of the now classic pair *modus/dictum* (see DICTUM). Thus Charles Bally:

An explicit sentence comprises . . . two parts: one correlates to the process that constitutes representation (for example, rain, a cure); we will call this, following the example of logicians, the *dictum*.

The other contains the key element of the sentence, namely, the expression of modality, correlative to the operation of the thinking subject. The logical and analytical expression of modality is a modal verb: both constitute the *modus*, which complements the *dictum*.

Modality is the soul of the sentence, it is constituted essentially by the active operation of the speaking subject. . . .

. . . the *modus* is the *theme*, and the *dictum* the substance of what is said in an explicit statement. . . . The *modus* and the *dictum* complement one another.

(Bally, *Linguistique générale et linguistique française*, §§28 and 32)

This is equally true of the pair "type/token" (see PROPOSITION, Box 4). Here, for example, is C. S. Peirce:

A common mode of estimating the amount of matter in a MS or printed book is to count the number of words. There will ordinarily be about twenty *the*'s on a page, and of course they count as twenty words. In another sense of the word "word", however, there is but one word *the* in the English language; and it is impossible that this word should lie visibly on a page or be heard in any voice, for the reason that it is not a Single thing or Single event. It does not exist; it only determines things that do exist. Such a definitely significant Form, I propose to term a *Type*. A Single event which happens once and whose identity is limited to that one happening or a Single object or thing which is in some single place at any one instant of time . . . such as this or that word on a single line of a single page of a single copy of a book, I will venture to call a *Token*.

(Peirce, *Collected Papers*, vol. 4, §537)

The same classic distinction informs Chomsky's duality of "competence" and "performance," which the author himself compares to the Saussurean pair:

> Linguistic theory is concerned primarily with an ideal speaker-listener, in a completely homogeneous speech-community, who knows its language perfectly and is unaffected by such grammatically irrelevant conditions as memory limitations, distractions, shifts of attention and interest, and errors (random or characteristic). ... To study actual linguistic performance, we must consider the interaction of a variety of factors, of which the underlying competence of the speaker-hearer is only one. ... We thus make a fundamental distinction between *competence* (the speaker-hearer's knowledge of his language) and *performance* (the actual use of language in concrete situations). Only under the idealization set forth in the preceding paragraph is performance a direct reflection of competence. In actual fact, it obviously could not directly reflect competence. ... The problem for the linguist, as well as for the child learning the language, is to determine from the data of performance the underlying system of rules that has been mastered by the speaker-hearer and that he puts to use in actual performance. ... The distinction I am noting here is related to the *langue-parole* distinction of Saussure.

> (Chomsky, *Aspects of the Theory of Syntax*)

Chomsky's distinction has the merit of being highly manipulable, and it is strengthened by its assumed close fidelity to its object. One might suspect, however, that this overly harmonious symmetry erases the interactive complexity of the problem that needs to be resolved.

This is why, downstream from Saussure, one of the most interesting studies appears to be the one proposed by Ludwig Jäger, which Thomas Scheerer summarizes as follows: what we are dealing with is a chiasmic classification based on the four concepts "actual/virtual" and "individual/social." So we have:

1. As far as the virtual (*in absentia*) is concerned, the distinction between, on one hand, an "individual" concept of a language (in the sense of subjective, internalized processes), corresponding to the Saussurean concepts of "treasure trove," "repository," "memory," and on the other hand, a social concept of language (in the sense of a social, semiological institution, whose value is intersubjective), corresponding to the Saussurean concepts of "social crystallization," "social secretion," "social product."
2. As far as the actual (*in praesentia*) is concerned, the distinction between, on one hand, an "individual" concept of speech (in the sense of subjective realizations of the possibilities given by the internalized and intersubjective potentials of language), and on the other hand, a "social" concept of speech (in the sense of an intersubjective—dialogical—production endowed with a new meaning, corresponding to the Saussurean concepts of "analogy" and of "parasemic creation").

The interesting aspect of this proposition is the concern to find a middle way, though not a reductive one, between the Saussurean duality proper, with its distinctions and its blind alleys, and the need for an order that does not sacrifice the complexity of the problem. This problem, once it has come to light, remains forever a source of torment, which from time to time generates illuminating conjectures.

II. From the Oneness of *Logos* to the Complexity of the Medieval Semantic Field

The difficulty of translating ancient texts into modern languages is dramatically illustrated by the terminological network that concerns us. On the one hand, we have the almost absolute oneness of *logos* in Greek, which by itself covers all the modern terms referring to the linguistic field, and even beyond, leaving just a small place for *glôssa*. In classical Latin, on the other hand, *logos* scatters into ten or more terms, whose meanings are more or less set. Medieval Latin inherits this diversity, with no real possibility of putting these terms into any order: indeed, it has to deal with a number of real legacies, via the transmission of texts, which come into conflict with specific and new terminological choices. These new choices are linked both to choices of translation in philosophical and religious texts (so, for example, it is *lingua* that appears in the Vulgate Latin as the expression used to talk about the *confusio linguarum*, but it is *locutio* that is retained for translating the famous passage from *De anima*, see section II.B.2, below), to theoretical choices in the elaboration of a particular doctrine (the opposition between *lingua* and *idiomata* in Roger Bacon), and to different uses of terms' former connotations, notably with the aid of some celebrated etymologies (see the one for *idioma*).

A. *Glôssa/logos: Langue/langage, parole,* and so forth

In ancient Greek, *logos* [λόγος] was a catchall word covering everything: it referred to a particular language or tongue, language in general, speech, and more generally discourse, but also the faculty of thinking and of speaking, and more generally relation (see LOGOS)—everything, that is, except for the tongue as an organ, for which the term was *glôssa* [γλῶσσα] (in Aristotle's biological treatises, for example). *Glôssa*, however, has the same kind of metonymic extension as *langue* in French: the tongue as an organ that is common to humans and animals (Homer, *Iliad*, 1.249, *Odysseus*, 1.332), and the tongue as an organ of speech (Hesiod, *Works and Days*, 707). So it can mean speaking as opposed to acting (Aeschylus, *Agamemnon*, 813), or feeling or thinking (Euripides, *Hippolytus*, 612; Lucien, *Pro lapsu inter salutendum* [*On a Mistake in Greeting*], 18). Since Homer, the term *glôssa* has also referred to the tongue we speak—understood generically to designate all language when the language spoken is Greek, or restrictively, when it is a foreign or barbarian tongue that is being alluded to, as idiom (*Iliad*, 2.804, 4.438; Herodotus, 1.57). "To speak a language" can be rendered as *glôssan nomizein* [γλῶσσαν νομίζειν], to have it in practice (Herodotus, 1.142), or *chrêsthai* [χρῆσθαι], to use it (4.109); and dialects are seen as "derivations" or "alterations" of a language, *tropous paragôgeôn* [τρόπουςπαραγωγέων] (1.142.8) (see TO TRANSLATE, section I). In rhetoric and poetics, particularly in Aristotle, *glôssai* are archaic or dialectal terms ("signal words" for Hardy, "borrowed names" for Dupont-Roc and Lallot; see WORD, II.B.1), as opposed to the "word" properly speaking (kurion [κύριον]), which can at times elevate the *logos*, and sometimes make it incomprehensible (*Poetics*, chaps. 21 and 22; in particular, 1458a 22–26). Finally, *glôssai* would later refer to the tongues of fire of the Pentecost.

It is worth noting that in Greek *glôssai* and *logoi*, in the plural, do not usually or primarily refer to the same reality as in the singular (*logos*: thought-speech, etc.; *logoi*, propositions, definitions; *glôssa*: tongue as an organ, and one language as distinct from another; *glôssai*: archaisms or obscurities).

Glôssa in the sense of "tongue" is distinct from the universality of the *logos* defining the humanity of humankind, in that it is linked to the differences between languages, and to human diversity. We tend therefore to reserve "language" (*langage*) for *logos*, and "tongue" (*langue*) for *glôssa*. In addition, we might be tempted to say that *parole*, in the Saussurean sense of an individual act, has no equivalent in ancient Greek, but this would be to forget that *logos* is first and foremost discursiveness, act, performance, and thus quite appropriate to designate a speech-act—but only insofar as it is a universally singular act defining the human (see SPEECH ACT).

- See Box 1.

B. The proliferation of terms for "language" in medieval Latin

- For classical Latin, see Box 2.

"Fiebat autem res non materno sermone, sed literis" (The conversation took place not in our mother tongue [*materno sermone*] but in Latin [*literis*]). This sentence from Guibert de Nogent's (d. ca. 1125) autobiography, *Monodiae*, allows us to understand at the outset the complexity of this semantic field in medieval Latin.

The notions collectively associated with the term "language" are at the confluence of ten or so words—*elocutio, eloquium, famen, idioma, lingua, linguagium, locutio, loquela, sermo, verbum, vox*—whose various meanings are generally wider than "language." This semantic field was of little interest to medieval lexicologists: it did not give rise to any of those differential verses so highly valued by the masters, nor to any substantial dictionary entries. Of these words, we will focus our attention on the most commonly represented in the medieval corpus.

1. Idiom (*eloquium, lingua, loquela, idioma, locutio, sermo*)

The terms in question share the meaning of "language of a group, idiom": the four privileged words having this meaning are *lingua* (*anglica, arabica, gallica, graeca, latina, romana,* etc.), *sermo* (*anglicus, hebraeus, latinus, maternus, sclavonicus*), *eloquium* (*arabicum, graecum, hebraeum, latinum*), and *idioma* (*arabicum, graecum, teutonicum*), while it is rarer to find *loquela* (*hebraica, latina, saxonica*) and *locutio* (*barbarica, latina*). The specific sense of *idioma*, "distinctive character," comes through in the expressions *idioma linguae, idioma linguae graecae, hebraeae, teutonicae*, and is retained after it acquires the more simplified meaning of "language," even if Robert of Melun (d. 1167) speaks, for emphasis, of *proprietas idiomatis hebraeae linguae*. So too the distinction in Peter Comestor (d. 1178; RT: *PL*, 198, col. 1653B) between *linguae* and *idiomata linguarum*: the apostles get their message across not only because of their mastery of languages, but also because of the dialects that are derived from them.

Idioma is used especially when one wishes to stress the difficulty of translating, whether it involves one of the three sacred languages or a vernacular language.

There is a wide consensus about the synonymy between several of these terms: Pierre Hélie (ca. 1150) uses *genus loquelae* and *genus linguae* indiscriminately, before qualifying them as *graeca, latina,* etc.; Boethius of Dacia (ca. 1270) posits an equivalence between *lingua* and *idioma* (grammatica in una lingua vel in uno idiomate [the grammar of one language or tongue]") but also posits the universality of grammar as a science, when he explains that "all languages are one single grammar [omnia idiomata sunt una grammatica]"; Peter Comestor (RT: *PL*, 198, col. 1623D) asserts an equivalence between *loquela* and *idioma* ("loquela tua id est idioma Galilaeae [and your speech of Galilee, that is to say]") in his commentary on Matthew 26:73. *Lingua* also signifies, by extension, but more rarely, the community formed by those who speak the same language (cf. Revelation 13:7): so Raoul of Caen refers to Tancredo, celebrated by all people (*populos*) in all languages (*linguas*).

2. Language, speech (*sermo, locutio, loquela*)

The meaning of "language" as the human ability to use vocal signs to communicate can be found in *sermo*, which thus translates *logos*—cf. the translation by Chalcidius of Plato's *Timaeus*, 47c: "Propter hoc enim nobis datus est sermo ut praesto nobis fiant mutuae voluntatis indicia" (Language has been given to us so we have a way to conveniently indicate our wishes to others). We also find it in *locutio*, for example, in the answer given by Boethius of Dacia to the question of knowing whether "grammar" is possessed naturally by men ("utrum grammatica sit naturaliter ab homine habita"): men who have never heard a human word spoken (*loquela*) are still naturally able to speak (*locutio vel grammatica*). He makes reference to Psammetichus's famous experiment, reported by Herodotus (for a more detailed history, see Launay, "Un roi, deux enfants et des chèvres," which unfortunately cites only very few texts in the original):

> Si homines aliqui in deserto nutrirentur, ita quod numquam aliorum hominum loquelam audirent nec aliquam instructionem de modo loquendi acciperent, ipsi suos affectus naturaliter sibi mutuo exprimerent et eodem modo. Locutio enim est una de operibus naturalibus, cujus signum est, quod instrumentum, per quod fit locutio, natura in nobis ordinavit.

> (If men were raised in a desert such that they never heard a word spoken by other men, and received no instruction as to how to speak, they would still naturally express their feelings, and in the same way. Language is indeed one of the natural faculties, and the sign of this is that the instrument by which language is produced is given to us by nature.)

> (Herodotus, *Histories*)

There is one universal *modus loquendi* (*idem apud omnes*, an expression that Aristotle applied to mental affects [*pathêmata tês psuchês* (πάθηματα τῆς ψυχῆς)]; see SIGN), here attributed to language, with the accidental differences explaining the diversity of languages (*idiomata*).

1

Sprache/Rede, langue/parole? Heidegger as a reader of the Greeks

Heidegger states, in §34 of *Being and Time*, in the course of an analysis of speech as existential: "The Greeks had no word for *langue* (*Sprache*), they understood this phenomenon 'from the beginning' as *parole* (*Rede*)." The difference established between *Sprache* and *Rede* is by no means self-evident, however—added to this initial difficulty is that of its translations into French, which vary considerably: translations either stress the opposition *langue/parole*, as in the version above by François Vezin, or, on the contrary, they join the terms together, as twin sisters opposed to *Rede*, as in the translation by Emmanuel Martineau: "The Greeks have no word for *Sprache* (*parole*, *langue*), they understood this phenomenon 'from the very first' in the sense of *parler* [act of speaking]."

The distinction *Sprache/Rede* is a classic one in German, and we find it notably in Goethe (*Dichtung und Wahrheit* [*Poetry and Truth*], pt. 2, bk. 10): "Schreiben ist ein Mißbrauch der Sprache, still für sich lesen ein trauriges Surrogat der Rede" (Writing is a misuse of language, reading quietly to oneself is a sad substitute for live conversation). It is to the ancient tradition, still prevalent in the Middle Ages, of reading out loud that Goethe contrasts the *stille für sich lesen = legere in silentio* (Saint Augustine), *tacite legere*, or *legere sibi* (Saint Benedict).

For Heidegger, however, the distinction between *Sprache* and *Rede* only takes on its full meaning after accounting for both (1) the interpretation of *logos* [λόγος] he proposes in the same text (§7) as apophantic, and (2) the existential structure of *Mitsein* (being-with). He is concerned with returning to the conditions of the ontological, and thus existential, possibility of speaking [*la parole*] as an ontological structure of *Dasein*. *Rede* still leaves open the possibility of *Gerede* (§35); of *parlerie*, "gossip" (Montaigne); of *bavardage*, "idle chatter" (Martineau's translation); or of the *on-dit*, "hearsay" (F. Vezin's translation).

The opposition between *Sprache* and *Rede* is so indecisive that the following paragraph (§35) can say: "Die Rede ... ist Sprache" (La parole ... est langage parlé [Speech ... is spoken language], Vezin; or, Le parler ... est parole [Speaking ... is speech], Martineau). Other statements from the same period move in a similar direction and join together rather than oppose *Sprache* and *Rede*, as, for example, in the *Gesamtausgabe* (*GA*; vol. 27), where we read:

> The Greeks, like all peoples of Southern Europe, lived far more intensely within the realm of public speech and conversation [*in der öffentlichen Sprache und Rede*] than we are used to. For them, thinking is discussing openly and publicly. Books were of no interest, and even less so newspapers.

For the Greeks, *logos* was not thought of independently from "dialogue" within a space we might call "rhetorical" (§29 of *Being and Time* describes Aristotle's *Rhetoric* as "the first systematic hermeutics of the everydayness of being-together") and "political," in the sense of the Aristotelian definition of the *polis* [πόλις], in the *Nicomachean Ethics* (2.7), defined as a "community of words and actions." In short, *Rede* lends itself better than *Sprache* to underlining the existential character of speech, insofar as it is experienced in the exchange of spoken words.

What Heidegger emphasizes in his own way is that "language" is not understood in an original, but rather, a derived mode when it is envisaged independently of what one is talking *about*, as well as of those "with whom" one is talking. In other words, the existential structures of being-in-the-world (*In-der-Welt-sein*) and being-with (*Mitsein*) constitute the sole originary ground within which a *language*, understood as "use of the language to express thoughts and feelings" (RT: *Dictionnaire de la langue française*), can be rooted.

We need to add to this the fact that Heidegger, going against a long tradition, reads in the *Peri hermeneias* of Aristotle something entirely different from a mention of "sounds produced by the voice"—the Latin translation (*ae quae sunt in voce*) is in this case more faithful to the words of the Stagirite (see SIGN, Box 1). The decisive element in the voice, for Heidegger, is not its sonorousness, as in "vocal production"; rather, "the humanity of the voice is primary in relation to the fact that it can convey a message" (Fédier, *Interprétations*).

In *Unterwegs zur Sprache* (*On the Way to Language*), Heidegger expresses wonder at the fact that the Japanese have no word for *Sprache* and are not bound to the "brilliant history of sonority in the human adventure of language" (Hagège, *L'homme de paroles*), or in other words, to phonetics. This is what is expressed by *koto ba* (spoken word): "flower petals of the *koto*—the appropriation that controls all that for which responsibility must be assumed over what grows and blossoms into flowers"), which "names something other than the meaning conveyed by the names which come to us from metaphysics: γλῶσσα, *lingua*, *langue* and *language*" (*GA*, vol. 12).

Pascal David

BIBLIOGRAPHY

Fédier, François. *Interprétations*. Paris: Presses Universitaires de France, 1985.

Figal, Günter. "Heidegger's Philosophy of Language in an Aristotelian Context: *Dynamis Meta Logou*." Translated by Drew A. Hyland and Erik M. Vogt. In *Heidegger and the Greeks: Interpretive Essays*, edited by Drew A. Hyland and John Panteleimon Manoussakis, 83–92. Bloomington: Indiana University Press, 2006.

Goethe, Johann Wolfgang von. *Dichtung und Wahrheit*. In vol. 22 of *Gesamtausgabe*. Munich: Boerner, 1973. Translation by Robert Heitner: *From My Life*. Edited by Jeffrey L. Sammons and Thomas P. Saine. 2 vols. New York: Suhrkamp, 1987.

Hagège, Claude. *L'homme de paroles: Contribution linguistique aux sciences humaines*. Paris: Fayard, 1985. Translation by Sharon L. Shelly: *The Dialogic Species: A Linguistic Contribution to the Social Sciences*. New York: Columbia University Press, 1990.

Heidegger, Martin. *Einleitung in die Philosophie*. Edited by Otto Saame and Ina Saame-Speidel. In vol. 27 of *Gesamtausgabe*. Frankfurt: Klostermann, 1996.

———. *Sein und Zeit*. 13th ed. Tübingen: Niemeyer, 1976. English translation by John Macquarrie and Edward Robinson: *Being and Time*. New York: Harper and Row, 1962.

———. *Sein und Zeit*. French translation by E. Martineau: *Être et temps*. Paris: Authentica, 1985.

———. *Sein und Zeit*. French translation by F. Vezin: *Être et temps*. Paris: Gallimard, 1986.

———. *Unterwegs zur Sprache*. Edited by Friedrich-Wilhelm von Herrmann. In vol. 12 of *Gesamtausgabe*. Frankfurt: Klostermann, 1985. Translation by Peter D. Hertz: *On the Way to Language*. New York: Harper and Row, 1971.

Weigelt, Charlotta. *The Logic of Life: Heidegger's Retrieval of Aristotle's Concept of "Logos."* Stockholm: Almqvist and Wiksell, 2002.

2

Lingua and *sermo* in classical Latin

Two words were used to mean "language" in classical Latin: *lingua* and *sermo*. *Lingua*, which originally applied to the organ of speech, referred to the linguistic material of a people, the communication tool everyone possessed because he or she belonged to such and such a community. *Sermo*, which originally applied to meeting and talking, to conversation, to discussion, to exchanging opinions, was used to refer to the perfected, mastered language:

> cum audisset Latronem declamentem, dixit: sua lingua disertus est; ingenium illi concessit, sermonem objecit.

> (after having heard Latronus orate: he speaks, he said, with an eloquent tongue: he agreed he had talent, he objected to his fine language.)

> (Seneca the Elder, *Controversiarum*, 2.12)

There is, however, another opposition between these two terms, which we can at least speculate is present in Varro. The author of, among other texts, two works with similar titles, the *De lingua latina* and the *De sermone latino*, Varro apparently had a bipartite conception of the description of Latin (though it is difficult to assess, insofar as we only have one small part of *De lingua latina*, and just a few slight fragments of *De sermone latino*). If, as the most detailed analyses of the plan of *De lingua latina* show, this treatise was a study of language as meaning, it is tempting to think that *De sermone latino* was, by contrast, a study of the material aspects of language. The rare testimonies we do have of *De sermone latino* do not contradict this hypothesis: they deal with questions of spelling, of accent, of archaic forms, even of meter. Are the two types of opposition compatible? What they have in common is perhaps the fact that language in its most immediate manifestation (*lingua*) essentially aims at meaning, while language in the aspects that can be mastered (*sermo*) implies an awareness of its form. This hypothesis is, however, entirely conjectural.

Marc Baratin

BIBLIOGRAPHY

Baratin, Marc. *La naissance de la syntaxe à Rome*. Paris: Éditions de Minuit, 1989.
Seneca, Lucius Annaeus. *The Elder Seneca Declamations*. Translated by M. Winterbottom. 2 vols. Loeb Classical Library. Cambridge, MA: Harvard University Press, 1974.
Varro, Marcus Terentius. *On the Latin Language*. Translated by Roland G. Kent. 2 vols. Loeb Classical Library. Cambridge, MA: Harvard University Press, 1938.

Abbon de Saint-German discusses the power of speech in his commentary on Proverbs 18:21 ("mors et vita sunt in manibus linguae") and explicitly breaks with the biblical metaphor on *lingua*, translating this expression as "id est in potestate loquele." *Lingua* never in fact appears in this context in the sense of "language"; when it is present in association with *locutio* or *loquela*, it is always confined to the sense of "physical organ." So it is said that the tongue (*lingua*) is the instrument of taste and of speech (*gustum et locutionem*, according to the Latin translation of *De anima*, 420b 5ff.; see WORD, III.B.1).

These three terms—*locutio*, *sermo*, and *loquela*—are also used by extension to designate the human ability to pronounce language distinctly, a faculty of which mutes are deprived (in Bede, Aldheim, Thietmar, Peter the Venerable, and Pierre Riga, among others). *Lingua*, with its double meaning of a physical organ of articulating sounds and of a system of vocal signs, clearly cannot be used in this type of context without misinterpretation or ambivalence.

3. The language of an author, style (*sermo, eloquium, locutio, lingua*)

The meaning of "a way of speaking, style, expression, language" is assumed by *sermo, eloquium*, but also *lingua*. So Remigius of Auxerre gives *sermo* as a synonym for *facundia*, while Hugh of Saint Victor puts it between *vox* and *intellectus*. We also find *sermo vulgaris* (in the sense of an informal language), while Giraud de Barri (*Expugnatio Hibernica*) states that he is renouncing his previous way of writing in favor of a "presentis idioma sermonis," assimilated to a "novus modus eloquentiae." In addition, the style, expression, or "language" of a writer is referred to as, for example, "sermo clarus, sermo nitidu, sermo exquisitus, sermo blandus; eloquium fluens, eloquium luculentissimum." Both *sermo* and *locutio* are used to characterize verse and prose forms of expression: so one would say *sermo metricus, sermo prosaicus*, and Raban Maur, transposing a verse text into prose, claims he is translating not another language, but another mode of expression (vol. 5 [dated 814]): "interpres . . . non alterius linguae sed alterius locutionis." So it is particularly interesting to find *lingua* in this context, in the sense of "style," "language": Vulfin, the author of the *Life of Saint Martin* (ca. 800), contrasts an expert and erudite language ("diserti eruditique sermonis eloquium") with the poverty of an arid style ("paupertas sterilis linguae"). In the twelfth century, Geoffroy of Saint Victor congratulates Saint Augustine on having used a refined language in expressing himself ("ad eloquentiam linguam das urbanam").

C. The mother tongue (*lingua materna*): From lost unity to multiplicity/diversity

1. *Nos Latini*

The men and women of letters in the Middle Ages spoke Latin so much that they referred to themselves as "Latins" (*nos Latini*). Latin was felt as such a factor of identity or identification by clerics and scholars that any other language was a foreign language (*lingua aliena*), whether it was one of the erudite languages (Hebrew, Greek, Arabic), or a vernacular language. For this reason, one refers to words transferred or translated (*translata*) into Latin as foreign words, whether they had been assimilated or not, that is, whether they had taken on a Latin ending (*nota*), or not (*peregrina*). Latin, according to Gilles of Rome, was thus an invention of philosophers, who wanted to create for themselves their "own idiom" (*proprium idioma*) as a way of compensating for the deficiencies of the vulgar language (*De regimine principium*, 2.2.c.7). For some, the divide was clearly located between clerics and lay people: clerics had a language (*ydioma*) that was "the same for all" (*idem apud omnes*—the term *ydioma*, like *modus loquendi* earlier, indicating the specificity of, on the one hand, the social group, and on the other, of the human race), and that one learned at school, whereas lay people had languages made up of words whose meaning was established conventionally (*ydiomata vocum impositarum ad placitum*), and that one learned from one's mother and family. Latin enabled one to return to the unity that was lost with Babel, and this unity was necessary for knowledge, whether profane or sacred. Even though Roger Bacon went as far as to say that he spoke Latin as his mother tongue (*lingua materna*), as he did English or French, the former would generally be set in opposition to the two latter. The mother tongue is, according to Bacon, devalued as a cultural language for the "Latins," because he judges it unable to express particular kinds of knowledge, like logic. But it assumes a surprisingly far higher status for other peoples, when he says, for example, that they turn away from Christianity because it is not preached in their mother tongues, and is thus not able to persuade them convincingly ("quia persuasionem sinceram non recipiunt in lingua materna"; *Opus Majus*, vol. 3). For Bacon, a substantially unified *lingua* is diversified accidentally into different *idiomata* (for example, Greek splits into Attic Greek, Aeolian, Doric, Ionian); if Latin is the same "from the furthest reaches of Puglia to the outer limits of Spain," each idiom has its own distinct traits (*proprietas*), which is precisely why it is called *idioma*, from *idion* (proper), from which the word *idiota* is derived, describing someone who is content with the properties of his idiom. *Idios* [ἴδιος], in Greek, is opposed to *koinos* [κοινός]: anything private is considered "idiot"; or to put it another way, idiom and the idiomatic are different from *logos*, in that the latter opens up human beings to the political (Aristotle, *Politics*, 1.1.1253a 1–18: see PROPERTY, and cf. LOGOS and POLIS). This *proprietas*, this genius that is proper to each idiom, and that includes not just its vocabulary but also its rhythmic and musical properties, makes any literal translation impossible. In certain passages the *idiomata* are seen as dialects, in relation to the mother tongue (and Thomas Aquinas refers in a similar way to *locutiones*), but elsewhere it is simply a matter of different usages, or ways of pronouncing the same language, with the identity of a language being guaranteed by a "substance" that precisely remains independent of its usages.

For Dante, *materna locutio*, which he also calls *vulgaris locutio*, is opposed to Latin (still referred to as *grammatica*), precisely because *materna locutio* has been learned naturally, without rules, by imitating the nurse, whereas Latin has been learned "artificially," that is, according to the rules of art (cf. *Republic*, 1.13). Because it is so difficult to learn, only a few acquire the knowledge of second/secondary means of expression (*locutio secundaria*), and these are only available to a few peoples, such as the Greeks (see ITALIAN, Box 2):

[V]ulgarem locutionem [Italian: *lingua volgare*] appellamus eam qua infantes assuefiunt ab assistentibus cum primitus distinguere voces incipiunt; vel, quod brevius dici potest, vulgarem locutionem asserimus quam sine omni regula nutricem imitantes accipimus. Est es inde alia locutio secundaria nobis, quam Romani gramaticam vocaverunt. . . . Harum quoque duarum nobilior est vulgaris: tum quia prima fuit humano generi usitata; tum quia totus orbis ipsa perfruitur, licet in diversas prolationes et vocabula sit divisa; tum quia naturalis est nobis, cum illa potius artificialis existat.

(I call "vernacular language" that which infants acquire from those around them when they first begin to distinguish sounds; or, to put it more succinctly, I declare that vernacular language is that which we learn without any formal instruction, by imitating our nurses. There also exists another kind of language, at one remove from us, which the Romans called *gramatica*. . . . Of these two kinds of language, the more noble is the vernacular: first, because it was the language originally used by the human race; second, because the whole world employs it, though with different pronunciations and using different words; and third, because it is natural to us, while the other is, in contrast, artificial.)

(*De vulgari eloquentia*, 1.2–4)

This passage poses many questions: Since Latin was in fact the mother tongue of the Romans, an argument Dante will return to precisely in order to legitimize the use of the vulgar tongue, why is Latin a *grammatica*, and more artificial (that is, the product of art) than the vulgar tongue for clerics in the Middle Ages? Moreover, the fact that he asserts here that the "vulgar" is the noblest tongue, whereas he said the opposite in the *Convivio*, 1.5.7–15, has led to extensive commentary, particularly when one needs to remember that the *De vulgari* was written in Latin and the *Convivio* in *volgare* (for a summary of these discussions, see V. Coletti, *Dante-Alighieri*). In the *Convivio*, three reasons are adduced in support of Latin's superiority. The first of these is its "nobility": Latin is perpetual and incorruptible, and this is what allows ancient writings still to be read today. Then, its "virtue": anything that achieves what it sets out to do to the highest degree possible is considered virtuous, and Latin is the vehicle that best allows human thought to become manifest, while the vulgar is unable to convey certain things. And finally, its "beauty": Latin is more harmonious than the vulgar, in that it is a product of art, and not of nature. Latin, or the *grammatica*, is in any case a human creation, thanks to its inventors (*inventores grammatice facultatis*), which is regulated (*regulata*) by a "common consensus" and is therefore impervious to any "individual arbitrary" intervention. This is why it is defined, recalling Bacon's idea of a substantial unity, as "a certain identity of language which does not change according to time and place" (quaedam inalterabilis locutionis idemptitas diversis temporibus et locis; *De vulgari*, 1.9.11). We see, then, how ordinary and everyday variations of different individual ways of speaking (*sermo*) are unable to affect Latin, which remains the same through the ages, this being a necessary condition of the transmission of ancient knowledge.

2. The *vulgaris locutio*

As far as the question of origins is concerned, God, says Dante, created a "certa forma locutionis"—Pézard translates

Dante's phrase into French as "certaine forme de langage" (certain form of language); Coletti's Italian version is "data forma di linguaggio" (given form of language); Imbach, again into French: "forme déterminée du langage" (determinate form of language)—at the same time that he created the first soul. "Form" here covers both the terms for things, the construction of these terms, and the pronunciation of these constructions ("Dico autem 'formam' et quantum ad rerum vocabula et quantum ad vocabulorum constructionem et quantam ad constructionis prolationem"). This original "certa forma locutionis" has been variously interpreted, either as the first language (Hebrew, which Dante also refers to as *ydioma*: "The Hebrew idiom was the one produced by the lips of the first speaker"; *De vulgari*, 6.6), or as a universal prelinguistic structure enabling the first languages to be generated, or as a type (form) of which concrete languages would have been species. If, according to *De vulgari*, this form of language was the one Adam used, in his *Paradiso* Dante says, on the contrary, that Adam spoke a language that died out before Babel (*Paradiso*, 26). This pre-Babelian form of language would have been used by "all languages of all speakers" (qua quidem forma omnis lingua loquentium uteretur) if there had been no Babel, the "tower of confusion," whereas it was only preserved by the sons of Heber: "After the confusion, it remained with them alone, so that our Redeemer . . . could use not the language of confusion, but the language of grace." After Babel, humans had to invent languages, or rather ways of speaking (*loquelae*) as it pleased them (*ad placitum*) (*De vulgari*, 1.9.6). It is worth noting, however, that in other passages, Adam seemed already to be using a language invented *ad placitum* (*Paradiso*, 26), and that for other writers of the time, this same *ad placitum* characteristic of language happened not after Babel, but after the Fall, as a punishment for man's original sin, and that deprived humans of the ability to use a language that would express naturally the quiddity of things (Henri de Gand).

The many different interpretations of *De vulgari* depend ultimately on the way the different terms of the linguistic semantic field are interpreted. Contrary to the traditional approach (as defended, for instance, by P. V. Mengaldo), which simply attributes this variation in vocabulary to a mere "stylistic variation" on Dante's part, thereby authorizing an analogous "stylistic variation" on the part of the translator, we think, along with M. Tavoni ("Ancora su *De vulgari*"), that Dante's choice of vocabulary is deliberate and plays a crucial role in the treatise, a role that is, moreover, confirmed by its statistical distribution. It is impossible to ignore the fact that *locutio* dominates chapters 1–5, *idioma* chapters 6–9, and *vulgare* chapters 10–19; that *lingua* appears only in the narration of Babel, in the coded syntagmas (8.1: *confusio linguarum*, 6.6: *lingua confusionis*) referring back to those of the Vulgate (Genesis 10 and 11) and those of several exegetes; and that *loquela* in turn is present only in this episode, in order to designate human speech, which starts out unified and is subsequently divided into so many tasks. The first chapters thus seem to be intent on defining the different modes of expression or of speech (*locutiones*), both vulgar and artificial, proper to human expression—what is "proper" to human expression being to manifest one's thoughts to another, according to the common definition (borrowed here) in Plato's *Timaeus*. Dante

then proceeds, with the term *idioma*, to embody historical modes of expression "proper" to an individual or a community, passing from the Hebrew *idiom* of Adam to the first idioms after Babel. We enter after Babel into the realm of vulgar, attested and contemporary historical languages, which are diverse and imperfect, variable and dispersed, and which necessitate two different modes of return to unity. The first is a scholastic mode: unity is regained through the invention, to be determined by scholars, of one, stable language of knowledge, the *grammatica*, or Latin. The second is the "illustrious" mode, through the establishment of the *volgare latium* that Dante first of all promoted in *De vulgari*, and then acted out in the *Commedia*. The different linguistic terms are not to be seen as applying to disconnected realities but as manifesting different points of view about one identical reality: thus Latin is envisaged first of all as an example of a regulated mode of expression (*locutio regulata*); then as an *idioma*, as the proper language of the Romans; and finally as *grammatica*, an artificial invention that comes after the scattering of Latin into the vernacular. Naturally, this tripartite arrangement does not imply any equivalence among these three terms. The difficulty, which the divergent readings of Dante's treatise illustrate remarkably well, is a methodological one: should we understand the vocabulary regarding "language" with reference to other terminological networks of the time, or give it a certain autonomy by weighing the value of each term within the text—or within his work as a whole? In the first case, which terminological networks would we make reference to, assuming we can even determine a coherence for each one: a theological, scriptural network? A Scholastic, philosophical network? A literary, grammatical, or rhetorical network? Such questions have to be considered by every interpreter and every translator, especially when one is dealing (as is the case with Bacon) with authors who are marginal or whose works fall outside conventional, established institutional circuits, and thus languages. What is at stake here is the very understanding of their project itself.

To conclude, we have a constellation of three terms, to return to Saussure's schema, in which one of the terms (*langage*) is charged with a negative role, a pure abstract generality that has to be excluded so as to allow for a free play between the two other terms (*langue/parole*). This play is open, complex, intense, and it works by continuous interaction, without any reduction or exclusion. We might describe this, then, as a complementarity, or even better, a polarity; a richly productive and powerful system, with multiple implications, and which has no need for explicit recollection to reproduce itself.

Irène Rosier-Catach
Barbara Cassin (II.A)
Pierre Caussat (I.B)
Anne Grondeux (I.A)

BIBLIOGRAPHY

Abbon de Saint-German. *22 Predigten*. Edited by U. Önnerfors. Frankfurt: Peter Lang, 1985.

Agamben, Giorgio. "Le lingue e i popoli." In *Mezzi senza fine: Note sulla politica*. Turin: Bollati Boringhieri, 1996. Translation by Vincenzo Binetti and Cesare Casarino: "The Language and the People." In *Means without End: Notes on Politics*. Minneapolis: University of Minnesota Press, 2000.

Aristotle. *Poetics*. Edited and translated by Stephen Halliwell. Loeb Classical Library. Cambridge, MA: Harvard University Press, 1995.

Auroux, S. *L'encyclopédie: "Grammaire" et "langue" au XVIIIe siècle*. Paris: Mame, 1973.

Bacon, Roger. *Opus majus*. Edited by John Henry Bridges. London: Williams and Norgate, 1900.

Bally, Charles. *Linguistique générale et linguistique française*. 3rd ed. Bern: Francke, 1950.

Beer, Jeanette M. A. "Medieval Translations: Latin and the Vernacular Languages." In *Medieval Latin: An Introduction and Bibliographical Guide*, edited by F.A.C. Mantello and A. G. Rigg, 728–33. Washington, DC: Catholic University of America Press, 1996.

Boethius of Dacia. *Boethii Daci Opera: Modi Significandi Sive Quaestiones Super Priscianum Maiorem*. Edited by J. Pinborg and H. Roos. Copenhagen: G. E. Gad, 1969.

Brownlee, Kevin. "Vernacular Literary Consciousness c. 1100–c. 1500: French, German and English Evidence." In *The Cambridge History of Literary Criticism*. Volume 2: *The Middle Ages*, edited by Alastair Minnis and Ian Johnson, 422–71. Cambridge: Cambridge University Press, 2005.

Chomsky, Noam. *Aspects of the Theory of Syntax*. Cambridge, MA: MIT Press, 1965.

Coseriu, Eugenio. *Sprachkompetenz: Grundzüge der Theorie des Sprechens*. Edited by Heinrich Weber. Tübingen: Francke, 1988.

Culler, Jonathan. *Ferdinand de Saussure*. Rev. ed. Ithaca, NY: Cornell University Press, 1986.

Dahan, Gilbert, Irène Rosier, and Luisa Valente. "L'arabe, le grec, l'hébreu et les vernaculaires." In *Sprachtheorien in Spätantike und Mittelalter*, edited by Stan Ebbesen, 265–321. Tübingen: Narr, 1995.

Danesi, Marcel. "Latin vs. Romance in the Middle Ages: Dante's *De vulgari eloquentia* Revisited." In *Latin and the Romance Languages in the Early Middle Ages*, edited by Roger Wright, 248–58. London: Routledge, 1991.

Dante Alighieri. *De vulgari eloquentia*. Edited and translated by Steven Botterill. Cambridge: Cambridge University Press, 1996.

———. *De vulgari eloquentia*. Translated to Italian by V. Coletti. Milan: Garzanti, 1991.

———. *Oeuvres complètes*. Translated by A. Pézard. Paris: Gallimard / "La Pléiade," 1965.

Geoffroy of Saint Victor. "The *Preconium Augustini* of Godfrey of St. Victor." Edited by Philippe Damon. *Medieval Studies* 22 (1960).

Gilles of Rome. *De regimine principium*. Frankfurt: Minerva, 1968.

Giraud de Barri. *Expugnatio Hibernica*. In vol. 5 of *Opera*, edited by J. F. Dimock. London: Longman, 1867.

Guibert de Nogent. *Monodiae*. Edited by E.-R. Labande. Paris: Belles Lettres, 1981.

Herodotus. *Histories*. Translation by John M. Marincola and A. de Sélincourt. New York: Penguin, 1996.

Holdcroft, David. *Saussure: Signs, System, and Arbitrariness*. Cambridge: Cambridge University Press, 1991.

Hugh of Saint Victor. *Hugonis de Sancto Victore Opera Propaedeutica*. Edited by R. Baron. Notre Dame, IN: University of Notre Dame Press, 1966.

Humboldt, Wilhelm von. *Schriften zur Sprachphilosophie*. Volume 3 of *Werke in fünf Bänden*. Darmstadt, Ger.: Wissenschaftliche Buchgesellschaft, 1979.

Imbach, Ruedi. *Dante, la philosophie et les laics*. Paris: Éditions du Cerf, 1996.

Jäger, Ludwig. "F. de Saussures historisch-hermeneutische Idee der Sprache: Ein Plädoyer für die Rekonstruktion des Saussureschen Denkens in seiner authentischen Gestalt." *Linguistik und Dialektik* 27 (1976): 210–44.

Koerner, E.F.K. "Saussure and the French Linguistic Tradition: A Few Critical Comments." In *Memoriam Friedrich Diez: Akten des Kolloquiums zur Wissenschaftsgeschichte der Romanistik Trier, 2.–4. Okt. 1975*, edited by Hans-Josef Niederehe and Harald Haarmann, 405–17. Amsterdam: Benjamins, 1976.

Launay, M. L. "Un roi, deux enfants et des chèvres: Le débat sur le langage naturel chez l'enfant aux XVIe siècle." *Studi Francesi* 72 (1980): 401–14.

Maur, Raban. *Monumenta germaniae historica, epistulae (in Quart)*. Vol. 5, *Epistolae Karolini aevi (III)*. 2 vols. Edited by E. Dümmler. Berlin: Weidmann, 1898–99.

Mazzocco, Angelo. *Linguistic Theories in Dante and the Humanists: Studies of Language and Intellectual History in Late Medieval and Early Renaissance Italy*. Leiden, Neth.: Brill, 1993.

Mengaldo, Pier Vincenzo. "Un contributo all'interpretazione di *De vulgari eloquentia* I, i–ix." *Belfagor* 5, no. 44 (1989): 539–58.

Milner, Jean-Claude. *L'amour de la langue*. Paris: Éditions du Seuil, 1978. Translation by Ann Banfield: *For the Love of Language*. Basingstoke, UK: Macmillan, 1990.

Olender, Maurice. *Les langues du paradis: Aryens et sémites, un couple providentiel*. Paris: Gallimard, 1989. Translation by Arthur Goldhammer: *The Languages of Paradise: Aryans and Semites, a Match Made in Heaven*. Rev. and augm. ed. New York: Other Press, 2002.

Peirce, C. S. *Collected Papers*. Edited by Charles Hartshorne and Paul Weiss. Cambridge, MA: Harvard University Press, 1933.

Raoul of Caen (Gesta Tancredi). *Gesta Tancredi in expeditione Hierosolymitana, auctore Rudolfo Cadomensi, ejus familiari*. Vol. 3 of *Recueil des historiens des croisades: Historiens occidentaux*. Paris: Imprimerie Nationale, 1866.

Récanati, François. *Direct Reference: From Language to Thought*. Oxford: Blackwell, 1993.

———. *La transparence et l'énonciation: Pour introduire à la pragmatique*. Paris: Éditions du Seuil, 1979.

Rosier-Catach, Irène. "Roger Bacon: Grammar." In *Roger Bacon and the Sciences: Commemorative Essays*, edited by Jeremiah Hackett, 67–102. Leiden, Neth.: Brill, 1997.

Sanders, Carol, ed. *The Cambridge Companion to Saussure*. Cambridge: Cambridge University Press, 2004.

Saussure, Ferdinand de. *Cours de linguistique générale*. Edited by Charles Bally and Albert Sechehaye, with Albert Riedlinger. Critical ed. by Tullio de Mauro. Paris: Payot, 1985.

Scheerer, Thomas M. *Ferdinand de Saussure: Rezeption und Kritik*. Darmstadt, Ger.: Wissenschaftliche Buchgesellschaft, 1980.

Tavoni, Mirko. "Ancora su *De vulgari eloquentia* I 1–9." *Rivista di letteratura italiana* 7 (1989): 469–96.

———. "The 15th-Century Controversy on the Language Spoken by the Ancient Romans: An Inquiry into Italian Humanist Concepts of 'Latin,' 'Grammar,' and 'Vernacular.'" In *The History of Linguistics in Italy*, edited by Paolo Ramat, Hans-Josef Niederehe, and Konrad Koerner, 23–50. Amsterdam: Benjamins, 1986.

———. "On the Renaissance Idea that Latin Derives from Greek." *Annali della Scuola Normale Superiore di Pisa*, ser. 3, vol. 16 (1986): 205–38.

———. "Renaissance Linguistics." In *Italian Studies in Linguistic Historiography*. Edited by Tullio de Mauro and Lia Formigari, 149–66. Münster, Ger.: Nodus, 1994.

———. "'Ydioma Tripharium' (Dante, *De vulgari eloquentia*, I 8–9)." In *History and Historiography of Linguistics*, edited by Hans-Josef Niederehe and Konrad Koerner, 233–47. Amsterdam: Benjamins, 1990.

Vulfin. *Life of Saint Martin*. Edited by F. Dolbeau. In *Francia: Forschungen zur westseuropäischen Geschichte*. Ostfildern, Ger.: Jan Thorbecke Verlag, 1984.

LAW, RIGHT

FRENCH	*loi, droit*
GERMAN	*Gesetz, Recht*
LATIN	*lex, jus*
SPANISH	*ley, derecho*

➤ *DROIT*, LEX, and CIVIL RIGHTS, FAIR, LIBERAL, POLITICS, RIGHT, RULE OF LAW, STANDARD, THEMIS

Most of the legal notions used in modern political philosophy come from a transcription in vernacular languages of terms originating in Roman law, and from its reception in medieval Europe. This transmission of Roman concepts was accompanied by a significant inflection of their meaning, but the translation conventions have nonetheless been stable enough that basic terms such as *lex* and *jus* have found equivalent terms in every language of continental Europe, and the distinction between *loi* and *droit* in French, for example (or *Gesetz* and *Recht* in German) has remained constant. The situation, however, is fundamentally different for the English language, in which, or in relation to which, translation problems have meant constant difficulties, both in the philosophical vocabulary as well as in legal texts. In schematic terms, the problem takes the form of a double ambivalence. English distinguishes between "law" and "right," with each corresponding to some of the aspects of *loi* (*Gesestz*) or *droit* (*Recht*), but the extension of the concepts is not the same. "Law" has a wider extension than *loi*, and even if "right" partly overlaps with the polysemy of *jus* or of *droit*, the use of the term "right," in the singular and the plural, refers more often to the specific dimension of *droit* that the French would term *droits subjectifs* (subjective rights; that is, freedom, property, etc.) attached to individual or collective subjects.

I. The Particularities of English Political Right(s)

A. The legal vocabulary of English

In the continental tradition, law (or *la loi* in French) is both a rule and a command given by an authority empowered to enact it; more specifically, *la loi* refers to a certain kind of norm, established by a particular power (legislative power), and regarded as higher than that of other sources of *droit* (regulations, jurisprudence, and so on), in accordance with criteria that can be material or formal. In this context, the basic problem is knowing what founds the higher authority of the law, and what can stem from its intrinsic characteristics (rationality, generality, publicness, and so forth), and from the identity of the founder of the law (the sovereign). The history of law is thus bound up with the parallel history of modern political rationalism and of state sovereignty. The dominant tendency today, particularly clear in France, is to qualify the reverence for the law, because of the threefold effect of the weakening of legislative power, the proliferation of legislative texts, and, above all, the progressive acceptance of the *contrôle de constitutionnalité des lois* (the constitutional review of laws; in other words, for the French *Conseil constitutionnel*, the "law as an expression of the general will" is only a law when it is in accordance with the Constitution, as it is interpreted by the *Conseil*). It is important to note, however, that this evolution is not in itself enough to transform the entire logic of the juridico-philosophical categories. It simply means that the characteristics previously attributed to the law as an "expression of the general will" are transferred to a certain type of law (the Constitution), enacted by a specific legislative power (the "constituent" power or lawmaker), while all of the difficulties associated with the modern doctrine of sovereignty simply take a different form (O. Beaud, *La puissance de l'état*). On the other hand, the extension of the concept of *loi* in French is limited at the outset by its relation to the concept of *droit*, which refers both to the legal order as a whole, and to the right of a subject, which may be defended in a court case; so whatever its position in the hierarchy of norms, *la loi* is only a source of *le droit*. In the English tradition, however, "law" refers to the legal order as a whole (like *le droit*, in other words), but it also retains some of the main connotations associated with *la loi*. Conversely, if "right" can sometimes also be understood in a general sense (if only because the adjective "right" means "just"), it more often has a far narrower sense, when used in the plural or singular, and in consequence it tends to be confused with "subjective" rights (R. Dworkin, *Law's Empire* and *Taking Rights Seriously*).

These difficulties are quite well known and have generated a number of conventional translations, most of which are easy to understand and apply. *Philosophie du droit*, or *Rechtsphilosophie*, is normally translated as "philosophy of law," even if it refuses to make law (ordinary or even constitutional) the primary source of right (but Hegel's *Rechtsphilosophie* is nonetheless sometimes translated as "philosophy of right" out of faithfulness to the German). A law enacted by a lawmaker authorized to rule on such questions becomes "statute law" (which already leads to several oddities: in order to explain the original meaning of article 6 of the "Déclaration des droits de l'homme et du citoyen" ["Declaration of the Rights of Man and the Citizen"] of 1789, for example, we would have to say that in "French law," "statute law" is the expression of the general will). The shortcoming of "statute law," however, is that it suggests too clear a distinction between a legislative power and other authorities, which is not always relevant, either because one is referring to periods in the past when such a distinction did not always have the same importance that it has in the modern age, or because the legal-philosophical reasoning itself leads us to bracket it. This leads to a common and long-standing expedient that consists of reverting to the plural of the word, which almost always refers to the legislative, or nomothetic, dimension of the "law": "the laws" will be one possible translation of *la loi*, of *lex*, or of *nomos*, and the title of Cicero's *De legibus* (On the laws), just as much as Plato's *Nomoi* (*Laws*), do not pose any particular problems of translation.

These conventions are useful, but they do not overcome all the difficulties. As far as ancient notions are concerned, it is unfortunate that both the *lex naturae* of Cicero and the *jus gentium* of Roman law have to be translated as "law." In the modern context, the dual meaning of "law" still poses several problems, as becomes apparent, for example, in reading Locke's *Second Treatise of Civil Government*. For Locke, the state of nature is not a state of lawlessness, because human beings are subjected to the "law of nature" (§6), which in French could be translated either as *droit naturel* (as Bernard Gilson does, in Locke, *Deuxième traité du gouvernement civil*) or as *loi naturelle*: only civil government, however, enables the birth of a "legislative power," which in turn allows the "Commonwealth" to be governed by an "establish'd, settled, known, Law" (§124). The function of statute law, or "establish'd law," will thus be to make "natural law" (*droit naturel*) sufficiently public for it to take on a force of obligation, and ignorance or partiality would deprive it of this force in the state of nature. But statute law cannot itself have any legitimate authority unless it conforms to the natural law instituted by God, which is thus imposed upon human lawmakers as a higher commandment (English translators and authors encounter similar difficulties when, for example, they need to distinguish between *lex naturae* and *jus naturae*, which leads them at times to use "right" as a translation of *jus* so that "law" can be a better equivalent of *lex*). These problems are ultimately encountered at every point in any translation into English or from English: the "history of law" will become "legal history," and the "lawyers" in American cinema are both jurists and men of law, while being very different from Philippe the Fair's *légistes*, the class of jurists charged with renewing Roman law in France and creating from it a uniform and centralized legal code.

So when we go from Latin or modern continental languages to English, we encounter difficulties that flow from a particular legal institution, and that have lasted to this day, as any jurist knows who has ever tried to translate into English a notion such as the German *Rechststaat* (which the French *état de droit* captures perfectly), or to find a continental equivalent of the English "rule of law." To clarify these difficulties, we will begin with a genealogical analysis of the particularities of the English legal lexicon, and then go on to examine the way in which the first modern philosophers adopted or, on the contrary, subverted this tradition, before looking finally at the later transformations of English-language *philosophie du droit*.

B. The spirit of English law

English history is part of the wider history of western Europe, shaped by the development of the modern nation-state, which subordinated political (royal) power to the rationality of law. In England, as in France, this process led on the one hand to the institutionalization of royal power, by distinguishing it from patrimonial or imperial control, and on the other to an increase in the predictability of law, by privileging a law common to the whole kingdom. Generally speaking, then, what is particular to England in this context can be presented in the following way: the courts of the kingdom (notably the Royal Court) played a major role in the unification of English law, producing a law that was both customary and based on case law, and that provided royal power with the centralized structure that was needed in order to govern, but without having to make the positive law decreed by the king the primary source of law. The history of English freedom runs parallel to that of the history of the acquisition by the "barons," and then by all British subjects, of "rights" that are opposable to royal authority, and that form the substance of the different English declarations, from the Magna Carta (1215) to the Bill of Rights (1689). The conceptual system of English law appears at first to be a process of giving form to this singular historical experience, according to a logic that is both very old and extremely durable. In this regard, Frederick Maitland notes that the use among the great English jurists of the twelfth and thirteenth centuries (for instance, Glanvill and Bracton) of Roman terms is itself somewhat uncertain, and that they do not differentiate clearly between *jus* and *lex* (F. Pollock and F. W. Maitland, *The History of English Law*, 1:175). The two senses of "law" refer to the duality of the common law of the courts, and the statute law imposed by the sovereign. Subjects can oppose their "rights" to the political power, but this power nonetheless exercises a legitimate authority over these subjects. So "law" refers to two concurrent conceptions of the formation of norm, with the English constitution ensuring they work together by an endlessly repeated miracle. "Common law" does not at first seem like a "judge-made law," because it is supposed to be simply "revealed" by a judge, who in this sense is the "mouthpiece of the law." This is what distinguishes it from statute law, which is "made" by an authority that is based on its own views concerning justice or the common good, and that requires no other justification than its political legitimacy. Common law is thus presented as a means of formalizing customs, whose long existence is a guarantee of their venerable nature, and it also favors

continuity, since the first rule in making laws is that of the "precedent" (*stare decisis*).

Common law is thus a fundamental element of the Ancient Constitution, which was supposed to have governed the English since time immemorial (and whose prestige would make it possible for the 1688 Revolution to be presented as a restoration of an originary and more authoritative set of laws). The remarkable feat of English history is to have forged its path toward the rationalization of law on this traditional legitimacy. The centralization of judicial decisions allowed a homogenous order to emerge out of the different customs, and the primacy of the precedent encouraged legal security and the predictability of decisions, which constituted the basis of the development of modern society. The authority of the precedent was not always absolute; as the great jurist William Blackstone noted, "[T]he doctrine of the Law is the following: precedents and rules must be followed, unless they are clearly absurd or unjust," which means that on the one hand, judgments must not depend on the opinions of judges but on the laws and customs of the country (*Commentaries on the Laws of England*, 1:69), and on the other hand, that the judge can and must reject "decisions that are contrary to reason (absurd), or to divine law (unjust)" (A. Tunc, "Coutume et 'Common Law'," 57).

The major effect of this type of elaboration of law, from the point of view of political philosophy, is to have inhibited the full affirmation of the doctrine of sovereignty, which, by contrast, characterized the development of politics in France. While French theorists of the monarchy, such as Bodin, tended to make the sovereign the ultimate, if not sole, source of the law, the English based the authority of political power on an original "common law," while at the same time giving their political community the means for their law to make "progress" toward modernity. This original mechanism explains the political differences between England—where the Crown was unable to appear as the vehicle for progress, and where the 1688 Revolution confirmed the power of the courts—and France, where the actions of successive parliaments had long discredited the idea of judicial power (A. V. Dicey, *Introduction to the Study of the Law of the Constitution*). It also had important philosophical consequences: it limited the rise of modern legislative rationalism based on the idea of a natural affinity between reason and the "law" made by the sovereign, which would by contrast become fully developed within the culture of the French Enlightenment.

But we must also add that the primacy of common law is only one of the two main aspects of the English constitution: although it is based on the tradition of common law, the constitution also presumes "the sovereignty of Parliament" (or of the "King in Parliament"). This sovereignty needs to be understood in the strongest sense of the term: the sovereignty of Parliament is absolute in the sense that no rule of law can oppose an act or a statute of the English Parliament, if this act has been legitimately adopted (cf., for example, W. Blackstone, *Commentaries*, 1:156–57, and Dicey, *Introduction*), and this will become established notably within the courts, where a statute has the power to repeal the rules of common law (Blackstone, *Commentaries*, 1:89) under certain formal conditions. Similarly, "rights" are essentially subjective rights, which may have appeared within a custom before being integrated into common law or recognized by a statute, but which are as such opposable to political authority.

This paradox of English public law comes from the absence of a written constitution. It originally derived from the primacy of the customary or semicustomary arrangements of the Ancient Constitution (whose spirit in this respect is the spirit of common law), but it also evolved into the affirmation of the full sovereignty of Parliament, the natural counterpart of the flexibility of the constitution. The difficulties are moreover magnified by the fact that modern "constitutionalism" (which implies the subordination of ordinary law to the constitution, through the control by the courts of the constitutionality of the laws) evolved in the wake of the American experience, and in a legal world dominated by English concepts. Nevertheless, a study of the development of the English-language philosophy of law would reveal a permanent opposition between two approaches, whose duality is an expression of the ambivalence of the English tradition. The predominant approach, which goes from Edward Coke to a writer such as Ronald Dworkin, could be seen as a progressive idealization of the experience of common law. However, the very fact that it is a "law," combined with the particular logic of the modern conception of sovereignty, also explains the stubborn persistence of a positivistic current of thought trend that always tends to subvert the dominant vocabulary of English legal philosophy. This positivistic approach, defended by Thomas Hobbes and Jeremy Bentham, survives in Austin and Hart. It should be said, however, that these two traditions have certainly communicated with each other, especially through the affirmation of the liberal concept of freedom as an absence of constraint, a conception that was largely adopted by the advocates of the approach that emerged out of common law, but certain elements of which come from Hobbes. In order to understand this development, while explaining the enduring legacy of untranslatable concepts that English law has transmitted to philosophy, we would do well to begin with common law and the debates to which it gave rise in English political thought.

C. Common law

In its strictest sense, the expression "common law" refers to the first of the three main traditional branches of English law, the other two being equity and statute law. Common law here means a law common to the different regions of the kingdom, a law that, before the courts, must always prevail over particular usage or customs, and that is the indissoluble basis of the authority of the king over all his subjects, while providing these subjects with the advantages of a single system of justice. Common law is first and foremost a customary, unwritten law (*lex non scripta*, as Blackstone puts it), whose authority is tied to its immemorial nature. It is also a scholarly law, whose fundamental rules prohibit any arbitrary modification, and the knowledge of which is acquired through a long and patient study of precedents. But common law is not only an original "legal system": it is also the foundation of the English political regime, insofar as it provides

the basis for understanding the powers and domains of the different political institutions.

The prestige that common law enjoys has made it the foundation of what we might call the English political idiom—and this prestige flows in the first place from common law's ability, over such a long period of time, to resolve in an original manner the main problems England has faced. Thanks to its law, this country with such a troubled history has been able to see itself as the product of a continuous and harmonious history, both profoundly different from that of other European monarchies and called upon ultimately to give lessons in freedom to other civilized nations. Indeed, in a now-classic work—*The Ancient Constitution and the Feudal Law*—J.G.A. Pocock showed how common law constituted the model from which the English elaborated the doctrine of the Ancient Constitution that was to become a point of reference in the seventeenth century for the adversaries of the Stuarts and thus contribute to the victory of a liberal interpretation of the English regime. By emphasizing the continuity of common law before and after the Norman conquest, the effects of this event were minimized, while limiting the rights imposed by force. By making common law the heart of English law, the authority of the empire, along with Roman civil law, was excluded, while the differences between the English monarchy (a "mixed regime") and French absolutism were foregrounded. These ideas were to be more fully developed during the revolutionary period, when the adversaries of the Stuarts readily invoked the permanence of English law and the immemorial nature of the Ancient Constitution to challenge the idea that royal power would be the main source of law, or that this power could change the law in whatever way it wished.

The fundamental premises of the apologists of common law are themselves based on principles that go back a long way. We can already find them, for example, in the work of John Fortescue, who in the fifteenth century distinguished very clearly between the absolute monarchy of the French, and the "limited" monarchy of the English, for whom the royal prerogative was limited by the courts, the main one being Parliament, which was considered to be primarily a court of justice. But it was above all in the seventeenth century that the classic doctrine of common law was formulated, notably around the ideas of Edward Coke, the rival of Sir Francis Bacon and of Matthew Hale (1609–76).

■ See Box 1.

The classic conception of common law implies a certain interpretation of the English constitution, according to which all political or legal institutions must be subject to the law, that is, to the order of the common law, as it is interpreted by the judges of the main courts. Even during Coke's time, though, this orthodoxy met with several objections, drawn from political and legal practice, or from new political doctrine. First of all, there were in fact several elements within the English institutions that appeared to contradict Coke's vision: the Court of Chancery could temper common law through equity; Parliament could change it radically through statutes that replaced the previous law, and the royal prerogative seemed to give the monarch a certain independence with respect to the statutes

1

Edward Coke (1552–1664)

Edward Coke was at the same time a judge, a parliamentarian, and a legal theorist. Several times a Member of the House of Commons, of which he was Speaker in 1592–93, he was also the attorney general in 1593–94, then chief justice of the Court of Common Pleas (1606) and lord chief justice of England. As a parliamentarian, he was opposed to the absolutist tendencies of James I (for which he was imprisoned in 1621), and it was in this context that he was the author in 1628 of the *Petition of Right*, one of the basic documents of "English freedoms."

Coke is generally considered the greatest representative of the common law tradition, which he interpreted as being halfway between the traditional doctrines of limitation of power and the principles of modern liberalism. In the conception of law that Coke advocates, the authority and the knowledge of the judge are simultaneously minimized and magnified. On the one hand, the judge is indeed not a legislator and he does not "make" laws (*judex est lex loquens*); his function is to "state the law" (*jus dicere*). In a sense, even if the identity of the legislator is problematic here, common law is certainly a law, which is acknowledged

by the judges whose authority it founds, and which expresses a higher rationality. On the other hand, we can know this law, and the reason that inspires it, only through the succession of different generations, and this knowledge calls for an "artifical reason" based on accumulated experience, and not only on reasoning. Law is thus a specialized knowledge, which is not to be confused with "natural reason" (*nemo nascitur artifex*), and judges are its privileged guardians. This is why they, and they alone, are in a position to reveal the always identical and always new meaning that common law assumes over time.

themselves. More generally, the traditional English conceptions were also confronted with the contemporary development of the doctrine of sovereignty, which had been familiar to French jurists since Bodin, but which was not entirely unheard of in England itself (where it would be reclaimed by the partisans of the reinforcement of royal power, but also by certain defenders of the Parliament). On this latter point, Coke, who was also a political actor, tended to reject the logic of sovereignty, which he saw as incompatible both with the logic of English law and with the rights acquired by the English since the Magna Carta. As for equity and the statutes, he presented them as complements of common law, revealed by the authorities constituted by common law itself. In this context, Parliament itself appears as a specific jurisdiction, made up of the king, the House of Lords, and the House of Commons, whose supreme status authorizes it to change the law by proposing new statutes, by repealing previous statutes, and even by modifying the content of common law. So while he thereby reaffirmed the superiority of Parliament over the king (the king only being fully legitimate as a "King in Parliament"), Coke managed to reconcile the primacy of Parliament with the "Rule of Law," and with his own antivoluntaristic conception of the making of laws. On the one hand, Parliament had the "power to abrogate, suspend, qualify, explain or make void [legislation that previous parliaments enacted], in the whole or in any part thereof, notwithstanding any words or restraint, prohibition or penalty [in previous legislation], for it is a maxim in the law of parliament, *quod leges posteriores priores contrarias abrogate*," and this power is "so transcendent and absolute, as it cannot be confined either for causes or persons within any bounds" (*Institutes of the Laws of England*, vol. 4). On the other hand, Parliament was simply acting here as a judge, who invoked ancient statutes, that is, "law, this universal law that the English have claimed as their heritage" (ibid.; see also F. Lessay, "Common Law," and J. W. Gough, *Fundamental Law in English Constitutional History*).

■ See Box 2.

D. The philosophical consequences of the doctrine of common law

Beyond the English constitution, the doctrine of common law implies something akin to a general theory or a philosophy of law, which is a priori opposed to *positivist* theories (which recognize as law only "positive law," that is, a law made by the sovereign, or someone authorized by the sovereign), without for all that having the same inflexibility as most theories of "natural law" because it is rooted within a legal tradition that valorizes the role of time and of history in the revelation of law.

As one contemporary historian notes (G. L. Postema, *Bentham and the Common Law Tradition*), the authority of precedent and of custom does not necessarily imply that all common law goes back to furthest antiquity. What is crucial, however, is that one can affirm continuity between the past and the present. Usage and custom have imposed rules by showing that these rules were both acceptable, because they were consonant with the public spirit, and reasonable because they were in accordance with common reason. This affirmation linking historical continuity and "reasonableness" is not without some ambiguity. One could, along with Coke, draw from it a particularist conception of legal reason, which emphasizes the internal coherence of jurisprudence built up patiently through "cases" resolved by judges, or through the law "stated" by judges. As we will see, this aspect of the theory (which is obviously connected to the judicial "corporatism" of Coke, and to his defense of the "artificial reason" of the judge) has been the favorite target of the great modern critics of common law since Hobbes. It is no doubt for this reason that subsequent authors emphasize on the contrary the affinity between common law and natural justice, in order to show that common law includes within it a certain number of the general principles that not only conform to custom, but also translate rational needs linked to the very nature of law. These two conceptions of reason at work within the law have in common the fact that they are a priori opposed to positivist theses, which place positive law, made by a legislator and not revealed by a judge, at

2

Equity

In English law, "equity" refers to one of the three fundamental sources of law (along with common law and statute law): the Court of Chancery can judge "in equity" and thereby protect rights that have not been recognized by ordinary courts (which have to follow the common law rigorously). The English term "equity" sometimes designates the classical philosophical notion (Aristotle's *epieikeia* [ἐπιείκεια]), and at other times a particular right, originally produced by a distinct court. In *A Dialogue between a Philosopher and a Student of the Common Laws of England,* Hobbes plays cleverly on the two senses of the word in order to suggest the superiority of royal justice (against which there is no appeal, since it is directly inspired by natural reason) over the justice of ordinary judges, whose action has to be able to be tempered by the action of the courts of equity.

BIBLIOGRAPHY

Raynaud, Philippe. "L'equalité dans la philosophie politique." *Égalité et équité: Antagonisme ou complémentarité.* Edited by Thierry Lambert et al. Paris: Economica, 1999.

Newman, Ralph A. *Equity and Law: A Comparative Study.* New York: Oceana Publications, 1961.

the forefront of the creation of law. This is why common law, whatever its ambiguities, appears as a privileged adversary of legal positivism, and why critics of this approach are often still led, even today, to repeat and rediscover the typical modes of reasoning of common law.

Conversely, the traditional theory of the English constitution itself offered a foothold for a positivist interpretation, through the idea of the supremacy of Parliament—or of the "King in Parliament." The argument made by Coke, who explained the power Parliament has to change the law by its statutes, and its power to modify these statutes indefinitely, as coming from the authority that it possesses in common law, can in fact quite easily be reversed. If there is an authority that is sufficiently powerful and legitimate to modify the rules of English law, it is difficult not to think that this authority is sovereign, and that its decisions are presumed to be more rational than those made by common judges, who are inspired by their "artificial reason." In addition, if the Chancery Court has the power to correct the rules of common law, and if the king is not entirely subordinate to the statutes, then it does seem that the legal order has a number of holes in it, which common judges are not the only ones able to fill. This observation led certain authors, for different reasons, to develop a number of critiques of common law. These critiques, drawing on the royal prerogative or the sovereignty of Parliament or, even more profoundly, on the idea that some sovereign power is necessary if there is to be any law at all, have brought about a complete overhaul of the doctrine of law. A systematic examination of these discussions is beyond the scope of this entry. Referring readers to the works on this subject by F. Lessay, G. J. Postema, and J.G.A. Pocock , we will simply attempt to show briefly the influence of these critiques of common law on the development of English political philosophy and on the philosophy of contemporary law, where the vocabulary itself echoes these foundational debates.

II. "Law" and "Right" According to Hobbes: Legal Positivism versus Common Law

A. The foundational debate

Chapter 14 of Hobbes's *Leviathan* (1651) opens with a distinction between the Right of Nature (*jus naturale*) and the Law of Nature (*lex naturalis*): whereas the right of nature "is the liberty each man hath to use his own power as he will himself for the preservation of his own nature," a law of nature "is a precept, or general rule, found out by reason, by which a man is forbidden to do that which is destructive of his life, or taketh away the means of preserving the same, and to omit that by which he thinketh it may be best preserved" (*Leviathan*, 1996). The object of this distinction is to show why people are necessarily led to "lay down the Right" they naturally have over all things in their natural condition, without also having to thereby contradict their nature. When they "lay down" their rights, they do not stop seeking to preserve nature and their life; however, taking account of the laws of nature that show us how to preserve ourselves in fact brings with it a radical change, since it marks the transition from freedom to obligation and obedience.

Hobbes is aware of being an innovator when he so clearly distinguishes right and law, as in the following passage:

> For though they that speak of this subject use to confound *jus* and *lex*, right and law, yet they ought to be distinguished, because right consisteth in liberty to do, or to forbear; whereas law determineth and bindeth to one of them: so that law and right differ as much as obligation and liberty, which in one and the same matter are inconsistent.

> *(Leviathan)*

As has often been pointed out, this transformation of the relationship between right and law places Hobbes at the precise intersection of two fundamental trends in modern politics, which are on the one hand liberalism, and on the other the absolutism expressed by the theory of sovereignty. Hobbes was one of the fathers of liberalism because he prioritized subjective rights and freedom, conceived as the absence of constraint, in his analysis of the constitution of the political bond, which set him in opposition both to the classical tradition and to modern republicanism. But he was also one of the thinkers of the absolute state, because he claimed to show that individuals can attain their primary objective (the preservation of their life) only by transferring almost all of their rights to the sovereign, against whom no resistance is allowed, besides escape or exile. These two aspects of Hobbes's thought are moreover linked, since the absolute power of the sovereign and his laws goes hand in hand with a transformation of the status of the law, whose function is no longer to guide individuals toward virtue or the good life, but, more modestly, to create the conditions in which subjects will pursue their own ends in order to attain an essentially private, and no doubt worldly, happiness. The function of the absolutist state is to create the conditions of what Benjamin Constant will later call the "freedom of the Moderns" (in "De la liberté des Anciens comparée à celle des Modernes," 1819). Apart from defending the authority of the State against sedition and unrest, of which the first English revolution was a good example, Hobbes's work aimed at a complete transformation of politics, which took the form of a profound change of the status of political philosophy, and a radical subversion of the tradition of common law.

Hobbes's explicit project was to demonstrate the priority of the sovereign and the law in the definition of "right," and this involved a certain devalorization of the role of the judge in favor of the lawmaker. No less remarkable, however, was that this devalorization was part of a larger effort to place the question of right and law within the proper domain of political philosophy. More than anything else, the political philosophy of the author of the *Leviathan* is primarily one of law and right, because it foregrounds the necessity of an impartial third party who is an outsider to the disputes between persons, and who can institute a legal bond between them, thanks to the capacity to impose decisions without contest. In this sense the sovereign, who determines the competence of the other authorities, is indeed a kind of supreme judge, whose function is first and foremost to ensure the reign of law. "The law" is simultaneously "law" and "right," and the higher authorities are indissolubly "jurisdictional" and "legislative" (as were Parliament or the "King in Parliament" in the English tradition). This is what is demonstrated in the continual play between *jus* and *lex* that Hobbes engages in, and of which we find an admirable example in chapter 24 of *Leviathan*: "Of the Nutrition and Procreation of a Commonwealth," that is, the production and distribution of raw materials, as well as the status of the colonies created by a republic in foreign countries. In this chapter, Hobbes defends the thesis that the law and its guarantee depend on the prior protection and authorization of the sovereign, and to support his theory he invokes the authority of Cicero who, although he was known as a "passionate defender of freedom," had to recognize (*Pro caecina*, XXV.70 and 73) that no property could be protected or even recognized without the authority of a "civil law" (*Leviathan*, chap. 24). Now, what Hobbes is translating here is clearly *jus civile*, a "right" rather than a "law," whose relationship to the "law of nature" is somewhat different in Cicero to how the author of the *Leviathan* interprets it. Conversely, this inflection of the classical terminology of *jus civile* to a meaning more favorable to the sovereign authority of the supreme lawmaker is accompanied by a symmetrical transformation of the status of the law, which Hobbes supports very cleverly by referring to the etymology of the Greek *nomos* (law), so as to give "law" back the meaning that *jus* had in Roman law, that is, the function of attributing to everyone what he or she is due (*suum cuique tribuere*), and of thereby guaranteeing justice (*justitia*) in these distributions:

Seeing therefore the introduction of propriety is an effect of Commonwealth, which can do nothing but by the person that represents it, it is the act only of the sovereign; and consisteth in the laws, which none can make that have not the sovereign power. And this they well knew of old, who called that Nomos (that is to say, distribution), which we call law; and defined justice by distributing to every man his own.

(Leviathan)

Significantly, this text is cited by Carl Schmitt, who sought to place Hobbes back into an imperial political tradition, foreign to both liberalism and "enlightened" absolutism (Schmitt, *The* Nomos *of the Earth in the International Law of the Jus Publicum Europaeum*).

B. Hobbes and the tradition of common law: The subversion of the English legacy

What are the consequences of this philosophy of right for the English legacy, and especially for the tradition of common law? The clearest text on this subject is without doubt the admirable *Dialogue between a Philosopher and a Student of the Common Laws of England*, in which Hobbes stages the opposition between the tradition of Coke and the new "law-centered" and rationalist philosophy. In this text, Hobbes clearly attributes to Coke the confusion between "law" and "right" (or between *lex* and *jus*), which he had denounced in the *Leviathan*. He also develops a powerful internal critique of the juridical tradition of common law, in order to show that the modern conception of sovereignty (attributed here to the king and not to Parliament) is the only one able to lend true coherence to the English legal system. To support his argument, he quotes Bracton ("the most authentic author of the common law") on several occasions, to show that the king is fully sovereign in the temporal order. He adds that, since England's break from Rome, the spiritual power also lies with the king, and he interprets the expression "King in Parliament" in a way that proscribes any dualism in the civil authorities. The main target of the *Dialogue* is obviously the power of judges under common law, which the dominant tradition claimed was based on the wisdom produced by the "artifical reason" acquired over the course of legal studies, and which Hobbes attacks in the name both of "natural reason" and of the authority of the legislator. On the one hand, there is no other reason than natural reason (*Leviathan*, 29), if it is true that "no man is *born* with the use of reason, yet all men may grow up to it as well as lawyers" (ibid., 38), and the knowledge of judges is no different from that which is used in other arts. On the other hand, the wisdom of judges is not in itself sufficient to give the force of law to their decisions, since "it is not wisdom, but Authority that makes a law" (ibid., 29). The laws of England were not made by law professionals, but "by the kings of England, consulting with the nobility and commons in parliament, of which not one of *twenty* was a learned lawyer" (ibid., 29). Borrowing an expression from the *Leviathan*, "auctoritas, non veritas, facit legem," Hobbes makes it clear that he considers doctrines that valorize laws produced or revealed by English jurisconsults as sophisms of the same kind as those of Platonic philosophers, religious fanatics, or defenders of papism: the claim to make truth or wisdom the source of the law is nothing other than the mask worn by all those attempting to usurp supreme power. In addition, as the *Dialogue* argues elsewhere, the reasoning of the philosopher appears in the eyes of the lawyer as the product of a privilege unduly conferred on statute law against common law, whereas the philosopher by contrast claims to "speak generally of law" (29) when he discusses the role of the kings of England in making English laws.

The Hobbesian reconstruction of the theory of law thus concludes by prioritizing legislation over any other source of law, and by strongly affirming the sovereignty of the king; the other constituent parts of Parliament are, for Hobbes, merely useful accessories without being in any way indispensable to the adoption of laws. This does not mean, however, that Hobbes abandons the entire former tradition, nor that he refuses judges any role in making laws, since his strategy always consists in starting from an internal critique of the contradictions of tradition in order to show that his own proposals are more likely to achieve the objectives that tradition claimed to be pursuing. First of all, as was noted earlier, the primacy of the legislator itself comes from its ability to state law, and to ensure its reign, by transcending the violent disputes that persist in the state of nature: Hobbes's sovereign (who is for him the king) remains in some ways a judge, just as the English Parliament was in the traditional theories of common law lawyers, and his action is therefore still related to the two senses of law (*Dialogue*, 46: "Since therefore the King is sole *legislator*, I think it also reason he should be sole supreme judge"). Hobbes also adapts the equivalence of reason and the common law to his own ends, even if he ironically reverses its meaning: where Coke's disciples would say that common law was "artificial" reason itself, Hobbes will say that natural reason was the true common law. As for the role of judges, it was certainly severely reduced, but not entirely denied. Hobbes grants the common law judge a certain normative power, which comes from the fact that the sovereign had affirmed from the outset that, "in the absence of any law to the contrary," customary rules, or those based on cases, would have the force of law (in the same way that "civil law," that is, Roman law, could be incorporated into English law, if the king so desired). Moreover, the judge is not necessarily more passive than in the traditional doctrine. In the *Dialogue*, the philosopher goes as far as to acknowledge, against his interlocutor, that the judge can without risk reject the letter of the law, as long as he does not reject its meaning and the intention of the legislator (30). And in *Leviathan*, Hobbes notes that the judge can complete civil law by the law of nature when positive law does not fully authorize a reasonable decision, even if he also has to refer, in the most difficult cases, to the higher authority of the legislator (chap. 26).

III. Two Philosophical Traditions

The greatness of Hobbes comes from that fact that he was the first to grasp what it was in the common law legacy that prevented the modern state from becoming fully developed, at the same time as he understood admirably the indissolubly emancipatory, rationalist, and absolutist nature of the "modern" conception of sovereignty. This is why, in the subsequent history of English-language thought, one finds a "Hobbesian" logic at work in all the thinkers who want to break with the legacy of common law lawyers, or who want to highlight the similarities between the English system and other forms of the modern state. Conversely, the conceptual schemas of common law reemerge spontaneously in all those who, for different reasons, want to limit the claims of the sovereign and the legislator in order to reaffirm historical rights, or to give the judge a privileged role in the protection of these "rights." This can be seen in the examples of Bentham and Hart, on the one hand, and of Hume, Burke, and Dworkin on the other.

A. Legal positivism in England

Jeremy Bentham (1748–1832) is without a doubt the main heir to Hobbes in England, even if his political opinions are clearly a long way from monarchic absolutism. Utilitarian anthropology is a continuation of the fundamental ideas of Hobbes, through the work of Helvetius and Holbach, and above all, Bentham, who shares the same critical perspective on the English tradition as the author of *Leviathan*. For Bentham, as for Hobbes, the objective is to rationalize English law by reducing the influence of judges in favor of the political authorities. Here again, this planned rationalization takes the form of an affirmation of the rights of natural reason against the judicial culture, by giving priority to the law understood as a commandment, and by a fundamental transformation of the principles of legitimation of the rules and usages of common law. Bentham's attitude is thus similar, *mutatis mutandis*, to that of Hobbes, as is shown by the way in which he interprets the authority of custom, or the rule of *stare decisis*. For traditional lawyers, the historical continuity of custom in itself had authority, whereas for Bentham, custom only truly becomes law when it is legalized, that is to say, sanctioned by the so-called lawgiver: the reasoning is the same as the one that, in Hobbes's *Dialogue*, founded the authority of the English courts on the authorization of the sovereign. Custom and the rule of the precedent have, in addition, a genuine advantage from a utilitarian point of view, which is that they guarantee, thanks to the continuity of law, the *security* that the citizen is looking for in the legal order. But for Bentham, this entails consequences that are the opposite of those drawn by traditional lawyers. For them, the continuity of custom created a presumption of rationality and of legality, but the judge, who would reason on the basis of the principles incorporated in common law, could sometimes break with precedents when it seemed that these precedents would lead to an "unreasonable" decision, which explains how the judge, without "making" a law (since he only "reveals" it), could play an innovative role (for example, Blackstone, *Commentaries*, 1.69–71). For Bentham, however, the judge could not reject a precedent without becoming a legislator, and without thereby creating retrospective laws, which would endanger the security of citizens (Postema, *Bentham and the Common Law Tradition*, 194–97 and 207–10). But the conflict between the letter of the law and the decisions of judges could also be seen as a symptom of the imperfection of the traditional English system, where the inflexibility of the rule of precedent increased the risk of the arbitrariness of judges, which led Bentham to propose a complete reform of English law, in which law-making and adjudication are each regulated by the principles of utility, in ways that borrow both from the Hobbesian tradition and, paradoxically, from certain elements of the common law tradition (c.f. ibid., 339–464). The same problems will also be addressed by the great English theoreticians of legal positivism such as John Austin (1790–1859) and especially Herbert L. A. Hart (1907–92), whose work has notably paved the way for a "positivist" interpretation of the fundamental elements of English law. In contrast to the classical doctrine whereby the judge only "revealed" the law, common law now appears as a "judge-made law," in which the judge could be led to institute new rules when the existing law does not allow a case to be resolved.

B. The legacy of common law

The main philosophical legacy of the traditional English lawyers is to be found in authors such as David Hume or Edmund Burke. These authors' interpretations of politics can be seen as philosophical transpositions of the models of common law, as is shown by their use of English history, their emphasis on the limits of individual reason, and their search for an "artificial reason" that would be irreducible to the simple application of "metaphysical" rules based on "natural reason" (Postema, *Bentham and the Common Law Tradition*, 81–143, and Pocock, *Politics, Language, and Time: Essays on Political Thought and History*, 202–32). Alongside this tradition—which we might call "conservative"—it is also worth noting the very evident presence of modes of thought based on common law in an author such as Dworkin, whose critique of Hart's positivism is clearly in the service of the great "liberal" causes of our time. Indeed, in Dworkin's view, law cannot be reduced to rules, since it also contains a set of principles that underlie the legal system while expressing a common morality. These are the principles that judges use when they seem to reject precedent or, more generally, when they appear to "create" law, as the "liberal" judges on the Supreme Court of the United States do, and this reasoning is very similar to Blackstone's. In the same way, Dworkin's emphasis on the "continuity" of law above and beyond the "apparent" reversals of case-based law, or even his thesis that every difficult case has only one right response (which assumes that bad decisions can only be "errors"), quite clearly echo the ideas of the great English lawyers. And this work, which is entirely dedicated to the defense of modernity, also reminds us that the success of common law was due to its capacity to present the most radical innovations as the consequences of faithful adherence to tradition.

So there is, in English-language philosophy of law, something irreducible to the other modern trends, which comes from the way it incorporated within philosophy the schemas of reasoning that emerge directly out of the legal tradition of common law. It is almost as if the English experience and the English language carried with them a particular vision of law, irreducible both to positivism and to the most dogmatic versions of natural law. But this tradition is itself shot through by constant internal tensions and has been the object, beginning with Hobbes, of radical critiques based on a projected rationalization of the state and society, which have allowed English thought and the "continental" trends to be brought closer together: Hobbes sometimes appears as a successor to Bodin, and Bentham as a reader of Holbach and Helvetius. Conversely, the schemas that have emerged out of common law are very much alive in authors who are sensitive to the particular role of the judge, whose importance is obvious in the democratic politics and the constitutional law of our times.

Philippe Raynaud

BIBLIOGRAPHY

Austin, John. *The Province of Jurisprudence Determined*. London, 1832.

Beaud, Olivier. *La puissance de l'état*. Paris: Presses Universitaires de France, 1994.

Blackstone, William. *Commentaries on the Laws of England*. Chicago: University of Chicago Press, 1979. First published in 1765–69.

Carrive, Paulette. "Hobbes et les juristes de la *Common Law*." Pp. 149–71 in *Thomas Hobbes: De la métaphysique à la politique*. Edited by Martin Bertman and Michel Malherbe. Paris: Vrin, 1989.

Cormack, Bradin. *A Power to Do Justice: Jurisdiction, English Literature, and the Rise of Common Law, 1509–1625*. Chicago: University of Chicago Press, 2008.

Dicey, Albert Venn. *Introduction to the Study of the Law of the Constitution*. Reprint of 8th ed. [1915]. Indianapolis, IN: Liberty Fund, 1982.

Dworkin, Ronald. *Law's Empire*. Cambridge, MA: Belknap, 1986.

———. *Taking Rights Seriously*. Cambridge, MA: Harvard University Press, 1978.

Edlin, Douglas E. *Common Law Theory*. Cambridge: Cambridge University Press, 2007.

Gough, John Wiedofft. *Fundamental Law in English Constitutional History*. Oxford: Clarendon, 1955.

Hart, Herbert Lionel Adelphus. *The Concept of Law*. Oxford: Oxford University Press, 1961.

Hobbes, Thomas. *A Dialogue between a Philosopher and a Student of the Common Laws of England*. Edited and with an introduction by Joseph Cropsey. Chicago: University of Chicago Press, 1971.

———. *Leviathan, or the Matter, Forme, and Power of a Common-Wealth, Ecclesiasticall and Civill*. Oxford: Oxford University Press, 1996. First published in 1651.

Lessay, Frank. "Common Law," in P. Raynaud et S. Rials (éd), *Dictionnaire de philosophie politique*, PUF, 1996.

Locke, John. *The Second Treatise of Government: An Essay Concerning the True Original, Extent and End of Civil Government*. 3rd ed. Edited, revised, and with an introduction by J. W. Gough. Oxford: Blackwell, 1976. First published in 1690.

Pocock, John Greville Agard. *The Ancient Constitution and the Feudal Law*. Cambridge: Cambridge University Press, 1987.

———. *Politics, Language, and Time: Essays on Political Thought and History*. Chicago: University of Chicago Press, 1989.

———. *Virtue, Commerce, and History: Essays on Political Thought and History, Chiefly in the Eighteenth Century*. Cambridge: Cambridge University Press, 1985.

Pollock, Frederick, and Frederic William Maitland. *The History of English Law*. 2 vols. Cambridge: Cambridge University Press, 1998. First published in 1895.

Postema, Gerald L. *Bentham and the Common Law Tradition*. 2nd ed. Oxford: Oxford University Press, 1989.

Raynaud, Philippe. "Juge." In RT: *Dictionnaire de philosophie politique*.

Saccone, Giuseppe Mario. "The Ambiguous Relation between Hobbes' Rhetorical Appeal to English History and His Deductive Method in a Dialogue." *History of European Ideas* 24 (1998): 1–17.

Schmitt, Carl. "Nehmen/Teilen/Weiden." Pp. 489–504 in *Verfassungsrechtliche Aufsätze aus den Jahren 1924–1954: Materialien zu einer Verfassungslehre*. Berlin: Duncker and Humbolt, 1958. Translation by G. L. Ulmen: "Appropriation/ Distribution/ Production: An Attempt to Determine from *Nomos* the Basic Questions of Every Social and Economic Order." Pp. 324–35 in *The Nomos of the Earth in the International Law of the Jus Publicum Europeaum*. New York: Telos Press, 2003.

Tunc, André. "Coutume et 'common law.'" *Droits* 3 (1986): 51–61.

LEGGIADRIA (ITALIAN)

ENGLISH	grace, beauty
FRENCH	*grâce, beauté, élégance, légèreté*
GERMAN	*Geschicklichkeit*

➤ *GRACE*, and ART, BAROQUE, BEAUTY, DISEGNO, MIMĒSIS, SPREZZATURA

Leggiadria, a now obsolete term referring to an affected elegance, comes from the Latin *levitus* and from Provençal. During the Italian Renaissance *leggiadria* came to express an almost natural grace that was in no way divine but anchored in worldly reality, situated at the point of equilibrium in a tension between the natural and the artificial. It found cognates in other Romance languages (cf. the Spanish *ligereza* and *ligero*, with the additional sense of "inconstant" or "unfaithful"), and would also be translated as *grâce*, "grace," *grazie*, *élégance, beauté*, "beauty." Toward the end of the sixteenth century, however, during the time of the Counter-Reformation, and when Italy lost its autonomy, the meaning of the term shifted: *leggiadria* came to mean instead a beauty in which the artificial prevailed over the natural, and thus became one of the most important qualities of the courtier in treatises on how to comport oneself. *Leggiadria* would thereafter refer to the ability to create a social circle at a distance from actual political conflicts, and was presented as a feigned spontaneity whose most appropriate expression was *sprezzatura* (an affected casualness), as in *Il Cortegiano* (*Book of the Courtier*) by Baldassare Castiglione (1528), which was widely read in the courts of Europe. In this new sense, it could be translated as *gaillardise* (high-spiritedness) and *Geschicklichkeit* (artfulness, skillfulness; formed from *Geschick*).

I. The Education of Nature?

The term *leggiadria* had its origins and was used most frequently in love poetry. It referred to feminine beauty, or to the elegance of animals that one could in principle train, since *leggiadria* had to do, in fact, with educating nature—to the point of making what was acquired appear as natural. This nuance of meaning is found throughout poetry written in vulgar language, from Dante to the Baroque poets. In Poliziano, for example, *leggiadria* is the very particular grace of a doe and of a loved woman, who are both characterized by a spontaneous but precious elegance:

> Ira dal volto suo trista s'arretra, e poco, avanti a lei, Superbia basta: ogni dolce virtù l'è in compagnia. Beltà la mostra a dito e Leggiadria.

> (The fateful anger leaves his face, and Vanity resists a little more when he is before her; every sweet virtue accompanies him. Beauty points to her, and so does *Leggiadria*.)

> (*Le Stanze*, I.45; *The Stanze of Angelo Poliziano*, trans. D. Quint)

In the fifteenth century, the term expressed a rather vague oscillation between the natural and the artificial. In the sixteenth century, with the demand for systematizing and classifying literary genres as political systems, a number of treatises on love or poetics were keen to distinguish between beauty, grace, and *leggiadria*. The most striking example is the dialogue entitled *Il Celso. Della bellezza delle donne*. Here, Agnolo Firenzuola, in drawing up a taxonomy of terms used to describe beauty, uses a false etymology in making *leggiadria* derive not from lightness but from law (*legge*):

> La leggiadria non è altro, come vogliono alcuni, e secondo che mostra la forza del vocabolo, che un'osservanza d'una tacita legge, fata e promulgata dalla natura a voi donne, nel muovere, portare e adoperare così tutta la persona insieme, come le membra particolari, con grazia, con modestia, con misura, con garbo, in guisa che nessun movimento, nessuna azione sia senza regola, senza modo, senza misura o senza disegno.

> (As many people would have it, and as the very force of the word suggests, *leggiadria* is nothing but the observance of a tacit law, which is created and promulgated by you women, so that you can move, carry, and compose your whole body, as well as all the individual parts of your body, with grace, modesty, measure, and discretion, so that no movement is unregulated, nor without manners, measure or design.)

> (*Il Celso*, Discourse I)

So *leggiadria* continued to refer to a more than graceful beauty, but it began to lose its lightness, so to speak: it needed to have rules, measure, and *disegno*. The balance between the natural and the artificial thus seemed to tip toward the artificial, or at the very least, toward the construction of a consistent and well-planned order. It was no coincidence that this requirement was particularly marked in the nascent genre of treatises on art, where the principle of the imitation of nature began to compete with the idea of something constructed according to the intentions of the author, and thanks to his artistic skill. Opinions were thus divided, with the emphasis sometimes on the natural, and at other times on the artificial, but humanists seemed to go more in the direction of the latter.

The balance between the natural and the artificial found in earlier uses of *leggiadria* was still retained in Cosimo Bartoli's 1550 Italian translation of Alberti's *De re aedificatoria*: wherever the humanist has used the Latin term *venustas* ("from the goddess Venus," hence the aesthetic quality bound with the pleasure derived from the observation of bodily beauty, and most famously translated into English by Henry Wotton, in the seventeenth century, as "delight") to refer to a certain order obtained by supplementing the inadequacies of nature itself, the translator chose the word *leggiadria*. *Leggiadria* conferred on beauty both its principle of order and harmony, and the power to complete the plans that nature had not been able to complete:

> La bellezza è un certo consenso, e concordantia delle parti, in qual si voglia cosa che dette parti si ritrovino, la qual concordantia si sia avuta talmente con certo determinato numero, finimento, e collocatione, qualmente la leggiadria ciò è, il principale intento della natura ne ricercava.

> (Beauty is a certain correspondence and harmony between parts, whatever the thing they are part of, this harmony being obtained by a determined measure, by an order, and an arrangement, in other words, *leggiadria*, which is the principal aim of nature.)

> (Alberti, *L'Architettura*; It. trans. by C. Bartoli, VI.2)

But if, in Bartoli's translation, nature remains the main point of reference, in the same year Vasari clearly characterized the beauty of *leggiadria* as being, above all, free from any measure: according to him, it exceeds nature and the rules of proportional harmony. Its champions were thus Raphael, Parmigianino, and Pierino del Vaga; those who condemned it were Paolo Uccello and Piero della Francesca, that is, the painters who were the most closely attuned to the "natural" universe.

II. The New Morality and the Virtue of Grace

The shift in *leggiadria*'s meaning toward the sense of "artificial" and even of "artifact" occurred more explicitly in the use of *leggiadria* in manuals for deportment from the second half of the sixteenth century. With Italy's loss of its autonomy, and the Counter-Reformation, a new morality of behavior was evolving within the courts: men of letters elaborated a rhetoric based on the carefully managed distance between one's inner-self and how one displayed oneself in public. *Leggiadria* therefore acquired a meaning close to that of *sprezzatura*, as illustrated by Baldassare Castiglione in *Il Cortegiano* (1528), which consisted of dissimulating the efforts of art behind an appearance of nonchalance. This morality would find its theoretical justification much later in Torquato Accetto's *La Dissimulazione onesta* (1641); for him, disguising spontaneity and one's own opinions was a means of survival. In many treatises during the Counter-Reformation, *leggiadria* in effect became what characterized the space between the private and the public, the innate and the acquired, sincerity and lying, which was also the realm of social savoir-faire, of the carefully negotiated distance where the particular sociability of *leggiadria* reigned, namely, in conversation. In his *Galateo* (1558), Giovanni della Casa thus placed *leggiadria* in the register of good manners. It was always at the heart of the activity of *communicare e usare*, or developing a relationship whereby two men became less of a stranger or enemy to one another. But it was also defined as attending to the imperfections of one's own body: without the elegance of a carefully looked-after body, beauty and goodness become divorced from each other. Jean de Tournes (1598) translated into French the definition of *leggiadria* that figures in the *Galateo*:

> L'élégance [leggiadria] n'est en quelque sorte rien d'autre qu'une certaine lumière qui se dégage de la convenance des choses qui sont bien composées et bien divisées les unes avec les autres et toutes ensemble: sans cette mesure, le bien n'est pas le beau, ni la beauté plaisante.
>
> (Elegance [leggiadria] is in many ways nothing but a certain light which is given off by the perfection of things which are well arranged and well divided between one another, and as a whole: without this meaure, the good is not beautiful, and beauty is not agreeable.)
>
> (Della Casa, *Il Galateo*; Fr. trans. J. de Tournes)

This was the sense in which *leggiadria* was translated and adapted in high society in the courts of Europe. However, its popularity was short-lived: Heinrich Wölflin (*Renaissance und Barok*, 1888) saw the disappearance of the world of *leggiadria* (*die graziöse Leichtigkeit*) as one of the major elements of the transition from the Renaissance to the Baroque period: the break with the Renaissance involved a taste for shapes, colors, and spiral forms supplanting the taste for contours, design, and lightness. In the eighteenth century, *leggiadria* was thus completely overshadowed by the distinction between grace and beauty in neoclassical artists such as Antonio Canova, Leopoldo Cicognara, and Ugo Foscolo: for them, art aspired to be almost godlike, and consequently could not be considered worldly. Schiller's aesthetics, in which grace was a matter of beauty in movement, seemed to borrow certain aspects of *leggiadria*—though in fact his notion of grace was intended as a basis for the synthesis between nature and suprasensible freedom. *Leggiadria*, though, makes no claims at all to transcend the real. Anchored in worldly reality, it suspends certain of the world's rules in order to create parallel words, caught within a fragile equilibrium between the artificial and the natural, and not in order to bring about the intervention of divine grace. Like Guido Cavalcanti, who in Boccaccio escapes from being chased by leaping "with great lightness" and landing on the other side of the Orto San Michele, *leggiadria* does not deny the necessity of the real, but merely looks for the supporting points from where it can perform an elegant, light leap, a saving little nothing. Italo Calvino adapts Boccaccio's story in his *Lezioni americane* (1988) when he recommends lightness to writers of the next millennium, as one of the major yet forgotten touchstones of Western literature, heir to the humanism of the Renaissance.

Fosca Mariani-Zini

BIBLIOGRAPHY

Alberti, Leon Battista. *De re ædificatoria*. Florence: Niccolò di Lorenzo Alamani, 1485. Translation by Cosimo Bartoli: *L'Architettura*. Florence, Torrentino, 1550. Translation by Giovanni Orlandi: *L'architettura / De re aedificatoria*. 2 vols. Edited by G. Orlandi. Introduction and notes by Paolo Portoghesi. Milan: Polifilo, 1966. Translation by Joseph Rykwert, Neil Leach, and Robert Tavernor: *On the Art of Building in Ten Books*. Cambridge, MA: MIT Press, 1988.

———.*On Painting and On Sculpture: The Latin Texts of "De pictura" and "De statua."* Edited and translated, with introduction and notes, by Cecil Grayson. London: Phaidon, 1972.

Castiglione, Baldassare. *Il cortegiano con una scelta delle opere minori*. Edited by Bruno Maier. Turin: Unione Tipografico-Editrice Torinese, 1955. First published in 1528. Translation by Charles S. Singleton: *The Book of the Courtier*. Edited by Daniel Javitch. New York: Norton, 2002.

Della Casa, Giovanni. *Il Galateo*. In *Prose di Giovanni della Casa e altri trattatisti cinquecenteschi del comportamento*. Edited by Arnaldo Di Benedetto. Turin: Unione Tipografico-Editrice Torinese, 1970. First published in 1558. Translation by Konrad Eisenbichler and Kenneth R. Bartlett: *Galateo: A Renaissance Treatise on Manners*. Introduction and notes by K. Eisenbichler and K. R. Bartlett. 3rd rev. ed. Toronto: Centre for Reformation and Renaissance Studies, 1994. Translation by Jean de Tournes: *Le Galatée*. Lyon, 1598; revised as *Galatée ou Des manières* by Alain Pons. Paris: Librairie Générale Française, 1988.

Firenzuola, Agnolo. *Celso*. "Dialogo delle bellezze delle donne." In *Opere*. Firenze: Sansoni, 1971. Translation by Konrad Eisenbichler and Jacqueline Murray: *On the Beauty of Women*. Edited by K. Eisenbichler and J. Murray. Philadelphia: University of Pennsylvania Press, 1992.

Poliziano, Angelo. *Stanze per la giostra, Orfeo, Rime: Con un' appendice di prose volgari*. Novaro, It.: Istituto Geografico de Agostino, 1969.

———. *The Stanze of Angelo Poliziano*. Translated by David Quint. Amherst: University of Massachusetts Press, 1979.

Vasari, Giorgio. *Le vite de più eccelenti architettori, pittori et scultori italiani*. 9 vols. Edited by Gaetano Milanesi. Florence: Sansoni, 1878–85. First published in 1586. Translation by Gaston du C. de Vere: *Lives of the Most Eminent Painters, Sculptors and Architects*. 10 vols. London, 1912–15; reissued New York: AMS Press, 1976.

LEIB / KÖRPER / FLEISCH (GERMAN)

ENGLISH	lived-body/body/flesh
FRENCH	*chair/corps*
GREEK	*sôma* [σῶμα] / *sarx* [σάρξ]
HEBREW	*bāsār* [בָּשָׂר]
ITALIAN	*carne/corpo*
LATIN	*corpus/caro*
SPANISH	*carne/cuerpo*

➤ *FLESH*, SOUL, and ANIMAL, CONSCIOUSNESS, DASEIN, ERLEBEN, GESCHLECHT, *LIFE/LEBEN*, LOGOS, PATHOS, PERCEPTION, QUALE, SUBJECT

Leib has two meanings, which depend on its privileged correlative term: when paired with *Seele* (soul), it corresponds to the currently accepted sense of the body as the home of sensory experience and fits into the common opposition of soul/body. Understood in terms of its relation to its close neighbor, *Körper*, its meaning is inflected and revitalized through its etymological connection to *Leben* (life). *Leben* means the vital, fluid, living, and dynamic side of corporeity, whereas *Körper* refers to the structural aspect of the body, that is, its static dimension. One is thus tempted to translate *Leib* (1) as "flesh" (*chair* in French, *carne* in Italian and Spanish), in order to emphasize this aspect of vital fluidity, and *Körper* as "body," when the two terms are being used together, especially in a Husserlian context; (2) as "body" whenever it is *Seele* that structures the meaning, in more classical contexts. But the problem one runs up against is the re-translation of *chair*—a key term in Merleau-Ponty—in the Germanic languages, where there is a more specific term: *Fleisch* (German), and *flesh* (English), which are usually translated into French as *viande* (meat). (Spanish and Italian present no such difficulty.) In addition, *chair* carries with it theological connotations, which leads one to question the way in which the concept took root in a Greco-Latin, or even Hebrew, context. Indeed, both Greek and Latin have two terms that one could comfortably retain as bi-univocal in translating *chair/corps* or *Leib/Körper*, namely, *caro/corpus* and *sarx/sôma*. But just as the transition from German to French does not allow for a simple transposition of one pair to the other, one is also faced with shifts of meaning in Latin and in Greek, or at any rate, inflections linked to the underlying axiology of each term, in ways that are moreover quite distinct in philosophy and in theology.

I. The Lexical and Etymological Dimensions

In present-day German, *Leib* refers to the stomach or the breast, as, for example, in expressions such as *Nichts im Leibe haben* (to have an empty stomach) and *gesegneten Leibes sein* or *die Mutterleib* (to be pregnant). More broadly, *Leib* corresponds to anything having to do with the intimacy of the body at its most vital: *harten Leib haben* (to be constipated); or sensorial: *am ganzen Leibe zittern* (to tremble all over). *Leib* is also used in expressions that mention the soul (*Seele*) or the heart (*Herz*): *kein Herz im Leibe haben* (not to have a heart), *mit Leib und Seele* (wholeheartedly), and *jemandem mit Leib und Seele ergeben sein* (to be devoted body and soul to someone). This suggests a proximity between *Leib* and the realm of "sensing" or "feeling," whether affective or sensorial.

The etymology reveals a common root between *Leib* and *leben* on the one hand, and *Leib* and *bleiben* on the other, going back to Middle High German (*lîp*, genitive *lîbes*). In the first case, *Leib* conveys the idea of a vital flow, proper to all living beings, which animates an inert body. In the second,

bleiben attests to the link between *Leib* and dwelling, residing, and the intimacy of a place. *Leib* is part of a specific Germanic context: *lîp* are those who have "stayed" (*die Geblebenen*), who have not fallen on the battlefield, as opposed to *wal*, those who have fallen, that is, heaven's chosen ones (*die Ausgewählten*), the heroes. The life/death polarization of the pair *lîp/wal* follows naturally (the living and the dead), even if it is not constitutive of the primary meaning.

One can therefore find this shared sense between *Leib* and *leben* in many almost tautological idiomatic expressions: *bei lebendigen Leibe verbrannt werden* (to be burned alive), *Leib und Leben einsetzen* (to risk life and limb), *das ist er, wie er leibt und lebt* (that's just like him). In short, the *Leib* aspect of the body is vital and alive: the inert aspect is the becoming-inert of *Leiche* or of *Leichnam* ("corpse" in English, *cadavre* in French), or the inertia of *Körper*, a solid, physical, and material body. So one speaks of "bodies" in the physical sciences, celestial bodies (*Himmelskörper*) in Aristotelian cosmology, and corpuscles (*Körpchen*) in quantum physics. Whenever *Körper* is used in a human context, it signifies an organic structure or a complexion (*Körper-Anlage-Beschaffenheit*), a stature or conformation (*-bau*), comportment or bearing (*-haltung*), and in any case, a static, functional, or quantifiable configuration (*-gewicht*, *-größe*, *-kraft*).

■ See Box 1.

II. *Leib* and Its Entry into Philosophy

This was twofold: first, in terms of *Leib's* paired relation to *Seele* (soul), and second, in terms of its quasi-oppositional relation to *Körper*, and thus its correlation with *Geist* (spirit) (RT: *Historisches Wörterbuch der Philosophie*).

The ways in which *Leib* fits into a Kantian and post-Kantian context, within idealism more broadly, and then into its critical reassessment by Nietzsche, illustrate this pairing: here, *Leib* comes to be linked to subjectivity. Kant's *Opus postumum*, for instance, makes *Leib* a formal a priori of the subject, and Fichte (*Die Tatsachen des Bewußtseins*) asserts that the materiality of the *Leib* is the absolute a priori of self-consciousness. Hegel's *Phenomenology of Spirit*, however, insists on the fact that the body (*Leib*) is the expression of an individual, but that this expression is already mediated; it is a sign produced by the body, but the body is not at the origin of the sign. For Schopenhauer (*Werke*), the *Leib* represents an immediate object and expresses the will. Nietzsche describes it as a "great reason" and even sees it as the vital principle of theoretical reason (*Also sprach Zarathustra*). In short, *Leib* in the German nineteenth century was associated with transcendental subjectivity, or it was related to the individual, physiological, or instinctual subject.

III. *Crux phaenomenologica*: The Disintegration of *Leib* as an Effect of the Diversity of Its Translations

The psychology of the time, which Husserl inherited, also used the term *Leib*, but in the context of a psycho-physical parallelism (as in the work of Fechner, Wundt, and Avenarius), or more precisely, of the reciprocity of the psychic and the physical (Stumpf). Apart from these authors, Husserl borrowed from Theodor Lipps the notion of empathy as an *immediate* sharing of the feelings of others. Rejecting the

1

Lebenswelt and *In-der-Welt-Sein*: "Lifeworld" and "being in the world"

➤ DASEIN, *MALAISE, WORLD*

The emphasis on *Lebenswelt*, or "lifeworld," in the later writing of Husserl corresponds to an internal exigency of Husserlian phenomenology: yet it also seems to correspond to the impact of a return of the writings of the disciple (Heidegger) on those of his master (Husserl), in particular the notion elaborated in *Being and Time* of *In-der-Welt-Sein*.

French translators have preferred to translate Heidegger's expression as *être-au-monde* (being-to-the-world) rather than *être-dans-le monde* (being-in-the-world) (Sartre). It is indeed best understood with reference to the German *In-sein* (*être à* [to be at/to]), where what is at issue is not so much the localization or placement of being-in-relation-to, as the delocalization, or even "removal" or moving (as in changing residence) (*déménagement*) in the Baudelairean sense: "It always seems to me that I should feel well in the place where I am not, and this question of removal is one that I discuss incessantly with my soul." "To be at/to" is also "to be exposed to," and not being able not to be exposed to, so that the title of prose poem 48 in Baudelaire's *Le spleen de Paris* captures perfectly both the centripetal and centrifugal tension of "being-in-the-world" (and in a language): "Anywhere out of the world."

Pascal David

BIBLIOGRAPHY

Heidegger, Martin. *Sein und Zeit*. 13th ed. Tübingen: Niemeyer, 1976. Translation by John Macquarrie and Edward Robinson: *Being and Time*. New York: Harper and Row, 1962.

analogical inference of Benno Erdmann, he conceived of empathy as the mediated (corporeal) manifestation of the lived experience of others.

Leib thus acquired the meaning of "body as it is lived," leading Anglo-Americans to opt for the expression "lived-body." But this translation has the disadvantage of placing corporeality in a reflexive framework (my body, lived by myself), when phenomenology aimed to short-circuit the distinction between inside and outside. We come across similar difficulties with the French expression *corps animé* (animate body), which considers *Leib* from a psycho-physical point of view. We have the reverse of the same difficulty with the translations *corps organique* (organic body) or *corps vivant* (living body), which are relevant for worldly, anthropological phenomenology, but that each time incline *Leib* in the direction of biology.

What are we to make, then, of the *corps propre* (one's own body) that is a theme from Maine de Biran through to the Merleau-Ponty of the *Phenomenology of Perception*, the "subject-body," which is one's own, as opposed to the "object-body," which scientists deal with? This distinction would easily render Husserl's distinction between *Leib* and *Körper*, but such a translation is almost tautological: in fact, a *Leib* is always "mine" (*mein Leib*), or "my own" (*Eigenleib*). Even with the expression *fremder Leib*, it is the other's mode of a belonging to him- or herself that is in play. Likewise, whenever Husserl talks about *Leibkörper* (literally, body of flesh), or about *körperlicher Leib* or *physischer Leib*, or even *Körperleib* (Husserliana, no. 13; Husserliana, no. 15), he does so in order to free subjectivation from the object-body (*Körper*). Although what is one's own is just as much a component of *Leib* as what is quick or living, *Leib* cannot be reduced to this. When Husserl talks about *Eigenleib*, it is so as to specify *Leib* as one's own, not to assimilate the one to the other. The translation of *Leib* by *corps propre* may confirm the links between Husserl and Merleau-Ponty, but it also opens the door to an improper linking of *Leib* with what is properly one's life. The network of composite words we find in Husserl is supplemented by a series of derived terms (*leiblich/Leiblichkeit/Verleiblichung/körperlich/Körperlichkeit/Verkörperung*); the bi-univocal correspondence between *Leib* and *Körper* proves all the more uneasy, given that the Romance languages use a single term to refer to the everyday meaning and the theological meaning of incarnation, while German speaks, in the latter register, of *Menschwerdung*.

In Husserl, the sphere of "ownness" refers to the first experience in which the lived experiences of consciousness are constituted and engendered: it has a genetic status as the original matrix of our corporeality. In French, the notion of *chair* (flesh) attempts to express the sensible *locus* that is irreducible to objective spatiality But is this use of the term *chair* appropriate to refer to the way *Leib* is inflected? Merleau-Ponty first privileges this term in *Le visible et l'invisible* (1964) in referring not to the body of others, but to the being of the world. To emphasize the carnal dimension of experience is to affirm the world's sensing (of itself). Thus, the French *chair* captures better than the English "being" a certain unity of experience (there is a flesh of being), whereas one's "own" body is individual. The Husserlian *Leib* also contains this unity of the experience that, without appearing, is concretized in the form of everyone's body.

This "non-appearing" or "non-apparent" (*in-apparaissant*) is not something that lies beyond. If *chair* does not appear, it is because we do not perceive it, we are not attentive to it—as happens with small perceptions in Leibniz. This emphasis on the labile, fluid, soft nature of *chair*, which downplays the structured-ness of the body, is unique to French, even though it takes as its point of reference the usual sense of the term (in French, the bones and *la chair* connected to blood are opposed to *la viande* [meat], or the soft substance of the body). *Fleisch* (German) and "flesh" (English) have this sense, and the German translators of Merleau-Ponty have, moreover, translated *chair* in this way, also using the word *Leib*. What is revealed here is the hypersensitive dimension of a human being (*chair* is what can be wounded, or can flourish), the intimate exchange between inside and outside, namely, the skin: only the skin can have *la chair de poule* (goose bumps; literally, chicken skin). What is more, whether we are talking about a fruit or about the skin's appearance, *la chair* harbors a network that is both mobile and firm, plastic and structured, endlessly reconfigured: the vitality of the body resides in its *chair*.

Michel Henry can thus proclaim this carnal sense of *Leib*, which is a different name for what he calls "auto-affection." And Didier Franck proposes, in his discussion of the analytic of *la chair* in *Chair et corps*, the idea of refusing to give this originary aspect any autonomous status, by articulating the invisible, or the inapparent, as that which constitutes visible appearing. So to translate *Leib* as *chair* brings out the tension between phenomenology and metaphysics, because of the originary non-appearing unity that the term conveys. This articulation that would become the horizon of Husserlian phenomenology, and Merleau-Ponty's thinking toward the end of his life, as well as Michel Henry's perspective, are situated within this framework.

This tension becomes problematic when the metaphysics inherent in *la chair* doubles as instinctual immanence and theological transcendence. As early as the twelfth century, *chair* had a strong theological resonance that is certainly present in the notion of the living body as a glorious body. In addition, *chair* also had an instinctual, even sexual connotation: to speak about a carnal union was to speak in more elegant terms of a sexual union. From the ambivalence of the living body as biological or theological, to the ambiguity of *la chair* as instinctual or spiritual, we remain caught within the duality of immanence and transcendence.

IV. The Horizon of the Ancient World: Latin, Greek, and Hebrew Roots

How are we to arrive at rational grounds for choosing a translation of *Leib* when faced with such a swarm of different decisions taken over the years? It would seem appropriate to reflect on the Greco-Latin roots of the notion. In each case we have a pair (*sarx/sôma* [σάρξ/σῶμα]; *caro/corpus*) that modern languages have transposed into "flesh"/"body," *chair/corps*, or *carne/cuerpo-corpo*. But do the theological or philosophical contexts that the classical sources reveal mitigate the difficulties in translating *Leib*?

A. The equivocality of the contexts of Paul and John: *Sôma, sarx, pneuma*

In his First Epistle to the Corinthians, Paul wavers between flesh (*sarx*) and body (*sôma*): after having distinguished between the different kinds of flesh in the animal world and then having differentiated the bodies in the cosmology of the ancients, he separates the psychic, animal body (destructible, despicable) from the spiritual, pneumatic body (glorious, powerful). *Sôma* is ambivalent, linked to sin, rejected or elevated to the glory of resurrection. Paul's *sôma* has no quality of its own. *Sarx*, however, is defined in the Epistles to the Romans and the Galatians as being opposed to the spirit (*pneuma* [πνεῦμα]), but it is not identified with the somatic body, since as something selfishly closed upon itself, the residue of a sin that is legalized within the law, and the source of death, its meaning is entirely negative (Rom 7:5–14; Gal 5:13–16). *Sarx* is understood in terms of a morality of abstinence, which gives it a worldly and finite meaning. This meaning of "flesh" as a manifestation of human finitude is also one we

find in Matthew 26:41 (or Mk 14:38): the Spirit is filled with love, but the flesh is weak.

In John 3:6, *sarx* and *pneuma* refer to two types of creation: "Flesh gives birth to flesh, but the Spirit gives birth to spirit." *Sôma* alone contains the possibility of a glorious self-transformation. *Sôma* alone can have an individuated and individuating status, while *sarx* is infra-individual: the asthenic flesh is thus contrasted with the force of the spirit. Yet this hypothesis (Husserl, *Thing and Space*) does not hold up, because (a) we are only dealing with one, asthenic, meaning of the flesh; and (b) the axiology of the spirit and of the flesh is supported by that of glory and sin. It is notable, however, that "the Word became flesh" (Jn 1:14) has quite a different valence: the "flesh of life" in John is a redefinition of finitude as the possible power of individuation. The distinction is thus not between flesh and spirit (and also not between Paul and John), but between the flesh of sin and the flesh of glory and life (Cyril of Alexandria, *Deux dialogues christologiques*).

B. The univocality of the philosophical context: *Soma, psuchê, nous*

In the context of Plato and Aristotle, where *sarx* and *pneuma* do not form a conceptual framework, the distinction *sôma/psuchê* [ψυχή], or "animate body"/"intellect" (*nous* [νοῦς]), is the one that prevails, and it is linked to a depreciation of the somatic that would continue through the modern era, up to and including Descartes. *Phaedo* (83d) and *Gorgias* (493a–b) describe *sôma* as a prison cell, a tomb (*sôma = sêma* [σῆμα]), whose sign is desire, and understand *psuchê* as a form of exile, its own executioner crucified on the body. Aristotle radicalizes what in Plato was not a duality—but rather the soul's desire through the body, and the soul's exile in the body—by an ontological break that universalizes pure divine thought (*nous*) and individualizes corporeal form: *psuchê* and *sôma* are thus correlates of each other, as "form" (*morphê* [μορφή]) and "matter" (*hulê* [ὕλη]), or "activity" and "passivity" (*De anima*, 430a 5).

This duality reappears in Descartes in the distinction between the *res extensa* and the *res cogitans* (*anima, mens*, and *cogitationes*). In short, the body (*sôma, corpus*) is ontologically insubstantial and is kept at a distance, as passive matter. Heidegger was therefore able to think of corporeality as ontic substantiality, so the Platonic and Aristotelian filiation is not the one we should retain if we wish to see corporeality as something productive.

C. The non-onto-theo-logical (Hebrew) dynamic of the flesh: *Bāsār, rūaḥ, nèfèš*

To understand the theological ambivalence of *sôma/sarx* (or of *corpus/carne*, in Tertullian), and the positive meaning it can have, we might turn to another context: in the Hebrew scriptures, neither the body nor the flesh are valued negatively. The flesh (*bāsār* [בָּשָׂר]), as a human composite of body and soul, is even privileged as a concrete *index* of the spirit (*nèfèš* [נֶפֶשׁ]). A human being is an organic unity sometimes referred to as *nèfèš*, sometimes as *bāsār*, with *rūaḥ* [רוּחַ] (breath, spirit of God, soul) linked to it.

As the RT: *Traduction oecuménique de la Bible* testifies, roughly half of the occurrences of *bāsār* are translated as *chair* (flesh) (137 out of 270), indicating a consistent use of this term, whereas *corps* (body) does not correspond to any unified conceptual register: it is designated by seventeen Hebrew terms, among them *bāsār* (28/270) and *ḥayyah* [חַיָּה] (2/3), out of a total of seventy-two occurrences. "Flesh," on the other hand, corresponds to only five terms in Hebrew.

Nowhere in the Judaic tradition is "flesh" reduced to the physical or organic body. Its spiritual dimension is even the basis from which a possible glorification of the body itself makes sense. Obviously, this dynamic sense of the flesh pulls it away from substantiality: with respect to this endorsement of the flesh, Christianity will then bear onward this non-onto-theological sense of the body to which the expression in John testifies: "the Word became flesh."

D. How to translate?

We are dealing with four distinct conceptual fields. Christianity and phenomenology emphasize the ambivalence of the corporeal: sinful/glorious (*sarx-caro/sôma-corpus*, and *Körper/Leib*). The two other fields are unequivocal—either positive (Judaism) or negative (philosophy).

In addition, there is no analogical or inverse relationship between one pair (*sarx/sôma*) and another (*Körper/Leib*), in which *sarx* would be to *Körper* what *sôma* would be to *Leib*, since *sôma* also has a negative sense and *sarx* a positive sense. In short, the pair *sarx/soma* (*caro/corpus*) is not on its own a discriminating difference. A further quality polarizes its relevance: the *modal* pair sin/glory. *Sarx* on its own is not evil, but the sin by which Paul qualifies it is, to such a point that this sin then comes to define *sarx*. On the other hand, following the Judaic meaning of "flesh," John makes it the flesh of life, which refers, as in the Old Testament, to the complete person—body, soul, and mind.

In this respect, one decisive historical point of reference is that of the German esotericists (Weigel, Oetinger, Baader), who make *Leiblichkeit* into a *geistige Leiblichkeit*, endowing the body-flesh with a spiritual life that Schelling would turn to his advantage, as the *body-flesh* that phenomenology would reactivate by relieving it of its substantial materiality, and by recasting it as a vital subjective dynamism.

The pair *Körper/Leib* allows for an operative distinction because of the inertia/life or objective/subjective polarities that the Greek and Latin pairs do not offer and that Hebrew alone allows for through the expanded sense of *bāsār*. So it is the *qualities* of *sôma-corpus* (sin/glory) and of *sarx/carne* (death/life) that come to be analogous with the qualities of *Leib/Körper* (subjective lived experience / inert objectivity).

We could say, then, that the *Leib/Körper* polarity is conceptualized without being terminological. In this respect, it is reasonable to follow Paul Ricœur's appeal to the economy of meaning (body/flesh), and the use of a single term to cover the different concepts that *Leib*'s history and uses disclose. If we go along with this principle, we will opt for a minimalistic translation of *Leib* as "body": we could also convey the phenomenological polarity by using the term "flesh," given that Husserl uses *Leib* in a distinctive way, associating it with *Körper*, and articulating it with *Seele*. Distinct terms are thus legitimized according to their usage. Either *Leib* (flesh) works phenomenologically in liaison with *Körper*, or *Leib* (body) is associated with the psychic: in German (*Leib und Seele*), just as in French (*âme et corps*), idiomatic expressions are available that make sense in everyday language.

By working with two usages, one more technical, and the other more everyday, we bring into play a salutary contextualization. By maintaining a distinction between *Leib* and *Körper* in French, one can account for the difference between corporeal appearing and carnal appearing. It is then that the philosophical emerges: the aim of the German compound nouns is to indicate the interweaving that is the only way one can conceptualize unity in difference. Further, does this articulation (as *corps* and as *chair*, or between a technical and an everyday term) not correspond to the double meaning of *Leib* (linked to *Seele*/opposed to *Körper*), which signals *Leib*'s entry into philosophy?

Natalie Depraz

BIBLIOGRAPHY

Avenarius, Richard Heinrich Ludwig. *Philosophie als Denken der Welt gemäss dem Princip des kleinsten Kraftmasses: Prolegomena zu einer Kritik der reinen Erfahrung.* 3rd ed. Berlin: Guttentag, 1917.

Cyril, Patriarch of Alexandria. *Deux dialogues christologiques.* Translated by G. M. de Durand. Paris: Éditions du Cerf, 1964. Translation of the second dialogue by John Anthony McGuckin: *On the Unity of Christ.* Crestwood, NY: St. Vladimir's Seminary Press, 1995.

Dodd, James. *Idealism and Corporeity: An Essay on the Problem of the Body in Husserl's Phenomenology.* Dordrecht, Neth.: Kluwer, 1997.

Erdmann, Benno. *Wissenschaftliche Hypothesen über Leib und Seele: Vorträge gehalten an der Handelshochschule zu Köln.* Cologne: M. Dumont-Schauberg, 1908.

Fechner, Gustav Theodor. *Elemente der Psychophysik.* 3rd ed. 2 vols. Leipzig: Breitkopf and Härtel, 1907. Translation by Helmut E. Adler: *Elements of Psychophysics.* Edited by David H. Howes and Edwin G. Boring. New York: Holt, Rinehart and Winston, 1966.

———. *Religion of a Scientist: Selections from Gustav Th. Fechner.* Edited and translated by Walter Lowrie. New York: Pantheon Books, 1946.

Fichte, Johann Gottlieb. *Die Tatsachen des Bewußtseins.* Edited by I. H. Fichte. Vol. 1 in *Nachgelassene Werke.* Bonn: Marcus, 1834.

Franck, Didier. *Chair et corps: Sur la phénoménologie de Husserl.* Paris: Éditions de Minuit, 1981.

Hegel, Georg Wilhelm Friedrich. *Phänomelogie des Geistes.* Edited by J. Hoffmeister. Berlin: Akademie Verlag, 1971. Translation by A. V. Miller: *Phenomenology of Spirit.* Oxford: Oxford University Press, 1977.

Henry, Michel. *C'est moi la vérité: Pour une philosophie du christianisme.* Paris: Éditions du Seuil, 1996. Translation by Susan Emanuel: *I Am the Truth: Toward a Philosophy of Christianity.* Stanford, CA: Stanford University Press, 2003.

Hübner, Kurt. "Leib und Erfahrung in Kants *Opus postumum.*" *Zeitschrift für philosophische Forschung* 7, no. 2 (1953): 204–19.

Husserl, Edmund. "Aus den Vorlesungen, Grundprobleme der Phänomenologie, Wintersemester 1910/1911." In *Zur Phänomenologie der Intersubjektivität,* edited by Iso Kern. Husserliana, no. 13. The Hague: Nijhoff, 1973. Translation by Ingo Farin and James G. Hart: *The Basic Problems of Phenomenology: From the Lectures, Winter Semester, 1910–1911.* Dordrecht, Neth.: Springer, 2006.

———. *Cartesianische Meditationen und Pariser Vorträge.* Edited by S. Strasser. The Hague: Nijhoff, 1973. Translation by Dorion Cairns: *Cartesian Meditations: An Introduction to Phenomenology.* The Hague: Nijhoff, 1977.

———. *Ding und Raum: Vorlesungen 1907.* Edited by Ulrich Claesges. Husserliana, no. 16. The Hague: Nijhoff, 1973. Translation by Richard Rojcewicz: *Thing and Space: Lectures of 1907.* Dordrecht, Neth.: Kluwer, 1997.

———. *Ideen zu einer reinen Phänomenologie und phänomenologischen Philosophie.* Edited by Karl Schuhmann (vol. 1) and Marly Biemel (vol. 2). 2 vols. Husserliana, nos. 3.1 and 4. The Hague: Nijhoff, 1977, 1952. Translation by W. R. Boyce Gibson: *Ideas: General Introduction to Pure Phenomenology.* London: Allen and Unwin; New York: Macmillan, 1931.

———. *Zur Phänomenologie der Intersubjektivität: Texte aus dem Nachlass, Dritter Teil, 1929–35.* Edited by Iso Kern. Husserliana, no. 15. The Hague: Nijhoff, 1973.

———. *Zur Phänomenologie der Intersubjektivität: Texte aus dem Nachlass, Zweiter Teil, 1921–28.* Edited by Iso Kern. Husserliana, no. 14. The Hague: Nijhoff, 1973.

Kant, Immanuel. *Opus postumum.* 2 vols. Edited by Königlich Preussischen Akademie der Wissenschaften. Vols. 21 and 22 in *Kants Gesammelte Schriften.* Berlin: De Gruyter, 1936–38. Translation by Eckart Förster and Michael Rosen: *Opus postumum.* Edited by Eckart Förster. Cambridge: Cambridge University Press, 1993.

Lipps, Theodor. *Ästhetik; Psychologie des Schönen und der Kunst.* 2 vols. Leipzig: Voss, 1914–20.

McGuckin, John Anthony. *St. Cyril of Alexandria: The Christological Controversy; Its History, Theology, and Texts.* Leiden, Neth.: Brill, 1994.

Midgley, Mary. "The Soul's Successors: Philosophy and the Body." In *Religion and the Body,* edited by Sarah Coakley, 53–68. New York: Cambridge University Press, 1997.

Nietzsche, Friedrich. *Also sprach Zarathustra.* Edited by Giorgio Colli and Mazzino Montinari. Vol. 4 of *Kritische Studienausgabe.* Berlin: De Gruyter, 1988. Translation by Adrian Del Caro: *Thus Spoke Zarathustra: A Book for All and None.* Edited by Adrian Del Caro and Robert B. Pippin. Cambridge: Cambridge University Press, 2006.

Ricœur, Paul. *Soi-même comme un autre.* Paris: Éditions du Seuil, 1990. Translation by Kathleen Blamey: *Oneself as Another.* Chicago: University of Chicago Press, 1992.

Schopenhauer, Arthur. *Sämtliche Werke.* Edited by Paul Deussen. 6 vols. Munich: Piper, 1911–13. Translation by T. Bailey Saunders et al.: *The Works of Schopenhauer.* Edited by Will Durant. Abridged ed. New York: Simon and Schuster, 1928.

———. *The World as Will and Presentation.* Translated by Richard E. Aquila with David Carus. 2 vols. Longman Library. New York: Pearson Longman, 2008–10.

Stumpf, Carl. *Leib und Seele: Der Entwicklungsgedanke in der gegenwärtigen Philosophie; Zwei Reden.* 2nd ed. Leipzig: Barth, 1903.

Welton, Donn, ed. *The Body: Classic and Contemporary Readings.* Malden, MA: Blackwell, 1999.

Wundt, Wilhelm Max. "Über psychische Kausalität." In *Zur Psychologie und Ethik: Zehn ausgewählte Abschnitte aus Wilhelm Wundt,* edited by Julius A. Wentzel. Leipzig: Reclam, 1911. Translation by Charles Judd: "Psychical Causality and Its Laws." In *Outlines of Psychology,* 352–72. 3rd rev. ed. Leipzig: Engelmann, 1907.

LËV [לֵב], LËVAV [לְבָב] (HEBREW)

ARABIC	*qalb* [القلب], *fu'ād* [الفؤاد], *lubb* [لبّ]
ENGLISH	heart
FRENCH	*coeur*
GREEK	*kardia* [καρδία]

➤ *HEART,* and CONSCIOUSNESS, ESSENCE, GEMÜT, GOGO, INGENIUM, INTELLECTUS, SAMOST' SOUL, BOX 4, TO TI ÊN EINAI, TRUTH, UNDERSTANDING

This word is common to Semitic languages. Its usage represents, as with many languages, a remarkable case of the metaphorical use of a part of the body, considered as central, in order to express the moral worth of an individual or the very essence of something.

Arabic has specific words for the heart as an organ (*qalb* [القلب], and less commonly *fu'ād* [الفؤاد]). In Hebrew *lëv* [לֵב] refers less to the organ than to the entire thorax (cf. 2 Sm 18:14ff.), with all of the entrails contained within the cavity that it forms. It is from the heart that the very source of life is said to spring (Prv 4:23; cf. 25:13). It is the seat of life force and the center of the psychic life in all its dimensions (cf. Maimonides, *Guide of the Perplexed,* I, 39). The heart is the source of perceptions (Dt 29:3), memory (Is 46:8 etc.; Jer 3:16, etc.), feelings, and desire—including courage (Ps 40:13), in the sense in which Rodrigue in Corneille's *Le* *Cid* is asked "*As-tu du coeur?*" (Do you have the heart?). There is nothing specifically Semitic about this. In Aristotle, too, the "heart" (*kardia* [καρδία]) is the end point of sensations, and the starting point of the movements of the organism (cf. RT: *Index Aristotelicus,* 365b 34–54). And in Egypt, from the Middle Empire on, a heart would be weighed postmortem, a procedure that was supposed to assess the moral worth of the dead person and thus to determine his fate in the afterlife. Attributing higher intellectual functions to the heart is something we find in Latin (cf. Cicero, *Tusculanes,* I, 9, 18), but this is not at all the case in Greek. The Bible talks about a wise and intelligent heart (Ps 90:2; Prv 15:14). In the Qur'ān, people who "have a strong heart" (*'ūlū 'l-albāb* [أولو الألباب] are those who are intelligent enough to decipher the signs of creation and to see in them traces of the presence of Allah (III, 190).

The meaning of "the innermost core," which allows one to speak of the "heart of something," is discreetly present in the Bible, which mentions, for example, the "heart" of an oak tree (2 Sm 18:14); it develops in medieval Hebrew and takes on a laudatory meaning under the influence of the Arabic *lubb* [لبّ], which can refer to the pit of a fruit and also to what is most pure about a thing, its quintessence.

Rémi Brague

BIBLIOGRAPHY

Maimonides, Moses. *The Guide of the Perplexed.* Translated, with introduction and notes, by Shlomo Pines. Introductory essay by Leo Strauss. Chicago: University of Chicago Press, 1964.

LEX / JUS (LATIN)

ENGLISH	right, law
FRENCH	*loi, droit*
GERMAN	*Recht*
GREEK	*nomos* [νόμος]
ITALIAN	*diritto*
SPANISH	*derecho*

➤ LAW, TORAH, and CIVILTÀ, *DROIT* [THEMIS], DUTY, FAIR, MORALS, PIETAS, RELIGIO, RIGHT/JUST/GOOD, *RULE,* SOLLEN

The Greek *nomos* [νόμος], implying at the same time the notions of sharing, or division, of the law, of right, and of obligation (see THEMIS), has no corresponding term in modern languages. The exception is present-day Greek, in which two distinct lexical terms still designate the law and division (more precisely "law" and "department": cf. RT: Mirambel, *Petit dictionnaire français-grec,* and RT: Pernot, *Dictionnaire grec moderne–français*)—and in which the root of the word *nomos* is declined as a series of terms referring to the law (so we have *nomiki,* the science of law [cf. RT: Kyriakides, *Modern Greek-English Dictionary*]; *nomika,* the study of law [cf. RT: Mirambel, ibid.]; *nomikos,* a lawyer [cf. RT: Mirambel, ibid., and RT: Pernot, ibid.]; and *nomodidaskalos,* a law professor [cf. RT: Alexandre et al., *Dictionnaire français-grec*]). The Romans, aware of the correspondence between *lex* and *nomos,* emphasized the fact that the Latin word referred to a free choice and not to an imposed division. Thus *lex* prefigures *jus* in that it expresses a political will linked to Roman imperialism. As for *jus*, it acquires its full meaning in its interaction with *directum* (the straight path, the correct way)—which through its popular usage produced, among other terms, "right," *droit*, *diritto*, *derecho*, and *Recht* (considered unhesitatingly as translations of *jus*)—and with *rex*, the one who draws lines and angles and who thus determines what is inside and outside, allowing for the construction both of the architectural town and of the city as Republic: hence *rex*, the "sovereign," the "king." In the context of the Roman Empire's military and political victory in Greece, we can see why the Greek *nomos* succumbed to the Latin *norma* (square), a linguistic phenomenon indicating a true Roman "squaring off" of ancient civilization.

I. From *Nomos* to *Norma*

The Greek *nomos* [νόμος] does not explicitly designate the law but rather the "portion assigned" (*nemein* [νέμειν], "to distribute"; see THEMIS) to something or someone, particularly in terms of its species or genus. So men, unlike animals, are assigned *dikê* [δίκη], "justice," and not violence ("So listen to justice [*dikês*], forget violence [*biês* (βίης)] forever: this is the law that the Cronid assigned [*nomon dietaxe* (νόμον διέταξε)] for men"; Hesiod, *Works and Days*, 275–76).

There is no distinction between the *nomoi* that regulate the universe and the *nomoi* of the city: indeed, the normative process that makes a certain type of mammal into a political animal takes the form of a determining structure of authority in which man is domesticated by the home before being civilized by the city. It is a matter of being shaped by the laws (*nomoi*) of the home (*oikos*; see ECONOMY and OIKONOMIA). Submission to the "laws of the home" was for pre-Christian antiquity the first stage of managing living beings, whether human, animal, or vegetable. The *oikos* (the *domus* in Latin) *domesticates* living beings, with only humans able subsequently to undergo the selective process of insertion into the city (Baud, *Le droit*). On the essential function of the laws of the home, one only need recall that the confrontation between Creon and Antigone, the most famous passage in ancient literature on the opposition between divine laws and those of the city, concerns the laws of the home that are dominated by funerary worship, which is ultimately related to the law of Zeus (Sophocles, *Antigone*, lines 440–601).

Linguistically, there is no relation between *nomos*, *lex*, and *jus*. The contact between Greek and Latin is indeed somewhat perverse, since the transition occurs by way of instruments of measure. In fact, the Greek *gnômôn* [γνῶμων] (which refers specifically to a sundial and a ruler) is the source of the Latin *norma*, a square, a term no doubt borrowed, via the Etruscan language, from the accusative of *gnômôn* (see RT: Ernout and Meillet, *Dictionnaire étymologique de la langue latine*, s.v.). *Nomos* is what is attributed through an act of sharing or division and designates justice as first of all the justness of a measure. Measuring tools, designed to be used by a builder, are the true interface between justness and justice. What we find here in the Greco-Roman world is clearly expressed in the Bible: "You shall do no wrong in judgment, in measures of length or weight or quantity. You shall have just balances, just weights, a just *ephah*, and a just *hin*" (Lv 19:35–36; an *ephah* was "a dry measure having the capacity of about 3/5 of a bushel or about 22 liters," and a *hin* was "a liquid measure having the capacity of about 1 gallon or about 3.8 liters";

RT: *Holy Bible, New International Version*). Neither should we forget the weight and name for money (*nomisma* [νόμισμα] in Greek, from *nomos* precisely, a point that Aristotle underlines in the *Nicomachean Ethics*, 5.8.1133a. 30ff.). This is why the balance, or set of scales, has become firmly established as an allegorical figure for human justice. It should come as no surprise that in ancient Roman law a transfer of property required the ritual presence of a bronze ingot and a set of scales (one acquired property *per aes et libram*, "with bronze and balance") nor that, in light of the intermediary situation of the laws of the home, an obligation could be created simply by writing in the account book of the father of the family (known as *expensilatio*).

The emergence of the "urbanistic" laws of the *urbs* and the "civic" laws of the *civitas* is thus identified with the addition of a metaphorical meaning to instruments that were first used to apprehend the physical world scientifically, then to organize space, and finally to build houses and design towns. In the city of the Republic, *norma* became a virtual form thanks to which man could make law out of the matter constituted by the society of animals already domesticated by the laws of the home. As for the *forma*, also derived from the Greek *gnômôn*, this referred to the mold, and especially the small mold, the *formula*, which gave a legal form to human relations: in classical Roman law, one could not bring about an action because one possessed a right, but one could have one's right recognized because a lender had anticipated the small mold of the *formula* and had placed a legal claim relating to the dispute within it.

There was thus a logical chain, but one that went from Greek to Latin, linking *nomoi* to *normae*, the norms of a civilization that agreed on its laws, and also, more generally, on what was beautiful, good, and just—these norms establishing within the city, through various sanctions (critique, ridicule, reprobation, banishment, and finally passing legal sentence), a system that frames society using squares and formulas.

■ See Box 1.

The *norma* became a linguistic vampire. Although it referred solely to the normative world, that is, the world of human activity, it became in modern languages the happy rival of *nomos*. *Nomos* is, of course, present in terms such as "economy" and "autonomy," as well as in a few neologisms in scientific jargon, but "anomaly" still seems almost a grammatical error when opposed to the formidable army of terms like "norms," "normal," "normality," "normalization," and so on. The linguistic failure of *nomos*—which conceals its conceptual permanence—could be explained by the political domination of the Greek world by a Roman civilization founded on the preeminence of law and which was determined that the wisdom of law (*jurisprudentia*) should prevail over every school of Greek philosophy.

II. *Lex*

Although *jus* and *lex* were unrelated to Greek vocabulary, the proximity of *lex* to *nomos* was not difficult for the Romans to perceive, and this was what allowed them to claim *jus* as something truly their own. In other words, what we call law always expressed, at a time when the Roman Empire referred to itself as the West, a normative system that constituted the

1

Gnômôn, metron, kanôn

➤ TRUTH, Box 2

A large number of nouns are derived from *gignôsko* [γιγνώσκω], "to learn to know by dint of effort" and, in the aorist, "to recognize, discern, understand" (RT: Chantraine, *Dictionnaire étymologique de la langue grecque*), such as *gnôsis* [γνῶσις] (search, enquiry, knowledge, gnosis), *gnômê* [γνώμη] (intelligence, judgment, decision, intention, maxim; the composite term *suggnômê* [συγγνώμη] signifies forgiveness; see PARDON), and *gnôma* [γνῶμα] (a sign of recognition). One of these terms, *gnômôn* [γνώμων], as an adjective described someone who discerns, understands, and judges; as a noun, *gnômôn* refers to "that which regulates or rules." It had many technical uses, whether it was a question of people, experts, inspectors (*hoi gnômones* [οἱ γνώμονες] are the guardians of the sacred olive trees; Lysias, *Orations* 7), or, especially, things or instruments that measured time and space: the needle on a sundial and the dial itself (Plutarch, *Morals*, 1006e; Herodotus, *Histories*, 2.109), a clepsydra or water clock (Athenaeus, *Deipnosophistae*, 42b), the sharp edge of a forest (Apollodorus of Damascus, *Poliorcetics*, 149.4), and above all a carpenter's square, which the Pythagoreans used to explain through representation how numbers are generated (a square [*gnomon*], that, as Aristotle emphasizes in the *Categories*, "surrounding a square, magnifies it without altering it" [15a 30]). It was the tool par excellence of astronomy, of geometry (the *gnômôn* in Euclid is the complementary parallelogram of another parallelogram or of a triangle), of arithmetics (the *gnômôn* is the odd factor of an even number, as 3 is in relation to 6), and the tool in ancient mathematics of the co-constitution of arithmetic and geometry. We switch with this single word from the most intellectual to the most concrete (the *gnômônes* are also the teeth by which one determines the age of a horse or a donkey; Xenophon, *On Horsemanship*, 3.1), from the operations of the mind to the instruments by which it is inscribed in the world.

The same type of semantic extension is true of the canon and the measuring stick.

Metron [μέτρον], "measure," from the same family as *mêtis* [μῆτις] ("cunning": see MÊTIS), refers equally to a measuring instrument (the surveyor's stick [*Iliad*, 12.422]); the measures of wine and water [*Iliad*, 7.471]), the factor in a product (Nicomachus of Gerasa, *Introduction to Arithmetic*, 83–84), as well as to the quantity measured, space, or time (sea, youth), in particular a verse or meter (as distinct from *melos* [μέλος] and *rhuthmos* [ῥυθμός]; Plato, *Gorgias*, 502c, and *Laws*, 2.669d). Above all, as "measure" it means a just measure (after Hesiod, *Works and Days*, 694, it is linked to *kairos* [καιρός]; see MOMENT). Aristotle emphasizes, for example, that "there is a *metron* for the size of a city, as for everything else, animals, plants, organs" (*Politics*, 7.4.1326a, 35–37)—in this case the size being equal to the distance a voice will carry. *Metron* as a (just) measure and *metriotês* [μετριότης], "moderation," are thus linked to *meson* [μέσον] and to *mesotês* [μεσότης], the (exact) middle, which are used to define virtue (*arêtê* [ἀρητή]; see VIRTUE; cf. Aristotle, *Nicomachean Ethics*, 2.1106b 24–28). From metric system to just measure then, mathematics and morality, via poetry and music, are intrinsically linked. But a more telling testimony than anything else of the impact in ancient times of the *metron* and the art of measuring (*metrêtikê* [μετρητική]; Plato, *Protagoras*, 356–357) is the celebrated phrase of Protagoras about man as measure and his violent reinterpretations: "man is the measure of all things [*pantôn chrêmatôn metron estin anthrôpos* (πάντων χρημάτων μέτρον ἐστὶν ἄνθρωπος)], of those which are that they are, and of those that are not that they are not" (80 B1 DK = Sextus, *Adversus mathematicos*, 7.60; see RES, Box 1; cf. Cassin, *L'effet sophistique*, 228–31 and 261–63). For the Plato of the *Laws*, it is God who is the measure (4.716c), and for the Aristotle of the *Nicomachean Ethics*, it is the *spoudaios* [σπουδαῖος], the good man, who

is in himself *kanôn* [κάνων] and *metron* (5.11.1136a 32–33).

With *kanôn*, we move this time from matter to operation. The *kanôn* is the stem of a reed or the stalk of a rush (*kanna* [κάννα]) and refers to any long and straight bar made of wood (the bars or handle of a shield, the keel or the centerboard of a boat, the stick of a distaff, the beam of a set of scales, the key of a flute, the posts of a bed), particularly the ruler and line of woodworkers and carpenters (Euripides, *Trojans*, 6; Plato, *Philebus*, 56b), from which we get rules, models, principles (Euripides, *Hecuba*, 602: "we know evil, when we have learned good as *kanôn*"). Bailly (RT: *Dictionnaire grec-français*) explains that in music, *kanôn* refers to a kind of tuning fork; in history, to the different ages; in grammar, to the rules and the model of verb declensions and conjugations: in short, from the canon of Polycletus to the classical catalogue of alexandrines, by way of the logic (*to kanonikon* [τὸ κανονικόν]) of the Epicureans, a canon always provides the rule. The word was borrowed by administrative Latin to designate a tax, and by the language of the church to refer to a rule, or a canon (RT: Chantraine, *Dictionnaire étymologique de la langue grecque*).

This set of terms, which explains why "no-one may enter if he is not a geometrician"—the words engraved above Plato's Academy—attests to the close relationship in Greek between mathematics and morality. The Latin synergy between architecture and law constitutes one of the possible triumphs of this Greek relation.

Barbara Cassin

BIBLIOGRAPHY

Cassin, Barbara. *L'effet sophistique*. Paris: Gallimard, 1995.

Robin, Léon. *La pensée grecque et les origines de l'esprit scientifique*. Edited by P.-M. Schuhl and G. A. Rocca-Serra. Expanded ed. with complementary bibliography. Paris: Albin Michel, 1973. First published in 1923.

foundation of civilization. Since Romans had agreed to refer to the art of "being together" as "civility" (*civilitas*) (Duclos, *De la civilité*), including being together within their civil law, the French elaborated, one after the other in the sixteenth and seventeenth centuries, the terms *civiliser* (to civilize) and *civilisation* (civilization) in order to refer, respectively, to a procedural act and to a legal situation: the fact of entering, and then of being within, a civil law (Starobinski, "Le mot civilisation"; see also CIVILTÀ). The romance languages followed suit, and

English registers the first usages of "to civilize" in this sense in the last years of the sixteenth century.

A. Inscribing *lex*

The Greeks also respected "unwritten laws," those *agraphoi nomoi* [ἄγραφοι νόμοι] that came down directly from a divine being and that were consonant with natural law, like those unprescribed laws of the family that Antigone obeys in disobeying Creon, and that, unlike written laws, could not be usurped by any tyrant (Aristotle, *Rhetoric*, 1.1373b 4–15; cf. Hoffmann, "Le *nomos*, 'Tyran des hommes'") On the other hand, the Romans inscribed within the West the mystique of the founding text, even before it was reinforced by their own adherence to a "religion of the Book."

Although it originally referred to a religious law, *lex* retained only traces of this origin in a few rare phrases. Unlike *jus*, the *lex* of the Romans was essentially human, first of all because it required some human work to give it its lapidary form (in the broad sense of what is engraved in stone or bronze), and because later on the Romans conceived that it could be incarnated by one man, the emperor. Unlike custom (*mos*), which presupposed a tacit common understanding, *lex* was what had to be engraved and displayed in the town. *Legem figere* means "to engrave the law in bronze or stone and display it in the forum"; *legem delere, perrumpere, perfringere* is "to erase," "get rid of," or "break the law" (RT: Ernout and Meillet, *Dictionnaire étymologique de la langue latine*, s.v. *lex*). *Lex* thus functioned as a kind of hinge connecting the materiality of the town (*urbs*) to the immateriality of the city (*civitas*), thereby confirming the link between architecture and law suggested by *norma*.

The most important *lex* for the Romans was the Law of the Twelve Tables, a written record from the fifth century BCE of the customs of a primitive and superstitious rural society, yet which Cicero presented as containing more wisdom than all of the schools of Athens (Cicero, *On the Orator*, 44). The Romans did claim to respect a natural law that could be discovered by "correct reason" (Cicero, *On the Republic*, 3), but they never missed an opportunity to point out that nothing was closer to correct reason than Roman law. With the Law of the Twelve Tables, the Romans went from engraving in stone to writing "within the heart." Indeed, Romans in Cicero's time learned the Law of the Twelve Tables as a rhyme (Cicero, *On the Laws*, 2.4), despite the fact that it had become an archaic text whose meaning was only understood, and even then imperfectly, by a small minority of scholars. Even though in the second century CE writers were still defending its wisdom (Gellius, *Attic Nights*, 30.1), the most important thing for the Romans was that the Law of the Twelve Tables was inscribed within the materiality of the town as well as in the legal truth of the city.

Engraved on the walls of the town, then in the hearts of the Romans, the *lex* was finally marked upon the emperor's body. Drawing the consequences from the fact that the emperor of the late Roman Empire had become the cornerstone of Roman law, and reappropriating a phrase that the Hellenistic monarchies had popularized (*nomos empsuchos* [νόμος ἔμψυχος]), Justinian's compilation transmitted to the West the idea that the emperor (and, thereafter, the pope, the king, the state, etc.) was a "living law" (*lex animata*; Justinian, *Corpus juris civilis*, *Novellae* 105.2, §4), which medieval jurists completed by adding that he had "all the archives in his heart" (a recurring theme in the entire work of Pierre Legendre; see in particular *L'empire de la vérité*).

B. *Nomos* and *lex*

Cicero thematized the relationship between *nomos* and *lex*. Like all Romans, and like everyone in the ancient world, his admiration for Plato knew no bounds, but it was not so great as to temper the pride he felt when he contemplated a Roman culture based on law and that, sustaining as it did an empire which had conquered Greece, could claim that its science and wisdom in law, or *jurisprudentia*, was a match for Greek philosophy (Cicero, *On the Orator*, 1.34.195, and *On the Republic*, 1.22 and 2.15). This was why he wanted to draw a clear distinction between *nomos* and *lex*. For him, then, the Greek *nomos* was a process of distribution, whereas the Roman *lex* was a deliberate choice:

> And so they believe that law is intelligence, whose natural function it is to command right conduct and forbid wrongdoing. They think that this quality has derived its name in Greek from the idea of granting to every man his own [*Graeco . . . nomine nomon suum cuique tribuendo appelatam*], and in our language it has been named for the idea of choosing [*ego nostra a legendo*]. For as they have attributed the idea of fairness to the word law, so we have given it that of selection [*ut illi aequitatis sic nos delectus vim in lege ponimus*], though both ideas properly belong to law.

> (Cicero, *On the Laws*, in Santangelo, "Law and Divination," n. 15)

Through its laws, Rome asserted itself as master of its destiny, an imperial destiny, which declared as one of its duties that of giving laws, *leges datae*, to the nations its conquered. The victorious general, or the governor appointed to administer the conquered territory, would generally give an engraved, public law, and the nations making up the empire were progressively identified by a *lex*, either original or given. Rome was sovereign judge of all other laws. So Justinian declared in 553, in *Novella* 146 of *Corpus juris civilis* that the Jews indulged in "senseless interpretations" of the Bible. Since it could not be linked to the "correct reason" of natural law, the Torah placed Jews outside the law. This is where we can locate the origin of Western anti-Semitism (Legendre, *Les enfants du texte*).

This ancient trajectory of the word *lex*, which led to its inscription within the *body* of the emperor, while also inversely pointing to an ethnic identity, explains why, as it traversed the Middle Ages, it could on the one hand refer to any fragment of what the medieval university called the Body of Roman Law (Justinian's *Corpus juris civilis*), and on the other hand could refer during the Frankish period to that which distinguished one people from another (the *lex* of the Salic Franks—the *Lex Burgundionum*, or Burgundian Laws—not to mention the *lex* of the different Gallo-Roman groups . . . and thereafter written by the barbarian king, whose subjects they had become!).

III. *Jus*

Finally, why do we talk about "law" (*droit*) when we are dealing with what is "legal" (*juridique*)? This important lexical question resists attempts to obscure it.

A. Of a so-called *jus naturale*

A great deal has been written by lexicographers on the origins of *jus*, which is so intimately bound up with Roman cultures (RT: Ernout and Meillet, *Dictionnaire étymologique de la langue latine*, s.v. *jus*; RT: Benveniste, *Le vocabulaire des insitutions indo-européennes*, vol. 2, chap. 3: "*Jus* et serment à Rome"). The indisputable connection to an oath (*jusjurandum*) firmly designates a religious expression that has the force of a law and a sacred expression of commitment. The desacralization of *jus* occurred over a long period of time. This took the form initially of making within the law a separate public law (*jus publicum*) containing everything to do with "sacred things, the priesthood and the public offices" (Justinian, *Corpus juris civilis*, *Digest*, 1.1.1, §2: "Publicum jus in sacris, in sacerdotibus, in magistratibus consistit"), and then by the medieval elaboration of canon law, which restricted public law to anything to do with public offices (Chevrier, "Remarques"). In addition, and quite understandably, imbuing *jus* with a religious meaning gave to the word, which expressed the law, an important political force. Linking the founding of a town to the existence of a city that had become an empire, Roman legal advisors created an indissoluble bond between *jus* and the political existence of Rome. Historians and Roman jurists transcribed the Ciceronian theory, according to which *lex* was at the origin of *jus*, into a patriotic register—thereby confirming our critical attitude when confronted by the bravura passages of the philosopher lawyer—and they have always emphasized the fact that the Law of the Twelve Tables was the sole "source of law," the *fons juris* of Rome, and of this empire that made the West.

The transition in Latin from *nomos* to *norma* established as a first principle that law, unlike justice, but like architecture, was necessarily man-made. This is why it is imperative to understand what Romans meant when they, before anyone else, talked about "natural law."

According to the author of Justinian's *Institutes* (1.2), which was written in 533 to train future jurists of the empire, "natural law is that which she has taught all animals" (*jus naturale est, quod natura omnia animalia docuit*) and "a law not peculiar to the human race, but shared by all living creatures, whether denizens of the air, the dry land, or the sea" (*nam jus istud non humani generis proprium est, sed omnium animalium quae in coelo, quae in terra, quae in mari nascuntur; Institutes of Justinian*, trans. modified—Ed.). As for what this *jus naturale* consists of, he only makes allusion to the union of male and female, to procreation, and to the education of the young. One essential text proves that we are dealing here not with what we would call law, but with what the Greeks referred to as the *nomos* that we have in common with animals: Demosthenes's *Against Aristogiton* (*Orations*), in which he defined as a *nomos* of nature [τῆς φύσεως νόμος] the fact that humans love their parents just as much as animals do (25.65).

So the *jus naturale* that Justinian's *Institutes* discusses does not belong to the normative world in which what we call the law operates but rather to the sphere of the most elementary of human observations. For *jus naturale* to come into the sphere of law properly speaking, one would have to have granted animals the legal status of persons. It is true that the philosophers of pre-Socratic antiquity, especially within the Pythagorean school, reflected deeply on the way in which one could conceive of justice between humans and animals (see on this point the groundbreaking work of Fontenay, *Le silence des bêtes*), but law has never taken this into account. Noxal surrender, whereby an animal that had caused injury was handed over to the victim of that injury, was nothing other than the vestige of the archaic principle according to which any living body could be materially committed to another in a relationship of obligation. However, because they considered that humans were clearly distinct from other animals, Roman legal advisors agreed that the child of a slave should never be kept by a usufructuary, yet the latter was perfectly entitled, at the end of his contract, to return the cow or mare but to keep the calf or the colt (Terré, *L'enfant de l'esclave*).

Justinian's *Institutes* was a pedagogical work that moved from the general to the particular in order to arrive at the real object of the study: Roman civil law. This didactic operation starts out with the *nomos* common to men and animals, for which there is only the noun *jus*, since the ultimate objective is *jus civile*. So natural law (*jus naturale*) is retained, although to be more precise, it only appears in the introduction to the rubrics (bk. 1, title 2), announcing what are in a sense the real legal topics, which are then defined in the first paragraph with a gradation in their relevance: "[L]aw is divided into the law of the people (common to all men) and civil law (particular to a given city)" (*jus autem civile vel gentium ita dividitur*). As we can see, true law excludes the *nomos* of nature, translated as *jus naturale*, and only comprises two parts: the law of the people (comprising the most common contracts), and civil law, the real subject of the treatise, which can finally be achieved through the rhetorical operation of going from the general to the particular. Indeed, even though the *Institutes* concede that the laws of Solon and Dracon might have once been considered as the civil law of the Athenians, it goes without saying that, in the spirit of the work, the true civil law is that of the Romans. This is testimony to the often scornful condescension that Roman legal advisors showed, much as Cicero himself had done (*On the Orator*, 1.44.97), whenever they mentioned the law of other cities, but it is also a consequence of the fact that, since Caracalla's edict of 212, all those living within the empire had become Roman citizens.

"What we call law has nothing 'natural' about it," writes Pierre Legendre, "any more that it constitutes an 'objective' phenomenon whose universal character is self-evident" (*Sur la question dogmatique*). Neither in Greek literature nor in Roman law do we find anything that is truly natural law. Whether it is a question of the unwritten laws (*agraphoi nomoi*) of the Greeks or of the *jus naturale* of the Romans, what we see is nothing more than a natural order guaranteed by a deity. Antigone appealed to Zeus's law in opposing Creon, and the Christianized empire of Justinian's time attributed "natural laws" to divine Providence, using a plural that reinforced the allegiance to the unwritten laws of the Greeks: "naturalia quidem jura . . . divina quadam providentia constituta" (the laws of nature. . . are established by divine providence; Justinian, *Institutes*, 1.2, §11). So quite logically, therefore, in 1140, the *Decree of Gratian*, the founding text of the new discipline of canon law (*jus canonicum*), opens with the following definition of natural law: "Natural law is what is contained in the Law [the Law of Moses: the Old Testament] and the Gospels" (*Jus nature est, quod in Lege et in Evangelio continetur; Decree of Gratian*, 1 d.a.c. 1). And following this same logic, Thomas Aquinas made natural law the means by which men approached a divine law that was beyond their intellect (Strauss, *Natural Right and History*).

B. *Jus* and *directum*

So in antiquity and in the Middle Ages in the West, divine laws (*lois divines*) absorbed natural law (*droit*) because law, properly speaking, was considered to be man-made. It was a necessarily human product because it was made using a ruler and a square. This was why the Roman *jus*, which was in fact visibly present as the root of several words associated with the "juridical," gave way to *directum* (RT: Du Cange, *Glossarium mediæ et infimæ latinitatis*, vol. 3, s.v. *directum*), from which were formed most of the terms in the West that refer to the law: *diritto* (Ital.), *derecho* (Sp.), *diretto* (Port.), *droit* (Fr.), *Recht* (Ger.), *right* (Eng.), and so on. Light is shed on the mystery if we take into consideration that the *Digest*, this monumental work that Justinian's compilers devoted to legal doctrine, ends with a concluding title (50.17), the "Rules of Ancient Law" ("De regulis juris antiqui"), and if we understand that the king (*rex*) is what links *regula* to *directum*. *Gnômôn* and *norma* opened up and circumscribed the space of norms, within which the *rex* designated rules, and prepared the way for what we today call law (*droit*). Before being a king, the *rex* is first and foremost the one who draws straight lines (RT: Benveniste, *Le vocabulaire des insitutions indo-européennes*, vol. 2, s.v. *Rex*), the one who makes a *directum*, that is, a straight line, using a *regula* or a ruler, the tool enabling one to rule (*regere*), that is, to "direct in a straight line," and then to "be a director or a commander" (RT: Ernout and Meillet, *Dictionnaire étymologique de la langue latine*, entry *rego*). The *rex* Romulus ploughed the first straight furrow, from which the town (*urbs*) and the city (*civitas*, the place of civil law) were built.

By distinguishing what was sacred from what was profane (at Rome there was a sacred inner space, the *pomoerium*, that one could not enter armed) and also by distinguishing what was Roman territory from what was not, the *rex* defined as well the extendable site of civil law within which the West was formed.

Jean-Pierre Baud

BIBLIOGRAPHY

Baud, Jean-Pierre. *Le droit de vie et de mort: Archéologie de al bioéthique*. Paris: Aubier, 2001.
Caillemer, Exupère. "Nomoi." In *Dictionnaire des antiquités grecques et romaines*, edited by C. Daremberg and E. Saglio, vol. 4, fasc. 1. Paris: Hachette, 1908.
Chevrier, Georges. "Remarques sur l'introduction et les vicissitudes de la distinction du 'jus privatum' et du 'jus publicum; dans les œuvres des anciens juristes français." In *Archives de philosophie du droit*, 5–77. Paris: Sirey, 1952.
Cicero, Marcus Tullius. *"On the Commonwealth" and "On the Laws."* Edited by James E. G. Zetzel. Cambridge: Cambridge University Press, 1999.
———. *Orations*. Edited and translated by John T. Ramsey, G. Manuwald, and D. R. Shackleton Bailey. Loeb Classical Library. Cambridge, MA: Harvard University Press, 2010.
Demosthenes. *Orations*. Edited by A. T. Murray. Loeb Classical Library. Cambridge, MA: Harvard University Press, 1939.
Duclos, Denis. *De la civilité: Comment les sociétés apprivoisent la puissance*. Paris: La Découverte, 1993.
Fontenay, Élisabeth de. *Le silence des bêtes: La philosophie à l'épreuve de l'animalité*. Paris: Fayard, 1998.
Gellius, Aulus. *Attic Nights*. Translated by J. C. Rolfe. Vols. 1–3. Loeb Classical Library. Cambridge, MA: Harvard University Press, 1927.
———. *Les nuits attiques*, IV. Translated by Y. Julien. Paris. Les Belles Lettres, 1998.
Gratian. *Corpus juris cononici*. Vol. 1, *Decretum*, edited by E. Friedberg. Graz, Austria: Akademische Druk–u. Verlagsanstalt, 1959.
Hesiod. *Works and Days*. In *The Homeric Hymns and Homerica*, translated by Hugh G. Evelyn-White. Cambridge, MA: Harvard University Press, 1914.
Hoffmann, Geneviève. "Le *nomos*, 'Tyran des hommes.'" *Droit et Cultures* 20 (1990): 19–30.
Justinian I. *Corpus juris civilis*. Edited by T. Mommsen and P. Krueger. Berlin: Weidmann, 1886.
———. *The Institutes of Justinian*. Translated by J. B. Moyle. 5th ed. Oxford: Oxford University Press, 1913.
———. *Justinian's Institutes*. Translated and with an introduction by Peter Birks and Grant McLeod. Ithaca, NY: Cornell University Press, 1987.
Legendre, Pierre. *L'empire de la vérité: Introduction aux espaces dogmatiques industriels*. Paris: Fayard, 1983.
———. *Les enfants du texte: Étude sur la fonction parentale des états*. Paris: Fayard, 1999.
———. *Sur la question dogmatique en Occident: Aspects théoriques*. Paris: Fayard, 1999.
Santangelo, Federico. "Law and Divination in the Late Roman Republic." In *Law and Religion in the Roman Republic*, edited by Olga Tellegen-Couperus, 31–56. Leiden, Neth.: Brill, 2012.
Starobinski, Jean. "Le mot civilization." In *Le temps de la réflexion*, vol. 4. Paris: Gallimard, 1983.
Strauss, Leo. *Natural Right and History*. Chicago: University of Chicago Press, 1953.
Terré, François. *L'enfant de l'esclave: Génétique et droit*. Paris: Flammarion, 1987.
Xenophon. *The Economist*. In *The Shorter Socratic Writings: "Apology of Socrates to the Jury," "Oeconomicus," and "Symposium,"* translated and with interpretive essays by Robert C. Bartlett, with Thomas Pangle and Wayne Ambler. Ithaca, NY: Cornell University Press, 1996.

LIBERAL, LIBERALISM

➤ CIVIL RIGHTS, CIVIL SOCIETY, ECONOMY, LAW, *LIBERTY*, LIGHT, PEOPLE, POLITICS, *POWER*, STATE, WHIG

The English term "liberalism" evokes a political and cultural tradition that has no real French equivalent, which makes the word difficult not so much to translate as to use correctly. There have, of course, been French liberals, but when all is said and done, they have been fairly distant from the English model, and ended up abandoning what constitutes its core feature, namely the individual. With its origins in the Glorious Revolution and in the work of John Locke, liberalism in the sense of an affirmation of the priority of individual liberties, and their protection against the abuses of the sovereign or the collectivity, represents a national cultural tradition that spread across the rest of Europe, and has found its fullest expression in the American Constitution. But it is not easy to grasp its meaning outside of this context. It refers to a set of attitudes and convictions rather than a doctrine whose contours are well defined. This can lead to complete misunderstandings: thus, liberal designates a progressive or social-democratic attitude in the United States, but in France the word signals an opposition to the welfare state. It seems perhaps more satisfactory to draw a distinction between the acceptance and the refusal of a certain modernity: "liberalism" would then designate an acceptance of market capitalism, of individualism, of permissive morals, and a refusal of nationalism and of the all-powerful state. Given the ideological and emotional charge of this language, we should perhaps content ourselves with describing certain of its contemporary usages that translators need to be aware of, and between which they will have to choose. For the sake of convenience we will make a distinction between a liberal "philosophy"; the political positions that lay claim to this philosophy; economic liberalism; and finally, a rather vaguely defined social and cultural attitude particular to the Anglophone world and to northern Europe.

The word "liberal," identical in contemporary English and French, is derived from the Latin *liberalis*, which designates that which relates to a person who is free (in contrast to a slave), and his physical or moral qualities ("noble, gracious, honorable, beneficent, generous"), as exemplified by the "liberal arts": see especially ART, II, BILDUNG, CIVILTÀ, *CULTURE*. The entry ELEUTHERIA has a discussion of the different paradigms used to think and express liberty, including the one derived from the French *liberté* (as opposed to "freedom"), from the root **leudh* (to believe), which is a root common to the Greek *eleutheria* [ἐλευθερία], the Latin *liberi* (children), *liberty*, or *liberal*. On the network freedom-nobility-virtue, see BEAUTY, Box 1, VIRTÙ, Box 1; cf. *LIBERTY*.

Politically, the term "liberal," which originally referred to the virtue of liberality, has only come into usage fairly recently; what has been called liberal since the nineteenth century are those political movements that defend the legacy of the English and American revolutions, that is, limiting the powers of the state in the name of the rights of the individual. This limitation is by way of various institutional arrangements, such as representative government, and the separation of powers, and always presumes a clear distinction between the "state" and "civil society." Liberalism in this sense rejects any integral political control of the economy, but does not rule out a certain redistribution of income. The French term *libéral*, which does not refer to the same tradition, cannot, of course, be superimposed on the English term: see below, and WHIG; see also *CONSERVATIVE*, and cf. CIVIL SOCIETY, LAW, POLITICS.

I. The Origins of Liberalism

As a complex cultural and political reality, liberalism seems to have a certain consistency at an intellectual level. But the myth of liberalism's intellectual unity has been shattered, and we now talk instead of liberalisms. We can at least distinguish between two historical forms, the second of which is better known. The first liberalism was the "liberalism of diversity" (W. Galston, "Two Concepts of Liberalism"), a legacy of the Protestant Reformation and the War of Religions, which took the form, particularly in Locke, of an appeal for tolerance with respect to the diversity of religious beliefs. It was based on a fear of civil war, whence the expression "liberalism of fear" (J. Shklar, *Ordinary Vices*), rather than on the idea of tolerance as a positive ideal. The second liberalism, "the liberalism of autonomy," emerged out of the Enlightenment and out of Kant's work. He justified tolerance in terms of an appeal to universal reason, as a factor that could ultimately unify humankind. So it would be wrong simply to equate liberalism with the Enlightenment. Beyond these distinctions, however, we can identify several constant features within liberal philosophy as it was championed, in different ways, by Kant, Humboldt, Benjamin Constant, John

Stuart Mill, Tocqueville, and, more recently, Isaiah Berlin, Karl Popper, and John Rawls.

Its most characteristic feature is the priority of individual freedom. In opposition to the ancient ideal of direct or participatory democracy, as exemplified by the thought of Jean-Jacques Rousseau, liberalism would instead represent modernity, with the "freedom of the Moderns" or the protection of the private sphere of individuals against any abusive interference, and it would defend the sovereignty of the individual for reasons that were both epistemological and moral. The epistemic foundation of liberalism, inherited from Locke and then redefined by Mill and Kant, and later by Popper, can be located in the affirmation of an intrinsic relation between the values of truth and of individual freedom. The access to truth appeared to be essentially linked to the individual's freedom of judgment and of inquiry, and to the absence of barriers inhibiting dialogue and discovery. The origin of this idea is to be found in Greek philosophy, in the Socratic ideal of the free man, of which liberalism is the direct descendant (certainly in Mill, at any rate). Far from being a society like any other, the liberal world will claim to establish an essential link to truth and reason. Its moral basis lies in the conception, inherited from Kant, of the person and of his or her inalienable rights, a conception that leads an author like Rawls to place justice and rights at the heart of liberalism:

> Each member of society is thought have an inviolability founded on justice or, as some say, on natural right, which even the welfare of every one else cannot override. . . . Therefore, in a just society the basic liberties are taken for granted and the rights secured by justice are not subject to political bargaining or to the calculus of social interests.
>
> *(A Theory of Justice)*

This priority of freedom leads to the defense of the theory that the power of the state and of government should be limited through the existence of a "Bill of Rights"; by establishing "checks and balances," the best known of which is "judicial review"; by the separation of church and the state; and by the secularization of political power—even when there is an "established" religion in place, as in Great Britain.

■ See Box 1.

It is only in recent times that liberalism has moved closer to democratic ideals. Indeed, liberalism traditionally mistrusted democracies, and was suspicious of the "despotism" of majorities, a mistrust that was articulated eloquently by Tocqueville. Since popular and electoral forms of democracy had shown themselves to be powerless in the face of the rise of fascism and totalitarianism, they were rejected in the twentieth century by liberalism as carrying within them the seeds of tyranny and of antiliberalism, as conveyed by the debatable notion of "popular sovereignty." This gave rise to the conception of a liberal democracy, in which constitutionalism tempers the errant behavior of elected majorities. But the weak point of liberalism, in contrast to the Republican ideal, remains therefore its failure to leave room for political participation (the "liberty of the Ancients"). It can lead only to social atomism, since its individualism deprives it of any true doctrine of citizenship, or of political community.

1

Checks, balances, and institutional restraints in the Anglo-Saxon world

➤ *JUSTICE*

a. Checks and balances

To the classic doctrine of the simple separation of powers (Montesquieu), the British constitutional practice has, since the eighteenth century, added the idea of the balance and control of powers by each other. The term "check" (untranslatable into French) refers to the capacity of control and prevention leading to an equilibrium, or to "balances." In the American Constitution, this principle of checks and balances has given the president the power, among others, to block legislation and to nominate judges to the Supreme Court; the Senate can ratify treaties; and the House of Representatives can itself initiate the process of impeaching the president, etc.

b. Judicial review

"Judicial review" first appeared at the beginning of the nineteenth century, as a typically American constitutional conception, and it has come to be part of most contemporary democratic regimes. Whenever there is a conflict between the executive, legislative, and judiciary powers, or between the regions (or states) and the central (or federal) power, or even between the citizens and the state, there is a higher moral authority (the Supreme Court, the Constitutional Council, etc.), which has the power to decide and to judge whether laws (or actions of the state, etc.) comply or not with the Constitution.

c. Judicial activism / judicial restraint

This concerns a fundamental dilemma of any constitutional philosophy, which could be expressed as follows: when should one accept the verdict of an election, and when should one intervene and defend what one believes to be the "principles" of the Constitution? Divided between activism (for example, at the time of the New Deal, which judges had condemned as anticonstitutional) and the duty to restraint with respect to legitimately elected powers, or of laws voted in Congress, magistrates in constitutional courts cannot lay claim to objectivity, and consider themselves as simple interpreters of the Constitution and of the fundamental laws. It is in this sense that one should understand the question of the "power of judges."

II. Liberalism as a Political Reality: "Radicals," "Conservatives," and "Liberals"

It is important to note, at the outset, that the term "liberalism" has only a relational meaning, as a function of the existence or absence of other political or social movements, in particular long-standing worker movements, and communist or socialist parties, which were established in the nineteenth century. In the exemplary case of the United States, where the three political families (conservatism, liberalism, radicalism) are different from those in Europe, and can only really be defined through their relations to each other, liberalism clearly occupies more or less the ground of the political left as it is understood in Europe.

Conservatives or, more recently, neo-Conservatives, correspond roughly to the European right wing, but with nuances that have to do with particularities of American history. There is no place in the imaginative world of this history for the ancien régime: while religion, notably Protestantism, plays a central role, even though the Constitution has broken away from the idea on any established religion. So American conservatives very much favor security and tough penal politics ("law and order"); they distrust the welfare state, in the name of both individual property and individual responsibility; they are worried about the difficulties that the institution of the family is undergoing, or about the decline of churches, and some of them are even inclined to support the positions of the religious right on questions such as abortion, prayer in school, or the anti-Darwinian teaching of creationism.

Radicals, in contrast to liberals, would correspond to the European extreme left, but their lack of a Jacobin tradition, and especially of any Leninist ideology, means they are most often fervent democrats who are very attached to the "formal liberties" (to certain of these, at any rate) that most of the "leftist" tendencies of the Old World do not really value. There is, moreover, a specifically American genealogy of radicalism, which aims to revive the democratic elements of the national tradition by harking back to figures such as Thomas Paine (during the Revolutionary era), or even the abolitionist Garrison: on closer examination, it becomes apparent that this radicalism owes a great deal to the "liberal" and puritanical roots of American democracy—hence, the quite accurate characterization of the American Revolution, by the historian Gordon S. Wood (*The Radicalism of the American Revolution*), as a "radical" revolution. In this context, we could justifiably see "liberals" as representing a moderate left. The following are, or were, all liberals: supporters of Franklin D. Roosevelt's New Deal, lawyers who have defended the rights of women and of blacks, advocates of a security policy that is more preventive than punitive, or even all those who accepted the profound changes that have affected the American way of life since the 1960s.

It goes without saying that, as is also the case with the original French distinction between right and left, the relational nature of these definitions means that the respective positions of the "liberals," "conservatives," and "radicals" on any specific problem can vary. Thus, for example, a certain activism on the part of the Supreme Court justices, which came across as conservative during the time when it blocked reforms deemed to be progressive, belongs now, on the contrary, to the shared "liberal" culture of the present age, marked by the historic role played by Chief Justice Earl Warren and his immediate successors (the fight against racial segregation, making abortion a constitutional right, and so forth); and conversely, most conservatives today would say they are in favor of a certain "judicial restraint" (see Box 1.c). The fact that liberalism is also a philosophical movement whose definition is itself an important matter of debate can complicate things even further, since politically conservative movements can be led to present themselves as liberal (see A. Bloom's foreword to L. Strauss, *Liberalism, Ancient and Modern*). Moreover, one could legitimately think that the respective positions are always essentially situated within a broader context, which remains that of liberalism in the wider sense, which is to say, a politics inscribed within the constitutional framework of a representative government.

The situation is obviously quite different in Europe, and particularly in France, where liberalism is historically the movement that has, one might say, *consciously* pursued the development of a "modern regime" based on the defense of individual freedoms and rights, while resisting the democratic excesses of the "tyranny of public opinion" and, above all, of socialism. Although it has its origins in England, it also had a number of very eminent representatives in France (Montesquieu, Constant, Tocqueville) and even in Germany (Wilhelm von Humboldt). Its golden age was in the nineteenth century, and it has appeared to be on the wane since then, with the progress of socialism, the establishment of worker and trade union traditions, and the rise of the postwar welfare state, all of which has led European liberalism to be more closely aligned with the conservative right. Margaret Thatcher's new right in Great Britain appropriated the term "liberal" and gave it a new meaning in order to wage war on both the welfare state and the paternalism of traditional conservatives. She thus introduced so-called liberal deregulatory and monetarist economic policies, which did not prevent her from reinforcing and centralizing the state in a way that was totally opposed to the liberal conception of politics. Liberals everywhere came to occupy a rather vague middle ground, along with the more moderate tendencies of the Christian Democrats (liberal parties can act as bridge parties, as in Germany—or be prevented from doing so because of the electoral system, as in Great Britain). Within a broader context, the situation in France is rather unique,

since liberals there have been led more and more to efface the individual from their preoccupations, and to come round ultimately to republicanism and statism (L. Jaume, *L'individu effacé*). If French "radicals" could no doubt place themselves somewhere between their American homonyms and "liberals," a further "leftism" (*sinistrisme*), to borrow René Rémond's expression, pushed them more toward the right with the development of socialist, and then communist, political parties.

It is clear in any case that, until quite recently, one had to be very cautious about transferring the American categories of "conservatism," "radicalism," and "liberalism" to discussions of French politics. Conservatism was weakened because many of its themes were taken over by the far-right party Action Française: the most liberal republicans, in the European sense of the term "liberal," certainly formed an important trend during the Third Republic, but they had no successors within subsequent political movements (only a few politicians aligned themselves with their politics).

III. Liberalism and the Market

Would it clarify matters, then, to link liberalism to a conception of society in which the market and "civil society," in Hegel's sense, would be the true agents of social organization, thereby making the role of the state secondary? This approach is tempting, since if we make the role of the state definitive, we end up with a split between individualist liberals and interventionist and centralizing antiliberals, on both the left and the right, which would perhaps correspond better to present-day transformations in French democracy and society. The market has, indeed, been conceived by some authors, the most famous of whom is Friedrich von Hayek, as a political principle that limits power, and thus as the source of a greater freedom of choice for individuals. But this conception has led to further confusions, and for this reason in English the term "libertarianism" is preferred to "liberalism."

■ See Box 2.

On the other hand, for social-democratic liberals, best represented by the philosopher John Rawls—but the economist

---

2

Libertarianism

Libertarianism represents the position that goes furthest in defending the minimal state, advocating a principle of nonintervention and of nonredistribution for the most disadvantaged, based on a theory of alternative justice—one of entitlements or freely acquired property rights (Nozick, *Anarchy, State, and Utopia*), without a principle of justice (for instance, a principle that would affirmatively mandate equality of opportunity, or that would establish the principle that certain needs are basic, and their fulfillment

equally so) that would act as a corrective of this initial distribution. A position such as this is inspired by the idea of the self-regulation of economic and social change, illustrated by the metaphor of the "invisible hand" of Adam Smith. It leans upon Vilfredo Pareto's principle of "optimality," that is, the existence of points of equilibrium in the market, and argues that the market by itself provides the criteria of justice: a distribution is optimal or just when there is one single individual whose position would be worsened

if distribution were modified to compensate for the situation of the most disadvantaged. Freedom of exchange is thus sufficient to ensure its justice, with any intervention of the state being unjust because it limits individual freedoms.

BIBLIOGRAPHY

Nozick, Robert, *Anarchy, State, and Utopia*, New York: Basic Books, 1974.

Van Parius, Philippe, *Qu'est-ce qu'une société juste?* Paris: Seuil, 1991.

John Harsanyi would also be a good example—it should be possible to reconcile social justice and the respect for individual freedoms. The market cannot by itself be the source of a principle of justice or redistribution; in order to respect equal freedoms for all, such a principle needs to be the object of an agreement on the part of those who can hope to profit from it, as well as of those who would see their benefits diminish. Liberalism has no hesitation, then, in placing itself within the great tradition of the social contract in arguing that the principles of economic justice (Rawls' second principle) are just if they can be the object of unanimous consent (that is, of a contract), and can be shown to benefit the most disadvantaged. Far from being subject to the laws of the market, contemporary liberalism justifies its limits in the name of social justice:

> A social ideal in turn is connected with a conception of society, a vision of the way in which the aims and purposes of social cooperation are to be understood.

> (Rawls, *A Theory of Justice*)

What is common, however, to the different expressions of the vague concept of economic liberalism is, as Bernard Manin has clearly shown, the idea of an order that would not result from a central power, and that would even in a way come to take its place, in order to free individuals from oppression. If the market is well used, it would appear as a source of emancipation like other dimensions of civil society, whose field of action extends well beyond the satisfaction of economic needs.

■ See Box 3.

IV. A Liberal Culture?

The term "liberalism" ultimately describes a cultural tradition that emphasizes the autonomy of individuals, their spirit of enterprise, their capacity for self-government, without the need to refer to a central power, certainly at an economic level, but no less at a social level, in the tradition of eighteen-century civil society in the English sense. This liberal conception of civil society is not the same as the *bürgerliche Gesellschaft* execrated by Marx, but conforms more closely to the *zivile Gesellschaft*, that is, the "public forum" within which citizens of a democracy organize themselves, communicate, act together, cooperate, and develop their potential, without necessarily going through the structures of the state, or through a centralized bureaucracy. This is a culture for which the world of associations, far from being marginal, is at the heart of the full development of the individual, and of his or her peaceful relationships with others. This social dimension of liberalism is often overlooked by those who understand individual freedom solely in terms of its tension with an external authority, as the "freedom to say no." This misunderstanding corresponds to a religious division within Europe, and the question can be clarified if we consider liberalism in light of Protestant values, in the sense in which an individual, according to these values, is conceived of as morally responsible for his choices, and as having no other judge for his acts than his own conscience. Permissiveness and individualism in liberalism are inseparable from what one could appropriately call an interiorized "moral code based on principles," as opposed to a "moral code based on authority," whereby the law is always external, and overshadows the agent. Depending on whether one admires or detests this tradition, whether one condemns it as permissive and as the source of social fragmentation and anomie, or whether one thinks of it as providing new sources of happiness and fulfillment, the term "liberalism" will be used with pejorative or positive connotations, and it is set in opposition either to totalitarianism and state violence or to the republic and social democracy, or even to "libertarianism" and the dangers of the anarchic development of the postmodern individual, as the American or Canadian "communitarians" emphasize.

Catherine Audard
Philippe Raynaud

BIBLIOGRAPHY

Berlin, Isaiah. *Liberty*. Edited by Henry Hardy. With an essay on Berlin and his critics by Ian Harris. Oxford: Oxford University Press, 2002.

Constant, Benjamin. *Principes de politique*. In *De la liberté des Modernes*. Paris: Hachette, 1980. *Principes de politique* was first published in 1818.

Galston, William. "Two Concepts of Liberalism." *Ethics* 105 (April 1995).

3
Communitarianism

➤ *COMMUNITY*, GENDER

An important critical movement in the United States and Canada has emerged to challenge classical liberalism: it is known as "communitarianism," a term one could translate into French, though awkwardly, by the neologism *communautarisme*. This movement aims not to defend traditional communities per se, but to recognize the modern individual's need for rootedness and identity. Just as the abstract and universalist philosophy of the Enlightenment was rejected by Hegel and by the political romanticism of Herder and Schleiermacher in the name of the value of traditions, community, *Gemeinschaft*, and a sense of history, so the contemporary communitarian critique of liberalism emphasizes the importance of individuals being rooted in communities, and of the concrete diversity of cultures, as well as of gender differences (feminist critiques).

BIBLIOGRAPHY

Berten, André, ed. *Libéraux et communautariens*. Paris: Presses Universitaires de France, 1997.

Taylor, Charles. *Multiculturalism: Examining the Politics of Recognition*. Princeton, NJ: Princeton University Press, 1994.

Walzer, Michael. *Pluralisme et démocratie*. Paris: Esprit, 1997.

———. *Spheres of Justice: A Defense of Pluralism and Equality*. New York: Basic Books, 1984.

Gautier, Claude. *L'invention de la société civile*. Paris: Presses Universitaires de Francs, 1993.

Halévy, Élie. *La formation du radicalisme philosophique* [1901–4]. 3 vols. Paris: Presses Universitaires de France, 1995.

Hartz, Louis. *The Liberal Tradition in America*. New York: Harcourt Brace Jovanovich, 1983.

Harvey, David. *A Brief History of Neoliberalism*. Oxford: Oxford University Press, 2007.

Hayek, Friedrich A. von. *The Road to Serfdom*. Chicago: University of Chicago Press, 1944. Translation by G. Blumberg: *La route de la servitude*. Paris: Presses Universitaires de France, 1985.

Jaume, Lucien. *L'individu effacé ou le paradoxe du libéralisme français*. Paris: Fayard, 1997.

Manent, Pierre. *Histoire intellectuelle du libéralisme*. Paris: Calmann-Lévy, 1987.

———. *Les Libéraux*. Paris: Hachette Littératures, 1986.

Manin, Bernard. *Principes du gouvernement représentatif*. Paris: Calmann-Lévy, 1995.

Mill, John Stuart. *On Liberty*. Edited by David Bromwich and George Kateb. New Haven, CT: Yale University Press, 2001. First published in 1858.

Pareto, Vilfredo. *Manuel d'économie politique*. Translated into French by A. Bonnet. Paris: Giard et Brière, 1909.

Popper, Karl. *The Open Society and Its Enemies*. London: Routledge and Kegan Paul, 1966.

Rawls, John. *A Theory of Justice*. Rev. ed. Oxford: Oxford University Press, 1999.

Renaut, Alain. *L'ère de l'individu*. Paris: Gallimard, 1989.

Rosanvallon, Pierre., *Le libéralisme économique*. Paris: Seuil, 1989.

Shklar, Judith. *Ordinary Vices*. Cambridge, MA: Harvard University Press, 1984.

Smith, Adam. *An Enquiry into the Nature and Causes of the Wealth of Nations*. Edited by R. H. Campbell and A. S. Skinner, general editors. Indianapolis: Liberty Classics, 1981. First published in 1776.

Strauss, Leo. *Liberalism, Ancient and Modern*. New York: Cornell University Press, 1988.

Wood, Gordon S. *The Radicalism of the American Revolution*. New York: Knopf, 1992.

LIBERTY

I. Domains and Models

1. The polysemy of the word "liberty" is a source of considerable difficulty. The adjective "free" (Fr. *libre*) covers a spectrum of nuances: it can be a synonym for "spontaneous," "unconstrained," "uninhibited" (so a body, for example, can be in "free fall"; see FORCE), and also for "independent," "autonomous," even "autarchic"; it can have the more technical sense of "indeterminate" or "indifferent," and so one might talk of a free choice that makes no difference either way, or of free will. One finds just as many nuances in most modern languages.

2. The question of liberty is a determining one for the constitution of subjectivity, and subsequently for psychology, even down to the word "subject" itself (in which one hears "subjection"); see SUBJECT and WILL, WILLKÜR; cf. CONSCIOUSNESS, DRIVE, ES, I/ME/MYSELF, UNCONSCIOUS.

3. For the moral dimension of liberty, see PRAXIS; cf. *DESTINY, DUTY, MORALS, OBLIGATION*.

4. The sense of "liberty" informs the political and social domains from the outset, beginning with the difference between free individual and slave: see in particular LIBERAL and BILDUNG, Box 1; see also CIVIL SOCIETY, HERRSCHAFT, LAW, POLIS, POLITICS, *POWER*, WORK.

Refer to ELEUTHERIA, I and Box 1 for the different clusters of meaning within the main linguistic networks: nature and growth; or culture and belonging to a group of friends; see also SVOBODA, one of the ways of saying "freedom" in Russian, which is formed from the Slavic possessive *svoj* [СВОЙ], analogous to *suus*.

II. From Greek to Latin

The main focus here, however, will be on two problems of translation from Greek to Latin, which allow for a better understanding of a certain number of particularities within the networks of modern languages.

A. From the Greek *eleutheria* to the Latin *libertas*

1. How does one get from the regulated development that characterizes the Platonic *eleutheria* [ἐλευθερία] to *libertas*, conceived of as the freedom of the will, when the very notion of "will" has no direct equivalent in Greek? Two entries respond to this question: ELEUTHERIA, which discusses the translation of Greek meanings of "freedom" in the Latin of the Church Fathers and of Scholasticism; and WILL, which reconstructs the medieval history of the formation of a terminological equivalent to the Greek *thelêsis* [θέλησις]: *voluntas* as the freedom to agree to or to reject the content of a judgment, or to act rationally for the general good. The secularization of this notion of will leads to the modern, Cartesian notion that "[t]here is no one who does not feel and does not experience will and freedom as one and the same thing, or rather that there is no difference between what is voluntary and what is free" (Descartes, *Meditationes de prima philosophia*, "Réponses aux troisièmes objections," in *Œuvres* [AT], 7:191.I.10–14).

2. On the changes that the vocabulary of the will undergoes in contemporary Anglo-Saxon philosophy, refer to WILL, Box 1; cf. CONSCIOUSNESS and SOUL.

B. The translation of *to autoexousion* by *liberum arbitrium*

1. The Latin *liberum arbitrium* (free will) replaced the Greek notion of authority over oneself with that of an indifferent choice between opposites, and thus locates the entire concept of liberty in this indifference of choice. In other words, the two determinations of "freedom," which, for us moderns, seem to be self-evident are as follows: a) the near synonymy of "free" and "voluntary," which means that any form of freedom is fundamentally determined as freedom of (the) will; b) the fact that the proper locus of freedom is to be found in election, that is, in a choice between opposites, such that freedom itself can be understood as freedom of the will (cf. Thomas Aquinas: "The proper act of free will is choice. For we may say that we have a free will because we can take one thing while refusing another. And this is to choose." *Summa theologica*, I, quarto 83, article 3, reply).

2. In this respect, the translation of the question of free will in turn leads to several decisive choices. In German, the term *Willkür* links from the start the matter of the freedom of the will to the autonomy of the will: The discussion of the Kantian problematic, which is inherited by our terminology, can be found in the entry WILLKÜR.

In Russian, the semantic play between the two words for "freedom"—*svoboda* [свобода] and *volja* [воля]—offers a different coupling of the relationship between the infinite nature of the will and the affective naturalness of motives, while the term *postupok* [поступок] refers to a free act, insofar as it can take the form of a commitment: see POSTUPOK and SVOBODA.

➤ ACT, PEOPLE, RIGHT/JUST/GOOD

| LIE

The French word for "to lie," *mentir* (derived from the Latin *mentiri*; the etymologies do not tell us much, including those related to Anglo-Saxon, English "lie," German *Lüge*), means to say something false with the intention of deceiving. Lies thus refer to the articulation of the true and the real, the logical and the ontological, but they involve an ethical register. One can find under TRUTH (in particular TRUTH, IV; see also, for the Russian, ISTINA and PRAVDA) a discussion of the antonyms of truth, one of which is the lie. The main dividing line falls between languages and traditions that fail to distinguish between error and lie (the Greek *pseudos* [ψεῦδος] might be from the root *bhes-, "to breathe," like *psuchê* [ψυχή], "the soul," or *phêmi* [φημί], "to say"), and do not reflect the Latin, then Christian, differentiation between the two.

I. Logic and Ontology

Refer to *FALSE* for the articulation between these two registers.

II. Ethics

Lying is a discursive act (see SPEECH ACT; cf. *ACT*) that makes a willful use of something false. The problem of intention, good or bad, is central: are there "good lies"? Is there a "right to lie"? See INTENTION, WILLKÜR. Lies are in this sense connected to a will that is judged from the outset as condemnable (see *GOOD/EVIL*, MORALS, *VALUE*), unlike aesthetic illusion (which is not): see *FICTION*, and cf. *APPEARANCE* (particularly DESENGAÑO, LEGGIADRIA, MIMÊSIS).

A "lie" brings into play the belief of the listener: see *FAITH*, GLAUBE; cf. CLAIM.

The devil is the "liar" par excellence: see DEVIL.

| LIEU (FRENCH)

The Latin *locus*, which means not only "place, location, site" but also "rank, situation," translates the Greek *topos* [τόπος]. In French, the word for place, *lieu*, has come to be used in a range of technical senses, particularly medical ("sick region," "genitalia") and rhetorical (*lieu commun*, or commonplace).

1. In aesthetics, refer to IN SITU, which reappropriates an archeological term to mean the fundamental trait of a work of art conceived in terms of its site. On the ontological relationship between a work of art and its place, see in particular LIGHT, Box 2, and cf. *IL Y A*.
2. On the rhetorical *topos*, see COMMONPLACE; cf. ANALOGY, COMPARISON, *IMAGE*, MIMÊSIS, TROPE, and more broadly, *DISCOURSE*, LOGOS, SPEECH ACT.

3. On place in relation to space and physics, see FORCE, MOMENT, NATURE, *TIME, WORLD*.
4. On place conceived of as an originary place of one's own, see HEIMAT, *IL Y A*, OIKEIÔSIS, PROPERTY, and SEHNSUCHT, Box 1, cf. *MALAISE*; see also DASEIN, LEIB, WELTANSCHAUUNG (*WORLD, 5, 6*); cf. PEOPLE/RACE/NATION and PRINCIPLE.

➤ SEIN

| LIFE / LEBEN

The French *vie* (life), deriving from the Latin *vita*, serves to designate existence, the type of life (a creature's ways of living and means of existence), the life story, biography, or model for living.

1. In the German ERLEBEN, as distinguished from *Leben*, one finds a reflection on how to separate out natural life—the Greek *zôê* [ζωή], see ANIMAL—from the reflective life that enables human experience and existence—the Greek *bios* [βίος], in the sense of mode or "species of life," and *aiôn* [αἰών], "the span of life." In addition, see AIÔN, DASEIN, ERLEBEN, *EXPERIENCE*, LEIB, cf. OLAM.
2. For the relation to death, as tied to human consciousness, see also CONSCIOUSNESS, *DESTINY, MALAISE*.
3. On the relationship between the mode of life and the means of existence, see BERUF, ECONOMY, ENTREPRENEUR, OIKONOMIA, *WISDOM*.
4. On the relation of "life" (*vie*) to narrative, to models, and to history, see HISTORY, *RÉCIT*, VIRTÙ; cf. SPECIES.

➤ GESCHLECHT, GOD, *HUMANITY*, PATHOS

| LIGHT / ENLIGHTENMENT

DANISH	*lys*
DUTCH	*licht*
FRENCH	*lumière, Lumières*
GERMAN	*Licht*; Old High German, *lio(t)ht; Aufklärung*
GREEK	*leukos* [λευκός], *phôs* [φῶς]
HEBREW	*haśĕkālâ* [הַשְׂכָּלָה]
ITALIAN	*luce, Lumi/illuminismo*
LATIN	*lux, lumen*
RUSSIAN	*svet* [свет]
SPANISH	*luz, Luces/Ilustración*

➤ BILDUNG, DOXA, ERSCHEINUNG, *IDEA*, ITALIAN, MADNESS, MIR, *REASON*, SVET

The Indo-European vocabulary for "light" refers to what is brilliant or resplendent, based on the idea of a free, clear space in the open air as opposed to a wooded and enclosed space.

Closely related to sight, a bodily sense granted privilege in the Western tradition, "light" serves as a paradigm for knowledge and reason. The term's use to describe the European movement known as the Enlightenment derives from Novalis, who employed it having in mind the new status of light in modern physics.

I. The Indo-European Vocabulary of Light

The set of terms expressing "light" in the modern European languages comes from the Indo-European root *leuk-, which gives us the Greek *leukos* [λευκός], "a luminous, brilliant white," and the Latin *lucere*, "to shine"; *lustrare*, "to illustrate"; and *luna*, "moon." The Indo-European vocabulary of light shows a remarkable proximity between the Greek, Romance, and Germanic families, even if the Greek only happens to be represented by *leukos* and its derivations (but see also Box 1).

■ See Box 1.

The adjective *leukos* [λευκός], like all those that in ancient Greek have to do with the vocabulary of color, refers less to whiteness itself than to its intensity, its brilliance. It describes marble, and "when the notion of brilliance is used it indeed seems to be related to *hêlios* [ἥλιος], [sun] [(*Iliad*, 14.185) and in the expression λευκὴ φωνή = λαμπρὰ φωνή [*leukê phônê = lampra phônê*], 'ringing voice' in Aristotle (*Topics*, 106a)" (RT: *Dictionnaire étymologique de la langue grecque*). We might compare this to *argos* [ἀργός] (from which the Latin *argentum* is derived), which is also used to describe the sheen of white (clay, the white of the eyes), expressed in this case as a rapid flash (lightning, horses, Ulysses's dog) and from which the Greek name "Argonauts" is formed (cf. RT: *Dictionnaire étymologique de la langue grecque*, s.v. *argos*).

In Latin, *lumen, -inis* (neut.; from *leuk-s-men > *louksmen > *lousmen > lumen) differs from *lux, lucis* (fem.) in that it must have originally referred to a means of lighting, a "light," with the concrete sense that the suffix *-men* gave to the formation. *Lux*, write Ernout and Meillet (RT: *Dictionnaire étymologique de la langue latine*), is light "considered as an activity, an active and divine force, particularly as the 'light of day' . . . . [L]ux is a more general term than *lumen*, and their uses do not overlap."

Under *leukos*, Chantraine (RT: *Dictionnaire étymologique de la langue grecque*) makes a connection to the Latin *lucus*, originally a "clearing," literally *laûkas*, "field" (Old High German *loh*, "clearing"). Ernout and Meillet (RT: *Dictionnaire étymologique de la langue latine*) note under *lucus*, with reference to the *lux* group (cf. also the possible but contested etymology of the French word *lucerne*, "skylight"; RT: *Dictionnaire étymologique du français*), that "[t]his Indo-European word designated a free and clear space, as opposed to a wooded one—woods and covers being the main obstacles to man's activity." These connections between the bright space of a clearing and the clarity of light are not self-evident. The English "light" (Lat. *lux*) is more strictly distinguished from its homonym "light" (Lat. *levis*), which is related to the German *leicht, lichten, Lichtung*, than in Continental cognates. Heidegger's thought can help us to think of lightness as a condition of light.

■ See Box 2.

1

Phôs, phainô, phêmi (light, showing [oneself/itself], speaking): An ultra-phenomenological Greece

➤ ERSCHEINUNG, *PHÉNOMÈNE*, PROPOSITION

Even though the term "phenomenology," as Heidegger remarks, does not appear historically until the eighteenth century (in Johann-Heinrich Lambert's *Neues Organon* of 1764), it belongs to the Greek epoch. *Phainomenon* [φαινόμενον], the middle participle of *phainô* [φαίνω], "what appears, by itself, from itself," and *logos*, "to say." In paragraph 7 of *Being and Time*, Heidegger recalls that *phainô* comes from *phôs* [φῶς], "light." But in truth, there is an even tighter etymological knot to be tied here. Chantraine (RT: *Dictionnaire étymologique de la langue grecque*) notes that *phainô* is formed from the Sanskrit root *bha*, which is semantically ambivalent, since it means both "to enlighten," "to shine" (*phainoi, phamí*), and "to explain," "to speak" (*phêmi* [φημί], *fari* in Latin); in other words, "saying" and "shining" are already mutually interdependent; there is already a phenomenology in the phenomenon itself.

Finally, *phôs* [φῶς], the same word as "light" aside from the accent (acute instead of perispomenon), also refers to a man, a hero, a mortal and was a common term in Homer's time. Its etymology is "obscure," Chantraine tells us (RT: *Dictionnaire étymologique de la langue grecque*). Yet, "if the dental inflection is secondary, there is a formal identity between the Greek nominative and the Sanskrit *bhas*, light, brilliance, majesty." "But," he adds, "from the semantic point of view, the connection is not so easy to make." Phenomenologically, it is, however, too good to be true: etymological evidence that joins together in the same dazzling term "light," "phenomena," and "man." Greek man is then the one who sees, as a mortal, the light (that of the day of his birth, of the return, of death), what appears in the light, phenomena, and the person who enlightens them by expressing them. The play on words between *allotrion phôs* [ἀλλότριον φῶς], now a perispomenon, from fragment 14 of the poem by Parmenides ("light from elsewhere," that is, the light that the moon has by borrowing it from the sun), and *allotrion phôs* [ἀλλότριον φῶς], with an oxytone accent, "the man from elsewhere," "the stranger" of the Homeric poems (for example, *Iliad*, 5.214, or *Odyssey*, 16.102, 18. 219), and its fate in Empedocles (fr. 45; RT: DK), are sufficient to confirm that the etymology, whether Cratylean or not, was understood. The two words resonate within each other, as they do in Homer's *Parmenides*, the epic poem on cosmology and philosophy.

We have here the common matrix of perception in Greece, both classical and romantic, and the theme that interested Heidegger so keenly: truth—if it is a mutual interdependence of appearing and of saying in human *Dasein*, both openness and finitude—seems to be a copy of, and a meditation on, this etymology.

Barbara Cassin

BIBLIOGRAPHY

Heidegger, Martin. *Sein und Zeit*. 13th ed. Tübingen: Niemeyer, 1976. Translation by John Macquarrie and Edward Robinson: *Being and Time*. New York: Harper & Row, 1962.

Parmenides. *The Fragments of Parmenides: A Critical Text with Introduction, Translation, the Ancient Testimonia and a Commentary*. Edited by A.H. Coxon, Assen: Van Gorcum, 1986.

———. *Parménide: Sur la nature ou sur l'étant: La langue de l'être*. Edited, translated, and commentary by Barbara Cassin. Paris: Éditions du Seuil, 1998.

2

Lichtung, "clearing," "bright space," "lightness"

Contrary to appearances, the German *Lichtung* does not come from *Licht*, "light," but from *leicht* (cf. Eng. "light"), which is from the verb *lichten*, "to lighten," "clear," "free." So the *Lichtung* in question in section 28 of *Being and Time* ("To say that it is 'illuminated' [*erleuchtet*] means that as Being-in-the-world it is cleared [*gelichtet*] in itself") in no way places *Dasein* within a "photological" tradition, nor does it take up again the Platonic metaphor of light. Returning in 1965 to these questions, in the text that would appear in 1984 as *Zur Frage nach der Bestimmung der Sache des Denkens*, Heidegger states:

The presence of what-is-present has as such no relation to light in the sense of brightness. But presence is referred to light [*das Lichte*] in the sense of the clearing [*Lichtung*].

What this word gives us to think about may be made clear by an example, assuming that we consider it sufficiently. A forest clearing is what it is, not because of brightness and light, which can shine within it during the day. At night, too, the clearing remains. The clearing means: At this place, the forest is passable.

The lightening [*Das Lichte*] in the sense of brightness and the lightening of the clearing [*Lichtung*] are different not only regarding the matter, but regarding the word as well. To lighten [*Lichten*] means: to render free, to free up [*freigeben*], to let free. To lighten belongs to light [*leicht*]. To render something light [*Leichtmachen*], to lighten something means: to clear away obstacles to it, to bring it into the unobstructed, into the free [*ins Freie*]. To raise [*lichten*] the anchor says as much: to free it from the encompassing ocean floor and lift it into the free of water and air.

Or again, in a seminar held jointly with Eugen Fink in 1966–67:

Haben Lichtung und Licht überhaupt etwas miteinander zu tun? Offenbar nicht. . . . Die Lichtung dürfen wir nicht vom Licht her, sondern müssen sie aus dem Griechischen heraus verstehen. Licht und Feuer können erst ihren Ort finden in der Lichtung.

(Do clearing and light have anything to do with one another? Evidently not. . . . We must not understand clearing from light, but we must understand it from the Greek. Light and fire can only find their place first in a clearing.)

("Seminar in Le Thor," *Gesamtausgabe*)

It is therefore a matter of going back from light to its nonvisual condition of possibility, which no longer has anything to do with the opposition of light and dark but precedes it as its a priori, as a "lightness of being" (as A. Schild's translation into French of Heidegger's expression in *Zur Frage nach der Bestimmung* has it: "légèreté de l'être"). The French translation of *Lichtung* as *allégie* (F. Fédier's translation), unlike *Lichtung*'s translations into French as *clairière* (clearing) or *éclaircie* (bright space) or into Spanish as *claridad* and *claro*, frees the term from the register of light, in accordance with Heidegger's indications.

BIBLIOGRAPHY

Fédier, François. *Regarder voir*. Paris: Les Belles Lettres, 1995.

Heidegger, Martin. *Zur Frage nach der Bestimmung der Sache des Denkens*. Edited by Hermann Heidegger. St. Gallen, Switz.: Erker, 1984. Translation by Richard Capobianco and Marie Göbel: "On the Question concerning the Determination of the Matter for Thinking." *Epoché: A Journal for the History of Philosophy* 14 (Spring 2010): 213–23. Translation by A. Schild: *L'affaire de la pensée*. Mauvezin, Fr.: Trans-Europe-Repress, 1990.

Heidegger, Martin, and Eugen Fink. *Heraklit: Seminar Wintersemester 1966/1967*. In *Gesamtausgabe*, vol. 15. Frankfurt: Klostermann, 1986. Translation by Charles H. Seibert: *Heraclitus Seminar, 1966/67*. Tuscaloosa: University of Alabama Press, 1979.

Sallis, John. "Into the Clearing." In *Heidegger: The Man and the Thinker*, edited by Thomas Sheehan. Chicago: Precedent, 1981.

Sallis, John, and Kenneth Maly, eds. *Heraclitean Fragments: A Companion Volume to the Heidegger/Fink Seminar on Heraclitus*. Tuscaloosa: University of Alabama Press, 1980.

II. Light, Sight, and Idea

In the vocabulary of Western thought, light enjoys an equally privileged position as the one that sight occupies among the five senses, to the point where sight serves as a common denominator of the other senses, as Saint Augustine noted:

Ad oculos enim videre proprie pertinet. Utimur autem hoc verbo etiam in ceteris sensibus, cum eos ad cognoscendum intendimus. Neque enim dicimus: audi quid rutilet, aut: olefac quam niteat, aut: gusta quam splendat, aut: palpa quam fulgeat: uideri enim dicuntur haec omnia. Dicimus autem non solum: uide quid luceat, quod soli oculi sentire possunt, sed etiam: uide quid sonet, uide quid oleat, uide quid sapiat, uide quam durum sit.

(Vision belongs properly to the eyes. But we use this term even for the other senses when we apply them to knowing. Yes, we do not say: "Listen to how this shines," nor: "Feel how this glows," nor: "Taste how resplendent this is," nor "Touch how bright this is." It is "see" that we use, indeed, in all these cases. Not only do we say: "See how this shines"—and the eyes alone can perceive this—but also: "See how this sounds, see how this feels, see how tasty this, see how hard it is.")

(*Confessions*, 10.35, 54)

What is expressed here is the primacy of sight, illustrated and reinforced by a common means of expression; we might even say a "photological" tradition. The brightness of the sun, called *leukos* [λευκός] by Homer (see above), will become, in the famous allegory of the cave in Plato (*Symposium*, 7), the analog of light received from the Idea of the Good, as opposed to the darkness, which reigns in the cave.

The light of the sun will remain in Descartes's programmatic text the paradigm for knowledge:

. . . cum scientiae omnes nihil aliud sint quam humana sapientia, quae semper une et eadem manet, quantumvis differentibus subjectis applicata, nec mejorem ab illis distinctionem mutuatur, quam Solis lumen a rerum, quas illustrat, varietate . . .

(. . . just as all sciences are nothing other than human wisdom, which always remains one and identical to itself, however different the subjects to which it is applied may be, and it receives no more diversity than the *light of the sun* from the variety of things its *illuminates . . .*)

(*Regulae ad directionem ingenii*, 1; my italics)

(On the sources of the "metaphor of a radiant sun to signify the universality of an omniscient understanding," cf. Jean-Luc Marion, in *Règles utiles et claires*: "Should we conclude that the 'solar' relationship of understanding to its truths is transposed, with Descartes, from the divine to the human?") It is not accidental that Descartes mentions the *naturali rationis lumen* (natural light of reason) at the end of the same Rule 1: a decisive shift occurs, in fact, from external light to the light of the human mind, as *lumen naturale = ratio*. This is the "light of reason" (Descartes), "the daylight of reason" (Boileau, *Art poétique*, 1.19), "the natural light of reason" (Leibniz, *Théodicée*, §120)—which is alone capable of lighting "someone who walks alone in the dark" (Descartes, *Discours de la méthode*). "Tremble in case the light of reason does not come," Voltaire will say in the following century (RT: *Dictionnaire philosophique*, "Abbé").

III. The *Aufklärung*/"Enlightenment"

A. The emergence of a *terminus technicus*

Combined with the advent of modern rationalism, the determination of reason as *lumen naturale* would lead to the characterization of the eighteenth century as the "age of Enlightenment" (Sp. *El siglo de las luces* and *Ilustración*; Ital. *Lumi/Illuminismo*; Fr. *Lumières*; but Ger. *Aufklärung*, from the adj. *klar*; Lat. *clarus*; Eng. *clear*). The expression *es klart auf* (*aufklaren*, with no vocalic alternation) is used first of all to describe the weather brightening up, the sky clearing, through a borrowing of the German from Dutch sailors (cf. RT: *Duden: Das Herkunftswörterbuch*). This was the origin of the transitive verb *aufklären*, in the sense of the English "to enlighten" (an *Aufklärer* is not only someone with an enlightened mind or a philosopher of the Enlightenment, but also someone who "lights the way" in the military sense of reconnaissance), and leads to the formation in the eighteenth century of the term *Aufklärung* as a philosophical concept, *terminus technicus*. In 1784, Moses Mendelssohn still felt the term was a neologism. This is how he puts it in his essay "Ueber di Frage: Was heißt aufklären?":

Die Worte *Aufklärung, Kultur, Bildung* sind in unsrer Sprache noch neue Ankömmlinge. Sie gehören vor der Hand bloß sur Büchersprache. Der gemeine Haufe versteht sie kaum. (3)

(The words "enlightenment," "culture," "education" are still newcomers to our language. At the present time they belong merely to the language of books. The common masses scarcely understand them.)

The term *Aufklärung*, however, still retains a close semantic, even lexical, relation to "light," as shown by the definition Wieland gives of it ("Sechs Fragen zur Aufklärung"):

Was ist *Aufklärung*?

Antwort: Das weiß jedermann, der vermittelst eines Paars sehender Augen erkennen gelernt hat, worin der Unterschied zwischen Hell und Dunkel, Licht und Finsternis besteht.

(What is *Aufklärung*?

Answer: this is what everyone knows who, *having eyes to see*, has learned by using them to recognize the difference between the bright and the dim, between *light* and darkness.)

(my italics)

Or again, in this statement by Lichtenberg:

Man spricht viel von Aufklärung und wünscht mehr Licht. Mein Gott, was hilft aber alles Licht, wenn die Leute entweder keine Augen haben, oder die, die sie haben, vorsätzlich verschließen.

(One talks a lot about *Aufklärung*, and one wishes for more light, but my God, what is the use of all the light you can wish for, if people either have no eyes to see, or if they do, close them on purpose.)

(Lichtenberg, *Sudelbücher*, 1:201)

It is proper for the light of reason to cast itself everywhere and thus to reject prejudices and superstitions in respect of which the *Aufklärung* claims to be a liberation (Kant, *Was ist Aufklärung?* 1783). The light of enlightened reason against the darkness of obscurantism—indeed, in German, the counterconcept of *Aufklärung* is *Schwärmerei*, a tricky word designating excessive, sometimes infantile, perhaps misguided enthusiasm or adulation.

- See Box 3.

B. Critique of the Enlightenment and the reductive conception of light in modern physics

Novalis, who was the author of *Apologie der Schwärmerei* (1788) and who thus of his contemporaries set himself apart from the *Aufklärer*, made a highly original link between the French, then German, movement of the Enlightenment and the new status of light being defined by modern physics as a mathematical science of nature. He thereby anticipated the critiques that Merleau-Ponty, in his *Eye and Mind* (chap. 3), would subsequently direct at Descartes's *Dioptrics*:

Das Licht war wegen seines mathematischen Gehorsams und seiner Frechheit ihr Liebling geworden. Sie freuten sich, daß es sich eher zerbrechen ließ, als daß es mit Farben gespielt hätte, *und so benannten sie nach ihm ihr großes Geschäft, Aufklärung.*

(Light had become their favorite theme because of its obedience to mathematics, and because of its insolence. They rejoiced at seeing that it is refracted rather than being iridescent [playing with its colors], *and it is from this that they gave the name Aufklärung to their great affair.*)

("Die Christenheit oder Europa," 1799)

Descartes indeed stated in Discourse 1 of his *Dioptrics* (6:85, ll. 1–4) that "in the bodies we name colored, colors are nothing but the different ways in which these bodies receive it [light] and send it back to our eyes."

3

Haśēkālâ [הַשְׂכָּלָה]

Haśēkālâ, [הַשְׂכָּלָה] sometimes retranscribed as *Haskālā*, comes from *śēkel* [שֵׂכֶל], "reason," "intellect," "discernment," "culture." Formed from a Hebrew root, this term is not strictly speaking a Hebrew translation of the German term *Aufklärung* nor of the English "Enlightenment," even if it refers to a movement closely associated with the Enlightenment. "Even though it is inspired by Enlightenment philosophy, its roots, its particular character, and its development, are entirely Jewish" (RT: *Dictionnaire du judaïsme*). The name "Age of Enlightenment" would in Hebrew be almost blasphemous, if only because of verses 3–5 of *bĕrēʾšît* (Genesis), where it falls not to man but to God to say of (and to) the light (*ʾôr* [אוֹר] "light," "sun," "morning," "brightness") that it be—Septuagint: [Γ ενηθήτω φῶς]; the Vulgate: "Fiat lux"; Luther (RT: *Die Bibel nach der Übersetzung Martin Luthers*): "Es werde Licht"; RT: *The Bible: Authorized King James Version*: "Let there be light"; Le Maistre de Sacy: "Que la lumière soit faite." The term "Haskalah," which is foreign to biblical Hebrew, first appeared in Germany in the 1760s and referred to a social and cultural movement in Judaism in Central and Eastern Europe that grew from the middle of the eighteenth century through the nineteenth. It expressed a more open attitude among Jews regarding their values and the way of life of their non-Jewish neighbors; the desire to emerge from the ghetto; and

the rejection of what we might today call a withdrawal into ethnic identity. In place of these, Haskalah favored an emancipation, even assimilation, that opposed both orthodox Judaism and Hasidism. Its emblematic figure was Moses Mendelssohn (1729–86), the author—notably—of a German translation of the Torah, yet one that was printed in Hebrew characters.

It was out of the Haskalah movement in Germany that a *Wissenschaft des Judentums*, or "science of Judaism," was born and was according to Steinschneider able to develop alongside an agnostic, even atheistic, position. Steinschneider, as Gershom Scholem asserts, "did not hide the fact that in his eyes the function of the science of Judaism consisted in burying the phenomenon with dignity." (Scholem had planned to write an article, which would in fact never appear, to be titled "Sebstmord des Judentums in der sogenannten Wissenschaft des Judentums" [The suicide of Judaism in what has been called the science of Judaism].) We should no doubt take into account, in this uncompromising judgment, Scholem's own position on what came to be known as the *Deutschjudentum*, a Judeo-German symbiosis, of which Hermann Cohen would become the most celebrated representative. How, though, was the sometimes frenzied anti-Judaism of the Enlightenment, sadly exemplified by Voltaire, compatible with a knowledge of

Judaism and with a recognition of the status (social, political, and legal) of European Jews? This was one of the inherent tensions of the Haskalah—at the same time, it was a dissemination of Jewish culture, even if it was in a vernacular language other than Hebrew or Yiddish, and the sowing of the seeds of an ideology that would come to deny it, embalming it if necessary and placing it outside the realm of the properly scientific. How could a "religion of reason," or a "religion considered within the limits of pure reason" (Kant), acknowledge the attested Revelation of Judaism, which we commonly refer to as Judeo-Christian? Cohen would attempt heroically to overcome this contradiction in his *Religion der Vernunft aus der Quellen des Judentums* (*Religion of Reason: Out of the Sources of Judaism*).

BIBLIOGRAPHY

Cohen, Hermann. *Religion der Vernunft aus den Quellen des Judentums*. Edited by Bruno Strauss. Wiesbaden: Fourier, 1988. Translation and introduction by Simon Kaplan: *Religion of Reason: Out of the Sources of Judaism*. Introductory essay by Leo Strauss. New York: Ungar, 1972.

Scholem, Gershom Gerhard. *Von Berlin nach Jerusalem: Jugenderinnerungen*. Frankfurt: Jüdischer Verlag, 1994. Translation by Harry Zohn: *From Berlin to Jerusalem: Memories of My Youth*. New York: Schocken, 1980.

Elsewhere (in a letter to Mersenne from December 1638, *Correspondance*, 2:469, ll. 1–2), Descartes would define light as a propulsion (*poussement*): "it is only this propulsion in a straight line which is called *Light*." So Novalis constructed a genealogy of the project of the *Aufklärung*, the Enlightenment, as well as of the name claimed for it, with reference to the history of the sciences, that is, by connecting this project to the new way in which modern physics was approaching the phenomenon of light. In French, the Enlightenment (*Les Lumières*) was also sometimes called *la lumière* (RT: *Dictionnaire de la langue française*, s.v. "lumière," meaning 13), as is attested by this statement from Voltaire (letter to Gallitzin, 14 August 1767, *Correspondance*), which is a counter-illustration to the genealogy proposed by Novalis: "It pleases me to see that an immense republic of cultivated minds is being formed in Europe: *light is communicating from all sides* [*la lumière se communique de tous côtés*]" (my italics).

So in the eyes of Novalis, it was on the basis of a simplistic (and reductive) conception of light, an optical narrowing particular to modern physics, that the word and the idea of the Enlightenment were able to germinate and flourish. Going against the grain of the very project of modern science as a mathematical science of nature, Novalis remained

here a witness to a Platonic, even Neoplatonic, or Plotinian understanding of light. He was not alone: Goethe exclaims, in a reply to Schopenhauer, "What are you saying! Light only exists when you see it? No! It is rather you who would not be there if light itself didn't see you" (*Gespräche*, 2:245).

Indeed, according to Plotinus, "What the soul must see is the light by which it is illuminated. For neither is the sun seen in another's light. How is this achieved? Take everything away" (*Ennead*, 5.3, 17, 28). "What we must see is what enables us to see; it is light which is the source of our gaze" (Hadot, *Plotin*), and not only its object. This is what is "solar" (*sonnenhaft*) about the eye, as Goethe will say at the beginning of a celebrated quatrain:

Wäre nicht das Auge sonnenhaft,
Wie könnten wir das Licht erblicken?

(If the eye were not sun-like,
How could we perceive light?)

(*Zur Farbenlehre*; translation modified)

One of the other repercussions of this shift from external, solar light to the "enlightenment" of the human mind would be a singular reevaluation of the light that is not produced by the human mind, or by reason: Swedenborg, Saint-Martin, and the *illuminism* movement would still use light as a frame of reference but in a completely different way.

Pascal David

BIBLIOGRAPHY

Augustine, Saint. *Confessions*. Translated by Henry Chadwick. Oxford: Oxford University Press, 1991.

Boileau, Nicolas. *L'art poétique*. Edited by Sylvain Menant. Paris: Flammarion, 1998.

Descartes, René. *Correspondance*. Vol. 2 of *Œuvres de Descartes*, edited by Charles Adam and Paul Tannery. Paris: Vrin, 1973.

———. *Dioptrics*. In *Discours de la méthode et essais*, vol. 6 of *Œuvres de Descartes*, edited by Charles Adam and Paul Tannery. Paris: Vrin, 1973. Translation by Paul J. Olscamp: *Optics*. In *Discourse on Method, Optics, Geometry, and Meteorology*, edited by Paul J. Olscamp. Indianapolis: Hackett, 2001.

———. *Discours de la méthode*. In *Discours de la méthode et essais*, vol. 6 of *Œuvres de Descartes*, edited by Charles Adam and Paul Tannery. Paris: Vrin, 1973. Translation by Desmond M. Clarke: *Discourse on Method and Related Writings*. London: Penguin, 2003. See also translation by Elizabeth S. Haldane and G.R.T. Ross: *Discourse on Method and Meditations on First Philosophy*, edited by David Weissman. New Haven, CT: Yale University Press, 1996.

———. *Regulae ad directionem ingenii / Rules for the Direction of the Natural Intelligence*. Edited and translated by George Heffernan. Amsterdam: Rodopi, 1998. Translation by Jean-Luc Marion: *Règles utiles et claires pour la direction de l'esprit en la recherche de la vérité*. The Hague: Nijhoff, 1977.

Eckermann, Johann Peter. *Gespräche mit Goethe in den letzten Jahren seines Lebens*. Edited by Otto Schönberger. Stuttgart: Reclam, 1994. Translation by John Oxenford: *Conversations of Goethe with Johann Peter Eckermann*, edited by J. K. Moorhead. Introduction by Havelock Ellis. New York: Da Capo Press, 1998.

Goethe, Johann W. von, and Johann Peter Eckermann. *Gespräche mit Goethe in den letzten Jahren seines Lebens: 1823–1832*. Vol. 2. Leipzig, 1836.

———. *Zur Farbenlehre*. 2 vols. Tübingen: J. G. Cottäschen, 1810. Translation by Charles Lock Eastlake: *Theory of Colours*. Cambridge, MA: MIT Press, 1982.

Hadot, Pierre. *Plotin ou la simplicité du regard*. Paris: Plon, 1963. Translation by Michael Chase: *Plotinus; or, The Simplicity of Vision*. Introduction by Arnold I. Davidson. Chicago: University of Chicago Press, 1993.

Leibniz, Gottfried Wilhelm von. *Théodicée*. In *Œuvres de Leibniz*, series 2, edited by M. A. Jacques. Paris: Charpentier, 1842.

Lichtenberg, Georg Christoph. *Sudelbücher*. In *Sudelbücher I*, vol. 1 of *Schriften und Briefe*, edited by Wolfgang Promies. Munich: Hanser, 1967.

Mendelssohn, Moses. "Ueber die Frage: Was heißt aufklären?" In *Was ist Aufklärung? Thesen und Definitionen*, edited by Ehrhard Bahr. Stuttgart: Reclam, 1974. Translation by Daniel O. Dahlstrom: "On the Question: What Does 'to Enlighten' Mean?" In *Moses Mendelssohn: Philosophical Writings*, edited by Daniel O. Dahlstrom. Cambridge: Cambridge University Press, 1997.

Merleau-Ponty, Maurice. *L'œil et l'esprit*. Paris: Gallimard / La Pléiade, 1964. Translation by Carleton Dallery: *Eye and Mind. The Primacy of Perception and Other Essays on Phenomenological Psychology, the Philosophy of Art, History and Politics*, edited by James M. Edie, 159–90. Evanston, IL: Northwestern University Press, 1964.

Novalis [Friedrich von Hardenberg]. "Die Christenheit oder Europa." In Vol. 3 of *Schriften*, edited by Paul Kluckhohn, Richard Samuel, Hans-Joachim Mähl, and Gerhard Schulz, 507–25. Stuttgart: Kohlhammer, 1967. Translation by John Dalton: *Christianity, or, Europe*. London: Chapman, 1844.

Schmidt, James, ed. *What Is Enlightenment? Eighteenth-Century Answers and Twentieth-Century Questions*. Berkeley: University of California Press, 1996.

Voltaire. *Correspondance*. Edited by Theodore Besterman. 13 vols. Paris: Gallimard / La Pléiade, 1977–87.

———. *Select Letters of Voltaire*. Translated and edited by Theodore Besterman. New York: Nelson, 1963.

———. *Voltaire in his Letters, Being a Selection of His Correspondence*. Translated by S. G. Tallentyre. Honolulu: University Press of the Pacific, 2004.

Wieland, Christoph. "Sechs Fragen zur Aufklärung." In *Was ist Aufklärung? Thesen und Definitionen*, edited by Ehrhard Bahr. Stuttgart: Reclam, 1974.

LOGOS [λόγος] (GREEK)

ENGLISH	discourse, language, speech, rationality, reason, reasoning, intelligence, foundation, principle, proportion, count, account, recount, thesis, tell, tale, tally, argument, explanation, statement, proposition, phrase, definition
FRENCH	*discours, langage, langue, parole, rationalité, raison, intelligence, fondement, principe, motif, proportion, calcul, rapport, relation, récit, thèse, raisonnement, argument, explication, énoncé, proposition, phrase, définition, compte/conte*
GERMAN	*Zahl, Erzählung*, cf. *legen/liegen/lesen*
HEBREW	*dāvār* [דָּבָר]
LATIN	*ratio/oratio, verbum*

➤ *DISCOURSE, REASON* and GREEK, HOMONYM, LANGUAGE, MADNESS, PREDICATION, PROPOSITION, RES, SENSE, SIGNIFIER/SIGNIFIED, SPEECH ACT, WORD

The Greek word *logos* [λόγος] has such a wide range of meanings and so many different usages that it is difficult to see it from the perspective of another language except as multivocal, and in any case it is impossible to translate it except by using a multiplicity of distinct words. This polysemy, sometimes analyzed as homonymy by grammarians, has usually been considered by modern commentators as a characteristic of Greek language and thought that relates, before all of the technical meanings, to the primordial meaning of the verb *legein* [λέγειν]: "to assemble," "to gather," "to choose." What is untranslatable here, paradigmatically, is the unity beneath the idea of "gathering together," a series of concepts and operations—mathematical, rational, discursive, linguistic—that, starting with Latin, are expressed by words that bear no relationship to one another.

One authoritative way of indicating this lost unity is to see it as inscribed within a play on words that incorporates this relationship etymologically, or even simply at the level of signifiers, as in the Latin *ratio/oratio* (the first comes from *reor*, which, like one part of *legein*, means "to count" then "to think"; the second, which according to a popular etymology is derived from *os, oris*, the "mouth," complements the first with the meaning of "speech"). In French the play is on *compte/conte*, which are both derived from *computare* but were certainly not distinguished from one another until the seventeenth century; in English there is an analogous play on "count"/"account"/"recount" and also on "tell"/"tale"/"tally"; in German, on *Zahl/Erzählung* and also on *legen/liegen/lesen*.

The other way one could proceed, which is not an alternative, is to import the word into one's own language: this culminates in the Heideggerian usage, which bears witness to philosophy's debt to Greek. Finally, to get the full measure of the polysemy of *logos* in the course of the word's history, we have to trace the connection between the first branching into *ratio/oratio* (or "reason"/"speech") and the *Logos* in John's Gospel, translated as *Verbum*, which refers back to the Hebrew *dāvār* [דָּבָר], and which means both the word and the thing, in this case, Christ as the word made man.

I. The History of the Language and Lexicography

The multiplicity of meanings of *logos* [λόγος] poses for the language historian the question of knowing whether we are dealing with a phenomenon of polysemy properly speaking (the proliferation of meanings that begins with a single etymological root) or of homonymy (a formal convergence that is produced from several homophonic etymological roots). As always in such cases, the question generates different answers depending on whether one looks at it from a synchronic perspective (how did the language users experience things?) or a diachronic perspective (what do we learn from an etymological investigation?).

■ See Box 1.

The unanimous view of modern etymologists is that what can appear from a synchronic point of view as a more or less accidental semantic convergence between homophonic roots (homonymy) must on the contrary be described as the effect of a diachronic differentiation in the original meaning of a single root λε/ογ-, thus as a phenomenon of polysemy. Where *logos* is concerned, a philological analysis of the occurrences in ancient Greek of the terms, both noun and verb forms, that are based on this root and comparison with the Latin leads us indeed to think that the fundamental sense of λε/ογ- is that of "collecting," "gathering," and "assembling" and that the use of the Greek verb *legô* [λέγω]—Latin, *lego*—in specific contexts is, for each of the languages, the source of differentiations that a priori are unforeseeable but that are in fact very real.

In Latin, it seems plausible that a syntagma like *legere oculis* (to take in with a glance) as applied to the graphic signs of a text or the names of a list gives us the origin of the meaning of "to read," which *lego* acquired in this language

---

1

Compound words and derivations: One or two roots?

In addition to the word λόγος itself, ancient Greek has more than two hundred compound nouns with -λογος/-λόγος as the second element. The sheer number, as well as the open-ended proliferation of this lexical group, suggest that the group itself is a good, if indirect, way of approaching an analysis of the term.

From a semantic point of view, this set of terms can easily be divided into two groups:

- In the first, -λογος refers to the notions of "gathering together," so we have σύλλογος: "gathering," "meeting," assembly"; and λιθολόγος: "stonemason" (who puts stones together).
- In the second, -λογος refers to the notion of "word," "speech," so we have διάλογος: "conversation," "dialogue"; and μυθολόγος: "storyteller."

In both cases, -λογος is clearly related to the verbal root λεγ-, which is able to convey the two meanings identified in the compound nouns: so σύλλογος} is related to συλλέγειν, "to gather," and διάλογος is related to διαλέγεσθαι, "to have a dialogue." Faced with this lexical range, a speaker of Greek might feel that his language had two homophonic roots of the form λε/ογ-, one meaning "to gather"—hereafter referred to as λε/ογ-1; and the other, "to speak," "to say"—hereafter referred to as λε/ογ-2.

Morphologically, the compound words with the ending -λογος can be separated, according to the general rules of Greek, into two conceptual categories:

a. those ending in -λογος, in which the unaccented λ can be interpreted as an *action noun*, for example, διάλογος, "conversation," "dialogue" (λε/ογ -2); σύλλογος, "act of putting together," "the result of

this act" (λε/ογ-1); φιλόλογος, this word having a "possessive" sense: "someone who cherishes the λ," "a lover of literature, a philologist" (λε/ογ-2); and

b. those ending in -λόγος, in which the accented λ can be interpreted as an *agent noun*, with the compound *X*-λόγος meaning "(someone) who λέγει *X*"; for example, μυθολόγος, "(someone) who tells stories" (λε/ογ-2); and λιθολόγος, "(someone) who puts stones together" (λε/ογ-1).

So it is the accent that allows us to determine that the "philologist" is a lover of language rather than someone who talks about love.

As we can see, the two types (a) and (b) allow for the two meanings identified of the root λε/ογ-. Moreover, all of those compound terms that are used to designate an agent—all of group (b) in theory, and several of the representatives of group (a)—in turn quite naturally provide the basis of a verb derivation ending in -εῖν (-εῖσθαι) and of an abstract noun derivation ending in -ία, designating the activity of the agent; for example:

- φιλόλογος → φιλολογεῖν, "to devote oneself to the study of literature" and φιλολογία, "the study of literature, philology"
- μυθολόγος → μυθολογεῖν, "to tell stories" and μυθολογία, "(*the act of telling stories)," whence "imaginary story"
- λιθολόγος → λιθολογεῖν, "to build by putting stones together" and λιθολογία, "the activity of a stone-mason"

The uniformity of the derivations produced in this series, which culminates in a

relatively technical vocabulary often designating activities relating to professions of one kind or another, undoubtedly helps to give a semantic unity to this range of terms containing the root λε/ογ- and in which the initial opposition we envisaged between λε/ογ-1 and λε/ογ-2 is blurred. Alongside the series of terms—such as, on the one hand, κακολόγος (a malicious gossip [person]), κακολογεῖν (to speak ill of someone), κακολογία (malicious gossip [noun]) and ἀντίλογος (someone who contradicts), ἀντιλογεῖν (to contradict), ἀντιλογία (contradiction) (λε/ογ-2); and on the other hand, ποιολόγος (a haymaker), ποιολογεῖν (to make hay), ποιολογία (haymaking), βοτανηλόγος (a botanist), βοτανηλογεῖν (to collect plants), βοτανηλογία (plant collecting) (λε/ογ-1)—where the two semantic fields are quite distinct, it is likely that for the linguistic sensibility of Greek speakers of different periods, the semantic values associated with -λογεῖν/-λογία fluctuated more or less whenever the designated activity linked the notion of "collecting," "assembling," "recording" (λε/ογ-1) with the notion of "a discourse on . . . ," "a theory of . . . " (λε/ογ-2). This was manifestly, and tendentiously, the case for "scientific" activities, in which a learned person with specialist knowledge would give a more or less theorized *discourse* on the objects or facts he had *collected*. Could we not say that the occupation of the ἀστρολόγος, someone who tells us about the stars, is also to record them for us? Or that the ἐτυμολόγος, who shows us through a kind of second-level discourse the ways in which words "say the truth," is not also a collector of *etymons*, and potentially, a compiler of ἐτυμολογικά (lists of etymologies)? And that the γενεαλόγος has to record previous generations before telling me my own ancestry?

without, however, losing its original meaning. This polysemy was retained all the way through to the Romance languages, in which—to give the example of French—*lire* (read), *relire* (reread), *élire* (elect), *dialecte* (dialect), and *collecte* (collect) sit happily alongside one another. In Greek, the Homeric uses of *legô*—*ostea legômen* [ὀστέα λέγωμεν], "let us gather up the bones" (*Iliad*, 23.239); *duôdeka lexato kourous* [δυώδεκα λέξατο κούρους], "he chose/assembled/counted twelve young men" (*Iliad*, 21.27); *leg' oneidea* [λέγ' ὀνείδεα], "reeled off / uttered curses" (*Iliad*, 2.222); and *su de moi lege theskela erga* [σὺ δέ μοι λέγε θέσκελα ἔργα], "gather together for me/enumerate for me / recount to me / tell me your marvelous exploits" (*Odyssey*, 11.374)—allows us to see clearly how the already frequent use of this verb in Homer (meaning "to assemble") and complemented by terms referring to linguistic entities (curses) or lending themselves to linguistic form ("accomplished exploits" → "things recounted") could have led to its more specific designation as a spoken *word*: "gather together" → "put into a row" → "count (out)" / "enumerate" → "(re)count" → "say." The compound Homeric verb *katalegein* [καταλέγειν] (and later on its nominal derivations *katalogos* [κατάλογος], then *katalogê* [καταλογή], "record," "register," "list," "catalogue") illustrates particularly well the flexibility and the contextual conditions in which the initial semantic value of the root λε/ογ- is modulated. An epic expression such as ἀλλ' ἄγε μοι τόδε εἰπὲ καὶ ἀτρεκέως κατάλεξον, "come now, tell me this, record / enumerate / recount calmly" (*Iliad*, 24.380 and 656; *Odyssey*, 1.169, etc.) is certainly a precious example of these "linguistic" contexts that, beginning with the prehistory of the Homeric text, have oriented the semantic evolution of the root λε/ογ.

These historical data, now well established, enable us to consider from a more accurate perspective the somewhat flexible and ultimately uncertain polysemy manifest in the Greek words belonging to the semantic family of *logos*. One point is worth emphasizing. The Greek *logos* retains, from the basic meaning "to gather" of the root λε/ογ- and as an almost indelible connotation, the semantic feature of being syntagmatic. Of all the well-known semantic variations of *logos*—"conversation," "speech," "tale," "discourse," "proverb," "language," "counting," "proportion," "consideration," "explanation," "reasoning," "reason," "proposition," "sentence" (see Box 3)—there is barely a single one that does not contain the original sense of "putting together": the constitution or consideration of a series, of a notionally complex set. As "counting" or "proportion," *logos* is never an isolated "number"; as "tale," "discourse," "proverb," "proposition," or "sentence," it is never (or only ever marginally) a "word," and so on. One only has to consider the relative semantic poverty of another root related to "saying," *Fεπ- (cf. *epos* [ἔπος], *eipein* [εἰπεῖν]), which is closely related to λεγ- in the auxiliary inflection of the verb *legô*, to understand how much the extraordinary richness of λε/ογ- owes to this "syntagmatic" dimension of its semantic field. Even if, as we know, etymology does not control indefinitely and absolutely the meaning that words can take on in the course of their history, it is important to keep in mind that the Greek *logos* is connected to a polysemic etymon in which the sememes "to gather" and "to say" are closely related. This has to be the starting point of any reflection on the history of *logos* as a philosophical term.

- See Box 2.

2

How do dictionaries translate *logos*?

Dictionaries, whether etymological or not, distinguish between two verbs: *legô* and **legô*, *étendre* (RT: Bailly, *Dictionnaire grec français*), "lay" (RT: LSJ) [by contrast, see Box 6]. The LSJ then gives for the first a single entry, divided into three main meanings: 1. "pick up," 2. "count, tell," and 3. (with the future and aorist 2) "say, speak."

The Bailly dictionary, basing its definitions on the distribution of usual moods and tenses, lemmatizes two verbs formed from the same root **leg-*, *rassembler* (to gather): the first means 1. "to gather," 2. "to pick," from which we get "to collect," "to sort out," "to count," and only later, "to enumerate," "to say one after the other"; the second straightaway means: 1. "to say," in the sense of "to speak," "to declare," "to announce," 2. "to say something," "to speak reasonably," 3. "to designate," and 4. "to signify"—before giving a number of more technical meanings ("to praise," "to recite," "to read out loud," "to organize," "to speak like an orator," "to move

a vote," etc., until 11. "to have someone say"). This series of dissonant meanings, entirely motivated by English dictionaries' desire for simplicity, is a symptom of the modern difficulty of discursively binding together a rational trajectory with a wide range of verbal statements. In French, the adjective *discursif* denotes both a rigorously ordered series, as well as a digression (RT: *Le nouveau petit Robert*), while *discursivité* is only first attested in 1966 in Michel Foucault's *Les mots et les choses* (RT: *DHLF*, vol. 1).

As for the noun *logos*, Bailly makes a distinction between two broad semantic fields, which become increasingly complex: A. *parole* (speech); B. *raison* (reason). The RT: LSJ, on the other hand, juxtaposes a series of entries: 1. "computation, reckoning"; 2. "relation, correspondence, proportion"; 3. "explanation"; 4. "inward debate of the soul"; 5. "continuous statement, narrative"; 6. "verbal expression or utterance"; 7. "a particular utterance, saying"; 8. "thing spoken of, subject matter." It is

noticeable that there is a transition from the mathematical (1–2), to the rational (recounting to the other and to oneself, 3–4), and then the linguistic (statement, utterance, or reference). In one case we start with speech and arrive, via reason, with its capacity to judge and evaluate, at the mathematical sense of "relation, proportion, analogy" (B.III.4 of Bailly, 4th and final sense in RT: Bonitz, *Index aristotelicus*); in the other, it is the mathematical that provides the starting point (RT: LSJ). The essential dissonance could thus be expressed as a double question: as the history of the language suggests (see above), was the mathematical sense primary, with relationality and proportionality serving as a paradigm, even a matrix, of a syntagmatic structure in general, in a line that ran from Pythagoras to Plato and then Neoplatonism? Or rather, from a structural perspective that is no doubt more Aristotelian (Bailly, Bonitz), is mathematical technique simply one application of the human *logos*?

II. The Polysemy of *Logos* Thematized and Used by the Greeks Themselves

The history of Greek philosophy can be described as a series of reinterpretations of the meaning of *logos* against a background of a still-active polysemy. What we find is a shift from one doctrine or systematics to another through a strategy of refocusing. From the pre-Socratics and the Sophists to Plato, from Plato to Aristotle, from Aristotle to the Stoics, and so on, the polysemy of *logos* is reorganized each time around a different matrix of meaning. We offer here merely a few examples.

A. From the power of speech (*logos*) to the correctness of the statement (*logos*)

From the Sophists to Plato, the sense of "speech" is very clearly devalued in favor of that of "rational statement." In his *Gorgias*, subtitled *On Rhetoric*, Plato shifts *logos* away from the field of discursiveness, which he assigns to rhetoric, and toward that of the rationality and correctness of statements, which he reserves for philosophy.

The Sophist Gorgias, in the *Encomium of Helen*, a famous speech that had the effect of absolving her before the whole of Athens of any blame for the Trojan war, defined *logos* as "a great sovereign [*dunastês megas* (δυνάστης μέγας)] who, with the smallest and most inapparent of bodies, accomplished the most divine acts [*theiotata erga apotelei* (θειότατα ἔργα ἀποτελεῖ)]" (82B11 DK, §8). The power of *logos*-as-speech (*discours*), which is greater than that of force, is thus linked to its performative effectiveness. More than simply saying what is, in accordance with the movement of revealing and of representational adequacy proper to ontology, *logos*-as-speech enacts what it says, and in particular produces the *polis* (see POLIS), the city, as a continuous discursive exchange and creation of consensus, which characterizes that political animal endowed with *logos* that is man (see *epideixis* in SPEECH ACT, I).

Socrates, in dialogue with Gorgias, begins with an apparently banal definition of rhetoric as the "art of speaking" (*technê peri logous* [τέχνη περὶ λόγους]; 450c). However, when he examines rhetoric more closely, he refuses to call it an art, describing it instead as *alogon pragma* [ἄλογον πρᾶγμα] (465a), an expression that we are compelled to translate, following Alfred Croiset (in his 1974 translation into French of *Gorgias* and *Meno*), as a practice or a thing "devoid of reason": that *logoi*-as-speech can redeem or recall the *alogon*-as-irrational is the mark of the Platonic operation that devalues and excludes from philosophy one meaning of *logos* in favor of another. Within this shift from one sense of *logos* to another a war is waged between philosophy and rhetoric, which constitutes one of the key points of access to the Greek world: "The most immoderate presumption of being able to do anything, as rhetors and stylists, runs through all antiquity in a way that is incomprehensible to us" (Nietzsche, "The History of Greek Eloquence").

The Platonic dialectic then reinvests each of the accepted senses of *logos* with new meaning. As the art of asking the right questions and giving the right answers to them, it is also the art of defending a thesis (*logos*), in which the musical sense of setting the tone, of finding the key or the dominant, is still resonant: it is the art of "reasoning" and "accounting for" (*logon didonai* [λόγον δόδιναι]); *logos*, or discourse as argumentation, is opposed to *muthos* [μῦθος], or discourse as narration. The ploysemy of *logos* is thus placed under the yoke of correct or rigorous statement (*orthos logos* [ὀρθὸς λόγος]), or of reasoning, as the very medium of philosophy: "[W]hen we ask men questions, and if we ask questions in the right way, these questions say by themselves everything as it is. Now if knowledge and correct reasoning [*orthos logos*] were not present within them, they would not be able to do this" (*Phaedo*, 73a8). This is the turn that Socrates thematizes in *Phaedo* (99e), when he declares himself tired of the materialist examination of existing things and maintains that one has to "take refuge in reasoning [*eis tous logous* (εἰς τοὺς λόγους)] and, within this reasoning, examine the truth of beings" (M. Dixsaut's French translation is "*raisonnement*," which she describes as a *cache-misère* [respectable outer garment, or better: a fig-leaf; *Platon: Phédon*], but this is nevertheless preferable to "proposition" [Hackforth, *Plato's Phaedo*]; *idées* [ideas] or *notions* [notions; Robin, *Plato's Œvres Complètes*], or "definitions" [Bluck, *Plato's Phaedo*]).

Logos, as a rational statement, entails analysis: "grammatical" analysis before it was invented—inseparable from dialectical activity with respect to forms and the five basic genres—is linked in the *Sophist* to the logical analysis of truth. *Logos* is the "first combination" (*hê protê sumplokê* [ἡ πρώτη συμπλοκή]; *Sophist*, 262c 5–6) made up of a noun and a verb and could be either true or false (263b): the meaning of *logos* as "statement" was therefore set at exactly the same time as the meaning of *onoma* as "name" (until then, *onoma* had meant, rather, a "word") and the meaning of *rhèma* [ῦῆμα] as "verb." Understood in this way, *logos* is perhaps the best way of designating definition itself: for the word or name "circle" (*onoma* [ὄνομα]), there is a corresponding *logos* made up of nouns and verbs: "something whose extremities are all at a perfectly equal distance from the center" (*ex onomatôn kai rhêmaton* [ἐξ ὀνομάτων καὶ ῥημάτων]; Letter 7, 342c).

B. The network of meanings of *logos* in Aristotle

In the philosophical "dictionary" that Aristotle proposes in Book Δ of his *Metaphysics*, there is no entry entitled *logos* that records and clarifies the uses of this word. Yet the word is caught within a multiplicity of networks that, even if they are primarily anchored in different places of his work, are used (without being thematized) within one and the same treatise. This is particularly true of *De anima*, and in analyzing these networks, we gain a better understanding of the extreme difficulty of a classic work such as this. Any interpretation of Aristotle is always faced with the choice of two approaches to the networks in which a work's key terms are embedded: either exploring the differences and revealing the gaps and conceptual shifts by using a multiplicity of heterogeneous translations (so Hamlyn, for example, states in the preface to his edition of *De anima*: "to prevent misunderstanding I have flagged all occurrences of the word by providing the translations with the subscript '$_L$'") or attempting to "make . . . available the source which motivates the different ways of meaning" (Heidegger, *Phänomenologische interpretationen*) by reinventing the scope of the Greek language within the target language.

A first network (*De anima*, 1 and 2), thematized in Book Z of the *Metaphysics*, links *logos* to *eidos* [εἶδος] ("form" as opposed to "matter"), to *to ti ên einai* [τὸ τί ἦν εἶναι] (quiddity, quintessence), and to *entelecheia* [ἐντελέχεια] ("act" as opposed to "power"), as well as to *horos* [ὅρος] (definition). So the soul is the *logos* of the body, as (for instance) ax-ness is the *logos* of the ax—and we should add that it is the *logos* of the soul to be *logos* of the body (see 412b 11–16). *Logos*, designating what gives form to a thing, thereby constitutes its definition: it is simultaneously "essence," "finality," "raison d'etre," "definition," and "account" (as the swarm of translations at 412b 10 testifies: "this is what the soul is," that is, *ousia . . . hê kata ton logon* [οὐσία . . . ἡ κατὰ τὸν λόγον]: "a substance . . . in the sense of form" [Barbotin]; "substance, that corresponding to the principle L" [*De anima*]; "substance as that which corresponds to the account of a thing" [Durrant]; "the substance which corresponds to reason" [Bodéüs]; "the essence insofar as it is expressed" [cf. Heidegger, *Questions II*]). Being par excellence and the expressible par excellence, physics and metaphysics, are thus onto-logically bound together and open the *Metaphysics* out onto the *Organon*.

A second network connects *logos*, "voice," "discursiveness," and "rationality" (*De anima*, 2.8 and 3.3) in several statements that make *logos* something proper to man. This network remits to two kinds of analysis: one is based in anatomy and physiology and specifies the type of linguistic articulation proper to the human *logos* (*The History of Animals*, 9.535a, 28–30, for example); the other, via the elaboration of expressiveness as articulated in the *Peri hermeneias* (4.16b 26: *logos . . . esti phônê sêmantikê* [λόγος . . . ἐστι φωνὴ σημαντική], "a vocal sound that has a conventional meaning") relates, by virtue of their connections to the right and the good and to living well, man conceived as an "animal endowed with *logos*" and man conceived as a "political animal" (*Politics*, 1.1.1253a 7–15). With the *phantasia logistikê* [φαντασία λογιστική] ("representation"—though not *aisthêtike* [αἰσθητική], "representation with the senses," as is the case with animals—but "rational" [Barbotin, among others], "calculating" [Bodéüs], or better still, "discursive," *De anima*, 3.10.433b 29–30), which conjoins imagination and persuasion, *De anima* brings together under the term *logos* domains that we would separate under the headings of, on the one hand, anatomy and physiology, and on the other, politics and ethics, but also rhetoric and poetics.

The third, more specific, network in the *De anima* defines "sensation" as a *logos*, in the mathematical sense of "relation," "proportion," a *ratio*: sensation (*aisethêsis* [αἴσθησις]), the name for the actual coincidence between a sensory organ (*aisthêtêrion* [αἰσθητήριον]) and an object sensed (*aisthêton* [αἰσθητόν]), is nothing other than the calculation of an average between contrasting qualities—for example, white/black to make gray. This is why "an excess of objects sensed destroys the sensory organs: for if the movement is too strong for the organ, the *logos* [the relation] is broken, and this is sensation" (*De anima*, 2.12.424a 30–31; cf. 3.2.426a 27–b 8). But the fact that *logos* is frequently translated as "form" (Barbotin) or "reason" (Bodéüs) does not facilitate this understanding, or our understanding generally.

The fourth network involves a semantic field that is barely distinct from the second network: at most it gives *logos*, when joined to *phasis* [φάσις] and *apophasis* [ἀπόφασις] ("affirmation" and "negation"), the specific meaning of "statement."

But what is new has to do with the subject capable of *legein*, of making statements: not man, but *aisthêsis* itself, including that of the *aloga*, or "beasts," *legei*. Sensation states what it senses by itself; sight says what it sees (white), but still it does not speak, it does not produce *logos*, that is, a grammatical statement, a predicative sentence ("Socrates is white"). So the perplexity remains as to which part of the soul it is that senses, and "one could not easily class it as *alogon*, nor as *logon echon* [λόγον ἔχον]" (*De anima*, 3.9.432a 15–17).

This survey of the meanings of *logos* makes their disjunction, as well as their systematization, apparent: so a gap remains between the mathematical *logos*, which calculates sensation, and the *logos* proper to man, who makes statements, constructs arguments, and unites and persuades citizens. It is as if the Greek language contributed to confusing, and thus to foreclosing, a certain number of questions that Aristotle, "compelled by truth," nevertheless persisted in asking.

C. *Logos* and Stoic systematics

The Stoics, unlike Aristotle, turned the polysemy of *logos* into a principle of their systematics. For them, *logos* thematically organized and unified the three parts of the philosophical *logos*: physics, ethics, and logic.

Physical *logos* is the rational and immanent order of the world (*kosmos* [κόσμος]), which is fully determined by causal relations without exception. The Stoics made a distinction between two fundamental cosmological principles that reproduced the strict division between acting and suffering: between matter (*hulê* [ὕλη]), which is a pure indeterminate principle, the absolute capacity to undergo, and *logos*, which is the source of the determination of everything. They called this *logos* "god," insofar as they considered it the demiurge, a driving force and formative power. Its physical name was "fire," a legacy of the Heraclitean *logos*: so for Zeno, this god was "an artistically working fire, going on its way to create; which is equivalent to a fiery, creative, or fashioning breath" (Diogenes Laertius, *Lives of Eminent Philosophers*). In addition, each living being, each body, each individual in the physical world, contained *logoi spermatikoi* [λόγοι σπερματικοί], seminal reasons, from which he developed, each one representing the singular reason of the fatal law according to which he would develop, provided the conditions he encountered were favorable. *Logos* justified the Stoic identification of nature—common nature as nature proper, fate, providence, and Zeus: it was well known the world over that, in Plutarch's words, "common nature and the common reason of this nature [ἡ κοινὴ φύσις καὶ ὁ κοινὸς τῆς φύσεως λόγος] are Fate, Providence and Zeus" (Plutarch, *Contradictions of the Stoics*, 34.1050b).

This identity was also a principle of Stoic ethics, a rational ethics that affirmed an identity between virtue, happiness, and the sovereign good. For Zeno, the end is a way of living in accordance with nature, itself identified as a way of living according to virtue, that is, a "way of living in accordance with the experience of the events which occur naturally." The order of the events is nothing other than fate, which is *logos* (Plutarch, ibid.).

In logic, *logos* was the faculty of reasoning that distinguishes men from animals. This is the faculty of giving reasons or providing causal relations or of accounting for (*logon didonai*) what we perceive by formulating our perceptive data, or of providing logical representations (*phantasiai logikai* [φαντασίαι λογικαί]) between them. In every case, what the faculty furnishes are human representations as distinct from animal representations; throughout, *logikos* indissociably means both rational and discursive.

■ See Box 3.

III. From Greek to Latin

A. *Logos / ratio, oratio*

The Latin term *ratio* does not cover all the senses of *logos*: it has neither the meaning of "gathering" nor the meaning of "speech." From the verb *reor* ("to count," "to calculate," and in popular usage "to think," "to estimate," "to judge"), and used less frequently than *puto* or *opinor*, the noun *ratio* did not produce many compound terms: *ratiocinor* is rare, and the adjective *rationalis* was not used before Seneca. It was out of the meanings of "counting" and "calculation," which *ratio* has in common with *logos*, and from the time of

Plautus (300 BCE), that all of the uses attesting to the values of "reasoning," "method," and "explanation" developed. This was why, when Cicero and Lucretius translated and expounded Greek philosophical doctrines, *ratio* was available to them as a term that was able to convey a large number of the meanings of *logos*. A given meaning could be made clearer with another noun, which was not added to *ratio* but qualified it, in pairs such as *ratio et consilium* (the plan, intention), *ratio et mens* (intelligence, the faculty of reason), *ratio et via* (method). To convey the sense of "speech," the term *oratio*, which is not etymologically related to *ratio* but is a remarkable homophone, allows us to hear the polysemy of *logos*, especially when it is paired with *ratio*.

1. The new coherence of Lucretius

The uses of the term *ratio* in the poem *De rerum natura* (*On the Nature of Things*) by Lucretius tended to reduce the polysemy of the term in order the reinforce the coherence of the Epicurean method and the didactic effectiveness of his exposition; this movement of reduction and unification of meaning is marked on the one hand by a recurrence of the

---

3

The polysemy of "logos" according to Greek grammarians

A marginal scholium of a manuscript of the *Technê grammatikê* by Dionysius Thrax, the text below should be taken for what it is: a more or less careful (there are several redundancies) and byzantine compilation of notes of different sources and dates. It does not, therefore, call for the same kind of exegesis as a deliberately constructed text. We offer it here as a kind of "exhibit" in a trial to show the extent to which the polysemy of *logos*, described here as equivocal or as a homonym, had struck Greek grammarians. In this respect, the zealous manner in which our scholiast provided as long a list of meanings as possible, even at the cost of occasionally repeating himself, is in itself a noteworthy symptom:

<Heliodorus>

Logos is used in many different senses: it is an equivocal word that can signify many things. *Logos* can mean

1. the rational capacity (ἐνδιάθετος λογισμός) that makes us reasonable, thinking beings (λογικοί καί διανοητικοί);
2. concern (φροντίς), cf. the expressions "it is not worthy of *logos*" or "I do not feel any *logos* about him";
3. consideration (λογαριασμός), cf. "the commander feels *logos* for his lieutenants";
4. justification (ἀπολογία), cf. "He gave a *logos* for that";

5. the general (*logos*) [ὁ καθόλου] that encompasses all parts of speech (μέρος λόγου);
6. definition (ὅρος), cf. "sentient living being," as the answer to the question "give the *logos* for animal";
7. the juxtaposition of words which express full meaning, that is syntactical *logos*, cf. "finish your *logos* [sentence]";
8. (*logos*) of expenses, sometimes called *logos* of the bank;
9. the (*logos* [relation]) of geometry, cf. "there is the same *logos* between two cubits and four cubits, as between a half and one cubit";
10. proportion (ἀναλογία), cf. "the *logos* of four to three is four thirds";
11. a good reason (τὸ εὔλογον), cf. "he did not do that without a good *logos*," meaning "with good reason" (εὐλόγως);
12. the conclusion that follows from premises [he then gives an example of a syllogism];
13. the fact of being rationally endowed (λογικὴ κατασκευή), when we say that men are endowed with *logos*, but not beings that are devoid of reason (ἄλογα);
14. potentiality (δύναμις), when we say that it is by virtue of a natural *logos* that animals have teeth and a beard, in other words, by virtue of natural and seminal potentialities;
15. the vocal form that is coextensive with thought (ἡ συμπαρεντεινομένη φωνὴ τῶ διανοήματι), cf. ἄπελθε [go away], which is a word (λέξις), insofar as it has a

meaning and also a *logos* because of the sense of the thought content that completes it;
16. that which expresses self-sufficiency (ὅ δηλοῖ τὸ αὐτοτελές), cf. what one says when something is missing from a statement: "finish your *logos*";
17. extension (*logos*), as a given type of completion, cf. "the *logos* of Demosthenes against Midias is beautiful";
18. book (βιβλίον), "lend me the book *Against Androtion*" [a speech by Demosthenes];
19. the relation between sizes (σχέσις τῶν μεγεθῶν), when we say that one size has the same *logos* in relation to another size, as some other size has in relation to some other size;
20. subject (ὑπόθεσις) [i.e., the summary of the plot], cf. "I am now going to read out the *logos* of the play and its didascalic [comic fragment]";
21. cause (αἰτία), cf. Plato [*Gorgias*, 465a]: "I do not call art an activity devoid of *logos* [ἄλογον πρᾶγμα]";
22. God, par excellence (κατ᾽ ἐξοχὴν ὁ θεός), cf. Jn 1.1: "In the beginning was the *logos*, and the *logos* was with God"; in other words, "the son of God, in the beginning, was exactly the same and equal to his Father."

(Dionysius Thrax, *Scholia in Dionysii Thracis artem grammaticam*, in *Grammatici Graeci*, vol. 1, fasc. 3) *vera ratio*, and on the other by a number of uses that cover several different Greek compound nouns that are based on *logos*: *logismos* [λογισμός], *epilogismos* [ἐπιλογισμός], *phusiologia* [φυσιολογία].

Vera ratio describes the Epicurean doctrine (see, e.g., *On the Nature of Things*, 1.498; 5.1117), whose truthfulness is proclaimed in opposition to the erroneous theories of Heraclitus (1.637) and of Anaxagoras (1.880). It is "just reasoning" that allows us to account for the movement of atoms (2.82; 2.229), and it is the advent of an explanation that will reveal a new aspect of the world:

Now, pay attention to the true doctrine.
An unheard of discovery will strike your ears.
A new aspect of your universe will be revealed.

(Nunc animum nobis adhibe veram ad rationem.
Nam tibi vehementer nova res molitur ad auris.
Accidere, et nova se species ostendere rerum.)

(Lucretius, *On the Nature of Things*, 2.1023–1025)

In these uses, *ratio* covers almost the only sense of *logos* that it does not have in Latin, that is, the sense of "speech"; it is the master's speech, the revealed word, this *logos* that, at the end of the *Letter to Herodotus* (Diogenes Laertius, 10.83), refers to the synthesis of the main points of this doctrine, which can lend a certain force to anyone who has memorized it.

On the other hand, *ratio* unifies several aspects of Epicurean natural science (*phusiologia*), whose objective is to "explain the causes of phenomena" (Diogenes Laertius, ibid., 10.78): *ratio* is thus often paired with *causa* (4.500, 6.1000), and sometimes replaces it (7.1090; the *ratio* of an epidemic). *Ratio* covers all natural laws (2.719) and, for this very reason, provides a general principle of explanation of nature: *ratio* is thus closely associated with *natura* in the expression *natura haec rerum ratioque*, which refers to the recent discovery by Epicurus of the system of nature and its explanation in Latin by Lucretius:

Lastly, this recent discovery of the system of nature, and today, indeed, I am the very first able to translate it into the language of our fathers.

(Denique natura haec rerum ratioque repertast nuper, et hanc primus cum primis ipse repertus nunc, ego sum in patrias qui possim vertere voces.)

(Lucretius, *On the Nature of Things*, 5.335–337)

The importance of this use is indicated in the syntagma that appears as a refrain four times in the poem (1.148, 2.61, 3.93, 6.41), *natura species ratioque*, "the sight and explanation of nature," or more precisely, "the explanation that accounts for phenomena" (*naturae species*, what nature makes manifest), but also "the explanation that proceeds by reasoning on the basis of phenomena." These glosses, which are not translations, are intended to remind us that *ratio* refers here to *logismos*, the reasoning by which the lessons of nature are explained (Diogenes Laertius, 10.75), or to *epilogismos*, through which we understand the end of nature (10.133). Two fundamental aspects of this methodical reasoning are thus conveyed by the single term

ratio. Nonetheless, the understanding of invisible things, perceived *dia logou* [διὰ λόγου] (10.47, 10.59, 10.62), is not expressed by *ratio*, but by *mens* (6.77) or by *injectus animi*, the mind's projection. Rational activity, when it covers any kind of perception, is thus directly related to the thinking and feeling subject, which no compound of *ratio* could express.

2. The nodal points of translation in Cicero

The uses of *ratio* in the Ciceronian corpus reveal at least two "nodes" of translation, which stand out against the banalization of the term as a result of what we might call a diffuse Stoicism. We find an example of this banalization in the brief exposition of the physical doctrine of Anaxagoras (*De natura deorum*, 1.26): the ordering of the world produced by the *nous* (fr. A38 RT: DK), the *diakosmêsis* [διακόσμησις], is translated by a phrase in which the group of words *vis ac ratio* describes the rational process set in motion, as if the *diachosmêsis* of Anaxagoras were the unfolding of an immanent rationality, the one postulated by the Stoics ("Anaxagoras . . . was the first to argue that the well-ordered organization of all things was a result of an infinite intelligence which had perfected their composition by proceeding *rationally* [*omnium rerum discriptionem et modum mentis infinitae* vi ac ratione *dissignari*]").

A first node occurs around the translation of *logikê* (*technê*) [λογική (τέχνη)], "logic": "in altera philosophiae parte, quae quaerendi ac disserendi quae logikê dicitur" (in the second part of philosophy, concerning the search for and exposition of arguments, which is called "logic"; *De finibus*, 1.22). We note here that *ratio* is not what technique is concerned with, but rather the method itself of *quaerere* and *disserere*: "logikên quam rationem disserendi voco" (*De fato*, 37).

The sense of "gathering," well attested for *logos* but not for *ratio*, is thus conveyed by the term *disserere*, "to connect words together, in the right order." *Ratio* has to do more with the unfolding, with the method of the process, as is made clear by this definition of *apodeixis* [ἀπόδειξις], or demonstration, translated as *argumenti conclusio* (giving form to an argument): "ratio quae ex rebus perceptis ad id quod non percipiebatur adducit" (the method that leads from perceived things to what was not perceived; *Academica*, 2.26).

According to another translation choice (which we find relates to the doctrine of Antiochus; *Academica*, 1.30–32), *ratio* is given a meaning that is closer to the sense of *logos* as "reason and discourse": logic is defined as "philosophiae pars, quae erat in ratione et in disserendo" (the part of philosophy that concerns the methods of reasoning and its exposition), and the object of dialectics is said to be "oratio ratione conclusa," discourse governed by the rules of argumentation.

The homophonic play of words *ratio/oratio* allows us to resolve, from a point of view that is here clearly marked by Stoicism, the impossible translation of the object of logic. However, the occurrences of this nonetymological pair (but which must have been perceived as etymological, to judge by Cicero's uses of the terms) help us to understand where the second difficulty lies.

When *ratio* and *oratio* are used together, they emphasize a mythical kind of coherence: the origins of eloquence in *De inventione* (1.2) and of the social bond in *De officiis* (1.50), are explained by the ability to handle *ratio* and *oratio*, whether in teaching or learning. This coherence is also the one that Stoic discourse aspires to, over and against moral suffering (*Tusculanes*, 4.60). But the dissociation between the two terms highlights their irreducible distinction, or the trap of the Stoic conception of language. When arguing against the Stoic Cato, Cicero states his disagreement at the level of words, *oratio*, while claiming to be in agreement with Cato about the main points of doctrine, the *ratio*: "Ratio enim nostra consentit, pugnat oratio" (we agree on doctrine, it is language which opposes us; *De finibus*, 3.10). Similarly, in Cicero's translation of the *Timaeus*, the inadequacy of all language, other than by "resemblance," to translate anything to do with gods and the creation of the universe (29c) is clearly marked thanks to the distinction between the *ratio* of the demiurgical god and the *oratio* that gives us its image—and yet both terms serve to translate *logos*.

The uses of *ratio* in Seneca's language are marked by an interpretation of the doctrine that limits man's participation in the reason of the world: the *animus* of god is wholly *ratio*, that of man is possessed by *error* (*Natural Questions*, preface, 14). Man's rationality is constitutive, and Seneca coins the adjective *rationalis*, which essentially covers the first manifestation of *logos* through the mastery of the spoken language: *infans irrationalis, puber rationalis* (the newborn infant is without reason [without speech], the child possesses reason; *Epistles*, 118.14). But if ratio is the *imitatio naturae* (ibid., 66.39), the conditions of this imitation are made more difficult by a general blindness that prevents us from perceiving the rational principles at work in nature and in the nature proper to man (ibid., 95). So the construction of the rational subject does not coincide with a progressive reinforcement of reason, but with a process of curing this blindness (ibid., 50). This interpretation, which systematically treats errors of judgment as an illness, privileges the vocabulary of care, and of the willingness or disposition to be cured (hence Seneca's interest in *bona mens* and *voluntas*).

B. From *Logos* to *Verbum*: The Gospel according to John

1. The *Logos*: Son of God, *ḥokmah* (wisdom) or *dāvār* (the spoken word)?

Logos appears seven times in the Gospel according to John in the New Testament (four times in the prologue to the fourth Gospel 1:1, 14; twice in John 1 1:1, 5:7; once in Rv 19:13). The term is translated canonically as "Word," or *Verbe* in French, which is a calque of the *Verbum* of the Vulgate.

John says that the *Logos* was "in the beginning" (John 1 1:1), even before the creation of the world, and it was through it that God created all things (1:3: "all things were made through him"). The *Logos* "was God" (1:1), as well as being a person distinct from God (1:2: "the Word was with God"). It is also called the "only Son" of God (1:14). What is specific to John's *Logos* is that it "became flesh and dwelt among us" (1:14): incarnation confers upon *Logos* the mission of communicating with men and of revelation to them, which is related to its current sense of "spoken word" in common Greek. We go from the organic nature of the *logoi spermatikoi* (seminal reasons) of the Stoics, a legacy of Aristotelian form, to the economy of persons and of filiation.

The ancient exegetes (e.g., Origen, Saint Augustine) were convinced early on of the continuity between the two Testaments. In this perspective, it was first of all the Wisdom of the Old Testament (*ḥokmah* [חָכְמָה]), translated as *Sophia* in the Septuagint), which prefigured the *Logos* of John: Paul (1 CE) was thus already calling the Son of God "wisdom of God" (1 Cor 1:24). There are many points that Wisdom and *Logos* have in common that allowed for this assimilation: both are created by God (Prv 8:22; cf. Jn 1:4); both represent life (Wisdom declares "for he who finds me finds life and obtains favor from the Lord" [Prv 8:35]; cf. the *Logos*: "in him was life, and the life was the light of men" [Jn 1:4]); both preexist creation ("The Lord created me at the beginning of his work, the first of his acts of old" [Prv 8:22]); and both constitute the means of creation (Wisdom is the worker, *technitis*, who makes everything that is [Prv 7:21 and 8:6]; and Jn 1:3 says of *Logos* that "all things were made through him"). Wisdom is even presented as spoken "from the mouth of the Most High" (Eccl 24:3), and in that regard, it reconnects with the usual meaning of *logos* and its communicative function.

Despite these convergences, John did not use *Sophia*, which is a translation of *ḥokmah*, to designate the Son of God but rather *Logos*, which is a translation of *dāvār*. Beside the difference in gender of the nouns (*Sophia* is a feminine term, unlike *Logos*, which is masculine and then appropriated as the Son of God), *Logos* covers a much greater semantic field than Wisdom, which is associated in Rabbinical tradition with the Torah, the written Law (cf. Eccl 24:23). *Dāvār* is, like *Logos*, the means of revelation (cf. Ex 3:14, where God reveals himself to men through his Word as the One and Only God), and above all, it is an active power.

- See Box 4.

2. *Logos*: *Verbum, sermo, ratio,* or *causa*?

a. *Logos, verbum,* and *sermo*

In the Latin versions of the Bible, two concurrent translations for the *logos* of the prologue of Jn 1:1 are attested depending on the geographical region: in North Africa, *sermo* was used (cf. Cyprian, *Ad Quirinum testimoniorum*, 2.3: "In principio fuit Sermo et Sermo erat apud Deum et Deus erat Sermo"). In Europe, however, it was *verbum* that prevailed (Novatian, *De Trinitate*, 30). Whether the term that was kept to translate *logos* was *verbum* or *sermo*, Christ was the spoken word. But *verbum* was more suited than *sermo*, which had strong connotations of internal plurality, for the unity and uniqueness of the Son of God. So in his *Tractatus in Johannis Evangelium* (*Tractates on the Gospel of John*, 108.3), Augustine comments on the passage from John 17:17 in the following terms:

> "Your discourse [*Sermo*]," he says, "is truth." What else did he say than "I am the truth"? For indeed, the Greek Gospel has *logos*, that which is also read there where it was said, "In the beginning was the Word [*Verbum*] and the Word was with God and the Word was God." And of course we know that the Word itself is the only-begotten Son of God, who "was made flesh and dwelt among us [*Et utique Verbum ipsum novimus unigenitum Dei Filium quod caro factum est et habitavit in nobis*]." And because of this [*verbum*] it could also be put here and in some codices has been put: "Your Word [*Verbum*] is truth," as in some codices even there it was written "In the beginning was the Discourse [*Sermo*]." But in the Greek,

4

The ambiguity of the Hebrew *dāvār* [דָּבָר], spoken word

The Hebrew word *dāvār* [דָּבָר] presents an interesting ambiguity, since it means both "word" and "thing"—this last, first of all in the sense of "fact," "event." This Semitic substratum explains certain oddities of the early Gospels, such as the angel's expression to Mary "no word [*rhêma* (ῥῆμα)] is impossible for God," or the words of the shepherds at the Nativity: "let us go see this word which has happened" (Lk 1:37 and 2:15). The same ambiguity exists in Arabic, where *amr* [الأَمْر] sometimes refers to the "matter at hand" (pl. *umūr* [أُمُور], sometimes to the command given (pl. *awāmir* [أَوَامِر]). In French, *chose* (thing) is a doublet of *cause* (cause, reason, case): *la chose* (thing) is what is *en cause* (the case) in a legal debate, and the thing one is talking about (*ce dont on cause*). The words *Ding* in German and "thing" in English both recall the *thing*, which was the name for an assembly of people where certain "things" would be on the agenda.

The ambiguity of the word makes sense in terms of the representation of creation as having issued forth from a divine command. This idea is found in the ancient Near East, perhaps as a result of the idea of thunder as a divine voice (cf. Sumerian *ENEM* = Akkadian *awātum*). It appears in the Bible: "By the word [*dāvār*] of the Lord the heavens were made" (Ps 33:6). It is implicit in the first story of creation at the beginning of Genesis. This creative word is hypostatized in Philo, who gives it the name *logos*. The term is used in John's Gospel to designate the word in which all things were created and that became flesh. The Latin translates this as *Verbum*, which refers in theology to the second person of the Trinity before his incarnation as Jesus Christ. The emphatic usage of "word" to refer to the poetic word, sometimes with a capital letter, represents a secularization of the idea.

A further representation comes to be grafted on to this meaning, whereby the word can *magically* act upon reality. To know the "answer to a mystery," or *mot* (word) *de l'énigme* in French, enables one to change things by returning to their verbal source. Things are like frozen words, which one can free up. This idea is echoed, finally, in a quatrain by Eichendorff: "a poem [*Lied*] lies dormant in all things" ("Wünschelrute"), and in Proust: "[W]hat lay hidden behind the steeples of Martinville must be something analogous to a pretty phrase" (*Swann's Way*, chap. 1).

One of the most famous plays on words in Western literature is based on the ambiguity of *dāvār* [דָּבָר]. In the first *Faust*, Goethe has his hero retranslate the opening of the prologue to John's Gospel: "in the beginning was *logos*." He rejects *Wort* (word), then *Sinn* (meaning), then *Kraft* (power), to settle in the end on *Tat* (act) (vv. 1224–37). This choice seems arbitrary, unless we understand that Faust begins with an implicit retroversion of his text, which is attentive to its Semitic substratum.

Rémi Brague

BIBLIOGRAPHY

Proust, Marcel. *Swann's Way*. Translated by C.K.S. Moncrieff and T. Kilmartin. London: Chatto and Windus, 1981

---

without any variation, both there and here, is *logos*. And so in truth, that is, in his Word, in his Only-Begotten, the Father sanctifies his own heirs and his coheirs [*Sanctificat itaque Pater in veritate, id est in Verbo suo, in unigenito suo, suos heredes ejusque coheredes*].

(Tractates on the Gospel of John)

The association made at the end of this passage between *Verbum* and *veritas* (truth) is not coincidental. It points to a popular etymology, traditionally attributed to Varro and that Saint Augustine adopts when he links *verbum* (the word) either to *verum* (true) or to *verum boare* (to proclaim what is true) (*De dialectica*, 6). One can probably see here another factor explaining the translators' choice of *Verbum* to translate the *Logos* of John.

b. *Logos* and *ratio*

Yet the church fathers would continue to question the possible translation of *Logos* by *Ratio*, which pointed to the divine Reason of the creative God.

For Tertullian (verses 150–222), who possessed an African version of the Bible in which the translation of *logos* as *sermo* was preferred, *logos* does not correspond to the Latin *verbum* but instead to the combination of *ratio* (reason) and *sermo* (speech). Indeed, although it is true (Tertullian maintains) that thought precedes the spoken word, that reason (*ratio*) is the substance of this spoken word (*sermo*), *ratio* is nonetheless expressed in the form of an inner spoken word.

This [reason] the Greeks call *Logos*, by which expression we also designate discourse [*sermo*]: and consequently our people are already wont, through the artlessness of the translation, to say that *Discourse* [*sermo*] *was in the beginning with God*, though it would be more appropriate to consider Reason of older standing, seeing that God is [not] discursive [*sermonalis*] from the beginning but is rational [*rationalis*] even before the beginning, and because discourse itself, having its ground in reason, shows reason to be prior as being its substance. Yet even so it makes no difference. For although God had not yet uttered his Discourse [*sermo*], he always had it within himself along with and in his Reason [*ratio*], while he silently thought out and ordained with himself the things which he was shortly to say by the agency of Discourse: for while thinking out and ordaining them in company of his Reason, he converted into Discourse that which he was discussing in discourse. [*Cum ratio enim sua cogitans atque disponens sermonem, eam efficiebat quam sermone tractabat*].

(Tertulliani adversus Praxean, §5)

In Augustine we find an analogous opposition between *Verbum*, as the creative Word of the Father, and *Ratio*, as the Reason immanent to God independently of all creation. But Augustine prefers *verbum* to *sermo* as a translation for *logos*, since the former term for him emphasizes, better than *ratio*, the notion of an effective Word, as we can see in the *De diversis quaestionibus* (*Eighty-Three Different Questions*, question 63):

"In the beginning was the Word." The Greek word *logos* signifies in Latin both "reason" [*ratio*] and "word" [*verbum*]. However, in this verse the better translation is "word" [*verbum*], so that not only the relation to the Father is indicated, but also the efficacious power with respect to those things which are made by the Word [*Sed hoc loco melius verbum interpretamur, ut significetur non solum ad Patrem respectus, sed ad illa etiam quae per Verbum facta sunt operativa potentia*]. Reason, however, is correctly called reason even if nothing is made by it.

In the *Tractatus in Johannis Evangelium* (1.10), Augustine considers this translation to be established, in spite of the potential ambiguity of the word *verbum*, which refers equally to the Word and to human spoken words. Rather than suggesting a better translation, the author is content to underline the difference between the *Verbum* of the Father and our human words (*verba*): "And whenever you hear: *In the beginning was the Word* [*In principio erat Verbum*], so that it does not make you think of something of little value—as you normally do when you hear talk of human words [*cum verba humana soleres audire*]—this is what you must think: *the Word was God* [*Deus erat Verbum*]."

c. *Logos* and *causa*

In the ninth century, John Scotus Erigena (810–877) also reflected on the notion of *Logos* in his *Periphyseon* (*On the Division of Nature*). In this text, he blends a number of Neoplatonic elements with his own Christology and argues that within the Word reside Ideas, that is, the first causes from which all things were created:

> The most primary reason of all things, which is simple and multiple, is God the Word. For it is called by the Greeks *logos*, that is, Word [*verbum*] or Reason [*ratio*] or Cause [*causa*] [*Nam a Grecis* logos *vocatur, hoc est verbum vel ratio vel causa*]. Therefore, that which is written in the Greek gospel, *en archêi în ho logos*, can be interpreted "In the beginning was the Word," or: "In the beginning was the Reason," or: "In the beginning was the Cause." For nobody who makes any one of these statements will be deviating from the truth. For the only-begotten Son of God is both Word and Reason and Cause, Word because through Him God uttered the making of all things [*verbum quidem quia per ipsum deus pater dixit fieri Omnia*]—in fact He is the Utterance of the Father and His Saying and His Speech [*immo etiam ipse est Patris dicere et dictio et sermo*], as He Himself says in the gospel, "And the speech which I have addressed to you is not Mine but His that sent Me" [*et sermo quem locutus sum vobis non est meus sed ipsius qui misit me*]. . . . Reason because He is the principal Exemplar of all things visible and invisible, and therefore is called by the Greeks *idea*, that is, species or form [*ratio vero quoniam ipse est omnium visibilium et invisibilium principale exemplar ideoque a Grecis* idea*, id est species bel forma dicitur*]—for in Him the Father beholds the making of all things He willed to be before they were made—; and Cause because the origins of all things subsist eternally and immutably in Him [*causa quoque est quoniam occasiones omnium aeternaliter et incommutabiliter in ipso subsistunt*].

(2.642b–642c)

With Meister Eckhart, the theology of the Word become even more complex. He devoted paragraphs 4 to 51 of his *Commentary on the Prologue of the Gospel of Saint John* to an exegesis of the expression *in principio erat Verbum*. Following Augustine, he proposed the equivalence between *Logos* and *Verbum et ratio* (§4). For him, *logos* is the first cause of all things (§12: "*causa prima omnis res ratio est, logos est, Verbum in principio*" [the first Cause of all things is Reason, Logos, the Word in the Principle]). He emphasizes the intellective nature of the Word (§38: "*Verbum, quod est ratio . . . in intellectu est, intellegendo formatur, nihil praeter intellegere est*" [the Word, which is reason . . . is in the intellect, is formed by knowing, is nothing but knowing]). Man, as intellect, can find himself again in the Word and can be reborn to his true divine nature, while the Father creates his Son in the human soul.

This use of *logos* in the language of theology to refer to the Son of God, the second person of the Trinity, is strikingly original. John deflected the term by wresting it from its usual noetic domain and dwelling on the Incarnation. Thereafter followed a period when the notion of causality, which was essential to the Christian conceptualization of creation, was eclipsed. Then the Latin of the medieval theologians reinvested *logos* with the profane values of Greek philosophy (the Platonic idea and the Stoic cause).

■ See Box 7.

IV. Vernacular Puns

A. English: "Tell," "tale," "tally"; "count," "account," "recount"

"Say," the most common word in English to express "saying," is not really polysemic and can only ever translate one of the meanings of *legein*. It competes with other families of words, in particular those around the verbs "tell" and "count," which like *legein*, open out onto more complex usages that are at once arithmetical, discursive, and performative.

(a) A first important and rather archaic meaning of "tell," which is still present, was that of "counting" or "enumerating"—saying or "telling" out the numbers one by one (one, two, three, etc.), a first form of counting that also interested Wittgenstein in the *Philosophical Investigations*. We find this usage in *Robinson Crusoe* in the following:

> He could not tell twenty in *English*; but he numbered them by laying so many Stones on a Row, and pointing to me to tell them over.

(Daniel Defoe, *Robinson Crusoe*, chap. 15)

This is what one does when one counts out coins, for example, or banknotes, and a "teller" in English is both someone who tells tales, as well as someone who counts money in a bank. (Automatic tellers dispense cash or tell customers the balance in their bank accounts.) The idea of counting is associated with the idea of saying (stating the numbers, one by one), and arithmetic is the ability to follow a series out loud, such as two, four, six. Conversely, the association of "tell" with "count" defines narration; hence, a "tale," as derived from a primary form of counting, like a series with stages that can be enumerated and well defined: serialized tales are of this kind.

"Tell" is specifically oriented toward the effect or intention of the spoken word and has the dimension of a speech *act*: "telling" is always something other than describing or stating and does not refer, as "say" almost always does, to a statement. So rather than "say," one will "tell a lie" or "tell the truth," and "tell" adds to the simple idea of speaking, the fact of pointing out (to tell the time), of announcing or informing, correctly or not; of letting others know. "Tell" also means to narrate or relate, as in to "tell tales" (the two words being closely linked). "Tell" sometimes suggests, again going beyond a descriptive use of language, confession or revelation, as in "to disclose," "to reveal" (cf. the expression "tell all"). Its usage also extends to cases where it is a matter of making distinctions, of showing discernment, as one *speaks* (tell friend from foe, tell right from wrong). So "telling" is distinct from the notion of stating and means "to *make* or *see* a difference" and "to have some criterion for" ("I can tell," or "How can you tell it's a goldfinch?" the example given by J. L. Austin in "Other Minds").

So we can identify two directions in the verb "tell": that of narrating or recounting and that of enumerating or counting (cf. the verb "tally"). The usages of the verb "tell" suggest two dimensions of *logos* that go beyond the simple description of what is: the "telling," the narrative saying, which is intended to have an effect on others (what Austin, in *How to Do Things with Words*, defined as the perlocutionary dimension of what is said); and the act of counting implied in any statement (which would be its illocutionary dimension). Whatever the case, it seems that the verb "to tell" and its usages highlight more than "to say" and more than its French equivalents, a performative dimension of spoken language that is inseparable from a conception of *logos* as performance.

(b) This duality, to which the false French pair *conter* (to tell) / *compter* (to count) curiously enough corresponds, is to be found in the compound words based on "count" (recount, account). (Romance languages in general play on this pun: see, for instance, Cervantes, *Don Quixote* 1.28, where Dorotea refers to the sad account of her woes: "el cuento, que no le tiene, de mis desdichas" (the story [*cuento*], which is uncountable [*que no tiene cuento*], of my sorrows). "To recount" in the strict sense means "to count again," but also "to narrate." "Account" can be used not only in the sense of "counting" (money) but also in the sense of "giving an account of" something or of "accounting for" (as in the Greek *logon didonai*, the "day of reckoning" is the last judgment). This is precisely how Locke uses the noun "account," which is why in the French translation, Pierre Coste (*Essai philosophique*) alternatively uses *compte* (tally) and *récit* (tale). This, of course, then poses the problem of translating into French the expression "accountable" for one's actions, where the French for "accountable" should be not, as Coste translates it, *responsable* (responsible), but rather *comptable* (countable) (as Étienne Balibar proposes in his version, in "Points-bilingues"). We can see here, then, how moral philosophy during this period of English philosophy is defined in economic terms.

The pairs "count"/"account" and "tell"/"tally" thus articulate a remarkable link connecting counting, saying, and debt. Stanley Cavell identifies a Shakespearean source of this problematic that links the economic to the moral. In his

essay on *A Winter's Tale* entitled "Recounting Gains, Showing Losses," he shows how Shakespeare's vocabulary is saturated with these double usages of "tell" and of "count," "account," "loss," "gain," "owe," "debt," "repay," etc. We can see how rich the economic lexicon already is in Shakespeare's language, but counting, or rather the impossibility of counting, takes on an added dimension, that of the inability to say, to express oneself, or to "tell." Leontes in *A Winter's Tale* is thus "unable to tell anything," to know and to say what counts, and Cavell, returning to the dual sense of *saying* and *knowing* in "telling," sees in this attitude an expression of skepticism itself—the impossibility of expression repeating the inability of counting, and of counting for others.

This usage of the pair "tell"/"count" closely links "saying" to categorizing, as in the expression "to count as." To "count something as" is to put it in a category or a semantic unit. Here again is Cavell: "how we determine what counts as instances of our concepts, this thing as a table, this other as a human. To speak is to say what counts" (*In Quest of the Ordinary*). To see a thing as this or that is to "count" it, in the literal sense, as one of these words (or concepts), or as one of those others. In *This New Yet Unapproachable America* (1989), Cavell reads Kantian, but also Emersonian, categories as the means by which we count things, that is, count a given thing as falling under a given word, and thereby, he concludes, "recount our condition." The term "recount" thus becomes untranslatable. (The French translation is forced to invent the verb *ra-compter* for "to recount"). The linguistic play surrounding "tell"/"count" would thus allow for a new definition of the categories (that is, of the application of concepts and words to the world) by the invention of a conception of *logos* that would at the same time, and indissolubly, be a narrating (recounting), a counting out of differences, and an accounting. So it is through the English language and its usages that the irreducibility of *logos* to a simple description of the world, or the irreducibility of description to statement, becomes apparent in very concrete ways.

B. German: *Legen, liegen, lesen*

The difficulty of translating *legein* and *logos* is a cornerstone of Heidegger's reflection on Greece, on language, and on philosophy, and it prompts a complex linguistic play in German. One of the starting points of this reflection is Heraclitus's fragment 50.

▪ See Box 5.

In discussing this fragment, Heidegger proposes retranslating *logos* and *homologein* by taking as a pivotal term the "literal" or "authentic" (*eigentlich*) meaning of *legein*.

> Wer möchte leugnen, dass in der Sprache der Griechen von früh an λέγειν reden, sagen, erzählen bedeutet? Allein es bedeutet gleich früh und noch ursprünglicher und deshalb immer schon und darum auch in der vorgenannten Bedeutung das, was unser gleichlautendes "legen" meint: nieder- und vorlegen. Darin waltet das Zusammenbringen, das lateinische *legere* als lesen im Sinne von einholen und zusammenbringen. Eigentlich bedeutet λέγειν das sich und anderes sammelnde Nieder- und Vor-legen. Medial gebraucht, meint λέγεσθαι: sich niederlegen in die Sammlung der Ruhe; λέχος ist das

5

Translating a pre-Socratic (Heraclitus, fragment 50)

A "fragment" is surrounded by an aura of meaning and depends on an interpretation of the whole that is more wished for than guaranteed. This is true of the very famous fragment of Heraclitus:

οὐκ ἐμοῦ ἀλλὰ τοῦ λόγου ἀκούσαντας ὁμολογεῖν σοφόν ἐστιν ἕν πάντα εἶναι

(Not after listening to me, but after listening to the account [*logos*], one does wisely in agreeing that all things are one.)

(Heraclitus, *Fragments*)

– A more rationalist interpretation understands *logos* in the sense of *Sinn*, "sense," "reason," and founds a pre-Stoic cosmic physics, in which *logos* produces the unity of the world; this is how we might read the German translation by Diels Kranz (RT: DK): "Haben sie nicht mich, sondern den Sinn vernommen, so ist weise, dem Sinne gemäss zu sagen [to say according to the meaning], alles sei eins." Dumont proposes, in French: "Si ce n'est pas moi, mais le Logos que vous avez écouté, il est sage de convenir qu'est l'Un-Tout" (If it is not me, but *Logos* that you listened to, it is wise to agree that One is All).

– A more discursive interpretation, defended for example by J. Bollack and H. Wismann, emphasizes the difference between signifier and signified, between saying and what is said: "L'art est bien d'écouter, non moi, mais la raison, pour savoir . . . dire en accord toute chose-une" (Art is indeed listening, not to me, but to reason, to know how . . . to say in agreement all one-thing). The commentary does not "rationalize"; quite the opposite: "To allow the signifier to act, Heraclitus asks that we listen to what is being said, without being limited by the intention of the speaker" (ibid.).

– An ontological interpretation, like the one Heidegger proposes, links *logos* to the unveiling of being: "Nicht mir, aber der Lesende Lege gehörig: Selbes liegen lassen: Geschickliches west (die lesende lege): Eines einend Alles [Belonging and lending an ear, not to me, but to the gathering Posing: leaving the Same laid out: something well-disposed spreads out its being (the gathering Posing): One uniting All]" ("Logos [Heraklit, Fragment 50]").

BIBLIOGRAPHY

Bollack, Jean, and Heinz Wismann. *Héraclite ou la séparation*. Paris: Éditions de Minuit, 1972.
Dumont, Jean-Paul, ed. *Les écoles présocratiques*. Paris: Gallimard / Folio, 1991.
Heidegger, Martin. "Logos [Heraklit, Fragment 50]." In *Vorträge und Aufsätze*, edited by Friedrich-Wilhelm von Hermann. Gesamtausgabe, vol. 7, 211–34. Frankfurt: Klostermann, 2000. Translation by David Farrell Krell and Frank A. Capuzzi: "Logos (Heraclitus, fragment B 50)." In *Early Greek Thinking*, translated by David Farrell Krell and Frank A. Capuzzi, 59–78. San Francisco: Harper & Row, 1975.
Heraclitus. *Fragments*. Translated by T. M. Robinson. Toronto: University of Toronto Press, 1987.
Maly, Kenneth, and Parvis Emad, eds. *Heidegger on Heraclitus: A New Reading*. Lewiston, NY: Edwin Mellen, 1986.

Ruhelager; λόχος, ist der Hinterhalt, wo etwas hinterlegt und angelegt ist.

(Who would want to deny that in the language of the Greeks from early on λέγειν means to talk, say, or tell? However, just as early and even more originally, and therefore already in the previously cited meaning, it means what our similarly sounding *legen* means: to lay down and lay before. In *legen* a "bringing together" prevails, the Latin *legere* understood as *lesen*, in the sense of collecting and bringing together. Λέγειν properly means the laying-down and laying-before which gathers itself and others. The middle voice, λέγεσθαι, means to lay oneself down in the gathering of rest; λέχος is the resting place; λόχος is a place of ambush where something is hidden, poised to attack.)

("Logos [Heraklit, Fragment 50]")

There are several comments one might make here.

In the first place, with regard to the Greek. Heidegger makes no distinction (in contrast with the standard etymology given by Frisk [RT: *Griechiches etymologisches Wörterbuch*] and by Chantraine [RT: *Dictionnaire étymologique de la langue grecque*]), between *λέγω, from the Indo-European root *legh- "to be lying down" (from which we get λέχος and λόχος, as well as *legen, liegen*, or the French *lit*) and λέγω, from *leg-, "to gather." This fusion or confusion is an essential part of his argument. Here the onto-logical privileging of the Greek *Logos* takes root by his raising the following question: "How does λέγειν, whose literal meaning is to lay out (*legen*), come to mean saying and speaking (*sagen und reden*)?" The answer concerns the being of language:

To say is λέγειν. This sentence, if well thought, now sloughs off everything facile, trite, and vacuous. It names the inexhaustible mystery that the speaking of language comes to pass from the unconcealment of what is present [*der Unverborgenheit des Anwesenden*], and is determined according to the lying-before of what is present as the letting-lie-together-before [*dem Vorliegen des Anwesenden als das beisammen-vorliegen-lassen*].

("Logos [Heraklit, Fragment 50]")

Logos, which is thus linked to the unveiling of *alêtheia*, is what allows the phenomenon to show itself as itself (*apophainesthai*; cf. *Sein und Zeit*, §7B).

What would have come to pass had Heraclitus—and all the Greeks after him—thought the essence of language expressly as Λόγος, as the Laying that gathers! Nothing less than this: the Greeks would have thought the essence of language from the essence of Being [*das Wesen der Sprache aus dem Wesen des Seins*]—indeed, as this itself. For ὁ Λόγος is the name for the Being of beings [*das Sein des Seienden*]. Yet none of this came to pass.

("Logos [Heraklit, Fragment 50]")

With *Logos* (and its capital letter), the Greeks "*inhabited* this being of language," but they never *thought* it, not even Heraclitus, who made it appear "for the time of a lightning flash."

In German, the same fusion/confusion is repeated, now pertaining to *legen* and *lesen*: "To lay [*legen*] means to bring to lie [*zum Liegen bringen*]. Thus, to lay is at the same time to place one thing beside another [*zusammenlegen*], to lay them together. To lay [*legen*] is to gather [*lesen*]" (ibid.). The present day meaning of *lesen* in German, "to read" (like the Latin *legere*), is therefore only a variation of the *lesen* that gathers together, gathers up, and shelters (cf. *Ährenlese*, "gleaning"; *Traubenlese*, "grape harvest"; *Lese*, "crop," "harvest"; *Auslese*, "selection"; *Erlesen*, "election"; *Vorlese*, "preselection"; etc.). Heidegger's German articulates the being of saying and the being of holding forth as a laying out, exactly as the Greek does.

■ See Box 6.

Barbara Cassin
Clara Auvray-Assayas
Frédérique Ildefonse
Jean Lallot
Sandra Laugier
Sophie Roesch

BIBLIOGRAPHY

Aristotle. *De Anima*. Translated by D. W. Hamlyn. Oxford: Oxford University Press, 1993.
———. *On the Soul, Parva Naturalia, On Breath*. Translated by W. S. Hett. Rev. ed. Loeb Classical Library. Cambridge, MA: Harvard University Press, 1964.

Augustine, Saint. *Eighty-Three Different Questions*. Translated by David L. Mosher. The Fathers of the Church, vol. 70. Washington, DC: Catholic University Press of America, 1982.
———. *Tractates on the Gospel of John*. Translated by John W. Rettig. 5 vols. Washington, DC: Catholic University of America Press, 1988–95.
Austin, John L. *How to Do Things with Words*. Oxford: Oxford University Press, 1962.
———. "Other Minds." In *Philosophical Papers*, edited by J. O. Urmson and G. J. Warnock, 83–84. 2nd ed. Oxford: Oxford University Press, 1970.
Balibar, Étienne. "Points-bilingues." In *Identité et différence*. Paris: Éditions du Seuil, 1997.
Bluck, R. S., trans. *Plato's Phaedo*. Indianapolis, IN: Bobbs-Merrill, 1955.
Bray, G. "The Legal Concept of Ratio in Tertullian." *Vigiliae Christianae* 31 (1977): 94–116.
Cassin, Barbara. *Aristote et le logos: Contes de phénoménologie ordinaire*. Paris: Presses Universitaires de France, 1997.
———. *L'effet sophistique*. Paris: Gallimard, 1995.
———. "Who's Afraid of the Sophists? Against Ethical Correctness." Translated by Charles T. Wolfe. *Hypatia* 15 (Fall 2000): 102–120.
Cavell, Stanley. "Recounting Gains, Showing Losses." In *In Quest of the Ordinary*, by Stanley Cavell. Chicago: University of Chicago Press, 1988.
———. *This New Yet Unapproachable America*. Albuquerque, NM: Living Batch Press, 1989. Translation by S. Laugier: *Une nouvelle Amérique encore inapprochable*. Paris: Éditions de L'Éclat, 1991.
Dictionnaire de théologie catholique. Alfred Vacant, Eugène Mangenot, and Emile Amann. Paris: Letouzey and Ané, 1923–50.
Diogenes Laertius. *Lives of Eminent Philosophers*. Translated by R. D. Hicks. London: Heinemann, 1925.
Dixsaut, Monique, trans. *Platon: Phédon*. Paris: Flammarion, 1991.
Ebbesen, Sten. *Greek-Latin Philosophical Interaction*. Aldershot, UK: Ashgate, 2008.
Erigena, John Scotus. *Periphyseon (On the Division of Nature)*, Book 3. Edited by I. P. Sheldon-Williams with the collaboration of Ludwig Bieler. Dublin: Dublin Institute for Advanced Studies, 1981.

6

Vernunft ist Sprache, λόγος: The three senses of *Wort*

If I were as eloquent as Demosthenes I would yet have to do nothing more than repeat a single word three times: reason is language, *logos*. I gnaw at this marrowbone and will gnaw myself to death over it. There still remains a darkness, always, over this depth for me; I am still waiting for an apocalyptic angel with a key to this abyss.

(Letter from Hamann to Herder, 8 August 1784, Heidegger, "Language")

The famous passage quoted by Heidegger, "Reason is language, λόγος," in the essay "Language" is dated 8 August. Hamann addresses Herder by putting himself in the position of Job in his mire (Job 30:6ff.); he refers to Herder's later *Ideas on the Philosophy of the History of Mankind*, which he has just received, as a *Lustgarden* (garden of pleasures) and only feels directly concerned by book 4, on the divine origin of language and the role of religion in the life of mankind. "*Vernunft ist Sprache, λόγος*" refers to the entire conception of creation in its two aspects—nature and history—as the word of God, in accordance with his reading of Genesis. This clear "language" that God speaks is made obscure (*finster*) by the fall; this is why intelligence only comes at the end of time, with the angel of the apocalypse, who will reveal its meaning, and not with a human *Clavis Scripturae* (*kritische Grübeley*). Reason is in the abyss of language, which is itself the veiled speech of God, a divine proffering that is the model of all creation. Herder's explanation is thus somewhat too short for Hamann; although it reintegrates reason with language, it does not see the divine word as being within language, whereas for Hamann the three are inseparable, and the logic of specialization that is particular to the modern world is unaware of this. To counter this logic of specialization (which Herder embodies, despite his critical stance toward it), Hamann suggests that we need to return to the three senses of *logos*, which are to be found also, he says, in the German *Wort*: reason (*Vernunft*), speech (*Sprache*), word (*Logos*). According to Hamann, this strategy could be put in terms of the rhetoric of Demosthenes, as *actio, actio*, and *actio* (adapting a passage in Cicero he was fond of, *De oratore*, 3.56.213; cf. *Orator*, 27.56). Through Luther's translation of the *Logos* in John's Gospel, Hamann sets out to rediscover the unity of reason and language, but especially their shared origin in the word of God. The reason of Modernity is absorbed in the divine word, *Wort* expressing simultaneously, in Protestant cultures, revelation and language. The defense of natural language is thus for Hamann a way to contain reason (*Vernunft*) and to subject it to the word. So for him, *Wort* is more a strategic reduction of *Logos* than an adequate translation, but it allows him to intervene in the three domains covered by this term.

Denis Thouard

BIBLIOGRAPHY

Heidegger, Martin. "Language." In *Poetry, Language, Thought*, edited by A. Hofstadter. New York: Harper and Row, 1971.

7

Glossolalia: From the unity of the word to plurality of tongues

"Glossolalia" is a technical expression referring to a variety of speech act whose name derives from the Greek term for speaking in tongues. Saint Paul may have been the first to define this linguistic practice. In his first letter to the Corinthians, he enjoins his addressees not to "speak into the air" (1 Cor 14:1–25). To "speak in tongues," Paul suggests, is how to forget the meaning of one's words. It is to abandon one's tongue for "tongues" and "obscure expressions," such that one becomes a "child in understanding" and a "barbarian . . . that speaketh unto a barbarian." In *The End of the Poem: Studies in Poetics*, Giorgio Agamben has commented that such speech consists not so much in the "pure uttering of inarticulate sounds" as in a " 'speaking in gloss,' that is, in words whose meaning one does not know." To hear such sounds is to know they mean something without knowing exactly what such a "something" might be; in other words, it is to discern an intention to signify that cannot be identified with any particular signification. Agamben notes that the traditional translations of the Greek text of Paul's letter fail to capture the full radicalism of the linguistic "barbarism" that it clearly describes. Whereas the King James version, following the Vulgate, has "If I know not the meaning of the voice, I shall be unto he that speaketh a barbarian, and he that speaketh shall be a barbarian unto me," a literal rendition would read otherwise on a single, decisive point: "If I know not the

meaning of the voice, I shall be unto he that speaketh a barbarian, and he that speaketh shall be a barbarian *in* me [*en hemoi*]." "The text's *en hemoi*," Agamben writes, "can only signify 'in me,' and what Paul means is perfectly clear: if I utter words whose meaning I do not understand, he who speaks in me, the voice that utters them, the very principle of speech in me, will be something barbarous, something that does not know how to speak and that does not know what it says."

One might well conclude that to speak in tongues is therefore to speak without speaking. For glossolalia begins where the canonical determinations of language end: at the point at which speech is irrevocably loosened from both its significance and its subject, as one experiences, within oneself, "barbarian speech that one does not know." It is an "unfruitful" state, in Paul's words, since it is one in which language is sundered from its semantic and intentional ends, suspended, "in unknown tongues," without the "profit" of a definite sense or purpose. But it is precisely this semantic sterility that also renders glossolalia stimulating for thought. What is speech loosened from its adherence to the rules of a particular language, from the will of an individual speaker, from the conventions of adult and native discourse? Giorgio Agamben may be the contemporary philosopher who has considered these questions with the greatest acuity, and he has suggested more than once that in such glossolalia one may discern

a fundamental dimension of language all too seldom considered as such: communicability without content, or, more simply, "gesture."

Daniel Heller-Roazen

BIBLIOGRAPHY

Agamben, Giorgio. *The End of the Poem: Studies in Poetics*. Translated by Daniel Heller-Roazen. Stanford, CA: Stanford University Press, 1999.
———. *Infancy and History: The Destruction of Experience*. Translated by Liz Heron. London: Verso, 1993.
———. *Language and Death: The Place of Negativity*. Translated by Karen E. Pinkus with Michael Hardt. Minneapolis: University of Minnesota Press, 1991.
———. *Means without Ends: Notes on Politics*. Translated by Vincenzo Binetti and Cesare Casarino. Minneapolis: University of Minnesota Press, 2000.
———. *Potentialities: Collected Essays in Philosophy*. Edited and translated by Daniel Heller-Roazen. Stanford, CA: Stanford University Press, 1999.
———. *Remnants of Auschwitz: The Witness and the Archive*. Translated by Daniel Heller-Roazen. New York: Zone Books, 1999.
———. *The Time That Remains: A Commentary on the Letter to the Romans*. Translated by Patricia Dailey. Stanford, CA: Stanford University Press, 2005.
Heller-Roazen, Daniel. "Speaking in Tongues." *Paragraph* 25, no. 2 (2002): 92–115.

Gilson, Étienne. *History of Christian Philosophy in the Middle Ages*. New York: Random House, 1955.

Grillmeier, Alois. *Jesus der Christus im Glauben der Kirche*. Freiburg, Ger.: Herder, 1979. Translation by John Bowden: *Christ in Christian Tradition*. 2nd rev. ed. 2 vols. London: Mowbrays, 1975.

Hackforth, R., trans. *Plato's Phaedo*. Cambridge: Cambridge University Press, 1955.

Hawtrey, R.S.W. " 'Ratio' in Lucretius." *Prudentia* 33 (2001): 1–11.

Heidegger, Martin. "Logos (Heraklit, Fragment 50)." In *Vorträge und Aufsätze*. 3rd ed., Pfulligen, Ger.: Neske, 1967. First published in 1954. Translation by David F. Krell and Frank A. Capuzzi: "Logos." In *Early Greek Thinking*. New York: Harper and Row, 1975.
———. *Phänomenologische Interpretationen zu Aristoteles: Einführung in die phänomenologische Forschung*. Edited by Walter Bröcker and Käte Bröcker-Oltmanns. *Gesamtausgabe*, vol 61. Frankfurt: Klostermann, 1985. Translated by Richard Rojcewicz: *Phenomenological Interpretations of Aristotle: Initiation into Phenomenological Research*. Bloomington: Indiana University Press, 2001.
———. "Vom Wesen und Begriff der PHYSIS. Aristoteles, Physik B, 1 (1939)." In *Wegmarken*, edited by Friedrich-Wilhelm von Hermann, 239–302. 3rd ed. *Gesamtausgabe*, vol. 9. Frankfurt: Klostermann, 1976. Translation by Thomas Sheehan and William McNeill: "On the Essence and Concept of Φύσις in Aristotle's Physics B, I." In *Pathmarks*, edited by William McNeill, 183–230. Cambridge: Cambridge University Press, 1998.

Keener, Craig S. *The Gospel of John: A Commentary*. 2 vols. Peabody, MA: Hendrickson, 2003.

Kertz, Karl G.S.J. "Meister Eckhart's Teaching on the Birth of the Divine Word in the Soul." *Traditio* 25 (1959): 327–63.

Léon-Dufour, Xavier. *Lecture de l'Évangile selon Jean*. 4 vols. Paris: Éditions du Seuil, 1988–96.

Libera, Alain de, and Emilie Zum Brunn. *Maître Eckhart: Métaphysique du verbe et théologie négative*. Paris: Beauchesne, 1984.

Locke, John. *Essai philosophique concernant l'entendement humain, où l'on montre quelle est l'etendue de nos connoissances certaines, et la manière dont nous y parvenons*. Translated by Pierre Coste. Amsterdam, 1700.

Long, A. A., and D. N. Sedley. *The Hellenistic Philosophers*. 2 vols. Cambridge: Cambridge University Press, 1987.

Nicolas, Christian. *Utraque lingua: Le calque sémantique: Domaine gréco-latin*. Louvain, Belg.: Peeters, 1996.

Nietzsche, Friedrich. "The History of Greek Eloquence." In *Friedrich Nietzsche on Rhetoric and Language*, edited and translated by Sander L. Gilman, Carole Blair, and David J. Parent, 213. New York: Oxford University Press, 1989.

Ojeman, R. "Meanings of 'Ratio' in the *De rerum natura*." *Classical Bulletin* 39 (1963): 53–59.

O'Rourke Boyle, Marjorie. "Sermo, reopening the conversation on translating in Jn 1, 1." *Vigiliae Christianae* 31 (1977): 161–68.

Plato. *Œuvres complètes*. Edited and translated by Leon Robin. 2 vols. Paris: Gallimard / La Pléiade, 1940.
———. *Plato* [in twelve volumes]. Translated by H. N. Fowler et al. Loeb Classical Library. Cambridge, MA: Harvard University Press, 1914–37.

Schindler, Alfred. *Wort und Analogie in Augustins Trinitätslehre*. Tübingen: Mohr, 1965.

Tertullian. *Tertulliani adversus Praxean liber: Tertullian's Treatise against Praxeas*. Translated by Ernest Evans. London: SPCK, 1948.

Weigelt, Charlotta. *The Logic of Life: Heidegger's Retrieval of Aristotle's Concept of Logos*. Stockholm: Almqvist and Wiksell, 2002.

Yon, Albert. *Ratio et les mots de la famille de reor: Contribution à l'étude historique du vocabulaire latin*. Paris: Champion, 1933.

LOVE / LIKE

CATALAN	*amistança*
FRENCH	*aimer, amour, amitié*
GERMAN	*lieben, mögen, Minne*
GREEK	*eran* [ἐρᾶν], *agapan* [ἀγαπᾶν], *philein* [φιλεῖν], *erôs* [ἔρως], *philia* [φιλία], *agapê* [ἀγάπη]
HEBREW	*'āhëv* [אָהֵב], *'ahavāh* [אַהֲבָה]
ITALIAN	*amare, voler bene a, piacere a*
LATIN	*amare, diligere, amicitia, caritas*
SPANISH	*amar, amistad*

➤ MORALS, NEIGHBOR, PATHOS, PLEASURE, SENSE, SOUL, VERGÜENZA, *VIRTUE*

Our present-day languages deriving from Indo-European ones are connected mainly with two major etymological types: for Romance languages, the Latin verb *amare*, which may be based on *amma* (mother), and for the Germanic group (with *lieben* and "love"), a Sanskrit root that has sometimes been associasted with the Greek *eros* [ἔρως], as well as with the Latin *libido*. But whatever the etymology may be, the various words all have a generic sense of equivalent extension, unless they are inserted into a system of opposition: the pair to "love" / "to like" in English; *mögen/lieben* in German. In French, *aimer* designates a whole spectrum of relationships and affects that ranges from sexuality and eroticism to more or less sublimated relationships between people, values, things, or behaviors (when one "loves" [*aime*], one can "make love," "be in love," "cherish," "like," etc.). The semantic indetermination that consequently characterizes these terms forces us to resort to complements or to circumlocutions that enable us to determine which kind of affect we are dealing with (in French, *aimer d'amitié* vs. *aimer d'amour*), and these complicate translation accordingly. This indetermination also leads to the reinvestment or invention of new words to specify a kind of love or object (in the New Testament, *agapê* [ἀγάπη], and its translation by *caritas*, the Germanic *Minne*, and in Catalan, Raymond Lully's *amistança*). From this point of view, the first of modern languages is Latin, since it combines in *amare* what are in Greek two completely distinct poles: on the one hand, *eran* [ἐρᾶν], *aimer d'amour*, "to (be in) love," a disymmetric relation of inequality and dissimilarity (active/passive)—a Platonic word whose extension determines an erotics of philosophy; on the other hand, *philein* [φιλεῖν], *aimer d'amitié*, "cherish," a relation of equality or commensurability and resemblance—an Aristotelian word that characterizes ethical and political bonds.

I. The Bipolar Schema: In Modern Languages, "to Love" Means Everything

The different affective modalities covered by the verb "to love" (or *aimer, lieben*, etc.) are located between the extremes of a bipolarity ranging from sensuality to intellect: depending on the context, the period, or the author, the meaning moves, in each language, now toward one extreme, then toward the other. To determine which of these two poles we are referring to, we are often obliged to resort to several kinds of qualification that take into account especially the nature of the affect involved, its intensity, or its object (one can love God, one's neighbor, one's wife, one's sexual partner, one's child, a close friend, something one will never see again, a landscape, chocolate, staying home). Thus the differentiation will be made by means of epithets, complements, expressions of modality (e.g., with sensual desire, eroticism, libido, or inversely, with respect, tenderness, friendship, sympathy, charity). But the dichotomy can also manifest itself as an antithesis between two different semantic fields: in German, *lieben* (love) and *mögen* (like), or *Liebe* and *Minne* (a poetic type of love); in Italian, *amare* and *voler bene a* (which includes the idea of a strong desire); whereas in French, *aimer* means both "love" and "like" and thus sometimes has to be further specified (*aimer d'amour, aimer bien*). However, even this antithesis is not always maintained. Thus, although the disjunction between "love" and "like" works for the differentiation by affect (I love you, *je vous aime* / I like her, *je l'aime bien*), the same is not true when it is a matter of intensity: to the question "Do you like cabbage?" one may very well reply "I love it" ("*J'adore ça!*" French says, using the same verb as for God) or "I am fond of it."

A. Dichotomies based on the nature and modalities of the affect

The bipolar character of the vocabulary of love is manifested especially through a series of pairs of opposites, the most common of which are those that distinguish between eroticized, sensual, or carnal love and romantic, tender, spiritual love, two affects whose interaction was analyzed by Freud; "concupiscent love" and deep affection for a friend (*amour d'aimitiè*), a classical distinction, especially since the time of Aristotle, Cicero, and Descartes; love as *affectus* and love as esteem, an opposition close to the one Malebranche establishes between "instinctual love" (*amour d'instinct*) and "rational love" (*amour de raison*); "pathological love" and "practical love," which Kant radically opposes to each other. We can add the dichotomy proposed by Pierre Rousselot regarding medieval authors: "physical love," which is governed by natural tendencies (*phusis* [φύσις]) that lead every being to seek its individual happiness, versus "ecstatic love," violent, independent of natural appetites, foreign to any personal interest and to any selfish inclination. This distinction is related to the one, also concerning the love of God, on which Fénelon and quietism base themselves when they oppose "mercenary love" to a "pure love" that pushes contempt of self and disinterestedness to the point of showing itself to be indifferent to the "impossible supposition" of damnation itself.

1. Sensual love and romantic love

Liebe, on the one hand, and *amour*, on the other, conjoin in their generic meaning the *amor/libido* bipolarity that the Latin substantives perfectly distinguish. But they do not proceed from the same source. When Freud opposes two forms of love that are expressed, one by tender or romantic feelings, and the other by directly sexual tendencies, he has no trouble in discerning, beneath *Liebe*, the force of the *libido*, sexual desire, which organizes itself, invests itself, transfers itself, sublimates itself (see DRIVE). On the other hand, for Lacan, *amour* is radically opposed to desire.

■ See Box 1.

2. From love to *tendresse* and sentimentality

In translating the opposition that Freud establishes between *sinnliche Liebe* and *Zärtlichkeit*, French translators render the latter term as *tendresse* (tenderness). *Tendresse* came into common use only in the seventeenth and early eighteenth centuries, being limited to the sense that it currently has, amorous feeling, whereas *amour* was also applied to sexual or eroticized love. The vocabulary of *tendresse* came to replace that of friendship (*amitié*), which had had since the sixteenth century the strong sense of "love" (*amour*), following on the adjective *tendre* (tender)—which, like the Latin *tener*, expressed the idea of youth, freshness, or delicacy, in the sense in which one speaks of "tender years" (*âge tendre*). In the French classical period, *tendre* was even used as a masculine noun to designate the love relationship, in particular in Mlle. de Scudéry's famous "Carte du Tendre" (Map of the Land of Tenderness).

■ See Box 2.

3. Bipolarities from the Middle Ages to Kant

Christian authors of the Middle Ages base themselves partly on Aristotle (*Nicomachean Ethics*, 8.2) and Cicero (*De amicitia*, §6) to oppose "concupiscent love" (*amor conscupiscentiae*) to "the love of friendship or good will" (*amor amicitiae seu benevolentiae*). The former, which ranges from the desire for the pleasures of the senses to the desire for divine benefits (which is related to what Kant was later to call *amor complacentiae*), consists in a selfish attraction to objects that provide us with delight or enjoyment and that we want to possess. The latter, whose definition is reminiscent of the Greek *eunoia* [εὔνοια], draws us toward a being whom we love for himself, whom we wish well, or whom we are happy to see possess this good. In his *Passions of the Soul* (§81), Descartes says that this "distinction" is traditional, but he thinks that "it concerns solely the effects of love" and that this does not imply a genuine duality in the essential definition of the latter, which is always, whatever its effects or objects might be, a mixture of concupiscence and good will. In the 1950s, in order to translate this distinction into contemporary language, some psychologists popularized the opposition between *amour captatif* and *amour oblatif* ("the desire to have and possess the object, to assimilate it and identify it with oneself," as opposed to the "desire to give oneself and lose oneself in the love object, to identify with it"; Maggini, Lundgren, and Leuci, "Jealous Love"). The latter is characterized by an altruistic propensity to sacrifice oneself in which Jacques Lacan discerned a form of egocentric aggressivity.

The resort to the bipolar schema was also established in the context of a question that remained acute throughout the history of conceptions of love, that is, the question of whether love is essentially a matter of sentiment and affectivity to the point of culminating in an absence of any moderation and the most irrational passion, or whether it must necessarily be in accord with reason and knowledge. Some medieval theologians had already adopted the traditional idea, which began with Origen and Saint Augustine and continued to Leibniz and Malebranche and which sees true love as having to be based on an exact appraisal (*aestimatio*) or discernment (*discretio*) of the value of its object. This intellectualist program, which finds its application particularly in the case of "ordinate love" ("Ille autem iuste et sancte vivit qui rerum integer aestimator est; ipse est autem qui ordinatam dilectionem habet" [Now he is a man of just and holy life who forms an unprejudiced estimate of things, and keeps his affections also under strict control]; Augustine, *On Christian Doctrine*, bk. 1, chap. 28). This thesis is in contrast to the doctrinal orientation of Bernard of Clairvaux, the bard of love as *affectus* and as the impulse of the heart escaping not only all measure but also all rational control. However, his friend and disciple William of Saint-Thierry elaborated a theory of "love-intellection," that is, a love regulated by knowledge. We find this idea, which was fairly widespread in the seventeenth century, in Descartes and especially in the works of Corneille. Descartes emphasizes, in fact, the importance of an intellectual appraisal of the value of the different objects of love. Thus he observes that love differs from other affections "by the esteem one has for what one loves, in comparison with oneself" (*Passions of the Soul*, §83) and that it is governed by "judgments that also lead the soul [*âme*] to join itself willingly with things that it considers good and to separate itself from those that it considers bad" (ibid., §79).

With Spinoza, we find once again, in a more original form, the idea of the rationality of the order of love, notably with regard to *amor Dei intellectualis*, which is for him the crowning achievement of reason. This love goes beyond reason itself and beyond law. It represents the plenitude of knowledge that prevents the soul from getting lost in the fog of affectivity or passion, a torment that Romanticism later magnified under the name of *Leidenschaft* (an ambiguous composite derived from *leiden*, "to suffer"—the substantive *Leiden* designating the Passion of Christ), whereas affectivity itself, developing in it as legitimately as that other natural force constituted by the imagination, permits it to overcome pure intellectualism.

■ See Box 3.

B. Dichotomies based on the object: The invention or reinvestment of other words

To the various binary oppositions we have just mentioned as enabling us to clarify the meaning, obviously so ambiguous, of the word "love" (and *amour*, *Liebe*, or *amore*), one can add others that take into account not the nature or modalities of the affect, but rather the object loved or its specific qualities. For example, the following: love of God / love of one's neighbor or oneself; filial love / love of country; earthly love / heavenly love (cf. Lucien's work on Marguerite de Navarre published under this title); self-love (egocentric love; Aristotle calls it *philautie*, Hugo of St. Victor calls it *amor privatus*) / altruistic love (according to Gregory the Great); homosexual love / heterosexual love. But the invention of other words is made necessary precisely when the object cannot

1

The Freudian and Lacanian dichotomies

In *Group Psychology and the Analysis of the Ego* (*Massenpsychologie und Ich-Analyse*, 1921), chap. 8, "Being in Love and Hypnosis" ("Verliebtheit und Hypnose"), Freud points out that the affective relationships that we designate by the term "love" (*Liebe*) represent such a vast "scale of possibilities" that the term is full of ambiguities: it can designate "the object-cathexis on the part of the sexual instincts with a view to directly sexual satisfaction . . . , what is called common, sensual love," as well as feelings of "affection" (*Zärtlichkeit*). At a certain stage of development, the latter are grafted onto the original libidinal current, inhibiting its drives toward sexual aims. In adolescence, the sensual current (*sinnliche Strömung*), which reappears with a certain intensity, enters into competition with "affectionate trends of feeling that persist" in such a way that the subject's future destiny will be marked by the existence between these two currents of either a genuine schism or a sort of harmony. In the first case, "A man will show a sentimental enthusiasm for women whom he deeply respects but who do not excite him to sexual activities, and he will only be potent with other women whom he does not 'love' and thinks little of or even despises" (cf. "A Special Type of Choice of Object Made by Men" ["Über einen besonderen Typus der Objektwahl beim Manne," 1910]). In the second case, a synthesis regarding the same erotic object is produced "between the unsensual, heavenly love and the sensual, earthly love," so that "[t]he depth to which anyone is in love, as contrasted with his purely sensual desire, may be measured by the size of the share taken by the aim-inhibited instincts of affection."

In his article of 1912 that was reprinted in *Contributions to the Psychology of Love* and called "On the Universal Tendency to Debasement in the Sphere of Love" ("Über die Allgemeinste Erniedrigung des Liebeslebens"), Freud mentions the rift observable in some men between the current of sensuality and that of affection. He states that psychoanalysis should allow such men to arrive at "a completely normal attitude in love" harmoniously combining the two tendencies. In reference to the last of the stages of libidinal development (after the oral, sadistic-anal, and phallic stages), some of Freud's disciples have theorized this as "genital love"—a notion that Jacques Lacan criticized, targeting those who, without regard for "the fundamentally narcissistic nature of all being in love (*Verliebtheit*) were able to so utterly deify the chimera of so-called 'genital love' as to attribute to it the power of

'oblativity,' a notion that gave rise to so many therapeutic mistakes" (*Écrits*). Perhaps it is because of such criticisms that the French often use the English term "genital love," as if to remind themselves that this "illusion" seduced chiefly Anglo-Saxon psychology.

Lacan adopted Freud's distinction but inflected it in the form of a radical opposition between *amour* and *désir*, the former being rigorously defined as "ignorance" of the latter and as being nothing more than "what substitutes for the sexual relationship." However, Freud maintained a link between the two, asserting that love is what enables the sexual appetite to revive after a certain period of non-desire following satisfaction, after what he calls "an interval free of desire." In Lacan, the word *amour* is thus made unequivocal by the fact that it signifies nothing other than de-eroticized sentimentality. Thus he posits a difference in nature between love thus defined and what has been excluded from it: desire. For Freud, on the contrary, what is called "spiritual love" is merely erotic love metamorphosed, in the best of cases, by sublimation, a process that redirects the infantile libido toward nonsexual cultural goals.

This radical Lacanian dichotomy is nonetheless tempered by the fact that for psychoanalysis, "love" designates not only the "choice of object" (*Objektwahl*) but also "transference love" (*Übertragungsliebe*), a phenomenon that is fundamental for the functioning of analytical procedures. It was after the failure of his treatment of his first hysterical patients that Freud theorized transference and, more precisely, transferential love as "resistance" to analysis. This love is transformed into an "indispensable requirement," its manipulation allowing the analyst to make "the patient's buried and forgotten love-emotions actual and manifest" (*die verborgenen und vergessenen Liebesregungen*)" ("The Dynamics of Transference" ["Zur Dynamik der Übertragung," 1912]; see also "Postscript," in *Fragment of an Analysis* [Dora]).

We can thus say that Lacan qualifies, on this subject, his opposition between *amour* and *désir*. While on the one hand he defines love as nothing more than "ignorance" of desire and the sexual, on the other hand he posits that love itself, as the motive force of transference, is a necessary condition for the analytical process: "At the beginning of the analytical experience, let us recall, was love" (*Le transfert*). Thus, this same seminar of 1960–61 was devoted almost entirely to the question of love. A minute analysis of Plato's *Symposium* provided Lacan with an opportunity to theorize the relations between *amour* and *désir* differently. From

the myth of the birth of the *daimon* Erôs, as he is mentioned in Socrates's and Diotima's speeches (*Symposium*, 202a), Lacan takes the formula "Love is giving what one does not have" (*Le transfert*), declaring: "We can say that the dialectical definition of love, as it is developed by Diotima, rejoins what we have tried to define as the metonymic function in desire" (ibid.).

BIBLIOGRAPHY

Freud, Sigmund. "Being in Love and Hypnosis." Chapter 8 of *Group Psychology and the Analysis of the Ego*, in vol. 18 of *The Standard Edition of the Complete Psychological Works of Sigmund Freud*, edited and translated by James Strachey, 111–16. London: Hogarth Press, 1955.

———. "The Dynamics of Transference." In vol. 12 of *The Standard Edition of the Complete Psychological Works of Sigmund Freud*, edited and translated by James Strachey, 97–108. London: Hogarth Press, 1958.

———. *Five Lectures on Psychoanalysis*. Translated by J. Strachey. New York: Norton, 1989.

———. *Fragment of an Analysis of a Case of Hysteria*. In vol. 7 of *The Standard Edition of the Complete Psychological Works of Sigmund Freud*, edited and translated by James Strachey, 3–112. London: Hogarth Press, 1953.

———. "Mass Psychology and the Analysis of the I." In *Mass Psychology and Other Writings*, translated by J. Underwood. London: Penguin, 2004.

———. "The Most Prevalent Form of Degradation in Erotic Life." In "Contributions to the Psychology of Love," chap. 4 of *Sexuality and the Psychology of Love*, edited by P. Rieff. New York: Touchstone, 1997.

———. "On the Universal Tendency to Debasement in the Sphere of Love." In vol. 11 of *The Standard Edition of the Complete Psychological Works of Sigmund Freud*, edited and translated by James Strachey, 177–90. London: Hogarth Press, 1957.

———. "A Special Type of Object Choice Made by Men." In vol. 11 of *The Standard Edition of the Complete Psychological Works of Sigmund Freud*, edited and translated by James Strachey, 163–76. London: Hogarth Press, 1957.

———. "The Technique of Psycho-analysis." In *An Outline of Psycho-analysis*, translated by J. Strachey. New York: W. W. Norton, 1970.

Lacan, Jacques. *Écrits*. Paris: Éditions du Seuil, 1966. Translation by B. Fink: *Écrits: The First Complete Edition in English*. New York: W. W. Norton, 2006.

———. *Le transfert*. Vol. 8 of *Le séminaire* (1960–61). Paris: Éditions du Seuil, 1991. Translation by C. Gallagher: *The Seminar of Jacques Lacan 8: Transference*. London: Karnac Books, 2002.

2

Affectionate, affection, sentimental

Starting from *tendresse* (tenderness) (or from the related forms *tendreur* and *tendreté*), which was initially understood literally—Vauvenargues still preferred the literal meaning, for example, regarding the "tenderness of meat"—the classical French language came, through the compassion inspired by the delicate or fragile nature of an object, to an attitude corresponding, in the subject, to a penchant henceforth designated by the word *tendresse* in the affective sense. In other languages this semantic shift took place on the basis either of the same Latin adjective *tener* (as in English with "tenderness," in Italian with *tenerezza*, and in Spanish with *ternura*) or of another word that had as its primary meaning the idea of weakness or delicacy (like *zart* in German, from which *Zärtlichkeit* is derived). Nevertheless, Kant, precisely in referring to the fragility of the feeling of friendship (*teneritas amicitiae*) in his "Doctrine of Virtue" (*The Metaphysics of Morals*, pt. 2, §46), paradoxically brings us back to the literal, pre-seventeenth-century sense of the French word *tendresse*. He states that "[f]riendship . . . is something so *tender* that if it is based on feelings [and not on principles and rules] it cannot for an instant be guaranteed against interruptions."

The semantic development of the French word *tendresse* can in fact be explained in two ways: either the object affected by tenderness in the pre-seventeenth-century sense of "weakness" inspires a sympathetic attention in others that is called upon to transform itself into a dynamics of love that will assume the name of *tendresse* in the affective sense; or such a passionate fire in the heart flaring up independently of any previous emotion is perceived as a typically feminine feeling, that is, one related to the sensitivity of the "weaker sex." But in both cases, we are dealing with the register of weakness, of inclination, that is, of *pathein* [παθεῖν], or what Spinoza calls the *animi pathema*, and even of defectiveness, for example, when one is said to have weakness for a person, an expression that corresponds to *prendre quelqu'un par son faible* (to attack someone at his weak point) and that leads to the notions of attraction, the traps of seduction, and charms from which someone suffers.

This avatar of the word *tendresse* is related to the modern meanings that were acquired at the same period by the noun *sentiment* and the epithet *sentimental*. The latter made its entrance, with the meaning it now has, through the 1769 translation of Laurence Sterne's *A Sentimental Journey*. The translator explained the word this way: "It has not been possible to render the English word 'sentimental' in French by any expression that might correspond to it, and it has therefore been left in English. Perhaps in reading it will be found that it deserves to be made part of our language." The adjective "sentimental" had only very recently appeared in English, in 1749, by derivation from "sentiment" (which had itself been borrowed from French in the fourteenth century), with its double meaning of opinion based on an evaluation that is more subjective than logical (according to the meaning that is found, for example, in David Hume's work) and a disposition belonging to the register of the heart and affectivity (and sometimes given a pejorative connotation, particularly emphasized in what is called *ressentiment*). German has adopted the epithet *sentimental* and the noun *Sentimentalität*, which has the meaning of "sentimentality" when it is preceded by the adjective *affektiert*.

BIBLIOGRAPHY

Sterne, Laurence. *Le voyage sentimental.* Translated by J. F. Frenais. 2 vols. Amsterdam, 1769.

3

"Pathological love" and "practical love" in Kant

The pair "pathological love" / "practical love" introduced by Kant at the beginning of the *Groundwork of the Metaphysics of Morals* (RT: Ak., 6:399), illustrates once again the bipolarity of the notion of love and the necessity of resorting to epithets. Kant's problem is the following: love seems to depend on sensibility alone, and as such it should be excluded from an ethics that posits that in principle an act has no moral value unless it is done out of duty. What then should we do with the duty of love expressed in the Old Testament: "You shall love your neighbor as yourself" (Lv 19:18; cf. Mt 22:39)? Kant was forced to recognize in "The Metaphysical Principles of Virtue" (pt. 2 of the *Groundwork*) that "a *duty to love* makes no sense" (RT: Ak., 6:401–2). The solution to this problem involves a distinction opposing "practical" love, which can be the object of a duty insofar as it resides in the will, to a "pathological love" depending on sensibility. "The Metaphysical Principles of Virtue" makes use of a parallel distinction between "charity" (*amor benevolentiae*) and "kindness" (*amor complacentiae*). In each case the distinction seeks to bring the principles of Kant's moral doctrine into conformity with the Scriptures: this attempt was given particular attention by the neo-Kantians, who in the early twentieth century reexamined the question of Kant's Christianity (cf. Bauch, "Luther und Kant").

BIBLIOGRAPHY

Bauch, Bruno. "Luther und Kant." *Kant-Studien* 4 (1900): 416–19, 455–56.

be confounded with any other, as for example, in the case of God or a person loved with an incommensurable love.

1. Conjugal *fides* and courtly love

In his famous book *Love in the Western World*, Denis de Rougemont opts to harden the opposition that manifested itself in the twelfth century between two forms of love: on the one hand, the love between Christian spouses, founded on a mutual *fides*, and on the other hand, "courtly love" (or *fin'amor*, "refined love," or "pure love" in Occitan), which he assimilates to the adulterous, murderous passion felt by the troubadour or the hero (notably Tristan) with regard to the "lady of his thoughts." However, the expression "courtly love" appeared in French only very lately, around 1880, in the work of Gaston Paris, whereas, to designate such a form of love, German had long had the untranslatable noun *die Minne*.

- See Box 4.

2. The New Testament between *eros* and *agapê*

Sometimes the disparity with which human love is confronted when it has as its object not a peer or an inferior but God himself is considered impossible to render using oppositional terms taken from the common vocabulary. When the Swedish Lutheran theologian Anders Nygren found himself in this situation, he compensated for this difficulty by appealing to the two Greek terms *erôs* [ἔρως] and *agapê* [ἀγάπη]. But he considered them as far more than simple polarities of love; between them he saw an opposition that broadened "to the point of becoming a philosophical antithesis" that presented itself as an irreconcilable conflict between "two fundamental motives" (*Agape and Eros*). Nygren indicates what is at stake through an epigraph borrowed from the Hellenist Ulrich von Wilamowitz-Moellendorff: "Although the German language is so poor that it has to use the single term 'love' [*Liebe*] in both cases, the two ideas [*erôs* and *agapê*] nonetheless have nothing in common." Believing that he saw in the Greek conception of *erôs* both a synthesis of nonpossession and possession, on the one hand, and on the other hand a demonic intermediary that allowed the subject to move from the crude forms of desire to truth and immortality, Nygren thought Christianity had radically overthrown this monist conception of love by promoting, in opposition to the Platonic *erôs*, the *agapê* revealed by the New Testament writings of Paul and John.

- See Box 5.

The special problem posed for theologians and mystics by the human soul's love for God also led them to invent specific words in their own vernacular languages, usually by derivation from a common word in these vernaculars or from a Latin word. That is what happened, precisely with regard to "love," in the work of the creator of philosophical and literary Catalan, Ramon Llull (ca. 1235–1315).

- See Box 6.

3. Lexical investments and reinvestments in Christian Latin

In fact, to translate the Hebrew *'āhēv*, which is applied to the love of God, Christian authors initially adopted relatively new terms, either Greek ones like *agapê* (whereas *agapan* [ἀγαπᾶν] is older) rather than *erôs* or *philia*, or Latin ones such as *caritas* rather than *amor*. In Latin, they even invented *dilectio*, built on the older verb *diligere*.

a. *Caritas* in the church fathers

The notion of *caritas* was established by the first Christian authors writing in Latin when they had to translate the Bible into that language. At that time they were dependent on Greek—that of the books of the New Testament and the translation of the Bible made by Alexandrian Jews (the Septuagint). As we have seen, the translators of the Septuagint, who had had three verbs to render the Hebrew verb *'āhēv*: *eran* [ἐρᾶν] (*erôs*), *philein* [φιλεῖν] (*philia*), and *agapan* (*agapê*), showed a marked preference for the last, probably because, having classically a much less determinate meaning, it lent itself to a semantic innovation corresponding to the stronger and deeper meaning of the Hebrew *'āhēv*. As G. Kittel and Friedrich's RT: *Theologisches Wörterbuch* notes in the article "*agapê*," "the old word *'āhēv* imbued the pale Greek word with its rich and yet precise meaning. . . . The whole group of words in the family of *agapan* received a new meaning through the translation of the Old Testament."

4

The Germanic *Minne*

Although the erotic ideal advocated by the Provençal troubadours and the *trouvères* in northern France has only recently been given the name of "courtly love" (which amounts to defining such an original experience by the place where it developed: the seigneurial or royal courts—*corteis*—of the period), in the Middle Ages the German language already had a specific term, *die Minne*, to designate this form of love and more particularly what characterizes it in its essence. Moreover, down to Wagner's *Tristan und Isolde*, we find it personified, in the same way as *fin'amor* in courtly literature, as the goddess of love (*Liebesgöttin*), as Lady Minne (*Frau Minne*).

According to the usual etymology (Lat. *memini*, "remember," and *mens*, "mind"), the noun *Minne* (like the verb *minnen* and the adjectives *minnig* and *minniglich*) emphasizes the presence of the beloved in the consciousness of the lover and the fact that this presence continues over time in the form of phantasm and memory. In short, *Minne* is love insofar as it occupies the lover's mind and leads him to resort to poetry, for instance, to testify to his psychic experience. The latter corresponds to the experience medieval theologians described, in order to stigmatize it, as *delectatio morosa*, that is, the habit of dwelling with pleasure on thoughts of the absent beloved. It is illustrated still more clearly by the passion that the courtly poet cultivates for the "lady of his thoughts," especially in the extreme situation of *amour de loin*. Thus, around this courtly adventure of *fin'amor*, the Germanic lexicon acquired the following components: *der Minnesang* (the poetry of the troubadours), *das Minnelied* (love song), *der Minnedichter* and *der Minnesänger* (troubadour), *der Minnedienst* (service to the lady), *der Minnetrank* (love philter). But the term *Minne* and the characteristics of Provençal "pure love" were also used by the thirteenth-century Flemish members of a lay sisterhood (the Béguines) in developing a theory of the love of God. For Hadewijch of Antwerp (d. ca. 1260), the love-experience designated by the expression *Minnemystik* included two phases. The first takes the form of an impetuous, passionate desire (*aestus amoris*; in Dutch, *orewoet*); this is the element of joy (*ghebruken*) in total union. The second is marked by an experience of ravishment and privation (*ghebreken*), of suffering and distress. However, this is more of an alternation; indeed, a coexistence of apparent contradictions corresponding to the antithetical feelings of joy and desolation in which courtly poetry saw the expression of the essential transcendence of love.

5
The "true" Christian notion of love according to Nygren

In his work *Agape and Eros*, Nygren maintains that even when it takes the form of "celestial love," the primary characteristic of Orphic or Platonic *erôs* is "aspiration, lust, desire" and remains ineluctably faithful to its basic nature as man's appetite for an object to be possessed, whereas the *agapê* celebrated in the New Testament is supposed to be essentially a gift of oneself, a totally disinterested descent, and for that reason a sacrifice of which God alone is capable. Moreover, Nygren seeks to identify the "transformations" to which, since the end of the Middle Ages, theology is supposed to have subjected the "true" Christian notion of love, which is *agapê*. It is supposed to have adulterated the latter by developing the theory of *caritas ordinata*, or "the order of love," that is, the order of a love that has the property of necessarily conforming to the value of the object itself. In Nygren's view, such a theory represents a "fatal synthesis" from which Luther was to seek to free theology and that amounts to including in *agapê* one of the essential elements of *erôs*, namely an interested desire motivated by the qualities that can be discerned in the love object.

The Scholastic adage according to which a thing must be loved in proportion to its value (*magis diligendum quia magis bonum*) would thus take us back to the kind of love that is traditionally described as mercenary and that is in reality radically foreign to the New Testament conception of love.

Nygren's work, which had a wide impact, has a weak philological basis. Interpreters pointed out, in particular, that unlike the Hebrew language, which had only the verb *'āhēv* [אָהֵב] and the noun *'ahav āh* [אַהֲבָה] to designate all forms of love (sacred or profane, noble or impure, selfish or disinterested, etc.), the Greek of the Septuagint had several words to render the diversity of these forms, such as *agapê*, *erôs*, and *philia*. Even when the Hebrew text refers to sensual love, the Septuagint prefers *erôs*—a word that is, moreover, extremely rare in the Septuagint as a whole—the term *agapê* (which the Latin Vulgate renders as *caritas*). It is the word *agapê* that we find in the most erotic passages of the epithalamium of the Song of Songs. Thus lines 7–10 in chapter 7, which express a passionate desire for the physical possession of the beloved, begin with these words: "How fair and pleasant you are, O love [*agapê*], delectable maiden!"

But if the term *agapê* has been thus used by the Greek Jews of Alexandria to designate forms of love other than spiritual love, and inversely, Christian authors have traditionally interpreted this biblical poem attributed to Solomon as an allegory of mystical love, that is no doubt because beneath the instability of the vocabulary, we can discern a certain semantic malleability and, more precisely, a certain legitimacy in passing from one kind of affect to another. Thus Nygren's "systematic" dichotomy would be replaced, as Paul Ricoeur puts it (in *Liebe und Gerechtigkeit*), by a "process of metaphorization" by virtue of which, for example, erotic love, *erôs*, has the power to signify and express *agapê*, thus rendering the real analogy that connects distinct affects.

BIBLIOGRAPHY

Nygren, Anders. *Agape and Eros*. Translated by Philip S. Watson. London: SPCK, 1953.
Ricoeur, Paul. *Liebe und Gerechtigkeit = Amour et justice*. Tubingen: J.C.B. Mohr, 1990.

6
Amistat and *amistança*

Catalan words ending in *-ança* or *-ància* designate the action of the verb and are derived from it. Thus *contemplança* means the action of contemplating (*contemplar*). In the case of *amistança*, the verb *amistansar* is not attested before 1373. It has two meanings: "reconcile," "make friends"; and "live in concubinage with." Thus it is because a third term is required alongside *amor* and *amistat*, and not by derivation, that Ramon Llull created the word *amistança*.

This term is never translated as "action of reconciling." Whereas in common usage *amistat* acquires the sense of amorous friendship outside marriage ("women's *amistat* is deceiving," Llull, *Blanquerna*, chap. 27), *amistança* is reserved for loyal, pure, disinterested friendship between two persons (Ausiàs March, poem 92: "But the other love, *amistança pura*, / After death its great strength endures . . ."). *Amistança* (whose character is emphasized by the use of *pura*) is felt by the poet for a dead woman. For the poet, who never mentions God's love or love for God, *amistança pura* constitutes the major elevated form of love. *Amistança* subsequently underwent the same development in meaning as did *amistat*: in the seventeenth century, the word could mean "concubinage."

For Llull, *amor* is reserved for God, along with the verb *enamorarse*, which frequently reinforces the verb *amar*. In his *Llibre d'amic et amat* (*The Book of the Lover and the Beloved*), he describes the *amor* of the *amic*; it is never a question of carnal *amistat*: "Blanquerna [the fictional author of the *Llibre*] wanted to make them [his hermit-readers] to love [*enamorar*] God." Similarly: "The *amic* says to the *amat*: You who fill the sun with spendor, fill my heart with love." In this context, *amistat* would have an unacceptable sexual connotation and *amistança* would be too human. The doublet *amic/amat* takes into account the intentionality of *amor* and the duality Ramon Llull considered constitutive of the love between man and God.

Dominique de Courcelles

BIBLIOGRAPHY

Llull, Ramon. *Blanquerna*. Translated from the Catalan with an introduction by E. A. Peers. London: Dedalus, 1988. First published in 1926.
———. *The Book of the Lover and the Beloved*. Edited by Kenneth Leech. Translated by E. A. Peers. London: Sheldon Press, 1978.

In their turn, Christian authors writing in Latin had to wonder how to render the word *agapê* as used in the Septuagint and in the New Testament. At that time, Latin had two verbs meaning "to love": *amare* (with the broad sense of amorous passion as well as that of disinterested affection) and *diligere*, and also two nouns, *amor* and *caritas*. *Caritas*, which we frequently find in Cicero and which later became an important term in the Christian Scriptures and in Christian theology, is derived from *carus*, which had the twofold meaning of what one "cherishes" and what is "of great price"—whence the proximity of the terms *charité* and *cherté* in French. *Caritas* adds to the meaning of *amor* that of esteem and respect, as we see, for example, in Seneca and especially in Cicero. For the latter, *amor* designates the affection two spouses or two brothers have for each other or that of parents for their children, but the use of *caritas* was considered preferable when speaking of the love one has for the gods, for the fatherland, for one's parents, for superior men, or for humanity, notably in the expression *caritas generis humani* (*De finibus*, 5.23, 65).

But the first Latin Christian authors adopted none of the words of this classical vocabulary to render the word *agapê* in the Septuagint and the New Testament. Thus in the first half of the third century, Tertullian and Cyprian of Carthage limited themselves to transcribing the word as such, as was also done with other Hellenisms, like *baptizein* [βαπτίζειν] and *charisma* [χάρισμα], that were permanently established. Nonetheless, in their commentaries on the Scriptures and in their theological writings, they tended to render the verb *agapan* by *diligere* and the substantive *agapê* by either *dilectio* (especially Tertullian), a word that had just appeared in the language of the Church, or by *caritas* (especially Cyprian). It was only later on, and mainly with Saint Jerome at the end of the fourth century, that the latter two terms entered into the translation of the Bible itself, but with a preference for *caritas*, which occurs 114 times as opposed to 24 times for *dilectio*. Thus, as Hélène Pétré points out, "the term which in everyday language served to designate the affections, and whose use Cicero had broadened in the expression *caritas generis humani*, expresses for Christians the highest virtue that contains both the love of God and love for humans." It is notably by *caritas* that the Vulgate renders *agapê* in the famous Pauline hymn in 1 Corinthians (13:1–8): "If I speak in the tongues of men and of angels, but have not *caritas* [King James: ". . . have not *love*"], I am a noisy gong or a clanging cymbal. . . . If I give away all I have, and if I deliver my body to be burned, but have not *caritas* I gain nothing. . . . *Caritas* never ends." Nonetheless, Augustine, for instance, sometimes declares that the three terms *amor*, *dilectio*, and *caritas* are more or less equivalent.

Among the church fathers, *caritas* designates the love man has for God and for his neighbor *propter Deum*, in conformity with the evangelical principle, as well as the love that is in God himself (*Caritas summa* or *Caritas in Deo*) and that is expressed particularly in the mutual relations among the three persons of God. In the Middle Ages, Peter Lombard (ca. 1100–60) maintained in his *Sentences* that *caritas* is a love so sublime that it can be conceived only as identical with the presence of God himself (and more precisely of the Holy Spirit) in the soul. At the end of the twelfth and the beginning of the thirteenth centuries, most theologians rejected this theory (which was officially condemned by the Council of Vienna in 1311–12) and made *caritas* a *habitus* in the Aristotelian sense of the term, that is, a peculiarly human capacity for action and merit, like faith and hope, over which it has precedence as the "mother of all virtues." These theologians thus came to distinguish this supernatural *caritas* from *dilectio naturalis*, or the love of God and one's neighbor, of which the first spiritual creatures (Adam, Eve, and the angels) were capable before the Fall—that is, without grace, a state that according to some writers corresponded to the state of pure nature.

In twelfth- and thirteenth-century theological summas, the treatises dealing with the virtue of *caritas* gave particular attention to the notion of *caritas ordinata*, or *amor discretus*, that is, supernatural love's property of conforming to the value of its object. This property derives from the diversity of the measure implied in the double commandment that demands that man love God "with all his heart" and his neighbor "as himself." Thus the *quantum* of love that serves as a basis for these two movements of incommensurable love is the one that one must have for oneself, *amor sui*, which Aristotle calls *philautia* (*Nicomachean Ethics*, 9.8) and Hobbes calls "self-love" (*Leviathan*, chap. 15). This Scholastic notion seems to be the origin of a proverb that is usually used ironically and is translated in French as "Charité bien ordonnée commence par soi-même." Other languages translate it more prosaically, omitting the dimension of *ordo amoris*. Thus in German, people say, "Jeder ist sich selbst der Nächste," and in English, "Charity begins at home."

b. From *caritas* to "charity"

In addition to the specifically theological meaning of the love of God and neighbor, in the third century *caritas* acquired the meaning of "gift" or "alms." In the tenth century it was gallicized in the form of *caritet* and then *charité*, which designated the theological virtue, particularly in its dimension of mercy and benevolence with regard to the poor and deprived. Thus this word was later adopted to designate congregations or associations (Brothers or Sisters of Charity, Ladies of Charity) that were especially attached to this form of religious devotion. Then the term was extended to the various manifestations of aid and assistance in social life (*vente de charité, bureau de charité*). The epithets *charitable* (sometimes used ironically) and *caritatif* derive from the word *charité*. *Caritatif*, which was relatively rare, came to be widely used in the twentieth century to refer to Catholic charitable movements, under the influence of the English "caritative," which was originally part of the vocabulary of political economy. Thus while retaining, especially for moral theology, its meaning of supernatural virtue turned toward God and neighbor, "charity" assumed more and more the restricted meaning of mercy, humanity, and philanthropy, whereas in modern times, debates about the theological virtue itself, notably those in which Fénelon and quietism were involved, are recentered more specifically on the believer's love of God, and more precisely on the question "in what sense it must be disinterested," as Malebranche put it in the subtitle to his treatise *De l'amour de Dieu* (1697).

The semantic evolution of the French word *charité* (like that of the Italian *carità*, the Spanish *caridad*, and the Portuguese *caridade*), in the sense of mercy as a feeling and benevolence as an act, is unknown in German. In German, the New Testament *agapê* (the supernatural love of God and neighbor) is rendered by *Liebe* (notably in 1 Cor 13:1–8, where the clause "If I . . . have not *agapê*" is translated by Luther as "wenn ich hätte der Liebe nicht") and charity toward one's neighbor, in a literal way, by *die Nächstenliebe*, but when it is a matter of the feeling of mercy and generosity, by *die Mildtätigkeit*, and for charitable action, by *die Hilfsbereitschaft* or *die Barmherzigkeit*.

Finding it easier than other languages to do without periphrases, German translates "mutual love" by *Gegenliebe*. Max Scheler even proposed the neologisms *miteinanderlieben* for "to love in mutual contiguity" and *Liebensgemeinschaft* for "community of love"—a reality that was, according to him, introduced into history by Christianity.

II. The Latin and Greek Vocabulary of Love

A. Latin: *Amare, amor, amicitia*

In Latin, as in modern languages, the uses of *amare* cover the whole spectrum of sexual, amorous, familial, and friendly relationships, so that the expression of a specific bond requires the adjunction of other terms. In Cicero's language, the implementation of distinctions through juxtapositions and contrapositions of other terms involves precise stakes, since it is a matter of defining, on the one hand, *amor* in relation to the tradition of the Platonic theory of love and, on the other hand, *amicitia* as a notion constructed on the basis of Roman practices. But the distinction between the two substantives is a constructed effect that is all the more obvious because they derive from *amare* (*De amicitia*, 27.100) and because it is *amor* that gives *amicitia* its name. In his *Tusculan Disputations* (4:68–76), quoting numerous examples of *amor* in the poets, Cicero tries to show that *amor* is usually "borne by desire" (*libidinosus*) and that this desire leads to an illicit sexuality (*stuprum*) or even to madness (*insania/furor*); consequently, one cannot "accord authority to love [*amori auctoritatem tribuere*]" as Plato does or accept the Stoics' definition, in which love is "the drive that moves us to make friendships on the basis of a vision of beauty" (*conatum amicitiae faciendae ex pulchritudinis specie*). Connoting *amor* in this way, Cicero refuses to accept the positive values of the Platonic theory of love, and he elaborates a notion of *amicitia* in which *amor* does not play a major role. In the dialogue *De amicitia*, he takes the various levels on which the bond of friendship was expressed in Rome as a basis for a definition of *amicitia* that includes, with numerous mediations, the Greek traditions, whose lexicon is in this case untranslatable. Friendship is a special relationship, the one that unites two great statesmen, Scipio and Laelius, which makes it possible to articulate the connections between political friendship and private friendship: the choice of the interlocutors allows Cicero to emphasize something to which the language itself testifies, namely the identity of the vocabulary of political relations and private relations.

Amicitia is an active relationship that is expressed above all in *benevolentia*, the will to act for the good of the friend, and it is precisely *benevolentia* that enables us to distinguish the bond of family relationship (*propinquitas*) from friendship: "Whereas you may eliminate [goodwill] from [family] relationship, you cannot do so from friendship. Without it, family relationship still exists in name, friendship does not" (translation modified). This active goodwill gives the service rendered (*prodesse*) and pleasure (*delectare*) equal weight, and they mutually correct each other: the attraction to the other may then be expressed by *amor* and *motus animi*; it grows and is confirmed only through the exchange of services (*beneficium*) and lasting attachment (*studium consuetudo*). The association of pleasure with services rendered seeks to refute both the Epicurean thesis that friendship arises from need and weakness and the conflations of friendship with flattery (*blanditia*) characteristic of relationships with a tyrant, in which the absence of *fides* and *caritas* are manifest. It is, on the contrary, a question of guaranteeing the equality of exchange that alone can provide pleasure: "There is nothing more pleasant than performing duties for one another with devotion" (nihil vicissitudine studiorum officiorumque jucundius). It is on this basis that the sweetness of private relationships can flourish (*suavitas-comitas-facilitas*).

B. Greek: The two poles of *eran* and *philein*

Greek distinguishes very clearly between two ways of loving, *eran* and *philein*. Thus it has a verb, and a whole terminological complex, for each of these poles, which most modern languages now differentiate only by means of adjuncts. *Eran* is presented as a passion that comes from outside, like Cupid's arrows, and is connected with desire (*epithumia* [ἐπιθυμία]), pleasure (*hêdonê* [ἡδονή]), and the enjoyment (*charis* [χάρις]) of an object; it designates an essentially dissymmetrical relation between an *erastes* who feels love and makes it (he is the Corneillian *amant* or, rather, *amoureux*, because it is never taken for granted that his love is shared) and an *eromenos* who is its object (the "beloved"). *Philein* ("to love as a friend," "to cherish," and "to like to . . .") is on the contrary an action or activity freely consented to and deployed from within an (ethical) character or a (political, social) position; it determines a relationship that is not always symmetrical but is in any case mutual and reciprocal, whether it is a matter of similarity, equality, or commensurability.

That is how we can understand, in the first cosmogonies, difference as an originary power between *erôs* and *philia* or *philotês* [φιλότης], both of which are usually translated by "love." Hesiod's *erôs* "softens the sinews" (*lusimelês* [λυσιμελής]; *Theogony*, 121) and intervenes to pass from parthenogenesis to the embrace of Earth and Sky (137ff.); in Parmenides's *Poem* (28B12 DK), *erôs* causes the elementary polarities to be deployed and dispersed. On the contrary, Empedocles's *philotês* unites similars with similars, which Discord (*neikos* [νεῖκος]) separates again (e.g., 28B22 DK).

But the peculiarly philosophical use of these terms is determined by Plato, on the one hand, and Aristotle, on the other. Plato seeks to capture *philein* under *eran* and proposes erotics as the very model of philosophy; Aristotle makes *eran* a special and accidental case of *philein* and describes in terms of *philia* the whole of the relations constitutive of the human world. We are justified in supposing that modern languages are rather Platonic, since they combine everything under the pole of the erotic, hierarchizing objects and affects.

▪ See Box 7.

1. *Eran* or dissymmetry: Plato's philosophy as a generalized erotics

Plato reveals the dissymmetry inherent in the erotic relationship connecting pederasty with Socratic dialectic and makes *erôs* a condition of philosophy. In *Lysis*, which is considered one of the dialogues of Plato's youth, Socrates's whole operation consists in treating *erôs* as if it meant *philia* or, to put it another way, in eroticizing *philia* (the subtitle of the dialogue is *peri philias*), so as to convince little Lysis that

7

An etymological romance: *Amare*, the maternal breast; *eran*, the male body; *philein*, the sociability of the bond

Etymological and semantic disputes rage about whether fantasies and repression are to be compared or distinguished.

Ernout and Meillet (RT: *Dictionnaire étymologique de la langue latine*) acknowledge the plausibility of the derivation of *amare* from *amma*, "mother," which is closely related to *amita*, "aunt," the father's sister, and of course to *mamma*, "nurse," "mother," "breast." On the other hand, *eran*, which also translates *amare*, tends to be on the side of the male. Chantraine (RT: *Dictionnaire étymologique de la langue grecque*) stands by an unknown etymology, rejecting, along with Benveniste (RT: *Le vocabulaire des institutions indo-européennes*), the series of comparisons proposed by Onians (RT: *Origins of European Thought*, p. 177, n. 2; p. 202, n. 5; pp. 472–80) and instead connecting "damp desire" (*pothos hugros* [πόθος ὑγρός]) and *erôs* with *hersê* [ἔρση], "the dew" (like *houreô*, "urinate," from the Sanskrit word for "rain," *varsa-*) and dew with the male, *arsên* [ἄρσην], which we find in the "sap" of "spring" (both designated by the Greek *ear* [ἔαρ], or in "spring," as in the Latin words for "man" (*ver* and *vir*).

Whatever the word's etymology may be, Onians suggests that the primary meaning of *eraô*, is "I pour out (liquid)," and in the middle voice, "I pour out myself." Dictionaries try to avoid this lexical oddity by distinguishing two *eraôs*, one meaning "to love" and the other, used only in compounds, meaning "to pour" (for *exeraô* [ἐξεράω], "pour out," "vomit"; Chantraine proposes a derivation from *era* [ἔαρ], which is preserved in *eraze* [ἔραζε], "on earth"). In general, dictionaries that take this path do not succeed in maintaining a clear separation (thus according to

RT: LSJ, *suneraô* [συνεράω] is a single verb with two meanings, "pour together" and "love jointly," and not two distinct verbs as in Bailly's RT: *Dictionnaire grec-français*). For Onians, the meaning of *eran* thus merges with that of *leibô* [λείβω], "pour drop by drop" (in the middle voice, *leibesthai* [λείβεσθαι], "to spread out," "to liquefy"), which he compares with *liptô* [λίπτω], *liptesthai* [λίπτεσθαι], "desire" (with its "lipidic" family of fat, gluey, shining) to the point of identifying *ho lips* [ὁ λίψ], "rainy wind"; *hê lips* [ἡ λίψ], "the running, the drop or libation"; and *lips* [λίψ], "desire." He then proposes a truly remarkable cluster combining liquid poured out (Gr. *leibein*, Lat. *libare*, "make a libation"), desire (Lat. *lubet* or *libet*, *libido*), love (Ger. *lieben*), and procreation and freedom (*Liber*, the Italic god of fertility; *liberi*, "children"; *libertas*, "liberty"), which he finds in the same form in the Saxon cluster *froda*, "foam"; *Freyr* and *Freyja*, the gods of love and fertility; and "free" and *frei*.

This is probably an etymological fiction and is censured at every step by Chantraine and Benveniste, who distinguish, for example, between *leibô* and *libare*, *liptô* and *libet/lubet*, "desire"; but their censure is also acrobatic, because to account for the "disturbing polysemy" of Latin *libare*, Benveniste has to retain from the ancient meaning of "pour a few drops" that of "take a very small part" (RT: *Le vocabulaire des institutions indo-européennes*, 2:209).

For *philein*, we must begin from the adjective *philos* [φίλος], which enters into the construction of several hundred words in the Greek lexicon; and since, Benveniste writes (ibid., 1:353), the debate about its origin is ongoing, "it is more important to

begin to see what it means." Benveniste starts over from the fact, "peculiar to a single language, Greek," that the adjective *philos*, which means "friend," also has, apparently as early as Homer, the value of a possessive: "mine, thine, his, etc." (*philos huios* [φίλος υἱός] means "his son," *philon êtor* [φίλον ἦτορ], "my heart" [*Iliad*, 18.307]; *phila heimata* [φίλα εἵματα], "your clothes" [*Iliad*, 2.261]). Nevertheless, the possessive does not constitute the matrix of the word's meaning. Benveniste finds the latter in the connection between *philos* and *xenos* [ξένος], in the "relationship of hospitality" through which a member of a community makes a foreigner his "guest": this is a reciprocal obligation that may be given material form in the *sumbolon* [σύμβολον] (a sign or token of recognition, for example, a broken ring, of which the partners have kept corresponding halves), which establishes a pact (*philotês*) that can be seen in the word *philêma* [φίλημα], "kiss." To translate *philein*, Benveniste resorts to a neologism: *hospiter* (ibid., p. 341; for example, *Illiad*, 6.15: "C'était un homme riche, mais il était *philos* aux hommes; car il hospitait [*phileesken* (φιλέεσκεν)] tout le monde, sa maison étant au bord de la route"). Rooted in the society's oldest institutions, *philos* thus designates a type of human relationships: "All those who are bound to each other by reciprocal duties of *aidôs* [αἰδώς] ("respect," see VERGÜENZA) are called *philoi*" (Benveniste, ibid., p. 341), since combatants who make a pact, including relatives, allies, servants, friends, and particularly those who live under the same roof (*philoi*)—that is, the wife, designated as *philê* when she is made to enter into her own home. In that very way the term acquires its affective value.

---

he should submit to his lover without shame (222b). That is why one of the central questions concerns the difference between active and passive, "the person who loves" and "the person who is loved," in a relationship of *philia* conceived on the model of that of *erôs*: "As soon as one man loves [*philei* (φιλεῖ)] another, which of the two becomes the friend [*philos* (φίλος)]—the lover of the one loved [*ho philôn tou philomenou* (ὁ φιλῶν τοῦ φιλουμένου)], or the loved of the lover [*ho philoumenos tou philountos* (ὁ φιλούμενος τοῦ φιλοῦντος)]?" (212b). The strategy consists in making "desire" (*epithumia*), *erôs*, and *philia* equivalent (221b–e) and in deducing the necessity of loving (*eran*) one's lover under cover of the reciprocity inherent in *philein*, which is expressed by the creation of the verb *antiphilein* [ἀντιφιλεῖν], "love in return": "Though [lovers] [*hoi erastai* (οἱ ἐρασταί)] love [*philountes* (φιλοῦντες)] their darlings as dearly as possible, they often imagine that

they are not loved in return [*antiphileistai* (ἀντιφιλεῖσθαι)], often that they are even hated" (212b–c). The fact that from the point of view of the *eromenos*, *philia* is thus simply a more suitable or socialized lure for *erôs* is clear in Socrates's recantation in the *Phaedrus*, where the seduced beloved sees himself in his lover as in a mirror: "he possesses that counterlove which is the image of love [*eidôlon erôtos anterôta* (εἴδωλον ἔρωτος ἀντέρωτα)], though he supposes it to be friendship rather than love, and calls it by that name [*erôs*]" (255d–e; cf. *Symposium* 182c, where the *erôs* of the *erastes* has as its complement the *philia* of the *eromenos*).

This play between *eran* and *philein* is particularly difficult to render in French: the French translation of both *philein* and *eran* by *aimer* erases any trace of the Platonic operation, as if French had already registered it. But in the Socratic dialogues, if *erôs* can take on the traits of *philia*, that is because *philia* is never more than one of the possible kinds of the comprehensive class of *erôs*. In the *Symposium*, Diotima explains to Socrates that through synecdoche, a name that is in reality the name of the whole has been limited to a small part (the erotic *erôs*, that of the *erastes*, the lovers): "You see, what we've been doing is to give the name of Love [*erôta* (ἔρωτα)] to what is only one single aspect of it [*tou erôtos ti eidos* (τοῦ ἔρωτός τι εἶδος)]; we make just the same mistake, you know with a lot of other names" (205b); so that one does not talk about *eran* in relation to those who love money, gymnastics, or wisdom, but rather about *philein*: whence "philosophy" (205d). It is understandable that this is naturally followed by the demonstration of a perfect continuity between the desire for sensual beauty and the love of the beautiful that in itself is *monoeides* [μονοειδές], "a single idea," a "unique form" (210b, 211e). The right path thus consists in "mounting the heavenly ladder, stepping from rung to rung—that is, from one to two, and from two to *every* lovely body, from bodily beauty to the beauty of institutions, from institutions to learning, and from learning in general to the special lore that pertains to nothing but the beautiful itself—until at last he comes to know what beauty is" (211c). Although this exposition of the asceticism of pederastic *erôs* practiced by Socrates (212b) is delivered by a foreigner, a woman, and a Sophist (the subject is beauty and speech, not the Good), it continued to define Platonism, Platonic love, and its process of sublimation. All the more because this asceticism itself is contagious, taught de facto, since Alcibiades, who is loved so "Platonically" by Socrates that he ends up pursuing him as a lover, notes that the *erastes* is not the person people think he is: in these dialogues in which the person who is questioned starts answering (Plato often plays on the proximity of *eromai* [ἔρομαι], "I question," and *erômai* [ἐρῶμαι], "I love"), Socratic irony consists in trading roles and making others who have been "bitten" by his philosophy (218a; 222b) fall in love with him. Thus erotic dissymmetry determines the practice of philosophy.

2. *Philein*: The equality of roles, equalization, and commensurability. Aristotle or an ethics and politics of friendship

To give a sense of the difference between *eran* and *philein*, we can begin again from the compounds *antiphilein* and *anteran* [ἀντερᾶν]. There is nothing more misleading than a parallel, for *anti*- sometimes indicates reciprocity: *antiphilein* means "love in return," "to return *philia* for *philia*," which in Aristotle refers to the very definition of *philos* ("*philos* is the person who loves [*ho philôn* (ὁ φιλῶν)] and who is loved in return [*kai antiphiloumenos* (καὶ ἀντιφιλούμενος)]"; *Rhetoric*, 2.4.1381a 1; Aristotle's and Cicero's uses [*redamare*, "love in return," *Laelius*, 14.49] thus function as displacements of the *Lysis* and returns to common usage) and sometimes antagonism. Before Plato, *anteran* meant essentially "compete in love," when the problematics of love was not deliberately inflected in terms of *philia* ; political office should be reserved for philosophers who do not seek power (see, e.g., *Republic*, 7.521b: "those who take office should not be lovers of rule [*erastas tou archein* (ἐραστὰς τοῦ ἄρχειν)], otherwise there will be a contest with rival lovers [*anterastai* (ἀντερασταί)]"). Compare Calame (*Poetics of Eros*), where in the apocryphal dialogue *Anterasti* (*The Rivals*), the rivalry concerns the dignity of the object of love, wisdom, or gymnastics.

Books 8 and 9 of *Nicomachean Ethics* (cf. *Eudemian Ethics*, 7, and *Rhetoric*, 2.4) testify to the breadth of the notion of *philia*: it designates all the positive, mutual relationships between the self and others, in the home and in civil and political society, on the basis of the bond between self and self. "Friendship" is the customary translation, but it is obviously untenable because it cannot cover this whole set of meanings that includes, in particular, love for those of one's own species ("philanthropy," 1155a 20; the master even has *philia* for a slave, insofar as the slave is a man, 1161b 6), the bond between parents and children (affection, paternal, maternal love / filial piety), husband and wife (tenderness, conjugal love), companions ("camaraderie" or "love" among *hetairoi* [ἑταῖροι]), age groups ("benevolence" in the elderly, "respect" among the young), mutual-aid relationships (charity, hospitality), trade and business (esteem, confidence, fairness), specifically political relations that are vertical (rulers' "consideration," subjects' "devotion") and horizontal ("sociability," "harmony"; thus *homonoia* [ὁμόνοια], "concord," "consensus" of citizens, is "political friendship," 1167b 2), and even the relationship between men and the gods (piety, indulgence). Thus it is, conversely, in Aristotelianism that *philia* becomes generic, and *erôs* becomes simply one of its species, based on the consideration of "pleasure" (*di' hêdonên* [δι' ἡδονήν]), 1156a 12), which is frequent among the young, just as friendships among older people are based on the "useful" (*to chrêsimon* [τὸ χρήσιμον], 1156a 10). But both of these are only "accidents" of the third and essential kind of *philia*: "friendship" properly so called, which is based on virtue (true friends are *kat' aretên* [κατ' ἀρετήν], "like in virtue," 1159b 4). Only the last expresses the essence of friendship, because it is situated from the outset in an exchange, a stable and equal reciprocity: "Now equality and likeness are friendship [*hê d' isotês kai homoiotês philotês* (ἡ δ' ἰσότης καὶ ὁμοιότης φιλότης)], and especially the likeness of those who are like in virtue" (1159b 2–4). Let us note also the peculiarity, which is consonant with *philein*, of the English expression "to like," whose etymology includes the idea of "similar to," in which affection and resemblance agree in the attraction of the same by the same.

Whence the clear relationship between *philia* and democracy, "for where citizens are equal they have much in common" (1161b 10). But when inequality is evident, and the superiority of one party over the other is constitutive of the relationship (man/woman, dominant/dominated, etc.), then it is "proportion that equalizes the parties and preserves the friendship" (to analogon isazei kai sôizei tên philian [τὸ ἀνάλογον ἰσάζει καὶ σῴζει τὴν φιλίαν]; 1163b 29f.); the inferior's *philia* compensates by its intensity and constancy the merit of the superior, for example, by returning in honor what he receives in money: "even unequals can be friends; they can be equalized" (*isazointo gar an* [ἰσάζοιντο γὰρ ἄν]; 1159b 2; cf. 7.15 and 16). This characteristic of commensurability enables us to understand why the institution of money (*nomisma* [νόμισμα], 1164a) depends on *philia*, and how, more generally, the passage to the symbolic makes it possible to acquit oneself of what is unacquittable with regard to relatives and with regard to the gods (e.g., 1163b 15–18).

■ See Box 8.

8

Aimance / "lovence"

Aimance, in spite of its romantic sound (parallel to "romance") and its association with ideas that trace back to amour courtois and the troubadours, is apparently a recent term. It was coined in 1927 by the French linguist and psychoanalyst Edouard Pichon, a figure who influenced Lacan. Aimance was interestingly picked up by the francophone Moroccan writer Abdelkebir Khatibi, who used it as a general title for his poetic works. It is from Khatibi, a close friend, rather than from Pichon, that Jacques Derrida borrowed the term. He used it extensively in his Politiques de l'amitié (1994), and when the work was translated into English as The Politics of Friendship in 1997, the translator, George Collins, coined the neologism "lovence."

The reference to Pichon is interesting, however, because his intention was to provide an equivalent for Freud's concept of libido that would avoid its overly sexualized connotations and point to a broader concept of object attraction, one that would not necessarily entail sexual satisfaction. Pichon's move was symptomatic of a general "French" resistance to "German" psychoanalysis in the name of a more civilized culture of sentiments. This appeal to the tradition of amour courtois and the troubadours formed part of a larger trans-European conflict over definitions of desire and sublimation (which is evident in C. G. Jung's critique of Freud's "hypersexualism").

In a sense, what Derrida performs in Politics of Friendship through the deconstructive reading of a philosophical tradition ranging from Aristotle to Nietzsche is a complete displacement of this ill-formulated sex/amour debate. One of Derrida's reasons for having recourse to a third term that is neither love nor friendship is to identify an indeterminate affect that circulates among modalities of love and friendship on a spectrum of sentiments that defy description or enumeration. Derrida's use of aimance parallels, in this respect, Freud's use of the category pulsion, with its neutralization of the active/passive opposition in desire. Aimance also fosters a phenomenology of the transference processes through which love, friendship, hostility, and rivalry are institutionally and sentimentally constituted and undone. This phenomenology of twoness (what Nietzsche in an extraordinary wordplay called Zweisamkeit, literally "loneliness-in-two") significantly questions the rigid distinction between the public and private spheres, as well as conventional, gendered views that sustain the "double interdiction" against friendship with and among women in the philosophical tradition. Recent reclamations in English of the word "amity" (as in Sharon Marcus's Between Women: Friendship, Desire and Marriage in Victorian England), to signal forms of female friendship and affection that fall outside heteronormative and same-sex vocabularies of love and sexual relation, might well be considered a fair approximation of the French aimance.

Étienne Balibar

REFERENCES

Derrida, Jacques. The Politics of Friendship. Translated by George Collins. London: Verso, 1997. First published in 1994.

Khatibi, Abdelkebir. "L'aimance et l'invention d'un idiome." In Œuvres. Vol. 2, Poésie de l'aimance. Paris: Éditions de la Différence, 2008.

Marcus, Sharon. Between Women: Friendship, Desire and Marriage in Victorian England. Princeton, NJ: Princeton University Press, 2007.

Pichon, Edouard. Développement psychique de l'enfant et de l'adolescent. Paris: Librairie de l'Académie de médecine, 1965.

In view of the heterogeneity of the paradigms of erôs and philia, we can gauge the scope of the problems and transformations that their translation by a single word presupposes.

Clara Auvray-Assayas
Charles Baladier
Philippe Büttgen
Barbara Cassin

BIBLIOGRAPHY

Aristotle. Nicomachean Ethics. Translated and edited by R. Crisp. Cambridge: Cambridge University Press, 2000.

Augustine, Saint. On Christian Doctrine. Translated by J. F. Shaw. Mineola, NY: Dover, 2009. First published in 1887.

Calame, Claude: The Poetics of Eros in Ancient Greece. Translated by J. Lloyd. Princeton, NJ: Princeton University Press, 1999.

Cicero, Marcus Tullius. De amicitia. Laelius: A Dialogue on Friendship. Translated by E. S. Schuckburgh. London: Macmillan, 1931.

Daumas, Maurice: La tendresse amoureuse XVI–XVIIIème siècles. Paris: Librairie Académique Perrin, 1996.

Diogenes Laertius. Vitae philosophorum. Edited by H. S. Long. 2 vols. Oxford: Oxford University Press, 1964. Translation by R. D. Hicks: Lives of Eminent Philosophers. Cambridge, MA: Harvard University Press, 1925.

Febvre, Lucien. Amour sacré, amour profane. Autour de l'Heptaméron. Paris: Gallimard / La Pléiade, 1944.

Ferrari, Giovanni R. "Platonic Love." In The Cambridge Companion to Plato, edited by R. Kraut, 248–76. New York: Cambridge University Press, 1992.

Hesiod. Theogony. Translated by Norman O. Brown. New York: Liberal Arts Press, 1953.

Kant, Immanuel. Critique of Practical Reason. Edited by M. Gregor. Cambridge: Cambridge University Press, 1997.

Le Brun, Jacques. Le pur amour. De Platon à Lacan. Paris: Éditions du Seuil, 2002.

Maggini, Carlo, Eva Lundgren, and Emanuela Leuci. "Jealous Love and Morbid Jealousy." Acta Biomedica 77 (2006): 137–46.

Mommaers, Paul, with E. Dutton. Hadewijch: Writer, Beguine, Love Mystic. Louvain: Peeters, 2004.

Nygren, Anders. Agape and Eros. Translated by Philip S. Watson. Chicago: University of Chicago Press, 1982.

Pétré, Hélène. Caritas. Étude sur le vocabulaire latin de la charité chrétienne. Louvain: Université Catholique, 1948.

Plato. Lysis. Translated by J. Wright. In The Collected Dialogues of Plato, edited by Edith Hamilton and Huntingon Cairns. Princeton, NJ: Princeton University Press / Bollingen, 1961.

———. Phaedrus. Translated by R. Hackforth. In The Collected Dialogues of Plato, edited by Edith Hamilton and Huntingon Cairns. Princeton, NJ: Princeton University Press / Bollingen, 1961.

———. Symposium. Translated by Michael Joyce. In The Collected Dialogues of Plato, edited by Edith Hamilton and Huntingon Cairns. Princeton, NJ: Princeton University Press / Bollingen, 1961.

Price, Anthony W. Love and Friendship in Plato and Aristotle. Oxford: Clarendon Press, 1989.

Ricoeur, Paul. Liebe und Gerechtigkeit = Amour et justice. Tübingen: J.C.B. Mohr, 1990.

Robin, Léon. La théorie platonicienne de l'amour. Paris: Presses Universitaires de France, 1964.

Rougemont, Denis de. Love in the Western World. Translated by M. Belgion. New York: Pantheon, 1956.

Rousselot, Pierre. The Problem of Love in the Middle Ages: A Historical Contribution. Translated by A. Vincelette. Milwaukee, WI: Marquette University Press, 2002.

M

MACHT, GEWALT (GERMAN)

ENGLISH   might, power, violence

➤ POWER and DROIT, FORCE, HERRSCHAFT, JETZTZEIT, RIGHT/JUST/GOOD, VALUE

When Luther comments on Romans 13 ("Let every person be subject to the governing authorities"), he writes that "one must not resist authority (*Obrigkeit*) by force (*Gewalt*), but only by confessing the truth" (*Weimar Ausgabe*, 11: 277). This interpretation underlines one of the connotations—rebellious force—that gradually, and especially toward the end of the Middle Ages, came to be added to the traditional meaning of *Gewalt*, which originally referred to the entire range of acts connected with the exercise of temporal power: administering, reigning, organizing (the root of the term goes back to the Latin *valere*). It is clear that the associated notions of *potestas* and of *vis* (force) are directly linked to this exercise of power, and because *Gewalt* implies the use of force, the meaning of the term moves easily, by extension, toward the idea of violence, that is, a rebellious, even revolutionary, force exerted against power (*Macht*). *Gewalt* and *Macht* thus share the idea of *potestas*, with *Gewalt* inflecting this idea toward *vis* and *violentia*, while *Macht* tends more toward *potentia*.

I. An Uncertain Division:
The Arbitrary and the Free Deployment of Force

It is not so much the etymology of these terms or the tradition of their usage that suggest or anticipate the semantic value they assume in philosophical reflections but rather a terminological decision that establishes a division at the heart of their fields of connotation, whose borders are blurred. When Kant calls *Macht* a "power which is superior to great hindrances," and *Gewalt* this same force "if it is also superior to the resistance of what is also endowed with *Macht*," we can say on the one hand that *Gewalt* is understood as a modality of *Macht*, and on the other that these definitions transpose what is normally a political and legal linguistic usage into the domain of nature. This well-known quotation is the beginning of paragraph 28 of the "Analytic of the Sublime" where Kant talks of natural force (which should be expressed rather by the term *Kraft*, referring to physical force in general, see FORCE). He simply wants to emphasize that the force of nature can be understood as a power that, on certain occasions, is unleashed and turns violent. This violence is understood as an avatar of power that, as such (that is, as *potentia*), is synonymous with possibility (here the connection with "potentiality" is of importance) in the broad sense of the term.

In contemporary usage *Macht* might be best understood in Max Weber's definition of the term: "Any possibility, within a social relationship, of imposing one's will, even in spite of a resistance, and regardless of what this possibility is based on" (*Wirtschaft und Gesellschaft*, 28). *Gewalt* in turn refers first and foremost to the exercise of a constraint (and it matters little

whether it is legitimate or not). The minimal distinction between the two notions comes down to the following: *Gewalt* always refers to the idea of "free" control of something or of someone; consequently, the connotations of arbitrariness, of instrumentalization, or of reification belong logically to this semantic field. *Macht*, on the other hand, refers essentially (if not exclusively) to the *vita activa*, to using one's will and establishing aims that one attempts to achieve. The connotations of *Macht* thus have more to do with autonomy and coherence of action, and its adequacy to the goals pursued, which implies that *Macht* inevitably requires legitimacy and recognition.

II. From *Potestas* and *Potentia* to *Macht* and *Gewalt*:
The Different Stages in the Critique of Domination

The evolution of the semantic fields of these two terms, which have continually cut across one another, has had at least three clearly identifiable phases.

The first has accompanied the formation of modern political forms of authority since the end of the Middle Ages, which have, with increasing concentration, placed the exercise of domination into the hands of the state apparatus. One effect of the reception of Roman law, and of conflicts between princes, imperial power, and papal authority, which appealed to divine omnipotence (*Allmacht*), has been to make the notions of *potestas* and of *potentia* increasingly abstract terms. This phase has ended with a distribution of "domination" among the state (which has been able to "monopolize the legitimate use of constraint" [M. Weber, *Wirtschaft und Gesellschaft*, 29]), civil society, the economy, and the remains of the different spiritual authorities.

The second phase concerns the vast domain of the legitimization of power and the use of force. In the article on *Gewalt* in his dictionary, Grimm points out that the meaning of "a misuse of power was barely formulated" in the Middle Ages: this sense of the term arises with the convergence of a concentration of powers, the move toward secularization, and the rationalization of the conception of law. It was only then that the terms of power and of constraining force departed from their status as normative notions expressing the legitimate need to conserve a *social* and political order, whose essentially Christian foundations were never questioned. *Gewalt* and *Macht* thus became either descriptive notions (whose connotations remained relatively "neutral"), or states of things that, while they had no clear and explicit justification, nevertheless aroused the suspicion that they were potentially illegitimate. From the sixteenth century onward, political thought would continually reflect upon the opposition between right and force, just as, in parallel, moral thought would oppose the "power" of reason to the "violence" of passions. The term *Gewalt* was interpreted from the perspective of natural justice, for example, as referring at the same time to the space of freedom belonging to each individual, the illegitimate intrusion of an individual into the private sphere of another individual, and the legitimate force that preserves this natural space of freedom. It is difficult to avoid noting how much *Macht*, in this semantic extension, can cut across each of the values attributed to *Gewalt*, with the one partial exception that the connotations of *Macht* are slightly less negative.

The third phase, in the eighteenth and nineteenth centuries, was the phase of contestation that came with the fact of power and force being concentrated in the hands of the apparatuses of the state and of domination. Revolutionary phenomena, modern wars, the analysis of the structure of society in terms of conflict and exploitation, the critique of law in the name of the ideological interests it served and whose "reality" it masked, all brought about a shift in the understanding of these two notions. They were no longer understood in the general context of law but became poles of social and political theories, whose objective was the critique of domination with a view to its redefinition, its control, or even its disappearance in history. At the same time these two terms were notions that became as much concepts of theoretical reflection as they were notions usurped for instrumentalized ends (revolutionary "violence" [*Gewalt*], for example, could be said to be "legitimate" from the perspective of an ideology of history judging the present in the name of a "scientifically" guaranteed future, based on a belief in the "power" [*Macht*] of the exploited classes).

When Fichte develops the idea, in his 1796 work *Grundlage des Naturrechts nach Prinzipien der Wissenschaftslehre*, that the "law must be a power (*Macht*)," and when he asks what the nature of this power should be, such that it goes beyond the law of the will of each individual, from a contractual perspective directly inspired by Rousseau, he will use the term *Übermacht*, which immediately becomes a synonym for *Übergewalt*, in other words, a superior power, or the supreme force/power of the law. The "common will" of the contracting parties must have a "superior power in view of which the power of each individual is incommensurably restrained, so that this will can be preserved beyond itself and ensure it is maintained: this is the force of the state (*Staatsgewalt*)" (ibid., 153). The only distinction one can make in the use of these two terms is that *Macht* here appears as more abstract and general, whereas *Gewalt* is explicitly referred to the *potestas executiva*, since then the use of force is concretely required for the constraining force of the law to be effectively realized.

In Hegel, as in Kant, the distinction between the two notions is thematized—"Force (*Gewalt*) is a manifestation of power (*Macht*), or it is power as exteriority" (Hegel, *Logik*, 2: 200). The *Enzyklopädie* (1830, §541) talks about *Staatsgewalt* in the same sense as Fichte and uses *Gewalt* to refer to the distribution of the power of the state into different powers (executive, legislative, judicial). When the *Enzyklopädie* discusses the state of nature (ibid., §502), however, *Gewalt* signifies less "force" than "freely disposing of something" (according to its first meaning):

> The law of nature—strictly so called—is for that reason the predominance of the strong (*Stärke*) and the reign of

force (*Gewalt*), and a state of nature a state of violence (*Gewalttätigkeit*) and wrong, of which nothing truer can be said than that one ought to depart from it. The social state, on the other hand, is the condition in which alone right has its actuality: what is to be restricted and sacrificed is just the willfulness and violence of the state of nature (*Gewalttätigkeit*).

> (*Encyclopaedia of the Philosophical Sciences,* trans. and with introduction by William Wallace, 1894).

However, in his *Philosophy of Right* §95 (cf. also §93 add.), Hegel will use *Gewalt* to designate constraint (*Zwang*), that is, the use of brute force against a natural existence that is an agent, the bearer or the product of will (the existence of a man, or what he has produced or built). But *Gewalt* also serves here as a synonym for "possession" (*Besitz*), which is defined by the fact of disposing externally of something in whatever way one wishes. This first level of possession will be overcome to reach the level of property (*Eigentum*), which is no longer defined in terms of free disposition but also of the right which of course guarantees this free disposition (within certain limits) over and against the arbitrary power of another person.

Marx will not depart radically from this distribution of connotations. His now celebrated expressions—"the proletariat must abolish political power when it is in the hands of the bourgeoisie. They must themselves become a power (*Gewalt*) and, first and foremost, a revolutionary power" ("Moralisierende Kritik und kritisierende Moral," 4: 338); "force (*Gewalt*) is the midwife of every old society pregnant with a new one. It is itself an economic power" (*Capital*, I, §8, chap. 31)—do not essentially modify the meanings of the two terms, and the differences between them are more of degree and of modality than of nature.

■ See Box 1.

III. *Macht* and *Gewalt*, "Power" and "Violence": Arendt and Benjamin on the Functions of Violence

There have been only two real and original departures from these meanings. The first of these is Walter Benjamin's use of the term *Gewalt*, in the extreme extension of its sense, that is, the violence against all tradition, to which he is not afraid of adjoining the adjective "divine" (*göttliche*) violence. The second is to be found in the decisive opposition between power (*Macht*) and violence (*Gewalt*) that Hannah Arendt develops in the essay bearing this title (*Macht und Gewalt*).

In his 1920 essay "Critique of Violence" (*Selected Writings*, vol. 1), Benjamin opposes the mythical, foundational, and conservative violence of law with divine, destructive, and purifying violence: "For only mythic violence (*schaltende Gewalt*), not divine, will be recognizable as such with certainty, unless it be in incomparable effects, because the expiatory power of violence is invisible to men. Once again all the external forms are open to pure divine violence, which myth bastardized with law. Divine violence may manifest itself in a true war exactly as it does in the crowd's divine judgment on a criminal. But all mythic, lawmaking violence (*verwaltende Gewalt*), which we may call 'executive,' is

1

The "will to power" ("*Wille zur Macht*") in Nietzsche

This expression, "will to power," first appears at the time Nietzsche was writing *Thus Spoke Zarathustra* in 1883, thus in the final phase of this thinking. It is understood first of all as another, more precise way of referring to what is commonly called life. But in Zarathustra itself, the "will to power" is directly related to the evolution of cultures across time and history, as a way of establishing control over the whole of phenomenal reality. This expression returns at several points in 1885, especially in *Beyond Good and Evil*, and refers there to the furthest level that our own reflection can reach when it attempts to interpret reality (what Nietzsche designates as the "original text"). So the "will to power" is the highest level attained by our hypotheses, and it thus becomes identified with philosophy as the attempt to think the totality of what is. The "will to power" thus refers to the general dynamic of our instincts, from the most basic to the most refined drives, to the dynamic of the body, and even that of the inorganic world. But we must never forget that instincts constantly adjust themselves and evaluate circumstances with a view to satisfying themselves and that they necessarily enter into conflict with one another. There are thus only transient and fragile states of equilibrium between these different movements, and this is what we call the "self," for example, or a "cause," or "knowledge," or "will." Since Nietzsche on the one hand says that "will" (*Wille*) is an exoteric term, that it does not exist as such—there is only an instinctual dynamic that is absolutely inseparable from the dynamic of the mind—and since on the other hand what he declares as his most profound thought is that of the "eternal return" (*ewige Wiederkunft*, an expression we find in 1882, before the notion of the "will to power" makes its appearance), we are entitled to consider the "will to power" as the "mask" of the eternal return. Nietzsche explains in a posthumous fragment (7 [54], end 1886–spring 1887) that the "supreme will to power" is the fact of "impressing upon becoming the character of being . . . that everything returns is the most extreme convergence between a world of becoming and a world of being."

In 1887 Nietzsche planned to write a book that would bear the title "Will to Power." He worked on this plan during the course of the year in 1888, explaining that, on the one hand, the 372 fragments mentioned in relation to this plan were only to help him clarify his own thoughts, and that any publication of them was consequently prohibited (letter to P. Gast, February 1888), and on the other hand, that this same project from then on was to be called "Transvaluation of All Values" (letter to F. Overbeck, 13 February 1888). In September of that same year, Nietzsche abandoned the expression "will to power" as a designation of what he was about to publish, and the foreword to the *Twilight of the Idols* was completed on 30 September, identifying this date as year one of the "transvaluation of all values." The different editions of the *Will to Power* that appeared after Nietzsche's death were simply compilations of posthumous fragments, grouped more or less coherently according to the themes defined by the successive teams at the Weimar Archives (under the aegis of Nietzsche's sister).

---

pernicious. Pernicious, too, is the law-preserving, 'administrative' violence that serves it. Divine violence (*göttliche Gewalt*), which is the sign and seal but never the means of sacred dispatch, may be called 'sovereign' (*waltende*) violence" (ibid., 252). This violence, whose conception is manifestly inspired by the ideas of Georges Sorel, is also said to be revolutionary; it is a "pure violence exerted on behalf of living beings against all life," it is a "liberation from all law," whereas mythical violence "imposes all at once both guilt and expiation." A manifestation of divine violence can be found in the element of "educative power" that is "outside of all law." In essence, the backdrop to this divine violence is a transposition of a conception derived from Jewish mysticism into terms that are Sorelian rather than Marxist (even though the idea of pure violence is very close to the Hegelian Marxist sense of *Gewalt* as negativity). This is Isaac Luria's cabalistic notion of the "breaking of vases," this catastrophe that is responsible both for the dispersion into the world of the sparks of evil and for the "exile" of God himself, the "divine contraction" whose consequence is creation itself. Divine violence is also manifested in the idea of the here and now (see JETZTZEIT), the potential sudden eruption of the messianic dimension at the heart of the mythical, and thus fallacious, continuity of time.

Arendt, for her part, opposes the domain of "force," that is, the domain of technology (production, and making the material means adequate to the ends), to that of "power,"

or of institution, supported by a greater or lesser number of individual wills. "Power" (*Macht, pouvoir*) is thus both the condition of any sociopolitical order and a finality in itself, whereas "force" (*Gewalt*, or violence) only has aims that change each time. In addition, power has no need for justification, but only for legitimacy, whereas force is never legitimate. The use of force can in certain circumstances be justified in terms of an anticipation of what it could achieve; power, in contrast, derives its legitimacy instead from the past, from a tradition. At the same time revolutions are only the results of redistributions of power, and force itself cannot set them in motion (its function being instead to introduce reforms). When "revolutionary violence" (*revolutionnäre Gewalt*), however, brings about a transformation of reality, it only achieves one result: "the world has become more violent (*gewalttätiger*) than it was before" (*Macht und Gewalt*, 80). Power is normative, while force as violence is instrumental; power is not identifiable with domination, since it is lacking constraint, manipulation, and conflict. Neither is defined by its capacity to overcome resistance (it does not pertain, as in Max Weber, to a relation of order and obedience). To refer to a "power without violence" (*gewaltlos*) is a pleonasm. Violence can destroy power; but it is absolutely incapable of creating power" (ibid., 57).

■ See Box 2.

Marc de Launay

2

"Forcing" (*Forçage*)

"*J'aimerais l'appeler un forçage, si scandaleuse-ment autoritaire soit la connotation du mot*" (I would prefer to call it [the psychoanalytic act, which 'forces' a particular sort of knowl-edge to appear] a forcing, however scandal-ously authoritarian the word may sound) (*Conditions*). So writes Alain Badiou, toward the end of his 1991 lecture "La vérité: forçage et innommable," thus hesitating ever so slightly around the problem of conceptual nomination, the problem, that is, of the rela-tion between the *word* ("la connotation du mot") and the *concept* this word is to *name* ("j'aimerais *l'appeler* un forçage," "*call it* a forc-ing"). Badiou's scruple is to the point: defined in French as "*l'action de forcer, de faire céder par force*," "the act of forcing, making some-thing occur on account of, or making some-thing bend to, a force," *forçage* is thick with connotations of violation, sexual violence, un-naturalness, and impropriety. To the degree that word and concept are never in a simple relation of exteriority to one another and that concept-invention is therefore always an *inventio* in the rhetorical sense, working with the *historicity* of the term in question, Badiou's well-founded scruple necessarily doubles as a provocation. After all, one might think of *forçage*, intuitively, as the very other of the idea of philosophy, a virtual synonym for the absence of reason; or, alternately, at a somewhat more advanced level of reflection, *forçage* might be understood as a figurative description of the philosophical malady par excellence, a kind of rapacious idealism that acknowledges no alterity, no gap between concept and object, forcing everything that stands in its path. The provocation is only heightened when one realizes that Badiou's concept of *forçage* bears upon nothing less philosophically central than the relation of truth to knowledge. Assuming that the provocation is not an empty one, what kind of philosophical situation might demand such a paradoxical alignment of *forçage* with values such as truth and knowledge? To what exigency does a concept of *forçage* respond? The fact that Badiou adapts *forçage* from Paul Cohen's mathematical technique of "forcing" does not lessen the paradoxicality of the con-cept or the urgency of the questions raised by its formulation. Similarly, other English-language usages such as "forcing bulbs" in horticulture or "forcing bids" in the game of bridge may give the term a technical inflec-tion, but they do not fundamentally alter its connotation. (Indeed, given philosophy's his-torical ambivalence to *technē*, these usages could hardly be said to prepare or anticipate a distinctly philosophical conceptualization of the term.)

Without further delay, let us turn back to the text of Badiou's lecture: *forçage* is "a matter of the point at which, although in-complete, a truth authorizes anticipations of knowledge, not statements about what is, but about what will have been if the truth reaches completion." Already in this brief description, not quite yet even a proper definition, questions of time and decision are clustered, somewhat unexpectedly, with the problem of epistemology, the problem of knowledge. It is to this knot that the para-doxical concept of *forçage* corresponds. As is by now well known, a truth for Badiou is an event in the robust sense, which means that it, by definition, eludes knowledge; *forçage* bears, in turn, on the knowledge *of* truth, the consequences of truth for a knowledge to which it nonetheless necessarily remains heterogeneous.

Because a truth cannot be *known*, it is undecidable and therefore subject to deci-sion. Yet the theory of *forçage* is not as such a decisionism. It is, rather, a paradoxical epis-temology of the *future effects* generated *by* groundless decisions—a meta-decisionism, perhaps. One decides on the basis of the fu-ture anterior—what *will have been* if the truth comes to completion, what *will have been* if the situation is altered to accommodate what was previously an anonymous multiple or subset. What this means, in practice, is the introduction of a new *name* into a situation, a name that corresponds to nothing in the cur-rent situation and therefore has no referential value in the present but instead "refers" to its "completed" existence in a "*situation à-venir*" (*Being and Event*).

Two additional points must be made concerning the technical aspects of *forçage*. The first is that of the paradox of "authorized anticipations of knowledge" or of *forçage* as "method" (*Conditions*). For the modern (i.e., Cartesian) theory of knowledge is founded on the notion of intuitive (or *sensible*) evi-dence; "method" as such was conceptualized precisely as a guard *against* anticipation. The initiation, under the sign of *forçage*, of an epistemology of "authorized antici-pation" is therefore remarkable to say the least. Second, and following from this point, the equivocal character of *forçage* in rela-tion to various twentieth-century philoso-phies of time is worthy of interest. On one hand Badiou's thought is premised on the non-self-identity and non-self-sufficiency of the historical present; and insofar as the event inaugurates a sequence, it might be said to "temporalize," to bring about a par-ticular acute sense of historicity. And yet, on the other hand, *forçage* effects a kind of

telescoping of the future into the present, a telescoping that necessarily drains the future of its futurity; the negation of the historical present thus ultimately leads for Badiou not to a heightened sense of temporality, but to an affect of *eternity*.

To round out this entry, several additional notes are in order. First, the equivocal relation throughout Badiou's *oeuvre* between *forçage* and force as such is worthy of note, though there is not room for an extended treatment here. In *Théorie du sujet* (1980), for instance, Badiou mobilizes *forçage* alongside Hegel's concept of *Kraft* from the *Wissenschaft der Logik*, using both to think the *rupture dialec-tique* between subject and structure. *Kraft* is theorized as the positing of externality, whereby the seemingly reactive subject, in *understanding itself to posit* the structure that seems to determine it, transforms struc-ture into a moment of its own development (*Théorie du sujet*). *Forçage* approaches the same problematic from a different angle, juxtaposing the classical logic of implica-tion ("p *implies* non-q"), which by definition cannot think rupture, with the logic of *for-çage*, according to which "p *forces* non-q" is a *contingent development from the absence of a constraint*, a consequence of the fact, in other words, that *nothing more powerful than p forces q* (Ibid.).

Thus Badiou can write the following, im-plicitly aligning force and *forçage*: "Between formal implication and *forcing* there lies all the ambivalence that the dialectic introduces in the old problem of determinism. The sub-ject's surrection is the effect of *force* within the place. This does not mean that the place implies it" (Ibid.). In *L'être et l'événement*, by contrast, the critique of political ontology leads to a *rejection* of the language of force, even as *forçage* becomes an ever more impor-tant theoretical construct. Badiou thus writes, in regard to Hobbes: "To suppose that the po-litical convention results from the necessity of having to exit from a war of all against all, and to thus subordinate the event to the ef-fects of force [*subordonner l'événement aux effets de la force*], is to submit its eventness to an extrinsic determination. . . . Politics is a *creation*, local and fragile, of collective hu-manity, it is never the treatment of a vital ne-cessity" (*Begin and Event*).

Second, the concept of *forçage* has an interestingly ambiguous psychoanalytic background. Though Badiou cites Lacan in his lecture on *forçage*, he does not cite any of the instances in which Lacan in fact writes of *forçage*, referring instead to the theory of the "half-saying" [*mi-dire*] of truth elaborated in *Seminar 17*. Badiou does suggest, however, that there may be a Freudian precedent to the concept in what he cites as *"frayage,"* a term rendered as "working-through" [*Durcharbeiten*] in the English translation of Badiou's essay (*Conditions*, 206/138). *"Frayage"* is in fact the term Jacques Derrida uses, on the basis of the French idiom *"se frayer un chemin,"* to translate Freud's *Bahnung* (pathbreaking, pioneering, forging), in his famous 1966 essay on "Freud and the Scene of Writing" (in *L'écriture et la différence*). Alan Bass in turn renders *frayage/Bahnung* as "breaching," a term that captures the implicit violence of the concept far more effectively than the comparatively euphemistic "facilitation" favored in the *Standard Edition*. The reference to *frayage* (*Bahnung*) thus not only

links *forçage* back to the discussions of "force and place" in *Théorie du sujet* but also points toward a comparison between Derridean *différance* and Badiouian *forçage* as distinct modes of "spacing" that find a common precedent in Freud's *Bahnung*.

Third, and finally, the question of a modernist *aesthetics* of *forçage* remains to be addressed. For Badiou writes in passing, in reference to Rimbaud and Mallarmé, of *"un forçage de la langue par avènement d'une autre langue à la fois immanente et créée"* (the forcing of language by the advent of another language at once immanent and created) or again, this time in relation to Beckett, of *"une invention dans la langue, un forçage poétique"* (an invention in language,

a poetic *forcing*) (*Petit manuel d'inésthétique, Beckett, l'écriture et la scène*). This conceptualization of *forçage* in fact resonates with the use made of the term by Lacan in *Seminar 23*, in which he writes, in reference to his own appropriation of knot-theory, of "the forcing of a new writing [*le forçage d'une nouvelle écriture*] . . . and the forcing of a new kind of idea [*et le forçage d'un nouveau type d'idée*]" (*Séminaire 23*). Lacan, however, draws attention to what Badiou does not—the status of mathematical formalization as such, here grasped under the sign of *forçage*, as a formidable intervention in the *aesthetics* of *philosophical* writing.

Daniel Hoffman-Schwartz

BIBLIOGRAPHY

Arendt, Hannah. *Macht und Gewalt*. Munich: Piper, 1970. Translation: *On Violence*. New York: Harcourt Brace, 1970.

Benjamin, Walter. *Gesammelte Schriften*. Edited by Rolf Tiedemann and Hermann Schweppenhäuser. 7 vols. Frankfurt: Suhrkamp, 1991.

———. *Selected Writings*. Edited by Marcus Bullock and Michael W. Jennings. 4 vols. Cambridge, MA: Belknap, 1996–2003.

Fichte, Johann Gottlieb. *Grundlage des Naturrechts nach Principien der Wissenschaftslehre*. In *Sämmtliche Werke*. Vol. 3. Edited by I. H. Fichte. Berlin: De Gruyter, 1965. First published in 1845. Translation by Michael Baur: *Foundations of Natural Right according to the Principles of the Wissenschaftslehre*. Edited by Frederick Neuhouser. Cambridge: Cambridge University Press, 2000.

Hanssen, Beatrice. *Critique of Violence: Between Poststructuralism and Critical Theory*. London: Routledge, 2000.

Hegel, Georg Wilhelm Friedrich. *Enzyklopädie der philosophischen Wissenschaften im Grundrisse*. Edited by Wolfgang Bonsiepen and Hans-Christian Lucas. In *Gesammelte Werke*. Vol. 20. Hamburg: Meiner, 1992. First published in 1830. Translation by Steven A. Taubeneck: *Encyclopedia of the Philosophical Sciences in Outline, and Critical Writings*. Edited by Ernst Behler. German Library. Vol. 24. New York: Continuum, 1990.

———. *Grundlinien der Philosophie des Rechts*. Edited by Klaus Grotsch and Elisabeth Weisser-Lohmann. In *Gesammelte Werke*. Vol. 14. Hamburg: Felix Meiner, forthcoming. Translation by T. M. Knok: *Outlines of the Philosophy of Right*. Edited and with introduction by Stephen Houlgate. Oxford: Oxford University Press, 2008.

———. *Wissenschaft der Logik, Erster Band: Die objektive Logik*. Edited by Friedrich Hogemann and Walter Jaeschke. In *Gesammelte Werke*. Vol. 21. Hamburg: Meiner, 1985. First published in 1832. *Wissenschaft der Logik, Zweiter Band: Die subjektive Logik*. Edited by Friedrich Hogemann and Walter Jaeschke. In *Gesammelte Werke*. Vol. 12. Hamburg: Meiner, 1981. First published in 1816. Translation by A. V. Miller: *Science of Logic*. London: Allen and Unwin, 1969.

Marx, Karl. *Das Kapital: Kritik der politischen Ökonomie*. 3 vols. In *Marx-Engels Werke*. Vols. 23–25. Berlin: Dietz, 1963–1983. Translation: *Capital*. 3 vols. In *Karl Marx and Frederick Engels Collected Works*. Vols. 35–37. New York: International Publishers, 1996–98.

———. "Moralisierende Kritik und kritisierende Moral." In *Marx-Engels Werke*. 4: 331–59. Berlin: Dietz, 1972. First published in 1847. Translation: "Moralizing Criticism and Critical Morality." In *Karl Marx and Frederick Engels Collected Works*. 6: 312ff. New York: International Publishers, 1976.

Weber, Max. *Wirtschaft und Gesellschaft*. Tübingen: Siebeck, 1922. Translation by Ephraim Fischoff et al.: *Economy and Society: An Outline of Interpretive Sociology*. Edited by Guenther Roth and Claus Wittich. 2 vols. Berkeley: University of California Press, 1978.

MADNESS / INSANITY

FRENCH	*folie, démence*
GERMAN	*Schwärmerei, Wahn; Unsinn, Verrücktheit*
GREEK	*mania* [μανία], *phrenitis* [φρενῖτις], *aphrosunê* [ἀφροσύνη], *paranoia* [παράνοια]
ITALIAN	*follia, pazzia; demenza*
LATIN	*furor, phrenesis; dementia, insania, insipientia*

➤ DRIVE, GENIUS, LOGOS, *MALAISE* [MELANCHOLY], MEMORY, MORALS, PATHOS, *PRUDENCE, REASON*, SOUL, *WISDOM*

The terminology of madness follows two distinct models in most languages. On the one hand, there is a positive model, which treats madness as a distinct entity subject to the highest valuations: thus Greek *mania* and, in another register, Latin *furor*, which indicate exceptional states. These persist in literary modernity in the ideas of inspiration, enthusiasm, and genius, as well as *Schwärmerei*, the extravagance in terms of which Immanuel Kant characterizes both the madness of Emanuel Swedenborg and that of dogmatic idealism. On the other hand, we also find a negative or privative model: madness and the insane are outside or past reason or even wisdom (*aphrôn, insipiens, insania, dementia*, from which come our terms "insanity," "dementia," "paranoia," and others). Unreason in this sense is in danger of being run together with irrationality (the *aphrôn* [ἄφρων] is the opposite of the *phronimos* [φρόνιμος], the morally sensible sage).

Cicero, with the goal of personally overseeing the shift from Greek vocabulary to Latin, opens the latter up to the symmetry of the health of the body and that of the soul. The medieval terminology of the subject confers a sort of technical value, even in theological controversies, upon terms like *insipiens* and *phreneticus*. The many terms of antiquity, which were initially based on Greek *mania* [μανία], were retained in modern languages until the advent of modern psychiatry, at the end of the eighteenth century, though at the cost of semantic shifts and new linguistic choices owing in particular to translations and definitions of Cicero, the Stoics, and Augustine.

I. Greek *Mania* and Its Modern Destiny: From Enthusiasm to Psychosis

A. The *mania* of philosophers and the *phrenitis* of doctors

Concerning *mania* [μανία], Boissier de Sauvages writes: "From the Greek *mainomai*, I am crazy, furious; in Latin, *furor, insania*; in French, *folie & manie*" (*Nosologie*, 7.389). The word is thus trapped in its equivalences in Latin and in French. We may consider it the most general, the most available, both in extension and in understanding (*mainomai* [μαίνομαι] answers to a Sanskrit root that means "to believe, to think," from which we derive both *menos* [μένος], "warrior spirit," and *mimnêskô* [μιμνήσκω], "I remember" (see MEMORY). *Mania* initially refers to what we tend to place under the vague word "madness," and continues to do so in ordinary language. In Hippocrates, we may say that mania is only found as a symptom, as are all changes of *êthos* [ἦθος], "character." It does not yet exist as a concept of sickness.

Plato describes four forms of divine madness (*mania*, *Phaedrus* 265b, and esp. 244–45). The first, inspired by Apollo, is mantic delirium, divination. The "moderns," says Plato, are the ones who, lacking a sense of beauty, introduced a *t* to the word and called the art of divination *mantikê* [μαντική] rather than *manikê* [μανική]. The second form is "telestic" delirium, given by Dionysus, who "accomplishes" (*teleô* [τελέω]) in the sense that he initiates one into mysteries. The third is the delirium inspired by the Muses, namely poetic delirium. The fourth form, a gift of Aphrodite or Eros, is that which incites love, *erôtikê mania* [ἐρωτική μανία]. This text, which ancient medicine carefully recalls, is of primary importance for understanding this medicine's definition of mania. Thus, Caelius Aurelian, a doctor in the fifth century CE (who is transposing a second-century doctor, Soranus of Ephesus, into Latin), writes:

> Plato, in the *Phaedrus*, declares that madness is twofold: one comes from a tension of the mind, having a cause or origin in the body, the other is divine or sent down, and is inspired by Apollo; now we call this divination.

(*Chronic Illnesses* 1.5, ed. Bendz, 144)

Continuing to cite the text of the *Phaedrus* in the *Chronic Illnesses*, Caelius is right to speak of the duality of madness. For whatever the number of distinctions Plato makes, alongside these "meaningful" madnesses, there is the sickness of madness. In fact, we may speak of a "double madness," a good one ("the greatest gifts come by way of madness," Plato, *Phaedrus* 244b) and a pathological madness. It is this duality that is put to the test in Euripides's tragedy *The Bacchae*.

Something happened, however, that we could not better show than by citing Galen. When he reads in a Hippocratic constitution (*Epidemics* 3 = RT: Littré, *Dictionnaire de la langue française*, 3:92) that "none of the frenetics had an attack of mania . . . but instead of that they were prostrate," he is perplexed. The conjunction of mania and *phrenitis* [φρενῖτις] is incomprehensible to him. Since Hippocrates cannot be wrong, Galen thinks we must give *phrenitic* a metaphorical sense. In truth, the Hippocratic text is a problem for him because a very important epistemological break had taken place, namely, the development of definitions of illnesses. As for the systematic contrast between *phrenitis* and *mania*, no doubt we must place it in the second half of the second century BCE. Thus, since diagnosis follows definition, we could not confuse *phrenitis*—that is, insanity with fever, *crocudismos* [κροκυδισμός] (the gesture of ripping out strands of tissue or blades of straw) and *carphologia* [καρφολογία] (permanent and involuntary movements of hands and fingers)—and *mania*, insanity without fever. With regard to this text, Galen has the same problems of translation and understanding as we do.

The determination and definition of illnesses like mania, *phrenitis*, or melancholy presuppose a certain number of complex cultural facts, including in particular: the constraint of the definition according to the model of philosophy and rhetoric; the definitive separation between illness of the body, reserved for doctors, and that of the soul, reserved for philosophers; the victory of soul-body dualism; and the triumph of the Stoic theory of passion as an illness of the soul (see PATHOS). Celsus attempted a new grouping. He classified under the notion or "genre" of *insania* the three major illness among which "madness" is essentially distributed, namely, *phrenitis*, melancholy (the fear and sadness attributed by Hippocratics to "black bile"), and *mania*. Why *insania*? We would be at a loss to give a semantic analysis, but a shift has occurred in any case from a positive entity, mania, to a privation, insanity, that authorizes and promotes the parallel between illness of the soul and illness of the body. The determinations of madness, or the ways of expressing it in the widest sense in Latin, are numerous. It seems indeed that this is Celsus's choice. The semantic field of madness is henceforth determined by the history of medicine.

B. Psychiatric frenzy and mania

These problems are not restricted to Greco-Roman antiquity. This is not only because these texts were well known and scrutinized through the middle of the nineteenth century, and play a role in the foundation of psychiatry, but also because a certain number of problems were dealt with in antiquity in a way that was decisive for psychopathology, and for the very meaning of the word "mania."

When psychiatry was created (at the end of the eighteenth century), the question of terminology returned. Philippe Pinel writes then: "The happy influence exercised on medicine recently by the study of other sciences can no longer allow giving the general name of madness, which may have an indeterminate scope, to insanity" (Pinel, *Traité médico-philosophique*). There are in his writings, however, two concepts of madness. One, in his *Nosographie philosophique*, corresponds to the tradition; another one, wider and newer in its definition, creates problems of categorization with the first, in his *Traité médico-philosophique* (128–29).

However, Pinel's student Esquirol wrote, in 1816, an article entitled "On Madness." In 1818, he wrote another, "On Mania," in which he returns to the classic definition: "Mania is a chronic affection of the brain, usually without fever, characterized by perturbation and exaltation of the senses, mind, and will." "I shall use," Vincenzo Chiarugi had written, on the other hand, "the word *insanity* [*pazzia*] without having to adopt a term taken from a foreign language, thus avoiding the risk of confusion and misunderstanding" (*Della pazzia in genere e in speczie*, trans. Mora).

Finally, outside of any medical context, it is prudent to avoid translating *mania* by "mania," since the English term is reserved for technical use; "madness," which remains the most general and least technical term, is used instead. It is common to see translators, out of a desire to avoid repetition, go so far as to translate *mania* by "frenzy." This is unfortunate, since in traditional nosography, *mania* is in fact opposed to "frenzy" (*phrenitis*). Translating *mania* by "delirium" should also be avoided, as since Pinel, we know that there are manias without delirium. *Mania* remains a technical term today, defined thus: "State of intellectual and psychomotor excitation, and exaltation of mood, with morbid euphoria, of periodic and cyclic evolution, entering the framework of manic-depressive psychosis" (RT: Postel, *Dictionnaire de psychiatrie*, s.v.).

■ See Box 1.

We may note, furthermore, that traditional nosography found itself overlaid, from the end of the eighteenth century on, with a "scientific" nomenclature derived from the medicalization of madness, henceforth defined as "mental illness." However, as Michel Foucault noted, between these two lexica of madness—that is, before the era of medicalization—an intermediate, purely descriptive terminology developed. A person was described as a "stubborn litigant," a "big liar," a "mean and quibbling" person, a "worried, despondent, and gruff mind":

> There is little sense in wondering if such people were sick or not, and to what degree. . . . What these formulae

indicate are not so much sicknesses as forms of madness perceived as *character faults* taken to an extreme degree, as though in confinement the sensibility to madness was not autonomous, but linked to a moral order where it appeared merely a disturbance.

> (Foucault, *A History of Madness,* 133)

II. The Latin Terminology: *Furor / Insania / Dementia*

A. Cicero as a translator of the Greeks

The uses of Latin terminology for madness are marked by the influence of Stoicism, the distinctions and analyses of which are taken up in contexts that are not strictly Stoic. Thus Cicero:

> I shall . . . follow the time-honoured distinction made first by Pythagoras and after him by Plato, who divide the soul into two parts: to the one they assign a share in reason, to the other none. . . . Let this then be our starting point; let us nevertheless in depicting these disorders employ the definitions and subdivisions of the Stoics who, it appears to me, show remarkable penetration in dealing with this problem.

> (Cicero, *Tusculan Disputations* 4.11, trans. King, 339)

A first attempt deals with the distinction of passions and illness, which the Greek groups under the general expression *pathê*:

1

Contemporary nosography

The conceptions of "madness" that were developed in antiquity did not find a place in the nomenclatures established by contemporary psychiatry, in which, for example, we find words or expressions like *aliénation mentale* (P. Pinel, 1797; "insanity" in English), *psychosis* (E. Feuchtersleben, 1844), *paranoia* (C. Lasèque, 1852) or *Verrücktheit* in German (W. Griesinger, 1845, then E. Kraepelin), *schizophrenia* or *dementia praecox* (E. Bleuler, 1908), and *phobia* (1880). In this new nosography, the denotations of ancient terms like *mania* [μανία], *phrenitis* [φρενῖτις], and *pathos* [πάθος] for the Greeks, or *furor*, *insania*, and *perturbatio* for the Romans (whose symptomatology generally went back to Hippocrates or Galen), often only retained from that point on a literary or popular usage.

The modern and contemporary nosography of madness relies on a wide variety of neologisms borrowed from Greek, such as "phobia" (from *phobos* [φόβος], illness whose primary symptom is a paralyzing and irrepressible fear when faced with an object or situation that in reality presents no danger; psychoanalysis refers to this rather as "anxiety hysteria"), "manic-depressive psychosis" (from the beginning of the twentieth

century, the third, after paranoia and schizophrenia, of the major current psychoses that is characterized by a disturbance of mood in which states of manic euphoria and fits of melancholy or depression alternate), "hysteria" (an eighteenth-century term; then, at the end of the nineteenth century, a collection of disorders that was initially believed to be related to eroticism originating in the uterus—from the Greek *hustera* [ὑστέρα]—and that relate to unconscious conflicts manifested by bodily symptoms and in the form of symbolizations), "paranoia" (from *paranoia* [παράνοια], a kind of systematic delirium in which interpretation predominates and which does not include intellectual deterioration; Freud saw it as a defense against homosexuality).

However, note that, alongside these various terms, psychiatry and psychoanalysis place emphasis on the idea of a *schize* or a defect in the personality of the subject, notably with regard to what is called "schizophrenia." This last term, by which Bleuler replaces the expression *dementia praecox* used by Kraepelin, comes directly from the Greek verb *schizô* [σχίζω], which means "to separate, split, dissociate," and which had already yielded "schism" in the sense of "separation." Thus schizophrenia

would be characterized by symptoms of mental dissociation, discordance of affects and frenzied activity that lead to a general withdrawal into oneself (autism) and a breaking off of contact with the external world. The same idea is found in the German noun *Spaltung* used by Freud, which French psychoanalysts translate by *clivage*, though often using it rather loosely, with the meaning of a dissociation of consciousness, or of the object, or of the ego—regarding this Freudian *Ichspaltung*, Lacan translates the expression as "refente du sujet" (*Écrits*, 842).

BIBLIOGRAPHY

Bleuler, Eugen. *Lehrbuch der Psychiatrie*. Berlin: Springer, 1916.

Ey, Henri. *Consciousness: A Phenomenological Study of Being Conscious and Becoming Conscious*. Translated by J. H. Flodstrom. Bloomington: Indiana University Press, 1978.

———. *Études psychiatriques*. 3 vols. Paris: Desclée de Brouwer, 1948–52.

Foucault, Michel. *History of Madness*. Edited by J. Khalfa. Translated by J. Murphy and J. Khalfa. New York: Routledge, 2006.

Kraepelin, Emil. *Lehrbuch der Psychiatrie*. 9th ed. Leipzig: Kraepelin and Lange, 1927.

Lacan, Jacques. *Écrits*. Paris: Seuil, 1966.

Terror, lusts, fits of anger—these belong, speaking generally, to the class of emotions which the Greeks term *pathê* [πάθη]: I might have called them "diseases," and this would be a word-for-word rending: but it would not fit in with Latin usage. For pity, envy, exultation, joy, all these the Greeks term diseases, movements that is of the soul which are not obedient to reason; we on the other hand should, I think rightly, say that these same movements of an agitated soul are "disorders," but not "diseases" in the ordinary way of speaking.

(Ibid., 3.7, trans. King, 233)

It is in the context of this general distinction that we must understand the etymological connection between *insania* (madness) and *insanitas* (ill health), on the basis of which Cicero develops the Stoic doctrine of passion/illness: "The word *insania* refers to a weakness and a sickness of the intelligence [*mentis aegrotatio et morbus*], that is, the ill health [*insanitas*] of a sick mind [*animus aegrotus*]" (ibid.). Thus the appeal to a play on etymology makes it possible to find a linguistic correlate of the symmetry between bodily and mental health, which is a philosophical construction. In this way, Cicero gives Latin a capacity that neither the general term *pathê* nor *mania* (which *insania* translates) has in Greek, at the expense of forcing Latin usage: whereas *sanus* may mean either healthy of body or healthy of mind, *insanus* only means "mentally ill / crazy."

Once this symmetry has been established, Cicero can interpret the only legal text from the classical period that refers to a person as a madman (*furiosus*), so that the oldest legal usage of the language coincides with the Stoic approach: *furor* is, just as much as *insania*, an imbalance of the mind, but it is such that it prevents one from fulfilling the obligations of life.

I cannot readily give the origin of the Greek term *mania*: the meaning it actually implies is marked with better discrimination by us than by the Greeks, for we make a distinction between "unsoundness" of mind, which from its association with folly has a wider connotation, and "frenzy." The Greeks wish to make the distinction but fall short of success in the term they employ: what we call frenzy they call *melancholia*, just as if the truth were that the mind is influenced by black bile only and not in many instances by the stronger power of wrath or fear or pain, in the sense in which we speak of the frenzy of Athamas, Alcmaeon, Ajax and Orestes. Whosoever is so afflicted is not allowed by the Twelve Tables to remain in control of his property; and consequently we find the text runs, not "if of unsound mind," but "if he be frenzied." For they thought that folly, though without steadiness, that is to say, soundness of mind, was nevertheless capable of charging itself with the performance of ordinary duties and the regular routine of the conduct of life: frenzy, however, they regarded as a blindness of the mind in all relations.

(Ibid., 3.11, trans. King, 237–39)

The distinction suggested on the authority of the Twelve Tables allows for a better account of what separates the state of fury of the great tragic heroes from the madness that the paradoxical definition of the Stoics attributes to the non-sages: this distinction does not exist in the verb *mainesthai*, which refers equally to the madness of Heracles, prophetic fury, and non-wisdom. The paradox "*hoti pas aphrôn mainetai* [ὅτι πᾶς ἄφρων μαίνεται]" is translated "*omnem stultum insanire*" (Cicero, *Stoic Paradoxes* 27). The choice of the Latin *stultus*, which does not connote madness, to render the Greek *aphrôn* [ἄφρων], whose most well-attested meaning is "demented/crazy," reinforces the effect of distinguishing them and expresses what is most characteristic of the Stoic doctrine of the passions: all passion comes from an error of judgment.

However, the distinction drawn does not simply dispose of *furor* as an illness of "great natures": Cicero refuses to attribute it to black bile, and presents it rather as a complete blindness that results from excess. In this way, he maintains the Stoic point of view by taking advantage of everything that, with regard to *furor*, connotes excess—from heroic fury to the self-dispossessions of erotic poetry—without appealing to a precise form of judgment. The term is also absent from the list of forms of anger that yields, in the Ciceronian translation, *ira*, *excandescentia*, *odium*, *inimicitia*, *discordia* (anger, irascibility, hate, enmity, resentment) (*Tusculan Disputations* 4.21).

B. *Furor* and *insania* in the Stoics

Cicero's attempts at drawing distinctions are largely adopted by Seneca, who nevertheless takes advantage of them to explore the confusion of moral and physical causes of collective disorder:

Between the insanity of people in general and the insanity which is subject to medical treatment, there is no difference, except that the latter is suffering from disease and the former from false opinions. In the one case, the symptoms of madness may be traced to ill-health; the other is the ill-health of the mind.

(Seneca, *Ad Lucilium epistolae morales* 94.7, trans. Gummere, 3:21–23)

However, *furor* and *insania* are used conjointly to refer to evils of body and mind, the evil of the individual in civilization: *furor* refers to a state of ingratitude that has become so general that it threatens the foundation of all social bonds ("*Eo perductus est furor ut periculosissima res sit benificia in aliquem magna conferre*," ibid., 81.31–32), or the blindness comparable to that of the clown who, having lost his sight, believed that the house had gone dark (ibid., 50). It is the state of all who can no longer perceive that they are affected, since the organ of judgment is too sick: Seneca's language exploits the symmetry between *insania* and *insanitas* more widely than Cicero does, to apply the Stoic paradox to a state of civilization: "We are mad, not only individually, but nationally [*non privatim solum sed publice furimus*]" (ibid., 95.30, trans. Gummere, 77).

III. Scholastic Expressions for Unreason and Christian Faith as "Madness"

A. The *fol*

From the eleventh century on, under the influence of the Gregorian reform and of Cluny, all the different components of European society came to be integrated into what was called Christendom. Those who were excluded—Jews, Saracens, heretics—ran the risk of being accused of thinking or acting "differently." Their deviance was then classified as a major defect of confusion or madness. In the vernacular, the "other" was called a *sot* (in Old French *soz, sos*, from the medieval Latin *sottus*, of unknown etymology), a maniac, a *dervé*, insane, *fol*. This last term, which would take up a prime position in the language of madness, comes from the Latin *follis*, which means "pouch of sealed leather, goatskin flask, balloon or bellows for fires." Only in the Middle Ages does it take on a derisive second meaning, designating a stupid person or idiot.

In their own academic disputes in Latin, theologians did not refrain from stigmatizing their adversaries as incapable of correct reasoning, stricken with *stultitia*, *amentia*, or *furor*. However, among the terms related to unreason or mental confusion that they exchanged in more or less insulting ways, there are two terms that assume, in the disputes, a properly technical sense: *insipiens* and *phreneticus*. The first is the Vulgate translation of the epithet *aphrôn*, found in the Septuagint in the incipit of Psalm 52 (53 today), which stigmatizes unbelief. This incipit, in effect, appears in Latin bibles in the following form: "*Dixit insipiens in corde suo: Non est Deus*" (The fool said in his heart: There is no God). This is why medieval iconography illustrating madmen or madness takes as its frame the illuminations of the letter *D*, which is the initial letter of this verse of the psalm.

B. The *insipiens*

Unlike *fol*, *insipiens* is etymologically close to the idea of mental derangement, coming from *sapio*, "to have taste, discernment," and from *sapiens* as a noun or adjective "sage," referring to the non-sage—someone whose reason is faulty. It is translated into French as *insensé*, that is, someone whose statements are contrary to good sense and whose mind wanders (from *sensus* and, in the language of the Church, *insensatus*, an adjective that evokes absurdity, stupidity, idiocy, like "nonsense" in English).

Yet, even though this same attitude of mind, this unreason, was also imputed to the Jews, guilty of not having recognized Jesus as the Messiah, it is Anselm of Canterbury who pronounces it of its most emblematic figure, the monk Gaunilo, for refusing to accept the proof of God's existence offered by the author of the *Monologion* and the *Proslogion*. When Anselm attacks him, especially in chapters 2 and 4 of the latter, he never refers to Gaunilo by name—only, and often, as the *insipiens*. He asks in particular how this fool par excellence "could say in his heart what cannot be thought [*quomodo insipiens dixit in corde suo, quod cogitari non potest*]." What "cannot be thought" is that God does not exist, once one has in one's mind the idea of a being such that it is impossible to conceive a greater one. It is necessary, indeed, that he exists both in thought and in reality ("*et in intellectu et in re*"). "Why then *did the fool say in his heart: God is not*, . . . unless it is because he is stupid [*stultus*] and foolish [*insipiens*]?" (See SENSE.)

C. The *phreneticus*

Among the most violent attributions the authors of the Latin Middle Ages hurled at their opponents, we also find *phreneticus*. Thus, in the twelfth century, Richard of Saint-Victor

defends the constricting character of his argument relative to the Trinity by falling back on dialectic: "This hard to break triple-bond by which any frenetic destroyer of our faith finds himself firmly chained [*unde phreneticus quivis fidei nostrae impugnator fortiter alligetur*]," *De Trinitate*, 3.5). Yet the term *phreneticus* comes here not from a scriptural source, but from the tradition of Augustine, himself well aware of ancient medico-psychological terminology.

The bishop of Hippo first recalls the clinical table (cf. Guimet, "*Caritas ordinata et amor discretus*," 226–28). *Phrenesis* (from the Greek *phrenitis*) is a mental illness that engenders the loss of reason and that, for example, leads the subject to laugh when he should cry (*Sermo 175*, 2.2, RT: *PL* 38.945). It is sometimes accompanied by delirium, visions, and extravagant divinatory phenomena (*De Genesi ad litteram*, 12.17.35–36, RT: *PL* 34.468). It is indicated by disorders such as fever, abuse of wine, and insomnia, and leads to crises that become increasingly violent as death approaches (*De quantitate animae*, 22.38, RT: *PL* 32.1057, 40.1058; *Ennaratio in Psalmum 58*, RT: *PL* 36.696). In all of these symptoms, the "frenetic" is contrasted with the "lethargic," who founders constantly in inertia and in sleep (*Sermo 87*, 11.14; RT: *PL* 38.538).

Augustine then puts this classic schema to a moral and spiritual use. In his eyes, the two components of *phrenesis*, confusion and violence, are found in particular in the case of the Jews. It is under the influence of a virulent furor that they, refusing the salvation brought to them by Christ, made themselves executioners. And it is with respect to their blindness that the Messiah begs divine forgiveness for them: "They know not what they do." Attributing this same pathological state to his other adversaries, the Donatists, Augustine suggests binding the *phreneticus* with constrictive arguments (*Sermo 359*, 8, RT: *PL* 39.1596), a remedy taken up by Richard of Saint Victor in attempting to restrain this lunatic by means of dialectic.

Nevertheless, the *phrenesis* of late antiquity and the Middle Ages is paradoxically rehabilitated in the romantic period, continuing into surrealism, by so-called frenetic literature, which, especially with Charles Nodier (1781–1840), is presented as a deliberate intensification of sensuality, passion, imagination, revolt, and fantasizing.

■ See Box 2.

IV. Kantian *Schwärmerei* and the Relation to Belief

A. The "swarm of bees"

Originally, the German noun *Schwärmerei* meant the agitation of bees, which move about without stopping; more precisely, on the one hand, it means the disorderly movements of each of the bees considered independently, and on the other hand, it means the compact flight of the swarm forming a group, equally uncontrollable. This double meaning made it possible to apply the term to religious beliefs that could be stigmatized as "wandering" and "sectarian." Thus it was often used by Luther starting in the 1520s to denounce the "left wing" of the Reformation, which condemned the flesh in an exalted manner, interpreting the Gospel of John (6:63) in a fanatical sense: "It is the spirit that quickeneth; the flesh profiteth nothing." *Schwärmerei* connotes the exalted

2

The Pauline praise of madness

The parable of the wise virgins and the mad virgins (Matthew 25:1–2) only invokes madness as a synonym of distraction, casualness, lack of foresight: "Five among them were mad and five prudent [*pente de ex autôn êsan môrai kai pente phronimoi* (πέντε δὲ ἐξ αὐτῶν ἦσαν μωραὶ καὶ πέντε φρόνιμοι)]."

It is in Paul that the paradoxical situation in virtue of which Christian faith is a form of madness radically opposed to reason and common wisdom is described (1 Cor. 1:23–25): "We declare a Christ crucified, scandal for Jews and madness for pagans [*ethnesin de môrian* (ἔθνεσιν δὲ μωρίαν)] . . . for what is madness of God is wiser than men [*hoti to môron tou theou sophôteron tôn anthrôpôn estin* (ὅτι τὸ μωρὸν τοῦ θεοῦ σοφώτερον τῶν ἀνθρώπων ἐστίν)]." Paul adds (1 Cor. 3:18): "If someone among you thinks himself wise in the way of the world, let him become mad [*môros genesthô* (μωρὸς γενέσθω)]." And later in the same epistle (4:10): "We are mad [*êmeis môroi* (ἡμεῖς μωροὶ)], we, because of Christ."

To express this idea of madness and scandal applied to devotion to the crucified Christ, Paul appeals to the term *môria* [μωρία], which, present notably in Aeschylus and Plato, is related to the verb *môrainô* [μωραίνω], which means, in the transitive sense, first "to dull" or "to stultify" (cf. Matthew 5:13: "If the salt becomes bland [*môranthê* (μωρανθῇ)] . . ."), then "to make mad." Thus the adjective *môros* [μωρός] has the primary sense of "dulled" or "insipid," and the secondary sense of "mad" or "insane." Translated into the Vulgate as *stultitia*, *môria* comes in composition in Greek terminology with *sophos* [σοφός] and *phrôn* [φρῶν] to yield *môro-sophos* [μωρό-σοφος] and *môro-phrôn* [μωρό-φρων], terms meaning equally "madly wise" and "wisely mad," as though they were especially apt to express the Pauline paradox.

imagination that moves outside of accepted paths, the uninhibited stubbornness of beliefs, and sectarian behavior. It is truly an untranslatable term, since neither Latin, nor English, nor French has a term with any sort of link to the image of the swarm of bees, in which the evocation of the isolated adventure of a dreamer meets up, contradictorily, with that of the fanaticism of an uncontrollable group. In French, the term is translated as *exaltation*, *fanatisme*, or *enthousiasme*, depending on the case. In German military terminology, the image of the swarm is also invoked to refer to the activity of a scout who is detached from the group on a personal adventure, as well as the compact but uncoordinated movement of a group of soldiers.

B. Kant: From Swedenborg's hallucinations to Leibniz's idealism

The term *Schwärmerei* was used until the eighteenth century in theological controversies to refer to heretics, schismatics, and innovators who deviated and disturbed the equilibrium and calm of the Church. All of these uses involve insulting or stigmatizing labels rather than a clear concept. Kant transforms the polemical usage into a concept when, in 1766, in the *Dreams of a Spirit-Seer, Explained through Dreams of Metaphysics*, he describes the thought of the visionary Swedenborg as deriving from *Schwärmerei*, contrasting it with Leibnizian idealism. In this work, Kant analyzes at length the system of beliefs and thoughts that, based on the idea of the unreality of death, allows the seer to communicate with the spirits from beyond, who speak to him in virtue of the ecstatic transformations of his senses. The sensory hallucinations are interpreted by Swedenborg as a message from angels and the Christ, which reveal to him the true order of things under the appearance of laws of nature. The content of the images in these visions, which dwell in him, is related by this "prophet of the other world" to the text of Genesis, of which Swedenborg claims to give the correct interpretation by arguing that his "internal being is open" and that he is therefore himself the oracle of the spirits.

The terminology of *Schwärmerei* is thus related, in 1766, to that of ghosts and interaction with spirits. If, as we have just seen, the extravagance of the speeches and practices of the seer do not give rise only to ridicule but also to conceptual elaboration, the link between extravagance, madness, and the belief in spirits gives Kant the opportunity to play with these different terms. Indeed, besides *Schwärmerei*, German has another term that comes from the life of insects to express the ideas that populate the heads of deranged individuals: *Hirngespinst* (in RT: *Ak.*, 2:926). *Spinnen* means "to spin." *Hirngespinst*, just as untranslatable as *Schwärmerei* (except perhaps by "chimera" or "fantasmagoria"), refers to having a spider in the brain, or, as is sometimes said more colloquially, "to have spiders in the belfry." However, the images of bees and spiders are conjoined in the *Dreams of a Spirit-Seer* in such a way that the reference to the extravagance of interaction with the spirits yields another term, *Hirngespenst*, by which Kant means the notion of a "ghost in the head." The system of these different terms is what also transforms the sense of the word *Wahn*, which thenceforth means not so much illusion, understood as perception of an appearance, as madness—and this sense is maintained in the *Critique of Pure Reason*. The word *Wahn* is thus distinguished from all of those that Kant uses, from the *Essay on Illness of the Head* (1764) through *Anthropology Considered from a Pragmatic Point of View* (1798), where he attempts to classify all the forms of mental derangement according to the faculties, perceptual or intellectual, that are affected. Besides the common forms of head and heart sickness, which range from stupidity (*Blödsinn*) to clownery (*Narrheit*), derangement (*Verkehrtheit*) is the inversion (*Verrückung*) of empirical notions. Delirium (*Wahnsinn*) is the disorder that strikes judgment at the point closest to this perceptual experience; dementia (*Wahnwitz*) is the upsetting of reason in its most universal judgments. Of course, the term *Wahn* is related to *Wahnsinn*, "delirium," and in 1766 Kant writes that what interests him about Swedenborg is the disturbance of judgment at its closest resemblance to perceptual disorder, that is, the latter's hallucinations. But *Wahn* gets its specific meaning from the philosophical discussion that links Swedenborg's delirium to that of reason in the idealism represented by Leibniz.

When Kant comments on Swedenborg's *Arcana Coelestia*, he insists on the fact that, more than the wild construction in itself, what *Schwärmerei* really consists in is consistent sensory hallucination, when it feeds the belief in the unreality of death and in the communication with spirits, and, last but not least, when it constructs a philosophy of nature as simple appearance, which enters into the minds of men through the conversations they have with spirits from the beyond. It is as an idealist theory of nature that Kant connects *Schwärmerei* to Leibniz's thought. He makes the connection since, in 1766, Kant challenges rationalists to say in what the difference between the two systems of thought consists. However, the reformulation introduced in 1781 in the *Critique of Pure Reason*, when he gives a transcendental definition of the modality of our judgments, retains the imprint of this closeness established in 1766 between *Schwärmerei* and Leibniz's thought. Kant distinguishes, in effect, that which "without being impossible in the sense of contradiction, cannot be counted among the things that are possible." There are two forms of this impossibility in the transcendental sense: the Leibnizian intelligible world, and the fanatical world system of the *Schwärmer*. Further, in the preface to the first edition of the *Critique of Pure Reason*, Kant creates a composite word that unites once again the ecstatics and the dogmatists, against which the critique of reason will teach us to preserve ourselves. The critical response that he brings to bear on the problems of metaphysics will not be content, he says, with "the extravagant-dogmatic desires for knowledge" ("*Zwar ist die Beantwortung jener Fragen gar nicht so aufgefallen, als dogmatischschwärmende Wissbegierde erwarten mochten,*" in RT: *Ak.*, 3:14).

We may note that Kant uses *Schwärmerei* as a synonym for *Fanatismus* when he insists on the practical function of the extravagance that determines the will in these cases. This explains why, in the *Critique of Practical Reason*, the term "fanaticism" is most often used to refer to the insane illusion of moral and political reformers who wish to convince us that a good determined in its content is the absolute achieved. The formalism of morality according to Kant has the function of avoiding the madness of the will that is fanaticism. And we know that, in the *Kritik der Urteilskraft* (Critique of the power of judgment, usually translated as "Critique of the faculty of judgment"), Kant returns to the closeness of enthusiasm and fanaticism. It is this usage of the term *Schwärmerei*, and not its meaning as strictly related to critical and transcendental themes, that is taken up by all the authors, writers, philosophers, and poets of the romantic era in Germany. Its mild forms make it equivalent to whim, but a whim that cannot be uprooted, that develops into fantasies or all-pervasive beliefs.

▪ See Box 3.

V. The Right to Madness

At the end of the Middle Ages, in a register similar to that of the Pauline dialectic between the madness and the wisdom of the Cross, several currents of thought attempted to give a positive view of madness using the same terms that had thus far been considered pejorative, or at least to mitigate their seriousness. The fifteenth century locked up the cargo of the insane in the strange "Ship of Fools" (*Narrenschiff*), which long wandered the rivers and canals of the Rhineland and Flanders. By contrast, Erasmus made his *Praise of Folly* (1509) the tool of a reversal that made it possible to see two very different aspects of all human things, one seeming glorious despite being pathetic (such as the conceits of scholars and theologians), the other held to be extravagant and contemptible, but in reality filled with a noble prudence and genuine wisdom. Montaigne does the same in making wisdom of madness and madness of wisdom. At the start of the seventeenth century, Cervantes's *Don Quixote* is a comic interrogation of the indefinite boundary between delirium and good sense, between enchantment and disillusionment (see DESENGAÑO). Fascinated by and basking in the feats of chivalry from old novels, the noble hidalgo of La Mancha leaves his village, wearing his armor, to make what he has read become real. In this way, though himself bewitched, he ends up bewitching the world and preserving truth through the lies of fiction.

In its turn, rationalism, especially that of Descartes and Spinoza, aims to banish the insane from the order of reason and to deny their psychic states any positive reality, whereas the *philosophes* of the Enlightenment make their position more nuanced by interpreting insanity as a ruse of nature that is only harmful past certain limits. The latter view clears of all charges, for example, the "literary madmen" of Raymond Queneau and Andre Blavier, and those who have given approval to what is called "the art of the mentally ill," inheritors of part of the positivity of Greek *mania*. However, the same attempt at understanding will underwrite the idea that madness can appear in anyone, even if its extravagance is not always perceptible.

Toward the end of the eighteenth century, indeed, the symbolic softenings attributed to Pinel with regard to the treatment of madness paradoxically liberate a highly vengeful language opposing the so-called scientific approach to psychiatry that accompanied them. Visiting the "lunatics" in a hospital, Charles Nodier, in *La fée aux miettes* (1832), defines the "madman" as "a discarded or chosen creature like you or me, who lives by invention, fantasy, and love in the pure regions of the intelligence." From romanticism to surrealism, with André Breton, Maurice Blanchot, and Michel Foucault, in relation to Gerard de Nerval, Comté de Lautréamont, Antonin Artaud, Vincent Van Gogh, Friedrich Nietzsche, and Friedrich Hölderlin, the claim "he is mad" is dropped in the face of the question, "Is he mad?" Thus, as Blanchot says about Hölderlin's extreme and genuinely schizophrenic fits:

> Madness would be a word perpetually in disagreement with itself, and thoroughly interrogative, so that it calls into question its possibility, and thereby, the possibility of the language which would compose it, hence the questioning as well, insofar as it belongs to the game of language . . . a language, as such, already gone mad.

(Preface to Jaspers, *Strindberg et Van Gogh*, trans. Holland)

Clara Auvray-Assayas
Charles Baladier
Monique David-Menard
Jackie Pigeaud

3
Freudian *Schwärmerei*

Curiously, we find the term *Schwärmerei* in Freud, in a very specific sense. It does not refer, in the writings of the founder of psychoanalysis, to any form of delirium, nor any belief, but to the stories that adolescents tell each other when they bestow a worshipful love upon someone of the same sex: oaths of fidelity, daily correspondence, declarations of the absolute. These whims or flames usually disappear as if by enchantment, says Freud in *Drei Abhandlungen zur Sexualtheorie* (Three essays on the theory of sexuality [1905], in *Gesammelte Werke*, vol. 5), and in particular when love for someone of the opposite sex appears. However, there again, the paradox of the *Schwärmerei* is to be an uncontrollable belief despite its fragility, and to construct an imaginary world in which one is ecstatic. As a result, the term *Schwärmerei* is also used by Freud in two other cases. The first is in the exalted love of what is called "the young (female) homosexual" for a mature woman of low morals, to whom she attaches herself. The seriousness of the passion is shown when, meeting her father one day while she is walking with the woman of her thoughts, she throws herself off a bridge that overlooks a railway ("The Psychogenesis of a Case of Homosexuality in a Woman," [1920], in *Standard Edition*, 18:145–72). In another case, Freud describes as *Schwärmerei* the dedication of martyrs who do not feel pain when they suffer for their God ("Psychical [or Mental] Treatment" [1890], in *Standard Edition*, vol. 7). He insists there on the transition that takes place, in these experiences, between the perverse components of drives and the self-sacrifice that ensures belief (see "On the History of the Psychoanalytic Movement," in *Standard Edition*, vol. 14).

BIBLIOGRAPHY

Freud, Sigmund. *Drei Abhandlungen zur Sexualtheorie*. First published in 1905. In *Gesammelte Werke*, vol. 5. Translation by J. Strachey: *Three Essays on the Theory of Sexuality*. New York: Basic Books, 2000.
———. *Gesammelte Werke*. 18 vols. London: Imago, 1940–52. Translation by J. Strachey: *The Standard Edition of the Psychological Works of Sigmund Freud*. Edited by J. Strachey. New York: W. W. Norton, 1989.

BIBLIOGRAPHY

Anselm, Bishop of Canterbury. *Basic Writings*. Translated by T. Williams. Indianapolis, IN: Hackett, 2007.
Blanchot, Maurice. "La folie par excellence." In K. Jaspers, *Strindberg et Van Gogh: Swedenborg et Hölderlin*. Paris: Minuit, 1953. Translation by M. Holland: "Madness *par excellence*." In *The Blanchot Reader*, edited by M. Holland, 110–28. London: Blackwell, 1995.
Boissier de Sauvages, François. *Nosologia methodica*. Amsterdam, Neth.: Sumptibus Fratrum de Tournes, 1763. French translation by M. Gouvion: *Nosologie méthodique, ou Distribution des maladies en classes, en genres et en espèces*. Lyon, Fr., 1772.
Brisson, Luc. "Du bon usage du dérèglement." In *Divination et rationalité*, 230–48. Paris: Seuil, 1974.
Chiarugi, Vincenzo. *Della pazzia in genere e in specie: Trattato medico-analitico. Con una centuria di osservazioni*. 3 vols. Florence: Carlieri, 1793–94. Reprinted Rome: Vecchiarelli, 1991. Translation by G. Mora: *On Insanity and Its Classification*. Introduction by G. Mora. Canton, MA: Science History Production, 1987.
Cicero. *Tusculan Disputations*. Translated by J. E. King. London: Heinemann, 1945.
David-Ménard, Monique. *La folie dans la raison pure: Kant lecteur de Swedenborg*. Paris: Vrin, 1990.
Derrida, Jacques. "Cogito et histoire de la folie." In *L'écriture et la différence*. Paris: Seuil, 1967. Translation by A. Bass: "Cogito and the History of Madness." In *Writing and Difference*, 36–76. London: Routledge, 2001.
Esquirol, Jean Étienne. *Des maladies mentales*. Paris: Baillière, 1838. Translation by E. K. Hunt: *Mental Maladies: A Treatise on Insanity*. Introduction by R. de Saussure. New York: Hafner, 1965.
Foucault, Michel. *History of Madness*. Edited by J. Khalfa. Translated by J. Murphy and J. Khalfa. London: Routledge, 2006.
Goldschmidt, Georges-Arthur. *Quand Freud voit la mer: Freud et la langue allemande*. Paris: Buchet-Chastel, 1988.
Guimet, Fernand. "*Caritas ordinata* et *amor discretus* dans la théologie trinitaire de Richard de Saint-Victor." *Revue du Moyen-Âge* (Aug.–Oct. 1948).
Iogna-Prat, Dominique. *Ordonner et exclure: Cluny et la société chrétienne face à l'hérésie, au judaïsme et à l'Islam, 1000–1150*. Paris: Aubier, 1998.
Jaspers, Karl. *Strindberg et Van Gogh: Swedenborg et Hölderlin*. Paris: Minuit, 1953.
Laharie, Muriel. *La folie au Moyen-Âge: XIe–XIIIe siècles*. Paris: Le Léopard d'or, 1991.
Pigeaud, Jackie. *Folie et cures de la folie chez les médecins de l'antiquité gréco-romaine: La manie*. Paris: Les Belles Lettres, 1987.
———. "La réflexion de Celse sur la folie." In *La médecine de Celse: Aspects historiques, scientifiques et littéraires*, 257–79. Saint-Étienne, Fr.: Publication de l'Université de Saint-Étienne, Centre Jean Palerne, 1994.
Pinel, Philippe. *Traité médico-philosophique sur l'aliénation mentale, ou la Manie*. 2nd ed. Paris: J. A. Brosson, 1809.
Plato. *The Collected Dialogues*. Edited by Edith Hamilton and Huntington Cairns. Princeton, NJ: Princeton University Press, 2005.
Seneca. *Ad Lucilium epistolae morales*. Translated by Richard M. Gummere. London: Heinemann, 1925.

| MALAISE (FRENCH)

➤ GOOD/EVIL

Malaise (the opposite of *aise* [ease] in French, from the Latin *jacere* [to throw], itself linked to the idea of dwelling, then to the idea of convenience and of pleasure), refers to a painful sensation, as much moral as physical, and in particular implies the more or less conscious, or more or less confused, perception of a dysfunction in the relationship between the soul and the body. The term *malaise* can cover a multitude of experiences of suffering, whether fleeting or chronic, slight or keen, that a person, but also a group, might undergo. An era, a language, a culture, or a nation can distinguish itself by naming, defining, or expressing its *malaise*, in literature as well as in philosophy.

I. A Dysfunction between Soul and Body

1. On the relationship between soul and body, the networks of affect and passion, see in particular CONSCIOUSNESS, DRIVE, GEFÜHL, GEMÜT, GOGO, LEIB, *PASSION*, PATHOS, PERCEPTION, PHANTASIA (and *IMAGINATION*), STIMMUNG, STRADANIE, UNCONSCIOUS, WUNSCH; cf., ANIMAL, LOVE, PLEASURE, SOUL, *SUFFERING*.

2. The physiological location in which malaise is rooted varies with the organic cause to which one attributes the dysfunction: so it could be the bile, see MELANCHOLY; the spleen, see SPLEEN; or the throat, see ANXIETY. The degree of its possible medical diagnosis and treatment varies as well: see MELANCHOLY; cf. GENIUS, MADNESS, PATHOS.

II. Sketch of a Typology of Different Kinds of *Malaise*

A. Individual suffering, ontological suffering, national suffering

Individual *malaise* can lead one to question one's relationship to being, and one's sense of belonging to the world; see ANXIETY, DOR, HEIMAT, Box 2, SAUDADE; cf. CARE, DASEIN, SORGE, *SOUCI*, and TRUTH, Box 8. It can also have a moral, religious, or social register, or bear witness to a whole era: see ACEDIA, SEHNSUCHT, SPLEEN.

In more general terms, these affects form part of a national cultural register, with the word used to designate them functioning as a password, even when it is "imported," like "spleen," for example: see ACEDIA, DESENGAÑO, DOR, SAUDADE, SEHNSUCHT, SPLEEN.

B. Models and expressions

A number of different temporal and spatial models are involved, one of the richest being the Greek *nostalgia*, always turning back to the past and seeking to return to the place of origin: see SEHNSUCHT, Box 1 and *NOSTALGIA*; cf. HEIMAT. But the future and the unknown beyond can be no less determining: see SAUDADE, SEHNSUCHT, cf. *DESTINY*.

The expressions of *malaise* and of pain are also significantly different from one another, implying syntactically the whole (Lat., *me dolet*, "I am suffering") or the part (Eng., "my foot aches"), and determining a relation to philosophy (*angst*, *Sehnsucht*), and/or to poetry (nostalgia, *saudade*, spleen), to literature (*desengaño*), or to silence (*acedia*): see all of these terms.

➤ PORTUGUESE, SVOBODA

MANIERA (ITALIAN), MANNER, STYLE

DUTCH	*manjer; handeling; wijze van doen*
FRENCH	*manière, faire, style*
GERMAN	*Manier; Stil*
ITALIAN	*maniera; stile*

➤ AESTHETICS, ART, BAROQUE, CLASSIC, CONCETTO, DISEGNO, GENIUS, GOÛT, INGENIUM, MIMÊSIS, ROMANTIC, TABLEAU

The word *maniera* as it was used in different languages, and understood in its different senses, was at the heart of the language of art criticism from the sixteenth to the end of the eighteenth century. It refers to the personal nature of an artist's work, to the taste of a whole school, and to the use of a formal language associated with a particular time and place (the Florentine manner, the Roman manner, the Flemish manner). When used with other adjectives (grand manner, strong or clashing manner) or with proper names (in the manner of Michelangelo, of Carrache, of Raphael), it refers to the modes of expression chosen by artists. It can take on a negative connotation: a mannered artist is one who copies a manner, who neglects to imitate nature. This diversity of meanings led to a number of substitutes (in particular *faire* in French, *Stil* in German, "style" or "stile" in English, all with different nuances), and finally to the word being abandoned at the end of the eighteenth century.

I. *Maniera* and the Origin of Art Theory

It seems that the word *maniera* first appeared in Italian art literature. The first known occurrence is in the *Libro dell'arte* by Cennino Cennini, written at the end of the fourteenth century: "Always attach yourself to the best master and, following him everywhere, it would be unnatural for you not to take on his manner [*sua maniera*] and his style" (chap. 25). *Maniera* is here the characteristic hallmark of an artist, his signature style, but also the particular qualities that could, paradoxically, be acquired by others. For Raphael, in his letter to Pope Leo X (in *Gli scritti*) on the conservation of ancient monuments, the term can suggest the formal characteristics of a monument: "The monuments of our time are known for not having a *maniera* that is as beautiful as those of the time of the Emperors, or as deformed as those of the time of the Goths," which he describes later on as "dreadful and worthless"; these Gothic buildings, he writes, are "*senza maniera alcuna* [without any manner]." It was, however, in Vasari's *Le vite* that *maniera* became a key term in the language of art criticism. The different meanings and the frequency of its use made it one of the richest notions of Vasari's text. *Maniera* referred to the particular character of a people (Egyptian *maniera*, Flemish *maniera*. . .), and to the different stages in the evolution of art history (*maniera antica*, *maniera vecchia*, *maniera moderna*). Each artist had his own *maniera*, comparable to writing, and it was also sometimes defined with the help of adjectives ("hard," "dry," "great"). *Maniera* was also something like an artistic recipe, used to express the nonrepresentable effects of nature: sculptors tried to find a *maniera* to represent horses. It was above all the hallmark of the greatest artists (with Michaelangelo the foremost among them) who knew how to surpass nature. It could, finally, be a form of infidelity to nature, a simple artistic practice.

This meaning became more clearly developed in the seventeenth century, and the most famous expression of a critique of *maniera* is without doubt that of Bellori, in his introduction to the life of Annibale Carracci:

> Artists, abandoning the study of nature, have corrupted art with *maniera*, by which I mean a fantastic idea, based on practice and not on imitation.
>
> (*Le vite*, 31; *Lives of the Modern Painters*, trans. A. S. Wohl)

An art that is too dependent on *maniera* is removed from nature, and must therefore be condemned.

II. The Double Meaning of "Manner" in European Languages

The adaptation of the word *maniera* was a determining factor in the transmission of the Italian conception of the work of art to the different countries in Europe. It is striking, then, that in Dutch art criticism, the term *manier* was used in combination with the term *handeling*, which had an equivalent meaning. So Van Mander (1604) talked about the *vaste stoute handeling* (the assured and bold manner) of painting, like the *vaste manier van Schilderen* of Cornelis van Haarlem. The word *manier* could also refer to a comparative art criticism: Van Eyck painted his draperies, according to Van Mander, *op de manier van Albertus Durerus* (in the manner of Dürer). Samuel van Hoogstraten, in his *Inleyding tot de hooge schoole des Schiderkonst* (Introduction to the high school of painting) (1678), uses different expressions incorporating the term— each with a slightly different meaning—within a span of two pages. He uses the word *manier* in a negative sense in talking about painters who adopt the habit of coloring "als of de dingen aen haere manier, en niet haere manier aen des aerd verbonden was" (as if things were dependent upon their manner, and not their manner dependent upon things). Yet the following chapter is entitled "Van der handeling of maniere van schilderen [Of handling or the manner of painting]," where *maniere* is spelled with an *e* at the end. In commenting on the word *handeling*, he talks about *wijze van doen* (way of doing), and the word *manier* in Holland indeed seemed to remain linked to the particular nature of the hand.

In France, the word had different meanings, and was used in different ways depending on the authors. Abraham Bosse, in his study of the manner of the greatest painters, adjudged that "if the natural was well copied according to the rules," there would not be so many different manners; but "because ignorance reigned for a period of time among the practitioners of this art, many of them as a result came to formulate manners that pleased their particular fancies" (*Sentiments sur la distinction des diverses manières de peinture* [Sentiments on the distinction between different manners of painting], 1649, p. 142). Manner was both the characteristic hallmark of an artist and a proof of whim opposed to nature. For André Félibien, manner was "the habit painters adopted in the practice of all the aspects of painting, whether it be composition, or design, or use of color" (*Des principes de l'architecture* [Principles of architecture], 1676). As he goes on to explain, "Painters normally adopt a habit that is related to the masters they have learned from, and whom they have wished to imitate. So we recognize the manner of Michelangelo and of Raphael in their students." Depending on which master or model a painter chose, the manner could be good or bad. As the result of this kind of training, manner was the equivalent of an "author's style," or the "writing of a person who frequently sends one letters" (ibid.). Roger de Piles borrows Félibien's definition and inflects it: "What we call Manner is the habit painters have adopted, not only in how they use the paintbrush, but also in the three main aspects of Painting" (*Conversations* [1677], unpaginated first draft of a dictionary). He eliminates the reference to the acquisition of manner from the masters, and goes on to compare manner to the "style and the writing of a man from whom one has already received a letter," whereas Félibien compares it to both. Although his formulation is close to Félibien's, Piles gives a wider sense to his definition. Manner was both a characteristic of the "hand" of an artist (handling a paintbrush, writing) and a characteristic of his mind (style). "All kinds of manner are good when they represent Nature, and their difference comes only from the infinite number of ways in which Nature appears to our eyes" (ibid.). Manner was the way in which

each artist interpreted nature personally, and not the result of a scholarly apprenticeship.

The negative meaning gradually prevailed, however. Within the Académie Royale de la Peinture et de Sculpture, manner was condemned in a lecture delivered in 1672 by Philippe de Champaigne, "Contre les copistes de manière" (Against artists who copy manner), which would be delivered five more times between 1672 and 1728. The topic would be taken up again in 1747 in a lecture by the comte de Caylus, "Sur la manière" (On manner), which would also be delivered four times over the next twenty years. While Champaigne restricted his condemnation to the lack of originality of the painters who appropriated the manner of others, Caylus defined manner as "a more or less happy failing . . ., a habit of always seeing in the same way . . ., a thing we put in place of nature to be approved, by means of an art that consists merely of its perfect imitation." Painters who were renowned for having no manner would be deserving of the greatest praise. The lecture by Charles Antoine-Coypel on the "Parallèle entre l'éloquence et la poésie" (Parallel between eloquence and poetry) (1 February, 1749; published in 1751), though, was more in the tradition of Roger de Piles:

> Everyone knows that in talking about different kinds of writing we use the word "style," which thus signifies figuratively the manner of composition or of writing. As painters each have their own manner of composing and writing with a paintbrush, they could use this word, just as orators do. But they simply call this large part of their art "manner." So when I say that this painting is in the manner of Raphael, I put in the art lover's mind an idea that is equivalent to what a man of letters would think if I said this speech is in the style of Cicero.

Most dictionaries from the second half of the seventeenth century, which were often compilations, systematically presented these two meanings of the word "manner," namely the way of doing things that characterized the works of a particular artist, and the artistic failing that consisted in "departing from what was true, and from nature." They would generally distinguish between "having a manner" and "being mannered," even though there was often no clear distinction between this latter expression, and "having a bad manner." When "manner," understood in the sense of "a way of doing," was qualified by other adjectives ("strong and deeply felt," "weak and effeminate," "gracious," and finally "gentle and proper"), it enabled a series of categories to be established into which one could place all of the greatest painters. As for the "great manner," it was defined as a knowing exaggeration that created a distance from the baseness of the natural. This expression characterized paintings in which nothing is small, in which details are sacrificed for the idea, and it was, above all, the definition of a genre of painting.

Artists themselves, however, remained critical and used the word "manner" in a predominantly negative sense. For the painter Michel-François Dandré-Bardon, "Manner is an improper assortment of exaggerated traits and of excessive forms" (*Traité de peinture* [Treatise on painting]). He goes on to explain,

> This definition states clearly enough that by manner we do not here mean the way of doing things, the style

that distinguishes one master from another master, for in this sense everyone has his own manner . . ., besides the shame of ignorance, nothing is more insulting to an artist than being called mannered.

Manner understood in this sense was condemned less forcefully by the engraver and secretary of the Académie, Charles-Nicholas Cochin, than it was by Dandré-Bardon. In a lecture delivered in 1777 at the Académie of Rouen, Cochin took "manner" to mean not "the manner of painting or of drawing," but everything that was at a remove from nature, every "convention learned or imagined that is not based on what is true, either because it comes from imitating the masters, or from our own mistakes" (*Discours sur l'enseignement des beaux-arts*). For him, manner was associated with the search for an ideal beauty that was superior to nature. But he was nevertheless keenly aware of the technical limits of painting, and considered that it "is very difficult, and almost impossible, not to be somewhat mannered in painting shadows" (ibid., 21). This assimilation of "manner" to convention led to the word entering ordinary language, as is illustrated by Diderot's essay "On manner," published in the *Salon* of 1767:

> It would seem, then, that manner, whether in social mores, or criticism, or the arts, is a vice of a civilized society. . . . Every person who departs from the appropriate conventions of his state and of his nature, an elegant magistrate, a woman who despairs and swings her arms, a man who walks in an affected manner, are all false and mannered.

> (*Les Salons*, 3:335–39)

III. The Search for a Substitute in French: *Faire* (*Technique*)

This negative sense of *manière* prompted critics to look for an alternative term to describe an artist's personal way of painting or of drawing. The word *goût* (taste) had been used since the sixteenth century as a synonym for *manière*, and dictionaries would systematically cross-reference the two terms. Expressions such as "painted with great taste" or "a picture that shows a great taste in painting," "a taste like Raphael's," and so on, would continue to be found in many texts of art criticism. By the seventeenth century, however, the meaning of the word *goût* had become too broad for it to be able systematically to replace the word *manière*. Charles Nicholas Cochin attempted to substitute the noun *faire* for *manière*, and indeed refused to use *manière* to refer to the technical qualities of a painting, which in his view were the only ones that mattered:

> One of the greatest beauties of art . . . is . . . the singular effect of the sentiment that moves an artist while painting; it is this artistry in the work, this assuredness, this masterly ease, that often distinguishes beauty, that beauty which arouses admiration, from mediocrity, that always leaves us cold. It is that *faire* [technique] (as artists call it) that separates the original of a great master from a copy, no matter how well executed, and that characterizes so well the true talents of an artist, that the smallest, even most uninteresting detail of the

painting reveals to the connoisseur that the piece must be the work of a great master.

> ("De l'illusion dans la Peinture [On illusion in painting]," 1771)

Faire, used in the sense in which Bosse and Piles use *manière*, was thus the subject of long, enthusiastic definition, which allowed Cochin to defend *faire* against the accusation that it described just a kind of mechanics. Even in poetry, he would say, *faire* is essential, and is what distinguishes Racine's *Phèdre* from Pradon's. Dictionaries, however, would mention the term only very briefly, and would refer to *manière*, thus demonstrating the other term's relative failure. Watelet, in the RT: *Encyclopédie* of Diderot and d'Alembert, considered it to apply to the "mechanism of the brush and the hand." Dandré-Bardon, in his *Traité de peinture*, instead preferred *beau-faire* (fine technique).

Watelet and Lévesque's *Encyclopédie méthodique: Beaux-Arts* (1788–92) attests to the aesthetic revolution that was taking place around 1790. In the entry "Illusion," Watelet reproduced in its entirety a lecture by Cochin in which the word *faire* is foregrounded. Lévesque, who was responsible for completing the dictionary after Watelet's death (1786), asked the painter Robin for an article on "Beau-Faire" (which, under the same heading "Faire," had followed the former entry by Watelet in Diderot's *Encyclopédie*). Robin radically condemned the term: "It is not, however, that good technique [*le bien-fait*] or bad technique [*le mal-fait*] in art do not have their charm and their unpleasantness; but woe betide anyone who does not see them as the least worthy or most insignificant vice of a work of art!" The failure of the word *faire* is linked to the failure of an aesthetics that wanted to emphasize the technical qualities of painting.

IV. The Emergence of the Notion of "Style"

The notion of "style," which would ultimately replace that of manner, emerged gradually in art theory. It was used above all comparatively, but from the seventeenth century, certain writers tried to give the word some of the meanings of *maniera*. Thus, for instance, this passage, cited approvingly in his notes by Nicholas Poussin, which he found in and borrowed from A. Mascardi's treatise *Dell'arte istorica* (Rome, 1636):

> La maniera magnifica in quattro cose consiste: nella materia overa argumento, nel concetto, nella struttura, nello stile. . . . Lo stile è una maniera particolare ed industria di dipingere e disegnare nata dal particolare genio di ciascuno nell'applicazione e nel uso dell'idee, il quale stile, maniera o gusto si tiene dalla parte della natura e dell'ingenio.

> (The magnificent manner consists of four things: the matter or argument, the idea, the structure, the style. . . . Style is a particular manner or talent in painting and in drawing, which comes from the particular genius of each person in the application and use of the idea. This style, or manner, or taste, are on the side of nature and genius.)

> (Notes cited in Bellori, *Le vite de' pittori, scultori et architetti moderni* [1672], 480)

Style, or the particular manner, is thus subordinate to the grand manner, and is inherent in a creative personality. Despite the confused nature of the language, Poussin and Mascardi are certainly trying to draw a distinction between two meanings of the word *maniera*: one that has to do with the particular character of an artist, and the other that is presented as a rhetorical category characterizing the painting.

In France, the notion of style had been used as a comparative term by Félibien and Piles. Coypel's lecture cited earlier ("Parallèle," 1751) helped to determine the meaning of the word *style* as it applied to painting. Style was a reflection of content, and Coypel established the traditional distinction for painting among the heroic and sublime style (that of the frescoes of Michaelangelo and of Raphael in the Vatican), the simple style (landscapes and animals), and the tempered style (the historical paintings of Alabani or Maratta, subjects that were more graceful than impassioned). Style characterized as much the subject as the way in which it was handled. This parallel influenced dictionary definitions, which all noted that style was an inherent part of composition and execution. While the word indicated a reflection of the genre and the content as far as the composition was concerned, and a formal quality as far as the artistic execution was concerned, it was almost never used in isolation; it could be heroic, simple, tempered, and so on, or dry, polished, assured, harsh, and so forth. The term remained fairly marginal in France, however, and it was the translations of English and German texts that would help make "style" into one of the key notions of art theory.

While Johann Georg Sulzer, in his *Allgemeine Theorie der Schönen Künste* (General theory of art), used *Manier* in a sense very close to the French and Italian meanings, the word *Stil* began to appear in Johann Joachim Winckelmann almost simultaneously, and in a much broader sense. Winckelmann in 1764 made reference to "dem verschiedene Stile der Völker, Zeiten und Künstler" (*Geschichte der Kunst des Altertums* [*History of the Art of Antiquity*]), which his French translator J. Huber rendered in 1789 as "les différents styles et les différents caractères des peuples, des temps et des artistes" (the different styles and the different characters of the people, the times, and the artists)." *Stil* borrows certain of the connotations of "manner," but eliminates the particular role of the artist. Styles are characteristic of peoples and times, like manners for Vasari. Winckelmann thus studied the Egyptian style, the Etruscan style, and identified four styles among the Greeks: *Älter Stil*, which could be translated as "ancient style" or "style of imitation"; *hohe Stil* or *Stil der Grosse*, sublime or grand style; *schöne Stil*, beautiful style; and finally *Stil den heinlichen oder den platten,* minor and vulgar style. "Style" for Winckelmann, and similarly for Anton Raphael Mengs, thus replaced "manner" as a means of talking about the formal characteristics of a civilization, while "manner" introduced a personal dimension.

In England, there was a similar shift: the reflection on "manner" referred to *connoisseurship*, and the word was used in the senses Abraham Bosse gave to it. "Manner" still had a positive connotation in Jonathan Richardson, but a much more ambiguous one in William Hogarth:

What are all the manners, as they are called, of even the greatest masters, which are known to differ so much from one another, and all of them from nature, but so many strong proofs of their inviolable attachment to falsehood, converted into established truth in their own eyes, by self-opinion?

(*The Analysis of Beauty*, [1753])

Joshua Reynolds reversed the terms, and used the term "manner" negatively:

[T]hose peculiarities, or prominent parts, which at first force themselves upon view, and are the marks, or what is commonly called the manner, by which that individual artist is distinguished. . . . A manner, therefore, being a defect, and every painter, however excellent, having a manner.

(*Discourses on Art*, 6th Discourse [1774])

Reynolds introduced the term "style," while he spelled "stile" and "style" in a somewhat unsystematic fashion. "Stile" could be the equivalent of "manner" in the sense of designating the ways in which a subject is expressed: "Stile in painting is the same as in writing, a power over materials, whether words or colours, by which conceptions or sentiments are conveyed" (2nd Discourse [1769]), whereas "the style" would refer to the rhetorical category to which the work corresponds: "The *Gusto grande* of the Italians, the *Beau idéal* of the French and the 'great style,' 'genius,' and 'taste' among the English, are but different appellations of the same thing" (3rd Discourse [1770]). But the two meanings and the two spellings are also used interchangeably: "And yet the number is infinite of those who seem, if one may judge by their style, to have seen no other works but those of their master, or of some favourite whose manner is their first wish and their last" (6th Discourse [1774]).

In the *Encyclopédie méthodique*, Lévesque devoted an entry of five-and-a-half columns to the word *Style* (as much as the two combined entries of *Manière* and *Maniéré* [Mannered]). His definition, which he acknowledged was essentially taken from the writings of Mengs and of Reynolds, was an attempt to synthesize the meaning of *Stil* in Winckelmann and Mengs, and the second sense of "style" in Reynolds: "The combination of all the elements that come together in the conception, the composition and the execution of a work of art make up what we call its style, and one might say that it constitutes the manner of being of this work" (Watelet and Lévesque, *Encyclopédie méthodique*, "Style").

So even though the word "style" had been used previously in art criticism, it was only through the detour of its translation that it became established within a critical metalanguage and replaced "manner," at the expense, however, of a narrowing of its semantic field. "Style" quickly assumed all of the meanings that until then had been associated with "manner," with the exception of the sense of practice pure and simple, which was seen as negative. It did not encompass the particular character of the hand of an artist, and subordinated painting to style as a means of expressing an idea. In the nineteenth century, however, the contradictory senses of "manner" reappeared in relation to the word "style," and brought into play at the same time the particular style of the artist, that of his time and his school, the mode of representation chosen, and the difference relative to a natural model. The nuances introduced by each artist in the use he made of this term make any single definition impossible, and leave translators no other solution but to adapt this catchall word to each of their respective languages so as to enrich their own treatises.

Christian Michel

BIBLIOGRAPHY

Bellori, Giovan Pietro. *Le vite de' pittori, scultori et architettori moderni*. Torino: G. Einaudi, 1976. First published in Rome, 1672. Translation by Alice Sedgwick Wohl: *The Lives of the Modern Painters, Sculptors, and Architects*. New York: Cambridge University Press, 2005.

Bosse, Abraham. *Le peintre converty aux précises et universelles règles de son art. Sentiments sur la distinction des diverses manières de peinture, dessin et gravure* . Edited by R.-A. Weigert. Paris: Hermann, 1964. First published in 1649.

Brusati, Celeste. *Artifice and Illusion: The Art and Writing of Samuel van Hoogstraten*. Chicago: University of Chicago Press, 1995.

Caylus, Anne Claude de. "Sur la manière et les moyens de l'éviter." In *Vies d'artistes du XVIIIe siècle. Discours sur la peinture et la sculpture. Salons de 1751 et de 1753. Lettre à Lagrenée*, edited, with introduction and notes, by André Fontaine. Paris: Laurens, 1910.

Cennini, Cennino. *Il libro dell'arte della pittura: Il manoscritto della Biblioteca nazionale centrale di Firenze, con integrazioni dal Codice riccardiano*. Edited by Antonio P. Torresi. Ferrara, It.: Liberty House, 2004. Composed betwen 1400 and 1437; first published in 1821. Translation and notes by Christiana J. Herringham: *The Book of the Art of Cennino Cennini: A Contemporary Practical Treatise on Quattrocento Painting*. London: Allen and Unwin, 1899.

Champaigne, Philippe de. "Contre les copistes de manière." In *Les Conférences de l'Académie royale de peinture et de sculpture au XVIIe siècle*, edited by Alain Mérot, 224–28. Paris: École Nationale Supérieure des Beaux-Arts, 1996.

Cheney, Liana de Girolami. *Readings in Italian Mannerism*. Foreword by Craig Hugh Smyth. New York: Lang, 1997.

Cochin, Charles-Nicolas. "De l'illusion dans la Peinture." In vol. 2 of *Œuvres diverses; ou, Recueil de quelques pièces concernant les arts*. Paris, 1771.

———. *Discours sur l'enseignement des beaux-arts prononcés à la séance publique de l'Académie des sciences, belles-lettres et arts de Rouen*. Paris: Cellot, 1779.

Coypel, Charles-Antoine. "Parallèle entre l'éloquence et la poésie." *Mercure de France* (May 1751): 9–38.

Dandré-Bardon, Michel-François. *Traité de peinture suivi d'un essai sur la sculpture*. Paris, 1765.

Diderot, Denis. "De la manière dans les arts du dessin." In vol. 3 of *Les Salons*, edited by Jean Seznec and Jean Adhémar. Oxford: Clarendon Press, 1963. Essay first published in 1767.

———. *Diderot on Art*. 2 vols. Edited and translated by John Goodman. Introduction by Thomas Crow. New Haven, CT: Yale University Press, 1995.

Eck, Caroline van, James McAllister, and Renee van de Vall, eds. *The Question of Style in Philosophy and the Arts*. Cambridge: Cambridge University Press, 1995.

Félibien, André. *Des principes de l'architecture, de la sculpture, de la peinture, et des autres arts qui en dependent: Avec un dictionnaire des termes propres à chacun de ces arts*. Paris, 1676.

Franklin, David. *Painting in Renaissance Florence, 1500–1550*. New Haven, CT: Yale University Press, 2001.

Hogarth, William. *The Analysis of Beauty*. Edited, with introduction and notes, by Ronald Paulson. New Haven, CT: Yale University Press, 1997. First published in 1753.

Hoogstraten, Samuel van. *Inleyding tot de hooge schoole des Schiderkonst*. Rotterdam, 1678. French translation and commentary by Jan Blanc: *Introduction à la haute école de l'art de peinture*. Geneva: Droz, 2006.

Mérot, Alain. *French Painting in the Seventeenth Century*. Translated by Caroline Beamish. New Haven, CT: Yale University Press, 1995.

Piles, Roger de. *Conversations sur la connaissance de la peinture et sur le jugement qu'on doit faire des tableaux*. Geneva: Slatkine, 1970. First published in 1677.

Raphael. *Gli scritti: Lettere, firme, sonetti, saggi tecnici e teorici*. Edited by Ettore Camesasca, with Giovanni M. Piazza. Milan: Rizzoli, 1994.

Reynolds, Joshua. *Discourses on Art*. Edited by R. R. Wark. New Haven, CT: Yale University Press, 1997. First published ca. 1774.

Smyth, Craig Hugh. *Mannerism and Maniera*. Introduction by Elizabeth Cropper. 2nd ed. Vienna: IRSA, 1992.

Sulzer, Johann Georg. *Allgemeine Theorie der schönen Künste: In einzeln, nach alphabetischer Ordnung der Kunstwörter auf einander folgenden, Artikeln abgehandelt*. 2 vols. Leipzig: Weidmann Reich, 1771–74.

Van Mandel, Karel. *Lives of the Illustrious Netherlandish and German Painters*. Vol. 1. Edited and translated by H. Miedema. Doornspijk, Neth.: Davaco, 1994.

Vasari, Giorgio. *Le vite de più eccelenti architettori, pittori et scultori italiani*. 9 vols. Edited by Gaetano Milanesi. Florence: Sansoni, 1878–85. First published in 1568. Translation by Gaston du C. de Vere: *Lives of the Most Eminent Painters, Sculptors and Architects*. 10 vols. New York: AMS, 1976.

Winckelmann, Johann Joachim. *Geschichte der Kunst des Altertums*. Darmstadt, Ger.: Wissenschaftliche Buchgesellschaft, 1993. First published in 1764. Translation by Harry Francis Mallgrave: *History of the Art of Antiquity*. Introduction by Alex Potts. Los Angeles: Getty Research Institute, 2006.

MATTER OF FACT, FACT OF THE MATTER

FRENCH   *fait, réalité*

➤ *FACT* and BELIEF, ENGLISH, NATURE, PROPOSITION, REALITY, SACHVERHALT, SENSE, TATSACHE, *THING*, TO TRANSLATE, *WORLD*

We will here be less interested in fact, than in the rather strange expression "matter of fact," which is found in English philosophy, and notably in Hume. "Matter" means (a) "material substance, thing" and (b) "affair, subject," and "matter of fact" thus in a sense replicates the word "fact." We might mention a number of typical common expressions, such as "for that matter," "a matter of time," "what's the matter with you?" but "matter" in its derived verbal form also indicates importance and implication: "no matter," "it matters." This specifically English double-meaning enables a number of clever plays on words, such as the title of Peter Geach's book *Logic Matters*, or Bertrand Russell's *What Is Mind? No Matter? What Is Matter? Never Mind*. It is an integral part of the semantics of the expression "matter of fact," which both refers to factuality and posits it as necessary and essential. This duality is found in the (absolutely untranslatable) inverted form of the expression, as it is used by the American philosopher W. V. O. Quine: "fact of the matter," which is a particularly forceful statement of factuality, while adding to this notion a physicalist dimension (the "fact of the matter" as a physical reality), but also, paradoxically, an ontological question.

I. "Matters of Fact"

"Matters of fact" (it is frequently in the plural in Hume) is normally translated into French as *faits* (facts), but also sometimes, with a surprising literalism, as *choses de fait* (factual things) (see the French translation of Book 1 of the *Treatise of Human Nature* by G. Tanesse and M. David, 1912; the term was retained in a recent edition by Didier Deleule). This translation, in addition to demonstrating the paradoxical nature of the expression "matter of fact," highlights the "hardness," or at least the reality of a fact defined in this way. It does seem at first sight as if for Hume the expression "matter of fact" means an empirical fact, a state of affairs, which is part of reality: "This is a matter of fact which is easily cleared and ascertained" (*Treatise of Human Nature*, 1.1 §7, 19). "Fact" and "reality" sometimes appear to be synonymous: "If this be absurd in fact and reality, it must also be absurd in ideas" (ibid.).

"Matters of fact" are thus questions that concern the existence of objects, and empirical reality:

> It is evident, that all reasonings from causes or effects terminate in conclusions, concerning matter of fact; that is, concerning the existence of objects or of their qualities.
>
> (*Treatise of Human Nature*, 1.3 §7, 94)

We have to add that these "matters of fact" are objects of "belief." They are "conceived" by us; we have an idea of them, but a particularly strong and lively idea. This liveliness defines belief, which "super-adds nothing to the idea":

> It is certain we must have an idea of every matter of fact which we believe. . . . When we are convinced of every matter of fact, we do nothing but conceive it.
>
> (Ibid., 1.3 §8, 101)

These are the two aspects we also find in the famous definitions of *Enquiry Concerning Human Understanding*, a work in which Hume draws a distinction between "matters of fact" and "relations of ideas." Facts, by contrast with relations of ideas, are not known by understanding alone: their opposite is always possible, and the certainty proper to them is different:

> All the objects of human reason or enquiry may naturally be divided into two kinds, to wit, *Relations of Ideas*, and *Matters of Fact*. . . . Matters of fact, which are the second objects of human reason, are not ascertained in the same manner; nor is our evidence of their truth, however great, of a like nature with the foregoing. The contrary of every matter is still possibility.
>
> (*Enquiry*, 25)

We might wonder first of all what Hume means in referring to the "contrary" of a fact when he has defined a fact as an empirical fact, and not as an idea, a belief, or a proposition (whose object is a fact). Here we encounter a peculiarity of "fact" that "encapsulates" a state of affairs and a proposition, a specific characteristic indicated by the English expression "that-clause": a fact is expressed in the form "that *p*," which refers both to a fact and to a proposition:

> *That the sun will not rise tomorrow* is no less intelligible a proposition, and implies no more contradiction, than the affirmation, *that it will rise*.
>
> (Ibid., 25–26)

"That the sun will not rise tomorrow" is an "intelligible" proposition, which can be affirmed, but also a fact (see SACHVERHALT). To believe a proposition is not to have a feeling of belief that would be attached to a given proposition, it is to "believe a fact," directly so to speak, which is indicated by the construction "believe that."

> If you were to ask a man, why he believes any matter of fact, which is absent; for instance, that his friend is in the country, or in France; he would give you a reason. . . . All our reasonings concerning fact are of the same nature.
>
> (Ibid., 26)

"That-clauses" of this kind have been subsequently explored by contemporary philosophers of language, notably Ramsey, Austin, Strawson, and Davidson, in order to challenge the idea that there are objective "facts" (see BELIEF, PROPOSITION) that are objects of belief, or of statements. So they explore expressions such as "true to the facts" and "unfair to facts," as well as the question of what we say when we "say that" (see "On Saying That" in Donald Davidson, *Inquiries into Truth and Interpretation*). What is at stake is knowing whether we can eliminate the notion of fact from the theory of language.

II. The Expression "Fact of the Matter"

In several well-known texts, Quine used the expression "fact of the matter," as a rather puzzling inversion of Hume's expression "matter of fact" (the reinvention of Humean naturalism being one of Quine's goals, Hume is naturally one of Quine's main philosophical points of reference). The expression, first used in a negative form ("no fact of the matter"), suggests that some questions have no reality or foundation. Quine expresses this idea in the context of his thesis concerning the indeterminacy of radical translation. The situation of radical translation is the case where we are dealing with a radically foreign language, with no dictionary or tradition of translation, nor any bilingual interpreter, and where a linguist has to compose a translation manual from his or her empirical observations of the verbal behavior of an indigenous people. According to Quine's thesis, there are several possible, empirically equivalent, and incompatible translations of one and the same expression. It is meaningless to ask which is *the* correct translation, the correct reconstitution of the foreign language. In *From a Logical Point of View*, he summarizes his method using the expression *ex pede Herculem*: we can reconstitute the statue of Hercules from his foot, but there is nothing from which the language can be reconstructed, no "fact of the matter," no (physical) reality that allows us to ask the question:

> In projecting Hercules from the foot we risk error, but we may derive comfort from the fact that there is something to be wrong about. In the case of the lexicon, pending some definition of synonymy, we have no statement of the problem; we have nothing for the lexicographer to be right or wrong about.
>
> (*From a Logical Point of View*, 63)

Quine explains the meaning of the expression in the context of a polemical exchange with Chomsky by comparing the indeterminacy of translation to the underdetermination of theories by their data. Just as several theories can account for the same set of empirical data, several theories of language can account for the same verbal behavior. Linguistic theory, as part of science, is underdetermined by the data of indigenous verbal behavior. But this is not sufficient to account for the indeterminacy of translation, which is a banal epistemological problem, since, as Quine explains, the indeterminacy of translation is *additional* to this empirical undeetermination:

> Though linguistics is of course a part of the theory of nature, the indeterminacy of translation is not just inherited as a special case of the under-determination of our theory of nature. It is parallel but additional.

(Reply to Chomsky, in *Words and Objections*, 303)

This is where the "fact of the matter" comes into play, with respect to empirical data as well, or even in a "physicalist" context, where reality is defined solely by the natural sciences: "This is what I mean by saying that, where indeterminacy of translation applies, there is no real question of right choice; there is no fact of the matter even to *within* the acknowledged under-determination of a theory of nature" (ibid.).

Translation has no "fact of the matter"; it translates "nothing." When a linguist thinks he has discovered something, he is only projecting his own hypotheses, "catapulting" himself, as Quine puts it, into a native language using the categories of his own language:

> There is no telling how much of one's success with analytical hypotheses is due to real kinship of outlook on the part of the natives and ourselves, and how much of it is due to linguistic ingenuity or lucky coincidence. I am not sure that it even makes sense to ask.

(*Word and Object*, 77)

There is no sense, or rather no reality (of "fact of the matter") to the question, since the translator, to a large extent, "reads" his or her own language into the native language. The absence of "fact of the matter" repeats in a particularly radical form Quine's critique of meaning: nothing is translated in translation, and no meanings or senses (see SENSE) of which the expressions in different languages would be the counterpart or the expression.

The "fact of the matter," as the redundant nature of the expression suggests, gestures toward a physicalist point of view, as Quine says in an article entitled "Facts of the Matter." If the question of translation—knowing which manual of translation is the "correct" one—is deprived of the "fact of the matter," it is because it has no physical relevance:

> My position was that either manual could be useful, but as to which was right and which wrong there was no fact of the matter. . . . I speak as a physicalist in saying that there is no fact of the matter. I mean that both manuals are compatible with the fulfillment of just the same elementary physical states by space-time regions.

("Facts of the Matter," in *Essays on the Philosophy of W. V. Quine*, 167)

A real difference for "fact of the matter" would be a difference in the way elementary physical states are distributed. However, we should not deduce from this that the

notion is just a physical one, which would weaken Quine's thesis. It is a naturalist notion (and here, very characteristically, the reference to Hume reappears): the notion of "fact of the matter" is intrinsic to scientific theory; this factuality is defined by our theory of the world, as a product of human nature. The "fact of the matter" is no longer a physical substratum ("a distribution of elementary physical states") that is independent of language, but also turns out to be, by an effect of *mise en abyme*, part of our conceptual schema: "Factuality, like gravitation and electric charge, is internal to our theory of nature" (*Theories and Things*, 23). The notion "fact of the matter" is itself to be considered immanently. This is Quine's conclusion in *Theories and Things*: "The intended notion of matter of fact is not transcendental or yet epistemological, not even a question of evidence; it is ontological, a question of reality, and to be taken naturalistically within our scientific theory of the world" (23).

So the truly radical nature of his notion of "matter of fact" comes to the fore in Quine's late texts: it refers not only to empirical evidence, like the Humean "matter of fact," but also to a radical ontological indeterminacy. "What counts as a fact of the matter" is, as such, subjected to indeterminacy: "We can switch our own ontology too without doing violence to any evidence, but in so doing we switch from our elementary particles to some manner of proxies and thus reinterpret our standard of what counts as a fact of the matter" (*Theories and Things*, 23).

Sandra Laugier

BIBLIOGRAPHY

Davidson, Donald. "On Saying That." In *Inquiries into Truth and Interpretation*, 93–108. Oxford: Oxford University Press, 1984.

Davidson, Donald, and Jaako Hintikka, eds. *Words and Objections: Essays on the Work of W. V. Quine*. Dordrecht, Neth.: Reidel, 1969.

Follesdal, Dagfinn. "Indeterminacy of Translation and Underdetermination of the Theory of Nature." *Dialectica* 27 (1973): 289–301.

Hume, David. *An Enquiry Concerning Human Understanding and Other Writings*. Edited by Stephen Buckle. Cambridge: Cambridge University Press, 2007. First published in 1748.

———. *A Treatise of Human Nature*. Oxford: Clarendon, 1978. First published in 1739–40.

Laugier-Rabaté, Sandra. *L'anthropologie logique de Quine: L'apprentissage de l'obvie*. Paris: Vrin, 1992.

Pitcher, George, ed. *Truth*. Englewood Cliffs, NJ: Prentice-Hall, 1964.

Quine, W. V. O. "Facts of the Matter." In *Essays on the Philosophy of W. V. Quine*, edited by Robert W. Shahan and Chris Swoyer. Norman: University of Oklahoma Press, 1979. Also in *American Philosophy from Edwards to Quine*, edited by R. W. Shahan, 176–96. Norman, OK: University of Oklahoma Press, 1979.

———. *From a Logical Point of View: Nine Logico-Philosophical Essays*. 2nd rev. ed. Cambridge, MA: Harvard University Press, 1980.

———. "Indeterminacy of Translation Again." *Journal of Philosophy* 84 (1987): 5–10.

———. "On the Reasons for Indeterminacy of Translation." *Journal of Philosophy* 67 (1970): 178–83.

———. "Replies." In *Words and Objections: Essays on the Work of W. V. Quine*, edited by Donald Davidson and Jaako Hintikka, 292–352. Dordrecht, Neth.: Reidel, 1969.

———. *Theories and Things*. Cambridge, MA: Harvard University Press, 1981.

———. *Word and Object*. Cambridge, MA: MIT Press, 1960.

Strawson, Peter S. "Truth." *Proceedings of the Aristotelian Society* 24 (1950): 129–56.

MEDIA / MEDIUM (of communication)

I. The Magic of Words

Here is Freud in 1890 on "Psychische Behandlung (Seelenbe-handlung)" for a medical manual whose title, *Die Gesundheit*, needs no translation:

> Wir beginnen nun auch den "Zauber" des Wortes zu verstehen. Worte sind ja die wichtigsten Vermittler für den Einfluß, den ein Mensch auf den anderen ausüben will; Worte sind gute Mittel, seelische Veränderungen bei dem hervorzurufen, an den sie gerichtet werden, und darum klingt es nicht länger rätselhaft, wenn behauptet wird, daß der Zauber des Wortes Krankheitser-scheinungen beseitigen kann, zumal solche, die selbst in seelischen Zuständen begründet sind.

> (*Gesammelte Werke*, 5:301–2)

The French edition of this text, translated and edited by Jean Laplanche, renders the paragraph:

> A présent, nous commençons également à comprendre la 'magie' du mot. Let mots sont bien les instruments les plus importants de l'influence qu'une personne cherche à exercer sur une autre; les mots sont de bons moyens pour provoquer des modifications psychiques chez celui à qui ils s'adressent, et c'est pourquoi il n'y a désormais plus rien d'énigmatique dans l'affirmation selon laquelle la magie du mot peut écarter des phénomènes morbides, en particulier ceux qui ont eux-mêmes leur fondement dans des états psychiques.

> ("Traitement psychique [traitement d'âme]")

Finally, here is Strachey's translation in the *Standard Edition*:

> Now, too, we begin to understand the "magic" of words. Words are the most important media by which one man seeks to bring his influence to bear on another; words are a good method of producing mental changes in the person to whom they are addressed. So that there is no longer anything puzzling in the assertion that the magic of words can remove the symptoms of illness, and especially such as are themselves founded on mental states.

> ("Psychical [or Mental] Treatment")

Even after setting aside the problems of translation in general and of the Freud translation in particular, we are left to wonder over Strachey's choice of the word "media" where Freud wrote *Vermittler* and the French translators opted for *instrument*—not because "media" works poorly, but because it works so well, perhaps better than the original. A *Vermittler* is a person who acts as a broker or intermediary; to suggest that words are the most important, *Vermittler* is to offer us a metaphor that evokes a person in a well-tailored suit working on commission. The French *instrument* presents still other challenges of interpretation, not metaphorical this time, but metonymic. The claim that words are instrumental in exercising influence is clear enough. But what about the claim that they are the "most important" instruments? Compared to what? The dictionary offers us such examples of the word *instrument* as "compasses" (*un instrument de bord*)

and "tractors" (*un instrument agricole*) but nothing that would make a compelling alternative to "words," which is what it would take for Freud's argument to make sense.

By contrast, the English word "medium" raises far fewer difficulties, and the ones it does raise are much more interesting. The RT: *Oxford English Dictionary* tells us that a medium is "any intervening substance or agency." We understand right away that Freud is arguing that of the various substances or agencies through which men and women seek to intervene in one another's lives—drugs, money, caresses, and so on—words are the most effective when it comes to producing beneficial changes in mental states. It would have been helpful if Freud had specified whether he meant spoken words or written words, or both, but that is a problem of argumentation rather than of language or translation. In short, the term makes it easier to understand Freud's claim and then to have an argument about it. After centuries of untranslatability, "medium" has been welcomed into French and German and a number of other languages for precisely this reason. It allows authors to join an argument long dominated by Anglo-American philosophy, social science, and industry.

II. A Wonderfully Perfect Kind of Sign-Functioning

The Latin adjective *medius* has roots in the Sanskrit *madhya* and the Greek *mesos*, all three terms meaning something like "in the midst" or "in the middle." One could be in the midst or middle of any number of things, some quite concrete—the distance from here to there—and others more abstract. Hence Quentin Skinner cites Cicero's maxim in *De officiis* that "our highest duty must be to act in such a way that *communes utilitates in medium afferre*—in such a way that the ideal of the common good is placed at the heart of our common life." This idea was taken up by Renaissance civic humanists, who held that classical virtues "ought to be in medio, in our midst; they ought indeed to be actively brought forth in medium, into the center of things" (*Visions of Politics*).

"Medium" approaches a recognizably modern sense when, in addition to being a place where ideas or affects can be brought forth, it becomes a way of bringing them forth. One of the first appearances of this notion is in book 2 of Bacon's *Advancement of Learning* (1605), where Bacon takes up Aristotle's claim that "words are the images of cogitations, and letters are the images of words." This may be true, he writes, "yet it is not of necessity that cogitations be expressed by the medium of words." Bacon mentions the gestures of the deaf and dumb, Egyptian hieroglyphs, and Chinese characters. One could even say it with flowers: "Periander, being consulted with how to preserve a tyranny newly usurped, bid the messenger attend and report what he saw him do; and went into his garden and topped all the highest flowers, signifying, that it consisted in the cutting off and keeping low of the nobility and grandees" (in *The Major Works*).

This argument may well have been influenced by Montaigne, who, in one especially beautiful passage in the "Apology for Raymond Sebond" (1580), reflected on the many forms of communication available to animals and men: "After all, lovers quarrel, make it up again, beg favors, give thanks, arrange secret meetings and say everything, with their eyes." Not only eyes, but heads, eyebrows, shoulders, and hands communicate "with a variety and multiplicity rivalling the tongue." Montaigne called these *moyens de communication* (John Florio's 1603 translation of the essay translates this as "meanes of entercommunication"). But there is a crucial difference between Montaigne and Bacon's theories of media: Montaigne is concerned to show the many ways men and women can communicate with one another; Bacon wants to find the most effective ways. The introduction of "medium" into English-language theories of communication shifted the grounds of philosophical debate toward pragmatic matters.

This shift was helped by the word's associations with natural philosophy, which classified media according to how they assisted or resisted whatever passed through them (e.g., light, magnetism). "When the Almighty himself condescends to address mankind in their own language," James Madison writes in Federalist Paper no. 37 (1788), "his meaning, luminous as it must be, is rendered dim and doubtful, by the cloudy medium through which it is communicated." Madison's pun neatly captures this conflation of the two senses of medium in English; such a pun would not have been possible in French or German (the French translation of 1792, usually attributed to Trudaine de la Sablière, misses it entirely by describing His will as "obscurcie par le voile dont elle s'envelope"; a translation of 1902 by Gaston Jèze does much better with "le nébuleux moyen par lequel elle est communiquée").

As chemical and mechanical technologies for reproducing words and images proliferated in the nineteenth century, so too did the sense that these technologies were members of the same conceptual family: the family of media. Thus a treatise on libel from 1812: "Libel in writing may be effected by every mode of submitting to the eye a meaning through the medium of words; whether this be done by manual writing, or printing, or any other method" (George, *A Treatise on the Offence of Libel*). The formula "medium of words" evokes Bacon, but the emphasis is now on the "symbolical devices," as the author calls them, rather than on the symbols themselves. The word "medium" could expand to include nearly anything that facilitated communication. In his 1864 account of the analytical engine, one of the first general-purpose computers, Charles Babbage explains that it functioned through the "medium of properly-arranged sets of Jacquard cards" (*Passages from the Life*)—the punch cards engineered by Joseph-Marie Jacquard to operate his automatic looms. By the turn of the twentieth century, the concept had expanded yet again to include new electrical means of communication. (On electrification's contribution to the unification of a concept of media, see Gitelman and Collins, "Medium Light.")

■ See Box 1.

This proliferation was such that Charles Sanders Peirce attempted to arrive at a formal definition in his 1906 essay "The Basis of Pragmatism in the Normative Sciences." What do all these media have in common? "A medium of communication is something, A, which being acted upon by something else, N, in its turn acts upon something, I, in a manner involving its determination by N, so that I shall thereby, through

A and only through A, be acted upon by N." He offered the example of a mosquito, which is acted upon by "zymotic disease," which it in turn transmits to a new host animal in the form of a fever. It was an odd example, logically and biologically, and Peirce recognized its oddness. "The reason that this example is not perfect is that the active medium is in some measure of the nature of a vehicle, which differs from a medium of communication in acting upon the transported object, where, without further interposition of the vehicle, it acts upon, or is acted upon by, the object to which it is conveyed." In other words, the mosquito did not simply transmit the zyme unchanged; it transformed the zyme into a fever. This logic of the parasite stood in contrast to a classically logocentric scenario: "After an ordinary conversation, a wonderfully perfect kind of sign-functioning, one knows what information or suggestion has been conveyed, but will be utterly unable to say in what words it was conveyed, and often will think it was conveyed in words, when in fact it was only conveyed in tones or facial expressions" ("The Basis of Pragmatism").

III. A Somewhat Cumbrous Title

Samuel Weber has argued that the modern era is characterized by a theological stance that attributes to media "the function of creatio ex nihilo." "The 'singularization' and simplification of the complex and plural notion of 'the media' would be a symptom of this theology" (*Benjamin's -abilities*). He credits this sacralization to Hegel, whose notion of mediation (*Vermittlung*) elevates the process to world-historical importance. However, it was not only, or even mainly, speculative philosophy that gave us "the media" as an uncountable noun with innumerable powers. It was Anglo-American social science.

By the beginning of the twentieth century, the recognition of a family resemblance between the various "implements of intercommunication" (to take another phrase of Peirce's) meant that they could be compared and contrasted in profitable new ways (Weber, ibid.). "The medium gives a tone of its own to all the advertisements contained in it," writes Walter Dill Scott, a student of Wilhelm Wundt, who was a professor of applied psychology at Northwestern University, in his *Theory of Advertising* of 1904. Scott made this remark in a section of his book entitled "Mediums," but this form was soon obsolete. The plural would vacillate in grammatical number before settling into a singular that could be labeled as "mass," "mainstream," "new," and so forth. Indeed, as late as the 1940s, it was still necessary to explain what one meant by "mass media." Julian Huxley, presiding over the newly formed UNESCO in 1946, announced that "Unesco is expressly instructed to pursue its aims and objects by means of the media of mass communication—the somewhat cumbrous title (commonly abbreviated to 'Mass Media') proposed for agencies, such as the radio, the cinema, and the popular press, which are capable of mass dissemination of word or image" (the English text of Article I reads "means of mass communication"; the French text, "organes d'information des masses").

The term "mass media" found its niche in scholarly articles by such influential American midcentury thinkers as Hadley Cantril, Harold Lasswell, and Paul Lazarsfeld.

1

Ordinateur/Computer/Numérique/Digital

For the advocates of a purity of the French language jeopardized by the multiplication of imports from English, computer science and digital culture have represented an important battleground because of the Anglo-American preeminence that has marked them since their beginnings in the 1940s. In their perspective, the adoption of terms like *ordinateur* and *informatique* to designate computer and computer science appeared as clear victories. These words not only sounded French, they also conveyed a different take on what computing was about. More recently, however, the line of demarcation has become less evident because of the ambiguity that surrounds the definition of *numérique* versus digital.

Ordinateur was proposed in 1955 by the Latin philologist and Sorbonne professor Jacques Perret, who had been asked by one of his former students to suggest French names for the new machines that IBM was about to commercialize in the country. Perret suggested *ordinateur*, which applied to the capacity of someone to arrange and organize. *Ordinateur* used to have strong religious connotations. According to the RT: *Le Littré*, the adjective had been applied to God bringing order to the world. It also designated the person in charge of ordaining a priest. But very few persons would be aware of this religious dimension, argued Perret, so that the name would essentially relate to the notions of ordering and accounting, just like the other French term, *ordonnateur*, which was used in the administration for officials with power to authorize expenditures. *Ordinateur* was from the start a success. It was even transposed in Spanish and Catalan as *ordenador* and *ordinador*. (It is however worth noting that most other Romance languages preferred to translate the word "computer": *calcolatore* in Italian or *calculator* in Romanian.) This success coincided with a major evolution in the public perception of computers. Whereas the first machines had been generally envisaged as mere computing devices, the accent was shifting toward their capacity to order logical propositions, a capacity that seemed to announce the possibility of an artificial intelligence. Thus, despite its French particularism, *ordinateur* was in profound accordance with a worldwide transformation epitomized by the 1968 science fiction film *2001: A Space Odyssey*. In charge of every aspect of the mission to Jupiter staged in the film, the HAL 9000, the ship's computer, was definitely more an *ordinateur* than a computing device.

Informatique was another major success. Coined in 1962 by a former director of the computing center of the French company Bull, Philippe Dreyfus, from the contraction of *information* and *automatique*, the term was officially endorsed during a cabinet meeting by President Charles de Gaulle, who preferred it to *ordinatique* to name the science of information processing (see Mounier-Kuhn, *L'informatique en France*). Around the same time, the German *Informatik*, the English "informatics," and the Italian *informatica* also appeared. But the French term has enjoyed a widespread use without equivalent in other countries. Since its adoption, first by the government, then by the French Academy, the term has evolved in two seemingly discrepant directions. On the one hand, it covers a much broader range of subjects and domains than was envisaged by its creator and early promoters. Beside computer science proper, it applies to information technology as well as to the entire computer industry. On the other hand, it retains a distinctive scientific flavor. In French, *informatique* seems to belong to the same disciplinary family as mathematics, thus putting the emphasis on the abstract dimension of computer science, on its logic and algorithmic content. It is worth noting that until recently, computer science was often associated with mathematics in the programs of study of French higher-education institutions. Such an association bore the mark of the long-standing approach of technology as an "application" of pure science, a conception epitomized by institutions such as the École Polytechnique. At this stage it would be tempting to contrast a French propensity toward abstraction when dealing with computer and digital subjects with a more concretely oriented English vocabulary. Browsing through the various official publications devoted to French alternatives to the use of English words and expressions (the feared *anglicismes*), such as the *Vocabulaire des techniques de l'information et de la communication* published in 2009 by the Commission Générale de Terminologie et de Néologie, the official committee for seeking such alternatives, seems to confirm such an opposition. The contrast between the French *numérique* and the English "digital" could easily pass for a typical instance of this divergent orientation. A closer examination reveals, however, a more confusing set of relations between the two terms, as if the full meaning of what is at stake in their contemporary use could be apprehended only by playing on the interwoven resonances that they evoke. This ambiguous relation might represent an incentive to question the opposition mentioned above between allegedly French and English approaches to computer and digital subjects.

Numérique versus "digital": both terms derive from a similar reference to numerals.

The French term is directly related to *nombre* and *numération*, whereas the English comes from "digit." Contrary to its French equivalent, "digit" refers to the concrete operation to count on one's fingers: *digitus* means "finger" or "toe" in Latin. The term "digital" is thus well adapted to the most recent evolution of computer culture, namely, its more and more concrete, almost tactile, turn. Conceived initially as mere electronic calculators, then as logical machines that could possibly become intelligent in the future, computers have become emblematic of a new cultural condition giving priority to the individual and his/her sensations and emotions. This evolution had been foreseen by Nicholas Negroponte, the founder of the Massachusetts Institute of Technology Media Lab—an institution devoted to the exploration of the new possibilities of interface between human and machine. In his 1995 book, *Being Digital*, Negroponte opposed the information age to the digital age about to unfold. According to him, whereas the former was all about anonymity, standardization, and mass consumption, the new cultural era would see the rise of individual experience and preferences.

The French *numérique* definitely misses this individual and sensory dimension. But the full scope of what is at stake in the rise of digital culture is perhaps better understood by playing on the extended resources that a comparison between English and French offer. The lack of direct tactile connotation of *culture numérique* is partly compensated by the fact that the adjective "digital" is more clearly related to fingers in the French language. It applies among other things to fingerprints: *empreintes digitales*. With the new importance given to biometrics in emergent digital culture, this connection matters. It reveals that what is at stake today is not only individual experience but also identification by institutions and corporations. From numbers to fingers and back, it becomes then interesting to work constantly on the border between French and English, on a moving threshold marked by disconcerting exchanges and uncanny inversions of meaning.

Antoine Picon

BIBLIOGRAPHY

Mounier-Kuhn, Pierre-Eric. *L'informatique en France de la seconde guerre mondiale au plan calcul: L'émergence d'une science.* Paris: Presses de l'Université Paris-Sorbonne, 2010.

Negroponte, Nicholas. *Being Digital.* New York: Alfred A. Knopf, 1995. Reprint, New York: Vintage Books, 1996.

But European philosophers resisted this tendency. Their attitude is summed up by Sartre in a fragment from his notebooks of 1947–48 entitled "The American Way: Technical Civilization, hence Generality": "This is what mass media, best seller, book of the month, best record, Gallup, Oscar, etc., tend to do," he wrote, leaving all the important words in English. "It is a matter of presenting to the isolated exemplar the image of the totality" (*Notebooks for an Ethics*). Back in Germany, Adorno also took his distance from a term that he had resorted to repeatedly while in exile. In "The Culture Industry Reconsidered," first delivered as a radio address in 1963, he argued that "the very word mass-media [*Massenmedien*], specially honed for the culture industry, already shifts the accent onto harmless terrain. Neither is it a question of primary concern for the masses, nor of the techniques of communication as such, but of the spirit which sufflates them, their master's voice." For Sartre, Adorno, and their contemporaries, "mass media" was less an untranslatable than an untouchable sullied by intellectual and institutional associations with American cultural imperialism. The entry in the current edition of the RT: *Dictionnaire de l'Académie Française* reflects this sense of its origins: "Média. n. m. XXe siècle. Abréviation de l'anglais des États-Unis mass media, de même sens."

This resistance was soon exhausted. In the late 1960s, the German publishers of Marshall McLuhan's *Understanding Media* settled on the weirdly operatic title *Die magichen Kanäle*. At the end of the century, a collection of McLuhan's writings appeared under the title *Medien Verstehen: Der McLuhan-Reader* (1998). In France, in the 1990s, Régis Debray launched the excellent *Cahiers de médiologie*, devoting issues to themes like theatricality and bicycles; more recently he started a review entitled, simply, *Médium*. Cognates like "multimedia," "remediation," and "mediality" proliferate globally. This reflects less the dominance of English than the collective urgency of an intellectual project. "For the moment," Jean-Luc Nancy writes, "it is less important to respond to the question of the meaning of Being than it is to pay attention to the fact of its exhibition. If 'communication' is for us, today, such an affair—in every sense of the word . . . —if its theories are flourishing, if its technologies are being proliferated, if the 'mediatization' of the 'media' brings along with it an auto-communicational vertigo, if one plays around with the theme of the indistinctness between the 'message' and the 'medium' out of either a disenchanted or jubilant fascination, then it is because something is exposed or laid bare" (*Being Singular Plural*).

Ben Kafka

BIBLIOGRAPHY

Adorno, Theodor W. "Résumé über Kulturindustrie." In *Ohne Leitbild*. Frankfurt: Suhrkampf Verlag, 1967. Translation by Anson G. Rabinbach: "Culture Industry Reconsidered." *New German Critique* 6 (Fall 1975): 12–19.

Babbage, Charles. *Passages from the Life of a Philosopher*. London: Longman, Green, 1864.

Bacon, Francis. *The Major Works*. Edited by Brian Vickers. Oxford: Oxford University Press, 2002.

Freud, Sigmund. "Psychische Behandlung (Seelenbehandlung)." In *Gesammelte Werke*, vol. 5. London: Imago Publishing, 1942. Translation by Jean Laplanche: "Traitement psychique (traitement d'âme)." In *Résultats, idées, problèmes I. (1890–1920)*. Paris:

Presses Universitaires de France, 1984. Translation by James Strachey: "Psychical (or Mental) Treatment." In vol. 7 of *The Standard Edition of the Complete Psychological Works of Sigmund Freud*, edited by James Strachey. London: Hogarth Press, 1953–74.

George, John. *A Treatise on the Offence of Libel, with a Disquisition on the Right, Benefits, and Proper Boundaries of Political Discussion*. London: Taylor and Hessey, 1812. Reprinted in *The Monthly Review* 73 (January–April) 1814.

Gitelman, Lisa, and Theresa M. Collins. "Medium Light: Revisiting Edisonian Modernity." *Critical Quarterly* 51, no. 2 (July 2009): 1–14.

Huxley, Julian. *Unesco: Its Purpose and Its Philosophy*. UNESCO Preparatory Commission, 1946. Links to these versions, along with Spanish, Russian, Arabic, and Chinese, can be found at http://www.onlineunesco.org/UNESCO%20Constitution.html (accessed 1 Sept. 2009).

Madison, James. Federalist Paper no. 37. In *The Federalist Papers*, by Alexander Hamilton, James Madison, and John Jay, edited by Terence Ball. Cambridge: Cambridge University Press, 2003. Translation by [Trudaine de la Sablière?]: *Le Fédéraliste, ou Collection du quelques écrits en faveur de la constitution proposée aux États-Unis*. Vol. 2. Paris: Chez Buisson, 1792. Translation by Gaston Jèze: *Le Fédéraliste (commentaire de la constitution des États-Unis)*. Paris: V. Girard & E. Brière, 1902.

Montaigne, Michel de. "Apology for Raymond Sebond." In *The Complete Essays*, translated by Michael Andrew Screech. New York: Penguin, 1993.

———. *The Essayes of Michael Lord of Montaigne*. Translated by John Florio. London: George, Routledge, 1886. First published in 1803.

Nancy, Jean-Luc. *Being Singular Plural*. Translated by Robert D. Richardson and Anne E. O'Byrne. Stanford, CA: Stanford University Press, 2000.

Peirce, Charles S. "The Basis of Pragmatism in the Normative Sciences." In *The Essential Peirce: Selected Philosophical Writings*, vol. 2 (1893–1913). Bloomington: Indiana University Press, 1998.

Sartre, Jean-Paul. *Notebooks for an Ethics*. Translated by David Pellauer. Chicago: University of Chicago Press, 1992.

Scott, Walter Dill. *The Theory of Advertising: A Simple Exposition of the Principles of Psychology in Their Relation to Successful Advertising*. Boston: Small, Maynard, and Company, 1904.

Skinner, Quentin. *Visions of Politics. Vol. 2: Renaissance Virtues*. Cambridge: Cambridge University Press, 2002.

Weber, Samuel. *Benjamin's -abilities*. Cambridge, MA: Harvard University Press, 2008.

MELANCHOLY

FRENCH	*mélancolie*
GERMAN	*Melancholie, Schwermut*
GREEK	*melagcholia* [μελαγχολία]
LATIN	*melancholia, furor*

➤ ACEDIA, DESENGAÑO, DOR, ES, FEELING, GEMÜT, GENIUS, INGENIUM, I/ME/MYSELF, LEIB, MADNESS, *MALAISE*, PATHOS, SAUDADE, SEHNSUCHT, SPLEEN, STIMMUNG

Although we can date the origin of what we know as modern psychiatry back to the work of Philippe Pinel—whose *Medico-Philosophical Treatise on Mental Alienation or Mania* (year IX, 1801) signaled both the autonomy of mental illness as a field of study separate from physiology and the application of new clinical and institutional practices to the treatment of patients—the study of mental illness, or of madness, as a discipline has a longer history that goes back to antiquity. The word "melancholy" at that time referred to a state of sadness and anxiety, without a fever, and most often accompanied by an obsession, or near delirium, this state being marked by an excess of black bile, which some authors considered to be the cause of the illness and others as a concomitant symptom.

The word "melancholy," then, comes originally from the Hippo-cratic theory of the humors (*melas* [μέλας]), "black"; *cholê* [χολή], "bile"), as well as from a chemical theory of fermentation and of vapors, and would continue to be understood more or less explicitly as such until the nineteenth century, even though "melancholy" tended by then to refer to a state of mental alienation that was increasingly distinct from physiology. By exploring the history of the term and the shifts in its meaning, we can thus identify four themes and points of reference to consider diachronically: the conception of humor, the symptom of obsession, lovesickness, and the nature of genius. The way in which we will discuss them will help us to differentiate between the major trends of English, German, and French psychiatry, and the typologies that they propose.

One might have thought that the general application in psychiatry of the assessment scales of humor—in its psychological sense, close to the Greek *thumos* [θυμός], and its disorders (*dusthumia* [δυσθυμία])—would have attenuated the former denotations of the term "melancholy." It seems, however, that modern approaches to melancholy—particularly as it is manifested in mourning, psychomotor slowing down, generalized negativism, or intellectual hyperlucidity—are on the contrary reviving the figures as they were used by writers in antiquity, in that they pertain more to actual psychological mechanisms than to simple semantic analogies.

I. The Ambiguity of the Concept

From the perspective of contemporary psychiatry, melancholy is something of a paradox, in that it has to take account both of the relativity of a nosology that has largely been superseded by our understanding of how complex affections are, and also of the uniformity of a semiology determined by the different scales of assessment of the symptoms (for the most part American) which European psychiatry is compelled to use as its points of reference. Nevertheless, melancholy still seems to elude any attempt at a definitive classification, as can be seen, for example, in the shift from *DSM III* (*Diagnostic and Statistical Manual of Mental Disorders*) (1980) to *DSM III-R* (1987), and then *DSM IV* (1994), which sees a modification of the diagnostic signs of melancholy, as well as in the CIM (Classification internationale des maladies de l'OMS), known as the ICD in English, which practically eliminates it.

The problem is not a new one, and Jean-Étienne Esquirol, in his work *De la lypémanie ou mélancolie* (On lypemania or melancholy) (1820), already wrote that "the word *melancholy*, widely used in ordinary language to express the habitual sadness of a few individuals, must be left to the moralists and poets, who do not have to be as rigorous as doctors with their expressions. This term can be retained and used to describe the temperament in which the hepatic system is predominant, and to refer to the disposition to obsessive ideas and sadness, while the word *monomania* expresses an abnormal state of physical or moral sensibility, with an unconscious and permanent delirium." Esquirol adopted the word *lypemania* (*lupê* [λύπη], "sadness") in place of "melancholy," and used the latter term to refer on the one hand to a disposition of the temperament—a permanent state (*hexis* [ἕξις]), a predisposition (*proclivitas*)—and on the other, to the open manifestation of the illness, a punctual, accidental state (*diathesis* [διάθεσις]), the manifestation of the ill (*nosos* [νόσος], *nosêma* [νόσημα]).

The interest of this ambiguity particular to "melancholy" as a term is expressed throughout the history of

psychiatry, whose origin can be traced back to the end of the eighteenth century with the practice of "moral treatment," via two paradoxical semiological forms, made up of contradictory traits, such as the signs of genius and of madness on the one hand, and the signs of what was permanent and accidental on the other. The dispositional characteristics of genius were thus manifestations of a humor that could just as easily lead to madness, as a result of a momentary disturbance of thymic equilibrium. Although European psychiatry is still relatively young, it does not for all that challenge the traditional historical sources from which it emerged, both medical and philosophical, however attentive it appears to be to international (for the most part originally American) systems of diagnosis. As testimony to this, we might take current debates, often inspired by psychoanalysis, about the meaning of the term "melancholy," in other words, about the specific signs that guide its classification in the three main traditional nosographic groups (neuroses, psychoses, and perversions). Already in 1915, at the beginning of his article "Mourning and Melancholia," Freud wrote: "Melancholia [*Melancholie*], whose concept [*Begriffsbestimmung*] fluctuates even in descriptive psychiatry, takes on various clinical forms the grouping together of which into a single unity does not seem to be established with certainty; and some of these forms suggest somatic rather than psychogenic affections." The study of the concept is further complicated if we take into account another tradition, in parallel with the medical history of the shifts in its uses and meanings, that is, the ethological tradition (*ethos* [ἔθος], "custom," but which also designates a set of cultural characteristics; see MORALS), which is no doubt more literary, but which still has an influence on the psychiatric approach. This is the very tradition that Esquirol advised leaving to the moralists and poets, and which draws on the mythical resources particular to different groups.

II. The Humoral Conception of Melancholy

The word "melancholy," as its etymology indicates, locates the affection it refers to within the Hippocratic theory of the four humors (black bile, yellow bile, phlegm, and blood), which persisted into the nineteenth century, even though interest in humoral theory waned in the second half of the seventeenth century as scholars and others switched their focus toward mental alienation, understood increasingly as a form of distraction or wandering. Indeed, around this time a number of works appeared which, imbued with the scholarship of the Renaissance, itself built upon Greek and Arabic sources, progressively made way for a more mentalist conception of obsession or *idée fixe*, the therapies for which took the form of purging and amusement or distraction (see CATHARSIS). So starting with the conception of a complex chemistry in which heating and fermentation were the main agents of transformation of natural elements, the Hippocratic description of temperament (one could be melancholic, choleric, phlegmatic, or sanguine) understood as a combination (*krasis* [κρᾶσις]) of the four humors (*chumoi* [χυμοί]), depending on how much of each of them was present in different organs, would be integrated into an already more modern conception of a pathology centered on mental disorders, and in relation to which humor would only be one cause among several others.

The first definition of melancholy is to be found in aphorism 23 of book 6 of the *Aphorisms* of Hippocrates: "If a fright or despondency (*dusthumia* [δυσθυμία]) lasts for a long time, it is a melancholic affection" (*The Genuine Works of Hippocrates*, Eng. trans. Francis Adams). And Galen, who resurrected humoral theory in the second century CE and can serve as a representative of Greco-Roman medicine, completed Hippocrates's definition as follows: "Melancholy is a sickness that damages the mind (*gnome* [γνώμη]), with a feeling of malaise (*dusthumia*) and an aversion toward the things that are most cherished, without a fever. In some of those who are ill, an abundant and black bile also attacks the esophagus, so much so that they vomit and at the same time their mind is considerably affected" (Galen, *Medical Definitions*, 19 K 416). One could not express better than in this description of melancholy, which is both etiological and semiological, the reciprocal influence of the soul and the body, as if, in this case, temperament (*krasis*) suffered from an excess of black bile which, damaging the stomach (*stomachos* [στόμαχος]), affected the soul in its vital energy. Melancholy indeed suggests a mental pathology with a double cause, in humoral chemistry and in an organic dysfunction. But Galen's definition does further work still. Although it is the excessive vapors of back bile that most often cloud the brain, the same result can be seen with the combustion of the other three humors, to such an extent that the term "melancholy" ends up referring not only to the harmful effects of black bile, but also to those of the other three humors when they are affected in the same way. So "melancholy" became a generic and representative term for madness, which comes from a complexion or temperament that, even though it remains natural, nonetheless predisposes an individual to this kind of distraction.

It was for this very reason that other writers, and in particular Aretaeus of Cappadocia, extended the semiology of melancholy well beyond the simple effects of black bile, to include a more multiform disorder of the understanding. Cicero, who favored this extension of the term, went as far as to translate the melancholy of the Greeks using the term *furor*, thus reducing melancholy to a "deep anger" or to a "fury," as J. Pigeaud explains in his seminal work *La maladie de l'âme*. In book 3 of his *Tuscalanae*, Cicero wrote: "The Greeks, indeed . . . have no one word that will express it: what we call furor, they call μελαγχολία [*melagcholia*], as if the reason were affected only by a black bile, and not disturbed as often by a violent rage, or fear, or grief. Thus we say Athamas, Alcmæon, Ajax, and Orestes were raving [*furere*]." And according to R. Klibansky, E. Panofsky, and F. Saxl, Cicero's intention was to "describe a convulsion of the soul which could not be gathered from the mere concept of 'atrabiliousness'" (*Saturn and Melancholy*).

This extension of the term "melancholy" still lies at the heart of the problematic in contemporary psychiatry, in the sense that some psychiatrists like to keep "melancholy" within the category of psychoses, whereas others prefer to consider it as a specific structure, and yet others still are keen to eliminate it from the nosology—but it does not originate with the Neo-Stoics (Hippocrates, Galen, and their followers). It was already present in Plato and Aristotle, who compared melancholy to the state of inebriation, and considered that the multiple forms of melancholy reproduced drunkenness's different degrees of distraction. Plato writes in *The Republic*: "Then a precise definition of a tyrannical man is one who, either by birth or by habit or both, combines the characteristics of drunkenness, lust, and madness (*melagcholikos* [μελαγχολικός])." And in the famous *Problem XXX*, Aristotle, or Pseudo-Aristotle, maintains that the word "melancholy," following the variety of manifestations of inebriation according to the nature of the individuals, designates the excessive and incomprehensible changes they undergo whenever too great a quantity of black bile is acting upon them, or whenever some external occurrence stimulates it too aggressively: "In most people then black bile engendered from their daily nutriment does not change their character, but merely produces an atrabilious disease. But those who naturally possess an atrabilious temperament immediately develop diverse characters in accordance with their various temperaments."

III. "From Humor to Mood": The Age of Quantitative Measure

As a result of these successive shifts in the meaning, then, the word "melancholy" does not refer to a precise pathological entity, and in this respect, its overwhelmingly diverse and extensive semiology makes it impossible to establish a definitive and stable nosology. It suggests an "essentially polymorphous" temperament, to borrow J. Pigeaud's expression from his commentary on *Problem XXX*, which possesses in their potential state "all the characteristics of all men." The numerous attempts at a psychiatric classification of melancholy have accordingly relied on privileging some aspect or particular mechanism. This has meant isolating such aspects or mechanisms from the whole range of manifestations of the illness so as to make them a distinctive sign that corresponds to a system of classification, whose relevant criteria can then be shared in advance. But the experimental studies that were conducted with a view to achieving this aim did not confirm the hypothesis of differential biological reaction, so researchers then focused their efforts on somatic treatments, in particular, medication using antidepressants. These positive studies are part of an active attempt to establish the meaning of the word "melancholy," retrospectively as it were, since it is according to how patients respond to the different treatments administered to them that researchers hope to confirm whether they can be classified as melancholic or depressive. In any case, we are forced to return to the need to determine international assessment criteria, one of whose manifest paradoxes is that they give renewed credibility to a humoral theory by trying to understand and measure melancholy according to a quantitative assessment scale.

Given the inherently variable nature of the nosography of melancholy, we cannot but be skeptical a priori of the many ventures nowadays to isolate analytically the symptoms of the identified affection in order to then evaluate them using a comparative scale of measure. Furthermore, to proceed in this way one would have to envisage a nosographic category sufficiently broad to cover all of the apparently characteristic signs of melancholy according to their intensity. This was the category of depression, and the debate surrounding the distinction between melancholy and depression, far from disappearing, has grown even more complex as a result.

It would also be worth looking more closely at diagnostic classifications, as well as the assessment scales of the intensity of the symptoms, in particular, those relating to the psychomotor disorder that is seen increasingly as an indication of melancholy. This is because they show, on the one hand, the mobility of the semiology of melancholy—and this is far from insignificant when it is sometimes assigned psychotic characteristics—and on the other hand, the interest there is in retaining the notion of humor (or mood, in the Anglo-Saxon tradition). Humor or mood in this sense is obviously different from the humoral theory of Hippocrates, and more closely resembles the Greek notion of *thumos* [θυμός], understood as the way in which one feels oneself, the self-perception of one's own relationship to the world, a kind of psychic coenesthesia (see CONSCIOUSNESS, Box 1). Anglo-Saxon psychiatry is most explicit in this regard, and uses the word "mood" for this "coenesthetic" humor. We are now far removed from the physical register in which the humors operated, however; no longer would the word "moisture" be in any sense applicable to this "coenesthetic" humor, though "moisture" is indeed related to the liquid humor in the Hippocratic sense and, for someone like Ben Jonson, already referred metaphorically to the general character of a man when all of his humors flowed in the same direction:

So in every human body,
The choler, melancholy, phlegm, and blood,
By reason that they flow continually
In some one part, and are not continent,
Receive the name of humours. Now thus far
It may, by metaphor, apply itself
Unto the general disposition:
As when some one peculiar quality
Doth so possess a man, that it doth draw
All his affects, his spirits, and his powers,
In their confluctions, all to run one way,
This may be truly said to be a humour.

(*Every Man Out of His Humour*, I.1)

In the same way, spleen would be considered as that vague and sad humor which, as in ancient times, comes from an accumulation of humor/moisture in the spleen, which was where black bile was to be found, according to many physicians (R. Blackmore, 1725). (See INGENIUM, Box 2, and SPLEEN.)

While contemporary psychiatry attempts to assess the intensity of certain characteristic signs of humor, or mood, with a view to establishing a psychiatric nosography that is intended to be universal, it approaches melancholy in a number of different ways. These alternative approaches include, on the one hand, phenomenological psychiatry, with its notion of endogeneity, which goes back to clinical observation of the behavior of the patient, and the description he himself gives of his mood, and on the other hand, psychiatry inspired by psychoanalysis, which identifies within the patient's discourse the psychic mechanisms underlying the formation of the symptoms. Here again, the meaning of the word "melancholy" will be subject to many modifications and shifts, depending on the methodological approach adopted. So phenomenological psychiatry will refer to melancholy as an illness of endogeneity by emphasizing its generic nature, and psychoanalytically inspired psychiatry will describe it as a narcissistic illness and will consider the nosological question as secondary. If the former approach is still attached to the notion of humor, this time in the sense of the inner sentiment of the unfolding of a personal history (*innere Lebensgeschichte*), the latter approach is attached to the various figures of melancholy, understood as formal models of psychic function, some of which are already to be found in the annals of modern psychiatry, dating from the end of the eighteenth century.

IV. The Clinical Tradition: The Age of the Great Classifications

A. *Endon, Stimmung, Schwermut*

Endogeneity, then, might provide a new interpretation of modern humor, as useful to positivist psychiatry (with the category of "endogenous depression") as it is to phenomenological psychiatry, which attempts to account for the notion of melancholy itself. Hubertus Tellenbach, heir to the great German phenomenological psychiatric trend of the first half of the twentieth century (with, among others, E. Strauss, V. E. von Gebsattel, and L. Binswanger), proposed a definition of endogeneity accompanied by its substratum: the *endon*, which we should no doubt understand as a formal schema that is useful for the overall configuration of the notion. The term "endogenous" appeared around the beginning of the twentieth century (A. Mechler), and was often a synonym for "constitutional," which did little to explain the nature of melancholy since other affections could also be related to it, in particular, psychoses and neuroses, which were said to have a "depressive basis." The term concerned the "disorders of the humor," or even the "vital feelings" in their stuporous or maniacal disturbances. This is where some located those affects whose anomalies derived from a primary organization of drives, and which were thus relatively independent from external events and psychological motivations. This simply indicates how vague the notion still was, and how it seemed to call out for a third etiological field alongside the somatic and the psychic. Indeed, Tellenbach's definition of melancholy is more an overall description than an actual definition: it emphasizes the importance of vital rhythms, and the coherence of their combination, in other words, their historial aspect:

By endogeny, then, we mean what emerges as the unity of the basic form in any life event [*als Einheit der Grundgestalt in allem Lebensgeschehen*]. The *endon* is by its origin the *phusis*, which opens out and remains within the phenomena of endogeny.

(*Melancholie*)

The word "melancholy" thereafter refers, in a phenomenological context, to an endokinesis, to a movement of the *endon*, or even a rupture with the *endon*, understood as a blockage of the basic manifestations of life (stupor, despondency, despair), a blockage that the individual endeavors to prevent by a defensive behavior focused entirely on a respect for, and conformity to, an established order (*Ordentlichkeit*). If Tellenbach's phenomenological approach to melancholy still reflects the relevance of German psychiatric thought, in spite of the pressure exerted by the obligation to apply international classificatory norms, it is because the humoral tradition has its roots not only in a clinical practice that attempts to analyze its manifestations, but also in a philosophical tradition that psychiatrists are not averse to exploiting in elaborating their theoretical models.

Like psychiatrists from the English-speaking world, German psychiatrists use an original term to designate modern humor: *Stimmung*, whose meanings have an even wider resonance than the corresponding English term, "mood" or "humor" in the nonphysical sense. *Stimmung* comes from *stimmen*, to make one's voice (*Stimme*) heard, to establish, to name (*bestimmen*, "to determine"), and to play an instrument in order to tune it. This latter meaning, when extended to humor, suggests the fact of putting oneself in a certain frame of mind (see STIMMUNG). The lexicon of the French translation of Tellenbach's work retains the following composite nouns: *Gestimmtsein* (being-in-a-mood); *Gestimmtheit* (color of the mood); *Verstimmung* (change of mood); and *Stimmbarkeit* (suppleness, affective mobility). The richness of this vocabulary (beyond its application to melancholy, which makes melancholy not so much a morbid entity as a frame of mind, or even a *typus*, as Tellenbach puts it) echoes in this sense the great movements of German psychiatry from the end of the nineteenth century. This tradition, beyond the clinical and nosographic conception of someone like Kraepelin in particular, was still very much in line with the work of J. Herbaert: a dynamic of associations of ideas in which the antagonisms between representations were related analogically to intracortical antagonisms. As far as melancholy specifically was concerned, the German classification made a distinction between a simple melancholy (*melancholia simplex*) and a stuporous melancholy (*melancholia errabunda, melancholia agitans sine active*); relative to these two forms, there were then a melancholy without delirium; a precordial melancholy; a delirious melancholy, which was also still called religious; and a hallucinatory melancholy, which was still called hypochondriacal. W. Griesinger, for example, follows this classification of melancholy (*Mental Illnesses*, 1845), and places melancholy properly speaking (*Melancholia*), along with hypochondria, in the more general category of "states of mental depression. Melancholy (*Schwermut*)." This latter term, a synonym for despondency or depression (*schwer*, "heavy, weighty," and *Mut*, "feelings, qualities, or states of mind"), conveys the main quality of humor, much as does the term "tristimania," coined by the American B. Rush in 1812, or *lypémanie* (lypemania), coined by J.-É. Esquirol in France in 1820, or L. Delasiauve's *dépression* (1860). From this perspective, and in order to distinguish *Melancholia* from simple *Schwermut*, R. Krafft-Ebing and H. Schüle would emphasize the accidental or nonaccidental nature of the etiological factor, as well as the presence or lack of anxiety. But it was E. Kraeplin who would foreground most explicitly the difficulty of establishing a stable semiology of melancholy, and of putting it in a relevant classificatory category.

B. Manic depression

French psychiatrists before Kraepelin had included melancholy in the group of thymic psychoses broadly named "manic depressive" (or what Farlet in 1851 called *folie circulaire* [circular madness], and Baillarger in 1854 called *folie à double forme* [double-formed madness]). Kraepelin, however, distinguished it clearly from manic depression up until 1913, when he included it in the eighth edition of his *Lehrbuch der Psychiatrie*, emphasizing the identity of the clinical symptoms of the two illnesses, even if the variations of mood in melancholy often remain very slight, to the point of being imperceptible. From that point on, manic depression constituted a disease in the same way that paranoia and schizophrenia did, and it encompassed all of the symptomatic variations of melancholy, of mania, and of the different combined states, as well as pure mono-symptomatic forms. The interest of such a classification as regards melancholy lay in what would henceforth appear to continue to distinguish it from other simple forms, that is, the integrity of ideation. From psychomotor inhibition to the state of stupor, from delirious ideas to confused states, three types of pure melancholy emerge, all characterized by an aggravation of what we might call a fullness of the idea, from the point of view of the mechanism; and by moral suffering and psychomotor inhibition, from the point of view of the classic syndrome.

Kraepelin's nosography remains a key reference point in the history of psychiatry, not just in Germany, but in Europe more generally, insofar as, according to a detailed semiology, all the simple forms of the illness are grouped under more general forms (so, for example, "pure melancholy" is under the form "manic depression" [*maniac-depressive Psychose*]), and thus retain their characteristics almost autonomously. For this reason, melancholy is still nowadays classed as manic depression or neurotic depression depending on the assessment of the disturbances of ideation, of the intensity of sadness and anxiety, as well as of the degree of psychomotor slowing, to use the modern expressions. The second half of the nineteenth century, and the start of the following century, witnessed an explosion of great German treatises in psychiatry, which were vast systems of classifications of mental illness that relied on the most detailed of semiological methods, drawn up during close clinical observation. The mechanisms of the different ideas, the very ones brought to light and favored by the organo-dynamist approach that would be developed in France, and even more so by psychoanalytically inspired psychiatry, could already be glimpsed as a number of metaphorical figures at work in these treatises. For melancholy, for example, one finds in the figures of the hole and of the cavity (T. Meynert, Freud), as well as the figure of the whirlwind and the spiral movement (H. Schüle, H. Emminghaus), characteristics of the loss of psychic investment, and of the flux of thought. After this, the psychosomatic or psychic mechanisms underlying the symptomatic manifestations would enter the definitions of mental affections at the expense of a semiology, whose endless reworkings made the establishment of a universal nosology extremely difficult.

V. Melancholy as a Paradigm of Narcissistic Illness

A. Melancholic discourse

In spite of the delirious or confused appearance that certain forms of melancholy can take, the illness that corresponds to this name is said to be distinguished from manic depression in that it preserves the integrity of intellectual processes, even if the full weight of the obsession often causes a patient to sink into extreme pathological behaviors, such as total mutism or systematic negativism. German psychiatry and French psychiatry attach a similar importance to the discourse of the patient through the repetitive figures he presents, and which is said to translate the nature of the affections from which it derives. In 1891 G. Dumas, in his medical thesis *Les états intellectuels dans la mélancolie* [Intellectual states in melancholy], makes a distinction between an organic melancholy and an intellectual melancholy, depending on the whether the state prior to melancholy was affective or intellectual, and according to the possible variations of the causal order, conceived as follows: organic facts, mental productions, and confused perceptions of these facts, or melancholy. Melancholy is thus less a pathology than a psychic operation whose aim is to justify the organic or affective disorders of which the patient continues to be aware. Melancholy would not simply have an organic etiology—which neither the Germans nor the French were yet able to do without—but also a rational logic. This logic prompts the patient to translate his impressions of diminution and of weakness into a type of discourse and behavior, which then precisely becomes part of the definition of melancholy. "In all cases," writes G. Dumas, "the affective effect, melancholy, appears to be merely the awareness of the movements made, the confused idea of the body. We are no longer in the presence of an ill-defined power succeeding an idea, and being expressed by physical organs; we are only ever dealing with intellectual states, ideas, images or sensations, and with physiological states." W. Griesinger, to whom G. Dumas refers in his thesis, had already emphasized this impression of great coherence that emerges from melancholic discourse. For Griesinger, this is a testimony to the mind trying to understand cenesthetic states or apparently inexplicable movements of the body, and which, in order to do this, conceives of logical arguments that are more or less removed from the lived context, more or less artificial in relation to the still uninterpreted affective base.

B. The mechanism of melancholy

We find in Germany as well as in France, besides an interest in nosology, a continued and no less powerful interest in the study of the particular forms of discourse of the patients, insofar as these forms might reveal the underlying etiological mechanisms of the different types of affections. Alongside the descriptive semiological description of melancholy, then, a morphological definition explaining the illness is also elaborated, in both Germany and France, whose medical traditions are nonetheless distinctly different: German alienists remained attached to the theory of the association of ideas since J. Herbart, who attributed to representations a force of attraction and repulsion, and French alienists remained attached to the organo-psychic approach of the Greco-Latin tradition. This organo-psychic influence is still largely present not only among French psychiatrists, but also more widely across the Mediterranean, insofar as it determines two otherwise unrelated directions for research and treatment of melancholy: the neuro-pharmacological approach, and the psychodynamic approach, whose essentially psychoanalytic points of reference are still very much alive in France. Melancholy then comes to be discussed in terms of mechanisms, and in this it follows Freud, who drew this conclusion from V. Tausk's lecture on melancholy on 30 December 1914:

> The essential criterion by which we must circumscribe the symptoms (which, in practice, never appear in their pure form) and the forms of illness is its mechanism. The observation of benign cases, offers, as Hitschmann mentioned, the only possibility of drawing up a chart of pure symptoms. If this is true, there is only one melancholy, which has the same mechanism, and which should be curable by psychoanalysis.

Freud's call for circumscribing and unifying the concept of melancholy was followed, however, in a less-than-unified way by psychoanalytically inspired psychiatrists. The result is a vast nosographic panorama within which melancholy shifts from being a manic-depressive psychosis to a major depression, and even a narcissistic illness (still described as an "illness of the ideal"). The 1914 formulation comes close to the category of "narcissistic neuroses" that Freud, in 1924, would distinguish from psychoses and neuroses, and of which for him melancholy was the paradigm: "We may provisionally assume that there must also be illnesses which are based on a conflict between the ego and the super-ego. Analysis gives us a right to suppose that melancholia is a typical example of this group; and we would set aside the name of 'narcissistic psychoneuroses' for disorders of that kind" ("Neurosis and Psychosis"; see *ES*). Psychiatric practice, while necessarily distinct from psychoanalytic practice in the sense that its primary aim is the medical objective of the disappearance of the symptom, through well-established therapeutic knowledge, nevertheless shares with psychoanalysis a recognition of those unconscious mechanisms identified by Freud, which it finds at the heart of the melancholic patient's discourse. Three such mechanisms are commonly encountered in psychiatric literature. They attach respectively to the figure of mourning, understood as an impossible psychic resolution; to the figure of a generalized negativism, which results in a logical, hyper-formalized discourse; as well, finally, as to the figure of a narcissistic rift, whose consequences would manifest themselves through a devalorization of one's self-image.

C. The figures of melancholy: Lovesickness

It is curious to note how similar contemporary figures of melancholy are to those that were already present in the history of the illness, from antiquity up through the seventeenth century, in the form of different kinds of melancholy, such as "divine melancholy" (Marsilio Ficino), "white melancholy or white bile" (Agrippa of Nettesheim), and even "amorous or erotic melancholy" (Jacques Ferrand and the authors of the various "Treatises on Lovesickness" of the seventeenth century).

If the ancients had already provided a good description of these different manifestations of melancholy, the Renaissance and the classical age established them as almost autonomous models. In this regard, "erotic melancholy" offers one of the most instructive examples, insofar as it provides the raw material for a number of specialized treatises written by doctors, as well as philosophers and theologians. We find many allusions in antiquity to the discomfort of the state of being in love (Hippocrates, Caelius Aurelianus, Rufus of Ephesus, Aretaeus of Cappadocia), either from *erôs* [ἔρως], or from *epithumia* [ἐπιθυμία], passionate longing, lust, desire (the latter, provided that we understand the transcendental movement that *epithumia* leads to as the overcoming through love of simple covetousness or bodily desire). And it is indeed the state of being in love, and its crisis of passion, which causes unreliability of judgment, as well as languor and the stupor that accompanies it when the absence of the object is felt all too cruelly. Aretaeus of Cappadocia tells of one such case when he describes an adolescent boy who, having sunk into melancholy and been abandoned by his doctors, was cured by the love of a young girl: "But I think, he added, that he was in love from the beginning and that, having been disappointed in his advances on the young girl, he became languorous, which made him appear melancholic to his compatriots" (quoted in J. Pigeaud, *De la mélancolie*). This passion thus gave way in the sixteenth and seventeenth centuries to a particular category of melancholy: "erotic melancholy," which was compared to a kind of "fury of love" or "amorous folly," an expression that a doctor such as Jacques Ferrand translates using the word *erôtomania* [ἐρωτομανία]. It could certainly be considered as an "illness of desire," an expression that would not really be anachronistic since the author specifically makes desire an efficient cause of the malady:

We therefore say that, according to this doctrine [the doctrine of Hippocrates], love or erotic passion is a kind of reverie, which is caused by an excessive desire to enjoy the loved object. Now, if this kind of reverie is without fever, and accompanied by ordinary fear and sadness, it is called melancholy. *Res est solliciti plena timoris amor* [Love is a thing that is filled with fear and worry].

(Ferrand, *Traicte de l'essence et guerison de l'amour et de la mélancolie érotique*)

Ferrand, following his master du Laurens, classifies melancholy as a kind of hypochondria, attaching to it the symptoms of the latter, such as stomach upsets and disorders associated with the organs. While he claims that the heart is the seat of the cause of the illness, the liver the seat of love, and the genitalia the seat of combined causes, the symptoms are said to be in the brain, which is responsible for the general alteration of one's mind and temperament. His contemporaries, in particular, A. de Laurens, J. Guibelet, T. Bright, and R. Burton, also respected this classification, and while none of their works was devoted to lovesick melancholy, they did discuss it in particular chapters. These authors, and especially Burton, talk in this regard of "heroic melancholy," an expression that is also mentioned by Ferrand, who traces it back to Arabic writers:

Avicenna, and the whole Arabe family, call this illness *Alhasch* or *Iliscus* in their language: Arnaud of Villanova [de Villeneuve], Gordon, and their contemporaries call it heroic or lordly Love, either because the ancient heroes or half-gods were greatly affected by this ill, as the Poets recite in their fables, or because the great Lords and Ladies were more prone to this illness than the people, or finally, because Love dominates and masters the hearts of lovers.

(Ferrand, *De la maladie d'amour ou mélancolie érotique*)

Now, the term "heroic melancholy" no doubt comes from a semantic confusion of the Greek *erôs* (love) with *herus, heroycus,* or *hereos* (words whose meaning has long eluded lexicographers), if not even with the Greek *hêrôs* [ἥρως] (hero), Arnaud de Villeneuve in the thirteenth century, in his *Liber de parte operativa* being the first to make this mistake, which was later adopted by Burton. Lovesick melancholia, the object of many specific treatises, is thus offered, from the point of view of mood or affect, as the model for a behavior characterized by a withdrawal of investment in the outside world, a turning in upon oneself, and a moral suffering fueled by feelings of self-deprecation and guilt. Mourning or separation merely provides melancholy with an opportunity to manifest itself; the illness is here understood as a constitutive mode of psychic structuration for some, and a physic-chemical anomaly for others, which are present well before any precipitating event. The fact remains that, as the works on "lovesickness" show so clearly, melancholy is affirmed as an "illness of desire," in the sense in which desire, attacked at its core, gives way as it collapses to a number of different expressive formulations, such as, for example, Seneca's *taedium vitae*, close to boredom, or even nostalgia (see SEHNSUCHT), understood in the seventeenth century as an illness of exile, or homesickness (J. Hofer, 1688).

To classify melancholy as a specific category of psychiatric nosography seems, then, to be an impossible task, given the different epistemological contexts that govern such a classification on the one hand, and the variability of symptomatological descriptions that work against any precise semiology on the other. However, alongside these descriptions, phenomenological and psychoanalytical trends continue to inform a different kind of practice, which is based on an approach toward the illness that, for phenomenology, focuses on the nature of the patient's temperament and on an awareness of his or her biographical history, and for psychoanalysis, focuses instead on unconscious mechanisms and psychic structuration. What is understood by melancholy is therefore understood in terms of the symptoms themselves which, first identified in antiquity, would nowadays be defined by a metaphorical displacement: mood and moral suffering, obsession and partial delirium, lovesickness and mourning, as well as the characteristic of genius, and the hyper-lucidity of a discourse reduced to a pathological authenticity. We might say that desire can no longer be sustained by narcissistic projection, for want of a sufficiently stable specular image, and that this originary failure points to a fundamental anomaly in the relationship to the other, the advent of which psychoanalytic metapsychology tries to reconstruct. Melancholy is a narcissistic illness, an illness of desire and of truth, in the sense that, as Freud states, the melancholic subject has come so close to this truth that it falls ill as a result (*Mourning and Melancholia*, 1915). Beyond the seduction of an eminently protean philosophical and literary discourse, melancholy defies any attempt at reductive classification in the field of psychiatry. It is thus held captive by the Aristotelian *kairos* [καιρός], if we are willing to understand this *kairos* as the opportunity offered to the temperament to manifest itself as a structural effect.

Marie-Claude Lambotte

BIBLIOGRAPHY

Aristotle. "Problem 30:1." In *Problems*. Translated by W. S. Hett and Harris Rackham. Rev. ed. Loeb Classical Library. Cambridge, MA: Harvard University Press, 1953–57.

———. "Problems." In *The Complete Works of Aristotle*, Bollinger Series 71. 2 vols. Edited by Jonathan Barnes. Princeton, NJ: Princeton University Press, 1984.

Binswanger, Ludwig. *Melancholie und Manie: Phänomenologische Studien*. Pfullingen, Ger.: Neske, 1960.

———. *Being-in-the-World: Selected Papers of Ludwig Binswanger*. Translated by Jacob Needleman. New York: Basic Books, 1963.

Burton, Robert. *The Anatomy of Melancholy*. Edited by Thomas C. Faulkner et al.; introduction by J. B. Bamborough. 6 vols. Oxford: Clarendon Press, 1989–2000.

Comay, Rebecca. "The Sickness of Tradition: Between Melancholia and Fetishism." In *Walter Benjamin and History*, edited by Andrew Benjamin, 88–101. New York: Continuum, 2005.

Dumas, Georges. *Les états intellectuels dans la mélancolie*. Paris, 1894.

Esquirol, Jean-Étienne. "De la lypémanie ou mélancolie [Ch. 8]." In *Des maladies mentales considérées sous les rapports médical, hygiénique et médico-légal*. 2 vols. Paris, 1838. Translation by E. K. Hunt, with an introduction by Raymond de Saussure: "Lypemania or melancholia [Ch. 8]." In *Mental Maladies: A Treatise on Insanity*. New York: Hafner, 1965. First published in 1845.

Ferrand, Jacques. *De la maladie d'amour ou mélancolie érotique*. Paris, 1623. Translation, critical introduction, and notes by Donald A. Beecher and Massimo Ciavolella: *A Treatise on Lovesickness*. Syracuse, NY: Syracuse University Press, 1990.

Freud, Sigmund. "Trauer und Melancholie." In *Freud-Studienausgabe III: Psychologie des Unbewußten*, edited by Alexander Mitscherlich, Angela Richards, and James Strachey, 183–212. 9th ed. Frankfurt: Fischer, 2001. Translation by James Strachey: "Mourning and Melancholia." In *The Standard Edition of the Complete Psychological Works of Sigmund Freud*. 14: 243–58. London: Hogarth Press, 1953–74.

———. "Neurosis and Psychosis." In *The Standard Edition of the Complete Psychological Works of Sigmund Freud*. Translated by James Strachey. Vol. 19. London: Hogarth Press, 1953–74.

Gowland, Angus. *The Worlds of Renaissance Melancholy: Robert Burton in Context*. Cambridge: Cambridge University Press, 2006.

Jackson, Stanley W. *Melancholia and Depression: From Hippocratic Times to Modern Times*. New Haven, CT: Yale University Press, 1986.

Jordan-Smith, Paul. *Bibliographia Burtoniana: A Study of Robert Burton's The Anatomy of Melancholy; with a Bibliography of Burton's Writings*. Stanford, CA: Stanford University Press, 1931.

Klibansky, Raymond, Erwin Panofsky, and Fritz Saxl. *Saturn and Melancholy: Studies in the History of Natural Philosophy, Religion, and Art*. New York: Basic Books, 1964.

Kraepelin, Emil. *Einführung in die psychiatrische Klinik: Zweiunddreissig Vorlesungen*. 2nd ed. Leipzig: Barth, 1905. Translation and introduction by Thomas Johnstone: *Lectures on Clinical Psychiatry*. New York: Hafner, 1968. First published in 1904.

Lambotte, Marie-Claude. *Le discours mélancolique de la phénoménologie à la métapsychologie*. Paris: Anthropos, 1993.

———. *Esthétique de la mélancolie*. Paris: Aubier, 1984.

Lussier, Martin. "'Mourning and Melancholia': The Genesis of a Text and of a Concept." *International Journal of Psycho-analysis* 81 (2000): 667–86.

Nunberg, Herman. *Minutes of the Vienna Psychoanalytic Society/Protokolle der Wiener Psychoanalytische Vereinigung, Volume 4 (1912–1918)*. New York: International Universities Press, 1918.

Pigeaud, Jackie. *De la mélancolie: Fragments de poétique et d'histoire*. Paris: Dilecta, 2005.

———. *La maladie de l'âme: Étude sur la relation de l'âme et du corps dans la tradition médico-philosophique antique*. Paris: Les Belles Lettres, 1981.

———. *Melancholia: Le malaise de l'individu*. Paris: Payot and Rivages, 2008.

Plato. *The Republic*. Translated and with an introduction by H.D.P. Lee. Harmondsworth, Eng.: Penguin, 1955.

Radden, Jennifer. *Moody Minds Distempered: Essays on Melancholy and Depression*. Oxford: Oxford University Press, 2009.

Simon, Jean Robert. *Robert Burton (1577–1640) et l'Anatomie de la mélancolie*. Paris: Didier, 1964.

Starobinski, Jean. *Histoire du traitement de la mélancolie, des origines à 1900*. Basel, Switz.: Geigy, 1960.

Tellenbach, Hubertus. *Melancholie*. 3rd ed. Berlin: Springer, 1961. Translation by Erling Eng: *Melancholy: History of the Problem, Endogeneity, Typology, Pathogenesis, Clinical Considerations*. Pittsburgh: Duquesne University Press, 1980.

Vidal, Fernando. "Jean Starobinski: The History of Psychiatry as the Cultural History of Consciousness." In *Discovering the History of Psychiatry*, edited by Mark S. Micale and Roy Porter, 135–54. New York: Oxford University Press, 1994.

MEMORY / FORGETFULNESS

FRENCH	*mémoire, oubli*
GERMAN	*Erinnerung, Gedächtnis, Vergessen*
GREEK	*mnêmê* [μνήμη], *mnêmosunê* [μνημοσύνη], *memnêmai* [μέμνημαι], *lêthê* [λήθη], *lêsmosunê* [λησμοσύνη]
LATIN	*subvenire, menini, obliviscor*

➤ CONSCIOUSNESS, DICHTUNG, HISTORY, *IMAGE*, MADNESS, MIMÊSIS, PARDON, PRESENT, SOUL, *TIME*, TO TRANSLATE, TRUTH, UNCONSCIOUS, VERNEINUNG

The specialized words denoting the faculty of mastering and actualizing the past, that is, memory-thought, split off from a group encompassing the activity of the mind in the broadest sense, and opening out onto many different associations, including warlike violence and delirium. The root *men-* covers everything to do with the mind in general, with *men* in *menos* [μένος] (force), and *man* in *mania* [μανία] (delirium), and for memory in Greek: *mimnêskomai* [μιμνήσκομαι], *mnêmê* [μνήνη], *mnêmosunê* [μνημοσύνη], and in Latin: *memini* and *memor, memoria*.

Memory has a double status: it can be referred to and invoked, or it can be experienced. There are different models for thinking memory. First and foremost of these is writing (Gr. *graphê* [γραφή]), with a trace that is left and then found again; imprinting (Gr. *tupos* [τύπος]); and a trail (Ger. *Spur*) that can be followed. We find, relatedly, the notion of a "treasure" trove, present in various models of thought (see the connotations of the Ger. *Gedächtnis*). When this memory-treasure is possessed, it lends itself to the progressive work of internalizing the world (see the Ger. *Erinnerung*), which is more dynamic than the different models of memory in the Romance languages. The close association of memory with gratitude is prefigured in the German language (*Dank*, "thanks," alongside *Gedanke*, "thought"), and thought is concentrated into acknowledgment (*reconnaissance*), to the point where knowledge (*connaissance*) becomes nothing more than a fixation on history (*Denken* as *Gedenken*, commemoration).

French clearly marks the duality between effective action and sudden, almost involuntary memory, by making a distinction between *se rappeler* (to recall) and *se souvenir* (to remember).

Forgetting has a constant relation to memory, which is not-forgetting, or a form of counter-forgetting, which then becomes a natural state, established through a selective effort of the mind. The English (forget) and the German (*vergessen*) suggest a kind of fluid power that carries away the traces of an experience, which is then out of reach. The effacement in the French word *oubli* (Low Lat. *oblitare*, "to erase, to efface") conveys the idea of a more controlled relation: here, effacement is an object of analysis in itself; forgetting ceases to be the counterposition of a methodically selective process of remembering or recollecting, and in artistic creation, it characterizes the condition of a decisive transition to another order of meaning.

I. Memory-Thought

A. The Greek and Latin roots: "Memory" and "mental"

Memory perhaps does not exist by itself, as a distinct intellectual faculty. The support it offers to man in his life is so central that it cannot be separated from the manifestations of thought in several of its forms. Thought represents to itself the choices it makes and endlessly recalls the paths and values it sets for itself. It becomes attached to what it knows, to what it knows it must not lose from sight, or to what one could not think, that is, what one could "forget." Memory and warlike force are thus closely related in language, and converge as two forms of concentration. Where they diverge is when action splits into two and becomes, in the language of tales and songs, the object of an autonomous reminiscence.

"I remember" is *memini* in Latin and *memnêmai* [μέμνημαι] in Greek, but historically these do not express the same thing. Both are perfect tenses, expressing a state, and are closely related through their linguistic genealogy. In Latin we find the same, rich root *men-* (all that is "mental"), denoting in a wider sense "the movements of the mind." The corresponding words in Greek, *menos* [μένος], "force," or the perfect tense *memona* [μέμονα], took on somewhat different meanings. In "to think forcefully," the object and intensity of a commitment was retained, and as a result one could hear a passion in it, and above all the ardor of being in combat, a will which, when one has it, is irresistible. One would like to have it when one encounters it in the enemy, and one can never acquire it when the primary and spontaneous manifestation of the fundamental value of courage is lacking. The force that is thereby revealed lays claim to its superiority; it creates the social order of the heroic world, and of the world before it.

The Latin words *memor*, "remembering," and *memoria*, "memory"—which has become a catch-all term in several languages—are based on the supplemental intensifier of yet another root, but which is also attached to *men-*, and which we find in *memini*. It highlights no less forcefully how closely interconnected, outside of any specialized sense, the art of "remembering" and the contents of "thought" are (we have the related word in Sanskrit, *smarati*, "to think," and in Greek, *merimna* [μέριμνα], "concern," with the intensification in the adjective *mermeros*

[μέρμερος], "causing concern"). Ernout-Meillet's RT: *Dictionnaire étymologique de la langue latine* mentions that the expressive value one hears in *memor* has, according to him, become "attenuated." It has had to go from a powerful energetic representation to the presence of a system of stabilized memory.

But one can still think differently about the faculty of memory. The Greek language developed an independent group from *mna-*, another form of the same root, alongside *men-* (mimnêskomai [μιμνήσκομαι], "to recall"; *mnêmê* [μνήμη], "memory"; *mnêma* [μνῆμα], "monument"; *mnêmôn* [μνήμων], "who remembers"). What happens is unusual. Memory staked out a terrain for itself within the order of spoken language, and it is hard not to connect this fact to the cultural importance of remembering the past, and to the formation of specialized castes who were guardians of a culture's own language, a language that was inherent in its poetry. This is the key distinction: two core meanings radiate out in different ways, with physical battle on one side and verbal ability on the other, and the overlapping play of these two meanings can be seen clearly in early texts.

B. Force and delirium: *Menos, mania*

Homer shows that memory in action is put in the service of the social order. The soothsayer instructs the hero, who defends the town and the kingdom. The intrusion of unbridled passions reveals that the order is doubly threatened, whether this order is manifest at home or on the battlefield, by the raw nature that reigns within. Rules against the evasion of forgetting within, and against fleeing from the excess outside, are invoked in consequence.

Rage is concentrated and deployed, as the uses of the verb *memona* [μέμονα] show in Homer's *Iliad*: the hero, Hector, gives in to his passion, which remembers itself as if it had been the sole object of his will, and merges with his force ("Remember," he says to the other Trojans, "your irresistible force [μνήσασθε] . . . [ἀλκῆς]"; 6.112). When the Trojans out of cowardice retreat in the face of war, they are embodied in the contrasting figure of Paris, and for a while the pleasures of lovemaking replace the heroic acts of war. Memory is associated with exhorting and actualizing social values, and forgetfulness with not respecting them. Helenos, the Trojans' soothsayer, exhorts the two leaders, Hector and Aeneas, to stop the warriors from throwing themselves into the arms of their women, to the great delight of their enemies (6.80–82). He shows that their army is divided; it destroys itself, whereas nothing stops the champion of the Greeks. Diomedes rages like a second Achilles, and no one can measure up to his force (*menos* [μένος], which has been transformed into pure delirium; he is mad, *mainetai* [μαίνεται]). Achilles is the son of a goddess, but Diomedes is truly delirious ("*all' hode liēn mainetai*" [ἀλλ᾽ ὅδε λίην μαίνεται]; 6.100ff.); no ordinary force of war can oppose him ("*oude tis hoi dunatai menos isopharizein*" [οὐδέ τίς οἱ δύναται μένος ἰσοφαρίζειν]; 6.101).

C. The two forms of forgetfulness: Too much or not enough intensity

Memory, as a creator of values, is implicitly defined in terms of a contradiction. Thought's freedom disengages itself from, but remembers, the constraints of the social order. The two domains touch and overlap, and it is as if the struggle brings out an inherent tension within language.

1. A thought without limits

Delirium in Greek, or *mania* [μανία], is always, in another form, "to think" (the same root *men-* with a zero vowel pattern): "the Greek *mainesthai* [μαίνεσθαι] is dissociated from the general notion and applies to a wild and furious passion" (RT: *Dictionnaire étymologique de la langue grecque*, s.v. *"mainomai"* [μαίνομαι]).

Delirium is freed from rage. Hector meets Diomedes, who is invincible. At the same time, the soothsayer urges him to go into the town so that he can implore the support of the protective goddess there. This is impossible, if not absurd, since Athena, as everyone knows, favors the Greeks.

Helenos had a vision of disaster the moment Diomedes appeared, a vision of an absolute force. With a disregard for all principle, this force makes no pretense of commanding or ordering, and simply prepares for a crushing defeat. Pure delirium, *mania*, fills the heart of this warrior. No one can do a thing against his rage, which is potentially limitless. Language historians have focused on the way in which passion and madness come together in this text, as if the poet were highlighting their linguistic kinship. Homer's verses here do reveal a certain excess (whether this is linguistically correct or inaccurate), related to what it means to put someone to death, outside of the social bounds that normally circumscribe the power to execute. Force is now helpless when faced with delirium since all the rules have been obliterated: the point of view that the text constructs leads to the discovery of a gaping hole, formed when collective memory is set aside. In its place we find the exorbitance of a form of thought that has no limits, and this becomes the basis on which memory is founded.

Ulysses, in his visit to Achilles, presents in the same way Hector's omnipotence as victor and conqueror, when he attempts to set fire to the Greek ships. Excess has a new master, and the gods give him free rein according to their will. They are playing with total annihilation, which will go in whatever direction they wish: "He leaves it up to Zeus and goes into a frightening delirium (*mainetai ekpaglôs pisunos Du* [μαίνεται ἐκπάγλως πίσυνος Δύ]) . . .; the rage which possesses him sweeps everything away (*kraterê de he lussa deduken* [κρατερὴ δέ ἑ λύσσα δέδυκεν])" (*Iliad*, 9.237–39). The soothsayer's vision is again overcome by the persuasion of Ulysses the orator. He goes immediately into a delirium. Nothing will now stop Hector, just as nothing stopped Diomedes; he is beside himself, in the grip of an acute fit of madness.

2. The perils of forgetfulness

Forgetfulness (*lêthê* [λήθη]) can come, though not from an excess of intensity, but from a failure to hold on to thought.

When he leaves the battle (in books 2 and 6) and returns to his mother, Hector does not want to drink the wine she offers him (6.258–62). "Do not break my limbs: I am afraid of forgetting force and combat" (*mê m' apoguiôsêis meneos, d'alkês te lathômai* [μή μ' ἀπογυιώσῃς μένεος, δ' ἀλκῆς τε λάθωμαι]); to forget is to lose. He does not want to lose his warrior-like force, and knows that he only has this force if he has a clear head, and in his heart, the force to think about

it, which is how he constitutes it. Forgetfulness opens the way for the opposite to happen, leading to loss, alienation, and disaster.

II. The Making of the Past

A. Making history and the war of memories

Remembered values concern the life of the cities in their present, but there is another more autonomous form of memory, which integrates the past. It is represented in the epic by a character such as Nestor, who is old and who remembers. He is the indispensable witness, who is present in both the *Iliad* and the *Odyssey*.

Actualizing the past relies on former conflicts and their political dénouements, which serve as models. The action itself verges on excess, and is in danger of being thereby weakened. Memory intervenes in the action, and is focused between these two poles. One of its forms consists of recalling the conditions of its incarnation. The other separates and distances itself from the action by imagining the form of the experiences of the past as if it were a matter first of all of knowing, and then acting.

The creation of meaning implies the distance of a past and of remembered facts. But since the masses are incommensurable and in a sense immemorial, and thus "unmemorable" (*amnêmoneutos* [ἀμνημόνευτος], or *unvordenklich* in German), as impossible to grasp as the present that passes, small and large societies, states, and communities within states, all construct various horizons, which are all more or less mythical. Through memory they transform what is known, which had already been transformed. What is historical are not facts, which can often be embroidered, but the fact that a tradition was at a certain moment in time rearranged and reorganized, reordered in such a way that the guiding principles, even the finality, are intelligible to us. This is how we can grasp the importance of memory in the world of Greek culture. It takes the form of mastering a tradition, and of a particular mnemotechnic that is necessary because of the extent of the historical corpus, which increases when all of the different regional actualizations of that tradition are added to it.

The stakes are extremely high. The struggles to preserve memory, of such immense importance in our times, are part of these traditions, within and between nations, which redefine their identities. Any event can be accepted, gaining a "right to memory," or on the contrary be repressed, or challenged, because it is out of place, embarrassing, or burdensome. So while historical knowledge is progressing and attaining a previously unknown degree of precision, it still remains shot through with taboos and things left unsaid, amnesias by command, political constraints, and the need to hold on to mythical beliefs. The past is both unknowable and available, and this is what we might call the war of memories.

B. Nietzsche: Becoming as ontology

Faced with an investigative openness that encompassed all areas and ages of the modern world, which was exposed to their arbitrary nature and forced certain choices, and at a time when historicism was in the ascendant, Nietzsche described history in terms of corresponding periods of superior dominance. While some periods stood out, they were all essentially seen as concentrations of energy. For Nietzsche, knowledge is all the richer for restricting itself to what is essential, which is constantly reborn and returns in identical form in the immensity of becoming.

The dialectical discussion of history and non-history in chapter 1 of the second part of *Untimely Meditations* ("On the Use and Abuse of History for Life" [*Vom Nutzen und Nachteil der Historie für das Leben*]) only apparently defends forgetting (*das Vergessen*). Nietzsche articulates an aporia: man is condemned to escape the forgetfulness of childhood (*die Vergessenheit*), and destined to know his past, yet this past crushes him. All that counts are the strong concentrations in which life is manifest. Nietzsche broadens the frame of reference, starting with the personal, progressing to the historical, the anthropological, and then to the evolution of all societies. He talks deliberately and insistently about "the creative force of an individual, of a people, of a civilization" (*die plastische Kraft eines Menschen, eines Volks, einer Kultur*) in order to encompass a totality, when he is in fact thinking of the embodiment of these forces in the superior individual, the super-man. The speculative categories of ontology are for him transferred to the history of the triumphant man who abandons himself to becoming. The forces of dispersion and becoming in all its diversity are turned back against themselves, and they produce their own negation. Through an accumulation of vital forces, in an almost biological sense, becoming is pushed to the point where it can acquire the name of "being," and paradoxically be immobilized at the moment of culmination. This is not so much a triumphant liberation from the weight that inhibits life, as a non-history.

Nietzsche adapts, develops, and reinterprets the historian Niebuhr's disenchanted conclusion on chance, where the eye of "the most powerful minds turned to the particular structure that commands their vision." He invests in a supra-historical (*überhistorisch*) perspective, as a science of the past in its totality. For Nietzsche, a lucid analysis should enable us to recognize the conditions in which a particular force was able to become a dominant one within the arbitrary circumstances of history. One immediate consequence of this is that knowledge of the past (historical phenomena as an object of knowledge, *Erkenntnisphänomen*) is no longer the objective; if this were the case, it would be dead ("*Ein historisches Phänomen, rein und vollständig erkannt und in ein Erkenntnisphänomen aufgelöst, ist für den, der es erkannt hat, todt*"). Knowledge is living (blind power is not wasted "for someone who is alive" [*für ihn, den lebenden*]), only when it is applied to the content it is useful to know, for anyone who can use it to his advantage. Science is nothing by itself, it is destined for those in power, and past regimes serve the regimes of the future. Memory is rehabilitated as a site of reincarnation or resurrection ("in the wake of a powerful new current of life, of a culture which is becoming" [*im Gefolge einer mächtigen neuen Lebensströmung einer werdenden Kultur*]). By emphasizing the superior concentration of forces ("*von einer höheren Kraft beherrscht*"), Nietzsche thus eliminates the meaning of history, and moves in the direction of freedom and utopia, although it is true that his vision of what might replace it, since it is overly intellectual, is no less "supra." It

frees itself from and leaves behind the stranglehold of the past, and responds to an expectation and desire to make the future ("*der Blick in die Vergangenheit drängt . . . zur Zukunft hin*"). Nietzsche's speculation is more realist: it considers the actualization of the forces in the course of a history that does not change and opens itself up to reincarnation. Memory is saved when its brilliance is recovered within this other messianism that he finds in the cyclical culminations of life. The remembered life of history is reaffirmed in the fulfillment of life ("*Historie zum Zwecke des Lebens*"), and individual moments are dissolved in the identity of a force. Memory then relates essentially, if not exclusively, to whatever force has been dominant; there is never anything inferior, and no projection into the future (see HISTORY).

C. Poetic memory: Mnemosyne and Lesmosyne

Memory is the mother of Muses, and Immortality is secondary. Remaking the past, conceived broadly as bringing together all human knowledge, was transformed in ancient societies when it was entrusted to specialists who brought the past alive through words and music. Memory became a professional activity, whose function was linked to feasts and celebration, and to a body of knowledge susceptible to invention, and to the reinventions of multiple horizons.

The word *mnêmê* [μνήμη], which will assume so much importance, is absent from Homer, and only once does he use the word *mnêmosunê* [μνημοσύνη], which gave its name to Memory, mother of the nine Muses, according to Hesiod's *Theogony* (l. 54). In a scene from the *Iliad* in which Hector, in his delirium, dreams of destroying the Greek ships, he again says that he has to keep the fire "in his memory" (*mnêmosunê tis . . . puros . . . genesthô* [μνημοσύνη τις . . . πυρὸς . . . γενέσθω]). The two forms of delirium, the desire for death and poetic power, are joined together. The poet shows, at this crucial moment of an illusion, that he knew the word and uses it. He makes the delirious hero into a poet like himself, arranging reality in his ecstasy as he likes, and at the same time shows that he has chosen to make him speak in this way.

Zeus, in the *Theogony*, makes love to Mnemosyne, and fathers the Muses over the course of nine nights, outside of the circle of the gods. When they are born, they find a home in a world apart, close to the summit of Olympus, where they share with the gods (while being separated from them) freedom from all cares, at an appropriate distance: this is the condition of song (vv. 53–67). The divine reproduces itself with the daughters of Memory; it re-creates itself within a zone of marvelous and unreal autonomy. The gods have access through voice to the joy that they feel from identifying themselves in this mirror, and men allow themselves, through the intervention of the Muses, to be transported far away; through them, they become part of the divine. Art makes them forget their misfortune, and through a temporary cessation of their cares, tears them away from the normal laws of an everyday temporality.

A second Olympus is established next to the gods, a domain of forgetfulness. After all, the gods themselves are involved in the affairs of mankind, whether they control them or not. Forgetting as a way of repairing evil becomes, more absolutely, the condition of the conquest of another world, where in theory nothing is ever forgotten, nothing good, but also nothing evil.

From the word *mnêmosunê*, the poet creates in this same passage the antithetical word *lêsmosunê* [λησμοσύνη] (v. 55), the power of forgetfulness that is communicated. This is not an "intentional paradox" (as West says of v. 55 [Hesiod, *Theogony*]). Forgetting is not the absence of memory, nor its effacement, but more positively, a tearing one away from the avatars of an ordinary alienating existence. Initiating us into the history of the world drives evil out of this world. The word is created not as a negation, but as an analogy and as an active counterpart to memory, a complementary power, which is said to possess the art of driving away misfortune, as Helen's drugs are able to do in volume 4 of the *Odyssey*. Lesmosyne provides a respite from sorrows and pains, and forgetfulness is her work of magic. This counter-term to memory is only attested once more that we know of in Greek literature, in the *Antigone* of Sophocles (v. 156), with the same allusion to an extraordinary overcoming of an ominous reality, the threat of nothingness.

D. The fiction of total knowledge

1. Homer's Muses

The Muses know everything, and represent the abstraction of an all-powerful art. Totality in space and time, in the world or in history, is part of a limitless superhuman memory.

When Homer asks for the help of the Muses, the daughters of Memory, he mentions a particularly precise knowledge, and above all a superlative distinction—"who was the first?" or "the best?": see, for example, *Iliad*, 2.760ff.: "These were the leaders of the Danaans and their lords. But who was far the best among them, do you tell me, Muse—best of the warriors and of the horses that followed with the sons of Atreus?" (*su moi ennepe, Mousa* [σύ μοι ἔννεπε, Μοῦσα]; Homer, *Iliad*). The information presupposes a choice; the Muses have the advantage of knowing everything, and the poet does not know it. The appeal is made to an absolute authority, and song renders even more problematic the knowledge to which poets lay claim. These invocations, through their forcefulness, confer the evidence of necessity upon the statement. It is flawless, without forgetfulness or simply true; the Greek of Homer's time has an adjective that expresses what is "true" by saying "that which is not evasive" (*alêthês* [ἀληθής]), that is, small totalities, every time (see TRUTH).

During the chariot race, old Phoenix is stationed at the finish line. He will be able to recall the race—in its entirety—and tell the truth ("*hô memneôito dromou kai alêtheiên apoeipoi*" [ὦ μεμνέῳτο δρόμου καὶ ἀληθείην ἀποείποι]; 23.361). It is not that he could hide the truth, but that he has to see everything to be able to make distinctions (this and not that), and indeed, the author analyzes the nature of his own speech by this means. He knows that the sum of knowledge that it implies is only a fiction or a construction, and thereby demonstrates the two aspects of absolute memory upon which it is itself based. It aspires to be whole, but the poet does not hide the fact that it is a fiction, pointing to its own limits and inadequacy. He knows that his art is an entirely artificial product, something made, precisely, through art.

2. Baudelaire's Andromache: Suffering considered as a Muse

In the age of modernity, the absolute power of memory as restitution is founded upon exclusion. Baudelaire's "Le cygne"

(The Swan) in *Les fleurs du mal* (Flowers of Evil) is an orchestration of the universal fecundity of exile and absence. Assimilation via the grandeur of failure, which is clearly situated within a Christian tradition, provides a new principle of unification. The modern poet confronts the immensity of literary tradition, and prefigures Mallarmé's *Le livre*, as well as Paul Celan.

In one of the most far-reaching explorations of the faculty of memory that has ever been undertaken, Baudelaire set out to make the widow, starting with Virgil's Andromache, and then going farther back to Hector's wife in Homer, a symbol of absence, welcomed and surpassed in the poetic pathos of a staged allegory. The mind has this power, and overcomes separation because it reconstitutes itself paradoxically in this separation: "*je pense à vous*," "*je ne vois qu'en esprit*," "*je pense à mon grand cygne*" (I think of you, I see only in my mind, I think of my great swan), then: "*Je pense à la négresse*" (I think of the negress): the movement extends to everything that has ever uprooted, exiled, excluded. This determinate absence retracing the fate of all that has not been, but which could or should have been, spreads its influence across every related language that is connected by similar exclusions. As it recalls in the midst of sorrow, the memory of memories is recomposed once again from one language to another (see MALAISE [MELANCHOLY, SPLEEN]). In response to the *immense majesté* (giant majesty) of the widow's grieving we have the fecundity of a "memory," which like the earth is already fertile, containing all that could ever have been said and written later on, as in various poetic projects of total synthesis:

Paris change! mais rien dans ma mélancolie
N'a bougé! palais neufs, échafaudages, blocs,
Vieux faubourgs, tout pour moi devient allégorie
Et mes chers souvenirs sont plus lourds que des rocs.

Aussi devant ce Louvre une image m'opprime:
Je pense à mon grand cygne, avec ses gestes fous,
Comme les exilés, ridicule et sublime
Et rongé d'un désir sans trêve! et puis à vous,
Andromaque . . .

Ainsi dans la forêt où mon esprit s'exile
Un vieux Souvenir sonne à plein souffle du cor!
Je pense aux matelots oubliés dans une île,
Aux captifs, aux vaincus!. . . à bien d'autres encor!

(Paris may change, but in my melancholy mood
Nothing has budged! New palaces, blocks, scaffoldings,
Old neighborhoods, are allegorical for me,
And my dear memories are heavier than stone.

And so outside the Louvre an image gives me pause:
I think of my great swan, his gestures pained and mad,
Like other exiles, both ridiculous and sublime,
Gnawed by his endless longing! Then I think of you,
Fallen Andromache . . .

And likewise in the forest of my exiled soul

Old Memory sings out a full note of the horn!
I think of sailors left forgotten on an isle,
Of captives, the defeated . . . many others more!)

(The Flowers of Evil)

Majesty, although wholly objective, is already the product of an immemorial poetic tradition, and it is this in fact that the poet rediscovers, that he recollects and analyzes. The different levels of the Alexandrine verses transpose the triumph over immediate experience into the most mediated layers of literary culture, whose words the poet allows to resonate in the poem, such as the three syllables of "Helenus." It is as if the most tragic separations were the source of all poetic creations, and conversely, that absence was only accessible via literature. The poet's own exile (*"dans la forêt où mon esprit s'exile"* [in the dim forest to which my soul withdraws]) connects him to all those who have ever been exiled. *"Un vieux souvenir sonne"* (An ancient memory sounds); there is only one, and when he has concluded this extended poetic exploration, he is as old as the world, recollecting every loss that has never been gathered in: *"Je pense"* (I think). By the end, it is everything and anything that the poet has fashioned into poetry because he has lost it. It is also a history of poetry, transformed by its Christian past. Suffering becomes a Muse, who knows everything, and the jubilant poet has a key that opens whatever he touches.

3. Mallarmé's break with tradition: The freeing of forgetfulness

With Mallarmé, the Orphic search for a truth hidden within language leads to a more marked break from previous poetic practices. The transition in his poetry from nothingness to a purer and more autonomous space of language means that he is concerned not only with the forgetfulness that the world has suffered through the ages, nor simply with the forgetfulness of the world as a condition of poetic creation, but with the forgetfulness of false forms of presence in the world, which are nevertheless celebrated poetically. Memory is displaced, and folds back upon itself.

This difference in tone and light can be seen in one of his key sonnets, "Le vierge, le vivace . . . ," which is almost certainly a programmatic and defining statement of his art, and which makes forgetfulness a condition of poetic song. It is not poetry itself, which could equally well glorify the immediacy of life, as it has done ad infinitum in the past. There exists another language, whose precision is quite different, one that is transferred and refined through rejection and negation. The poetic élan and desire to overcome separation that we find previously are transported elsewhere, into something more absolute. These are still maintained in order to counter forgetfulness in memory, but memory now re-emerges on the other side of the nakedness of effacement, and performs a radical break with the world. Memory traces harden in this Orphic language as it becomes abstracted within a third space, and as it rises up out of this poetry that is stripped bare. The passage through negation was a necessary one.

Poetry in the figure of a swan leaves behind it *"ce lac dur que hante sous le givre / le transparent glacier des vols qui n'ont pas fui"* (Beneath the frost of a forgotten lake / Clear flights of glaciers not fled away; trans. John Holcombe). The world of life is thus divided, and also leaves behind the raw matter of frozen traces: *"Un cygne d'autrefois se souvient"* (In past magnificence of another day / The swan remembers). It remembers its lost glory as in a mirror: if it escapes, it is because it has resisted and not given in to incantation and

celebration. Its poetic means have transported it elsewhere, and forgetfulness is the line that is crossed by verbal transcendence, with art finding a way to create for itself another world.

Forgetfulness is the primary condition of poetic creation. In the same way, *Vergessen* in German, in Celan's poetry, is the very movement of words being uprooted, and deliberately becomes part of traditions of language in order to make them say something else. The distant separation from the world of the senses that forgetfulness represents is, then, a rejection of the language that evokes this world; it is a space of both transgression and freedom. All that has ever been said can be said again, and is saved from effacement by a system of references that is each time created anew.

III. Models of Thought

A. Writing

One of the key questions in psychology and gnoseology is that of knowing how memory works. What do we retain, and why do we retain in such different ways, not primarily according to the history of each individual, but when we consider more generally the lesser or greater power of the faculty of memory itself? Plato, before Freud, chooses writing as the model.

1. Plato: Memory and knowledge

All men are different and have their own unique mark. However, when Plato analyzes the error of this proposition, the model proves to be inadequate, and he literally makes signs fly. If inscription was originally engraved, it will subsequently become volatile.

Plato first introduces the psychological or intellectual function of memory, without the recourse to anamnesis, in his *Theaetetus* dialogue, during the discussion of erroneous judgment. He admits "for the sake of argument" that the "ideas" or impressions formed in our minds leave an imprint on something, like a block of wax that we have within us, on which an impression (or *ekmageion* [ἐκμαγεῖον]) is made. It is as if we were reproducing the sigil of a ring within our souls. So there is nothing to stop us having such representations, whether true or false, valid or invalid. Plato's model includes a selection stage—forgetting occurs when the inscriptions are erased and lost (191d)—and an explanation of the inequality among men, which he says is due to the volume and quality of the impregnable mass we each possess (191c). He also makes the connection with cultural memory, which we would call collective memory, so we might describe it as the presence of Memory. It is indeed true that everything is written and discussed using memory, and Plato's model is thus a necessary one (see EIDÔLON).

What we still need to consider, however, is the case where an error is not a matter of correctly identifying an object, but of mistakenly making a false substitution in the order of knowledge available to us. The wax tablet no longer works as a model when we imagine the possibility of not representing something to ourselves that we in fact know very well. Knowledge eludes us if we consider that there is such a thing as a false opinion, and that "we are capable of not knowing what we know." In the dialogue, Socrates introduces an important semantic distinction between having at one's disposal ("possessing," *kektêsthai* [κεκτῆσθαι]), and having concretely in one's hand (*echein* [ἔχειν]), as we would hold a stylus (197b). What we need, more than an erasure or simple virtuality, is a wider effective presence, but a presence that is not actualized. Socrates is thus led, once he presents this deeper understanding of the complex reality of the dynamics of memory in the course of his reasoning, to propose another image. He imagines an enclosure, with a large variety of captive birds that would live in this aviary, whether in large swarms, or in small groups, or even on their own: each has been imagined to conform to the logical structures of thought. The owner tries to catch the one he needs, but does not always succeed. What he wants is there, but he cannot get it—"such that he does not catch and hold in his hands what he had possessed for a long time" (*ha palai ekektêto* [ἃ πάλαι ἐκέκτητο]; *Theaetetus*, 198d).

If Homer, who knew this text well, says *kear* [κέαρ] (or *kêr* [κῆρ]) for "heart," instead of *kardia* [καρδία], as Plato does, this is because he means "wax," *kêros* [κηρός], hiding it by means of the phonic association of poetry: we have to know how to interpret according to the *Cratylus*, and look for wax (*kêros*) in the word "heart" (*kêr*). Memory figured as wax is the "heart" of the soul (*Theaetetus*, 194c), and receptivity is thus defined and attributed to a fundamental technique, like that of the poets. It retains all impressions and ideas, imprinted as a seal is imprinted: the magic of an infinite number of seals is indeed a gift that memory, the mother of the Muses, has made to the human soul (191d).

2. Freud: Writing within the unconscious

Freud's great discoveries—infantile sexuality and repression, and the role of the memory attached to them—can be figured as a kind of writing, as Freud himself does. The history of the transmission of this writing resembles that of his texts, with the phases that precede it, and it follows the period of latency that separates us from the dramas of our inhibited early development. It is the impressions of this resistance and the wounds left behind that enable us to go backward in time, to decipher the "text," and to correct deviations.

The object of the kind of reconstructive memory (*Gedächtnis*) that the psychoanalytic cure attempts to perform exists as a form of writing. For Freud, a language has been primordially engraved in the body, at an age when the infant was merely responding to the urges of its drives and instincts. The infant bears the marks of this phase, like a sigil that has been imprinted, determining its history, or even culture, at a stage that is paradoxically the most vital and energetic of its existence. The deviations from accidents to this natural history set in place an equally primal negation, and they make the body into a text that can be read—or not read.

Freud invokes the model of inscription from the outset, in the founding text of the famous letter to Fliess of 6 December 1896 (no. 52 = 112), written just as he makes his extraordinary discovery. Freud uses the term "writing down" (*Niederschriften*), as if there were within the different layers of the soul a scribe who recorded the perceptions or the accidents and impressions, and put them down on paper, so as to fix them precisely. The basic principle consisted of rigorously separating out consciousness from this memory (*Gedächtnis*), which was buried, and made up of successive inscriptions and different layers. As they are superimposed, there is a process of transcription (or of translation, *Übersetzung*), which is also a kind of rewriting (*Umschrift*), and Freud here also uses the word "transcription" (*Überschrift*). The scribe "transcribes."

According to the model sketched out in his letter, Freud suggests a transcription of the material that was retained in the first level, and made up of pure signs of perception. This transcription first takes place in a second layer, which is defined by the state of non-consciousness (*Unbewußtsein*), then in a third, which is characterized as "pre-consciousness" (*Vorbewußtsein*). This latter phase is dependent on representations of words, communicating with our official ego, and precedes the subsequent development of a "consciousness of thought" (*Denkbewußtsein*). The work of translation takes place at each moment of transition from one phase of life to another, and it occasionally goes wrong. The inhibitions that it runs up against explain the origin of neuroses. There are "residues" or "surviving" remainders. Freud's terminology is innovative and bold. It suggests that something "survives" its previous stage (*Überleben*), and that these survivors are thereafter elements out of place. The different modes of writing enter into conflict, and normal development is arrested. Traumas can be understood as "fixations" in the strong sense of the term, hard obstacles that are the result of something that has not passed through or that did not work properly. Repression (*Verdrängung*) is in no sense the same as forgetfulness, but it is rather conceived as a resistance that redirects the "thrust" (*Drang*) of the drive, as if into a blind alley. It is through a kind of rereading, using the verbal representations acquired during the third stage prior to puberty, that one can go back and reactivate the unconscious. This return through memory is reparative, and can possibly bring about a recovery since the earlier repression may not have been firmly established at the following stage and can be eliminated. A partially intelligible memory opens up a path into the registers and archives of the unconscious, and enables a phased interpretation of the amnesia with the help of a memory. Dimly remembered perceptions, which are nevertheless conscious, force open the door leading to the essential mysteries of early childhood life (see DRIVE and VERNEINUNG).

3. Bergson: The traces of lived experience in involuntary memory

In the chapter on "The Two Forms of Memory" Henri Bergson draws a distinction between, on one hand, a memory that eludes representation, as if it has been learned, and that is revealed to be a rationalist prejudice, an ideology inhibiting the perception of, on the other hand, another kind of memory, one that is "spontaneous" and "perfect from the outset." As he says about this second sort of memory, "time can add nothing to its image without disfiguring it" since it is a possession that is properly our own. Although time moves forward in its duration, it retains "in memory its place and date." The terms Bergson uses here are important since what counts is "a memory" (*souvenir*) that must not become "foreign to our past life," that is, alienated by everything else, by external influences.

Ernst Cassirer, in the third volume of his *Philosophie der symbolischen formen*, reproached Bergson for not having considered the intuition of time as a more global functional unity, which would include all of the different directions of our perception and our consciousness, future as well as past. Bergson's dissociation of the horizon of memory from the horizon of expectation did not seem legitimate to Cassirer, but these are no doubt two equally valid points of view, and one does not necessarily have to absorb the other.

Bergson wrote *Matter and Memory* at the same time Freud was making his discoveries. What is under debate in both cases is the identity and irreducible experiences of an individual person. Philosophy opens the way for a new form of "self" through the notion of involuntary memory, Proust's reading of which produced a novelistic exploration that was unprecedented in its psychological depth. The fracturing of perspectives was fruitful, and almost fatal for the chosen domain of investigation (we might recall Epicurus, who was already attempting to construct intellectually a trouble-free art of living, in his search for *ataraxia* [see GLÜCK and PLEASURE]). Knowledge of the past becomes a distinct act; it belongs to us, and is devoid of anxiety. We are ultimately indebted to Freud's work for this principle.

Bergson isolates spontaneous memory, as distinct from learned memory, which is part of learning the mechanisms that are indispensable to our role as social actors. He analyzes lived experience and discovers the succession of unitary and irreducible monads of which it is made up. The work of memory is not freely organized, but is preformed in the history of the subject, who provides the self with a multitude of "dates," each one complex. The self tries to find its way among these, hoping to identify the things that count and that he has already retained. His memory will thus be made up of a multitude of memories, which are specifically limited to the experience of the person who lives with them.

4. Benjamin: Layer memory

Walter Benjamin describes the value of Proust's search in terms of its transcendental dimension. The self, in recollecting itself, discovers its being by recognizing the different stages of awareness of what it is doing. As a translator of Proust, Benjamin in a short text "Ausgraben und Erinnern" (Excavation and Memory) retranslates the work of uncovering. He compares it to an archeologist's analysis of the layers of soil: "he will be like a man who digs" (*wie ein Mann der gräbt*). In doing so, he liberates images, which are the buried treasures of our past, provided the digger, or searcher, can indicate the place and the process of discovery: "being epic and rhapsodic in the strictest sense, recollection as true *Erinnerung* has to provide at the same time an image of the person remembering." The act is illuminated in the silhouette of the digger. The image is elevated to the status of a symbol, and Benjamin breaks down into its constituent elements the German "synonym" for *Denkbild* (alongside *Sinnbild*; the title *Denkbild*, borrowed from a series of texts, groups together the disparate texts). By digging down into a word, we learn that what we remember is the image of the "thought" that penetrates this word. The word *Denkbild* has its tradition, and Herder, for example, wrote: "learn to understand these symbols [*diese Denkbilder*]," that is, those images in which thought is held fast (see BILD).

B. Memory as a storehouse

1. German, between the actualization of the past and accumulation, *Erinnerung* and *Gedächtnis*

There are two words in German with quite different values, *Erinnerung* and *Gedächtnis*, to which the French terms *souvenir* and *mémoire* only partially correspond. The first indicates an action, within the individual confines of a person's inner self, as if actualizing one of a thousand possible memories. The second, closer to a cerebral capability than to the soul, calls to mind a casket and its treasures because of the suffix and the analogies one could make between *Gedächtnis* and a word such as *Behältnis*, a box. An object is enclosed and if one has a "good" memory, it is that much more safely preserved. This intensifier is formed from the root of the verb *denken* (to think), through an apophonic play on words. The basic tenses of *denken* are the preterite *dachte*, and the participle *gedacht*, which one could associate with the idea of a cover and a roof (*Dach*). The faculty of memory is in a sense multiplied in this shelter where everything that has been thought is gathered together.

2. Hegel: The concept and its associations

For Hegel, memory becomes an integral part of the dynamics of the unfolding of Spirit. The dimension opened up by language with the word *Erinnerung* allows Hegel to situate memory, and to deepen the link that connects it to the successive structures of history. He understands it, in the *Phenomenology of Spirit*, as a movement toward a superior, and more "inner" appearance, of substance when it is exposed to truth. The movement of interiorization becomes an *internal* memory, or *Erinnerung*. As substance acquires greater depth through this attention to the past, the science of memorized history is founded. Elsewhere, the progression of world history is presented as self-examination and self-discovery. Absolute spirit folding itself back upon its own foundation is translated by a turn of phrase borrowed from religious practice: *insichgehen*, "to enter into oneself." Interiorization encompasses traditional self-examination and the entire dimension of self-reflection.

3. Poetic memory integrated into the philosophical system: *Erinnerung* and *Andenken*

The *Phenomenology* integrates early Greek poetry into the evolution of self-consciousness. The pathos of the poet enables him to escape from domination by raw nature. This is an effect of developing one's memory, *mnêmosunê*, in which a movement of reflexive thought becomes manifest, involving a reconsideration of one's given state (*Besinnung*) and the acquisition of an internal reference. Interiority includes the interiorized memory (*Erinnerung*) of the immediacy of the previous stage, which is thus overcome. It was still deprived of freedom, and with writing, as well as music, the phase including the liberation of consciousness reaches a second level.

The function of memory brings with it the painful rift of poetry. For Hölderlin, who experiences this rupture as a retreat of the gods of antiquity, his last hymns, entitled *Memory* (*Andenken*) or *Mnemosyne*, suggest the primordial role of the poet: it is his "fidelity" (*Treue*) that preserves. Poetry aspires to reconcile the alien with what is properly one's own, all the while acknowledging concrete differences, and under the threat of memory's collapse.

4. Heidegger's double interiorization

The movement traced by Hegel is taken up again by Heidegger. In his *Kant* from 1929 (*Kant und das Problem der Metaphysik*), Heidegger reinterprets the anamnesis of earlier visions of the soul in Plato in terms of fundamental ontology. He presents it now as a founding act of the human condition of being-there (*Dasein*): "It is indeed a question of remembering again, of anamnesis (*wie der Erinnerung*), as Plato says: but authentic 'remembering' (*Erinnerung*) must at all times interiorize the interiorized object." This doubling of Hegelian interiority may seem surprising ("*das Erinnerte verinnern*"), but the word incorporates an analysis of the concept and moves beyond a tautology by a dimension opened up by the word, which divides the concept. What is "recalled" is not called by consciousness, but comes forth and imposes itself. The object is nothing other than the essential finitude of *Dasein*; it comes and takes hold of what opens itself to finitude. The movement is thus reversed, and the notable difference is that the interiorization is not properly speaking an interiorization of the self, as it was for Hegel. From a more theological perspective, welcoming the fundamental truth defines the authentic existence of the self. Memory will be a matter, then, of "letting [fundamental truth] more and more come to us," in its innermost possibility, where innermost means constitutive or foundational. Memory is determined as a form of re-collection. *Erinnerung*: no other word in any other language would allow one to think and translate this re-collection, and taking it one step further, interiority will be given to the truth itself that encompasses it. German culture based on Lutheranism ultimately focuses on this doubled reintegration of its primary movement.

5. Heidegger's Hölderlin: Truth concentrated into
Andenken and *Verdankung*, the words for memory

After 1934, Heidegger locates "what thinking is" in the sphere of language. His argument unfolds notably in his meditations on and paraphrases of Hölderlin's poem "Mnemosyne," which for him prefigures a source of poetic effusion that relates less to historically determinate memory than to a call emanating from thought itself. In Hölderlin's poem we see a number of words merge together, like *Andenken*, or memory in the sense of a thought that is attached to an object (*An-denken*), or a concentrated accumulation, like *Andacht des Andenken*, where in addition to memory we have, with the apophony, religious fervor or contemplation or, by means of another vector, gratitude in the archaism *Gedanc*, in *Dank* and *Verdankung*: one could easily get lost or go under. It is no doubt as a reaction against Heidegger's emphatic and expansive call for an original thinking, that Paul Celan, in his own semantic network, so clearly connected the word "thought," *Denken*, to the constant memorability of historical truth, assigning to it another kind of origin by playing one "thought" off against another. The title of one of his poems, "Andenken," refers to the most deliberately personal experience.

C. Paul Celan: The breath of memory

Poetry, like art, can be experimental. A short poem, from *Breathturn*, presents memory, inherent in the matter of all poetic language, as able to come alive on its own through a particular effect of concentration. It is as if, reproducing itself by a breath, it were the creator of everything.

The text encompasses a singular moment, marked by an exceptional happiness in which everything is sketched out and writes itself. There is nothing supernatural about the effect of this moment of grace, but as always with Celan, it charts a new path. The poem is composed in a process of self-understanding and self-discovery. A fist (poetry) closes on the emblematic device it is grasping, though these are only stones or pieces of gravel. Poetic speech is in the stones:

DEN VERKIESELSTEN SPRUCH in der Faust,
vergißt du, daß du vergißt,
am Handgelenk scießen
blinkend die Satzzeichen an
durch die zum Kamm
gespaltene Erde
kommen die Pausen geritten
dort, bei
der Opferstaudede,
wo das Gedächtnis entbrennt
greift euch der Eine
Hauch auf.

(THE SILICIFIED SAYING in the fist,
you forget that you forget,
blinking, the punctuation marks
crystallize at the wrist,
through the earth
cleft to the crest
the pauses come riding,
there, by
the sacrifice-bush,
where memory catches fire,
the One Breath
seizes you.)

The "you" is the poet, and an "I" is addressing him. The hand of the "you" is holding the pen, and it is associated here with the reduction of writing and the rendering-rhythmical of nothingness. The blaze of memory itself is absorbed by the virtuality of a speaking that would conform to it entirely.

The debris has been shaped. A piece of glass calls out and attracts punctuation marks, is given form and structure. The movement of concentration is sketched: the earth cracks open, and a ridge bursts forth. A moment of suspension thus rises up out from the verbal magma. It assumes a figure thanks to the pauses, and absence itself folds back on itself. The expectation of something taking a fixed form condenses the incandescence of memory, so it is no longer either the circumscribed object, or any faculty that is unfolding within language, but it is caught within an involuted movement and lets out a simple breath. This unique breath takes hold of the signs, and at the same time of the poet, who in this instance "forgets to forget," as he usually does.

The paradox is only an apparent one. The disconnectedness from the horizons that are set out suggests disappearance, followed by a return of everyday meanings. The dead, in their muteness, find a place where they can be "unforgotten" (*unvergessen*; see the poem "Still Life" [*Stilleben*]). Differentiation is specific: the survivors from the work of selection are exempted from methodical forgetting, they are its raison d'être and its negation. The word "memory" comes alive, and is expressed in its condensation, it speaks to itself.

IV. Forgetfulness as a Condition of Memory

A. The words for forgetfulness and memory: Connotations of different languages

Memory has a double status in modern languages. It is either invoked or experienced. How this duality is translated in each language is essential since it results from the fact that the past, whether lived or imagined, personal or collective, is both always there and absent. It is forgotten, or on the contrary comes to meet us and imposes itself, which is why there is a constant crossover between invocation and visitation.

The range of associations relating to the ways one establishes a past or distant event, in one's mind or body, covers a broad spectrum beyond the specialized words.

In French, the abstract value of the intensifier *rappeler* (to remind; *appeler intensément*, to call intensely) appears very early on in the language, in the sense of "to bring to consciousness or memory." It is the origin of the pronominal expression *se rappeler* (to recall; before 1673), which then begins to compete with *se souvenir de* (to remember), derived from the Latin *subvenire*, "to come to the aid of, to help," then "to come to mind, to occur." The impersonal expression *il me souvient* (I recollect) and the intransitive are older than the pronominal verb *se souvenir* (fourteenth century), which became established in parallel with *se rappeler*. In the one case, help comes by itself, it is experienced passively as a gift; the other conveys the idea of effort and the notion of success or of sovereignty, which is perhaps even magical. We can indeed remember the dead, and so enter into the unknown. "Calling" is also expressed in German as *in Erinnerung rufen*. French, though, emphasizes the act, or actualization, and does not directly link the verbal activity to the site itself of memory, nor to the faculty of memory, nor to a present knowledge. In English, for example, "to remember" is also related more to "remembrance" than the act of memory is to the matter itself that is remembered.

To forget is to not reach, or on the contrary to lose, and can also be an absolute tabula rasa. The etymology of the German word for forgetting, *Vergessen*, like the English "forget," expresses failure or falling short. The search or pursuit has amounted to nothing, the prize has eluded us. In fact, the German ear, because of a phonic play of assonances, associates forgetting with a more widespread loss, by way of the verb meaning "to pour," *giessen* (*ich vergass*, "I forgot"; *ich vergoss*, "I poured out"). It is the opposite of the horn of plenty, a current that sweeps us away. The French word *oubli* does not convey this same dynamism.

The French verb *oublier* goes back to the popular Latin *oblitare*, present in all popular Gallo-Roman dialects, though alongside the more eloquent verb *desmembrar* used in the Southwest (Sp., archaically, said: *desmemorar*), based on *memorare*, to "unremember." In classical Latin, *oblivisci*, along with the participle *oblitus*, is considered a metaphor borrowed from writing (see Bréal, then Ernout and Meillet). The word is related to *oblinere*, "to efface, wipe out," and is also associated with *levis*, "smooth" (from the Gr. *leios* [λεῖος]), implying the absence of any roughness and difference, things being reduced to a white powder. French retains something of this perhaps in the idea of a flat vacuity, and Mallarmé connected the word *oubli* to *aboli* (abolished), which opens out onto nothingness.

■ See Box 1.

B. Forgetfulness within memory

Forgetfulness, with its power to tear one away from fullness of meaning, offers a means of perpetuating memory. Memory thinks, but only manages to do so through forgetting if instead of signifying loss, flight, or abandonment, memory allows us on the contrary to reconstitute a reference. We choose what counts.

While in French one thinks about someone (*pense à quelqu'un*), or has a thought for someone (*une pensée*), in

---

1

French, between thought and dream

While other languages, such as English, German, Spanish, or Italian, only have one word for dream (Ger. *Traum*, Sp. *sueño*, Ital. *sogno*), French has two: on the one hand, *songe* (from the Lat. *somnium*), and on the other *rêve*, derived either from a form of the Latin *rabies* (rabies) or from the popular Latin for "vagabond," *exvagus*, or according to others from a form of Gallo-Roman, *exvagares*, from *exvadere*, "to go out." "Delirium" overlaps with "escape" in our imagination, unless one is in fact superimposed on the other. As well as the "interpretation of dreams (*rêves*)," French also has the expression "key to our dreams (*songes*)," and this singular duality has its own history. *Songer*, the verbal form, has a noble lineage. Its values can be situated in a context of quite wide semantic freedom. The word oscillates between the rigor of focused thought (*songez-y bien*, "pay close attention to this, think it over carefully"), and the vagueness of the imagination (*à quoi songes-tu donc?* "what are you dreaming about?"). The evolution of the language meant that it rather dominated the field, referring on the one hand to the rational operation of "thinking," derived in Romance languages from the Latin intensive *pensare*, "to weigh," which connects reflexive activity to evaluation and appreciation, not present in *songer*, and on the other hand, suggests the opposite world of dream experiences. The lexical unity became fractured and split off in two different directions. *Penser* gained the upper hand over *songer*, pushing *songe* into the realm of illusory appearance. *Rêve*, which was used to mean delirium or ecstatic extravagance, has only recently supplanted *songe*, without eliminating it entirely, however, such that when one is *songeant*, one is sometimes thinking, concentrating, or recalling, and sometimes one is dreaming, or letting oneself be carried away.

German the verb *denken* also means "to remember," to the point where no distinction is made between the two verbs, as one does in more formal language with the prefix *ge-* in *gedenken*, which denotes the reverence of a solemn and ritual commemoration. Celan, who makes the extermination of the Jews the central focus of his poetry, uses one word for the other, thinking for remembering, and restricts its meaning, binding thought and memory together. This is a limit case, and perhaps an exemplary one. To think is to "enter forgetfulness"—as one enters a religion—in order to recall, to think about nothing but the object, which never moves away and which shapes the form of every content, whatever it may be, which is created by history. "Thoughts" (*Gedanken*) will thus be determined and structured from within by the power of verbal creation. French is unable to say this because thought and memory are not similarly bound together, nor linked to gratitude (*Dank*), as they are in English as well ("think" and "thank"). But they were originally, if thought was first of all formed by life returning back to its past, where it was expressed and described. Reflection developed within the autonomy of language which, turning upon itself, masters its own inventiveness.

We can envisage not holding on to one meaning, as a deepening of our understanding of an event in its duration, as if it were a response, an echo, a replica. However, to be free of a (heavy) past—something life demands as time progresses: *this* responds to a very different, and contrary, objective. In this case, the present remains shaped by a choice, and imposes a certain way of doing things, a judgment, a practice, and a politics.

▪ See Boxes 2 and 3.

Jean Bollack

2

Erinnerung (recollection) and *Gedächtnis* (memory) in Hegel

The German word *Erinnerung* (recollection) is based on the verb *erinnern* (to recollect)—literally, "to interiorize"—and signifies the internalizing act whereby one remembers some particular thing one knows or has encountered in the past. *Gedächtnis* (memory), on the other hand, derives from the verb *denken* (to think) and suggests a remembering capacity involving an abstract or generalizing element associated with thinking. The distinction between *Gedächtnis* and *Erinnerung* in Hegel's philosophical system has been traced to Aristotle's treatise *De memoria et reminiscentia*, which was posited as the source of the differentiation of two kinds or modes of memory in medieval philosophy from Augustine to Duns Scotus (see RT: *Etymological Dictionary of Greek*).

Erinnerung is differentiated from *Gedächtnis* in the context of Hegel's analysis of representation (*Vorstellung*) in the *Encyclopedia of Science* as the transition from perception or intuition (*Anschauung*) to thinking (*Denken*). Representation is divided into three stages with intellect progressing from *Erinnerung* (recollection) to *Einbildungskraft* (imagination) and *Gedächtnis* (memory). Here is the passage from paragraph 451 of the *Encyclopedia*:

a. The first of these stages we call recollection (inwardization) in the peculiar meaning of the word according to which it consists in the involuntary calling up of a content that is already ours. Recollection forms the most abstract stage of intelligence operating with representations. Here the represented content is still the same as in intuition; in the latter it receives its verification, just as, conversely, the content of intuition verifies itself in my representation. We have, therefore, at this stage a content that is not only intuitively perceived in its immediacy, but is at the same time recollected, inwardized, posited as mine. As thus determined, the content is what we call image.

b. The second stage in this sphere is imagination. Here there enters the opposition between my subjective or represented content, and the intuitively perceived content, of the object. Imagination fashions for itself a content peculiar to it by thinking the object, by bringing out what is universal in it, and giving it determinations that belong to the ego. In this way imagination ceases to be a merely formal recollection (inwardization) and becomes a recollection that affects the content, generalizes it, thus creating general representations or ideas. Since at this stage the opposition of subjectivity and objectivity is dominant, the unity here of these determinations cannot be an immediate unity as at the stage of mere recollection, but only a restored unity. The manner in which this restoration takes place is that the intuitively perceived external content is subjugated to the mentally represented content that has been raised to universality, is reduced to a sign of the latter content which is, however, thereby made objective, external, is imaged.

c. Memory is the third stage of representation. Here, on the one hand, the sign is inwardized, taken up into intelligence; on the other hand, the latter is thereby given the form of something external and mechanical, and in this way a unity of subjectivity and objectivity is produced that forms the transition to thought as such.

According to a traditional interpretation, the developmental, historical movement of *Geist* (spirit) in Hegel involves a flowing, cumulative process in which particular *Erinnerungen* are converted into the generality of *Gedächtnis*. This relation is still to be found in the interplay of recollection and memory in Bergson, according to which *souvenir* adds up to *mémoire*: "*Il n'y a pas de conscience sans mémoire, pas de continuation d'un état sans l'addition, au sentiment présent, du souvenir des moments passés. En cela consiste la durée. La durée intérieure est la vie continue d'une mémoire qui prolonge le passé dans le présent*" (*Essai sur les données immédiates de la conscience*). The same pattern can be discerned in the hermeneutic model of experience of Hans-Georg Gadamer, despite his critique of the synthesizing movement of Hegel's dialectic. From the perspective of hermeneutic consciousness "the real" (*das Wirkliche*) or "real experience" (*wirkliche Erfahrung*) is handed down "out of the truth of recollecting" (*aus der Wahrheit des Erinnerns*).

In an influential lecture delivered at Harvard University in 1980 and published later in the posthumous collection of essays entitled *Aesthetic Ideology*, Paul de Man proposed an interpretation of the relationship between *Erinnerung* and *Gedächtnis* in Hegel that challenged the traditional view. De Man approaches Hegel's *Lectures on Aesthetics* and in particular the crucial distinction between symbol (*Symbol*) and sign (*Zeichen*) by way of the account of *Erinnerung* and *Gedächtnis* in the *Encyclopedia*. De Man starts with the following description of the interaction between thinking (*Denken*) and perception or intuition (*Anschauung*): "Thought subsumes the infinite singularity and individuation of the perceived world under ordering principles that lay claim to generality. The agent of this appropriation is language." A corresponding movement is discerned by de Man on the level of representation in the transition from recollection to memory in the *Encyclopedia*. For de Man, in contrast to Bergson, there is memory only without recollection: "memory effaces remembrance (or recollection)," he argues, "just as the I effaces itself" by entering into or being appropriated by the generality of language. "The faculty that enables thought to exist," de Man continues, "also makes its preservation impossible." Thus, he concludes, Hegel's *Lectures on Aesthetics* are "double and duplicitous": they represent the efforts of *Gedächtnis* and the order of the sign to preserve aesthetics by sweffacing the singularity of *Erinnerung* that is the basis of Hegel's symbolic concept of art. Thus, the famous statement by Hegel—"art for us is a thing of the past"—could be translated on the basis of de Man's interpretation as "*Erinnerung* for us is a matter of *Gedächtnis*."

On the occasion of de Man's death in 1983, Jacques Derrida delivered a series of lectures later published as *Mémoires for Paul de Man* that were in part an extension of the reinterpretation of *Erinnerung* and *Gedächtnis* just sketched. Derrida is especially interested in elaborating an affirmative dimension to de Man's critique of Hegel. "We are quite close here," Derrida observes at one point, "to a thinking memory (*Gedächtnis*) whose movement carries an essential affirmation, a kind of engagement beyond negativity, that is to say, also beyond the bereaved interiority of introjection (*Erinnerung*): a thinking memory of fidelity, a reaffirmation of engagement." Thought, Derrida writes, is not "bereaved interiorization; it thinks at boundaries, it thinks the boundary, the limit of interiority." Thus, for Derrida, thinking affirms itself at the limit of Hegel's distinction between *Erinnerung* and *Gedächtnis*.

Kevin McLaughlin

BIBLIOGRAPHY

Bergson, Henri. *Essai sur les données immédiates de la conscience.* Edited by Arnaud Bouaniche. Paris: Presses Universitaires de France, 2007.

Translation by F. L. Pogson: *Time and Free Will: An Essay on the Immediate Data of Consciousness.* Mineola, NY: Dover Publications, 2001.

Bloch, David. *Aristotle on Memory and Recollection: Text, Translation, Interpretation, and Reception in Western Scholasticism.* Leiden: Brill, 2007.

Bormann, C. von. "Erinnerung." In *Historisches Wörterbuch der Philosophie*, vol. 2. Edited by Joachim Ritter. Basel: Schwabe Verlag, 1972.

de Man, Paul. "Sign and Symbol in Hegel's Aesthetics." In *Aesthetic Ideology*. Minneapolis: University of Minnesota Press, 1986. 91–104.

Derrida, Jacques. *Mémoires for Paul de Man.* Translated by Cecile Lindsay, Jonathan Culler, and Eduardo Cadava; translations edited by Avital Ronell and Eduardo Cadava. New York: Columbia University Press, 1986.

Gadamer, Hans-Georg. *Truth and Method.* 2nd rev. ed. Translated by J. Weinsheimer and D. G. Marshall. New York: Crossroad, 1989.

Hegel, G.W.F. *Philosophy of Mind* (*Part III of the Encyclopedia of the Philosophical Sciences*). Translated by William Wallace, together with the *Zusätze* in Boumann's 1845 edition, translated by A. V. Miller and with foreword by J. N. Findlay. Oxford: Oxford University Press, 1971.

3

Erfahrung (German)—Experience (English)

Experience (*Erfahrung*) which is passed on from mouth to mouth is the source (*Quelle*) from which all storytellers have drawn. . . . "When someone goes on a trip, he has something to tell about," goes the German saying, and people imagine the storyteller as someone who has come from afar. But they enjoy no less listening to the man who has stayed at home, making an honest living, and who knows the local tales and traditions.

Walter Benjamin, "The Storyteller"

Translated by the English word "experience," *Erfahrung* derives from the verb *fahren* (signifying "to go" or "to travel") and contains the sense of knowledge to which one has come through something like a journey. *Erfahrung* is thus rooted in the concept of a knowledge attained from observations made in the course of an event or an encounter. This knowledge is not limited to the person making the observations but rather includes those to whom it can be passed along and handed down as part of a tradition. The evidence of *Erfahrung* is communicable; it is knowledge that can be imparted and learned. "Learning" is another signification of *Erfahrung* in the sense both that one learns something from one's own experience and that one can learn of something communicated by someone else, for example, through a letter or a newspaper: "*durch einen Brief, durch die Zeitung etwas erfahren.*" The adjective *erfahren* is applied to those who are skillful, expert, or practiced in a particular occupation, such as a skillful doctor (*ein erfahrener Arzt*) or an expert tradesman (*ein erfahrener Fachmann*). Unlike the obsolete signification of the English word "experience" or the sense carried still today by the French word *expérience*, *Erfahrung* does not include the scientific meaning of what we now call "experiment" (from the Lat. *experiri* and the Gr. *empeiria* both based on roots signifying "to try"). Nevertheless the path by which *Erfahrung* travels to become a crux in modern German philosophy in the work of Immanuel Kant passes by way of the experimental method developed in natural science during the early modern period.

As with "experience," the philosophical origins of *Erfahrung* are traced to the concept of *empeiria* in Aristotle, especially to his *Metaphysics*, where it is defined as the specifically human capacity or faculty produced by memory: "The animals other than man live by appearances and memories, and have but little of connected experience; but the human race lives also by art and reasonings. Now from memory experience is produced in men; for the several memories of the same thing produce finally the capacity for a single experience" (980b). The product of memory, Aristotle specifies, experience is knowledge of the particular (what the Scholastics would later call *cognitio singularium*), rather than the general, which is the domain of art (981a). This definition of experience as the capacity for knowledge of the

(continued)

(continued)

particular produced by memory in human beings is cited and recited throughout medieval and early modern philosophy from Albertus Magnus and Thomas Aquinas to Thomas Hobbes and Christian Wolff.

The new scientific theory advanced by Francis Bacon in the seventeenth century with its emphasis on experimentation reinterpreted the concept of experience in effect by reaching back to its etymological roots and insisting on the connection to "trying" and "trial." Most importantly, Bacon argued that experience was not a faculty or capacity but rather a method and a process—not an ability but a way to come to knowledge. Bacon differentiated between *experimentia vaga* and *experientia ordinata* and asserted the superiority of regulated experiment over vague experience as the true path to knowledge. Bacon's distinction in the word "experience," more precisely in the Latin word *experientia*, of these two significations is suggested by the nineteenth-century English translation of the *Novum Organum* (1720) that remained a standard for more than a century: "And an astonishing thing it is to one who rightly considers the matter, that no mortal should have seriously applied himself to the opening and laying out of a road for the human understanding direct from the sense, by a course of experiment (*experimentia*) orderly conducted and well built up, but that all has been left either to the mist of tradition, or the whirl and eddy of argument, or the fluctuations and mazes of chance and of vague and ill-digested experience (*experimentia*)." The two senses discovered by Bacon in the single Latin word *experientia* that are translated into English in this passage as "experience" and "experiment" correspond in German to *Erfahrung* and *Versuch*. The Grimms' dictionary (RT: *Deutsches Wörterbuch*) traces the emergence of *Versuch* in the sense of a scientific experiment to seventeenth-century natural science and cites Wolff's allusion in the early eighteenth century to the distinction between *gemeine Erfahrungen* (ordinary experiences), on the one hand, and *Versuche* (experiments), on the other.

The most important condition for the emergence of *Erfahrung* as a pivotal concept in modern German philosophy was the development of the empiricist theory of experience by John Locke in *An Essay Concerning Human Understanding* (1690) and David Hume in *An Enquiry Concerning Human Understanding* (1748). Locke and Hume returned to and reworked the Aristotelian sense of *empeiria* as a human faculty, rather than deriving from it a method of scientific trial in the

manner of Bacon. Instead of being produced by memory, however, experience for the empiricists was the result of perception. The human capacity for experience, according to these theories of "understanding," is a potentiality to be receptive to inner and outer impressions. The empiricists made the radical claim that receptivity was the source, not just of knowledge of the particular, but of all knowledge. Bacon had ordained that the experimental method was to begin with what he called *experientia literata*—emphasizing the indispensable work of the experimental scientist who writes down and archives the results that form the basis of his "interpretation of nature" (*interpretatio naturae*). At the hands of the empiricists nature writes itself down on human beings who become their own archive. Thus we come into the world, as Locke famously says, as a "white paper, void of all characters, without any ideas" and nature inscribes itself on us as experience.

The ground shifts in Kant's project for a transcendental critical philosophy. With the appearance of the *Critique of Pure Reason* in 1781 *Erfahrung* breaks free of the empiricist context and takes up a position that inaugurates the speculative tradition in German thought and redefines the philosophical landscape of the West. *Erfahrung* for Kant is the result not of receptivity to sense impressions but of the ability to judge inner and outer objects that affect the mind. Transcendental critique is, in other words, concerned with experience as a possibility—with "our mode of cognition of objects insofar as this is to be possible a priori." Kant thus begins the exposition of *Erfahrung* in the first part of the first *Critique* with the deduction of space and time as elements in which the appearance of objects—of experience—becomes possible. Although it does not come from experience, the knowledge to which we come in transcendental critique is *of* experience, specifically, of the possibility of experience. Kant's theory of *Erfahrung* is therefore not to be understood as simply turning away from empirical experience—it might be more accurately described as a translation of this experience into the *Erfahrung* of transcendental critique.

Erfahrung in Kant was the key source of the revival of interest in his work during the second half of the nineteenth century. In the German context, for example, Hermann Cohen's study of this topic, *Kants Theorie der Erfahrung* (first published in 1871 and in a revised and expanded second edition in 1885), became a canonical work among the Neo-Kantians, in particular, those centered at the University of Marburg. At one point in his interpretation Cohen underlines the following sentence at the beginning of the

introduction to the second edition of the first *Critique* as encapsulating Kant's critique of British empiricism, and in particular of Hume: "But although all our cognition commences (*anheben*) with experience," Kant writes, "yet it does not on that account all arise (*entspringen*) from experience." The difference that the transcendental turn makes, Cohen observes, can be understood as the distinction between *anheben* (commencing or beginning) and *entspringen* (arising or springing from) in this assertion. The first part of this sentence acknowledges the skepticism of Hume's insistence on experience as the ground of knowledge; but the second part makes room for the transcendental thesis that sense impressions do not represent the "final formal element of experience." *Erfahrung* also includes a dimension—Cohen calls it an "extension" (*Ergänzung*) or a "complement" (*Complement*)—of a priori possibility. We can have knowledge of objects that we do not encounter in the space and time of a psychological process, Kant proposes, by "only what we ourselves lay into them" (*nur was wir selbst in sie legen*). Cohen glosses: "What kind of ground is it that we ourselves ground? It should be not a beginning but a springing from (*Entspringen*), but this springing from occurs indeed out of a spring (*Quelle*) that we ourselves dig. . . . In ourselves lies the springing point (*Springpunkt*) of all knowing."

Among the most important philosophical developments in the twentieth century that derive from the return to Kant's theory of *Erfahrung* is Walter Benjamin's literary and social criticism. Although he was influenced, especially in his early work, by the writings of Cohen and his student, Ernst Cassirer, Benjamin was by no means an adherent of Neo-Kantianism, much less a mere follower. Cohen and his colleagues in Marburg believed that the "extension" that is the source of *Erfahrung*—its originary possibility—could be discovered and described scientifically through the application of the non-Euclidean geometry of spacetime. Benjamin's early essay, "Two Poems by Friedrich Hölderlin" (1914–15) shows some signs of experimentation along these lines. Yet in another essay from this same early period, "On the Program for the Coming Philosophy" (1917), Benjamin harshly criticizes what he regards as the mechanically "empirical" concept of *Erfahrung* promulgated on the basis of Kant (indeed, he calls this concept "Kantian"). When the question of *Erfahrung* resurfaces in his writings of the 1930s, in particular, in his critical essays such as "Experience and Poverty" (1933), "The Storyteller" (1936), and "On Some Motifs in

Baudelaire" (1939), Benjamin explicitly refers to Henri Bergson's critique of Kant's theory of *Erfahrung*, especially as it extends from Bergson's early work translated as *Time and Free Will: An Essay on the Immediate Data of Consciousness* (1889) to *Matter and Memory* (1896). Bergson's critique in the former of Kant's transcendental deduction of space and time in the first *Critique* becomes the basis of the concept of memory developed in the latter. What especially attracts Benjamin's attention is that Bergson's theory of memory offers an account of the dynamic communicability of experience. Bergsonian *mémoire*, Benjamin proposes, reveals that "*Erfahrung* is matter of tradition"—this, he goes on to explain, constitutes the "philosophical structure" of *Erfahrung*. At this point Benjamin draws on a Hegelian topos and distinguishes between, on the one hand, experience as *Erfahrung*, which is based on *Gedächtnis* (the German translation offered for Bergson's *mémoire*), and, on the other, a kind of experience he calls *Erlebnis* (citing Wilhelm Dilthey), which is derived from *Erinnerung* (a word employed by Hegel to characterize an interiorizing form of subjective memory that has been translated into English as "recollection"). The specific connection between experience and memory in Benjamin's theory of *Erfahrung* is articulated through his manipulation of these four terms for which English equivalents have proven elusive.

If Benjamin's theory of *Erfahrung* attempts to emancipate itself from the scientific concept of experience advanced by Cohen and the Neo-Kantians, on the one side, it also seeks to free itself from the antiscientific concept of experience proposed by Bergson, on the other. It is therefore important to take note of how Benjamin departs from the Bergsonian project of providing an account of experience, and in particular the experience of time (*la durée*) as it is truly lived. Unlike Bergson, whose critique of Kant argues that true experience occurs in a temporality fundamentally different and apart from spatial extension—indeed, Bergson sees spatialization as the hallmark of the inauthentic, mechanized time of science—Benjamin insists repeatedly on what he calls the "interpenetration" (*Durchdringung*) of time and space. According to a similar logic, Benjamin describes the experience of the "standardized, denatured existence" of the mechanical time against which *Matter and Memory* is directed itself as an *Erfahrung* and goes on to suggest that Bergson's work communicates knowledge of an experience he avoids in the form of an image of what Benjamin calls "large-scale industrialism." The communicability of this image derives, in other words, from what does not take place in the time and space of a cognitive experience. The knowledge communicated by this image springs, not from an object that appears within a psychological process of perception, but from what we ourselves—or perhaps, more specifically, Benjamin himself—lays into this source. This inserting of an "extension," which Benjamin proceeds to characterize as a "synthetic" process in his comments on the interpenetration of involuntary and voluntary memory in the fiction of Marcel Proust, is the basis of an *Erfahrung* of which "only a poet can be the adequate subject." In this sense Benjamin finds in the poetry of Baudelaire and in the novel of Proust, but also in the wanderings of the "historical materialist" in his late study of nineteenth-century Paris the transcendental *Erfahrung* opened up by Kant.

Kevin McLaughlin

BIBLIOGRAPHY

Aristotle. *Metaphysics*. 2 vols. Translated by W. D. Ross. Oxford: Clarendon Press, 1924.

Bacon, Francis. *New Organon*. In vol. 8 of *The Works of Francis Bacon*. Collected and edited by James Spedding, Robert Leslie Ellis, and Douglas Denon Heath. Cambridge: Riverside Press, 1863. 59–350.

Benjamin, Walter. "On the Program for the Coming Philosophy" and "Two Poems by Friedrich Hölderlin." In *Selected Writings*, vol. 1. Cambridge, MA: Harvard University Press, 1996.

———. "Experience and Poverty." In *Selected Writings*, vol. 2. Cambridge, MA: Harvard University Press, 1999.

———. "The Storyteller" and "On Some Motifs in Baudelaire." In *Selected Writings*, vol. 3. Cambridge, MA: Harvard University Press, 2002.

Cohen, Hermann. *Kants Theorie der Erfahrung*, 2nd ed. Berlin: F. Dümmler, 1985.

Gadamer, Hans-Georg. *Truth and Method*. 2nd rev. ed. Translated by J. Weinsheimer and D. G. Marshall. New York: Crossroad, 1989.

Inwood, Michael. "Memory, Recollection and Imagination." In *A Hegel Dictionary*. Oxford: Blackwell, 1992.

Kambartel, Friedrich. "Erfahrung." In *Historisches Wörterbuch der Philosophie*, vol. 2. Edited by Joachim Ritter. Basel: Schwabe Verlag, 1971–2005.

Kant, Immanuel. *Critique of Pure Reason*. Translated by Paul Guyer and Allen W. Wood. Cambridge: Cambridge University Press, 1998.

BIBLIOGRAPHY

Assmann, Jan. *Das kulturelle Gedächtnis: Schrift, Erinnerung und politische Identität in frühen Hochkulturen*. Munich: Beck, 1992. Translation by Rodney Livingstone: *Religion and Cultural Memory: Ten Studies*. Stanford, CA: Stanford University Press, 2006.

Baer, Ulrich. "Landscape and Memory in the Work of Paul Celan: 'To Learn the Language of the Place.'" In *Semiotics*, edited by C. W. Spinks and John Deely, 111–23. New York: Peter Lang, 1996.

Baudelaire, Charles. *The Flowers of Evil*. Translated by James McGowan. Oxford World Classics. Oxford: Oxford University Press, 2008.

———. *Œuvres completes*. Vol. 1. Edited by C. Pichois. Paris: Gallimard / La Pléiade, 1976.

Benjamin, Walter. "Ausgraben und Erinnern." In *Gesammelte Schriften*, edited by T. Rexroth, 4:400ff. Frankfurt: Suhrkamp, 1991.

———. "Denkbilder." In *Gesammelte Schriften*, edited by T. Rexroth, 2:305–438. Frankfurt: Suhrkamp, 1991. Translation by Rodney Livingstone et al.: "Ibizan Sequence" and "Thought Figures." In *Walter Benjamin: Selected Writings, Volume 2, 1927–1934*, edited by Michael W. Jennings, Howard Eiland, and Gary Smith, 553–737. Cambridge, MA: Harvard University Press, 2005.

Bergson, Henri. *Matière et mémoire: Essai sur la relation du corps à l'esprit*. Paris: Presses Universitaires de France, 1965. First published in 1896. Translation by Nancy Margaret Paul and W. Scott Palmer: *Matter and Memory*. New York: Dover Publications, 2004. First published in 1912.

Bloch, David. *Aristotle on Memory and Recollection: Text, Translation, Interpretation, and Reception in Western Scholasticism*. Leiden: Brill, 2007.

Cassirer, Ernst. *Philosophie der symbolischen formen*. 2nd ed. 4 vols. Vols. 1–3: Oxford: Cassirer, 1923; vol. 4: Berlin: Cassirer, 1931. Translation by Ralph Manheim: *The Philosophy of Symbolic Forms*. Introduction by Charles W. Hendel. 4 vols. New Haven, CT: Yale University Press, 1953–96.

Celan, Paul. "Atemwende." In vol. 2 of *Gesammelte Werke*. 5 vols. Frankfurt: Suhrkamp, 1983. First published in 1967. Translation by Pierre Joris: *Breathturn*. Los Angeles: Sun and Moon Press, 1995.

———. "Stilleben." In *Von Schwelle zu Schwelle*. Vol. 1 of *Gesammelte Werke*. Frankfurt: Suhrkamp, 1983. Translation by David Young: Marick Press, 2010.

Freud, Sigmund. *Briefe an Wilhelm Fließ 1887–1902*. Edited by J. M. Masson. Frankfurt: Fischer, 1986.

———. *The Complete Letters of Sigmund Freud to Wilhelm Fliess, 1887–1904*. Translated and edited by Jeffrey Moussaieff Masson. Cambridge, MA: Belknap Press, 1985.

Hegel, G.W.F. *Phänomenologie des Geistes.* Edited by Eva Moldenhauer and Karl Markus Michel. Vol. 3 of *Werke.* Frankfurt: Suhrkamp, 1970. Translation by A. V. Miller: *Phenomenology of Spirit.* Oxford: Oxford University Press, 1977.

Heidegger, Martin. "Andenken." In *Erläuterungen zu Hölderlins Dichtung.* Frankfurt: Klostermann, 1996. 79–151. Translation and introduction by Keith Hoeller: "Remembrance." In *Elucidations of Hölderlin's Poetry.* Amherst, MA: Humanity, 2000. 101–74.

———. *Kant und das Problem der Metaphysik.* Vol. 3 of *Gesamtausgabe.* Frankfurt: Klostermann, 1991. Translation by Richard Taft: *Kant and the Problem of Metaphysics.* 5th ed. Studies in Continental Thought. Bloomington: Indiana University Press, 1997.

Hesiod. *Theogony.* Edited by M. L. West. Oxford: Oxford University Press, 1966.

Homer. *Iliad.* Translated by A. T. Murray, revised by William F. Wyatt. Cambridge, MA: Harvard University Press, 1999.

Mallarmé, Stéphane. "La vierge, le vivace . . ." In *Œuvres completes.* Vol. 1. Edited by B. Marchal. Paris: Gallimard / La Pléiade, 1998.

Nietzsche, Friedrich. *Die Geburt der Tragödie. Unzeitgemässe Betrachtungen I–IV. Nachgelassene Schriften 1870–1873.* Edited by Giorgio Colli and Mazzino Montinari. Vol. 1. *Kritische Studienausgabe.* Berlin: De Gruyter, 1980. Translation by Walter Kaufmann: "The Birth of Tragedy." In *The Birth of Tragedy and The Case of Wagner.* New York: Random House, 1967.

———. *Untimely Meditations.* Translated by R. J. Hollingdale. Cambridge: Cambridge University Press, 1983.

Ricoeur, Paul. *La mémoire, l'histoire, l'oubli.* Paris: Éditions du Seuil, 2000. Translation by Kathleen Blamey and David Pellauer: *Memory, History, Forgetting.* Chicago: Chicago University Press, 2004.

Weinrich, Harald. *Lethe: Kunst und Kritik des Vergessens.* Munich: Beck, 2005. Translation by Steven Rendall: *Lethe: The Art and Critique of Forgetting.* Ithaca, NY: Cornell University Press, 2004.

MENSCHHEIT, HUMANITÄT (GERMAN)

ENGLISH	humanity
FRENCH	humanité, sentiment d'humanité
LATIN	humanitas

➤ HUMANITY, and ANIMAL, BILDUNG, GESCHLECHT, MITMENSCH, MORALS, OIKEIŌSIS, PEOPLE/RACE/NATION

Belonging to the human race (*Menschengeschlecht*), the fact of being a human and of being part of humanity (*Menschentum*), does not necessarily mean that one shows one's humanity, or that one is moved by a sense of humanity (*Humanität*). The relatively recent introduction into German of the term *Humanität* (which is not, however, in the Grimms' dictionary) answers the need to make an even more rigorous distinction between the quality of a human being (*Menschlichkeit*) and the virtue of "humanity," since *Menschlichkeit* and *Humanität* can quite easily be confused. But mankind (*Menschheit*) considered as an ethical horizon, and ideal, is in its turn distinct from a simple belonging to the human race.

I. Human, Human Nature:
From *Humanitas* to *Humanität/Menschlichkeit*

The classical Latin *humanitas* does not refer to the human race, but contrasts that which pertains to human nature to everything animal, and then by extension refers more precisely to what characterizes human nature and its behaviors, and finally, its virtues and distinctive qualities. This broad range of meanings is illustrated by Cicero. Even though we first see with him the emergence of a "universal society of humankind" ("*societas universalis humanitatis,*" *De finibus*

3.19.62), humanity is still envisaged from the Aristotelian perspective of the political nature of man as endowed with language. Yet the term also refers to a series of qualities and virtues, to the extent that we can see a convergence of the two meanings in the attempt to bring together rhetoric, philosophy, history, and law in a single educational program. Although Cicero confessed that he did not really know what man was, or what his essence might be (*De finibus* 5.33), and thus does not strictly speaking allow us to see his thinking as anticipating "humanism," it would be possible to deduce from it, as Leonardo Bruni did in the fifteenth century, the notion of *studia humanitatis*.

■ See Box 1.

The medieval Christian tradition emphasizes the opposition between *humanitas* and *divinitas*, and makes the first term a synonym for everything that has to do with finitude and imperfection, without putting into question the primary meaning of human nature. Molière can thus have his theatrical pedant, Métaphraste, say, "*Si de parler le pouvoir m'est ôté, / Pour moi j'aime autant perdre l'humanité*" (If the power of speech were taken from me / I would just as well lose my humanity: *Le dépit amoureux,* 2.8), in the same sense that Pascal, speaking of Christ, writes, "*Sachant que nous sommes grossiers, il nous conduit ainsi à l'adoration de sa divinité présente en tous lieux par celle de son humanité présente en un lieu particulier*" (Knowing how gross we are, he thus conducts us to the adoration of his divinity, present in all places, by that of his humanity, present in a particular place: *Provincial Letters,* letter 16). Furthermore, the Grimms' *Deutsches Wörterbuch* (RT) takes *humanitas* as its point of reference both for the entry *Menschheit* and for *Menschlichkeit*, but it is precisely this dependency on Latin that Fichte challenged in the fourth of his *Addresses to the German Nation* (1807), criticizing the use of the term *Humanität*. His reaction to the importation of a foreign term was based on the argument that the development of the particular language and thought of the German people had in reality nothing to do with imported terms that were grafted on artificially, especially if the languages from which these terms were borrowed could not compete with the German language in their originality. French was, according to him, too dependent upon Latin, whereas German was perfectly capable of thinking the notion of humanity by giving it its own expressions: *Menschheit, Menschlichkeit,* and *Menschenfreundlichkeit* (which subsumes the idea of kindness, benevolence to others, and philanthropy, in its literal etymological sense). This explicit argument barely disguised the subtext: Fichte was reacting against a French model imported through the Academy of Berlin, which proposed a universalist ideal of humanity, when it was Napoleon's armies that undertook to impose this ideal, by refusing any German specificity. In addition, *Humanität* was too directly linked to a Roman Catholic semantic and cultural context, whose "universalism" was opposed head-on to the Lutheranism that founded the German language.

It was all the more surprising that the Grimms' dictionary, which dates from the first half of the nineteenth century and, as we saw, does refer to the Latin *humanitas*, does not record *Humanität* (RT: Jacob and Wilhelm Grimm, *Deutsches Wörterbuch*). *Humanität,* after all, was already present, sixteen years

1

The complex architecture of *humanitas* in Latin humanism

The Latin term *humanitas* first appeared around 80 BCE (the first instances of its use are in the *Rhetoric to Herennius* [2.24, 26, 50; 4.12, 23], anonymous and of uncertain date, and in Cicero's *For Publius Quinctius* §§51 and 97). At that time it meant a brotherly disposition based on the feeling of belonging to the same species, the *genus humanum* (*humanitas* would not signify "humanity" in this latter sense until the Christian authors; cf. Saint Jerome, *Letters*, 55.3, 4). The concept subsequently assumed the full extent of its meaning with Cicero, who elaborated a theory of both individual and collective human development through culture, particularly the liberal arts and literature, which explains the direct link between the modern term "humanities" and its original Latin meaning. Beginning with his speech *Pro Roscio Amerino* (Roscius was accused of parricide in 80 BCE), Cicero reflects first of all on the specificity of the human as opposed to the state of savagery, and then goes on to discuss the fundamentally enriching effects of civilization, which turn man into a cultural being, in contrast to the forms of barbarism, which abandon him to the state of nature verging on animality (see the speech *On Behalf of Archias the Poet*, and the treatise *De republica*, in particular 1.28). *Humanitas* thus establishes itself as a set of characteristics that supposedly define what a civilized man is, as opposed to what he is not, and from which follow certain duties he has to observe in his relation to himself, and to his fellow humans (this is the theme of Cicero's treatise *On Duties*).

We have, then, a complex architecture, under the constant threat of destruction from the poles against which *humanitas* is defined; animality, savagery, barbarism, monstrosity. *Humanitas* can only be preserved through our constantly exercising the human duties of solidarity, of justice, and of mercy (the term *humanitas* covers all of these meanings). Exercising these duties requires us to draw from the wellspring of the cultural memory to which humanity has consigned its own definitions of values (in philosophical discourse, in particular), and the illustration of its principles (notably through historical exempla). This accounts for the importance of the humanities, whose role is not a decorative but a constitutive one. In two exemplary texts, Cicero thus appeals both to the sense of community created in sharing the same culture, and to the adherence to the values of this culture. He does this, on the one

hand, in the speech *On Behalf of Archias the Poet*, when he asks the Romans not to exclude the foreign poet from its civic body, and on the other, in the programmatic letter to his brother, the governor of the province of Asia (*To His Brother Quintus* 1.1), when he urges him to show the greatest *humanitas* toward those he administers in Greece. In each case, *humanitas* is opposed to the force of exclusion represented by *acerbitas*, or a harshness verging on cruelty, and *saevitia*, which is one of the characteristics of a moral monster (see Seneca, *On Anger* and *On Clemency*). Anti-*humanis* is then defined as *immanis*: this adjective, the antonym of *manis* (good), refers generally to all that is out of proportion, and thus frightening, or monstrous. This is particularly true of the animal nature of wild beasts, *ferae*, an animality that, when transferred to men, denies all humanity by inverting its values. Seneca thus says of Caligula ("To Polybius," *On Consolation*, 17.5–6) that he "savored in the misfortunes of others the most inhuman consolation [*alienis malis oblectare minime humano solacio*]," a perfect perversion of the motto of Latin humanism we find in Terence (*The Self-Torturer* 77): "I am a man, and I deem nothing pertaining to man foreign to me [*homo sum, humani nil a me alienum puto*]," an even more eloquent echo of which we find in Seneca himself, who defines *humanitas* (*Letters* 88.30) as "not thinking of any misfortune as foreign [*nullum alienum malum putat*]."

It is worth adding the following clarifications to this very general presentation:

1. The contribution of the Greeks was, of course, a determining one (see Cicero's avowed debt, *To His Brother Quintus* 1.27–28). The sense of the unity of humankind is no doubt as old as man, but beyond this immediate awareness, we recognize within the idea of a necessary fraternity between the members of a same species the Greek *philantrôpia*, which was associated with *paideia* through the cultural side of the Roman *humanitas* (the difference being that the intellectual training to which *humanitas* refers is that of a fully developed man, and not the early training of the child, *pais*, as he is being taught). The originality of the Roman term, which has no equivalent in Greek, was first and foremost to associate the two words within a unitary, balanced conception of man. However, this lexical balance would not last a generation, and in the widest sense of the term,

humanitas would be, generally speaking, the invention of the generation of Cicero and Varro, and would lose its complexity during the Roman empire, when it was reduced either to *philantrôpia* or to *paideia* (see Aulus Gellius, *Attic Nights* 13.17). We can see here the effects of a generation that had been brought up with the cultural contributions of Hellenism, and that expected culture, perceived in its universality, to provide new tools for understanding the drama of contemporary events, and to remedy these by preserving the best of the national tradition, the *mos maiorum*, that is, those aspects in the historical evolution of Rome which marked the full development of civilized man (see Novara, *Les idées romaines*, 1:165–97).

2. Historical relativism has a philosophical counterpart: recent studies have thus emphasized how closely the Roman construction of *humanitas* was bound up with the imperial politics of Rome (see Paul Veyne, "*Humanitas*: Les Romains et les autres," in Giardina, *Les idées romaines*, 421–59; and Braund, "Roman Assimilations," 15–32). The alleged universality of the concept of *humanitas* in fact imposed the model of the Roman equipped with a Greco-Roman culture, gradually dominated by the Latin language, and imbued with the values of the *mos maiorum*. This model worked first of all by casting everything incompatible with it into the void of savagery and barbarism, and then by offering itself as a tool for integrating the conquered populations into the body of the empire through a process of harmonious romanization, which was synonymous with civilization, pure and simple.

3. Roman thinkers were not, however, unaware of any properly universal claims made in the name of *humanitas*. This surfaces specifically in regard to slavery, and with the influence of Stoicism; the limit of this universalism can be seen, however, in the absence of any questioning of slavery, even though slaves were recognized as men (see Cicero, *On Duties* 1.41 and 150, and especially Seneca, *Epistles* 47). Stoicism even provided the means for thinking what appears to us as a contradiction, by making the slave an employee in perpetuity who was looked after by his master. More generally, philosophical

(continued)

(continued)

cosmopolitanism, which in theory eradicated all inequalities of status, was in no way aiming to overthrow the political and social frameworks of the time, but cultivated respect for the existing structures and institutions by projecting human equality into the ideal state of a utopian City of Wise Men. It is nonetheless remarkable that the philosophical discourse on slavery certainly defined man in terms of the freedom to act well the role given to him by Fortune—a freedom, however, that was seen against the backdrop of a primary enslavement. Every man is a slave to his destiny and also, with the exception of ideal wise men, a slave to his own passions, a secondary enslavement that is ultimately worse than any other because it is voluntary, and involves one's own self-abasement (cf. Cicero, *Paradoxa Stoicorum* 5, on the theme "Only the wise man is free"; and Seneca, *On Tranquility of Mind* 10. 3: "All life is slavery"). Perhaps the Roman *humanitas* testifies not only to an imperialist pragmatism, and to an all-too-human inability to free oneself from the social and institutional framework of a given culture, but also, by contrast to the optimism of contemporary human rights, to an ancient sense of the fragility of human affairs and the weakness of man, who can never be helped enough by the whole of human culture in his attempts to escape a degradation that is often of his own making.

François Prost

BIBLIOGRAPHY

Bauman, Richard A. *Human Rights in Ancient Rome*. London: Routledge, 2000.
Braund, Susanna Morton. "Roman Assimilations of the Other: *Humanitas* at Rome." *Acta Classica* 40 (1997): 15–32.
Giardina, Andrea, ed. *L'uomo romano*. Rome: Laterza, 1989. Translation by Lydia G. Cochrane: *The Romans*. Chicago, IL: University of Chicago Press, 1993.
Novara, Antoinette. *Les idées romaines sur le progrès d'après les écrivains de la République: Essai sur le sens latin du progrès*. 2 vols. Paris: Les Belles Lettres, 1982–83.

before the *Addresses to the German Nation*, in Herder's great work, *Ideas for a Philosophy of the History of Mankind* (Ideen zur Philosophie der Geschichte der Menschheit), book 4, chapter 4: "I would hope to be able to capture in the term humanity [*Humanität*] everything I have said up until now on the superior formation of man in terms of reason and freedom. . . ." The title of this chapter is explicit: "Man is formed with a view to humanity and religion." *Humanität*, moreover, is emphasized throughout this book, and, like *humanitas* in Cicero, although it is never given a positive definition, Herder's *Humanität* includes everything that enables man to rise above his empirical ground, as well as everything that is aimed for in this movement of overcoming, since humanity is the "finality of mankind": the future of reason is to establish a "lasting humanity."

II. "Humanity" (*Menschheit*) as an Ethical Ideal?

Kant also draws a distinction between *Humanität* and *Menschlichkeit* on the one hand, and *Menschheit* on the other. In the appendix to the second part of the *Critique of Judgment* (§60, "Of the Methodology of Taste," *Critique of the Aesthetic Power of Judgment*), Kant reminds us in discussing the humanities that they are so called "because humanity [*Humanität*] means on the one hand the universal feeling of participation [*Teilnehmungsgefühl*] and on the other hand the capacity for being able to communicate [*mittheilen*] one's inmost self universally, which properties taken together constitute the sociability that is appropriate to humankind [*Menschheit*]." But the problem is no longer one of a semantic differentiation between an originally Latin term and a German term, since Kant introduces a double meaning of the term *Menschheit*. For animality also exists within man, and is opposed to "the idea of humanity [*Menschheit*] that he bears in his soul as the archetype of his actions" (*Critique of Pure Reason*, "Transcendental Dialectic," 1.1, trans. Guyer and Wood, 397), since one cannot determine "the highest degree of perfection at which humanity must stop . . . however great a gulf must remain between the idea and its execution" (ibid.). Humanity is thus both what characterizes man as an "object of experience" and the ideal of his freedom, "*humanity* raised in its Idea" (*Conflict of the Faculties*, §1, General Remark, "On Religious Sects," trans. Gregor, 105). *Menschheit*, then, referred both to a generic humanity, and to what it is within humanity, and only within humanity, that makes it no longer a fact, but a gradual evolution toward an ethical ideal: it is at the very core of this generic humanity that the driving force of its evolution is situated. Defined as freedom, this driving force is generic humanity's final cause, humanity perfected and reconciled, humanity having made real the idea that (by its very nature) it also *is*.

Borrowing this double Kantian sense, Hermann Cohen emphasizes that in Kant, the term both is "equivalent to a rational being," and has a "universalist, cosmopolitan meaning." Cohen, moreover, links Kant to Herder:

> Herder, who was a rebellious and thus ungrateful disciple of Kant, still engaged with his thought . . . through the idea of humanity . . . it is no coincidence that he was also the author of *On the Spirit of Hebrew Poetry*. He recognized the spirit of humanity in the earliest texts of the Old Testament. . . . This was an important intuition which guided Herder in his general conception of the spirit of the Bible: he recognized the messianism in the principle of monotheism.
>
> (*Religion of Reason*, chap. 13:
> "The Idea of Messiah and Humanity," §11)

Three perspectives converge at a sort of future vanishing point: politics has as its ideal the confederation of States, driven by the spirit of cosmopolitanism that ultimately tends toward the disappearance of nation-states, then of sovereign states. The spirit is based on the properly ethical aspiration to the ideal of a reconciled humanity, that is, an *ethics* that coincides with culture to the extent that it would render *religion* useless, since religion will have been, as a messianic monotheism, the revelation of the meaning of these ideals in the figure of the Messiah. (Christianity and Judaism are not fundamentally opposed if Noah is recognized as "the first Messiah," and if one accepts the essential role played by the prophets in the constitution of the historical and moral ideal of humanity; the real and irreducible point of divergence is, of course, the fact of accepting or refusing Jesus as the Messiah.) Cohen, who is openly hostile to the idea of miracles, does not imagine the Messiah other than in the secularized and rationalized form of a coincidence between the ideal and the real, between the *fieri* and the *factum*; he knows that it is not a matter of a promised effective reality, but of a tendency, of an asymptote. Unified humanity is merely an ideal: monotheistic messianism is its historical expression, and Kantian ethics and cosmopolitanism are its rational formulation. The feeling of humanity—Cohen makes no distinction between *Humanität* and *Menschlichkeit*—is an essential virtue since it is thanks to this virtue that humankind (*Menschentum*, which is merely *Menschengeschlecht* as far as science is concerned) has access to humanity (*Menschheit*), that is, to the true meaning of what would be the progress of humanity.

In Nietzsche's thought, the potential confusion between the different terms used to designate humanity (*Humanität* and *Menschheit*) and the human (*das Menschliche* and *das Humane*) becomes the object of constant critical attention. Nietzsche denounces, in the folding back of *Menschlichkeit* onto *Humanität*, one of the most enduring effects of Christianity on the way we conceive of the human, and the most telling sign of how Christianity has supplanted antiquity. Indeed, it is in studying closely what constituted the humanity of the Greeks, from a philological and historical perspective, that the deceptive, cunning (*witzig*) nature of this folding back becomes apparent. This study enables us to understand the extent to which the idea of the human (*das Menschliche*) becomes confused as soon as one banishes everything that Christianity designates as inhumanity (*Inhumanität*):

> The human [*das Menschliche*] which Antiquity shows us should not be confused with the human [*das Humane*]. . . . The human [*das Menschliche*] of the Greeks consists in a certain naivety by which, for them, are distinguished man, the State, art, society, the rights of war and of peoples, the relations between the sexes, education, looking after the home; this is precisely the human [*das Menschliche*] as it manifests itself everywhere, among all peoples, but for them, with no mask and inhumanly [*in einer Unmaskirtheit und Inhumanität*], which one must not overlook if one is to draw any lesson from it.
>
> (Nietzsche, frag. 3 [12], March 1875,
> in "Notes for 'We Philologists' ")

III. Man and Inhumanity

This confusion is in essence due to the fact that the idea of *Humanität* aims to separate man from nature. Reestablishing the meaning of *Menschheit* assumes that one can show how much "the natural qualities, and the properly called 'human' [*menschlich*] ones have grown up inseparably together" (Nietzsche, "Homer's Wettkampf"). One can thus no longer

make any distinction between man and nature. But to get rid of this folding back means taking away from humanity (*Menschheit*) any teleological meaning. Indeed, it is when one considers that humanity (*Menschheit*) is never sufficiently human (*Humane*) that one makes one or the other a goal:

> Man, not humanity [*die Menschheit*]. Humanity [*die Menschheit*] is much more a means than an end. It is a question of the type: Humanity [*die Menschheit*] is only material of experience, the enormous excess of what has not succeeded, a field of rubble.
>
> (Nietzsche, frag. 14 [8])

And also:

> In our present humanity [*Menschheit*] we have attained a considerable degree of humanity [*Humanität*]. The very fact that we are generally not aware of it is already a proof.
>
> (Nietzsche, frag. 15 [63])

This attachment to the idea of *Humanität* in Nietzsche's late writings, and the regret they express that there is never enough humanity, become a symptom of decadence.

Marc Crépon
Marc de Launay

BIBLIOGRAPHY

Cohen, Hermann. *Die Religion der Vernunft aus den Quellen des Judentums*. Leipzig: Fock, 1919. Translation by Simon Kaplan: *Religion of Reason out of the Sources of Judaism*. Introduction by Simon Kaplan. Introductory essays by Leo Strauss, Steven S. Schwarzschild, and Kenneth Seeskin. Atlanta, GA: Scholars Press, 1995.

Fichte, Johann Gottlieb. *Reden an die deutsche Nation*. Edited by Immanuel Hermann Fichte. In *Fichtes Werke*, 7:257–501. Berlin: De Gruyter, 1971. Originally published in 1808. Translation by R. F. Jones and G. H. Turnbull: *Addresses to the German Nation*. Edited by George Armstrong Kelly. New York: Harper and Row, 1968.

Herder, Johann Gottfried. *Ideen zur Philosophie der Geschichte der Menschheit*. Edited by Wolfgang Pross. 2 vols. In *Werke*, vol. 3. Munich: Hanser, 2002. Translation by T. Churchill: *Outlines of a Philosophy of the History of Man*. New York: Bergman, 1800.

Kant, Immanuel. *Anthropology from a Pragmatic Point of View*. Edited and translated by Robert B. Louden. Cambridge: Cambridge University Press, 2006.

———. *The Conflict of the Faculties* [Der Streit der Fakultäten]. Translated and introduction by Mary J. Gregor. New York: Abaris, 1979.

———. *Critique of the Power of Judgment*. Edited and translated by Paul Guyer and Eric Matthews. Cambridge: Cambridge University Press, 2000.

———. *Critique of Practical Reason*. Edited and translated by Mary Gregor. Cambridge: Cambridge University Press, 1997.

———. *Critique of Pure Reason*. Edited and translated by Paul Guyer and A. Wood. Cambridge: Cambridge University Press, 1997.

———. *Kants Gesammelte Schriften*. Edited by Königlich Preussische Akademie der Wissenschaften. Berlin: De Gruyter, 1902–.

———. *The Metaphysics of Morals*. Edited and translated by Mary Gregor. Introduction by Roger J. Sullivan. Cambridge: Cambridge University Press, 1996.

Nietzsche, Friedrich. *Digital Critical Edition of the Complete Works and Letters*. Based on the critical text by Giorgio Colli and Mazzimo Montinari (Berlin: De Gruyter, 1967–). Edited by Paolo D'Iorio. http://www.nietzschesource.org

Osamu, Nishitani. "Anthropos and Humanitas: Two Western Concepts of 'Human Being.'" In *Translation, Biopolitics, Colonial Difference*, edited by Naoki Sakai and Jon Solomon, 259–73. Hong Kong: Hong Kong University Press, 2006.

Wood, Allen. *Kant's Ethical Thought*. Cambridge: Cambridge University Press, 1999.

MERKMAL (GERMAN)

ENGLISH	mark
FRENCH	*marque distinctive, marque, note*
ITALIAN, SPANISH	*marca*
LATIN	*nota*

➤ *CONCEPT*, LOGOS, MOMENT, OBJECT, PREDICATION, PROPERTY, REALITY, REPRÉSENTATION, RES, SACHVERHALT, SENSE, SIGN, *THING* (RES), TROPE

The German *Merkmal* is generally considered as a term from Gottlob Frege's philosophical idiolect. Indeed, the word appears in contrast to *Eigenschaft* (property) in the *Grundlagen der Arithmetik* (Foundations of arithmetic) from 1884, when he introduces a new theory of predication (§53). According to this theory—readily reformulated with the help of a standard example in the history of logic—in a proposition such as "man is an animal," "animal" will not be analyzed in Fregean terms as a property of man, but as a "mark" of the concept of man. However, *Merkmal* is not only a technical term belonging to a particular philosophy; it is at the intersection of two series, whose initial convergence, and then progressive divergence, are linked to a fact of translation between Greek and Latin that is worthy of a philosopher's attention. More than its English or French equivalents, the clarity of the oppositions that structure its domain of application in German allow it to describe the aforementioned "intersection," its sources, its mechanisms, and its philosophical stakes. The first series is the one denoted by the synonymous pair *Merkmal-Zeichen* (sign); the second, which corresponds to Frege's usage, is the one denoted by the antonymous pair *Merkmal/Eigenschaft*. These two series do not normally have any necessary meeting point. Their intersection can only be explained by other philosophical languages: before becoming part of Frege's idiom in opposition to *Eigenschaft*, the notion of *Merkmal* had a protohistory, entailing a certain number of shifts in the understanding of what a concept, a judgment, and an object of judgment are, and how they are expressed in "languages." This is what we will reconstruct briefly here.

I. *Merkmal* and *Zeichen*, "Mark" and "Sign"

The synonymous pair *Merkmal-Zeichen* has its origin in the Latin of Boethius, in this case via the translation of the first chapter of *Peri hermêneias* (On interpretation) (16a2–7), in which Aristotle puts in place what has come to be known, since C. K. Ogden and I. A. Richards, as the "semantic triangle." In the Latin version, Boethius in fact translates two distinct Greek words, *sumbolon* [σύμβολον] and *sêmeion* [σημεῖον], as the same Latin word, *nota*:

Sunt ergo ea quae sunt in voce earum quae sunt in anima passionum notae et ea quae scribuntur eorum quae sunt in voce. Et quemadmodum nec litterae omnibus eaedem, sic nec eadem voces; quorum autem hae primorum notae, eaedem omnibus passiones animae sunt, et quorum hae similitudines, res etiam eaedem.

(Spoken words are the symbols of mental experience and written words are the symbols of spoken words. Just as all men have not the same writing, so all men have not the same speech sounds, but the mental experiences, which these directly symbolize, are the same for all, as also are those things of which our experiences are the images.)

(*Aristoteles latinus*, 2.1–2, p. 5 [4–9]; trans. Edghill)

(See SIGN, and on the current options for translating the Greek original, Box 1 there). Boethius's translation doubly modifies the relation of meaning according to Aristotle: first, through the (relative) elimination of what was conveyed by the distinction between *sumbolon* and *sêmeion*, and second, by bringing signifying and noting closer together. This explains the paired set of terms we find among certain medieval commentators of the *Peri hermêneias*, between *nota* and the speaker on the one hand, and *signum* and the interlocutor or listener on the other. (Cf. the text by Robert Kilwardby, cited in SIGN: "dicendum quod differunt nota et signum, quia nota est in quantum est in ore proferentis, set signum est in quantum est in aure audientis" (We will reply that *nota* and *signum* are different, because *nota* is used for what is in the mouth of the speaker, but *signum* for what is in the ear of the listener), and the commentary by I. Rosier-Catach). The replacement of *nota* by the pair *sumbolum/signum* in Guillaume de Moerbeke's medieval translation of the text plays no part in the genesis of the first series of *Merkmal*; many logicians had become used to reorganizing the semantic triangle with *signum* well before this translation. So there are two all-encompassing linguistic mechanisms in Latin, based on the neutralization of *sumbolon/sêmeion*, that account for the alternation between *Merkmal* and *Zeichen* in common philosophical usage in German, and that identify a mark and a sign (as they also do, more or less, in everyday language): the system of *nota*, and the system of *signum*. "To be a mark of" and "to be a sign of" are considered synonymous, by virtue of the simple fact that *Zeichen* contains, depending on the context, the same dimension of notification as the French *signe* (sign; signifier [in French] can have the meaning of "to let know," "to notify"; "donner un signe de" [to give a sign of] is synonymous in French with "donner une marque de"; and so on; cf. the analogous expression "signify" in English: "I signified my assent . . ."; and the use of "signify" and "signifyin'" in the African American tradition). To this is added, however, the transitivity of the posited relationship that Aristotle articulates in the "semantic triangle," and that subsequently acquires a historial dimension. Aristotle's formulation generally appears among Scholastics in the form of a saying based on *signum*: "Quicquid est signum signi est signum signati" (Anything that is the sign of a sign is the sign of its signified)—meaning that the vocal sound (Aristotle's *phônê* [φωνή]), insofar as it is the sign of the "passions" or the "affections of the soul" ("pathêmata tês psuchês [παθήματα τῆς ψυχῆς]"), is therefore also the sign of the things signified (the *pragmata* [πράγματα]) by these passions. There is, though, another expression attested as early as the twelfth century, "Nota notae est nota rei" (The *nota* of a *nota* is the *nota* of the thing), which initially has the same meaning as the first formulation, since it simply says the same thing in the language of Boethius's translation. But it will progressively assume a new meaning, explaining how *Merkmal* becomes part of a configuration we might describe as "pre-Fregean," which will lead to the opposition between *Merkmal* and *Eigenschaft*.

II. Marks of Concepts / Marks of Things

By positing that "animal" is not a property of "man," but a *Merkmal* of the concept of man, a Fregean means that *animal* is a "part" of man, or more precisely, that animal is a "part" of the concept *man*, whereas, for example, it is a "property" of the concept *man* to "have *n* individuals," and a property of a given individual to "fall under the concept *man*" (which is expressed in the single proposition that the concept has an extension: multiple individuals "fall under the concept"). In a letter published in 1941 (cf. *Unbekannte Briefe Freges*, ed. Steck, 9), Frege himself explains that the mereological and intensional relation of the marks to the concepts they constitute is comparable to the relation that stones have to the house that they are used to build, and that consists of this building ("Ich vergleiche die einzelnen Merkmale eines Begriffes den Steinen, aus denen ein Haus besteht" [I compare the individual marks of a concept to the stones from which a house is built]). In an article from 1903 on "The Foundations of Geometry" (373), the parts of a concept are presented, in a less visually figurative way, as its "logical parts [*logische Teile*]." The question that interests us here is not the origin of this new meaning of *Merkmal*, but rather this: what makes possible, even facilitates, the transition from the pair *Merkmal-Zeichen* to the opposition *Merkmal/Eigenschaft*?

A part of the history of *Merkmal* was traced by Kasimir Twardowski in a essay from 1894, *Zur Lehre vom Inhalt und Gegenstand der Vorstellungen* (On the theory of content and of the object of representations).

- See Box 1.

It is, however, in a text by Adolf Reinach from 1911, *Die obersten Regeln der Vernunftschlüsse bei Kant* (The supreme rules of reasoning in Kant), that we can find the most original indication of the trajectory that *Merkmal* takes before Frege. This trajectory, however, takes a surprising material form in the radical change of understanding that the Scholastic saying undergoes: "Nota notae est nota rei." When Reinach presents the two main rules of reasoning according to Kant, he refers to the 1672 text *Die falsche Spitzfindigkeit der vier syllogistischen Figuren* (The false subtlety of the four syllogistic figures), and makes a distinction between "the general rule of all affirmative reasonings" and "the general rule of all negative reasonings." The first, R1, is: "Ein Merkmal vom Merkmal ist ein Merkmal der Sache selbst" (A mark of a mark is a mark of the thing itself); the second, R2, is: "Was dem Merkmal eines Dinges widerspricht, widerspricht dem Dinge selbst" (What contradicts the mark of a thing contradicts the thing itself). These rules show that, in the "pre-Fregean" use of the term, *Merkmal* is related to "things," or rather to "the/a thing," and not, as in Frege, to "concept" (*Begriff*) as a part of the concept. Moreover, judgment is defined in relation to "things" in Kant's short text: "Etwas als ein Merkmal mit einem Dinge vergleichen, heißt Urteilen" (Comparing something as a mark to a thing is called judging). How should we therefore translate *Merkmal*? Reinach offers a fortuitous indication for a francophone translator when he makes explicit reference to the "Scholastic sayings adapted by Kant" in his two rules: in other words, for R1, "nota notae est etiam nota rei ipsius" (The *nota* of a *nota* is also the *nota* of the thing itself), and for R2, "repugnans notae repugnant rei ipsi" (What contradicts *the nota* contradicts the thing itself) (cf. Reinach, *Die obersten*

1

Merkmal, moment, "trope"

Paragraph 13 of Kasimir Twardowski's *Zur Lehre vom Inhalt und Gegenstand der Vorstellungen* (On the content and object of presentations) is devoted to *Merkmal*. In referring to the term, Twadrowski does not distinguish between *either* the level of the concept *or* the level of things, but between the level of representation (*Vorstellung*) and that of the object of representation. On this point, he mentions the "eminent authorities" who paved the way for our understanding of the "mark." The first is Kant, and the introduction to his *Logic*, from which he gives a long quotation:

> A distinctive mark is, on a thing, what constitutes a part of the knowledge of this thing, or even a partial representation, which amounts to the same, insofar as it is considered as the basis of the knowledge of the entire representation. . . . All thought is nothing other than the fact of representing itself using distinctive marks.

> (In Husserl and Twardowski, *Sur les objets intentionnels*, 171)

The second authority is the Aristotelian Adolf Trendelenburg, if we accept Twardowski's rewriting of the definition proposed in his *Logische Untersuchungen* (2:255): a *Merkmal* is "that which forms the concept in the thing [*Sache*]." Twardowski comments, "Although the meaning of this definition . . . appears to be rather unclear," it can be justified by "making it more explicit that what is understood by distinctive marks is what 'in the thing' provides the necessary material from which the concept of this thing is formed. What corresponds in the thing to the concept are the distinctive marks of this thing" (in Husserl and Twardowski, *Sur les objets intentionnels*, 172; it is worth noting the distinction he makes between *Sache* [thing as affair, matter] and *Dinge* [thing as object]).

The third authority is Albert Stöckl (*Lehrbuch der Philosophie*, vol. 1, §75):

> What we understand by distinctive marks are generally all the moments by which an object is recognized as what it is, and is distinguished from all other objects.

> (In Husserl and Twardowski, *Sur les objets intentionnels*, 172)

Merkmal is thus a veritable conceptual "exchanger": with Trendelenburg, it brings together Kant's "mark," the world of representation, and Aristotle's "part of *logos* [λόγος]," the world of essences; with Stöckl, it opens out onto the Husserlian notion of "moment" (see MOMENT), and thus onto the notion of "trope," since the *Rotomomente* (moments of the color red), the *individuelle Röte* (individual reds) of, or in, a red thing, are defined as *Einzelfall* (particular cases) of the *Spezies Röte* (redness species), and for Husserl (*Logische Untersuchungen*, vol. 1, §§31, 34, 39) clearly correspond to the tropes of recent trope theory (see TROPE).

BIBLIOGRAPHY

Husserl, Edmund, and Kazimierz Twardowski. *Sur les objets intentionnels (1893–1901)*. Translated into French by J. English. Paris: Vrin 1993.

Stöckl, Albert. *Lehrbuch der Philosophie*. Mainz, Ger.: Kirchheim, 1868.

Trendelenburg, Friedrich Adolf. *Logische Untersuchungen*. Reprint. Hildesheim, Ger.: Olms, 1964. First published in Leipzig, 1870.

Regeln, 51 n. 2). The obvious translation into French of *Merkmal* would thus be *note* (note), via the Scholastic Latin. This choice, though, was not uniformly adopted, and *marques* (marks) and *marques distinctives* (distinctive marks) are found more commonly. The use of *marques* in this context has an illustrious precedent. Gottfried Leibniz, writing in French, presents the (Scholastic) notion of a "nominal definition" by proposing that it "explique le nom par les marques de la chose" (explains the name by the marks of the thing) (cf. *Die philosophischen Schriften*, 5:18): the German and the French are here in agreement. But we can find other equivalents, pertaining to a different field. In the *Logique* (Logic) of his *Cours de philosophie*, published in Louvain in 1897, Desiré Mercier uses the term *caractères* to illustrate an *idée inadequate*: "L'idée inadequate nous présente l'objet au moyen de caractères qui ne suffisent pas à nous le faire distinguer de tout autre" (An inadequate idea presents an object to us by means of characters that are insufficient to distinguish it for us from any other object; *Cours de philosophie*, 83). We thus have several pairs expressing the same basic distinction: the distinction *nota/res*, the German pair *Merkmal/Ding*, and the French pairs *marques/choses* and *caractères/objet* (see OBJECT). What in fact is *la chose/Ding* that Kant as well as Leibniz discuss? It is an open question: *la chose* can refer either to man (common or universal), or to this man (singular or particular), or to Ø man (man as neither universal nor particular, what Kant himself sometimes calls *Gegenstand*, in the sense of the "matter" [Ger. *Materie*] of the concept, in other words, the *res* that is neutral, or indifferent to particular or universal, as opposed to the individual *Gegenstand* existing in intuition [Ger. *Anschauung*]). If we consider that Ø "man" refers to the whole set of "marks" taken "in itself" (Man in himself), the universe of *Merkmal* is connected to that of the "triplex status naturae" or the "triplex respectus essentiae" (*in se*, *in anima*, *in re*), that of the "indifference of the essence" (see UNIVERSALS).

Kant's rules R1 and R2 open out onto another problematic: the one inaugurated by Aristotle when he postulates in the *Categories* that "as far as definitions are concerned, the first species include the definition both of the species and of the genera, and the definition of the species includes that of the genus," and that, "in the same way, species and individuals also include the definition of the differences." In order to justify this affirmation, Aristotle introduces a rule that recalls R1: "Everything that can be said of the predicate can also be said of the subject [*hosa gar kata tou katêgoroumenou legetai, kata tou hupokeimenou rhêthêsetai* (ὅσα γὰρ κατὰ τοῦ κατηγορουμένου λέγεται, κατὰ τοῦ ὑποκειμένου ῥηθήσεται)]" (*Categories* 3b4–5, trans. Cooke). Besides the paralogisms that are easily dismissed, such as "Socrates is a man, man is a species, therefore Socrates is a species," the problem for commentators is that of the status of the "predicates of predicates" in Aristotle. (See, among others, the thirteenth-century *Fallaciae ad modum Oxoniae* [ed. Kopp, 106–7], which explains that this paralogistic type of reasoning constitutes the third mode of error of the figure of expression, based on a mistaken *commutatio* of the *quale quid*—"described," Greek *poion ti* [ποιόν τι]—as *hoc aliquid*, "this something," Greek *tode ti* [τόδε τι]; the author of the *Fallaciae* exposes the error in the analytical language of the *suppositio*: in the major, *homo* has a

"simply confused [*confusa tantum*]" supposition, and means something that is described; in the minor, it has a "determinate [*determinata*]" supposition, and means "this something"; see SUPPOSITION.) Aristotle touches on the question on several occasions, particularly when he discusses certain predicates of Man in himself (Ø man) that do not apply to man plain and simple (this man or that man)—for example, "immobile being" (cf. *Topics*, E.7, 137b3–10). The clearest passage is, however, in *Metaphysics*, M.4, 1079b3–11, in which he contrasts the theory of Ideas with a "pre-Fregean" argument: if there is an Idea of the circle, a Circle in itself, the Idea of the circle will have to contain all the marks of the essence of the circle as well as the property of "being an Idea (of)." To what part of the essence will this be added? Remarkably, the note by Tricot (*Métaphysique*, 2:738), based on the commentary by Bonitz, quotes the passage in which Bonitz uses the term *nota* to refer to the constitutive elements of the Idea.

The "pre-Fregean" thesis is clearly expressed by Leibniz when, faced with the paralogism "animal est genus, Petrus est animal, ergo Petrus est genus" (Animal is a genus, Peter is an animal, therefore Peter is a genus) (of the kind *poion ti / tode ti*), he replies that the major is not universal, since Ø animal is not a genus ("maiorem non esse universalem, neque enim is qui est animal est genus," *Defensio Trinitatis*, in *Die philosophischen Schriften*, 4:120), which, as Angelelli points out, amounts to saying that " 'genus' is not a mark of 'animal' " (*Studies on Gottlob Frege*, 149 n. 56). We also find this thesis prefigured in Albert the Great, when he explains that in "homo praedicatur de pluribus," the referents of "man" do not have the property of being the predicates of many ("nihil est in appellatis ipsis quod de pluribus praedicatur"), since the predicate "to be the predicates of many" is contingent on the form "man" without being contingent on its referents ("tale enim praedicatum contingit formae, ita quod non contingit appellatis," *Metaphysica*, 7.2.1, ed. Geyer, p. 339, 24–29).

III. *Merkmal* and *Urteil*, "Mark" and "Judgment"

A recurrent difficulty of the notion of judgment as an act of "linking marks together" (*Merkmalsverknüpfung*), governed by Kant's rules R1 and R2, is distinguishing between R1, the rule of *Categories* 3b 4–5, and the rule of the "Dictum de omni." For some authors, there is no difference between the two: "To say: 'If *A* is an attribute of every *B*, and *B* an attribute of every *G*, *A* is an attribute of every *G*,' is the same as saying: 'Everything that can be affirmed of the attribute must be affirmed of the subject' " (Tonqueduc, *Critique*, 54). Others who regularly use the notion of "mark," like Husserl, reject the formulation "Nota notae est nota rei" (cf. *Logische Untersuchungen*, vol. 1, §41). Starting out from the definition of "judgment" as "linking marks together," we cannot fail to notice the difference that exists between this approach and the "logical" approach to judgment, as it is discussed in the second edition of the *Critique of Pure Reason*. There, Immanuel Kant indeed points out that he has "never been able to satisfy [himself] with the explanation that the logicians give of a judgment in general: it is, they say, the representation of a relation between two concepts [*die Vorstellung eines Verhältnisses zwischen zwei Begriffen*]," because it "fits only categorical [*kategorische Urteile*] but not hypothetical [*hypothetische*] and disjunctive [*disjunktive*] judgments (which latter two do not contain a relation of concepts but of judgments themselves [*als welche letztere nicht ein Verhältnis von Begriffen, sondern selbst von Urteilen enthalten*])" (*Critique of Pure Reason*, 2nd ed., §19, trans. Guyer and Wood, 251). This implies, among other "troublesome consequences," that the "widespread doctrine of the four syllogistic figures" in effect "concerns only [*betrifft nur*] the categorical inferences [*die kategorischen Vernunftschlüsse*]" (ibid., 251 n. 1). It is also worth noting that this same passage introduces the notion of an "objectively valid" relation of judgment, defining it thus:

Diese beiden Vorstellungen sind im *Object* d.i. ohne Unterschied des Zustandes des *Subjects*, verbunden und nicht bloß in der Wahrnehmung (so oft sie auch wiederholt sein mag) beisammen.

(These two representations are combined in the *object*, i.e., regardless of any difference in the condition of the *subject*, and are not merely found together in perception [however often as that might be repeated].)

(Ibid., 252 [emphasis added])

With this Object/Subject opposition, we can see that the idea of "combination in the object," which up to a point is very close to R1, invests the "thing" (*Ding*) with a new coefficient, which belongs to the universe of the *Critique* and which assumes the distinction between "empirical intuition" and the "originary synthetic unity of apperception" (the "unity of transcendental apperception"). The change in the lexicon of judgment goes hand in hand with a change in the lexicon of the object.

Alain de Libera

BIBLIOGRAPHY

Albertus Magnus [Albert the Great]. *Metaphysica, Pars II: Libri 6–13*. Edited by Bernhard Geyer. In *Alberti Magni Opera Omnia*, vol. 16, part 2. Münster, Ger.: Aschendorff, 1964.

Angelelli, Ignacio. *Studies on Gottlob Frege and Traditional Philosophy*. Dordrecht, Neth.: Reidel, 1967.

Aristotle. *The Categories*. Translated by Harold P. Cooke. Loeb Classical Library. Cambridge, MA: Harvard University Press, 1973.

———. *De interpretatione vel Periermenias*. In *Aristoteles Latinus*, vol. 2, parts 1–2, edited by Lorenzo Minio-Paluello. Bruges, Belg.: Desclée de Brouwer, 1995.

———. *Métaphysique*. Translated by Jean Tricot. 2 vols. Paris: Vrin, 1991.

Barnes, Jonathan. "Property in Aristotle's *Topics*." *Archiv für Geschichte der Philosophie* 52 (1970): 136–55.

Bonitz, H. *Aristotelis Metaphysica*. 2 vols. Bonn: Marcus, 1848–49.

Cunningham, Stanley B. "The Metaphysics of the Good." In *Reclaiming Moral Agency: The Moral Philosophy of Albert the Great*, 93–112. Washington, DC: Catholic University of America Press, 2008.

Frege, Gottlob. *Die Grundlagen der Arithmetik: Eine logisch mathematische Untersuchung über den Begriff der Zahl*. Edited by Christian Thiel. Centennial ed. Hamburg: Meiner, 1986. Translation by J. L. Austin: *The Foundations of Arithmetic: A Logico-Mathematical Enquiry into the Concept of Number*. 5th rev. ed. Evanston, IL: Northwestern University Press, 1980.

———. "Über die Grundlagen der Geometrie." *Jahresbericht der Deutschen Mathematiker-Vereinigung* 12 (1903).

———. *Unbekannte Briefe Freges über die Grundlagen der Geometrie und Antwortbrief Hilberts an Frege*. Edited by M. Steck. Sitzungsberichte der Heidelberger Akademie der Wissenschaften, Mathematisch-naturwissenschaftliche Klasse, part 2. Heidelberg: Veiss, 1941.

Gates, Henry-Louis. *The Signifying Monkey: A Theory of African-American Literary Criticism*. New York: Oxford University Press, 1988.

Husserl, Edmund. *Logische Untersuchungen*. Edited by Ursula Panzer. Husserliana 19. The Hague: Nijhoff, 1984. Translation by J. N. Findlay: *Logical Investigations*. 2 vols. London: Routledge and Kegan Paul, 1970.

Kant, Immanuel. *Critique of Pure Reason*. Translated and edited by P. Guyer and A. Wood. Cambridge: Cambridge University Press, 1998.

Kopp, Clemens. "Die 'Fallaciae ad modum Oxoniae': Ein Fehlschlußtraktat aus dem 13. Jahrhundert." Dissertation. Cologne, 1985.

Leibniz, Gottfried. *Die philosophischen Schriften von G. W. Leibniz*. Edited by C. J. Gerhardt. 7 vols. Reprint. Hildesheim, Ger.: Olms, 1960.

Porphyry. *Isagoge: Texte grec, translatio Boethii*. Translated by Alain de Libera and Alain-Philippe Segonds. Introduction and notes by Alain de Libera. Paris: Vrin, 1998. Translation by Jonathan Barnes: *Porphory's Introduction*. With commentary by Jonathan Barnes. Oxford: Oxford University Press, 2003.

Reinach, Adolf. *Die obersten Regeln der Vernunftschlüsse bei Kant*. Edited by Karl Schuhmann. Munich: Philosophia, 1989.

Rosier-Catach, Irène. *La parole comme acte*. Paris: Vrin, 1994.

Tonquédec, Joseph. *La critique de la connaissance*. Paris: Beauchesne, 1929.

Twardowski, Kazimierz. *On the Content and Object of Presentations: A Psychological Investigation*. Translated and introduction by R. Grossmann. The Hague: Nijhoff, 1977.

MÊTIS [μῆτις] (GREEK)

ENGLISH   ruse, skill

➤ *RUSE*, and ART, *DESTINY*, DOXA, INGENIUM, MEMORY, *PRUDENCE*, *SOPHISM*, TALAṬṬUF, TRUTH, UNDERSTANDING, *WISDOM*

Mêtis [μῆτις], in ancient Greek, covers a wide semantic field, including the idea of practical intelligence, of astuteness, of a supple mind. This mental category had only sporadically caught the attention of scholars (Carlo Diano) before the groundbreaking book by Marcel Detienne and Jean-Pierre Vernant, *Les ruses de l'intelligence. La mêtis des Grecs* (*Cunning Intelligence in Greek Culture and Society*). The word derives from a verbal root that means "to measure" (Gr. *metron* [μέτρον], *mêtra* [μήτρα], "measure"; see LEX, Box 1). It is linked to the important root *med-, whose meaning Benveniste defines as follows: "to take the appropriate measures with authority" (RT: *Le vocabulaire des institutions indo-européennes*; see RT: *Dictionnaire étymologique de la langue grecque*, s.v. "medô"). This root offers a number of terms signifying measure, moderation, and modality (Lat. *modus*), as well as the attention of someone who "meditates," dominates, rules, decides (Gr. *medomai* [μήδομαι], "to attend to"; but also *mêdomai* [μέδομαι], "to meditate a plan, to have in mind"), including in the field of law and "medicine." *Mêtis* characterizes—for better or for worse; between omnicompetence and charlatanism—the posture adopted by the Sophists, "at the intersection between the traditional mêtis and the new intelligence of the philosopher" (Detienne and Vernant, *Les ruses de l'intelligence*). It was destined to become a category in contemporary anthropology, and is associated with the Anglo-Saxon category of the trickster, as well as with Lévi-Strauss's notion of *bricolage*.

Through a number of interconnected studies, M. Detienne and J.-P. Vernant sketched out a vast panorama that presents the whole range of mental attitudes covered by the term *mêtis* (astuteness, flair, shrewdness, foresight, feigning, disguise, resourcefulness, attention, vigilance, etc.), as well as the role of *mêtis* in a series of functions and strategies employed by the gods, by men, and by animals.

The book begins by analyzing the figure of the Oceanid Mêtis, "Prudence" (this is P. Mazon's chosen French translation in Hesiod's *Theogony*), the first wife of Zeus, who, in an unforeseen move that is more cunning than astuteness itself, grabs her and swallows her while she is already pregnant with Athena (*Theogony*, ll. 886–900). Mêtis, which is no less fundamental than in the Orphic version, is added to force, and in the case of Zeus, renders him unbeatable.

The semantic field of *mêtis* is covered by many other notions, such as that of a trap (*dolos* [δόλος]), of disguise, and above all of *technê* [τέχνη] (art, skill, and the technical crafts), of *kairos* [καιρός], or "the opportune moment" (see MOMENT), of *poros* [πόρος] (open passage), and of *apatê* [ἀπάτη] (ruse, deception; see TRUTH, Box 6). It is under the aegis of this vast semantic field that a number of different strategies are developed in hunting, fishing, war, etc., and used by the gods (especially Athena and Hephaistos), by men (blacksmiths, sailors, etc.), and by animals (the octopus, the fox, etc.). A new horizon is thus invented, opening out onto aspects and ideologies of ancient Greece that had been unknown, and that are symbolized by the practical intelligence of Athena, who distinguishes herself from the master of horses and of the sea, Poseidon, precisely because she uses technique, or *mêtis*, to make the farmer's plow, the bit for the horse's teeth, or the tiller to guide ships.

The section of the book dealing with Chronos, Zeus, and the epic heroes, Menelaus, Antilochus, and, above all, Ulysses, is based on the great epic texts and a number of examples from Greek tragedy. For *mêtis* is essentially a term from the *epos*, and although the comic theater of Aristophanes is full of ruses, the word never appears, just as we never find it in Herodotus, except in a quotation from Homer, nor in Euripides, and very rarely elsewhere in Greek tragedy. This accounts for the many recent studies devoted to the analysis of *mêtis*, particularly in the *Odyssey*, linking the notion to the polytropism of Ulysses, with his "thousand tricks," as well as to the ironic and treacherous writing of Homer's text itself (P. Pucci).

■ See Box 1.

The word *mêtis* is sometimes used in its Odyssean sense by modern critics. Thus, James C. Scott, in *Seeing Like a State* (1999), uses this word to describe the ingeniousness of traditional resourceful peasants who are good with their hands and able to adapt to changing situations, as opposed to rational and scientific technicians, who are abstract and who prefigure industrial agriculture and globalization.

Pietro Pucci

1

Ulysses: "My name is no-one," the first dramatization of *mêtis*

➤ ESTI, *NEGATION, NOTHING, PERSON, WITTICISM*

Ulysses and his traveling companions are imprisoned on their return journey by the man-eating Polyphemus, who, instead of offering them hospitality, devours them two at a time for his meals. How Ulysses carries out his "finest plan" (*aristê boulê* [ἀρίστη βουλή]; *Odyssey*, 9.98) is well known: he offers wine to Cyclops to get him drunk, blinds him while he is asleep using a stake he has hardened in the fire, and he and his companions escape from the den once he has removed the rock from the entrance, each of them hanging underneath a sheep's stomach. But this audacious plan, which entails tricking a monster, would not succeed without a preparatory ruse involving words, and which can be read in the Greek text through what Victor Bérard called "a cascade of puns." All of these puns revolve around the relationship between *outis* [οὖτις] and *mêtis*.

Outis, from the negative particle *ou* [οὐ] (no, not) and the indefinite pronoun *tis* [τίς] (someone), is the hero's name that Odysseus declares to Polyphemus to be his own: "*Outis* [οὖτις], No-one, is my name. I am called *Outis*, No-one, by my mother, my father, and all my companions" (366–67). So that when his neighbors the Cyclops, awakened by the screams of Polyphemus, ask him: "Is one (*mê tis* [μή τίς]) of the mortals coming to steal your flock? Is someone (*mê tis* [μή τίς]) killing you by ruse or by force?" (406), the monster can only reply: "My friends, no-one is killing me (Outis me kteinei [Οὖτίς με κτείνει])"

(408). However, because of the Greek syntax of negation, the sentence as a whole is to be understood, from the point of view of Polyphemus for whom No-one is the name of someone, to mean: "[It is] No-one [who] is killing me by ruse and not by force" (Outis me kteinei dolôi oude biêpsin [Οὖτίς με κτείνει δόλῳ οὐδὲ βίηψιν]), whereas the Cyclops, for whom no-one is negative, have to understand it to mean: "No-one is killing me, neither by ruse nor by force." The negative particle *ne* in the French "*ne … personne*" (no-one) is particularly useful in translating the Greek here since it is linked to the primarily positive meaning of *personne*, so if Polyphemus had been a good Frenchman, he might well have made himself understood. The chorus continues: "If no-one uses force on you" (ei mên dê mê tis se biazetai [εἰ μὲν δή μή τίς σε βιάζεται]) (410), it is because Zeus is inflicting an illness on you, and no-one can do anything about it. Now, in this response, just as immediately before in their questions, they rely upon the other negative particle, not *ou*, a factual negation, but *mê* [μή], the prohibitive negation, also known as "subjective" negation. This sort of negation is indeed very characteristic of Greek, implying a will or thought, and one finds it essentially in other moods than the indicative as a means of expressing all the nuances of prohibition, of deliberation, of want, and of regret, or, as in this case, of eventuality or of virtuality: *ei mê tis se biazetai*.

This is where, in focusing on this construction that is so attuned to the subtleties of negation, we find the really telling relationship to *mêtis*. No longer *mê* (negative particle) *tis* (someone), as two words, but *mêtis*, this time as a single word, the celebrated *mêtis* of the Greeks, their practical and cunning wisdom, embodied in the figure of Odysseus, who has any number of tricks up his sleeve. When he sees the Cyclops heading away, Odysseus laughs into his beard and rejoices in his heart: "It is my name that tricked him, and my irreproachable wit" (hôs onom' exapatêsen emon kai mêtis amumôn [ὡς ὄνομ' ἐξαπάτησεν ἐμὸν καὶ μῆτις ἀμύμων]) (414). And he uses the word again in book 20, exhorting his heart to be patient: "How courageous you were, in waiting until the *mêtis* released me from this den where I thought I would die!" (20–21).

One can understand why the *mêtis* of Odysseus, like that of Homer, as an effective mastery of speech, and of the very grammar and syntax of language, and as a play on being and non-being, were the heroic models for Sophistic rhetoric, which philosophers considered to be such a deceptive and scandalous art.

BIBLIOGRAPHY

Bérard, Victor, trans. and ed. *L'Odyssée "poésie homérique."* 2 vols. Paris: Les Belles Lettres, 1963.

BIBLIOGRAPHY

Détienne, Marcel, and Jean-Pierre Vernant. *Les ruses de l'intelligence: La mètis des Grecs*. Paris: Flammarion, 1974. Translation by Janet Lloyd: *Cunning Intelligence in Greek Culture and Society*. Atlantic Highlands, NJ: Humanities, 1978.

Diano, Carlo. *Forma ed evento: Principii per una interpretazione del mondo greco*. Venice: Pozza, 1952.

Faraone, Christopher A., and Emily Teeter. "Egyptian Maat and Hesiodic Metis." *Mnemosyne* 57 (2004): 177–208.

Ferretto, Carla. "Orione tra 'Alke' e 'Metis.'" *Civiltà Classica e Cristiana* 3 (1982): 161–82.

Goldhill, Simon. *The Poet's Voice: Essays on Poetics and Greek Literature*. Cambridge: Cambridge University Press, 1991.

Holmberg, Ingrid Elisabeth. "The Sign of Metis." *Arethusa* 30 (1997): 1–33.

Piccirilli, Luigi. "Artemide et la *mètis* di Temistocle." *Quaderni di Storia* 13 (1981): 143–46.

Pucci, Pietro. *Odysseus Polytropos*. Ithaca, NY: Cornell University Press, 1987.

Richlin, Amy. "Zeus and Metis: Foucalt, Feminism, Classics." *Helios* 18 (1991): 160–80.

Scott, James C. *Seeing Like a State*. New Haven, CT: Yale University Press, 1999.

Solomon, Jon. "One Man's Metis: Another Man's Ate." In *Hypatia: Essays in Classics, Comparative Literature, and Philosophy Presented to Hazel E. Barnes on Her Seventieth Birthday*, edited by William M. Calder et al., 79–90. Boulder: University of Colorado Press, 1985.

Schein, Seth L. "Odysseus and Polyphemus in the *Odyssey*." *Greek, Roman and Byzantine Studies* 11 (1970): 73–83.

Slatkin, Laura M. "Composition by Theme and the *Mêtis* of the *Odyssey*." In *Reading the Odyssey: Selected Interpretative Essays*, edited by Seth L. Schein, 223–55. Princeton, NJ: Princeton University Press, 1996.

MIMÊSIS [μίμησις]

FRENCH	*imitation, représentation*
GERMAN	*Nachahmung, nachmachen, kopieren, nachbilden*
ITALIAN	*imitazione, rassimiglianze; rittrare*
LATIN	*imitatio, similitude*

➤ IMITATION, and ACTOR, ANALOGY, ART, BEAUTY, COMPARISON, DESCRIPTION, DICHTUNG, DOXA, HISTORY, *IMAGE* [BILD, EIDÔLON], *IMAGINATION* [PHANTASIA], INGENIUM, PLEASURE, PRAXIS, REPRÉSENTATION, TRUTH

Since the Renaissance, the translation and interpretation of the term *mimêsis* [μίμησις] have been the source of important philosophical and theoretical debates that have played a crucial role in the history of artistic thought. The development of the theory of art, first in Italy in the fifteenth and sixteenth centuries, then in France in the seventeenth century, is fundamentally indebted to the Greek definition of art, in the general sense of *techne* [τέχνη] and the restricted sense of *poiêsis* [ποίησις], as a mimetic activity. And that definition, on each occasion, for the French as for the Italians, raised the same questions. In what does artistic imitation consist? What distinguishes it from resemblance, copy, reproduction, and illusion? What is its function: is it in the service of lies or the truth, pleasure, or knowledge? What is its object: is it nature or the idea, the visible or the invisible, the inner world or outer reality? All these questions are inscribed within a problematic largely determined by the semantic ambiguity of the concept of *mimêsis* in Greek philosophy. They correspond to the dual orientation given to the problematic of *mimêsis* by Plato and Aristotle, that is, to the opposition between a concept elaborated with reference to a pictorial model, giving *mimêsis* the meaning of "resemblance," and a concept elaborated with reference to a theatrical model, giving *mimêsis* the sense of "representation." This opposition between two meanings of *mimêsis*, between Platonic and Aristotelian *mimêsis*, is in a way constitutive of the

theory of imitation that developed starting in the Renaissance and that dominated thinking about art for several centuries. It is found in the idea of *imitazione*, as well as in those of imitation and *Nachahmung*, but by way of numerous transformations that affected its meaning deeply. The Italian theorists reinterpreted *mimêsis* on the basis of the idea of *imitatio*, transmitted by the Latin that they continued to use. And it was on the basis of the theory of *imitatio* that they developed a theory of *imitazione*. It was subsequently on the basis of the idea of *imitazione*, and in opposition to it, that the French in turn appropriated the Aristotelian theory of *mimêsis*. And the critique of *mimêsis* that developed in Germany at the end of the eighteenth century was in fact a calling into question of the French doctrine of imitation that had dominated European thought since the seventeenth century. All these displacements, adaptations, and "translations" from one language to another did no more, in a sense, than develop one of the aspects of the concept of *mimêsis* and exploit its prodigious semantic richness.

I. *Mimêsis* in Plato and Aristotle

A. Theater or painting?

Like other words of the same family (*mimêtês* [μιμητής], *mimeîsthai* [μιμεῖσθαι], etc.), *mimêsis* [μίμησις] is related to the noun *mîmos* [μῖμος]. Initially the term referred only to mime, dance, music, in other words, to activities aimed at expressing an inner reality and not at reproducing external reality. Its application to the visual arts was concomitant with the semantic shift that took place in the fifth century when it began to designate the reproduction of the external world. That new use would play a crucial role in the orientation Plato would give to the problematic of *mimêsis*. The philosophical elaboration of the concept of *mimêsis* was in fact born of a reflection on painting and sculpture. To be sure, the first sense of *mimêsis* subsists in Plato, who persisted in applying the term to music, dance (*Laws*, 7.798d), and the theater. We thus find the theatrical origin of *mimêsis* in the distinction between *mimêsis* and *diêgêsis* [διήγησις], mimetic discourse corresponding to the forms of tragedy and comedy, as opposed to a simple narrative in which the poet recounts in his own name, without hiding behind a character (*Republic*, 3.392c–394d). But such uses, which remain traditional, themselves stemmed from the establishment of a new sense of *mimêsis* based on a reference to the visual arts, and more specifically to painting, that is, a mimetic activity whose characteristic is to imitate outer reality and to do so in an image. The pictorial origin of the concept of *mimêsis* as elaborated by Plato thus inscribes the analysis of the concept in a field far removed from the one to which it was linked by the theatrical origin of the word. The problem no longer concerns the identity of the subject, the confusion between the actor and the author (as in the case of theatrical *mimêsis*), but the identity of the object, that is, the relation of the image (*eidôlon* [εἴδωλον]) to its model. The fact of connecting the question of *mimêsis* to that of the image gives *mimêsis* the sense of resemblance or likeness, and the definition of *mimêsis* as resemblance allows one to condemn pictorial *mimêsis* as a false and bad likeness, that is, to reject it in the name of the very criterion that it served to elaborate. To be sure, Plato did not reject all forms of pictorial *mimêsis*, as is evidenced by the division he establishes in *The Sophist* between two sorts of *mimêsis*: a *mimêsis eikastikê* [μίμησις είκαστική] and a *mimêsis phantastikê* [μίμησις φανταστική] (235d–236c). The first consists of reproducing the model by respecting its proportions and imbuing each part with the appropriate colors: an art of the accurate copy. The second, on the other hand, involving above all works of large dimensions (which thus need to be viewed at a distance), deforms the exact proportions and uses colors that do not correspond to those found in reality. This mimetic does not seek to reproduce the real as it is, but as it appears to the spectator given his point of view—"these artists give up the truth in their images (*tois eidôlois* [τοῖς εἰδώλοις]) and make only the proportions that appear to be beautiful, disregarding the real ones" (*ou tas ousas summetrias, alla tas doxousas einai kalas* [οὐ τὰς οὔσας συμμετρίας ἀλλὰ τὰς δοξούσας εἶναι καλάς]) (236a 4–6)—and it is there, of course, that we find lodged the art of sophistry, always considered "relativistic" (268c–d). It is a mimetics that does not reproduce being but appearance: a "phantastics," then, which is translated as the art of the "simulacrum" or of "illusion" (see PHANTASIA): it is, in keeping with good Platonic doctrine, to be condemned under the double heading of imprecision and deception, simultaneously because it is at a remove from truth and because it would have us believe its truth. Now there is "a great deal of this kind of thing in painting" (*pampolu . . . kata tên zôgraphian* [πάμπολυ . . . κατὰ τὴν ζωγραφίαν]) (236b 9). The quality of the *mimêsis* is to be gauged by the standard of its reference, evaluated in terms of accuracy and exactitude, that is, as a function of criteria that belong to the realm of knowledge and truth: in the arts of imitation, "it is first of all equality, whether of quality or quantity, that gives truth or rightness (*tên orthotêta* [τὴν ὀρθότητα])" (*Laws*, 2.667d 5–7).

This strictly referential conception of *mimêsis* nonetheless poses several problems with relation to the image—that is, as soon as one applies it to the type of imitation on which the Platonic theory of *mimêsis* is, in fact, based. The criteria of good *mimêsis* in the sense of likeness cannot be those of *mimêsis* in the sense of reproduction. An image that would reproduce the dimensions and all the characteristics of its model would no longer be an image but an identical duplicate of the original. One would no longer have Cratylus and the image of Cratylus, but two Cratyluses:

> Then you see, my friend, that we must find some other principle of truth in images ("*allên chrê eikonos orthotêta zêtein*" [ἄλλην χρὴ εἰκόνος ὀρθότητα ζητεῖν]), and also in names; and not insist that an image is no longer an image when something is added or subtracted. Do you not perceive that images are very far from having qualities which are the exact counterpart of the realities which they represent ("*hosou endeousin hai eikones ta auta echein ekeinois hôn eikones eisin*" [ὅσου ἐνδέουσιν αἱ εἰκόνες τὰ αὐτὰ ἔχειν ἐκείνοις ὧν εἰκόνες εἰσίν])?
>
> *Cratylus*, 432c 7–d 2

B. Resemblance or representation?

How is the resemblance of an image to be thought? How are we to think that other accuracy that presupposes the existence of a deviation between the product of the imitation and the object imitated? How are we to reconcile the referential definition of *mimêsis* with the idea that the imitation can be accurate while being inadequate to its model? This properly conceptual difficulty, evidence of a tension between contradictory demands, is already inscribed in the language. As R. Dupont-Roc and J. Lallot observe in the notes accompanying their translation of Aristotle's *Poetics*, whatever the difference between Aristotelian and Platonic *mimêsis*, there is "a feature common to verbs of imitation in the two authors: the fundamental ambivalence of the accusative of an object—affected (= model) or effectuated (= copy)—constructed with those verbs." And it is precisely in order to *preserve* that ambivalence that they chose to translate *mimeîsthai* by *représenter* and not by *imiter*: "unless there be elements in the context allowing one to discriminate, 'to represent (*représenter*) a man' offers the same ambiguity as *mimeîsthai anthrôpon* [μιμεῖσθαι ἄνθρωπον], whereas the traditional translation by *imiter* (to imitate) abusively selects an interpretation of the accusative as it does that of the model." This grammatical ambiguity, which allows one to focus the verb on the imitation as well as on the object imitated, is in agreement with the dual descent, both philological and philosophical, of the concept of *mimêsis,* that is, with the fact that its meaning was constituted to a twofold reference—both theatrical and pictorial. Those two lines of descent determine two distinct ways of envisaging the object of *mimêsis*. The first, which opens onto a space of fiction, leads one to connect the mimetic activity with its product, the object that Dupont-Roc and Lallot call the "object effectuated," which is given to be seen and heard in its actual presence—as in a theatrical performance (*représentation*). The second, which opens onto a world of images, connects it, on the contrary, with its model, what they call the "object affected," an object whose presence is duplicated in paint on an illusory mode—as in a pictorial imitation. It is plainly that second sense that is dominant in Plato, but without annulling the effects of the other line of descent, which continues to affect the Platonic tradition. The tendency is in some sense reversed in Aristotle, who reinserts the meaning of *mimêsis* into the realm of poetics. As Ricoeur has written, in *mimêsis*, according to Aristotle, "one should not understand . . . a reduplication of presence, as might be understood of Platonic *mimêsis*, but the break which opens up the space of fiction" (*Temps et récit*).

■ See Box 1.

Just as the theatrical genealogy of *mimêsis* comes to disturb, in Plato, the coherence of a construction based on a visual paradigm, the Aristotelian analysis of poetic *mimêsis*, in a movement that is similar but reversed, is haunted by the question of the pictorial image, which draws the problematic of *mimêsis* in an entirely different direction. The comparison with painting invoked by Aristotle on innumerable occasions, and which attests to the underlying (but active) presence of the pictorial reference, is not made without raising several difficulties. Poetic *mimêsis*, as defined by Aristotle, is, as is known, a *mimêsis* of action: it concerns "the imitation [representation] of men in action (*prattontas* [πράττοντας])" (*Poetics*, 2.1448a 1). Representing action means representing a plot (*muthos* [μῦθος]): "the Plot is the imitation of the action—for by plot [*muthos*] I here mean the arrangement of the incidents" (6.1450a 2). This correlation between *mimêsis*

1

The translation of *mimêsis* as "representation" in Aristotle

One of the strongest aspects of R. Dupont-Roc and J. Lallot's translation into French of Aristotle's *Poetics* is indeed the way it takes into account the dual philological and philosophical natures of the questions raised by the translation of *mimêsis*. The reasons they give to justify their choice of translating *mimêsis* as representation are of course first and foremost philological: "We can now see why, against an entire tradition, we chose to translate *mimeîsthai* not as 'to imitate' but as 'to represent': the decision was thus made on the basis of the theatrical connotations of this verb, and above all the possibility, as is also the case with *mimeîsthai*, of having the complement be either the 'model' object or the produced object—whereas 'to imitate' excluded the latter, which is the most important." But this choice also reflects a properly philosophical concern to account for the specificity of the Aristotelian conception of *mimêsis* in relation to the Platonic one, that is, a concern to resolve the many confusions and misinterpretations produced by the translation of *mimêsis* in the two authors as "imitation." Their translation thus has the great advantage of clarifying a conceptual difference by inscribing it into a lexical distinction,

that is, of clarifying retrospectively the Greek text itself. But it also adds a further degree of complexity to a history that is already fairly complicated, and the meaning of "representation" nowadays is indeed no less equivocal than the meaning of "imitation" was then. If "imitation" pulls *mimêsis* towards "resemblance" by conceiving of it as part of a problematic that was based on the paradigm of the image, "representation" draws us on the other hand to a theory of the sign founded on a linguistic model. Its present-day meaning has largely been determined by a history that has its origins in the seventeenth century, notably with the logicians of Port-Royal, and that was extensively developed in the twentieth century in the field of discourse theory. If the theatrical connotation of representation is still there in the everyday usage of the term, it has to a large extent disappeared from theoretical usage, where its connotation is primarily semiotic, including the application of the word to the analysis of the pictorial image. The way in which the term is nowadays used pervasively in art criticism, where it tends to replace the term "image," is particularly interesting in this respect. To think the image as representation amounts to thinking the

image as sign, and thus to obliterating its specifically visual dimension, which is still present in the word "imitation." It is thus hardly surprising that the translation of *mimêsis* as "representation" is consonant with certain recent analyses that have been undertaken in the context of the philosophy of language, independently of any philological or historical concern. So Kendall Walton, for example, in the opening pages of his book *Mimêsis as Make Believe*, is careful to warn his reader that the word *mimêsis*, as he uses it, has to be understood in the sense of representation, that is, without reference to any theory of resemblance or imitation. He immediately goes on to say, however, that if the meaning of *mimêsis* corresponds for him to that of "representation," it is in the particular sense that he himself gives to the term "representation"! It was doubtless in order to avoid all of these ambiguities that Walton preferred to return to the Greek term, but without translating it.

BIBLIOGRAPHY

Aristotle. *La poétique*. Translated by R. Dupont-Roc and J. Lallot. Paris: Éditions du Seuil, 1980.
Walton, Kendall. *Mimêsis as Make Believe*. Cambridge, MA: Harvard University Press, 1990.

---

and *muthos* by way of plot results in giving primacy to plot over characters in the definition of tragedy: "The plot (*ho muthos* [ὁ μῦθος]), then, is the first principle, and, as it were, the soul of a tragedy; Character (*ta êthê* [τὰ ἤθη]) holds the second place" (6.1450a 38–39). The comparison with painting, which intervenes immediately following this sentence, justifies that hierarchy by establishing a parallel between outline and plot, on the one hand, and color and character, on the other: "A similar fact is seen in painting. The most beautiful colors, laid on confusedly, will not give as much pleasure as the chalk outline of a portrait." But this comparison, which is in some sense structural and which establishes a hierarchical correspondence between the parts entering into the composition of a poem and those entering into the composition of a painting, agrees poorly with the one developed in chapter 2, again on the subject of character. It rests on an entirely different distinction that, in this case, calls into play the idea of resemblance or likeness:

Since the objects of imitation are men in action, and these men must be either of a higher or a lower type . . ., it follows that we must represent men either as better than in real life, or as worse, or as they are. It is the same in painting. Polygnotus depicted men as nobler than they are, Pauson as less noble, Dionysius drew them true to life. Now it is evident that each of the modes

of imitation above mentioned will exhibit these differences, and become a distinct kind in imitating objects that are thus distinct.

2.1448a 1–9; trans. S. H. Butcher

If the definition of *mimêsis* as a *mimêsis* of plot or action links poetry to history—from which it is distinguished, moreover, since actions are represented on stage by characters who are themselves in action—*mimêsis* of character, on the contrary, leads one to a linkage with painting, and more precisely with a genre of painting that raises in the most pointed manner the question of likeness, namely, that of portraiture. This twofold reference—to history and portraiture—attests anew to the impossibility of giving an unequivocal definition of *mimêsis*. If the *mimêsis-muthos* link fully justifies the translation of *mimêsis* as "representation," the existence of that other link, between *mimêsis* and portraiture, attests to the permanence, in Aristotle, of an interpretation of *mimêsis* in terms of image and thus of likeness, which would justify an occasional return to translating *mimêsis* as "imitation." As is the case in chapter 4, in which Aristotle suspends the Platonic condemnation of artistic imitation by assigning from the outset a cognitive function to the pleasure procured by mimetic activity, a tendency said to be inscribed in human nature. This pleasure in recognition, which, for Aristotle, lies at the source of knowledge, is directly linked to the existence of images, that is, to grasping a likeness or resemblance: "Thus the reason why men enjoy seeing a likeness *chairousi tas eikonas horôntes* [χαίρουσι τὰς εἰκόνας ὁρῶντες]) is that in contemplating it they find themselves learning or inferring, and saying perhaps, 'Ah, that is he'" (1448b 15).

C. Nature or history?

The definition of art in general and of painting in particular has often received legitimacy, notably in the sixteenth and seventeenth centuries, through the authority of Aristotle. Even at present, numerous interpreters see clear evidence of the influence of the Stagirite on the constitution of the theory of art. Yet although that theory does indeed borrow its elements from Aristotle, there is no basis for attributing to him such a determination of art. It conflates in a single idea definitions that, in Aristotle, belong to quite different registers. It associates with painting, and more generally with the arts in the modern, artistic sense of the term, that is, to activities that belonged, for Aristotle, to the realm of poetics, the definition that the philosopher gives for *techne* (τέχνη) in the *Physics*: "Generally speaking, art (*techne*) either executes what nature is impotent to effectuate or imitates it. . . . If, then, artificial things are produced with a view to a certain end, it is clear that this is equally the case for the things of nature; for in artificial as well as in natural things, antecedents and consequences have between them the same relation" (2.8.199a.15). Poetic *mimêsis* is referred by Aristotle not to nature but to history; it is an imitation of human actions (*mimêsis praxeôs* [μίμησις πράξεως]). Attributing to Aristotle the idea according to which art, in the artistic sense, is an imitation of nature thus implies a transfer of meaning from the realm of physics to that of poetics, from art in the sense of *techne* to art in the sense of *poiêsis* [ποίησις]. The translation of *techne* as *ars*, then as "art," the fact that Greek does not possess a term to designate what we call "art" in the sense of the fine arts, that is, the fact that it conflates in a single term two things that European languages, since the Renaissance, have strained to distinguish, namely, the art of the artist, the painter or sculptor, and the art of the artisan or worker (a distinction renewing one established in the Middle Ages between the liberal arts and the mechanical arts; see ART) are certainly not unrelated to this transfer. And that in itself would undoubtedly not have been possible if the meaning attributed by Aristotle to *mimêsis, mimeîsthai*, when those words refer to images and not plots, had not in some way included a space to welcome and incorporate it. The fusion, in a new conception of art, of *mimêsis* in the sense of an imitation of actions and *mimêsis* in the sense of an imitation of nature may have received its authority from the secondary sense that *mimêsis* has within the *Poetics* itself. We are dealing here with one of the multiple transformations that allowed the *Poetics*, starting with the Renaissance, to become a foundational text for the theory of painting. It effectively allowed one to reassign priority to the pictorial paradigm in the definition of *mimêsis*. And also to take advantage of the possibilities offered by the synthesis previously effected in the Middle Ages, by way of the word *ars*, between the definition of *techne* given in the *Physics*, where *techne* is opposed to *phusis* [φύσις], and the one found in the *Nicomachean Ethics*, where

techne is distinguished from *praxis,* those two terms then corresponding to two different modes of regulated and finalized activity: "the disposition to act accompanied by a rule [τῆς ποιητικῆς ἕξεως]" (6.4.1140a 3–5; see PRAXIS). The theory of imitation, as it was to develop in the Renaissance and the classical age, would give a new meaning to the link between the idea of art and that of rules by redefining the rule within an artistic realm that affirmed and was intent on defending its autonomy in relation to the domain of "mechanical" activities. The misinterpretation of the Aristotelian idea of *mimêsis* was thus not the cause, but in fact the effect of the labor of reinterpretation that the transformation of the artistic domain (and the new stakes with which art was charged) made necessary.

▪ See Box 2.

II. From the Imitation of the Visible to the Expression of the Invisible: The Powers of the *Imago*

In chapter 1 of his book published in 1637, *De pictura veterum libri tres,* a veritable *summa* of humanist thinking about art, Franciscus Junius enumerates the different definitions of imitation. After citing chapter 4 of the *Poetics,* the preface to *Eikones,* and book 2 of the *Life of Apollonios* by Philostratus, he writes: "In any event, for grammarians, image (*imago*) means what proceeds from imitation (*imitago*)." This sentence bears witness to the transformation visited on the idea of imitation through the transition from *mimêsis* to *imitatio,* as a result of the connection established in Latin between *imitatio* and *imago.* In this sense, the history of *imitatio* becomes inseparable from that of *imago.*

Imago belongs to the same semantic field as *simulacrum, signum, effigies,* and even *exemplar* and *species.* Signifying the imitation of a portrait, the word *imago* was applied to the image of the deceased. It designated the mask made from the imprint of a face. Initially referring to ancestral cults, it also designated, in classical Latin, the image of the gods, associated with terms referring to the realm of the sacred. The transformation of the meaning of *imago* in the course of the Middle Ages by the theological problematic of the image would simultaneously modify the meaning of *imitatio* by inscribing it in a new network of signification articulated around the idea of likeness, but a likeness or resemblance that was also thought in new terms, as evidenced by the extraordinarily complex use of "similitude" and its offshoots. The meaning taken on by *imitatio* in the fourteenth century, for example, in the expression *imitatio Christi,* illustrates the amplitude and the nature of this transformation. The use of *imitatio* refers in this case to a problematic of resemblance that developed from a reinterpretation of *imago,* the relation of son to father and that of man to God, giving a radically new meaning to the term. The idea according to which man had been created in the image of God required one to no longer think of the resemblance of the *imago* solely in terms of a copy, but also in terms of an analogy.

Under the influence of Neoplatonic doctrines (Boethius, Scotus Erigenus, and above all the School of Chartres), analogical thinking would bring about a complete re-elaboration of the meaning of *imitatio* as applied to artistic activities. To a theorist of the Middle Ages, the artist seeks to imitate the

2

Alberti's window

The new definition of painting that was developed during the Renaissance would mean that these different and initially heterogeneous levels of meaning were able to coexist, and this coexistence would sometimes bring with it certain contradictions. Far from being a sign of logical inconsistency, these contradictions in fact attested to the difficulty that the first theoreticians of art had in combining the two senses of *mimêsis* in a fully unified theory. The definition of a painting as an "open window," which we find in book 1 of Alberti's *De pictura*, is in this respect exemplary, particularly in light of the endless misunderstandings to which it has given rise. For Alberti, this window frames a narrative representation; it does not open out onto nature but onto a story: "First of all about where I draw. I inscribe a quadrangle of right angles, as large as I wish, which is considered to be an open window through which I see the story (*historia*) I want to paint" (English translation, slightly modified; in the Italian translation of his treatise, Alberti uses the word *storia* which, like *historia*, corresponds to Aristotle's *muthos* [on the two versions of Alberti's treatise, see BEAUTY]). But this definition does not match the one we find elsewhere in the text, where pictorial representation is characterized by its function of showing, that is, its function as an image: "No one would deny that the painter has nothing to do with things that are not visible. The painter is concerned solely with representing (*repraesentare*) what can be seen." This explains how this analogy with the window could have been interpreted in a sense that was completely alien to Alberti's thought, as a window opening out onto the visible world, like those *vedute* one comes across in so many Renaissance paintings. We find the same ambivalence in Poussin a century later. In one of his last letters, he defined painting as "an imitation, made up of lines and colors on some surface, of whatever is visible under the sun" (letter to Fréart de Chambray, 2 March 1665). But elsewhere he writes that "painting is nothing but the imitation of human actions," this second definition of imitation conforming to the Aristotelian idea of poetic *mimêsis*, since it was in fact a translation of a sentence by Torquato Tasso, which Poussin contented himself with copying out by replacing the word "poetry" with the word "painting."

BIBLIOGRAPHY

Alberti, Leon Battista. *On Painting*. Translated by J. Spencer. New Haven, CT: Yale University Press, 1970.

Poussin, Nicolas. *Correspondance de Nicolas Poussin*. Paris: Fernand de Nobèle, 1968.

visible world created by God as the creative work of God, to create in the image of God by prolonging the activity of nature. The relations between human creation and divine creation are governed by a principle of concordance and similitude, resting on the application of the rules of harmony, proportion, symmetry, and clarity, which the artist discovers in himself as in nature, and which allow him to attain that beauty which is nothing other than the visible manifestation of the divine splendor. The artist imitates not only *natura naturata*, but also *natura naturans*. As Panofsky writes, "the thesis according to which art imitates nature as much as possible or rather imitates according to nature, means that a parallel (but not a relation) is being set up between art and nature: art (under which rubric one must naturally and perhaps principally understand as well the *artes* that are foreign to the three arts based on drawing) does not imitate what nature creates, but works in the manner in which nature creates, pursuing, through specific means, objectives that are themselves defined, by realizing determined forms in materials that are themselves determined" (*Idea*). The visible form achieved by the artist is the material expression of a form immanent to his mind or imagination (*fantasia*) that the artist discovers in his contemplation of the visible world. In imitating the visible, art expresses the invisible. Commenting on a sentence of Robert Grosseteste: "Forma est exemplar ad quod respicit artifex ut ad ejus imitationem et similitudinem formet suum artificium" (The form is the idea that the artist has in sight in order to produce the imitations and likenesses of his art)," Edgar De Bruyne writes as follows: "The material work does not necessarily and faithfully copy the visible form . . . but inevitably it expresses the representation of what the artist conceives in his soul. It is that spiritual model that the form imitates above all else" (*Etudes d'esthétique médiévale*). As Saint Bonaventure writes, with reference to the classical theories of rhetoric: "Dicitur imago quod alterum exprimit et imitator" (It is said that the image expresses something other than what it imitates) (quoted by De Bruyne). The transformation of *imitatio* in relation to that of *imago* adds to the horizontal definition of imitation as outer likeness a twofold dimension, both vertical and in depth, expressiveness being characterized as a movement from inner to outer and from low to high. The first consequence of this transformation is to allow theologians to resolve in a manner favorable to images the thorny question that had been raised by the iconoclasts and that would be endlessly renewed until the Council of Trent, namely, the question of the worship of images (see OIKONOMIA). The second is plainly to furnish a major argument for legitimating artistic activity. The theoretical labor of Scholastic thought consisted of giving substance, an ontological dimension, to concepts such as *imago* or *forma* and to confer on them a properly theological function.

III. From *Imitatio* to *Imitazione*: Renaissance Theories of Art

It was thus this rather complicated history, extending over several centuries, that the humanist thought of the Renaissance would inherit. It was on that basis that the Italian theoreticians returned to the Greek and Latin texts that they discovered in the original, those of Aristotle, Plato, Horace, and Cicero. They were related to the problematic of *mimêsis* through the mediation of a field in which the idea of *imitatio* was gradually inscribed.

A. Hesitations in vocabulary

The definition of art as imitation first developed in the domain of the visual arts, giving to *imitare, imitazione*, the meaning of likeness, an image faithful to visible reality. The idea that art was to imitate nature appeared among painters and theoreticians of painting at the beginning of the fifteenth century. It is found in Alberti (*De pictura*, III, 1435), Ghiberti (*I commentarii*, 1436), and even in Leonardo, who stated that the painting most deserving of praise was that which was faithful to the thing imitated ("conformità co'la cosa imitata") (*Trattato della pittura*, fragment 411, in *Libro di pittura*). It was not until the second half of the sixteenth century and the dissemination of Aristotle's *Poetics* that the concept of imitation would be applied to the poetic arts, thus taking on a new meaning. (The first Latin translation of the *Poetics* from the original, by Lorenzo Valla, appeared in 1498; the Greek text was printed for the first time in 1503. In the second half of the sixteenth century, numerous translations in the vernacular appeared, accompanied by commentaries, along with poetics of Aristotelian inspiration.)

How is one to reconcile Aristotelian *mimêsis* with the idea of *imitatio* and above all with that of *imitazione* as it is expressed in the realm of painting? That conceptual difficulty first presented itself as a problem of translation. How was one to translate *mimêsis*? If *imitatio*, borrowed from classical Latin, finally prevailed in Renaissance Latin, certain translators nonetheless hesitated with regard to that term as an adequate rendering of the sense of *mimêsis*. It was thus that in 1481, the translator of Averroes opted for *assimilatio*, while Fracastoro, in the following century, anticipating the solution proposed by Depont-Roc and Lallot, thought that one could opt for either "imitation" or "representation": "sive imitari, sive representare dicamus" (*Naugerius*; *sive de Poetica dialogues*). The complete triumph of *imitatio* and its Italian derivative, *imitazione*, which would in turn give birth to the French and English variants of *imitation*, would not be sufficient to remove all those hesitations. The transition to the vernacular would be accompanied by numerous distinctions attesting to the permanence of the difficulties encountered. In his *Tratatto delle perfette proporzioni*, published in 1567, Vicenzo Danti, basing himself on the Aristotelian distinction between poetry and history, thus proposed to reserve *imitare* for art and to use *ritrarre* to designate an imitative likeness, one that reproduces things as one sees them. (*Ritrarre* from the Lat. *ritrahere*, "to pull backward"—as in Fr. *retirer* [withdraw] or *retrait*—initially had the general meaning of representing, describing, recounting; applied to painting, it took on the meaning of a representational likeness.) Already in Ceninni, one encounters the expressions *retrarre da natura* or *ritrarre naturale* (*Il libro del arte*). As for Castelvetro, the author of an Italian translation of Aristotle's *Poetics*, published in 1570, which would be strenuously challenged by the French during the following century, he chose to translate *mimêsis* as *rassomiglianze*, resemblance, and not as *imitazione*.

■ See Box 3.

B. Imitate nature or the idea?

These divergences found in the Italian translators, whether translating into Latin or the vernacular, illustrate the extreme diversity of conceptions competing (and doing so without cease) over a span of several centuries. The uncontested reign of the idea of imitation from the Renaissance to the end of the eighteenth century would never imply the existence of a systematic and unified theory of imitation.

As previously stated, the problem of imitation was first posited in the realm of painting before being taken up and formulated in very different terms by theoreticians of poetics. Was one to imitate nature or the idea, an external model or an inner model, the real or the beautiful? Ought the painter to seek to render visible reality as faithfully as possible, in

---

3
The resemblance of the portrait

The use of the word *ritratto*, derived from *ritrarre*, to refer to a portrait illustrates the richness of the identification between portrait and resemblance that made the portrait the paradigm of resemblance, and thus of painting as a lifelike image (just as the words *po(u)rtraire* and *po(u)rtraiture* were used in the seventeenth century to mean painting in general). But this identification also explained why the portrait came to be considered as an inferior genre in terms of the hierarchy of genres elaborated in the light of Aristotle's *Poetics*, and which implied the primacy of narrative painting. How could the status of the portrait as a genre be defended from the perspective of Aristotelian criteria? It was precisely in order to resolve this difficulty that an author such as Mancini proposed making a distinction between two types of portrait: *il rittrato simplice*, or simple portrait, conforming to the Platonic definition of *mimêsis eikastikê* [μίμησις εἰκαστική], which "expresses nothing more than the dimension, proportion, and resemblance of the thing it imitates (*similitudine della cosa que imita*)," and *il rittrato con azione et espressione d'affetto*, or portrait with action and passion, in which there is "besides resemblance (*similitudine*), action and passion, which is imitated (*imitandosi*) by representing (*rappresentar*) the mode of this passion (*il modo di quell'affetto*)" (Mancini, *Considerazione sulla pittura*). Of course, the variety of terms used by Mancini—*similitudine*, *imitare*, *rappresentar*—and the link between action and passion, which connects the problematic of action to that of the expression of emotions, attest to the changes that the Middle Ages and the Renaissance brought to bear on Aristotle's *mimêsis*, as well as Plato's. But this distinction between two genres of portrait, as foreign as it is to Aristotle's thought, was a response to the difficulty that originates with the double meaning Aristotle gives to *mimêsis*, depending on whether he relates the term to discourse or to the image. Roger de Piles would also invoke Aristotle in describing the portrait genre, yet used a different argument: "If painting is an imitation of nature, it is doubly so with respect to the portrait, which not only represents man in general, but such and such a man in particular" (*Cours de peinture par principes*).

BIBLIOGRAPHY

de Piles, Roger. *Cours de peinture par principes*. Paris: Gallimard / La Pléiade, 1989. First published in 1708.

Hénin, Emmanuelle. *Ut pictura theatrum*. Geneva: Droz, 2004.

Mancini, Giulio. *Considerazione sulla pittura*. Rome: Accademia nazionale dei Lincei, 1956–57. First published ca. 1620.

its details and with its imperfections, or, on the contrary, to render visible that ideal image of beauty that exists only in the mind or the imagination, on the model of the perfect orator as described by Cicero in a passage of the *Orator* that all theoreticians of painting would refer to for centuries (see BEAUTY and DISEGNO)? However important it was, the influence of Neoplatonism and Ciceronianism on thinking about art during the Renaissance is insufficient to explain the existence, or even the meaning, of such a series of questions. Like all questions addressed to painting, they have their source, first of all, in the very history of that art. They refer to what might be called painting stories, in this case to those of two paintings of Zeuxis, recounted by Pliny. In one, Zeuxis had painted grapes that were so well imitated that birds swooped down on the canvas. In the other, he had the most beautiful virgins of Crotona pose for him. Unable to find perfect beauty in a single model, he had borrowed from each what she had that was most beautiful. These two tales would long assume paradigmatic value in reflections on the idea of imitation in the field of painting. The first legitimates a realist interpretation of imitation as likeness, and would be constantly invoked by all those who praised the illusionary powers of painting (the mirror and the monkey are two traditional emblems of painting). The second functions in favor of a more intellectualist conception of imitation, submitting *imitazione* to the *idea* and the *concetto*, and whose purpose is no longer to give an illusion of the real through a faithful likeness with things, but to attain perfection and beauty (see CONCETTO). Thus did Alberti, referring to the story of Zeuxis and the virgins of Crotona, recommend to the painter to imitate several models because it is impossible to find perfect beauty in a single body. Such was the method used by Raffaello, as he confessed in a letter to Castiglione on the subject of the difficulty he had in finding a model to paint his Galatea: "Since there is a penury of good judges and beautiful women, I make use of a certain idea (*certa idea*), which comes to my mind (*mente*)." It is that *certa idea* discussed by Raffaello that the artist imitates through his *disegno*. To defend "il primato del disegno" in painting, as the Florentines did, implies a Platonic (or rather Neoplatonic) conception of imitation as imitation of a mental representation to which the painter relates as to a model in his imitation of things. Reviving a theological problematic developed in the Middle Ages, Zuccaro would go so far as to make of the *disegno interno* an imprint of divinity, a *segno di dio*, and thus to define painting as an activity that consists not in imitating things but in acting in a way resembling God (*L'Idea de' pittori, scultori, et architetti*; see DISEGNO).

C. To imitate is not to lie: The problem of fiction

Adopted by theoreticians of poetics, the idea of imitation would undergo a certain number of transformations that would affect in turn the pictorial conception of imitation. First, because they often expressed themselves in Latin, and even while writing in Italian, they would think of *imitazione* as a translation of *mimêsis* and *imitatio*. Associated with the translation and interpretation of texts, consideration of the subject took on a more scholarly cast. Moreover, it was inevitable that the application of the principle of imitation to the language arts would inflect its meaning in a new direction. For a poet, imitating does not mean the same thing as

for a painter. He imitates with words, not images. His imitation, contrary to the painter's, cannot be conceived in terms of resemblance. The theory of *disegno* was in this respect characteristic of the reversal effected by *ut pictura poesis*, that is, by the comparison between painting and poetry (see COMPARISON); by referring image to *idea*, to *concetto*, it defined pictorial imitation on the model of poetic imitation.

This dissociation between imitation and likeness is at the origin of most of the problems posed by the idea of imitation in the field of poetics. How is one to reconcile the definition of poetry as imitation with the various licenses that are part of poetic invention? Does not the referential character of the idea of imitation contradict that right to be all-daring that Horace ascribes to the poet? Some did not hesitate to denounce the perils of a theory that imposed far too narrow limits on artistic activity. The poet, Patrizi would say, is not an *imitator* but a *facitor, facitor* being in this case a perfect equivalent for the Greek *poietes* (*Della poetica*). The opposition between *imitator* and *facitor* nonetheless raises a genuine problem. The poet does indeed fabricate fictions. Whereas the idea of imitation allows one to ascribe to art a function relating to knowledge and thus to truth, the idea of fiction implies one relating to mendacity and falsehood. In the Middle Ages, Isidore of Seville had labored to distinguish *falsum* from *fictum*, but his distinction had barely left a trace. In the Renaissance and the seventeenth century, a number of theoreticians of art would continue to speak of the beautiful lies—or even the innocent lies—of art, thus using for the benefit of art the very argument that had long served, and would continue to serve, to condemn it.

D. Imitating the masters: The problem of invention

The conception of imitation elaborated in the Renaissance on the basis of readings of Aristotle, Horace, and Cicero enabled a partial resolution of the opposition between imitation and fiction. Poetic invention can be legitimated by the authority of ancient authors. But that very authority brought to the fore a new difficulty that radically transformed the elements of the problem of *mimêsis* and formulated it in new terms. Imitation was no longer conceived solely with reference to nature but also in relation with the ancients, whose works were posited as models of the imitation of nature. The imitation became in a way an imitation to the second degree, the imitation of an imitation: art was to imitate art in order to imitate nature. This notion according to which art was to rest on an imitation of the masters constituted the true novelty of the theory of imitation as it developed in the framework of humanism. But it would also give rise to a number of reservations, particularly among artists and theorists invoking a Platonic conception of art, such as those of the Academy of Florence, who were rather hostile to the principle of imitation. Although they recognized a pedagogical value in the imitation of the ancients, they refused to regard the ancients as unsurpassable models to whom the artist was to submit. The debate provoked by the idea of a model in the realm of poetry was thus in all ways analogous to one previously evoked on the subject of painting, even if it was formulated in different terms. The story of Zeuxis took on paradigmatic value not only for the painter but also for the poet, on the condition that the beauties of art be substituted for those of nature. No model was perfect enough for it to have sufficed for the artist to imitate it in order to achieve beauty. This is why it was necessary to imitate several models and above all to imitate them with discernment, as Pico wrote in the course of the polemic that pitted him against Bembo on the idea of imitation: "Imitandum inquam bonos omnes, non unum aliquem, nec omnibus etiam in rebus" (I say that one must imitate all good writers, not merely one, and not in everything). It is not in authors who wrote before him that the poet finds the source of his inspiration, he said, but in a "certain inner idea" (*idea quaedam*), which is not without evoking the *certa idea* of Raffaello. To the normative conception of imitation defended by Bembo, Pico thus opposed a critical relation to the tradition compatible with the freedom of the poet and his originality: "Inventio enim tum laudatur magis, cum genuine est magis, et libera" (Since the more an invention is free and original, the more is it worthy of praise). Conceived as *inventio*, imitation was transformed into true emulation, allowing the artist to surpass his models and to create works superior to those of the past. In authors writing in Latin, *imitatio*, moreover, was gradually cast aside to the benefit of *inventio*. That term, borrowed from rhetoric, did not have the modern sense of inventing. *Inventio* harmonized with the idea of imitation, as opposed to *creatio*, which belonged to the lexicon of theology.

IV. From *Imitazione* to *Imitation*: French Aristotelianism

A. The ends of imitation

The *Poetics* played a major role in the birth and development of the theory of art in France in the seventeenth century. Whether defining art in general or various forms of artistic representation, pondering the nature of tragedy or that of historical painting, establishing the rules governing the composition of a dramatic poem or those intervening in the composition of a painting, classical theorists for the most part sought inspiration in Aristotle and borrowed most of their categories from him. They did not, however, have at their disposal a French translation of the *Poetics* until 1671, the date on which Norville's version appeared, followed in 1692 by Dacier's. It was thus initially by way of Italian translations, whether in Latin or in the vernacular, that Aristotelian thinking on art penetrated into France, as well as by way of Italian (but also Dutch) exercises in poetics, such as those of Daniël Heinslus (*De tragediae constitutionae*, 1511) or Gerald Jan Vossius (*De artis poeticae*, 1647), which would have a great influence on French thought. Even when they read Greek, the French related to Aristotelian *mimêsis* by way of its re-elaboration via the idea of *imitatio* and *imitazione*.

Those translations were the object of a certain number of critiques whose stakes broadly exceeded the framework of a narrowly philological dispute. In contesting the interpretation of *mimêsis* given by the Italians, what was at stake was also affirming the originality of the French theory of artistic imitation, along with the superiority of French over Latin and Italian. The principal reproach addressed to the Italians was having obscured Aristotle's text as a result of not knowing anything about the art of the theater. Most interpreters, Corneille wrote, explained it only "from the perspective of grammarians or philosophers. Since they had more experience of study and speculation than of the theater, reading them can make us more erudite, but will not shed much light on which we can depend for success in the theater" (*Discours de l'utilité du poème dramatique*). Corneille's refusal to dissociate theory from practice attests to a change in perspective that affected the entire range of reflection about art in the seventeenth century. Whether focused on theater or painting, aesthetic theory developed in France on the basis of art and was elaborated principally by artists. The redefinition of the idea of imitation was largely a function of this very specific feature of aesthetic theory in France. If imitation was always posited as a principle, it was above all conceived as a problem, or rather as a set of problems that it fell precisely to artists to solve. Now the nature of those problems (as of the solutions given them) was itself determined by the subordination of the principle of imitation to the pleasure principle, which displaced the idea of imitation by integrating it into a problematic that was no longer one of the causes of art, but rather of its effects. Painting is an imitation, Poussin would say, and "its end is delectation" (letter to Fréart de Chambray, 2 March 1665). For the French, if imitation did indeed define the nature of art, it was not its aim. The sole aim of art was to please, and it was always in terms of that aim that the principle of imitation was conceived. Its application was entirely subject to that finality. Defining artistic imitation thereupon consisted in determining the rules through which imitation could achieve that goal: "The principal rule is to delight and to stir the emotions," wrote Racine in his preface to *Bérenice*. "All the others have been forged only to satisfy that first one." Corneille, like many others, did not, moreover, hesitate to ascribe that notion to Aristotle at the beginning of his first *Discours* on dramatic poetry: "Even though the sole aim of dramatic poetry for Aristotle was to delight the audience."

■ See Box 4.

This definition of imitation in terms of pleasure illustrates the influence exercised by thinking about rhetoric on artistic theory. It effectively has its source in the hierarchy established by Cicero between the finalities of the art of oratory: *docere* (to instruct), *delectare* (to delight), *movere* (to move), and which gives pride of place to *movere*. The application of the Ciceronian problematic to the realm of the poetic and visual arts would be accompanied in France by numerous debates attesting to the same difficulties as those already encountered by theoreticians of rhetoric in aligning the necessities of *docere* with the exigencies of *movere*. If some went so far as to call into question the pedagogical and moral purpose of art, all were in agreement in denying it priority and in affirming with Racine that the principal rule of art was to delight and to stir the emotions. Which does not at all mean that they refused to ascribe to art a value rooted in knowledge. On the contrary, since that value was attributed to pleasure itself, as in La Fontaine, whose art was undoubtedly the best example of that harmonious and perfectly balanced synthesis between the exigencies of pleasure and those of knowledge, which corresponded to the classical ideal of perfection.

4

Pleasure: From the cause to the aim

In his concern to restore the truth of Aristotle's text, Dacier would denounce what in his eyes was a completely erroneous interpretation of the idea of *mimêsis*, particularly in the commentary accompanying the famous passage from chapter 4, which he translated as follows: "There are two main causes, both quite natural, which seem to have produced poetry; the first is imitation, a quality innate to men, since they differ from the other animals in that they are all inclined toward imitation, it is by means of imitation that they learn the first elements of the sciences, and all imitations give them a singular pleasure." The commentary concerns the final point:

> The most learned commentators of Aristotle have made a very considerable error here in taking these words as an explanation of the second cause they

give for poetry, as if Aristotle said: And the second is that all imitations give them pleasure. Aristotle was incapable of saying something whose meaning was so mistaken, and of giving to one effect two causes that are only a single cause. It is as if one said that two causes make a plant cultivated by a gardener grow: the first is that he waters it, and the second is the pleasure he takes in watering it. There is no one to whom this does not appear absurd. This philosopher says, then, that the first cause of Poetry is imitation, to which men are naturally inclined, and since this inclination, however natural it is, would be useless if men took no pleasure in producing imitations, he adds: and in which they take a singular pleasure.

Dacier, *La Poétique d'Aristote*

If the mistake of learned commentators was in believing that pleasure was the second cause that Aristotle attributes to imitation (when it in fact is the tendency to rhythm and melody), Corneille's mistake was even greater since it consisted of turning this cause into an aim, and even of making it the sole aim of art. But this "mistake," which was the foundation of all classical aesthetics, was an extremely productive one in the field of art.

BIBLIOGRAPHY

Dacier, André. *La poétique d'Aristote: contenant les règles les plus exactes pour juger du poème héroïque, & des pièces de théâtre, la tragédie & la comédie.* Amsterdam: George Gallet, 1692.

B. Imitating according to nature and the true

What is a good imitation? How to distinguish between imitation and likeness? What does it mean to imitate nature? What is the nature of the model to be imitated? Although the French raised the same questions, on the whole, as their Italian predecessors, they nonetheless posed them in a palpably different manner. That difference was not solely a function of the political and institutional conditions in which reflection on art developed in France, but also of the existence of a new theoretical, philosophical, and scientific context; it involved epistemological changes affecting the entirety of concepts around which the theory of artistic *mimêsis* had always been articulated. And, in the first place, that of the image. The idea of representation, as it was elaborated in France, resulted in calling into question the traditional definition of the image in terms of resemblance, thus necessitating a different manner of conceiving of images. It was indeed the new concept of representation that underlay the comparison frequently invoked by Descartes between idea and image. When he stated that ideas were "like images of things," or even "like pictures or paintings," that did not mean that ideas resembled things but that they were related to things in the same manner as images that imitated the appearance of things, that is, through representation. All of this presupposed a radically new conception of the image, based on the idea of the sign and no longer on resemblance. As Descartes writes in *La dioptrique*, an image does not need to resemble that which it is an image of in order to represent it, and often even "to be more perfect, insofar as they are images, and to better represent an object, they ought not to resemble it, like those engravings which, being composed of but a bit of ink scattered here and there on paper, represent to us forests, cities, men, and even battles and storms." This problematic of the sign and representation would be broadly developed by the logicians

of Port-Royal, who would notably apply it to the problem of the Eucharist: the bread and wine represent the body of Christ but do not resemble it. But it was plainly in the realm of painting that its effects would be most conspicuous, giving a new orientation to the debates that had until then inspired the idea of imitation.

▪ See Box 5.

The other transformation clearly concerns the concept of nature, which took on a new sense in the seventeenth century, both on the physical and the metaphysical levels. If the word "nature" continued to designate the visible world for painters, it became charged at the same time with numerous meanings that combined in a more or less confused or contradictory way in the language of artists. It was at times taken in an empirical sense, as a synonym of observable reality, at others in a rational sense, as a synonym of essence, rule, law, at still others in a normative sense, as a synonym of beauty and truth, and most of the time in all those senses simultaneously. It referred as much to the object of artistic imitation as to the effects which that imitation sought to produce. In all cases, it implied the idea of a model, whether the model to be imitated or as a model for imitation.

The re-elaboration of the idea of imitation on the basis of a problematic of representation, like the new significations attributed to the word "nature," explain the fact that the definition of art as an imitation of nature did not have the same meaning for the French as for the Italians. More Aristotelian than Platonist, the French were less interested in the powers of the idea than in the necessity for rules (of composition, construction, design, color, etc.). As Cartesians, they thought that even the most extravagant fictions originate in a "certain mix and composition" of parts that are not "imaginary, but true and existent," as Descartes puts it in his first *Meditation*, taking as his example precisely the bizarre and extraordinary forms that painters invent in their works: "This art in general," Félibien wrote about painting, "extends to all manners of representing entities that are in nature. And although painters occasionally have formed some that are not natural, like the monsters and grotesques that they invent, which are nonetheless composed of parts known and taken from different animals, it cannot be said that they are pure effects of the imagination" ("Préface aux Conférences de 1667"). Just as they refused to oppose imitation and imagination, the French did not see a contradiction between a concern for exactitude in the observation of reality and the application of analytic criteria in the elaboration of representation. The opposition between realist imitation and ideal imitation was absorbed into a conception of imitation far less dogmatic than is commonly thought and that submitted imitation to criteria of selection and correction that were no longer ideal but rational. One must imitate nature through reasonable choice, as Le Brun would say. That reasonable choice meant that artistic imitation was to satisfy simultaneously the rules of art, the exigencies of truth (whence the importance given at the Academy to the study of anatomy, proportion, geometry, perspective) and those of verisimilitude and decorum.

■ See Box 6.

C. Representing action

If the definition of artistic imitation according to its modalities (nature and truth) was, as we have seen, rather flexible, that which defined it as a function of its object was far more normative. It consisted in defining art as a representation of human actions. Taking up the Aristotelian definition of poetic *mimêsis*, the French applied it to the full range of the arts, not only the poetic arts, but also sculpture, painting, and even ballet. For the French, as for Aristotle, imitating an action meant first of all representing the plot or what was called the *fable* (the term with which most translators of the *Poetics* rendered *muthos*). The first effect of that definition of art in the realm of painting would be the establishment of a hierarchy of genres dominated by historical painting, that is, by narrative painting. But imitation was not solely concerned with plot; as in Aristotle, it also took as its object character, the passions, sentiments, what the seventeenth century would call *mores* (a term utilized to translate the *êthos* [ἦθος] of the *Poetics*). It was thus that Claude François Ménétrier wrote:

> Ballet does not imitate solely actions; it also imitates, according to Aristotle, passions and customs, which is more difficult than the expression of actions. This imitation of the customs and affections of the soul is based on impressions that the soul makes naturally on the body, and on the judgments we make of the customs and inclinations of persons on those inner movements.
>
> *Des ballets anciens et modernes*

This text also illustrates the transformation to which the classical theoreticians subjected Aristotelian *mimêsis*. It will be noted that on the subject of actions Ménestrier employs the terms "imitation" and "expression" indiscriminately.

5

The resemblance of the portrait (bis)

It is hardly surprising that the effects of this new concept of representation should manifest themselves most clearly in relation to the portrait. If a good portrait is lifelike, what defines the lifelike resemblance of a portrait? Félibien gave a completely original answer to this question, which the Italians had already asked themselves, and which recalled Descartes's analysis. "How is it," Félibien asks, "that a mediocre painter is sometimes more successful in painting a lifelike portrait than an experienced and learned man? . . . Be aware that what often appears as a lifelike resemblance in these mediocre portraits is nothing but that. . . . From the moment, by some sign, an image is formed in our mind which is in some way related to a thing we know, we immediately believe that we find in it a great resemblance, even though, in looking at it more closely, it was often nothing more than a rather weak idea."

Félibien, *Entretiens sur les vies*

BIBLIOGRAPHY

Félibien, André. *Entretiens sur les vies et les ouvrages des plus excellents peintres anciens et modernes*. Paris: Les Belles Lettres, 1987.

6

Decorum

"Decorum" has the same meaning as it does in Latin, that is, appropriateness. In the artistic field, decorum has, like *prepon* [πρέπον] in Greek rhetoric, a double meaning; it is determined both upstream and downstream, so to speak. The first determination is referential in nature: the rule of decorum requires that characters are represented in a way that is in keeping with their state, their situation, their nature: a king could not be expressed or be clothed in the same way as a peasant, each passion has to be represented in a manner that befits the state of the person, etc. The second is moral and social in nature. Representation has to be in keeping with the moral sentiments of the spectators, it must not shock them, and it has to respect the rules of propriety. Furetière only mentions this second meaning in his dictionary (RT: *Dictionnaire universel, contenant généralement tous les mots français tant vieux que modernes, et les termes de toutes les sciences et des arts*): " Decorum: A Latin, then French word, which is expressed in this proverbial saying: to observe decorum, meaning to respect all the rules of polite society."

The use of the word "expression" as an equivalent of "imitation" conveys the new manner in which the action/passion relation was conceived in the seventeenth century.

■ See Box 7.

The problems raised by the representation of history were the object of numerous debates in the seventeenth century, in the domains of both theater and painting. Such discussions called into play the same distinction between likeness and representation that we have already encountered with regard to portraiture, but in a somewhat different manner. Does the fact of imitating history in accordance with nature and the truth, as required by the principle of imitation, demand of the artist that he faithfully respect historical truth, or can he deviate from it should it enter into conflict with the necessities of representation, that is, with the nature and truth of art? That question led to a rather lively exchange between Philippe de Champaigne and Le Brun on the subject of Poussin's painting, *Eliézer et Rébecca*. Whereas Champaigne reproached Poussin for not having "treated the subject of his painting with all the faithfulness of history, since he had eliminated from it any representation of the camels mentioned by history," Le Brun thought to the contrary that the painter was right to take that liberty with history, "that the camels had not been eliminated from the painting without solid consideration; that Monsieur Poussin, constantly seeking to refine and to unburden the subject of his works and to bring forth in an agreeable manner the principal action being treated, had rejected the bizarre objects that might debauch the eye of the spectator and amuse it with minutia" (Academic Lecture of 7 January 1668).

But it was surely in the realm of poetry that the representation of history raised the most difficulties. For poetry represents history by way of fiction. Faithfulness to history thus poses two problems of a rather different nature for the poet. The first involves the difference between resemblance and representation: as in painting, a faithfulness to history may enter into conflict with necessities imposed by the rules of art. The second no longer brings into play the autonomy of art, but rather that of the artist: a respect for history imposes constraints that may be incompatible with the freedom of the poet, that is, with his right to dare anything. This problem plainly concerned the powers of the artist in general, be he painter or poet. But in France, as previously in Italy, it was envisaged essentially with reference to the activity of the poet,

and that precisely because it was born of a reflection on the idea of fiction, and fiction fell under the rubric of poetry and not painting, which raised in turn the question of illusion—dramatic poetry presenting the particularity of bringing into play simultaneously the pictorial question of illusion and the poetic question of fiction.

Reconciling these various exigencies was not always possible, but the freedom of the poet also consisted in casting aside all contradictions, as may be seen in the case of Corneille, who, in his prefaces, did not hesitate to resort to the most disparate arguments, in keeping with the needs of the play in question. It was thus in the name of the rules of art, and consequently the necessities of representation, that he justified the liberties he had taken with history in *La Mort de Pompée*, where he opted to "reduce to two hours what had transpired over two years." One rediscovers here the Aristotelian distinction between poetry and history. This did not prevent Corneille elsewhere from invoking historical truth, and thus the necessities of resemblance, but on this occasion to justify freedoms taken with the rule of verisimilitude or plausibility ("the truth is not always plausible") and that of morality (i.e., of catharsis in the moral sense as understood in the seventeenth century), which demanded that criminals inspire horror and crime be always punished. That argument from resemblance, which is a pictorial argument, was developed at length in the dedication to *Médée*, precisely on the basis of a comparison between poetry and painting:

> Poetry and painting have this in common, among many other things, that one often makes beautiful portraits of an ugly woman, and the other beautiful imitations of an action that should not be imitated. In portraiture, it is not a matter of wondering whether a face is beautiful but whether it bears a resemblance; and in painting, one should not consider whether behavior is virtuous but whether it is similar to that of the person being introduced; it consequently evokes for us good and bad actions indiscriminately, without offering us the latter as an example; and if it wishes to impose a measure of horror on us, it is not at all because of their punishment, which it does not affect to show us, but because of their ugliness, which it attempts to represent to us naturally.

However different they be, the justifications of *Pompée* and *Médée* are not at all incompatible. They both express the same

---

7

Expression

The word *expression* entered the French vocabulary of painting around 1650, and this new usage remained for a long time without an equivalent term in other languages (*espressione* was still absent from Baldinucci's *Vocabulario toscano dell arte del disegno* in 1681). *Expression* was used first of all in the general sense of the expression of the subject of a painting, that is, as a synonym for representation. But it quickly took on a second, more restricted meaning, referring to the representation of passions. Le Brun thus made a distinction between general expression, which "is a naïve and natural resemblance of the things one wishes to represent," and particular expression, "which indicates the movements of the heart, and makes visible the effects of passion" (*Conférences académiques* of 7 April and 5 May 1668 on *L'Expression des passions*). The first meaning would gradually disappear in favor of the second, making way for the distinction representation/expression.

refusal to subject art to extrinsic constraints, whether they be the constraints of historical truth or those that morality and society are intent on exercising over representation.

D. To imitate is not to copy:
From the idea of invention to that of originality

This will to autonomy explains the interest brought to the question of the imitation of masters, which had resulted in the polemic between Pico and Bembo. But here too the position of the French was less dogmatic than is often believed. They were unanimous in acknowledging that imitation of the masters played an essential role in the education of a painter, sculptor, or writer. It is in imitating art that one learns to imitate according to nature and truth, that is, that one becomes an artist oneself. But the imitation of art cannot be conflated with artistic imitation in the strict sense; it is its necessary but by no means sufficient condition. It was thus that Philippe de Champaigne lashed out at those he called "copyists of a manner," who "limit themselves servilely to copying the particular manner of an author, taken as their aim and as the sole model they need consult. They judge on the basis of that author alone the manner of all others and have no eyes to discern the beauties and various agreements that nature offers for our imitation" (Academic Lecture, 11 June 1672). In the image of Zeuxis, one must imitate several models and not one alone, and, as Pico already said, do so with discernment, which meant, for the French, by imposing on oneself nature and truth as a rule. But it was above all another motif that was taken up in the seventeenth century to characterize the artist's approach: that of the bee gathering from all flowers to produce a honey that is its alone. Like the bee, the artist was to borrow from different masters in order to become finally his own master, that is, in order to find a manner belonging to him alone. This is precisely the manner in which La Fontaine describes what may be called his poetic method. After acknowledging the extreme diversity of his sources of inspiration, he mocks the "foolish herd" of servile imitators who "follow like real sheep the shepherd of Mantua": "I make use of him in a different manner, and, letting myself be guided, often make bold to strike out on my own. I will always be seen to practice this custom; my imitation is in no way a form of slavery" (*Épître à Mr l'Évêque de Soissons*). This proclamation of independence and freedom is all the more important in the case of La Fontaine in that he was a partisan of the ancients.

The quarrel of the ancients and the moderns, which developed over the last decades of the seventeenth century, did in fact change the nature of the debates over the imitation of masters. The partisans of the moderns did not call into question the idea of imitation, but rather that of the masters, French artists of the century of Louis XIV being for them infinitely superior to those of the past, which included not only the Greeks and Romans, but also the Italians of the Renaissance. Whether partisans of the ancients or the moderns, everyone in the seventeenth century defined artistic imitation in the same way—with reference to nature and truth. They thus all made the same distinction between genuine artistic imitation and that of servile imitators content with merely imitating the manner of someone else. Those who defended the ancients did not present them as models to imitate, but as

models in imitating according to nature and truth. And it was precisely for the same reason that the partisans of the moderns refused to consider the ancients as models, because they did not imitate according to nature and the truth, contrary to the French, they claimed, whose success on this point was without example in the past. "Voiture did not model himself on anyone," wrote Charles Perrault; the art of La Fontaine, he said, "is of an entirely new species," and there is not a single one of his inventions "which has a model in the writings of the Ancients" (*Parallèle des anciens et des modernes*). The idea of invention, constantly associated since the Renaissance with that of imitation, no longer had the merely rhetorical sense of *inventio*; it also took on the meaning of novelty, which in turn gave a new meaning to the idea of imitation by inscribing it in a problematic that was no longer, as in Pico, one of emulation, but of originality: "Never has anyone," wrote Perrault about La Fontaine, "more deserved to be regarded as original and of the first of his kind" (*Les hommes illustres*).

E. From a regulating principle to a normative principle:
The idea of imitation in the eighteenth century

Although reflection on the idea of imitation was pursued in the eighteenth century, it no longer aroused the same passions as in the previous century. First, because such reflection now developed outside the sphere of practicing artists, among theoreticians of art approaching the idea of imitation from an exclusively theoretical angle and no longer as in the seventeenth century, under its twofold—theoretical and practical—aspect. Escaping from the artists, reflection about art became more systematic, as may be illustrated by the title of the abbé Batteux's work, published in 1746: *Les beaux-arts réduits à un seul principe* (The fine arts reduced to a single principle). The generalization of the principle of imitation to the full range of the fine arts was thus accompanied by a theoretical hardening that transformed what was a rather supple regulating principle, intervening in the training of artists, for the classics, into a simultaneously normative and explanatory universal principle, which claimed to account for all forms of art. In addition, the emergence of an aesthetic of sentiment and an aesthetic of nature (both linked to the rise of new forms of sensibility and to transformations in the idea of nature) resulted in giving pride of place to a definition of art as the imitation of nature to the detriment of all other definitions, and at the same time giving that definition a sense rather removed from the one it had in the seventeenth century. One no longer thought, as did Boileau, that "there were no longer serpents or odious monsters who, once imitated by art, were unable to please the eyes" (*Art poétique*). The preference now went to imitating the beauties of nature, in pleasing tones of verisimilitude and decorum. This new conception of the idea of imitating nature, accompanied by a disaffection regarding the great genres (tragedy, historical painting), plainly rendered most of the thinking of the previous century on the subject of the relations between nature and history out of date. In art as in philosophy, nature would henceforth be opposed to history. One would have to wait for David for the Aristotelian definition of art as the representation of human actions to regain a second wind in painting.

These various transformations affecting the idea of imitation did not prevent the authors of the eighteenth century from voicing the same convictions on a number of scores as their predecessors. And specifically concerning the necessity of distinguishing the imitation of art from all other forms of imitation, resemblance, or reproduction. Developing thought on the nature of the senses and the role of sensations thus led theoreticians of art to radically pit artistic imitation against illusion. As Marmontel wrote in the article "Illusion" in the *Encyclopédie*, what is called theatrical illusion or pictorial illusion are but "demi-illusions," "the pleasure taken in art being a function of that tacit and inchoate reflection that warns us that it is but a feint." The specific nature of artistic imitation is expressed in the specific nature of the pleasure which that imitation procures for us. It was thus through another perspective—that of the analysis of sensations—that the theorists of the eighteenth century rediscovered the Aristotelian idea, which lay at the heart of classical doctrine, according to which the pleasure produced by *mimêsis* was a pleasure specific to *mimêsis*.

V. *Nachahmung*: The Calling into Question of *Mimêsis*

The use of the term *nachahmen* (to imitate) posed a problem in Germany already in the first half of the eighteenth century, and was the symptom of a lexical malaise that was fueled by the more general crisis of the Aristotelian principle of *mimêsis*. More and more authors, such as J. J. Winckelmann and J. G. Herder, attempted subtle differentiations in order to rescue the word from any confusion with its pejorative correlates, *nachmachen* and *kopieren* (to copy, to reproduce). But such subterfuges barely fooled anyone. At the end of the eighteenth century, it was no longer those correlates that were contested, but the word *nachahmen* itself. Over and again, Jean Paul and F. Schlegel associated *Nachahmung* (imitation) with mere copying, an evolution concluded by A. W. Schlegel with his peremptory refutation of the axiom *ars imitatur naturam*. Art was not obliged to imitate nature. The word *nachahmen*, in his view, would henceforth be supplanted by the terms *bilden* (to fashion, to give form to) and *darstellen* (to represent).

A. A latent lexical malaise (1700–1760)

It was only after 1700 that the principle of *mimêsis*, which had so broadly occupied Italy, England, and France since the Renaissance, began to be debated in Germany. But at the time the discussion began, the formula *ars imitatur naturam* could no longer be taken for granted since each of the terms in the axiom had been invested with multiple meanings. Imitation could be understood at times as strict reproduction, at others as an inventive recomposition of the real and nature, at times as *natura naturata*, and at others as *natura naturans*. As of the 1740s there was thus a deep linguistic malaise regarding the use of the word *nachahmen* (to imitate), with attempts alternately to save it at whatever cost or to burden it with negative virtualities. If, still in the middle of the century, recourse to the word *Nachahmung* seemed stripped of ambiguity and difficulty for J. C. Gottsched or J. E. Schlegel ("a poet is a skillful imitator of all things in nature" [ein geschickter Nachahmer aller natürlichen Dinge]; Gottsched, *Versuch einer kritischen Dichtkunst*), such was not the case for J. J. Bodmer, J. J. Breitinger, or G. E. Lessing. "The terms *faithful* and *beautified* [*getreu und verschönert*],

used with regard to imitation and nature as subject of imitation [*Nachahmung*], are subject to many misunderstandings," Lessing announced in 1768 in his *Hamburgische Dramaturgie*.

■ See Box 8.

At times invested with Aristotelian dignity, at others associated, on the contrary, with the minimally prestigious register of the copy (*nachmachen, kopieren*), the notion of *Nachahmung* issued in increasingly subtle lexical differentiations, which constitute a problem for the translator. In this regard Winckelmann's use of the term is eloquent. Whereas he had made of imitation the core and very title of his first essay, "Gedanken über die Nachahmung der griechischen Werke in der Malerei und Bildhauerkunst" (Reflections on the Imitation of Greek Works in Painting and in Sculpture) of 1755, Winckelmann would use it in his subsequent texts only with increasing embarrassment. In 1759, he undertook to distinguish genuine imitation (*nachahmen*) from mere copying (*nachmachen*):

> To personal thought, I oppose the copy (*das Nachmachen*), but not at all imitation (*die Nachahmung*): by the term *copy* I understand a slavish tracing (*knechtliche Folge*). In imitation, on the contrary, what is imitated, if handled with reason, may assume an other nature, as it were, and become one's own (*gleichsam eine andere Natur annehmen und etwas eigenes werden*).

> *Erinnerung über die Betrachtung der Werke der Kunst*

The lexical discomfort is evident. Following Winckelmann, Herder attempted a subtle distinction between *nachahmen* as a transitive verb, the synonym of slavish copying, and *nachahmen* as an intransitive verb, designating imitation proper. "*Einen nachahmen* signifies, in my view, to imitate the subject, the work of others; *einem nachahmen* signifies, on the contrary, to borrow from an other his manner of treating that subject, or a comparable subject" (Einen nachahnem heißt, wie ich glaube, den Gegenstand, das Werk des andern nachahmen; einem nachahmen aber, die Art und Weise von dem andern entlehnen, diesen oder einen ähnlichen Gegenstand zu behandeln) (quoted from J. and W. Grimm, RT: *Deutsches Wörterbuch*, vol. 13, s.v. "Nachahmen"). Restitution into French becomes complex: one would have to translate the transitive *nachahmen* as *copier, reproduire servilement* (slavish copying), and the intransitive *nachamen* as *s'inspirer, rivaliser avec* (to be inspired by, etc.). For Winckelmann and Herder, the strategy was the same: it was a matter of inventing a kind of negatively charged yet extremely close twin of *nachahmen*, such as *nachmachen* or *einen nachahmen*, in order to save the word *Nachahmung* from its disastrous possibilities. But the lexical ruse barely fooled anyone, and it was the term *Nachahmung* itself that ended up with the blemish of the slavish epigone.

B. *Nachahmen* and the decline of the principle of imitation around 1800

Later developments bear this out. In subsequent decades it was not only words of the same family (*kopieren, nachmachen, nachbilden*) that became suspect, but the semantic matrix

8

The critique of the idea of the imitation of nature in Lessing

The use that Lessing made of *Nachahmung* was consistent with his general methodology in art theory: he availed himself of the notion, but in order to point out its internal contradictions. As he said, if one applied literally the principle of imitation of nature that Breitinger and Batteux were so attached to, then the worst deformities would pass for art, and perfect harmony of proportions would be something very unusual:

> The example of nature which has to justify the connection between the most solemn seriousness and the most frivolous gaiety, could equally well be used to justify any dramatic monstrosity that would be unstructured, disconnected, and lack all common sense. The imitation of nature (*Die Nachahmung der Natur*) should absolutely not be the principle of art (*Grundsatz der Kunst*); or rather, if it had to remain so, art would thereby cease being art, or at least high art. . . . According to this way of thinking, the most artistic work would be the worst, and the most mediocre would be the best.
>
> Lessing, *Hamburgische Dramaturgie*, §70, 1 January 1768 (1769)

Lessing was not attacking the principle of imitation as such, but the imitation of nature. If the imitation of nature is the essence of art, then one has to follow this to its logical conclusion. A perfect reflection of reality can only reflect back to us representations and images that are often ugly, even hideous. The strict application of the principle of imitation of nature produces the opposite of what it is aiming for, namely, beauty, and thus loses all validity as an artistic principle. In his essay *Laocoön*, the word *Nachahmung* reappeared, but in relation to the modes of representation in painting: "Painting employs wholly different signs (*Zeichen*) or means (*Mittel*) of imitation (*Nachahmungen*) from poetry, —the one using forms and colors in space" (Lessing, *Laocoön*). Lessing retained the word *Nachahmung*, which seemed the most appropriate to express the quest for the ideality of the beautiful, and thus for the essence of art itself. So *Nachahmung* was not rejected, but it did not really have the status of an artistic and aesthetic concept. When he discussed painting in *Laocoön*, he identified more with *Darstelling*, representation. The other, far vaguer meaning made allusion to the poetic and pictorial models of the ancients. *Nachahmung* was not yet explicitly opposed to *mimêsis*; without being actually empty in terms of content, the word expressed at best a concession to the worship of the classical ideal of beauty. In other words, it still had some legitimacy because of the authority of Winckelmann, but its theoretical validity had become so problematic that only the aesthetics that were taking shape in Germany could give it back its productive capacity.

Jean-François Groulier

BIBLIOGRAPHY

Lessing, G. E. *Hamburgische Dramaturgie*. Stuttgart, Alfred Kröner Verlag.
———. *Laocoön*. Translated by Ellan Frothingham. BiblioBazaar, 2009.

itself: *nachahmen*. The attack came above all from the Romantic school and its surroundings.

- See Box 9.

In his *Vorschule der Asthetik* (*Pre-School of Aesthetics*) (1804), Jean Paul adopted Herder's lexical distinction between a transitive and intransitive use of *nachahmen*, but brought it to an abrupt close:

> Does the expression *die Natur nachahmen* mean the same thing as *der Natur nachahmen,* and is repetition imitation? Verily, the principle that consists in faithfully following nature scarcely makes sense.
>
> (Aber ist denn einerlei, die oder der Natur nachzuahmen, und ist Wiederholen Nachahmen?—Eigentlich hat der Grundsatz, die Natur treu zu kopieren, kaum einen Sinn.)
>
> *Vorschule der Asthetik*, §3

In 1785, in order the better to disqualify imitation, Jean Paul made of *nachahmen* a synonym pure and simple of *kopieren*: "The imitation of nature is not yet poetry since the copy cannot contain more than the original" (Die Nachahmung der Natur ist noch keine Dichtung, weil die Kopie nicht mehr enthalten kann als das Urbild) (*Uber natürliche Magie der Einbildungskraft* [On the Natural Magic of the Imagination]). More and more frequently associated with the terms *wiederholen, kopieren, nachäffen*, the word *nachahmen* has the French reader hesitating between several translations: *répéter, copier, singer,* or *imiter*. Between F. Schlegel, who, on the subject of imitation, spoke of "artificial counterfeits" of Greek works (*künstliche Nachbildungen* in the first edition, changed to *Künstliche Nachahmungen* in later editions, *Uber des studium der griechischen Poesie* [On the Study of Greek Poetry]), and Novalis, who, in a letter to his brother Karl, probably dating from 1800, stated peremptorily that poetry was at the strict antipodes to imitation, the status of the word *Nachahmung* continued to be degraded and the span of translations to broaden. In 1801–2, A. W. Schlegel put a radical halt to the discussion. In his *Vorlesungen über schöne Literatur und Kunst* (Lectures on Literature and the Fine-Arts) delivered at the University of Berlin, he offered a systematic refutation of the Aristotelian principle of *mimêsis*:

> Aristotle had posited as an unchallengeable principle that the fine arts were imitative (*die schöne Künste seien nachahmend*). This was precisely the case on the condition that one meant by it a simple thing: they have something imitative (*es komme etwas Nachahmendes in ihnen vor*); but it was imprecise if it meant, in the sense in which Aristotle himself understood it, moreover, that imitation constituted their entire essence (*die Nachahmung mache ihr ganzes Wesen aus*).. . . Numerous moderns have subsequently transformed this principle into the following axiom: art must imitate nature (*die Kunst soll die Natur nachahmen*). The imprecision and ambiguity

9

Formative imitation in Karl Philipp Moritz

By the end of the eighteenth century, imitation no longer implied the idea of a rational order inherent in nature, or that was particular to a system of artistic rules. It was faced with a dual process: on the one hand, the increasing subjectivization of all aesthetic categories, and on the other, the development of a new concept of nature. Art was seen from that point on as having to produce works in accordance with a principle of autonomy analogous to the autonomy that was immanent to living organisms. So a work of art had to be accomplished as a dynamic, internal, and autonomous process. But for Moritz, this movement was not at all, as it was for Goethe, part of an investigation of nature as such. Or rather, art and nature were connected as part of a whole that was analogous to the cosmos of the Greeks and that closely conditioned them. Art should in effect aim to find the language of nature, either through imitation or through symbolism. The aesthetic orientation of Moritz was thus as far removed from the rationalism of Breitinger as it was from the exclusively artistic vision of Winckelmann or of Lessing. It was the enthusiasm and mysticism of the whole that inspired the thought of Moritz: the essential criterion of beauty could only be something

that was perfectly finished or accomplished (*Vollendete*). But this beauty was itself only one moment of a movement tending toward the apprehension of the whole. According to him, if we do not possess the concept of what is right or good in an ethical sense, we cannot grasp in its fullness the idea of a formative imitation (*die bildende Nachahmung*), to the extent that this imitation is immanent to the creative faculty of the beautiful as it is manifest in a work of art:

Die eigentliche Nachahmung des Schönen unterscheidet sich also zuerst von des moralischen Nachahmung des Guten und Edlen dadurch, dass sie, ihrer Natur nach, streben muss, nicht, wie diese in sich hinein, sondern aus sich heraus zu bilden.

(So the imitation of what is properly speaking beautiful is first of all distinct from the moral imitation of the good and the noble in that it has to strive, according to its nature to form an image that is not, like this imitation, an image in itself, but to form its image out of itself.)

Moritz, Über die bildende Nachahmung des Schönen

The "aus sich heraus zu bilden" (to form its image out of itself) dissipates the ambiguity of the sentence. Formative imitation has nothing in common with imitation as Lessing, for example, understood it; it is a *poiesis*, inspired by a *Bildungskraft*, a formative power. *Nachahmung* is all the more untranslatable since Moritz uses the word by defining it as what it is not, that is, an activity of the creative imagination. The break with the artistic tradition of imitation was thus complete; Moritz envisaged an idealization of beauty involving as much a mystical experience as an aesthetic experience. It was, however, in function of this new and sometimes obscure meaning that the aesthetic orientation of German Romanticism would be determined.

Jean-François Groulier

BIBLIOGRAPHY

Moritz, Karl Phillip. *Über die bildende Nachahmung des Schönen*. In *Schriften zur Ästhetik und Poetik*, Tübingen: Niemayer, 1962. First published in 1788.

of the terms "nature" and "imitate" have provoked the greatest misunderstandings and led to the most diverse contradictions.

For A. W. Schlegel, the symptoms of the inadequacy of the term *nachahmen* were numerous. In Batteux, for example, who postulates that art ought to imitate beautiful nature, or elsewhere that art ought to imitate it as more beautiful, the word "imitate" is incorrect "since one either imitates nature as it is, in which case it is possible that the result will not be beautiful, or one gives it a beautiful form *(man bildet sie schön)*, and one is no longer dealing with imitation *(so ist es keine Nachahmung mehr)*. Why not say straightaway: art should represent the beautiful *(Warum sagen sie nicht gleich: die Kunst soll das Schöne darstellen)*?" The word *nachahmen,* an incorrect term that translates in this case the incorrect notion of imitation in Batteux, ought simply to be eliminated. And Schlegel concludes: "A more accurate formulation of the principle would be: art ought to give a form to nature *(die Kunst muß Natur bilden)*." *Bilden* and *darstellen* would replace *nachahmen.* With enough untranslatability, the untranslatable is voided.

VI. Realism or Conventionalism: New Perspectives

The concepts of reference, correspondence, and resemblance, which were at the origin of various theories of imitation, have by now become quite problematic. The idea of imitation, as it functioned for centuries through numerous transformations, assumed that the object was given in

experience and that the representation might adequately refer to reality. "To perceive similarities," wrote Aristotle, "is to give evidence of a sagacious mind" (*Rhetoric*, 3.11.5). That proposition, which defined resemblance as a condition of the possibility of representation, possessed the value of an axiom in theories of art until the nineteenth century. The naïve realism underlying conceptions of representation based on the idea of resemblance has largely been called into question by the epistemology and analyses developed in particular by various philosophies of language. Nelson Goodman radicalized a conventionalist position, ending up in a relativism. For him, what links A and B consists in a relation between elements that may be totally heterogeneous, and that relation brings about a symbolic productivity every bit as efficacious as traditional resemblance of an Aristotelian sort: "Almost any picture can represent anything" (*Languages of Art*). The principle according to which the representation of reality must rest on resemblance to the thing represented is thus based more on a belief than on logical arguments. This conception of representation was born of an aesthetic reflection on the functions of metaphor, but was extended to the whole gamut of symbolic creations of art by basing itself on a new theory of reference. Ernst Gombrich opposed what he called the "extreme conventionalism" of Nelson Goodman and defended the existence of "a real visual resemblance" with recourse to contemporary research in psychology, anthropology, and philosophy on the subject of perception. Without denying the importance of codes and what Goodman calls "inculcation" in the process of recognizing visual representations, Gombrich rejects the idea that images representing nature would be no more than conventional signs in the same way as linguistic signs. There exist for him relations of similarity between the visual space of the painting and the nature of the object represented (cf. "Image and Code: Scope and Limits of Conventionalism in Pictorial Representation," in *The Image and the Eye*). But such bonds of resemblance exclude all realist reference to the object since the most realistic representation already presupposes an extended apprenticeship and rigorously determined cultural and social frames of reference. One thus ends up, in most such inquiries, with a paradoxical situation, since the devaluation of imitation as the central concept of aesthetics has given rise to numerous theories on what was at the very foundation of that concept, that is, resemblance, reference, and representation. Contrary to reflection on art in the nineteenth century, contemporary aesthetics no longer rejects imitation in the name of creative freedom or a radical autonomy of artistic invention, but by virtue of a foundational conviction according to which every act of reference—by perception and above all by language—to reality eliminates any possible homology or isomorphism between discourse and reality. Determined in relation with logic, thus disposing of new epistemological and metacritical models, aesthetics sees itself as necessarily implicated in the debate over realism and anti-realism. The question of realism thus conditions the determination of values, the objective properties of a work, the beautiful, and colors as much as it does that of representation, reference, and resemblance, that is, a large part of the field of aesthetics. This does not at all mean that the concept of imitation has lost all validity and that it is presently stripped of all expressive value, including in the domains of pure copying and artistic forgery. It is through a more precise analysis of the functions of reference that the idea of imitation can conserve its meaning.

Jacqueline Lichtenstein
Elisabeth Decultot

BIBLIOGRAPHY

Alberti, Leon Battista. *On Painting and On Sculpture: The Latin Texts of* De pictura *and* De statua. Edited, translated, introduction, and notes by Cecil Grayson. London: Phaidon, 1972.

Aristotle. *La poétique.* Translated, edited, and notes by R. Dupont-Roc and J. Lallot. Paris: Éditions du Seuil, 1980.

Auerbach, Erich. *Mimêsis: Dargestellte Wirklichkeit in der abendländischen Literatur.* 2nd ed. Bern: Francke, 1959. Translation by Willard R. Trask: *Mimêsis: The Representation of Reality in Western Literature.* New Introduction by Edward W. Said. 50th anniversary ed. Princeton, NJ: Princeton University Press, 2003.

Batteux, Charles. *Les Beaux-Arts réduits à un seul principe. Principes de la littérature.* Vol. 1. Lyon, 1802. First published in 1746. Translation by John Miller: *A Course of the Belles Lettres, or the Principles of Literature.* London, 1761.

Bensaude-Vincent, Bernadette, and William R. Newman, eds. *The Artificial and the Natural: An Evolving Polarity.* Cambridge, MA: MIT Press, 2007.

Blumenberg, Hans. *Die Lesbarkeit der Welt.* Frankfurt on the Main: Suhrkamp, 1981.

———. "'Nachahmung der Natur': Zur Vorgeschichte der Idee des schöpferischen Menschen." In *Wirklichkeiten in denen wir leben: Aufsätze und eine Rede.* Stuttgart: Reclam, 1981. 55–103. First published in 1957. Translation by Anna Wertz: "'Imitation of Nature': Toward a Prehistory of the Idea of the Creative Being." *Qui Parle* 12 (2000): 17–54.

Boileau, Nicolas. *Art poétique.* Chant III in *Œuvres.* Paris: Gallimard / La Pléiade, 1966.

Bruyne, Edgar de. *L'Esthétique du Moyen Âge.* Louvain: Éditions de l'Institut supérieur de philosophie, 1947. Translation by Eileen B. Hennessy: *The Esthetics of the Middle Ages.* New York: Ungar, 1969.

———. *Études d'esthétique médiévale.* 3 vols. Bruges: De Tempel, 1946.

Cennini, Cennino. *Il libro del arte.* Milan: Longanesi, 1984. First published in 1437.

Corneille, Pierre. *Discours de l'utilité du poème dramatique.* In *Œuvres completes.* Paris: Éditions du Seuil, 1963.

Descartes, René. *Œuvres et lettres.* Edited by A. Bridoux. 2nd exp. ed. Paris: Gallimard / La Pléiade, 1953.

———. *The Philosophical Writings of Descartes.* Translated by John Cottingham, Robert Stoothoff, Dugald Murdoch, and Anthony Kenny. 3 vols. Cambridge: Cambridge University Press, 1988.

Félibien, André. *Entretiens sur les vies et sur les ouvrages des plus excellents peintres anciens et modernes: Entretiens I et II.* Edited, introduction, and notes by René Démoris. Paris: Les Belles Lettres, 1987.

———. "Préface aux Conférences de 1667." In *Les Conférences de l'Académie royale de peinture et de sculpture.* énsb'a, 1996.

Fracastoro. Girolamo. *Naugerius; sive de Poetica dialogues.* Bari: Laterza, 1947. First published in 1555.

Ghiberti. *I commentarii.* Florence: Giunti, 1988. First published in 1436.

Gombrich, Ernst. *The Image and the Eye.* Oxford: Phaidon, 1982.

———. "The 'What' and the 'How': Perspective Representation and the Phenomenal World." In *Logic and Art: Essays in Honor of Nelson Goodman,* edited by Richard Rudner and Israel Scheffler, 129–49. Indianapolis: Bobbs-Merrill, 1972.

Goodman, Nelson. *Languages of Art: An Approach to a Theory of Symbols.* 2nd ed. Indianapolis: Hackett, 1976.

Gottsched, Johann Christoph. *Versuch einer kritischen Dichtkunst.* 4th ed. Leipzig, 1751.

Hohner, Ulrich. *Zur Problematik der Naturnachahmung in der Ästhetik des 18 Jahrunderts.* Erlanger: Palm and Enke, 1976.

Isidore, of Seville. *The Etymologies.* Translated by Stephen A. Barney et al. Cambridge: Cambridge University Press, 2006.

Jauss, Hans Robert, ed. *Nachahmung und Illusion.* Munich: Eidos, 1969.

Jean Paul. *Über natürliche Magie der Einbildungskraft.* In *Werke.* Edited by Norbert Miller. Vol. 4. Munich: Hanser, 1962. 195–205.

———. "Vorschule der Ästhetik." In *Werke.* Edited by Norbert Miller. Vol. 5. Munich: Hanser, 1963. 7–456. Translation by Margaret R. Hale: *Horn of Oberon: Jean Paul Richter's School for Aesthetics.* Detroit: Wayne State University Press, 1973.

Junius Franciscus. *De pictura veterum libri tres.* Amsterdam, 1637. Translation: *The Literature of Classical Art,* Vol. 1, *The Painting of the Ancients.* Edited by Keith Aldrich, Philipp Fehl, and Raina Fehl. Berkeley: University of California Press, 1991.

La Fontaine, Jean de. *Épître à Mr l'Évêque de Soissons.* In *Œuvres completes.* Paris: Éditions du Seuil, 1965. First published in 1687.

Leonardo. *Tratatto della pittura,* fragment 11. In *Libro di pittura.* Florence: Giunti, 1995.

Lessing, Gotthold Ephraim. *Hamburgische Dramaturgie.* Edited by K. L. Berghahn. Stuttgart: Reclam, 1981. Translation by Helen Zimmern: *Hamburg Dramaturgy.* New introduction by Victor Lange. New York: Dover, 1962. First published in 1890.

Mancini, Giulio. *Considerazioni sulla pittura.* 2 vols. Rome: Accademia nazionale dei Lincei, 1956–57. First published in 1620.

Ménétrier, Claude François. *Des ballet anciens et modernes selon les règles du théâtre.* Chez René Guignard, 1682. Repr. Geneva: Minkoff-Reprints, 1972.

Mérot, Alain, *Les Conférences de l'Académie royale de peinture et de sculpture au XVIIe siècle.* Paris: École Nationale Supérieure des Beaux-Arts, 1996.

Panofsky, Erwin. *Idea.* Paris: Gallimard / La Pléiade, 1989.

Patrizi, Francesco. *Della poetica.* Edited by Danilo Aguzzi Barbagli. 3 vols. Florence: Instituto nazionale di studi sul rinascimento, 1969–71. First published in 1586.

Perrault, Charles. *Les hommes illustres qui ont paru en France pendant ce siècle avec leurs portraits au naturel.* Geneva: Slatkine Reprints, 1970. First published in 1696–1700.

———. *Parallèle des anciens et des modernes.* Geneva: Slatkine Reprints, 1979. First published in 1688–96.

Poussin, Nicolas. *Correspondance de Nicolas Poussin.* Paris: Fernand de Nobèle, 1968.

Preisendanz, Wolfgang. "Mimêsis und Poiesis in der deutschen Dichtungstheorie des 18. Jahrhunderts." In *Rezeption und Produktion zwischen 1530 und 1730: Festschrift für G. Weydt,* edited by W. Rasch, 537–52. Bern: Francke, 1972.

———. "Zur Poetik der deutschen Romantik I. Die Abkehr vom Grundsatz der Natur-nachahmung." In *Die Deutsche Romantik. Poetik, Formen, Motive*, edited by H. Stef-fen, 54–74. Gottingen: Vandenhoeck and Ruprecht, 1967.

Quatremère de Quincy, Antoine Chrysostome. *Essai sur la nature, le but et les moyens de l'imitation dans les beaux-arts*. Paris, 1823. Translation by K. C. Kent: *An Essay on the Nature, the End, and the Means of Imitation in the Fine Arts*. New York: Garland, 1979.

———. *De l'imitation*. Introduction by Leon Krier and Demetri Porphyrios. Brussels: Archives d'architectures modernes, 1980.

Raffaello. Letter to Castiglione. In *Lettere di diverse eccellentissimi huomini*. Edited by Lodovico Dolce. Venice: Appresso Gabriel giolito de Ferrari et fratelli, 1554.

Ricoeur, Paul. *Temps et récit*. Vol. 1. Paris: Éditions du Seuil, 1993.

Santangelo, Giorgio. *Le epistole "De imitazione" di Giovanfrancesco Pico della Mirandola e di Pietro Bembo*. Florence: Nuova Collezione di testi umanistici inediti o rari, 1954.

Schlegel, August Wilhelm. *Vorlesungen über Ästhetik I (1798–1803)*. Edited by E. Behler. Kritische Ausgabe der Vorlesungen. Vol. 1. Paderborn: Schöningh, 1989.

Schlegel, Friedrich, *Über das Studium der griechischen Poesie*. Edited by E. Behler. Kritische Friedrich-Schlegel-Ausgabe. Vol. 1. Paderborn: Schöningh, 1958. 217–67. Translation, edited, and critical introduction by Stuart Barnett: *On the Study of Greek Poetry*. Albany: State University of New York Press, 2001.

Scott, Izora, ed. and trans. *Controversies Over the Imitation of Cicero in the Renais-sance: With Translations of Letters Between Pietro Bembo and Gianfrancesco Pico, On imitation. . .* Davis: Hermagoras, 1991. First published in 1910.

Tasso, Torquato. *Discorsi dell'arte poetica et del poema eroico*. Bari: Laterza, 1964. First published in 1587. Translation by Mariela Cavalchini and Irene Samuel: *Discourses on the Heroic Poem*. Oxford: Clarendon, 1973.

Tatarkiewicz, Wladislaw. *A History of Six Ideas: An Essay in Aesthetics*. Translated by Christopher Kasparek. The Hague: Nijhoff, 1980.

Winckelmann, Johann Joachim. "Erinnerung über die Betrachtung der Werke der Kunst." In *Kleine Schriften*, edited by W. Rehm, 149–56. Berlin: De Gruyter, 1968.

———. *Essays on the Philosophy and History of Art*. Edited, translated, and intro-duction by Curtis Bowman. 3 vols. Bristol: Thoemmes, 2001.

———. "Gedanken über die Nachahmung der griechischen Werke in der Malerei und Bildhauerkunst." In *Kleine Schriften*, edited by W. Rehm, 27–59. Berlin: De Gruyter, 1968. Translation by Elfriede Heyer and Roger C. Norton: *Reflections on the Imitation of Greek Works in Painting and Sculpture*. La Salle: Open Court, 1987.

Zuccaro, Federico. *L'idea de' pittori, scultori, et architetti*. In *Scritti d'arte di Federico Zuc-caro*. Florence: L. S. Olschki, 1961. First published in 1607.

MIR [мир, мір] (RUSSIAN)

ENGLISH	world, peace, peasant commune
FRENCH	*monde, paix, commune paysanne*
GERMAN	*Welt, Friede*
GREEK	*kosmos* [κόσμος], *eirênê* [εἰρήνη]
LATIN	*mundus, pax*

➤ *PEACE*, *WORLD*, and CIVIL SOCIETY, OIKEIÔSIS, PRAVDA, SECULARIZATION, SOBORNOST', SVET, SVOBODA

The presence in Russian of two homonyms, *mir* [мир] (peace) and *mir* [мир] (world), raises an etymological problem: Was it a matter of two distinct terms at the outset? Need we imagine one of the two semantic veins as derived from the other, or should we imagine two derivations diverging from a common notion? Moreover, was that homonymy used by writers in order to bring to light or create an intersection between the "peace" field and the "world" field? Finally, how do we situate *mir* [мир], the name of an institution, the "peas-ant commune," in relation to "peace" and "world"?

I. *Mir* (World) and *Mir* (Peace): A Fertile Ambiguity

The Russian language inherited from Old Slavonic two mas-culine nouns *mir*—one signifying "peace" (and translating regularly the Greek *eirênê*), the other signifying "world" (and translating regularly the Greek *kosmos*). The two words are perfect homonyms. Insofar as spelling is concerned, the custom—in printed texts and in nineteenth-century cursive—was to distinguish them through use of a normal Cyrillic *i* for *mir* [мир] (peace) and a "dotted" *i* (theoretically reserved for the notation of an *i* before a vowel) for *mir* [мір] (world). That distinction did not survive the spelling re-form of 1917, which eliminated a certain number of letters from the Russian alphabet, including the dotted *i*: the two versions of *mir* have since been spelled identically, as they had been written in Old Russian texts until the eighteenth century. It happens that Vladimir Mayakovsky published in 1916, just prior to the reform, his great poem against the war that was then ravaging Europe, "Vojna i mir": the spell-ing of *mir* (with a dotted *i*) indicated that the title was to be understood as "War and the Universe" (which is how Claude Frioux translates it into French), even though the expres-sion echoes the title of Tolstoy's novel, *War and Peace*. And in fact, in Mayakovsky's poem, it is not a matter of contrasting war and peace but of describing the suffering inflicted by war on the world. In editions published during the Soviet era, after the spelling reform, the two titles cannot be dis-tinguished in print.

As a rule, context allows one to distinguish between the two *mir*s: the two homonyms are indeed two different words, and it is entirely appropriate for dictionaries to treat them in two separate entries. The autonomy of each of the terms is notable in their offshoots: only *mir* (peace) gives rise to a verb, *mirit'* [мирить] (to reconcile), whence comes *smirit'* [смирить] (to appease, tame). And although it is true that the adjective *mirovoj* [мировой], which most often means "worldwide," can also have the meaning of "relative to peace" (in the expression *mirovoj sud'ja* [мировой судья], "justice of the peace"), and it is also true that the Old Sla-vonic *mrinu* and the Old Russian *mirni* translates *tou kosmou* [τοῦ κόσμου], *kosmikos* [κοσμικός], and *mundi*, as well as *tês eirênês* [τῆς εἰρήνης] and *pacis*, at least the modern Russian form of that adjective, *mirnyj* [мирный], no longer means anything other than "peaceful."

It is precisely because the two *mir* nouns can no longer be confused that one can play on their homophony to pro-duce poetic or rhetorical effects, as in the saying *V mire žit', s mirom žit'* [В мире жить, с миром жить] ([If one wants] to live in the world, [one must] live in [observing the] peace) (RT: *Tolkovyǐ slovar' zhivogo velikorusskogo iazyka*, s.v. *mir* 1); or in the poet Yesinin's line, *k miru vsego mira* [к миру всего мира] (for the peace of the whole universe), an appeal dat-ing from 1917 (see Pascal, *Civilisation paysanne en Russie*); or even in the Soviet slogan *mir miru!* [мир миру!] (peace to the world!), which merely takes up the prayer from the Menologion of Novgorod (twelfth century): *mir vsemu miru podazd'* [мир всему миру подаздь] (give peace to the entire world) (RT: *Materialy dlia slovaria drevnerusskogo iazyka*, s.v. *mir*); or even in the translation of the Gospel according to John (14:27):

Mir ostavljaju vam, mir moj daju vam, ne tak kak mir
daët ja daju vam.

[Мир оставляю вам, мир мой даю вам, не так как
мир даёт я даю вам.]

[Εἰρήνην ἀφίημι ὑμῖν, εἰρήνην τὴν ἐμὴν δίδωμι ὑμῖν· οὐ
χαθὼς ὁ χόσμος δίδωσιν ἐγὼ δίδωμι ὑμῖν.]

(I leave you peace; I grant you my peace; I give it to you,
not as the world gives it.)

The situation of *mir*, on the linguistic level, is thus entirely
different from the one encountered with *volja* [воля], for example, which at times means "will" and at others "freedom"
(as can be seen in the names of two political groups of the
late nineteenth century, *Zemlja i volja* [Земля и воля], "Land
and Freedom," and *Volja naroda* [Воля народа], "the Will of
the People"). In the case of *volja*, we are not dealing with two
homonyms, but with a single word, whose semantic range
includes notions that, in other languages, are rendered by
two distinct signifiers. Moreover, the "freedom" denoted by
volja is to be understood as the free exercise or unimpeded
deployment of the will. It is distinguished from freedom as
personal autonomy, which is denoted by *svoboda* [свобода];
volja translates *thelêma* [θέλημα], but *svoboda* translates *eleutheria* [ἐλευθερία] (RT: *Materialy dlia slovaria drevnerusskogo
iazyka*). See SVOBODA.

■ See Box 1.

II. The Idea of "Bond": *Mir* and *Sobornost'*

On the linguistic level, however, what requires reflection is
not the differentiation of the semantic status of *mir* (world),
but the relation between *mir* (peace) and *mir* (world). Although it is true that in the history of Russian (and even
in Old Slavonic) we are dealing with two distinct terms,
one cannot but wonder whether the two *mir*s are linked by
a common etymology. It is generally believed that in the
prehistory of common Slavonic there must have existed a

1

War and Peace: The duality of *mir* and the polysemy of "world"

If, in the case of the two versions of *mir*,
the translator-interpreter needed only to
decide between "peace" and "world," his or
her task, for the most part, would be easy.
There are, however, ambiguous situations.
Circumstances and context allow listeners to
choose the interpretation best suited to their
mood, without it necessarily being that of the
speaker. One example (studied by Bočarov in
1980) is offered by Tolstoy in *War and Peace*
(vol. 3, pt. 1, chap. 18). It is the summer of 1812.
Napoleon's armies are invading Russia. Natasha is at services and hears the great *ekten'ja*
[ектенья] (responsive prayer) of the liturgy
of Saint John Chrysostom. Here is the translation of the passage in the Pléiade edition:

> Le diacre s'avança sur l'ambon ... et ...
> entonna d'une voix haute et solennelle
> la prière: — Prions en paix le Seigneur
> — Oui, songea Natacha, prions tous
> ensemble, sans distinction de classes,
> sans inimitié, unis dans un amour frater-
> nel! — Prions le Seigneur pour la paix
> d'en haut et le salut de nos âmes. Pour le
> monde des anges et de tous les esprits
> incorporels qui vivent au-dessus de nous,
> comprenait Natacha.

The deacon came out to the ambo ...
and, ... began loudly and solemnly to
read the words of the prayer:

> "In peace let us pray to the Lord."
> "As one world—all together, without
> distinction of rank, without enmity, but
> united in brotherly love—let us pray,"
> thought Natasha.

> "For the peace from above and for the
> salvation of our souls!"
> "For the world of the angels and the
> souls of all the bodiless beings who dwell
> above us," Natasha prayed.

The situation is more complex than is implied
by Uspenskij's analysis (to which Bočarov refers)
and the French translation. In the Russian editions published during Tolstoy's lifetime and,
more generally, before the spelling reform, all
occurrences of *mir* are written мір (world). If
the French and English translators thus render the deacon's first exclamation, "mirom
gospodu pomolimsja [мíром господу
помолимся]," as "let us pray in peace," it is
because they seek in a way to correct Tolstoy
so as to make him conform to the Greek text,
which says: "en eirênê tou kuriou deêthômen
[ἐν εἰρήνῃ τοῦ χύριου δεηθῶμεν]," thus: "in
peace [*eirênê*], let us pray to the Lord." But, to
judge by the spelling, *mirom*, an adverbial form
of *mir*, is to be understood as "together, so as to
form a world." The deacon (according to Uspenskij, to whom Bočarov refers) is addressing the
praying community insofar as it is a unanimous
totality or world. Natasha, for her part, does not
transpose "peace" into "world," as the translations would lead us to believe, but draws out
of "world" the idea of love, which orients us
toward "peace." The deacon's second exclamation ("o svysnem mire I o spasenij dus našix [о
свысьнем мíре и о спасений дус нашіх]")
is faithful to the Greek—despite the spelling—
only if one interprets it as a prayer for peace
from on high (*anôthen* [ἄνωθεν]). But Natasha

imagines praying for the spirits who are in the
world above. Between the deacon and Natasha, there is not exactly a misunderstanding;
one cannot say that she has mistaken the
sense of his words, or of the Greek. The homonymy creates an ambiguity here that legitimizes both translations simultaneously, and
that consequently can be reconciled. Such a
situation is possible only because the semantic
fields of the two versions of *mir*, even though
the terms are lexically distinct, intersect, or
even because each projects onto the other an
aura of connotations. Thinkers on the subject
of *sobornost'* [соборность] have insisted on
this, as we shall see below: the world is not
truly a *mir* unless it is a gathering of unanimous
human beings, united by a feeling of mutual
belonging, of forming a coherent and harmonious whole based on an agreement between
its parts and that whole, as well as on the inner
peace of each of its individuals. So strong is
the hold of the group, thus constituted, on its
members that they have no other horizon than
the group itself: the entire world can be nothing other than the projection of the group. A
desire for peace inspires agreement, which is
both the structure of the world and the necessary condition for its achievement.

Such at least is the ideal of the world. But
mir in the sense of "world" has taken on, in
Russian (as it had even in Old Slavonic), all
the values that have become those of Greek
kosmos, Latin *mundus*, French *monde*, Spanish and Italian *mundo*, and German *Welt*. The
world is also what is "mundane," the domain
of the secular, profane, and here-below, in

opposition to the spiritual world, the world above. (Thus Pleberio, in Fernando di Rojas's 1499 *Tragedia de Calixto y Melibea (La Celestina)*: "¡Oh vida de congojas llena, de miserias acompañada! ¡Oh mundo, mundo!" [Oh life, filled with pains, accompanied by miseries! Oh world, world!].) *Obmirščenie* [обмирщение] is the fact of entering into agreement with the powers of this "world": old-believers reproach the church for accepting the reforms advocated by the state in the seventeenth century, and for "yielding to the world" (on the attitude of the church toward the "mundane" world, see Bulgakov, *Pravoslavie*).

Here too, Tolstoy's novel offers an example of the paradoxical advantage a writer can draw on, not only from the homonymic relation of the two versions of *mir*, but from the polysemous nature of *mir* as "world." To go back to Bočarov's analyses: before the invasion of Napoleon's armies and the ensuing war, certain of the principal characters led a worldly life (*mirskaja žizn'* [мірская жизнь]) in society that seemed to them painful and artificial. Pierre Bezukhov gets mired down and sullies himself "in the world," reproaching himself for being a "man of the world" (*mirskoj čelovek* [мірской человек]). Similarly, Nikolai

Rostov finds peace only after distancing himself from "worldly life" (in this case, his civilian existence) and rejoining his regiment, which seems a monastery to him, the image of a pure world. What prompts dissatisfaction and discomfort with the mundane world of secular life is that it embodies dispersion, disorder, and incoherence. The social and secular (*mirskoj* [мірской]) world is opposed to the cosmic (*mirovoj*) world, whose heroes are open, in moments of total solitude suited to mystical perception, to an intuition—of the unity of the universe. The world as cosmos is opposed to the world of profane society as heaven is opposed to earth, but also as the harmony of the totality is opposed to fragmentation and chaos. In other words, the world is a cosmos to the extent that it is agreement. The remarkable fact—for the structure of the novel *War and Peace*—is that this world of harmony, based on friendship and thus on peace between the elements that constitute it, is revealed to the characters of the novel when there is war: in order to confront the ordeals of war, society rejects dissension, pettiness, and various forms of selfishness or secular social existence in order to form here below a spiritual community in the image of the

cosmic world, one in which individuals come to feel that they belong directly to the cosmic totality; their worldly existence, their social determinations, are abolished. It will be seen how, in the title *Vojna i mir* (*War and Peace*), *mir* does not only mean "peace," but refers as well to the "world" and the contrasts between the profane or secular world and a cosmic world identified with the spiritual world.

BIBLIOGRAPHY

Bočarov, S. "Le terme *mir* dans *Vojna i mir*." *Actes du colloque Tolstoï aujourd'hui*. Paris: Institut d'Études Slaves, 1980.

Bulgakov, Sergeï Nikolaevich. *Pravoslavie: Očerki učenija pravoslavnoj Cerkvi*. 2nd ed. Paris: YMCA, 1985. Revised translation by Lydia Kesich: *The Orthodox Church*. Crestwood, NY: St. Vladimir's Seminary Press, 1988.

Tolstoy, Leo. *La guerre et la paix*. Translated by Henri Mongault. Paris: Gallimard / La Pléiade, 1952. Translation from Russian to English by Richard Pevear and Larissa Volokhonsky: *War and Peace*. New York: Knopf, 2007. First published in 1869.

Uspenskij, Boris Andreevich. "Vlijanie jazyka na religioznoe soznanie [The influence of language on religious conscience]." *Trudy po jazykovym sistemam* 4 (1969).

mir signifying "peace" that would have split into two terms, one conserving the original sense, the other taking on the sense of "world." According to Antoine Meillet (RT: *Le slave commun*), the model for this transition from "peace" to "world" was furnished by the administrative Latin of the Roman Empire: *pax romana* became an expression designating all the territory ruled by Roman peace. Similarly, Old Slavonic translated the Greek *kosmos* by (*visi*) *miru*, "(all) the peace," the entire domain of peace, and thus the world. The term *mir* would have been borrowed from *mihr* in an Iranian language, perhaps Scythian, a form deriving from ancient Iranian **mithra*, represented in Avestan by *miqra*. The Sanskrit Vedic *mitra* regularly corresponds to the latter term. We are thus confronted with an Indo-Iranian etymon *mitra* (RT: *Ėtimologicheskiĭ slovar' russkogo iazyka*, s.v. *mir*). In Avestan as in Vedic, the noun can be neutral or masculine. In Vedic Sanskrit, *mitra*, neuter, signifies "friendship," "alliance" (and also, curiously, "friend"). Mitra is also the name of a major divinity in the Vedic pantheon, the god of friendship, friendship personified. In Avestan, *miqra* means "contract" and, as a proper noun, designates the god who reigns over all that partakes of the good, of order and light. Meillet (RT: *Etudes sur l'étymologie et le vocabulaire du vieux slave*) and, following him, Benveniste (RT: *Le vocabulaire des institutions indo-européennes*) and Dumézil, maintain that the original meaning of Indo-Iranian **mitra* is "agreement, friendship resulting from a contract." From a morphological point of view, **mitra* is the instrument or agent through which the **mi-* operation is achieved. The meaning of that verbal root

may thus be a subject of speculation. It may be a matter of the Indo-European root **mi-* (to change) and (to exchange), represented notably by the Sanskrit **mi-* (to alter) and *mith-* (alternate) and the Latin *muto* (to change), *mutuus* (reciprocal): the contract on which the friendship denoted by **mitra-* is based is itself the formalization of an exchange of benefits. But the existence of other Indo-European **mi-* roots—allowing one to trace other semantic lines of transmission for **mitra-* (and thus for *mir*)—have been posited: a **mi-* (to attach) would allow us to understand **mitra-* as a "bond," originally a material bond, and secondarily a bond understood as the constitutive obligation inherent in a contract. The Greek *mitra* [μίτρα] (belt) would be a borrowing from an Iranian form that would have retained that concrete sense (RT: *Dictionnaire étymologique de la langue grecque*, s.v. "Frisk"). Certain etymologists acknowledge as well a root in **mi-* that would be at the origin of the Sanskrit *mayas* (sweetness), and the Old Slavonic *milu* (likable) (RT: *Etudes sur l'étymologie et le vocabulaire du vieux-slave*). That last etymology would make the Indo-European **mitra* a far more affective form of friendship than one resulting from either a binding obligation or exchanges regulated contractually. (Jan Gonda rejects the notion that *mitra-* is a term for "contract.")

These speculations on the ultimate etymology of *mitra* are not unrelated to the more or less explicit (or more or less refined) analyses of the terms *mir* (peace) and *mir* (world) conducted by Russian authors. Florensky (*The Pillar and Ground of the Truth*) states outright that the two versions of *mir* cannot be dissociated, in the sense that "the idea of *mir*, of the world, is based on the notion of a concordance of parts, harmony, and unity. The world is a coherent whole; it is the *mir* of the beings, things, and phenomena it contains." In other words, with peace and agreement being the condition of the world, and the world being the space constituted by peace, it is the sense of "peace" (order, harmony, coherence) that is primary. This idea underlies the doctrines positing that *sobornost'* (solidarity) is the foundation of the human world, and that *sobornost'* is an expression of love as the realization of an inner principle that is supernatural and prevails over empirical nature: it is the principle of divine truth. And inversely:

> . . . the principle of truth [*pravda* (правда)], which is the foundation of society as community [*obščestva* (общества)], the principle of the submission of human passions and natural tendencies to the will and force of God, is necessarily achieved as love [*ljubov'* (любовь)], total inner unity of the human being, a unity without which the union and coordination that empirically determine the nature of the community are impossible.

> (Frank, *The Spiritual Foundations of Society*)

For Frank, as is known, this genuine community, "this spiritual organism is what is understood—in the deepest and most general sense—by the word 'church' (*tserkov'* [церковь]). Thereby, we arrive at the affirmation that at the foundation of all community, as the means and creative principle of that community, there is necessarily the Church." Thus, the "world is to melt without residue into the Church. . . . The entire world is to become without residue the world in God, but God cannot take his place without residue in the world" (ibid.). He continues:

> Social life is constituted by a constant struggle between the principle of solidarity and the principle of individual freedom, between the power [*vlast'* (власть)] that protects the interests of the whole and anarchical tendencies, between centripetal and centrifugal forces. . . . It is only when those two principles find support in a third principle . . . , the service of God, the service of absolute truth, that they achieve agreement and are lastingly reconciled.

The social world becomes a community, the *mir* of the secular world becomes a church only when that reconciliation, which is a pacification (*primirenie* [примирение]), has completed its work. It may be noted, in taking up the question of the original meaning of *mir* anew, that if the harmony of the whole is a form and consequence of the love that the constitutive parts of that whole bring to God, then that social bond cannot be interpreted as a system of exchanges regulated by contract.

Thus the ideologues of *sobornost'* adopt as their own, and with considerable insistence, Tönnies's opposition between *Gemeinschaft* and *Gesellschaft* (see CIVIL SOCIETY, Box 1). It is clearly in society as *Gesellschaft* that the parts are reciprocally adjusted through the effect of laws or forces that are imposed on them and remain, in a sense, external in relation to them. In *Gemeinschaft*, on the contrary, the unity is internal,

and the solidarity organic. But in point of fact, Frank further notes, in the case of a human society, even beneath the external modifications appropriate to *Gesellschaft*, one detects the presence of an internal solidarity characteristic of *Gemeinschaft*. Adapting the teaching of Khomyakov on the nature of the unity of the church, Frank, in *The Spiritual Foundations of Society*, affirms that *sobornost'* is based on a relation of love. If the ideal is to act so that the human world might melt into the Church, through the effects of pacification, it must also be recognized that the principle of love or organic solidarity is indispensable, even if it is invisible, for every society.

III. *Mir*, Peasant Commune and Utopia—Slavophiles and Socialists

The theme of *sobornost'*, which implies a reflection on the "peace" component and the "world" component in the unitary notion of *mir*, also includes considerations about a third sense of the word: *mir* as the name of a specific institution, the peasant commune, also called *obščina* [община]. The real institution that corresponded to *mir* taken in this sense was the object, between 1840 and 1930, of various intellectual battles bearing directly on the characteristics (and thus on the fate) of Russian society, and that ultimately involved the nature of the social bond and the very status of the political. Before indicating briefly the stakes of those debates, we may note that in all dictionaries, *mir* as "peasant commune" is presented as an aspect of *mir* as "world," a circumstance confirmed by the spelling of the word prior to the reform: each "peasant commune" is a world in itself, a whole whose cohesion is ensured by extremely powerful customs of solidarity. It was this *mir* as "peasant commune" that Toporov had in view in his remarks (in "Iz nabljudenij nad etimologiej slov mifologiceskogo xaraktera") on the etymology of the term: "The god Mitra is the one who gathers men in a social structure, a *mir*, it might be said, borrowing a term from Russian social tradition." This way of defining the group wanted by Mitra takes into account, Toporov says, the "natural [or etymological] bond" between the Indo-Iranian **mitra* and the Russian *mir*.

What sort of totality-collectivity are we dealing with in the peasant *mir*? Intellectuals became truly aware of the importance of this kind of social organization only after the German traveler August von Haxthausen published the results of his investigation of the Russian agrarian regime. The Slavophiles opted to see in the *mir* described by Haxthausen the *mir* mentioned in the juridical texts of Kievian Russia (notably the *Russkaja pravda* of the thirteenth century). By 1856, the Russian political philosopher Boris Chicherin had shown that this was an error: in Kievian Russia, the peasants of a commune (in the sense of a territorial circumscription) formed a *mir*, that is, they met periodically to designate their magistrates, who were responsible for the police and relations between the commune and the outer world, the prince and the lords of the manor (see Eck, *Le Moyen Âge russe*). Although the Kievian *mir* also had to administer lands not yet assigned, the peasant was free to dispose of the lands he worked as he wished. In contrast, the *mir* Haxthausen observed was the true holder (if not the owner), administrator, and assigner of the land worked by the peasants (Eck, ibid.). According to Klyuchevsky, the characteristic features of this mir-obscina—obligatory equalization of the lots assigned to each household, complete power of the commune over the peasant, the commune's vouching (out of solidarity) for the payment of taxes—were not explicitly established until the seventeenth century (*Socineniya*, vol. 2).

■ See Box 2.

The peasant *mir* was an extraordinarily persistent and fertile ideological (if not philosophical) theme in Russian thought of the second half of the nineteenth century. The defense and illustration of the *mir* was one of the principal motifs of the Slavophile trend.

Thus I. Kireevskij saw in the *mir* a society whose cohesion was ensured by a fundamentally moral bond. The Russia of times past, "authentic" Russia, unaltered by reforms imitated from the West, was united by that moral bond "into a single vast *mir*, a nation in which faith, land, and custom were shared by all" (quoted in Walicki, *Slavophile Controversy*). The *mir* was a unity grounded in the intimate adhesion of individuals and the integrating force of religion and of shared moral convictions. As opposed to this, organization imposed by an external law, where social relations result from rational contracts combined with legal guarantees, was, for C. S. Aksakov, artificial and bad. An autonomous sphere of the juridical and the political existed: it was entirely in the hands of the monarch and the state. It was external to the life of the people as

organized, in accordance with its inner truth, in the community of the *mir*; the freedom to be defended was not the power for the people to intervene in political affairs, but the right to be free from politics (Walicki, *History of Russian Thought*). The *mir* was, like the church whose counterpart it was within society, a form of common life that combined unity and freedom and whose law was love (Walicki, *Slavophile Controversy*, quoting Khomyakov).

The Slavophiles were not alone in exalting the *mir*. In the camp of the adversaries of autocracy, those who dreamed of a democratic Russia and were inspired in large measure by the revolutionary doctrines and movements of Western Europe, Alexander Herzen, in 1846, was also discovering first the importance, then the positive value of the *mir*. The *mir* was not just a remnant from a precapitalist order. It was also the germ and the model of a socialist organization for the whole of Russia. The hope of Herzen and his "populist" disciples that socialism might come to Russia without necessarily passing through a capitalist phase was based on the existence of the *mir*. Herzen, like the Slavophiles, was horrified by the disasters that the Industrial Revolution, and more generally capitalism, had inflicted on entire populations, but, unlike the Slavophiles, his aim was not to preserve or restore old structures, but to "preserve the commune and render the individual free." That combination defined his ideal of "Russian socialism" (see Malia, *Alexander Herzen and the*

2

History of the *mir*

Whatever its antiquity, and whatever the variations and obscurities of the agrarian codes before and after the abolition of serfdom in 1861, the commune appears as the natural form of peasant life. This is a kind of proverb among peasants of the Russian plain: "the land is with the *mir*" (*zemlja mirskaja* [земля мирская]) (see Lewin, *Making of the Soviet System*; and ibid., for an analysis of juridical debates concerning the *mir*).

The principal function of the *mir* is the periodic redistribution of land among households, in accordance with the manpower provided by each household or the number of mouths to be fed. A scrupulous concern for egalitarian justice brought the *mir*, in its allocation of plots of land, to take into account quality of soil, configuration of terrain, and distance from the village. In addition, one had to yield to all the constraints inherent in the practice of triennial crop rotation, applied to all the lands in the commune. Each household thus received a lot composed of narrow strips of land, which were dispersed and frequently impractical to till with a harnessed plow, but the resultant distribution was rigorously and minutely egalitarian. The lands associated with each household did not form a single block, but consisted of

parcels surrounded by other parcels belonging to other households. Labor was necessarily and at all times collective. The division of lots resulted from decisions, which were always unanimous, taken after tumultuous discussions by family heads convened in general assemblies (*sxod* [сход]). The *mir* system was further reinforced after the 1861 reform: it was to the *mir* that the responsibility fell for buying and administering the lands that large landholders were obliged to cede to the peasants once they were liberated. In the eyes of many economists, however, the *mir* was an insurmountable impediment to agricultural development and thus to the capitalist modernization of Russia. The Stolypin reforms, after the failure of the revolution of 1905, aimed to break the framework of the commune and to favor the emergence of a class of land-owning peasants, intent, in order to get rich, on taking initiatives, working hard, and employing a salaried workforce. These reforms were largely successful: on the eve of the 1917 revolution, almost half the peasant families of European Russia had left their *mir*, and the peasants had become individual farmers. But the upheavals of civil war and the changes triggered by the reform of 1918 ("land to the peasants!") resulted in the *mir*

being reconstituted, and a good number of peasants who had left their communes returned. For more than a decade, the Soviet government allowed the *mir* to subsist, even as it sought to invigorate the class struggle in the villages and to favor soviets of poor peasants. It was only with generalized collectivization (elimination of the kulaks, establishment of *kolkhozes* and *sovkhozes*) at the beginning of the 1930s that the *mir* disappeared. (Concerning the vitality of the *mir* during the first years of the Soviet regime, see Pascal, *Civilisation paysanne en russe*; Lewin, *Paysannerie et le pouvoir soviétique*.)

BIBLIOGRAPHY

Lewin, Moshe. *The Making of the Soviet System: Essays in the Social History of Interwar Russia*. New York: Pantheon, 1985.

———. *La paysannerie et le pouvoir soviétique 1918–1930*. Paris: Mouton, 1966. Translation by Irene Nove, with John Biggart: *Russian Peasants and Soviet Power: A Study of Collectivization*. New York: W. W. Norton, 1975.

Pascal, Pierre. *Civilisation paysanne en Russie: 6 esquisses*. 2 vols. Lausanne: Éditions l'Âge d'Homme, 1969–73. Translation by Rowan Williams: *The Religion of the Russian People*. London: Mowbrays, 1976.

Birth of Russian Socialism; Walicki, *History of Russian Thought*). It stemmed from a critique, not only of capitalism, but also of the idea that only capitalist society, by engendering the forces that would destroy it, could give birth to socialism and, additionally, that what would follow capitalism would necessarily be socialism. For Herzen, the paths of history were not traced in advance (see Berlin, *Russian Thinkers*).

Among the adversaries of the *mir* one finds, principally, as of 1861, all the partisans of the transformation of Russia into a modern country: functionaries, economists, entrepreneurs. For them, the *mir* was one of the principal causes of the economic, social, cultural, and—in a certain sense, moral—backwardness of the Russian peasantry (see Besançon, *Être russe au XIXe siècle*). But the "populist" or (later) "socialist-revolutionary" vision of the *mir* (which would be criticized as late as the 1920s by the economist Cajanov, the partisan of a society founded on familial peasant property, see Kremnev, *Puteshestvie moego brata Aleksei*) was above all attacked by the Marxists. They rejected the utopia of a socialism carried forward by the peasant masses and constructed on the model of the *mir*; for them, the mission of leading the revolution that would achieve the transition to socialism fell to the industrial proletariat, the product of capitalism. It should be remembered, however, that as of the 1860s, Marx, and then Engels, when questioned by the Russian populists (notably by Danielson, the translator of *Capital*), on several occasions offered answers less categorical than, and more distant from, what was in the process of becoming Marxist orthodoxy. In their preface to a Russian edition of the *Communist Manifesto* in 1882, they wrote: "If the Russian revolution becomes the signal for a workers' revolution in the West, so that the two revolutions complement each other, the current model of Russian common property can become the starting point for a communist revolution" (quoted in Rubel, *Marx, critique du marxisme*). In sum, according to Marx, the enclosed, ahistorical, and specifically Russian "world" that was the Russian peasant *mir* could be saved and could preserve Russia from capitalism only if it were caught up in the history of a properly "worldwide" revolution.

Charles Malamoud

BIBLIOGRAPHY

Berlin, Isaiah. *Russian Thinkers*. London: Hogarth, 1978.
Besançon, Alain. *Être russe au XIXe siècle*. Paris: Colin, 1974.
Eck, Alexandre. *Le Moyen Âge russe*. Preface by Henri Pirenne. 1933. 2nd ed. The Hague: Mouton, 1968.
Florensky, Pavel. *Stolp i utverzhdenie istiny: Opyt pravoslavnoj teoditsei v dvenadtsati pis'makh*. Moscow: Lepta, 2002. Translation by Boris Jakim: *The Pillar and Ground of the Truth*. Introduction by Richard F. Gustafson. Princeton, NJ: Princeton University Press, 1997. First published in 1914.
Frank, Semen L. *Duxovnye osnovy obščestva*. New York: Posev, 1988. Translation by Boris Jakim: *The Spiritual Foundations of Society: An Introduction to Social Philosophy*. Athens: Ohio University Press, 1987.
Frioux, Claude. *Maïakovski*. Paris: Éditions du Seuil, 1961.
Gonda, Jan. "Mitra and Mitra: The Idea of Friendship in Ancient India." *Indologica Taurinensia* 1 (1973): 71–107.
Haxthausen, August, Freiherr von. *Studien über die innern Zustände, das Volksleben und insbesondere die ländlichen Einrichtungen Russlands*. 6 vols. Hanover, 1847–52. Translation by Eleanore L. M. Schmidt: *Studies on the Interior of Russia*. Edited by S. Frederick Starr. Chicago: University of Chicago Press, 1972.
Heller, Léonid, and Michel Niqueux. *Histoire de l'utopie en Russie*. Paris: Presses Universitaires de France, 1995.
Klyuchevsky, V. O. *Socineniya*. Vol. 2 of *Kurs russkoĭ istorii*. Ann Arbor, MI: J. W. Edwards, 1948. Translation by C. J. Hogarth: Vol. 2 of *A History of Russia*. 5 vols. London: J. M. Dent, 1911–31.
Kremnev, Ivan (pseudonym of A. V. Chaianov). *Puteshestvie moego brata Aleksei*. Moscow: Gosudarstvennoe izdatel'stvo, 1920. Translation by Robert E. F. Smith: "The Journey of My Brother Alexei to the Land of Peasant Utopia." In *The Russian Peasant, 1920 and 1984*, edited by Robert E. F. Smith, 63–108. London: Cass, 1977.
Malia, Martin. *Alexander Herzen and the Birth of Russian Socialism*. Cambridge, MA: Harvard University Press, 1961.
Mayakovsky, Vladimir. "Vojna i mir." In *Poèmy*. Moscow: Prosveshchenie, 1974. Translated as: "War and the World." In vol. 2 of *Selected Works in Three Volumes*. Moscow: Raduga, 1986. First published in 1916.
Pascal, Pierre. *Civilisation paysanne en Russie: 6 esquisses*. 2 vols. Lausanne, Switz.: Éditions l'Âge d'Homme, 1969–73. Translation by Rowan Williams: *The Religion of the Russian People*. London: Mowbrays, 1976.
Rubel, Maximilien. *Marx, critique du marxisme: Essais*. Paris: Payot, 1974. Translation by Joseph O'Malley and Keith Algozin: *Rubel on Karl Marx: Five Essays*. Edited by Joseph O'Malley and Keith Algozin. Cambridge: Cambridge University Press, 1981.
Tolstoy, Leo. *Vojna i mir*. Moscow: Zakharov, 2000. Translation by Richard Pevear and Larissa Volokhonsky: *War and Peace*. New York: Knopf, 2007. First published in 1869.
Toporov, V. N. "Iz nabljudenij nad etimologiej slov mifologiceskogo xaraktera [Observations on the etymology of words of a mythical nature]." *Etimologija* (1967).
Walicki, Andrzej. *A History of Russian Thought from the Enlightenment to Marxism*. Stanford, CA: Stanford University Press, 1979.
———. *The Slavophile Controversy: History of a Conservative Utopia in Nineteenth Century Russian Thought*. Oxford: Clarendon Press, 1975.

MITMENSCH (GERMAN)

ENGLISH   fellow human
FRENCH   *autrui*

➤ *AUTRUI*, and ACTOR, I/ME/MYSELF, MENSCHHEIT, NEIGHBOR, PARDON, SUBJECT, WELT, *WORLD*

Of recent use in philosophy, the *Mitmensch* (literally, the man-with-me), who is not simply "the other," but not really "others" per se, is situated at the heart of a complex configuration, where it is caught between an undifferentiated alter ego—an other (*alius*) who is indeed someone, but not just anyone (that is, the *thou* or *you* of the dialogical relation)—and the "neighbor," in the sense conferred on the term by the Decalogue. The distinct orientations taken by those using the term, and the theological or religious impregnation of the word, have contributed to the difficulty of translation—a difficulty all the more remarkable in that reflection on the *Mitmensch* has found an echo in France in various debates that oppose diverse conceptions of the functions of *autrui* (others).

Although the term attested to by Adelung in 1777 (RT: *Versuch eines vollständigen grammatisch-kritischen Wörterbuches der hochdeutschen Mundart*) is immediately understandable in common parlance, where it designates simply "any person sharing with me the human condition"—"Meine Glückseligkeit kann ohne Liebe meiner Mitmenschen nicht bestehen" (My happiness cannot exist without the love of those with whom I share existence), wrote Schiller, and similarly

Voss: "du Frei muß werden sobald zu Vernunft er gelangte der Mitmensch!" (any other man, as soon as he gains access to Reason, must be free!)—it appears in philosophy from the outset as a concept. The two initial orientations given to the word (by Hermann Cohen in 1919, then, ten years later, by Karl Löwith) are different, but it is not their difference that makes for the difficulty of finding an equivalent for the term; the translation of *Mitmensch* in French as *autrui*, which is undoubtedly the only reasonable and suitable rendering, in no way allows the term to be shorn of its ambiguities. In addition, there exists, in the historical context in which the concept was formed, a dimension that was from the outset theological, in which the word subsumed simultaneously a "neutral" sense—*Mitmensch* does indeed signify any other person who shares the same condition as me—and a plainly religious sense. Bultmann, throughout his long career, also employed the word to designate not exactly *der Nächste*, but the other human being whom my practical behavior must consider not as a *Nebenmensch* (literally, the man alongside [me]), but, precisely, as a *Mitmensch*, in such manner that I can as a consequence understand the meaning of the commandment that will make of the *Mitmensch* (which everyone has the right to be for me) a fellow human. Conversely, Jesus, the eminent fellow human, is in reality, under the figure of Christ, the paradigm of the *Mitmensch*.

Two general axes can be described from a historical, as well as a thematic, point of view: on the one hand, the phenomenological lineage initiated by Löwith, a student of Husserl and then of Heidegger, which leads to the French phenomenology of Sartre and Merleau-Ponty, and which is continued by Deleuze; on the other, the ethico-religious orientation of Cohen, adapted by Buber to an extent, which emerged in the idea of the "other" in Lévinas. Nevertheless, Deleuze's critique of the Sartrean alter ego (see "Michel Tournier et le monde sans autrui") was executed against a backdrop of phenomenology, just as Lévinas's "other" was similarly rooted in a renewal of phenomenology (see "La trace de l'autre"). Thus it is that the notion of *autrui*, "others," in French, which confirms, without in any way resolving this foundational semantic duality, can give but an approximate equivalent of *Mitmensch*, and its principal virtue lies precisely in the ambiguity that is retained in French, even though it remains altogether mute, at least on first hearing, in relation to the religious dimension, which was the initial breeding ground of the notion.

I. From *Nebenmensch* (the Man beside Me) to *Mitwelt* (a Shared World): A Place for the *Mitmensch* (Hermann Cohen, Karl Löwith)

The systematic origin of the concept comes from an inflection implemented by Cohen toward the end of his life, when he returned to the arguments he originally put forth in *Ethik des reinen Willens* (1904) in order to show its limits and to acknowledge the specificity of religion, which, until then, had not received an independent status. Cohen had shown that there could be no pure morality without the second person, the *Nebenmensch*. But the *Nebenmensch*, if it remains captive to the limits of the concept of plurality, does not satisfy the exigencies of the concept of the non-self, "for which reason one prefers to it the more precise

concept of the other. The other is not an other; on the contrary, in his precise correlation, he is in a relation of continuity with the *I*. The other, the alter ego, is the origin of the ego" (*Ethik des reinen Willens*, chap. 4). This moral conception would undergo a substantial deepening and transformation when Cohen, in 1918, wrote *Die Religion der Vernunft aus den Quellen des Judentums* (published in 1919). The initial problem he posed turns on the limits of morality, and it is a matter of showing that there exists, beyond the "it" or "he" that constitutes the exclusive horizon envisaged by the realm of the practical, a "thou" whose singularity escapes the notion of the alter ego. Because it lifts humanity out of all that is empirical and available to the senses, ethics is constrained to look past concrete individuality in order to objectivize the ego at the higher level of abstract humanity. Religion finds the basis of its legitimacy from a systematic point of view, and the basis of its specificity with regard to reason, as soon as it brings to the fore the irreducible singularity of a "thou" that is no longer an alter ego, the *Nebenmensch*, but rather the *Mitmensch*. The suffering of others, in its singularity, confronts the "I" with its responsibility for the suffering that it inflicts by sinning, and the particular objectivization of the inflicted harm that is manifested in the suffering of the other is what constitutes self-consciousness—and the source of religion. Moreover, the correlation between man and a God whose uniqueness Cohen emphasizes cannot be sustained logically if that "man" is not understood in his own radical uniqueness—but a uniqueness that is not identical with the absolute unity of the divine. It is thus solely a matter of the individual considered in his or her extreme singularity, that is, of the other (*autrui*), which is at once like oneself and altogether other: the *Mitmensch* henceforth opposed to the *Nebenmensch*. It is thus not by chance that the central chapter of *Die Religion der Vernunft aus den Quellen des Judentums* (*Religion of Reason out of the Sources of Judaism*) is devoted to the subject of forgiving, the act that exceeds—par excellence—the limits of morality (a sphere that knows genuine reparation only in the law) and that reveals the singularity of the relation between "I" and "thou" that operates below the relations between *Nebenmenschen* and that only functions between *Mitmenschen* as between "I" and God: "The hypothesis that the alter ego and the other (*autrui*) might be identical is precisely the prejudice of contemporary thought. . . . The alter ego is not at all the *other*. It is experience itself that rejects that identification."

For Löwith, in his doctoral thesis "Das Individuum in der Rolle des Mitmenschen" (The individual in the role of *Mitmensch*), the notion of *Mitmensch* intervenes in the analysis of the structure of being-together (*Miteinandersein*), which implies that one makes a distinction between a world, an environment (*Umwelt*), and a shared world (*Mitwelt*). "Others do not encounter each other originally as suspended objects whose characteristics would partake of the person, but in a relation of man to the world, thus an 'intramundane' relation, a world considered as a 'shared world,' in the perspective of the surrounding world" (*Sämtliche Schriften*, vol. 1, chap. 2, in which the reference to §24 of Heidegger's *Being and Time* is explicit). It is because humans are so essentially a part of the world that they profoundly determine its nature, and this world that is accessible to me is not only humanly structured in the sense of a world shared by others, it is also my world, and it is first of all with regard to myself that it can be characterized as a world shared, which in turn is oriented as a function of a self for whom other people are others. Thus the shared world, if it is encapsulated in a specific other person, becomes for me a "thou." Löwith, who examined in particular Feuerbach's *Principles for a Philosophy of the Future*, thus sought to account for the equivalence posited by that author: "the world or thou." And the "thou" does not represent only the shared world, but the entire world. In the conclusion of his thesis, in which Löwith cites Stirner, he reinforces the idea of the uniqueness of every "I" living at the center of its world with its "property," that is, with what is proper or belonging to it. But he emphasizes still more forcefully that one's own world is always also a world shared, and that every radical individuality is also, by dint thereof, a personality (in the Latin sense of *persona*), that is, a "role" for others. It is that role that is also defined by the term *Mitmensch*. The condition of possibility of that duality between the individual and the other that coexists in every human being rests on the modality of being human: he or she is independently an other because he or she is independent of his or her own nature. From one's being, no specific obligation to be can be deduced other than the obligation to be a *Mitmensch*, that is, a personality that results from the relation between each individual and the others, a relation from which one can in no way escape. This necessity of the *Mitwelt* determines that of the *Mitmensch*, and what results from this phenomenology of being-together is an individual-person duality that is considered as ultimate, but that remains primarily oriented as a function of the ego.

II. Other People between Structure and Transcendence: Legacy of the *Mitmensch* in France (from Sartre to Ricœur)

A deepening of this perspective occurred in Merleau-Ponty (as in Deleuze by way of a critique of the Sartrean theory of the alter ego developed in *L'être et le néant*), one that develops an abstract mode of the notion of *others* that no longer designates a particular modality of the other individual and becomes rather a structure of the field of perception. In a working note of November 1959 (*Le visible et l'invisible*), Merleau-Ponty writes: The self-other relation to be conceived . . . as complementary roles of which neither can be held without the other being held as well: masculinity implies femininity, etc. Fundamental polymorphism in relation to which it is not mine to constitute the other *in the face of* the Ego: it is already there, and the Ego is conquered from it." Exactly a year later, one finds—in a note titled "autrui" (others)—these sentences, which seem to be returning to Löwith's thesis (which Merleau-Ponty had not yet read, although he had promised himself to do so): "*Autrui* is not so much a freedom seen *from without* as destiny or fate, a subject competing with a subject, but it is caught in a circuit that binds it to the world, as ourselves, and thereby also into a circuit that binds it to us—And that world is *common* to us, is an interworld—And there is transitivism through generality" (*Le visible et l'invisible*). The

critique of Sartre is quite present in what lies behind these reflections (ibid.):

> If access to *autrui* has entered into a constellation of others . . . it is difficult to argue that the other is nothing other than the absolute negation of myself, for when it comes to absolute negation, there is only one, which absorbs into itself all rival negations. Even if we have a *principal other* . . . the mere fact that it is not a unique other obliges us to understand it not as absolute negation, but as modalized negation, i.e., ultimately, not as what contests my life, but as what gives it form. . . . [T]he problem of others [is not to be posed] as that of access to a different mode of negativization but as that of initiation to a symbolic and typology of others whose *being for itself* and *being for others* are reflexive variants, and not essential forms.

Thus *autrui* would be less related to the Sartrean alter ego, "the gaze of the other that robs me of the world," and more to a structure.

Similarly, Deleuze granted to Sartre—but in order to immediately strip him of it—the merit of having wanted to make of *autrui* a structure irreducible to subject or object: ". . . but since he defined that structure by the gaze, he lapsed into the categories of object and subject, by making of *autrui* he who constitutes me as an object when he looks at me." *Autrui* is defined from the outset as a "structure of the field of perception" such that "it is not myself, but *autrui* as a structure that renders perception possible." And that structure is not one among others since *autrui* conditions the whole of the field. The fundamental effect of the presence of others "is the distinction of my consciousness and its object," a distinction that occurs simultaneously in space and in time (all quotations from "Michel Tournier et le monde sans autrui"). More generally, Deleuze (ibid.) contests the manner in which philosophical dualism correctly articulates the categories of the functioning of the field of perception and the variations of objects within that field and the subjective syntheses exercised on perceptual matter:

> The true dualism is entirely elsewhere: between the effects of the "structure of *autrui*" in the perceptual field, and the effects of its absence. . . . In defining *autrui* . . . as the expression of a possible world, we make of it . . . the *a priori* principle of the organization of the entire field of perception according to categories; we make of it the structure that permits the functioning as well as the "categorization" of that field.

In 1967, in the re-edition of his *En découvrant l'existence avec Husserl et Heidegger*, Lévinas included an unpublished text, "Langage et proximité," which took its place among a series of texts titled "Raccourcis" [Shortcuts], taking up the essential aspects of the theses developed in his *Totalité et infini*. One finds in that previously unpublished text the famous passage about the caress, which tends to bring to the fore the gaps in our intentional understanding by distinguishing cognitive understanding from the ethical relation to the real:

> Perception is a proximity with being which intentional analysis does not account for. The sensible is

superficial only in its role being cognition. In the ethical relationship with the real, that is, in the relationship of proximity which the sensible establishes, the essential is committed. Life is there. . . . The poetry of the world is inseparable from proximity par excellence, or the proximity of a neighbor par excellence. And it is as though by reference to their origin in the other [*Autrui*], a reference that would obtain as an a priori structure of the sensible, that certain cold and "mineral" contacts are only privately congealed into pure information or pure reports.

Another one of the *raccourcis*, "Enigme et phénomène" (1965), quite plainly refers to the legacy of Hermann Cohen, where *autrui*—understood in terms of the infinite as what refers us to an originary anteriority, which never becomes a presence or is incarnate—"solicits by way of a face, the term of my generosity and my sacrifice. A Thou is inserted between the I and the absolute He." It will be understood that *autrui* is what regulates an essential asymmetry between oneself and the other, who is always closer to God than oneself is. Lévinas thus represents a radical attempt to bring into coexistence, in the notion of *autrui*, a profoundly revised version of the phenomenological tradition and the initial ethico-religious dimension. Paul Ricœur, in showing the limits of that perspective, which grants a radical exteriority to *autrui*, recalls that:

> . . . the theme of exteriority reaches the end of its trajectory, namely, the awakening of a responsible response to the beckoning of the other, only by presupposing a capacity to receive, discriminate, and acknowledge. . . . In order to mediate the openness of the Same to the Other and the internalization of the voice of the other in the same, must not language contribute its resources of communication, and thus of reciprocity, as is attested to by the exchange of personal pronouns . . . which reflects a more radical exchange, that of the question and the answer, in which the roles are endlessly reversed?

> (*Soi-même comme un autre*)

Autrui, then, again becomes the other, and there is an end of hypostasizing, on the basis of the category of alterity, at times as a radical and infinite singularity, at others as a general, originary, and abstract structure of the field of perception. The *Mitmensch* becomes anew *das Andere*.

Marc de Launay

BIBLIOGRAPHY

Bultmann, Rudolf. *Glauben und Verstehen*. Tübingen: J.C.B. Mohr, 1993.
Cohen, Hermann. *Ethik des reinen Willens*. Introduction by Steven S. Schwarzschild. 5th ed. In vol. 7 of *Werke*. Hildesheim, Ger.: Olms, 1981. Originally published in 1904.
———. *Die Religion der Vernunft aus den Quellen des Judentums*. Leipzig: Fock, 1919. Translation and introduction by Simon Kaplan: *Religion of Reason out of the Sources of Judaism*. Atlanta: Scholars Press, 1995.
Deleuze, Gilles. "Michel Tournier et le monde sans autrui." In *Logique du sens*. Paris: Éditions de Minuit, 1969. Translation by Mark Lester with Charles Stivale: *The Logic of Sense*. Edited by Constantin V. Boundas. New York: Columbia University Press, 1990.
Gibbs, Robert, ed. *Hermann Cohen's Ethics*. Leiden, Neth.: Brill, 2006.
Heidegger, Martin. *Sein und Zeit*. 13th ed. Tübingen: Niemeyer, 1976. Translation by John Macquarrie and Edward Robinson: *Being and Time*. New York: Harper and Row, 1962.
Husserl, Edmund. *Cartesianische Meditationen und Pariser Vorträge*. Edited by S. Strasser. The Hague: Nijhoff, 1973. Translation by Dorion Cairns: *Cartesian Meditations: An Introduction to Phenomenology*. The Hague: Nijhoff, 1977.
Lévinas, Emmanuel. "La trace de l'autre" and "Langage et proximité." In *En découvrant l'existence avec Husserl et Heidegger*. Paris: Vrin, 1967. Translation by Alphonso Lingis: "Language and Proximity" in *Collected Philosophical Papers*. Dordrecht, Neth.: Martinus Nijhoff / Kluwer, 1987.
Löwith, Karl. *Mensch und Menschenwelt*. Edited by Klaus Stichweh and Marc B. de Launay. In vol. 1 of *Sämtliche Schriften*. Stuttgart: Metzler, 1981.
Merleau-Ponty, Maurice. *Le visible et l'invisible: Suivi de notes de travail*. Edited by Claude Lefort. Paris: Gallimard, 1964. Translation by Alphonso Lingis: *The Visible and the Invisible: Followed by Working Notes*. Edited by Claude Lefort. Evanston, IL: Northwestern University Press, 1968.
Ricœur, Paul. *Soi-même comme un autre*. Paris: Éditions du Seuil, 1990. Translated by Kathleen Blamey: *Oneself as Another*. Chicago: University of Chicago Press, 1992.
Sartre, Jean-Paul. *L'être et le néant*. Paris: Gallimard, 1943. Translation by Hazel E. Barnes: *Being and Nothingness: An Essay on Phenomenological Ontology*. Introduction by Mary Warnock. London: Routledge, 2003.

MOMENT, MOMENTUM, INSTANT

DANISH	*øjeblik*
FRENCH	*moment, instant, occasion*
GERMAN	*der Moment, das Moment, Augenblick*
GREEK	*kairos* [καιρός], *rhopê* [ῥοπή]
ITALIAN, SPANISH	*momento*
LATIN	*momentum*

➤ AIÔN, AUFHEBEN, DASEIN, *DESTINY*, FORCE, HISTORY, JETZTZEIT, PRESENT, *TIME*, WITTICISM

"Moment" has two meanings that are derived from one another: a technical (mechanical) meaning and a temporal meaning. The mechanical meaning is the Latin *momentum*, and refers concretely, via Archimedes, to the small quantity that tips the scales. The temporal meaning is a movement that determines a before and an after that are irreducible the one to the other. This sudden bursting through of time into space is a key to understanding the Greek *kairos* [καιρός], which is translated, among other things, as "moment."

Modern languages are characterized by their tendency to forget the technical meaning in everyday usage, which focuses on the temporal determination of a small lapse of time (cf. the article "Moment" in Diderot and d'Alembert's *Encyclopédie* [RT: *Encyclopédie ou Dictionnaire raisonné des sciences, des arts et des métiers*]: "A moment does not last long: an instant is even shorter"). They specify the technical meaning differently and in parallel with the temporal meaning.

German has, in addition, differentiated the technical meaning from the temporal meaning by gender: Hegel makes the technical meaning a speculative usage that requires a reorganization of its distinction from the temporal meaning. The philosophical lexicon of the other languages adapts the Hegelian usage ("moment" as instance, or level of reality) through translation.

I. *Momentum* (Lat.), *Rhopê* (Gr.), and Their Translations

The technical meaning of the Latin word *momentum* is prior to the meaning of a small interval of time. *Momentum* refers then to a particular magnitude linked to movement. The redefinition of the category of movement by Galileo and Newton led to a linguistic distinction being established in modern languages, different from one language to the next, between a dynamic meaning and a static meaning, which are merged together in Latin.

Even in its technical sense, *momentum*, which is derived from *movimentum* (from *movere*, "to move"), does not have an univocal meaning. This polysemy reflects a difficulty encountered from the thirteenth century onward in translating the Greek term *rhopê* [ῥοπή], a term used in Book 4 of Aristotle's *Physics* (216a13–20) and in the *Commentary* written by Eutocius (sixth century) from the book of Archimedes known in English as *On the Equilibrium of Planes* (cf. *Archimedis opera omnia cum commentariis Eutoccii*, 264, 13–14).

In Aristotle and in Eutocius, *rhopê* designates the tendency that a body naturally has to move at a speed proportional to its weight (or its lightness in Aristotle). But in the work of Archimedes cited, *rhopê* has the meaning, when considering a set of scales, of a weight that can tip the scales one way rather than the other. It is still a tendency, but it results then from the combination of the weight and the distance between the fulcrum and the beam of the scales. Some translators who use *momentum* in order to designate the first meaning of *rhopê* have to then use another term (for example, *pondus*) when they want to signify the second meaning. Yet this usage is far from being a general one, since Vitruvius, in Book X of *De architectura* (1486), describes *momentum* as the combined effect of the weight and of the distance traveled. What is more, *momentum* is also used in the Middle Ages to translate the Greek term *to kinêma* [τὸ κίνημα], which is found in Book VI of Aristotle's *Physics* (I.232a9–10, and 241a4) and which there designates the indivisible quantum of a movement that has already occurred.

At the end of the sixteenth century, the technical meaning of *momentum* is thus threefold: (a) a natural tendency toward movement as an effect of gravity (dynamic meaning); (b) the product of weight times distance (what we might call the term's *statistical* meaning); (c) a small quantity of movement. These three senses make only an implicit reference to the movement of the fulcrum of a set of scales when it tips: *momentum* contains the contradictory idea of a (static) equilibrium and its (dynamic) rupture as an effect of an infinitesimal cause.

These three meanings can be found, mixed and distributed (according to the particular distortions of each language), in the technical usage that many modern European languages make of the derivations of the Latin word *momentum*, namely the following: *moment* in French, "momentum" and "moment" in English, *momento* in Spanish and Italian, and *das Moment* in German.

In modern French, *moment* refers to the result of a precise mathematical operation, which consists of constructing the vectorial product of the vector position of a material point by a vector having this point as its origin: one calls this the moment of the vector (in relation to the origin chosen in order to identify the position). Since force as Newton defines it is a vector applied to the material point on which it acts, one can define through this operation the *moment* of a force. Meaning (b) is privileged here, as well as a mathematical

conception of mechanical quantities, emphasizing their construction. By analogy, the quantity called in French *moment cinétique* (kinetic moment), constructed in the same way with the slight difference that the force is replaced by the quantity of movement (defined as the product of mass and velocity, a vectorial quantity), *should* be called the "moment of the quantity of movement." This is not the case, however, though the adjective *cinétique* added to *moment* is intended to remind one of this link with the velocity of the moving body, and to make the notion of *moment* a kinetic, even dynamic, one.

In English, there are two words derived from the technical meaning of the Latin *momentum*: "momentum," which is imported directly, and "moment," which is a translation of the Latin term. "Momentum" in English refers to what in French is called the "quantity of movement." This usage comes after Newton, who discusses what he calls the "quantity of motion" and, in Latin, *quantitatis motus*. The English "moment," as in French, refers to the vectorial product of the vector position by another vector. So one finds in English the expression "moment of a force"; in the literature of the time, the expression "moment of momentum" designates what in French is called "kinetic moment."

The importation of *momentum* into English comes in response to a conceptual concern to underscore the dynamic connotation that Newton's second law confers on the "quantity of motion." This law is still called the "fundamental principle of dynamics," and states that the variation of the quantity of motion of a moving body is equal to the force applied to this body. The English "momentum" thus denotes an impulse and retains in part meaning (a) of its Latin homonym, while modifying it, since the English "momentum" is a result of applying an external force and is not inherent in the body (because of its gravity). What is more, the English term introduces a type (c) nuance, in that Newton's law is a differential law and thus deals with infinitely small quantities.

French then makes a distinction between two concepts, one dynamic and the other static, using two clearly different words (*quantité de mouvement* and *moment*), and thereby emphasizing the mode of construction of the physical quantities concerned, whereas English, which uses two phonetically adjacent terms, retains some trace of the Latin polysemy. We are dealing not only with two conceptions of the relationship between mathematics and physics, but more profoundly with two different intuitive representations of movement: it is not insignificant that movement is a quantum in French, and an impulse in English. The difficulty this distinction had in becoming established will be confirmed by the fact that in classical French (notably in the aforementioned RT: *Encyclopédie*), *moment* sometimes designates the "quantity of movement." The *Encyclopédie* article "Mechanics" even reproduces a strange line of argument that attempts to justify, with regard to the set of scales, the use of a single term for two different notions.

The German *das Moment* is used more or less identically to *moment* in French. The moment of a force is *das Kraftmoment*. Since the term for quantity of moment, however, is *Impuls* (previously *Bewegungsgrösse*, "quantity of movement"), the kinetic moment is, more logically than in French, called *Impulsmoment*. Yet *das Moment* has a more dynamic connotation than *moment* in French, as can be seen in the expression *Drehmoment*, literally "moment of rotation," to refer to the kinetic moment.

The present-day usage of the term *momento* in Italian is closely related to the usage of *moment* in present-day French. We should, though, note one meaning of *momento* that is of fundamental historical importance: the meaning Galileo gives to it between 1593 and 1598 when he establishes a link—which had been unthinkable before then, and that no other language borrowed—between meanings (a) and (b) above. This convergence of meanings corresponds to an abortive attempt by Galileo to derive the dynamic from the static without the intermediary of the kinematic, based on a parallel between a set of scales and an inclined plane:

> Momento e la propensione di andare al basso, cagionata non tanto dalla gravità del mobile, quanto dalla disposizione che abbinno tra di loro i diversi corpi gravi.
>
> (Moment is the propensity to go downwards, caused not so much by gravity as by the disposition that the heavy bodies have between them.)
>
> (*Mechanics*, 2nd definition, cited in K. Lasswitz, *Geschichte der Atomistik vom Mittelalter bis Newton*)

II. *Kairos*

The Greek word *kairos* [καιρός], which can correspond to the French *moment*, in the sense of *bon moment* (right moment), *moment opportun* (appropriate moment), *occasion* (opportune moment) (cf. the title of the novel by Crébillon fils, *The Night and the Moment*), refers to a nonmathematizable singularity. Latin rhetoric (Quintilian, *Institutio Oratoria* III.6.26; V.10.43) thus distinguishes between *tempus generale* or *chronos* [χρόνος], a time linked to history and likely to be dated, and *tempus speciale* or *kairos*, a distinct time that is either periodically repeated (a favorable season in a natural cycle, or

an auspicious moment that is favorable for a certain kind of action in people's lives), or that occurs unpredictably, and it is thus expressed as *tempus per opportunitatem* (*G. Fabii Laurentii Victorini explanationum in rhetoricam Ciceronis libri duo*, ed. Halm, I.21) or as *occasio* (ibid., I.27).

▪ See Box 1.

The specificity of the Greek word, which accounts for the scope of its application, comes from its originally spatial meaning, referring to a crucial cutting or opening point, as in the adjective *kairios* [καίριος], found only in the *Iliad*, and which applies to the flaw in a breastplate, hinge, or fitting (IV.185; XI.439; VIII.326), and to the bony suture of a skull (VIII.84), all places where a blow to the body could be fatal and would decide one's fate. So Euripides speaks of a man "struck in the *kairos*" (*Andromache*, 1120). This may perhaps explain how in Latin the skull's "temple" (*tempus, -oris*), "time" (*tempus, -oris*), and the (architectural) "temple" (*templum*) are related to *temnô* [τέμνω], "to cut" (cf. *temenos* [τέμενος], "enclosure, sacred place, altar").

According to the hypothesis put forward by Onians, the usual word *kairos* ([καιρός], with an acute accent) and the technical term *kairos* ([καῖρος], with a circumflex) are one and the same, with the difference of accents used to mark, as it often does, a semantic specification. *Kairos* with the circumflex belongs to the vocabulary of weaving and refers to the braid that regulates and separates the threads of a warp, often paired with the mechanism that holds up the top part of the work: *kairos* determines the spacing between even and odd threads, which allows for the interweaving of warp and weft. In the same way, *kairos* in the usual sense of the term suggests the opening of something discontinuous in a continuum, the breach of time in space, or of temporal time in spatialized time. In medical vocabulary it is a moment of crisis, and the interlacing or combination of circumstances

---

1

Longue durée

The concept of *longue durée* was the centerpiece of Fernand Braudel's writing, and it is intimately linked to his vision of historical time. Precisely because it is a complex concept, it is usually not translated into other languages, including English.

Braudel uses *durée* to signify "temporalities," for his principal concern is to establish multiple temporalities in the analysis of social reality. He starts from the assumption that for the past 250 years, at least in history and the social sciences, there were really only two possible temporalities: one espoused by nomothetic social scientists who assert that there exist universal general laws about social behavior that hold true across all of time and space, and the other subscribed to by idiographic historians who reject the notion of universal general laws and insist on particular hermeneutic insights into social reality.

Braudel argues that both approaches are false and misleading. There exist in his view other temporalities—neither universal nor particular—that provide a better understanding of the past and the present. He names four of them: *structure* (or *longue durée*); *conjoncture* (or *moyenne durée*); *événement* (or *courte durée*); and *très longue durée*. For Braudel, *l'histoire événementielle* (eventual history) corresponds to the particularist time of idiographic historians and *très longue durée* designates the eternal time of the nomothetic social scientists. His own work takes place in the space of *longue durée*—long-lasting but not eternal realities—as well as in the time of *conjonctures* (cyclical process within *structures*).

All of these terms pose translation problems in English, whether as nouns or adjectives. While *événement* is easily rendered

as "event," there is no English equivalent of *événementiel*. I have recommended "episodic" as a term that captures the essential element, that of brief, observable phenomena. *Conjoncture* has cognate equivalents in all European languages, except English. The English term "conjuncture" is primarily used to signal a meeting-point of two phenomena and is close to an "event." The French (and other European-language) meaning of *conjoncture* is that of a medium-length curve going either up or down (an A-phase and a B-phase). "Cyclical" time might be the closest in equivalence. As for *très longue durée*, it is best left in French. After all, Braudel says of it, "If it exists, it must be the time of the wise men (*sages*)."

Immanuel Wallerstein

in politics and history. It expresses timeliness (thus the [appropriate] measure, brevity, tact, convenience) and opportunity (thus advantage, profit, danger), or any decisive moment that is there to be seized, normatively or aesthetically, as it passes by—and seized sometimes even by the hair, since *kairos* is often figured as a young man who is bald or has the back of his head shaved, but who has a long forelock in front. Thus, in Pindar, *kairos* is used to characterize words, both expertly fired and well woven, which hit their mark (*Nemean Odes*, 1.18; *Pythian Odes*, 1.81, 9.78).

The attention given to *kairos* defines a certain type of rhetoric, that of Alkidamas, or of Isocrates and the Sophists, and characterizes rhetorical improvisation (Greek *epi tôi kairôi* [ἐπὶ τῷ καιρῷ], Latin *ex tempore*), of which Gorgias was, according to Philostratus, the initiator (*Vitae Sophistarum*, I, 482–83).

III. *Der Moment / Das Moment*

German decouples the meanings that are simultaneously present in the Latin *momentum*, and redistributes them not onto two different words, but onto two genders of the same word, one of which is adapted by the vocabulary of speculative philosophy. *Der Moment*, in the masculine, refers to a more or less long interval of time, and *das Moment*, in the neuter, originally has the physical meaning of *momentum*. The German philosophical lexicon from Kant onward produced an additional meaning based on *das Moment*, that of cause, or factor, or component of a whole, considered or not in terms of its temporal succession. From there, it became a technical term of speculative philosophy, adopted as such by other languages, including French. This term, created and coined by philosophical language, leads to two questions. The first is the question of the relationship between the mechanical and the speculative meanings of *das Moment*.

▪ See Box 2.

This process itself, to refer here only to language and mechanics, is still never thought independently of time (cf. the verbs used by Hegel: "to put an end to" and "to preserve," as described in Box 2). This is what Marx shows, by contrast, in his attempt after the *Grundrisse* to no longer think in terms of the "moments" of economic processes that should instead be freed from a surreptitious eschatology, and from the correspondence between temporal succession and the movement of the concept as postulated by Hegel.

2

Moment (Ger.) in *The Science of Logic*

The most apposite text here is the commentary on *aufheben* that concludes the first chapter of *The Science of Logic*, in other words, the text par excellence in which the generality of a statement feeds on the particularity of an idiom. Its generality is linked first of all to its immediate environment, since this passage concludes the stage of the logic where the most abstract notions intervened, that is to say, *being*, *nothingness*, and *becoming*, and it appears at the moment when *becoming* both ends and is preserved in its being-there (*Dasein*). Hegel then proceeds to his own objective, analyzing the phenomenon that has just occurred, the *Aufheben*, saying his intention is to discuss "one of the most important concepts in philosophy," of which the movement from *becoming* to being-there is only an example (see AUFHEBEN). Hegel here offers a sort of note on the terminology, focusing on the verb *aufheben* (rather than the noun *Aufhebung*) in its accepted senses and different usages. If *aufheben* holds our attention, it is because of the "delightful" phenomenon that "speculative thought" observes in a particular language, German: the same verb offers the two opposite meanings of "stop, bring to an end" and "preserve, maintain." Nevertheless, to be able to think other than "from the lexical point of view," it is necessary to show how "a language has come to use one and the same word for two opposite determinations," by examining what happens in the thing itself in question. It to this end that Hegel introduces the term *Moment*:

> Etwas ist nur insofern aufgehoben, als es in die Einheit mit seinem Entgegengesetzten getreten ist: in dieser näheren Bestimmung als ein Reflektiertes kann es passend Moment genannt werden. Gewicht und Entfernung von einem Punkt heißen beim Hebel dessen mechanische Momente, um der Dieselbigkeit ihrer Wirkung willen bei aller sonstigen Verschiedenheit eines Reellen, wie das ein Gewicht ist, und eines Ideellen, der bloßen räumlichen Bestimmung, der Linie.

> (Something is sublated only insofar as it has entered into unity with its opposite; in this closer determination as something reflected, it may fittingly be called a "moment." In the case of the lever, "weight" and "distance from a point" are called its mechanical "moments" because of the sameness of their effect, in spite of the difference between something real like weight, and something idealized, such as the merely spatial determination of "line.")

> (*Wissenschaft der Logik*, 114; trans. G. di Giovanni, *The Science of Logic*, 82)

It is clearly a matter of comparing two distinct domains: the speculative domain, within which the *Aufheben* operates, and the mechanical domain, in which one calculates moments of force. *Moment* is presented here as a borrowing, a "Latin expression" used by "technical philosophical language." In the *Aufheben* of speculation, as in the *Moment* of mechanics, the opposites—elimination and preservation, the real and the ideal—work together.

So Hegel uses a Latin word *momentum*, Germanized simply as *Moment*, to explain to German readers how a German word works, and what is more, an everyday German word. This is a rather curious operation. The equivalence proposed at the beginning of his commentary between *das Aufgehobene* (the substantivized past participle of *aufheben*) and *das Ideelle*, mentioned in the passage cited, ought to suggest the existence of a stronger link between the *Aufheben* and the *Momente*—the very one that the conclusion establishes when it mentions "the meaning and the more precise expression that being and nothingness acquire when they are moments." At this point, *Momente* can be defined as what the process of *Aufheben* is composed of.

BIBLIOGRAPHY

Hegel, Georg Wilhelm Friedrich. *Wissenschaft der Logik*. Frankfurt: Suhrkamp, 1831. Translation by George di Giovanni: *The Science of Logic*. Edited by di Giovanni. Cambridge: Cambridge University Press, 2010.

In philosophical discussion, *das Moment* thus goes back to the configuration of the Latin *momentum* and its multiple mechanical and temporal meanings. The problem then is not so much that *das Moment* has a temporal meaning. (In French translation one hears this temporal aspect necessarily in *moment*, even though the translation proves rather awkward in certain contexts in which the speculative meaning prevails, as we can see in this passage from Jaspers: "*Der Augenblick hat in sich zum Beispiel ein* [neuter] *Moment der Angst* [the instant contains for example the moment of anxiety]" (116). The problem is rather one of knowing how to translate *der Moment* differentially, now that a good part of the temporal meaning is contained within *das Moment*.

The second question thus has to do with the translation into French or other languages of *der Moment* and of the system of nouns that are used in German to express the lapse of time in its unequal durations. Whereas French has only the pair *instant/moment*, German has three terms to work with: *der Moment*, *das Moment* with its temporal connotations, and *der Augenblick*. The "opposition" (*Gegensatz*) between *Zeitmoment* and *Augenblick* (Jaspers, *Psychologie der Weltanschauungen*, 114) follows a completely different logic than the opposition *moment/instant*. *Augenblick* alone has the sense of "lived instant," whereas *der [Zeit]moment* can in some instances refer not to a moment but to an instant as an objective division, a unit of measurement of time (ibid., 111: *der objective Zeitmoment* [the objective moment of time]; *ein beliebiger,*

willkürlich gewählter Moment [any moment, chosen at random]). So the particular translation difficulties of *der/das Moment* end up revealing the autonomy of the reflection on *Augenblick*.

■ See Box 3.

IV. *Augenblick/Instant*

German represents an instant not as an immobile point on a line (*in-stans*) but as an organic movement, the blink of an eye. The German *Augen-blick* suggests both the quickness of a glance and the light that this look retains (cf. the poem by Schiller, "Die Gunst des Augenblicks" [The favor of the moment]). The word literally means both a "look" and a "closing of the eyes"; it is the blinking of an eye staring at its object, then by extension the "short duration" of this closing, which is generally agreed to be "indivisible" (RT: *Versuch eines vollständingen grammatisch-kritischen Wörterbuches der hochdeutschen Mundart*, 1792 edition, in the article "Augenblick," 1:col. 561).

This particular metaphor does not necessarily entail any difference in usage with respect to the French: the pair *Moment/Augenblick* works much like the French pair *moment/instant*, with the second term in each being reserved for the description of a lapse of time so brief that it eludes measurement. However, while French usage requires the addition of an epithet when instant refers to anything other than an objective division of time (see, for example, G. Bachelard, *L'Intuition de l'instant* [Intuition of the instant], 36: "*un instant*

3

An English Hegelianism? "Moment" in John Stuart Mill

It is curious to note that John Stuart Mill, in his *System of Logic* (published in 1843, or about ten years after the text by Hegel cited earlier, *The Science of Logic*) problematizes the notion of "moment" in more or less the same way that Hegel does. In a chapter discussing the "Conditions of a Philosophical Language," Mill first of all recalls the dynamic meaning of "moment." Then, emphasizing the truth it contains and which concerns the conservation of something unknown (since the product of the velocity of a body and its mass does not refer to anything experientially real), he assigns it a role that assumes its full importance in the use of fictions, as he conceives it in Book V. This notion, which Mill begins by critiquing, is now reoriented so that it can be accepted on other conditions than those stipulated previously. The whole play of the theory of fictions used by utilitarians lies in the awareness that a term only apparently intends something in experience, but that it should not be rejected for this reason, provided one is no longer deluded about its

illusory transcendence, because it retains an indirect power to determine things.

It was already a received doctrine that, when two objects impinge upon one another, the momentum lost by the one is equal to that gained by the other. This proposition it was deemed necessary to preserve, not from the motive (which operates in many other cases) that it was firmly fixed in popular belief; for the proposition in question had never been heard of by any but the scientifically instructed. But it was felt to contain a truth; even a superficial observation of the phenomena left no doubt that in the propagation of motion from one body to another, there was something of which the one body gained precisely what the other lost; and the word momentum had been invented to express this unknown something. The settlement, therefore, of the definition of momentum, involved the determination of the question, What is

that of which a body, when it sets another body in motion, loses exactly as much as it communicates? And when experiment had shown that this *something* was the product of the velocity of the body by its mass, or quantity of matter, this became the definition of momentum.

(*A System of Logic*, vol. 2)

Given its logical and philosophical context, this analysis, rooted in physics and part of a theory of fictions, obviously calls to mind the equivalent of the *Moment* of the *Aufheben* in Hegel's *Logic*. What is strange about this analogy is that it probably occurs without Mill's being aware of it himself, despite his interest—a mixture of acerbic critique and restrained admiration—in German philosophy.

BIBLIOGRAPHY

Mill, John Stuart. *A System of Logic, ratiocinitive and inductive: Being a connected view of the principles of evidence, and methods of scientific investigation.* London: J. W. Parker, 1843.

4
Øjeblik in Kierkegaard

➤ ANXIETY

The instant, which is in Søren Kierkegaard the object of a series of original developments in the register of existentiality, cannot be assimilated to any of the points of *chronos*: past, present, future. Of the two terms in Danish, *moment* and *øjeblik*, the first can refer, outside of speculative philosophy, to all of the moments of a whole or of a natural or historic process. It is important, though, to mention one not-insignificant usage, since body and soul are said to be two "moments" of a synthesis, with the mind being the third term. The question of the third, posed when the two "moments" are the temporal and the eternal (*Kierkegaard's Writings*, 7:185), leads precisely to the concept of *øjeblik*, which is usually preferred to *moment* in order to connote the existential dimension. After Kierkegaard's great works in which the instant is a cornerstone of the analysis of the aesthetic and ethical stages, the concept is elaborated philosophically in two books published in 1844: *Philosophical Fragments* and *The Concept of Anxiety*, notably in chapter 3.

Without the instant, which comes from God himself in time, "everything would have remained Socratic" (*Kierkegaard's Writings*, 7:53), and the paradox whereby time and eternity touch one another would have been missed. Or to put it another way, everything would have remained in the hands of "negation, transition, mediation, these three masked, suspect and secret agents which [in Hegel's *Logic*] set everything in motion" (ibid., 7:181). The Christian impulse of reflection leads Kierkegaard to base himself, to the contrary, on a number of solid philosophical pillars (Socrates, the Platonic *exaiphnês* [ἐξαίφνης], the idealist philosophy of religion) to develop the concept of an instant to its fullest extent, at the risk of "a productive misunderstanding" (W. Beierwaltes, "Exaiphnês oder," 282).

The "instant" is a term that produces an image—"Atom and blink of an eye" (*Kierkegaard's Writings*, 7:187; 1 Cor. 15:52)—and refers to the end of time while expressing eternity. How should we interpret this "first attempt to suspend time"? For the Greeks, eternity is the past, to which we can only accede by moving backward. For Judaism, history and the future become decisive. But it is Christianity, Kierkegaard maintains, that first introduces both an absolute qualitative difference, and a contact, between time and eternity. The future, far from being conceived as a result of the past, is "a whole of which the past is a part" (cf. Merleau-Ponty, *Phénoménologie de la perception*, 471). But for this

to obtain, the instant has to be posited concretely, so that an "ambiguity" can appear: the ambiguity "in which time intercepts [tears: *afskaere*] eternity, and eternity penetrates time" (*Kierkegaard's Writings*, 7:188). The instant, as the "fullness of time" (Gal. 4:4, cited in 7:18, 189), the "making eternal of the historical, and the making historical of the eternal" (7:58), means that the eternal is "the future which returns like the past" (*Kierkegaard's Writings*, 7:58, 15:92).

Just as Leucippus did for space, Plato posed the question of movement in time. His achievement is to have thereby discovered *exaiphnês* (RT: LSJ: "on a sudden," "the moment that") and its suddenness. However, his "metaphysical" approach can make it only a "mute atomic abstraction" (*Kierkegaard's Writings*, 7:183). While doing justice to the Greeks (5:20), Kierkegaard continues, we should define more precisely this "strange [*atopon* (ἄτοπον)] thing" that has no place, this pure in-betweenness (*mellem*), or interval between motion and repose, this *kat' exochên* [κατ᾽ ἐξοχήν] transition, "which is in no time." It could be a matter of "what is happening behind the back of consciousness" (*Lectures philosophiques de Søren Kierkegaard*, ed. and trans. H.-B. Vergote, 304, 321). Taken out of its physical and metaphysical context, and transferred to the field of existentiality on the basis of what is "dogmatically" given, this transition falls into the realm of possibility (ibid., 300). It conditions the play of categories of leap, decision, repetition, and contemporaneity, where the concept that is being worked is the instant as opposed to reminiscence, disjunction as opposed to mediation.

Understood in this way, *øjeblik* is, in opposing ways, at the center of the analyses of faith and anxiety, where it appears that the primacy of the future and the vertigo of freedom give the dimension of the possible, of pure in-betweenness as power, its full scope. As "the One which both is and is not," the instant of "the anguishing possibility of power . . . a higher form of non-knowledge . . . in a higher sense, is and is not" (*Kierkegaard's Writings*, 7:146, 183). The instant is both temporal (a transition) and "outside of time."

Since the conception of time is decisive in the determination of the stages of existence (aesthetic, ethical, religious), the concept of an instant will become the object of three original variations, marked by a rhythm of increasing potentiality.

The aesthetic instant, the beautiful "poetic" moment, is "the eternal instant of joy"

(*Kierkegaard's Writings*, 2:272). It is eternal because, once all concern about external contingencies is eliminated, "it is everything" (3:401; 10:278). But since it is unable to instigate a history, aesthetic passion "runs aground on time" (10:234 ff.).

"The aesthetic is in man that by which he is immediately what he is; ethics is that by which he becomes what he becomes" (*Kierkegaard's Writings*, 4:162). The models of this becoming are conjugal love and social action, which involve duration, continuity, and history. It is through the instant of resolute choice of the self that ethical individuality "uses time for its own ends" (10:235).

Different from aesthetic and ethical eternity, as well as from the abstract eternity of the Hegelian *Logic*, the eternity in question in the Christian religious sphere determines the third application of the concept of *øjeblik*. If the master is greater than the occasion, it is because the "absolute Fact" (*Kierkegaard's Writings*, 7:93) has happened, through which is given, in time, the condition that allows the paradoxical instant to be confronted, when thought is summoned to discover "what it cannot think" (7:35).

Because the ethics of autonomy is only a "transient sphere" (*Kierkegaard's Writings*, 9:438), the paradoxical instant, compared to the immediacy of the aesthetic instant, this "parody of eternity" (7:186), represents a new immediacy. But these two instants share a passion for eternity which, however different they may be from one another, are not the eternity of "the human in general," of unconditional duty and of the suspended power of the absolute choice of self. When Kierkegaard entitles his last polemical writings against established Christianity *The Instant*, he is evoking this "category of great importance in that it opposes pagan philosophy, and an equally pagan speculation in Christianity" (7:183ff.).

BIBLIOGRAPHY

Beierwaltes, Walter. "Exaiphnès oder: Die Paradoxie des Augenblicks." *Philosophisches Jahrbuch* 74 (1967): 271–83.

Colette, Jacques. "Instant paradoxal et historicité." Pp. 109–34 in *Mythes et Représentations du temps*. Paris: Centre National de la Recherche Scientifique, 1985.

Kangas, David J. *Kierkegaard's Instant: On Beginnings*. Bloomington: Indiana University Press, 2007.

Kierkegaard, Søren. *Lectures philosophiques de Søren Kierkegaard*: *Kierkegaard chez ses contemporains danois*. Edited and translated

by Henri-Bernard Vergote. Paris: Presses Universitaires de France, 1993.
———. *Skrifter*. 26 vols. Edited by Niels Jørgen Cappelørn et al. Copenhagen: Gad, 1997. Translation by Howard V. Hong and Edna H.

Hong: *Kierkegaard's Writings*. 26 vols. Princeton: Princeton University Press, 1978–98.
———. *Søren Kierkegaard's Journals and Papers*. Edited and translated by Howard V. Hong and

Edna H. Hong, with Gregor Malantschuk. 7 vols. Bloomington: Indiana University Press, 1967–78.
Merleau-Ponty, Maurice. *Phénoménologie de la perception*. Paris: Gallimard, 1945.

fécond" [a fertile moment]), it is the other way round in German, where *Augenblick* alone refers immediately to a lived instant. Jaspers underlines the fact that "the word *Augenblick* describes something completely heterogeneous in what remains identical in the formal concepts of time, namely the full and the empty [*das Erfüllte und Leere*]." This leads to the following terminological distinction: "The atom of time [*Zeitatom*] is of course nothing, but the instant [*Augenblick*] is everything" (*Psychologie der Weltanschauungen*, 108–17). In this phrase Jaspers summarizes the entire process by which *Augenblick* has come to be endowed with a powerful poetic and aesthetic force. Poetry in particular develops the theme of the small bit of eternity contained within an instant (cf. Goethe, *Faust*, I.V.73), while for Lessing *Augenblick* becomes an original aesthetic concept, a timely moment that is distinct from *kairos* in that it crystallizes a temporal sequence, including the future, instead of disrupting it: "Painting, in its compositions in which several times coexist, can make use of only one single moment [*Augenblick*], and because of this must choose the fullest one, from which what precedes and what follows will be most easily understood" (G. E. Lessing, *Laokoon*, in *Werke*, 2:89).

The difficulty comes into sharper focus when a claim is made, so to speak, on all of the particular elements that have been mentioned. In Heidegger's *Sein und Zeit*, the term first appears in two key paragraphs marking the transition to originary temporality (§65 and §68). *Augenblick* is then used to determine the characteristics of the "authentic present" insofar as it is maintained in the future and the having-been.

In der Entschossenheit . . . wird [die Gegenwart] in der Zukunft und Gewesenheit gehalten. . . . Die in der eigentlichen Zeitlickheit gehaltene, mithin eigentliche Gegenwart nennen wir den Augenblick.

(In the decision . . . the present is maintained within the future and the having-been. This present maintained within authentic temporality, thus the authentic present, we name the instant.)

(*Being and Time*, §69, 338)

In this respect, *Augenblick* is explicitly distinguished from the *Jetzt*, the *now* of derived temporality that understands time as a receptacle, a *milieu* within which one instant follows another in succession. *Instant*, by the sheer weight of its etymology, thus appears as an uneasy translation for *Augenblick*, which indicates a present that is not itself within time, and a present in which nothing happens, since

it alone is what can enable *Dasein* to open itself to a being "in a time."

We come back, then, to the problem of the metaphoricity proper to *Augenblick*. The adverbial expression "in the blink of an eye" offers a valid equivalent, but it cannot in any case systematically replace a noun. The meaning of Adelung's comment that *Augenblick* should be understood figuratively even though it is never, or hardly ever, used literally, can now be fully appreciated: "instant," unlike *Augenblick*, does not translate the metaphor, and designates a different conception of time, while "blink of an eye" translates the metaphor, but does not express time.

- See Box 4.

Françoise Balibar
Philippe Büttgen
Barbara Cassin

BIBLIOGRAPHY

Archimedes. *Archimedis opera omnia cum commentariis Eutoccii* [On the equilibrium of planes]. Edited by J. L Heiberg. Leipzig: Teubner, 1972. Teubner edition first published in 1915.

Bachelard, Gaston. *L'intuition de l'instant: Étude sur la Siloë de Gaston Roupnel*. 3rd ed. Paris: Stock, Delamain, & Boutelleau, 1932.

Friese, Heidrun, ed. *The Moment: Time and Rupture in Modern Thought*. Liverpool, UK: Liverpool University Press, 2001.

Gallet, Bernard. *Recherches sur kairos et l'ambiguïté dans la poésie de Pindare*. Bordeaux, Fr.: Presses Universitaires de Bordeaux, 1990.

Galluzzi, Paolo. *Momento: Studi Galileiani*. Rome: Ateneo and Bizzarri, 1979.

Heidegger, Martin. *Sein und Zeit*, Tübingen: Niemeyer, 1986. First published in 1927. Translation by John Maquarrie and Edward Robinson: *Being and Time*. New York: Harper Row, 1962.

Jaspers, Karl. *Psychologie der Weltanschauugen*. Berlin: Springer, 1925.

Lasswitz, Kurd. *Geschichte der Atomistik vom Mittelalter bis Newton*. Vol. 2. Leipzig: Voss, 1890.

Lessing, Gotthold Ephraim. *Laokoön*. In vol. 2 of *Werke*. Frankfurt: Deutscher Klassiker Verlag, 1967.

Sipiora, Phillip, and James S. Baumlin, eds. *Rhetoric and Kairos: Essays in History, Theory, and Praxis*. Albany: State University of New York Press, 2002.

Stephenson, Hunter W. *Forecasting Opportunity: Kairos, Production, and Writing*. Lanham, MD: University Press of America, 2005.

Trédé, Monique. *Kairos: L'à-propos et l'occasion (le mot et la notion, d'Homère à la fin du IVe siècle avant J.-C.)*. Paris: Klincksieck, 1992.

Victorinus, Q. Fabius Laurentius. *Q. Fabii Laurentii Victorini explanationum in rhetoricam Ciceronis libri duo*. Edited by Carolus von Halm. Leipzig: Teubner, 1863.

Wägenbaur, Thomas. *The Moment: A History, Typology, and Theory of the Moment in Philosophy and Literature*. New York: Peter Lang, 1993.

Ward, Koral. *Augenblick: The Concept of the 'Decisive Moment' in 19th- and 20th-Century Western Philosophy*. Aldershot, UK: Ashgate, 2008.

Wilson J. R. "Kairos as Due Measure." *Glotta* 58 (1980): 177–204.

MOMENTE (GERMAN)

➤ MOMENT, STIMMUNG, *TIME*

We say of a musical work that it corresponds to a form made up of *Momente*, according to the German expression in use since the nineteenth century, whenever the sequence is itself conceived as an accumulation of *Momente*. This becomes, then, the standard term for a musical unit of time. Stockhausen gave a complex compositional meaning to the term, which has had a determining influence on contemporary music and musical terminology.

For the Germans, particularly Schubert, musical *Momente* referred to those parts (*Stücke*) that are not composed with the aim of developing a form extended across several different times but that, on the contrary, indicate a brevity that itself constitutes an autonomous unit of time. The notion of *Momente* in the compositional sense of the term appeared between 1958 and 1960 in the work of Karlheinz Stockhausen. In the first case, *Momente* is translated as "moments," and the temporal division of the work into moments refers to a distinct musical genre. In the second case, the term *Momente* is retained as a proper name that is used to conceptualize a unique experience that simultaneously affects melodic structure, timbre, and duration (*Momente* in Stockhausen are "individual passages of a work . . . regarded as experiential units"; Sadie, *New Grove Dictionary*).

In his work entitled *Momente* (finished on 21 May 1962 in Köln) for soprano, four choral groups, and thirteen instrumentalists and based on the Song of Solomon and songs by Blake and Bauermeister, Stockhausen explains that this notion of *Momente* slows him to "form"

> something in music which is as unique, as strong, as immediate and present as possible. Or I experience something. And then I can decide, as a composer or as the person who has this experience, how quickly and with how great a degree of change the next moment is going to occur.
>
> (*Karlheinz Stockhausen on Music*)

Stockhausen refers to three clearly distinct types of *Momente* that, as the work takes form, end up acting upon each other. First of all, in terms of the melody, the *Moment* has to do with the work on heterophonia, the play that is internal to the arrangement of the pitch of each note. Here, the spoken voice, articulated and not sung, takes precedence. The *Moment* increases the already equivocal meaning of the voice. Then, in terms of timbre, this reaches its high point in the treatment of the men's choir and percussion sections so as to produce consonants, hisses, and loud noises; this less discursive *Moment* is intended to introduce an entropic sequence within a more articulate extension or duration. Finally, there is the *Moment* that refers to duration as an alternation between polyphonic sequences and silences; the sense of a new *Moment* is a result of a deliberate break in the musical flow created by the female voices.

> I would thus understand by Moment any formal unit that has, in a given composition, a personal and strictly assignable characteristic. I could also say: any autonomous thought. The concept is thus qualitatively determined,

taking into account a given context (as I said, in a given composition), and the duration of a moment is one of the properties among others of its mode of being.

> (Stockhausen, "Momentform")

This explains the importance of the plural, *Momente*, which emphasizes the large number of operations and, at the same time, their singularity and function. It is worth noting that this conception of articulated composition in *Momente* brings forth variables, permutable elements—in short, what the composer calls a polyvalent form. These are variables of dynamics, statistical divisions of sounds in a global duration: the collective form of the *Moment*. The procedures are there to reveal the mutable functions of the *Momente* in all their power as inserts. Three other works by Stockhausen take up the question of *Moment* and of the *Momentform*: *Kontakte* (1958), *Carré* (1959–60), and *Gruppen* (1958). *Momente* in the sense in which Stockhausen uses the term would from that point on become part of contemporary musical terminology.

Danielle Cohen-Lévinas

BIBLIOGRAPHY

Sadie, Stanley, ed. *The New Grove Dictionary of Music and Musicians*. 2nd ed. 29 vols. London: Macmillan, 2001.
Stockhausen, Karlheinz. "Momentform." *Contrechamps* 9 (1988): 111–12.
———. *Karlheinz Stockhausen on Music: Lectures and Interviews*. Collected by Robin Maconie. London: Marion Boyars, 1989.

MORAL SENSE

FRENCH   *sens moral*
GERMAN   *sittliches Bewusstsein*

➤ MORALS, SENSE, and COMMON SENSE, CONSCIOUSNESS, ENGLISH, PERCEPTION, PRAXIS, RIGHT/JUST/GOOD, *VIRTUE*

We can date the invention and philosophical usage of the term "moral sense" to Shaftesbury, and more particularly to Hutcheson. The tradition of a philosophy of moral sense is more generally constituted within the Anglo-Scottish philosophy of the eighteenth century. Moral sense associates the understanding of morality with a moral sensibility. It consists of a set of innate dispositions. It is also a look of approval or disapproval of a given action. However, the recourse to the term "sense" allows us to envisage practical reason playing some role, a moral activity that is far more than the faculty of perceiving good or evil.

The expression "moral sense" is a relatively recent invention. As a term in the lexicon of philosophical discourse, it is generally attributed to Shaftesbury's *An Enquiry Concerning Virtue* (1699). A hotly disputed notion in the eighteenth century, the moral sense is invoked less often in debates on moral philosophy of the times than in everyday language. We say of someone with very firm principles of good and evil that he is "a man with a developed moral sense."

If the philosophical and ordinary meanings of moral sense always suggest a certain presence of morality within a man, they refer more to a set of moral questions than to a simple doctrinal position.

"Moral sense" was established as a term primarily in order to take the side of naturalism in morals; "moral sense" refers to a set of dispositions that are innate to morality, a capacity that preexists all conventions. This relation to the discernment of good and evil takes the form of an ability to perceive the moral quality of actions, a sense. According to Thomas Burnet, man has a natural awareness of good and evil, which can be understood as a moral sense: "I understand by natural conscience a natural sagacity to distinguish moral good and evil, or a different perception and sense of them" (*Remarks on Locke*).

The existence of a natural sensibility in morality is in many ways reinforced in the definition Hutcheson gives of "moral sense." Moral sense is not used to perform a good deed but rather to be sensitive to the moral qualities of an action and to approve of them. Hutcheson proposes a morality of the spectator and not of the agent: moral sense for him designates a perception that becomes an approval or disapproval of an action: "A Determination of our minds to receive the simple Ideas of Approbation or Condemnation, from Actions observ'd" (*An Enquiry Concerning Virtue*).

It nonetheless remains the case that from these perspectives, moral sense is above all linked to a receptiveness of the human mind in practical matters. Does this expression not also hold out the possibility that one may exercise one's moral reason by intervening in one's own actions? Thus, in Shaftesbury, moral sense refers to an ability to form adequate representations of good. Sense is not reduced to the faculty of perceiving; it is to be understood as a "reflected sense" (*Characteristics*), an instance of the control and examination of moral representations. "Moral sense" and, more often, "sense of right and wrong" constitute a second-order affection, or even the mind's disposition to examine sensations, actions, or received passions. Man "is capable of having a Sense of Right or Wrong; a Sentiment or Judgment of what is done through just, equal, and good Affection" (*Characteristics*). Moral sense is reason based on the perceptive naturalness of actions and passions.

In our time, Charles Taylor's critique of moral naturalism barely mentions the place of moral sense. It is directed, rather, toward the role of naturalist epistemology, whose model incites us to seek "criteria" for morality. In contrast to this approach, Taylor asserts the need to have recourse to moral intuitions, to what motivates us morally, without appealing to moral sense, which is instead a means of apprehending morals independently of science ("Explanation and Practical Reason").

Fabienne Brugère

BIBLIOGRAPHY

Burnet, Thomas. *Remarks on Locke*. Edited by G. Watson. Doncaster: Brynmill Press, 1989. First published in 1699.

Hutcheson, Francis. *An Inquiry into the Original of our Ideas of Beauty and Virtue, in Two Treatises, I. Concerning Beauty, Order, Harmony, Design; II. Concerning Moral Good and Evil*. 5th ed. London: 1753.

Shaftesbury, Anthony Ashley Cooper. *Characteristics of Men, Manners, Opinions, Times*. Vol. 2, *An Enquiry Concerning Virtue*. Hildesheim: Olms, 1978. First published in 1711.

Taylor, Charles. "Explanation and Practical Reason." In *Philosophical Arguments*. Cambridge, MA: Harvard University Press, 1995.

MORALS / ETHICS

FRENCH	*morale, éthique*
GERMAN	*Sitten, Sittlichkeit, Moralität*
GREEK	*ethos* [ἔθος], *êthos* [ἦθος]
LATIN	*mores, moralitas*

➤ BERUF, DUTY, LAW, *LIBERTY*, MENSCHHEIT, MORAL SENSE, *RELIGION*, *VIRTUE*, WERT

"Morals" (from the Latin *mores*, "customs") and "ethics" (from the Greek *êthos* [ἦθος], "character"), like their equivalents in the other modern languages, generally refer to the rules that make up the norms of human behavior. They are distinguished, both within one language and from one language to another, in terms of two types of problem. The first is the problem of the subject and its conduct, whether as an individual or as a community. The second concerns the nature of what "morals" designate: as a simple description, the designation "morals" refers to nature and to history; as a prescription, it dictates laws, and establishes values, whether good or bad. How these four dimensions (individual and collective, descriptive and prescriptive) are linked constitutes the arena in which the differences between languages are played out.

One might think that "morals," of Latin etymology, is the exact equivalent of "ethics," of Greek etymology, and that these twin terms coexist with the same meaning in the main modern European languages, including English, even if the Greek term is, as usual, more erudite and more technical (like "corporeal" and "somatic," for example). This is wrong on two counts: on the one hand, however unstable and confused these differences are, "morals" and "ethics" do not nowadays share the same field of application, and their distinction is sometimes even a doctrinal *topos*; on the other hand (and this is a paradoxical chiasmus that is often not recognized as such), it is often ethics that are invoked with reference to mores, as a reflection on social norms and conduct, whereas "morals" refers primarily to the individual—if not to his "character" (*êthos*), then at the very least to the question of his freedom of choice.

We can find in the organization of the Greek terminology as it was first established by Aristotle, as well as in the way in which Cicero justified his choices of translation, two causes that may to some extent account for the paradox of the modern usage.

I. *Ethos* [ἔθος] as "Habit" and *Êthos* [ἦθος] as "Character": What Are Ethics?

Two competing nouns developed in Greek from *eiôtha* [εἴωθα], "I am in the habit of" (Sanskrit *svada-*, "character, penchant, habit"; cf. Latin *suesco*, with probably the same root *swedh-* as *ethnos*, a "people"): *ethos* [ἔθος] and *êthos* [ἦθος]. Both have the same original meaning, "custom," but they evolved in different ways.

Ethos came to mean "habit, custom, usage" and refers, for example, to "the custom of the city [*ethos tês poleôs* (ἔθος τῆς πόλεως)]" (Thucydides 2.64); *ethei* [ἔθει] is thus opposed to *phusei* [φύσει], "by nature" (so Aristotle, in the *Nicomachean Ethics* 10.9, 1179b20ff., contrasts the doctrines of those who think we are good "by nature, by habit, by teaching," cf. 1154a33).

Êthos, with an eta [η], refers first in the plural to the places where animals and men habitually stay ("The familiar places and the horses' pasture [ἤθεα καὶ νομόν]," *Iliad* 6.511), and in the singular, to one's habitual way of being, or disposition, or nature. The word falls within the category of what we might therefore call "psychology" (one is, for example, "sweet-natured [*praios to êthos* (πϱᾷος τὸ ἦθος)]," Plato, *Phaedrus* 243c3–4; or, like Pandora, "of a deceptive character [*epiklopon êthos* (ἐπίκλοπον ἦθος)]," Hesiod, *Works and Days* 67, 78).

■ See Box 1.

In Aristotle, *êthos* becomes part of the terminological language of poetics: the "characters" (*êthê*), which allow us to describe the characters in action, are one of the six elements of tragedy, along with the story, *muthos* [μῦθος]; expression, *lexis* [λέξις]; thought, *dianoia* [διάνοια]; spectacle, *opsis* [ὄψις]; and song, *melopoia* [μελοποΐα] (*Poetics* 6.1450a5–10). It is above all part of the terminology of rhetoric: the "character" (*ethos*) of the orator, along with the passion (*pathos* [πάθος]) of the listener and the *logos* [λόγος] itself in its persuasiveness, constitute the three "technical proofs," that is, those which depend on art itself, unlike those, like testimonial accounts, which have an external origin (*Rhetoric* 1.2, 1356a): the good orator indeed not only should study characters (*theôrêsai ta êthê* [θεωϱῆσαι τὰ ἤθη], 1356a22) as part of his training, as Plato's *Phaedrus* had already suggested, so as to adapt his speech to his audience, but also should himself display a character that has been appropriately adapted, and that corresponds to the particular character of the political regime in which he is speaking ("We should ourselves possess the character particular to each constitution [*ta êthê tôn politeiôn hekastês* (τὰ ἤθη τῶν πολιτειῶν ἑκάστης)]," *Rhetoric* 1366a12), so as to inspire confidence (*pistis* [πίστις]) and to induce persuasion (*pistis*, again). This explains, then, the connection between rhetoric and "ethics" (proofs—still *pistis*—come, says Aristotle, "by means of speech that is not only demonstrative, but 'ethical' [*di' êthikou* (δι' ἠθικοῦ)]," *Rhetoric* 1366a9ff.), as well as the fact that political science, which determines what constitutes the properly human good, can be an architectonic for both rhetoric and ethics (*Nicomachean Ethics* 1.1, 1094a26–b7).

Where Aristotle is particularly innovative, however, as the title of his *Ethics* (*en tois Êthikois* [ἐν τοῖς Ἠθικοῖς], *Politics* 4.1295a36ff.) by itself indicates, is in using the adjective *êthikon* [ἠθικόν] to mark out an entirely separate area of philosophy. This partition, which has become an accepted part of philosophy programs, was institutionalized in the Stoic description of the parts of philosophy (see Diogenes Laertius, *Proemium* 18). As a way of defining it, Aristotle chose to reinterpret the two terms, and to make *êthos* (character) a consequence of *ethos* (habit):

> Ethical virtue [*hê êthikê* (ἡ ἠθικὴ), sc. *aretê* (ἀϱετὴ), literally, excellence of character] for its part [that is, as distinct from *aretê dianoêtikê*, excellence of thought, intellectual virtue] arises as an effect of habit [*periginetai* (πεϱιγίνεται): is born or comes "around and following from"], which is how its name is formed, as a slight variation of *ethos*. It is plain from this that none of our ethical virtues arises [*egginetai* (ἐγγίνεται): is born or comes "within"] within us by nature.

> (*Nicomachean Ethics* 2.1, 1103a17–19; cf. *Eudemian Ethics* 1220a39–b3)

The stakes here are very high: for Aristotle, it is question of determining as accurately as possible the place of nature in ethics: "Neither by nature, then, nor contrary to nature do virtues arise in us; rather we are adapted by nature to receive them, and are made perfect by habit" (*Nicomachean Ethics* 2.1, 1103a23–26). The interplay between *êthos* and *ethos* anchors virtue in practice, both through the political habits that are contracted because of a good constitution, and through individual exercise of virtue; in other words, virtue is a *technê* [τέχνη], a "know-how":

> The virtues we get by first exercising them, as also happens in the case of the other arts [*technai*]. For the things we have to learn before we can do them, we learn

---

1

Heraclitus, *êthos anthrôpôi daimôn* [ἦθος ἀνθρώπῳ δαίμων]

➤ DAIMÔN, DESTINY

The wide range of interpretations proposed for fragment B119 of Heraclitus, *êthos antrôpôi daimôn* (variously rendered in English as "The character of man in his guardian spirit" [W. S. Graham], "Character for man is destiny" [Kathleen Freeman], "A man's character is his fate" [Jonathan Barnes]), allows us to understand how strange *êthos* can seem to us, and *daimôn* [δαίμων] no less so. It is generally understood that man's fate is engraved in his personality (*sein Eigenart*, as Diels-Kranz translates it in German), whether this is seen as reflecting his destiny (Antigone is born Antigone), or indicating his responsibility (the only fate we have is the one we

make for ourselves). Jean Bollack, basing his analysis on the twin terms *ethos-êthos*, "habit"-"character," notes that these two interpretations rely on an anachronistic representation of "character," of the kind one would find in the thirteenth century, whereas the Greek does not make "character" something virtual that can be dissociated from a way of being (and he ultimately draws a different conclusion from this, *Héraclite*, 382ff.). Martin Heidegger, in his *Letter on Humanism* (trans. Capuzzi, 256), places so much emphasis on the common etymon that he proposes to read it as:

> Man dwells in the nearness of god.

BIBLIOGRAPHY

Bollack, Jean, and Heinz Wismann. *Héraclite ou la séparation*. Paris: Minuit, 1972.

Darcus, S.M.L. "*Daimon* as a Force in Shaping *Ethos* in Heraclitus." *Phoenix* 28 (1974): 390–407.

Heidegger, Martin. "Brief über den Humanismus." In *Wegmarken*, edited by Friedrich-Wilhelm von Herrmann, *Gesamtausgabe*, 9:313–64. Frankfurt: Klostermann, 1976. Translation by Frank Capuzzi and J. Glenn Gray: "Letter on Humanism." In *Basic Writings*, edited by David Farrell Krell, 2nd rev. and expanded ed., 217–65. San Francisco, CA: HarperSanFrancisco, 1993.

by doing them, for example, men become builders by building and lyre-players by playing the lyre.

(Ibid., 1103a31–34)

This text is often compared to the one in Plato's *Laws*: his Athenian, in making his program of education, already joins together *êthos* and *ethos*, character and habit, but in stipulating that it is during infancy, and even in the mother's womb, that "more than at any other time the character is engrained by habit [*emphuetai . . . to pan êthos dia ethos* (ἐμφύεται . . . τὸ πᾶν ἦθος διὰ ἔθος)]" (*Laws* 7.792e; cf., for example, *Nicomachean Ethics*, trans. Tricot, 87 n. 3). This overlooks the fact that what is at stake is deliberately reversed: where Plato comforts the naturalist by arguing that habit is innate, Aristotle neutralizes what is given to us naturally by arguing for a responsible practice.

Most of the difficulties and even confusions between customs and morals, between morals and ethics, stem from this initial chiasmus, which anchors ethics in habit more than in character, in culture and practice more than in nature. The proof of this is that most philosophers who have attempted to define the terms in their own languages, like Cicero or G.W.F. Hegel, have tried to find a set of problematics equivalent to the Greek, thus placing the task of translation at the heart of their reflection.

II. *Mores*

If the reflection on "ethics" in the Greek language is focused on the close link between *êthos* and *ethos*, in Latin the problem of the basis of "morals" is exacerbated by the fact that the same term refers in the singular (*mos*) to habit, and in the plural (*mores*) to character. These two domains are all the more closely interrelated because Latin authors would themselves continually question the relationship between *mores* and *mos*. So it would be helpful to begin by clarifying the different meanings of the term, both in the singular and in the plural, and to underline how culturally specific the linguistic usage is in our theoretical reflection.

Mos (in the singular) refers in its most widely accepted sense to one's usual manner, to habit insofar as it characterizes the agent of the action, whether this agent is singular (thus Chrysippus proceeds, in one work, "in his usual manner," *more suo*: Cicero, *De republica* 3.12), plural (thus Numa respected "the old way in which Greek kings did things [*mos vetus Graeciae regum*]" in legal matters: Cicero, *De republica* 5.3), or even an anonymous collectivity (thus Cicero's grandfather's house was small, "in the ancient manner [*antiquo more*]," *Laws* 2.3). The latter two examples cited themselves suggest the slippage in meaning from a characteristic habit to that particular form of habit that "tradition" represents, a meaning frequently conveyed when the term is in the singular, but also in the plural. An example of this would be *mos*, which tolerates the sort of deception that is proscribed by the law of nature, according to Cicero (*De officiis* 3.69); likewise, what Cicero in *Laws* (2.23) calls "our traditions," *nostri mores*, constitutes, along with Numa's laws, the frame of reference when he elaborates his code of law in religious matters. "Ancestral tradition" thus constitutes the *mos* par excellence, and the most complete manifestation of habit elevated to a system of reference.

The term as it applies to the characterization of an individual denotes first in the plural all of the habits that define a behavior, what we call someone's "character," insofar as it is what this individual's "morals" are based on. So Latin does not separate exteriority—behavior as objective action—from interiority—the set of dispositions that constitute the motivation for the behavior. This is not to say, however, that Latin authors were unaware of any such distinction. When it is needed, this clarification is generally made by connecting the term *mores* to other terms that circumscribe the extension of the concept. We might highlight two types of such paired expressions: either *mores* are considered in terms of the exteriority of the action, and are then associated with terms like *vita* (life, way of life; cf. Cicero, *De republica* 1.10, 16; 2.21), *instituta* (the principles of life; cf. Cicero, *De officiis* 1.120), or *consuetudo* (habit; cf. Cicero, *De republica* 3.17); or "character" is prioritized in the way one understands *mores*, and in this case the associated terms are *ingenium*, *indolis*, and *natura*, three terms denoting temperament as a natural disposition (cf. Cicero, *De officiis* 1.107ff., 3.16; Seneca, *De ira* 1.6.1, 2.15.1). So the Latin reflection on *mores* constantly brings into play two realms: on the one hand, the realm of habit perceived in terms of its formality, or almost its arbitrariness; on the other, a naturalistic realm prior to any formalization, compared by Seneca (*De ira* 2.15.1–2) to a land out of which the moral dispositions of a human being emerge.

In a philosophical context, such a dual approach tends to overlap with the classical Greek dichotomy of law and nature (*nomos/phusis*). Two examples of analysis we come across in Cicero will show how the reflection on *mores* might be structured around these poles. In book 3 of *De republica*, the character Philus returns to an argument first made by the neoacademician Carnedes asserting that justice does not, in nature, have its foundation in a social instinct. Philus emphasizes in particular that the "morals" of men can in fact be reduced to habits (*consuetudines*) and to instituted forms of behavior (*instituta*) that are based on nothing more than the arbitrariness of a custom passing itself off as a law, as is demonstrated by the multiplication of habits and behaviors into an infinite number of forms depending on the number of different peoples, as well as their variability over time. Conversely, the character Lelius in *De amicitia* (the very same person who in *De republica* responds to Philus's speech, and who comes to the defense of justice) continually draws *mores* and *natura* closer together, with the primary aim of countering the utilitarian theory of friendship that the Epicureans propose: for Lelius, it is the accord between good natures, manifested by harmony of *mores*, that founds and sustains the feeling of affection (*caritas*) from which authentic *amicitia* develops.

The confrontation of these two texts highlights a profound ambiguity in the Latin conception of *mores*, which is divided between a descriptive approach toward the "morals" noted, and a prescriptive approach aimed at sanctioning "good morals." The linguistic usage can help us to understand how this division works: one tendency is toward using such terms as *consuetudo*, *usus* (usage), and *instituta*, whenever it is a matter of seeing *mores* in terms of their objectivity and their potential variability, whereas the term *mores* itself is more often than not used on its own whenever it is a matter of defining a moral norm, or of seeing how one measures up to the proposed norm. Because of this tendency, the polemical use of the term *mores* in Philus's speech is intended precisely to disqualify the idea that these "morals" are anything more than *instituta*. Looking at it from the opposite perspective, the term *mores* is almost always used from a moral point of view to stigmatize any transgression of an ethical rule: the *mores* that are thereby denounced are thus not perceived in neutral terms, from a descriptive point of view, but as the opposite or negative of what "good morals" should be. The use of the term thus illustrates the imperative of the norm in the very statement of its negation, as in the speech on the tyrant, presented as a figure who is antithetical to all human and civic values—for example, in book 2 of Cicero's *De republica*, or again in Seneca's *De clementia*.

Mores thus pose a problem for the principle of "morals," which results on the one hand from a confusion of the perspectives of (external) morals and (internal) character, and on the other from the description of what is given, and the prescription of a norm. This confusion can be explained in large part by an ancient conception of the person, the complete philosophical expression of which we find in Cicero (*De officiis* 1.107–21). This exposition is substantially indebted to the Stoic philosopher Panaetius, but, beyond the particularities of doctrine, reflects an approach to the person that is characteristic of the dominant aristocratic milieux in the Greco-Roman world (see Gill, "Personhood and Personality," 169–99). The person is thus defined as a synthesis of two pairs of "roles" (the term *persona* refers to a mask, and later by extension to a theatrical role: it translates *prosôpon* [πρόσωπον] in Greek): the first pair comprises the "common" *persona* of a rational being and the "singular" *persona* made up of our individual temperament and sensibility; the second pair joins the *persona* that is imposed on us by fate or birth and the circumstances of our life, with the *persona* given by the deliberate choice of a career. This schema therefore combines on the one hand, without explicitly analyzing their potential conflict, the objective determinations of a given character and the rational imperatives that prescribe a universal morality, and on the other hand, the internal motives related to the *natura* of each person, and the external behaviors conditioned by institutions and social functions (see PERSON).

The relationship to *mos* as "tradition" provides a key, though, to understanding the Latin conception of *mores*, as can be judged by looking at three accounts: the political philosophy of Cicero (*De republica, Laws*), the historiography of Titus Livius (books 1 to 5, from the founding of Rome by Romulus to its symbolic refounding by Camillus), and the practical morals of Seneca (*De ira, De clementia*). In all three cases, individual or collective *mores* (the *mores* of a people or of a social group) are conceived with reference to a Roman tradition that provides an evaluative norm through concrete models that embody a mind governed by virtue. *Mores*, in the plural, are thus intended both to exemplify and to consolidate a singular *mos*, a historic and cultural reality that has gradually been elaborated and unified through the accumulation of acts of behavior, and of examples of character in the course of historical time. For Roman man, there is no real place for any conflict between fact and norm, outside

and inside, singular and collective, and the purpose of the *mores* is to reproduce within the plurality of experiences the essence of a *mos* that brings together these opposites. Any conflict is precisely the sign of moral monstrosity embodied by perverse, seditious, or tyrannical figures (for example, Tarquin the Elder, Spurius Maelius, Appius Claudius the decimvir, the emperor Caligula), whose singular "character" has the effect of dissolving the cohesion of the social body by their private or political "morals," which go against the *mos*.

III. *Mœurs*, Morals, Ethics: Between Descriptions of Individual or Collective Rules of Behavior, and Prescriptions of Norms

In the French language, the division between *les mœurs* and *la morale* seems to become accentuated, and to make a hard and fast separation between the descriptive and the normative. *Les mœurs* are the rules of behavior of a people or of an individual, and a critical judgment is needed to know whether they are good or bad, accepted or prohibited, since they could equally well be both. *La morale*, on the other hand, only includes rules of good behavior. They determine and codify, more or less systematically, what is good and what is acceptable (so for this reason one does not speak of *mauvaise morale*, but of *mauvaises mœurs* [bad moral conduct]). This being the case, the difference between the terms is also part of a broader discursive division, or even a conflict, between disciplines. *Mœurs* and *morale* do not only each designate a different content (whether descriptive or prescriptive), but also are opposed to each other as two different approaches to human behavior (anthropological and sociological or theological and confessional): so the choice of the first term could imply the refusal of any theoretical or normative approach, whereas preference given to the second term could be the sign of a claim to universality.

The growing fortunes of the notion of ethics need to be understood in the context of this dilemma. This notion seems to be reserved for a normative approach toward human behavior that aims to go beyond its description, and is at the same time not based on any official dogma (particularly religious dogma), or any moral catechism. The different composite terms derived from ethics, what are known as applied ethics (bioethics, environmental ethics, professional ethics), attempt to lend a rational legitimacy to the production of criteria of decisions and rules of conduct in each particular domain.

A. *Les mœurs*: From psychological analysis to anthropological investigation and sociological study

The description of *mœurs* is presented initially as a resistance to moral prescription and prediction. However, in the transition from the language of the moralists to the essays of the Enlightenment, the object itself of this description changes, and the meaning of the term modulates.

1. The knowledge of *mœurs* still plays a part, in the *Réflexions ou sentences et maximes morales* (1765) of La Rochefoucauld, in drawing a "portrait of man's heart" (preface to the 1765 edition, in Lafond, *Moralistes du XVIIe siècle*, 232). Already with La Bruyère's *Les caractères ou les mœurs de ce siècle* (1688), however, this knowledge becomes the

object of an investigation intended to describe different human types. The more this investigation extends to include the diversity of social classes, and then of peoples, the less possible it becomes to think of this as a prescriptive project. Moral rules and principles are abandoned in favor of the freedom of the reader, who himself draws the lessons from the portrait, the investigation, or the history that are proposed to him. Whereas La Rochefoucauld, in spite of his visible retreat from any Christian moral prediction, presents his maxims as "the summary of a moral code conforming to the thinking of several Church Fathers" (in Lafond, *Moralistes du XVIIe siècle*, 232), La Bruyère emphasizes: "These are moreover not maxims that I wished to write: they are like moral laws [*comme des lois dans la morale*] and I confess that I have neither the authority nor the genius to be a legislator. . . . Those who write maxims ultimately want to be believed: I am willing to accept, on the contrary, that people say of me that sometimes I have not observed well, provided that as a result people observe better" (preface to *Les caractères*, in Lafond, *Moralistes du XVIIe siècle*, 695). So the proliferation of points of view on human behavior, and the recognition of social and geographical diversity, are not just a question of knowledge. Replacing *la morale* with *les mœurs* gives the subject back the liberty to constitute himself as a moral subject, allowing him to move freely between description and prescription. For the philosophers of the Enlightenment, this freedom will become an even more important juncture in their approach to the question of human behavior. One of the principles of the Enlightenment was to relate the constitution of a moral subject to its environment (geography); this philosophical principle thus authorized the transition from psychology to anthropology—even if this meant searching for the signs of humanity's moral unity within the diversity of morals. As Rousseau put it in *Émile*:

Cast your eyes on all the nations of the world, go through all the histories. Among so many inhuman and bizarre cults, among this prodigious diversity of morals and characters [*cette prodigieuse diversité de mœurs et de caractère*], you will find everywhere the same ideas of justice and decency, everywhere the same notions of good and bad.

(Rousseau, *Émile*, 4:597, trans. Bloom, 288)

2. This search for unity does not preclude, however, understanding morals in their historical context; in fact, quite the opposite. This leads to the second fundamental change that came about as a result of the philosophy of the Enlightenment: moral prescriptions are also derived from a philosophy of history. This is what the link between Voltaire's *Essai sur les mœurs et l'esprit des nations* (Essay on the morals and customs [or *intelligence*] of nations) and his epistemological reflections on history amply demonstrates (see, for example, the article "History" in RT: Diderot and d'Alembert, *Encyclopédie ou Dictionnaire raisonné des sciences, des arts et des métiers*).

3. This does not mean, though, that all constraint disappears. In moving from *la morale* to *les mœurs*, what is also transformed is the relationship of politics to human behavior. Examining one's moral conscience and controlling the conformity of practices to the rules that determine beliefs are replaced by a policing of morals that is not content to discipline the bodies of individuals, to organize and pacify society, but goes further and seeks to control and orient the way in which populations evolve. This policing of *mœurs* accompanies the diversification of those forms of knowledge that participate actively in the normalization of these regulated behaviors.

▪ See Box 2.

B. *La morale*: Between rational foundation, Christian apologetics, and positivist sociology

Confronted with the domination of *les mœurs*, of the forms of knowledge to which this domination gives rise, and of the controls that discipline them, the idea of *morale* can only appear as a resistance to the diversity and the shifting historicity of the rules of behavior. This resistance is likely to assume two opposing forms.

The first form of opposition is that of a rational foundation. We find a conclusive sign of this opposition in the fate that befalls each of these two terms (*mœurs* and *morale*) in Descartes's *Discourse on Method*. Whereas *mœurs* (as well as *voyages*) are eliminated because of the uncertain nature of the knowledge associated with them, *la morale* is presented as a set of necessary rules by which one should lead one's life. In principle, these rules should be obtained following a deductive process that does not draw in any way on experience, but in the absence of an immediate rational foundation, a *morale par provision* is established, a provisional *morale* whose essential characteristic is precisely that, far from being reduced to a conformity to *les mœurs*, it has to include other rules.

The second form of opposition makes *la morale* the object of an apologetic discourse. It links the defense of *la morale* to the existence of a dogma. This is why it refuses to come down on the side of either the rational foundation of *la morale*, or the acceptance of the diversity of *les mœurs*. Pascal thus makes the relativity of *les mœurs* an argument against nature as much as against reason: "The corruption of reason is shown by the existence of so many different and extravagant customs [*mœurs*]. It was necessary that truth should come, in order that man should no longer dwell within himself" (ed. Lafuma, no. 600, p. 584, trans. Trotter). There is in consequence no legitimate *morale* beyond one inspired by religion: "It is right that a God so pure should only reveal Himself to those whose hearts are purified. Hence this religion is lovable to me, and I find it now sufficiently justified by so Divine a morality [*une si divine morale*]. But I find more in it" (ibid., no. 793, p. 600, trans. Trotter). This duality is of major importance, since it means that *la morale* is always suspected of having the shadow of a Christian God cast over it.

This leads to the temptation to lend the term an unprecedented residual and positivist definition, turning *la morale* simultaneously into a set of social facts, comparable to

2

Biopolitics and the policing of *mœurs*

Replacing moral prescription with the description of *mœurs* is a prominent feature in the emergence of what Michel Foucault called a "society of normalization." The biopolitics that organizes this society by controlling hygiene, health, the family, and sexuality is made possible by the fact that it is based less on a system of preestablished rules and moral precepts, or on theological dogma, than on a series of forms of knowledge and of controls that not only regulate the lives of individuals, but also conflate themselves in a global subject: the population. The notion of *mœurs*—which becomes the object of an actual science (cf. Lévy-Bruhl, *La morale et la science des mœurs* [Ethics and moral science], 1903)—thus ensures the articulation between the

disciplining of the body (the singular) and the normalization or regularization of this population (the collective). It is also what allows a part of this population to be designated and identified as outsiders, and to apply a politics of exclusion to them. So the description or caricature of the different moral codes of behavior (*mœurs*) of a given population is a systematic component of racist discourses.

This is all the more true in that the naturalization of *mœurs*—unlike *la morale*, which is used, on the contrary, as a criterion to distinguish man from animals—allows for a blurring of the borders between humanity and animality. As soon as one can refer to the *mœurs* of animals, and describe a population in terms of its *mœurs* as differing, or

deviating, from the norm, the comparison with such and such an animal species is easily made. Thus Voltaire writes about albinos in his *Essai sur les mœurs et l'esprit des nations*: "The only human thing about them is their stature, and their faculty of speech and of thought is far removed from our own."

BIBLIOGRAPHY

Clark, Stephen R. L. *The Political Animal: Biology, Ethics, and Politics*. London: Routledge, 1999.

Foucault, Michel. *Il faut défendre la société: Cours au Collège de France, 1975–1976*. Edited by Mauro Bertani and Alessandro Fontana. Paris: Seuil, 1997. Translation by David Macey: *Society Must Be Defended: Lectures at the Collège de France, 1975–76*. Edited by Mauro Bertani and Alessandro Fontana. New York: Picador, 2003.

---

religious facts, legal facts, and so on; the science of these facts; and the application of this science. This is what Lucien Lévy-Bruhl proposes in a key passage in *Ethics and Moral Science* (1903):

Even if we leave aside the old conception of "theoretical *morale*," the word *morale* still has three senses between which we must carefully distinguish.

1. The term *morale* is applied to conceptions, judgments, sentiments, usages as a whole, which relate to the respective laws and duties of men among themselves, recognized and generally respected at a given period and in a given civilization. It is in that sense that we speak of a Chinese *morale*, or a contemporary European *morale*. The word designates a series of social facts analogous to other series of facts of the same kind, religious, juridical, linguistic, etc.
2. The science dealing with those facts is called "ethics" [*morale*], just as the science dealing with phenomena of nature is called "physics." In that way, ethical science is opposed to natural science. But while "physical" is used exclusively to designate the science of which the object is called "nature," the word *morale* is used to designate both the science and the object of the science.
3. The applications of the science may be called "ethics" [*morale*]. By "progress of ethics" [*progrès de la morale*], a progress of the art of social practice is understood: for instance, a fuller justice realized by men in their relations with each other, more humanity in the relations between the different classes of society, or in those between nations. This third meaning is plainly separated from the two preceding, which differ equally between themselves. Hence there are inextricable confusions, and particularly the result that moral philosophy [*la philosophie morale*]

today, similar in that point to the natural philosophy of the ancients, discusses purely verbal problems, and overlooks real problems.

(Lévy-Bruhl, *Ethics and Moral Science*, trans. Lee, 81)

What this two-pronged attack (religious on the one hand, positivist on the other) renders problematic is the prospect of a rational foundation of practical norms. So it traces the path of a third term, which appears later and which, without restricting the discourse on behavior to a moral catechism or an anthropological and sociological investigation (and thus subsuming the normative within the descriptive), does not reject the rational determination of norms for conduct.

C. Ethics

The appearance of the term "ethics," at first more technical than the terms formed on *mors*, emphasizes this division between knowledge of nature (even if it is the second nature of habits) and the systematization of duties, without collapsing the second into the dogmas of religion. What is significant in this respect is the fact that "ethics" was only used initially to refer to (to translate) the philosophical works of antiquity, as opposed to moral catechisms (thus La Bruyère, for example, in the *Discours sur Théophraste*, refers to Aristotle's *Ethics*). But the growing (and recent) fortunes of the term come above all from the impossibility of using the notions of *morale* and *mœurs* to designate the imposition of practical norms in domains that one does not imagine to be governed solely by economic or technical imperatives: the environment, business, enterprise. To speak about bioethics, environmental ethics, or business ethics is thus, in theory, to take into account the need to have available determinate norms by which decisions can be taken in circumscribed domains and in precise circumstances. In theory, this normative register should be based neither on an anthropological or sociological description of the rules of behavior specific to a given domain, nor on an external catechism. The difficulty comes from the fact that such independence is never clearly demonstrable. Applied ethics cannot easily prove that they do not ratify the morals and interests of a given milieu (professional or otherwise), or that they do not introduce, in a disguised form, some (religious or political) catechism. We can thus legitimately ask whether "ethics," used so as to avoid saying *mœurs* or *morale*, does not in reality say the same thing as one or the other of the two terms. But "ethics" can also refer to the combination of the two, independent of any religious dogma: the universal and abstract dimension of a moral concern that cannot be easily defined, and the diversity of its fields of application.

▪ See Box 3.

IV. *Sitte, Sittlichkeit, Moralität*

The German language distinguishes between the descriptive (nature) and the prescriptive (law), but also between the individual and the communitarian, which are the principles from which philosophy establishes its terms. Thus Kant rigorously separates morals (*die Sitten*) from morality (*Moralität*). This disjunction consecrates and completes the one that rationalism and Enlightenment philosophy had established in the French language, and does not essentially displace its opposition, except to clarify under what absolute conditions the prescriptive is freed from the descriptive, and morality from anthropology. It is for this reason that it does not pose any major problem of translation.

The same cannot be said of the more radical attempt to rejoin what the different languages had so well taken apart, namely in Hegel's accomplished efforts to think through the conjunction of nature, history, and the law. In the *Philosophy of Right*, he sets the notion of *Sittlichkeit* in opposition to *Moralität*. *Moralität* is effectively defined first of all by its failures. The term refers less to the set of rules of conduct that an individual gives himself, and in which he realizes his freedom abstractly, than to the very interiorization of these rules, their possession by a free will. *Moralität* is thus wholly on the side of the law that the autonomous subject gives himself, and it says nothing of the effective laws of conduct shared by a community of men. In the process, *Moralität* involves two kinds of forgetting: (1) the necessarily collective or communitarian dimension of the rules of conduct (the subject of *Moralität* can only be an abstract individual); and (2) what these rules owe to shared habits whose repeated exercise becomes second nature.

The notion of *Sittlichkeit* reintroduces these two dimensions. *Sittlichkeit* of course implies morals (*die Sitten*), insofar as they come from habit and constitute a second nature, though Hegel makes it clear that, contrary to the usage the French moralists might have made of it in the seventeenth century, it cannot be a matter of rules of conduct or of individual virtues. So *Sittlichkeit* has nothing in common with the naturalization of character invoked in the discourse on *mœurs* of these moralists. But the division of *mœurs* is part of *Sittlichkeit* precisely, and only, to the extent that within it, one can realize a concrete freedom, and in that respect it brings together what until then had been separate: *Sitten* and *Moralität*.

▪ See Box 4.

It is this forced conjunction (a conceptual and semantic tour de force) that Nietzsche would attack, denouncing in the *Sittlichkeit der Sitte* the illusion that consists of attributing a new dignity to manners and customs, and of forgetting that at the source of *Sitte*, one finds in reality nothing other than the sacrifice of the individual for the benefit of the collective whole, and a calculation: the preference for a durable advantage over an ephemeral advantage. So Nietzsche writes in §9 of *The Dawn of Day*, entitled, precisely, *Begriff der Sittlichkeit der Sitte* (Conception of the morality of customs): "Morality is nothing else (and, above all, nothing more) than obedience to customs, of whatsoever nature they

---

3

La valse des éthiques (The dance of ethics)

La valse des éthiques is the title Alain Etchegoyen chose for a work in which he analyzed and lamented the contemporary excess of applied ethics: business ethics, whose aim is to propose to employees a system of values that can help boost performance; and bioethics, and its various offshoots. His book is symptomatic of an interplay between ethics and morals, and in effect expresses a nostalgia for a prescriptive and universal morality, Kantian in nature (*die Moralität*), that motivates his critique of these different local ethics:

> *La morale* [morality] is a categorical imperative: ethics is a hypothetical imperative. This distinction is a telling one.

Either the action is determined by an unconditional imperative that is imposed categorically: conscience in this case acts out of duty. This should be considered *morale*. Or the action is determined by a hypothesis that imposes a behavior on it, which we might also term an imperative of prudence. In this instance we are dealing with ethics.

(*La valse des éthiques*, 78)

What "ethics" designates, then, according to Etchegoyen, is a vague moral concern that has trouble masking a whole series of compromises with the interests of the moment. We might wonder, then, how far the criticism he levels at ethics reproduces, almost as a caricature, the opposition between *Moralität* and *Sittlichkeit*—especially given, as Jean-Pierre Lefebvre writes in the glossary accompanying his French translation of Hegel's *Phenomenology of the Mind*, that "this term [ethics] is currently undergoing an evolution in French that collapses the traditional meaning of ethics and that of *Sittlichkeit*."

BIBLIOGRAPHY

Etchegoyen, Alain. *La valse des éthiques*. Paris: Bourin, 1991.
Hegel, Georg Wilhelm Friedrich. *Phénoménologie de l'esprit*. Translated by Jean-Pierre Lefebvre. Paris: Aubier, 1991.

4

Sittlichkeit, das Sittliche: Translating Hegel

It should come as no surprise that the translation into French of *Sittlichkeit* has proved problematic for all who have attempted it, nor that translators have found so many words to convey its absolute singularity. Thus Derathé translates *Sittlichkeit* as *vie éthique* (ethical life: Hegel, *Principes de la philosophie du droit*). Labarrière and Jarczyck (in *Le syllogisme du pouvoir*), like Kervergan (in his translation of *Principes de la philosophie du droit*), use the neologism *éthicité* (ethicity). Fleischmann speaks (in *La philosophie politique de Hegel*) about *morale réalisée* (realized morality). Symptomatically, Lefebvre (translator of *Phénoménologie de l'esprit*) constructs an entire circumlocution to account for the untranslatability of the term, "*souci des bonnes mœurs et de la coutume* [concern for good morals and for customs]," while he translates the adjective *sittlich* as *éthique* (ethical).

This awkwardness in translation immediately brings to mind the chiasmus between ethics and morals described earlier. The choice of *éthicité* or of *vie éthique* is intended to make us hear the *ethos* (habit) in *Sittlichkeit* that morality, in the Kantian sense of the term, had bracketed off. In the translation of §151 of the *Philosophy of Right*, which explains the meaning not of *Sittlichkeit*, but of the ethical element (*das Sittliche*), with reference to the sharing of these same *Sitten* (manners and customs), the French translators Pierre Jean Labarrière and Gwendoline Jarczyck put *Sitte* in quotation marks, and refer it to the Greek *ethos*. The ethical element of the habit then becomes "*une seconde nature qui est posée à la place de la volonté première simplement naturelle et est l'âme, la signification et l'effectivité pénétrant son être-là, l'esprit vivant et présent là—comme un monde dont la substance n'est qu'ainsi comme esprit*" (a second nature that is put in place of first, simply natural will, and is the soul, the meaning, and the effectiveness penetrating its being-there, the spirit that is living and present there—like a world whose substance is only as it is insofar as its spirit: Hegel, *Principes de la philosophie du droit*). With this second nature, we are well and truly in an Aristotelian register, but with the important difference that the conformity to customs, to manners, to *Sitten*, is also an entirely conscious act of freedom: it is in terms of this free consciousness that the term *Sittlichkeit* should be understood.

The choice of *vie éthique* or *éthicité* to translate *Sittlichkeit* is thus understandable, even if it is not certain whether these terms are indeed the most appropriate to make us hear the Greek *ethos*, or whether the Aristotelian meaning is not lost in the adventures and misuses of the term *éthique*. One would have to pass over and above French and Latin in order to grasp, within the French language, the Greek origin of the term. One would also have to forget about the original confusion between *ethos* and *êthos* initiated by Aristotle. It is true that Hegel himself plays around with Aristotle's categories and gets lost in them, when he translates, in the notes in the margin of his copy of *Philosophy of Right*—another sign of a complex legacy and of an impossible translation—*êthos* as *Sitte* (*mœurs*), and *ethos* as *Gewohnheit* (habit).

BIBLIOGRAPHY

Fleischmann, Eugène. *La philosophie politique de Hegel*. Paris: Plon, 1964.
Hegel, Friedrich. *Phénoménologie de l'esprit*. Translated by J. P. Lefèvre. Paris: Aubier, 1991.
———. *Principes de la philosophie du droit*. Translated by R. Derathé. Paris: Vrin, 1982.
———. *Principes de la philosophie du droit*. Translated by J. F. Kervergan. Paris: Presses Universitaires de France, 1998.
Labarrière, Pierre Jean, and Gwendoline Jarczyck. *Le syllogisme du pouvoir*. Paris: Aubier, 1989.

may be. But customs are simply the traditional way of acting, and valuing. Where there is no tradition there is no morality; and the less life is governed by tradition, the narrower the circle of morality. The free man is immoral, because it is his will to depend upon himself and not upon tradition" (*Dawn of Day*, trans. Kennedy, 14). It is more than likely that Nietzsche's text is very closely working away at the Hegelian construction, and he in fact rejects precisely what, for the author of the *Philosophy of Right*, was the specificity of *Sittlichkeit*, namely freedom.

V. *Ethik*

The notion of *Sittlichkeit* does not allow us, however, to account for the conflicts that can appear in the formation of habits and character (in the sense of *ethos*), between theological principles or prescriptions concerning action, and practical social or professional imperatives. Thus the need, for Max Weber, for another term: *Ethik*, which he uses throughout his work to account for the precepts that result from this conflict and that determine this particular *ethos*, and which he uses as well in the title of his book, *Die protestantische Ethik und der "Geist" des Kapitalismus* (*The Protestant Ethic and the "Spirit" of Capitalism*). In this work, the notions of "ethics" and *ethos* are clearly articulated in relation to one another. "Ethics" is the set of prescriptive rules that, precisely, lend to the conduct of Protestant capitalists the character of an *ethos*. This articulation enables Weber to analyze in these terms the idea that it is everyone's duty to increase their capital:

> Truly what is here preached is not simply a means of making one's way in the world, but a particular ethic. The infraction of its rules is treated not as foolishness but as forgetfulness of duty. That is the essence of the matter. It is not mere business astuteness, that thing is common enough, it is an ethos. *This* is the quality which interests us.

> (Weber, *The Protestant Ethic and the "Spirit" of Capitalism*, trans. Parsons, 51)

So what Max Weber understands by Protestant ethics cannot be reduced to a deduction of pure reason, in the sense of *Moralität*, nor to the rationality of the State, in the sense of *Sittlichkeit*. Taken in these terms, *Ethik* only exists as the systematic reconstruction of an ideal type. It is in this sense that there can be a capitalist ethics, a politico-social ethics, or a "rational ethics of the profession" (see BERUF). It is in this sense, too, that we can refer to a bourgeois *ethos*, or an "*ethos* of the rational bourgeois enterprise."

To speak of *Ethik* is nevertheless ipso facto, and more generally, to go beyond the descriptive stage and to adopt a purely reflective, even systematic point of view. This is particularly true of Cohen's *Ethik des reinen Willens* (Ethics of pure will), in which *Ethik* designates the systematization of *Sittlichkeit*.

■ See Box 5.

Barbara Cassin
Marc Crépon
François Prost

5

Cohen's *Ethics of Pure Will*

In his *Ethik der reinen Willens* (Ethics of pure will, 1904), Hermann Cohen explicitly critiques Kant's division between morality (*Moralität*) and legality (*Gesetzlichkeit*): on the one hand, Kant makes law the center of gravity of ethics, but on the other, he makes a distinction between morality and legality. Kant also separated the philosophy of right from ethics:

> Mann könnte denken wenn die Legalität des Gesetzes so gleichbedeutend wird mit dem Zwange des Rechtes, dass dadurch der Sinn des Gesetzes für die Ethik ausser Zweifel gestellt würde; dass es als das schlechthin allgemeine Gesetz von der Maxime als dem subjektiven Bestimmungsgrunde, unterschieden werde. Indessen wenn sonach das Sittengesetz als das Gesetz der Gemeinschaft und der Menschheit, aller Isoliertheit des Individuums engegentritt, worin unterscheidet es sich alsdann von dem Gesetze des Rechts, bei welchem es sich doch auch um Jedermann handelt? Es entsteht bei dieser Unterscheidung zwischen Recht und Sittlichkeit der schwere Zweifel, dass die reine Sittlichkeit vielmehr leer sei; und dass sie, von der Lehrart abgesehen, in der Hauptsache doch nichts Anderes als die Religion besage und bedeute.

> We might think that, if the legality of the law becomes synonymous with the constraint exerted by right, the meaning of the law for ethics would thus be guaranteed.... However, if the moral law [*Sittengesetz*], as a law of the community and of humanity, is opposed to any particularity of the individual, how would it be distinct from the law of right, whose competence extends to each and every one of us? Establishing a difference in this way between right and morality [*Sittlichkeit*] sows a seed of serious doubt: pure morality would then seem to be empty and, in essence ..., it would be and would mean nothing other than religion.

> (Cohen, *Ethik der reinen Willens*, 254)

The only other passage in which Cohen uses the *Fremdwort* (foreign word) *Moralität* emphasizes the fact that he does not consider legality in opposition to morality, but that morality has to be "recognized as being an immanent force of legality," and that if this link were removed, ethics would remain deprived of what would be, by analogy, the *factum* of science; the consequence of such a failure would be that ethics would fall either within the domain of psychology, or into the hands of religious exclusivity.

For Cohen, the distinction is thus between ethics and morality (*Sittlichkeit*), without it being a matter of a fundamental conceptual opposition; rather, it is first and foremost a problem of the logic of the system. Within the system, precedence is given to reason (*Vernunft*), and thus to logic, since it alone is able to determine the purity needed to clear the principles of thought of all representation, and consequently of ensuring that thought is truly autonomous when dealing with intuition and the data it carries. At the highest level of the system, one could establish an equivalence between reason and rational interest; understanding, which attempts to draw out the rational principles of the natural sciences (the lower level being the experience of nature), corresponds to reason, and ethics, from which right (the analogon of mathematics) and the law (the analogon of experience) are derived, corresponds to the interest of reason. In addition, ethics is the logic of the sciences of the mind (or the moral sciences), since the problems that come under its competence are the individual, totality, the will, and action.

This is why Cohen is also opposed to Hegel: because his logic would also encompass ethics. Whereas Hegel does consider as distinct the idea of *Sollen* (should be), he establishes an equivalence between the concept and the being. So, for him, the idea would be the development of the concept, and would remain a prisoner of being, which would also then encompass that which should be. Cohen opposes to this form of pantheism an equivalence between ideas (ideas are the prescriptions of the practical use of reason) and what should be.

Ethics is the science of pure will: the fact that the term comes from the Greek *ethos* [ἔθος] simply means that this science has not broken free from one of its problems, that of customs and manners (*Sitten*). But these customs are not the content of morality (that is, *Sittlichkeit*, as the content of the will, in the same way that nature is the content of thought), and were this not the case, this morality would seem to have as its basis the nature of the subject—something that Cohen rejects. Morality, rather, has right and justice as its objectives. From the point of view of its relationship with religion, ethics requires that religion be demythologized, since it is simply the historical form through which ethics has gradually found its way into general culture. The level of customs (*mœurs*) thus remains that of particularity and plurality, that is, the level of society; whereas the level of totality—that of the State (that which enables morality to be realized), and, further down the line, that of the confederation of States—is only affected by morality under a particular aspect. This aspect is morality, inasmuch as it is assimilated into an ethics whose ultimate horizon, the level of the unity of humanity, that is, the ideal, can only be thought from the perspective of the "pure" interpretation that ethics gives of Hebraic messianism. Cohen indeed refuses to grant religion any autonomy, as he does thought, will, and feeling (the feeling of the aesthetic): at most, religion has a "specificity" within the system (Marc de Launay).

BIBLIOGRAPHY

Cohen, Hermann. *Ethik der reinen Willens*. Berlin: Bruno Cassirer, 1904.

BIBLIOGRAPHY

Aristotle. *Organon*. Translated by J. Tricot. 6 vols. Paris: Vrin, 1970.

Bobzien, Susanne. *Determinism and Freedom in Stoic Philosophy*. Oxford: Clarendon, 1998.

Cohen, Hermann. *Ethik des reinen Willens*. Introduction by Steven S. Schwarzschild. 5th ed. In *Werke*, vol. 7. Hildesheim, Ger.: Olms, 1981.

Ferrary, Jean-Louis. "Le discours de Philus (Cicéron, *De republica* III, 8–31) et la philosophie de Carnéade." *Revue des Études Latines* 55 (1977): 128–56.

Gill, Christopher. "Personhood and Personality: The Four-Personae Theory in Cicero, *De officiis I*." *Oxford Studies in Ancient Philosophy* 6 (1988): 169–99.

Griffin, Miriam T. *Seneca: Philosopher in Politics*. New ed. Oxford: Oxford University Press, 1992.

Griffin, Miriam T., and Jonathan Barnes, eds. *Philosophia Togata: Essays on Philosophy and Roman Society*. Oxford: Clarendon, 1989.

———. *Philosophia Togata II: Plato and Aristotle at Rome*. Oxford: Clarendon, 1997.

Hahm, David E. "Plato, Carneades, and Cicero's Philus (Cicero, *Rep.* 3.8–31)." *Classical Quarterly*, n.s. 49 (1999): 167–83.

Hegel, Georg Wilhelm Friedrich. *Grundlinien der Philosophie des Rechts*. Edited by Klaus Grotsch and Elisabeth Weisser-Lohmann. In *Gesammelte Werke*, vol. 14. Hamburg: Felix Meiner, 2011. Translation by T. M. Knox: *Outlines of the Philosophy of Right*. Edited with introduction by Stephen Houlgate. Oxford: Oxford University Press, 2008.

Irwin, Terence. *The Development of Ethics: A Historical and Critical Study*. 2 vols. Oxford: Oxford University Press, 2007.

Kant, Immanuel. *Die Metaphysik der Sitten*. Originally published 1797. Edited by Königlich Preussischen Akademie der Wissenschaften. In *Kants Gesammelte Schriften*, vol. 6. Berlin: De Gruyter, 1907. Translation by Mary Gregor: *The Metaphysics of Morals*. Edited by Mary Gregor. Introduction by Roger J. Sullivan. Cambridge: Cambridge University Press, 1996.

Laks, André, and Malcolm Schofield, ed. *Justice and Generosity: Studies in Hellenistic Social and Political Philosophy*. Proceedings of the Sixth Symposium Hellenisticum. Cambridge: Cambridge University Press, 1995.

Levi, Anthony. *French Moralists: The Theory of the Passions, 1585 to 1649*. Fair Lawn, NJ: Oxford University Press, 1965.

Lévy, Carlos. *Cicero Academicus: Recherches sur les Académiques et sur la philosophie Cicéronienne*. Rome: École française de Rome, 1992.

Lévy-Bruhl, Lucien. *La morale et la science des mœurs*. Paris: Alcan, 1903. Translation by Elizabeth Lee: *Ethics and Moral Science*. London: Constable, 1905.

Lafond, Jean, ed. *Moralistes du XVIIe siècle: De Pibrac à Dufresny*. Paris: Laffont, 1992.

Moriarty, Michael. *Fallen Nature, Fallen Selves: Early Modern French Thought II*. Oxford: Oxford University Press, 2006.

Nietzsche, Friedrich. *The Dawn of Day*. Translated by J. M. Kennedy. London: George Allen and Unwin, 1924.

———. *Morgenröthe*. Edited by Giorgio Colli and Mazzino Montinari. In *Kritische Gesamtausgabe*, part 5, vol. 1. Berlin: De Gruyter, 1971. Translation by R. J. Hollingdale: *Daybreak: Thoughts on the Prejudices of Morality*. Edited by Maudemarie Clark and Brian Leiter. Cambridge: Cambridge University Press, 1997.

Pascal, Blaise. "Pensées." In *Œuvres complètes*, edited by Louis Lafuma. Paris: Seuil-L'Intégrale, 1963. Translation by W. F. Trotter: *Pensées*. Mineola, NY: Dover, 2003. Originally published in 1958. Translation by Roger Ariew: *Pensées*. Indianapolis, IN: Hackett, 2005.

Powell, J.G.F., ed. *Cicero the Philosopher: Twelve Papers*. Oxford: Oxford University Press, 1995.

Rousseau, Jean-Jacques. *Émile*. In *Œuvres complètes*, vol. 4. Paris: Gallimard-Pléiade, 1969. Translation by Allan Bloom: *Emile: or, On Education*. Introduction and notes by Allan Bloom. Harmondsworth, Eng.: Penguin, 1991.

Rueff, Martin. "Morale et mœurs." In *Dictionnaire européen des Lumières*, edited by Michel Delon. Paris: Presses Universitaires de France, 1997. Translation by Gwen Wells: *Encyclopedia of the Enlightenment*. Edited by Michel Delon and Philip Stewart. Chicago, IL: Fitzroy Dearborn, 2001.

Striker, Gisela. *Essays on Hellenistic Epistemology and Ethics*. Cambridge: Cambridge University Press, 1996.

Voelke, André-Jean. *L'idée de volonté dans le stoïcisme*. Paris: Presses Universitaires de France, 1973.

Voltaire. *Essai sur les mœurs et l'esprit des nations*. Edited by René Pomeau. 2 vols. Paris: Garnier, 1963. Translation by Anonymous: *The General History and State of Europe*. 3 vols. London, 1754–57.

Weber, Max. *Die protestantische Ethik*. Edited by Johannes Winckelmann. 6th ed. 2 vols. Gütersloh, Ger.: Mohn, 1981–82. Translation by Talcott Parsons: *The Protestant Ethic and the Spirit of Capitalism*. Reprint. New York: Dover, 2003. Translation by Stephen Kalberg: *The Protestant Ethic and the Spirit of Capitalism*. Introduction by Stephen Kalberg. 3rd ed. Los Angeles, CA: Roxbury, 2002.

| MOTIONLESS

"Motionless" is, along with "silent," one of the possible translations of the German *still*, a topos of classical aesthetics: see STILL, and AESTHETICS, CLASSIC, SUBLIME. Cf. *SERENITY, WISDOM*.

See also, on movement in general and on the immobility of Aristotle's Prime Mover, ABSTRACTION, II, *ACT, DYNAMIC, FORCE*, Box 1, MOMENT, STRENGTH.

➤ GOD, *NEGATION, NOTHING*

NAROD [народ] (RUSSIAN)

ENGLISH	people
FRENCH	*peuple*
ITALIAN	*popolo*
LATIN	*gens*

➤ PEOPLE, and *CULTURE*, *GENRE*, MIR, PRAVDA, RUSSIAN, SOBORNOST', SVOBODA

The Russian noun *narod* [народ] is derived from *rod* [род], "family line, species, genus." *Narod*, exactly like "people," signifies both the population of a country and "the lower classes, the common people." For Slavophiles, *narod* has the elevated sense of the "spiritual unity" of the nation, and a large part of the Russian intelligentsia idealizes it as a natural and organic element, the "authentic life" of the people. Although it was a cliché in both czarist Russia and the Soviet Union, *narod* took on a less ideological meaning in the work of Bakhtin, who related it to the notion of *narodnaja kul'tura* [народная культура], popular culture.

I. *Narod* and *Gens*

The root *rod* [род], which in Slavic languages has supplanted the Indo-European radical *gen*, essentially signifies "birth." In modern Russian the term has the different senses of "clan, tribe, parents"; "family, line, generation"; "species, genus" (or "gender" in the grammatical sense) (RT: *Slovar' russkogo iazyka* [Dictionary of the Russian language]). All these meanings refer to entities (things or individuals) that have been created or put into the world together. In the derived term *narod* [народ] (people), the prefix *na-* still connotes more the totality of the individuals (put into the world together or unified).

In *The Russian Religious Mind*, Georgi Fedotov highlights the importance of the continuing veneration of the *rod*—a veneration that goes back to paganism and more particularly to the "cult of the dead as the ancestors of an eternal kinship community." "The Latin people and the Celtic clan," Fedotov writes, "are only pale images of social realities that were once alive. In Russian language and life, the *rod* is full of vitality and vigor." A typical linguistic manifestation of this vitality is the use of family names as polite forms of address: "The terms 'father,' 'grandfather,' 'uncle,' and 'brother,' as well as the corresponding feminine terms, are used in the language of Russian peasants to address both known and unknown individuals." In this way "all moral relationships between individuals are raised to the level of blood kinship." In Russian, family relationship is rendered by *rodstvo* [родство], an abstract nominalization of *rod*.

This linguistic habit of extending kinship relations to everyone sheds a particular light on the roots of Russian communalism and explains the importance of notions like *mir* [мир] (village community), *sobornost'* [соборность] (conciliarity), *obščestvo* [общество] (community), etc.: for Slavophiles, the archaic cult of the *rod*, to which *narod* clearly refers, is one of the characteristics of Russian civilization.

II. *Natsija*, *Narod*, and *Narodnitčestvo*

Observers of nineteenth-century Russian society repeatedly emphasized that the nobles (*dvorjane* [дворяне]) and the people (*narod*) often seemed to be two separate nations: their clothes, their manners, even their language—everything was different. The Russian word *natsija* [нация] (nation), which comes from the Polish *nacja* (RT: *Ètimologičeskij slovar' russkogo jazyka* [Etymological dictionary of the Russian language], vol. 3), was created during the time of Peter the Great, whose reforms produced a sharp division within Russian society between cultivated people and the *narod*. In its contemporary acceptation *natsija* signifies "a community of people unified by a language, territory, economy, and a common mentality, developed historically" (RT: *Slovar' russkogo iazyka*, vol. 2). As for *narod*, it means "the population of a state" but also "the lower classes, the common people" (RT: *Tolkovyĭ slovar' zhivogo velikorusskogo iazyka* [Explanatory dictionary of the living language of Great Russia], vol. 2).

For Slavophiles, *narod* has an elevated sense, whereas *natsija* is neutral in value. Slavophilism is essentially an ideological reaction to the modernization of Russia and particularly to the gap between the nobles and the *narod*. Slavophiles have concentrated on the Russian way of organizing life in the village community (*mir*) and on the interpretation of the law as truth and justice (*pravda* [правда]). This way of living was contrasted with Western standards of formal law (cf. Kireevski, *Polnoe Sobranie Sočinenii* [Complete works], 1: 115–16). The patriarchal Russian village was considered the true origin of the nation's life and strength, the incarnation of traditional national virtues. Slavophiles regarded themselves as full participants in this patriarchal life and did not want to detach themselves from the *narod*, which for them expressed the spiritual unity of all Russians.

The idealization of peasants is connected with guilt feelings on the part of the intelligentsia, whose privileges depended chiefly on the maintenance of serfdom; the term itself (*intelligentsija* [интеллигенция]) appeared around 1860 in the work of Piotr Boborykin and passed from Russian into other European languages (RT: *Great Soviet Encyclopedia*, vol. 10). The idea that intellectuals have a duty to the people found its practical development in the *narodničestvo* [народничество] movement. *Narodničestvo* is usually rendered in French, very inexactly, as *populisme*, and in English by "populism." An English translator of Berdyayev explains *narodničestvo* as "the movement that in 19th-century Russia was based on the feeling of an obligatory devotion to the general interests of the common folk" (Berdyayev, *Slavery and Freedom*). A *narodnik* [народник] is someone who "believes in the *narodničestvo* and practices it" (ibid.). During the 1860s and 1870s many *narodniks* "went to the people." They took up residence in the countryside in order to devote themselves to bringing civilization to the people and improving their lives, seeking to overcome the gap between the intelligentsia and the *narod*. The ideals of *narodničestvo* inspired a few generations of passionate advocates who became physicians and schoolmasters in the villages.

Narodničestvo found expression in Russian literature of the second half of the nineteenth century, notably in the work of Tolstoy and Dostoyevsky. For Tolstoy, the simple, everyday life of the common people was endowed with a high moral and religious value: only in the common people was there true life, the life that allows the individual to arrive at salvation and "Resurrection" (*voskresenie* [воскресение]), to borrow the title of one of his well-known novels. Similarly, Dostoyevsky, exploring the nature of the "Russian character" (*russkij xarakter* [русский характер]), believed, in an almost religious way, in the Russian *narod* as the ultimate moral value.

III. Berdyayev, *Narod*, and *Ličnost'*

Berdyayev, on the contrary, adopts a personalist point of view and disapproves of the excessive cult of the *narod*, which he considers an obstacle to the development of subjectivity and individuality. *Narodničestvo*, he writes, "does not exist in the West, it is a specifically Russian phenomenon. Only in Russia can one find this perpetual opposition between the intelligentsia and the people [*narod*], this idealization of the people that becomes almost a religion, this quest for truth and God in the people" (Berdyayev, *Mirosozertsanie Dostoevskogo*). According to Berdyayev, *narodničestvo* reveals a weakness rather than a strength among the cultivated Russian elite:

> [T]he intelligentsia's tendency to seek its integrity solely in the "organic life" of the *narod* shows its lack of spiritual autonomy. Russian *kollektivizm* [коллективизм] and *sobornost'* have been considered a great advantage of the Russian people (*russkogo naroda* [русского народа]), the one that has raised it above European nations (*nad narodami Evropy* [над народами Европы]. But in reality this means that the person (*ličnost'* [личность]) and the personal spirit have not yet been awakened in the Russian people (*v russkom narode* [в русском народе]), and that the person is still too immersed in the natural element of the life of the people.

IV. *Narod*, Carnival, Laughter:
The Notion of *Narodnaja Kul'tura* in Bakhtin

It is not surprising that *narod* plays the role of a major ideological cliché. In Soviet ideology *narod* was the general term that served to designate the workers, kolkhozians (workers on collective farms), and the "working intelligentsia" (*trudovaja inteligensija* [трудовая интеллигенция]). Its abstract nominalization, *narodnost'* [народность], was inscribed in the two famous trinities of Russian cultural history: along with autocracy (*samoderžavie* [самодержавие]) and orthodoxy (*pravoslavie* [православие]), it composed the formula of official nationalism in Russia at the end of the nineteenth century, and along with ideological conviction (*partijnost'* [партийность]), it constituted the dogmatic definition of "socialist realism" as an artistic genre. The cliché "socialist realism" was created in the USSR in the 1930s to define in an official way the method of Soviet literature.

Socialist realism is "an aesthetic expression of the socialist conception of the world and of man" (RT: *Great Soviet Encyclopedia*, vol. 24/1).

In Mikhail Bakhtin we find a counterideological use of the term *narod*. Bakhtin introduces the notion of "popular culture" (*narodnaja kul'tura* [народная культура]) or "comic popular culture" (*narodnaja smexovaja kul'tura* [народная смеховая культура]). Popular culture gives people a specific view of the world that is opposed to official or serious culture. For Bakhtin the twofold, serious/comic view of the world is an intrinsic characteristic of human civilization. The paradigmatic event of popular culture is the popular festival, the carnival. Carnival is a universal event, democratic and egalitarian. During the festival "life is subject only to [carnival's] laws, that is, the laws of its own freedom [*zakony svobody* (законы свободы)]" (Bakhtin, *Rabelais and His World*). Carnival "does not acknowledge any distinction between actors and spectators," Bakhtin writes, "because its very idea embraces all the people [*on vsenaroden* (он всенароден)]" (ibid.). The adjective *vsenarodnyj* [всенародный] poses a real problem of translation: it has been rendered in French by the expression "*fait pour l'ensemble du peuple*," and also by "*qui est le bien de l'ensemble du peuple*" (*L'Œuvre de François Rabelais*). In a sense, both translations are correct; *vsenarodnyj*, formed on the basis of *narod* and the prefix *vse-* (omni-), which expresses universality, means literally "omni-popular, shared by all." We must understand this term by putting it on the same level as Solovyov's *sobornost'* (uni-totality) and *vseedinstvo* [всеединство] (omni-unity = uni-totality).

However, Bakhtin turns the Slavophile vocabulary away from its ideological aim. As an actor in the carnival, the *narod* is a natural element, no longer a "mysterious, foreign, and seductive" force, as it is in Berdyayev (*Mirosozertsanie Dostoevskogo*, 169). It is gay and joyous. It is a spontaneous element in which the individuality and subjectivity of the modern period have not yet been separated from each other. It involves neither a person opposed to society nor a difficult shaping of personality that requires a return to the *narod*, as is the case in the *narodničestvo* of the nineteenth century. The person is unified with the *narod* in an organic manner: Bakhtin speaks of the "body of the *rod* [*rodovoe telo* (родовое тело)]" in Rabelais (Bakhtin, *Tvorčestvo Fransua Rable*). The expression *rodovoe telo*, in which the adjective *rodovoe* is derived from *rod*, is in fact another untranslatable expression: the French translator renders it as "corps procréateur" (Bakhtin, *L'Œuvre de François Rabelais*) and the English translator as "ancestral body" (*Rabelais and His World*, 19, 322–24). In fact, Bakhtin writes that in Rabelais's work, Pantagruel is the image of the "people's body [*vsenarodnoe telo* (всенародное тело)]" (*Tvorčestvo Fransua Rable*, 359, *Rabelais and His World*, 341). Carnivalesque culture is a spontaneous element that undoes all seriousness, including official ideology.

> As opposed to the official feast, one might say that the carnival celebrated temporary liberation from the prevailing truth and from the established order; it marked the suspension of all hierarchical rank, privileges, norms, and prohibitions.

> (*Rabelais and His World*, 10)

Bakhtin underscores the indissoluble and essential connection between the extra-official laughter of the popular feast and freedom (*svoboda*) (*Rabelais and His World*, 71–73). Thus, under the Stalinist regime humanism took the form of an anti-autocratic *narodničestvo*:

> Growth and renewal are the dominant motifs in the figure of the people (*narod*). The people (*narod*) is the newborn child fed on milk, the newly planted tree, the convalescent and regenerated organism.

> (Ibid., chap. 6)

If we now return to the twofold meaning of "people" (see PEOPLE), both the body of citizens and the mass of the excluded, we see that it is more the second term of this opposition on which thinking about the *narod* is based. The history of the intelligentsia connects the word with the diverse strategies deployed for getting closer to or distinguishing oneself from the *narod* (insofar as it has neither the same education nor the same culture)—unless it is, as in Bakhtin, to foil the ideological instrumentalization that these strategies themselves imply.

Zulfia Karimova
Andriy Vasylchenko

BIBLIOGRAPHY

Bakhtin, Mikhail Mikhailovich. *Tvorčestvo Fransua Rable i narodnaia kul'tura srednevekov'ia i Renessansa*. 2nd ed. Moscow: Khudozh, 1990. Translation by Helene Iswolsky: *Rabelais and His World*: Cambridge, MA: MIT Press, 1968. Translation by A. Robel: *L'Œuvre de François Rabelais et la Culture populaire au Moyen Âge et sous la Renaissance*. Paris: Gallimard, 1970.

Berdyayev, Nicolai. *Mirosozertsanie Dostoevskogo* [World of Dostoyevsky]. Moscow: Zakharov, 2001. Translation by Donald Attwater: *Dostoievsky*. New York: New American Library, 1974.

——. *O rabstve i svobode čelovka*. Paris: YMCA, 1972. First published in 1939. Translation by R. M. French: *Slavery and Freedom*. New York: Scribner, 1944.

Fedotov, Georgii. *The Russian Religious Mind*. Vol. 1. Cambridge, MA: Harvard University Press, 1946.

Kireevski, Ivan. *Polnoe Sobranie Sočinenii*. Vol. 1. Moscow: University of Moscow, 1910.

Klechenov, Gennadii. "The 'Narod' and the Intelligentsia: From Dissociation to 'Sobornost'." *Russian Studies in Philosophy* 31, no. 4 (1993): 54–70.

Kovalev, Vitalii. "The 'Narod,' the Intelligentsia, and the Individual." *Russian Studies in Philosophy* 31, no. 4 (1993): 71–82.

NATURE

GERMAN	*Natur, Aufgang*
GREEK	*phusis* [φύσις]
LATIN	*natura*
RUSSIAN	*priroda* [природа], *natura* [натура]
SPANISH	*naturaleza*

➤ ART, *CULTURE*, ERSCHEINUNG, ESSENCE, ESTI, FORCE, LIGHT, MIMÊSIS, *TO BE*

The Latin translation of the Greek *phusis* [φύσις] by the Latin *natura*, from which are derived most of the words designating "nature" in European languages, can be considered an inconsequential event in Western history—or, on the contrary, a major event—with great historical import. Heidegger never ceased to problematize this translation as it had never been problematized before, though

that led him to render the Greek *phusis* as *Aufgang*, "opening up," "emergence," rather than by *Natur*, "nature." To gauge the significance of Heidegger's gesture we must, however, move beyond the pseudo-opposition between a supposedly Greek nature-growth and a supposedly Roman nature-birth. Setting himself the task of determining *phusis* as the movement of a thing's coming to be by itself (whence physics), Aristotle turns first to etymology to make this term signify in its original sense:

> "Nature" [*phusis*] means (1) the genesis [*genesis* (γένεσις)] of growing things [*tôn phuomenôn* (τῶν φυομένων)]—the meaning that would be suggested if one were to pronounce the *u* in *phusis* long.

> (*Metaphysics*, 5.4. 1014b 17–19)

Aristotle explicitly connects *phusis* with *phuô* [φύω], *phuesthai* [φύεσθαι], "to grow, raise, cause to be born, to develop," the verb coming from the Indo-European root **bhu-*, from which also come the Latin *fui*, the French *fus*, the English "[to] be," and the German *bin, bist*, in the conjugation of the verb *sein* in the present indicative, which until the fourteenth century included forms that have now disappeared, <wir> *birn*, <ihr> *birt*, replaced respectively by *sind* and *seid*, which, like the Latin *sum*, come from a different Indo-European root.

This connection of *phusis* with the idea of "growth" may nonetheless seem as insufficient as it is incontestable, for we must still ask how "growth" is understood. Heidegger proposes to move back from the idea of "grow" to the allegedly more originary idea of "flowering" (Ger. *das Aufgehen*), which can itself be traced back phenomenologically to an "appearance":

> The other Indo-European radical is *bhu, bheu*. To it belong the Greek *phuô* [φύω], to emerge [*aufgehen*], to be powerful [*walten*], of itself to come to stand and remain standing. Up until now this *bhu* has been interpreted according to the usual superficial view of *physis* [φύσις] and *phuô* [φύω] as nature and "to grow" [*wachsen*]. A more fundamental exegesis, stemming from preoccupation with the beginning of Greek philosophy, shows the "growing" to be an "emerging," which in turn is defined by presence [*Anwesen*] and appearance [*Erscheinen*]. Recently the root phy- [φυ] has been connected with pha- [φα], *phainesthai* [φαίνεσθαι]. *Physis* [φύσις] would then be that which emerges into the light [*das ins Licht Aufgehende*], *phyein* [φύειν] would mean to shine, to give light therefore to appear. (Cf. *Zeitschrift für vergl. Sprachforschung*, vol. 59.)

> (Heidegger, *Introduction to Metaphysics*, 59)

Heidegger problematizes, in an unprecedented way, the age-old translation of Greek *phusis* by Latin *natura* and its different derivatives in European languages, in contrast, for example, to Husserl, who declared at the beginning of his Vienna lecture that in Greek antiquity nature is "what the ancient Greeks considered nature [*was den alten Griechen als Natur galt*]." Nonetheless, the Slavic languages constitute a notable exception: while Russian uses *natura* [натура] in the sense of "the essence of a being," *natura rerum*, natural phenomena taken as a whole are designated instead by the term *priroda* [природа], from *rod* [род], which is close to the meaning of German *Geschlecht*: "generation, line, race, species" (see GESCHLECHT).

Breaking with a long tradition, or rather a long obstruction, Heidegger proposes, then, to reinterpret *phusis* not as "nature" (from Latin *nasci*, "to be born"), but as *Aufgang*, an "opening-up" or "emergence." But contrary to a commonly held view, Heidegger does not oppose a *natura*-"birth" to a *phusis*-"growth" that he considers more originary; rather, the line of demarcation runs between *phusis* on one hand, and *natura* as birth and growth combined on the other. While nature designates a sector of the existent (in pairs of oppositions in which the other term may be culture—nature/culture—history, art, super-nature [grace], etc.), *phusis* names instead the "how" (desinence-sis: *phu-sis*) in accord with which everything appears. It is a name for Being, not for the existent. In short: "nature" is ontically oriented, and *phusis* is ontological. Reinterpreted in its original acceptation, the term *phusis* seems to Heidegger to be "*das Grundwort des anfänglichen Denkens* (the basic word of beginning thought)" (*Heraklit*, 101).

■ See Box 1.

Rather than Homer, it is Heraclitus who constitutes the source on which Heidegger constantly drew for the meaning of *phusis*, and notably fragment 123: *phusis kruptesthai philei* [φύσις κρύπτεσθαι φιλεῖ]. This fragment has often been translated as "Nature likes to hide itself." Heidegger renders it this way: "Das Aufgehen dem Sichverbergen schenkt's die Gunst," or "Das Aufgehen schenkt die Gunst dem Sichverbergen" (*Heraklit*, 110)—"It is to withdrawal [to the movement of withdrawing] that unclosing grants its favor." Or, in Jean Beaufret's French translation of the German translating the Greek: "Rien n'est plus propre à l'éclosion que le retrait" (*Dialogue*, 1, 18). Here it is no longer a matter of "nature" but of an internal tension, an "unapparent harmony," in the Heraclitean sense, between veiling and unveiling, occultation and disocculation, or between sheltering and unsheltering. That is probably why Heidegger notes that the term *phusis* is "perhaps untranslatable" (*vielleicht unübersetzbar*), following this passage:

> We still leave untranslated the fundamental word: *phusis*. We do not say *natura* and *Nature*, because these names are too equivocal and loaded—and, in short, because they acquire their nominative force only from a very special and very slanted interpretation of *phusis*. We have in fact no word for conceiving in a single expression the mode of deployment of *phusis* as it has been clarified up to this point. (We try to say *Aufgang*—the rise of what rises by opening—but we remain powerless to give to this word, without intermediary, the plenitude and determination it needs.)
>
> (Heidegger, *Wegmarken*, 259; *Questions II*, 208–9)

■ See Box 2.

Pascal David

1

Homer, *phusis* and *pharmakon*

➤ LOGOS

The first known occurrence of *phusis* is found in Homer. The word, a hapax, is uttered by Hermes in an enigmatic passage that deals especially with the *pharmakon* [φάρμακον] and the language of the gods:

> So spoke Argeïphontes, and he gave me the medicine (*pharmakon*), which he picked out of the ground, and he explained the nature of it to me (*kai moi phusin autou edeixe* [καὶ μοι φύσιν αὐτοῦ ἔδειξε]). It was black at the root (*rhizêi* [ῥίζῃ]), but with a milky flower (*anthos* [ἄνθος]). The gods call it *moly*. It is hard for mortal men to dig up, but the gods have power to do all things.
>
> (*Odyssey*, 10. 302–306)

The word *pharmakon* (from **pharma*, which it is tempting to connect with *pherô* [φέρω], "plant that grows in the earth," RT: *Dictionnaire étymologique de la langue grecque*, s.v.) means both "remedy" and "poison" ("medicinal herb, drug, treatment, philter, potion, spell, dye, color, cleaning agent, reagent, tanner," etc.; the *pharmakos* [φαρμακός, accent on the omicron] is a scapegoat, an expiatory victim, whereas the *pharmakos* [φάρμακος, accent on the alpha] is a poisoner, a magician). This ambivalence allows the word to designate in a perfectly appropriate way the *logos* [λόγος] that causes pain or enchants, produces terror or courage (Gorgias, *Eulogy of Helen*, 82B 11 DK, §14), and also writing, as a remedy/poison for memory (Plato, *Phaedrus*, 274e; see Derrida). But in Homer, Hermes's *pharmakon* is a *pharmakon esthlon* [φάρμακον ἐσθλόν] (v. 286, 292, a "plant of life," says Bérard, "good," "courageous," like a Homeric hero), capable of saving Odysseus from Circe's *pharmakon*, which transforms men into swine—but brings Odysseus into her bed. Among the gods this good *pharmakon* is called *môlu* [μῶλυ], which sounds like a "loan-word of unknown origin," but later designates a kind of garlic (RT: *Dictionnaire étymologique de la langue grecque*). It is this *pharmakon* whose *phusis* Hermes explains to Odysseus. By translating *kai moi phusin autou edeixe* as "*il m'apprit à connaître*" ("he taught me to know"), Victor Bérard skillfully uses an elision to avoid the difficulty, whereas Homer says "and he explained the *phusin* of it to me." Wolfgang Schadewaldt, on the other hand, renders *phusis* in this passage by *Wuchs*, a word from the same family as the verb *wachsen*, "to grow," and thus goes back to the idea of growth (*Die Odyssee*, 176: "*und wies mir seinen Wuchs*"). In any case, *phusis* is, like the idea of *pharmakon* itself, contradictory or ambivalent: the root is black, the flower white. Language of the gods, language of humans, difficult to understand for mortals, but easy for the all-powerful; black but white; remedy and poison: the textual terrain of *phusis* requires careful attention.

Barbara Cassin and Pascal David

BIBLIOGRAPHY

Derrida, Jacques. "La pharmacie de Platon." In *La Dissémination*. Paris: Éditions du Seuil, 1972. Translation by Barbara Johnson: "Plato's Pharmacy." In *Dissemination*, 61–171. Chicago: University of Chicago Press, 1981.

Homer. *The Odyssey*. Translated by A. T. Murray. 2 vols. Loeb Classical Library. Cambridge, MA: Harvard University Press, 1966–1974. Translation by Victor Bérard: *L'Odyssée*, edited by Victor Bérard. Paris: Les Belles Lettres, 1974. First published in 1924. Translation by Wolfgang Schadewalt: *Die Odyssee*. Zurich: Artemis, 1966.

2

Supernatural

➤ *GRACE, SVET* (Box 1)

At the beginning of his commentary on Book II of Aristotle's *Physics* (in *Questions II*), Heidegger mentions, among the antithetical oppositions in which "nature" is one of the terms, "nature/grace," adding between parentheses: *"Über-natur"* (super-nature). Although the adjective *surnaturel* has become common parlance in French, the same is not true of the substantive *surnature*, and the least one can say is that it is hardly used outside the vocabulary of theologians, so that we are more inclined to nominalize the adjective and speak of the "supernatural," at the price of an abusive confusion, in ordinary usage, with the "paranormal." A mystery remains to be explained: why is there this strange absence? To understand it, we have to examine the history of the "supernatural." This history has been written, from the point of view of the history of dogma, by Henri de Lubac, in his classic study *Surnaturel—Études historiques*, which forms a trilogy with two other works: *Augustinisme et théologie moderne* and *Le Mystère du surnaturel*. According to *Augustinisme et théologie*

moderne (315n2), it was Scheeben who introduced the word *Übernatur* ("super-nature") in a technical sense, distinguishing it from the supernatural, but de Lubac adds: "Although this distinction does not appear to have been widely adopted, one cannot, in our view, make Scheeben entirely responsible for the currently widespread usage that incorrectly replaces *surnaturel* by *surnature*." The appearance of the term *Übernatur* seems to go back, in the German language, to Rhineland mysticism: "Suso once speaks of an *'übernatur'* (*Das Büchlein der ewigen Weisheit* [*A Little Book of Eternal Wisdom*], Part 2, chap. 24), but it does not seem that this word came into widespread use" in German (*Surnaturel*, 405). It appears to have been in the ninth century, in "the Carolingian translations of Pseudo-Dionysius by Hilduin and John Scotus Erigena, that *supernaturalis* made its true entrance into theology," an entrance that was to be followed by a long eclipse: "Its use, which remained rare until the middle of the thirteenth century, became widespread only after St. Thomas

Aquinas" (ibid., 327). The word seems to have been shaped by the Greek *huperousios* [ὑπερούσιος] (Didymus the Blind, Pseudo-Dionysius), and thus has a very distant origin in the equation *phusis = ousia* [οὐσία] mentioned by Aristotle (*Metaphysics* 5.4, 1015a 12–15).

BIBLIOGRAPHY

Lubac, Henri de. *Augustinisme et théologie moderne.* Paris: Aubier, 1965. Translation by Lancelot Sheppard: *Augustinianism and Modern Theology.* London: Chapman, 1969.

——. *Le mystère du surnaturel.* Paris: Aubier, 1965. Translation by Rosemary Sheed: *The Mystery of the Supernatural.* London: Chapman, 1967.

——. *Surnaturel: Études historiques.* New ed. Edited by Michel Sales. Paris: Desclée de Brouwer, 1991.

Milbank, John. *The Suspended Middle: Henri de Lubac and the Debate Concerning the Supernatural.* Grand Rapids, MI: Eerdmans, 2005.

Suso, Henry. *A Little Book of Eternal Wisdom.* Translated by Walter Hilton. Norwood: Angelus, 1910.

BIBLIOGRAPHY

Aristotle. *The Metaphysics.* Translated by Hugh Tredennick. Rev. ed. 2 vols. Loeb Classical Library. Cambridge, MA: Harvard University Press, 1936.

Heidegger, Martin. "Alétheia (Heraklit, Fragment 16)." In *Vortrage und Aufsätze.* Edited by Friedrich-Wilhelm von Hermann. *Gesamtausgabe.* 7: 249–74. Frankfurt am Main: Klostermann, 2000. Translation by David F. Krell and Frank A. Capuzzi: "Aletheia (Heraclitus, Fragment B 16)." In *Early Greek Thinking*, 102–23. New York: Harper and Row, 1975.

——. *Einführung in die Metaphysik.* Edited by Petra Jaeger. *Gesamtausgabe.* Vol. 40. Frankfurt: Klostermann, 1983. Translation by Gregory Fried and Richard Polt: *Introduction to Metaphysics.* New Haven, CT: Yale University Press, 2000.

——. *Heraklit.* Edited by M. S. Frings. *Gesamtausgabe.* Vol. 55. Frankfurt: Klostermann, 1979.

——. "Logos (Heraklit, Fragment 50)." In *Vorträge und Aufsätze.* Edited by Friedrich-Wilhelm von Hermann. *Gesamtausgabe.* 7: 211–34. Frankfurt: Klostermann, 2000. Translation by David Farrell Krell and Frank A. Capuzzi: "Logos (Heraclitus, fragment B 50)." In *Early Greek Thinking*, 59–78. San Francisco: Harper and Row, 1975.

——. "Vom Wesen und Begriff der PHYSIS. Aristoteles, Physik B, 1." In *Wegmarken.* Edited by Friedrich-Wilhelm von Hermann. *Gesamtausgabe.* 9: 239–302. Frankfurt: Klostermann, 1976. Translation by Thomas Sheehan and William McNeill: "On the Essence and Concept of Φύσις in Aristotle's *Physics* B, I." In *Pathmarks*, edited by William McNeill, 183–230. Cambridge: Cambridge University Press, 1998.

Husserl, Edmund. "Die Krisis des europäischen Menschentums und die Philosophie." In *Die Krisis der europäischen Wissenschaften und die transzendentale Phänomenologie: Ein Einleitung in die phänomentologische Philosophie.* Edited by Walter Biemel. *Husserliana.* 6: 314–48. The Hague: Nijhoff, 1954. Translation by David Carr: "Philosophy and the Crisis of European Humanity." In *The Crisis of European Sciences and Transcendental Phenomenology*, 269–99. Evanston, IL: Northwestern University Press, 1970.

Schoenbohm, Susan. "Heidegger's Interpretation of *Phusis* in *Introduction to Metaphysics.*" In *A Companion to Heidegger's* Introduction to Metaphysics. Edited by Richard Polt, 143–60. New Haven, CT: Yale University Press, 2001.

NEGATION

The word "negation"—like the Latin *negatio,* from *nego, negare* ("to say no" and "affirm that [. . .] not [. . .]," "deny," "reject")—designates both the term, particle, or negative operator ("not," "no," "nothing," "no one") and an utterance or proposition that is opposed to assertion, or to a given assertion, and whose truth value is thus the inverse of that of affirmation.

I. Negative Words and How to Designate What Is Not the Case

1. See *NOTHING* (ESTI) for the formation and meaning of negative terms in various languages See also *PERSON, II.4.*
2. On the relationship to being, see OMNITUDO REALITATIS, REALITY; cf. *TO BE* (ESTI).
3. On the relationship to the Other, see NEIGHBOR; cf. TO TRANSLATE, Box 1.
4. On the experience of negation and the relationship to nonbeing, see ANXIETY; cf. DASEIN, *MALAISE.*

II. The Operations of Negation

1. On the logical procedure that makes possible the construction of an assertion or a negation, and on their truth value, see PROPOSITION and TRUTH; see also NONSENSE, PRINCIPLE (in particular PRINCIPLE, I.C on the principle of noncontradiction) and SENSE; cf. *FALSE,* IMPLICATION, *LIE,* SPEECH ACT. Concerning the fact that

two negations are not necessarily equivalent to an assertion, see PORTUGUESE and ESTI I, IV.

2. On the procedure of extenuation and the passage to the negative, especially in theology, see ABSTRACTION, Box 1.

3. On the dialectical force of the negative and of negativity, see AUFHEBEN; cf. ATTUALITÀ, PLASTICITY, PRAXIS.

4. On the procedure of denial, in which negation leads to an awareness of a content, see VERNEINUNG; cf. DRIVE, ENTSTELLUNG, and more generally ES, UNCONSCIOUS, WUNSCH.

5. On erasure and oblivion, see MEMORY; cf. AIÔN, ERZÄHLEN, HISTORY.

➤ *ABSURD, FICTION*, MATTER OF FACT

NEIGHBOR

ARABIC	*jar* [جار]
FRENCH	*prochain*
GERMAN	*Nächste*
GREEK	*plêsion* [πλησιον]
HEBREW	*re'a* [רֵעַ]
ITALIAN	*prossimo*
LATIN	*proximum*
SPANISH	*prójimo, vecino*

➤ *AUTRUI*, and ACTOR, I/ME/MYSELF, MENSCHHEIT, MITMENSCH, PARDON, SUBJECT, WELT, *WORLD*

The English word "neighbor," based on the prefix "nigh-" (denoting proximity in time or space) and the suffix "boor" (a dweller or place of dwelling, as in "bower" or "abode"), brings three distinct but overlapping conceptual clusters into philosophy and critical theory. First, and most important, is the religioethical register of the Neighbor, which derives from the biblical injunction to "love your neighbor as yourself" (originally found in Lv 19:18, and quoted and referred to elsewhere, e.g., Mt 22:39, Mk 12:31, Lk 10:27, Jas 2:8, Rom 13:9). This Neighbor connotes an unspecified category of fellow human beings (and sometimes animals) whom we are obligated to "love," usually understood as implying responsibility or care. Islam too refers to "the neighbor" (*al-jar*) as a figure of special obligation and ambiguous determination (see Qur'an, Surah Al-Nisah 4:36, and the Maariful commentary by Mufti Muhammad Shafi); the Arabic *jar* [جار] is closely related to the Hebrew *gar* (to dwell) and thus to *ger* (a proselyte, resident Gentile, or stranger). The religious figure of the Neighbor passes readily into secular culture and ethics, where it is often presented as the emblem of a universal ideal, and sometimes as equivalent to the "other" of the so-called Golden Rule: "do unto others as you would have them do unto you." This is a weak parallel, however, since the Levitical injunction does not necessarily imply reciprocity, and some interpreters (such as Kierkegaard and Levinas) have insisted on its asymmetry. The figure of the Neighbor as a privileged object remains very active in philosophy and psychoanalysis, as well as in vernacular ethics.

Second, we can distinguish a more general sociopolitical concept of *neighbors*, based on propinquity, spatiotemporal proximity, or contiguity. If the Neighbor is the embodiment of a religioethical ideal, neighbors are transient figures who contingently occupy that position. The modern discussion of sociopolitical neighbors and the neighborhood begins with Weber, Tönnies, Durkheim, and Simmel and continues in contemporary sociology, political theory, public policy, and urban planning. In his first inaugural address in 1933, Franklin D. Roosevelt announced his administration's Good Neighbor Policy, which was intended to improve relations with Latin America in the reflexive logic of the Levitical commandment. For Roosevelt, the good neighbor "resolutely respects himself and, because he does so, respects the rights of others." Robert Frost's famous line, "Good fences make good neighbors," with its problematics of the border, could serve as the sociopolitical neighbor's motto. If the "good neighbor" at minimum is one who observes boundaries and respects obligations, neighbors may also provide mutual assistance or share conviviality—but unlike the religioethical Neighbor, the value of reciprocity here remains paramount. Positive, negative, and ambivalent representations of neighbors can occasionally be found in modern literature (e.g., Rilke, Kafka, Thomas Berger), whereas in popular culture, from Donald Duck to David Lynch, the figure of the "bad neighbor" (whether merely annoying or downright threatening) is much more common. The sociopolitical idea of neighbors implies the existence of a *neighborhood*, usually a territorial vicinity or social grouping based on shared resources, interests, or problems; the neighborhood is an informal mode of association situated between the intimacy of the family and the public concerns of the polis. A neighborhood may involve no more than a vaguely defined geographical area, or it can organize itself as a quasi-political entity, a "neighborhood association," for the sake of common issues or goals. Moreover, the rise of the Internet has allowed for the easy development (and even easier dissolution) of virtual "neighborhoods" that fulfill neighborly functions such as the exchange of information, opinions, and phatic gestures.

Third, we can identify a mathematical set of meanings of *neighboring*, which is often associated with the derivative terms "neighborhood" and "nearest neighbor" and is current in topology, set theory, graph theory, systems theory, cellular automata theory, game theory, and various branches of information technology. The mathematical concept of the neighborhood was introduced by David Hilbert in his definition of planes in *Foundations of Geometry* (app. 4) and developed by Felix Hausdorff in his foundational work on set theoretical topology. Generally speaking, the neighborhood of a given point is defined as a collection of elements or points with certain specific properties in relation to that point, depending on the particular axiomatization. The mathematical notion of the neighborhood describes modes of place and proximity but is not limited to classical Euclidean, or "metric," models of space. The neighborhood of a point in metric space involves those points that are less than a certain distance from it, whereas in topological space, a neighborhood can be specified without such metrics, allowing for concepts such as "being near" and "infinitesimal closeness" and producing a much more general theory of abstract spaces. If distance is a key idea in the theory of metric space, the neighborhood has an analogous function in topological space, which can be deformed without altering the structure of its neighborhoods. Several branches of social and biological sciences make use of theories of neighborhoods in their models, including social network analysis, mathematical sociology, and a branch of molecular embryology known as topobiology. And several philosophers, including Alain Badiou, Gilles Deleuze, Felix Guattari, and Manuel DeLanda, have used mathematical neighboring for political, social, and other conceptual functions.

In all three of these contexts, the Neighbor and "neighboring" involve a degree of ambiguity or indeterminacy. The question of who is included in the category of the Neighbor is vigorously argued in Judaism, Christianity, and Islam. In social theory and political discourse, neighbors constitute a zone of indistinction between friends and enemies, the familiar and the strange, where alliances are contingent and hospitality easily slips into hostility. In popular culture, such neighbors are often represented as social irritants or comic foils, symptomatic of the permeability of private and public space, of real and virtual neighborhoods. Religioethical and sociopolitical concepts of the neighbor tend to be nonsystematic and informal in their fundamental concepts, and this is one reason why the neighbor has occasioned such complex and controversial histories of hermeneutical, ethical, and philosophical speculation. Mathematical accounts of neighboring, on the other hand, strive to formalize concepts such as adjacency, connectedness, and approximation by means of such fundamental set theoretical distinctions as that between parts or regions of a set, on the one hand, and groups of particular elements or members of a set, on the other.

These three meanings fused (some would say confused) in the English word "neighbor" are distinguished by two or more terms in other European languages. The religioethical Neighbor of the Hebrew Bible and the New Testament is usually translated as *prochain* in French—"Tu aimeras ton prochain comme toi-même" (Ostervald, *Traduction de la Bible*, 1724) and *Nächste* in German—"Du sollst deinen Nächsten lieben wie dich selbst" (Luther, *Biblia, das ist, Die gantze Heilige Schrifft, Deudsch*, 1545). *Prochain* derives from *proche*, meaning "close" or "nearby," from the vulgar Latin *propeanus* and the classical *prope*. In the New Vulgate translation, the neighbor of Leviticus 19:18 is *proximum*, the "closest" (although in earlier Latin editions *amicum*, "friend," was used). The Greek term used already in the Septuagint is *plêsion* [πλησιον], also signifying nearness. The German *Nächste* is the substantive of the adverb *nächstens*, meaning "soon" or "near," again implying physical proximity or temporal imminence. In German, *der Nächste* means generally "the next one" (as in *Du bist der Nächste*, "You're next"), and specifically the neighbor to whom one is obligated, but it is not used to refer to the sociopolitical neighbor. This next-door neighbor is *der Nachbar* (masc.) and *die Nachbarn* (fem.), terms very close to the English "neighbor." The French equivalents are *le voisin* (masc.) and *la voisine* (fem.), which come from the Latin *vicinus*, meaning "near" and derive from *vicus*, meaning "a quarter or district of a town." The mathematical concept of neighboring often borrows the language of sociopolitical usages, so

in French the word for a topological neighborhood is *voisinage* (in German, however, a distinct word is used, *Umgebung*, meaning "surroundings" or "environment"). In comparison with French and German, the English word "neighbor" may appear promiscuous in its condensation of three distinct semantic fields; but it also suggests the possibility of productive conceptual interimplications among the three ideas.

The original formulation "love your neighbor as yourself" (*v'ahavtah le're'akha kamokha* [וְאָהַבְתָּ לְרֵעֲךָ כָּמוֹךָ]) in the Hebrew Bible (Lv 19:18) has led to a complicated history of interpretations and a polemic between Judaism and Christianity. The verse is lexically and grammatically ambiguous: Who is referred to as "neighbor" (*re'a*)? What is meant by "love" (*ahav*)? And what is implied by the reflexive term "as yourself" (*kamokha*)? The use of the preposition ל here, indicating "love to" rather than "love of" or "for" the neighbor, is unusual; and the particle ו that connects this line to the previous verse can imply equally conjunction (and) or disjunction (or), each involving distinct, even opposed, interpretive consequences. The word *re'a* [רֵעַ]—usually but not invariably translated in this context as "neighbor"—derives from the primitive root *ra'ah*, which means to "pasture," "tend," "graze," or "feed," without the connotations of proximity that emerge in European languages. *Re'a* is used in a variety of senses in the Torah, and its reference in Leviticus 19:18 is unclear—does it apply exclusively to fellow Jews, or are other people included? The dominant strand of Jewish interpretation of the commandment, from Onkelos (second century CE) through Maimonides (twelfth century) up to the Emancipation (1848), has argued that *re'a* is limited here to other Jews; and indeed, in some of its other biblical appearances, the word seems to refer exclusively to fellow Israelites. But at still other points *re'a* is not confined in this way: in Exodus 11:2, for example, *re'a* refers to the Jews' Egyptian neighbors; elsewhere it seems to figure idolaters or even idols (Jer 3:1), and in Psalm 139 it seems to signify "thought" or "will." Modern Jewish commentators (cf. Simon) have argued for a broader understanding of Leviticus 19:18, often citing the thirteenth-century French rabbi Menachem Ha-Meiri as evidence of a universalist ethics of the neighbor in Judaism, but this may in part be due to pressure from competition with Christianity.

It is not surprising that Christianity, in its Pauline mission to the Gentiles, presents an expansive interpretation of the Neighbor. Already in the parable of the good Samaritan in Luke (10:25–37), the question, who is my neighbor? (*kai tis estin mou plêsion* [και τις εστιν μου πλησιον]) seems controversial: in contrast with the Kohen and the Levite, who pass by without helping a "half dead" man in the road (perhaps due to religious prohibitions against priestly contact with a corpse?), the Samaritan—an Abrahamic sect with heterodox beliefs and practices, hence similar to Christianity—assists the injured man with unlimited generosity, instituting an almost saintly paradigm of the good neighbor, one that is implicitly opposed to Jewish legalism and tribalism. Beyond its polemical function, the parable has significant philosophical implications: first, it poses the neighbor as a *question*—that is, as a topic for debate, a problem, or idea—moreover, one with political implications, in the suggested politico-theological opposition of Judaism and Christianity as particularist and universalist communities. Second, the neighbor here is now a *subjective* position, which is expressed as the imperative of becoming a neighbor rather than treating others as neighbors—a dialectical inversion of earlier biblical references, where the neighbor was invariably presented as a grammatical and ethical object. If the question at the beginning of the parable is, who is the neighbor (whom I should love)? by the conclusion, the question is implicitly reframed as, who am I (who should love my neighbor)?

While Christianity tends to expand the inclusiveness of the category of neighbor, it also limits or focuses the sense of "love" in the Levitical verse by translating it into Greek as *agape* (*caritas* in Latin; both words are often translated into English as "charity"), which does not have the sexual implications of *eros* or the philosophical sense, beginning with Aristotle, of *philia*. The Hebrew word that appears in the injunction, *ahav* [אָהַב], is used for all kinds of love, from erotic to spiritual, from the most illicit to the most hallowed. The rabbinic tradition has been especially elaborate in its accounts of the vast number of particular duties implied by "love" in Leviticus 19:18, including acts intended to alleviate the suffering of others, to increase other people's enjoyment, and to minimize the friction of everyday social relations. It is worth noting, too, the unexpected uses made of the commandment as a proof text in a number of Talmudic contexts, including discussions of sexual relations and capital punishment. In Tractate *Niddah*, for example, it is argued: "A man is forbidden to perform his marital duty in the day-time, for it is said, *But thou shalt love thy neighbor as thyself.* But what is the proof? . . . He might observe something repulsive in her and she would thereby become loathsome to him" (17a). And the imperative of establishing the least painful methods of execution is asserted in Tractate *Kethuboth* and elsewhere by citing the commandment: "Scripture said, But thou shalt love thy neighbour as thyself—choose for him an easy death" (37b). Although these references to Leviticus 19:18 are not presented as interpretations of the commandment, they suggest that the neighbor can accommodate both the most intimate and the most public interpretations and that ambivalence and even death are by no means foreign to its account of neighbor love.

In the Gospels, the injunction to love the neighbor is always paired with that to love God (from Dt 6:5), and the two commandments are frequently linked in later Christian accounts of neighbor-love, as well as in numerous Jewish sources, as the supreme religioethical principle. Saint Augustine argues that the naturally occurring love of self must be transformed or corrected by love of God, and only then can we love our neighbor appropriately. Hannah Arendt points out that for Augustine it is only from the perspective of a self-love that has passed through self-denial that authentic neighbor-love is possible: "It is not really the neighbor who is loved in this love of the neighbor—it is love itself" (*Love and Saint Augustine*). Arendt argues that for Augustine, neighbor-love does not establish the natural community of a neighborhood but instead *isolates* both the neighbor and the self, who are alone together with God.

For philosophy the most important Christian account of neighbor-love, however, is Saint Paul's: "Owe no one anything, except to love one another; for the one who loves

another has fulfilled the law. The commandments . . . are summed up [*anakephalaioutai* (ἀνακεφαλαιουται)] in this word, 'Love your neighbor as yourself.' Love does no wrong to a neighbor; therefore, love is the fulfilling [*plêrôma* (πληρωμα,)] of the law" (Rom 13:8–10). In calling neighbor-love the "summation," or literally, "recapitulation" of the law, Paul is repeating the rabbinic commonplace, associated as well with Jesus, that it represents the moral essence of Judaism, as it will in Christianity. But when Paul calls neighbor-love the "fulfilling" of the law, he is saying something much more radical. This notion of *plêrôma* has often been taken as a key statement of Christian supersessionism, the assertion that Jewish "law" (and Judaism as such) is *replaced* by Christian "love," as the conclusion of an earlier moment and the imminence of a new one. According to Giorgio Agamben, Paul's account of neighbor-love as *plêrôma* is a process that leads not to epochal transformation but rather to the fulfillment of the law in each moment, "a messianic recapitulation, something inseparable from the messianic fulfillment of times." Alain Badiou argues that Paul reduces the multiplicity of the law to the single injunction to love the neighbor insofar as it avoids the law's dialectics of prohibition and transgression in its pure positivity and because "it will require faith in order to be understood . . . because *prior to the Resurrection, the subject, having been given up to death, has no good reason to love himself.*" For Badiou, self-love, in its fidelity to the event of the resurrection, *instantiates* a subject; to love the neighbor "as yourself" thus is the work of a faithful subject whose love enacts the "*force* of salvation." In his 1987 lectures on Paul, Jacob Taubes emphasized Paul's disconnection of the commandments to love God and the neighbor in this passage; Paul's exclusion of love of God, Taubes argues, must be understood as an "absolutely revolutionary act," the critique of the function of God the Father, anticipating both Nietzsche and Freud and opening a new political theology of the neighbor.

From the eighteenth century, philosophy has taken up the biblical tradition of the Neighbor, often as an emblem of ethical reason as such. In *The Groundwork of the Metaphysics of Morals* (1785; in *Practical Philosophy*), Kant presents neighbor-love as a paradigm of practical reason based on the will, rather than mere inclination. In the *Critique of Practical Reason* (1788), he claims that neighbor-love is not only a particular "law of love" but also the "kernel of all laws," the expression of the asymptotic goal of "the moral disposition in its complete perfection"—the "love for the law" (5:83–84). And in the *Metaphysics of Morals* (1797), echoing the common complaint that love cannot be commanded, Kant argues that neighbor-love must be understood as a practice of "benevolence (practical love)," not an affective state. Nevertheless, Kant grants the injunction to love the neighbor the status of a metaethical principle and calls it one of the fundamental "subjective conditions" of the concept of duty (6:399). As "the duty to make others' *ends* my own (provided only that these are not immoral)," neighbor-love for Kant expresses the duty of Duty itself, beyond any particular religious conviction or ethical objective (6:450)—indeed, Kant barely mentions the neighbor in his *Religion within the Limits of Reason Alone* (1793), as if the topic rightfully belongs to philosophy.

For Hegel, however, Kant's account of ethics and neighbor-love, remains, we might say, "too Jewish." In *The Spirit of Christianity and Its Fate* (1799; in *On Christianity*), Hegel criticizes "Kant's profound reduction of what he calls a 'command' (love God first of all and thy neighbor as thyself) to his moral imperative." For Jesus, Hegel argues, neighbor-love is "a command in a sense quite different from that of the 'shalt' of a moral imperative." Kant's imperative, like the notion of a commandment in Judaism, implies a split between an "is" and an "ought" (as well as "reason" and "inclination"); neighbor-love, however, is purely an *is* (*ein* Sein), or what Hegel calls, in a remarkable phrase, "a modification of life" (*eine Modifikation des Lebens*), and is formulated as a commandment only because life requires form in order to be expressed. In the subsection on "Observing Reason" in *Phenomenology of Spirit* (1807), Hegel returns to neighbor-love as an example of reason's claims for "immediate ethical certainty" (parallel with his earlier discussion of consciousness's "sense-certainty"): "Another celebrated commandment is 'Love thy neighbor as thyself.' It is directed to the individual in his relationship with other individuals and asserts the commandment as a relationship between two individuals, or as a relationship of feeling [*Empfindung*]." But this "feeling" must involve an *act*, and this act must be reasoned, in the service of my neighbor's well-being [*Wohl*]: "I must love him *intelligently*" (*ich muß ihn mit* Verstand *lieben*). The immediacy and necessity claimed for the commandment are imperiled by the impossibility of knowing the conditions of my neighbor's well-being with any certainty; indeed, Hegel argues, only the state can determine the nature of "intelligent, substantial beneficence" (*verständige wesentliche Wohltun*), and the individual's act of neighbor-love is both trivial in comparison with the state's and always potentially in conflict with it. Hence, as a commandment, neighbor-love is merely an empty, formal universality; any content given to it is contingent and uncertain. But while the commandment cannot claim concrete universality, Hegel insists that "in its simple absoluteness, it represents *immediate ethical being* [*unmittelbares sittliches Sein*]," prior to and in excess of the empty oppositions between subject and object, content and form, as well as individual and state.

This tension between formal universality and immediate ethical being is played out in the nineteenth century and later. Of special note is Kierkegaard's lengthy discussion in *Works of Love* (1847), which is organized into three inflections of the commandment: "You *shall* love," "You shall love *the neighbor*," and "You shall love the neighbor." For Kierkegaard, neighbor-love is the only form of love that is essentially free, paradoxically, *because* it is commanded. Whereas erotic love and friendship are bound to the compulsions of desire and the vicissitudes of affection, the imperative to love the neighbor liberates the subject, who must make a radical and existential decision, *either* "preferential love" *or* neighbor-love. This choice, moreover, is the condition of possibility of any authentic form of love, including "self-love," which is limited by neighbor-love rather than by its foundation. In its uncanny proximity, the neighbor questions the self-identity of both subject and object. The neighbor, Kierkegaard writes, "in itself is a multiplicity," unlike the necessary individuality

of the friend or the lover; the neighbor, moreover, is *generic*, without the particularity that characterizes the object of preferential love. Hence some commentators (including Adorno) have accused Kierkegaard of eliminating the neighbor as a living person altogether, leaving only the abstract idea of "the human"; indeed, Kierkegaard argues that the most unselfish and freest love is for the *dead*, who have none of the distracting traits of living individuals. In an essay from 1940, Adorno argues that the "impotent mercifulness," "severed from social insight," of Kierkegaard's doctrine of neighbor-love reflects the failure of social relations in modernity, "the deadlock which the concept of the neighbor necessarily meets today. The neighbor no longer exists."

In later modernity, we find increasing suspicion of the injunction to love the neighbor—that it is an ideological ruse, the very motto of bad faith. For Nietzsche, neighbor-love is symptomatic of the failure of *self*-love: "Your love of the neighbor is your bad love of yourselves," both narcissistic and self-loathing. Rather than love of the neighbor, Nietzsche follows philosophical tradition by urging love of the friend—not, however, because the friend is "closer" to the subject than the neighbor—indeed, if anything the neighbor is too close: "Do I recommend love of the neighbor to you? I prefer instead to recommend flight from the neighbor [*Nächsten-Flucht*] and love of the farthest [*Fernsten-Liebe*]. . . . I wish you were unable to stand all these neighbors and their neighbors [*allerlei Nächsten und deren Nachbarn*] . . . [T]hose farther away pay for your love of your neighbor; and even when you are together five at a time, always a sixth one must die" (*Thus Spoke Zarathustra*). Nietzsche argues that neighbor-love is unjust: to love *this* neighbor is always to sacrifice some other neighbor who happens to be farther away; but even more, neighbor-love gives up on "the farthest"—the possibility of encountering the new, the unknown, the yet to come. As if reformulating the Levitical injunction, Nietzsche writes, "Let the future and the farthest be for you the cause of your today: in your friend you shall love the overman as your cause" (*in deinem Freunde sollst du den Übermenschen als deine Ursache lieben*). In its distance, the friend is the locus of the coming "overman," who is not an idealization of the specular "self" but rather the "cause" of what the subject may become.

If for Nietzsche the neighbor is too close, for Freud, the neighbor is too distant, not near enough to one and one's interests, and thus undeserving of love. In his impassioned critique of neighbor-love in *Civilization and Its Discontents*, he writes, "My love is something valuable to me which I ought not to throw away without reflection. . . . If I love someone, he must deserve it in some way. . . . He deserves it if he is so like me in important ways that I can love myself in him; and he deserves it if he is so much more perfect than myself that I can love my ideal of my own self in him" (*Standard Edition*, 21:109). Love *is* narcissistic for Freud, hence one both can and must love only those with whom one can identify, insofar as there is a limited economy of love and to squander it recklessly would be irresponsible and at the expense of those with a rightful claim to it. Moreover, the call to neighbor-love conceals the truth of civilization's "discontents," the aggressivity in excess of any self-interest or economy: "The element of truth behind all this, which people are so ready to disavow, is that . . . their neighbor is for them not only a potential helper or sexual object, but also someone who tempts them to satisfy their aggressiveness on him, to exploit his capacity for work without compensation, to use him sexually without his consent, to seize his possessions, to humiliate him, to cause him pain, to torture and kill him" (*Standard Edition*, 21:111).

For Freud and Nietzsche, the injunction to neighbor-love emblematizes the ethical and social contradictions that fret the project of Enlightenment and hence requires ironic unmasking as ideology. But the intensity of their critical attention and the striking degree of animus that fuels it suggests that the neighbor is not merely one more moral cliché among many but instead a special source of anxiety and trauma, to be returned to as a resource for thinking. For a series of philosophers and psychoanalysts in later modernity, including Rosenzweig, Levinas, and Lacan, this disturbing element in the neighbor and the injunction to neighbor-love exceeds the dialectics of religion and secular reason precisely as the residue of those logics and as something caught up in them but not fully explainable in the terms of either.

In his seminar of 1959–60, *The Ethics of Psychoanalysis*, Lacan suggests that Freud's critique of neighbor-love reveals a fundamental truth about *jouissance*, the traumatic enjoyment that the subject both repudiates and secretly treasures. Lacan connects Freud's discussion of the Neighbor in *Civilization and Its Discontents* with his account of the *Nebenmensch*—literally the "next person," the first other encountered by the subject—in his early *Project for a Scientific Psychology* (*Standard Edition*, vol. 1). At the heart of the *Nebenmensch* is what Freud calls *das Ding*, the unsymbolizable "thing" that constitutes the kernel of exteriority, the other's *jouissance*, at the heart of subjectivity. Lacan argues that Freud repudiates the commandment to love the neighbor not merely as naïve or impractical but also as a manifestation of the "obscene" demands of the superego for excessive enjoyment. It is this account of the neighbor that allows Lacan to formulate an ethics of psychoanalysis that avoids the problematic (discovered by Saint Paul) that the moral law itself *produces* desire and transgression in its very attempt to limit them. In this ethics, to love the neighbor's *jouissance* as one's own would be to encounter the strangeness of one's desire. More recently, Lacan's account of the neighbor has been a recurrent topic in the work of Slavoj Žižek, Eric Santner, and Kenneth Reinhard. Žižek's numerous essays, talks, and chapters on the topic express his ambivalence: "Smashing the Neighbor's Face"; "Love Thy Neighbor? No Thanks!"; "Fear Thy Neighbor as Thyself"; and "The Only Good Neighbor is a Dead Neighbor!" For Žižek, as well as for Santner and Reinhard, the neighbor persists as a key locus of political theological insight even after its disenchantment and death in modernity.

In this work on the political theology of the neighbor, Lacan is supplemented by that of the German Jewish philosopher Franz Rosenzweig. The figure of the neighbor is an exemplary locus for what Rosenzweig calls "the new thinking," which is in excess of the dialectic of faith and reason. In *The Star of Redemption* (1919), Rosenzweig sees neighbor-love as the purely human means of enacting redemption according to the two paths represented by Judaism and Christianity. The "Jewish" mode of neighbor-love involves the instantaneous transformation of love of self into love of the neighbor, which thereby immediately realizes eternity; the "Christian" mode

is the world-historical expression of redemption through the progressive expansion of local congregations into universal empire. In each case, the neighbor is the "anyone" whose proximity is coordinate with the imminence of redemption, which is always "not yet" and ever unfolding "from one neighbor to the next neighbor." Rosenzweig's ideas on the neighbor respond to those of his teacher, Hermann Cohen, one of the founders of the Marburg School of neo-Kantianism. In *Religion of Reason* (1919), Cohen tried to reconcile Jewish legalism with Kantian ethics. Cohen had already vigorously defended the universalism of the Jewish account of the neighbor in 1888, when he testified in a defamation suit against an anti-Semitic school teacher who had claimed that Judaism authorizes discrimination against Gentiles; this testimony along with three other essays of Cohen's on the neighbor were collected and published by Martin Buber after Cohen's death.

Buber's own reflections on the neighbor and the "I–Thou" relationship were in turn influential in Emmanuel Levinas's work on the neighbor (although Levinas was critical of the reciprocity of Buber's model). The neighbor is a crucial topic in both Levinas's "Jewish" and "philosophical" writings, including his major work, *Otherwise Than Being* (1974), in which it represents an originary proximity that determines the subject as responsible and fundamentally indebted to the other: "Proximity is thus *anarchically* a relationship with a singularity without the mediation of any principle, any ideality. What concretely corresponds to this description is my relationship with my neighbor. . . . [I]t is an assignation of me by another, a responsibility with regard to men we do not even know." For Levinas, the neighbor figures the preontologically ethical constitution of the subject in its nonreciprocal relationship to the other. According to Levinas, the obligation to love the neighbor is a debt that can never be amortized and for which I am unjustly persecuted: no person can take my place and assume my ethical burden, but I am called to assume the place of all other neighbors. For Levinas, the radical asymmetry of the relationship to the religioethical Neighbor must be distinguished from the equality and interchangeability that define sociopolitical neighbors; in this sense, the injunction to love the neighbor is both *descriptive* and *prescriptive*—it is both the condition of subjectivity as such and an imperative to sociopolitical action.

Levinas's account of the neighbor can be understood as a critique of Heidegger's notion in *Being and Time* of *Mitsein*, or "being-with," which, many critics have argued, is not for Heidegger a social or ethical relation but rather the originary structure of *Dasein*. In his later work, the proximity of *Mitsein* develops into a discourse of nearness, the neighbor, and the neighborhood—concepts that do not readily correspond to the ideas of the neighbor we have described so far but which we might call ontological neighboring. As Derrida points out, whereas in *Being and Time* the "nearness" of *Dasein* to being is *ontic*, in Heidegger's later writings proximity is *ontological*: "Whence, in Heidegger's discourse, the dominance of an entire metaphorics of proximity . . . a metaphorics associating the proximity of Being with the values of neighboring, shelter, house, service, guard, voice, and listening" ("The Ends of Man"). In the "Letter on Humanism" (1946), for example, Heidegger writes that "man is the neighbor of being" (*Der Mensch ist der Nachbar des Seins*;

Basic Writings), and in "The Nature of Language" (1957), he writes that "Thinking . . . goes its ways in the neighborhood of poetry. It is well, therefore, to give thought to the neighbor, to him who dwells in the same neighborhood" (*On the Way to Language*). Derrida criticizes Heidegger's account of *Dasein*'s proximity as merely one more version of humanism, the "proper" of man, and asks, "Is not this security of the near what is trembling today?" The theme of the neighbor persists in Derrida's writings, including his posthumous *The Animal That Therefore I Am* (2006), where he criticizes the tradition, from Aristotle to Heidegger, of regarding animals as "*all the living things* that man does not recognize as his fellows, his neighbors, or his brothers." Derrida suggests that animals epitomize the uncanny otherness of the neighbor: "[N]othing will have ever given me more food for thinking through this absolute alterity of the neighbor or of the next (-door) than these moments when I see myself seen naked under the gaze of a cat."

The mathematical concept of the neighborhood is central to a series of key oppositions that run through the work of Deleuze and Guattari, including that between "striated" (or metric) and "smooth" (or nonmetric) spaces in *A Thousand Plateaus* (*Mille plateaux*, 1980). These oppositions derive in part from Pierre Rosenstiehl and Jean Petitot's distinction between hierarchical "arborescent" societies (which they describe via the so-called friendship theorem, where, for any group of "friends," there is exactly one "dictator" who coordinates the system and is everyone's "friend") and "acentered," or nonmetric "rhizomatic" systems based on *neighbors*, "in which," according to Deleuze and Guattari, "communication runs from any neighbor to any other, the stems or channels do not preexist, and all individuals are interchangeable, defined only by their state at a given moment." Unlike the static system of "friends" (which Deleuze and Guattari associate with the classical "*philo*-sopher"), a neighborhood is a *becoming*, "a zone of proximity [*zone de voisinage*] and indiscernibility, a no-man's-land, a nonlocalizable relation sweeping up the two distant or contiguous points, carrying one into the proximity [*le voisinage*] of the other—and the border-proximity [*voisinage-frontière*] is indifferent to both contiguity and to distance." In *What Is Philosophy?* (1991), Deleuze and Guattari propose a "geophilosophy" of neighbors: if the Greek philosophical society of "friends" leads to the capitalist society of "brothers," geophilosophy organizes itself in terms of *neighbors*: "a concept is a heterogenesis—that is to say, an ordering of its components by zones of neighborhood."

If for Deleuze and Guattari a concept as such is a "neighborhood," a loose assemblage of valences and vectors, for Badiou the neighborhood is a particular *concept*, with precise mathematical and political implications. In *Theory of the Subject*, Badiou develops the mathematical idea of the neighborhood into a dialectical materialism through the distinction between algebra and topology (1982; from seminars delivered in 1975–79). For Badiou, materialism involves two types of dialecticity drawn from mathematics: the algebraic disposition, based on identity, belonging, and reflection; and the topological disposition, based on the asymptote, adherence, and the remainder. Algebra, which is a "combinatory materialism," studies the relations between the elements of a set according to laws of "composition" (such as association or commutativity) in terms of the belonging or *membership* of elements. Topology, according to Badiou, arises from the need to grasp movement and place in order to specify concepts such as location, approximation, continuum, and differential. Rather than individual elements, topology examines *parts* or subsets; it aims at "what happens when one investigates the site of a term, its surrounding, that which is more or less 'near' to it. . . . If the master concept of algebra is that of the law (of composition), topology is based on the notion of neighborhood." Whereas algebra is a science of identifying and naming a particular element, topology involves *dis-identification* or de-particularization: what applies to one point in a topology *must also apply to other neighboring points*. Topology does not describe individual elements but rather *collectives*; in a "neighborhood," Badiou writes, "the element is the point of flight for a series of collectives. The individual has no other name than its multiple adherences" (*Theory of the Subject*). The notion of locating elements in overlapping clusters as "neighborhoods" tends toward the "expansion of the local" as more and more elements are potentially each other's "neighbor." Badiou makes the political implications of this model explicit: "the working class may be the first neighborhood—already very vast—of a factory revolt. You will thus obtain . . . wider neighborhoods. . . . The intersection of these two neighborhoods is nothing less than the form of internationalism immanent to the term 'revolt'" (*Theory of the Subject*). The topological concept of a neighborhood thus suggests a principle of political collectivization other than citizenship (whose models are paternal and fraternal and based on genealogy and friendship): the neighbor is not a "member" of a state defined by socioeconomic coordinates but is, instead, a *part* of a loosely aggregated neighborhood.

Badiou's account of the potentially infinite expansion of the neighborhood involves Paul Cohen's concept of a "generic" set produced by the technique known as "forcing" (ideas that are central in Badiou's *Being and Event*.) By "forcing" a "generic extension" of a set, a new set is produced that is nonconstructable, that is without external unifying predicates—thus not a proper set at all under Gödel's criterion of constructability. As its name suggests, a generic set is only *minimally* described: "[T]he generic essentially resembles the topological, which . . . disindentifies the element in favor of its neighborhoods" (*Theory of the Subject*). In political terms, Badiou associates such a "forced" generic neighborhood with the possibility of the proletariat itself. If a generic set is a neighborhood in which individual elements are indiscernible and the limit function is approximate, the authentically political neighborhood is essentially *generic*, an open collective whose parts are always in excess of its members. In the final chapter of *Theory of the Subject*, "Topologies of Ethics," Badiou proposes an ethics of exposure, of openness, where "justice" and "courage" are presented as functions of the neighborhood: justice relativizes the law—it arises from the "topologization of algebra," in which "the neighborhood subordinates the elementary to itself. Justice is the *blurring of places*, the opposite, therefore, of the right place." Courage, on the other hand, interrupts the relativized law for the sake of the excess, the remainder, "thus dividing the prescription of the place by *completely* investing its neighborhoods. All courage amounts to passing through there where previously it was not visible that anyone could find a passage." Finally, Badiou's topological concept of the virtues of the neighborhood provides a precise model for the political idea called *communism*: the neighbor is the subject of communism, subtracted from the state—the common or generic subject, whose adherences are minimally specified and infinitely expansive.

Kenneth Reinhard

BIBLIOGRAPHY

Adorno, Theodor. "On Kierkegaard's Doctrine of Love." *Studies in Philosophy and Social Sciences*. 8 (1940): 413–29.

Agamben, Giorgio. *The Coming Community*. Translated by Michael Hardt. Minneapolis: University of Minnesota Press, 1993.

———. *The Time That Remains: A Commentary on the Letter to the Romans*. Stanford, CA: Stanford University Press, 2005.

Arendt, Hannah. *Love and Saint Augustine*. Chicago: University Of Chicago Press, 1998.

Augustine, Saint. *On Christian Doctrine*. Mineola, NY: Dover Press, 2009.

Badiou, Alain. *Saint Paul: The Foundation of Universalism*. Stanford, CA: Stanford University Press, 2003.

———. *Theory of the Subject*. Translated by Bruno Bosteels. London: Continuum, 2009.

Berger, Thomas. *The Feud*. New York: Little Brown, 1989.

———. *Neighbors*. New York: Simon & Schuster, 2005.

Cohen, Hermann. *Der Nächste: Vier Abhandlungen über das Verhalten von Mensch zu Mensch nach der Lehre des Judentums*. Saarbrücken, Ger.: Verlag Dr. Müller, 2006.

———. *Religion of Reason: Out of the Sources of Judaism*. Atlanta: American Academy of Religion, 1995.

DeLanda, Manuel. *Intensive Science and Virtual Philosophy*. London: Athlone Press, 2002.

———. *A New Philosophy of Society: Assemblage Theory And Social Complexity*. London: Continuum, 2006.

Deleuze, Gilles, and Felix Guattari. *A Thousand Plateaus: Capitalism and Schizophrenia*. Translated by Brian Massumi. Minneapolis: University of Minnesota Press, 1987.

———. *What Is Philosophy?* New York: Columbia University Press, 1996.

Derrida, Jacques. *The Animal That Therefore I Am*. Edited by Marie-Louise Mallet, translated by David Wills. New York: Fordham University Press, 2008.

———. "The Ends of Man." In *Margins of Philosophy*, translated by Alan Bass. Chicago: University of Chicago Press, 1982.

Edelman, Gerald. *Topobiology: An Introduction To Molecular Embryology*. New York: Basic Books, 1993.

Freud, Sigmund. *The Standard Edition of the Complete Psychological Works of Sigmund Freud*. Translated and edited by James Strachey et al. 24 vols. London: Hogarth Press, 1953–74.

George, Nick, and Milt Schaffer. *The New Neighbor* (a Donald Duck cartoon). Directed by Jack Hannah. Burbank, CA: Walt Disney Productions, 1953.

Hausdorff, Felix. *Set Theory* (*Grundzuge der Mengenlehre*). Berlin: Springer, 2002.

Hegel, Georg W.F. *On Christianity: Early Theological Writings*. Translated by T. M. Knox. New York: Harper Torchbooks, 1961.

———. *Phenomenology of Spirit*. Translated by A. V. Miller. Oxford: Oxford University Press, 1979.

Heidegger, Martin. "Letter on Humanism." In *Basic Writings*, translated by David Farrell Krell. New York: Harper Modern Classics, 2008.

———. "The Nature of Language." In *On the Way to Language*, translated by Peter D. Hertz. New York: Harper Collins, 1982.

Hilbert, David. *The Foundations of Geometry*. Translated by E. J. Townsend. 2nd ed. Chicago: Open Court, 1910.

Kant, Immanuel. *Practical Philosophy*. Edited and translated by Mary J. Gregor. Cambridge: Cambridge University Press, 1999.

Kierkegaard, Søren. *Works of Love*. Edited and translated by Howard V. Hong and Edna Hong. Vol. 16 of *Kierkegaard's Writings*. Princeton, NJ: Princeton University Press, 1998.

Lacan, Jacques. *The Seminar of Jacques Lacan, Book 7: The Ethics of Psychoanalysis*. Translated by Dennis Porter. New York: W. W. Norton, 1992.

Levinas, Emmanuel. *Otherwise Than Being*. Translated by Alphonso Lingis. Pittsburgh, PA: Duquesne University Press, 1998.

Lynch, David, director. *Blue Velvet*. Wilmington, NC: De Laurentis Entertainment Group, 1986.

Nietzsche, Friedrich. *Thus Spoke Zarathustra*. Translated by Adrian Del Caro. Cambridge: Cambridge University Press, 2006.

Putnam, Robert D. *Bowling Alone: The Collapse and Revival of American Community*. New York: Simon & Schuster, 2001.

Reinhard, Kenneth. "The Ethics of the Neighbor: Universalism, Particularism, Exceptionalism." *The Journal of Textual Reasoning* 4 (November 2005). http://etext.lib.virginia.edu/journals/tr/volume4/TR_04_01_e01.html

Ricœur, Paul. "The *Socius* and the Neighbor." In *History and Truth*. Evanston, IL: Northwestern University Press, 1965.

Rilke, Rainer Maria. *Die Aufzeichnungen des Malte Laurids Brigge*. Leipzig: Insel Verlag, 1910.

———. *Das Stunden-Buch; Geschichten vom lieben Gott*. 1900/1904. In *Gesammelte Werke in fünf Bänden*. Vol. 2, *Gedichte II*. Frankfurt: Insel Verlag 2003.

Rosenstiehl, Pierre, and Jean Petitot. "Automate asocial et systèmes acentré." *Communications* 22 (1974): 45–62.

Rosenzweig, Franz. *The Star of Redemption*. Madison: University of Wisconsin Press, 2005.

Sampson, Robert J., Jeffrey D. Morenoff, and Thomas Gannon-Rowley. "Assessing 'Neighborhood' Effects: Social Processes and New Directions in Research." *Annual Review of Sociology* 28 (2002): 443–78.

Shafi, Maulana Mufti Muhammad. *Maariful Qur'an*. Translated by Mufti Taqi Usmani. 8 vol. Karachi, Pakistan: Maktaba Darul-Uloom, 1998–2003.

Simmel, Georg. *Soziologie: Untersuchungen über die formen der Vergesellschaftung*. Berlin: Duncker & Humblot, 1908.

Simon, Ernst. "The Neighbor (*Re'a*) Whom We Shall Love." In *Modern Jewish Ethics: Theory and Practice*, edited by Marvin Fox, 29–56. Columbus: Ohio State University Press, 1975.

Sorkin, Michael, and Joan Copjec. *Giving Ground: The Politics of Propinquity*. New York: Verso, 1999.

Taubes, Jacob. *The Political Theology of Paul*. Stanford, CA: Stanford University Press, 2003.

Tönnies, Ferdinand. *Community and Society*. New Brunswick, NJ: Transaction Publishers, 1988.

Weber, Max. "The Neighborhood: An Unsentimental Economic Brotherhood." In Vol. 1 of *Economy and Society*, edited by Guenther Roth and Claus Wittich, 360–63. Berkeley: University of California Press, 1978.

Žižek, Slavoj, Eric Santner, and Kenneth Reinhard. *The Neighbor: Three Inquiries in Political Theology*. Chicago: University of Chicago Press, 2006.

NEUZEIT / MODERNE (GERMAN)

ENGLISH   modern times, modern age, modernity
FRENCH   *temps modernes, âge moderne, modernité*

➤ BAROQUE, BILDUNG, CLASSIC, HISTORY, PRESENT, ROMANTIC, SECULARIZATION, STATO, *TIME*

In contrast to the *antiqui/moderni* pair, the German *Neuzeit* is part of an idea of historical periodization that divides history into three ages: antiquity, Middle Ages, and *Neuzeit*. Since the nineteenth century the term has designated the period that follows the Middle Ages, a period that is fundamentally open to the present and whose temporal limits seem ill defined. Unlike *die Moderne* (which French and English translate, as they do *Neuzeit*, by *modernité*, "modernity"), which generally refers to the nineteenth century and more particularly to its aesthetics, *Neuzeit*, which was coined at the same time, indicates first of all the feeling of a profound change in all domains of life such as might have been experienced by the humanists of the "Renaissance" who were made the pioneers of this "modernity" (Burckhardt). The chronological extension of the term ranges, with many variations, from the Italian Renaissance to the century of industrialization, and indeed down to our own time.

Since Ranke proposed the historiographic practice and theory known as *Historismus*, the notion of *Neuzeit* has undergone additional differentiations (into subperiods such as *Frühe Neuzeit, jüngere Neuzeit, neueste Neuzeit*); on the other hand, *Neuzeit* correspondingly has lost its initial connotations and has become simply a term of historical periodization. It is in that form that the notion of *Neuzeit* was definitively established (in the middle of the twentieth century) in history, sociology, and the history of philosophy. It is also increasingly argued that this historical period should be closed by assigning it an end. Here, however, the debate becomes philosophical, and German then prefers to use the term *Moderne*, which usually shifts the discussion to the value of modernity. French has no way to render this shift in emphasis.

The first use of *Neuzeit* is found in the Grimm brothers' dictionary (1884), where it is opposed to the *Vorzeit* (literally, "the earlier period") and illustrated by a verse written by the young revolutionary Freiligrath in 1870, in which he describes himself as "a feverish and impassioned child of the *Neuzeit* who still longs a little for the older [time] (*die alte* [*Zeit*])." Here the word expresses a feeling of renewal (*Neu-zeit*, literally, "new time"), an upheaval affecting all life and all people, contemporaries' excitements and fears; it is applied to the present time, but it also situates the individual in the dynamics of history that carries everyone along with its forward thrust, that is, in general progress. In French this is rendered by the expression *les temps modernes* rather better than by the word *modernité*.

I. *Neuzeit*: The Historiographical Determinants

A series of events traditionally marks the beginning of the *Neuzeit*: the discovery of America in 1492, that is, the opening up of a closed world to a potentially infinite universe; Luther's proclamation of his ninety-nine theses and the beginning of the Reformation in 1517; and the invention of the printing press. The interpretation of some of these events has given rise to intense debates, particularly in the case of the Reformation, in which Nietzsche saw a regressive protest against the Italian Renaissance (*The Antichrist*, §61), and on which Troeltsch offered a more qualified judgment balancing the Reformation's traditional (that is, for him, Lutheran) elements against the innovative (Calvinist) ones (*Die Bedeutung des Protestantismus für die Entstehung der modernen Welt*, 1911).

However, a consensus among historians has emerged, defining the *Neuzeit* on the basis of a certain number of dominant traits inchoately emerging well before 1500, that enables us to discern a long-term historical configuration (*longue durée*). Among these traits is the invention of printing and the consequent opening up of a "public space" (*Öffentlichkeit*): the communication media that were developed starting in the sixteenth century are described in German as *neuzeitlich* and not *modern*, the latter word being reserved for the technical innovations of industrialization in the

nineteenth and twentieth centuries. To this is usually added the transition from feudalism to a capitalist economic model, the development of a new social class—the bourgeoisie—and the formation of modern states. Various concepts have been tried out, associated, and opposed to provide a more complete explanation of this process of turning societies into states: in addition to the well-known processes of absolutism and "disciplinarization" (*Zivilisationsprozess*, with the different nuances introduced into it by Michel Foucault and Norbert Elias), the pair formed by the concepts of secularization and confessionalization (*Säkularisierung, Konfessionalisierung*) (see SECULARIZATION) characterizes the whole of historical writing about the Germanic Holy Roman Empire and establishes itself as one of the most remarkable components of thinking about the *Frühe Neuzeit*.

II. *Frühe Neuzeit, Neuere Zeit, Neueste Zeit*: Problems of Periodization

Economic and political historians differentiate *Neuzeit* into three or four phases. The first, that of the *Frühe Neuzeit*, goes from about the time of the first Italian city-states to the end of the Thirty Years' War, and led to a new order in Europe (1350–1650). The second phase is described as *neuere Zeit* or *jüngere Neuzeit* and is marked by the formation of a modern subject and the ideals of the Enlightenment. It is generally said to extend as far as the French Revolution, emphasizing the advent of the bourgeoisie as a historical actor. Industrialization and its effects constitute the essential trait of the third period, designated as *neueste Zeit*. This tautological redundancy (*neu, Neuzeit, neueste Zeit*, etc.) shows that the notion of *Neuzeit* always implies an awareness of the historical relativity of every period (R. Vierhaus, "Vom Nutzen," 14). Of these expressions only *Frühe Neuzeit*, which designates the period between about 1450 and 1650 and is sometimes extended as far as 1800, has been unanimously adopted.

The problems of defining and delimiting a *Neuzeit* period have led to extensive historiographical reflection. Thus, this concept has been connected with the notion of crisis (Aston, *Crisis in Europe*) and with the suggestion, made by Hans Blumenberg and others, that well-defined historical periods are separated by transitional periods. The idea of a "threshhold between periods" (*Aspekte der Epochenschwelle*) or even of a "threshold century" (*Vierhaus*, ibid., 21), allows us to abandon the search for the exact limits of the *Neuzeit* and conceive it instead as a set of diverse changes and as a plural, open process (ibid., 23). The same can be said of Reinhard Koselleck (in Brunner, Conze, and Koselleck, *Geschichtliche Grundbegriffe*, 1: xiv–xv); introducing the idea of a time when modernity was "getting into the saddle" (*Vorsattelzeit*), in which the "process of translating" "classical topoi" into "modern [*neuzeitlich*] conceptuality" took place, he makes a differentiation that other historians have adopted in their periodizations of German history) (cf. H. Schilling, *Aufbruch und Krise*).

III. *Neuzeit*, Nature, and the Divine

The historiography of the *Neuzeit* accords a large place to the transformations of science. For Romano Guardini, the change in the notion of nature and the philosophy of nature is the essential characteristic of the *Neuzeit* (*Das Ende*, 35ff.). Drawing on Goethe, he considers modern man a stranger in the midst of nature, which no longer is, of course, in any way divine. Ernst Cassirer went so far as to make central to his thinking about the *Neuzeit* the idea of a modern individual who has to resituate himself in relation to this unknown universe (*Individuum und Kosmos*). For Cassirer, the *Neuzeit* begins somewhere between Nicolas of Cusa's theory of knowledge and ignorance and Giordano Bruno's materialism. Bruno is also one of the main figures of the *Neuzeit* for Hans Blumenberg (*Die Legitimität*), even though Blumenberg chooses the name of Copernicus to mark the turning point of modern times and the "pathos" of this revolution (*Die kopernikanische Wende* and *Kopernikus im Selbstverständnis der Neuzeit*, 343). Man is no longer at the center of the world; his "ex-centricity" entails his cosmological and theological deracination (*Entwurzelung*), compensated by a theoretical "curiosity" (*curiositas, theoretische Neugier*) that constitutes, as it were, the signature of the *Neuzeit*. The notion of *Neuzeit* is thus paired with that of secularization, which Blumenberg, in opposition to Carl Schmitt, seeks to liberate from a long tradition of interpretation that makes of it a "category of historical illegitimacy" (*Kategorie geschichtlichen Unrechts*).

- See Box 1.

IV. *Neuzeit, Moderne*

Although in German the adjective *modern* is replacing *Neuzeit* with increasing frequency, the substantive *Moderne* remains uniquely applicable to the historical period that begins around the middle of the nineteenth century. In addition, the concept of the *Moderne* appears along with the art and literature of this period, and its theorizations are always aesthetic in nature—from Friedrich Vischer, who sees in it "the union of the ancient and the romantic" (*Aesthetik oder Wissenschaft*, §467), to Theodor Adorno, who describes

modernity as "the art of the most advanced consciousness" (*Ästhetische Theorie*, 57; on Baudelaire's "*beau moderne*" and the philosophical interpretation of modernity, see Vincent Descombes, *Philosophie*, and Jürgen Habermas, *Der philosophische Diskurs* [1988]). On the other hand, after World War II the word *Neuzeit* seems to have lost its optimistic connotations and has been reduced to a neutral historical term, whereas the word "modern" still reflects the idea of a positive progress. In the debate over postmodernity and neo-structuralism that flourished in Franco-German philosophical dialogue during the 1980s, it was the term *Moderne* that was used. The *Moderne*, setting aside the notions that are associated with it (subjectivity, autonomy, self-foundation) and the criticism that has been directed at them, is conceived fundamentally as a project, and this introduces into it a component of reflexivity that is absent in the notion of *Neuzeit*, at least in its current usage (cf. Habermas, "Die Moderne," 1980); this might be the philosophical specificity of *Moderne* in relation to *Neuzeit*. At a time when the project of modernity is being challenged, the fate of the notion of *Neuzeit* thus seems to have dwindled in philosophy and to retain its pertinence only in historiographical debates about the periodization of modernity. However, given the richness of these debates, it could be that the speculative power of the concept of *Neuzeit* will remain. Moreover, the originality of Blumenberg's philosophical project can also be gauged by the maintenance of the term *Neuzeit*, which signals a different periodization of modernity by taking as its starting point the Renaissance rather than the Enlightenment and the Industrial Revolution, unlike thinkers concerned with the *Moderne*. The difference between Blumenberg and Habermas thus begins with their choice of words. The problem of French *modernité* would then be that it cannot account for this bifurcation.

Gisela Febel

1

Vor tid, nutiden (Danish)

These terms, which are rendered as "our time," "the present time," "the epoch," and other analogous expressions, appear in almost all the works in which Kierkegaard characterizes his period. The latter is subjected to criticism for having lost the sense of the individual man's (*Enkelte*) concrete possibilities because it has not undertaken the task of the "subjective existent thinker." The "epoch" is dominated philosophically by speculation and socially by mass culture (the press). This also affects Christianity, Denmark's official religion. Being aware of one's times to the point of denouncing their vices is to confront the incomprehension of the present generation and abandon all hope of being admired.

The tactic to be adopted consists in deceiving one's surrounding world ("*Mundus vult decipi, decipiatur ergo*": 2: 229, 9: 313, 16: 33), making them hear the voice of the isolated man who stigmatizes the failings of the epoch. Kierkegaard might have said, like Hamlet, "The time is out of joint." But he would have done so without believing that he was called upon to "set it right." For his "time," he wants to be only a "corrective" (*correctiv*) (17: 276, 19: 43). Whether it is a matter of thought, literary mores, or religion, the task of the subjective thinker is simply to describe the stages of existence, their specific temporality, in order to make the reader "attentive" (14: 79, 86) to the dangers of "leveling" (*Nivellering*) (5: 153) and

of jealousy that levels (8: 184, 202, 225). This is not unrelated to Heidegger's analysis of mediocrity (*Durchschnittlichkeit*) or of "one" (*man*) and leveling (*Einebnung*) (*Sein und Zeit*, §27).

Jacques Colette

BIBLIOGRAPHY

Heidegger, Martin. *Sein und Zeit*. Tübingen: Niemeyer, 1963.
Kierkegaard, Søren. *Skrifter*. Edited by Niels Jørgen Cappelørn et al. 26 vols. Copenhagen: Gad, 1997–. *Kierkegaard's Writings*. Edited by Howard V. Hong and Edna H. Hong. 26 vols. Princeton, NJ: Princeton University Press, 1978–1998.

BIBLIOGRAPHY

Adorno, Theodor W. *Ästhetische Theorie*. Edited by Gretel Adorno and Rolf Tiedemann. In *Gesammelte Schriften*. Vol. 7. Frankfurt: Suhrkamp, 1970. Translation by Robert Hullot-Kentor: *Aesthetic Theory*. Edited and with introduction by Robert Hullot-Kentor. Minneapolis: University of Minnesota Press, 1997.

Aston, T. H., ed. *Crisis in Europe, 1560–1660*. Introduction by Christopher Hill. New York: Basic Books, 1965.

Blumenberg, Hans. *Aspekte der Epochenschwelle: Cusaner u. Nolaner*. Frankfurt: Suhrkamp, 1976.

———. *Die Genesis der kopernikanischen Welt*. Frankfurt: Suhrkamp, 1975. Translation by Robert M. Wallace: *The Genesis of the Copernican World*. Cambridge, MA: MIT Press, 1987.

———. *Die kopernikanische Wende*. Frankfurt: Suhrkamp, 1965.

———. *Kopernikus im Selbstverständnis der Neuzeit*. Mainz, Ger.: Akademie der Wissenschaften, 1965.

———. *Die Legitimität der Neuzeit*. Frankfurt: Suhrkamp, 1966. Translation by Robert M. Wallace: *The Legitimacy of the Modern Age*. Cambridge, MA: MIT Press, 1983.

Brentano, Franz. *Geschichte der Philosophie der Neuzeit*. Edited and with introduction by Klaus Hedwig. Hamburg: Meiner, 1987.

Brient, Elizabeth. *The Immanence of the Infinite: Hans Blumenberg and the Threshold to Modernity*. Washington, DC: Catholic University of America Press, 2002.

Burckhardt, Jacob. *Die Kultur der Renaissance in Italien: Ein Versuch*. Edited by Konrad Hoffmann. Stuttgart: Kröner, 1985. Translation by S.G.C. Middlemore: *The Civilization of the Renaissance in Italy*. Introduction by Peter Gay. Afterword by Hajo Holborn. New York: Modern Library, 2002.

Cassirer, Ernst. *Individuum und Kosmos in der Philosophie der Renaissance*. 5th ed. Darmstadt, Ger.: Wissenschaftliche Buchgesellschaft, 1977. Translation by Mario Domandi: *The Individual and the Cosmos in Renaissance Philosophy*. Introduction by Mario Domandi. Philadelphia: University of Pennsylvania Press, 1963.

Descombes, Vincent. *Philosophie par gros temps*. Paris: Éditions de Minuit, 1989. Translation by Stephen Adam Schwartz: *The Barometer of Modern Reason: On the Philosophies of Current Events*. New York: Oxford University Press, 1993.

Gadamer, Hans Georg. "Postmoderne und das Ende der Neuzeit." *Vortrag 1992*. Heidelberg, 1996. Audiocassette.

Guardini, Romano. *Das Ende der Neuzeit: Ein Versuch zur Orientierung; Die Macht: Versuch einer Wegweisung*. Mainz, Ger.: Matthias-Grünewald, 1989. Translation by Joseph Theman and Herbert Burke: *The End of the Modern World: A Search for Orientation*. Edited and with introduction by Frederick D. Wilhelmsen. Chicago: Regnery, 1968.

Habermas, Jürgen. *Der philosophische Diskurs der Moderne: Zwölf Vorlesungen*. Frankfurt: Suhrkamp, 1985. Translation by Frederick G. Lawrence: *The Philosophical Discourse of Modernity: Twelve Lectures*. Introduction by Thomas McCarthy. Cambridge, MA: MIT Press, 1987.

———. "Die Moderne—ein unvollendetes Projekt." In *Kleine politische Schriften 1–4*, 444–64. Frankfurt: Suhrkamp, 1980. Translation: "Modernity: An Unfinished Project." In *Habermas and the Unfinished Project of Modernity: Critical Essays on* The Philosophical Discourse of Modernity. Edited by Maurizio Passerin d'Entrèves and Seyla Benhabib, 38–58. Cambridge, MA: MIT Press, 1997.

Hegel, Georg Friedrich Wilhelm. *Vorlesungen über die Philosophie der Geschichte*. Edited by Eva Moldenhauer and Karl Markus Michel. In *Werke*. Vol. 12. Frankfurt: Suhrkamp, 1970. Translation by John Sibree: *The Philosophy of History*. Rev. ed. New York: Willey, 1944.

Koselleck, Reinhart. *Kritik und Krise. Eine Studie zur Pathogenese des bürgerlichen Welt*. Frankfurt: Suhrkamp, 1979. *Critique and Crisis: Enlightenment and the Pathogenesis of Modern Society*. Cambridge, MA: MIT Press, 1988.

———. "Neuzeit." In *Vergangene Zukunft. Zur Semantik moderner Bewegungsbegriffe*. Frankfurt: Suhrkamp, 1979. Translation by Keith Tribe: "Neuzeit." In *Futures Past: On the Semantics of Historical Time*, 222–54. Introduction by Keith Tribe. New York: Columbia University Press, 2004.

Nietzsche, Friedrich. *Der Antichrist*. Edited by Giorgio Colli and Mazzino Montinari. In *Kritische Studienausgabe*. Vol. 6. Berlin: De Gruyter, 1980. Translation by Judith Norman: "The Anti-Christ." In *The Anti-Christ, Ecce Homo, Twilight of the Idols, and Other Writings*, edited by Aaron Ridley and Judith Norman, 1–67. Cambridge: Cambridge University Press, 2005.

———. "Vom Nutzen und Nachteil der Historie für das Leben (Unzeitgemäße Betrachtung II)." In *Die Geburt der Tragödie. Unzeitgemässe Betrachtungen 1–4*. Edited by Giorgio Colli and Mazzino Montinari. *Sämtliche Werke, Kritische Studienausgabe*. Vol. 1. Berlin: De Gruyter, 1980. Translation by R. J. Hollingdale: "On the Uses and Disadvantages of History for Life (Second Untimely Meditation)." In *Untimely Meditations*, 57–124. Cambridge: Cambridge University Press, 1983.

Schilling, Heinz. *Aufbruch und Krise: Deutschland 1517–1648*. Berlin: Siedler, 1988.

———. *Religion, Political Culture, and the Emergence of Early Modern Society: Essays in German and Dutch History*. Leiden, Neth.: Brill, 1992.

Troeltsch, Ernst. *Die Bedeutung des Protestantismus für die Entstehung der modernen Welt*. Munich: Oldenbourg, 1928. First published in 1911. Translation by W. Montgomery: *Protestantism and Progress: The Significance of Protestantism for the Rise of the Modern World*. Philadelphia: Fortress, 1986.

Vierhaus, Rudolf. "Vom Nutzen und Nachteil des Begriffs 'Frühe Neuzeit.' Fragen und Thesen." In *Frühe Neuzeit—Frühe Moderne? Forschungen zur Vielschichtigkeit von Übergangsprozessen*. Edited by Rudolf Vierhaus. Göttingen, Ger.: Vandenhoeck and Ruprecht, 1992.

Vischer, Friedrich Theodor. *Aesthetik oder Wissenschaft des Schönen*. Hildesheim, Ger.: Olms, 1975. First published in 1848.

NONSENSE

FRENCH	*non-sens, absurdité*
GERMAN	*Unsinn, Sinnlosigkeit*
SPANISH	*disparate, sinsentido*

➤ *ABSURD*, and ENGLISH, INGENIUM, *NEGATION*, PRINCIPLE, PROPOSITION, *SENS COMMUN* [COMMON SENSE, SENSUS COMMUNIS], SENSE, SIGN, SIGNIFIER/SIGNIFIED, SPEECH ACT, TRUTH, *WITTICISM*

Why is it generally difficult to translate "nonsense" as the French expression *non-sens*? Why has it not been possible, until recently, to bring the "positive" dimension of "nonsense" into French or German? To answer these questions we have to examine the development of the expression, particularly in contemporary English, and the gradual explication and even philosophical rehabilitation of nonsense: to determine, so to speak, the different senses of non-sense. For the analytical tradition, it is particularly important to distinguish radical nonsense or the absurd (cf. the German adjective *unsinnig*) from a nonsense that is the absence of meaning or emptiness (cf. Ger. *sinnlos*) and which accordingly raises the question of a (normative) definition of the meaningful. But we can also try to move beyond this distinction, as did, in various ways, Wittgenstein's grammatical philosophy.

I. Natural Conception / Philosophical Conception of "Nonsense"

We can distinguish, following Cora Diamond in her essay "What Nonsense Might Be," two conceptions of nonsense. They are defined superficially by what "nonsense" is opposed to: "good sense" and "sense." The English word "sense" has precisely these two uses (cf. Jane Austen's title, *Sense and Sensibility*, which is rendered in French by *Raison et Sentiments*, but which refers to both sense and the sensible; also recall the adjective "no-nonsense," which means "solidly reasonable"). "Sense" is thus the exact opposite of "nonsense," and the identification of these two conceptions of nonsense in a single expression is no doubt characteristic of English.

Among the British empiricists, notably Hume, nonsense is opposed first of all to reason (in the sense of "good sense," "common sense"); it is associated with the absurd and the ridiculous and sometimes simply with an absence of seriousness. Hume is fond of the expression "talking nonsense," which he occasionally uses in a critical way:

> Does a man of sense run after every silly tale of witches or hobgoblins or fairies, and canvass particularly the evidence? I never knew any one that examined and deliberated about nonsense.

> (*Letters of David Hume*, vol. 1, no. 188)

Or again, in a letter to Strahan:

> Since Nonsense flies with greater Celerity, and makes greater Impression than Reason; though indeed no particular Species of Nonsense is so durable. But the several Forms of Nonsense never cease succeeding one another; and Men are always under the Dominion of some one or other, though nothing was ever equal in Absurdity and Wickedness to our present Patriotism.

> (Ibid., vol. 2, no. 455)

The "natural" sense of nonsense is thus at first sight something like "absurd" or "contradictory." In *Leviathan*, Hobbes identifies absurdity and nonsense: man has not only the privilege of reason, he writes, but also "the privilege of absurdity, to which no living creature is subject, but men only. And of men, those are of all most subject to it that profess philosophy" (chap. 5). But Hobbes also develops an initial, quite elaborate linguistic theory of nonsense. He distinguishes between two types of nonsense in expressions:

> One, when they are new, and yet their meaning not explained by definition; whereof there have been abundance coined by Schoolmen and puzzled philosophers. Another, when men make a name of two names, whose significations are contradictory and inconsistent. . . . For whensoever any affirmation is false, the two names of which it is composed, put together and made one, signifie nothing at all.

> (*Leviathan*, chap. 4, §21–24)

For example, the expressions "round quadrangle" or "incorporeal substance" are meaningless, "meere sound"; here we are dealing with radical nonsense, since Hobbes does not limit himself to saying that the expression refers to no object, that it has no meaning (it is a "senselesse and insignificant word"); it is empty, it signifies nothing.

Here we have a first glimpse of the transition from the natural conception (nonsense = absurdity) to a philosophical or linguistic conception of nonsense, the two conceptions remaining closely linked:

> And therefore if a man should talk to me of a round quadrangle . . . or of free-Will, I should not say he were in an Errour ; but that his words were without meaning; that is to say, Absurd.

> (Ibid., chap. 5, §22)

For Hobbes, nonsense is a capacity of the human species ("the privilege of Absurdity") that is as distinctive as the capacity for laughter (cf. *Leviathan*, chap. 6); we will see that the two are not unrelated.

II. Philosophers and the Natural Conception of Nonsense

The natural conception is developed in Annette Baier's article "Nonsense," which presents six categories:

1. what is obviously false, and "flies in the face of the facts";
2. semantic nonsense, that is, the case in which one doesn't know what one is talking about, in which the utterance is "wildly inapposite";
3. phrases that imply category mistakes; e.g.: "This stone is thinking about Vienna," or this passage from Lewis Carroll: "He thought he saw a Garden-Door / That opened with a key; / he looked again, and found it was / A Double Rule of Three";
4. word sequences that are composed of familiar terms but have an "oddball and unclear syntactical structure." Thus the expression Carnap cites in the classification of nonsense he offers in his famous essay "The Elimination of Metaphysics through Logical Analysis of Language": "Caesar is and";
5. statements that are produced by taking a "respectable" statement and replacing one or more of its words (but not too many) with meaningless words that cannot be translated into the familiar vocabulary, while at the same time retaining a recognizable structure. An example proposed by G. E. Moore: "Scott kept a runcible at Abbotsford"; another, by Carnap, in his *Logical Syntax of Language*: "Piroten karulieren elatisch"; and by Frege, in his *Über die Grundlagen der Geometrie*: "Jedes Anej bazet wenigstens zwei Ellah." We see that these examples of nonsense arouse a certain creativity among philosophers, even those who are the least imaginative. The literary examples of this kind of nonsense are countless: obviously Lewis Carroll, or, in German, Christian Morgenstern (what commentators call "nonsense lyrics" inspired by Mauthner; see Jacques Bouveresse, *Dire et ne rien dire*);
6. "Mere gibberish."

Obviously it is conception 5, which was broadly exploited by Lewis Carroll, that is the most fascinating one from the translator's point of view. The translations of Carroll's "Jabberwocky" no doubt vary more than those of "normal" sentences, but they can be made without difficulty and in accord with well-defined rules, as is shown by the following example:

> All mimsy were the borogoves.
> (Tout flivoreux vaguaient les borogoves.)

> (Parisot)

> (Enmîmés sont les gougebosqueux.)

> (Warrin, in *The Annotated Alice*)

In reality, this category of nonsense illustrates the independence of meaning from syntax, as is shown by Chomsky's ultrafamous example, "Colorless green ideas sleep furiously," which, though nonsensical, can still be translated.

But category 4 is equally central for contemporary philosophical reflection: it is used in the philosophy of language to distinguish two types of nonsense, one radical (category 6), and the other, a syntactical or categorical nonsense, which consists in putting together words that do not go together.

III. The Battle over Philosophical Nonsense

A. The substantial conception of nonsense

Philosophical nonsense is inseparable from the idea of linguistic rules that determine the limits of meaning, of what can be said. Many interpreters think they find such an idea in Wittgenstein's *Tractatus logico-philosophicus*. But this is instead a later conception that can be found, for example, in the work of Rudolf Carnap and Bertrand Russell, and it is radically different from the natural conception. It assumes that we have to mark off nonsense, that is, pseudo-propositions (*Scheinsätze*), from meaning, from what can be said.

In "The Elimination of Metaphysics," Carnap distinguishes two kinds of meaningless pseudo-propositions:

i. those that contain one or more words without meaning;
ii. those that contain only words that have meaning but are arranged in such a way that no meaning emerges from them.

According to Carnap, metaphysical nonsense can sometimes be reduced to nonsense of type (i). But usually a metaphysician knows perfectly well what he means by each of his words, and the critique of metaphysics bears on nonsense of type (ii). Type (i) is pure nonsense; it is literally unintelligible. Type (ii) nonsense is substantial nonsense: we know what each part of the proposition means—the problem is the composite that they form.

> In saying that the so-called statements [*Sätze*] of metaphysics are *meaningless* [*unsinnig*], we intend the word in its strictest sense . . . a sequence of words is meaningless if it does not, within a specified language, constitute a statement. It may happen that such a sequence of words looks like a statement at first glance; in that case, we call it a pseudo-statement.

> ("Elimination of Metaphysics")

For Carnap, logical syntax specifies which combinations of words are acceptable and which are not. The syntax of natural language allows the formation of nonsense (ii), in which there is a "violation of logical syntax." Here we see the emergence of a specific, philosophical conception of nonsense:

> Let us take as examples the following combinations of words:

> 1. "Caesar is and"
> 2. "Caesar is a prime number."

> Since (2) looks like a statement yet is not a statement, does not assert anything, expresses neither a true nor a false proposition, we call this word sequence a "pseudo-statement." . . . This example has been so chosen that the nonsense is easily detectable. Many

so-called statements of metaphysics are not so easily recognized to be pseudo-statements. The fact that natural languages allow the formation of meaningless sequences of words without violating the rules of grammar, indicates that grammatical syntax is, from a logical point of view, inadequate.

> (Ibid.)

The nonsense thus obtained is not due to one or another word's lack of meaning but rather to the meanings themselves that these words have and that fail to combine to "make sense." The rules of ordinary language are different from the rules of logical or philosophical syntax. Thus for Carnap there are "varieties" of nonsense—not only the absurd or radical nonsense but also the logically impossible.

This so-called substantial conception of nonsense, apparently inspired by Wittgenstein and his idea of the "limits of meaning," is in reality profoundly opposed to his conception of nonsense as sense.

B. *Sinnlos/unsinnig*

Frege and Wittgenstein have a conception much closer to the natural one and recognize only one kind of nonsense. This is what is called the austere conception of nonsense, and it can be opposed to Carnap's substantial conception. Wittgenstein's conception, particularly in the evolution from his earlier to his later philosophy, provides interesting perspectives.

The question of nonsense, including the question of the different kinds into which nonsense may be divided, becomes central in the philosophy of language starting with Wittgenstein's *Tractatus* and his use of Frege's definition of sense (see SENSE, V). Nonsense understood as an absence of meaning is at the center of the contemporary conception of logic. Frege identifies sense and thought (*Gedanke*), a thought being a special kind of sense, a propositional sense. The important point for Frege is not to conceive the sense/nonsense distinction on the model of the true/false distinction. There are true or false statements and thoughts: a statement is true (or false) when it expresses a true (or false) thought; but there is no thought without meaning nor a statement that is meaningless because it is supposed to express a meaningless thought. For Frege, there are no logically faulty thoughts: they are not thoughts at all. This idea is picked up by Wittgenstein in the *Tractatus*, where it plays a central role in the definition of nonsense and the illogical: "Thought can never be of anything illogical [*wir können nichts Unlogisches denken*], since, if it were, we should have to think illogically [*unlogisch denken*]" (3.03, trans. Pears and McGuinness).

Let us recall that the *Tractatus*'s goal is to determine the limits of language by the limits of nonsense:

> Die Grenze wird also nur in der Sprache gezogen werden können und was jenseits der Grenze liegt, wird einfach Unsinn sein.

> (It will therefore only be in language that the limit can be drawn, and what lies on the other side of the limit will simply be nonsense.)

> (*Tractatus,* preface, trans. Pears and McGuinness)

Scientific propositions alone are meaningful (*sinnvoll*). Tautologies and contradictions are meaningless (*sinnlos*) because they do not represent a given state of affairs, but they are not nonsense (*Unsinn*) because they are part of language and symbolism.

Tautologie und Kontradiktion sind sinnlos.

(Tautologies and contradictions lack sense.)

(*Tractatus*, 4.461, trans. Pears and McGuinness)

Tautologie und Kontradiktion sind aber nicht unsinnig.

(Tautologies and contradictions are not, however, nonsensical.)

(Ibid., 4.4611)

Metaphysical propositions, however, are radically nonsensical (*unsinnig*):

Die meisten Sätze und Fragen, welche über philosophische Dinge geschrieben worden sind, sind nicht falsch, sondern unsinnig. Wir können daher Fragen dieser Art überhaupt nicht beantworten, sonder nur ihre Unsinnigkeit feststellen.

(Most propositions and questions, that have been written about philosophical matters, are not false, but senseless. We cannot, therefore, answer questions of this kind at all, but only state their senselessness.)

(*Tractatus*, 4.003, trans. Ogden and Ramsey)

As is shown by the enigmatic passage that (almost) concludes the *Tractatus*, it is of the utmost importance to understand that these propositions are not nonsensical, which does not mean that we must understand them: precisely, it is radically impossible to understand them. This is Wittgenstein's text:

Meine Sätze erläutern dadurch, dass sie der, welcher mich versteht, am Ende als unsinnig erkennt, wenn er durch sie—auf ihnen—über sie hinausgestiegen ist. (Er muss sozusagen die Leiter wegwerfen, nachdem er auf ihr hinaufgestiegen ist.)
Er muss diese Sätze überwinden, dann sieht er die Welt richtig.

(Ibid., 6.54)

Here is the Ogden and Ramsey translation into English:

My propositions are elucidatory in this way: he who understands me finally recognizes them as senseless [*unsinnig*], when he has climbed out through them, on them, over them. (He must so to speak throw away the ladder, after he has climbed on it.)
He must surmount these propositions; then he sees the world rightly.

Compare Pears and McGuinness:

My propositions serve as elucidations in the following way: anyone who understands me eventually recognizes them as nonsensical, when he has used them—as

steps—to climb up beyond them. (He must, so to speak, throw away the ladder after he has climbed up it.)
He must transcend these propositions, then he will see the world aright.

For Wittgenstein, then, surmounting these propositions means recognizing them to be metaphysical and without meaning (*unsinnig*). Whence the temptation that long guided the reading of Wittgenstein's work: it was thought that there was a kind of understanding of nonsense that showed itself instead of saying itself and that metaphysics had its paradoxical place in this "showing." We cannot ignore the deliberately Kantian side of the *Tractatus*'s project. The goal is to set a limit (*Grenze*) to thought, in a project similar to that of a critique of pure reason: a resumption of the Kantian project (drawing a line of demarcation between science and nonscience), expressed here in terms of nonsense: setting the limits of sense (see Strawson's book on Kant's first critique, *The Bounds of Sense*) by delimiting the domain of what can be said. But such an approach falls far short of Wittgenstein's project and his conception of nonsense, as the preface to the *Tractatus* shows:

[T]he aim of the book is to draw a limit to thought, or rather—not to thought, but to the expression of thought: for in order to be able to draw a limit to thought, we should have to find both sides of the limit thinkable (i.e. we should have to be able to think what cannot be thought).
It will therefore only be in language that the limit can be drawn, and what lies on the other side of the limit will simply be nonsense.

(Trans. Pears and McGuinness)

One cannot set a limit to thinking because in order to do so, one would have to specify what cannot be thought, nonsense, and thus grasp it in some way in thought. But there can be no statements regarding what one cannot speak about, not even meaningless statements that might mean something if they had sense. Hence the limit will be set "within" language (that this can be done is what the book is going to show). Once this limit has been set, what remains beyond directly intelligible statements (beyond scientific propositions) will be pure nonsense. This means that Wittgenstein excludes precisely the idea that certain statements are nonsense but might nonetheless indicate something that cannot be said. There is therefore only one kind of *unsinnig* nonsense: it is the "austere" conception of nonsense.

What is the source of nonsense? Wittgenstein warns us against "the most fundamental confusions of which the whole of philosophy is full" (3.324). The philosopher often allows himself to be hypnotized by the existence of a single sign (*Zeichen*) for two objects. But the fact of sharing a sign cannot be considered characteristic of the objects themselves (3.322). What matters is not the sign itself, but rather that of which the sign is the perceptible side (3.32), namely, the "symbol" (*Symbol*), which determines the meaning of the proposition (3.31). Then how can the possibility of access to the symbol be conceived? Wittgenstein's response is very important and constitutes the connection between his earlier and his later philosophies: "In order to recognize the symbol in the [am] sign we must consider the significant use [*sinvoller Gebrauch*]" (3.326).

This "significant use" is the only experience we have of meaning, and it is the criterion of what is and what is not nonsense. Thus, as early as the *Tractatus*, the borderline between sense and nonsense is determined by neither the "empirical content" of logical positivism nor a kind of transcendent authority that is supposed to set the limit of thought: it is determined by usage. In reality, the theory of usage that characterizes all of Wittgenstein's later philosophy is already present in the theory of nonsense in the *Tractatus*. An expression without meaning is an expression to which I, myself, do not give meaning.

Thus Wittgenstein explains "the correct method in philosophy":

> The correct method in philosophy would really be the following: to say nothing except what can be said, i.e. propositions of natural science—i.e. something that has nothing to do with philosophy—and then, whenever someone else wanted to say something metaphysical, to demonstrate to him that he had failed to give a meaning to certain signs in his propositions.
>
> (*Tractatus*, 6.53, trans. Pears and McGuinness)

A statement without meaning is not a particular kind of statement: it is a symbol that has the general form of a proposition and that has no meaning because we have not given it one. This reduces the distinctions between *sinnlos/bedeutungslos/unsinnig*—which is nonetheless philosophically central. Here is Wittgenstein again: "Wird ein Zeichen *nicht gebraucht*, so ist es bedeutungslos. Das ist der Sinn der Devise Occams" (3.328). The standard French translation of this proposition, by Pierre Klossowski, renders *nicht gebraucht* as *ne pas utilisé* (not used). Etienne Balibar's unpublished, much more careful translation has instead: "Un signe dont on n'a *pas l'usage*, n'a pas de signification non plus" (A sign whose usage one does not have or know, also has no meaning). Ogden and Ramsey translate Wittgenstein's proposition this way: "If a sign is *not necessary* then it is meaningless. That is the meaning of Occam's razor." And Pears and McGuinness: "If a sign is useless, it is meaningless. That is the point of Occam's maxim." In translation, the range of senses covered by "Wird ein Zeichen nicht gebraucht," extraordinarily, runs from "not used" to "use not known" to "not necessary" to "useless."

We come back once again—both in Wittgenstein's argument, and in our understanding of the different ways in which the *Tractatus* has been translated—to meaningful use (*sinnvoller Gebrauch*). But usage is not prescribed by anything other than usage itself. "We cannot give a sign the wrong sense" (5.4732, trans. Pears and McGuinness).

No sense can be illegitimate (*unrecht*) once it is given, that is, as soon as we give sense to this or that sign. As for metaphysical nonsense, when the sign ceases to be used in conformity with its habitual usage, that does not mean that what has been said has defined a new use for it. It is in this absence of definition, not in the sense of a formal definition but in the sense of a factual absence of giving meaning, that nonsense arises.

That, as we have seen, is what *Tractatus* 6.53 (trans. Ogden and Ramsey) underscores: "[W]hen someone else wished to say something metaphysical, to demonstrate to him that he has given no meaning to certain signs in his propositions."

Nonsense as such then produces an elucidation: the person who understands the author of the *Tractatus* understands that his propositions are nonsense, and it is in understanding this that he is illuminated.

> Meine Sätze erläutern dadurch, dass sie der, welcher mich versteht, am Ende als unsinnig erkennt.... Er muss diese Sätze überwinden.
>
> (My propositions are elucidatory in this way: he who understands me finally recognizes them as senseless.... He must surmount these propositions.)
>
> (Ibid., 6.54)

We must note here a slight strangeness in expression: we always think we remember this conclusion of Wittgenstein's as "the person who understands these propositions understands that they are nonsense." But what Wittgenstein wrote in a last-minute evasion is "he who understands *me*" (*welcher mich versteht*) (our emphasis). He thus chooses to draw attention to the difference between understanding someone and understanding what he says. It is a matter not only of understanding that Wittgenstein's propositions are nonsense, but also of abandoning the idea of understanding them "*qua* nonsense." The elucidation provided by this nonsense is the comprehension of their author—Wittgenstein.

C. Nonsense and language games

In the *Philosophical Investigations*, Wittgenstein develops his conception of nonsense by concerning himself with another kind of nonsense that is connected with the fitting (*treffend*) character of an utterance in its context. It is important to situate this conception, as Diamond does, in relation to the earlier one. Wittgenstein's later philosophy seeks to define "nonsense" by the absence of a "language game" (*Sprachspiel*) in which the expression can be used. "Nonsense" is thus defined once again but in a new sense, by usage.

> When a statement is called senseless [*ein Satz ... sinnlos*], it is not as it were its sense that is senseless [*so ist nicht sein Sinn sinnlos*]. But a combination of words is being excluded from the language, withdrawn from circulation.
>
> (*Philosophical Investigations*, §500)

Or in a 1935 lecture (in English):

> Though it is nonsense to say "I feel his pain," this is different from inserting into an English sentence a meaningless word, say "abracadabra," and from saying a string of nonsense words.
>
> (*Wittgenstein's Lectures*)

And thus we are tempted to see an evolution in Wittgenstein toward a more pragmatic conception of nonsense, defined no longer by rules of logic, but by rules of usage. In reality—and that is what is shown by the predominance and centrality of the idea of nonsense in his later philosophy as well—an expression that is misused, and hence is excluded from language, is nonsense; it is not a sense used in a way that is wrong, absurd, or inadequate. That is what some commentators (like Charles Travis in *The Uses of Sense*) define in the later Wittgenstein as sensitivity to significance in usage (S-use sensitivity): the meaning of a word is also defined by its later and possible uses. For Wittgenstein, whether in his early or his later philosophy, there is no intermediary between sense and nonsense, even if there are diverse kinds of nonsense, just as there are diverse kinds of meanings or ways of meaning.

IV. "Nonsense," *Witz*, Philosophical Grammar, and Ordinary Language

Up to this point, we have examined nonsense in its "logical" and grammatical sense; it remains to consider poetic and comic nonsense, which we have already touched upon in relation to Lewis Carroll. How can we define the comic quality of nonsense? Specialists in nonsense as a literary genre generally resist the tendency to identify nonsense with an absence of sense: nonsense is instead the absence of a certain sense, for example, common sense or reason, that is subverted in nonsense.

In this context we can distinguish, following Wittgenstein, three uses of the notion of sense: (1) the primary notion of sense; (2) the notion of a secondary sense, proposed by Wittgenstein in §11 of the second part of the *Philosophical Investigations* (e.g., the use of "fat" or "yellow" in the statements "Wednesday is fat" and "the vowel 'e' is yellow") and derived from the primary sense; (3) the complex of *Sinnerlebnisse* or *Bedeutungserlebnisse* (experiences of meaning, which are central in the later Wittgenstein) that accompany use and that, despite their name, are seen as nonlinguistic experiences. However, *Bedeutungserlebnisse* do not play a major role in the definition of poetic or comic nonsense. Thus we can define poetic or comic nonsense in the framework of a sensitivity to meaning and of a lived experience of meaning ("*das Erleben der Bedeutung*," that must be distinguished from *Bedeutungserlebnisse*) (see ERLEBEN)—which Wittgenstein has in mind in speaking of someone who is "meaning-blind," incapable of feeling (appreciating) the humor of jokes. "If you didn't *experience* the meaning of words, then how could you laugh at puns [*Wortwitze*]?" (*Letzte Schriften*, vol. 1, §711).

The meaning-blind person (*Bedeutungsblind*; cf. *Remarks* [*Bemerkungen*], vol. 1, §202) is indeed blind to nonsense—in any case to the specific type of nonsense that we find in poetry and humor and that thus has more to do with meaning than is commonly thought.

Wittgenstein remarks that "even a nonsense-poem [*ein Unsinn-Gedicht*] is not nonsense in the same way as the babbling of a child" (*Philosophical Investigations*, §282; Klossowski translates *Unsinn-Gedicht* into French as "un poème de 'non-sens'").

Wittgenstein compares three statements—"a newborn child has no teeth," "a goose has no teeth," and "a rose has no teeth"—and notes that even if the last seems truer or more certain that the other two, it seems less meaningful. However, there is always a way to give it meaning by imagining adequate conditions of use (*Philosophical Investigations*). In Wittgenstein's later philosophy, there are no inherently meaningless expressions or ones to which we cannot give meaning, only expressions to which we do not want to give meaning: we can give them one, someday, and include them in a language game. Every combination of words can, if we wish, be "put into circulation." From this point of view, Wittgenstein's later philosophy no longer has anything to do with a normativism of meaning and opens the way toward a positivity of nonsense.

The new attention Wittgenstein gives to the ordinary facts of grammar and language makes him particularly sensitive to nonsense, to *Witz* and wordplay, and to their meaning. He notes: "Aptitude for philosophy resides in the ability to receive a strong and lasting impression from a fact of grammar" (*Big Typescript*).

This aptitude also determines the capacity for humor, and more particularly for wit, because it draws our attention to curious properties of language. Wittgenstein cites Lichtenberg in this connection and takes an interest in how we understand Lewis Carroll's poems.

> Let us consider the witty meaning [*witzige Bedeutung*] that we give to Carroll's grammatical games. I could ask: why do I think a grammatical word-play [*Witz*] is profound in a certain sense? (And this is naturally philosophical profundity.)
>
> (*Wiener Ausgabe*, vol. 3, quoted in Bouveresse, *Dire et ne rien dire*)

Wittgenstein discerns the proximity between *Witz* and philosophy in their common ability to appreciate, as it were, the salt of language. He is supposed to have once said that one could imagine a philosophical work consisting entirely of jokes (without, for all that, being facetious). The *Witz* is another, more amusing way of "knocking one's head against the barrier of language"—a task that defines philosophy. This is how Jacques Bouveresse puts it:

> A philosophical proposition and a grammatical *Witz* both have a direct relation to the question of the limits of meaning, and seem to be opposed to each other a little as the pleasure of nonsense is to what might be called by contrast the pain, impotence, and frustration of nonsense. It has been said that the witticism, as analyzed by Freud, could be considered a successful lapsus. Wittgenstein sometimes seems to suggest that a philosophical proposition might resemble an involuntary witticism.

How can *Witz* draw our attention to language and yet have a profundity of the same kind as that of grammar itself? It is because it is characterized precisely by the impossibility of determining what constitutes the comic—the container or the content, thought or language:

> We receive from joking remarks a total impression in which we are unable to separate the share taken by the thought-content from the share taken by the joke-work. . . . We do not know what pleases us and what we are laughing about.
>
> (Freud, *Jokes*, 8:94)

The Freudian theory of wit maintains that the joke, which begins as simple play, is rapidly put into the service of the inclinations and drives of psychic life that have to overcome obstacles and inhibitions to express themselves. It is clear that this has something in common with philosophy, particularly when it becomes grammatical and shows the inseparability of thought and language. This transition to grammar is inseparable from a certain nonsense or even buffoonery: we find with pleasure in Wittgenstein efforts to transgress the rules of the grammar of language in the broad sense (of its usages), which draw our attention precisely to these rules. "Why can't a dog simulate pain? Is he too honest?" (*Philosophical Investigations*, §250). Another example Wittgenstein gives is that of someone who writes at the top of an official document: "Place: here. Date: now." Here again this attention to nonsense and the equivocal may remind us of Freud. Freud observes that "Jokes do not, like dreams, create compromises; they do not evade the inhibition, but they insist on maintaining play with words or with nonsense unaltered," presenting it as meaningful. "Nothing," he continues,

> distinguishes jokes more clearly from all other psychical structures than this double-sidedness and this duplicity in speech. From this point of view at least the authorities come closest to an understanding of the nature of jokes when they lay stress on "sense in nonsense [*Sinn im Unsinn*]."
>
> (Freud, *Jokes*)

For Freud the "joke-work" (*Witzwerk*) consists precisely in finding sense in nonsense and thus in giving a meaning, not discovering it. Freud defines *Witz* as "sense in nonsense" (see SIGNIFIER/SIGNIFIED and INGENIUM, Box 3). Superficial nonsense is used in the *Witz* to express a thought that is important but that one does not necessarily want to, or cannot, approach. The *Witz* is thus never radical nonsense (*Unsinn* as defined above). An explicit contradiction or obvious falsity cannot constitute a witticism: "The scandal begins when the police put an end to it" (Kraus); or, to take a recent example, "In the interest of our relationship, let's not have one" (*Ally McBeal*). In taking an interest in the traps set by language, and also in its profoundly and naturally ordinary character, Wittgenstein's philosophy (and later Austin's, which is fertile in wit and nonsense) specified an essential relationship that *Witz* maintains with philosophical grammar: that is, their ability to express both a problem and its solution as already present before our eyes: we simply hadn't looked or listened carefully enough to recognize them.

Sandra Laugier

BIBLIOGRAPHY

Baier, Annette. "Nonsense." In vol. 5 of *The Encyclopedia of Philosophy*, edited by Paul Edwards. New York: Macmillan, 1967.

Bouveresse, Jacques. *Dire et ne rien dire: L'illogisme, l'impossibilité et le non-sens*. Nîmes, Fr.: Chambon, 1997.

Carnap, Rudolph. "Die Überwindung der Metaphysik durch logische Analyse der Sprache." *Erkenntnis* 2 (1932): 219–41. Translation by Arthur Pap: "The Elimination of Metaphysics through Logical Analysis of Language." In *Logical Positivism*, edited by A. J. Ayer, 60–81. Glencoe, IL: Free Press, 1959.

Carroll, Lewis. *Alice's Adventures in Wonderland*. Edited by Selwyn H. Goodacre. Berkeley: University of California Press, 1982.

——. *The Annotated Alice (Alice's Adventures in Wonderland and Through the Looking-Glass)*. Introduction and notes by Martin Gardner. New York: Meridian Press, New American Library, 1960.

——. *The Hunting of the Snark: An Agony, In Eight Fits*. Edited by Barry Moser. Berkeley: University of California Press, 1983.

——. *Œuvres*. Translated by Henri Parisot. Paris: Gallimard / La Pléiade, 1990.

——. *Through the Looking-Glass and What Alice Found There*. Edited by Selwyn H. Goodacre. Berkeley: University of California Press, 1983.

Cheung, Leo K. C. "The Disenchantment of Nonsense: Understanding Wittgenstein's *Tractatus*." *Philosophical Investigations* 31, no. 3 (2008): 197–226.

Deleuze, Gilles. *Logique du sens*. Paris: Minuit, 1969. Translation by Mark Lester with Charles Stivale: *The Logic of Sense*. Edited by Constantin V. Boundas. New York: Columbia University Press, 1990.

Diamond, Cora. "Throwing Away the Ladder." In *The Realistic Spirit: Wittgenstein, Philosophy, and the Mind*. Cambridge, MA: MIT Press, 1991.

——. "What Nonsense Might Be?" In *The Realistic Spirit: Wittgenstein, Philosophy, and the Mind*. Cambridge, MA: MIT Press, 1991.

Frege, Gottlob. *The Frege Reader*. Edited by Michael Beaney. Oxford: Blackwell, 1997.

Freud, Sigmund. *Der Witz und seine Beziehung zum Unbewussten. Studienausgabe*, vol. 4. Frankfurt: Fischer, 1970. Translation by James Strachey: *Jokes and Their Relation to the Unconscious*. In vol. 8 of *The Standard Edition of the Complete Psychological Works of Sigmund Freud*, edited by James Strachey. London: Hogarth, 1953–74.

Hobbes, Thomas. *Leviathan: Authoritative Text, Backgrounds, Interpretations*. Edited by Richard E. Flathman and David Johnston. New York: W. W. Norton, 1997.

Hume, David. *The Letters of David Hume*. Edited by J.Y.T. Grieg. Oxford: Clarendon, 1932.

Leijenhorst, Cees. "Sense and Nonsense about Sense: Hobbes and the Aristotelians on Sense Perception and Imagination." In *The Cambridge Companion to Hobbes's "Leviathan,"* edited by Patricia Springborg, 82–108. Cambridge: Cambridge University Press, 2007.

Mulhall, Stephen. *Wittgenstein's Private Language: Grammar, Nonsense, and Imagination in "Philosophical Investigations," Sections 243–315*. Oxford: Clarendon, 2007.

Schulte, Joachim. *Wittgenstein: Eine Einführung*. Stuttgart: Reclam, 1989. Translation by William H. Brenner and John F. Holley: *Wittgenstein: An Introduction*. Albany: SUNY Press, 1992.

Strawson, Peter. *The Bounds of Sense: An Essay on Kant's "Critique of Pure Reason."* London: Routledge, 2002.

Travis, Charles. *The Uses of Sense*. Oxford: Clarendon, 1989.

Wittgenstein, Ludwig. *Letzte Schriften über die Philosophie der Psychologie / Last Writings on the Philosophy of Psychology*. Translated by C. G. Luckhardt and Maximilian A. E. Aue, edited by G. H. von Wright and H. Nyman. 2 vols. Oxford: Blackwell, 1992.

——. *Logisch-philosophische Abhandlung = Tractatus logico-philosophicus: Kritische Edition*. Edited by Brian McGuinness and Joachim Schulte. Frankfurt: Suhrkamp, 1989. Translation by C. K. Ogden and F. P. Ramsey: *Tractatus logico-philosophicus*. London: Routledge and Kegan Paul, 1922. Translation by D. F. Pears and B. McGuinness: *Tractatus logico-philosophicus*. London: Routledge, 1974. First published in 1961. Translation by Pierre Klossowski: *Tractatus logico-philosophicus, suivi de Investigations philosophiques*. Paris: Gallimard, 1961.

——. *Philosophical Investigations*. Translated by G.E.M. Anscombe. 3rd ed. New York: Macmillan, 1968.

——. "Philosophy." In *The Big Typescript, TS 213*, edited and translated by C. Grant Luckhardt and Maximilian A.E. Aue, §86–93. Malden MA: Blackwell, 2005.

——. *Remarks on the Philosophy of Psychology: Bemerkungen über die Philosophie der Psychologie*. Edited by G.E.M. Anscombe, G. H. von Wright, and H. Nyman. Chicago: University of Chicago Press / Oxford: Blackwell, 1980. Vol. 1, translated by G.E.M. Anscombe, edited by G.E.M. Anscombe and G. H. von Wright. Vol. 2, translated by C. G. Luckhardt and Maximilian A. E. Aue, edited by G. H. von Wright and H. Nyman.

——. *Wiener Ausgabe*. Edited by Michael Nedo. 8 vols. Vienna: Springer, 1993–.

——. *Wittgenstein's Lectures (1932–1935)*. Edited by A. Ambrose. Oxford: Blackwell, 1979.

NOSTALGIA

A certain number of terms that serve to designate uneasiness or malaise, experienced as characteristic of a culture or a national genius, find an equivalent in the word "nostalgia": *nostalgie* (Fr.), *saudade* (Port.), *dor* (Rom.), and *Sehnsucht* (Ger.). The component of quest and exile, including existential exile outside oneself, displacement in all senses of the word, is in fact predominant in the term "nostalgia," whether it is linked to solitude (*saudade*), to the suffering connected with an impossible desire (*dor*), or to an aspiration to something entirely different (*Sehnsucht*). See DOR, SAUDADE, SEHNSUCHT, and, more broadly, *MALAISE* (ACEDIA, ANXIETY, MELANCHOLY).

On the Greek model of nostalgia as "suffering of, or for, the return," see SEHNSUCHT, Box 1.

➤ HEIMAT, PORTUGUESE, STIMMUNG, STRADANIE

NOTHING, NOTHINGNESS

The expressions designating what does not exist are constructed in different ways, both within a single language and from one language to another. French, for example, immediately sets in competition a positive term and a negative term. The positive term, *rien*, derives from Latin *rem*, the accusative of *res*, *rei*, which originally designated a good, property, or personal effect (see RES and *THING*). The negative term, *néant*, also derives from Latin, but it is composed of a negative particle (*nec*, *ne*) applied, depending on the hypothesis, to the positive *entem* (the accusative of *ens*, "not a being") or to the positive *gentem* (the accusative of *gens*, "not a living being").

I. Positive Nouns / Negative Nouns

1. The main positive nouns designating what does not exist are, in addition to the Iberian *nada*—derived from Latin (*res*) *nata*, the past participle of *nasci*, meaning "to be born" (see PORTUGUESE and cf. SPANISH)—the French words *rien* and *personne*. The positive use of the feminine noun *une rien* has been gradually replaced by the nominalization of the pronoun and the adverb that commonly serve as negative auxiliaries, *rien*, *un rien*: "The word offers a short version of the evolution of the etymological meaning of *chose* inverted as *néant* (c.1530)" (RT:*DHLF*), which did not fail to have a philosophical impact: see RES; cf. REALITY, *TO BE*, VORHANDEN. In an analogous way, *personne*, formed on the basis of the positive *persona*, or the actor's mask (which is certainly not an anodyne entity), designates any given human being a "person," and, in correlation with *ne*, acquires the negative value of "no one": see PERSON. Consult MÊTIS, Box 1, "Odysseus: My name is No-One," for an example of a pun on *personne* that implies both the difference, which is fundamental in Greek, between negation and privation (*ou/mê*), and the connection in French between the expression of negation and the so-called *ne explétif*; on the latter, see ESTI, Box 4.
2. The majority of the terms designating what does not exist are composed of a negation bearing on a positive term that does not, moreover, designate the same thing, depending on the languages concerned (Gr. *ouden/mêden*, Lat. *nihil*, Fr. *néant*, Ger. *Nichts*, Eng. "nothing"; cf. Gr. *outis/mêtis*, "not someone," Lat. *nemo*, "not a man," Eng. "nobody," and so forth). Thus in Greek it is *hen*, "one," that is negated (see MÊTIS, Box 1); in Latin it is supposed to be the *hilum*, a minuscule black dot at the end of a broad bean (*ni-hil*; RT: *Dictionnaire étymologique de la langue latine* citing Festus); in German, it may be a *Wiht* (little demon), unless it is *Wicht*, from *Wesen* (essence) (cf. ESSENCE); in English, it is "thing."
3. Further reflection takes into consideration the degree of freedom in certain languages that construct, by means of an erroneous division, a new positive on the basis of the negative compound: that is what happens in Democritus's Greek (68 B 56 DK [see RT: DK]), which proposes *den* (a false division of *ouden*, which is normally divided into *oude-hen*, "not even one"), an amalgam of the last letter of the negative particle and the negated positive. German can render Democritus's *den* in a similar way, reactivating a term used by the Rheinland mystics, *das Ichts* ("Das Ichts existiert um nicht mehr als das Nichts," RT: DK translation of Democritus's fragment whose French equivalent would be "Le *éant* n'existe pas plus que le néant"). See ESTI, IV.B.

II. Derivations and the Combinatory System

We find here and there a certain number of remarkable disparities that give rise to major translation problems.

1. In some languages and in some cases, a term (noun, adjective, or verb) may be negated in several ways that stipulate different modes of nonexistence and refer to different paraphrases: this is the case in particular for the difference between negation and privation, which is fundamental in Greek, for example (*ouden*, *mêden*; see ESTI, II, IV.A, and MÊTIS, Box 1), and the different ways of indicating presence and the possession implied by privation (absence of something, through lack ["a-logical"], defect ["il-logical"], exteriority ["de-mentia"], extenuation, and so forth). On the way in which a negative or privative term is formed by means of a particle or a prefix, see—in addition to ESTI, and COMBINATION AND CONCEPTUALIZATION—GERMAN and the study of the *Lust-Unlust* pair under PLEASURE, II.C. See also TRUTH (particularly for the Greek *alêtheia*, which Heidegger renders by *Unverborgenheit*), UNCONSCIOUS, and cf. MADNESS.
2. The rules of derivation, combination, and syntax related to negative terms produce texts that are characteristic of certain languages and particularly difficult to translate into other languages; this is the case, for example, of the German derivation that moves from the adverb *nicht* to the substantive *Nichts*. Regarding this set of problems, particularly illuminating examples will be found under ESTI. See also PORTUGUESE, and cf. ANXIETY, AUFHEBUNG, PRINCIPLE.

See also *NEGATION* and, in particular, VERNEINUNG.

➤ *FALSE*, NONSENSE

OBJECT, OBJECTIVE BEING

FRENCH   *objet, être objectif*
GERMAN   *Objekt*
GREEK   *antikeimenon* [ἀντικείμενον]
LATIN   *obiici, obiectum; esse obiective*

➤ ERSCHEINUNG, ES GIBT, GEGENSTAND, INTENTION, PERCEPTION, *PHÉNOMÈNE*, REALITY, REPRÉSENTATION, SEIN, SUBJECT, TATSACHE, *THING*, *TO BE*, TRUTH, VORHANDEN

The word "object," like the concept to which it refers, has not always existed. But we constantly project it into texts to which it is alien.

I. The *Antikeimenon*, or Thought without Object

Must it not be admitted that even if the word is lacking, the concept of object is as old as philosophy itself? In reality, Plato and Aristotle did not fail to analyze the faculties' relationship to their terminus, but they did not have an independent word for doing so. Whereas it is absent in the original Greek, translators introduce it—projecting onto ancient authors, through a retrospective illusion, our Latin vocabulary inherited from medieval philosophy.

When Plato speaks of the faculties and of "that to which they are related," he always uses a clumsy paraphrase. Of course, he mentions the relationship between a capacity for knowledge or desiring and the order of the things that this capacity knows or desires. But he describes them only by manipulating syntax: thirst will never be the desire for "anything other than that of which it is its nature to be, mere drink" (*Republic* 4.437e, trans. Shorey; Chambry renders this in French as "elle ne saurait être le désir d'autre chose que de son *objet* naturel" [emphasis supplied]).

Plato (or rather Socrates's interlocutor Glaucon) goes on: "Each desire in itself is of that thing only of which it is its nature to be [the desire]" (ibid.; Chambry renders this as "chaque désir pris en lui-même ne convoite que son *objet* naturel pris en lui-même" [emphasis supplied]). Similarly, "Science, which is just that, is of knowledge which is just that, or is of whatsoever we must assume the correlate of science to be" (ibid., 4.438c; Chambry translates this as "ou de l'objet, quel qu'il soit, qu'il faut assigner à la science" [emphasis supplied]). To distinguish a faculty, Socrates says, "I look to one thing only—that to which it is related [*eph' hôi*] and what it effects" (5.477d; Chambry: "je ne considère que son objet et ses effets"). Here we see how flexible the Platonic connection is, limiting itself to a relative pronoun, and how plodding and awkward a literal translation seems; how much clearer and necessary appears the projection of the term "object" so as to explain the sense of Plato's text. It remains that this kind of translation introduces into Plato a concept that has no semantic foundation. On the contrary, for Plato, the corresponding terms always come "in pairs of twins" (*Theatetus*

156b1). The powers of the soul and that of which they are the powers are correlative; but in this correlation, what Plato calls a "power" (*dunamis* [δύναμις]) has no terminological correlate in the order of things. What our translations call the "object"—anachronistically, but in accord with an interpretation almost inevitable for a modern mind—remains anonymous in Plato. Aristotle, who was more inclined to classify, regroups the powers and what they take as their themes in a larger category, that of opposites. The powers (*dunameis*) are distinguished according to their specific activities, and the activities, in turn, according to their opposites (*antikeimena*): "And by opposites, I mean food, what is perceptible, or the intelligible" (*De anima* 2.4, 415a20). Although the operations are primary, "we might inquire whether the search for their opposites [*antikeimena*] ought not to precede them, for example, the sensible before the sensitive faculty, and the intelligible before the intellect" (ibid., 1.1, 402b15; the 1982 edition of Tricot's French translation adds a note: "The word *antikeimena* thus signifies here the objects of sensation and intelligence"). *Antikeimenon* is given first a local meaning, that of "opposite," as is shown in Aristotle's *De caelo*, where it designates the lowest place and the highest place, situated at the two extremes of an imaginary axis connecting them: "Fire and earth move not to infinity but to opposite points [*antikeimena*]" (*De caelo* 1.8, 277a23; cf. 2.2, 284b22; see Bonitz's remarks in his *Index Aristotelicus* of 1870, 64a18). Each faculty is distinguished from another by its particular operations, since the activity precedes the power and constitutes its specificity: "The activity of the sensible object and that of the percipient sense is one and the same activity" (*De anima* 3.2, 425b25). But beforehand, each activity is determined by its reference to its opposite, that is, by the type of specificity that affects each of the faculties of the mind: they are *opposita*, as James of Venice correctly rendered the term (ca. 1130).

Shall we say, then, that Aristotle has found a name for what remains unnamed in Plato? Should we interpret *antikeimenon* as signifying the opposition of the object with regard to the power? Here there is a retrospective illusion to which we could easily succumb. But Aristotle's thought does not prefigure the medieval and modern concept of the object, as if the generality of his language held the rest of history in its secret folds and paved the way for later distinctions, or as if later interpreters succeeded in arriving at the truth of a meaning that was latent but already secretly present, and of which they are the heirs.

In the first place, Aristotle does not absorb the Platonic expression into a more precise vocabulary; he limits himself to situating the relationship of correlation observed by Plato in a still more general classificatory concept. The *antikeimenon* is a very broad class of correlates that are only a particular case: "The term 'opposite' is applied to contradictories, and to contraries, and to relative terms, and to privation and possession, and to the extremes from which and into which generation and dissolution take place" (*Metaphysics* Δ.10, 1018a20–21). And the correlate is itself a genus whose species include the relation of "the measurable to the measure, and the knowable to knowledge, and the perceptible to perception" (ibid., Δ.15, 1020b31–32). Far from containing in embryonic form the distinctions with which the concept of *obiectum* is charged, the Aristotelian notion of *antikeimenon* merely allows a regrouping: it places the cognitive correlation in a hierarchy of more general terms.

Moreover, a correlative relation is symmetrical: it can be reversed, and knowledge can thus become in turn the opposite of the knowable (*Categories* 10.11b29–30; cf. 7.6b34–36). The medieval and modern concept of object is asymmetrical: one would never say that knowledge is "the object of the known." The sense of "opposite" is thus far broader than that of the later term "object": opposition signifies a general, reciprocal relationship that is larger than the particular case of the powers of the mind and of their theme; it therefore does not define the status of the term in question by the faculty. What a power knows is first of all the thing itself, not an object defined by its pure correspondence with the faculty. The faculty is determined by the being, and it is not the object that defines the faculty (*Metaphysics* Δ.15, 1021a26–b3; I.6, 1057a7–12).

II. *Obiectum,* or the Obstacle before the Eyes

The word "object" designates the act of something presenting itself as opposite or standing over against, the Latin *obiici.* Here again, should we say that the word that designates it, and thus the concept that accompanies it, is already present in Latin antiquity?

Classical Latin already has the past participle of *obiicio,* "to throw or place before, to be opposite, to set against"; and Tacitus, in *Germania,* refers to women in combat "using their breasts as shields [*obiectu pectorum*]" (8.1). Latin also uses the masculine substantive *obiectus,* which is derived from *obiicio,* to refer to "what is set before" or what "stands before" (an *obstant*), an "obstacle," a "spectacle," and more precisely, an "apparition," a "phenomenon." But the invention of the neuter noun *obiectum* corresponds to a new conceptual requirement.

This requirement proceeds first of all from the theory of perception, when it implies an activity of the powers of the mind. For Augustine, who adopts the Platonic theory of vision, the latter is engendered by the encounter between the look, which emanates from our eyes, and color, which emanates from the thing. Our eye emits a ray "by which we touch everything that we see. . . . If you want to see further, and some body interposes itself [*interponatur*], the ray collides with the body set in front of it [*corpus obiectum*] and it cannot pass beyond it toward what you want to see. . . . You want to see a column, a man stands in the middle of your field of view, your look is blocked" (Augustine, *Sermo* 267, 10.10; RT: *PL* 38, col. 1262). Here the *obiectus* is the *obstant,* the body interposed between the eye and the thing to be seen, the obstacle that puts the terminus of my movement, the theme pursued by my operation, out of reach. The *obiectus* hinders the activity of sight; it is not the latter's objective. The past participle *obiectum* does not designate the thing looked at,

but that which, thrown before the eyes, breaks the axis of the look, violates the transparency of its seeing.

By a paradoxical consequence of this active theory of vision, however, its terminus is always an obstacle that limits by its shadow the ray of pure light emitted by the eye; and reciprocally, the obstacle is an *obiectum.* Thus Pseudo-Grosseteste, commenting on this passage in Augustine around 1230, substantializes the past participle: "The mental ray that comes out of the eye is not affected by the external object [*non immutatur ab obiecto extra*]" (Baur, *Die Philosophischen Werke des Robert Grosseteste,* 255.15–19). Here it is no longer an adjective designating a quality but very probably a neuter and a subsistent term. Contraposition is no longer an accident of perception, its inevitable reverse; instead, it indicates a positive property of the visible.

The concept of object is constructed when the term *obiectum* combines two determinations: the older meaning of interposition, and the new one, in conformity with the Aristotelian problematics, of the terminus to which a power is relative. The use of the term is solidified and determined in Pseudo-Grosseteste:

> But it is further added that, whether for natural appetite, or for the deliberative faculty, there exist different objects and different motors. Thus there also exist different acts and different powers.
>
> (Pseudo-Grosseteste, in Baur, ibid., 264.42–44)

Even if Pseudo-Grosseteste is the only writer to produce the concept of object in its nascent state, in presenting his sources (Augustinian and Aristotelian), we cannot exclude the possibility that it is a tool that was forged in the Faculty of Arts and anonymously spread by it (several attestations between 1225 and 1230 allow us to suggest this: e.g., the *Summa duacensis* [ed. Glorieux, 43 and 49] and the *De anima et de potenciis eius* [ed. Gauthier, 223, 232, 244, and 250]). It appears for the first time in the title of the anonymous *De potenciis animae et obiectis* (between 1220 and 1230; ed. Callus, 147–48).

It is in Philip the Chancellor's *Quaestiones de anima* that the concepts of subject and object are related to each other for the first time:

> Una [potentia] enim simpliciter est quae est una in subiecto et obiecto, duplex quae est una in subiecto, duplicata in obiecto.
>
> (For [a power] that is absolutely unique is [the power] that is in the subject and the object, and it reduplicates that which is one in the subject but reduplicated in the object.)
>
> (Philip the Chancellor, *Quaestiones de anima,* ed. Keeler)

The object not only is the interposed obstacle, but also is clearly recognized as the theme specific to the act of knowing; it even serves to distinguish the diverse faculties, because it is anterior to them. Thus Grosseteste thinks he is allowed, when citing the text of Aristotle's *De anima,* to translate *antikeimena* not by *opposita,* as James of Venice had, but by *obiecta.* This is the translation that became standard in the second half of the thirteenth century, and was adopted in William of Moerbeke's version of *De anima*.

With the fusion of Aristotle's psychology and the Augustinian theory of vision, a decisive turning point is reached: the faculties of the mind are no longer open to the driving and multiform manifestation of the being with which they are identified in the act of knowing, but are determined by the prior nature of their specific object. What is known is no longer the face of the thing itself, but the obstacle with which the look collides, that deprives its activity of its own transparency. Knowledge is no longer a simple reception of an actual being by the power moved, but rather the ricochet of a ray emitted by the intellect that is reflected back to it after having bounced off its terminus. It is no longer the direct confrontation of the thing known and the knowing intellect, bound together by a common act, but the reverberation of sight on the "objectness" that has clothed the thing with a characteristic stratum. The thing known emerges as an object; the problem of knowledge is gradually detached from the being of the thing. Truth is henceforth transformed into an adequation between the powers of the mind and the corresponding objects:

> Some *habitus* are in the mind qua *habitus*, and thus they are by themselves in the mind or in man; there are others that are there as objects [*in ratione obiectorum*], and such is truth and falsity, because they are thrown before [*obiiciuntur*] the understanding.
>
> (Bacon, *Questiones supra libros prime philosophie Aristoteles*)

III. *Esse Objective*, or the Ontology of Objects in General

The concept of *esse obiective* (objective being) lexicalizes this development: what is present to pure thought is not imprinted there as a perception passively received through the senses, but as the terminus of an act of seeing: it is present as the object of our representation: "Once this thing is known as it is in nature, it shines objectively within, in the understanding itself" (Henry of Ghent, *Quodlibet* 5, quest. 26, f. 205 N ; cf. 5, quest. 14, f. 175). Objective being refers to the being of the thing as it is targeted by our representation, thus both as immanent (represented) and transcendent (representing). The understanding agent, when it encounters the external thing, produces the object in the understanding as a real accident in the mind. It thus gives it the status of a universal: the form "man" can be attributed to all men. The object is not a being received, but is constituted in the intellect and by the intellect: "For our act of intellection, we have an internal object, even if to feel we need an external object" (*Quodlibet* 13, art. 2, §[20] 60, ed. Alluntis, 470). And Duns Scotus emphasizes that the being of the thing remains the same, whether its object exists or not: the objective being of Caesar is identical whether he is absent or existent. Objective being is universal, abstract, immanent to the spirit.

Thus Duns Scotus constructed the main characteristics of the modern theory of objective being, or of objective reality, as it is developed down to Suárez, Descartes, and Kant: "What is objective is that which constitutes an idea, a representation of the mind, and not a subsistent and independent reality" (RT: *Vocabulaire technique et critique de la philosophie*, s.v. *Être objectif*).

The invention of the term "object" and its compounds shows how illusory it would be to assume that concepts are eternal, how dangerous and yet stubbornly persistent is the retrospective illusion of interpreters and translators who slip the new concept into ancient texts, and how much the fundamental concepts of metaphysics are connected with the evolution of the vocabulary that makes it possible to name them.

▪ See Box 1.

Olivier Boulnois

1

Quine and qualia

➤ TO TI ÉN EINAI

Philosophical debates about qualia cluster around two broad positions: the acknowledgment of irreducible, phenomenal properties of subjective experience on the one hand, and the characterization of such properties as eliminable or epiphenomenal on the other. Of the many problems at issue in these debates, one concerns the accessibility of such private, introspective experiences to public, intersubjective linguistic reports. Because qualia are often treated as nonextensional and nonrepresentational, they trouble both (traditionally analytic) philosophies of language that correlate linguistic meaning with empirical content, and (traditionally continental) philosophies of language that emphasize the irreducibility of discourse.

The philosophy of W.V.O. Quine (1908–2000) can be daunting in its many guises, here resembling Rudolf Carnap's logical positivism, there anticipating Jacques Derrida's deconstruction, and always recalling a pragmatic tradition running from Charles Sanders Peirce to John Dewey. Strictly speaking, there is no Quine on qualia. His most influential writings largely predate now conventional discussions of inverted color spectra or brilliant neurophysiologists in black-and-white rooms, reflecting instead mid-century behaviorist approaches to psychological considerations and resembling, in this regard, the later Ludwig Wittgenstein's private language argument. For Quine, behaviorism constitutes a methodological necessity in the study of language: "In psychology one may or may not be a behaviorist, but in linguistics one has no choice" (Quine, *Pursuit of Truth*, 37–38). Quine's thought thus appears to resemble more closely the latter of the two positions referred to above, tending more toward the reduction or elimination of phenomenal properties than toward their recognition or affirmation.

Given its explicitly extensionalist, physicalist, and behaviorist commitments, it is not surprising that Quine's philosophy would largely ignore qualia, or at least remain implicitly agnostic regarding the existence of phenomenal properties not subject to linguistic representation or empirical

(continued)

(continued)

verification; yet even as Quine's philosophy of language presents a challenge to the purported ontology of qualia, it preserves the challenge that qualia present to the philosophy of language, although in displaced form. Consider a classic example in expositions of qualia. Seeing a turquoise patch feels a certain way to me that it may not feel to you. This property of "what it is like," for me, to see turquoise exemplifies the qualitative aspect of a subjective experience. Now, although you and I may undergo different experiences while seeing turquoise, we will likely both be able to produce the word "turquoise" upon being asked the name of the color that we see—likewise for drinking coffee, having a headache, and so on. While on a private, phenomenal level, we might experience very different things, on a public, linguistic level, our behavior coincides. By these lights, verbal behavior is too crude an instrument to detect more subtle differences in subjective properties. However, Quine shows, most notably through his "principle of indeterminacy of translation," how the language of physical objects itself faces equally significant difficulties (*Word and Object*, 27). Quine imagines a linguist attempting to produce a handbook for translating a hitherto unknown language. A rabbit appears, and a native speaker utters "Gavagai." Our field linguist writes "rabbit" in his notebook as the translation of "Gavagai." Yet in thus correlating what Quine calls "stimulus meaning" with "occasion sentences," and in accordingly translating "Gavagai" as "rabbit" by virtue of a perceived sameness of stimulus meaning, our linguist assumes the native speaker's language is similar enough to our own that there is cognitive synonymy between his conception of rabbit and ours. As Quine points out, however, there is no way of knowing, based on observed linguistic behaviors alone, whether the speaker means "rabbit" or "rabbithood" or "stages of rabbits" or even "the rabbit fusion."

This indeterminacy characterizes for Quine all acts of translation, and it applies not only to our translations between languages but also to our simplest referential correlations between words and things: the indeterminacy of translation leads to the inscrutability of reference. Thus the threat that qualia represent for behaviorist, materialist, or functionalist philosophies of language—as when diverging experiences of a color fail to register in the common verbal behavior that those same experiences prompt—remains present in Quine's work, which relocates the vagaries of mental properties in the world of physical objects. The threat thus emerges from within physicalist discourse itself rather than arriving from the other side of an explanatory gap in the form of phenomenal discourse. If physicalist discourse can be seen as necessarily insufficient for representing phenomenal properties, Quine extends this line of reasoning, demonstrating the indeterminacy of physicalist discourse even in representing physical objects. Radical translation, he notes, "begins at home" ("Ontological Relativity," 46).

For Quine, translational indeterminacy and referential inscrutability necessitate philosophical holism, which stresses the underdetermination of language by reality, or of science by experience. Quine rejects reductionism as an unexamined dogma of empiricism: "Our statements about the external world face the tribunal of sense experience not individually but only as a corporate body. . . . The unit of empirical significance is the whole of science" (Quine, "Two Dogmas," 41–42). Inasmuch as one can translate his statements about the external world into positions on mental properties, one might say that Quine would be skeptical of qualia not because they can be reduced or eliminated, but because they represent in themselves an atomistic, reductionist approach to complex phenomena.

Quine's holism prompts his pragmatism. He describes phenomenal and physicalist conceptual schemes as mutually constitutive and mutually irreducible: for each, the other plays the role of "a convenient myth" (Quine, "On What There Is," 18). Quine does not seek to eliminate phenomenal properties, but neither does he go so far as to grant them an autonomous existence independent of physicalist conceptions. In choosing which ontological framework to adopt under what circumstances, Quine advocates "tolerance and an experimental spirit," one that bears in mind "our various interests and purposes" (ibid., 19). Such a spirit allows that science admits, and must admit, of certain conceptual or theoretical posits that are at once irreducible and mythic, and in fact are irreducible because they are mythic: "Physical objects are conceptually imported into the situation as convenient intermediaries—not by definition in terms of experience, but simply as irreducible posits comparable, epistemologically, to the gods of Homer" (Quine, "Two Dogmas," 44). This line of reasoning extends not simply to physical objects and Homeric gods, but also to forces, irrational numbers, and classes of classes. And, one imagines, to qualia. Quine does not evade the challenge that putatively intrinsic properties of phenomenal experience pose to physicalist discourse about external objects. His is not a naive physicalism. Instead, he advocates a holist, pragmatist approach to the difference between physicalist and phenomenal ontological commitments and conceptual frameworks. To "quine qualia," in this regard, amounts less to materialist elimination than to pragmatic tolerance (cf. Dennett, "Quining Qualia," 42–77).

Michael LeMahieu

BIBLIOGRAPHY

Dennett, Daniel C. "Quining Qualia." In *Consciousness in Contemporary Science*, edited by A. J. Marcel and E. Bisiach. Oxford: Clarendon, 1988.

Quine, W.V.O. "Ontological Relativity." In *Ontological Relativity and Other Essays*. New York: Columbia University Press, 1969.

———. "On What There Is." In *From a Logical Point of View*, 2nd rev. ed. Cambridge, MA.: Harvard University Press, 1980. First published in 1948.

———. *Pursuit of Truth*. Rev. ed. Cambridge, MA.: Harvard University Press, 1992.

———. "Two Dogmas of Empiricism." In *From a Logical Point of View*, 2nd rev. ed. Cambridge, MA.: Harvard University Press, 1980. First published in 1951.

———. *Word and Object*. Cambridge, MA.: MIT Press, 1960.

BIBLIOGRAPHY

Bacon, Roger. *Questiones supra libros prime philosophie Aristoteles*. In *Opera hactenus inedita Rogeri Bacon*, edited by R. Steele and F. Delorme, vol. 10. Oxford: Clarendon, 1930–32.

Baur, Ludwig, ed. *Die Philosophischen Werke des Robert Grosseteste, Bischofs von Lincoln*. Münster, Ger.: Aschendorff, 1912.

Bonitz, Herman. *Index Aristotelicus*. Berlin: G. Reimeri, 1870.

Boulnois, Olivier. "Être, luire et concevoir: Note sur la genèse et la structure de la conception scotiste de l'*esse objective*." *Collectanea Franciscana* 60 (1990): 117–35.

De potenciis animae et objectis. Edited by D. A. Callus. *Recherches de Théologie Ancienne et Médiévale*, no. 19 (1952).

Dewan, Lawrence. "'Objectum': Notes on the Invention of a Word." *Archives d'Histoire Doctrinale et Littéraire du Moyen Âge* 48 (1981): 37–96.

Gauthier, René Antoine, ed. "Le traité *De anima et de potenciis ejus* d'un maître ès arts (c. 1225)." *Revue des Sciences Philosophiques et Théologiques*, no. 66 (1982).

Glorieux, Palémon, ed. *La 'Summa duacensis' (Douai 434): Texte critique avec une introduction et des tables*. Paris: Vrin, 1955.

Henry of Ghent. *Quodlibet*. Edited by F. Alluntis. Madrid: Biblioteca de Autores cristianos, 1968.

Kobusch, Theo. "Objekt." In RT: Ritter and Gründer, *Historisches Wörterbuch der Philosophie*, 6:1026–52.

Philip the Chancellor. *Quaestiones de anima*. Edited by L. W. Keeler. Münster, Ger.: Aschendorff, 1937.

Plato. *Plato in Twelve Volumes*. Vols. 5–6, *The Republic*. Translated by Paul Shorey. Cambridge, MA: Harvard University Press, 1969.

———. *La république*. Translated into French by Émile Chambry. Paris: Les Belles Lettres, 1931; 10th ed., 1996.

| OBLIGATION

"Obligation"—from Latin *obligo*, "to attach" (*ligo*) "to" or "against" (*ob*)—has, like the Latin word *obligatio*, a strong meaning that is juridical (a commitment made by the parties, a guarantee or security deposit) and moral (mental commitment, responsibility, moral bond, constraint).

I. Obligation and Legal Bond

The legal, social, and religious system connecting obligation, norm, and law is explored in the entries for LEX and PIETAS (the disposition to perform one's office, or the feeling of duty) and RELIGIO (which "ties together" men and gods), so far as Latin is concerned; for Greek, see THEMIS, Boxes 1, 2 (see also KÊR and the complex vocabulary of destiny, which includes *anagkê* [ἀνάγκη], "necessity, constraint"). The other side of the tradition, the Arab and Hebrew one, is explored in the entries for TORAH (see also Hebrew BERĪT, "covenant"). The German *Pflicht* (from *pflegen*, "to care for") translates *obligatio* and *officium*: see SOLLEN and cf. BERUF. For English, see FAIR, LAW, and RIGHT/JUST/GOOD. Finally, the Russian SOBORNOST', which is translated by "conciliarity," designates the kind of gathering-together that connects people, beyond "catholicity," in Russian culture (cf. OIKONOMIA, PRAVDA).

See *DROIT*; cf. *DESTINY*.

II. Obligation and Moral Duty

The expression of moral obligation is connected with that of duty. Thus it is joined with the expression of debt, and thereby with fault and possibility: see DUTY and cf. PARDON; see also ASPECT and *PROBABILITY*.

The connection between having a duty to be and having a duty to do is explored on the basis of German; see SOLLEN. The terminological network thus rejoins that of will: see WILLKÜR and WILL; and that of value: see WERT and cf. *VALUE*.

On the relationship to the act as a moral act, see MORALS, POSTUPOK; cf. *ACT, GOOD/EVIL,* and *PRUDENCE*.

➤ *ALLIANCE, COMMUNITY, CONCILIARITY,* SECULARIZATION

OIKEIÔSIS [οἰκείωσις] (GREEK)

ENGLISH	appropriation
FRENCH	*appropriation*
GERMAN	*Zueignung*
ITALIAN	*attrazione*
LATIN	*conciliatio, commendatio*

➤ *APPROPRIATION*, and HEIMAT, I/ME/MYSELF, LOVE, OIKONOMIA, PROPERTY, TRUTH

"Appropriation" is the literal translation, which has become inevitable, of the Stoic term *oikeiôsis*, derived from the verb *oikeioô* [οἰκειόω], "to make familiar" and later "to make specific to, to appropriate"; "to appropriate to oneself" in the reflexive sense, "related to the family, to the estate; belonging to the family," whence "proper to." *Oikeiôsis* is opposed to *allotriôsis* [ἀλλοτρίωσις], "alienation," and designates what nature has originally "appropriated or attached to us or conciliated with" us. The term also has an affective dimension that is very poorly rendered by "appropriation."

Providing the transition from the physical to the ethical, the notion of *oikeiôsis* [οἰκείωσις] is used by the Stoics in two different arguments, which makes understanding and translation even more difficult. This notion suggests that living beings do not seek primarily pleasure, but instead what is "appropriate" to each of them, starting with the preservation of their own constitutions. This entails a certain form of self-esteem and implies that in accordance with this tendency or primary impulsion (*prôtê hormê* [πρώτη ὁρμή]), we can posit for rational beings this double equation: living in accord with nature = living in accord with reason = living in accord with virtue. But *oikeiôsis* also has the purpose of founding relationships of justice between human beings by ensuring that self-esteem founds love for one's relatives, a love that must be understood as love for their own good, and which is destined to broaden to encompass all rational beings, thus founding in nature the social bond, or even the cosmopolitanism cherished by the Stoics, whether this is merely a cosmopolitanism of the wise, as in the older Stoicism, or that of all human beings, as in Panetius and later writers.

It is informative to compare the most recent French translation of the canonical statement of the thesis, as it is given by Diogenes Laertius, with the presentation offered by Cicero:

> The living being's primary impulse is, they say, to preserve itself, because from the outset nature appropriates it [to itself], as Chrysippus says in the first book of his treatise *On Ends*, when he says that for every living being the chief object that is proper to him is his own constitution and the consciousness he has of it.

> (L'impulsion première [τὴν πρώτην ὁρμήν] que possède l'être vivant vise, disent-ils, à se conserver soi-même [τὸ τηρεῖν ἑαυτό], du fait que la nature dès l'origine l'approprie (à soi-même) [οἰκειούσης αὐτὸ τῆς φύσεως ἀπ' ἀρχῆς], comme le dit Chrysippe au premier livre de son traité *Sur les fins*, quand il dit que pour tout être vivant l'objet premier qui lui est propre [πρῶτον οἰκεῖον] est sa propre constitution [σύστασιν] et la conscience [συνείδησιν] qu'il a de celle-ci.)

(*Lives of Eminent Philosophers*)

When an animal is born, it is spontaneously appropriated to itself [*ipsum sibi conciliari*], . . . interested in preserving itself [*commendari ad se conservandum*], and loving its own constitution, as well as everything that is likely to preserve this constitution [*et ad suum statum eaque quae conservantia sunt eius status diligenda*].

(Dès que l'animal est né, il est spontanément approprié à lui-même [*ipsum sibi conciliari*], . . . intéressé à se conserver soi-même [*commendari ad se conservandum*] et à aimer sa propre constitution ainsi que tout ce qui est propre à conserver cette constitution [*et ad suum statum eaque quae conservantia sunt eius status diligenda*].)

(*De finibus*)

Leaving aside the way in which this argument is presented in our two authors—a priori proof in Chrysippus, proof by effects in Cicero—we can observe that contrary to his usual practice, Cicero does not give the Greek term *oikeiôsis*, or even its Latin equivalent, but instead leaves it to his interpreters to give priority to *conciliatio* (literally, "association," "union") or *commendatio* (literally, "recommendation"). Cicero's exposition regarding the other aspect of this notion, that of justice, underscores what in Christianity would be called "love for one's neighbor," and uses only the term *commendatio* (*De finibus*, 3.62–63). We can now understand why, perhaps deviating somewhat from the literal meaning of the Greek, French translators have preferred, as did É. Bréhier in his edition of the Stoics for the Bibliothèque de la Pléiade, to use the verbs *attacher* and *adapter* in rendering Diogenes Laertius's canonical statement, whereas R. D. Hicks, the English translator of the Loeb Classical Library edition, opted for "endear," because he translated *oikeion* by "dear." That also explains why M. Pohlenz's translation of *Oikeiôsis* by *Zueignung* was rendered in Italian by *attrazione* (trans. O. De Gregorio).

These variations obviously show that, to cite two of the most recent and most authoritative editors and translators of Hellenistic literature, A. Long and D. Sedley, "any translation [loses] something of the original."

Jean-Louis Labarrière

BIBLIOGRAPHY

Arnim, Hans Friedrich August von, ed. *Stoicorum veterum fragmenta*. 4 vols. Stuttgart: Teubner, 1968. First published in 1903–24.

Bees, Robert. *Die Oikeiosislehre der Stoa*. 2 vols. Würzburg, Ger.: Königshausen und Neumann, 2004–5.

Bréhier, Émile, trans. *Les Stoïciens*. Edited by Pierre-Maxime Schuhl. Paris: Gallimard / La Pléiade, 1962.

Brunschwig, Jacques. "The Cradle Argument in Epicureanism and Stoicism." In *The Norms of Nature*, edited by Malcolm Schofield and Gisela Striker, 113–44. Cambridge: Cambridge University Press, 1986.

Cicero. *De finibus*. Translated by F. J. Martha. Paris: Les Belles Lettres, 1967.

Diogenes Laertius. *Vies et doctrines des philosophes illustres*. Translated by R. Goulet. Paris: Livre de Poche, 1999.

Goldschmidt, Victor. *Le système stoïcien et l'idée de temps*. Paris: Vrin, 1953.

Inwood, Brad, and Pierluigi Donini. "Stoic Ethics." In *The Cambridge History of Hellenistic Philosophy*, edited by Keimpe Algra et al., 675–738. Cambridge: Cambridge University Press, 1999.

Long, Anthony A., and David N. Sedley. *The Hellenistic Philosophers*. 2 vols. Cambridge: Cambridge University Press, 1987.

Pembroke, S. G. "Oikeiôsis." In *Problems in Stoicism*, edited by A. A. Long, 114–49. London: Athlone, 1971.

Pohlenz, Max. *Die Stoa: Geschichte einer geistigen Bewegung*. 2 vols. Göttingen, Ger.: Vandenhoeck und Ruprecht, 1948–49. Translation by O. De Gregorio: *La Stoa*. 2nd ed. Florence: Nuova Italia, 1978.

Schofield, Malcolm. "Social and Political Thought." In *The Cambridge History of Hellenistic Philosophy*, edited by Keimpe Algra et al., 739–70. Cambridge: Cambridge University Press, 1999.

Striker, Giserla. "The Role of *Oikeiôsis* in Stoic Ethics." *Oxford Studies in Ancient Philosophy* 1 (1983): 145–67.

OIKONOMIA [οἰϰονομία] (GREEK)

ENGLISH economy
FRENCH *économie*

➤ ECONOMY, *IMAGE* [BILD, EIDÔLON], MIMÊSIS, MOMENT, OIKEIÔSIS, SECULARIZATION, SOBORNOST', SVET, *WORLD*

The term *oikonomia* [οἰϰονομία] is a nodal concept in Christian thinking about the image (*eikôn* [εἰϰών]). To understand it, we have to analyze its semantic history over the nine centuries that preceded its triumph. The Apostle Paul, who inherited the classical notion of *oikonomia* (Xenophon, Aristotle), chose the term to designate in his Epistles the totality of the level of the Incarnation. Its apparent polysemy is the origin of the disparity in its translations. Thus the profound unity of a regulative concept was veiled, legitimizing any relationship between the spiritual world and the temporal world. Intended to justify the adaptations of the Law to everyday and historical reality, the patristic economy supported all the modalities of management and administration in the visible world. The doctrine of the image sealed this pragmatic unity with an astonishing modernity.

I. From Xenophon and Aristotle to Paul

Patristic literature owes the introduction of the term "economy" to Paul's Epistles, in which we find *oikonomia* [οἰϰονομία] used to designate the economy of the Pleroma, or the divinity taken in the plenitude of its perfection (Eph 1:10), the economy of grace (3:2), and the economy of mystery (3:9). In the Epistle to the Colossians (1:25), Paul speaks of the economy of God (*oikonomia theou* [οἰϰονομία θεοῦ]). In modern French translations, the word is never rendered literally; instead we sometimes find *accomplissement*, sometimes *plan*, *dessein*, or *réalisation* (RT: *Traduction oecuménique de la Bible*). The person entrusted with this accomplishment is the *diakonos* [διάϰονος] or *oikonomos* [οἰϰονόμος], translated by *intendant* or *ministre*, the Vulgate having opted for *actor*. For Paul, it is a matter of borrowing from the Greek language a term that up to that point designated the management and administration of goods and services in domestic life and of importing the model of the private economy into the public economy, into the life of the city. That is in fact the sense in which both Xenophon and Aristotle use the word *oikonomia*.

Before them, Hesiod dealt in his *Works and Days* with the familial economy in a rather poetic way. In the *Republic* (4 and 5) and in the *Laws* (4 and 8), Plato used *oikonomia* to construct philosophically a figure of administration in the ideal city. The Platonic economy is the science of the management of goods and persons in a state led by a sage endowed with temperance (*sôphrosunê* [σωφροσύνη]) and justice (*dikaiosunê* [δικαιοσύνη]). Access to these cardinal virtues passes through education and requires the exercise of dialectic conceived as the art of dialogue that leads to knowledge. The legislating faculty is nothing other than the *logos* [λόγος], that is, discursive rationality.

The objective of Xenophon and Aristotle is entirely different. Both of them deal with practical problems connected with the everyday reality of the family and the city and do not venture into literary or utopian terrain. As a result, in both thinkers *oikonomia* becomes a crucial notion in the sense that it determines the site of a confrontation between political realism and justice. In *The Economist*, Xenophon analyzes all the elements of the management of wealth and goods in the context of the family farm.

> SOCRATES: Tell me, Kritoboulos, is economy [οἰκονομία] the name of a certain kind of knowledge [ἐπιστήμης], like medicine, the art of forging or carpentry . . . ? Could we say, then, that it is a task [ἔργον] of economy?
> KRITOBOULOS: It seems to me that it is the task of a good economist [οἰκονόμου] to administer his household well.
> SOCRATES: And someone else's household, if it is entrusted to him—couldn't he administer it as he does his own? A competent carpenter [τέκτων] could work for another person as he does for himself. Thus someone who is familiar with economics [οἰκονομικός] will have the same ability. . . . Hence a person who knows this art [τὴν ταύτην τέχνην ἐπισταμένῳ], even if he has no property of his own, can earn a salary by administering another person's household [οἰκονομοῦντα] as he would by building it.

(Xenophon, *The Economist*, 1.1–4)

As Leo Strauss puts it, "the administrator of an estate may be good or bad at management. But the economist (*oikonomikos*), that is, a person who has mastered the art of administering his estate, is ipso facto a good manager" (*Xenophon's Socratic Discourse*). In the debate between Socrates and Kritoboulos in Xenophon's work, the concept of *oikonomia* is in fact inhabited by the inevitable tension between the calculus of optimization and ethical requirements, an art of acquisition without war coupled with a providential conception of nature. In the rest of the debate, Socrates discusses further the management of wealth and the correct measures to take in order to ensure the prosperity of households and of the city.

In Aristotle's *Economica* (*Oikonomikos*), things become clearer: neither providence nor utopia is at issue, but rather a detailed consideration of actual practices and their results. In the private domain, Aristotle remains quite close to Xenophon, but when he moves to the public domain, economic concern is inseparable from political concern. *Oikonomikos* no longer designates a person but rather a mode of rationalized relations of the real that is closer to a judgment of (dialectical) probability than to a metaphysical concern. The function of judgment is entrusted to the proper usage of the *doxa* [δόξα]. The analysis of tricks thus finds its place here. Economics is

a practice, both strategic and tactical, in the service of power and the accumulation of wealth. Its means are judged by their results.

■ See Box 1.

All this was inherited by the church fathers after Paul's suggestion that the Incarnation be assimilated to a plan for managing and administering humanity's secular reality by the divinity. Translations give a very confused picture of the term's polysemy since the word *oikonomia* sometimes disappears, and sometimes, put between quotation marks, is the subject of an awkward commentary on an accidental homonymy. However, the systematic unity of the term is essential for anyone who wants to understand the operative efficacy of *oikonomia*. The disparate translations show the uneasiness felt by Christians when faced with a Christological operator of opportunism. It is true that *oikonomia* changes meaning every time its use requires an inflection, but what constitutes the founding unity of polysemy itself is precisely its militant resistance to any kind of rigor (*akribeia* [ἀκρίβεια]) or univocalness in interpretation.

II. Patristic Polysemy: Economy and Incarnation

The polysemy of *oikonomia* does not reflect a semantic evolution since all the term's meanings have coexisted and operated simultaneously since the first centuries of the Christian era. In the eighth century, a crucial turning point linked economy with the debate on the legitimacy of the icon in patristic literature. It was in connection with the crisis provoked by the iconoclastic emperors (724) that the defenders of the image ("iconophiles") constructed the conceptual unity of the economy. In this way the definition of an operator that provides for uninterrupted management of heaven's interests and earthly goods is revealed and completed in all its philosophical and political breadth.

■ See Box 2.

A. Divine economy and ecclesiastical institution

The term *oikonomia* is used in patristic literature in its classical sense of the management and administration of goods and people or to designate responsibilities and offices within the ecclesiastical institution. The Incarnation, that is, the divine will to resort to the visible and historical, becomes the model for human management and administration of the secular space by those who are considered its stewards (*oikonomoi*). Paul is the founder of the system of incarnational economy. The *oikonomia* opens up the operative space of the new law which, in the image of Christ, is composed of infractions and transgressions that Paul was the first to declare (Rom 2:29; 2 Cor 3:6) to be the realization of the spirit of the law in opposition to its letter (Eusebius, *Histoire ecclésiastique*, RT: *PG*, vol. 20, col. 308C; Dio Chrysostom, *De sacerdotio*, 6.7.40). Consequently, the word *oikonomia* designated the person of Christ as well as the whole narrative of his life, passion, resurrection, and beyond, as far as the future completion of the providential plan of redemption (Athanasius, RT: *PG*, vol. 25, col. 461B, and vol. 26, col. 169A; Justinian, RT: *PG*, vol. 6, col. 753B; Irenaeus, RT: *PG*, vol. 7, col. 504B; Gregory of Nazianzus, RT: *PG*, vol. 36, col. 97C; Gregory of Nyssa, RT: *PG*, vol. 45, col. 137B).

1

Chrematistics and economy

The first question is whether the art of getting wealth [*chrêmatistikê* (χρηματιστική)] is the same as the art of managing a household [*oikonomikê* (οἰκονομική)] or a part of it, or instrumental to it. . . . Now it is easy to see that the art of household management is not identical with the art of getting wealth, for the one uses [*porisasthai* (πορίσασθαι)] the material which the other provides [*chrêsasthai* (χρήσασθαι)]. For the art which uses household stores can be no other than the art of household management.

(Aristotle, *Politics*, 1.8.1256a3–13)

Of the art of acquisition [*eidos ktêtikês* (εἶδος κτητικῆς)] then, there is one kind which by nature [*kata phusin* (κατὰ φύσιν), sc. war and hunting] is a part of the management of a household, insofar as the art of household management must either find ready to hand, or itself provide, such things necessary to life, and useful for the community of the family or state, as can be stored. . . . And so we see that there is a natural art of acquisition which is practiced by managers of households [*oikonomois*] and by statesmen [*politikois* (πολιτικοῖς)], and what is the reason of this.

(1257b27–38)

And thus we have found the answer to our original question, whether the art of getting wealth is the business of the manager of a household and of the statesman or not their business?—viz. that wealth is presupposed by them. For as political science does not make men, but takes them from nature and uses them, so too nature provides them with earth or sea or the like as a source of food. At this stage begins the duty of the manager of the household [*oikonomos*], who has to order the things which nature supplies.

(1258a19–25)

In book 1 of the *Politics*, Aristotle distinguishes two economic systems: one that remains closely connected with nature and undertakes to store up, manage, and make profitable the products necessary to life (economy); the other, unlimited, which seeks only the acquisition of wealth (chrematistics) and requires ethical vigilance because of the substitution of money for goods themselves (commerce). These two systems concern both domestic economy and political economy. The *Economics*, an Aristotelian treatise, adopts this distinction but chooses to accord its specifically political place to the acquisition and

growth of power by appropriation and growth of goods. In the *Economics*, chrematistics is no more than a set of financial techniques and strategies. We should note that in the *Politics* (1258b), on the chrematistic side of economy, the profitability of investments produces an interest called *tokos* (τόκος), which provides Aristotle with an opportunity to condemn usury as an activity opposed to nature (*para phusin* [παρὰ φύσιν]). This may seem surprising, since he observes that this productivity is homonymic with the procreation of children (*homoia gar ta tiktomena tois gennôsin auta estin* [ὅμοια γὰρ τὰ τικτόμενα τοῖς γεννῶσιν αὐτὰ ἐστιν]). Christianity was, on the contrary, to exploit this homonomy positively in an ecclesial economy that takes as its model engenderment and filiation on the basis of the fecund womb of the mother of God, named *Theotokos* [Θεοτόκος]. In classical thought, reflection on economy was often inseparable from an agricultural model, and the fundamental concern always remains that of a rational harmony between *oikonomia* and *phusis* [φύσις], between economy and nature. The Christian construction of economy breaks with any natural model in order to define a symbolic system of theologico-political power.

2

The crisis of the image: The iconoclastic period (724–843)

For almost a century, the Byzantine Empire was shaken by a theologico-political conflict in which what was at stake was the legitimacy of the image and the monopoly that institutions could have over it. The iconoclastic emperor Leo III decreed (724) the destruction of all religious images, which were to be replaced by imperial figurations and the decorations of profane art. The church entered this conflict in which the foundation of its temporal power was involved, and triumphed in 843, with the "solemn restoration." It was on the occasion of this historical convulsion that Christian theologians and philosophers produced the first doctrine of the image. This remarkable philosophical innovation, in a world that was heir to Judaism and Greek thought, which were not very favorable to visible things (out of fidelity to the rigor of ontological questioning), was carried out in the name of Economy. It was through the renewal of the uses of this term and through the play of its polysemy that the first Western thinking about the image began, the first iconology.

From the moment that the Incarnation becomes a long-term design that necessarily includes the most radical test of reality, namely, mortality, *oikonomia* becomes the model of every adaptation of human management to the providential level, the operating concept that relates spiritual requirements to the exercise of temporal power. In other words, it is the concept of the adaptation of means to ends in virtue of which the "occasion" (*kairos* [καιρός]; see MOMENT) is judged in terms of utility or efficacy. It is not a matter of either jurisprudence or casuistry, because its foundation remains unshakably Christological; in fact, the person of Christ cannot be considered as a particular case treated as an exemplum. It is thus a kind of eschatologically founded pragmatism. This finalized adaptation is based on organic analogies of which the most foundational is again of Pauline origin: the identification of the body of Christ with the body of the church (1 Cor 12:31). Henceforth, the ecclesiastical institution becomes the *oikonomos* of the accomplishment and all the means it uses to lead the *oikoumenê* [οἰκουμένη], that is, all inhabited lands, to the triumph of Christianity are justified by the divinity of the ends and the harmony of a natural order. The church has thus made a transition from the domestic *oikos* [οἶκος] to the cosmological *oikos* in order to extend to the whole universe the science of management and administration of the divine patrimony, creation. The divine economy is the natural model of all exchange and all consumption.

B. *Dispositio* and *dispensatio*

In light of the tensions in classical thought, we can understand why the church soon found itself facing the following question: how far can the adaptation of means to ends be taken? How far can trickery and the temporary abandonment of evangelical principles lead us to agree that the ends are more important than the requirement of justice and love? Debates on this subject were frequent, whether it was a question of the strategies to be used for conversion, pedagogical tricks, or pious lies.

To better delimit the semantic space of *oikonomia*, we have to start over from its Christological foundation as it derives from Paul's use of the word. The *Oikonomia* of God is Christ, the filial incarnation. From this follows a Trinitarian use (Hippolytus, RT: *PG*, vol. 10, col. 808A, 816B, 821A), which is rendered in Latin sometimes by *dispositio*, and sometimes by *dispensatio*, depending whether the emphasis falls on the system as the structure of divinity (Tertullian) or on its dynamics as productive of meaning and history. Tertullian adds to the Latin terms the transliteration of the Greek (in the form of *oeconomia*) to designate the Trinitarian dimension of the filial mystery (RT: *PL*, vol. 2, col. 158A). *Dispositio* makes it possible to shed light on the naturalistic dimension of *oikonomia*, which covers the whole of creation, and thus simultaneously *phusis* [φύσις], *kosmos* [κόσμος], and *sustasis* [σύστασις]—that is, nature, the universe, and the organic system (Clement of Alexandria, RT: *PG*, vol. 8, col. 1033A–B). The body is included in this providential, ordered structure of the world, and *oikonomia* thus inherits the Stoic conception of the cosmos. *Dispositio* is a structural concept, whereas *dispensatio* is a functional concept. *Dispensatio*, a dispensation and a development in the visible, covers the historical effects of the divine will and action in the world and the adaptation of its investments to its creature. The concept of accounting for expenditures, profits, and losses finds here its theological foundation.

We shall say immediately what the goods are that are dispensed [*chorêgia tôn agathôn* (χορηγία τῶν ἀγαθῶν)] that come to us from the Father through the Son: in order to continue in existence, every nature in creation, whether it belongs to the visible world or the intelligible world, needs divine solicitude [*epimeleias* (ἐπιμελείας)]. That is why the demiurge Word, the only begotten God, grants his help in proportion to each one's needs [*hekastou chreias* (ἑκάστου χρείας)]. In addition, he provides resources [*epimetrei tas chorêgias* (ἐπιμετρεῖ τὰς χορηγίας)], varied and of all kinds, according to the diversity of his debtors, distributing them proportionately to each one [*summetrous hekastôi* (συμμέτρους ἑκάστῳ)] in accord

with the necessity of his needs [*kata ton tês chreias anagkaion* (κατὰ τὸν τῆς χρείας ἀναγκαῖον)].

(Basil of Caesarea, *Traité du Saint-Esprit*)

This dispensation raises, for ecclesiastical management, the question of profitability and balanced accounts in the distribution of benefits and in the distribution of rewards and punishments (cf. Kotsonis, *Problèmes de l'économie ecclésiastique*).

The translation given priority in the Vulgate is *dispensatio*, which covers both *phusis* and *pronoia* [πρόνοια], that is, nature and providence. Thus it is used by Clement (RT: *PG*, vol. 8, col. 809B), Origen (RT: *PG*, vol. 11, col. 277A), Gregory of Nyssa (RT: *PG*, vol. 45, col. 126C) and Maximus the Abbot (RT: *PG*, vol. 90, col. 801B). The harmony of the world is open to all ways of adapting means to ends in order to obtain consensus (*homologia* [ὁμολογία]). Thus the term "economy" designates prudence (*phronêsis* [φρόνησις]), as in Origen and Athanasius (RT: *PG*, vol. 25, col. 488B) or Theodore of Studion (RT: *PG*, vol. 99, col. 1661C); pedagogical strategy and the manipulation of minds, as in Origen (RT: *PG*, vol. 13, col. 496B); trickery and all stratagems that make possible the adjustment of silence and rhetorical procedures, as in Gregory Nazianzus (RT: *PG*, vol. 36, col. 473C) or Basil (RT: *PG*, vol. 32, col. 669A); and finally lies (*apatê* [ἀπάτη], *kalê apatê* [καλὴ ἀπάτη]), as in John Chrysostom (RT: *PG*, vol. 48, col. 630ff.).

C. "Economize the truth"

Letter 58 from Gregory Nazianzus to Basil of Caesarea perfectly illustrates the question of the pastoral economy in its management of opportunity. Basil, confronting heretics, cleverly dissimulates, for strategic reasons, the rigor of the Trinitarian dogma in order to avoid a conflict that would threaten the unity of the church in the provinces affected by heresy. Not being in a strong position, Basil keeps partially silent. Accused of cowardice by the more rigorous, he receives this letter of support from his friend.

It is better to economize the truth [οἰκονομηθῆναι τὴν ἀλήθειαν] by yielding a little to the circumstances, as one does to a cloud [ὥσπερ νέφει τινὶ τῷ καιρῷ], rather than compromise it by making a public declaration that reveals everything. . . .

The audience did not accept this economy. They cried that it was the result of the managers of cowardice [οἰκονομούντων δειλίαν] and not of discourse. As for you, divine and holy friend, teach us how far we must go in the Theology of the Spirit, what terms we must use, how far we must be economical [μέχρι τίνος οἰκονομητέον] to maintain these truths when confronted by our contradictors.

(Gregory of Nazianzus, *Lettres*)

The difficulties raised by putting a theological concept in the service of politics mobilized the church fathers and theologians when Christian charity had to be reconciled with the desire for hegemony and conversion. It was entirely possible to make economy the foundation of an active conception of tolerance. But this did not happen, and strategic accommodation won out, to the point of accepting a certain Machiavellianism.

Pontifical management of human affairs yielded historical examples in which the respect for the Gospels no longer inspired the hierarchy's decisions. The penitential economy then came to the rescue for sinners.

The wealth and ambiguity of the term's polysemy provide an adequate explanation for the prudent silence of the church, which never produced an overall thematic work on this dangerously ambivalent term. That God and his creature meet on the "economic" terrain of a mutual accommodation clearly emerges from the texts without ever being the object of a conceptual mobilization. The sole testimony to a thematic definition occurs in a lost work of Eulogios that we know through Photius's review of it. Eulogios seems to have taken into account only the semantic field of accommodation and opportunity.

- See Box 3.

III. The Iconic Economy

Starting in the eighth century, in connection with the crisis of images unleashed by the iconoclastic emperors, the defense of the icon was entirely constructed on the economic interpretation of the Incarnation. The management and administration of visible things became the cornerstone of ecclesiastical politics. An enemy of the icon can be called an *iconomachos* as well as an *economachos*, because in Greek the two words are pronounced in the same way, *ikonomachos*. Thus the enemy of the icon is a tormentor of Christ, the enemy of the church and the universal plan of redemption. The iconic *oikonomia* thus gathers together the entire semantic field of *oikonomia* in a unifying doctrine that supports all the productions of images. In fact, the icon celebrates the Incarnation and institutes the production of visible things as *mimêsis* [μίμησις] of all God's providential operations. The strategic, pedagogical, and political adaptation of means to ends practiced by the institution is part of the divine adaptation to the system of visibility.

To elaborate the iconic specificity of the *oikonomia*, the church fathers opposed it to *theologia* [θεολογία], that is, to the Jews' literal fidelity to the Mosaic Law. Economy is the mark of the new law, the end of biblical prohibitions and of subjection to the letter (Theodore of Studion, RT: *PG*, vol. 99, col. 353D). There followed moments of crisis within the church when the *oikonomia* became, to the indignation of the most rigorous minds, the justification for lies, abuses, and crimes committed in the name of legitimate ends. Economy conflicts with *akribeia*, that is, with the literal respect for the Law. The "holy economy" inevitably began to feed the polemic directed against the Jews. Enemies of the Incarnation and the image, they are at the same time accused of practicing a diabolical management of goods and profits. Their relationship to money bears the signs of their damnation.

We can now understand in a different way the difficulty faced by Christian translators who chose to give priority to the disparate with the entirely economical goal of concealing the "ideological" unity of a term that threatened the spiritual purity of practices. Translating the word *oikonomia* as "economy" every time it occurred might reveal only too clearly the political goals of a temporal power that no longer felt it was faithful to the ethical requirements of the Gospels. This explains the countless footnotes warning the reader against the deviations of what is presented as an accidental homonymy that could give rise to serious misunderstandings. The anxiety is well founded: it is exactly the same thing at issue in the secular and religious senses of *oikonomia*, namely, of legitimating all the means necessary for the management and administration of the visible world with a view to salvation while respecting the indestructible unity of an institution. *Oikonomia* is not a homonym, but a unified concept in the service of unification.

- See Box 4.

Marie-José Mondzain

3

Eulogius's distinctions

The lost treatise by Eulogius was probably contemporary with the debates about the Monophysite and Nestorian heresy (fifth century), that is, with an era in which the rigorous defense of dogmatic truths endangered the unity of the church. Therefore, it was necessary constantly to seek the best possible "compromises" between spiritual fidelity and political aims. This "compromise" is "economy" and requires a pragmatic adaptation within a vigilance that remained theoretical. This treatise is the only Byzantine work that seems to have attempted a synthesis of "economic" operations.

Eulogius draws a triple distinction within the notion of economy as it is recognized by the church, and he shows that it is only by not aligning themselves with none of the three that they [the heretics] have arrived at a

formless mixture of impiety through the alliance they have made between the excesses of their heresies. To begin with, Eulogius says that the principle of economy does not recognize just anyone as a judge and arbiter of its realization, but instead chooses them among the servants of Christ, among the dispensers [*oikonomous*] of the divine mystery and among those who legislate from episcopal sees. In addition, it is a proper principle that exercises the economy when the dogmas of the faith are not subjected to any attack by it.

Often a circumstantial economy [*proskairos oikonomia* (πρόσκαιρος οἰκονομία)] is established for a limited time by admitting and retaining a few givens that were not supposed to be in order to allow the true faith to recover

its durable power and tranquility. . . . The second economy concerns words. Thus when the church's dogmas are well established and expressed in different terms, we agree in order to say nothing about certain words, especially if they are not serious reasons for scandal for those whose intention is sufficiently upright. . . .

A third mode of economy concerns the frequent case in which people do not take into account a decree that has been promulgated, and promulgated precisely against them, without the authority of the true dogmas being thereby lessened.

(Photius, *Bibliothèque*)

BIBLIOGRAPHY

Photius. *Bibliothèque*, vol. 4, codex 227. Translated by R. Henry. Paris: Les Belles Lettres, 1965.

4

Nikephoros: The iconophile synthesis

It was probably through the crisis of the image that the operational unity of the concept of *oikonomia* was constituted. Explicitly bringing together under a single term the Incarnation, political management of goods and persons, and the stakes involved in iconic figuration made *oikonomia* the key element in a symbolic construct. Economy synthesizes doctrinally the evangelical message and the life of the institution. Patriarch Nikephoros was a vehement and exemplary spokesman for this view in the ninth century:

> Even before taking up the question of icons, through the view that he [the iconoclast] expresses publicly, he allows his plan to be divined without waiting to turn it in the famous way that we know. Now see the logical consequence that is maintained between his conception and everything that precedes. In fact, he

has first discussed the two natures and hypostases, and then, suddenly carried away by arrogance and passion, he jumps abruptly and without order to icons and prototypes. He could offer no better proof that the whole discussion that he has carried on has had, from start to finish, no goal other than to do violence both to the sacred symbols of our faith and to the whole Economy of our Savior Jesus Christ, and he has merely thrown himself still further into revolt against Christ.

> (Nikephoros the Patriarch, *Discours contre les iconoclastes*, [*Antirrhétiques* 1, 224C–225A])

Nikephoros's *Antirrhetici* are the most important of the iconophile works, and they were written in the ninth century. In them, the term "economy" is used thirty-nine times

to identify very closely the defense of the Incarnation with that of the image. These polemical treatises responded to the iconoclastic interpretation of economy, which claimed that after the Resurrection, respect for the evangelical message was the only legitimate responsibility of the church's theology and its hierarchy, whereas the temporal economy fell to the secular political power of the emperor. The interpretation of *oikonomia* thus became a political stake in which the separation of powers was central. The church triumphed by bringing together under a single term the secular issues of the visible, power, and wealth.

BIBLIOGRAPHY

Nikephoros the Patriarch. *Discours contre les iconoclastes*. Translated by M. J. Mondzain. Paris: Klincksieck, 1991.

BIBLIOGRAPHY

Basil of Caesarea. *Traité du Saint-Esprit*. Translated by B. Pruche. Paris: Éditions du Cerf, 1947.

Chrysostom, John. *Perí hierōsýnēs = De sacerdotio*. Edited by J. Arbuthnot Nairn. Cambridge: Cambridge University Press, 1906. Translation and introduction by Graham Neville: *Six Books on the Priesthood*. London: SPCK, 1964. Translation, editing, introduction, and notes by Anne-Marie Malingrey: *Sur le sacerdoce: Dialogue et homélie*. Paris: Éditions du Cerf, 1980.

Eusebius of Caesarea. *The Ecclesiastical History*. Translated by Kirsopp Lake and J.E.L. Oulton. 2 vols. Loeb Classical Library. Cambridge, MA: Harvard University Press, 1957–59.

Gregory of Nazianzus, *Lettres*. Vol. 1. Translated by P. Gallay. Paris: Les Belles Lettres, 1964.

Kotsonis, J. *Problèmes de l'économie ecclésiastique*. Translated by P. Dumont. Gembloux, Belg.: Duculot, 1971.

Mondzain, Marie-José. *Image, icône, économie*. Paris: Éditions du Seuil, 1996. Translation by Rico Franses: *Image, Icon, Economy: The Byzantine Origins of the Contemporary Imaginary*. Stanford, CA: Stanford University Press, 2005.

Richter, Gerhard. *Oikonomia: Der Gebrauch des Wortes Oikonomia im Neuen Testament, bei den Kirchenvätern und in der theologischen Literatur bis ins 20. Jahrhundert*. Berlin: De Gruyter, 2005.

Strauss, Leo. *Xenophon's Socratic Discourse*. Ithaca, NY: Cornell University Press, 1970.

Xenophon. *Oeconomicus*. Translated by E. C. Marchant. In *Xenophon in Seven Volumes*. Vol. 4. Loeb Classical Library. Cambridge, MA: Harvard University Press, 1923.

'ŌLĀM [עוֹלָם] (HEBREW)

ENGLISH **world**
FRENCH *monde*

➤ WORLD [WELT], and AIÔN, *HUMANITY*, *LIFE*, PRESENT

Among the words that designate the world, some emphasize the order of things, like the Greek *kosmos* [κόσμος] and the

Latin *mundus*. Others accentuate the presence of the subject, his being-in-life. The world is what one comes into at birth, and what one leaves at death. That is the case for English "world," German *Welt*, and Dutch *vereld*, in which the etymology is easier to discern: the length of life (cf. Eng. "old") of a man (Lat. *vir*; Ger. *wer*- in *Werwolf*, "wolfman," "werewolf"). The Hebrew word for "world" is currently *'ōlām* [עוֹלָם]. It is present in the Bible, but probably not in this sense, even in a late text like Kohelet (Ecclesiastes) 3:11. There is another, temporal sense, that of indefinite duration, usually in fixed expressions such as *'ōlām* [עוֹלָם], "to have an indeterminate future," whence "for all time," or *me-'ōlām* [מֵעוֹלָם], "for a time whose beginning is unknown," "since a moment which is not known," whence "forever."

The substantive, used in a constructed state as a quasi-adjective, designates the most remote antiquity (Dt 32:7, etc.). Indetermination is the principle that is supposed to explain the word's probable etymology through a root meaning "to hide": the distant past and future lie outside our knowledge.

The meaning "period, era, eon" evolves from the idea of an eschatological change that will distinguish an era still to come (*hā-'ōlām ha-bā'* [הָעוֹלָם הַבָּה]) from the present era (*hā-'ōlām ha-zèh* [הָעוֹלָם הַזֶּה]). Since in this future era, "everything" will have to be changed, the word designating the period takes on the meaning of its content: that of "world," a meaning that it retained in the later history of the language, and that passed, through the intermediary of Aramaic, into the Arabic (*'ālam* [عالم]).

In the first century CE, the formula "come into the world" is found, with the sense, for humans, of "to be born," or for things, "to appear." This is the case in the Greek Old Testament (Wis 2:24; 14:14), the New Testament (Jn 1:9; 13:1; 16:33), and the Talmud, where the expression "those who come into the world [בָּאֵי עוֹלָם]" designates all humans (e.g., Rosh Hashanah, 16a; the targum of Kohelet 1:4). It is also the case in pagan authors (Dio Chrysostom, 12.33); *On the Sublime*, 35.22). Biblical Greek renders this meaning either by *kosmos* [κόσμος] or by *aiôn* [αἰών]. This word has the twofold advantage of a certain phonetic proximity and a clear semantic relationship, the Greek word having designated, quite early in its evolution, the span of a life, and the Hebrew word being capable of signifying, for its part, "in perpetuity," in the sense of "for the whole of life" (Dt 15, 17, etc.).

Rémi Brague

| OMNITUDO REALITATIS

ENGLISH   the whole of reality
FRENCH   *le tout de la réalité, le tout inclusif de la réalité*
GERMAN   *der Inbegriff aller Realität, die Allheit aller möglichen Pradikäte*

➤ REALITY, *WHOLE*, and DASEIN, ESSENCE, GERMAN, GOD, *NEGATION*, RES, SEIN, *TO BE*, TO TI ÊN EINAI, VORHANDEN

Omnitudo realitatis, the Kantian formula that defines the ideal of pure reason—the idea of a being that includes within itself the whole of reality, without its being necessary to make a decision regarding the existence of a being of such an eminent superiority"—is no doubt the best proof of the differentiated sense of the term "reality" in Kant's critical work. Here, *Realität* is a simple calque of the Latin *realitas*, in the sense of the real content (*Sachheit*), of positive and exhaustive determinability ("total possibility"), against the background of which the determination of each existing thing stands out. The formula finds its meaning only in reference to Christian Wolff and Scholastic uses of the tem *realitas*, the very ones that were to make possible the first thematic opposition of existence understood as *Wirklichkeit* (actuality) to reality (*Realität*). This opposition is the core of Kant's critique of the ontological argument, insofar as the concept of God as *ens originarium, ens summum, ens entium*, although it is truly—but only within the bounds of reason—the "concept of supreme reality" that contains within itself "the whole of reality" does not for all that imply existence (*Dasein*). For Kant, *Dasein*, like being (*Sein*) or "positing," is not a "real" predicate, that is, one that can be "understood" in the set of "realities" through which the *ens realissimum* (see REALITY, and the distinction *Realität/Wirklichkeit*) are wholly defined.

Through this strange locution (*omnitudo realitatis*) we see in miniature, as it were, the extent to which Kant's breakthrough still had to struggle with the late Scholastic terminology of German academic metaphysics. The same can be said about many classic philosophical texts in Latin that require a kind of retroversion to Greek. In translating "German classical philosophy" we must not ignore this historical density of the concepts, even though they are elaborated by contraposition to *Fremdwörter*.

I. The Classical Meaning of the Kantian Formula: The Supremely Real Being

Kant introduces, in the framework of the Transcendental Dialectic, and as an ideal of pure reason, the idea of a total reality (*omnitudo realitatis, Allheit der Realität*), which corresponds to the principle of complete determinability: "*alles Existierende ist durchgängig bestimmt*" (everything which exists is completely determined). "In accordance with this principle, each and every thing is therefore related to a common correlate, the sum [*Inbegriff*] of all possibilities," that is, "to the *totality* (*universitas*) or sum of all possible predicates" (*Critique of Pure Reason*, A 573/B 601). Thus, to such a complete determination corresponds a concept we can never represent (*darstellen*) *in concreto* and whose proper place is pure reason itself. The latter, through its demand in principle for the complete determination of every thing (*Ding*), a demand that is itself based on the idea of the "sum-total of all possibility" (*Inbegriff aller Möglichkeit*), forms the concept of an individual object (*einzelner Gegenstand*) that is completely determined through the mere idea and must therefore be entitled an *ideal* of pure reason (ibid., A 574/B 602), which is also the idea of an *omnitudo realitatis* or an *ens realissimum*: the unique "thing" (*Ding*), completely determined by itself, which must be represented as an "individual" (ibid.). The possibility of that which thus contains within itself "all reality" (*alle Realität*) is to be considered "originary" in relation to the derived character of the "possibility of things" (*Möglichkeit der Dinge*), whose diversity is directly connected with the specific manner in which they "limit" the supreme reality (*höchste Realität*) that forms, as it were, its "substrate" (ibid., A 576/B 604). This supreme reality may also bear the more traditional names of *ens originarium, ens summum, ens entium* (originary being, supreme being, being of beings). Naturally, this is only an Idea—Kant even calls it a "fiction" (*Erdichtung*) (ibid., A 580/B 608)—that cannot be hypostatized in the concept of a Supreme Being.

II. "Reality," "Possibility," and "Quiddity" in the Work of Christian Wolff

In the Kantian vocabulary the formula *omnitudo realitatis* goes back beyond Wolff and Leibniz to the Scholastic use of the term. In his *Philosophia prima sive ontologia* (1730), Christian Wolff defined the "thing" and its "reality" in these terms:

> Quicquid est vel esse posse concipitur, dicitur res, quatenus est aliquid; ut adeo res definiri possit per id, quod est aliquid. Unde et realitas et quidditas apud scholasticos synonyma sunt.

> (Everything that is or that we can conceive being is called a thing, insofar as it is something; thus the thing could be defined by the fact that it is something. That is why, among the Scholastics, reality and quiddity are synonymous terms.)

(Wolff, *Philosophia prima*, §243)

Wolff had already posited, in his 1729 "German Metaphysics" (*Deutsche Metaphysik*), that "*Alles was seyn kann, es mag würklich seyn oder nicht, nennen wir ein Ding*" (Everything that can be, whether it is actually real or not, we call "thing") (§16). In Wolff's work, the distinction between *realitas* and *existentia*—the one that characterizes the tradition that Duns Scotus inaugurated—is also confirmed by this addition to §243: "*E.g., arbor et ens dicitur et res. Ens scil. si existentiam respicis; res vero, si quidditatem*" (Of a tree we say, for example, that it is an existent and a thing. An existent if we consider its existence; a thing, if we consider its quiddity). However, we must note another, broader use of the term *realitas* to designate, as in the *Theologia naturalis* (1736–37), everything that can be understood as truly inherent in any existent whatever ("*quicquid enti alicui vere inesse intelligitur*," 2: 5). In conformity with this new meaning, *existentia* (whether necessary or contingent) can then be itself considered a *realitas*. But if, as an inherent reality (*inesse alicui*), existence can be attributed as one property among others, it is nonetheless not identified with actuality or effectivity.

III. Existence as a Complement of Possibility, *Existentia* as *Actualitas*

In his "German Metaphysics" of 1719, Wolff discussed existence (understood as a complement or "fulfilling" of possibility) in terms of actuality (*Würklichkeit*):

Es muß also außer der Möglichkeit noch was mehrers dazu kommen, wenn etwas seyn soll, wodurch das Mögliche seine Erfüllung erhält. Und diese Erfüllung des Möglichen ist eben dasjenige, was wir Würklichkeit nennen.

(However, something additional must still be added, if something is supposed to be, whereby the possible receives its fulfillment. And this fulfillment of the possible is precisely what we call actual reality. [That is, actuality or existence.])

(Wolff, *Deutsche Metaphysik*, §14)

Used adverbially, the term *wirklich* (*würklich*) determines the mode of being present (being-there) or existent (*vorhanden*):

Weil die Welt nicht würklich da ist . . . die Welt ist würklich außer unserer Seele vorhanden.

(Because the world is not "really" present . . . the world really exists outside our minds [that is, it is actually present in front of us].)

(Wolff, *Vernünftige Gedanken*, §942–43)

This use of the term *Wirklichkeit* is in fact merely a translation of the Latin *actualitas*, understood as a determination of existence. Rudolf Goclenius, in his famous *Lexicon philosophicum*, observed, in the article "Actualitas": "*Actualitas prima, qua res existit, dicitur Esse; Paul. Scal. ita loquitur cum Barbaris, quorum haec est distinctio*" (We call being the primary actuality through which a thing exists; that was what Paul Scaliger called it, repeating this barbarous Scholastic distinction). Wolff says more precisely: "*Esse ens dicitur, quatenus est possibile: existere autem, quatenus actu datur*" (The existent is called being, insofar as it is possible; but we say that it exists insofar as it is given in the act or "actually given") (*Philosophia prima sive ontologia*, §874n). In this primary actuality, we can easily recognize the Aristotelian *energeia* [ἐνέργεια] (see PRAXIS), which is distinct from the essence or the formality that defines this or that being.

IV. *Realitas,* Realities, and Negations

Alexander G. Baumgarten and Georg Friedrich Meier, who on this point are quite closely dependent on Wolff, use the term *realitas* in the same sense. *Realitas* is used in the context of the general analysis of "determinations" (*notae et praedicata*) and combines all the positive conceptual characteristics that can be attributed to a thing through opposition to negative determinations (*negationes*) (Baumgarten, *Metaphysica*, §§34, 36; Meier, *Metaphysik*, §46). *Negationes* are thus directly opposed to *realitates* (Baumgarten, *Metaphysica*, §135), and the existent as such, or at least the existent that is conceived as *ens perfectum, positivum, reale*, is defined by the set of *realitates* that compose it, among which may figure existence or actuality (*actualitas*), understood as *complementum possibilitatis*:

Cum in omni ente sit realitatum numerus, omne ens habet certum realitatis gradum.

(As there are a certain number of realities in every existent, every existent contains a certain degree of reality.)

(Baumgarten, *Metaphysica*, §248)

Of course, for Baumgarten as for the Wolff of the *Theologia naturalis*, existence is to be counted among realities, since it contributes to complete determination (*complementum*) of what is (*Philosophia prima*, §172–73) :

Existentia non repugnat essentiae, sed est realitas cum ea compossibilis.

(Existence does not reject essence, but is instead a reality that is compossible with it.)

(Baumgarten, *Metaphysica*, §66)

Existentia est realitas cum essentia et reliquis realitatibus compossibilis.

(Existence is a reality compossible with essence and with all other realities.)

(Ibid., §810.)

But existence, thus understood as a "reality," opens another dimension, that of actuality or *Wirklichkeit* (we have already seen how the latter term imposed itself on Wolff). Thus, Baumgarten can now write: "*Omne actuale est interne possibile, seu posita existentia ponitur interna possibilitas*" (everything that is actual is intrinsically possible, which means that existence being posited, internal possibility is as well) (ibid., §8), which Hegel was to "translate" very naturally as "*Was wirklich ist, ist möglich*" (what is actually real is possible) (*Wissenschaft der Logik*, ed. G. Lasson, 2: 381).

Thus *realitates* considered as positive determinations, which are themselves susceptible of degrees, constitute so many *entia realia*, and in principle they can all be applied to a concrete thing (the *ens reale* in the strict sense) in which they are inherent; then we understand that all realities, as perfections raised to the highest degree (*plurimae maximae realitates*), may coincide in one and the same being which, containing within itself the *omnitudo realitatis*, will be the *ens realissimum*:

Omnes realitates sunt vere positivae, nec ulla negatio est realitas. Ergo si vel maxime conjugantur in ente omnes, numquam ex iis orietur contradictio. Ergo omnes realitates sunt in ente compossibiles. Ergo enti perfectissimo convenit omnitudo realitatum, earumque, quae ullo in ente esse possunt, maximarum.

(All realities are truly positive, and no negation is a reality. Thus if all realities are combined to the highest degree in the existent, no contradiction will ever result. All realities are therefore compossible in the existent. Hence the complete totality of realities—and the maximal ones that may be in a given existent—is appropriate for the most perfect existent.)

(Baumgarten, *Metaphysica*, §807)

V. The Kantian Thesis: Being as Positing

We see clearly all that is at stake in the thesis that makes existence a "reality." It is the most economical formulation and, as it were, the core of the ontological argument: we can affirm the existence of God as soon as existence has been established as a real predicate, for otherwise, as Baumgarten once again emphasizes:

Deus non actualis esset ens omnibus realitatibus gaudens, cui quaedam tamen deesset.

(God would not be the actual [or effective] existent enjoying all realities, since he would lack one of them.)

(Baumgarten, *Metaphysica*, §807)

Here we find once again the ancient ontological argument, set forth this time in Wolffian concepts, the very conceptual system that Kant was to criticize as early as 1763, refusing both to make existence and being-there (*Dasein*) a real predicate or to count it among the realities that belong to a thing or constitute it, and to make God the concept including all realities. Saying that being (*Sein*) is not a real predicate (*reales Prädikat*) or that it adds no "reality" to the concept of a thing leads Kant to define it as "positing": "*Es ist bloß die Position eines Dinges, oder gewisser Bestimmungen an sich selbst*" (It is merely the positing of a thing, or of certain determinations, in themselves) (*Critique of Pure Reason*, A 598/B 626). Thus the propositions "God is omnipotent" and "God exists" can no longer be analyzed in terms of predication, as if it sufficed to distinguish (as in Meister Eckhart) between propositions of the third and second adjacents. There is no proposition of the second adjacent, or rather, when we say "God exists," "we attach no new predicate to the concept of God, but only posit the subject in itself with all its predicates" (*Critique of Pure Reason*). Existence or actuality adds nothing ("*Das Wirkliche enthält nichts mehr als das Mögliche*" [The real contains no

more than the possible], ibid.). What is entirely lacking here is a common measure or additivity.

The remaining, irreducible heterogeneity of being and reality governs Kant's thesis of being as *Position* (positing). It is certainly permissible to see in this, as Heidegger does, the distant echo of a Scholastic doctrine transmitted by Suárez: "It suffices to consider this word 'existence' to see in the *sistere* [*ex-sistere*], in placing, the connection with *ponere* and positing: *existentia* is the *actus quo res sistitur, ponitur extra statum possibilitatis*" ("La thèse de Kant sur l'être," *Questions II*, 110; *Nietzsche*, 2: 417ff.; Heidegger, "Kant's Thesis about Being"). But we can also focus our attention, not on this uniformly continuous history ("From Anaximander to Nietzsche"), but on the Kantian rupture with the Scotist tradition.

Jean-François Courtine

BIBLIOGRAPHY

Baumgarten, Alexander Gottlieb. *Metaphysica*. 7th ed. Hildesheim, Ger.: Olms, 1963. First published in 1779.

Corr, Charles Anthony. "The *Deutsche Metaphysik* of Christian Wolff: Text and Transitions." In *History of Philosophy in the Making*, edited by Linus J. Thro, 113–20. Washington, D.C.: University Press of America, 1982.

Hegel, Georg Wilhelm Friedrich. *Enzyklopädie der philosophischen Wissenschaften im Grundrisse*. §1-244. In *Die Wissenschaft der Logik*, edited by Wolfgang Bonsiepen and Hans-Christian Lucas. *Gesammelte Werke*. Vol. 20. Hamburg: Meiner, 1992. First published in 1830. Translation by A. V. Miller: *The Science of Logic*. London: Allen and Unwin, 1976.

Heidegger, Martin. "Kants These über das Sein." In *Wegmarken*, edited by Friedrich-Wilhelm von Hermann. In *Gesamtausgabe*. Vol. 9: 445–80. Frankfurt am Main: Klostermann, 1976. Translation by Thomas Sheehan and William McNeill: "Kant's Thesis about Being." In *Pathmarks*, edited by William McNeill, 337–64. Cambridge: Cambridge University Press, 1998.

———. *Nietzsche*. Edited by Brigitte Schillbach. 2 vols. In *Gesamtausgabe*. Vol. 6. Frankfurt am Main: Klostermann, 1996–97. Translation by David Farrell Krell: *Nietzsche*. 4 vols. New York: Harper and Row, 1979–87.

Kant, Immanuel. *Kritik der reinen Vernunft*. Edited by Königlich Preussischen Akademie der Wissenschaften. In *Kants Gesammelte Schriften*. Vols. 3–4. Berlin: De Gruyter, 1902–. Translation by Paul Guyer and A. Wood: *Critique of Pure Reason*. Edited by Paul Guyer and A. Wood. Cambridge: Cambridge University Press, 1997.

Meier, Georg Friedrich. *Metaphysik*. 4 vols. Preface by Michael Albrecht. Hildesheim, Ger.: Olms, 2007. First published in 1755–59.

Wolff, Christian. *Deutsche Metaphysik: Vernünftige Gedanken von Gott, der Welt und der Seele des Menschen, auch allen Dingen überhaupt. Gesammelte Werke*. Vol. 10. Hildesheim, Ger.: Olms, 1983. *Metafisica Tedesca, con le Annotazione alla Metafisica Tedesca*. Edited by Raffaele Ciafardone. Milan: Bompiani, 2003.

———. *Philosophia prima sive ontologia*. New ed. Edited by Jean École. *Gesammelte Werke*. Part 2, vol. 3. Hildesheim, Ger.: Olms, 1962. First published in 1736.

———. *Theologia naturalis*. Edited, with introduction, notes, and index by Jean École. 3 vols. *Gesammelte Werke*. Part 2, vols. 7–8. Hildesheim, Ger.: Olms, 1978–81. First published in 1739–41.

PARDON / FORGIVE

FRENCH   *pardon*
GERMAN   *vergeben*
GREEK   *suggignôskein* [συγγιγνώσκειν]
LATIN   *ignoscere, remittere*
SPANISH   *perdonar*

➤ DUTY, *FALSE,* MEMORY, THEMIS

In most European languages, the verb "to pardon," or "to forgive," is a compound of "give" with an intensive preverb and is modeled on late Latin *perdonare*: thus *vergeben* (Ger.), *pardonner* (Fr.), *perdonar* (Sp.). The pardon, as a supplement to giving, is a way of escaping the rigorous calculus of crime and punishment. However, antiquity expresses "pardon" in terms of knowledge: the Greek *suggignôskein* [συγγιγνώσκειν] and Latin *ignoscere* are compounds of verbs meaning "become acquainted with" (*gignôskein* [γιγνώσκειν], *noscere*); yet the two paradigms are antithetical: the Greek understands the pardon as shared knowledge (*sun*, "with"), whereas in Latin "pardon" belongs to the register of ignorance and the refusal to know (*in-*, no doubt privative). The moral and political implications of these two attitudes differ considerably.

I. Donation and Pardon

In most modern languages, both Romance and Germanic, "to pardon" is a transposition of Late Latin *perdonare*, which is, moreover, attested only once (in Romulus's *Aesop*, around the fourth century). The verb is not a direct compound of the Latin *dare* (give) but derives, through the noun *donum*, from *donare* ("to donate," and in particular, "to absolve," "to favor"). A pardon, as the intensive preverb indicates, has the structure of a completion or an excess, of a surplus of donation. It makes an exception in the accountability of debt and justice, which apportions punishment to the crime in accord with a strict retribution derived from the *lex talionis*.

By itself, "giving" or "donating" already implies a movement beyond equality and reciprocity: according to the definition in *Le nouveau petit Robert*, the French word *donner* means *abandonner*, to give something to someone "without receiving anything in return." Similarly, the archaic economy of the potlatch, brought to light by Marcel Mauss, implies a "gift/counter-gift" circulation that goes beyond commercial exchange: "in the things exchanged in the potlatch, there is a virtue that forces the gifts to circulate, to be given and given back" (*Essai sur le don*). The munificence of the counter-gift constantly begins a new debt that perpetuates the process of "expense," to adopt Georges Bataille's expression. This excess constitutive of the gift and its systematics is, however, not of the same order as that involved in the pardon. Instead of initiating an infinite chain, the pardon is instead a cutting off, or "de-cision," like a decision handed down by a court. But pardoning is not, like punishing, a matter of

balancing accounts; it is on the contrary a matter of agreeing to clear an account even if it is in deficit, even if it is not clear. A fault is remitted (*remittere veniam*) just as the International Monetary Fund remits a debt or a judge remits a sentence, to "clear the account." This is shown in the Lord's Prayer, in which the verse "Forgive us our trespasses as we forgive those who trespass against us" translates the accountant's Latin: *dimitte nobis debita nostra* (forgive us our debts), which is itself modeled literally on the Greek: *aphes hêmin ta opheilêmata hêmôn* [ἄφες ἡμῖν τὰ ὀφειλήματα ἡμῶν] (lit. "remit, release our debts"; see Matt 6:12–15).

There is, however, an alternative way to proceed. We might consider that with forgiveness, the final reckoning is, in the end, simply extended. New, initially extrinsic elements do come into play here: the request for forgiveness ("Forgiveness? Have they ever asked us for forgiveness?" Jankélévitch, *L'imprescriptible*), repentance ("If [your brother] sins against you seven times in the day, and turns to you seven times and says, 'I repent,' you must forgive him," Luke 17:3). All this evidence of good will, in fact, generates a new but no less exact accounting: one that balances the request for and the granting of forgiveness, which we could describe as "Abrahamic" and which functions even in the great public representations of repentance (Ricœur, *La mémoire*).

What significance should then be assigned to completion, to the surplus constitutive of the "par-don"? Can we still say that forgiveness clears an account in deficit? Yes, and in at least two modes of excess. First, because the Gospel's hyperbole in commanding us to love our enemies or to turn the other cheek produces an offer of "absolute," or "mad," forgiveness that always goes beyond the request and may merge with a structure of renewal analogous to that of the potlatch (this would in any case be worth thinking about). Also, as Jacques Derrida stressed, because there is something "unpardonable" and "imprescriptible": a pardon is really a pardon—the perfection of the gift—only when it pardons the unpardonable, remits the imprescriptible (the Shoah, which we no longer dare introduce with "for example"); only the impossible pardon is truly nonaccountable and in conformity with its concept.

II. Forgiveness and Grace: Theological-Political Verticality

To account for the inadequation of every model of exchange, even if it is noncommercial, Paul Ricœur chooses to emphasize the "vertical disparity between the profundity of the offense and the loftiness of the forgiveness" (*La mémoire*). This vertical disparity, which for him constitutes the authentic singularity of forgiveness, has to do with the possibility of "detaching the agent from his act": "you are better than your acts," says this "liberating word" (see Matt 18:18, "Whatever you bind [*alligaveritis*] on earth shall be bound [*ligata*] in heaven, and whatever you loose [*solveritis*] on earth shall be loosed [*soluta*] in heaven," where *solvere*, "to unbind," "to dissolve," "to absolve," translates the Greek *luein* [λύειν].

This strong conception is without any doubt theological-political. There is the one who pardons, on high, who possesses the sublime ability to originate anew, to re-create, and there is the one who is pardoned, down below, because he has offended and fallen (although the etymology of *culpa* is unknown, *fallere*, from which "fault" and "false" are derived, is generally connected with the Greek *sphallô* [σφάλλω], "to cause to fall," or with Old High German *fallan*, "to fall," and *peccare*'s first meaning is "to stumble," "to make an error"). Clearing every account is a gracious remission. Only grace can in fact settle the account in deficit: first of all, the efficacious grace of God, however it is transmitted (although the state of innocence was lost with Adam, "baptismal grace" is substituted for it, and in the case of mortal sin, "penitential grace"); then, modeled on it or legitimated by it, the ruler's clemency (from the Latin *clemens*, "gently sloping"), which is never more than the human transposition of God's grace. This condescension of grace, which is sometimes unbearable, is in any case exercised in the disparity of a dual relationship.

III. To Forgive: Not to Know or to Understand?

This vertical disparity is in perfect conformity with the conception of the pardon that is expressed in classical Latin. On the other hand, it is not compatible with the Greek pardon.

The verb "to pardon" corresponds to the Latin *ignoscere*—a verb for which *venia* (indulgence, favor, grace) serves as a substantive (*veniam dare, petere*, "to grant," "to request pardon," whence our "venial" sin). Latin grammarians saw in *ignoscere* a compound with a privative prefix, derived from *noscere*, "become acquainted with," "recognize" (perfect *novi-*, "know"), as is shown for example by the gloss *ignoscere: non noscere* (Loewe, *Prodromus*, quoted by RT: *Dictionnaire étymologique de la langue latine*); but there is also a verb *ignorare*, which means "not to know," "to be ignorant of." There is thus a complex interplay among ignorance, denial, and pardon, as is shown for example by this remark of Seneca's regarding a slap received by Cato: "He did not get angry, he did not take revenge for the insult, he did not even forgive it [*ne remisit quidem*], but he denied the fact—there was more magnanimity in not recognizing than in pardoning [*majore animo non agnovit quam ignovisset*, with the play on the two compounds *ad-nosco*, 'recognize,' 'admit' and *ignosco*]" ("On Constancy," 14.3). In any case, it is clear that the kind of ignorance involved in the Latin pardon is connected with the sovereign decision not to remember, to forget, to "grant amnesty"; the anecdote reported in "On Anger" (2.32.2) concludes with these words of Cato's: "I do not recall that I have ever been struck" (*non memini . . . me percussum*). There is magnanimity and high-mindedness in the wise man who haughtily pardons, and this condescendence is entirely founded on a denial of knowledge.

The Greek *suggignôskein* [συγγιγνώσκειν] takes us into a completely different world: instead of being connected with ignorance or forgetting, forgiveness has to do with shared knowledge. *Suggignôsken* means literally "become acquainted with" and thus generally "to share knowledge" (knowledge that may be a mistake [Thucydides, *History of the Peloponnesian War*, 8.24.6] or the secret of a conspiracy [Appian, *Civil Wars*, 2.6]); and, in the middle voice, when one shares knowledge with oneself, "to be conscious of " (Lysias, *Discourses*, 9.11); whence: "to be of the same opinion," "to consent" (when making a transaction or a treaty), "to recognize," "to confess" (thus Sophocles's Antigone says: "Once I suffer I will know that I was wrong"; *Antigone*, v. 1018); and finally, "to have a fellow feeling with another" (RT: LSJ), "pardon": this is the most common meaning among the Greek tragedians (e.g., Sophocles, *Electra*, 257; Euripides, *Helen*, 1105). Moreover, the noun *suggnôme* [συγγνώμη] always has this sense of "pardon," "forgiveness," "indulgence." It is by understanding together, that is, by entering into the other person's reasons, by intellectual action and not by compassion, that a Greek pardons or forgives.

- See Box 1.

The prefix *sun-* (with) in the Greek *suggignôskein* invalidates the essential characteristic of the modern pardon, as well as that of Latin ignorance: it cannot imply any vertical disparity. On the contrary, pardon/comprehension takes place in the horizontality of a "with" that belongs, not to the theological-political domain, but to the political alone. The relationship is no longer dual but plural, implying a "we," or even a city, that the pardon redefines. Furthermore, the offense is not seen as a fall, but rather as a failure, *hamartia* [ἁμαρτία], *hamartêma* [ἁμάρτημα] (from *hamartanein* [ἁμαρτάνειν], "miss the target"; thus both "make a mistake" and "commit an offense"). Aristotle underlines this with regard to this definition of virtue as mean:

> [I]t is possible to fail [*hamartanein*] many ways . . . while to succeed [*katorthoun* (κατορθοῦν)] is possible only in one way . . . —to miss the mark [*apotuchein tou skopou* (ἀποτυχεῖν τοῦ σκοποῦ)] is easy, to hit it [*epituchein* (ἐπιτυχεῖν)] is difficult.
>
> (*Nicomachean Ethics*, 2.6.1106b28–33).

Thus we are faced with two heterogeneous models clearly reflected in the Latin and Greek words: an exemption when confronted by a failure, which uses the superior's refusal to recognize to clear an account in deficit and start over from zero; and an intellectual sharing that redefines the space of a "we."

Barbara Cassin

BIBLIOGRAPHY

Arendt, Hannah. *The Human Condition*. 2nd ed. Chicago: University of Chicago Press, 1998.

Aristotle. *The Nicomachean Ethics*. Translated by David Ross. Revised with an introduction and notes by Lesley Brown. Oxford: Oxford University Press, 2009.

Bataille, Georges. *The Accursed Share: An Essay on General Economy*. Translated by Robert Hurley. Vol. 1. New York: Zone, 1988.

———. *La part maudite: Essai d'économie générale. La consumation*. Paris: Minuit, 1967. First published in 1949.

Derrida, Jacques. "Le siècle et le pardon" (interview with Michel Wieviorka). In *Foi et savoir: Suivi de "Le siècle et le pardon,"* 101–33. Paris: Éditions du Seuil, 2000. Originally published as "Le siècle et le pardon" in *Le Monde des Débats* 9 (1999): 10–17. Translation by Michael Hughes: "On Forgiveness." In *On Cosmopolitanism and Forgiveness*. London: Routledge, 2001.

Jankélévitch, Vladimir. *Forgiveness*. Translated by Andrew Kelley. Chicago: University of Chicago Press, 2005.

———. *L'imprescriptible: Pardonner? Dans l'honneur et la dignité*. Paris: Éditions du Seuil, 1986.

1

Aristotle: *Suggnômê* as understanding and broad-mindedness

In the *Nicomachean Ethics* (6.11), Aristotle counts *suggnômê* ("judging with," "compassion," "remorse," "sympathy") among what are called the "intellectual virtues" (*dianoêtikas* [διανοητιϰάς]), in contrast to the "moral virtues," which have to do with character, *êthikas* [ἠθιϰάς] (on this distinction, see ibid., 1.13). It is connected with *sunesis* [σύνεσις], "junction" (from the verb *suniêmi* [συνίημι], "bring or send together," "approach," "understand," with the same preverb *sun-* as in *suggnômê*), which is translated by "intelligence"; and it is defined in relation to *gnômê* [γνώμη], the faculty of knowing (this is obviously *gnômê* as in *suggnômê*, which is rendered by "judgment," "resolution," and covers "good sense" and "common sense" (the common sense expressed in proverbs, *gnômai* [γνῶμαι]) as well as "intention" and "verdict." *Gnômê* and *suggnômê* both refer not to the just man (*to dikaion* [τὸ δίϰαιον], who distributes in accord with equality or corrects and equalizes proportionally), but rather to equity (*hê epieikeia* [ἡ ἐπιείϰεια]), which, being at the heart of justice, corrects the just man according to the law by taking into account singularities and cases (ibid., 5.14). One quotation will suffice

to explain how "pardon" is anchored in comprehension, discernment, and broad-mindedness and why it proves difficult to translate into French as well as English.

What is called judgment [*sens* in J. Voilquin's French translation; *bon sens* in Gauthier–Jolif's], in virtue of which men are said to "be sympathetic judges" [some manuscripts read *eugnômonas* (εὐγνώμονας); *qu'ils ont un bon jugement*, in J. Tricot's French translation] and to "have judgment, [*echein* . . . *gnômên* (ἔχειν . . . γνώμην)]," is the right discrimination of the equitable [*hê tou epieikous . . . krisis orthê* (ἡ τοῦ ἐπιειϰοῦς . . . ϰρίσις ὀρθή)]. This is shown by the fact that we say that the equitable man is above all others a man of sympathetic judgment [*suggnômonikon* (συγγνωμονιϰόν), "understanding"; *favorablement disposé pour autri* in J. Tricot's French translation; *l'homme qui, entrant dans le sens des autres, est porté à leur pardonner* in J. Barthélémy Saint-Hilaire's translation], and identify equity with sympathetic

judgment about certain facts [*to echein . . . suggnômên* (τὸ ἔχειν . . . συγγνώμην); *de montrer de la largeur d'esprit* in J. Tricot's translation]. And sympathetic judgment is judgment which discriminates what is equitable [ἡ δὲ συγγνώμη γνώμη ἐστὶ ϰριτιϰὴ τοῦ ἐπιειϰοῦς ὀρθή] and does so correctly; and correct judgment is that which judges what is true.

(*Nicomachean Ethics*, trans. Ross, 6.11)

BIBLIOGRAPHY

Aristotle. *Éthique à Nicomaque*. Translated by J. Barthélémy-Saint-Hilaire. Revised by A. Gomez-Muller. Paris: Librairie Générale Française, 1992. Translated by R. A. Gauthier and J. Y. Jolif. 2nd ed. Louvain, Belg.: Publications Universitaires, 1970. Translated by Jean Tricot. 7th ed. Paris: Vrin, 1990. Translated by J. Voilquin [1940]. Paris: Flammarion, 1965.

———. *The Nicomachean Ethics*. Translated by David Ross. Revised with an introduction and notes by Lesley Brown. Oxford: Oxford University Press, 2009.

———. "Should We Pardon Them?" Translated by Ann Hobart. *Critical Inquiry* 22 (1996): 552–72.

Lacoste, Jean-Yves. "Pardon." *Dictionnaire d'éthique et de philosophie morale*. Edited by Monique Canto-Sperber, 1069–75. Paris: Presses Universitaires de France, 1996.

Mauss, Marcel. *Essai sur le don*. In *Sociologie et anthropologie*. 10th ed. Paris: Presses Universitaires de France, 2003. First published in 1950. Translation by Ben Brewster: *Sociology and Psychology: Essays*. London: Routledge & Kegan Paul, 1979.

Ricœur, Paul. *La mémoire, l'histoire, l'oubli*. Paris: Éditions du Seuil, 2000. Translation by Kathleen Blamey and David Pellauer: *Memory, History, Forgetting*. Chicago: University of Chicago Press, 2004.

Seneca. "On Constancy." In *Seneca: Moral Essays*, vol. 1. Edited by T. E. Page et al. Translated by John W. Basore. The Loeb Classical Library. London: Heinemann, 1928.

Sophocles. *Antigone*. Translated by R. Fagles. In *Sophocles: Three Theban Plays*. New York: Viking, 1982.

PARONYM, DERIVATIVELY NAMED, COGNATE WORD

FRENCH	*paronyme*
GERMAN	*Paronym, nachbenannt*
GREEK	*parônumos* [παρώνυμος]
ITALIAN	*denominativo*
LATIN	*denominativum*

➤ ANALOGY, CONNOTATION, ESSENCE, HOMONYM, PRÉDICABLE, PREDICATION, SENSE, SUPPOSITION, WORD

"Paronym" is the usual translation of the Greek *parônuma* [παρώνυμα], used by Aristotle in the first chapter of the *Categories* (1a12–15): "Things are said to be named 'derivatively' which derive

their name from some other name, but differ from it in termination (*ptôsis* [πτῶσις]). Thus the grammarian derives his name from the word 'grammar,' and the courageous man from the word 'courage'" (trans. E. M. Edghill in *Basic Works of Aristotle*). The differing translations of the substantive or adjective term in various European languages bear witness to a difficulty that is not merely linguistic. The problem raised by *parônumos* [παρώνυμος] for the translator/interpreter has to do with the fact that while the term does not initially play a metaphysical role in Aristotelian discourse, it acquires a preponderant role in the tradition of interpreting Aristotle, which makes it a kind of hidden source of the history of metaphysics.

I. The Status of Paronyms, between Words, Things, and Concepts

Boethius translated *Categories* 1a12–15 this way:

Denominativa vero dicuntur quaecumque ab aliquo, solo differentia casu, secundum nomen habent appellationem, ut a grammatica grammaticus et a fortitudine forti.

(Finally, we call denominatives all those which, differing from another thing solely by the "case," receive their appellation in accord with [its] name: thus from grammar grammarian, and from courage, courageous.)

(*Aristoteles Latinus*, 5, 15–17)

Denominativa seems to mark a clear difference from *sumpta* (derived names)—and rightly, because for Aristotle, *parônuma* [παρώνυμα] are, like homonyms and synonyms, things, and not terms. The difficulty arises from this parallelism: in modern, non-Aristotelian usage, synonymy and homonymy concern linguistic units. Ultimately, this displacement, which began in the Middle Ages, cannot fail to spill over onto the perception of the status of paronymy, its function, and the stakes that it involves within the Aristotelian horizon. Another difficulty has to do with the fact that in classical Latin, *appellatio, appellare,* and *appellatum* refer to both "the named" (a man named "Peter") and to the "calling" or naming ("who is called Peter"), that is to say, to two different facts: the fact of naming (calling someone "Peter") and the fact of bearing the name "Peter." Hence the dimension of the derivation of the name (the de-nominative) raised in the determination of the Aristotelian paronym—a thing that takes its name from another thing through a kind of double derivation (real, where the courageous is a declination of courage, and verbal, where the word "courageous" is an inflection, bending, shifting, of "courage")—is either illegible or redundant in Boethius's translation (and its French revision by Jules Tricot).

■ See Box 1.

Paronyms being adjectives, and, in logic, concrete accidental terms, the question of the meaning of paronymic terms was the object of lively controversies from the Middle Ages to the seventeenth century. Two main positions opposed each other: that of Avicenna and that of Averroës. Avicenna's thesis (*Logica* I, 1508, folio 9va) was summarized and rejected by Averroës in his *Long Commentary on the Metaphysics* (text 5, comm. 14): "He [Avicenna] says that 'white' in 'Socrates is white' signifies primarily the subject and secondarily the accident, but quite the contrary is the case: 'white' signifies primarily the accident and secondarily the subject. In fact, it is of the essence of the accident to exist in a subject." Averroës's thesis was adopted by most thirteenth-century philosophers: the common opinion was that "white" signifies whiteness *in recto* and the subject *in obliquo* (cf., e.g., Dietrich of Freiburg, *De accidentibus,* chap. 13, p. 72). Avicenna's doctrine, conveyed through the theory of connotation, established itself thanks to Ockham, with a few lexical differences. Thus Marsilius of Inghen, a follower of Buridan, uses the term "material signified" to refer to the subject (for which alone the term substitutes) and "formal signified" to refer to what the term "connotes" or "signifies connotatively," whereas Buridan himself used the term *appellatio* in preference to *connotatio.* In the seventeenth century, Averroës's theory became dominant, combined this time with a distinction between "distinct" signification and "vague" signification. Its paradigm is the discussion of "connotation" in the *Port-Royal Grammar,* which adopts, in this context, the medieval distinction between "direct" (*in recto*) signification and "oblique" (*in obliquo*) signification:

> I have said that adjectives have two significations: one distinct, which is that of the form; and the other vague, which is that of the subject. But it must not be concluded therefrom that they signify more directly the form than the subject, as if the most distinct signification were also the most direct. For on the contrary it is certain that they signify the subject directly, and as grammarians say, *in recto,* though more vaguely, and they signify the form only indirectly, and grammarians again say, *in*

1

Modern translations

Modern translations of Aristotle's *Categories* generally adopt the Boethian interpretation. A few English versions use "derivatively named" (H. P. Cooke, trans., *Aristotle, The Categories, On Interpretation*; E. M. Edghill, trans., *The Works of Aristotle, I: Categoriae and De interpretatione*). In French, the same goes for R. Bodéüs (*Catégories* [2001], 3): "In addition, we call 'derived' [*dérivées*] all things that are distinguished from each other by inflection and have the appellation corresponding to their name. Thus from the knowledge of letters derives the literate and from courage the courageous"; others (including K. Oehler, German trans.; J. L. Ackrill, English trans.; and D. Pesce, Italian trans.) prefer, like J. Tricot, to stick to the "Greek" term, as does E. Rolfes, who uses the formula "Paronym (*nachbenannt*)" (in *Aristoteles, Kategorien*). However, they all clearly imply that what is "denominated" (*nach-benannt*) after another thing is indeed a thing, and not a word. Owens justifies the calque of the Greek (*The Doctrine of Being in the Aristotelian Metaphysics,* 330). For him, the distinction made in English between

"denominative" and "derivative" is not pertinent, because both apply to words. The best translation of *parônuma* is thus "*paronyms,*" according to Owens: "Derivative in this application would refer only to the word, not the thing. Denominative likewise applies only to the words. . . . There is in English no term for this notion." Modern translations do not interpret the calque of Latin *denominativa* in the same way. For us, this means that the philosophical ambiguity of the Aristotelian notion of "paronymy," which is connected with its position intermediary between "homonymy" and "synonymy" (which was to produce its effects at the beginning of the invention of the analogy of being; see ANALOGY), is doubled, indeed covered over, by the ambiguity of the French *dénominatif* or English "denominative," which are torn, but in a different way than the Aristotelian paronym, between words and things.

BIBLIOGRAPHY

Aristotle. *Aristoteles, Kategorien. Neu übersetzt und mit einer Einleitung und erklärenden Anmerkungen versehen.* German translation by E. Rolfes. Leipzig: Felix Meiner, 1920.

———. *Aristotle, The Categories, On Interpretation.* 2nd ed. Translated by H. P. Cooke. London: Loeb Classical Library, 1938.

———. *Catégories.* French translation by R. Bodéüs. Paris: Les Belles Lettres, 2001.

———. *Categories, and De interpretatione.* Translated by J. L. Ackrill. Oxford: Oxford University Press / Clarendon Press, 1963.

———. *Catégories; De l'interprétion.* French translation by J. Tricot. Paris: Vrin, 1966.

———. *Kategorien.* German translation by K. Oehler. Berlin: Akademie-Verlag, 1984.

———. *Le Categorie.* Italian translation by D. Pesce. Padua: Liviana Ed., 1966.

———. *The Works of Aristotle, I: Categoriae and De interpretatione.* Translated by E. M. Edghill. Oxford: Oxford University Press, 1928. Reprinted in 1963.

Owens, Joseph. "Aristotle on Categories." *The Review of Metaphysics* 14 (1960/61): 73–90.

———. *The Doctrine of Being in the Aristotelian Metaphysics.* Toronto: Pontifical Institute of Medieval Studies, 1951.

olbliquo, though more distinctly. Thus white, *candidus*, signifies directly something having whiteness; *habens candorem*; but in a very vague way, not indicating in particular any of the things that can have whiteness; and it signifies whiteness only indirectly; but in a way just as distinct as the word whiteness, *candor*, itself.

(*Grammaire de Port-Royal*, 3rd ed., II.2 / A. Arnauld, *Grammaire générale et raisonnée*)

The metaphysical issue is first of all the relationship between Plato and Aristotle. Expressing in language (that of "de-nomination") and in a quasi-Platonic way the relation of a concrete thing to a form that is, so to speak, declined in it, Aristotelian paronymy is also the hollow place marked out within a mechanism—the distinction of homonyms, synonyms, and paronyms—linking words and things, crossing their respective properties. Neither words, nor things, nor concepts, but in a sense all three at once, the entities (*parônuma*) that, in the Aristotelian tradition, are involved in the definition of paronyms—this grammarian and this grammar, connected by a desinence that does not really pertain to things, but that is not simply an aspect of words—thus appear as the sign of an originary indecision in the Aristotelian system of categories, between a Platonism that is residual but confined to language, and an inchoate Aristotelianism that has not yet found its level of action. The interpretation of the term *parônumos* requires elucidating the status of the *ptôsis* [πτῶσις] (case, desinence, inflection) both in Aristotle, and in his commentators taking into account the complex role *ptôsis* was to play, in late antiquity and the Middle Ages, in the constitution of a so-called Aristotelian metaphysics that gradually came to center on the notion of an "analogy of being."

"Paronymy," the structure to which the term *parônumos* refers in the *Categories*, is described this way by C. H. Kahn (*The Verb "Be" in Ancient Greek*): "Paronymy is a four-term relation between two things, A and B, and two corresponding words, 'A' and 'B' (the 'names' of these things), such that 'A' differs from 'B' by a minor morphological deviation." We see that a single term can thus cover simultaneously two relations, A/B and 'A'/'B,' as well as their own relation to each other, A/B ≡ 'A'/'B.' The reader of Aristotle's ancient and medieval interpreters cannot fail to wonder what, in the texts he has before his eyes, founds A/B ≡ 'A'/'B,' and if it is founded, whether this "foundation" is truly "Aristotelian." From this point of view we must keep in mind that for Aristotle, not every term morphologically derived from another term refers to a "paronymy": "human" or "the human" is not a paronym of "man" or of "humanity." As is clearly shown by *Categories* 8, 10a27–b11, "paronymy" does not concern just any concrete term relative to the corresponding abstract or just any adjective relative to a substantive: paronymy has to do only (1) with concrete accidental terms considered from the point of view of the property that they signify and of the substance that possesses them; and, by that very fact, (2) with the relationship of ontological dependency connecting an accident with a substance. From this point of view, "paronymy" thus cannot be understood independently of the diverse medieval interpretations of *Metaphysics* z 1, 1028a10–20 (the accident

is not *ens*—an existent—but *entis*, something of an existent), representing the accident (according to Aristotle) as an "inflection of substance."

- See Box 2.

II. Paronymy between Analogy and Emanation

This interpretation of the accident as an "inflection" must also be kept in mind when stressing the central role played by "paronymy" in the late antique interpretation of Aristotle's *Metaphysics*. "Paronymy" is involved in the genesis of the theory called "the analogy of being" (*analogia entis*). The phenomenon can be described as the establishment of the homonyms *aph' henos* (ἀφ' ἑνός] (coming from something unitary, "unity of provenance" [Lat. *ab uno*]) and the homonyms *pros hen* [πρὸς ἕν] (in view of something of one, "focal unit" [*ad unum*]), or more simply *pros hen legomena* [πρὸς ἕν λεγόμενα], placed by Greek commentators on Aristotle in a median position between homonyms and pure synonyms, in the very place concurrently occupied, but for other reasons, by Aristotle's *parônuma*.

- See Box 3.

The appearance of what is called the "theory of analogy" assumes that at a given moment, the "intermediaries" *aph' henos* and *pros hen* (or some of their properties) were collected under the rubric "homonyms by analogy," and that this occurred either by displacing paronyms or by absorbing them or certain of their properties. Whoever its author, this act—which by its very violence caused to merge or be superimposed in a single place phenomena as different as the focal meaning, paronymy in the strict sense, and the ontological derivation—has had two distinct posterities. The most famous and most studied is the theory of the analogy as being characteristic of the Arabo-Latin age (which began with Avicenna's and Averroës's translations of the so-called Arabic Aristotle). Within this horizon, *denominatio* is gradually marginalized by the notion of *analogia* or absorbed by it in increasingly complex formulations. But despite all this, we must not purely and simply identify "analogy" and "paronymy," as some contemporary interpreters have done (cf. Hirschberger, "Paronymie und Analogie bei Aristoteles"). In the Greco-Latin age of metaphysics, when the problem of the unification of the multiple meanings of being does not play a leading role, the notion of *denominatio* (= "paronymy") intervenes in an entirely different context. Boethius uses it to resolve a specific problem formulated in the *De hebdomadibus*: "Quomodo substantiae in eo quod sint bonae sint cum non sint substantialia bona"—that is, to determine "how, assuming that they are good (since they tend toward the good and are thus like it in some way), things that exist—substances—are good in their very being without however being substantially good." This question is in no way Aristotelian. In fact, in both his problem and his solution, Boethius inaugurates, through "paronymy," a radical displacement of Aristotelian ontology: he introduces, through his mediation, the Christian-Platonic idea of a stream, a flow (*fluxus, defluere*) of existing things, "secondary goods" proceeding from the will of the first Good. Boethius's thesis was that existing things are good neither in their essence nor through participation, but by

2

Ptôsis

The noun *ptôsis* is not attested in Greek before Plato. A noun of action based on the radical of *piptô* [πίπτω], "to fall," *ptôsis* means literally "a fall": the fall of a die (Plato, *Republic*, X.604c), or of lightning (Aristotle, *Meteorology*, 339a3). Alongside this basic value (and derived metaphorical values: "decadence," "death," and so forth), in Aristotle the word receives a linguistic specification that was to have great influence: retained even in modern Greek [*ptôsê* (πτώση)], its Latin translation by *casus* allowed it to designate grammatical "case" in most modern European languages. In fact, however, when it first appears in Aristotle, the term does not initially designate the noun's case inflection. In the *Peri hermeneias* (chaps. 2 and 3), it qualifies the modifications, both semantic and formal (casual variation) of the verb and those of the noun: "[he] was well," "[he] will be well," in relation to "[he] is well"; "about Philo," "to Philo," in relation to "Philo." As a modification of the noun—that is, in Aristotle, of its basic form, the nominative—the case (*ptôsis*) differs from the noun insofar as, associated with "is," "was," or "will be," it does not permit the formation of a true or false statement. As a modification of the verb, describing the grammatical tense, it is distinguished from the verb that oversignifies the present: the case of the verb oversignifies the time that surrounds the present. From this we must conclude that to the meaning of a given verb (e.g., "walk") the case of the verb adds the meaning [*prossêmainei* (προσσημαίνει)] of its temporal modality ("he will walk"). Thus the primacy of the present over the past and the future is affirmed, since the present of the verb has no case.

But the Aristotelian "case" is a still broader, vaguer, and more elastic notion: presented as part of expression in chapter 20 of the *Poetics*, it qualifies variation in number and modality. It further qualifies the modifications of the noun, depending on the gender (chap. 21 of the *Poetics*; *Topics*) as well as adverbs derived from a substantive or an adjective, like "justly," which is derived from "just." The notion of case is thus essential for the characterization of paronyms.

Aristotle did not yet have specialized names for the different cases of nominal inflection. When he needs to designate them, he does so in a conventional manner, usually by resorting to the inflected form of a pronoun—*toutou* [τούτου], "of this," for the genitive, *toutôi* [τούτῳ], "to this," for the dative, and so on—and sometimes to that of a substantive or adjective.

In the *Prior Analytics*, Aristotle insists on distinguishing between the terms (*horoi* [ὅροι]) that "ought always to be stated in the nominative [*klêseis* (κλῆσεις)], e.g. man,

good, contraries, but the premises ought to be understood with reference to the cases of each term—either the dative, e.g. 'equal to this' [*toutôi*, dative], or the genitive, e.g. 'double of this' [*toutou*, genitive], or the accusative, e.g. 'that which strikes or sees this' [*touto* (τοῦτο), accusative], or the nominative, e.g. 'man is an animal' [*houtos* (οὗτος), nominative], or in whatever other way the word falls [*piptei* (πίπτει)] in the premiss" (trans. A. J. Jenkinson, *Analytica posteriora*, I.36, 48b, 41). In the latter expression, we may find the origin of the metaphor of the "fall"—which remains controversial. Some commentators relate the distinction between what is "direct" and what is "oblique" [as pertains to grammatical cases, which may be direct (*orthê ptôsis*) or oblique (*plagiai ptôseis*), but also to the grand metaphoric and conceptual register that stands on this distinction] to *falling* in the game of jacks, it being possible that the jack could fall either on a stable side and stand there—the "direct" case—or on three unstable sides—the oblique cases. In an unpublished dissertation on the principles of Stoic grammar, Hans Erich Müller proposes to relate the Stoic theory of cases to the theory of causality, by trying to associate the different cases with the different types of causality. They would thus correspond in the utterance to the different causal postures of the body in the physical field. For the Stoics, predication is a matter not of identifying an essence (*ousia* [οὐσία]) and its attributes in conformity with the Aristotelian categories, but of reproducing in the utterance the causal relations of action and passion that bodies entertain among themselves. It was in fact with the Stoics that cases were reduced to noun cases—in Dionysius Thrax (TG, 13), the verb is a "word without cases" (*lexis aptôton*), and although *egklisis* means "mode," it sometimes means "inflection," and then it covers the variations of the verb, both temporal and modal. If Diogenes Laertius (VII.192) is to be believed, Chrysippus wrote a work *On the Five Cases*. It must have included, as Diogenes (VII.65) tells us, a distinction between the direct case (*orthê ptôsis*)—the case which, constructed with a predicate, gives rise to a proposition (*axiôma*, VII.64)—and oblique cases (*plagiai ptseis*), which now are given names, in this order: genitive (*genikê*), dative (*dôtikê*), and accusative (*aitiatikê*). A classification of predicates is reported by Porphyry, cited in Ammonius (*Commentaire du "De Interpretatione" d'Aristote*, 44, 19f.).

Ammonius (ibid., 42, 30f.) reports a polemic between Aristotle and the Peripatetics, on the one hand, and the Stoics and grammarians associated with them, on the other.

For the former, the nominative is not a case, it is the noun itself from which the cases are declined; for the latter, the nominative is a full-fledged case: it is the direct case, and if it is a case, that is because it "falls" from the concept, and if it is direct, that is because it falls directly, just as the stylus can, after falling, remain stable and straight.

Although *ptôsis* is part of the definition of the predicate—the predicate is what allows, when associated with a direct case, the composition of a proposition—and figures in the part of dialectic devoted to signifieds, it is neither defined nor determined as a constituent of the utterance alongside the predicate.

In Stoicism, *ptôsis* seems to signify more than grammatical case alone. Secondary in relation to the predicate that it completes, it is a philosophical concept that refers to the manner in which the Stoics seem to have criticized the Aristotelian notion of substrate [*hupokeimenon* (ὑποκείμενον)] as well as the distinction between substance and accidents. *Ptôsis* is the way in which the body or bodies that our representation [*phantasia* (φαντασία)] presents to us in a determined manner appear in the utterance, issuing not directly from perception, but indirectly, through the mediation of the concept that makes it possible to name it/them in the form of an appellative (a generic concept, man, horse) or a name (a singular concept, Socrates). Cases thus represent the diverse ways in which the concept of the body "falls" in the utterance (though Stoic nominalism does not admit the existence of this concept—just as here there is no Aristotelian category outside the different enumerated categorial rubrics, there is no body outside a case position). However, caring little for these subtleties, the scholiasts of *Technê* seem to confirm this idea in their own context when they describe the *ptôsis* as the fall of the incorporeal and the generic into the specific [*ek tou genikou eis to eidikon* (ἔκ τοῦ γενικοῦ εἰς τὸ εἰδικόν)].

In the work of the grammarians, case is reduced to the grammatical case, that is, to the morphological variation of nouns, pronouns, articles, and participles, which, among the parts of speech, accordingly constitute the subclass of *casuels, a "parts of speech subject to case-based inflection*" [*ptôtika* (πτωτικά)]. The canonical list of cases places the vocative [*klêtikê* (κλητική)] last, after the direct [*eutheia* (εὐθεῖα)] case and the three oblique cases, in their "Stoic" order: genitive, dative, accusative. This order of the oblique cases gives rise, in some commentators eager to rationalize (Scholia to the *Technê*, 549, 22), to a speculation inspired by "localism": the case of the place from which one comes (in Greek, the genitive) is supposed "naturally" to precede that of the place where one is (the dative), which itself "naturally" precedes that of the place where one is going (the accusative). Apollonius's reflection on syntax is more insightful; in his *Syntax* (III.158–88) he presents, in this order, the accusative, the genitive, and the dative as expressing three degrees of verbal transitivity: conceived as the distribution of activity and passivity between the prime actant (A in the direct case) and the second actant (B in one of the three oblique cases) in the process expressed by a biactantial verb, the transitivity of the accusative corresponds to the division "A all active—B all passive" (A strikes B); the transitivity of the genitive corresponds to the division "A primarily active/passive to a small degree—B primarily passive/active to a small degree" (A listens to B); and the transitivity of the dative, to the division "A and B equally active-passive" (A fights with B). The direct case, at the head of the list, owes its prmacy to the fact that it is the case of nomination: names are given in the direct case. The verbs of existence and nomination are constructed solely with the direct case, without the function of the attribute being thematized as such. Although Chrysippus wrote about *five* cases, the fifth case, the vocative, seems to have escaped the division into direct and oblique cases. Literally appelative [*prosêgorikon* (προσηγορικόν)], it could refer not only to utterances of address but also more generally to utterances of nomination. In the grammarians, the vocative occupies a marginal place; whereas every sentence necessarily includes a noun and a verb, the vocative constitutes a complete sentence by itself.

Frédérique Ildefonse

BIBLIOGRAPHY

Aristotle. *Analytica priora*. Translated by A. J. Jenkinson. In the *Works of Aristotle*, vol. 1, edited and translated by W. D. Ross, E. M. Edghill, A. J. Jenkinson, G.R.G. Mure, and A. Wallace Pickford. Oxford: Oxford University Press, 1928.

———. *Poetics*. Edited and translated by Stephen Halliwell. Cambridge: Harvard University Press / Loeb Classical Library, 1995.

Delamarre, Alexandre. "La notion de *ptōsis* chez Aristote et les Stoïciens." In *Concepts et Catégories dans la pensée antique*, edited by Pierre Aubenque, 321–45. Paris: Vrin, 1980.

Deleuze, Gilles. *Logique du sens*. Paris: Minuit, 1969. Translation by Mark Lester with Charles Stivale: *The Logic of Sense*. Edited by Constantin V. Boundas. New York: Columbia University Press, 1990.

Dionysius Thrax. *Technē grammatikē*. Book I, vol. 1 of *Grammatici Graeci*, edited by Gustav Uhlig. Leipzig: Teubner, 1883. English translation by Thomas Davidson: *The Grammar*. St. Louis, 1874. French translation by Jean Lallot: *La grammaire de Denys le Thrace*. 2nd rev. and expanded ed. Paris: CNRS Éditions, 1998.

Frede, Michael. "The Origins of Traditional Grammar." In *Historical and Philosophical Dimensions of Logic, Methodology, and Philosophy of Science*, edited by E. H. Butts and J. Hintikka, 51–79. Dordrecht, Neth.: Reiderl, 1977. Reprinted, in M. Frede, *Essays in Ancient Philosophy*, 338–59. Minneapolis: University of Minnesota Press, 1987.

———. "The Stoic Notion of a Grammatical Case." *Bulletin of the Institute of Classical Studies of the University of London* 39 (1994): 13–24.

Hadot, Pierre. "La notion de 'cas' dans la logique stoïcienne." Pp. 109–12 in *Actes du XIIIe Congrès des sociétés de philosophie en langue française*. Geneva: Baconnière, 1966.

Hiersche, Rolf. "Entstehung und Entwicklung des Terminus πτῶσις, 'Fall.'" *Sitzungsberichte der deutschen Akademie der Wissenschaften zu Berlin: Klasse für Sprachen, Literatur und Kunst* 3 (1955): 5–19.

Ildefonse, Frédérique. *La naissance de la grammaire dans l'Antiquité grecque*. Paris: Vrin, 1997.

Imbert, Claude. *Phénoménologies et langues formulaires*. Paris: Presses Universitaires de France, 1992.

Pinborg, Jan. "Classical Antiquity: Greece." In *Current Trends in Linguistics*, edited by Th. A. Sebeok. Vol. 13 in Historiography of Linguistics series. The Hague and Paris: Mouton, 1962.

3

The commentators' arbitrage

The transfer of "intermediary" homonyms to the problem of the unification of the multiplicity of the meanings of being, probably begun as early as Alexander of Aphrodisias, was well documented by sixth-century commentators writing in Greek (against Porphyry who, in the *Isagoge*, declared in favor of a strict homonymy of being). Among these commentators, we may mention especially Elias, who explicitly rejects Aristotle's and Porphyry's thesis regarding being (strict homonymy), and clearly declares in favor of the unity of origin and the unity of end:

> [T]he existent is divided neither into a homonymous vocal sound (as Aristotle says in the *Categories* and Porphyry says in the *Isagoge*), nor as a genus into species (as Plato says), but according to the origin and the end.
>
> [διαιρεῖται τοίνυν τὸ ὂν οὐχ ὡς ὁμώνυμος φωνή (ὥσπερ ἐν Κατηγορίαις ᾿Αριστοτέλης καὶ νῦν ὁ Πορφύριος εἴρηκεν), οὐδὲ ὡς γένος εἰς εἴδη (ὥσπερ ὁ Πλάτων εἶπεν), ἀλλ' ὡς τὰ ἀφ' ἑνὸς καὶ πρὸς ἕν].
>
> (Élias, *In Porphyrii Isagogen*, in *Commentaria in Aristotelem Graeca*, 18.1:70, 18–21)

BIBLIOGRAPHY

Élias. *In Porphirii Isagogen*. In vol. 18, book 1, of *Commentaria in Aristotelem Graeca*. Edited by A. Busse. Berlin: G. Reimer, 1900.

their very origin, because their being has been willed by the Creator and "emanates" or "flows" from his will; it was left for the theologians of the Greco-Latin age to give his thesis a definitive form by drawing more explicitly on the Neoplatonic harmonics of the structure of *denominatio*. This act was clearly accomplished by Boethius's commentator Gilbert of Poitiers, when he reformulated the thesis of *De hebdomadibus* by positing that since they emanate from the will of the *primum Bonum*, secondary goods can be called good (*bona*) "according to a denomination" (*denominative*).

The formula is anything but banal. In fact, "to be said denominatively" does not signify here the derivation of the name from a thing qualified on the basis of the corresponding quality—as "white is derived from whiteness, grammarian from grammar, or just from justice"—any more than the simple formation of a (concrete) noun on the basis of another (abstract) noun. This Boethian real predication expresses a causal relationship close to what Plato called "eponymy." The first medieval attempt to carry out a metaphysical reorganization of the system formed by *Categories* 1, 2, 5, and 8, the Porretan theory of *denominatio*, provided the overall physiognomy of the first age of medieval metaphysics before the arrival of the metaphysics of analogy based on the corpus of writings on nature by Aristotle and his Arab interpreters.

According to Gilbert of Poitiers, "denomination" concerns a precise aspect of reality: the dimension of being-caused. That is why most of the examples used to illustrate it are technical. The being concerned is an *opus*, the result of an action, a *factum*. Although, as we have pointed out, Aristotelian paronymy did not apply to terms such as "human" or "the human" relative to "man" and "humanity" (but rather to concrete accidental terms like "white") the Porretan notion of *denominatio* is, in contrast, illustrated in an exemplary way by the term *humanum*. For Gilbert and the Porretan logicians the term *humanum* can indeed be attributed formally to a living being, as in *animal humanum*, but it is attributed denominatively to a fabricated product, as in *opus humanum*, because—and here we come back to the notion of *denominatio* understood as causal emanation—it emanates or has emanated (*fluxit*) from an agent whose being is human. As we see, what is said to be "according to a *denomination*" is here opposed above all to what is attributed "formally." The same distinction is found in all the medieval texts that, in the Arab-Latin age of metaphysics, oppose, as does Avicenna (*Logica*, Venice, 1508, fol. 3 vb), univocal predication and denominative predication (see PRÉDICABLE, PREDICATION).

III. Paronymy and *Suppositio*

Paronymy, as an instrument for two distinct metaphysical theories, the Boethian theory of "emanation" and the Arab-Latin theory of "analogy," is also crucially involved in the origin of the logical theory of signification and reference, as one of the places where the theory of *suppositio* developed. The opposition between the noun "man" and the noun "grammarian" has an important place in Anselm of Canterbury's *De grammatico*, in which it illustrates the distinction between, on one hand, nouns that, like *homo*, are both principally (*principaliter*)—that is, first—significative and principally appellative of a substance; and on the other hand, nouns like *grammaticus*, which present a different semantic structure. For Anselm (De *grammatico*, in *Opera omnia*, 1:156), what distinguishes "man" from "grammarian" is that in the first case the substance is both signified and named *principaliter*, that is, directly (per se), whereas in the second case, the case of the "grammarian," the substance is named but not properly (*proprie*) signified, that is, per se, and that the quality signified properly is not named (we note that the explanation provided here would be more difficult to give in German, where the same term, *Benennung*, opposed to *Bezeichnung*, "signification," is used to designate appellation in the Aristotelian sense of "denomination" and appellation in the sense of nomination, that is, of "reference" [= Frege's *Bedeutung*]). In other words, the noun "grammarian" names the substance

that it signifies *per aliud* and signifies per se an accident that it does not name.

Anselm's theory was developed by the grammarians and logicians of the twelfth century, who substituted for Anselm's pair *per se-per aliud* the pair *principaliter-secundario* (principally–secondarily) (cf. *Promisimus*, ed. L. M. de Rijk, 2:258; Abelard, *Dialectica*, ed. L. M. de Rijk, 113 and 596). These authors say that the denominative "signifies principally" the quality or form from which it is derived (*sumptum*) and only secondarily the subject that it "names" (*nominat*). This formulation's goal is to resolve the traditional question arising from the patent disagreement of the two main authorities of the high Middle Ages in matters of semantics: Priscian, for whom every noun "signifies a substance and a quality," and Aristotle, for whom "a noun like whiteness signifies only the quality." The Ockhamist theory of the synonymy of abstract and concrete nouns (*Summa logicae*, I.6) is part of the same horizon. Going back to Avicenna's distinction between univocal predication and denominative predication, Ockham posits that the synonymy of the concrete and the abstract is valid principally in the category of substance, because in the case of substances there is no real distinction between the subject itself and what makes it what it is (the sole difference residing "in the manner in which nouns signify" [*in modo significandi*]). On the other hand, this synonym is not valid in the case of denominatives like "white" and "whiteness," because these terms cannot have the same *suppositio*, the former necessarily "supposing for" (substituting for, taking the place of) the subject of the accident, and the latter for the accident itself (*Summa logicae*, I.5).

Alain de Libera

BIBLIOGRAPY

Abelard, Peter. *Dialectica: First Complete Edition of the Parisian Manuscript.* 2nd rev. ed. Edited and with an introduction by L. M. de Rijk. Assen, Neth.: Van Gorcum, 1970.

Anselm, Archbishop of Canterbury. *De grammatico.* In vol. 1 of *Opera omnia*, edited by Franciscus Schmitt. 6 vols. Stuttgart: Frommann Verlag–Bad Cannstatt, 1968–84.

———. *The Major Works.* Edited and with an introduction by Brian Davies and G. R. Evans. Oxford: Oxford University Press, 1998.

———. *Promisimus.* In *The Origin and Early Development of Early Terminist Logic*, vol. 2 of *Logica modernorum*, edited by Lambertus Marie de Rijk. Assen, Neth.: Van Gorcum, 1967.

Aristotle. *Basic Works of Aristotle.* Translated by E. M. Edghill. Edited by R. Mckeon. New York: Random House, 1941.

———. *The Categories; On Interpretation; Prior Analytics.* Translated by Harold P. Cooke and Hugh Tredennick. Cambridge, MA: Harvard University Press / Loeb Classical Library, 1973.

Arnauld, Antoine. *Grammaire générale et raisonnée [Texte imprimé], contenant les fondemens de l'art de parler expliquez d'une manière claire et naturelle. . . et plusieurs remarques nouvelles sur la langue françoise.* Paris: P. Le Petit, 1660.

Ashworth, E. J. "Language and Logic." In *The Cambridge Companion to Medieval Philosophy*, edited by A. S. McGrade, 73–96. Cambridge: Cambridge University Press, 2003.

Aubenque, Pierre. "Les origines de la doctrine de l'analogie de l'être: Sur l'histoire d'un contresens." *Les Études philosophiques* 33, no. 1 (1978): 3–12. Translation by Zeki H. Bilgin: "The Origins of the Doctrine of the Analogy of Being: On the History of a Misunderstanding." *Graduate Faculty Philosophy Journal* 11 (1986): 35–45.

———. "Sur la naissance de la doctrine pseudo-Aristotélicienne de l'analogie de l'être." *Les Études philosophiques* 3/4 (1989): 291–304.

Code, Alan. "Aristotle: Essence and Accident." In *Philosophical Grounds of Rationality: Intentions, Categories, Ends*, edited by Richard E. Grandy and Richard Warner, 411–39. Oxford: Clarendon, 1988.

Dietrich of Freiburg. *De accidentibus*. In *Opera Omnia, Schriften zur Naturwissenschaft, Briefe*, edited by Maria Rita Pagnoni-Sturlese, Rudolf Rehn, Loris Sturlese, and William A. Wallace. Vol. 4 in *Corpus philosophorum teutonicorum medii aevi*. Hamburg: Meiner, 1985.

Ebbesen, Sten. "Boethius as an Aristotelian Scholar." In *Aristoteles: Werk und Wirkung*, vol. 2, edited by Jürgen Wiesner, 286–311. Berlin: de Gruyter, 1987.

Grice, Paul. "Aristotle on the Multiplicity of Being." *Pacific Philosophical Quarterly* 69 (1988): 175–200.

Hirschberger, J. "Paronymie und Analogie bei Aristoteles." *Philosophisches Jahrbuch* 58 (1960): 191–203.

Kahn, C. H. *The Verb "Be" in Ancient Greek*. Indianapolis, IN: Hackett, 2003.

Lewis, F. A. *Substance and Predication in Aristotle*. Cambridge: Cambridge University Press, 1991.

Owen, G.E.L. "Logic and Metaphysics in Some Earlier Works of Aristotle." In *Aristotle and Plato in the Mid-Fourth Century*, edited by Ingemar Düring and G.E.L. Owen, 163–90. Gothenburg Swed.: Almqvist and Wiksell, 1960.

Rijk, Lambertus Marie de. *Logica Modernorum: A Contribution to the History of Early Terminist Logic*. Vol. 2 Assen, Neth.: Van Gorcum, 1962–67.

Simplicius of Cilicia. *On Aristotle's "Categories 1-4."* Translated by Michael Chase. Ancient Commentators on Aristotle. Ithaca, NY: Cornell University Press, 2003.

William of Ockham. *Summa logicae*. Vol. 1 of *Opera philosophica*, edited by Philotheus Boehner, Gedeon Gál, and Stephanus Brown. St. Bonaventure, NY: Cura Instituti Franciscani, Universitatis S. Bonaventurae, 1974. Translation and introduction by Michael J. Loux: *Ockham's Theory of Terms, Part I of the Summa Logicae*. Notre Dame, IN: University of Notre Dame Press, 1974.

PASSION

"Passion"—which is derived via the Latin *passio* from the verb *patior* (*pati, passus sum*), "to suffer, endure, resign oneself to, allow"—is one of the possible translations of the Greek *pathos* [πάθος], from *paschein* [πάσχειν], "to receive an impression or sensation, to undergo treatment, to be punished." It emphasizes the passivity of the mind or the subject, which undergoes what comes to it from outside, whereas other translations, such as Latin *perturbatio* or French *émotion*, stress mobility and agitation. In the entry PATHOS the systems and stakes connected with this initial difference in emphasis between the passive and the kinetic are discussed.

I. Passion and Action

We customarily oppose the logical, grammatical, and ontological categories of acting and undergoing, of active and passive, of subject and object. But the vocabulary of philosophy constantly challenges, from one language and period to another, the distinctions it makes: see in particular AGENCY, DRIVE, INTENTION, *LIBERTY*, NATURE, OBJECT, PERCEPTION, SENSE, I.A, SUBJECT, WILL; cf. *ACT*, ACTOR.

II. Passion and Suffering

1. Passion designates first of all the passions of the soul, the perturbations, or even illnesses that affect, as Descartes said, "the union of the soul and the body" and constitute, as it were, the irrational substance of human life: see DRIVE, FEELING, GEFÜHL, GEMÜT, MADNESS, STIMMUNG; cf. *DISPOSITION*, ES, *MALAISE, REASON, TO SENSE*, UNCONSCIOUS.

2. Passion refers to love, on the one hand, and to suffering, on the other: see LOVE, PLEASURE. The Russian word STRADANIE brings into play the relationship between activity and passion along with the redemptive value of suffering (cf. Ger. *Leidenschaft* [passion], from *leiden* [suffer]: *Die Leiden des jungen Werthers* are the sufferings/passions of the sensitive young man); see also WORK, and cf. BERUF.

   On the "Passion" of Christ, which is connected with the Incarnation, see also BOGOČELOVEČESTVO, GOD, OIKONOMIA.

3. On the relationship between wisdom and passion, the use and regulation of the passions, the idea of an ability to resist, of a constancy or courage of the soul, see GLÜCK (particularly GLÜCK, Box 1), MORALS, PHRONĒSIS, PIETAS, VIRTÙ, *WISDOM*.

PATHOS [πάθος] (GREEK) / PERTURBATIO (LATIN)

ENGLISH	emotion, feeling, passion
FRENCH	*passion, émotion*
GERMAN	*Affekt, Begierde, Hang, Leidenschaft*
GREEK	*epithumia* [ἐπιθυμία], *orexis* [ὄρεξις], *pathêma* [πάθημα], *pathos* [πάθος], *thumos* [θυμός]
ITALIAN	*emozione, passione, sentimento*
LATIN	*affectus, emotio, morbus, passio, perturbatio*

➤ *PASSION,* and *ACT*, CATHARSIS, DRIVE, FEELING, GLÜCK, I/ME/MYSELF, LEIB, *LIBERTY*, LOVE, MADNESS, *MALAISE*, PLEASURE, SOUL, STRADANIE, *TO SENSE*, WILL, *WISDOM*

Psychic life is movement. The mind moves. Psychic life is passion. The mind is, in fact, moved. The vocabulary of feeling in European languages is organized around these two poles: on one hand, the idea of a turbulence, a becoming, an instability—something starts moving and transforms itself; there is a psychic activity; on the other hand, such an activity is the effect of an external cause to which the mind finds itself exposed, which it undergoes, passively. Something happens to it and transforms it. Agitation is the form that passivity takes. Thus in Greek, we have *thumos* [θυμός], *epithumia* [ἐπιθυμία], *orexis* [ὄρεξις], but also *pathos* [πάθος], *pathêma* [πάθημα]. In Latin, *emotio, perturbatio*, on the one hand; *morbus, passio, affectus*, on the other hand. In French, *sentiment* and *passion* and *émotion*. In English, "feeling," "passion," "emotion." What is at stake theoretically here—the choice between a kinetic or passionate conception of feeling—can be understood in the context of a history of decisions regarding the way to translate the ancient words into modern languages. Discussions of the concepts often take the form of linguistic commentaries; for example, when Cicero translates the Greek *pathos* by the Latin *perturbatio* instead of *morbus*, or when Augustine criticizes this translation. This tension still determines our contemporary problematics, including that of psychoanalysis.

I. From *Epithumia* to *Pathêma*

Affective life is an excess of movement, a movement that is simultaneously spontaneous and reflexive: an impulsive response, a reaction, whose active and imperious aspect is emphasized. The metaphorical figure of such an activity is the horse, which, in Plato, represents the desiring soul: a spirited animal sensitive to the beauty of bodies and things that can be possessed and which, in their presence, displays an extraordinary energy that is difficult to contain. Rage and courage are also a horse full of spirit and energy. This characterization in terms of movement is inseparable from the idea that sense experience is in general an experience of change, of becoming, of the impermanent. As sensations—and just like other sensations/perceptions—pleasure and pain belong to the domain of what moves and never stops. Plato uses *pathos* [πάθος] and *pathêma* [πάθημα] only when he wants to emphasize the sick, morbid, incurable nature of the affects, their pathological side. His dominant lexicon is that of motivity.

The Aristotelian vocabulary shifts the accent to the "pathetic" aspect of affects. Ethics and rhetoric are based on the possibility of acting on the mind, one's own or those of others, in order to produce effects that are called, therefore, *pathêmata*. Instead of the Platonic obsession with turbulence and anxiety, in Aristotle we find an entire technique of influence or manipulation. Rage, love, hatred, shame, indignation are all responses that are both reasonable and irrational. They are reasonable because they are motivated by a thought, irrational because the thought is accompanied by a bodily change like cold, heat, tears, trembling. Each passion corresponds to a precise idea that is pertinent in a certain situation: the idea of having suffered an inopportune offense, coupled with the desire for revenge, triggers what is called "rage" (*orgê* [ὀργή]). The anticipation of a danger is manifested in what is called "fear" (*phobos* [φόβος]). The cognitive and intellectual nature of the emotion justifies the recentering of affective vitality around the concept of passivity: passion is what I am made to think, thus to feel. Passion is the echo of the world's contingency in my understanding and my body. Passion is my way of interacting with what surrounds me and happens to me. What happens around me touches me, what is done to me affects me, what is said to me moves me. My passivity is my vulnerability with regard to what is external to me, to the milieu in which I live. Inevitable, passion is thus not pathological: on the contrary, suffering is healthy, it is cathartic.

The word *pathos* was definitively established with the Stoics. In a theory that reinforces, on one hand, the cognitive conception of feeling and that proposes, on the other, a model of wisdom and happiness defined by impassiveness, passion becomes, still more clearly than for Aristotle, the subject's reaction to the world. A cognitive operation effects the mediation between me and what happens to me: consent (*sugkatathesis* [συγκατάθεσις]). I always have to say yes or no to my representations, perceptions, thoughts. Thus I am carried away by fury only if I say yes to the thought of an offense received and the anticipation of my vengeance. I am seized by panic only if I ratify the overestimation of a danger. I get angry and tremble only if I approve the beliefs of which rage and fear are the somatic effects. I am therefore responsible for my passions: what I feel, I want to feel with my assent. Such a theory makes voluntary the movements by which the mind

allows itself to be carried away; accepts, in fact, to allow itself to be carried away. Nothing is more voluntary than passivity that is consented to and complicit with passion.

II. From *Pathos* to *Perturbatio*

It is on this point that the translation from Greek into Latin becomes a significant decision. In the *Tusculan Disputations*, Cicero asks how best to translate into Latin the concept that the Greek Stoics express by *pathos*. *Pathos* should be rendered by *morbus* if one wants a literal translation. *Morbus*, "illness," would convey the meaning of what befalls you and puts you in an unhealthy state of suffering. To *morbus*, however, Cicero prefers another word, *perturbatio*: "Quae Graeci [πάθη] vocant, nobis perturbationes appellari magis placet quam morbos" (These movements that the Greeks call *pathê*, we prefer to call perturbations rather than illnesses), he writes (*Tusculan Disputations*, 4.4.10; cf. *De finibus*, 3.35). He defines *perturbationes* as swirling, jerky movements of the mind, contrary to reason. *Perturbationes* are the worst enemies of the mind and of a tranquil life (*Tusculan Disputations*, 4.15.34).

Why does Cicero prefer—*nobis magis placet*—to call "perturbations" what the Greeks call illnesses or passions? For a series of reasons. The first is respect for Latin usage, *consuetudo*. Cicero notes that in the common language, Latins call *perturbationes* all the states that the Greeks call *morbi* (ibid., 3.4.7). But does that mean that we must take ordinary language as our guide, without reflection? No, because the choice of *perturbatio* is the correct one: "Nos autem hos eosdem motus concitati animi recte, ut opinor, perturbationes dixerimus" (We, I think, are right in calling the same motions of a disturbed soul perturbations; ibid.). (As is often the case, here Latin is a more accurate, more appropriate language than Greek—thus Cicero.) Consequently, it is preferable not to render the Greek word for word: *verbum a verbo* (ibid.). It is better—*magis placet*—to replace *morbus*, which would be the literal translation, by *perturbatio*. But substituting *perturbatio* for *morbus* means substituting *perturbatio* for *pathos*, and thus, in a way, correcting the Greek, reinventing the pertinence of the philosophical vocabulary and making it more reasonable.

In a commentary that shows the complexity of the translation decisions he makes, Cicero justifies choices that are linguistic and philosophical. Another argument against a literal translation of *pathos* by *morbus* is that *morbus* is synonymous with *aegritudo*, which means "suffering," "sorrow," "distemper." With an acute sense of exactitude, the Romans reserve *aegritudo* for pain, by analogy with bodily illness, whereas the Greeks call *pathê* all the movements of the soul, including those that are agreeable, such as desire and sensual pleasure. Thus translation offers an opportunity for a criticism of the source language, whose lexicon is presented as generic and contradictory. Pleasure and desire are not illnesses, Cicero observes, because one does not suffer from them. The translation of *pathos* by *morbus* is adequate for a specific perturbation, the one that is rightly called *aegritudo*, "distemper" (ibid., 3.10.22).

The more he enters into probing explanations of the vocabulary of the passions, which he tries to transform into emotion, the more Cicero unveils an ambitious strategy: reforming a metaphorical field. The language of ancient psychology and ethics seems to him to be dominated by the paradigm of the body, of medicine, and hence of illness. But although this model works well as regards the perturbation that concerns him most, pain, it does not lend itself to the expression of the concept of affectivity in general. *Morbus* is not a good term because *pathos* is not a good idea—philosophically speaking. Why? Because for Cicero the history of the mind goes back to Plato and even further, to Pythagoras. First Pythagoras and then Plato had analyzed the structure of the *psuchê* [ψυχή] into two parts, one the basis of a distinctive characteristic, movement. Whereas one part is tranquil and constant, calm and placid, the other part is full of *motus turbidi*, movements and maelstroms, such as rage or desire (ibid., 4.4.10). It was this very precise concept of mobility, unrest, and inconstancy that was to resurface in the Latin word. Cicero took advantage of his role as a creative translator, as a fabricator of neologisms and importer of Greek notions, to refresh the philosophical memory that had faded in the Greek vocabulary. In Latin, a new language, we find on the surface of the word the originary signified that theory had always identified as essential in affective life: the idea of perturbation. In the Latin language, a work in progress that translators were shaping by the choices they made, words were to be, in sum, more appropriate, more adequate to notions. If it is a question of naming a *motus turbidus*, because that is the pertinent definition, then it must be called *perturbatio*.

Through the decisions it requires, the act of translating offers an opportunity to find the correct word, to improve the fit between word and concept. Reformulating in another language makes it possible to bring out a forgotten or underestimated meaning and thus to amend an incoherent usage. Cicero seems to reproach the Greeks, from Pythagoras to Zeno, for not having preferred to *pathos* a word like *tarachê* [ταραχή] (alarm; see *Lysias* 6.35), for example, just as he has chosen *perturbatio* rather than *morbus*. It seems to him, in fact, that ancient ethics always thought "emotion" when it used the word "passion." In the commentaries accompanying his lexical choices, we can discern his criticism of Stoicism: whereas he rejects the obsessional nosography of the classification of the *pathê*, he notes their tumultuous nature. However—and translation comes in here—the kinetic metaphor should have priority over the medical metaphor. Cicero observes that all the Stoics, and notably Chrysippus, tried very hard to compare the illnesses of the mind with those of the body. Let us instead examine more closely what the thing itself contains (*ea quae rem continent pertractemus*), he suggests. What has to be understood is the fact that perturbation is always in movement: *intellegatur igitur perturbationem . . . in motu esse semper* (ibid., 4.10.24). Perpetual movement is thus the "thing" (*res*) whose essence the word *perturbatio* expresses. Moreover, Zeno had already defined a perturbation as a "commotion" (*commotio*) contrary to reason (ibid., 4.6.1). In doing so, he situated himself in the Pythagorean and Platonic tradition that identifies wisdom with peace of mind (ibid., 4.4.10). However, the Greeks, including Zeno, called this *perturbatio*—which they defined (wrongly) as a *commotio*—a *pathos*.

A worn-out language failed to render adequately an essential idea. Another language was now able to rediscover such a semantic characteristic. The word *perturbatio* echoes what is in fact a *perturbatio*, echoes the thing that the word *pathos* obscures. In this particular case, the translation is an interpretation. It is a retrospective lesson in pertinence. It is also a reshaping of the history of philosophy. The preference for the metaphor of movement rather than for that of illness is part of a historiographical strategy. The Stoics, Cicero maintains, were right to center affectivity on movement. They understood that this was the essential point: a direct line could be traced to Pythagoras and Plato. On the other hand, the Aristotelians forgot it, and their ethic of moderate passions is dangerously tolerant. Saying that the affects are emotions makes it possible to see them as leaps into the void and as slippery slopes, that is, as movements that it becomes impossible to stop and that thus have to be prevented, rather than assisting them with moderation. The fact that *perturbatio* is a *commotio*, a turbulence, an excitation—a metaphoric leap, a plunge, a collapse—has consequences for the way in which the remedy is conceived. Although some illnesses are incurable, medical language is, by definition, a language of healing. In physics, on the other hand, what falls cannot stop midway; what slips will not come back up the slope; a person who drifts out to sea will no longer be able to swim back. We treat an illness when it is not an incurable plague, but we *avoid* falling off a cliff, because such a movement cannot be controlled. We avoid diving into a current that will carry us out to sea, where we lose our footing. We avoid starting down a slippery slope (ibid., 4.18.41). In short, it is imperative to block emotions from the outset, before they are born, for they force their way forward by themselves (*ipsae se impellunt*). It is they that move, that make you move, that move you.

Cicero adduces Stoic arguments against Aristotelian arguments, taking the precautions that a good skeptic requires. These are efficacious, ad hominem arguments. Nonetheless, he does not conceal his approbation, even if it is critical, for the "virility" of Stoic morality and his scorn for the softness of Aristotle's language and thought. Peripatetic *ratio* and *oratio* lack vigor (they are *enervatae*); for Cicero, the Stoic discourse wholly centered on prevention is necessary. On one condition, however: it has to adopt a more rigorous tone, strengthen still further the insistence on the irresistible, ineluctable, incurable aspect of the *motus turbidus*. To do so, and especially in order to deepen the contrast with Aristotle and his moderation, the Stoic *oratio* has to be reconciled with its contents, its *ratio* has to become intolerant: it has to be inflected toward the mechanics of movement. The vocabulary of physics is a vocabulary of the irreversible. The Latin translation of *pathos* by *perturbatio* reestablishes the pertinence of this vocabulary for ethics. In the words of a new language, philosophy and the philosophical vocabulary are once again in accord.

III. From *Perturbatio* to *Affectus*

Cicero reorganizes the vocabulary of the passions around their motivity and their tumult, in contrast with the immobility of reason. He does this through a translation and the commentaries that accompany it. This translation is discussed at length in Saint Augustine's *The City of God*. Reflection on the best way to interpret Greek *pathos* and to render it in Latin leads to the Christian turning point in the psychology of the affective. Between Cicero and Augustine, we therefore remain in the continuity of a single language, Latin, but we put back in question the pertinence of the Stoic vocabulary and the lexical transfer from the Greek.

The passions that the Greeks call *pathê*, Cicero called *per-turbationes*, Augustine writes, but most people call them *passiones* (*City of God*, 14.8.1). Thus we should avoid adopting Cicero's term *pertubatio* without precautions; it is an idiosyncratic translation, a single author's translation. It is better to adopt the general use of *passio*, or still better, to use the term *affectus*, because the latter allows us to speak of the emotions without applying to them a systematically and exclusively negative connotation. Since *per-turbatio* echoes, so to speak, the definition of *motus turbidus*, it is a term saturated with philosophical scorn. It is the right word in a theory of virtue that turns on *apatheia* [ἀπάθεια], "impassiveness"; and in an ethics in which "good" is only a synonym of "reasonable" and in which every form of affectivity is disqualified. Augustine, however, rejects the Stoic ideal of the imperturbable sage who is supposed not to be disconcerted, irritated, or moved by anything. For him, persons who never enjoyed themselves, never wished for anything, never suffered, and were afraid of nothing would be, ultimately, insensitive to good and evil. Christian morality requires us to love God, to desire good and hate evil. Contrition for sins committed and the fear of punishment are indispensable. How can we believe without fervor, how can we repent without tears? What would charity be without compassion, or fear without trembling? The Christian is a being of flesh and blood, a being who would lose his humanity if he pretended to a rigor that is nothing more than arrogance and vanity (ibid., 14.9.6). The Christian knows that after the Fall he was condemned to sin and that therefore he must feel and suffer. He knows that passions are the result of original sin, a memory of the lost Eden. The affects are only the perversion of a will that was once absolutely good but has now become good or bad. The relationship with good and evil is entirely affective: the emotions make us sin, but they are also our sole path to salvation. It is not reason that will save us.

Rejecting the identification of the good with *a-patheia* means rejecting the idea that every movement is troubling, that every emotion is a *motus turbidus*. Consequently, this amounts to rejecting *per-turbatio*, a term that in Cicero's language preserves the hard core of Stoic ethics. Augustine chooses *affectus* because it is neutral: we are affected by upright feelings if we lead an upright life; we have perverted feelings if our lives are perverted (ibid., 9.6). It is only the city of the impious, that is, unbelievers, that is shaken (*quatitur*) by bad (*pravi*) affects, which are illnesses and perturbations (*tamquam morbis ac perturbationibus*). Passion perturbs when there is no faith, for a perturbation is an affect, but in its negativity (ibid., 14.10. 26–27, 14.12.31).

By preferring *affectus*, Augustine returns to the use of *pathos*. On the one hand, he criticizes the Stoic intransigence of which Cicero had made himself a spokesman. On the other hand, he places passivity, rather than movement, back at the heart of feeling. By endorsing another Stoic idea, namely that we voluntarily consent to our representations, he insists on the exteriority of what touches us,

excites us, terrifies us. We are affected by a cause, in the sense that we are invested by it, that it can put us in this or that disposition (*afficere*). Therein consists the failure of our will, of that perfect mastery, of that total freedom of choice that Adam and Eve perverted long ago. Now our will has gone off track (*perversa voluntas*). By allowing ourselves to be invaded by a pleasure or a pain, we are saying yes to something that we should reject. But we say yes because our will is now split, divided, and can take the wrong turn. Passion—that is, the finitude that makes us human—resides in this possibility of error, of this inflection of the will that allows itself to be influenced, carried away, convinced.

IV. Modern Transpositions: "Endeavor," *Trieb*

European languages transparently translate the words whose Greek and Latin history we have sketched. The texts we have chosen, namely those by Aristotle, the Stoics, and Augustine, are constantly referred to in the conceptual and linguistic debates that punctuate the later history of the philosophy of the passions. In this long history, the work of Thomas Hobbes marks a critical moment that is of particular interest and can be compared with that in which Cicero found himself .

■ See Box 1.

Like Cicero, Hobbes is aware of the importance of choosing the right word when he transposes into his language concepts that come from texts written in another language. And as was the case for Cicero, for Hobbes the problem arises in an acute form when he discusses the vocabulary of the passions:

> These small beginnings of motion, within the body of man, before they appear in walking, speaking, striking and other visible actions, are commonly called endeavours.
>
> (*Leviathan*, 1.6)

"Endeavor" is thus the generic term for this initial movement that is the condition of all desire and all repulsion. Appetite (desire) and aversion form a pair of contraries on which depend the passions, all of which can be analyzed and classified in one of these two categories (ibid):

> These words, appetite and aversion, we have from the Latins; and they both of them signify the motions one of approaching, the other of retiring. So also do the Greek words for the same, which are *hormê* and *aphormê*.

"Appetite" and "aversion" are English translations of *appetitio* and *aversio*, which render, in turn, *hormê* [ὁρμή] and *aphormê* [ἀφορμή]. As a reader of Cicero, Hobbes adopts a vocabulary of the passions that we find in its Stoic version in the *Academica* (*Lucullus*, 8.24; cf. *De fato*, 17) and at the very heart of the Epicurean vocabulary in *De finibus*. For Hobbes, the human being's cognitive, affective, and moral functioning is thus explained by two movements: a movement that impels us toward the object that causes it and a movement that repels us from such an object. These are the two endeavors—appetite and aversion—of which all the passions are only particular modifications. The requirement of clarity is fulfilled and the ease of translating from Greek and Latin into English is accompanied by a serene reference to the past. In these ancient languages, truth advances naturally, and the

1

Hobbes and translation

➤ TO TRANSLATE

Hobbes regards translation as a test of philosophical clarity and validity. Faced with a Scholastic tradition that in the middle of the seventeenth century continued to use Latin, he had the greatest scorn for this disfigured and worn-out Language, which no longer even corresponded to the great Roman models:

> The writings of School divines are nothing else, for the most part, but insignificant trains of strange and barbarous words, or words otherwise used than in the common sense of the Latin tongue; such as would pose Cicero, and Varro, and all the grammarians of ancient Rome.
>
> (*Leviathan*, 4.46)

This usage cut off from common sense and grammar produced an esoteric, foreign language that no longer meant anything. To this barbarous language, which was neither authentically ancient nor truly modern, the author of the *Leviathan* issued a challenge (ibid.): just try to translate it!

> Which if any man would see proved, let him (as I have said once before) see whether he can translate any School divine into any of the modern tongues, as French, English, or any other copious language.

That would be the only way to see if these "insignificant trains of strange and barbarous words" actually meant anything. If the translation of them was intelligible, it would have been proved that they were already meaningful in Latin. If not, it would have been proved that they were meaningless (ibid.):

> Which insignificancy of language, though I cannot note it for false philosophy, yet it hath a quality, not only to hide the truth, but also to make men think they have it, and desist from further search.

Thus translatability becomes a criterion of truth. Precisely at the point where philosophical practice becomes a dissection of arguments to test their coherence and validity, the fact of translating acquires the status of an experimental method. It is an operation, an action on a text, whose result proves a hypothesis or replies to a question. In this work, considered foundational for the British tradition, philosophy becomes analytic thanks to translation. The requirement of clarity and intelligibility entails a linguistic commitment: it is not so much a matter of writing in modern languages—Hobbes himself wrote in both English and Latin—as of *being able* to translate.

BIBLIOGRAPHY

Hobbes, Thomas. *Leviathan: Authoritative Text, Backgrounds, Interpretations*. Edited by Richard E. Flathman and David Johnston. New York: W. W. Norton, 1997.

---

modern languages have only to take hold of these clear and distinct ideas. "For nature itself does often press upon men those truths, which afterwards, when they look for something beyond nature, they stumble at" (*Leviathan*, 1.6). The "trains of words" (see Box 1) pass from one language to another: this proves the lucidity of true philosophy. Hence they have passed the test of modernity.

Hobbes thus carries out a task different from Cicero's, but he shares with his Roman mediator a concern to establish links. Philosophy must not remain confined to a foreign idiom. The latter has to be either appropriated or rejected. To translate is to understand and make understood. To translate is to clarify. It is therefore not surprising to see translation become a crucial enterprise for the Enlightenment.

Among the last contemporary avatars of the tension between external passivity and internal agitation, we may mention the way in which psychoanalysis conceptualizes this same oxymoron (see DRIVE and I/ME/MYSELF). Psychoanalysis makes a radical break with philosophy. The unconscious and especially the phenomenon of repression shift the problem of activity and passivity to another, more complex level. However, the same tension is at work. Here, there is a triple passivity of which the ego must become aware: first, the one that puts it at the mercy of the drives (*Triebe*), that is, the quantities of energy in movement and tending toward discharge; second, the one that it undergoes with regard to the super-ego, to the law that has been internalized and become unconscious; and finally, the impotence that the ego experiences in the symptom. The drive is a stimulus, but it acts chiefly through a phantasmatic resurgence. It is life, activity, desire to be, but also repetition, compulsion, reflex. The language of physics allows Freud to express the oxymoron of an activity that is all the more active because it is governed by a neurotic constraint, a necessity all the more imperious because its manifestations are *patho*logical, led on by the *pathos* of the repressed that is returning. The desire that formerly underwent repression, the desire whose realization in an act or in a movement has been inhibited, becomes, through this inhibition itself, infinitely powerful, insistent, "active." Hyperactive now, because it was formerly passive.

Giulia Sissa

BIBLIOGRAPHY

Aristotle. *The "Art" of Rhetoric*. Translated by John Henry Freese. Loeb Classical Library. Cambridge, MA: Harvard University Press, 1975.

———. *The Nicomachean Ethics*. Translated by H. Rackham. New and rev. ed. Loeb Classical Library. Cambridge, MA: Harvard University Press, 1975.

Augustine, Saint. *The City of God*. Translated by Marcus Dods. Peabody, MA: Hendrickson, 2009.

Cicero, Marcus Tullius. *Tusculan Disputations*. Translated by J. E. King. Loeb Classical Library. Cambridge, MA: Harvard University Press, 1960.

Hobbes, Thomas. *Leviathan: Authoritative Text, Backgrounds, Interpretations*. Edited by Richard E. Flathman and David Johnston. New York: W. W. Norton, 1997.

James, Susan. *Passion and Action: The Emotions in Sixteenth-Century Philosophy*. Oxford: Oxford University Press, 1997.

Kahn, Charles. "Discovering the Will: From Aristotle to Augustine." In *The Question of Eclecticism*, edited by John M. Dillon and A. A. Long, 234–59. Berkeley: University of California Press, 1988.

Konstan, David. "The Concept of 'Emotion' from Plato to Cicero." *Méthexis* 19 (2006): 139–51.

Nussbaum, Martha. *The Therapy of Desire*. Princeton, NJ: Princeton University Press, 1994.

Plato. *Phaedrus*. In *Euthyphro, Apology, Critic, Phaedo, Phaedrus*, translated by Harold North Fowler. Loeb Classical Library. Cambridge, MA: Harvard University Press, 1971.

Rorty, Amelie O. "From Passions to Emotions and Sentiments." *Philosophy* 57 (1982): 159–72.

| PEACE

"Peace" is one of the possible translations of the Russian *mir* [мир], which means simultaneously "peace," "the world," and "the peasant community": see MIR; cf. RUSSIAN and SOBORNOST', and *CONCILIARITY*. This can be compared with *svet* [свет], which designates simultaneously the world and light: see SVET and cf. LIGHT, PRAVDA, *WORLD* [WELT].

➤ *ALLIANCE*, HERRSCHAFT, LOVE, MACHT, PLEASURE, POLITICS

| PEOPLE

FRENCH   *le peuple, les gens*

➤ PEOPLE/RACE/NATION, *PERSON*, and AGENCY, BEHAVIOR, COMMON SENSE [*SENS COMMUN*, SENSUS COMMUNIS], ENGLISH, LIBERAL, NAROD, POLITICS, WHIG

The ambiguity of the English word "people"—which refers to both an indivisible unity and a plurality or federation of individuals, to the point that the term is dissolved in an impersonal plurality ("people say") or even turned into a pronoun ("they say")—is particularly interesting, the two senses being used alternatively and even coexisting in English philosophical and political language. The passage to American English is even more significant than in other cases, because the twofold use of the word and the transformation of its meaning played a central role in the definition of political power at the time of the American Revolution.

I. "People," Singular and Plural

"People" was originally synonymous with "folk" (a word associated with "race," "nation," "tribe"; cf. Ger. *Volk*), and initially referred to a unit. The development of the term's usage is marked on the grammatical level by the passage to the plural in the conjugation of the verb of which "people" is the subject ("people say," "people want"). This is a possibility specific to English, in which "people" can be both singular and plural. In seventeenth-century English, and especially in the field of political philosophy (Hobbes, for example), the people constitute a unity ("All the duties of sovereigns are implicit in this one phrase: *the safety of the people* is the supreme Law"; *On the Citizen*, ch. 13), the body of citizens, which can be divided into parts. But the term coexists with the common and very loose use of "people" in the plural ("people are to be taught"; *Leviathan*, ch. 2). We also sometimes find a plural "peoples" ("the common-peoples minds"; ibid.), which clearly shows the indeterminacy of the word. These linguistic facts make particularly complex the definition of the relationship between individual and people, the word "people" referring both to a unit and to a plural conglomerate.

To this is added another, nonspecific meaning (see PEOPLE/RACE/NATION) of the people as a class that is oppressed or in a relationship of inferiority, a meaning that has the same dimensions (both protesting and despising) as the French word *peuple*. We may note that a new and odd sense has appeared in English that radically inverts this one: "people" in the sense of celebrities, as in the case of the magazine *People*.

II. "People" and the American Innovation

This ambiguity between the singular and the plural is related to the assertion that the people is simultaneously one and multiple, as is clearly indicated in the expression "We the people." Thus we read at the beginning of the 1787 U.S. Constitution: "WE, THE PEOPLE of the United States, in order to form a more perfect Union ... do ordain and establish this CONSTITUTION." For Hamilton and Madison (see *Federalist Papers* nos. 39 and 46), the "people" is "the great body of the people," and it is in it that resides the sole source of sovereignty: "The fabric of American empire ought to rest on the solid basis of THE CONSENT OF THE PEOPLE" (Hamilton, *Federalist Papers*, no. 22). "The ultimate authority resides in the people alone" (Madison, *Federalist Papers*, no. 46). The question of this consent is basic to the whole of American thought specific to democracy: how to conceive the consent of the people, that is, of each individual, to society? This problem is connected with the ambiguity of the word "people," which the Federalists were paradoxically to resolve by proposing a twofold definition: the people can be either a group of "individuals composing a single English nation" or a group of individuals "forming distinct and independent English states." The political organization is defined as a "compound" divided into a federal and a national power, the people remaining the supreme authority that delegates its power.

Madison (ibid.) particularly insisted on this absolute sovereignty of the people, which is the "common superior" of the federal and state governments, and thus "the ultimate authority." Thus is affirmed the great principle of the original right to power vested in the people. James Wilson argued that the people of the United States disposed of and exercised its primitive rights, and it alone *delegates* (Hamilton, *Federalist Papers*, no. 23) its powers. According to the Federalists, all power resides in the people, and not in the government of the states. The now vaunted basis of federalism, the "mixed character" (Madison, *Federalist Papers*, no. 39) of political power, is thus inseparable from the idea of the delegation of power by the people, which has the authority to delegate power to its agents and to form a government that the majority believes will contribute to its happiness, the transcendent power of the people being competent to form the kind of government the people considers likely to produce its happiness. The redefinition of power reveals itself here to be connected with a redefinition of what a constitution consists in: it is not the definitive organization of a power, because at any time the people can rescind—without resorting to revolution—its delegation of power to a defective government and can subject its constitution to renewed debate. The constitution is thus based on the "assent and ratification of the people of America," but the people are conceived "not as individuals composing one entire nation, but as composing the distinct and independent states to which they respectively belong": "It is to be the assent and ratification of the several States, derived from the supreme authority in each State—the authority of the people themselves" (Madison, *Federalist Papers*, no. 39).

Thus the essential duality of "people" implicit in the definitive passage from the singular to the plural (cf. "themselves") is carried out in the Federalist project. The multiplicity of interests (of the individuals) that compose the people become compatible with the common interest through the multiplication of the centers of power. It is this phenomenon of the fragmentation of power that Gordon Wood has defined as the "disembodiment" of power (*Creation of the American Republic*). The paradox is that the people exercises its sovereignty in and through this very disembodiment. According to Wood, this is clearly related to a radical transformation of the meaning of the word "people" and of the relationship to politics in general following the overthrow of the old Whig concepts. When the American Revolution began, the people were considered a homogeneous entity in rebellion against the rulers. But under the pressure of reality, the idea gradually emerged of a non-homogeneous people without any genuine unified interest. Thus Americans transformed the people in the same way that the British had transformed rulers a century earlier: they broke the relationship of interest among individuals (Wood, ibid.).

In conclusion, the political stake involved in the redefinition of "people" becomes clear. Politics could no longer be defined, Wood says, as a battle between rulers and the people: "In the future, political struggles would be internal to the people, they would oppose the diverse groups and diverse individuals that sought to create inequality on the basis of their equality" (ibid.).

We see that this new sense of "people" sums up the American innovation in politics (even if much could be said about its possible perversions; cf. Wood's concluding chapter, which seems to deplore a disconnection of the social and the political and perhaps a lasting impoverishment of political thought in America), in its desire to truly implement the classical idea of popular sovereignty. Thus in the United States, the people as a source of power—which we find in the use of the term in the sense of "electorate" or, in the judicial field, in the expression "the People vs. X")—was to coexist with the "people" having divergent community interests (black people, my people) or simply "people" in an indeterminate, pronominal way (people say), and even, in more casual language, "he's good people."

Sandra Laugier

BIBLIOGRAPHY

Hamilton, Alexander, James Madison, and John Jay. *The Federalist Papers*. Edited by Clinton Rossiter. New York: New American Library, 1961.

Hobbes, Thomas. *Leviathan: Authoritative Text, Backgrounds, Interpretations*. Edited by Richard E. Flathman and David Johnston. New York: W. W. Norton, 1997.

———. *On the Citizen*. Edited and translated by Richard Tuck and Michael Silverthorne. Cambridge: Cambridge University Press, 1998.

Patterson, Thomas E. *We the People: A Concise Introduction to American Politics*. 7th ed. New York: McGraw-Hill, 2008.

Wootton, David, ed. *The Essential Federalist and Anti-Federalist Papers*. Indianapolis. IN: Hackett, 2003.

Wood, Gordon. *The Creation of the American Republic*. Chapel Hill: University of North Carolina Press, 1969.

PEOPLE / RACE / NATION

FRENCH	*peuple, race, nation*
GERMAN	*Volk, Rasse, Nation*
GREEK	*dêmos* [δῆμος], *genos* [γένος], *ethnos* [ἔθνος], *laos* [λαός], *ochlos* [ὄχλος], *plêthos* [πλῆθος], *hoi polloi* [οἱ πολλοί]
LATIN	*populus, gens, natio, plebs*

➤ CIVIL SOCIETY, *DROIT*, GENRE, GESCHLECHT, LAW, NAROD, OIKONOMIA, PEOPLE, POLIS, POLITICS, *STATE*

What the terms "people," "race," and "nation" have in common is that they designate types of geographical and historical, cultural, social and/or strictly political community. The difficulty of translating them has to do with the fact that from one language to another, and within each language from one period to another, they do not necessarily refer to the same types of membership, or distinguish, intersect, or share them in the same way. Hence by translating *dêmos* [δῆμος] or *populus* as "people," *ethnos* [ἔθνος], *natio*, or the plural *gentes* by "nation(s)," *genos* [γένος] or *genus* by "race," we fall victim to a retrospective illusion that projects onto Greek or Latin notions, ambiguities, and problematics that do not belong to them.

Thus *dêmos*, like *populus*, designates both citizens as a group and the least wealthy (and sometimes the most numerous), least educated, and least noble part of that group, but never a natural and/or historical component of human diversity. But this is often the case for the notion of "people," and still more for that of *Volk* (*Völker*), the uses of which give priority, on the contrary, to a community of birth or a shared history. Inversely, *ethnos*, *natio*, or *gentes* never had a political meaning (they do not imply any kind of citizenship), whereas the history of the term "nation" is understood as a history of its gradual articulation with the notion of the state, although its ethnic sense does not disappear.

Finally, the idea of race, although fluctuating (as a component of human diversity, as a social category), remains inseparable from various theories that make the war of the races the motive force in history—something the terms *genos* or *genus* never connoted.

I. People, Race, Nation

A. "People"

The Chevalier de Jaucourt's article on "People" (*Peuple*) in the RT: *Encyclopédie ou Dictionnaire raisonné des sciences, des arts et des métiers* testifies to the fact that the word is dauntingly polysemous: "People: a collective noun that is difficult to define because different ideas about it are formed in diverse places, in diverse times, and depending on the nature of events." In reality, efforts to define the word "people" turn on a twofold ambivalence: that between a political creation and a natural or historical given, and that between citizens and the masses positively or negatively valued. The modern definition of "the people" as a political creation and in this case, a contractual institution—a definition that stems from Rousseau—thus collided from the outset with a double resistance: "the people" is also a factual reality anterior to the contract; moreover, the word sometimes designates the part of the population that, because of its poverty or lack of education, is excluded from the exercise of sovereignty.

1. The act through which a people is a people

Determining the meaning of "people" involves first of all the question of its origin or foundation, as is shown by Rousseau's polemical attack on Grotius: "A people, says Grotius, can give itself to a king. So that according to Grotius, a people is a people before giving itself to a king. That very gift is a civil act, it presupposes a public deliberation. Hence before examining the act through which a people elects a king, it would be well to examine the act by which a people is a people" (*The Social Contract*, I.5; trans. J. T. Scott in *The Major Political Writings of Jean-Jacques Rousseau*). But the fact that the people has no political existence and therefore cannot deliberate before being instituted as such by the contract does not mean that it did not previously exist. On the contrary, the institution of the people as a political body is conceived all the more strongly when gauged by the distance between a point of departure and a point of arrival, a first form of community (a first "people") and the form that gives this first people sovereignty. This is shown with particular clarity by the three chapters that deal with the people in *The Social Contract* (II.8–10):

> What people, then, is suited for legislation? One that, while finding itself already bound by some union of origin, interest, or convention, has not yet borne the true yoke of laws. One that has neither deeply rooted customs nor supersitions; . . . finally, one that combines the stability of an *ancient people* with the docility of a *new people*.

> (trans. J. T. Scott, *Major Political Writings*; emphasis added)

Thus the foundation of the people as a political body does not erase its natural or historical origin. On the contrary, it is based on the first bonds that define it. Although there is in the polysemic unity of "people" a persistent ambiguity that is difficult to eliminate, a glance back at Greek and Latin makes it easy to understand: the unity of "people" asserts, in a monothetic way, the transition, and even the consubstantiality, between the natural (geographical and historical) reality of the people as *ethnos* [ἔθνος], or even as *genos* [γένος], and the political reality of the people as *dêmos* [δῆμος]. The phrase "first people," or "original people," has in fact, none of the meanings that covered by *dêmos* or *populus* (see *infra*). It corresponds far more to what the Greek terms *ethnos* and *genos* suggest. As a result, if one had to give impossible Greek or Latin equivalents for the terms of Rousseau's formula summing up the problematics of sovereignty, we would probably arrive at the following definition of the contract: the act by which a people (*ethnos, natio*) is a people (*dêmos, populus*).

This confusion, which has major consequences, is still more manifest as soon as the notion is made plural. Then it is almost impossible to make a distinction between peoples and nations—understood as the anthropological components of human diversity. In *The Social Contract*, as in the *Discourse on the Origin and Basis of Inequality among Men*, Rousseau uses both terms in the plural in an undifferentiated way, sometimes in the same sentence. Thus in the famous note 10 in the latter work: "there are whole peoples that have tails like four-footed animals." No doubt some writers, like Buffon or Voltaire, tried to distinguish between peoples and nations on the basis of the degree of political organization, but the distinctions vary and are reversed from one author to another.

2. The people: A body of citizens or a mass of outcasts?

For the philosophers of the Enlightenment, "the people" was also that part of the population that was in fact deprived of political rights and thus totally dominated. The second ambivalence thus is located not at the level of the foundation, as a problem of political philosophy, but in ordinary language. Depending on whether it is evaluated positively or negatively, it testifies to the force of social prejudices or to the insufficiency, and even the hypocrisy, of the contractualist definiton of "the people," so long as too numerous and too massive inequalities continue to exist within the body politic. The whole question is who belongs to the people and who, on the contrary, claims the right to except himself from it. Thus Abbé Coyer could deplore (in his *Dissertations pour être lues*, 1755; the first of these "dissertations" is on the old word *patrie*, the second on the nature of the people) the fact that the people saw itself constantly shrinking: "The people used to be the general estate [*l'état général*] of the nation, simply opposed to the great and the nobles. It included farmers, workers, artisans, merchants, financiers, men of letters and men of law." In fact, that is what Vauvenargues might have had in mind when he wrote, "The people and the nobility do not have the same virtues, or the same vices." But in the eighteenth century, "the people" was no longer defined by opposition to the nobility, but by opposition to the Third Estate. The bourgeosie's increasing power, and its desire not to be confounded with the mass of the people, led to an increasingly narrow perception and definition of "the people." It seems that everyone wanted to distinguish himself, and first of all Rousseau, who did not escape the rule when he wrote in his *Confessions*: "Born into a family superior in its manners to the common people, I had learnt only wisdom from my relations, who had shown me honourable examples, one and all" (II.66, trans. J. M. Cohen). The meaning of "people" is here quite close to the one that *le public* acquired in French at about the same time, understood as the formless, restless mass that included neither the nobles nor the members of the *parlements* nor yet even the merchants; a mass that was characterized not only by its lack of education and its potential violence but also by its association with labor. However, taken in this sense, the people was also lauded and even glorified in revolutionary literature: thus Jean-Paul Marat praised it when he asked whether the people or the bourgeoisie was the defender of the Revolution: "In the state of war in which we find ourselves, there is only the people, the common people so despised and so little despicable, that can inspire respect in the enemies of the revolution" (*Textes choisis*, 217).

Going back to the Greek and Latin shows that this ambivalence is found in *dêmos* and *populus*, whose use tends sometimes toward *plêthos* [πλῆθος] and *plebs*, but here as well the evaluation can be either positive or negative. However, it is worth noting that no political construction, even the most democratic, succeeds in completely and permanently reducing this opposition between the body of citizens and de facto outcasts. That is why, on the fringes of the thought that institutes the people, a discourse that makes it an object of compassion permanently subsists.

■ See Box 1.

1

People, the masses, and collective man in Gramsci

The question whether "people" refers to a body of citizens or to a group of outcasts still influences the problematic nature of the relationship between the philosopher and the people. Whereas in the first case the intellectual is not distinguished from the people (or at least does not ask whether he is), in the second case he is forced to reflect on the conditions under which he can address the people. This is particuarly clear in Gramsci's thought. In his work, the Italian word *popolo* appears to be linked to two complementary problems, that of philosophy, and that of revolution. The conceptual and terminological elaboration differs, opening in one case on the equivalence between people, the masses, and the uneducated, and in the other on the idea of a collective man. In his reflection on philosophy, Gramsci uses indifferently *popolo* (people), *massa*, (masses), and *i semplici* (the uneducated). Among the factors that explain the persistence of a philosophical trend is its adoption by the people's common sense (*senso comune*). If there is a popular conception of philosophy, it is not unconnected with "specialists' philosophies," despite the gap between the intellectual elite and the masses. The relation between the two groups centers on the idea of the conscious direction of action. Described by Gramsci as the "healthy core of common sense," it can be developed into a "unitary and coherent whole" and it is in this very development that resides "so-called scientific philosophy" (*Gramsci dans le texte*, 137). But the common meaning is itself only "a chaotic aggregate of disparate conceptions in which one can find whatever one wants" (307). Thus, popular philosophy must not be confused with philosophy as conceptual criticism. The relationship is mediated, and must be elaborated all the more because, in Gramsci's view, philosophy undergoes a metamorphosis when it is diffused among the masses: it can be experienced by them only as a faith (158).

Moreover, the people's point of view is the yardstick by which philosophies should be evaluated. Thus some philosophies prove to be hostile with regard to the people. They help keep the people ignorant and do not offer it the means to acquire conscious direction of its action. This is the case of idealism, whose distance with respect to the people is manifested in the rejection of "cultural movements that want to 'go to the peoples'; or again of "Jesuitized Christianity, transformed into a pure narcotic for the popular masses [*le masse popolari*]" (140, 155). In addition, the people's point of view is made the criterion of

a true "philosophy of *praxis*" (an expression that Gramsci uses to refer to communism in a veiled way, in order to keep his texts from being censored), so that it does not suffer from the weakness of "philosophies of immanence." The latter, for example in the work of Benedetto Croce and Giovanni Gentile, were not able to "create an ideological unity between the low and the high, between the 'uneducated' and the intellectuals [*i 'semplice' e gli intelletuale*]" (140). To establish the conditions for this unity between the low and the high, Gramsci seems at first to resort to a simple tactic: considering that all philosophy tends to become the common sense of a given milieu, no matter how restricted it might be, he recommends investing in a thought that is already that of common sense, in order to endow it with the "coherence" and "sinew of individual philosophies." However, this investment is itself conditioned by the "'felt' demand for contact with the 'uneducated'" (142). Thus, this is not a simple tactic, because in this "felt demand" we can clearly discern the political dimension of this philosophy of *praxis*: it depends on a commitment to "fight modern ideologies in their most refined form in order to be able to constitute one's own group of independent intellectuals and to educate the popular masses, whose culture was medieval" (255–56).

This commitment shifts us toward political questions that open up a new view of the people that involves analyzing the conditions for revolution. The success of the latter depends, according to Gramsci, on the consensus of the masses and their participation. The notions of the masses and the uneducated, which serve to describe from a cultural point of view the internal division of the people, are reinterpreted and put in the service of a unified vision that opposes the people as a whole to a minority of intellectuals and specialists. In an essay written in 1926, "Some Aspects of the Southern Question," Gramsci notes the fracture lines separating peasants and workers, cities and rural areas, proletariat and intellectuals. He defines the revolutionary project on the basis of these fractures: given the divisions and the necessity of not making a "passive revolution," a revolution without the people, the political ambition must at first be limited to the project of a revolution on the national scale. To carry out a successful revolution, it is thus necessary to achieve a "cultural-social unity [*unità cultural-social*] that causes a large number of scattered wills, whose goals are heterogeneous, to be welded together to attain the same

end, on the basis of a single, common conception of the world" (*Gramsci dans le texte*, 173). In the first of the notebooks devoted to the topic of "The Modern Prince," Gramsci takes up the figure of Machiavelli, who conceived, according to Gramsci, the movement of a people and the process of forming a collective will:

> Throughout the book, Machiavelli discusses what the Prince must be like if he is to lead a people to found a new State; the argument is developed with rigorous logic, and with scientific detachment. In the conclusion, Machiavelli merges with the people, becomes the people; not, however, some "generic" people [*si fa popolo, si confonde col popolo, ma non con un popolo "genericamente" inteso*], but the people whom he, Machiavelli, has convinced by the preceding argument— the people whose consciousness and whose expression he becomes and feels himself to be, with whom he feels identified.
>
> (trans. Q. Hoare and G. N. Smith, *Selections from the Prison Notebooks*)

A new notion emerges from this reflection. It expresses what the people must become in the revolution: the "collective man [*uomo collettivo*]" (*Gramsci dans le texte*, 173). It appears as the key formula for revolutionary thought and action, but it also takes us back to Gramsci's thinking about the philosophy of *praxis*. The task of this philosophy, of its intellectuals, is to create the social-cultural unity of a people. In this sense, the "people" can be conceived as the key concept in Gramsci for connecting thinking about philosophy with thinking about revolution.

Marie Gaille-Nikodimov

BIBLIOGRAPHY

Gramsci, Antonio. *Gramsci dans le texte*. Edited by F. Ricci and J. Bramant. Translated into French by J. Bramant, G. Moget, A. Monjo, and F. Ricci. Paris: Éditions Sociales, 1953.
———. *The Gramsci Reader: Selected Writings, 1916–1935*. Edited by David Forgasc. Introduction by Eric Hobsbawm. New York: New York University Press, 2000.
———. *Opere*. 12 volumes. Turin: Einaudi, 1947–71.
———. *Selections from the Prison Notebooks*. Edited and translated by Quentin Hoare and Geoffrey Nowell Smith. New York: International Publishers, 1971.

B. "Nation": The body of the king and the body of citizens

The polysemy of "people" is further aggravated by the fact that its different senses are recuperated by "nation" as the latter term, through a whole series of mutations, acquires a rigorous political meaning; and all the more so because the meaning of "nation" becomes a historical and political issue. Under an absolute monarchy, the nation is initially summed up in the body of the king—the whole of his subjects insofar as they are his subjects. Thus the glory of the nation, so often invoked, is nothing other than the power of the king. That is what Rousseau points out in the *Jugement sur le projet de paix perpétuelle* (Judgment of the program for perpetual peace): "Every occupation of kings or of those to whom they entrust their functions is intended to realize two goals: to extend their domination abroad and to make it more absolute within. Any other design is either related to one of these or merely serves as a pretext for them. Such are the public good, the happiness of his subjects, the glory of the nation" (*Œuvres complètes*, 2:592).

The politicization of the idea of the nation can be understood, then, as a series of efforts to break it away from its identification with the person of the absolute monarch. At first, the monarchical definition is opposed by an attempt to restore to the nation the sense of a historical community of customs and culture, and to turn against the king's power the rights that his origin gives him. That is what is involved in the various theses like the one defended by Henri de Boulainvilliers in *Essais sur la noblesse de France* (1732), which undertake to distinguish two nations on the basis of their origins: the descendents of the Gauls conquered by the Romans, and the nobility descended from the Franks. Taken in this sense, the nation can no longer define all the subjects of a monarch, connected physically and legally with the king's body, but that does not imply the unity of a territory either. As a nation, the nobility transcends state boundaries. Thus the nobles of all countries can claim to belong to an original community (of birth) in order to proclaim the rights of the nation that they constitute in opposition to other nations.

The nobility's historical appropriation of the term "nation" met with resistance on the part of the Third Estate, which was to turn the meaning and the use of the term in another direction. Against the nobility's speculations, the Third Estate at first sought to regain control of the term "nation" by identifying it with the unity of a territory bounded by frontiers and subject to a common set of laws and government. That is, for example, what the article "Nation" in the RT: *Encyclopédie* does. Then the goal is to make the nation the source of sovereignty and the owner of the crown, the government, and public authority: "In a word, the crown, the government, and public authority are goods of which the body of the nation is the owner and of which the rulers have the usufruct," Diderot wrote in the article "Autorité public." And, reversing the terms of the monarchical definition, he adds in his *Observations sur le Nakaz*: "There is no true sovereign other than the nation." But it was especially with the Abbé Sieyès's pamphlet *Qu'est-ce que le tiers-état?* ("What is the Third Estate?") that "nation" took on an essentially political and legal meaning. For Sieyès, a nation is defined both by its political ability to subsist—which requires particular works

(exploitable and exploited resources) and public functions (the army, the judiciary, the administration, the church)—and by its juridical existence: "a body of associates living under a common law and represented by the same legislature." To the extent to which the Third Estate itself is capable of providing this subsistence, of performing these functions, and constituting such a body, it forms "a complete nation" (*Qu'est-ce que le tiers-état?*, 31). The nobility, on the contrary, imprisoned in its privileges and its idleness, is outside the common order, the common law. It forms, Sieyès wrote, "a separate people in the great nation." Thus the semantic relationship between "people" and "nation" was shattered: the political dimension was no longer reserved for the former and history for the latter, but the other way around. This idea of a "complete nation" led first to the articulation of the idea of the nation with that of the state. Saying that the Third Estate is a complete nation does not mean that the nobility is excluded from the nation, but only that the Third Estate is capable by itself of assuming all the functions of the state that give the nation its unity.

C. "Race": A biological given or a social class?

It remains that the political sense of "nation" does not put an end to the other meanings that the term has been able to acquire, starting with the meaning of a community of customs and language constituting, independently of any political unity, a part of human diversity—a subject of study for anthropology and history. That is why in translations that sometimes involve the retrospective illusion, *ethnos* or *genos* (see below) is occasionally rendered, especially in the nineteenth century but still today, by "nation." Some discourses and some theories even explicitly oppose this relative "denaturalization" and "dehistoricization" of the notion, preserving its dimension of a natural and/or historical community. But then it is confused with "race." It is particularly in the works of historians who make race the engine of history at the same time that they construct the idea of national history, such as Augustin Thierry's *Lettres sur l'histoire de France* (1820, 1827), that we find this ambiguity between a strictly political and legal meaning of "nation" and its identification with a natural community. But "race" is also polysemous, and its use to designate the human communities of antiquity (through historical description or translation) is subject to just as much confusion. The philosophical use of the notion of race was initially linked, in the seventeenth century, with the broadening of anthropology (previously limited to humany anatomy and psychology) to describe the varieties of the human species—as in Buffon's *Histoire naturelle de l'homme* or Voltaire's *Essai sur l'histoire générale et sur les moeurs et l'esprit des nations*. The notion of race was then used in a double register, descriptive and explanatory, which gave rise to numerous polemics, like the one between the polygenists and the monogenists. Ostensibly, the question is whether the differences for which this notion is supposed to account (differences that are primarily morpholigial, such as skin color or the shape of the face) are original or derived—whether several races of human beings appeared simultaneously on Earth or at least independently of one another, or on the contrary they derive from a common source that contained them all in embryonic form. In reality, the goal is almost always to show the superiority of one race over the others.

But the word "race" has still another meaning, and the difference it designates is not always and exclusively ethnic. In the nineteenth century, two meanings existed alongside one another: the first is the broad, open one that is implied by the theme of the war of the races that recurs in the discourse of historians. Races are not necessarily ethnically determined components but may also be social or cultural groups. In fact, Marx praised Augustin Thierry—the theoretician of the war of races as the engine of history (*Sur l'antipathie de race qui divise la nation française*)—as the "father of class struggle in French historiography" (letter to Engels, 27 July 1854). Here, "race" referred to distinct groups that, although they inhabited (or had inhabited) the same territory, had not been able to mix, for reasons that were not only ethnic but also cultural or social in nature. In the second sense, races are natural, biologically determined components of human diversity. Then we see how ambiguous it is to translate *genos* or *genus* by "race." The translation is, of course, legitimate when "race" is situated in the tradition of natural history, to which *genos* in part belongs. But "race" also implies divisions that are too historically and ideologically determined to be transposable, and it suggests, at the price of a real retrospective illusion, that they have always been conceived that way.

- See Box 2.

II. *VOLK*, "NATION"

A. *Volk*

Volk, unlike "people," and also unlike *dêmos* and *populus*, has the pejorative sense of "rabble" only in exceptional cases. This is connected with another of its characteristic traits: the word designates only marginally, in an exclusively political and juridical way, a body of citizens, and it refers to the natural basis of the political body rather than to this body itself. This basis may both be presented as an obstacle to the rational and political constitution of this body and exhibited, indeed sacralized, as the main reason for opposing it.

1. *Volk*: An obstacle to the Commonwealth

That is so shown first of all by the complexity and complementarity of the definitions of *Volk* given by Kant in his *Metaphysical First Principles of the Doctrine of Right* (the first part of his *Metaphysics of Morals*) and his *Anthropology from a Pragmatic Point of View*. Significantly, it is in the latter and not the former that we find a rigorous definition of *Volk*:

> By the word *people* [*Volk*] (*populus*) is meant a *multitude* of human beings united in a region [*die in einem Landstrich vereinigte Menge Menschen*], in so far as they constitute a *whole*. This multitude, or even the part of it that recognizes itself as united into a civil whole [*einem bürgerlichen Ganzen*] through common ancestry [*gemeinschaftliche Abstammung*], is called a *nation* [*Nation*] (*gens*). The part that exempts itself from these laws (the unruly crowd within this people [*die wilde Menge in diesem Volk*]) is called a *rabble* [*Pôbel*] (*vulgus*).

> (trans. R. B. Louden, *Anthropology from a Pragmatic Point of View*, 213)

Kant connects *Volk* with *populus*, but gives it a sense that is both narrower and vaguer than that of the Latin term. It designates, as it were, the first degree of union, before any recognition of a common origin, and a fortiori of a common fate. To indicate a meaning similar to that of Cicero's *populus*—that is, a political meaning—Kant thus had to introduce other terms, this time in the *Doctrine of Right*:

> This condition of the individuals within a people [*dieser Zustand der Einzelnen im Volke*] in relation to one another is called a *civil* condition [*bürgerlicher Zustand*] (*status civilis*), and the whole of individuals in a rightful condition, in relation to its own members, is called a *state* [*Staat*] (*civitas*). Because of its form, by which all are united through their common interest in being in a rightful condition [*im rechtlichen Zustande*], a state is called a commonwealth [*das gemeine Wesen*] (*res publica latius sic dicta*).

> (trans. M. J. Gregor, *Metaphysics of Morals*, §43, 89)

But it is above all Kant's definition of the contract that manifests most clearly how much he reserves *Volk* to designate the natural element of the body politic. Unlike Rousseau, he does not say that the contract is "the act by which a people is a people," but rather "the act by which

---

2

The malaises of ordinary language

In French, an ambivalence persists in the different uses of the term *race* in ordinary language.

1. To say of someone that *il a de la race* or *il est racé* is first of all to reproduce a class judgment. Moreover, the expression has no meaning other than the one that attributes "class" to some person or other. But it is also to claim that there is a natural foundation for social distinctions;

it is to seek in the *genos* a justification for inequality.

2. Inversely, the interdiction that weighs on the word *race*, taken in its ethnological sense, testifies to its basis in natural history. To avoid *race* is to refuse to reduce human diversity to a given of natural history. The races, it will be said, are good for animal species (in the sense of breeding), not for humans. And it is true that the history of the term is partly linked with the blurring

of these boundaries and with the lifting of the moral interdictions that are attached to them. Speaking of human *races* as we speak of *races animales* used to be a way of justifying the fact that relationships between these different species of men (in this case, colonizers and colonized) could be as violent as those that organized the animal realm. Thus we will prefer to use the term *ethnie* (ethnicity), which preserves or restores the division between humanity and animality.

a people forms itself into a state is the *original contract*. Properly speaking, the original contract is only the idea of this act" (ibid., §47, 91–92). The definition of the contract makes it possible to distinguish the "people conceived as subject" (the mass of individuals) from the "people unified itself" (the people considered as a state). However, it will be noted that as soon as *Volk* no longer has the natural meaning given it by anthropology, a paraphrase is necessary, as well as a resort to Latin, as if Kant did not have confidence in the German language's ability to express these matters of public law.

As a final sign of Kant's reluctance to give *Volk* a juridical meaning, we must mention the doubts he expresses regarding the legitimacy of using the expression *Völkerrecht* to designate the right of nations, in other words, his refusal to make peoples (*Völker*) the subject of international law. What is involved in this law are the relations not among peoples but among states:

> The right of *states* in relation to one another (which in German is called, not quite correctly, the right of nations, but should instead be called the right of states, *jus publicum civitatem*) is what we have to consider under the title *Völkerrecht*.
>
> (Ibid., §53.114)

2. *Volk*: Nature and history versus reason and law

What appears in Kant as a semantic reluctance (he finds the term *Volk* unsuitable) becomes in other writers a way of resisting any rational and juridical conception of the body politic. The naturalness and historicity of the *Volk* were opposed in principle to any attempt to reduce the people to relationships of law. Thus Herder defends the people against the state

in his *Ideen zur Philosophie der Geschichte der Menschheit* [Ideas for the philosophy of the history of humanity] (1784/91;):

> Nature raises families; the most natural state is therefore also *one* people, with one national character [*ein Volk, mit einem Nationalcharakter*]. . . . [A] people is as much a plant of nature as a family, only with more branches.
>
> (*Ideen* in *Johann Gottfried Herder Sämtliche Werke*, ed. B. Suphan et al., 13:384)

The people (*Volk*) is thus conceived as a natural organism whose divisions can result only from a politics of violence. And government has no legitimacy except insofar as it belongs to this organism. But this strong naturalization of the notion of the people is also a historicization of it. It is, in fact, for the people to cultivate its specificity in the course of a history that, far from implying any attachment to its original nature (Kant), on the contrary preserves it. It is in this perspective that we should understand the development of several notions derived from *Volk* that put the unity of the people under the sign of its historicity, even its antiquity, or under that of its naturalness.

■ See Box 3.

3. The erasure of social inequalities

This mutually exclusive naturalization and historicization of the *Volk* erases the tension between the juridical body of the citizens and individuals or groups whose social and political situation excludes them from that body. As a result, the object of compassion is shifted: it is no longer the most wretched part (the uneducated and impoverished people) that arouses pity, but rather the people as a whole (*das Volk*),

---

3
The ideology of *Volk* and *Volkstum*

On the basis of *Volk* have been created *Urvolk* (aboriginal people), *Volksgeist* (spirit of the people), *Volkslied* (folksong), and *Volkstum* (people-ness), which never refer to either a legal determination of the people or to the people as the group composed of the wretched and excluded. That is why the expressions "folksong" or "popular element" are not suitable translations of these German words. Of all these words, *Volkstum* is the most untranslatable. Coined by Ludwig Jahn in 1810 (in a work entitled precisely *Deutsches Volkstum*), it designates the strength given a people by its organic unity and makes the latter the source of its sovereignty. *Volkstum* is in fact in tension with *Königtum* (royalty). Let us add that this substance (or element) of each people is also the principle of its opposition to all others, and that its greater or lesser importance determines its ability to dominate others;

"What is it that makes England and France the leading world powers? Nothing other than the *Volkstum* that is constantly reborn in the midst of the greatest upheavals" (cf. *La langue source de la nation*, ed. P. Caussat et al., 134). But *Volkstum* is only one example among others of the different terms that can be forged by a nationalist ideology on the basis of the word *Volk*—as was shown by Victor Klemperer analyzing, day by day, the rhetoric of *Volk* and its derivatives in the discourse of the Nazis.

BIBLIOGRAPHY

Barbour, Stephen. " 'Uns knüpft der Sprache heilig Band': Reflections on the Role of Language in German Nationalism, Past and Present." In "*Das unsichtbare Band der Sprache*": Studies in German Language and Linguistic History in Memory of Leslie Seiffert, edited by John L. Flood, Paul Salmon, Olive Sayce, and Christopher Wells, 313–32. Stuttgart: Heinz Akademischer, 1993.

Bauman, Richard, and Charles L. Briggs. *Voices of Modernity: Language Ideologies and the Politics of Inequality*. Cambridge: Cambridge University Press, 2003.

Caussat, P., D. Adamski, and M. Crépon, eds. *La langue source de la nation: Messianismes séculiers en Europe centrale et orientale (du XVIIIe au XXe siècle)*. Hayen, Belg.: Mardaga, 1996.

Faye, Jean Pierre. *Langages totalitaires: Critique de la raison narrative*. Paris: Hermann, 1972.

Jahn, Friedrich Ludwig. *Deutsches Volkstum*. 1813. Hildesheim, Ger.: Olms, 1980.

Klemperer, Victor. *LTI—Notizbuch eines Philologen: An Annotated Edition*. Notes and commentary by Roderick H. Watt. Lewiston, NY: Mellen, 1997. Translation by Martin Brady: *The Language of the Third Reich: LTI-Lingua Tertii Imperii: A Philologist's Notebook*. London: Continuum, 2006.

whether this compassion has to do with the people's insufficiently recognized language, spoken and written, its insufficiently developed culture, the absence of international recognition, or the actual existence of a cultural or political domination. The register of the people's self-pity certainly constitutes an element in the rise of nationalism that cannot be ignored.

Nietzsche notes that such a perspective constitutes a genuine break with a whole tradition inherited from antiquity:

> To differentiate between government and people, as if two separate spheres of power, one stronger and higher, the other weaker and lower, were negotiating and coming to agreement, is a bit of inherited political sensibility that still accords exactly with the historical establishment of the power relationship in *most* states. When, for example, Bismarck describes the constitutional form as a compromise between government and people, he is speaking according to a principle that has its reason in history (which is, of course, also the source for that portion of unreason, without which nothing human can exist). By contrast, we are now supposed to learn (according to a principle that has sprung from the *head* alone, and is supposed to *make* history) that government is nothing but an organ of the people, and not a provident, honorable "Above" in relationship to a habitually humble "Below."
>
> (trans. M. Faber and S. Lehmann, *Human, All Too Human*, 215)

Nietzsche challenges the unitary definition of "people" and in connection with his repeated criticisms of democracy as the weak's revenge and domination, *Volk* usually has the meaning of *vulgus* or *plebs* in their pejorative sense.

B. "Nation"

Nonetheless, in German *Volk* does not cover by itself the whole of the naturalness of the body politic. Although it designates a group gathered in a single territory, another term is necessary to designate a community of birth. The latter is, as we have seen, the precise meaning that Kant gives to the term *Nation* in his *Anthropologie in pragmatischer Hinsicht* (*Anthropology from a Pragmatic Point of View*). Except for when in *The Doctrine of Right* he wants to refer in a more political sense to the community of birth, the bond of kinship implied by the Latin terms *gens* or *natio*, Kant uses a lengthy paraphrase to avoid using *Nation*:

> As natives of a country, those who constitute a people [*Volk*] can be looked upon analogously to descendants [*nach der Analogie der Erzeugung*] of the same ancestors [*von einem gemeinschaftlichen Elternstamm*] (*congeniti*) even though they are not. Yet in an intellectual sense and from the perspective of rights, since they are born of the same mother (the republic) [*von einer gemeinschaftlichen Mutter (die Republik)*], they constitute as it were one family (*gens, natio*), whose members (citizens of the state) are of equally high birth.
>
> (trans. M. J. Gregor, *Metaphysics of Morals*, I, §53, 114; translation modified)

Once again, Kant resorts to Latin to designate the political character of the bond of birth, as if he could not count on the German term to do so.

In reality, *Nation* was at that time already being used as part of a strategy to which Kant could not subscribe. For authors like Herder, the nation is a community of birth, to be sure, but it is much more than that. It is an organic whole, a unity both natural and historical, and its customs, traditions, language, and religion, as well as its feelings and imagination, are all subject to the same process of development. In this regard it is the object of a veritable sacralization that has nothing to do with attachment to common legal norms. Nations constitute a division of humanity foreseen by divine Providence: "The Creator alone is the only one who conceives the full unity of any one and of all nations [*die ganze Einheit einer, aller Nationen*], in all their great diversity without thereby losing sight of their unity" (*Auch eine Philosophie der Geschichte zur Bildung der Menschheit* [1774]; trans. I. D. Evrigenis and D. Pellerin, *Another Philosophy of History for the Education of Mankind*, 26).

Thus we can see in what a complex system of illusions we find ourselves entangled when Herder uses this same term, *Nation*, in referring to the Roman Empire's violent treatment of the communities it conquered: "The walls that separated the nation from other nations were broken down, the first step taken to destroy the national characters of them all, to throw everyone into one mold called 'the Roman people'" (ibid., 23). Herder gave the form *Nation* an atemporal dimension that perpetuated it.

III. *Dêmos*, *Ethnos*, *Genos*, and Their Translations

In Anatole Bailly's Greek-French dictionary (RT: *Dictionnaire grec-français*) we find the same sequence, *race-peuple-nation* (as well as *tribu*, and also *classe*, *caste*, *sexe*, along with strange compounds such as *race de peuples* and *famille de peuples*) to render both *ethnos* and *genos*; and in any case *peuple* is one of the translations proposed for each of the three terms *dêmos*, *ethnos*, and *genos*. Thus the tripartite *race, peuple, nation* division as such does not constitute a significant system of differences in Greek: the Greek words in question evoke quite different series that distinguish them from one another or complicate them in different ways.

A. *Genos*: From the biological to the political (*genos* and *polis*, "race" and "city") and the logical (*genos* and *eidos*, "genus" and "species")

Genos, from *gignesthai* [γίγνεσθαι] ("to be born," and then "to become, to occur") had first of all the biological meaning of "birth, origin, descent." It signifies "race, stock," that of the gods (Hesiod's *Theogony*) and that of mules, and within the human "genus" (*genos anthrôpôn* [γένος ἀνθρώπων]), it takes on the narrower sense of "ancestry, kinship." In Homer, a person introduces himself in terms of his *genos* ("My *genos* is Ithaca and my father is Odysseus," says Telemachos, *Odyssey* XV.267), and Greek tragedies focus on the *genos*—the "family" of the Atreids, for instance. Thus *genos* functions as an equivalent of the two Latin words *genus* and *gens* (Greek *gennaios* [γενναῖος]: "noble, high-born"). It therefore connects the biological with two types of series, (1) sociopolitical and (2) logico-ontological.

1. The first series shows that birth is basic to social organization. Émile Benveniste describes how the "three concentric divisions of ancient Greece" (*Origines de la formation des noms en indo-européen*, 1:257, cf. 1:316), *genos, phratria* [φρατρία], and *phulê* [φυλή], which are analogous to Latin *gens, curia,* and *tribus*—along with the quantification stipulated in Solon's Athenian constitution, that thirty "clans" make a "phratry," and three phratries make a "tribe"—broaden the fraternity of blood to a military solidarity (Homer, *Iliad*, II.362 f.) and then an institutional one. Genealogical divisions are then rearranged into a "nomenclature of territorial divisions" (É. Benveniste, *Le vocabulaire des institutions indo-européennes*, 1:310) and embedded in sequences such as *oikos* [οἶκος], *kômê* [κώμη], *polis* [πόλις] (household, village, city-state).

For a long time, the essential question was as follows: what is the place of the genealogical and the "genic" in politics? One answer—which Plato attributed, not without irony, to Aspasia, a courtesan who was loved by Pericles and who is supposed to have influenced his famous funeral oration—makes the *genos* the foundation of the *polis*: the excellence of Athens comes from the Athenians' *eugeneia*, represented by the myth of their "autochthony" (their ancestors, they say, were born from the soil itself of their "motherland"): "This good birth [*eugeneia* (εὐγένεια)] has as its first foundation the origin [*genesis* (γένεσις)] of their ancestors [*progonôn* (προγόνων)], who, instead of being immigrants and engendering their descendants [*ekgonous* (ἐκγόνους)] metics . . . were autochthons" (*Menexenus*, 237b; cf. 245d); it is the *isogonia* [ἰσογονία], the "equality of birth" of all these "brothers" that provides a natural basis for the *isonomia* [ἰσονομία], the "equality before the law" established by law among Athenian citizens (239a).

Aristotle's answer consists, on the contrary, in distinguishing among orders. The *genos*, the line of biological descent, takes in politics the form of the *oikos* (the home) and of the *oikia* [οἰκία] (the family or household: man, wife, children, animals, servants). The *polis* is conceived as the outcome of successive local regroupings, several households forming a village (the "village" or *kômê* is a "colony," *apoikia* [ἀποικία], an extension-externalization of the family, *oikia*), and several villages forming a city (*Politics*, I.2,

particularly 1252b16f.): the geographical land is substituted for the patriotic myth. At the same time, the "political" establishes from the outset an order radically distinct from the "domestic" or "economic" order, whose goal is no longer to "live" but to "live well" (*eu zên* [εὖ ζῆν]) (1252b30): it is neither the unity of place (*topos* [τόπος]) nor the *genos* of the inhabitants, their common origin, that can guarantee the identity of a *polis*, but only the *politeia* [πολιτεία], the "political constitution" itself (III.3).

- See Box 4.

2. The *genos*, thus relieved of its mythical, epic, and tragic freight, opens out onto another kind of series that is properly philosophical, and makes the transition from genealogy to logic and ontology. The terminology elaborated in terms of natural history (the "class" of animals) lends itself to categorial uses. Established by Aristotle by means of the distinction *genos/eidê* [εἴδη] genus/species, it is reexamined by Plotinus and Porphyry, who try to elaborate on this transition.

- See Box 5.

B. *Ethnos* and *dêmos*: Geography and politics

Ethnos designates a more or less stable group of individuals, soldiers, or animals that is characterized by a common *ethos* [ἔθος] ("habits," "customs," from the same root **swedh-*) and that is distinguished from the *genos* as "foreign" (*othneios* [ὀθνεῖος])—thus in Rome, *ta ethnê* [τὰ ἔθνη] referred to the peoples of the provinces, and in the New Testament, it refers to the Gentiles as opposed to the Hebrews. *Dêmos*, which is generally related to *daiomai* [δαίομαι] (to divide up), signifies in Homer "country, territory" (for example, *Iliad* V.710: "The Boeotians who lived on a very fertile land [*dêmon* (δῆμον)]"); in Athens, the *demes* (divisions of tribes) were part of the administrative topography, and then the inhabitants of this country ("to the misfortune of your father, your city, and all your people [*dêmôi* (δήμῳ)]") (ibid., III.50); finally, perhaps because they lived in the countryside, it refers to the "common people," as opposed to the powerful (when Odysseus sees a "king or notable hero" [ibid., II.188]; "when he sees a man of the people [*dêmou andra* (δήμου ἄνδρα)]") (ibid., II.198). While *genos* implies a

---

5
The genera of being: Genealogy or logic: Porphyry and his translation

➤ ANALOGY, HOMONYM, PRÉDICABLE, PRINCIPLE, *TO BE*

The basic problem that determines the whole doctrine of the analogy of being can be formulated in terms of the semantics of the *genos*: how important a role is played by the Platonic and Neoplatonic genealogical meaning in the logical meaning that Aristotle established in the *Organon*? In Aristotelian theory, each science is the science of a single genus of being, but being is not genus, so that the recurrent problem arising from Aristotelianism can be formulated as follows: are the categories genera of being or are they multiple meanings indicating heterogeneous domains?

It is in Porphyry's *Isagoge* that the semantic stake is clearest. Porphyry opposes Plotinus, who, in the sixth book of the *Enneads*, "genealogized" Aristotle's categories the better to Platonize them. Porphyry re-Aristotelianizes them: Porphyry's genealogical tree does not have a single summit—there is no supreme genus like the Stoics' *ti*, nor are there any lowly rootlets to feed the superb tree. There is no process of engenderment, no hierarchical procession that allows us to pass logically to the individual, even if the tree is often designed to lead from the *genus generalissimum* to the *species specialissima* (A. de Libera, *La querelle des universaux*, 46). However, Porphyry takes into account the influence of the genealogical meaning when he distinguishes the meanings of *genos*: "genus is thus expressed in three ways, and it is the third with which philosophers are concerned." The three ways are (a) "the multiplicity of those who draw their origin from a single principle" (example: "the genus of the Heraclids" designates those who have Heracles as an ancestor); (b) "the principle

of each individual's birth," whether this concerns the father (Heracles for Hyllos) or the homeland (Athens for Plato); (c) "'genus' is also used in another way: it is that beneath which the species is ranked, perhaps named in this way in imitation of the preceding meanings; in fact, the genus of which we are speaking is a sort of principle [*archê* (ἀρχή)] for what is beneath it, and seems to embrace all the multiplicity [*plêthos*] that is under it." Meaning (c) goes back to the literal definition given in Aristotle's *Topics*: "genus is what is predicable [*katêgoroumenon* (κατηγορούμενον)] relative to the question 'what is?' [*en tôi ti esti* (ἐν τῷ τί ἔστι)]" (*Isagoge*, I.5), or, "A 'genus' is what is predicated in the category of essence of a number of things exhibiting differences in kind." (*Topics*, I, 5, 102a31 f.; trans. W. A. Pickard-Cambridge), with the example of the "animal" (or the "living being," *zôion* [ζῷον]) as the genus for "man." We will emphasize Alain de Libera's notes: "Here there is an unavoidable translation difficulty in French: since Porphyry claims to illustrate the various meanings of 'genus,' we are forced to use the term, even if the words *race* or *lignée* would probably be preferable" (*Isagôgê*, 38, n. 11) for meanings (a) and (b). And especially, the relation to the "properly philosophical" meaning: "Here it is as if Porphyry were stressing the resemblance between . . . the properly Aristotelian philosophical acceptation—the relation of genus to species—[and] the 'ordinary,' or at least nontechnical meanings of the term in order to overcome the opposition Aristotle himself makes between the genealogical meaning and the genus-species relation" (ibid., 39, n. 19).

In opposition to Plotinus's refutation, Porphyry thus outlines a Plotinization of Aristotle by regenealogizing the meaning of *genos*. But he does so the better to carry out the final movement, which is that of disjunction: by opting for the radical homonymy of being (*Isagôgê*, II, 10), Porphyry refuses to "suture the Aristotelian doctrine of categories by means of a genealogical notion of genus, understood as an 'analogical' unity, *aph' henos* [ἀφ' ἑνός]" (ibid., 39). The disjunction of the meanings of *genos* and the homonymy of being are connected; to promote the genealogical meaning is to support the analogical procession that engenders on the basis of a unique principle, against the logical and categorial sense necessary for the homonymic disjunction. In a certain way, the difficulties of translating Porphyry into French are what corroborate the power of the homonymy for us today.

BIBLIOGRAPHY

Aristotle. *Posterior Analytics*. Translated by Hugh Tredennick. Cambridge, MA: Harvard University Press / Loeb Classical Library, 1976.

———. *Topics*. Translated by W. A. Pickard-Cambridge. Available at http://classics.mit.edu/Aristotle/topics.html (last accessed 10 June 2013).

Libera, Alain de. *La querelle des universaux: De Platon à la fin du Moyen Age*. Paris: Éditions du Seuil, 1996.

Porphyry. *Isagoge: Texte grec, Translatio Boethii*. Translated by Alain de Libera and Alain-Philippe Segonds. Introduction and notes by Alain de Libera. Paris: Vrin, 1998. Translation and commentary by Jonathan Barnes: *Introduction*. Oxford: Clarendon Press, 2003.

community of origin, *ethnos* implies a community of mores and *dêmos* implies a community of territory that culminates in a political structure.

In Aristotle's *Politics* we find, repeated over and over, the most rigorous expression of the difference between *ethnos* and *dêmos*. *Ethnos* is first contrasted, in virtually all its occurrences, with *polis* (city, state). In the technical sense, the *ethnê* designate the "peoples" (*peuples*; cf. J. Aubonnet's translation) or "tribes" (*peuplades*; cf. P. Pellegrin's translation) or "nations" (*nations*; cf. J. Tricot's translation) that have not yet reached the stage of the accomplished city, provisionally or definitively. This question, heavy with ideology, is subject to debate, depending precisely on one's interpretation of the natural historicity of the city and whether one gives priority to the break or the continuity with the family and the village:

"The cities were first governed by kings, as the *ethnê* still are today" (Aristotle, *Politics*, 1252b19f.).

That is why the term is used above all to designate barbarian groups, all of which are characterized by a lack of differentiation and can be despotically hierarchized, and which do not know this form of political equality by reciprocity (being alternately governors and governed)—the only one that can preserve differences from being erased by uniformity:

It is not like a military alliance [*summachia* (συμμαχία)]. The usefulness of the latter depends on its quantity even where there is no difference in quality [*to auto tôi eidei* (τὸ αὐτὸ τῷ εἴδει)] (for mutual protection is the end aimed at), just as a greater weight of anything is more useful than a less (in like manner, a state differs from a nation [*ethnos*], when the nation has not its population [*to plêthos* (τὸ πλῆθος)] organized in villages, but lives an Arcadian sort of life); but the elements out of which a unity is to be formed differ in kind. Wherefore the principle of compensation [*to ison to antipeponthos* (τὸ ἴσον τὸ ἀντιπεπονθός)], as I have already remarked in the *Ethics*, is the salvation of states.

(Ibid., II.1261a24–31; trans. B. Jowett in *Basic Works of Aristotle*, 1147)

Ethnos, a geographical and not a political term, has to do in particular with a theory of climates. It is the word used by Hippocrates when he examines, in his treatise on *Airs, Waters, and Places*, the effects of climate on the temperament and customs of all species of human beings: "I want to explain now how Asia and Europe differ from each other in every respect, and in particular with regard to the physical appearance of their peoples [*peri tôn ethneôn tês morphês* (περὶ τῶν ἔθνεων τῆς μορφῆς)], in which they are distinct and do not at all resemble each other" (XII, 1). This was, of course, the term Aristotle adopted (*Politics*, VII.7) to distinguish the *ethnē* of cold regions such as Europe, who are full of courage (*thumos* [θυμός]) but lacking in intelligence (*dianoia* [διάνοια]) and skill (*technē* [τέχνη]), and are thus free but not organized into cities (*apoliteuta* [ἀπολίτευτα], 1327b26), from those of Asia, who are inversely endowed (with *dianoia* and *technē*, but not *thumos*), and are consequently subjected or enslaved, with, in the middle, the *genos* of the Greeks, "the race of Hellenes," which is endowed with both courage and intelligence, and lives freely and politically. But this *genos* consists of *ethnē* that are more or less balanced and more or less politically virtuous—Pierre Pellegrin, when dealing with the Greeks, shifts, unaccountably, from *peuplades* to *peuples* (1327b34), and entitles his study "Le caractère national: Qualités des peuples selon le climat"—though once again the rigor of the terms can only be etymological or conventional. However that may be, *ethnos* designates the geographical and very precisely ethological component of human diversity, in contrast to both the community of origin (*genos*) and the political structure (*polis, politeia*).

▪ See Box 6.

Dêmos, unlike the words that serve to translate it (*populus, peuple*, people, *Volk*), is one of the three terms that from earliest classical antiquity belonged exclusively to the vocabulary of politics. Sometimes it designates the body of citizens who make up the *polis* (and from which are excluded by definition those who have no political rights, and in particular women, children, and slaves, whatever the system), and sometimes, exactly like "the people" and unlike the *Volk*, the most "deprived" among them (*aporoi* [ἄποροι]), who are also always, as if by accident, the most numerous. In this latter sense, other words bearing more negative connotations are sometimes substituted for *dêmos*: *plêthos* (from *pimplêmi* [πίμπλημι], "to fill," like *polus* [πολύς], "numerous"), "the multitude, the crowd," or even "the rabble" that Xenophon contrasts with the *dêmos* (*Constitution of Athens*, 2, 18), and in the plural *ta plêthê* [τὰ πλήθη], "the masses," those whom, according to Plato, a demogogic Sophist would never fail to persuade (*Gorgias*, 452e); or again *ochlos* [ὄχλος] (*ochleô* [ὀχλέω] means both "to move" and "to disturb, harass," probably from **wegh-*, like "vehicle" and "wave"), the masses in disorder, the tumult of the crowd (*Gorgias* again, where Plato makes the meanings circulate among "popular assemblies," for instance the tribunals [454b] and the ignorant crowd [458–59]). Similarly, Latin writers played on *plebs* and *turba*.

This double polarity of *dêmos* is clearly connected with the polemics regarding democracy: the least bad of all possible governments, the government of all for all, or else a degenerate system that inevitably leads to power being seized by the most vile (*phauloi* [φαῦλοι]), the common people, as opposed to the good people (*spoudaioi* [σπουδαῖοι] from *spoudê* [σπουδή], "zeal"). Aristotle writes the history of democracy, drawing on the Sophists to rehabilitate the *dêmos* as *plêthos*, the people as multitude.

▪ See Box 7.

IV. *Populus, Plebs, Gens*

The former genealogical names lose their institutional and social meaning and become a nomenclature for territorial divisions. Each language proceeds to rearrange its terminology. The way in which this transformation takes place in the different languages is extremely informative, because languages do not have the same way of being Indo-European.

> Latin is Indo-European in its fidelity to earlier usage, to the vocabulary of institutions, even when this vocabulary covers new realities; Greek is Indo-European in an inverse way, through the persistence of the primitive model organizing a new series of designations.

(É. Benveniste, *Le vocabulaire des institutions indo-européennes*, 1:310sq.)

6

Dêmos / laos: "People" / "people"

Many Greek words that are not related to each other are translated by "people," which tells us something about the vagueness of the modern term. For example, *phulon* [φῦλον] ("tribe," "race," from *phuô* [φύω], "push"), alongside *genos* or *ethnos*. Above all, as Émile Benveniste has noted (*Le vocabulaire des institutions indo-européennes*, 2:90), we translate without distinction two words that have absolutely different meanings and refer, as early as the Homeric poems, to historically distinct realities: *dêmos* and *laos* [λαός]. *Laos*, frequently used in the plural, without any corresponding term outside Greek, can be traced back to the Achaean period; it designates the people insofar as it bears arms (thus neither old men nor children) and implies the personal relation of a group to a leader whom it follows: thus Menelaos is a "shepherd of peoples." *Dêmos*, which goes back to the Dorian invasion, and thus to a more recent date, implies on the contrary, as we have seen, a fixed relationship to a territory, and designates not a military community but the stability of a politicizable or political body.

7

Dêmos and *plêthos*: Democracy and the plurality of citizens

➤ POLIS

To frame the problem, let us sketch a table of the different kinds of government or constitutions (*politeiai* [πολιτεῖαι]), that is, of the different types of governments (*politeumata* [πολιτεύματα]) set forth by Aristotle in Book 3 of the *Politics*. The "true" forms of government, listed according to the number and quality of the governors, may, as in Plato, undergo deviations regarding the goals that make them move from concern for the *koinon* [κοινόν] (public good, common interest,) to the selfishness of the *idion* [ἴδιον] (specific or private interest): then they change their names.

Government	True government (public good, *to koinon sumpheron* [Gr.])	Deviation (parekbasis) (private good, *to idion* [Gr.])
By one	Monarchy	Tyranny
By a few	Aristocracy	Oligarchy
By many	*Politeia*	Democracy *hoi polloi* [οἱ πολλοί] *to plêthos* [τὸ πλῆθος]

The central enigma, which is well known, has to do with the fact that the true form of government by the many does not really have its own name: it is called just *politeia*. Democracy, government by the people, is of this kind and is only the deviated form of it; it is defined as the government "that seeks the advantage of the poor (*pros to sumpheron to tôn aporôn* [πρὸς τὸ συμφέρον τὸ τῶν ἀπόρων])" (*Politics*, III.1279a9). Whence the prudence of Solon, the legislator par excellence: "Solon, himself, appears to have given the Athenians only that power of electing to offices and calling to account the magistrates which was absolutely necessary; for without it they would have been in a state of slavery and enmity to the government. All the magistrates he appointed from the notables and men of wealth" (II.12.1274a15–19, and III.11.1281b31f.; trans. B. Jowett in *Basic Works of Aristotle*). However, the *dêmos*, precisely because it is *plêthos* (mass, number), has thereby an intrinsic quality capable of conferring on democracy an unparalleled virtue and of making government by the many the government par excellence. This promotion is based on the very definition of the city, which for Aristotle, contrary to Plato, is not initially unified and hierarchized like the body or the mind, but multiple and synthetic like a chorus or a symphony, so that "in the virtue of each the virtue of all is involved" (VII.13.1332a38):

> But a state is a composite [*tôn sugkeimenôn* (τῶν συγκειμένων)], like any other whole made up of many parts [*sunestôtôn d' ek pollôn moriôn* (συνεστώτων δ' ἐκ πολλῶν μορίων)]; these are the citizens, who compose it [*hê gar polis politôn ti plêthos estin* (ἡ γὰρ πόλις πολιτῶν τι πλῆθος ἐστὶν)]. It is evident, therefore, that we must begin by asking, Who is the citizen, and what is the meaning of the term?

> (*Politics*, III.1.1274b38–41; trans. B. Jowett in *Basic Works of Aristotle*)

Quantity thus becomes a quality and justifies giving this *plêthos* the sovereign power:

> For the many [*tous pollous* (τοὺς πολλούς)], of whom each individual is but an ordinary person, when they meet together [*sunelthontas* (συνελθόντας)] may very likely be better than the few good, if regarded not individually but collectively [*ouch' hôs hekaston, all' hôs sumpantas* (οὐχ' ὡς ἕκαστον, ἀλλ' ὡς σύμπαντας)], just as a feast to which many contribute is better than a dinner provided out of a single purse. For each individual among the many [*pollôn gar ontôn* (πολλῶν γὰρ ὄντων)] has a share of virtue and prudence, and exactly like a crowd [*to plêthos*], when they meet together, they become in a manner one man, who has many feet, and hands, and senses; that is a figure of their mind and disposition (*ta êthê kai tên dianoian* [τὰ ἤθη καὶ τὴν διάνοιαν]). Hence the many [*hoi polloi*] are better judges than a single man of music and poetry; for some understand one part, and some another, and among them they understand the whole.

> (Ibid., 1281a42–b10; translation by B. Jowett modified)

Thus is justified the fact that "the mass of citizens" (*to plêthos tôn politôn* [τὸ πλῆθος τῶν πολιτῶν]), that is, "all those who have neither wealth nor title to virtue," participate in the deliberative and judicial powers:

> When they meet together their perceptions are quite good enough, and combined with the better class they are useful to the state (just as impure food when mixed with what is pure sometimes makes the entire mass more wholesome than a small quantity of the pure would be), but each individual, left to himself, forms an imperfect judgment.

> (Ibid., 1281b34–38, trans. B. Jowett)

Probably no one has ever praised the democratic deviation more subtly.

BIBLIOGRAPHY

Cassin, Barbara. "De l'organisme au pique-nique." Pp. 114–48 in *Nos Grecs et leurs modernes*. Paris: Seuil, 1992.

A. *Populus*

Whether we connect the word *populus* with the Indo-European root **pel-/ple-* (Greek *plêthos*, Latin *plenus*) or with an Etruscan origin, it is recognized that it initially had a military meaning: *populus* designated the mass of infantrymen, and other words have retained a trace of this meaning, such as the Latin deponent verb *populari*, which means "to sack or devastate." With the reorganization of the military and the *comitiae*, the term *populus* lost this meaning and came to apply to the citizenry as a whole, gathered together in the centuriate assembly. *Civitas* was later added to *populus*, reinforcing the idea of collectivity. But in Cicero's philosophical works these two notions are articulated in a more complex way.

> A people [*populus*] is not just any assembly of individuals brought together in just any way [*non omnis hominum coetus quoquo modo congregatus*], but the gathering of a multitude, carried out by virtue of an agreement regarding the law and a community of interests [*coetus multitudinis juris consensu et utilitati communione sociatus*].

> (*De republica*, I.25, 39)

Originally, then, there were no isolated individuals, but a human group. Then, according to Cicero, it was the agreement regarding law (*consensu juris*)—and not individual interests or historical affinities—that "informed" the association, whereas the application of this agreement realized "the common interest." Far from amounting to a collection of individual wills, and even independently of them, the *populus* thus appears as a collectivity structured by these two objective, specific bonds. Such a definition, which allows us to move beyond the moral-political dualism, emphasizes the natural foundation of the social bond; it also establishes an abstract idea of the public good; and finally it gives the *populus* a very strong juridical value as an independent organism that the Greek *dêmos* never had, a value that we find again in another definition of the *populus* as a *corpus ex distantibus*, "a body formed of disparate elements" bound together by the bond of law alone (Seneca, *Letters to Lucilius*, 102, 6).

■ See Box 8.

For Cicero, the *populus* precedes conceptually the *civitas*, its institutional form, and the *res publica*, its patrimonial dimension (Peppe, "La nozione di *populus*," 318): "Omnis populus qui est talis coetus, omnis civitas quae est constitutio populi, omnis res publica quae populi res est" (Every people, that is, the assembly I have described, a city that is the political organization of a people, a state that is the commonwealth; Cicero, *De republica* I.26, 40). Whereas all citizens participate in the commonwealth insofar as they form a group, as *cives*—that is, as individuals having citizenship and thus forming a part (*pars*) of the people—they share unequally in the government. It is for the mixed constitution, the historically determined *constitutio populi*, to set the rules for the attribution of power within the *res publica*. Thus inequalities emerge at the level of the *civitas*—where *populus* designates, in a narrower way, the whole of the citizens grouped together.

Far from being merely theoretical, this latter sense of the word *populus* reflects the state of Roman society from the third century BCE onward, a society that recognized the legal equality of all citizens, patricians, and plebeians, but that, on fiscal principles, made the people a constitutional actor with limited power and managed by "good people," that is, the Senate (and the magistrates)—as is suggested by the city's signature: *Senatus populusque romanus*. In this context one can probably speak of popular sovereignty. But apart from the appearance in the second century BCE of a democratic trend, it cannot be denied that a large part of Roman society tended to make the popular assembly the sole subject of power, which was, as it were, delegated to the magistrates (Cicero, *De officiis*, I.34, 124). Moreover, it was to be one of the ideological foundations of the Principate, and Seneca defined the monarch as a person "invested with the powers of the people in order to exercise them on the people" (*potestas populi in populum data*) (*Letters to Lucilius*, 14, 7).

The political definition of the people takes into account only adult male citizens. Does that mean the women and children, who were nonetheless citizens, were excluded from it? In reality, *populus* sometimes also designates the whole of the citizenry. What difference is there, Julian wonders, between the laws, received after the people's judgment (*judicio populi*), and "what the people has approved without any text [*ea quae sine ullo scripto populus probavit*]?" (*Digest*, I.3.32.1). This equivalence between *leges* and *mores*, which reflects the ambivalence of the word *populus*, characterizes the whole of the production of Roman law (F. Gallo, "Produzione del diritto e sovranità popolare nel pensiero di Giuliano").

B. Populus, plebs

These three definitions (an organism bound together by law, an assembly of citizens, the totality of the citizenry) clearly distinguish *populus* from *plebs*. From a legal point of view, the term *plebs* groups together the *proletarii*, initially those who are outside the *populus*—that is to say, outside the legions—whence the archaic formula *populus plebsque* (the *populus* and the *plebs*). Later on, the *plebs* was gradually integrated into the *populus*, but the term *plebs* retained its exclusive meaning of a group outside the patrician families (Gaius, *Institutiones*, I.3; Aulus Gellius, *Attic Nights*, X.20, 5). Under the Republic, the word designated more generally all those who did not belong for tax purposes to the upper orders (senators and knights in Rome, decurions in the provinces). Thus *plebs* ended up designating "the popular masses," "the common people," and was sometimes synonymous with

---

8

Cicero and Saint Augustine

Cicero's definition was criticized at length by Saint Augustine (*De civitate Dei*, II.17–19; XIX.21–24). "When man does not serve God, what justice can there be in man? There is therefore not that common acknowledgment of right [*jus*] that makes a multitude of men a people." And further on, "What can be the true interest [*utilitas*] of those who live in impiety, as anyone lives who betrays the service of God for that of demons?" Augustine is thus led to propose a new definition: "Populus est coetus multitudinis rationalis rerum quas diligit concordi communione sociatus" (a people is an assemblage of reasonable beings bound together by a common agreement as to the objects of their love) (*City of God*, XIX.24; trans. M. Dods, 706). Thus conceived, the *populus* is not a legal but a cultural unit; it is defined, not by a legal form, but by an ethical content, love for the same values and for God. No doubt Augustine recognized that historical peoples and even pagans had the right to bear this name: that is the case of the people of Rome in times of peace. But from his point of view, the Christian community is the authentic people and the spiritual city the true city. However, for Augustine, Cicero's presupposition is that the people is an organized community, not a juxtaposition of individuals, and the connection with *civitas* remains fundamental.

BIBLIOGRAPHY

Augustine. *City of God*. Translated by M. Dods. New York: Modern Library, 1950.

"the poor" (Cicero, *De republica* II.39; *De legibus*, II.50). In this sense, the word had numerous equivalents: *multitudo, turba*, and also *vulgus*, which refers to the lowest part of the *plebs*. These terms, accompanied by a depreciative adjective, often took on a moral connotation: *multitudo indocta, vulgus imperitorum, plebs et infima multitudo* (uneducated masses, ignorant multitude, plebeians and common people) (Cicero, *Pro Murena*, 38 and 70; *Pro Milone*, 95). With this twofold moral and sociological connotation, *plebs* comes closer to the Greek *plêthos*, while *populus* renders *dêmos*.

However, exceptions to this distinction emerged toward the end of the Republic, especially in the political vocabulary, where *populus* was often used to refer to the *plebs* (for example in Sallust or Livy). Under the Empire, the confusion increased because of the collapse of the *populus*'s powers. This confusion is also found in Greek texts of the period, where *dêmos* ends up expressing the idea of the crowd or "rabble" (Cassius Dio, 74, 13).

■ See Box 9.

C. *Populi, natrones, gentes*

Referring to a group of citizens, *populus* also had an international dimension. The jurist Gaius (*Institutiones*, I.1) defined the *jus gentium* as the natural law that governs "all the peoples" of the earth (*omnes populi*). Through this meaning, *populi* approaches *gentes* or *natiunes*, but these notions in fact diverge on an essential level.

Gens designates neither a political group nor the work of a legislator, but rather an assembly of men—"a *multitudo* that has issued from the same origin or was constituted after having separated itself from another nation [*natio*]," according to Isidore of Seville (*Etymologiae*, IX.2.1). Although its members often bear the same name (Cicero, *Topics*, 29), the group is not genetically homogeneous (*Grand Dictionnaire Encyclopédique Larousse*, s.v. "Nomen," 443), whether it is a Patrician clan (Greek *genê*) whose ancestor is often mythical, or one of the various peoples who compose the human race. As for *natio*, from *nascor*, "to be born," it suggests more the idea of a natural origin or a common territory: "It is a group of men who have not come from elsewhere, but were born in the same place" (RT: *De verborum significatu quae supersunt*, s.v. "Natio"). In any case, *natio*, like *gens*, is outside the civic sphere. From these nonpolitical groups that usually lived under the direction of a chief, the Romans clearly distinguished the *populus* and its institutional form, the *civitas*, in which man manifested his liberty. "All peoples [*nationes*] can endure servitude,

but not our city [*civitas*]," wrote Cicero (*Philippics*, X.10, 20). And for him, the *populi* are those who are organized into *civitates*; it is in this sense that they have their own law, a *jus civile* (*De officiis*, I.23) distinct from the *jus gentium*. Pointing out the different degrees (*gradus*) in Roman society (*De officiis*, I.53; III.69), Cicero lists the whole of the human species; then the noncivic groups, those that have in common a name (*gentes*), birth or place (*nationes*), language (*linguae*); and finally the *civitas*. In doing so, he situates the city less in a genealogical conception than in a universe constructed legally and alien to ethnic or geographical determinations.

Christians used *nationes* (Greek *ta ethnê*) to designate pagans. In this they were simply imitating the Roman model: just as, for the law of the Empire, the *nationes* are outside a *civitas* and foreign to the *populus romanus* (Gaius, *Insitutiones*, I.79), so in the Christian vocabulary the term designates those who are outside the *civitas christiana*, the *populus Dei*.

At the end of this itinerary, we can better understand what risk is involved in superimposing "race" and *genos*, "nation" and *ethnos*, and with them all the terms that designate human communities in various languages. It is the danger of the retrospective illusion. Beyond careless translations, an implicit philosophy of history is at stake. Thus the systematic use of "nation" to translate this or that Greek or Latin term organizes nothing less than the "nationalization" of all the communities of antiquity, that is, the construction of this particular form of community as an object of universal history, just as the use of "race" or *Rasse* extracts this notion from the historical and ideological contexts in which it emerged, in order to confer on it an ahistorical validity.

Marc Crépon
Barbara Cassin
Claudia Moatti

BIBLIOGRAPHY

Aristotle. *Politics*. Translated by Benjamin Jowett in *Basic Works of Aristotle*, edited by R. McKeon. New York: Random House, 1941. Translation by J. Aubonnet: *Politique*. Paris: Les Belles Lettres, 1960–1989). Translation by Pierre Pellegrin: *Les Politiques*. Paris: Flammarion, 1990. Translation by J. Tricot: *La Politique*. Paris: Vrin, 1970.

Benveniste, Émile. *Origines de la formation des noms en indo-européen*. Paris: Maisonneuve, 1935; reprint 1984.

———. *Le vocabulaire des institutions indo-européennes*. Edited by Jean Lallot. 2 vols. Paris: Éditions du Minuit, 1969.

Gallo, Francesco. "Produzione del diritto e sovranità popolare nel pensiero di Giuliano (a proposito di *D*. I, 3, 32)." *IURA* 36 (1985): 70–96.

Gaudemet Jean. "Le people et le gouvernement de la république romaine." *Labeo* 11 (1965): 147–92.

9

Populus and *popularis*

Contrary to French, in Latin it is difficult to discern an absolute reciprocity between "people" and "popular." Nonetheless, in the conflictual context of the late Republic, a development begins: the *populares*, the leaders of the democratic party, define themselves as the representatives of the *populus* as a whole and as sovereign, whereas their adversaries depreciate them as demagogues who are seeking the favor of the *plebs* and the slaves. This debate clearly seems to prefigure the way *populus* and *plebs* approached one another under the Empire, whereby *populus* reconnects with its derivative, *popularis*.

Herder, Johann Gottfried. *Auch eine Philosophie der Geschichte zur Bildung der Menschheit.* First published in 1774. Translation by Ioannis D. Evrigenis and Daniel Pellerin: *Another Philosophy of History for the Education of Mankind.* Indianapolis, IN: Hackett, 2004.

———. *Ideen zur Philosophie der Geschichte der Menschheit.* In vol. 13 of *Johann Gottfried Herder Sämtliche Werke*, edited by B. Suphan et al. Berlin: Weidmann, 1887. *Ideen* first published in 1784/91.

Kant, Immanuel. *Anthropologie in pragmatischer Hinsicht.* Vol. 7 of *Kants Gesammelte Schriften*, edited by Königlich Preussischen Akademie der Wissenschaften. Berlin: de Gruyter, 1902. Translation by Robert B. Louden: *Anthropology from a Pragmatic Point of View.* Edited by R. B. Louden. Cambridge: Cambridge University Press, 2006.

———. *Metaphysics of Morals.* 2nd ed. Translated by M. J. Gregor. Cambridge: Cambridge University Press, 1996.

Marat, Jean-Paul. *Textes choisis.* Paris: Éditions Sociales, 1975.

Moatti, Claudia. *La raison de Rome: Naissance de l'esprit critique à la fin de la République (Ile-Ier siècle avant Jésus-Christ).* Paris: Éditions du Seuil, 1997.

Momigliano, Arnaldo. "The Rise of the Plebs." In *Social Struggles in Archaic Rome: New Perspectives on the Conflict of the Orders*, edited by K Raaflaub, 174–97. Berkeley: University of California Press, 1986.

Nietzsche, Friedrich. *Human, All Too Human.* Translated by M. Faber and S. Lehmann. Lincoln: University of Nebraska Press, 1984.

Peppe, Leo. "La nozione di *populus* e le sue valenze: Con una indagine sulla terminologia pubblicistica nelle formule della *evocatio* e della *devotio*." In *Staat und Staatlichkeit in der frühen römischen Republik: Akten eines Symposiums, 12. –15. Juli 1988, Freie Universität Berlin*, edited by Walter Eder, 312–43. Stuttgart: Steiner, 1990.

Rousseau, Jean-Jacques. *Confessions.* Translated by J. M. Cohen. London: Penguin, 1953.

———. *The Major Political Writings of Jean-Jacques Rousseau.* Translated by John T. Scott. Chicago: University of Chicago Press, 2012.

———. *Œuvres complètes.* 2 vols. Paris: Gallimard, 1959–69.

Sieyès, Emmanuel Joseph. *Qu'est-ce que le tiers-état?* Paris: Presses Universitaires de France, 1982. First published in 1789.

Yavetz, Zvi. *Plebs and Princeps.* New Brunswick, NJ: Transaction Books, 1988.

PERCEPTION / APPERCEPTION

FRENCH	*perception, aperception*
GERMAN	*Empfindung, Wahrnehmung, Apperzeption*
GREEK	*katalêpsis* [κατάληψις]
LATIN	*perceptio, comprehensio, aperceptio*

➤ BEGRIFF, CONSCIOUSNESS, EPISTEMOLOGY, ERSCHEINUNG, GEFÜHL, I/ME/MYSELF, LEIB, OBJECT, PATHOS, *SENS COMMUN*, SENSE, TRUTH, UNCONSCIOUS

The noun "perception" had difficulty establishing itself in modern philosophical French. In Decartes, it retains the meaning of its antecedent, the Latin *perceptio*, which makes it a kind of intellectual operation, but a certain awkwardness is discernible in its usage, which explains why the more common verb *apercevoir* is frequently preferred to it. A tension between the noun and the verb was rapidly established because of the ambiguity of the latter, which can designate any act of knowing, the current meaning of sense perception being only one possibility among others. For Descartes, the common root of all these meanings is situated in consciousness's reflexivity, which is supposed to be present in all these operations: it is this presupposition that was attacked by Leibniz on the grounds that every perception is not necessarily conscious. Leibniz's critique of

Descartes gave rise in French to a new pair of opposites, *perception* and *aperception* (perception accompanied by consciousness). This linguistic innovation and its transposition into German was the origin in Kant of a new economy of representation (*Vorstellung*) involving *Wahrnehmung*, *Empfindung*, and *Apperzeption*.

I. Perception as an Operation of the Understanding: "Apperception" and "Perceive," from the Noun to the Verb

The Latin verb *percipere*, which originally meant, in the literal sense, "to take," "to gather," "to receive," and then, by transposition, "to feel," "to experience," "to learn," "to know," gave rise to the noun *perceptio* translating the Greek term *katalêpsis* [κατάληψις], which derived from the vocabulary of Stoic philosophy and designated a comprehensive grasping of the reality of the thing given in its representation (see Cicero, *De finibus bonorum et malorum*, 5.76, and *Academica*, 2.107: *perceptio* is a synonym of *cogitatio*, "thought," and *comprehensio*, "comprehension" or "a gathering together in thought of what truly is"; see BEGRIFF, Box 1).

Thus *perceptio* could be used in medieval philosophy to designate a philosophically formed concept, conferring in return on the verb *percipere* the correlative meaning of "receive into knowledge."

In modern philosophy, perception acquired the status of the fundamental relation between the knowing subject and what becomes an object for the subject. Descartes designates by perception all the cogitations of which the mind is the subject:

> Sunt deinde alii actus quos vocamus cogitativos, ut intelligere, velle, imaginari, sentire, etc., qui omnes sub ratione communi cogitationis, sive perceptionis, sive conscientiae conveniunt.
>
> (There are other acts, which we call "cogitative" [such as understanding, willing, imagining, sensing, etc.], all of which have in common the one feature of thought or perception or consciousness.)
>
> (*Meditationes de prima philosophia*)

However, in a narrower sense, Descartes excludes the will from the field of perception, which is identified solely with the operation of the understanding, including when it implies imagination or sensibility:

> Omnes modi cogitandi . . . ad duos generales referri possunt: quorum unus est perceptio, sive operatio intellectus; alius vero volitio, sive operatio voluntatis. Nam sentire, imaginari, et pure intelligere, sunt tantum diversi modi percipiendi.
>
> (All the modes of thinking that we observed in ourselves may be related to two general modes, the one of which consists in perception, or in the operation of the understanding, and the other in volition, or the operation of the will. Thus sense-perception, imagining, and conceiving things that are purely intelligible, are just different methods of perceiving.)
>
> (*Principia philosophiae*, pt. 1, principle 32)

The detours taken by the French translator of the *Meditationes* show that at that time "perception" was not easily or directly acceptable in French. Its more familiar substitutes were abandoned in favor of the new, technical term only in the two contexts of the *Meditationes*, where *perceptio* is thematized as such. In addition, this thematization introduces the duality of a perception considered sometimes as an intellectual operation or purely mental in nature and sometimes as an operation mediated by the senses and involving the body.

■ See Box 1.

In the same way, Abbé Picot, the French translator of the *Principia philosophiae*, hesitated to use *perception* every time he encountered the Latin *perceptio*. In part 1, principle 32, he uses *perception* in the title, but in the body of the article he uses the verb instead of the noun, writing: "*l'une [de nos façons de penser] consiste à apercevoir par l'entendement*" (one [of our ways of thinking] consists in perceiving through the understanding). Similarly, in principle 45, he accepts *perception* in the title, but in the text he prefers to substitute *connaissance* (knowledge) (as in principles 46 and 48). In principle 35, *intellectus perceptio* is simply reduced to *l'entendement* (the understanding).

Perception is absent from Descartes's first writings in French: *Le Monde*, the *Dioptrique*, and the *Discours de la Méthode* (but *apercevoir* is frequent in *Le Monde* and is also used in the *Dioptrique*, in a sense for which French would now use *percevoir*: "*les corps que nous apercevons autour de nous*" [the bodies that we apperceive around us; *Œuvres*, 6:87]; "*les qualités que nous apercevons dans les objets de la vue*" [the qualities that we apperceive in the objects of vision; *Œuvres*, 16:130]; "*apercevoir la distance*" [apperceive distance; *Œuvres*, 6:137], etc.). Not until the *Passions of the Soul* (1649) did Descartes use the word *perception* as a philosophical term legitimated by its usage (see art. 17 and 19–25). Applied to the mind, the opposition between action and passion coincides with that between the will and the "*perceptions ou connaissances*" that the mind "*reçoit des choses qui sont représentées par elle*" (receives

from things that are represented by it). Perception derives from this a twofold character: (1) it is a reception, which implies a passivity of the mind, even when it is the mind itself that is the cause of its own perceptions: "*Bien qu'au regard de notre âme, ce soit une action de vouloir quelque chose, on peut dire que c'est aussi en elle une passion d'apercevoir qu'elle veut*" (Although in regard to our soul it is an action to desire something, we may say that it is also one of its passions to perceive that it desires); (2) perception represents something that is of the mind itself, or of the body, or of external things. Thus it always has a referential function, through which "we relate" our perceptions to objects outside us, or to our body, or to our mind (titles of arts. 23, 24, 25).

Nonetheless, and this was the conclusion of the Second Meditation's analysis of the lump of wax, every perception includes the mind's perception of itself. The previously mentioned equivalence between thought, perception, and consciousness has an entirely general import: in the Cartesian sense, every perception is conscious and thus so is the perception that the perceiving subject has of himself. That is why Descartes, like his translators, makes perception the equivalent of the act that is expressed by the reflexive verb *s'apercevoir*: the operation through which the subject perceives (*s'aperçoit de*) something is always also the operation through which the subject perceives him- or herself.

II. Leibniz: The Opposition "Perception"/"Apperception"

It was precisely in order to contest this equivalence that Leibniz was led to introduce a terminological and conceptual distinction between perception and apperception:

> The passing condition, which involves and represents a multiplicity in the unit [*unité*] or in the simple substance, is nothing but what is called Perception, which is to be distinguished from Apperception or

---

1

From Latin to French: "Perception" in the translation of Descartes's *Meditations*

A difficulty arose in translating the Latin vocabulary transmitted by Scholasticism into a French acceptable to Descartes's contemporaries. *Perception* was established only gradually, being justified at first on the basis of the more obvious and familiar meaning of the verb *s'apercevoir*, in the sense of "recognize," "become aware of." In the original Latin version of the *Meditations* (*Meditationes de prima philosophia*, 1641), *perceptio* occurs twenty-one times. To translate these, the Duke of Luynes's French translation (published in 1644) uses *perception* only six times. Elsewhere, the translator uses *connaissance* (six times), *notion* (three times, once in the phrase *connaissance ou notion*), *sentiment* (two times, once in the phrase *perception ou sentiment*), and finally *intelligence, conception, idée* (once each); we also find the

verbal transposition *connaître et concevoir*, and even, for *recta rerum perceptio* (lit., "the correct perception of things"), the periphrase *le droit chemin qui peut conduire à la connaissance de la vérité*.

The verb *percipere* is preponderantly translated by *concevoir* (thirty-one times) and, more rarely, by *connaître* and *apercevoir* (five occurrences each), and even by *comprendre* (four instances). We occasionally find *recevoir* ("in the mind," or "through the senses"), *sentir, ressentir, penser, entendre*, and also the periphrase *avoir la notion de*. . . . The translator uses *perception* nine times, of which seven occur, remarkably, in two precisely localized contexts. First, three times, in the Second Meditation, in the famous passage in which the analysis of the perception of a bit of wax is supposed to yield the conclusion that the

human mind is always involved in any perception or knowledge of a body and that it is in this regard "easier to know," or "more notable," than the body. In the first occurrence, the translator is careful to justify his use of an unusual word, offering a definitional explanation: "its perception [of the bit of wax], or else the action through which it is perceived [*par laquelle on l'aperçoit*]," an action that turns out to be nothing other than an intellectual operation or a "mental inspection" (*inspectio mentis*).

The four other occurrences come in the Sixth Meditation, but this time in order to provide the equivalent of *sentiment*, which is taken to refer to knowledge derived from the senses. Finally, this last meaning occurs two more times, as a rendering not of *perceptio* but of *comprehensio sensuum* and *sensus*.

Consciousness. . . . In this matter the Cartesian view is extremely defective, for it treats as non-existent those perceptions of which we are not consciously aware.

(*Monadology*)

To make room for these perceptions that we do not perceive and that can be described as unconscious, Leibniz characterizes perception ontologically in its universality as a form of the relationship of the multiple to the true unity, which is that of the simple substance or monad: "It suffices that there be a variety in unity in order for there to be a perception. . . . Perception is for me the representation of the multiple in the simple" (Letters to Bourguet, *Die philosophischen Schriften*, 3:581, 574). According to this description, perception designates the mutual relation that connects the world with each simple substance that represents it from a singular point of view and with a varying degree of clearness and distinctness: every perception includes the infinite in such a way that the hierarchy of beings is ordered in accord with the explicitation that they are capable of recognizing in the internal multiplicity of their representation. Thus "natural perception" can be distinguished, then "perception accompanied by memory," and finally "perception accompanied by consciousness," or the perceiving subject's reflection on himself. In this regard, the different levels of perception are part of a much more general notion of which they constitute the species, which is that of expression, and which Leibniz sought to distinguish from knowledge:

One thing expresses another, in my usage, when there is a constant and regular relationship between what can be said about one and about the other. It is in this way that a projection in perspective expresses a geometrical figure. Expression is common to all the forms and is a genus of which natural perception, animal feeling, and intellectual knowledge are species. In natural perception [*perception naturelle*] and feeling it suffices that what is divisible and material and is found dispersed among several beings should be expressed or represented in a single indivisible being or in a substance which is endowed with true unity. The possibility of such a representation of several things cannot be doubted, since our soul provides us with an example of it. But in the reasonable soul

this representation is accompanied by consciousness, and it is then that it is called thought. Now this expression takes place everywhere, because every substance sympathizes with all the others and receives a proportional change corresponding to the slightest change which occurs in the whole world, although this change will be more or less noticeable as other bodies or their actions have more or less relation with ours.

(Letter to Arnauld, 9 October 1687, in *Philosophical Papers and Letters*)

Although the Leibnizian vocabulary establishes with great clarity the distinction between perception in the general sense and apperception understood as conscious, reflective perception, the transposition of this lexicon into another language cannot be made without difficulty.

■ See Box 2.

Although the German verb *wahrnehmen* is translated in French by *s'apercevoir*, *Wahrnehmung* can ultimately render *perception* only at the price of abandoning the formal universality of Leibniz's definition and returning to a construction in which all perception implies consciousness of the reference to its object. But this does not amount to a return to Descartes's position, because the perceived object can only be the object of sensation, and the notion of a purely intellectual perception fades away. Kant's vocabulary testifies to the completion of this transformation.

III. Kant's Vocabulary: *Vorstellung, Wahrnehmung, Empfindung, Apperzeption*

Kant situates perception (*Wahrnehmung*) in a generic domain of which "representation" (*Vorstellung*) constitutes the first, indefinable term: as a "state of mind" (*blosse Bestimmung des Gemüts*), the representation includes a subjective aspect (what Descartes called a mode or way of thinking, *modus cogitandi*) and at the same time it has an objective reference to what it is for the subject, the presentation of what is in front of (*vor*) him. Perception is a representation accompanied by consciousness (see also *Logik* [*Logic*], introduction, §8, in RT: Ak., 9:64): to perceive (Ger. *wahrnehmen*, Lat. *percipere*) is "to represent something to oneself consciously" (*sich mit Bewusstsein etwas vorstellen*); if it is related to the subject as a "modification of his

---

2

From French to German: The case of Leibniz's *Monadology*

Heinrich Köhler, the German translator of Leibniz's *Monadologie* (1720; originally published in French in 1714), must have constantly associated the Franco-Latin term *perception* with the equivalent that he gave for it, *Empfindung*, which implicitly emphasizes its receptive or felt character: "*ce qu'on appelle la* perception, *qu'on doit distinguer de l'aperception ou de la conscience*" (art. 14) becomes "*welches man die* Empfindung *oder* Perception *nennet die man von der*

Apperception *oder von dem* Bewusst sein *wohl unterscheiden muss.*" On the other hand, to translate the verb *s'apercevoir* Köhler used *wahrnehmen*, which later yielded the substantive *Wahrnehmung*, which in turn became the accepted translation of *perception*. Thus "*les perceptions dont on ne s'aperçoit pas*" is rendered as "*die* Perceptiones *oder* Empfindungen *deren man sich nicht bewusst ist, und welche man nicht wahrnimmt.*" In article 23, "*on s'aperçoit de ses perceptions*"

is rendered as "*seine* Empfindungen *und* Perceptionen *wiederum wahrnimmet.*"

BIBLIOGRAPHY

Leibniz, Gottfried Wilhelm. *Monadologie: Französisch und Deutsch.* Translated by Heinrich Köhler, edited by Dietmar Till. Frankfurt: Insel, 1996.

———. *Monadology.* Translated by Nicholas Rescher. Pittsburgh: University of Pittsburgh Press, 1991.

state," it is sensation (Lat. *sensatio*, Ger. *Empfindung*), and if it is related to the object, it is knowledge (Lat. *cognitio*, Ger. *Erkenntnis*) (*Kritik der reinen Vernunft*, A [1781] 320 / B [1787] S 376, in RT: Ak.). As such, perception thus implies three terms: a consciousness, the sensation that determines this consciousness, and the object appearing in the sensation, which is also called a phenomenon (see ERSCHEINUNG). If the latter is taken as the starting point, it can be said that "when combined with consciousness, it is called perception" (*Erscheinung, welche, wenn sie mit Bewusstsein verbunden ist, Wahrnehmung heisst*; ibid., A 120); but if instead consciousness is taken as the starting point, then "[p]erception is empirical consciousness, that is, a consciousness in which sensation is to be found" (*Wahrnehmung ist das empirische Bewußtsein, d.i. ein solches, in welchem zugleich Empfindung ist*; ibid., B 207), which can also be put this way: "The consciousness of an empirical representation is called a perception" (*Prolegomena to Any Future Metaphysics*, §10). Sensation as such, which is henceforth termed *Empfindung*, is the state of the subject whose sense receptivity is affected by the object, which thereby presents itself as a phenomenon (*Kritik der reinen Vernunft*, A 19 / B 33, in RT: Ak.). But perception requires, in addition to consciousness, a way of synthesizing the diversity that it contains (the internal diversity of the matter of sensation present in each perception and the diversity of the "dispersed and isolated" perceptions themselves; A 120); this synthesis is first of all the work of the imagination, which "constitutes a necessary ingredient of perception itself" (ibid.), but the unity that makes it possible is none other than the unity of self-consciousness, for which Kant adopts the Leibnizian term "apperception" (*Apperzeption*).

The terminological equivalence between "self-consciousness" (*das Bewusstsein seiner selbst*) and apperception makes the latter "the simple representation of the 'I'" (*die einfache Vorstellung des Ich*) (ibid., B 68). But this completely general acceptation is valuable because it enables us to differentiate two levels of self-consciousness and apperception. On the one hand, self-consciousness as a determination of the changing state of the subject in the flux of internal phenomena will be called "empirical apperception. On the other, the unchanging consciousness of an identical "I think," one and invariant ("It must be possible for the 'I think' to accompany all my representations") and the necessary and a priori condition of all consciousness, will be called "pure apperception" (*reine Apperzeption*) (ibid., B 131–32). The former is a self-consciousness that is simply subjective (a consciousness of the empirically determined internal state of the subject), whereas the latter expresses an objective self-consciousness (a unity necessary for the foundation of any concept of the object and of any judgment expressing the universal validity of phenomena in an experience).

IV. The End of Theories of Apperception: Perception and the Body

"The consciousness of myself as original apperception" (ibid., A 117) is also "an act of spontaneity" (ibid., B 132): it is in this sense that Fichte rehabilitates, in opposition to Kant's terminology, the authentic meaning of "intellectual intuition" (*intellektuelle Anschauung*) as an immediate, non-sensible representation of the activity of the "I" (second introduction to *Grundlage der gesamten*). In the *Phenomenology of*

Mind, Hegel constructed an alternative theory of *Wahrnehmung* that differs from others in that it is based on the etymology of the term, "take for true" (*Wahr-nehmen*, "per-ceive," *per-cipio*).

■ See Box 3.

Herbart's criticism of Fichte and Kant, which reduces apperception to the observation of perceptions that have already been formed in the mind and makes it the representation of "I," a result and no longer an origin of the synthesis of representations in consciousness, marked the end of the philosophical use of the term "apperception" (*Psychologie als Wissenschaft*). On the other hand, perception became a major theme in the philosophy of knowledge and psychology throughout the nineteenth century before becoming central to the interests of phenomenology in Husserl's work and in its later developments. The most widespread contemporary view is then that, as Merleau-Ponty put it, "to perceive is to make something present to oneself with the help of the body" (*Le primat de la perception*). In this sense, "perception" retains some trace of the meaning it had in the work of seventeenth-century philosophers—inasmuch as "perception" leans on representation, here reinterpreted as "presence"—but the corporeal basis of access to the world prevents it from being assimilated to a pure "mental inspection."

Michel Fichant

BIBLIOGRAPHY

Arbini, Ronald. "Did Descartes Have a Philosophical Theory of Sense Perception?" *Journal of the History of Philosophy* 21 (1983): 317–38.

Belaval, Yvon. "La perception." In *Études leibniziennes: De Leibniz à Hegel*. Paris: Gallimard, 1976.

Brandom, Robert B. "Leibniz and Degrees of Perception." *Journal of the History of Philosophy* 19 (1981): 447–79.

Descartes, René. *Meditationes de prima philosophia*. In vol. 7 of *Œuvres*, edited by C. Adam and P. Tannery. Paris: Vrin, 1996. Translation by Roger Ariew and Donald Cress: *Meditations, Objections, and Responses*. Indianapolis, IN: Hackett Publishing, 2006.

———. *Œuvres*. Edited by C. Adam and P. Tannery. 11 vols. Paris: Vrin, 1996.

———. *Passions of the Soul*. In vol. 1 of *The Philosophical Writings of Descartes*, translated by John Cottingham, Robert Stoothoff, and Dugald Murdoch. Cambridge: Cambridge University Press, 1988.

———. *Principia philosophiae*. In vol. 8a of *Œuvres*, edited by C. Adam and P. Tannery. Paris: Vrin, 1996. Translation by E. S. Haldane and G.R.T. Ross: *Philosophical Works of Descartes*. New York: Dover, 1967.

Fichte, Johann G. Second introduction to *Grundlage der gesamten Wissenschaftslehre*. Vol. 1 of *Johann Gottlieb Fichte's sämtliche Werke*, edited by J. H. Fichte, 472 and 476. Berlin: Veit, 1845. Translation by Peter Heath and John Lachs: *The Science of Knowledge*. Cambridge: Cambridge University Press, 1982.

Guyer, Paul. *Kant and the Claims of Knowledge*. Cambridge: Cambridge University Press, 1987.

Herbart, Johann Friedrich. *Psychologie als Wissenschaft, neu gegründet über Erfahrung, Metaphysik und Mathematik*. Königsberg, Ger.: Unzer, 1824–25.

Kant, Immanuel. *The Cambridge Edition of the Works of Immanuel Kant*. Edited by Paul Guyer and Allen W. Wood. Cambridge: Cambridge University Press, 1992–.

———. *Critique of Pure Reason*. Edited and translated by Paul Guyer and Allen W. Wood. In *The Cambridge Edition of the Works of Immanuel Kant*, edited by Paul Guyer and Allen W. Wood. Cambridge: Cambridge University Press, 1997.

Kulstad, Mark. "Some Difficulties in Leibniz's Definition of Perception." In *Leibniz: Critical and Interpretive Essays*, edited by Michael Hooker, 65–78. Minneapolis: University of Minnesota Press, 1982.

3

Wahrnehmung: Hegel's lexical play

➤ TRUTH

For a reader accustomed to Leibnizian and Kantian distinctions, the beginning of Hegel's *Phenomenology of Mind* is puzzling because it simply ignores the *Empfindung/Wahrnehmung* pair, that is, the coexistence of sensation and perception in the act of knowing. In Hegel, what precedes *Wahrnehmung* is called *sinnliche Gewissheit* (sense-certainty). It is no longer a question of the relation between sensation and perception—understood as a return to the principle, a movement from the compound (the manifold of sensation) to the simple (the synthesis of the manifold in consciousness, and then the unity of the "I")—but rather of a two-stage process that implements diverse ways of registering truth in consciousness. Each of these two stages produces its own figure of truth, "its truth" (in the case of perception, the thing: the thing is the truth of perception), but they have in common the same aspiration to *capture* truth. The first sentence of the chapter "Perception," which sums up what has been said about sense-certainty, should also be read as a play on the verb *nehmen*, "to grasp or take":

> Die unmittelbare Gewissheit nimmt sich nicht das Wahre, denn ihre Wahrheit ist das Allgemeine; sie aber will das Diese nehmen. Die Wahrnehmung nimmt hingegen das, was ihr das Seiende ist, als Allgemeines.

> (Immediate certainty does not make the truth its own [does not *seize* the truth], for its truth is something universal, whereas certainty wants to deal with [to *seize*] the *This*. Perception, on the other hand, takes [*seizes*] what exists for it to be a universal.)

> (*Phenomenology of Mind*, emphasis added)

Sense-certainty concerns a singularity, a "this," but its own dialectic reveals that the latter is a universal, insofar as "here" is always a "set of other 'heres'"; perception, on the contrary, immediately takes the thing for a universal and corresponds to good sense (ibid., p. 160), for which the world is a world of things. French translators of *Phenomenology* have all rendered the insistent repetition of the verb *nehmen* here (cf. the translations by J.-P. Lefebvre, p. 103, and J. Hyppolite, p. 93; Hyppolite accentuates this even more by rendering the initial *nimmt sich* as *prendre possession*). But in Hegel, *nehmen* can be used in different ways that mark the advance from sense-certainty to perception. Whereas *sinnliche Gewissheit* seeks "to take," "to capture without mediation," *Wahrnehmung* is a "taking for" (*nimmt . . . als*), and more precisely, a "taking-for-true" (*Wahrnehmen*). It therefore explicitly presupposes an activity, or reflection, of consciousness; and, because perception is a "taking for," the perceiving consciousness also raises the possibility of illusion (*Täuschung*), understood as the particular form of non-truth that it invents and opposes to the truth of the thing and its properties (*Eigenschaften*), of the One and the universal, of taking and reflection, everything that Hegel calls the *Sophisterei* (sophistry) of perception and that finds a provisional solution in the "sphere of understanding" (ibid., p. 175).

The difficulty faced by the French translator is lexical: he cannot render Hegel's play on the decomposition of the verb *wahrnehmen*. To render the inversion *sein Nehmen des Wahren*, referring to consciousness (consciousness's *seizure* or capture of truth), Lefebvre offers what is probably the closest approximation: "*sa captation du vrai*" (p. 110), *captation* bringing out the *capere* in *percipere* (Hyppolite, p. 102, translated this as "*sa préhension du vrai*"); but the two nouns, put back in the correct order, do not coalesce to form a verb, as they do in German (*das Nehmen des Wahren* is an inversion of *wahrnehmen*). In French, *perception* is not necessarily the *véri-captation* that Hegel makes us hear in *wahr-nehmen*:

no more is the English "perception" anything lexically like "truth-capturing" or "truth-seizure."

But for all that, Hegel's play on the verb *nehmen* is, on the whole, translatable into French; on the other hand, what remains to be clarified is the internal coherence of the itinerary leading from Leibniz to Hegel. The history of theories of perception in Germany is a Franco-German history, as is clearly shown by the neologism *aperception*, a French term forged by the German Leibniz and acclimated in Kant's language. Hegel's initiative, which involves stressing for the first time the etymology of *Wahrnehmung*, constitutes a direct response to this tradition. It seeks to exclude from the word every trace of a partly French past, and operates at the very moment that Hegel opposes a paradigm of truth and certainty to an analysis of the different instances or organs of knowledge. In this sense, the substitution of the *Gewissheit/Wahrnehmung* pair for the old *Empfindung/Wahrnehmung* pair provides a good illustration of the methods of language and thought that Hegel deployed to move from a theory of knowledge (see EPISTEMOLOGY) to a doctrine of science.

Philippe Büttgen

BIBLIOGRAPHY

Hegel, Georg Wilhelm Friedrich. *Phänomenologie des Geistes*. Edited by Eva Moldenhauer and Karl Markus Michel. Vol. 3 of *Werke*. Frankfurt: Suhrkamp, 1970.

———. *Phenomenology of Mind*. Translated by J. B. Baillie. London: Allen and Unwin, 1910.

———. *La phénoménologie de l'esprit*. Translated by Jean Hyppolite. Paris: Aubier, 1941.

———. *Phénoménologie de l'esprit*. Translated by Jean-Pierre Lefebvre. Paris: Aubier, 1991.

———. *Phenomenology of Spirit*. Translated by A. V. Miller. Oxford: Oxford University Press, 1977.

Laporte, Jean Marie Frédéric. *Le rationalisme de Descartes*. Paris: Presses Universitaires de France, 1950.

Leibniz, Gottfried Wilhelm. *Monadology*. Translated by R. Latta. Oxford: Oxford University Press, 1898.

———. *Philosophical Essays*. Edited and translated by Roger Ariew and Daniel Garber. Indianapolis, IN: Hackett, 1989.

———. *Philosophical Papers and Letters*. Translated and edited by Leroy Loemker. 2nd ed. Dordrecht, Neth: Reidel, 1969.

———. *Die philosophischen Schriften*. Edited by Carl I. Gerhardt. Hildesheim, Ger.: Olms, 1960. First published 1875–90.

Merleau-Ponty, Maurice. *Phénoménologie de la perception*. Paris: Gallimard, 1945. Translation by Colin Smith: *Phenomenology of Perception*. New York: Routledge, 2002.

———. *Le primat de la perception et ses conséquences philosophiques, communication et discussion à la Société française de philosophie, 23 novembre 1946*. Grenoble: Cynara, 1989.

Muralt, André de. *La conscience transcendantale dans le criticisme kantien: Essai sur l'unité d'aperception*. Paris: Aubier, 1958.

Patterson, Sarah. "Clear and Distinct Perception." In *A Companion to Descartes*, edited by Janet Broughton and John Carriero, 216–34. Malden, MA: Blackwell, 2008.

Pucelle, Jean. "La théorie de la perception extérieure chez Descartes." *Revue d'Histoire de la Philosophie et d'Histoire Générale de la Civilization* 3 (1935): 297–339.

Thiel, Udo. "Leibniz and the Concept of Apperception." *Archiv für Geschichte der Philosophie* 76, no. 2 (1994): 195–209.

Wilson, Catherine. "Confused Perceptions, Darkened Concepts: Some Features of Kant's Leibniz-Critique." In *Kant and His Influence*, edited by George MacDonald Ross, 73–103. New York: Continuum, 2005.

PERFECTIBILITY

FRENCH   *perfectibilité*
GERMAN   *Perfektibilität, Vervollkommenheit*
LATIN   *perfectibilitas*

➤ BERUF, BILDUNG, GLÜCK, GOD, HISTORIA UNIVERSALIS, *HUMANITY*, I/ME/MYSELF, *LIBERTY*, OIKONOMIA, *RÉVOLUTION*, *VIRTUE*

Although the adjective *perfectibilis* appeared in 1612, it was only in 1755 that Rousseau and Grimm brought the noun *perfectibilité* into French. The term spread throughout Europe in the second half of the eighteenth century, and was the object of multiple refractions that often interpreted it, contrary to Rousseau, as a necessary tendency toward perfection—so that it tended to be identified with improvement ("perfection," *Vervollkommnung*). In the 1790s it became established with the sense of "indefinite perfectibility," that is, as a major concept in the philosophies of history that were attracting the most attention; then people spoke, without further specification, of "the system of perfectibility." This success nonetheless seems to have been ephemeral. On the one hand, "Progress" having become an objectively obvious fact, it was pointless to assert its objective necessary condition; on the other hand, in order to be conceived rationally, it could not be entirely "indefinite," that is, absolutely indefinable, or dangerously utopian.

I. From the Faculty of Self-Improvement to Indefinite Improvement

Initially, perfectibility appears as a "faculty of self-improvement," that is, as a kind of metafaculty on which the development of all the other faculties depends (Rousseau, *Discours sur l'origine de l'inégalité des hommes*). Its main characteristics are the following: (1) it is peculiar to human beings—to the individual and to the species; (2) its actualization is fortuitous—it depends on "circumstances"; (3) it is ambivalent insofar as it makes possible both insights and errors, both virtues and vices—the actualization of perfectibility therefore does not mean improvement because it signifies that one can "either come closer to the perfection inherent in his species, or move farther from it to the point of degeneration," and, in fact, our first steps have always "led far beyond nature" (Melchior and Grimm, *Correspondance littéraire*); (4), finally, it is "almost unlimited" (Rousseau, *Discours sur l'origine de l'inégalité des hommes*). In France, during the subsequent thirty years, the concept was subjected to an extreme overdetermination.

Helvétius changed the status of the concept and then its definition. In 1758, he related this metafaculty to a principle of which it is only the consequence, namely, "the kind of concern that the absence of impression produces in the mind," that is, the fear of boredom (*De l'esprit*, III, chap. 5). In 1773, in the summary of *De l'homme*, he reverses the reflexive mode of the formulation: the reactive faculty of self-improvement becomes basically the passive faculty of "being improved": "As a result, the human mind is susceptible of perfectibility, and in men who are commonly well-organized, the inequality of talents can only be a pure effect of the difference in their education" (*De l'homme*, summary IV; cf. II, chap. 23). People are thus perfectible in the sense that they are "educable," passively subject to the actions of their enlightened rulers, in conformity with a certain materialism.

But the concept could also be appropriated by challenging one or another of its secondary characterizations. For example, it is possible to deny that perfectibility is peculiar to humans, and to make it a property of every living being. Then it becomes a cosmological concept, and that is just how Bonnet understands it in his *Palingénésie philosophique*: "Would a philosopher deny that an animal is a perfectible being, and perfectible in a limited degree?" Why then should we not think that oysters might one day attain knowledge of their creator? But it is just as possible to deny that this perfectibility is ambivalent and unlimited. In this sense, in 1765 Voltaire expressly declared, in opposition to Rousseau: "He [man] is perfectible; and from this it has been concluded that he has perverted himself. But why not conclude that he has perfected himself to the point where nature has marked the limits of his perfection?"

Here, perfectibility no longer has much to do with a subjective faculty; it is absorbed into the historical fact of human progress, of multiple and reversible advances. It was for Condorcet, in the 1780s, to homogenize the latter in a single, irreversible process destined to be achieved in the cumulative and endless succession of generations: thus appears in France the "indefinite perfectibility" that is the vector of the *Esquisse d'un tableau historique des progrès de l'esprit humain* (1795), and which Condorcet retrospectively attributed to the Turgot of 1750 (*Œuvres*). When Auguste Comte carefully distinguished the adequate concept of *perfectionnement* (improvement) from "the chimerical conception of an unlimited perfectibility" (*Cours de philosophie positive*, XLVIIIe), he was trying to eliminate a concept that was both useless and perilous: improvement without perfectibility is progress in order.

II. On *Perfektibilität* as a Tendency to Perfection

In Germany, things took a quite different, much more theological form; here, we have to recall Matthew 5:48: "You, therefore, must be perfect, as your heavenly Father is perfect."

In 1756, Moses Mendelssohn translated Rousseau's *Second Discourse*; he rejected the neologism *Perfektibilität* and stuck to "Vermögen, sich vollkommener zu machen" (the ability to make oneself more perfect) (Rousseau, *Abhandlung von dem Ursprunge*). He justifies this choice in the long letter he sent the same year to Lessing, in which *Vermögen* becomes *Bemühung, Bestreben*, that is, an effort, an aspiration to come as close as possible to the "model of divine perfection" (das Muster der göttlichen Volkommenheit). *Perfectibilité* thus translated turns against Rousseau: far from being satisfied to be a savage as long as circumstances allow him to do so, the human being always already aspires to the perfection of which God is the paradigm. This view was to be decisive.

On 21 January 1756, Lessing replied to Mendelssohn, rejecting his translation and substituting for it *Perfektibilität*, by which he meant "the property by virtue of which a thing can become more perfect, a property that characterizes all things in the world and that is absolutely necessary for their perseverance" (die Beschaffenheit eines Dinges darunter, vermöge welcher es vollkommener werden kann, eine Beschaffenheit, welche alle Dinge in der Welt haben, und die zu ihrer Fortdauer unumgänglich nötig war). (*Sämtliche Schriften*). This was probably an attempt to substitute a Spinozist translation of *perfectibilité*, understood at that time as a thing's pure power of persevering in its being, for the Leibnizian translation that Mendelssohn proposed as the internal principle of a continuous and necessary aspiration to perfection, that is, to a constant and harmonious improvement of one's natural powers (*Kräfte*).

But it was Mendelssohn who won out. Perfectibility, which had been a reactive faculty, now became a spontaneous tendency, a sort of eminently positive instinct that was henceforth constantly opposed to Rousseau. In 1764, in *Über die Geschichte der Menschheit* (On the history of humanity), it was certainly in opposition to Rousseau that Isaac Iselin translated *perfectibilité* by *der Trieb zur Vollkommenheit* (the impulse to perfection) in order to make it the basis for a veritable theodicy of history in which the latter tends to be identified with progress itself (*Fortschritt, Fortgang*): naturally inclined to perfection, the human race is destined to have a natural development in which Oriental sensibility, Mediterranean imagination, and finally Nordic reason succeed each other. In 1722, in his *Versuch über das erste Prinzipium der Moral*, J.M.R. Lenz sought to base morals on two major principles: "the impulse to perfection and the impulse to happiness" (der Trieb nach Vollkommenheit und der Trieb nach Glückseligkeit). For Lenz as well, Rousseau contradicted himself when he asserted that the human being, by essence perfectible, finds happiness in the tranquility of the state of nature. In reality, happiness is the state most in conformity with perfection, that is, with the optimal development of the strengths and faculties with which humans, like any living being, are naturally endowed. And in 1777, in the eleventh of his *Philosophische Versuche über die menschliche Natur und ihre Entwicklung* (Philosophical essays on human nature and its development), J. N. Tetens explains perfectibility anthropologically: Rousseau's *Vervollkommenheit* is far too indeterminate and it has to be connected with something other than itself, namely, with the spontaneity that characterizes every living being. "Perfectible spontaneity" (*perfektible Selbsttätigkeit*) characterizes humans to the highest point in the sense that they are destined to become autonomous with regard to their environment, more slowly, but also more fully, than the animal individual. Moreover, it is significant that Tetens understands this process as an "impulse to development" (*Trieb zur Entwicklung*): once again, perfection finalizes perfectibility.

Thus it is still the same schema that is found invested in multiple fields—historical, moral, anthropological. But we see that is also still ambiguous, for if perfectibility thus becomes the mute impulse that leads humans to perfection, it is still a task, a vocation (*Beruf*), and that is why it is so important to become adequately aware of it. We must therefore draw attention to the reflexive form of the verb: perfectibility is the duty that a person has, as a subject, to *perfect oneself*, and progress is thus nothing other than the accomplishment of that tendency (obligation) extended to the species as a whole. But when in the following century Hegel, in an act comparable to Comte's, challenges *Perfektibilität* as "something just as deprived of determination as change in general," essentially "without purpose or goal" (ohne Zweck und Ziel) (*Die Vernunft in der Geschichte* [*Reason in History*]), he does not do so because he opposes progress, but because he refuses to leave it to an indeterminacy similar to that of the old concept of Providence (*Grundlinien der Philosophie des Rechts* [Elements of the Philosophy of Right], §343).

III. From "Perfectibility" to the Withering Away of Government

The first English translation of Rousseau's *Second Discourse* appeared in London in 1761 (DOI, 1755). From the outset, it adopted "perfectibility" to designate what becomes a faculty of improvement, and the translation published by Becket in London in 1767 followed suit. However, pending a more detailed study, it seems that the term did not really "take" until the 1790s.

Scottish thinkers clearly avoided it because they were trying to conceive a typical history of civil institutions which, far from setting aside the facts, resulted on the contrary from their inductive superimposition: the natural history of humanity is an abstraction from national histories. The violent criticism of the *Second Discourse* with which A. Ferguson's *Essay on the History of Civil Society* (1767) opens is, in this respect, just as significant as the solemn homage paid to Montesquieu further on (I, 10). To avoid the neologism "perfectibility," he said that "man is susceptible of improvement and has in himself a principle of progression, and a desire of perfection" (I, 1), on the condition that this be interpreted to mean that the fortuitous pressure of circumstances is indispensable to the actualization of this principle. Here we see the appearance of the major concept of improvement, whose least bad translation into French would probably be *perfectionnement*, (in contrast to German *Vollkommenheit/Vervollkommnung*, English does not construct an analogous noun on the basis of "perfection"). And in the Scottish "improvement," we can probably also hear the verb "to prove" (in the sense of testing or trying out) because it is in fact a basically empirical process that is carried out through successive adjustments and readjustments to the previously mentioned circumstances.

Instead, it is to the English Protestant dissidents that we must turn to find something comparable to what the Germans were working out at this time. In 1767 Richard Price attributed a natural "improvableness" to humans (*Four Dissertations*; cf. Laboucheix, *Richard Price, théoricien de la révolution américaine*), and the following year Joseph Priestley averred that the human species was "capable of an unbounded improvement" (*Essay on the First Principles of Government*). In this context, "improvement" refers to an absolutely endogenous process that as such requires only an absence of obstacles in order to actualize itself: "It is a universal maxim, that the more liberty is given to every thing which is in a state of growth, the more perfect it will become." The point is now not to discern the typical course of nations, but to affirm that human progress is the immanent work of society as opposed to government: the latter has no task other than to provide the conditions by ensuring a maximum liberty of discussion in the millenarian perspective of a fulfillment of all things in which truth will finally shine forth in vivo for those who have been able to prepare themselves for it. Humans are "perfectible" in the sense that by themselves, politically authorized and morally obliged to freely examine ideas, they move from truth to truth toward the heavenly Jerusalem.

Thus, as in Germany, perfectibility becomes a spontaneous tendency to improvement of which progress is the irresistible manifestation. And again as in Germany, this tendency is a duty of which one must become aware. The difference arises from the fact that, on the one hand, the temporality in which it is expressed is clearly that of an eschatology, and on the other hand, and especially, it justifies a devaluation of politics as such: because humans are perfectible, their improvement is up to them, not to government. When William Godwin chose to use the term "perfectibility" in his *Enquiry Concerning Political Justice* (1793), he sought to radicalize the latter orientation at the expense of the former: it is for humans to improve themselves infinitely until they can, in this world, do without any government at all.

In the first edition of his book, Godwin's use of the term remains allusive, and he limits himself to declaring that "there is no characteristic of man which seems, at least at present, to distinguish him so eminently, or to be of such great importance in all the branches of moral science, as perfectibility" (*Political and Philosophical Writings*). In the 1796 edition, he is more precise: "By perfectible, it is not meant that he [man] is capable of being brought to perfection. But the word seems sufficiently adapted to express the faculty of being continually made better and receiving perpetual improvement; and in this sense it is here to be understood."

Thus the human being, first as a rational animal, then as moral being, will gradually, constantly, and indefinitely improve him- or herself if existing institutions, chiefly government, do not prevent doing so. It is necessary and sufficient to allow the tendency toward truth that essentially characterizes humans to develop freely. But here it is no longer a question of a collective resurrection, but rather of an absolutely secular perfectibility that guarantees—in the long term, of course—that government will simply wither away: after all, if people are indefinitely perfectible, that is because when they are fully grown-up, they have to govern themselves, without any coercion being required. Thus once again perfectibility is supplanted by progress, and it is no accident that Godwin prefers the expression "progressive nature," though progress is then the promise of a happy anarchy. We can understand

why T. R. Malthus reacted so violently in the first edition of his *Essay on the Principle of Population*.

The history of the concept of perfectibility consists of two stages: Rousseau's concept of "perfectibility" was first transformed into a spontaneous tendency to seek perfection, and then set aside in the name of Progress, as a kind of useless and even embarrassing scaffolding. Thus perfectibility was not a preliminary version of progress, but on the contrary what had to be concealed in order to be able to conceive progress in entirely diverse modalities depending on the context. It is hardly surprising, therefore, that Rousseau's neologism now appears to us as an enigma to which we never tire of returning.

Bertrand Binoche

BIBLIOGRAPHY

Affeldt, Steven G. "Society As a Way of Life: Perfectibility, Self-Transformation, and the Origination of Society in Rousseau." *Monist* 83 (2000): 552–606.

Behler, Ernst. "The Idea of Infinite Perfectibility and Its Impact upon the Concept of Literature in European Romanticism." In *Sensus Communis: Contemporary Trends in Comparative Literature/Panorama de la situation actuelle en littérature comparée*, edited by János Riesz, Peter Boerner, and Bernhard Scholz, 295–305. Tübingen: Narr, 1986.

———. *Unendliche Perfektibilität: Europäishe Romantik und Französische Revolution*. Paderborn, Ger.: Schöningh, 1989.

Beyssade, Jean-Marie. "Rousseau et la pensée du développement." In *Entre forme et histoire: La formation de la notion de développement à l'âge classique*, edited by Olivier Bloch, Bernard Balan, and Paulette Carrive, 195–214. Paris: Meridiens Klincksieck, 1988..

Bonnet, Charles. *Palingénésie philosophique*. Lyon, Fr.: Bruyset, 1770.

Buck, Günther. "Selbsterhaltung und Historizität." In *Geschichte: Ereignis und Erzählung*, edited by Reinhart Koselleck and Wolf-Dieter Stempel, 29–94. Munich: Fink, 1973.

Chonaill, Siobhan Ni. "'Why May Not Man One Day Be Immortal?': Population, Perfectibility, and the Immortality Question in Godwin's Political Justice." *History of European Ideas* 33 (2007): 25–39.

Comte, Auguste. *Cours de philosophie positive*. Vol. 2. Paris: Hermann, 1975.

Condorcet, Jean-Antoine-Niclas. *Œuvres*. Paris: Firmin-Didot, 1847.

Ferguson, A. *Essay on the History of Civil Society*. Edinburgh: Edinburgh University Press, 1966.

Frankel, Charles. *The Faith of Reason: The Idea of Progress in the French Enlightenment*. New York: Octagon Books, 1969. First published in 1948.

Godwin, William. *Political and Philosophical Writings*. London: Pickering, 1993.

Hegel, G.W.F. *Die Vernunft in der Geschichte*. Hamburg: Meiner, 1955.

Helvétius, Claude Adrien. *De l'esprit*. Paris: Fayard, 1989.

———. *De l'homme*. Paris: Fayard, 1989.

Hornig, Gottfried. "Perfektibilität: Eine Untersuchung zur Geschichte und Bedeutung dieses Begriffs in der deutschsprachigen Literatur." *Archiv für Begriffsgeschichte* 24, no. 1 (1980): 221–57.

Iselin, Isaac. *Über die Geschichte der Menschheit*. Zurich: Orell, Gessner, Füsselin, 1770.

Koselleck, Reinhart. "Fortschritt." In *Geschichtliche Grundbegriffe: Historisches Lexikon zur politisch-sozialen Sprache in Deutschland*, edited by Otto Brunner, Werner Conze, and Reinhart Koselleck, vol. 2, 375–84. Stuttgart: Klett, 1972–97.

Laboucheix, Henri. *Richard Price, théoricien de la révolution américaine, le philosophe et le sociologue, le pamphlétaire et l'orateur*. Montreal: Didier, 1970. Esp. 192–205. Translation by Sylvia and David Raphael: *Richard Price as Moral Philosopher and Political Theorist*. Oxford: The Voltaire Foundation at the Taylor Institution, 1982.

Lenz, J.M.R. *Versuch über das erste Prinzipium der Moral*. In vol. 2 of *Werke und Briefe*. Leipzig: Insel, 1987.

Lessing, Gotthold Ephraim. *Sämtliche Schriften*. Leipzig: Göschen, 1857.

Lovejoy, Arthur O. *The Great Chain of Being: A Study of the History of an Idea*. New York: Harper and Row, 1960. Chap. 9. First published in 1936.

Malthus, T. R. *Essay on the Principle of Population*. London: Johnson, 1798.

Melchior, Friedrich, and Baron Grimm. *Correspondance littéraire*. Paris: Garnier, 1877. First published in 1755.

Mendelssohn, Moses. *Gesammelte Schriften*, Leipzig: Brockhaus, 1843.

Muller, Virginia L. *The Idea of Perfectibility*. Lanham, MD: University Press of America, 1985.

Passmore, John Arthur. *The Perfectibility of Man*. London: Duckworth, 1970.

Politzer, Robert L. "A Detail in Rousseau's Thought: Language and Perfectibility." *MLN* 72 (1957): 42–47.

Pollin, Burton Ralph. *Education and Enlightenment in the Works of William Godwin*. New York: Las Americas, 1962.

Price, Richard. *Four Dissertations*. London: A. Millar and T. Cadell, 1767.

Priestly, Joseph. *Essay on the First Principles of Government*. 2nd ed. London: Johnson, 1771. First published in 1768.

Rousseau, J.-J. *Abhandlung von dem Ursprunge der Ungleichheit unter den Menschen, und worauf sie sich gründe, ins Deutsche übersetzt . . .* Berlin: Voss, 1756.

———. *Discours sur l'origine de l'inégalité des hommes*. In *Œuvres completes*. Paris: Gallimard / La Pléiades, 1964

Schandeler, Jean-Pierre. *Les interprétations de Condorcet: Symboles et concepts (1794–1894)*. Oxford: Voltaire Foundation, 2000.

Spadafora, David. *The Idea of Progress in Eighteenth-Century Britain*. New Haven, CT: Yale University Press, 1990. Chaps. 6 and 7.

Tetens, J. N. *Philosophische Versuche über die menschliche Natur und ihre Entwicklung*. In *Sprachphilosophische Versuche*. Hamburg: Meiner, 1971.

Tubach, Frederic C. "Perfectibilité: Der zweite Diskurs Rousseaus und die deutsche Aufklärung." *Études germaniques* 15, no. 2 (1960): 144–51.

Voltaire. *Essai sur les moeurs*. Paris: Garnier, 1963.

PERFORMANCE (FRENCH)

"Performance," a term borrowed from English (first recorded in English in the fifteenth century), is one of the French translations of the English word "happening," in which what happens is an oeuvre-event that involves an audience: cf. WORK, Box 2.

It is also one of the established translations of Greek *epideixis* [ἐπίδειξις], which designates a rhetorical performance, especially epideictic. The entry SPEECH ACT explores the vocabulary of performativity, which is especially dependent upon English linguistics (J. L. Austin), in different languages. See also LANGUAGE (particularly LANGUAGE I.A, on the distinction between "competence" and "performance" introduced by Chomsky); cf. LOGOS.

In any case, whether in logic or in aesthetics, a performance is an event (see *EVENT*) that is connected with a context and a moment in time (see MOMENT, II), and that refers to an act (see *ACT* [AGENCY, PRAXIS]).

➤ ART, *IL Y A*, PLASTICITY, *PERSON*

PERSON

I. Person and Persona

"Person" comes from the Latin *persona* (from *personare*, "resound"), which initially designated an actor's mask (Gr. *prosôpon* [πρόσωπον], "that which faces the eyes, the countenance"), the character played, and the actor himself (Gr. *hupokritês* [ὑποκριτής], "he who replies," or "he who interprets"; whence English "hypocrisy," which passes from the register of imitation to that of artifice):

see ACTOR and MIMÊSIS. From the outset, "person" inherited a twofold semantic extension in modern languages:

1. "Person" belongs to the register of grammar (the "persons" as subjects of the verb, "personal" pronouns): see ACTOR, Box 1, ES, and I/ME/MYSELF.
2. "Person" belongs to the domain of law, which opposes "things" and "persons": see *DROIT* [LEX], *THING* [RES, SACHVERHALT]; cf. CIVIL RIGHTS.

II. Person and Subject

1. To these two registers must be added the theological register, via the work on the question of the Trinity, and the difference between *hypostasis* and *huparxis* [ὕπαρξις]: see ESSENCE, GREEK, II.C, and SUBJECT, Box 5.
2. The articulation of these registers paves the way for the adoption of the term "person" to designate in a privileged way, starting in the seventeenth century, the individual subject of thought and action, and by extension, subjectivity in general: see CONSCIOUSNESS, *IDENTITY* [SAMOST', SELBST], SOUL, SUBJECT; cf. AGENCY.
3. In French, *personne* and *personnalité* draw from the registers of psychology and morality. *Personnalité* is a more abstract term that now commonly has, in addition to a juridical sense, a psychological sense (the primary character of an individual) and the moral sense of a free and autonomous individual: see on the one hand GENIUS, INGENIUM, *PASSION,* and on the other hand *AUTRUI* [DRUGOJ, MENSCHHEIT, NEIGHBOR], MORALS, WILLKÜR. On the ethics of the person and "personalism," see the study of Russian *ličnost'* [личность] in RUSSIAN, POSTUPOK (free act), SOBORNOST' (conciliarity).
4. Finally, on the negative sense of "person," *personne*, as a pronoun used in some Romance languages, see *NOTHING*; and, on the Greek wordplay *mêtis/outis* [μῆτις/οὖτις], used by Odysseus, see MÊTIS, Box 1; cf. ESTI, *NEGATION*.

PHANTASIA [φαντασία] (GREEK)

ENGLISH	imagination, fancy, appearing
FRENCH	*imagination, image, (re)présentation*
GERMAN	*Phantasie, Einbildungskraft*
LATIN	*visum, imago, imaginatio*

➤ *IMAGINATION* [FANCY], and *APPEARANCE*, CONCETTO, DOXA, ERSCHEINUNG, *IMAGE* [BILD, EIDÔLON], INGENIUM, LIGHT, MIMÊSIS, PERCEPTION, *PHÉNOMÈNE*, REPRÉSENTATION

The standard translation of the Greek *phantasia* [φαντασία] by "imagination" raises more problems than it solves, if only because it resorts to a calque of Imperial Latin *imaginatio*, which was unknown to Cicero, for whom an *imago* was still chiefly a portrait (*De finibus*, V.1.3). The modern translation of *phantasia* by "representation," which is increasingly accepted, is certainly preferable because it does not refer to a notion, the imagination, which for us designates something quite different from what the Greeks might have meant by *phantasia*, but it does not make room for what is at the heart of *phantasia*: appearing.

I. *Phantasia*, Apparition, and Representation

The translation difficulties reflect the no less great difficulties involved in determining what the Greeks might have meant by *phantasia*: they have to do both with the polysemy of the Greek term, which is connected with the development of the Greek language itself, and with the complex and varied usage that Greek philosophers made of it. Let us explain at the outset that if *phantasia* must be related to *phainô* [φαίνω], "to make appear in the light" (*phôs* [φῶς]—and still more, to the middle-voice verb *phainomai* [φαίνομαι], "to come into the light, to appear"—it is also related to *phantazomai* [φαντάζομαι], "to become visible, to appear, show itself" (*phantazô* [φαντάζω], "to make visible, present to the eye or to the mind" it does not exist in the active mood before the Hellenistic period and does not acquire the sense of "to imagine" until the first or second century CE, when, for example, it appears in the author of the *Treatise on the Sublime* [Pseudo-Longinus] and in Alexander of Aphrodisias. We see immediately that the term originally had very little to do with our modern "imagination," whether reproductive or creative, and probably still less with Malebranche's *folle du logis* (madwoman in the house) or with Pascal's *maîtresse d'erreur et de fausseté* (mistress of error and falsity). Moreover, didn't Herodotus use the verb *phantazomai* to mean simply "show itself" (*Histories*, IV.124, where he says that the Persians no longer saw the Scyths because they had disappeared—*aphanisthentôn* [ἀφανισθέντων]—and no longer showed themselves—*ouk eti ephantazonto* [οὐκ ἔτι ἐφαντάζοντο])?

Thus we can understand Aristotle's famous statement: "As sight [ὄψις] is the most highly developed sense, the name *phantasia* has been formed from *phaos* [φάος], because it is not possible to see [ἰδεῖν] without light" (*De anima*, III.3.429a.2–4; trans. J. A. Smith in *Basic Works of Aristotle* 9). The Stoics, adopting the same etymology, added the following: "*phantasia* gets its name from the word 'light' [φῶς]," and in fact just as light allows us to see both itself and what it envelops, *phantasia* allows us to see both itself and what has produced it" (Aetius, IV.12–15; Sextus Empiricus, *M.*, VIII.162). The view peculiar to the Stoics (*phantasia* is *index sui*), and the fact that, according to Aristotle (*De anima*, III.7.431a.16–17; 8, 432a.9–10), "the soul never thinks without an image" (*phantasma* [φάντασμα])—Barbotin renders

this in French as *sans image*, Bodéüs better as *sans représentation*—are marks of *phantasia*'s reliability: therefore we can only be astonished by any interpretation tending to reduce *phantasia* to what governs internal visual images alone in the absence of any object, images (*phantasmata*) that are supposed, moreover, to be usually false (so that *phantasmata* is then rendered by "illusions," whence our modern "phantasm"). In any event, this interpretation absolutely contradicts the Aristotelian definition of *phantasia* as "a movement resulting from an actual exercise of a power of sense" [ὑπὸ τῆς αἰσθήσεως τῆς κατ' ἐνέργειαν] (*De anima*, III.3.429a.1–2). If we stress this etymology and the connection between *phantasia* and *phainesthai*, we are not directed first of all to visual, "pictorial" mental images but rather to what has to do with apparition, with becoming apparent, with the presentation of an external entity thus brought to light, indeed, with the simple presentation of real things—which may very well be things *heard* rather than *seen*.

- See Box 1.

If Hobbes was very aware of the difficulties of moving from Greek to Latin, the Romans themselves had to experience them directly. Republican Latin, practiced by the author to whom we owe many of our translations of Greek notions, namely Cicero, had only three terms that could be used to render *phantasia*: (1) *imago*, which designated primarily a portrait, but could also refer to mental images, such as those used in mnemonic techniques; (2) *imitor*, which meant mainly to imitate in the attempt to reproduce an image, and which "translated" the Greek verb *eikazô* [εἰκάζω], which meant "to make a portrait, to represent by means of a drawing or painting," whence "to resemble"; (3) *imaginosus*, "subject to hallucinations."

We can now understand the difficulties Cicero encountered in translating the Greek word *phantasia*. On the one hand, probably to emphasize that the Stoics' *phantasia* referred to the representation that "is engraved, struck, and impressed on the basis of an existing object in conformity with that object in such a way that it would not be produced if the object did not exist" (*De legibus*, VII.50), he resorted to the Latin word *visum* (*Academica*, I.40), which is usually translated by "representation," but which signifies primarily "the thing seen." But on the other hand, he also used *visio* and *imago* to render the Epicureans' *eidôlon* (*De divinatione*, II.120;

1

Hobbes and the difficulties of moving from Latin to Greek

Thus we are a priori very far from any idea of a representation in the absence of an object and still further from any assimilation of *phantasia* to Hobbes's "decaying sense" (in the Latin version, *sensio deficiens, sive phantasma dilutum et evanidum*) (*Leviathan*, I.2). Whatever we moderns may owe to this conception and whatever we may think of this possible comparison, we have to note that

Hobbes saw clearly that *imaginatio* very imperfectly translated as *phantasia*:

> For after the object is removed or the eye shut, we still retain an image [*imaginem*] of the thing seen, though more obscure than when we see it. And this is it the Latins call *imagination* [*imaginatio*] from the image made in seeing, and apply the

same, though improperly to all the other senses. But the Greeks call it *fancy* [*phantasia*], which signifies *appearance* and is as proper to one sense as to another. [The Latin words between brackets are those used by Hobbes himself in the Latin version of the book, *De Cive*, 1641.)

(*Leviathan*, I, 2)

De finibus, I.21), that is, the *simulacrum*, to borrow Lucretius's Latin (see IMAGE and SPECIES), which is the replica of the bodies emanating from themselves and producing in us an "image" (*phantasia*, which here takes on a strong sense close to *phantasma*, because this term, which presents a further difficulty, not only designates a faculty but can also designate what results from that faculty).

It is not until Imperial Latin, then, that we find *imaginor* and its derivatives, beginning with *imaginatio*. *Imaginor* and *imaginatio*, however, render the late meanings of *phantazô* and *phantasia*. This is shown by the following statement by Quintilian (first century CE), casually made in the course of a discussion of the ways of eliciting emotion:

> The Greeks call [phantasia] [φαντασία] (we could well call it *visio*) the faculty of representing to ourselves the images of absent things, to the point that we have the impression that we are seeing them with our own eyes and holding them in front of us [per quas imagines rerum absentium ita repraesantur animo ut eas cernere oculisac praesentes habere videamur].

> (*Institutio oratoria*, VI.2. 29)

Quintilian still proposes to translate *phantasia* by *visio*, but the definition he gives it is already far more "modern": it seems to be modeled, even in the appeal to emotion, on the definition given in the *Treatise on the Sublime* (XV), when Pseudo-Longinus emphasizes that in his age (probably the first century CE), the term *phantasia* is used regarding passages in which writers, orators, and poets, acting out of enthusiasm and passion, seem to have seen so vividly what they are describing that they succeed in bringing it before the eyes of their audiences. Thus *imaginatio*, which also does not at first refer to our modern conception of the imagination, can translate *phantasia*, but, strictly speaking, this translation is relevant only for a few late occurrences of *phantasia*. Later still, William of Moerbecke seems to have realized this in his *translatio vetus* of Aristotle's *De anima*, since he does not hesitate to decline *phantasia* and *phantasma* in Latin, as if they were untranslatables, a usage followed by Thomas Aquinas in his commentary, which nonetheless sometimes uses *imaginatio* as well (*In Aristotelis librum de anima*, 644–45, where we see the marvelous usage *phantasiantur* in the context of a discussion of the seeming prudence of ants and bees). However, a century earlier *phantasia* was essentially pejorative and designated something that was related to apparitions, phantoms—which could also be designated in Greek by *phantasma* because of its relationship to *phasma* [φάσμα], "vision, specter, phantom" (see, for example, Aeschylus, *Seven against Thebes*, v. 710, for *phantasma*; *Agamemnon*, v. 274, for *phasma*).

II. Appearing and Appearance

Although—or because, as it would probably be more correct to say—*phantasia* refers first of all to that which appears, it is nonetheless true that it can also refer to a mental image that is very likely to be false, or to pure appearance. It was Plato who gave this turn to the notion, to which it cannot, however, be reduced. Trying to understand thought, *dianoia* [διάνοια], as the mind's

internal, silent dialogue with itself (*Theatetus*, 189e–190a; *Philebus*, 38b–40b), Plato distinguishes between the pure phenomenon of thought, which he characterizes as *doxa*, and thought that presents itself to the mind through the intermediary of sensation (*aisthêsis* [αἴσθησις]). It is this second form of thought, a mixture of opinion and sensation, that he chooses to call *phantasia* or to designate by *phainetai* (Diès translates it in French as *j'imagine*, but literally it means "it appears"), emphasizing that inevitably it will sometimes be false (*Sophist*, 2633e–246b).

■ See Box 2.

While it is true that in Plato and Aristotle what appears through *phantasia* may be subject to doubt, *phantasia* cannot be reduced to this aspect. This is evident in the Stoics, but it is also the case in Aristotle, for whom the spectrum of the *phantasmata* ranges from the true ones, which are necessary for thinking, to the false or illusory ones, such as appear in dreams, hallucinations, and all situations in which the conditions of perception are difficult, by way of the *phantasmata* at work in local movement, in which the role of *phantasia* is to make the object in question appear to be desirable so that one moves toward it. Ultimately, what radically separates Aristotle from Plato with regard to the reliability of *phantasia* is the former's express desire to distinguish it clearly from judgment: just because the sun appears (*phanetai* [φαίνεται]) to me to have a one-foot diameter does not mean that I will believe that it is smaller than the Earth we live on (*De anima*, III.3.428a–24b.10). Thus Aristotle regularly connects *phantasia* with the impersonal *phainetai*, "it appears," explaining that these terms have to be understood in their literal and not their derived ("metaphorical" in Aristotle's vocabulary) senses. *Phainetai* could in fact be used in Greek to signify anything that "appears," whether it appears by virtue of *phantasia* (the literal sense, according to Aristotle) or by virtue of something else, like sensation or thought (derived senses, according to Aristotle). In other words, just as we can say "it appears" to signify what emerges from an argument, or simply to mean "it seems," the same goes for Greek, with *phainetai* (and it is interesting that Aristotle himself does not fail to do so, as in *De anima*, III.10.433a.9, where *phanetai* introduces the conclusion of an argument that appeals precisely to *phantasia*). It is in this sense that we must understand this statement: "If then imagination [*phantasia*] is that in virtue of which an image [*phantasma*] arises for us, excluding metaphorical uses of the term" (*De anima*, III.3.428a.1–2), only what appears by virtue of *phantasia* deserves to be called *phantasma*, and not, as for Plato or in ordinary language, everything that appears or seems to be by virtue of sensation, opinion, or thought.

III. Appear to, Appear as

"Thus it appears" that if *phantasia* refers first of all to what appears, whether what appears is true or false (despite their redistribution of terms, the Stoics were hardly innovative from this point of view), we cannot identify it with our modern "imagination," a notion that has in addition the disadvantage of emphasizing an activity on the part of the subject, whereas in Greek it is rather a matter of receiving.

2

Plato's ambiguity, Aristotle's precision, and the Stoics' redefinitions

➤ SUBLIME

Three texts that echo each other allow us to gauge more accurately the oscillations in the philosophical use of a single family of words and the difficulty of translating them.

Plato writes the following:

> SOCRATES: If a man sees objects that come into his view from a distance [πόρρωθεν] and indistinctly, would you agree that he commonly wants to decide [κρίνειν] about what he sees?
> PROTARCHUS: I should.
> SOCRATES: Then the next step will be that he puts a question to himself.
> PROTARCHUS: What question?
> SOCRATES: "What is that object which catches my eye [φανταζόμενον] there beside the rock under a tree?" Don't you think that is what he would say to himself, if he had caught sight of some appearance [φαντασθέντα] of the sort?
> PROTARCHUS: Of course.
> SOCRATES: And then he would answer his own question and say, if he got it right, "It is a man."

(*Philebus*, 38c–d; trans. R. Hackforth in *Collected Dialogues of Plato*)

Aristotle writes this:

> [E]ven in ordinary speech, we do not, when sense functions precisely with regard to its object [οὐδὲ λέγομεν], say [ἐνεργῶμεν ἀκριβῶς περὶ τὸ αἰσθητόν] that we imagine it to be a man [ὅτι φαίνεται τοῦτο ἡμῖν ἄνθρωπος], but rather when there is some failure of accuracy in its exercise.

(*De anima*, 428a.10–12; trans. J. A. Smith in *Basic Works of Aristotle*)

Regarding Stoicism, we read,

> [Chrysippus said that we have to distinguish *phantasia*, *phantaston*, *phantastikon*, and *phantasma*]. . . . The *phantaston* [usually translated by "object represented"] is what produces *phantasia* [the "representation"]. . . . The *phantastikon* [usually translated by "imagination" or "imaginary"] is an empty movement, an affection that occurs in the mind without any *phanataston* having given rise to it. . . . The *phantasma* ["imaginary object"] is that to which we are drawn in this empty movement of the *phantastikon*.

(Aetius, *Placita philosophorum*, IV.12.1–5)

The situation described by Plato clearly refers to what appears to *X* or *Y* as this or that, in the presence of the object. As a result, the conditions of perception govern the veracity or reliability of what appears to us, and it is therefore misleading, to say the least, to translate *phainetai* in French by *j'imagine*, as Diès did in his translation of the *Sophist*, 264a.

Similarly, when Aristotle, preparing to criticize Plato's definition of *phantasia* as a mixture of sensation and opinion, virtually quotes the *Philebus* in seeking to distinguish *phantasia* from sensation, the French translator Barbotin senses the necessity of rendering *phainetai* by *paraît* in his rendering of Aristotle's *De anima*, but he nonetheless thinks he has to add *l'image*, which spoils everything. The sentence put between quotation marks in Aristotle's text—an obvious allusion to the passage in the *Philebus* quoted earlier—should be rendered in French not as "cela nous paraît être l'image d'un homme," as Barbotin has it, but rather as something like "cela nous paraît être un homme," because it is the object itself that appears to be this or that, and the better the conditions of perception, the better the apparition will be.

Finally, the Stoics undertook a redistribution of terms by separating the *phantasma* from *phantasia* and making it responsible for everything that produces illusions. But by a strange reversal of the situation, we can nonetheless conclude that this act bore a new conception of the imagination as creative, to which Pseudo-Longinus and Philostratus testify: Orestes's visions, which the Stoics always associated with the *phantasmata* of the *phantastikon* (cf. Sextus Empiricus, *Adversus mathematicos*, VII.170, 244, 249; VIII.63, 67), were to become the very model of literary creation, Euripides having seen the Furies and succeeded in making us see what he had "imagined" [ἐφαντάσθη] (*On the Sublime*, XV.2).

BIBLIOGRAPHY

Plato. *Philebus*. Translation by R. Hackforth: *Philebus* in *Collected Dialogues of Plato*, edited by E. Hamilton and H. Cairns. Princeton, NJ: Princeton University Press, 1961.
———. *Le Sophiste*. Translated into French by Auguste Diès. Paris: Les Belles Lettres, 1925.

"Representation" is better, but it has in turn the disadvantage of stressing what presents itself "again," which may, of course, be the case but is not necessarily the case. Whence the way of writing it in several languages: "(re)presentation." But this is hardly satisfying, since what it is most important to preserve is the connection with *phainomai* and *phantazomai*, while at the same time finding a family of terms from the same root to translate *phantasma*, *phantaston*, and *phantastikon*, and to refer both to mental images (pictorial or not) and to simple apparitions, to dream-images and hallucinations and other phantoms or shades—the least of the paradoxes certainly not being that a term derived from the word "light" can also signify "shade."

"Appear" is undoubtedly the key word that allows us to define more precisely what the Greeks understood by *phantasia* (provided, that is, that it is not identified with appearance taken in a pejorative sense, with mere semblance). In fact, though it is not necessary to appeal to Wittgenstein's "seeing as," since Plato already provided us with the means, we must understand *phantasia*, no matter which *phantasma* it should cause to appear, as a structure with a twofold complement governing the fact that something, whatever it is, appears to X or to Y *as* this or that.

▪ See Box 3.

Jean-Louis Labarrière

3
The reappearance of "phantasm" on the basis of the vocabulary of psychoanalysis

As used by translators of Freud, "phantasm" is supposed to render the German *Phantasie*, that is, the idea of the products of the imagination through which the ego tries to escape the grasp of reality (such as daydreams) and that are often closely related to the unconscious. This term (along with its adjective *phantasmatic*), which reappeared in the vocabulary of psychoanalysis, is now widely used in ordinary language. Despite the fact that in medical French *fantasme* was occasionally used as early as 1836 in the sense of visual hallucination, and that in the 1906 edition of the *Nouveau Larousse illustré* it is soberly defined as a "chimera that is formed in the mind," in 1926 it is still absent from the eighth edition of the RT: *Dictionnaire général de la langue française*.

Resurfacing in French psychoanalytic literature over the course of the first third of the twentieth century, *fantasme* reconnected with the persistence in everyday popular speech of the Latin *phantasma*, a late transcription of the Greek word given the same spelling, which signified an image presented to the mind by an extraordinary phenomenon and that remained linked with *phantasia*, a term that initially designated the mental operation accompanying such an image, and only later "shade" or "phantom." *Phantasma* established itself in Imperial Latin in the form of *fantauma*, from the Ionian Greek *phantagma* and the Massalian Greek *phantôma*. This *fantauma* from what is now southern France is found again in the twelfth-century French *fantosme*, with the meaning of "vision of a person from the other world" or "phantom," and then "illusion" and "daydream." In Romance languages, the Italian and Spanish *fantasma* very clearly retains this twofold meaning, first of specter and then of mental image, whereas in French the two medieval terms *fantosme* and *fantasie* long continued to designate an extraordinary vision (*fantosme*) and the power of imagination (*fantasie*).

These last two terms are found in German in the form of *Phantom* (in English "phantom," and by extension, "deceptive image, illusion") and *Phantasie* (the word "imagination"). The pride of place that Freud gives to *Phantasie* led the first French psychoanalysts to translate the term by a word new to French, or newly rehabilitated in French usage: *fantasme*. However, *Phantasie* designates less the power of imagining (*Einbildungskraft*) than the imaginary world and the whole of its contents, the creative activity of dreams, images, and visions to which the mind lends itself and that are expressed by the verb *fantasieren* (substantialized in the form of *das Fantasieren*). So that as Laplanche and Pontalis note in their *Vocabulary of Psychoanalysis*, the French *fantasme* "does not correspond exactly to the German [*die Phantasie*], in that it has a more restricted extension; *fantasme* refers to a specific imaginary production, not to the world of fantasy or imaginative activity in general" (trans. D. Nicolson Smith). Nonetheless, although it was psychoanalysis that actually established the term *fantasme* in French—but by assigning it a more restricted meaning than German *Phantasie*—the corresponding concept has spread within the discipline to multiple levels or modalities (for instance: primal fantasy, *fantasme originaire*, *fantasme de séduction*, conscious and unconscious phantasm, the "family romance," and so forth)—whether they come from Freud, Jung, Lacan, or Melanie Klein. But today the use of *fantasme* has moved far beyond the field of psychoanalysis, in which it was born in the early twentieth century.

It remains that in French, and especially in English, "fantasm" or "fantasy" are sometimes written "phantasm" or "phantasy," the school of Melanie Klein seeing in this—inappropriately, it seems—a way of distinguishing the unconscious phantasm (*phantasy*) from the conscious phantasm (*fantasy*). Independently of this interpretation, the British publishers of the Standard Edition of Freud's complete works, who generally opted for *phantasy*, justified, in these somewhat awkward terms, the distinction between the two spellings:

Phantasy is adopted here on the basis of a discussion in the *Oxford English Dictionary*, which comes to this conclusion: "In modern usage, the terms *fantasy* and *phantasy*, despite their phonic identity and their etymology, tend to be apprehended as being distinct, the predominant sense of the former being "caprice, whim, fantastic behavior," whereas [the predominant sense of] the latter is "imagination or hallucinatory representation." Consequently, *phantasy* will be understood here with the technical meaning of a phenomenon concerning the psyche. But *fantasy* may also be used in certain appropriate occurrences.

(*Standard Edition*, 1:24)

Thus the difference from their French colleagues (for whom *phantasme* and *fantasme* have the same meaning), and also from their Italian colleagues (who use *fantasia* or *fantasma*) and Spanish colleagues (*fantasía* and *fantasma*), Anglo-Saxon psychoanalysts seem to insist on establishing a real distinction between *fantasy* and *phantasy*, the latter term being seen as closer, by its spelling, to the German *Phantasie* and indicating, in their view, a specific dependence, in relation to Freudian vocabulary, on the concept that is supposed to correspond to it.

Charles Baladier

BIBLIOGRAPHY

Freud, Sigmund. *The Standard Edition of the Complete Psychological Works of Sigmund Freud*. 24 vols. Edited by John Strachey et al. London: Hogarth Press, 1953–74.
Laplanche, Jean, and Jean-Bertrand Pontalis. *Vocabulary of Psychoanalysis*. Translated by D. Nicolson Smith. New York: Norton, 1974. First published in France in 1967.

BIBLIOGRAPHY

Armisen, Mireille. "La notion d'imagination chez les Anciens." *Pallas* 15/16 (1979–80): 11–51 / 3–37.
Aristotle. *De anima*. Translation by J. A. Smith: "On the Soul." In *Basic Works of Aristotle*. Edited by R. McKeon. New York: Random House, 1941.
Birondo, Noell. "Aristotle on Illusory Perception: Phantasia without Phantasmata Source." *Ancient Philosophy* 21 (2001): 57–71.
Blumenthal, H. J. "Neoplatonic Interpretations of Aristotle on 'Phantasia.'" *Review of Metaphysics* 31 (1977): 242–57.

Bundy, Murray Wright. *The Theory of Imagination in Classical and Medieval Thought*. Urbana: University of Illinois Press, 1927.
Castoriadis, Cornelius. "The Discovery of the Imagination." *Constellations* 1, no. 2 (1994): 183–213.
Cocking, John M. *Imagination: A Study in the History of Ideas*. London: Routledge, 1991.
Fattori, Marta, and Massimo Bianchi, eds. *Phantasia~Imaginatio*, Rome: Ateneo, 1988.
Flory, Dan. "Stoic Psychology, Classical Rhetoric, and Theories of Imagination in Western Philosophy." *Philosophy and Rhetoric* 29, no. 2 (1996): 147–67.

Heil, John F., Jr. "Aristotle's Objection to Plato's 'Appearance': De anima 428a24–b9." *Ancient Philosophy* 23 (2003): 319–35.

Imbert, Claude. "Théorie de la représentation et doctrine logique dans le stoïcisme ancien." In *Les Stoïciens et leur logique*, edited by Jacques Brunschwig. Paris: Vrin, 1978.

Labarrière, Jean-Louis. "De la 'nature phantastique' des animaux chez les Stoïciens." In *Passions and Perceptions*, edited by Jacques Brunschwig and Martha Nussbaum, 225–49. Cambridge: Cambridge University Press, 1993.

———. "Des deux introductions de la *phantasia* dans le *De anima*, III, 3." *Kairos* 9 (1977): 141–68.

———. "Jamais l'âme ne pense sans phantasme." In *Aristote et la notion de nature*, edited by P.-M. Morel, 149–179. Bordeaux, Fr.: Presses Universitaires de Bordeaux, 1997.

Labarrière, Jean-Louis, ed. "Aristote —Sur l'imagination." *Les Études philosophiques* 1 (1977).

Lycos, Kemon. "Aristotle and Plato on 'Appearing.'" *Mind* 73 (1964): 496–514.

Manieri, Alessandra. *L'Immagine poetica nella teoria degli antichi*. Pisa, It.: Istituti Editoriali e Poligrafici Internazionali, 1998.

Modrak, Deborah K. W. "Φαντασία Reconsidered." *Archiv für Geschichte der Philosophie* 68 (1968): 47–69.

Nussbaum, Martha C. "The Role of *Phantasia* in Aristotle's Explanation of Action." In *Aristotle's "De motu animalium."* Princeton, NJ: Princeton University Press, 1978. 221–69.

Osborne, Catherine. "Aristotle on the Fantastic Abilities of Animals in *De Anima* 3.3." In vol. 19 of *Oxford Studies in Ancient Philosophy*, edited by David Sedley, 253–85. New York: Oxford University Press.

Schofield, Malcolm. "Aristotle on the Imagination." In *Aristotle on Mind and the Senses*, edited by G.E.R. Lloyd and G.E.L. Owen, 99–141. Cambridge: Cambridge University Press, 1978.

Vernant, Jean-Pierre. "Image et Apparence dans la théorie platonicienne de la Mimêsis." *Journal de Psychologie* 2 (1975). Reprinted as "Naissance d'images." In *Religions, histoires, raisons*. Paris: Maspero, 1979. 105–37.

Watson, Gerard. *Phantasia in Classical Thought*. Galway, Ire.: Galway University Press, 1988.

Wedin, Michael V. *Mind and Imagination in Aristotle*. New Haven, CT: Yale University Press, 1988.

| PHÉNOMÈNE (FRENCH)

The word *phénomène* (in Greek, *phainomena* [φαινόμενα]) was introduced into French by Renaissance astronomers to designate the stars and constellations that shine so visibly to the eye. Today its philosophical usage lies at the intersection of the object and subject, between manifestation and consciousness.

I. *PHAINOMENON*, "PHENOMENON"

The English word "phenomenon," like its analogues in other languages, including French and German, is a calque of the Greek *phainomenon* [φαινόμενον], a participle of the middle voice verb *phainesthai* [φαίνεσθαι] meaning "to show, shine, appear, become visible, show itself as." We find the same Indo-European root *bh(e)ə₂*- (illumine, shine) in *phôs* [φῶς] (light), in *phantasia* [φαντασία] (imagination, representation), and also in *phêmi* [φημί] (to say). See LIGHT, Box 1, and PHANTASIA, cf. IMAGINATION.

Phainomenon retains a certain ambiguity. Sometimes the term designates that which "appears" or seems to appear as this or that, without really or truly being so (thus a *phainomenos sullogismos* [φαινόμενος συλλογισμός] is one that "merely seems to reason" [Aristotle, *Topics*, 1.100b25]); other times, it designates what we call, properly, "phenomena,"

that is, obvious and constraining events, such as natural phenomena, that are sometimes remarkable and for which we have to account (*apodounai ta phainomena* [ἀποδοῦναι τὰ φαινόμενα] [Aristotle, *Metaphysics* Λ 1073a36–37]). The well-founded phenomenon has to be distinguished from the imaginary phenomenon, and it is legitimate to speak of the "reality of phenomena" (Leibniz, *De modo distinguendi phaenomena ab imaginariis*). See APPEARANCE, IMAGE.

II. *Phänomen/Erscheinung*

Unlike German, French has only a single term; as a result, it is difficult to render in French the subtle difference that may exist between *Phänomen* and *Erscheinung*, unless we resort to the term *apparition* for the latter (Leibniz still writes *phaenomena sive apparitiones*) or create the improbable term *parence* (jargon used by a few translators of Heidegger). In Kant, for whom everything that is the object of a possible experience is a phenomenon, the latter is opposed to the *noumenon*, but also to the thing in itself (*Ding an sich*) and, like *Erscheinung*, to *Schein* (deceptive appearance, illusion). See ERSCHEINUNG, GEGENSTAND; cf. OBJECT, REALITY, RES, *THING*.

III. *Phénomène, Conscience, Phénoménologie*

In French, the technical term *phénomène* designates everything that appears to consciousness. In this sense, phenomena are to be described first, without seeking laws, causes, or hidden principles. It is in accord with this meaning of the term that Descartes wrote in the *Principles of Philosophy* (III.4), "I shall give a brief description of the phenomena whose causes I claim to seek." See CONSCIOUSNESS; cf. I/ME/MYSELF, REPRÉSENTATION, SUBJECT.

Phenomenology (Ger. *Phänomenologie*, introduced by Lambert; see LIGHT, Box 1), especially Husserlian phenomenology, constructs a lexicon that makes it possible to reconfigure the relationship between phenomenon and consciousness. See EPOCHÊ, ES GIBT, INTENTION; cf. ERLEBEN, PLASTICITY.

| PHRONÊSIS [φρόνησις] (GREEK)

ENGLISH	prudence, wisdom, practical wisdom
FRENCH	*prudence, sagesse, sagesse pratique, intelligence, intelligence pratique, sagacité*
GERMAN	*Klugheit, praktische Vernunft*
ITALIAN	*prudenza, ragione pratica*
LATIN	*prudentia*
SPANISH	*prudencia*

➤ *PRUDENCE, VIRTUE,* and ARGUTEZZA, INGENIUM, MADNESS, MÊTIS, PRAXIS, PRUDENTIAL, SORGE, SOUL, VIRTÙ, *WISDOM*

The set of possible translations of the Greek term *phronêsis* [φρόνησις] shows the extension of its semantic field in ancient Greek, the development of this notion, and the redistributions to which it gave rise in Greek philosophy, as well as its advent in philosophies in European languages on the basis of its Latin translation by Cicero as *prudentia*. Originally designating thought, without emotion or desire being necessarily excluded, *phronêsis*, which was long not distinguished from *sophia* [σοφία], "wisdom," knowledge, scientific knowledge," as Plato and even Aristotle often show, came to designate a virtue, an "excellence" (see VIRTÙ, Box 1), exercised in the practical domain. Traditionally included among the four "cardinal" virtues, along with courage, justice, and temperance (or moderation), phronêsis nonetheless has a special status. It is a "dianoietic" or "intellectual" virtue (Aristotle), and even a "science" (the Stoics); but it is also an attitude or behavior that is involved in both private and public affairs—in short, it is, as is usually said, a kind of "practical knowledge." Every smart manager is a "prudent" person (phronimos [φϱόνιμος]); to be such a person "virtuously" or, better, to be one in a "virtuoso" manner, one also has to know how to anticipate the future and not limit oneself to a timid management style. From this point of view, the Greeks' "prudence" has almost nothing to do with the "prudence in business" to which Descartes alludes in his prefatory epistle to the French translation of the *Principles*, where he seeks to distinguish it from the wisdom with which philosophy must be conducted. We can take as an indication of this complexity the fact that Cicero himself, who normally translates phronêsis by prudentia, nonetheless sometimes renders this first of the four virtues by the phrase sapientia et prudentia (*De officiis* 1.15–16) when he wants to distinguish it from the three other cardinal virtues by its status as the intellectual virtue.

I. *Phronêsis* as Thought

The word *phronêsis* is derived from the verb *phroneô* [φϱονέω], which, broadly speaking, means "to be intelligent, to think, to have feelings" (cf. RT: *Dictionnaire étymologique de la langue grecque*, s.v.). In Homer, "thought" (*phronêsis*) or "thinking" (*phronein* [φϱονεῖν]) resides in the *thumos* [θυμός], the "breath," which is itself, according to Onians (see SOUL, Box 3), contained in the *phrenes* [φϱένες], the "lungs." Onians (RT: *Origins of European Thought*) consequently notes that whereas in Homer, *phronein* may in fact designate the intellectual aspect of thought, as it does in later Greek (thus Agamemnon "thinking [*phroneonta* (φϱονέοντα)] in his mind [*thumos*] things that were not to be realized," *Iliad* 2.36–37), this verb nevertheless has a broader sense that also includes the emotions and desire. This is shown again, later on, by the verse in Sophocles's *Philoctetes* (1078) in which Neoptolomos hopes that Philoctetes will change his *phronêsis* with regard to his companions: "Meanwhile, perhaps, he may come to a better mind [*phronêsin*] concerning us" (trans. Jebb, 208). Here we see that *phronêsis* does not refer to a purely intellectual act, but rather to the sense of the term "thought" that we still find in expressions such as "have a thought for," "our thoughts are with you," and so on.

Plato himself, who clearly emphasized the intellectual determination of *phronêsis*, is still dependent on this polysemy. Thus, after having strongly maintained that the body and the attachment to pleasure that may result from it hobble the development of *phronêsis*, "intelligence, thought," which, as seekers of the truth, we ought to cherish, because it alone is worth the effort and will make us truly virtuous (*Phaedo* 65a, 66a–e, 68a–b, 69a–c), Plato, in the same dialogue, nonetheless classifies it alongside sight, hearing, and analogous functions when the blessed are concerned (111a3–4). Similarly, in the *Theatetus* (161c), he says that Protagoras, whom some might consider the equal of the gods in wisdom and knowledge (*sophia*), in reality has no more *phronêsis* (judgment, intelligence) than a tadpole. However,

it remains that Plato, more than any earlier philosopher, clearly distinguishes what belongs to *phronêsis* from what belongs to the body and its "entrails." Thus in the *Timaeus* (71d–e), the "appetitive" part of the soul (*to epithumêtikon* [τὸ ἐπιθυμητικόν]), the one that is associated with hunger, thirst, and all bodily needs, is lodged under the *phrenes* so as to be kept as far as possible from the part that deliberates, thinks, and reflects, which is lodged in the head, itself separated from the rest of the body by the neck. Stressing the fact that this appetitive part of the soul participates neither in the *logos* [λόγος] nor in *phronêsis* (*Timaeus* 71d), Plato even maintains that our conceivers made the liver so that it might be impressed by "images" (*phantasmata* [φαντάσματα]), and this also makes dreams and divination possible. As force of mind, *phronêsis*, like thought and reflection, is thereby clearly opposed to *aphrosunê* [ἀφροσύνη], "dementia," and the proof is, Plato says, that no man in possession of his *nous* [νοῦς] (see UNDERSTANDING, Box 1), his (good) senses, is capable of divination. Only someone whose *phronêsis*, "capacity for reflection," is impaired in one way or another can succeed in divination (71e). The turn toward the intellectual aspect of the semantic field is thus very clear, and is also shown by the fact that in Plato, *phronêsis* and *sophia* are often used as synonyms: they belong to the domain of thought, intelligence, knowledge, wisdom. This is still sometimes the case in Aristotle as well, not only in his "early" writings, such as the *Protrepticus*, but also in the *Metaphysics* (Γ.5, 1009b13, 18, 32); M.4, 1078b15), notably when he reproaches the "ancients" for not having been able to distinguish between *phronêsis*, "thought," and sensation (cf. *De anima* 3.3, 427a17–22, where we find the same association as in Plato between the *noein* [νοεῖν], "thought," and *phronein*, "intelligence").

Nevertheless, as Aubenque has shown in his magisterial book *La prudence chez Aristote*, Plato's usage must not mask the "traditional" sense of the term *phronêsis*. In fact, although the word *phronêsis* commonly designated thought in a very general sense, it designated as well, and perhaps especially, thought or intelligence in a more specific sense, namely, to use a formula that Aristotle would not reject, "the understanding of human affairs." By this is meant both a certain kind of knowledge, the one that concerns precisely human affairs, which are changing and variable, and a certain kind of reasoning and behavior with regard to "life." This attitude, we might say, is rooted in a solid experience that makes the person who has it "wise": a person who is called a *phronimos*, a "prudent, intelligent, sagacious" person, will be able to gauge situations, anticipate them, and cope with them thanks to his experience and discernment. That explains why Aristotle sought to base himself on this "popular wisdom" in seeking, in opposition to Plato, to distinguish a person who is "wise" in the sense of having scientific knowledge, from a person who is wise in the sense of "prudent."

■ See Box 1.

II. *Phronêsis* as a Virtue

When in the *Republic*, Plato adopts a four-part classification that was apparently already in use in his time, he hesitates, in designating what we usually translate as "wisdom," between

1

And Thales fell

Thales, who is supposed to have been the first of the Seven Sages of Greece to have borne the fine name of *sophos* [σοφός], is said to have fallen into a well while he was looking at the heavens, causing him, moreover, to be mocked by his servant. Plato reports the anecdote in the *Theatetus* (174a), where he uses it to poke fun at ignoramuses with slaves' souls who mock true sages, the philosophers who, even if they may in fact fall into a well and look silly, in reality possess true knowledge of the things of this world, namely, the knowledge that makes one truly free. It is also recounted by Montaigne, who gives it a quite different, juicier interpretation:

> I feel grateful to the Milesian wench who, seeing the philosopher Thales continually spending his time in contemplation of the heavenly vault and always keeping his eyes raised upward, put something in his way to make him stumble, to warn him that it would be time to amuse his thoughts with things in the clouds when he had seen to those at his feet.
>
> ("Apology for Raimond Sebond," in *The Complete Essays of Montaigne*, trans. Frame, 402)

(N.B.: Montaigne follows here the version of the anecdote given in Diogenes Laertius, *Lives of the Eminent Philosophers* 1.34, in which the servant deliberately leads Thales to a hole that she has previously dug.)

Unlike Plato, Montaigne thus adopts, and radicalizes, the point of view of the "popular opinion" that Aristotle mentions in order to convey the distinction he is trying to make between *sophia* and *phronêsis*: knowledge of things of a theoretical order is not of the same nature as knowledge of things of a practical order. The possession of the former in no way entails possession of the latter, as Thales's fall into the well clearly shows (*Nicomachean Ethics* 6.7, 1141bff.). That is why Thales can be considered a *sophos*, but not a *phronimos*.

Even when *sophia* wants to take revenge on the servant, and prove that she, *sophia*, is capable of practical applications, this does not guarantee her the status of *phronêsis*. *Sophia* can be practically effective without being ethically virtuous. That is the meaning of the anecdote reported

in the *Politics* (1.11, 1259a6–23). Thales performed an *epideixis* [ἐπίδειξις], a "demonstration," a display of *sophia* (a19; see SPEECH ACT): having predicted, thanks to his astronomical knowledge, that there would be an abundant olive harvest, he gave deposits for the use of all of the olive presses, and then rented them out again at the rate he wanted, thus inventing the monopoly and chrematistics, and proving that "philosophers can easily be rich if they like, but . . . their ambition is of another sort" (1259a16–18, trans. Jowett). *Phronêsis* is not the same thing as *sophia*, even when the latter is applied; and the Aristotelian sage, whether he is a *phronimos* or a *sophos*, knows it in a way quite different from the Platonic *sophos*.

BIBLIOGRAPHY

Aristotle. *The Basic Works of Aristotle*. Edited by R. McKeon. Translated by B. Jowett. New York: Random House, 1941.

Montaigne, Michel de. *The Complete Essays of Montaigne*. Translated by D. M. Frame. Stanford, CA: Stanford University Press, 1965.

---

sophia and *phronêsis* (see, for example, *Republic* 4.427e versus 433b). Furthermore, *phronêsis* can also designate both the understanding as an ability to reflect in a general way (4.432a) and the understanding as an intellectual ability distinct from bodily abilities (5.461a). In other words, the terminology is still far from being fixed, and no matter what turn Plato tried to give to this notion, it remains that in his work, *phronêsis* continues to have multiple meanings.

A. Aristotle's work

It is in the sixth book of Aristotle's *Nicomachean Ethics* that *phronêsis* is first clearly treated as a virtue or "excellence." It is not that Aristotle was the first to consider *phronêsis* a virtue, but that he gave this notion a special sense, basing himself on popular usage while at the same time radically reformulating things. Aristotle's contribution is characterized by at least three features:

a. a sharp break with Plato's intellectualist turn;
b. a clear distinction between the respective domains of *sophia* and *phronêsis*; and
c. a redistribution of the four virtues (which, since Saint Ambrose, it has been customary to call "the four cardinal virtues"), namely, prudence (*phronêsis/prudentia*), courage (*andreia* [ἀνδρεία] / *fortitudo*), justice (*dikaiosunê* [δικαιοσύνη] / *iustitia*), and temperance or moderation (*sôphrosunê* [σωφροσύνη] / *temperantia-moderatio*; Cicero

translates *sôphrosunê* by both *temperantia* and *moderatio*, and even by *modestia* or *frugalitas*; cf. *Tusculan Disputations* 3.16–18).

■ See Box 2.

1. The new classification of the virtues

In the *Nicomachean Ethics*, Aristotle adopts a distinction that was current in the Academy, but was also traditional, between the irrational part of the soul (which he limits for his current ethical inquiry to the desiring part of the soul, *to orektikon* [τὸ ὀρεκτικόν], sometimes simply called "the ethical part," *to êthikon* [τὸ ἠθικόν], *Nicomachean Ethics* 6.132, 1144b15) and its rational part, the *logos* being properly possessed by the latter, whereas the former (at most) listens to the *logos* and obeys it. Then he distinguishes first the "moral virtues"—or, to give them their true name, the "virtues of character" (*êthikai aretai* [ἠθικαὶ ἀρεταί])—which are those of the desiring part of the soul, from the "intellectual virtues" (*aretai dianoêtikai* [ἀρεταὶ διανοητικαί]), which are those of the part to which the *logos* is specific. Courage, justice, and temperance are thus ranked among these moral virtues or virtues of character that one acquires in early childhood, because character or temperament (*êthos* [ἦθος]) is shaped and strengthened through habit (*ethos* [ἔθος]: ibid., 2.1, 1103b17–19; the same play on words is already found in Plato, *Laws* 7.792e; see MORALS). On the other hand, *phronêsis* and *sophia* are ranked not only among

2

The four cardinal virtues

Plato, though he did not necessarily invent it, makes use of the four-part classification "wisdom (*sophia* or *phronêsis*), justice, courage, temperance." The Stoics call these four virtues "primary" (*tas prôtas* [τὰς πρώτας]: Diogenes Laertius, *Lives of the Eminent Philosophers*, 6.92; the term *phronêsis* was then adopted to designate the most important of them); but the expression "cardinal virtues" was not used by the Greek philosophers. Saint Ambrose uses this term to designate the civil virtues that every good Christian must possess in addition to the three theological virtues, namely, faith, hope, and charity. In fact, he usually calls them "principal" virtues (*principales*), and in this we can see a relic of Stoicism. However, Saint Ambrose enumerates seven "principal virtues": the Spirit of wisdom and intelligence, the Spirit of counsel and strength, the Spirit of knowledge and piety, and the Spirit of holy fear (*De sacramentis*, 3.2.8–10; *De mysteriis*, 7.42). Finally, defining *moderatio* as the virtue that tempers justice, Saint Ambrose considers it for that reason to be the most beautiful of all (*De paenitentia*, 1.1.1–2).

the intellectual virtues that are acquired through experience (*empeiria* [ἐμπειρία]) and are obviously indispensable so far as *phronêsis* is concerned, but also among those acquired through education (*didaskalia* [διδασκαλία]: *Nicomachean Ethics*, 2.1, 1103b14–17).

2. The distinction between *sophia* and *phronêsis*

When he takes up the study of the intellectual virtues (*Nicomachean Ethics* 6.2), Aristotle begins by subdividing the properly rational part into a "scientific" part (*to epistêmonikon* [τὸ ἐπιστημονικόν]) and a "calculative" part (*to logistikon* [τὸ λογιστικόν]), also called "opinionative" (*to doxastikon* [τὸ δοξαστικόν],1144b14; it is less a matter of calculating in the literal sense of the term than of making conjectures). The scientific part of the soul is the domain of theoretical things, that is, those that cannot be other than they are—in other words, necessary things, which are the only ones that can be made the object of truly scientific study, precisely because they are necessary. The excellence of this part is called *sophia*, or "wisdom," as it is usually translated. The calculative part of the soul, on the other hand, is the domain of things that can be other than they are, that is, contingent things—and, very specifically, within this domain it is the sphere of "human affairs" (*ta anthrôpina pragmata* [τὰ ἀνθρώπινα πράγματα]), "things to be done" (*ta prakta* [τὰ πρακτά]), that is the ambit of the calculative part of the soul. The excellence of this part is called *phronêsis*. Emphasizing the radical heterogeneity of these two domains, Aristotle thus breaks up what Plato had tried to unify: *sophia*, which understands nothing about the domain of things to be done, does not govern *phronêsis*; and *phronêsis*, insofar as man is not the most excellent thing in the world, does not govern *sophia*. The "conflict of faculties" is thus settled.

As a result, in contrast to the moral virtues, the "intellectual" virtues do not form a homogeneous whole. Let us not delude ourselves, therefore, regarding the intellectual character of Aristotelian *phronêsis*: *phronêsis* and the set of moral virtues form a whole, an autonomous domain, that of practical life (see PRAXIS), which cannot be reduced to scientific knowledge properly so called. The proof of this is that Aristotle already presupposes *phronêsis* in the famous definition of moral virtue as "a state of character concerned with choice [*hexis proairetikê* (ἕξις προαιρετική)], lying in a mean [*mesotês* (μεσότης)], i.e., the mean relative to us, this being determined by a rational principle" (*Nicomachean Ethics* 6.2, 1106b36–37,

trans. Ross). For this definition concludes this way: "And by that principle by which the man of practical wisdom [*phronimos*] would determine it." Thus Aristotle underscores the essential role of the prudent man in the very definition of moral virtue: it is the prudent man who determines the mean, the "happy medium." Incarnated in the *phronimos*, *phronêsis* thus intervenes long before it is defined as such within the study of the intellectual virtues (ibid., 6.5–9).

3. *Phronêsis* and its field of action

Aristotelian *phronêsis* thus occupies a rather special place that continues to be of great interest to modern thinkers (see PRAXIS, PRUDENTIAL). It is a virtue, but it is also a certain kind of knowledge, a certain kind of understanding: the understanding of practical things. Generally speaking, its domain is that of "doing." That is why Aristotle does not hesitate to classify it among the "productive sciences" (*poiêtika* [ποιητικά], *Eudemian Ethics* 1.5, 1216b18; he is using the term "science" [*epistêmê* (ἐπιστήμη)] in a broad sense), even though *phronêsis* is distinct from *poiêsis* [ποίησις] in the sense of *technê* [τέχνη], because it does not "produce" anything external to itself (*Nicomachean Ethics* 6.4; see PRAXIS). But *phronêsis* is indeed "productive," because contrary to the theoretical sciences, knowledge is not its only end. Only *phronêsis* governs action. If Aristotle bases himself on the fact that we recognize as "prudent" a person who manages his own affairs as well as possible, he immediately reworks this popular meaning by noting that "we think Pericles and those like him to be prudent men [*phronimous*] because they are capable of seeing [*dunantai theôrein* (δύνανται θεωρεῖν)] what is good for them and for men in general" (ibid., 6.5, 1140b7–10). This is a clear break with Plato, who did not hold statesmen in high esteem, and Aristotle further emphasizes it by observing that "political wisdom and practical wisdom are the same state of mind" (ibid., 6.8, 1141b23–24). Once it is established that *phronêsis* is the art of deliberating well concerning the means to an end, Aristotle explains that it is especially a knowledge of particular things and is thereby closer to sensation than to knowledge in the strict sense. That is why, he says in substance, a young man may very well be an excellent mathematician—mathematics never involves, after all, anything but "discourse"—but he cannot be a good politician, because that requires experience, and thus time (ibid., 6.9, 1142a11–20).

B. The new Stoic order

In proportion to their dogmatism or absolute rationalism—for them, the wise man's knowledge is an unshakeable knowledge that covers every domain, all of them closely interwoven with the others, and the great majority of men must be considered a bunch of good-for-nothings (*phauloi* [φαῦλοι])—the Stoics make *phronêsis* as a virtue the "knowledge [*epistêmê*] of bad things, of good things, and of what is neither good nor bad" (Diogenes Laertius, *Lives of the Eminent Philosophers* 7.92). The founder of the school, Zeno of Citium, who was still influenced by Socratic monism, went back beyond Aristotle to the Socratic conception of the unity of virtue-knowledge. Then *phronêsis*, whose name could be preserved, was merely one of the multiple versions of this virtue-knowledge, even if, by basing oneself on Plutarch, one could probably attribute a certain precedence to it: it was part of the definition of each virtue, which means that the *phronêsis* that enters into the definition of each of the virtues had to be distinguished from *phronêsis* "in the special sense." Thus, whereas courage is "prudence in domains requiring endurance, and moderation is prudence in domains requiring a choice, prudence in the strict sense [*tên d' idiôs legomenên phronêsin* (τὴν δ' ἰδίως λεγομένην φρόνησιν)] is prudence in domains concerning distribution" (Plutarch, "On Stoic Self-Contradiction" 1034a, in RT: *The Hellenistic Philosophers*).

Although this first conception did not persist among the Stoics, they did continue to reject Aristotle's sharp distinction among domains, which was itself founded on a monist psychology: "They suppose that the passionate and irrational part is not distinguished from the rational part by any distinction intrinsic to the nature of the soul, but that the same part of the soul, which they call thought and the directive part [*dianoian kai hêgemonikon* (διάνοιαν καὶ ἡγεμονικόν)], becomes a virtue or a vice insofar as it completely reverses itself and changes in the passions and alterations of its habitus or character, and that it contains nothing irrational in itself" (Plutarch, "On Moral Virtue" 441d, in RT: *The Hellenistic Philosophers*). Even if it continued to use the word *phronêsis* and to make it a virtue, Stoicism could not tolerate the existence of an autonomous and heterogeneous domain of science, as is found in Aristotle. That is why when Chrysippus, for example, seems to adopt the traditional classification of the four "cardinal" virtues, which the Stoics called "primary" virtues (see Box 2), he insists at the same time on their strong cohesion: "[The Stoics] say that the virtues are in a relationship of mutual implication [*antakolouthein allêlais* (ἀντακολουθεῖν ἀλλήλαις)], not only because anyone who has one of them has them all, but also because a person who accomplishes an action in accord with one of them accomplishes it in accord with them all" (Plutarch, "On Stoic Self-Contradiction" 1046e, in RT: *The Hellenistic Philosophers*). Similarly, Chrysippus continues to maintain that all virtue is knowledge, even if each virtue is a different kind of knowledge.

C. *Phronêsis* and *prudentia*

In choosing to translate *phronêsis* by *prudentia*, Cicero heard in the latter an echo of *providentia*, the art of foreseeing. *Prudentia* is in fact derived from *providentia* (*pro-video*, "to see ahead, foresee"; cf. RT: *Dictionnaire étymologique de la langue latine*). From this point of view, he was certainly not wrong, because we can read in Aristotle that "it is to that which observes well the various matters concerning itself that one ascribes practical wisdom [*phronimos*]. . . . This is why we say that some even of the lower animals have practical wisdom, viz., those which are found to have a power of foresight with regard to their own life" (*Nicomachean Ethics* 6.7, 1141a25–28, trans. Ross). But while Aristotle based himself on popular beliefs, Cicero relies on the strict Stoic definitions of *sophia* and *phronêsis* when he translates the latter by *prudentia*: "By *prudentia*, in Greek [*phronêsis* (φρόνησις)], we mean a virtue different from *sapientia*: prudence is the knowledge of what is to be desired and avoided; wisdom, which is, as I have said, the supreme virtue, is the knowledge [*scientia*] of things divine and human, which includes communal and social bonds between the gods and men" (*De officiis* 1.153). Thus even when Cicero, following in the footsteps of Panetius and middle Stoicism, maintains that *honestum*, "honorable conduct," which is the foundation of all morality, derives from one of the four virtues the Stoics considered primary, he nonetheless stresses that these four virtues are "interconnected and interwoven" (ibid., 1.15). Moreover, since it is in this passage that Cicero translates the first of these virtues by *sapientia et prudentia*, defining it as "the quest for and discovery of the true," we see that he clearly remains dependent on Stoic rationalism.

Given that this definition of *prudentia* became common in the world of Greco-Roman antiquity—it was retained by Augustine: "Prudence [*prudentia*] is the knowledge [*scientia*] of the things that must be desired and the things that must be avoided" (*On Free Will*, 1.13.27)—we might see in this a good reason not to resort to the translation by "prudence" when it is a matter of Aristotelian *phronêsis*. However, it must be noted that Thomas Aquinas, who discusses *prudentia* at length in his *Summa theologica* (IIa, IIae, qu. 46–56) from an Aristotelian point of view, did not bother with this difficulty and avoided the obstacle presented by the authority of Augustine—*prudentia* is a virtue, and knowledge is contrasted with virtue (qu. 47, art. 4)—by saying that the latter "understood knowledge in the broad sense of any act of right reason [*ibi large accipit scientiam pro qualibet recta ratione*]" (ibid.). Similarly, when he reaffirms, following Aristotle, that "prudence intimates action" (*Nicomachean Ethics* 6.11, 1143b8, where we read that *phronêsis* is "imperative," *epitaktikê* [ἐπιτακτική]), Aquinas once again gets around Augustine, who seems to limit *phronêsis* to "knowing how to be wary of the hazards that threaten action" (qu. 47, art. 8).

Today, of course, prudence is seldom defined in any but this Augustinian manner, as caution—for example, when driving a car. But the French translation of *phronêsis* by *sagesse*, "wisdom," is no better (French speakers will often say that a child is *sage*, and in France *comités de sages* are empanelled to give direction on matters of policy: is it not as if these *sages* could be expected to provide wise advice because they are not engaged in action?), and has, moreover, the great disadvantage that we then have to wonder how to render *sophia* and *sophos*. Translators who refuse to render Aristotle's *phronêsis* by "prudence" (*prudencia*, *prudenza*, etc.), whether because of its "technical" translation in Cicero, the meaning this notion acquired in Kant (in whose work "prudence" is no more than "cleverness," *Klugheit*), or unfortunate modern meanings of the term, end up splitting "wisdom" into two: on the one hand, "wisdom" as such, to translate *sophia*, and on the other, "practical wisdom" or "practical reason" (*praktische Vernunft*, *ragione pratica*). There is no lack of resources; in French, the translation of *sophia* by *philosophie* and *phronêsis* by *sagesse* has even been proposed (Gauthier and Jolif, *Aristote*).

III. *Phronêsis, Sophia,* and *Sôphrosunê*

The translation problems that arise from the twofold Greek and Latin tradition, as well as the development of the terms "wisdom" and "prudence" in our languages, are obviously not simple issues. The difficulty has to do with what the "moderns" as well as the "ancients" call "wisdom" (*sagesse*). One symptom of this is the definition of the "Sage" that we find in Furetière's dictionary: "A philosopher who, through the study of nature and past events, has learned to know himself, and to conduct his actions well. Plutarch wrote a fine *Treatise on the Banquet of the Seven Sages*. The Sage has passions and moderates them. The Stoics, seeking to create a Sage, only made a statue of him" (RT: *Dictionnaire universel*). But since, for the notion of wisdom (*sagesse*), Furetière refers first of all to God's knowledge, and then to the knowledge that humans can acquire through the study of physics and morality, it is remarkable that through this very barb directed at the Stoics, it seems that one point in their doctrine is reaffirmed: wisdom is not only the superior art of living of a person who knows how to shelter himself from what torments other people—Montaigne's famous "soft pillow"—but primarily a knowledge of a theoretical order that, because it is theoretical, proves the basis for a self-knowledge that enables us to conduct our actions well. (It would, moreover, suffice to add dialectics to physics and morality to obtain the three inseparable parts of the Stoic system that constitute the Stoic Sage's virtues.)

A. *Phronêsis, aphrosunê, sôphrosunê*

This difficulty is illustrated by both Aristotle and the Stoics, to whom we owe our heritage with regard to *phronêsis*, a peculiar heritage in the sense that in antiquity, it was the Stoic heritage that prevailed and that ended up allowing the philosophy of modern times to reduce the Aristotelian heritage to almost nothing, whereas for our contemporaries, it is the Aristotelian heritage that seems to be the most interesting (cf. Pellegrin, "Prudence"). But that is to forget that in both cases, it is primarily a question of "virtue" and of what has to be called "wisdom" (*sagesse*). In this sense, if we recall that what Plato opposed to *phronêsis* as "wisdom" or "knowledge" was *aphrosunê*, "madness" (*Timaeus* 71e), it will not be without interest to note that when the Stoics oppose to the primary virtues the primary vices, which they define, consistently with their exposition, as "ignorances [*agnoias* (ἀγνοίας)] of things of which the virtues are the sciences [*epistêmai*]" (Diogenes Laertius, *Lives of the Eminent Philosophers* 7.93), it is again

aphrosunê (*sottise* in the French translation of Diogenes Laertius, ed. and trans. Goulet-Cazé) that, as a "primary" vice, is the contrary of the "primary" virtue *phronêsis*. Of course, we do not speak Greek better than do the Greeks, but we might have expected *aphrosunê* to be opposed not to *phronêsis* but to *sôphrosunê*, that other "primary" virtue that since Cicero we have translated as "temperance" or "moderation," and whose task it is to regulate bodily pleasures, chiefly those of touch and taste, according to Aristotle (*Nicomachean Ethics* 3.13–15; the moderation of the ancients will be opposed to Christian "concupiscence," which has so much to do with vision).

Aphrosunê is not opposed to *sôphrosunê*, however, but characteristically to *phronêsis*, "wisdom," "virtue," or "knowledge." It was the term *akolasia* [ἀκολασία], a word that designates literally the character of that which has not been pruned and has grown all by itself, that the Greeks usually opposed to *sôphrosunê* (cf. Plato, *Republic* 4.431b; Aristotle, *Nicomachean Ethics* 3.15; Diogenes Laertius, *Lives of the Eminent Philosophers* 7.93). The whole question, as Plato and all his posterity said, is education, the crucial period being when the child is learning to control his body (*Republic* 2.377a–b). This explains Aristotle's strange play on words: "That is why we call temperance [*sôphrosunê*] by this name; we imply that it preserves one's practical wisdom [*hôs sôizousan tên phronêsin* (ὡς σῴζουσαν τὴν φρόνησιν)]" (*Nicomachean Ethics* 6.5, 1140b12): one may very well be dissolute and a good mathematician, be drunk and still know that two plus two equals four; but one cannot be both dissolute and prudent.

B. Understanding the Aristotelian circle and contemporary questions

For some of our contemporaries who are quick to seek in Aristotle the solution to the problems we face in dealing with G.W.F. Hegel's strong criticisms of Immanuel Kant and moral formalism, Aristotle is supposed to have developed a formidable circle between *phronêsis* and the three other main moral virtues: we cannot be morally virtuous without prudence, Aristotle says, or prudent without moral virtue (*Nicomachean Ethics* 6.13, 1144b30–32; 10.8, 1178a14–19). But this is to forget that in Aristotle, *phronêsis* is above all a virtue or "excellence," and not just any form of "practical reason," even if it is an "intellectual" virtue. The apparent paradox has to do with the fact that the person who ensures the choice of the happy medium defining moral virtues, namely the prudent person, cannot exist without first having moral virtue, and in particular the moral virtue Aristotle considers the most important of all, *sôphrosunê*, temperance or moderation. But this is a matter of education. The explanation is not at all paradoxical, even in appearance: although moderation is necessary to guarantee the correctness of practical judgments, no such guarantee is necessary to ensure the correctness of theoretical or mathematical judgments, for example. That is why, following in this respect Plato's adage, Aristotle puts such stress on the necessity of giving children a proper upbringing: the desiring part of the soul has to be accustomed to obeying the properly rational part, which will acquire all of its value when the time comes for reason to govern. The virtue of prudence is thus established only in someone who is moderate; in return, moral values, including moderation, with time become authentic virtues and not simple habits, the results of previous training. Aristotle is not caught in a logical circle here; he uses this entailment to guarantee that *phronêsis* will be a virtue, and not mere smartness or terrible skill (*deinotês* [δεινότης], *Nicomachean Ethics* 6.13, 1144a26–34). For, understood as practical intelligence seeking to adjust means to ends, *phronêsis* can indeed be related to the form of wily, tricky intelligence that Détienne and Vernant have so well described in their famous book on the Greeks' *mêtis* [μῆτις] (*Les ruses de l'intelligence*; see MÊTIS). Odysseus's ruses, or those of the octopus, thus sketch the portrait of a certain type of *phronimos*, the "crafty devil." That is why, according to Aristotle, "practical reason" and "deliberative procedures" are in no way proofs of the morality of the person deliberating. Without moral virtues, and first of all moderation, *phronêsis* is no longer a virtue and retains of that characterization—of its status as a virtue—only the worst: the art of adjusting means to ends. In other words, "the end does not justify the means," but it is not for reason—or even for what some of our contemporaries would like to call "practical reason," meaning by that Aristotelian *phronêsis*, and not Kant's *praktische Vernunft*—to ensure the rectitude of the ends: that is a matter of desire—but of a "moderate" desire.

Jean-Louis Labarrière

BIBLIOGRAPHY

Aristotle. *Aristote: L'éthique à Nicomaque*. Edited and translated by R.-A. Gauthier and J.-Y. Jolif. Paris: Nauwelaerts, 1970.

———. *Basic Works of Aristotle*. Edited by R. McKeon. Translated by W. D. Ross. New York: Random House, 1941.

Aubenque, Pierre. *La prudence chez Aristote*. Paris: Presses Universitaires de France, 1963.

Détienne, Marcel, and Jean-Pierre Vernant. *Les ruses de l'intelligence: La mètis des Grecs*. Paris: Flammarion, 1974. Translation by Janet Lloyd: *Cunning Intelligence in Greek Culture and Society*. Atlantic Highlands, NJ: Humanities Press, 1978.

Diogenes Laertius. *Vies et doctrines des philosophes illustres*. Edited and translated by Marie-Odile Goulet-Cazé et al. Paris: Librairie générale française, 1999.

Labarrière, Jean-Louis. "La philosophie morale d'Aristote." In *Dictionnaire d'éthique et de philosophie morale*, edited by M. Canto-Sperber. Paris: Presses Universitaires de France, 1996.

———. "Sagesse et temperance." In *Dictionnaire d'éthique et de philosophie morale*, edited by M. Canto-Sperber. Paris: Presses Universitaires de France, 1996.

———. "La servante de Thalès riait-elle à bon droit?" *Autrement* 20 (1996): 41–56.

Long, Christopher P. "Contingent Knowledge: *Phronêsis* in the *Ethics*." In *The Ethics of Ontology: Rethinking an Aristotelian Legacy*, 131–52. Albany, NY: SUNY Press, 2004.

Pellegrin, Pierre. "Prudence." In *Dictionnaire d'éthique et de philosophie morale*, edited by M. Canto-Sperber. Paris: Presses Universitaires de France, 1996.

Rosen, Stanley. "Phronesis or Ontology: Aristotle and Heidegger." In *The Impact of Aristotelianism on Modern Philosophy*, edited by Riccardo Pozzo, 248–65. Washington, DC: Catholic University of America Press, 2004.

Segvic, Heda. "Aristotle on the Varieties of Goodness," "Aristotle's Metaphysics of Action," and "Deliberation and Choice in Aristotle." In *From Protagoras to Aristotle: Essays in Ancient Moral Philosophy*, edited by Myles Burnyeat, introduction by Charles Brittain, 89–171. Princeton, NJ: Princeton University Press, 2009.

Sophocles. *The Complete Plays of Sophocles*. Translated by R. C. Jebb. New York: Bantam, 1967.

PIETAS (LATIN)

ENGLISH	piety, pity, filial piety
FRENCH	*piété, pitié, piété filiale*
GERMAN	*Frömmigkeit, Mitleid*
GREEK	*eusebeia* [εὐσέβεια]
ITALIAN	*pietà, pietà filiale*
SPANISH	*piedad*

➤ PITY, and DUTY, GOD, *JUSTICE*, LOVE, MENSCHHEIT, MORALS, PARDON, RELIGIO, VIRTUE

The Romance languages, and also English, have words such as *piété* (Fr.), *pietà* (Ital.), *piedad* (Sp.), and *piety* (Eng.) that seem to translate transparently the Latin *pietas* but do not take into account the meaning the Latin word had in the Roman world. That is because the semantic referent of "piety" has come to be limited exclusively to the religious domain as it has been marked out by Christianity. Today, the gap can be seen in the fact that in French the doublet *piété/pitié* has been constituted from a single etymon and that in the parallel doublet in English, "piety"/"pity," the forms thus related took on clearly distinct semantic values as early as the seventeenth century. However, the situation is different in Spanish and Italian, where the use of a single signifier for these two signifieds makes *piedad* and *pietà* more polysemous words. On the other hand, the German words *Frömmigkeit* and *Mitleid* are not derived from the same etymon, nor even from a single one, and thus they are not formally related in any way. *Frömmigkeit*, based on the adjective *fromm*, signifies "pious" in the sense in which one is "imbued with religious consciousness," "submissive to God's will," with which is connected the idea of profit, also found in the Middle High German *vrum, vrom*. *Mitleid*, which means "pity," is composed in the same way as "compassion" (from Lat. *compassio*, Gr. *sumpatheia* [συμπάθεια]) and refers to the fact of "suffering with," of "sharing others' suffering." The Latin *pietas* is based on the adjective *pius*, which relates it etymologically to the Italic languages and probably to *purus* (pure), the original sense of *pius* being perhaps "with a pure heart," in relation to the verb *pio* (to purify; cf. RT: *Dictionnaire étymologique de la langue latine*). But independently of etymological questions, we should restore to *pietas* its own semantic referent, which was first of all pagan and then gradually became Christian, before we consider the evolution of this notion in modern languages.

I. *Pietas*, a Roman Virtue

The Romans thought that they were distinguished from other peoples chiefly by the virtue of *pietas*: "[S]ed pietate ac religione atque hac una sapientia quod deorum numine omnia regi gubernarique perspeximus, omnis gentis nationesque superavimus" ([B]ut by the piety and religion and that unique wisdom through which we have understood that the world is directed and governed by the power of the gods, we have surpassed all other peoples and nations; Cicero, *De haruspicum responsis*, 9.19, in *Orations*). Thus *pietas* enters Cicero's politico-religious philosophy, and then the ideology of the Principate, whose beginnings saw the emergence of the figure of *pius Aeneas*, and as such, "[*pietas*] alone [being able] to indicate the good accord between gods and men because it signifies first of all the concord between the sons and the father, between citizens and the prince . . . , insofar as the destiny of Rome was, for five centuries, to merge with that of the emperor, [it] was to become the basic virtue of Roman history" (Meslin, *L'homme romain*, chap. 5).

Thus *pietas* can be defined as the "feeling of duty," or more exactly as the "disposition to fulfill one's duty toward that to which one owes it," that is, the three constituted entities that are the three spheres of origin and membership in society for the Roman: the family; the homeland (see Cicero, *De inventione* [*On Invention*], 2:66: "pietatem, quae erga patriam aut parentes aut alios sanguine conjunctos officium servare moveat" [piety, which forces us to fulfill our duty to our homeland, our family, and all those who are linked to us by blood]); and finally the gods (see Cicero, *De natura deorum* [*On the Nature of the Gods*], 1.41: "Est enim pietas justitia adversus deos" [Piety is justice toward the gods]). Republican *pietas* was replaced by the *pietas* that is due the emperor, notably in the imperial cult and that is itself relayed by the emperor's *pietas* toward the gods, his relatives, and the citizens of the empire (Ulrich, *Pietas*). The different forms of *pietas* are thus related to these three domains of application. Most often, it is the moral character of this notion that prevails in the different acceptations of the word, but its affective character is also perceptible in drama, for example, in the comedies of Plautus and Terence, and in the epistolary genre. There remained something in this term that attached to the notion of a code, a moral code, for instance; but that *pietas* was somehow "coded" does not necessarily mean that it was cold or rigidified by morality (such are the clichés often governing our image of the Romans), for here it is a matter of expressing love for a father, a mother, a daughter, a brother. . . .

The semantic field of *pietas* includes essentially the terms *honestas*, *dignitas*, and *conscientia*, as far as the subject's internal disposition (Fugier, *L'expression*), and also *officium* and *religio* as the subject's dispositions to a practice and as the exercise of that practice itself. Other terms help determine the meaning of *pietas*. Thus *fides*, as "dictorum conventorum constantia et veritas" (fidelity and sincerity in the words and commitments made; Cicero, *De officiis* [*On Duties*], 1.7), brings out the pertinence of the criterion of membership and origin in the notion of *pietas*. *Voluntas* (see Cicero, *Pro Plancio*, 80: "Quid est pietas nisi voluntas grata in parentes?" [What is piety if not a grateful disposition toward one's parents?]) shows that it is a question of an internal disposition (here, *grata*) relating to others. Finally, *justitia*—which is part of the definition of *pietas* (see Cicero, *De natura deorum*, 1.41, according to a formula that probably goes back to Posidonios), just as *dikaiosunê* [δικαιοσύνη] is part of that of *eusebeia* [εὐσέβεια] (see Plato, *Euthyphro*, 12e)—indicates that this virtue involves performing a duty.

The Greek term *eusebeia*, to which *pietas* corresponds, has a great similarity to the Latin term, since the exercise of this virtue does not apply solely to the gods, but also to family and homeland. However, a first difference between the two terms has to do with the fact that *pius* probably originally meant "with a pure heart," whereas *eusebês* [εὐσεβής], "who respects the gods and their laws," is based on *sebomai* [σέβομαι], "to feel a respectful fear" (RT: *Dictionnaire étymologique de la langue grecque*). A second difference arises especially from the fact that *pietas* is an object of reflection peculiar to Latin authors. For the Romans, the fact that Rome had extended its empire so universally, seeing it as an application of justice in the world of that time in which human realities (*res humanae*) and divine realities (*res divinae*) mutually determined each other, could be explained only by their unfailingly loyal, traditional,

ritual practice of all the forms of duties. Cicero's philosophy (see in particular *De republica*, 1.46.70 and 2.2.4; *De natura deorum*, 3.2.5; *De officiis*, 1.17.53–57) accounts in this way for the fact that in Rome the familial, civic, and religious domains merged in the representation of the sacred character of the Roman lineage. Taken together, the different entities to which *pietas* applied sketch out a continuum that a certain etymological play emphasizes. Thus, *pietas* is exercised toward one's *parentes* and relatives, then toward the homeland, *patria*, which has been received from these *parentes*, and goes back to that of the *patres* and beyond to that of the *majores*. The *parentes* include the *pater*, that is, the *paterfamilias*, one of the representatives of the sequence of generations through which the heritage is made. The word *patres* is also understood politically, the *patria* representing a Rome populated and defended by the heads of families, the *patres*. Finally, the *majores* are those who have given Rome its gods and its cults; thus they have a role in the "miracle" of the origin of Rome, which was later manifested in its conquest of the world, and they transmitted this *mos majorum* that the exercise of precisely this *pietas* from generation to generation is supposed to perpetuate. After Cicero, it was in the succession of the sovereigns of the empire, and of the lineages that "went back" to the heroes and gods (Mars and Venus, Apollo, Hercules, and Jupiter), that the miraculous and sacred character of the Roman lineage was then transmitted.

II. *Pietas, Piété*, and *Pitié*

Under Emperor Constantine, at the time of the official recognition of Christianity (313 CE), the Christian author Lactantius undertook a dialectical reflection against Cicero, whose remarks he discussed and deployed in order to combat his pagan contemporaries. Let us note first that he reconsiders the etymology of *religio* that Cicero had proposed and that he does so by referring to *pietas* in *Divinae institutiones* [*Divine Institutes*], 4.28 (RT: *PL*, vol. 6; see RELIGIO). But above all, in seeking to invalidate the pagan *pietas* by giving the term a new meaning, Lactantius makes reappear as in a photographic negative, so to speak, the conceptual unity peculiar to pagan *pietas*, a *pietas* that is simultaneously familial, sociopolitical, and religious. He defines *pietas*, in fact, in the chapter of his *Divinae institutiones* that is entitled "De justicia": "[S]i ergo pietas est cognoscere deum, cujus cognitionis haec summa est ut colas, ignorat utique justitiam qui religionem non tenet" ([P]iety consists in learning to know God, and if this knowledge is summed up in worshiping him, someone who does not observe the religious worship of God surely is ignorant of justice; ibid., 5.14.12). Lactantius, opposing the Roman religion inherited from the *majores*, defends the religion of the human family that has issued from the same God and Father (ibid., 3.9.19): "pietas autem nihil aliut quam Dei parentis agnitio" [piety is nothing other than the knowledge of God (qua) Father]; the creator of the first couple, who were the parents of a single lineage, of a universal genealogy ("Nam si ab uno homine quem deus finxit omnes origimur, certe consanguinei sumus" [If, in fact, we have been born from this unique man whom God has assuredly made, we are all of the same blood]; ibid., 6.10.4), and thus share a single, identical Christian *pietas* (see also ibid., 2.11.19, 5.6.12, 6.9.21, etc.). Lactantius thereby delimits new contours and introduces new traits into the meaning of *pietas* that include *affectus, misericordia,* and *humanitas.*

A century after Lactantius, Augustine reconsidered the meaning of *pietas* and defined the meaning that was henceforth to prevail in Christianity. Having become a gift (the gift of the Spirit: Is 11:2; 1 Cor 12:1, as Tertullian notes, *Adversus Marcionem*, 3.17.3, and *Adversus Judaeos*, 9.26) and a virtue of the Christian religion, *pietas* also becomes the *vera pietas* that he seeks to define, permanently setting in history and the history of the language the mark of Christian dogma on this element of the Latin lexicon. Alongside the common uses of *pietas* applied by his contemporaries ("dicitur . . . more vulgi") to the accomplishment of duties toward parents or the needy, Augustine distinguishes *pietas* as designating "in the literal sense [*proprie*] the *cultus Dei,* the worship of God" (*Civitas Dei,* 10.1), which is based on the three theological virtues: "qui autem vera pietate in Deum, quem diligit, credit et sperat" (he who, with true piety, believes in God, hopes in him, and loves him; ibid., 5.20). It is this Christian definition of *pietas* that we repeatedly find in medieval literature (Bon and Guerreau-Jalabert, "*Pietas*"). For example, Saint Bernard writes: "[P]ietas est cultus Dei qui constat ex tribus: fide, spe et caritate" ([*Pietas*] is the worship due to God, consisting in three things: faith, hope, and charity; RT: *PL,* vol. 183, *Sententiae,* 3.21). Cicero's definitions were, of course, still frequently cited during the Middle Ages, but the overall logic of the notion of *pietas* and the meaning it had in the Latin of the pagans had, in fact, disappeared. On the other hand, Jerome's translation of the Bible shows that in the late fourth and early fifth centuries, efforts were being made to distinguish a *pietas*-worship that included the domain of Christian religion from another *pietas* which was seen as merely an *affectus* that was, in short, too human or too "pagan." This is the distinction that is the origin of the *piété*/*pitié* doublet in French and the "piety"/"pity" doublet in English, even if its semantic differentiation was established only in the seventeenth century, probably under the influence of the Latin of Christian theologians and of the Church.

In the eleventh century, Old French, as a vernacular language, had two words derived from *pietas,* namely *pitié* and, as a loan word, *piété.* But if this doublet existed formally, the meanings were not yet clearly distinguished: the two terms "appear as synonyms, and both have the meaning of the modern word *pitié*" (Bon and Guerreau-Jalabert, "*Pietas*"), and it was only in the middle of the sixteenth century that a semantic distinction between them appeared and was established in the following century. But at the same time that *piété* was defined as "affection and respect for God and holy things," the term was extended to mean "respectful affection for relatives and the dead" (RT: *Dictionnaire universel*), and the expression *piété filiale,* or "filial piety" (a Latinism, modern dictionaries note), came into use. Contemporary French—in which *piété* is understood primarily as "a fervent attachment to God: respect for religious beliefs and duties" or, like its avatar in the pagan, polytheistic domain, "a feeling of respect for the gods, for religious practices" (being distinguished from *pitié* as "a sympathy that arises from the sight of the sufferings of others and makes us wish them to be relieved")—is thus at least in part heir to this semantic structuring (Bon and Guerreau-Jalabert, "*Pietas*"), which is also found in the two German terms *Frömmigkeit* and *Mitleid*—a circumstance that makes the Latin *pietas* at times very difficult to translate into German today.

The Italian *pietà* in particular poses translation difficulties. In Curzio Malaparte's narrative entitled *La Pelle* (*The Skin*), *pietà*'s polysemy plays a significant role. This novel is imbued with the idea that the modern (*moderno*) Christianity of the American liberators of Italy (following the Second World War), which was full of solidarity but lacking in pity, contrasts with the Neapolitans' piety, into which enters their atavistic pity for other people and for themselves: it is a Christian pity (*pietà cristiana*). Thus the novel describes the "crazy pity" (*pazza pietà*), the "ferocious pity" (*feroce pietà*) of desperate men and women tearing themselves away from the wretched remains of dead bodies that "pity and love" (*pietà e affetto*) make them think they recognize but that becomes "piety and love" (*pietà e affetto*) when these men and women gather to practice the funerary rites over the dismembered cadavers. But there is a play on the double sense of *pietà* that can probably also be found in the French technical term in (Christian) art, *pietà,* borrowed from the Italian, which finally replaced, at the end of the nineteenth century, the synonymous designation *Vierge de pitié* or *Pitié.* And there remains in French, as in most Romance languages, a trace of the *pitié* that also used to mean *piété* in the old expression *mont-de-piété, Monte di Pietà* (It.), or *monte de piedad* (Sp.): pawnshop.

Blandine Colot

BIBLIOGRAPHY

Ball, Robert. "Theological Semantics: Virgil's *Pietas* and Dante's *Pietà*." In *The Poetry of Allusion: Virgil and Ovid in Dante's Commedia,* edited by Rachel Jacoff and Jeffrey T. Schnapp, 19–36. Stanford, CA: Stanford University Press, 1991.

Bon, Bruno, and Anita Guerreau-Jalabert. "*Pietas*: reflexions sur l'analyse sémantique et le traitement lexicographique d'un vocable médiéval." *Médiévales* 42 (2002): 73–88.

Cicero, Marcus Tullius. *Back from Exile: Six Speeches upon His Return.* Translated by D. R. Shackleton Bailey. Chicago: Scholars Press, 1991.

———. *On Duties.* Translated by Walter Miller. Loeb Classical Library. Cambridge, MA: Harvard University Press, 1913.

———. *On Invention; The Best Kind of Orator; Topics.* Translated by H. M. Hubbell. Loeb Classical Library. Cambridge, MA: Harvard University Press, 1949.

———. *On the Nature of the Gods; Academics.* Translated by H. Rackham. Loeb Classical Library. Cambridge, MA: Harvard University Press, 1933.

———. *Orations: Pro Archia Poeta; Post reditum in senatu; Post reditum ad quirites; De domo sua; De haruspicum responsis; Pro Plancio.* Translated by N. H. Watts. Loeb Classical Library. Cambridge, MA: Harvard University Press, 1979.

Colot, Blandine. "'Latin chrétien' ou 'latin des chrétiens': Essai de synthèse sur une terminologie discutée." In *Moussyllanea: Mélanges de linguistique et de littérature anciennes offerts à Claude Moussy,* edited by B. Bureau and C. Nicolas, 411–19. Louvain: Peeters, 1998.

———. "*Pietas*, argument et expression d'un nouveau lien socio-religieux dans le christianisme romain de Lactance." In *Studia patristica,* edited by M. F. Willes and E. J. Yarnold, 23–32. Vol. 34. Louvain: Peeters, 2001.

Fugier, Huguette. *L'expression du sacré dans la langue latine.* Paris: Les Belles Lettres, 1963.

Lactantius. *Divine Institutes.* Translated by Anthony Bowen and Peter Garnsey. Liverpool: Liverpool University Press, 2003.

Meslin, Michel. *L'homme romain.* Paris: Hachette, 1978.

Saller, Richard P. "*Pietas*, Obligation and Authority in the Roman Family." In *Alte Geschichte und Wissenschaftsgeschichte,* edited by Peter Kneissl and Volker Losemann, 393–410. Darmstadt: Wissenschaftliche Buchgesellschaft.

Ulrich, Theodor. *Pietas (pius) als politischer Begriff im römischen Staate bis zum Tode des Kaisers Commodus.* Breslau: Marcus, 1930.

Wagenvoort, Hendrik. *Pietas: Selected Studies in Roman Religion.* Leiden: 1980.

PITY

The doublet *pitié/piété* renders in French the meaning of the Latin virtue par excellence, *pietas*, which designated the feeling of duty toward the gods, ancestors, and the homeland, and later came to refer to the emperor's benevolence. See also PARDON, RELIGIO. On the relationship between humans and God, see *ALLIANCE*; cf. in particular *DESTINY, GOD, HUMANITY, SECULARIZATION*. On the vocabulary of duty, see *OBLIGATION*; cf. in particular DUTY, MORALS, SOLLEN, *VALUE,* WILLKÜR.

➤ LOVE

PLASTICITY

FRENCH   *plasticité*
GERMAN   *Plastizität*
GREEK   *plassein* [πλάσσειν]

➤ ART, AUFHEBEN, BEAUTY, *FICTION, FORM,* GERMAN, I/ME/MYSELF, SPEECH ACT, SUBJECT

It was around the turn of the nineteenth century that the neologism *plasticity* (*plasticité, Plastizität*) made its official appearance in European languages. It joined two already existing words formed on the same root (the Gr. *plassein* [πλάσσειν], "to model or shape"): first, the noun *plastics* (*la plastique, die Plastik*), designating the art of elaborating forms, and more particularly, sculptures; second, the adjective *plastic* (*plastique, plastisch*), which signifies on the one hand "capable of changing form" (like wax or clay), and on the other hand "capable of giving form" (like the plastic arts or plastic surgery; see ART, Box 2). Plasticity qualifies precisely the double aptitude for receiving and producing form.

Hegel was the first to note the frequent but indeterminate use his contemporaries made of this term, and undertook to give it a conceptual value. The two contradictory meanings of receiving and giving form allowed him to situate *Plastizität* in the register of speculative terms with two opposed meanings that were to have great influence on later thought, which found itself obliged, as it were, to invent referents for them. In the case of plasticity, this invention consists of an exportation. Hegel tears it away from its native domain, art, and assigns to it its true domain of validity, the development of subjectivity. Then the essential task of translating the subject is incumbent upon plasticity.

I. Between the Rise and Annihilation of Form: The Meanings of Plasticity

"Plasticity" articulates several meanings, and can thus be broken down into a series of equivalents that never retain more than one characteristic. "Malleability" and *Bildsamkeit* qualify the simple register of receptivity to form. "Formation," "information," *Einbildung*, and *Durchbildung* emphasize only the process of giving form. To be sure, one of the essential aspects of plasticity is indeed its receptiveness to impression: the word "plasticity" designates the ability to be shaped or modeled, including by culture or education (*la plasticité de l'enfant*), and also the ability to adapt or evolve (the plasticity of the brain, the *vertu plastique du vivant*). Nonetheless, while the adjective "plastic" is opposed to "rigid" or "fixed," it does not mean "polymorphous." Something that is plastic retains

form; for example, once shaped, marble cannot recover its initial form. This ability to preserve impressions is precisely what distinguishes plasticity from elasticity, and separates the malleable from the protean.

Thus we can understand why a certain synthetic material that appeared in the early twentieth century was called "plastic": it is capable of taking various forms and properties depending on the uses for which it is intended, but once it is molded, it nonetheless suspends the virtuality of its metamorphoses.

This fidelity to form, in which receptivity and activity are combined, enables us to understand two other recent and apparently contradictory meanings of the term "plastic," one in the realm of histology, the other in that of explosives. In histology, "plasticity" designates the ability of tissues to re-form themselves after having been injured (healing). "Plastic" also refers to a powerful explosive substance. It is as if plasticity put violence at the very heart of regeneration: the ability to receive a form, indeed to re-form tissue after a wound, via the necessity of enduring the explosion of an initial state: the formless, an inadequate or outdated form.

II. Hegel and the Plasticity of the Subject

Hegel sees in plasticity a means, both synthetic and disruptive, of qualifying in a perfectly adequate way the development of subjectivity, that is, the process of self-determination (*Selbstbestimmung*). In the preface to the *Phenomenology of Mind* he writes: "only that philosophical exposition can manage to become plastic in character which resolutely sets aside and has nothing to do with the ordinary way of relating the parts of a proposition." The "parts of a proposition" designate here the subject, the copula, and the predicate. If, according to Hegel, philosophy had up to that point lacked plasticity, that was because it had always considered the subject non-plastic, that is, purely and simply passive, receiving its accidents or predicates from outside, without producing them itself. Conversely, philosophy has conceived the act of predication as a pure and simple imposition of form, an arbitrary movement, a transition (*Übergehen*) between juxtaposed terms consisting in relating the predicate to a subject that remains fundamentally foreign to it. "Usually the subject is first set down as the fixed and objective self; from this fixed position the necessary process passes on to the multiplicity of determinations or predicates." That is why subjectivity, and consequently philosophy, have not yet found their true form.

Excluding this kind of ordinary relationship between the parts of a proposition requires us to break with an excessively narrow understanding of predication that misses the essential point, namely, the mutual determination of the terms themselves that make it possible. The philosophical proposition nonetheless makes this determination manifest insofar as in it subject, copula, and predicate appear as immediately identical. As an example, Hegel takes the proposition "God is Being" as paradigmatic of every philosophical assertion. What is the subject, what is the predicate? And how could one proceed in a linear way from one to the other? "Thinking," Hegel says, "instead of getting any farther with the transition from subject to predicate, in reality finds its activity checked [*gehemmt*] through the loss of the subject, and it is thrown back [*es erleidet . . . einen Gegenstoß*], on the thought of the subject because it misses this subject." This has to do with the fact that the concept—or the speculative content of the proposition—immediately enters into contradiction with its own form insofar as it resists its predicative prolongation. It then deserts it to "return into itself."

For Hegel, this retreat is the real reason that philosophical texts are difficult. The difficulty is not due to the highly technical level of the discourse, but to the strange character of propositions that at first appear to be tautological (the terms of the proposition seem to be equivalent) and heterological (they seem to mean something different from what they say since their own content escapes them). However, this retreat of the concept into itself is an essential moment that prepares the passage from the simply predicative understanding of the proposition to its authentically speculative understanding.

At this point in regression, the subject loses its fixed form. In the first stage of its plasticity it becomes malleable to the point of not having any form. Nonetheless, Hegel says, this retrograde movement does not last: "it is necessary ... that this return of the concept into itself be represented [*dargestellt*]." Having returned to the originary point where it rids itself of all forms, the subject is projected forward to give form—that is, to embody itself in a particular determination. In this way it affirms itself both as subject and as its own predicate: that is the meaning of self-determination. The plasticity of the subject characterizes its capacity to receive and to form its own content—in a word, to self-differentiate itself.

- See Box 1.

The plastic operation constituted by self-determination thus presupposes that the subject is malleable: it has to be capable of ridding itself of its initial form. It also includes a moment of formation: the subject forms its accident by particularizing itself. The synthesis of these two instances, carried out precisely by plasticity, intervening between the rise and annihilation of form, is both a virtuality of explosion (in his article on natural law, Hegel compares the process of mental self-determination to the action of a bomb) and a promise of reparation: meaning, injured by the initial conflict between the content and the form of the proposition, is finally healed, and the philosophical proposition is finally healed.

If "plasticity" had finally to be translated, if its power of translation had to be translated, we might turn to the word "tone" and its derivatives ("tonic," tonality). Etymologically and literally, "tone" (Gr. *tonos* [τόνος]) means "tension," and more precisely "good tension, midway between softness and hardness." Whence its double field of application, medical (in medicine, "tone" refers to the consistency of healthy tissue) and musical. Translated in tonic terms, plasticity appears to be a thing's power of transformation, as Hegel says in the *Science of Logic* (§189), "in its form itself," that is, its ability to sculpt its own becoming.

III. Nietzsche and the Ethical Value of Plasticity

Nietzsche unexpectedly continues along the line of speculative idealism by radicalizing the Hegelian definition of plasticity—the relationship of the subject to the accident, that is, to the event as well. In plasticity, Nietzsche sees the affirmation of becoming. In the second of his "untimely meditations" he declares:

There is a degree of sleeplessness, of rumination, of the historical sense, which is harmful and ultimately fatal to the living thing, whether this living thing be a man or a people or a culture.

To determine this degree, and therewith the boundary at which the past has to be forgotten if it is not to become the gravedigger of the present, one would have to know exactly how great the *plastic power* of a man, a people, or a culture is: I mean by plastic power the

---

1

"Plastic individualities"

Hegel's exportation of the concept of plasticity (see ART, Box 2) from aesthetics into philosophy requires a mediation, which is provided by the concept of Greek "plastic individualities" (*plastische Individuellen*). By this expression Hegel means great historical figures like "Pericles, Phidias, Plato, and especially Sophocles, but also Thucydides, Xenophon, Socrates" who attained in life what statues realize in matter itself: the incarnation of the spiritual. Living sculptures, these are "exemplary" or "substantial" figures. Like statues, "plastic individualities" give body to the mind while at the same time allowing it to be imbued by the Thing itself. Receiving and giving meaning, they are qualified as *selbstdeutende*, self-interpreting.

It is in referring to this auto-exegetical operation characterizing classical art and the Greek mode of being in general that Hegel comes to elaborate the concept of a specifically philosophical plasticity, the mode of being of subjectivity, and first of all the plasticity of the philosophizing subject. In the preface to the *Science of Logic* (1831), Hegel appeals directly to his reader's plasticity: "A plastic presentation [*plastischer Vortrag*] requires a plastic sense of reception and comprehension [*einen plastischen Sinn des Aufnehmens und Verstehens*]." This plastic sense of comprehension requires that the subject allow itself to be dispossessed of its initial form in order to become itself a formative power, that is, an

interpreter. Then the plasticity of the universal subject (*Selbst, Soi*), the specific imprint of subjectivity, which distinguishes it from every other kind of support, is in fact its ability to inform itself, that is, to hold the middle in the perpetual tension of a dialectical uneasiness, between evanescence and petrification.

BIBLIOGRAPHY

Hegel, G.W.F. *Cours d'esthétique*. Vol. 2. Translated by J.-P. Lefebvre and V. von Schenck. Aubier, 1996.
———. *The Science of Logic*. Translated by George Di Giovanni. Cambridge: Cambridge University Press, 2010.

capacity to develop out of oneself in one's own way; to transform and incorporate into oneself what is past and foreign, to heal wounds, to replace what has been lost, to recreate broken moulds.

Later on, plasticity, as life force and regeneration, as a midpoint between an excess of sensitivity and absolute indifference, even appears as an antidote to resentment:

> Ressentiment itself, if it should appear in the noble man, consummates and exhausts itself in an immediate reaction, and therefore does not poison: on the other hand, it fails to appear at all on countless occasions on which it inevitably appears in the weak and impotent. To be incapable of taking one's enemies, one's accidents, even one's misdeeds seriously for very long—that is the sign of strong, full natures in whom there is an excess of the power to form, to mold, to recuperate and to forget. . . .

Genealogy of Morals, First Essay, Section 10

It is clear that plasticity constitutes for Nietzsche a fundamental storehouse of meaning for a new conception of subjectivity that would free it from the form—simultaneously too vague and too strict—of the *cogito* in order to reveal its explosive and creative aspect.

Catherine Malabou

BIBLIOGRAPHY

Hegel, G.W.F. *Aesthetics: Lectures on Fine Art*. Vol. 2. Translated by T. M. Knox. Oxford: Clarendon Press, 1998.

———. *The Encyclopedia Logic, with the Zusätze: Part I of the Encyclopaedia of Philosophical Sciences with the Zusätze*. Translated by Theodore F. Geraets, W. A. Suchting, and H. S. Harris. Indianapolis: Hackett, 1991.

———. "On the Scientific Ways of Treating Natural Law, on its Place in Practical Philosophy, and its Relation to the Positive Sciences of Right." In *Political Writings*. Translated by H. B. Nisbet. Cambridge: Cambridge University Press, 1999.

———. *Hegel's Science of Logic*. Translated by A. V. Miller. Atlantic Highlands, NJ: International Humanities Press, 1969.

———. *Phenomenology of Mind*. Translated by J. B. Baille. Repr. New York: Harper, 1971. First published in 1910.

———. *Phenomenology of Spirit*. Translated by A. V. Miller. Oxford: Clarendon Press, 1977.

Lyotard, Jean-François. *The Differend: Phrases in Dispute*. Translated by Georges Van Den Abbeele. Minneapolis: University of Minnesota Press, 1988.

Malabou, Catherine. *The Future of Hegel: Plasticity, Temporality, and Dialectic*. Translated by Lisabeth During. New York: Routledge, 2005.

Nancy, Jean-Luc. *The Speculative Remark: One of Hegel's Bons Mots*. Translated by Céline Surprenant. Stanford, CA: Stanford University Press, 2001.

Nietzsche, Friedrich. [*On the Genealogy of Morals*.]

· *On the Genealogy of Morality*. Translated by Carol Diethe. New York: Cambridge University Press, 2007.

· *On the Genealogy of Morals*. Translated by Walter Kaufmann and R. J. Hollingdale. New York: Vintage Books, 1989.

· *Première dissertation*. Translated by C. Heim. In *Œuvres philosophiques complètes*, edited by I. Hildenbrand and J. Gratien, vol. 7, 236. Paris: Gallimard, 1971.

———. *Unfashionable Observations*. Translated by Richard T. Gray. Stanford, CA: Stanford University Press, 1998.

———. *Untimely Meditations*. 2nd ed. Translated by R. J. Hollingdale. Cambridge: Cambridge University Press, 1997.

Wake, Peter. "Nature as Second Nature: Plasticity and Habit." In *The Normativity of the Natural*. Edited by Mark J. Cherry. Dordrecht: Springer, 2009.

▌PLEASURE

ENGLISH	pleasure, enjoyment, delight
FRENCH	*plaisir, jouissance*
GERMAN	*Lust, Wohlgefallen, Vergnügen*
GREEK	*hêdonê* [ἡδονή], *chara* [χαρά], *chairein* [χαίρειν], *terpsis* [τέρψις], *euphrosunê* [εὐφροσύνη]
ITALIAN	*piacere, diletto, gusto, godimento*
LATIN	*suavitas, voluptas, delectatio, fruitio*
SPANISH	*goce, gozo, placer*

➤ BEAUTY, DRIVE, GLÜCK, GOÛT, LOVE, *MALAISE*, PATHOS, PHRONÊSIS, PRAXIS, SENSE, SUBLIME, *SUFFERING*, UTILITY

In the main European languages, the vocabulary of pleasure is determined by the heritage of Platonism. Archaic Greek distinguishes between the pleasure of existence (*chairein* [χαίρειν], "to feel joy"; *euphrainô* [εὐφραίνω], "to charm") and pleasure in the object (*terpein* [τέρπειν], "to sate, to enjoy"; *hêdesthai* [ἥδεσθαι], "to find pleasure in"; adj., *hêdus* [ἡδύς], "pleasant," "to qualify the object"). But philosophy chooses to combine all these terms under a generic term: *hêdonê* [ἡδονή]—which renders *voluptas*, pleasure (*plaisir, piacere*, etc.), *Lust*—determined as "the" pleasure in the object par excellence, the pleasure that the body takes in food or in love. Then all pleasure, enclosed in the two dominant systems, pleasure/pain and desire/lack, could be reduced to this yardstick in order to be devalued.

This reduction had several decisive effects on the use of these words in the history of philosophy. For one thing, it led to semantic inventions and refashionings. Sometimes, in fact, distinctions were made either to emphasize a pleasure that is noble or sublimated because of its subject (the Aristotelian god whose act is *hêdonê*; the Kantian soul capable of disinterested *Lust*, as opposed to the *Vergnügen* of the senses) or because of its object (the Spinozist series *titillatio, laetitia, gaudium*). At other times, lower pleasures are rehabilitated to change the relationships between desire and pleasure (*delectatio morosa*) and pleasure and pain (*Lust/Unlust*) and the distinctions between sensible and intelligible, body and soul (delight, joy). On the one hand, it produces a "moral" effect regarding the proper use of pleasures: this is the regime of the "metretic," of moderation, from Aristotle to Foucault.

I. From the Pleasure of Existence to Pleasure in the Object

A. The Greek system: *Charis, euphrosunê, terpsis/hêdonê*

In Homer, the pleasure par excellence is the pleasure of existence, the satisfaction taken in existing fully, which is expressed both as harmony with the outside (*chairein* [χαίρειν], *charis* [χάρις]) and as endogenous harmony (*euphrainô* [εὐφραίνω], *euphrosunê* [εὐφροσύνη]). For example, Odysseus, weeping at Alkinoos's feast, explains, in verses that can only be under- or overtranslated, what is "most beautiful" for him: "I say there is no goal more pleasurable [*telos chariesteron* (τέλος χαριέστερον)] than the good cheer [*euphrosunê*] that imbues a whole group" (*Odyssey*, 9.5–6). The French translator Bérard renders this as "Le plus cher objet de tous mes voeux, je te jure, est cette vie de tout un peuple en bon accord," while Jaccottet renders it as "Croyez-moi en effet, il n'est pas de meilleure vie que lorsque la gaieté règne dans tout le peuple." The verb *chairein* means "to be delighted," "to take pleasure" (in one's heart, in one's mind), and the noun that corresponds to it, *chara* [χαρά], which is frequent in the tragedians, for example, signifies joy in the fullest sense. *Charis*, the deverbal of *charein*, has two main types of meanings. First, it is the life force in its plenitude and superabundance (what Hegel would call *Lebendigkeit*, "liveliness" or "vitality"): the "grace," in the sense of "charm," of a woman; the "virile splendor" of the warrior; the "majesty" and "glory" of kings—in short, the brilliance, whatever it might be, that makes a person radiant (thus, before Odysseus appears before Nausicaa or Penelope, "Athena gilded with grace his head and shoulders"; *Odyssey*, 6.235, 23.162, etc.); similarly, adolescence is "the most graceful time of young manhood" (*chariestatê hêbê* [χαριεστάτη ήβη], ibid., 10.279). It is also "grace" in the sense of "favor" (including the "favors" granted by women: "The ancients called *charis* woman's spontaneous consent to the male"; Plutarch, "On Love," 751e) and "gratitude" that prevails in the feasting and presides over the exchange; the verb *charizesthai* [χαρίζεσθαι] means "to be pleasing to someone," "to gratify" (cf. the common prepositional turn of phrase genitive + *charin* [χάριν]: "for the pleasure of," e.g., *legein logou charin*, "to speak for the pleasure of speaking" [Aristotle, *Metaphysics*, 4.5, 1009a 21], and the Latin *gratia* + ablative [see RT: *Le vocabulaire des institutions indo-européennes*, 1:201]). Thus, in each occurrence of *charis*, it is a question of a pleasure that is attached to the person himself and not to objects or activities.

The myth tells us this in its own way: the "beautiful *Charis*" is the hospitable wife of Hephaistos (*Iliad*, 18.382), and the *Charites*, the three Graces born of Zeus and the daughter of Oceanus, live with the Muses on Olympus (Hesiod, *Theogony*, 64.907–11) and "accompany all the gods" (Homer, "To Aphrodite," v. 95). Their name indicates that they are divinities of beauty and seduction, of abundance, of the power of nature: Thalia (lit. "young shoot," "abundance," "feast"), Agleia (lit. "brilliant," "radiant"); as for the third, Euphrosune (from *eu* [εὖ], "good," and *phrên* [φρήν], "mind"), her name directly expresses the pleasure of existence and, par excellence, the merriment of feast and the banquet, the "good humor," well-being, and joie de vivre that, as we have seen, "imbues a whole group" when "the feasters up and down the houses are sitting in order / and listening to the singer, and beside them the tables are loaded / with bread and meats, and from the mixing bowl the wine steward / draws the wine and carries it about and fills the cups" (*Odyssey*, 9.7–10).

- See Box 1.

In the *euphrosunê* of the banquet, the pleasure of existence is already connected with enjoyment of the object. The verb *terpein* [τέρπειν] (more often used in the mediopassive *terpesthai* [τέρπεσθαι]) also designates the joy of the feast, pleasure that is simultaneously physical, social, and aesthetic and that is enjoyed with food, music, and song (e.g., *Odyssey*, 8.45). It expresses essentially the idea of full satisfaction ("to find full satisfaction of one's desire": Chantraine [RT: *Dictionnaire étymologique de la langue grecque*], following Latacz [*Zum Wortfed "Freude"*]; the Greek term can be related to Sanskrit *tarpayati*, "to be satisfied"), which explains the extent of its application—from sexual relations to knowledge. This idea of plenitude helps us understand why *terpesthai* expresses particularly well the pleasure taken in nonmaterial things and in activities that have to do with togetherness, that involve

play, and that produce harmony. Thus the Muses, by singing for Zeus, "rejoice his great spirit" (*humneusai terpousi megan noon* [ύμνεῦσαι τέρπουσι μέγαν νόον]; Hesiod, *Theogony*, 37), and *terpsis* expresses the irresistible, lethal charm of the Sirens' singing (*Odyssey*, 12.52.186–8: "for no one else has ever sailed past this place in his black ship / until he has listened to the honey-sweet voice that issues / from our lips; then goes on, well pleased [*ho terpsamenos* (ὅ τερψάμενος)], knowing more than ever"). A formula of Democritus also reflects this particular sense of *terpein*: "*tôn hedeôn ta spaniôtata ginomena malista terpei* [τῶν ἡδέων τὰ σπανιώτατα γινόμενα μάλιστα τέρπει]" (among pleasing things, we enjoy most those that come most rarely; B 232, RT: DK). *Terpsis* is thus characterized as a pleasure taken in the exercise of one's faculties and in registering nonmaterial objects, without the constraint of need—more than a pleasure, a bliss.

The substantive *hêdonê* [ἡδονή] is not found in Homer, but the adjective *hêdus* [ἡδύς] (pleasant) is, regularly designating pleasant objects and primarily, once again, the pleasures of the table: eating and drinking. Etymologically, a *hedus* is someone who has good taste: Chantraine (RT: *Dictionnaire étymologique de la langue grecque*) relates *hêdomai* (= *domai*) to the Sanskrit *svadate*, "to take good taste" (whence the Latin *suavitas*), and Greek also has the verb *hêdunô* [ἡδύνω], which means "to season," whence "to charm." This pleasure, irreducible because it is initially linked with the satisfaction of natural needs, can also turn out to be harmful because of the negative counterparts of the object of pleasure (as for the Cyclops, who "was terribly / pleased with the wine he drank [*hêsato d'ainôs hêdu poton pinôn* (ήσατο δ' αἰνῶς ἡδὺ ποτὸν πίνων)]"; *Odyssey*, 9.353–4, the only occurrence of the verb *hêdesthai* in Homer). On the whole, the archaic uses of *hêdesthai* and of *hêdus* refer to physical pleasure and involve contact, whether it is a matter of touching or of taste (cf. RT: LSJ, s.v. [ἡδονή] 2), connecting the feeling with an object that is its cause and is thus qualified as *hêdus*.

Prodicus, following Plato (*Protagoras*, 337c, 358a; cf. Aristotle, *Topics*, 2.112b 22–24), still makes a careful distinctionbetween the *charis* and the *terpsis* of the *hêdonê*—too careful, because this lexical detail runs counter to the Platonic operation, which consists in merging all pleasures under the generic term *hêdonê* (which becomes established in the fourth century) the better to depreciate them ontologically. In the *Philebus* (On Pleasure [*Peri hêdonês*]), Plato deliberately puts *charein* or *chara*, *terpsis*, and *hêdonê* all on the same level (11b 4–5 and 19c 7), concluding with the depreciation of *chairein* ("all the oxen and horses and every other animal that exists tell us so by their pursuit of pleasure [*chairein*]"; 67b 1–2; Hackforth translation). The unification of pleasures under *hêdonê* is accompanied by an ontological hierarchization of true, pure pleasures on the one hand and impure pleasures on the other. In both cases, Plato analyzes *hêdonê* on the model of the satisfaction of physical needs: it is pleasure-repletion (*plêrosis* [πλήρωσις]; cf. *Gorgias*, 493d–494e), impure pleasure being a pleasure associated with pain, whereas pure pleasure, taken, for example, in things that are always beautiful in themselves, is presented as a sublimated pleasure, involving a fulfillment unaccompanied by need or suffering (*Philebus*, 50a 1–51b 7). Consequently, a happy life is no

1

Chaire, or how to greet

Comparing the two great traditional formulas of salutation, each of which connotes a different priority in the shared perception of the world, is very informative.

The Greek expression is *Chaire* [Χαῖρε], "Rejoice!" "Be glad (you're alive)!" That is, Lucian tells us, a formula that Homer always used, not only when people saw each other for the first time, but even when they separated and hated each other. In its classical sense, the term obviously refers to joy, and in particular to the joy of victory (*charma* [χάρμα] is the "desire for combat" and, with a concrete value, the word designates a "lance point" [Stesichorus, fr. 267 Page; cf. RT: *Dictionnaire étymologique de la langue grecque*]), and the first to use it is supposed to have been either Philippides, the messenger from Marathon, exhaling the word with his last breath, or Cleon, addressing the Athenian people after the Battle of Sphacteria (424 BCE). Pleasure and joy in life are certainly implied, as is shown by the criticism of the common epistolary formula found at the beginning of the *Third Letter* attributed to Plato: "[Plato] to Dionysius, Joy [*Chaire*]! Is it the best form of salutation to wish you 'joy' as I have, or would it be better if I were to follow my usual

custom [*eu pratte* (εὖ πράττε)] and bid you 'Do well'?" ("act well," "succeed," which Bailly renders in French, emphasizing the "success" aspect, by *bonne chance*, and Brisson, more correctly and emphasizing the moral condition of happiness, by a play on words: "[com] porte-toi bien"; Diogenes Laertius, 3.61). "That is the salutation that I use when I write to my friends. You of course descended to flattery and addressed even the god at Delphi in these very terms . . . and wrote, they say, 'Joy to you [*Chaire*]. Keep ever the pleasant life of a tyrant'" (*Collected Dialogues*).

It is an inappropriate flattery, because, as the *Charmides* (164e) notes, the god at Delphi addresses humans with a "far superior salutation" when he says "Know thyself" instead of *Chaire*, in order to exhort them "not to rejoice, but to be wise" (or "moderate": *sôphrônein* [σωφρωνεῖν]). Finally, Pythagoras, among others, is supposed to have chosen to say *Hugiaine* [Ὑγίανε], "Health," implying at the same time acting well and joy. This formula, generally reserved for saying farewell, is already very Roman.

In Latin, when one arrives, one says *aue* or *haue* (this may be an adaptation of a Punic

word, according to Ernout and Meillet, RT: *Dictionnaire étymologique de la langue latine*, who report that "the formulas of salutation are often borrowed"), and when one leaves one says *vale* ("Be well," "Good health," from *valere* "to be strong," "to be powerful," physically, but also socially). We may compare this with the beautiful wish for peace that is daily expressed in Hebrew and in Arabic and with the most banal wish for a "good" period of time (*bonjour*, *bonsoir*, "good morning," *buenos días*, or even *bonne continuation*), which usually serves as a salutation—or a farewell—in our modern European languages.

BIBLIOGRAPHY

Diogenes Laertius. *Lives of Eminent Philosophers*. Translated by R. D. Hicks. Loeb Classical Library. Cambridge, MA: Harvard University Press, 1972.

Lucian. "A Slip of the Tongue in Greeting." In *Lucian*, Vol. 6. Translated by K. Kilburn. Loeb Classical Library. Cambridge, MA: Harvard University Press, 1960–67.

Plato. *The Collected Dialogues of Plato*. Translated by L. A. Post and edited by E. Hamilton and H. Cairns. Princeton, NJ: Princeton University Press / Bollingen, 1961.

longer linked with pleasure, with *hêdonê*, but with wisdom, with *phronêsis* [φρόνησις] (see PHRONÊSIS) (12b).

The major later conceptualizations attempt, each in its own way, to go beyond or to undo the framework thus sketched out by Plato; in doing so they nonetheless follow Plato, concerning whom it is right to emphasize that, as always, he goes beyond himself. In Aristotle and Epicurus, the term *hêdonê* prevails, but it is reinvested, at least in part, as pleasure in existence. Aristotle separates *hêdonê* from its bodily model (see Plato, *Republic*, 9.584c): pleasure, felt by the mind alone, even if the source of the affect is bodily (cf. *Nicomachean Ethics*, 10.2), is primarily connected with life (*zôê* [ζωή]) and with *energeia* [ἐνέργεια], the activity, or actuality, that defines it (10.4.1175a 12). It follows that no pleasure is movement or becoming, because pleasure is "perfect, complete in its form [*teleion to eidos* (τέλειον τὸ εἶδος)] at every moment" (10.4.1174b 5–6). *Hêdonê* completes the act as an end given over and above (it is added "as the bloom of life is added to those who are at the acme of their strength [hoion tois akmaiois hê hôra (οἷον τοῖς ἀκμαίοις ἡ ὥρα)]"; 10.4.1174b 10) and acquires its value from the act itself to which it is joined. That is why the happy life of wisdom is also the most pleasing (10.7.1177a 4: "pleasure has to be mixed with happiness"); the greatest pleasure is that of the act of thinking, and the prototype of this is the pleasure of the first mover, pure act ("its actuality is also pleasure"; *Metaphysics*, 50.7.1072b 15). But the most complete reversal is carried out by Epicurus, who proceeds to redifferentiate *hêdonê* positively, neither devaluing

nor sublimating physical pleasure because he recognizes it, on the contrary, as the prime good ("the pleasure of the belly [*tês gastros hêdonê* (τῆς γαστρὸς ἡδονή)] is the principle and root of all good"; *Athenaea* 546F, RT: *The Hellenistic Philosophers*). The prime pleasure is the pleasure of movement (*kata kinêsin* [κατὰ κίνησιν]), which alleviates suffering. The result is a second type of pleasure, a stable pleasure (*katasthêmatikê* [καταστηματική]), which corresponds to the calming itself, the absence of pain in the body (*aponia* [ἀπονία]) and the absence of disturbance in the mind (*ataraxia* [ἀταραξία]). This stable pleasure is the true principle of happiness as state of pleasure, the pleasure of existing. The use (*chreia* [χρεία]) of pleasures must enable us to include the various kinds of pleasure in the stable unity of a life. The stability of the body thus makes possible the pure pleasures of the mind, consisting in an autonomous movement of the mind alone, which express themselves in the vocabulary of *chara* and *euphrosunê* and reinvest them. "Epicurus, in his treatise *On Choices*, puts it this way: 'The absence of [mental] disorder and the absence of pain are static pleasures, whereas joy and gaiety are perceived in the act in a movement [ἡ μὲν γὰρ ἀταραξία καὶ ἀπονία εἰσὶν ἡδοναί· ἡ δὲ χαρὰ καὶ ἡ εὐφροσύνη κατὰ κίνησιν ἐνέργει βλέπονται]'" (Diogenes Laertius, *Lives*, 10.136).

B. *Voluptas*

In Latin, the adjective *hêdus* and the noun *hêdonê* are translated, in conformity with their etymology, by *suavis* and *suavitas*. But Cicero prefers the term *voluptas* (which, according to RT: *Dictionnaire étymologique de la langue latine*, may derive from *volo*, with a broadening *p* from the Greek *elpomai*, which means "to hope," "to wait for something"), asserting that *voluptas* renders the Greek *hêdonê* in Latin more precisely than any other word (*De finibus*, 2.13).

In philosophical Latin, the vocabulary of pleasure is completely dominated by the role played by Epicureanism in Rome. Epicureanism was disseminated by Lucretius, whose *De rerum natura* begins by celebrating Venus as the mother of the nine Egyptian divinities, the Enneads, and as the pleasure of men and gods alike ("Aeneadum genetrix, horminum divomque voluptas"; *De rerum natura*, 1.1). The term *voluptas* is used in most occurrences as the exact equivalent of the Epicurean *hêdonê*, and the context is that of ethical doxography (see particularly Cicero, *De finibus* and *Tusculan Disputations*, and Seneca, *De vita beata* and *De beneficiis*).

Voluptas, as the principle and end of Epicurean doctrine, is opposed to *labor* and *dolor*; these are the choices open to *virtus*. The conventional images in which *voluptas*, "pale and painted," serves as a foil to a tanned and robust *virtus*, covered with dust and watching over institutions (Seneca, *De vita beata*, 8), are so many variations on Prodicus's apologue showing Hercules at the intersection of vice and virtue (Cicero, *De officiis*, 1.118). Here, the condemnation of Epicurean *voluptas* draws on elements that Roman civic morality borrowed from Cynicism and Stoicism and reduces the meaning of the term to physical pleasures. But neither Cicero nor Seneca limits himself to this meaning: they both know that the word *voluptas* can also express the pleasure of the search for truth or aesthetic pleasure; and when they use the word with these meanings, they do not differ from the Epicureans, for whom *voluptas* is both the most physical pleasure (that of the newborn child and the dissolute person) and the most moralized pleasure (that of the sage who makes the suffering of a mortal illness disappear by remembering with pleasure conversations with friends). Seneca assumes this ambiguity when he uses, to evoke the joys provided by making friends, the words *delectatio*, *jucunditas*, and *oblectamentum* (*Epistulae*, 9). He even goes so far as to reject the restrictive sense given *voluptas* by the Stoics, resorting instead to the common use (ibid.: the pleasure of reading a friend's letter). This use is already documented in Cicero, who mentions the peasant's *voluptas* in seeing the natural growth of plants and the *voluptas* of aging writers who contemplate their works (*De senectute*, 50). Similarly, the vocabulary of aesthetic pleasure used in the part of *De oratore* devoted to *movere* (i.e., how to move the audience; 2.18.121) makes the transition from the pleasure of the senses to the pleasure of judgment with the terms *venustas, suavitas*, and *lepos* (ibid., 3.46.181).

But Cicero's refutation of the doctrine of pleasure depends on a series of distinctions: first of all, it is important not to confuse a being's primary tendency to preserve itself with the "constitutive pleasure" that the Epicureans accorded to the infant and the sage. It is also necessary to distinguish a neutral state of the body, the absence of pain (*indolentia*), from the movements aroused by *voluptas* (whereas the Epicureans defined pleasure by the cessation of suffering). Finally, *voluptas* has to be characterized by a potential for excess, whereas the Epicureans postulated that the body set natural limits to pleasure. To forestall this

moralization of the body—and also to keep his fellow citizens from preferring the *voluptas* of contemplation to political work—Cicero tried to establish a linguistic distinction between the pleasures of the body and those of the mind, but it is not clear-cut. This attempted distinction—whose stakes are philosophical and political—involves a reorganization of the vocabulary of pleasure that claims to be based on the meanings of words documented by the founders of Latin literature. This is shown quite clearly by a passage in *De finibus* (2.13–14):

> What I mean by *voluptas* is exactly what he [Epicurus] means by *hêdonê*. . . . No Latin word can be found which captures a Greek word more exactly than *voluptas* does. Everyone in the world who knows Latin takes this word to convey two notions: elation in the mind [*laetitia in animo*], and a delightfully sweet arousal in the body [*commotionem suavem jucunditatis in corpore*]. This elation is described by one character in Trabea as "excessive mental pleasure" [*voluptatem animi nimiam*] and by another in Caecilius when he tells us he is "glad with every gladness" [*omnibus laetitiis laetum*]. But there is the following difference: the term "pleasure" [*voluptas*] is applicable to the body as well as the mind (in the latter case it is an example of vice according to the Stoics, who define it as "the irrational exulting of a mind that takes itself to be enjoying some great good"), whereas elation [*laetitia*] and joy [*gaudium*] are not applicable to the body. Every Latin speaker takes pleasure [*voluptas*] to consist in the perception of some delightful stimulation [*cum percipitur ea, quae sensum aliquem moveat jucunditas*]. The term "delight" [*jucunditas*] may, if you wish, also be applied to the mind, since "to delight" [*juvare*] can be used in either case, as can "delightful" [*jucundus*], which is derived from it. It must, however, be understood, that someone might say, "I am so elated [*tanta laetitia auctus sum*] that everything is in a whirl," and someone else might say, "Truly my mind is now in torment." The former is wildly delighted, the latter racked with pain, but there is room in the middle for neither joy nor anguish. Likewise, in the case of the body, between the enjoyment of the most sought after pleasure, and the agony of the most intense pains, there is the condition that is free of either.

Although the distinctions proposed by this text have been hardened by the requirements of polemics, they nonetheless helped influence all the uses of the vocabulary of pleasure in Cicero's readers, from Seneca to Augustine.

II. From Desire to Pleasure: *Delectatio*, "Delight," *Lust*

A. *Delectatio*, or the snares of interiorized pleasure

Plato had already conceived the so-called impure *hêdonê* on a physiological model as repletion or satisfaction of a lack that is in itself painful: the fact that suffering preceded or accompanied pleasure sufficed, in his view, to deprive it of any claim to constitute a good. But on the one hand, "pure" *hêdonê* persisted; on the other hand, the quest for moderation was still possible. If the pleasures of food or sex tended, in fact, to enslave desire (*epithumia* [ἐπιθυμία]), which they aroused and disappointed in an endless spiral, temperance allowed one to escape the panic of pleasure-seeking desire. Thus *hêdonê* ceases to have a pejorative value here only when it is either repressed or transposed into the search for truth. But with Christianity, the status of pleasure with respect to desire changed in a significant way: far from seeing in it a pure *appetitus* that finds pleasure only when it has attained its object, moralists saw desire as being already imbued with pleasure. That is what is at stake in the medieval debates on the problem of *delectatio morosa*.

- See Box 2.

The development of this problem also corresponds to an inflection of the concept of *delectatio* that also involves the etymology of the term. The Latin *delectatio*—from which the Old French *delit* (pleasure), modern French *délice*, and English "delight" derive—comes, in fact, from *lax* (*lacio*), which means "trap" or "snare"—whence *delicere*, "to catch someone in one's nets." These nets may remain sensible in nature, *delectatio* as such then being not at all suitable for the wise man. Nonetheless, *delectare vel conciliare* (to please or conciliate) is the second of the goals of ancient rhetoric, according to Cicero, the first being *docere* (to instruct), and the third *movere* (to move), or *flectere* (to persuade). Augustine distinguishes

two aspects in *delectatio*: first, the attraction an object exercises on the mind (he repeatedly bases this on a quotation from Virgil's *Bucolics* [2.65]: "Trahit sua quemque voluptas" [His (desire for) pleasure draws each one on]), and second, the joy the will takes in possessing the desired object. Augustine, who often plays, as do later Christian authors, on the alliteration between *dilectio* and *delectatio*, points out that the latter is precisely what the former seeks in its object and that therefore there can be no love without delight: "Non enim amatur nisi quod delectat" (*Sermon*, 159, RT: *PL* 38, col. 869). Regarding this alliteration, we can note that in modern Italian the same word, *diletto*, signifies "beloved" or "darling" when it is an epithet and "charm," "attraction," or "pleasure" when it is a noun: that is because it derives from *dilectus* in the first case and from *delectatio* in the second, whereas *dilettante* participates in both meanings and in this double etymology.

In addition, Augustine acknowledges an intellectual delight (*delectatio mentis*), holy and celestial, which he puts in opposition to earthly or physical delight (*delectatio carnis*), both being part of *appetitus*. Thus for Scholastic theologians, *appetitus* oscillates between two extreme types of pleasurable things: the *delectabile sensibile* (pleasurable sensation) and the *summum delectabile* (greatest pleasure). When, in

---

2

Delectatio morosa

In the field of moral philosophy, the close relationship between pleasure and desire has opened up a set of problems that Christian theologians have called *delectatio morosa* since the second half of the twelfth century. This expression, when translated into French as *délectation morose*, leads to a kind of misinterpretation. The epithet *morosa* refers here not to a complacent pleasure in some "morose" thought, but rather to the pleasure that the imagination savors deliciously as it is expectantly waiting (Lat. *moratur*) in the desire for an object that remains absent because it is inaccessible or prohibited.

The conception of such a *delectatio* inherent in desire itself represents an important turning point in relation to the conception of desire in late Greek antiquity. For Plato in particular, bodily appetites and sensuality are irremediably insatiable, whether they involve—according to the triad mentioned in the *Republic* (580e) and destined to become traditional—food, drink, or erotic pleasures, to which we must add money as a means of acquiring such pleasures. In relation to each of these objects, the desiring mind, like the Danaides with their pierced jar, sees what it is waiting for constantly escaping it: the more it seeks to fill itself up, the more it empties out. Desire, except in the case of someone whose object of desire is wisdom, is thus

condemned to be repeatedly reborn, always remaining unsatisfied and insatiable. But drawing on the Gospel according to which "everyone who looks lustfully at a woman has already committed adultery with her in his heart" (Mt 5:28), Christian authors problematized this relationship between pleasure and desire in an entirely different way. They wanted to consider—and denounce, since in their view it involved forbidden lusts—less the insatiability of desire than the presence of pleasure within it, as if the simple imaginary representation of the desired object procured an enjoyment analogous to that of actual possession. It was in the context of a debate on the degree of culpability that might burden the spontaneous movement of sensuality (*primus motus sensualitas*) before the will's explicit consent that the moralists developed, especially in the Middle Ages, the topos of *delectatio morosa* to produce a veritable psychology of the pleasure that is supposed to be provided by complacent savoring of the imaginary representation of a prohibited act.

But as we have said, the expression *delicatio morosa*, which by itself evoked the gloomy idea of culpability only for Christian morality (which was later to criticize this psychic attitude as "sinning through thought"), raises a translation problem in languages such as English and French, in which the epithet

"morose" generally serves to quality a morbid state imbued with sadness or despondent rumination. The Latin word *morosus*, in fact, has a double etymology: when written with the first syllable long, it derives from *mos, moris* (character trait, with a pejorative connotation of being difficult, somber, and acrimonious); when written with the first syllable short, it comes from the verb *moror, -aris* (to linger, to wait) and from the noun *mora* (delay, stop, pause). Since French and English have retained (except in the case of the contemporary use of *moratoire* and "moratorium," respectively) only the meaning corresponding to the first etymology, it is very difficult for them to understand the medieval epithet *morosa*, which refers to the second meaning and qualifies the joy that one can draw, in one's own heart, from desire itself. In Italian, on the other hand, where *morosità* means "delay" (particularly in acquitting oneself of a debt or an obligation), and where the French *morosité* or English "moroseness" is rendered by *malinconia* or *tristezza*, and in Spanish, where *morosidad* also means "delay" and *moroso* means "lazy" ("morose" being translatable by *taciturno*), the true meaning of the Scholastic *delectatio morosa* is more easily accessible, namely the meaning of a complacent pleasure that the mind takes in entertaining at length the fantasy of the desired object.

speaking of *delectatio morosa*, these authors draw attention to the snares connected with the stasis of desire that lingers (*moratur*) on the image of the object, we understand how *delectatio* came to be predestined, as it were, to qualify aesthetic delight: the delight one takes in the object with relative indifference to its existence or its possession. Thus in his definition of painting, Poussin declares that the goal of this art is delight (*délectation*), understood, following the critics of the late sixteenth century, as the delight of the mind and not that of the senses (*Lettres et propos sur l'art*).

B. "Delight" and the distancing of the reality of suffering

In the English term "delight," the idea of lingering is combined with that of the distancing in relation to pain that characterizes, according to Edmund Burke, the aesthetic and transaesthetic feeling of the sublime. Burke was probably the first to distinguish clearly, beyond indifference and the pure forms of pain or pleasure, a "relative displeasure" that arises from a distancing of pleasure and is called, depending on the case, "grief" or "disappointment," and a "relative pleasure" that accompanies the slow disappearance of suffering. Lacking an available word, Burke calls the latter "delight," explaining the intensity inherent in it by the underlying idea of a victory over pain. His contrast between delight and pleasure runs counter to common usage, and he sums it up this way:

> Whenever I have occasion to speak of this species of relative pleasure, I call it *Delight*; and I shall take the best care I can, to use that word in no other sense. I am satisfied that the word is not commonly used in this appropriated signification; but I thought it better to take up a word already known, and to limit its signification, than to introduce a new one which would not perhaps incorporate so well with the language. I should never have presumed the least alteration of our words, if the nature of the language, framed for the purposes of business rather than those of philosophy, and the nature of my subject that leads me out of the common track of discourse, did not in a manner necessitate me to it. I shall make use of this liberty with all possible caution. As I make use of the word *Delight* to express the sensation which accompanies the removal of pain or danger; so when I speak of positive pleasure, I shall for the most part call it simply *Pleasure*.
>
> (*A Philosophical Enquiry*)

C. *Lust* and the *Lust/Unlust* pair

The initial meaning of the German word *Lust* does not seem to have been "pleasure." Like the English "lust," it derives from the Indo-European **lutan*, which means "to submit," "to bend," and is supposed to have originally designated only a more or less resistable inclination. But whereas English "lust" has retained the restricted meaning of "unbridled desire," "cupidity," or "craving," the semantic range of the German term extends from "appetite," "sexual desire" (*Ich habe Lust von dir* always means "I want you"), or "fantasy" to all the forms of satisfaction. In short, the semantic field of *Lust* extends beyond the sensible affect of pleasure to designate the desire that is *Lust*'s origin and effect.

In its philosophical usage, *Lust* is frequently followed by *Unlust*, without it being very clear whether *Lust* arises of its own accord or from the suppression of *Unlust*. *Unlust* poses a translation problem still more complex than *Lust*: Is the negation logical or real? Does it designate the absence of desire (indifference), reverse desire (repulsion), relative displeasure (grief), or positive displeasure (pain)? The register of *Unlust* is very broad.

1. *Lust* and *Unlust* in Kant

Kant makes *Lust* a genus within which he distinguishes two species, sensible and intellectual: the former divided into sensual and aesthetic, and the latter into theoretical and practical subspecies. Hence, there are several sources of ambiguity in translations. When we read in French versions of the *Critique of Judgment* that the feeling of respect for moral ideas "n'est pas un plaisir" (is not a pleasure), we have to realize that Kant does not use *Lust* here, but rather *Vergnügen*, a term that could be rendered in French by *contentement* to take into account the root of the adverb *genug*, which means "enough," "sufficiently." A purely physical pleasure constitutes the core of *Lust*. But as soon as we seek to connect it with concepts or Ideas, don't we lose sight of the aspect of organic comfort? How can the most individually subjective sensible affect be combined with a universal representation? Kant shifts the meaning of *Lust* in a decisive way by giving it a de jure universality in the domain of aesthetics. Refusing to see in it the cause or effect of the representation, he promotes it to the rank of a "predicate of a representation": the exclamation "It's beautiful!" can then be a judgment in the absence of any concept. Now we have to understand that alongside aesthetic *Lust*, we find what Kant calls teleological *Lust*. The first type of *Lust* is connected with the mode of the object's presentation; the second considers its end or its concept, which, without determining the object, nonetheless makes reflection on its content possible.

If in these two cases the translation by "pleasure" is insufficient, that is because of *Lust*'s tendency to maintain or reproduce the representative state that it provides. *Lust* is both pleasure and the desire for pleasure; the pleasure received is interwoven with the pleasure desired. That is not the case in the practical domain, where *Lust* is correctly translated by "pleasure," since the German term is connected with the realization of an intention and not with the desire for a subjective state. Let us stress, in this regard, the historical import of the linguistic division that leads Kant to choose desire-pleasure, *Lust*, to designate the faculty of aesthetic judgment, reserving *Begierde* (from *Gier*, "avidity") to signify desire-will, under the legislation of practical reason.

It will be noted that the *Lust/Unlust* opposition in the physiological register leads Kant, in a framework derived from Stahl, Hoffman, Haller, and Burke, to distinguish between the feeling of life being advanced and that of life being constrained: the latter is an essential preoccupation, since an uninterrupted joy might soon lead to death from overstimulation. In the aesthetic order, a tempered, direct, and positive pleasure is contrasted with a violent, indirect, and negative pleasure. The beautiful will then function to produce *Lust*, as a kind of favor, while the sublime will ensure the rise of *Lust* from *Unlust*, thus granting the witness of the sublime a sort of coerced privilege (see SUBLIME). The subject finds himself forced to experience the intense pleasure of the sublime, whereas in his taste for the beautiful, he freely enjoys the harmony of the representative state and of the communicability of a feeling connected with a representation. We have to observe that, when the sublime is involved, the translation of *Lust* by "pleasure" becomes a particular source of misunderstanding: in English and French, the idea of pleasure is disconnected from that of desire, where the idea of pleasure remains linked with favor and does not tolerate well the presence of a constraint.

2. *Lust* and *Unlust* in Freud

Under the impact of Kant's speculations on sensual pleasure and aesthetic pleasure, *Lust* and *Unlust* henceforth tended to be associated with a pair of oppositions—no longer in order to stigmatize, in the Platonic manner, the impurity of their alliance, but rather that the effects of their rivalry might be recognized: *Lust* and *Unlust* are less final causes consciously determining action than efficient causes implementing mechanisms of appropriation or avoidance. Thus Freud recognizes in *Lust* and *Unlust* the principles of psychic life that mark the paths to be followed or avoided and regulate the psychic apparatus's functioning.

More than that, Freud, presupposing a form of continuity between the initial functions and the superior functions of the mind, considers judgment as the "appropriated evolution" of absorption into the ego and of expulsion from the ego. "Affirmation—as a substitute for union—belongs to Eros; negation—a result of rejection—belongs to the drive to destruction" ("Negation"). Instinctive repulsion already prefigures a concerted rejection, and although *Unlust* may risk slipping into the form of destructive misunderstanding from which repression springs, it nonetheless constitutes the germ of the symbol of negation. *Lust* and *Unlust* are thus two opposed sources of judgment: those of the judgment of attribution, which concerns the (good or bad) property attributed to a thing, and those of the judgment of existence, which posits the existence or nonexistence of a reality peculiar to my representation (see VERNEINUNG).

But since the affective process is forced to actualize itself more in repulsion than in assimilation, Freud tends to credit *Unlust* with a more important role than *Lust*. Conceiving negation in terms that are no longer solely dynamic but also economic, he seeks to grasp the stages of the transformation of desire and stresses the capacities of *Lust* and especially *Unlust* for metamorphosis and their "sublimating possibilities," noting especially the relation between preliminary pleasure and the activity of thinking. The problems Freud encounters in his theory of sublimation thus have a great affinity with those encountered with regard to the sublime: they have to do with the complex relationships that thought processes entertain with the flow of *Lüste* and *Unlüste*, which are constantly refashioned under the impact of various influences but may be endowed with an intensity to which the subject has no choice but to adapt.

While the motives of pleasure can be inventoried, repulsion and the desire for pleasure, inciting the psychic apparatus to movement, elude critical observation and force us to rethink the hidden coherence of actions and thoughts

under the category of destiny. Thus we could oppose *Lust* with *hêdonê* as a more or less evanescent affect, presupposing the implementation of complex and partially unconscious mechanisms, to the enjoyment of goods belonging to determinate hierarchies and leading to appropriative behaviors.

III. Pleasure, Enjoyment, Fruition

A. The juridical and affective senses of "enjoyment"

The French word *jouissance* appeared in the fifteenth century as a derivative from the verb *jouir*. At first, it had the juridical sense of drawing from a property all the benefit it was supposed to provide. In the seventeenth century, this initial meaning was applied to the notion of usufruct, the right to make use of a good belonging to someone else. But in the meantime, at the beginning of the sixteenth century, *jouissance* also acquired the meaning of intense sensual pleasure, especially sexual pleasure. In French, as in other Romance languages, the conjunction of these two meanings took place under the primacy of the lexical lineage *gaudium/gaudere*. Thus it may seem surprising that the word *jouissance* (like the Italian *godimento* or the Spanish *goce* and *gozo*) first came into use in its juridical sense and only later acquired its hedonistic sense: in reality, this linguistic fact marks a break with the Latin vocabulary, which separated quite sharply the register of *jouissance*-pleasure—with *voluptas, gaudium, suavitas, delectatio,* and *dulcedo*—from that of *jouissance*-law—with *possessio, usus,* and *fructus* (the latter term also having, however, the initial meaning).

German analogously makes use of two distinct lexical series to mark the difference between the enjoyment that provides pleasure (*Genuss, Behagen, Wohlgefühl, Lust, Freude*—and, more particularly, sensual enjoyment, *Sinnengenuss* and *Wollust*) on the one hand, and on the other hand, the enjoyment of one's own property, which is expressed notably by *Besitz* (possession), *Benutzungsrecht* (right to enjoy), or *Nutzung* (use, enjoyment). However, between these two registers there is a kind of hinge word: *Genuss*, which covers both meanings, as does *jouissance* in French. But it should be noted that it acquired only by extension, and with more difficulty, the sense of *jouissance*-pleasure, because, having the same etymology as *Nutzen* (utility, profit, fruit, benefit), it was originally marked by the juridical sense of "use" (like *Gebrauch*), "possession," and "usufruct."

In English, the distinction between the two meanings seems less clear than in German; "enjoyment" in the juridical sense is expressed by "use" or "possession," and also by "fruition" (which recalls the semantic duality of Lat. *fructus*), and finally, perhaps under foreign influence, by "enjoyment" (to enjoy certain rights), which thus takes us back to the lineage of *gaudere*.

In any event, whether in expressing legal enjoyment a language starts out from a term that originally belonged to the juridical vocabulary (like the Ger. *Genuss*) or from a term belonging to the vocabulary of affectivity (like the Fr. *jouissance*), it is a question of having or possessing something, insofar as that is opposed to feeling pleasure in something. Thus when the RT: *Diccionario de autoridades* of the Spanish Royal Academy attributes to the verb *gozar* the following meanings: "1. To have and possess something, like dignity, the right of earlier birth, or an income; 2. To draw pleasure and joy from something; 3. To know a woman carnally; 4. To feel a strong pleasure, sweet and agreeable emotions," the objective sense of the first meaning is supposed to prevail over the subjective meanings of the second and fourth.

It thus appears that in the languages we have just mentioned, the same word ends up designating "enjoyment" in both its objective and subjective senses. There is enough proximity between them so that one can easily—and indifferently—pass from enjoyment as the right of possession situated beyond the principle of pleasure/displeasure to enjoyment as an experience from which one receives an intense pleasure in the thing possessed, in which one makes another person (or oneself) the object of one's own *fruitio*. However, the etymology of the word is not without importance, because here it is not just isolated nouns that are contrasted, but different semantic constellations. Thus *Genuss* refers directly to the vocabulary of use or possession (*Nutzung, Benutzung*, etc.), whereas *jouissance* spontaneously evokes pleasure and joy (*gaudium*) with the verb *jouir* (and especially the imperative: *Jouis!* which Lacan considers *surmoïque* [super-egoish]). In French, the verb *jouir*, taken in the intransitive sense, leads to the substantive *jouisseur*, which designates a person who seeks life's pleasures, especially sensual pleasures. German calls such a person a *Geniesser* (from *Genuss*) or a *Lebemann* ("playboy," always in the masculine!), whereas Italian calls him a *gaudente*, reserving *fruente* (*di*) for a person who enjoys a good. In English, a *jouisseur* is a "sensualist," and often the French term itself is used.

The relationship between enjoyment-pleasure and enjoyment-law has been refashioned in contemporary thought, particularly under the influence of Marxism and psychoanalysis, in a way that seeks to merge these two classic meanings in a notion of enjoyment endowed with an unprecedented extension making it thereby possible to rehabilitate the freedom of the inclination to enjoy and the right to have full use of oneself. In particular, this attempt constitutes the central motif of the "paradoxical economy" set forth by Georges Bataille in *La part maudite* (1949). For Bataille, "becoming aware of the crucial meaning of an instant in which growth (the acquisition of something) is resolved in an expense is precisely self-consciousness, that is, a consciousness that no longer has anything as its object" and man is given back the free enjoyment of himself. This is a thesis that seems to be a speculative repetition of an "ecstasy" that the author mentioned in *L'expérience intérieure* (1943): "At that moment, I thought that this dreamy pleasure would not cease belonging to me, that I would live from that moment on, endowed with the power to enjoy things in a melancholy way and to breathe in their delights" (*Inner Experience*).

Among the reworkings of the concept of enjoyment in which contemporary thinkers have engaged, we must give a special place to the one that Jacques Lacan introduced into the field of psychoanalysis, which poses a problem for any translator. It even seems that the French word *jouissance* was included in the 1988 edition of the *Shorter Oxford English Dictionary* simply because in this unusual sense, it seemed untranslatable in English. Not only does the Lacanian concept of *jouissance* break away completely from the register of pleasure, but in addition, although it was elaborated on the basis of the juridical vocabulary, it detaches itself from all the conventionally accepted meanings in any domain whatever of language.

- See Box 3.

B. Enjoyment and "fruition"

Understood in the subjective sense of full satisfaction, the French term *jouissance* is an exact translation of Saint Augustine's *fruitio*. Augustine borrows from Stoic eudaemonism the contrast between this register of *frui* (enjoy) or of the goal and that of the *uti* or means (make use of), and the idea that the only true enjoyment is that of the supreme good. For Jansen, simple *delectatio* represented a first-order *affectus*, especially when it accompanied love; but the true goal of this *affectus* is *fruitio*, which is congress with the beloved object for its own sake and which thus constitutes the final fruit (*fructus*) of love at the same time as its quiescence (*quies*); whence the interest of this notion for quietism and the mystics in general, who speak of "fruitful union." In this sense, in French the archaic term *fruition* is still sometimes found in the literary language: "Ô fruition paradisiaque de tout instant!" (A. Gide, *Journal*, quoted in the *Trésor de la langue française*, s.v. "Jouissance").

"Fruition" continues to be used in English, but in the sense of "realization," "concretization" related to "fruit" and "fruitful," which recall the proximity of the Latin *frui* to *fructus*. The Italian *fruire* and *fruizione* (enjoyment, especially of a right or a benefit) remain loyal to this etymology, but to designate an intense pleasure, Italian resorts to the verb *godire* and the substantive *godimento*, which have the same origin as the French *jouissance*, namely the Classical Latin verb *gaudere*, via the intermediary of Vulgar Latin **gaudire*. Old French *joïr* (in Provençal, *jauzir*)—from which the noun *jouissance* emerged in the sixteenth century—had the meaning of "welcome warmly" and "gratify [someone] with one's love," and then, already in the twelfth century, in the indirect transitive form, that of "possessing a good" and "getting full satisfaction from any kind of possession." When the word *jouissance* appeared with its twofold meaning of "the possession of a good or a right" and "joy or intense pleasure," it corresponded through the latter meaning to *gaudere*, whereas the former meaning connected it, paradoxically, with the signified of *frui*. The same phenomenon that makes it possible to move seamlessly from the meaning "pleasure" or "amorous joy" (cf. the "joy" of the troubadours) to that of a right that one appropriates (another person being expropriated of it) and that one can claim—or vice versa—is found in several other European languages, notably in the Romance languages, such as Italian, with *godimento*, and Spanish, with *goce* and *gozo*.

IV. The Pleasures: Nomenclatures, Usages, Scales

A. The legacy of *placeo* and *placo*

While the German word *Lust* and, in a way, the English "pleasure," have a twofold meaning (pleasure/desire), we cannot say that the French *plaisir* is itself perfectly simple semantically. It, too, retains a sense that is close to "desire" and "will"; more precisely, "what it pleases someone to do or to command." This was the sense that established itself in

3

Jouissance according to Lacan

Although Freud himself mentioned *jouissance* (*Genuss*) with regard to both the satisfaction (*Befriedigung*) of vital needs and the fulfillment of a desire (*Wunscherfüllung*), it was Lacan who made this notion, constantly connected with either sexual pleasure or with the exercise of a right, a concept that is now considered important in the field of psychoanalysis. In an initial step, he distinguished it sharply from pleasure, placing *jouissance* at the foundation of his theory of perversion, understood no longer in the classic and pejorative sense of "sexual perversion," but instead as one of the three major components of psychic functioning alongside neurosis and psychosis. The perverse structure is characterized by the subject's obedience to the command of a law that he mocks while at the same time annihilating himself in this submission. In a second step, Lacan introduced the concept of *jouissance* into his theory of the difference of the sexes by distinguishing between phallic *jouissance* and feminine *jouissance* and by presupposing, on the one hand, that in humans desire is constituted by its relation to words, and on the other hand, that "there is no sexual relationship"; that is, that the subject, in the sex act, encounters neither the object of his desire that the other seems to him to represent nor the fulfillment that he expected to receive from such an experience. Thus the foreign translator who tries to find in his own lexicon of pleasure a term corresponding to *jouissance* as Lacan understands it finds that with Lacan one is always dealing with a very particular form of satisfaction, or at least with a satisfaction that is other than fully satisfactory. Everything seems to proceed from the exceptional *jouissance* experienced by the symbolic Father, the leader of the primal horde to whom the possession of all women is attributed and whose memory gives rise, in all other men, to the phantasm of an inaccessible, forbidden place of "absolute *jouissance*." These other men will experience no *jouissance* other than the "phallic *jouissance*" that is subjected to the flaw of castration and that is consequently irreducibly marked by lack, and not by the plenitude usually connoted by this term.

This masculine *jouissance* arouses the specter of "another *jouissance*" that is different from absolute *jouissance* and from phallic *jouissance*, and that Lacan suggests has been given to woman. The position of the latter in the field of sexuality consists in the fact that she is "not-all" (*pas-toute*) subject to the phallic logic of the castration complex, and that she exceeds, to that extent, such a determination. This excess, which is not simply complementary to masculine *jouissance*, constitutes a "supplement" with respect to the latter, but in woman it leads to a particular form of division (between "phallic *jouissance*" and the "other *jouissance*," "this *jouissance* that she is not all, that is, that makes her somewhat absent from herself, absent as subject"). Thus the gap between the sexes can be defined in the following way: "As such, [*jouissance*] is destined to these different forms of failure that constitute castration, for masculine *jouissance*, and division, so far as feminine *jouissance* is concerned" (*Le savoir du psychanalyste*, unpublished, 4 November 1971). But the supplementary *jouissance* peculiar to women (about which they cannot say anything and that is felt in particular by women who are mystical) is also experienced as *jouissance* of the Other, and, precisely, of the lack in the Other ("Dieu et la jouissance de la femme").

This diversity of the forms of *jouissance* and the two major traits that they have in common—namely, the relation each of them has with the impossible and their radical distinction from the vagaries of the register of pleasure (feelings, emotions, affects)—means that different languages encounter great difficulties in translating the Lacanian term *jouissance*. Italian generally resorts to *godimento*. Spanish oscillates between *goce* (delight) and *gozo* (pleasure), some translators preferring the latter word, which seems to them more restrictive than the former in relation to the imagined complete satisfaction. Other languages, such as English, limit themselves to putting the French word *jouissance* between quotation marks or in italics.

BIBLIOGRAPHY

Lacan, Jacques. "Dieu et la jouissance de la femme." In *Le Séminaire*. Vol. 20, *Encore*. Translation by Bruce Fink, edited by Jacques-Alain Miller: *On Feminine Sexuality, the Limits of Love and Knowledge*. New York: W.W. Norton & Company, 1999.

Old French, especially in such locutions as *à son plaisir* ("at will," from the Latin *gratum*) and *bon plaisir* or *à plaisir* (as it pleases, as much as one wants), which have survived down to our own time and to which the German adjective *beliebig* corresponds. The latter, which means, both as an adjective or a pronoun, "any" and, as an adverb, "at will," "at discretion," "as much as one wants," comes from the verb *belieben* (to find good, to desire, to love) and from the substantive *Liebe*, words that derive from the Indo-European root that in Latin produced *libet* and then *libido*. This line of signification seems to be the very one that Freud follows when he considers the libido as the equivalent of hunger in the register of sexuality and defines it as the appetite for an object whose enjoyment satisfies the goal of the sex drive. Jung himself, even as he desexualized it, made the libido an appetite or an "interest" reaching forward (see DRIVE, Box 2).

The Latin verb *placere*, which probably began as an impersonal verb meaning "it seems good," "it pleases," "it has been decided" (*placitum est*), corresponded to the causative *placo* (I try to please), which is related to the French expression *j'apaise* (I calm, conciliate). Along that line, the noun *placitio* (the action of pleasing) was marked by the graphic and phonic proximity of *pax*, so that *placidus* ceased to have the meaning "pleasant" and took on that of "calmed" or "peaceful." This shift can already be seen with Saint Jerome. However, even in the thirteenth century, the old sense remained: thus Albert the Great translated the Augustinian notion of amorous knowledge (*notitia cum amore*) by the expression *notitia placida* (*Commentarii in I Sententiarum*, dist. 27, art. 8). This semantic movement associating the idea of pleasure with that of quiescence or satisfaction is found in the German word *Befriedigung*, which means "contentment," "satisfaction," and derives from *Friede* (archaic form of *Frieden*, "peace"). We can even see in it a lexicographic concordance with the fact that Freud conceives pleasure as the relief of a tension, that is, as a "negative pleasure," as opposed to pain.

In addition to the meaning of "pleasant feeling," the French word *plaisir* also has, by metonymic derivation—and only since the fifteenth century—the concrete meaning of that which produces such an affective state. Thus we speak of the *usage des plaisirs* (the use of pleasures).

■ See Box 4.

However, as early as Greek antiquity, thinking about pleasures opens out, beyond their different categories or possible nomenclatures, onto the use that can or must be made of them and on their "moral problematization," as Michel Foucault has studied it in the second volume of his *History of Sexuality*. As he emphasizes, the place the subject gives to pleasures is essentially a matter of ethics, that is, of the relationship to oneself or of "concern with the self." Among the Greeks, the *aphrodisia* [ἀφροδίσια] are not acts listed in catalogues in which their legitimacy, or, on the contrary, their degree of deviation, of gravity and culpability, are evaluated, as Christian manuals of confession later tried to do. We can thus say that "what is at stake in the ethical system of the *aphrodisia* is the dynamic ensemble consisting of desire and pleasure associated with the act":

> What seems in fact to have formed the object of moral reflection for the Greeks in matters of sexual conduct was not exactly the act itself (considered in its different modalities), or desire (viewed from the standpoint of its origin or its aim), or even pleasure (evaluated according to the different objects or practices that can cause it); it was more the dynamics that joined all three in a circular fashion (the desire that leads to the act, the act that is linked to pleasure, and the pleasure that occasions desire).

It follows that the morality of the *aphrodisia* is a question of measure or moderation and of the supervision of sexual practices, of the desires that lead us to them, and of the pleasures that they provide us. Immorality in this area is excess, intemperance, disorder. But the objective is not to do away with pleasures and desires. On the contrary, we must use desire to maintain the sensation of pleasure and use need to revive desire (a little, as when Freud says that the affective bond of love is what, during the "intervals free of desire," enables this desire to arise again). Nonetheless, contrary to what Foucault seems to think, this connection between desire and pleasure was not entirely unknown to Christian moralists, who developed, notably in the Middle Ages, the topos of the *delectatio morosa*.

B. From *jucunditas* to "jubilation"

Although Latin terms such as *suavitas, voluptas, delectatio,* and *placere* have persisted almost as such in Romance languages, several other terms have been lost, especially in French. That is the case for *jucundus*, whose posterity concerns Italian in particular. This adjective—which was first and especially used by Cicero and Seneca, means "pleasant," "agreeable," and comes from *juvo* (to give pleasure to)—later yielded the noun *jucunditas* (joy). In Christian Latin, a popular etymology connected *jucunditas* with *jocus* (joke) and caused the word to be transformed into *jocunditas*. But the composite sense of "joke" and "joy" or "pleasure," which French could translate by *jeu* and *joie* or *plaisir*, is rendered much more clearly and without requiring a periphrasis by the Italian *giocondità*: the latter benefits, in this case, from the phonic relationship between *gioia* (joy) and *gioco* (joke, game). Nevertheless, contemporary Italian dictionaries generally give the sense of "gaiety"; that is, they emphasize play more than pleasure. However rich its past may have been, in contemporary languages the

---

4

Pleasure and pleasures (*aphrodisia* and *venerea*)

In French, grammar marks in a special way the transition from pleasure as an agreeable affective state to pleasure understood as something from which one draws satisfaction, usually sensual. This metonymic use of *plaisir* can be expressed by an adjectival phrase modifying a place (*un lieu de plaisir*), a time (*une soirée de plaisir*), or a person (*un homme de plaisir*). We also find it when the substantive is determined by a definite article and remains in the singular (e.g., *rechercher le plaisir*, or in the partitive, *se donner du plaisir*), but even more frequently when it is in the plural. Then it may retain a generic meaning or be constructed with a complement specifying a place or a time (*les plaisirs de Capoue*) or else a kind of pleasure (*les plaisirs de la chasse, du sport, de l'amour*).

Apropos of amorous pleasures, which are not limited to the sex act as such and which are described in Christian pastoral literature as "pleasures of the flesh" or "forbidden pleasures," we can note that French, no doubt like many other modern languages, is usually obliged to make use of periphrasis, whereas ancient languages such as Sanskrit, Greek, and Latin have a specific word for this purpose. Thus in Vedic literature, the word *kama* designates the pleasure of the senses or of sexual activity, even if it also covers, by extension, the whole semantic field of love. Still more clearly, in Greco-Roman antiquity there was a particular word to designate physical love: in Greek, the verb *aphrodisiazein* [ἀφροδισιάζειν] (to indulge in sexual pleasures, in the active voice in the case of a man, and in the passive voice in the case of a woman); in Latin, the neuter noun *venus, -eris* (sexual desire and pleasure), which has an exact counterpart in Sanskrit with *uanah* (desire). Each of these two Greek and Latin terms acquired that specific meaning because it had come to personify the divinity—Aphrodite or Venus—presiding over such pleasures (*ta aphrodisia* [τὰ ἀφροδίσια], among the Greeks; *venerea*, among the Romans).

Unlike these ancient languages, our contemporary ones do not have a specific, stable term to designate sexual pleasures, unless we resort to the language of triviality: in French, *la bagatelle, la gaudriole, la baise* (or more obscene, particularly because it designates the sex act itself—the verb *foutre* [from the Lat. *futuere*], which was especially favored by Sade). Italian resorts to the adjunction of a qualifier, for example, in *godimento venereo* ("sexual [literally, 'venereal'] pleasure"). As for the term *érotisme*, invented by Restif de la Bretonne in 1794, it designates a tendency, an interest, or a modality relating to physical love rather than to the pleasures themselves that are specific to the latter.

field of pleasure and joy is covered by a plurality of terms that are semantically quite close to each other. Thus in French, in addition to *plaisir* and *délectation*, we find *satisfaction, volupté, contentement, agrément, plaisance* (archaic), *complaisance, joie, allégresse*, and *jubilation*. In German, the most common words are *Lust, Vergnügen, Freude, Gefallen, Behagen*, and *Genuss*. To these Kant adds *Wohlgefallen* (*Critique of the Power of Judgment*, §3), which has the sense of "satisfaction," but he also uses *Vergnügen*, which the translators of the French Pléiade edition render by *plaisir* but which comes from *genug* (enough) and *Genügen* (sufficiency, satiety) and corresponds instead to *contentement*.

English has a very comparable distribution of terms, which Bentham takes into account when he distinguishes in "Table of the Springs of Action" fifty-four synonyms of "pleasure." Among them are "gratification," "enjoyment," "fruition," "joy," "delight," "delectation," "merriment," "mirth," "gaiety," "content," "comfort," and "satisfaction."

Some of these French, German, and English words are particularly related to the expression or manifestation of pleasure and joy. This is the case, for example, of "jubilation," a notion whose meanings can range from belligerent shouting or the sound of a battle trumpet to mystical ecstasy and narcissistic pleasure. Its Latin spelling, *jubilatio*, is borrowed from the Hebrew term that designates the ram's horn (*yôbhei*), the trumpet that is blown for great and solemn events and whose sound is translated, in the Septuagint, by the Greek *alalagmos* [ἀλαλαγμός] (from the verb *alalazein* [ἀλαλάζειν]), which means "war cry." In the Christian world, *jubilatio* came to designate an inner joy (close to "spiritual intoxication") that may be externalized in songs or cries (*jubilus* is the name given to singing exercises bearing on the last syllable of "alleluia" or on the whole of the word). Augustine saw in it the expression of an inexpressible spiritual delight, whereas Cassiodorus considered *jubilare* a synonym of *juvare* and *delectare*, emphasizing that this *copiosa mentis exultatio* (abundance of joy) is the outer manifestation of an ineffable mental pleasure. This term is found in the Romance languages and even in German, with *jubilieren*, which is, however, doubled by *frohlocken* (to rejoice).

C. Taxonomies within the semantic field of "pleasure"

We have already seen how Cicero tried to specify the meaning of the Latin word *voluptas* by means of other words that designate sensations or feeling concerning the body or the mind (*laetitia, gaudium, jucunditas*). However, the distinction between pleasure and joy, for example, remains rather poorly defined. Since this instability within a semantic field as extensive as that of pleasure concerns all languages, the translation of a term from one of them into another often raises problems. In the philosophical vocabulary, we can see this in particular in the rather fluctuating way in which the ternary hierarchy adopted by Spinoza is translated into French.

■ See Box 5.

The great diversity of pleasure's semantic field seems so universal that Bentham, seeking to determine it in English, ended up forging the concept of "fruitfulness" to designate a pleasure's ability to produce further pleasures: fruitfulness is enjoyment extended to the technical sense of a structural property of affectivity. This demonstrates the English language's specific ability to confer on fictive entities, beginning from real entities, a degree of supplementary reflexivity by giving them the suffix *-ness*. An entity is said to be real when, in a given case or in discourse, we intend to attribute existence to it, whereas a fictive entity is one to which we do not attribute a true existence. Thus for Bentham, pleasure and pain are real entities qua sensations that are not preceded by any other. However, pain takes precedence over pleasure in that it is usually felt more strongly. It follows that pleasure has a more "reflexive" character than pain and that the word "lust," for example, which is considered to refer to a real entity, can genera te "lustfulness," "luxury," "luxuriousness," etc.

Consequently, English's propensity to create substantives from verbs—gerunds such as "well-being"—also leads to the calculation of pleasures. To make verbs into substantives is to make it possible to classify them, as Bentham does when in "Table of the Springs of Action" he enumerates fifty-four

---

5

The register of pleasure and joy in Spinoza's translators

In the Latin text of Spinoza's *Ethics* (pt. 3, prop. 22.1, and prop. 18.2), we find the following descending gradation: *gaudium, laetitia*, and *titillatio*. The last term, which Spinoza associates with *hilaritas* (in the sense of "joyfulness"), corresponds in Descartes to the *chatouillement des sens* (the tickling of the senses), about which he says that it is "followed so closely by joy . . . that most people do not distinguish between them" (*Passions of the Soul*, §94). But German translators, for whom, according to Ritter's *Wörterbuch*, *die Lust* designates not the feeling of mere

pleasure, but that of joy, also use the word *Lust* to render Spinoza's *laetitia*, whereas they render the stronger word *gaudium* by *Freude*.

French translators generally render *laetitia* by the Cartesian term *joie* and *titillatio* by *plaisir*, and more precisely, by *plaisir local* or *chatouillement*. But then it is harder for them to render *gaudium*: C. Appuhn opts for *épanouissement* and R. Misrahi for *contentement*, as do R. Caillois and B. Pautrat, whereas P. Macherey, who sees *gaudium* as a *passion joyeuse*, prefers *satisfaction*. The

problem for German translators, who were able to render *laetitia/gaudium* satisfactorily by *Lust/Freude*, is then to translate the inferior term in the gradation as *titillatio*, whereas in French, if one considers *plaisir* correctly rendered by *titillatio* and *laetitia* by *joie*, resources seem to be lacking for *gaudium*.

BIBLIOGRAPHY

Descartes, René. *The Passions of the Soul*. Translated by Stephen Voss. Indianapolis, IN: Hackett, 1989.

synonyms of the term "pleasure," including a certain number of neologisms:

1. Gratification; 2. Enjoyment; 3. Fruition; 4. Indulgence; 5. Joy; 6. Delight; 7. Delectation; 8. Merriment; 9. Mirth; 10. Gaiety; 11. Airiness; 12. Comfort ; 13. Solace; 14. Content; 15. Satisfaction; 16. Rapture; 17. Transport; 18. Ecstasy; 19. Bliss; 20. Joyfulness; 21. Gladness; 22. Gladfulness; 23. Gladsomeness; 24. Cheerfulness; 25. Comfortableness; 26. Contentedness; 27. Happiness; 28. Blissfulness; 29. Felicity; 30. Wellbeing; 31. Prosperity; 32. Success; 33. Exultation; 34. Triumph; 35. Amusement; 36. Entertainment; 37. Diversion; 38. Festivity; 39. Pastime; 40. Sport; 41. Play; 42. Frolic; 43. Recreation; 44. Refreshment; 45. Ease; 46. Repose; 47. Rest; 48. Tranquillity; 49. Quiet; 50. Peace; 51. Relief; 52. Relaxation; 53. Alleviation; 54. Mitigation.

By means of a nomenclature of this kind (he draws up several others, notably for "desire"), Bentham does not seek to classify pleasures in order to hierarchize them for the purposes of action or politics, according to the degree of truth or value attributed to one or another of them. In his view, it is difficult to maintain that some pleasures are truer than others. Pleasure and, still more, pain, are only principles that have "authority" over our behavior, and play, within our actions, the role of motivating forces. They may be used as guides—fallible ones, in any case—to help us construct a world, either one of physical objects or one of interpersonal relations. They are thus fundamental to the whole of the "springs of action." Hence the "fictive" or "reflexive" character of pleasures does not prevent us from considering them as neither good nor false, neither true nor false. The principle of utility, which postulates the quest for the greatest happiness for the greatest number, leads us to put them in a logical and quantitative form, to subject them, by means of multiple rules, to a calculus (see UTILITY). Thus when they are treated as nouns, the diverse pleasures constituted as entities can have a quantity, an intensity, a duration, a probability, a distance or proximity, a fecundity, and a purity that make them quantifiable, "associable," capable of being subjected to laws and of entering into such calculations.

Charles Baladier
Clara Auvray-Assayas
Jean-François Balaudé
Barbara Cassin
Jean-Pierre Cléro
Baldine Saint Girons

BIBLIOGRAPHY

Augustine, Saint. *On Christian Doctrine*. Translated by R.P.H. Green. Oxford: Oxford University Press, 1999.

Baier, Annette. "Master Passions." In *Explaining Emotions*, edited by Amelie O. Rorty, 403–23. Berkeley: University of California Press, 1980.

Bataille, Georges. *Inner Experience*. Translated by L. A. Boldt. Albany: State University of New York Press, 1988.

———. *La part maudite*. Paris: Éditions de Minuit, 1949. Translation by Robert Hurley: *The Accursed Share*. 3 vols. New York: Zone Books, 1991–93.

Bentham, Jeremy. "Table of the Springs of Action." In *Deontology; Together with A Table of the Springs of Action; and the Article on Utilitarianism*. Edited by Amnon Goldworth. Oxford: Clarendon Press, 1983.

Brunschwig, Jacques, and Martha Nussbaum, eds. *Passions and Perceptions: Studies in Hellenistic Philosophy of Mind*. Cambridge: Cambridge University Press, 1993.

Burke, Edmund. *A Philosophical Enquiry into the Origin of Our Ideas of the Sublime and Beautiful*. Edited by Adam Phillips. Oxford: Oxford University Press, 1998.

Cicero, Marcus Tullius. *De finibus bonorum et malorum*. Cambridge, MA: Harvard University Press, 1951. Translation by R. Woolf: *On Moral Ends*. Cambridge: Cambridge University Press, 2001.

———. *Ethical Writings of Cicero*: *"De Officiis" (On Moral Duties); "De Senectute" (On Old Age); "De Amicitia" (On Friendship)*, and *"Scipio's Dream."* Translated by Andrew P. Peabody. Boston: Little, Brown, and Co., 1887.

———. *Tusculan Disputations*. Translated by J. E. King. Cambridge, MA: Harvard University Press, 1945.

Descartes, René. *The Passions of the Soul*. Translated by Stephen Voss. Indianapolis, IN: Hackett, 1989.

Diogenes Laertius. *Lives of Eminent Philosophers*. Translated by R. D. Hicks. Loeb Classical Library. Cambridge, MA: Harvard University Press, 1972.

Foucault, Michel. *History of Sexuality*. Vol. 2, *The Use of Pleasure*. Translated by Robert Hurley. New York: Vintage, 1988.

Freud, Sigmund. "Being in Love and Hypnosis." In *Group Psychology and Analysis of the Ego*. Translated by James Strachey. New York: Liveright, 1951.

———. "Negation." In vol. 19 of *The Standard Edition of the Complete Psychological Works of Sigmund Freud*, edited by John Strachey, 233–39. London: Hogarth Press, 1953–74.

———. *Three Contributions to the Theory of Sex*. In *The Basic Writings of Sigmund Freud*. Translated and edited by A. A. Brill. New York: Modern Library, 1995.

Gosling, J.C.B. *The Greeks on Pleasure*. Oxford: Clarendon Press, 1982.

Haliwell, Stephen. *The Aesthetics of Mimesis*. Princeton: Princeton University Press, 2002.

Hesiod. *Theogony, Works and Days, Shield*. Translated by Apostolos Athanassakis. 2nd ed. Baltimore: Johns Hopkins University Press, 2004.

Homer. *The Odyssey*. Translated by Richmond Lattimore. New York, Harper and Row, 1967.

———. "To Aphrodite." In *The Homeric Hymns*, translated by Apostolos Athanassakis. 2nd ed. Baltimore: Johns Hopkins University Press, 2004.

Kant, Immanuel. *Critique of the Power of Judgment*. Translated by Paul Guyer and Eric Matthews. Cambridge: Cambridge University Press, 2001.

Lacan, Jacques. "Dieu et la jouissance de la femme." In *Le Séminaire*. Vol. 20, *Encore*. Paris: Éditions du Seuil, 1975.

Latacz, Joachim. *Zum Wortfed "Freude" in der Sprache Homers*. Heidelberg: Winter, 1966.

MacLachlan, Bonnie. *The Age of Grace: Charis in Early Greek Poetry*. Princeton, NJ: Princeton University Press, 1993.

Marcuse, Herbert. *Eros and Civilization: A Philosophical Inquiry into Freud*. Boston: Beacon Press, 1955.

Nasio, Juan-David. *Five Lessons on the Psychoanalytic Theory of Jacques Lacan*. Translated by David Pettigrew and François Raffoul. Albany: State University of New York Press, 1998.

Plato. *Philebus*. Translated by R. Hackforth. In *Collected Dialogues of Plato*, edited by E. Hamilton and H. Cairns. Princeton, NJ: Princeton University Press / Bollingen, 1961.

Plutarch. "On Love." In *Moralia*. 15 vols. Loeb Classical Library. Cambridge, MA: Harvard University Press.

Poussin, Nicolas. *Lettres et propos sur l'art*. Edited by Anthony Blunt. Paris: Hermann, 1964.

Russell, Daniel C. *Plato on Pleasure and the Good Life*. Oxford: Clarendon Press, 2005.

Seneca. *Four Dialogues*. Warminster, UK: Aris and Phillips, 1994.

———. *Moral Essays*. Loeb Classical Library. Cambridge, MA: Harvard University Press.

———. *Opera omnia, quae supersunt*. Edited by Friedrich E. Ruhkopf. 5 vols. Leipzig: 1797–1811.

Spinoza, Baruch. *Ethics*. Translated by G.H.R. Parkinson. Oxford: Oxford University Press, 2000.

Taylor, C.C.W. *Pleasure, Mind, and Soul: Selected Papers in Ancient Philosophy*. Oxford: Oxford University Press, 2008.

Weinman, Michael. *Pleasure in Aristotle's Ethics*. New York: Continuum, 2007.

PLUDSELIGHED / DESULTORISK (DANISH)

ENGLISH   suddenness/desultory
FRENCH   *soudaineté / sans suite, décousu*
GERMAN   *Plötzlichkeit/desultorisch*

➤ *INSTANT* and CONTINUITET, DAIMÔN, DASEIN, DEVIL, *EVENT*, EVIGHED,
I/ME/MYSELF, JETZTZEIT, MOMENT, *TIME*

The terms *Pludselighed* and *Desultorisk* occur in Kierkegaard along with *Evighed* and *Continuitet*. The absence of continuity (*Desultorisk*) takes on a special character when it occurs suddenly (*Pludselighed*), for example, when evil abruptly arises (*Œuvres complètes*, 4:37), as is suggested by the description of the demonic.

"If one reflects on its content, the demonic is determined as closing in on oneself; if it takes time into account, it is determined as the sudden" (ibid., 7:226). Lawless, foreign to the continuity of natural phenomena, the demonic is not of a somatic but rather of a psychic nature. It appears and disappears suddenly, in the rhythm of a suddenness (*Pludselighed*) that consists in the "abracadabra continuity of one who communicates only with himself" (ibid., 7:227). Like Mephistopheles it arises suddenly, being nothing other than itself, without content, like a shade that has died of boredom, given over to "continuity in nothingness" (ibid., 7:229).

The Kierkegaardian approach to time (like other categories instrumentalized in experience, such as the interval or the interstice in the sense of *inter-esse*) is marked by the restless oscillation between two movements or antagonistic terms, between humor and irony, tragedy and comedy, doubt and confidence, seriousness and joking. Regarding temporality, this "pendular movement" (*Pendulbevaegelse*) (*Journal*, 1:83) regulates the valorization and depreciation of the permanent and the sudden. As Kierkegaard writes, "Continuity in alternation governs the privilege of "the first time," of the semelfactivity of "what occurs only once," like "first love") or the Incarnation (*Œuvres complètes*, 10:76, and 4:36–38). This does not exclude the supremacy of "the second time" (*Journal*, 2:226, *Œuvres complètes*, 15:301–2; 17:171), which is not without analogy to Stendhal's second crystallization, but whose source is biblical: "Behold, I make all things new" (Rev. 21:5).

In its very ambiguity oscillation expresses the paradoxical aspect of discontinuity, as a fact, which gives time all its weight, its concrete continuity. In this we can see a kind of echo of the Platonic *atopon*: the nontemporal supremely active in time is the *exaiphnês* [ἐξαίφνης], the sudden, which interrupts mediation, not without having the value of *metaxu* [μεταξύ], of articulation or connection that, nonetheless, annihilates neither the tenor of the difference nor the violence of the collision.

In Kierkegaard, terms with a temporal resonance are frequently the origin of thematics that are deployed in very diverse registers. Thus the fact of being discontinuous is often denoted by the adjective *desultorisk* ("inconsistent, disjointed"). Thought's leaps are *desultorisk* (Hamann, *Œuvres complètes*, vol. 7): the incomprehensibility with regard to Abraham (vol. 3), the fragmentation of the posthumous writings (vol. 1), the seducer's moves (vol. 3), the

moments of aridity that, in the weary soul of the mystic, alternate with luminous moments (vol. 4), the irruption of evil (vol. 4). Continuity, on the contrary, is due to the ethical instant (vol. 2) of decision, to the recollection that maintains an eternal continuity (vol. 9). The aesthetician leads conquests, but since he is "incapable of possessing" (vol. 4), he can only "bend eternity in time in fantastic ways" (vol. 7). In continuity, the ethicist has the ardor of a conqueror, but also the humble patience to constantly acquire possession.

The sudden (*Plugselighed*) character of the *exaiphnês*, of the lightning bolt (*Blitz*) are found again in the brusque eruption of obscurity of madness, of death, of the shadows on Golgotha (vol. 15), of the demonic. Sudden also is the strange passage from the singular existent to the fantastic I of speculation. But suddenness provokes not only fear or astonishment. The emergence of a new quality (sin or grace, vol. 13), the light and gliding arrival of the favorable moment (*kairos* [καίρος], vol. 16) also occur with suddenness (see MOMENT).

Jacques Colette

BIBLIOGRAPHY

Bohrer, Karl H. *Plötzlichkeit. Zum Augenblick des ästhetischen Scheins*. Frankfurt: Suhrkamp, 1981.
Kierkegaard, Søren. *Journal* (extracts). Translated by K. Ferlov and J.-J. Gateau. 5 vols. Paris: Gallimard, 1942–61. Vol. 1, rev. and expanded ed., 1963.
———. *Kierkegaard's Writings*. 26 vols. Princeton, NJ: Princeton University Press, 1978–2000.
———. *Œuvres complètes*. Translated by P. H. Tisseau and E. M. Jacquet-Tisseau. 20 vols. Paris: L'Orante, 1966–86.

POETRY

I. *Poiêsis* and *Praxis*

The English word "poetry" (archaic, "poesy") derives, via Latin, from the Greek *poiêsis* [ποίησις], from *poiein* [ποιεῖν] (to make, produce), referrring to the production of an object, as distinguished from *praxis* [πρᾶξις], from *prattein* [πράττειν] (to do, act) referring to an action that is its own end. On this fundamental difference between *poiêsis* and *praxis*, see PRAXIS; cf. *ACT* [AGENCY, ATTUALITÀ, SPEECH ACT], ACTOR, MORALS, WORK.

II. Poetry and Literature

1. In the entry for German DICHTUNG (from *dichten*, "to invent" and "to compose a poem"), which can be rendered by both "literature" and "poetry," the difference in the demarcations of the domains of discourse are examined. See also ERZÄHLEN, *FICTION*, HISTORY, LOGOS.
2. On the relationship between poetry and prose, and the connection with figures, see SUBLIME, and COMMONPLACE, COMPARISON, TROPE; cf. MIMÊSIS, *STYLE*.

➤ CATHARSIS

POLIS [πόλις], POLITEIA [πολιτεία] (GREEK)

ENGLISH   city-state, state, society, nation
FRENCH   *cité, État, société, nation*

➤ *STATE* [DEMOS/ETHNOS/LAOS, STATE/GOVERNMENT, STATO], and CIVIL RIGHTS, CIVIL SOCIETY, ECONOMY, *GOVERNMENT*, OIKEIŌSIS, OIKONOMIA, PEOPLE, POLITICS

The word *polis* [πόλις] is considered untranslatable: city-state, state, society, or nation? But is it the word that is untranslatable in our languages, or the reality that it designates, which has no equivalent in our civilization? *Polis* designates the "political community" peculiar to a stage in Greek civilization. But the fact that today we still cannot designate anthropological reality in general without appealing to the word *polis* shows that it is not easy to distinguish between translating words and establishing correspondences between things or deciding between Greek particularity and human universality.

Politeia [πολιτεία] seems to pose different problems: the *politês* [πολίτης] being a member of the *polis* (hence the citizen), *politeia* designates either, distributively, the citizens' participation in the city-state as a whole, and thus "citizenship," or collectively, the organization of citizens into a whole, and thus "constitution" or "regime." But there again, it is difficult to separate historical realities from the concepts philosophy bases on them since that is the title Plato gives to his main work on politics—the *Republic* (*Politeia*)—and the name that Aristotle gives to a particular *politeia* among all those that seem to him possible.

I. *Polis* and Political Philosophy

The *polis* [πόλις] is first of all a political entity peculiar to archaic and classical Greek civilization between (at least) the eighth and the fourth centuries BCE, connecting a human community and a determinate territory. Whereas other peoples lived in empires having an "ethnic" identity (e.g., the Persians), the originality of the Greeks in the classical period was that they lived in small, free communities (the Athenians, the Lacedaemonians, the Corinthians, et al.) having no unity other than political. Thus every city-state enjoyed territorial sovereignty, made its own laws (according to its *politeia* [πολιτεία]), and was protected by its own gods. Three governmental institutions were common to all the city-states: a large Assembly that brought together all or part of the *polites* [πολίτες] ("citizens," which was never synonymous with "residents," because minors, foreigners, "metics," women, and slaves were excluded); one or more smaller councils, generally entrusted with preparing and executing the decisions made by the Assembly; and a certain number of public offices (the *archai* [ἀρχαί], magistracies), exercised in alternation by certain people. The *politeia* specific to each *polis* defined the way these different bodies were recruited and their powers. Nonetheless, during the classical period, the *poleis* were distinguished from each other by whether they had adopted a democratic or an oligarchic *politeia*. In the former case, as in Athens, the Assembly brought together all the citizens and decisions were made by majority vote after a debate in the course of which everyone had an equal right to speak; in addition, everyone had an equal opportunity to take part in the councils and in most of the tribunals and magistracies (except the military and financial ones) through

simple drawing of lots. In oligarchic city-states, only some of the members of the *polis* could take part in governmental organs and magistrates were chosen by election.

This singular historical reality constituted by the *polis* can be designated by the term "city-state" so long as the *polis* is not confused with the city (in Greek: *astu* [ἄστυ]), which was only a part of the city-state. But the problem is not only linguistic, it is philosophical from the outset because political philosophy was born in the *polis* as a "reflection" on the *polis* itself, both as the community of the Greeks and a way of life for men, and as a critical investigation into the *politeiai*, the different real or possible ways in which citizens could live together. It is from this interweaving of the singular and the universal, of the historical and the conceptual, of the real and the possible, that arise the difficulty of translating and the philosophical fertility of these notions of the *polis* and the *politeia*.

II. *Polis*: State, Society, Nation?

The difficulty of translating *polis* is less a matter of language than of history. No modern political entity is identical with the ancient *polis*. We usually live in states, each of which has legal sovereignty over a community of individuals, families, and classes called "society," and whose members feel themselves to be united by a similarity in language, culture, and history called "nation." However, although the Greek *polis* appeals to the three elements of legal system, social interdependence, and historical identity, it is nonetheless distinguished from what we call a "state," "society," or "nation."

Every Greek felt connected to his *polis* by an attachment so strong that he was often prepared to sacrifice his time for its administration and his life for its defense, and he feared the punishment of exile more than any other. Nonetheless, this feeling was not exactly national, if by "nation" we mean a community of language and culture (what the Greeks called *ethnos* [ἔθνος], and which they distinguished precisely from *polis*), not exactly patriotic, since it is less a relationship to a "native land," to a territory, than what the Greeks called *chôra* [χώρα], an awareness of belonging to a human community bound together by a shared past and a future to be constructed in common.

Each community was welded together by institutions that had a sovereign power over the whole of its members and its constituent groups. This relates the *polis* to the modern state, if we understand thereby the authority that "successfully claims a monopoly on the legitimate use of violence" (Weber, *Politik als Beruf*).However, a *polis* is not exactly a "state," the concept of which is correlative to that of the individual and "society." The state appears as an omnipotent, anonymous, and distant legal institution against which individual liberties must—always and again and again—be defended: the state is "they" against "us"—and "we" are individuals, or society. The same was not true in the *polis*: the pressure exercised by the *polis* is still exercised by "us," as such, by the community as a whole. To this extent, the freedom of the individual is gauged not by his independence with regard to the state but by the collectivity's dependence with regard to him, that is, to his participation in the *polis*.

The *polis* is thus first of all a community with a transgenerational permanence and a transfamilial identity, whose members feel a solidarity transcending all ties of blood.

In this sense, it is related to a "society." But it is not a "society" in the modern sense, for two complementary reasons. First of all, negatively, because for the Greeks, social and economic relations belonged to the sphere of the *oikos* [οἶκος] and not to that of the *polis*—that is, they were private, not public matters. Second, the *polis* is not a neutral context of exchange or of the circulation of goods, but rather the center of a historical experience, past and future, real or imaginary; in other words, the unity of this community did not arise from the interdependency of its members, but from action with a view to administering or defending it: it was a political unity.

The *polis* is thus neither a nation, nor a state, nor a society. It does not exist negatively, by inadequation, but positively, by definition. What constitutes the *polis* is the identity of the sphere of power (which for us concerns the "state") and the sphere of community (which for us is organized into "society"), and it is to this unity that each individual feels affectively bound (and not to the "nation"). Thus we can understand why the first political thinkers were able to take it as both their object and their model: while being aware of the singularity of the *polis*, they saw in it the concept of a "political community" in general. Thus according to Plato, Protagoras thought that men have to live in *poleis* because they lack other animals' biological qualities that fit them for the struggle for life, and thus have to unite by showing the virtues necessary for life in common (Plato, *Protagoras*, 320c–322d). Plato sees the *polis* as deriving from the necessity that humans cooperate and specialize (*Republic*, 2.369b–371e). Aristotle sees man as being by definition a "political animal" (*Politics*, 1.1253a 1–38), that is, "one who lives in a *polis*," and by that we must understand not only a "social animal," but also a being that can be happy only if he can freely decide, with his peers, what is right for their common life. It is as if the particularity of the *polis*, in which the sphere of the community merges with that of power, had made political thought as such possible. That is why the *polis* is neither the state nor society, but the "political community."

III. *Politeia*: Citizenship and Regime

This particularity also explains the dichotomy of the meanings of *politeia*. If the *politês* is a person who participates in the *polis*, the *politeia* may be either the subjective bond of the *politês* to the *polis*, that is, the way in which the *polis* as a community distributes among those whom it recognizes as its participants (the "citizenry"), or the objective organization of the functions of government and administration, that is, the way in which the power of the *polis* is collectively guaranteed (the "form of government" or the "constitution"). The first meaning is anterior and corresponds to the single use of the word in Herodotus (*Histories*, 9.34), who offers, moreover, without using the term *politeia*, the oldest classification of "forms of government" (3.80–83), depending on the number of those who govern: a single individual ("tyranny"), several ("oligarchy"), or all ("isonomy"). However, it is the second meaning that was to prevail in political thought, for example, with the *Poleitai of the Lacedaemonians* or the *Poleitai of Athens*, two texts transmitted in the corpus of Xenophon's works, or the "Collection of *Poleitai*" assembled by Aristotle, and of which only that of Athens is extant. Given that all these cases involve a kind of a posteriori codification, the term "constitution" seems to be the most appropriate translation of *poleitai*, on condition that it not be taken to imply any notion of a basic law written a priori. On the other hand, when Plato (*Republic*, 8) and then Aristotle (*Politics*, 3.6–7) classify and compare *poleitai*, they are concerned above all to discern in each case the fundamental principle on which the organization of power in the *polis* rests, and the term "form of government" seems more adequate.

However, neither of these translations is sufficient because one of Aristotle's *poleitai*, the one in which power is assumed by all citizens with a view to the common good, is called precisely *poleiteia* ("republic"? "constitutional regime"?), as if it incarnated, as it were, the essence of any *politeia*, by combining the two senses of the word: according to this *politeia*, in fact, all those who belong to the citizenry, and thus to the *politeia*, have the right to participate in the administration of the *politeia*.

> The words constitution (*politeia* [πολιτεία]) and government (*politeuma* [πολίτευμα]) have the same meaning, and the government, which is the supreme authority in states (*to kurion tôn poleôn* [τὸ κύριον τῶν πόλεων]), must be in the hands of one, or of a few, of the many (*ê hena ê oligous ê tous pollous* [ἢ ἕνα ἢ ὀλίγους ἢ τοὺς πολλούς]). The true forms of government (*politeias* [πολιτείας]), therefore, are those in which the one, or the few, or the many, govern with a view to the common interest; but governments which rule with a view to the private interest (*to idion* [τὸ ἴδιον]), whether of the one, or of the few, or of the many, are perversions. For the members of a state (*politas* [πολίτας]), if they are truly citizens (*tous metechontas* [τοὺς μετέχοντας]), ought to participate in its advantages (*koinônein tous sumpherontas* [κοινωνεῖν τοὺς συμφέροντας]). Of forms of government in which one rules, we call that which regards the common interests, kingship or royalty; that in which more than one, but not many, rule, aristocracy; and it is so called, either because the rulers are the best men, or because they have at heart the best interests of the state (*polei* [πόλει]) and of the citizens (*tois koinônousin autês* [τοῖς κοινωνοῦσιν αὐτῆς]). But when the citizens at large administer the state for the common interest, the government is called by the generic name—a constitution [ὅταν δὲ τὸ πλῆθος πρὸς τὸ κοινὸν πολιτεύηται συμφέρον, καλεῖται τὸ κοινὸν ὄνομα πασῶν τῶν πολιτειῶν]. And there is a reason for this use of language.
>
> (*Aristotle, Politics*, 3.7.1279a 25–39)

But where translations of *politeia* by "constitution" or "form of government" are clearly inadequate is when the titles of the political works of numerous Greek thinkers, first of all Plato, have to be translated. These "Republics" do not limit themselves to presenting the functioning of a form of government, but found an overall project of common life, including programs of education, the organization of labor and leisure, moral rules, etc.: another proof, if one be needed, that the *polis* is indeed the unity of the community and power, two agencies that are for us divided between the state and society.

Francis Wolff

BIBLIOGRAPHY

Aristotle. *The Politics, and the Constitution of Athens*. Edited by Stephen Everson. Cambridge: Cambridge University Press, 1996.

Benveniste, Émile. "Two Linguistic Models of the City." In *Problems in General Linguistics*. Translated by Mary Elizabeth Meek. Coral Gables: University of Florida Press, 1971.

Herodotus. *The History*. Translated by David Grene. Chicago: University of Chicago Press, 1987.

Plato. *Protagoras*. Translated by Stanley Lombardo and Karen Bell. Indianapolis: Hackett, 1992.

———. *The Republic*. Translated by G.M.A. Grube. Indianapolis: Hackett, 1974.

Weber, Max. *Politik als Beruf*. Munich: Duncker and Humblot, 1919. Translation by Gordon C. Wells and edited by John Dreijmanis: *Politics as a Vocation*. In *Max Weber's Complete Writings on Academic and Political Vocations*. New York: Algora, 2007.

Xenophon. "Constitution of the Lacedaemonians," and "Constitution of the Athenians." In *Scripta Minora*. Translated by E. C. Marchant and G. W. Bowersock. Loeb Classical Library. Cambridge, MA: Harvard University Press, 1968.

POLITICS, POLICY

➤ CIVIL SOCIETY, DEMOS/ETHNOS/LAOS, ECONOMY, GEISTESWISSENSCHAFTEN, *GOVERNMENT*, POLIS, *STATE*, STATE/GOVERNMENT

In French, the noun *politique* refers to two orders of reality that English designates as two different words, "policy" and "politics." In one sense, which is that of policy, we speak in French of *la politique* to designate "an individual's, a group's, or a government's conception, program of action, or the action itself" (Aron, *Democracy and Totalitarianism*): it is in this sense that we speak of *politiques* of health or education or of Richelieu's or Bismarck's *politiques* in foreign affairs. In another sense, which translates as the English word "politics," *la politique* designates everything that concerns public debate, competition for access to power, and thus the "domain in which various *politiques* [in the sense of "policy"] compete or oppose each other" (ibid.). This slight difference between French and English does not generally pose insurmountable problems, because the context usually suffices to indicate which meaning of *politique* should be understood, but in certain cases it is nonetheless difficult to render in French all the nuances conveyed by the English term, or, on the contrary, to avoid contamination between the two notions that English distinguishes so clearly. On the basis of an examination of the uses of the two words in political literature in English, we will hypothesize that their respective semantic fields are not unrelated to the way in which scholarly theories (and academic institutions) conceive what French calls *la politique*.

I. "Politics" and "Policy" in Philosophy

In contemporary academia, the domain of politics designates first of all an essential part of the field of "political science": the study of the forms of political competition, in accord with methods that arose from the analysis of pluralist regimes, but which can be transposed to the analysis of authoritarian regimes to shed light on conflicts among different opinion- or interest-groups that pursue opposed projects and distinct policies. Studies of electoral sociology (as well as analyses of other forms of political participation—demonstrations, petitions, activism, and so forth) belong to this domain, along with all kinds of studies on political parties, the recruitment of governing elites, and, more generally, on the competitive and/or agonistic dimension of the regimes or political systems studied (see, for example, Campbell et al., *The American Voter*). But there also exist scientific approaches to policy that seek to bring out the conditions in which a particular policy can be implemented by a state, an administration, or, by extension, some kind of organization (a company may have a policy of investment, training, and so forth); significantly (insofar as it is a question of public organizations), this study of policy is generally called in French *analyse des politiques publiques*, in order to compensate for the indeterminacy of the word *politique* (for a general presentation, see Muller and Surel, *L'Analyse des politiques publiques*). As always in the social sciences, we find here a great diversity of approaches and theoretical oppositions to which we may give a political, even a partisan, meaning; but there is nonetheless a certain consensus in political science, at least in English-speaking countries, that has to do with the relations between scholarly discourse and common representations. The distinction between politics and policy is considered natural, even and especially when one inquires into the relations between them: the choice of a policy in a given sector obviously depends on politics, but that makes it only all the more useful to distinguish between the two notions. More deeply, most classical studies in political science have in common a combination of a certain confidence in the notions that have emerged from the common consciousness and an effort to critique and demystify the latter's most naïve or most widespread representations. With regard to the analysis of political life, sociology has constantly sought, with varying success, to shed light on the gap between classical democratic principles (popular sovereignty, the expression of the enlightened citizen) and the real functioning of representative regimes, which are in many respects oligarchical, and which very easily tolerate a certain political passivity; it could also be shown that many classical analyses, like that of "party identification" in *The American Voter*, draw their persuasive force from the fact that they tend to dissipate the democratic prejudices on which democratic regimes live. (If identification with a party is a crucial element in electoral choices, that is not because it increases political consciousness, but on the contrary because it makes political participation easier by relieving voters of having to form their own opinions on every question). The analysis of public policies, which has developed in the wake of decision studies, is primarily concerned with explaining the gaps between the intentions of decision-makers and the results of their actions, as well as the general opacity of decision-making processes themselves (Leca, in Grawitz and Leca, *Traité de science politique*, vol. 1). The dominant trends in political science are thus based on what might be called a non-Bachelardian epistemology that emphasizes the continuity between the common consciousness and scientific knowledge, and that probably reflects a more or less conscious adherence to the values of pluralistic democracy: that is no doubt what explains, *a contrario*, the reservations about this kind of political science expressed by French thinkers who reject this kind of naiveté and stress the discontinuity between science and common sense in order to bring out more clearly the oligarchical dimension of pluralistic regimes (see, for example, Lacroix, "Ordre politique et ordre social," in *Traité de science politique*, vol. 1). Whatever one thinks of these debates, the existence of a political sphere in which conflict and public deliberation are the conditions of legitimate public action is not an eternal given of human life: it is in this sense that the great Hellenist Moses I. Finley could say, "Politics in our sense rank among the rarer activities in the pre-modern world. In effect, they were a Greek invention, more correctly perhaps, the separate inventions of the Greeks and of the Etruscans and/or Romans" (*Politics in the Ancient World*). The duality between policy and politics is also significant for political philosophy, insofar as the latter can hardly be understood without taking into account the distinction between the logic of command and the logic of deliberation. Most contemporary political philosophies, which implicitly accept the postulates of free-market economics (even if, as in the work of J. Habermas, to appeal to its ideals against its actual functioning), tend to privilege politics while at the same time including the policy dimension in the general framework of strategic action that often borrows from economic analysis. In other, more classical philosophies, politics may be conceived, in a rather Aristotelian way, with reference to its architectonic function, but also to the role played in it by public deliberation and the civic bond, which also assumes that its domain is irreducible to the particular goals that guide the policy of particular communities (see, for example, Oakeshott, *On Human Conduct*).

II. Politics and Policy

The oscillation of contemporary practical philosophy between the celebration of the civic ideals of liberated communication and the public sphere, on the one hand, and the general prestige of theories of rational choice, on the other, no doubt shows that the distinction English makes between the two dimensions of what French calls *la politique* involves more than a simple linguistic usage. However, this distinction does not suffice to exhaust the study of politics, which has led some authors to speak of the political as a concept that cannot be reduced to politics. In the work of Carl Schmitt, who introduced "the political" in his 1932 book *Der Begriff des Politischen* (*The Concept of the Political*), this distinction was framed as a polemic against liberalism, which tended, according to him, to reduce the specificity of "the political" to the advantage of the ethics-economy polarity, making "the political" the means of limiting ethical constraints to the benefit of individual freedoms. Schmitt's theses are indissolubly scientific and normative (even polemical); from the scientific point of view, the problem is to find the fundamental distinction in the political order equivalent to good and evil in the moral order, beautiful and ugly in the aesthetic order, and profitable and unprofitable in the economic order. But this quest is itself a way of discrediting liberal civilization, which underestimates the major role conflict plays in the constitution of political unities: "The specific distinction of the political, to which political acts and motives can be traced, is the discrimination between friend and enemy" (ibid.). The political is thus irreducible to culture, economics, or

ethics, because it truly appears only when crucial problems are involved whose resolution may require violent clashes. This conception, which reflects the author's hostility to the Treaty of Versailles and the ideology of the League of Nations, implied a radical criticism of the cosmopolitan and humanitarian ideals inherited from liberalism, and had dangerous aspects that Schmitt himself illustrated by supporting, for a time, the Nazi regime. But it would be unfair to see in this an appeal for a general subordination of human existence to the requirements of the political, itself reduced to violent conflict: the political is only one of the spheres of human action, in which, moreover, conflict is only one possibility that defines the limits of rationalization and not the ordinary forms of life. Strictly speaking, Schmitt's theory does not imply general war or conquest, even if in principle it excludes the achievement of perpetual peace—which would mark the end of all political existence *stricto sensu*, and which, in the real political world, is in fact the theme that makes it possible to criminalize some political actors, who are presented as enemies of peace and humanity (ibid.).

In itself, then, the idea of a distinction between the political and politics, which would enable us to conceive the political dimension of human life transhistorically, does not necessarily entail a complete or literal adoption of Schmitt's themes, but it does suggest that the political is endowed with a dignity superior to that of politics, either because it is distinguished from everyday politics, or because it is the specific object of philosophy and grand theory, whereas most of the social sciences can hardly rise above the level of the empirical study of political life. In this sense, the concept of the political is no doubt part of the common fund of contemporary philosophy. (For a line of inquiry fairly close to Schmitt's, see Freund, *L'Essence du politique*; for an approach faithful to the Aristotelian tradition, see Vullierme, *Le Concept de système politique*.)

Philippe Raynaud

BIBLIOGRAPHY

Aron, Raymond. *Démocratie et totalitarisme*. Paris: Gallimard, 1965. Translation by Valence Ionescu: *Democracy and Totalitarianism*. Edited by Roy Pierce. Ann Arbor: University of Michigan Press, 1990. First published in English by Praeger, New York, in 1969.

Campbell, Angus, Philip E. Converse, Warren E. Miller, and Donald E. Stokes. *The American Voter*. Chicago: University of Chicago Press, 1960.

Finley, M. I. *Politics in the Ancient World*. Cambridge: Cambridge University Press, 1983.

Freund, Julien. *L'Essence du politique*. Paris: Sirey, 1965.

Grawitz, Madeleine, and Jean Leca, eds. *La science politique, science sociale. L'ordre politique*. Vol. 1 of *Traité de science politique*. Paris: Presses Universitaires de France, 1985.

Habermas, Jurgen. *Between Facts and Norms: Contributions to a Discourse Theory of Law and Democracy*. Translated by William Rehg. Cambridge, MA: MIT Press, 1996.

Muller, Pierre, and Yves Surel. *L'Analyse des politiques publiques*. Paris: Montchrestien, 1998.

Oakeshott, Michael. *On Human Conduct*. Oxford: Clarendon Press, 1991.

Schmitt, Carl. *The Concept of the Political*. Translated by George Schwab. Chicago: University of Chicago Press, 2007.

Vullierme, Jean-Louis. *Le Concept de système politique*. Paris: Presses Universitaires de France, 1989.

PORTUGUESE

A Baroque Language

➤ BAROQUE, DASEIN, *DESTINY*, FICAR, HÁ, *MALAISE* [SAUDADE], MANIERA, *POETRY*, SPANISH

The Portuguese language, by virtue of its flexible syntax, the inversions of its punctuation, and its fondness for excess and rhetorical figures, is a baroque language. The characteristic traits of its philosophies—a penchant for aesthetic, metaphysical, existential, and "sensationist" questions—and the interweaving of its thought with literature derive from this original stamp. Although Portuguese literature has reached maturity, Portuguese philosophy, held back by the influence of Latin, has emerged only in recent centuries. Thus no one knows whether the baroque will persist or whether the philosophical language of the classics, which Portuguese is absorbing with the voracity of its "anthropophagic reason," will take it in new directions. With its very concrete expressions, its vitalism with regard to fundamental questions, and its aura of occultism, it is a language that overthrows the traditions of Western thought.

I. The Idea of the Baroque

"The finite sea may well be Greek or Roman, / Portuguese is the infinite ocean" (Pessoa, *Message*). The bonds connecting the Portuguese language with the idea of the baroque are circular and in some sense umbilical. "Baroque" comes from a word in the Portuguese goldsmith's art, *barroco*, which refers to irregular pearls, the rarest ones, whose obvious impurity gives them a high value, an additional mystery that cannot be grasped by reason and that invites us to go beyond it. Portuguese also uses *barroca* to refer to a cliff that overhangs an abyss, an escarpment produced by marine erosion that is unstable because it is made of clay, *barro*, a formless matter that has nonetheless retained the artisanal, biblical meaning of transcendence, like the lascivious flesh that can be brought to life by the divine breath. Before it spread to Italy and all of Europe during the Counter-Reformation of the seventeenth and eighteenth centuries, the baroque style was already emerging at the end of the fifteenth and sixteenth centuries in the symbols of the Manueline style, that last breath of the Gothic in Portugal. Its emblem is the armillary sphere, a globe containing brass rings representing the circles of the heavens and symbolizing the voyages that discovered new worlds in the East and West. With the ornamental exuberance of the maritime motifs in Lisbon's monasteries and palaces, which already overflow their Gothic skeletons and shed the melancholy greenish light of *saudade*, "Portugal offers us the archetype of the Baroque" (Ors, *Lo Barroco*), and along with it, the secret meaning of the spiritual history of Portugal. According to António Quadros (*O espírito da cultura portuguesa*), Portuguese writing "is viscerally baroque, expressing the sinuous, spiralling, spontaneous, dynamic, unpredictable, and creative practice of nature." This conception of natural writing—writing as nature creates—which contemplates the mystery of an insinuating and veiled order, is described this way by António Vieira, the "prince" of baroque prose:

> What are these celestial expressions and words? The words are the stars, the expressions are their composition, their order, their harmony, and their course. Consider how the way of preaching in the heavens is in accord with the style that Christ taught on earth. In both cases, it is a matter of sowing: the earth sown with wheat, the sky sown with stars. One must preach as if one were sowing, not as if one were paving or tilling. Ordered, but like the stars: *Stellae manentes in ordine suo.* All the stars are in order, but it is an order that inspires, not a laborious order. God did not make the heavens in the form of a checkerboard of stars, as preachers make a sermon a checkerboard of words.

> (*Sermão da sexagésima*)

Vieira's original baroque was opposed to the affected mannerism of some seventeenth-century Dominicans who tried to imitate Góngora or slavishly followed petrified rhetorical manuals. But first of all, it was opposed to the straight and antithetical order of which the checkerboard is the quintessential image and to the Cartesian linearity of classical reason. Therefore it is not surprising that in a culture as rationalistic and measured as the French, the term "baroque" was given so many pejorative connotations: "irrégulier, bizarre, inégal" (RT: *Dictionnaire de l'Académie Française*); "le superlatif du bizarre" (RT: *Encyclopédie méthodique*); "d'un bizarrerie choquante" (RT: *Dictionnaire de la langue française*); "qui est d'une irrégularité bizarre, inattendue" (RT: *Le nouveau petit Robert*). *Le nouveau petit Robert* confirms this bias by the synonyms it suggests: "biscornu, choquant, étrange, excentrique, irrégulier." Pellegrin outlines an explanation: this is a "defensive reflex" against "dangerous imperialism and the Counter-Reformation, the privileged vehicles of the baroque, of Roman and Jesuitical origin" ("Visages, virages, rivages du baroque").

The idea of the baroque defines thinking in the Portuguese language. We encounter this baroque question several times. First, in the interweaving of philosophy and art, since it is from art that we draw the idea of the baroque. Then in the intersection of the diachrony of language and so-called eternal philosophical problems: What does it mean to characterize a whole language by a privileged period, the baroque? Is there a crucial moment that henceforth determines in Portuguese a structure of writing and its philosophy? And this leads us to a final question, How do particular linguistic events peculiar to Portuguese provide access to a philosophical perspective, that is, to universal questions?

II. Between Art and Philosophy

A. A metaphysics of sensations

In Portuguese, thought inclines toward questions that have to do with art, aesthetics, and feelings. This also holds for Spanish and even Italian, whether we see in this the influence of the sea or that of the sun, Camus would say, on southern peoples. But thinking i n Portuguese inclines toward art and feelings even when it decides to speculate metaphysically. It produces "a metaphysics of sensations," to use an expression taken from Fernando Pessoa's *Sensationist Manifestos* and adopted by José Gil. This speculation is, moreover, often treated physiologically, as a special case of malaise: "Metaphysics is the result of an indisposition" (Pessoa, *Poesia de Álvaro de Campos*).

Metaphysics is usually approached from an existential point of view and deals with problems in philosophical anthropology, such as the feelings basic to nostalgia and melancholy (*saudade, fado*) or the moral ambiguity of sensual pleasure and of ecstasy.

■ See Box 1.

It is once again an existential perspective that marks the ontology of the difference between *ser* and *estar*; most languages have only the verb "to be." A question raised by some Iberian translators of Heidegger, who want to make him say in Spanish what German does not allow him to say; or by those who, like António Quadros, want to base the history of metaphysics on linguistic and cultural facts:

[T]he philosophy of existence, preceded, moreover, by the work of Kierkegaard and by that of the Iberian thinkers Unamuno and Leonardo Coimbra, emerges systematically in Germany with the thought of Heidegger and Karl Jaspers, as a reaction against the idealist absolutizing of a Being without qualities and blind to the concrete conditions of existence. These philosophers labored to distinguish between being in itself and being in the world, which the Portuguese language renders directly in the distinction between *ser* and *estar*.

(*O espírito da cultura portuguesa*)

The immediacy of the existential problematics conveyed by common usage, in Portuguese as in Spanish, is explored much further through the mediation of literature than through strictly philosophical speculation.

B. A philosophy inscribed in literature

"If a brilliant idea occurs to you, / it's better to write a song. / It has been proven that it is possible / to philosophize only in German" (Caetano Veloso, "Lingua," a song on his CD *Velô*). Portuguese thought, which is essentially baroque, often prefers to express itself by means of the art of the sermon, the novel, or poetry, as if the straightforward form of the philosophical treatise were unable to tame its overflowing vitality. Bernardo Soares, one of Fernando Pessoa's aliases, attributes this to the sonority of the language, and especially that of its vowels:

That hieratic movement of our clear majestic language, that expression of ideas in inevitable words, like water that flows because there's a slope, that vocalic marvel [*assombro vocálico*] in which sounds are ideal colours—all of this instinctively seized me like an overwhelming political emotion. And I cried. Remembering it today, I still cry. Not out of nostalgia for my childhood, which I don't miss, but because of nostalgia for the emotion of that moment, because of a heartfelt regret that I can no longer read for the first time that great symphonic certitude.

I have no social or political sentiments, and yet there is a way in which I am highly nationalistic. My nation is the Portuguese language.

(*The Book of Disquietude*)

An Italian noticed this as well: "There is no harmonic system comparable to the vocalic complexity of the Portuguese language which, including pure, nasal, and diphthongued vowels, has 43, forty-three voices—I say!"

1

Fado

➤ DESTINY

The word *faco*, from Latin *fatum*, refers first of all to fate or destiny, the irruption of time that thrusts the event into the midst of presence. This was undoubtedly understood as the result of the utterance (Lat. *fari, fabula*, Port. *fala*) of the gods decreeing directly what is and what will be without the symbolic intermediary of human language. For humans this is the irreversible condition in which they find themselves from birth on, the set of possibilities that cannot be transcended and that lead inexorably to death. Thus it is also the real power that marks human finitude. From this is derived a second meaning peculiar to Portuguese: *fado* is the melancholy feeling of the consciousness of this finitude and especially of its inexorability. Thus it is a feeling, or rather a disposition, that has its origin in a special metaphysical comprehension, probably drawn from some Stoic echo and from the Arab prophetic

tradition. We can find in it an analogy with the late Roman Empire: a spiritual maturity that was achieved at the moment of economic and political decline. For Portugal, it was the overseas empire that collapsed; the Portuguese language remains, pluralized in its idioms, over five continents.

Fado makes sensible an existential condition consisting in a feeling of weariness and aimless drifting. It is an often discreet melancholy by which one allows oneself to be borne along in places frequented specifically in order to experience it by listening to its expression: the most traditional kind of song in Portugal draws both its name and its inspiration from it. Fernando Pessoa describes it this way:

All poetry—and song is an assisted poetry—reflects what the soul lacks. Thus the songs of sad peoples are gay, and the songs of gay peoples are sad.

But *fado* is neither gay nor sad. It is an episode of interval. Before existing, the Portuguese soul conceived *fado* and desired everything without having the strength to desire it.

Strong minds attribute everything to Destiny; only weak ones trust personal will, because it does not exist.

Fado is the weariness of the strong soul, Portugal's scornful glance at the God it believed in and that immediately abandoned it.

In *fado*, the gods return, legitimate and distant.

("O fado e a alma Portuguesa")

BIBLIOGRAPHY

Pessoa, Fernando. "O fado e a alma Portuguesa." *O Notícias Ilustrado*, 2nd series, no. 44, 14 April 1929.

(Vincenzo Spinelli, quoted in António Quadros, *O espírito da cultura portuguesa*). The number is correct, but he exaggerated the singularity: Greek, which moreover invented the vowels that the Phoenician alphabet lacked, has as many; Greek does not have the nasal diphthongs (*ão, ães, ões*), but Portuguese does not make the quantitative distinction between long and short vowels [ε/η, o/ω]. If we add to this all the tonic riches explored by the Greeks in meter and by the Portuguese in rhyme, we understand that their first philosophers were poets. In Portuguese, a rhyme can appear in the last and in the penultimate syllable of a word: *rime aguda* (acute) for words whose tonic syllable is the final, like *parangolé*; *rime grave* for words whose tonic syllable is the penultimate, divided into masculines like *fado* and feminines like *fada*; and *rime esdrúxula* (lit., bizarre), for words in which it is the antepenultimate, such as *âmago*. In French, on the contrary, rhymes are more mnemonic supports than musical notations, since they are borne essentially by the last phonetic syllable.

But this aesthetic penchant does not concern prosody alone. If a positivist philosopher like Euclides da Cunha, having decided to write an essay on the messianism of the man of the desert, ended up writing, despite his philosophical and scientific pretensions, an emblematic novel—*Os sertões*—that is because the theme, deploying antithetical ideas, along with the vocabulary and expressions of the language, carried him away.

Thus the most significant philosophers writing in Portuguese are to be found in its literature, as if the latter were the primary way of grasping knowledge and existence:

> The preponderance of the improvised over the functional, the predominance of verve over argumentation, the prevalence of partying over work, the precedence of ritual over planning, the prejudice of the taboo against efficiency, the choice of superstition in preference to rationality, of thought in preference to knowledge, are the priorities that challenge the rigid parameters of evaluation, resist the constant rules of order, and reject the general principles of progress.

> (Carneiro Leão, "Tiers Monde")

These great philosophers of Portuguese literature, or if one prefers, these literary writers of its philosophy, are found far more frequently than philosophers who present themselves as such.

This explains why António Vieira, for example, is sometimes reduced to being no more than a Jesuit preacher of the seventeenth century, and yet, as "a faithful mirror of the baroque mentality, Vieira is considered the greatest representative of classical Portuguese prose" (RT: *Le nouveau dictionnaire des auteurs*, 3:3319)—"classical" because he is a model of the baroque style, of course.

But the man who fought from the pulpit the expulsion of the Jews in the Old World and against the enslavement of blacks and Indians in the New, the man who knew that to make its way into people's stubborn understanding a good idea needs true rhetoric much more than good arguments is only rarely considered a philosopher:

> Não está a coisa no levantar, está no cair : Cecidit. Notai uma alegoria própria da nossa língua. O trigo do semeador, ainda que caiu quatro vezes, só de três nasceu ; para o sermão vir nascendo, há-de ter três modos de cair. Há-de cair com queda, há-de cair com cadência, há-de cair com caso. A queda é para as coisas, a cadência para as palavras, o caso para a disposição. A queda é para as coisas, porque hão-de vir bem trazidas e em seu lugar; hão-de ter queda : a cadência é para as palavras, porque não hão-de ser escabrosas, nem dissonantes,hão de ter cadência : o caso é para a disposição, porque há-de ser tão natural e tão desafetada que pareça caso e não estudo : Cecidit, cecidit, cecidit.

> (It is not a matter of rising but of falling: *Cecidit*. Observe an allegory specific to our language. The sower's wheat, although having fallen four times, rises up only three times: in order that the sermon rise, it has to fall in three senses: it has to fall in the fall, it has to fall in the cadences, it has to fall in the coincidences. The fall is for subject matter, cadence for words, coincidence for arrangement. The fall is for the subjects discussed, because they have to be well prepared and in their proper place; they will have a "fall." Cadence is for the words, because they must be neither scabrous nor dissonant; they must have a "cadence." Coincidence is for arrangement, for it must be so natural, so free of affectation, that it resembles a "coincidence" rather than something studied: *Cecidit, cecidit, cecidit*.)

> (Vieira, "Sermão da sexagésima")

C. Rhetoric and concrete expressions in ordinary language

Repetition, excess, ostentation, play with mirrors, *mise en abyme*, and rhetorical figures are frequent, both in ordinary, everyday language and in more formal registers.

Negation, whose placement is relatively free, can be repeated for emphasis without reversing the polarity of the sentence. Two negations do not equal an affirmation. For example, *Não sei não* (I don't know at all) is a stronger form of *Não sei* or *Sei não* (I don't know).

In sentences with compound negations, a simple negation can also be added without changing the meaning: *Eu nunca disse nada a ninguém* (I've never said anything to anyone) is equivalent to *Eu não disse nunca nada a ninguém* and even to *Eu nunca não disse nada a ninguém*. The polarity is reversed only if the simple negation is placed immediately before the compound negation: *Eu não nunca disse . . .* (It is not true that I have never said . . .).

Syntactical inversions are frequent, and ambiguity is always felt to be closer to the real than the reasonable is, as in the expressions the realist writer Nelson Rodrigues likes to use that twist the common logic of meaning. He operates with an extremely flexible syntax that he bends in several different directions. The title of one of his tragedies, *Perdoa-me por me traíres*, (Pardon me for the fact that you are betraying me) reverses the expected *Perdoa-me por te trair* (Pardon me for betraying you) and loses in English (and in French) half the mirror-play and ambiguity of the original, which makes use, in order to carry out its twists, of the ellipsis of the subject and the personal infinitive conjugated in the second person singular.

■ See Box 2.

The nonfinite modes—the infinitive, the gerund, and the participles—which are usually the most abstract in modern languages, are more concrete in Portuguese. In addition to the infinitive, which may be conjugated according to grammatical persons, the participle is frequently used in several verbal expressions: with *estar*, "to be" (*estou cantando*, I am singing), *andar*, "to walk" (*ando comendo*, I've been eating), and *vir*, "to come" (*venho acreditando*, since I have believed). Like the continuous tenses in English, which is also a very concrete language, the participle determines the imperfective aspect of actions. Brazilian Portuguese, which is closer to Latin usage, often uses the participle in circumstantial complements such as *O garoto ouvia a história sorrindo* (The boy listened to the story smiling), whereas in Portugal people frequently prefer the more modern prepositional form of the infinitive: *A sorrir, o garoto ouvia a história*. Its use reminds us strikingly of the use of the participle in Greek, which is so important for worldly temporal relationships that Plato made it the name of this relationship: participation. Another passage from Vieira, chosen by Raymond Cantel, shows that "the personal infinitive makes a more concrete presentation possible," and, with the abundance of participles, makes us "feel better the cost and the difficulty" of the action:

[T]em o Holandês rebelde de se perturbar, vendo as nossas tropas de quatro Portugueses, e quatro negros marcharem tantas léguas de dificultosíssimos caminhos, sem camelos, nem elefantes, que lhes levem as bagagens, e andarem livres, e intrepidamente em suas campanhas, talando, e abrasando tudo apesar de seus presídios.

([T]he rebellious Dutchman has to be concerned to see our troops of four Portuguese and four blacks march [*marcharem*] so many leagues over such difficult roads, without camels or elephants to carry their baggage, and march [*andarem*] free and intrepid through their countrysides, razing and ravaging everything, despite their shackles.)

(Cantel, *Les sermons de Vieira*)

Portuguese occults words and even whole phrases by means of ellipses, the supreme figures of the baroque, often indicated by a series commas. It hides still more: sometimes, the whole conclusion of an idea is left up to the reader by the abundant use of ellipsis points. Skepticism? Insinuation? Esotericism? It is up to the reader to decide. Consider this bilingual title of André Coyné's bilingual book, *Portugal è um ente . . . De l'être du Portugal* (Portugal is an existent . . . On the being of Portugal), whose punctuation conceals and announces the subject's secrets.

Receptive to mysteries, sometimes mystical and messianic, Portuguese culture indulges madly in its numerous revivals of Sebastianism: the belief in the advent of a fifth universal empire (according to Daniel's interpretation of Nebuchadnezzar's dream), more spiritual and ideal, when there shall be an upheaval of the heavens and the earth, or the land and the sea, with the mythical return of the young king Sebastian of Portugal, who disappeared mysteriously at the Battle of Alcácer Quibir, in 1578, which was won by the Moors. Thus he became the "hidden king," an emblem of the mystical spiritual power, in prophecies (as in *The History of the Future*, which caused Vieira to be accused of making prophecies and for which he was imprisoned from 1665 to 1667) and in

---

2

The personal infinitive

The personal infinitive is a nominalizable verbal form, like any infinitive, and temporally indeterminate, but it is conjugated in all three persons of the singular and plural. It may or may not have a grammatical subject, but the real subject that underlies the verbal action is indicated by the verb ending. It is used when one wants to express this subject:

cantar (my singing, "my to sing")
cantares (your [fam.] singing, "your to sing")
cantar (his/her singing, "his/her to sing")
cantarmos (our singing, "our to sing")
cantardes (your singing, "your to sing")
cantarem (their singing, "their to sing")

To translate this into French, Italian, or Spanish, languages in which the infinitive usually takes on the function of a noun, the Portuguese expression may be attached to a grammatical person by adding a possesive adjective (*mon chanter*, *mi cantar*, etc.). Doing so is stylistically clumsy, but it avoids ambiguities. Consider this extract, in a truly untranslatable baroque style:

O quereres e o estares sempre a fim
do que em mim é de mim tão
desigual
faz-me querer-te bem,
querer-te mal
bem a ti, mal ao quereres assim
infinitivamente pessoal
e eu querendo querer-te
sem ter fim
. . .

(Your willing and desiring
what in me is
so different from me
makes me wish you well,
wish you ill,
well to you, ill to your
willing, so
infinitively personal
and I want to want you
infinitely
. . .)

(Caetano Veloso, "O Quereres")

BIBLIOGRAPHY

Togeby, Knud. "L'Énigmatique infinitif personellel en portugais." *Studia Neophilologica* 27 (1955): 211–18.

Veloso, Caetano. "O Quereres." *Velô*. Universal Distribution 824024, 1998, compact disc. Album originally released in 1984.

numerous secret societies: the Templars, Rosicrucians, etc. (see SAUDADE).

D. The masks of philosophy

Although they did not speculate directly, writers, novelists, and poets nonetheless liked, in a manner somewhat resembling Plato or Diderot, to make their characters philosophize. The cynical philosopher Quincas Borba, a character created by the nineteenth-century writer Machado de Assis, resembles Voltaire's Pangloss with his system of humanitism, which describes all human action as part of a single vital organism:

> *Humanitas*, he said, the principle of all things, is nothing other than the same man, distributed over all men. . . . Thus, for example, the headsman who executes a condemned man can excite the vain clamor of poets; but substantially, it is *Humanitas* that corrects in *Humanitas* an infraction of the law of *Humanitas*.
>
> (*Posthumous Memoirs of Brás Cubas*)

This spurious organicism cuts across the heterogeneous philosophies maintained by Fernando Pessoa's aliases: personalities or characters, the personae of an author who enjoys describing writers when this author writes texts—art completely displacing the monist status of truth and exploding the idea of subjectivity's self-identity. In this same vein, Guimarães Rosa's Riobaldo speculates on the loftiest problems of metaphysics and morals in his language that is semi-illiterate but full of lived experience:

> At first, I did my damnedest, and didn't think about thinking, I had no time for that. I lived a hard life, like a live fish in the frying pan: someone who's wearing himself out doesn't get all worked up. But now, seeing that I've got time, and no little worries, I just lie about. And I've discovered this taste for speculating on ideas. Does the devil exist or not?
>
> (Guimarães Rosa, *Grande Sertão: Veredas*)

It is a fine gloss in popular language but uses a vocabulary drawn from the oldest Western traditions, and in particular from the Aristotelian thesis about the connection between leisure and theoretical activity.

III. The Structure and Diachrony of the Baroque in Portuguese

It is hard to decide whether the baroque is a style that structurally determines Portuguese or is simply a stage in its history—a very long stage, to be sure, since its effects have persisted more than four centuries. There are arguments on both sides. In any case, it was, is, or will turn out to have been a style or a period for the constitution of Portuguese, just as the Renaissance was for Italian, classicism for French, or Romanticism for German.

A. Portuguese among Romance languages

Portuguese is the youngest of the neo-Latin languages—according to the Brazilian poet Olavo Bilac (1865–1918): "Latium's last bloom, uncultivated and beautiful"—delayed in its constitution as the national language by the Arab occupation up to the twelfth century. Originally a dialect of the region around the city of Porto, it was recognized officially only in 1256, by King Denis. That is no doubt why it is one of the modern languages closest to Latin. And that is not without importance in philosophy. The study of Latin remained obligatory in Brazilian and Portuguese secondary schools until the 1970s; all authors writing in Portuguese, except the very youngest, know it quite well. Jesuit scholasticism as a whole benefits from it. Vieira, one of the first philosophical writers in Portuguese, quotes the Vulgate in his sermons, as we have seen, without any pedantry. It was only with the expulsion of the Jesuits by the enlightened despotism of Prime Minister Pombal, at the end of the eighteenth century, that Portuguese replaced Latin in the university and the academic world. Plombal's reforms did a great deal to impose the Portuguese language: from the prohibition on the use of other languages in the colonies (lanugages such as Tupi, still widely spoken in Brazil at that time) to the adoption of a program of educational reform inspired by the works of the philosopher and linguist Luis António Vernay, a follower, in his own way, of John Locke's theories of knowledge.

B. A structural effect

The historical proximity of Latin marks the Portuguese language structurally, not only in its vocabulary but also in its syntax, which remains halfway between the old, inflected language and modern languages without declinations. Except for personal pronouns, Portuguese no longer declines words, but their syntagmatic positions in the sentence are nonetheless not fixed. There is a great syntactical mobility, which leads to problems of ambiguity—which is either explored or resolved by an abundant use of commas. All these elements of position and coordination dispose the Portuguese language to the rhetorical figures of the baroque: inversions, ellipses, syllepses, chiasmas, reiterations, etc. If the period is the absolute king of the classical sentence, the comma—twisted, sinuous, doubtful, concessive, reversing—dominates baroque discourse as a whole. Cunha and Cintra's RT: *Nova gramática do português contemporâneo* (New grammar of contemporary Portuguese) lists about twenty different uses.

The punctuation of Portuguese depends on its general way of constructing sentences. The long sentence full of subordinate clauses is very frequently used. There are even novels consisting of a single sentence, such as Raduan Nassar's *Um copo de cólera* (A glass of choler/cholera), a monologue in which punctuation is eliminated and the pauses are determined by the reader's need to breathe. The same oral eloquence is found in Haroldo de Campos's *Galáxias* (Galaxies), a poem that, when read aloud, calls for the rhythm of the *repentistas*, performers who challenge each other verbally until the improvised inspiration of their verses (their life) is finished. But in most cases, the long sentence does not eliminate punctuation; on the contrary, it multiplies commas, semicolons, colons, dashes.

A single example will suffice—a sentence from Carneiro Leão's *Third World* and his own free translation of it into French ("Tiers Monde"), which forgoes the baroque figures of the Portuguese original:

Todo passo é uma aventura de originalidade: passeando pela essência do real, nossos passos caminham pela originariedade do caminho, caminhar e caminhada.

(Every step is an adventure in novelty/originariness: strolling through the essence of the real, our steps walk upon the originality of the path, to walk walked.)

Car chaque pas est une aventure. En se promenant à travers l'essence de la réalité, nos pas cheminent dans l'originalité du chemin.

(Every step is an adventure. In strolling through the essence of reality, our steps walk in the novelty/originariness of the path.)

Originalidade and *originariedade* are both translated by *originalité*; *caminho, caminhar*, and *caminhada* become simply *chemin*; and the untranslatable paronymy *passo, passear* is lost. The sentence is divided into two.

C. A season of language

The fact that Portuguese is a young language may mean not that it owes it flexible syntax to a definitive structure but instead that it is still open to unexpected changes. Will these changes take place, freezing the language in a more rigid structure, or will it retain the characteristic traits of the baroque? Modern languages have generally gone through a process of maturation that involved the translation of classical Greek and Latin texts. During and after these great waves of translation, some of the most significant writers and philosophers in each language arose because they wanted to compete with the ancient models or detach themselves from them. The quarrel of the ancients and the moderns in France and the German Enlightenment and Romanticism are examples of this. Portuguese has not yet finished this task of translating the ancients; it is still at the beginning. Although some translations of Plato and the pre-Socratics have been published, the same cannot be said of translations of Aristotle, for example, which are often simply modeled on English or French translations.

Is the acquisition of the classics preparatory to the advent of a language that is itself more classical? Brazil is developing an "anthropophagic reason," propagated in literature by the concretist movement of Augusto de Campos, Haroldo de Campos, and Décio Pignatari, Brazilian semiologists and poets who have been exercising their neobaroque influence since the foundation in 1952 of a group called Noigandres (the flower that leads ennui astray). Oséki-Dépré offers this comment on Haroldo de Campos's work *De la raison anthropophagique. Dialogue et différence dans la culture brésilienne*:

> . . . in total accord with Oswald de Andrade's "anthropophagic reason," which he conceives as "the thought of the critical devouring of the cultural and universal legacy elaborated not on the basis of the subjected and reconciled perspective of the 'noble savage,' but on that of the disabused point of view of the 'bad savage' who devours whites, the cannibal." Haroldo de Campos makes explicit and confirms the idea of the "anthologist" attitude of transcreation, a "translation that presents itself

as a radical operation," a translation of form, of the "mode of intentionality," of the "aim" of a work, to speak in Benjaminian terms. . . .

Whether it be through transcreation or through intertextuality, "anthropophagic reason" is realized in the same perspective: discovering and disseminating the new text, broadening the poetic range of the Portuguese language, expanding the literature, in a renovated language, through the virtual and organically new poetic information.

("Le concret baroque")

After all, nothing prevents a language thoroughly crisscrossed by the appropriation of the classics from producing pages that remain just as rampant, twisted, curvy, sensual, baroque.

Portuguese, perhaps by its existential and sentimental tendencies, or perhaps by its heterogeneous syntax, overthrows the abstract status of some universal philosophic notions. The important role played by the information of the aspectual details of verbs, which even multiplies copulative verbs (see FICAR and SPANISH) and which gives time a very humanized, lived, carnal character, undermines the rigid architecture of a very rectilinear reason. In this language, concepts are never columns of cold, white, eternal marble; instead, they are curves sensually shaped in soapstone, like those sculpted by Aleijadinho, which do not even try to conceal the ravages of time.

Portuguese express the passage of time and the presence of death, especially because they feel them and usually suffer from them. Sadness, nostalgia, and lassitude are the shifting and swampy ground on which they establish their foundations. If sensual pleasure arises, that is only the result of this awareness of the brevity of life. Therefore it is not surprising that philosophy written in Portuguese tends toward a metaphysics of sensations, more aestheticizing and existential, more inclined toward worldly, human problems, and that more logical or mathematical abstraction has little success. The recent impact of analytical philosophy, which is stronger in Brazil than in Portugal, might turn philosophy toward a simpler and more rigid syntax, although it is closely linked to English-language sources and limited to academia. So long as the spirit of the language remains under the spell of melancholy and the sensual pleasure of the times, universities and philosophical institutions seem to be permanently supplanted by the arts and by literature, which are more sensitive to human experience. Unless, through an inversion that draws thought from the sensations of existence, philosophical abstraction might be perceived as the product of an extreme nostalgia without an object. Then thought would recognize as its own this area that is guarded only by the muses and the Horae, the seasonal gods:

Vi que não há Natureza,
Que Natureza não existe,
Que há montes, vales, planícies,
Que há árvores, flores, ervas,
Que há rios e pedras,

Mas que não há um todo a que isso
   apparpertença,
Que um conjunto real e verdadeiro
É uma doença das nossas idéias.

(I've seen that there is no Nature,
That nature does not exist,
That there are hills, valleys, plains,
That there are trees, flowers, pastures,
That there are rivers and stones,
But that there is no whole to which all this belongs,
That a true and genuine whole
Is a disease of our ideas.)

(Pessoa, *Collected Poems of Alberto Caeiro*)

Fernando Santoro

BIBLIOGRAPHY

Campos, Haroldo de. *Galáxias*. São Paulo: Editora Ex Libris, 1984.

Cantel, Raymond. *Les sermons de Vieira: Étude du style*. Paris: Ediciones Hispano-Americanas, 1959.

Carneiro Leão, Emmanuel. "Tiers Monde." *Sociétés* 2, no. 2 (February 1986): 3–4.

Costa, João, ed. *Portuguese Syntax: New Comparative Studies*. New York: Oxford University Press, 2000.

Guimarães Rosa, João. *Grande Sertão: Veredas*. Rio de Janeiro: Editora Nova Fronteira, 2006. First published in 1956. Translation by James L. Taylor and Harriet de Onis: *The Devil to Pay in the Backlands*. New York: Knopf, 1963.

Levenson, Jay A. *The Age of the Baroque in Portugal*. New Haven, CT: Yale University Press, 1993.

Machado de Assis, Joachim Maria. *The Posthumous Memoirs of Brás Cubas*. Translated by Gregory Rabassa. Oxford: Oxford University Press, 1999.

Ors, Eugeni d'. *Lo barroco*. Madrid: Tecnos, 1993.

Oséki-Dépré, Inês. "Le concret baroque." In *Galaxies*, by Haroldo de Campos, translated by Inês Oséki-Dépré. La Souterraine, Fr.: La Main courante, 1998.

Pellegrin, Benito. "Visages, vivrages, rivages du baroque." In *Figures du baroque*, edited by Jean-Marie Benoist and Suzanne Allen. Paris: Presses Universitaires de France, 1983.

Pessoa, Fernando. *The Book of Disquietude*. Translated by Richard Zenith. Manchester: Carcanet, 1996.

———. *The Collected Poems of Alberto Caeiro*. Translated by Chris Daniels. London: Shearsman Press, 2007.

———. *Fernando Pessoa & Co.: Selected Poems*. Translated by Richard Griffin. New York: Grove Press, 1998.

———. *A Little Larger Than the Entire Universe: Selected Poems*. Translated by Richard Griffin. New York: Penguin, 2006.

———. *Message*. Translated by Jonathan Griffin. London: Menard Press, 1992.

———. *Poesia de Álvaro de Campos*. Lisbon: Ática, 1944.

———. *Selected Prose of Fernando Pessoa*. Translated by Richard Zenith. New York: Grove Press, 2001.

Quadros, António. *O espríto da cultura portuguesa*. Lisbon: Sociedade de Expansão Cultural, 1967.

———. *A idéia de Portugal na literatura portuguesa dos últimos 100 anos*. Lisbon: Fundação Lusíada, 1989.

Spinelli, Vincenzo. *A língua portuguesa nos seus aspectos melódico e ritmico*. Lisbon: Quandrante, 1940.

Veloso, Caetano. "Lingua." On *Velô*. Universal Distribution 824024, 1998, compact disc. Album originally released in 1984.

Vieira, António. "Sermao da sexageima" [Sermon for Sexagesima]. In *Obras Completas*, vol. 1. Porto: Lello, 1951. First published in 1655.

———. *Sermões*. 2 vols. São Paulo: Hedra, 2000.

———. *Sermon of Saint Anthony to the Fish and Other Texts*. Translated by Gregory Rabassa. Dartmouth, MA: University of Massachusetts Dartmouth Press, 2009.

POSTUPOK [поступок] (RUSSIAN)

FRENCH   *action, acte libre, engagement*

➤ *ACT,* and DASEIN, DRUGOJ, DUTY, ISTINA, *LIBERTY, PERSON,* PRAVDA, PRAXIS, RUSSIAN, SAMOST', SVOBODA, *TO BE*

The Russian word *postupok* [поступок] has been rendered in French by *action* and by *acte*. However, *action* corresponds to the Russian *dejstvie* [действие], and *acte* corresponds to the Russian *akt* [акт]. Both translations are thus insufficient. *Postupok* designates a singular, personal action that presupposes responsibility, not necessarily a morally good act, but an "ethical act." According to Mikhail Bakhtin's philosophy of the act, *postupok* is carried out from the position specific to each individual—what Sartre was to call *engagement*.

I. Action: From *Dejstvie* to *Postupok*

The Russian term *dejstvie* [действие], "voluntary manifestation of an activity," is the equivalent of the French *action*. Unlike *dejstvie*, *akt* [акт] refers to an action that is more technical than voluntary and connotes the action's completion (RT: *Tolkovyĭ slovar' zhivogo velikorusskogo iazyka*, 1:9). *Dejstvie* is the modern neuter form of the old elevated word *dejanie* [деяние], derived from the verb *dejati* [деяти], "act" (see RUSSIAN, "L'opposition diglossique en russe"). *Dejanie* corresponds to the Greek *pragma* [πρᾶγμα], and to the Latin *actus, actio* (RT: *Materialy dlia slovaria drevnerusskogo iazyka*, 1:800). In Old Russian *dejati* also meant "touch" and "speak" (Sreznevskiĭ, *Materialy*, 1:800–802), but these meanings have now disappeared. Until the beginning of the twentieth century, the term *postupok* [поступок] was presented in dictionaries as equivalent to *dejanie* (RT: *Tolkovyĭ slovar'*, 3:348; RT: *Etymological Dictionary of the Russian Language*, 409).

The word *postupok* comes from the Old Russian noun *postup* [поступ], "movement, action, act" (Sreznevskiĭ, *Materialy*, 2:1270) and, finally, the verb *stupat* [ступать], "to walk, pace." Etymologically, *postupok* thus means "the step one has taken." In contemporary everyday language, the term means "intentional action," "an individual's behavior" (RT: *Slovar' russkogo iazyka*, 3:326). Thus, even in its prephilosophical usage, *postupok* refers to a singular, personal action; it is thus the best translation of Greek *praxis*, in the sense of an individual's act (e.g., in Aristotle).

II. Three Levels of *Postupok* in Bakhtin

The contemporary philosophical meaning of *postupok* has been influenced by Mikhail Bakhtin's ethical existentialism. In his unfinished work, *Toward a Philosophy of the Act*, he connects the crisis in contemporary philosophy (he was writing in the early 1920s) with its inability to move beyond the limits of the theoretical world. According to Bakhtin, only the philosophy of the ethical act (*postupok*) can constitute a first philosophy capable of surmounting the split between culture and life.

Bakhtin elaborates the concept of *postupok* on three levels.

1. The absolute level combines singularity (*edinstvennost'* [единственность]) and participation (*pričastnost'* [причастность]). Bakhtin's starting point is the fact expressed by the assertion "I am." This fact has two

aspects, the singularity of individual existence—it is I who am—and its participation—I am to be.

> *Et ego sum* (*I ja—esm'* [И я—есмь]), I too, exist actually (*dejstvitel'no* [действительно]) . . . I, too, participate in Being in a once-occurrent and never repeatable manner: I occupy a place in once-occurrent Being that is unique and never-repeatable, a place that cannot be taken by anyone else and is impenetrable for anyone else.

> (Bakhtin, *Toward a Philosophy*, 40)

One must therefore understand the singularity of a person as his non-coincidence with everything that is not himself.

The word *esm'* in the expression *ja esm'* ("I am") is the archaic Slavonic (and therefore elevated) form of the verb *est'* [есть], the infinitive of which, *byt'* [быть], is the root of the word *bytie* [бытие] ("to be"). Moreover, *bytie* is the elevated term in the opposition *bytie/suščestvovanie* [существование] ("existence") (see ISTINA). To stress the absolute character of the fact of the "singular participation" of a person in Being, Bakhtin introduces the metaphor of the "non-alibi in Being" (*ne-alibi v bytii* [не-алиби в бытии]). Man has no moral alibi: he can escape neither his own singularity nor his unique place. It is on this non-alibi in being that the duty to act is based:

> That which can be done by me can never be done by anyone else. The uniqueness and singularity of present-on-hand Being is compellently [*sic*] obligatory.

> (Ibid.)

2. The level of existential choice is situated between responsibility (*otvetstvennost'* [ответственность]) and duty (*dolženstvovanie* [долженствование]). However, duty is not absolute in character. One can in fact choose to assume responsibility for one's own existence or to ignore it and become an impostor (*samozvanets* [самозванец]). Only the acceptance of responsibility creates duty.

> Duty is possible only where there is a recognition of the existence [*bytie*] of a singular person within himself. . . . The responsible act [*postupok*] is an act [*postupok*] based on the recognition of one's constraining singularity.

> (Ibid., 113)

3. The ontological level concerns the act (*postupok*) and the event (*sobytie* [событие]). The singularity of a person is definitively realized only in a responsible act:

> The act [*postupok*] constitutes once and for all the actualization of the possible in the singular.

> (Ibid., 103)

However, according to Bakhtin, the being in which I participate cannot be reduced to the world of my act alone. The ultimate subject of moral philosophy is "the being-event" (*bytie-sobytie* [бытие-событие]), the world of the intersubjective event. The Russian prefix *so-*, the equivalent of Latin *co-*, designates a common characteristic of being. By its etymology

sobytie is "common being, common existence, co-existence." Bakhtin metaphorically actualizes the term *bytie-sobytie*:

> The real being-event [*bytie-sobytie*] is determined not in and by itself, but precisely in relation to my own constraining singularity: If the "face" of an event is determined from the unique place of a participative self, then there are as many different "faces" as there are different . . . [individual poles of subjective responsibility.]

> (Ibid., 45)

The whole set of personal worlds creates a unique event.

The word *sobytie* comes from the verb *sbyvat'sja* ([сбываться], "to be realized"). Another meaning that is clearly present in *sobytie* is thus that of the realization of the singular existence of the Self (see SAMOST'). It is only in the world shared with others that this realization takes place: in *sobytie* the individual makes his singular place a responsible step (*postupok*) toward others (see SVOBODA and DRUGOJ).

Thus the *postupok* is the responsible act through which a person participates in being. From the point of view of values, the *postupok* cannot be subordinated to the goals, desires, or needs of which it is the realization. Unlike the act considered by analytical philosophy, the *postupok* is a value in itself, that is, an ultimate value: "The act [*potupok*] is a final accounting, an ultimate, deepened conclusion" (ibid., 103). That is why, according to Bakhtin, only the *postupok* unites the world of culture with that of life.

Andriy Vasylchenko

BIBLIOGRAPHY

Bakhtin, Mikhail. *Toward a Philosophy of the Act*. Translated by Vadim Liapunov. Austin: University of Texas Press, 1993.

| POWER, POSSIBILITY

"Power" derives from Latin *posse*, which itself goes back to the adjective *potis*, meaning "powerful, master of" (on the Indo-European root **poti-*, which designates the leader of a group, family, clan, or tribe; cf. Gr. *posis* [πόσις], "spouse," *despotês* [δεσπότης], "master of the house," *potnia* [πότνια], "mistress"). However, the Latin verb, and in particular the impersonal *potest*, from which derived in the time of Quintilian the learned adjectives *possibilis* and *impossibilis*, created to translate Greek *dunatos* [δυνατός] and *adnunatos* [ἀδύνατος] (from *dunamis* [δύναμις], "strength"; see DYNAMIC), expresses, like the impersonal Greek *dunatai* [δύναται], "possibility" (*fieri potest ut*, "it may happen that"). Thus *pouvoir* operates in the area between, on the one hand, possibility as a logical category modality (*possibilitas*) that is distinct from the impossible, the contingent, and the necessary, and that is connected with potentiality as an ontological category (*potentia*) determining the real or the actual, and, on the other hand, power (*potestas*) in the moral and political sense, to establish a relationship with duty and authority. The interferences between these two major meanings, logico-ontological and ethicopolitical, within the diverse linguistics systems, are particularly noticeable in the entries DUTY and WILLKÜR, I.C.

I. Power, Possibility, Potentiality

A. Logical modality

On the expression of possibility as a category of modality, in its relation to negation and time, see, for example, ASPECT, INTENTION, *NEGATION, NOTHING,* PRÉDICABLE, PRESENT, PRINCIPLE, VERNEINUNG, WUNSCH.

Cf. *PROBABILITY* [CHANCE], and *DESTINY.*

B. Ontological modality

The "possible" is taken first of all in the sense of what is "potential" as opposed to what is actual: see *ACT, I* (esp. PRAXIS and FORCE, on the matricial difference *dynamis/energeia* [ἐνέργεια]). Something that is "physically" possible satisfies the general conditions of experience: see *EXPERIENCE, IL Y A,* NATURE, *PHÉNOMÈNE* [ERSCHEINUNG]; cf. EPISTEMOLOGY. In a certain ontological perspective, possibility merges with reality (*realitas*): see in particular ATTUALITÀ, REALITY, RES ; cf. ESSENCE, SPECIES.

II. Power and Political Power

Power is nothing other than the ability to act and, more precisely, to act in an effective way in pursuing goals: see *ACT, II* [PRAXIS].

Political power designates the ability to make others act in a specific way, even if this requires coercion; thus it differs from authority: see *AUTHORITY* and HERRSCHAFT.

On the relation between *potentia* and *potestas,* power and violence, see MACHT; cf. LEX, PIETAS, RELIGIO. Generally speaking, power is of considerable importance in modern moral and political philosophy, which stresses freedom more than virtues and the ability to coerce more than authority: see *LIBERTY* [ELEUTHERIA, POSTUPOK, SVOBODA], *OBLIGATION* [SOLLEN], *VIRTUE* [VIRTÙ], WILL, WILLKÜR; cf. *DROIT,* LAW, MORALS, *STATE.*

➤ GOD, SECULARIZATION

PRAVDA [правда] (RUSSIAN)

ENGLISH	righteousness, justice, truth
FRENCH	*justice, équité, vérité*
GREEK	*dikaiosunê* [δικαιοσύνη]
LATIN	*justitia*

➤ *JUSTICE,* THEMIS, TRUTH, and *DROIT,* ISTINA, LAW, MIR, POSTUPOK, PRAXIS, SOBORNOST', SVET

The word *pravda* [правда], despite the unambiguous nature of the equivalents used to translate it: "truth," *vérité, Wahrheit*—designates not only truth but also justice. The accent falls chiefly on the latter meaning when we examine words that have the same root: *pravo* [право] (law), *spravedlivost'* [справедливость] (justice, equity), *pravosudie* [правосудие] (justice, correct judgment). But *pravda* is not a homonym: its meaning resists a complete separation of the notions of *istina* [истина] (truth) and *spravedlivost'* (justice), of theory and practice. *Pravda* is never used to designate scientific truth. We can gauge the effects of untranslatability by the fact that *pravda* is usually rendered by "truth," neglecting its initial semantic field: justice, legitimacy, law, equity.

I. Slavic *Pravda* and Indo-European "Justice"

The Slavic word *pravda* [правда] corresponds to the Greek *dikaiosunê* [δικαιοσύνη] and the Latin *justitia.* It is formed on the Slavic root *prav,* "straight, just" (RT: *Ėtimologicheskiĭ slovar' russkogo iazyka* [Etymological dictionary of the Russian language], 352). The most plausible etymology traces *prav* back to Indo-European **pro-vos,* related to Latin *probus,* "good, honest" (*probhus*), Sanskrit *prabhús,* "exceptional, superior," and Anglo-Saxon *fram,* "strong, active, courageous." In Old Church Slavonic, Bulgarian, Ukrainian, and Russian, the first sense of *pravda* is "justice" and the second "truth"; in Serbo-Croatian, *prâvda* means "legal prosecution, trial"; in Slovene, *pravdâ* means "regulation, law, legal action"; *pravda* in Czech and Slovak and *prawda* in Polish have analogous connotations. In contemporary Russian the word *pravednik* [праведник], "just man," goes back to Old Church Slavonic and corresponds to Greek *dikaios* [δίκαιος] ("just"), *hagios* [ἅγιος] ("saint"), *martus Christou* [μάρτυς Χριστοῦ] ("martyr to Christ"). To the antonym *nepravda* [неправда] correspond *adikia* [ἀδικία], *anomia* [ἀνομία], "injustice."

Logically, the word *pravda* should occupy a central place in the philosophical dictionary of the language to which it belongs. But if we try to find the article "Pravda" in the five-volume philosophical encyclopedia published in the USSR, we have to acknowledge its absence. Why? This silence, which distances itself from the title of the periodical *Pravda,* the official voice of the authoritarian regime, leads far beyond ideological considerations and the circumstances of place, time, or censorship, and allows us to take another approach to classical theologico-political problems. The historian and philosopher George Fedotov, who emigrated to the United States after the Second World War, offers the following explanation: "The Russian word *pravda* has a particularly rich meaning: it can mean 'justice,' 'righteousness,' and even 'truth.' And we certainly encounter it through its contrary, *nepravda* (injustice) at every step of the way in the annals of relations between powers" (*Russian Religious Mind,* 2: 171).

Translations do not betray us when *pravda* renders the Greek *dikaiosunê* in the Septuagint or *dikê* [δίκη] in Heraclitus or Sophocles (Antigone's *dikê* is rendered as *pravda*). Classical expressions such as "the sun of *pravda*"—*sol justitiae*—reflect a traditional ethico-cosmological analogy whose essence is revealed by the principle according to which "the world holds together thanks to the just." The inverse is presupposed to be true: the just themselves depend on the analogy between the order of the world (*mir* [мир]) and the order of the city so long as this analogy lasts. Once this traditional bond was broken by modern physics, the semantic stability of *pravda* was affected, and first of all, its proverbial practical character. In the standard dictionary of V. I. Dal', *pravda* is defined as "truth in action, truth manifested, the good; justice done, equity." In the examples Dal' gives, the accent is clearly on active participation and the act as such: "Practice justice and *pravda*," "fight for *pravda*," "live in accord with *pravda*"; and *pravdivost'* [правдивость] (a substantive derived from *pravda,* signifying conformity with *pravda* and usually translated by "veracity, sincerity") is explained as "complete adequation between utterance and action." Many expressions of this kind remain alive in the Russian language today, going back to expressions that bear witness to the lasting influence of the first translations into Slavic of the liturgy, the psalms, and the Scriptures made by Cyril and Methodius in the ninth century, hundreds of years before the Latin Vulgate passed into other vernacular languages. The main instrument of literacy was the Book of Psalms, and learning to read conveyed this analogy between the order of the created world and that of the city.

■ See Box 1.

II. *Pravda* and the Gap between "Legality" and "Legitimacy"

The semantic development of *pravda* did not undergo the systematic and direct influence of Roman law. The limits of the word were not determined within a system of codified notions, so that a series of obstacles to radical inquiry into its relationships with jurisprudence in the strict sense of the term did not arise. But history provides unquestionable proof that these relations had all their meaning from the outset: *pravda* is a key notion in vernacular law and gave its name to the oldest collection of laws set down in writing by the East Slavs, *The Russian Pravda* (eleventh century). Although the modernization of legal terminology changed the semantics of *pravda*, its legal sense was not erased but given a superior status. At the same time that he asked Leibniz to draw up a system of social classification for his empire, Peter the Great ordered Feofan Prokopovich to define the emperor's absolute legal power in a document entitled *The Pravda of the Monarch's Will* (1722; we see in this text the direct influence of Hobbes and Pufendorf). Can *pravda* in this title be rendered as "legitimacy"? This translation was to be contested more than once. In response to the absolutist version of a radical rationalization of law, there followed a no less radical reaction on the part of the Russian Jacobins led by Colonel Pestel (hanged 1825), who entitled his constitution *The Russian Pravda*. But can *pravda* be translated here by "constitution"? This historical question was answered in the negative by the unsuccessful attempts to limit the monarch's *pravda* constitutionally—until the revolution of 1905.

Questions of this kind do not reduce the philosophical and philological problems of translation to historical and political problems. By relativizing our representation of the immutable essence of the word *pravda*, we discover its now concealed semantic dimensions, which have remained at the stage of unrealized possibilities. Untranslatable today, they represented potentialities of translation in the network of European idioms; but the course of revolutions has led to their not being actualized. However that may be, confronted by this massive forgetfulness, it is important to emphasize that the original legal meaning of the word *pravda* has passed through all sorts of vicissitudes, including the 1917 revolution's systematic destruction and abolition of the Czarist regime's legal institutions and the traditional linguistic representations of justice.

III. The Bipolarity *Pravda/Istina*

Law and ethics designate practical philosophy as the domain for the positive application of the notion of *pravda*; the negative definition of the limit of this notion's use is provided by the theory of knowledge and the natural sciences: the latter operate with *istina* [истина] and not *pravda*.

Modern sciences sometimes reject the word *pravda* and sometimes eliminate its immediate semantic context, as in "promises, oaths, injunctions, commands, decrees, regulations, laws, contracts, judgments, witnesses" (Uspensky, *Jazykovaja situacija Kievskoj Rusi*). Ancient philosophy broadened the domains in which the word "law" (*nomos*, [νομός]) could be applied by transferring it by analogy from the *polis* [πόλις] to the *kosmos* [κόσμος], from the human world to the natural world. Starting in the seventeenth century, under the influence of advances in mechanics, the analogy was turned around: the concept of "physical" law, following the demonstration of its unprecedented effectiveness in describing material objects, began to determine the conception of justice and "social physics." Naturalism was erected into a social project. Of the different aspects of action—"who?" "where?" "when?" "how?"—naturalism absolutized the one most distant from humans and circumstances: "what (to do)?" The leveling of the dimensions constitutive of *pravda*—references to the person and the situation ("opportunity" [καιρός], see MOMENT, II; Aristotelian "equity" [ἐπιεικής], see THEMIS, IV)—made *pravda*

1

The Slavic liturgical language

In the twentieth century R. Jakobson and N. Trubetskoy demonstrated the fundamental linguistic and liturgical role played by Cyril and Methodius in constituting the lexicon of the principle Slavic notions. Their hermeneutics was explicitly developed in the course of the controversy in Venice in 867 regarding "the heresy of three languages," in which translation into the Slavic language was accused of infringing on the sacred character of the three "untranslatable" liturgical languages: Hebrew, Greek, and Latin. The innovation of Cyril and Methodius was taken over in Hussite translations (fourteenth century),

had repercussions on vernacular translations throughout Europe at the time of the Reformation, and finally led to the liturgical reform adopted by Rome in the twentieth century, as well as to the proclamation of Cyril and Methodius as patrons of united Europe (1980).

But what is paradoxical today is the situation of the Slavic language itself (in which an important role is assigned to the word *pravda*): just as in the case of Latin until recently, a discussion is going on concerning Slavic's untranslatable character (see RUSSIAN). In the precise case of the word *pravda*, its liturgical use has retained, in the language of

Dostoevsky and Pasternak, traditional semantic strata that disappear when it is translated by the "secular" words "justice" and "truth."

BIBLIOGRAPHY

Jakobson, Roman. *Selected Writings*. Vol. 6: *Early Slavic Paths and Crossroads*. New York: Mouton, 1985.

Trubetskoy, Nikolai Sergeyevich. *Obščeslovianskiy element v russkoj kulture* [The pan-Slavic element in Russian culture]. In *Histoire. Culture. Langue*. Moscow: Éd. Progress, 1995.

———. *Travaux du Cercle linguistique de Prague*, no. 8. Prague, 1939.

entirely dependent on an *istina* interpreted instrumentally. But that did not eliminate the bipolarity between *istina*, which corresponds to the question of "being," and *pravda*, which corresponds to the question of "ought to be." For instance, *istina* notes the "physiology" of a disease affecting an individual or a society; *pravda* moves to the question of what must be, in opposition to what must not be. The necessity of actively realizing *pravda* takes on a particularly menacing character when it is reduced to the practical application of an already known *istina*. Separating *pravda* from the concrete "who" (fundamentally inaccessible) and from the concrete "where" (which localizes knowledge), made it more abstract and manipulable. At the turn of the twentieth century, the "conflict of faculties" ended with the belligerent domination of the natural sciences and the Russian nihilists' notion that it was possible to apply to society schemas as rigid as Mendeleev's periodic table of elements. This model represses the semantic plurality of the term *pravda* illustrated by the proverb "to each his own *pravda*."

IV. The Short-Circuit between *Pravda* and Violence

The revenge of *pravda* in a space geometricalized by science takes on a moral and universal character. Tolstoy's protest against violence is not limited to a devastating criticism of the police state, war, and the military but is also directed against the judicial system, whose function of limiting violence cannot be performed without resorting to violence. What is required is the implementation of a radical separation between the *pravda*-pardon of the Gospels and the *pravda*-vengeance of the pagans. The petition that Solovyov and Tolstoy addressed to Alexander III in 1881 on behalf of regicide terrorists provides a historical example: "Using violence to render justice means admitting that *pravda* itself is powerless. Contemporary revolution shows by its acts that it acknowledges that *pravda* itself is powerless. But in reality *pravda* is strong, although the violence of contemporary revolution betrays its impotence" (Solovyov, *Smysl sovremennyx sobytij*, 38).

The abolition of slavery in America and in Europe (including Russia, in 1861) explains in part the elevated level of hopes for justice and goodwill during this period. Solovyov ironically sums up this irrational leap into naturalistic argumentation in the following syllogism: "Man is descended from the apes, therefore let us love one another." The fear that the "sources of the self" (to adopt Charles Taylor's title) might go bankrupt or become insolvent is connected with the gap that opens between the moral precept and the one who formulates it in a "sermon on the mount," on the one hand, and the space in which people try to put it into practice, on the other. The major factor of space—from the Baltic to the Pacific—has a considerable influence on the topos of *pravda*, subjecting it to a linear logic and the leveling that we find in the revolutionary *tabula rasa*. Geographers have calculated that the dimensions of Nicholas II's empire amounted to one-sixth of the earth's surface. The globalization of an egalitarian system of justice in this world without limits and borders sheds light on the implacable logic described in Dostoyevsky's *The Devils* and put into action by Bolshevism. The determination expressed by his characters, who set out to erase evil as such on the continent, does not

lead to the emergence of "the new man" but is transformed into vengeance taken on anything that resists them. On the way to revenge, justice deteriorates into mere vengeance. Twisted in this way, *pravda* does not cut the Gordian knot of violence but finds itself still more tightly bound by it, losing its natural ally, freedom.

All or nothing, thesaurus or *tabula rasa*, those are the two poles of the controversy between Solovyov and nihilism. The argument of Solovyov's work *Opravdanie dobra* (1896 [The justification of the good]) seeks to demonstrate the conjunction of civil liberty (law) and freedom of conscience (morality) in *pravda*. Opposing Tolstoy's juridical nihilism, Solovyov writes concerning *pravda*:

> Here we have a term which alone embodies the essential unity of the juridical and moral principles. . . . In all languages, moral and juridical notions are expressed either by the same terms or by terms derived from the same root . . . *dikê* and *dikaiosunê*, *jus* and *justitia*, as in Russian, *pravo* [право] (law) and *pravda*, in German *Recht* and *Gerechtigkeit*, in English *right* and *righteousness*. The two meanings are distinguished by suffixes. Cf. also the Hebrew ṣèdèq [צֶדֶק] and ṣedāqāh [צְדָקָה].

> (Solovyov, *Justification of the Good*, 317)

Solovyov defines *pravda* as "the right relation toward everything" (ibid., 136); it is the universal principle of his philosophical system.

For his book *L'Idée russe*, written in French, Solovyov quotes and translates the Slavophile Axakov's judgment regarding the transformation of the administrative structures of the church into a department of the state apparatus: "For the ideal of a truly spiritual government (*pravlenie* [правление], inner *pravda*) has been substituted by that of a purely formal and external order (*pravda*, *ordre*)" (191). Why did Solovyov translate *pravda* by the French word *ordre*? The translation difficulty arises in part from the noncorrespondence between two incongruent elements: on the one hand, external and internal *pravda* in Russian, and on the other hand, *justice-institution* and *justice-vertu* in French. In an article written in German, "The Russian Worldview" (1925), Siméon Frank, the greatest of Solovyov's disciples, emphasized that

> The Russian language has a very characteristic word that plays an extremely important role in the whole structure of Russian thought—from the popular way of thought to creative genius. This untranslatable word is *pravda*, which designates simultaneously the *istina* and moral and natural law, just as in German the word *richtig* designates something appropriate or adequate on both the theoretical and the practical levels.

The unity of *pravda* and *pravo*, broken and presented as archaic by the nihilist point of view, was reconstituted by Solovyov and Frank. In response to the charge of archaism, they undertook an archeology of *pravda*.

V. Projects Seeking to Move beyond the Theory/Practice Opposition with the Help of *Pravda*

In the modern period the untranslatability of the word *pravda* is connected with the separation between the *vita activa* and the *vita contemplativa* (Hannah Arendt). The invention of "technology" (of the concept and of the phenomenon, as is shown by the school of Alexandre Koyré) is determined by the fact that the paradigm of the divergence between *technê* [τέχνη] and *epistêmê* [ἐπιστήμη] in Plato and Aristotle is replaced by that of their convergence in Descartes and Bacon. The axiomatics of "practical philosophy" and of basic concepts is transformed by terminological "practicism" as the decisive criterion of scientific theories and ideological doctrines. Dependence on a technological invention like the printing press paves the way for a political instrumentalization of *pravda*.

After Kant's two *Critiques*, setting rigorous limits to "theoretical reason" and "practical reason," three paths leading toward their synthesis emerged in European philosophy: the aesthetic-anthropological (Schiller), the politico-speculative (Hegel), and the socio-historical (Marx).

a. The aesthetic synthesis of Schiller's Russian followers tended to unify practical good and theoretical *istina* within the concept of *pravda*: that is the specificity of the "message" of the Russian novel and the leitmotiv of literary and social criticism (beyond the cleavages between conservatives and revolutionaries). The way in which N. K. Mikhailovsky formulated this idea has gone down in the annals of the radical intelligentsia:

Every time the word *pravda* occurs to me, I cannot help marveling at the extraordinary beauty it contains. This word exists, it seems, in no other European language. Only the Russian language, it appears, designates truth and justice by the same word, so that they seem to merge in a grandiose unity.

(Mikhailovsky, *Écrits*)

b. The Slavic Hegelians' political synthesis tends to unify truth and justice in the concept of the state. But while in Germany the state is defined by the philosophy of right (*Recht*), in Russia it is defined by the philosophy of *pravda* (legitimacy-justice). The short-circuiting of the concepts of state and *pravda* characterizes the utopia of the right-wing Hegelians. Thus the ideologues of "Eurasianism" reconceptualized *pravda* in statist terms. In 1921 the Eurasianist historian M. Shakhmatov concluded his study "The Pravda State (Essay on the History of Statist Ideals in Russia)" (in *Evrazijskij Vremennik* [Eurasian annals], 4 (1925): 304) with the following diagnosis:

Contemporary Europe has moved away from the "*Pravda* state." Some of its elements have been preserved only in England, where religion and law, law and ethics, have not yet been completely separated.

This kind of diagnosis conflates two orders of "untranslatability." The rationalization of the jurisprudence of various European traditions has not made the concepts *pravda*/*Recht*/"law" identical (whence the reference to a "traditional" England; see LAW). In addition, within the limits of the Russian language, one cannot formulate *pravda* in juridical terms, which in Europe are determined by the separation of religion, morality, and law, and especially of force and law.

c. "The unity of theory and practice" proclaimed by Marxism-Leninism is the main cause of the latter's success in Europe, which seeks in vain the aforementioned unity. Marx returned the Aristotelian concept of *praxis* to the center of philosophy, reorienting it toward a "technology of history." Marxism promised humanity that it would make political action intelligible in the present and historical theory intelligible in the past and the future, and it replaced the Bible in the libraries of the intelligentsia. But at the same time the biblical notion of *pravda*, which was full of forgotten eschatological promises, retained for the Russian intelligentsia its value as a symbol of a new synthesis. After the 1905 revolution it was subjected to criticism by thinkers who had broken with Marxism, such as N. Berdyayev, P. Struve, S. Bulgakov, S. Frank, et al. To the intelligentsia's *pravda*, Berdyayev opposed the "philosophical *istina*" and called for a search for a different synthesis, "a synthesis that responds to the intelligentsia's legitimate and positive need for an organic unification of theory and practice, of *pravda-istina* with *pravda-justice*) (Berdyayev, "Intelligentskaïa pravda," 29). But in accord with Lev Shestov's pessimistic analysis, *pravda* is helpless to resist the expansion of Utopia, that is, of a system of hypertheoretical responses to hyperpractical questions.

VI. The Difficulties of Retroversion: Justice-*Pravda*-Truth

Introduced by Saint-Simon and Fourier, the expression "social justice" is rendered in Russian by *pravda*. A century of the development of revolutionary ideas was also to confer on both the social idea and its lexical form a semantic freight absent in Western sources. In the nineteenth century, the word *pravda*, even without the adjective "social," was loaded with an explosive connotation. It was a challenge to the old semantic order. This connotation is easily discernible in what Dostoevsky wrote when he was a young follower of Fourier; it is modified substantially, though it has not entirely disappeared in his last works, where he warns against the revolutionary obsession. It is around the word *pravda* that the web of the (meta)juridical trials in *Crime and Punishment* and *The Brothers Karamazov* is woven. *Pravda* provides the axis of the "Pushkin speech" (1880), which is considered Dostoyevsky's intellectual testament (Heidegger's "European Nihilism," for example, opens with a quotation from this speech). If we take into account the major semantic enrichment of the notion, retranslating *pravda* into French by resorting to the initial concept of "social justice" would be reductive and unacceptable. But translating *pravda* into French by *vérité* is an example of "untranslatability" that deprives the reader of the references that intersect in the search for "justice" in France and in Russia (francophone Russian intellectuals cross French ideas with Old Church Slavonic). Dostoyevsky writes:

Truth [*pravda*] is not outside yourself, but in yourself; find it in yourself, subject yourself to yourself, dominate yourself yourself, and you will see the truth [*pravda*]. It is not in things, this truth [*pravda*], it is not outside you or somewhere beyond the seas, it is above all in your own work on yourself. Overcome yourself, repress yourself—and you will be free as you have never dreamed of being free, and you will undertake a great work, and make others free, and find happiness, for your life will be filled with joy and you will finally understand your people and its sacred truth [*pravda*].

(Dostoyevsky, *Diary of a Writer*, 1356)

VII. *Pravda*: A Word That Has the Force of Law and That Goes beyond the Law

As a universal laboratory always in search of *pravda*, literature has powerfully contributed to shaping the idea: the "word" (*slovo* [слово]) replaces the judge and the supreme law (note that *slovo* is an "untranslatable": it means both "word" and "discourse," "address," "saying," and refers back to *logos*).

"Starting with Gogol, Russian literature sets out in quest of *pravda*, and teaches us how to achieve it" (Berdyayev, *Origins of Russian Communism*). Vladimir Solovyov said that, before the defeat at Sevastopol, Gogol's *Dead Souls* was for Russia the "Last Judgment." The notion of *pravda* was then associated with the Inspector General (*Revizor*) in the old Czarist regime. *Pravda*, like the Inspector General, penetrates all the cells and affairs of the capital and the provinces of the empire, revealing his analytical power and imposing his fundamental criteria. *Pravda* and *Revizor* travel incognito. "One must not cheat with words"—this maxim of Gogol's was used by Solovyov as an epigraph to the article written toward the end of his life about the question of freedom of conscience in the Russian Empire. The imbroglio of lies that characterized the relations among the state, the church, society, the secret police, literature, censorship, the universities, and the educational system became particularly unbearable in light of the judgments made by Gogol, Dostoyevsky, Leskov, Saltykov-Shchedrin, Tolstoy, and Chekhov. The paralysis of the legal system and the imperial government's tendency to infringe the law at all levels of the administrative hierarchy much more radically than in other European cultures led to distrust of the judicial system, whereas confidence in verbal judgment increased. The word that does justice—*pravda*—is not presented as a commentary on or a complement to existing law, or even as its competitor, but as a tribunal in the absence of law, as the legislator of an alternative justice. Assigned this function, the word is endowed with new potentialities revealed by the challenges and ordeals of Russian and Soviet history; for the same reasons, it is less developed than it is in countries that have not experienced totalitarianism. This is a historical reason for the difficulty of translating *pravda* as the uprightness of verbal judgment, of the word invested with the power to make final, authoritative decisions.

Solovyov sought to examine from a philosophical point of view the theme of decision-making responsibility that constitutes the (non)correspondence of word and action in great empires. According to him, the Second Rome, the thousand-year-long Byzantine Empire, fell because of the contradiction between a pagan conception of the state inherited from the First Rome and the commands of Christ, affirmed in words but ignored in acts. It was this same contradiction that deprived Ivan the Terrible's "Third Rome" of legitimacy. According to Solovyov, Peter the Great's revolution destroyed less the organic unity of old Russia than

it unmasked the hypocrisy concealing the contradiction between pious words and impious actions. The concept of contra-diction (*protivo-rečie* [противоречие]) thus recovered its initial practical meaning (more concrete than in Hegelian logic). *Mutatis mutandis*, we can say that for *pravda* the "criterion of contradiction in practical philosophy" established by Solovyov is just as fundamental as the Aristotelian principle of non-contradiction is for *istina* in theoretical philosophy.

Solovyov reintroduced, above and beyond German idealism, the initiative of carrying out the mutation of European practical philosophy; according to him, this project went back to Patristics, from Origen to Saint Augustine and Maximus the Confessor—in numerous Slavonic translations of Pseudo-Dionysius, *Pravda-Dikaiosunê* is one of the names of God. Moreover, we must emphasize the radical difference between this project and those of Kierkegaard and Nietzsche, which are analogous to it in other respects, seeking the transformation of Western metaphysics. The point of departure for Solovyov and Dostoyevsky is not the isolated individual whose freedom breaks the bonds uniting people to each other and appears to be "irrational" with regard to universal reason but the verbal relationship between free beings, the verbal bond that counts on shared freedom and on a life open to the paradox of *pravda*.

VIII. *Nepravda*: Principle and Effect of "Newspeak"

Nepravda is the key word that allows us to characterize an ideological regime that systematically falsifies its discourse. In his novel *1984* George Orwell gave a precise description of the fundamental relation that links *nepravda*—lawlessness—to terror directed against traditional "untranslatabilities" and against formal logic (on the pediment of the "Ministry of Pravda," we can read the slogan "War is Peace"). The path that leads to social arbitrariness passes by way of a semantic mutation of the vocabulary. The cleavage between two words derived from the same root, *pravo* (law) and *pravda*, is the result of the implementation of Soviet newspeak. In the twentieth century remarks concerning the original meaning of *nepravda* ("crime, infraction of the law") disappeared from dictionaries. Dal'''s dictionary (1881) has this to say about *nepravda*: "any illegitimate, violent action contrary to conscience; vexation, unjust judgment, iniquity. . . . Latin equivalents: *injuria, injustum, improbitas, inaequitas*." But Dal' explains the change in *nepravda* and *pravda*—which he regards as contemporary:

The meaning of these words has been deformed almost before our very eyes, because now they have become synonyms of "lie" (*lož* [ложь]) and "truth" (*istina*). . . . But originally *istina* referred solely to intellectual notions, while *pravda* referred to moral qualities, and that is why our first body of laws was called *The Russian Pravda*.

(Dal', *Tolkovyĭ slovar'*, 2: 529)

What is emphasized here is a specific historical stage in the rationalization of *pravda*, the breaking of its ties with the juridical and moral spheres; these ties have been significantly loosened but are still perceptible in the uses of its antonym. In the article "Criminal Act" in Brockhaus and

Efron's encyclopedic dictionary (RT: *Entciklopediceskij slovar'* [Encyclopedic dictionary], vol. 25), "crime" and *nepravda* are considered equivalents, specifying the forms of juridical *nepravda*: criminal *nepravda* and civil *nepravda*. Soviet dictionaries completely rejected the juridical sense of *nepravda* and reduced its moral content to a minimum. We might say that the extreme narrowing of the word's meaning corresponded to an extreme broadening of the reality of *nepravda* in a criminal state. In response to the Soviet dictionaries, George Fedotov wrote:

> The word *pravda* can reply to those who have not totally forgotten the meaning of this word. The *pravda* that is on the way to exile opposes participation in the general *nepravda*, in unjust proceedings, edification, work, or deeds at the bottom of which lies a fundamental *nepravda*.

> (*Tiažba o Rossii*, 200–201)

IX. Exile for *Pravda, Philo-dikaia, Philo-xenia*

The refusal to participate in a "collective *nepravda*" organized in a systematic fashion through the implication of everyone in a collective crime and responsibility is the initial act of George Fedotov's philosophy of exile. He adds a particular topological accent to the ancient and modern theme of the exit from the totalitarian "cave," that of "exile for *pravda*":

> It is easy to be exiled for *pravda*; but it is difficult to live for *pravda* in exile. *Pravda* is not like statues of the gods that one can take along when fleeing Troy in flames. It has to be permanently vivified, felt again and again in the heart and mind. Otherwise it withers, leaving only a shell of desiccated words.

> (Ibid., 203)

How can one reply when words like "freedom," "democracy," "equality," and "justice" were so discredited during the period between the two world wars? One response, a difficult one, is exile, as an act and as an object of reflection, as a historical phenomenon specific to the twentieth century, that of "displaced persons." Hannah Arendt expressed her high esteem for Fedotov's thought in her book *The Origins of Totalitarianism*, and his liberal philosophy and critique of Soviet pseudo-*pravda* were developed in America by M. Karpovitch and M. Malia. In the liberal tradition the reestablishment of the connection between freedom and *pravda* (after their divorce in Marxism-Leninism) takes on a decisive importance, even if its price is exile. Fedotov analyzes the historical relevance of the Gospels' encouragement of "those who are persecuted in the name of justice [*pravda*]." "Exiled" (*izgnannye* [изгнанные]) and "persecuted" (*gonimye* [гонимые]) are words that have the same root in Russian. The same goes for the two kinds of emigration, the one that moves "toward the outside" and the one that moves "toward the inside." The topology of exile manifested externally, visible to all, discovers and offers a chance to reveal to the world the vast, invisible archipelago of "internal exile." Its reality is denied by the ideologues of the new regime and written off by Western adversaries of communism. In both cases, the revolution's *tabula rasa* is simply accepted as a given recognized by everyone. Fedotov deconstructs this a priori assumption that serves as the basis for all debate about communism. Instead of discussing the claims made about this *tabula rasa* that was the USSR, covering about one-sixth of the planet's surface, Fedotov examines it as a palimpsest and deciphers the lines and meanings that have been effaced. Hegelians on both the right and the left (A. Kojève, G. Lukács) followed the course of the Absolute through history by reading the collective letters published in the newspaper *Pravda*; Fedotov, on the contrary, scrutinized the "effaced" and silent destiny of those who, despite the party's orders, did not sign these letters, who crossed their names off the lists of the historical *nomenklatura*, who deprived their families of any place in the sun of Humanity. The rigorous distinction between the concepts of the "sense of history" and *pravda* gave these people effaced by the winners' history a right to exile. "The *Pravda* of the Defeated" is the title of a programmatic article of 1933, in which Fedotov contrasts two opposed philosophies of history: the Hegelian and the Augustinian. The reexamination of the latter is guided by an axiom: the smallest movements toward good or evil are impossible to erase. Hospitality accorded to those who have no place in either the political system or the idealist system is situated in a hermeneutics of the palimpsest: "To bet on those who are today without power, who hide in 'the caves and burrows' of Soviet life, on those whose voices do not reach us, but of whom, in truth, neither Russia nor the 'the entire world are worthy,' let us dare to bet on these unknown people, in full awareness of the risk we are taking: that is Pascal's wager, the wager of faith, the wager without which no one's life is worth living" (*Tiažba o Rossii*, 313).

An internal emigré, Osip Mandelbaum established the link between exile in the name of *pravda* and the topological analysis of Dante's *Inferno*. The word *pravdo-ljubie* [правдолюбие] (*philo-dikaia*) refers us to a semantic matrix analogous to the one Émile Benveniste described in the combination of *philos* and *xenos* (see LOVE). The paradigmatic example of *philo-dikaia* was provided by the radical hospitality granted by the Glagolev family in 1941, in Kiev, to a Jewish family in danger of being shot by the Nazis. The Glagolevs gave their guests their house, their passports, and their name. An important document about this has been published: Father Alexis Glagolev, *In the Name of His Friends* (*Novy Mir*, no. 10, 1991). Here hospitality becomes synonymous with solidarity in exile. Paul Celan used Marina Tsvetayeva's formulation of *philo-dikaia* as an epigraph: "Poets are youpins." Here *philo-xenia* and *philo-dikaia* are one and the same thing. Such a topology of *pravda* is at the antipodes of the utopia of the "pravda-state."

X. The Paradox of *Pravda*

In the American translation of the *Great Soviet Encyclopedia* in thirty-five volumes—which is among the great dictionaries, being both a reference work and a unique testimony to the period of the cold war—the word *pravda* is translated as "truth." No reference is made to justice, right, or righteousness. This biased translation of a biased article devoted to the newspaper with the largest circulation on earth represents the tip of the iceberg: the British called this encyclopedia "lies in alphabetical order."

At the opposite of this pole of lexicographic falsification, we find the simple absence of an entry for *pravda* in the five-volume *Philosophical Encyclopedia*. The figure of the unsaid is an expressive one, the sign revealing the situation of the hostage concept in the post-Stalinist vocabulary. The void where the article on *pravda* should be in the *Philosophical Encyclopedia* can be understood not as a lacuna in a text invested with ideological authority but as a rip or tear and a manifestation of the palimpsest on *pravda* on which Fedotov, from his exile in Paris, made his Pascalian wager.

The catastrophe in Chernobyl in 1986 and the official lies about it revealed to millions of people the Achilles' heel of the Soviet system: "the fear of *pravda*," "pravdaphobia" (Struve, *Pravdobojazn'*, 101–3). Who is afraid of *pravda*?—that is the slogan of the liberating discourse of *glasnost'* [гласность] (another untranslatable term, made ordinary by the "public voice" or by "transparency"). We are witnessing the collapse of the experiment with the "artificial eclipse" of the sun of *pravda*. Justice-truth regarding communism not only brings out the fundamental contradiction between words and acts; more profoundly, there is the contradiction between the word and its double in "newspeak." The collapse of the word-idol leads to that of the word-usurper, which excludes verification by means of question and answer. Elaborated by the works of M. Bakhtin and S. Averintsev, the critique of monologic discourse—the rejection of the other—and the philosophy of dialogue enter into civic discourse.

The empires of the twentieth century have not erased once and for all dialogue and tension between the two constitutive poles of Europe: the *istina* of Athens and the *pravda* of Jerusalem. Socrates's ability to deliver a speech about truth (*istina*) during his trial presupposed a real legal framework that forbade his being interrupted by blows or by torture. In Jerusalem *istina* presupposes *pravda* in a significantly different sense. Like *pravda*, the Hebrew word *'Èmèṯ* combines the meaning of "truthfulness" (*istinnost'* [истинность]) with that of "accuracy" and "justice" (Averintsev, *Sophia-logos*, 396). The corresponding French terms, *justesse* and *justice*, show the lasting influence of the translation of the Psalms. French leaves open the possibility of this semantic identity, for example in the expression "*c'est juste*," meaning "it is true." But the contrast between this marginal performative in French and a fundamental notion in the Slavic languages shows what a great philosophical task is faced by the translator. The paradox of *pravda* is not limited to the declination of justice and truth in a single word. The meaning of *pravda* is anterior to the distinction between the practical and the theoretical. But the bipolarization that characterizes these notions today leads to the formation of a discourse incapable of including the translation of the word *pravda*. Its resistance to translation indicates that *pravda* is irreducible to concepts and refers us back to the philosophical tradition of *docta ignorantia*. In his work *The Unknowable*, Simeon Frank demonstrates the link uniting *pravda* with this tradition, which goes back to Nicholas of Cusa and the writings of Pseudo-Dionysius. *Pravda*'s apophatic horizon here encounters Socrates's awareness of his ignorance. The classic formula *inattingibile inattingibiliter attinguntur* (understanding through an awareness of the incomprehensible character of something) describes *pravda*. The criticism of the limits of translation is transformed into a way of understanding the untranslatable. Frank writes:

> We cannot speak of a superior *pravda*, express it as such with our concepts, because it speaks about itself, expresses and reveals itself silently; and we have neither the right nor the ability to express this self-revelation adequately by means of our thought; we must remain silent before the grandeur of *pravda* itself.

> (Frank, *Unknowable*, 313)

Hegel described the modern world as a way of life in which the newspaper had been substituted for the morning prayer; in the twentieth century the newspaper *Pravda* tried to put into practice the ultimate consequences of this substitution or "revolution in communication." To those who seek to interpret the postcommunist, atheistic world, the problem of the untranslatability of this key concept suggests the following strategy: not offering an overall interpretation of the "totalitarian system," not deducing the meaning of the word *pravda* from the concept of "totalitarianism," but reversing the point of view—questioning ideologies that claim to include theory and practice, past and present, *vita contemplativa* and *vita activa*, by opening up to the paradoxes of *pravda*.

Constantin Sigov

BIBLIOGRAPHY

Arendt, Hannah. *The Human Condition*. Chicago: University of Chicago Press, 1998.

Averintsev, Sergei. *Sophia-Logos: Slovar'*. Kiev: Dukh i Litera, 2000.

Bakhtin, Mikhail. *Toward a Philosophy of the Act*. Translated by Vadim Liapunov. Austin: University of Texas Press, 1993.

Berdyaev, Nicolai. "Intelligentskaïa pravda i filosofskaïa istina." In *Vekhi. Iz Glubiny*. Moscow: Pravda, 1991.

———. *The Origins of Russian Communism*. Translated by R. M. French. Ann Arbor: University of Michigan Press, 1960.

Dostoyevsky, Fyodor. *The Diary of a Writer*. Translated by Boris Brasol. New York: Charles Scribner's Sons, 1949.

Fedotov, George. *The Russian Religious Mind*. Vol. 2: *The Middle Ages: The Thirteenth to the Fifteenth Centuries*. Cambridge, MA: Harvard University Press, 1944–46.

———. *Tiažba o Rossii* [The dispute over Russia]. Paris: YMCA Press, 1982.

Frank, Simeon L. *The Unknowable: An Ontological Introduction to the Philosophy of Religion*. Translated by Boris Jakim. Athens: Ohio University Press, 1983.

Malia, Martin. *Russia under Western Eyes: From the Bronze Horseman to the Lenin Mausoleum*. Cambridge, MA: Harvard University Press, 1999.

Shestov, Lev. *Athens and Jerusalem*. Translated by Bernard Martin. Athens: Ohio University Press, 1966.

———. *Dostoevsky, Tolstoy, and Nietzsche*. Translated by Bernard Martin and Spencer E. Roberts. Athens: Ohio University Press, 1969.

Solovyov, Vladimir. *Divine Sophia: The Wisdom Writings of Vladimir Solovyov*. Translated by Boris Jakim, Judith Kornblatt, and Laury Magnus. Ithaca, NY: Cornell University Press, 2009.

———. *Justification of the Good: An Essay on Moral Philosophy*. Translated by Nathalie A. Duddington. London: Constable, 1918.

———. "Smysl sovremennyx sobytij [The meaning of current events]." In *Écrits en deux volumes*, 34–38. Moscow: Pravda, 1989.

Struve, Nikita. "Pravdobojasn' [Pravdaphobia]." *Vestnik* [*Le Messager*] 2 (1986): 147.

Uspensky, Boris. *Jazykovaja situacija Kievskoj Rusi i eë znacenie dlja istorii russkogo literaturnogo jazyka* [Linguistic situation in Kievan Rus and its importance for the study of the Russian literary language]. Moscow: MGU, 1983.

Walicki, Andrzej. *Legal Philosophies of Russian Liberalism*. Oxford: Clarendon Press, 1987.

PRAXIS [πρᾶξις] (GREEK)

ENGLISH   praxis, practice, action, agency
FRENCH   *praxis, pratique, action*
GERMAN   *Praxis*
ITALIAN   *prassi*

➤ *ACT* [ATTUALITÀ, TATSACHE], AGENCY, ART, *EXPERIENCE,* EXPERIMENT, I/ME/
MYSELF, LOGOS, PATHOS, PLEASURE, *POETRY* [DICHTUNG], *PRUDENCE,*
SUBJECT, *THING* [RES], VIRTÙ, VORHANDEN, WORK

The term *praxis* [πρᾶξις]—always seen in modern languages as
imported from Greek, even though German and to a certain extent
Italian have naturalized it (*die Praxis* [with a German plural, *die
Praxen*], *la prassi*)—is central in contemporary philosophy, where it
designates, depending on the case, an alternative to the points of
view and values of being of *logos* [λόγος] or language, of theory or
speculation, of form or structure, and so on. It refers, then, either
to an Aristotelian version (*Nichomachean Ethics*) that opposes it to
poiêsis [ποίησις] and relates it to an ethics and a politics of "prudence" (*phronêsis* [φρόνησις]), or to a Marxist version (*Theses on
Feuerbach*) that identifies it with the effort to transform the existing
world rooted in labor and class struggle (*umwälzende* or *revolutionäre Praxis*). Between these two poles there is a Kantian version of
the practical element of action (*das Praktische*) and the "primacy of
practical reason," which, by assigning to philosophy an infinite task
of moralizing human nature (a task called "pragmatic" [*pragma-
tisch*]), consummates the break with naturalism and prefigures the
dilemmas of collective historical action. If all of these points of view
continue to provide indispensable reference points for philosophy,
that is because they correspond to ways of thought, to irreducible
political and metaphysical choices that nonetheless constantly
intersect and confront one another: in this way, an "ambiguity of
praxis" has been constituted transhistorically and poses a problem
for philosophy that is just as unavoidable as the "ambiguity of
being."

Two key problems arise from *praxis* [πρᾶξις]. First, should it be
translated? Second, to what language does it belong, Greek or
German? These two problems are not really separable: they define
an exemplary process of appropriation that essentially comes down
to the Marxist transformation of the Aristotelian category, by way of
a Kantian or post-Kantian problematics. Most of the connotations
attached to the use of *praxis* now come not directly from the Greek
source, but from German uses of the term, especially post-Marxist
ones, that have been sufficiently naturalized to constitute an autonomous reference competing with the Greek or overdetermining
its heritage to the point of sometimes making paradoxically difficult
a "Hellenism" that might otherwise seem unproblematic, as in the
case of Hannah Arendt.

We will examine first Aristotle's constitution of the *praxis-poiêsis-
epistêmê* [πρᾶξις-ποίησις-ἐπιστήμη] triad and its transformation
into *praxis-poiêsis-theôria* [πρᾶξις-ποίησις-θεωρία], in order to
determine its anthropological meaning. Then we will show how the
Marxist thesis—which argues that *Praxis* provides a criterion of truth
or reality for both the idea and the social power of emancipation—
condenses the tensions of a "philosophy of practice" developed by
German idealism in the wake of Kant. We will also note indications
of another classic way of connecting "theory" with "practice" that
stretches from Francis Bacon to positivism (Auguste Comte), by
way of the French Encyclopedists. Finally, we will compare a few

great twentieth-century returns to the problem of *praxis* (including
projects for reconstituting a "philosophy of praxis") that either try
to fulfill the promises of Marxism (Georg Lukács, Antonio Gramsci,
Jean-Paul Sartre, and, by antithesis, Louis Althusser), or seek to
propose an alternative to its political conception (Jürgen Habermas,
Hannah Arendt), or to modify the term's semantic value in order to
locate it, along with nature, morality, and history, in the element of
institution and usage (Ludwig Wittgenstein).

I. The Aristotelian Conceptualization and Its Ambivalence

The Greek noun *praxis* is one of the nouns of action corresponding to the verb *prassô* [πράσσω] (to go all the way the
end of, to cross; and then to complete, to accomplish; and,
more generally, to do or to act), alongside *pragma* [πρᾶγμα],
which is more concrete: *praxis* is usually rendered in English
as "practice," "experience," "custom" (in French as *action* [ac-
tion], in the sense of *exécution, entreprise, conduite* [execution,
enterprise, conduct]), and *pragma* by pragmatics (in French,
chose, affaire [thing, object], or, in the case of the plural, *ta
pragmata*, as *les faits* [facts] but also *les affaires, les choses de la
vie* [business, the things in life]). See in RES, Box 1.

All uses of the term *praxis* in philosophy (its translations and nontranslations) are determined by the powerful
Aristotelian concept introduced in the *Nicomachean Ethics*,
where it is one of the main themes. It is by virtue of the privileged position of *praxis* in Aristotle's thought that Aristotle's
work ended up shaping the "practical philosophies" centered on an ethical concern with a teleology of the good (*telos*
[τέλος]), (*agathon* [ἀγαθόν]) with all of the compounds with
eu [εὖ], and with individual and collective "value" or "excellence" (*aretê*) [ἀρετή], traditionally translated as "virtue." At
a certain point, "practical philosophy" was transformed into
"the philosophy of practice": a shift made possible by the
heft of the classical term *praxis*.

A. The system of Aristotelian *praxis*

Praxis is inseparable from the ramified uses of the verb
prattein [πράττειν] and its qualifications as established
in the first lines of the *Nicomachean Ethics*: "*ta prakta* [τὰ
πρακτά]," actions (1.1, 1094a1); "*to d' eu zên kai to eu prattein* [τὸ δ' εὖ ζῆν καὶ τὸ εὖ πράττειν]," good living and
good acting (1.1, 1095a19); "*hoi de charientes kai praktikoi*
[οἱ δὲ χαρίεντες καὶ πρακτικοί]," men of culture and men
of action—practically synonymous with political action:
"*hoi politikoi* [οἱ πολιτικοί]" (1.3, 1095b22); "*to dikaio-
pragein* [τὸ δικαιοπραγεῖν]," acting in accord with justice
(1.8, 1099a19); and so on.

These uses have two basic types of extension and intension. On the one hand, there is the "broad" type, which we
would today call "formal," in which *praxis* connotes everything that has to do with action and operation (in contemporary philosophical English, the term "agency" is used)
and that consequently is opposed to mere dispositions and
to an "inactive" or speculative kind of life: "*epeidê to telos
estin ou gnôsis alla praxis* [ἐπειδὴ τὸ τέλος ἐστὶν οὐ γνῶσις
ἀλλὰ πρᾶξις]" (Since the goal is not knowledge, but action:
Nicomachean Ethics 1.1, 1095a5–6). What all of these uses have
in common is their emphasis on the form of the "exercise,"
the duration, repetition, and assiduity of which ensures the

improvement of results or of the agent's abilities. That is why, even when *praxis* is opposed to knowledge or discourse, it nonetheless connotes them, as soon as they require repeated exercise and a learning process (2.3). In many passages, *praxis* or *prattein* could not be better translated than by "application" or "exercise": "*haper ek tou pollakis prattein ta dikaia kai sôphrona periginetai* [ἅπερ ἐκ τοῦ πολλάκις πράττειν τὰ δίκαια καὶ σώφρονα περιγίνεται]*" (*A development that can come only from assiduous exercise of justice and wisdom:* 2.3, 1105b4–5).

On the other hand, the uses of *praxis* and the whole register of the "practical" are clearly connected—in a way we might call substantial—to a specified domain, which is that of approved behaviors. The latter, in turn, are organized around two poles: one that is specifically ethical and concerns the quality or value of individuals and their behavior, and another that is political (politics being, Aristotle tells us, the "organizing" or "fundamental" (*architektonikê*) discipline, and the object of the treatise on ethical virtues being "political in a way": "*politikê tis ousa,*" 1.1, 1094b11), that is, relative to the city, to the way in which people act there toward others and on each other. The two sides of the term thus merge in the idea of "making oneself" by acting for the common good in accord with the virtue of *phronêsis* [φρόνησις], "prudence" or "practical intelligence." This is the ideal of self-sufficiency or *autarkeia* that is suitable, not for a "solitary animal," but for man, who is "political by nature" (1.5, 1079b8–11)—an autarky that is, however, as we shall shortly see, likely to be quite differently reinvested.

■ See Box 1.

B. The tripartite classification of *praxis, poiêsis, and epistêmê/theôria*

Aristotle begins by distinguishing among *praxis, technê* as *poiêsis,* and *epistêmê* in order to valorize the field of *praxis* and the virtue or excellence that is peculiar to it (*phronêsis,* examined in book 6 of the *Nicomachean Ethics*). He then shifts the opposition by substituting *theôria* for *epistêmê,* which sublimates its meaning and reverses the corresponding evaluation. He situates *theôria* at the limits of the human, as is indicated by its contact with divinity—for example, in book 10, which is devoted to the question of pleasure. Later thinkers tended, on the one hand, to erase the difference in point of view between the two triads—that is, to make *theôria* (which gradually lost its theological connotations) a simple equivalent of *epistêmê*—and, on the other hand, to reduce—not without exceptions and resistances, even within great systems—the ternary point of view to a dualist one, a simple opposition between "theory" and "practice."

The first triad (*praxis-poiêsis-epistêmê*) is constructed in the first lines of the *Nicomachean Ethics* (1.1, 1094a1), "*pasa technê kai pasa methodos, homoiôs de praxis te kai proairesis* [πᾶσα τέχνη καὶ πᾶσα μέθοδος, ὁμοίως δὲ πρᾶξίς τε καὶ προαίρεσις]*" (Every art and every inquiry, and similarly every action and pursuit), and resumed a few lines later, "*praxeôn kai technôn kai epistêmôn* [πράξεων καὶ τεχνῶν καὶ ἐπιστημῶν]*" (Actions, arts, and sciences: 1094a7, where *technê* [τέχνη] is definitional for *poêsis*). In this triad, there are in reality two-times-two pairs. On the one hand, there are *poiêsis* and *praxis,* the faculty

---

1

The metaphysics of *praxis*

The relation of the concept of *praxis* to the doctrine of power and the act (whose principles are set forth in Book Theta of Aristotle's *Metaphysics*) is complex. Here we will note two important themes correlated with the terminology repeatedly used in the *Nicomachean Ethics*.

The first concerns the relation between *praxis* and *energeia* [ἐνέργεια], a term designating "being in actuality" or the full realization of an essence or form that has found its proper matter, which, in the *Nicomachean Ethics,* designates the being of man, of which *praxis* itself is a part. *Energeia* is in itself "practical" in its phenomenological relation to exercise, continuity (cf. *Nicomachean Ethics* 2.1, 1103a31–32: "The virtues we get by first exercising them, as also happens in the case of the arts as well [*tas d' aretas lambanomen energêsantes proteron, hôsper kai epi tôn allôn technôn* (τὰς δ' ἀρετὰς λαμβάνομεν ἐνεργήσαντες πρότερον, ὥσπερ καὶ ἐπὶ τῶν ἄλλων τεχνῶν)],*" and

disposition (*hexis* [ἕξις]) that results from practical activity becomes in turn its condition of possibility, in accord with a "virtuous" circle (2.2, 1103b29–30): "We must examine the nature of actions, namely how we ought to do them; for these determine also the nature of the states of character that are produced [*anakaion episkepsasthai ta peri tas praxeis, pôs prakteon autas; hautai gar eisi kuriai kai tou poias genesthai tas hexeis* (ἀναγκαῖον ἐπισκέψασθαι τὰ περὶ τὰς πράξεις, πῶς πρακτέον αὐτάς· αὗται γάρ εἰσι κύριαι καὶ τοῦ ποιὰς γενέσθαι τὰς ἕξεις)]*."

It is "practical" also in its ontological relation to life (*zôê* [ζωή]), understood as a nonbiological realization of the human, from which come the collusive formulations that combine *energeia* and *praxis* (1.6, 1098a12–14: "We state the function of man to be a certain kind of life, and this to be an activity or actions of the soul implying a rational principle [*anthrôpou de tithemen ergon zôên*

tina, tautên de psuchês energeian kai prazeis meta logou (ἀνθρώπου δὲ τίθεμεν ἔργον ζωήν τινα, ταύτην δὲ ψυχῆς ἐνέργειαν καὶ πράξεις μετὰ λόγου)]*"; 10.6, 1176b5–7: "Those activities are desirable in themselves from which nothing is sought beyond the activity. And of this nature, virtuous actions are thought to be [*kath' hautas d' eisin hairetai aph' hôn mêden epizêteitai para tên energeian. toiautai d' einai dokousin hai kat' aretên praxeis* (καθ' αὑτὰς δ' εἰσὶν αἱρεταὶ ἀφ' ὧν μηδὲν ἐπιζητεῖται παρὰ τὴν ἐνέργειαν. τοιαῦται δ' εἶναι δοκοῦσιν αἱ κατ' ἀρετὴν πράξεις)]*." Thus *energeia,* which is for Aristotle the supreme mode of being, is in a sense conceived on the model of practice (*praxis*) and its "virtue." But this proposition is very ambivalent, because it can also be understood as meaning that we must seek "beyond *praxis* proper," at a higher level of generality, the "active" perfection that the concept of *praxis* allows us simply to approach.

of making and the faculty of acting, both of which differ from *epistêmê* in that they belong to the domain of *genesis* [γένεσις] (becoming, engendering) and of contingency ("*ti tôn endechomenôn kai einai kai mê einai* [τι τῶν ἐνδεχομένων καὶ εἶναι καὶ μὴ εἶναι]," the essence of the things whose essence is to be "capable of being or not being." 6.4, 1140a12–13). The notions of contingency and becoming remain crucial even where *poiêsis* and *praxis* are used to underscore the "rational" (associated with a "reasoned state" [6.4, 1140a3–5] or "true course of reasoning" ["*hexis meta logou alêthous* (ἕξις μετὰ λόγου ἀληθοῦς)," 6.4, 1140a10, 20], one to produce and the other to act). Contingency, or proceeding case-by-case, distinguishes *poiêsis* and *praxis* from *epistêmê*, which deals with the necessary and the general.

But on the other hand, *praxis* is paired with *epistêmê* in contradistinction to *poiêsis*: in fact, it is only in making (*poien ti* [ποιεῖν τί], "making something") that there is a product (*ergon*) to be added, later and outside it, to *energeia*, to the implementation, to the activity itself, so that the product is more important than the activity: "Where there are ends apart from the actions, it is the nature of the products to be better than the activities" ("*beltiô pephuke tôn energeiôn ta erga* [βελτίω πέφυκε τῶν ἐνεργειῶν τὰ ἔργα]," 1.1, 1094a5–6). In other words, "While making has an end other than itself [*telos . . . heteron* (τέλος . . . ἕτερον)], action cannot; for good action [*eupraxia*] itself is its end [*telos*]" (6.5, 1140b6–7). (Tricot renders this in French as "*la bonne pratique étant elle-même sa propre fin*" [good practice being in itself its own end] to show that *eupraxia* involves both success [successfully completing the action] and a good action [acting well]). We have to grant that "action and making are different kinds of things" (6.4, 1140a2). *Praxis* involves the "shaping of man by man" (and for man); it is the whole set of activities guided by the virtue of "prudence" (*phronêsis*, 1140b1), through which human individuals construct the world of their social relations: "We consider that those can do this who [like Pericles] are good at managing households or states" ("*einai de toioutous hêgoumetha tous oikonomikous kai tous politikous* [εἶναι δὲ τοιούτους ἡγούμεθα τοὺς οἰκονομικοὺς καὶ τοὺς πολιτικούς]," 1140b10).

Insofar as it is essentially *energeia*, tending to nothing other than its own improvement, *praxis* approaches *epistêmê*; but through its orientation in relation to the singular, acting "case by case" depending on the *kairos* (see MOMENT), it differs from *epistêmê* and to some extent goes beyond it (1141b14–15: "Nor is practical wisdom [*phronêsis*] concerned with universals only—it must also recognize the particulars; for it is practical, and practice is concerned with particulars" ("*oud' estin hê phronêsis tôn katholou monon, alla dei kai ta kath' hekasta gnôrizein; praktikê gar, hê de praxis peri ta kath' hekasta* [οὐδ' ἐστὶν ἡ φρόνησις τῶν καθόλου μόνον, ἀλλὰ δεῖ καὶ τὰ καθ' ἕκαστα γνωρίζειν· πρακτικὴ γάρ, ἡ δὲ πρᾶξις περὶ τὰ καθ' ἕκαστα]"), and it is very precisely political in that regard ("Political wisdom and practical wisdom are the same state of mind," 1141b23). It is this political *praxis* that comes closest, at this stage, to the ideal of *autarkeia* [αὐτάρκεια]: "By self-sufficient [*autarkes* αὔταρκες], we do not mean that which is sufficient for a man by himself, for one who

lives a solitary life, . . . since man is born for citizenship" (1.5, 1097b8–11).

C. From Practical-Political Autarky to Theoretical Autarky

Yet this presentation, which was to have immense influence (down to Machiavelli and the classical doctrines of *prudentia* and the art or skill peculiar to politics: *Staatsklugheit*, and even *raison d'État*, and so on), is questioned in book 10 of the *Nicomachean Ethics*, which discusses the relation between pleasure and activity (10.4, 1174b23: "*teleioi de tên energeian hê hêdonê* [τελειοῖ δὲ τὴν ἐνέργειαν ἡ ἡδονή]," pleasure completes—or "finalizes," as we might now say—the activity). Aristotle is then led to reconstruct the question of *autarkeia* so as to detach it from its political model ("living well" inseparable from "acting well") and to identify it with intellectual contemplation, with "the life of the mind": "the self-sufficiency that is spoken of must belong most to the contemplative activity" ["*legomenê autarkeia peri tên theôrêtikên* [sc. *diagôgên*] *malist' an eiê* [λεγομένη αὐτάρκεια περὶ τὴν θεωρητικὴν <sc. διαγωγὴν> μάλιστ' ἂν εἴη]," 10.7, 1177a27). Clearly, *praxis* is not subjected to the constraint of the matter on which the maker has to impose form, nor to the needs of the user who "orders" a product of technology, but it is still burdened with external dependencies: above all, social relations themselves, that is, the structure constitutive of the political sphere. In pursuing his ends, a politician depends on his fellow citizens (*politai* [πολίται]), his friends (*philoi* [φίλοι]), and his equals or peers (*homoioi* [ὅμοιοι]).

It is rather surprising to see Aristotle reversing his earlier judgments here: what appeared to be a completion becomes a lack; ethical-political *praxis* still depends on *poiêsis*, because it produces not objects, but effects external to it. As a result, *theôria* becomes a genuine *praxis*: "Nothing arises from it [theoretical excellence] apart from the contemplating, while from practical activities [or excellences, *aretai* [ἀρεταί]], we gain more or less apart from [*peripoioumetha* (περιποιούμεθα), from *poiein*] the action" (10.7, 1177b1–4). Ultimately, it is by conforming to the paradigm of *praxis* that *theôria* comes to take its place.

But in reality, it is the definition of man himself that has changed. We are no longer in the immanence of the shaping of man by man, but in the break that relates the human (or rather, exceptional individuals) to the divine—which, according to a typically Aristotelian intellectualism, can only involve *theôria*; science as the contemplation of first principles and first causes, and the kind of life that corresponds to it, entirely devoted to thought and detached from any utility or efficacy. Obviously, in this perspective (or is this only a typically "modern" reaction?), the notion of *autarkeia* or self-sufficiency is associated in a contradictory way with a representation of the beyond on which human happiness is supposed to depend. But Aristotle's idea is that speculative activity brings the human individual into the divine world of complete self-sufficiency, which thus realizes a transcendence of activity beyond the opposition between acting and disposition, or action and passion (10.7, 1177b27–28: "It is not insofar as he is a man that he will live so, but insofar as something divine is present in him" ("*ou gar hêianthrôpos estin houtô biôsetai, all' hêi theion ti en autôi huparchei* [οὐ γὰρ ᾗἄνθρωπός ἐστιν οὕτω βιώσεται, ἀλλ' ᾗ θεῖόν τι ἐν αὐτῷ ὑπάρχει]"). And yet this transcendence, or this aptitude for transcending the "purely human," is precisely the "specifically human" (1178a5–7): "That which is proper to each thing is by nature best and most pleasant for each thing; for man, therefore, the life according to reason is best and pleasantest, since reason more than anything else *is* man" ("*to gar oikeion hekastôi têi phusei kratiston kai hêdiston estin hekastôi; kai tôi anthrôpôi dê ho kata ton noun bios, eiper touto malista anthrôpos* [τὸ γὰρ οἰκεῖον ἑκάστῳ τῇ φύσει κράτιστον καὶ ἥδιστόν ἐστιν ἑκάστῳ· καὶ τῷ ἀνθρώπῳ δὴ ὁ κατὰ τὸν νοῦν βίος, εἴπερ τοῦτο μάλιστα ἄνθρωπος]"). *Theôria* is *energeia* par excellence, more free of passivity even than *praxis* itself because *praxis* remained a contradictory essence, involving a conflict between independence and dependency.

II. The Marxist Reversal:
Preconditions, Alternatives, Irreversibility

Karl Marx's *Theses on Feuerbach* introduces the other concept of *praxis*, in which the Greek is transliterated and linked to an entirely different relationship between politics and metaphysics.

■ See Box 2.

It is certainly not impossible in this case to hear echoes of Aristotelian "practical philosophy" (as elaborated in the Nicomachean Ethics), which Marx read with admiration and commented on throughout his life. There is something here like an inversion of the doctrine of the excellence of *theôria*, (seen as "mystical" perhaps), and a return to the primacy of *praxis*, which is to be definitively situated in the political sphere of immanence (even at the cost of a transformation of the ideal of *autarkeia* or self-sufficiency into a principle

of humanity's self-transformation through history or *Selbstveränderung*). But this very formulation, with its Hegelian and Kantian overtones, indicates that one or more intellectual revolutions have occurred that we must mention here.

Very schematically, there are four preconditions for the understanding of this formulation of *praxis*. The first, purely negative, is the fact that, in the course of the centuries intervening between the *translatio philosophiae* from Athens to Rome and the final establishment of European philosophies in vernacular languages, the Greek term *praxis* did not find any genuine Latin translation, with the result that the reactivation of this or that aspect of Aristotle's problematics was always accompanied by recourse to the Greek word or to a transcription of it (such as "practice" and, a fortiori, the Italian *prassi*). *Actio*, in particular, is not such a translation, but rather is a term that has its own field of application (especially in the physical and oratorical domains; see ACTOR). The same goes, of course, for "theory." The second precondition, viewed through the category of "idealism" to which Marx assigns the development of the "active side" of philosophy, involves the opposition, accorded crucial importance by Kantianism and post-Kantianism, between a practical point of view and a speculative point of view. This opposition will lead to a significant but paradoxical and evanescent use of the word *Praxis* (as a virtually German word). Here we see the mark of the "end of classical German philosophy" that Friedrich Engels identified with the Marxist revolution when the *Theses of Feuerbach* were published posthumously. The third precondition consists of the tendency to pose the theory/practice opposition in German idealism against the more or less concurrent one in the French tradition that culminated in positivism. We find traces of this opposition within Marxism itself, down to the present time. The fourth and last

---

2

Karl Marx, *Theses on Feuerbach*

The first thesis of Karl Marx's *Theses on Feuerbach* states:

The main defect of all hitherto-existing materialism . . . is that the Object, actuality, sensuousness, are conceived only in the form of the object, or of contemplation, but not as human sensuous activity [*sinnlich menschliche Tätigkeit*], practice [*Praxis*], not subjectively. Hence it happened that the active side [*die tätige Seite*], in opposition to materialism, was developed by idealism—but only abstractly, since, of course, idealism does not know real, sensuous activity as such [*die wirkliche, sinnliche Tätigkeit*] . . . [Feuerbach] therefore regards the theoretical attitude as the only genuinely human attitude, while practice is conceived and defined only in its dirty-Jewish form of appearance [*in ihrer schmutzig jüdischen*

Erscheinungsform]. Hence he does not grasp the significance of "revolutionary," of "practical-critical," activity [*der "praktisch-kritischen" Tätigkeit*].

The second thesis states:

The question of whether objective truth [*gegenständliche Wahrheit*] can be attributed to human thinking is not a question of theory but is a practical question [*eine praktische Frage*]. Man must prove the truth, i.e., the reality and power, the this-sidedness [*Wirklichkeit und Macht, Diesseitigkeit*] of his thinking, in practice [*in der Praxis*]. The dispute over the reality or nonreality of thinking that is isolated from practice is a purely scholastic question.

The third thesis states:

The coincidence of the changing of circumstances [*Ändern der Umstände*] and of

human activity or self-change [*der menschlichen Tätigkeit oder Selbstveränderung*] can be conceived and rationally understood only as revolutionary practice [*revolutionäre Praxis*].

The eighth thesis states:

All social life is essentially practical. All mysteries that lead theory to mysticism find their rational solution in human practice and in the comprehension of this practice [*in der menschlichen Praxis und in dem Begreifen dieser Praxis*].

Finally, the eleventh thesis states:

Philosophers have hitherto only interpreted the world in various ways [*verschieden interpretiert*]; the point is to change [*ändern*] it.

precondition lies in the coherence of the Marxist problematic of idealism's reversal, a product of the peculiarly "philosophical" moment to which the *Theses* belong. Idealism was never to be purely and simply recanted, but instead set aside in the process of constituting "historical materialism." It would subsequently re-emerge as a subject of debate in contemporary interpretations of Marx.

A. *Praxis* in German idealism

Praxis's central position in German idealism may be due to the conjunction of one of Kant's titles (that of an essay of 1793, "On the Common Saying: This May Be True in Theory but It Does Not Apply in Practice [*Praxis*]," often abridged as *Theory and Practice*) and the role he (and his successors) assigned to "practical philosophy" as a doctrine of the supreme (moral) goals of reason. But a paradox arises almost immediately. Although Kant makes systematic use of the adjective *praktisch* (in his terms "practical reason" or "pure practical reason"), his only use of *Praxis* as a substantive occurs in the essay mentioned above. As has been explained by translators and commentators on this text (Alexis Philonenko), it is in this essay that Kant sets forth his conception of the role of judgment in the moral and political domain. This was of course in response to the adversaries of the French Revolution who were inspired by Edmund Burke and who made institutional tradition the indispensable guide to political wisdom, *Staatsklugheit*. Kant, as the author of the three *Critiques*, adopted the word *Praxis* and the "commonplace" that is attached to it by the very writers he is criticizing (the "popular" philosophers and the jurists and theorists of government of the Enlightenment). Thus, he assumed an academic legacy of the eighteenth century, even if he did not invest it with his own intentions.

Kant nominalizes *praktisch* in the form of *das Praktische*, "the practical" or "the practical element." For him, it is a matter of showing that this element does not reside in prudence or skill (*Klugheit*, *phronêsis*), because the latter concerns the intelligent arrangement of means and ends, or a "technique" and the conditions of its effectiveness, whereas *das Praktische* resides solely in morality. It thus determines the "concept of freedom," and emerges as a "supra-sensible" principle inseparable from the categorical imperative. The practical element proper is thus not *technisch-praktisch*, but *moralisch-praktisch*. In a different context, Kant terms "pragmatic" the kind of anthropological research that studies the passage from the laws of practical reason to experience, so as to control the "pathological" element introduced by our sensible nature, and that thus controls disciplines such as pedagogy, applied morality, and politics, and in certain regards the philosophy of history as well (on all of this, see RT: Eisler, *Kant-Lexicon*, s.v. "Pratique," 829–30). Kant's philosophy thus forges a new concept of the practical, and accords it a central place in philosophy (a "primacy," as Kant calls it), in relation to a pragmatic "task" (see SOLLEN) of moralizing human relationships or of an imperative to transform the world (which we find again, literally, in Marx, even if he conceived its realization quite differently). Kant makes the human race both the (transcendental) "subject" and the (empirical) "object" of this self-transformation and makes it "responsible" (as in the essay *Was ist Aufklärung?*

humanity is made responsible for its own state of subjection). But within this very primacy, Kant guarantees the persistence of the deduction and the speculative principle identified with Reason.

What change was made by "post-Kantian" systems in this regard? Neither Johann Gottlieb Fichte nor G.W.F. Hegel thematized a theory/practice opposition or made conceptual use of the term *Praxis*. They did, however, help enrich it after the fact by emphasizing both the dimension of the act and activity (*Tat*, *Tätigkeit*, *Handlung*, *Tathandlung*; see TATSACHE), and that of efficacy and reality (*Wirkung*, *Wirklichkeit*; see REALITY). Though act-activity and efficacy-reality both belong to what Marx called "idealism" itself bound up with the problematic of the will, they pull it in diametrically opposed directions.

That said, between Kant and the radical essayists of the period preceding the revolutions of 1848 (the period Germans call the *Vormärz*), there was another conjuncture, in which the idea of the "emancipation of humanity," (which is inseparable from the "goals of practical reason" as determined by critical philosophy), was aligned with the idea of a "transformation of the historical conditions" of human existence (including both knowledge and production or action). In this context the word *Praxis* took on these different valences, which are at once "subjective" and "objective," and which expressed their fusion in a new "critical and revolutionary" concept of experience (according to the expression later used by Marx to characterize its dialectic). From this point of view, Marx's writings (especially between 1843 and 1847) appear to be less an "exit" (*Ausgang*) than a culmination of the movement of "classical German philosophy" (Engels, *Ludwig Feuerbach and the Outcome of Classical German Philosophy*).

B. "Theory" and "practice" from Bacon to French positivism

Alongside the German—Kantian and post-Kantian—constitution of the "philosophy of practice," an entirely different formation developed in the French intellectual sphere, one that culminated in the positivist conception of the relations between "theory" and "practice" as systematized by Auguste Comte. Contemporary epistemology, both in its logical empiricist and its historical aspects, is heir to this tradition. To understand its importance and intrinsic connection with the "social status of modern science" (Canguilhem, "Le statut social de la science moderne"), we must go back to the *Encyclopédie*, and most specifically, to the inspiration it drew from the work of Francis Bacon. Bacon had designated *scientia activa* or *operativa* as the terms for a method derived from experience, a method drawn on for the indefinite expansion of the powers of humanity, freed from "fictions" or "idols," and from speculative forms of Scholasticism (but not, for all that, radically anti-Aristotelian: on the contrary, it contained in embryonic form a first great convergence between nature and artifice, between *poiein* and *prattein*). Bacon had in fact employed the Greek *praxis* in a few places in the *Novum organum* (ed. Ellis and Spedding, 1:180, 268, 270, etc.) to show that recourse to experience did not divert study from its object, but constituted the sole means of "augmenting" it or bringing something "new" to it. The French Encyclopedists, who had the advantage over Bacon of coming after the development of a

(Galilean-Newtonian) mathematical physics, and in particular of a mechanics to which some of them made fundamental contributions, constructed on this basis a new epistemology set forth in Jean le Rond d'Alembert's *Discours préliminaire* and in the *Encyclopédie* articles "Application" (by d'Alembert) and "Art" (by Denis Diderot) (RT: Diderot and d'Alembert, *Encyclopédie ou Dictionnaire raisonné des sciences, des arts et des métiers*). These latter reflect for the first time the technological connection (they did not use the term "technology," which was invented in the early nineteenth century) between the science of physicists or chemists and the art of engineers. Military as well as civil technology thus lost the status of an "enterprise" (that is, of an adventure; see ENTREPRENEUR) and acquired that of a "systematic practice" whose principles are formulated by science, but which provides them with the indispensable complement of experience in the field.

In the section on the classification of the sciences in his preface to the *Metaphysical Foundations of Natural Science* (1784), Kant introduced this new dimension of applied knowledge under the name of a "systematic art." But he continued to relegate it to an empirical domain, from which the a priori basis of the pure sciences—that is, mathematics—was definitively detached. It was Auguste Comte, in the second lecture of the *Discours sur l'esprit positif* (1844), to conceptualize the connection, simultaneously reciprocal and dissymmetrical, that mathematization, the experimental method, and technology had established between "theory" and "practice." This connection, conceived as the relation between the abstract and the concrete, is both internal to the classification of the positive sciences, in accord with a progression from the simple to the complex (from mathematics to sociology), and external to their objective, which is properly speculative (a term that in Comte is synonymous with "theoretical") insofar as knowledge of the laws governing phenomena makes it possible to predict (and indeed, in the simplest cases, to calculate) the technical results in the field of "productive operations." From this comes the synthetic formula that, according to Comte, expresses the general relation between science and art (or "industry," a term adopted by Saint-Simon's followers): "from science to prediction; from prediction to action." Comte notes that the "two systems" formed by the "whole of our knowledge of nature" and by the "knowledge of the procedures that we deduce from it in order to modify it" are at once "essentially distinct in themselves" and inseparable. He remarks that although from the "dogmatic" point of view, the simple necessarily precedes the complex and the abstract precedes the concrete, in accord with a deductive relationship, the same is not true from the historical point of view. The problems whose solution can be provided only by theory must first be identified in practice, even when the latter, since the dawn of civilization, had supposedly been accessible only under the veil of a "theological" or magical way of thinking. The more complex the domain of phenomena, the longer it would take to transcend these beginnings and arrive, in the contemporary period, at the domain of sociological phenomena to which political practice is addressed.

It is well known that Marxism and positivism were at odds in their methods and objectives (even if they had a common source in Saint-Simonianism and, through that, the French tradition of the Encyclopedists). *Praxis* and practice thus governed two distinct philosophical paradigms, especially in the French context. However, since such situations in the history of ideas never actually exclude intersections, there were some substantial ones, both on the side of positivism (think of the dialectical ferments that Karl Popper, on his own admission, drew from his intensive reading of Vladimir Lenin's *Materialism and Empirio-Criticism*, 1908) and on the side of Marxism (think of Louis Althusser's conception of the "epistemological break," influenced by Gaston Bachelard's recasting of Comte's positivism).

C. Marxist *praxis*

The "Young Hegelians" who reintroduced the term *praxis* into philosophy (at the junction of philosophy and politics), were of course circumscribed by the limit of the Hegelian system. But they transgressed this limit in reaffirming the primacy of a (revolutionary and creative) subjectivity over and against the apparent objectivism of "the end of history" and the legitimation of state institutions (the latter, as in Hegel, imbued with liberalism). They also assigned fundamental importance to critique, which for them entailed not only the deconstruction of onto-theology, but also a questioning of the established order's values. That is why they turned toward the Kantian heritage radicalized by Johann Gottlieb Fichte and F.W.J. von Schelling. In his *Prolegomena zur Historiosophie* (1838), August von Cieszkowski invented the expression "the philosophy of *praxis*," to which he gave the meaning of an "auto-activity" (*Selbsttätigkeit*) or liberation of action that opens up the historical space of transformation and self-conciousness. In his opuscule of 1841, *Die europäische Triarchie* (The European triarchy), and his 1843 article *Philosophie der Tat* (Philosophy of action), Moses Hess (who was for a few years the closest interlocutor of Marx and Engels) systematized this idea of a free, collective *praxis* that bore the "future" of mankind, and associated it with a socialist credo. Hess also opposed it to another *praxis* that was materialist and "Judaic" in the sense that German Protestantism gave to this term, that is, oriented toward self-interest rather than toward universal emancipation; cf. his opuscule "Uber das Geldwesen" (1843). An ethical and political division thus passes through the heart of *praxis*, separating the world's two movements of appropriation and transformation. For his part, Arnold Ruge (the co-founder with Marx of the *Deutsch-Französische Jahrbücher*, whose single issue was published in Paris in 1844) used *praxis* in the sense of the "philosophy of work." All of these references are not only crucial for understanding the underlying allusions in the *Theses on Feuerbach* (which must in this regard be read as a cryptic formulary); they also shed light on the powerful tension that never ceases to influence Marx's thought and that his use of the word *praxis* encompasses. He is also seeking to open a breach for the future in the enclosure of objective spirit and the institutions of bourgeois society. In this sense, he is in search of a form and a subject for "revolutionary" action (which he later thought he had found in the proletariat and workers' socialism); but for all that, he cannot resign himself to abandoning the perspective of reality. He wants to extract emancipatory auto-activity (or the realization of freedom) from the element of pure will, thus allowing its activism to become "materially" a transformation of the world. For that to happen, it has to be inserted into the development of social relationships and conflicts, and, in the final analysis, into the development of material life (and its "modes of production"). The Marxist use of the term *praxis* is thus both something inherited from the Young Hegelians and a criticism of their understanding of it. *Praxis* thus has a rather tenuous status in Marx's work as well as in that of the later Marxists.

The concept of *praxis* is central to the *Theses on Feuerbach* (written in 1845, at the same time as *The German Ideology*, and published posthumously in 1888), of which it is clearly the keystone; in return, the *Theses* systematically deploy its different aspects. But Marx had already resorted to the same term, or to the adjective "practical" (*praktisch*), especially in the series of essays written in 1843 and 1844: *On the Jewish Question, Correspondence with Ruge, Contribution to the Critique of Hegel's Philosophy of Right* (all of which had appeared in the *Deutsch-Französische Jahrbücher*), and *The Holy Family* (written in collaboration with Engels). The "settling of accounts" with the representatives of post-Hegelian liberal philosophy (Bruno Bauer) and anthropological communism (Ludwig Feuerbach) would contribute to reversing the idea of *praxis*. Initially, the idea was still negatively connoted, as shown by the allusion (in *On the Jewish Question*, which is loaded with anti-Semitic stereotypes) to "the practical spirit," that is, to the supposedly self-interested spirit of Judaism. This "practical spirit" was set up in contrast to a Christian idealism whose trace is still found in the first of the theses on Feuerbach. Now, on the contrary, *praxis* becomes irreducible to any single representation; it forms the model of transformative action—of action capable of emancipating humanity—on the condition that it include dialectically, as part of its own determination, what appeared to be its contrary, or what it had to transcend, namely, the "sensible," the real or material being of "social relationships." This real or material being of social relations is the "actual essence" of man (sixth thesis). Marx will insist that its historical development coincides with the activities and productive powers of labor (consciousness of their being a function or expression that is more or less autonomized). There is a certain equivalence, then, between the "proletariat" as a "universal" class or agent of "human revolution" (beyond the simply "political" bourgeois revolution) and *praxis* as a historical development that involves replacing the "weapons of criticism" with the "criticism of weapons."

We have to acknowledge, however, that this equivalence, which had the performative effect of founding a "new materialism" irreducible to the sensualism of the Enlightenment, turned out to be fragile in its original construction; for, Marx, once past a certain stage in his thinking, would abandon the terminology of the argument and, most notably, the reference to *praxis*. We also have to recognize, after the fact, that the shift in terrain that this equivalence proclaimed is on the agenda more than ever. It governs the constant quest (constitutive of the Marxist point of view in philosophy) for an "encounter" between the science of historical material conditions and the insurrectional power of emancipatory movements. It also informs a great deal of contemporary philosophical research dealing with the limits of representation and the philosophical genre itself.

We can discern three reasons, legible in Marx himself, for the introduction of this rupture into philosophy. The first has to do with the fact that "practical activity," that is, thought as the true "differential of history" (instead of consciousness or morality), abolishes the classical distinctions between *praxis* and *poiêsis* that itself governed the possibility of making *theôria* autonomous. As result, the assignment of the bearers of these peculiarly human authorities, agencies, or "powers of acting" to classes or isolated social types, defined once and for all (men of action, producers, intellectuals, or contemplatives), is put back in question.

The second reason, which the second of the *Theses on Feuerbach* formulated with peerless vigor, has to do with the fact that the problematic of truth has now been torn away; not from the element of thought, but from the transcendence of thought with respect to its conditions, (a transcendence constituted on the model of a theological dualism). Marx will bring truth closer to *Diesseitigkeit*, a term that is difficult to translate but that is perfectly legible in its theological provenance. It refers to this world as opposed to the beyond, as well as to what philosophers have called "the world," "experience," "the things themselves," "labor," "the everyday," and so on. To inscribe this orientation, which is both immanent and productive, in the philosophical tradition (a tradition, it is true, that is subterranean rather than dominant), Marx sometimes refers, in the same spirit, to Vico's formula: "*verum esse ipsum factum*" (The truth is what is made).

Finally, the third reason for this philosophical rupture is that practical activity or *praxis* (soldered to the poïëtic, and inclusive of theory) is originally social, or, better, "transindividual." This means that the element of reciprocal action or relation always already forms the condition of its possibility. This opens up, at least in principle, the program of a transcendence of metaphysical oppositions between the singular and the universal or between the subject and the object (initially reduced by Marx to man and nature: *praxis* is the "humanization of nature and the naturalization of man," that is, it is the real history of society—the theme of *The German Ideology*).

III. After Aristotle and Marx: Dilemmas of the Contemporary Philosophy of Action

The history of philosophy does not include modes of thought or languages that ever went out of date. Every conceptual coherence that has once been constituted can be reactivated, which does not mean that it will be reactivated in the same form. One of the causes of this shifting resides in the effect of the irreversibility of translations or re-creations of which certain words bearing a fundamental question have been the object. This is precisely the situation in which we find ourselves with regard to *praxis*. To conclude this genealogical outline, we will indicate two types of terminological difficulty. One concerns, within the Marxist tradition itself or in close association with it, the resurgences of the idea of a "philosophy of *praxis*" in the twentieth century. The other concerns the obstacles that, in other contemporary philosophical trends, stand in the way of using the term *praxis* (including in the form of "returns to Aristotle" or "returns to

Kant") because of its appropriation by Marx (and that testify by that very fact to the power of this appropriation). The exceptions appear all the more significant.

A. Antonio Gramsci and the "philosophy of *praxis*"

The expression "philosophy of *praxis*" is one of the leitmotifs of Gramsci's *Prison Notebooks* (*Quaderni del carcere*), a fragmentary work that many people regard as a "refoundation" of Marxist philosophy, written in Fascist prisons between 1926 and 1937 and published with varying classifications after 1945.

It has to be recognized that in some respects, *praxis* was a coded expression intended to deceive the censors. But "philosophy of action," coined in Italian in a naturalized form (*filosofia della prassi*, which is neither the more usual *pratica* nor a quotation of a foreign expression), sums up well the orientation of the intellectual enterprise undertaken by the martyred communist leader and conceived by him as a radicalization of historicism (*storicismo assoluto*). To understand the importance of that enterprise, we have to situate it in a double context, that of the "critical" recastings of Marxism and that of the Italian Hegelianism characterized by an "actualist" orientation (Giovanni Gentile).

Paradoxically, the most influential of the texts of twentieth-century "critical Marxism" before Gramsci—namely, Georg Lukács's *Geschichte und Klassenbewußtsein* (*History and Class Consciousness*)—is a book that was renounced by its author after it had been condemned by the Third International, and that one might therefore expect to have been forgotten. On the contrary, it inspired the whole development of the Frankfurt School from Adorno and Horkheimer to Habermas, and various dissident philosophical movements within the countries of "real socialism." Here we would mention the "Budapest School" (see *Individuum und Praxis: Positionen der 'Budapester Schule,'* by Georg Lukács, Agnes Heller, and Ferenc Feher [1975], cited in RT: Labica and Bensussan, *Dictionnaire critique du marxisme*, s.v. *Praxis*, 912; the Yugoslavian "Praxis" group (particularly Gajo Petrovic), publishers of a journal of the same name since 1965; not to mention other, non-Marxist philosophies [Martin Heidegger]). Analogous to Gramsci's later elaboration, though pursuing quite different directions, Lukács's early work attests to the resurgence of an antinaturalist point of view (opposed to the interpretation of historical materialism as economic determinism) in Marxism, contemporary with the crisis of imperialism (the First World War), Soviet-style or "councilist" revolutions (not only in Russia, but also in Germany, Hungary, and Italy), and the quest for new forms of alliance between intellectuals and the working masses (a point of view that rapidly lost out within the official communist movement). Lukács's whole enterprise in *History and Class Consciousness* is directed against the reification" (*Verdinglichung*) of thought and action in forms of commercial rationality extended by capitalism to all spheres of life, and the juridical, technological, and scientific objectivism that, according to Lukács, constitute its ideological counterpart. However, confronted by this generalized alienation, which has first to be conceived in its essence, the possibilities of criticism, resistance, and revolutionary overthrow do not reside in pure willpower, but in the constitution of society (particularly its immanent negative

form, its "dissolution," of what Marx called, after Hegel and Schelling, an "identical subject-object" of history, none other than the proletariat itself). The proletariat's "class consciousness," also called "practical consciousness" (that passes immediately from being to action without stopping at the stage of abstract representation), thus figures the obverse and necessary product of capitalist reification. The resort to this sociopolitical category of class consciousness, not found in Marx, demonstrates that in the unity of contraries in the "subject-object," it is the subject that prevails. (This also corresponds to a rupture of the symmetry postulated by Marx in the *Theses on Feuerbach* between the transcendence of pure naturalism and that of pure humanism, to the advantage of the latter.) That is why Lukács always speaks of *praxis* as a "*praxis* of the proletariat," where the proletariat forms the ultimate empirical reference, but also incarnates the mythic movement of universal history and its end in a messianic "actor" that is both singular and omnipresent.

Gramsci's adoption of the expression "*filosofia della prassi*" has a very different genealogy that extends over a longer period. As has been pointed out by André Tosel (who has studied its history in a complete and subtle way), it was first forged by Antonio Labriola in the context of a historicist variant of the Second International's Marxism. This claimed Giambattista Vico as one of its ancestors and emphasized the "morphogenesis" of societies that results from their internal conflict. The most decisive contribution to the Gramscian genealogy was, however, made by Gentile.

■ See Box 3.

The pronounced influence of Gentile's "actualism" on Gramsci's conception of the philosophy of *praxis* is now becoming better known, even if the degree of its impact or the variety of its modalities remain the subject of passionate controversy (especially in Italy). "Actualism," was read by Gramsci as a typical figure of *coincidentia oppositorum*, a tragic mark of the relations between philosophy and politics in the great "European civil war" of the twentieth century. At the time of the revolution of the councils in Turin, Gramsci himself began by practicing a vitalist, activist, and spontaneist Marxism influenced by Georges Sorel's concepts of "proletarian violence" and the general strike (the latter seen as the specific form of the masses' intervention in history). The later notion of *praxis* that Gramsci worked through in the *Prison Notebooks* was much more indebted to his novel reading of Machiavelli. Here, the action of the revolutionary party was compared to that of a "new Prince" seeking to transform the "passive revolutions" of contemporary society prompted by capitalist modernization into a "national-popular will." Gramsci also did a re-reading (to which a very attentive reception of American "pragmatism" also contributed) of the Hegelian organic conception of the state in terms of cultural hegemony and the democratization of culture, where violence and education contribute to a single dialectic. What emerges is the idea of a process that is by definition unfinished and uneven. This process seeks to bring about the conditions for a collective *praxis* or a historical initiative on the part of the masses, manifest as a latent possibility inhering in the power relations of social structure. It essentially takes the form of a tendential transition

3
"Marx in Italics": Labriola, Gentile, and the *filosofia della prassi*

➤ ATTUALITÀ

In the work of Antonio Labriola, *prassi* designates specifically the fact that the "work of thought" (which includes science and philosophy) is part of the "work of history" (which is itself rooted in the history of the organization of labor). This insistence on work and this effort to generalize its notion unquestionably bear traces of Marx, but Aristotelian accents are not absent from Labriola's formulations when he seeks to express *prassi*'s political and anthropological meaning: "For historical materialism, becoming . . . is reality itself; just as the *prodursi* [self-production] of man, who rises above the immediacy of (animal) life to achieve perfect liberty (which is communism), is real" (*La concezione materialistica della storia* [1896]).

Labriola's texts were the object of a prolonged debate between two great representatives of the Italian idealism shaped by Hegel. Whereas Benedetto Croce, in a spirit that is fundamentally more Kantian than Hegelian, grants priority to *pratica*, Giovanni Gentile, the leader of neo-Hegelianism (and the future official philosopher of fascism) adopts the expression *filosofia della prassi*. Gentile exhumed the *Theses on Feuerbach* and demonstrated their importance, thus making himself the defender of a revolutionary interpretation of Marxism against both its social-democratic spokesmen (Labriola) and against its liberal critics (Croce). For Gentile, Marxism, even in its specialized economic developments, is a "great" philosophy, not so much of history as precisely of practice, that is, of the transformative action that expresses the intervention in history of a constitutive subjectivity that is simultaneously immanent to becoming and destructive of the continuity of time. It is to this theoretical view of *praxis* in terms of permanent revolution, which he perceives as an "inverted idealism," that Gentile seeks to oppose his own spiritualist conception, to which he was to give the name "actualism" (cf. *Teoria generale dello spirito come atto puro,* a reply to Croce's *Logica come scienza del concetto puro*).

The Hegelianism to which Gentile adheres cannot be constructed without understanding and going beyond Marx's notion of the ontological identity of thinking and acting. In this combination we can once again hear "activist" accents (a radical critique of the idea of "passivity" and thus of any determination of action by its "given" conditions and circumstances) that proceed more from the Fichtean tradition (to which Gentile is also close in his formalization of the principle in terms of the affirmation of the "I," the *lo assoluto*, the subject of "the pure act"). But ultimately, the objective of actualism, which Gentile was to imagine he could implement in the framework of the "total state" founded by Mussolini, resides in the institution of "society's permanent self-education," which would be the very form of the spirit's concrete becoming, and, in this sense, *praxis* par excellence.

BIBLIOGRAPHY

Croce, Benedetto. *Logica come scienza del concetto puro*. Edited by C. Farinetti. Naples, It.: Bibliopolis, 1996. First published in 1905.
———. *Filosofia della pratica: Economia ed etica.* First published in 1907. Bari, It.: Laterza, 1973.
Gentile, Giovanni. "La filosofia della prassi." In *La filosofia di Marx*, new ed. Florence: Sansoni, 1974. First published in Pisa, It., 1894.
———. *L'atto del pensare come atto puro.* Florence: Sansoni, 1937. First published in 1911.
Labriola, Antonio. *Saggi sulla concezione materialistica della storia.* Edited by E. Garin. Bari, It.: Laterza, 1965.
Tosel, André. *Marx en italiques: Aux origines de la philosophie italienne contemporaine.* Mauvezin, Fr.: TER, 1991.

---

between the passivity that class domination imposes on "subaltern" social groups (what Gramsci calls "the economico-corporative stage") and the "intellectual and moral reform" that is supposed to allow them to become actors in their own history (and in this sense seems to return strictly to the Aristotelian definition of motion: "The fulfillment of what is potential *as* potential"). But here we are concerned not with a "pure act," but rather, according to a correction made by Gramsci himself in the *Prison Notebooks*, with an "impure act," "real in the most profane and mundane sense of the word," that is, inseparable from a matter that imposes its constraints on it. The "optimism of the will" and "pessimism of the intelligence"—the ethical components of an actualized and dialecticized *phronêsis*—also characterize the point of view of Gramscian *praxis* and forbid us to confuse absolute historicism with subjectivism or totalitarianism.

B. Phenomenological problematics

Contemporary, post-Marxist mutations of *praxis* are not limited to the Hegelian tradition. On the contrary, among the most interesting are those that emerge from the encounter with phenomenology (the problematics of Edmund Husserl and Martin Heidegger in particular), and which critique the exclusive orientation toward consciousness or speculative conceptions of existence. The important figure here is obviously Jean-Paul Sartre.

In the two volumes of the *Critique of Dialectical Reason*, of which only the first (*The Theory of Practical Ensembles*, 1960) was completed and published before his death, Sartre combined many sources of philosophical inspiration: not only Husserl, Heidegger, and Marx, but also Hegel, Kierkegaard, and other less obvious ones, Fichte and Bergson, not to mention countless other important figures in historiography and the human sciences. The central notion he elaborates is that of *praxis*: first as an "individual *praxis*," and then as a "historical *praxis*," via the essential mediation of the "group" (in accord with different institutional or spontaneous modalities that may be ephemeral, such as the movement of revolutionary crowds bound together by an "oath" like the Tennis Court Oath of 1789, or enduring, like social class, with its representative organizations). Sartre studies programmatically two movements or transitions: "from individual *praxis* to the practico-inert," and "from the group to history." Here we find again, even if under other names, the problematics we have already encountered (particularly that of reification, which Sartre connects with the original figure of the "seriality" of actions and groups). But Sartre was clearly also working out a new conception.

An essential part of this new conception proceeds from what had preoccupied Sartre in his earliest writings: the necessity of establishing, against the transcendental tradition in which phenomenology was initially situated, a gap between the structure of consciousness as a field of "views" oriented toward objects (an essentially "immanent" structure that, in his 1937 article *Transcendence of the Ego*, Sartre went so far as to compare to Spinoza's substance, as a production of its own modes) and the structure of the subject-ego, not as a source of consciousness, but as something essentially transcending consciousness, a representative for it. Arguably the *praxis* that occupied him later on, after he had declared that Marxism was the "horizon that cannot be transcended for the philosophy of our time," was a deepening of this gap within subjectivity, and as such a way of positing an immanent intentionality prior to all consciousness, and by that very fact exceeding it. That is why the movement of totalization that, according to Sartre, constitutes the structure of history's intelligibility, and that runs through class struggle and leads to its transcendence, can only be rooted in *praxis*, even if it does so only in a negative or aporetic fashion. That is the other great originality of Sartre's conception of *praxis*: insofar as it must always proceed from individuals, while at the same time aiming at their unification or fusion in a community, it is fundamentally lost, or, as Sartre puts it, "stolen" from its own subjects. In Sartre's radically conflictual and ultimately very Hobbesian model of human history, *praxis* can be realized only by alienating oneself. It seeks the impossible: "to make history" out of the conditions of passivity and dependency, or the dominant institutions themselves. As Marx said, in a passage of the *Eighteenth Brumaire of Louis Bonaparte* that Sartre never tired of interpreting, "Men make their own history, but they do not make it arbitrarily, in conditions they themselves have chosen." *Praxis*,

for Sartre, will never abandon the pursuit of this impossible "liberation" from the inertia or adversity that is inherent in it. *Praxis* is the "despite everything" of the human condition.

■ See Box 4.

C. The determinations of Marxism without its "horizon"

One can suppose that the concern to escape Marxist determinations of *praxis* and its horizon accounts for why there is a resistance within a number of contemporary philosophical trends to adopting the terminology of *praxis*, even where it would seem natural to do so. A case in point would be when there is a "return to Aristotle," either from the perspective of an ethics of prudence and judgment, or from that of a regulation of discourses and their public use. We will mention a few examples that are especially interesting because they also bring out problems of translation and idiomatic singularity.

1. Pragmatism without practice

We might wonder why the term "practice" is so little theorized by American "pragmatism," a philosophy founded on the recourse to experience, action, and practice. The term "pragmatism" was invented by Charles Sanders Peirce, adopted by William James and John Dewey, and later modified by Peirce, who, after it came into common use, rejected it in favor of "pragmaticism," as is shown by the following passage in the *Collected Papers*:

> His [the writer's] word "pragmatism" has gained general recognition in a generalized sense that seems to

---

4

Althusser: "Practices" versus *praxis*

The influence of Lukács's and Gramsci's theories, and especially the influence of the Sartrean conception of *praxis*, helps us understand why the other great representative of French philosophical Marxism in the 1960s, Louis Althusser, radically rejected the concept. Althusser's conception of Marxist philosophy clearly also proceeds from a critical reading of Hegel, a reading whose program the *Theses on Feuerbach* formulated as "new materialism." It owes to Gramsci and, through him, to Machiavelli a radical conception of the equivalence of theory and politics. But Althusser, who participated in the structuralist adventure and was determined to ferret out in their furthest recesses the germs of subjectivism and historicism that prevented the constitution of a materialist science of revolution, refused to see in *praxis*, and particularly in the "dialectic" of human works and material or institutional inertia, any more than spiritualist dualisms in a new garb. Moreover, Althusser speaks not so much of "practice" as of "practices"

(including "theoretical practice," operating on the generality of concepts). He seeks, it seems, to provide a theoretical account of their analogy (in the sense in which metaphysics spoke of the analogy of being) on the model of a "generalized production," consequently reducing *prattein* to *poiein* (and as we have seen, a certain French positivist-productivist tradition is not alien to this possibility). On closer inspection, however, we see that he does so in a very strange way, leading to a theoretical account that is as original in its own way as that of Sartre, to which it is opposed term for term. Theory is one kind of practice among others. Every practice is internally "overdetermined" by all the others, which it presupposes even as it represses them, in a "totality with a dominant" (*totalité à dominante*) that is subject to constant variations. A practice is "productive" not so much of "objects" or externalized results as of "effects" that are consubstantial with it (a typically structuralist thesis, but in *Capital* Marx had spoken of the "twofold

character of labor" and shown that the effect of the latter is not solely to produce merchandise but also to reproduce social relationships): "effects of knowledge," "effects of society," "effects of subjectivity," even "effects of transference" (in the field of the unconscious), and so on. A practice is essentially a "struggle," on the model of the class struggle (and for Althusser, within its horizon), or a union of contrary tendencies: understanding and misunderstanding, production and exploitation, identification and distancing (in Brecht's sense). It can be maintained that with these paradoxical characteristics, *poiein* has been essentially transformed into a complex form of *prattein*—although as a "process without a subject," if not without an agent (or "agency").

BIBLIOGRAPHY

Althusser, Louis. *Pour Marx*. Paris: François Maspero, 1965.

Lecourt, Dominique. *La philosophie sans feinte*. Paris: J. E. Hallier / Albin Michel, 1982.

argue power of growth and vitality. The famed psychologist, James, first took it up, seeing that his "radical empiricism" substantially answered to the writer's definition of pragmatism, albeit with a certain difference in the point of view. . . . But at present, the word begins to be met with occasionally in the literary journals, where it gets abused in the merciless way that words have to expect when they fall into literary clutches. . . . So then, the writer feels that it is time to kiss his child good-by and relinquish it to its higher destiny; while to serve the precise purpose of expressing the original definition, he begs to announce the birth of the word "pragmaticism," which is ugly enough to be safe from kidnappers.

(Peirce, *Collected Papers*, 5:414)

The word *praxis* never appears in Peirce, and "practice" is hardly examined, even though it is used quite often in established expressions ("in practice," "the practice of"). The language of pragmatism is rather that of facts (including "facts of consciousness"), experience (including "pure experience"), and behavior ("conduct," notably in Dewey and Mead). Practice is defined only by the recourse to facts, and by the passage to the practice with which theories are confronted, as is shown by typical expressions such as "practical application" and "application to practice" (ibid., 2:7). From an "Aristotelian" point of view, we have here a kind of reversal of *praxis* and *pragmata*. For example:

The value of Facts to it [science], lies only in this, that they belong to Nature; and Nature is something great, and beautiful, and sacred, and eternal, and real. It therein takes an entirely different attitude toward facts from that which Practice takes. For Practice, facts are the arbitrary forces with which it has to reckon and to wrestle. Science . . . regards facts as merely the vehicle of eternal truth, while for Practice they remain the obstacles which it has to turn, the enemy of which it is determined to get the better. Science feeling that there is an arbitrary element in its theories, still continues its studies . . .; but practice requires something to go upon, and it will be no consolation to it to know that it is on the path to objective truth—the actual truth it must have.

(Ibid., 5:589)

The emphatic recourse to Practice here hardly conceals the absence of a problematization of the concept, indeed, its depreciation in relation to true science—a paradox in a philosophy that calls itself "pragmatism," but prefers to think in terms of facts and truth, and not of "practice."

2. Habermas: From *praxis* to "communicative action"

Educated within the Frankfurt School, of which he at first appears to be one of the followers, influenced by American functionalism and by the "linguistic turn" of the 1960s, and politically supportive of Kantian-inspired constitutionalism and cosmopolitanism, Jürgen Habermas began his career by adopting a "critical" opposition between technique and practice. To the former he ascribed, in a way reminiscent of Lukács, *epistêmê* or "objective" science. To the latter, or *praxis*, in the "German" sense of the term, he ascribed both

a set of movements affirmative of natural law, and a battle against alienation, commodity fetishism, reification "projected into the public sphere [*Öffentlichkeit*]" where they become the object of debates and declarations, in such a way as to lead to an ideal of community. He then retranslates into Marxist language Max Weber's distinction between action determined by an end (*zweckrationales Handeln*) and reasonable action in relation to values (*wertrationales Handeln*), giving strong preference to the latter. But when Habermas finally finds the specific concept of his philosophy, which expresses the connection between discursive forms and juridical norms in the development of "civil society," while at the same time articulating it with the "lifeworld" (*Lebenswelt*, a concept of Husserlian origin)—that of "communicative action" (*Theory of Communicative Action*, 1981)—he abandons the use of the term *praxis*. No doubt in his view the latter retains connotations too closely connected with decision theory and exclusively associated with the representation of the history of civil society as a development of the capitalist divison of labor and the market; in short, with everything culminating in a valorization of social antagonism detrimental to the production of a social consensus on the fundamental values of democracy.

3. Arendt and "action"

The most important case for our purposes is that of Hannah Arendt, because she directly confronts the anthropological problem of recasting conceptions coming out of Aristotle and Marx. Arendt has a detailed knowledge of Marx's work. She is continually carrying on a critical dialogue with it, especially when she takes up an original position in a "neoclassical" trend of political thought that seeks to reformulate the ideal of *phronêsis* (which she also calls, referring to Kant as much as to Aristotle, "judgment"). Her aim in doing so is to defend the autonomy of political goals against both ideological totalitarianisms and socioeconomic reductionisms (and, a fortiori, against their collusion). The central concept in Arendt's thought, provisionally systematized in *The Human Condition* (1958), is "action."

Arendt's conception of action, which underlies her construction of the relations between the different "spheres" of human existence (intimacy, the private sphere, the public sphere, the sphere of knowledge), and her critique of a modernity that has witnessed the triumph of utilitarian values (those of the *animal laborans* in search of material happiness) over the *vita contemplativa* and the *vita activa* itself, is set forth in another "triad" of which action constitutes the fragile apex: labor-work-action. How is this related to the Aristotelian triads we examined at the outset? And to the Marxist conceptualization of social practice?

These two questions are difficult to treat separately. Arendt has apparently expelled *theôria* from her topics, and split the concept of *poiêsis* in two (drawing a distinction between *technê* and *poiêsis*, corresponding respectively to *labor*, which is supposed to reproduce the conditions of animal life or "well-being" and culminates in the ideal of consumer society, and to *work*, which is supposed to inscribe the mark of humanity on the duration of the world, or to guarantee the primacy of artifice over nature, through technology and especially through art). This new division (corresponding to the distinction between "arts" and "crafts" in the subtitle of the *Encyclopédie* [RT: Diderot and d'Alembert, *Encyclopédie ou Dictionnaire raisonné des sciences, des arts et des métiers*] and intended to promote them)—makes it possible to situate the Marxist conception of social practice not only outside the field of "action" or *praxis*, but also within the product of art and art itself, in the pure immediacy of making, and thus within the domain of "craft," and the whole tradition stemming from John Locke that makes human labor the measure of value.

Nevertheless, Arendt does not use the term *praxis* to designate the conception of the world held by the ancients, and by Plato and Aristotle in particular, except as an untranslatable "Greek word." Nor does she seek simply to restore the Aristotelian point of view. This has to do not only with her desire to write in ordinary language, but also with her desire to introduce into the concept of "action" an element completely unknown to the ancients: historicity, in the form of the various kinds of uncertainty in human affairs, the constitutive function of representations or appearances in political activity (which affects the workers' movement itself), the creative function of speech acts (pardons, promises, declarations), the loss of traditions that forces people periodically to start their political history over again, and finally, the development of institutions qua necessary conditions of *theôria* (or the *vita contemplativa*). These characteristics of historicity are certainly completely different from those described by Marx; indeed, they are exactly opposite to them. But precisely for that reason, we find ourselves here in the field of a genuine (and interminable) confrontation with Marx (though Arendt's very simplified presentation of him resembles a caricature): one *praxis* versus another, except that the word *praxis* is, for reasons both contextual and symbolic, "crossed out."

4. The originality of Wittgenstein's *Praxis*

Finally, the only one of the great protagonists of the philosophical adventure of the twentieth century in whose work the term *Praxis* plays an important and original role—even if it is not, strictly speaking, thematized— is Wittgenstein. For him it is, of course, a German word, apparently in common use. Only readers who are aware of the history of philosophy and are involved in various ideological disputes will wonder about its relationship to the Aristotelian, Kantian, post-Kantian, and Marxist meanings of the term.

For Wittgenstein, the word refers first of all to the use of language, which in his later philosophy he opposes to the reduction of language to logic carried out in the *Tractatus Logico-Philosophicus*: "*Dies ist leicht zu sehen, wenn Du ansiehst, welche Rolle das Wort im Gebrauche der Sprache spielt, ich meine, in der ganzen Praxis der Sprache*" (You can easily see this if you consider what role the word plays in the use of language, I mean, in the practice of language taken as a whole: *The Brown Book* [*Eine philosophische Betrachtung*], 157). Wittgenstein also constantly refers to "the practice of language games" (*die Praxis des Sprachspiels*). Wittgenstein's later philosophy thus represents a passage from theory to practice (the term *praktisch* is frequently used) through the attention given to playing language games ("*in der täglichen Praxis des Spielens* [in the daily practice of playing]": *Remarks on the*

Foundations of Mathematics), and to actual, "everyday" usage. It is interesting that in the *Brown Book*, which is a kind of English version of *Eine philosophische Betrachtung*, Wittgenstein systematically uses "practice" as an equivalent of the German *Praxis*.

Praxis is thus defined as the context that gives meaning to words: "*Nur in der Praxis einer Sprache kann ein Wort Bedeutung haben*" (Only in practice in a given language can a word have meaning: *Remarks on the Foundations of Mathematics*); "*Die Praxis gibt den Worten ihren Sinn*" (Practice gives words their meaning: *Remarks on Colour*). The nature of this context is what is constantly debated by Wittgensteinians and post-Wittgensteinians: Is it linguistic, or social and institutional (cf. John Searle, Kenneth Jon Barwise)? Sociologists of science (D. Bloor) and ethnomethodologists thus make extensive use of Wittgenstein in their arguments that seek to situate knowledge in social practices.

But it is in Wittgenstein's reflection on the "rule" that the notion of *praxis* plays the most specific role. The idea of *praxis* indicates the repetition inherent in the rule, as in every kind of usage: for Wittgenstein there is no rule that is applied only once: "*Ist, was wir 'einer Regel folgen' nennen, etwas, was nur ein Mensch, nur einmal im Leben, tun könnte?*" (Is what we call "obeying a rule" something that it would be possible for only *one* man to do, and to do only *once* in his life? *Philosophical Investigations*, §199); "*Um das Phänomen der Sprache zu beschreiben, muß man eine Praxis beschreiben, nicht einen einmaligen Vorgang*" (In order to describe the phenomenon of language, one must describe a *Praxis*, not a one-time event: *Remarks on the Foundations of Mathematics*). In the *Philosophical Investigations*, Wittgenstein states that "'obeying a rule' is a practice [*eine Praxis*]" (§202) and "not an interpretation [*eine Deutung*]" (§201). And a little earlier, in §199, he indicates that there are all kinds of practices that involve "obeying a rule [*Regel*]." This does not mean that every practice is governed by rules, but inversely, that the meaning of systems of rules cannot be completely described without referring to the connections established between the different "practices" to which they belong and between these practices and "forms of life" (*Lebensformen*) specific to them, even though they vary indefinitely and can be attributed either to individuals or to groups.

In fact, the word "practice" does not suffice to render the plasticity of this horizon of reality and everyday exercise to which Wittgenstein confines the philosophical aporias of meaning and modality (how can we conceive the contingency of the necessity of rules?). Wittgenstein also has to use the words "action" or "activity" (*Tätigkeit*), and especially "use" or "usage" (*Gebrauch*: "*In der Praxis des Gebrauchs der Sprache,*" *Philosophical Investigations*, §7), in both the sense in which one uses a tool and the sense in which one conforms to a tradition (unless one transgresses it). We do not first "understand a rule" and then, possibly, "apply" it; we make "use" of it. "The use of the word in practice is its meaning" (*The Blue and Brown Book*, 68). Thus *praxis* has not simply descended into the "here and now," it has been disseminated in the multiplicity of common experiences that envelop discursive activity. In the *Tractatus Logico-Philosophicus*, philosophy is defined as activity and not as theory: "*Die Philosophie ist keine Lehre, sondern eine Tätigkeit. Ein philosophisches Werk besteht wesentlich aus Erläuterungen*" (Philosophy is not a theory but an activity. A philosophical work consists essentially of elucidations: 4.112). Elucidation defines the philosopher's activity, and thereby defines the ethical value of the *Tractatus*— or, as Wittgenstein frequently says, its "therapeutics" of thought, which is pursued in a different way in his later philosophy through the emergence of *Praxis*. Wittgenstein uses the term *praxis* more frequently than "therapy," which appears only once in the whole of his work, or even than "activity" (*Tätigkeit*), which we still find in the writings of the intermediary period ("*Das Denken heißt eine Tätigkeit*" [Thinking is an activity]: *Philosophical Grammar*), but which is later entirely replaced by *Praxis*.

Two final remarks. First, when returned to dependency on the *Praxis* that implements it, the "rule" is no longer subject to the great metaphysical opposition between a descriptive proposition or assertion and an imperative or prescription. The distinction between the normative and the theoretical is qualified, which makes it easier to approach the problematics of "discursive practice," the speech act, or the truth effect. Next, and as a consequence, the most pertinent confrontation, in the end, is not with Aristotle or Marx, but with Kant. In the *Critique of Practical Reason*, Kant wrote: "A practical rule is always a product of reason because it prescribes action [*vorschreibt die Handlung*] as a means to an effect, which is its purpose" (RT: Ak., vol. 5). In Wittgenstein's work, the "rule," before prescribing an action or its goal, must be stated in the context of an action, that is, of a use, of a practice or *praxis*. Otherwise it will have no effect, and consequently no "meaning." There is no doubt here that, despite all the differences, comparisons might be made with other problematics of use (like that of Foucault: "the use of pleasures") or of activity (like that of the "ergologues about whom Yves Schwartz writes). But Wittgenstein is the only one to speak of *praxis* with a sublime unawareness of the historically acquired ambiguity of the notion.

Étienne Balibar
Barbara Cassin
Sandra Laugier

BIBLIOGRAPHY

Arendt, Hannah. *The Human Condition*. 2nd ed. Chicago, IL: University of Chicago Press, 1988. First published in 1958.

Bacon, Francis. *Novum organum*. Translated by James Spedding et al. Edited by James Spedding, Robert Leslie Ellis, and Douglas Denon Heath. New ed. London: Longmans, 1872.

———. *The Philosophical Works of Francis Bacon*. Edited by J. M. Robertson. London: Routledge, 1905.

Ball, Terence, ed. *Political Theory and Praxis: New Perspectives*. Minneapolis: University of Minnesota Press, 1977.

Bensussan, Gérard. *Moses Hess, la philosophie, le socialisme (1836–1845)*. Paris: Presses Universitaires de France, 1985.

Bernstein, Richard. *Praxis and Action*. Philadelphia: University of Pennsylvania Press, 1971.

Canguilhem, Georges. "Le statut social de la science moderne." Unpublished lectures given at the Sorbonne, Paris, 1961–62.

Cieszkowski, August. "Prolegomena to Historiography." In *Selected Writings of August Cieszkowski*, translated and edited by André Liebich. Cambridge: Cambridge University Press, 1979.

Comte, August. *August Comte and Positivism: The Essential Writings*. Edited by Gertrud Lenzner. Chicago, IL: University of Chicago Press, 1975.

De Giovanni, Biagio. *Marx e la constituzione della Praxis*. Bologna, It.: Capelli, 1984.

Engels, Friedrich. *Ludwig Feuerbach and the Outcome of Classical German Philosophy*. Edited by C. P. Dutt. New York: International Publishers, 1941.

Gramsci, Antonio. *Prison Notebooks*. Translated by Joseph A. Buttigieg and Antonio Callari. 3 vols. New York: Columbia University Press, 1992–2007.

Habermas, Jürgen. *Theory and Practice*. Translated by John Viertel. Boston, MA: Beacon Press, 1974.

———. *The Theory of Communicative Action*. Translated by Thomas McCarthy. 2 vols. Boston, MA: Beacon Press, 1984–87.

Hess, Moses. *Die europäischer Triarchie*. Leipzig: Otto Wigand, 1841.

———. "Über das Geldwesen." In *Philosophische und socialistische Schriften, 1837–1850*, edited by Wolfgang Mönke. Berlin: Akademie-Verlag, 1980.

Höffe, Otfried. *Praktische Philosophie: Das Modell des Aristoteles*. Berlin: Akademie, 1996.

James, William. *Pragmatism, a New Name for Some Old Ways of Thinking: Popular Lectures on Philosophy; The Meaning of Truth: A Sequel to Pragmatism*. Cambridge, MA: Harvard University Press, 1978.

Kant, Immanuel. *Critique of Practical Reason*. Translated by Mary Gregor. Cambridge: Cambridge University Press, 1997.

Labica, George, ed. *Karl Marx: Les thèses sur Feuerbach*. Paris: Presses universitaires de France, 1987.

Lukács, Georg. *History and Class Consciousness*. Translated by Rodney Livingstone. Cambridge, MA: MIT Press, 1971.

Macherey, Pierre. *Comte: La philosophie et les sciences*. Paris: Presses universitaires de France, 1989.

Marx, Karl. *Selected Writings*. Edited by David McLellan. Oxford: Oxford University Press, 1977.

Peirce, Charles Sanders. *The Collected Papers of Charles Sanders Peirce*. Edited by C. Hartshorne and P. Weiss. 6 vols. Cambridge, MA: Harvard University Press, 1931–35.

Rubinstein, David. *Marx and Wittgenstein: Social Praxis and Social Explanation*. London: Routledge and Kegan Paul, 1981.

Sartre, Jean-Paul. *Critique of Dialectical Reason*. Translated by Quintin Hoare. 2 vols. New York: Verso, 2004–6.

Schwartz, Yves. "Philosophie et ergologie." *Bulletin de la Société Française de Philosophie* 94, no. 2 (April–June 2000).

Tosel, André. *Praxis: Vers une refondation en philosophie marxiste*. Paris: Éditions sociales, 1984.

Vérin, Hélène. *Entrepreneurs, Entreprise: Histoire d'une idée*. Paris: Presses Universitaires de France, 1982.

Wittgenstein, Ludwig. *The Blue and Brown Books*. Oxford: Basil Blackwell, 1958.

———. *Philosophical Grammar*. Translated by Anthony Kenny. Berkeley: University of California Press, 1974.

———. *Philosophical Investigations*. Bilingual edition. Translated by G.E.M. Anscombe. Oxford: Blackwell, 2001.

———. *Philosophical Remarks*. Translated by Raymond Hargreaves and Roger White. Oxford: Blackwell, 1975.

———. *Remarks on Colour*. Translated by Lina McAlister. Berkeley: University of California Press, 1978.

———. *Remarks on the Foundations of Mathematics*. Translated by G.E.M. Anscombe. Cambridge, MA: MIT Press, 1967.

———. *Tractatus Logico-Philosophicus*. Translated by D. F. Pears and B. F. McGuiness. London: Routledge and Kegan Paul, 1974.

PRÉDICABLE

FRENCH   *prédicable*
GREEK   *katêgoroumenon* [κατηγορούμενον]
LATIN   *praedicabile*

➤ CATEGORY, ESSENCE, LOGOS, PARONYM, PREDICATION, PROPERTY, SUBJECT, SUPPOSITION, *THING, TO BE,* TO TI ÊN EINAI, UNIVERSALS

A certain confusion prevails among translators of Aristotle regarding the fundamental terms of onto-logic: *katêgoroumenon* [κατηγορούμενον], *katêgorêma* [κατηγόρημα], and *katêgoria* [κατηγορία]. Although J. Tricot, basing himself on a few actual uncertainties in Aristotle's text, considers them as practically synonyms, it seems preferable to distinguish them in principle in a strict manner, in conformity with a certain medieval usage, reserving "predicable" (Lat. *praedicabile*) for *katêgoroumenon*, "categoreme" (Latin *categorema* [vs. "syncategoreme"]) for *katêgorema*, and "category" or "predicament" (Latin *categoria, praedicamentum* [see *CATEGORY*]), for *katêgoria*. In a sense, this clarification does violence to the texts, because it is obvious that the Greek *katêgoroumenon* means both "predicate" and "predicable." However, modern logic and ontology use Latin (that is, Franco-Latin, Anglo-Latin, Germano-Latin, etc.) more than Greek, and we cannot consider negligible the decisions made by "Latinity" since the sixth century to "enlist" the Aristotelian-Porphyrian technical idiom. The term *praedicabile* was introduced by Boethius in his translation of Porphyry's *Isagoge* to render *katêgoroumenon*, which Marius Victorinus, the first translator of the work, had earlier rendered by *appellativus*. Although it is not always easy to recognize in Aristotle Porphyry's distinction between "predicate" and "predicable" (we will see that some medieval thinkers did not consider it pertinent), it exists in Aristotle and is discussed in the *Categories*. One has to pay attention to this in order to estimate accurately the horizon, foundations, and stakes involved in the debate between nominalism and realism from the Middle Ages to the present—realism presupposing, today as always, the reification of the relations between "predicables" (that is, the "realization" of "Porphyry's Tree"), whereas nominalism presupposes the neutralization of the difference between *praedicamentum* and *praedicabile*.

I. Predicate and Predicable

In *Categories* (1b.10-12), once he has posited the classification of four kinds of beings—secondary substances, primary substances, universal accidents, particular accidents—by permutation of the relations *kath' hupokeimenou legesthai* [καθ᾽ ὑποκειμένου λέγεσθαι] ("to be said of a subject") and *en hupokeimenôi einai* [ἐν ὑποκειμένῳ εἶναι] ("to be in a subject"), which constitutes the complete inventory of the "things that there are," Aristotle formulates a general rule according to which "when something is predicated (*katêgoreitai* [κατηγορεῖται]) of something else as of a subject (*hôs kath' hupokeimenou* [ὡς καθ᾽ ὑποκειμένου]), everything that is said (*legetai* [λέγεται]) of the predicable (*katêgoroumenou* [κατηγορουμένου]) will also be said [ῥηθήσεται] of [this] subject (*hupokeimenou* [ὑποκειμένου])." The expression "be predicated of something as of a subject" does not mean "be attributed to a subject" in the sense in which one says that in a proposition the predicate is attributed to the logical subject by means of a copula ("S is P"), but rather the relation existing between a "predicable" and what is "subjected" to it in the serial order that constitutes a genus—the

very type of relation that was later to be articulated in what is called "Porphyry's Tree." To illustrate this general law, Aristotle takes two examples (1b.12–15): that of "man" predicated of "this man" (a man), and that of "animal," which, according to the rule, is also predicated of the individual man, since the individual man is both a man and an animal. The meaning of the rule is that when one thing—man (a species)—is predicated of another—individual man (a primary substance)—"as of a subject," what is predicated of it—animal (a genus)—is predicated of it and of its subject. To present this rule, Aristotle does not employ the terms "genus" and "species," but that is indeed what he has in mind, as is shown by the definitive formulation in chapter 5 of the *Categories* (3b.2–7), based on the general formula of 1b.10–12: "the definition of the species and that of the genus are applicable to the primary substance." In his *Commentary* on the *Categories* "by question and answer" Porphyry explains the meaning of Aristotle's expression "to be predicated of something as of a subject": it means "to be stated by it as being part of its essence" (see *Isagoge et in Aristotelis categorias commentarium*, ed. A. Busse, 80.5 f.). Thus there is a clear distinction between the "predicate" in the logical sense of the term, the predicative part of a proposition, and "what is predicated" in the sense of the "predicable." In a proposition such as "Socrates is walking," the term "walking" is predicated of the term "Socrates" (which is the logical and grammatical subject of the sentence), but it is not "predicated as of a subject" because it does not express a constituent of its essence. On the other hand, as Porphyry emphasizes, in the statement "Socrates is [a] man," "man" is predicated of "Socrates" as of a subject, for if we ask, "What is Socrates?" the correct answer (that is, the *logos* [λόγος] expressing his being) is this: "He is a man." In "Socrates is a man," "man" is thus both predicate and predicable. What Aristotle has in mind in 1b.10–15 is thus a relation of "predicability" based on another relation, that of "subordination," which means that what is predicated of a predicable Y as of a subject is also predicated of that of which Y is predicated as of an individual subject X. The complete schema of the relation of predicability, corresponding to the vertical relations established on "Porphyry's Tree," is thus:

$$Z \rightarrow Y$$

$$Y \rightarrow X$$

$$Z \rightarrow X$$

(where Z designates a genus, Y a species, X an individual, and → the relation "to be predicated of . . . as of a subject"). This schema articulates entities that are ontologically subordinated to each other within the single genus (X is subordinated to Y, which is subordinated to Z). The same thesis is set forth in *Isagoge* 2.§14: "of everything of which the species is predicated, of that, necessarily, will also be predicated the genus of the species, etc."

Porphyry goes on to define the three "predicables" implied in the relation of subordination:

Genus: Genus signifies what is predicable of several things differing in genus, relative to the question "what is it?"

([τὸ κατὰ πλειόνων καὶ διαφερόντων τῷ εἴδει ἐν τῷ τί ἐστι κατηγορούμενον.])

(Busse, ed., 82.6–7)

Species: Species signifies what is predicable of several things differing in number, relatively to the question: "what is it?"

([τὸ κατὰ πλειόνων καὶ διαφερόντων τῷ ἀριθμῷ ἐν τῷ τί ἐστι κατηγορούμενον.])

(Ibid., 82.10–11)

Difference: A difference is what is predicated of several things differing in species, relative to the question "how is the thing?"

([τὸ κατὰ πλειόνων καὶ διαφερόντων τῷ εἴδει ἐν τῷ ποῖόν τί ἐστι κατηγορούμενον.])

(Ibid., 82.19–20)

On this basis, Porphyry analyzes the relation between essence, animal, and man—the essence is not subordinated to anything, since it is "highest" (there is nothing anterior to it); the animal is a species in relation to the essence and a genus in relation to man; man is a species in relation to the animal and the essence—and then he explains that the relations among the three are determined by the rule that stipulates that what is "higher" is predicated on what is "lower" "synonymously" (sunônumôs [συνωνύμως]), a key term in the Aristotelian theory of predication. Next he introduces a distinction between "constitutive" differences (sustatikai [συστατικαί]) and "divisive" differences (diairetikai [διαιρετικαί]). This set constitutes the foundation of what "Porphyry's Tree" presents for the analysis of the genus "substance" or "essence."

II. The Five Predicables

In addition to what he says in the Categories, Aristotle also sets forth the theory of predicables in Topics: 1.4, gives their "division"; 1.5 their "definition"; 1.8, the justification for this division; 1.6., 6.1, and 7.5, the analysis of their relations. Aristotle's list of predicables has four entries: definition, property, genus, and accident ([ὁρισμός, ἴδιος, γένος, συμβεβηκός]). Porphyry's, on the other hand, lists five: genus, species, difference, property, and accident ([γένος, εἶδος, διαφορά, ἴδιος, συμβεβηκός]). If we juxtapose Aristotle's and Porphyry's lists, we see that the Isagoge refashions Aristotle's division in two ways: (1) by substituting difference for definition; and (2) by adding species to the initial list.

Medieval commentators did not fail to stress this elimination of definition. In his Summa logicae, William of Ockham gave it a special chapter at the end of his analysis of "Porphyry's five predicables." He even added three chapters on description, descriptive definition, and the terms "defined" and "described," based on John of Damascus's Dialectica. In this way he reconnected, at a distance, with a central element of Neoplatonic exegesis, in which the distinction between orismos [ὁρισμός] (definition), logos [λόγος] (statement, formula), and hupographê [ὑπογραφή] (description), which is not made explicit in the Isagoge (although it is used in it),

is the object of careful elaboration (cf. William of Ockham, Summa logicae, 1:26–29).

Aristotle himself draws from his list an initial modified list; the final list in the Topics is an elaboration of an earlier table with four terms including genus, property, accident, and difference, which Aristotle modified by reducing difference to genus: "the differentia too, applying as it does to a class (or genus) should be ranked together with the genus" (Topics, 1.4.101b.18–19); (2) by dividing property into two parts, one of which, signifying "the essential of the essence" (to ti ên einai [τὸ τί ἦν εἶναι]), is definition, while the other, not signifying it, is the only one called "property" (to idion [τὸ ἴδιον]).

By restoring "difference" to its list of predicables, the Isagoge combines Aristotle's two lists, analyzing definition, which is eliminated from the new list, into its two constituents: genus and difference. The introduction of species alongside genus, difference, property, and accident is a change in perspective with regard to the Topics that has been criticized by some interpreters. In his book on Aristotle, W. D. Ross severely criticizes Porphyry's revision: "Porphyry later muddled hopelessly [Aristotle's classification of predicables] by reckoning species as a fifth predicable" (Aristotle, 2nd ed., 57). This modification is easily explained, however; the Isagoge is an introduction to the Categories, and its function is to explain, within the limits of the skopos [σκοπός] (subject) of the Categories, the elements of ontology that they contain. As we have seen, the relation genus-species-difference-individual is the backbone of the Categories. In choosing species, Porphyry is performing his work as an interpreter: he exchanges the perspective of the Topics for that of the Categories. In the Topics, Aristotle examines only propositions (premises or problems) that have a general term as their subject: species thus does not figure on his list; in the Isagoge, on the other hand, Porphyry adds propositions having an individual term as their subject, and thus species necessarily figures on his list. This broadening of the typology of propositions results from an ontological decision: Porphyry Platonizes Aristotle's theory of predicables as it is set forth in the Topics. However, this Platonization is consistent with the theoretical content of the Categories. Porphyry Platonizes Aristotle only at points where he is still Platonic or, at least, "Platonizable."

Having already mentioned the definitions of genus, species, and difference proposed in the Commentary on the Categories (Busse, ed., 82), we will cite here from the Isagoge only those of property and accident:

Property

Greek: [καὶ γὰρ ὃ μόνῳ τινὶ εἴδει . . . ταῦτα δὲ καὶ κυρίως ἴδιά φασιν, ὅτι καὶ ἀντιστρέφει.]

Boethius: et id quod soli alicui speciei. . . . Haec autem proprie propria perhibent esse, quoniam etiam convertuntur.

([A property is] what belongs to a species alone [. . .] [Properties] are precisely those [traits] which, according to [philosophers] are called properties in the strict sense, because they can be converted.)

(trans. J. Barnes)

Accident

Greek: [συμβεβηκός ἐστιν ὃ ἐνδέχεται τῷ αὐτῷ ὑπάρχειν ἢ μὴ ὑπάρχειν, ἢ ὃ οὔτε γένος ἐστὶν οὔτε διαφορὰ οὔτε εἶδος οὔτε ἴδιον, ἀεὶ δέ ἐστιν ἐν ὑποκειμένῳ ὑφιστάμενον.]

Boethius: Definitur autem sic quoque: accidens est quod contingit eidem esse et non esse, vel quod neque genus neque differentia neque species neque proprium, semper autem est in subiecto subsistens.

(df 1 Accident: An accident is what can belong or not belong to the same thing.

df 2 Accident: or else it is that which is neither genus, nor difference, nor species, nor property, but which always subsists in a subject.)

(trans. J. Barnes)

In Porphyry, definition "df 2 Accident" corresponds to "df 1 Accident" in Aristotle, who also offers, in the *Topics*, two definitions:

Greek: [Συμβεβηκὸς δέ ἐστιν ὃ μηδὲν μὲν τούτων ἐστί, μήτε ὅρος μήτε γένος, ὑπάρχει δὲ τῷ πράγματι· καὶ ὃ ἐνδέχεται ὑπάρχειν ὁτῳοῦν ἑνὶ καὶ τῷ αὐτῷ καὶ μὴ ὑπάρχειν.]

Boethius: Accidens autem est quod nichil horum est, neque diffinitio neque proprium neque genus, inest autem rei et contingit inesse cuilibet uni et eidem et non inesse.

(*Topica*, trans. Boethii in *Aristoteles latinus*, 11.1–2)

df 1 Accident: An accident is something which, though it is none of the foregoing, i.e., neither a definition nor a property nor a genus—yet belongs to the thing.

(*Topics*, 1.5.102b.4–5; trans. J. Barnes)

df 2 Accident: something which may possibly either belong or not belong to any one and the self-same thing.

(*Topics*, 1.5.102b.6–7; trans. J. Barnes)

Porphyry's definition differs from Aristotle's by the addition of *aei de estin en hupokeimenôi huphistamenon* [ἀεὶ δέ ἐστιν ἐν ὑποκειμένῳ ὑφιστάμενον] (but which always subsists in a subject), and this was to pose numerous problems for medieval thinkers.

III. "Predicable" and "Universal"

The distinction between "predicable" and "universal" is difficult to formulate. In one sense, there is no difference between these terms, since both designate the five entities that tradition has also called "five voices" [πέντε φωναί], extrapolated from the heading of one of the chapters in the *Isagoge* about the "common properties of the five voices" (*Peri tês koinônias tôn pente phônôn* [Περὶ τῆς κοινωνίας τῶν πέντε φωνῶν]). These five entities—Apuleius speaks of five *significationes*, while Marius Victorinus speaks of *partes* or *res*,

and Boethius, in the first edition of his commentary on the *Isagoge* also uses the term *res*—being universally predicable, it may seem pointless to distinguish in this case between "predicable" and "universal." The terminist logicians of the thirteenth century, however, made a series of definitions that fully justify, from their realist point of view, a distinction between the two terms. According to them, "predicable" has two meanings: strictly speaking, a "predicable" is what "is predicated on several [things]"; in the broad sense, it is "what is predicated on a thing or of several [things]." Thus "predicable" and "universal" are synonyms, in the strict sense of "predicable." They differ from one another, however, in that the predicable is defined by "being said" (*dici*) whereas the universal is defined by "being [in]" (*esse in*): "differunt in hoc quod praedicabile definitur per dici, universale autem per esse" (Peter of Spain, *Tractatus*, 2.§1.17). In this analysis, the predicable is thus "what is by nature capable of being said of several [things] [*quod aptum natum est dici de pluribus*]." The former is a term, the second a thing or property.

■ See Box 1.

The pair *dici* versus *esse in* is not congruent with the two relations used in the *Categories* to produce the four classes of things: primary and secondary substances, particular and universal accidents. In the *Categories*, the relation *kath' hupokeimenou legesthai* [καθ' ὑποκειμένου λέγεσθαι] (to be said of a subject) is the mark of universality, whereas *en hupokeimenôi einai* [ἐν ὑποκειμένῳ εἶναι] (to be in a subject) is that of accidentality. The meaning of the words *dici* and *esse* in the terminist definition is thus either different from the Aristotelian meaning or it is unsuited to the situation. Moreover, the nominalists rejected, as a categorial error, the use of the notion "to be in" with regard to the universal.

In the fourteenth century the terminist thesis was redefined on the basis of the theory of "supposition" (see SUPPOSITION). "Predicable" and "universal" are both metalogical or metalinguistic terms that designate other terms, including concepts and signs. In his *Summulae* (in fact a commentary on Peter of Spain's *Tractatus*), Jean Buridan explains that "according to the literal meaning of the words" Peter's thesis is false. One cannot say that the universal and the predicable are the same thing, but only that the terms "universal" and "predicable" are convertible. They differ, however, *secundum rationem*. In his explanation of this difference, Buridan, as a nominalist, erases the distinction initially made by Aristotle and Porphyry between predicate and predicable. "Predicate" (*praedicatum*) and "subject" (*subjectum*) are relative terms. The same goes for "predicable" (*praedicabile*) and "subjectable" (*subicibile*). A term is said to be "predicable" insofar as (*ea ratione*) it is "suited by nature to be predicated of a subject," while it is said to be "subjectable" insofar as (*ea ratione*) it "signifies equally several things and is suited to substitute for several things, without regard to the fact that it functions as a subject or as a predicate." For Buridan, a universal term is thus not defined as such by *esse in*. A universal "is in nothing." The expression *esse in* must be understood in the sense of "to be predicated truly and affirmatively."

The same metalinguistic redefinition of *esse in* as *praedicari vere et affirmative* appears in Ockham. In his commentary on the *Isagoge*, even the passage on the "subsistence" of the

1

Inhaerere/inesse: The ambiguities of the expression of inherence

➤ PREDICATION, Box 3, TERM

The word "inhere" is used to render the two Latin verbs *inhaerere* and *inesse* without attending to the fact that they may have different meanings. In medieval texts *inesse* is used to indicate the fact that an accident is in a substrate, *inhaerere* being usually employed in the logical context of predication to indicate the quality signified by the predicate insofar as it is attributed to the subject, insofar as it is signified as being in the subject. The distinction seems to go back to Boethius, and to the developments of his thought proposed by Abelard. Boethius generally uses the verb *inesse* to describe the inherence of an accident, of a quality, for example, in a subject. The verb can thus signify an accident that inheres (*inest*) in a subject. But Boethius also uses the verb *inhaerere* repeatedly in his *De topicis differentiis* to describe the relations between terms, between the "subject term" and the "predicate term":

In praedicativa quaestione dubitatur an subiecto termino praedicatus in inhaereat.

(In a predicative question, we ask whether the predicate inheres in the subject term.)

(*De topicis differentiis*, 1177B; trans. E. Stump)

Here the question is how to determine, in a given proposition, which of the four "modes of inherence" is the one in accord with which the predicate term is predicated on the subject term (*quisnam modus sit quattuor inhaerendi*, 1186C), that is, whether the predicate is predicated of the subject qua genus, definition, property, or difference (1179A–B). Although Boethius does use *inhaerere* for relations between terms, this relation seems to depend on a real relation, which he indicates by the verb *inesse*:

In predicative questions one is asking nothing other than whether the subject inheres (*inhaereat*) in the predicate. If it is in (*inesse*), we must ask whether it is in qua genre, accident, property, or definition. And if it is not in, the question disappears. In fact, what is not in, is not either as an accident, or as a definition, or as a genus, or as a quality. But if it proves to be in, the question remains which of the four modes of inherence (*modus inhaerendi*) is involved.

(*De topicis differentiis*, 1186C; trans. E. Stump)

In his commentary on these passages, Abelard sought to clarify this terminological confusion. As a nominalist, he makes a clear distinction between real relations between things and relations between terms, which constitute the true object of dialectic. Thus he distinguishes between an "inherence of things" (*inhaerentia rerum*) and "inherence of words, of names" (*inhaerentia vocum*), discerning two questions in Boethius's original question as to whether "the predicate term inheres in the subject term." The "inherence of things" concerns the real relations between things: since every predication indicates a "coupling" of things or essences (see in PREDICATION, Box 3), it indicates that what is denoted by the subject term is identical to what is denoted by the predicate term. These real relations are thus not indicated by "being in" (*inesse*) but rather by identity, because "in every predicative affirmation we affirm that something *is* something (ibid.):

In the questions, "Is Socrates a man?" or "Is Socrates white?" we are asking whether the predicate inheres (*inhaereat*) in the subject.

(*De topicis differentiis* , 275; trans. E. Stump)

Elsewhere, Abelard speaks of the "coherence" of two matters (*cohaerentia*) in the first case, and of the "adjacency" or "adherence" of a form to a matter in the second (*Dialectica*, 329). On the other hand, the "inherence of names" concerns the different modes indicating the relations between the subject and predicate terms, for example relations of identity for property or definition, of superiority for genus, and so forth. In this sense, asking whether the predicate inheres (*inhaereat*) in the subject amounts to inquiring into the mode in which it suits (*conveniat*) the latter. For example, when Boethius explains that "when something is posited as being in (*inesse*) something, it can be superior," it is clear, Abelard says, that the question is not whether the "animal" thing is superior to the "man" thing, since they are really identical, but rather to see if, in saying *homo est animal* the term "animal" is superior to the term "man," which determines that the former is genus in relation to the latter, and the same goes, *mutatis mutandis*, for the three other predicables. In fact, he concludes, in asking this question about the modes of inherence, "Boethius really wanted to speak of the

terms of which the proposition is composed, rather than of the things that they signify" (*Super topica glossae*, 270; cf. *Dialectica*, 165–66, "Edition super porphyrium"). The truth of the proposition "snow is white" depends on real relations between things; to determine whether the accident is in (*inest*) the subject, we have to ask whether one thing (snow) is identical with another thing (this white) and not with this essence (whiteness); but the topical relations depend on relations between terms—and Abelard is here in open opposition to his realist teacher William of Champeaux, who maintained that they concerned real relations between things.

The distinction between these two meanings of the term *inhaerere* is mentioned apropos of other questions. For example, in discussing adverbs of modality, Abelard explains that they cannot qualify real inherence (the modality *de sensu*, later called *de re*), but only verbal inherence: in the proposition "Socrates possibiliter est episcopus" ("Socrates could be a bishop") one cannot speak of the real inherence (or "coherence") of bishop in Socrates (because Socrates is, at the time one speaks, a layperson), which is still clearer in the example "Socratem impossibile est esse lapidem" ("It is impossible that Socrates is a stone"). In opposition to William of Champeaux, who was a partisan of an interpretation of modalities *de dicto*, Abelard maintains that modality acts on the level of *enuntiatio*, and refers to the manner in which the predicate term is joined to the subject term (*Dialectica*, 191–98, *Glossae super peri hermeneias*, 484).

Irène Rosier-Catach

BIBLIOGRAPHY

Abelard, Peter. *Dialectica*. Edited by Lambertus Marie de Rijk. Assen: Van Gorcum, 1956. 2nd rev. ed. 1970.
———. "Editio super porphyrium." pp. 3–42 in *Scritti di logica*, edited by Mario Dal Pra. Florence: La Nuova Italia, 1969.
———. *Glossae super peri hermeneias*. Part 3 of *Logica "ingredientibus."* Turnhout, Belg.: Brepols, 2010.
———. *Super topica glossae*. Part 7 of *Logica "ingredientibus."* In *Scritti di logica*, edited by Mario Dal Pra. Florence: La Nuova Italia, 1969.
Boethius. *De topicis differentiis*. English translation by Eleonore Stump. Ithaca, NY: Cornell University Press, 2004.

accident in a subject is redefined in this way: according to Ockham, the second definition of "accident" merely elaborates on the first, because in the expression *semper autem est in subjecto subsistens* ("is always also subsisting in the subject"), *subsistere* means *praedicari*. For Ockham, the meaning of the second definition of "accident" in Porphyry is thus purely "logical":

> df 2 Accident: omne praedicabile de multis, quod neque est genus neque species neque differentia neque proprium, et non praedicatur de omnibus sed de aliquibus praedicatur et de aliquibus non, est accidens, hoc est contingenter praedicabile.

> (Everything that is predicable of several subjects and is neither a genus nor a species nor a difference nor a property, and which is not a predicable of all subjects but is predicable of some and not of others, is contingently predicable.)

> (*Expositio in librum Porphyrii de praedicabilibus*, 2:99, 30–34)

The neutralization of the distinction between predicable and universal, to the advantage of the meaning of "predicable" (= a term is universal when it "signifies several things"), is a characteristic of nominalism, whether medieval or modern.

Alain de Libera

BIBLIOGRAPHY

Ammonius. *Ammonii in Porphyrii Isagogen sive V Voces*. Edited by Adolf Busse. Commentaria in Aristotelem Graeca 4.3. Berlin: G. Reimer, 1891.

Apuleius. *The Logic of Apuleius, Including a Complete Latin Text and English Translation of the Peri Hermeneias of Apuleius of Madaura*. Translated by David Londey and Carmen Lohanson. New York: E. J. Brill, 1987.

Aristotle. *"Categories" and "On Interpretation."* Translated by J. L. Ackrill. Oxford: Clarendon Press, 1963.

———. *Topica*. Vol. 5.1–3, in *Aristoteles latinus*. Latin translation by Boethii (Boethius). Edited by Minio-Paluello. Brussels: Desclée de Brouwer, 1969. English translation by Jonathan Barnes: *Topics*. In *Complete Works of Aristotle*, edited by J. Barnes. Princeton, NJ: Princeton University Press, 1984. French translation by Jacques Brunschwig. *Topiques*. Edited, and with an introduction, by J. Brunschwig. Paris: Les Belles Lettres, 1967.

Barnes, Jonathan. "Property in Aristotle's *Topics.*" *Archiv für Geschichte der Philosophie* 52 (1970): 136–55.

Brunschwig, Jacques. "Sur le système des 'prédicables' dans les *Topiques* d'Aristote." pp. 145–57 in *Energeia: Etudes aristotéliciennes offertes à Mgr. Antonio Jannone*. Paris: J. Vrin, 1986.

Buridan, Jean. *Summulae de praedicabilibus*. Edited by L. M. de Rijk. Nijmegen: Ingenium, 1995.

Code, Alan. "Aristotle: Essence and Accident." pp. 411–39 in *Philosophical Grounds of Rationality: Intentions, Categories, Ends*, edited by Richard Grandy and Richard Warner. Oxford: Clarendon Press, 1986.

Ebbesen, Sten. "Boethius as an Aristotelian Scholar." In *Aristoteles, Werk und Wirkung*, vol. 2, edited by J. Wiesner. Berlin: W. de Gruyter, 1987.

Elias [olim Davidis]. *Eliae in Porphyrii Isagogen et Aristotelis Categorias Commentaria*. Edited by Adolf Busse. Commentaria in Aristotelem Graeca 18.1. Berlin: G. Reimer, 1900.

Evangeliou, C. "Aristotle's Doctrine of Predicable and Porphyry's Isagoge." *Journal of the History of Philosophy* 23, no. 1 (1985): 15–34.

John XXI, Pope. *The Summulae logicales of Peter of Spain*. Edited by Joseph Patrick Mullally. Notre Dame, IN: University of Notre Dame Press, 1945.

Matthews, Gareth B., and Sheldon Marc Cohen. "The One and the Many." *Review of Metaphysics* 21, no. 4 (June, 1968): 630–55.

Peter of Spain. *Tractatus*. Edited by L. M. De Rijk. Assen, Neth: Van Gorcum, 1972.

Porphyry. *Aristoteles latinus*. In *Isagoge, translatio Boethii accedunt isagoges fragmenta M. Victorino interprete*, edited by L. Minio-Paluello. Bruges: Desclée de Brouwer, 1966.

———. *Isagoge*. French translation by Alain de Libera and Alain-Philippe Segonds. Introduction and notes by Alain de Libera. Paris: J. Vrin, 1998.

———. Introduction to *Isagoge*. Edited by A. Busse in *Isagoge et in Aristotelis categorias commentarium*, CAG 4.1. Berlin: Reimer, 1887. English translation by E. J. Warren: *Porphyry the Phoenician: Isagoge*. Toronto, ON: Pontifical Institute of Medieval Studies, 1975. English translation, with commentary, by Jonathan Barnes: Introduction to *Isagoge*. Oxford: Oxford University Press, 2003.

Ross, W. D. *Aristotle*. 2nd ed. London: Methuen, 1930.

Simplicius. *Commentaria in Aristotelem Graeca*. Vol. 8. Edited by K. Kalbfleisch. Berlin: G. Reimer, 1907.

———. *On Aristotle's Categories 1-4*. Translated by Michael Chase. Ithaca, NY: Cornell University Press, 2003.

———. *On Aristotle's Categories 5-6*. Translated by Frans A. J. de Haas and Barrie Fleet. Ithaca, NY: Cornell University Press, 2001.

———. *On Aristotle's Categories 7-8*. Translated by Barrie Fleet. Ithaca, NY: Cornell University Press, 2002.

———. *On Aristotle's Categories 9-15*. Translated by Richard Gaskin. London: Duckworth, 2000.

William of Ockham. *Opera philosophica*. Vol. 2 of *Expositionis in libros artis logicae proemium et expositio in librum Porphyrii de praedicabilibus*. 7 vols. St. Bonaventure, NY: Franciscan Institute, 1974–88.

———. *Summa logicae*. 3 vols. Edited by Philotheus Boehner. St. Bonaventure, NY: Franciscan Institute, 1951–54. Translation by Michael J. Loux: *Ockham's Theory of Terms: Part I of the Summa logicae*. Notre Dame, IN: University of Notre Dame Press, 1974. Translation by Alfred J. Freddoso and Henry Schuurman: *Ockham's Theory of Propositions: Part II of the Summa logicae*. Notre Dame, IN: University of Notre Dame Press, 1980.

PREDICATION, PREDICATE, ATTRIBUTE

FRENCH	*prédication, prédiquer, attribuer*
GERMAN	*Aussage, aussagen*
GREEK	*katêgoria* [κατηγορία], *katêgorô* [κατηγορῶ]
ITALIAN	*attribuzione, attribuire*
LATIN	*praedicatio, praedicare*

➤ ANALOGY, *CATEGORY, CONCEPT* [BEGRIFF, CONCEPTUS], ESSENCE, ESTI, HOMONYM, LOGOS, PARONYM, PRÉDICABLE, PROPOSITION, SUBJECT, TERM, *TO BE*, UNIVERSALS

"Predication" designates the logical form par excellence: the attribution of a predicate to a subject in a proposition is the basic unit of classical logic. The canonical predicative form defining the association of two concepts, subject and predicate, is traditionally presented as the connection of two terms (or "extremes") by means of a copula (lexicalized by the verb "to be"), expressed by the formula "S is P." This analysis is generally traced back to Aristotle—not entirely correctly, however. In fact, the three expressions that appear in his work to designate predication are *huparchein* [ὑπάρχειν] (belong to), *legesthai* [λέγεσθαι] (be said of), and *katêgoreisthai* [κατηγορεῖσθαι] (be predicated of), so that the copula has the function of implementing the imposed/supposed equivalence of *huparchein*, *legesthai*, and *katêgoreisthai*. This assimilation is consummated in all the summae of medieval logic, and the predominance of the tripartite analysis of logical form into "S is P" gives the impression that the distinction "subject"-"predicate," which derives from the *hupokeimenon* [ὑποκείμενον]–*katêgorêma* [κατηγόρημα] pair, is universal.

Thus it was on the basis of the "Aristotelian" conception of predication and its tripartite analysis of propositional form as it was established in the Middle Ages, following Boethius's Latin translations, that the tradition developed and then, starting with G. Frege, threw into crisis—to the advantage of the "function"—the logical theory of predication. The problems encountered by a translator of ancient and medieval texts on logic, which were simply extended in pre-Fregean logic, are thus all concentrated on the avatars of *katêgoreisthai/legesthai*. Here we will discuss only the main difficulties—*praedicatio in quid* versus *praedicatio in quale*; *praedicatio ut de subjecto* versus *praedicatio ut in subjecto*; *praedicatio univoca* versus *praedicatio denominativa*—before returning to the problem of the copula.

I. The "Aristotelian" Conception

Aristotle's three ways of designating predication, *huparchein* [ὑπάρχειν] ("belong to"; Ger. *kommen zu*), *legesthai* [λέγεσθαι] ("be said of"; Ger. *ausgesagt werden*), and *katêgoreisthai* [κατηγορεῖσθαι] ("be predicated of"; Ger. *behauptet werden*), must all be understood on the basis of *huparchein*, at least insofar as predication proper is concerned, occurring in the context of syllogistic reasoning, and thus in that in which the basic unit is the proposition understood as a "premise." In fact, although since the Middle Ages all propositions have commonly been analyzed in the so-called Aristotelian form—"A is B"—Aristotle himself never writes "A *estin* B" (A is B) (except in presenting defective arguments or acknowledging ordinary usage), but only "*to* A *huparchei tôi* B" (the A belongs to B), in series such as "If [the] A belongs to all B, and if [the] B belongs to all C, then [the] A belongs to all C." Naturally, since the same thesis can be expressed using *legesthai*, as Aristotle himself does in the *Prior Analytics*, I.4.25b, 35n.), basing himself on the definition of the *dictum de omne* ("That one term should be included in another as in a whole [*en holôi* (ἐν ὅλῳ)] is the same as for the other to be predicated of all of the first. And we say that one term is predicted of all of another, whenever no instance of the subject can be found of which the other term cannot be asserted") (I.24b, 28.n.; trans. A. J. Jenkinson), the Aristotelian conception of predication on the basis of *huparchein* can easily be reduced to a form that is simpler and easier to handle "in languages": the copula "is" functions to implement the so-called equivalence of *huparchein*, *legesthai*, and *katêgoreisthai*.

This assimilation, which is found in all medieval treatises on logic, is taken further by another assertion in the *Prior Analytics* (I.37, 49a.n.): "The expressions 'this belongs to that' and 'this holds true of that' have to be understood in as many different ways as there are different categories," interpreted as meaning that for Aristotle in various propositions the copula has as many meanings as there are categories (Bochenski, *A History of Formal Logic*). The predominance of the tripartite analysis of the logical form into "S is P" gives the impresssion that the distinction "subject"-"predicate," which arises from the *hupokeimenon* [ὑποκείμενον] – *katêgorêma* [κατηγόρημα] pair (see PRÉDICABLE and SUBJECT), is universal. That is how the Stoic distinction between *ptôsis* [πτῶσις] and *katêgorêma* is understood: the "inflections," that is, the terms or proper nouns (*onomata* [ὀνόματα]) and general terms (*prosêgoriai* [προσηγορίαι]) that, in a statement, designate an object, being transcribed as "subjects," and the *katêgorêmata*, that

is, the terms that attribute a property to these subjects being transcribed as "predicates" (cf. M. Pohlenz, *Die Stoa*). G. Schenk, commenting on Diogenes Laertius (VII.70), thus writes that among the Stoics, "the normal form of the statement/proposition is the case in which the subject is presented in its fundamental form, that is, the one in which the connection is made by means of a nominative" (Als normale Form der Aussage betrachten sie den Fall, wo das Subjekt sich in seiner Grundform aufrecht erhält, d.h. die Verbindung in einem Nominativ vollzogen wird [*Zur Geschichte der logischen Form*, in *Einige Entwicklungstendenzen von der Antike bis zum Ausgang des Mittelalters*, 1:216]; see section V of this entry).

In his translations of Aristotle, Boethius (ca. 480–524/25 CE) uses *praedico* to render *katêgorô* [κατηγορῶ], and *praedicatio* to render *katêgoria* [κατηγορία], which is also rendered by *praedicamentum*. The word *praedicatio* appears, of course, in a great variety of contexts. It raises no particular problem; it is the distinctions that it involves that require explanation in some cases. In the Scholastic vocabulary, *praedicatio* appears in a great variety of contexts in expressions such as *praedicatio essentialis* versus *praedicatio accidentalis*, *praedicatio per essentiam* versus *praedicatio per accidens*, and *praedicatio per se* versus *praedicatio per aliud*, which are so many unproblematic calques of Aristotle's technical language. Other uses of *praedicare* can be easily explained: *in abstracto* versus *concretive*, *in plurali* (or *pluraliter*) versus *in singulari* (or *singulariter*), *negative* versus *positive*, *per prius* versus *per posterius*, *simpliciter* versus *secundum quid*. On the other hand, some uses of *praedicatio/praedicare*, although also of Aristotelian origin, raise genuine problems. For example, *in quid* (or *in eo quod quid*, or *in eo quod quid est*) versus *in quale* (of *in quale quid*, or *ineo quod quale*) or *de ut de subjecto* versus *ut in subjecto* and *de univoce* versus *denominative*. For the first group, the difficulty concerns only the translation, because the conceptual content is clearly accessible; for the second group, it is the notion itself that poses a problem, the translation difficulty disappearing as soon as the content is identified.

II. Predication *In Quid* / Predication *In Quale*

The expression *praedicatio in eo quod quid est* (or *in eo quod quid sit praedicari*) first appears in Marius Victorinus (ca. 280–365), the translator of Porphyry's *Isagoge*, which was later popularized by Boethius's translations of Aristotle's *Organon* and by the *Logica vetus*. That is the case, for example, of the definition of genus in Aristotles' *Topics* (I.5.102a31–32): "Genos esti to kata pleionôn kai diapherontôn tôi eidei en tôi ti esti katêgoroumenon" [Γένος ἐστὶ τὸ κατὰ πλειόνων καὶ διαφερόντων τῷ εἴδει ἐν τῷ τί ἐστι κατηγορούμενον], which Victorinus renders in Latin by "Genus autem est quod de pluribus et differentibus specie in eo quod quid est praedicatur." J. Brunschwig's French translation ("Est genre un attribut qui appartient en leur essence à plusieurs choses spécifiquement différentes" [Genus is an attribute that belongs in its essence to several specifically different things; *Topics*]), as well as J. Tricot's ("Est genre l'attribut essentiel applicable à une pluralité de choses différant entre elles spécifiquement" [Genus is the essential attribute that applies to a plurality of things differentiated among themselves in specific ways; *Topics*]), although very clear, allow us to discern a certain confusion with regard to the basic formula of essential predication: *en tôi ti esti katêgoreisthai* [ἐν τῷ τί ἐστι κατηγορεῖσθαι]. It is this expression that raises the greatest problems for the translator. The formula "to be predicated" (*en tôi ti esti* [ἐν τῷ τί ἐστι]), introduced by Aristotle and later adopted and established by Porphyry, contains a reference to the idea of a question. What is predicated *en tôi ti esti* is what is predicated to answer the question "What is that thing?" The answer to the question is the *ti esti,* which, insofar as it is expressed in a definition, is the *to ti ên einai* [τὸ τί ἦν εἶναι] (see TO TI ÊN EINAI). The Latin *praedicare in eo quod quid est*, like the Greek *en tôi ti esti katêgoreisthai*, thus means "be predicated as to what is," "be predicated by indicating the 'what it is'"—that is, "be predicated in the rubric 'What is?'" or "be predicated in the relationship of *ti esti*," in short: "to be predicated relative to the question 'What is?'" In the Middle Ages, the Boethian expression was often abbreviated to *praedicari in eo quod quid*, and then to *praiedicari in quid*. The meaning is clear: the reference is to essential predication.

However, if we want to retain the technical aspect of Scholastic language, we find ourselves somewhat perplexed. A first solution is that adopted by medieval thinkers, conveyed by J. Biard in his translation of Ockham's *Summa logicae* (I, chap. 20): "Le genre est ce qui se prédique de plusieurs choses différentes par l'espèce, en en indiquant la quiddité" (Genus is what is predicated of several things differing in species, indicating the quiddity). This makes it possible to avoid using the term "essence," which is in fact better to reserve for *to ti ên einai*—and that is why Biard also uses the Franco-Latin expression *se prédiquer in quid*. Another medieval solution, adopted by O. Boulnois in his translation of Duns Scotus (*Sur la connaissance de Dieu et l'univocité de l'étant*), is *se prédiquer dans-le-quoi*. The same difficulty arises, still more acutely, for the expression *in eo quo quale si praedicari*. This formula is particularly notable in the *Isagoge*, VIII.§5, where Porphyry explains the way in which difference is predicated: "eti to men genos en tôi ti estin, hê de diaphora en tôi poion ti estin, hôs eirêtai, katêgoreitai" [ἔτι τὸ μὲν γένος ἐν τῷ τί ἐστιν, ἡ δὲ διαφορὰ ἐν τῷ ποῖόν τί ἐστιν, ὡς εἴρηται, κατηγορεῖται], which Boethius translates as "amplius genus quidem in eo quod quid est, differentia vero in eo quod quale quiddam est, quemadmodum dictum est, praedicatur." With the most natural translations of *en tôi poion ti estin* (*in eo quod quale sit*) and *en tôi ti estin* being "to be predicated relative to the question 'What is?,'" we can render the passage by "In addition, genus is predicated relative to the question 'What is' and difference, relative to 'How is?'—as has been said." Translating the passage with "to be predicated *in quale*" (to be predicated in what it is) is another possibility. In his French translation of the passage, J. Tricot proposes the following: "Le genre est inhérent à l'essence, tandis que la différence rentre dans la qualité" (Genus is inherent in essence, whereas difference is included in quality). Warren's English translation gives the following: "Further, as has been said, genus is predicated essentially, but difference qualitatively." For the definition of difference ("difference is what is predicated of several things differing in species, relative to the question 'How is the thing?'"), Tricot once again renders *en tôi poion* by "in the category of quality." This seems a poor solution even if it is not basically incorrect. What matters is still to use the vocabulary to make as clear as possible the distinction between the questions "What is X?" (*quid*

est? [which bears on the essence or the essential]) and "How is X?" (*qualis est?* [which bears on the *poion ti*]) incorporated by Aristotle and Porphyry in the definition of the two types of predication, the matrix of the distinction between essential predication and accidental predication, detailed in another form in the following distinctions: "predication as of a subject" versus "as in a subject" and "univocal predication" versus "denominative predication."

III. "Predication as of a Subject" versus "Predication as in a Subject"

The distinction between *praedicatio ut de subjecto* and *praedicatio ut in subjecto* raises no translation problems. However, the meaning of the notions is more difficult to grasp, especially when *praedicatio ut in subjecto* is replaced in the Scholastic language by *praedicatio denominativa* (see PARONYM). We can describe the phenomenon this way: the Aristotelian theory of predication, as it is set forth in the *Categories*, is based on a distinction between "beings that are said of a subject" and "beings that are in a subject." This distinction is often obscured by modern translations. The reason for this is twofold: on the one hand, the confusion of PS "be said of a subject" and Pp "be a predicate in a proposition," and on the other hand the relative homonymy (or only partial synonymy) of PS "be said of a subject" and P*S "to be predicated of a thing as of a subject."

The expression "be said of a subject" appears for the first time in the *Categories* (1a20–21): "Of things themselves some are predicable of a subject, and are never present in a subject" [τῶν ὄντων τὰ μὲν καθ᾽ ὑποκειμένου τινὸς λέγεται, ἐν ὑποκειμένῳ δὲ οὐδενί ἐστιν]. They designate a property (*kath' hupokeimenou legetai*), which, combined with the other (*en hupokeimenôi einai*), makes it possible to distribute beings in four classes. Contrary to what one might expect, "be said of a subject" does not mean "function as a predicate in a proposition" but rather "be applied to a plurality," that is, "be universal," and even, for the same reason, "be capable of functioning as a predicate in a proposition" (in fact, a particular cannot be predicated). Interpreting "be said of a subject" as meaning "be a predicate" is reverse cause and effect: it is because it is applied to a plurality that what is said of a subject is capable of then being a predicate in a proposition. The expression *kath' hupokeimenou legetai* designates the property that makes it possible to distinguish universals from particulars—*en hupokeimenôi einai* designating, for its part, the property that makes it possible to distinguish substances from nonsubstances.

In chapter 2 of the *Categories*, Aristotle thus based on these two relations the classification that allows him, by permutation, to classify, as the commentators (introducing at the same time a distinction between substance and accident that Aristotle had not previously mentioned) were to say, the "four kinds of beings": universal substances, particular nonsubstances, universal nonsubstances, and particular substances—which characterizes each existing substance as not being in a subject (all nonsubstance), being in a subject (all universal), being said of a subject (all particular), and not being said of a subject. This theory of the "four combinations" was made more precise by Porphyry, and then, among the Romans, by Boethius (under the title *quatuor complexiones*), with a distinction between universal substance, particular substance, universal accident, and particular accident (cf. RT: *PL*, vol. 64, cols. 169–71), which can be represented as follows:

Said of a subject	In a subject	
+	+	universal accident
-	+	particular accident
+	-	universal substance
-	-	particular substance

Although the distinction between PS "be said of a subject" and Pp "be a predicate in a proposition" is not always recognized or correctly rendered by modern translations, what both distinguishes and unites PS "be said of a subject" and P*S "be predicated of a thing as of a subject" is still less clear. The reason is that this distinction is from the outset neither comprehensible nor sharply defined, and moreover it is not uniformly maintained in Aristotle or his commentators. To grasp its import, we have to first see that it operates in the horizon of a distinction between intracategorial predication and transcategorial predication. Then we have to understand that although the theory of predication sought by Aristotle in the *Categories* has as its main goal to explore the first of these two forms of predication, that is, P*S, the meaning of P*S appears on the basis of two rules mentioned in the inverse order of their presupposition: the first in accord with the logical order (notated here as R1), which defines the "synonymy" of predication within the same category, formulated in 2a19–21, whereas the second (R2), which defines its "transitivity," is formulated in 1b10–11. The meaning of P*S thus appears only by combining the stipulations of R1 and R2—that is, once Aristotle's formulas have been put back in their true logical order.

R1 says [φανερὸν δὲ ἐκ τῶν εἰρημένων ὅτι τῶν καθ' ὑποκειμένου λεγομένων ἀναγκαῖον καὶ τοὔνομα καὶ τὸν λόγον κατηγορεῖσθαι τοῦ ὑποκειμένου]. J. Tricot translates this as follows: "Il est clair, d'après ce que nous avons dit, que le prédicat doit être affirmé du sujet aussi bien pour le nom que pour la définition" (It is clear, after what we have said, that the predicate ought to be affirmed by the subject and equally for the noun and the definition). This translation, which omits *tôn kath' hupokeimenou legomenôn*, does not allow us to grasp the function of R1. By giving R1, Aristotle formulates, without saying so explicitly, the first characteristic of intracategorial predication: attribution (*sunônumos* [συνωνύμως]). What R1 means in fact is that in the case in which two entitites x and y belong to the same category and y is predicated of x, the definition of y and "y" (that is, the term designating y) are both predicated of x. The problem for the translator and reader of 2a19–21 is that Aristotle does not make it clear that R1 holds for the entities belonging to the same category. Nonetheless, what R1 defines, namely what 3a33–34 calls "predication by synonymy" is, in Aristotle's view, the fundamental trait of intracategorial predication valid for "synonymous" things, those that have, according to the first chapter of the *Categories*, like an ox and

a man, the same name ("animal") and the same *logos* [λόγος]. The difficulty of 2a19–21 is thus that in R1, "be said of a subject" does not have the same meaning as in PS: *tôn kath' hupokeimenou legomenôn* does not designate all things that are applicable to several things (that is, all universals, whether substances or accidents), but rather a subset of these things, those that apply to other things "according to the name and the definition" (in other words, only secondary substances and differences). Even if this cannot be directly formulated in a translation, in order to understand R1 properly, we must then see that its main expression—the "things said of a subject"—refers to neither Pp nor PS, which, unfortunately, is not possible once P*S has been introduced.

■ See Box 1.

It is in R2 that P*S is introduced. This may explain why Aristotle presents this rule, which is logically posterior to R1, before the latter. R2 has to do with the transitivity of intracategorial predication. There again, Aristotle does not specify this. On the other hand, he uses the expression P*S, which supports his whole theory of predication. The intervention of P*S in 1b10–11 is neutralized by Tricot's translation. The text says, "ὅταν ἕτερον καθ' ἑτέρου κατηγορῆται ὡς καθ' ὑποκειμένου, ὅσα κατὰ τοῦ κατηγορουμένου λέγεται, πάντα καὶ κατὰ τοῦ ὑποκειμένου ῥηθήσεται." Tricot offers this translation: "Quand une chose est attribuée à une autre comme à son sujet, tout ce qui est affirmé du prédicat devra être aussi affirmé du sujet" (When a thing is attributed to another thing as it is to its own subject, everything that is affirmed as belonging to the predicate must also be affirmed as belonging to the subject). The function of R2 is to explain that in the case in which three entities, x, y, z, "belong to the same category," that x is predicated of y by synonymy and that y is predicated of z by synonymy, x is predicated of z. The problem raised by this rule is that of correctly interpreting the expression "be predicated of a subject," which assumes that what has been said in R1 has been introduced into it. This necessity is more or less well emphasized in the main translations.

■ See Box 2.

The problem of R2 is not, in fact, the variety of expressions used to render the series *kathêgorêtai/legetai/rhêthêsetai*—namely, for *kathêgorêtai*: est attribué, praedicatur, è predicata, "is predicated," "will be said," gilt; for *rhêthêsetai*: devra être affirmé, dicentur, saranno dette, "will be predicable," "will be said," gelten (muß), gelten (wird)—but rather the implicit claim that it conveys, that is, that it is valid only for realities belonging to the same category. The transitivity of predication emphasized by R2 has only an intracategorial validity; it holds only in the context of synonymous predication (defined by R1).

The significance of the system formed by R1 and R2 is thus properly understood only if one grasps the import of the difference between PS and P*S. Even if, in fact, the expressions "be said of x" and "be predicated of x as of a subject" are often treated as though they were interchangeable, it remains that in the *Categories* the main function of P*S is to explain the predicative relation of secondary substances or of differences to their subjects. This is made explicit in three theses set forth in *Categories* 5.

1

The translations of the First Rule (Aristotle, *Categories*, 2a19–21)

[φανερὸν δὲ ἐκ τῶν εἰρημένων ὅτι τῶν καθ' ὑποκειμένου λεγομένων ἀναγκαῖον καὶ τοὔνομα καὶ τὸν λόγον κατηγορεῖσθαι τοῦ ὑποκειμένου].

"Manifestum est autem ex his quae dicta sunt quoniam eorum quae de subjecto dicuntur necesse est et nomen et rationem de subjecto praedicari." (trans. Boethius, *Aristoteles Latinus*)

"È chiaro da quello che si è detto che anche il nome e la definizione delle cose

che son dette di un soggetto è necessario che siano predicati del soggetto." (trans. M. Zanatta)

"It is plain from what has been said that both the name and the definition of the predicate must be predicable of the subject." (trans. E. M. Edghill)

"It is clear from what has been said that if something is said of a subject both its name and its definition are necessarily predicated of the subject." (trans. J. L. Ackrill)

"Aus dem Gesagten erhellt, daß bei solchem, was von einem Subjekt ausgesagt wird, der Name und der Begriff gleichmäßig von dem Subjekt ausgesagt werden müssen." (trans. E. Rolfes)

"Aufgrund des Gesagten ist klar, daß bei dem, was von einem Zugrundeliegenden ausgesagt wird, sowohl der Name als auch die Definition von dem zugrundeliegenden prädiziert werden müssen." (trans. K. Oehler)

2

Translations of the Second Rule (Aristotle, *Categories*, 1b10–11)

"ὅταν ἕτερον καθ' ἑτέρου κατηγορῆται ὡς καθ' ὑποκειμένου, ὅσα κατὰ τοῦ κατηγορουμένου λέγεται, πάντα καὶ κατὰ τοῦ ὑποκειμένου ῥηθήσεται."

"Quando alterum de altero praedicatur ut de subjecto, quaecumque de eo quod praedicatur dicuntur, omnia etiam de subjecto dicentur." (trans. Boethius)

"Quando una cosa è predicata di un'altra come di un soggetto, tutte quelle cose

che son dette del predicato saranno dette anche del sogetto." (trans. M. Zanatta)

"When one thing is predicated of another, all that which is predicable of the predicate will be predicable also of the subject." (trans. E. M. Edghill)

"Whenever one thing is predicated of another as of a subject, all things said of what is predicated will be said of the subject also." (trans. J. L. Ackrill)

"Wenn etwas von Etwas als seinem Subjekt ausgesagt wird, so muß alles, was von dem Ausgesagten gilt, auch von dem Subjekt gelten." (trans. E. Rolfes)

"Wenn das eine von dem anderen als von einem Zugrundeliegenden ausgesagt wird, wird alles, was von dem Ausgesagten gilt, auch von dem Zugrundeliegenden gelten." (trans. K. Oehler)

Porphyry seems to have been the first philosopher to see the importance of the difference beteen PS and P*S. In his *Commentary* on the *Categories* "by question and answer," he explains clearly the meaning of P*S: "be predicated of a thing 'as of a subject' means 'be stated of a thing as being part of its essence' or as 'constituting its essence'" (trans. S. K. Strange, *On Aristotle's Categories*). As a reader of Porphyry, Boethius transmitted this interpretation to the Romans. That is why in his work essential predication, intracategorial predication, is usually called *praedicatio ut de subjecto* in opposition to accidental, transcategorial predication, which is called *praedicatio ut in subjecto*. Porphyry, rather than Aristotle, seems to have been the origin of this expression. In any case, it is these two varieties of predication that we find expressed in the Middle Ages by the pairs univocal predication / denominative predication and essential/accidental:

> There are two kinds of predication: one is univocal, as when we say that Socrates is a man, because man is predicated of Socrates truly and unequivocally [*vere et univoce*]; the other is denominative, as when whiteness is predicated of man, in fact, the man is said to be white and having-whiteness, but he is not said to be whiteness [*dicitur enim homo albus et habens albedinem nec dicitur esse*

albedo]. Similarly, if we say that a body is white and that a color is white, the definition of the predicate is not predicated equally of the two subjects.

> (Avicenna, *Logica* [Venice, 1508], f. 3vb.)

IV. "Univocal Predication" versus "Denominative Predication"

The reformulation of predication "as of a subject" as "univocal" predication continues Porphyry's *kath' hupokeimenou* interpretation in the form of "essential" predication. On the other hand, the notion of "denominative" predication emphasizes the original Aristotelian notion of accidental attribution. The source of Avicenna's terminology is clear: the passage in the *Topics* (II.2.109b4–8) in which, concerning the attribution of genus to species, Aristotle himself distinguishes predication "by synonymy" from predication in a "paronymic" form—a distinction that J. Brunschwig renders in French by means of the *univoque/dérivée* pair and J. Tricot by *d'une façon synonyme / dans sa forme dérivée*:

> [L]'attribution d'un genre à son espèce ne se fait jamais sous une forme dérivée: les genres se prédiquent toujours de manière univoque à leurs espèces, puisque

les espèces admettent à la fois le nom et la définition de leur genre.

(The attribution of a genus to its kind is never done under its derived forms: genus is always predicated in a uniform way to its species, whereas species allow for both the name and the definition of their genus.)

(Fr. trans. J. Brunschwig, *Topiques*)

[L]e prédicat tiré du genre n'est jamais, dans sa forme dérivée, affirmé de l'espèce, mais c'est toujours d'une façon synonyme que les genres sont affirmés de leurs espèces.

(The predicate taken from the genus is never, in its derived form, affirmed in the species, but it is always in a way synonymous.)

(Fr. trans. J. Tricot, *Topiques*)

The distinction between these two kinds of predication, which develops the basic intuition of *Categories*, 5.3b7–9, allows Aristotle to define the attribution of the accident as "paronymic" (or, as Brunschwig translates it, based on *l'utilisation d'une expression dérivée*):

[E]n disant que le blanc est coloré, on ne présente pas l'attribut comme un genre, puisqu'on utilise une expression dérivée [*parônumôs legetai* (παρωνύμως λέγεται)]; on ne le présente pas non plus comme un propre ou comme une définition, puisque *définition* et *propre* n'appartiennent à aucun autre sujet, alors qu'il existe bien d'autres choses colorées que le blanc, par exemple un morceau de bois, une pierre, un homme, un cheval; il est donc clair qu'on le présente comme un accident.

(In saying that white is colored, one does not present the attribute as a genus, since one is using a derived expression [*parônumôs legetai* (παρωνύμως λέγεται)]; nor does one present it as something proper or as a definition, since "definition" and the "proper" belong to no other subject; even though there are many colored things other than white, for example, a piece of wood, a stone, a man, a horse. It is clear that one presents it as an accident.)

(Fr. trans. J. Brunschwig, *Topiques*, II.2.109b8–12)

The expression *parônumôs legetai* appears in the *Categories*, 8.10a27–31, regarding the distinction between *poiotêtes* [ποιότητες] and *poia* [ποιά], qualities and *qualia*: Aristotle explains that a *quale* is "something spoken of paronymically"—that is, about which one speaks "using a paronym"—(when the initial quality has a name) or "in some other way" (when the initial quality does not have a name). An important aspect of the Aristotelian vocabulary is that paronymic attribution, which is characteristic of accidental predication, and designation by derivation, which is characteristic of the formation of a concrete noun, are covered by the same expression, *parônumôs legetai*. This is not perceptible in Tricot's translation (cf. *Catégories* 8.10a27–31):

Sont donc des qualités les déterminations que nous avons énoncées ; quant aux choses qualifiées, ce sont

celles qui sont dénommées d'après ces qualités, ou qui en dépendent de quelque autre façon.—Ainsi dans la plupart des cas, et même presque toujours, le nom de la chose qualifiée est dérivé [de la qualité]: par exemple, blancheur a donné son nom à blanc, grammaire à grammairien, et justice à juste.

(Qualities are thus determinations that we have enunciated: as to qualified things, they are those that have been named after qualities, or that depend on them in some other way. In most cases, almost always in fact, the name of the qualified thing is derived from the quality: for example, whiteness gives a name to white, grammar to the grammarian, and justice to the concept of the just.)

In *Categories*, 8, the examples of morphological derivation provided by Aristotle are whiteness/white, grammar/grammarian, and justice/just. The first already appeared in *Categories*, 5, the second in *Categories*, 1, in the definition of "paronyms" (*parônuma* [παρώνυμα]), the third replacing the courage/courageous pair that is also introduced in *Categories*, 1. In *Categories*, 5, the example of the color white serves to distinguish primary substance, secondary substance, and accident "from the point of view of signification." Primary substance signifies a *tode ti* [τόδε τι]. Substance, or rather secondary essence, seems to signify a *tode ti* because of the "form of its appellation"; in reality, it signifies a *poion ti* [ποιόν τι], because the subject to which it is attributed is multiple and not unique, as in the case of primary substance. In this respect it is comparable to an accident, which also signifies a *poion ti*. There is, however, a difference between them: the accident signifies the *poion* absolutely (*haplôs* [ἁπλῶς]); the species (*eidos* [εἶδος]) and the genus (*genos* [γένος]) do not signify it absolutely, "they delimit the *poion* in relation to the *ousia*," that is, they signify an *ousia* in one way or another. Once again, Aristotle's play on *poion* is not rendered by Tricot, who, interpreting the text on the basis of Boethius's Latin translation, uses the abstract *qualité* and the term *qualification* (cf. *Catégories* 5.3b13–21, 15):

Pour les substances secondes, aussi, on pourrait croire, en raison de la forme même de leur appellation, qu'elles signifient un être déterminé, quand nous disons, par exemple, homme ou animal. Et pourtant ce n'est pas exact: de telles expressions signifient plutôt une qualification, car le sujet n'est pas un comme dans le cas de la substance première ; en réalité, homme est attribué à une multiplicité, et animal également.—Cependant ce n'est pas d'une façon absolue que l'espèce et le genre signifient la qualité, comme le ferait, par exemple, le blanc (car le blanc ne signifie rien d'autre que la qualité), mais ils déterminent la qualité par rapport à la substance : ce qu'ils signifient, c'est une substance de telle qualité.

(For secondary substances, as well, one might assume, by virtue of the form of their appellation, that they signify a determinate being, when we say, for example, man or animal. And yet, that is not quite right: such expressions actually signify a qualification, because the subject is not one, as in the case of the primary substance. In reality, man is attributed to a multiplicity, and so is animal. Thus there is no absolute way in which species and genus signify a quality, as in the case of the color white (because white means nothing other than a quality); but both determine the quality in relation to substance: what they signify is the substance of a given quality.)

The convergence in *Categories*, 1, 5, and 8, of the level of attribution, that of derivation, and that of signification in a single terminological network is noteworthy. We observe, however, that derivative names and paronyms must not be purely and simply identified. All paronyms are derivative, but all derivatives are not paronyms—since Boethius, Latin has drawn a distinction between *sumpta* and *denominativa* (see PARONYM).

V. The Problem of the Copula

The dominance of the "Aristotelian" analysis of logical form suggests that it is natural to interpret the structure of the proposition on the basis of the verb "to be." This pseudo-naturalness has been strongly denounced in the modern period, in terms that have now become almost scholastic: the confusion between the existential and the predicative senses; the verbal illusion that consists in believing that the verb "to be," detached from the terms that follow it, has the same function in judgments of relation as in predicative judgments, leading to the inevitable reduction of the former to the latter. Some writers have attributed to the "Aristotelianization of the mentality of the countries bordering on the Mediterranean" (cf. L. Rougier, *La métaphysique et le langage*, 105) the responsibility for this major "corruption" of logic (cf. Geach, "History of the Corruptions of Logic," 44–61). Up until Frege's challenge to the formula "S is P," there have been two opposed, dominant models of predication: Aristotle's, based on the attributive proposition, and the Stoic model, often said to have made the most radical challenge to the attributive model of predication. Even overlaid by the language of "subject" and "predicate," the Stoic theory seems in fact to be a complete reversal of the so-called natural schema. For the Stoics, the "subject" has only a complementary value; being both an inflection of the verb and a case of the noun, it is what "completes" the *katêgorêma*, "an [expressible] incomplete *lekton* [*ellipês lekton* (ἐλλιπὴς λεκτόν)] awaiting completion" (cf. P. Aubenque, "Herméneutique et ontologie," 103: "It [the Stoic subject] is a *ptôsis*, a kind of inflection of the verb, whereas in Aristotle, the subject-form is the *onoma* itself, and not a case of the noun"). This devaluation of the attributive sentence is accompanied by an ontological choice: "Stoic ontology is an 'ontology' without Being; it perceives the world as a succession of events in search of subjects, and not as a juxtaposition of stable existents awaiting attributes" (ibid.; cf. P. Hadot, "La notion de cas dans la logique stoïcienne," 109–12; see PARONYM, Box 2, and SIGNIFIER/SIGNIFIED).

Medieval writers' choice of the Aristotelian analysis, which ensured the victory of the attributive proposition, had important consequences:

By introducing the verb to be as the copula, that is, as an explicit operator of synthesis (whereas any verb, Aristotle himself notes, has the power to exercise this synthetic function), Artisotle tips the balance of the proposition toward the subject. The verb "to be," having only a weak meaning, cannot bear the weight of the proposition, which then shifts toward the *hupocheimenon*, which is declared to be the *ousia*, that is, "beingness" [*étantité*] proper, which its identification with the *sub-jectum*, the substrate, leads it to be translated in Latin correctly as *sub-stantia*, that is, the subsistent and permanent basis perduring under the variability of the attributes. In a parallel manner, the predicate, which in the verbal phrase is the action or event expressed by the verb, is reduced to an attribute, that is, to an accident of the subject, which is "essential" only because it is substantial.

(Ibid., 102–3)

■ See Box 3.

Although it did not take place, for good reason, in the context of a European language, Arabic reflection on the Aristotelian logical schema deserves notice. Averroës, for example, strongly emphasizes that "in Arabic one can form an apophantic statement on the basis of two nouns without a connecting verb, a nominal statement being no less predicative than a statement containing a verb." To do justice to the Aristotelian analysis, he thus resorts to the notion of "potential" interpreted in the sense of "implicit," and presents the tripartite product of the nominal statement as an explicitation/actuation. Of the three notions imported in a predication (Ar. *ḥaml* [الحمل])—the subject (Ar. *mawḍūʿ* [موضوع]), the predicate (Ar. *maḥmūl* [محمول]), and the relation (Ar. *nisba* [نسبة]), which links the subject and the predicate—two are explicit (the subject and the predicate), while the other (the relation) is implicit. To make the relation explicit, one can resort either to the word *huwa* [هو] (him) or to *mawğūd* [موجود] (existent). In this sense, one will say, "Zayd is just." The copula is thus not a "necessary part" of the premise (which one obtains through analysis), it is in it only potentially, and serves only to make explicit or to lexicalize the connection between subject and predicate, "by compensating for a linguistic defect" (because "in Arabic there is no word designating this kind of connection, whereas it exists in other languages," *Commentary on the "De interpretatione*," §19). The "third element" is thus only an "addition."

In modern logic, essentially starting with Frege, the copula is no longer considered solely as an unnecessary addition but as a useless and misleading one. The analysis of the proposition in two terms, subject and predicate, connected (or separated) by a copula, has been denounced by many modern thinkers as the result of a projection of the linguistic asymmetry of the (grammatical) subject and predicate into ontology or logic themselves (in the Aristotelian manner, I can say "Socrates is a man," not "the/a man is Socrates"). It is generally thought that this deficit is made up starting with Frege (cf. M. Dummett, *Frege's Philosophy of Language*). For Frege, a proposition such as "Two is a prime number" is vitiated by "the inexactitude of its linguistic expression," the use of the copula "making it appear that something is added to the object and to the concept, as if the relation of subsumption were a third element." Without returning to the Stoic schema of incompletion and completion (the verb-predicate

3

Copula in Medieval Logic

➤ PRÉDICABLE, Box 1

It was in the Middle Ages that the notion of the copula was fully worked out, within a system in which there was a problematic connection between the distinction between the existential meaning and the predicative meaning of the verb "to be," in the form of the distinction between *secundum* and *tertium adjacens*; the conflict between the predicative sentence and the verbal sentence; and the distinction between two types of predication: identity and inherence. In order to grasp all the elements in this system and the way in which they are related, we have to go back to a specific passage in the *Peri hermêneias* in which Boethius and, following him, the grammarians and logicians of the eleventh century interpreted these problems, introducing a new terminology.

Although the verb *copulare* is ordinarily used by Boethius as a synonym of *conjungere* or *componere*, in the sense of "conjoin" or "connect," with terms or things as its object, starting at the end of the eleventh century we see it take on a very particular meaning in the analysis of predication. The grammarians and commentators on Priscian's *Institutiones grammaticae*, followed by Abelard a few decades later, introduced the idea that the verb is characterized by a "coupling value" (*vis copulandi*), a property that allowed it to connect the subject and the predicate; this property is clearly inspired by the definition Aristotle gives of the verb in the *Peri hermêneias*, and it led to the introduction of the terms *copula* and *verbum copulativum*. For example, we read the following in an anonymous commentary from the early twelfth century:

> Praedicativa propositio est illa quae alia praedicatum et subjectum, ut "homo est animal," subjectum ut "homo," praedicatum ut "animal," et "est" praedicatum ut "animal," et "est" copula quae copulat ista duo.

> (A predicative proposition is a proposition in which there is a predicate and a subject, like "man is an animal," a subject "man," a predicate "animal," and "is," which is the copula coupling the two.)

> (Iwakuma, "*Introductiones dialecticae artis secundum magistrum G. Paganellum*")

Similarly, in Abelard:

> Haec est autem proprietas, quod verbum semper est nota, id est copula praedicatorum de altero, id est copulativum est praedicatorum, quae praedicata de altero quam de ipsis verbis copulantibus

necesse est praedicari. Nunquam enim verbum copulativum praedicati subici potest, ut "lego" vel "legis" vel "legit" nunquam alicui potest in propositione subici, sed praedicari, quando scilicet gemina vi fungitur [copulantis] scilicet et praedicati.

> (It is a matter of a property, that the verb is always the mark, that is, the term that couples the predicates with something else [to the other term, the subject], that is, it has the property of coupling the predicates; and these predicates have to be predicated of something other than the verbs that couple themselves. In fact, the coupling verb can never be the subject of the predicate, for example, "I read" or "you read" can never be the subject in a proposition, but always the predicate, when they have a double value, both of coupling and of predicate.)

> (*Super Peri hermeneias*)

This passage in Abelard is taken from the grammarians that preceded him: they introduced the idea that every verb has a double value, a value of coupling (*vis copulandi*) and a value of predicate (*vis praedicati, vis verbi*) that corresponds to its particular meaning. The same holds for the verb "to be," which has this value of coupling, or substantive value (whence its name of *verbum substantivum*, "substantive verb"), and its own value, which is, depending on the author, an existential or a specifically semantic value (see R. W. Hunt, "The Introductions to the 'Artes' in the Twelfth Century").

This double value was to play a role in the analysis of predication. When the verb "to be" is in *secundum adjacens*, the two values are active, a value of copula and a value of predicate (it couples the thing that it signifies). But the case in which it is in *tertium adjacens*, when there is predication of an accident, such as *Socrates est albus* (Socrates is white), is harder, the question being whether it can have a purely connective function, to the exclusion of its existential value. This elicited divergent interpretations. The grammarians and Abelard considered this kind of proposition to be susceptible of two analyses, even though they disagreed regarding the priority to be attributed to each, and Abelard himself was to modify his position on this point. First, there is a "coupling of essences" (*copulatio essentiae*) signified by the terms "subject" and "predicate": the verb "to be" "signifying all essences *qua* essences, it has property of coupling all essences"; it "couples" the essence or "thing" Socrates with "this white thing," with the meaning "this white thing Socrates is that

white thing"—this initial analysis originates in the "substantive value" of the verb "to be" (*ex vi substantivi*). Second, the quality signified by the predicate *albus*, namely whiteness, *albedo*, is signified as inhering in the subject Socrates—this second analysis has for its cause the nature of the predicate (*ex vi praedicationis*). These two analyses, which we juxtapose here, were to be the origin of two major, and separate, analyses of predication in the Middle Ages: the theory of identity, according to which the predicate is taken in extension, predication amounting to positing an identity between what the subject denotes and what the predicate denotes; and the theory of inherence, according to which the predicate is taken intentionally, predication amounting to positing the inherence of the quality in the subject. It should be noted that this particular usage of the term *copulare* to designate the connection of the "things" denoted by the subject and the predicate originates in the interpretation of an extremely problematic passage in *Peri hermêneias*, 3, which Boethius translates this way:

> Ipsa quidem secundum se dicta verba nomina sunt, et significant aliquid—constituit enim qui dicit intellectum, et qui audit quiescit—sed si est vel non est, nondum significat. Neque enim "esse" signum est rei vel "non esse," nec si hoc ipsum "est" purum dixeris. Ipsum quidem nihil est, consignificat autem quandam compositionem, quam sine compositis non est intelligere.

> (In themelves, verbs are in reality nouns, and they signify something—the person who is speaking constitutes in fact an act of understanding, and the one who listens can rest (for the signification is completed, he expects nothing more)—but they do not yet signify that something is or is not. Neither "being" nor "not being" is a sign of a thing, if one says "is" all by itself. It is, in fact, nothing, but it consignifies a composition that cannot be understood without the component terms.)

> (Aristotle, *Peri hermêneias* 3.16b20–25, trans. Boethius in *Aristoteles Latinus*)

This passage is of capital importance for the developments regarding the substantive verb (does it mean something or not?) and the notion of "consignification" (see CONNOTATION). Boethius, in opposition to Porphyry, thinks that Aristotle means to say here, not that the verb "to be" has no meaning, but that it does not yet signify the true and the false. In order to explain why it realizes its signification only in conjunction with the terms it serves to link, Boethius introduces a distinction between two uses, depending on whether it is employed alone or in conjunction with a predicate. It is in this context that, in the first commentary on the *Peri hermêneias*, Boethius uses the term *copulare* to mark the connection of things signified by the subject and the predicate (*duas res copulat atque componit*). In the second commentary, we find the analysis of what was later called the "coupling of essences," both for predications *de secundo adjacente*, like *Socrates est*, which can be glossed as "Socrates is one among those who exist" (*Socrates aliquid eorum est quae sunt*), and in predications *de tertio adjacente*, like *Socrates philosophus est*, which is interpreted as making it possible to conjoin "Socrates" and "philosophy," but also signifies that Socrates participates in philosophy, this second value then being transformed into the signification of an inherence of the quality in the subject. It is in relation to this value of "coupling" or "conjunction" that Aristotle's statement is justified, even when it is in *secundum adjacens*, Boethius explains: the verb "to be" "has a value of conjunction, not of thing [*vim conjunctionis cujusdam obtinet, non rei*]"; here Boethius adopts a formulation of Porphyry's: "it designates no substance" (*nullam*

substantia monstrat) (cf. Boethius, *Commentarii in librum Aristotelis Peri hermeneias*).

On the basis of this passage and the commentaries of the grammarians, Abelard made a clear distinction between *copulare* and *praedicare*, which is coherent with his position on universals: since there is no whiteness *qua* essence, but only individual whitenesses and white things, in saying *Socrates est albus* we can only "predicate whiteness in adjacency, and white, or, in other terms, what is affected by whiteness, in an essential way"; whiteness is thus *predicated* in the sense in which one means that whiteness inheres in the subject, but Socrates is *coupled* with this white thing or with this thing that is affected by whiteness. Each term used here has a precise meaning: the adjective *albus* is "conjoined" with the verb, it "predicates" an adjacent form, and "couples" the "foundation of whiteness that it denotes" (*fundamentum quod nominat*); the accidental form is predicated, but it is the substrate in which it is found and which the term "accident" denotes or "names" that is coupled (whence the gloss: Socrates is what is affected by whiteness). It is because of the imperfect nature of the verb "to be," and because it can never be a "pure copula," that this essential or existential value is always present, along with this "coupling of essences" leading to the

positing of an identity or an identification of two singular existing things, denoted by the subject and the predicate (Abelard, *Super Peri hermeneias*).

Irène Rosier-Catach

BIBLIOGRAPHY

Abelard, Peter. "Glossae Super *Periermenias Aristotelis*." In *Peter Abaelards Philosophische Schriften. I. Die Logica "Ingredientibus". 3. Die Glossen Zu Peri Ermhneias*, edited by Bernhard Geyer, 306–504. Münster: Verlag der Aschendorffschen Verlagsbuchhandlung, 1927.

Aristotle. *Peri hermêneias*. In *Aristoteles Latinus* II 1–2. *De Interpretatione vel Periermenias*. Translatio Boethii, Specimina Translationum Recentiorum. Edited by L. Minio-Paluello. Bruges, Belg.: Desclée, de Brouwer, et Cie., 1965.

Boethius. *Commentarii in librum Aristotelis Peri hermeneias*. Edited by K. Meiser. Leipzig: B.G. Teubner, 1877/1880.

Hunt, R. W. "The Introductions to the 'Artes' in the Twelfth Century." In *Collected Papers on the History of Grammar in the Middle Ages*, edited by G. L. Bursill-Hall. Amsterdam: Benjamins, 1980.

Iwakuma, Y. "Introductiones dialecticae artis secundum magistrum G. Paganellum." In *Cahiers de l'Institut du Moyen Âge grec et latin*, no. 63, 1993.

being "completed" by a *ptôsis*), Frege, thanks to the notions of unsaturation and saturation, carries out the same reduction of the useless "third": "the unsaturation of the concept has as its effect that the object that performs the saturation adheres immediately to the concept, without needing a particular connection" (cf. G. Frege, *Über Schoenlies*).

Alain de Libera

BIBLIOGRAPHY

Aristotle. *Aristoteles Latinus*. Vols. 1–3, *Topiques, translatio Boethii*. Edited by L. Minio-Paluello. Bruges, Belg.: Desclée de Brouwer, 1969.

———. *Le Categorie*. Translated and edited by Marcello Zanatta. Milan: Biblioteca Universale Rizzoli, 1989.

———. *Categories*. Translated by J. L. Ackrill. Oxford: Oxford University Press / Clarendon, 1975. Translation by E. M. Edghill: *Categories* in vol. 1 of *The Works of Aristotle*, edited W. D. Ross and J. A. Smith. Oxford: Oxford University Press, 1928.

———. *Catégories*. Translated and edited by F. Ildefonse and J. Lallot. Paris: Éditions du Seuil, 2002. Translation by Jules Tricot: *Catégories*. In vol. 1 of *Organon*. Paris: Vrin. 1984.

———. *Kategorien*. Translated and edited by Klaus Oehler. Berlin: Akademie Verlag, 1984.

———. *Organon*. Translated by J. Tricot. Paris: Vrin, 1946–60.

———. *Prior Analytics*. Translated by A. J. Jenkinson in *Basic Works of Aristotle*, edited by R. McKeon. New York: Random House, 1941.

———. *Topica*. Translated by E. S. Forster. Cambridge, MA: Harvard University Press / Loeb Classical Library, 1989.

———. *Topiques*. Translated and edited by Jacques Brunschwig. Paris: Les Belles Lettres, 1967.

Aubenque, Pierre. "Herméneutique et ontologie: Remarques sur le *Peri hermêneias* d'Aristote." In *Penser avec Aristote*, edited by A. Sinaceur, 93–105. Toulouse: Érès, 1991.

Averroës. *Averroës' Middle Commentaries on Aristotle's "Categories" and "De Interpretatione."* Translated, with notes and introduction, by Charles E. Butterworth. Princeton, NJ: Princeton University Press, 1983.

———. *Commentaire moyen sur le "De Interpretatione."* Translated, with notes, by A. Benmakhlouf and S. Diebler. Paris: Vrin, 2000.

Bäck, Allan. *Aristotle's Theory of Predication*. Leiden, Neth.: Brill, 2000.

Barnouw, Jeffrey. *Propositional Perception: Phantasia, Predication, and Sign in Plato, Aristotle and the Stoics*. Lanham, MD: University Press of America, 2002.

Bochenski, J. M. *A History of Formal Logic*. Translated by I. Thomas. New York: Chelsea, 1961.

Bréhier, Émile. *La théorie des incorporels dans l'ancien stoïcisme*. Paris: Vrin, 1962.

Brunschwig, Jacques. *Papers in Hellenistic Philosophy*. Translated by Janet Lloyd. Cambridge: Cambridge University Press, 1994.

de Rijk, Lambertus Marie. *Logica modernorum*. Vol. 2.1 of *The Origin and Early Development of the Theory of Supposition*. Assen, Neth.: Van Gorcum, 1967.

Dummett, Michael. *Frege's Philosophy of Language*. London: Duckworth, 1973.

Duns Scotus. *Sur la connaissance de Dieu et l'univocité de l'étant*. Translated by O. Boulnois. Paris: Presses Universitaires de France, 1988.

Ebbesen, Sten. "Boethius as an Aristotelian Scholar." In vol. 2 of *Aristoteles Wirk und Wirkung*, edited by J. Wiesener, 286–311. Berlin and New York: Walter de Gruyter, 1987.

Frege, G. *Über Schoenlies: Die logischen Paradoxien der Mengenlehre*. In *Kleine Schriften*, edited by H. Hermes, F. Kambartel, and F. Kaulbach. Hamburg: Meiner, 1969.

Geach, P. T. "History of the Corruptions of Logic." In *Logic Matters*. Los Angeles: University of California Press, 1972.

Gochet, Paul. *Esquisse d'une théorie nominaliste de la proposition*. Paris: A. Colin, 1972.

Hadot, P. "La notion de cas dans la logique stoïcienne." *Actes du XIe Congrès des sociétés de philosophie de langue française*. Neuchâtel, Switz.: La Baconnière, 1966.

John XXI, Pope. *The "Summulae logicales" of Peter of Spain*. Edited by Joseph Patrick Mullally. Notre Dame, IN: University of Notre Dame Press, 1945.

Newton, Lloyd, ed. *Medieval Commentaries on Aristotle's "Categories."* Leiden, Neth.: Brill, 2008.

Nuchelmans, Gabriel. *Theories of the Proposition: Ancient and Medieval Conceptions of the Bearers of Truth and Falsity*. Amsterdam: North-Holland, 1973.

Pohlenz, Max. *Kleine Schriften*. Vol 1 of *Die Begründung der abendländischen Sprachlehre durch die Stoa*. Hildesheim, Ger.: Olms, 1965.

———. *Die Stoa*. Göttingen, Ger.: Vandenhoeck und Ruprecht, 1948.

Porphyry. *Einletung in die Kategorien*. Translated by E. Rolfes. Hamburg: Felix Meiner, 1958. First published in 1925.

———. *Introduction*. Translated, with commentary, by Jonathan Barnes. Oxford: Oxford University Press, 2003. Translation by Edward W. Warren: *Isagoge*. Toronto, ON: Pontifical Institute of Mediaeval Studies, 1975. Translation by Steven K. Strange: *On Aristotle's Categories*. London: Duckworth, 1992.

———. *Isagoge*. Translated into French by Alain de Libera and Alain-Philippe Segonds. Introduction and notes by Alain de Libera. Paris: J. Vrin, 1998.

———. *Isagoge*. Translated into Italian, with introduction and commentary, by Bruno Maioli. Padua: Liviana, 1969. Translation, with introduction and commentary, by G. Girgenti: *Isagoge*. Milan: Rusconi, 1995.

———. *Isagoge, translatio Boethii accedunt isagoges fragmenta M. Victorino interprete*. Vol. 1, books 6–7 of *Aristoteles Latinus*, edited by L. Minio-Paluello. Bruges, Belg.: Desclée de Brouwer, 1966.

———. *Isagoge et in Aristotelis Categorias Commentarium*. Edited and introduced with notes by A. Busse. Berlin: G. Reimer, 1995. First published in 1887.

Rougier, L. *La métaphysique et le langage*. Paris: Denoël, 1973.

Schenk, G. *Zur Geschichte der logischen Form*. Vol. 1 of *Einige Entwicklungstendenzen von der Antike bis zum Ausgang des Mittelalters*. Berlin: VEB Deutscher Verlag der Wissenschaften, 1973.

Strawson, Peter. *Subject and Predicate in Logic and Grammar*. London: Methuen, 1974.

Surdu, Alexander. *Aristotelian Theory of Prejudicative Forms*. Hildesheim, Ger.: Olms, 2006.

William of Ockham. *Summa logicae*. 3 vols. Edited by Philotheus Boehner. St Bonaventure, NY: Franciscan Institute, 1951–54. English translation by Michael J. Loux: *Ockham's Theory of Terms: Part I of the Summa logicae*. Notre Dame, IN: University of Notre Dame Press, 1974. French translation by Joël Biard: *Somme de logique*. Mauvezin, Fr.: Trans Europe Repress, 1988.

PRESENT, PAST, FUTURE

DANISH	*præsentisk, nuværende, tilkommende*
FRENCH	*présent, passé, futur*
GERMAN	*gegenwärtig, anwesend, Gegenwart/Anwesenheit ; vergangen/gewesen; zukünftig*
GREEK	*paron* [παρόν], *parelthon* [παρελθόν], *mellon* [μέλλον]
LATIN	*praesens, praeteritum, futurum*

➤ *TIME*, and ASPECT, COMBINATION AND CONCEPTUALIZATION, ENGLISH, ESSENCE, ESTI, HISTORY, MEMORY, MOMENT, *TO BE*, TO TI ÊN EINAI

Is our way of dividing up time into past, present, and future determined by the divisions made in languages, that is, by the different systems of grammatical tenses? Derived from Benveniste, the question can be fully answered only by attentively examining these systems, and in particular the different expressions of aspect. Several approaches open up, however, in the words themselves that express, in different languages, the parts of time and/or grammatical tenses: an archeology of the Greek tripartite division of time, which is anything but obvious on first inspection, will be followed by an examination of the differentiations internal to

modern languages, the twofold past and present in German (*vergangen/gewesen, Gegenwart/ Anwesenheit*), and the twofold future in French (*futur/avenir*).

I. Time and Grammatical Tenses

In English and in French, "past," "present," and "future" designate both grammatical tenses and temporal zones, or, to put it another way, tenses (Lat. *tempora*) within time (Lat. *tempus*), but this is far from being the case in all languages. The tripartite division of time into past, present, and future, which can be traced back as far as Homer only with many qualifications, is found in the verbal systems of the Indo-European languages, even if the future, which issued from an ancient desiderative present, is a late formation (Gr. *opsomai* [ὄψομαι], "I want to see, I am going to see, whence I shall see"; and in addition the Indo-European expresses above all an aspectual value). The constitution of a future tense signals the development in the Greek verb of the expression of time, which had become more important in Greek than in Indo-European in general (cf. Meillet, *Aperçu d'une histoire de la langue grecque*). Linguists have often pointed out how "aberrant" German is in this respect; an expression like "I shall become" is rendered by *Ich werde werden* (on the rather unnatural "clumsiness" of the expression of the future in German, cf. Vendryès, *Langage*, who also notes that "it is a general tendency of language to use the present in relation to the future: an old present serves as a future in Russian, in Welsh, in Scottish Gaelic, and elsewhere").

Here we touch on questions related to the way philosophical speculation is connected with the establishment of grammatical categories. Was Aristotle unconsciously guided by the "categories" of the Greek language, as Benveniste claimed ("Catégories de pensée et catégories de langue," in *Problèmes de linguistique générale*), or did he rediscover something of which his language was the depository, thus ultimately confirming the accuracy of his analyses, as Trendelenburg (*Geschichte der Kategorienlehre*) and then Brentano (*De la diversité des acceptions de l'être d'après Aristote*) had maintained? It is interesting to see that diametrically opposed conclusions could be drawn from a single fortunate coincidence. This problem, which we will have to limit ourselves to mentioning in passing, nonetheless finds expression in the diversity of names given to the parts—grammatical and physical or experienced—of time.

From problems connected with the thematization of time, grammatically and philosophically tripled, we must distinguish those raised by the various appellations relative to the past and the future in particular. What is it that differentiates the German terms *vergangen* and *gewesen*, *Gegenwart* and *Anwesenheit*? Why does French have two words for the future, *futur* and *avenir*?

II. The Tripartite Division of Time

In §168 of his RT: *Syntaxe grecque*, J. Humbert introduces the system of tenses in Greek in the following way:

> Grammarians have accustomed us to mentally divide time into three zones: past, present, and future. We have in our minds a very spatial representation of time: it is supposed to be imaged as a line without limits, running

from left to right: the line which, on the left, constitutes the past, is segmented over a certain distance that is our present, and then continues to the right, extending indefinitely into the future. This abstract conception, which makes time something realized, is said to be even more inexact in Greek than in other languages.

While it is not essentially linear, despite the Aristotelian analogy of the line, the tripartite division of time appears very early in the world of ancient Greece. In the *Iliad* (1.5.70), Homer says that the seer Calchas knows "the present, the future, the past" [τά τ᾽ ἐόντα τά τ᾽ ἐσσόμενα πρό τ᾽ ἐόντα]. We note that these times are not listed successively, and that here the reference is less to times than to what they bear, what is conveyed by them. In reality, this verse does not, strictly speaking, distinguish times but rather (intratemporal) existents, and it resorts, remarkably enough, to the same substantivized present participle in the neuter plural (*eonta*) to characterize what P. Mazon's translation renders respectively by *le présent* and *le passé*, whereas Homer refers, more literally, to "what is, what will be, and what is earlier," just as does Hesiod, in whose *Theogony* the same expressions are found in the same order (*Theogony*, 38). In Parmenides's *Poem* (8.5), the "is" is described this way: "it never was nor will be, for it is in the present" [οὐδέ ποτ᾽ ἦν οὐδ᾽ ἔσται, ἐπεὶ νῦν ἔστιν]. All we have to do is identify being with being-present, even if that means splitting the latter between what was and what will be, for time itself to be conceived, Montaigne wrote, as "necessarily divided into two," between "what has not yet come into being" and "what has already ceased to be":

> And as for these words *present, immediate, now,* on which it seems that we chiefly found and support our understanding of time, reason discovering this immediately destroys it; for she at once splits and divides it into future and past, as though wanting to see it necessarily divided in two.

> *Essais*, II

- See Box 1.

In the archaic period, various verbal roots coexisted that did not belong to "this coherent and complete system that we call a conjugation," namely, "a set of themes each expressing a 'time' or a mode of the process and being deduced from each other by simple morphological procedures" (Chantraine, *Morphologie historique du grec*, §175). The aspectual value of the Greek verb in the aorist arises from considerations other than the simple concern to situate action on a temporal axis as past, present, or future. In the *Georgics*, Virgil seems to echo Homer when he speaks of the seer Proteus embracing things "quae sint, quae fuerint, quae mox ventura trahantur" (which are, have been, and will soon occur in the future). The classical discussion of what Plato's *Timaeus* calls the "parts" or "divisions" of time—*merê chronou* [μέρη χρόνου]—saying of "eternal substance" that "it was, it is, and it will be" [ἦν ἔστιν τε καὶ ἔσται] (37e 3–6), is given by Aristotle in the *Physics* (4, chap. 10), where it is the instant (*to nun* [τὸ νῦν]) that discriminates the *parelthon* [παρελθόν]/past from the *mellon* [μέλλον]/future. In late antiquity, finally, Augustine acknowledges the usual tripartite division, even though he sees in it no more than an unfortunate habit that has been only too much used and abused: "Dicatur etiam: tempora sunt tria, praeteritum, praesens et futurum, sicut abutitur consuetudo; dicatur etiam" (Let it be said too, "there be three times, past, present, and to come": in our incorrect way; *Confessions*, 11.20, 26).

Antiquity thus was at first unaware of, and then thematized and investigated, the tripartite division of time into past, present, and future that is familiar to us. To conceive the genesis of this division means, however, going back to the initial lack of obviousness on the basis of which it was forged, even if that means agreeing with Augustine that the effect of obviousness that it seems to have enjoyed since late antiquity is unfortunate.

III. The Two Pasts: *Vergangen* and *Gewesen*

"The past is never dead, it is not even past": this statement of Faulkner's, quoted by Hannah Arendt (*Between Past and Future*), well emphasizes what it is about the past that is irreducible to what is only *passé, dépassé, trépassé* (to use

---

1

The sense of time

In the *Dictionnaire complet d'Homère et des Homérides* published by Napoléon Theil N. and Hippolyte Hallez-D'Arros in 1841, we read:

[ὀπίσω] [*opisô*]: *adv.* 1) with reference to place: behind . . . 2) with reference to time, *lit. what is still behind, what cannot be seen* . . . [ἅμα πρόσσω καὶ ὀπίσσω ὁρᾶν], to see at once the present and the future, *literally* things that are behind, *that is,* which have not yet

reached us and which will come, *that is,* the future; *it is always in this sense that Homer uses* [ὀπίσσως], the past, he calls [τὸ ἔμπροθεν] *what has already passed by us; as for* [πρόσω], *they are the things that are before us,which we have so to speak at hand* [τὰ ὑπὸ χεῖρα].

[πρόσω] [*prosô*]: *adv.* 1) with reference to space: before, in front of, in advance . . . 2) with reference to time: before, in advance, *that is,* the past *and not the*

future, *according to an error that I see shared by people who are nonetheless very competent; this has to do with the fact that the Greeks did not represent time as a river they have gone up; for them, time flowed in the opposite sense; the waters ahead of them were the ones that had passed by them and were, consequently, the past; those they had behind them were the future; many examples from Homer support my view.*

Apollinaire's expression). Whereas Descartes could assert that "when one is too curious about things which were practised in past centuries, one is usually very ignorant about things which are practised in our own time" (*Discourse on Method*), a modern historian—Marc Bloch, for example—would insist not so much on what separates past and present as on what connects them ("The past may very well not dominate the present altogether, but without it the present remains incomprehensible"; *L'Étrange défaite*), or on their interpenetration (*Apologie pour l'histoire*).

What is past, insofar as it no longer exists, corresponds to the German *vergangen*, "past" in the sense of "over." *Vergangen* is the past participle of the verb *vergehen*, "to pass [by or away]," with an idea of decay contained in the prefix *ver-*, "pass" in the sense in which it is said that time passes (*vergeht*). But what is past in the sense in which it has not ceased to be corresponds to the German *gewesen*. The prefix *ge-*, which is used to form the past participle of many verbs, here indicates collection or recollection in a recapitulating presence. Hegel's formula, "Wesen ist, was gewesen ist," does not mean that the "essence" is "what has been." This literally exact translation of Hegel's remark makes no sense, seeing that the last words of the "Doctrine of Being" in the *Science of Logic* determine essence as "being insofar as it is the fact of not being what it is, of being what it is not": an essence is that in which being is collected, but internalized, which, no longer being, has not ceased to be, or to put it in Hegelian terms, "the truth of being." The essence (*Wesen*) is not "l'être [entendu] comme cet être purement-et-simplement intériorisé" that is being "rassemblé avec soi dans sa négation," as P.-J. Labarrière and G. Jarczyk render it on the last page of the "Doctrine of Being" (Hegel, *Science de la logique*). Here the essential is involved in the interpretation given between brackets, which blocks the very movement of "logic" as it animates, from within, Hegel's remark: not being *understood* other than it was earlier, as if the point were merely to vary the meanings of a single term, but instead *promoting itself* to the rank of essence by virtue of its own movement.

Unlike French, German includes in its conjugation of the verb *sein* (to be) both being (*Sein*) and essence (*Wesen* in *gewesen*). Hegel does not fail to insist on this repeatedly in the *Science of Logic*, especially at the very beginning of the "Doctrine of Essence": "The [German] language has preserved in the verb *sein* the *Wesen* [essence] in the past participle *gewesen*; for the essence is past being, *but intemporally past*" (1812 edition; emphasis supplied). At this point, Hegel separates *gewesen* from *vergangen*, that is, from what is purely and simply over, and brings it closer to the *Wesen* that is heard in it, so that the past is thereby detached from its temporal dimension, to express itself, as it were, *sub specie aeternitatis*.

Meditating in his own way on the relationship between *gewesen* and *Wesen*, Schelling regretted that "in the German language the old verb *wesen* [has] gone out of use (it is found only in the past tense—in the form *gewesen*)" (*Schellings Werke*). Heidegger returned to this point as well:

I understand what has been and has not ceased to be [*das Gewesene*] in the following way: just as the mountain

range [*das Gebirge*] is the group of mountains, being-having-been is what gathers being in its unfolding.

Second seminar on Kant at Cérisy in 1955

This reflection on the properties of German is accompanied, in many writers, by a meditation on the Greek heritage. To what point is temporality a constitutive dimension of Greek knowledge as essentially retrospective, and to what point is the past far from purely and simply disappearing by slipping into the non-being of what has been and is no more—that is what is shown not only by Platonic anamnesis, and by the emphasis put on a mythical past, but even by the name of knowledge, [οἶδα] ([*Ϝοῖδα]), like "having seen," from the same root as the Latin *video*, the German *wissen*—as Schelling pointed out (*Historical-Critical Introduction to the Philosophy of Mythology*) before Heidegger: "The perfect tense 'I have seen' is the present tense of 'to know'" (*Holzwege*; cf. RT: *Dictionnaire étymologique de la langue grecque*, s.v.). The enigma of the temporal constitution of knowledge, which is traced in a way by the genealogy at the beginning of book A of Aristotle's *Metaphysics*, culminated in the expression Aristotle created, *to ti ên einai* [τὸ τί ἦν εἶναι], Latin *quod quid erat esse*, *quidditas*, "being-what-it-was." For a discussion of what Aristotle designates by this "strange title" and of its supposed prehistory (Antisthenes, Solon), see Aubenque, *Le Problème de l'être chez Aristote* and his claim: "It is . . . idea, so profoundly Greek, according to which every essential view is retrospective, that seems to us to justify the *ên* [ἦν] ("was") of the *to ti ên einai* [τὸ τί ἦν εἶναι]." The vocabulary of Aristotelian ontology is thus illuminated by a tragic source; but we may also think of the grammarians' imperfect of discovery (RT: *Syntaxe grecque* §180, rem.), to which Aubenque also refers (see TO TI ÊN EINAI).

IV. The Two Presents: *Gegenwart* and *Anwesenheit*

Grammatically speaking, the present is not a univocal category in the various European languages. It exists in English in a form called the "present progressive" that considers the process in its unfolding. Descartes's *cogito, ergo sum*, generally translated in English as "I think, therefore I am," should probably be rendered instead as "I am thinking, therefore I am," which has the advantage of bringing out the fact that existence, far from being deduced from thought, is already present in the very act of *cogitatio*: *cogito = sum cogitans*. The present progressive reinjects the present participle into the indicative.

In French, the term *présent* is as polysemous as the German term *Gegenwart*. The French *présent* indicates (a) the time at which things occur, (b) that in the presence of which we find ourselves (Ger. *Anwesenheit*), (c) that which we witness, indeed that which is present to us, or what we receive, in the sense in which sensibility is thoroughly determined as receptivity to a given (as in Kant), and in the sense in which the phenomenon of phenomenology is what is visible in its being-given (*Gegebenheit*, Husserl).

As for the German term *Gegenwart*, which seems at first to designate the attitude consisting in confronting (*gegen*) in expectation (*-wart*), in resolutely awaiting what will come of the encounter, the RT: *Deutsches Wörterbuch* saw in this an "inconceivable contradiction," that of a presence that is expressed only by anticipation, a tending toward what it calls for; unless we should discern in it a futurity immanent in every present. Moreover, we should note that the term *Gegenwart* itself presupposes a relationship between past and present that is not one of strict continuity, but rather of opposition. The present is less what follows the past, in a peaceful, continuous flow, than what is strong enough to oppose the past and break away from it, in the promising discontinuity begun by this rupture. In the "genealogy of time" that he proposes in his *Ages of the World* (*Die Weltalter*, 1811–15), Schelling obviously understands *Gegenwart*, in all its antithetical dimension, in relation to *Gegensatz*, *Entgegensetzung* (opposite, opposition): "Der Mensch, der sich seiner Vergangenheit nicht entgegenzusetzen fähig ist, hat keine, oder vielmehr er kommt nie aus ihr heraus, lebt beständig in ihr" (The man who is not capable of opposing his past has none, or rather he never emerges from it, lives constantly in it). The present can thus be conquered only through a living and conflictual relationship of antagonism to the past, beyond any attachment to the past that does not allow the past to be constituted as such. For the present understood in this way, the *avenir* is *à-venir*, *avenant*.

But to the French *présent* and its presence also corresponds the German *Anwesenheit*, which bears the hidden harmony of being and time. How is this German term composed? According to Jean Beaufret, Heidegger noticed "one day"

that to the Platonic and Aristotelian name of being, *ousia*, which also means, in ordinary language, a peasant's property, directly corresponds, from this point of view, the German *Anwesen*, but on the other hand, nothing is closer to the neuter *Anwesen* than the feminine *Anwesenheit*, in which the ending -*heit* brings to language, making it shine, so to speak, that which in *Anwesen* still remains opaque. Thus *Anwesenheit* says: the pure brilliance of *Anwesen*. But on the other hand *Anwesenheit* is synonymous with *Gegenwart*, and thereby also says that what shines, when the Greek name of being (*ousia*, as the *apheresis* of *parousia*) resounds, is essentially of the present.

Dialogue avec Heidegger

The interference, given in the word itself, between the present defined in opposition to the past or to the future, on the one hand, and the present in its presence by opposition to absence, on the other hand, was to lead Heidegger, notably in *Being and Time*, to emphasize a concordance of times in the heart of the present, such that it subverts the traditional relation of the subordination of time (and of the *nunc fluens* [the now that flows away]) to eternity (as *nunc stans* [the now that remains]). So that "past and future meet or rather correspond to each other in an entirely different way than the adverb 'successively' indicates." Beaufret continues: "Present, past, and future, far from following one another, are *ek-statically* contemporary within a world in which the present is not the passing instant but extends as far as a future corresponds to a past."

The German *Gegenwart*, to designate the present, shows a futurity immanent in the present. The present is thus drawn toward the future, which illumines it in return. The being of

the human being cannot be said in the present because it is illuminated on the basis of the being-mortal of the person who says "I am." "I am," *ich bin*, which is however no longer the German translation of the Cartesian *ego sum* (= *ich bin vorhanden*, I am occurrent, as is also this bit of wax that you see there), but corresponds instead to the Latin *sum moribundus* (*Heidegger Gesamtausgabe*). Thus in Heidegger, it is on the basis of the future that time is, or rather matures, ages.

■ See Box 2.

V. *Futur* and *Avenir*

Etymologically, the French word *futur*, from the Latin *futurus* (fated to be), is related to *fus* ([je] *fus*), Latin *fui*, and thereby to the Indo-European root **bhu-* (to grow), whence the Greek *phuô* [φύω], "to cause to be born, to cause to grow" (whence *phusis* [φύσις]; see NATURE; cf. Aristotle, *Metaphysics*, D.4.1014b 16–17), German *bin*, English "be" (cf. RT: *Dictionnaire étymologique du français*). As an autonomous grammatical category, the future is, as we have seen, a relatively late development. In some languages (German, Russian), the future is more apt to be expressed by a near future with a desiderative value: "I am going to go" or "I want to go," rather than "I shall go." In modern Greek, the future is formed by adding [θα] before the present indicative, the abbreviation of [θέλω νά], "I want" (RT: *Aperçu d'une histoire de la langue grecque*). In English, which has no future paradigm in its verbal morphology, a modal distinction persists in the distinction between the two auxiliaries "shall" and "will." In French, the personal morphemes of the future are derived from the present tense indicative of the verb *avoir*: modern French *chanterai* (I shall sing) comes from Vulgar Latin *cantaraio* and Classical Latin *cantare habeo*, "I have the prospect of singing" (RT: *Grammaire de l'ancien français*). According to D. Maingueneau (RT: *Précis de grammaire*), in language there is a "fundamental dyssemmetry between the past and the future: the future is a projection on the basis of the present, and is radically modal . . . , whereas the past, that which is over and done, gives priority to the aspectual dimension. The future is always supported by the wills, hopes, fears, etc. of subjects." So much so, in fact, that in Old French the verb *voloir* (to will or desire) is sometimes used in the future instead of the present, which highlights its modal function because of its perspective *sémantèse*, as in the *Prose Tristan*, 216, 15: "Et li rois . . . quant il entent cest parole, il descent et s'en vet a la fosse, car il voudra veoir qui cil est qui dedenz gist [qui donc est celui qui repose là-dedans]" (cf. RT: *Grammaire de l'ancien français*). Let us add that today, grammarians see the future as including the form previously called "the conditional" in the form of a "future II," belonging to the same "tiroir." Ultimately, the future does not exist as an original grammatical form.

French *avenir* corresponds to German *Zukunft* (and to Dan. *tilkommende*): the *avenir* is *à venir* (to come) and *Zu-kunft* is derived from *kommen* (to come). But French has two terms, *futur* and *avenir*, whereas the German *Futurum* refers only to the grammatical category of verb tenses. *Futur* and *avenir* are not synonyms, but opposites in terms of modality: *futur* indicates only what will be, while *avenir* indicates what might be. In this sense, the *futur* is thus the suspension of the *avenir*,

2

Præsentisk/nuværende: Presence in Kierkegaard's Danish

Præsentisk is a neologism in Danish that was apparently coined by Kierkegaard, the usual terms being *nuværende* (being now) and *nærværende* (being near, before the eyes, current). It refers to presence (*Nærværelse*) to oneself: *sig selv præsentisk* (*Either/Or*), as opposed to absence (*Fraværelse*). Total self-presence is defined as "being today," as the exclusion of unhappiness: the "blessed God who eternally says 'today'" [*idag*] (*The Lily of the Fields and the Bird of the Sky*). Whereas the absence of the past and the future signifies perfection, presence (*praesentes dii*) is that of a "powerful support" (*kraftige Bistand*) (*The Concept of Fear*). In *The Most Unhappy* (*Den Ulykkeligste*, 1843), the pseudonymous author tells a story (similar to Kafka's *The Hunter Gracchus*) that extends, under the sign of lived temporality, Hegel's analysis of the unhappy consciousness. Hegel's *Phenomenology of Spirit* describes the unhappiness of the divided (*entzweit*) consciousness, which is absent from itself because it lives separately, without the horizon of union, marked by a doubling (*Verdoppelung*) that cannot be unified. It is the consciousness animated by pious fervor (*Andacht*), nostalgia (*Sehnsucht*), and a hope that is never fulfilled, without presence (*ohne Erfüllung und Gegenwart*). To explore concretely the forms of absence from

oneself (*sig selv fraværende*), Kierkegaard analyzes in terms of temporality this consciousness, which, according to Hegel, has its essence, the content of its own life, outside itself. That is what leads him to oppose to the present of the past and the present of the future the pluperfect (*plus quam perfectum*) and the future anterior (*futurum exactum*), in which there is nothing present. Whence the portrait of individualities that memory or hope makes unhappy. Nonetheless, the man of hope's absence from himself includes "a happier deception" than that of the man deceived by memories. For the former, the future, the infinite of the possible, remains, whereas the latter turns toward a past that was not the presence of anything. But "the most unhappy man" is the one who experiences both misfortunes. Since the two passions oppose each other, he is the theater of the powerlessness that consists in "not having time at all" (*slet ingen Tid*).

To this is opposed "repetition, the serious aspect of reality and existence," a repetition that is "the interest of metaphysics, and at the same time the interest against which metaphysics fails" (*Repetition*). The privilege of the present signifies that true life is in the instant and not in the state. Whatever the forms of life, the existential stages, might be, it is in

each instant that their meaning is given, in the event itself through which it is contracted (*pådrage*). This holds for joy as well as for despair, for fear and for serenity, "each instant (*ethvert Øjeblik*) being "real" (*virkelig*) only in the "present time" (*nærværende Tid*) of a "relationship to oneself" (*Forholdet til sig selv*) (*The Sickness unto Death*). As is shown by a passage in Kierkegaard's *Journal* for 1847–48 (*Papirer*, VIII A 305), this *præsentisk* moment involves freedom, and thus tends toward the future (see EVIGHED).

Jacques Colette

BIBLIOGRAPHY

Kierkegaard, Søren. *Samlade Vaeker*. Edited by A. B. Drachmann, J. L. Heiberg, and H. O. Lange. Copenhagen, 1920–36. Translation: *Kierkegaard's Writings*. 26 vols. Princeton, NJ: Princeton University Press, 1978–2000.

———. *Papirer*. Edited by P. A. Heiberg and V. Kuhr. 20 vols. Copenhagen, 1909–48.

———. *The Last Years: Journals, 1853–1855*. Edited and translated by Ronald Gregor Smith. London: Collins, 1965.

———. *Kierkegaard's Journals and Notebooks*. 2 vols. General editor, Bruce H. Kirmmse, edited by Niels Jørgen Cappelørn et al. Princeton, NJ: Princeton University Press, 2007–8.

given that it conceives the latter only as what proceeds anticipatively from the present and not what comes to the present in an unanticipated way. Thus the *avenir* differs from the *futur* as the possible differs from the real.

Fundamentally, it may be that the understanding of the verbal system on the basis of the tripartite division past-present-future was outdated, grammarians now tending to consider as aspectual values that used to be considered, wrongly, strictly temporal.

From this brief survey we can conclude that there is a certain homogeneity in the verbal system of Indo-European languages (even if the future infinitive, for example, is hardly found outside ancient Greek), but also a remarkable heterogeneity in the diverse expressions of times and tenses (Ger. *Zeiten* and *Tempora*) in the few languages examined here. In each case a certain division of reality is made, but this division (to which, moreover, both the French term *temps* and the German *Zeit* are etymologically related [see *TIME*]) is rarely the same.

Contemporary phenomenology has sought to rethink the unitary focal point prior to the tripartite division we have studied, while at the same time acknowledging the latter, and even trying to provide it with a rigorous foundation: either,

following Husserl, in the ego-pole radiating from its "living present" and its retentions and protentions, or, following Heidegger, in the contemporary character of ekstases. This seems to be what led Sartre to see in the tripartite classification past-present-future a kind of triple profusion or triple attachment, even when it does not present itself as such, whether in the triple synthesis of the "Transcendental Deduction" in Kant's *Critique of Pure Reason* (apprehension, reproduction, recognition) or in Nietzsche's division of history into antiquarian, monumental, and critical.

Pascal David

BIBLIOGRAPHY

Arendt, Hannah. *Between Past and Future*. New York: Penguin, 1961.

Aubenque, Pierre. *Le Problème de l'être chez Aristote*. Paris: Presses Universitaires de France, 1962.

Augustine. *The Confessions of Saint Augustine, Saint Bishop of Hippo*. Translated by E. B. Pusey. New York: Modern Library, 1949.

Beaufret, Jean. *Dialogue avec Heidegger*, Vol. 4. Paris: Éditions de Minuit, 1945. Translation by Marc Sinclair: *Dialogue with Heidegger*. Bloomington: Indiana University Press, 2006.

Benveniste, Émile. *Problems in General Linguistics*. Translated by Mary Elizabeth Meek. Coral Gables, FL: University of Miami Press, 1997.

Bloch, Marc. *Strange Defeat*. Translated by Gerard Hopkins with an introduction by Maurice Powicke and Georges Altman. New York: Norton, 1968.

———. *Apologie pour l'histoire*. Paris: A. Colin, 1949.

Brentano, Franz. *On the Several Senses of Being in Aristotle*. Edited and translated by Rolf George. Berkeley: University of California Press, 1981.

Chantraine, Pierre. *Morphologie historique du grec*. Paris: Librairie C. Klincksieck, 1961.

Descartes, René. *Discourse on Method*. In *Philosophical Works of Descartes*. Translated by E. Haldane and G.R.T. Ross. New York: Dover, 1955.

Hegel, Georg Wilhelm Friedrich. *Hegel's Science of Logic*. Translated by A. V. Miller. London: Allen and Unwin, 1969.

Heidegger, Martin. *Being and Time*. Translated by Joan Stambaugh. Albany: State University of New York Press, 1996.

———. *Heidegger Gesamtausgabe (GA)*. Series edited by Vittorio Klostermann. Vol. 20, edited by P. Jaeger, 1979, 2nd ed., 1988, 3rd ed., 1994.

———. *Off the Beaten Track [Holzwege]*. Translated by Julian Young and Kenneth Haynes. Cambridge: Cambridge University Press, 2002.

———. *What is Called Thinking?* New York: Harper and Row, 1968.

Hintikka, Jakkao, and Simo Knuuttila, eds. *The Logic of Being*. Dordrecht: D. Reidel, 1986.

Luchte, James. *Heidegger's Early Philosophy: The Phenomenology of Ecstatic Temporality*. London: Continuum, 2008.

Meillet, A. *Aperçu d'une histoire de la langue grecque*. Paris, C. Klincksieck, 1965.

Montaigne. *Essais*, Vol. 2. Edited by P. Villey. Paris: Alcan, 1922. Translation by D. M. Frame: *The Complete Essays of Montaigne*. Stanford, CA: Stanford University Press, 1958.

Schelling, Friedrich Wilhelm Joseph von. *The Ages of the World*. Translated by Jason M. Wirth. Albany: State University of New York Press, 2000.

———. *Historical-Critical Introduction to the Philosophy of Mythology*. Translated by M. Richey and M. Zisselsberger. Albany: State University of New York Press, 2007.

———. *Philosophie der Mythologie*. Edited by Andreas Roser and Holger Schulten. Stuttgart: Frommann-Holzboog, 1996.

Tredelenburg, Adolf. *Geschichte der Kategorienlehre*. Hildesheim, Ger.: Olms, 1979. First published ca. 1846.

Vendryès, Joseph. *Language: A Linguistic Introduction to History*. Translated by Paul Radin. New York: A. A. Knopf, 1925.

Valpy, F.E.J. *The Etymology of the Words of the Greek Language in Alphabetical Order*. London: Longman, Green, Longman and Roberts, 1860.

PRINCIPLE, SOURCE, FOUNDATION

FRENCH	*principe*
GERMAN	*Satz, Grundsatz, Prinzip, Principium, Anfangsgrund, Grund*
GREEK	*archê* [ἀρχή], *aitia* [αἰτία]
LATIN	*principium*

➤ LAW, MACHT, NATURE, PROPOSITION, *REASON*, SACHVERHALT, SENSE, SOLLEN, *THING, WORLD*

The principle, *archê* [ἀρχή], *principium*, is what begins and dominates, the two meanings being connected in both Greek and Latin. It is a generating element of being and/or a point of departure for knowledge. The Aristotelian distinctions are determining: principles and causes (*archai kai aitiai* [ἀρχαὶ καὶ αἰτίαι]), principles and axioms or hypotheses (*axiômata* [ἀξιώματα], *hupotheseis* [ὑποθέσεις]); but they do not pose any translation problem. In German, however, the paradigm of the beginning (*Prinzip*) is reduplicated in that of the foundation (*Grund*). The Kantian distinctions overthrew the Aristotelian nomenclature by introducing a sharp distinction between the logical and analytical domain, on the one hand, and the transcendental on the other hand. The logical meaning, which proceeds from the *Posterior Analytics*, was shaken up by

the various axiomatics that emerged between the end of the nineteenth century and the beginning of the twentieth: *Grundsatz* was then used in the sense of the initial laws of a formal system on the basis of which a certain number of theorems, propositions, *Sätze*, can be derived.

I. *Archai* and *Archê*

A. The ambiguity of *archê* and *telos*, *principium* and *finis*

Archê [ἀρχή] derives from the verb *archô* [ἄρχω], which in Homer means both "begin" (to take the lead or initiative: *êrche hodon* [ἦρχε ὁδόν], "he showed the way," *Odyssey*, 8.107; *archein polemoio* [ἄρχειν πολέμοιο], "begin the fighting," *Iliad*, 4.335) and "command" (*Iliad* 16.65); then it was used especially in the middle voice, *archesthai* [ἄρχεσθαι]; we can easily understand how the latter meaning emerged from the former, either because the leader was the first to act (cf. its uses in religion, music, and dance) or because he walked in front (RT: *Dictionnaire étymologique de la langue grecque*). *Archê* thus signifies both the beginning (principle, point of departure, for example, *euthus ex archês* [εὐθὺς ἐξ ἀρχῆς], from the beginning) and command (responsibility, authority, power, magistracy, for example, *archên archein* [ἀρχὴν ἄρχειν], exercise a responsibility). From "archaism" to "archetype" or "architecture" its numerous combined forms emphasize one and/or the other of these two meanings. A philosophy of the origin may thus be based on the way in which the beginning is decisive in Greek.

The Latin *principium*, from *princeps* (a combination of *primum* and *capio*, literally, "he who takes first," "he who occupies the first place"), has the same ambiguity (the *principium*, like the *archê*, of a discourse is its exordium; cf. RT: *Handbuch der literarischen Rhetorik*); the plural, *principia*, which designates the front lines of an army, is used, like the Greek *archai*, to signify both the parts from which a whole is formed (*principia rerum*), and natural impulses (*principia naturae*; Cicero, *De officiis*, 1.50) or the foundations of law (Cicero, *De legibus*, 1.18; cf. Gaffiot, s.v.).

The corresponding antonyms are no less ambiguous. Greek *telos* [τέλος] signifies achievement, in the sense of achieving an end (in the sense of goal or purpose); it is seconded by *teleutê* [τελευτή], which belongs to the same family, to signify the end in the sense of cessation or conclusion (in particular, death). The Latin *finis* covers the whole of this semantic field, and we still see this in English "end" and French *fin*: it signifies first limit, boundary, frontier, like the Greek *horos* [ὅρος] (which RT: *Dictionnaire étymologique de la langue grecque* relates to the Homeric *ouron* [οὖρον], furrow), which, in its abstract or logical meaning, is rendered precisely by "de-finition"; and then "cessation, the end" (*res finem invenit* [the thing is finished]) no less than "goal" (*domus finis est usus* [the goal of a house is to be used]; Cicero, *De officiis*, 1.138, renders exactly the final cause, the *hou heneka* [οὗ ἕνεκα], Aristotle's "that for which") and the culmination (*fines bonorum et malorum* [the supreme degree of goods and evils], Cicero, *De finibus*, 1.55). Cicero, precisely in *De finibus*, comments on the richness of the Latin term:

Sentis me, quod τέλος Graeci dicunt, id dicere tum extremum, tum ultimum, tum summum ; licebit etiam finem pro extremo aut ultimo dicere.

(You see, what the Greeks call *telos*, I sometimes call extremity, sometimes ultimate degree, and sometimes culmination; but I could say end instead of extremity and ultimate degree.)

3.26

B. *Archai* and *aitia* (principles and causes) / *archê* et *protasis*, *thesis, hupothesis, axiôma, aitêma, horismos* (principle and premise, thesis, hypothesis, axiom, postulate, definition)

It is common, then, to all beginnings to be the first point from which a thing either is or comes to be or is known.

to prôton einai hothen ê estin ê gignetai ê gignôsketai [τὸ πρῶ τον εἶναι ὅθεν ἢ ἔστιν ἢ γίγνεται ἢ γιγνώσκεται].

Aristotle, *Metaphysics*, D.1.1013a 17–19

A distinction is traditionally drawn between the principles of being (*principia essendi, principia realia*) and principles of knowledge (*principia cognoscendi*): Bonitz (RT: *Index aristotelicus*, s.v. *Arkhê*), for example, setting aside the univocal meanings of *initium* (used chiefly in meteorological or biological texts) and *imperium* (used chiefly in rhetoric and politics), arranges the occurrences of the term in Aristotle under these two rubrics.

Principia realia are the Pre-Socratics' *archai*, which Aristotle classifies, in book A of the *Metaphysics*, thereby providing the matrix of later doxographies, and even for an initial history of philosophy. The *archêgos* [ἀρχηγός], or "founder," of this kind of theory was Thales, for whom water was the sole *archê* of all things (A.3.983b 19–22): this type of *archê*, whether single or multiple, belongs to the order of the *stoicheion* [στοιχεῖον], of the "element" (b 11), that is, of the material cause. Aristotle reinterprets these principles to show how they prefigure and confirm his own systematics of causes: Anaxagoras's *nous* [Νοῦς], Empedocles's Love and Hate, as efficient causes (*archê kinêseôs* [ἀρχὴ κινήσεως]; 7.988a 33), the Platonic Ideas as embryonic formal causes, the One and the Good as final causes. These *archai* are *aitiai*, and in this case there is no difference between principles and causes (988b 16–21) or, more precisely, as chapter Δ of the *Metaphysics* explains, "all causes are beginnings" (5.1013a 17).

The *principia cognoscendi*, "principles of knowledge," are one of the three constitutive elements of any demonstrative science, namely: "(1) that which it posits; the subject genus whose essential attributes it examines; (2) the so-called axioms, which are primary premises of its demonstration; (3) the attributes, the meaning of which it assumes" (*Posterior Analytics*, 1.10.76b 11–16). Principle and cause are clearly connected in scientific knowledge because to know something is to know its cause:

We suppose ourselves to possess unqualified scientific knowledge of a thing [ἐπίστασθαι ἕκαστο] ... when we think that we know the cause on which the fact depends [τήν δ' αἰτίαν ... δι' ἣν τὸ πρᾶγμά ἐστιν], as the cause of that fact and of no other [ὅτι ἐκείνου αἰτία ἐστί], and, further that the fact could not be other than it is [καὶ μὴ ἐνδέχεσθαι τοῦτ' ἄλλως ἔχειν].

Posterior Analytics, 1.2.71b 9–12

The causes of the fact are thus the premises (*protaseis* [προτάσεις], from *pro-teinô* [προ-τείνω], "tend toward") of the demonstration, that is, the causes of the conclusion, and constitute the "specific principles" (*hai archai oikeai* [αἱ ἀρχαὶ οἰκεῖαι], 71b 23) of the knowledge of the fact: "a 'basic truth' in a demonstration is an immediate proposition" (*protasis amesos* [πρότασις ἄμεσος]), (72a 7–8), that is, a proposition (*apophansis* [ἀπόφανσις]) that is affirmative, *apophasis* [ἀπόφασις], or negative, *kataphasis* [κατάφασις]; see PROPOSITION), and is not preceded by any other.

However, the *Posterior Analytics* makes very precise distinctions among the different kinds of principles (book 1, chaps. 2 and 10): the protasis is a "thesis" (*thesis* [θέσις], from *tithêmi* [τίθημι], "to set or posit") when it is not necessary to have it in order to learn something; in the contrary case, it is an "axiom" (*axiôma* [ἀξίωμα], from *axioô* [ἀξιόω], "evaluate, believe to be right or true"). The thesis thus has a limited validity, while the axiom has a general validity. When a thesis rules on the existence of its object, it is a "hypothesis" (*hupothesis* [ὑπόθεσις], from *hupo-tithêmi* [ὑποτίθημι], "put on top of, suppose"; see SUBJECT), and if the hypothesis is contrary to what the student thinks (or if the student has no opinion about it), then it is a "postulate" (*aitêma* [αἴτημα], from *aiteô* [αἰτέω], "to ask, demand") (10.76b 30–31); when a proposition does not rule on the existence of its object, it is a simple "definition" (*horismos* [ὁρισμός], from *horizô* [ὁρίζω], "limit") (2.72a 20–24).

However, the common denominator of all these kinds of principles remains: "there will be no scientific knowledge of the primary premises" (*Posterior Analytics*, 2.19.100b 10–11); the principles are undemonstrable primary truths: "Whereas the rest can be demonstrated by the principles, the principles cannot be demonstrated by something else" (*Topics*, 8.3.158b 2–4). In this sense, there are two kinds of truths: secondary truths, established syllogistically—these are conclusions obtained thanks to the presence of a middle term (*to meson* [τὸ μέσον]) in two premises, a middle term that established the proportion between them and thus makes it possible to produce a third proposition—and primary truths, which are the only ones called "principles."

C. The question of the first principle

To understand what an *archê*, in the singular, really is, however, we must determine what resists this convenient classification enabling us to situate the physical (the principles of being) on the one hand, and the organon (the principles of knowing) on the other, but leaves room between the two for metaphysics in its relation to the scientific nature of knowledge (Aubenque, *Le problème de l'être chez Aristote*). All the complexity or hesitation constitutive of Aristotelian ontotheology can be expressed in terms of *archê*: is the knowledge sought, which deals with the *prôtê archê* [πρώτη ἀρχή], the theology of book Λ of the *Metaphysics*, according to which "on such a principle [viz. God], then, depend the heavens (*ek toiautês ... archês êrtêtai ho ouranos* [ἐν τοιαυτῆς ... ἀρχῆς ἤρτηται ὁ οὐρανὸς]) and the world of nature" (Λ, 7.1072b 14)? Or is the knowledge of being qua being described in book Γ of the *Metaphysics*, according to which the principle that "is the most certain of all" (*bebaiotatê ... pason* [βεβαιοτάτη ... πασῶν], is also the best known, *gnôrimôtatê* [γνωριμωτάτη], and it is *anupotheton* [ἀνυπόθε τον], not depending on any previous postulate), the one that has passed on to posterity under the name of the principle of non-contradiction, which is formulated as follows: 'it is impossible for any one to believe the same thing to be and not to be'" (*Metaphysics*, Γ, 3.1005b 19–20)? A science that is universal because it is primary, and deals with the *ousia prôtê*, primary substance, insofar as it is a first principle, or a science, first because general, which deals with the whole of being and first principles?

In any case, God and non-contradiction are both simultaneously principles of being and principles of intelligibility, ontological. Non-contradiction is clearly a logical law because it defines the truth condition of a demonstrative construction (arguments, syllogisms) and of a terminological construction (propositions), and, still more crucially, because it requires us to signify something when we speak (univocality and definition; see HOMONYM); it is also, as Heidegger emphasizes, a law of being that affirms "nothing less than this: the essence of the existent consists in the constant absence of contradiction" (*Nietzsche*). The Leibnizian principle of reason is also expressed, very explicitly, in the *Monadology*, for instance, as a principle of being and as a principle of discourse ("no fact can be real or existent, no statement true, unless there be a sufficient reason why it is so and not otherwise"; §32).

The principle is at once the cause and the reason for first truths as the middle term is both cause (the Scholastics' *principium essendi*, Kant's *Realgrund*) and reason (the Scholastics' *principium cognoscendi*, Kant's *Idealgrund*) of the syllogism ("A cause in the realm of things corresponds to a reason in the realm of truths"; Leibniz, *Nouveaux essais*, book 4,chap. 17).

- See Box 1.

II. *Principia*, Laws, Common Notions

While recognizing that the notion of principle has several meanings, Descartes refused to grant an exclusive privilege to the principle of non-contradiction; he tries to justify his use of the plural in the title of his *Principia philosophiae*:

It is one thing to seek a common notion that is so clear and so general that it can serve as a principle for proving the existence of all Beings, all *Entia*, which we will discover later on; and another to seek a Being whose existence is better known to us than any other, so that it can serve as a principle for knowing them.

Letter to Clerselier, June or July 1646

As an example of the first sense of "principle," Descartes gives the example of the principle of non-contradiction, which he formulates as follows: "impossibile est idem simul esse et non esse" (it is impossible for the same thing to be and not to be at the same time). But he refuses to reduce every kind of principle to this one because this principle does not produce true knowledge; it merely confirms truths we already know: "For it may happen that there is no principle in the world to which all things can be reduced; and the way in which other propositions are reduced to this one: *impossibile est idem simul esse et non esse*, is superfluous and useless." That is why in order to know we must turn to other principles: "in the other sense, the first principle is that our mind exists, because there is nothing whose existence is better known to us."

The *Principia philosophiae* date from 1644; they give us useful, not superfluous principles; they are "first causes" and include both "the principles of human knowledge" (the first part) and "the principles of material things" (the three other parts). These two types of principles are both clear and distinct, but the former are called "principles" *stricto sensu*; the latter relate to "what is most general in physics" and are called "laws of nature" or "rules" in accord with which changes in nature take place, as well as the other laws of nature formulated in articles 37–40 of the second part of the *Principia*. These laws "established in nature" are "imprinted upon our minds" in the form of "common notions" (Descartes, *Discours*, V). What is required of the principle is that it not promote an enterprise of reducing truths to a first notion. In reality, there are several innate common

---

1

Petitio principii

In Greek, to "beg the question" is *aiteisthai to en archê* [αἰτεῖσθαι τὸ ἐν ἀρχῇ] (Aristotle, *Metaphysics*, Γ.4.1006a 15–16), "to ask what is in the principle." Every first principle as such is necessarily undemonstrable. To demand (*aitein* [αἰτεῖν]) that it be demonstrated is a sign of the lack of education, *apiaideusia* [ἀπαιδευσία], characteristic of the Sophists—"for not to know of what things one should demand demonstration, and of what one should not, argues want of education (*esti gar apideusia* [ἔστι γὰρ ἀπαιδευσία])" (*Metaphysics*, 4.1006a 6–8). Thus Aristotle does not propose a "demonstration" (*apodeixis* [ἀπόδειξις]) of the principle of non-contradiction, but rather a "negative demonstration" or refutation

(*elegchos* [ἔλεγχος]; 1006a 18), so that the adversary of the principle bears all the responsibility for the demand: it is he who will be allowed to speak first so that by stating his rejection, he says something that is significant for himself and for others and thus always already obeys the principle that he claims to deny (1006a 18–27) (cf. Cassin and Narcy, *La Décision du sens*; see HOMONYM).

Principle and *petitio principii* refer to the problem of the ultimate foundation. The necessity of a stopping point (*anagkê stenai* [ἀνάγκη στῆναι]) has the force of a postulation. That is why Heidegger can see in the *petitio principii* not a logical error but a founding act.

Petere principium, in other words, tending toward the foundation and its foundation, is the single and unique step taken by philosophy, the step that moves beyond, ahead, and opens up the only domain within which a science can be established.

Heidegger, "Ce qu'est et comment se détermine la *phusis*"

BIBLIOGRAPHY

Cassin, Barbara, and Michel Narcy. *La Décision du sens*. Paris: Vrin, 1989.

Heidegger, Martin. "Ce qu'est et comment se détermine la *phusis*." French translation by F. Fédier: *Questions II*. Paris: Gallimard / La Pléiade, 1968.

notions (Euclid's *koinai ennoiai* [κοιναὶ ἔννοιαι]) whose use is so constant that it is no longer governed by systematic discernment on our part; principles in the sense of common notion-axioms are then in our minds as it were virtually or implicitly, in the manner of "the propositions suppressed in enthymemes, which are omitted not only outside our thought but also within it" (Leibniz, *Nouveaux essais*, book 1, §4). The principle fulfills its function when, on the one hand, it is so obvious that it cannot be denied, and on the other hand, it allows us to recognize the deductions that depend on it, in other words, the laws. Let us emphasize that this vocabulary is not always used: Descartes sometimes calls the three laws of movement "principles" (*Principia*, II, §36); similarly, Leibniz gives the name of "law" to the principle of the conservation of energy (*Discours de métaphysique*, §17). Along with Newton's *Principia*, we have here an effort to systematize natural philosophy; in Newton's work, principles are everything that allows us to account for the "first and last sums and ratios of nascent and evanescent quantities" (*Philosophiae naturalis principia mathematica* [1687]), which includes not only the "definitions" and "axioms or laws of movement" that Newton places before the first book, but also the lemmas and theorems of the three books of the *Principia*.

III. "Principle," "Foundation," "Source," "Original": Principles and the Connection of Ideas

Locke takes up the notion of principle in arguing against the theory of innate ideas. At the beginning of the *Essay Concerning Human Understanding*, he notes that "it is an established opinion amongst some men, that there are in the understanding certain *innate principles*: of primary notions, *koinai ennoiai*" (book I, chap. 2, §1). His refutation bears on both speculative and practical principles, taking the ironic form of a critique of the argument from authority: the schoolmasters and teachers maintaining the thesis that there are innate ideas postulate as "the principle of principles ... *that principles must not be questioned*" (I, 4, 24). The obviousness of some general propositions and the general consent to which they give rise do not, however, transform these general propositions into innate propositions. Moreover, the most general propositions, such as "what is, is" or "it is impossible for a thing to be and not to be" do not by themselves advance knowledge; on the one hand, the ideas of which they are composed—the ideas of identity and impossibility—are far from clear to everyone; on the other hand, in the best of cases they have only an argumentative value and serve to "stop the mouths of wranglers" (IV, 7, 11). In the transformation of general maxims into principles Locke discerns a survival of the dialectical method that consists in starting from the *endoxa* [ἔνδοξα], from generally accepted propositions, in disputes. But accepting such maxims does not imply that knowledge has to recognize them as principles:

> And then these Maxims, getting the name of Principles, beyond which men in dispute could not retreat, were by mistake taken to be the Originals and the Sources, from whence all knowledge began, and the Foundations whereon the sciences were built.
>
> IV, 7, 11

Locke prefers to use the terms "source" and "foundations" when discussing what seems to him to be the starting points for human knowledge: "perhaps we should make greater progress in the discovery of rational and contemplative knowledge, if we sought it in the fountain, *in the consideration of the things themselves*" (I, 4, 23). This "fountain" consists in simple ideas: sensation and reflection. The advance of knowledge is measured, then, by the agreement or disagreement of our ideas, and not by the status of principle that we confer on general propositions of the type "what is, is."

Hume, having recognized the difficulty of finding principles, emphasizes that we must substitute for conjectures imposed on nature or the mind a knowledge of the principles that would enable us to connect phenomena with each other in a regular way: such a project involves the analysis of the origin of our ideas (*An Enquiry Concerning Human Understanding*, §2) and knowledge of their derivation. Hume's analysis is not limited to a morphology of our ideas that divides them into ideas of reflection and ideas of sensation. He radicalizes Locke on the question of principles by questioning not only the source of knowledge but also its origin. His analysis is thus more genetic, and accords to the notion of origin, and to its corollary, the notion of derivation, such importance that this general maxim can be formulated:

> That all our simple ideas, in their first appearance, are derived from simple impressions, which are correspondent to them, and which they exactly represent.
>
> *A Treatise of Human Nature*, book 1, chap. 1, §1

IV. *Principium, Grundsatz, Prinzip, Satz, Grundgesetz*

A. Kantianism and post-Kantianism

In the French translation of Kant, *principe* may render six German words that the philosopher frequently uses and sometimes distinguishes: *Satz, Grundsatz, Prinzip, Principium, Anfangsgrund, Grund*. This translation is perfectly legitimate in some instances: it would be pointless, pedantic, and erroneous to render *Satz des Widerspruchs* as *proposition de contradiction*. But the impoverishment of the Kantian vocabulary has sometimes corresponded to an absence of conceptual distinctions that results in major lacunae and even interpretive confusions.

Within Kantianism, the terminology just described is used in the following contexts:

1. The *principium* retains the meaning of "principle" as beginning and command. It is a specification of the "principle" (*Prinzip*) to which Kant denies, in its generality, any value as a foundation for knowledge: "The term 'principle' [*Prinzip*] is ambiguous, and commonly signifies any knowledge which can be used as a principle [*Prinzip*], although in itself, and as regards its proper origin, it is no principle [*Prinzipium*]" (*Critique of Pure Reason*, B 356). On the other hand, the *Prinzipium* is valid in the legislative order (*Gesetzgebung*) because in this case we are in fact the authors, the source itself (*die Ursache*) of the laws, which are "entirely our own work" (B 358).

2. Principles in the sense of *Grundsätze* (sing. *Grundsatz*) are used by Kant in two ways:

a. First, they are the formal "fundamental propositions [*Grundsätze*] of the sensible world" (1770 Dissertation, §14 and 15), or space and time: they indicate the impossibility of the Leibnizian reduction of principles to the principle of identity and to the "great principle" (reciprocally related to the latter) according to which the predicate is in a subject (*praedicatum inest subjecto*; letter from Leibniz to Arnaud, 14 July 1686).

b. Second, the fundamental a priori propositions (*Grundsätze*) of the understanding found the possibility of knowledge and are in this sense "rules for the objective employment of the former [the categories]" (*Critique of Pure Reason*, A 161/B 200). They are foundational and take the form of "axioms of intuition," "anticipations of perception," "analogies of experience," and "postulates of empirical thought in general." They are demonstrable and their formulation is followed by a proof. Their theoretical role is to found the possibility of knowledge, their critical role is to break with the assimilation of "first principles" to "first causes": we cannot arrive at the notion of cause through a simple concept. "If the reader will go back to our proof of the principle of causality . . . he will observe that we were able to prove it only of objects of possible experience" (B 289).

The post-Kantian and anti-Kantian traditions both radicalize this point of view, especially in matters of logic; not only are first principles no longer first causes, but they are not necessarily connected with intuition to found knowledge. The question is: how can a subjective principle like intuition found objectivity, how can it realize the necessity that only a judgment can contain? B. Bolzano indicates that necessity is related first to the judgment, where concepts and, indirectly, our intuitions and representations, are connected with each other. In the *Beyträge zur einer begründeteren Darstellung der Mathematik* (partial French translation in J. Laz, *Bolzano critique de Kant*), Bolzano notes his reservations regarding Kant's foundation of synthetic judgments on intuitions, even if they are a priori:

It is well known that some people have been shocked by these a priori intuitions of critical philosophy. For my own part, I willingly concede that there must be a certain reason (*Grund*) completely different from the principle of contradiction, for which the understanding joins, in a synthetic judgment, the predicate to the concept of subject. But that this reason might be, and be called, an intuition, and what is more, a pure intuition in the case of judgments a priori—that I do not find clear.

3. The principles (*Prinzipien*) of reason have a regulative value through which reason is "interested" in the constitutive use of the fundamental propositions (*Grundsätze*) of the understanding. This interest gives them a subjective character that leads Kant to consider them as "maxims" (*Maximen*) instead. Their role is to give a "systematic or rational unity" to knowledge, and in

this sense they are "logical." Kant distinguishes three of them: (1) "a principle [*Prinzip*] of the *homogeneity* of the manifold under higher genera"; (2) "a principle [*Grundsatz*] of the *variety* of the homogeneous under lower species"; and (3) "the *affinity* of the concepts—a law [*Gesetz*] which prescribes that we proceed from each species to every other by gradual increase of the diversity" (*Critique of Pure Reason*, A 657/B 685).

We see here that the Kantian nomenclature, which is recapitulated in terms of "principles" (*Prinzipien*) of homogeneity, specification, and continuity, blurs for the translator and the French interpreter the initial distinction between *Grundsatz* and *Prinzip* (*Principium*). This is because the concepts of "fundamental proposition" (*Grundsatz*) and "principle" (*Prinzip*) are given different meanings depending on whether the context in which they are used is formal logic or transcendental logic. In the transcendental register, only the understanding has fundamental propositions (of which, as the "faculty of rules," it is the origin), whereas only reason has these (unconditioned) principles of which it is the source. In formal logic, *Grundsatz* designates a proposition to which we have gone back, and which, *a parte ante*, is thus not founded on an anterior proposition, whereas *Prinzip* designates the ability to derive, *a parte post*, other propositions. For traditional logical principles such as the principle of identity and the principle of contradiction, Kant uses the term *Sätze* (*Satz*, proposition) to indicate that these principles do not have foundational value, and that they are therefore only "criteria" of truth: "*The principle of contradiction* must therefore be recognized as being the universal and completely sufficient *principle of all analytic knowledge*; but beyond the sphere of analytic knowledge it has, as a *sufficient* criterion of truth, no authority and no field of application" (A 151/B 191). Mathematical philosophers of the nineteenth century like Bolzano retained the same terminology in speaking of the principles of identity and contradiction—*Satz der Einerleiheit* and *Satz des Widerspruches*—but far from being simple criteria of truth, these principle-propositions were considered as the universal source of all analytical judgments. On the other hand, the principle of reason (*Satz vom Grunde*) is for Kant a synthetic proposition that accounts for judgments. This principle assumes the intuition of time and yet, as Bolzano once more points out, "it is also valid where there is no time" (§8), namely, when the existence of noumena has to be justified.

From both the logical and transcendental points of view, the distinction between *Satz*, *Grundsatz*, and *Prinzip* is thus not merely reasonable: on the one hand, if a proposition can play the role of principle, a principle, since it can be founded on a superior proposition, is not necessarily a fundamental proposition; on the other hand, transcendental fundamental propositions have their source in the understanding, while principles have theirs in reason. Here we see the root of a possible confusion. In a logical sense, the understanding has principles and reason has fundamental propositions, which in a transcendental sense would be contradictory; if the logical sense is taken for the transcendental sense, the critical nomenclature and the architectonics that underlie it will be upset: reason will already be involved in the "Analytic of the Understanding," but that would destroy the enterprise of Criticism, if it is true that, according to a Kantian leitmotif, its systematicity is the foundation of its scientific character.

In the strictly practical (moral) domain, the vocabulary used in the *Critique of Practical Reason* is explicitly mathematical: "definition," "theorem," "axiom," "postulate," "law" (*Gesetz*), and this may seem surprising, coming from a thinker highly critical of the mathematical method in philosophy, and all the more so because this mathematical usage is adopted for an essential term in the Kantian vocabulary, that of "formula" (*Formel*), which is substituted for "principle" in referring to morality:

> A reviewer who wanted to find some fault with this work [*The Foundation of the Metaphysics of Morals*] has hit the truth better, perhaps, than he thought, when he says that no new principle of morality is set forth in it, but only a new formula [*kein neues Prinzip der Moralität, sondern nur eine neue Formel*]. . . . But whoever knows of what importance to a mathematician a formula is, which defines accurately what is to be done to work on a problem, will not think that a formula is insignificant and useless which does the same for all duty in general.

Critique of Practical Reason

It is possible to grasp the reasons for this change: on the one hand, it is only a matter of setting forth the doctrine, an exposition that has to be dogmatic; hence the formulas expressing the objective principles of knowledge constitute the fundamental propositions of transcendental philosophy. The latter thus produces a formulaic representation of the principles of knowledge: a system of statements which, through successive transformations, must return to the initial statements, those of the doctrinal empirical sites (letter to Markus Hertz, 26 May 1789). On the other hand, Kant maintains even in this lexicon a distinction between mathematics and philosophy since he reserves *Definitionen* for the former and *Erklärungen* for the latter.

Thus Kant, seeking to conceive a genuinely philosophical revolution that resembles only by analogy the revolution in physics, nonetheless found himself led back to a dangerous proximity to mathematics. In this return, to which the terms "principle" and "formula" testify, we can see the sign of how difficult it is to conceive a specifically philosophical demonstration. This difficulty is the constitutive knot that modern philosophical reflection seeks to undo when it inquires into its status as truth.

- See Box 2.

B. Frege: *Grundgesetz, Grundsatz, Axiom, Definition*

The term *Grundgesetz*, commonly used by Frege, can be translated as "basic law." This translation unfortunately preserves only one aspect of the German term *Grund*, which means both "basis" and "reason." In the preface to his *Begriffschrift* ("Concept Notation," 1879), Frege divides all truths that require a foundation (*Begründung*) into two kinds: those whose proof is entirely logical and those that are based on the facts of experience. The notion of basis or foundation is thus intimately connected, in German, with those of reason and proof: the basic laws are "the deepest reasons" (*die tiefsten Gründe*)

that constitute the justification (*Berechtigung*) for our assent" (*The Foundations of Arithmetic*, §3). In the domain of logic, the basic laws are general (*allgemein*) and "neither lend themselves to nor require a proof (*Beweis*)." Here Frege is directly borrowing one of Leibniz's formulas, though he does not cite him (*Nouveaux essais*, book IV, chap. 9, §3). The fact that *Grundgesetze* cannot be proven is connected with their "obvious" (*selbstverständlich*) character (*Basic Laws of Arithmetic*, vol. 2, §60; Frege apparently uses the adjective *einleuchtend* in the same sense: cf. *The Foundations of Arithmetic*, §90). Finally, the basic laws are often described as *Urwahrheiten* (first truths): cf. *The Foundations of Arithmetic*, §3.

In Frege, the notion of basic law is opposed to those of definition (*Definition*), axiom (*Axiom*), and theorem (*Lehrsatz*). In "Logic in Mathematics" (1914), Frege states that definitions, although important from a psychological point of view, are not essential to logic: they are simple abbreviations. A basic law is thus not a definition that bears on the signs used. Despite the fact that Frege often treats them as propositions (*Sätze*), basic laws, axioms, and theorems are not linguistic in nature. In his mature writings, Frege clearly indicates that they are thoughts (*Gedanken*) independent of the mind and of language. The notion of basic law also differs from that of axiom, but in a more subtle way. Every axiom is a basic law, and thus a primary truth, but the reciprocal statement is not true. A law is an axiom when it is used as the point of departure for a system of inferences. On the basis of axioms and rules of inference, one can derive a set of theorems (*Lehrsätze*). A primary truth considered as an axiom in one system can be considered a theorem in another, and vice versa ("Logic in Mathematics").

In relation to the Kantian tradition, the originality of Frege's notion of basic laws is twofold. First, Frege thinks that the comprehension of axioms does not depend on intuition but on inference, that is, on the ability to derive theorems from axioms in accord with the order of proof, and also on the correlative ability to go back from the theorems to the axioms. No source of intuitive knowledge, spatiotemporal or other, is required to grasp the obvious character of the axioms. Second, while Frege thinks that logical laws are purely general, he believes he can derive from them the existence of numbers considered as "objects," whereas Kant thought that only sense intuition can present objects to the understanding (*Critique of Pure Reason*, A 51/B 75).

In his introduction to the *Foundations of Arithmetic* (*Die Grundlagen der Arithmetik*, 1884), Frege states three principles (*Grundsätze*) that guide his inquiry. The first advocates separating "the psychological from the logical, the subjective from the objective." The second is that "we must find out what words mean (*bedeuten*) not in isolation but taken in their context." This is what we now call the Fregean principle of contextuality. Finally, the third principle prescribes that we "never lose sight of the difference between concept and object." These methodological principles must not be confused with the laws of Fregean conceptual notation. For example, the distinction between object and concept cannot be formulated within the logical system; it only "shows itself" in the correct use of the symbolism, which does not allow the denotation of a concept by means of an expression suited to an object.

2

Principle of reason, *Satz vom Grund*

In 1955–56, Heidegger gave, under the title *Der Satz vom Grund*, a series of lectures at the University of Freiburg that took as their theme the "great" Leibnizian principle, the *principium magnum, grande et nobilissimum*: the *principium (sufficientis) rationis*, the one that answers the fundamental question (*Grundfrage*) formulated notably in the *Principes de la nature et de la grâce fondés en raison* (§7): "'Why is there something rather than nothing?'... assuming that things must exist, we must be able to account for *why they must exist this way*, and not otherwise." Starting from the standard formulation of the principle *nihil est sine ratione*, Heidegger highlights the most rigorous statement of the *principium rationis* as *principium reddendae rationis*: what requires that this be accounted for? To whom? By whom? The lectures as a whole are thus presented as a long variation on a theme: that of the translation of *principium rationis—Satz vom Grund*; a variation with repetition, transposition, change in accentuation, "alternation of tones," so as to hear, in accord with all its harmonies, echoes, and resonances (*Anklänge*) what is said by the "principle": *Grundsatz*, fundamental proposition, or rather "ground proposition," since it—as a thesis or positing of the ground—is the ultimate presupposition of language and truth understood as propriety of judgment. The *principium rationis—Satz vom Grund*, understood as *Grundsatz*—is thus what makes the ground of every proposition: *der Satz vom Grund als Grund des Satzes*. The whole procedure of the lecture is then, by playing on accentuation (*Tonart*), to retranslate or reinterpret, in accord with other possibilities of the language, the *Satz* as a "leap" (*Sprung*) and as a "movement" in the musical sense of the term, and *ratio*, reason/*Grund*, as *Grund*, ground, abyssal ground (*Grund—Abgrund*). The powerful motif of play (*Spiel*) runs like a leitmotif from one end to the other of the lectures, which conclude with this surprising transposition of fragment 52 of Heraclitus (see also AIÔN, I.A):

[αἰὼν παῖς ἐστι παίζων]...

(*Seinsgeschick, ein Kind ist es, spielend*...)

(The fateful sending of being is a child who plays...)

Der Satz vom Grund

The text can thus be presented explicitly as a play on words (*Wortspielerei*) laboriously woven and intended to reinvest the principle in an ultimate paratactic reformulation:

Sein und Grund : das Selbe ./ Sein: der Ab-grund.

(Being and ground: the Same. / Being: the abyss.)

To play the game, or to accompany the movements of this game (*Sätze dieses Spiels*), is also, regressing from German to Greek, to understand Being/Ground as *logos* [λόγος], or to emphasize the abyss between the *rationem reddere* characteristic of the *principium* and the *logon didonai* [λόγον διδόναι] that is heard "with Greek ears" (!):

etwas Anwesendes in seinem so und so Anwesen und Vorliegen darbieten, nämlich dem versammelnden Vernehmen.

(offer what enters in presence in its unfolding in presence so or so—and offer it to the grasp that collects)

Jean-François Courtine

BIBLIOGRAPHY

Heidegger, Martin. *The Principle of Reason*. Translated by Reginald Lilly. Bloomington: Indiana University Press, 1991.

In an essay entitled "Der Gedanke" ("Thought," 1918), Frege asserts that logic must seek to discover the laws of being true (*Gesetze des Wahrseins*). However, he adds that the word "law" is ambiguous. People speak of moral or political laws in a normative or prescriptive sense, whereas the laws of being true are primarily descriptive; they refer to an ontological domain independent of natural processes and psychological representations. We can nonetheless draw from them "prescriptions (*Vorschriften*) for opinion, thought, judgment, reasoning." In this sense, the laws of logic, or of being true, are also laws of thought (*Denkgesetze*).

Ali Benmakhlouf
Fabien Capeillères
Barbara Cassin
Jérôme Dokic

BIBLIOGRAPHY

Aubenque, Pierre. *Le Problème de l'être chez Aristote*. Paris: Presses Universitaires de France, 1962.

Bolzano Bernard. *Beyträge zur einer begründeteren Darstellung der Mathematik*. Prague: Caspar Widtmann, 1810.

———. "Contributions to a Better-Grounded Presentation of Mathematics." In *The Mathematical Works of Bernard Bolzano*, edited by Steve Russ, 83–137. Oxford: Oxford University Press, 2004.

Descartes, René. *Principles of Philosophy*. In *The Philosophical Writings of Descartes*. 3 vols. Translated by John Cottingham, Robert Stoothoff, and Dugald Murdoch, vol. 3 including Anthony Kenny. Cambridge: Cambridge University Press, 1988.

Frege, Gottlob. *Concept Script, a Formal Language of Pure Thought Modelled upon that of Arithmetic*. Translation by S. Bauer-Mengelberg: *From Frege to Gödel: A Source Book in Mathematical Logic, 1879–1931*. Edited by J. van Heijenoort. Cambridge, MA: Harvard University Press, 1967.

———. *The Foundations of Arithmetic: A Logico-Mathematical Enquiry Into the Concept of Number*. 2nd rev. ed. Translated by J. L. Austin. Oxford: Blackwell, 1974.

———. *Nachgelassene Schriften*. Edited by H. Hermes, F. Kambartel, and F. Kaulbach. Hamburg: Felix Meiner, 1969.

———. *Posthumous Writings*. Translated by P. Long and R. White. Chicago: University of Chicago Press, 1979.

Gaffiot, Félix. *Dictionnaire latin-français*. New edition revised and expanded by P. Flobert (ed.). Paris: Hachette, 2000.

Heidegger, Martin. *Nietzsche*. Pfullingen: Neske, 1961. Translation by David Farrell Krell: *Nietzsche*. 4 vols. San Francisco: Harper and Row, 1979–82.

Hume, David. *An Enquiry Concerning Human Understanding*. Edited by L. A. Selby-Bigge, 3rd edition revised by P. H. Nidditch. Oxford: Clarendon Press, 1975.

———. *A Treatise of Human Nature*. Edited by David Fate Norton and Mary J. Norton. Oxford: Oxford University Press, 2000.

Kant, Immanuel. *Critique of Practical Reason*. 6th ed. Vol. 5 of AK. Translated by T. K. Abbott. London: Longmans, 1967. First published in 1879.

———. *Critique of Pure Reason*. Translated by Paul Guyer and Allen Wood. Cambridge: Cambridge University Press, 1998.

———. *Critique of Pure Reason*. Translated by N. Kemp-Smith. London: Macmillan, 1958.

————. *Gesammelte Schriften*. Edited by the Akademie der Wissenschaften. Berlin: Reimer, 1902–13.

Laz, Jacques. *Bolzano critique de Kant*. Paris: Vrin, 1993.

Leibniz, Gottfried Wilhelm. *Monadology*. In *Philosophical Essays*. Translated and edited by Roger Ariew and Dan Garber. Indianapolis: Hackett, 1989.

————. *The Monadology and Other Philosophical Writings*. Translated by R. Latta. London: Oxford University Press, 1898.

————. *New Essays on Human Understanding*. Translated by Peter Remnant and Jonathan Bennett. Cambridge: Cambridge University Press, 1981.

————. *The Leibniz-Arnauld Correspondence*. Edited and translated by H. T. Mason. Manchester: Manchester University Press, 1967.

————. *Discourse on Metaphysics*. In *Philosophical Essays*. Translated and edited by Roger Ariew and Dan Garber. Indianapolis: Hackett, 1989.

Locke, John. *An Essay Concerning Human Understanding*. Edited by P. H. Nidditch. Oxford: Clarendon Press, 1975.

Newton, Isaac. *The Principia: Mathematical Principles of Natural Philosophy: A New Translation*. Translated by I. B. Cohen and Anne Whitman. Berkeley: University of California Press, 1999.

PROBABILITY

"Probable" is related to proof (*probare*, "try out, test") and approbation (*probus*, "solid, upright, honest"). Thus it operates in several registers, epistemological, logical, and rhetorical, and it opens out onto ontology as well as aesthetics and ethics.

I. Proof and Probability

1. The vocabulary of proof and demonstration is examined under EPISTEMOLOGY, IMPLICATION, and PRINCIPLE. Also see TRUTH.
2. More precisely, "probability" and its calculation are discussed on the basis of the English term "chance," in contradistinction to "probability"; see CHANCE.
3. The expression of the probable, which is connected with the possible and the contingent as a distinct modality of the necessary, is attached to one of the senses of "owe/ought": see DUTY; cf. SOLLEN, WILLKÜR. See also, regarding linguistic expression, ASPECT.
4. The probable then merges with the possible, by contrast with the actual: see *ACT, POWER*.
5. Finally, the probable is related to dialectical demonstrations. See DOXA, II.C especially.

II. Probability and Verisimilitude

1. In rhetoric, the probable (Greek *eikos* [εἴκος]) is connected with what appears, and it belongs first of all to the vocabulary of the image and the imagination: see EIDÔLON, Box 1; cf. *APPEARANCE* [DOXA], *IMAGE, IMAGINATION* [FANCY, PHANTASIA], TRUTH.
2. It is attached in a privileged way to commonplaces. See COMMONPLACE; cf. COMPARISON and supra, I.4.
3. It is connected with aesthetic imitation: see MIMÊSIS concerning the relation between the true and the verisimilar in theories of art; cf. ART, PLASTICITY. On the discursive modalities then put in operation, see DICHTUNG, ERZÄHLEN, *FICTION*, HISTORY.
4. It implies faith and belief. See *CROYANCE* [BELIEF, GLAUBE].

➤ *DIALECTIC, FALSE, LIE*

PROGRESS

Derived from the Latin *progressus* (walking forward), the word "progress" designates an improvement related to time, and it may refer to the individual and/or to history.

I. Progress and Self-Improvement

The reader will find under PERFECTIBILITY a study of the passage, in various traditions, from "improvement" (*perfectionnement, Vervollkommnung*) and progress.

See also BILDUNG, *CULTURE,* MENSCHHEIT, VIRTÙ.

II. Progress and History

On the interpretation that can be given to a history oriented toward a goal or determined in its course by an origin that governs its development, see HISTORIA UNIVERSALIS; see also CIVILIZATION, CORSO, NEUZEIT, SECULARIZATION.

III. Ethics, Economics, and Politics

On the boundary between the individual and the collective, see BERUF, ENTREPRENEUR, and OIKONOMIA. See also, in the aesthetic domain, WORK, Box 1 especially.

➤ *DESTINY,* GEISTESWISSENSCHAFTEN, HISTORY, *TIME*

PROPERTY

FRENCH	*propriété, propre*
GERMAN	*Eigenschaft, Eigentum, eigen*
GREEK	*idiotês* [ἰδιότης], *to idion* [τὸ ἴδιον], *idios* [ἴδιος]
LATIN	*proprietas, proprius*

➤ COMPARISON, EREIGNIS, I/ME/MYSELF, OIKEIÔSIS, PRÉDICABLE, PREDICATION, *SELF,* TRUTH, UNIVERSALS

The term "property," in the abstract sense of a thing's mode of being, has a twofold origin, theological and juridical, which can still be discerned in the French expressions *amour propre* or *biens propres* (private property).

This twofold origin goes back to the general meaning of "proper" as the unsoiled, the intimate. This Latin genealogy (calqued by the French *propre* and the English "proper") is reduplicated by a Germanic genealogy that derives from *Eigenschaft* (property), from *eigen* (own), from *Eigentum* (property [in the sense of what one owns]). The connection between "proper" and "property" thus seems to be more than an accident in a single language; it seems to be a constant.

The Latin etymology traces *proprius* to *pro privo* (privately, RT: *Dictionnaire étymologique de la langue latine*, 540). *Proprius* is equivalent to *perpetuus* (ibid., 539): what is proper to an individual is a permanent characteristic of that individual. *Proprietas* is a relatively late derivative from *proprius*, with the twofold sense of possession and characteristic: it is a "calque of *idiotês*" which is found in Cicero (ibid., 540). The Greek *idios* [ἴδιος] is related to what is private, proper to someone, whether it be a good or a mode of being, by contrast with what is public (*koinos* [κοινός]). *Idiotês* [ἰδιότης] designates property, the proper character of something, and *idiôtês* [ἰδιώτης], for which there is no Latin calque, designates both the private citizen as opposed to the public man, and the nontechnician, the "idiot" in contrast to the specialist (cf. RT: *Le Vocabulaire des institutions européennes*, 1:328 ; see ART, and LANGUAGE, II.B.1). *Idios* is based on the Indo-European root **swe-d*, from which is derived *suus* (his); **swe* (which appears not only in **swe-d* but also in *swe-t*, connected with *étes* [Fr., *allié*], and in **swe-dh*, connected with *ethos* [ἔθος]), on the one hand "implies membership in a group of 'one's own,' and on the other it specializes the 'self' as individuality" (ibid., 1:332). The logical sense of *idion* [ἴδιον], "the proper, own" is strictly determined in Aristotle: "A 'property' [*idion*] is a predicate which does not indicate the essence of a thing [*to ti ên einai*, (τὸ τί ἦν εἶναι)], but yet belongs to that thing alone, and is predicated convertibly of it [*monôi d'huparchei kai antikatêgoreitai tou pragmatos* (μόνῳ δ' ὑπάρχει καὶ ἀντικατηγορεῖται τοῦ πράγματος)]" (*Topics*, 1.5.102a.18–19; trans. W. A. Packard-Cambridge in *Basic Works of Aristotle*). Along with genus, definition, and accident, property is one of the predicables (ibid., 1.5; see PRÉDICABLE and TO TI ÊN EINAI). J. Brunschwig comments, "When a property is attributed to a subject, the name (of the subject) is attributed to everything to which the formula (of the property) is attributed, and the formula (of the property) is attributed to everything to which the name (of the subject) is attributed" (Brunschwig, Introduction to *Topiques*, by Aristotle, 122).

In English, "property" is derived from "proper." A proper name is one that is proper to the individual (the French *nom propre* appears in 1549 as a modernization of the Old French *propre nuns*, which appears around 1155 [RT: DHLF]). The proper name is the one that is appropriate[d] to the individual. In this sense, "God" is an archetypal proper name: it is perfectly appropriate[d]. In French, *propre* has two meanings, the second a late development (1842, RT: DHLF) that is attributed to a person who bathes frequently and includes two derivatives with distinct senses: A: *propriété*, and B: *propreté* (in Walloon French it has been appropriated for "cleaning"). Sense A is present in the expression *le propre de X*, meaning "the essence of X"—for example, "le propre de la puissance est de protéger" (Pascal). Sense B is the origin of a general sense of "good order" and came to designate hygiene only later on—in the seventeenth century, a dinner or a garden could be said to be *propre* in the sense of appropriate for a situation or use, suitable: "Personne ne l'embarrasse, tout le monde lui convient, tout lui est propre" (La Bruyère). What sense A and B have in common is the idea of suitability (Greek *prepon* [πρέπον]; see MIMÊSIS, Box 6).

German distinguishes among *Eigenschaft*, *Eigentum*, and *Eigenheit* ("peculiarity"): an *Eigenschaft* is shared by several individuals (for example, "being red"), whereas an *Eigenheit* is possessed by a single individual (for example, "being myself"). In the seventeenth century, *Eigenschaft* appeared as a translation of *qualitas* and *attributum*, and was part of the vocabulary of technical philosophy established by Wolff in particular: "That which is uniquely and solely founded in the essence of a thing will be called a property [*Eigenschaft*]." Medieval and later mysticism in the Rhineland and in Flanders exploited the semantic affinity of the derivatives of *eigen*: it is just as much a matter of renouncing possessions as of

transcending both general and individual qualities (Suso's noble man is literally a "man without qualities" [*Eigenschaften*]). In this sense Musil's "Man without Qualities" descends from the "noble man" of Meister Eckhart and Suso. In this context, the juridical term *Aneignung* (a German translation of *appropriatio*) designates much more than taking material possession, the acquisition of an egoity (self-hood) or even an ipseity; and the ascetic and then mystical path is identified with disappropriation (syn.: detachment, abnegation, deprivation), which means renouncing what we have of our own, whether it be properties or possessions: "The monk must not only renounce ownership of material things, but also that of his own will [*proprietati propriae voluntatis*]" (quoted in RT: *Historisches Wörterbuch der Philosophie*, 335–36), but also "the doctrine of the cynical philosophers which was the spirit of disappropriation" (Voltaire). In the contemporary period, Heidegger reappropriated the proper, *Eigentlichkeit* (genuineness, authenticity) and *Ereignis* (propriation, event; see EREIGNIS). The abstract philosophical concepts *Eigenschaft*, property, and *propriété* thus have not only a juridical origin but also an ascetic origin.

Frédéric Nef

BIBLIOGRAPHY

Aristotle. *Topics*. Bks. 1 and 8. Translation by W. A. Packard-Cambridge: *Topics*. In *Basic Works of Aristotle*, edited by R. McKeon. New York: Random House, 1941. Translation with commentary by Robin Smith: *Topics*. Oxford: Clarendon Press, 1997.

Brunschwig, Jacques. Introduction to *Topiques*, by Aristotle. 1:vii–cxlviii. Paris: Les Belles Lettres, 1967.

PROPOSITION / SENTENCE / STATEMENT / UTTERANCE

FRENCH	*proposition, phrase, énoncé*
GERMAN	*Satz, Rede, Aussage*
GREEK	*protasis* [πρότασις], *logos* [λόγος], *phasis* [φάσις], *apophasis* [ἀπόφασις], *apophansis* [ἀπόφανσις], *logos apophantikos* [λόγος ἀποφαντικός], *thesis* [θέσις], *axiôma* [ἀξίωμα]
LATIN	*propositio, praemissa, oratio, oratio enuntiativa, sententia, elocutio, enuntiatio, sermo*

➤ DICTUM, *ÉNONCÉ*, INTENTION, LOGOS, PREDICATION, PRINCIPLE, SACHVERHALT, SENSE, SIGN, SIGNIFIER/SIGNIFIED, SPEECH ACT, SUPPOSITION, TERM, TROPE, TRUTH, WORD

The term "proposition" designates a complex unit intermediary, in the analysis of language, between the "word" or the "term" on the one hand, and "discourse" on the other. The "word" is the minimal unit endowed with meaning; combined with other words, it constitutes the sentence (see WORD, which itself can be analyzed as a SIGNIFIER/SIGNIFIED; see also HOMONYM). The "term" is more precisely the product of the decomposition of the proposition (see TERM). "Discourse" is the signifying totality constituted notably by propositions (see LOGOS and LANGUAGE).

A basic unit of logical syntax, the proposition is also the crossroads of philosophical semantics. The analysis of its constituents, subject and predicate (or more classically, subject, copula, and attribute; see PREDICATION), governs the semantics of terms, meaning and reference being originally approached as expressions of the "subject" function (see SUPPOSITION and SUBJECT). The question of the meaning or of the signified of the proposition opens in turn onto the notion of the "stateable" (see DICTUM), and onto all the problems of reference (see SENSE), deriving from the relation among intention (see INTENTION), objectivity, or state of affairs (see GEGENSTAND and SACHVERHALT) and truth-value (see TRUTH).

The "proposition" remains an enigmatic and even contested entity, however. Is it a matter of a thing or a matter of a word? That is the whole problem. Those who reject the existence of propositions and those who accept it are not talking about the same thing, the former thinking of the entities signified and the latter of the signifying forms. The semantic definition of the proposition as a subject ("bearer") of "true" or "false" predicates is rejected by all who believe that it is sentences in a given language that are true or false. Focusing on the meaning of the word "proposition" in modern philosophical texts involves confronting a network formed by the moving triad "proposition"-"statement"-"sentence" in its relations with the notions of "fact" or "state of affairs." If this is the case, it is the status itself of the set of these distinctions as it has been handed down by tradition in languages that has to be clarified.

Two kinds of ambiguity are connected with "proposition." The first has to do with the fact that in languages such as French, German, and English, the respective semantic fields of French *proposition*, German *Satz*, and English "proposition" are not completely congruent and refer to distinct terminological complexes. This leads to certain disparities that stubbornly confuse the reader of texts on logic, like the twofold meaning of the German *Satz*—"proposition" (*Satz* comes from *setzen*, "to pose") and "principle"—to which testify, for example, the use of the formula *Der Satz vom Grund* to render *principe de raison* (*principium reddendae rationis*), or the translation of the Aristotelian title *Peri hermêneias* [Περὶ ἑρμηνείας] by *Lehre vom Satz* (theory of the proposition; see PRINCIPLE and TO TRANSLATE). The confusion is at its height when the French term *proposition* is used to render Gottlob Frege's *Satz*, as opposed to its content, *Sinn* or *Gedanke*, which is rendered in English by "proposition."

The second ambiguity is connected with the difficulties specific to the Greek and Latin philosophical languages: *propositio* is in fact a Latin term that is ambiguous from the start, because it means both a statement (*oratio*) signifying the true and the false, and a statement serving as a premise for a demonstration. Latin-speaking logicians derived *propositio* from *pro alio positio*, an etymology according to which the proposition ultimately appears as a statement calling for another—the conclusion to be drawn (*pro alio, id est pro conclusione habenda*). Thus they exploited the possibility offered by Latin of expressing what was already contained in the Greek *protasis* [πρότασις], whose Aristotelian technical sense (the major premise in both an argument and a proposition) remains imbued with the idea of a question proposed (and thus to be established or verified), but also common, nonphilosophical senses corresponding to a spectrum ranging from "set in advance" (a period of time) to "place someone in the first rank" (in order to speak in the name of a group or to protect someone).

The two sorts of ambiguity are difficult to distinguish, and there is a tendency to impute to the "genius of the language" what in fact has to do with the history of idiolects: in any case, we have to take into account the effects of ancient terminologies on the technical

languages of logic and the modern philosophy of language. There are two keys to this exploration: make an inventory, starting with Greek and Latin, of the concurrent words belonging to other registers of analysis (grammar, rhetoric, dialectic) and conveying other pairs of theoretical and doctrinal oppositions; and look into the recurrent questioning—found in modern philosophy, but pertinent very early, as is shown by fourteenth-century debates about "propositions composed of things" or "real propositions"—bearing on an archetypal problem: namely, whether it is propositions or statements that are primarily the bearers of the true and false—"one of the most important subjects that future philosophy of language will have to discuss" (Bar-Hillel, "Universal Semantics and Philosophy of Language," 17).

I. What Is a *Propositio*?

A. Greek retroversions:
The ambiguity of Aristotle's *protasis* and the Stoics' *axiôma*

In the course of a translation from Greek, many terms are rendered by "proposition." For example, there is a first group of words around *phasis* [φάσις] (from *phêmi* [φημί], "to say"), which means "saying, speech, sentence"; but when *phasis*, neither entirely the same nor entirely different, is understood as connected with *phainô* [φαίνω] (make luminous, bring to light; and, in the middle voice, be luminous, be shown [as]), it means "denunciation, accusation," or "appearance of a star, phase of the moon." *Apophasis* [ἀπόφασις], when the prefix before *phainô* indicates its provenance, means "declaration, explanation, response, report, judicial decision, inventory" (to limit ourselves to Bailly's Greek dictionary, RT: *Dictionnaire grec français*); but, when *apo* denotes distance, *apophasis*, which is then supposed to come from *apophêmi* [ἀπόφημι], means "negation." *Apophansis* [ἀπόφανσις], which is clearly derived from *phainô*, means "explanation, declaration," and it designates, for example, a "property inventory." Another candidate is *protasis* [πρότασις] (throw ahead), which refers to the question proposed, the proposition, the premise. Yet another is *thesis* [θέσις], from *tithêmi* [τιθήμι] (set or lay), which refers to the action of instituting, or to convention, affirmation, or positing. Still another is *axiôma* [ἀξίωμα], from *axioô* [ἀξιόω] (evaluate, assess, believe to be right or true), which signifies price, consideration, resolution, principle, proposition. To these words we must still add *logos* [λόγος], one of the best candidates for any translation in the discursive and logical domain, which founds what modern logic can see only as the matrix of the greatest confusions (see LOGOS).

But the major fact crucial for the comprehension of the history and semantics of "proposition" is the conjunction of *protasis*, in the technical sense of the "premise" of a syllogism, with *apophansis* (or its developed expression, *logos apophantikos* [λόγος ἀποφαντικός]), "declarative statement," starting with the Latin translations of Aristotle; this is the point that determines the meaning of *propositio* and founds the ambiguity of "proposition." We can assume that this Latin confusion was made possible, or favored, by Aristotle's broad use of *protasis*: by itself, as it is explained in the *Analytics*, *protasis* has almost the same sense as *propositio*. The term is in fact defined in the first lines of the *Prior Analytics* (1.1, 24a16–17) as a *logos kataphatikos ê apophatikos tinos kata tinos* [λόγος καταφατικὸς ἢ ἀποφατικός τινος κατά τινος] (a sentence affirming or denying one thing of another). At the same time, all kinds of *protases* (universal, particular, or indefinite, dialectical or demonstrative) are qualified as "syllogistic" (24a28): the *protases* or "premises" are "that on the basis of which there is a syllogism," "that of which it is made" (cf. 1.25, 42a32: every syllogistic conclusion "follows from [*ek*] two premises and not from more than two"). The commentators gloss the etymology of *protasis*, "that which one holds out and proposes first" (cf. Bonitz, RT: *Index aristotelicus*, citing Ammonius, s.v.), from which emerges the *apodosis*, "given," deduced, from them. And the syllogistic premise will be "demonstrative" (*apodeiktikê* [ἀποδεικτική], the object of the *Analytics*) "if it is true" (*ean alêthês êi* [ἐὰν ἀληθὴς ᾖ], 24a30): since in *De interpretatione*, the true and the false are characteristics of the *logos apophantikos* as the affirmative or negative connection between a noun and a verb (17a2–3 and 8–10), we see that the superimposition is carried out without further question.

We will limit ourselves to locating a few sets of problems.

1. The *phasis-apophasis-apophansis* complex by itself leads to certain difficulties in the Aristotelian terminology that interpreters are not always able to monitor.

- See Box 1.

2. The development of the vocabulary from Plato and Aristotle to the Stoics ended up settling on *axiôma* as the best candidate for a term to be translated as "proposition" in the corpus of the grammarians and logicians. The Aristotelian *axiôma* is a "principle on the basis of which a demonstration is conducted," and thus that others are asked to accept (that is the definition given by Bonitz [RT: *Index aristotelicus*], who refers to *Posterior Analytics* 2.72a17; see PRINCIPLE, I.B), and it can be rendered precisely by modern "axiom." On the other hand, the Stoics' *axiôma* is defined, in a way very similar to the way *logos apophantikos* is defined in *De interpretatione*, as "what is true or false" ("*axiôma de estin ho estin alêthes ê pseudos* [ἀξίωμα δέ ἐστιν ὅ ἐστιν ἀληθὲς ἢ ψεῦδος]," Diogenes Laertius 7.65; cf. RT: Long and Sedley, *The Hellenistic Philosophers* 34A, 1:202 and 2:204). "The 'complete sayable'" ("*lekton autotelês* [λεκτὸν αὐτοτελές]": Sextus Empiricus, *Adversus mathematicos* 8.74 = RT: Long and Sedley 34B, 205; see SIGNIFIER/SIGNIFIED, II) is, as Long and Sedley say, the "basic material of Stoic logic" (ibid.; on the difference between Aristotle's logic and that of the Stoics, see in particular SIGN). The meaning of "judgment," "demand"—indeed, of "requirement" or "claim" (see CLAIM), which is discernible in the verb *axioô*—is emphasized by Diogenes Laertius, but English and French translations elect to use "propose" and "proposition": "Someone who says 'it is light' seems to be proposing that it is light [*axioun dokei to hêmeran einai* (ἀξιοῦν δοκεῖ τὸ ἡμέραν εἶναι)]. Then, if it is light, the proposition put forward [*to prokeimenon axiôma* (τὸ προκείμενον ἀξίωμα)] proves to be true, and if not, it is revealed to be false" (7.75 = RT: Long and Sedley 34E). Latin translators give *effatum* (Seneca, *Letters to Lucilius* 117.13 = RT: Long and Sedley 33E; Cicero, *Academica* 2.96 = RT: Long and Sedley 37H; Cicero also gives *enuntiatum* and *enuntiatio*, see RT: Long and Sedley

33E), but the translation by "'proposition' is much the least misleading," Long and Sedley assert (205). In fact, according to them, once the characteristics that belong to the linguistic act have been eliminated from *axiôma*, "no serious confusion need arise in attributing to the Stoics a doctrine of propositions" (206), a theory that anticipates significant characteristics of contemporary theories, and in particular the paradoxes of reference according to Bertrand Russell (207–8; see below, III; and see SENSE, SPEECH ACT, and IMPLICATION).

B. *Propositio,* or the seizure (*arraisonnement*) of the apophantic by the syllogism

In the "Summas" of thirteenth-century terminist logic, the definition of the *propositio* always contains two formulas: (1) "*propositio est oratio verum vel falsum significans*" (A proposition is a statement signifying the true or the false), and (2) "*propositio est oratio secundum quod ponitur in praemissis ad aliquid probandum*" (A proposition is a statement insofar as it is formulated in premises to prove something). The writers of logical summas thus put under the same term what Boethius called *oratio enuntiativa* or *enuntiatio*, namely Aristotle's *logos apophantikos*, and what Aristotle generally calls *protasis* in the *Prior Analytics*.

1. *Propositio-praemissa*

Let us begin with the second meaning, which is backed in both Latin and Greek by an etymology: "proposition" is used in the sense of "positing in order / with a view to the conclusion to be drawn [*dicitur propositio quasi pro alio posito, idest pro conclusione habenda*]" (cf. Nicholas of Paris, *Summa Metenses*, in De Rijk, ed., *Logica modernorum* 2.1, p. 452). We should note that in some texts, such as the *Posterior Analytics* (1.2, 71b20–22), Aristotle defines scientific demonstration without mentioning *protasis*. This silence is maintained in James of Venice's Latin translation (*Aristoteles Latinus*, 4.1–4, ed. Minio-Paluello and Dod, 7.16–18), which gives: "*Si igitur est scire ut posuimus, necesse est et demonstrativam scientiam ex verisque esse et primis et inmediatis et notorioribus et prioribus et causis conclusionis*" ("*anagkê kai tên apodeiktikên epistêmên ex alêthôn t' einai kai prôtôn kai amesôn kai gnôrimôterôn kai proterôn kai aitiôn tou sumperasmatos* [ἀνάγκη καὶ τὴν ἀποδεικτικὴν ἐπιστήμην ἐξ ἀληθῶν τ' εἶναι καὶ πρώτων καὶ ἀμέσων καὶ γνωριμωτέρων καὶ προτέρων καὶ αἰτίων τοῦ συμπεράσματος]"). However, it is broken in modern translations. Jules Tricot (in *Organon*, 8) renders this as "*Si donc la connaissance scientifique consiste bien en ce que nous avons posé, il est nécessaire aussi que la science démonstrative parte de prémisses qui soient vraies, premières, immédiates, plus connues que la conclusion, antérieures à elle, et dont elles sont les causes.*" Seidl (*Aristoteles: Zweite Analytiken*) gives: "*Wenn nun das wissenschaftliche Verstehen solcher Art ist, wie wir ansetzen, dann erfolgt notwendig die beweisende Wissenschaft aus [Prämissen], die wahre, erste, unmittelbare, bekanntere, frühere und ursächliche sind in Bezug auf die Konklusion.*" Other, more rigorous translators use the term "things," as does Barnes (*Aristotle's Posterior Analytics*, 3): "If, then, understanding is as we posited, it is necessary for demonstrative understanding in particular to depend on things which are true and primitive and immediate and more familiar than and prior to and explanatory of the conclusion." "Premises"? Or "things"? Or,

1

Phasis, apophasis, apophansis, kataphasis: Problems of Aristotelian terminology

➤ LIGHT, Box 1

In his *Organon*, Aristotle establishes the technical vocabulary of classical logic relative to words and terms, sentences and propositions, arguments and syllogisms (see LOGOS, SENSE, TERM, WORD). This contribution, which was decisively precise, nonetheless included a certain number of ambiguities, due especially to the subsistence of nonterminological uses. Two main difficulties concern the intermediate level.

1. *Apophasis/apophansis* and *apophasis/kataphasis*

A first difficulty has to do with the possible confusion of two signifieds of a single signifier that are dangerously close because they belong to the same semantic field: *apophasis* can mean either "declaration" or "negative statement." Whether there was originally a single root (as Chantraine seems to think, RT: *Dictionnaire étymologique de la langue grecque*, s.v. *phainô*) or two roots that are phonetically distinct and semantically convergent (*pha-* [φα-] / *phê-* [φη-], which designates above all the expression of thought, the assertion of an opinion in speech; and *fan*, which means, depending on the diathesis, "to be luminous" or "to make luminous," the latter being specified in certain compounds with the sense of "to manifest through language, to declare"), we seek in it the source of the confusion. Related to *apophanein*, *apophasis* means, in Demosthenes, for example (47.45), the "sentence uttered," and in Aristotle, "assertion," "declaration" (*Rhetoric* 1.8, 1365b27: "*kuria estin ê tou kuriou apophasis*," "Sovereign is the declaration of the sovereign body," which varies depending on the object; and, in the greatest proximity to the *gnômê* or *doxa* [see DOXA], *Metaphysics* Δ.8, 1073a16: "*memnêsthai dei tas tôn allôn apophaseis*," "We must recall the declarations made by others"). Related to *apophaskô* (Sophocles, *Oedipus Rex* 485) and *apophêmi* (Sophocles, *Oedipus at Colonus* 317), *apophasis* takes on the sense of "negative statement," in contradistinction to *kataphasis*, the "affirmative statement" with which it is already associated in Plato's *Sophist* (263e). The two meanings do coexist in Aristotle, but the danger is less serious than it seems. Aristotle, in accord with his linguistic policy of "de-homonymization" (see HOMONYM), largely wards off the danger by establishing *apophansis* (with its derivative, *apophantikos*) as the stable technical designation of "assertion" in the sense of "predicative statement" in general, and by reserving *apophasis* for negation or the negative statement, as

opposed to *kataphasis*, "affirmation, affirmative statement," both constituting an *antiphasis* or "contradiction." Thus in chapter 6 (17a23–26) of the *Peri hermêneias*, we find the following:

> Esti d'hê men haplê *apophansis* phônê sêmantikê peri tou ei huparchei ti ê mê huparchei, hôs hoi chronoi diêirêntai. *Kataphasis* de estin *apophansis* tinos kata tinos, *apophasis* de estin *apophansis* tinos apo tinos.

To be perfectly clear, this statement is nonetheless difficult to translate, as is shown by Tricot's version, whose internal incoherences are easy to emphasize:

> La *proposition* [*apophansis*] simple est une émission de voix possédant une signification concernant la présence ou l'absence d'un attribut dans un sujet, suivant les divisions du temps. Une *affirmation* [*apophasis*] est la *déclaration* [*apophansis*] qu'une chose se rapporte à une autre chose; une · négation [*kataphasis*] est la *déclaration* [*apophansis*] qu'une chose est séparée d'une autre chose.

> The simple *proposition* [*apophansis*] is a vocal utterance possessing a meaning related to the presence or absence of an attribute in a subject, according to divisions in time. An *affirmation* [*apophasis*] is the *declaration* [*apophansis*] that one thing is related to another thing; a *negation* [*kataphasis*] is the *declaration* [*apophansis*] that one thing is separated from another thing.

No doubt it would be more judicious to always render *apophansis* by *énoncé* (statement: *Categories and On Interpretation*, trans. Ackrill, 46–47), but translators always abandon the attempt to make the reader hear the connection, explicit in Aristotle and heavily emphasized by Heidegger, between *apophansis* and *apophainesthai*, "to show on the basis of" ("*epei de esti kai to huparchon apophainesthai hôs mê huparchon*," "But since it is also possible to make appear not to belong what belongs"). The text of *Peri hermêneias* (17a26–28) seeks, following these remarks, to make explicit the definition of the true and the false characteristic of the apophantic register (see below, and TRUTH).

2. The meanings of *phasis*

The astronomical sense of *phasis* (cf. *phainesthai*) appears once in Aristotle's *Meteorology* (1.6, 324b34). In all other occurrences—more

than fifty, chiefly in the *Organon* and the *Metaphysics*—*phasis* (cf. *phanai*) has the following meanings, in decreasing order of frequency:

a. It is used as a synonym of *kataphasis* opposed to *apophasis*; thus in *Metaphysics* Γ.4, 1008a9–10: "*peri tas allas phaseis kai apophaseis homoiotropôs*" (And all other assertions and negations are similarly compatible). (This text then proceeds with the presentation, three times in a row, of the verbal pair *phêsai kai apophêsai*, "affirm and deny"; see also *Prior Analytics* 37a12, 51b20, 33, etc.; *Sophistical Refutations* 180a26, b30; *De anima* 430b26; *Topics* 136a5–6 [with the very unusual play on *phasis* and *tês phaseôs idion*], 163a15, etc.).

b. It is used as a generic synonym of *apophansis*, except that it has more to do with propositional than apophantic logic, as in the recurrent expression "*hai antikeimenai phaseis*"—for example, *Metaphysics* Γ.6, 1011b13–14: "*bebeiotatê doxa pasôn to mê alêteis hama tas antikeimenai phaseis*" (The firmest opinion of all is that the opposed statements are not simultaneously true). In the same vein, see *Peri hermêneias* 12.21b17–18.

c. Finally, *phasis* is used twice in the *Peri hermêneias* to designate the semiotic status of a "separate part of the *logos*," a noun or verb "isolated" (*kechôrismenon*) from its phrastic context. "A sentence is a significant portion of speech, some parts of which have an independent meaning, that is to say, as an utterance [*hôs phasis*; Ackrill renders this as 'expression'], though not as the expression of any positive judgment [*all' ouch' hôs kataphasis*]. Let me explain. The word 'human' has meaning, but does not constitute a proposition, either positive or negative. It is only when other words are added that the whole will form an affirmation or denial" (4.16b27–30). Aristotle thus proposes to call the noun and the verb "an expression [*phasis*] only" ("*to men oun onoma kai to rhêma phasis estô monon*," 5.17a17–18). Instead of following Bonitz in seeing this as the *princeps* use, to which Aristotle does not limit himself (RT: *Index aristotelicus*, s.v. *phasis*), the simplest thing to do is probably just to say that when he characterizes the type of signification of a phrastic constituent that, detached from a construct that may be either a *kataphasis* or an *apo-phasis*, loses thereby all assertive capacity, Aristotle falls back, in order to designate what remains of meaning, on what remains of *kataphasis-apophasis* when the verbal prefixes that make them a species of assertive statement have been removed, namely, *phasis*.

For example, to signify *hôs phasis* when we say "[the] man" or "is in good health" is thus to present the listener with a signifier bearing a lexical signified that he recognizes, but that provides him with no information regarding what is or is not. We might render *phasis* here by "mention," but we would at the same time be abandoning the relationship to the family of terms.

---

perhaps, "principles"? The word is used by translators immediately following the passage above (71b22–23): "*sic enim erunt et principia propria ei quod demonstratur*" (James of Venice); "*c'est à ces conditions, en effet, que les principes de ce qui est démontré seront aussi appropriés à la conclusion*" (Tricot); "for in this way the principles will also be appropriate to what is being proved" (Barnes). The choice between "premises," "things," and "principles" hardly matters. Here it suffices to see that the French and German resort to "premise," *Prämisse*, rather than "proposition" or *Satz*. Then it is "premise," a calque of the Scholastic Latin *praemissa* (a neuter plural considered as a feminine singular, from *praemitto*, "to send on ahead"), that relieves *propositio* of its ambiguity.

2. *Propositio—oratio enuntiativa*

The first meaning finds its starting point in a quite different corpus, that of the *Peri hermêneias* (4.16b33–17a4):

> Esti de logos hapas men sêmantikos . . . apophantikos de ou pas, all' en hôi to alêtheuein ê pseudesthai huparchein. Ouk en hapasi de huparchei, hoion hê euchê logos men, all' out' alêthês oute pseudês. [Ἔστι δὲ λόγος ἅπας μὲν σημαντικός . . . ἀποφαντικὸς δέ οὔ πᾶς, ἀλλ' ἐν ᾧ τὸ ἀληθεύειν ἢ ψεύδεσθαι ὑπάρχειν. Οὐκ ἐν ἅπασι δὲ ὑπάρχει, οἷον ἡ εὐχὴ λόγος μέν, ἀλλ' οὔτ' ἀληθὴς οὔτε ψευδής.]

When one reads this passage in Tricot's French translation, it provides a definition of the proposition that every reader will consider to be of cardinal significance:

> Tout discours n'est pas une proposition, mais seulement le discours dans lequel réside le vrai ou le faux, ce qui n'arrive pas dans tous les cas: ainsi la prière est un discours, mais elle n'est ni vraie ni fausse.

> Not every discourse is a proposition—only that in which truth or falsehood dwell, and this is not universally the case. Prayer, for instance, is a form of discourse, but it is neither true nor false.

When Boethius translates it, he gives *oratio enuntiativa*: "*enuntiativa vero non omnis [oratio], sed in qua verum vel falsum inest; non autem in omnibus, ut deprecatio oratio quidem est, sed neque vera neque falsa*" (*Aristoteles latinus*, 2.1–2, ed. Minio-Paluello, 8.8–10). The lexicon of propositionality thus includes not only what has to do with the elements of the syllogism, with the syllogistic *protasis*, but also what has to do with the possibility of saying the true and the false. Depending on the author, this double register refers to a simple "distinction of reason": the same *oratio* is called *enuntiatio* when it is considered "alone and absolutely" ("*quando per se sumitur et absolute*"), and *propositio* when it is related to the conclusion to be proved or inferred

("*quando ordinatur ad aliquam conclusionem probandam vel inferendam*": William of Sherwood, *Introductiones*, ed. Lohr, 222). For some writers, it is the whole system that is based on such a distinction of reason. As Lambert of Auxerre put it (*Logica*, ed. Alessio, 12):

> Ista nomina: enunciatio, dictio, [as]sumptio, quaestio, conclusio, propositio, idem sunt realiter, nam una et eadem oratio secundum rem et secundum substantiam potest nominari hiis nominibus realiter, unde solum differunt secundum rationem.

> These names—"utterance," "word," "[hypo]thesis," "question," "conclusion," "proposition"—are the same thing, really, for it is one and the same thing, regarding substance, namely discourse [or: the utterance], which can really receive all these names. All that differs only in reason.

The *logos apophantikos* is approached in various ways by modern translations. Participating in the "reduction of the apophantic to the predicative" emphasized by Heidegger (*Sein und Zeit*, §44; see TERM), Tricot translates, as we have seen, by duplicating the substantive: "*Tout discours n'est pas une proposition, mais seulement le discours dans lequel réside le vrai ou le faux.*" Rolfes, who starts from *Rede* (discourse), proposes, elliptically, a verbal formation, *aussagen* (state), corresponding to the noun *Aussage* (statement, French *énonciation*, Italian *enunciazione*):

> Dagegen sagt nicht jede [Rede] etwas aus, sondern nur die, in der es Wahrheit oder Irrtum gibt. Das ist aber nicht überall der Fall. So ist die Bitte zwar eine Rede, aber weder wahr noch falsch.

> On the other hand, not every [discourse] states something, but only the one that includes in itself truth or falsity. But this is not always the case. A request [a prayer] is a discourse, but is neither true nor false.

> (Aristoteles, *Kategorien: Lehre vom Satz*, German trans. Rolfes, 97–98)

Similarly Zanatta: "*Ma non ogni [discorso] è enunciativo, bensì quello nel quale sussiste il dire il vero o il dire il falso. E non in tutti quanti i discorsi sussiste: per esempio, la preghiera è sì un discorso, ma non è né vera né falsa*" (*Della interpretazione*, 85). Ackrill, on the other hand, opposes "sentence" and "statement-making sentence": "Every sentence is significant . . ., but not every sentence is a statement-making sentence, but only those in which there is truth or falsity. There is not truth or falsity in all sentences: a prayer is a sentence but is neither true or false. [The present investigation deals with the statement-making sentence]" (*Aristotle's Categories and De interpretatione*, trans. Ackrill, 45–46).

In choosing to use two nouns (*discours, proposition*), Tricot thus removes from the *logos apophantikos* the apophantic dimension preserved (only in appearance, if we follow Heidegger) as *enonciation* by other translations (note that he even directly translates *apophansis* by *proposition* in the first lines of *De interpretatione* [16a22]; Ackrill renders it by "statement").

Logos	*Apophansis*	*Logos apophantikos*
Oratio	*Enuntiatio*	*Oratio enuntiativa*
Discours	*Énonciation*	*Proposition*
Sentence	Statement	Statement-making sentence
Rede	*Aussage*	*Satz, indikative Rede*
Discorso	*Enunciazione*	*Discorso enunciativo*

Up to a certain point, contemporary controversies over the truth-value bearer are programmed in the wake of equivalencies noted in the table here. The polysemy of the term *logos*, which includes the notions of "sentence" and "statement"—crucial in the modern debate—among its many meanings, is not the only thing involved; more profoundly, the logical *arraisonnement* of the *logos*, which claims that the *enuntiatio*, or *oratio* (= *logos*) qua "bearer of truth-values," is fundamentally "ordered to the syllogism [*ordinata ad sillogizandum*]" and not only "apt to be ordered in a syllogistic argument [*ordinata in sillogizando*]"—a theme that flows from the "ordering" of Aristotle's logical corpus, and results from the recursive reading of the *Organon*, from the "scientific" syllogism (*Posterior Analytics*), the more complex, to the simplest, the *oratio* and its ingredients, the noun and the verb (*De interpretatione*).

The difficulties of the European logical vocabulary also depend, however, on the idiolects specific to each philosophical tradition ("continental" or "analytical"), and even to each philosophy. The recent English translation of an important sixteenth-century work, the *De significato propositionis* by the Oxford philosopher Richard Brinkley, under the title *Theory of Sentential Reference*, expresses the philosophical point of view of the translator, M. J. Fitzgerald, who reserves, for theoretical reasons, the English term "proposition" for what is "expressed" in a sentence. In this case, it is the whole theoretical apparatus stipulating that "two sentences that express the same proposition have the same truth-value," or that "sentences have their truth-values in virtue of the proposition they express," which is present in the background, that poses a problem—a philosophical problem, not a problem of comprehension or translation. In the case of *De significato propositionis*, the translator's choice, once it is made fully explicit, amounts to reserving the word "proposition" for the signified of what the Latin expresses by *propositio*, and what he expresses by "sentence." The same goes for principles such as "nonsynonymous sentences express distinct propositions": the problem is how to know to what the word "proposition" refers—for example, an abstract entity, Frege's "sense" (*Sinn*)—and to determine on that basis the nature of the difference between "sentence" and "proposition" that is supposed by every user of this principle. Using such principles in a philosophical commentary on a medieval work, as many English-speaking interpreters of Brinkley and his contemporaries do, involves attributing to the ancients distinctions that are themselves far from being unanimously accepted in modern philosophy.

II. How Should Linguistic Units of Reference Be Defined?

A. The "sentence" in Latin antiquity

Propositio is not the only way of designating in Latin a complex unit endowed with meaning. In classical Latin the term belongs, in accord with the influence of the syllogism, to the rhetorical and dialectical registers rather than to the grammatical register. In nontechnical works, there are numerous terms that can be applied to a linguistic unit of the phrastic type: in particular, *sententia*, which derives from *sentire*, "to feel, to experience a sensation or feeling," designates in general an opinion, a way of seeing, a view that one expresses, an idea and, by extension, the form that this idea takes, which means that *sententia* can correspond contextually to what is called a sentence (but often signifies, more particularly, a maxim or aphorism, and thus the "twist" or witticism that concludes the sentence; see SENSE and ARGUTEZZA). As for *oratio*, which derives from *orare*, "to utter a ritual formula, a prayer, a plea," it is applied to language, and more specifically to prepared language, to eloquence, style, and particularly to prose, but also to more limited achievements—discourses, oral expositions—and hence, but very rarely in these nontechnical works, to still more limited wholes that may coincide with units of the phrastic type. These are only coincidental effects.

Alongside these general uses, technical texts in which language is analyzed present linguistic units whose classification depends on precise theoretical choices. Three domains are concerned: rhetoric, dialectic, and grammar. (Metrics, which we may consider in the Latin domain as a subset of grammar, has to do with preoccupations that are too particular to be taken into account here.)

1. The rhetorical "period"

The standard linguistic unit is the "period," *periodos* [περίοδος] in Greek, literally a "path that goes around" (perimeter wall, revolution of the stars, etc.), which Aristotle defines in his *Rhetoric* as a "sentence [*lexis* (λέξις); see SIGNIFIER/SIGNIFIED and WORD] that has a beginning and an end by itself and an extent that can be taken in at a single glance [*megethos eusunopton* (μέγεθος εὐσύνοπτον)]" (3.9, 1409a36–38). The Latins rendered it by the loan word *periodus* or by the calques *ambitus* and *circuitus*, or again by various adaptations, such as *circumscriptio*, *comprehensio*, and *continuatio*, which mark the unit and the whole thus "circumscribed" or "embraced," or the continuity of the whole formed. This period may be constituted by subsets: the member (*membrum*) and the phrase (*incisum* or *incisio*), which have no absolute definition, but only a definition relative to the whole of which they are the constituents. In general, a period forms a sentence (but not necessarily: a succession of questions and responses can form a period). However that may be, the criteria determining the period clearly distinguish it from the sentence:

> first, because of the context in which it appears,
> that of the oratorical discourse: the period has no
> application outside this context and is absolutely
> inseparable from it;

second, because of its dimension, which is necessarily developed—the simple combination of the elements that are indispensable but sufficient to constitute a sentence would never suffice to form a period ("A period has a minimum of two parts [*habet periodus membra minimum duo*]," Quintilian says);

finally, because of the reference to rhythm, both in the consideration of the relative volume of the various parts of the period (whence an ascending, descending, or staccato rhythm, etc.), and in the fundamental importance attributed to the combination of the syllabic quantities at the end of the period, that is, the clausula: the presence of a clausula is part of the definition of the period.

Another unit, the *propositio*, appears in the context of rhetoric, but in uses that are shared with dialectic, and that we therefore have an interest in examining here in the framework of this other discipline.

2. Dialectical terminology

The standard linguistic unit in the domain of dialectical terminology is what the Greeks, and in particular the Stoic tradition (cf. I.A above), call *axiôma*, the assertion, a linguistic unit that can be true or false. The Romans resorted to various translations to render this unit: Varro, in the first century BCE, cites *profatum*, a proposal that was not adopted, and *proloquium* (which had already been used a generation earlier by Aelius Stilon, and was known to Cicero, but which did not persist either). For his part, Cicero cites *pronuntiatum* (later abandoned), *enuntiatum* (which we find in Seneca in the first century CE and in Apuleius in the second century CE), and *enuntiatio* (still present in the fourth and sixth centuries in Donatus and Boethius). Varro (cf. Aulus Gellus, *Attic Nights* 16.8) defines the *proloquium* as "an assertion or a sentence in which there is nothing lacking [*sententia in qua nihil desideratur*]," but this criterion of completeness is isolated: the criterion of determination cited is generally the ability to be true or false (even if the point is debated regarding assertions in the future tense). In opposition to this sense of *axiôma* as the true-or-false assertion, Martianus Capella (fourth century), in his book on dialectic, creates the term *eloquium*, as opposed to *proloquium*, to designate utterances that are neither true nor false (orders, questions, etc.). These other types of utterance are usually related to the term *oratio* (*oratio imperativa, interrogativa*, etc.), whose generality lends itself to all kinds of specification.

The term *propositio* represents what is "posed," what is "advanced," the "thesis." In the syllogism, where three structural elements (major, minor, conclusion) are distinguished, the *propositio* is thus the major (strictly speaking, what is "posed" or "posited"). The criterion is unity of content: the *propositio* is a proposition in the sense in which it is a statement that sets forth a single idea ("*x* killed *y*"). As a result, when a single statement implies that "*x* killed *y* and wounded *z*," Quintilian speaks, in the plural, of *propositiones*. This plural shows that the *propositio* cannot be confused with the sentence.

3. Grammatical analysis

Grammatical analysis is constructed on the basis of a hierarchy of units: *littera, syllaba, dictio* or *pars orationis, oratio* (or its

rare variant, *elocutio*). Each level results from the combination of units from a lower level and itself constitutes an element of the unit at a higher level. In this perspective, the categories of words are *partes orationis* ("parties du discours," to use the French calque). This means only that words are an inferior unit in relation to *oratio*, which results, in most cases, from a combination of words. The *oratio* has as its sole specificity in relation to the word its ability to be "complete": in accord with the Stoic problematic, the *oratio* is complete or incomplete. That being the case, the nature of this completion, syntactical or semantic, or even pragmatic, remains open, and is not analyzed, except to a certain extent by Priscian at the very end of classical antiquity. The *oratio plena* is thus a construct that incontestably coincides with the sentence (or, when only a reply is involved, with a phrasoid expression), but before Priscian, nothing is said about the nature of this construct, except that it is complete. In short, whereas the sentence is opposed to the proposition, one forming an independent construct, the other a virtually dependent construct, the completion of the *oratio* is opposed to its "incompletion." What is an incomplete utterance? Originally, among the Stoics, it was a predicate when it is alone, without a point of application (that is, without a subject), but later on it was more generally any utterance in which something is lacking. Some grammarians even added intermediate levels. Thus Servius speaks, regarding an utterance including a pronoun (subject) and a verb, of a "semi-complete" utterance: it lacks something, which in this case is of the order of reference (a determinate referent for the pronoun and an object of the predicate verb). In fact, according to the progressive schema in which it is situated, the *oratio* is understood in a problematic of part and whole: there are "parts of the *oratio*" (categories of words), and the *oratio* itself, composed of these parts, is incomplete or complete. Whereas the sentence is understood in a problematic of independence with regard to dependence, the *oratio* is understood in a problematic of the achieved in relation to the unachieved. (Medieval posterity sought to specify the nature and modalities of this completeness.)

More vague than *oratio*, among the grammarians (e.g., Diomedes or Charisius) *sermo* sometimes designates a linguistic sequence that can constitute what we call a sentence, but these are either general uses, with the meaning "remark," or very specialized uses, probably in the Stoic perspective of the predicate as a propositional kernel, with *sermo* ending up being equivalent to the verb alone. Here we find again the difference in point of view that opposes the ancients to the moderns on this point: whereas the notion of the sentence advanced in early modern grammar sought to discover where the construct examined stops (and thus what the framework and conditions of its independence are), the ancients sought to discover where this construct began (from which comes the problematics of incompletion, that is, of the "not yet" in relation to the complete utterance).

B. The medieval criteria for defining *oratio*: *Congruitas/perfectio*

The definition of the sentence, *oratio* (but "sentence" is, as we have seen, only one of the possible equivalents of *oratio*; see also LOGOS, III.A), took place in the Middle Ages on the basis of various criteria inherited from both Aristotle and Priscian, but profoundly rethought to take into account the formal, semantic, and pragmatic aspects of the utterance, which are not always mutually compatible.

1. The principle of composition

Consider Aristotle's and Boethius's definition (*De interpretatione* 4.16b26): "*Logos esti phônê sêmantikê hês tôn merôn ti sêmantikon esti kechôrismenon, hôs phasis all' ouch hôs kataphasis* [Λόγος ἐστὶ φωνὴ σημαντικὴ ἧς τῶν μερῶν τι σημαντικόν ἐστι κεχωρισμένον, ὡς φάσις ἀλλ' οὐχ ὡς κατάφασις]"; "*Oratio est vox significativa, cuius partium aliquid significativum est separatum (ut dictio, non ut adfirmatio)*"; "A sentence is a significant spoken sound some part of which is significant in separation, as an expression not as an affirmation" (Ackrill); "*Le discours est un son vocal [possédant une signification conventionnelle] et dont chaque partie prise séparément présente une signification comme énonciation et non pas comme affirmation [ou négation]*" (Tricot). The distortion of the equivalences shows quite clearly the general weakness of the linguistic vocabulary. The essential criterion is composition. Various problems arise: (1) How can we distinguish the sentence from the compound noun (for instance, the noun *respublica*)? Usually we distinguish, in the first place, the simple noun (*domus*), which is composed of parts that can themselves be significant (*do* = I give; *mus* = mouse), but whose meaning does not contribute to that of the whole; in the second place, the compound noun, composed of parts that contribute to the meaning of the whole, but lose their meaning in the whole, so that the meaning is simple—Boethius says that in the compound, the parts "consignify"; and in the third place, the *oratio*, composed of parts that retain, in the compound, their full meaning. (2) This definition is often associated with a principle of compositionality, which posits that the meaning of the whole must be constructed on the basis of that of its parts. This raises a problem in the case of utterances that are figurative or include metaphorical uses. In such cases—as, for example, in the expression *prata rident* (The prairies are flowering)—it is inversely on the basis of the meaning of the whole that we can understand that *ridere* does not have its ordinary meaning of "laugh," but rather the transferred meaning of *florere*. Some authors maintain that in cases of this sort, we must understand the meaning in an overall way, without bringing in the principle of compositionality. They go so far as to conclude that figurative utterances are "instituted," whereas institution was generally reserved for simple units alone (a position held notably by Abelard).

2. The criterion of semantic completeness (producing an intellection)

The criterion of semantic completeness was forged on the basis of the *Peri hermêneias* (*On Interpretation*) 3.16b19–22: "*auta men oun kath' hauta legomena ta rhêmata onomata esti kai sêmainei ti, histêsi gar ho leêgôn tên dianoian, kai ho akousas êremêsen, all' ei estin ê mê oupo sêmainei* [αὐτὰ μὲν οὖν καθ' αὑτὰ λεγόμενα τὰ ῥήματα ὀνόματά ἐστι καὶ σημαίνει τι, ἵστησι γὰρ ὁ λέγων τὴν διάνοιαν, καὶ ὁ ἀκούσας ἠρέμησεν, ἀλλ' εἰ ἔστιν ἢ μὴ οὔπω σημαίνει]"; "*ipsa quidem secundum se dicta uerba nomina sunt et significant aliquid—constituit enim qui dicit intellectum, et qui audit quiescit—sed si est vel non est nondum significat*"; "*En eux-mêmes et par eux-mêmes ce qu'on appelle les verbes sont donc en réalité des noms, et ils possèdent une signification déterminée (car en les prononçant on fixe la pensée de l'auditeur, lequel aussitôt la tient en repos), mais ils ne signifient pas encore qu'une chose est ou n'est pas*" (Tricot); "When uttered just by itself a verb is a name and signifies something—the speaker arrests his thought and the listener pauses—but it does not yet signify whether it is or not" (see TERM, Box 1).

Boethius and medieval thinkers draw from this the idea that it is the "constitution of an intellection" that is the criterion of the utterance—or of the complete utterance. This may be interpreted as a semantic completeness: if the utterance produces an intellection, then it is "completed" (*perfectus*: we will see later the consequences of this interpretation, which makes it possible to transgress the criterion of formal completeness). In addition, a principle of compositionality is constructed at the same time: as Boethius says, if one hears a noun, the moment it is spoken an intellection is constituted, but our mind is still in suspense; if then we hear the verb, at the moment when the last syllable is pronounced, then our intellect can rest easy. The principle of the constitution of meaning is parallel on the level of the sentence and on the level of the word: it is only when the final syllable of *imperritus* (who is without fear) is pronounced that the mind can rest, so far as simple intellection is concerned. The listener's mind progresses in a linear way as the syllables are pronounced (cf. Boethius, *In Peri hermêneias* 2). Some twelfth-century authors try to determine the precise moment when the meaning of the utterance is produced, with the paradox that if it is when all the parts have been pronounced, then it signifies when it no longer exists. Others maintain that the utterance signifies while it is being uttered, the meaning being realized at the last moment of the pronunciation ("*in ultimo puncto illius prolationis*"), which is the first instant in which it produces a complete intellection. We find a comparable position in the discussions of the theologians as to the moment when the meaning of the utterance of the Eucharistic conversion is produced, and therefore when the conversion itself is produced (see SPEECH ACT). Once pronounced, the parts no longer exist qua vocal form, but only in their genus, which is quantity. Abelard proposes a solution rather analogous to the one that we find later in Duns Scotus: we constitute the intellection of the utterance by remembering that its parts. To say that a sentence signifies thus means simply that the mind of someone forms an intellection of it by a process of assembling the partial intellections (*recollectio*; see de Libera and Rosier, "Les enjeux logico-linguistiques").

■ See Box 2.

Medieval texts hesitate to give priority to one or the other of these two criteria, formal completeness or semantic completeness. A formalist approach like that of the thirteenth-century Modists privileges the former: formal completeness entails semantic completeness, or in other terms, grammaticality automatically implies semanticity. *Congruitas* indicates a construction's degree of correctness, *perfectio* an utterance's degree of completeness (requiring the presence of a *suppositio* and an *appositio*); the Modists excluded *proprietas*, or semantic compatibility: the compatibility (*convenientia*) or noncompatibility (*repugnantia*) of the signifieds does not have to be taken into account by grammar. By expelling from their domain non-sense, illustrated by examples such as "capa categorica" ("a categorical—or

2

The definition of *oratio* according to Priscian

Priscian gives the following definition of the statement: "*Oratio est ordinatio dictionum congrua, sententiam perfectam demonstrans*" (The statement is a correct combination of words indicating a complete meaning: *Institutiones grammaticae*, in RT: Keil, *Grammatici latini*, 2:53.28–29). Thus labeled, this definition describes *oratio* first of all as a correct combination, which for Priscian implies that it includes a noun and a verb and that, in addition, the rules of agreement are respected. The semantic characteristic comes in only secondarily: the statement must indicate a complete meaning. The difficulty was to arise from the juxtaposition of the two criteria, formal and semantic. But according to another reading of the text, the definition goes this way: "*ordinatio, congruam perfectamque sententiam demonstrans*." The

combination that characterizes the statement is not qualified, whereas the meaning it conveys is: it must be complete and finished. This is a less frequent variant, but one that is nonetheless based on the Greek text of the scholia on the *Technê grammatikê*, and that may go back to Apollonius (*Grammatici graeci*, ed. Hilgard, vol. 1, fasc. 3, p. 214.5). The question is whether the adjective *congrua* is related to the combination of words (a reading supported by other passages in Priscian; RT: Keil, *Grammatici latini*, 3:201.1 or 208.25: "*est enim oratio comprehensio dictionum aptissime ordinatarum*" [The statement is in fact a group of words ordered in a completely suitable way]), or to the meaning. In the latter case, it is the criterion of formal semantic completeness that is primary. According to Priscian, this implies that we must find

on the formal level principles that account for this completeness, even if they are not ordinary rules, as in the case of figurative or elliptical statements. Thus even a simple word like *honestas* can be considered complete and thus acceptable as a reply to the question "*Quid est summum bonum in vita?*" (What is the supreme good in life?). Hence it is intelligibility that governs grammaticality (Baratin, *La naissance de la syntaxe à Rome*). The copyists' hesitations regarding the choice of the variant *congrua* or *congruam* testify here to the difficulty of choosing between the formal criterion and the semantic criterion in defining the *oratio*.

BIBLIOGRAPHY

Grammatici graeci. Edited by Alfred Hilgard. Hildesheim, Ger.: Olms, 1965.

---

affirmative—hat," an incongruous association of a metalinguistic adjective with a nonmetalinguistic substantive), the Modists thus tried, as Noam Chomsky did, famously, by means of the exemplary phrase "colorless green ideas sleep furiously," to found a syntax that dispenses with any reference to the lexical meaning of the units. Other attempts to articulate formal and semantic criteria resulted in accounts that favor the pragmatic dimension of language—as in the works of the intentionalist grammarians of the thirteenth century, who were inspired by both Priscian ("Every construction must be related to the intellection of the expression," *Institutiones grammaticae* 17.187) and Aristotle (the principle of the "constitution of intellection" that satisfies the listener): an utterance must be judged acceptable if it corresponds to the speaker's deep intention, and if it can be interpreted and recognized as such by the listener, whether it is grammatical or not. Thus a substantive such as *aqua*, uttered alone, is not an *oratio perfecta*; but if water has to be sought when a house is on fire (a particular intonation would be required), then it acquires the status of *oratio perfecta*, corresponding adequately, by its elliptical form, to the speaker's state of panic. Inversely, a grammatically correct utterance that does not correspond to the speaker's intention will accordingly be rejected (see *actus exercitus* in SPEECH ACT).

C. Correctness / completeness / truth

The connection of these different criteria with the notion of truth is carried out mainly in the context of logic. In the philosophical tradition that concerns us, cases of ill-formed utterances give rise to the problem of how to determine whether such utterances (*orationes*) thereby lose the status of a proposition (*propositio*), that is, if an ill-formed sequence is automatically deprived of truth-value: such malformations include grammatical incorrectness (such as "*homo est alba*" ["man is white" or "a white woman," where a masculine

noun is connected with a feminine adjective]), semantic redundancy, and the semantic incompatibility of the constituents composing the subject or predicate groups, the impossibility of assigning a reference (e.g., "*omnis Socrates*," which violates the rule according to which a distributive sign can be applied only to a common term whose extension is greater than two; or, again, "*omnis phoenix*" [all phoenix]— the phoenix existing, by definition, as a unique entity at a certain moment in time, like "*omnis sol*" [all sun]); or cases of empty reference, such as "*Asinus rationalis currit*" (A rational ass runs; cf. Ebbesen, "The Present King of France"; de Libera, *La référence vide*). This last case can be analyzed in various ways: a proposition such as "*Asinus est rationalis*" (The ass is rational) is generally considered false; but "*Asinus rationalis currit*" may be analyzed as incorrect (*incongrua*); or as correct but asemantic or *impropria* (incapable of producing an intellection); or as nonreferential (*rationalis* not being able to perform its function of determining the substantive, and thus preventing the group from "supposing" something); or, sometimes, as false. The "implication of a possible falsehood" ("*Homo qui est albus currit* [The man who is white runs]," if there is no white man: the fact that there are white men, implied here, is possible, even if that is not the case) is distinguished from the "implication of an impossible falsehood" ("*Asinus qui est rationalis*" [The ass that is rational]," the distinction having consequences that are analyzed in diverse ways, in terms of correctness or of truth; see IMPLICATION). The question of empty reference was the subject of lively debate in the thirteenth century: Can one say, "Homo est animal, nullo homine existente" (Man is an animal, no man existing)? Is this sentence false or ill-formed, because it cannot give rise to an intellection, the subject itself not being able to give rise to an intellection and/or to have a denotation (cf. de Libera, "Roger Bacon et la référence vide," and *La référence vide*)? This case, where it is impossible to assign a reference to one of the terms because of the state of the world and of the moment of predication, is often compared with the cases previously described in which "empty reference" occurs because of the incompatibility of a proposition's constituents (as in *asinus rationalis*). The notion of *congruitas/incongruitas* is always clearly distinguished from that of *veritas/falsitas*: if we consider that a proposition cannot be true unless it is well formed, it is obvious that there are well-formed propositions that are not true, and that one cannot say of all ill-formed propositions that they are false (since some of them cannot have truth-value).

▪ See Box 3.

Medieval thinkers' reflections on the construction, correctness, completeness, and proper formation of utterances (*orationes*) thus brings into play the great possible options in the analysis of language, since we can take an interest in the utterance itself (with its formal or semantic properties), or in its production (taking into account the speaker's intention), or in its interpretation (considerations on the freedom of the interpreter), the problem then always being to determine whether an ill-formed or uninterpretable utterance is still an utterance, and if only well-formed utterances can be true or false.

III. From "Proposition" to "Utterance": The Competition of Idiolects

Friedrich Ludwig Gottlob Frege played a key role in the constitution of what might be called the modern system of the proposition. At the beginning of his monograph *La norme du vrai* (The norm of truth) on the philosophy of logic, Pascal Engel describes this system as follows: (1) The proposition is what can be true or false, and has a truth-value: truthbearer. (2) The proposition is the meaning of a sentence, and is clearly distinguished from the latter. A sentence is a series of signs, a proposition is what a sentence expresses. (3) The proposition is the content of what is said or conveyed by a certain speech act, what the sentence "does." (4) The proposition is the content of a certain psychological state.

How can so many different senses of the word "proposition" coexist?

A. Frege and his translations—*Satz/Gedanke: Proposition/pensée* (French) or "sentence"/"proposition" (English)?

In his articles "Über Sinn und Bedeutung" (Sense and reference) and "Der Gedanke" (Thought), Frege, after defining the sense and reference of proper names, inquires into "the sense and reference of a whole declarative sentence [*Behauptungssatz*]." Such a sentence, he tells us, "has a thought as its content":

> Wir fragen nun nach Sinn und Bedeutung eines ganzen Behauptungssatzes. Ein solcher Satz enthält einen Gedanken.

> ("Über Sinn und Bedeutung," 32)

Here Frege clearly distinguishes the *Satz*, the "sentence," from the content or thought (*Gedanke*) expressed by this *Satz* (see SENSE, BELIEF). The content or *Gedanke* turns out, later in the text, to be the sense (*Sinn*) of the sentence. Frege emphasizes the objectivity of thought and thus of sense, which can, he says in a famous note, be common properties of several subjects and are thus clearly distinct from the psychological content, like Bernard Bolzano's "proposition in itself" (*Satz an sich: Wissenschaftslehre*, 1.19).

> Ich verstehe unter Gedanken nicht das subjektive Tun des Denkens, sondern dessen objektiven Inhalt, der fähig ist, gemeinsames Eigentum von vielen zu sein.

> By a thought I understand not the subjective performance of thinking but its objective content, which is capable of being the common property of several thinkers.

> ("Thought," in *The Frege Reader*, 156n)

3

Congruitas

> ➤ TRUTH

The word *congruitas* can be rendered rather well by "correctness," "congruence," "proper formation," and *congruus* by "correct, congruent"; we also find Latin (*in*) *competens*. In grammar, *incongruitas* refers essentially to the rules of proper formation, which imply formal marks (agreement) or syntactical characteristics (modes of signifying); in logic, it refers exclusively, or in addition to these first rules of proper formation, to the rules of proper formation that make use of the semantic traits of the constituents. The terms "proper formation" and "well/ill formed" render the two meanings fairly well. Let us note that *constructio congrua* can mean either the correct process of construction, or the result of the process (and, in that case,

constructio can be equivalent to *oratio*). Writers discuss the conformity (*conformitas*) or the nonconformity (*discrepantia*) of accidents and modes of signification; of the compatibility (*convenientia*) or incompatibility (*repugnantia*) of semantic traits; *proprietas* is given a privileged place on the semantic level: an expression is said to be *impropria* if, for example, it includes a term taken in a figurative or inadequate sense (it is not taken in the literal or "proper" sense). *Nugatio* (a term that may have no modern equivalent) refers to improper formation on the semantic level; in its strict sense, it covers pointless semantic redundancies (e.g., *homo animal* [man animal], *homo rationalis* [man endowed with reason], *corvus niger* [black

crow], *homo v*the incompatibilities of the semantic traits of the constituents (e.g., *spero dolorem* [I hope pain], *homo irrationalis* [man without reason]). The term *perfectus* is difficult to translate; the notion of *perfectio*, defined in the twelfth century on the basis of Aristotle's *Metaphysics* Δ.16, 1021b21–25, in Averroës's reading, is well summed up in the adage "*perfectum est cui nihil deest quod ei sit necessarium*" (The perfect is that in which nothing of what is necessary to it is lacking); it covers both completeness and "perfection" (cf. the *perfective* in grammar) in the sense of the English adjective "achieved" (see ASPECT). This double meaning can be rendered by the term "completeness," but not by the corresponding adjective "complete."

In conformity with the philosophical tradition, Claude Imbert, in her translation of Frege's "Über Sinn und Bedeutung," chooses to render *Satz* in French as "proposition." If we compare this translation with English ones, we encounter an interesting problem. In Frege, the *Sinn*, as the objective content of the sentence, is clearly distinguished from the sentence itself. But in the first translations and adoptions in English of the Fregean distinction, it is the objective content of the sentence, the *Gedanke* or *Sinn*, not the sentence (*Satz*) itself but what it signifies, that is rendered by "proposition." Simply translating *Satz* into French as *proposition* can create a difficulty, but translating *Gedanke* into English by "proposition," as is done in this case, raises other, still more serious problems. The translation choices made in the first half of the twentieth century, starting with the spread of the philosophy of language (of which Frege is the founding father), have several consequences for the status of propositions:

1. Propositions are "detached" from sentences as a result of the twofold translation of *Satz*: *Satz* as a sentence (for example, systematically in Rudolf Carnap, first in the English translation of *Logische Syntax der Sprache* [*The Logical Syntax of Language*], and then in *Meaning and Necessity*), and *Satz* as "proposition," understood as the meaning of the sentence or as expressed by the sentence.
2. Propositions are closely connected with meaning (*Sinn*) and thoughts (*Gedanken*), and become abstract, objective entities. These entities are then considered not only as "what is signified," but also as "what is named" by sentences.

The first English translation of the passage from Frege previously cited thus reads: We are now going to inquire into the sense and the nominatum of a whole declarative sentence. Such a sentence [*Satz*] contains a proposition [*Gedanke*].

(Feigl and Sellars, *Readings in Philosophical Analysis*, 89)

The *Satz/Gedanke* pair, which in French becomes *proposition/pensée*, is here translated by "sentence"/"proposition," not without incoherence and difficulty, because in the subsequent sentence we find:

Is this thought [*Gedanke*] to be regarded as the sense [*Sinn*] or the nominatum [*Bedeutung*] of the sentence?

Whereas the note concerning the objectivity of thought is, with a certain lack of appropriateness, translated as:

By proposition [*Gedanke*] I do not refer to the subjective activity of thinking [*Tun des Denkens*], but rather to its objective content.

It is clear that what caught the attention of the translators and philosophers who introduced Frege's thought to the United States in the 1940s was the objective, desubjectivized character of the Fregean *Gedanke*. This led to their reluctance to translate this term by "thought," which it seems impossible to objectivize in this way. But this is perhaps to underestimate the theoretical impact Frege achieved, especially in the

note, by affirming the existence of a thought independent of its bearer and not psychological. The English translation of *Gedanke* by "proposition" might at first seem to jump to conclusions; but far from being audacious, it draws back before the idea of a thought that is not "thought by someone." The shared form of the noun ("thought") and the participle ("it is thought"), which is more obvious in English than in other languages, may play a role here—and it may also be that English-language philosophy finds it especially difficult to integrate an anti-psychologizing mode of thought.

B. *Gedanke,* "proposition" (English), *phrase* (French)

The transposition of *Gedanke* as the English "proposition" allows us to clearly differentiate the proposition both from the mental or psychological act of thinking, and from the sentence, of which the proposition becomes the content or the objective meaning, common not only to different thinkers, but also to different languages. We find a very clear exposition of this double view in Alonzo Church: the proposition (1) is not the particular declarative sentence, but rather the content of meaning that is common to the sentence and its translation into another language, and (2) is not the particular judgment, but the objective content of the judgment, which can be the common property of several people.

The proposition thus turns out to be an abstract proposition, the object designated by the sentence. It will be noted that Bolzano arrived at a similar theoretical result by using a single term, distinguishing between "proposition" (*Satz*) and "proposition in itself" (*Satz an sich*), which does seem to cover the transition from particular sentences to propositions. In such a perspective, the sentence/proposition relation also emerges in the type/token distinction, the proposition being a type of which the different sentences expressing it are occurrences or tokens. That is what seems to be shown by the example, frequently used in this context, of a sentence and its translation (Time flies / *Tempus fugit*) as expressions of a single proposition.

■ See Box 4.

We can see how the notion of proposition, established in such a context, would later be exposed to all of the criticisms aroused by the idea of translation. The passage into a foreign language is in fact crucial in Church's argument regarding propositional attitudes (*Introduction to Mathematical Logic*): if the object of a belief was a sentence, for example, the utterance of a propositional attitude "I believe he is here" would be equivalent to "I believe the sentence 'he is here.'" To translate such statements correctly, we have to consider that it is the proposition qua abstract object, and not the sentence, that is the object of belief or of any other propositional attitude or act; thus there is a radical difference between the token sentence and the abstract proposition.

In "standard" analytical philosophy, beginning in the 1940s, we thus find a basic unit of expression, the sentence, which, when it is endowed with a meaning, expresses a complete thought, and is then defined as a declarative sentence—in which we find the Aristotelian and medieval problematic of the *logos apophantikos* and of completeness. Sentences are conceived (in a reformulation of Frege's theory) as names. This may seem rather unnatural, Church says, insofar as the

4
"Type"/"token" (English), *type/occurrence* (French)

➤ SIGN, SPECIES

The distinction between "type" and "token," invented by the American philosopher C. S. Peirce, plays an essential role in linguistics and in the philosophy of language. A "token" of a sign is a particular, physical occurrence of this sign, whereas its "type" is, depending on the point of view, the class of the actual or possible occurrences of this sign. The token is a specific utterance of a given linguistic expression, itself considered as a type. The expressions themselves can be considered as tokens of a proposition or of a meaning "type," at least according to a certain approach to signification.

The basic text is found in Peirce's *Collected Papers*. Peirce notes that on a page printed in English, one can find "about twenty *the*'s on a page." There are in one sense twenty "the's," and in another sense a single word "the": "There is but one word 'the' in the English language; and it is impossible that this word should lie visibly on a page, for the reason that it is not a Single thing or Single event." It is "such a definitely significant Form" that Peirce defines as a "Type." The individual object or event (a given word, a given line on a page) will be a "Token." The token is thus a "Sign of the Type" and "hence of the object that the Type signifies." The token is an "instance" of the type. There are twenty instances of the type "the" on a page (see Peirce, *Collected Papers*, 4:537 [article written for *The Monist,*1906]).

Peirce's distinction had a remarkable influence on later developments. In a review of Wittgenstein's *Tractatus logico-philosophicus*, F. P. Ramsey noted that the use of *Satz* in the *Tractatus* has an ambiguity that Russell's concept, for example, is lacking, and that could have been avoided by using the type/token distinction (review of the *Tractatus logico-philosophicus*, in *Mind* 32 [1924]: 464–78). The distinction is also adopted in a fertile way in Ogden and Richards's influential book *The Meaning of Meaning* (1923) (see SPEECH ACT, in particular IV.B).

On the linguistic level, we can note that linguistic "types" and "tokens" have different statuses: types belong to "competence," whereas tokens belong to "performance" (see SPEECH ACT).

One of the most interesting extensions of the distinction is found in semantics. The sentence itself (disregarding the debate concerning the proposition) can be considered a type or a token: each time someone utters the sentence "The cat is on the mat," we have a new instance of this type-sentence.

Peirce's distinction also has fertile uses in the philosophy of mind (see SOUL). A distinction is drawn between types and instances of mental states, and this distinction founds "token physicalism"—translated into French by Récanati and Rastier as *physicalisme occasionnel*—a materialist theory according to which the identification of mental states with cerebral states can be established only at the level of instances. "Every instance of a mental state is an instance of a cerebral state, but (according to *physicalisme occasionnel*) that does not mean that a type of mental state can be reduced to a type of cerebral state" (F. Récanati, in RT: *Vocabulaire des sciences cognitives*, s.v. "Type/token").

BIBLIOGRAPHY

Ogden, C. K., and I. A. Richards. *The Meaning of Meaning*. London: Kegan Paul, 1923.
Peirce, C. S. *Collected Papers*. Cambridge, MA: Harvard University Press, 1958.

use of sentences is not in principle to "name something," but to "make an assertion" (ibid., 24). Thus we must distinguish an assertive use and a nonassertive use of sentences. Considering sentences as names, we can inquire into their denotation and meaning. Their denotation is an abstract object, namely, their truth-value (true or false); their meaning is "that which is grasped when we understand the sentence, or . . . that which two sentences in different languages must have in common in order to be correct translations each of the other" (ibid., 25). We can grasp the meaning of a sentence without knowing its denotation (truth-value), but knowing (thanks to its meaning) that it has a truth-value. Then we have this new version of Frege (ibid., 26):

Any concept of truth-value, provided that *being a truth-value* is contained in the concept, and whether or not it is the sense of some actually available sentence in a particular language under consideration, we shall call a proposition, translating thus Frege's *Gedanke*.

We arrive at a radical theory of the proposition as abstraction, entirely detached from the linguistic entity that is the sentence. Church recognizes, lucidly, that this is a characteristic of English, where in nontechnical usage "proposition" has long signified the meaning, not the sentence (ibid.):

This is the happy result of a process which, historically, must have been due in part to sheer confusion between the sentence itself and the *meaning* of the sentence. It provides in English a distinction not easily expressed in other languages, and makes possible a translation of Frege's *Gedanke* which is less misleading than the word "thought."

C. "Proposition-statement" (*Satz*) versus *Tatsache, propositions* versus *faits*

Bertrand Russell uses the word "proposition" in an entirely different sense, far removed from Church's translation of Frege's *Gedanke*, to designate the description of a state of affairs (see SACH-VERHALT). A sentence is associated not only with a meaning, but also with a fact: it is not solely expressive, but also indicative. The denotation of the proposition is seen as a state of affairs, and not a truth-value: its truth-value will be determined by its relation to a state of affairs. In "On Denoting" (1905), Russell rejects the Fregean conception of meaning in order to assert that the only important dimension of a proposition is its "denotation" (see SENSE). He distinguishes between a "verbal expression" and a "proposition" (as a logically structured unit composed of elements). A proposition, just like a verbal expression, has no meaning, only (in certain cases) a denotation that depends on its "denoting phrases" and its logical structure.

■ See Box 5.

5
Real propositions and states of affairs: The current relevance of the medieval debate

Some realist logicians of the fourteenth century acknowledged the existence of "propositions of things" or "real propositions" (*propositio in re*). This theory shifts into reality itself the question of the relation between proposition and reality. In so doing, it anticipates certain modern reflections on the state of things as the denotation of the proposition. In the thirteenth century, the text of Aristotle's *Categories* 14b21–22 was paraphrased as *"res est causa veritatis orationis"* (The *res* is the true cause of the statement), which poses the problem of how to interpret *res*: as an individual thing or as a state of things (see SACHVERHALT). The notion of a "proposition composed of things" seems to have been invented by Gauthier Burley, William of Ockham's main adversary. For Burley, the "ultimate signified" of mental propositions must be something real. Since this can be neither the individual thing supposed by the subject and the predicate, nor—on pain of infinite regress—a "complex of concepts," it can be only a "complex of things"—and it is this composite that he calls a "real proposition": *"Ergo in rebus est aliquod compositum cuius subiectum est res et praedicatum similiter, quod dicitur propositio in re."* Contrary to the nominalists and almost all of his contemporaries, Burley thus distinguished not three but four kinds of proposition: the written proposition (*in scripto*), the oral proposition (*in voce*), the mental proposition (*in mente*)—also called "conceptual" (*in conceptu*)—and the real proposition (*in re*). The point of departure for the theory of the real proposition is Aristotelian: the goal is to determine "what corresponds" in reality to "complex truth," that is, to the "intellectual" combination and separation Aristotle mentions when he defines the true in the logical sense of the term by positing that "he who thinks the separated to be separated and the combined to be combined has the truth" (*Metaphysics* Θ.10, 1051b3–4), or when, in the *Categories* 14b21–22, as translated by Boethius, he posits that *"ex eo quod res est vel non est oratio dicitur esse vera vel falsa"* (From this it follows that whether a proposition is true or not depends on whether the thing is true or not). Burley's originality is to have taken this as a basis for seeking a "truthmaker" in a "reality" seized and rationalized as a "real proposition composed of things." The argument in favor of the real proposition is founded on a principle common to many medieval theories of truth as correspondence: in order for a proposition *in mente*, *in prolatione*, or *in scripto* to be true, "it must really be so, as in the proposition that signifies it [*oportet quod sit in re sicut propositio significat*]." This assertion presupposes another: that *there is something*, in reality, that is such that the proposition signifies it. This "something" is the real proposition, also called a "complex thing" (*res complexa*), a "connected being" (*ens copulatum*), or, more simply, a "composite" (*compositum*). Burley's main theoretical justification is given in his *Middle Commentary* of ca.1310 on the *De interpretatione*: "Res significata per istam 'homo est animal' non dependet ab intellectu nec etiam veritas istius rei; immo ista esset vera etsi nullus intellectus consideraret. Et ista similiter 'Chimaera est Chimaera' esset vera, etsi numquam aliquis intellectus consideraret." If neither the signified nor the truth of a proposition depend on the intellect, that is because what is signified by the proposition is the truthmaker of the proposition, and this signified is a complex reality independent of our activity of thought: a state of things, a fact, or a complex object.

BIBLIOGRAPHY

Burley, Walter. "Walter Burley's Middle Commentary on Aristotle's *Perihermeneias*." Edited by S. Brown. *Franciscan Studies* 33 (1973): 45–134.

Cesalli, Laurent. "Le réalisme propositionnel de Walter Burley." *Archives d'Histoire Littéraire et Doctrinale du Moyen Âge* 68 (2001).

Miverley, Guillaume. *Compendium de quinque universalibus*. In *Johannes Sharpe, Quaestio super universalia*. Edited by Alessandro D. Conti. Florence: L. S. Olschki, 1990.

Pinborg, Jan. "Walter Burleigh on the Meaning of Propositions." In *Medieval Semantics: Selected Studies on Medieval Logic and Grammar*, edited by S. Ebbesen. London: Variorum Reprints, 1984.

A new concept of the *Satz* emerges in Wittgenstein's *Tractatus logico-philosophicus*, which is generally translated into English and French by "proposition": the *Satz* is indissolubly the expression-demonstration of a meaning (and in that way, Fregean) and a depiction (*Abbildung*; see BILD and DESCRIPTION) of a state of affairs (and in that way, Russellian). It is defined as a "perceptible expression of thought":

4.3.1. Im Satz drückt sich der Gedanke sinnlich wahrnehmbar aus.

In a proposition a thought finds an expression that can be perceived by the senses.

We see that Wittgenstein rejects the interpretation of the proposition as an abstract entity, and makes the *Satz* a propositional sign "that can be perceived by the senses [*sinnlich wahrnehmbar*]." He also rejects the idea that a proposition's denotation is a truth-value, without abandoning the connection Frege established between *Gedanke* and *Satz*. The notion of the meaning of the proposition turns out to be central in the *Tractatus*. For Wittgenstein as for Russell, the proposition is a function of components, that is, of expressions (*Ausdrücke*). But for Wittgenstein (and here he differs from Russell), the proposition does not refer to a complex object; it has a meaning (whereas names have only a denotation), which is what we know when we understand a proposition, the state of affairs it depicts. It is in fact a state of affairs (*Sachverhalt*) and not an object that has here the absolute independence that defines logical atomism (Russell). The proposition thus acquires a logical and ontological priority. The *Tractatus* connects sense (*Sinn*) and reference or denotation (*Bedeutung*) in a different way from Frege, by defining the proposition (*Satz*) both by thought (*Gedanke*) and by fact (*Tatsache*).

4.021. Der Satz ist ein Bild der Wirklichkeit: denn ich kenne die von ihm dargestellte Sachlage, wenn ich den Satz verstehe.

A proposition is a picture of reality: for if I understand a proposition, I know the situation that it represents.

4.022. Der Satz zeigt seinen Sinn. Der Satz zeigt, wie es sich verhält, wenn er wahr ist.

A proposition shows its sense. A proposition shows how things stand if it is true.

4.024. Einen Satz verstehen, heisst, wissen was der Fall ist, wenn er wahr ist.

To understand a proposition means to know what is the case if it is true.

D. "Proposition" / "statement" / "sentence"

Understood in this way, the proposition (*Satz*) raises in a new way the question of the relationship to facts, as is shown by the way English translators of *Satz* hesitate between "proposition," "sentence," and "statement." The deployment of the different translations of *Satz* results in a complex table of the "meanings" that the word "proposition" can take in French and English. The proposition (*Satz*) understood as a depiction of a state of affairs, or "saying that," does not name a fact, it *states* it. The proposition should then be called (as it is by J. L. Austin) a statement. A proposition expresses a meaning, it states . . . what? A fact. It is this idea of fact as what is asserted, stated, that can determine, in a minimalist way, truth as correspondence, as is shown by the expression "It is a fact that . . ." A fact, from this point of view, is defined as a true statement (as is shown, according to Austin, by the parallel "to be a truth" / "to be a fact"). Thus a statement is, extending the *Satz*, a problematic notion, falling between the sentence and the fact.

Such a theorization of the statements/facts pair is found in diverse forms in Russell and G. E. Moore. We can, however, inquire into the status of these facts, which are not simple situations, but are also "objective," and ask if they are not subject to certain criticisms formulated with regard to propositions/thoughts understood in Frege's sense. To assert a fact is to make an assertion. To state a proposition is to make an assertion. F. P. Ramsey was one of the first to criticize, in "Facts and Propositions," what he called the "linguistic muddle," which is connected with the idea of truth, but which is also associated with the idea both of the proposition and of fact. To say that a proposition is true, or that it corresponds to the facts, is simply to state that proposition, to make that assertion. Thus there is no need for facts, or propositions, or truth. This "redundancy theory" of Ramsey's (see TRUTH, V.B) has been subjected to a number of criticisms, but its radicality has continued to make it interesting.

It was probably Quine who struck the fatal blow to propositions, and thus to facts. The thesis of the indeterminacy of translation (see TO TRANSLATE, Box 4) already constituted a challenge to the Fregean *Gedanke*, and even to the very notion of meaning itself: there is no entity intermediary between two linguistic expressions that are translated from each other, and that express each other. There are always several possible translations, and indeterminacy. This criticism could be formulated in Quine, as in Ramsey, on the basis of the question of truth, in a passage in the *Philosophy of Logic* that draws attention to a new configuration of the terms "statement," "sentence," "utterance," and "proposition":

> When someone speaks truly, what makes his statement true? We tend to think that there are two factors: meaning and fact.
>
> Quand quelqu'un dit vrai, qu'est-ce qui fait que son assertion est vraie? Nous avons tendance à croire que deux facteurs sont en jeu: la signification et le fait.
>
> (Quine, *Philosophy of Logic*, 1)

It is this tendency that Quine criticizes. If a German utters the declarative sentence "*Der Schnee ist weiss,*" we are tempted to say that his sentence is true by virtue of its meaning (the meaning of the German sentence is that snow is white) and the fact (that snow is white), because "the fact of the matter is that snow is white." But here there is a redundancy or, as Quine puts it, a "philosophical extravagance": Why resort to two elements that are not only identical (they both state that snow is white), but also useless? We have the declarative sentence, and snow is white; why appeal to "intangible intervening elements"? This is a "hollow mockery." Quine's violent objection to propositions (a tendency that, according to him, "cannot be excused") is motivated by the indeterminate status of meanings and the impossibility of establishing and defining a relation of synonymy between sentences.

> Meanings of sentences are exalted as abstract entities in their own right, under the names of propositions. These, not the sentences themselves, are seen as the things that are true or false. These are the things that are known or believed.
>
> (Ibid., 2)

Quine's critique of propositions and facts is accompanied by a linguistic analysis and a justification of his constant choice to speak of sentences and not propositions. French translators of Quine often render "sentence" by *énoncé*, following a well-established usage in French translation of contemporary texts on the philosophy of logic.

> Philosophers' tolerance toward propositions has been encouraged partly by ambiguity in the term "proposition." The term often is used simply for the sentences themselves, declarative sentences. . . . Some philosophers . . . have taken refuge in the term "statement."
>
> (Ibid.)

Or, still more systematically, in a recent translation of a passage that sums up the whole problematic:

> What are true or false, it will be widely agreed, are propositions. But it would not be so widely agreed were it not for the ambiguity of "proposition." Some understand the word as referring to sentences meeting certain specifications. Others understand it as referring rather to the meanings of such sentences. What looked like wide agreement thus resolves into two schools of thought: for the first school the vehicles of truth and falsity are the sentences, and for the second they are the meanings of the sentences. . . . It seems perverse to bypass the visible or audible sentences and to center upon sentence meanings.
>
> (Quine, *Pursuit of Truth*, 77)

It is amusing to note that the French translation, by rendering "sentence" as *énoncé*, makes, by also seeking consensus, the same error as the one pointed out by Quine in the passage itself regarding the consensus choice of "proposition." In French, *énoncé* also introduces an ambiguity, being a kind of intermediary between "sentence" and "statement" (cf. *énoncer que...*). But the use of "statement," as Quine clearly saw, is an "evasive use": "statement" means something different from "sentence," and designates, since coming into use by the Oxford philosophers, an act.

> I gave up the word [statement] in the face of the growing tendency at Oxford to use the word for acts that we perform in uttering declarative sentences. Now by appealing to statements in such a sense, instead of propositions, certainly no clarity is gained.
>
> (Quine, *Philosophy of Logic*, 2)

Thus we must once again examine the new vocabulary targeted here by Quine, which, according to him, perpetuates the mythology of propositions. In reality, we could also maintain that the introduction of the new terms "statement" and "utterance" takes a further step in the critical task (begun by Ramsey and Quine) of abandoning propositions in favor of sentences. The relation of the proposition-type to the sentences-tokens that, according to the traditional doctrine, express it could be set in parallel with the relation of the sentence to its real occurrences (utterances). For ordinary language philosophers, the primary objection to propositions is that a sentence-type can have different truth-values, and of course different meanings, in its different concrete occurrences. It is clear that the theory of performatives and speech acts developed by Austin and later generalized by John Searle poses a radical challenge to these concepts of truth and meaning (see SENSE, SPEECH ACT, TRUTH). We will limit ourselves to a few remarks on the vocabulary designating linguistic units, which becomes more complex here. The proposition/sentence pair, a development of the German *Satz*, becomes a system, sentence-statement-utterance, whose terms are combined in various ways. We have to recognize (cf. Quine's critique) that the notion of "statement" (like that of "utterance"), initially proposed as a minimal term (like French *énoncé*), rapidly acquired, through the theory of speech acts that made use of it, an inevitable theoretical importance. The two terms have been used to indicate the dimension of doing involved first in certain utterances (performatives), and then in all utterances. Of course, this can be seen not as a performative dimension of all utterances, but, trivially, as the action implied in the very fact of making an utterance: the difficulty remains, as we see, to find the term that is as neutral and minimal as possible, and that is what, at least initially, was sought in "statement," "utterance," and *énoncé*. We can see some of these difficulties at the beginning of *How to Do Things with Words*. Austin begins with "statement" to criticize the idea that assertions are always descriptive, and thus the equivalence of statement and proposition:

> It was for too long the assumption of philosophers that the business of a "statement" can only be to "describe" some state of affairs, or to "state some fact."...Not all "sentences" are (used in making) statements.
>
> (*How to Do Things with Words*, 1)

"Statement" is difficult to translate into French. In French it tends to be translated as *affirmation*, which is a problem, just as is *assertion*, because the expression "state a fact" is more natural than *affirmer un fait*, and *a fortiori* is more natural than *asserter un fait*. We can also note the equivalence between "state a fact" and "make a statement," which institutes the connection between statement and fact, but also defines the statement as an action (unlike "sentence" and "proposition"). In a note, Austin adds:

> It is, of course, not really correct that a sentence ever *is* a statement: rather, it is *used* in *making a statement*, and the statement itself is a "logical construction" out of the makings of statements.
>
> (Ibid.)

The difficulty of translating the "makings of statements" indicates the problem: an assertion, like a proposition, is supposed to be an abstraction elaborated on the basis of the tokens constituted by acts of making statements. Moreover, there are utterances (the French translations usually give *énonciations*, which better renders the oral character of the utterance than does *énoncé*; German translates this by *Äußerung*) that are not statements; "many utterances look like statements" but "do not state a fact." These "pseudo-statements" refer and are comparable to the *Scheinsätze* defined by Carnap. The basic unit that includes all the others is thus said to be the utterance.

> We shall take, then, for our first examples some utterances which can fall into no hitherto recognized *grammatical* category save that of "statement."
>
> (Ibid., 4)

The utterances that interest Austin are such that to utter the sentence is not to describe or state, it is to *do* (see SPEECH ACT, IV). This is what defines the "performative," which is short for "performative [or performatory] utterance [or sentence]." Here is established the relation, rather close in Austin, between "utterance" and "sentence." Utterances include sentences, without the difference between them being clearly marked, which attenuates their immediately spoken character (the "speech act"): "What are we to call a sentence or an utterance of this type?" (ibid., 6). "Utter a sentence" and "make [or issue] an utterance" are not very different. "Utterance" makes it possible to play on the verb "to utter" and on constructions like "uttering" and "utterer" (cf. Grice, *Utterer's Meaning*). It is with Austin's definition of the utterance that the idea of the proposition as an entity disappears. There is no longer an object separate from the utterance, so to speak, no type of which it would be the token: what is said is absorbed into the saying, what is said does not exist independent of its occurrence and its utterance.

French has the good fortune of having a basic terminology for this vocabulary, established by Austin himself in the paper he presented at Royaumont in 1958, "Performatif-constatif," which he had written himself in French (the English version, "Performative-Constative," published after his death, was translated by Geoffrey Warnock and is less colorful than the original). Austin uses *énoncé* for "utterance," *assertion* for "statement," and *effectuer* for "perform." We could take our inspiration from these choices, even if *assertion* lacks part of the factual dimension of "statement," and *énoncé* lacks the physical dimension of "utterance." Similarly, Austin himself translated "speech act" into French as *acte de discours*, which seems in fact more adequate than *acte de langage*, which has since been generally adopted.

There are numerous philosophical meanings of the term "proposition" that have been sedimented in various contemporary uses. Defined semantically in terms of true or false, a proposition no longer has any apparent relationship with the *logos-apophansis-logos apophantikos* complex inherited from Aristotle. It is an extra- or translinguistic entity: a sentence is French or Turkish; a proposition is not and cannot be either. An *énoncé*, like a sentence, is always in a language. The French *proposition* (German *Satz*, English "proposition") seeks to transcend this linguistic difference, to define a content of language or an independent thought. This semantic definition of the proposition is rejected by everyone who thinks that it is the sentences of a given language that are true or false—"It is what human beings *say* that is true and false" (Wittgenstein, *Philosophical Investigations*, §241). Others purely and simply reject "propositions," seen as mythical beings subsisting independent of thoughts and sentences (as Russell puts it, "a proposition is only a symbol," "propositions are only sentences in the indicative," "propositions are shadows, they are nothing"). Focusing on the meaning of the word "proposition" (*Satz*, etc.) in modern philosophical texts means being confronted, as we can see, with theories rather than with linguistic fluctuations, and sometimes with a departure from usage. But the constant passage from one language to another allows us to bring out the polysemies and to eliminate the ambiguity from words in languages, as when *protasis* becomes *praemissa* and *propositio*, or *Satz* becomes simultaneously "statement," "utterance," and "sentence."

Marc Baratin
Barbara Cassin
Sandra Laugier
Alain de Libera
Irène Rosier-Catach

BIBLIOGRAPHY

Aristotle. *Aristoteles Latinus*. Volume 2.1. Edited by L. Minio-Paluello. Paris: Desclée de Brouwer, 1965.

———. *Aristoteles Latinus*. Volume 4.1–4. Edited by L. Minio-Paluello and B. G. Dod. Paris: Desclée de Brouwer, 1968.

———. *Aristoteles: Zweite Analytiken*. Translated by H. Seidl. Amsterdam, Neth.: Rodopi, 1984.

———. *Aristotle's Posterior Analytics*. Translated by Jonathan Barnes. Oxford: Clarendon, 1975.

———. *Categories and On Interpretation*. Translated by J. L. Ackrill. Oxford: Clarendon, 1963.

———. *Della interpretazione*. Translated by M. Zanatta. Milan: Rizzoli, 1992.

———. *Kategorien: Lehre vom Satz*. Translated by E. Rolfes. Hamburg: Felix Meiner, 1925. 2nd ed., 1958.

———. *Organon*. Translated by J. Tricot. 6 vols. Paris: Vrin, 1950–69.

Austin, John L. *How to Do Things with Words*. Oxford: Clarendon, 1962.

———. "Performative-Constative." Translated by Geoffrey Warnock. In *The Philosophy of Language*, edited by John R. Searle, 13–22. London: Oxford University Press, 1971.

———. *Philosophical Papers*. Oxford: Clarendon, 1962.

———. *The Philosophy of Language*. Edited by John R. Searle. London: Oxford University Press, 1971.

Ayer, Alfred J. *Language, Truth and Logic*. London: Gollancz, 1953.

Baratin, Marc. *La naissance de la syntaxe à Rome*. Paris: Minuit, 1989.

Bar-Hillel, Yehoshua. "Universal Semantics and Philosophy of Language." In *Substance and Structure of Language*, edited by Jaan Puhvel. Berkeley: University of California Press, 1969.

Benmakhlouf, Ali. *Bertrand Russell: L'atomisme logique*. Paris: Presses Universitaires de France, 1996.

Bolzano, Bernard. *Wissenschaftslehre*. Sulzbach, Ger.: Seidel, 1837. Translation by Rolf George: *Theory of Science*. Edited by Rolf George. Oxford: Oxford University Press, 1972.

Brinkley, Richard. *Richard Brinkley's Theory of Sentential Reference: "De significato propositionis" from Part V of His* Summa nova de logica. Translated and edited by Michael J. Fitzgerald. Leiden, Neth.: Brill, 1987.

Burley, Walter. *Commentarius in librum Perihermeneias Aristoteles*. In "Walter Burley's Middle Commentary on Aristotle's *Perihermeneias*," edited by S. Brown. *Franciscan Studies* 33 (1973): 45–134.

Carnap, Rudolf. *The Logical Syntax of Language*. Translated by Amethe Smeaton. London: Kegan Paul, 1937.

———. *Meaning and Necessity*. Chicago, IL: University of Chicago Press, 1956.

———. "Überwindung der Metaphysik durch logische Analyse der Sprache." *Erkenntnis* 2 (1932): 219–41. Translation by A. Pap: "The Elimination of Metaphysics through Logical Analysis of Language." In *Logical Positivism*, edited by A. J. Ayer. New York: Free Press, 1959.

Church, Alonzo. *Introduction to Mathematical Logic*. Vol. 1. Princeton, NJ: Princeton University Press, 1956.

Colloque philosophique de Royaumont. *La philosophie analytique*. Paris: Éditions de Minuit, 1962.

De Rijk, Lambertus Maria, ed. *Logica modernorum*. Vol. 2.1, *The Origin and Early Development of the Theory of Supposition*. Assen, Neth.: Van Gorcum, 1967.

Dummet, Michael. *Frege's Philosophy of Language*. London: Duckworth, 1973.

Ebbesen, Sten. "The Present King of France Wears Hypothetical Shoes with Categorical Laces: Twelfth-Century Writers on Well-Formedness." *Medioevo* (1982): 91–113.

Élie, Hubert. *Le signifiable par complexe: La proposition et son objet: Grégoire de Rimini, Meinong, Russell*. Paris: Vrin, 2000. Originally published ca. 1937.

Engel, Pascal. *La norme du vrai*. Paris: Gallimard, 1989.

Feigl, Herbert, and Wilfrid Sellars, eds. *Readings in Philosophical Analysis*. New York: Appleton Century-Crofts, 1949.

Frege, Gottlob. *The Frege Reader*. Edited by M. Beaney. Oxford: Wiley-Blackwell, 1997.

———. *Nachgelassene Schriften*. Edited by H. Hermes, F. Kambartel, and F. Kaulbach. Hamburg: Felix Meiner, 1969. Translation by P. Long and R. White: *Posthumous Writings*. Chicago, IL: University of Chicago Press, 1979.

———. *Translations from the Philosophical Writings of Gottlob Frege*. Edited and translated by P. Geach and M. Black. 3rd ed. Oxford: Blackwell, 1980.

———. "Über Sinn und Bedeutung." *Zeitschrift für Philosophie und Philosophische Kritik* 100 (1892). French translation by Claude Imbert: *Écrits logiques et philosophiques*. Paris: Seuil, 1971.

Gochet, Paul. *Esquisse d'une théorie nominaliste de la proposition*. Paris: A. Colin, 1972.

Grice, H. P. "Utterer's Meaning and Intentions." *Philosophical Review* 78 (1969). Reprinted as chap. 5 in *Studies in the Way of Words*. Cambridge, MA: Harvard University Press, 1989.

Hyder, David. *The Mechanics of Meaning: Propositional Content and the Logical Space of Wittgenstein's Tractatus*. Berlin: De Gruyter, 2002.

Katz, Jerrold. *Propositional Structure and Illocutionary Force: A Study of the Contribution of Sentence Meaning to Speech Acts*. New York: Crowell, 1977.

Kneepkens, C. H. "On Medieval Syntactic Thought with Special Reference to the Notion of Construction." *Histoire Épistémologie Langage* 12, no. 2 (1990): 139–76.

Lambert of Auxerre. *Logica*. Edited by Franco Alessio. Florence: La Nuova Italia, 1971.

Laugier, Sandra. *L'anthropologie logique du Quine*. Paris: Vrin, 1992.

———. "Frege et le mythe de la signification." In *Phénoménologie et logique*, edited by Jean-François Courtine. Paris: Presses de l'École normale supérieure, 1996.

Libera, Alain de. "Roger Bacon et la référence vide: Sur quelques antécédents médiévaux du paraoxe de Meinong." In *Lectionum varietates, Hommage à Paul Vignaux*, edited by J. Jolivet et al., 85–120. Paris: Vrin, 1991.

———. *La référence vide: Théories de la proposition*. Paris: Presses Universitaires de France, 2002.

Libera, Alain de, and Irène Rosier. "Les enjeux logico-linguistiques de l'analyse de la formule de la consécration eucharistique." *Cahiers de l'Institut du Moyen Âge Grec et Latin* 67 (1997): 33–77.

Nuchelmans, Gabriel. *Theories of the Proposition: Ancient and Medieval Conceptions of the Bearers of Truth and Falsity*. Amsterdam, Neth.: North-Holland, 1973.

Perler, Dominik. *Der Propositionale Wahrheitsbegriff im 14. Jahrhundert*. Berlin: De Gruyter, 1992.

Pinkster, Harm. *Latin Syntax and Semantics*. London: Routledge, 1990.

Pitcher, George, ed. *Truth*. Englewood Cliffs, NJ: Prentice-Hall, 1964.

Prior, A. N. *The Doctrine of Propositions and Terms*. Edited by P. T. Geach and A.J.P. Kenny. London: Duckworth, 1976.

Quine, W.V.O. *From a Logical Point of View*. Cambridge, MA: Harvard University Press, 1953.

———. *Philosophy of Logic*. Englewood Cliffs, NJ: Prentice Hall, 1970.

———. *Pursuit of Truth*. Cambridge, MA: Harvard University Press 1990.

———. "Russell's Ontological Argument." In *Essays on Bertrand Russell*, edited by E. D. Klemke. Urbana: University of Illinois Press, 1971.

———. *Word and Object*. Cambridge, MA: MIT Press, 1960.

Ramsey, Frank P. "Facts and Propositions." *Proceedings of the Aristotelian Society*, supp. vol. 7 (1927): 153–70.

———. *The Foundations of Mathematics and Other Logical Essays*. Edited by R. B. Braithwaite, with a preface by G. E. Moore. London: Routledge and Kegan Paul, 1965.

Recanati, François. *La transparence et l'énonciation*. Paris: Seuil, 1978.

Rosier, Irène. "La définition de Priscien de l'énoncé: Les enjeux théoriques d'une variante, selon les commentateurs médiévaux." In *Grammaire et l'histoire de la grammaire: Mélanges à la mémoire de Jean Stefanini*, edited by Claire Blanche-Benveniste, André Chervel, and Maurice Gross, 353–73. Aix-en Provence, Fr.: Université de Provence, 1988.

Russell, Bertrand. *My Philosophical Development*. London: Routledge, 1955.

Searle, John R. *Speech Acts*. London: Cambridge University Press, 1969.

Sherwood, William, fl. *Introductiones in logicam*. Edited by Charles H. Lohr. *Traditio* 39. Also published in *William of Sherwood's Introduction to Logic*. Translated with an introduction and notes by Norman Kretzmann. Minneapolis: University of Minnesota Press, 1966.

Wittgenstein, Ludwig. *Philosophical Investigations: Fiftieth Anniversary Commemorative Edition*. Translated by G.E.M. Anscombe. Oxford: Wiley-Blackwell, 2001.

———. *Tractatus logico-philosophicus*. Translated by D. F. Pears and B. F. McGuiness. London: Routledge and Kegan Paul, 1974.

PROPOSITIONAL CONTENT

This is one of the possible translations of the German *Sachverhalt*, which in everyday language designates the "facts of the case." But this translation emphasizes the propositional formulation of the object of judgment at the expense of the properties of the objects of experience. The other, no less frequent translation as "state of affairs" suffers from the inverse defect. See SACHVERHALT.

Here we are dealing with a logical terminology connected with the greatest questions (the relation thing-word-mind and the definition of truth), which makes the transition from a medieval Latin term (DICTUM) that emerged from Stoicism in its competition with Aristotelianism (see *lekton* [λεκτόν] under SIGNIFIER/SIGNIFIED, II) to the German of the late nineteenth century and early twentieth century, which

opens onto contemporary English and American analytic philosophy, and for which French produces descriptive translations that make the problem obvious.

See, on the one hand, DICTUM, INTENTION, PROPOSITION, SENSE; on the other hand, ERSCHEINUNG, *FACT*, GEGENSTAND, *IL Y A*, MATTER OF FACT, OBJECT, TATSACHE, *THING* [RES], *TO BE*; finally, TRUTH.

➤ *STATE OF AFFAIRS*

PRUDENCE

"Prudence" derives from the Latin *prudentia*, in which Cicero still heard *providentia*, the "foresight" that characterizes "providence." The Latin word, which was connected with a civilization based on law (*jurisprudentia*; see LEX, II.B), seeks to render the Greek *phronêsis* [φρόνησις], which designates practical wisdom, both intellectual (*phronein* [φρονεῖν], "to think," *phrenes* [φρένες], "lungs"; cf. SOUL, Box 3 and cf. *HEART*) and moral: see PHRONÊSIS for an exploration of the interpretations and translations of this key term in the various linguistic systems (in particular, German *Klugheit*). See MORALS, *VIRTUE, WISDOM*. Cf. LOGOS, MÊTIS, UNDERSTANDING.

The term has been reinvested in contemporary English, with prudential ethics connected to economics: see PRUDENTIAL; cf. MORAL SENSE, RIGHT/JUST/GOOD, UTILITY.

➤ DUTY, ECONOMY, GLÜCK, INGENIUM, *SENS COMMUN, VALUE*

PRUDENTIAL / PRUDENCE

FRENCH	*prudentiel, prudence*
GERMAN	*Klugheit*
GREEK	*phronêsis* [φρόνησις]
LATIN	*prudentia*

➤ *PRUDENCE* [PHRONÊSIS], *WISDOM*, and ECONOMY, FAIR, OIKONOMIA, PLEASURE, PRAXIS, UTILITY, VIRTÙ, WUNSCH

The adjective "prudential" does not present any genuine translation problem. But in relation to the introduction into contemporary philosophical language of this technical term borrowed from economics, it is interesting to inquire into the connection between this term and its philosophical ancestors. What contemporary exponents (mainly English speaking) of rational choice theory understand by "prudential" too easily assumes that the dilemmas regarding the nature of practical reason have been resolved, in the sense in which the great classical conceptions of *phronêsis* and *prudentia*, from Aristotle and Cicero to Kant and Sidgwick, tried to understand it. These dilemmas are still being debated by writers who, even when they draw on both traditions, try, like James Griffin, to reevaluate the relations between prudential virtues and ethics or to derive all of ethics from prudential reason, like David Gauthier or John Rawls in his early work.

I. From the Reason for Acting to Self-Interest and Anticipation

Philosophers used to understand the notion of prudence in three dimensions. In the first place, it was understood as providing reasons for acting that, while not necessarily being moral in the sense of the categorical imperative of duty, are nonetheless good reasons. Here, "good" means what enables us to realize maximally our essence (Kant) or our happiness (the utilitarians). Prudence, Kant writes, is "skill in the choice of means to one's own highest welfare" (*Foundations of the Metaphysics of Morals*, §2). Because of this relationship to happiness, prudential reason is distinguished from instrumental reason or technics, whose end, in the Kantian vocabulary, is not real but only possible (the imperative of prudence, *Klugheit*, is an assertive hypothetical and not a problematic one). In a second sense, the domain peculiar to prudence is limited to self-interest. The whole difficulty proceeds from how this limit is interpreted: is it selfishness or self-esteem that takes the Other equally into consideration? Sidgwick asks whether the imperatives of prudence are compatible with the utilitarian maxim of rational good will or with the axiom of justice or equity, and this indicates that the question is far from being resolved (*Methods of Ethics*). The third characteristic of the notion resides in its relation to temporality. Prudence is the contrary of the kind of short-term, irrational thinking that Mill calls "expediency" (*Utilitarianism*). It presupposes a capacity for rational anticipation, complex modes of reasoning to evaluate one decision in relation to another—for example, an immediate advantage in relation to one that is greater but more distant. We must not forget that the Latin *prudentia* comes from *providentia*, that is, "foresight."

II. The Rational Agent's Interests

In the technical sense conveyed by the term "prudential," we see shifts taking place in the three directions we have indicated. First, we as ideal rational agents on whom economic theories are based are interested solely in maximizing our utility, that is, our expressed preferences, and not our happiness, a notion that has been abandoned on the grounds that it is too "normative." The conception of the growth of a pleasant state of mind is replaced by the economics of welfare; pleasure or happiness is replaced by the satisfaction of desires or preferences, even if we do not always desire what makes us happy. Second, in accord with methodological individualism, we as rational agents are interested only in our own satisfaction; the Other is taken into account only in estimating the chances of succeeding in negotiating or threatening. We are in an individualist, conflictual model in which cooperation is chosen only because it will maximize our chances (the prisoner's dilemma). The self-contradictions of self-love and self-esteem are eliminated. Finally, as Jean-Pierre Dupuy ("Prudence et rationalité") rightly points out, the economic model's conception of temporality reverses the flow of time in the sense that arguments are made on the basis of what would have happened if decision X had been made earlier, leading to a result that will never occur, because in the meantime we will have taken care to make a more advantageous decision.

Catherine Audard

BIBLIOGRAPHY

Aristotle. *Nicomachean Ethics.* Books 2–4. Translated with an introduction and commentary by C. Taylor. Oxford: Oxford University Press, 2006.

———. *Nicomachean Ethics.* Books 8 and 9. Translated with a commentary by M. Pakaluk. Oxford: Oxford University Press, 1999.

Dupuy, Jean-Pierre. "Prudence et rationalité." In *Une prudence moderne?* Edited by P. Raynaud and S. Rials. Paris: Presses Universitaires de France, 1992.

Gauthier, David. *Morals by Agreement.* Oxford: Clarendon Press, 1986.

Griffin, James. *Well-Being.* Oxford: Clarendon Press, 1986.

Hariman, Robert, ed. *Prudence: Classical Virtue, Postmodern Practice.* University Park: Pennsylvania State University Press, 2003.

Kant, Immanuel. *Foundations of the Metaphysics of Morals.* Translated by L. W. Beck. Indianapolis, IN: Bobbs-Merrill, 1959.

———. *Groundwork of the Metaphysics of Morals.* Translated by Mary McGregor. Cambridge: Cambridge University Press, 1997.

Mill, John Stuart. *Utilitarianism.* 2nd ed. Edited by G. Sher. Indianapolis, IN: Hackett, 2000.

Rawls, John. *A Theory of Justice.* Cambridge, MA: Harvard University Press, 1971.

Sidgwick, Henry. *The Methods of Ethics.* 7th ed. London: Hackett, 1981.

Q

QUALE, QUALIA

FRENCH *quale, qualia*
GERMAN *Quale, Qualia*
LATIN   *quale, qualia*

► CONSCIOUSNESS, ERLEBEN, PERCEPTION, PROPERTY, REPRÉSENTATION, SOUL, SUBJECT

The term "quale" (plural "qualia") refers to the qualitative properties of experience insofar as they elicit in the subject the experience of a distinctive impression. This blue that I perceive, this pain felt, this coffee fragrance, are "qualia."

Since the middle of the twentieth century several words have been competing as designations of these properties: they have been called "subjective qualities" or "sensuous qualities," "phenomenal properties" or "phenomenological properties," or even immediate impressions ("raw feels"; see Herbert Feigl's 1967 book *The Mental and the Physical*). The Latin word prevailed in English-language philosophy, and has been adopted in German and French translations, probably because of the symmetry with the *quantum/ quanta* pair, one representing a qualitative differential, the other a quantitative differential.

In many uses of the term, "qualia" refers to singular events, such as the manifestation of a pain at a given moment (Casati, "Qualia") or to instantiated (that is, nonrepeatable) singular properties (this way of suffering here and now being necessarily different from all others). Other uses of "qualia" refer to general properties of such events (for example, the intensity or the type of pain). In this use, the concept of "quale" does not coincide with the notion of secondary quality: the term can be applied to primary qualities such as forms as well as to secondary qualities such as colors, because, for example, one can have an objective experience of "seeing" a square form (different from the experience of "touching" a square surface).

The word "quale" cannot be used interchangeably with the term "sensation" insofar as, unlike a sensation, a quale cannot be treated in a quantitative or relational manner. Moreover, the word can be applied to data that are not strictly sensorial, such as the impression of knowing or that of imagining: some philosophers maintain that mental states of the propositional type (such as believing that P or desiring that Q) also give rise to qualia that are at the origin of the subject's understanding of what the mental state in question is.

It seems indisputable, at least at first sight, that some of our mental states have qualia in the sense that they give rise to a distinctive qualitative impression. It is often thought that conceding this point amounts to recognizing that there are facts to which subjects have a privileged epistemic access, and which they can know in an infallible way, or at least with an exclusive authority. But how can we explain the privileged status of the access enjoyed by subject of the experience relative to the knowledge of corresponding objective properties such as temperature, form, and length, which is in each case eminently subject to error?

One of the ways of responding to this difficulty consists in treating qualia as a domain that cannot be reduced to any physicalist approach (Chalmers, *The Conscious Mind*). The quale thus becomes a weapon in a dualist argumentative apparatus. The other way consists in maintaining, inversely, that the existence of qualia does not threaten the monist materialist conception of the world, while at the same time recognizing that a functionalist explanation (that is, an analysis based on the causal relations between an object giving rise to qualia and the subject's dispositions to believe or to act) cannot be given for qualia. It is, in fact, emphasized that qualia are by nature "intrinsic" properties that cannot be explained by a differential and relational approach. One of the ways of showing this is to imagine that a subject has a deviant experience of color in which the colors of the spectrum are reversed. Given that language learning is not affected by the intrinsic characteristics of experience, the anomaly of this subject's qualia could not be discerned by someone else, or detected by a relational analysis of the functionalist type (Block and Fodor, "What Psychological States Are Not"). Similarly, no one could discover the anomaly of a subject who was totally deprived of qualia but who gave the same verbal and behavioral responses as a subject capable of qualitative experience.

A final argument draws from the discovery of qualia the proof of functionalism's incompleteness as a theory of the mental. Let us imagine that a subject named Mary has lived in a black-and-white world but has learned everything one can know about the perception of colors. Let us further suppose that one day Mary emerges from this colorless world and sees a red object: it seems indisputable that Mary thus discovers a new fact. We must therefore conclude that the functionalist analysis does not offer a complete explanation of mental events (Jackson, "What Mary Did Not Know").

These arguments led adversaries of dualism to make numerous attempts to show either that a nonfunctionalist explanation of qualia is possible (for example, by studying the properties of the neurons that implement them), or that qualia are the object of practical knowledge and not of conceptual knowledge; or, finally, that qualia are a myth of which science must rid itself (Dennett, "Quining Qualia"; Tye, *The Imagery Debate*).

Joëlle Proust

BIBLIOGRAPHY

Block, Ned, and Jerry Fodor. "What Psychological States Are Not." *Philosophical Review* (1972): 159–81.

Casati, Roberto. "Qualia." In *Vocabulaire de sciences cognitives*, edited by O. Houdé, D. Kayser, O. Koenig, J. Proust, and F. Rastier. Paris: Presses Universitaires de France, 1998.

Chalmers, David. *The Conscious Mind*. Oxford: Oxford University Press, 1996.

Clémentz, François. "Qualia et contenus perceptifs." pp. 21–56 in *Percepion et Inter-modalité. Approches actuelles de la question de Molyneux*, edited by Joëlle Proust. Paris: Presses Universitaires de France, 1997.

Dennett, Daniel. "Quining Qualia." pp. 42–77 in *Consciousness and Contemporary Science*, edited by A. Marcel and E. Bisiach. Oxford: Oxford University Press, 1988.

Jackson, Frank. "What Mary Did Not Know." *Journal of Philosophy* 83 (1986): 291–95.

Shoemaker, S. "A Case for Qualia." In *Contemporary Debates in Philosophy of Mind*, edited by Brian McLaughlin and Jonathan Cohen. Oxford: Blackwell, 2007.

Tye, Michael. *Ten Problems of Consciousness*. Cambridge, MA: MIT Press, 1995.

QUIDDITY

"Quiddity" is a technical termed modeled on the Scholastic Latin *quidditas* (*quiditas*) and translating the Aristotelian *to ti ên einai* [τὸ τί ἦν εἶναι] (we also find a Latin calque, which is purely descriptive and grammatically ill formed: *quod quid erat esse*): see TO TI ÊN EINAI and ESTI, SEIN, *TO BE*. The term *quidditas* was introduced by Latin translations of Avicenna's *Metaphysics*. It was later overdetermined as a response to the question *quid sit* (what is?), as opposed to the question *an sit* (is it?), which is said to have produced *anitas*, a word that soon disappeared. While quiddity refers to the essence as it is articulated in the definition, the *anitas* refers to existence, or rather to the *quod est*, "what it is." See ESSENCE, OMNITUDO REALITATIS, and cf. PREDICATION, REALITY, RES.

➤ *ACT, IL Y A*, SPECIES

R

REALITY

FRENCH	*réalité*
GERMAN	*Realität, Wirklichkeit, Wesenheit, Sachheit*
ITALIAN	*realtà, realtà effettiva, effettualità*
LATIN	*realitas, actualitas, forma, formalitas, entitas,*
	entitas quidditativa
SPANISH	*realidad, efectividad*

➤ *ACT*, ATTUALITÀ, ERSCHEINUNG, ESSENCE, *FICTION*, GEGENSTAND, OBJECT, SACHVERHALT, TATSACHE, *THING* [RES], *TO BE*, TO TI ÊN EINAI, TRUTH

The term *realitas*, a neologism coined by Duns Scotus, does not pose translation problems as such, and it was easily transcribed into European languages. On the other hand, the conceptual identity that it posits between "reality," "formality," "quiddity," and "internal possibility" leads—over the long term, even after Kant—to a complete redistribution of the ontological vocabulary; thus we find, depending on the traditions, which sometimes overlap in the same author, the equivalence of reality and the quidditive content (*Sachheit*) and also the association of reality with factuality, or even of reality with actuality. Thus German academic metaphysics, faithful to Duns Scotus's and Suárez's reforms, retranslated the vocabulary of actuality (*actualitas, esse in actu*) into the register of objective reality (*Wirklichkeit*) to the point of creating a pseudo-doublet: *Realität/Wirklichkeit*.

Whereas in most European languages, even if to very different degrees, the term "reality" is characterized by an apparently irreducible ambiguity between essence and existence. The few historical itineraries proposed here allow us to illuminate some inflections and to avoid some misinterpretations produced by a retrospective reading.

I. Duns Scotus's Inventions of *Realitas*

In its first, Scholastic meaning, the term *realitas* was not associated with the adjective *realis* or the expression *esse reale*, in the sense of what exists as posited outside its causes, but instead with *res*, understood in its broadest sense. Thus it was a technical term and an abstract notion that designated precisely the essence, or rather the essentiality, of the *res* as such in abstraction from existence. It was, it seems, starting with Henry of Ghent and especially Duns Scotus that the term *realitas* appeared in the Scotist tradition. Its meaning was initially defined in the context of the doctrine of formalities, that is, of the traits or "notes" constitutive of a determinate essence. Although *formalitas* is not itself a *res*, it nonetheless corresponds to a reality; that is, to a unitary and consistent determination that can be objectively apprehended by the mind (the *entitas quidditativa* that classical German philosophy rendered by *Wesenheit*, "essence," or rather, "essentiality"), thus helping to make explicit an essence or a quiddity (Duns Scotus, *Ordinatio* 3, dist. 22, n. 5,

in *Opera omnia*; see TO TI ÊN EINAI). Of course, the *realitates* or *formalitates* have no separate existence and thus no defined ontological status; they subsist only in and through the *res* (thus *realitates* are always *realitates rei*), from which, however, they are distinguished formally *a parte rei*. Thus they provide the foundation for a "real" distinction (i.e., of one thing in relation to another); in other words, for a distinction that is neither actual nor potential, but only virtual or merely formal.

■ See Box 1.

In the Scotist tradition, *realitas* is thus a term broader than *res* and has an indifferent ontological status with respect to objective reality. Reality or formality is in fact independent of the intellect:

> Et ideo potest concedi quod ante omnem actum intellectus est realitas essentiae qua est communicabilis, et realitas suppositi qua suppositum est incommunicabile; et ante actum intellectus haec realitas formaliter non est illa.

> (And we can thus grant that anterior to any act of intellect there is the reality of the essence, through which it is communicable, and the reality of the subject through which the subject is non-communicable; and that anterior to the act of intellect, this latter reality is not formally the former [reality].)

> (Duns Scotus, *Ordinatio* 1, dist. 2, pt. 2, qu. 1–4, n. 403,
> in *Opera omnia*, 2:357)

Understood in this way, reality is radically separated from the *fictum*, or the rational entity, and far from being purely and simply conflated with the *res*, it is composed of formal notes (*formalitates*) or reasons (*rationes*) that distinctly constitute the complete essence of the *res*, considered as such, in the multiplicity of its aspects or its intelligible determinations:

> Quodlibet commune et tamen determinabile, adhuc potest distingui, quantumcumque sit una res, in plures realitates formaliter distinctas, quarum haec non est illa.

> (Everything that is common and yet determinable can, however, be distinguished, insofar as it is a thing, into several formally distinct realities, one of which is not the other.)

> (Duns Scotus, *Ordinatio* 2,
> dist. 3, qu. 6, n. 15, in *Opera omnia*)

The *res positiva* thus is initially not the individual and singular reality posited *extra intellectum* (outside the intellect, in the nature of things), but rather what is presented to the mind as a *realitas*; that is, as a mental content (*Sachbestand*)

1

Res essentialis vs. *realitas actualis*: The reformulation of the distinction between essence and existence in Petrus Aureolus

The use of *realitas* as a synonym of *entitas* or *formalitas* is much more doctrinal (in conformity with Scotist hyperrealism) than lexical, and this is shown especially by an author like Petrus Aureolus, who was often close to Duns Scotus but did not hesitate to criticize him severely. When, in his *Commentary on the Sentences* (*Scriptum*, dist. 8, qu. 21), he takes up the question whether there is a real distinction between essence and existence—a question whose classical formulation had been established by Giles of Rome—Petrus Aureolus can propose the apparently Scotist thesis that "no thing really differs from its reality. If it did differ, it would already be another reality, and thus not its own" (nulla res differt realiter a sua realitate. Si enim differt, jam est alia realitas, et per consequens non sua; *Scriptum*, dist. 8, qu. 21, n. 60); the term *realitas*, which can be understood in the sense of *realitas essentiae* or *res essentialis*, actually has a quite different meaning, quite close to what we would now call "objective reality" (*realitas actualis*). In a long and complex argument, initially intended to show negatively that it is not possible to distinguish between being and essence, Petrus Aureolus illustrates his thesis ("esse lapidis est sua realitas" [he being of a stone is its reality]), drawing on a demonstration *ad absurdum* from which the ambiguity inherent in the neologism *realitas* clearly emerges: on the one hand, the formality constitutive of an essence or a nature, which can be grasped in its indifference with respect to existence, or rather in comparison with

haecceitas (*Ordinatio* 2, dist. 3, pt. 1, qu. 5–6, n. 187, in Duns Scotus, *Opera omnia*, 7:483), and on the other hand, the objective existence of an actual "reality":

> Et si dicatur quod res sumitur dupliciter, uno modo pro re essentiali — et sic non est verum quod esse lapidis sit sua realitas—, vel pro realitate actuali, et sic est verum ; unde in lapide actualiter existente sunt duae realitates, una quidem essentialis puta lapiditas, et alia accidentalis puta actualitas; siquidem hoc non valet, quoniam realitas essentialis lapidis aut habet quod sit realitas ex ipso esse, aut habet seipsa et sine esse. Si habet sine esse quod sit realitas extra nihil et in rerum natura, ergo res sine esse potest esse extra nihil et in rerum natura ; quod est contradictio. Si vero habet quod sit realitas non a se sed per esse, aut esse imprimit suam realitatem et ita erit efficiens et imprimens, quod est impossibile; aut non imprimit suam realitatem sed eandem communicat, et tunc habetur propositum quod esse est realitas essentiae, indifferens ab ea.

> (And if it is said that the term "thing" is taken in two senses: on the one hand, in the sense of an essential thing—and then it is not true that the being of a stone is its reality—, and on the other hand, in the sense of actual reality, then it is true; it follows that in the stone actually existing, there are two realities, one essential, namely stoniness, and the other accidental, namely actuality;

yet the inference is not valid because either the essential reality of the stone is such that it is reality on the basis of the being itself, or it is reality in itself and independently of being. If it is possible that independently of being, it is a reality, outside of nothing and [posited] in the nature of things, then the thing will be able to be outside of nothing and in the nature of things, independently of being, which implies a contradiction. But if it is such that it is reality not by itself, but thanks to being, then either being shapes its reality and will be an efficient and shaping cause, which is impossible, or it does not shape its reality, but communicates it, and in this case we arrive at the thesis sought, namely that being is the reality of essence, and not different from the latter.)

> (*Scriptum*, dist. 3, §14, n. 31–32)

Given the difficulty of such a passage and its translation, we can easily gauge the importance of the conceptual re-elaboration that affects the terms "reality," "being," and "actuality" here, which are likely to shift to the side of essence or of existence that will be qualified precisely as "actual."

BIBLIOGRAPHY

Aureolus, Petrus. *Scriptum super primum Sententiarum*. Edited by Elgius M. Buytaert. St. Bonaventure, NY: Franciscan Institute, 1956.

Duns Scotus, John. *Opera omnia*. Vatican City: Typis Polyglottis Vaticanis, 1950–.

whose own content and internal rigor suffice to distinguish it essentially from the *res ficta*, or chimera. This elaboration of the Scotist doctrine of the *realitas* was doubtless carried out through Henry of Ghent's analysis of the *ens ratum* (*Quodlibet* 9, qu. 3, in corp., in *Opera omnia*) and led to a new determination of *ratitudo* (*Ordinatio* 1, dist. 36, qu. 1, n. 48, in *Opera omnia*, 6:290). (See RES, Box 3.)

The *res* understood *a ratitudine* thus designates a quidditative reality (*realitas quidditativa*) heir to Avicenna's essence or common nature ("equinitas est equinitas tantum" [equineness is nothing other than equineness]; *Metaphysics*, vol. 5, chap. 1) and distinct from both fiction and objective, or actual, reality (*realitas actualis existentiae*)—the reality that is already defined, before Kant, as posited. Thus Duns Scotus, by apprehending reality as formality, seeks to move beyond the negative determination, which is too broad, that Henry of Ghent gave of it, simply by opposing it to the *purum nihil*:

Sciendum quod omnium communissimum omnia continens in quodam ambitu analogo est res sive aliquid sic consideratum ut nihil sit ei oppositum, nisi purum nihil, quod nec est, nec natum est esse in re extra intellectum, neque etiam in conceptu alicujus intellectus, quia nihil est natum movere intellectum nisi habens rationem alicujus realitatis.

(It must be known that what is most common, including everything in itself, in accord with an analogous circle, is the thing or the some-thing, considered in such a way that nothing is opposed to it except pure and simple nothingness, which is not and cannot be outside the intellect, in the nature of things, and which is not in the concept of some understanding, either, because nothing is apt to set the understanding in movement except what has the reason of some reality.)

(Duns Scotus, *Quodlibet* 7, 1, in *Opera omnia*)

According to this same Scotist logic, the *entitas individuans*, or even the *proprietas individui*, which constitutes the *haecceitas* (the "thisness") of every singular being, will ultimately be defined as *realitas*, and even as *ultima realitas entis*.

II. The Influence of Duns Scotus on the Classical Age

Down to Bolzano and Peirce, the influence of this Scotist usage was considerable: we find a very clear testimony to this in the seventeenth century, in Micraelius's *Lexicon philosophicum terminorum philosophis usitatorum* (col. 1203–5):

> Realitas est aliquid in re. Ideoque in unaquaque re possunt multas realitates poni. . . . Realitates interim distinguendae sunt a re, in qua sunt. Sic in homine est realitas rationalitatis, animalitatis, substantialitatis.

> (Reality is something in the thing. So that in each thing several realities may be posited. . . . The realities must be distinguished from the thing in which they are. Thus the reality of rationality, animality, and substantiality is present in man.)

Thus, in a tradition that was still very much alive in the seventeenth century, but which our retrospective overestimation of the Cartesian "break" too often obscures, *realitas*, *aliquitas*, *essentia*, and *quidditas* remained almost synonymous notions (*Ordinatio* 1, dist. 3, qu. 1, n. 302, in *Opera omnia*, 3:184). Outside the Scotist tradition, Godfrey of Fontaines (in 1285 a professor of philosophy in Paris, where he continued to teach until 1304), seeking to define in turn the creature's eternal mode of being in the divine understanding, spoke of *realitas*, the latter now being determined as *realitas objectiva* (objective reality), that is, a reality that could be considered, prior to any existential positing, in its *esse objective* (objective being), that is, as something confronting the intellect and being capable of being an object for it:

> . . . . sicut ipsa realitas et essentia vel quidditas creaturae ab aeterno etiam non solum est essentia et quidditas realis in potentia et in esse cognito, sed in actu secundum esse essentiae reale et quidditativum. . . . Quare oportuit eas importare aliquam realitatem, quae esset obiectum verum et reale intellectus divini realiter differens a suo exemplari. . . .

> (Reality and the essence or the quiddity of the creature is from eternity not only a real essence and quiddity with the potential of being cognized, but an actual existing being of essence, according to the real and the quidditative. And so it was necessary to introduce some reality, which really would be the real and true object of the divine intellect differing from a copy.)

> (Godfrey of Fontaines, *Les quodlibet* 9, qu. 2)

All these propositions remain rigorously unintelligible if we understand by them, in the sense that now seems obvious, the terms "reality," "real," "object."

With the Scotist notion of reality, we are in fact not merely very distant from, but actually at, the antipodes of the modern notion of existence or objective reality (*Wirklichkeit*). From this point of view, even the *ultima realitas*, that is, the last characteristic trait that makes an *entitas quidditative* (quidditative entity) an *entitas ut haec* (an entity distinct from all others and ultimately characterized by its *haecceitas*) and that thus contributes to individuation, is still of a conceptual nature and does not include within itself the *essere existere* (being of existing or what existing is). Étienne Chauvin, in his *Lexicon rationale seu thesaurus philosophicus* (1692), perfectly summarized the Scotist use of the term—still defended by his late disciples (J. Poncius [J. Punch], 1603–1673; B. Mastrius, 1602–1673; B. Bellutius, 1600–1670) and also transmitted to academic metaphysics, notably by Suárez—by defining it in these terms:

> Realitas est diminutivum dictum a re. Et a Scotistis, qui primi vocis hujus inventores fuere, distinguitur a re: quod res sit id quod per se potest existere et non sit pars rei: realitas autem sit aliquid minus re. Et ideo ponunt in unaquaque re plures realitates, quas alio nomine appellant formalitates: in homine v.g. plures realitates ex Scotistarum sententia, puta esse substantiae, esse viventis, animalitas, et ultima denique realitas, per quam constituitur esse hominis, tanquam per differentiam ultimam, et ea est rationalitas.

> ("Reality" is a term derived from *res* ["thing"]. "Reality" is distinguished by the Scotists, who were the first to invent this term, from the *res*, because the *res* is what can exist by itself and is not part of something else; whereas a reality is something less than the thing. That is why they posit in each thing several realities that they also call by another name: "formalities." In man, for example, according to Scotist doctrine, there are several realities, for example the being of substance, the being of the living, animality, and finally the ultimate reality through which the being of man is constituted, as by an ultimate difference, and that is rationality.)

III. Descartes and the "Objective Reality" of the Idea

If one wants to understand and assess the decisions, both doctrinal and terminological, made by the great authors of the seventeenth century (Descartes, Spinoza, Leibniz, Malebranche, et al.), one has to always keep in mind this backdrop constituted by the then-prevalent Scotist usage, because it is in relation to it that deviations that have become invisible for us are defined. In Descartes, the term *realitas* is always associated with a determining adjective (formal reality, objective reality, subjective reality) and connected with the problematics of the idea. Descartes's first use of the formula *realitas objectiva* regarding the idea is found in the Third Meditation (*Œuvres*, 7:40.15 and 41.4), and it immediately called for explanations that were repeated in his correspondence and in the replies to queries. The formula itself is not new, but it is the meaning Descartes gives it that causes the difficulty, or rather it is the Cartesian context in which it appears. Let us summarize very briefly an extremely well-known line of argument: *Sum res cogitans*, "I am a thing that thinks," and the *modi cogitandi* are in me as in a subject. I have abandoned, as hyperbolic doubt forces me to do, the hypothesis—that is, the positing of *res extra me*—from which ideas are supposed to proceed and which they are supposed to resemble. The path that Descartes is trying to blaze is very narrow: "*alia via mihi occurrit*"—

But there is yet another method of inquiring whether any of the objects of which I have ideas within me exist outside of me. If ideas are taken as certain modes of thought [*cogitandi modi*], I recognize amongst them no difference or inequality, and all appear to proceed from me in the same manner; but when we consider them as images [*tanquam rerum imagines*], one representing one thing and the other another, it is clear that they are very different one from the other.

(Meditations, in Œuvres, 7:40.5)

How can these ideas be distinguished? Here a new, internal principle has to be found, a principle of diversification or unequalization among ideas, and this implies considering the idea as a representative form, essentially referred to an immanent content. Thus for Descartes the idea is always something mental, but it nonetheless presents itself at first as representative, which amounts to saying that, within the hypothesis of hyperbolic doubt, it is then or first of all representative of nothing (*nihil, nulla res*, in any case in the sense of the *res extra animam*). Such a use of the term "idea" to designate the content of human thought was completely unprecedented and must therefore have led to numerous misunderstandings. Thomistic Scholasticism usually reserved the term "idea" for the eternal archetypes in which God thinks things. According to the most common Scholastic doctrine, in fact, God knows things by conceiving his own essence as imitable; thus he has a representative and purely intelligible knowledge of them.

For Descartes, in contrast, the idea is a thing thought (*res cogitata*) that includes, as such, a double reality: on the one hand as *modus cogitandi* (and in the sense that all ideas are to be put on the same level), and on the other hand as a representative form that apprehends a determinate content and an intelligible reality that is sui generis:

Per realitatem objectivam ideae intelligo entitatem rei repraesentae per ideam, quatenus est in idea.

(By the objective reality of the idea, I mean that in respect of which the thing represented in the idea is an entity, in so far as that exists in the idea.)

(Œuvres, 7:161.4–6)

The reality of the idea is precisely the entity that is in turn a positive "thing"; even if it is an *ens deminitum* (a diminished being), yet it is not nothing, but something to which the principle of causality, taken in all its universality, can still be applied (*Meditations, Reply to Second Objections, Axioma 3, Œuvres*, 7:165.7–9). And if it is also true (*Axioma* 4) that "whatever reality or perfection exists in a thing [*realitas sive perfectio in aliqua re*], exists formally or else eminently in its first and adequate cause," then it appears that the *realitas objectiva* of our ideas cannot escape this general principle until the discovery of the idea of "a being supremely perfect" that "possesses so much objective reality (that is to say participates by representation in so many degrees of being and perfection)" that it necessarily requires an absolutely perfect cause (*Œuvres*, 7:41.24–29). Thus, thanks to the Cartesian transposition of the Scotist doctrine of the production of things in God in accord with their *esse intelligibile*, the idea considered

in its objective reality is neither a *fictum quid* nor an *ens rationis*, but indeed a *reale aliquid, quod distincte concipitur* (neither something fictive nor a rational entity, but indeed something that is real and conceived distinctly [ibid., 7:103.10–13]).

IV. Spinoza, Leibniz: Perfection and the Requirement of Existence

In the *Principia philosophiae cartesianae*, in which he faithfully sets forth the Cartesian doctrine of the *realitas ideae*, Spinoza stresses the hierarchized differentiation of the objectively represented content of the idea as soon as the latter is considered in its *realitas objectiva*: "[I]llam scilicet [ideam], quae objective continet esse et perfectionem substantiae, longe perfectiorem esse, quam illam, quae tantum objectivam perfectionem alicujus accidentis continet" (This idea that contains objectively the being and perfection of substance is far more perfect than that which contains only the objective perfection of any accident whatever; *Opera*, 1:153.29–154.2). Thus Spinoza, like Descartes, and following Duns Scotus, also explains *realitas* as *entitas* (ibid., 1:154.27–31), and even in the *Ethics*, *realitas* is still associated with *perfectio* (*Ethics*, in *Opera*, vol. 2, def. 6). For Leibniz as well, the ancient meaning of *realitas*, in conformity with the Scotist tradition in the broad sense, remains guiding and determining: reality does not primarily characterize the worldly object exterior to consciousness, but rather the content or tenor of what it apprehends as quiddity, or essence, or of what is objectively present in it. We see this especially in Leibniz's definitions of perfection, which always bring in the concept itself of *realitas*:

Ego definire malim perfectionem esse gradum seu quantitatem realitatis seu essentiae.

(I prefer to define perfection as the degree or quantity of reality or essence.)

(Die philosophische Schriften, 1:366)

Perfectio est essentiae gradus seu quod quid plus habet essentiae vel realitatis, eo est perfectius.

(Perfection is the degree of essence, that is, what has more essence or reality is thereby more perfect.)

(Quoted in Bodemann, Die Leibniz-Handschriften, 124)

Perfectio est gradus [seu quantitas] realitatis.

(Perfection is the degree [or quantity] of reality.)

(Textes inédits, 1.11)

Thus the reality does define something positive (*aliquid positivum et absolutum*), in proportion to the essence, even if this reality, precisely insofar as it pretends or aspires to existence in accord with its degree of perfection, requires a really—or, better, an actually—existing foundation: "[F]or if there is a reality in essences or possibilities, or in eternal truths, this reality must be founded on something existing and actual, and consequently in the existence of the necessary being" (*Monadology*, §44; cf. *Theodicy*, §184).

But what does "reality" mean in such a remarkable passage? It is not opposed to the possible as the actual is to the virtual: instead, it is the reality of the possible in the divine understanding;

that is, the reality of its substance, its peculiar tenor or determinateness. The reality is from the outset conceived as *essentia* or *realitas possibilis*, and it is as such that it appears as *exigentia existentiae*. Thus the reality, far from being opposed to the possible as a category of modality, constitutes its very being or the "lesser being."

> Omnia possibilia, seu essentiam vel realitatem possibilem exprimentia, pari jure ad existentiam tendere pro quantitate essentiae seu realitatis, vel pro gradu perfectionis quam involvunt.

> (All possibles, that is, everything that expresses an essence or a possible reality, tend, by the same right, toward existence, in function of the quantity of essence or reality, or the degree of perfection that they include.)

> (*De rerum originatione radicali*, in *Die philosophische Schriften*, 7:10)

Thus when Leibniz identifies *realitas* and *cogitabilitas*, or even reduces the former to the latter ("nihil aliud realitas quam cogitabilitas" [reality is nothing other than cogitability]; *Die philosophische Schriften*, 1:271), he is only drawing the ultimate conclusions from the movement that leads by stages from the essence or real perfection through Suárez's *essentia realis* to the possible defined as noncontradictory, thinkable (*cogitabile in universum quatenus tale est*; Leibniz, *Opuscules et fragments inédits*).

V. *Realitas*—"Reality"

However, we also find in Leibniz certain uses of the term *realitas*, or still more clearly, uses of the adjective *realis*, that anticipate the post-Kantian meaning of the word. For instance, distinguishing real phenomena from imaginary ones, Leibniz wonders, in his correspondence with Clark, about the reality of space and time; space and time cannot in fact be reduced to the *ordo possibilium existentiarum*, because neither one nor the other contain any *realitas* when abstracted from the divine immensity or eternity:

> Spatium, quemadmodum et tempus, nihil aliud sunt quam ordo possibilium existentiarum, in spatio simul, in tempore successive, realitasque eorum per se nulla est, extra divinam immensitatem atque aeternitatem.

> (Space and in a certain way also time are nothing other than the order of possible existences, simultaneously in space, successively in time, and their reality in themselves is null, outside the divine immensity and eternity.)

> (*Leibnizens mathematische Schriften* , 7:242)

> Sciendum est ante omnia, Vim quidem esse quiddam prorsus reale, in substantiis etiam creatis; at spatium, tempus et motum habere aliquid de ente rationis, nec per se, sed quatenus divina attributa, immensitatem, aeternitatem, operationem aut substantiarum creatarum vim involvunt, vera et realia esse.

> (It must be known first of all that force is something completely real, even in created substances; whereas space, time, and movement have something of the

rational entity, and are not by themselves real and true things, but only insofar as they include divine attributes, immensity, eternity, the operation or the force of created substances.)

> (*Specimen dynamicum*, in *Leibnizens mathematische Schriften*, 6:247)

Thus reality comes to designate, by opposition to the rational entity or the purely apparent, phenomenal being, what truly or actually exists, independent of the knowledge that a conscious subject may have of it. Perhaps we may see in this a distant anticipation of the new meaning of the term *realitas* that gradually established itself in English philosophy of the seventeenth and eighteenth centuries, when the term "reality" became a synonym of "existence," even if we still frequently encounter, especially in Berkeley, the classical expressions "reality of ideas," "reality of notions"—which can be interpreted in the direct line of the Scholastic tradition—to emphasize the truth or validity of ideas. However, the latter already refers to the reality of things that corresponds to the modern use of the term, taken as a synonym of "objectivity" (*Principles of Human Knowledge*, §33–36, in *Works of George Berkeley*; Locke, *An Essay*, bk. 2, chap. 22:30–32; bk. 4, chap. 4).

Whereas David Hume, in his *A Treatise of Human Nature* ("Of the Ideas of Space and Time," bk. 1, pt. 2), clearly opposes "reality" and "possibility": "the reality, or at least possibility, of the idea of a vacuum, may be proved by the following reasoning. . . ." Here reality is distinguished, as a modality, from possibility, whereas in the German academic tradition (so-called *Schulmetaphysik*), *Realität* (*realitas*) is always on the side of possibility. Let us also note that in Hume, to limit ourselves to him, the term "reality" appears most often in an adverbial form to indicate what is "in fact and reality," just as the adjective "real" is associated with the words "positive" and "existent" ("thing real and positive"; "something real and existent").

VI. The Kantian Heritage:
Reality / Objective Reality, *Realität/Wirklichkeit*

Kant succeeds in keeping together two entirely heterogeneous meanings of "reality": one referrring, as a category of quality, to the Scholastic, and ultimately Scotist, use of the term; the other gesturing, as *objektive Realität* or *objektive Gültigkeit* (objective reality, objective validity), not backward toward a completely atypical Cartesian usage, but rather forward, toward the idea, obvious for us today, of objectivity. However, the first authors of the post-Kant period quickly put an end to this difficult tension: either, with Fichte and Schelling, by making the term "reality" (*Realität*) bear all the weight of positivity and positing, to the point of lending it the lexically completely unexpected meaning of unconditionality (*Unbedingheit* vs. *Ding*) or activity/actuality; or, with Hegel, by substituting for it, in this reference to actuality or to "energy," the term *Wirklichkeit*, "objective reality," whose emphatic use, not very much in accord with common usage, must then be justified.

A. The plurality of Kantian meanings

Kant's work certainly constitutes a decisive turning point in the history of the meanings of the term "reality" (*Realität*), for if it still bears witness to the Scholastic meaning, shaped essentially by Scotism, of the Latin term *realitas*, on which the loan-word *Realität* is modeled, it introduced at the same time, through the notions of "objective reality" and "realization" (*Realisierung*), the modern meaning of the term as it later came to be used almost uncritically. For Kant, reality is a category of quality (*Critique of Pure Reason*, A 80/B 106), and not of modality, according to a usage that goes back, beyond Wolff, to Suárez and ultimately to Duns Scotus, since it designates the determination or qualitative determinacy of a *res* (its content-as-a-thing, *Sachverhalt*). The Latin term, which figures again in the *Critique of Pure Reason* (B 602 ff.), has as its equivalent strict *Sachheit* (which we will take care not to translate into French by *choséité*) in the sense of an external, physical thing (*Ding*).

But Kant is also the thinker who, thanks to complementary adjectival determinations (objective reality, empirical reality, subjective reality, etc.), is at the origin of the meaning that is now the most common: the real, in the dominant sense of the term "reality," is what is autonomous, independent of subjective conditions and of the process of knowledge—in short, external to the knowing subject and therefore endowed with an extramental being. Kant is, finally, the thinker who inaugurated, no doubt indirectly, an essential distinction that is peculiar to Germanic languages between *Realität* and *Wirklichkeit*.

After Kant, the problem of reality bears most often on the being-in-itself of things, in abstraction from knowing, in the tradition of Cartesian doubt relative to the reality of the external world. In truth, Descartes spoke of existence and never of reality in the sense of objective reality (*Meditationes*, Meditation 6: "De rerum materialium existentia et reali mentis a corpore distinctione" [The existence of material things, and the real distinction between mind and body]), whereas in the Kantian attempt at a "demonstration of the reality of the external world" (*Critique of Pure Reason*, B 274 ff.), it is always a matter, through the refutation of idealism, of demonstrating the *Wirklichkeit*, the "objective reality" of things outside oneself and independent of the inner sense. It is with the expression *objektive Realität* that we rediscover the common problematics of what is objectively given in sense experience:

> Wenn eine Erkenntnis objektive Realität haben, d.i. sich auf einen Gegenstand beziehen, und in demselben Bedeutung und Sinn haben soll, so muß der Gegenstand auf irgend eine Art gegeben werden können.

> (If knowledge is to have objective reality, that is, to relate to an object, and is to acquire meaning and significance in respect to it, the object must be capable of being in some manner given.)

> (Kant, *Critique of Pure Reason*, A 155 /B 194)

Thus only perception (*Wahrnehmung*) is capable of providing the matter (*Stoff*) of our concepts, and it is also perception that is the "sole mark of actuality" (*Wirklichkeit*) (ibid., A 225/B 273). Knowledge therefore cannot have objective reality, that is, relate its concepts to objects insofar as an object is given through the senses. If the object is given, "the *possibility of experience* is, then, what gives objective reality to all our *a priori* modes of knowledge" (ibid., A 156 /B 195). There is therefore

objective reality (*objektive Realität*) only insofar as the relation of our concepts to an object (*Gegenstand, Objekt*) is provided or attested. What makes the objective reality of a concept is surely its relation to the object given in a possible experience, but, as Heidegger in particular emphasized, the concept itself, considered in its real content (*Sachgehalt*), includes within itself, in a latent or implicit manner, this reference to actuality and existence (*Phenomenological Interpretation*). With regard to space or time, empirical reality is opposed to "absolute reality" (Kant, *Critique of Pure Reason*, A 35/B 52) and defines their "objective validity" (*objektive Gültigkeit*) with respect to all the objects that can ever be given to our senses (ibid.). To say of time, for instance, that its reality is subjective thus means that if we abstract from the subjective conditions of empirical intuition, it is no longer anything: its reality is subjective, that is, directly related to inner experience. Although as a general rule, and particularly when he associates reality, substantiality, and causality, Kant denies these concepts any meaning capable of determining an object outside their use in possible experience (ibid., A 677 /B 705, A 679/B 707); he also sometimes defines the reality of ideal concepts by distinguishing them from rational entities or pure chimeras.

B. Fichte and Schelling: The fundamental ontological distinctions of the German language

In the *Grundlage der gesamten Wissenschaftslehre* (*Foundations of the Entire Science of Knowledge*, 1794), Fichte notes, in a not very Kantian way:

> The Ego can determine itself only as reality [*Realität*], because it is posited purely and simply as reality . . . and no negation is posited in it . . . every reality [*Realität*] is posited in the Ego, but the non-Ego is opposed to the Ego. . . . Every non-Ego is negation [*Negation*], and it thus has no reality in itself [*es hat gar keine Realität in sich*].

> (*Science of Knowledge*, pt. 1, §2)

And it is no doubt echoing Fichte that Schelling uses the term *Realität* in *Vom Ich als Prinzip der Philosophie oder über das Unbedingte im menschlichen Wissen* (*Of the I as the Principle of Philosophy or, On the Unconditional in Human Knowledge*; 1795): here, "reality" designates not the "thing" (*Ding*), but the unconditioned (*das Unbedingte*):

> The philosophical formation of languages, whose major traits remain perceptible especially in the original languages, is a genuine marvel produced by the mechanism of the human mind. Thus our German word *bedingen* ("to condition"), along with its derivatives . . . is in fact an excellent term, of which it might almost be said that it includes the whole treasury of philosophical wisdom. *Bedingen* designates the action by which any thing becomes a *Ding* ("thing"), whence it follows at the same time that by itself nothing can be posited as a *Ding*, in other words, that an unconditioned thing [*ein unbedingtes Ding*] is a contradiction in terms. The unconditioned is in fact what cannot be transformed into a thing, can never become a thing [*zum Ding werden, zum Ding gemacht sein*].

> (*Of the I*, §3)

The subtitle of *Of the I* is *On the Unconditional in Human Knowledge*, and its initial purpose was defined in these terms: "etwas zu finden, das schlechterdings nicht als Ding gedacht werden kann" (to find something that simply cannot be conceived as a thing), that is, what provides human knowledge with its "reality" (*Realität*). A little later in the same work (§15, n. 3), Schelling comes back to the privilege of language—the German language—when it is a matter of ontological distinctions as fundamental as those that concern being, existing, reality, and objective reality:

It is striking to observe that most languages have the advantage of being able to distinguish absolute being [*das absolute Sein*] from all conditioned existing [*bedingtes Existiren*]. Such a differentiation, which is found in all primitive languages, refers back to an originary ground which, as soon as language is first elaborated, has already determined this differentiation, without people even being aware of it. But it is no less striking to observe that most philosophers still do not make use of this asset offered by their language. Almost all of them use the words "be," "be there," "existence," "actuality" [*Sein, Dasein, Existenz, Wirklichkeit*] almost as if they were synonymous. However, the word "be" obviously expresses pure, absolute being-posited [*das reine, absolute Gesetzt-sein*], whereas existence [*Dasein*] already designates etymologically a posited being that is conditioned, limited [*ein bedingtes, eingeschränktes Gesetztsein*]. And yet people commonly talk, for example, about the existence of God [*Dasein Gottes*], as if God could actually be there, that is, in a conditioned, empirical way . . . . Someone who can say of the absolute Ego: "It is actual" [*wirklich*] knows nothing about it. *Sein* expresses being posited as absolute whereas *Dasein* expresses a being posited as conditioned in general, whereas *Wirklichkeit* expresses a being posited as conditioned in a determinate way, by a determined condition.

A lexical consideration that is extended in the *Briefe über Dogmatismus und Kritizismus* (*Letters on Dogmatism and Criticism*):

It is nonetheless striking to note that the German language already makes such a precise distinction between the actual [*das Wirklichkeit*] (what is given in sensation or has an effect on me, and on which I have a retroactive effect [*auf mich wirkt und worauf ich zurückwirke*]), the being-there [*das Daseiende*] (what is there in general, that is, in space and time), and being (what is purely and simply by itself, independently of any temporal condition).

(Sixth Letter, n. 1, in *Historisch-Kritische Ausgabe*, ser. 1, 3:77–78)

C. Reality as a positive ontological category

After Kant, it was the distribution of *Realität* and *Wirklichkeit* in the framework of the categories of quality and modality, respectively, that gradually tended to become blurred. In this process, Kant's critique of the ontological argument and his determination of being as positing (*Setzung, Position*) must certainly have played a crucial role: if Fichte, for example, in the *Grundlage der gesamten Wissenschaftslehre* (1794), continued to oppose reality and negation directly by associating reality, identity, possibility, and essentiality, he quickly emphasized as well that reality, which has its ultimate source in the Ego, must, like the latter, be defined in terms of activity and positing:

If we abstract from all judging as determined acting, and if we consider solely the mode of the human mind's action given through this form, we obtain the category of reality [*die Kategorie der Realität*]. Everything to which the proposition A = A can be applied has reality [*Realität hat*] precisely insofar as this form is applied. What is posited by the simple positing of anything (posited in the Ego) is reality [*Realität*] in it, is its essence [*Wesen*].

(*Grundlage*, 2:261)

These quotations from Fichte and Schelling show how on the one hand Kant's usage (reality vs. negation) is faithfully maintained, and on the other, how a new theoretical and conceptual proximity is established: that between reality and activity (*Aktuosität*, Leibniz would have said) that no doubt constitutes an indispensable historical mediation here. Thus Fichte notes (ibid.): "Aller Realität Quelle ist das Ich. Erst durch und mit dem Ich ist der Begriff der Realität gegeben" (The Ego is the source of all reality. It is only through and with the Ego that the concept of reality is given). If the Ego is understood as activity (*Thätigkeit*), self-positing (*Sich-setzen*), the conclusion is inevitable: "Alle Realität ist thätig; und alles thätige ist Realität. Thätigkeit ist positive Realität" (All reality is active; and everything that is active is reality. Activity is positive reality).

In his *System des transcendentalen Idealismus* (1800), Schelling also associates reality, egoity, and self-positing activity: "Das Ich ist Prinzip der Realität, das Objekt hat abgeleitete Realität . . . es gibt einen höheren Begriff als den des Dinges, nämlich den des Handelns, der Tätigkeit" (The Ego is the principle of reality, the object has a derivative reality . . . there is a higher concept than that of the thing, namely action, activity; *Historisch-Kritische Ausgabe*, vol. 9, bk. 1). Hegel, in his *Science of Logic*, also adopts Kant's distinction only to subvert it by reintroducing the moment of negation into the very heart of reality as a category of quality as soon as the latter is determined.

D. Actual reality, *Wirklichkeit*

Hegel's famous formula in the preface to the *Elements of the Philosophy of Right* (*Grundlinien der Philosophie des Rechts*, 821): "[W]hat is real [*wirklich*] is rational [*vernünftig*], and what is rational [*vernünftig*] is real" is no more obvious in German than in its English translation, as is amply shown by the criticisms to which it was soon subjected (Von Thaden, Haym, et al.) and especially by Hegel's repeated clarifications. This clearly indicates that the Hegelian meaning of the term *Wirklichkeit*, even if it draws on the same resources of the German language and the paronymic series *Werk, wirken, Wirkung, wirklich, Wirklichkeit, Verwirklichung* . . . , was initially constructed theoretically. In the addition to section 142 of the *Encyclopedia of the Philosophical Sciences* (1817–30, in *Werke*, vols. 8–10), Hegel denounces the trivial opposition between "idea," "correctness," "truth," and "actuality," taken in the sense of "sensible external existence":

> Ideas are not simply lodged in our heads, and the idea in general is not something so powerless that its realization [*Realisierung*] depends on our good will to be achieved [*bewerkstelligen*] or not achieved, but it is instead what is at the same time absolutely efficient and also actual [*das schlechthin Wirkende zugleich und auch Wirkliche*].

Thus actuality will not be confused with reality, nor the actual with the real, first of all because we must distinguish the actual from simple appearance, *Erscheinung* (*Science of Logic*), and second because, according to the proper use of the language, "we hesitate to recognize as a poet or statesman someone who cannot accomplish anything substantial and rational, like a true poet [*wirklicher Dichter*] or a genuine statesman [*wirklicher Staatsmann*]" (*Encyclopedia*, addition to §142). Philosophy, in contrast to common sense, will thus not oppose the idea or ideality to actual reality but will recognize in the Idea only what is "true" and will consider it as *energeia* [ἐνέργεια], as "the interior which is absolutely outside [*das Innere, welches schlechthin heraus ist*], and consequently as the unity of the inside and the outside, or like actuality, in the emphatic sense of the word, the one to which we refer here" (ibid.). Returning once again to the formula in the preface to the *Elements of the Philosophy of Right*, in the introduction to the second version of the *Encyclopedia* (§6), Hegel explains that it is important to distinguish in existence (*Dasein*) what is mere appearance (*Erscheinung*) from what is only partly *Wirklichkeit*. Here again, we must distinguish "the aspect of things that does not deserve the emphatic name of actuality," the contingent, the possible, being-there, the existence of actuality. Regarding the emphatic sense of "actuality," we can rely on the economical formulation in the *Encyclopedia*:

> Actuality is the unity, which has become immediate, of essence and existence, or of the inside and the outside. The exteriorization of the actual is the actual itself [*die Äusserung des Wirklichen ist das Wirkliche selbst*], so that in it there also remains an essential element [*ebenso Wesentliches bleibt*], and it is an essential element only insofar as it is in an immediate external existence [*in einer unmittelbarer äußerlicher Existenz*].
>
> (*Encyclopedia*, 1817, §91)

That is, for Hegel, the true reconciliation or rather the transcendence of the opposition between Plato and Aristotle: the Idea (*idea*, [ἰδέα, εἶδος]) become actual (*energeia* [ἐνέργεια]). And Hegel clarifies the thesis, repeated in the *Science of Logic*:

> Earlier, being [*Sein*] and existence [*Existenz*] were presented as forms of the immediate; being is in a general way immediacy and not reflected, and passage [*Übergang*] into the Other. Existence is immediate unity of being and reflection; that is why it is appearance [*Erscheinung*], it proceeds from the ground and returns to it [*kommt aus dem Grunde und geht zu Grunde*]. The actual is the being-posited of this unity, Relationship [*Verhältnis*] become

identical itself; it is consequently exempt from the passage [into the Other], and its exteriority [*Äußerlichkeit*] is its energy [*Energie*]; it is reflected in the latter in itself; its being-there is only the manifestation of itself [*die Manifestation seiner selbst*], not of an Other.

This commentary, which is rather dense, provides the essential clues that allow us to understand in what way the "emphatic" Hegelian thematization of *Wirklichkeit* in a sense merely extends the terminological use established by Christian Wolff and so-called German academic philosophy, and it thereby also reconnects with one of the classical motifs of existence understood as *ex sistere, poni extra causas*, but it also and especially constitutes Hegel's genuine newness. It is the newness of a beyond-phenomenology that is not limited to appearance (*Erscheinung*) in its indefinite movement of coming into existence and perishing, but attempts to apprehend exteriority itself as "energy" (*Wirksamkeit*): actuality is manifest and manifestation, manifestation of nothing other than oneself, and manifestation in oneself; that is, it is also "reflection." The *Science of Logic* (*Wissenschaft der Logik*) explains that

> [w]hat is actual can act [*was wirklich ist, kann wirken*]; its actuality makes something known by what it brings forth [*seine Wirklichkeit gibt etwas kund durch das, was es hervorbringt*]; its being-in-relation to the Other is the manifestation of itself [*die Manifestation seiner*].

The reader will have recognized here the highest Hegelian figure of the mind, the one that makes it possible to conclude the *Encyclopedia*'s "philosophy of mind" in its last chapter ("Absolute Spirit") with a long quotation from Aristotle's *Metaphysics* (50.7.1072b 18–30).

Jean-François Courtine

BIBLIOGRAPHY

Berkeley, George. *The Works of George Berkeley, Bishop of Cloyne*. Edited by A. A. Luce and T. E. Jessop. 9 vols. London: Thomas Nelson and Sons, 1948–57.

Bodemann, Eduard, ed. *Die Leibniz-Handschriften der Königlichen Oeffentlichen Bibliothek zu Hannover*. Hannover, Ger.: Hahn, 1805.

Chauvin, Étienne. *Lexicon rationale sive thesaurus philosophicus*. Rotterdam, Neth.: Apud Petrum vander Slaart, 1692.

Descartes, Réné. *Œuvres*. Edited by C. Adam and P. Tannery. 11 vols. Paris: Vrin, 1969.

———. *The Philosophical Works of Descartes in Two Volumes*. Edited and translated by E. S. Haldane and G.R.T. Ross. Vol. 2. New York: Dover Publications, 1934.

———. *The Philosophical Writings of Descartes*. Translated by John Cottingham et al. 3 vols. Cambridge: Cambridge University Press, 1988.

Duns Scotus, John. *Opera omnia*. Vatican City: Typis Polyglottis Vaticanis, 1950–.

———. *Philosophical Writings: A Selection*. Translated with introduction and notes by Allan Wolter. Indianapolis, IN: Hackett, 1987.

———. *Quaestiones super libros Metaphysicorum Aristotelis*. Edited by R. Andrews et al. 2 vols. St Bonaventure, NY: Franciscan Institute, 1997. Translation by Girard J. Etzkorn and Allan B. Wolter: *Questions on the Metaphysics of Aristotle*. 2 vols. St. Bonaventure, NY : Franciscan Institute, 1997–98.

Fichte, Johann Gottlieb. *Grundlage der gesammten Wissenschaftslehre*. Vols. 1 and 2 of *J. G. Fichte: Gesamtausgabe der Bayerischen Akademie der Wissenschaften*. Edited by Erich Fuchs, Reinhard Lauth, Hans Jacobs, and Hans Gliwitzky. 40 vols. Stuttgart-Bad Cannstatt: Frommann, 1964–.

———. *The Science of Knowledge*. Edited and translated by Peter Heath and John Lachs. Reprint, Cambridge: Cambridge University Press, 1982.

Godfrey of Fontaines. *Le huitième quodlibet*. Edited by M. de Wulf and J. Hoffmans. Louvain, Belg.: Institut supérieur de Philosophie de l'Université, 1924.

———. *Les quodlibet cinq, six et sept*. Edited by M. de Wulf and J. Hoffmans. Louvain, Belg.: Institut supérieur de Philosophie de l'Université, 1914.

Hegel, Georg Wilhelm Friedrich. *Elements of the Philosophy of Right*. Translated by H. B. Nisbet and edited by Allen Wood. Cambridge: Cambridge University Press, 1991.

———. *Science of Logic*. Translated by A. V. Miller. London: Allen and Unwin, 1969.

———. *Werke*. Edited by Eva Moldenhauer and Karl Markus Michel. 20 vols. Frankfurt: Suhrkamp, 1971.

Heidegger, Martin. *The Basic Problems of Phenomenology*. Translated by Albert Hofstadter Bloomington: Indiana University Press, 1982.

———. *Phenomenological Interpretation of Kant's* Critique of Pure Reason. Translated by Parvis Emad and Kenneth Maly. Bloomington: Indiana University Press, 1997.

Hume, David. *A Treatise of Human Nature*. Edited by David Fate Norton and Mary J. Norton. Oxford: Oxford University Press, 2000.

Kant, Immanuel. *Critique of Practical Reason*. Translated and edited by Mary Gregor. Cambridge: Cambridge University Press, 1997.

———. *Critique of Pure Reason*. 2nd ed. Translated by N. Kemp-Smith. New York: Macmillan, 1933.

Leibniz, Gottfried Wilhelm. *Opuscules et fragments inédits de Leibniz. Extraits des manuscrits*. Edited by Louis Couturat. Paris: Presses Universitaires de France, 1903. Reprint. Hildesheim, Ger.: Olms, 1961.

———. *Philosophical Essays*. Translated and edited by Roger Ariew and Dan Garber. Indianapolis, IN: Hackett, 1989.

———. *Philosophical Papers and Letters*. 2nd ed. Edited and translated by Leroy E. Loemker. Dordrecht, Neth.: D. Reidel, 1969.

———. *Die philosophischen Schriften*. Edited by C. I. Gerhardt. 7 vols. Berlin, 1875–90. Reprint. Hildesheim, Ger.: Olms, 1965.

———. *Leibnizens mathematische Schriften*. Edited by C. I. Gerhardt. 7 vols. Berlin, 1849–63.

———. *Textes inédits d'après les manuscrits de la Bibliothèque provinciale de Hanovre*. Edited by Gaston Grua. 2 vols. Paris: Presses Universitaires de France, 1948.

Locke, John. *An Essay Concerning Human Understanding*. Edited by P. H. Nidditch. Oxford: Clarendon Press, 1975.

Micraelius, Johann. *Lexicon philosophicum terminorum philosophis usitatorum*. 2nd ed. Stettin, 1662.

Paulus, Jean. *Henri de Gand: Essai sur les tendances de sa métaphysique*. Paris: Vrin, 1938.

Schelling, Friedrich Wilhelm Joseph. *Historisch-Kritische Ausgabe*. Edited by Jörg Jantzen, Thomas Buchheim, Jochem Hennigfeld, Wilhelm G. Jacobs, and Siegbert Peetz. 40 vols. Stuttgart: Frommann-Holzboog, 1976–.

———. *Of the I as the Principle of Philosophy, or On the Unconditional in Human Knowledge*. In *The Unconditional in Human Knowledge: Four Early Essays 1794–96*. Translated with commentary by F. Marti. Lewisburg, PA: Bucknell University Press, 1980.

Spinoza, Baruch. *Complete Works*. With translations by Samuel Shirley. Edited by Michael L. Morgan. Indianapolis, IN: Hackett, 2002.

———. *Opera*. 2nd ed. Edited by C. Gebhardt. 5 vols. Heidelberg: Carl Winters, 1972.

| REASON

The English word "reason" and the French word *raison* are both formed on the basis of *reor* (to count or calculate), whence "think, believe." The Latin verb translates the Greek *legein* [λέγειν], two of whose principal meanings it retains, but only two: "count" and "think." The third principal meaning of the Greek term, "speak, discourse," which designates a third type of putting into relation and proportion, is rendered by other Latin series (*dicere, loquor, orationem*, or *sermonem habere*), so that ultimately the Greek word *logos* [λόγος] is approached by Latin philosophers by means of a syntagm, *ratio et oratio* (reason and discourse). Each vernacular fragments the meaning of *logos* into a greater or lesser

plurality of meanings, each represented by one or more specific words. The first question, from the point of view of the difference of languages, is thus that of the breadth of the meaning of "reason" or its equivalents, and of the systems diffracting the meanings of *logos* and then of *ratio*. A presentation of this will be found under LOGOS (see also LANGUAGE, PROPOSITION, WORD).

But another complex of problems immediately arises. The Latin *ratio* absorbs the meanings of other Greek terms, such as *nous* [νοῦς] (mind) and *dianoia* [διάνοια] (intelligence), which are also translated in other, more technical ways, such as *intellectus*; so that "reason," in the sense of "rationality," is a comprehensive term, whereas "reason" in the sense of "intellect" or "understanding" is a singular and differentiated faculty. However, none of the comprehensive terms or systems of opposition coincides with those of another language, which are moreover changing. Under INTELLECTUS one will find a way of conceiving these divergences on the basis of the polysemy of *intellectus* and of the Latin pair *intellectus/ratio* (cf. INTELLECTUS, Box 2), which is related to the Greek *nous/dianoia*, and opens onto other theoretically marked systems such as the Kantian pair *Verstand/Vernunft*. This should be complemented by the entries for INTELLECT and UNDERSTANDING.

I. Reason and Rationality

A. Man, animal, god

Since Aristotle's definition of man as an "animal endowed with *logos*," which Latin writers rendered by *animal rationale*—omitting the discursive dimension—reason, or the *logos*, is a specific difference that defines man by his difference from other living beings and/or his participation in a divine or cosmic nature: see LOGOS and ANIMAL, *DISCOURSE*, SPEECH ACT; cf. GOD, *HUMANITY*, NATURE, *WORLD*. On the discursive dimension properly so called, see also *ÉNONCÉ*, INTENTION, LANGUAGE, SENSE, SIGN, SIGNIFIER/SIGNIFIED, TO TRANSLATE, WORD.

See also POLIS, and BILDUNG, *CONSENSUS*, POLITICS concerning the other Aristotelian definition of man as a "political animal."

B. Reason and madness

Reason is opposed to madness understood as "dementia." On the privative vocabulary that is one of the possible ways of describing madness, see MADNESS; cf. *MALAISE*.

More broadly, reason is conceived in terms of difference from what does not belong to its domain and falls outside its immediate law, but which man may, in certain ways, share with other animals, such as sensation, passion, imagination, and possibly memory: see PERCEPTION, *IMAGINATION* [BILD, FANCY, PHANTASIA], MEMORY, PATHOS, *TO SENSE* [FEELING, GEFÜHL].

See also discussions on the way in which psychoanalysis conceives and names these relations: DRIVE, ENTSTELLUNG, ES, UNCONSCIOUS, VERNEINUNG, *WITTICISM*, WUNSCH.

C. Rationality and the principle of intelligibility

Rationality, defined by the *logos*, is connected with logic as the art of speaking and thinking, and with its founding principles. Under PRINCIPLE, the principle of noncontradiction (see also HOMONYM) is explored, as well as that of the principle of reason (*principium reddendae rationis, Satz vom Grund*). More broadly, see PREDICATION, SUBJECT, *TO BE,* TRUTH; cf. ABSTRACTION, *ABSURD, THING,* UNIVERSALS.

Finally, rationality functions as a principle of the intelligibility of the world and history, particularly in Hegel: see ATTUALITÀ, AUFHEBEN, CLAIM, GERMAN, HISTORIA UNIVERSALIS, LIGHT, PERFECTIBILITY, PLASTICITY, *RUSE,* SECULARIZATION; cf. II.C of this entry.

II. The Partitions of Reason

A. Semantic diffractions

Although there is no language that retains under a single word all the meanings of *logos* (except by bringing *logos* into the language in question), the distribution of these meanings is more or less close to Latin. For the classical French word *raison*, which maintains almost all the Latin meanings (including the mathematical sense of proportion: *raison d'une série, raison inverse*), a contemporary French-German dictionary proposes the following terms: *Vernunft, Verstand* (rational faculty; see UNDERSTANDING and also II.B of this entry), *Billigkeit* (acceptability; cf. CLAIM), *Recht* (law, right), *Recht haben* (to be right; see LEX, RULE OF LAW; cf. DUTY, MACHT), *Grund* (ground, foundation), *Satz vom Grund* (principle of reason; see PRINCIPLE), *Ursache* (cause; cf. DASEIN, GEGENSTAND, RES, *THING*), *Anlass* (motive), *Erklärung* (explanation; see GERMAN, TO TRANSLATE, UNDERSTANDING), *Rechenschaft* (calculation, account), *Genugtuung* (satisfaction; see PLEASURE), *Firma* (firm; cf. ENTREPRENEUR), *Proportion, Verhältnis* (proportion, relation) (*Hand-Wörterbuch*, F-D, D-F, Weis-Mattutat, Klett-Bordas, 1968). This example shows that the whole of the vocabulary is thus mobilized.

B. Reason and faculties

We can distinguish between two interfering systems: the first designates reason, identified with thought in general, in its relationship to a bodily and/or mental instance; the second situates reason in a hierarchy of faculties whose organization it determines.

Regarding the first system, as it is expressed in various languages, see SOUL (where one will find studies of the main distortions, especially around English "mind," German *Geist*, and French *esprit*, along with the main metaphors that serve to express the mental in ancient Greek, Latin, and Hebrew), CONSCIOUSNESS, *HEART*. We will emphasize especially the ways of designating reason and mind that appear to be the most irreducible from one language to another: thus Greek LOGOS, MÊTIS, Latin INGENIUM, Basque GOGO, and German GEMÜT; cf. Italian CONCETTO, and GENIUS; see also FRENCH and GERMAN.

Regarding the second system, and the partitions that do not coincide, see UNDERSTANDING (under which the Kantian vocabulary is set forth, and in particular the distinction *Verstand/Vernunft*), and INTELLECT, INTELLECTUS, *INTUITION*, REPRÉSENTATION, SENSUS COMMUNIS.

C. Speculative reason, practical reason

From Plato and Aristotle to Kant and beyond, two great domains of rationality have been distinguished: theory, or speculative reason, and practice.

Regarding the former, see especially II.B of this entry; cf. AESTHETICS, EPISTEMOLOGY, GEISTESWISSENSCHAFTEN.

Regarding the latter, see ART, DUTY, GLÜCK, *LIBERTY*, MORALS, PHRONÊSIS, PRAXIS, WILL, *WISDOM*; cf. *ACT*, and I.C of this entry.

➤ *CROYANCE*, UTILITY

RÉCIT

The French word *récit*, from Latin *recitare*, which means "to read out loud (a law, a document, a letter), give a public reading" (*citare* means first of all "set in motion," whence "lift one's voice in song"), is one of the ways of designating narrative. Under ERZÄHLEN the reader will find a comparison of the French and German terminological systems. See also ROMANTIC.

In addition, *récit* is one of the possible translations of a certain number of Greek words, in particular *muthos* [μῦθος], which, when distinguished from *logos* [λόγος] (rational language), can also be rendered in French by *mythe*; when distinguished from *ergon* [ἔργον] (act), by *parole*; when distinguished from *diêgêsis* [διήγησις] (simple narration), by *récit dialogué*; when distinguished from *êthos* [ἦθος] (character), by *fable*; when distinguished from *historia* [ἱστορία] (narrative of facts), by *fiction*: see HISTORY, LOGOS, MIMÊSIS. See also DESCRIPTION (on the various ways of "showing" and the vocabulary of *ekphrasis* [ἔκφρασις], see DESCRIPTION, Box 1), DICHTUNG, *FICTION* (and on the vocabulary of the "plastic," see ART, PLASTICITY), *STYLE*.

➤ *PHÉNOMÈNE*, REALITY, SPEECH ACT, *THING*, TRUTH

REFERENCE

"Reference" (from the Lat. *referre*, "to report, relate") is, along with "denotation," one of the accepted translations of the German *Bedeutung* as distinguished from *Sinn*: see especially SENSE, V. On the relationship to the referent, particularly in regard to the medieval semantics of *suppositio*, see SENSE, III.B, and SUPPOSITION; cf. INTENTION, SACHVERHALT, SIGN.

➤ *AUTHORITY*, OBJECT, REALITY, *RÉCIT*, SIGNIFIER/SIGNIFIED, WORD

RELIGIO (LATIN)

ENGLISH   religion
FRENCH   *religion, culte, crainte*

➤ *RELIGION*, and CROYANCE [BELIEF, GLAUBE], *DESTINY, DROIT, FAITH*, GOD, LEX, PIETAS, SIGN, THEMIS, *WORLD*

It is on the basis of the use of the term *religio* in Latin philosophers that we can understand the extension given the word in the Christian West. In Classical Latin, the meanings of *religio* never exactly coincided with those attested for the term "religion" in English and French, which designates both a set of practices of worship and the beliefs on which the latter are based. It was Christianity that unified the distinct uses of the word *religio* and defined it in relation to an object of belief, as it is expressed by the use of the objective genitive *religio veri Dei* (the religion of the true God). But if Christianity's original contribution consisted in giving a doctrinal content to the term, it was the Roman philosophers of the first century BCE (Cicero and Lucretius) who changed the word's spheres of use, and it was their polemics that established in the Latin language the oppositions that were taken up again by their Christian readers, Lactantius, Arnobius, and Augustine.

I. From Reading Signs to Worshiping the Gods

In its most frequent uses, *religio* designates the scrupulous attention given to signs, whether these are manifestations external to the individual or, on the contrary, modifications on the psychological level, such as fear, doubt, or apprehension, which prescribe decisions or prevent us from making them. Used in this way, the term *religio* does not apply exclusively to the sphere of relations with the gods; on the other hand, it is not the same as respect for codes or prescriptions. These codes are in fact not rigorously fixed and the possibilities of error are great, to judge by the numerous anecdotes related by Roman historians (see Scheid, *Religion et piété à Rome*). The evaluation of what should be done thus remains subjective, and flows from an estimate that may be mistaken, and never excludes fear.

When *religio* covers the whole of the practices of worship, as is shown by Cicero's definition, "religio, id est cultus deorum" (religion, that is, the worship of the gods) (*De natura deorum*, 2.8), we can assert that this synthetic use of the term is the consequence of taking a philosophical position. This emerges clearly from the whole of the text from which this definition is drawn. It is a Stoic who is speaking, and who wants to prove—against his Epicurean and Neo-Academic interlocutors—that the Stoic doctrine is the only one capable of coinciding with Roman practices, or rather, of making them intelligible: with this in mind, he seeks to grasp the unification of the meanings of *religio* by using the term in six distinct ways:

> Caelius tells us how Flaminius met his death at Lake Thrasimene because he neglected the signs (*religione neglecta*) and caused great damage to the state. . . . Those who have obeyed the injunctions that were signified to them (*qui religionibus paruissent*) have made the state prosper. If we compare our institutions with those of foreign peoples, we will discover that we are equal or even inferior in every other respect, but for religion, that is, the worship of the gods, we are far superior. And in truth, respect for the rites exercised such power (*tanta religionis vis*) over our ancestors that some generals fulfilled the vows they had made to the gods on behalf of the state—their heads veiled and uttering the set words—by committing suicide. . . . Gracchus, who had nonetheless held the elections and realized that the affair was going to arouse fears among the citizens as a whole (*in religionem populo venisse*), reported the results to the Senate. . . . Thus this man who was above all others in wisdom preferred to admit a mistake that he could well have concealed rather than associate the state with any impiety (*haerere in re publica religionem*);

the consuls immediately gave up their powers rather than keep them a moment longer in defiance of religious prescriptions (*contra religionem*).

> (Cicero, *De natura deorum*, 2.8–11)

II. The *Religio/Superstitio* Opposition

This unification of the diverse uses of *religio*—which authorizes the uniqueness of the term—is also realized by means of the opposition between *religio* and *superstitio*. The distinction between the two terms, which resulted from efforts to define it made by philosophers and not by the guardians of the rites, made it possible to give a positive content to *religio* at a time when Lucretius, on the contrary, was using *religio* exclusively to designate the fearful observation of uncomprehended rites that is generally translated by "superstition": *turpis religio* (2.660), *antiquae religiones* (6.62). It was in opposition to this sense given to *religio* by Lucretius that we must assess the definition Cicero offers in *De divinatione*:

> It is not true that in suppressing superstition we are also suppressing religion. On the one hand, we act wisely when we maintain the ancestors' institutions by preserving rites and festivals, and on the other hand, the beauty of the world and the order of the heavenly phenomena force us to recognize that there is a superior and eternal nature that the human race must honor with its veneration.

> (Nec vero superstitione tollenda religio tollitur. Nam et majorum instituta tueri sacris caerimoniisque retinendis sapientis est, et esse praestantem aliquam aeternamque naturam, et eam suspiciendam admirandamque hominum generi pulchritudo mundi ordoque rerum caelestium cogit confiteri.)

> (*De divinatione*, 2.148)

The content given to *religio* associates the respectful preservation of the rites—because they were instituted by the ancestors—with the principal cause, according to the Greek philosophical tradition, of the formation of the belief in the divine, namely, admiration for the order and beauty of the world.

It is on the basis of this definition that we can understand the way Christian writers developed the word *religio*, even though they did not use the same criterion for distinguishing between religion and superstition: it is not how the gods are honored but which gods are honored that is crucial: "Religion is the worship of the true, superstition is the worship of the false" (religio veri cultus est, superstitio falsi). What matters is what one worships (*quid colas*), and not the way in which one does it (*quemadmodum colas*) (Lactantius, *Divine Institutions*, 4.28).

When attempts were made to show through etymology how *religio* could designate both a practice and what qualifies it in contrast to superstition, the transformation of the Latin word came into play. In the dialogue in the *Nature of the Gods*, the Stoic proposed in fact this twofold etymology: "those who, for days on end, prayed and sacrificed so that their children might survive (*superstites essent*), have been called superstitious (*superstitiosi*) . . . but those who examined carefully and, so to speak, gathered together (*tamquam relegerent*) everything that is related to the worship of the gods were called religious (*religiosi*), from the word *relegere*." This etymology emphasizes that which, in *religio*, refers to the scrupulous observation of the rites and associates their practice with the knowledge of its foundations: *relegere* means to gather together and reread to understand, as Varro did at the same time in his *Antiquitates rerum humanarum et divinarum*.

III. *Religio, Pietas, Sanctitas, Fides*

Another etymology was proposed by Lactantius, who emphasized instead the "bond":

> Hoc vinculo pietatis obstricti Deo et religati sumus: unde ipsa religio nomen accepit, non, ut Cicero interpretatus est, a relegendo. . . . Diximus nomen religionis a vinculo pietatis esse deductum quod hominem sibi Deus religaverit et pietate constrinxerit, quia servire nos ei ut domino et obsequi ut patri necesse est.

> (It is by this bond of piety that we are attached and bound to God. It is from this that religion has received its name, and not, as Cicero claimed, from the word *relegere*. . . . We have said that the word "religion" was deduced from the bond of piety, because God binds man to him and attaches him by piety, since we must necessarily serve him as a master and obey him as a father.)

> (*Divine Institutions*, 4.28.3–12)

Although Lactantius's etymology seems less well founded than that of the Stoics (see RT: *Le Vocabulaire des institutions indo-européennes*), it allows us in any case to understand the critical moment when the term *religio* included all the relations with the gods, in a synthesis of the juridical and moral links that entered into the definition of the word in the classical period.

By using the vocabulary of the bond, *vinculum-religare-constringere*, Lactantius emphasized the importance of *pietas*. In Classical Latin, *pietas* designates a type of relation that assumes that one performs the duties connected with the recognition of a juridical (and not natural) link, that of a son to his father, in particular. Thence proceeded the definition "pietas est justitia adversus deos" (piety is justice toward the gods) (*The Nature of the Gods*, 1.116). It was also the legal relationship that prevailed in *sanctitas*, covering everything that is protected by the sanction of the laws (*sanctire*). In addition to *pietas* and *sanctitas*, *fides* clearly defines the juridical sphere in which the relations of *religio* are defined: *fides* designates, on the basis of the protection that the victor owes to the vanquished, the guarantee provided by the state or by the gods who are implored "pro fidem deum." It was these three terms, associated in fluid semantic configurations, that allowed the elaboration of the definition proposed by Lactantius.

The inflection undergone by these three terms took place on the basis of a transfer of human relations to relations with the gods. In the particular case of *fides*, the inflection consisted in exploiting another field, that of rhetorical persuasion: to elicit the audience's confidence (*fides*), to obtain its assent (*fides*). The transition from persuasion to belief passed through the vocabulary of knowledge: "fides est firma opinio" (Cicero, *Partitiones oratoriae*, 9). Thus *opiniones* can designate all the kinds of knowledge the ancestors had

of the gods, and these kinds of knowledge, as such, were just as immutable as the rites instituted: "I shall defend the beliefs that our ancestors transmitted to us regarding the immortal gods, the rites and the practices of worship" (opiniones quas a majoribus accepimus de dis immortalibus, sacra, caerimonias religionesque) (*De natura deorum*, 3.5).

On the other hand, in classical usage we find no equivalent of a "belief in something." "The gods exist (or not)" is a proposition that is attached to a declarative verb, indicates a decision (*placet* [*De natura deorum*, 1.62]) or, finally, develops, in the Epicureans and Stoics, the content of a "pre-notion" (see ibid., 1.44–45; 2.13). As the object of an affirmation or negation, the proposition "the gods exist" cannot be governed by *credere*, whose epistemological value is too weak in Classical Latin. The closest approximation for an element of belief is the verb *suspicari* (to suspect, conjecture): "You blamed those who . . . , seeing the world . . . , suspected the existence of an excellent and eminent nature . . . [suspicati essent aliquam excellentem esse praestantem naturam]. But you, what masterpiece can you show us that makes you conjecture the existence of the gods [ex quo esse deos suspicere]?" (ibid., 1.100).

Clara Auvray-Assayas

BIBLIOGRAPHY

Cicero. *The Nature of the Gods*. Translated by P. G. Walsh. Oxford: Oxford University Press, 1998.

———. *Cicero on Divination: De divinatione, Book 1*. Translated with introduction and historical commentary by David Wardle. Oxford: Clarendon Press, 2006.

Lactantius. *The Divine Institutes, Books I–VII*. Translated by Sister Mary Francis McDonald. Washington, DC: Catholic University of American Press, 1964.

Scheid, John. *Religion et piété à Rome*. Paris: La Découverte, 1985.

———. *An Introduction to Roman Religion*. Translated by Janet Lloyd. Bloomington: Indiana University Press, 2003.

Wagenvoort, Henrik. *Pietas: Selected Studies in Roman Religion*. Leiden, Neth.: Brill, 1980.

| RELIGION

"Religion" is borrowed from the Latin *religio* (scrupulous attention), which is sometimes connected with the notion of "bond," from *religare* (bind), and sometimes with that of "collection, collect," from *relegere* (recollect), and includes a set of ritualized relations with the gods, but also relations of a juridical and moral order. Regarding the Latin word and its crucial Christian inflection, see RELIGIO and PIETAS; cf. LEX.

More generally, see the following:

1. On the relation between humans and the god(s), and on the representation of the sacred, see *ALLIANCE, BOGOČELOVEČESTVO, DEMON* [DAIMÔN, DUENDE], DEVIL, GOD; cf. *DESTINY, HUMANITY*.

2. On the relation between humans, the god(s), and the world, and on the mediation of the church, see also BERUF, SECULARIZATION, SOBORNOST' (and on Orthodox Christianity, *CONCILIARITY*); cf. *WORLD* [SVET, WELT].

3. On the vocabulary of belief, and on the relation between faith and reason, see *CROYANCE* [BELIEF, GLAUBE], REPRÉSENTATION.

REPRÉSENTATION (FRENCH)

ENGLISH   representation
GERMAN   *Vorstellung, Repräsentierung, Vertretung*
LATIN   *repraesentatio*

➤ BEGRIFF, CONSCIOUSNESS, DRIVE, ERSCHEINUNG, INTENTION, MIMÊSIS, PERCEPTION, PHANTASIA, *REASON*, SACHVERHALT, SENSE, SOUL, TRUTH, WILL

The term *représentation* can designate a relation, an action, or a vehicle of representation. The German terms *Repräsentierung* and *Vertretung* are used mainly to designate the action or relationship of representation. In Kant a *Vorstellung* implies a relation of representation, but it also has the characteristics of a vehicle. According to Frege, a *Vorstellung* is a secondary vehicle that has no intrinsic representative value. Moreover, he uses the term *Vertretung* in a different sense, to designate a logical relation between a concept and the object that "takes its place." The English term "representation," like the corresponding French term, has often been opposed to "presentation" (*présentation*). We also speak of mental or internal representations, by opposition to linguistic and iconic representations.

I. The Open Texture of the Term *Représentation*

The open texture of the term *représentation* is the main problem involved in using it to translate a philosopheme in a foreign language: the concept that it expresses is only partially determined and has optional marks (in the sense of Frege's *Merkmale*, that is, characteristics that every object that is subsumed under a concept has to have; see MERKMAL) that are sometimes mutually incompatible. The use of this term thus raises questions that the philosopher and translator have to answer if they intend to use it in a coherent way. It is useful to distinguish two groups of pertinent questions, even though this list is not exhaustive.

A. *Représentation*: A relationship, an action, or a vehicle?

The first question concerns the ontological status of representation. The term *représentation* can be considered the nominalization of the verb "to represent." In that case it designates either a simple relationship or the (relational) action of being represented. In general, a representation is a representation *of* something. The notion of representation thus typically includes the idea of a relationship. Since Brentano this notion has been associated with that of intentionality, understood here as a representation's property of referring to something other than itself (or simply to itself, in the borderline case of a self-reflexive representation such as: "The present sentence is false"). The simplest logical form of a representation is a dyadic relationship: "*x* represents *y*" or "*x* represents *y* to itself." In the first case, *x* is the vehicle of the representation (which may be a proposition, a mental state, an image, or a picture), and *y* is what is represented (a thing or a state of affairs). In the second case, *x* is the subject of the representation, and no independent vehicle is mentioned. We can combine these two schemas in a single form that figures representation as a triadic relationship: "*x* represents *y* for *z*," where *x* is the vehicle of representation, *y* is what is represented, and *z* is an interpreter, or, in Peirce's theory, an "interpretant," that is, an additional sign produced in the mind of the interpreter (cf. Peirce, *Elements of Logic*, §208; see SIGN, IV.A).

The term *représentation* can also be used to designate, not the relationship of representation, but one of the possible terms of this relationship, namely its vehicle. Then we speak of a representation as an entity (proposition, mental state, picture, etc.) that represents something, possibly for someone. In this sense a portrait, for example, not only implies a relation of representation with its model, but "is" itself a representation. This use, which is very common, may lead to confusion. In general, the vehicle of a representation is an entity external to the relationship of representation, in the sense in which the vehicle can be characterized independently of the fact that it enters into a relationship of representation. Thus we can identify a picture, for example, by its material properties (size, shape, colors), independently of the fact that it represents something. In other cases this condition of exteriority is not fulfilled, which leads to an abusive reification of the representation: the latter becomes the postulated term of a relation of representation without its being possible to characterize it otherwise.

B. The meaning of "re-"

Another set of questions concerns the indirect or mediate character of representation. The term *représentation* suggests, because of the prefix "re-," that what is represented is also capable of being simply "presented," that is, that the representation of something is based on the assumption that it is at least possible to present it as well. The distinction between presentation and representation can be understood in a temporal sense if, for example, we emphasize the fact that a representation must be caused by a presentation. But the repetition can also be understood in a logical sense. For example, it is sometimes thought that the representation involves a predicative or quasi-predicative articulation: *x* is represented as an *F* (as a man, as a table), where *F* is a predicate that characterizes or "typifies" what is represented. The representation itself is supposed to be "ante-predicative," that is, anterior to the distinction between what is represented and the way in which it is represented.

II. The Kantian Paradigm: *Vorstellung, Repräsentierung, Vertretung*

The German terms *Vorstellung, Vertretung*, and *Repräsentierung* are all often translated by *représentation*. If the translation of Kant's writings did not inaugurate the translation of *Vorstellung* (from *vor-stellen*, literally, "place before") by *représentation*, it at least established it. In fact, Kant defines the technical concept of *Vorstellung* by means of the ordinary verb *vertreten*, which suggests "moving in front of something" (*vor etwas treten*), and of which the corresponding noun is *Vertretung*: the *Vorstellung* is a "determination (*Bestimmung*) in us that we relate to something else (which it represents [*vertritt*], so to speak, in us)" (letter to Beck, 4 December 1792, Ak. 11: 395, cf. Freuler, *Kant*, 46). Moreover, Kant frequently uses instead of *Vorstellung* the Latin term *repraesentatio*, from which *Repräsentierung* directly issued. Kant distinguished two main types of conscious representation: the singular representation or intuition (*repraesentatio singularis, Anschauung*), and the general representation or concept (*repraesentatio generalis, Begriff*) (See ANSCHAULICHKEIT, BEGRIFF).

Kant's usage of the term *Vorstellung* is not only compatible with the semantic profile of the English term "representation" but responds explicitly to the main questions left open by the latter. First, every representation is intrinsically directed toward an object: "All representations have, as representations, their object" (*Critique of Pure Reason*, A 108). The *Vorstellung* is an element in an intentional relationship of representation. Second, the *Vorstellung* is "in us," that is, it is intrinsically subjective or psychological. Finally, the *Vorstellung* presupposes a certain distinction between the object represented and the way it is represented, which Kant calls the "content" (*Materie* or *Inhalt*) of the representation.

Nonetheless, the association of the first two marks of the Kantian concept of representation can give rise to a certain intellectual tension. Whereas Kant uses the terms *Vertretung* and *Repräsentierung* especially to designate the action or relation of representation, he uses the term *Vorstellung* to designate a mental state, a determination in us that has the value of representation. But how can something be both "in us" and imply a relation to an object represented "outside us"? Either Kant's *Vorstellung* has an intrinsic value of representation, in which case it would be wrong to reify it, or it is only a vehicle of the representation and can be characterized independently, though evidently Kant does not do so. About two hundred years later, Frege was to resolve this tension in an admirably rigorous way.

III. Frege Twists *Vorstellung*

Frege often twists Kant's vocabulary. In a note to the *Foundations of Arithmetic* (cf. §26, note 2), he criticizes Kant for having associated the term *Vorstellung* with two very distinct meanings. In the subjective sense a representation is sensible in nature and is like a mental image. In the objective sense it has nothing to do with the sensible and is logical in nature. To avoid confusion Frege reserves *Vorstellung* for the designation of the subjective representation.

Later on, in *The Thought: A Logical Investigation* (*Der Gedanke: Eine logische Untersuchung*, 1918), Frege gives the term *Vorstellung* a more general meaning. In this essay Frege recognizes three ontological domains—three "worlds" or "realms" (*Reiche*) of entities having different modes of existence. The first world is the external world (*Außenwelt*), which contains among other things all natural and thus objective entities. The second world, which is internal (*Innenwelt*), is that of psychological entities, which Frege divides into *Vorstellungen* and *Entschlüsse* (volitions). Representations include sense impressions, the creations of the imagination, sensations, emotions, sentiments, states of mind, inclinations, and desires. Finally, the third world is that of thoughts (*Gedanken*), whose constituents are the "senses" (*Sinne*) of linguistic expressions. Frege explains that *Vorstellungen*, like thoughts, are not accessible to sense perception, but that, unlike thoughts, they belong to the content of consciousness and necessarily have a "bearer" (*Träger*, that is, the subject of the representations).

No doubt the translation of *Vorstellung* by *représentation* is inevitable here, but it presents a difficulty: Frege's *Vorstellungen* do not have the property of intentionality, which seems to be the obligatory mark of our term *représentation*. Sense impressions, for example, are incapable of opening us to the outside world. The sensation of redness is a representation of redness only in the sense in which one speaks of the dancing of a waltz: just as dancing a waltz does not consist in putting oneself in relation to the object "waltz," having an impression of redness does not put the subject in relation with the quality "redness." Only thoughts (*Gedanken*), which do not belong to the content of consciousness, are capable of breaking the circle of our internal representations. But thought does not need *Vorstellungen* to be conveyed: the main vehicle of thought is public language—linguistic representations. Frege's English translators have preferred to translate *Vorstellung* by "idea" rather than "representation," but the difficulty just mentioned does not thereby disappear: an idea is still the idea "of" something that is in principle distinct from the idea itself.

A possible solution to this difficulty consists in interpreting Frege's *Vorstellung* as a secondary vehicle of thought, and thus as a term independent of certain relations of conceptual representation. The *Vorstellung* fulfills the condition that we set for an entity to be considered as a vehicle: it can be characterized independently of its value of representation, that is, as an element of consciousness accessible to introspection. Consequently, a sense impression, or a mental image, can represent an object only with the support of an appropriate conceptual background:

> The predicate "true" is not properly attributed to the representation itself, but rather to the thought that this representation depicts a certain object.
>
> (Daraus ist zu entnehmen, dass eigentlich nicht der Vorstellung selbst das Prädikat *wahr* zuerkannt wird, sondern dem Gedanken, dass sie einen gewissen Gegenstand abbilde.)
>
> (Frege, *Nachgelassene Schriften*, 142)

This interpretation, to which Dummett (*Origins of Analytical Philosophy*) drew attention, certainly does not diminish the essential differences between Kant's and Frege's notions of the *Vorstellung*, but it does justify to a certain extent the translation of Frege's *Vorstellung* by *représentation*.

IV. Frege and the Paradoxes of *Vertretung*

Frege uses the verb *vertreten* in a sense very different from that of *vorstellen*. In "On Concept and Object," Frege formulates the following famous paradox: although the city of Berlin is a city and the volcano Vesuvius is a volcano, the concept "horse" is not a concept. In Frege's view the expression "the concept 'horse'" can designate only an object, because it occupies the grammatical position of subject. An object is a complete entity, closed in upon itself, whereas a concept is by nature essentially incomplete or predicative. It follows that it is impossible to designate a concept directly, that is, by means of a singular expression, for the latter would necessarily lack the incomplete character of the concept. Frege then suggests that the singular expression "the concept 'horse'" designates a special object that "represents" or "takes the place of" (*vertretet*) the concept that one vainly sought to designate directly. In the *Basic Laws of Arithmetic* (1893–1903), Frege explains that this object is none other than the extension of the concept, or more precisely what

Frege calls its "truth-value range." As Philippe de Rouilhan has pointed out (*Frege*, 60), the extension is the *représentant* (*Vertreter*) of the concept in the category of objects. (Note the still more marked legal connotation in the English translation of Frege's book, where *vertreten* is rendered as "to go proxy for.")

Even if *vertreten* has been translated here as "represent" (de Rouilhan himself speaks of the "paradoxes of representation"), we must keep in mind the rigorous distinction that Frege makes between *vertreten* and *vorstellen*. He uses the verb *vertreten* principally to designate a purely logical relation that owes nothing to the psychological world. The noun *Vertretung* must thus be understood as being merely the nominalization of the verb *vertreten*. On the other hand, the expression *(sich) vorstellen* signifies "to have representations," where the latter are (as we have seen) essentially psychological entities.

V. "Presentation," "Representation," and "Mental Representation"

The English term "representation," like the French *représentation* and the German *Repräsentierung*, sometimes connotes an absence of immediacy. Thus, we can understand the contrast, to which Husserl draws attention in *Ding und Raum* (1907, 13–15), between the object of perception, which is there in the present and, as it were, in person (*als leibhafter*), on the one hand, and the object of imagination or belief, which is only "represented" (*vorgestellt*). Jacques Bouveresse (*Langage, perception*, 1: 54) has asked (but cf. Pacherie, "Théories représentationnelles") whether a model of perception, seen as constructing "internal representations" of the environment could really do justice to this observation by Husserl. Perception does indeed have an intentional object, but the latter seems to be intended directly, without being mediated by an internal representation.

The critique of the notion of internal representation is not peculiar to phenomenology. In the cognitive sciences an important school of thought has since the 1980s opposed the "cognitivist" paradigm incarnated by Fodor's "Representational Theory of Mind." According to this theory, our cognitive access to reality is mediated by "mental representations" that Fodor conceives as essentially symbolic—this is the hypothesis of the "language of thought." Fodor's detractors have criticized the "intellectualist" character of the representational theory of mind, which multiplies mental representations, arguing that essentially practical or nonrepresentational capacities provide a better account of an organism's intelligent interaction with its environment (cf. Cantwell-Smith, "Situatedness/Embeddedness"; Von Eckardt, "Mental Representations").

On the purely lexical level, however, the terms "presentation" and "representation" are not always seen as contraries. For example, John Searle considers presentations as kinds of representations. According to Searle, most if not all intentional states are representations of states of affairs. Presentations are thus representations that are characterized by their "direct," "immediate," and "involuntary" character. Visual experience, for instance, is better described as a presentation than as a representation, even though in reality it is both at once:

> The visual experience ... does not just represent the state of affairs perceived; rather, when satisfied, it gives us direct access to it, and in that sense it is a presentation of that state of affairs.

> (Searle, *Intentionality*, 46)

According to Searle's taxonomy, memory and propositional attitudes such as belief, desire, and previous intention are only simple representations, whereas perceptive experience and intention in action are also presentations.

Searle observes that it is not "natural" to describe perceptive experience as a representation because "if we talk that way it is almost bound to lead to the representative theory of perception" (ibid.). According to this theory, the perceiving subject does not perceive a physical object directly, but indirectly; his immediate perception is mediated by a "sense-datum" that can only represent the object.

Generally speaking, the critique of internal (or mental) representation can take several forms. For example, one can ask what the cognitive status of internal representations is, and especially whether the subject's cognitive access to what is represented has to pass by way of a cognitive access to the representation itself. If our only cognitive access to reality is representational in nature, an affirmative answer to this question seems to lead to an infinite regress (cf. Judge, *Thinking about Things*).

A very different criticism, which is independent of the preceding one, concerns the thesis that what we call "representation" necessarily involves a propositional articulation, whereas perception is "ante-predicative" (Husserl, *Erfahrung und Urteil*). Once again, this thesis presupposes a semantic choice. From a strictly lexical point of view, there is no objection to considering perception, no matter how immediate, as a "representation" (*représentation*, *Repräsentierung*) of its object.

Jérôme Dokic

BIBLIOGRAPHY

Bouveresse, Jacques. *Langage, perception et réalité*. Vol. 1 of *La Perception et le jugement*. Nimes, Fr.: Jacqueline Chambon, 1995.

Cantwell-Smith, Brian. "Situatedness/Embeddedness." In *The MIT Encyclopedia of Cognitive Science*. Edited by Robert A. Wilson and Frank Keil, 769–70. Cambridge, MA: MIT Press, 1999.

Clapin, Hugh, ed. *Philosophy of Mental Representation*. Oxford: Oxford University Press, 2002.

Cummins, Robert. *Meaning and Mental Representation*. Cambridge, MA: MIT Press, 1989.

Dickerson, A. B. *Kant on Representation and Objectivity*. Cambridge: Cambridge University Press, 2004.

Dummett, Michael. *Origins of Analytical Philosophy*. London: Duckworth, 1993.

Fodor, Jerry. *The Language of Thought*. Cambridge, MA: Harvard University Press, 1975.

———. *Representations*. Cambridge, MA: MIT Press, 1981.

Frege, Gottlob. *The Foundations of Arithmetic: A Logico-Mathematical Enquiry into the Concept of Number*. Translated by J. L. Austin. 2nd ed. Oxford: Blackwell, 1978. First published in 1884.

———. "Logik." In *Nachgelassene Schriften*. Edited by H. Hermes, F. Kambartel, and F. Kaulbach. Hamburg: Felix Meiner, 1969. Translation by P. Long and R. White: *Posthumous Writings*. Chicago: University of Chicago Press, 1979.

———. "On Concept and Object." In *Translations from the Philosophical Writings of Gottlob Frege*. 3rd ed. Edited and translated by Peter T. Geach and Max Black. Oxford: Blackwell, 1980. First published in 1892.

———. "The Thought." In *Logical Investigations*. Translated by Peter T. Geach and R. H. Stoothoff. Edited by P. T. Geach. New Haven, CT: Yale University Press, 1977. First published in 1918.

Freuler, Léo. *Kant et la métaphysique spéculative*. Paris: Vrin, 1992.

Husserl, Edmund. *Erfahrung und Urteil: Untersuchungen zur Genealogie der Logik*. Prague: Academia Verlagsbuchhandlung, 1939. Translation by James S. Churchill and Karl Ameriks: *Experience and Judgment: Investigations in a Genealogy of Logic*. Revised and edited by Ludwig Landgrebe. Evanston, IL: Northwestern University Press, 1973.

———. *Ding und Raum. Vorlesungen 1907*. Edited by Ulrich Claesges. The Hague: Martinus Nijhoff, 1973. Translation by Richard Rojcewicz: *Thing and Space: Lectures of 1907*. Edited by Richard Rojcewicz. Dordrecht, Neth.: Kluwer, 1997.

Judge, Brenda. *Thinking about Things: A Philosophical Study of Representation*. Edinburgh: Scottish Academic Press, 1985.

Kant, Immanuel. *Correspondence*. Translated and edited by Arnulf Zweig. Cambridge: Cambridge University Press, 1999.

———. *Critique of Pure Reason*. Translated by Paul Guyer and Allen Wood. Cambridge: Cambridge University Press, 1998.

Pacherie, Élisabeth. "Théories représentationnelles de l'intentionnalité perceptive et Leibhaftigkeit de l'objet dans la perception." *Archives de philosophie* 58, no. 4 (1995): 577–88.

Peirce, Charles Sanders. *Elements of Logic*. Vol. 2 of *Collected Papers*. Edited by C. Hartshorne and P. Weiss. Cambridge, MA: Harvard University Press, 1965.

Rorty, Richard. *Philosophy and the Mirror of Nature*. 30th anniversary ed. Princeton, NJ: Princeton University Press, 2009.

Rouilhan, Philippe de. *Frege et les paradoxes de la représentation*. Paris: Éditions de Minuit, 1988.

Searle, John. *Intentionality: An Essay in the Philosophy of Mind*. Cambridge: Cambridge University Press, 1983.

Von Eckardt, Barbara. "Mental Representation." In *The MIT Encyclopedia of Cognitive Science*. Edited by Robert A. Wilson and Frank Keil, 527–29. Cambridge, MA: MIT Press, 1999.

RES, ENS (LATIN)

ARABIC	*šay'* [شيء], *ma'nā* [المعنى]
ENGLISH	thing, something
FRENCH	*chose, quelque chose*
GERMAN	*Ding, Sache, etwas*
GREEK	*chrêma* [χρῆμα], *pragma* [πρᾶγμα], *ti* [τι], *ousia* [οὐσία], *on* [ὄν], *onta* [ὄντα]
ITALIAN	*cosa, qualcosa*
SPANISH	*cosa, algo*

➤ THING and ESSENCE, GEGENSTAND, HOMONYM, INTENTION, LOGOS, *NEGATION*, *NOTHING*, OBJECT, REALITY, SACHVERHALT, SEIN, SENSE, SIGN, SIGNIFIER/ SIGNIFIED, *TO BE*, WORD

Perhaps nothing fated the Latin word *res* to have such a long philosophical career—extending from Cicero to Franz Brentano's "reism" by way of Latin Scholasticism and German academic metaphysics of the seventeenth and eighteenth centuries—except its remarkable indeterminacy. This career allowed it, in passing through rhetoric and the fields of economics, law, logic, and finally metaphysics, to position itself not only as a possible equivalent of the Greek term considered the most common, *to on* [τὸ ὄν], "being" or "the existent," but also to overflow, so to speak, in the direction of the opposition between *aliquid* and *nihil*, "something" and "nothing," to the point of erecting itself into an absolutely primary or supertranscendental term. In another aspect of its semantics, the derivatives *realis* and *realitas* opened up the field of formality and possibility.

I. The Stoics and Aristotelian Semantics: *Pragma*, from the Thing Itself to the Incorporeal

The philosophical history of the word *res* doubtless parallels rather closely that of the Greek term *pragma* [πρᾶγμα], whose meaning was initially legal and rhetorical (Aristotle, *Topics* 1.18, 108a21; *Rhetoric* 3.14, 1415b4). *Pragma* designates the fact or affair that must be discussed, debated, and judged in a trial ("*die Streitsache, um die es vor Gericht geht*"; Wieland, *Die aristotelische Physik*, 170), and not only the material and individual reality given or immediately present. That is why this same term can also characterize what is indicated by a word or proposition, the meaning or state of affairs in question. That is certainly how Plato uses it in letter 7.341c: *to pragma auto* [τὸ πρᾶγμα αὐτό] does not signify the thing in itself, but rather the matter at issue, the "problems" debated, or the "subject" in dispute (as rendered in Joseph Souilhé's translation of Plato's letters). And it is legitimate to see in this passage of Plato the final anchoring point of the phenomenological maxim—as Husserlian as it is Heideggerian: "*Zur Sache selbst.*" The Latin translators, from Boethius to William of Moerbeke, did not find it difficult to render these different meanings by using the expression *res ipsa*.

Thanks in particular to Boethius's translations of the *Peri hermêneias*, the opposition *logos/pragma* [λόγος/πρᾶγμα] passed quite naturally into Latin, the term *res* not designating exclusively a singular material reality that is external and transcendent with respect to discourse. Let us also recall that in the famous opening of the *Peri hermêneias*, where Aristotle distinguishes between *pragmata* [πράγματα] and *pathêmata tês psuchês* [παθήματα τῆς ψυχῆς], the affections of the mind that reflect them and whose vocal forms (*phônai* [φωναί]) are symbols or signs, the term *pragmata* refers more to states of affairs than to material and singular things (see SIGN)—cf. Aristotle, *Metaphysics* Δ.29: it is proposed here that "the diagonal of a square is commensurate with the side" (*to tên diametron einai summetron* [τὸ τὴν διάμετρον εἶναι σύμμετρον]), or that "you are sitting" (*to se kathêsthai* [τὸ σὲ καθῆσθαι], 1024b19–20), as examples of statements of a state of affairs (*pragma*), of a "being such and such," always false, or sometimes true, sometimes false (see De Rijk, "*Logos* and *Pragma* in Plato and Aristotle").

This also allows us to correct the too-frequent interpretation of the famous passage in Aristotle's *Sophistical Refutations* (165a6–16) where he points out that we cannot bring into the discussion "the things themselves that are being debated" and that we must instead "use words as symbols" ("*epei gar ouk estin auta ta pragmata dialegesthai pherontas, alla tois onomasin anti tôn pragmatôn chrômetha hôs sumbolois*" [ἐπεὶ γὰρ οὐκ ἔστιν αὐτὰ τὰ πράγματα διαλέγεσθαι φέροντας, ἀλλὰ τοῖς ὀνόμασιν ἀντὶ τῶν πραγμάτων χρώμεθα ὡς συμβόλοις]"). The expression "the things themselves" does not refer primarily to an extra-mental and a-semantic reality—a stone, an ox, or an ass (which in fact it would often be difficult to bring into the discussion)—but to the affair at issue ("*die Sache, um die es in der Aussage geht; . . . etwas, worum es in der Rede geht*," Wieland, *Die aristotelische Physik*, 159–60). (Against this view, see HOMONYM, II.B.3).

■ See Box 1.

1

Ways of saying "thing" in Greek

➤ LAW, Box 1; PRAXIS; SEX, Box 1; VORHANDEN

If we start with the ways of saying "thing" in vernacular languages—for example, French *chose*—the most common retroversion is obviously the neuter, and particularly the neuter of nominalized participles, which is rendered, more or less, by adding *chose* or *objet* (see, for example, *aisthêton*, in SENSE, Box 1, on the article *to*; cf. I/ME/MYSELF, Box 2, on *auto*), or again the neuter of the relative pronouns and demonstratives (Ildefonse and Lallot innovate by proposing for the relatives at the beginning of Aristotle's *Categories*: "On dit homonymes les *items* [*hôn* (ὧν)] qui n'ont de commun qu'un nom"). But these are merely expletive "things," by default and by projection (see OBJECT). The same can be said of the indefinite *ti* [τι], which functions, when accented, like an interrogative (What? Which?): it has no equivalent other than "something" (*kalon ti* [καλόν τι], "something beautiful"), even when it designates, in the Stoic doctrine, that strange and remarkable supreme genre, "the something" (*to ti* [τὸ τι], quid: Seneca, letter 58.24; *res*, Cicero also says: see here, III), which includes both the bodies and the incorporeals and which Plotinus considers "incomprehensible" (*Enneads* 6.1.25.6–10).

In Greek, however, there are direct, "semanticized" ways of designating what French designates by *chose* in the full sense, *via* the Latin senses of *res* and *causa*, even if there is, as we shall see, no equivalence between them. Two words were in competition, *pragma* [πρᾶγμα] and *chrêma* [χρῆμα].

Pragma derives from *prassô* [πράσσω]. In Homer it is used only intransitively, in the sense of "go all the way, go all over," but in general it is transitive: "to achieve, accomplish, work on, deal with a matter, practice" (RT: Chantraine, *Dictionnaire étymologique de la langue grecque*, s.v.). More concrete than *praxis* [πρᾶξις], whose primary meaning is "activity" (see PRAXIS), *pragma* designates the motive or result of this activity: the thing as related to an action, the task, the affair, the concrete reality, the object. In the singular, it indicates both the subject matter (what is at issue), and what is actual and real, what is the case—in both senses, the thing itself (*auto to pragma* [αὐτὸ τὸ πρᾶγμα]) is involved, and it is very close to what *res* means in its primary senses, from the juridico-economic to the object of thought. But the plural, *ta pragmata*, is clearly more concrete: it designates "the realities" of the external world in which we act, namely the things that have occurred, the "facts," and the things we deal with, "affairs," whether public or private. It is the most common philosophical term for the objects in the world, including natural realities, insofar as living and knowing human beings are implied ("If external things [*ta pragmata*] are numerous and in movement toward each other," Melissus, 30A5; RT: DK 1:260, 974a25, for example). Moreover, that is why one cannot endorse Pierre Hadot's previously mentioned interpretation of the opening of Aristotle's *Sophistical Refutations*: if in this passage Aristotle regards homonymy as the radical illness of language, that is because there are more "things" than words, more concrete realities with which we have to deal than words at our disposal in natural language (cf. Cassin, *L'effet sophistique*, 344–47, and 386–87 n. 8). We can compare this "reality" connected with practice to *Wirklichkeit*, which is also connected with a *Wirken*, with the actuality of an implementation (see REALITY, VI), on at least one point: *pragmata* and *Wirklichkeit* are both distinguished by a pure, simple, ontologically immediate "given," that of the *phainomena* [φαινόμενα], the *onta* [ὄντα], "phenomena," "beings," the "things" that emerge on their own, appear and remain there, without reference to any operation at all (see ERSCHEINUNG, ESTI, and LIGHT, Box 1).

The other term, *chrêma*, implies human beings still more strictly. It is connected with a very large family derived from *chrê* [χρή], "it is necessary," in the sense of "there is need," and is centered on *chraomai* [χράομαι], "seek the use of something," "resort to for one's own use." Often seen as connected with *cheir* [χείρ], "hand" (and linked, by Heidegger himself, with *vorhanden*; see VORHANDEN), but also often connected with *chairô* [χαίρω] "enjoy" (RT: Chantraine, *Dictionnaire étymologique de la langue grecque*, s.v. *chraomai*, 1275), *chraomai* means "make use of," whether it is a matter of borrowing from a neighbor or questioning the god by consulting an oracle (*chrêsmos* [χρησμός] designates the reply), with the earlier sense of "lack, desire," and the later sense of "have a relationship with someone, become addicted to, undergo." Let us note, as testimony to the breadth of the theme, the adverb *parachrêma* [παραχρῆμα], "immediately" (literally, "ready for use"), and alongside the noun of action *chrêsis* [χρῆσις], the substantive *chreia* [χρεία], "use," which designates both a service or function (military "service") and a grammatical and rhetorical use (the *chreia* is the exploitation of commonplaces in an oratorical exercise). We see that *chrêma* names the thing insofar as it is used and counts, the poet, Plato says—*Ion* 534b—is "a light thing [*chrêma*], winged and sacred": it is because he is part of a chain that leads from the god and the muse to the rhapsode and the listener, in which he constitutes a particularly noteworthy functional link); in the plural, *ta chrêmata* [τὰ χρήματα] usually signifies "wealth, resources" (in modern Greek, *chrêma* means "money"): *chrêma* is, Gernet notes, "the very type of the economic notion" (*Droit et institutions*, 11 and n. 32). This definition of the "thing" by its use and function, like that of wealth by expenditure, is very frequent in the texts, from Antiphon (the miser who steals the *chrêmata*, riches, buried under a tree, and must console himself this way: "When it was yours, you didn't make use of it either" [*oud'* . . . *echrô* (οὐδ' . . . ἐχρῶ)], RT: 87B54 DK; cf. Cassin, *L'effet sophistique*, 325–26) to Aristotle: "The use of riches [*chrêsis* . . . *chrêmatôn* (χρῆσις . . . χρημάτων)] seems indeed to be spending them and giving them away [*dapanê kai dosis* (δαπάνη καὶ δόσις)]" (*Nicomachean Ethics* 3.4, 1120a4–9).

Chrêmata is thus the word that, in Anaxagoras's famous fragment "*homou panta chrêmata ên* [ὁμοῦ πάντα χρήματα ἦν]" ("All things were together," RT: 59B1 DK, 2:32, 11), and in Protagoras's equally famous fragment "*pantôn chrêmatôn metron estin anthrôpos* [πάντων χρημάτων μέτρον ἐστὶν ἄνθρωπος]" ("Man is the measure of all things," RT: 80B1 DK, 2:263, 3–4), is always rendered by "things" (*alle Dinge*, RT: DK). We see that a certain precaution is called for. In particular, it cannot be taken for granted that the reference is to phenomena and beings, according to the equivalences proposed by Sextus Empiricus (*Outlines of Pyrrhonism* 1.216) and endorsed by Heidegger, the better to make Anaxagoras and Protagoras Parmenidean pre-Socratics, Protagoras simply giving a fine moderation to the unveiling of *alêtheia* [ἀλήθεια] (cf. Cassin, *L'effet sophistique*, 108–10 and 225–36). It seems more accurate to say that the man of *chrêmata*, taken in a general economy of flux and expenditure, seeks to determine *pragmata*, to delimit them by his activity, to stabilize them into a world. In any case, this is to take seriously the clues that words and their use in the texts persist in giving us.

In the singular, from *pragma* to *res*, the consequence is good, even if the inventive sequel of history belongs only to *res*. But in the plural we have to distinguish, without counting the "items," at least two series of "things" in Greek: those that are given, and belong to the domain of the phenomenon of and phenomenology; and those that are acted, and are connected with the implication of human

(continued)

(continued)

beings as practitioners and users. The latter, which are called *pragmata* and *chrêmata*, lie outside the history of ontology.

Barbara Cassin

BIBLIOGRAPHY

Aristotle. *Catégories.* Translated and edited by Frédérique Ildefonse and Jean Lallot. Paris: Seuil, 2002.

———. *Categories and On Interpretation.* Translated by J. L. Ackrill. Oxford: Clarendon, 1963.

Cassin, Barbara. *L'effet sophistique.* Paris: Gallimard, 1996.

Gernet, Louis. *Droit et institutions dans la Grèce antique.* Paris: Flammarion, 1982.

Sextus Empiricus. *Outlines of Pyrrhonism.* Translated by R. G. Bury. Loeb Classical Library. London: W. Heinemann, 1933.

For their part, the Stoics, according to Sextus Empiricus (*Adversus mathematicos* 8.11–12; RT: *SVF* 2:166; RT: Long and Sedley, *The Hellenistic Philosophers*, 33B, 2:191), distinguished among the signifier (*to sêmainon* [τὸ σημαίνον]), that is, the vocal form or utterance (*phônê* [φωνὴ]), the signification (*to sêmainomenon* [τὸ σημαινόμενον]), which is the *pragma*, the conceptual content or the intentional object indicated by the voice ("*auto to pragma to hup' autês <phônês> dêloumenon* [αὐτὸ τὸ πρᾶγμα τὸ ὑπ' αὐτῆς <φωνῆς> δηλούμενον]"), "the actual state of affairs revealed by an utterance," the "intension" (De Rijk, "*Logos* and *Pragma* in Plato and Aristotle"), and its extralinguistic correlate: the external substrate, *to ektos hupokeimenon* [τὸ ἐκτὸς ὑποκείμενον], namely, the event, *to tugchanon* [τὸ τυγχάνον] (on the referent, see De Rijk, "*Logos* and *Pragma* in Plato and Aristotle"; on the name-bearer, see RT: Long and Sedley, *The Hellenistic Philosophers*, 1:197; see also SIGNIFIER/SIGNIFIED). Max Pohlenz pointed out that according to Hellenistic usage, *ta tunchanonta* [τὰ τυγχάνοντα] should be understood as an abbreviation of *ha tugchanei onta* [ἃ τυγχάνει ὄντα], "that which is," "which is met with" (Pohlenz, *Die Stoa*, 2:22; see Hadot, "Sur les divers sens du mot *pragma* dans la tradition philosophique grecque," in *Études de philosophie ancienne*, 61–76). See also Box 1.

II. The Latin Legal and Economic Heritage: *Res/Bona, Res/Causa, Res/Verba*

If there is a specifically Latin and prephilosophical history of the term *res*, it probably concerns the sphere of goods (*bona*), possession, wealth, or interest, as we see in Roman comedy (Plautus, *Pseudologus* 338: "It is not in your interest [*ex tua re non est*]"), or in common expressions such as *rem augere* (increase one's fortune) or *in rem esse alicui* (to be in someone's interest). This latter meaning is probably in conformity with the etymology, if it is true that the term is related to Sanskrit *revan* (wealth), as Ernout and Meillet claim (RT: *Dictionnaire étymologique de la langue latine*, s.v. *res*). This legal-economic meaning is presupposed by numerous compound expressions: *res sua, aliena, privata, publica, venalis, extra commercium, mobilis, immobilis, in patrimonio, extra patrimonium*, and even *res corporalis*, to designate a material, sensible, tangible thing by opposition to incorporeal *res*, such as the right to property (Gaius, *Institutiones* 2.12–14). In the juridical domain, we can distinguish between the *res* (the affair in general, the facts) and the *causa* (the charges or indictment, with regard to which the guilt or innocence of the accused has to be determined): *de re et causa iudicare*: Cicero, *Partitiones oratoriae* 9.30; *De finibus* 1.5.15, 2.2.5, 2.2.6).

In the general context of Latin rhetoric, the term *res* designates in an indeterminate way the subject matter of a discourse (*res de qua agitur*), so that it is the orator's peculiar task to set forth a question or a subject (*rem exponere, rem narrare*). If it fails to understand the subject or the *status quaestionis* (the *res subiectae*: Quintilian, *De institutione oratoria* 2.21.4), rhetoric risks falling into mere rambling about everything and nothing (Cicero, *De oratore* 1.6.20: "*Oratio . . . nisi subest res ab oratore percepta et cognita, inanem quandam habet elocutionem et paene puerilem*" (A speech, if it is not supported by a fund of precise knowledge, will be no more than a vain and frivolous display of words). But the word *res* (just like the Greek *pragma*) can also refer to thoughts, as in this description of the *oratio* given by Quintilian: "*Orationem . . . omnem constare rebus et verbis*," to which correspond respectively *inventio*, when it is a matter of *res* = thoughts, and *dispositio*, when it is a matter of discourse properly so called. Thus judicial rhetoric classically distinguishes between the "affair" that is to be judged and the *circumstantiae rei*—the examination of the circumstances being clarified in turn through questions that refer to the Aristotelian categories, *quid? quale? quantum? ad aliquid?*—whereas the rhetorical tradition also classifies the *loci* in relation to the opposition between *res* and *persona* (Quintilian, *De institutione oratoria* 5.10.23; Cicero, *De inventione* 1.24.34).

III. *Res* and *Corpus*

Despite a few passages in Tertullian that connect being a thing with corporeality, it does not seem that the *res* was understood from the outset as *solida* or associated with the body. In fact, Tertullian's use of the word *substantia* (*substantia corporis*) and the definition that he gives of it—"*cum ipsa substantia corpus sit rei cuiusque*"—militates rather in favor of the essential indeterminacy of the *res*, after it has concealed its original economic connotation (cf. Moingt, *Théologie trinitaire*, which includes a valuable index and lexicographic repertory). It was probably the indeterminacy of the term that made possible such a deliberate attempt to transpose or explain the Greek *ousia* [οὐσία]: "*Quomodo dicetur οὐσία— res necessaria, natura continens fundamentum omnium?*" Seneca asked in his famous letter 58, which begins by deploring the poverty of the Latin vocabulary when one seeks to set forth Plato's philosophy: "*Quanta verborum nobis paupertas, immo egestas sit, numquam magis quam hodierno die intellexi*" (How poor our vocabulary is, in fact, poverty-stricken. Never have I understood this as I have today).

In his *Topics*, Cicero also plays on the generality of a term that can designate both things that are ("*earum rerum quae sunt*"), like *fundum, penus, aedis, parietem, pecudem*, and so on, and intelligible things ("*earum quae intelleguntur*") without any *substantia corporis*, such as *ususcapio, tutela, agnatio*:

unum earum rerum quae sunt, alterum earum quae intelleguntur. Esse ea dico quae cerni tangive possunt, ut fundum aedis, parietem stillicidium, mancipium pecudem, supellectilem penus cetera; quo ex genere quaedam interdum vobis definienda sunt . . . Non esse rursus ea dico quae tangi demonstrarive non possunt, cerni tamen animo atque intellegi possunt, ut si usus capionem, si tutelam, si gentem, si agnationem definias; qualium rerum nullum subest quasi corpus . . .

(One group includes things that are, the other those that are intelligible. I say that the former are things that can be seen and touched, such as land, a house, a wall, a gutter, a slave, and large livestock, small livestock, furniture, provisions, etc.; in this group some elements remain to be defined. On the other hand, I say that these realities are not things that cannot be touched or pointed to, but are things that can nonetheless be seen and understood by the mind, such as property rights, trusteeship, clan, consanguinity, and anything else that lacks any bodily substrate.)

(Cicero, *Topics* 26–27)

Lohmann emphasizes that when Cicero translated the Stoic doctrine, presenting it as self-evident and making the *ti* its most general concept, he naturally used the term *res*: the *res* could easily be divided into things that are (*quae sunt*) and those that are intelligible (*quae intelliguntur*); it is legitimate to say that the latter do not exist ("Vom ursprünglichen Sinn der aristotelischen Syllogistik," in *Lexis*, 1:205–36). However, the opposition between the two languages, on which Lohmann based his argument, must be at least qualified, if we consider, for instance, this passage from Dionysius Thrax's *Ars grammatica* (*Grammatici Graeci* 1.1, ed. Uhlig, 24.3): "The noun is a part of speech that can be declined, signifying a body [*sôma*] or an incorporeal entity [*pragma*]: a body like 'stone' or an incorporeal like 'education'" (quoted in Pierre Hadot, *Études de philosophie ancienne*). "We may regret being obliged to translate *pragma* by 'incorporeal' [*incorporel*], a term that is obviously unrelated to the etymology of *pragma*, but any other translation seems completely impossible," Hadot concluded. But another translation is not in fact entirely impossible if we consider Donatus's Latin translation (RT: Keil, ed., *Grammatici Latini*, 4:355.5), which Hadot himself quoted in a note: "*Pars orationis cum casu corpus aut rem proprie communiterve significans*" (The part of speech that, when declined, signifies literally or in a general way the body or the incorporeal [*res*]). This generality and indeterminacy also explain why the term *res*, in the plural, was able rather naturally to translate the Greek *onta* [ὄντα], and why it acquired a clearly differentiated meaning only through the determinants that accompanied it or secondary oppositions that came into play only against the background of a neutral primary meaning. Thus it became possible to use the expression *res gestae* to designate the events related by a historian, and a more precise meaning could be defined using an adjective that assumes the whole semantic burden ("*res publica, res divina, res familiaris, res militaris, res navalis, res rustica, res naturalis, res adversae, res secundae*"), or again one could distinguish, by opposition, between *res* and *sermo*, *res* and *verbum*

(on this canonical opposition, see especially Cicero, *De natura deorum* 1.16, ed. Pease, 1:168 and note). The Augustinian version (*De doctrina christiana*, 2.1–4) of this latter opposition remained classical throughout the Middle Ages, but it was already found in Cicero, Quintilian, and Boethius.

IV. From Augustine to Abelard: *Res/Signa* and *Res/Verba*

The Augustinian distinction is remarkable in that it is based on a general primary meaning of *res*: all things, apprehended in a way that remains completely undetermined, without any distinction of region, status, or mode of being. Thus it is the poorest and most extended term, which can be at first grasped only negatively: "*Proprie autem nunc res appelavi, quae non sunt ad significandum aliquid adhibentur, sicuti est lignum, . . . pecus, atque huiusmodi cetera*" (I have just called "things" that which is not used to signify something, for example, wood, stone, livestock, and other realities of the same kind: *De doctrina christiana* 1.2.2). In other words, it is a question here of apprehending things that are only things, and not also "signs," like "the wood that Moses cast into the bitter waters."

Everything that can be taught can in turn be divided up in relation to this primary opposition between *res* and *signa*, or between *res* and *verba*, since a word is first defined by its transitive function of signification (*De magistro* 4.7), and it is part of the nature of the sign that it refers to something other than itself, that is, ultimately, to an external reality: "*res autem ipsa, quae iam verbum non est, neque in mente conceptio*" ("The thing itself, which is not already a word or a mental conception"), according to the (pseudo-Augustinian) *Principia dialecticae* (chap. 5).

To be sure, the sign itself is always a thing-sign ("*ita res sunt, ut aliarum etiam signa sint rerum*"), and it must always have a certain concrete reality (*vox, dictio, intellectus*), precisely in order to fulfill its signifying and transitive function, namely, referring to something else, in function of a polarity that no doubt plays a determining role: the polarity of the inside and the outside, pursuing the relationship in language between the thing (signified)—*res*—and the linguistic sign. Certainly, from the Augustinian point of view, signs cannot be reduced to the linguistic sign, in its phonic or mental reality, but must also include both natural signs and the *signum sacrum* constituted by the *sacramentum*, in its secondary and overdetermined opposition to the *res*.

In the plural, and when associated with *natura, ordo*, or *proprietas*, the word *res* designates the totality of created things (humans, animals, material realities), as in John Scotus Erigena, who uses the expression *universitas rerum*. But the meaning of the term can be further broadened to designate something in general (*aliquid*)—"*solemus enim usu dicere rem, quidquid aliquo modo dicimus esse aliquid*" (We are accustomed, through usage, to call "thing" what we say is in some way something: Anselm, *Epistula de incarnatione verbi* 2, p. 12.5–6, ed. Schmitt)—or an abstract "reality."

Also in Anselm, the distinction between *enuntiatio* and *res enuntiata* testifies to this general meaning of *res* as designating a state of affairs. Particularly in *De veritate*, Anselm examines what constitutes the truth of an utterance, even when the utterance denies that something is; but in this case, the utterance can still be said to be true, since "*etiam quando negat esse quod non est. . . , sic enuntiat quemadmodum res est"* (Even when it denies being to that which is not . . . it says that the thing is; ed. Schmitt, 2.177.17).

When Peter Abelard wonders, particularly in his *Dialectica*, about the meaning of the proposition (his *dictum*; see DICTUM), he determines the objective content of the act of thought as a *quasi res* that can itself refer, through various intellections and the corresponding *dictiones* (for example, *cursus*, *currit*), to the same "thing," without the latter being a singular external *res*. Jolivet, in his valuable *Notes de lexicographie abélardienne*, has examined in detail several passages in the *Logica ingredientibus* in which we see how the word *res* changes meaning and is thus modified by a remarkable ambiguity, since it can designate, in a "nonrealist" way, not only the singular, subsistent "thing," but also the signified of a proposition or of universal terms: in fact, the *res propositionis* may not correspond to any *res subiecta* (Jolivet, "Éléments pour une étude," in *Aspects de la pensée médiévale*, 203–32).

V. Avicenna and the Translations of Avicenna: *Wuğūd*

But in addition to the analyses by Augustine, Anselm, and Abelard, one of the major events in the history of the word *res* in the Latin West was certainly the production of direct or indirect translations of the *Šifā'* [الشفاء] of the *Metaphysics* of Ibn Sina, or, as he is more commonly known in the West, Avicenna. In book 1, chapter 5, and in book 5, chapter 1, Avicenna set out to define the existent (*al-Wuğūd* [وجود], *ens*; see VORHANDEN, Box 1) and the thing (*al-šay'* [الشيء], *res*), as well as their primary divisions. These are "the ideas that are inscribed in the mind by a first impression," "the things most capable of being represented by themselves." The existent and the thing (*ens* and *res*) are at the origin of all representation, and thus attention can be drawn to them, they can be highlighted, but they cannot be known in the strict sense, since the names and signs that would be used to do so would be secondary and more obscure than they are. Referring more particularly to the "thing," we can describe it as "that about which something is said" ("*res est de quo potest aliquid vere enuntiari*," *Liber de philosophia prima*, 1.33.37–38).

Such a thing does not necessarily exist among concrete subjects, however; it suffices that it be intended or posited in the mind ("*potest res habere esse in intellectu, et non in exterioribus*"). What defines it, in fact, is first of all the "*certitudo qua est id quod est*," the certainty (*ḥaqīqa* [حقيقة]) that provides it with an *esse proprium* (*Liber de philosophia prima*, 1.34.55–56, 35.58). Thus the concept of the thing differs from that of the existent (*ens*) or the actual: the thing (*res*) is defined in each case by its own *certitudo*: the *quidditas* (*māhiyya* [ماهية]) through which the thing is what it is. Chapter 1 of book 5, which deals with "general things and their mode of being" ("*de rebus communibus et quomodo est esse earum*"), confirms this analysis by highlighting the original status of the signified as such (for example, the famous *equinitas tantum*, which is neither universal nor singular but is indifferent with regard to ulterior specifications, that is, without condition of being general, particular, and so on.

Definitio enim equinitatis est praeter definitionem universalitatis nec universalitas continetur in definitione equinitatis. Equinitas etenim habet definitionem quae non eget universalitate, sed est cui accidit universalitas. Unde ipsa equinitas non est aliquid nisi equinitas tantum; ipsa enim in se nec est multa nec unum, nec est existens in his sensibilibus nec in anima, nec est aliquid horum potentia vel effectu, ita ut hoc contineatur intra essentiam equinitatis, sed ex hoc quod est equinitas tantum.

(For the definition of equineness is not the definition of universality and universality does not enter into the definition of equineness. In fact, equineness has a definition that does not need the definition of universality, but universality comes to it. In itself, it is neither one nor several, existing neither in reality nor in the mind, nor in one of these potential or actual things, in the sense that that would enter into equineness, but only insofar as it is equineness.)

(*Liber de philosophia prima*, 5.1.29–36, ed. Van Riet, 228)

(N.B. On all of this, see de Libera, *La querelle des universaux*, particularly 201–2; see also, regarding the doctrine accepted in the Latin Middle Ages as that of the nondifferentiation of essence, de Libera, *L'art des généralités*, 576ff.)

Avicenna posits (1.5.34–35) that "for every thing there is a nature by which it is what it is." Thus a triangle, for instance, has a "certitude by which it is a triangle, just as whiteness has one by which it is whiteness." The essence therefore includes a proper being distinct from existence as it is affirmed in a judgment. Avicenna's thesis thus posits the following equivalence: own certitude (*ḥaqīqa*), proper being, quiddity (*māhiyya*), to which is opposed being, or rather existence (*al-wuğūd*) in the sense of affirmation (*intentio esse affirmativi*) (cf. Goichon, *La distinction*, 31–35). In Latin, the series becomes *certitudo propria—esse proprium—quidditas*, and that is what makes possible the doctrine of an *esse essentiae*, a proper being of the essence capable of being apprehended beyond being or nonbeing ("outside being"; *außerseiend*, to borrow Meinong's vocabulary; see SEIN). Thus it is possible to consider the animal in itself, to consider its essence per se, in abstraction from everything that is accidental to it: taken itself, the essence is, as we have seen, neither general, nor universal, nor particular, nor singular; neither is it (and this is no doubt the central point) in the mind or outside the mind. By the being that is proper to it, the animal is "neither individual, nor one, nor multiple," but only animal ("*ex hoc esse animal tantum*"—"*equinitas est tantum equinitas*"). This is a thesis whose influence—even if it was based on a misunderstanding, as de Libera suggests (*L'art des généralités*, 588)—was entirely remarkable starting in the second half of the thirteenth century, when everyone was discussing the well-foundedness and import of the difference between *esse essentiae* (*esse essentiale*, *habituale*, *quidditativum*) and *essen existentiae* or *esse actuale* (Thomas Aquinas, Henry of Ghent, Duns Scotus, and others).

■ See Box 2.

VI. The Scholastic Distinctions: *Res a Reor, Res Rata*

But let us now return to the Latin thirteenth century: medieval thinkers tried to reduce the dangerous polysemy of the

2
Šay', "thing," and *šay'iyya*, "reality"

Jolivet has shown in a very convincing manner ("Aux origines") that the Arabic terms *šay'* and *šay'iyya* [الشيئية] (thingness, or rather, reality) had their own history, quite independent of the Aristotelian *pragma* [πρᾶγμα] and connected with the debates in Islamic theology regarding the nonexistent, of which we still find an echo, after Avicenna, in Šahrastānī ("L'inexistant est-il une chose ou non?"), but whose more distant background goes back to al-Kindi and al-Fārābī and to the positions of the Muslim practice of theological debate known as *kalam,* for which the "thing" is what is known and everything nonexistent is a "thing."

It is from this "formal ontology" centered on the "thing," as it is elaborated on the basis of al-Fārābī and Ibn Sīnā, that algebra developed, outside Aristotelian epistemological frameworks, as a science common to arithmetic and geometry, bringing in the "thing," *res* (al-*šay'*), as something unknown that can designate either a number or a geometrical magnitude (Rashed, "Mathématiques et Philosophie"). Thus are sketched the outlines of a new ontology in which one can speak of an object without definite characteristics, and even know it, but not represent it exactly. In the Latin translations of Arabic works on algebra that began to appear at the beginning of the thirteenth century, the term that was finally adopted to designate the unknown was thus *res* (*res ignota*), whereas in books on mathematics written in Italian, the word *cosa* appeared in the following centuries (cf. G. Crapulli, "Res e cosa (cossa)," and C. Costable and P. Redondi, "Sémantèse de res / cosa / cossa," in Fattori and Bianchi, *Res*).

BIBLIOGRAPHY

Fattori, Marta, and Massimo Bianchi, eds. *Res, IIIe Colloquio Internazionale del Lessico Intellettuale Europeo.* Lessico intellettuale europeo, vol. 26. Rome: Ateneo, 1982.

Jolivet, Jean. "Aux origines de l'ontologie d'Ibn Sina." In *Études sur Avicenne,* edited by Jean Jolivet and Roshdi Rashed, 11–28. Paris: Belles Lettres, 1984. Also published in *Annuaire de l'École Pratique des Hautes Études,* section 5 (Sciences religieuses), 84:389–94, 85:381–86, 86:373–79, 88:401–5.

Rashed, Roshdi. "Mathématiques et philosophie chez Avicenne." In *Études sur Avicenne,* edited by Jean Jolivet and Roshdi Rashed, 29–35. Paris: Belle Lettres, 1984.

Šahrastānī, al-. "L'inexistant est-il une chose ou non?" In *Nihaya,* edited by A. Guillaume, chap. 7. Oxford: Oxford University Press, 1934.

term *res* by proposing a three-part division that became traditional in a history that continued down to the seventeenth century among representatives of what has been incorrectly called "late" or even "belated" Scholasticism, because of a powerful retrospective illusion that insists that we adopt, without any critical distance, the thesis that there was a Cartesian break and a new *Instauratio magna,* forgetting that the seventeenth century could legitimately be described as the golden age of Scotism.

Bonaventure, in his *Commentary on the Sentences* (1250–52), thus proposes a three-part classification of the meanings of *res* that remained classical for all Scholasticism:

Dicendum quod res accipitur communiter et proprie et magis proprie.—Res, secundum quod communiter dicitur, dicitur a reor, reris; et sic comprehendit omne illud, quod cadit in cognitione, sive sit res exterius, sive in sola opinione.—Proprie vero dicitur res a ratus, rata, ratum, secundum quod ratum dicitur esse illud quod non tantummodo est in cognitione, immo est in rerum natura, sive sit ens in se, sive in alio; et hoc modo res convertitur cum ente.—Tertio modo dicitur res magis proprie, secundum quod dicitur a ratus, rata, ratum, prout ratum dicitur illud quod est ens per se et fixum; et sic res dicitur solum de creaturis et substantiis per se entibus.

(We shall say that the term *res* can be understood in the general sense, in the strict [*proprie*] sense, and in the most strict [*magis proprie*] sense.—The term *Res* said in general is said on the basis of *reor, reris* [reckon, calculate, think, believe], and thus includes everything that comes to knowledge, whether it be an external thing or a thing present only in thought [the equivalent of the Aristotelian *doxaston* (δοξαστόν) contradistinguished from the *epistêton* (ἐπιστητόν), *Posterior Analytics* 2.33, 88b30–31].—But the strict sense of *res* is *a ratus, rata, ratum,* on the basis of what is confirmed and established, since we call *ratum* [ratified] what is not only in knowledge but in the nature of real things, whether we speak of the existent in itself or in another; and in this sense the term *res* is convertible with the term *ens.*—Thirdly, and in the strictest sense, *res* is related to *ratus, rata, ratum,* when what is called *ratum* is what is existent by itself and fixed; and thus *res* is said only of creatures and of existents subsisting by themselves.)

(In *Opera omnia,* 2, dist. 37, dub. 1, p. 2:876a)

It is a remarkable passage, but also one that presents a challenge for translation because of its fantastic etymologies and its repetition of the same term with a different accentuation: *ratum/ratum.* The most surprising part of all this is that although the etymology of the word *res* is more or less clear (it goes back to Indo-Iranian), the verb *reor, reri, ratus sum, reri* has no known etymology and is in any case not related to *res.* From *pro rata parte,* a common expression in classical Latin, the jurists drew the term *ratihabitio,* the ratification that is involved in dividing up a heritage, for example; and the expression *ratum facere aliquid* became established in the sense of "ratify," "approve" (RT: Ernout and Meillet, *Dictionnaire étymologique de la langue latine*). Thus we can understand why *ratum* could be taken in the sense of what is confirmed or ratified by the mind. The shift in meaning must have seemed natural, if we consider that on the other hand, *ratio,* in the sense of "reckoning" and "calculation," is connected with *reor, reris,* even in the common expressions *rationem reddere* and *rationem habere.* But counting up one's wealth (*res*) is clearly different from ratifying through thought. The *magis proprie* meaning, that of accentuated *ratum,* can then be seen as characteristic of what is fixed and firm (*ratum et firmum*), actually or "really" ratified.

The influence of the three-part classification indicated here was to be all the more remarkable because Bonaventure is no doubt also the writer who introduced or coined the term *ratitudo* to clarify the third meaning:

Res dicitur a reor, reris, quod dicit actum a parte animae; et alio modo res venit ab hoc quod est ratus, quod dicit stabilitatem a parte naturae; et sic res dicit stabilitatem sive ratitudinem ex parte entitatis.

(*Res* is related to *reor, reris*, when it refers to an act on the part of the mind; and on the other hand, *res* is related to what is *ratus* [ratified], which refers to stability on the part of nature; and thus *res* refers to stability or ratification on the part of the entity.)

(Bonaventure, *Opera omnia*, 1, dist. 25, dub. 3, p. 446b)

■ See Box 3.

Henry of Ghent (d. 1293) distinguishes the *res secundum opinionem*, which is purely mental, from the *res secundum veritatem*, which is characterized by its internal certitude and thus moves from the contingent to the necessary, from the psychological to the metaphysical. This is again a *res a ratitudine* corresponding to an extra-mental reality (*aliquid extra intellectum*) that possesses the certitude by which it is a certain thing (cf. Paulus, *Henri de Gand*, 23–25).

The major distinction established by Henry of Ghent can thus be formulated as follows:

Res primo modo est res secundum opinionem tantum, et dicitur a reor, reris, quod idem est quod opinor, opinaris, quae tantum res est secundum opinionem, quoad modum quo ab intellectu concipitur, scilicet in ratione totius, ut est mons aureus, vel hircocervus, habens medietatem cervi et medietatem hirci.

(The *res* in the first sense is a *res* only according to opinion, and it is related to *reor, reris*, which is the same thing as *opinor, opinaris*, and it is only a thing according to opinion, according to the way in which it is conceived by the intellect, namely according to the reason of a (composite) whole, like a golden mountain or a goat-stag, which is half goat and half stag.)

(Henry of Ghent, *Quodlibeta*, 5.2, fol. 154D; 7.1, fol. 258B)

Duns Scotus (1265–1308), who also sought to reduce the ambiguity of the term *res*, presented first a tripartite classification in the *Quodlibeta* (q. 3, n. 2), but he later distinguished, in opposition to Henry of Ghent, a twofold figure of *ratitudo*, which thus took over for the *certitudo* that Avicenna attributed to quiddities: "*Unaquaeque enim res habet certitudinem qua est id quod est*" (*Ordinatio*, 1.3.2, Vatican ed., 3:184.14–17). The neologism *ratitudo* had a prodigious career down to Francisco Suárez's *Disputationes metaphysicae* (4.2 n. 2). Some writers, like Petrus Aureolus (d. 1322), tried to reduce the series of distinctions to a fundamental polarity between essence and existence:

Res sumitur dupliciter, uno modo pro re essentiali—et sic non est verum quod esse lapidis sit sua realitas—, vel pro realitate actuali, et sic est verum; unde in lapide actualiter existente sunt duae realitates, una quidem essentialis, puta lapiditas, et alia accidentalis, puta actualitas.

(*Res* is taken in two senses, on the one hand for the essential *res* [synonym of *essentia*], and then it is not true that the being of a stone is its reality—, and on the other for the actual reality, and in this case, it is true; consequently, in the stone that actually exists, there are two realities, namely "stoniness" and another, accidental reality, namely, actuality.)

(*Scriptum super primum Sententiarum*, 1.1.21 n. 60)

Other authors, on the contrary, multiplied the subdivisions in order to make place for rational entities or chimeras.

We find an echo of this as late as a "Cartesian" Dutch writer, Johannes Clauberg (1622–60), in his *Exercitationes et epistolae varii argumenti*:

Mens quando rem eandem considerat, ut est extra notionem in seipsa, et ut est in notione repraesentata, videt hoc aliquid esse fundamentale, notionem autem suam aliquid umbratile et intentionale. Unde res etiam seu ens absolutum rectissime dividitur, quod sit vel fundamentale, quod specialiter et *kat' exochên* [κατ' ἐξοχήν] reale dici solet, quod primo et propriissime est et producit aliquid, etc., vel intentionale, quod non est nec facit aliquid solide et proprie sicut reale (fundamentale) et est tamen quasi umbra et similitudo illius, quae nos illud facit cognoscere, unde communiter notio vel idea appellatur.

(The mind, when it considers one and the same thing, whether as it is in itself and outside the concept, or as it is represented in the concept, sees clearly that in the first case this something is fundamental, whereas its concept is something obscure and intentional. That is why the thing, or if one prefers, the existent taken absolutely, is most properly divided in the following manner: either it is fundamental, and is usually called real in the specific and quintessential sense, that is, what is firstly and most properly, which produces something, etc.; or else it is called intentional, insofar as it is not and does not make anything solid and proper, as does what is real (fundamental), and yet it is like shadow and a resemblance of the latter, and this allows us to know it, and that is why it is commonly called a concept or idea of the thing.)

(Clauberg, *Exercitationes*, 16, in *Opera omnia philosophica*, 621)

However, in the same work, Clauberg also proposed a four-part classification:

Res primo sumitur latissime pro omni cogitabili, nam quicquid sub cogitationem nostram cadit, sive verum sive fictum, sive possibile sive impossibile, sive actuale sit, interdum rei nomine appellatur. Nec dubitatur, quin accidens hoc significatu latissimo res dici queat.—Secundo res accipitur minus late pro omni eo quod est aliquid, non nihil, et sic reale ens opponitur enti rationis, . . . nempe ubi Authores sub illa (reali) modalem quoque distinctionem complectuntur . . . —Tertio stricte sumitur

3

Res rata, res a reor, ratitudo, Ding a denken

Medieval thought understands *res* as a supplementary transcendental, another name of being. Thomas Aquinas explains the doublet *ens* (being) and *res* (thing) on the basis of the two concepts of essence and existence: "The name *res* is derived from the quiddity," but since the essence can have a singular being outside the mind or a being apprehended in the mind, the name of "*res* is related to both of them: to what is in the mind, insofar as the *res* is based on *reor, reris*, and to what is outside the mind, insofar as the *res* signifies a being whose nature is solid (*ratum*) and firm" (*Sentences*, 1, d. 25, q. 1, a. 4, ed. Mandonnet, 3:612). Thus "being" refers directly to that which has the act of being (*esse*), but *res* refers to the quiddity both insofar as it is thought (*res a reor, reris*) and insofar as it exists (*res rata*). The *res* can be either the thing thought or the existing thing, but it is not what bears the full weight of Thomist metaphysics, which is oriented toward the being's act of being.

With Henry of Ghent, on the contrary, it is the *res* that is primary. For Henry, the definition of the *res* covers the double determination of the possible: that which is simply conceivable, that is, logically noncontradictory, or that which has a certain solidity in its possibility, that is, that which is real insofar as it has an essence. The first sense covers everything that is not pure nothingness, every object of opinion, including chimeras, fictions, possible worlds that will never be realized. The second sense designates what has an essence, that is, what has an idea, a positive model in divine thought. The two meanings of *res* must be opposed: the *res a reor, reris* ("think, believe, consider, imagine"), namely, the *res* in the etymological sense, which designates every object of opinion, whether it is endowed with an essence or not, and the *res ratitudine* (*ratitudo* is a medieval neologism designating solidity), namely, the *res* that has a certain solidity and designates the essence whose model is in God.

The intention of every created thing [*res*] insofar as it is so called on the basis of "I think, you think" [*reor, reris*] must be distinguished from the being of essence, which is appropriate to it insofar as it is a nature and an essence, and a thing [*res*] so called on the basis of its solidity [*a ratitudine*].

(Henry of Ghent, *Summa quaestionum ordinariarum*, art. 21, q. 4 response; 1.127, O)

This ambiguity of *res* conceals a hesitation regarding the interpretation of the nature of metaphysics: should being be conceived simply as the correlate of our representation that is the most primordial because it is the most universal, or as possible because it imitates a divine model and through it participates in its essence? Is it simply the representation of the logically possible (noncontradictory), including fiction, chimeras, secondary intentions, and so on, or the representation of the real possible (founded in a relation to divine nature)? This fundamental hesitation between a logic of representation and a metaphysics of participation, which we also find in the theory of analogy peculiar to Henry of Ghent, was ended by Duns Scotus. For him, the *res* endowed with a real possibility does not draw the latter from a relation to God, but from the solidity specific to quiddity, which is open to essence or existence. What is it that founds the intelligibility of the real? What kind of being should be assigned to the intelligible? Not pure fiction, forged by imagination or opinion, but genuine possibility, which has a being that is *ratum*, solid (*res a ratitudo*), and not purely thought (*res a reor*). It is a "being that is from the outset distinct from fictions, that is, from what is open to the being of essence or the being of existence" (Duns Scotus, *Ordinatio*, 1.36.48, Vatican ed., 6:290). Being is truly *ratum* only by its own solidity—because this being is of one kind and that being is of another kind: it is formal coherence that founds noncontradiction, and not the other way around; relayed by divine omnipotence, it opens out onto a production in existence.

Suárez presupposes this analysis of the two senses of *res* when he writes:

The *res* is predicated quidditatively, because it signifies a true and solid [*rata*] quiddity that is taken absolutely, and that is not coordinated with existence [*esse*].

(*Disputationes metaphysicae*, 2.4.2, in *Opera omnia*, 88)

The most proper name of being is precisely *res*, that is, the order of quiddities, that which is open to being. "*Res* indicates only the quiddity of the thing taken formally, and the solid [*rata*] or real essence of the being" (*Disputationes metaphysicae*, 3.2.1, in *Opera omnia*, 107). Here, reality means not actual existence, but a formal perfection of essence.

Still more audacious, Clauberg, in his *Ontosophia* (§§7–8), combines the etymologies, harmonizing Greek, Latin, and German to the point of identifying the *res* with the pure representable:

Aio *omne ens posse dici*, hoc est, nominari, voce viva vel scripta enuntiari. Hinc, *Sache*—res—a sagen, dicere. . . . Ipsum: res, si non a reor, est a ῥέω, loquor. . . . Praetera, *omne ens potest cogitari* seu intelligi, ideoque *cogitabile et intelligibile* appellatur. . . . *Ding,*—res—et *denken*— cogitare—eiusdem sunt originis.

(*Metaphysica de ente, quae rectius ontosophia*, quoted in Courtine, *Suárez et le système de la métaphysique*, 261)

This fantastic study in comparative etymology is obviously untranslatable.

Olivier Boulnois

BIBLIOGRAPHY

Aquinas, Thomas. *Sentences*. Edited by Pierre Mandonnet and Fabien Moos. Paris: Lethielleux, 1929.

Courtine, Jean-François. "Realitas." In *Historisches Wörterbuch der Philosophie*, edited by Joachim Ritter and Karlfriend Gründer, 8:177–88. Basel, Switz.: Schwabe, 1971–2007.

———. *Suárez et le système de la métaphysique*. Paris: Presses Universitaires de France, 1990.

Duns Scotus. *Ordinatio*. Rome: Editio Vaticana, 1963.

Honnefelder, Ludger. "Die Lehre von der doppelten ratitudo entis und ihre Bedeutung für die Metaphysik des Johannes Duns Scots." In *Deus et homo ad mentem J. Duns Scoti*, Acta Tertii Congressus Scotistici Internationalis Vindabonae, 28 Sept.–2 Oct. 1970. *Studia scholastico-scotistica* 5 (1972): 661–71.

res pro substantia, atque ita res opponitur modo, distinctio realis opponitur modali proprie dictae. . . . —Quarto strictius adhuc reale opponitur intentionali, quo sensu etiam res et signa rerum distinguuntur, nec interim negatur intentionale ens esse aliquid, prout signa etiam non sunt nihil. Hanc vocis illius acceptionem si respiciamus, dicere possumus, dari nonnulla accidentia, quae non sint realia, sed intentionalia, dari alia plurima, quae realia sint.

(The res is taken first in the broadest sense, for everything that can be thought, for everything that falls under our thought, whether it be true or fictitious, possible or impossible, or actual, nonetheless receives the name of thing. There is no doubt that in this broadest possible signification the accident can also be called a "thing."—In a second sense, res is understood less broadly as referring to everything that is something, not nothing, and thus the real being is opposed to the rational entity, as is still the case in authors who subsume the modal distinction into the first (real one). . . .—In a third sense, res is taken as substance, and thus it is opposed to mode, whereas real distinction is opposed to modal distinction properly so called. . . .—In a fourth sense, and in a still stricter way, the "real" is opposed to the intentional, and in this sense things are distinguished from signs of things, without, however, denying that intentional being is something, insofar as signs are also not nothing. Considering this latter meaning of the term, we can say that there are a few accidents that are not real, but intentional, and that there are many others that are real.)

(Clauberg, *Exercitationes*,
43, in *Opera omnia philosophica*, 665)

There are many writers, however, who, in spite or because of these multiplying distinctions, maintain as the fundamental meaning of res the concrete object existing outside the mind as a singular individual. Such is the *res secundum esse*: the *res posita*, that is, the *res singularis* (William of Ockham, *Sentences*, 1, dist. 2, q. 7): "*Omnis res positiva extra animam eo ipso est singularis*" (Every positive reality [existing] outside the mind is by that very fact singular).

VII. *Res* as a Transcendental and Supertranscendental Term

The broadening of the term *res* and its extension beyond even the meaning of *ens* defined as *ens ratum* (firm, stable, and ontologically ratified) tend to make it a transcendental term, and even the first among transcendental terms. In any case, res is counted among the transcendental terms starting with Gerard of Cremona. Thomas Aquinas sometimes assimilates *res* and *ens* (*Summa theologica*, 1a, q. 48, a. 2), even if in his thematic exposition of the transcendentals he carefully distinguishes between the two terms (*De veritate*, q. 1, a. 1). In his *Disputationes dialecticae*, Lorenzo Valla seeks to reduce the six transcendentals to *res* as the first and principal of them all: "*Ex his sex, quae nunc quasi de regno contendunt non aliter res erit rex, quam Darius.*" In fact, *aliquid* can be analyzed or explained as "*alia res*," *unum* as "*una res*," and so on. In this

transcendental meaning that dominates all other convertible properties, nothing is any longer opposed to *res*, except precisely nothing or nothingness: "*nihil habet repugnans nisi ipsum nihil*" (*Disputationes dialecticae*, book 1, in *Opera*, 646–48).

Even if they explicitly criticize Valla's anti-Aristotelian thesis, many writers, such as Fonseca (1528–99) and Suárez, unhesitatingly make *res* a transcendental term on the same footing as *ens*, or even a complete synonym of the latter: "*Sex porro transcendentia esse dicuntur, Ens, Unum, Verum, Bonum, Aliquid, Res*" (Fonseca, *Institutionum dialecticarum libri octo*, book 1, chap. 28, ed. Ferreira Gomes). Suárez, having cited the common thesis of the five transcendentals or passions convertible with being, nonetheless adds: "Many writers think that *res* is a more essential predicate [*magis essentiale praedicatum*] than being itself" (*Disputationes metaphysicae*, 3.2.1), without, however, expressing deep disagreement with this thesis, since, as he himself says, "*solum dicit de formali rei quidditatem, et ratam seu realem essentiam entis*" (The *res* simply and formally designates the quiddity of the thing, that is, its real and ratified essence).

On the other hand, Chrysostome Javelli, in his *Tractatus de transcendentibus*, part of a *Totius philosophiae compendium* published in Lyon in 1563 (1:460, col. 1), maintains a more Thomistic distinction: "*Ens sumitur ab esse, Res autem a essentia*" ("The participle 'being' is taken from the verb 'to be,' the thing [is taken] from the essence"). Whence he concludes, rather oddly, that *ens* can be said of both *ente reali* and *ente rationis*, whereas on the other hand, the *res* is said only of *entia realia*, that is, those that "have essence of quiddity." Thus the *res* can be identified with being (*ens*) only if the latter is understood (and this was to be the basis for Suárez's thesis against Thomas Cajetan) in the nominal sense, in the sense of "*ens nominaliter sumptum*." In the *Disputationes*, Suárez drew all the consequences of the distinction between the two meanings of "being": the *ens* taken as a participle and *ens* taken as a noun—a distinction, let us note, that is no more discernible in Latin than it is in French or English (at least so far as the present participle of the verb "to be" is concerned, whereas French has distinguished, at least since Claude Favre de Vaugelas, between the participle as an invariable form and as a qualifying or verbal adjective: *différant/différent*, *excellant/excellent*, *divaguant/divagant*, and so on).

Ens (being), insofar as it derives directly from the verb *sum*, is understood as a participle that names the *actus essendi* or the act of existing: to be and to exist are the same. ("*Quae opinio fundata est in significatione vocis ens; derivatur enim a verbo sum, estque participium eius; verbum autem sum, absolute dictum, significat actum essendi, seu existendi: esse enim et existere idem sunt*," Suárez, *Disputationes metaphysicae*, 2.4.1).

Of course, the same term (*ens*) can also be explained as "*ens nominaliter suptum*" (*ens ut nomen*), if we note that this time it signifies properly and adequately "*id quod est*," "that which is." But "*id quod est*" can in turn be understood as that which has, or rather exercises, the act of being or existing—in other words, that which is being in the sense of existing: what is *actu* (in actuality) or what is *potentia* (potentially), that which is being because it can be, because it is already the possible subject of a true predication, as when one says of man in general that he is an animal, leaving aside the question whether he is or is not *actu*, whether he exists, whether he is being ("*significat ergo adaequate 'ens,' id quod est . . . , id est, quod habet actum essendi seu existendi, ut idem sit ens, quod existens; dicit ergo ens de formali esse seu existentiam, quae est extra rerum quidditatem*"). However, Suárez rejects the thesis (here attributed to Domingo de Soto) according to which being cannot be predicated quidditatively or essentially (*in quid*) on everything, because it always implies a reference to being as disposition or way of holding oneself ("*habitudo ad esse*"), understood this time as an "act of being" ("*actus essendi*") that can be participialized ("*être participé*") by the created existent, while remaining external to its essence:

> dicit ens semper esse participium verbi *sum* sicut existens, verbi *existo*, et de formali significare esse, de materiali vero, quod habet esse postea vero declarat, ens non solum significare quod actu est, sicut existens, sed quod est actu vel potentia, quia de homine non existente vere dicitur esse ens, sicut esse animal vel substantiam, et nihilominus concludit ens non dici quidditative de rebus, praesertim creatis, quia dicit habitudinem ad esse, quod est extra essentiam creaturae.

> (According to [de Soto], "being" is always used as a participle of the verb "to be," as "existing" is used as a participle of the verb "to exist," and formally it signifies being, but materially it signifies what has being; then he clarifies his thesis by saying that "being" signifies not only what actually is, in the sense of existing, but what is in actuality or in potentiality, for, of a man who does not exist, it can be truthfully affirmed that he is a being, just as he is an animal or a substance, and yet he concludes that "being" is not said quidditatively of things, and especially of those that are created, since it signifies a relation to being that is external to the essence of the creature.)

(Suárez, *Disputationes metaphysicae*, 2.4)

Reaffirming the *habitudo ad esse* within the nominal meaning of being necessarily leads to opposing *ens* and *res*: the *res*, unlike the *ens*, can be predicated *in quid* of everything that is (that is, also of what is not actual), because it signifies nothing other than the quiddity itself, in its absolute truth ratified by the understanding, without the intervention of any further ordination to being or to existing. The same is not true of "being," which never signifies quiddity taken absolutely, but always "*sub ratione essendi*," that is, insofar as it can be ("*id quod est potentia*"), in the sense of what can receive the *esse* ("*Et in hoc constituit differentiam inter ens et res, quod res quidditative praedicatur, quia significat quidditatem veram et ratam absolute, et sine ordine ad esse; ens autem non praedicatur quidditative, quia non significat absolute quidditatem, sed sub ratione essendi, seu quatenus potest habere esse,*" *Disputationes metaphysicae*, 2.4.2). Without following the logic of his argument to its final implications, which would lead him to make the *res* an instance (one does not dare to say an "entity") more vast than existence, because it includes both existence and quiddity—the *esse essentiae* of the (pseudo-)Avicennian tradition—and to break the convertibility of the transcendentals, in order to make the

"thing" a supertranscendental term, Suárez limits himself here to identifying *ens* and *res* simply and purely: the two terms differ only nominally, through their linguistic origin (*in etymologia nominum*):

> Unde obiter colligo, ens in vi nominis sumptum, et rem, idem omnino esse seu significare, solumque differre in etymologia nominum; nam res dicitur a quidditate, quatenus est aliquid firmum et ratum, id est non fictum, qua ratione dicitur quidditas realis; ens vero in praedicata significatione dicit id quod habet essentiam realem; eamdem ergo omnino rem seu rationem realem important.

> (Whence I also conclude that "being" [*ens*], taken as a noun, and "thing" [*res*] are absolutely identical or signify the same, and that the only difference is in the etymology of the two terms. For the *res* is used on the basis of the quiddity, insofar as it is something firm and ratified, that is, nonfictitious, and that is why it is called "real quiddity"; whereas being [*ens*] names, in the meaning under consideration, what has a real essence; they thus refer to the same *res* or to the same real reason.)

(Suárez, *Disputationes metaphysicae*, 2.4.2)

The true background of this continuing tendency—which has been called "essentialist" (Étienne Gilson)—to make the *ens* a transcendental term is once again Henry of Ghent's previously mentioned analysis that tends to make *res* an absolutely general term, identical to the *etwas*, to the "something," to the *aliquid* in the sense of the non-*nihil*. Clauberg in particular had seen this very clearly when he interpreted "*res in latissima acceptione*" as "*Intelligibile seu Cogitabile*" (*Exercitationes*, 45, in *Opera omnia philosophica*, 2:668), that is, as a supertranscendent term or as "supertranscendental," without there being any reason to distinguish here between the two adjectives (cf. Doyle, "Supertranscendental Nothing").

Thus the philosophical history of the word *res* clearly leads, as Kobusch has shown ("Das Seiende als transzendentaler oder super-transcendtaler Begriff"), to making the *ens rationis* the most general concept defining the sphere of the thinkable (*cogitabile*), within which is secondarily delimited the domain of the *ens reale*, which itself merges with the possible understood as noncontradictory (*potentiale obiectivum*). If philosophically the Latin *res* was initially used to translate the Greek *pragma* [πρᾶγμα], in late Scholasticism and in *Schulmetaphysik*, it is usually understood as a transposition of the indeterminate *ti* [τι]. That is why a few authors who were not content to classify *res* among the transcendentals or to make it the first among them imagined a new, still more general category, that of supertranscendental terms that are perfectly illustrated by French *chose*, Latin *aliquid*, or German *etwas*.

Jean-François Courtine

BIBLIOGRAPHY

Anselm, Saint, Archbishop of Canterbury. *Basic Writings*. Edited and translated by Thomas Williams. Indianapolis, IN: Hackett, 2007.

———. *Epistula de incarnatione verbi*. Edited by Franciscus Salesius Schmitt. Bonn: Sumptibus Petri Hanstein, 1931.

Augustine, Saint, Bishop of Hippo. *Against the Academicians* and *The Teacher*. Translated with introduction and notes by Peter King. Indianapolis, IN: Hackett, 1995.

———. *The First Catechetical Instruction* [De catechizandis rudibus]. Translated and annotated by the Reverend Joseph P. Christopher. Westminster, MD: The Newman Bookshop, 1952.

———. *On Christian Teaching*. Translated with introduction and notes by R.P.H. Green. Oxford: Clarendon, 1995.

———. *The Works of Saint Augustine: A Translation for the Twenty-First Century*. Translated with notes by Edmund Hill. Edited by John E. Rotelle. Brooklyn, NY: New City Press, 1990–.

Avicenna [Ibn Sīnā]. *Liber de philosophia prima, sive scientia divina*. 3 vols. Edited by S. Van Riet. Theoretical introduction by G. Verbeke. Louvain: Peeters, 1977–83.

———. *The Metaphysica of Avicenna (Ibn Sīnā): A Critical Translation-Commentary and Analysis of the Fundamental Arguments in Avicenna's* Metaphysica *in the* Dānish nāma-i 'Alā'ī (The Book of Scientific Knowledge)*. Translated by Parviz Morewedge. New York: Columbia University Press, 1973.

———. *Al-Shifa*. Edited by G. C. Anawati and Sa'id Zayed. Cairo, Egypt: Organisme général des imprimeries gouvernementales, 1960.

Aureolus, Petrus. *Scriptum super primum sententiarum*. Edited by Elgius M. Buytaert. 2 vols. St. Bonaventure, NY: Franciscan Institute, 1956.

Bonaventure, Saint Cardinal. *Opera omnia*. Edited by Collegii a S. Bonaventura. 10 vols. Quarrachi. 1882–1902.

———. *The Works of Bonaventure: Cardinal, Seraphic Doctor, and Saint*. Translated from the Latin by José de Vinck. 5 vols. Paterson, NJ: St. Anthony Guild Press, 1960–70.

Brunschwig, Jacques. *Papers in Hellenistic Philosophy*. Translated by Janet Lloyd. Cambridge: Cambridge University Press, 1994.

———. "Stoic Metaphysics." Chap. 8 in *The Cambridge Companion to Stoicism*. Edited by Brad Inwood. Cambridge: Cambridge University Press, 2003.

Cicero. *De natura deorum*. Edited and translated by A. S. Pease. Cambridge: Cambridge University Press, 1965. Translation by P. G. Walsh: *The Nature of the Gods*. Oxford: Oxford University Press, 1998.

Clauberg, Johann. *Opera omnia philosophica*. Edited by Johannes Theodor Schalbruch. 2 vols. Hildesheim, Ger.: Olms, 1968.

De Rijk, Lambertus Marie. "*Logos* and *Pragma* in Plato and Aristotle." In *Logos and Pragma: Essays on the Philosophy of Language in Honour of Professor Gabriel Nuchelmanns*, edited by L. M. De Rijk and H.A.G. Baakhuis. Aristarium Supplementa 3. Nijmegen, Neth.: Ingenium, 1987.

———. *Through Language to Reality: Studies in Medieval Semantics and Metaphysics*. Edited by E. P. Bos. Northampton, Eng.: Variorum Reprints, 1989.

De Rijk, Lambertus Marie, and H.A.G. Baarkhuis. *Logos and Pragma: Essays on the Philosophy of Language in Honour of Professor Gabriël Nuchelmans*. Nijmegen, Neth.: Ingenium, 1987.

Dionysius Thrax. *Ars grammatica*. In *Grammatici Graeci* 1.1, edited by G. Uhlig. Leipzig: B. G. Teubner, 1883.

Doyle, James Patrick. "Supertranscendental Nothing: A Philosophical Finisterre." *Medioevo, Rivista di Storia della Filosofia Medievale* 24 (1998): 1–30.

Duns Scotus. *Opera omnia*. Vatican City: Typis Polyglottis Vaticanis, 1950–.

Fattori, Marta, and Massimo Bianchi, eds. *Res, IIIe Colloquio Internazionale del Lessico Intellettuale Europeo*. Lessico intellettuale europeo, vol. 26. Rome: Ateneo, 1982.

Fonseca, Pedro da. *Instituições dialécticas: Institutionum dialecticarum libri octo*. 2 vols. Translated and edited by Joaquim Ferreira Gomes. Coimbra, Port.: Universidade de Coimbra, 1964.

Goichon, Amélie-Marie. *La distinction de l'essence et de l'existence d'après Ibn Sina (Avicenne)*. Paris: Desclée de Brouwer, 1936.

Gutas, Dimitri. *Avicenna and the Aristotelian Tradition*. Leiden, Neth.: Brill, 1988.

Henry of Ghent [Henrici de Gandavo]. *Opera omnia*. 38 vols. Leiden, Neth.: Brill, 1979.

———. *Quodlibeta*. Leuven, Belg.: Leuven University Press, 1979. Translation by Roland J. Teske: *Quodlibetal Questions on Free Will*. With an introduction and notes by Roland J. Teske. Milwaukee, WI: Marquette University Press, 1993.

Hadot, Pierre. *Études de philosophie ancienne*. Paris: Belles Lettres, 1998.

Javellus, Chrysostomos. *Totius philosophiae compendium*. Lyons, Fr.: 1563.

Jolivet, Jean, and Roshdi Rashed, eds. *Études sur Avicenne*. Paris: Belle Lettres, 1984.

Kobusch, Theo. "Das Seiende als transzendentaler oder super-transcendtaler Begriff: Deutungen der Univozität des Begriffs bei Soctus und den Scotisten." In *John*

Duns Scotus, Metaphysics and Ethics, edited by L. Honnefelder, R. Wood, and M. Dreyer, 345–66. Leiden, Neth.: Brill, 1996.

Kretzmann, Norman, Anthony Kenny, and Jan Pinborg, eds. *The Cambridge History of Later Medieval Philosophy*. Cambridge: Cambridge University Press, 1982.

Libera, Alain de. *L'art des généralités: Théories de l'abstraction*. Paris: Aubier, 1999.

———. *La querelle des universaux: De Platon à la fin du Moyen Âge*. Paris: Seuil, 1996.

Lohmann, Johannes. *Lexis, Studien zur Sprachphilosophie, Sprachgeschichte und Sprachbestimmung*. Vol. 2.1. Schauenberg, Switz.: Verlag von Moritz, 1951.

Maurer, Armand A. *Medieval Philosophy*. Toronto: Pontifical Institute of Medieval Studies, 1982.

Meinong, Alexius. "The Theory of Objects." In *Realism and the Background of Phenomenology*, edited by Roderick M. Chisholm, 76–117. Glencoe, IL: Free Press, 1960.

Moingt, Joseph. *Théologie trinitaire de Tertullien*. 4 vols. Paris: Aubier, 1966–69.

Paulus, Jean. *Henri de Gand: Essai sur les tendances de sa métaphysique*. Paris: Vrin, 1938.

Plato. *Œuvres complètes*. Vol. 13, part 1 (*Lettres*). Translated by Joseph Souilhé. Paris: Belles Lettres, 1926.

Pohlenz, Max. *Die Stoa: Geschichte einer geistigen Bewegung*. 2 vols. Göttingen, Ger.: Vandenhoeck and Ruprecht, 1959.

Suaréz, Francisco. *Disputationes metaphysicae*. 2 vols. Hildesheim, Ger.: Olms, 1965. Translation by John P. Doyle: *The Metaphysical Demonstration of the Existence of God: Metaphysical Disputations 28–29*. Edited by John P. Doyle. South Bend, IN: St. Augustine's Press, 2004.

Valla, Lorenzo. *Opera omnia*. Turin: Bottega d'Erasmo, 1962.

Wieland, Wolfgang. *Die aristotelische Physik: Untersuchungen über die Grundlegung der Naturwissenschaft und die sprachlichen Bedingungen der Prinzipienfoschung bei Aristoteles*. Göttingen, Ger.: Vandenhoeck and Ruprecht, 1970.

| RÉVOLUTION

Révolution derives from Latin *revolvere* (turn back), and originally designated in particular the return by which a celestial body comes back to the starting point on its orbit: it is the basis of the cyclical conception of time, from Plato to Nietzsche's "eternal return," in contrast to linear time. See AIÔN, *CONTINUITY*, *ETERNITY*, MEMORY, MOMENT, PRESENT, *TIME*, WELT; cf. EPISTEMOLOGY, FORCE.

In political history, the word has come to designate a sudden change (cf. German *Umwälzung*, "upheaval") but does not imply a return to the point of departure. However, revolution is still contrasted with evolution, which has to do with continuity and the line. French hesitates between *révolution* and *évolution* to translate the kind of movement that is expressed by the Italian *mutazione*, notably in the work of Machiavelli: cf. VIRTÙ.

More generally, on the way of expressing progress, whether linear or cyclical, see CORSO, HISTORIA UNIVERSALIS, NEUZEIT, PERFECTIBILITY; cf. GLÜCK, HISTORY, *PROGRESS*. On the relation between the two conceptions of time and human practice, see PRAXIS; cf. AUFHEBEN, PLASTICITY.

Finally, on the revolutions that have marked European history and their singularity, see LIBERAL, PRAVDA, RULE OF LAW, WHIG. In a more metaphorical or more philosophical sense, see, for example, SUBJECT, LIGHT; cf. EUROPE, TO TRANSLATE.

➤ *DROIT*, POLITICS, *SOCIETY*

RIGHT / JUST / GOOD

FRENCH   *bien, juste, bon*
GERMAN   *gut, wohl, recht*

➤ *DROIT*, *GOOD/EVIL* [GUT], and FAIR, *JUSTICE*, LAW, PRUDENTIAL, TRUTH, UTILITY

The French translator of English terms for "good" is always in danger of being confronted by cases in which the contrast between "right" and "good" seems to be one between *bien* and *bien*. French does not make a sharp distinction between *le bien* and *le bon*, the imperative and the attractive, whereas English has two distinct series that correspond quite clearly to two aspects of the good. Moreover, where French clearly distinguishes between *le bon* and *le juste*, with the former emphasizing individual or collective interest and the latter universal moral law, English is less clear on the distinction between "right" and "just," since "rightness" can mean both *rectitudo* and *justitia*.

I. The Three Meanings of "Just"

First of all, "just" has a cognitive meaning, that of French *juste*, in the sense of "correct," "exact," or "true." Nonetheless, the English noun corresponding to French *justesse* is not "justice" but "rightness," whence the intervention of the Anglo-Saxon lexicon (*recht / right*, straight), which complicates matters. "Right" and "just" are, then, more or less interchangeable with each other, and except for a few nuances, with "good," which also has a cognitive sense (as in French, where a *bonne réponse* is *correcte* or *juste*). In this sense, the antonym of all three words—"good," "right," and "just"—is "wrong," in the sense of "erroneous."

The second sense of "just" is the moral sense, and here again, the distinction from "right" and "good" is imperceptible. The virtue of justice, Latin *rectitudo*, corresponds well to English "rightness," meaning "moral rectitude." "Right" is used chiefly to qualify "good" actions, while "good," like "just," is used more to describe the character of the virtuous agent. But this resemblance is misleading. "Right" has a much broader semantic field and comes to designate not only the conduct of the virtuous man, but also what is good, the moral criterion in general in contrast to the morally wrong. As for "good," it also has a nonmoral sense, the "good" in the sense of what satisfies appetites and natural desires, of happiness and well-being; and the passage from natural properties to moral properties has been, as we know, one of the thorniest debates in moral philosophy ever since Hume. It is at this point that the most serious translation problems arise, because there is no French equivalent for "right" (and especially no noun corresponding to "rightness") with this prescriptive sense. However, the meaning of this distinction as expressed by Henry Sidgwick, who was a disciple of both Kant and Mill, is entirely clear:

We have regarded this term ["rightness"], and its equivalents in ordinary use, as implying the existence of a dictate or imperative of reason which prescribes certain actions either unconditionally, or with reference to some ulterior end. . . . It is, however, possible to take a view of virtuous action in which . . . the moral ideal [is] presented as attractive rather than imperative . . .

substituting the idea of "goodness" for that of "rightness" of conduct.

(*Methods of Ethics*, bk. 1, chap. 9, §1)

Finally, the semantic fields of "right" and "just" differ completely from one another because a third sense of "just" is "fair," "equitable," a meaning absent in the case of "right." On the other hand, "right" has the meaning of "a just claim or title" (Fr., *droit*), as in the expression "rights and duties." One of the most important debates in English-language moral and political philosophy concerns the relations between right and good (in French, between *le juste* and *le bien*), whence the exemplary difficulties raised by this quotation from Michael Sandel:

The priority of the right means, first, that individual rights cannot be sacrificed for the sake of the general good (in this it opposes utilitarianism), and, second, that the principles of justice that specify these rights cannot be premised on any particular vision of the good life.

(*Liberalism and the Limits of Justice*)

This can be rendered in French as: "La priorité du juste veut dire, tout d'abord, que les droits individuels ne peuvent être sacrifiés au bien général (en ce sens elle s'oppose à l'utilitarisme) et, ensuite, que les principes de justice qui spécifient ces droits ne peuvent être déduits d'aucune vision particulière de la vie bonne."

II. The Relations between "Right" and "Good"

In the passage quoted above, Sidgwick contrasts the "attractive" meaning of the moral criterion, or "goodness," with its imperative meaning, or "rightness." This distinction seems quite clear. If "right" has to be translated into French as *bien*—for example, in the expression *le critère du bien et du mal*—and not by *juste* or *droit* or *correct*, and if its antonym is clearly "wrong" (Fr., *mal*), that is because it designates what must be done: it conveys the imperative, coercive, aspect of morality, the sense of duty and obligation. In contrast, "good" designates the attractive aspect of morality, what should be desired or wished, *le bon*. It is entirely inadequate to simply add, as one might be tempted to do in French, that "right" designates *le bien* (the "moral" good) and not *le bon*, because for Sidgwick and most other English philosophers, what French calls *bon* is just as moral as what French calls *bien*, but differently. On the other hand, such a distinction within morality is unacceptable if, like Kant, one thinks that "good" in the sense of "desirable" has no place in morality (see GUT):

"Well-being" [*Wohl*] or "woe" [*Übel*] indicates only a relation to our condition of pleasantness or unpleasantness . . . . But good or evil always indicates a relation to the will so far as it is determined by the law or reason.

(*Critique of Practical Reason*)

It is because the English tradition has always refused to practice this exclusion that it draws the line of demarcation not between *le bien* and *le bon*, but between *le juste* and *le bon*. English "rightness" is thus paradoxically closer to the

German *Gut* in this opposition, and in a French translation of Sidgwick's text, it should be rendered by *le bien*. From this we can conclude that "goodness" and "rightness" can be rendered only by *le bien* in these two cases, which seems to be a good example of untranslatability.

Another way of posing the problem is to say not that "good" designates the attractive, the desirable, but that it must be distinguished from "right" because it leads to a series of questions that are of a different order and are just as constitutive of morality: those that bear on ends in themselves, on what has intrinsic value, independently of the actions and desires of the human subject. The confusion of these two senses of "good" is avoidable if we distinguish between the adjective "good," which has this sense of intrinsic value, and the noun "good," which retains the ordinary sense of French *bon*. This kind of confusion is responsible, according to G. E. Moore, for the "naturalist sophism" that can be attributed to the Utilitarians, who make moral ends dependent on human desires and appetites. On this point, Kant would agree with Moore. Here is how Moore proposes to articulate "right" and "good," which can be translated here only by *bon* and *bien*, respectively, contrary to what Utilitarianism prescribes:

> The word "right" is very commonly appropriated to actions which lead to the attainment of what is "good" . . . . But Bentham's fundamental principle is that the greatest happiness of all concerned is the right and proper end of human action. He applies the word "right" to the end, not only to the means . . . which is a naturalistic fallacy.

> (*Principia ethica*, §14)

III. "The Priority of the Right over the Good"

The most troublesome case is that of the expression "the priority of the right over the good," which is untranslatable into French, and not solely because French lacks an equivalent for "right," but also because of English's lack of rigor. This expression has acquired two meanings that are related to each other but are still distinct and that have never been clearly explained because of the shifts we have already noted between "right" and "just." The first meaning concerns Rawls's liberal critique of the Utilitarians and their refusal to derive the right from the good. It contrasts "teleological and deontological doctrines" (see Box 1). The other meaning concerns the critique of liberalism made by the "communitarians," the question of the independence of the norms of justice from common values and the "common good," to adopt Habermas's vocabulary. The expression "the priority of the right over the good" thus comes to mean the priority of justice over the good, as in the remarks by Michael Sandel quoted above.

A first meaning is, as we have indicated, that of the priority of duty, of what must be done, over the good or happiness. Above all, it marks the priority of the question of freedom and moral autonomy over submission to the realization of a *summum bonum* given in advance by human nature. In this sense, the priority of *le bien* over the *le bon* is the fundamental thesis of an individualistic morality for which the capacity for individual justification through a social contract is the sole criterion of the validity of norms. This is a position parallel to the definition of the true by consensus and no longer by correspondence to a state of affairs external to judgment. But in what does this priority consist? Is it a logical priority—do we need the concept of "right" to constitute that of the "good"? That would presuppose that if this priority is not respected, there exist behaviors, organizations, etc. that are "good" without being morally right—which is absurd, whereas what is meant is that the imperative sense of the right has priority over the attractive sense of the good.

■ See Box 1.

IV. The Relations between "Right" and "Just"

The other source of confusion comes from the fact that English seems to slide, without much rigor, from "right" toward "just," from *rectitudo* toward *justitia*. New ambiguities are then created that are sources of confusion but also enrichments. This kind of slide can make it possible to leave the context of the moral analysis of the criterion of good and evil and to operate on a broader playing field, that of distributive

---

1

Teleological theories and deontological theories

Moral theories differ depending on how they articulate *right* and *good*. For teleological theories such as ancient moral theories of happiness (Epicureanism, Stoicism, etc.) or Utilitarianism, the right (the good in the sense of what must be done) is derived from the good that is supposed to be an end, a *telos* given in advance and independently of consciousness, such as pleasure or happiness, that one should seek to maximize. For deontological theories like those of Kant or Rawls, on the contrary, the right is posited independently of the good, since it is impossible to sacrifice the imperatives of duty to those of the individual or general welfare, and the autonomy of the right reflects the autonomy of the individual. However, we must qualify this analysis. According to deontological theories, the existence of a *telos*, a Sovereign Good, necessarily threatens individual freedom, whence this break between *good* and *right*. But this is certainly not the case. For Mill, for instance, it is clear that the right is a collective norm compatible with human freedom and happiness and that this independence of the one from the other is absurd. The *telos*, the good that is to be maximized, is itself dependent on an imperative: the duty to consider impartially the overall good of all the individuals concerned. The distinction between teleological and deontological theories is thus not found primarily in the priority, or not, of the right with respect to the good, as is often said, but rather in the break between moral imperatives and the hypothetical maxims of prudence and happiness, in the independence of the right—that is, of a certain idea of the person, of the person's freedom, in relation to the natural order.

justice, which includes politics and economics. That is the meaning of the well-known debate between liberals and communitarians, that is, between John Rawls, on the one hand, and Taylor, Sandel, and MacIntyre on the other. Contemporary liberal doctrine affirms, with Rawls, the independence of the principles of distributive justice with regard to the conceptions of a society's good. That is the meaning of the remarks by Michael Sandel quoted above.

What is demanded by the communitarian critique of the priority of the right over the good and of procedural ethics, as they are found in both Utilitarianism and Rawlsian theory, is a certain return to Aristotle against Kant, the possibility of restoring a substantial historical and social content to "right" by deriving it from the traditions, the conceptions of the good of a community, and no longer solely from the individual interest. Because of this slide from "right" to "just," the French reader may well not really perceive what is at stake here. The essential point at issue concerns a culturalist and historicist critique of procedural liberalism. The difference between the two senses of *bien* that we have seen above—senses that are conflated in French, but clearly distinguished in English—is that "good" refers to particular conceptions of individual or communal good. But are they good in a universal way, that is, "right" for humanity as a whole? That is why in reality the debate is about universalist justice and local justice, about what is good for me and my group, or about what might constitute a "human right." That is exactly what Rousseau means when he says that "the General Will is always right [*droite*], but it is not always good [*bonne*]" (*Du contrat social*, 2.3). He opposes *le droit* and *le bon*, which would be the best way to translate the conflict between the particularity and self-interest of the individual or the group, on the one hand, and the universality of the rule or the moral criterion, on the other.

Catherine Audard

BIBLIOGRAPHY

Hare, Richard. "Ethical Theory and Utilitarianism." In *Utilitarianism and Beyond*, edited by A. Sen and B. Williams. Cambridge: Cambridge University Press, 1982.

Kant, Immanuel. *Critique of Practical Reason*. Translated by L. W. Beck. New York: Liberal Arts Press, 1956.

Larmore, Charles. *The Morals of Modernity*. New York: Cambridge University Press, 1996.

Moore, G. E. *Principia ethica*. Cambridge: Cambridge University Press, 1993. First published in 1903.

Rawls, John. *Political Liberalism*. Rev. ed. New York: Columbia University Press, 2005.

———. *Theory of Justice*. 2nd ed. Cambridge, MA: Harvard University Press, 1999.

Rousseau, Jean-Jacques. *Du contrat social*. Edited by Bruno Bernardi. Paris: G. F. Flammarion, 2006. Translation by Donald A. Cress: *On the Social Contract*. In *The Basic Political Writings*, edited by Donald A. Cress and David Wootton. 2nd ed. Indianapolis, IN: Hackett, 2012.

Sandel, Michael, ed. *Justice: A Reader*. Oxford: Oxford University Press, 2007.

———. *Liberalism and the Limits of Justice*. Cambridge: Cambridge University Press, 1982.

Sidgwick, Henry. *The Methods of Ethics*. 7th ed. Preface by John Rawls. London: Hackett, 1981. First published in 1874.

Sen, Amartya. *The Idea of Justice*. Cambridge, MA: Harvard University Press, 2009.

Taylor, Charles. "Le juste et le bien." *Revue de Métaphysique et de Morale* 1 (1988): 33–56.

ROMANTIC

FRENCH   *romantique*
GERMAN   *romantisch*

➤ BAROQUE, CLASSIC, DESCRIPTION, DICHTUNG, ERZÄHLEN, *IMAGINATION*, LOVE, MANIERA, MIMÊSIS, NEUZEIT, PERFECTIBILITY

The term "romantic" first appeared in England about 1650; in the form *romantisch* it first established itself in German around 1700 and came into wide use after 1760. *Romantique* entered French in 1776 and was soon adopted by Rousseau. The word owes its morphological homogeneity to a common Latin root. The terms "romantic"/*romantisch*/*romantique* all come from the old French *roman* (or *romanz*), which designated both a particular literary genre and a particular linguistic mode: a verse narrative in a Romance language, that is, in the vernacular, as opposed to Latin. But this homogeneity stops at the formal level. Each passage into a new language gave rise to important shifts in meaning. In its initial English form the term had an essentially aesthetic meaning. "Romantic" is very close to French *romanesque* or *pittoresque* and thereby involves a particular intepretation of the principle of *mimêsis*. In the course of its second wave of diffusion in late eighteenth-century Germany, it added a new historical and critical meaning. Not only is German *Romantisch* related to *romanhaft* and *malerisch*, but it also designated a cultural era, the Middle Ages and Renaissance, a specific intellectual exercise (*romantisieren*), and soon a literary school (*Romantik*). After these multiple European peregrinations the word seemed oddly elusive, which may explain why French writers of the early nineteenth century were reluctant to adopt it.

I. As in a Romance

From the medieval *roman courtois* and *roman de chevalerie*, nourished by the Arthurian legend, down to Honoré d'Urfé's pastoral romance *L'Astrée* (1607–24), the French word *roman* designated a fantastic genre close to the fable. From this semantic matrix the English word "romantic," which appeared about 1650, inherited its first meaning: *romanesque*, that is, invented, imaginary, fictive. Although in England the word rather quickly lost its explicit connection with the world of the *romanesque*, the German term *romantisch* retained it for a long time.

Already present during the first wave of the word's introduction into German, which was carried out especially from Switzerland by J. J. Bodmer and J. J. Breitinger, the synonymous doublet *romantisch*/*romanhaft* continued to be used until the end of the eighteenth century. C. M. Wieland, who played a central role in the spread of the term *romanhaft*, regularly used the two terms interchangeably. Connected with the fabulous genre of the romance, the word also reflects the latter's aleatory popularity. In the late seventeenth and early eighteenth centuries, when the romance was attacked for its excessive implausibility, the terms "romantic"/*romantisch* usually meant "chimerical, false, fabricated," a negative connotation that disappeared in the course of the eighteenth century with the rehabilitation of new novelistic forms.

Having thus issued from a strictly literary sphere, the word "romantic" was nonetheless soon applied metaphorically to other kinds of experience: the perception of a landscape presented as real, the expression of an intimate feeling (a romantic land, romantic love), all uses that, by their disconcerting variety, seem to discourage any effort to give a precise definition. This astonishing diversity requires a shift in the definition from the sphere of the object to that of the subject. What is "romantic" is what is perceived by the subject as being like a romance. At the heart of the notion there is thus less an intrinsic quality of the object than a quality of the way the object is experienced. That is what C. Brentano says in his romance *Godwi* (1800–1802): "The romantic is thus a lens" (*Das Romantische ist also ein Perspectiv*) (2:258). If "romantic"/*romantisch* implies a relation to the subject, it presupposes in addition a specific relation to art and to nature, or more precisely, a strict reversal of the traditional principle of *mimêsis*. In romantic experience nature is perceived through the prism of art (literature or painting). In other words, for the romantic way of seeing things, it is no longer art that imitates nature, but nature that imitates art.

This is the mechanism that explains the precocious application of the term to a privileged domain: the landscape. When it appeared in England in the second half of the seventeenth century, "romantic" was frequently used to define landscapes that reminded the spectator of those in a novel or a picture. Very widely used by English theorists of the aesthetic (J. Addison, Shaftesbury) and in eighteenth-century travel narratives, this use soon became common in Germany, where it remained alive for a very long time. K. P. Moritz, F. Schiller, W. von Humboldt, and J. W. Goethe all deliberately resorted to it. For example, in Goethe's *Sufferings of Young Werther* we read:

> How glad we were when we discovered, at the beginning of our acquaintance, our mutual affection for this spot, which is in truth one of the most romantic that I have ever seen portrayed by an artist.

> (Wie freuten wir uns als wir im Anfang unserer Bekanntschaft die wechselseitige Neigung zu diesem Plätzchen entdeckten, das wahrhaftig eins von den romantischsten ist, die ich von der Kunst hervorgebracht gesehen habe.)

> (Goethe, Bk. I, letter of 10 September; Eng. trans. B. Q. Morgan, London: John Calder, 1957, 75)

From this connection with art, the adjective "romantic" drew a special relationship with painting. Still more than to literary reminiscences, it is to pictures that romantic experience refers. "Romantic"/*romantisch* very often means "picturesque"/*malerisch*. Claude Lorrain, Nicolas Poussin, G. Dughet, and especially S. Rosa are constantly cited as models underlying the perception of a real landscape. Thus a craggy region of New Zealand reminds G. Forster of a painting by Rosa, just as H. Walpole is reminded of this same painter by a tortuous Alpine landscape. It is not surprising, then, that the fortunes of this word, which constantly grew all through the eighteenth century, coincide with the fashion of the English garden. Like the term "romantic"/*romantisch*, the English garden is based on a reversal of the traditional concept of *mimêsis*: nature must be organized like a painting, pictorial or linear, but the intervention of art must be concealed as much as possible. Moreover, the great theorists of the English garden (U. Price, H. Walpole, T. Whately) made extensive use of the term "romantic." Following them, C.C.L.

Hirschfeld suggests that to make a garden "romantic," one should place rocks in it, imitating the paintings of S. Rosa, along with poetic inscriptions and paintings in the grottos that adorn it (*Theorie der Gartenkunst*, 1779–85). The experience of the romantic landscape cannot be understood without this explicit or implicit substratum of literary and pictorial references.

II. A Notion of Cultural History

From its matrix relation to the romance, "romantic"/*romantisch* took not only an aesthetic meaning but also a historical and cultural meaning. Since "romance" designated an ancient literary genre, the adjective derived from it was used to designate the chronological period that saw this genre's birth and development: the Middle Ages and Renaissance.

The appearance of this meaning in the 1760s was due to Thomas Warton, formulated in particular through the notion of romantic poetry, medieval poetry connected with peculiar cultural components (the Christian tradition, the gothic universe, etc.) Although this historical meaning appeared for the first time in England, it was in Germany that it truly took root and developed over the long term. It is as though, during the great wave of the diffusion of the word *romantisch* in the last third of the eighteenth century, German had drawn toward cultural history a notion that had up to that point been reserved in England chiefly for the literary and aesthetic domain. In this change J. G. Herder played, alongside C. M. Wieland, a central role. In the 1760s Herder frequently used the expressions *romantischer Taten* (romantic acts), *romantischer Charakter* (romantic character), and even *romantischer Fabelgeist* (the romantic spirit of the fable) to define the quintessence of the romantic period. One thing, however, is striking in the use of this word: its great imprecision. Under the category "romantic" Herder lumps together the Middle Ages and the Renaissance, along with the Scots, the Normans, the Arabs, and the Provençals. If the "romantic era" thus had very fluctuating chronological and geographical boundaries, it nonetheless had one constant: its opposition to antiquity and to modern neoclassicism. A distant avatar of the Quarrel of the Ancients and the Moderns, the antithesis *antik/romantisch* or *klassisch/romantisch* became structuring in late eighteenth-century Germany. In his essay "Der Ähnlichkeit der mittlern englischen und deutschen Dichtkunst" ("The resemblance of medieval poetry in English and German") (1777), Herder thus contrasts the freedom of medieval ballads and romances, romantic forms that have fallen into oblivion, with the regularity of ancient meter, caricatured in the modern period in French classical versification (9:522ff).

III. Critical Discipline

Used by Herder in an essentially aesthetic and historical sense, in the work of Novalis the term *romantisch* took on still another dimension. For Novalis and a whole generation of writers, it became a general concept designating a particular way of apphrehending the world, an intellectual exercise.

In addition to the traditional uses, which are very present in his writings, in 1797–98 Novalis coined a series of words that gave their root, *romantisch*, a new meaning. The first of these, *romantisieren*, designates a process of poeticizing the world:

> The world must be romanticized. . . . This operation is still entirely unknown. By conferring on secret things an elevated meaning, on the everyday a mysterious prestige, on the known the dignity of the unknown, on the finite the appearance of the infinite, I romanticize them.
>
> (Die Welt muß romantisiert werden. . . . Diese Operation ist noch ganz unbekannt. Indem ich dem Geheimen einen hohen Sinn, dem Gewöhnlichen ein geheimnisvolles Ansehn, dem Bekannten die Würde des Unbekannten, dem Endlichen einen unendlichen Schein gebe, so romantisiere ich es.)
>
> (Novalis, *Philosophical Writings*, vol. 2, §4, no. 105)

Thus invested with a very general critical dimension, the word *romantisch* soon came to designate a discipline or science called *Romantik* by analogy with other fields of knowledge (*Physik, Mathematik, Grammatik,* etc.). Just as there is a *Physiker* or a *Grammatiker*, so there is a *Romantiker*. The subject of this new discipline is life, or rather, what amounts to the same thing, the romance, since "we live in a colossal romance" ("*Wir leben in einem kolossalen Roman*"):

> Life is something like colors, sounds, forces. The Romantic studies life as the painter, the musician, and the specialist in mechanics study color, sound, and forces.
>
> (Das Leben ist etwas, wie Farben, Töne und Kraft. Der Romantiker studiert das Leben, wie der Maler, Musiker und Mechaniker Farbe, Ton und Kraft.)
>
> (Novalis, *Philosophical Writings*, vol. 3, §9, nos. 853 and 1073)

For Novalis the *Romantiker* is a person who succeeds in living his life like a romance, that is, poetically (*Fragmente und Studien*, 1797–98, no. 188, in *Philosophical Writings*). Disseminated through the publication of Novalis's works by F. Schlegel and L. Tieck (1802), these neologisms were soon being used by many writers.

IV. Overlapping Meanings

Far from excluding each other, these diverse historical and critical meanings never ceased to intersect, and around 1800 they conferred on the word *romantisch* an unusual density. At the confluence of these semantic traditions stood Friedrich Schlegel. Having started from Herder, but being a great reader of Novalis, he made a central contribution to the definition of the word. In his essay "*Über das Studium der griechischen Poesie*" ("On the study of Greek poetry"), written in 1795, he opposes, like Herder but in a way very favorable to the ancients, ancient poetry, which is beautiful, objective, natural, cyclical, and finite, to romantic poetry, which is infinite, subjective, artificial, progressive, and sometimes mixed with ugliness. However, though he is still very critical with regard to the romantic period, that is, the Middle Ages and the Renaissance, he reverses this judgment in his later writings. In the Athenäum fragments (1798), the infinite progressivity of romantic poetry is presented as a

privilege of modernity, and superior in this respect to that of antiquity, which remains ineluctably prisoner to a cycle of apotheosis and decline. In the tradition of Herder, then, Schlegel makes this term both a key notion in cultural history (*romantisch* designates the culture of the Middle Ages and the Renaissance) and a component of the antinomic pair "antiquity"/"modernity." But Schlegel soon gave it a much broader meaning. Although, of course, it was still connected with the literature of the twelfth to the sixteenth centuries, for him the concept of "romantic poetry" quickly came to include contemporary works (Goethe's *Wilhelm Meister's Apprenticeship*, L. Tieck's *Franz Sternbald's Wanderings*) and was also extended to include ancient authors (Homer, Aeschylus, Plato, Horace, and Virgil), and even included all the existing literary genres. At the end of this itinerary, the term *romantisch* designated neither more nor less than the essence itself of all poetic activity. It was endowed with a truly universal meaning in which all the earlier antinomies were dissolved: Herder's opposition between antiquity and modernity, and the oppositions between prose and verse, between romance and poetry. That is what is expressed in Athenäum fragment no. 116:

> Romantic poetry is a progressive, universal poetry. Its aim isn't merely to reunite all the separate species of poetry and put poetry in touch with philosophy and rhetoric. It tries to and should mix and fuse poetry and prose, inspiration and criticism, the poetry of art and the poetry of nature, and make poetry lively and sociable, and life and society poetical; poeticize art. . . . It embraces everything that is purely poetic, from the greatest systems of art, containing within themselves still further systems, to the sigh, the kiss that the poeticizing child breathes forth in artless song. . . . It alone can become, like the epic, a mirror of the whole circumambient world, an image of the age. . . . The romantic kind of poetry is the only one that is more than a kind, that is, as it were, poetry itself: for in a certain sense all poetry is or should be romantic.
>
> (F. Schlegel, Athenäum fragment 116, in *Friedrich Schlegel's Lucinde*, 175–76)

It was in this sense, saturated with diverse meanings, that the word *romantisch* spread from 1800 onward. Jean Paul's *Vorschule der Ästhetik* (Preparatory course in aesthetics) (1804, §22) provides a surprising example of this overlapping of meanings. In the tradition stemming from Herder, Jean Paul tells us, *romantisch* applies chiefly to the medieval and Christian era, as opposed to antiquity, but it does not in any way exclude Greekness. Moreover, in the English tradition it designates a landscape with romantic or pictorial qualities but also defines a way of apprehending the world, in accord with the meaning that Novalis gives the word. Finally, in the tradition stemming from Schlegel, *romantisch* also refers to the very essence of poetry.

To these multiple meanings another was added in the first decades of the nineteenth century. *Romantisch*, having become a term commonly used by a whole generation of writers (the Schlegel brothers, Tieck, Novalis, Brentano, Eichendorff, et al.), ended up designating this group. It must be emphasized that this use of the adjective, applied to a still quite recent school of writers, was actually very polemical. It was usually found in the adverse camp, that is, among the "classical writers" gathered around Goethe, or in F. Bouterwerk and J. H. Voss, who began in 1800 a very virulent campaign against the Schlegel group. In terms of literary history, the word *romantisch* thus emerged from these multiple mutations as a strangely equivocal term. In the German of the early nineteenth century, it could refer, in a very broad sense, to the whole poetic production of humanity since antiquity, the literature of the Middle Ages and Renaissance, the literature of the modern period down to the nineteenth century, or, finally, a contemporary school that arose at the very end of the eighteenth century.

V. The Importation of the Term into France

It is probably these multiple senses that explain the reluctance of French writers to adopt the word. *Romantique* does not appear in French until 1776, in P. Letourneur's introduction to a translation of Shakespeare, and then in an essay by the Marquis de Girardin, "De la composition des paysages," dated 1777.

In both cases it is in direct reference to the English meaning of the term that the adjective is adopted. Rousseau endorses this borrowing in the fifth chapter of his *Reveries of a Solitary Walker* (*Les Rêveries d'un promeneur solitaire*, 1782) when he describes the shores of Lake Biel-Bienne as "more wild and romantic than those of Lake Geneva" (*plus sauvages et romantiques que celles du lac de Genève*). Despite what is said by Letourner, who was trying to justify the invention of the word by emphasizing its radical difference from *romanesque*, the adjective *romantique* had difficulty prevailing over its rival. In the 1792 *Encyclopédie méthodique* and the 1798 edition of the *Dictionnaire de l'Académie française*, it appears only as an anglicized doublet of *romanesque*, used especially in relation to landscapes, in the sense of "similar to a romance" or, by extension, "picturesque." Rousseau himself, a few pages after using the word, speaks of "*romanesques rivages*." If the word *romantique* certainly found supporters (Senancour, Stendhal, L. S. Mercier), it seems not to have been seen as really French until the early nineteenth century.

The first wave of the term's spread in English having met with a certain resistance, the second wave in German was far more defining, both by its breadth and by the shift in meaning that it carried out: the word "romantic" moved from an essentially aesthetic and literary meaning to one in the domain of cultural history. It was A. W. Schlegel's definition that established itself in France, as it did elsewhere in Europe, especially after his lectures on dramatic art and literature (delivered in Vienna in 1808; published 1809–11 as *Über dramatische Kunst und Literatur*), which were published in French translation in 1814. In a somewhat simplified paraphrase of his brother Friedrich's reflections, A. W. Schlegel attached the concept of *Romantik* to the modern cultural era inaugurated in the Middle Ages, marked by the Christian tradition, and characterized by an infinitely progressive literature that was open to a mixing of the genres. The romantic era can be understood only as the antithesis of the ancient era. Picked up by Madame de Staël, this historical-cultural meaning was also filled out by Charles de Villers, a great mediator between

France and Germany, who connected the romantic era with both the late Latin that gave rise to the Romance languages and the medieval period. In the early nineteenth century, in the absence of an accepted adjective relating to the Middle Ages, *romantique* often meant "medieval." In 1810 Villers even tried to import a direct translation of the German noun *Romantik*, in the form of *la romantique*, to designate medieval poetry and its main characteristics. But this attempt failed, and the adjective long remained without a nominal form. The term *romanticisme*, proposed by Stendhal as a calque of the Italian *romanticismo* (see especially his *Racine et Shakespeare*, 2:113–21), was not adopted; by 1824 it had disappeared from his vocabulary. Paradoxically, it was the adversaries of this trend, and especially the members of the Académie française, who, in their determination to discredit this aesthetics, popularized the term *romantisme* in the 1820s. *Romantisme* signifies first of all a genre, based on the medieval model, and then, by extension, the contemporary movement that had made itself that genre's defender (a definition that was to be adopted by literary historians). In the preface to his play *Cromwell*, Hugo was able to use the noun without fearing that he would be misunderstood.

In England, Germany, and France the currently dominant sense of the word "romantic" bears hardly any trace of the three original meanings, aesthetic, historical, and critical. This rich multitude has been reduced to two main senses. For the most part "romantic" refers to a set of rather vague themes (melancholy, mystery, imagination, etc.) and, in a more precise sense that comes essentially from literary historians, to the group of writers who wrote about and exemplified these themes in the late eighteenth and early nineteenth centuries. But here again translation difficulties persist. Goethe, whom historians of German literature consider a virulent adversary of Romanticism, is commonly placed in France under the banner of the German Romantics.

Élisabeth Décultot

BIBLIOGRAPHY

Baldensperger, Fernand. "Romantique, ses analogues et ses equivalents. Tableau synoptique de 1650 à 1810." *Harvard Studies and Notes in Philology and Literature* 19 (1937): 13–105.

Brentano, Clemens. *Godwi oder das steinerne Bild der Mutter. Ein verwilderter Roman von Maria*. In *Werke*. Vol. 2. Edited by F. Kemp, W. Frühwald, and B. Gajek. Munich: Hanser, 1963.

Eichner, Hans, ed. *"Romantic and its Cognates. The European History of a Word*. Toronto: University of Toronto Press, 1972.

Gotthard, Helene, and Richard Ullmann. *Geschichte des Begriffes "Romantisch" in Deutschland*. Berlin: Ebering, 1927.

Herder, Johann Gottfried von. "Der Ähnlichkeit der mittlern englischen und deutschen Dichtkunst." In *Sämtliche Werke*, 9: 522–35. Edited by B. Suphan. Berlin: Weidmann, 1877–1913.

Immerwahr, Raymond. *Romantisch. Genese und Tradition einer Denkform*. Frankfurt: Athenäum, 1972.

Jauss, Hans Robert. *Literarische Tradition und gegenwärtiges Bewußtsein der Modernität*. In *Literaturgeschichte als Provokation*, 11–66. Frankfurt: Suhrkamp, 1970.

Lacoue-Labarthe, Phillippe, and Jean-Luc Nancy. *L'Absolu littéraire. Théorie de la littérature du romantisme allemand*. Paris: Éditions du Seuil, 1978.

Lovejoy, Arthur O. "The Meaning of 'Romantic' in Early German Romanticism." Part 1: *Modern Language Notes* 31 (1916): 385–96; Part 2: *Modern Language Notes* 32 (1917): 65–77.

Novalis. *Philosophical Writings*. Translated and edited by Margaret Mahony Stoljar. Albany: State University of New York Press, 1997.

———. *Pollens and Fragments: Selected Poetry and Prose of Novalis*. Translated and edited by Arthur Versluis. Grand Rapids, MI: Phanes Press, 1989.

———. *Schriften*. 5 vols. Edited by P. Kluckhohn and R. Samuel. Stuttgart: Kolhammer, 1960–88.

Paul, Jean. *Vorschule der Ästhetik*. In *Werke*, vol. 5. Edited by Norbert Miller. Munich: C. Hanser, 1959–85.

Plug, Jan. *Borders of a Lip: Romanticism, Language, History, Politics*. Albany: State University of New York Press, 2003.

Schlegel, August Wilhelm. *Course of Lectures on Dramatic Art and Literature*. Translated by John Black. 2nd ed. New York: AMS Press, 1973.

Schlegel, Friedrich. *"Athenäums"—Fragmente: und andere Schriften*. Stuttgart: Philipp Reclam, 2005.

———. *Friedrich Schlegel's Lucinde and the Fragments*. Translated by Peter Firchow. Minneapolis: University of Minnesota Press, 1971.

———. *On the Study of Greek Poetry*. Translated and edited by Stuart Barnett. Albany: State University of New York Press, 2003.

Stendhal. *Racine and Shakespeare*. Translated by Guy Daniels. New York: Crowell-Collier Press, 1962.

RULE

"Rule" derives from Latin *regula*. On the *regula*, a ruler serving to square things, and connected with "straight" (*directum*) and with the power of "ruling" (*rex*), see LEX (cf. *DROIT*), with LEX, Box 1 on the Greek network of equivalences, which opens not onto the problematics of law but onto that of the proper measure (see PHRONÊSIS and TRUTH, Box 1).

Règle is, along with *critère*, one of the accepted French translations of English "standard," designating what serves to evaluate and then to regulate experience in a more regional manner than law: see STANDARD, and cf. the constellation of the same family around STAND. The term is applied in all domains: as a rule of taste, of morality, or of production; the "standard" is a norm of evaluation or use that is determined by conformity (standardization). See ECONOMY, GOÛT, UTILITY; cf. ART, DUTY, LAW, MORALS, *OBLIGATION, VALUE*.

On the relation between "regular" and "secular," see SECULARIZATION; cf. BERUF, OIKONOMIA.

➤ *CULTURE, EXPERIENCE*

RULE OF LAW

FRENCH   *État de droit*
GERMAN   *Rechtstaat*

➤ CIVIL SOCIETY, DUTY, HERRSCHAFT, LAW, LIBERAL, MACHT, POLIS, POLITICS, SOLLEN, *STATE*

The concept of the rule of law, long viewed with disdain by philosophers who saw it as a purely legal or even ideological notion, enjoys considerable prestige in contemporary thought, which corresponds to the recent developments in internal democratic politics and international law. The end of the twentieth century saw the fall of West European conservative regimes (Spain, Portugal, Greece), the rise of constitutional courts in most democracies, the collapse of communist regimes in central and eastern Europe, and, finally, the sometimes problematic emergence of an international law that is designed to limit the sovereignty of states by making it possible, under certain conditions, to impose sanctions against governments that are guilty of flagrant violations of fundamental rights. It is no doubt possible to consider all of these heterogeneous but convergent processes under the concept of the rule of law, insofar as they all yield a contrast between totalitarian, authoritarian, and arbitrary states and a superior model defined by its conformity with the law—although it is not clear whether this entails simply the existence of a duly agreed-upon hierarchy of norms or, more radically, the subordination of states to metalegal norms such as the Rights of Man. We may note that the agents of these transformations themselves often referred to the concept of the rule of law to legitimate their actions, whether they were governments of countries in transition to democracy, constitutional courts, or even the last communist leaders when they were attempting to save something of the regimes they had been in charge of (Mikhail Gorbachev wished to establish in the Soviet Union a "Socialist rule of law"). Contemporary political philosophy has for the most part gone along with this movement, presenting itself as a philosophy of law (A. Renaut and L. Sosoe, *Philosophie du droit*), attempting to show the irreducibility of the rule of law (a creation of Western Europe) to a "police state" (B. Kriegel, *L'État et les Esclaves*), or seeking a synthesis between a radical theory of democracy and the liberal tradition of the rule of law (J. Habermas, *Between Facts and Norms*). Nevertheless, even today the notion of the rule of law remains problematic in numerous ways. The main questions are those of the origins of the concept of a rule of law (which goes back to the Germanic doctrine of the *Rechtstaat*, which appears in a very different context from that of France), of its operational value (contested on grounds offered both by Carl Schmitt and Hans Kelsen), and its translatability into English (where the concept of the rule of law refers both to a different division between right and law and to constitutional agencies that are not reducible to the "continental" models).

I. The German Doctrine of the *Rechtstaat*

The French expression "état de droit" is a translation of the German *Rechtstaat*, which first occurs in the nineteenth century to describe the progressive process of the framing and limitation of the state by the law and which was believed to be at work in the German State. As noted by Jacques Chevallier, "[T]his common objective nevertheless covers rather different visions of the State and the law" (*L'État de droit*, 11), running from the simple functional requirement of a state acting by means of the law to subtantial requirements concerning the content of the law, as well as the formalist idea of a state subject to law. The formula is moreover put forward both by liberal legal thinkers like R. von Mohl, who seek to limit the sphere of action of the state and hence to protect individual liberty, and by others, less ambitious or more conservative, who simply wish to rationalize the domination of the state by normalizing the relations between it and the administration with those administered. In the end, the formalist conception won out, since it made it possible to subordinate the administration to the law by opening avenues of legal recourse against it, while at the same time presenting the subjection of the state to the law as a product of self-limitation (which requires no ultimate reference to legal norms superior to those posed by the State). On one hand, the rule of law is contrasted with the police state (*Polizeistaat*), in which the law is only the instrument of an administration that may impose obligations upon those administered without being bound by higher norms. On the other hand, the rule of law is the fruit of a free (but rational) self-limitation of the state, the true subject of law, whose domination (*Herrschaft*) is at its origin a subjective law before which it is not possible to have public law, but whose immanent finality is to create law and rule by it (note here that the expression "self-limitation" translates several German words—*Selbstverpflichtung, Selbstbindung, Selbstbeschränkung*—which all contain the idea that the state imposes duties, obligations, or limits on itself; see R. Carré de Malberg, *Contribution à la théorie générale de l'État*, 231).

The *Rechtstaat* thus appears as an irreducibly liberal and statist concept, one that fits rather well in the German political philosophical tradition as developed from Kant to Hegel. The liberal aspect appears in the form of the demand that those administered be protected in their relationship to the state, but also, more radically, by the clear affirmation of principles of constitutionalism. The respect for higher norms is imposed not only on the administration and the executive power but also on the legislative power itself, which is subordinate to a nation's Constitution, according to a scheme that may easily be transposed from an empire to a liberal-democratic state (as is the case with current German basic law). The statist aspect is manifested by the absence of any superconstitutional norms (unlike what is supposed to happen today), by the rather emphatic claim of the originary power of the state (which goes along with the superiority of internal law over international law—which is also a product of the self-limitation of sovereign states), and more concretely by the autonomy of administrative law (which derives from the state's privilege of fixing its own rules that it follows in interactions with individuals). The theory of the *Rechtstaat* is also part of the general framework of the construction of public law centered on the state, which is inseparable from the development of the empire. We may note here that, by insisting on the state's originary power in respect of the nation, the theorists of self-limitation also dispute the claims of the Romantics and the historical school of law, while at the same time breaking with any patrimonial conception of the state and clearly distinguishing it from those doing the governing (cf. J. Chevallier, *L'État de droit*, 14–21). It would nevertheless be unfair to see here a uniquely German doctrine, since the theory of the rule of law is also pertinent to other nations of continental Europe, and more generally wherever the problem of the synthesis between affirmation of public law and the liberal limitation of state power is posed. This is illustrated by reception of the German doctrine in France, where it was eventually taken up by Raymond Carré de Malberg, despite the suspicion toward a theory that seemed to legitimate the imperial regime and that was opposed to the conception of the nation-state inherited from the French Revolution (*Contribution à la théorie générale de l'État*, 21–43).

French debates over the problem of the rule of law are not purely theoretical; they are, in fact, tightly set within the national and international political context of the beginning of the twentieth century. The authors who are most critical of the German doctrine, like Léon Duguit or, somewhat less so, Maurice Hauriou, are above all concerned to distinguish the state from the law, in order to guarantee the submission of the former to the latter. For Duguit, this is done by a twofold criticism of the doctrine of sovereignty and legal individualism, considered effects of subjectivism, against which he offers the rule of law as the only real foundation of an objective law, which is founded on social solidarity and opposed to both the state and to individuals. The state is thus not self-limiting, since it is not a legal subject, nor is its limitation based on the subjective laws dear to liberals (P. Raynaud, "Léon Duguit et le droit naturel"). For Hauriou, the law is also clearly distinct from the state, but the doctrine of self-limitation nevertheless retains some force for understanding the development of freedoms: "Logically, the self-limitation of the State appears to be an absurdity. Historically, it is the constitutional truth" (*Précis de droit constitutionnel*, 101). For its French defenders, most prominently Carré de Malberg, the rule of law appears both to be a contemporary expression of the ideals of the French Revolution (which makes it possible to contest the German priority on this point while also legitimating the French adoption of a German theory; see, for example, Carré de Malberg, *Contribution à la théorie générale de l'État*, 448n5) and as a powerful instrument for criticizing the constitutional mandate of the Third Republic. The French regime of the time, indeed, guaranteed the legality of the actions of the executive, or the administration, with more rigor than in Germany since it "subordinates to the laws even those administrative acts which do not pertain to the citizens as individuals." However, on the other hand, the French Constitution "has not reached the perfection of the rule of law" since it does not prohibit the legislator from "derogating the general rules consecrated by existing legislation" by particular laws, and because, above all, the legislator is not subordinate to the Constitution except by checks on the constitutionality of the laws, which makes it difficult to protect individual freedoms against the legislator (ibid., 492). At the same time, Carré de Malberg takes up the theory of self-limitation and translates it into the French language of sovereignty, giving what might be called a liberal version of legal positivism, while at the same time rejecting the German conception of the relations between the state and the nation. From the perspective of French constitutional law, the state cannot be the legal personification of the nation (cf. Raynaud, "Droit naturel et souveraineté national"). The debate between these views continued for a long time in the subsequent history of the doctrine, since they brought up fundamental questions, both theoretical and practical (J. Chevallier, *L'État de droit*; P. Raynaud, "Des droits de l'homme à l'État de droit"; M.-J. Redor, *De l'État légal à l'État de droit*). We may note, to conclude, that between the German version of the theory of *Rechtstaat* and the transposition made by Carré de Malberg, continuity wins out over discontinuity. In both cases, the synthesis between liberal concerns and public laws is effected by a legal positivism and the liberal theory of the self-limitation of the state, and the theory of the rule of law, which makes it possible to reinforce the guarantees of those subject to the law and to extend the actions of the courts, is used as a "solid support in the doctrinal construction of a fully flourishing administrative law" (J. Chevallier, *L'État de droit*, 32). Conversely, the main theoretical criticisms of the state bear, on the one hand, on its liberal component, and on the other, on the theory of self-limitation. In addition, the difficulty of translating the notion of the rule of law into English is linked historically to the weakness of administrative law in England.

II. The Criticisms of the Rule of Law

As it originated in the project of providing a liberal rationalization of the state, the notion of the rule of law was the object of various criticisms, many of which are antiliberal or antidemocratic, but some of which are, on the contrary, democratic and anti-authoritarian in spirit.

On the antiliberal side, the most radical and developed criticism is doubtless to be found in the work of the German jurist Carl Schmitt (1888–1985), whose considerable writings cannot be separated from his activities against liberal democracy. This viewpoint led him to support the Third Reich for a time (after he had, during the Weimar Republic, demanded the prohibition of the Nazi Party, though in the service of an authoritiarian transformation of the constitution in force at the time; see Beaud, *Les Derniers Jours de Weimar*). In Schmitt's major work *Constitutional Theory* (1928), the discussion of the principles of the "bourgeois rule of law" aims at revealing the implicitly polemical or partisan character of the notion of the rule of law, while at the same time uncovering its inability to account for what the modern liberal state retains of politics. If we were to take the expression of the rule of law literally, "we could call a rule of law any State which faultlessly respects the objective law in place and the existing subjective rights." This would lead to an application of this notion to the most powerless political forms and even the most archaic ones, forms in which the rights acquired would be scrupulously respected at the expense of the very conditions of the political existence and security of the state. "In this sense," Schmitt writes, "the old German Reich, the Roman Empire of the German Nation, was a perfect *Rechtstaat* at the time of its dissolution; its character as a *Rechtstaat* was the manifestation and the instrument of its political collapse" (*Constitutional Theory*). However, the contemporary meaning of the notion is in fact essentially polemical: the rule of law is opposed to the rule of might (*Machtstaat*), as well as to the police state and the welfare state and to "any other type of State which is not focused simply on maintaining the legal order" (ibid.). Finally, if we aim to give a more precise meaning to the notion, we find the principles of liberal constitutionalism, where the respect for fundamental (individual) rights is based on the division of power of the state (ibid.), which leads to various organizational criteria such as the principle of legality, the fixed division of political powers and the independence of the judiciary, which end in the general predominance of jurisdictional forms (*allgemeine Justizförmigkeit*) in the life of the state (ibid.). Schmitt's reservations about this conception of the state focus first on its unilateral character, which leads to misjudging the specifically political dimension of the legal order, which rests on sovereign choice and not simply on a "system of legal norms aimed at preserving the individual against the state" (ibid.). Schmitt suggests thus that the liberal state is either hypocritical or incapable of understanding itself, except by seeing that the rule of law itself presupposes a prior decision in its own favor—the liberal principle, which simply demands limitations on power, being silent on the question of the different forms of

government (ibid.). In other texts, Schmitt refers to the institutionalist dimension of the law, equally misunderstood by the doctrine of the rule of law in his opinion, which is unilaterally attached to the simple normative idea of the law as a system of abstract rules (see, for example, *On the Three Types of Juristic Thought*, a summary of his lectures from 1934).

While Schmitt's theories may be seen as a reactivization of the authoritarian aspects of the German conception of the state against liberal tendencies at work in the rule of law, those of Hans Kelsen, who affirms the identity between the state and the law, may be, on the contrary, considered as an effort to emancipate the normative idea of the predemocratic notions retained by the idea of state self-limitation.

Kelsen is known as one of the major representatives of legal positivism and, as such, is often the subject of ritualized and misguided criticisms, which bear on the supposed inability of positivists to criticize positive law where it is manifestly unjust or oppressive, where instances of the latter simply indicate the impossibility of basing the necessity of obedience to the law in the law itself, as well as the ultimately nonlegal character (since it is moral and/or political) of the fundamental norm from which positive law is derived. Defining the law as a type of constraint, Kelsen is led to include extremely shocking facts (see, for example, *Pure Theory of Law*). However, this must be seen as the expression of an attempt to deconsecrate the legal order, which is also, for the democratic Kelsen, perhaps the prior condition of a definition of the effective conditions of the preservation of freedoms. As for the identity of the state and the law, it leads Kelsen to a vigorous critique of the theory of self-limitation (or rather of self-obligation, *Selbstverpflichtung*), which shows that it relies on circular reasoning, since the authority of the state presupposes a norm that makes it a subject of the law empowered to lay down further norms. In this sense, every state is a *Rechtstaat*, and "it is impossible to think of a State which is not subordinated to the law," since "the State only exists in state actions, that is, actions accomplished by human beings and which are attributed to the State as a legal norm" (H. Kelsen, *Pure Theory of Law*). Thus, "the term *Rechtstaat* is a pleonasm" (ibid.). Kelsen notes, however, that in fact the expression *Rechtstaat* is often used as a simple synonym for democratic states guaranteeing legal security, which he denies distinguishes them at all from authoritarian states. As a practicing jurist, Kelsen, who was also a major democratic theorist, was one of the promoters in continental Europe of constitutional oversight. This oversight, which makes it possible to subordinate the legislative power to the fundamental norm, is one of the most powerful loci of the development of what may be called the rule of law. The anti-imperial orientation of Kelsen's doctrine, which inspires his critique of self-obligation, is equally visible in another fundamental claim in favor of the "pure theory of law," that of the unity of international and internal law, which is obviously in contradiction with the claims of the jurists of the Empire. Kelsen's best readers did not miss the point of this doctrine: in his most virulent period, Carl Schmitt denounced normativism as being essentially liberal and antipolitical (*On the Three Types of Juristic Thought*). A thinker like Raymond Aron, who, while liberal, was also a realist thinker about international relations, confessed his preference for the theory of self-limitation (even though it cannot provide a basis for the "obligatory force" of the law, this theory is "a formalization of historico-social reality"; see Aron's *Peace and War*).

III. "Rule of Law" in English

While the German notion of *Rechstaat* may be easily translated into most continental languages, its translation into English raises important problems that are not merely linguistic. The most common translation of *Rechtstaat* or *état de droit* is "rule of law," whose connotations are nonetheless rather different. From a linguistic point of view there is the problem of there being two meanings of "law," which corresponds to both the French *droit* and *loi*, whereas what would be called in French *droits subjectifs* are called "rights" in English. More importantly, the legal-political content of the concept of the "rule of law" is different from that of the *état de droit*. The notion of the "rule of law" refers more to substantial and procedural criteria of the legitimacy of governments and legal norms than to the formal coherence of a system of state norms. It means, on the one hand, that in the organization of the *government* the law must be placed above people (according to a classic idea going back to Greek thought), on the other, that legislation and legal processes must bear certain procedural qualities (cf. the American notion of "due process of law," usually translated into French as *procédure équitable*). Thus, where the *état de droit* urges above all a means (the hierarchy of norms) that are supposed to yield a certain result (freedom), the "rule of law" defines the result much more precisely, but does not indicate the means for achieving it (M. Troper, "Le concept d'État de droit," 63). The difficulty is, in fact, compounded by the English origins of the notion, given the degree to which the English Constitution is out of conformity with contemporary norms of constitutionality. The classic author in this regard is the great jurist A. V. Dicey (1835–1922), who showed that English rule rests on a subtle balance between the sovereignty of Parliament (which does not allow for constitutional oversight of the laws) and the "rule of law" (which demands that the administration derive from common law and that the functionaries shall be, like any other citizen, responsible before ordinary tribunals, which is incompatible with the continental and especially French idea of administrative law). The consequence of this doctrine is that, on one hand, the United Kingdom is not an *état de droit*, lacking oversight of the constitutionality of laws, and that on the other, France does not live under the rule of law, since it has an administrative law with a special jurisdiction (see D. Mockle, "L'État de droit et la théorie de la *Rule of Law*"). The practical repercussions are less serious today than at the beginning of the twentieth century, given the liberal evolution of administrative law and the importance of American constitutionalism in the culture of jurists and English-speaking philosophers of law. Nevertheless, it remains the case that British and American authors do not mean the same thing by "rule of law" that continental jurists or philosophers mean by *état de droit*. Indeed, this is why the most rigorous among them translate *Rechtstaat* by "constitutional government" and not by "rule of law" (Troper, "Le concept d'État de droit," 54).

Philippe Raynaud

BIBLIOGRAPHY

Aron, Raymond.: *Paix et guerre entre les nations*. 2nd ed. Paris: Calmann-Lévy, 1984. Translation by R. Howard and A. Baker Fox: *Peace and War: A Theory of International Relations*. Garden City, NY: Doubleday, 1966.

Beaud, Olivier. *Les Derniers Jours de Weimar. Carl Schmitt face à l'avénement du nazisme*. Paris: Descartes et Cie, 1997.

Carré de Malberg, Raymond. *Contribution à la théorie générale de l'État*. Paris: CNRS, 1962. First published in 1920.

Chevallier, Jacques. *L'État de droit*. 3rd ed. Paris: Montchrestien, 1999.

Dicey, Albert Venn. *Introduction to the Study of the Law of the Constitution*. Indianapolis: Liberty Fund, 1982; reprint of the 8th edition published in London by Macmillan in 1915. First edition published in 1889.

Duguit, Léon. *Traité de droit constitutionnel*. 5 vols. 3rd ed. Paris: Boccard, 1927–30.

Habermas, Jürgen. *Between Facts and Norms: Contributions to a Discourse Theory of Law and Democracy*. Translated by W. Regh. Cambridge, MA: MIT Press, 1996.

Hauriou, Maurice. *Précis de droit constitutionnel*. 2nd ed., reprint. Paris: CNRS, 1965. First published in 1929.

Kelsen, Hans. *General Theory of Law and State*. Translated by A. Wedberg. Reprint. Cambridge, MA: Harvard University Press, 1949. First published in 1945.

———. *Pure Theory of Law*. Translated by M. Knight. Berkeley: University of California Press, 1960.

Kriegel, Blandine. *L'État et les esclaves*. 3rd ed. Paris: Payot, 1989. Translation by M. A. LePain and J. C. Cohen: *The State and the Rule of Law*. Princeton, NJ: Princeton University Press, 1995.

Mockle, Daniel. "L'État de droit et la théorie de la *Rule of Law*." *Cahiers de droit* (Montréal) 35, no. 4 (December 1994): 823–904.

Pennock, J. R., and J. W. Chapman, eds. *Constitutionalism*. New York: New York University Press, 1979.

Raynaud, Philippe. "Droit naturel et souveraineté nationale. Remarques sur la théorie de l'État chez Carré de Malberg." *Commentaire* no. 22 (1983): 384–93.

———. "Des droits de l'homme à l'État de droit chez les théoriciens français classiques du droit public." *Droits* no. 2 (1985): 61–73.

———. "Léon Duguit et le droit naturel." *Revue d'histoire des facultés de droit et de science juridique* no. 4 (1987): 169–80.

Raz, Joseph. "The Politics of the Rule of Law." *Ratio juris* 2 (1989): 1–16.

Redor, Marie-Joëlle. *De l'État légal à l'État de droit. L'évolution de la doctrine publiciste française 1879–1914*. Paris: Economica, 1992.

Renaut, Alain, and Lukas Sosoe. *Philosophie du droit*. Paris: Presses Universitaires de France, 1992.

Schmitt, Carl. *Constitutional Theory*. Translated by J. Seitzer. Durham: Duke University Press, 2008. German text first published in 1928.

———. *On the Three Types of Juristic Thought*. Translated by J. Bendersky. Westport, CT: Praeger Publishers, 2004.

Troper, Michel. "Le concept d'État de droit." *Droits* no. 15 (1992): 51–63.

Waldron, Jeremy. "The Rule of Law in Contemporary Liberal Theory." *Ratio juris* 2 (1989): 79–96.

———. *The Law*. London: Routledge, 1990.

| RUSE

In French, *ruse*, from Latin *recusare* (to reject, refuse, protest against), is first of all a hunting term that designates a trick used by game animals to throw dogs off the scent and escape hunters (RT: *DHLF*). Various elements come into play.

I. Human Ruse, Divine Ruse

The Greek *mêtis* [μῆτις], the strategy used by the octopus, by Odysseus, by the sophist, and by Zeus, is connected with practical intelligence in a complex system that includes measure (*metron* [μέτρον]; see LEX, Box 1) and premeditated planning (cf. *medomai* [μέδομαι]; see MÊTIS).

TALAṬṬUF [تلطّف] designates Allah's ruse, whose subtlety combines grace and machination (see GRACE), and makes use of evil in order to do good, as Hegel's Spirit does in history (die List der Vernunft). See TALAṬṬUF. Cf. AUFHEBEN, *DESTINY*, HISTORY, OIKONOMIA, PLASTICITY.

II. Ruse, Skill, Wisdom

More broadly, "ruse" implies an inventiveness in means-ends relationships characteristic of artistic and mechanical skill; see ART, I, INGENIUM, Box 1 on Arabic *hads* [الحدس] and Greek *agchinoia* [ἀγχίνοια], ITALIAN, VI; cf. ARGUTEZZA, CONCETTO, GENIUS, MIMĒSIS.

This kind of know-how is connected with practical wisdom, see *PRUDENCE* [PHRONÊSIS, PRUDENTIAL], VIRTÙ, *WISDOM*; cf. MORALS.

➤ *DECEPTION, REASON, SOPHISM*

RUSSIAN

Diglossic Opposition in Russian

➤ ASPECT, AUFHEBEN, BOGOČELOVEČESTVO, *GOOD/EVIL*, GREEK, MIR, POSTUPOK, PRAVDA, SVOBODA

Diglossic opposition characterizes philosophical discourse in Russian. Diglossia is the coexistence in a single society of two languages that have different values, as opposed to bilingualism, in which two languages are on the same level. "Good," "truth," "knowledge," "action," and "time," for instance, present themselves in the form of organized oppositions in accord with the linguistic model of diglossia. The semantics of this opposition is based on the representation of two "worlds," one "low" and the other "high," so that the concepts concerned are rendered by two terms, one referring to the low world and the other to the high world. The relation between the two worlds is a dynamic process of realizing and sublating one world in the other. Since it is the "person" (*ličnost'* [личность]) that carries out this process, Russian philosophy is often described as personalist. The conceptual schema of the two worlds is the basis on which Russian philosophy has developed an ontology that cannot be separated from either anthropology or ethics.

I. Diglossia and the Russian Language: Linguistic and Historical Elements

Modern Russian is not a homogeneous language. Today, it includes two different types of elements, Slavonic and Russian. When the East Slavs were Christianized at the end of the tenth century, two languages coexisted in this linguistic community. The first was Old Slavonic, an ecclesiastical language based on a Macedonian dialect that was used to translate the Greek texts of the Gospels. It was imported along with Christianity into the Kiev state of the East Slavs. From the outset, in addition to its initial function as an ecclesiastical idiom, this language had assumed, as was usually the case in the Middle Ages, the role of the language of theology, literature, and science—in short, the language of civilization. We are accustomed to giving this language the name of Russian Slavonic or simply Slavonic (Ungeaun, "Le russe littéraire," 44).

The second language, which was clearly opposed to Slavonic, was popular, everyday Russian. This was, first of all, the language that was spoken daily. But it was more than that. From the beginning there were two domains in which Russian alone was accepted as a written language: administrative and judicial documents and private correspondence. The spoken language was thus the one used, not only in legislation and legal proceedings, but also in every document that had anything to do with the legal or juridical aspect of things, so that the language of the laws had become a chancellery language in the broad sense of the expression.

The East Slavs, and particularly the Russians, thus made use of two different written languages: a so-called chancellery language, which was indigenous, Russian; and a literary language, Slavonic. This dualism, this distinction in principle between chancellery language and literary language, is a characteristic trait of Russian history and language (ibid.).

In modern Russian, which is a mixed language, there is a functional semantic and stylistic opposition between Slavonic and Russian elements. The Ouspensky-Hüttl-Folter theory of reference explains this mixed character of modern Russian in relation to the diglossia that characterized the linguistic situation of the Kiev state. It is on the basis of this situation of diglossia that we can try to understand the "two worlds" schema that constitutes an important theme in Russian philosophy. The two languages of different values in this case are, on the one hand, the language of everyday conversation, and on the other, a quite codified language that is learned through formal apprenticeship and serves as the vehicle for a body of written texts that are highly respected; this latter language is the written language par excellence, and it is considered to be superior by the speaker himself. It is called the "high language" (H), as opposed to the everyday, "low language" (L). According to C. Fergusson, to whom we owe this concept, the conditions of diglossia are as follows:

1. there is a large literary corpus close to the language of ordinary communication, and this corpus incorporates the community's fundamental values;
2. only a small elite of the community receives formal education and has access to this corpus;
3. a long period of time (from one to several centuries) separates the time when conditions (1) and (2) are met from that when the situation of diglossia is established.

In the Ouspensky-Hüttl-Folter theory Slavonic, the ecclesiastical language, is obviously the high language, and Russian, the everyday language and also the chancellery language, is the low language.

The interpenetration of Slavonic and Russian during this first period produced a third language, Russian Slavonic, an intermediary language from which modern Russian emerged.

Fergusson stresses that:

A striking characteristic of diglossia is the existence of a large number of lexical pairs composed of an item H and an item L, and which refer to common concepts in frequent use in both the H language and the L language; the semantic field of each term is about the same, but the use of one or the other immediately marks the oral or written utterance as H or L.

(Fergusson, "Diglossia")

According to Ouspensky-Hüttl-Folter, the diglossia of the Russian language, in its initial state, explains the semantic and stylistic oppositions between Slavonic and Russian elements in modern Russian. As an example of this, let us take the concept of "face." The word that corresponds to it in Slavonic is *litse*, and in Russian *litso* [лицо]. During the first period (from the eleventh to the fourteenth century), the forms of Slavonic and Russian differed morphologically but were semantically equivalent. Both designated the face of God as well as the human face. Then came the emergence of diglossia as such, and the Russian word became a "marked" form designating solely the human face, while the Slavonic word continued to designate both the divine and the human face, so that in order to make a discourse "high," it sufficed to replace the Russian *litso*, which means only "human face," with its Slavonic equivalent, which means both "face of God" and "human face."

It was after the "second Bulgarian influence" in Russia (end of the fourteenth century and beginning of the fifteenth) that Slavonic and Russian forms ceased to be equivalent. Slavonic was henceforth distinct from Russian because the speaker did not use Russian forms to create Slavonic ones but learned Slavonic as an independent system. However, Slavonic words, with their peculiar physiognomy, became words in the Russian language, within which they were regarded as "high." Modern Russian emerged from this Russian Slavonic, which mixed the Slavonic forms with Old Russian.

The texts show that there was a close relationship between the subject dealt with and the linguistic key in which it was described. The linguistic difference between the Slavonic word and the Russian word corresponds to the difference between true ("high") reality and empirical ("low") reality, between objective and subjective knowledge. Analogies can be found in the opposition between Greek *gnôstês*/*histôr* [γνώστης/ἵστωρ] and the opposition between German *kennen*/*wissen*. In Russian these correspond to the two ways of saying "knowledge": *znati* [знати] (Slavonic), and *vedat'* [ведать] (Russian). Thus, Russians use Slavonic terms in speaking of angels and Russian terms in speaking of humans, but Slavonic terms are also used when speaking of man as the image of God. This correlation between the theme and the verbal key provides the linguistic model of the conceptual schema of the "two worlds" in Russian philosophical thought.

In late seventeenth-century Russia Slavonic words became autonomous to a certain extent, developing new meanings under the influence of other European languages, particularly French. These new meanings tended to be abstract, metaphorical, poetic, and sublime. Thus Slavonic forms differentiated themselves from Russian ones and became "marked" in turn: Slavonic *litse* no longer meant both "human face" and "face of God" but was now restricted, by direct opposition to Russian *litso* ("human face"), to the meaning "face of God." Modern Russian thus uses Slavonic forms to express abstract and poetic concepts.

Thanks to this diglossic play, when Russian seeks to develop its vocabulary, especially its intellectual vocabulary, it can do so in two ways. If it enriches its vocabulary by Europeanizing itself, it thereby affirms its autonomy with respect to Slavonic. But if it enriches its vocabulary by drawing on Slavonic, which has itself been enriched and modernized, then it presents Slavonic as autochthonous and asserts its identity with respect to other European languages. In general, diglossia, and the particular twist it gives to relations between Russian and European languages, is one of the roots of Russian untranslatables.

II. Dialectic Revised by Diglossic Thought: The "Two Worlds" Conceptual Schema

Because of the semantic and stylistic opposition of Slavonic and Russian elements, the Russian language gives rise to the "two worlds" conceptual schema. The objective situation of diglossia generates a diglossic thought that develops independently of the Slavonic or Russian origin of the terms it uses. It is appropriate to use this schema in analyzing Russian philosophical discourse. We will call thinking based on this kind of opposition "diglossic": it transposes the linguistic model of diglossia to the conceptual level.

The Russian philosophical language was constituted in the 1830s and 1840s, at the same time as modern Russian literature. Unlike the language of literature and journalism, whose development was shaped by the French model, the Russian philosophical language was shaped by German idealism (Schelling, Hegel). Our hypothesis is that Russian philosophy was constituted at that time on the basis of German dialectic interpreted in the framework of diglossic thinking.

The diffusion of Hegelian philosophy in Russia did not begin with the *Phenomenology* or the *Logic*. The first of Hegel's works to be translated into Russian were the *Philosophy of History*, the *Aesthetics*, and the *Philosophy of Religion*, which dealt with themes more directly connected with traditional Russian problems (Koyré, "Hegel en Russie," in *Études sur l'histoire*). Essentially, Russian thought takes two things from Hegel's philosophy: first, dialectical contradiction, and second, the idea of the rationality of the real.

1. Here, for example, is how diglossic thought interprets the concept of dialectical contradiction to make it conform to the "two worlds" schema. Consider the translation of the German word *aufheben*. Two words are used, *snimat'* [снимать] and *primirjat'* [примирять] (Hegel, *Complete Works*, vol. 9). *Snimat'* is a neologism whose literal meaning is "remove," "deduct," and even "disconnect" (a currently common meaning is "take a photograph"). *Primirjat'* corresponds to the German *versöhnen*, "to reconcile." "Reconciliation" is a transition from "conflict" to "peace": the root of the word *pri-mir-jat'* is the word *mir* [мир], which means "peace." Each of the Russian terms is an aspect of the polysemy of *aufheben*: the first is a word coined ad hoc, the second a word in ordinary, practical language. Hegel himself justified in advance this double translation by using *versöhnen* as a synonym of *aufheben*, but only with regard to human action (for example, in his *Philosophy of Religion*). In Russian the expression "the reconciliation [*primijat'*] of contradictories in unity" (ibid., vol. 3) thus

coexists with this other expression "the disconnection [*snimat'*] of contradictories in unity" (ibid.). But these two expressions are in fact distributed in accord with the diglossic schema of the high world and the low world. For example: "the concreteness of the thing is the unity of all its aspects and the reconciliation of all its oppositions" (Belinsky, *Complete Works*, vol. 11): this sentence refers to the high world; in fact, the notion of peace (*mir*), which is inseparable from that of *kosmos* [κόσμος], has religious connotations. Thus we see that a word in the ordinary language is used to express the high world.

2. Diglossic thought is also at work in the value hierarchy of the terms constitutive of any contradiction, for example, the opposition "individual"/"society," which plays a central role in the work of Vissarion Belinsky (1810–1847). It was in large measure because of the latter that Hegelianism ceased to be something discussed in salons and coteries and became a major event in intellectual history (oddly enough, Belinsky knew no German). Applying what the *Philosophy of Right* says about rational reality—"*Was wirklich ist, das ist vernünftig*" (Whatever is real is rational), Hegel, *Grundlinien der Philosophie*, 14)—he presents the individual/society dialectic as a process of reconciliation with reality ("*Versöhnung mit der Wirklichkeit*," Hegel, *Vorlesungen*, vol. 2).

Personality (*ličnost'* [личность]) is particular and contingent. Its mode of existence is the mirage and nothingness. Society is the highest reality. Compared with the universal, which alone is real, the individual is nothing. Personality is the negation of society, because society as a reality constitutes the positive; its negation is an anomaly, a "disease," as opposed to the healthy state. But as a rational being man is universal and necessary. That is why we must reconcile ourselves with rational reality. A man who has not been thus reconciled becomes a mirage and an "apparent nothingness" (Belinsky, *Complete Works*, 3: 341: "Reality . . . demands that man make complete peace with it, . . . or else it will crush him"). Belinsky always gives a positive sense to words like "real," "universal," and "rational," which have for him "an almost sacred coloring" (Tchizevskij, *Gegel*). Thus he contrasts "the domain of pure reason" with "common vulgar reason," and this contrast corresponds to the Hegelian opposition between reality and existence. Belinsky explains that the more one has universality, the more alive one is, and that a person who has no universality is a "living cadaver." For Hegel, reality is higher than existence ("*die Wirklichkeit steht auch höher als die Existenz*," *Wissenschaft der Logik*, 2: 169). But for Belinsky, this "higher" belongs to the high world and necessarily has the value of "better," to the point that the inequality of the terms of the opposition blocks the dialectical process itself. The fact that *ličnost'* belongs to the low world may explain its political use in the expression "personality cult." Khruschev was able to attack Stalin as a promoter of his "personality" because *ličnost'*, far from being a positive term, as "personality" is in English and French, has to "supersume" all the negative values of the individual. The critique of the

personality cult is thus still a matter of Hegelian-Marxist orthodoxy, but it is anchored in diglossic thought.

3. However, diglossic thinking does not imply remaining in dualism. The third specifically Russian characteristic is the development of the dialectical contradiction into a "(re)conciliation of all oppositions," for example, in the work of Alexander Herzen (1812–1860).

According to Herzen, Kant's achievement was to have shown the existence of antinomies within reason. The Kantian heritage has penetrated the mind of modern man in the form of a permanent battle between consciousness and habit, logic and narrative, thought and action, philosophy and history (Herzen, *Works in Two Volumes*, vol. 1). The Hegelian dialectic sublimates "all" these oppositions by achieving the unity of things in a movement for which the organization of the Russian lexicon provides the model. However, this kind of opposition between thought and reality is only one type among others: the theoretical type. There still remains the deeper dualism between theory and practice. The latter finds its definitive resolution only in man's personal "action." Herzen's conception of action differed from the one that was common at the time of the Left Hegelians. It is not a directly political or social action; nor is it "practice." Personal action is the element of a "language," because it has a symbolic sense and refers to something other than itself. What is this language?

Herzen's model is nothing other than the "two worlds" schema. The "low" world is the one represented by science as a language of abstraction and generalization. The "high" world is that of a science that penetrates "into the brain and the blood" (ibid.) and is manifested only in free and rational "action" (Slavonic *dejanie* [деяние]); it is the world of life or of "living truth." These actions constitutive of *ličnost'*, of the "person," are the language of history. The will of the people as a historical subject is based on the personal freedom of the *ličnost'*. The person creates (Slavonic *tvorit'*) his actions as well as his morality ("The truly free man creates his morality," Herzen, *Works in Seven Volumes*, vol. 5). In the framework of history, free action, the scientific word, is the *odejstvotvorenie* [одействотворение] of science, that is, its "actualization-creation." *Odejstvotvorenie* is a neologism invented by Herzen, probably on the basis of the German *verwirklichen*, which does not exist in modern Russian (it is a neologism like *entelecheia* [ἐντελέχεια] in Aristotle).

The oppositions that exist in the "low" world "resolve-disconnect" themselves in the Hegelian sense, but the opposition between the low and the high worlds cannot be "dissolved." Rather, it is "reconciled" (*primirjat'*), because reconciliation is the disconnection of the high toward the high, and this reconciliation takes place in free and rational action or *odejstvotvorenie*.

A few explanations regarding the use of this term: "In the context of action [Slavonic *dejanie*], reason and the heart are integrated in *odejstvotvorenie*" (Herzen, *Works in Two Volumes*, vol. 1). The verb *odejstvotvorjat'* [одействотворять] is a word composed of *dejstvie* [действие] ("action") and *tvorit'* [творить] ("create"). The verb *tvorit'*, "create like God the Creator," refers to the high world. The verb *dejstvovat'* [действовать] ("act") is an erudite equivalent of the authentically Russian verb *delat'* [делать] ("to do"), which refers to the low world. In Slavonic we find the verb *dejati* [деяати] ("act"), one of the derivatives of which is *dejanie* ("action"). Thus *dejanie* signifies action that is aimed at the high world, or high action.

The Slavic verb has two aspects, the perfective (which considers action from the point of view of its result) and the imperfective (which takes the process into account). *O-dejstvovat'* ("animate by action or for action," "make actual or efficacious," "realize") is the imperfective corresponding to the perfective *dejstvovat'*. The morphological structure of this verb thus reflects the transformation of the imperfective into the perfective, and then the transformation of this perfective base into a new imperfective by adding the form *tvorjat'*, from the verb *tvorit'* ("create") (in accord with the schema *o-dejstvovat'* [pf] > *o-dejstvotvorit'* [pf] > *o-dejstvo-tvorjat'* [impf]).

The imperfective obtained in this way clears the way for the process on the basis of what is already the result of an earlier process. The lexical means for obtaining this "imperfectivization" consists in making use of a verb from the high register: "create," which is added to "to make" from the first process. The total process thus includes both the first process and its completion (in other words, it is a "creation" that includes both the "making" and the product): this verbal form is in itself an eminently Hegelian actualization.

Thus the translation of the sentence considered in relation to the "two worlds" schema is presented in the following way: in the personal action of *ličnost'*, which is the "high" action as opposed to the actions of the reason and the heart, which are "low" actions, reason and the heart are integrated into the process that separated them from the low world in order to draw them, in a creative way, toward the high world.

This example is a good illustration of the general case. The reconciliation between the two worlds is the process that brings out what has already been achieved in the low world and carries it toward the high world. As a rule human action, which is at the same time language, carries out this reconciliation, which constitutes the reality of the high world. On this foundation alone all oppositions are reconciled in the framework of a synthetic unity. The "two worlds" schema provides the basis on which Russian philosophy develops an ontology that is separated from neither anthropology nor ethics. That is how diglossic thinking transforms the Hegelian dialectic, the relation between the perfective and the imperfective being itself subjected to this "supersumption" to the benefit of the imperfective.

III. The "Good" in the Two Worlds: The Diglossic Opposition between *Dobro* and *Blago*

The approximate French equivalent of the *dobro/blago* opposition is *bonté* (the quality of what is morally good)/ *bonheur* (happiness). French dictionaries translate both words as *bien*. The Greek *eu* [εὖ] has been translated as *blago* [благо] (Slavonic) or by *dobro* (Russian), whereas *agathos* [ἀγαθός] and *kalos* [καλός] have always been translated by *dobro* (RT: *Leksikologija i slovoobrazovanije drevnerusskogo jazyka* [Lexicology and word formation of the Old Russian language], 174).

The *dobro/blago* opposition was first applied in Russian philosophy by Vladimir Solovyov (1853–1900), in his fundamental work *Opravdanie dobra* (1897). The standard French translation of this title is *La Justification du bien*. Solovyov's starting point is the heritage of the dualism of Kantian ethics, namely the opposition between the motives of human action and the moral law, between the real world and the world of duty. Human action thus has two registers, that of the actual and empirical, and that of the normative. In this double register how is the distribution between the Slavonic term, *blago*, and the Russian term, *dobro*, carried out?

In our sublunary world *dobro* qualifies the ideal norm of the will, whereas *blago* designates the object that is the source of felicity. We seek to acquire this goodness that is called *dobro*, while *blago* is a grace that we enjoy or hope for. Insofar as it concerns human action, the actual accomplishment of duty, *dobro* belongs to the low world, even though the ideal to be attained (duty) concerns the high world. Thus the dialectical process aims at the realization of *dobro* and the unity of *blago* and *dobro*. To achieve this, Solovyov says, we have to show *dobro* as *pravda* (ibid.): therein consists *opravdanie dobra* [оправдание добра], the "justification" or "realization of the good." What does that mean?

The word *pravda*, from which *opravdanie* is constructed, is common to Slavonic and Russian. Its semantic field includes the promise, the oath, the rule, the command, the contract, the law. The starting point is the idea of a "divine order," a contract between God and man. Thus *pravda* corresponds to high reality, spiritual reality (Ouspensky, *Kratkij očerk*). In Russian the term has two meanings: "justice" and "truth." For Solovyov, who appeals to Russian linguistic intuition (ibid.), justice is nothing other than true reality.

The verb *opravdyvat'* [оправдывать] ("justify") is an imperfective of the perfective *opravdat'* [оправдать] (lit., "render justice"). The term *opravdanie* is the active noun drawn from the latter verb. The formula *opravdanie dobra* ("justification of good") can be interpreted in two ways, depending on whether the noun's genitive complement is understood as objective or subjective. Objective: the *dobro* is the object of a justification, a human realization in the low, sublunary world. Subjective: the good is the subject of the justification and takes an active part in the process that develops between the two worlds, the world in which *dobro* is distinct from *blago* and, on the other hand, the world in which they merge.

According to Solovyov, the expression "show the *dobro* as *pravda*," the literal meaning of *opravdanie dobra*, does not mean "show the *dobro* as justice" but rather "show the *dobro* as true reality." In this sense the *dobro* is the active *dobro* (subjective genitive) that unifies *dobro* and *blago*. As such, it is the state of God, "beatitude" (*blaženstvo* [блаженство]), the Russian word derived from *blago*.

Opravdanie dobra, that is, the accomplishment and realization of *dobro*, takes place only insofar as the divine Spirit really appears in humanity; and this realization merges with *blaženstvo* ("beatitude"). Humanity as "person" (*ličnost'*) is realized in history as the true bearer of the real ethical order, the perfect organization of the world, the universal

Church suitable for receiving the divine Spirit. The actions of this general person thus become a kind of language because they acquire a symbolic sense. Humanity, insofar as it performs this task, becomes "divino-humanity" (*bogočelovečestvo* [бого-человечество]).

In Solovyov's work the low world is the historical world, and the high world is that of beatitude and divino-humanity. The process of *opravdanie* accomplishes the transition from the former to the latter. The vehicle of this transition, the low agent, is humanity, but its true motor is *dobro* itself. *Dobro*, which first constitutes in the normative sphere in the low world, becomes actually real in the high world, through *opravdanie*. This process transforms the low agent (humanity) into a high agent (divino-humanity) and unites *dobro* and *blago* in the form of *blaženstvo* (beatitude). Thus the expression *opravdanie dobra* must be translated as "the (true) realization of the good," understanding "realization" in two senses: (1) the passage to the state of concrete reality, and (2) correct perception (cf. English "realize"). The "accomplishment of the good," beatitude, is the good realized. This dual conception of the good shows with the greatest force the irresistible propensity of Russian thought to formulate its notions in religious terms or, more exactly, in hierarchized dualities, thus taking advantage of the diglossia that characterizes the history of the Russian language.

Charles Malamoud
Valentin Omelyantchik

BIBLIOGRAPHY

Belinsky, Vissarion Grigoryevich. *Complete Works*. 13 vols. Academy of Sciences of the USSR, 1956.

———. *Selected Philosophical Works*. Moscow: Foreign Languages Publishing House, 1948.

Fergusson, Charles. "Diglossia." *Word* 15.2 (1959): 325–40.

Hegel, Georg Wilhelm Friedrich. *Complete Works* [in Russian]. 30 vols. Edited by A. Herzen. Moscow, 1954–1965.

———. *Grundlinien der Philosophie des Rechts*. Hamburg: Meiner, 1955.

———. *Vorlesungen über die Philosophie der Religion*. Hamburg: Meiner, 1966.

———. *Wissenschaft der Logik*. Hamburg: Meiner, 1966.

Herzen, Alexander. *Works in Seven Volumes*. Edited by F. Pavlenkov. Saint Petersburg, 1905.

———. *Works in Two Volumes*. Moscow: Mysl, 1985.

Hüttl-Folter, Gerta. "Diglossia v Drevnei Russi." *Wiener Slavistisches Jahrbuch* 24 (1978): 108–23.

Koyré, Alexandre. *Études sur l'histoire de la pensée philosophique en Russie*. Paris: Vrin, 1950.

Ouspensky, Boris. *Kratkij otcherk istorii russkogo literaturnogo jazyka* [Outlines of a history of literary Russian]. Moscow: Nauka, 1994.

———. "K voprosu o sistemetičeskikh vzaimootnošenijakh sistemno protivipostavlenykh tserkovno-slovianskikh i russkikh form v istorii russkogo jazyka." *Wiener Slavistisches Jahrbuch* 22 (1976): 92–100.

Shein, Louis, ed. and trans. *Readings in Russian Philosophical Thought: Logic and Aesthetics*. The Hague: Mouton, 1973.

Tchizevskij, Dimitri Ivanovich. *Gegel v Rossii* [Hegel in Russia]. Moscow: Foreign Languages Publishing House, 1939.

Ungeaun, B. O. "Le russe littéraire est-il d'origine russe?" *Revue des études slaves* 44 (1965).

Walicki, Andrej. *A History of Russian Thought from the Enlightenment to Marxism*. Translated by Hilda Andrews Rusiecka. Stanford, CA: Stanford University Press, 1979.

SACHVERHALT, SACHLAGE, OBJEKTIV (GERMAN)

ENGLISH	state of things, state of affairs, positive fact
FRENCH	état de chose, état-de-chose, contenu propositionnel
GREEK	pragma [πρᾶγμα]
LATIN	status rerum, status quaestionis, dispositio rei, complexe significabile

➤ STATE OF AFFAIRS and DICTUM, ERLEBEN, FACT, GEGENSTAND, INTENTION, MATTER OF FACT, OBJECT, PROPOSITION, PROPOSITIONAL CONTENT, SEIN, SENSE, TATSACHE, THING [RES]

Although in German *Sache* is a generic term designating the thing (in the physical sense, or the thing in question during a debate or trial), philosophical language has extended this concept, which has since Husserl designated both physical things and values, things for use, mathematical idealities, and the correlates of complex propositional forms. The same holds for the derivative forms *Sachlage* and *Sachverhalt*, which in everyday German designate the circumstances but in the philosophical language designate how things behave (*wie die Sachen sich verhalten*), which is translated into French as *état de chose* or, more terminologically, *état-de-chose*, and into English as "state of things" or "state of affairs." This translation masks the difficulty of grasping what these terms mean because they seem to denote properties or relations peculiar to objects of experience, even though they actually refer to the object of the judgment or of the propositional formulation. Similarly, the concept of the *Objekt* introduced by Meinong designates not the correlate of an experience but that of an act of judgment. The problem thus proceeds from the fact that all these terms have to do, not with the general problematics of objectivity, but with the specific question of the intentional object of judgment.

I. The Juridical Origin of *Sachverhalt*: The *Status Rerum*

The concept *Sachverhalt* has its origin in the juridical lexicon: it is derived from the legal notion of *status*, understood in the expression *status rerum* as the state of affairs in question, as contrasted with the *status homini*, which designates a person's status (free or slave). More precisely, the expression *status rerum* is found in judicial rhetoric, where it is defined as the object of litigation (*Streitfrage*), which is moreover one of the original meanings of *Sache* in German. Thus we read in the *Lexicon totius latinitatis* ("Status," 478): "*status dicitur quaestio, quae ex prima causarum conflictione dicitur*" (the question arising from the primary conflict of legal cases is called the *status*). For example, if the conflict of cases is defined by the contradictory assertions "A killed B" and "A did not kill B," then the *status* is defined as the question of whether A killed B. This juridical origin of the term *Sachverhalt* on the basis of *status* understood as *quaestio* no doubt explains the formation of the German word: the substantive *Verhalt* is not common in German (the nominalized infinitive *das Verhalten*,

"behavior," is used instead), and *Sachverhalt* is probably an abbreviation of a question as to "how a thing behaves" (*wie die Sache sich verhält*).

In this context there is already a shift of the sense of *status* from the real things about which a judgment is made toward the object of judgment itself, since *status* is correlative to the *narratio* and the argumentation: the object of litigation can be determined only by the establishment of the facts (*Sacherzählung*), and the judgment handed down is the conclusion of a series of arguments bearing on the facts (*sachliche Argumentation*). That is the sense in which the term is used by Quintilian:

> Quod nos statum, id quidam constitutionem vocant, alii quaestionem, alii quod ex quaestione appareat.

> (That which I call the *basis* [*status*], some style the *constitution* [of the object of litigation], others the *question* [of the object of litigation], and others again *that which may be inferred from the question.*)

> (Quintilian, *Institutio oratoria*, III, 6, 2, 409)

In detaching itself from the specifically juridical field, the term *status* underwent an extension that anticipates the modern meaning of *Sachverhalt* as "state of affairs"; initially reserved for the object of litigation, with which the pleas made by the prosecution and the defense were connected, it came to designate all the properties of a thing:

> Translate ponitur frequentissime pro modo, quo quaeque res stat, condicione, qualitate fortunae, loco, ordine.

> ([The expression "status"] is very frequently used to translate how each thing stands, its condition, external circumstances, place, order.)

> (RT: *Lexicon totius latinitatis*, 478)

In the German juridical lexicon the corresponding terms constitute a series of related concepts (*Rechtverhältnis, Sachstand, -lage, -verhalt, -verhältnis, Streitstand, Tatbestand*, that is, the state of affairs, the circumstances relevant to a case, a cause, a trial), in which *Sachverhalt*, whose meaning was initially close to that of *Tatbestand* (at first equivalent to the *corpus delicti*, but then restricted to the first part of the juridical *status*, which sets forth the conditions of the law's application), is gradually detached from this purely formal meaning and comes to designate all the concrete facts that make up the *Tatbestand*: "*der konkrete Lebensfall, der juristisch beurteilt werden soll*" (the concrete life-case that has to be decided by law) (E. Beling, *Grundzüge des Strafrechts* [Foundations of criminal law], 1930). On all this, see B. Smith. "Sachverhalt," in RT: *Historisches Wörterbuch der Philosophie*.

II. The Logical Origin of *Sachverhalt*: The *Complexe Significabile*

The second origin of the concepts of *Sachverhalt* and *Objektiv* is found in the way that Aristotle and medieval thinkers analyzed the relation between the proposition and its object, and especially in Gregory of Rimini's doctrine of the *complexe significabile*. The general issue at stake has to do with the determination of the object of the proposition: is it in the things themselves and their properties, or in the meanings that designate states of affairs? From this point of view, we can distinguish two stages: the first identifies the object of judgment no longer with the thing denoted but with the *complex* relationship between the thing and its properties; the second makes this complex no longer a real state residing in things but a complex *signification*.

a. In Aristotle's *Categories*, *pragma* [πρᾶγμα] designates not simply the thing, but the state of affairs described by a judgment that confirms the latter and gives it the status of truth (*Categories* 4b5–10, 12b5–15, and 14b19–23). This distinction is extended in some medieval theories of truth, which make the object of a proposition not the things themselves that are the denotation of nouns, but the *dispositio rerum*, that is, the relationship of things (substances, properties, accidents) to each other, in short, a state of affairs, a way of being, a "mode of behavior": the object of the judgment "A is B" is not "A" but the "being B of A." Thus we read in Thomas Aquinas that "*dispositio rei est causa veritatis in opinione et oratione*" (the state of affairs is the cause of truth in opinion and discourse) (*In duodecim libros*, IX, 11), and in Abelard's *Dialectica* we read that:

> non itaque propositiones res aliquas designant simpliciter, quemadmodum nomina, immo qualiter sese ad invicem habent, utrum scilicet sibi conveniant annon, proponunt. . . . Unde quasi quidam rerum modus habendi se per propositiones exprimitur, non res aliquae designantur.

> (Propositions do not designate simply random things, as names do, but set forth the way in which they behave with respect to each other, whether they are in accord with each other or not. . . . And thus what is expressed by propositions is, so to speak, the mode of things' behavior, the things themselves are not designated.)

> (*Dial.* 160.23–36)

b. Gregory of Rimini's doctrine, set forth in his *Commentary on the Sentences*, gives the complex the status of a *signified complex* and no longer that of a real complex: knowledge bears not on the proposition stated, or simply on the real object to which it refers, but on the adequate signified of the proposition (*significatum*); it is not only the proposition (*veritas in dicto*) or the thing with its mode of being (*veritas in re*) that is true, but also the signified of the proposition (*veritas in essendo*): neither the statement "A is B" (man is white) nor the thing denoted "A" in its "being–B" (man, whiteness), but the stateable complex or what is signified by complex "A to be B" (man to be white). Thus the object of a

demonstration is neither the conclusion stated, nor the external thing it concerns, but the total and adequate signified of the conclusion.

In this way, the relation between a thing and a property, which is translated in German by *Sachverhalt*, acquired the status of "complex objective meaning": it is not simply a subjective act of the mind connecting the thing with its predicates but actually an object, and an object of another type than a simple denotation (the existent, the external thing) or a complex denotation (the real state of affairs). The essential consequence of this is the extension of the concepts of thing, being, or "something" (*res, ens, aliquid*), that is, the extension of the concept of "object in general" beyond that of "external thing," because the signified complex is indeed an "object" of a certain kind but one that is irreducible to an external thing, namely an ideal object distinct from any real object. "Man to be animal" is not something like the animal itself, but it is not nothing; it is not a being, but it is nonetheless an object.

III. A Series of Equivalents: *Satz an sich* (Bolzano), *Sachverhalt* (Stumpf-Husserl), *Objektiv* (Meinong)

The term *Objektiv* was introduced by Alexius Meinong in his book *Über Annahmen* to designate the correlate of a judgment. In section 14 he examines the genealogy of this concept as it had been traced by A. Marty and recognizes as antecedents of the *Objektiv* Bolzano's "proposition in itself," Carl Stumpf's "state-of-affairs," and Brentano and Marty's "content of judgment" (*Urteilsinhalt*). This genealogy allows us to clarify the double basis of *Objektiv* in the intentional analysis of significations as ideal objects and in the intentional analysis of judgment and its correlate, and to situate it in the tradition of the medieval *complexe significabile*.

A. *Objektiv* and *Satz an sich*: Meinong and Bolzano

In Bolzano's work the concept of a "proposition in itself" or "objective proposition" combines the properties of objectivity, complexity, and completeness: on the one hand, like all subjective thought, it is distinct from any real statement, and unlike external things, it has no real existence, no spatiotemporal individuation but only an ideal, omnitemporal objectivity; on the other hand, unlike "concepts in themselves" (*Vorstellungen an sich*), which are both its simple parts and elementary signifieds, it has the property of bivalency, that is, of truth and falsehood; it is an ideal signified, bivalent and complex, the objective correlate of the stated proposition or of the subjective thought. "A square is round" designates an objective proposition, even though no real or noncontradictory object corresponds to it (cf. *Wissenschaftslehre* [*Theory of Science*, 1837], §19, and introduction to the *Grössenlehre* [*Theory of Magnitudes*, 1833], II, §2). The concept of *Satz an sich* thus defines one of the dimensions of the *Objektiv*, that of the ideality of signification.

B. *Sachverhalt* and *Objektiv*: Stumpf, Brentano, Meinong

The other dimension, that of the correlation between judgment and its "object," hails from Stumpf and Brentano. In the 1906 treatise *Erscheinungen und psychische Funktionen* [*Phenomena and psychic functions*], Stumpf, having defined "functions" as lived experiences other than the contents of sensation (acts of attention, unitary understanding, judgment, and also desire, will, etc.), seeks to define the correlates produced by these acts. Thus the act of unitary understanding has as its correlate a quality-of-form, the act of synthetic understanding as a whole, and the act of judgment a content-of-judgment to which Stumpf gives the name *Sachverhalt*. Brentano recognized, he tells us, that

> dem Urteil ein spezifischer Urteilsinhalt entspreche, der vom Vorstellungsinhalte (der Materie) zu scheiden sei und sprachlich in "Daß-Sätzen" oder in substantivierten Infinitiven ausgedrückt wird. . . . Ich brauche für diesen spezifischen Urteilsinhalt den Ausdruck *Sachverhalt*.

> (to the judgment corresponds a specific content-of-judgment that must be distinguished from the content-of-representation (matter) and that is expressed in language by subordinate clauses with "which" or by nominalized infinitives. . . . To designate this specific content of judgment, I use the expression "state-of-affairs.")

> (Stumpf, *Erscheinungen*, 29–30)

Meinong denied the equivalence between Stumpf's *Sachverhalt* and Bolzano's *Satz an sich*, on the one hand, and his concept of *Objektiv*, on the other: such an assimilation would in fact reduce the *Objektiv* to "psychic constructs" (*psychische Gebilde*, in *Über Annahmen*, §14) and would thus situate itself on the side of the subjective or psychological; if the state-of-affairs is a construct produced by the creative synthesis (*einer "schöpferischen" Synthese*) of psychic functions, it is nonetheless not a content included in consciousness and is not identified with these subjective functions; on the contrary, it is a new object requiring a grasping that involves going outside consciousness (*ein Hinausgreifen*). This new object is strictly correlative to the function of judgment and does not exist in itself, independently of the latter; in Husserlian terms, it is the intentional correlate of the act of judgment:

> Aber der Sachverhalt kann nicht für sich allein, unabhängig von irgendeiner Funktion unmittelbar gegeben und damit auch real sein . . . die Gebilde aber sind Tatsachen überhaupt nur als Inhalte von Funktionen.

> (But states-of-affairs cannot be immediately given in isolation, independent of any function, and be thereby real . . . constructs are facts insofar as they are contents of functions.)

> (Ibid., 32)

C. *Objektiv* and *Gegenstand*: Meinong

It is in Meinong's treatise *Über Annahmen* that the state-of-affairs designated by the term *Objektiv* finds its most systematic theoretical formulation and its most rigorous use in the framework of a generalized theory of objects (*Gegenstandstheorie*) that includes significations as ideal objects:

> In unserem Beispiele finden wir neben einem Gegenstande, über den geurteilt oder der beurteilt wird, noch einen anderen, der "geurteilt wird." . . . Objekt fällt also hier mit dem zusammen, was beurteilt, Objektiv mit

dem, was geurteilt wird. Insofern hat das Urteil also nicht einen Gegenstand, sondern deren zwei, von denen sonach jeder Anspruch hätte, "Urteilsgegenstand" zu heißen.

> (In our examples we find, alongside the object of a judgment or assessment, another object, which is "judged." . . . Thus here *Objekt* merges with that which is assessed and *Objektiv* with that which is judged. To this extent, the judgment has not a single objective correlate but two, both of which could lay claim to be called object-of-judgment.)

> (Meinong, *Über Annahmen*, §8, 14)

Here, *Gegenstand* is the genus designating the correlate of an act or a lived experience of which *Vorstellungsgegenstand* and *Urteilsgegenstand* are the species, the correlates of representation and judgment respectively. Meinong's goal is to show the specificity of the latter with respect to the former, and he does so by calling the former *Objekt* (denotation, reference, or real object represented) and the latter *Objektiv* (the meaning or complex signification that is the aim of judgment). Thus in the statement "there is snow outside," the object is "snow" and the "objective" is "that there is snow."

Let us clarify the terminological question. If Meinong rejects the concept "content of judgment" (*Urteilsinhalt*) employed by Stumpf, Brentano, and Marty, that is because metaphorically the term *Inhalt* makes the *Objektiv* something contained within the subjective lived experience of judgment, whereas it is an object grasped by the judgment:

> Ganz unnatürlich scheine mir aber, dabei so weit zu gehen, daß man [das Objektiv] in einem Erlebnis deshalb wollte "enthalten" sein lassen, weil es durch dieses erfaßt wird. Das Erfaßte ist vielmehr der Gegenstand des erfassenden Erlebnisses. . . . Objektive können nicht Urteilsinhalte heißen, weil sie nicht Inhalte heißen können.

> (It seems to me very artificial to go so far as to try to see [*das Objektiv*] as "contained" within an experience because it is grasped by means of the latter. What is grasped is rather the object of the grasping experience. . . . The Objectives cannot be called contents-of-judgment because they cannot be called contents.)

> (Ibid., §14)

The Objective is thus indeed an object, but far from being an object of an existing (*wirklich, daseiend*) representation, it is an ideal object, of a superior order, characterized not by existence but by pseudo-existence, a-temporality, or non-temporal persistence (*Persistenz*). Meinong expressed it by the term *Bestand*, which operates in a double register: on the one hand, it means "state of affairs," like *Sachverhalt*; on the other hand, it comes from the verb *bestehen* (to subsist) and designates what subsists outside of time, as opposed to *Gegenstand*, that is, the object that subsists in time. Although each of the two possible translations of *Bestand* ("state of affairs" and "subsistent") leaves out one of these two characteristics, the latter translation is preferable, not only because the context insists on the a-temporality common to the Objective and to all ideal objects (*ideale Gegenstände*), but also in order to avoid the redundancy with *Sachverhalt*.

> Bestände unterscheiden sich von Existenzen . . . darin, daß sie an keine Zeitbestimmung gebunden, in diesem Sinne ewig oder zeitlos sind. Das gilt natürlich auch vom Objektiv.
>
> (Subsistents differ from existents in that they are not bound by any temporal determination, and in this sense they are eternal or a-temporal. That also holds, of course, for the Objective).
>
> (Ibid., §11)

Thus "3 > 2" is a subsistent, an omnitemporal object, and paradoxically judgments bearing on temporal existence ("this table exists now") concern a-temporal Objectives, because time belongs solely to judgment and not to its correlate.

Finally, the properties that classical logic attributed to statements belong to Objectives: the two formal paradigms of Objectives are being ("A is") and being such (*Sosein*, "A is B"). Objectives are positive or negative (ibid., §12), and they admit of modalities (ibid., §13). But the nominal identity of these properties must not mask the difference between those of the Objective and those of the subjective judgment: the truth of judgment (*Wahrheit*) is a grasping of the actuality of the Objective (*Tatsächlichkeit*), its possibility, that of the verisimilitude of the Objective (*Wahrscheinlichkeit*).

D. From *Sachverhalt* to *Wertverhalt*, *Wertsachverhalt*, etc.: Husserl

The concept of *Sachverhalt* was also adopted by Husserl and Adolf Reinach, further extending Meinong's problematics. In Husserl's work it is part of a universal theory of the objective correlates of judgment (formal ontology) *qua* species of categorial objects distinct both from acts of judgment and things experienced (*Dinge*):

> Das Objektive des urteilenden Vermeinens nennen wir den beurteilten Sachverhalt; wir unterscheiden ihn in der reflektierten Erkenntnis vom Urteilen selbst, als dem Akte, in dem uns dies oder jenes so oder anders zu sein erscheint.
>
> (What plays the part of object to judgment and opinion we call the *state of affairs judged*: we distinguish this in reflex knowledge from the *judging* itself, the *act* in which this or that appears thus or thus.)
>
> (Husserl, *Logische Untersuchungen,* V, § 28, Hua XIX/1)

From this point of view, the category of state-of-affairs undergoes an extension of meaning, for it can be the correlate of other kinds of acts (of nominalization as "the being-P of S," of wishing, of questioning, etc.) and designates all objects other than those of simple representation, hence the universal object of formal ontology as a doctrine of the modes of the "something."

It is on this basis that we can pose and resolve the problems of translation: namely, both the complex character of the *Sachverhalt* (insofar as it is the correlate of a complex intention, implying a judgment or a predicative structure that may be ramified) and its quasi-universal extension to all the objective correlates of judgments (insofar as it is a correlate of diverse types of acts, judgments that are axiological, aesthetic, eidetic, etc.). Thus the term *Sachverhalt* has been translated into English, with reference to the Latin locutions *status rerum sive quaestionis* and *dispositio rei* as "state of things" and "state of affairs," and the latter has become standard since its first use in the English translation of Husserl's *Logische Untersuchungen* in 1905—reappearing later in the translations of Wittgenstein (*Tractatus logico-philosophicus*, 1922) and in Russell's works on objectives, facts, and propositions (*The Philosophy of Logical Atomism*, 1918; *Analysis of Mind*, 1921), and then in G. Bergmann (*Logic and Reality*, 1964) and in R. M. Chisholm's work on the ontology of state-of-affairs (*Person and Object*, 1976). However, the expression "state of affairs" is equivocal in that it can designate both a simple positive state of fact and the complex correlate of a judgment, whereas the meaning of *Sachverhalt* refers exclusively to the latter. Thus Boyce Gibson adopted, in his much later translation of Husserl's *Ideen* (1931), the translation "positive fact," which, referring to the first sense, is unacceptable because by depriving *Sachverhalt* of its character of complex predicative formation (which makes it a "predicatively formed affair-complex"), it falls back on *Sachgehalt* (which designates everything that has a concrete content) or *Zustand* (that is, the momentary state of a thing or of an ego in general) and makes impossible its extension to all sorts of possible judgments.

Husserl's vocabulary includes several terms that testify both to the predicative origin and to the possibility of extending *Sachverhalt* to the various kinds of judgment: thus (cf. *Ideen*, I, §95; Hua III/1, 220–21) an axiological judgment has as its object a *Wertsachverhalt* or *Wertverhalt*, that is, not the simple state-of-affairs present in the act of evaluation as having a value (*der werte Sachverhalt*, e.g., the betrayal of Jesus by Judas considered as evil), but the value of the state-of-affairs (the evil character of this betrayal) *qua* specific correlate of an axiological judgment based on the awareness of a state-of-affairs (the betrayal of Jesus by Judas); thus again (*Ideen* I, §6, Hua III/1, 19) the act of judgment concerning a correlation between essences (and not between facts) has as its proper correlate the eidetic state-of-affairs (*eidetische Sachverhalt*) designating either the ideal relation between essences as a subsistent object (*das Bestehende*) of judgment or the truth of this relation, which suffices to show that the meaning of the *Sachverhalt* is not limited to the positive fact; finally, since the activity of predication can be complex (because it can qualify objects that are themselves already nominalized states-of-affairs, e.g., "the betrayal of Jesus by Judas is an evil action"), its proper object is a *Sachverhalt* of a higher level because it results from a stratification of acts of grasping, predication, and nominalization, and this *Sachverhalt* then bears the name of *Sachlage*, which, translated into French by *situation* (which has the same drawback as "positive fact" in the case of *Sachverhalt*, namely that it eludes the predicative origin of the object in question), corresponds to the affair-complex, that is, to the complex state-of-affairs.

E. *Sachverhalt* and *Tatbestand*: Adolf Reinach

Reinach refines the characterization of *Sachverhalt*, which he clearly contrasts with the relation between objects that provides its factual material (*der sachliche Tatbestand, der Dingtatbestand*, in which *Bestand* has an opposite meaning to that of the one it had in Meinong, where it designates an objective substrate that is singular and concrete and not an ideal subsistent), as well as the ideal meaning intended by judgment. Reinach specifies the set of characteristics that distinguish it from things or worldly objects: the state-of-affairs is "apprehended" by a grasp of reality rather than being intuited in a perceptive manner, as are singular things. It is situated in a "logical and ideal" relation of antecedent to consequent rather than in a real and preddiscursive relation of cause and effect, like worldly realities. It admits modalities such as the possible, the necessary, the contingent, and so on and finally, it can be positive or negative, whereas concrete things are simple existent and do not admit of negativity ("Zur Theorie," §9).

This reaffirmation of the status of the *Sachverhalt* as ideality encourages us to be very prudent with regard to the French equivalent "*état-de-chose*" or "*état de chose*," which, while it stresses the relational character of *Sachverhalt*, nonetheless affirms neither its predicative origin (because an *état de chose*, e.g., the color of a rose, can be perceived, whereas the *état-de-chose* "the being-colored of the rose" is exclusively a correlate of judgment) nor its nonworldly status (since both a thing and a state can be worldly realities, whereas the *état-de-chose* is an ideality). Even so, we are not likely to find a more truly adequate translation.

Dominique Pradelle

BIBLIOGRAPHY

Abelard, Peter. *Dialectica*. 2nd rev. ed. Assen, Neth.: Van Gorcum, 1970.
Aristotle. *Categories and On Interpretation*. Translated by J. L. Ackrill. Oxford: Clarendon Press, 1963.
Bolzano, Bernard. "On the Mathematical Method." In *On the Mathematical Method and Correspondence with Exner*. Edited by Paul Rusnock and Rolf George. Amsterdam, NY: Rodopi, 2004.
———. *Theory of Science*. Edited by Rolf George. Oxford: Oxford University Press, 1972.
Cairns, Dorion. *Guide for Translating Husserl*. The Hague: Nijhoff, 1973.
Élie, Hubert. *Le complexe significabile. La proposition et son object; Grégoire de Rimini, Meinong, Russell*. 2nd ed. Paris: Vrin, 2000.
Husserl, Edmund. *Formal and Transcendental Logic*. Translated by Dorion Cairns. The Hague: Nijhoff, 1969.
———. *Husserliana. In Gesammelte Werke*. Edited by H. L. van Breda. The Hague: Nijhoff, 1950–.
———. *Ideas Pertaining to a Pure Phenomenology and to a Phenomenological Philosophy*. 3 vols. Translated by F. Kersten, R. Rojcewicz, and A. Schuwer. The Hague: Nijhoff, 1980–.
———. *Logical Investigations*. Translated by J. N. Findlay. London: Routledge and Kegan Paul, 1970.
Meinong, Alexius. *Gegenstandstheorie*. In *Gesamtausgabe*. Vol. 2. "The Theory of Objects." In *Realism and the Background of Phenomenology*, edited by Roderick M. Chisholm, 76–117. Glencoe, IL: Free Press, 1960.
———. *Über Annahmen*. In *Gesamtausgabe*. Vol. 4. Graz, Aus.: Akademie Druck und Verlagsanstalt, 1968–78. First published in 1909. Translation by James Heanue: *On Assumptions*. Berkeley: University of California Press, 1983.0
Quintilian. *The Institutio Oratoria of Quintilian*. 4 vols. Translated by H. E. Butler. Loeb Classical Library Series. Cambridge, MA: Harvard University Press, 1953–59.
Reinach, Adolf. "Zur Theorie des negativen Urteils." In *Münchener Philosophische Abhandlungen*, edited by A. Pfänder. Leipzig: J. A. Barth, 1911. Translation by Barry

Smith: "On the Theory of Negative Judgment." In *Parts and Moments: Studies in Logic and Formal Ontology*, edited by Barry Smith, 315–78. Munich: Philosophia Verlag, 1982.
Smith, Barry. "Introduction to Adolf Reinach's 'On the Theory of the Negative Judgment.'" In *Parts and Moments: Studies in Logic and Formal Ontology*, edited by Barry Smith, 289–314. Munich: Philosophia Verlag, 1982.
Stumpf, Carl. "Erscheinungen und psychische Funktionen." In *Abhandlungen der königlich preussischen Akademie der Wissenschaften*. 4: 1–40. Berlin: G. Reimer, 1906.
Thomas Aquinas. *In duodecim libros Metaphysicorum Aristotelis expositio*. In *Opera Omnia*. Vol. 8. Turin: Marietti, 1964. Translation by John P. Rowan: *Commentary on Aristotle's Metaphysics*. Rev. ed. Notre Dame, IN: Dumb Ox Books, 1995.

SAMOST' [самость] (RUSSIAN)

ENGLISH	self, selfhood, ipseity
FRENCH	*soi, ipséité*
GERMAN	*Selbst, Selbstheit*
GREEK	*ousia* [οὐσία]

➤ *SELF* [SELBST], and ACTOR, BOGOČELOVEČESTVO, CONSCIOUSNESS, DRUGOJ, ES, ESSENCE, I/ME/MYSELF, ISTINA, LËV, *PERSON*, POSTUPOK, RUSSIAN, SOUL, STAND, SUBJECT, SVOBODA, UNCONSCIOUS

The Russian word *samost'* [самость], a nominalization of the reflexive pronoun *sam* [сам], "myself" ("yourself," "himself," etc.) is the literal equivalent of English "ipseity." In the fifteenth century, *samost'* was nonetheless used in the sense of "essence" (*ousia* [οὐσία]). In modern Russian *samost'* can mean "the base, the center of the individual" and serve as a translation of French *soi*, English "self," or German *Selbst*. However, there is a diglossic tension between an ascetic meaning of *samost'* as an obstacle to the deification of the human being and a meaning derived from Jungian psychoanalysis as "the true self," the goal of personal development. The current tendency to neutralize the opposition between the two meanings reflects a unified, "onto-practical" vision of personal selfhood.

I. *Samost'* as *Ousia* and as "Monad"

The first known occurrence of the word as a philosophical term goes back to the anonymous fifteenth-century treatise on logic known as *Logika iudejstvujuščix* [The logic of those who practice Judaism]. The manuscript is a translation from the Hebrew and is thought to be an exposition of the logical ideas of al-Fārābī (Neverov, *Logika iudejstvujuščix*, 6), but the Hebrew original has not been found. The exposition follows more or less the content of Aristotle's *De interpretatione*. The Aristotelian distinction between essence (*ousia* [οὐσία]) and accident (*sumbebêkos* [συμβεβηκός]) is rendered in Slavonic by a distinction between *samost'* and *priključenie* [приключение], which means "occurrence, accident": "When one says 'man is living and white,' there is a difference between the relation [*prikosanie* (прикосание)] of living to man and the relation of whiteness to man: whiteness [is related to man] by accident [*po priključeniju* (по приключению)], and living by essence [*po samosti* (по самости)]."

In modern Russian the term that renders *ousia* is *suščnost'* [сущность] (Ukrainian *sutnist'* [сутність]), the nominalization of *suščee* [сущее], "that which is" (Greek *to ontôs on* [τὸ ὄντως ὄν]) (see also ISTINA). Although today *samost'* is no longer used in the latter sense, the term nonetheless retains the ontological connotations of *ousia*. Thus, to introduce the term *samost'* in his work *Nepostižimoe* [The inconceivable] (1939), Simeon Frank (1877–1950) leaves the field of subjectivity: "By *samost'*, we do not mean here the subject [*subjekt*] or the "self" [*ja*] . . . and still less the person [*ličnost'*]" (Под "самостью" мы разумеем здесь не "субъект" или "я" . . . и тем более не "личность"). (*Nepostižimoe*, 332). For Frank *samost'* is first of all "singular being" or "separate being": "The self [*samost'*] is *certain* uni-totality [*vseedinstvo*], one uni-totality among others [*odno iz vseedinstv*], but it is not uni-totality in general—uni-totality as such [*kak takovoe*]—and it is found precisely outside the latter "("Самостъ" есть некое всеединство, одно из всеединств, которое, однако, не есть всеединство вообще—всеединство как таковое—и имеет себя именно вне последнего) (ibid., 333–34). This reference to *vseedinstvo* [всеединство], "uni-totality," gives *samost'* the character of a monad: each singular being is separate and eo ipso reflects the totality of the Absolute (Frank speaks of "the monadic form of being," ibid., 334–35). Moreover, Frank does not relate *samost'* to German *Selbst*, but rather to *das Eigene*, "the proper, what is one's own" (ibid., 333, 338; see PROPERTY). We note that the Slavic term *sobstvo* [собство], "the person," a old synonym of *samost'* that designates both individuality and membership (see SVOBODA), is in fact the abstract nominalization of the adjective *sobtsvennyj* [собственный], "proper, own" (German *eigen*). On the other hand, starting in the eleventh century *sobstvo* was used as an equivalent of the Greek *hupostasis* [ὑπόστασις], which means both "essence" and "person" (*Kneževič*; see ESSENCE). All this still further reinforces the ontological connotations of *samost'*.

II. *Samost'* as Ipseity

Samost' is an exact translation of English "selfhood," French *ipséité*, and German *Selbstheit*. Thus Paul Ricoeur's preface to his book *Soi-même comme un autre*, entitled "La question de l'ipséité," is rendered in the Ukrainian translation as "Pytannia pro samist'" (Ukrainian translation, 7; cf. *Soi-même comme un autre*, 11). *Samist'* is also used in the Ukrainian translation of Emmanuel Levinas's *Entre nous*: "Tout savoir de l'ici est déjà savoir pour moi qui suis ici. Le savoir se fonde sur l'ipséité" becomes "Bud'-jake znannia 'tut' je vzhe znanniam dlia mene, perebuvajučogo tut. Znannia gruntujet'sia na samosti" [Будь-яке знання "тут" є вже знанням для мене, перебуваючого тут. Знання грунту Ється на самості] (Ukrainian translation, 31–32). Similarly, *samist'* translates "selfhood" in John Crosby: *The Selfhood of the Human Person* becomes in Ukrainian *Samist' liuds' koji osoby* (Ukrainian translation, 29 f.).

III. *Samost'* as "Self"

However, starting in the nineteenth century, the term *samost'* reappeared to render *Selbst* in Russian translations of classical German philosophy. This meaning has been preserved down to the present. Thus in Hegel's *Naturphilosophie* (to take an example that does not concern human subjectivity) we find the expression *das Selbst des Organismus*, "the organism's self" (Hegel, *Vorlesungen über die Naturphilosophie* [1842], 597), which is translated into Russian as *samost' organizma* [самость организма] (Russian translation, 499).

The same translation of *Selbst* appears with the more abstract meaning: "*Das Selbst ist in seinem Dasein, in seiner Gestalt in sich reflektiert*" (*Vorlesungen*, 597) and becomes "*Samost' v svoëm naličnom bytii, v svoëm obraze reflektirovana v samoe sebja*" [Самость в своём наличном бытии, в своём образе рефлектирована в самое себя] (Russian translation, 441). Similarly, we find *samost'* in the translations of Feuerbach (e.g., *Istorija filosofii* (History of philosophy), 1: 293, 318–20; 2: 31, 60, 68) and often in Heidegger (*Filosofskij*, 403–4; *Vremia i bytie* (Being and time), 442). As concerns the derivative terms in Heidegger, *Ich-selbst* is rendered by *ličnaja samost'* [личная самость], "the *samost'* of the person," and *Man-selbst* by *bezličnaja samost'* [безличная самость], where the prefix *bez-* designates the negation of the "I." However, *Selbstsein* is rendered by *bytie Ja* [бытие Я] or by *samobytie* [самобытие], but never by *bytie samosti* (*Filosofskij*, 403–4). On the other hand, outside the context of German philosophy, the French *Soi* and English "self" are usually translated into modern Russian by *Ja* [я] (the pronoun "I" as a philosophical term, often capitalized, in italics or between quotation marks). Because of the abstract character of *samost'*, Russian (like Ukrainian) avoids as much as possible its use to render "self" (*Selbst, Soi*). In the recent Russian edition of MacIntyre's *After Virtue*, we find *Ja* used as the equivalent of "self" (*èmotivistskoe Ja* [эмотивисцкое Я]: "the emotivist self"; *geroičeskoe Ja* [героическое Я], "the heroic self," and so on. (MacIntyre, *Posle dobrodeteli*, e.g., p. 48, 173). *Samist'* is missing in the list of equivalents of "self" offered by the *English-Ukrainian Philosophical Vocabulary* (RT: *Anglo-Ukrajins'kyj filosofs'kyj slovnyk*, 219). On the other hand, the list contains *Ja* (I); *ja sam* [я сам] (I myself); *sutnist'* (essence); *osoba* [особа] (the person), a term with the same root as *svoboda* [свобода] (see SVOBODA); *istota* [істота] (living being), from the same root as *istina* [истина] (see ISTINA). The *Soi* in Ricoeur's *Soi-même comme un autre* is rendered in Ukrainian by the reflexive pronoun *sam* [сам], "myself" (yourself, himself); since *soi* and *soi-même* are both rendered by *sam*, translators are sometimes forced to explain between parentheses which French term is involved: (e.g., Ricoeur, Ukrainian translation, *Soi-même*, 10–11). Let us note in passing that the Ukrainian and Russian grammars, which have too many indirect cases, are not well adapted to expressing the distinction between French *je* and *moi*, so that the translation of Ricoeur sometimes requires giving the French terms: "*ja* (*moi*)" or "*ja* (*je*)," or again "*ja* (*moi-même*)" (e.g., ibid., Ukrainian translation, 10, 17; see I/ME/MYSELF).

IV. The Translation of Jung: *Samost'* as Center of the Person

However—and this constitutes a genuine translation difficulty—in certain contexts "self" (*Selbst, Soi*) can be rendered only by *samost'* (or *samist'* in Ukrainian). Thus "self" used in the context of Carl Jung's analytical psychology is always translated by *samost'*. In two encyclopedias of psychology recently translated from English, *samost'* is the only term used to render Jung's *Selbst* (Frager and Fadiman, *Ličnost'*, 97–98; Hall and Lindzey, *Teorii ličnosti*, 88–89), whereas in other authors—particularly William James, Alfred Adler, Ludwig Binswanger, George Kelly, Carl Rogers, and Abraham Maslow—"self" is translated by *Ja* (Frager and Fadiman, *Ličnost'*; Hall and Lindzey, *Teorii ličnosti*). Although "self-actualization" is rendered in Russian by *samoaktualizatsija* [самоактуализация] (Frager and Fadiman, *Ličnost'*, 447–48, 491–95), the equivalent of the "ideal self" is *ja-ideal'noe* [я-идеальное] or else *ideal'noe ja* [идеальное я] (ibid., 446–47; Ross and Nisbett, *Čelovek i situatsija*, 274). But in Jung, as in Adler, Binswanger, Rogers, and Maslow, "self" refers to the wholeness of the person and signifies "the base, the center of the individual." Why, then, is there this disparity in the translations? The reason may be linked to the ontological connotations of the self as a term in Jungian psychology: like Plato's *ousia*, Jung's "self" often signifies "the essence" of the human being, whereas to other modern psychologists and psychoanalysts, it signifies more the image, the idea, the idealization, than an ontological concept. On the other hand, if we understand therapy and analysis as participation in the creation of an authentic self at the deepest level (that of both the therapist and the patient)—that is, as "ontological practice" or "ontopractice," Russian *ontopraktika* [онтопрактика], a neologism introduced by Igor Vinov in the collection *Practical Psychology* (RT: *Praktyčna psyxologijav konteksti kul'tur*, 77ff.)—a whole psychological theory will become an ontology of the person. Whence perhaps this new tendency to use *samost'* systematically in the sense of "the heart of the person and the center of his individual nature," beyond the limits of the exclusively Jungian context (RT: *Psixologija ličnosti*, 42, 67, 81, 82, 88, 150, 163), particularly in Maslow's and Rogers's theories of self-actualization (ibid., 108, 160, 206).

V. Ascetic Discourse:
Samost' as "Low" Self / *Serdtse* as "High" Self

However, in contemporary Russian thought there is a discourse that denies the importance of the realization of the self and uses *samost'* to signify the "low" self. Orthodox asceticism, both Byzantine and Russian, affirms the necessity of an "elimination of the self" (Rus. *preodolenie samogo sebja* [преодоление самого себя], Gr. *kinêsis huper phusis* [κίνησις ὑπὲρ φύσις]) as the condition of the transfiguration of the person in the act of the "deification" (Rus. *obožhenie* [обожение], Gr. *theôsis* [θέωσις]) of man (Florovsky, *Izbrannye bogoslovskie stat'i* [Collected theological articles], 60 ; see BOGOČELOVEČESTVO). In ascetic discourse *samost'* refers to the self that is to be eliminated. Thus Sergei Averintsev, a contemporary representative of ascetic discourse, disapproves of *samoljubie* [самолюбие], "self-esteem": "The ill will [*zlaja volja*] of the 'self' [*samosti*] seeks to subjugate the Other, to engulf his person [*ličnost'*]. . . . That is bizarre and dreadful" (Злая воля "самости" стремится поработить ближнего, поглотить его личность. . . . Это странно и страшно) (*My prizvany v obščenie* [We are called upon to communicate], 406–7.). Similarly, in Sergei Zarin's monumental work *Asceticism according to Christian Doctrine* (1907), we do not find the usual terms of analytic psychotherapy—*samorealizatsija* [самореализация] (self-realization) or *samoosuščestvlenie* [самоосуществление] (self-actualization); on the other hand, we find *samootverženie* [самоотвержение] (repudiation of the self), *samootrečenie* [самоотречение] (self-renunciation), *samoprotivlenie* [самопротивление] (resistance to the self),

samoprinuždenie [самопринуждение] (self-restraint), and so on (691).

To designate the center of human spiritual life, ascetic discourse uses the term *serdtse* [сердце] (neuter gender), "the heart," the equivalent of the Hebrew *lëv* [לֵב] (see LĒV) and the Greek *kardia* [καρδία]. In addition, the influence of neo-Platonism and especially the practice of hesychast asceticism gave the term mystical and spiritual connotations. The Greek term *hêsuchia* [ἡσυχία], which initially meant "tranquility," acquires in Byzantine Orthodox literature the meaning of "ascetic contemplation, in retreat and renunciation" (Averintsev, *Poetika rannevizantiĭskoĭ literatury* [The poetics of the first Byzantine literature], 258).

The essence of hesychasm as a spiritual practice is the transformation of the soul toward a state that is "open and ready for grace" (Khoruzhy, *K fenomenologii askezy* [On the phenomenology of asceticism], 105). Hesychast asceticism sees the heart, *kardia*, as "the existential and energetic center of the human being, the seat in which all the energies of man come together: strengths, aspirations, feelings, intentions" (ibid.). But to obtain the integrity of the *kardia* (the "high" self), one must first renounce oneself (the *samost'*, the "low" self).

This Orthodox ascetic discourse was adopted in the modern age by the "philosophy of the heart" (Russian *filosofija serdtsa* [философия сердца]. From the etymological point of view, the Russian word *serdtse* (Czech *srdce*, Polish *serce*, Ukrainian *sertse* [серце]) has the connotations of its Biblical Greek equivalent, *kardia*: the root *serd/sred* refers to the position within or at the center of a space. The list of terms with the same root includes the Russian *seredina* [середина] (middle, interior), *sreda* [среда] ("Wednesday," day in the middle of the week), *sredotočie* [средоточие] (center, crucial point), the adjective *srednij* [средний] (middle), and the adverb *posredi* [посреди] (among, at the center of) (Florensky, *Pillar and Ground*, 269).

Gregory Skovoroda (1741–1796), the founder of the "philosophy of the heart," found his *hêsuchia* in the life of the "itinerant philosopher" (Ukrainian *mandrovanyj filosof* [мандрованиŭ філософ]). Pamfil Jurkevytch (1826–1874) and Pavel Florensky (1882–1937) rearticulated in modern Russian the theological conceptions of the Church Fathers regarding the central role of *serdtse* in human spiritual life (see in particular Jurkevytch, *Filosofskie proizvedenija* [Philosophical works], 69–103; Florensky, *Pillar and Ground*, 267–71). Finally, in the work of Boris Vycheslavtsev (1895–1967), the "philosophy of the heart" found its psychoanalytic interpretation.

VI. Boris Vycheslavtsev: *Samost'* as "the True Self"

Vycheslavtsev uses the notion of *samost'* to move beyond the dualism of the *homo noumenon* and the *homo phenomenon* (Vycheslavtsev, "Serdce v xristianskoj i indijskoj mistike" [The heart in Christian and Indian mysticism], 81). He quotes Pascal's *Pensées*: "*Où est donc ce moi, s'il n'est ni dans le corps ni dans l'âme?*" (Where is this self, then, if it is neither in the body nor in the mind?) (Vycheslavtsev, *Ètika preobražënnogo èrosa* [The ethics of Eros transfigured], 259; cf. Pascal, *Pensées*, 141). According to Vycheslavtsev, "this self" of Pascal's is only *Ja sam* (I myself) or *samost'* (Vycheslavtsev, *Ètika*, 119, 259).

The *samost'* is not the body [*telo* (тело)], it is not the mind [*duša* (душа)], nor consciousness [*soznanie* (сознание)], nor the unconscious [*bessoznatel'noe* (бессознательное)], nor the person [*ličnost'*], nor even the spirit [*dux* (дух)]. What is it then? It is not "something," not "the thing" [*predmet* (предмет)], not the object [*ob'ekt* (объект)] or the idea. It is the infinite passage beyond itself [*za predely samoj sebja* (за пределы самой себя)], transcendence [*transtsenzus* (трансцензус)] and freedom [*svoboda*].

(Ibid., 258)

Both knowledge and action are attributed to *samost'*; it is the bearer of wholeness and the center of personal freedom:

Freedom [*svoboda*] is a creation *ex nihilo*, a creation that emerges by itself. . . . It is in this "by itself" [αὐτὸ κινοῦν] that the essence (*suščnost'*) of the self [*samost'*] and the I [*Ja*] lies.

(Свобода есть творчество из ничего, оно возникает само собой [αὐτὸ κινοῦν]. . . . В этом "само собой" и заключается сущность самости, сущность Я.)

(Vycheslavtsev, *Serdce*, 83)

When Vycheslavtsev relates *samost'* to *svoboda*, "freedom," we have to remember that *sobstvo*, the synonym of *samost'* that expressed individuality and membership, is from the same root as *svoboda*: both derive from *svoj* [свой], "my (your, his, our, your, their) own" (see SVOBODA). We can articulate the linguistic intuition that makes Vycheslavtsev's synthesis possible: "I myself" (*ja sam*, the Self proper) is "my own" (*svoj*), and it is thereby that I am free (*svoboden* [свободен]).

VII. The Paradox of the Person: A Dialogue between Asceticism and Psychotherapy?

Vycheslavtsev was the conduit for Freud's psychoanalysis and for Jung's work (he was the first to publish Jung in Russia). In his main work, *Ètika preobražënnogo èrosa*, he criticizes Freud's "naturalism" and proposes a Platonic interpretation of the sublimation (Greek *anagôgê* [ἀναγωγή]) of Eros as an ascension toward the ontological "sublime"—to the "superior levels of being" (109–14; see SUBLIME, Box 3).

By introducing the concept of *samost'*, Vycheslavtsev refers directly to Jung's *Selbst* (ibid., 263–64). Vycheslavtsev's *samost'*, which "transgresses the opposition between the conscious and the unconscious (ibid., 264), clearly refers to the discourse of analytical therapy. Vycheslavtsev draws a distinction between "detached" *samost'* (*otrešënnaja* [отрешённая]) and "incarnated" *samost'* (*voploščënnaja* [воплощённая]). *Samost'* can thus be understood in two ways. First, it can be taken in itself, in its "essence" (Vycheslavtsev gives the Greek *ousia* and the German *Wesen* as synonyms); as such, it never acts and, as a result, is not capable of sinning (Vycheslavtsev, *Serdce*, 79). But it can also be considered "in the real world, the one in which each of us acts . . . referring to a singular way of living and behaving" (ibid., 79); in this second meaning, *samost'* is *serdtse*, "the heart" of the living human:

The Christian self, or the heart [*serdtse*], is not the detached self [*otrešënnaja samost'*], which is irresponsible;

on the contrary, it is the incarnate self [*voploščënnaja samost'*], which is present everywhere, penetrates everything, and thus it is responsible [*otvetstvennaja*; see POSTUPOK] for everything.

(Христианская самость (сердце) ни есть отрешённая самость, ни за что не ответственная; нет, это воплощённая самость, всюду присутствующая, и потому за всё ответственная.)

(Ibid., 77)

This last sentence is a veritable program: by identifying "incarnate *samost'*" with the *serdtse*, Vycheslavtsev seeks to combine the discourse of psychotherapy with that of asceticism. At the same time, by distinguishing incarnate *samost'* from *samost'* as essence, *ousia*, and *Wesen*, he opposes the two practices—psychotherapy and asceticism—to abstract metaphysical discourse. Thus, it is the *serdtse* of the Church Fathers and not the *Selbst* of the philosophers that is "the true self."

In the first chapter of *Slavery and Freedom*, Berdyayev refers to the "fundamental paradox of the existence of the person":

The person [*ličnost'*] must create itself, enrich itself, acquire a universal content, achieve its unity and integrity in every aspect of its life. But to do so it must first exist [*byt'*]. . . . The person [*ličnost'*] is at the beginning of its path, and yet it is only at the end of the path.

(Личность должна себя созидать, обогащать, наполнять универсальным содержанием, достигать единства в цельности на протяжении всей своей жизни. Но для этого она должна уже быть. . . . Личность в начале пути, и она лишь в конце пути.)

(*Slavery and Freedom*, chap. 1)

If Berdyayev is right, the opposition between "low" *samost'* and "high" *samost'* is not so much diglossic as ontological; it refers to the real tension between the actual self and the possible self (see MacIntyre's analogous distinction between "human nature as it is" and "human nature as it could be" (Russian translation, 75). Both psychotherapeutic discourse and ascetic discourse accept the existence of this "vertical" dimension. But asceticism emphasizes the radical character of the transformation and one's inability to realize the latter without God's help, whereas the actualization of the self in analytical therapy is a natural (*estestvennyj* [естественный]) and terrestrial process. In the context of self-actualization, *samost'* can thus become the "high" term. On the contrary, in Orthodox ascetic discourse, which puts maximal emphasis on the ontological rupture between "the self" and "the true self," using *samost'*/*serdtse* to render this opposition, *samost'* plays the role of the "low" term. The question of the modern, unified meaning of *samost'* remains for the moment unresolved. Perhaps the diglossic tension can be surmounted without reducing the "vertical" dimension and falling into self-importance (*samodovol'stvo* [самодовольство]) and self-admiration (*samoljubovanie* [самолюбование]). One might think that the current tendency to neutralize diglossic tension does not entail giving up the "vertical" dimension of the human being but rather creating, through a dialogue between asceticism and analytical therapy, a unified, "ontopractical" vision of personal selfhood.

Andriy Vasylchenko

BIBLIOGRAPHY

Averintsev, Sergei. *My prizvany v obščenie*. In *Sofija—Logos. Slovnyk*. Kiev: Dukh i Litera, 2000.

———. *Poetika rannevizantiĭskoĭ literatury*. Moscow: Nauka, 1977.

Berdyaev, Nicolai. *The Realm of Spirit and the Realm of Caesar*. Translated by Donald A. Lowrie. New York: Harper and Brothers, 1952.

———. *Slavery and Freedom*. Translated by R. M. French. New York: Charles Scribner's Sons, 1944.

Crosby, John F. *The Selfhood of the Human Person*. Washington, D.C.: Catholic University of America Press, 1996. Translation into Ukranian in *Samist' liuds 'koji osoby, jak vona rozkryvaet'sia u moral'nij svidomosti*, in *Dosvid liuds'koji osoby*. Lviv: Svičado, 2000.

Feuerbach, Ludwig. *Gesammelte Werke*. Edited by Werner Schuffenhauer. Berlin: Akademie Verlag, 1981–.

Florensky, Pavel. *The Pillar and Ground of the Truth*. Translated and annotated by Boris Jakim. Princeton, NJ: Princeton University Press, 1997.

Florovsky, Georges. *Izbrannye bogoslovskie stat'i*. Moscow: Probel, 2000.

———. *Ways of Russian Theology*. Translated by Robert L. Nichols. Vols. 5 and 6 of *Collected Works of Georges Florovsky*. Edited by Richard S. Haugh. Belmont, MA: Nordland, 1972–.

Frager, Robert, and James Fadiman. *Personality and Personal Growth*. 4th ed. New York: Longman, 1998. Translation into Russian by M. Vasil'eva et al.: *Ličnost': Teorii, èksperimenty, upražnenija*. St. Petersburg: Prajm-Evroznak, 2001.

Frank, S. L. *Nepostižimoe*. In *Socinenija*. Moscow: Pravda, 1990.

Hall, Calvin S., and Gardner Lindzey. *Theories of Personality*. 2nd ed. New York: John Wiley and Sons, 1970. Translation into Russian by I. B. Grinchpun: *Teorii ličnosti*. Moscow: Aprel-Press, 1999.

Hegel, Georg Wilhelm Friedrich. *Philosophy of Nature* (Part 3 of the *Encyclopaedia of Philosophical Sciences*). 3 vols. Translated by Michael John Perry. London: Allen and Unwin, 1970.

Heidegger, Martin. *Being and Time*. Translated by Joan Stambaugh. Albany: State University of New York Press, 1996.

Jurkevytch, Pamfil. *Filosofski proizvedenija*. Moscow: Pravda, 1990.

Khoruzhy, Sergei. *K fenomenologii askezy*. Moscow: Izdatel'stvo gumanitarnoj literatury, 1998.

———. *O starom i novom*. St. Petersburg: Aleteja, 2000.

Levinas, Emmanuel. *Entre Nous: On Thinking-of-the-Other*. Translated by Michael B. Smith and Barbara Harshav. New York: Columbia University Press, 1998.

MacIntyre, Alasdair. *After Virtue. A Study of Moral Theory*. Notre Dame, IN: Notre Dame University Press, 1981. Translation into Russian by V. Tselitchchev: *Posle dobrodeteli*. Moscow: Akademičeskij Proekt, 2000.

Mead, George Herbert. *Mind, Self, and Society*. Chicago: University of Chicago Press, 1934.

Neverov, S. *Logika iudejstvujuščix*. Universitetskije Izvestija, Kiev: Tipografija Imperatorskogo Universiteta Sviatogo Vladimira 8 (1909).

Pascal, Blaise. *Pensées*. Translated by A. J. Krailsheimer. Harmondsworth, UK: Penguin, 1966.

Ricoeur, Paul. *Oneself as Another*. Translated by Kathleen Blamey. Chicago: University of Chicago Press, 1972. Translation into Ukranian by V. Andruschko and O. Syrtsova: *Sam Jak inšyj*. Kiev: Dukh i Lietera, 2000.

Ross, Lee, and Richard E. Nisbett. *The Person and the Situation. Perspectives of Social Psychology*. New York: McGraw Hill, 1991. Translation into Russian by V. V. Rumynsky: *Čelovek i situatsija*. Moscow: Aspekt Press, 2000.

Vycheslavtsev, Boris. *Ètika preobražënnogo èrosa*. Moscow: Respublika, 1994.

———. "Serdce v xristianskoj i indijskoj mistike." *Voprosy Filosofii* 4 (1990): 62–87.

———. *Večnoe v russkoj filosofii*. Moscow: Respublika, 1994.

Zarin, Sergei. *Asketizm po pravoslavno-xristianskomu učeniju*. Moscow: Palomnik, 1996.

SAUDADE (PORTUGUESE)

CATALAN	*anyoransa*
FRENCH	*nostalgie*
GERMAN	*Sehnsucht*
LATIN	*desiderium*
SPANISH	*soledad*

➤ *MALAISE, NOSTALGIA*, and ACEDIA, DASEIN, DESENGAÑO, DOR, ERLEBEN, INTENTION, LOVE, MELANCHOLY, PORTUGUESE, SEHNSUCHT, SPLEEN

Saudade is presented as the key feeling of the Portuguese soul. The word comes from the Latin plural *solitates*, "solitudes," but its derivation was influenced by the idea and sonority of the Latin *salvus*, "in good health," "safe." A long tradition that goes back to the origins of Lusophone language, to the thirteenth-century *cantiga d'amigo*, has repeatedly explored, in literature and philosophy, the special feeling of a people that has always looked beyond its transatlantic horizons. Drawn from a genuine suffering of the soul, *saudade* became, for philosophical speculation, particularly suitable for expressing the relationship of the human condition to temporality, finitude, and the infinite.

I. A "Matrix Expression"

In all languages, there are expressions that are "mothers," words that conceal and at the same time reveal a long and mysterious experience that is supra-individual and trans-temporal . . . *Saudade*, an untranslatable word of Galician-Portuguese origin . . . is precisely one of the "mother" expressions to which Goethe referred. . . . Starting out from the original experience of *soledade* or *soidade*, the [Portuguese] people arrived at the experience of *saudade*. Solitude is there found to be potentially transcendable through love. From another point of view, the present is found in it in the form of eternity, attached to the past by memory, to the future by desire.

(Quadros, *A idéia de Portugal*)

Saudade proceeds from a memory that wants to renew the present by means of the past in a loving soul that is restrained by the limits of its condition, whatever that might be. A concise definition of *saudade* appears in the treatise *The Origin of the Portuguese Language* (*Origem da língua portuguesa*, 1606) written by Duarte Nunes de Leão: "Memory of a thing with the desire for this same thing" (quoted in Botelho and Braz Teixeira, *Filosofia da saudade*). Endowed with a structural ambiguity, this feeling is located at the intersection of two affections that present absence: the memory of a cherished past that is no more and the desire for this happiness, which is lacking. Pleasure and anxiety: the result is a displaced, melancholic state that aspires to move beyond the finitude of the moment and the errancy of distance. "It is a suffering that we love, and a good that we suffer . . . " (Melo, *Epanáfora amorosa*).

But for all that, *saudade* is not so much a complex aspiration to the beyond, to the distant object of love, as it is a tender malaise of a body drawn out by the mind, corporal ecstasy itself. The tenderness of the common expression "to die of *saudades*" is explored in Tom Jobim's song "Samba do avião": "My soul sings / I see Rio de Janeiro / I am dying of *saudade*."

The song expresses the emotion felt regarding a return, a mix of anxiety and happiness that precedes the moment of arrival. *Saudade* is not something that is merely melancholy and solitary, felt at a distance from the beloved, but is also felt on meeting the beloved, as if all the accumulated pain were cathartically released in an instant of ecstasy, the instant of salvation. This may explain the very particular route taken in Portuguese by the Latin words *solutes/solitudes*.

II. Etymology, Myth, and History

In its archaic form, *soidade*, the word is found in the *cantigas d'amigo* sung by the thirteenth-century troubadours, which are the first texts in Portuguese literature. These are complaints, initially by women, deploring the absence of the beloved who has left to go to war or on crusades or on voyages of discovery and conquest beyond the seas. The origin of *soidades*, as well as of the Spanish word *soledades*, is the Latin plural *solitates* (solitudes), whose original signified is better preserved in Portuguese in the singular *solidão* (Lat., *solitas*) and in the poetic form *solitude* (Lat., *solitudo*). The abstract plural is used as a singular: *saudade* and *saudades* are used interchangeably.

The form *saudade* is found once in a fourteenth-century codex, but it began to spread, according to Carolina de Vasconcelos, only in the sixteenth century, in the years following the legendary Portuguese defeat at the battle of Alcácer Quibir. It was there that the Portuguese lost their king, Sebastian, who disappeared in the fighting, and since a successor could not be found, they subjected themselves to the Spanish crown. This battle produced a collective feeling of mourning and hope that has characterized the Portuguese soul ever since. Messianic legends developed that prophesied the king's return and the redemption of the Portuguese nation by *saudade*. The *History of the Future*, by the Jesuit António Vieira, which recounts the advent of a fifth universal empire ruled by a returned King Sebastian, is the best example of this. The figure of the *Encoberto* (the Veiled, the Hidden King) as a hypostasis of the feeling of *saudade* has been repeatedly discussed, notably by the existentialist philosopher Leonardo Coimbra.

The passage from *soidade* to the more melodious word *saudade* is explained, hypothetically, by the popular influence of the verb *saudar* (greet) and of the words *salvo* (safe) and *saúde* (health), which derive from the Latin *salvus/salutate*, as is shown by the still common habit of greeting people by sending *saudades*. A letter that is arbitrarily attributed to Camõens but that probably dates from his period (sixteenth century), explores this ambiguity:

Por usar costume antigo
Saúde mandar quisera
E mandara se tivera . . .
Mas . . . amor dela é inimigo
Pois me deu em lugar dela
Saudade em que ando,
Saudades cem mil mando . . .
E não ficando sem ela.

(Out of an old habit
I'd like to have sent you my salutation
And I'd have sent it if I'd had it . . .

But . . . love is its enemy
For instead it gave me
Saudade that I am suffering,
Saudades a hundred thousand I send . . .
And still have more here with me.)

(Quoted in Vasconcelos, *A saudade portuguesa*)

However, the religious idea of salvation was not involved in *saudade* before the existentialist and mystical poets and philosophers of the Portuguese renaissance, the nationalist and messianic cultural movement of the early twentieth century that accompanied the establishment of the republic in Portugal. Leonardo Coimbra and Teixeira de Pascoaes, the founder of the review *A Águia*, made this feeling an existential foundation, indeed a goddess, with a special religion and form of worship.

Saudade is thus associated with the most important events in Portuguese history and with most of its myths of origin. Ulysses is presented as the mythical founder of Lisbon (*Olisipolis*—the city of Ulysses): he is supposed to have founded it in a dream, without ever going there. A hero marked by nostalgia, the suffering of the return, he is also supposed to be the mythical ancestor of the *saudade* felt by the navigators wandering the globe and their wives who waited for them. All the departures for the *Reconquista*, the Templars' quest for the Holy Grail, the Crusades, the great maritime discoveries, and twentieth-century migrations accumulated to produce a diaspora that separated the people from their beloved, their families, their villages, and their country. This desire for the beyond that leads the Portuguese to leave is experienced as the effect of *saudade* and produces an archetypal reminiscence and desire.

III. Universality and the Existential Approach

When the Portuguese needed to define the specific characteristics of their nation, the theme returned. Thus when Portugal's difference from Spain was to be affirmed and the autonomy of its territory assured; when the Roman Catholic Church exceeded, with the Jesuits and the Inquisition, the limits of a properly spiritual power; when the French Enlightenment attracted the intellectuals in Coimbra; when the English made their capitalist industrial expansion felt; or, more recently, when the question of joining the European Union came up, whether in order to assert a national character or to justify a more cosmopolitan position, *saudade* has always been central. From the most scholarly philological discussions to the most chauvinist nationalist messianisms, trends, positions, and opinions diversify and clash: "The Lusitanian soul is concentrated in a single word, where it exists and lives like the reflection of the immense sun in a tiny dewdrop" (Teixeira de Pascoaes, *O Espírito lusitano ou o saudosismo* [1912], in Botelho and Braz Teixeira, *Filosofia da saudade*). The untranslatability of *saudade*, both the word and the feeling, accompanies Portuguese history from Dom Duarte (King Edward) of Portugal's first reflection on the theme: "And yet this name *suidade* seems to me so appropriate that neither Latin nor any other language I know has anything similar for such a meaning" (*Leal Conselheiro* [The Loyal Counsellor], chap. 25; written in 1438). In French, the words *nostalgie, désir, manque,* and *mélancolie* are used; in Catalan, *anyoransa*; Latin has *desiderium*, analyzed by Augustine and Spinoza, while German has *Sehnsucht*—but even the Spanish word *soledad*, whose origin is identical, does not really have the same meaning.

This singularity nonetheless indicates an existential approach to the human condition; it gives rise to a phenomenological analysis and thereby becomes capable of universality. *Saudade*, like anxiety, brings out human beings' relationships to the world. The medieval notion of *intentio* (see INTENTION) is thus reinvested by the phenomenology of *saudade*:

[I]n the act of *saudade* [or the act that is *saudoso*] are given [*dão-se*] the existence of being for the subject and the existence of the subject for being, or, to put it in the Scholastic vocabulary, that for which there is *saudade* is, from a certain point of view, *esse in*, that is, an event that is given [*se dá*] in an individualized consciousness and, from another point of view, *esse ad*, that is, an intentional relation with the absent and desired object. Thus if *saudade*'s going-into-itself [*ensimesmar-se*] implies the categorial determination of existence as *saudade* (*vivência saudosa*) in psychological life as a whole, its going-out-of-itself [*exsimesmar-se*] implies the complex problem of the forms, nature, and ontological place of the objects that the person who feels *saudade* [*o saudoso*] would like to see actualized.

(joaquim de Carvalho, "Problemática da saudade" [1950], in Botelho and Braz Teixeira, *Filosofia da saudade*)

With the idea of intention, the whole human condition unfolds in the time and the manner in which they are related to their own finitude. Silvio Lima describes this tension, this tense folding-back in the dimensions of presence, which tends toward the past in the memory and toward the future by desire:

Consciousness in *saudade* [the consciousness that is *saudosa*] suffers in the present from the privation of something past, but it suffers because it aspires to the return [*regresso*], to enjoy once again [*refruição*] the "lost paradise" and because it thus prefers it to the elimination of the obstacles that produce *saudade* [obstacles that are *saudozantes*]. Without this permanent flame of aspiration, *saudade-saudade* will not take place [*não se dará*]; the simultaneous *complexus* of three dimensions has to take place in the dimension of the present: the present inhales the past, and, in futurition, exhales it.

("Reflexões sobre a consciência saudosa," *Revista Filosófica* 44 [1955], in Botelho and Braz Teixeira, *Filosofia da saudade*)

The object that produces *saudade* determines in each case an existential, cultural, aesthetic, religious, metaphysical position (the *saudades* for a lover, a country, a time, this or that idea, etc.); inversely, everything, from literature to religion and politics, is capable of an interpretation modulated by *saudade*. This is the case for diverse philosophies, in their differences of period and language—from Plato's theory of the desire for the Beautiful through reminiscence of its idea to the transcendence of metaphysics by a return to the pre-Socratic origins of thought—the whole history of

philosophy can be woven and deconstructed in the shadow of this delectable melancholic passion.

Fernando Santoro

BIBLIOGRAPHY

Botelho, Alfonso, and António Braz Teixeira, eds. *Filosofia da saudade*. Lisbon: Imprensa Nacional, 1985.

Coyné, André. *Portugal é um ente*. Lisbon: Fund. Lusíada, 1999.

Duarte (Edward of Portugal). *Leal Conselheiro . . . Seguido do Livro da Ensinança de bem cavalgar toda sela*. Edited by J.-I. Roquette. Paris: Versions J.-P. Aillaud, Monlon et Cie., 1842. Revised in 1854.

Jobim, Antonio Carlos "Tom." "Samba do avião." On *The Wonderful World of Antonio Carlos Jobim*. Warner Bros. Records WS 1611. 1965.

Lourenço, Eduardo. *O labirinto da saudade: Psicoanálise mítica do destino português*. 3rd ed. Lisbon: Publicações Dom Quixote, 1988.

———. *This Little Lusiitanian House: Essays on Portuguese Culture*. Selected and translated by Ronald W. Sousa. Providence, RI: Gávea-Brown, 2003.

Melo, D. Francisco Manoel de. *Epanáfora amorosa*. Vol. 3 of *Epanáforas de vária história portuguesa*. Lisbon, 1660.

Quadros, António. *A idéia de Portugal na literature portuguesa dos últimos 100 anos*. Lisbon: Fund. Lusíada, 1989.

Vasconcelos, Carolina Michaëlis de. *A saudade portuguesa*. Porto: Renascença Portuguesa, 1922.

SCHICKSAL / VERHÄNGNIS / BESTIMMUNG (GERMAN)

DUTCH	*schicksel*
ENGLISH	fate, destiny
FRENCH	*destin, fatalité, destination*

➤ *DESTINY*, [KÊR], and BERUF, ES GIBT, GESCHICHTLICH, GOD, HISTORY, LIBERTY, PROPERTY, STIMMUNG

Schicksal and *Verhängnis* refer to a "sending" or "destiny" over which we ultimately have no control, even if they are not the same as strict fatality. The addressee nonetheless assumes responsibility for the way in which he is to acknowledge their receipt in that which, from Kant to Fichte in particular, was involved in the essential concept of *Bestimmung*—a destination or vocation that is also determination proper.

In the German vocabulary of destiny, the concept of *Schicksal* (Kant, *Critique of Pure Reason*, A 84–B 117) owes its name, borrowed from the Dutch *schicksel*, to the verb *schicken*, "to send," "to destine," from which is also derived *Schickung*, "dispensation," as the action of dispensing, and *Geschick*, the result of this action. In spite of Kant's charge of usurpation, or groundlessness, the term *Schicksal* was nonetheless rehabilitated by German Idealism in the horizon of Greek tragedy (Hölderlin, Schelling) or Christianity (Hegel), where it was defined as "the consciousness of oneself, but as an enemy" (Nohl, *Hegels theologische Jugendschriften*, 283).

To destine is first of all to attach solidly, as when a sailor secures (Latin *destinat*) to the mast the yards that hold the sail. Then it is to assign or attribute a share. Destiny is thus what its addressee (*destinataire*) receives as his share, without his playing any role in this process or being able to question the share he has been assigned.

(Beaufret, *Dialogue*, 3:11)

The French terms *destin* and *destinée* suggest sending and reception, but the German verb *schicken* is related to *geschehen*, "to happen," whence *Geschichte*, "history," which Luther still called (in the neuter) *das Geschicht*. Here we still hear an echo of *das Geschick*, the thing that is sent to us, and even a *Schickung*, or the dispensation of which man is not the actor but the receiver. It is in this sense that Schelling distinguished, in a letter of 8 April 1850 to Maximilian II of Bavaria, between metaphysics, the awareness that humans can acquire by their own lights, and the metaphysical (*das Metaphysische*), which falls to the share of man in virtue of a "divine dispensation (*göttliche Schickung*), which alone remains" (quoted in David, *Schelling*, 9).

We must distinguish *Verhängnis* and *Bestimmung* from *Schicksal*. *Verhängnis*, "fatality," is understood as designating "that from which a human destiny is suspended (*hängen*, "hang")." Understood during the Reformation in the sense of divine providence (*göttliche Fügung*), during the Enlightenment *Verhängnis* is used as a synonym of *Schicksal*, but since then it has taken on an essentially negative meaning, sometimes synonymous with "disaster." Schelling seems to play on the proximity and difference between the two terms when he writes, at the beginning of the tenth of his *Philosophical Letters on Dogmatism and Criticism*, in a passage that is tricky to translate:

> Man hat oft gefragt, wie die griechische Vernunft die Widersprüche ihrer Tragödie ertragen konnte. Ein Sterblicher—vom Verhängniß zum Verbrecher bestimmt, selbst gegen das Verhängniß kämpfend, und doch fürchterlich bestraft für das Verbrechen, das ein Werk des Schicksals war!

> (It has often been asked how Greek reason was able to bear the contradictions of its tragedy. A mortal—destined by fate to become a criminal, struggling himself against such a fate, and yet dreadfully punished for a crime that was the product of destiny!)

> (Schelling, *Schellings Werke*, 1:336)

Here the three concepts of *Schicksal*, *Verhängnis*, and *Bestimmung* ("destination," in the sense of intention or determination, essentially a Kantian and Fichtean term) seem to converge. However, *Bestimmung* escapes the idea of destiny in two ways. First, in one sense, because it expresses the "determination" of every thing, of each thing that determines it to be what it is, thus linking "determinism," to action exercised on it from the outside, thereby connecting it with the whole universe. Second, in another sense, because it qualifies man's "destination," that is, his freedom par excellence, as the action he exercises on himself in the ethical-practical field, in response to the call of a "voice"—German hears in *Bestimmung* the word *Stimme*, "voice"—that Kant calls "the iron voice of the categorical imperative." In the first instance, *Bestimmung* can be said of everything and is similar to *Bestimmtheit*, the "determinacy" that, in Hegel's German, qualifies a property, a characteristic of the being concerned; in the second instance, it is said of man as a rational being. Always obliged to choose, French does not help us understand that the passage from one meaning to another constitutes, for example, the whole itinerary of Fichte's "popular" work

known in French as *La destination de l'homme* (*Die Bestimmung des Menschen*; [The vocation of man]), a *destination* that is also, in the first, "Spinozist" part of the text, a "determination"—even if, as has been noted, "Fichte's originality in relation to tradition has to do with the fact that for him complete determination is not a theoretical given but a practical imperative (in French as well, *être bien déterminé* is a synonym of *vouloir*)" (j.-F. Marquet, "Fichte et le problème de la *Bestimmung*," in *Restitutions*, 19). The problem grows when, still in French, we relate *Bestimmung* as *destination* to *Schicksal* as *destin*: with regard to the latter, destination always says either too much (universal determinism) or too little (individual freedom). Here the lexical relationship based on *destiner* conceals an abyss of meaning and perhaps even a paradigm change in German philosophy of the first decade of the nineteenth century, during the period separating criticism from idealism. This transformation is the one that, from Kant's and Fichte's *Bestimmung*, and perhaps in order to get rid of its ambiguity, leads to Hegel's *Schicksal*. Then we can better understand the emergence at this point of new objects for speculation that Kant would never have included in his idea of philosophy: Greek tragedy and the "spirit" of Christianity.

Pascal David

BIBLIOGRAPHY

Beaufret, Jean. *Dialogue with Heidegger: Greek Philosophy*. Translated by Mark Sinclair. Bloomington: Indiana University Press, 2006.

David, Pascal. *Schelling. De l'absolu à l'histoire*. Paris: Presses Universitaires de France, 1998.

Kant, Immanuel. *Critique of Pure Reason*. Translated by Paul Guyer and Allen Wood. Cambridge: Cambridge University Press, 1998.

Marquet, Jean-François. *Restitutions: Études d'histoire de la philosophie allemande*. Paris: Vrin, 2001.

Nohl, Herman. *Hegels theologische Jugendschriften*. Tübingen: Mohr, 1907.

Schelling, Friedrich Wilhelm Joseph von. *Philosophical Letters on Dogmatism and Criticism*. In *The Unconditional in Human Knowledge: Four Early Essays 1794–1796*. Translated by F. Marti. Lewisburg, PA: Bucknell University Press, 1980.

Snow, Dale E. *Schelling and the End of Idealism*. Albany: State University of New York Press, 1996.

SECULARIZATION

FRENCH	*sécularisation, profanation*
GERMAN	*Säkularisation, Säkularisierung, Verweltlichung*
ITALIAN	*secolarizzazione*

➤ BERUF, BILDUNG, BOGOČELOVEČESTVO, DESENGAÑO, GOD, NEUZEIT, PIETAS, PRAXIS, RELIGIO, ROMANTIC, SOBORNOST', STATO, WELT

The word "secularization," derived from ecclesiastical Latin *saecularis* (an epithet that stems from *saeculum* in the sense of "world" or "worldly life"), comes into use in French around 1567 as part of the lexicon of canon law. As an expression of an antinomy between the religious world and the profane world, it gradually comes to be understood as a general process governing the whole of culture as it is modernized. Such "rationalization" coincides with the "disenchantment of the world" (*Entzauberung der Welt*), a condition engendering multiple responses and attempts at redress: among them, "laicity" (a strict separation of religion and public affairs), political secularism, and desecularization. In each case the initial opposition between sacred and profane remains in play and enriches the term's meaning.

I. Secularization According to Canon Law and *Verweltlichung*

The Justinian Code, which dates from around 533, mentions the opposition between *saeculum* (*a saeculari conversatione recedere* or *saeculo renuntiare*) and *vita sanctimonialis* (I.3.54). This general distinction between those who live "in the world" (*saeculum*) and those who live "in the clergy" is explained by another distinction within the ecclesiastical world between the status of those who belong to the ordinary clergy and that of monks and others who have taken monastic vows. This distinction is the one adopted for the most part by canon law when it distinguishes the regular clergy (the religious who are subject to a conventual rule) and the secular clergy. From another point of view, within the ecclesiastical sphere governed by canon law, the formal transfer of rights to monastic goods to a secular authority or the return of a monk or other religious to the secular clergy is distinguished from the act through which ecclesiastical goods in general are transferred to the strictly secular sphere, a transfer that is then designated by the term *profanatio*. The "profanation" of a sacred reality concerns first of all the Eucharastic host when it is made the object of a commercial transaction which, because it is inappropriate and confuses the registers of the sacred and the profane, amounts to "profaning" it.

The *Codex juris canonici* as it was promulgated in 1917 designates by the term "secularization" both the passage of a member of the regular clergy to the secular clergy—a simple exclaustration that does not break the vows taken by the religious—and, on the other hand, the return of a cleric, monastic or secular, to secular life—a complete secularization that releases him from his vows because he is leaving the clergy. In the sphere of canon law, secularization does not imply that the status of persons, privileges, or goods is modified to the point that they change in nature, becoming strictly profane. Such a transformation in nature implies the intervention of the pope, who alone, as the Vicar of Christ, *sicut Deus in terra*, has the capacity to make such a transformation.

The origin of the derivative use of the term "secularization" is the Treaty of Westphalia (1646). At the end of the Thirty Years' War, the question of the transfer of ecclesiastical goods to certain Protestant *Länder* had to be dealt with. In the first volume of his *Négociations secrètes touchant la paix de Münster et d'Osnabrück* (1725), Jean Le Clerc sums up the situation this way: "We have to make use of ecclesiastical goods to compensate those who will lose something for the love of peace, they [the goods] could not be more appropriately alienated." The French emissary, the Duke of Longueville, chose, for diplomatic reasons, to use the term "secularization" to qualify this transfer of property. In so doing he was responding to several simultaneous constraints. First, he sought to avoid offending Catholics by using a canon law expression that would create the illusion that the goods of which they would be deprived would not change in nature, even though that was in fact the case; thus it was not necessary to request papal intervention. Second, he tried to make it clear to Protestants that these goods were not only secularized but in fact "made profane" (*profanisés*). The use of the

latter term, which did not imply a transformation in nature, implied that the Lutherans also represented a church—which the duke did not, however, recognize, contrary to the desires of the Evangelical *Länder*, who understood that in this case "secularization" meant simply "making profane."

The German terms *Säkularisation* (or *Säkularisierung*) and *Verweltlichung* (literally, "making worldly") have their origin in the terminological ambiguity characteristic of these negotiations in 1646, as well as in the many commentaries to which they later gave rise. In Germany, the term *Säkularisation* became synonymous with anti-Catholic measures that implied in particular the alienation of ecclesiastical goods to the benefit of the secular sphere. This use became more widespread under the reign of Frederick II, who wanted to "secularize," that is, to "render profane" (*profaniser*) certain convents (letter to Voltaire, 24 March 1767, and Voltaire's reply, 5 April 1767), and after the treaty of Lunéville and the cession of the left bank of the Rhine to France in 1801, and especially in 1803, with the great "secularizations" that put an end to the Holy Roman Empire. It is to this latter event and to the reactions that it aroused among the first German Romantics that the term owes its further extension and its entry into philosophical terminology: "secularization" implied opposition to the Christian conception of the world, to the Christian order governing earthly life—it being understood that Christianity was identified with Catholicism, whereas Lutheranism was perceived as one of the most perfidious agents of this secularization. The term thus became an essential one in the Romantic philosophy of history.

II. From the Romantic Reaction to Hegel and Marx: *Verweltlichung* and *Säkularisation*

Joseph Freiherr von Eichendorff's *On the Consequences of the Suppression of the Territorial Authority of Bishops and Convents in Germany*, published in 1818, along with Novalis's essay "Europe or Christianity," is one of the very first testimonies to a very strong reaction to the consequences of what the author imputes to the Enlightenment: the criticism of traditional understanding had destroyed the authority of faith, which was supposed to be founded on a temporal basis (real property and political power) to play, through ecclesiastical institutions, a pacifying and charitable role, realizing on earth a reconciliation that anticipated the Redemption. "The secularization of the states and of ecclesiastical goods," Eichendorff writes, "is a misfortune that has struck Germany." The Romantic reaction did not, however, see secularization as a process that would end in a complete dechristianization; on the contrary, those who, like Schlegel and Novalis, believed in the beneficial action of the secret Catholic societies to which they belonged, envisaged the future of Europe as an ascent toward a new spiritual era, a final synthesis of history punctuated by the ages of the Father (the Revelation), the Son (the Reformation), and the Holy Spirit (the Redemption). Secularization was thus not understood as a radical *Verweltlichung*.

In his *Lectures on the History of Philosophy* (*Vorlesungen über die Geschichte der Philosophie*, in *Sämtliche Werke*, 19:190, 207), Hegel introduced the notion of *Verweltlichung* as a qualification of the historical movement that extends from the end of the Middle Ages to the French Revolution by way of

Scholasticism and the Reformation: the (Catholic) church was brought into a critical situation by the work of the Scholastics, who applied rational and finite notions to an absolute content; the crisis took the form of an increasingly sharp dissociation between the spiritual and the temporal (or "earthly") spheres. And, through the critical slant of the Reformation that deprived the papacy of its spiritual authority—after kings had asserted against it their *potestas* in the form of political sovereignty (especially in England)—the modern era that began with the rational form of the state constitutes the reconciliation of the spiritual and the temporal in the concept of freedom: this concept realizes the spiritual content of Christianity and makes it consubstantial with actual reality. The truth of Christianity is realized in the modern state, which incarnates the principle of Christian freedom (*Lectures on the Philosophy of History* [*Vorlesungen über die Philosophie der Geschichte* in *Sämtliche Werke*, vol. 11]). The realization of Spirit in history is accompanied by the total *Verweltlichung* of the church.

In his letter to Hegel of 22 November 1828, Ludwig Feuerbach seeks to pursue further "the realization and *Verweltlichung* of the ideal," to the point of the total dissolution of any theological dimension in anthropology (*Principles of the Philosophy of the Future*, 1843). And, at the same time, Marx proceeded in the same way to seek to outdo Hegel in his "Introduction to the Critique of Hegel's Philosophy of Right" (1843) and in his famous "Theses on Feuerbach" (1844; theses IV, VI, VII, and VIII). In a letter to Ruge written in September 1843 Marx describes the current reform in philosophy this way: "Philosophy has been secularized [*verweltlicht*], and the most striking proof of this is that philosophical consciousness itself has entered into the painful struggle, not with respect to the outside, but within its own heart" (*Marx-Engels Werke* 1:344). However, we must note that the "Introduction to the Critique of Hegel's Philosophy of Right" concludes with an initial definition of the proletariat that is not based on a sociological analysis or a political economy, but solely on a "messianic" construction of the history to come in which the proletariat will be called upon to play a Christological and soteriological role: it is the redeemer of humanity at the end of history as we have known it, that is, the proletariat is the historical way that human beings emerge from their alienation and can be reconciled, here on earth, with there true nature.

Richard Rothe was the first writer in Germany to identify Hegelian *Verweltlichung* with *Säkularisation*. In his *Theologische Ethik* (Theological ethics), he conceives the notion in the framework of a universal salvation history, and, like Hegel, thinks that the Reformation contributed to the "secularization" of Christianity. But he also thinks that in freeing itself from the (Catholic) church, Christian life did not cease to be Christian as it entered into a (Protestant) political and moral era. This is because the movement of history is governed by a kind of constant rebalancing: as the church is secularized, it Christianizes the state and "desecularizes" it to the same degree. The church was thus cast as a provisional form of the Christian spirit; with the state being another one. The validity, then, of a Christian theodicy, conceived as underlying universal history (*Vorlesung über die Geschichte der Kirche und des christlichen Lebens* [Lecture on the history of the Church and the history of Christian life]), is preserved.

The term *Säkularisation* acquired an extension sufficiently vast to allow it to be identified, in the perspective of the progressive positivism of the late nineteenth century, with progress itself (for example, in J.-M. Guyau's *L'irréligion de l'avenir* [Irreligion of the future]). The separation of church and state is governed by the idea that the natural end of historical development, of which secularization is the corollary, is the secularization of public life, whereas religion is limited to the private domain governed and controlled by the principle of the freedom of opinion and belief.

It was in the twentieth century that debates around the problem of secularization became most intense, and not just in reaction to the gradual political and institutional separation of church and state. It was, of course, in Germany—where a general obligation to pay taxes to support the churches persisted—that this problem was and remains most acute, for it responds to central aspects of "modernity": the gradual disappearance of the religious framework of life, and the role of the churches, and religious culture more generally, in ways of life.

III. Secularization and the Disenchantment of the World According to Weber

Although he avoids extending his analysis to the whole of world history, Max Weber characterizes the evolution of Western culture by the notion of rationalization (*Rationalisierung*), coupled with that of generalization. The rationalization that began, particularly, in the monotheistic form of religion has as its corollary a disenchantment of the world (*Entzauberung*) that means, first of all, the abandonment of magical beliefs regulating behavior. But on the one hand, Weber does not consider rationalization and religion to be systematically antinomic, on the contrary; on the other hand, disenchantment is not a synonym of either rationalization or secularization:

> There are essentially two complementary criteria that make it possible to evaluate the degree of rationalization achieved by a religion: first, to what extent it has rid itself of magic, second, what degree of systematic unity it has attained in the relations between God and the world, and correlatively, in its own ethical relations with the world.

> (*Gesammelte Aufsätze zur Religionssoziologie*, 1:512)

Disenchantment and rationalization may even be opposed:

> Action governed by magical representations often has a character that is subjectively far more rational in its goal than any non-magical "religious" behavior, precisely insofar as with the growing disenchantment of the world religiousness is forced to accept significations (for example, emotional or mystical ones) that are (subjectively) more irrational in their goals.

> ("Über einige Kategorien der verstehenden Soziologie," in *Gesammelte Aufsätze zur Wissenschaftslehre*, 433)

That is why Talcott Parsons's identification of *Entzauberung* and rationalization in his English translation of *The Protestant Ethic* is mistaken. Weber rarely uses the term "secularization," and it is rather Weber's readers who created amalgams, whereas Weber himself always remained very prudent in his handling of the term, which cannot be seen as an engine of universal history understood from a teleological point of view. His examination of the tendencies of modernity led him to observe that despite partial secularizations and a growing generalization, and despite a disenchantment that is often their corollary, religion (or religions) are not doomed to inevitable disappearance. At most we find a deep indifference to the essential contents of the sphere of religious worship, but not a twilight of the gods.

IV. Troeltsch's Corrective and Modern Theology

Ernst Troeltsch, who notes that the most decisive fact in modern history is the secularization of the state (whose engine is the secularization of religious individualism and whose philosophical foundations are utilitarianism and British skepticism), and who acknowledges that the belief in progress peculiar to the modern conception of history is a secularization of Christian eschatology, is nonetheless the first to oppose an excessive extension of the identification of modernity with secularization. He emphasizes, on the contrary, the fact that religious contents resist any secularization and that religion is not an economic ideal. There can be a secularization *lato sensu* only if the content thus "secularized" is itself governed by a genuine rejection of religion, parallel to the religious rejection of the world. Troeltsch does not begin, like Weber, from sociological and statistical considerations regarding the fact that capitalism is more widespread in regions where Calvinism was dominant, but from the content of the religious doctrines that determine the institutional forms (churches, sects, mysticisms) through which religion enters into direct relation with the world. A kind of internal secularization even began within the Catholic religion when Scholasticism took the Stoic theory of natural law as a basis for an attempt to synthesize natural ethics and revelation, suggesting that the decalogue might be identified with the *lex naturae*. Nonetheless, Troeltsch advocates an antagonistic vision of the relations between religion and world history, with the intention of preserving the critical potential contained in the religious institutional forms that have least compromised with the temporal sphere.

We find in Karl Barth the same prudence with regard to the generalized conception of secularization: "Where are the windows of the divine world that are supposed to open onto our social life?" ("Der Christ in der Gesellschaft," in *Gesammelte Vorträge*, 36), and especially in Friedrich Gogarten, who inverts the point of view: the condition for faith is precisely that the world be secular. Gogarten's concern is to distinguish faith from its proselytizing justification, which is always in danger of slipping into ideology. The radicality of disenchantment does not triumph over a faith that remains—to use an expression of Rudolf Bultmann's—a paradox, but it emphasizes its purity: it does not proceed from the world; even if it has to refuse to be a flight outside the world, it is irreducible to an anthropological conception of the opposition between the sacred and the profane. Secularization

remains a necessary element of faith; but Gogarten introduces the notion of secularism (*Säkularismus*) to designate an immanentist perversion, the abusive ideologization of temporal powers that are supposed to provide salvation on earth (this notion is nonetheless very close to what is meant by *gnosis*).

V. The German Pair *Verweltlichung-Säkularisation* and the French Pair *Sécularisation-Laïcité*

The most recent discussion, Hans Blumenberg's critique of Karl Löwith's position, contributes nothing new to the definition of the term, but does clarify what it designates. Löwith is certainly right to show how Voltaire, for example, "secularized" Bossuet's conception of Providence by seeking to substitute a vision of strictly immanent progress; by doing so, he transferred into the secular sphere thought contents that were all borrowed from the Christian spiritual sphere; but it cannot be directly concluded from this that modern history is a history of secularization whose theological origin can finally emerge purified after beliefs in progress have revealed the ambiguity of their origin and that of their ideological applications. Blumenberg tries to bring out a different, more empirical genealogy of progress in the extension of reality that scientific theory enables us to master and in that of actual scientific method. Giving up the attempt to explain the totality of universal history makes it possible to avoid a conceptual formation that remains metaphorical.

German usage retains the *Verweltlichung-Säkularisation* pair, which has, for the time being, been stabilized, but must constantly be explained, depending on whether one understands the terms in the perspective of a philosophy of history or in the more limited framework of a sociology or a precise historical analysis. In French, the problem arises as soon as *sécularisation* is identified with *laïcisation*: *laïcité* can be understood as a consequence of secularization *lato sensu*, that is, as the normal outcome of a historical process that began with the Enlightenment and was actualized in the formation of the modern liberal state, or as an imperfect solution to the problem of secularization, since *laïcité*, if it remains "neutral," affects only one aspect of social life, but thus acknowledges the existence of a permanent cultural tension, since no religion can bear being reduced to the ranks of simple private opinion. On the other hand, if this *laïcité* is understood as "interventionist," that is, if the state seeks to make common cause with what it believes to be a just tendency of history, it will be in danger of infringing upon the fundamental freedoms enjoyed by the private sphere, thus changing the nature of a constitutional principle that is essential to any republic. It is this dilemma and this contradiction that are the deep moving force behind a constant renewal of the modern debate.

Marc de Launay

BIBLIOGRAPHY

Atchley, J. Heath. *Encountering the Secular: Philosophical Endeavors in Religion and Culture*. Charlottesville: University of Virginia Press, 2009.

Barth, Karl. "Der Christ in der Gesellschaft." In *Gesammelte Vorträge*. Zollikon, Ger.: Evangelischer Verlag: 1950.

Blumenberg, Hans. *The Legitimacy of the Modern Age*. Translated by Robert M. Wallace. Cambridge, MA: MIT Press, 1983.

Feuerbach, Ludwig. *Principles of the Philosophy of the Future*. Translated by Manfred Vogel. Indianapolis, IN: Hackett Publishing Company, 1966.

Gauchet, Marcel. *The Disenchantment of the World: A Political History of Religion*. Translated by Oscar Burge. Princeton, NJ: Princeton University Press, 1997.

Gogarten, Friedrich. *Verhängnis und Hoffnung der Neuzeit, die Säkularisierung als theologisches Problem*. Stuttgart: Friedrich Vorwerk Verlag, 1953. Translation by Thomas Wieser: *Despair and Hope for Our Time*. Philadelphia: Pilgrim Press, 1970.

Guyau, J.-M. *L'irréligion de l'avenir*. Paris: Alcan, 1887.

Hegel, Georg Wilhelm Friedrich. *Vorlesungen über die Geschichte der Philosophie* [*Lectures on the History of Philosophy*]. Vols. 17–19 of *Sämtliche Werke*, edited by H. Glockner. Stuttgart: Frommann, 1927–40. *Lectures* first published 1805–6.

———. *Vorlesungen über die Philosophie der Geschichte* [*Lectures on the Philosophy of History*]. Vol. 11 of *Sämtliche Werke*, edited by H. Glockner. Stuttgart: Frommann, 1927–40. *Lectures* first published 1837.

Löwith, Karl. *Meaning in History*. Chicago: University of Chicago Press, 1949.

Lübbe, Hermann. *Säkularisierung. Geschichte eines Ideenpolitischen Begriffs*. Freiburg, Ger.: K. Alber, 1975.

Marx, Karl. *Marx-Engels Werke*. 1st of 43 vols. Berlin: Dietz, 1956.

Rothe, Richard. *Vorlesung über die Geschichte der Kirche und des christlichen Lebens* [Lecture on the history of the Church and the history of Christian life]. Heidelberg, 1875.

Taylor, Charles. *A Secular Age*. Cambridge, MA: Harvard University Press / Belknap Press, 2007.

Troeltsch, Ernst. *Historicism and Its Problems*. Tübingen: Verlag von J.C.S. Mohr (Paul Siebeck), 1922.

———. *Protestantism and Progress: The Significance of Protestantism for the Rise of the Modern World*. Philadelphia: Fortress Press, 1986.

Weber, Max. *Gesammelte Aufsätze zur Religionssoziologie*. 3 vols. Tübingen: Siebeck, 1988. First published in 1920.

———. *The Protestant Ethic and the Spirit of Capitalism*. Translated by T. Parsons. London: Routledge, 1992.

———. "Über einige Kategorien der verstehenden Soziologie." In *Gesammelte Aufsätze zur Wissenschaftslehre*. Tübingen: Siebeck, 1951. First published in 1913.

SECURITAS (LATIN)

ENGLISH	security, tranquility, carelessness
FRENCH	*sécurité, sûreté, incurie*
GERMAN	*Sicherheit, Sorglosigkeit*
GREEK	*asphaleia* [ἀσφάλεια], *ataraxia* [ἀταραξία], *akêdeia* [ἀκήδεια]
ITALIAN	*sicurezza, trascuratezza*

➤ CERTITUDE, DASEIN, SEIN, SORGE, *SOUCI* [CARE], STATE, STATO

The semantic career of *securitas* is as long as it is ambivalent. The word is constructed from the prefix *se-* (removal from), the common noun *cura* (concern, care, anxiety), and the suffix *–tas*, which denotes a state of being. Hence, the primary meaning of *securitas* is "the condition of being removed from care." Since *cura* is itself ambivalent—expressing either something troubling (anxious concern, nervous fear, burdensome worry) or something beneficial (careful attentiveness, loving diligence, well-intentioned administration)—*securitas*, precisely as the removal of *cura*, may designate a state that is either profitable or harmful. When *securitas* implies the elimination of a vexing problem, it clearly denotes a good; however, should the term entail the eradication of conscientious attention, it expresses a state of heedlessness. To be without care is to be protected or vulnerable, safe or negligent, carefree or careless.

I. Tranquility and Safety

In the mid-first century BCE, *securitas* emerges in the philosophical writings of Cicero. Here, the *cura* implicitly cancelled is generally negative; that is, *securitas* names the alleviation of psychological disturbances and therefore represents the Latin translation of any number of ideals promulgated in Hellenistic moral philosophy that also feature a negating prefix, such as Epicurean *ataraxia* [ἀταραξία] (being free of perturbations) or Stoic *apatheia* [ἀπάθεια] (being free of bothersome passions; see *De officiis* 1.69). Cicero also employs *securitas* as a synonym for the *euthumia* [εὐθυμία] (cheerfulness) celebrated by Democritus (*De finibus* 5.23). Seneca continues this trend by regularly equating *securitas* with the *beata vita* (blessed life) of the philosopher (*Epistles* 92.3). In both authors, *securitas* denotes the "peace of mind" (*tranquillitas animi*) associated with the private life, far from the oppressive concerns and worries of the political sphere. The removal of *curae* corresponds to the philosopher's withdrawal from the forum.

It is only with the collapse of the Roman Republic that the sense of *securitas* begins to be employed in a decidedly public fashion. Throughout the Imperial period, the word denotes military or governmental protection—not a condition to be enjoyed privately, away from the city, but rather within the city's sheltering walls. Previously, in republican usage, meanings of civil defense were instead expressed by *salus* (which yields the English "safety" and "salvation"). Following the accession of Augustus, *securitas* therefore suffers its first semantic split, between an inner, subjective sense of composure and an external, objective sense of shielded safety.

The latter, Imperial meaning should no longer be understood exclusively as a translation of Hellenistic *ataraxia* or *apatheia*, but rather as an extension of another privative term in Greek: *asphaleia* [ἀσφάλεια] (steadfastness, stability; literally, prevention [*a-*] from stumbling or falling [*sphallein*]). A term with clear conservative connotations, *asphaleia* is the guarantee that institutions will not crumble, that they will continue to persist like the "eternally steadfast [*asphales*] abode of the gods" described by Homer (*Odyssey* 6.42) or the "infallible [*asphalê*] statutes of the gods" invoked by Sophocles's Antigone (*Antigone* 454). Accordingly, Velleius Paterculus, writing nearly eight decades after Cicero's late works, uses *securitas* to describe the emperor's achievement in removing the threat of civil war (*Historiae romanae* 2.89).

II. Certainty, Conviction, and Negligence

With the post-Augustan conflation of *securitas* and *salus*, as well as the link to *asphaleia*, the concept of *securitas* moves well beyond issues of emotional tranquility and physical protection to include cognitive dispositions like "certainty" and "intellectual conviction," where the "concern" of falsehood no longer diminishes one's position. Yet, in addition to these positive senses, *securitas* can also be understood as the negation of *cura* as "attentiveness" or "diligence." Quintilian, for example, resorts to the term *securitas* to denote "carelessness" among his students (*Institutio oratoria* 2.2.6). Seneca, too, although he generally aligns *securitas* with Stoic "imperturbability" (*apatheia*), finds occasion to use the same term to mean "idleness" and "negligence" (e.g., *De beneficiis* 5.12.2). Even already in Cicero, one can glimpse misgivings concerning an otherwise vaunted ideal. In *De amicitia*, "removal of care" (*securitas*) severs an individual from interpersonal relationships that define the best and most pleasing aspects of human life (*De amicitia* 47). The allure of a transcendent, philosophical position may on the surface promise a carefree, unbothered existence, but in the inescapably immanent reality of our lives, both in the world and among others, any such promise seduces us to a carelessness that renders virtue impossible.

Augustine introduces the term into Christian discourse by emphasizing a crucial point: "true security" (*firma securitas*) is only possible posthumously with God, that is, in the eternally blessed state in which the saved will at last be removed from the anxiety that constitutes the present realm of earthly existence (*Confessions* 2.6.13). To be utterly secure in this world would threaten our security insofar as it would offer a deceptive resting point, when the only valid resting point should be in divine grace. Augustine is cognizant of the political and social ramifications: for example, he observes how the Roman Republic degenerated into weakness and reckless complacency after its glorious triumph in the final war against Carthage (*City of God* 3.21). To fail to recognize one's vulnerability is to suffer from the carelessness of a security that leaves one more vulnerable than ever.

The pejorative sense of *securitas* as "negligence" persists throughout Christian usage, which tended to associate the word with a caricatured portrayal of Epicureanism, not necessarily aligned with *ataraxia*, but rather with *akêdeia* [ἀκήδεια] (indifference, torpor; literally, the negation of care [*kêdos*]). Following Gregory the Great, Christian theologians ultimately define *akêdeia* as "sloth," one of the seven mortal sins stemming from pride and invariably ending in "melancholy," where all occupation, spiritual as well as physical, is supplanted by detrimental boredom, lethargy, and complete insouciance. Hence, Robert Burton, in *The Anatomy of Melancholy*, warns that "many a carnal man is lulled asleep in perverse security" (Part 3.4, 2.6).

Positive connotations of *securitas* in the Christian era are missing from political and religious discourse but do persist in some legal contexts, where the term serves as an ideal of guarantee in oaths, pledges, and contracts. When *securitas* resurfaces in civil and theological thought during the Reformation, it again betrays the ambivalence that has always characterized its usage. Martin Luther distinguishes public security—a good provided by secular governments and their magistrates—from individual security, symptomatic of the slothful and the proud, who neglect careful examination of scripture or are wrongly confident of their state of grace.

Meanwhile, the positive sense of security as protection is established as a central topic in modern political philosophy, from Niccolò Machiavelli's readings of Livy to Thomas Hobbes's discussion of the sovereign's covenant and John Locke's securement of liberty through the "bonds of civil society." Later still, the eighteenth-century economic theories of the Physiocrats use a concept of security to maintain the profitability of open markets. With the rise of nineteenth-century nationalism, state security is elevated to prominence,

paving the way for the abuses of state apparatuses in the century that follows.

III. Allegories of Care

Philosophical approaches—loosely gathered under the rubric of existentialism—raise suspicions about the idealization of security and its implicit elimination of care: Søren Kierkegaard's reflections on anxiety, Friedrich Nietzsche's genealogies, and even Martin Heidegger's fundamental ontology criticize a purely theoretical position detached from the world—a metaphysical attitude that should be exposed as a defensive flight, as a strategy that seeks false tranquility in objectivity. The destructive—or deconstructive—impulse discernible in this work aims to deprive the substantial subject of any sure, noncontingent foundation, like the *fundamentum inconcussum* that René Descartes envisioned against radical doubt. In a similar spirit, philosophical anthropologists like Helmut Plessner define all human institutions as security projects that aim to remedy or compensate for mankind's essential lack of instinctual capabilities, and hence conceive philosophical critique as a mode of *Entsicherung*, a "desecuring" that vividly removes the "safety catch" (*Sicherung*) of conventional patterns of thought in order to prepare the ground for a more secure security.

In his famous analysis of "care" (*Sorge*) as the "Being of Being-There [*Dasein*]," Heidegger cites a fable recorded by the first-century Roman grammarian Hyginus (*Fabulae* 220; Heidegger, *Being and Time*, §42). The story relates the creation and naming of mankind. A personification of *cura* forms a figure from muddy clay, and Jupiter, upon request, animates it with his spirit. A debate over the creature's name ensues: Cura wants to name it after herself, but Jupiter insists that he should be so honored. After Earth (*Tellus*) herself appears to make her own case, the three contestants appeal to Saturn, who judges that after death, the spirit should return to Jupiter and the body should go back to Tellus, but as long as the creature lives, it should be possessed by Cura. As for the name, it should be called *homo* (mankind), since it was formed out of the *humus* (soil). Heidegger offers this fable as a "pre-ontological document" that illustrates *Dasein*'s self-interpretation within the horizon of temporality. Yet, he neglects to stress that the terms of the story further spell out mankind's relation to security. If mankind is consigned to the realm of Cura for the duration of life, then an absolutely secure state—a condition that is purely "removed from care" (*se-cura*)—is only possible posthumously, when the body rests in the fixity of the Tellurian grave and the spirit enjoys the freedom of Jupiter's heaven.

The promise of perfect security therefore rests on a negation of time, which includes the negation of human mortality, be it the lifelessness of physical death or the im-mortality of eternity. Political critics of security, in line with a Lockean tradition, frequently lament the well-known trade-off that purchases protection with the sacrifice of certain liberties. Yet, one could cite an even more insidious consequence: the dream of absolute security does not simply take away one's freedom but also threatens to remove the time-bound mortality that defines human existence. Hence, Jean Baudrillard characterizes the booming security industry as "state blackmail," which converts all manners of accidents, diseases, and threats into "capitalist surplus profit"—"the worst repression, which consists in dispossessing you of your own death" (*Symbolic Exchange*, 177). For Baudrillard, an "immortal life" is a contradiction in terms, an ideologically driven oxymoron. To live is to be able to die; and security technologies, which forestall this potential end, end up defusing potentiality, foreclosing future contingencies, and therefore preventing life itself from living.

IV. Vigilance

It is not necessary to accept Baudrillard's radical judgment to recognize that the concern for security is always a concern for being without concern. The desire to protect oneself and others, the need according to the law of self-preservation to foresee and preempt danger, the commitment required to locate threats and remedy vulnerabilities, all ostensibly demand carefulness and caution, vigilance and ingenuity, usually by implementing a capacity to calculate risk and assess probability. One cannot be without care. Perhaps no one understood this better than Franz Kafka, the one-time officer and safety expert at the *Arbeiter-Unfall-Versicherungs-Anstalt* in Prague. In his short story "Der Bau" (The burrow), the tiny foraging animal knows that the protection of his day-to-day life requires constant awareness. His fortification is left vulnerable by design, which forces him to remain watchful. Paradoxically, it is the structure's lack of total impenetrability that ensures the inhabitant's capacity for self-defense. His mortality saves his life.

John T. Hamilton

BIBLIOGRAPHY

Baudrillard, Jean. *Symbolic Exchange and Death*. Translated by I. H. Grant. London: Sage, 1993. Originally published as *L'échange symbolique et la mort* (Paris: Gallimard, 1976).

Conze, Werner. "Sicherheit, Schutz." In *Geschichtliche Grundbegriffe: Historisches Lexikon zur politisch-sozialen Sprache in Deutschland*, edited by O. Brunner, W. Conze, and R. Koselleck, 8 vols., 5:831–62. Stuttgart: Klett, 1972–97.

Der Derian, James. "The Value of Security: Hobbes, Marx, Nietzsche and Baudrillard." In *On Security*, edited by R. D. Lipschutz, 24–45. New York: Columbia University Press, 1995.

Dillon, Michael. *The Politics of Security: Towards a Political Philosophy of Continental Thought*. London: Routledge, 1996.

Neocleous, Mark. *Critique of Security*. Montreal: McGill-Queen's University Press, 2008.

Schrimm-Heins, Andrea. "Gewißheit und Sicherheit: Geschichte und Bedeutungswandel der Begriffe certitudo und securitas." *Archiv für Begriffsgeschichte* 34 (1991): 123–213.

| SEHNSUCHT, SEHNEN (GERMAN)

ENGLISH   nostalgia, yearning, longing
FRENCH   *nostalgie, aspiration*

➤ *MALAISE, NOSTALGIA*, and DOR, DRIVE, GEFÜHL, HEIMAT, I/ME/MYSELF, PATHOS, ROMANTIC, SAUDADE, SOUL, WUNSCH

German lexicographers like to emphasize that the verb *sich sehnen* and the corresponding noun, *Sehnsucht*, are words that have no equivalents in other European languages. Since these words—frequently used in everyday language and almost too common in poetry after 1750—are not at first sight among the technical terms of philosophy, no one is offended by the fact that they may give rise to very diverse translations into French (*nostalgie, aspiration, désir ardent*, etc.). On closer inspection, however, these terms bear a philosophical freight to which we should pay attention. *Das Sehnen* (is this aspiration or nostalgia?) is one of the central terms in the first version of Fichte's *Wissenschaftslehre* (1794–95). *Sehnsucht* is also at the heart of the thinking of Friedrich von Schlegel, who notes in his *Philosophy of Life* (*Philosophie des Lebens*, 1827) that philosophy might be defined as a "doctrine or science of nostalgia" ("Lehre von der Sehnsucht, oder Wissenschaft der Sehnsucht," in *Kritische Friedrich von Schlegel Ausgabe*,10: 33).

I. The "Sentimental" Origin of *Sehnsucht*

The verb *sich sehnen*, whose etymology is obscure, appeared in Middle High German only after the eleventh century and means "languish, torment oneself, desire, sigh for something." In the middle of the seventeenth century, le lexicographer Justus Georg Schottel gave as its equivalent the Latin *cupidine ardere* (RT: *Deutsches Wörterbuch*, art. "Sehnen"). *Sich sehnen* was used extensively by courtly poets, especially in referring to the torments of love. This "sentimental" origin deeply influenced the verb and the noun *die Sehnsucht* (a compound with the suffix *–sucht*, which designates a sickly state): thus it referred to the suffering of a person consumed by desire.

A. The indeterminacy of the object of desire

The terms *sehnen* and *Sehnsucht* are centered on the desiring subject and on the pain that he feels (*ardere*) and not on the object of his desire, which remains relatively indeterminate. *Sehnen* and *Sehnsucht* designate a tension, a subject's aspiration to change his state. When the object of desire is specified, an abstract and immaterial term is generally used (*Sehnsucht nach Ruhe, nach der Heimat, nach Geborgenheit* [the desire for peace, for the homeland, for security]). In *Sehnsucht* the crude and even brutal aspect that lust (*das Begehren*, the desire to possess) may take on is in a way abolished or sublimated. From this point of view, we might say that it is an ennobled (spiritualized) form of desire, which probably also explains the inflation of *Sehnsucht* in German poetry between 1750 and 1850.

B. The difference between *Sehnsucht* and nostalgia

These characteristics of *Sehnsucht* allow us to compare it with "nostalgia"—which is one of the terms most frequently used by translators when they seek to render the German word. The accent put on the subject's suffering, along with the vague and immaterial aspect of that to which he aspires, seems to suggest that "nostalgia" and *Sehnsucht* are equivalent to each other. But nostalgia is, properly speaking, the longing for a return, the suffering connected with the desire to go back to what one has previously known (see Box 1). *Sehnsucht* is not connected with a return; the idea associated with it is primarily that of a departure ("Ah! To be able to leave as they do / Into that marvelous summer's night!" Eichendorff writes in his poem "Sehnsucht," vv. 7–8). Whereas *Sehnsucht* is turned toward a distant goal and often concerns the future rather than the past, nostalgia is an elegiac sentiment and manifests itself in the form of regret. Littré's French dictionary does not list a meaning of *nostalgie* that is not turned toward the past: that is why *nostalgie* is a very imperfect translation of *Sehnsucht*. In fact, a use of the French word *nostalgie* that is more temporally open does not appear until the middle of the nineteenth century. In one of his prose poems, Baudelaire refers, for example, to cigars that "make the soul nostalgic for unknown countries and joys" (Baudelaire, "Le joueur généreux" [1864]). In French this use remains, however, marginal: the idea of a tendency toward the past remains closely connected with the word *nostalgie*, which thus remains faithful to its etymology.

■ See Box 1.

II. The Term's Philosophical Freight

A. Fichte: *Das Sehnen*, the aspiration of the self

It is in this lexical landscape that the reflections of Fichte and the Romantics about *Sehnsucht* developed in Germany, along with Hegel's rigorous critique of the notion. *Das Sehnen* played an important role in the first version of Fichte's *Wissenschaftslehre* (1794–95). The word is usually translated into French by *aspiration*, but the reference is to an aspiration that is a feeling, or else to a nostalgia that is an aspiration. For Fichte the constraints and limitations imposed on the Ego lead it to reflect on what impels it irresistibly toward objects external to itself.

We call such a determination in the Ego an aspiration (*Sehnen*); a tendency (*Trieb*) toward something absolutely unknown, which manifests itself only as a need (*Bedürfnis*), a disquiet (*Unbehagen*), a void (*Leere*) that seeks to fulfill itself and which does not indicate what

would allow this fulfillment. The Ego feels an aspiration; it feels a lack in itself.

(Fichte, *Gesamtausgabe*.)

In his *System of Ethics* (*System der Sittenlehre*, 1798), Fichte similarly defines *das Sehnen* as the indeterminate sensation (*Empfindung*) of a need (that is, one that is not determined by any concept of an object) or as a "feeling (*Gefühl*) of a need that we do not ourselves know. We lack something, but we don't know what."

Aspiration, nostalgia directed toward the future, is precisely what permits the Ego to feel within itself the existence of an outside. It is only through *das Sehnen*, Fichte writes, that "the Ego is pushed outside itself; it is only by *das Sehnen* that an outside world is revealed within the Ego" (ibid.). Whereas the feeling of constraint forces the Ego to perceive itself solely as a passive figure (it undergoes limitation), "in the feeling of aspiration it is also perceived as active" (ibid.). In this context *das Sehnen* is a powerful source of energy that drives the Ego to transform the outside world: "The object of *das Sehnen* is something other, something that opposes the existent. In *das Sehnen*, ideality and tendency toward reality are intimately connected" (ibid.). Here we should emphasize that it is the choice of the nominalized verb *das Sehnen* that allows Fichte to confer a dynamic and active value on a lexical field that originally stressed the subject's suffering.

B. The infinity of Romantic *Sehnsucht*

The idea that *das Sehnen* has a genuine creative power was adopted by the authors of the early Romantic period. The privilege that it acquired in Fichte's theory of knowledge was transferred to the more psychological or anthropological

---

1

Nostos and nostalgia

The English word "nostalgia," like the French *nostalgie*, was "borrowed by physicians (1759) from the modern scientific Latin *nostalgia*, coined in 1678 by the Swiss physician J. J. Harder." And this Latin term was invented to translate "the Alemannic *Heimweh*, the 'homesickness' [see HEIMAT] felt by the Swiss who were abroad, especially mercenaries" (RT: DHLF, s.v.). "Nostalgia" thus derives from Swiss Latin, coined on the basis of Greek—even if the compound term is not itself Greek—*nostos* [νόστος] ("return") and *algos* [ἄλγος] ("suffering, pain"), on the model of medical terms that describe diseases in terms of the organ affected, such as "neuralgia" and "lumbago."

Nostos is derived from *neomai* [νέομαι] ("to come back, return") and comes from a root whose active meaning is supposed to be "to save": this is shown in particular by the name *Nestor*, "one who comes safely home, who succeeds in bringing back his army" (see Chantraine's

comparisons with Germanic, Old High German, and Anglo-Saxon, and with the Sanskrit *násate*, "to approach, unite with" RT: *Dictionnaire étymologique de la langue grecque*).

Nostos appears, obviously, in Homer's *Odyssey*. A *nostimos* [νόστιμος] is "one who is capable of returning": the question is whether Odysseus—and then Telemachus who has gone in search of him—is a *nostimos* (IV, 806; XIX, 85), or whether he has been deprived (*apheileto* [ἀφείλετο]) of "the day of return" (*nostimon êmar* [νόστιμον ἦμαρ], I, 168, 354), whether he has lost it (*ôileto* [ὤλετο], *apólese* [ἀπώλεσε], I, 168, 354). In the first lines of Book I, the motif is already presented:

By now, all the survivors, all who avoided headlong death were safe at home [*oikoi* [οἴκοι]], escaped the wars and waves.
  But one man alone . . . his heart set on his wife and his return [*nostou*

kechrêmenon êde gunaikos (νόστου κεχρημενον ἠδὲ γυναικός)]—Calypso, the bewitching nymph, the lustrous goddess, held him back.

(*Odyssey*, trans. R. Fagles, I, 13–18)

Calypso, the "enveloping, the covering," loves and cares for Odysseus, promises him that he will be "immortal and young forever"; but as Odysseus tells Alcinous, "she never won the heart inside me, never. / Seven endless years I remained there, always drenching / with my tears the immortal clothes Calypso gave me" (VII, 97–99).

Here we see the complex motif that links nostalgia not only with the desire for return and with the tedium of separation from home but also to the obstacle, to the desire of the other, and to the desire for immortality.

Barbara Cassin

term *Sehnsucht*. In one of his last writings, Friedrich von Schlegel makes the feeling of *Sehnsucht* the source of almost "everything that is grand and beautiful in the domain of the spirit" (Schlegel, *Kritische*, 10: 33; in addition to the texts cited here, cf. especially ibid., 11: 123; 12: 392, 430f.). In his work *Die Anweisung zum seligen Leben oder auch die Religionslehre* (*The Way towards the Blessed Life; or, the Doctrine of Religion*), Fichte himself had made "longing (*Sehnsucht*) for the eternal" a kind of vital principle, "the deepest root of all finite existence" (Fichte, *Gesamtausgabe*). Nothing can quench this inner thirst in man: "the object of true *Sehnsucht* can only be inaccessible," Goethe wrote (*Dichtung und Wahrheit*, 10: 54; see also *Hamburger Ausgabe*, 7: 240, and the poem *Selige Sehnsucht* [Blessed longing] in ibid., 2: 19, first stanza: "Don't tell anyone about it, except the wise / For the crowd is quick to mock: / I want to praise the Living / Who longs to die in the flame"—but we must emphasize that Goethe distances himself from all this praise of nostalgic longing).

Fichte, and then Schleiermacher and Friedrich von Schlegel, conferred on this principle a strong metaphysical and religious dimension: for Schlegel, *Sehnsucht* is "a vague feeling of the deepest longing" (*ein unbestimmtes Gefühl des tiefsten Verlangens*), which no truly terrestrial object, or even any ideal, could satisfy, since it is directed toward the eternal and more generally toward the divine" (Schlegel, *Kritische*, 10: 32). (In his famous *Dialogue on Poetry* [*Gespräch über die Poesie*, 1800], the young Schlegel had already emphasized that *Sehnsucht* constantly renews itself (ibid., 2: 284; cf. Lacoue-Labarthe and Nancy, *L'Absolu littéraire*, 290). True *Sehnsucht* knows no limits, but instead, "climbing step by step, never ceases to rise further" (*Philosophy of Language and the Word*, 1828–29, in Schlegel, *Kritische*, 10: 398). It is hardly surprising to learn that, by means of a circular movement entirely characteristic of Schlegel's thought, this engine that drives us toward the divine is itself of divine origin (ibid., 10: 33).

C. Hegel: *Sehnsucht* and the unhappy consciousness

By emphasizing the dynamic aspect of *Sehnsucht*, Romantic thought thus tends to erase somewhat the element of suffering and passivity. For Hegel this longing is, on the contrary, one of the chief manifestations of the unhappy consciousness. In the *Phenomenology of Mind*, the depreciation of *Sehnsucht* is part of the criticism of Fichte and the Romantic thinkers. When we consider the unhappy consciousness as pure consciousness,

> it takes up towards its object an attitude which is not that of thought; but rather (since it is indeed in itself pure thinking particularity and its object is just this pure thought, but pure thought is not their relation to one another as such), it, so to say, merely gives itself up to thought, devotes itself to thinking (*geht an das Denken hin*), and is the state of Devotion (*Andacht*). Its thinking as such is no more than the discordant clang of ringing bells, or a cloud of warm incense, a kind of thinking in terms of music, that does not get the length of notions, which would be the sole, immanent, objective mode of thought. This boundless pure inward feeling comes to have indeed its object; but this object does not make its appearance in conceptual form, and therefore comes

on the scene as something external and foreign. Hence we have here the inward movement of pure emotion [*Gemüth*] which feels itself, but feels itself in the bitterness of soul-redemption. It is the movement of infinite Yearning [*Sehnsucht*], which is assured that its nature is a pure emotion of this kind, a pure thought which thinks itself as particularity—a yearning that is certain of being known and recognized by this object, for the very reason that this object thinks itself as particularity. At the same time, however, this nature is the unattainable "beyond" which, in being seized, escapes or rather has already escaped.

(Hegel, *Phenomenology of Mind*, 257–58)

We find the same point of view and the same implicit criticism of Fichte, Schleiermacher, Schlegel, and Schelling not only in Hegel's analysis of the "beautiful soul" that "flees contact with actuality" and whose sole activity is "languishing" (*das Sehnen*) (ibid., 354), but also in his *Aesthetics*, where he citicizes the modern tendency to privilege the distant:

> The Greeks' divine, correct way of thinking did not consider going out toward the distant and indeterminate [*das Hinausgehen ins Weite und Unbestimmte*], in the manner of the modern sentiment of nostalgia [*Sehnsucht*], as the *nec plus ultra* for man, but rather as a kind of damnation, and relegated it to Tartarus.

(Hegel, *Sämtliche Werke*, 13: 55)

In the *Aesthetics* Hegel also condemns the "languorous nostalgia" (*Sehnsuchtigkeit*, a depreciative derivative coined by Hegel) of the Romantic authors who wanted to rediscover the naïveté of popular poetry (ibid., 14: 202) and of Novalis, a nostalgia "that does not consent to lower itself to actual action and actual production, because it fears being soiled by contact with finitude" (ibid., 12: 221).

Christian Helmreich

BIBLIOGRAPHY

Baudelaire, Charles. "Le joueur généreux." [1864], in *Petits poèmes en prose*, edited by Robert Kopp, 99. Paris: Gallimard, 1973. Poem first published in 1864.

Corbineau-Hoffmann, A. "Sehnsucht." In *Historisches Wörterbuch der Philosophie*. Edited by Joachim Ritter and Karlfriend Gründer. Basel, Switz.: Schwabe, 1971–2007.

Fichte, Johann Gottlieb. *Fichte: Early Philosophical Writings*. Translated and edited by Daniel Breazeale. 2nd ed. Ithaca, NY: Cornell University Press, 1993.

———. *Gesamtausgabe der bayerischen Akademie der Wissenschaften*. Edited by R. Reinhard. Stuttgart: Frommann-Holzboog, 1962.

———. *Œuvres choisies de philosophie première. Doctrine de la science (1794–1797)*. Translated by A. Philonenko. 3rd ed. Paris: Vrin, 1990.

———. *The System of Ethics in accordance with the Principles of the Wissenschaftslehre*. Edited and translated by Daniel Breazeale and Günter Zöller. Cambridge: Cambridge University Press, 2005.

———. *The Way Towards the Blessed Life; or, the Doctrine of Religion* [*Die Anweisung zum sieligen Leben, oder auch die Religionslehre*]. Translated by William Smith. In *The Popular Works of Johann Gottlieb Fichte*, edited by Daniel Breazeale. Bristol, Eng.: Thoemes Press, 1999.

Goethe, Johann Wolfgang von. *Dichtung und Wahrheit*. Vol. 12 of *Werke, Hamburger Ausgabe*. Edited by Erich Trunz. Munich: Beck, 1981. *Works. English & German*. New York: Suhrkamp/Insel , 1983–.

———. *Poetry and Truth from My Own Life*. Translated by Minna Steel Smith. London: G. Bell, 1930.

Hegel, Georg Wilhelm Friedrich. *Aesthetics: Lectures on Fine Art*. Vol. 2. Translated by T. M. Knox. Oxford: Clarendon Press, 1998.

———. *Phänomenologie des Geistes*. Edited by Wolfgang Bonsiepen and Reinhard Heede. Hamburg: Meiner, 1980. Translation by J. R. Baillie: *Phenomenology of Mind*. Rpt. New York: Harper, 1967. First published in 1910.

———. *Sämtliche Werke*. 26 vols. *Jubiläumausgabe*. Stuttgart: F. Fromman, 1927–1940.

Hogrebe, Wolfram. "Sehnsucht und Erkenntnis." In *Fichtes Wissenschaftslehre 1794. Philosophische Resonanzen*, 50–67. Frankfurt: Suhrkamp, 1995.

Homer. *Odyssey*. Translated by R. Fagles, Harmondsworth, Eng.: Viking Penguin, 1996.

Lacoue-Labarthe, Philippe, and Jean-Luc Nancy. *L'Absolu littéraire*. Paris: Éditions du Seuil, 1978.

Pöggeler, Otto. *Hegels Krikit der Romantik*. Munich: W. Fink, 1999.

Schlegel, Friedrich von. *Kritische Friedrich von Schlegel Ausgabe*. 35 vols. Edited by E. Behler. Munich: F. Schöningh, 1958–2002.

———. *The Philosophy of Life and Philosophy of Language in a Course of Lectures*. Translated by A. Morrison. London: H. G. Bohn, 1847.

SEIN / SOSEIN / AUSSERSEIN (GERMAN)

ENGLISH   being / being so / beyond being

➤ *TO BE*, and DASEIN, ES GIBT, *FICTION*, GEGENSTAND, INTENTION, *NOTHING*, OBJECT, REALITY, REPRÉSENTATION, RES, SACHVERHALT, WERT

In the post-Kantian era, the vocabulary of being was redistributed within the horizon of the object, in conformity with the Kantian injunction to substitute an "analytic of pure understanding" for the "pretentious name of ontology." The phenomenon, which was already present in neo-Kantianism, in Lotze, and in Nathorp, would know a development particularly rich in distinctions in the school of Franz Brentano, where the elucidation of the doctrine of intentionality (see INTENTION) would meet up with the Bolzanian problematic of "representations without object" (*gegenstandlose Vorstellungen*). As a consequence a significant sector of German and Austro-Hungarian philosophy would revisit the Hegelian division between *Realität* and *Wirklichkeit*, reality and effectivity (see REALITY), and introduce or redefine a new lexicon that, even as it harkened back to ancient tradition (Porphyry, Boethius, Latin Scholasticism of the thirteenth century), would impose on various European languages a difficult terminological innovation exemplified in Alexius Meinong's distinction between *Sein*, *Sosein*, and *Aussersein*.

I. Being and Object-Being: From Ontology (the Science of *On Hê On*) to the Theory of the Object (*Gegenstandslehre*)

In his *Metaphysics*, through generalization and universalization, Aristotle distinguished the mode of knowledge that focused universally on being as being, or rather, on the existent only insofar as it can be characterized as existent, from all other regional or specialized sciences, which envisage existents only *en merei* [ἐν μέρει], according to a determined perspective and by selecting a "sample." By 1888, against an explicitly neo-Kantian horizon, Paul Nathorp had already retranscribed Aristotle's ontological investigations in terms of objects:

That supreme (because most general and most abstract) object is, as we learn in the fundamental concept of the "object in general" (*Gegenstand überhaupt*), for it is thus

that we are able, so to speak, in Kantian terms, to restore the Aristotelian *on hê*.

(Natorp, "Thema und Disposition der aristotelischen Metaphysik," 39)

K. Twardowski, in his celebrated short work of 1894 (*Zur Lehre vom Inhalt und Gegenstand der Vorstellungen*, Vienna, 1894), similarly repeated Aristotle's gesture, retranslating it into a lexicon of object and objecthood, as it was opened up at the time by a consideration of representation (*Vorstellung*) in its complex intentional structure, oriented as it was toward a content (*Inhalt*) and an object (*Gegenstand*):

What particular sciences are concerned with, to be sure, are nothing but the objects of our representations (*die Gegenstände unserer Vorstellungen*). . . . On the other hand, a science which draws into the circle of its considerations all objects, those that are physical, organic and inorganic as well as those that are psychical, those that are real (*realen*) as well as those that are not real (*nicht realen*), those that exist as well as those that do not exist, and which searches for the laws obeyed by those objects in general—and not just a determinate group of them—, such is metaphysics. . . . Such is the meaning of the venerable definition according to which metaphysics is the science of the existent as such (*Wissenschaft vom Seienden als solchen*).

(Twardowski, *Zur Lehre*, 39)

The theory of the object would thus take over from metaphysics, or more precisely from ontology, even if the process as evoked here by Twardowski is plainly rudimentary as compared to the complex and subtle deployment of *Gegenstandtheorie* (1904), in which Meinong would attempt far more judiciously to distinguish between "theory of the object" and "ontology" and to situate ontology itself, in the Aristotelian tradition, as a restricted segment in a far more comprehensive consideration of the *Gegenstand* and its modalities.

A. Translating being into the lexicon of objecthood

If Twardowski did not resolutely move the theory of the object outside of metaphysics, constituting it as an extra-ontological doctrine, it was no doubt because he had retained the classical identification, dating from Thomas Aquinas, between (*On Truth*, 1, 1) *ens* and *aliquid*:

Der Gegenstand ist etwas anderes als das Existierende; manchen Gegenständen kommt neben ihrer Gegenständlichkeit, neben Beschaffenheit, vorgestellt zu werden (was der eigentliche Sinne des Wortes "essentia" ist), auch noch die Existenz zu, anderen nicht. Sowohl was existiert ist ein Gegenstand (*ens habens actualem existentiam*) als auch, was nur existieren könnte (*ens possibile*), ja selbst was niemals existieren, sondern nur vorgestellt werden kann (*ens rationis*), ist ein Gegenstand, kurz, alles was nicht nichts, sondern in irgend einem Sinne "etwas" ist, ist ein Gegenstand. Thatsächlich erklärt die Mehrzahl der Scholastike "aliquid" für gleichbedeutend mit "ens," und zwar im Gegensatz zu denjenigen, welche ersteres als ein Attribut des letzteren auffassen.

(The object is something other than an existent: to numerous objects, in addition to their objectity, to their capacity to be represented (which is the literal meaning of the word "essentia") there attaches existence as well, and to others, not. An object can be what exists (*ens habens actualem existentiam*) as what could exist (*ens possibile*), and even what could never exist, but only be conceived (*ens rationis*); an object, in sum, is everything that is not nothing, but is in any sense "something," an object. In point of fact, a majority of the scholastics regard "aliquid" as a synonym of "ens," and that in opposition to those who regard the former as an attribute of the latter.)

(Twardowski, *Zur Lehre*, 37–38)

B. Object and existence

Bertrand Russell, for his part (and the point is worth emphasizing), wrote in the *Principia Mathematica* in 1903:

Being is that which belongs to every conceivable term, to every possible object of thought—in short to everything that can possibly occur in any proposition true or false, and to all such propositions themselves. ... "A is not" implies that there is a term: A, whose being is denied, and hence that A is. ... Numbers, the Homeric gods, relations, chimeras and four-dimensional spaces, all have being, for if they were not entities of a kind, we could make no propositions about them. Thus being is a general attribute of everything, and to mention anything is to show that it is. Existence, on the contrary, is the prerogative of some only among beings.

(Russell, Allen & Unwin, 1937, 2nd ed., 136)

He rejoins in this passage the long tradition which, from Thomas Aquinas to Kant, distinguishes, in the critique of the ontological argument, being or entity (*aliquid*) and existence, which cannot be counted among the predicates of reality (see DASEIN).

II. Object and Something
(*Gegenstand, Etwas, Bestand*)

The reference to the doctrines of Scholasticism and the metaphysics of Aristotle was initially intended, within the economy of Kazimierz Twardowski's essay (*Zur Lehre*), to specify the meaning of the term "object" (*Gegenstand*), but ended up opening onto "something" (*etwas*) whose status and whether or not it depended on an intentional or constitutive subject were both unknown:

An object can be approximately described in the following manner: anything that can be represented by a representation, acknowledged or rejected by a judgment, desired or detested by an affective act we call an object. Objects are real or not real (*real oder nicht real*); they are possible or impossible; they exist or do not exist. They all have in common the fact of being able to be or not be an object (*Objekt*) (but *not* an intentional object), of psychical acts and are designated in language by a name ...; considered as a family (*Gattung*), they form the *summum genus* that finds its customary expression in language

in "something" (*etwas*). All that is "something," in the broadest sense, is so called, first of all, in relation to a subject that thinks it, but, subsequently, independently of that object, an "object" (*Gegenstand*).

(Ibid., 40)

Alexius Meinong, more resolutely still than Twardowski in his essay of 1894, took up in his own terms the project of a theoretical treatment of the object as such, in a move that generalized and extended it beyond ontology, assumed to be too narrow because too linked to actuality (*Wirklichkeit*) (see REALITY).

For Meinong if one is to elaborate a general science of the object, it is consequently important to distinguish it from metaphysics, which is not universal enough to encompass the complete treatment of the *reiner Gegenstand* (pure object) (*Übergegenstandstheorie*, in *Gesamtausgabe*, vol. 2). Traditionally, metaphysics is undoubtedly concerned with everything that is, but that totality is confused with the set of all that exists, including what has existed or will exist; but that set is infinitely small compared with the totality of *Erkenntnisgegenstände* (objects of knowledge). Limited to the real, to what exists, has existed, or will exist, metaphysics is fundamentally always *Daseinsmetaphysik* (metaphysics of being-there, of existence). From this it follows that it is legitimate to distinguish a *daseinsfreie Metaphysik* (a metaphysics freed from existence), which it would be appropriate to rebaptize, in order to avoid all confusion, a "theory of the object." The theory of the object should include in particular ideal objects having a certain consistency (*Bestand*) and of which it can be said that they subsist (*bestehen*), but which nonetheless do not exist (*existieren*), which are nothing actual (*wirklich*), such as number, equality, difference, etc. Meinong thus eschews Twardowski's awkwardness in seeking to determine the *Gegenstand* as *summum genus*: the desire to define the object formally is without meaning, he notes, since both *genus* and *differentia* are lacking, if it is true that everything is object (*alles ist Gegenstand*).

It is thus important to proceed to a broadening of the sphere of the object beyond even that of being and nonbeing, a broadening intent on breaking with the ontology of Aristotelian tradition, in conformity with the provocative and paradoxical formula: "es gibt Gegenstände, von denen gilt, daß es dergleichen Gegenstände nicht gibt" (Meinong, *Gesamtausgabe*, 2: 490).

Before proposing a translation, let us attempt to unravel the paradox of the formula, whose backdrop is constituted by the distinction, at the heart of the vocabulary of being, among:

- *existieren*, which applies to objects said to be real or actual;
- *bestehen*, which is applied to "objectives" (*Objektive, Sachverhalt* [see SACHVERHALT]);
- *Sosein* (so-being), which applies to nonreal, but possible, entities, such as a "golden mountain," concerning which it is always permissible to determine the being-such or so-being, independently of being (*Sein*);
- *Außersein* (outside-being), which applies to contradictory entities such as a "square circle," entities that are not purely and simply nothing but retain in themselves an ultimate positional residue.

Whereas metaphysics limited itself to what effectively exists, it befell the theory of the object to bring fully to light the independence of *Sosein* (so-being) in relation to its indifference in relation to being, beyond being, and nonbeing.

The neologism *Außersein* is thus intended first of all to resolve the paradox of the governing formula, as Meinong explains in *Über Annahmen*:

Our grasp (*Ergreifen*) finds in objects something pre-given (*etwas vorgegeben*), without its being necessary to take into account the matter of knowing how the question of their being or nonbeing is decided. In this sense, "there are" also objects that are not, which I attempted to designate by an expression that is a bit barbarous, but I could not find a better one: namely, the "outside-being" (*Außersein*) of the pure object. The term is a response to the effort to interpret the strange "*es gibt*," which can not, it appears, be denied even to the objects most foreign to being (*seinsfremdeste Gegenstände*), without it becoming necessary to resort to a third type of being, in addition to existence (*Existenz*) and subsistence (*Bestand*). But since then I have on more than one occasion had the very distinct sense that such an effort could not come to terms with the specific positivity (*eigentümliche Positivität*) that appears to be a function of the pre-given character (*Vorgegebenheit*) of any object available in theory to being grasped and conceived. It is upon consideration of this point that I am obliged to envisage expressly the eventuality of there possibly being, beyond existence and subsistence, a third mode, which can no longer be called being, and which, finally, must be characterized as something related to being (*etwas Seinsartiges*) in the broadest sense of the term. What remains to be decided is precisely the question of knowing whether this *Außersein* ("outside-being") itself is an ontological determination or if it indicates only that such a determination is lacking.

(Meinong, *Gesamtausgabe*, 2nd ed., 4:79–80)

The principle of the independence of so-being or suchness (*Sosein*) is to be understood first of all in this sense: the fact that an object has properties in no way implies that that object itself *is*, that is, that it exists *extra mentem* or *extra causas*. But that weak version of the principle of independence is insufficient to characterize the position defended by Meinong, since it simply brings us back to the Scholastic, pre-Kantian position of *realitas*. In the strong version of the thesis, independence is a property of the object in relation to mind and its intentions; the object, considered in what should no longer be termed its "being," unless in a sense that is too broad and inadequate, is indeed "apprehended," "but precisely not constituted": not being constituted, neither does the object have the classic status of objective being, which always ultimately turns on the extra-mental *res* and is distinguished from the *ens rationis*. If it is not possible to give a formal definition of the object, etymology can come to our aid: for the *Gegen-stehen* (standing against) of the *Gegen-stand* brings us back to the lived experience of apprehending the object (should we say the *ob-stant*?), an experience that cannot be envisaged as *constitutive* in any sense at all. Meinong insists

on the anteriority of the object as such (*objeto*, entity, Grossmann) independently of the question of knowing whether we are dealing with an object, which might trivially be called real, with an ideality, or with a being of reason, in its status a *fictum*, *figmentum* (see *FICTION*).

In relation to apprehension (*dem Erfassen gegenüber*), the *object* (*Gegenstand*) is what is in every case *logically anterior*, even when the object in question logically comes after apprehension. This is why apprehension can never create its object or even modify it, but can merely select it, so to speak, by extracting it from the multiplicity of what has been given in advance (at least as foreign to being).

(Meinong, *Personal Presentation*)

Thus the principle of the independence of so-being or suchness finds its true bearing only if applied not only to possible objects but also to *impossibilia*, once it is accepted that the suchness of an object is not affected by its nonbeing (*Nichtsein*); such nonbeingness (*Nichtseiendes*) suffices to procure for the judgment apprehending it its "nonbeing."

If I say "blue does not exist," I am thinking only of blue and not of a sample of blue or of the qualities and possibilities that it might present. It is as though blue should possess being *in the first place* (*erst einmal*), before any possibility of raising the question of its being or non-being. ... Blue or any other object is in some sense given prior to our decision concerning its being, and it is given in a way that does not prejudge its non-being. ... In order to be able to affirm that a given object is not, it appears that the object must be understood, in a sense, *in advance* (den Gegenstand ... erst einmal ergreifen) in order to speak of its nonbeing, or, more precisely, to defend or deny the attribution of nonbeing to that object.

(Meinong, "Theory of Objects")

Indeed, if, concerning any "given" object, I am to judge that it is not, it is necessary that I be able to apprehend the object in a first instance in order to attribute to it the predicate of nonbeing, or more precisely to impute or deny that predicate to it. It is thus necessary to introduce still another level or understanding of "being," in addition to those of existence or subsistence; one that was first named by Meinong "quasi-being" (*Quasisein*), then "beyond being and nonbeing" (*jenseits von Sein und Nichtsein*), which is appropriate to the pure object, or even exterior to being, outside-being (*Außersein*). Being is exterior to the pure object, as opposed to so-being or suchness: "What is in no way foreign to the object and constitutes, to the contrary, its true essence, resides in its suchness, which adheres to the object, whether it be or not be [Dasjenige, was dem Gegenstand in keiner Weise äußerlich ist, vielmehr sein eigentliches Wesen ausmacht, besteht in seinem Sosein, das dem Gegenstande anhaftet, mag er sein oder nicht sein]."

III. *Es Gibt, Es Gilt*

One must keep in mind the irreducible dimension of donation, of being given, even pre-given, if one is to interpret rigorously Meinong's paradox: "Es gibt Gegenstände, von denen gilt, daß es dergleichen Gegenstände nicht gibt."

It is a paradox whose translation is only apparently obvious. We may say, with Findlay, that "there are objects concerning which it is the case that there are no such objects," while completely losing sight of the subtle interplay between the first *geben*, the *gelten*, and the second *geben*. Let us begin with the *gelten*, recalling, in the present context, the distinctions of H. Lotze:

> We shall call actual (*wirklich*) a thing that *is,* in opposition to another that *is* not; actual is also an event taking place (*ein Ereigniß welches geschieht*) or which has taken place, in opposition to another that fails to occur; actual a relation that subsists (*besteht*), as opposed to one that does not subsist; finally, we call actually true (*wirklich wahr*) a proposition of *value* (*ein Satz welcher gilt*) as opposed to one whose validity (*Geltung*) is still in doubt.
>
> (Lotze, *Logik vom Erkennen,* 511)

Gelten, in this case, understood as a kind of actuality, corresponds to a meaning of being (ὄν, εἶναι) said to be veracious but which applies here to propositions ("Wahrheiten *sind* nicht, sondern *gelten* nur [truths *are* not, but only bear value]," ibid., 578). The problematic horizon in which Meinong's terminological and doctrinal decision is situated is quite clear: *gelten* corresponds to the veritative sense of being: "it is true that . . ."; "it is the case"; "it is thus." The last *es gibt*, in the articulation of the paradox, can be understood in the broadest and most common sense of being: "there are objects for which, it is the case: such objects are not, do not exist." Thus the truly problematic element in the formulation of Meinong's paradox is the first *es gibt*, which is very poorly rendered by the French *il y a* or the English "there is." In point of fact, with that *es gibt* we are in the presence of an elementary figure—as tenuous as might be liked, reduced to almost nothing, but precisely not to nothing at all—of the gift or of being given.

■ See Box 1.

IV. The Extra-Ontological

It remains, in the strict framework of the theory of the object, that the ultimate rule—imposing itself a priori as a final instance—is this singular "given": objects for which it is *valid* to claim that they are not, and of which, thus composed, in their being-so or suchness, *there are none*; such objects cannot *be,* or better, being (*das Sein*) cannot be attributed to them in a judgment, neither as a property, nor as an accident. And yet that irreducible given or pre-given—it "resists," and that characteristic might well be the final word concerning *Außersein*—must be understood in the strong sense: it imposes itself on us, offering itself a priori to every act of apprehension, it is that from which, in a quasi-empirical manner, we must necessarily take off. This is why Meinong can adopt for his

---

1

Heidegger's *es gibt*

➤ ES GIBT, *IL Y A*

Far be it from us, needless to say, to entertain the grotesque idea of linking *es gibt* in Meinong with the Heideggerian *es gibt*, as it appears, well before the final variations of *Zeit und Sein,* in *Sein und Zeit,* in order to indicate—in quotation marks that need be interpreted, moreover—that being "is" not, but that "there is" being.

It was not Meinong, but Emil Lask who engaged the young Heidegger on the path of *es gibt*; his first course at Freiburg (1919, in *Gesamtausgabe,* 56–57, *Zur Bestimmung der Philosophie*) proposes, in fact, a long analysis of *es gibt,* which begins with a variation on *gelten* (ibid., 50ff.), before opening onto the question: "Gibt es das 'es gibt'?" [Is there a "there is"?]. Emil Lask envisaged the category of *Es-geben* ("there being") as that of reflection (reflexive *Gegenständlichkeit*). Opening on to pure objectality prior to any determination of an object (Lask, *Logik der Philosophie,* 130, 142, 162), that is, as the elementary category of a "something" (*etwas*) that constitutes the minimum required for anything apt to be subsequently presented as a categorically defined object; thus the *il y a,* "there is," of pure objectality, is opposed, "objected," to reflection so that the latter can be exercised. The "something" (*etwas*) or "it" (*es*) of *es gibt* thus furnishes a material still "logically bare," "a-logical," and prior to any possibility of applying formal categories.

But it may also be wondered to what extent the question elaborated by Heidegger in the 1919 course "Gibt es das 'es gibt'?" echoes the critique formulated by Paul Natorp in his revised edition—which was known to Heidegger—of Husserl's *Ideen I* (*Logos,* 7: 224–46, 1917–1918)—the original given or the final giving, which furnished Husserl with his "principle of principles" (*Ideen I,* 24):

> daß jede originär gebende Anschauung eine Rechtsquelle der Erkenntnis sei, daß alles, was sich uns in der "Intuition" originär . . . darbietet, einfach hinzunehmen sei, als was es sich gibt, aber auch nur in den Schranken, in denen es sich da gibt.
>
> ([The principle of principles affirms] that every originary presentive intuition is a legitimizing source of cognition, that everything originarily (so to speak, in its "personal" actuality) offered to us in "intuition" is to be accepted simply as what it is presented as being, but also only within the limits in which it is presented there.)

Natorp opposed the very process of thought in its discursiveness:

> *Der Prozeß selbst ist das "Gebende"* für die . . . "Prinzipien"; nur so "gibt" es, "gibt" sich (wie andere Sprachen sagen) Gegebenes.
>
> (*The process itself is what "gives". . .* in relation to principles; it is only thereby that there is, that the given (as is said in other languages) is given.)
>
> (In Husserl, *Wege der Forschung,* ed. H. Noack, Darmstadt: Wissenschaftliche Buchgesellschaft, 1973, 43)

There can thus be no "completed presentation or giving (*fertige Gegebenheit*)," which would be like a polar star for thought; such fixed stars, as Natorp emphasizes, are never more than planets of a higher order: "So ist nichts, sondern wird nur etwas 'gegeben' [thus nothing is 'given,' but all that is given is such only insofar as it becomes it]" (ibid., p. 42).

own purposes the idea of a philosophy that would begin from below, that is, from what is irreducibly given, even if foreign to being (*außerseiend*). There is thus given, but outside-being, this which is valid and is true: certain objects are not, and that in such manner that their "beyond being-and-non-being" is itself capable of being given. Meinong, in fact, strained to give a more easily acceptable formulation of his "paradox" by introducing the singular concept of *Außersein*, which was precisely intended to reduce the paradox: "He who is inclined to paradox might very well say that there are objects concerning which it can be affirmed that there are none."

The obvious solution for neutralizing the paradox—one against which the theory of the object was precisely elaborated—would consist in interpreting the first *es gibt* (there are objects) in the trivial sense of an existence in representation or of a pseudo-existence: certain objects are or are possible, for instance, in the divine intellect; others, which are not, have being only in and through representation, as *entia rationis* or *intentionalia*; their "being" is reduced to *objective esse* or pseudo-existence.

■ See Box 2.

But for Meinong the thesis of nonexistence never refers merely to representation or being-represented but indeed to an object, say, *x*, about whose being or non-being it is wondered: "if I am to be able, concerning an object, to judge that it is not, it would appear that I am under the necessity of initially apprehending the object in order to be able to assign to it the predicate of non-being." Or to state it in other terms, and more rigorously: to the objective (or to the state of things: *das Objektive*) that "A is not A" or to the nonbeing of A, a being must nonetheless be attributed, be it only through appeal to the analogy of the relation between the whole and the part (medieval thinkers, grounding themselves in the resources of the infinitive proposition, were able to paraphrase things economically: "objectum hujus 'Deus est Deus' est 'Deum esse Deus'; et hujus 'homo est albus' ... significatum est 'hominem esse album.' ... Hujus 'homo non est asinus' objectum est 'hominem non esse asinum'" (Adam Wodeham, in Perler, *Satztheorien*, 296–98). We translate, with emphasis: "the object of this, that is, the state-of-things described by the proposition 'God is God' is 'God-to-be-God'; and the complex signified of the proposition 'the man is white' is 'man-to-be-white'; the object or state-of-things of the proposition: 'man is not a donkey' is 'man-not-to-be-donkey.'"

Taking the objective (*das Objektive*) for the whole, if it be, it is necessary that the part, the objectity or *objectum*

2

Rābiṭa (رابطة)

For the word *rābiṭa*, coming from the verb *rabaṭa* (ربط), which means "to connect," the following meanings are listed in dictionaries: "nexus," "tie," "bond," "relation," "league." It has been used specifically in philosophy to translate the Latin word *copula* or the Greek *sumplokê*, which designated the verb "to be," which connects, in different conjugated forms, the subject and the predicate in a proposition under the canonical form "S is P." Aristotle considered such a form to be a logical canon, insisting that if a proposition, for example, "Socrates walks," does not appear under such a form it should be restored to its authentic logical structure (subject, copula, predicate) which is "Socrates is walking."

Why insist on transforming "Socrates walks" into "Socrates is walking"? To manifest the ontological import of what is affirmed, namely that the individual substance Socrates has predicated the attribute "to be walking," which expresses his "posture." And we know that "posture" is precisely one of the ten categories of being, defined by Aristotle as the most fundamental ways in which being is said. The verb "to be" in its different forms is then a crucial element in Aristotle's logic which has been rightly characterized by Robert Blanché as an "onto-logic."

The first translators of Aristotle's *Analytics* into Arabic were fully aware of the profound connection between his logic and his ontology and therefore of the necessity to have a linguistic element indicating the relation between the subject and the predicate. As philosophers in the Muslim world, from Al-Fārābī to Averroës, have explained, in the apophantical assertion in which the subject is a noun and the predicate also a noun, there must be expressed a verb, or any linguistic element serving as a verb, to indicate the relation of the predicate to the subject. And as they well remarked, too, there does not exist in Arabic, unlike, for example, Indo-European languages, a word for that kind of (onto-logical) relation. In Arabic (as in Hebrew), the copula is not expressed in the present tense, and it is more natural to say "Socrates an animal" than "Socrates *is* an animal." In linguistic terms the language uses the zero copula form.

In order to maintain the formal equivalence between the canonical form of Aristotle's logical proposition and its Arabic rendition, the pronoun or a word meaning "existing" is considered as the *rābiṭa* playing the role of the verb "to be." Thus "Socrates *huwa* hayawān," literally meaning "Socrates, he, an animal," or "Socrates *mawjūdun* hayawānan," literally meaning "Socrates is existing as an animal," will be the translations of "Socrates is an animal."

To translate a philosophical tradition into a language unfamiliar with it leads to these sorts of accommodations. The Hellenizing philosophers from the world of Islam realized that in the case of the *rābiṭa*, as well as in other instances. An interesting paradox concerning the copula is found in the rendition of the apophantical assertion in the present tense. Islamic philosophers were concerned to preserve the ontological weight of the copula, in this instance, but their usage undermined it. To have the pronoun serve as a copula is to reduce the latter to a *formal* sign, to being the simple *indication* of a relation. And it is perfectly possible then to see that as a prefiguration of the modern disjunction that will occur in the history of logic between that discipline and ontology, when the copula became a simple sign of relation (represented by an algebraic symbol) defined by certain formal properties.

Bachir Diagne

BIBLIOGRAPHY

Blanche, Robert. *La logique et son histoire d'Aristote à Russell*. Paris: Armand Colin, 1970.
Elamrani-Jamal, Abdelali. *Logique aristotélicienne et grammaire arabe*. Paris: Vrin, 1983.
Mahdi, Muhsin. "Language and Logic in Classical Islam." In *Logic in Classical Islamic Culture*. Edited by Gustav E. von Grunebau, 51–83. Wiesbaden, 1970.

(*Gegenstand*), also be, in a certain manner. From the objective of nonbeing, if it be, there consequently flows the being of objectity. This, it will be agreed, is less to resolve than to deepen the paradox, leading one to posit, if not a third type, at least a third level of being, beyond existence and subsistence, the very one that Meinong himself had at one point called "quasi-being," were it not that such being ("quasi-being") could no longer be opposed to a nonbeing of the same type.

"Can we still," Meinong asks, "call being a being to which no nonbeing, in principle, would be opposed?" ("Theory of Objects"). Are we not rather obliged to give up the analogy between whole/part or even complex/constitutive element and objective/objectity, positing that if the objective of a nonbeing—by which we understand: the being of that objective—is not "assigned to the being of its object," it is because being and nonbeing are not situated at the level of the object. Or more appropriately phrased: that the pure object is beyond being and nonbeing, or that it is foreign to being (*außerseiend*). We are naturally dealing here with the pure object or the object as such—in the minimalism of its *gegenstehen*—a circumstance that in no way contradicts the fact that a specific absurd object (a round square or a goat-deer) bears within itself evidence of its nonbeing, even as ideality does that of its nonexistence. In transferring the full doctrinal difficulty onto the term *Außersein*—which, we have just seen, cannot be simply transcribed into a "beyond being and nonbeing"— Meinong would reduce the paradox with which his name is associated:

> What might be appropriately called the principle of beyond-being of the pure object (*Außersein des reinen Gegenstandes*) definitively dissipates the apparent paradox that furnished the initial motive for the establishment of that principle "the principle of the independence of *Sosein* in relation to *Sein*."
>
> (Ibid.)

It thus follows from the principle of indifference that being or nonbeing do not belong to the nature of the object: the latter is beyond being and nonbeing; it is *außerseiend*, beyond being, outside-being. In truth, if one takes the expression literally, it must be understood that it is less the object that is outside the sphere of being, a sphere to which one is naturally inclined to accord special status, regarding it as primordial, than the couple being/nonbeing that is outside the object: "Sein wie Nichtsein dem Gegenstand gleich äußerlich ist."

Such is the price to be paid for a complete de-ontologization of the object as such.

> If someone, for example, judges that a *perpetuum mobile* does not exist, it is nonetheless quite clear that the object (*Gegenstand*) to which existence has been thus denied must necessarily have properties and even characteristic properties without which the conviction of its non-existence could not have either meaning or justification.
>
> (Meinong, *Über Annahmen*, 12, in *Gasamtausgabe*, 4:79)

It is thus important not to retreat in the face of a conclusion directly opposed to the metaphysical tradition of Avicenna, Aquinas, and Duns Scotus:

> Being is thus precisely not the only condition that would allow the process of knowledge to find its first angle of attack. It is, on the contrary, itself just such an angle of attack. But nonbeing, it turns out, is just as good a one.
>
> (Meinong, "Theory of Objects," 77)

Jean-François Courtine

BIBLIOGRAPHY

Cavallin, Jens. *Content and Object. Husserl, Twardowski, and Psychologism*. Dordrecht, Neth.: Kluwer, 1997.

Findlay, John Niemeyer. *Meinong's Theory of Objects and Values*. Oxford: Clarendon Press, 1963.

Grossmann, Reinhardt. *Meinong*. London: Routledge and Kegan Paul, 1974.

Lask, Emil. *Die Logik der Philosophie und die Kategorienlehre*. 3rd ed. Tübingen: Mohr, 1993.

Lotze, Hermann. *Logik: Drei Bücher vom Denken, vom Untersuchen, und vom Erkennen*. Edited by G. Gabriel. Hamburg: Felix Meiner, 1989. Translated as: *Logic, in Three Books, of Thought, of Investigation, and of Knowledge*. Edited by Bernard Bosanquet. Oxford: Clarendon Press, 1888.

Meinong, Alexius. "The Theory of Objects." In *Realism and the Background of Phenomenology*, edited by Roderick M. Chisholm, 76–117. Glencoe, IL, Free Press, 1960.

———. *Über Annahmen*. Vol. 4 of *Gesamtausgabe*. Graz: Akademie Druck und Verlagsanstalt, 1968–78. Translation by James Heanue: *On Assumptions*. Berkeley: University of California Press, 1983.

Natorp, Paul. "Husserls 'Ideen zu einer reinen Phänomenologie.'" *Logos, Internationale Zeitschrift für Philosophie der Kultur* 7 (1917–18): 224–46.

———. "Thema und Disposition der aristotelischen Metaphysik." *Philosophische Monatshefte* 24 (1888): 37–65, 540–74.

Peña, Lorenzo. *El ente y su ser*. Universidad de Leon, Secretariado de Publicaciones, 1985.

Perler, Domink, ed. *Satztheorien. Texte zur Sprachphilosophie und Wissenschaftstheorie im 14. Jahurhundert, Lateinisch-Deutsch*. Darmstadt: Wissenschaftliche Buchgesellschaft, 1990.

Russell, Bertrand. *The Principles of Mathematics*. 2nd ed. London: Allen and Unwin, 1937.

Schubert Kalsi, Marie-Luise. *Alexius Meinong on Objects of Higher Order and Husserl's Phenomenology*. The Hague: Nijhoff, 1978.

Twardowski, Kazimierz. *On the Content and Object of Presentations: A Psychological Investigation*. Translated by R. Grossmann. The Hague: Nijhoff, 1977.

SELBST (GERMAN)

ENGLISH	self
FRENCH	*soi, soi-même*

➤ *SELF*, and COMBINATION AND CONCEPTUALIZATION, CONSCIOUSNESS, GERMAN, I/ME/MYSELF, *PERSON*, SAMOST', SUBJECT

The root *Selbst* is found in the composition of a large number of philosophical concepts, particularly in Hegel's philosophy, where *Selbstbewusstsein* (self-consciousness) occupies a central and decisive position. Its status as a prefix, which is the most common case, leaves open the question of the relation between the various components of those concepts: is it, for example, a case of consciousness functioning, as it were, on its own, "with complete autonomy," or simply of consciousness having itself as its object? The translation of *selbst* has frequently "oscillated" between those poles, and it would be hard for it to do otherwise.

German etymology sheds light, if any be needed, on the hesitations of translators. *Selb-* is an adjective that is declined (giving *derselbe, dieselbe, dasselbe*: the "same" in the sense of identity), stemming from a root that was undoubtedly a reflexive pronoun (from the family of French *se*), whose adverbial form *selbs* becomes *selbst* in Luther, whereas the transformation of the adverb into a noun (*das Selbst*) intervenes at the very beginning of the eighteenth century, on the model of "the self" in English.

It appears that the use of the concept (a noun) was originally religious: it designated the "odious self," sinful ego, agent of corruption. That negative echo was immediately audible in *selbstisch*, constructed by analogy with *selfish*.

Compounds with *selbst* as a prefix are numerous and common. In philosophy we find in particular *selbstständig, Selbstständigkeit* (autonomous, autonomy), *Selbstbestimmung* (self-determination), *Selbstbetrug* (self-deception), *Selbstbewegung* (spontaneous motion), *Selbsterhaltung* (self-conservation), *Selbsterkenntnis* (self-knowledge), *Selbstgefühl* (feeling of selfhood), *Selbstkritik* (self-criticism), *Selbstmord* (suicide), *Selbstsucht* (egotism), *selbsttätig* (automatic), *Selbstzweck* (containing its end within itself). Depending on the second part of the compound, *selbst* designates the autonomous nature of the operation (*selbstständig, selbsttätig*) or its reflexive object (*Selbstsucht*), or even both simultaneously (*Selbstmord*), which is the most frequent case.

A considerable number of these uses are found in French compounds beginning with *auto-*, with the undoubted exception of those cases in which the second component contains in sufficient measure the dimension of active or operative autonomy for *selbst* in its first sense to be plainly redundant and for the prefix to immediately imply its status as object. Such is the case for *Selbstgefühl* and *Selbstbewusstsein*. In Hegel in particular, in the *Phenomenology*, the transition from simple consciousness to self-consciousness occurs in the very notion of object of consciousness, which functions as subject from the outset but is finally discovered to be such in the chapter thus titled.

The conventional translation of *das Selbst* is "the Self" (Fr. *le Soi*). To be completely rigorous, we would be obliged, however, to indicate that on the one hand, this translation is redundant in relation to that of the reflexive forms of the personal pronoun (corresponding to *sich* in both the accusative and the dative), which the translator regularly needs in order to translate *sich, an sich, für sich, in sich,* etc. Finally, as both adjective and adverb, the root *selb* strongly connotes identity or, if one prefers, the identity of what is the "same" (*die Sache selbst*: the thing itself, *dieselbe Sache*: the same thing), or even what is not to be distinguished from its essence: in the sense of "properly speaking." In French one can thus envisage restoring the connections between self-sameness and identity by reinforcing the *Soi* with the adverb *même*, which presents the interest of leaving the bare reflexive forms available for translating *sich*. *Das Selbst* would thus be "*le Soi-même*"—(the) Oneself—in French, with a capital since "*soi-même*" would have to be retained for *sich selbst*, which is quite frequent!

This configuration is sustained in German by the possibility of using the nominative form of the personal pronoun as a noun (*das Ich*: "the I," as it has been translated in French since Rimbaud (*le Je*), although previously rendered as *Moi* or *Ego*), whereas French—generally unbothered by declensions—has specialized the form: *moi, toi,* and *soi* for such uses. In contrast, *das Selbst* thus becomes a kind of synonym for the concept of the subject: it is the impersonal subject (but not the "id") and thus also the essence. This concept has consequently become the special reserve of phenomenology. It will be noted that Kant makes scant use of it and prefers the classical paradigm derived from Greek—*die Autonomie*—to *Selbstständigkeit*. Current German usage has specialized the noun *das Selbst* in descriptions of behavior: "the *I* conscious of itself."

Jean-Pierre Lefebvre

BIBLIOGRAPHY

Hegel, Georg Wilhelm Friedrich. *Phenomenology of Spirit.* Translated by A. V. Miller. Oxford: Clarendon Press, 1977.

| SELF

At certain moments in its history, the term "self" has posed some interesting problems for translators of philosophy. In 1700 Pierre Coste, the French translator of Locke's *Essay on Human Understanding,* proposed the innovative *soi* in order to simultaneously insist on the reflexive dimension contained in the English *self* and take his distance, following Locke himself, from the *moi* (or ego) introduced by Descartes and Pascal: see CONSCIOUSNESS. Coste also used *soi-même*. That Anglo-French innovation, characteristic of the turn in classical metaphysics toward subjectivity, currently raises four sorts of problems:

1. its relation to the syntax and semantics of European languages
2. associations between *mêmeté* and *ipséité* (to invoke Paul Ricoeur's terminology) in the history of the problematic of identity since its formulations in Greek: see in particular I/ME/MYSELF, Box 2; IDENTITY
3. speculative elaborations of the "subject substance," particularly in German and Russian; see SELBST, SAMOST; cf. SUBJECT, SUPPOSITION
4. fluctuations in the topographical model of the psyche as renewed by psychoanalysis; see ES; cf. DRIVE, UNCONSCIOUS

➤ *IDENTITY, PERSON*

| SEMIOTICS, SEMIOLOGY

FRENCH	*sémiotique/sémiologie*
GERMAN	*Semiotik*
GREEK	*sēmeiōsis* [σημείωσις]

➤ LANGUAGE, and SENSE, SIGN, SIGNIFIER/SIGNIFIED, SPEECH ACT, THING

The existence of the doublet "semiotics/semiology" is derived from the difference in traditions from which each term stems. Semiotics

(*Semiotik*, cf. Lambert, "Semiotik") refers to the Stoic and medieval tradition upon which C. S. Peirce drew, influencing the entire pragmatist tradition (although Peirce himself preferred "pragmaticist" in order to distinguish his thought from James's pragmatism) invoked by C. Morris; whereas semiology derives from Saussure's RT: *Cours de linguistique générale* (1916). There is no established convention regarding the use of the terms, which vary according to schools. Hjelmslevians, for instance, use semiology for everything relating to language and semiotics for everything relating to the general study of signs, whereas Saussurians like J.-L. Prieto retain the broadest extension for the term "semiology." In 1969, however, the International Association of Semiotics recommended using the term "semiotics" for cases entailing a broader extension.

For Saussure, semiology is "a science that studies the life of signs within social life; it would be part of social psychology and, consequently, of general psychology. . . . It would teach us what signs consist in and what laws regulate them. . . . Linguistics is but a part of that general science" (RT: *Cours de linguistique générale*).

The term "semiotics" comes from Locke, who divides science into *Physica, Practica,* and *Semeiotike* (*Essay Concerning Human Understanding,* 4.21.1–4). He identifies semiotics in part with logic: "it is aptly enough termed also Logike, logic: the business whereof is to consider the nature of signs the mind makes use of for the understanding of things, or conveying its knowledge to others." In his "Semiotik" (1764), J. H. Lambert adopts Locke's term but grants "semiotics" a broader extension: it describes all sorts of signs, even if the orientation remains fundamentally cognitive. Peirce uses three terms: "semeiotics," "semeiotic," and "semiotic." Semiotics would be an extension of logic; it is "often identified with logic" ("Ideas, Stray or Stolen, about Scientific Writing [1904]," in *The Essential Peirce: Selected Philosophical Writings,* 2:327); "logic is the study of the essential nature of signs" (ibid., 2:311). The definition of semiotics is as broad as possible: "What I call, semiotic, namely, the doctrine of the essential nature and fundamental varieties of possible semiosis" (Peirce, *Collected Papers,* vol. 5, §488; from statements recorded in 1907). Semiosis (a term which he claims he has borrowed from the "Greek of the Roman period") is, according to him, "the action of practicing any sort of sign" ("Pragmatism [1907]," in *The Essential Peirce,* 2:411). According to Peirce, logic comprises three branches: speculative grammar (a term borrowed from modal logic), critic logic, and methodeutic (a word Peirce preferred to "methodology"). It was speculative grammar that included the general theory of signs. Morris ("Foundations of the Theory of Signs" in *Signs, Language and Behavior*) defines semiotics as a general theory of signs that includes syntax (sign / sign relations, the study of the formal conditions of meaning of combinations of signs), semantics (sign / object relations, the study of the conditions of interpretation), and pragmatics (sign / user relations). R. Carnap (*Meaning and Necessity*) adopted this trichotomy. In Peirce, semiotics tends to be identified with a general grammar of signs, whereas Morris distinguishes different components within semiotics, including the grammatical component.

Émile Benveniste ("Sémiologie de la langue") has interpreted the opposition between Saussurean semiology and Peircean semiotics as a paradigm reflecting the division intrinsic to language itself between a "semiotic mode" and a "semantic mode." The term "semiotics" is thus redefined: "Semiotics designates the signifying mode specific to the linguistic SIGN and constituting it as a unit."

Frédéric Nef

BIBLIOGRAPHY

Benveniste, Émile. "Sémiologie de la langue." Pp. 43–66 in vol. 2 of *Problèmes de linguistique générale.* Paris: Gallimard La Pléiade, 1974.

Carnap, Rudolph. *Meaning and Necessity.* Chicago: University of Chicago Press, 1947.

Lambert, Johann Heinrich. "Semiotik." In vol. 3 of *Neues Organon.* Berlin: Akademie-Verlag, 1990. *Neues Organon* was first published in 1764.

Locke, John. *An Essay Concerning Human Understanding.* Edited by P. H. Nidditch. Oxford: Clarendon Press, 1975.

Morris, Charles. "Foundations of the Theory of Signs." In vol. 1, pt. 2 of *International Encyclopedia of Unified Science.* Chicago: University of Chicago Press, 1938.

———. *Signs, Language and Behavior.* New York: Prentice Hall, 1946.

Peirce, Charles Sanders. *Collected Papers.* 8 vols. Edited by C. Hartshorne and P. Weiss. Cambridge, MA: Harvard University Press / Belknap Press, 1960–66.

———. *Selected Philosophical Writings, 1893–1913.* Vol. 2 of *The Essential Peirce.* Edited by the Peirce Edition Project. Bloomington: Indiana University Press, 1998.

Prieto, Luis-José. *Pertinence et Pratique. Essais de sémiologie.* Paris: Éditions de Minuit, 1975.

Tejera, V. *Semiotics from Peirce to Barthes.* Leiden: Brill, 1988.

SENS COMMUN / COMMON SENSE

I. Ambiguity of "Common Sense"

"Common sense" is an ambiguous notion, between a technical sense originating in Aristotle and referring to sensibility and the convergence of sensations, and a more common meaning referring to "good sense" and the community of men. In point of fact, the expression can be traced back to at least two Latin versions:

1. *Sensus communis,* which translates *koinê aisthêsis* [κοινὴ αἴσθησις] ("perception common" to several senses) comes from Aristotle and involves, on the one hand, the way in which the different senses communicate with each other and, on the other, the way in which one senses what one senses (*sunaisthesis* [συναίσθησις]): see SENSE, I.B, CONSCIOUSNESS, I. *Sensorium commune* is another translation of Aristotle's *koinê aesthêsis,* interpreting it as linked to its own organ, contrary to what Aristotle affirms. Concerning the Scholastic notion and its transition through Arabic, see SENSUS COMMUNIS; cf. *IMAGINATION* [PHANTASIA], INTENTION, PERCEPTION.

2. *Bona mens,* which can be found, for example, in Seneca, and designates correct judgment and even the wisdom that every member of the human community is apt to share. One is thus involved with the positive aspect of Greek *doxa* [δόξα] and, within the individual subject, with "good sense" (resulting in a veritable crisscross between French and Latin usage) and the "natural light" invoked by Descartes or the *gesunder Menschverstand* (healthy understanding): see DOXA, LIGHT, PHRONÊSIS, UNDERSTANDING, *WISDOM.*

Concerning the more directly political aspect of such community, see *COMMUNITY, CONSENSUS, SOCIETY* and cf. LOGOS, MENSCHHEIT, MORALS.

II. "Common Sense" and "Ordinary Life"

The Anglo-Scottish tradition, originating in Shaftesbury and Reid, tended toward a "philosophy of common sense" whose moral and epistemological aspects, converging toward an original analysis of sociability, it developed: see MORAL SENSE and COMMON SENSE; cf. UTILITY. On the link between sociability and "esprit," in the sense of wit, joke, and humor, see NONSENSE and INGENIUM, Box 2. The philosophy of common sense leads to a privileging of the "ordinary": ordinary language and ordinary life; see CLAIM, ENGLISH; cf. MATTER OF FACT, SENSE, V, and SPEECH ACT, IV.

➤ AESTHETICS, COMMONPLACE, GOÛT, PERCEPTION

SENSE / MEANING

FRENCH	*sens*
GERMAN	*Sinn, Bedeutung, Gefühl, Empfindung*
GREEK	*aisthêsis* [αἴσθησις], *nous* [νοῦς], *dianoia* [διάνοια], *sêma* [σῆμα]
ITALIAN	*senso*
LATIN	*sensus, sententia, vis, intellectus, significatio*
SPANISH	*sentido*

➤ CONNOTATION, FEELING, GEFÜHL, HOMONYM, INGENIUM, INTELLECT, INTELLECTUS, INTENTION, LOGOS, MORAL SENSE, NONSENSE, PATHOS, PERCEPTION, *REASON, SENS COMMUN* [COMMON SENSE, SENSUS COMMUNIS], SIGNIFIER/SIGNIFIED, SPEECH ACT, *TO SENSE*, UNDERSTANDING

"Time is the meaning [*le sens*] of life—*sens* as one might say the direction or sense [*sens*] of a current of water, of a sentence, of a fabric, of the sense [*sens*] of smell." That sentence of Paul Claudel (quoted by Cuvillier, *Vocabulaire philosophique*, s.v. "Sens") suggests that the polysemy of *sens* is not random.

The polysemy of the Latin *sensus* lies at the origin of those to be found in the Romance and Anglo-Saxon languages (Fr. *sens*, It. *senso*, Sp. *sentido*, Eng. "sense," Ger. *Sinn*). The semantic field of *sensus*, toward the end of the classical age, articulated three major meanings: (1) sensation, sense perception; (2) understanding, intellectual perception; (3) signification. The articulation did not exist before then: in Greek, the register of *aisthenasthai* [αἰσθάνεσθαι], "to sense," "to perceive," "to notice" (1), is absolutely distinct from that of *semainein* [σημαίνειν], " to signify or mean" (3). And yet it was under the rubric of a Greek term, *nous* [νοῦς], emergent from the second meaning above, that of intellectual perception, that the church fathers, who rendered it as *sensus*, would unify the set.

Moreover, the polysemy did not necessarily evolve in the same fashion later on. One observes two sorts of phenomena. On the one hand there are cases of contamination between the various meanings of "sense," something like a potentially unified semantic flux; this is all the more palpable in French (and, later on, in Italian and German) in that "sense" takes on the additional valence of "direction," so much so that *le bon sens* in French simultaneously denotes "the right direction" and "common sense," which consequently end

up connoting each other (see COMMON SENSE). On the other hand, there are frequently, in any given language, one or several ways of saying one of the senses of "sense," which results in a distinction available to philosophical appropriation, such as between *Sinn* and *Bedeutung*, or "sense" and "meaning." Finally, the articulation between sensation and intellect produces an entire intermediate complex, from inner sense to moral sense, by way of sensitivity and sentiment, that is caught up in the constituted network of each language ("sense," "sentiment," "feeling" [see FEELING], or *Gefühl, Empfindung* [see GEFÜHL]).

I. Greek: Heterogeneity and Amplitude

When one departs from the polysemy of the French *sens*, and already from the Latin *sensus*, what is retrospectively striking in the Greek is, on the contrary, the heterogeneity, without any apparent transition in either language or classical doctrine, between, on the one hand, the register of sense or intellectual perception, or of the external or internal knowledge it might bring, and, on the other hand, the register of sign and signification. The unity that would be effected under the sign of *nous* between outer sense, inner sense, and literal sense was not envisaged, and was perhaps impossible to envisage, in Aristotelian terms at the time the semantic was being theorized as such.

A. The scope of *aisthêsis*

On the other hand, the term *aisthêsis* has an extremely large range of meanings, which makes it difficult to translate with a single term. It is a derivative of *aisthanomai* [αἰσθάνομαι], and the construction of that verb is already revealing: with the genitive, like verbs denoting a sensory act (with the exception of vision), it generally means "to perceive" something; with an object in the accusative, it means "to understand" (Thucydides, 5.26.5), and with the genitive of origin of the person from whom one has information, it means "learning something from someone"; in all cases it implies that one "perceives something" or "perceives that," that one "realizes" (Thucydides, ibid.: "being of an age to realize that," speaking of one's own experience of the war; see CONSCIOUSNESS, Box 1); so much so that when one employs it absolutely, it ends up meaning that one is in possession of one's faculties, of common sense (Thucydides, 1.71.5: *hoi aisthanomenoi* [οἱ αἰσθανόμενοι], "people of common sense [*gens de bon sens*]," Bailly [RT: *Dictionnaire grec français*] advises, whereas J. de Romilly's translation in 1958 gives us no less reasonably "men who will know [*les hommes qui sauront*]").

1. "Hearing" and "sensing"

According to Chantraine (RT: *Dictionnaire étymologique de la langue grecque*), *aisthanomai* comes from *aïô* [ἀΐω] (as witnessed above all in the participle in Homer), based on the Sanskrit *avih*, like the Latin *audio*, which means "to hear," "to perceive" (and less frequently, "to listen, "to obey"). We touch here on the "linguistic" privilege of one or another model of sensation. Thus it is that hearing, more than vision, is initially the determinant sense for Greek *aisthêsis* (Bailly takes the example of Thucydides, 6.17.6: *akoêi aisthanomai* [ἀκοῇ αἰσθάνομαι], "I perceive by hearing, I hear it said"). On the other hand, the French *sentir*, from the Latin *sentire*, is specialized as "perceiving by smell" and "exhaling an odor."

(The RT: *DHLF* mentions *senteur* [scent] and, in game hunting, *sentement*, which designates the sense of smell of hunting dogs and the odor they detect.) To sum up, such examples make manifest the merger or fusion between subject and object in sensation, a link thematized by Aristotle in *aisthêsis* (see below, I.A.3). But the difference in paradigm between *aisthanomai*, which is initially "auditory," and *sentir* (to sense), which becomes "olfactory," can also shed light on the the displacement effected from *aisthêsis* to *nous* when we move on to the Latin *sensus*. Indeed, the Greek *nous*, which Bailly proposes to translate in French equivalents or cognates of "intelligence, mind [*esprit*], thought, sagacity, wisdom, common sense, intention, soul, heart, sentiment, will, desire" (I omit the rather frequent translation as "intuition," which takes us this time to the paradigm of vision—Latin, *intueri*, "to see"— which also informs Greek *theory* or *idea* [see SPECIES]), is essentially linked to the French word *flair*, the ability of dogs to smell; and it is precisely this "olfactory" sense that will give us *sensus*.

2. The system of hierarchies

That difference in model—ears or nose?—is complicated by a gnoseological hierarchy. The Aristotelian system gave us the lasting outline of the framework within which *aisthêsis* and *nous* could be differentiated, namely, a hierarchy of living beings and their faculties, which is deployed in *De anima*. Aristotle distinguishes three types of living beings: vegetables (*phuta* [φυτά], see NATURE, Box 1), which possess only the ability to nourish themselves (*to threptikon* [τὸ θρεπτικόν]); animals (*zôia* [ζαῷ], see ANIMAL), which possess the faculty of "sensing" (*to aisthêtikion* [τὸ αἰσθητικόν], which opens onto that of desiring, *to orektikon* [τὸ ὀρεκτικόν], see WILL and PHANTASIA); and men ("and"—he says—"any other similar or superior being"), who possess in addition the ability to think (*to dianoêtikon to kai nous* [τὸ διανοητικόν τε καὶ νοῦς]) (*De anima*, 2.3.414a 29-b 19). The distinction between the "dianoetic," discursive intelligence ("which moves through," *dia* [διά], while scenting), and the "noetic," intuitive intelligence ("which scents"), is not pertinent at this level of descriptive generality, but *nous* is plainly the term of maximal scope and complexity, at once the final instance, subsuming all the others, and a separate and sovereign instance, linked to what is divine in man ("the *nous* that becomes all things and the *nous* that produces them all" [ibid., 3.5.430a]; see INTELLECTUS). This is why *aisthêsis* and *nous* are structurally linked: "the soul is analogous to the hand; for as the hand is a tool of tools [*organon . . . organôn* (ὄργανον . . . ὀργάνων)], so the mind is the form of forms [*ho nous . . . eidos eidôn* (ὁ νοῦς . . . εἶδος εἰδῶν)] and sense the form of sensible things [*kai hê aisthêsis eidos aisthêtôn* (καὶ ἡ αἴσθησις εἶδος αἰσθητῶν)]" (ibid., 3.432a 1-3). But we touch here on a limit that calls into play the range not only of the notions of *nous* and *eidos* [εἶδος], but, more directly, that of the notions of *aisthêsis* and *aisthêton* [αἰσθητόν].

3. *Aisthêsis* as the joint act of the sentient and the sensed

The amplitude of the *aisthêsis* is deployed and thematized in *De anima*. For us it is a function of the fact that within it the subjective/objective alternative is always already transcended. In fact, *aisthêsis* designates simultaneously (a) the faculty of sensing or "sensitivity" characterizing certain living beings; (b) the exercise of that faculty, or "perception"; (c) its distribution, linked or not to the organs of the senses (each of the five "senses," then, which, insofar as they are located in an organ are said to be *aisthêtêrion* [αἰσθητήριον], but also the notorious "common sense"); (d) finally, the affections or pathemes produced by the objects of the senses, the "sensations." The synchrony of these uses—sensitivity, perception, sense, sensation—with the remarkable conjunction of the active and the passive is one of the effects of the definition of *aisthêsis* as a "single act [*mia . . . energeia* (μία . . . ἐνέργεια)] of the sentient-sensing [*tou aisthêtikou* (τοῦ αἰσθητικοῦ)] and of the sensible-sensed [*aisthêton*, cf. the "double sense" for us of the verbal adjective in -*tos*]" (*De anima*, 3.2.426a 16–17), and as the active coinciding of the organ of sense (*aisthêtêrion*) and the sensed (*aisthêton*), each of those two elements, like hearing and sound, which will become subject and object, being identical to the other, "though retaining their being" (ibid., and 3.2.425b 26–28; Cassin, *Aristote et le logos*; see SUBJECT, OBJECT, and PATHOS), in a "crossing over" that would not be lost on Merleau-Ponty.

■ See Box 1.

B. *Koinê aisthêsis* and common sense

Koinê aisthêsis [κοινὴ αἴσθησις], which is rendered as "common sense," designates in Aristotle not a sixth sense but rather the fact of feeling simultaneously at least two sensations (*aisthêseis* [αἰσθήσεις]) arriving through two distinct sensory channels (*aisthêseis* [αἰσθήσεις]). This results in two extremely important consequences:

a. On the one hand, a transversalization of the sensations specific to each sense, namely color, and this specific color, for sight; and odor, and this particular odor, for smell. We thus arrive at a perception of what is "commonly sensed" [*idia aisthêta* (ἴδια αἰσθητά)], which each of the senses has us sensing alone solely by accident: these include movement, rest, size, number, unity (*De anima*, 3.1.425a 14–16; cf.2.6.418a, 17–18). Above all, one arrives at a recognition of an object through a synthesis of impressions sensed in isolation by the individual senses, which are, for their part, always true: such synthesis makes it possible to name things, but it also enables errors—yellow and bitter: is it "bile"? (ibid., 3.1.425b 1–4; see TRUTH, Box 7 and Cassin, *Aristote et le logos*). Whence the dual meaning of *sentirei* in Latin, "to sense" (*percipere*) and "to judge" (*judicare*), which can be understood, for example, through Albertus Magnus's commentary on *De anima* ("odorare est sentire et judicare odorem," quoted in Spinosa, "Sensazione e percezione").

b. On the other hand, sensation of sensation (one "realizes"—in which we rediscover the Homeric sense of *aisthanesthai* [αἰσθάνεσθαι]—that one senses, one senses that one senses), an auto-affection or "consciousness of (sensing)," which can be called "aperception" (see, in addition to *De anima*, 3.2.425b 12 ["since we sense that we see and that we hear. . ."], *De somno*, 255a 15; cf. *sunaisthêsis* [συναίσθησις] in Alexander of Aphrodisia [Spinosa, "Sensazione e percezione"]; see PERCEPTION and CONSCIOUSNESS). It is to the extent that sensing is a

1

Aisthêton

➤ OBJECT, SIGNIFIER/SIGNIFIED, II.

It is not easy to render Greek philosophical texts dealing with sensation, despite the terminological equivalences that appear to be imperative: such is the case of *sensible* (in French) for *aisthêton*, [αἰσθητόν], of *visible* for *oraton* [ὁρατόν], etc. The reason for this is in fact less lexical than grammatical. Ancient Greek tends to transform verbal adjectives or participles into nouns with great ease and disposes of a singular or plural neutral for designating without any more precision than that which it is discussing. In addition the verbal adjective in -*tos* generally marks possibility, like Latin adjectives in -*bilis*, but it occasionally retains from its origin the meaning of a passive past participle (cf. Lat. *audi-tus*).

This yields particularly concise formulations, which lead translators to issue glosses in order to be clear, at the risk of philosophical anachronisms. They are frequently tempted to restore to *sensible* its adjectival status by having it modify the word "thing" or, worse yet, "object," thus introducing surreptitiously into ancient thought a distinction between subject and object that would not appear until

our classical age. In Aristotle—and he would be widely followed in this—it is the *sensible* that acts on the senses and realizes them in imitation of itself. The "sensible" is thus defined through the sensation it affords and the sense through the "sensible" offered by it (sight by the visible, hearing by sound . . .), in keeping with a conceptual circularity that dispenses with opposing subject to object.

French extricates itself from such concision through a certain roughness of style and one or two additional elements. In *De sensu et sensibilibus* (440a 18–19), R. Mugnier renders "ὥστ' εὐθὺς κρεῖττον φάναι τῷ κινεῖσθαι τὸ μεταξὺ τῆς αἰσθήσεως ὑπὸ τοῦ γίνεσθαι τὴν αἴσθησιν" as "par suite, il vaut mieux déclarer sur-le-champ que c'est l'intermédiaire indispensable à la sensation qui, par le mouvement reçu du sensible, produit la sensation." In English, translating appears to be more difficult. J. I. Beare feels obliged to abandon the term "sensible" and to resort to paraphrase: "So that it were better to say at once that visual perception is due to a process set up by the perceived object

in the medium between this object and the sensory organ."

It appears that the difficulty in English is increased by the current meaning of "sensible," which ordinarily does not refer to an immediately sensory register. "Sensible" designates either a reasonable person (the French *sensé*) or even, with reference to clothes or shoes, to practical things in which one feels good. One has to force one's language if one is to translate the Greek word by word, or else be resigned to paraphrase. And such is also the case for French *sensible* in the sense of "what is given to be felt or sensed," which is hard to convey in English.

Gérard Simon

BIBLIOGRAPHY

Aristotle. *On Sense and the Sensible*. In *The Works of Aristotle*, translated by J. I. Beare. Oxford: Clarendon Press, 1931.
———. *De sensu et sensibilibus*. In *Petits traités d'histoire naturelle*, translated by René Mugnier. Paris: Les Belles Lettres, 1953.

matter of judging that common sense will be conceived (by Albertus Magnus, for instance) as the first of the "inner senses" (Spinosa, "Sensazione e percezione").

In Aristotle, what is "commonly sensed" forms a well-defined list and is the effect of a perception mediated by at least two simultaneous senses, and is, as a result, vulnerable to error. In Plato, where the phrase "common sense" does not appear, the possibility of comparing and "grasping what individual senses have in common" (*to koinon lambanein peri autôn* [τὸ κοινὸν λαμβάνειν περὶ αὐτῶν]; *Theaetetus*, 185b) is related directly to the soul, without the mediation of any sense organ, as a "faculty exercised through language" [*hê dia tês glôttês dunamis* (ἡ διὰ τῆς γλώττης δύναμις); ibid., 185c]. In each case, there does not exist a "common sense" that can be isolated from the other senses and linked to its own organ (*sensorium commune*). But we can, without doubt, understand on that basis a *sensus communis* as a common manner of sensing and appreciating (Cicero, *De oratore*, 1.12; 2.68), which can be vulgar and in error or replete with "good sense" and a "sense of what is fitting" (Seneca, *De beneficiis*, 1.12.3) and linked to ordinary language as the expression of a *consensus* (see SENSUS COMMUNIS and COMMON SENSE).

C. An intersection with *semainein*?

Is there, in our journey, no point of contact between the register of sensitivity/sensibility and that of signification?

a. The semantic is touched on with the description of sensation as a relation, *logos* [λόγος], which is

determined in each case by contrasting qualities. It is thus the breadth of the term *logos* that must be investigated (see LOGOS). Indeed, *aisthêsis*-sensation *legei* [λέγει] "speaks," in the sense of "adds up," "evaluates," to the extent that it is nothing other than a singular proportion, an assessing, between contraries: as in gray, which I sense as being nothing but a *logos* of black and white (*De anima*, 2.12.424a 17-b 3 and 3.2.426a 27-b 29); see Cassin, *Aristote et le logos*). Thanks to the *aisthêsis koinê*, one can recognize and name (*legein* [λέγειν]) an object one senses while running the risk of being in error (this yellow and that bitterness gives us "bile"). One thus obtains a descriptive statement (*logos*) that is close to a definition (*logos*) of the perceived object. But, to pursue our example, one does not for all that know what "bile" "means" (*sêmainei* [σημαίνει]). On the other hand, we are in a realm of "signals" in the Homeric and pre-Aristotelian sense: yellow signals bile, at the risk of a misinterpretation.

b. From another point of view, the relation between the "aisthêsis" in the sense of sensitivity/sensibility, and the discursive/semantic is constructed within the black box of the soul in *De interpretatione*, which brings into relation sounds of the voice, states of the soul, and things of the world (see SIGN, Box 1). Place is made for the intention and meaning of the *nous* as a *sensus* to be understood simultaneously as receptivity, intentionally directed at the object, and as emission, intending to submit to the convention of meaning as it is put in place on the basis of the principle of noncontradiction in Book Γ of the *Metaphysics* (to speak is to say something that has a meaning and only one, for oneself and for others, see PRINCIPLE, I.C and HOMONYM, II.B.3; see also INTENTION).

But the entire complex is surely not constructed around a single term that we might translate as *sense*, given the present scope of that word for us.

II. The Unitary Polysemy of *Sensus*: Triple Sense and Semantic Flux

The polysemy of *sensus* is linked to the Greek terms *aisthêsis*, *dianoia*, *nous*, and the tendentially unitary semantic flux characterizing it is the expression of the philosophical debate over the relations between sensation and knowledge.

The three registers determining the senses of *sensus* are organized according to four levels of analysis that long remained implicit: the physiological level, the psychological level, the gnoseological level, and the logico-linguistic level. *Sensus*, as "sensation," "sense perception," thus includes at the physiological level the sense of "sensation" as the biological functioning of a sense organ, the passive motion of the organ under the impulse of external objects, and the sense of "sense organ." At the psychological level, *sensus* additionally includes the meaning of "faculty of the senses" (senses of sight, of hearing, etc.) (*aisthêsis*, see above, I. A; see as well PATHOS). *Sensus*, as "comprehension," "intellectual perception," participates in the gnoseological level and includes the meanings of "consciousness" (see CONSCIOUSNESS), "intention" (see INTENTION), "sentiment," "opinion" (Lat. *sentential*, which is also derived from *sentire*), and of "thought," "judgment," "mind," and "intellect," implying a second phase of mental elaboration of the data furnished by sensation. *Sensus*, as "signified," "signification," is situated at the logico-linguistic level and includes the senses of "idea," "concept," "mental concept," to the extent that every sense perception that involves the intellect entails an interpretation of sense data as well as the attribution of mental concepts to data furnished by sensation and expressed through the mediation of linguistic signs.

A. Sites of polysemy

Translations and commentaries of Greek texts of late antiquity and the Middle Ages are quite revealing as to the polysemy of *sensus*. In the Epistles of Saint Paul (New Testament, Latin translation, fourth–fifth centuries) and in the Latin *Asclepius* (ca. fourth century), the correspondence between *sensus* and *nous*, as "intention," "thought," "mind," "intellect," leads to the acknowledgment of an overall semantic similarity within the Greco-Latin couple. Thus Saint Paul, referring to the "reprehensible thoughts in which God has plunged the pagans," says "tradidit eos Deus in reprobum sensum" (*paredôken autous ho theos eis adokimon noun* [παρέδωκεν αὐτοὺς ὁ θεὸς εἰς ἀδόκιμον νοῦν]; Rom 1:28): then, referring to the "peace of God that surpasses all understanding": "et pax Dei quae exuperat omnem sensum" (*kai hê eirênê tou theou hê huperechousa panta noun* [καὶ ἡ εἰρήνη τοῦ θεοῦ ἡ ὑπερέχουσα πάντα νοῦν]; Phil 4:7); or, further on, referring to the thought of God and his counsel: "Quis enim cognovit

sensum Domini aut consiliarius eius fuit?" (*Tis gar egnô noun Kuriou? Hê tis sumboulos autou egeneto?* [Τίς γὰρ ἔγνω νοῦν Κυρίου ; ἢ τίς σύμβουλος αὐτοῦ ἐγένετο]; Who has known the mind of the Lord or who has been his counselor?).

In *Asclepius*, the hermetic work, on the other hand, *sensus-nous* designates the intellect, the superior human faculty that allows humans to partake of the divine:

Sed de animalibus cunctis humanos tantum sensus (nous) ad divinae rationis intelligentiuam exornat, erigit atque sustollit.

(Of all living things, consciousness equips only the human, exalts it, raises it up to understand the divine plan.)

(Copenhaver, ed., *Hermetica*, chap. 6, ll. 8–10)

The text continues:

Unde efficitur ut, quoniam [homo] est ipsius una compago, parte, qua ex anima et sensu (nous), spiritu (pneuma) atque ratione divinus est velut ex eolementis superioribus inscendere posse videatur in caelum, parte vero mundane, quae constat ex igne (et terra), aqua et aere, mortalis resistat in terra.

(Whence, though mankind is an integral construction, it happens that in the part that makes him divine, he seems able to rise up to heaven, as if from higher elements— soul and consciousness, spirit and reason. But in his material part—consisting of fire (and earth) water and air—he remains fixed on the ground, a mortal.)

(Ibid., chap. 10, ll. 22–26)

We can similarly compare:

Gratias tibi summe, exsuperantissime . . . condonans nos sensu (nous), ratione, intelligentia: sensu ut te cognoverimus; ratione, ut te suspicionibus indegamus; cognitione, ut te cogniscentes gaudeamus.

(<ch>arin soi oidamen . . . charisamenos hêmin noun <log>on gnôsin; noun me<n>, hina se noêsômen, logon <de hin>a se epikalêsômen, gnôsin hina epignôsômen. [<χ>άριν σοὶ οἴδαμεν . . . χαρισάμενος ἡμῖν νοῦν <λόγ>ον γνῶσιν νοῦν μὲ<ν>, ἵνα σὲ νοήσωμεν, λόγον <δὲ ἵν>α σὲ ἐπικαλήσωμεν, γνῶσιν ἵνα ἐπιγνώσωμεν.])

(We thank you, supreme and most high god, by whose grace alone we have attained the light of your knowledge . . . by giving us the gift of consciousness, reason, and understanding: consciousness, by which we may know you; reason, by which we may seek you in our dim suppositions; knowledge, by which we may rejoice in knowing you.)

(Ibid., chap. 10, l. 41)

This usage would subsequently spread to the Greek and Latin church fathers: Saint Irenaeus (*Adverses haereses*, bk. 2, chap. 13, §3), Tertullian (*Adversus Praxean*, chap. 6), or Saint Jerome (*S. Hieronymus presbyteri opera*, chap. 3, l. 549).

On the basis of the *sensus-nous-intellect* correspondence, the overall affinity between the semantic fields of *sensus* and *nous* can be observed. The two terms are, in fact, articulated according to the three senses of (1) sense perception, (2) intellectual perception, (3) signification, to the extent that they express in general the complex and articulated world of humans in relation to the world, a person endowed with body and mind facing a world both available to the senses and intelligible. *Sensus* and *nous* diverge according to a polarized semantic outcome, *sensus* coming to signify principally sensory perception and signification, and *nous*, intellectual perception and signification. The perceptual (and consequently "immediate") nature of cognitive understanding obtained through sensory as well as intellectual perception (which is thus distinguished from abstract and discursive—or nonintuitive—knowledge) remains the connotation common to both terms. The tripartite polysemy of *sensus* is indicated in the earliest Scholasticism: in an anonymous commentary on *Asclepius*, dating from the twelfth century (Vat. Ott lat. 811) (*sensus corporei, intellectus, significatio*) and in the alphabetical dictionary of the Bible of Alanus of Lille (twelfth century; *Dictiones dictionum theologicarum*, in RT: *PL*, vol. 210, col. 941B) (*intellectus, significatio*).

B. Semantic continuity via the cognitive value of the senses

The triple meaning of *sensus*—(1) sensation, (2) comprehension, (3) signification—is articulated in keeping with an essential semantic continuity, which is the expression of fundamental doctrines, both ancient and medieval, about the cognitive value of the senses. Those doctrines are in turn themselves conditioned by different conceptions of the nature of the human soul.

Sensus, as passive corporeal sensation (1a), entails a reduction of knowledge to sensation characteristic of the sensualist and materialist tendencies of antiquity (the atomism of Democritus, the Epicureans, the Stoics, and, in part, the Sophists), for which the corporeal nature of the soul, whatever its subtlety, reduces the cognitive process in its totality to a contact between bodies. *Sensus* as sensory perception (1b) but also as intellectual perception (2) names different ways of reducing sensation to an act of the soul, a reduction with differing connotations for Aristotle and Aristotelianism and for Plato and the Neoplatonists, according to the status of the human soul, which is at times the form of the body, at others a spiritual substance.

Medieval commentaries, translations, and texts offer clear evidence of this semantic differentiation, which, from the perspective of terminology, is articulated in two phases: (a) a rendering explicit of the polysemy of Aristotelian and Platonic *aisthêsis* along with *sensus communis*; and (b) the Neoplatonic notion of *dianoia* (with John Scotus Erigena, ninth century) and *sensus interior*, opening onto *sensus litteralis* and the third meaning of sense.

1. *Aisthêsis* and *sensus communis*

The commentary on Aristotle's *De anima* composed by Albertus Magnus (thirteenth century) underscores the simultaneously passive and active nature of Aristotelian *aisthêsis*: passive modification, but also an acquisition of potentiality, consciousness of sensing, sensory judgment (above all in the *koinê aisthêsis*, see above and SENSUS COMMUNIS):

Et ad hoc dicimus, quod odorare non est absolute pati a sensibili percepto, sed potius odorare est sentire et judicare odorem, quod est secunda sensus perfectio, et non est tantum pati, sed etiam operari aliquid.

(We say to this that apprehending an odor is not absolutely to suffer from what has been perceived by the senses, but more exactly that to apprehend an odor is to sense and judge the odor, which constitutes the second perfection of sense, and that it is not only to suffer but equally to effectuate something.)

> (Albertus Magnus, *De anima*;
> cf. Aristotle, *De anima*, 2.12.424b 18–20)

The soul as form of the body is what guarantees the sensory contribution to knowledge, according to Aristotle's moderate empiricism, within which Albertus Magnus articulates explicitly the notion of *sensus* as sensory perception (1b), which had remained implicit in the Aristotelian *aisthêsis*.

In the medieval version of Plato's *Phaedo*, Henry Aristippus of Calabria (twelfth century) translates *aisthanomai* not only as *sentire*, but also as *sensu percipere* and *sensu concipere* (perceive/conceive through the senses), with the intention of emphasizing the purely instrumental role of the corporal sphere in sensation. The translator thus contributes to making manifest the Platonic reduction of sensation to a sensory perception that, in this case and as opposed to Aristotle, is the prerogative of a purely spiritual soul, which is temporarily linked to a radically heterogeneous and inferior body through whose intervention the soul cannot be in any way altered. In keeping with the situation of sensation in Plato, the soul, on the one hand, makes use of the bodily organs as instruments for conserving the body and perceiving the sensory world; but, on the other hand, sensation is never anything but a stimulus that awakens in the soul the memory of intelligible realities that it has previously known:

Possibile enim hoc eciam apparuit, sensu percipientem quid [aisthomenon ti] vel videntem vel audientem vel aliquem alium sensum sumentem, diversum quid ab hoc animo concepisse, quod oblivione deletum erat, cui hoc assimilatum est simile existens vel cui dissimile.

(Here indeed is the possibility that has clearly appeared to us: when someone perceives through the senses, sees, hears, apprehends a thing through some other sense, he conceives, based on that thing, something else that had been erased by forgetting, and which is brought in contact with the first, whether it resembles it or not.)

> (*Plato latinus: Phaedo*, 76a 1–4, p. 31)

2. *Dianoia, sensus interior,* and *sensus litteralis*

In the tripartite division of the faculties of the human soul in the image of the divine Trinity, John Scotus Erigena distinguishes two faculties in the *motus compositus* of sense as set forth by Maxim the Confessor. The first—*sensus exterior, aisthêsis,* sensation and sensory perception (or *sensus 1*)—is foreign to the divine image in man, since it is an intermediary between the soul and the body. The second—*sensus interior, dianoia,* intellectual perception (or *sensus 2*)—is nothing other than reason and intellect: it is the organ of the "division of nature," since, in an Aristotelian manner, it divides and rejoins—and even distinguishes and reorganizes—images of natural specific objects, effects and signs of universal causes, channeling them to the unity of causes by way of reason and intellect:

> et si quis intentius graecae linguae proprietatem perspexerit, duorum sensuum in homine proprietatem reperiet. In ea enim NOUS intellectus dicitur, LOGOS ratio, DIANOIA sensus, non ille exterior sed interior; et in his tribus essentialis trinitas animae ad imaginem Dei constitutae subsistit. Est enim intellectus, et ratio, et sensus, qui dicitur interior et essentialis; exterior vero, quem corporis et animae copulam diximus, AISTHÊSIS vocatur.

> (But, if one examines more closely the semantics of the Greek language, one discovers that the word is not univocal and that it encompasses two distinct meanings. For in the Greek language, the intellect is called *nous*, reason *logos*, and sense *dianoia*, and this word does not at all designate external sense, but inner sense; and it is in those three components that the essential trinity of the soul, created in the image of God, subsists. The trinity of the soul is thus composed of intellect, reason, and sense, which is called the inner and essential sense, whereas the outer sense that we have defined as the conjunctive link between body and soul is called *aisthêsis*.)

(Erigena, *Periphyseon*, bk. 2, p. 98, ll. 20–26)

In Erigena, *sensus interior* is thus situated entirely in the higher sphere of the soul and is purely spiritual, and it is also *dianoia* by virtue of the semantic affinity with *nous* in the sense of "signification" (*sensus* 3). In the biblical hermeneutics of the Greek church fathers, *dianoia* is indeed the *sensus litteralis*, the sense of Scripture. It is thus the case that in Origen, the sense (*sensus*) of Scripture is the *nous tôn graphôn* [νοῦς τῶν γραφῶν], in conformity with the Christian doctrine with the four meanings of Scripture (cf. Origen, *De principiis*, 3, sub indice).

■ See Box 2.

III. The Exuberance of the Latin Lexicon of Signification

Against the backdrop of this unitary flux, the Latin lexicon of the third sense of "sense" would undergo exceptional diversification. When the question of meaning or signification became an object of specialized study, medieval thinkers would attempt to specify each of its aspects (primary and secondary sense, lexical and grammatical sense, etc.), and traditional terms were redefined by the place they occupied in a network in which new terms were being forged (e.g., *significatio* vs. *suppositio* or vs. *consignificatio*). This specialization was linked to problematics that would make a significant reappearance in analytic modernity.

A. *Sensus, sententia, vis, significatio, intellectus*

The term *sensus* is caught up as one in a set of nouns bearing the idea of signification (*sententia, vis, significatio, intellectus*), related as it is to a series of verbs (*sentire, valere, significare, intellegere*) that are frequently difficult to distinguish. That

set underwent constant reorganization, with predictable instances of interference between the third (gnoseological) and fourth (logico-linguistic) levels. It was only when networks were established that contrasting values attained a measure of precision.

The evolution of the two derivatives of *sentire* is delicate. The term *sensus* gradually came to supplant *sententia* during the Roman era, in the sense of "mental disposition," taking on a generic value, while the specialization of *sententia* in the lexicon of law ("sentencing") and politics ("advice" given to the Senate) explains its use as "authorized, profound, authentic signification" (see Box 2). In grammatical tradition, *sententia* was chosen to translate the Greek *dianoia*, and occasionally *lekton* [λεκτόν] as well, to denote a thought insofar as it can be expressed in a composite linguistic sequence, whence the extension of the term to the sequence itself. That choice contributed to the disappearance of the difference between Stoic and Aristotelian terminologies (Nuchelmans, *Theories of the Proposition*). The term was used systematically when it was a matter of the expression of a complete meaning (*sententia perfecta, plena*), whether to define a logical proposition (cf. Varro: "proloquium est sententia, in qua nihil desideratur"; quoted by Aulus Gellius, *Attic Nights*, 16.8) or a grammatical sentence (cf. Priscian's definition: "oratio est ordinatio dictionum congrua, sententiam perfectam demonstrans" [a sentence is a correct sequence of words, manifesting a complete meaning], *Grammatici latini*, vol. 2, p. 53, l. 28; see *lekton* in SIGNIFIER/SIGNIFIED, II and PROPOSITION, Box 2). In rhetoric, *sententia* was applied more broadly to ideas that constitute a speech, to an opinion expressed (in which it translates the Greek *doxa* [δόξα]), or to whatever constitutes the substance or deep meaning of a text (or of a sentence or a word—although this last use was less frequent as of the time of the Empire and rare in the Middle Ages), the sense, as well, to be probably attributed to a text in opposition to the one assigned to it by an adversary (cf. Cicero, *Rhetoric to Herennius*, 2.13). It is in this sense that it can be opposed to the letter of the text (*scriptum, littera*) and also to the *sensus* most immediately associated with it. A *sententia* thus being the reading to be retained of a passage or a text—Boethius, for example, speaks of *sententia Aristotelis* or Bérenger of *sententia catholice ecclesie*—the term designates by extension an authoritative text, resulting in those collections of systematically organized excerpts, anthologies of *sententiae* such as those of Peter Lombard in theology, which would elicit comment throughout the Middle Ages.

The different meanings of *significatio*—"the act of indicating," "indication or mark (of approval, above all)," "signification, meaning"—parallel those of the verb *significare*, from which it originated (a compound of *signum* and *facere*), "to indicate (through signs)," "to make known," "to announce or presage," and "to mean." Starting from what was originally an intransitive use, as in Plautus, for instance ("to make signs"), the verb became transitive, taking as its object the content intended by the signs ("to be a sign of"). If Latin possessed the verb *signare* in the first sense ("to make a mark"), it created a verb that was not modeled on any Greek term for the second sense, even if *significare* surely benefited from the

2

The different "meanings" of texts

The Latin vocabulary of exegesis was established gradually in Christian patristics, then in medieval Scholasticism, while borrowing from Hellenistic and Jewish exegeses (the bibliography is abundant, see Dahan, *Exégèse chrétienne*). Although the opposition between the letter and the spirit grounds a distinction between two moments of the reading of a text, the content of the distinction and the terms that express it are far from unambiguous. Already in the patristic era, *littera*, for example, could either refer to the explicit or manifest content of the expression (which might, moreover, not have any) or include the figurative or metaphorical sense, the *figura* (which can elsewhere form part of spiritual exegesis; see Bureau, "Littera"). *Litterae* thus designates for Saint Augustine both the letters of the alphabet and "letters," that is, the text to be read (*divinas litteras*), whence the analogy between the two apprenticeships of reading: "that which teaches how to understand Scripture is similar to that which teaches the letters [*similis est tradenti litteras*], that is, to the master who teaches how to read" (*De doctrina christiana*, prooemium 8).

In the beginning of the twelfth century, Hugh of Saint Victor presented in a precise and enduring manner the distinction between *littera*, which corresponds in the strict sense to the analysis of the text, *sensus*, which takes the historical context into account, and *sententia*, which derived the theological teaching of the passage; he explained that every text was to have at least two of those three "senses," and certain have three:

> Illa narratio litteram et sensum tantum habet, ubi per ipsam prolationem sic aperte aliquid significatur, ut nihil aliud relinquatur subintelligendum. Illa vero litteram et sententiam tantam habet, ubi per ex sola pronuntiatione nihil concipere potest auditor nisi addatur expositio. Illa sensum et sententiam habet, ubi et aperte aliquid significantur, et aliquid aliud subintelligendum relinquitur quod expositione aperitur.

> (Only the letter and the sense are possessed by the narrative in which, through its mere utterance, something is signified sufficiently clearly for nothing ambiguous to subsist. The narrative which has only letter and signification is one of which nothing can be understood when it is heard as merely articulated, unless an explanation is added to it. Finally, the narrative possessing sense and signification in which one thing is signified clearly and another left as an implication to be revealed after an explanation.)

> (*Didascalicon*, 6.8)

The work of exegetes is situated at three levels: labor of comprehension, of exposition, and also of "criticism," since even as they render the text before their eyes explicit, they are obliged to judge and evaluate it in terms of correctness [*congruitas*], ultimately deciding whether to complete its letter, to rectify its apparent meaning, in order finally to declare its true meaning. In point of fact, the *littera* is not necessarily "complete or perfect [*perfecta*]"; it can also be superabundant or elliptical, and even incomprehensible or incorrect [*incongrua*] "if it is not resolved in another letter" (*Didascalicon*, 6.9). Moreover, even if the signification of its words is clear (*significatio aperta*), the *sensus* can be correct or incorrect (*congruus*, *incongruus*) or be revealed to be "unbelievable, impossible, absurd, false," for example, in Psalm 79:7, "They devoured Jacob." On the other hand, the *sententia divina* "is never absurd, never false, and contrary to the *sensus* containing many contradictions, does not admit any incompatibility [*repugnantia*]; it is always correct/coherent [*congrua*], always true" (ibid.).

The *littera*, or *sensus litteralis*, in the broad sense, comprises three levels of meaning (*littera*, *sensus*, *sententia*) and is massively opposed to "spiritual" interpretation (which is also called mystical, or allegorical, in the broad sense). In fact, Thomas Aquinas says, whereas scientific texts depend on men, who have at their disposition only words, God has the power to make use of a dual mode of signification; he can simultaneously call on words and realities (*duplex significatio, una per voces, alia per res quas voces significant*), and, for that reason, Scripture will have several senses (*plures sensus*): "The signification [*significatio*] through which words signify concerns the literal or historical sense [*sensus litteralis seu historicaus*]; the signification through which the realities designated by words designate still other realities concerns the mystical sense [*sensus mysticus*]" (*In Epistolam ad Galatas*, in *Opera omnia*, 21:230). Exegetes generally recognize in the latter three levels of meaning: the moral or anthropological sense, which transmits moral teachings; the allegorical sense (the term being taken here in the narrow sense), which refers to truths of faith relative to the church; and the anagogical or mystical sense, referring to future life. Those three levels of meaning, which determine the spiritual sense, thus constitute, along with the literal sense, what are called the four senses of Scripture.

The sacred text is thus characterized by this accretion or stratification of levels of meaning, the essential opposition being the distinction between the literal and the spiritual sense conveyed by numerous images (for example, the nut and its shell): the debates between exegetes deal with the domains covered by each, the primacy to be accorded to one or the other, the relations they entertain with each other (continuity or discontinuity), the nature of the "hermeneutical leap" allowing one to pass from the first to the second, to move beyond what the text says to attain a truth lying beyond words.

BIBLIOGRAPHY

Bureau, Bruno. "Littera: 'sens' et 'signification' chez Ambroise, Augustin et Cassiodore." In *Conceptions latines du sens et de la signification*, edited by Marc Baratin and Claude Moussy, 213–37. Paris: Presses de l'Université Paris-Sorbonne, 1999.

Dahan, Gilbert. *L'exégèse chrétienne de la Bible en Occident médiéval, XIIe–XIVe siècle*. Paris: Cerf, 1999.

Hugh of Saint Victor. *Didascalicon*. Edited by Charles Henry Buttimer. Washington, DC: Catholic University of America Press, 1939.

Lubac, Henri de. *Medieval Exegesis*. Translated by Mark Sebanc. Grand Rapids, MI: W. B. Eerdmans, 1998.

Valente, Luisa. "Une sémantique particulière: La pluralité des sens dans les Saintes Écritures (XIIe siècle)." In *Sprachtheorien in Spätantike und Mittelalter*, edited by Sten Ebbesen, 12–32. Tübingen: Gunter Narr, 1995.

meanings of *semanein*: "to make a sign," "to reveal," "to manifest," "to denote," meanings that are found again in philosophical Latin, particularly when the subject is divination. In that perspective, the act of "mean-ing" can be as much that of the sign, to which intentionality, a predisposition to indicate, to point toward something, is attributed, as that of an individual seeking to manifest that intentionality by means of a sign (cf. Brachet, "Réflexions sur l'évolution"). In medieval Latin, that double valence, which is not found in the French verb *signifier*, was preserved, including in treatises of semantics, a situation well expressed in an anonymous treatise of logic from the end of the twelfth century:

> "Significare" applied to an expression and to the person using it [*utens*] is not the same thing, as is habitually said. When one says that "such a person expresses a thing through an expression [*significant rem per vocem*], this means: "uses a sign and a mark of the thing with the intention of producing a sign concerning the thing" [*utitur signo et nota rei cum intentione faciendi signum de re*]. And *significare* predicated in this sense is in a way to act, considered in relation to the person forming the expressions. But when it is said of expressions, the word does not predicate an action, but rather a relation or a similarity, and a fitting of the sign, in so much as it is a sign, in relation to what it signifies [*relatio . . . signi ad signatum*]. . . . To say of an expression that it signifies the thing [*vocem significare rem*] is to say that the expression makes a sign of the thing [*vocem facere signum de re*]: here "to make" does not mean "to act" [*agere*], but "to make a sign" [*signum facere*], that is, "to be a mark" [*notam esse*]. As a result, "to signify" is not the same thing for the user as for the expression. Indeed "to signify," with reference to a speaker, announces the so-called action of expression, the relation or mutual fit of sign and signified.
>
> (*Tractatus de proprietatibus sermonum*, in De Rijk,
> *Logica modernorum*, 2:710–11)

Significatio is the term that appears to have been used in a technical way to address the intrinsic semantic properties of a word or an expression, more rarely of a sentence or speech (in which cases there is a preference for *sententia* or *sensus*), for example, of its polysemy (*significatio duplex*) or of the evolution in meaning it has undergone.

Vis served as a translation of the Greek *dunamis* [δύναμις] in speaking of the virtue of a plant, the effectiveness of a remedy, the value of a coin, and, by analogy, the meaning of a word or a sentence—it is a noun linked to the verb *valeo*, which renders as the Greek *dunamai* [δύναμαι]. Cicero frequently used the expressions *vis verborum* and *vis verbi* (for the value or meaning of words), which would be the subject of an extremely precise development in Augustine's *De dialectica*: the word is instituted as a function of a certain (immediate or mediate) relation to the thing; its pronunciation will thus provoke a sensory impression in the listener, which will induce an intellectual impression dependent either on the nature of the word (the "softness" or "harshness" of its sound, for instance), on the thing it signifies, or on both. Thus it is, according to Augustine, that the "force" proper (*vis*) of words is constituted (*De dialectica*, chap. 7, §14), a force that can be impeded as a result of obscurities or ambiguities that Augustine would describe in minute detail. A word's *vis* can be understood only to the extent that the word is a sign, the sign of something for someone; it is thus a function of its ability to move the listener: the *vis* thus retains its "dynamic" connotation, since it is not the *significatio* associated with the word that is important, but "its force" and consequently what it produces as meaning in the listener: "Vis verbi est qua cognoscitur quantum valeat autem tantum quantum movere audientem potest" [The *force* of a word is that whereby the extent of its efficacy is learned. It

has efficacy to the extent to which it is able to affect a hearer; *De dialectica*, chap. 7, §12]. In the thirteenth century, Henry of Ghent, in his reading of this passage, would further emphasize this connotation: "Vis verbi est qua agitur quantum valet." This nuance of efficacy would be quite marked in texts of the Middle Ages when, particularly in the context of sacramental theology, *vis* and *virtus* would be occasionally interchangeable, when the *vis* or *virtus significandi* of a word (its signifying value or force) would mesh with the *vis* or *virtus sacrificandi* of the sacramental sign (its sanctifying value or force), defined as "doing what it says" (see SIGN and SPEECH ACT). For the grammarians, the *vis* was the semantic force of a word—whether it is "signifier" or "consignifier" as in the case of conjunctions—which explains its constructive potentials, with different cases, for example.

Intelligere, originally meaning "to comprehend," appeared frequently in Cicero, then underwent a slippage in its passive form (*intelligetur*) toward "to understand," "to mean." What is "understood" by a term can be not only its obvious sense but also something that is connoted, implied, insinuated (see TERM, Box 1). It is always a matter of the sense received—or that one should receive if one follows the authorized interpreter. The passive *innuitur* was a further step toward the implicit, since the verb was often used in the Middle Ages in a theological context when a word applied to a divine reality was analyzed as the bearer of a supplementary value in relation to its ordinary sense (see CONNOTATION). The noun *intellectus* first took on the meaning of "sense," "signification" with Seneca (*Naturalis quaestiones*, 2.50.1). Boethius used *intellectus* as an equivalent of *passiones animae* the *pathêmata tês psuchês* [παθήματα τῆς ψυχῆς] of the first chapter of *Peri hermeneias*: "[V]oces quiden significant intellectum, ipsas autem voces litterae significant. Sunt autem intellectus passiones." (Sounds of the voice signify intellections, but the letters signify those sounds themselves. And the intellections are the passions of the soul), whence the triad: *voces, intellectus, res*. The term *intellectus* would thus designate simultaneously the intellection of a word and the concept (without any linguistic connotation) until the introduction of the term *conceptus* (see INTELLECTUS and CONCEPTUS), and also the intellectual faculty, the intellect. The polysemous nature of the word was well perceived in the Middle Ages. Intellections are never mechanically produced by words; they imply an activity indicated by the term *intelligere*.

B. The technicality of the medieval semantic lexicon

The developments of medieval semantics produced an entire range of technical terms, with precise meanings, arrayed in three different directions.

1. "Meaning"/"reference"

First, a distinction was established between meaning and reference, an opposition absent as such in antiquity, as is plain from the undifferentiated use of *significare*, *ostendere*, or *designare* or from the imprecision of the term *res* as the object of those verbs, at once "signified" and "referent" (see Roesch, "Res et verbum"). As of the end of the eleventh century, it was linked to a reflection on paronyms, which was pursued on the basis of Aristotle's *Categories*, and on the *nomen appelativum*, a designation for the "common noun" by the grammarians, ending up (for the grammarians and for Anselm) in *De grammatico*, with the distinction between *significare* and *appellare*:

> Grammaticus non significat hominen et grammaticam ut unum, sed grammaticam per se et hominem per aliud significant. Et hoc nomen quamvis sit appellativum hominis, non tamen proprie dicitur ejus significativum; et licet sit significativum grammaticae non tamen est ejus appelativum.

> ("Grammarian" does not signify "man" and "grammar" in a single unit, but it signifies "grammar" by itself and "man" by something else." And that name, even though it is what a man is called, does not, however, properly speaking, signify him; and although it may signify grammar, it is not what grammar is called.)

> (Anselm, *De grammatico*, 12.4.231–4.241)

The proper object of the *Categories*, Anselm concludes, is to show what terms "signifiy" and not what they "call" or "name" (ibid., 12.4.5122, 12.4.5144, 12.4.604). The grammarians and the logicians would use the doublet *significatio* and *nominatio*: the noun "man" "names" the substance and "signifies" the quality, whereas the pronoun has solely the function of "nomination," since it can be applied "to all referents" (*ad omne suppositum pertinet*). It names a substance in so far as it is determined by the quality of rationality and mortality. Similarly, *album* "names" the body by signifying whiteness; it signifies principally whiteness and secondarily the body. Such analyses vary according to whether one is a realist or a nominalist: depending on whether or not one admits the existence of the universal "whiteness," one will accept either the proposition that the name "names" such whiteness or that it merely signifies it (see De Rijk, *Logica Modernorum*, and Fredborg, "Speculative Grammar"). Toward the second half of the twelfth century, the distinction would be stabilized by logicians with the couple *significatio* and *suppositio* on the basis of a consideration of polysemy: *significatio* is stable, fixed by imposition; *suppositio* is variable, dependent on contextual elements; *canis* ("sea dog"/"constellation" is an *ambiguous* term since different meanings are a function of different impositions, whereas *homo* (in the statements *homo est species* [man is a species], *homo est nomen* [man is a name], *homo currit* [a man is running]) is *univocal*, the semantic variations being contextually determined and with constant signification (see PARONYM; SUPPOSITION; WORD, Box 4; HOMONYM).

2. Primary meaning, proper sense vs. secondary sense
Second, a network of terms was introduced in order to think through the distinction between what a term signifies primarily and what it implies or connotes secondarily (see *translatio* in TO TRANSLATE and CONNOTATION).

3. Signification vs. modes of signifying
The distinction between signification and the way of signifying developed as part of speculative grammar and theology; it allowed for a new way of thinking about the relations between being, thought, and language, as well as the different questions they raise, in particular that of the arbitrary, conventional, or natural character of language.

In the semantics of the thirteenth century, the linguistic unit *homo* was analyzed as being constituted by (1) a lexical signified (*significatum speciale*); (2) a general signified (*significatum generale*) or essential general mode of signifying, which accounts for its categorization as a part of speech (a noun); (3) specific essential modes of signifying, which account for its categorization as a type (noun, a common name); and (4) accidental modes of signifying, establishing its accidents (masculine, nominative, etc.).

- See Box 3.

The opposition between modes of signifying and signifieds is deployed in speculative grammar on four levels: (1) on the ontological level: the mode of signifying refers to

---

3

The sources of the notion of "mode of signification"

The notion of "mode of signification" has several distinct sources, which, before converging, combined to create several terminological confusions.

A. *Modus significandi* was initially the general characteristic of a part of discourse: the use has its origin in the *institutiones grammaticae*, in which Priscian explains that parts of discourse are not distinguished by formal properties (such as case), but by "properties of signification," that is: general semantic characteristics (e.g., a name or noun signifies substance and quality).

B. *Connotata*, then *modi significandi*, would later be used to designate what would subsequently be designated more precisely as *modus significandi accidentalis*: on the basis of the Aristotelian notion that the verb "consignifies" time, grammarians very early on had the idea of defining most accidents as secondary significations to be added to the principal signification (e.g., person, mood, etc.) (see CONNOTATION).

C. In a different register, *modus significandi*—which would be better rendered as "manner of signifying"—is what distinguishes two terms with the same semantic root and different endings, and specifically paronyms (see PARONYM): thus "white" and "whiteness" signify the same "thing" (whatever the ontology invoked) but differ in their manner of signifying, since they signify in an abstract or concrete mode.

In all these cases, and as is the case for consignification, the mode or manner of signifying refers to a signification that is not the principal or lexical signification but rather is either an additional signification (*significare cum*: *homo* signifies "man" and at the same time one or another property) or a manner of signifying (*significare sic*: "white" signifies whiteness insofar as it exists in a particular case). It will be noted that in cases (A) and (B), what are at stake are second-order or metalinguistic properties, but in case (C), first-order or semantic properties.

the property or mode of being of the thing, the signified to the thing; (2) on the semantic level: the modes of signifying ground the grammatical properties, the signifieds, the lexical properties—whence the idea of a double articulation, or institution, of language, the first, through which the *vox* becomes a signifying word (*dictio*; see WORD), and the second, through which it becomes a co-signifying part of speech, endowed with a mode of signifying; (3) on the epistemological level: grammar deals only with modes of signifying, logic with signifieds; (4) finally, it is the linguistic order that justifies (3): grammatical properties explain the construction and congruence of statements, the object of grammar; signifieds are the foundation of truth, the object of logic.

The Modists sought to justify the notion of *modus significandi* philosophically: every *modus significandi* corresponds to a property of things, or *modus essendi*, and to a conceived property, or *modus intelligendi*. The Aristotelian triad *voces/passiones/res* was duplicated in this system of three *modi*: *significandi, intelligendi, essendi.* This was true only for certain authors, for whom the modes of signifying were signs of *modi intelligendi*, which were signs of *modi essendi*. Others, inspired by Avicenna, supported the identity of modes: the same common nature (e.g., the property of movement) could exist in three different forms—as existing, as conceived, and as signified. In all cases, the modes of signifying, corresponding to modes of being, were quite distinct from the signifieds, which corresponded to things themselves. A single "thing" (pain) might exist in reality, might be conceived, and might be signified, being associated with either the property of movement (the verb: *doleo*) or the property of repose (the noun: *dolor*). The question of arbitrariness was thus thought through again: there was no relation of motivation or dependence between the grammatical category of a word (or of any of its accidents) and its lexical signified, since in theory any *thing* could be signified on any mode. The question of arbitrariness, moreover, underwent a kind of proliferation: it became imperative to simultaneously think about the relation between the various formal components of a linguistic unit (its modes of signifying); the relation of those components to the properties of the things on which they were grounded; and the relation of the grammatical components to the semantic components, etc. Whereas, in the Aristotelian tradition, *voces* represented the realm of convention and variation, and *intellectus* and *res* the realm of what was "identical for all," the Modists staged the coup of positing within language *modi significandi* that were substantially "identical for all," any difference being situated at the mere "accidental" level of "vocal" expression, thus affirming that a genuine "science of language," endowed with a universal subject, could exist. The nominalists of the fourteenth century would reproach them for that claim.

In theology, the notion of *modus significandi* was used as of the twelfth century to characterize simultaneously the semantic behavior of nouns and the mental operation corresponding to the use of nouns. Used for the analysis of speech about God, the notion of the signifying mode allowed one to think about the disparity between being and language, between what God *is* and what can be said of Him, a distinction already strikingly articulated at the end of the twelfth century by Alain de Lille when he distinguished

between *proprietas essendi* and *proprietas dicendi*: "Deus vere est, sed non vere esse dicitur" (God is in truth, but he cannot be said to be in truth). The principle of the correspondence between thought and language (*sicut intelligitur, sic significatur*) can be turned into a noncorrespondence grounding a negative theology: just as we cannot think God, we can not speak him either (*sicut non intelligitur, ita nec significatur*). That noncorrespondence, initially analyzed in terms of distinct connotations (for example, *just*, if said of God, connotes the cause; if said of man, it connotes the effect [see CONNOTATION]), was subsequently theorized in terms of signifying modes: we signify God, said Saint Bonaventure (to choose an example), not as he is, but as we conceive him, the modes of signifying corresponding to those modes of understanding and knowing. Starting with the reading of Pseudo-Dionysius and the idea that perfections, which are precontained in God, exist in him in a certain mode and are received by each creature commensurately with what it is, in keeping with its measure of "intellective receptivity," the notion will be inflected: Albertus Magnus, then Thomas Aquinas, could thus distinguish in the name designating perfection (e.g., *bonitas*) between the "thing signified" (*res significata*), which is perfection itself, and its mode of reception, on which the name's "signifying mode" is dependent. Nouns of perfection are thus improper at the level of signifying mode (*quantum ad modum significandi*), since, being invented by men, they correspond to their mode of thought and to things as they are able to conceive of them; at the level of the thing signified (*quantum ad rem significatam*), they are suited specifically to God, since justice is first of all, *per prius*, in God before existing, *per posterius*, in man (see TO TRANSLATE, IV and ANALOGY). For Thomas, as for other theologians, these "signifying modes" characterizing creatures are marked, inscribed in names themselves: verbs and participles, for instance, imply a temporality intrinsic to their signifying mode, but that temporality does not at all concern the thing signified as such.

IV. Modern Convergences between the Three Senses of "Sense"

Between the seventeenth and eighteenth centuries, three privileged witnesses allow us to understand how the three senses of "sense" have been articulated in the modern period.

A. Descartes and the degrees of "meaning"

In the middle of the seventeenth century, Descartes, in his *Replies to the Sixth Objections to the Meditations*, article 9, still felt the need to distinguish three degrees, three meanings of "sense," in order to be able to evaluate their degree of certitude with precision. In order to do so, he restricted the true and proper notion of meaning, and, consequently, its infallible character, to the first two degrees, namely: the first, the movement of the bodily sense organ under the pressure of external objects; and the second, the perception of sounds, odors, colors, pleasure, and pain, which stems from the union of body and soul in the mind. Descartes, on the other hand, reserved for the intellect alone the third degree, which was commonly attributed to the senses and included an evaluation, a cognitive judgment as to objects of the senses expressed during sensory impressions, a judgment that could be true or false.

The Cartesian distinction refers implicitly to three of the four different levels of analysis (see above, II) that had long been superimposed and crisscrossed in the historical debate surrounding the nature and validity of sensations. With regard to those three levels, Descartes still felt a need for clarification, and he assigned them respectively to the realms of the physiology of sensation, to the psychology of sensation, and, finally, to the gnoseological aspect of the question.

B. Vico and the *sensus/sentientia* link

There emerges from the texts a semantic flux revealing a continuity, in some respects unexpected, linking the principal meanings of *sensus*: sensation and sensory perception, intellectual perception, signification. Light is cast on this by linguistic analysis via the *sensus/sentientia* nexus: *sensus* is successively a sense organ, a faculty, the act of feeling, consciousness of feeling and thus *sentientia*, opinion, cognitive judgment bearing on what has been sensed.

In the modern period, at the beginning of the eighteenth century, Vico understood the full historical and philosophical import of philologico-linguistic analysis. Even as he attributed, in radical fashion, a fundamentally empiricist attitude to all the thinkers of antiquity (including the Platonists), Vico properly recognized in the *sensus/sentientia* derivation the linguistic expression of a very precise school of thought bearing the sensualist stamp, in contrast to the occasionalism of Malebranche and deriving from the Platonic-Augustinianism to which Vico adhered. The Latins, Vico observed with implicit reference to the degrees of "sense" distinguished by Descartes, "understand by the term *sensus* not only external senses, such as sight, and inner senses, that is: those of the soul, such as pleasure, pain, and boredom; but they also name *sensus* judgments, deliberations, and desires" (*De antiquissima Italorum sapientia*). Proof of this is offered by certain linguistic expressions in which *sentientia* is used for *judgment* or *opinion* (ibid. chap. 7, §1):

Latini sensus appellatione non solum externos, ut sensus videndi, ex. gr., et internum, qui *animi sensus* dicebatur, ut dolorem voluptatem, molestiam, sed judicia, deliberationes et vota quoque accipiebant: *ita sentio, ita judico; stat sentientia, certum est; ex sentientia evenit, uti desiderabam; et in formulis illud: ex animi tui sentientia.*

(Under the term *sense*, the Latins included not only the external senses (for example, the sense of sight) and inner sense (such as pain, pleasure, and worry) which they called *animi sensus* (*sense of the soul*), but also judgments, deliberations, wishes; so in Latin, to say *ita sentio*, (*I sense that it is so*) means I judge that it is so; to say *stat sentientia* (*my sentiment holds that*) means I am certain that; to say it turned out *ex sentientia* (*it turned out in keeping with my sentiment*) means it turned out as I desired. And among their legal formulas is the expression *ex animi tui sentientia* (*in keeping with your soul's sentiment*).)

And he linked the Platonists with the Stoics by virtue of their conception of reason as an ethereal and extremely pure sense, all the while recalling the materialism of the Epicureans, for whom thinking was sensing or feeling, and the empiricist psychology of the Aristotelians, who considered that the human mind perceives only by way of the senses (ibid.):

An igitur, quia antiqui Italiae philosophi opinati sint mentem humanum nihil percipere nisi per sensus, ut Aristotelaei; vel eam non nisi sensum esse, ut Epicuri asseclae; vel rationem sensum quendam aethereum ac purissimum, ut Platonici Stoicique existimarunt? Et vero Ethnicarum sectarum nulla, quae mentem humanam omni corpulentia puram agnorunt. Et ideo omne mentis opus sensum esse putarint; hoc est quicquid mens agat vel patiatur, corporum tactus sit.

(Accordingly, is this because the ancient philosophers of Italy were of the opinion that the human mind perceives nothing except through the senses (as was deemed the case by the *Aristotelians*); or that it is nothing but sense (as was deemed the case by the *followers of Epicurus*); or that reason is a kind of ethereal and most pure sense (as was deemed the case by the *Platonists* and the *Stoics*)? Indeed, there was no pagan sect which acknowledged the human mind to be pure of all corporeality. And the reason for this is that they regarded the operation of the mind to be entirely a function of sense.)

To this pagan metaphysic of sense, Vico opposed his own Christian metaphysic (ibid.):

Sed nostra religio eam prorsus incorpoream esse docet: et nostri metaphysici confirmant, dum a corporibus corporea sensus organa moventur, per eam occasionem moveri a deo.

(But our religion teaches that the mind is absolutely incorporeal, and our metaphysicians confirm that when the bodily sense organs are moved by bodies, through this occasion the mind is moved by God.)

C. Clauberg and the rereading of the *aisthêsis/dianoia* relation

It was during the modern period that the central importance of the relation between *aisthêsis* and *dianoia* would be confirmed, and it would occur, not at all by chance, in Cartesian circles, for the seventeenth century was also characterized by a renewed interest in the investigations of psychophysiology and the debate over the limits and conditions of human knowledge through an examination of the faculties of the soul. But the reconsideration of *aisthêsis* and *dianoia* occurred in this case through an interesting rereading.

In his systematic commentary concerning Cartesian doctrine on the three degrees of sense (for Descartes, see above, IV.A), Johannes Clauberg specified that the term *sensus* must be understood as the second of the three meanings indicated, namely, the perception of the soul united with the body:

Atque ego tibi assentior et addo, hanc mentis perceptionem, quae toto genere differt a corporis motu praecedente, proprie stricteque sensum nuncupari.

(I am in agreement with you and I add that such perception of the soul, which differs absolutely from the movement of the body preceding it, is properly and strictly termed *sense*.)

(De cognitione Dei et nostri)

"To sense" is thus, properly speaking, "to perceive" ("sensum proprie esse ac dici quam diximus perceptionem" [sense proper and properly speaking is what we have called "perception"]; ibid.), "to think" ("clarissime intelligo, quomodo recte philosophantibus sentire sit cogitare" [I understand as clearly as possible that for those who philosophize correctly to sense is to think]; ibid.); and, in support of this Cartesian thesis, he affirms that according to *Physicus* (Strato of Lampsacus), *aisthêsis* and *dianoia* coincide. Clauberg writes, "Idem esse dixerit [Strato Lampsacenus] *aisthêsin kai dianoian*, id est, sensum et cogitationem mentis" (Strato of Lampsacus has said that *aisthêsis* and *dianoia* are one and the same thing, that is, the sense and thought of the mind). Strato, Theophrastus's successor at the head of the Lyceum, interpreted Aristotelian thought in an empiricist and naturalist sense and cast himself as the theoretician of "sensory demonstration" (*apodeixis aisthêtikê* [ἀπόδειξις αἰσθητική]), developing a psychology of the reciprocal dependence of sensation and intellect (see Repellini, "Il Liceo e la cultura alessandrina").

Clauberg, for his part, tended to read Strato's affirmation in the Cartesian manner: as a reduction of sense to thought. The question of the Cartesians was, Are seeing and sensing the province of the eye or of the mind? (*Sitne mens quae videt, an oculus, an aliud quid?* [Is it the mind that sees or the eye, or something else?]; *De cognitione Dei et nostri*); and the reply was as follows: to sense is the domain of the mind in unity with the body, for to sense is to perceive, entailing attention, apprenticeship, on the part of the mind, in the movements provoked in the brain by the action of external bodies on the sense organs. Wherein we note the ascendancy of the Platonic-Augustinian doctrine: "Et maxime illud Aristotelis Probl. 33 sect. 11 . . . unde dictum Mens videt, mens audit" (This is above all what Aristotle says in the *Problems* . . . where it is said that the mind sees, the mind hears; ibid.); or further still: "Hunc [secundum gradum sensus] dico esse apprehensionem atque attentionem mentis, in ea cerebri parte, ad quam omnes externorum sensuum motus deveniunt, immediate residentis atque operantis" (I say that this [the second degree of sense] is the apprehension or attention of the mind, which resides and operates in immediate fashion in that part of the brain where all the movements of the external senses finally arrive; ibid.).

V. Sinn/Bedeutung, "Meaning," "Sense"

The rest of the story autonomously develops the lexicon of the third sense of "sense"—a complex story implicating analytic philosophy as well as phenomenology and hermeneutics. The contemporary break is owed to Frege and the "invention" of the *Sinn/Bedeutung* difference, in which the contest between German and English is joined.

We can, in fact, date the emergence of the concept of "sense," *Sinn*, which, from its inception, was distinguished from "reference," *Bedeutung* (or "denotation," as Claude Imbert translated it into French in 1971), to Frege and his

fundamental article *Über Sinn und Bedeutung* (1892). The *Sinn* of a sentence or word is a distinct public entity belonging to or associated with a statement, whereas the *Bedeutung* is the reality designated by the sentence or word.

Although Frege's doublet structures the whole of reflection on signification in the twentieth century, it does not allow easy translation. It is crucial to recall that analytic philosophy had its inception, from the beginning of the century, in a translation into English of a distinction formulated in German. The English word "meaning," like the French word *signification*, is ambiguous, at times meaning *Sinn*, at others *Bedeutung*, and the fraught nature of ordinary usage is such that the word endlessly overrides the distinction. The massive transfer (occurring, for historical reasons, during the years 1930–40) of the philosophy of language and theories of signification from German to Anglo-Saxon philosophy brought all the dimensions and discussions of "sense" and "reference" to bear on the notorious term "meaning" and thus transformed the linguistic question of signification in its double valence (sense and reference) into the central and single philosophical problem of analytic philosophy.

A. From empiricism to *Sinn/Bedeutung*

1. The vague sense of "meaning" before Frege

The problem of a distinction between sense and reference is not posed in a framework in which language is assumed to refer to mental objects or ideas: *meaning* is a relation between words and objects that can be either external or internal. It is of little consequence under such circumstances to know whether someone like Hobbes had a referential or ideationist theory of signification since, in a sense, he didn't have any at all, the sign-relation he evoked being a nonlinguistic relation (mental discourse produces verbal language, "put into words" [*Leviathan*, pt. 1, chap. 7]). "Meaning" is a vague term, mental in cast, that designates the relation between words and objects or ideas designated as much as those objects or ideas themselves, as in Locke, for whom "significations" are ideas (*An Essay concerning Human Understanding*, bk. 4, chap. 2, §4, §7). It is not surprising that all of the philosophy of language in the twentieth century, following what is known as the linguistic turn, sought to criticize this notion of "meaning" defined as idea in order to reconceive it in terms of language. More dubious are those readings that project a theory of signification (sense, reference) in the contemporary sense onto those classical thinkers or, worse yet, who discover in them arguments for rementalizing sense (see Hacking's justified critique, *Why Does Language Matter to Philosophy?*).

One should not, however, neglect the fact that there is a sense of "meaning" at the very heart of British empiricism that is not that far removed from contemporary usage—a properly linguistic—but also critical—sense. Hume thus envisaged in his *Enquiry concerning Human Understanding* (§2) a means for "discounting" the sense-laden use of a philosophical term. The term that would not have any would be impossible to derive from an impression. The link between the two senses of "sense"—"sensation" and "meaning"—may well have been forged here, not between (mental) idea and signification, but between impression (sensation) and signification (sense). It would seem that only a critique, which is central in Hume, of what Quine would call "the idea idea" (*From a Logical Point of*

View) could open the path to a clear concept of signification. One finds in this passage in Hume the outline of a critique of the statements and terms of metaphysics via the criterion of signification (to be charged with or stripped of meaning) that would be brought to completion by Carnap. Similarly, but by virtue of a different approach, Berkeley, in his introduction to *A Treatise concerning the Principles of Human Knowledge*, criticizes abstract general ideas by advancing this argument:

There is no such thing as one precise and definite signification annexed to any general name, they all *signifying* indifferently a great number of particular ideas.

There emerges here the critique of what Quine would call the "myth of meaning," the problem being not only to define meaning but also to isolate and fix it.

▪ See Box 4.

4

"Import"/"sense," "meaning," "signification"

English has at its disposal many more words than French for conveying what French calls *sens* and *signification*: "sense," "signification," "meaning," "appellation," and "import." Every sentence or proposition has a sense or meaning, which may vary from one individual to another, or from one community to another. "Sense" is dependent on "import," but cannot be confused with it, since "import" is more "objective" than sense. "Import, not discourse," as Bentham put it laconically (*Essay on Language*). As with the importation of a commodity or a service into an economic system, the "import" is at once the entry of a sign into a linguistic system and the drift that is initiated within it once that inaugural event occurs and that it is possible to retrace in a relatively objective manner. Entry and drift may be overlooked by "meaning" and "sense," which are entirely synchronic in orientation; on the other hand, "import" cannot be discussed without implying an awareness of the diachrony of meaning. What etymology seeks to reactivate is plainly the "import," a term that is almost untranslatable in French other than by the expression *sens etymologique*, which is an overtranslation.

I. The economic and dynamic sense of "import"

However original it may be, English, like all languages, is composed of borrowings from other languages:

In the stock of words of which the English language is composed, a very considerable, not to say the largest, portion, are borrowed from some one or other of several foreign languages; in some instances at a very early date, in others at different points of time from the remotest down to the most recent.

(Bentham, *Essay on Language*)

The import dynamic consists of a more or less forced entry into a system and the provoking of a perturbation—with the ongoing

necessity of reequilibrating the system. The import is also the transmission of that initial shock, to the extent that it can be preserved. The import is what is conveyed within the language; it is, in a translation, what one seeks to transfer from one language to another, without, however, any hope of guaranteeing the absolute identity of what is being transferred.

II. The diachronic dimension of the "import"

One thus perceives the difference that exists between "import," on the one hand, and "sense" or "meaning," on the other: the philosophers, who speak in the language that they study and in which they conduct their analyses, strain to achieve awareness of the import, which is radically forgotten by those who, being mystified or hypnotized by the object, imagine they are grasping a meaning that they forge without knowing or mastering it. The import is what philosophers attempt to retrieve through their etymological labor, which reverses the historical order, since, in starting with a fiction, which always has sense and meaning, they aim at the actual entity from which it is derived. "Import" and "original" are constantly linked by Bentham: whatever the case for originality, the import can be grasped only indirectly, by questioning the immediate meaning.

In every language, words are found in clusters growing out of the same root. Whatsoever be the cluster to which the word in question belongs, the comprehension a man has of its import is comparatively imperfect, if it includes not a more or less general acquaintance with the whole cluster to which it belongs.

(*Essay on Language*)

It is that path, both logical and historical, that philosophers must be able to retrace if they are to fulfill the task that John Stuart Mill assigned to intellectuals, that of knowing the sources of the words with which they speak:

To common minds, only that portion of the meaning is in each generation suggested, of which that generation possesses the counterpart in its own habitual experience. But the words and propositions lie ready to suggest to any mind duly prepared the remainder of the meaning. Such individual minds are almost always to he found; and the lost meaning, revived by them, again by degrees works its way into the general mind.

(*A System of Logic*, bk. 4, chap. 4)

Bentham subtly distinguishes between what he calls "logical history," which ideally reconstructs the order in time as well as the logic of "removes," that is, the order of fictive entities in their degrees of distance from real entities, and "chronological history," which designates the far more chaotic course of time but which philosophers should also understand if they are intent on grasping the reality of the import rather than submitting to what fallaciously appears of it in meaning:

Language has its logical and its chronological history: its logical history shows what must have been the order of formation among the elements of language—shows it from the nature of man, shows it from the circumstances in which all men are placed, shows it from circumstantial evidence. The chronological history of language shows what has actually been.

(*Essay on Language*)

It may be said that the notion of import, as developed in these remarks, stems from "Benthamian," rather than from the English, language and derives its meaning only within a thematic specific to Bentham. In actuality, Mill mentions it as well (e.g., in *A System of Logic*, bk. 1, chap. 5, in order to deal with the meaning of propositions) and is familiar with the problematic, although

(*continued*)

(continued)

he does not always articulate it with terminological distinctions as systematic as those found in Bentham. Curiously, like Hume, he utilizes it more often as a verb, in the logical sense of "entailing" or "implying." It should unfortunately be added that when Mill specifically retains the noun, the French translator of *A System of Logic*, Peisse, pays no attention to it and treats "import" as though he were dealing with "meaning"; on occasion, he even overlooks the term completely and leaves it out—but it is not easy to proceed differently.

Jean-Pierre Cléro

BIBLIOGRAPHY

Bentham, Jeremy. *Essay on Language*. In vol. 8 of *The Works of Jeremy Bentham*. 11 vols. Edinburgh: Bowring, 1838–43. Reprint, New York: Russell & Russell, 1962.

Mill, John Stuart. *Essays on Ethics, Religion and Society*. In vol. 10 of *Collected Works of John Stuart Mill*, edited by J. M. Robson. Toronto: University of Toronto Press, 1963–91.

———. *A System of Logic Ratiocinative and Inductive*. Vols. 1 and 2 of *Collected Works of John Stuart Mill*, edited by J. M. Robson. Toronto: University of Toronto Press, 1963–91. Translation by L. Peisse: *Système de logique*. Brussels: Mardaga, 1988.

2. Frege's invention

The distinction introduced by Frege created an objectivist break within a rather confused semantic field. Indeed, neither *Bedeutung* (denotation or reference, the object designated) nor *Sinn* (the meaning of the proposition, the thought it expresses) was defined by Frege in terms of ideas or mental content (see the text *Der Gedanke* [*Thought*], 1919). Frege was not content to transform or perfect the concept of sense: he invented it, breaking with the entire philosophical tradition of determining meaning in mental—or, in any event, prelinguistic—terms. He objectified *Sinn* (as he did thought, *Gedanke*, with whose definition he is associated) as absolutely independent from the thinking or speaking subject. The introduction of *Sinn* (along with that of *Bedeutung*) thus effected a depsychologization of questions relating to language—that may have been subsequently attenuated by translations of *Sinn* as "meaning"/"sense" or *sens/signification* (in French).

A further difficulty, of which Frege was aware, was then raised by the universality of sense and its independence of specific languages. *Sinn* ("original *Sinn*" in the pun much appreciated by English-language philosophers in the 1960s) was originally defined as the common endowment of languages and a cultural invariant, thus bearing the seeds of its own critique within itself, specifically by way of the problematics of translation and, more generally, of linguistic difference and relativity.

3. Wittgenstein's new distinctions and the confusion of the English translations

In the tradition initiated by Frege, the critique of "meaning" in the mental or psychological sense would continue. Wittgenstein, in *Tractatus logico-philosophicus*, would take up and modify the *Sinn/Bedeutung* distinction. According to the *Tractatus* (3.3), only a proposition (*Satz*) has a meaning (*Sinn*), a name or a primitive sign has a denotation (*Bedeutung*) and represents (*vertritt*) the object. The English translation of the *Tractatus* (1922) by C. K. Ogden employs "meaning" for *Bedeutung*, creating a lasting ambiguity. Bertrand Russell, in his introduction, thus has "meaning" serve for both the sense of the proposition (*Satz-Sinn*, 3.11) and the denotation of the component sign. All those translations would contribute to a standard interpretation of the *Tractatus*, which has only recently begun to be cast off in order to reestablish the bond between the first and second philosophies of Wittgenstein.

Another source of confusion and slippage is the Wittgensteinian distinction between *unsinnig* and *sinnlos* (4.461, 4.4611), which are translated respectively as "nonsensical" and "without sense." Tautology and contradiction are deprived of sense: they are *sinnlos*, but not nonsensical, *unsinnig*. They do not present a state of things but are nonetheless part of language. In various interpretations of Wittgenstein by the Vienna Circle, *sinnlos* became what was radically deprived of sense and consequently to be excluded from language (see NONSENSE). In *Overcoming Metaphysics*, Carnap thus makes the transition from the absence of the *Bedeutung* of the term (no empirical content) to the absence of the sense of its statements (impossible linguistic constructs). In reducing the distinction between sense and denotation, thought and empirical content, one obtained a kind of hybrid for which the term "meaning" (which would become *signification* in philosophical French) worked rather well. "Meaning" thus became the criterion for distinguishing between statements deemed acceptable or not in the framework of a scientific philosophy. Every problem of knowledge became translatable as a problem of meaning.

The basis for such a criterion for distinguishing between statements endowed with meaning or not resides in what has been called a verificationist theory of meaning, which defines the meaning of a proposition (with Schlick) as the method of its verification. That concept of meaning was now in turn a (curious) retranslation of a proposition in the *Tractatus* (Ogden translation):

Einen Satz verstehen, heisst wissen was der Fall ist, wenn er wahr ist.

(To understand a proposition is to know what the case is when it is true.)

In point of fact, Wittgenstein, far from suggesting a method of verification, was affirming the effective bond between meaning and truth. For example (4.022):

Des Satz zeigt seinen Sinn. Der Satz zeigt, wie es sich verhält, wenn er wahr ist.

(The proposition shows its sense. The proposition shows how it is, when it is true.)

It is remarkable that this superimposition of meaning on truth (on the possibility of being true or false) should subsequently become a determination of meaning in terms of originary experiences, which is rather removed from the perspective of the *Tractatus.*

B. Indeterminacy of the translations

1. The ambiguities of "meaning" and "sense"

The contrast between the distinction proposed by Frege, which has become classic, indeed structural, in analytic philosophy, and ordinary English, which is characterized by the flexibility with which "meaning" is used, is considerable. *Sinn*, like *Bedeutung*, fell prey from the outset to a certain indetermination in translation, being rendered on some occasions as "sense" or on others as "meaning," or even as "denotation" or *significatum*. It may seem curious that "meaning" is utilized indifferently to translate *Sinn* and *Bedeutung* by philosophers (Russell is the most striking example) who elsewhere take up on their own (or at least are familiar with) Frege's distinction. It was only once "reference" and "denotation" were imposed as translations of *Bedeutung* that a first clarification of the status of "meaning" was achieved: "meaning" would partake rather of the realm of *Sinn* (as in Quine, see below, C.2).

C. Imbert translated *Bedeutung* in French as *dénotation* in order to bring into relief the full force of Frege's gesture. The translation did not really catch on in French, which, following the most frequent usage in English, prefers *référence* in as much as some would distinguish between "denoting" and "referring" (Bertrand Russell, Peter Strawson). In an edition of Frege's *Nachlass*, still other translators recently decided to translate *Bedeutung* as *signification* in French (and not as *référence*, which would be closer to standard English usage). As P. de Rouilhan has noted,

> To be sure, what Frege designated in his day as *Bedeutung* is what we French-speaking logician-philosophers today designate as "référence." But what logico-philosophical German designated in Frege's day as *Bedeutung* is what we today designate as "signification." It is not for us to rectify Frege's deviations (about which Husserl complained) in relation to his own language (by which we mean not a certain idiolect, but the language of a certain community). It befell us to transpose them into our own, and that is what we were able to do as simply as possible by translating *Bedeutung* as "signification."
>
> (Intro. to Frege, *Écrits posthumes*)

That choice, however, introduces a *sens/signification* doublet in French, which seems insufficiently clear and scarcely differential.

It was on the translation of *Sinn* by "sense" (in English) and *sens* (in French) that agreement was easiest to achieve. To be sure, the term itself was subject to an ambiguity, this time common to English and German, as well as to French, namely the "semantic" sense and the "sensory" sense of sense. (It is perhaps here, in the analytic field, that the origin of the verificationist definitions of meaning, particularly in the interpretation of the *Tractatus* by the Vienna Circle, is to be found.) Evidence is provided by Strawson's *The Bounds of Sense*, an influential work devoted to Kant's first *Critique*: Strawson introduced a "principle of significance" that transformed the problem of the limits of knowledge and sensibility into a semantic question: that of the limits of sense (of the domain in which our questions make sense). His position, extremely influential in analytic philosophy, was given clear and radical form in the last sentence of that work, in which he affirmed the impossibility of according meaning to a question beyond the limits of our language: "We lack the words to say how it would be without them."

The Bounds of Sense thus represents a turning point wherein the empiricist theme of the limits of our sensibility shades into the logico-linguistic theme of the limits of our language and thus of meaning, what Strawson and later Quine would call our "conceptual scheme." That history has recently been summarized by Hilary Putnam, who describes the transition effected by analytic philosophy from radical empiricism to semantic theories, followed by its more recent return to theories of perception and the senses in "Sense, Nonsense, and the Senses" (1995). In point of fact, the dual sense of "sense" reflects the dual heritage of analytic philosophy and all the ambiguity of its constitution: it lays claim to the heritage of British empiricism (for which, to borrow Quine's pun, "only sense makes sense" [*Theories and Things*]), even as it remains the Anglo-Saxon continuation of what Alberto Coffa has defined as "the semantic tradition" stemming from Frege and Carnap, whose investigations focused on sentences or statements as semantic units. The efforts of historians currently underway in the United States on the origins of analytic philosophy and logical empiricism will perhaps result in an understanding of how that dual (empiricist and semantic) tradition, when added to the specifically American tradition of pragmatism, succeeded in producing the multiplicity of theories of signification and in maintaining, in most cases, its twofold dimension.

Superimposed on the entire complex, finally, is "sense" in the sense of "good sense," "rationality." An illustration may be found in the title of Austin's *Sense and Sensibilia*, which refers to Jane Austen's *Sense and Sensibility* (translated into French as *Raison et Sentiments*).

2. Ogden and Richards and the "meaning of meaning"

Reflection on the "meaning of meaning" runs through the entirety of analytic philosophy, as evidenced by the celebrated book of Ogden and Richards, *The Meaning of Meaning*, which was published in 1923 and composed in stages, starting in 1910. It is a volume that is somewhat forgotten at present (or at least it was until a recent reedition with a preface by Umberto Eco) but that exerted considerable influence in its day. Putnam, for instance, would take up Ogden and Richards's title in his famous article "The Meaning of 'Meaning'" (with the extra quotation marks making all the difference), in which he sketches out—as a critique of Frege's *Sinn*—a causal theory of reference.

Ogden and Richards's book, even as it situates itself in the Frege-Wittgenstein line of ascent, plays on the diversity of senses ascribable to "meaning." For them, "meaning" designates both Frege's *Sinn* and his *Bedeutung*. The English translation of *Tractatus logico-philosophicus* (1922), which was Ogden's, uses "meaning" for *Bedeutung* and "sense" for *Sinn*.

The Ogden–Richards volume claims to be simultaneously a presentation of the different "meanings of meaning" and a critique. But the book does not always elude the objections it formulates against philosophical theories of meaning, notably in its elaboration of an "emotive" theory of signification, which was inspired by Wittgenstein and which would prevail in analytic—and particularly moral—philosophy during the 1940s.

In chapter 8 of their book, Ogden and Richards lodge an attack against the inflation within Anglo-Saxon thought of the different senses of "meaning," of which they list at least sixteen uses. This omnipresence of the word "meaning" is for them a sign of inadequate reflection with regard to the functions of symbols, a clarification of which would be imperative in keeping with their will to found a new semiotics (which would serve to inspire Charles Morris, one of the introducers of the Vienna Circle in the United States; see SEMIOTICS). Among the uses that are classified and criticized in *The Meaning of Meaning*, two (beside the well-known sense of "importance") are deserving of our attention. On the one hand, an "intentional" usage, which is facilitated by the English gerund (mean-ing) and which yields a noun-form of the verb "to mean"—as in "What I meant was . . . " (analyzed on p. 192), designates both the signification and the intention of a proposition; that dual dimension of "meaning" enables an easier assimilation of theories of intentionality by the philosophy of language. On the other hand, a "perceptual" usage, which was criticized by Ogden and Richards for its imprecision, particularly in Sellars (in an article in *Mind* and in his volume *Critical Realism*), for whom "meaning" is added to the content of perception or serves to structure it. It is in this connection that they note that

> the one inevitable source of misunderstanding and disagreement, the omnipresence of the term Meaning, was allowed to pass unchallenged. It seems to have been accepted without question into the vocabulary of American philosophy, for use on all occasions of uncertainty.
>
> (*The Meaning of Meaning*)

It was naturally in psychology that Ogden and Richards found the most misleading forms of that usage as well as of the meaning-perception association, but they also launched an attack on philosophers close to the analytic trend, such as Moore and Dewey, who "all have their own uses of the word, obvious yet undefined" (ibid.).

Finally, they advanced for the first time a dimension of meaning that might be called anthropological: the term "meaning" is omnipresent in Malinowski, whose texts on meaning in anthropology are included in an appendix to *The Meaning of Meaning*. "Meanings," in the plural, refers to cultural diversity (pluralities of signification, expression, and language). Everything thus becomes a search for meaning (in sociology and anthropology, Weber and Malinowski adopted an elaborated form of the concept of *Sinn*):

> All this shows the wide and complex considerations into which we are led by an attempt to give an adequate analysis of meaning. Instead of translating, of inserting simply an English word for a native one, we are faced by a long and not altogether simple process of describing

wide fields of custom, of social psychology and of tribal organization which correspond to one term or another. We see that linguistic analysis inevitably leads us into the study of all the subjects covered by Ethnographic field-work.

> (Malinowski, "The Problem of Meaning")

This anthropological dimension of meaning would be developed in the positions of Quine, positions based on a circumstance of radical translation (see TO TRANSLATE, Box 3).

Ogden and Richards thus proposed a recasting of the notion of meaning, which can be associated in their work with the emergence of pragmatics. Their principal references for such a renewal, enumerated and described successively, were, in order, Husserl, Russell, Frege, Gomperz, and, finally, Peirce. The London lectures (1922) delivered by Husserl, and particularly their abstracts in English, were cited to bring into relief his theory of "meaning." That was obviously the translation used by Ogden and Richards for *Bedeutung* when they presented several excerpts from *Logical Investigations*, a circumstance relevant to the extent that in those passages Husserl makes rather undifferentiated use of *Sinn* and *Bedeutung*. Here, too, it will be seen how the use of "meaning" allows one to associate, as though naturally, the two dimensions distinguished by Frege and which the English language had such trouble differentiating clearly.

C. The crossing of the Atlantic

1. The adaptation of the vocabulary of Viennese empiricism, or how "meaning" slipped from *Sinn* to *Bedeutung*

A crucial moment in the history of "meaning" in the twentieth century was the introduction in the 1930s in the United States, during the immigration of philosophers of the Vienna Circle expelled by Nazism, of an entire lexicon belonging to Viennese empiricism. It was through Carnap, brought to the United States by Quine, who had met him in Europe in 1933, that Frege's distinction in the transformed version just evoked would be introduced. Quine, who had *The Logical Syntax of Language* translated into English, played a crucial role. In *Logical Syntax*, *Bedeutung* and *Sinn* are both rendered by "meaning" ("sense [or meaning]," §14, theorem 14-4). In presenting Carnap's work and his project of "philosophy as syntax," Quine called "meaning" *Bedeutung* and, as of 1934, articulated the idea of a description of language that would have recourse to neither sense nor denotation (which, along with Carnap, he would subsequently propose to call "intension" and "extension" but which both thinkers would continue to reject). Thus it was that "meaning," from "sense," became in a way, through its Atlantic crossing and the beginnings of the critique of the notion of signification, "reference."

2. Quine and the "myth of meaning"

In a series of theses that would figure at the center of American philosophy for decades (1950–80), Quine waged an assault on the "myth of meaning." He was not aiming only at a certain confused use of "meaning," in the manner of Ogden and Richards, but also proposed a more radical critique directed first of all at the "meaning" of linguists ("The Problem of Meaning in Linguistics," in *From a Logical*

Point of View). Now despite the self-proclaimed fidelity of Quine to Frege, Quine's critique challenged the founding father of analytic philosophy by attacking what had been one of the achievements of Frege's semantics: the ideality of meaning.

The celebrated thesis of the indeterminacy of translation (is a *gavagi* a rabbit? see *Word and Object*, chap. 2; see also TO TRANSLATE, Box 3) was initially an attack against the *meanings* of the linguists, the significations of the mentalists, the semantics of Carnap, and even the *Sinn* of Frege: there is no more an empirical signification than there is analyticity, no more a mental meaning than there is a shared fixed point between languages. But—and this is a consequence that Quine himself calls "unexpected"—his thesis no less calls into question reference itself, the matter of knowing *what* I am speaking *about*, with the thesis of ontological relativity and inscrutability or, to use Quine's most recent expression, the indeterminacy of reference. The radicalism of this critique has not always been well received by post-Quinians, who have attempted to restore different ways of meaning (e.g., Davidson, who attempts to reconstruct meaning on the basis of the concept of truth as defined by Tarski) or to show that Quine's thesis would be tantamount to making all language impossible (Putnam).

The confusion of dualities—intension/extension, sense/reference—within "meaning" was thus paradoxically justified a posteriori or, at the very least, explained in the shared critique of those entities undertaken by the philosophy of language starting in the 1960s. The extent to which these skeptical theses are currently debated in America is well known. It is therefore a matter of some oddity that it was in France (and in French) that Quine first presented his thesis of the indeterminacy of translation (in 1958, at the Royaumont colloquium), under the title "Le mythe de la signification," in which the word *signification* could, in fact, accommodate all the senses (and also all the impasses) of "meaning." There remained a considerable difficulty: the relation between "to mean" and "meaning."

D. "Must we mean what we say?"

The absence of a standard translation of "meaning" in French, and more generally the dual character as noun and verb of "meaning," was highlighted in the following sentence by Quine: "One can perhaps talk of meaning without talking of meanings. An expression means; *meaning* is what it does" (*Theories and Things*).

Whereupon Quine made reference to French, which he deemed superior: *cela veut dire*. But it is clear that the verbal, or active, character of "meaning" confers a supplementary dimension on the English term (as in the untranslatable expression "to make sense" as well). Moreover, the verb "to mean" is untranslatable in French: *signifier* is too technical; *vouloir dire*, often inadequate, introduces an intentional aspect in certain contexts. Now all reflection on ordinary language in English-language philosophy of language after Wittgenstein is centered on this dual use of "mean" and the immediate relation between "mean" and "meaning," which is absent from French and German. To signify is to mean, but is every signification intentional? And is meaning—*vouloir dire*, wanting to say—always wanting to say *something*, expressing

an intention? The problem of such meaning (*meinen*) was already raised in the *Tractatus* (5.62) in relation to solipsism:

> Was des Solipsismus nämlich *meint* ist ganz richtig, nur lässt es sich nicht sagen.
>
> (What solipsism *means* is quite precise, only it cannot be uttered.)

Translated by Ogden: "what solipsism *means*." We are confronted here with a *meinen* that partakes of neither *Sinn* nor *Bedeutung* and that is well rendered by the French *veut dire*. Wittgenstein's meaning (or *vouloir dire*) is not an attempt to say otherwise than through language something that cannot be said clearly: for Wittgenstein, if an expression is without meaning, it has none "anywhere." As Diamond put it: "There is not a thought shorn of sense that would be expressed by a proposition shorn of sense" (*The Realistic Spirit*; see NONSENSE). It is a point that Wittgenstein would express in the *Philosophical Investigations*: "When one says that a phrase has no meaning, it is not, so to speak, that its meaning has no meaning." This brought him to determine the meaning of our ordinary statements, and such is the question that opens *The Blue Book*: "What is the meaning of a word?"

Therein lies the whole question of ordinary-language philosophy, which began with the second Wittgenstein, who proposed that meanings should no longer be sought elsewhere, outside language, but rather at our feet, as it were: in our daily usage. That emergence in the second Wittgenstein of a new concept of the verb "to mean" guided the choices of the French translators of the last edition of *The Blue Book*, in which, for meaning, the translators proposed *sens* and for the verbal form, *vouloir-dire* instead of *signifier*. Thus was laid out an entire line of translation of "meaning" altogether different from the previous semantic tradition and that would follow Wittgenstein's celebrated indication: "meaning = use." "Meaning," or *vouloir-dire* in French, would be determined by what I *do* with language. The whole of J. L. Austin's method, which was a radical critique of the traditional analytic notion of signification (first in his article, "The Meaning of a Word" [1940], then in his theory of the performative), was based on a new kind of inquiry into meaning as *vouloir-dire*; knowing what we mean is knowing "what we say when," what our relation to a statement is in the complete discursive situation.

In *Must We Mean What We Say?* Stanley Cavell has pressed the question of intentional (or unintentional) meaning furthest. He delves into the claim of the ordinary-language philosophers Wittgenstein and Austin to say and know what we say and what we mean. Cavell shows that such (intentional) meaning—*vouloir-dire*—can be determined only through a consideration of the language community and its judgments. "We" are those who say what we mean, but who is this *we*, and what is it that grounds *my* relation to it? Cavell's conclusion is radical: *I* am the only possible source of meaning, which emerges from our agreement ("to signify" or "to mean" is *übereinstimmen*, to harmonize or resonate together) and, in circular fashion, serves to found it and is founded on it alone. To accept to signify or mean is to accept that agreement and to be accepted by it. The question of meaning is thus transformed: it is no longer one of the boundary between sense and nonsense, of language's capacity to mean something, but, on the contrary, one of the refusal of expression and meaning, which is precisely that of skepticism. "Why do we attach significance to *any* words and deeds, of others or of ourselves? . . . How can anything we say or do count as doodling, be some form of nonsense; and why is all the rest condemned to meaning?" (Cavell, *The Claim of Reason*; see COMMON SENSE, and also, for the Aristotelian background, which often goes unnoticed, HOMONYM, II.B.3 and above, I.A.3). For Cavell, it is the repression of this dimension of meaning that may well have been accomplished by the whole of contemporary thought about sense, the various definitions and critiques of signification being but the masks donned by our refusal of expression. "A fantasy of necessary inexpressiveness would solve a simultaneous set of metaphysical problems" (ibid.). For Cavell, what is thus repressed is plainly not the idea of intention or intentionality, whose past and present philosophical fortunes (see INTENTION) are well known, but the power of language itself to mean, making of me, so to speak, the bearer of its meaning. From this point of view, Cavell has pursued in his way the labor of depsychologizing meaning inaugurated by Frege and Wittgenstein, continued by Austin, and occasionally voided in various contemporary determinations (and even critiques) of signification.

■ See Box 5.

Barbara Cassin
Sandra Laugier
Alain de Libera
Irène Rosier-Catach
Giacinta Spinosa

BIBLIOGRAPHY

Albertus Magnus, Saint. *De anima*. In *Opera omnia*, edited by Clemens Stroick. Münster, Ger.: Aschendorff, 1968.

Anselm, Saint. *De grammatico*. In *Opera omnia*, edited by Francis S. Schmitt. Edinburgh: Nelson, 1946.

Aristotle. *The Complete Works of Aristotle: The Revised Oxford Translation*. Edited by Jonathan Barnes. Princeton, NJ: Princeton University Press / Bollingen, 1984.

Ashworth, E. J. *Studies in Post-Medieval Semantics*. London: Variorum Reprints, 1985.

Augustine, Saint. *De dialectica*. Edited and translated by B. Darrell Jackson. Dordrecht, Neth.: D. Reidel, 1975.

Austin, J. L. *Philosophical Papers*. Oxford: Clarendon Press, 1962.

———. *Sense and Sensibilia*. Oxford: Clarendon Press, 1962.

Baker, Gordon P. *Wittgenstein, Frege, and the Vienna circle*. Oxford: Blackwell, 1988.

Bouveresse, Jacques. *Dire et ne rien dire: L'illogisme, l'impossibilité et le non-sens*. Nîmes, Fr.: Jacqueline Chambon, 1997.

Brachet, Jean-Paul. "Réflexions sur l'évolution sémantique de *significare*." In *Conceptions latines du sens et de la signification*, edited by Marc Baratin and Claude Moussy, 29–39. Paris: Presses de l'Université Paris–Sorbonne, 1999.

Carnap, Rudolph. *The Logical Syntax of Language*. London: Routledge & Kegan Paul, 1937.

Cassin, Barbara. *Aristote et le logos*. Paris: Presses Universitaires de France, 1997.

Cavell, Stanley. *The Claim of Reason*. Oxford: Oxford University Press, 1979.

———. *Must We Mean What We Say?* Cambridge: Cambridge University Press, 1969.

Clauberg, Johannes. *De cognitione Dei et nostri*. In *Opera omnia philosophica*. Hildesheim, Ger.: Olms, 1968. First published in 1691.

Coffa, Alberto. *The Semantic Tradition from Kant to Carnap*. Cambridge: Cambridge University Press, 1991.

Copenhaver, Brian P., editor. *Hermetica: The Greek Corpus Hermeticum and the Latin Asclepius in a New English Translation*. Cambridge: Cambridge University Press, 1992.

Cuvillier, Armand. *Vocabulaire philosophique*. Paris: Armand Colin, 1956.

5
Feeling

A vast complexity in aesthetics, philosophy, and psychology, "feeling" evokes everything from physical sensation to emotional affect. Henry Mackenzie's *The Man of Feeling* (1771) epitomized the eighteenth-century "cult of sensibility," an answer to scientific positivism, material economics, and military might. Romanticism gave "feeling" cognitive and philosophical heft. In a succinct essay "On Gusto" (1816), describing "power or passion defining any object," William Hazlitt argued for "truth in feeling"—this power and truth at once reorganizing rational epistemologies and purging for masculine aesthetics the stigma of feminine weakness and effeminate sensibility. The Hazlitt-admiring poet John Keats equated "feeling" with knowledge itself: "we read fine things but never feel them to the full until we have gone the same steps as the Author"; if he bristled at William Wordsworth's poetic didacticism, he admired his poetic power in making his reader "feel the 'burden of the Mystery'" in his "dark passages" (letter to John Hamilton Reynolds, 3 May 1818, quoting "Tintern Abbey"). As he lay dying, he wrote of his "feeling of my real life having passed" and, paradoxically, of his still keen "feeling for light and shade, all that information (primitive sense) necessary for a poem" (letter to Charles Brown, 30 November 1818).

Wordsworth blazoned a poetics of feeling in his preface to the second edition of *Lyrical Ballads* (1800), setting this as a principle opposite to narrative action, a value superior to rational understanding, a science in itself, and an antidote to the "degrading" popular appetite for works of "outrageous stimulation." Careful to say that the poet is one who has "thought long and deeply," he identified "All good poetry [as] the spontaneous overflow of powerful feelings," and his poetry as one in which "feeling . . . gives importance to the action and situation, and not the action and situation to the feeling."

This import and power are not uncontested. To Mary Wollstonecraft, women were degraded by "false sentiments and overstretched feelings" at the expense of salutary "natural emotions" and rational maturity (*A Vindication of the Rights of Woman*, 1792). Coleridge argued that feeling was but one element for poetic imagination—a "power" revealed "in the balance or reconciliation of opposite or discordant qualities": "a more than usual state of emotion, with more than usual order; judgement ever awake and steady self-possession, with enthusiasm and feeling profound or vehement." The "genius" of creating images "modified by a predominant passion," moreover, requires remoteness from "personal sensations and experiences"; Shakespeare's power entails "the alienation . . . the utter *aloofness* of the poet's own feelings, from those of which he is at once the painter and the analyst" (*Biographia Literaria*, 1817). This standard sustains T. S. Eliot's high modernist maxim that "Poetry is not a turning loose of emotion, but an escape from emotion"; he wasn't advocating emotional vacuity, only crucially "personal emotions" (*Tradition and the Individual Talent*, 1917). The question is never resolved. Beat poets would revivify the pulse of feeling, both in the extravagant shaping of poetry on the page and in energetic performances on the stage.

Susan Wolfson

De Rijk, Lambertus Maria. *Logica Modernorum*. Vol. 2, *The Origin and Early Development of the Theory of Supposition*. Assen, Neth.: Van Gorcum, 1967.

———. *Through Language to Reality: Studies in Medieval Semantics and Metaphysics*. Edited by E. P. Bos. Northampton, UK: Varorium Reprints, 1989.

Diamond, Cora. *The Realistic Spirit*. Cambridge, MA: MIT Press, 1991.

Erigena, John Scotus. *Periphyseon* [*De divisions naturae*]. Translated by I. P. Sheldon-Williams. Dublin: Dublin Institute for Advanced Studies, 1972.

Fattori, Marta, and Massio Luigi Bianchi, eds. *Sensus-sensatio. VIII Colloquio internazionale del lessico inteletuale Europeo*. Florence: Leo S. Olschki, 1996.

Fredborg, Karin Margareta. "Speculative Grammar in the 12th Century." In *The Cambridge History of Twelfth Century Philosophy*, edited by Peter Dronke. Cambridge: Cambridge University Press, 1988.

Frege, Friedrich L. G. *Écrits posthumes*. Translated by P. de Rouilhan and C. Tiercelin. Nîmes, Fr.: J. Chambon, 1999.

———. *Nachgelassene Schriften*. Edited by H. Hermes, F. Kambartel, and F. Kaulbach. Hamburg: Felix Meiner, 1969. Translation by P. Long and R. White: *Posthumous Writings*. Chicago: University of Chicago Press, 1979.

———. *Translations from the Philosophical Writings of Gottlob Frege*. 3rd ed. Edited and translated by P. Geach and M. Black. Oxford: Blackwell, 1980.

Garcea, Alessandro. "Gellio e la dialettica." *Memorie dell'Academia delle Scienze di Torino* 24 (2000): 53–204.

Hacking, Ian. *Why Does Language Matter to Philosophy?* Cambridge: Cambridge University Press, 1975.

Hamlyn, David Walter. *Sensation and Perception: A History of the New Philosophy of Perception*. London: Routledge & Kegan Paul, 1961.

Henry Aristippus. *Plato latinus: Phaedo*. Edited by L. Minio Paluello and H. J. Drossart Lulois. London: Warburg Institute, 1950.

Irenaeus, Saint. *Adversus haereses*. Books 1 and 2. In *Sancti Irenaei episcopi Lugdunensis libri quinque adverses haereses*, vol. 1, edited by W. W. Harvey. Cambridge: Cambridge University Press, 1857.

Jerome, Saint. *S. Hieronymus presbyteri opera. Part 1, Opera exegetica. 6: Commentarii in prophetas minores*. Vol. 2, *Commentarii in prophetas Naum, Abacuc, Sophoniam, Aggaeum, Zachariam, Malachiam*. Turnhout, Belg.: Brepols, 1970.

Kretzmann, Norman, Anthony Kenny, and Jan Pinborg. *The Cambridge History of Later Medieval Philosophy*. Cambridge: Cambridge University Press, 1982.

Libera, Alain de, and Irène Rosier. "La pensée linguistique médiévale." In *Histoire des idées linguistique*, Vol 2. Liège, Belg.: Mardaga, 1992.

Malinowski, Bronislaw. "The Problem of Meaning in Primitive Languages." In *The Meaning of Meaning*, C. K. Ogden and I. A. Richards, 451–510. London: Routledge & Kegan Paul, 1923.

Marmo, Costantino. *Semiotica e linguaggio nella scolastica: Parigi, Bologna, Erfurt, 1270–1330, la semiotica dei Modisti*. Rome: Instituto Palazzo Borromini, 1994.

Merleau-Ponty, Maurice. *L'œil et l'esprit*. Paris: Gallimard, 1964. Translation by Carleton Dallery, revised by Michael B. Smith: "Eye and Mind." In *The Merleau-Ponty Aesthetics Reader*, edited by Galen A. Johnson and Michael B. Smith. Evanston, IL: Northwestern University Press, 1992.

Moussy, Claude. "Les vocables Latins servant à desigper le sens et la signification." In *Conceptions latines du sens et de la signification*, edited by Marc Baratin and Claude Moussy, 13–27. Paris: Presses de l'Université Paris–Sorbonne, 1999.

Nuchelmans, Gabriel. *Theories of the Proposition. Ancient and Medieval Conceptions of the Bearers of Truth and Falsity*. Amsterdam: North-Holland, 1973.

Ogden, Charles Kay, and Ivor Armstrong Richards. *The Meaning of Meaning*. London: Routledge & Kegan Paul, 1923.

Pinborg, Jan. *Die Entwicklung der Sprachtheorie im Mittelalter*. Münster, Ger.: Aschendorff, 1967.

Putnam, Hilary. *Philosophical Papers, II*. Cambridge: Cambridge University Press, 1975.

———. "Sense, Nonsense, and the Senses." *Journal of Philosophy* 91, no. 9 (1994): 445–517.

———. *Words and Life*. Cambridge, MA: Harvard University Press, 1994.

Quine, W.V.O. *From a Logical Point of View*. Cambridge, MA: Harvard University Press, 1953.

———. *Theories and Things*. Cambridge, MA: Harvard University Press, 1981.

———. *Word and Object*. Cambridge, MA: MIT Press, 1960.

Repellini, Ferruccio F. "Il Liceo e la cultura alessandrina." In *Storia della filosofia*, vol. 1, edited by P. Rossi and C. A. Viano. Rome: Laterza, 1993.

Roesch, Sophie. "Res et verbum dans le De Lingua Latina de Varrón." In *Conceptions latines du sens et de la signification*, edited by Marc Baratin and Claude Moussy, 65–80. Paris: Presses de l'Université Paris–Sorbonne, 1999.

Rosier, Irène. "*Res significata* et *modus significandi*. Les enjeux lingistiques et théologiques d'une distinction médiévale." In *Sprachtheorien in Spätantike und Mittelalter*, edited by Sten Ebeesen, 135–68. Tübingen: Gunter Narr, 1995.

Ruello, Francis. *Les noms divins et leurs "raisons" selon saint Albert le Grand, commentateur du "De divinis nominibus."* Paris: Vrin, 1963.

Schaeffer, John D. *Sensus Communis: Vico, Rhetoric, and the Limits of Relativism*. Durham, NC: Duke University Press, 1990.

Soulez, Antonia, ed. *Manifeste du cercle de Vienne et autres écrits*. Paris: Presses Universitaires de France, 1985.

Spinosa, Giacinta. "Sensazione e percezione tra platonismo e aristotelismo: Semantica greca del sensus medievale." In *Sensus-sensatio, VIII Colloquio internazionale del lessico inteletuale Europeo*, edited by Marta Fattori and Massio Luigi Bianchi. Florence: Leo S. Olschki, 1996.

Strawson, Peter. *The Bounds of Sense*. London: Methuen, 1973.

Valenta, Luisa. "'Cum non sit intelligibilis, nec ergo significabilis.' Modi significandi, intelligendi e essendi nella teologia del XII secolo." *Documenti e Studi Sulla Tradizione Filosofica Medievale* 11 (2000): 133–94.

Vico, Giambattista. *De antiquissima Italorum spaientia*. In *Opere filosofiche*, edited by P. Cristofolini. Florence: Sansoni, 1971. First published in 1710. Translated by Jason Taylor: *On the Most Ancient Wisdom of the Italians*. New Haven, CT: Yale University Press, 2010.

Wittgenstein, Ludwig. *The Blue and Brown Books*. Oxford: Basil Blackwell, 1958.

———. *Philosophical Investigations*. Bilingual ed. Translated by G.E.M. Anscombe. Oxford: Blackwell, 2001.

———. *Tractatus logico-philosophicus*. Translated by C. K. Ogden. London: Routledge & Kegan Paul, 1922. Translated by D. F. Pears and B. F. McGuiness. London: Routledge & Kegan Paul, 1974.

Wolfson, Harry A. "The Internal Senses in Latin, Arabic and Hebrew Philosophical Texts." *Harvard Theological Review* 28 (1935): 69–133.

SENSUS COMMUNIS (LATIN)

FRENCH   *sens commun*

➤ *SENS COMMUN*, and COMMON SENSE, *IMAGINATION* [PHANTASIA], I/ME/MYSELF, INTELLECT, INTELLECTUS, INTENTION, MEMORY, PERCEPTION, SENSE, SOUL, TRUTH, UNDERSTANDING

The Scholastic notion of "common sense" was fixed in its principal directions with the medieval Latin translation of the section of Avicenna's *The Cure* dedicated to the treatise *De anima*. It thus presupposes Avicenna's classification of the inner senses into five instances, each situated in a different location in the brain, and designated respectively by the terms: (a) common sense, (b) imagination, (c) imaginative (in animals) or cogitative (in men), (d) estimative, (e) memory.

The inclusion of common sense, or of the function attributed to it, in a classification of internal senses is not totally an innovation of Avicenna (contrary to the assertion of Wolfson, "The Internal Senses in Latin, Arabic, and Hebrew Philosophic Texts). In point of fact, in the treatise *Ideas of the Citizens in the Virtuous City*, al-Farabi already distinguished a *principal sensory faculty*, "one in which the perceptions of the five senses are joined, as if the five senses were so many informants, each charged with a variety of information from a different region of the kingdom," and an *imaginative faculty*, "retaining sensations after their disappearance from the senses, judging sensations, possessing total power over them, separating them from each other and combining them." Since that treatise was unknown in the West, it was Avicenna and he alone who introduced the so-called peripatetic division of the cognitive faculties among the Latins.

The distinction of the five inner cognitive faculties of *inner senses* is governed by a more fundamental distinction opposing *forma sensibilis* and *intentio sensibilium* (cf. Avicenna, *Liber de anima, seu Sextus de naturalibus*, 1.5). Inner and outer senses in fact have two objects of perception: (1) forms, such as the length of a thing, which is initially grasped by the outer senses, then transmitted to the inner sense; (2) what Avicenna calls the "intention of a sensory object," which is a content directly grasped by the inner sense without an external sense having perceived it—which is what happens, for example, when a lamb perceives the threat represented for it by a wolf. This threatening aspect, which is not directly perceived by the outer senses, is the wolf's *intentio* (*ma'na* [المعنى]), to be distinguished from its form, which normally provokes spontaneous avoidance or flight.

Common sense is the first of the inner senses. In book 1, chapter 4, Avicenna incidentally calls it the faculty of *bantasia* [بنطاسيا], that is, "common" sense, but he speaks only of "common sense" when dealing with it *ex professo* in chapter 1 of book 4. *Bantasia* translates the Greek *phantasia* [φαντασία]. That term may be disconcerting to the extent that [the] common sense in Avicenna is a receptive instance, "centralizing the data of different sensations," in Verbeke's felicitous phrase. In point of fact, as originally defined by Avicenna, the function of [the] common sense is, prima faciae, to "receive all the forms that the five senses transmit to—and imprint upon—it." But that is not its only function. Avicenna's common sense is not only the faculty capable of "simultaneously grasping the objects of the different sensory faculties" (a statement, it may be noted in passing, that transposes into the realm of faculties Aristotle's remark in *De anima*, 3.1.425b 1ff. on a "common sensation" produced when there is a *simultaneity of sensation relative to the same object*), but is also "the principle from which said sensory faculties emanate" (3.8) and "to which they subsequently return with their booty" (5.8). Above all, (the) common sense plays a role in what, for lack of a better term, may be called the "transformation" of sensation into perception—a role quite distinct from that of the faculty that follows it, imagination (Lat. *imaginatio*, Ar. *Khayal* [الخيال]), which is to "retain what (the) common sense permanently receives from the five senses, after the disappearance of the sensory input in question (*post remotionem sensibilium*)." The "form" of the straight line traced by the fall of a raindrop: such is the product of the imagination, the effect of a retention of what has been grasped by (the) common sense and the outer sense, the effect of "endowing with form" or of a "formation" of the two series of data, one imaginary, in the sense of *bantasia*, and the other real. That is why the retensive imagination is also called *formans*, *vis formans*, and *virtus formalis* (*al-musawwira* [المصوّرة]). Common sense and "formative" imagination are anatomically distinct: (the) common sense is located in the first cavity of the brain, the imagination at the extremity of the anterior ventricle.

Imagination should not be confused with the "imaginative" faculty (*al-mutakhayyila* [المتخيّلة]), the third inner sense, called (*vis*) *cogitative* (*al-quwwat al-mufakkira* [القوة المفكرة]) in man. The role of this cogitative or imaginative faculty is to separate or combine the images retained by the imagination, to divide and compose images: it is itself located in the brain's central cavity, "ubi est vermisae" (where the worm lies). This is followed by the estimative faculty, situated in the extremity of the central cavity of the brain and whose object is *intentiones* unperceived through the intermediary of the outer senses. Memory, situated in the brain's posterior cavity, fulfills the same function of retention in relation to the estimative faculty as the imagination in relation to [the] common sense. It will be noted that the system of cognitive functions or inner senses does not account for the processes of *intellectual* knowledge.

■ See Box 1.

Alain de Libera

1

"Common sense," "sensation," "perception" according to Avicenna

In his *Liber de anima*, 1.5, Avicenna explains the role of common sense in the transformation of sensation into perception. Take the case of a drop of water that falls while tracing a straight line. The external sense (sight) allows only the "form of what is "facing" it (literally, what is *obstant*, what *ob-jects*) to be imprinted in itself, but what faces it appears "as a point, not a line." The external sense thus does not perceive the straight line traced by the falling drop. At instant *T*, it grasps only the position occupied by the droplet at instant *t*: "He cannot see it twice at the same time, but he sees it only there where it is" (non videt eam bis, sed videt eam ubi est). This is where common sense intervenes:

At the precise moment [= *t*] at which the form of the drop (transmitted by sight) is imprinted in "common sense" and withdraws from it, but before the form (deposited in common sense) has entirely disappeared, two powers are exercised simultaneously: the external sense grasps the drop of water where it is (*ubi est*); the common sense perceives it as though it were (still) where it was (*quasi esset ubi fuit*) and as though it were (solely) where it is (*quasi esset ubi est*). What it perceives is thus a *distensio recta*, the trace of a straight line.

Two remarks: common sense does not perceive the thing where it is, which is the business of the external sense; what it grasps is not real, but on the order of *bantasia*. It grasps a movement, that is: it relates to the thing *as though* it were in two distinct locations—the one it occupied and the one it occupies. Given the fact that the forms of the external sense follow each other in the common sense and the forms of common sense in turn follow each other, an instance is required to apprehend both, retaining and conserving them, "when the thing (*res*) has passed (*abiit*)": this is the role of imagination, *imaginatio*.

BIBLIOGRAPHY

Avicenna. *Liber de anima, seu Sextus de naturalibus*. Edited by S. Van Riet. Leiden, Neth.: Brill, 1968.

———. *Avicenna's Psychology: An English Translation of Kitāb al-najāt, Book II, Chapter VI*. Translated by F. Rahman. London: Oxford University Press, 1952.

Davidson, Herbert Alan. *Alfarabi, Avicenna, and Averroes, on Intellect: Their Cosmologies, Theories of the Active Intellect, and Theories of Human Intellect*. New York: Oxford University Press, 1992.

Verbeke, G. "Introduction to the Psychological Doctrine of Avicenna." In *Liber de anima . . .* , 49–59. Edited by Simone Van Riet. Louvain, Belg.: Peeters Publishers, 1972.

Wisnovsky, Robert, ed. *Aspects of Avicenna*. Princeton, NJ: Princeton University Press, 2001.

Wolfson, H. A. "The Internal Senses in Latin, Arabic, and Hebrew Philosophic Texts." *Harvard Theological Review* 28 (1935).

| SERENITY

"Serenity," and its adjectival form "serene," comes from the Latin *serenus*, "calm, without clouds" (with perhaps an evocation of the first meaning of "dry," as from Gr. *xeros* [ξερός]), used to describe skies as much as faces.

"Serenity" is the English translation generally adopted for the German *Gelassenheit*, a term belonging to the vocabulary of mysticism (where *Gelassenheit* signifies a sort of special, even ecstatic, abandon brought on in the proximity of God). Serenity, as a meditative quality by way of *Gelassenheit*, also relates to the notion of the historical in Heidegger's conception of *Seinsgeschichte*, or History of Being: see GESCHICHTLICH and HEIMAT; cf. *DISPOSITION, II,* SORGE.

More generally, "serenity" abuts the idea of felicity (see GLÜCK; cf. *HAPPINESS*) as well as being a related effect or corollary state of wisdom (see *WISDOM*).

➤ STILL

| SEX, GENDER, DIFFERENCE OF THE SEXES, SEXUAL DIFFERENCE

FRENCH	*sexe, genre, différence des sexes, différence sexuelle*
GERMAN	*Geschlecht, Gender, Geschlechterdifferenz, Differenz der Geschlechter*
GREEK	*genos* [γένος]
LATIN	*genus*
SWEDISH	*Kön, Genus*

➤ DRIVE, GENDER, *GENRE*, GESCHLECHT, MENSCHHEIT

Gender became a philosophical concept in Anglo-Saxon thought during the 1970s. Despite the analogy, to translate as *genre* (in French) or *genero* (in Spanish) proves to be ambiguous, whereas German adopts the English form *Gender*, which it allows to coexist as *Geschlecht*, which can be rendered by "sex" as well as by "gender." Raising as many problems as it attempts to solve, the concept of gender is balanced by the classic phrases *différence des sexes* (in French) and "sexual difference." The first is common in French, German, and Italian, but does not exist in English, which has at its disposal only "sexual difference" and "sex."

I. The Invention of the Concept of "Gender"

"Gender": the word is old, but the concept is new. The appearance in 1968 of Richard Stoller's book *Sex and Gender* marked the beginning of a terminological and philosophical debate that is far from over. The title seemed to say it all in its seemingly obvious distinction between biological sex and social gender. That heuristic scheme, with its opposition between the biological and the social, allows for multiple and contradictory interpretations, but presupposes an epistemological framework that should not be forgotten. Nature and culture designate an opposition, or rather a tension, in the analysis of the relation between the sexes—of the *différence des sexes*, as is said, for instance, in French. There are thus three terms in play: "sex," "gender," and "difference of the sexes." In a context that is both philosophical and political, the end of the twentieth century acknowledged that the physiology of the sexes, whose very reality is problematic, is no more than a support for the individual and collective identification of men and women, and that as a result a critique of sexual assignments imposes a new terminology. The beginning of the twentieth century had succeeded in disassociating sexual beings, "men" and "women," from their alleged attributes, both masculine and feminine, with an eye to a greater flexibility of identification. A century later, feminist thought is conceptualizing the critique of sexual duality. "Gender" is the key word, and it must be understood as a philosophical proposition. A decision has been reached to symbolize, by way of the concept of gender, the necessity of thinking the difference of the sexes. The delineation of that notion is thus a contemporary philosophical event.

That event is first of all a challenge, one born of a difficulty that is epistemological because it is terminological. The word "sex," despite its seemingly transnational character (with its links to Lat. *secare*, to cut), is a term whose interpretation spans from the extremely concrete to the extremely abstract. The English language denotes above all the biological and the physical with the word "sex"; French, on the other hand, understands the word as much in terms of sexual life as of the sexuated character of humanity. In brief, "sexual difference" (in English) refers to the material reality of the human condition, whereas *différence des sexes* (in French) includes an abstract and conceptual partition of the species. *Différence sexuelle* coexists in French with *différence des sexes* and thus allows for an understanding of the distinction between the two: *différence sexuelle* presupposes a difference between the sexes and thus gives a definition of the difference, whether in terms of biology (via the natural sciences) or philosophy (the object of speculation on the feminine); *différence des sexes*, on the contrary, implies an empirical recognition of the sexes independent of any definition of content. German offers other perspectives with the generic term *Geschlecht*, a word that covers the empirical and the conceptual. Unlike the situation in French, the single German word *Geschlecht* (see GESCHLECHT) designates both sex and gender. American feminist thought thus "invented" the concept of gender for lack of an adequate tool for thinking about the sexes, a thought of two in one, for lack of a formalizing thought about the sexes. The realism of the word "sex" entailed neither a theoretical elaboration nor a subversive vision. But if "gender" was thus promoted to the rank of a theoretical concept, the word (from the Gr. *genos*, Lat. *genus*) was not new in the language, whence the question of determining how other languages received that terminological and conceptual proposition (see PEOPLE, III).

II. "Gender," *Genre Humain*, and Grammatical Gender

French was confronted with a multiplicity of terms and expressions. Contrary to the case in English, *genre* in French designates not only grammatical gender; it also serves to name the species, the *genre humain*, mankind. *Genre* thus designates both the sum total of human beings and the sexuation of the species into two categories. (It may be noted in passing that *genre humain* and *espèce humaine* are distinct but occasionally overlapping expressions, even if, as is the case for *Geschlecht* and *Gattung* in German, the former is more political and the latter more zoological.)

Given the polysemous relation between the human *genre* and grammatical *genres*, the importation of "gender" was met with a certain opaqueness. In short order, it appeared that "gender" was yielding to a translation in the plural (*genres*), as if returning to its origin in grammar. That situation calls for two remarks: the slippage toward grammatical gender reintroduced, at maximal distance from an abstract and neutral framework,

a strictly sexuated duality; simultaneously, grammar, with its two, and even three, genders—masculine, feminine, and neutral—might be the ideal medium for a fluid elaboration of thought about the sexes. The attempt at abstraction by way of "gender" in the singular would find its legitimacy in a return to the plural. Grammar would be the right way to find the balance between biological sexes and social sex, nature and culture. Nothing would be privileged, neither the fact of two different sexes nor the arbitrariness of individual attributions. But sex itself, like sexuality, would seem to disappear as a result. Might gender be an epistemological fig leaf?

■ See Box 1.

III. The Uses of Gender

All this does not suffice for the imposition of a new concept. It is plausible that the need for a doublet of the word "sex" proved more or less urgent depending on the language. If "genre" has been imposed in the common language, the terms to which it is opposed are not equivalent from one language to the next. English has solely "sexual difference," whereas French can use, with a variety of nuances, *différence sexuelle*, *différence des sexes*, and even *différence de sexe*. German as well makes use of the term *Geschlechterdifferenz* or *Differenz der Geschlechter*. To the extent,

---

1

Masculine, feminine, neuter

The existence of the category of grammatical gender is at the origin of a certain number of difficulties in translation that are experienced when an effort is made to translate a text from a language, such as English, in which most words do not enter into masculine/feminine categories, into another, such as French, in which, on the contrary, all words partake of one gender or the other. There are cases in which translating a "neutral" word (without gender assignment) by a word that necessarily has one adds to the text a connotation absent from the original. This difficulty is particularly perceptible when, for one reason or another, untranslated English words are introduced into French discourse. If, for example, one wants to spell out the difference in meaning between the words "soul" and "mind" (see SOUL), one is quite "naturally" led to write *la soul* and *le mind*, thus attributing to English words the grammatical gender of the words that commonly translate them into French (*âme* and *esprit*, in this case). But in so doing, one adds to the delineation of differences of meaning a difference of gender that does not exist in English and that is spontaneously interpreted as a supplementary difference in meaning. That addition is anything but trivial since, in French, categories of grammatical gender bear an implicit sexual connotation. This leads to complaints concerning the "sexism" of one language or

another (in fact, of all of them)—complaints that linguists categorically reject, arguing that languages do not obey semantic criteria.

This difficulty, linked to an unconscious sexualization of words in languages possessing masculine and feminine grammatical genders, may be linked to a remark by Aristotle (*On Sophistical Refutations*, 1.14.173 b 17–22) according to which, to the extent that the feeling of anger is a feature of heroes, and thus eminently virile, one commits a solecism in speaking in the feminine (the word *he menis* [ἡ μῆνις], which means "anger," is feminine). The *Iliad*, consequently, should have opened with reference to Achilles's wrath in the masculine. Aristotle here refers to the distinction proposed by Protagoras (Aristotle, *Rhetoric*, 3.5.1407b 6) between the genders of nouns (*tagene ton onomaton* [τὰ γένη τῶν ὀνομάτων]; concerning *genos* [γένος], see PEOPLE, III.A), which can be either "male" (*arrena* [ἄρρενα], which translates less literally as masculine) or "female" (*thelea* [θήλεα], feminine) or, finally, neither male nor female, as "things, useful objects" (*skeu* [σκεύη], also designated in Gr. as *ta metaxu onomata* [τὰ μεταξὺ ὀνόματα], names between the two, which yields neuters, from the Lat. *ne-uter*, neither one nor the other).

The determination of gender proposed by Protagoras is explicitly sexuated (as the words "male" and "female" bear witness). It is based

on the notion that the male/female division operates in the realm of words in the same way as in that of beings (living and inanimate "things"). "In the same way" should be understood in two different senses. First, in the sense that the operation of division into two classes no more exhausts the full set of words than it does that of "things": it always leaves a residue, a remainder of words and "things" that fail to enter into either of the two categories. Then, in the sense that the division of words into the three generic categories (one of which is defined as the residue of the other two) reproduces identically that of "things": female words designate female things; male words designate male things. Finding it strange and even scandalous that "anger" (*colère*) is feminine is conceivable only within the framework of that hypothesis, in which words, if they do not resemble the things they designate, are nonetheless marked with gender by the nature, male or female, virile or feminine, of those things: it suffices (theoretically) to know the meaning of a word to determine its grammatical gender, either directly (if it be masculine or feminine) or by default (for neuter nouns).

It is enough to utter this thesis to see that it does not have universal bearing. Even English, which also possesses three generic determinations, is removed from Protagoras's model. The masculine/feminine opposition plays a secondary role in it since it intervenes only after the division between humans and nonhumans, among "things" themselves, has been effected, and is applied, in the realm of words, only to those designating humans, in the strictest sense: persons, to whom it is possible to ascribe a biological gender—in which case grammatical gender fuses (in theory) with biological gender. It is consequently unthinkable that the word designating in English the wrath of heroes might be of masculine gender: one cannot define the biological gender of wrath with which its grammatical gender might be confused. A word's sense helps in determining its grammatical gender only if its meaning reveals that one is dealing with a person: "queen," which designates a person, is necessarily feminine. Gender effects, whether masculine or feminine, are extremely discreet in English: the gender of the noun designating a person affects neither the adjective nor articles, whether definite or indefinite, associated with it; only pronouns in the singular ("he" or "she") indicate the (biological) gender of the person designated. It can be said that the English language takes almost no cognizance of grammatical gender: all words, except for a few exceptions ("man," "woman," "king," "queen"—and, to be sure, "ship"), are neuter, without gender. From that circumstance to the claim that it does not know of the difference of sexes the distance is considerable. But it will be understood that those speaking a language in which almost all nouns are without gender, and in which the (male/female) difference of sexes never affects any words other than those designating persons, have felt the need not to overlook the slightest occasion to emphasize that difference—be it at the price of artificiality, as in the case of the increasingly frequent use of "he or she" to designate human beings. It will also be appreciated that it is within the English (and/or American) language—a language in which biological and grammatical gender, for humans, coincides—that the concept of "gender" (see GENDER) emerged. One may wonder whether "gender," the social construction of sexual identities, is not intended to compensate for the absence of grammatical gender. For individuals speaking a language possessing genuine grammatical

genders live in a world in which the feminine/masculine distinction, even if it is not semantically determined (we shall see that this is not generally the case), is nonetheless omnipresent and contributes in part to the (broadly social) formation of masculine and feminine identities. Whether we like it or not, the fact that the word *fleur* (flower) is in the feminine in French influences the concept of the feminine gender (generally, not merely grammatically) entertained by those who express themselves in that language. In brief, the language establishes between gender and grammatical gender a series of cross-references that are unthinkable in English.

Linguistics opposes to such imprecise considerations—which amount to claiming that conceptions of the world forged by individuals cannot be the same depending on whether the language they speak and write does or does not dispose of genuine grammatical genders—the rigorous thesis according to which languages are formal systems whose construction does not depend on the meaning of words, and which thus do not obey any semantic determination (with grammatical gender not offering an exception to the rule, which is a version of the celebrated "arbitrary nature of the sign"). French and German are generally invoked in support of this argument. In German, a language of combinations par excellence, there exists an entire series of rules allowing one to know the gender of a noun from its morphology: the suffixes *-lein* and *–chen* are (in general) marked as neuter; the prefix *Ge-* renders neuter the noun in which it enters into combination—at least when one is dealing with a word produced by combination; nouns whose ending is in *-ung, -heit, -keit, -schaft,* and *-erei* are feminine, etc. Similarly, in French, a study by experts on the learning of French by English-language speakers (Tucker, Lambert, and Rigault, 1977) revealed that the attribution of gender was based—at a rate of 85 percent—on formal (and more precisely phonological) criteria. In such cases, it is the last phoneme of a noun that confers its grammatical gender (limited to two possibilities: masculine/feminine). If such correlations are indisputable, it remains nonetheless the case that they involve empirical rules, valid only 85 percent of the time, resulting more from

statistical findings than from genuine analysis (as is the case in German), which would alone allow for an understanding of how children who do not know where the end of a word is located determine the gender of nouns with great assurance. On the other hand, one understands quite easily the allures of this kind of result for linguists. It appears to be a confirmation of the thesis according to which languages are purely formal systems, and a weapon to be used against those who object, incorrectly to all appearances, that languages are not constructed rationally. Science analyzes that objection as the effect of a narcissistic wound (language, because it is a purely formal system, pays no heed to sexual difference, however important it be for the species), like those produced by the Copernican revolution, the theory of evolution, and psychoanalysis.

That being the case, the question raised at the outset (of how an individual expressing himself in French manages not to ascribe the feminine grammatical gender to the English word "soul" and thereby a feminine nature to what it designates) remains no less valid. It is indeed possible that grammatical gender is determined by formal considerations; nonetheless, once it is constructed it produces effects. How would one not infer, if only unconsciously, that what the English word "mind" designates is masculine in nature, since it is translated into French by a masculine word? One might also pose the question as follows: what conceptions of "soul" and "mind" are entertained by the Anglophone speaker? Does he perceive in the word "soul" the traditionally feminine characteristics that a Francophone speaker, albeit in spite of himself, senses in it? How can one translate from one language to another without taking into account the quasi-silent connotations induced by the existence or absence of grammatical gender?

Françoise Balibar

BIBLIOGRAPHY

Corbett, Greville G. *Gender*. Cambridge: Cambridge University Press, 1991.

Tucker, Richard G., Wallace Earl Lambert, and André Rigault. *The French Speaker's Skill with Grammatical Gender*. The Hague: Mouton, 1977.

however, that *Geschlecht* means simultaneously "sex" and "gender," German has been obliged to provide a double for *Geschlecht,* thus resorting to *Gender*. Swedish proceeds similarly with *Kön* and *Genus*, invoking the Latin word, as has long been the case in German, to serve as a concept. The question, then, is no longer one of translating "gender," which has become a transnational word, but of not being able to translate correctly into English *différence des sexes* or *Geschlechterdifferenz*. "Sexual difference" (in

English) implies reference to characteristics, qualities, and definitions of difference that go considerably beyond a conceptual use preceding any position regarding content.

■ See Box 2.

To this may be added, outside of any considerations related to research, the importance given to the use of "gender," notably during the Fourth World Conference on

2

"Sex" and "sexual difference"

An account of the way that "sex" is woven into the philosophical vocabularies of Europe needs to be more than an account of the theoretical and terminological innovations of the late twentieth and early twenty-first centuries. It needs to include what Fraisse calls the "extremely concrete" as well as the "extremely abstract" meanings of the word, not least because they may not be separable. In the routine employment of the concept of "sex" in the vernacular European philosophies, from the seventeenth century onward, we should note one initial peculiarity: even where the words are as linguistically incongruent as the English "sex" and the German *Geschlecht*, when the context is unambiguous the presumption in translation is that they refer to the same thing, precisely because that "thing" was *itself* taken for granted as a natural fact; neither the object of a philosophical analysis nor the site of a philosophical problem. When Kant compares "the fair sex," *das schöne Geschlecht*, with *das männliche Geschlecht*, (*Observations on the Feeling of the Beautiful and Sublime*), the apparent transparency of the presumption of the natural fact of sex difference (the distinction between male and female) is the abstract equivalent that facilitates the linguistic exchange between the particulars "sex" and *Geschlecht*, no questions asked.

However, Fraisse claims that the apparent equivalence between "sex" and *sexe* is false, for within the French *sexe* there is a distinction between sexual difference/*différence sexuelle* and *la différence des sexes*, where the former refers concretely—contentfully—to the "material reality of the human condition," the empirical domain of the biological and the physical, and the latter—a philosopheme—to an abstract conceptual division. The "realism" of the English "sex," it is said, refers only to the former. The sex/gender distinction is then the answer to the felt need for the distinction between sexual difference/*différence sexuelle* and *la différence des sexes*, but in opposing cultural "gender" to natural "sex" the difficulty in thinking sex in English as *la différence des sexes* remains. In fact the English phrase "sexual difference," as opposed to balder talk of "sex," only began to appear in Anglophone feminist theory as a mark of the reception of the psychoanalytically influenced and literary feminist theory from France (notably that of Kristeva, Irigaray, and Cixous) that was often mistakenly identified as "French feminist theory" tout court. This terminological innovation in English was not always a result of critical reflection on the conceptual distinction between "sex" and "sexual difference"; as such it continues to sow

confusion. From this point of view the English "sex" is a plain and stodgy pudding, the just desert, perhaps, of an empiricist philosophical tradition. As empirical datum, sex is outside the philosophical arena, or it is an only illegitimate interloper there, as Kant's sexism seems to show. But this, in effect, protects "sex" from any critical, philosophical scrutiny by virtue of its naïve everydayness, or forecloses the possibility of an investigation into that everydayness itself. It presumes that the discrete biological meaning of the English "sex" makes it a word that is in itself politically and ideologically innocent, and that sex only loses this innocence in the uses to which it is put.

But "sex" is much more complicated than this, and part of its complexity is precisely its guise of simplicity. While apparently referring to a value-neutral, merely biological natural division in kind, it always in fact means more than this. The recognition that this semantic peculiarity is also a political problem is at the heart of Beauvoir's *The Second Sex*. In the first chapter Beauvoir attempted to disaggregate the existential concepts of man and woman from the biological, or better zoological, concepts of male and female, arguing that the latter—the terms of sex difference or sex in the English sense—were inadequate foundations for the explanation of the specificity of the latter. But she did so in the context of the recognition that this is indeed—even in French—how the terms of sex tend to function. Her attempt to determine the meaning of sex existentially was pitched against the assumption—common to both popular discourses and philosophy—that biological sex determines what it is to be a woman. This presumption is fully part of the meaning of sex (or *sexe*, or *Geschlecht*).

"Sex" is not so much the fact of the exclusive division of the human species into male and female as the *presumption* of this fact and, importantly, the presumption of the *efficacy* of this fact. That is, the popular concept of "sex"—casually employed by most modern European philosophers at one time or another (consider, for example, Rousseau's remark in *A Discourse on the Origin of Inequality*, "Aimables et vertueuses citoyennes, le sort de votre sexe sera toujours de gouverner le nôtre," or Locke in *Some Thoughts Concerning Education*, "The principal aim of my Discourse is, how a young Gentleman should be brought up from his Infancy ... where the difference of Sex requires different treatment, 'twill be no hard matter to distinguish")—is constituted by the presumption that there just is a naturally determined sex duality (the exclusive division into male and female) and that this duality is also naturally determining.

It is becoming increasingly obvious that this presumed exclusive duality is empirically inadequate to the observable phenomena. Thus, for some, the very fact of sex difference is put in doubt. But this only reveals the persistence of the presumption relatively independently of the facts—whatever they may be—allowing us to see, according to both Christine Delphy and Monique Wittig, that "sex" is a *political* term that mandates a hierarchical social division.

For Fraisse, the range of meanings of "sex" ("from the extremely concrete to the extremely abstract") belies its apparently transnational character. But to the extent that "sex" refers to more than an innocent empirical datum it *is* a "transnational" term because it carries a transnational presumption. Now, "transnational" does not mean "transhistorical." But the transnational assumption of sex quickly leads us to presume, further, that it does—to presume that the modern concept of sex has always been with us. To take just one example, English translators and commentators, feminist and otherwise, have tended to assume that the (very broadly speaking) modern concept of sex is central to the discussion, in Plato's *Republic*, of whether females can or should be part of the ruling Guardian class. The translation of Plato's *genos* as "sex" is simultaneously both the symptom and the cause of this presumption: "Then if men or women as a sex [*to tōn andrōn kai to tōn gunaikōn genos*] appear to be qualified for different skills or occupations," I said, "we shall assign these to each accordingly; but if the only difference apparent between them is that the female bears [*to men thēlu tiktein*] and the male begets [*to de arren ocheuein*] we shall not admit that this is a difference relevant for our purpose, but shall maintain that our male and female Guardians [*tous te phulakas hēmin kai tas gunaikas*] ought to follow the same occupations" (454d–e). The word *genos*, which is sometimes translated as sex, means, primarily, race or stock or kin, and also offspring, tribe, generation, and kind. To the extent that "sex" is a general term, naming a specific kind of difference, a specific feature of both male and female or the principle of division between them, there is nothing like an equivalent term in classical Greek. Each time *genos* is used in the *Republic* in relation to men or women or male or female it is attached to one or the other in order to specify men or women or male or female as a class in distinction from this or that man or woman or male or female animal. There is no singular term like "sex" to refer to a distinction in kind between men and women or male and female. Indeed the very broad generality of the concept of a *genos*, which may refer indifferently to any content (the *genos* of this, that, or the other—it does not matter), is most unlike the very narrow specificity of the concept of sex, which is identical with its limited content, designating what kind of categories "male" and "female" are. The considerable grammatical and semantic differences between the two terms *genos* and "sex" mean, therefore, that the translation of the former as the latter effects a conceptual transformation. The very basis of Socrates's argument concerning the possibility of female Guardians is the refusal to privilege any kind of difference, the distinction between any groups of *genē*—kinds of kinds—except that between Guardian, auxiliary and producer themselves. In translating *genos* as "sex" we introduce a special kind of kind, an emphasis on a special kind of difference, which is merely one difference among others in the text of the *Republic* itself. "Sex" cannot, strictly speaking, be translated backward into classical Greek. The fact that "sex" is nevertheless a standard translation for *genos* in book 5 of the *Republic* is a symptom of the common presumption that underlies its translatability in modern thought.

Can sex, in this sense, be contained behind a semantic *cordon sanitaire*, separated off from associated words? If, as Fraisse says, the French *sexe* includes the meanings of both sexual difference/*différence sexuelle* (i.e., the English "sex") and *la différence des sexes*, can the philosopheme float freely in the refined air of extreme abstraction? No. To think *la différence des sexes* is to think its relation to, and not merely its distinction from, "sex."

Stella Sandford

BIBLIOGRAPHY

Beauvoir, Simone de. *Le Deuxième sexe*. Paris: Gallimard / La Pléiade, 1976. Translation by Constance Borde and Sheila Malovany-Chevallier: *The Second Sex*. New York: Alfred A. Knopf, 2010.

Delphy, Christine. "Penser le genre: Quels Problèmes?" In *Sexe et genre: de la hiérarchie entre les sexes*. Edited by Marie-Claude Hurtig et al. Paris: Éditions du CNRS, 1991. Translation by Diana Leonard: "Rethinking Sex and Gender." *Women's Studies International Forum* 16, no. 1 (1993).

Dorlin, Elsa. *Sexe, genre et sexualités*. Paris: Presses Universitaires de France, 2008.

Fraisse, Geneviève. *La Différence des sexes*. Paris: Presses Universitaires de France, 1996.

Kant, Immanuel. *Beobachtungen über Das Gefühl des Schönen und Erhabenen*, "Von dem Unterschiede des Erhabenen und Schönen in dem Gegenverhältnis Beiderbecke Geschlecht." Verlag du Leipzig, 1913.

———. *Observations on the Feeling of the Beautiful and Sublime*, Section Three, "Of the Distinction Between the Beautiful and Sublime in the Interrelations of the Two Sexes." Translated by John T. Goldthwait. Berkeley: University of California Press, 1960.

Sandford, Stella. *Plato and Sex*. Cambridge: Polity, 2010.

Wittig, Monique. "The Category of Sex." In *The Straight Mind and Other Essays*. Boston: Beacon Press, 1992.

Women (1995), which took place in Beijing under the aegis of the United Nations, and which allowed the internationally consecrated expression "women's rights" to be replaced by the notion of "gender." In Africa currently, including French-speaking countries, "gender and development" is a theme of discussion. The linguistic shift has thus occurred from "woman" to "gender" (and no longer only from "sex" to "gender"). The recourse to "gender" allows the noun "woman" to no longer serve as a general category in characterizing research and efforts on the subject or as a way to define a commitment. In French-speaking Africa, the term is offensive to the extent that it also means that the "woman" question is a relation between the sexes, men and women, as much as a demand for equality. Europe is also, as such, a laboratory. The use of "gender" has been generalized but not in a uniform way. The English word has been superimposed in phrases specific to each language as well as in the expressions "gender equality" (a synonym for "equality of the sexes") and "gender perspective" (translated in French as *dimension de genre*). "Gender" in English thus subsists within other languages, which is paradoxical, given the European desire for exhaustive translation. Yet "gender" persists in designating a social (as opposed to biological) dimension. Thus discrimination against a pregnant woman would not be categorized as "gender discrimination," but rather as "sexual discrimination." The words "man" and "woman" would be used to designate the "sex."

IV. Epistemology and Historicity

Feminist inquiry has become sharper with the refinement of its vocabulary. The first step was breaking with the dominant tradition subsumed in the aphorism Freud borrowed from Napoleon ("Anatomy is destiny"), and showing what it is, in the relation between the sexes, that distinguishes the "natural" biological fact from the "cultural" social construction. In a second phase, it became possible to dissociate the two realities completely and to affirm that gender no longer had anything to do with sex, that each of them was produced and not given, and that maintaining the link, however contradictory it might be, between the two, was a residue of prejudicial essentialism. The objective was to liberate individual and collective identities from all norms. But if "sex" entailed a reference to "sexuality," could "gender" encompass the dimension of sexual life? Some would claim that "gender" conjures away the provocation entailed by the fact that sex is still present, while others, on the contrary, would see in it the basis for a possible liberation. Doing away with the word "sex" is not, to be sure, a trivial matter.

The fact is that the hierarchical distinction between "sex" and "gender" is more similar to the link between fact and concept than to the dualism opposing nature and culture. The political problem is thus compounded by an epistemological problem: is the heuristic scheme between two contradictory terms pitted against each other still pertinent? Is not the critique that makes use of that schema held hostage to it to the extent that it validates it? The opposition between nature and culture is a conceptual framework specific to the modern era: does compounding it with a tension between reality and concept change anything? Should not thinking nourished by feminist inquiry and action invent a new framework, a new problematic for the question of the difference of the sexes? Should we not respond differently to the opposition between the biological and the social (and to that between "sex" confronting "gender" as much as "gender" confronting "sex") than through a dualism, however roughed up it might be? The difficulty of the debate over sex and gender is a function of the fact that it remains imprisoned in a problematic of identity:

the quest for (or the critique of) identity appears to be the fundamental question. Yet a different question might modify the perspective—that of otherness. For in excessively debating the identity of sexuated beings too little is said of their relation, of the relation to the other and to others. Yet that relation—the sexual relation, social relations, relations of domination or emancipation—is historical. The historicity of the difference of the sexes might serve as a guiding thread—historicity construed as a critique of atemporal representations of the sexes as well as a situating of the sexes in the factory of history.

In conclusion, we return to the distinction between "sexual difference" and French *différence des sexes*, those two formulations enjoyed by the French language and with which philosophy has not refrained from playing. With the expression "sexual difference," the duality of the sexes is endowed with a content, multiple—but always distinct—representations of the masculine and the feminine. With *différence des sexes*, the duality entails neither affirmation of meaning nor proposition of value: it is an empty determination. Therein lies its essential value.

Geneviève Fraisse

BIBLIOGRAPHY

Bussman, Hadumod, and Renate Hof, eds. *Genus. Zur Geschlechterdiffernz in den Kulturwissenschaften*. Stuttgart: Alfred Kröner, 1995.

Butler, Judith. *Gender Trouble: Feminism and the Subversion of Identity*. New York: Routledge, 1990.

Derrida, Jacques. "Geschlecht, différence sexuelle, différence ontologique." In *Psyché*. Paris: Galilée, 1987. Translation by Ruben Berzdivin: "'Geschlecht,' Sexual Difference, Ontological Difference." In *A Derrida Reader*. Edited by Peggy Kamuf. New York: Columbia University Press, 1991.

Diotima (Research Group). *Il pensiero della differenza sessuale*. Milan: La Tartaruga, 1987.

Fraisse, Geneviève. *La Différence des sexes*. Paris: Presses Universitaires de France, 1996.

Irigaray, Luce. *An Ethics of Sexual Difference*. Translated by Carolyn Burke and Gillian C. Gill. Ithaca, NY: Cornell University Press, 1993.

Laqueur, Thomas Walter. *Making Sex: Body and Gender from the Greeks to Freud*. Cambridge, MA: Harvard University Press, 1990.

Mathieu, Nicole-Claude. *L'Anatomie politique: Catégorisations et idéologies du sexe*. Paris: Côte-femmes, 1991.

Meade, Teresa A., and Merry E. Wiesner-Hanks. *A Companion to Gender History*. Malden, MA: Blackwell, 2004.

Moi, Toril. *What is a Woman? And Other Essays*. Oxford: Oxford University Press, 1999.

Rubin, Gayle. "The Traffic in Women: Notes on the 'Political Economy' of Sex." In *Toward an Anthropology of Women*. New York: Monthly Review Press, 1975.

Scott, Joan. *Gender and the Politics of History*. New York: Columbia University Press, 1988.

Stoller, Robert. *Sex and Gender. On the Development of Masculinity and Femininity*. New York: Science House, 1968.

SHAME

Shame is one of the accepted translations for the Spanish *vergüenza*, a moral and social feeling related to the look of the other, and that corresponds to some extent to the Greek *aidôs* [αἰδώς]: see VERGÜENZA. Cf. SPREZZATURA.

More generally, on moral philosophy in general, see MORALS, and DUTY, HAPPINESS [GLÜCK], *VALUE, VIRTUE* [PHRONÊSIS, VIRTÙ].

On the relationship to the fear inspired by God or the gods, see in particular *ALLIANCE* [BERÎT], RELIGIO, PIETAS, SECULARIZATION, THEMIS; cf. *DROIT*, LAW.

On the relationship to decency and to sex, see GENDER, PLEASURE, SEX.

▶ *AUTRUI, BEHAVIOR, COMMUNITY*, GEMÜT, *MALAISE*

SIGN, SYMBOL

FRENCH   *signe, symbole*
GERMAN   *Zeichen, Zeigen, Sinnbild, Symbol*
GREEK   *sêma* [σῆμα], *semeion* [σημεῖον], *sumbolon* [σύμβολον]
LATIN   *signum, nota, symbolum*

▶ ANALOGY, COMPARISON, *IMAGE*, IMPLICATION, LOGOS, MERKMAL, MIMÊSIS, NONSENSE, SEMIOTICS, SENSE, SIGNIFIER/SIGNIFIED, SPEECH ACT, TERM, UNIVERSALS, WORD

"Sign," as a being or thing, encompasses a great diversity of fields. If, in an Augustinian perspective, every sign is first of all a thing, a thing is not necessarily a sign, even if it can always, to an extent, become one (*De doctrina Christiana*, 1.2.2); thus, for example, for Christians the events recorded in the Old Testament, *res gestae*, are "signs" of the New Testament (*De doctrina Christiana*, 3.22–23). Sign thus partakes of an elaborate setup, which inscribes it as part of a network with realities that, in a way, proceed from it. Signification, variously interpreted. Grounded or motivated in the course of history. The delimiting of the respective fields of "sign" and "symbol" is one of the most problematic of the networks deployed in various languages, from the inaugural distinction of *semeion* [σημεῖον] and *symbolon* [σύμβολον] in Greek to the German formation *Sinnbild* (literally, meaning [*Sinn*]-image[*Bild*], in which *Sinn* betrays in addition a sensory dimension), used, for example, by E. Cassirer to designate the "symbol" as what ensures the transition from image to meaning. Such diverse networks, however, can be identified only by detecting certain mutations from the Latin, and even neo-Latin, *signum*, which allows the "sign" to communicate with the "term," in accordance, for example, with the "categoreme" vs. "syncategoreme" axis, and have the word *signum* designate—at a certain stage of the development of medieval logic—what are today called "quantifiers." From the medieval "sign [of quality]" to the modern "quantifiable symbol," there are transitions, but they count less than delineating the sets that they link. In what follows, we will present the essential, starting with the Aristotelian send-off, joining up, by way of the Stoic moment and the distortion it induced, with the major oppositions constructed in the Middle Ages around several polarities, whether regarding sources—Aristotle vs. Augustine—or the conceptual structures they convey or propose to recast in their entirety, such as the distinction between natural signs and conventional signs, and, more discretely, and affecting the "sign" itself, that between "sign of" and "sign for," in which the intersubjective dimension of the sign is explicitly thematized.

I. Greek Vocabulary of the Sign: Several Problematic Nodes

A. *Sêma* and *sumbolon*

Homer and Hesiod do not use *semeion*, but two words, *sêma* [σῆμα] and *sumbolon* [σύμβολον], which can also be translated by "sign," but whose concrete meaning and social usage are quite pronounced.

Sêma, from which would develop *semeion* [σημεῖον], to "signify or mean" (see SENSE), says sign in the sense of "signal" (to begin a battle, *Odyssey*, 21.231; as a presage sent by the gods, 20.3, for instance), as a "landmark" (sign on a trail allowing one to rediscover one's way, *Iliad*, 10.466; points of demarcation, *Odyssey*, 8.192), and more generally, a "sign of recognition" guaranteeing the trustworthiness of an identity or a message (such as the mark made by each warrior on lots to be drawn [*Iliad*, 7.189], what is conveyed by Bellerophon's tablet—first traces of writing [6.176ff.] and above all the secret, shared by husband and wife alone, of the conjugal bed carved from an olive tree whose roots were still in the ground [*Odyssey*, 23.202]). It is eminently the sign by which one recognizes a grave: the "tomb" (*Odyssey*, 2 or 11.75) and such is the meaning with the pun on *soma* [σῶμα]/*sêma*, "body/tomb," which can be found from Orpheus (B3 DK) to Philolaos (B14 DK). It was undoubtedly in Parmenides's *Poem* that the relation between signal and signification made its appearance, at the time of the constitution of the identity of the existent, with the description of the *semata* [σήματα] (8.2) which, "landmarks" on the road to the verb "to be," are nothing other than the predicates of the beings to be found within it, semantemes as much as semes (unengendered, imperishable, whole, one, continuous, etc.) (see ESTI). *Sêma* refers us to something other than itself, which it signals in a more or less constant or natural manner, thus leaving room for interpretation.

Sumbolon, from *sum-ballo* [συμ-βάλλω], "to throw together" (in which it is "together" that is to be emphasized), has a far more precise meaning. It too is a "sign of recognition," but it originally designated quite materially the parts of an astragal or of any other object divided in two and whose readjustment would bear witness to an old relation between guests (Euripides, *Medea*, 613), between an exposed child and his parents (Euripides, *Ion*, 1386), then between all sorts of parties to a contract. *Sumbolon* will also be used for a token (tesserae of a citizen who votes and receives remuneration, seats at the theater), a passport, a receipt, a guarantee, a contract, or a treaty. The relation between the whole and the material parts of a *sumbolon* is thus the visible sign of a convention between parties to a contract.

B. *Semeion*

1. The Aristotelian send-off

There are, in the corpus of Greek philosophy, two nodes of problems concerning the notion of the sign and the relation of signification, a circumstance that accounts for the variation in translations of terminology as well as the incompatibility between definitions subsequently.

The first pertains to the meaning to be given to the first sentences of chapter 1 of Aristotle's *De interpretatione*, a canonical text that structures for the entire tradition the relation between language (both written and spoken), affections of the soul, and things, and entails in particular that the status of the variation *semeion/sumbolon* be determined. The second relates to the incompatibility of the terminology introduced by the Stoics, whose highly elaborate theory of the sign is from the time of the very first commentaries a source of unending contamination for that of Aristotle, opening, to all appearances, onto concepts of a more immediate modernity (*semeion*, "sign," but also *semainon* [σημαίνον], "signifier," *semainomenon* [σημαινόμενον], "signified," *lekton* [λεκτόν], "expressible," *tugchanon* [τυγχάνον], "referent") (see SIGNIFIER/ SIGNIFIED, II).

- See Box 1.

A characteristic of the *semeion* should be noted: the "variable geometry" of its nature. A *semeion* is as much an

empirically observable thing, a "symptom" of an illness in an investigation, as a premise, apt to appear in a demonstration. In both cases, the *semeion* allows one to move to (or to deduce), with more or less certainty, something (a phenomenon or a proposition) other than itself.

We can thus understand the definition of the *semeion* in the *Prior Analytics*, 2.27: "A sign means a demonstrative proposition necessary or generally approved: for anything such that when it is another thing is, or when it has come into being the other has come into being before or after, is a sign of the other's being or having come into being," (trans. A. J. Jenkinson), in relation to the rhetorical difference that is probable (*semeion*)/demonstrative (*tekmerion* [τεκμήριον]), and the use of *semeion* ("here is an index of it") in the remainder of chapter 1 of *De interpretatione* (in 16a, 16). This is a corroboration of the possible (but not necessary) "naturalness" of the *semeion*.

This is particularly clear in Stoicism, linked to the transformation of the "subject" of signification, which is no longer the word, as in Aristotle, but only the complete *logos* (see WORD). Milk as a "sign" of giving birth is thus simultaneously the nourishing liquid present in the mother's breast (one of Aristotle's examples) and the proposition: "that woman has milk" is the premise of the valid conclusion in the *sunêmmenon* [συνημμένον]: "that woman gave birth" (which is the adaptation of the Aristotelian example by Sextus).

2. The Stoic definition of the *semeion* and the taxonomy of signs according to the "demonstrability" of the object

The sign may be said in two manners (*legetai dichôs* [λέγεται διχῶς]), in the general and the specific sense (*koinôs te kai idiôs* [κοινῶς τε καὶ ἰδίως]); in the general sense: this is what seems to show something (*ti dêloun* [τι δηλοῦν]), to the extent that we are accustomed to name a sign what serves to renew the object that has been observed in conjunction with it (*pros ananeôsin tou sumparatêrêthentos autôi pragmatos* [πρὸς ἀνανέωσιν τοῦ συμπαρατηρηθέντος αὐτῷ πράγματος]); in the specific sense: it is what is indicative (*endeiktikon* [ἐνδεικτικόν] of an object that is not apparent ("unshown," *tou adêloumenou pragmatos* [τοῦ ἀδηλουμένου πράγματος]).

(Sextus Empiricus, *Adversus mathematicos*, 8, chap. [*pros Logikou*, 143–44])

From this definition flows the fundamental distinction between two kinds of signs, which structures the Skeptics' presentation and critique of dogmatic Stoic semiology, as proposed in chapter 3 of book 8 of *Adversos mathematicos*. We shall leave aside things that are manifest (*enargê* [ἐναργῆ]), which are in need of no more than their own evidence, and thus do not partake of the realm of signs. There can be signs only of things that are not apparent (*adêla* [ἄδηλα]), on the condition, however, that they not be "absolutely not evident" (*kathapax adêla* [καθάπαξ ἄδηλα], for instance, the number of grains of sand in the Libyan desert) since in that case they escape by definition all apprehension whatsoever. There will thus be a sign of things that are "occasionally not evident" (*pros kairon adêla* [πρὸς καιρὸν ἄδηλα], such as Athens when I am in Libya), or rather "naturally not evident" (*phusêi adêla* [φύσει ἄδηλα],

1

Sign/symbol/image

The major options in translating *De interpretatione*, 1.16a 3–8

Ἔστι μὲν οὖν τὰ ἐν τῇ φωνῇ τῶν ἐν τῇ ψυχῇ παθημάτων σύμβολα, καὶ τὰ γραφόμενα τῶν ἐν τῇ φωνῇ. Καὶ ὥσπερ οὐδὲ γράμματα πᾶσι τὰ αὐτά, οὐδὲ φωναὶ αἱ αὐταί· ὧν μέντοι ταῦτα σημεῖα πρώτων [πρώτων: Minio-Paluello, generally followed / πρώτως: all manuscripts expect one; Ammonius], ταὐτὰ πᾶσι παθήματα τῆς ψυχῆς, καὶ ὧν ταῦτα ὁμοιώματα πράγματα ἤδη ταὐτά (Aristotle, *De interpretatione*, 16a 3–8).

Translations have had to administer two series of differences: that between *ta en têi phônêi* (literally, what there is in the voice), *ta graphomena* (what is written), on the one hand, and *phônai* (the sounds of the voice), *grammata* (letters), on the other hand; that, above all, between *sumbolon* (symbol), *semeion* (sign), *homoiôma* (image, representation). Two major interpretive options can be distinguished, depending on the thrust of *prôton* or *prôtos*. According to the first option, shared with virtual unanimity by Greek, Latin, Arabic, and modern translators and commentators, written and spoken words are signs "in the first instance" (*hôn, prôtôn,* or *prôtôs*) of affections of the soul, and, in the second instance, of the things themselves that those affections represent. Tricot follows the English translator Ackrill, in adopting the first option:

Sounds emitted by the voice are symbols of states of the soul, and written words the symbols of words emitted by the voice. And just as writing is not the same for all men, neither are spoken words the same, even though the moods of which those expressions are the immediate signs (*hôn . . . prôtôn.* Ackrill maintains the reading but instead translates the adverb *prôtôs*: "but what these are in the first place signs of—affections of the soul" - identical for all, regardless of editorial choices) as are identical the things of which those moods are the images.

Words are the direct signs of affects and the indirect signs, precisely via those affects, of things. The significant difference, as Ammonius emphasizes, occurs between, on the one hand, things and affects, which are the same for all since they are linked by a natural relation of resemblance that we are unable to change, and, on the other hand, sounds and letters, which are not the same for all, as is proven by the difference between languages, and which are linked to each other,

as with affects and things, by a conventional relation of signification. From which it follows that there can be no fundamental difference between *semeion* and *sumbolon* (vocal sounds, says Ammonius in 1934, are *sumbola kai sêmeia*, "symbols and [or: that is] signs" of thoughts): one can understand that tradition would follow Boethius into the abyss in his proposal to translate each case as *notae*, and that Pierre Aubenque, would deplore the lack of rigor in Aristotle's terminology (*Le problème de l'être chez Aristote*).

The second option, quite recently elaborated, even though it draws on certain commentaries of Ammonius and Boethius (see Kretzmann and Pépin) understands that one is dealing in these sentences with two interlocking or nesting descriptions of language: sounds of the human—but also animal—voice (*tauta*, 6) are first of all natural signs (the adverb *prôtôs* modifies *sêmeia*) of affections of the soul and only subsequently, in the case of articulated speech specific to humans and thus in the context of differences between languages, become conventional symbols (*sumbola*) of those affections, just as letters are conventional symbols of articulated sounds. The translation then becomes something like:

But it should be known that sounds emitted by the voice are symbols, affections that are in the soul, and the traces of them that are written are symbols of the sounds emitted by the voice. And just as written letters are not the same for all men, emanations of voice are not the same either; on the other hand, what those sounds emitted by the voice are first of all signs of, that is, affections of the soul, are the same for all, just as the things those affections resemble are the same.

This second option presents the obvious interest of working the terminological differences rather than crushing them.

Whatever, however, the version retained, the overall movement from *logos* to soul, and from soul to things, remains, in all cases, unchanging and paradigmatic: *De interpretatione* deploys in its very first lines the classic structure informing phenomenology and remains a founding document of language:

things	phenomeno
soul	---
words	logy

The soul's mediation effects the transition from things to words; phenomenology appears clearly as a question of transitivity:

the phenomenon reveals itself in language, allows itself to be spoken and written, on two conditions: that it "pass" into the soul, and that the soul "pass" into the *logos*.

It is true that this dual condition also constitutes a dual problem: is it certain that the mediation of the soul does not partially conceal things, and that in turn that of the *logos* does not in some way skew the affections of the soul? In order to render the "phenomenological method" of his investigation perceptible, Heidegger, in paragraph 7 of *Sein und Zeit*, proposes an exploration of the concept of phenomenon, then of the concept of *logos*, resulting in a "provisional concept of phenomenology" such that the reader is gradually stripped of his classical prejudices and arrives at a more Hellenic and Aristotelian understanding of the term. But such a guiding thread can also be followed in reverse (see TRUTH, SENSE); one is obliged to admit that this phenomenological structure is, always already and already in Aristotle, covered over and layered in the constitution of objectivity. In other words, transitivity is ultimately guaranteed only by making of showing a sign, of *logos* a judgment, of unveiling an adequation, and of the phenomenon an object. Might a Greek phenomenology, however much the paradigm of phenomenology, be undiscoverable?

BIBLIOGRAPHY

Ammonius. *Ammonii in Porphyrii Isagogen sive V Voces*. Edited by Adolf Busse. Berlin: G. Reimer, 1891. CAG, IV, 3.

Aristotle. *Categories and On Interpretation*. Translated by J. L. Ackrill. Oxford: Clarendon Press, 1963. Translation in French and notes by J. Tricot: *Aristote, Organon I: Categories, II: De l'Interprétation*. Paris: Vrin, 1997.

Aubenque, Pierre. *Le problème de l'être chez Aristote*. 2nd ed. Paris: Presses Universitaires de France, 1966.

Cassin, Barbara. *Aristote et le logos*. Paris: Presses Universitaires de France, 1997.

Kretzmann, Norman. "Aristotle on Spoken Sound Significant by Convention." In *Ancient Logic and Its Modern Interpretations*. edited by J. Corcoran, 4–21. Dordrecht: Reidel, 1974.

Pépin, Jean. "Sumbola, sêmeia, homoiômata. À propos de *De interpretatione* 1 16a 3–8 et *Politique* VIII 5, 1340a 6–39." In *Aristoteles Wirk und Wirkung*. Edited by P. Moraux. Vol. 1, *Aristoteles und seine Schule*. Berlin: De Gruyter, 1985.

Whitaker, Charles W. A. *Aristotle's De Interpretatione: Contradiction and Dialectic*. Oxford: Clarendon Press, 1996.

for example, the idea of intelligible pores or an infinite void outside the cosmos).

In the first case, the sign is "commemorative," *hupomnêstikon* [ὑπομνηστικόν], since it merely links two perceived items whose connection (*sumparatêrêsis* [συμπαρατήρησις]) has already been frequently observed, and one of which, that is then recalled, is temporarily absent, according, moreover, to any temporal modality whatsoever: a scar, sign of the past, recalls a wound; smoke, sign of the present, evokes fire; a blow to the heart, sign of the future, announces death. It will be understood that the study of signs can concern simultaneously what we call a sign, the thing that serves as a sign (smoke in relation to fire), and the *sunêmmenon*, the reasoning in the form of "if . . . then," characteristic of Stoic logic ("if there is smoke, there is fire"; see IMPLICATION). In the second case, the sign is said to be "indicative," *endeiktikon*: it contains in itself the entire demonstration since what is signified is by its nature not observable in itself, so that "it is directly on the basis of its specific nature and constitution, almost by emitting a vocal sound (*monon ouchi phônên aphien* [μόνον οὐχὶ φωνὴν ἀφιέν]). That it is said to signify what it is indicative of." Thus the movements of the body are signs indicative of the existence of the soul, which by its nature is not available to the senses. One part of Sextus's anti-dogmatic effort consisted in radically separating the two kinds of signs, maintaining the commemorative sign whose dependability we experience and live every day, but dismissing the pretentions of the indicative sign, by exposing the aporia of its concept. In so doing, the Skeptic first revealed the Stoic systematic, and transmitted a corpus of examples or cases that would continue to be commented on and developed by an Aristotelian semantics against which they were, nonetheless, elaborated.

3. The Aristotle/Stoic distortion and its reading by Heidegger

Heidegger's judgment here is interesting in more than one respect. (1) It establishes two eras of the sign: Aristotle, during the great age of the Greeks, understood the *Zeichen* as a *Zeigen*: as a self-display and a license to appear against a backdrop of *alêtheia* [ἀλήθεια]. The Stoics understood the sign as a designation (*Bezeichen*) according to a structure of reference. On one hand, phenomenology; on the other, linguistics. (2) In *De interpretatione*, *sumbola*, *sêmeia*, and *homoiômata* are to be—provisionally, but essentially—considered as synonyms since they are first of all three modes of self-revelation, saying how the phenomenon "unshelters itself" in the soul, the soul in the voice, and the voice in letters.

But that strong interpretation should no doubt be resisted. In point of fact, the difference between *dêloun,* "showing," and *sêmainenein,* "signifying," as thematized by Aristotle, already implies a mutation in the notion of the sign: "Nothing is by nature a word, but only when it becomes a symbol (*sumbolon*); in point of fact, unarticulated sounds (*agrammatoi psophoi* [ἀγράμματοι ψόφοι], which are not written) like those of beasts, do indeed show something (*dêlousi ge ti* [δηλοῦσί γέ τι]), "but not one is a word" (*De interpretatione*, 16a 16–19). One moves with Aristotle from *sêmainein* [σημαίνειν], an action verb with ontological transitivity (Heraclitus, B93: the Delphic oracle "neither says nor conceals, but makes a sign [*oute legei oute kruptei alla sêmainei* (οὔτε λέγει οὔτε κρύπτει ἀλλὰ

σημαίνει)]"), to *sêmainein* having as its subject a word: "the word signifies the fact of being or not being that (*to einai ê mê einai todi* [τὸ εἶναι ἢ μὴ εἶναι τοδί]")" (*Metaphysics*, 4.1006a 28–30). To the extent that signification is a natural indicator referring to the impressions of the soul, it cannot distinguish man from animal (*Politics*, 1.1253q 1–18). But it can do so as soon as it is *kata sunthêkên* [κατὰ συνθήκην], by convention, constituted as a human *logos*. At that point, it is no longer man, but the word "man," which means something, namely, the *logos* [λόγος] that makes it explicit, provides its definition (cf. Cassin, *La décision du sens*).

It will be seen how it all holds together—the *semeion/sumbolon* difference, the *dêloun/sêmainein* difference, the transition to words as the subjects of meaning: the "linguistic" is there in Aristotle as much as in the Stoics. It is thus not so much in the phenomenological opening or closure that the difference between Aristotle and the Stoics will be situated as in the very definition of what is a phenomenon and of what it is that means. On the one hand, with Aristotle, the analysis, oriented by the substance-subject (see SUBJECT, I), into word-units (*onomata* [ὄνοματα]) bearing meaning and combination via the "with" (the *sun* [σύν] of syntax and syllogism); on the other, with the Stoics, analysis into units of action rather than substances, into complete statements rather than into words, and into hypothetical arguments rather than syllogisms (the *sun* of the *sunêmmenon*, which links an "if" with a "then"): it is no longer the *onoma* but the *logos* that constitutes the signifying unit. Two types of phenomena and two types of linguistics, but one is no less linguistic than the other. Once again, the *sêmeion* is variable in its geometry.

II. *Signum* and the Intersubjective Dimension

A. Greek tradition and Roman innovation

Beyond its assumption of the *semeion/sumbolon* doublet and its numerous versions up to Boethius's translation of *De interpretatione*, Roman civilization loaded the *signum* with semantic charges that were at times directly adapted from Greek and at others more adjusted to the resources of Latin. Among the numerous meanings of *signum* that interfere, in classical Latin tradition, with the logico-linguistic uses in the broader field of the "semiotic," to the point of recurring as examples of "signs" in medieval typologies more or less directly inspired by Augustine (see Roger Bacon on this point), one finds those of the "insignia" and the (painted or sculpted) "image." *Signa*, in point of fact, designates the insignia "that distinguish the divisions of an army" (whence *signifer*, found in the medieval astrological notion of "sign-bearing heavens," prolonging the equivalence of *signa* and *sidera*, typical of Roman civilization, attested to by [among other sources] Varron's *De lingua Latina*, 7.14: "Signa dicuntur eadem et sidera. Signa quod aliquid significant" [stars are also called signs—signs because they signify something]). That specifically military sense presides—at the limits of "miracle," "presage," and annunciatory sign—over the presentation of the Cross as a "sign" in the story of Emperor Constantine ("in hoc signo vinces"). But we also find *signum* at the heart of *sigillum* (small image or statuette; seal, signature), in a register in which properties of different rank are combined, going from the material level of branding (the "mark" imposed on the herd as a sign of possession—*pecora signis notare*) to the ideal level of iterability (the *sigillum* and the operation it authorizes, the *sigillatio*, representing par excellence the iterability of the sign). It is not by chance that "sigillation" (no doubt borrowed from *Timaeus*, 50c–d, extends through an Aristotelian casting of Plato's doctrines, in *Metaphysics*, 1.6.987b–988a, in which the term *ekmageion* [ἐκμαγεῖον] has gone directly into Latin in the form of *etymagium, echmagium*) plays, in Ammonius, the role of a paradigm or explanatory model of the production of the various types of "forms," implied by the theory of "universals":

> Imagine a ring, with an imprint (*tis ektupôma* [τις ἐκτύπωμα]) [representing], for example, Achilles, along with numerous slabs of wax; suppose that the ring imprints its seal on the slabs of wax; suppose now that someone comes along later and looks at the slabs of wax, observing that all [the imprints] come from a single seal; he will have the imprint in himself, that is, in his discursive faculty [ἐχέτω παρ' αὐτῷ τὸν τύπον ὅ ἐστι τὸ ἐντύπωμα ἐν τῇ διανοίᾳ]; it can thus be said that the seal on the ring is "prior to the multiples" [ἡ τοίνυν σφραγὶς ἡ ἐν τῷ δακτυλιδίῳ λέγεται πρὸ τῶν πολλῶν εἶναι]; that the imprint in the slabs of wax is "in the multiples" [ἡ δὲ ἐν τοῖς κηρίοις ἐν τοῖς πολλοῖς], whereas the one that is in the discursive faculty of the person who has imprinted is "posterior to the multiples" and "posterior in the order of being" [ἡ δὲ ἐν τῇ διανοίᾳ τοῦ ἀπομαξαμένου ἐπὶ τοῖς πολλοῖς καὶ ὑστερογενής]. Well, such is what must be understood in the case of types and species.

> (Ammonius, *In Porphyrium Isagoge*; see UNIVERSALS)

Everything in this complex is taken up somewhat helter skelter in medieval tradition, meshing with deep associative networks serving as vehicles for Aristotelico-Boethian semantics. It is those networks that need to be analyzed in order to gauge the phenomena induced by the polysemous nature—including in its (theological, medical, astrological) transdisciplinary aspects—of the Greco-Latin doublet *semeion/signum*, in the languages of philosophy.

B. The stakes of the *signum* in medieval tradition

The stakes entailed by the introduction of the term *signum* were considerable since it was a matter, under Augustine's influence, of introducing the intersubjective dimension of the relation to the other, whereas the Aristotelian tradition was interested above all in the relation between words, things, and thoughts, as was well expressed by the word *nota*, "mark," used by Boethius in his translation of Aristotle (as well as his commentary on his thought), *De interpretatione* 1.16a.3–8.

Signum, in medieval semantics, has three fields of meaning. First, it retains the old sense of "proposition" playing a specific role in an argument. In its second (and most common) sense of "sign," it should be related with the word *nota*. The third sense is that of "logical sign."

A contamination between the Augustinian tradition of *signum*, which was dominant in theological texts, specifically in sacramental theology, and the peripatetic tradition of the *nota* can be observed on several occasions, notably in Albertus Magnus. Taking up various developments pursued in the context of sacramental theology, Roger Bacon attempted an integration of the two traditions, resulting in a general semiological system, unified by the notion of *signum*, attempting to integrate all types of signs, linguistic and non-linguistic, inferential and iconic, conventional and natural, and adding to the array of reflections on the relation to the signified, derived from Aristotle, others on the relation to the speaker/interpreter, inspired by Augustine.

1. *Signum* and inference

The first meaning of *signum* has no linguistic connotations and refers to the grounds of an inference. In such cases the medieval reference is first of all to Aristotle's *Prior Analytics* (2.27), then to the first book of his *Rhetoric*. Peter of Spain thus defines the *signum* as *propositio inferens*, that is, as the antecedent of a conditional. The *signum* thus serves as a necessary inference between the antecedent and its consequence, as opposed to the plausible or *ycos* (from Gr. *eikos* [εἰκός], copied, but not translated, into Latin; see EIDÔLON), which refers to the probable character of the proposition in itself (*Tractatus*, 5.3). Albertus Magnus, in his commentary on the *Prior Analytics*, adapts the classical Augustinian definition of the sign (see infra), and injects into it the idea of inference, which it did not contain: the *signum* is that which, on the basis of the image that it offers to the senses by itself, brings forth something other than itself to knowledge, that is, supplies something else, that can be inferred from it (*Liber priorum analyticorum* 2.7, 8). A *signum* is thus a demonstrative proposition from which one can infer a necessary or probable conclusion (see Marmo, "Bacon, Aristotle (and Others)").

2. *Signum* and *nota*: The translation of *Peri hermeneias*

Boethius, translating the first chapter of Aristotle's *Peri hermeneias*, uses the term *nota*:

> Sunt ergo ea quae sunt in voce earum quae sunt in anima passionum notae et ea quae scribuntur eorum quae sunt in voce. Et quemadmodum nec litterae omnibus eaedem, sic nec voces; quorum autem hae primorum notae, eaedem omnibus passiones animae sunt, et quorum hae similitudines, res etiam eaedem.

> (16a 2–7; *Aristoteles Latinus*, 1–2)

There is thus a relation of *nota* simultaneously between vocal expressions (or rather "ea quae sunt in voce," what is in a vocal expression) and *passiones animae* (the marks or impressions that things leave in the mind) and between written expressions and vocal expressions; and a relation of *similitude* between *passiones animae* and things. It will be noticed that at the end of this first chapter, the Latin translation uses the term *signum* in an argumentative sense that is often found in Boethius: a statement can be based on an example or on a fact that constitutes a (supplementary) sign of its acceptability, an "index" (cf. Aristotle, *De interpretatione*, 16a 16, cited supra).

William of Moerbeke restored the original Aristotelian opposition by opposing *symbola* and *signa*, thus leaving aside the term *nota*. He did so both in his translation of the *Peri hermeneias*, "Sunt quidem igitur que in voce earum que in anima passionum *symbola* et que scribuntur eorum que in voce. Et sicut neque littere omnibus eedem, sic neque voces eedem; quorum tamen hec signa primum, eedem omnibus passiones anime, et quarum hee similitudines, res iam eedem" (Aristotle *Latinus*, 2.1–2), and in that of Ammonius's commentary on that text, which was completed in 1268. Thomas Aquinas would make abundant use of the latter text in his own commentary, but would continue to comment on Boethius's translation, even as he preferred to use the term *signa* (*Expositio Libri Peri hermeneias*), which serves as a gloss for *nota* in its two meanings: "sunt note, id est signa." That gloss, which could already be found in other Parisian authors of the middle of the thirteenth century, such as Nicholas of Paris, was by no means a given.

The opposition between the Augustinian and Aristotelian perspectives is apparent in the commentary proposed by Robert Kilwardby, and adopted by Albertus Magnus, concerning the first chapter of *Peri hermeneias*, with the distinction between *signum* and *nota*:

> Postea queritur propter quia dicitur ea que sunt in voce sunt NOTE et non signa, et hoc ut iuxta hoc pateat differentia inter notam et signum. Et dicendum quod differunt nota et signum, quia nota est in quantum est in ore proferentis, set signum est in quantum est in aure audientis: quod patet per hoc quod signum est quod se offert sensui, aliud derelinquens intellectui. Quia igitur species intelligibilis in anima in quantum significanda est alteri dicitur "passio" in anima eius qui loquitur, melius dicit, sunt note quam signa.

> (It will then be wondered why he said that what is in the expression is a *mark* [*nota*] and not a *sign* [*signum*], and consequently what is the difference between *nota* and *signum*. It will be answered that *nota* and *signum* differ, since *nota* is used for what is in the mouth of the speaker, but *signum* for what is in the ear of the listener: this appears clearly when it is said that the sign is that which is offered to the senses, while depositing something for the intellect [a modified version of the definition of *De doctrina Christiana*, see below]. Since, then, the intelligible species in the soul, insofar as it is to be signified to another, is called "passion" in the soul of the one who speaks, the author was well advised to say that these are *marks* rather than *signs*.)

> (Robert Kilwardby, *Super Peri hermeneias* [ca. 1240], quoted by Rosier, *La parole comme acte*)

The distinction is important: *nota* is situated on the side of the speaker, and takes into account the production of signs based on the intelligible species that it forms in the mind and that constitutes its "marks," which corresponds, according to the author, to the meaning of the passage. Moreover, this is Thomas Aquinas's understanding, when he insists, on the basis of Ammonius and the *Politics*, on the fact that *voces* are made so that man, a "political and social animal," can express to others the knowledge (*notita*) that he has acquired of things. On the other hand, *signum* conveys the reception of the expression by the listener. The introduction of

an intersubjective dimension appears clearly influenced by Augustine, and is explicitly based on his definition of the sign. Whereas *nota* is situated in the series that includes the verbs *notare, connotare*, whence its meaning of "mark," *signum* is placed among terms indicating signification.

Augustine's definitions of the signs were broadly known and commented on in the Middle Ages in chapters devoted to sacramental theology. The best known was certainly that of *Doctrina Christiana* (2.1.1: "signum est res praeter speciem quam ingerit sensibus, aliud aliquid ex se faciens in cogitationem venire" [the sign is a thing which, in addition to the impression that it leaves on the senses, brings forth, therefrom, something more to thought]), which is taken up in the *Sententiae* of the theologian Peter Lombard in the middle of the twelfth century, with the division between *signa data* and *signa naturalia* (*Sententiae*, 4.1.5–6; see infra). If we occasionally find this definition in the thirteenth century, or that of the *De dialectica* (5: "signum est quod et se ipsum sensui et praeter se aliquid animo ostendit" [the sign is that which simultaneously presents itself to the senses and something other than itself to the mind]), cited in various texts, it appears in distorted form, attributed to different authors.

3. "Sign of" and "sign for"

It was with Roger Bacon that the Aristotelian and Augustinian traditions would be articulated in a new manner. Roger Bacon did indeed base his reflections on the thought of theologians such as Richard Fishacre and Bonaventure, even as he incorporated the contributions of commentaries on *Peri hermeneias*, but also examples borrowed from the *Analytics*.

Starting from the definition in *De doctrina Christiana*, the Dominican Richard Fishacre (ca. 1240), followed by Bonaventure, then by Roger Bacon in his astonishing treatise *On Signs* (1268), would introduce the idea that the sign (or more precisely the term "sign") is characterized by a dual relation—a relation to what it means (termed the "accusative relation") and a relation to the individual for whom it means (termed the "dative relation"). For the theologians, the first was essential: in the context of sacramental theology, it was important to say that the relation of the sacramental sign to its signified (grace) was inscribed in the institution of the sign by Christ, and could not be modified, independently of the way in which it was received. Bacon, on the contrary, would regard the dative relation as having priority: even if the sign possesses a given meaning at the moment of its institution, if it is not received as a sign, the sign remains a sign only in its substance, but is not a sign in act. This implies that the relation to the signified is entirely dependent on the will of the speaker and the interpreter, who freely define and redefine it with every utterance.

■ See Box 2.

4. Natural signs and signs that are *ordinata*

Bacon then proposes a general typology of signs that integrates linguistic and non-linguistic signs. He distinguishes natural signs (comprising three types: through inference, similarity, and relation of cause to effect) and signs that are *ordinata* or *data*, following Augustine; then he divides the latter, following Aristotle this time, into instituted

2

Fishacre/Bacon: The doubly relational nature of the sign

Drawing on Augustine, Richard Fishacre elaborated the notion that the sign is by nature a relative entity, and that two relations are implied, the relation to the signified and the relation to the interpreter. Roger Bacon would adopt that idea. The opposition between the two authors bore on the primacy of the two relations, Roger Bacon viewing the relation to the interpreter (producer/receiver) of the sign as essential since it befalls him to determine what the signified of the sign will be.

Richard Fishacre, *Commentary on the First Distinction of the Fourth Book of Sentences*:

It will be said that the noun *sign* is a relative. Among the names of relatives, some signify a single relation, others a dual relation. Single, as in *is placed*, dual as in *given*, since the word says simultaneously a relation to the person who gives and to who receives. In the same way *gleam* signifies a single relation, to what gleams, and *illuminate* a dual relation. Consequently, in my opinion, *sign*—if the word is understood in the strict sense—signifies a first relation to the signified (*ad significatum*) and a second relation to the person for whom it signifies (*ad eum cui significat*), and that dual relation is contained in the definition that has been posited (that of *De doctrina Christiana*): the relation to the signified through the clause *something else* (*aliud*), namely: the signified, and the relation to someone for whom it signifies (*ad aliquem cui significat*), through the clause *coming to knowledge* (*in cognitionem venire*). Just as *given* signifies what is through someone and for someone (*ab aliquo et alicui*), just so is the sign a sign of something and for someone (*alicujus et alicui*). The relation to the signified is the one that is most essential to the sign. Thus, since that relation depends on a relation that is either nature or will, the sign is split into a natural sign, such as smoke, which is a sign of fire, and a given or instituted sign, such as the noun *man,* which is the sign of such a thing. The relation to him for whom the sign signifies is occasionally permanent, which is manifest for instituted signs: it is

by virtue of the will of whoever realizes the institution that the word *man* always signifies that specific thing. Occasionally that relation is not permanent: such is the case for smoke, which can be considered as a thing in itself and not insofar as a fire is its cause, in which case it is not at all a sign, since one of the two relations is lacking; but if it is considered insofar as fire is its cause, from that point of view it is entirely a sign. Now, it should be seen that the two relations are permanent for instituted signs, and this by virtue of their institution, but neither of those relations is essential to the sign. But on the contrary, for natural signs, the relation to the signified is essential, and thus perpetual, since it is of the essence of every creature to be caused by God, and thus to be a sign of Him.... But the relation of natural signs to the person for whom they signify is neither essential nor perpetual, but accidental. Created things are, in fact, not only made to signify the Creator. Consequently, when a word is understood or apprehended, it is immediately apprehended as a sign for the person who apprehends it, since words are made solely in order to signify, whereas when I apprehend a created thing, it is not immediately apprehended as a sign for whoever apprehends it, but frequently as a thing.

Roger Bacon, *De signis* (1268):

The sign is in the predicament of relation and is spoken of essentially in reference *to the one for whom it signifies* (*ad illud cui significat*). For it posits that thing in act when the sign itself is in act and in potency when the sign itself is in potency. But unless some were able to conceive by means of this sign, it would be void and vain. Indeed, it would not be a sign, but would have remained a sign only according to the substance of a sign. But it would not be a definition of the sign, just as the substance of the father remains when the son is dead, but the relation of paternity is lost. And even if the sound of a voice,

a circular indication, or any other thing is imposed in act on a thing with which it is in relation, and instituted in such manner that it can represent it and signify it for others, nonetheless if that for which it signifies is not in act, it is not a sign in act but a sign in potency only. It is, in fact, different being imposed in act, which permits signifying for whomever it be, from being a sign in act. The verb *signify* is essentially and principally related to what acquires something, namely a thing signified by a dative, rather than a thing signified by an accusative. And for that reason, it refers only accidentally to the thing to be signified, that is, an object of knowledge for knowledge. One can indeed not conclude: "The sign is in act, and thus the thing signified exists," since non-beings can be signified by words as much as beings can, unless we intend that the being necessarily demanded by the signified is solely in the intellect and the imagination.

The sign is that which, offered to *the senses or to the intellect,* represents itself to that intellect, since not every sign is offered to the senses as the common definition of sign supposes. However, on the testimony of Aristotle, another kind is offered only to the intellect. He states that the *passiones anime* (concepts/species) are signs of things (*signa rerum*), and such *passions* are a habit of the soul and species (representations/intentions) of the thing (*species rerum*) existing for the soul, and therefore they are offered only to the intellect so that they represent external things to that intellect.

BIBLIOGRAPHY

Fredborg, Karen Margareta, Lauge Nielsen, and Jan Pinborg. "An Unedited Part of Roger Bacon's 'Opus Majus': 'De signis.' " *Traditio* 34 (1978): 76–136.

Rosier, Irène. *La parole comme acte*. Paris: Vrin, 1994.

Rosier-Catach, Irène. *La parole efficace: Signe, rituel, sacré*. Paris: Éditions du Seuil, 2004.

signs resulting from a deliberation (signifying in a conceptual mode), whether linguistic or non-linguistic, and signs that signify naturally (signifying in an affective mode). The phrase "natural sign" is ambiguous and covers quite different relations of meaning. In a first sense, it characterizes a kind of relation between sign and signified based on a natural link, which may be causal, mimetic, or iconic in nature. In a second sense, the reference is to a "type of production" of the sign, which is "natural" when it occurs in a non-deliberate manner, as is the case for screams, moans, and manifestations by animals, which escape the control of reason. The confusion between the two uses is facilitated by the fact that, in both cases, the sign signifies without the intervention of a prior will by the "institutor of speech" or the intention of a specific speaker. In *De signis*, Bacon renders this distinction explicit by placing the first case under the rubric of "natural signs" and the second under that of "signs signifying naturally."

- See Box 3.

3
Natural signs: Conventional and voluntary

This distinction is used to translate two oppositions that do not, in fact, coincide. The first is drawn from Augustine's *De doctrina Christiana* (2.1, 2): "signorum alia sunt naturalia, alia data" (among signs, some are natural, others are "given"). The second is constructed on the basis of Aristotle's *De interpretatione,* as interpreted in the Middle Ages, for example, by Petrus Hispanus (*Tractatus*): "vocum significativarum alia significativa ad placitum, alia naturaliter" (among vocal expressions some are intentionally meaningful, others naturally so). In Augustine, it is a matter of an opposition between, on the one hand, signs that "without intention or desire to signify, allow to be known, by themselves, something more than what they are in themselves," and, on the other hand, those that "all living beings address to each other to reveal, as much as they can, the motions of their soul, that is: all that they feel and all that they think." Augustine gives as examples, for the first case, smoke signaling fire, the pawprint indicating the passage of an animal, or even the irritated face of a man that conveys his feelings: each of these signs reveals what it means "without wanting to," and because we are accustomed, says Augustine, to associate "from experience" the two things being related. Roger Bacon would specify that in this first case the sign-relation is based on a natural relation between two things, a relation that might be, for him, one of interference, of similarity, of effect to cause. Augustine's *signa data* were produced in order to generate a thought or intellection, "to transfuse into the mind of an other what the individual producing the sign bears in his mind," thus Scripture, which was revealed in order to be interpreted, or the sound emitted by a cock in order to let his chicks know he has found food. These are signs that are not necessarily conventional, but were produced intentionally, or at least in order to be acknowledged. They are the result, according to Roger Bacon, of a deliberation and a choice. On the other hand, the opposition between words signifying *naturaliter* and *ad placitum* rests essentially on the criterion of *institution* and Boethius, and the Middle Ages following his lead, made use, for *ad placitum*, of the expressions *positione* or *ad positionem* (by [im]position) or even *voluntaria, ex institutione*; these expressions signify by virtue of an institution, and are thus not "the same for all" (*eadem apud omnes*), unlike signs signifying naturally. This distinction allows, on the one hand, for a distinction between nouns, verbs, sentences, that signify by virtue of such a process of institution, from other expressions (*voces*) that signify "by nature" (*natura*), without institution, such as the moans of the sick or the barking of a dog. But it is also used to distinguish written and oral expressions, intellections and things, and in this case it is not a matter solely of signification. Written and oral expressions are *secundum positionem* because they depend on an institution (*secundum hominum positionem*), and as a result they are not identical for different populations and are subject to variation. Conversely, intellections and things are by nature since they are identical for all and cannot be modified. It is because things are identical for all, and intellections are similar to things that the latter are equally identical for all. It will be perceived that the expression "by nature" is in fact applied by Boethius to two types of very different things, moans and barks, on the one hand, and intellections and things, on the other. Those two sets are deserving of the negative characteristic of not being the work of an institution. But the first covers vocal productions which, for Augustine, might partake of *signa data* (e.g., barking, insofar as it is intentional), the second realities that are not as such signs; were one to consider the relation of similitude of intellections to things, intellections would then be classified among the *signa naturalia*.

Roger Bacon articulates the two distinctions jointly, and proposes an overall schema in which it appears clearly that the Augustinian distinction trumps the Aristotelian distinction:

1. *signa naturalia* (e.g., smoke-fire; intellections-things, etc.) (= natural 1)
2. *signa data*
   2.1 *significativa ad placitum* (e.g., words, signs, etc.)
   2.2 *significativa naturaliter* (e.g., moans, barking of dog) (= natural 2).

A sign being a relational entity, it is not its substance that gains it entry into one or another of these categories, but the type of relations it entertains with the thing that it signifies, it being understood that it may entertain several such relations. A sign that is identical in substance can thus be considered in two different ways, in accordance with the nature of its relation with the thing it signifies. Consider the case of the dog's bark: it can be considered as either natural 1: I hear a dog and infer that there is an animal barking (the signification is produced because one is accustomed to associating an effect with a cause, or recognizing a relation of "concomitance" between the two events; but the bark was not produced in order to generate that thought; or as natural 2: the bark is a sign produced by a dog in order to manifest its anger (as Abelard puts it, it is, so to speak, the sign God gave dogs in order to do so, just as he gave men conventional language). This is exactly Augustine's position regarding facial expressions, which can involuntarily convey a movement of the soul or be produced "truly in order to be a sign," and thus intentionally (*De doctrina Christiana*, 1.2.2, 3). This is also how we may distinguish, along with Roger Bacon, the fact that the cock crows (*gallum cantare*), a natural sign (in the first sense) of dawn, and the crowing of the cock (*cantus gallli*), used to indicate that nourishment has been found.

The confusion between the two senses of "natural" is manifest in numerous discussions and obscures several classifications.

The term "conventional" is used erroneously to render the Latin *signa data* (Roger Bacon also uses *ordinata*): these are signs that living beings give each other (or are given) and that they employ intentionally. Augustine, moreover, uses other terms to designate the voluntary act that allows men to agree on the signification of signs (*consensio, placitum*; cf. *De doctrina Christiana*, 1.2.34, 37; 35, 38). *Ad placitum* can be translated as "conventional" only for certain authors; if the expression always refers to a deliberate decision to attribute a value to words or signs, that decision can be seen as a primal instituting process (*institutio, impositio*), occurring once and for all, and "counting as a law" for a given linguistic community, but also as a tacit—daily and thus perpetually renewed—act dependent on the "good will" of each interlocutor, an act which, for Roger Bacon, amounts to effectuating a new imposition of the sign, allowing a renewal of its meaning.

Bacon thus reinterprets the first chapter of *Peri hermeneias* in a rather personal manner, criticizing traditional interpretations, which he deems reductive (*De signis*, 166): thoughts are the natural signs (*signa*) of things and vocal sounds are the conventional signs of thoughts even as written words are the conventional signs of vocal sounds. In addition, vocal sounds are also the natural signs of their own images in the mind of the speaker, simultaneously by inference (one sees the sign, one infers from it that there exists an image of the sign in the mind), by similitude (the oral word is in conformity with its mental image), by relation of cause and effect (the vocal sound is the effect of its mental image). The vocal sounds are in a relation of natural sign to the image of the thing (one infers from the existence of the vocal sign that there has been a knowledge of the thing, and thus an image of it), and not, as Aristotle and Boethius seemed to maintain, in a relation of conventional sign, since the vocal sign signifies conventionally only the thing—Bacon here is taking a stand against those who thought that the word signifies first the concept and secondarily the thing in the "great controversy" (to use Duns Scotus's subsequent expression) that divided medieval thought. Finally, there exists a relation of natural sign from the image of the thing to the thing. That last relation may be at the origin of the idea later elaborated by Ockham that concepts are the natural signs of things.

5. *Signum* and logical function

Signum in a third sense designates terms that have a logical function, notably quantifiers. Boethius, commenting on *Peri hermeneias* (chap. 7), speaks of determinations (*determinationes*) or additions indicating particularity or universality (*adjectiones particularitatis/universalitatis*), which determine the quantity of a proposition, that is, which arrange for the universal thing signified by the determinate noun to be taken in its universality, with *omnis* (all), or, on the contrary, in a partial manner (*in partem*), with *quidam* (a certain, indefinite). Insofar as the quality of the proposition is concerned, Boethius uses the expression "particle of negation" (*particula negationis*). At the beginning of the twelfth century, Abelard and Garlandus Compotista commonly speak of *signa* as much for quantity (*signa universalitatis, particularitatis, quantitatis*) as for quality (*signa negationis*) (Abelard, *Glossae Super Peri Hermeneias*: "The signs of quantity, that is, of universality and particularity, like the signs of quality, that is, of affirmation and negation like 'est' and 'non est' are such that they allow one to know and to manifest respectively the universality and particularity of propositions and the property of affirmation or negation since such signs render the proposition universal and particular, and in the latter case, affirmative or negative"). Abelard also speaks of *signum consecutionis* for conjunction. He discusses whether such *signa*, which are "determinations" for Boethius, merit the name of "parts of discourse" (*partes orationis*), even if they cannot be called *termini*, an expression appropriate solely to subject and predicate (*Dialectica*).

During the same period, the grammarian Guillaume de Conches distinguished four varieties of names, and included in the last category those names that signify "ways of speaking about things" (*modi loquendi de rebus*), like *omnis, quidam, aliquis, nullus* (all, a certain, some, none), which the dialecticians, he says, call *signa propositionum* (in De Rijk, *Logica, modernorum*, vol. II/I). In terminist logic, this use of *signum* would be maintained, with *signa* thus constituting a subset of syncategoremes. The author of the *Summe metenses* (middle of the thirteenth century) justifies this term by saying that the *signa* are thus called because they signify the mode of signifying or supposing possessed by the *terminus* to which they are adjoined, grounding that affirmation on the Augustinian definition of the sign. Although every word is a sign, according to Aristotle, who says that words are signs of intellections ("voces sunt signa intellectuum"), such words can be called signs by antonomasia because they are "signs of signs" (*signa signorum*). The author thus emphasizes the particular character of such words, which refer not to things, but to other words (see INTENTION). He thus distinguishes signs that signify things, whether substance or accident, from those that signify other signs, by signifying either a mode of signifying terms of substance or a mode of supposing terms of accidents (De Rijk, *Logica modernorum*, vol. II/I).

III. The Place of the Symbol: From *Symbolum* to *Sinnbild*

The "symbol," by definition, implies simultaneously a difference—there are two distinct partners in a convention—and a bond—the two elements of the symbol must be able to be joined together. The connection, in turn, can be arbitrary (a mathematical symbol) or motivated according to different modalities (similitude, analogy, a "natural" relation, water as the symbol of purity) and its interpretation can be conventional and coded (scales as a symbol of justice) or more open to individual choice (Todorov, *Théories du symbole*). This initial complexity, illustrated, for example, by the confused and inconclusive discussion of the word's definition in Lalande's classic dictionary (RT: *Vocabulaire technique et critique de la philosophie*), and leading to the suggestion, in Umberto Eco's words (*Semiotics and the Philosophy of Language*), that the "symbol is simultaneously everything and nothing," has had considerable impact on the way in which its opposition to the sign has been described. But from negative theology to the theories of art of the first German Romanticism, what has always been at stake in the symbol has been the articulation of the finite and the infinite.

A. The Neoplatonic heritage

1. Dissimilarity and negative theology

During the Latin Middle Ages, the *symbolum* was felt to derive from the Dionysian tradition: it was indeed transmitted by way of the first chapters of Pseudo-Dionysius's *Celestial Hierarchy*, and various commentaries on that text, including primarily those of John Scottus Eurigena and Hugh of Saint Victor.

Symbols are first of all sensorial realities in the material world that constitute intermediaries allowing men to ascend toward the supernatural (cf. Hugh of Saint Victor: "symbolum est collatio formarum visibilium ad invisibilium demonstrationem" [the symbol is the conjoining of visible forms of reality in order to demonstrate invisible realities]; RT: *PL*, vol. 175, col. 941B). It is because materials available to the senses are resemblances, copies of such realities (cf. John Scottus: "per symbola, hoc est per signa sensibilibus rebus similia" [through the intermediary of symbols, that is, signs available to the senses and similar to things],"in which the glossing of *symbola* as *signa* will be noted) that they can lead an individual to hidden *mysteria*, as though "taking him by the hand," following a *materialis manuductio*. Symbols are veils (*velamina*) that conceal the mysteries they signify and, as a result, John Scottus specifies, constitute "exercises" for the human soul, which attempts to accede to them thereby. "Symbols" thus include the images in the Bible as well as the types of the Old Testament or the sacraments of the New, but additionally, for John Scottus, all the realities of the created world, natural realities and even artistic creations.

It will thus no longer be said that symbols are at once similar, insofar as they are copies, and dissimilar, insofar as they are of an inferior level, to the thing signified: there are indeed two kinds of symbols, the similar and the dissimilar, of which the latter are less deceptive than the former, then two kinds of utterance, the affirmative and the negative, of which the latter are less false than the former (cf. John Scottus, *Expositions,* 3.3.156BC: "just as negation is prior to affirmation in meaning, so dissimilar and absurd images are prior to images and manifestations of divine things"). Privilege is thus accorded in a single swoop to dissimilar images and negative theology. Subsequent reflection on divine names would clearly distinguish, starting with Pseudo-Dionysius (*Celestial Hierarchy*, 2.3.140Cff.), "symbolic names, such as *leo, lapis* (lion, stone), from "mystical" names, such as *sapientia, bonitas, essentia* (wisdom, goodness, essence).

The former, designating realities of the sensory world, are never "appropriate" for God, and can be applied to him only metaphorically, according to a process of *translatio*, established by way of an intermediate term (it is because of the lion's *strength*, also attributed to God, that he is called a *lion*; see *translatio* under TO TRANSLATE, IV). It is solely concerning the latter, whose purpose is the expression of essential properties, that the question will be raised of determining whether they are equivocal, univocal, or analogous to those same names when used for creatures. If the latter, through their semantic content, seem to approach divine truth more closely, the former are nonetheless more true *as signs*, being posited from the outset, through the dissimilarity that characterizes them, as pure signs, without risk of passing for true and adequate expressions. Albertus Magnus and Thomas Aquinas would clearly contrast those two types of names, explaining that the thing meant was suited, for the former, *per prius* to creatures and, for the latter, *per prius* to God, with the former being called *metaphoricie* and the latter *proprie* as a function of analogy, even though, at the level of their modes of signifying, all names are equally improper since instituted at the outset to signify the realities of the world of creation (see ANALOGY, HOMONYM).

2. "Sign" or "symbol" in Augustine:
The arbitrariness of translations

The Dionysian use of the *symbolum* can be related with certain affirmations of Augustine, for example, when he considers created realities as *vestigia trinitatis*, as a set of signs "referring to the sole *res* that cannot subsequently become a *signum*, which is God" (*De Trinitate*, 6.10.12; cf. Maieru,

"*Signum* dans la culture médiévale"). But we would do well to insist on the fact that Augustine made massive use of the term *signum:* numerous studies of "medieval universal symbolism" are absolutely incoherent in the use they make of the term "symbol" to read Augustine, translating *signum* capriciously as "sign" or "symbol," and the verb *significare* as "to signify" or "to symbolize," introducing arbitrary divisions within the different types of *signa* in order to distinguish a subset corresponding to "symbols." Thus Chydenius, in a frequently cited article, declares without giving justification that intentional signs given by men and by God can be called "symbols," but natural signs or intentional signs produced by animals cannot. Similarly, he introduces a distinction between *interpretative* and *descriptive* symbols, a distinction which, despite the efforts of the author to superimpose them, does not overlap with any of the Augustinian distinctions, such as those between *signa naturalia* and *data* or between *signa propria* and *translata*. Augustine's definition of *signum*, so often cited and explicated in the Middle Ages, is invoked by certain commentators as that of the "symbol," or even of the "sign-symbol." Although it is frequently said that Augustine's *signum* "absorbed the values of the symbol" (Ladner, "Medieval and Modern Understanding of Symbolism"), there has never been an inquiry into the philosophical or theological consequences of the fact that in Augustine's text, we are dealing at this juncture with only one term, namely, *signum*.

Signum is the signifier associated, either naturally or conventionally, with a precise, determinable, and identifiable signified, even if it is invisible or inaccessible, like God or grace, and even if that signified may be polymorphous or ambiguous. There is an intended order in the world, with things referring to each other according to a pre-established "plan"; things are made to be interpreted so that man can rediscover the meaning that they have been associated with or that he has associated with them in the case of voluntarily instituted signs, like the kiss exchanged to seal a peace or the wreath of foliage (*circulus vini*) to indicate wine in a tavern. This is the case for all signs, whether they be words or things referring to other things (thus "ox" signifies the animal, which itself signifies Christ). The criteria according to which one attempts to define the "symbol" in reality function, in the case of medieval authors, as so many criteria allowing one to discriminate between different types of signs—for instance, the criterion of similarity for natural signs; the same holds for functions judged characteristic of the "symbol," such as "recognition within a community," which is a function of the "sign."

In the context of sacraments, and thus contrary to the translating habits of the moderns, the term *symbolum* is never used, and use is made exclusively of the Latin *signum*, grounded in Augustine's definitions, whereas as of the sixteenth century the term "symbol" would be employed for the external form of the sacrament. Modern commentators of medieval texts, however, frequently render the Latin *signum* as "symbol," which inflects the thought of the era markedly; whereas the Augustinian *signum*, developed and extended in medieval definitions, situated the sacrament in its dual function of knowledge (providing access to invisible realities) and operativity (producing what it allows one to know, grace; see

SPEECH ACT, III) along with intersubjectivity (a sign produced by someone for someone), the use of the term "symbol," in this context, places the accent on the sacrament as a "password," an instrument of recognition and identification (cf. in this sense Chauvet, *Symbol and Sacrament*).

∎ See Box 4.

B. "Symbol," *Sinnbild*, "allegory" in German idealism and early Romanticism

From Kant to Hegel, the major area for reflection on the symbol is the philosophy of art. During that period, the concept of the symbol appears as a metaphysical solution to the problem of the unification of the finite and the infinite—the

---

4

Symbolum: A rereading of *Metaphysics* on the basis of Augustine and Averroës

The exceptional use of *symbolum* to speak of language in its simultaneously intersubjective and conventional dimensions in the Middle Ages is linked to the quite remarkable convergence of three different sources, resulting in the affirmation: "sermo omnis symbolum est" (all speech is symbolic). The first of these sources is a passage from Aristotle's *De sensu et sensato* (1.437a 12–15), notably used by Albertus Magnus in the *De voce* question of *Summa de creaturis*, written in Paris around 1246. Albertus inquires whether intelligible form is necessarily in the word and draws on our passage in order to argue in the affirmative: what passes (*transit*) from master to pupil-listener are not words without meaning, but meaningful words, since, as Aristotle claims, "hearing plays an accidental role in knowledge: meaningful discourse (*sermo*) is the cause of knowledge, not by itself, but in an accidental manner, by virtue of the fact that it is composed of words: and every noun is a symbol" (nominum unumquodque symbolum est).

Henri de Gand inquires in several articles of his *Summa questionum ordinarium*, written in 1292–93, as to the possibility of knowing, signifying, and naming God. His investigation is no longer merely one of the truth or of the property of signification or nomination, but far more one of the possibility of *transmitting to others* such knowledge, in the event it should prove possible, of signifying to others something by means of signs that might manifest it, which is an altogether novel question, clearly inspired by the Augustinian perspective in which the author situates himself. Signs, explains Henri de Gand, are established by convention to signify something and can transmit only what they have been imposed on. But in order to function as "symbols" between speaker and listener, the thing signified must be known to both and they must have something intelligible in common, which is problematic in the case of speech about God. The entire argument can be summarized as the affirmation that every noun (or vocal verb; or discourse [*sermo*]) is a symbol. Henri draws, on the one hand, on the passage from *De sensu et sensato* already mentioned. He associates it explicitly, on the

one hand, with *De doctrina Christiana* (2.24, 37; 25, 38), passages in which Augustine insists on the fact that signs signify "non natura, sed placito et consentione significandi," and, on the other hand, with a famous passage of Aristotle's *Metaphysics* (4.1006a 28ff.), on the principle of contradiction (see HOMONYM and PRINCIPLE). The reference to this passage cannot be understood if one reads the first Latin translations (cf. *translatio anonyma, Aristotes Latinus*), but only if one consults the Arabo-Latin version:

> Primum igitur omnium istorum est concedere quod sermo aut negat aliquid, aut affirmat ali-quid, et dignum est existimare quod hoc primum solum manifestum. *Et necesse est ut sermo loquentis fit signum de aliquo apud ipsum, et apud alium, si aliquid dicit.* Quoniam, si hoc non fuerit, non poterit disputare neque secum, neque cum alio.

> (In the first place, we should begin by considering, among all things, that speech either denies something or affirms something, and it should be estimated that only the first opinion is manifest. *And it is necessary that the speech of the one speaking become a sign of something, simultaneously for him and for others, if he wants to say something.* Indeed, were this not the case, he could debate neither with himself nor with others.)

Averroës comments on this passage, explaining that the discourse of the speaker must signify something that is simultaneously in his mind and in that of his listener, and which must be intelligible for both interlocutors, failing which there can be no discussion:

> Dicamus igitur quod necesse est homini concedere quod sermo dicentis, idest quod sua loquela, significat illud, quod est in ejus anima apud ipsum, et apud ipsum cum quo loquitur, sed ille qui loquitur dicit aliquod intelligibile, quod si illud, quod dicit, non fuerit intelligibile apud ipsum et apud audientem, non fit disputatio, neque ad ipsum, neque ad alterum.

> (We shall thus say that it is necessary to concede that the speaker's discourse, that is: what he says, signifies precisely what is in his soul for himself, and for the one with whom he is speaking, and that he who speaks utters something that is (an) intelligible, because, if what he said were not intelligible, both for himself and for his listener, there could be no discussion, neither with himself nor with others.)

Henri de Gand paraphrases the passage from the *Metaphysics* by glossing *signum* as *symbolum*, adapting the formula from *De sensu et sensato*, and insisting on the fact that for there to be transmission of meaning it is necessary for the thing signified to be known both to the speaker and to the listener, so that hearing the sign might provoke in the listener a rememoration of the thing that the noun signified for the speaker and with which it had been associated by imposition:

> Quia nomen sive verbum vocis universaliter debet esse symbolum inter duo, scilicet (inter add. I) loquentem et illum cui loquitur, sic ut res significata modo quo imponuntur nomina ad significandum, sit in se nota utrique, et quod nomen ad significandum ipsam rem ut talis est, sit institutum.

> (Because the noun or verb should be universally a symbol between two individuals, namely, between the one who speaks and the one who is spoken to, so that the thing signified, in the mode according to which nouns were imposed to signify, be known by both, and the noun instituted to signify the thing as it is.)

> (*Summa quaestionum ordinarium*, art. 73, q. 9, ll. 34–35; cf. also art. 20, q. 1)

Duns Scotus would recall this opinion while himself reflecting on the divine names (*Reportata Pariensia*, I, d. 22).

BIBLIOGRAPHY

Scotus, Duns. *Reportata Pariensia*. Edited by L. Wadding. Paris, 1639; repr. Paris, 1891–95.

humanly knowable form of the absolute. In a general manner, that union is understood, in opposition to the idea of convention or the arbitrary, as manifesting a secret affinity between the essence of the finite and that of the infinite—the former revealing itself capable of sheltering, in its very finitude, the divine, the latter able to reveal fully the life that animates it only by becoming embodied in finite reality.

1. A *Versinnlichung* (transition into the sensorial) of the Idea

The conditions of the idealist and Romantic comprehension of the symbol are posited by Kant in §59 of the *Critique of Judgment* (1790). On the one hand, indeed, he presents the symbol (*Symbol*) as a *form of intuition*: just as schematization is a "hypotoposis" or presentation (*Darstellung*) of concepts of understanding, "symbolism" "places before us," although in a manner that is only *analogical*, the concepts of reason or Ideas—and to that extent, it allows, if only indirectly, a "transition onto the sensorial" (*Versinnlichung*) of the Idea. Kant thereby intentionally took his distance from the Leibnizian use of the notion of the symbol, insofar as the latter assimilated *cognitio symbolica* to knowledge through signs and opposed it to intuitive knowledge (cf. Leibniz, *Meditationes de cognitione, veritate et ideis*, 1684). In addition, the intuition that we have of the Idea in the symbol is, according to Kant, *merely* indirect and analogical (in the strict sense of an identity of relations): an organism can symbolize a free polity to the extent that I judge the kind of relation between the parts of an organism to be identical to the kind of relation between the citizens of a free polity. But there is no resemblance or community of being between the freedom of a polity and organicity: the latter allows me to *think* the former, but not to *know* its essence. Symbolism thus partakes of an activity of judgment by a subject concerning an Idea which, by definition in Kant, remains a regulating horizon, not a constitutive force of reality.

On the basis of the Kantian definition, two tendencies emerge in the use of the notion: one that insists on the *presence* of the Idea in its symbolic embodiment, or even on the fusion of the universal and the particular in the symbol, the other that insists more on the *inadequacy* of the symbol to the Idea that it presents, thus bringing it closer to a mere sign. Those two tendencies, both emerging from the problem of the "presentation" (*Darstellung*) of the absolute in the finite, are opposed to each other, but can, on occasion, fuse in a paradoxical manner.

2. *Sinnbild* and *Andeutung*

The correspondence between Schiller and Goethe, between 1794 and 1797, was the site of an interpretation of the *Symbol* no longer merely as an analogical intuition of the Idea, but rather as a way of knowing the Idea insofar as it is present in a living manner in the sensorial reality that it organizes. According to Goethe, the symbol manifests the Idea on its own, but indirectly: symbolic objects "appear to be there solely for themselves (*bloß für sich*) and are, however, meaningful (*bedeutund*) to their very depths" (*On the Objects of the Plastic Arts*, 1797). On the other hand, allegory refers to the idea as something external to itself, destroying the interest taken in the sensorial presentation itself, which is no more than a simple intermediary allowing for the direct comprehension of the idea. Allegory is but the translation into images of the concepts of understanding, whereas the symbol has the Ideal as its inner organic principle. The intellectual proximity between Goethe and Schiller was undoubtedly an essential factor in the formation of the Schellingian concept of the symbol (cf. Goethe's letter to Schelling of 29 November 1803), defined in his *Lecture on the Philosophy of Art* (1802). Schelling insists there, in a rather Goethean spirit, on the identification of being and meaning in the symbol: "the finite [here] is at the same time the infinite itself, and does not merely mean it (*nicht bloß es bedeutend*)" (*Sämmtliche Werke*, V). Given that circumstance, the German word *Sinnbild* seems particularly suited to designate the compenetration or identity of the Idea and its presentation in the symbol since the latter, which presents the absolute in art, must be as concrete as the image (*Bild*) and yet as universal and charged with meaning (*Sinn*) as the concept. In allegory, on the other hand, the particular does no more than signify (*bedeuten*) the general. In a general way, the classical aesthetic of Goethe and Schelling thus has a tendency to bring the allegory closer to the sign (*Zeichen*).

Parallel to that organic understanding of the symbol, which tends to assimilate the presentation of the Idea to a real presence, there developed a conception in which the symbolic unity of the finite and the infinite appears like a goal situated at infinity rather than an actually realized embodiment. It appeared notably in what Friedrich von Schlegel called both "symbol" (*Symbol*) and "allegory of the infinite" (*Allegorie des Unendlichen*). All beauty is allegorical, and allegory for Schlegel is the tendency toward the absolute in the finite itself: "Every allegory signifies God (*bedeutet Gott*), and one can speak of God in no other than in an allegorical way" (*KFSA*, XVIII, 347, no. 315). Beyond what it actually presents, and which is always insufficient from the perspective of infinity, art makes a sign (*andeutet*) toward the absolute, which it can never truly render present: the symbol is understood here as an indication (*Andeutung*) or allusion. Creuzer, in his *Symbolism and Mythology of the Ancient Peoples* (1810–12) similarly insists on the inadequacy of the finite symbolic form to the essence of the idea that it manifests, "the incongruity of the essence with the form" (*Incongruenz des Wesens mit der Form*). He delineates, moreover, in an original manner the distinction between symbol and allegory with the help of the category of time: the former gives us instantaneously the intuition of the idea, whereas the latter reveals its meaning to us over the course of a gradual intellectual process. Hegel, finally, despite his opposition to Romanticism and to Friedrich von Schlegel on a number of points, nonetheless characterized symbolic presentation, in his *Lectures on Aesthetics* (1820), in terms of its inadequacy (*Unangemessenheit*) to the very essence of the Idea. The symbolic is in fact the first form of the artistic manifestation of the absolute, that is, the Idea would thereafter yield itself in a form available to the senses; but because the content of the idea itself was as yet indeterminate, symbolic figures, for instance, in Egyptian art, allow us to anticipate or intuit the absolute, instead of rendering it truly present: "the symbol (*Symbol*), although it ought not—like the merely external and formal sign (*wie das bloß äußerliche und formelle Zeichen*)—be entirely inadequate to its meaning, ought nonetheless, inversely, in order to remain a symbol, not render itself totally suited (*angemessen*) to it either" (*Werke*). Plenitude of sensory presence is the privilege of classical Greek art (i.e., what Schelling called . . . symbolic art). But in the final analysis, the presentation of the Idea in art, and thus in the immediacy of a sensory figure, can never be fully adequate to its essence, which is perfectly revealed only in its concept rendered explicit by philosophy.

Karl Wilhelm Ferdinand Solger (1780–1819), a philosopher close to the first wave of Romanticism, whose thought, drawing its inspiration largely from Schelling, simultaneously presented a certain proximity to the thought of Hegel, developed, in his dialogue *Erwin* (1815), a conception of the symbol in which the two tendencies evoked come together. On the one hand, the symbol is indeed the full and entire presence (*Gegenwart*) of the idea in a finite reality; on the other hand, the intimate link between the symbol and *irony* manifests to a similar degree the persistence of an infinite distance or inadequation between the idea and its symbolic embodiment. Irony is indeed the state of mind of the spectator of a work of art (but also the moment of the life of the idea itself) in which he (or it) recognizes that the realization of the idea in a finite figure, the only means of its embodiment, can only and simultaneously coincide with its denaturation.

IV. Neologisms and Redefinitions

In semiotics, the meaning given to the "symbol" by Peirce is generally retained: that of a purely conventional relation, dependent on neither a relation of contiguity (as opposed to the index) nor a relation of resemblance (as opposed to the icon), whereas Saussure inversely uses the term "sign" to indicate a conventional, arbitrary, and necessary relation between signifier and signified which, in the symbol, are for him, to the contrary, linked by a "rudimentary natural bond." For Wittgenstein, finally, the accent placed on the symbol, "use without meaning," at the expense of the sign, which is no more than its perceptible face, constituted an essential element of his critique of metaphysics, opening onto a philosophy of ordinary language.

A. Peirce's taxonomies

In Baldwin's *Dictionary of Philosophy and Psychology*, C. S. Peirce, under the entries "sign," "index," and "symbol," provides convenient definitions. A "sign" is "anything that determines anything else (its interpretant) to refer to an object to which it refers itself (its object) in the same fashion, the interpretant becoming in turn a sign, and so forth until infinity." "Index" and "symbol" are types of "signs." An "index" is a sign that does not refer to an object so much because of an analogy or a similarity as because of a "dynamical (including spatial) connection both with the individual object, on the one hand, and with the senses or memory of the person for whom it serves as a sign, on the other hand." A "symbol" is "a sign that is constituted as a sign purely by the fact that it is used and understood as such, whether the habit be natural or conventional, without consideration for the motives that have governed its choice." In the manuscript on trichotomies of signs (ca. 1903), Peirce situates this distinction of three types of signs within a more general classification. If every symbolic situation has a triadic structure, by virtue of the ontological principle of differentiation of Firstness, Secondness, and Thirdness, one ought to distinguish in a ternary manner not only signs, but

also the divisions of signs themselves. Peirce thus distinguishes the following divisions: (1) depending on the sign in itself (*qualisign, sinsign, legisign*); (2) depending on the sign and its object (*icone, index, symbol*); (3) depending on the relation of the sign to its interpretant (*rheme, dicisign, dicent sign*). For example, the *qualisign* is determined as a type of sign manifesting a firstness (whose quality is the paradigm). In this perspective, which is the only correct one and which consists of deriving Peirce's semiotics from his metaphysics and not the reverse (cf. Tiercelin, *La pensée-signe*), the icon is a dual category (it considers the sign-object relation) of Firstness. An icon is a sign that refers to its object by virtue of a similarity to that object. The index is a dual category of Secondness and the symbol a dual category of Thirdness.

In his manuscript, Peirce defines the symbol more precisely:

> A symbol is a sign which refers to the object that it denotes by virtue of a law, usually an association of general ideas, which operates to cause the symbol to be interpreted as referring to that object.

The symbol, to the extent that the law is human, is conventional. The symbol, by virtue of the legal causality of its denotation, is a legisign, that is, a sign that is a law (cf. "Every conventional sign is a legisign"). The symbol is simultaneously open to an extension and a limitation in comparison with icons and indices. The extension is the symbol's capacity to specify the qualities of the objects denoted (an icon resembles its object by virtue of a community of quality, but without specifying it, and an index does not include a descriptive element necessary for that specification—an example: a footprint denotes a presence, but does not specify its qualities; for that, recourse would be needed to natural language, which is an assemblage of symbols, with the possible exception of deictics, which can be considered as indices and metaphors taking the place of icons). The symbol plays an indispensable role in major operations of thought: abduction, deduction, demonstration. In that sense, the symbol is the very life of reality and of science:

> A symbol is an embryonic reality endowed with power of growth into the very truth, the very entelechy of reality.

> (*New Elements,* ca. 1904)

The limitation is that the symbol can only denote types of objects and not occurrences. A footprint denotes an individual event, but the symbol "donkey" denotes the donkey in general and not Balthazar or Fanchon; "red" denotes the property "red" in general. In his semiotics, Peirce thus carefully distinguished the "sign," the general concept of all signifying relations, declined according to the ontological categories of the real world, from the "symbol," which is a kind of sign denoting, by virtue of its legal character, the universal and the general (see SEMIOTICS).

B. Wittgenstein: On the symbol as use endowed with meaning

It is altogether remarkable to discover a distinction parallel to the one introduced by Peirce, but independently, in Wittgenstein. Wittgenstein cautions us (*Tractatus*, 3.324) against "confusions of which philosophy is full." The philosopher frequently allows himself to be mesmerized by the existence of a single sign (*Zeichen*) for two objects. Yet a shared sign cannot be regarded as a characteristic of the objects themselves (3.322), and, what is important is not the sign itself but that of which it is the perceptible aspect (3.32), namely, the symbol (*Symbol*). A symbol is thus any part of the proposition that characterizes and determines its sense (3.31).

How are we to conceive of the possibility of an access to the symbol? Wittgenstein's answer is crucial for all of his later philosophy:

In order to recognize the symbol in the sign we must consider the significant use.

(3.326)

It is the "significant use" that constitutes the symbol. The error of philosophy and metaphysics, allowing themselves to be taken in by the play of signs, is to believe frequently that where there is a common sign, there is a common symbol, thus neglecting essential distinctions inscribed in language use and the "perceptible" reality of the symbol. Thus already in the *Tractatus*, the limit between sense and nonsense is determined neither by "empirical content," nor by a kind of transcendent instance that would trace the limit of thought, nor by a reality with which our speech would be obliged to enter into conformity through its structure. It is determined by use:

In the language of everyday life it very often happens that the same word signifies in two different ways—and therefore belongs to two different symbols—or that two words, which signify in different ways, are apparently applied in the same way in the proposition.

Thus the word "is" appears as the copula, as the sign of equality, and as the expression of existence; "to exist" as an intransitive verb like "to go"; "identical" as an adjective; we speak of *something* but also of the fact of *something* happening.

(In the proposition "Green is green"—where the first word is a proper name and the last an adjective—these words have not merely different meanings but they are *different symbols*.)

(3.323)

Far from the "realist metaphysics" currently attributed to the early Wittgenstein, it would be negligence regarding the sign/symbol distinction that would constitute the fundamental reason for metaphysical errors.

■ See Box 5.

Barbara Cassin
Mildred Galland-Szymowiak
Sandra Laugier
Alain de Libera
Frédéric Nef
Irène Rosier-Catach

5
The symbolic in psychoanalysis

1. *Symbol*, *Symbolik*, and *Symbolbildungen* in Freud

The use of the notions of *symbol/symbolic* dates back to the origins of Freudianism. In the text *Project for a Scientific Psychology* (*Entwurf einer Psychologie*, 1895), Freud already uses the term *Symbol* (*das Symbol*) to describe the (normal or pathological) phenomenon in which an element takes the place of another, the association between the two not always being manifest. Among the examples given by Freud, one finds that of the soldier who "sacrifices himself for a piece of colored cloth on a pole because it has become the symbol of his native country," or of "the knight who fights for a lady's glove" (*The Origins of Psychoanalysis*). What is at stake in such cases are "symbol formations" (*Symbolbildungen*) that belong to normal life. In the hysterical symbol, the phenomenon is realized in a different manner. "The hysteric whom A causes to cry does not know that it is only because of an association between A and B in which he himself does not play any role in her psychic life. In such a case, the symbol has completely replaced the object."

In chapter 6 of *The Interpretation of Dreams* (*Die Traumdeutung*, 1900), in the section titled "Representation by Symbols in Dreams" (Die Darstellung durch Symbol im Traume). Freud develops the idea according to which dreams use "the symbolic" (*die Symbolik*) in order to conceal representations of latent dream thoughts, most often sexual in origin. He adds that

This symbolism (*diese Symbolik*) does not belong to the dream itself, but to the activity of unconscious representation—particularly among commonfolk, and it can be found in folklore, myths, legends, colloquial phrases, the wisdom of maxims and in jokes circulating among the people more completely than in dreams.

Freud thus used the term "symbol" to designate a kind of constant signification appearing in formations of the unconscious, notably in dreams: for example, "a hat as a symbol of a man (or of male genitals)" (*des männliches Genitales*) or the "genitals represented by buildings, stairs, and shafts" (*Darstellung des Genitales durch Gebäude, Stiegen, Schachte*),

etc. (see the index of symbols at the end of the work). Freud adds:

We characterize a constant relation of this kind between an element of the dream and its translation as symbolic, the dream element itself as the symbol of the unconscious thought in the dream.

("Die Symbolik im Traum," in *Vorlesungen zur Einführung in die Psychoanalyse* (1917), in *Gesammelte Werke*, vol. XI)

Nonetheless, Freud's use of the notions of "symbol" and "symbolic" is not precisely stable. In the text cited above, Freud affirms:

It should also be granted that the boundaries of the concept of symbol are currently difficult to define with precision in relation to substitution, representation, etc. The limits are unclear, since it even is related to allusion.. . . It will thus be seen that a symbolic relation is a comparative connection of a very particular sort, and

(continued)

(continued)

whose bases we have not yet clearly apprehended. Perhaps in the future we will find clues leading to this unknown.

In essence, the symbol is thus one thing put in the place of another. The fact that there is a hidden connection between the symbol as such and the thing signified implies that this relation can also be deciphered, as happens in unconscious formations (dreams, symptoms, parapraxes, and jokes). It should be noted, however, that Freud himself has reservations concerning the symbolics of "invariant translations": "Interpretation depending on a knowledge of symbols is not a technique that can replace the associative technique or measure up to it." Jacques Lacan emphasizes that this constitutes a break with Jung and the idea of an archetype established from the beginning:

This exteriority of the symbolic in relation to man is the very notion of the unconscious. And Freud constantly demonstrated that he was faithful to it as to the very principle of his experience. As is shown by the point on which he broke outright with Jung, that is, when the latter published his "Metamorphoses of the Libido." For an archetype is tantamount to making of the symbol a flowering of the soul, and that is crucial. . . . But what should be said, in conformity with Aristotle, is that it is not the soul that speaks, but man who speaks with his soul."

("Situation de la psychanalyse en 1956,"
Écrits)

2. The Symbolic in the Teaching of Jacques Lacan

For Jacques Lacan, the nominal form "the symbolic" takes on more precise contours, borrowing from linguistics (the arbitrary nature of the sign and the articulation of signifier and signified from Saussure, metaphor and metonymy from Jakobson) and, initially, from structural anthropology (Lévi-Strauss). From structural anthropology Lacan has taken in particular the notion of a "symbolic system":

Every culture can be considered as a set of symbolic systems, of which language, rules of marriage, economic relations, art, science, and religion are of the first rank.

(Lévi-Strauss, "Introduction à l'œuvre
de Marcel Mauss")

It is with that grid that Jacques Lacan undertook a return to the Freudian roots of psychoanalysis, formulating the axiom that he would argue until the end of his teaching: "The unconscious is structured like a language." That axiom lies at the basis of his elaboration of the "symbolic" register, with its equivalence between symptom and metaphor, desire and metonymy.

From the outset of his teaching, Lacan constructed his notion of the symbolic in relation with two other "registers" from which it could not be dissociated, the imaginary and the real. Although he had already used the word "symbolic" in his text "The Mirror Stage" in 1949, it was not until 1953, in the lecture "Le symbolique, l'imaginaire, et le réel" and in "Fonction et champ de la parole et du langage en psychanalyse," that he elaborated it in all its complexity. In "Le symbolique," Lacan writes:

It is indeed in this manner that the symbolic at play in the analytic exchange is to be understood, to wit: what we discover, and what we speak about over and again, and which Freud manifested as its essential reality, whether it be a matter of actual symptoms, parapraxes, and whatever be inscribed; it is still and always a matter of symbols and even of symbols specifically organized in language, and thus functioning on the basis of equivalents of signifier and signified: the very structure of language.

The "symbolic" thus becomes the very center of the analytic experience, inseparable from other elaborations, such as the "Name-of-the-Father," "phallic signification," "paternal metaphor," "foreclosure." The Oedipus complex constitutes the fundamental operation determining the subject's insertion in the symbolic order.

Lacan reinterprets the Freudian Oedipus complex, dividing it into three logical phases: in the first phase, "the subject identifies in the mirror with the object of the mother's desire"; in the second phase, "the father intervenes fully as the agent of privation of the mother"; and in the third phase, "the father can give the mother what she desires (the phallus), and is able to give it to her because he has it" (*Les formations de l'inconscient*). "What is the symbolic path? It is the path of metaphor," writes Lacan. It is the "paternal metaphor," the result of the Oedipus complex, that establishes for the subject any possibility of signification ("phallic signification"): in the paternal metaphor, it is a matter of "the substitution of the father as symbol, or signifier, in place of the mother."

The phallus is thus the psychoanalytic symbol par excellence—"the pivot of the entire subjective dialectic." It is the "signifier of a lack," which regulates for the subject the realm of the dialectic of demand and desire.

Insofar as it is a symbol, it cannot be confused with the biological organ.

The non-inscription of the "Name-of-the-Father" (foreclosure, *Verwerfung*) characterizes psychosis: "What is rejected in the symbolic order, in the sense of *Verwerfung,* reappears in the real (*Les psychoses*).

Throughout his teaching, Lacan gave different emphasis to the three registers. In the beginning, he devoted his efforts to the elaboration of the register of the imaginary. As of 1953, he concentrated on bringing the symbolic into greater relief, until the early 1970s, when he began to deepen his elaboration of the real, which, contrary to the symbolic, "emerges as excluding meaning" (1977).

Although Lacan modified his theory of the symbolic as he developed that of the "real," and the notions linked to that register—such as that of *jouissance* (bliss)/*jouis-sens*—he never abandoned the tripartite conception of psychic structure. In the seminar "R.S.I." (1974–75), he presented the three registers in terms of the topological figure of the Borromean knot: "The definition of the Borromean knot starts at three; you break one of the rings and they are free, all three of them, that is: the two other rings are set free" (unpublished seminar, session of 10 December 1974).

Elisabete Thamer

BIBLIOGRAPHY

Freud, Sigmund. *Gesammelte Werke*. 18 vols. Frankfurt: Fischer: 1940–52. Translation: *The Standard Edition of the Complete Psychological Works of Sigmund Freud*. 24 vols. Edited by J. Strachey. London: Hogarth Press, 1953–66.
———. *The Complete Letters of Sigmund Freud to Wilhelm Fliess, 1887–1904*. Translated and edited by Jeffrey Moussaieff Masson. Cambridge, MA: Belknap Press of Harvard University Press, 1985.
———. *The Interpretation of Dreams*. Vols. 4–5 of *The Standard Edition*, see above.
———. *The Origins of Psychoanalysis*. New York: Basic Books, 1954.
Lacan, Jacques. *Autres écrits*. Paris: Éditions du Seuil, 2001.
———. *Écrits*. Paris: Éditions du Seuil, 1966. Translation by Bruce Fink: *Écrits*. New York: W. W. Norton, 2007.
———. *Le séminaire*, Book III, *Les psychoses*. Edited by J.-A. Miller. Paris: Éditions du Seuil, 1981.
———. *Le séminaire*, Book V, *Les Formations de l'inconscient*. Edited by J.-A. Miller. Paris: Éditions du Seuil. 1988.
———. "Le symbolique, l'imaginaire, et le réel." *Bulletin de l'Association freudienne internationale* 1 (1982).
Lévi-Strauss, Claude. "Introduction à l'œuvre de Marcel Mauss." In *Sociologie et anthropologie* by Marcel Mauss. Paris: Presses Universitaires de France, 1993.

BIBLIOGRAPHY

Abelard, Peter. *Glossae Super Peri Hermeneias*. Corpus Christianorum Continuatio Mediaevalis, 206. Turnhout: Brepols, 2010.

Ammonius. *Ammonii in Porphyrii Isagogen sive V Voces*. Edited by Adolf Busse. Berlin: G. Reimer, 1891. CAG, IV, 3.

Aquinas, Saint Thomas. *In Aristotelis libros Peri hermeneias et posteriorum analyticorum exposition, cum textu et recensione leonine*. Turin: Marietti, 1964. Translation by Jean T. Oesterle: *Aristotle: On interpretation. Commentary by St. Thomas and Cajetan (Peri hermenias)*. Milwaukee: Marquette University Press, 1962.

———. *Sancti Thomae Aquinatis, Doctoris Angelici, Opera omnia / iussu impensaque Leonis XIII P. M. edita*. Vol. 1. Rome: Ex Typographia Polyglotta S. C. de Propaganda Fide, 1882–.

Aristotle. *Aristoteles Latinus. II, 1–2 De interpretatione vel Periermenias*. Bruges: Desclée de Brouwer, 1995.

Arnauld, Antoine, and Claude Lancelot. *La grammaire générale et raisonnée*. Edited by H. E. Brekle. Stuttgart: Frommann, 1966. First published in 1660. Translation: *A General and Rational Grammar*. Menston: Scolar Press, 1968.

Arnauld, Antoine, and Nicole Pierre. *The Art of Thinking: Port-Royal Logic*. Translated, with an introduction by James Dickoff and Patricia James and a foreword by Charles W. Hendel. Indianapolis: Bobbs-Merrill, 1964.

Augustine, Saint. *On Christian Doctrine*. Translated by R. P. H. Green. Oxford: Oxford University Press, 1999.

Ax, Wolfram. *Laut, Stimme und Sprache*. Göttingen: Vanderhoeck and Ruprecht, 1986.

Baratin, Marc, and Françoise Desbordes. *L'Analyse linguistique dans l'antiquité classique*. Vol. 1 of *Les théories*. Paris: Klincksieck, 1981.

Boethius. *Commentaries on Aristotle's De interpretatione*. 2 vols. Edited by Karl Meister. New York: Garland, 1987.

Boulnois, Olivier. "Représentation et noms divins selon Duns Scot." *Documenti e studi sulla tradizione filosofica medievale* 6 (1995): 255–80.

Cassin, Barbara. "Parle si tu es un homme." In *La décision du sens*. Edited by Barbara Cassin and Michel Narcy. Paris: Vrin, 1989.

Cassirer, Ernst. "The Dialectic of the Mythical Conscience." Part V of *Mythical Thought*. Vol. 2 of *The Philosophy of Symbolic Forms*. Translated by Ralph Manheim. Preface and introduction by Charles W. Hendel. New Haven: Yale University Press, 1953–96.

Chauvet, Louis-Marie. *Symbol and Sacrament: A Sacramental Reinterpretation of Christian Existence*. Translated by Patrick Madigan and Madeleine Beaumont. Collegeville, MN: Liturgical Press, 1995.

Chydenius, Johan. *The Theory of Medieval Symbolism*. Helsinki: Helsingfors, 1960.

Coffa, Alberto. *The Semantic Tradition from Kant to Carnap*. Cambridge: Cambridge University Press, 1991.

Creuzer, Georg Friedrich. *Symbolik und Mythologie der alten Völker, besonders der Griechen*. Hildesheim, Ger.: Olms, 1973.

Dahan, Gilbert. *L'exégèse chrétienne de la Bible en Occident médiéval, XIIe–XIVe siècle*. Paris: Éditions du Cerf, 1999.

De Rijk, Lambertus Marie. *Logica Modernorum: A Contribution to the History of Early Terminist Logic*. 2 vols. Assen: Van Gorcum & Company, 1962–67.

Diamond, Cora. *The Realistic Spirit*. Cambridge, MA: MIT Press, 1991.

Eco, Umberto. *Semiotics and the Philosophy of Language*. Bloomington: Indiana University Press, 1984.

Eco, Umberto, et al. "On Animal Language in the Medieval Classification of Signs." In *On the Medieval Theories of Signs*, edited by Umberto Eco and Costantino Marmo, 3–41. Amsterdam: Benjamins, 1989.

Fédier, François. *Interprétations*. Paris: Presses Universitaires de France, 1985.

Galland-Szymkowiak, Mildred. "Le symbole chez Solger, ou l'existence de l'idée." In *L'Ésthetique de Karl Solger, symbole, tragique et ironie*, edited by A. Baillot, 67–97. Tusson: Du Lérot, 2002.

Hamesse, Jacqueline. "Signum dans les lexiques médiévaux ainsi que dans les texts philosophiques et théologiques anteriéurs à Thomas d'Aquin." In *SIGNUM*, edited by Massimo Luigi, 79–93. Florence: Leo Olschki, 1999.

Hegel, G. W. F. *Werke*. Edited by Eva Moldenhauer and Karl Markus Michel. Frankfurt am Main: Suhrkamp, 1969–79.

Heidegger, Martin. *On the Way to Language*. Translated by Peter D. Hertz. New York: Harper and Row, 1971.

Hobbes, Thomas. *Part I of De Copore* [*Elementorum philosophiae section prima de corpore*]. Translated by A. P. Martinich. New York: Abaris Books, 1981.

Imbert, Claude. *Phénoménologie et langues formulaires*. Paris: Presses Universitaires de France, 1992.

Janke, Wolfgang. "Das Symbol." *Philosophisches Jahrbuch* 76 (1968): 164–80.

Jungius, Joachim. *Logica Hamburgensis*. Edited by Rudolf Meyer. Hamburg J. J. Augustin, 1957. First published in 1638.

———. *Logicae Hamburgensis additamenta*. Edited by W. Risse. Göttingen: Vandenhoeck and Ruprecht, 1977.

Ladner, Gerhart B. "Medieval and Modern Understanding of Symbolism: A Comparison." *Speculum* 54, no. 2 (1979): 223–56.

Laugier, Sandra. *Wittgenstein: Métaphysique et jeux de langage*. Paris: Presses Universitaires de France, 2001.

Leibniz, Gottfried Wilhelm. *Philosophical Papers and Letters*. Edited and translated by Leroy E. Loemker. 2nd ed. Dordrecht: D. Reidel, 1969.

———. *Philosophical Texts*. Edited and translated by R. S. Woolhouse and Richard Francks. Oxford: Oxford University Press, 1998.

Maierù, Alfonso. "Signum dans la culture médiévale." In *Sprache und Erkenntnis im Mittelalter*. 2 vols. Edited by J. P. Beeckmann et al. Berlin: De Gruyter, 1983. 1:51–72.

———. "*Signum* negli scritti filosofici teologici fra XIII e XIV secolo." In *SIGNUM*, edited by Massimo Luigi, 120–41. Florence: Leo Olschki, 1999.

Manettie, Giovanni. *Theories of the Sign in Classical Antiquity*. Translated by Christine Richardson. Bloomington: Indiana University Press, 1993.

Marache, Maurice. *Le symbole dans la pensée et l'œuvre de Goethe*. Paris: Nizet, 1960.

Marmo, Costantino. "Bacon, Aristotle (and Others) on Natural Inferential Signs." *Vivarium* 35, no. 2 (1997): 135–54.

———. *Semiotica e linguaggio nella scolastica: Parigi, Bologna, Erfurt, 1270–1330, la semiotica dei Modisti*. Rome: Instituto Palazzo Borromini, 1994.

Meier-Oeser, Stephan. *Die Spur des Zeichens. Das Zeichen und seine Funktion in der Philosophie des Mittelalters und der fruhen Neuzeit*. Berlin: Freie Universität, 1997.

Nuchelmans, Gabriel. *Theories of the Proposition: Ancient and Medieval Conceptions of the Bearers of Truth and Falsity*. Amsterdam: North-Holland, 1973.

———. *Late-Scholastic and Humanist Theories of the Proposition*. Amsterdam: North-Holland, 1983.

———. *Judgment and Proposition from Descartes to Kant*. Amsterdam: North-Holland, 1983.

Peirce, Charles Sanders. *Collected Papers*. 8 vols. Edited by C. Hartshorne and P. Weiss. Cambridge, MA: Belknap Press of Harvard University Press, 1960–66.

———. *The Essential Peirce: Selected Philosophical Writings*. 2 vols. Bloomington: Indiana University Press, 1993–98.

Pépin, Jean. "Aspects théoriques du symbolisme dans la tradition dionysienne. Antécédents et nouveautés." In *Simboli e simbologia nell'alto medioevo*. Spolète, 1976. 33–66.

Rosier, Irène. *La parole comme acte*. Paris: Vrin, 1994.

———. "Res significata et modus significandi. Les enjeux linguistiques et théologiques d'une distinction médiévale." In *Sprachtheorien in Spätantike und Mittelalter*, edited by Sten Ebeesen, 135–68. Tübingen: Gunter Narr, 1995.

———. "Henri de Gand, le De dialectica d'Augustin, et l'imposition des nom divins." *Documenti e studi sulla tradizione filosofica medievale* 6 (1995): 145–253.

———. *La parole efficace: Signe, rituel, sacré*. Paris: Éditions du Seuil, 2004.

Schelling, F. W. J. von. *Sämtliche Werke*. Stuttgart: Cotta, 1856.

Schlegel, Friedrich von. *Friedrich Schlegel—Kristische Ausgabe seiner Werke (KFSA)*. Edited by Ernst Behler, Jean-Jacques Anstett, and Hans Eichner. Berlin: Ferdinand Schöningh, 1958–.

Schlesinger, Max. *Geschichte des Symbols. Ein Versuch*. Hildesheim, Ger.: Olms, 1967.

Short, T. L. *Peirce's Theory of Signs*. Cambridge: Cambridge University Press, 2007.

Soerensen, Bengt Algot. *Symbol und Symbolismus in den ästhetischen Theorien des 18. Jahrhunderts und der deutschen Romantik*. Copenhagen: Munksgaard, 1963.

Spade, Paul Vincent. "Some Epistemological Implications of the Burley-Ockham Dispute." *Franciscan Studies* 35 (1975): 212–22.

Thomasius, Christian. *Einleitung zur Vernunftlehre*. Hildesheim, Ger.: Olms, 1968.

Tiercelin, Claudine. *La pensée-signe. Études sur C. S. Peirce*. Nîmes: J. Chambon, 1993.

Todorov, Tzvetan. *Théories du symbole*. Paris: Éditions du Seuil, 1977.

Wittgenstein, Ludwig. *Tractatus Logico-Philosophicus*. Translated by D. F. Pears and B. F. McGuiness. London: Routledge and Kegan Paul, 1974.

Wolff, Christian. *Vernünftige Gedanken von den Kräfften des menschlichen Verstandes*. In *Gesammelte Werke*, vol. 1, pt. 1. Hildesheim, Ger.: Olms, 1965. First published in 1713. Translation: *Logic, or, Rational Thoughts on the Powers of the Human Understanding*. Hildesheim, Ger.: Olms, 2003.

█ SIGNIFIER / SIGNIFIED

FRENCH	*signifiant/signifié*
GERMAN	*Bezeichnendes, Bezeichnung/Bezeichnetes*
GREEK	*sêmainon* [σημαῖνον], *sêmainomenon* [σημαινόμενον], *lekton* [λεκτόν]
ITALIAN	*significante/significato*
LATIN	*signans/signatum, effatum, enuntiatum, dictum*
SPANISH	*significante/significado*
SWEDISH	*uttryck/innehåll*

➤ DICTUM, HOMONYM, INGENIUM, LANGUAGE, LOGOS, NONSENSE, SACHVERHALT, *SENSE*, SIGN, *WITTICISM*, WORD

That a sign is composed of a signifier and a signified is something that we moderns believe we owe to Saussure, but that Jakobson, for instance, attributes to the Stoics. The Stoics, however, latch their doublet to a terminological and doctrinal innovation, that of the *lekton* [λεκτόν] (expressable, utterable), which no longer is present as such in modernity. The use of the term "signifier," as of the doublet "signifier/signified," eminently anti-Aristotelian (see SENSE and WORD) up to and through its adaptation by Lacan, derives from ontological presuppositions and linguistic conceptions so heterogeneous that it has produced no end of slippages and generated countless misinterpretations.

What is the meaning, what are the major reinterpretations of "signifier/signified" (are "signifier" and "signified" dissociable or not, of the same nature or not, implying or not a third term and according to what relation?), and how is this readable in the way in which they are said and in the definitions they receive?

I. History of the Couple? Mythic Precursors

The couple seems so obvious that it is recurrently projected as deriving from the authority of a host of precursors: Aristotle/the Stoics, Augustine, Port-Royal. The idea that the couple "signifier/signified" comes from Port-Royal has its origin in Michel Foucault's presentation of the classical theory of the sign (*The Order of Things*). It was then, according to the author, that a "binary disposition of the sign" was substituted for "an organization which, in different modes, had been ternary from the time of the Stoics and even the first Greek grammarians" according to different modalities: first, the tripartite Stoic division, "signifier, signified, 'conjuncture' (*tugchanon* [τυγχάνον])" (see below); and second, the one put in place during the Renaissance and based on the notion of similitude ("similarities linking the marks to the things designated"). In Foucault's presentation of the classical notion of the sign, however, only representation will be at stake, and not the reorganization of the allegedly Stoic couplet, as confirmed by quotations from Port-Royal, and notably the definition of the sign as containing "two

ideas, one of the thing that represents, the other of the thing represented" (I, chap. 4). In concluding, Foucault adopts the idea that the "binary theory of the sign" is based on the "link between a signifier and a signified," even as he notes that that link "can only be established within the general medium of representation." That binary disposition presupposes that "the sign is a representation doubled and redoubled on itself," since "the signifier has as its sole content, function, and determination what it is that it represents . . . [and that] that content is indicated solely in a representation that is given as such," as is well illustrated by the example of the tableau. Thus is revealed the homogeneous nature of the sign and the signified, excluding "the possibility of a theory of signification." The connection between a theory of signs and a theory of ideas, which is determinant in Saussure, is similarly evoked by Foucault concerning the debate between Destutt de Tracy and Gerando. The relation to Saussure is ultimately spelled out in the conclusion only because of the "psychologistic" definition he gives of the sign, and of the "rediscovery" of its binary nature.

The same precursors are to be found in Lacan, who gets them from Jakobson (see below). And the novelty of Lacan himself is thus serialized in terms of its exceptionality by Jean-Claude Milner:

> From a strictly morphological point of view, Saussure could have sought inspiration in the *semainonta/semainomena* doublet found in Aristotle and the Stoics, or in the *signans/signatum* doublet found in Saint Augustine. But in French, he does indeed appear not to have had a predecessor. The fact that the signifier is on the active side and the signified on the passive side does not appear to have been thematized before Lacan.

> (*Le périple structural*, 42 n. 13)

The mythic precursors are indeed both precursors and mythical: we will analyze the Greek terminology of the Stoics, in its innovation in relation to Aristotle, then the Latin doublet found in Augustine, not in itself since the doublet is foreign to his theories of meaning, but in the posterity based on his theories, the semiology of the sacraments.

II. "Signifier"/"Signified" in the Stoics: The Invention of the *Lekton*

The Stoics, unlike Aristotle, innovated a terminological use of the doublet *sêmainon* [σημαῖνον] / *sêmainomenon* [σημαινόμενον] (signifier/signified). This is why they are often perceived as the first precursors of Saussurean linguistics. From the point of view of the theory of language, the difference between Aristotle and the Stoics was pinpointed with greatest precision by Ammonius, who commented on Aristotle in the fifth century CE: "Nouns and verbs signify thoughts," says Ammonius, corroborating the traditional interpretation of the beginning of *De interpretatione* [see SIGN], "and one need invent nothing other between thought and thing, as is posited by the men of the Portico and that they choose to call the 'sayable' (or the 'expressable,' *lekton* [λεκτόν])" (17, 25-18).

A. The constitutive relation of signification: "signifier" (*sêmainon*) / "signified" (*sêmainomenon, lekton*) / "referent" (*tugchanon*)

"The Stoics [claimed] that there are three things linked together (*tria suzugein allêlois* [τρία συζυγεῖν ἀλλήλοις]): the signified, the signifier, and the referent (*to te sêmainomenon kai to sêmainon kai to tugchanon* [τό τε σημαινόμενον καὶ τὸ σημαῖνον καὶ τὸ τυγχάνον])" (Sextus Empiricus, *Adversus mathematicos*, 8.11–12, SVF [Stoicorum Veterum Fragmenta] 2.166).

It was initially the very word *sêmainon* (signifier) that the Stoics were the first to press into terminological service: "The signifier is the vocal sound, for instance, 'Dion' (*tên phônên, hoion tên Diôn* [τὴν φωνὴν, οἷον τὴν Δίων]) (ibid.)." A. A. Long and D. N. Sedley (*The Hellenistic Philosophers*) propose "utterance," and J. Brunschwig and P. Pellegrin (*Les philosophes hellénistiques*) opt for "émission vocale" (on the meaning of *phônê*, see WORD). The signifier, or *phônê*, which is emitted and heard, in its bodily materiality, shows or manifests (*dêloô* [δηλόω]) a signified.

> The signified (*sêmainomenon*) is *auto to pragma* [αὐτὸ τὸ πρᾶγμα], the thing in question manifested by the vocal sound, and which we understand, for our part, when it is presented to our thought by the vocal sound, whereas those who do not speak our language do not understand it even though they hear the vocal sound.
>
> ([σημαινόμενον δὲ αὐτὸ τὸ πρᾶγμα τὸ ὑπ' αὐτῆς δηλούμενον καὶ οὗ ἡμεῖς μὲν ἀντιλαμβανόμεθα τῇ ἡμετέρᾳ παρυφισταμένου διανοίᾳ, οἱ δὲ βάρβαροι οὐκ ἐπαΐουσι καίπερ τῆς φωνῆς ἀκούοντες.])

(Sextus Empiricus, *Adversus mathematicos*)

Auto to pragma ("the thing in question"; see RES) is rendered by M. Baratin and F. Desbordes (*L'Analyse linguistique dans l'Antiquité Classique*) as "contenu de pensée" (thought content); A. A. Long and D. N. Sedley (*The Hellenistic Philosophers*) opt for "the actual state of affairs." What is essential, whatever the tension between subjectivization and objectivization, is to avoid the confusion between objects of the world and the referent, *tugchanon* (see SACHVERHALT). "As for the *tugchanon*, it is the corresponding external object—Dion itself in this case (*tugchanon de to ektos hupokeimenon, hôsper ho Diôn* [τυγχάνον δὲ τὸ ἐκτὸς ὑποκείμενον, ὥσπερ ὁ Δίων])." To *tugchanon*, literally "what is found there" (whence Foucault's translation as *conjoncture* [*The Order of Things*]), is also subject to interpretative nuances: *référent* (Baratin and Desbordes, *L'Analyse linguistique*), "name-bearer" (with an *onomatos* as direct object elided [Long and Sedley, *Hellenistic Philosophers*, 2:197, cf. 1:201]), *porteur du nom* ("bearer of the name" [Brunschwig and Pellegrin, *Les philosophes hellénistiques*]). The link with Gottlob Frege's *Bedeutung* comes from Benson Mates, then from A. A. Long, quoted by J.-B. Gourinat (*La dialectique des stoïciens*, 114 [see SENSE]): the *tugchanon* designates, in any event, the external substrate (*hupo keimenon* ["extended below"], which is correctly translated as "object," but which designates no less clearly the substrate subject; see OBJECT, SUBJECT), which is corporeal, physical, and corresponds to what is emitted by the voice: "Dion"/Dion.

Of those three components, Sextus continues, "[T]wo are corporeal, the vocal sound and the referent (*toutôn de duo men einai sômata, kaithaper tên phônên kai to tugchanon* [τούτων δὲ δύο μέν εἶναι σώματα, καθάπερ τὴν φωνὴν καὶ τὸ τυγχάνον]), but the third is incorporeal, the signified of 'utterable' thought content (*hen de asômaton, hôsper to semainemenon pragma, kai lekton* [ἕν δὲ ἀσώματον, ὥσπερ τὸ σημαινόμενον πρᾶγμα, καὶ λεκτόν]."

The Stoic invention of the "signifier/signified" doublet thus presents two characteristics: (a) the doublet cannot work without a third term, on the order of the referent; (b) the signified is not called only *sêmainemenon* ("signified"), since the Stoics invent another name for it as well, *lekton*, as if to mark their own invention. The *lekton*, which is "incorporeal" (and that also designates it as a Stoic innovation), manifests the anti-Aristotelianism of the Stoic theory of language, which otherwise, with signifier and referent assimilated to word and thing, might pass for Aristotelian.

B. *Logos* and *lekton*

The neologism *lekton* is a nominalization of the verbal adjective from the verb *lego* [λέγω] (to say). The impossibility of translating *logos* [λόγος] unambiguously encounters, in Stoic logic, the difficulty of understanding and translating *lekton* (see LOGOS). The *lekton* is defined as "what subsists according to" or "in conformity with a logical representation" (*to kata phantasian logiken huphistamenon* [τὸ κατὰ φαντασίαν λογικὴν ὑφιστάμενον]) (Diogenes Laertius, *The Lives and Opinions of Eminent Philosophers*, VII.63). This definition is given greater precision by Sextus (*Adversus mathematicos*, 8.70), and one understands, after reading current translations unable to convey the meaning of terms with the common root *leg-* (in this case, that of Gourinat, *La dialectique des stoïciens*), why matters are difficult to understand: the Stoics "say that what is utterable [*lekton*, i.e, 'available to discourse'] is what has reality in a rational representation [*logiken*, 'discursive representation']; and that a rational representation is one in which what is represented can be manifested by language [*logôi parastêsai* [λόγῳ παραστῆσαι], 'manifested by discourse']."

What is designated by this concept, for which we dispose of a large variety of ancient and modern translations? The difficulty for recent translators of *lekton* lies less in their choice of verb—there is general agreement, with Baratin and Desbordes, who render *lekton* as *énonçable* (cf. *L'Analyse linguistique*, 72–73), on using the verb *énoncer* in French for *legein* [λέγειν]—than in the question of knowing whether or not the concept entails a nuance of virtuality. Is it a matter of *dicible, exprimable, énonçable* (ibid.)—Long and Sedley translate *lekton* as "sayable"; Brunschwig and Pellegrin as *dicible*—or of *dit* (Long, *Language and Thought in Stoicism*, 77; C. Imbert, "Théorie de la représentation et doctrine logique dans le stoïcisme ancien," 247)?

The *lekton* appears as a correlate of the verb *legein*, in the sense in which Aristotle speaks of a correlate (*antikeimenon* [ἀντικείμενον]) for a relative term: the slave is thus slave of the master and the master master of the slave; knowledge is knowledge of the knowable and the knowable is knowable by knowledge; sensation is sensation of what can be sensed and what can be sensed can be sensed by sensation. In point of fact, as Claude Imbert (ibid.) indicates, the *lekton* must be understood within the series relating to the act of uttering, *legein, lexis* [λέξις] / *lekton*, parallel to the series of representation, *phainomai* [φαίνομαι], *phantasia* [φαντασία] / *phantaston* [φανταστόν], of intellection, *noein* [νοεῖν], (*noeisthai* [νοεῖσθαι]), *noêsis* [νόησις] / *noêton* [νοητόν], of sensation, *aisthanesthai* [αἰσθάνεσθαι], *aesthêsis* [αἴσθησις] / *aisthêton* [αἰσθητόν]. Such series allow one to indicate the role of the object of knowledge within the very movement of knowing. Concerning all these cognitive acts and for all sensory activities, one may note the same division within the word "action" as it pertains to the actor and as it pertains to the result of the action, that is, its accomplishment in the object.

Lekton is thus to be understood as *aisthêton* (see SENSE, I and Box 1), *noêton, phantaston*. What remains to be understood is the difference between *lekton, lexis*, and *logos*. It appears that *logos* is distributed into a couplet in two different ways:

1. First in relation to *lexis*, within the part of the dialectic concerned with *phônê*, understood within the division of the signifier: the *lexis* is *phônê eggrammatos* [φωνὴ ἐγγράμματος], "a voice articulated in letters," without for all that being necessarily endowed with meaning, whereas the *logos*, for its part, as utterance or discourse, is simultaneously voice, articulation, and bearer of meaning (see WORD, II.B.2).

2. Secondly in relation to *lekton*, involving the relation between the study of *phônê* and the study of "signifieds." In this second doublet, the distinction between *logos* and *lekton* advances neither by way of articulation, nor by the relation to *phônê*, nor by the distribution of the signifier. If *logos*, as opposed to *lexis*, is necessarily a bearer of meaning, it is because of the *lekton*. Whereas the *lexis* concerns the articulation of the signifier, the *lekton* conceptualizes the discursive situation productive of meaning in the framework of the utterance: the Stoics would distinguish between the meaning that is thought of a given situation (the *nooumenon pragma* [νοούμενον πρᾶγμα]) and the meaning of what is said that exposes it discursively, its *lekton*, which exists in the reality of the act of utterance.

As Gilles Deleuze proposes in *The Logic of Sense*, the *lekton* is nothing other than the sense or the meaning. However, it is not a matter of meaning in general, or of the meaning of a term, but always of the meaning of a statement or a sentence (it can be the meaning of a term only to the extent that a term is always understood by the Stoics as that of an incomplete sentence). That it is a matter of the meaning of a sentence is attested to by the distinction specific to the field of signifieds (cf. Diogenes Laertius, *The Lives and Opinions of Eminent Philosophers*, VII.63), between the "sayable" or "complete saying" (*lekton autoteles* [λεκτὸν αὐτοτελές])—and the "sayable" or "incomplete saying" (*lekton ellipes* [λεκτὸν ἐλλιπές])—for example, one "written," concerning which we ask: "Who?" It is indeed the reference to the meaning of the complete sentence (*lekton autoteles*) that determines the completeness or incompleteness of a linguistic sequence. The distinction between such completeness and incompleteness is part of logic, the study of signifieds. Logical analysis in terms of *lekta*, like the distinction between complete

"sayables" (*lekta autotelê* [λεκτὰ αὐτοτελῆ]) and incomplete "sayables" (*lekta ellipê* [λεκτὰ ἐλλιπῆ]), brings the dimension of the sentence into relief by making explicit the constructability of the complete sentence, separating considerations of syntax properly speaking from the analysis of truth values (true or false).

The distinction between truth and falsity nonetheless intersects with the distinction between complete and incomplete *lekta* in the following way: "it is the 'sayable' that is true or false, but not any 'sayable' at random, since there exist cases that are complete and others that are incomplete" (Sextus Empiricus, *Adversus mathematicos*, M.7.12). What is called an assertion (*axiôma* [ἀξίωμα], see PROPOSITION) partakes of the complete variety of the "sayable," and it is precisely the assertion that Sextus characterizes in these terms: "What is true or false is an assertion (*axiôma estin ho estin alêthês hê pseudos* [ἀξίωμά ἐστιν ὅ ἐστιν ἀληθὲς ἢ ψεῦδος])" (ibid.). The incomplete "sayable," on the other hand, is neither true nor false. Syntactical rules governing the construction of a sentence allow one to add to it what it lacks in order to achieve completeness and, if among the different varieties of the sayable that are complete, an assertion is generated to situate it simultaneously as true or false.

The difference between *logos* and *lekton* is justified by way of the separation between the two parts of the Stoic dialectic: the study of signifiers, on the one hand, the study of signifieds, on the other. *Logos*, however much it partakes of language, is not without a body. The *lekton*, on the other hand, is incorporeal: without the specific *logos* whose "meaning effect" it is, the *lekton* does not exist; it "subsists." How are we to understand the production of an effect of meaning during a speech act? How not to exist before existing without being a potentiality or virtuality? Therein lies precisely what the Stoics call "subsisting" (*huphistanai* [ὑφιστάναι]) for the *lekton*, which exists (*huparchein* [ὑπάρχειν]) only at the moment that the sentence is uttered. The *lekton* would thus be understandable as the sayable/said.

■   See Box 1.

C. Latin (non)translations of *lekton*

A passage from Letter 117 of Seneca (117.13; K. Hülser, *Die Fragmente zur Dialektik der Stoiker*, 892) lists the different Latin translations that have been proposed to designate the "what I am talking about" corresponding to the sentence "Cato is walking," which is not a body, but a "declarative fact concerning a body": *effatum, enuntiatum, dictum*. When he explains that "what is said (*quod nunc loquor*) is not a body," Seneca is certainly thinking of the *lekton*, a particular case of which he is considering, the one that is *enuntiativum*, the *axiôma*; this corresponds to other usages in Latin, in which *effatum* and *enuntiatum* explicitly rendered the Greek *axiôma* (see PROPOSITION); compare to this passage cited by Gabriel Nuchelmans:

> "Sunt," inquit, "naturae corporum, tamquam hic homo est, hic equus"; has deinde sequuntur motus animorum enuntiativi corporum. Hi habent proprium quiddam et a corporibus seductum tamquam "video Catonem ambulantem": hoc sensus ostendit, animus credidit. Corpus

1

The Stoic incorporeal

According to the testimony of Diogenes Laertius (*The Lives and Opinions of Eminent Philosophers*, 7.140), "what is capable of being occupied by bodies, without it actually being the case" may be defined as incorporeal. The Stoics recognized four incorporeals: time, place, emptiness, and the *lekton*.

The distinction between body and incorporeal (*asômaton* [ἀσώματον]) partakes of the Stoic theory of causality and its originality. Whereas the body, in keeping with the Platonic definition of being as potency (*dunamis* [δύναμις]; Plato, *The Sophist*, 247e), may be defined as what is able to act or to suffer, the incorporeal is defined by inactivity and impassiveness: "The incorporeal, in their view, by nature does not act or undergo anything" (Sextus Empiricus, *Adversus mathematicos*, 8.263). More precisely, "No incorporeal interacts with a body, nor a body with an incorporeal, but a body with another body" (Nemesius, SVF [Stoicorum Veterum Fragmenta] 1.117; Long and Sedley, *The Hellenistic*

Philosophers, 45.C). Now, a body is a cause for another cause of an incorporeal effect: "Every cause is a body and is a cause for a body of an incorporeal [effect], for example: a scalpel, which is a body, is a cause for the body that is wood of an incorporeal [effect], the predicate 'to be burned'" (Sextus Empiricus, *Adversus mathematicos*, 9.211). Émile Bréhier's analysis of this passage is worth retaining:

When the scalpel slices the flesh, the first body produces on the second not a new property, but new attribute, that of being cut. The attribute does not designate any real quality. . . . [It] is always, on the contrary, expressed by a verb, which means that it is not a being but a manner of being. . . . This manner of being is located, in some sense, at the limit, at the surface of the being and it cannot change its nature; it is, in truth, neither active nor passive, since passivity would presuppose a corporeal nature undergoing an action.

It is purely and simply a result, an effect not to be classified among beings.

[The Stoics distinguish] radically, something that no one had done before them, two levels of being: on the one hand, deep and real being, which is force; on the other hand, the level of facts, which are played out at the surface of being and constitute an endless multiplicity of incorporeal beings.

(*La théorie des incorporels dans l'ancien stoïcisme*, 1–2)

The originality of the Stoic theory of causality lies in this "rupture of the causal relation" (G. Deleuze, *The Logic of Sense*), which joins causes with each other and effects with each other; it also lies in the fact that principle and cause are not incorporeals; they are active and productive, and thus corporeal. The incorporeal is not the higher degree of reality, and corporeal reality is in no way its degradation.

est quod video, cui et oculos intendi et animum. Dico deinde: "Cato ambulat. Non corpus," inquit, "est quod nunc loquor, sed enuntiativum quiddam de corpore, quod alii effatum vocant, alii enuntiatum, alii dictum."

("There are," it is said, "certain natural classes of bodies; we say: 'This is a man,' 'this is a horse.'" Then there attend on the bodily natures certain movements of the mind which declare something about the body. And these have a certain essential quality which is sundered from the body; for example: "I see Cato walking." The senses indicate this, and the mind believes it. What I see, is a *body*, and upon this I concentrate my eyes and my mind. Again, I say: "Cato walks." "What I say," they continue, "is not a body; it is a certain declarative fact concerning a body—called variously an 'utterance,' a 'declaration,' a 'statement.'")

(*Theories of the Proposition*, 108)

These terms cannot translate precisely the Greek *lekton*, the terms *effatum, enuntiatum,* and *dictum*, indicating solely the content of a *complex* linguistic sequence. The perspective, in point of fact, has changed. The Stoic focus on the notion of predicate, and the distinction between complete (*autoteles*) and incomplete (*ellipes*) *lekton* has disappeared and given way to an opposition between simple and complex: thus does Augustine, in *De dialectica*, contrast *verba sumplicia* with *verba conjuncta,* while distinguishing among the latter those that have a complete meaning. Whereas for the Stoics the incomplete *lekton* was a predicate, for Augustine one arrives at an incomplete sequence of words (*verba conjuncta*) by excising, for example, from the complete sequence *homo festinans in*

montem ambulat (a man in a hurry walks toward the mountain) the verb *ambulat* (M. Baratin, *La naissance de la syntaxe à Rome*, 408–13).

Because of this opposition between the simple and the complex, it appears that "the sayable," which is to be found only in Augustine's *De dialectica*, cannot be regarded as a translation of *lekton*: it is, in fact, introduced as a pendant of *dictio* in the remarkable series *verbum, dicibile, dixtio, res* (see WORD, Box 3); it thus corresponds to the mental content of a simple word, which is occasionally said by Augustine to be prior to the utterance of the word (*dictio*), occasionally simply contained in the word, and at still other times to be understood by it in the mind of the listener. Here too the perspective has changed: meaning is no longer realized, as with the Stoics, solely in the *lekton autoteles*. There can be meaning, and thus a junction between form and content, at the level of the simple word. The *dicibile*, despite the suffix *-ibile*, which normally indicates potentiality, is thus capable of existing either as a potential or an act. It is perhaps on the basis of this term that the term *enuntiabile* would be forged, a term that would be used in the Middle Ages, along with *dictum*, to designate that content, but insofar as it belongs to the *enuntiatio* or the proposition (see DICTUM).

The term *sententia*, on the other hand, designates the content expressed in a linguistic sequence, which can be either simple or complex; in most cases, it is a rendering of the Greek *dianoia* [διάνοια], particularly for the grammarians, but it is clear that it can also render the Greek *lekton*—that dimension of thought insofar as it is expressed by words being so strong for the Romans that they occasionally use the term for expression itself. As evidence of all these difficulties, we shall adduce in conclusion Aulus-Gellius, who, giving the Greek definition of *axiôma*—*lekton autoteles apophanton hoson eph' hautôi* [λεκτὸν αὐτοτελὲς ἀπόφαντον ὅσον ἐφ ' αὐτῷ] ("an intrinsically declarative complete statement")—specifies that "I have foresworn translating, since I would have had to use new and unknown words, which would have shocked our ears." And he continues by giving Varro's "excellent definition": *proloquium est sententia in qua nihil desideratur* ("an assertion is a statement in which nothing is lacking"), in which *sententia* has taken the place of *lekton* (Aulus-Gellius, *Attic nights*, XVI.8; cf. G. Nuchelmans, *Theories of the Proposition*, chap. 7, and A. Garcea, "Gellio e la dialettica," 125–35).

III. *Signans/Signatum*

In medieval Latin, the term *signum* is often ambiguous and designates either the sign in its entirety or only the signifier, for which we also find *signans*, in opposition to the signified *signatum*. The elaboration of Augustine's *De dialectica*, which distinguishes *dictio* and *dicibile*, but within a system of four terms including as well *res* and *verbum* (see WORD, Box 3), would remain virtually unknown subsequently. As far as complex entities are concerned, the terminology is occasionally unstable: even though, at the time the terminology was created in the twelfth century, the *dictum* ("what the proposition says") was distinguished from its "name," the *appelatio dicti* (for example, *Socratem currere* is the name of the corresponding *dictum*), the terms *dictum* and *enuntiabile* at times designate the signifier and at others the signified of the proposition, such imprecision compounding the one frequently observed in the term *propositio* itself (see DICTUM and SACHVERHALT).

■ See Box 2.

IV. Saussurean Metalanguage and Its Translations

A. The elaboration of Saussure's terms

The *Cours de linguistique générale* (hereafter referred to as CLG) (1916) of Ferdinand de Saussure (1857–1913) is a posthumous

---

2

The *signans/signatum* doublet and the theory of sacrament

The *signans/signatum* (signifier/signified) doublet appears in the very precise context of the definition of "sacraments" in the twelfth century. Peter Lombard, whose *Sentences* would remain the basis of the teaching of theology as of the second half of the twelfth century, begins his treatise of sacraments as follows:

> What is a sacrament? Augustine, in Book 10 of *The City of God* [CCIm 47, 277]: "A sacrament is a sign of a sacred thing (*sacrae rei signum*)." It is also said that a sacrament is a "sacred secret" . . . in such manner that the sacrament is a sacred signifier and a sacred signified (*sacrum signans et sacrum signatum*). But at present we shall deal with the sacrament insofar as it is a sign.

(*Sentences*, Book 4.1.c.2, p. 232)

The definition of the sacrament as a "sign," understood here as a signifier ([*signans*), is the result of a long history. The first Christian rites, such as the laying on of hands, unction for the ill, which were initially perceived as distinct rites, which were first called *mustêria* [μυστήρια], this term designating as well, as in all initiatic practices, the hidden mysteries or designs of God. Until Augustine, the terms *mysterium* and *sacramentum* would be used in both senses. Under the influence of the Greeks and Origen, the symbolic value of the rite was accorded prime importance, but this opened on to "symbolic" exegetical reading more than to a redefinition of the sacrament. It was by developing this allegorical reading that Augustine made of the *sacramentum* a

synonym of *signum*. The facts and episodes of the Old Testament were not simply to be known, but to be interpreted in their value as signs, that is, as granting to be known something *other* than what they were in themselves. Christian sacraments are signs referring to a signified, the *res sacramenti*, which was, for Augustine, essentially the commemoration of Christ, and they were in addition bearers of multiple symbolic values, such as the purification associated with baptismal immersion. For him, the sacramental effect, grace, was the *virtus* or *vis sacramenti*, but was not its signified, whereas subsequently, when the sacrament would be defined as "effectuating what it means," signified and effect would coincide (see SPEECH ACT). The distinction between *signum* and *res* was at the heart of Augustine's analysis: every teaching bears either on signs or on things, and things can be said only by signs. Certain things are only things, others are simultaneously things and signs, and signs can be such only if they are used to signify something other than themselves (see SIGN). Christian sacraments are thus indeed signs, and "sacred signs," visible or sensory forms providing access to invisible realities; and, like all signs, they refer to a *res*, which is in this case *res sacra*, with which they entertain a situation idiosyncratic to them, a relation of "similitude" (concerning the distinction between *dicibile* and *res,* see WORD, Box 3).

Despite Augustine, it was the definition of sacrament as "mystery" that would

endure for several centuries. The stakes in the redefinition of the sacrament as "sign" were associated with a very precise debate on the nature of the Eucharistic conversion. Berenger of Tours, in the eleventh century, argued that the bread and wine continued to be such after consecration, but were transformed from pure things (*res*) into signs, signs of the body and blood of Christ. Bread and wine changed their status but were not annihilated. Whereas, when Moses's staff was changed into a serpent, there was the new presence of a serpent that had not existed before, in this case there was not, Berenger maintained, a new thing that began to be, since Christ exists for all eternity. He emphasized the relational nature of the sign: what acts as a sign is necessarily *ad aliquid*, and consequently in relation with a signified. I can thus not be accused, Berenger protested, of saying that the bread and wine would be *only* sacraments; indeed, since I posit that they become signs, I am necessarily positing at the same time the *res sacramenti*. The body of Christ could not be that *res* if the sign were totally annihilated. The sign (*signum*) and the signified (*signatum, res*) must be distinct, and it can thus not be said that the sacrament *is* the body of Christ. Despite the condemnation of Berenger, this discussion would have a great influence. It was with reference to it that theologians of the following generation would speculate as to whether the sacrament was a "signifier" (*signum, signans, significans*) or a "signified" (*res significata, signatum, significatum*), and, in the case of the Eucharist, a "figure" (*figura*) or "truth" (*veritas*). It was in this context that *signans/signatum* or *significans/significatum* first appeared as a pair. The difference between the two pairs is impossible to determine with precision: in manuscripts, in fact, and varying with historical periods, a common abbreviation can be used ambiguously and interpreted, in keeping with the habits of the publisher, as *sign-* or *signific-*. To be sure, the two possibilities existed, but the pertinence of their difference was not necessarily reflected by the very different conditions of the manuscripts currently available to us. It should be emphasized that these terminological pairings were virtually never applied to the linguistic sign: if *significatum* or *res significata* were frequently used for the signified, it was most commonly done for the signified of a word (*dictio, vox*), more rarely of a sign (*nota, signum*). It will be understood that the pairing appeared in a context in which it was a matter of resolving an essential point: Was the sacrament *signans, signatum*, or both simultaneously?

Despite the assignment, drawing upon Peter Lombard, and in a durable manner, of the sacrament to the category of signs, the question would continue to be raised, with certain authors accepting, against Augustine, the notion that a sign can be a sign or form of itself, and there is not necessarily a difference between a sign and a signified (cf., for example, Innocent III, *De sacramento altaris*, RT: *PL*, vol. 217, col. 881D: "Sacramentum autem actem active et passive dicitur, quasi sacrum signans et sacrum signatum . . . Corpus Domini, cum utroque modo dicitur sacramentum, est scarum signum et sacrum signatum" [The sacrament may be said in both active and passive manner, as sacred signifier and sacred signified. . . . The body of the Lord, since the sacrament may be said according to those two modes, is sacred signifier and sacred signified].). Augustinian terminology would result in a new distinction, allowing one to oppose what is *sacramentum tantum* (for example, bread and wine, or the water of baptism), *sacramentum et res* (the body of Christ, *res* in relation to the sign, *sacramentum* in relation to the mystical body that it signifies, or the character imprinted by baptism), and *res tantum* (the mystical body).

Irène Rosier-Catach

BIBLIOGRAPHY

Féret, Henri-Marie. "'Sacramentum Res' dans la langue théologique de saint Augustin." *Revue des sciences philosophiques et théologiques* 29 (1940): 218–43.

Montclos, Jean de. *Lanfranc et Bérenger. La controverse eucharistique du XIe siècle*. Louvain, Belg., "Spicilegium sacrum lovaniense," études et documents, fasc. 37, 1971.

Rosier, Irène. "Langage et signe dans la discussion eucharistique." In *Histoire et Grammaire du sens. Hommage à Jean-Claude Chevalier*, edited by Sylvain Auroux, Simone Delesalle, and Henri Meschonnic, 42–58. Paris: Armard Colin, 1996.

———. *La parole efficace: signe, rituel, sacré*. Paris: Éditions du Seuil, 2004.

Van Den Eynde, Damien. "Les définitions des sacraments pendant la première période de la théologie scolastique." *Antonionanum* 24, nos. 1 and 4 (1949): no. 1: 3–78, 182–228, no. 4: 439–88.

publication based on notes of his students who attended the courses given by the linguist between 1907 and 1911 at the University of Geneva. Saussure's metalanguage was based on stipulative definitions. In certain cases he gives a new technical definition of a term or expression with established usage—and even "takes up a traditional word and makes it serve reverse ends" (Milner, *Le périple structural*, 31)—and, in other cases, he forges terminological innovations in order to avoid ambiguities linked to terms used in ordinary language.

First of all, "the linguistic sign unites not a thing and a word but a concept and an acoustic image" (Saussure, CLG [1966]): the relation of designation between language and the world, or, less crudely, between the sign and its referent, must not be confused with the relation of signification intrinsic to the sign. This refusal of the principle of nomenclature, which presupposes a prior reserve of things designated by a label and implies that the meaning of a word corresponds to a fragment of reality, is as perfectly compatible, contrary to what is frequently affirmed, with Aristotle as with the Stoics: each did indeed carefully distinguish between the indication of an outside, or referentiality, and the signification required by the internal functioning of the sign as such (see SIGN). On this point there is a line of transmission that goes from Aristotle to the Stoics to Saussure, even if the articulation between those two relations is not identical.

It was only at the end of his third course, in 1913, that Saussure forged the terms "signified" and "signifier" to replace, respectively, those of "concept" and "acoustic image." That terminological choice was felicitous, since it brought into relief the dependence of that couple in relation to the totality of the sign:

> We propose to . . . replace *concept* and *acoustic image* respectively with *signified* and *signifier*; those latter terms have the advantage of marking the opposition which separates them either from each other or from the totality of which they form a part.

(CLG)

Here the Aristotelian legacy has been abandoned. For Aristotle, in point of fact, to signify was to signify something, and the sign taken as a whole was to be analyzed only in its relation to what it signified, not as an internal duality signaling a pair of participles (*signifiant, signifié*) that are, moreover, if not unfindable in his thought, at least not terminological in intent (*sêmainonta* [σημαίνοντα] / *sêminomena* [σημαινόμενα]) (see *De interpretatione*, I, commented on in SIGN, Box 1). On the other hand, the pair of terms *semainon/semainomenon* is indeed Stoic, and that is why Stoicism, in its very anti-Aristotelianism, is frequently said to be a precursor of Saussurean linguistics. In point of fact, the pair of terms is Stoic, but their coupling is already less so. For the first Stoic observation is that one can have a signifier without a signified (for those who don't "understand" the language), whereas the linguistic entity considered by Saussure exists solely as two-in-one (the "chemical compound" of the signifier and the signified, on the model of water composed of oxygen and hydrogen [CLG], one side for thought, the reverse side for sound to be segmented and cut apart on the sheet of paper that language is [ibid.]). Which brings us to another difference: the Saussurean signifier and signified are homogeneous, both being "psychical"—Saussure specifying carefully that with the signifier we are not dealing with the "material sound, something purely physical," but with the "psychical imprint of that sound," which is present as well in the inner conversation that we hold with ourselves "without moving either our lips or our tongue" (ibid.); so much so, moreover, that Saussure will be able to characterize the signifier (understood, it is true, as value and difference, opening consequently onto a comparative systematic foreign to simple signification) as an incorporeal: "In its essence, the linguistic signifier is not at all phonic; it is incorporeal, constituted, not by its material substance but solely by the differences that separate its acoustic image from all the others" (ibid.). The Stoic signifier and signified, on the contrary, are heterogeneous: the first, contrary to Saussure's signifier, is a body, whereas the second is a thought-content, which, depending on one's perspective, may be more or less incorporeal or embodied (the *sêmainom-enon* properly speaking designates the thought-content embodied in a signifier, but it is an incorporeal *lekton* insofar as it is only virtually uttered, and a *pragma* independently of all embodiment [Baratin, *La naissance de la syntaxe à Rome*]. The Stoic connection between signifier and signified is thus thoroughly dynamic, linked not to an "abstract conception of language" (Imbert, "Théorie de la représentation"), but to the event of speech acts that incorporate and embody what is sayable, such that each of the two series, signifiers and signifieds, has its degrees and its autonomy.

"Those who have been formed by Saussure literally no longer understand texts from before Saussure. Saussure rendered the Stoics opaque . . . he rendered Saint Augustine opaque . . . he rendered Arnauld and Nicole opaque and, with them, if Foucault is right, all of classical philosophy by instituting a symmetrical and reciprocal model of the sign" (Milner, *Le périple structural*). In Saussure, in point of fact, one does not begin with two separate entities (sign/thing, signifier/signified) arbitrarily joined, but from a single one, the sign, which is divided by analysis into "two faces." It is the absence of all relation between those two faces ("suppose that one designs a figure on the front side, it is clear that it entertains no 'relation' with the figure one might eventually design on the reverse side" [Milner, *Le périple structural*]) that is encapsulated in the word "arbitrary": as Milner notes, "one should not confuse the arbitrariness characterizing a certain type of relation and the arbitrariness characterizing the absence of all relation" (ibid.).

This is why the concept of *value* appears to be central in Saussure's theoretical edifice. Given that signs are not delimited in advance, how is one to end up with an association of a signifier and a signified? One must begin with a solidary totality, the system, in order to grasp the linguistic units. That association can occur only through speech, which is, in a sense, the external document of language (CLG). The segmentation of elements into signs implies a comparison of different manifestations of the alleged element in different surroundings. For instance, the phonic sequences *donne-moi ton porte-plume* (give me your pen-holder) and *cet animal porte plume et bec* (that animal has feathers and a beak) constitute different units as a function of their difference in value. With this method, one arrives as much at signs shorter than the word, such as suffixes and inflexions, as at signs longer than the word, namely: syntagms. It is value that effects the delimitation of signs and the association of signifier and signified. Value is characterized as relative, differential, and negative: a linguistic unit exists only in relation to other units, and by virtue of what surrounds it (cf. CLG). It is important not to confuse the conceptual aspect of value with *signification*, which is the counterpart of the auditory image and which, consequently, is equivalent to the concept or the signified (ibid.). In the contrary case, one regresses back into the principle of nomenclature, which takes the "word as an isolated and absolute whole" (ibid.). Value is above all determined by signs that belong simultaneously to a system.

B. How to translate Saussure?

Should translators attempt to inject French terminology onto a preexisting terminology in the target-language, or should they attempt to forge a vocabulary even as they obey the linguistic system of the language concerned? To translate the words *signifiant* (signifier) and *signifié* (signified), they can follow Saussure's logic and begin with the (French) word *signifier* in the target-language, from which they will derive the signifiers for the terms *signifiant* and *signifié*. This can be explained by the principle of motivated arbitrariness: in this case there is partial agreement of the associative series concerning the signifier and the signified, in function of a systematic solidarity.

Here are various translations of Saussure's lexicon, as well as subsequent commentaries that translators have offered on the subject. Consider the chart below:

Cours de linguistique générale	Grundfragen der allgemeinen Sprach-wissenschaft H. Lommel (1931)	Course in General Linguistics W. Baskin (1959)	Course in General Linguistics R. Harris (1983)	Curso de lingüística general A. Alonso (1945)	Corso di linguistica generale T. De Mauro (1967)	Kurs i allmän lingvistik A. Löfqvist (1970)
French	German	English I	English II	Spanish	Italian	Swedish
Signe	Zeichen	Sign	Sign	Signo	Segno	Tecken

Cours de linguistique générale	Grundfragen der allgemeinen Sprach-wissenschaft H. Lommel (1931)	Course in General Linguistics W. Baskin (1959)	Course in General Linguistics R. Harris (1983)	Curso de lingüística general A. Alonso (1945)	Corso di linguistica generale T. De Mauro (1967)	Kurs i allmän lingvistik A. Löfqvist (1970)
Concept	Vorstellung	Concept	Concept	Concepto	Concetto	Begrepp
Image acoustique	Lautbild	Sound image	Sound pattern	Imagen acústica	Immagine acoustica	Ljudföreställning
Signifié	Bezeichnetes	Signified	Signification	Significado	Significato	Innehåll
Signifiant	Bezeichnendes/ Bezeichnung	Signifier	Signal	Significante	Significante	Uttryck
Arbitraire	Beliebigkeit	Arbitrary	Arbitrary	Arbitrario	Arbitrarietà	Godtycklighet
Valeur	Wert	Value	Value	Valor	Valore	Värde
Signification	Bedeutung	Signification	Meaning	Significación	Significazione	Betydelse

Key words concerning the Saussurean linguistic sign with their principal European translations.

At present, there is only one translation of the *Cours de linguistique générale* into German, dating from 1931. Herman Lommel was the first to reconstitute Saussurean terminology in a European language. In the German linguistic tradition, the established notions of *Lautbild* and *Vorstellung* preceded the Saussurean notions of "acoustic image" and "concept," which was propitious for the translation of the latter pair (cf., for example, Hermann Paul, *Prinzipen der Sprachgeschichte*, 1880). The equivalents of the terms "signifier" and "signified" were molded from the verb *bezeichnen* following the French model. One thus arrived, on the one hand, at *Bezeichnetes*, the neutral form of the past participle, and, on the other, at *Bezeichnendes*, the neutral form of the present participle, or indeed at *Bezeichnung*, through nominalization of a verbal form, those two last terms being used with a certain looseness insofar as the designation of the signifier is concerned. In the postscript of the second edition of Lommel's version (1967), Peter von Pohlenz judged that a new translation of the *Cours* was needed, which might take into account the evolution of linguistic terminology. He alternately used the gallicized forms of *Signifikant* and *Signifikat* to designate *signifiant* and *signifié*. One also encounters the terms *Zeichenausdruck* (expression of the sign) and *Zeicheninhalt* (sign content).

W. Baskin (*Course in General Linguistics*, 1959), the first translator of the *Cours de linguistique générale* into English, appears not to have encountered any problems with regard to terminology concerning the sign. It is true that in his day, translations of the Saussurean terms had already been established in Anglophone linguistics. Nonetheless, in his translation of the *Cours* in 1983, R. Harris effected a considerable renewal of Saussure's terminology. He claimed that translators and commentators had done a disservice to Saussure's thought because of their poor translations (*Course in General Linguistics*, 1983, xiii). According to Harris (ibid., xv), the term "sound image" proposed by Baskin to render "image acoustique" suggests the combination of a written word and a spoken word, as though the words had been stored in the brain in quasigraphic form. In its place, Harris prefers "sound pattern," an expression that, according to him, better translates the auditory impression constructed by the mind. As far as the translation of *signifié* and *signifiant* are concerned, Harris renounces the terms "signified" and "signifier," opting respectively for "signification" and "signal." The term "signification" can be easily confused with the term "meaning," which in turn is an equivalent of the French term *signification*. As for the use of the term "signal" to designate the *signifiant*, it is not particularly successful, since in suggesting that the sound is the bearer of a message, the word omits the psychical nature of the signifier. These idiosyncratic choices do not appear to have met with much favor from linguists, with the result that in his translation of Saussure's third course, on the basis of manuscript sources, Harris (*Saussure's Third Course*, 1993) reformulated the terms under the labels "signified element" and "signifying element." The translator justified this terminological fluctuation in terms of the difference of the two audiences to whom the two translations were addressed: that the translation of the published *Cours de linguistique générale* was intended for students wishing to become acquainted with a classic text of linguistics, whereas that prepared from manuscript sources was addressed to specialists apt to understand a more elaborate metalanguage (*Saussure's Third Course*, xvii). The infidelities of Harris's translation compared with Baskin's should be attributed to Harris's concept of translation. For according to him, translation is an analysis and an interpretation rather than a rendering (ibid., *Saussure's Third Course*, xx).

In as much as it is a Germanic language, Swedish functions in a manner identical to German. In the Swedish linguistic literature, there now appears to be a pedagogical tendency to substitute ordinary terms for technical terms. To translate the terms *signifié* and *signifiant*, A. Löfqvist, the translator of the *Cours de linguistique générale* into Swedish, opted for a translation offering the reader a fallaciously facile access to the text. In ordinary language, the term *uttryck* used to designate the *signifiant* has the sense of "expression, form." The dictionary defines *uttryck* as "audible sign" along with other meanings. The word thus has the same shortcoming as the term "signal" in English. *Signifié* is translated by a term as dubious as its counterpart, namely the word *innehall*, which in English would give "content." Yet that usage, which follows the model of the German terms *Zeichenausdruck* and *Zeicheninhalt*, is currently sacrosanct in Swedish. Bertil Malmberg implicitly voiced disapproval of that terminology by substituting the terms *betecknat* (signified) and *betecknande* (signifier), derived from the verb *beteckna*, which better obeys Saussure's logic. In the literature, one also encounters the pair *signalerade* and *signalerande*.

The Romance languages accommodated the French terminology without difficulty. The translator of the *Cours de linguistique generale* into Spanish, Amado Alonso, does not discuss any difficulties translation might raise in relation to the theory of the sign. The Italian translator, on the other hand, is more murky on the subject. In the preface to his Italian translation, Tullio De Mauro claims to have respected the structure of the sentences and the vocabulary of the original (cf. *Corso di linguistica generale*, xxi). The use of the words *significant* and *signifié* as nominal participles did not have a precedent in French before Saussure. It was, above all, with the translation of the term *signifié* from the verb *significare* that the Italian translator encountered difficulties. The notion of *significato* already existed in the language, but was the equivalent of the French *signification*, a term that the Italian translator did not hesitate to render as *significazione*, a rather rarely used word that referred rather to the act or the effect of the verb *significare*. In his commentary on the *Cours*, moreover, De Mauro concludes that "it is not clear that Italian, possessing as it does a familiar word like *significato* to render without difficulty Saussure's *signifié*, derives any advantage from it." The Spanish translator was also confronted with this terminological problem since the word *significado* is synonymous with *significación*. This allowed De Mauro to conclude that given "the facile linguistic equivalence, the Saussurean notion [of the *signifié*] would be subject to all the 'vagueness and indefiniteness' . . . connoted by the familiar word *significato* and, in other languages, by words like *Sinn*, *Bedeutung*, 'meaning,' *signification*, etc." (*Corso di linguistica generale*).

V. Psychoanalytic Terminology

A. "What is the signifier?"

What is the signifier? Jacques Lacan offers this explanation:

The signifier—as promoted by the rites of a linguistic tradition that is not specifically Saussurian, but goes back as far as the Stoics and is reflected in Saint Augustine's work—must be structured in topological terms. Indeed, the signifier is first of all that which has a meaning effect (*effet de signifié*), and it is important not to elide the fact that between signifier and meaning

effect there is something barred that must be crossed over.

("To Jakobson," in *Encore.
The Seminar of Jacques Lacan*, trans. B. Fink)

Lacan, who inherited the precursors discovered by Jakobson, reconceived the signifier outside of linguistics, as part of his psychoanalytic *linguisterie*: he inverted the Saussurean schema of signified/signifier (Saussure: signified/signifier [*Cours de linguistique générale*]; Lacan: S/s, "which is read: signifier over signified" ["The Instance of the Letter in the Unconscious, or Reason Since Freud," in *Écrits*, trans. B. Fink]). In thus placing the signifier above the bar, he promoted the autonomy of the signifier, which he understood "in the active sense" (Milner, *Le périple structural*) as a "signifying" or *signifiance*" and not as signification ("what has the effect of being signified" would not be able to be linked to a signified that it would express). Lacan is thus able to insist on the bar: if "the unconscious is structured like a language" (see *Encore*, trans. B. Fink, 15), it is in the sense that the bar strikes the speaking subject who does not know what he or she is saying ("the fact that the *S* and the *s* of Saussure's algorithm are not in the same plane, and man was deluding himself in believing he was situated in their common axis, which is nowhere" ["The Instance of the Letter in the Unconscious, or Reason since Freud," in *Écrits*, trans. B. Fink, 430–31]). The Lacanian rereading of Freud thus works as a recentering on the signifier, linked to dreams ("from the first chapter of the *Traumdeutung*, [Freud] brings to the forefront that *the dream is a rebus*, and no one notices it" [*Le séminaire*, Livre 4: *La relation d'objet*, 294]), to jokes ("it does not appear to have been noticed that the analysis of jokes begins with the diagram of the analysis of a phenomenon of condensation, the word *famillionaire*, a fabrication based on the signifier, via the superimposition of *familiar* and *millionaire*" [ibid.]). The signifier or, more precisely, "signifying activity" (*du signifiant*), which insists on the symptom, characterizes a subject in the manner of a symbolic nominalization ("determining the acts, words, and destiny of a subject unbeknownst to him," in the radical formulation of E. Roudinesco and M. Plon [RT: *Dictionnaire de la psychanalyse*, s.v. "Signifiant"]). "My definition of the signifier (there is no other) is as follows: a signifier is what represents the subject to another signifier. This latter signifier is therefore the signifier to which all the other signifiers represent the subject—which means that if this signifier is missing, all the other signifiers represent nothing. For something is only represented to ("The Subversion of the Subject and the Dialectic of Desire in the Freudian Unconscious," in *Écrits*, trans. B. Fink, 693–94]): this definition manifests the manner in which active and passive, subject and signifier, have switched their traditional places.

B. The play of the signifier and the existence of the real

The place occupied by the signifier in psychoanalysis opens onto a perception of language that is completely different from that of (classically Aristotelian) philosophy. "The giant of language recovers its stature at being suddenly delivered from the Gulliverian bonds of meaning" ("Situation de la psychanalyse en 1956," in Lacan, *Écrits*, 470). This is intrinscally linked to the analyst's way of listening to the punctuation of therapy: "We repeat to our students: 'Beware of understanding!' . . . Let one of your ears grow as deaf as the other should be acute. And that's the one you should focus on listening to sounds or phonemes, words, locutions, maxims, without omitting pauses, scansions, interruptions, periodic expansions and parallelisms, for there is where the word-to-word of translation is prepared, without which analytic intuition has neither basis nor object" (ibid., 471).

It is, however, not so easy to take leave of Aristotle. Thus in the seminar on object relations (*Le séminaire*, Livre 4: *La relation d'objet*), which was held in 1956–57, Lacan hesitates, as Freud himself did in *Jokes and Their Relation to the Unconscious*, between according privileged status to the signifier's relation to sense or to *nonsense*. The signifier is linked to sense or meaning insofar as it is vulnerable to effects of homonymy, that is, multiple meanings (see HOMONYM): as Lacan emphasizes with regard to Little Hans and his horse, "the symptomatic signifier is so constituted that its nature is to cover in the course of development multiple signifieds, and as different as can be. Not only is it its nature to do so, but that is its function" (*Le séminaire*, Livre 4: *La relation d'objet*, 288). Analyzed in these terms, the signifier promotes the invention and creation of meaning: "Man, because he is man, is confronted with problems which are as such problems of signifiers. The signifier, in fact, is introduced into the real by its very existence as a signifier, because there are words which are spoken, sentences which are articulated and follow each other, joined by a medium, a copula on the order of *why* or *because.* Thus it is that the existence of the signifier introduces into the world of man a new meaning" (ibid., 293).

But occasionally Lacan insists instead on the manner in which the signifier, far from creating meaning, annihilates it:

> All that Freud would subsequently elaborate consisted in demonstrating the effect of annihilation, the veritably destructive, disruptive character of the play of the signifier in relation to what can be called the existence of the real. In playing with the signifier, man persistently calls into question his world, unto its very roots. The value of the joke, and what distinguishes it from the comic, is its capacity to play on the fundamental meaninglessness of every use of meaning. At any moment, it is possible to call into question every meaning insofar as it is based on a use of the signifier. In point of fact, that use is in itself deeply paradoxical in relation to all possible signification, since it is that very use which creates what it is intended to sustain.
>
> (*Le séminaire*, Livre 4: *La relation d'objet*, 294)

From Freud's *Jokes and Their Relation to the Unconscious*, read as a new version of Gorgias's *Treatise of Non-Being*, Lacan gleans the destruction and disruption of the existence of the real (and for reasons similar to those of Gorgias). It is necessary and sufficient to show that meaning, or the sphere of being, ontology, and so forth, rests on a *husteron proteron* [ὕστερον πρότερον], a "latter before," that can be called "paradoxical": only the use of the signifier creates meaning, or further still, being is an effect of speech. "It is that very use which creates what it is intended to sustain," and that is why everything is subject to collapse: "it becomes quite *funny*, with all that that word *drôle* may contain in the way of strange resonances" (*Le séminaire*, Livre 4: *La relation d'objet*, 295; see INGENIUM, NONSENSE, and SPEECH ACT).

■ See Box 3.

Barbara Cassin
Frédérique Ildefonse
Carita Klippi
Irène Rosier-Catach

3

"Signifier," *lekton*, and *point de capiton* (quilting point)

We need to grow accustomed to handling schemata scientifically adapted from an ethic— in this case that of the Stoics—of the signifer and the *lekton*. And one sees immediately that *lekton* does not afford a good translation. One keeps it in reserve and plays a bit with the signified, more accessible and more hospitable to those who find themselves in it, in the illusion that their thoughts on the subject might be worth anything more than garbage.

I say to whomever is prepared to hear it, since such an articulation presupposes a discourse having already registered its effects, effects of the *lekton* precisely. For it is from the practice of a doctrine in which it is demonstrated that the insistence of what is uttered is not to be held as secondary in the essence of speech that my term

the *point de capiton* or quilting point takes shape. Wherein *lekton* comes to be translated in a way agreeable to me, without my boasting about it, being far more than an expert on Stoicism a stoic from the get-go when it is a matter of determining what might be taken up anew of it.

(Lacan, preface to the French paperback edition of *Écrits* [1969])

The Stoic signifier, considered as *lekton*, would be translated as *point de capiton* or "quilting point." This is because the *lekton* effectively blocks the "incessant sliding of the signified beneath the signifier" characterizing Saussure's linguistics:

All experience argues against it, which had me speaking, at a certain moment

of my seminar on psychoses, of "quilting points" required by that schema to account for the dominance of the letter in the dramatic transformation that dialogue can effect in the subject.

(Lacan, "L'Instance de la lettre dans l'inconscient," in *Écrits*, 502–3)

This understanding of the signifier as *lekton* makes in particular for the difference between the meanings of metaphor and metonymy for Jakobson and Lacan. Jakobson situates metaphor and metonymy "of the signifying chain," Lacan specifies, as "the substitution of one signifier for another for the one, and the selection of a signifier in its sequence for the other. From which it follows (but only for Jakobson: for me

(continued)

(continued)

the result is different) that the substitution is by way of similarities, the selection by way of contiguities" ("Radiophonie," Question 3, in *Autres écrits*, 415–16). For Lacan, what counts is rather the manner in which, within the chain, a signifier is knotted or stitched to the signified in order to produce signification: and there lies the *lekton*, "which renders legible a signified . . . ; it is what I termed the 'quilting point' [or *point de capiton*] in order to illustrate what I will call the Saussure effect of disruption of the signified by the signifier, specifying that it corresponded quite precisely to my esteem for the mattress-audience reserved for me, since I was, of course, at Sainte-Anne, albeit composed of analysts" (ibid.).

The rest of the signifying operation would later become the object *a*, the unassignable cause of desire, which disables the causal relation at the very moment in which it brings it into play. Defined in terms of the nonbiological object of the Freudian drive, which finds its bodily contingency in the erogenous zones (interruptions finding "favor in the anatomical trait of a margin or an edge" [*subversion du sujet et dialectique du désir dans l'inconscient freudien*] in *Écrits*, 817), it is outside of language but gives it its overall consistency. The object *a*, condition of the unconscious, is characterized as being "incorporeal," a term attributed explicitly by Lacan to the Stoics: "Let us render their due to the Stoics for having managed with this term—incorporeal—sign wherein

the signifier exercises its hold on the body" ("Radiophonie," in *Autres écrits*, 409). Or more clearly still, and exactly at the same time: "Where to situate it, this object *a*, the principal incorporeal of the Stoics? In the unconscious or is it elsewhere? Who is to know?" (*Autres écrits*, 402).

The *point de capiton* is an operator, and *a* is what remains afterward, on the model of a catalyst. It would appear that the topological model of the cross cap, which allowed Lacan to transcribe what clinical practice taught him, authorized him after the fact to read in the Stoics, no doubt thanks to his discussions with Jakobson, what the Stoic *lekton* anticipated of his own theory.

Jean-Jacques Gorog

BIBLIOGRAPHY

Ax, Wolfram. *Laut, Stimme und Sprache*. Göttingen, Ger.: Vanderhoeck and Ruprecht, 1986.

Baratin, Marc. *La naissance de la syntaxe à Rome*. Paris: Éditions de Minuit, 1989.

Baratin, Marc, and Françoise Desbordes. *L'Analyse linguistique dans l'Antiquité Classique*. Vol. 1 of *Les théories*. Paris: Klinscksieck, 1981.

Bréhier, Emile. *Chrysippe et l'ancien stoïcisme*. Paris: Presses Universitaires de France, 1951.

———. *La théorie des incorporels dans l'ancien stoïcisme*. Paris: Vrin, 1962.

Brunschwig, Jacques. "En quel sens le sens commun est-il commun?" In *Corps et âme—Sur le "De anima" d'Aristote*. Edited by Gilbert Romeyer Dherbey and Cristina Viano. Paris: Vrin, 1996.

Brunschwig, Jacques, and Pierre Pellegrin. *Les philosophes hellénistiques*. Paris: Flammarion, 2001.

Burnyeat, Myles. Introduction to *Theaetetus of Plato*. Indianapolis, IN: Hackett, 1990.

Cassin, Barbara. *L'Effet sophistique*. Paris: Gallimard / La Pléiade, 1996.

Deleuze, Gilles. *The Logic of Sense*. Translated by Mark Lester with Charles Stivale. Edited by Constantin V. Boundas. New York: Columbia University Press, 1990.

Foucault, Michel. *The Order of Things: An Archaeology of the Human Sciences*. New York: Pantheon Books, 1970. Translation of *Les mots et les choses*, first published in Paris by Gallimard / La Pléiade in 1966.

Frede, Michel. "The Stoic Notion of a Lekton." In *Companions to Ancient Thought 3: Language*, edited by Stephen Everson, 109–28. Cambridge: Cambridge University Press, 1994.

Garcea, Alessandro. "Gellio e la dialettica." *Memorie dell'Academia delle Scienze di Torino* 24 (2000): 53–204.

Goldschmidt, Victor. *Le système stoïcien et l'idée de temps*. Paris: Vrin, 1953.

Gourinat, Jean-Baptiste. *La dialectique des stoïciens*. Paris: Vrin, 2000.

Hülser, Karlheinz. *Die Fragmente zur Dialektik der Stoiker*. 4 vols. Stuttgart-Bad Cannstatt, Ger.: Frommann-Holzbook, 1987.

Ildefonse, Frédérique. *Les Stoïciens*. Vol. 1 of *Zénon, Cléanthe, Chrysippe*. Paris: Les Belles Lettres, 2000.

Inwood, Brad, and Lloyd Gerson, trans. and eds. *The Stoics Reader*. Indianapolis, IN: Hackett, 2008.

Imbert, Claude. *Phénoménologie et langues formulaires*. Paris: Presses Universitaires de France, 1992.

———. "Théorie de la représentation et doctrine logique dans l'ancien stoïcisme." In *Les Stoïciens et leur logique*, 223–39. Paris: Vrin, 1978.

Jakobson, Roman. "Quest for the Essence of Language." In *On Language*, edited by Linda R. Waugh and Monique Monville-Burston, 407–21. Cambridge, MA: Harvard University Press, 1990. Essay first published in 1966.

Lacan, Jacques. *Autres écrits*. Paris: Éditions du Seuil, 2000.

———. *Écrits*. Paris: Éditions du Seuil, 1966. Translation by Bruce Fink: *Écrits*. New York: W. W. Norton, 2007.

———. *Le séminaire. Livre 4: La relation d'objet*. Edited by Jacques-Alain Miller. Paris: Éditions du Seuil, 1975.

———. *Le Séminaire. Livre 20: Encore*. Edited by Jacques-Alain Miller. Paris. Éditions du Seuil, 1975. Translation by Bruce Fink: *Encore. The Seminar of Jacques Lacan*. New York: W. W. Norton. 1999.

———. *Speech and Language in Psychoanalysis*. Translated by Anthony Wilden. Baltimore: Johns Hopkins University Press, 1968.

Lohmann, Johannes. *Musiké und Logos. Aufsätze zur griechischen Philosophie und Musiktheorie*. Stuttgart: Musikwissenschaftliche Verlagsgesellschaft, 1970.

Long, Anthony A. "Language and Thought in Stoicism." In *Problems in Stoicism*, edited by Anthony A. Long, 75–113. London: Athlone Press, 1971.

Long, Anthony A., and David Sedley, eds. 2 vols. *The Hellenistic Philosophers*. Cambridge: Cambridge University Press, 1987.

Milner, Jean-Claude. *Le périple structural: Figures et paradigme*. Paris: Éditions du Seuil, 2002.

Nuchelmans, Gabriel. *Theories of the Proposition. Ancient and Medieval Conceptions of the Bearers of Truth and Falsity*. Amsterdam: North-Holland, 1973.

Paul, Hermann. *Prinzipien der Sprachgeschichte*. Tübingen, Ger.: Niemeyer, 1968.

Saussure, Ferdinand de. *Corso di linguistica generale*. Translated into Italian by Tullio De Mauro. Bari, It.: Laterza, 1967.

———. *Cours de linguistique générale*. Edited by Charles Bally and Albert Sechehaye, with the collaboration of Albert Riedlinger. Paris: Payot, 1966. Translation by Wade Baskin: *Course in General Linguistics*. New York: McGraw Hill, 1959. Translation, with annotations, by Roy Harris: *Course in General Linguistics*. London: Duckworth, 1983.

———. *Curso de lingüística general*. Translated into Spanish by Amado Alonso. Buenos Aires: Losada, 1945.

———. *Grundfragen der allgemeinen Sprachwissenschaft*. Translated into German by Herman Lommen. Berlin: De Gruyter, 1967.

———. *Kurs i allmän lingvistik*. Translated into Swedish by Anders Löfqvist. Staffanstorp, Swed.: Cavefors, 1970.

———. *Troisième Cours de linguistique générale (1910–1911) d'après les cahiers d'Émile Constantin*. Oxford: Pergamon Press, 1993. Translation by Roy Harris: *Saussure's Third Course of Lectures on General Linguistics (1910–1911), from the Notebooks of Émile Constantin*. New York: Pergamon Press, 1993.

Sextus Empiricus. *Against the Logicians*. Translated by R. G. Bury. Cambridge, MA: Harvard University Press / Loeb Classical Library, 1935.

SILENT

"Silent" is, along with "motionless," one of the possible translations of the German *still*, a topos of classical aesthetics: see STILL, and AESTHETICS, CLASSIC, SUBLIME. Cf. *SERENITY, WISDOM*.

➤ *NOTHING*, WORD IV.A

SOBORNOST' [соборность] (RUSSIAN)

ENGLISH   conciliarity, conciliation
FRENCH   *conciliarité, collégialité, communauté, solidarité*

➤ *CONCILIARITY*, and BOGOČELOVEČESTVO, MIR, NAROD, OIKONOMIA, PRAVDA, RELIGIO, RUSSIAN, SAMOST', SECULARIZATION

Sobornost' [соборность], since Khomiakov, has designated the collegial nature of the Church, its capacity to surmount the individual even as it respects the freedom of each person. A Slavophile concept par excellence, it quickly exceeded the limits of theology and currently refers to a fundamental quality of Russian life, Russian thought, and even Russian culture.

I. The Church: Place of Assembly and Not of Dogma

The translation of the word might be "conciliarity" or even "synodality" to the extent that the councils of the Church are called in Russian *sobor* [собор], from the root *bor-*, which means "to take," and from the prefix *so-*, which means "with." The *sobor* is the assembling of the entire Church. It also designated in Russian the assembly of the land of Russia in the person of its representatives elected by the different estates of the Old Regime, boyars, merchants, clerics, peasants, and that assembly was called *Zemskij Sobor* [земский собор]. Ecumenical councils were called *vselenskie sobory* [вселенские соборы]. Finally, since the cathedral in which the bishop officiates is not considered primarily in Orthodoxy as a place of teaching, a *cathedra,* but as a place of assembly for the people of believers, it too is designated by the word *sobor*, which might in such circumstances be translated as a church or "college of clerics." But in Russian *sobor* can be immediately supplemented with *kafedral'nyi* [кафедральный], which comes from *cathedra* and refers to the notion of the place where dogma is proclaimed.

II. A Lay Theologian and Soldier, Alexis Khomiakov

The term *sobornost'* [соборность], destined to undergo a great extension, was used for the first time—in order to define the nature of orthodoxy—by a lay theologian of the nineteenth century, Alexis Khomiakov (1804–60), who was also an officer, a poet, and a dramatist. The term thus comes from the expanded lexicon of religion. It quickly became a key word in Russian Slavophile thought, before being broadened to political, philosophical, and literary thought. It can be translated as "free and unanimous collegiality." In 1989 a current theoretician of semiology, Viatcheslav Vsevolodovich Ivanov, a member of the last Supreme Soviet of the U.S.S.R., issued an appeal to the spirit of *sobornost'* so that Russia might move

harmoniously from one political regime to another. Works on *sobornost'* in Russian literature and thought appear daily.

Sobornost', along with *pravda* [правда] (justice-truth) and *narodnost'* [народность], is thus one of the major concepts through which Russia would differentiate itself from the Occident, which is regularly accused of rationalism and individualism. *Narodnost'* designates the national popular spirit, while *sobornost'* is the spirit of unity through the freedom of individuals.

■ See Box 1.

In German the distinction forged by Tönnies in 1887 between *Gesellschaft* and *Gemeinschaft* partakes of the same typology, essentially distinguishing between the abstract categories of social science and concrete, living categories, in brief, between a written contract and the living union that needs no contract. (Yuri Lotman expresses astonishment that even as mystical a saint as Francis of Assisi needed to sign a contract with his wolf [Lotman, " 'Dogovor' i 'vručcenie sebja' kak arxetipičeskie modeli kult'tury," 3: 345]). Between the Western state and the family, which the collective life of the Slavic community resembles according to Slavophiles, there lies all the difference between *Gesellschaft* and *Gemeinschaft* (see CIVIL SOCIETY, Box 1).

III. *Sobornost'* and Catholicity

It is thus in a text in French by Khomiakov that the first more or less complete elaboration of the notion of *sobornost'* (in the broad and abstract sense of "unanimous and free collegiality through the spirit") is to be found. The text is *Quelques mots par un chrétien orthodoxe sur les communions occidentales à l'occasion d'une brochure de M. Laurentie* (Paris, 1853). The author signs with the name Ignotus. He announces that he is taking up his pen to defend the "orthodox Catholic church" from unjust accusations, *catholique* in this case being the French translation of the word *sobornost'* [соборность]. In another article, a letter to the editor of *Union chrétienne* "on the meaning of the words *catholique* and *sobornyj* with reference to a speech by Father Gagarin, a Jesuit," Khomiakov returns to the definition of the word. Gagarin had reproached the Orthodox for translating the word *katholikos* [ϰαθολιϰός] in the Nicene Symbol with a dull term, lacking in energy, *sobornyj*, which has many other uses, meaning additionally what partakes of the "kathedra," the synod, or even the social. In the Nicene Symbol, the word is *katholikos*; the Russians translate *sobornyj*, with the term *catholique* being reduced to designating the Roman Church and thus restricting the concept to a kind of space or territoriality. Khomiakov thus takes up the term, tears it away from the Roman Church, and deliberately creates the category "Catholic Orthodox." Shortly thereafter Khomiakov took up his pen anew in French to write to the editor of the *Union chrétienne* in a polemic against one of his compatriots who had become a Jesuit, Father Gagarin. The latter had criticized the Russian term *sobornyj* for its murkiness and imprecision. Gagarin had observed that the Russian term designated a reality that invoked simultaneously synod, *cathedra*, and society itself. Catholicism was a merely geographical universality, Khomiakov responded, whereas *sobornost'* is a universality of the spirit, he continued, resorting to an argument customarily addressed to Protestants.

1

Narodnost'

Narodnost' is one of the three components of the famous definition of Russia given by Count Ouvarov, minister of Nicolai I, "Autocracy, orthodoxy, *narodnost'*." It is impossible to translate by a single word the reality designating the bond between official power and the people, above all its intermediaries; it defines the simultaneously popular and national character of the Russian monarchy.

The myth of *narodnost'* has as a complement that of the exclusion of the Russian intelligentsia, which flees like Aleko in Pushkin's poem, "The Prisoner of the Caucasus"—a theme developed by Slavophiles and above all by Dostoyevsky in his Pushkin speech (1881).

BIBLIOGRAPHY

Dostoevsky, Fydor. *A Writer's Diary.* 2 vols. Translated and annotated by Kenneth Lantz. Evanston, IL: Northwestern University Press, 1993–94.

It was thus in the context of a polemic with a fugitive from Orthodoxy that the broadening of the word occurred: individualistic Western thought could not achieve a complete grasp of being; only *sobornost'* managed that, since it is not the mere addition of components of the synod, but "organically surmounts their exclusion and their enclosure in a gnoseological limitation" (Skobtsova, *Khomiakov*, 41). Even *yourodstvo* [юродство] or "folly in Christ"—a form of asceticism quite characteristic of Russian piety: the fool for Christ simulates madness, renounces his property and hygiene, denounces the hypocrisy of the powerful (the best known was the Blessed Vassily, in the sixteenth century, buried in Red Square in Moscow)—is, in the East, part of the gnoseological process. In the West the participation of madness and disorder in the creation of order is strictly impossible and forbidden. For love participates in it in the Slavic East, it possesses a force and a gift, whereas in the West it is reduced to a law. The constraining principles of law and dogma are part of Western religious and philosophical thought, whereas freedom is integrated into *sobornost'*. It is a matter of a unity-freedom that is not imposed, but experienced by all in the act of *sobornost'*.

IV. The Divine Humanity of Solovyov

Vladimir Solovyov, the son of a great historian of Russia and a disciple of Khomiakov but destined to become a more eminent philosopher, developed this notion in that of "pan-humanity" or "humano-divinity." Through that concept Solovyov wanted to reintegrate harmony into the whole of humanity. In his view it was a matter of establishing a "total interpenetration of the individual and collective principles, the inner coincidence between maximal development of the personality and social unity at its most complete" (Solovyov, *Lectures*). There would thus be born a free collectivity whose thinking would be one, but not forced.

Solovyov spoke of the principle of *obscinnost'* [общинность], which is the social principle of the life of the *mir* [мир] in economic solidarity, without the imposition of collectivism. It is well known that the *mir*, or village collective, which proved as solidary when confronted with taxes or conscription as it had confronting landlords, was the object of an intense polemic in Russia, with some seeing in it the promise of a future communism, linked to primitive communism and organically bound to Russian rural life, and others seeing in it

the dictatorship of the strongest over the weakest within a village assembly held by the kulaks.

- See Box 2.

V. Toward an "Ecclesialization" of the World

The theologian Sergei Bulgakov reminds us that, from the etymological point of view, *peasant* in Russian does not mean pagan, as in French, but (on the contrary) Christian (*krest'janin* [крестьянин]). This is not random. The new Russian thought of the Silver Age at the beginning of the twentieth century, influenced by the thinking of Marxists converted to idealism, then to Christianity, like Father Sergei Bulgakov himself, insisted on the cosmic character of man, on the necessity of promoting a Christian socialism, a reconciliation of man and nature through a flourishing of the economic energy of man by way of Christianity and even the Church, the world being called on to become increasingly church-like or ecclesiastical (a translation of the Bulgakovian neologism *otserkovlenie* [оцерковление]), even in the sphere of the economy. Orthodoxy, bereft of a monarchical principle and even of any strictly ecclesiastic spirit, is called on to promote economic democracy. *Sobornost'* or the collegial spirit (such is C. Andronnikof's translation of the word in Bulgakov's *Orthodoxy*) is not a democracy, but it includes a democratic spirit within it, and particularly in the economic domain. Bulgakov was plainly influenced by Dostoyevsky, who said that Orthodoxy was "our Russian socialism." Long before the *Esprit* movement, thinkers of the Silver Age thus indicated the path to a Christian economics integrating communism and marrying it to the freedom of the individual. The inspiration of the Church of *sobornost'* gathering the faithful in the free union of the Church was destined to exercise its influence throughout the world. Nicolas Berdyayev interpreted the idea for the French Catholics of the Franco-Russian Rencontres group and later for Emmanuel Mounier's *Esprit* movement.

Another Orthodox thinker, Father Pavel Florensky, who perished in the gulag, declared in his very singular book, titled *The Pillar and Ground of the Truth*, that Orthodoxy had invented a sacrament of fraternization that issued in a specific rite, the ritual of "adelphopoeisis," a half-ecclesiastical, half-popular rite consisting in the exchange of crosses and the taking of an oath of loving friendship. The rite confirmed that there was to be nothing in the Orthodox Church that was not general, nor anything that was to be private. Neither

2
Obscinnost'

➤ MIR

Obscinnost' marks the predestination of Russia to primitive communism—based on mutual assistance and a refusal of property—to be found in the old social institution of *mir* or the peasant collectivity that administers lands, distributes them, and represents the community in the face of political power. This ancient Slavic institution is considered as what differentiates Russian society, which is collectivist, from that of the individualist West. The *mir* in the strict sense subsisted for a few years at the beginning of the Soviet era and was then replaced by the *kolkhoz* and its principle of constraint.

Privatsache nor impersonal law, which corresponds to the spirit of *sobornost'*.

VI. Nicolas Berdyayev between *Sobornost'* and Personalist Socialism

Berdyayev, in his book on Khomiakov's thought, insists on the gnoseology of the founder of Slavophile thought: "Being is given solely to ecclesiastic awareness of universal communion. Individual consciousness is unequipped to grasp the Truth" (Berdyayev, *Aleksei Stepanovich Khomiakov*, 2:127). But Berdyayev reproached the theologian for not having succeeded in connecting that "great idea of universal communion [*sobornost'*]" with cosmology and with the "soul of the world" (ibid.), as Solovyov did. A philosophy of integral spirit, a quest for concrete being, such are the original paths of Russian philosophy, according to Berdyayev, that derive from the theological concept of *sobornost'*.

Berdyayev's thought passed through quite contradictory phases, going from an aristocratic stance advocating inequality to a Khomiakovian conception of familial communion, in a society that was above all land-based, that is, linked to the *zemščina* [земщина], which might be translated as the "voice of the land," a concept quite different from the voice of the people: "the Russian *zemščina* is organic; it is not divided into classes that struggle with antagonistic wills" (ibid., 201). The land must be the czar's councilor and allow the consensus of the land to ascend to him; the *zemskaja duma* [земская дума] is the representative of the land, and not of the social classes in conflict. A strange and brief reappearance of this conception was seen in the last Supreme Soviet, that of *perestroika*, to which a certain number of Slavophile thinkers (or thinkers taken with that tendency) (Sergei Averintsev and Viatcheslav S. Ivanov) had been elected. For them political decisions became the fruit of a consensus. Berdyayev writes that the entire history of Russia is dependent on a relation of the land (*zemlja* [земля]) to power. The Saint Petersburg interlude, which inserted the bureaucracy between the czar and the land, was a catastrophe. Peter the Great ordered that writing was to be done with the door open: writing was not to be an isolated and seditious act, but an act before all and sundry—familial, transparent, and public.

VII. Current Broadening of the Concept

Sobornost' is without contest one of those imprecise concepts in which the originality, attractiveness and—for others—the repulsiveness of Russian thought lie. The word is untranslatable in its polysemy—in theology and politics throughout Russian history, where it always functions as a mark of the originality of Russian or Orthodox "togetherness."

It is currently to be found applied to such fields as literature, as in the book of a Moscow scholar, Ivan Esaulov, on "the category of *sobornost'* in Russian literature." The author analyzes the principle of *sobornost'* in the work of Pushkin, and particularly by way of the theme of the paradoxical solidarity between men, for example, between the brigand and future insurgent and the young nobleman in "The Captain's Daughter." The criterion has long been applied to the work of Tolstoy. The encounter between Pierre Bezukhov and the simple moujik Platon Karataev in *War and Peace* is a sample of *sobornost'*. The world perceived by Pierre at that juncture is a round, cosmic world, in which everything is linked by a paradoxical organic bond that is not beholden to reason. Petya Rostov feels in the depth of his being the *sobornost'* that unites all soldiers, even the crudest of them, and which is revealed with the emperor's arrival in Moscow, when Petya hurls himself forward shouting "Hurrah," while a service of thanksgiving is held in the cathedral. The sacristan who saves Petya from the tumult on that occasion, and mounts him on King-Cannon, which can still be seen in the Kremlin, describes what is happening in the cathedral and uses the term *soborne* [соборне] on several occasions, meaning "solemnly, all together, pontifically," but whose "meaning remained obscure for Petya." Petya does not understand the word's meaning, but he lives it intensely since he throws himself into the colorful crowd and shares all its emotions; and his enthusiasm will be even greater when he subsequently joins the army, that great family in which his brother Nicolas already feels as good as in his father's house. Petya's death—one of the most forceful episodes in all of Tolstoy's work—is also a high point of intense connection of all with all, of lived *sobornost'*. But the episode is treated musically, as though one were hearing a fugue, in which each instrument played its own motif. "And without finishing it, melded with another that initiated almost the same motif, then with a third, and a fourth; then they all fused into a single motif, separated out again, only to fuse anew, at times in a solemn religious chant, at others in a song of victory that was dazzling in its luminosity" (Tolstoy, *War and Peace*).

VIII. Immersion in the Living

Tolstoy's fugue accompanying the death of the youngest hero of *War and Peace* is the secular transposition of an old Russian Orthodox church chorale, the *sobornost'*:

It is only by immersing ourselves in ourselves, by seeking our own mystical roots in the total organism, that we experience our own *sobornost'*, that we know our self as non-self. In the atmosphere of ecclesiastic love, in the experience of the sacramental mysteries, our particularity is surmounted and collectivism fails to occlude *sobornost'*.

(Bulgakov, *Light without Decline*)

Georges Nivat

BIBLIOGRAPHY

Berdyayev, Nikolai. *Aleksei Stepanovich Khomiakov*. Farmborough, UK: Gregg International, 1971.

Bulgakov, Sergii. *The Orthodox Church*. Translated by Elizabeth S. Cram. London: Centenary Press, 1935.

———. "Protopresbyter Sergii Bulgakov: Hypostasis and Hypostaticity: Scholia to *The Unfading Light.*" Revised translation by Anastassy Brandon Gallaher and Irina Kukota. Edited by Anastassy Brandon Gallaher and Irina Kukota. Introduction by A. F. Dobbie Bateman. *St Vladimir's Theological Quarterly* 49, nos. 1–2 (2005): 5–46.

Esaulov, Ivan E. *Kategorija sobornosti v russkoj literature*. Petrozavodsk, 1995.

Florensky, Pavel. *The Pillar and Ground of the Truth*. Translated and annotated by Boris Jakim. Princeton, NJ: Princeton University Press, 1997.

Khomiakov, Alexei S. *On Spiritual Unity: A Slavophile Reader: Aleksei Khomiakov, Ivan Kireevsky, with Essays by Yury Samarin, Nikolai Berdiaev, and Pavel Florensky*. Translated and edited by Boris Jakim and Robert Bird. Hudson, NY: Lindisfarne, 1998.

———. *Quelques mots par un chrétien orthodoxe sur les communions occidentals à l'occasion d'une brochure de M. Laurentie*. A. Franck, 1853.

Lotman, Yuri. " 'Dogovor' i 'vručcenie sebja' kak arxetipičeskie modeli kult'tury." In *Izbrannye stat'i*. Vol. 3. Tallin, 1993.

Skobtsova, Ekaterina. *Khomiakov*. Paris: YMCA Press, 1929.

Solovyov, Vladimir. *Lectures on Divine Humanity*. Revised and edited by Boris Jakim. Hudson, NY: Lindisfarne, 1995.

SOCIETY

"Society" is borrowed from the Latin *societas* (association, meeting, community, society), which can designate participation in a commercial enterprise as well as an alliance or political union: a *socius* is a partner and, no doubt, according to the etymology, a comrade in war. Latin *societas* was used to render the Greek *koinônia* [κοινωνία], from *koinos* [κοινός] (common, public); on the relation between "community" and "society," see POLIS, COMMUNITY, II.

The term "society" acquired precise meaning rather late, through a series of oppositions whose development scans the history of political and social thought since the end of the eighteenth century and which generally tend to relativize the position conferred by philosophy to politics in the human sphere: "civil society" forms spontaneously and is distinguished from the state; social relations are distinguished from political ties, and, for sociology, are their cause rather than their effect; the "individual" is at once cause and effect of society; the "social" or the "societal" cannot be reduced to the "economic": we have explored, under the rubric "civil society," the set of networks at play, both ancient (*koinônia politike* [κοινωνία πολιτική], *societas civilis*) and modern (in particular the distinction *Gemeinschaft/Gesellschaft*, in CIVIL SOCIETY, Box 1). See also CIVIL RIGHTS, ECONOMY, OIKONOMIA, PEOPLE, POLITICS, SOBORNOST', *STATE*.

On the relation between society and sociability, see CIVILTÀ and *CIVILITY, CIVILIZATION, CULTURE, WITTICISM*; cf. FRENCH and ITALIAN.

➤ ENTREPRENEUR, GEISTESWISSENSCHAFTEN, *HUMANITY*, *POWER*

SOLLEN (GERMAN)

FRENCH   *devoir, obligation*

➤ *OBLIGATION*, and BERUF, *DESTINY*, DUTY, LAW, *LIBERTY*, MORALS, PIETAS, TATSACHE, *TO BE, VALUE*, WERT, WILLKÜR

Etymology traces the "modal auxiliary" *sollen* to the noun *Schuld* (debt, guilt) and the Latin *debere, solvere*; on the other hand, *Pflicht*—a noun formed from the verb *pflegen*, "to take care of something," and, by extension, "to have the habit of"—is traced back to the idea contained in the Latin *colere*, "to take care of, to cultivate." Whereas *Pflicht* translates as *officium* or *obligatio*, always referring to a content of what is to be accomplished, *sollen* refers from the outset to a fundamental level, at once an obligation to be and to do, posing the problem of its relation to being, with a resultant insistence on either ethical function or logical (and even ontological) status. This ambiguity has been noted as underlying the expression "naturalist paralogism" ("from what is one cannot deduce what ought to be"), which is said to be grounded in Hume (*Treatise on Human Nature*, III, I, 1, conclusion). But it is rather starting with Kant, and up until his critique by Lask and Rickert, as well as by Scheler, that this dual usage has been deployed in all its acuity.

Translating Exodus 20:13, Luther renders the Hebrew *lo' tireṣāḥ* [לֹא תִּרְצָח] as "Du sollst nicht töten (Thou shalt not kill)." The commandment is not formulated according to the order of objective necessity that would be expressed through the modal auxiliary *müssen*, but according to the register of what is assumed to be, the behavior one is assumed to adhere to without necessarily succeeding in doing so. Similarly, in Galatians, 3:19, *ti oun ho nomos* [τί οὖν ὁ νόμος] is rendered as "Was soll nun das Gesetz?" The nuance introduced by *sollen* is halfway between necessity and recommendation, between imperative command and advice.

I. *Sollen* before *Pflict*:
Duty and Duty-to-Be in Kant and Fichte

It is in this semantic tradition that Kant's use of the nominal verb *das sollen* is inscribed: practical philosophy is a discipline in which "it is not a matter for us of proceeding to the subsumption of the principles of what effectively takes place, but of the laws of what is supposed (*soll*) to happen, even if it never does" (*Foundations of the Metaphysics of Morals*). The understanding latches exclusively onto the principles of the structure of being *sive natura*, of being as it is, as it is by necessity; now the *Sollen* depends on "its own order which heeds only ideas," so that what ought to happen thus has no empirical cause (cf. *Prolegomena to Any Future Metaphysics*, 53). The *Critique of Pure Reason* (B 576) explains it without ambiguity: "[Reason] creates for itself, with perfect spontaneity, its own order following the ideas to which it adapts empirical conditions and according to which it goes as far as to proclaim as necessary actions which never occurred," since natural conditions (including the senses) "cannot produce obligation (*Sollen*), but only a will that is far from being necessary, is always conditioned, and to which, on the contrary, the obligation (*Sollen*) proclaimed by Reason opposes a rule and a measure, and even an interdiction and an authority." It comes as no surprise that the practical and speculative interest of reason is summarized in three questions (*Critique of Pure Reason*, B 833): "What can I know? What should I do? [Was soll Ich tun? What am I supposed to do?] and "What do I have a right to hope?" The presence of *Sollen* is at once the sign of human finitude and the awareness of that finitude, an awareness that seeks to remedy it: "For a being in whom Reason is not the sole principle determining will, the [practical] rule constitutes an imperative, that is, a rule defined by an obligation (*Sollen*) expressing the objective constraint that dictates action, and it signifies that if Reason determined will completely, the action would occur without fail according to that rule" (*Critique of Practical Reason*). In the intelligible sphere, *Sollen* and *Tun* would not be distinct, any more than the will would need to determine itself as a function of categorical imperatives or skill in terms of hypothetical imperatives. *Sollen* thus makes sense only for beings equally determined by their senses, and the limits of our capacities will not dispense us from obeying that *Sollen*, since "we are supposed (*sollen*) to become better" (*Religion Within the Limits of Reason Alone*).

The transcendental critique thus opens onto a primacy of the duty-to-be, which it presupposed in a way since the critique made sense only against the backdrop of a finitude that it explores systematically; in addition it is that duty-to-be as duty-to-do that determines the general regimen of action and subtends the conception of duty (*Pflicht*) as *officium* or *obligatio*, a task or concrete obligation. Since a duty (*Pflicht*) performed by inclination, compassion, etc., has no moral value, and the only duty worthy of such value is one that forces us "to become better"—that is, to act against all our penchants, contrary to every search for benefit or interest, without at all taking into consideration the happiness or effects produced by our action—the duty-to-do (*Sollen*) is indeed the organizing axis on which duty (*Pflicht*) is inscribed, even as it is subordinated to it. To the extent that Kant refuses the possibility of there actually being a "conflict of duties" (*Metaphysics of Morals*) ("A collision of duties and obligations is not at all thinkable"), the details of the practical prescriptions constituting the content of an obligation are, from the logical point of view, fully as subordinate as the action necessary to fulfill them is to the general register of *Sollen* (both duty-to-be and duty-to-do, simultaneously). The difference between duties of virtue (*Tugendpflichten*)—in which an end and a duty coincide—and juridical duties (*Rechtspflichten*)—which are to submit to the maxim according to which neither the self nor another can be means for the other—as well as the distinction between morality and legality (and consequently the distinction between internal and external obligation) remain under the aegis of the promulgation by pure Reason of ends partaking exclusively of the duty-to-be.

Fichte adopted for the most part this use and value of Kant's *Sollen* while radicalizing its importance with regard to the pure self and freedom: "Free being ought (to be/do) (*soll*); for obligation (*Sollen*) is precisely the expression of the determination of freedom" (*System der Sittenlehre* [1798], in

Werke, ed. De Gruyter, 4:60). As in Kant, the *Sollen* is the characteristic of the self as finite Reason, but the fact that man is equally a pure ego implies that "he ought (*soll*) to be what he is simply because he is. . . . He ought to be what he is because he is a pure ego" (*Lectures on the Vocation of the Scholar* [1794]). Fichte thus insists on the process-like nature of the *Sollen*, "an 'ought' (*soll*) is itself in its deepest being a genesis, and it demands a genesis. . . . It is the absolute postulate of a genesis" (*Wissenschaftslehre* [1804], 22nd lecture), even if it is not exclusively a matter of the moral approximation of the good in the practical realm; the meaning of *Sollen* is broadened to the whole of action, whatever it be:

> I ought [to do] (*ich soll etwas*) something signifies that I ought to produce it from myself or—since it imposes on me an undoubtedly infinite aim to the extent that *is* not ever and, on the contrary, can never ever but ought to be—if I could not realize it fully, I would, however, always do in such matter as to find myself in the approximation of that aim.
>
> (Fichte, *System des Sittenlehre*, 4:66)

II. *Pflicht* and *Sollen*: Contradictions and Reversals from Hegel to Nietzsche

Beyond Schelling's critique, which is obviously opposed to the idea that there would be a possible passage between the finite ego and the infinite (the absolute ego), it is above all Hegel who refuses this conception of *Sollen*: "What universally holds value is also universally valid; what ought to be *is* in fact also, and what is only supposed to be without being has no truth" (*Phenomenology of the Spirit*). Further still, the "inadequation of being to what ought to be" is the origin of evil (*Encyclopedia*, 472), and "the substance that knows itself to be free, at the core of which the absolute duty-to-be is as well and just as much being, finds its reality in the form of the spirit of a people" (ibid., 514).

Schopenhauer breaks with the dignity of meaning conferred on *Sollen* and, in his eyes, *Pflicht* and *Sollen* are almost synonymous in their shared status as *relative notions*: the only difference between the two terms is a function of the juridical status of each individual (cf. *Über die Grundlage der Moral*, 4). Thus the slave knows only *Sollen*, to the extent that he has no rights and thus has no duty (*Pflicht*) incumbent on him. Nietzsche would take up this analogy between *Sollen* and *Pflicht*, but by introducing a decisive stylistic inflection: the first chapter of the first book of *Thus Spake Zarathustra* opens with the well known text on the "Three Metamorphoses," in which the dragon baptized "Thou-shalt," blocking the path of the lion who says "I want," is opposed to the creation of new values; he thus embodies the values of the past, lays claim to the everlasting, whereas the lion incarnates the strength needed to "create itself freedom, and give a holy Nay even to duty (*Pflicht*)." The lion has strength only in negation and refusal, and one needs the innocence and absence of memory of the child to affirm a new beginning. The refusal of "thou-shalt" tends to the affirmation of new values, to the conversion of all values; now that last imperative again implies the entire series of *du sollst*, that will continually punctuate the text of *Zarathustra*. Nietzsche quite plainly

takes up the Lutheran rhetoric of the translation of the Decalogue to apply it to a new tablet of values, so that what was
on the order of duty (*Pflicht*) belongs resolutely to the past,
whereas what was on the order of duty-to-be is concealed by
Sollen, allows it to escape that past and open itself up to the
future of transformed values, which are just as (and, in fact,
altogether more) demanding.

III. *Sein, Sollen, Gelten*: Problems of the Ontology of Duty from Franz Brentano to Heinrich Rickert

But that exclusively ethical use of *Sollen*, in fact, merely emphasizes the ambiguity concealed by its meaning from the
outset, since it signifies the duty-to-be as well as the duty-
to-do. It was more or less at the same time that Brentano
attempted to establish the idea of moral knowledge, and reflected, in a logical perspective, on the values that govern action: thus the commandment "thou shalt not kill" can quite
well be interpreted, on the one hand, as an interdiction on
murder, that is, as partaking of a judgment that disqualifies
murder universally and in general, and, on the other hand,
as a corollary interdiction, but one that is no longer universal, on killing. The judgment disqualifying murder in general
also disqualifies the act of killing but without, however, banning it in certain circumstances. To the judgment "killing is
bad" is added another, "all murder is forbidden," which no
longer exactly partakes of the duty-to-do or the duty-to-be,
but of a judgment concerning the absolute value of life
(cf. F. Brentano, "Zur Lehre von der Relativität der abgeleiteten Sittengesetze" [2 September 1893]). That same ambiguity is found in the *Ethik des reinen Willens* (1904) by Hermann
Cohen to the extent that, concerned with emphasizing the
difference between being and the duty-to-be, and grounding
ethics on *Sollen*, he could not avoid granting a value of being
to the duty-to-do: "It is in the duty-to-be (*Sollen*) that the
value of being of the ethical resides. . . . Without *Sollen*, there
would be no will, but only desires. Through *Sollen*, the will
achieves and conquers true being" (*Ethik*, 7:27).

It was precisely against the insistence on distinguishing
duty-to-be and being that Emil Lask undertook to redefine the relations between *Sollen* and value: "It appears to
be a simple explanation of the concept of value to affirm
that value is what *ought* absolutely *to be* although it *is* not
always ("Hegel in seinem Verhältnis zur Weltanschauung
der Aufklärung" [1905], in *Gesammelte Schriften*, vol. 1). The
Sollen or normative characteristic is a predicate of value; it
designates but an aspect of it and is in no way identical to
it. *Sollen* (or the norm) does, in fact, not only designate the
essence of value but also its relation to reality, its realization.
Lask would establish a distinction as a more subtle relation
between duty-to-be and being: being is identical to the *logical content* of validity, "being is a 'being worth' (*Gelten*)" (*The
Logic of the Philosophy and Doctrine of Categories,* in *Gesammelte
Schriften*, 2:118). More precisely, "the logical form is identical
only to the being of the existent, just as a theoretical content of worth (*geltend*), participant in value and duty-to-be,
coincides with it" (ibid., 273). The distance is thus less between being (of the existent) and duty-to-be than between
pure duty-to-be and impure duty-to-be, that is, between a
value (*Gelten*) partaking of duty-to-be and the category of
being, which is altogether determined and partakes equally

of duty-to-be. The objectivity of being coincides with *Sollen*
as a *category*, which is also quite determined. Lask refuses to
ascribe *Gelten* to a subject endowed with a will to know, since
"from the point of view of its adherence to a value, *all* subjectivity would appear as 'practical,' 'autonomous' behavior, as
a will devoted to value for value's sake, as the subordination
of a *Sollen* in the name of *Sollen* itself" (*System des Logik*, in
Gesammelte Schriften, 3:95).

In his intervention at the international philosophy
colloquium of 1908 ("Is there a primacy of practical Reason in logic?" in *Gesammelte Schriften*, 1:347–56), Lask quite
naturally criticized the thesis until then defended by Rickert,
according to which a duty-to-be would precede being by
maintaining a Kantian division between pure and practical
Reason. That critique would bring Heinrich Rickert to undertake a profound revision of his *Der Gegenstand der Erkenntnis*
(as he acknowledged in his preface to the third edition, 1915).
He did not hesitate to describe as a Copernican revolution
at the heart of the concept of judgment (*Der Gegenstand der
Erkenntnis*, 1927) the fact that henceforth it would no longer
be the effective real that would be the Archimedean point
of a judgment on reality, but the duty-to-be harbored by the
necessity of bearing a judgment. In a judgment of the "that
is (quite) real" sort, the *that*, the content, is the subject of the
judgment to which the form reality should (*soll*) be ascribed
as predicate:

> It is not around *reality* that the knowing ego-subject
> "gravitates" . . . , but around theoretical *value* that he
> must gravitate if he is to recognize that *reality*. Thus
> the concept of the effective real enters, concerning the
> form "reality," into a necessary relation with the con-
> cept of duty-to-be and evaluating subject . . . for "real"
> quite properly signifies or simply *is* the content that
> ought (*soll*) effectively to be affirmed or admitted.

> (Ibid.)

IV. *Werturteil* and *Pflichturteil, Sollen* and *Pflichtsollen*: Max Scheler and the Material Ethics of Values

In his "Material Ethic of Values," Scheler rejects the idea
that value judgments would express "instead of a bond
of being a bond of duty-to-be . . . or that, more generally,
every value judgment must necessarily be based on the
lived experience of a 'duty-to-do' (*Sollen*), whatever it be.
In point of fact, the moral meaning of propositions such
as 'this image is beautiful' or 'that man is good' is not at
all that this image or that man ought (*sollen*) to be something" (*Formalism in Ethics*). Otherwise put, value judgments
of the type simply describe a state of things that, in certain
cases only, present themselves with a dimension of obligation ("That man ought [*soll*] to be good"), which then signifies that an "idealization" preceded the judgment. The
value judgment is not reducible to a "judgment of obligation" (*Sollurteil*) for the simple reason that the domain of
the former is far more vast than that of the latter. One can
thus not reduce being to a duty-to-be, and even less to a
duty-to-do. This is all the more the case in that Scheler posits as a principle that every duty-to-do (*Sollen*) ought to be
grounded in values that alone ought to be (*sollen*), but also
ought not to be (ibid.)

Since there exists no duty-to-do whose matter would simply be existence, there is always, pitted against the "duty-to-be," a "duty not to be," that should be characterized as a quality different from obligation itself and distinguished strenuously from the "duty-to-be of a non-being." . . . Duty-to-be is applied to positive values, non-duty-to-be to negative values.

(Ibid.)

On its own, *Sollen* cannot determine what positive values are; it affirms them by opposing them to negative values: "Every *Sollen* . . . is oriented toward the exclusion of non-values, and not toward the position of positive values" (ibid.) From this, Scheler deduces that every proposition that expresses a *Sollen*

rests on a positive value, but does not itself contain that value. What "ought to be" is never originally the existence of the good, but simply the non-existence of evil. It is thus impossible for any duty-to-be whatsoever to contradict the judgment of what is positively good or might depend on that judgment. If I know, for example, what it is good for me to do, "what I ought to do" is of little concern to me. For me to *ought,* I must first know what is good. But if I know immediately and fully what is good, that effective knowledge equally determines (and in an immediate way) my will without my having to pass through the intermediary of an "I ought."

(Ibid.)

This is the perspective on which Scheler bases his resumption of Hegel's critique of the Kantian and Fichtean conception of *Sollen*:

The attitude of an ethic of this sort is such that it can attain positive values only *through reference* to negative values. . . . But if one adds to it a tendency to conflate ideal duty-to-be with the duty-to-be of obligation (*Pflichtsollen*), or to derive ideal duty-to-be itself from the duty-to-be of obligation, one arrives at a peculiar species of negativism and simultaneously at a fear of seeing all existent moral values enter into contact with reality, a fear of every effective realization of the good in action and in history.

(Ibid.)

Marc de Launay

BIBLIOGRAPHY

Brentano, Franz. *The Origin of Our Knowledge of Right and Wrong*. Edited by Roderick Chisholm. Translated by Roderick M. Chisholm and Elizabeth H. Schneewind. London: Routledge and Kegan Paul, 1969.

———. "Zur Lehre von der Relativität der abgeleiteten Sittengesetze." In *Vom Ursprung sittlicher Erkenntnio*. Hamburg: Mainer, 1969.

Cohen, Hermann. *Ethik der reinen Willens*. Hildesheim, Ger.: Olms, 1981.

Cohen, Hermann, Marc B. de Launay, Carole Prompsy, et al. *Cohen, Natorp, Cassirer, Windelband, Rickert, Lask, Cohn: Néokantismes et théorie de la connaissance*. Paris: Vrin, 2000.

Lask, Emil. *Gesammelte Schriften*. 3 vols. Tübingen: Mohr, 1923–24.

Rickert, Heinrich. *Der Gegenstand der Erkenntnis*. Tübingen: Mohr, 1927.

Scheler, Max. *Formalism in Ethics and Non-Formal Ethics of Values: A New Attempt toward the Foundation of an Ethical Personalism*. Translated by Manfred S. Frings and Roger L. Funk. 5th rev. ed. Evanston, IL: Northwestern University Press, 1973.

———. *Gesammelte Werke*. Bern: A. Francke, 1954.

Stratton-Lake, Philip. *Kant, Duty, and Moral Worth*. London: Routledge, 2000.

SOPHISM, SOPHIST

"Sophism" is a borrowing from Latin *sophisma*, itself the transliteration of Greek *sophisma* [σόφισμα]. The Greek term designates first of all an ingenious invention, a skillful expedient such as that of Prometheus stealing fire to help mortals, Ulysses playing on words to escape the Cyclops (see MÊTIS, Box 1), or even Thales monopolizing the presses (see PHRONÊSIS, Box 1). It thus has a connection to know-how (*technê* [τέχνη]) and ruse: see ART, I, MÊTIS, and it refers to qualities of inventiveness denoted by the Latin *ingenium* and that the Renaissance, particularly in Italy, would rediscover in the form of ingenious subtlety (see ARGUTEZZA, CONCETTO). The connotations of the term may vary from wisdom (*sophisma* and *sophistês* [σοφιστής] and "sophist" have the same root as *sophia* [σοφία], meaning "wisdom, knowledge," and *sophos* [σοφός], meaning "sage") to trickery (see TRUTH, Box 7, which specifies the kind of "deception" produced by a sophism), to insolent pretention (*hubris* [ὕβρις], "insolence, excess": see VERGUENZA, II; *apaideusia* [ἀπαιδευσία], "bad upbringing": see PRINCIPLE, Box 1).

I. Sophism and Logic: "Sophism," *Sophisma*, "Fallacy"

Sophistical discourse implies a privileging of the powers of language, an awareness of its efficacy and performativity, linked to what will constitute rhetoric: see SPEECH ACT, I, LOGOS, II.A). That awareness implies critique of the pretentions of ontology to speak the truth by conforming to what is: see TRUTH, I; cf. ESTI, *IL Y A*.

But starting with Plato and then with Aristotle, sophistical thought would be devoted to sophistry, in the sense of fallacious reasoning, in other words, reasoning that is not only false but also intentionally deceptive: see HOMONYM; and, more generally, it is linked, at all levels, with deceptive appearances: see DOXA, EIDÔLON, MIMÊSIS (cf. *APPEARANCE, IMAGE*).

In the Middle Ages, a *sophisma* is a proposition intended to test the validity of a rule or a distinction, and *sophismata* [σοφίσματα] are disputes organized around a proposition, making use at the level of literary form and Scholastic practice of certain of the gains of Aristotle's *On Sophistical Refutations*: in addition to HOMONYM, see TROPE, and cf. CONNOTATION, SUPPOSITION.

In English, note should be made of the distinction between "fallacy," which designates an error in reasoning that has all the appearances of truth, and "sophism," which denotes additionally an intention to deceive, with the difficulty that "fallacy" is the received translation for medieval *sophisma*, which is more ambiguous (cf. French *fallacieux* and Latin *fallax*, TRUTH, IV.B.2); see, for example, RIGHT for use of the syntagm "naturalistic fallacy," rendered in French as *sophisme naturaliste*; see the bibliography of TROPE for the use of *fallacy* in the titles of medieval works; see also SOLLEN.

II. Sophism and Politics

Hegel says of the Sophists that they were "the masters of Greece," in the sense of pedagogues and teachers, but also in the sense of being politically powerful, dominating through the power of language and the establishment of the political per se; see, in addition to LOGOS, II.A and RES, Box 1, SPEECH ACT, I, TRUTH, Box 2, and *CONSENSUS*, PRAXIS, VIRTÙ.

➤ *DIALECTIC, DISCOURSE*, DOXA, SENSE, SIGN, SIGNIFIER/SIGNIFIED, *WISDOM*

SORGE (GERMAN)

FRENCH	*souci*
GREEK	*phrontis* [φροντίς]
	merisma [μέρισμα]
LATIN	*sollicitudo*

▶ CARE [*SOUCI*], DASEIN, *IL Y A*, *MALAISE*, PATHOS, PHRONĒSIS, *TO BE*

Although there is, prior to Heidegger, an entire—and, to be frank, rather problematic—"prehistory" of the concept of care (Plato, Aristotle, Seneca, Saint Paul, Hyginus, Saint Augustine), an identification of sources does not suffice to illuminate the ontological structure elaborated by Heidegger under this rubric. The question of the rooting of the concept in tradition—but in which tradition, precisely?—is currently a matter of debate.

A key term in Heidegger's thought, at the center of which it designates nothing less than the being of *Dasein* (according to the title of §41 in *Being and Time*), and indeed its "arch-structure" (*Urstruktur*), *Sorge* speaks the being of *Dasein* to the extent that "it is a matter" (es geht um). The "care" in question here should thus be separated from our ordinary understanding of the term (as in the Fr. *avoir des soucis*, to have worries; note, moreover, that *souci* comes from the Lat. *sollicitare*, to agitate, shake forcefully, trouble, whereas *Sorge* is related to Lat. *servare*, to preserve, keep, like Eng. "sorrow," from Old Eng. *sorg*, Middle Eng., *sorge*, but which took on the meaning of "chagrin," "affliction"). Insouciance (*Sorglosigkeit*) is itself a deficient mode of *souci*, far more than its opposite. It partakes no less of *souci*, "care," understood as an ontological structure, than of anxious care.

The existential-ontological interpretation of *Dasein* as care finds its "pre-ontological" basis in fable 220 of Hyginus, on which Goethe, by way of Herder, drew in elaborating part 2 of his *Faust* (cf. *Being and Time*, 42). Emphasizing that the orientation of his analysis of care is related to a study of Augustinian anthropology, on a basis furnished by Aristotelian ontology, Heidegger specifies: "Already in Stoicism, *merisma* [μέρισμα] was a stable term, which is found in the New Testament, and which the Vulgate translates as *sollicitudo*." According to Rémi Brague, however:

This is an error: Bultmann notes (art. "Merimnao," etc. of the *TWNT*, IV, 594) that "it is remarkable that the term is absent from Stoicism, where it is replaced, among others, by *phrontis*." The latter term is, in fact, found in the doctrine of the passions (cf. *SVF*, III, p. 100 sq.). But it is scarcely elsewhere than in two passages of Seneca [*Letters to Lucilius*, 121, 17 and 124, 14] that it becomes a concept. For more details on the historic origin of the concept of *Sorge*, cf. Heidegger, *Prolegomena zur Geschichte des Zeitbegriffs* (*GA*, 20), 418–20. Heidegger's error appears to come from an article by K. Burdach, which he cites in a note on p. 47.

Brague, *Aristote et la question du monde*

The question of determining whether "Heidegger sought, with the concept of 'care,' to bring to light a hidden source of Aristotle's thought" (Brague, *Aristote et la question du monde*), specifically, deepening *phronēsis* [φρόνησις] in the direction of *phrontis* [φροντίς], or rather, on the contrary, whether

Being and Time was connected in this regard to "the philosophical tradition of 'care for the self,' a tradition whose origin is Platonic" (Larivée and Leduc, "Saint Paul") remains a subject of debate, even if the former hypothesis strikes us as plainly more convincing. One should also undoubtedly add to the discussion a sentence from Aristotle's *Rhetoric* (in which *Being and Time*, 29, sees "the first systematic hermeneutic of the everyday with being-with-others"), which articulates *phrontizein* [φροντίζειν] (caring for) with the manner specific to "everydayness" of relating to death:

ἴσασι γὰρ πάντες ὅτι ἀποθανοῦνται, ἀλλ᾽ ὅτι οὐκ ἐγγύς, οὐδὲν φροντίζουσιν.

(All men know that they are going to die, but since it is not imminent, they are not concerned by it.)

Rhetoric, 2.5.1382a 26–27

Pascal David

BIBLIOGRAPHY

Aristotle. *On Rhetoric: A Theory of Civic Discourse*. Translated, with introduction, notes, and appendixes by George A. Kennedy. New York: Oxford University Press, 1991.

Brague, Rémi. *Aristote et la question du monde: Essai sur le contexte cosmologique et anthropologique de l'ontologie*. Paris: Presses Universitaires de France, 1988.

Heidegger, Martin. *Being and Time*. Translated by Joan Stambaugh. Albany: State University of New York Press, 1996.

———. *History of the Concept of Time: Prolegomena*. Translated by Theodore Kisiel. Bloomington: Indiana University Press, 1985.

———. *Logik—Die Frage nach der Wahrheit*. In vol. 21 of *Gesamtausgabe*. Frankfurt: Klostermann, 1975–.

Hyginus. *The Myths of Hyginus*. Translated and edited by Mary Grant. Lawrence: University of Kansas Press, 1960.

Larivée, Anne, and Alexandra Leduc. "Saint Paul, Augustin et Aristote comme sources gréco-chétiennes du souci chez Heidegger—Élucidation d'un passage d'*Être et Temps* (§42, note 1)." *Philosophie* 69 (2001): 30–50.

SOUCI

Souci comes from Latin *sollicitare* (to agitate strongly), which is composed of *sollus* (whole) and *citus*, from *cieo* (to put into motion); after designating above all "amorous preoccupation," the term became in its contemporary use a quasi-synonym of "problem." In philosophy, it refers not merely to a passing preoccupation, or a difficulty, but to what Heidegger took to be the very characteristic of *Dasein*, of human being-there: see ANXIETY, DASEIN, and cf. *MALAISE*.

1. To the extent that *Dasein* is that being for which its very being is to be in question, this preoccupation with its very being, which is not the Platonic "care for the self," becomes a fundamental ontological structure, rendered in French by *souci*: see SORGE; cf. *IL Y A, TO BE*.

2. The translation of *Sorge* into English as "care" (from the Gothic *Kara* [chagrin, whence sorrow] and not from the Latin *cura* [care, particularly the administration of public affairs]), aside from being as unsatisfactory as the French version, underscores the difficulty for the Francophone reader of grasping the nuance present in the English doublet "care"/"solicitude";

see CARE, in which one will find reflections on the "ethics of care," the "feminine" deconstruction of a morality of justice (cf. *JUSTICE*, MORALS).

3. For the relationship between "care" and "security," both internal and external, and particularly with reference to classical philosophy, see SECURITAS.

SOUL, SPIRIT, MIND, WIT

BASQUE	*gogo*
FRENCH	*âme, esprit*
GERMAN	*Seele, Geist, Gemüt, Witz*
GREEK	*psuchê* [ψυχή], *dianoia* [διάνοια], *thumos* [θυμός], *phrenes* [φρενές]
HEBREW	*rûah* [רוּחַ], *nešâmâh* [נְשָׁמָה]
ITALIAN	*mente, ingenio, anima*
LATIN	*mens, anima, animus, ingenium*
SPANISH	*mente, ingenio, alma*

➤ BELIEF, CONSCIOUSNESS, GEMÜT, GOGO, INGENIUM, INTELLECT, INTELLECTUS, I/ME/MYSELF, MEMORY, PATHOS, PERCEPTION, *SELF* [SELBST, SAMOST], SENSE, SUBJECT, UNDERSTANDING, WILL

Philosophers' use of terms in the various European languages that designate "mental reality" and refer its manifestations to a substrate or unitary field of experience seems at first to pose only problems of translation that are connected with partially divergent etymologies or with conflicts between doctrines (mentalism, physicalism, reductionism, and so forth). This is, however, a prejudice established by textbook presentations of a philosophical "psychology" still dominated by a dualism that is manifested at least methodologically and has been widely accepted since the beginning of the nineteenth century. But this prejudice dissolves as soon as we become aware of the irreducible contradictions concealed by the nonequivalence of the paradigms of the "mental" in the classical philosophical languages. The first symptom of this is the lack in French of a simple equivalent of the Latin *mens*. The great philosophers do not treat these contradictions negatively, as obstacles to pure "thinking about thinking," but positively, as a means of gaining access to the complexity of the mind's relationship to itself (often through multilingual philosophers' efforts to translate such terms, as in the case of Descartes, Leibniz, or Kant).

Rather than seek to reconstitute here a complete genealogy of these concurrent paradigms, we will carry out two reductions (two successive theoretical "zooms," as it were). On the one hand, we will concentrate on the translation problems and the tensions characteristic of the classical metaphysics inaugurated by Cartesianism, which continues to shape the horizon of the doctrines of Hume, Kant, and Hegel, and even of phenomenology. We will emphasize their historical originality between two types of naturalism: the naturalism of ancient doctrines of the *psuchê* [ψυχή] and the *anima*, which has been preserved despite medieval onto-theology's transformation of its meaning, and the naturalism of experimental psychologies or of contemporary "philosophy of mind." On the other hand, we will reduce the examination of this metaphysical period of transition to the clarification—on the basis of their terminology itself—of a major opposition between Descartes's and Locke's points of view, in relation to a persistent tradition (unfortunately perpetuated by many contemporary presentations of the origins of

the mind-body problem) that sees in them the founders of the same theoretical trend.

The presentation of classical metaphysics will stress first the centrality of a problematic of a self-presence immediately given in thought (or in its own immanence, for which Locke and Kant recast the notion of experience or *Erfahrung*), which is denoted by the term *mens*, rendered in French as *esprit*, or by the term "mind" rendered in German as *Gemüt* or *Seele*. But this problematic struggles with the limitations of its own intellectualism or mentalism, which is sometimes discernible in the order of the sign and communication, and sometimes in the order of affectivity; it reappears in the form of a "remainder of soul" in contradiction with the general movement of the desubstantialization of mental reality that is reflected in fluctuations in language and that anticipates revolutions in contemporary thought (notably in psychoanalysis, which is paradoxically closer to the way the Greeks problematized the insistence of the bodily in the psychic than metaphysical thought ever was).

There is a clear opposition between the language of Descartes and that of Locke on this subject. Descartes's use of both *âme* and *esprit* to render in French his concept of the Latin *mens* surrounds, so to speak, the central ideal of a self in the first person (*ego sum res cogitans*) radically deprived of interiority (except in the form of an "image of the body" internal to thought itself). For Locke, by contrast, this interiority (or "fold" of reflection) is the object of the system of correlations that he establishes among the three fundamental (and founding) concepts of philosophical "psychologism": mind, consciousness, and self, all of them *stricto senso* untranslatable.

Around this central opposition, we will study the relationships between linguistic divergences and the philosophical aporia of "thinking about thinking" through the study of the particularly significant cases of Spinoza, Leibniz, and Berkeley, which illustrate the opposed ways in which the seventeenth- and eighteenth-century philosophers tried to combine reflection on the power of representation with reflection on the autonomy of the individual willing subject, whether with respect to immanence or with respect to transcendence, thus making the terminology of *esprit* irreducibly polysemous.

Finally, having thus arrived at the threshold of modernity, we will situate in counterpoint the debates surrounding the idea of a philosophy of mind aroused by contemporary Anglo-American thought. These debates are inseparable from terms with novel meanings that are difficult to translate into languages other than the very idiomatic English of the analytical tradition. But there, too, we will show that there are tensions, in particular the one that contrasts the great return of the psychologizing point of view (which has become inseparable from the debate on the various degrees of "physicalism" or "reductionism" authorized by cognitive psychology based on neurophysiology) with Wittgensteinian criticism and its logico-anthropological interpretations, which carry into the language of the philosophy of mind a Fregean problematic of the *Geist* in the sense of a "thought of content" and arrive at a paradoxical de-psychologization of psychology. It might seem that here we are dealing with a repetition of the opposition between Cartesianism and Lockean psychologism, with the qualification that in the "philosophy of mind" the interiority of the mind has basically been turned into an observable exteriority, and that in Wittgenstein the dimension of experience has moved toward a kind of praxis [πρᾶξις]: that of the uses of language, on which the description of the manifestations of mind is itself dependent. Thus we are confronted not so much by a repetition as by a revival whose formulations are henceforth inscribed within the framework of a single dominant idiom and its more or less approximate national translations.

I. The "Mental": A Catchall?

In modern languages, the notion of the "mental" (derived from Vulgar Latin *mentalis*, which itself derives from *mens*, designating the superior part or, for Christian theology, the immortal part, of the soul, *anima*) has come to cover a vast domain of experiences or phenomena that our spontaneous dualism opposes to the field of the physical or the biological. Apart from its use as a substantive in French, it is more or less rigorously identified with the technical term "psychic," which competes with it (particularly in psychoanalytic discourse, but Freud himself used the expressions *seelischer Apparat* and *psychischer Apparat* more or less interchangeably, both of them being rendered in French translations by *appareil psychique* [psychic apparatus] and occasionally by *appareil mental* [mental apparatus]). It has certainly benefited from the support provided by its association in English with the word "mind," which also derives etymologically from *mens* (*memini* [to remember, to cause to come to mind]; see MEMORY), and which frequently recurs in the discussion of the mind-body problem, that is, in the problematic of the psycho-physical or psycho-physiological correspondences that form the horizon of contemporary cognitivism.

■ See Box 1.

This tendency toward standardization should not prevent us from seeing that the term "mental" is a catchall from both the logical and the philological points of view. It has gradually absorbed semantic chains that have been distinct from one another since antiquity, some of them concerning the parts of the living organism and its behavior, others the structure, hierarchy, and destiny of souls, and still others the phenomena of consciousness and their relationship to intellectual processes and the perception of personal identity. The grouping of the meanings of the mental that is characteristic of what might be called modern psychologism in European culture (including a transcendental psychologism) has not, however, taken place in the same way in all languages, in particular because each language has its own terms for the powers of thought and imagination, or for the interiority of the self (in Italian, *ingenio*, or in German, *Gemüt*: see INGENIUM, GEMÜT).

However, *Geist*, *Gemüt*, and *Witz* are obviously no more subdivisions of the more general meaning designated by French *esprit* (even if Kant sometimes refers to French uses of this term) than the meaning of *âme* is distributed over *Seele* and *Gemüt*.

Similarly, French is led to translate by the single word *âme* the Latin terms *animus*, *anima*, and *mens*, but it also translates *mens* as *esprit*, thus creating an ambiguous relation with *spiritus* (whereas English has "the mind," and Italian and Spanish *mente*). German *Geist* is rendered in English by either "spirit" or "mind" (not to mention "ghost"), whence the two successive translations of Hegel's title: one psychologizing (*The Phenomenology of Mind*), which in the body of the text (at the beginning of chapter 4) couples the term with the adjective "spiritual" ("With this we already have before us the notion of *Mind* or *Spirit*"); the other theologizing (*Phenomenology of Spirit*). Finally, there are two terms in French (*âme*, *esprit*), whereas English has three ("mind," "soul," "spirit") or even four, with the archaic "wit" (see Box 1 in this entry), and this results in certain difficulties such as the ambiguity of the notion of *philosophie de l'esprit*, which is used in French to render the new "philosophy of mind."

■ See Box 2.

It can be suggested that these discrepancies themselves express different conceptions or perceptions of the mental that are both rooted in the culture and conceptualized by the history of philosophy. This idea, which may be combined with a precise philology, is nonetheless debatable in several respects.

First of all, it presupposes what is to be proved: the relative autonomy, uniform horizon, and permanence of the mental or psychic domain that the Greek, Latin, German, French, English, and other European-language words are said to designate and describe and among which a network of approximate translations is established. One of the fundamental contributions made by R. B. Onians (in his great book *The Origins of European Thought* [1951]) is to have challenged these postulates while at the same time illuminating in exciting ways the anthropological and cosmological notions originally covered by certain words (*phrēn* [φρήν], *thumos* [θυμός], *anima*, *genius*, and so forth). In other words, different corporal schemas, even if breath is privileged, can lead to the notion of mind (see Boxes 3, 4 in this entry).

Second, this idea can designate the referential signified or the general horizon of complementarities and substitutions only by means of expressions that themselves belong to this field and that reflect a certain, historically dated way of conceiving its organization. The same goes, obviously, for modern expressions such as "life" or "mental reality," "psyche," "psychical life," and so on.

Finally, this idea neglects or marginalizes the paradox to which all dictionaries attest, namely the fact that over time a given term in one language, for example, *Gemüt* in German, can be given virtually all the equivalents in each of the others: *âme*, *caractère*, *esprit*, *pensée*, *humeur*, and so forth (an amazing example that can be considered emblematic here is provided by the Basque *gogo*—see GEMÜT, GOGO), and the fact that the paradigmatic oppositions constantly reverse their value (for example, *âme* and *esprit* in relation to immanence and transcendence, materiality and immateriality).

This is not the place to discuss the whole development of the terminology of the "soul" and "spirit" in various European languages to how it has been sedimented and renewed from antiquity to the present time, as well as the problems of transfer and equivalence that have resulted from it (see UNDERSTANDING and INTELLECT, INTELLECTUS). But we will examine two major successive moments that crucially shaped the terminology of the "mental," even though they are very heterogeneous: Descartes's awkward position between several languages and several "souls" and Locke's invention of the "mind"—the first great attempt to define the "interiority" of thought, immediately accessible to itself, which antiquity had situated only as a divine ideal of wisdom or beyond death, and

1

"Mind," "soul," "body": The example of Hume

English has three words, "mind," "soul," and "spirit," where French has only two (âme, esprit). Modern, nonreligious works on what the French call esprit clearly prefer the term "mind." But it has to be recognized that the three terms are to a large extent interchangeable, since some expressions have become almost phrasal (as when Hume refers to the "passions of the soul" [A Treatise of Human Nature, 395] and not of "passions of the mind," just as in French one speaks of passions de l'âme, that is, without thinking of the religious sense or the moral value of soul). Here we will be concerned chiefly with the example of Hume, which is both representative of the classical problem and particularly helpful in understanding its repercussions in contemporary philosophy.

If we try to discern Hume's intentions, we see the meanings distributed rather insistently as follows:

"Mind" is opposed to "spirit" by its different relationship to "body." There are in Hume countless uses of the phrase "mind or body" (Treatise, 439) or "mind and body" (ibid., 453, 489) that imply, if not an identity of mind and body, at least the possibility of a similar theoretical treatment of them corresponding to a certain resemblance between the objects. It would be harder to say "spirit and body" or "spirit or body" precisely because "spirit" indicates a nonphysical principle in humans or participation in a nonmaterial or even immaterial reality.

"Mind" and "body" are associated through a certain resemblance, if not a community, of "frame and constitution" (ibid., 488, 583). Just as the body is a system of organs, the mind is an integrated set of perceptual laws, or of impressions and ideas, whose limits are no more fixed than the ectoderm fixes the precise limits of a body in its environment or designates the surface that provides access to what is external to this body. When Hume asserts that "mankind [is] nothing but a bundle or collection of different perceptions, which succeed each other with an inconceivable rapidity, and are in a perpetual flux and movement" (ibid., Treatise, 252), he is returning—through Indo-European men, included in "mankind"—to a very old sense of the word "mind," and this allows him to problematize the limits of this "bundle or collection," its self and its incorporeal nature. In any case, etymological dictionaries emphasize the possibility that English "mind" may have its origin in Indo-European men or

man, which means "make use of one's mind," "think" (see MEMORY). Consider, for instance, the article "mind" in RT: The Oxford Dictionary of English Etymology (577) and also in Origins: An Etymological Dictionary of Modern English (Routledge [1966], 404). The latter, while emphasizing that the derivation of "man" from man (think) has been discredited, nonetheless adds that it can be proven to be correct. The second edition of the Oxford English Dictionary (11:284) adopts a closely related position. The Barnhart Dictionary of Etymology (H. W. Wilson [1988]) says the same thing. It is the functioning of laws that produces the true limits of the mind, which is in itself limitless.

In order for "spirit" to recover its original material meaning—in his Chrestomathia, Jeremy Bentham reminds us of its proximity to "breath," spiritus—it has to be plural; then, in the form of "spirits" (Hume, Treatise, 420–23, 427) it frequently confuses translators who are led astray by the expressions "in high spirits" and "in low spirits," forgetting the material sense of the "animal spirits" that in the eighteenth century were still thought to circulate in our nervous system.

"Mind" is the term that privileges the psyche least and allows us to adhere more strictly to the descriptive and explanatory. On the other hand, "spirit" is primarily a term of valorization, against materiality, against dependency on the laws, against spatiality and temporality. It is easier to say "in the mind" or "into the mind" (Hume, Treatise, 420–21, 426, 441, 446, 453), "out of the mind," or even "on the mind" or "upon the mind" (ibid., 410, 422, 473, 527) than "in the spirit," or "out of the spirit," expressions that become completely absurd insofar as the notion of "spirit" implies a real separation from the body. The abstract tendency of "spirit" is seen particularly in the difficulty of using "human spirit" to refer to the human mind, whereas French forces the speaker to use the expression esprit humain in this context. On the other hand, in English it is easy to speak of the "human mind" (ibid., 423), even if it involves redundancy, as the previously mentioned Indo-European root suggests. Human beings share "spirit" with the angels, whether the term is used seriously or ironically.

The metaphysical tendency of "soul" is different from that of "spirit," in that it plays a role less in an opposition between different kinds of substance than in a reflection on destiny, with a much more marked religious connotation (even though Hume speaks of

"supreme spirit or deity"). We never speak of the immortality or immateriality of the mind, but only of the immortality or immateriality of the soul (Hume, Treatise, I.4.§5). The nature of the "soul" is the explicit object of "metaphysical disputes" (ibid., 236); this is not exactly the case for "mind" or even for "spirit." It is "human souls" that correspond (592) and have a "simple essence." On the other hand, the "mind" evolves only by stages, configurations, and situations for which a dynamics can account. "[The] mind runs along a certain train of ideas" (406); "the mind naturally runs on with any train of action, which it has begun" (565). "Mind" is opposed topically to "spirit," dynamically to "soul."

Finally, far from opposing itself to its objects, the mind is supposed to have a tendency to subject them to the laws that govern itself. Thus the mind, in its theoretical activity, "balances contrary experiments" (Hume, Treatise, 403); we would hardly see "soul" or "spirit" engaged in a similar process of imitating their objects.

The greater value accorded "soul" or "spirit" at the expense of "mind" can also be seen in the way spiritual force is described. No matter how physical it is, the word "strength," which is used to qualify the vigor of a body, is nonetheless more often applied to "spirit" and "soul" than to "mind" (Hume, Treatise, 433–35), because of its relative archaism in comparison with the term "force," which is felt to belong to a modern dynamics more likely to be applied to "mind" and to the discovery of its laws. The word "force" is less valorized, less loaded with affectivity than "strength" or "vigor," just as "mind" is less valorized than "spirit" or "soul," which remain inseparable from a philosophy dominated by affectivity and moral values. It is for "soul" to have the old aristocratic virtues of vigor, "courage and magnanimity" (ibid., 434) and to seek out suitable adversaries in the quest for a grandeur which the philosopher of mind, who has read Cervantes, hardly believes in anymore (435).

Jean-Pierre Cléro

BIBLIOGRAPHY

Bentham, Jeremy. Chrestomathia. Edited by M. J. Smith and W. H. Burston. Oxford: Clarendon Press, 1983.
Hume, David. A Treatise of Human Nature. Edited by L. A. Selby-Bigge and P. H. Nidditch. Oxford: Clarendon Press, 1978. First published 1739–40.

2

The ambiguity of the expression *philosophie de l'esprit*

The French expression *philosophie de l'esprit* refers to two theoretical orientations that are foreign to each other (P. Engel, *Introduction à la philosophie de l'esprit*). The first refers to the doctrine of philosophers attached to mind-body dualism, such as Louis Lavelle and René Le Senne. From this point of view, a materialist philosophy of mind would be a contradiction in terms. The second refers to a thematic field rather than to a doctrine—the mental, and not the spiritual. The philosophy of mind understood in this sense is interested in the nature of mental phenomena and in their relations with behavior; recently, it has also examined their relations with cerebral phenomena. So conceived, the philosophy of mind has always constituted a domain of philosophical interest—the analysis of the faculties of the mind (sense perception, memory, imagination) or relations between the body and the mind. However, a domain was not constituted explicitly under this name until the second half of the twentieth century, in the wake of the philosophy of language.

The term *philosophie de l'esprit* nonetheless remains subject to ambiguity insofar as it is applied to two different types of reflection (these two types corresponding, as might be expected, to very different styles of argumentation). The first, inspired by the so-called ordinary language tradition or by Husserl's phenomenology, conceives the philosophy of mind as a purely conceptual analysis based on the common experience and understanding of states of consciousness (Ryle, *The Concept of Mind*; Hornsby, *Simple Mindedness*). The second holds that the philosophy of mind can develop fruitfully only by including in its reflection scientific knowledge regarding the mind and the brain (Engel, *Introduction à la philosophie de l'esprit*). Willard Van Orman Quine's rejection (in his "Two Dogmas of Empiricism") of the distinction between analytical propositions, which are true by virtue of their meaning, and synthetic propositions, which are true by virtue of experience, has led many analytical philosophers to turn to the cognitive sciences to raise the classical problems of philosophy (such as the nature of self-knowledge or of representation) in a way that is enriched by, and compatible with, the contributions of these sciences. Today, some phenomenologists challenge Husserl's antipsychologism by seeking to naturalize the concept of consciousness (Petitot, Varela, and Pachoud, *Naturalizing Phenomenology*).

The development of the cognitive sciences has certainly favored the development of a naturalistic philosophy of mind by making available to philosophy information that stimulates its reflection on the nature of the mental. But we must not confuse naturalistic philosophy of mind with the philosophy of psychology or with cognitive philosophy. The former produces original arguments intended to naturalize traditional philosophical concepts (Rey, *Contemporary Philosophy of Mind*), whereas the philosophy of psychology offers a critical evaluation of the analyses and methods applied in psychology (Grünbaum, *Validation in the Critical Theory of Psychoanalysis*). Cognitive philosophy, on the other hand, participates directly in scientific activity by contributing to the development of concepts or by proposing experimental schemas (Dennett, *Consciousness Explained*).

Joëlle Proust

BIBLIOGRAPHY

Dennett, Daniel C. *Consciousness Explained*. Boston: Little, Brown and Company, 1991.
Engel, Pascal: *Introduction à la philosophie de l'esprit*. Paris : La Découverte, 1994.
Grünbaum, Adolf: *Validation in the Clinical Theory of Psychoanalysis*. Psychological Issues, no. 61. Madison, CT: International Universities Press, 1993.
Hornsby, Jennifer: *Simple Mindedness: In Defense of Naïve Naturalism in the Philosophy of Mind*. Cambridge, MA: Harvard University Press, 1997.
Petitot, Jean, Francisco Varela, and Bernard Pachoud, eds. *Naturalizing Phenomenology*. Stanford : Stanford University Press, 2000.
Quine, Willard Van Orman. "Two Dogmas of Empiricism." In *From a Logical Point of View*. New York : Harper and Row, 1953. 20–46.
Rey, George: *Contemporary Philosophy of Mind*. Oxford: Blackwell, 1997.
Ryle, Gilbert: *The Concept of Mind*. London : Hutchinson, 1949.

that contemporary philosophy, psychology, and neurophysiology have, it seems, lost again, either in the depths of the unconscious or in the objectivity of behavior and brain processes.

- See Boxes 3 and 4.

Our hypothesis is that "translation problems" are characteristic of a "threshold" of modernity that extends, roughly speaking, from Descartes to Hegel, and whose Lockean, Humean, and Kantian stages must be considered decisive. The "psychology" or "noology" of antiquity was either transmitted from Greek and Latin in accord with a terminology that is now part of history, or it arose from a more general problem whose importance we are only beginning to see (cf. once again Onians and Box 3 in this entry): that of the conceptions of the human animal peculiar to a civilization whose experiences, and hence modes of thought, are now very distant from us (which does not mean that they are not capable of being rethought and brought up-to-date). So far as contemporary disciplines are concerned, we can acknowledge that the translation of their terminology is largely a matter of convention (at least within the European or Western sphere), even if it may be enlightening to understand the connotations of certain terms in their original languages (see Box 6 on Wittgenstein and the "philosophy of mind").

On the other hand, so far as the metaphysics of *âme* and *esprit*, of *mens* and "mind," *ingenium,* and *Gemüt* and *Geist* in the early modern period is concerned, what is untranslatable or imperfectly translatable clearly manifests the confrontation of the strategies deployed to "think thought" in the context of a revolutionary anthropology. "Homo cogitat," Spinoza posits as an axiom at the beginning of the second part (*De mente*) of his *Ethics*, but what does "think" mean? And precisely what thinks in "man"? These questions, to be sure, are no longer the ones we ask. But we cannot claim that they have disappeared from our horizon. It is no accident that they were asked—in this diversity—at a time when philosophy was emerging from an apparent linguistic uniformity, passing into vernaculars and seeking a new universality that would include them (so that Latin itself became, in Descartes and Spinoza, one idiom among others).

3

Onians's Greeks: *Thumos, âme-sang* and *psuchê, âme-souffle*

One of the effects of Onians's work is to force us to retranslate ancient texts, particularly those of Homer and the tragedians: we can no longer accept, for example, the translation of the cry repeated by the Furies in Aeschylus's *Eumenides, thumon aie, mater Nux* [θυμὸν ἄιε, μᾶτερ Νύξ], literally "inspire me with breath, Mother Night," as "Hear me, Mother Night" (*The Oresteia*, trans. I. C. Johnston). Onians's whole method (unlike that of Bruno Snell, for instance) consists in interpreting in a radically nonmetaphysical way words and expressions referring to the body, that is—and this is the order followed in his work and emphasized in the title—"spirit," "soul," "world," "time," and "fate." This brings out two ancillary characteristics: on the one hand, thoughts and emotions are rooted in the body, or in modern terms, there is no separation between *res cogitans* and *res extensa*; on the other hand, the body is not entirely the same as our own, we no longer have the same organs as Homeric heroes. As a result, not only must translations be revised, but some translations are impossible.

Using etymology and cross-references like a detective, Onians sets out to find "the seat of consciousness." The spiritual part of our being, thought, intelligence, or mind, is designated primarily by the word *thumos* [θυμός], "which appears to be something vaporous," a "breath," a "vapor" fed by the ferment of the blood, a "blood-soul" (cf. Onians, *Origins of European Thought*, I.2, esp. 39–40). Onians connects *thumos* with *thumaio* [θυμιάω], "to smoke" (Chantraine [RT: *Dictionnaire étymologique de la langue grecque*] mentions instead *thuô* [θύω], with a long *u*, "rush furiously forward," like the wind, for instance, and distinguishes it from *thuô* [θύω], "to sacrifice," which is used chiefly to refer to offerings that are burned and that smoke). *Thumos* denotes the heart, ardor, courage, the hero's combative enthusiasm; hot, it is contained in the *phrenes* [φρενές] and the *prapides* [πραπίδες], which designate not the "diaphragm," as the word is commonly translated, nor the "pericardium" (for *phrên*, RT: LSJ gives "midriff, heart, mind" and "will, purpose"; for *prapides* it gives "midriff, diaphragm," and "understanding, mind"), but rather the "lungs," thick, dense, spongy (Onians, *Origins of European Thought*, I.3, esp. 55, 68); death destroys and breaks the *thumos*. Close to the *thumos*, the *êtor* [ἦτορ], situated in the *phrenes* but also in an organ that can be either the heart or the stomach (called *kardia* [καρδία], *kradiê* [κραδίη]) and is responsible for respiration, the heartbeat, and the pulse. Stimulated by the emotions, it laughs, and when one speaks to oneself, one

is speaking to it as one does to the *thumos* (ibid., 105; see CONSCIOUSNESS, Box 1).

Both words, *thumos* and *êtor*, differ from the *psuchê* [ψυχή], another way of referring to the breath, this time in the sense of respiration, breathing (the Indo-European root **bhes-*, "to breathe," as for *phêmi* [φημί], "say"): this "breath-soul" in contradistinction to the "blood-soul" constituted by the *thumos*, is cold and situated in the head; in Homer it designates particularly the separated soul of the dead that escapes the body like a puff of smoke (*Iliad*, XXI.100), flies away like a moth or bat (*Odyssey*, XXIV.6), or a dream (*Odyssey*, XI.222), to live in Hades in the form of an *eidôlon* [εἴδωλον], "phantom," that preserves the form or "image" (see EIDÔLON and MIMÊSIS), and as a *skia* [σκιά], shade (Onians, *Origins of European Thought*, II.1, 119–23; cf. the *nekuia* [journey to the underworld], *Odyssey*, XI, where translator V. Bérard regularly renders both *psuchê* and *skia* as "shade" [*ombre*], and *thumos* by "soul" [*âme*], for example, pp. 204–24).

Finally, *noos* [νόος] or *nous* [νοῦς] (which Onians associates with *neomai* [νέομαι], "I go," *neô* [νέω], "I swim"), described as "in" the *thumos*, defines it "as in a sense a current consists of but defines air or water" (Onians, *Origins of European Thought*, 107); with the result that it is valorized as "intelligence, intellect," while remaining less manifestly material than the *phrenes*. Basically it is something like a "current of consciousness" that perceives through the senses ("It is the *nous* that sees and it is the *nous* that hears; all the rest is deaf and blind" (see Onians, ibid., 108; see UNDERSTANDING, Box 1).

Conflations of organs, "mental" distinctions that remain indiscernible for us: Homer's world can explain our own (it allows us, Onians emphasizes, to understand what we are saying, the beliefs that persist in our traditional expressions and acts—we "swallow" what someone says, a poet is "inspired," the last kiss given a dying person always collects only the *psuchê* that escapes, etc.), but it cannot coincide with our world.

This distance between Homer's world and ours is connected in particular with the fact that we have inherited a whole philosophical reworking that, as early as Plato and Aristotle, hierarchizes and unifies complementary powers in terms of *dunameis* [δύναμεις], all of these powers belonging to the *psuchê*, in other words, to "faculties of the mind." *Psuchê* becomes a generic term covering *nous* and *thumos*, and takes on new distinctions like the one between *dianoia* [διάνοια] (literally, "what crosses the *nous*," translated as

"intelligence, thought, project") or *epithumia* (literally, "what is on the *thumos*," translated as "desire" or "the desiring faculty"). In the course of the *Republic* and the *Timaeus*, a tripartite analogy is constructed that holds both for each individual's *psuchê*, for his body, and for the social body—or should we say the social soul?—constituted by the city-state (*politeia* [πολιτεία], see POLIS). At the top is *logistic*, which "decides" (*ho logos* [ὁλόγος], *to logistikon* [τὸ λογιστικόν], *to bouleutikon* [τὸ βουλευτικόν], see LOGOS), that is, the head, and thus the guardians or the philosopher-king, everything that has to do with *logos, nous, dianoia*, rational decision, destined to be immortal; in the middle, the humors, ardor, or the thymic part (*to thumoeidês* [τὸ θυμοειδής]), that is, the chest and thorax, with the heart, lungs, diaphragm, and thus the warriors or guardians who "provide help" (*to epikourêtikon* [τὸ ἐπικουρητικόν]); at the bottom, the desiring faculty (*to epithumêtikon* [τὸ ἐπιθυμητικόν]), or the lower abdomen, between the diaphragm and the navel, and thus producers and merchants who nourish and create wealth (*to chrêmatistikon* [τὸ χρηματιστικόν]). Each person has his own virtue: the top is "wise" (*sophos* [σοφός]); the middle "courageous" or "virile" (*andreios* [ἀνδρεῖος]), and the bottom "tempering" (*sôphron* [σώφρων]); as for the structure itself, it is "just" insofar as each faculty, like each entity, remains in its place (cf. *Republic*, IV.434c–444e; IX.580d–581e; see also the anatomy lesson in the *Timaeus*, 69d–76e, and the myth in the *Phaedrus*, 256a–b, 253c–254e). The organic has thus become an ethical-political diagram.

With Aristotle and the natural sciences, the hierarchy internal to the soul, which also creates a hierarchy among souls, becomes the theme of a hierarchy of species: the soul, Aristotle says very simply, is "not a body, but something bodily (*sôma men gar ouk esti, somatos de ti* [σῶμα μὲν γὰρ οὐκ ἔστι, σώματος δέ τι]), *De anima*, II.2.414a.20–21). To a given body belonging to a genus and species corresponds a soul endowed with a given faculty or potentiality, and not necessarily all of them. Thus plants (*ta phuta* [τὰ φυτά], "what grows") have only the "nutritive faculty" (*to threptikon* [τὸ θρεπτικόν]). Some living beings (*ta zôia* [τὰ ζῷα], see ANIMAL) also have the "sensitive faculty" (*tò aisthêtikon* [τὸ αἰσθητικόν]) and at the same time, through the sense of touch, the "appetitive faculty" (*to orektikon* [τὸ ὀρεκτικόν]), which includes *epithumia* [ἐπιθυμία], *thumos*, and *boulêsis* [βούλησις], desire, ardor,

(continued)

(continued)

and will, that is, very precisely the Platonic tripartite division, thus forcibly concentrated under the appetite that flows from sensation. Some animals have in addition the "faculty of moving in accord with the place (*to kata topon kinêtikon* [τὸ κατὰ τόπον κινητικόν]). Finally a very small number, humans in any case, also have the "thinking faculty" (*dianoêtikon, logismon kai dianoian* [διανοητικόν, λογισμὸν καὶ διάνοιαν])—"as for the theoretical faculty (*peri de tou theôretikou* [περὶ δὲ τοῦ θεωρητικοῦ], intelligence or speculative

intellect, that is another question" (*De anima*, II.3.414a.29–41b.14).

These terminological reinvestments testify to the fact that the distance among Greeks, between the heroic body and the rational animal, is no smaller than that between the Greeks and us.

Barbara Cassin

BIBLIOGRAPHY

Aeschylus. *The Oresteia*. Translated by Ian C. Johnston. Arlington, VA: Richer Resources Publications, 2007.

Homer. *Odyssée*. Translated by Victor Bérard. Paris: Gallimard / La Pléiade, 1973. Translation first published in 1924.

Onians, Richard Broxton. *The Origins of European Thought: About the Body, the Mind, the Soul, the World, Time and Fate*. Cambridge: Cambridge University Press, 1951.

Snell, Bruno. *Die Entdeckung des Geistes. Studien zur Entstehung des europäischen Denken bei den Griechen*. Göttingen, Ger.: Vandenhoeck and Ruprecht, 1975. Translation by Thomas Gustav Rosenmeyer: *The Discovery of the Mind: In Greek Philosophy and Literature*. New York : Dover, 1982.

4
"Soul" and Hebrew *nèphèš* [נֶפֶשׁ], *rûah* [רוּחַ], and *nešāmā* [נְשָׁמָה]

The word designating the soul, *nèphèš* [נֶפֶשׁ], is often derived from the idea of "breath," and more precisely from the respiration, the vital breath whose presence signals life, and which leaves the body at the moment that one dies or "expires." In that regard, Semitic languages do not differ from Greek. In its first written occurrence (*Iliad*, I.3), Greek *psuchê* [ψυχή] is already specialized in the sense of "soul." On the other hand, the Hebrew *nèphèš* is still attested in concrete senses: "gullet" (Is 5:14b; Pr 27:7) or "breath" (Job 41:13). The word is employed chiefly in reference to humans; the *nèphèš* of God is almost never mentioned. This soul is the seat of all mental, intellectual, and emotive activities (cf. Maimonides, *Guide for the Perplexed*, I.41). Whatever has a soul is therefore "animate," alive; the word is used to designate life, as when one says "don't leave a soul alive." It is frequently used, as the word *èsèm* [עֶצֶם], "bone" is also used, as a reflexive pronoun (e.g., 1 Sm 18:1). To do something to one's soul is to do it to oneself, to one's self.

The Hebrew word for "spirit," *rûah* [רוּחַ], has a multitude of meanings, and efforts

have been made to distinguish among them in the exegetes and also in the philosophers (cf. Maimonides, *Guide*, 1.40; Hobbes, *Leviathan*, III.34; Spinoza, *Tractatus theologico-politicus*, 1). The etymology allows us to clarify matters somewhat: originally, *rûah* meant "wind." It still has this meaning in the Gospel of John, which says (in Greek, however), that the *pneuma* [πνεῦμα] blows wherever it wishes. Moreover, an old image sees the wind as God's breath (Ps. 18:16b). It is this meteorological rooting that makes it possible, in certain contexts, to distinguish *rûah* from *nèphèš*: the former is a breath exterior to the organism. But as a result, the word can be used to designate what comes from outside, invading and filling the organism. The outside can be the absolute Other; thus we often speak of God's "spirit," and almost never of his "soul." To be filled with the spirit is reserved for certain exceptional individuals: it descends upon the "judge" and makes him go completely berserk, usually in order to help him play his political role as the

dictator who saves the people (Jgs 3:10, 6:34, 11:29), sometimes in a private matter (Jgs 14:6, 9). The spirit is laid upon the prophet (1 Sm 10:6). The king represents a kind of institutionalization of *rûah*: in him, the effects of the spirit are permanent (Jgs 16:13). The idea of artistic inspiration is discreetly anticipated. It is attributed, not to an inspiration coming from the Muses, as in Greece (Hesiod, *Theogony*, 1.31), but from the divine spirit, given to Betsalel, the artisan of the temple (Ex 31:3).

Nešāmāh [נְשָׁמָה], derived from a verb probably meaning "to pant" (Isaiah 42:14), also designates the vital breath. Thus God breathes into the human form that he has just shaped the breath (*nešāmāh*) of life, and man becomes a living "soul" (*nèphèš*) (Gn 2:7). However, *nešāmāh* is used only with reference to humans, whereas *nèphèš* is also used for animals. It is also as well in the sense of "to be alive" (e.g., Dt 20:16). The Septuagint usually renders it by *pnoê* [πνοή], "breath."

Rémi Brague

II. Descartes and the Problem of Multiple *Âmes*

A. Latin-French reciprocity

With Descartes, we might hope to find a simple situation. At the center of his metaphysics there is a formula he uses in the *Discourse on Method* and repeats in the French translation of the *Meditations*: "this self, that is, my soul (*âme*) through which I am what I am." But how can we understand this strange equivalence literally? The textual evidence may be complicated by the fact that Descartes writes in two

languages between which there is a notorious terminological discrepancy in the area of psychology.

It is important to understand that Descartes' relationship to these two idioms is not unilateral but rather circular or reciprocal. The philosopher who sometimes calls himself René and sometimes Renatus did not write (and think) first in Latin and then translate himself into French, but neither did he write first in French and then seek, in order to communicate his thoughts, a Latin equivalent. It is easy to see that while Descartes's French retains Latin rhetorical patterns and transposes a terminology taken from the ancients and from Scholasticism (for example, "subject" [*sujet*] for *subjectum*, which is moreover rare), his very classical Latin (more that of the Jesuit schools than that of the universities) sometimes coins expressions that have a French background. Some of his texts were written first in Latin, others in French. There is no hierarchy between them. Translations were made in both directions, usually under the author's supervision. The discrepancy between the two idioms overdetermines the expression of a doctrine that evolves over time as it coheres into a system and is confronted by unanticipated questions and objections.

Should we conclude, then, that the relationship between *mens*, *esprit*, and *âme* poses a problem of translation? If that is the case, Descartes provides an explicit solution, but the question is whether he is able to maintain it throughout. In Latin, he rejects the word *anima* and chooses the word *mens*, to which he gives the meaning of *res* (i.e., *substantia*) *cogitans*. When he writes in French, he uses *âme* in the same sense, despite the etymology, but has to explain it. But in the translations from Latin to French, he authorized the use of *esprit* (particularly in the *Meditations*, translated by the Duke of Luynes), even though in the end it was the equivalence *mens* = *âme* that was finally made official, as it were (*Replies to Objections, Principles of Philosophy*). However, the difficulties, which were not to be inconsequential for later Cartesianism, arose from four facts: (1) the word *anima* is not totally proscribed, it is found in the "paratext" of the *Meditations*; (2) the term *mens* itself gives rise to ambiguities, because the meaning Descartes gives it is contrary to the traditional one (especially in the Augustinian and Thomist tradition); (3) the fluctuation of the "authorized" translations of *mens* between *âme* and *esprit* is not purely a matter of convention: each of these terms has connotations that affect the core of the theory, and this also means that in a way neither of the two terms is quite right; (4) *anima* reappears in the Latin translation of Descartes's last work, the *Passiones animae*: a translation that is, admittedly, posthumous, but whose basis has to be sought in the work itself.

B. The ever-immortal *anima*

An examination of the titles under which Descartes's *Meditations* were published is intriguing. In Latin (first edition 1641): *Renati Descartes Meditationes de prima philosophia in qua* [sic] *Dei exsistentia et animae immortalitas demonstratur*; (second edition 1642): *R. D. Meditationes de prima philosophia, in quibus Dei exsistencia et animae humanae a corpore distinctio demonstrantur*; in French (1647): *Les méditations philosophiques de René Descartes touchant la première philosophie dans lesquelles l'existence de Dieu et la distinction réelle entre l'âme et le corps de l'homme sont démontrées*. In the rest of the text, including the intermediary subtitles, Descartes systemically uses *mens* (*Meditatio Secunda: De natura mentis humanae. Quod ipsa sit notior quam corpus*; *Meditatio Sexta: De rerum materialium exsistentia, et reali mentis a corpore distinctione*); the French translation systematically renders *mens* by *esprit*, except in this last subtitle (*Méditation sixième: De l'existence des choses matérielles, et de la réelle distinction entre l'âme et le corps de l'homme*). The dedicatory epistle to "Messieurs le Doyen et Docteurs de la Sacrée Faculté de Théologie de Paris" also uses *anima/âme*, whereas

the abridged edition of the *Meditationes* alternates between *animae immortalitas* and *mentis immortalitas*.

From this we might conclude that the use of *anima* is a *captatio benevolentiae* directed toward theologians imbued with Scholasticism. Without ignoring this reference to the conditions of "the art of writing" in the French classical age, we can complement it with an intrinsic interpretation. The formula closest to the doctrinal content of the *Meditations* is obviously the one that refers to the "real distinction" (that is, the distinction in substance) between the soul/mind and the body, for which only the appropriate term is *mens*, in the Cartesian sense. The text suggests that this thesis is a logical presupposition of the thesis regarding immortality (which is not demonstrated). But from one to the other there is a leap that Descartes is not able to evade or reduce. Only the expression *animae immortalitas* really has an accepted theological meaning, and it connotes "first philosophy" (as was indicated by the first Latin title). Descartes can dispense with it only by abandoning not only the hope of being understood by orthodox thinkers but also a whole part of his doctrine (in particular the claim in the Third and Fourth Meditations that there is a resemblance between human nature and the Divine, and perhaps also the claim that there are "innate ideas" that God has placed within us as "seeds of truth").

C. *Mens*, "soul/mind," and the act of *ego cogitans*

What then is the problem raised by the meaning of the word *mens*, and what indirect light could the translations of this term by "soul" and "mind" shed on it? In the same year, 1644, the Latin translation of Descartes's *Discourse of Method* appeared, in which *âme* (soul) is translated by *mens*, as well as the French versions of the *Meditationes* produced by Luynes (who renders *mens* by *esprit*) and by Clerselier (who renders *mens* by *âme*), and finally the Latin *Principia*, in which Descartes gives his system a "definitive" expression. He clearly settles his choice on the *mens/âme* couple, objecting as early as 1641, in a letter to Mersenne, to the "ambiguity" of *anima* (which confuses the vegetative or motor principle with a faculty of thought, bringing *res cogitans* back into the sphere of "animation" and "organization," as in Aristotle, where the soul is the "form of the body"—an objection that is repeated and explained in the *Responses to the Second and Third Objections*). However, since the eighth and ninth principles of the first part of the *Principia* collect under the rubric of the *âme* (*mens*) the totality of the modes of thought (*cogitatio*), including sensation, as "actions" separate from the body, one might wonder why in the French *Meditations* he accepts without correction the translation by *esprit* (which also includes paradoxical echoes of the body: consider "animal spirits" and the alchemical use of the term in the sense of "subtle matter").

We see two reasons for this. The first, which is stylistic and philosophical, is that in this way Descartes is able to establish a connection between the characteristic expressions of his metadiscourse that reflect the nature of the activity or mental exercise called "meditation" (in particular *mente concipere* [conceive in (my) mind], *inspectio mentis* [inspection of the mind], *in ipsa mente* [(ideas found) in the mind itself], *in meipsum mentis aciem converto* [I reflect on myself], etc.) and the expressions of the doctrinal discourse regarding the nature of thinking thing (*res cogitans*). Paradoxically, in seventeenth-century French only the word *esprit* makes it possible to refer to the subject of meditation, that is, to the reality or actuality (or even the performativity) of thought thinking itself, which Descartes also calls the understanding, and which in his first, unfinished essay, the *Rules for the Direction of the Mind*, he had called in Latin *ingenium*). Here the term *âme* paradoxically seems to have a spiritual and even mystical meaning, as it later did in the work of Malebranche.

But this leads us to a deeper reason that we can try to approach by the *via negativa*. In fact, neither *âme* nor *esprit* is really suitable, because in Descartes *mens* designates not only the "substance" whose whole essence consists in thinking (or whose essence merges with its "principal attribute," *cogitatio*), but also connotes the presence of the subject in his thought, or the fact that thought grasps its own essence only in the first person. Thus one would have to be able to designate immediately by *mens*, or by one of its translations, not only the subject of thought as a "thing," but also the fact or "act" itself of the *cogito*, or better yet, the *ego sum cogitans*. This is, strictly speaking, impossible, but Descartes never ceased to seek to approximate it through a series of formulas in Latin and French, two of the most remarkable of which are the one in the *Discourse*, part 4, already cited (see I/ME/MYSELF): "This self, that is, the soul, through which I am what I am," which in the Latin version becomes *Adeo ut ego, hoc est mens*, and the one in the Second Meditation, *Quid autem dicam de hac ipsa mente, sive de me ipso?* rendered as "What shall I say about this mind, that is, about myself?" We see that Descartes, at the precise moment when this ipseity is recognized, formulated in order to name "the thing that thinks" a generalized equivalence that also proves that none of the necessary terms is sufficient, and that singularly qualifies the importance of the fact that from one language to the other, their correspondence cannot be exact (if Luynes had accepted *âme*, he would have had four terms out of four, not three out of four):

sum igitur praecise tantum res cogitans, id est, mens, sive animus, sive animus, sive intellectus, sive ratio, voces mihi prius significationis ignotae.

(Thus I am, strictly speaking, only a thing that thinks, that is, a mind, an understanding, or a reason, which are terms whose meaning was previously unknown to me.)

(Descartes, Second Meditation; trans. Lunes)

What the oscillation between *âme* and *esprit*—the first term more theological, the second more epistemological—ultimately shows is that they no more translate an original Latin *mens* than the latter truly renders their signifieds, which is impossible as such and in any case is irreducible to the form of a "substantive," since it refers to an action: the act of thinking (oneself) in the first person, inevitably implying a short circuit between the utterance and the act of enunciation. The French and Latin names circle around the sought-after signification.

D. "The passions": An eclipse of the mind

There remains the problem raised by the translation of Descartes's last work: *The Passions of the Soul* (*Les passions de l'âme*,

1649). In Latin, the book becomes *Passiones animae, per Renatum Descartes, gallice ab ipso conscriptae, nunc autem in exterorum gratiam latina civitate donatae. Ab H. D. M. j. u. l.* It is true that this translation (made by Henri Desmarets, and brought out a few months later by the same publisher as the original Latin version, Elzevier) was not reviewed by Descartes, who had just died. Once again a contextual explanation offers itself, this time with reference to the tradition of philosophical and medical works on the passions, a tradition to which Descartes belongs and that goes back to antiquity (*pathê* [πάθη] or *pathêmata tês psuchês* [παθήματα τῆς ψυχῆς], a Platonic and Aristotelian expression transmitted through Stoicism; see PATHOS). But this explanation merely deepens the paradox. At the heart of the treatise we find one of the theses that justified the privilege accorded to the word *mens*: the "indivisibility" of the soul into parts that are distinct, and a fortiori hierarchical, which is reaffirmed in principle 47 ("For there is in us only one soul, and this soul has in itself no diversity of parts: it is the same that is sensitive and rational, and all its appetites are wills"). Which means that in the *Discourse*, the *Meditations*, and the *Principles* the soul that is affected by the passions is always, in principle, the "thing" or *res* that "thinks." It is just that here a new, "passive" modality of cogitare is explored in detail. But beneath this doctrinal continuity, a shift has taken place. On the one hand, the renewed criticism of the physical representation of the soul as a system of organic parts or functions has as its correlate a singular insistence on their qualitative diversity or on the ethical inequality of the individuals with whom the souls are identified: there are "great souls" and "low or vulgar souls," as Descartes's correspondence with Princess Elizabeth explains in counterpoint. Once again, a stylistic feature encounters a theoretical question. On the other hand, and above all, the self-certainty that is at the heart of the Cartesian doctrine assumes here an unforeseen form that practically inverts the preceding one. As in the Sixth Meditation, it is the paradox of the "union" of two absolutely distinct substances that is the object of analysis. But whereas the Sixth Meditation concentrated its attention on the intellectual clarity of the "distinction" (even in perceptual illusions), *The Passions of the Soul* is devoted to the moral properties of the confused experience we have of the substantial union. This human body that we "are" not, is nonetheless not foreign to us: an idea that is intellectually obscure but indubitable as a sensation or feeling. Therefore if we try to imagine a translation such as *passiones mentis* we can see its insufficiency and even its impossibility.

This does not mean that the translation by *anima* is satisfactory. Descartes has not returned to an Aristotelian conception of the soul as the "form of the body." Nor has he returned to the theological tradition (on the contrary, the ethics of the *Passions* is clearly antitheological, and the underlying metaphysics includes blasphemous aspects, in particular in its too-human reconstitution of the mysteries of the Incarnation). He has defined a new field of experience in which there is still "thought" but not, strictly speaking, "understanding." The real question is why he did not use the language of the "heart," which is that of the tragedians and moralists, and which intersects with some of the key notions in his ethics ("generosity"), especially when they concern the analogy of the relation to oneself and the relation to others (which Descartes subsumes under the single notion of "esteem"). The answer is probably that this term is too closely connected with the discourse of the mystics. Nonetheless, it is difficult to avoid the impression that there is a correspondence between the enigma (the conjunction of the body and the soul) subsisting at the heart of the system and the impossibility of unambiguously designating the subject of thought. For this strange proximity of spiritualism and materialism, which will persist in Descartes's posterity, no learned or ordinary language, no system of translation, can offer any more than an approximation.

III. Fluctuations in the Seventeenth and Eighteenth Centuries

A description of the place of the terms *âme* (soul) and *esprit* (mind) in French philosophers and essayists of the seventeenth century would probably be very revealing of the configurations or "points of heresy" (as Foucault would say) that characterized the philosophical discourse of that time. In large measure, it either proceeds from Descartes or expresses a position with regard to his work, but in accord with strategies that are always overdetermined. In particular, nothing would be more erroneous than to assign once and for all either of the two terms to the camps that were henceforth to confront each other: materialists and spiritualists, rationalists and empiricists.

A. Resolving the irreducible contradictions of Cartesianism

It is the "Augustinians" who want to push dualism to the extreme and who privilege the word *esprit* (La Forge, who published Descartes's work and continued it with his *Traité de l'esprit de l'homme* [1666]). For his part, Malebranche uses the word *âme* to refer both to the "foundation of the soul" and the "foundation of being" (which is God himself), while at the same time reversing the Cartesian *cogito* (for him, the soul is essentially obscure to itself, and the "inner feeling" through which it becomes conscious of its existence is practically described in the terms that in Descartes characterized as the union of mind and body). Because he wants to overthrow the religious doctrine of the Creation and the Fall, La Mettrie coins, in the spirit of Locke, the expression "natural history of the soul (*âme*)" (1745), which in Rousseau's *Confessions* becomes the "history of my soul," in the sense of the history of "my life." But Helvétius gives the title *De l'esprit* (1758) to a work in which he seeks to base the enterprise of Enlightenment on a generalized sensualism.

Most astonishingly of all, perhaps, Condillac (*Essai sur l'origine des connaissances humaines*, 1746; *Traité des sensations*, 1754) systematically uses the language of the "soul" (*âme*) and its "operations." Here he is probably following Coste's classical translation of Locke (1700), which renders "mind" sometimes by *âme* and sometimes by *esprit*, but—contrary to what we would do today—with a prevalence of the former term (the article "*Âme*" in the *Encyclopédie*, which refers to Voltaire's commentary on Locke, tends to do the same). It would also be worthwhile to explore another hypothesis, that of the Cartesian heritage, since Condillac pursues his analysis by moving back toward a pure sensation that represents the original conflation of body and thought before the understanding is constituted.

Thus we would have an essential link in the continuity of a "French" doctrine of the union of the soul and the body as an irreducible mode of perception, a doctrine that extends from Descartes to Merleau-Ponty, passing through Malebranche, Maine de Biran, and Bergson, and that remains profoundly foreign to the psychophysical issues of the "mind-body problem."

But still more important is the question of the adjustments made to the terminology of the soul and mind in the context of opposing attempts to resolve the contradictions of Cartesianism: in Latin, by Spinoza, from an anthropological point of view determined by his politics of freedom; in French, by Leibniz, from a metaphysical point of view oriented toward a new theology of salvation.

Spinoza radically desubstantializes the mind/soul, which becomes a "finite mode" of the attribute "thought" (one of those that characterizes, on equal terms, the intelligibility of substance) and in the course of his work this leads him to definitively reject *anima* in favor of *mens* (cf. E. Giancotti-Boscherini, "Sul concetto spinoziano di Mens"). But his primordial interest in the question of "individuation" at all levels of nature and life, and especially the degree of the individual's autonomy with respect to the parts that compose him and to the collectivities that include him, leads Spinoza also to retain the "old" term *ingenium*, which is applicable to human individualities as well as to "historical" individualities (states, cities, social classes). In the unfinished *Tractatus politicus*, he makes this the equivalent of a *quasi-mens*, which is not so much a "collective soul" or a "spirit of the people" as an institutional "unanimity" indissociable from the power of the people and its political resistance to dissolution.

Leibniz also puts the question of the individual or unity at the center of his philosophy, but he does so in order to invent a new ontology of substantial individuality. Writing his systematic treatises in French (in particular, the *Monadologie* of 1714), he institutes a relation between *âme* and *esprit* that is both inclusive and hierarchical. The old adage *omnia sunt animata*, whose meaning had been enriched by contemporary Neoplatonism (Thomas More, Ralph Cudworth) allows him to maintain that to every "monadic" individual corresponds an *âme*, that is, a perception of itself and an "appetition," that is, a tendency to act or develop. However, only certain souls (especially human souls, but also others that are of equal or superior status) have a "clear" perception, in various degrees, of themselves and of their volitions (In his *Nouveaux essais sur l'entendement humain*, written in 1703 but not published until 1765, Leibniz, coining an astonishing neologism to translate Locke's "consciousness," calls this a *consciosité*, or, in his definitive terminology, an *apperception*). It is these souls that deserve to be called *esprits* and that, in the preestablished harmony of creation, subordinate all others to themselves in order to realize the immanent goal.

■ See Box 5.

B. "Mind" or "Spirit": The case of Berkeley

In his *Essay Concerning Human Understanding* (1690), Locke made consciousness the essential characteristic of the mind, and self-consciousness the new name for the human subject (see CONSCIOUSNESS). On the contrary, Berkeley (like Leibniz)

5

The mind-body problem

What is the place of the mind and consciousness in the natural order? The problem of the relations between the mind and the body is traditionally conceived as the question of the substance that composes each of them. If we adopt a dualism of substances, the difficulty consists in understanding how two distinct substances—the mind, whose essence is thought, and matter, whose essence is extension—could have a distinct causal relationship, for instance, in the case of action. The hypothesis of a possible interaction between substances, defended by Descartes, seems difficult to maintain given the autonomy of substances. Leibniz's solution is psycho-physical parallelism, according to which there are no direct causal relations between physical and mental events. The two series of events develop in parallel. The synchronization of the two series requires recourse to a mediating principle such as divine Providence. Leibniz's theory is not dualistic because according to him there are no material substances.

Another monist solution of the problem is provided by Spinoza: there is only one substance, of which mind and matter are "two aspects" or attributes. Psycho-physical parallelism derives from the fact that the events of each attribute express one and the same essence of the same substance.

Contemporary authors have explored the Spinozist solution using new means: Bertrand Russell (*The Analysis of Mind*) and Michael Lockwood (*Mind, Brain, and the Quantum*) set out to defend a "neutral monism," whereas other authors favor a "property dualism" that is compatible with a materialist monism (B. O'Shaughnessy, *The Will: A Dual Aspect Theory*) or not (D. Chalmers, *The Conscious Mind*). What is specific to the contemporary way of working out the problem is the introduction of concepts that seek to define the nature (psycho-biological or logical) and modal force of the dependency linking the mental and the physical. The difficulties of translation proceed from the abundance of specialized neologisms as well as from the adoption, in various senses, of notions that are simply homonymous, such as "reduction," "materialism," or "physicalism." Mental phenomena are said to "supervene on"—depend systematically on—physical nature in the sense that any mental difference assumes the existence of a corresponding physical difference. Donald Davidson ("Mental Events") has reintroduced into the contemporary debate on the mind-body problem the emergentist conception of the mental. The interest of the concept of "supervenience" is that it allows us to conceive the relationship between mind and brain as a dependency *without reduction*. It has been the object of numerous technical distinctions (strong, weak, or global supervenience; see J. Kim, *Supervenience and Mind*).

"Physicalism" is the general term that designates the idea that mental phenomena supervene upon physical-biological nature. There are several ways of understanding physicalism, depending on the form given to the dependency between the mind and physical nature. "Type physicalism," also called "psycho-physical reductionism," is the strongest form of physicalism, and was defended as late as the 1970s (D. Armstrong, *A Materialist Theory of the Mind*). "Token physicalism" was adopted by functionalists attached to the multi-realizability of mental states (N. Block, "Antireductionism Slaps Back"). Davidson supports a related position, with the thesis of "anomal monism": every mental event is identical with an occurring physical event, but does not give rise to any psycho-physical law; in other words, the identity of brain and mind is not invariant relative to the type of mental event in question.

Philosophers continue to seek a solution to the problem that is compatible with physicalism but makes it possible to escape the threat of making mental phenomena, and especially representations, simple epiphenomena without any causal role (Engel, "Actions, raisons et causes mentales").

Joëlle Proust

BIBLIOGRAPHY

Armstrong, David. *A Materialist Theory of the Mind*. London: Routledge and K. Paul, 1968.

Block, Ned. "Antireductionism Slaps Back." *Philosophical Perspectives* 11 (1997): 107–32.

Chalmers, David J. *The Conscious Mind*. Oxford: Oxford University Press, 1996.

Davidson, Donald. "Mental Events." In *Essays on Actions and Events*. Oxford: Clarendon; New York: Oxford University Press, 2001. 207–24.

Engel, Pascal. "Actions, raisons et causes mentales." *Revue de Théologie et de Philosophie* 124 (1992): 305–21.

Kim, Jaegwon. *Supervenience and Mind*. Cambridge: Cambridge University Press, 1993.

Lockwood, Michael. *Mind, Brain and the Quantum*. Oxford: Blackwell, 1992.

Nagel, Ernst. *The Structure of Science*. London: Routledge and Kegan Paul, 1961.

O'Shaughnessy, Brian. *The Will: A Dual Aspect Theory*. Cambridge: Cambridge University Press, 1980.

Russell, Bertrand. *The Analysis of Mind*. London: Allen and Unwin, 1921.

defends a rigorous theocentrism. We should therefore not be surprised that Berkeley challenges the primacy of consciousness. What in Leibniz leads to a broadening of the concept of the mind to include unconscious thought, which underlies and explains consciousness (see PERCEPTION), in Berkeley leads to a tendency to dissolve the idea of consciousness in favor of that of representation or phenomenon. He avoids the very term "consciousness," but sometimes uses the adjective "conscious," and constantly uses "perception" and "reflection." Why is there this reversal with respect to the usage then prevalent?

We can propose the following hypothesis. In Berkeley's thought, there is no need for a self-identical consciousness to give unity to experience by operating on simple ideas and forging complex ideas of relations: the relations are already given with the phenomena themselves, they are part of the perceptive complex, in the form of habitual connections or associations between thing-ideas. We can even go so far as to suggest, as Husserl does in his lectures on *Philosophie première*, that "things refer to each other by associative-inductive means," that is, they are structured as signs and form, as it were, a language immanent to things (not a mental language, but rather a language-object). Thus the field of phenomena indicates its own meaning, or is given along with it.

This kind of immanence of meaning or of the unity of phenomena, which is inherent in the perception of their connections, does not in any way eliminate the function of the *subject* or *ego*: on the contrary, it affirms the latter *qua* activity. The subject is both the receiver of all perceptions and the spiritual actor in all decisions or volitions, and consequently of all projects ("[M]an is a project of himself rather than a memory of himself," writes Geneviève Brykman, adding, "there is no doubt that Berkeley sought at the same time to move beyond Locke's point of view, from which personal identity is an identity of consciousness" [*Berkeley et le voile des mots*, 100]).

To this characteristic of the subject Berkeley attaches once again the name of "spirit." Brykman (*Berkeley*, 94f.) shows that in Berkeley there is a fundamental tension between "mind" and "spirit" (terms that are both translated into French as *esprit*), which is connected with the (re)discovery of "spiritual reality" as the unity of existence, thought, and will ("So long as I exist or have any idea, I am eternally willing: to acquiesce in my present state is to will," Berkeley writes in one of his manuscripts):

> The spirit is then designated, no longer as *mind*, but as *spirit* and image of God as pure act. But this is not to say that one conception of the spirit is abandoned for another; it is to say that to a dangerously skeptical conception Berkeley adds a thesis that is very bold, but more acceptable for a churchman. And if we suppose that that there is a dualism in Berkeley, the dividing line does not run between the spirit and ideas, but within the spirit itself, between a set of perceptions (mind) and an act (spirit): on the one hand the human mind tends to be a simple set of visible minima more or less regularly related to other sensible minima; on the other hand, the human spirit is a series of acts or volitions that accompany the given. Is there any more relation between these two statuses and denominations of the finite mind than there is between the mind and the body in other philosophies? Yes, at first sight, and yes, in a sense. But in the end, Berkeley posits the theoretical interdependence of active and passive things. And whereas in the most widespread conception of the relations between the mind and the body, the immortality of the soul is posited on the basis of the independence of the soul with regard to bodily phenomena, Berkeley makes "perceived things" conditions of possibility for the implementation of acts of the mind.

> (G. Brykman, *Berkeley*, 94–95)

Just as the perceiving subject is not fundamentally a "consciousness"—at least in the sense that Locke had just given this term—personal identity, the "ego," or "I" that is caught in this tension, cannot be considered a "self-consciousness." Does that mean that we must go so far as to consider the subject or personal identity (the sense of the word "I") as a "fiction," as Hume was to propose not long afterward in his *Treatise on Human Nature* (1740, I.IV.§Vi, 342f., and Appendix, 758f.; see Box 1 of this entry)? Even though Berkeley referred to the role of imagination in the cohesion of experience, his system's extreme propositions, as well as his theological orientation, were to lead him to another outcome. "The immanence of the perceiving subject in the field of perceptions," or of "idea-things" (a formulation much more satisfactory than the immanence of perceptions and thus of things to the subject's field of consciousness

maintained by Husserl), leads to a permanent difficulty in extracting the subject from the world and from his sensations. Inversely, the identification of "I think" with an "I want" leads to a tendency to consider the subject as the creator of his own world, or a tendency to solipsism—despite the reflection that shows me, by analogy, the existence of other minds. "Apart from the imagination, there is no way of distinguishing the mind from the whole of things perceived, nor the spirit from the undifferentiated power of God" (G. Brykman, *Berkeley*, 96).

IV. Locke and the Isolation of the "Mental"

But of all the questions that arise at the intersection of language and theory, the most fundamental is that raised by Locke's attempt to isolate the "mental" (representations, operations, faculties) as an autonomous field of subjectivity that is observable or objectifiable. Here we will focus on the aspects of the terminology that reflect Locke's effort to inaugurate, after Descartes but in a completely different way, a problematics of the activity of thought disengaged from traditional substantialism, while at the same time remaining irreducible to materialist reductionism. These aspects are all the more interesting because having put them at the heart of a new theoretical idiom, as distant from Latin as from the French of the "Republic of Letters," Locke used them to achieve an amazingly coherent semantics that set its stamp on the modern philosophy of the subject and has remained essentially recognizable over the centuries (see CONSCIOUSNESS and I/ME/MYSELF).

A. "Mental"/"verbal"

Locke founded psychologism in philosophy (and set it on the road toward the transcendental attitude) by carrying out in advance a kind of "anti-linguistic turn" based on the isolation of meanings that are "anterior" to linguistic signs and depend solely on the association of ideas and the relationships of agreement or disagreement that they entertain with them or with their objects—in the final analysis, the objects of sense perception reflected in the "ideas of sensation" that form the matter of all intellectual activity. He systematically opposes "mental propositions" to "verbal propositions," and "mental Truths" or "Truths of Thought" to "verbal Truths" or "Truths of words," the former element in these oppositions providing the criterion of the latter. From the outset, the concept of "mind" refers to the whole of the operations of the "mental" faculties internal to thought, in contrast to verbal expressions, which are secondary and external because they are conventional. The opposition between the mental and the verbal (Vulgar Latin *mentalis* versus *verbalis*) is just as common in Arnauld and Nicole's *Logique de Port-Royal* (1662).

This parallel brings out an irremediable lacuna in French, which has no substantive corresponding to "mind," making the English concept untranslatable. Naturally, Locke is aware of the etymological link between "mind" and Latin *mens*, which facilitates the immediate expression of his conceptions of mind as the seat of consciousness and of memory and recollection as the criterion of personal identity, leading him to attempt modernity's most complete "secularization" of Augustinian interiority.

B. "Mind"/"understanding"

On this basis we can try to clarify the complex relations between the terms "mind" and "understanding" in Locke's work. The title of the *Essay Concerning Human Understanding* refers to the latter term; in this respect it can be compared to Spinoza's unfinished treatise *De intellectus emendatione*, and it inaugurates a tradition that will also include Hume (*An Enquiry Concerning Human Understanding*). But on reading Locke's work, we may feel that the respective ranges of the two terms fluctuate. The field of "intellectual" operations obviously exceeds the purely "mental" to include all the acquisitions of knowledge and reason that have as their condition the verbal expression and communication of ideas. Inversely, when Locke presents mental functioning as divided into a passive side that is characterized by the acquisition of ideas ("perception," in the broad sense) and involves the understanding, and an active side that is characterized by acts of will—the understanding becomes only one part of the mind.

In reality, the two terms are fundamentally coextensive, and this reflects Locke's profound "intellectualism" and "cognitivism," but it also allows him to couple all associations of ideas with a virtual double in the form of an affective process. On the one hand it is mind itself that develops by incorporating into its functioning the instruments of language, whose use and meaning it determines. On the other hand—as the analysis of the relations among will, uneasiness, and desire discussed in chapter 21 ("Of Power") in Book II of *Essay Concerning Human Understanding* shows—the will is not so much an autonomous faculty as the resultant of the mind's intrinsic activity, which is already reflected in the constant succession of its thoughts, and which is subsumed under the notion of uneasiness.

Unlike other seventeenth- and eighteenth-century conceptions of the "understanding," in Locke "mind" refers, not to a receptacle of ideas or a system of faculties, but to a logico-psychological "machine" in movement. The differential between passivity (sensation, perception) and activity (operations, reflection, desire) is constitutive from the outset, which also makes it possible to understand how it is transformed throughout human existence in a constant process of acquisition and appropriation, while at the same time preserving an essential identity.

C. "Mind," "consciousness," "self"

The heart of Locke's conceptualization is constituted by the relations of mutual presupposition that are established among mind, consciousness, and the self, three notions that Locke either invented as concepts or completely reworked. They are already combined in a formula in the *Essay* (II.1.19) that has remained canonical as a definition of consciousness: "Consciousness is the perception of what passes in a Man's own Mind."

Mind and consciousness, notions that are developed in terms of operations, faculties, and "powers," on the one hand, and perception and the "internal sense" on the other, are only the two sides of a single process of *reflection*, which constitutes the basis of the intellectual operations carried out on ideas to produce new ideas and the essence of

thought's "self-presence." This reciprocity allows Locke to transform the Cartesian metaphysical proposition according to which the "mind always thinks" into a phenomenological axiom: the mind cannot think without knowing what it thinks (without being conscious of its thoughts: "as *thinking* consists in being conscious that one thinks," *Essay*, II.1.19), thus opening the way toward a radical critique of substantialism in both its animist and spiritualist forms (the mind is neither soul nor spirit) and in its materialist form (the mind is not the body, or at least their connection is merely hypothetical).

Consciousness and self are just as indissociable (so that in Locke "consciousness" is always already "self-consciousness," a term that he introduced into philosophy: in 1700, his French translator Coste still found it untranslatable). Consciousness has as its foundation a reflexive identity of thought or a logico-psychological principle of identity (every perception is also a perception of perception), but the self (conceived by Locke in terms of the individual's continual *appropriation* of his own ideas, and through them, of his actions) is nothing other than the continuity of consciousness. This unity of self and consciousness (which Leibniz immediately declares to be unacceptable, in view of the obscure or unconscious nature of most of the ideas that enter into the "complete notion" of each of them) essentially founds not only the separation of individual consciousnesses, each of which has its own, irreducible identity (and consequently the necessity of tolerance, or of freedom of conscience), but also each person's responsibility (within the limits of his or her self-consciousness, whose "pathologies," such as the phenomena of double personalities, Locke begins to explore). Thus it is the basis for a theory of the "identity of a person" that is as important for morality, religion, and politics as it is for the metaphysics and "psychology" it makes possible. The term itself is introduced, in this sense, by Wolff in 1732 (*Psychologia empirica*) and 1734 (*Psychologia rationalis*).

Finally, self and mind are also reciprocal concepts. Their equivalence with the notion of consciousness would suffice to show this formally, but the meaning of this fact can be seen when we understand that it covers the coincidence of the time of the mind's operations ("the train of ideas," the mind's inability to remain durably focused on a single idea, and especially the "logical time" of associations) and the time of retention or memory, in which these operations are summed up at every moment (except for those lost to memory) and which enables every mind to perceive itself as identical to itself over time. This phenomenological coincidence is ultimately what Locke calls *experience*, which is essentially an "experience of consciousness," that is, an internal experience that replicates external experience and makes possible its progressive development or its "appropriation of the world." The concept of experience, of the "operations of our own Mind" that involve "observing in our selves" (*Essay*, II.1.4), thus contains the permanent possibility of a subjectification *and* an objectification of ideas, which are like the two folds of a single interiority. That is the way interiority presents itself to itself, raised to the level of a concept, which sums up the mutual relations of mind, self, and consciousness.

V. The Remainder of the *Âme* on the Threshold of Modernity

The questions that arise at the intersection of these readings converge on the localization of a "remainder"—but not, strictly speaking, something inexpressible, since it is precisely through words that we can approach it. If we start once again from Locke's constitution, under the name of "mind," of a field of "inner experience" where the operations of thought are dominated by consciousness, we will discover among our principal authors striking discrepancies and term-for-term oppositions whose radicalness shows that they are situated within a common "moment," or rather that they constitute that moment by their very conflict.

A. From psychological positivity to the transcendental illusion: The "internal sense," *das Innere*

Both Locke and Kant refer to "self-consciousness" (*Selbstbewusstsein*) and the problematics of experience (*Erfahrung*), but what is in Locke a kind of self-deployment of a positivity becomes in Kant the site of a transcendental illusion, and thus also the reason for the shift in philosophy toward a critical register that seeks to define limits for reflective activity. Whereas in Locke consciousness as the "internal sense" is that which gives the subject to itself immediately, in Kant it is instead that which makes the subject inaccessible to itself. This does not mean that this field of experience ceases to be the site of truth. On the contrary, this is why what might be called the Lockean "thing in itself" (the substance of soul, whether material or immaterial, repressed into the realm of the unknowable by the theorizing of the conscious mind) haunts Kant's discourse more than ever. Following the example of Wolff, who had used the word "soul" (*Seele*) to translate "mind" into German, Kant restores to the idea of the soul part of the phenomenality of thought, which allows it to attribute to itself both permanence and identity (hence "personality"). And Kant makes interiority itself (*das Innere*: a notion that, in a crucial passage of *The Critique of Pure Reason*, he declares to be "amphibological" because it seeks to represent as a "space" something that contradicts exteriority, and thus spatiality) an *explicandum* and not an explanation. Therefore it is not the natural dimension of psychic processes but rather consciousness's "self-image," a structural or superficial effect produced by the "internal sense," whose deep origins remain "hidden" as Kant says in the chapter of the "transcendental schematism." One of the consequences of this is that Kant, though he provided an ample stimulus for "scientific" psychology and psychologism (from Herbart to Piaget), did not contribute to them, directing his attention instead toward a moral ("pragmatic") constitution of anthropology.

B. "Uneasiness" and interiority effect in the union of soul and body

The common view of Descartes as the father of all modern philosophies of consciousness results from a misunderstanding (partly encouraged by Kantian readings) that imputes to him Lockean theorems that were in fact developed against him (see CONSCIOUSNESS). But what remains fascinating when we read Descartes after Locke is that even though both thinkers insist on the "irreducibility" of acts of thought and the possibility of describing intellectual operations in an autonomous way (the question as to whether their "matter" comes solely from sensation or in part from "innate" ideas being in this respect secondary), they hold entirely different views regarding the question of "interiority." We cannot help being struck by Descartes's "nonpsychologism," that is, the care with which he avoids referring to an interiority of thought corresponding to the constitutive exteriority of bodies (whose "principal attribute" is extension). That is to say, in Descartes, immanence and interiority are not the same. His position was radicalized by Spinoza. The question thus raised has fed into all of modern and contemporary philosophy: that of Hegel (whose *Geist* is the perfect example of the internalization into itself of all experience, and the plane of the immanence of all cultural productions), but also that of Husserl and William James, and finally, through Sartre's great essay on "The Transcendence of the Ego," Deleuze, who constantly refers to the latter. Up to our own day, post-Cartesian and post-Lockean philosophies have offered different answers to the question of how the "interiority" of reflection and the subject's "immanence" in thought are connected.

But this statement must be immediately qualified. In Descartes there is an effect of interiority in thought, but this effect is not a matter of pure thought; it corresponds to the experience of "union" (where, as we have seen, the idea of the *anima* returns parasitically on *mens*), in which Descartes himself says that the soul thinks "as if it were the body," that is, through sensation it projects itself within its envelope and its form. An extreme, paradoxical experience that is, nonetheless, simply human experience if, as Descartes's letters to Princess Elizabeth and his *Passions of the Soul* suggest, its principal and permanent modality is so-called substantial union.

This is a typical example of what might be called "the remainder of the soul" in its Cartesian form. But one could also say that the concept of "uneasiness" is the name of this remainder in Locke's philosophy, especially if we note that "uneasiness" connotes all the "borders" of interiority, where pure mental reality proves to be at least virtually dependent on what is outside it: pure or originary sensation, which Kant was to designate as a limit of representation, and the linguistic sign, which is social in essence. Perhaps it is even dependent on its "repressed" (individual corporeal or spiritual substance, "body and soul," from which proceed affects that exceed, even with consciousness, the intellectuality of its "ideas").

These questions draw attention to the semantic uncertainties internal to each system as well as to the problems of untranslatability between theoretical traditions, which are inseparable from the idioms in which philosophers work and which they work on. We believe them to be ultimately indissociable.

C. The threshold of modernity and the contemporary configuration

With great caution, we could thus suggest that the "remainder" circulating among philosophers of the seventeenth and eighteenth centuries, even though it did not correspond to any unambiguous signified, nonetheless designated the problematic unity of a series of "questions at the limits" that are constitutive of mental or intellectual reality. For example: the questions of the relation between activity and passivity (or, in the language of the time, "will" and "understanding," and also "concept" and "intuition"), questions of the relationship between intellectuality (representation, perception, idea) and affectivity (desire, feelings, passions) that in the seventeenth and eighteenth centuries put understanding outside itself, if they did not provide access to its vital sources (*conatus*), and finally questions about the sign and symbol, at the intersection of reflection on language, nature, and artifice ("civility," "sociability"), the products of artistic "genius," which constantly challenge the individualism dominant in seventeenth- and eighteenth-century thought by causing to rise up once more within the soul or mind a determination that is both preindividual and transindividual.

The threshold of modernity is this singular moment marked by the gradual decline of the influence of ancient schemas (philosophical, but also religious or medical) of the division and hierarchization of the "parts of the soul," with their social and cosmological implications, which Christianity continually tried to appropriate in order to give them a supernatural meaning. The attempt to conceive the *mens* as the totality of the soul, not as the name of its indivisibility, against the tradition that made it (in competition with *intellectus*; see INTELLECTUS) one of the equivalents of the Platonic and Aristotelian *nous* [νοῦς], is particularly representative in this respect.

At this point, the objective of a "thought of thought" changes radically in meaning. In Aristotle the *noēsis noēseôs* [νόησις νοήσεως] had essentially the meaning of a *reflexivity* whose perfect or exhaustive figure could be conceived by philosophy only as an ideal situated "outside itself" in the totality of the world and the divine. Among the moderns, starting with Descartes and especially Locke and Kant, it corresponds to a "subjectivization" of thought that brings thought back "to itself," but at the cost of the imperfection or finitude of reflection, and thus the existence of a "remainder" situated in the depths of the mind or on its margins. And even Hegel, who thinks he can reconstitute an absolute ("absolute spirit," *absoluter Geist*; "absolute knowledge," *absolutes Wissen*) by making logic and history converge in a single "dialectic" or union of contraries, and who is thus able to quote literally (in the conclusion to the *Encyclopedia of the Philosophical Sciences*, §577) Aristotle's formula (*Metaphysics,* XII.1072b.18–30) that identifies the divine with "the pure act," precisely insofar as it is a "thought of thought," while at the same time conferring on it a radically new meaning (that of the culmination of a historical *Bildung* of the spirit, of an education or transindividual culture), does not really escape this configuration. In particular, we could try to show this by interpreting the persistent discrepancy in his thought between the notions of "consciousness" (*Bewußtsein*) and "spirit" (*Geist*): for while consciousness undeniably provides the phenomenological model of the "self" (*Selbst*) that is essentially the spirit (which makes it a "subject"), the latter, through its "objectivity" and its "substantial" depth, remains irreducible to consciousness. In this respect Hegel is still part of what we call here the "threshold."

But neither is the threshold of modernity continuous with our contemporary configuration. The latter is itself certainly constituted in accord with a plurality of trends, the most extreme seeming to be represented:

1. by an objectivist, naturalistic isolation of the "mental," whether within a psycho-physiological perspective or not. Dependent on Locke's formulation, with the "cognitive sciences" and the new "philosophy of mind" it seeks to move beyond the limits Locke assigned to the observation of mind;

2. in the area of Freudian psychoanalysis and its various "topics," by an apparent return to the multiplicity of structures (or "partial souls") characteristic of the ancient point of view, but in radically new conditions that have emerged from the combination of the clinical hypothesis of the unconscious and a modern problematics of the subject, which obliges us to inquire anew into the continuity of the notions of *psychè* and the psyche. As if each of the old terms now prescribed its own path (see ES);

3. by a critique of individualism and the autonomy of the subject, which is oriented either toward a sociology or anthropology of the "institutions of meaning" (Descombes) or toward post-phenomenological hermeneutics, and which seems in these ways to explore the various connotations of *Geist* in the sense of "culture" (see BILDUNG and GEISTESWISSENSCHAFTEN).

■ See Box 6.

Étienne Balibar

6

Wittgenstein's critique of the mental or, once again, on a few difficulties in translating the expression "philosophy of mind": "Philosophy of mind" and psychology

I. The "mind"? With what is the "philosophy of mind" concerned?

In contemporary philosophy, the term "mind" raises a problem of translation, as is shown by the difficulty of delimiting a French domain of the *philosophie de l'esprit* that would be the equivalent of the English philosophy of mind. Advocates of the current *philosophie de l'esprit* in France (Joëlle Proust, Pierre Jacob, Pascal Engel) have implicitly decided that *philosophie de l'esprit* is the same thing as the "philosophy of mind": all one has to do—referring to a few well-chosen ordinary usages (*état d'esprit, l'esprit de...*)—is to get used to the expression, so that it ceases to be a neologism and becomes natural as a result of being heard and institutionalized. This is supposed to provide a way out of the transitional period in which the use of the word *esprit* is problematic because it is still associated, sometimes (like the German term *Geist*) with a spiritualist and metaphysical tradition, and sometimes with the new mentalist tradition.

The philosophy of mind concerns first of all what might be called "mental phenomena" or phenomena of the mental. The French word *mental* might in fact provide a better translation of "mind" than *esprit* does, if nominalizing the adjective *mental* did not raise certain doubts (and were not, in French, associated with moral connotations, notably in sports vocabulary, where it thrives: *un mental d'acier*). Speaking of mental phenomena, or simply of *le mental*, allows us to evade the question of the status of the mind: the mind is to be conceived not as a metaphysical or psychological entity, but as what the philosophy of mind is concerned with, namely a set of phenomena to be examined without preconceptions, using the tools at our disposal: "the field of philosophy that concerns the nature of mental phenomena and its manifestations," to adopt the expression with which a recent presentation of the *philosophie de l'esprit* begins (D. Fisette and P. Poirier, *Philosophie de l'esprit, état des lieux*, 11).

This apparently neutral starting point conceals several preconceptions, as the words "nature" and "manifestations" indicate. Samuel Guttenplan's recent and already classic *Companion to the Philosophy of Mind* (1994) also takes a project of description as its point of departure: "What things or phenomena count as mental, as showing the presence of minds?" (6).

There follows a list of phenomena considered common and ordinary: the ability to learn, perceiving, acting intentionally, understanding language, etc. Thus, the philosophy of mind is concerned with everything that is a manifestation of the mind, without prejudging the nature of this mind, but prejudging that all kinds of things (a large part, indeed the totality, of our activities and capacities) are "manifestations" of this mind or "show its presence." Such a thesis draws part of its strength from the fact that only "mind" (and not "spirit") is concerned, and everything becomes more natural because of the vagueness of the term in the English-language philosophical tradition.

The uncritical use of the term "mind" thus leads us to accept the idea that we commonly attribute beliefs, intentions, and mental states, and the next step is to define the status, contents, nature (physical, mental, both, or other), and so forth, which are now the classic objects of the *philosophie de l'esprit*. The problem of defining the mind, as Wittgenstein emphasizes, is thus the point of departure, "the first step":

How does the philosophical problem about mental processes and states and about behaviourism arise? —The first step is the one that altogether escapes notice. We talk of processes and states and leave their nature undecided. Sometime perhaps we shall know more about them—we think. But that is just what commits us to a particular way of looking at the matter. For we have a definite concept of what it means to learn to know a process better. (The decisive movement in the conjuring trick has been made, and it was the very one that we thought quite innocent.)—And now the analogy which was to make us understand our thoughts falls to pieces. So we have to deny the yet uncomprehended process in the yet unexplored medium. And now it looks as if we had denied mental processes. And naturally we don't want to deny them.

(trans. G.E.M. Anscombe, Philosophical Investigations, §308)

II. The "linguistic turn" and philosophy of mind

Regarding the philosophy of mind, there is much talk of a new paradigm and a turning point in contemporary philosophy that is supposed to succeed the "linguistic turn" that took place at the beginning of the twentieth century. The philosophy of mind is to replace, as it were, the philosophy of language and move beyond it, drawing on the advances in the cognitive sciences during the same period. Here again we encounter certain difficulties; the philosophy of mind has been constructed, over the past thirty years, "on" the achievements of the philosophy of language, even if it has rejected some of its elements. After the linguistic turn and the mentalist turn, the "mind" is no longer what it was in the nineteenth century, and the renewed interest in mental phenomena cannot be detached from the linguistic and psychological dimensions of such phenomena.

The work of an author like Wittgenstein belongs as much to the philosophy of mind as to the philosophy of language (see D. Stern, *Wittgenstein on Mind and Language*). For Wittgenstein, it is the idea itself of something of which these phenomena would be the "manifestation," or whose existence is shown by these phenomena (an idea that founds the very definition of the philosophy of mind) that is problematic and misleading. Whence the importance of an examination of language, which cannot be rendered obsolete by the progress of the sciences of the mind. What counts for him is the investigation of *the ways we use language* (grammatical investigation), the ways we use words like "think,"

"remember," "see," "attend to," etc., which are obscured by images—common to psychology and philosophy—of internal processes, of belief, of *esprit* that block our access to the usage of the word the way it is, to the description of its uses. Wittgenstein does philosophy of mind through philosophy of language.

III. Folk psychology, scientific psychology, psychology without psychology

A particularly important dimension of contemporary philosophy of language is its critical relation, from the outset, to psychology. That is why in order to delimit a domain of the philosophy of mind it does not suffice to advocate a simple rehabilitation of psychology, as has recently been done in France (P. Engel, *Philosophie et Psychologie*).

The material common to the philosophy of language and psychology (what we usually call our "states of mind") might accredit the notion, greatly favored by contemporary mentalists, that there is a "folk psychology" (often called "popular psychology") that might serve at least as a database for scientific psychology. According to these authors, our vocabulary and psychological propositions have not yet attained the level of elaboration characteristic of scientific theories, and hence are part of a "naive psychology." This naive psychology consists in describing, explaining, and predicting human behavior in terms of interactions among beliefs, desires, and intentions. Psychologists think that folk psychology functions, for example, by attributing beliefs—since *ordinarily* we say: "X believes that Y has the intention to . . . ," and so forth. However, one might ask in what way "X believes that" involves attributing a mental entity, namely a belief (see BELIEF), to Y. The passage—an elementary stage in the philosophy of mind—from our ordinary expressions ("X believes that") to the claim of an attribution of beliefs to a mind is part of a clever strategy, as Vincent Descombes has shown in *La denrée mentale*:

First, the mentalist dogma is presented to us as being extremely commonplace: as if it were equivalent to a simple recognition of the existence of a psychological dimension in human affairs. Who would deny that people have opinions and desires, except the old-fashioned, narrow-minded behaviorist whom everyone mocks? What obscurantist would deny that neurological research is of interest for psychology? . . . Who would deny the platitude: people act on the basis of what they think they know and what they want to obtain? But in the final analysis, the reader is surprised to

(continued)

(continued)

learn that by accepting these not very contestable truths he has accepted, one after the other, the elements of a metaphysics of the mind.

We can discern in Wittgenstein a project of speaking about the mind in "nonpsychological" terms. His interest is always, almost obsessively, in the "phenomena of the mental," which he calls *geistig* or *seelisch* (it matters little which, he says). "And now it looks as if we had denied mental processes (*geistige Vorgänge*). And naturally we don't want to deny them" (*Philosophical Investigations*, §308). To deny the existence of the mental is already to lend it *more credit* than would a procedure that—to borrow an expression from his *Tractatus logico-philosophicus*—would speak of the self, of psychology, "in a non-psychological (*nicht-psychologisch*) manner." Wittgenstein's approach is a philosophical one that involves psychology (of mind) without accepting the philosophy of spirit. As Cavell has shown in *The Claim of Reason*, Wittgenstein's perspective is not a simple negation of the existence of mental states, but a reinvention of psychological problems, their reformulation as questions of linguistic usage, their membership in a community of language. In *Must We Mean What We Say?* Cavell describes this specificity of Wittgenstein's approach (70):

> The implication is not that I cannot know myself, but that knowing oneself—though radically different from the way we know others—is not a matter of "*cognizing*" (classically, "intuiting") mental acts and particular sensations." (emphasis added)

Wittgenstein's later philosophy is a radicalization of the *logical* project of the *Tractatus*: to bring out the necessity that presides over our utterances in ordinary language regarding psychology, which has nothing to do with the necessity of positing entities of which these utterances are supposed to be the manifestation. This leads Cavell to a famous formulation:

> We know about the efforts of philosophers such as Frege and Husserl to undo the "psychologizing" of logic (like Kant's undoing of Hume's psychologizing of knowledge): the shortest way I might describe a book such as the *Philosophical Investigations* is to say that it attempts to undo the psychologizing of psychology, to show the necessity controlling our application of psychological and behavioral categories; even, one could say, show the necessities in

human action and passion themselves. And at the same time it seems to turn all of philosophy into psychology—matters of what we call things, how we treat them, what their role is in our lives.

(Ibid., 91)

The project of Wittgenstein's *Investigations* pursues in another way that of the *Tractatus*: the exploration of the mind. A psychological investigation that can be accomplished only in a nonpsychological way. In this sense, paradoxically, the whole of Wittgenstein's work can be conceived as belonging to the context of the philosophy of mind, but a philosophy of mind in which mind is defined nonpsychologically. The origin of such a conception (as Cora Diamond shows in *The Realistic Spirit*) is found in Frege, in a remarkable expression in his article "Der Gedanke":

> Not everything is an idea. Otherwise psychology would include within itself all the sciences, or at least it would have supreme authority over all the sciences. Otherwise, psychology would also reign over logic and mathematics. But it would be impossible to more seriously misunderstand mathematics than by subordinating it to psychology. Neither logic nor mathematics has as its task to study souls (*Seelen*) or the contents of consciousness of which the individual is the bearer (*Träger*). Instead, we could assign them the task of studying the mind (*Geist*): the mind, not minds.

("Der Gedanke: Eine logische Untersuchung" [Thought: A logical investigation])

If logic is not concerned with individual minds, it is not because it denies psychology: it is because thought or mind—*Geist*—is wholly defined by the laws of logic. It is logic that defines what a mind is. Wittgenstein borrowed this point from Frege to define a depsychologized philosophy of mind.

Thus the problematic passage from *Geist* to "mind" is an interesting nodal point in the history of analytical philosophy: its rementalization, which has been largely achieved in English-language philosophy over the past few decades, neglects this Fregean-Wittgensteinian definition of the mind to base itself in an unexploited way on another tradition, the mentalist tradition of mind. Whence all the recent work by English-speaking philosophers inspired by Wittgenstein (Cavell, then Diamond) who suggest a nonmentalist concept of mind. Thus Diamond borrows from Frege the idea that there is no more a thought without meaning than there is an illogical mind:

But *the* mind has no fuzzes and no logically confused thoughts . . . and so far as philosophy deals with *the* mind, it will not have, internal to its subject matter, any distinction between the fuzzy and the sharply defined, or between the nonsensical and what makes sense.

(*The Realistic Spirit*, 2)

The propositions of logic, even if they say nothing, deal with the mind, and it is *nowhere else*.

[T]he *Tractatus* does not break the connection in Frege between *the* mind and logic-and-mathematics. The connection emerges this way: the propositions of logic and the equations of mathematics show what Wittgenstein calls "the logic of the world," and that *is* for them to show the possibilities that belong to the mind or the self considered in a nonpsychological way.

(Ibid., 2)

Philosophy will speak (in a nonpsychological manner) of the mind in its analysis of ordinary propositions or in its presentation of the general form of the proposition (Wittgenstein, *Tractatus*, 5.47). For Wittgenstein, we learn more about the mind through these analyses than through psychology—but this implies a transformation of philosophy that will lead to a definition of the mind by usage:

> Everything is already there in . . ." How does it come about that this arrow → *points*? Doesn't it seem to carry in it something besides itself? "No, not the dead line on paper; only the psychical thing, the meaning, can do that." –That is both true and false. The arrow points only in the application that a living being makes of it. This pointing is *not* a hocus-pocus which can be performed only by the soul.

(*Investigations*, §484)

To give up the mythology of the mind is to seek what one expected from these entities (the mind, the soul, the mental, whatever) in language itself. Examining usage means this: seeing nothing in usage that isn't already there, and not explaining it by the mind. This sums up the "depsychologization of psychology" carried out by Wittgenstein, which might thus be extended to the mind: the immanent definition of the mind by our (its) usage. Parodying the well-known Wittgensteinian slogan "meaning as use," we might say "mind as use."

Sandra Laugier

BIBLIOGRAPHY

Cavell, Stanley. *Must We Mean What We Say?* 2nd ed. Cambridge: Cambridge University Press, 2002.
———. *The Claim of Reason*. Oxford: Oxford University Press, 1979.
Descombes, Vincent. *La denrée mentale*. Paris: Éditions de Minuit, 1996.
Diamond, Cora. *The Realistic Spirit, Wittgenstein, Philosophy, and the Mind*. Cambridge, MA: MIT Press, 1991.

Engel, Pascal. *Philosophie et psychologie*. Paris: Gallimard, 1996.
Fisette, D., and P. Poirier. *Philosophie de l'esprit, état des lieux*. Paris: Vrin, 2001.
Frege, Gottlob. "Der Gedanke: Eine logische Untersuchung." *Beiträge zur Philosophie des Deutschen Idealismus* 1 (1918–19): 58–77.
Guttenplan, Samuel, ed. *A Companion to the Philosophy of Mind*. Oxford: Blackwell, 1994.

Stern, David. *Wittgenstein on Mind and Language*. Oxford: Oxford University Press, 1995.
Wittgenstein, Ludwig. *Philosophical Investigations*. Translated by G.E.M. Anscombe. Reprint. Oxford: Blackwell, 1997.
———. *Tractatus Logico-Philosophicus*. Translated by D. F. Pears and D. F. McGuinness. Introduction by B. Russell. London: Routledge and Kegan Paul, 1974.

BIBLIOGRAPHY

Arnauld, Antoine, and Pierre Nicole. *Logique de Port-Royal*. First published in 1662. Translation by J. V. Buroker: *Logic, or, The Art of Thinking*. 5th ed. Edited by J. V. Buroker. New York: Cambridge University Press, 1996.
Balibar, Étienne. "'Ego sum, ego existo': Descartes au point d'hérésie." *Bulletin de la Société Française de Philosophie* 3 (1992).
Berkeley, George. *The Works of George Berkeley, Bishop of Cloyne*. Edited by A. A. Luce and T. E. Jessop. London: Nelson, 1948; Nendeln, Liechtenstein: Kraus Reprint, 1979.
Besnier, Bernard. "Esprit." in *Les notions philosophiques: Encyclopédie philosophique universelle*. Paris: Presses Universitaires de France, 1990.
Bodei, Remo. *Geometria delle passioni: Paura, speranza, felicità, filosofia e uso politico*. Milano: Feltrinelli, 1991.
Brown, Deborah J. *Descartes and the Passionate Mind*. New York: Cambridge University Press, 2008.
Brykman, Genevieve. *Berkeley et le voile des mots*. Paris: Vrin, 1993.
Deprun, Jean. *La philosophie de l'inquiétude en France au XVIIIème siècle*. Paris: Vrin, 1979.
Descartes, René. *Correspondance avec Elisabeth*. Edited by J. M. Beyssade. Paris: Flammarion, 1989. Translation by J. Cottingham, R. Stoothoff, D. Murdoch, and A. Kenny: "Correspondence with Elisabeth." In vol. 3, *The Correspondence*, of *The Philosophical Writings of Descartes*. Cambridge: Cambridge University Press, 1991.
———. *Discours de la méthode*. Edited by E. Gilson. Paris: Vrin, 1967. Translation by D. A. Cress: *Discourse on the Method for conducting one's reason well and for seeking truth in the sciences*. Indianapolis: Hackett, 1998.
———. *I principi della filosofia*. Translated by P. Cristofolini. Turino: Bollati Boringhieri, 1992. Translation by R. P. Miller: *Principles of Philosophy*. New York: Springer, 1984.
———. *Passiones animae*. Edited by J. R. Armogathe and G. Belgioioso. Lecce, It.: Conte editore, 1997. First published in 1650. English translation by S. H. Voss: *The Passions of the Soul*. Indianapolis: Hackett, 1989.
Descombes, Vincent. *Les institutions du sens*. Paris: Éditions de Minuit, 1996.
———. *The Mind's Provisions: A Critique of Cognitivism*. Translated by S. A. Schwartz. Princeton, NJ: Princeton University Press, 2001.
Giancotti Boscherini, Emilia. "Sul concetto spinoziano di Mens." In *Ricerche lessicali su opere di Descartes e Spinoza, Lessico Intellettuale Europeo III*, edited by G. Crapulli and E. Giancotti Bsoscherini. Rome: Edizioni dell'Ateneo, 1969.
Hegel, Georg Wilhelm Friedrich. *The Phenomenology of Mind*. Translated by J. B. Baillie. Rev. ed. New York: Macmillan, 1931. First published in 1910.
———. *Phenomenology of Spirit*. Translated by A. V. Miller. New York: Oxford University Press, 1977.
———. *Philosophy of Mind: Translated from the Encyclopedia of the Philosophical Sciences*. Translated by W. Wallace. New York: Cosimo Classics, 2008.
Husserl, Edmund. *Erste philosophie*. Vol. 8 in *Husserliana*. Haag, Neth.: Nijhoff, 1950. First published in 1923–24.
———. *The Essential Husserl: Basic Writings in Transcendental Phenomenology*. Edited by D. Welton. Bloomington: Indiana University Press, 1999.

Kambouchner, Denis. *L'Homme des passions: Commentaires sur Descartes*. Paris: Albin Michel, 1995.
Locke, John. *An Essay Concerning Human Understanding*. Edited by P. H. Nidditch. Oxford: Clarendon Press, 1979.
Merleau-Ponty, Maurice. *The Incarnate Subject: Malebranche, Biran, and Bergson on the Union of Body and Soul*. Translated by P. B. Milan. Edited by A. G. Bjelland Jr. and P. Burke. Amherst, NY: Humanity Books, 2001.
———. *L'Esprit Mind/Geist*. Vol. 2 of *Methodos: Savoirs et textes*. Villeneuve d'Ascq, Fr.: Presses Universitaires du Septentrion, 2002.
Onians, R. B. *The Origins of European Thought: About the Body, the Mind, the Soul, the World, Time, and Fate*. New York: Arno Press, 1951.
Raulet, Gérard. "Esprit-Geist." In *Au jardin des malentendus: Le commerce franco-allemand des idées,* edited by J. Leenhardt and R. Picht. Arles, Fr.: Actes Sud, 1997.
Sartre, Jean-Paul. *La transcendance de l'ego: Esquisse d'une description phénoménologique*. Paris: Vrin, 1988. First published in 1936. Translation by A. Brown: *The Transcendence of the Ego: A Sketch for a Phenomenological Description*. London: Routledge, 2004.
Solignac, Aimé. "NOYS and MENS." In vol. 11 of *Dictionnaire de la spiritualité*. Paris: Éditions Beauschesne, 1980.
Winkler, Kenneth P. *The Cambridge Companion to Berkeley*. New York: Cambridge University Press, 2005.
Wolff, Christian. *Psychologica empirica*. In part 2 (Lateinische Schriften), vol. 5, of *Gesammelte Werke*. Hildesheim, Ger.: Olms, 1968. First published in 1732.
———. *Psychologica rationalis*. In part 2 (Lateinische Schriften), vol. 6 of *Gesammelte Werke*. Hildesheim, Ger.: Olms, 1968. First published in 1734.

SPANISH

The Spanish Singularity: The Pair of *Ser* and *Estar*

➤ DASEIN, ESSENCE, FICAR, *IL Y A* [ES GIBT, ESTI, HÁ], NEIGHBOR, PREDICATION, SEIN, *TO BE,* VORHANDEN, WORD ORDER

Spanish has two different, non-synonymous words—*ser* and *estar*—to express the semantic complex that other languages group under the verbs "to be," *sein*, and *être*. This pair (which allows for a distinction, more or less, between the stable and the circumstantial at the level of predication) is in the first instance a feature of everyday language. Its philosophical importance is nonetheless evident. On one hand, its existence implies considerable linguistic and conceptual difficulties for the appropriation, in Spanish, of the traditional ontological vocabulary. Discussions originating in the Spanish-speaking community about the translation of the

Heideggerian vocabulary are a good example. On the other hand, the expressive possibilities of the pair are also a source of difficulty when it comes to translating them into other languages. This aspect of the question is illustrated by the constitution of a conceptual network expressed by etymologically related terms (*estar, bienestar*, and Ortega y Gasset's *circun-stancia*), the reworking of the primary sense of a common phrase for theoretical reasons (Zubiri's *estar siendo*), and, finally, the suggestion of *estar* by certain Latin American thinkers as the expression of a more basic and fundamental vision of the world than that associated with being.

I. *Ser/Estar* in Everyday Spanish

In Spanish, most of the semantic contents and functions of the Latin verb *esse* are executed by two different verbs: *ser* (whose conjugation derives directly from *esse* but also from *sedere*, "to be seated") and *estar* (from Lat. *stare*, "to be standing"). Originally meaning "to stand up," "to remain in place," or "to remain immobile," *stare* thus gave rise to one of the verbs that may serve as a copula in Castilian attributive constructions. Portuguese and Catalan had a similar evolution to that of Spanish. Italian also adopted *stare* as an independent form and uses it in certain constructions that it shares with Castilian, but not as a copula. Finally, the conjugation of the French verb *être* integrated a part of that of the Latin *stare* (for the imperfect, for example) but did not develop it as an independent form.

In contemporary Spanish, it is possible to separate at least two different uses of the pair. *Ser* and *estar* in effect have both an absolute usage, which treats them as predicates on their own, modified or unmodified by an adverb or an adverbial expression, and a copulative usage, according to which, on the contrary, they serve as a link between a subject and its predicate.

In its absolute use, the verb *ser* can make for the expression of the existence of an object or a person, though it rarely does (*ella es y eso me basta* [she is and that is enough for me]). Along the same lines, but very commonly used, it is a synonym for the verbs "to arrive," "to take place," or "to happen" (*el crimen fue de noche* [the crime took place at night]). The verb *estar*, for its part, has above all a locative value and is used to note the position or the place where the subject is, physically or in a figurative sense. Thus, phrases such as "he is not there," "the apple is on his head," or "you are in my heart" will always be constructed with *estar*. Similarly, a construction with an adverb of state or an equivalent expression ("we are fine," "the neighbors are in perfect harmony," etc.) will necessarily use this verb (*estamos bien, los vecinos están en perfecta armonía*, etc.).

These absolute uses, however, pose no special problems for translation. They are fixed values that are rather well determined, which may be taken up in any language without any loss of major nuance. The same cannot be said of the copulative use of *ser* and *estar*. In effect, the inherent economy and precision of this use are not easily transposed into languages that do not have the pair. Insofar as they are verbs that relate a subject and a predicate, *ser* and *estar*, far from being simple syntactic auxiliaries, presuppose important changes in the content of the sentence. They effectively determine the mode of belonging of the predicate to the subject by

opposing, respectively, the habitual with the occasional, the classificatory with the singular, the regular with the sporadic, and/or the abstract with the concrete. One may say, for example, of a fruit that it is green, using *ser* to indicate that its surface presents that color in a *permanent* way. On the other hand, *las uvas están verdes* (the grapes are green)—with *estar*—refers immediately to the transitory and complete state of the maturation of the fruit, that is, to a group of properties that result from and are part of a process, and that, as such, are liable to change.

■ See Box 1.

The possibility of distinguishing between these different modes of belonging is open, in theory, to any predicate. Common usage, however, is much more restricted. Normally, if the predicate is expressed by a noun, the attribution is made with *ser*. On the other hand, if the predicate is an adjective, Spanish-speakers will habitually use both verbs. Often, they will knowingly try to distinguish between what they consider to be an indelible or constant trait of the subject and one that presents itself as changeable. Sometimes, however, usage is less rigorous. Both *eso es permitido* and *eso está permitido* (that is permitted) are used, but normally only *ser* will be used to say "that is obligatory."

II. *Ser/Estar* and Heideggerian Terminology

The existence of this pair naturally had consequences for the appropriation of traditional philosophical vocabulary. The problem can be laid out in simple terms: how should we translate the occurrences and the cognates of a word as philosophically rich as *être* (or its "equivalents" in other Western languages) into a language that, like Spanish, usually spreads its meanings and functions out over two different terms? One way to approach the problem is to ignore the existence of the pair and its possibilities by reducing it to one of its members. For etymological reasons, the term chosen for such a reduction is traditionally *ser*. In fact, Spanish (just like other Romance languages) already has a panoply of terms (*ente, entidad, esencia*, etc.) that are etymologically related to forms of the Latin *esse*, which allows it to express a large part of the ontological vocabulary.

With regard to the Heideggerian vocabulary, this route was taken by José Gaos, the first translator of *Sein und Zeit* into Spanish. To render the vast series of expressions, verbal or nominal, taken on by *sein* (for example, *Sein, Seinsfrage, Dasein, Zu-sein, Seinsart*), he effectively created a network of equivalences where, practically, only the word *ser* is present (*ser, pregunta que interroga por el ser, ser-ahí, ser relativamente a, forma del ser*, respectively). In his *Introducción a "El ser y el tiempo" de Martin Heidegger* (1971), Gaos justifies some of his choices, notably that of *ser ahí*:

> Since we must distinguish between *Dasein* and its *Existenz*, and the latter has all the rights to the translation *existencia*, we must give another to *Dasein*. Which? Only the "literal" translation, the "calque" "*ser ahí*" is capable of reproducing the chief ideas according to which the *being there* is its *there*, and the latter is, as such, place, since it possesses the "existential constitution" contained by "*to find oneself*" and "*to comprehend*," which, in turn, is constituted as a "projection," etc.

1

Ser/estar—essential/accidental

One of the traditional ways of defining the copulative usage of this pair of words consists of referring it to the opposition between essential and accidental (see, among other works, RT: *Diccionario de construcción*, 3:1076, and Vañó-Cerdá, *Ser y estar + adjetivos*). With *ser*, one would express the essential attributes of the subject; with *estar*, by contrast, it would be a matter of simple accidents. However, if one takes it in a strict sense, this opposition turns out to be of quite a different order.

First of all, the copulative usage of *ser/estar* concerns every type of attribute expressed by an adjective. Thus, for example, it

is perfectly possible to say of a man that he is pale (and therefore to predicate an accidental condition) using either *ser* or *estar*. Next, the opposition essential/accidental constitutes, in its ordinary usage, a dichotomy of mutual exclusion. The same attribute belonging to the same subject therefore cannot be an accident and be part of its essence. This strict antithesis does not apply to the current usage of the pair of verbs. Nothing prevents Maria from receiving both predicates: *estar bella* and *ser bella* at the same time.

In reality, rather than establishing some sort of classification of attributes or

properties, the current usage of the pair obliges us to distinguish two perspectives arising from different locutions. In using *ser*, the speaker seeks to articulate a fact he habitually encounters or supposes he may habitually encounter; with *estar*, on the contrary, he places the accent on the singular or transitory character of this same fact.

BIBLIOGRAPHY

Vañó-Cerdá, Antonio. *Ser y estar + adjetivos: Un estudio sincrónico y diacrónico*. Tübingen: G. Narr, 1982.

(Puesto que hay que distinguir entre el *Dasein* y su *Existenz*, y ésta tiene todos los derechos a la traducción *existencia*, hay que dar a aquél otra. ¿Cuál?... Sólo la "literal," el "calco" "ser ahí" resulta capaz de reproducir las capitales *ideas* de que el *ser ahí* y de que éste es como tal *lugar* como tiene la "constitución existenciaria" integrada por el "encontrarse" y "el comprender," éste constituido a su vez como "proyección," etc.)

(Gaos, *Introducción*)

All of these reasons internal to the Heideggerian text cannot hide the genuine problem, however. In Spanish, as just mentioned, the verb used for expressing the position of a given subject, the fact for someone of "existing in a certain place" (RT: *Diccionario del uso del español*), is not *ser* but *estar*. A second possibility then opens up: instead of ignoring and reducing the pair, we could use each of the members as Spanish syntax demands. To translate *Dasein*, for example, we find in RT: *Vocabulario filosófico* a synthesis of various propositions using *estar* and a justification of these choices.

Although José Gaos ... used the verb *ser* to translate *Dasein* (inventing the expression *ser ahí*), other philosophers have suggested expressions based on *estar* to translate it. Thus *estar en algo* [*estar* in something] (Xavier Zubiri), *el humano estar* [the human *estar*] (Pedro Laín-Entralgo), *estar en el ahí* [*estar* in the there], or simply *el estar* (Manuel Sacristán). Gaos's reasons for using *ser* to translate *Dasein* are well-founded, since they relate to a system of assignments and equivalents constructed for translating *Sein und Zeit*. ... But we can understand why other authors chose *estar* to translate *Dasein*: the presence of the demonstrative *da* implies that *estar* is the appropriate Spanish term, since it immediately and without violence evokes the spatiotemporal character given to *Sein* by the *da*.

Although the solution for *Dasein* adopted by Jorge Eduardo Rivera—the most recent translator of *Sein und Zeit* into Spanish—consists in preserving the German term, his version is nonetheless a good example of this approach. To

give a few examples, *Mitsein* is rendered by *coestar*, *In-sein* by *estar-en*, or again, *In-der-Welt-sein* by *estar-en-el-mundo*. Even while aiming to preserve the technical character of the Heideggerian vocabulary, the translator thus chose to respect the habitual usage of the pair in Spanish. Sometimes, however, his choices are also inspired by considerations that go beyond grammar. This is the case with the translation offered for *Vorhandenheit* or *Vorhandensein*: *estar-ahí*. The expression had already been used by the Spanish translators of H.-G. Gadamer's *Wahrheit und Methode* (*Verdad y método*, 319n29), who used it to render *Dasein* in presenting Gadamer's Heideggerian project. According to Rivera, however, if *estar-ahí* can effectively translate *Dasein*, it is not in the sense introduced and discussed by Heidegger, but rather in the sense that the term already had in classical German and that corresponded to the Latin *existentia* (Heidegger, *Sein und Zeit*). Given that, since *Vorhandenheit* is used by Heidegger to clarify this traditional sense of *Dasein* (*Sein und Zeit*, §9), it should be translated by the phrase *estar-ahí*.

It is in this same, nonreductive spirit that we may understand the commentaries, halfway between translation and interpretation, by the Spanish philosopher and essayist Julián Marías. In his essay "Estar a la muerte" (*Obras completas*, 3:172–73), he effectively examines two different examples taken from Heideggerian terminology: the concepts of *Sein zum Tode* and of *In-der-Welt-sein*. The existing translations of the first copied, artificially, the German syntax. A suggested alternative was therefore "ser para la muerte" (to be for death)—which, according to Marías, "despite its literary deficiency, unduly forces the original, emphasizing the 'mortalism' ... often attributed to Heidegger" more than necessary—but also "ser a muerte" ("to be to the death," as in "fight to the death") or "ser relativamente a la muerte" (to be relative to death). However, no suggestion takes into account the existence of a common phrase in Spanish that, according to the author, captures the sense of the Heideggerian word with inflicting "any linguistic or conceptual violence" upon it. This phrase is *estar a la muerte*, as in the title of the article. The expression normally refers to the fact of finding oneself in imminent danger of death. Yet, with *Sein zum*

Tode, it is precisely a matter of "taking this condition of man of which he is only aware when this imminence makes itself particularly salient and raising it up to a category of human life, to an 'existential' as Heidegger himself says" (se trata de elevar a categoría de la vida humana, a "existencial," como dice el propio Heidegger, esa condición del hombre, de la que éste no se da cuenta más que en caso en que la inminencia es especialmente acusada; Marías).

With *In-der-Welt-sein*, the problems of translation are even more flagrant, simply because in Spanish, "with or without the hyphens," the literal version, *ser en el mundo*, does not make sense. *Estar* is used instead, in order to indicate "without equivocation the inclusion . . . in everything which is a place, a space," which would yield, very naturally, *estar en el mundo*. What is more, the use of the verb *estar* presupposes, again according to Marías, a sort of engagement with the real that fits perfectly with the concept of German philosophy. In effect, "while *ser* may refer to a simple way of being, not necessarily real . . . , *estar* necessarily refers to reality: no doubt Ophelia 'is' [*es*] pale, but only a woman who 'is' [*está*] pale can be real" (mientras el "ser" puede apuntar a un mero modo de ser, posiblemente irreal . . ., el "estar" remite necesariamente a la realidad: quizá Ofelia "es" pálida, pero no puede ser sino real la mujer que "está" pálida; ibid.).

III. *Estar, Bienestar,* and *Circun-stancia*

The problems of translation related to the pair also work in the other direction: what should a translator do with an occurrence of *estar* when a Spanish-speaking author takes advantage of its specificity with regard to *ser*? In Ortega y Gasset, for example, we find at least two passages where the locative value of *estar* (practically absent from the verb *ser*) is highlighted. Both passages develop and make precise a notion that is central to the philosopher's thought: "circum-stance."

The first passage is found in the author's fourth lesson on metaphysics (*Unas lecciones de metafísica*). The analysis of the concept of life leads him to posit as a sine qua non condition of any act of self-consciousness the idea that man, necessarily and essentially, "finds himself surrounded by what is not himself, finds himself in an outline, in a circum-stance, in a landscape" (se encuentra rodeado de lo que no es él, se encuentra en un contorno, en una circun-stancia, en un paisaje). Our relations with this Other consist first in the fact, for us, of being (*estar*) in it. But what does *estar* mean in this instance? It is not, as for an object, a matter of a relationship of part to whole, since there is no homogeneity between the I and the spatio-temporal and social envelope of its circumstances. Rather, the radically unique character of each I (an "I who lives his life, and this life which the I lives is lived by no other, *even if all the contents of the two lives had been identical*") imposes a profound heterogeneity. *Estar*, thus, in this very precise case, "is for me to exist in this other than me, it is therefore to exist outside of me, in an unknown land, it is to be [*ser*] fundamentally foreign, since I am not a part of that where I am [*estoy*, from the verb *estar*], I have nothing to do with it" (es existir yo en lo otro que yo, por tanto, es existir fuera de mí, en tierra extraña, es ser constitutivamente forastero, puesto que no formo parte de aquello donde estoy, no tengo nada que ver con ello; ibid.).

These reports of total alienation between the I and its circumstance do not remove the possibility of an interaction, or more precisely, an intervention of the former with regard to the latter. This is in effect what comes out of the *Meditación de la técnica y otros ensayos sobre ciencia y filosofía*. Here the philosopher, seeking to clarify the concept of human need, contrasts *estar* with *bienestar*, "well-being." The first, proper to the animal, corresponds to an atechnical adaptation to the world, to an appropriation of the latter that limits itself to providing for the objective needs of life. The second, on the other hand, "implies the adaptation of the environment to the will of the subject," the transformation into a subjective need of what, objectively, may present itself as superfluous. In effect,

> objective biological needs are not, by themselves, needs for him [sc. man]. When he finds himself limited to these, he refuses to satisfy them and prefers to extinguish himself. They only transform themselves into needs for him when they present themselves as conditions of "*estar* in the world," The latter, in turn, is only necessary under a subjective form, that is, because it makes "*bienestar* in the world" and the superfluous possible.
>
> (las necesidades biológicamente objetivas no son, por sí, necesidades para él. Cuando se encuentra atenido a ellas se niega a satisfacerlas y prefiere sucumbir. Sólo se convierten en necesidades cuando aparecen como condiciones del "estar en el mundo," que, a su vez, sólo es necesario en forma subjetiva, a saber, porque hace posible el "bienestar en el mundo" y la superfluidad.)
>
> (*Meditación de la técnica*)

The occurrences of *estar* in these two passages may be translated in French by the verb *être* (which has a clear locative value) or by more punctual and plastic expressions like *se trouver* and *se placer*. In doing so, however, we would erase certain nuances of the original, notably the etymological affiliation that *estar* and *circonstance* have in the first case (a relation emphasized from time to time by Ortega y Gasset by separating the two components of the latter word by a hyphen) or between those terms and *bienestar*, in the second. Nevertheless, this loss is not too serious, since it is situated at the level of the signifier: the central idea (the ineluctable and problematic belonging of the individual to his context) would be preserved regardless. The situation, however, is different when the author, besides taking advantage of the materials of his language, manages to reshape the meaning from the possibilities it offers. The following example may illustrate this.

IV. *Estar Siendo*

In his treatise *Sobre la esencia*, the Spanish philosopher Xavier Zubiri uses an expression constituted by both members of the pair, one in the infinitive and one in the gerundive. It is *estar siendo*, a nominalized verbal phrase, that enables him to express duration (*duración*), one of three "dimensions according to which the real presents itself to us [*está plasmado*] from its interiority into the intrinsic exteriority of its characteristics [*notas*]"; the two other dimensions being richness—the abundance of characteristics—and their solidity or stability.

From a linguistic point of view, the phrase does not entail any transgression of Spanish syntax. *Estar*, in effect, is playing the rather banal role of auxiliary. Added to any gerundive verb, it enables the expression of the durational aspect of an action. We could therefore translate it, literally, by "being in the course of being." However, in reality, the interpretation that Zubiri himself offers of this *estar* blocks this kind of analysis from the start. The role of auxiliary is in effect completely left behind, mixing inextricably with values that depend, rather, on the copulative usage.

As a statement of the real character of things, the features [*notas*] actualize it in a well-determined formal relationship, a relationship which we could call the "*estar siendo*," putting the accent on "*estar*." Let us recall that *stare*, "*estar*," sometimes had the meaning of *esse* in Classical Latin, "*ser*," but in a "strong" sense. It thus entered some Romance languages as an expression for being, not in any particular sense, but "physical" reality as "physical." In this manner *esse*, "*ser*," became restricted exclusively to its sense as a grammatical tool: the copula. It is only on rare occasions that "*ser*" allows us to distinguish the profound and the permanent from the circumstantial, which will then be expressed with "*estar*"; to say of someone that "he is" a sick person ["*es un enfermo*] or that he "is" sick ["*está* enfermo]—these are two different things. However, this is no exception to what we just said, as the original nuance is perfectly perceptible. For the circumstantial, precisely because it is circumstantial, envelopes the "physical" moment in its realization, whereas the "is" ["*es*" of *ser*], profound and permanent, denotes rather the "mode of being" ["*modo de ser*"] and not the "physical" character. This is why the expression "*estar siendo*" is, perhaps, that which best expresses the character of "physical" reality which belongs to every real thing and which, from an intellective point of view, is approved in the statement.

(En cuanto constatación de la índole real de la cosa, las notas actualizan a ésta en un respecto formal precisamente determinado, un respecto que podríamos llamar el "estar siendo," cargando el acento sobre el "estar." Recordemos que stare, estar, tenía a veces en latín clásico la acepción de esse, "ser," pero en un sentido "fuerte." Pasó así algunas lenguas románicas para expresar el ser no de una manera cualquiera, sino la realidad "física" en cuanto "física." Con lo cual el esse, ser, quedó adscrito casi exclusivamente a su sentido de útil gramatical, la cópula. Sólo raras veces expresa el "ser" lo hondo y permanente a diferencia de lo circunstancial, que se expresa entonces en el "estar"; así cuando se dice de fulano que "es" un enfermo, cosa muy distinta de decir de él que "está" enfermo. Pero esto quizá tampoco hace excepción a lo que acabamos de decir, sino que el matiz primitivo es perfectamente perceptible. Porque lo circunstancial, precisamente por serlo, envuelve el momento "físico" de su realización, al paso que el "es" hondo y permanente denota más bien el "modo de ser,"

no su carácter "físico." Por esto la expresión "estar siendo" es, tal vez, la que mejor expresa el carácter de realidad "física" de que está dotada toda cosa real, y que intelectivamente se ratifica en la constatación.)

(Sobre la esencia)

Estar siendo thus does not only express something like the act of existing *in general* in duration. In effect, as Zubiri says immediately afterward, this dimension does not concern "'*mera*' *realidad*," "pure and simple" reality, the indeterminate abstraction of being. Rather, *estar siendo* aims to express the flow of a very concrete mode of existence, that of belonging to what the author calls "physical reality," that is, to the real character of *that which*, continually and presently actualizing itself in rich and stable features (*notas*), presents itself to us as a fully determined "such." Yet, if the phrase constitutes for the author the most appropriate expression of this "tality" (*talidad*, a neologism made from *tal*, "such"), this is because it is possible for him to give back to the *estar* that composes it a strong and peculiar sense by using the resources of his language. This sense belongs to it by right, but a purely grammatical analysis would be incapable of bringing it out. Zubiri's *estar siendo* is, beside, a clear example of an untranslatable in the wide sense of "that which one is never done translating." The literal version, "to be currently being," though not incorrect properly speaking, nevertheless loses the connotation that the author wishes to use it to express. A paraphrastic version—"to be currently being here and now," for example—might capture it, but we would then lose the plasticity and simplicity of the original. The idea that the phrase expresses is, in fact, already deeply anchored, materially and semantically, in a peculiarity of its source language. Sometimes, however, taking advantage of these peculiarities leads to another type of untranslatable and generates expressions that, purely and simply, are not to be translated. The use that some Latin-American thinkers have for the verb *estar* can illustrate this possibility.

V. *Ser* versus *Estar* in Latin-American Philosophy

One can sometimes perceive a certain pride in texts by Spanish speakers about the pair of terms—sometimes colored with irony, sometimes clearly serious—in their combined expressive possibilities. Julián Marías, for example, in "Estar a la muerte," remarks, not without humor: "I believe that the Germans would exchange one of the provinces we left them for the verb *estar*" (the paper was written in 1953), adding that "if their language had this verb, in addition to *ser*, German philosophy and hence all of modern philosophy would be different." For others, the pair comes from the "interior form of the language," in the sense that Wilhelm von Humboldt gave that expression. It would thus constitute a specific feature of Spanish, contributing to the creation of a vision of the world that was proper and almost exclusive to the Spanish-speaking community (Navas-Ruíz, *Ser y estar*).

However, this sentiment of "pride," fruit of the impression of possessing something unique that may yield unanticipated possibilities, probably finds its most systematic expression among certain representatives of self-styled

"Latin American philosophy" (a branch of Catholic thought, politically engaged and inspired by diverse philosophical sources). Carlos Cullen's article "Ser y estar: Dos horizontes para definir la cultura" illustrates this point of view well.

In it the author distinguishes, in relatively simplistic fashion, two different approaches to the notion of culture. The first, derived from modernity but strongly anchored in Greek thought, is a "code of interpretation of human activity in all its manifestations, which is structured on the basis of a core of meaning furnished by 'the effort of being' [*esfuerzo de ser*]" (ibid.). This is the ontological perspective, or the perspective of *ser*. Cullen distinguishes two moments in its constitution. The first, structured around notions of the transcendental subject and experience, leads to a concept of culture based on progress and accumulation. Action, freed of all "immediacy," is thus identified with the necessary and the universal. We must wait for the "masters of suspicion" (Marx, Nietzsche, and Freud) in order for this model to reach a crisis. In a second moment, in effect, human activity is no longer conceived of as being the inevitable and always purified product of the consciousness of a transcendental subject. It constitutes, rather, the very foundation of all consciousness and any notion of subjecthood.

This crisis, however, does not indicate a decisive break, according to Cullen. It does not presuppose a change in paradigm and gives rise instead to a sort of extension of the modern approach. If, on one hand, "culture is no longer a code," it remains, however, only "the very possibility of structuring codes"; if, on the other hand, the "heroes, sages, and geniuses" who illustrate modernity have disappeared, it is only to be replaced by their "immense creative power" (ibid.). The true crossing of the boundary of *ser* (an approach to culture that, according to Cullen, is no longer proto-ontological but pre-ontological) can only come from a new boundary, that of *estar*. This is a matter of "the meaning acquired for man and his activity from a vital core which imposes itself 'as pure and simple *estar*, nothing more' [*como mero estar, no más*]" (ibid.). Over and against a historical and temporal conception of culture, this boundary offers the soil (*suelo*) as the principal referent. It thus gives rise to a "geo-culture," an expression of the rootedness (*arraigo*) in this soil, founded on "great history"—that of the provisional and the immediate—whose "subject" is none other than the people. It is also a matter of a culture characterized by its *negativity*, since it must reject the Western codification of human actions, hitherto dominant.

This boundary of *estar* is not a simple theoretical construction for Cullen. It is in fact the very one "which is alive in 'deepest America,' the America which falls just shy of any effort to be Western, which is in the process of slowly engulfing the effort of being, that is, which teaches us to read events starting with the soil, to write history into *estar*, to wait while already being its fruit" (es el vigente en la "América profunda," la que está más acá de todo esfuerzo por ser occidentales, la que lentamente va fagocitando el esfuerzo por ser, es decir, nos va enseñando a leer los acontecimientos desde el suelo, inscribir la historia en el estar, esperar estando el fruto; ibid.).

Several years later, J. C. Scannone published the article "Un nuevo punto de partida en la filosofía latinoamericana." Here again it is a matter of distinguishing a way of looking at the world characterized by strong notions such as identity and necessity—the territory of *ser*—with a perspective able to integrate the provisional and the indeterminate—the territory of *estar*. This antagonism, which claims to be, above all, the expression of an experience, is nevertheless already present, according to the author, in "the philosophical potentialities of the Spanish language (and languages like Portuguese)," in which "*estar* has a more local and circumstantial sense, where it signifies being firm (upright), but ready to begin moving, and does not express the essence in itself of things as does, by itself, the verb *ser*."

In the end, both Cullen and Scannone refer, as to their developments concerning the notion of *estar*, to the work of the Argentine Rodolfo Kusch. A genuine inspiration behind Latin-American philosophy, this thinker was, in his vast œuvre, most interested in the problems concerning culture and identity of Native Americans. He would admit, however, at the end of his life, that it was the concept of *estar* "which haunted [him] all through [his] work. It is a matter of *estar* being something prior to *ser* and which has the deep meaning of becoming" (De ahí el concepto de estar. Me ha obsediado durante toda mi producción. Se trata del estar como algo anterior al ser y que tiene como significación profunda el acontecer; quoted in Cullen, "Ser y estar," 44n5). It is thus in the work of Kusch that we find, for the first time (in *América profunda*, 1962), the doctrine of the priority of *estar* in relation to *ser*. It is also Kusch who creates a large number of the dichotomies (uncultured/cultured, stench/purity, deepest America/the West, etc.) that provide him with content and allow him to express its consequences. As with his descendents, this domain of *estar* (supposedly older and more authentic) is rooted for Kusch in a conception of the world that is peculiar to Latin America, whose main features are already to be found in pre-Columbian civilizations.

With this type of treatment, a step is taken with regard to what we have seen for Zubiri. Here, there are no longer translation problems, simply because the expression *estar* (replete with connotations, near or far from the original sense) becomes itself irreplaceable. This peculiarity of Spanish is not just a resource for expressing an idea. It is simultaneously both the starting point and the heart of reflection. From that point on, paradoxically, *estar* is transformed from its verbal form into a sort of a proper noun. Its sense becomes fixed, and despite its earlier possibilities, however rich, it comes to denote only a specific doctrine. It is to be hoped that the feeling of "pride" that seems to have given it momentum will be modified slightly. One may be "proud" or not of *being called* Juán or María, but that has little to do with the fact of *being* Juán or Mariá.

Alfonso Correa Motta

BIBLIOGRAPHY

Cullen, Carlos. "Ser y estar: Dos horizontes para definir la cultura." *Stromata* 34 (1978): 43–52.

Gadamer, Hans-Georg. *Wahrheit und Methode*. Tübingen: Mohr, 1965. Translation by A. Agud Aparicio and R. de Agapito: *Verdad y método*. Salamanca, Sp.: University of Salamanca, 1988.

Gaos, José. *Introducción a "El ser y el tiempo" de Martin Heidegger*. Mexico City: Fondo de Cultura Económica, 1951.

Heidegger, Martin. *Sein und Zeit*. Tübingen: Niemeyer, 1953. Translation by J. E. Rivera Cruchaga: *Ser y tiempo*. Santiago, Chi.: Editorial universitaria, 1997.

Marías, Julián. "Estar a la muerte." In *Obras completas*, vol. 3. Madrid: Revista de Occidente, 1959.

Navas-Ruíz, Ricardo. "Ser y estar: Estudio sobre el sistema atributivo del español." *Acta Salmenticensia: Filosofía y Letras*17, no. 3 (1963).

Ortega y Gasset, José. *Meditación de la técnica y ostros ensayos sobre ciencia y filosofía*. Madrid: Revista de Occidente, 1982.

———. *Unas lecciones de metafísica*. Madrid: Revista de Occidente, 1974. Translation by M. Adams: *Some Lessons in Metaphysics*. New York: Norton, 1970.

Scannone, J. C. "Un nuevo punto de partida en la filosofía latinoamericana." *Stromata* 36 (nos. 1–2) (1980): 25–47.

Vaño-Cerdá, Antonio. *Ser y estar + adjetivos: Un estudio sincrónico y diacrónico*. Tübingen: G. Narr, 1982.

Zubiri, Xavier. *Sobre la esencia*. In *Estudios filosóficos*. Madrid: Sociedad de estudios y publicaciones, 1985. First published in 1962. Translation by A. Robert Caponigri: *On Essence*. Washington, DC: Catholic University of America Press, 1980.

SPECIES, FORMA, EXEMPLAR, EXEMPLUM

> FRENCH   *aspect, apparence, exemple, forme, idée, modèle*
> GREEK   *eidos* [εἶδος], *idea* [ἰδέα]

➤ *IDEA, FORM* and ART, ESSENCE, *IMAGE*, MIMĒSIS, REPRÉSENTATION, SOUL, *TO BE*

The Latin translations of the terms *eidos* [εἶδος] and *idea* [ἰδέα]—as used in the specific context of Plato's writings—should be appreciated in terms of the full panoply of choices available to interpreters given that, in effecting transfers from one language to another, what is sought is not literal translation, unanimously scorned in classical Rome, but a global restitution of meaning. In the precise case of these two words, choices in translation indicate first of all different stages in the reception of Platonic doctrine, and bear witness in particular to a plainly "artificialist" inflection of the Platonic doctrine of ideas, under the crucial influence of the *Timaeus*. But what is at stake here is not a linear history proceeding by successive additions and rectifications: the translation proposed by Cicero, which privileges the Latin *species*, was maintained by neither Seneca nor Apuleius. Inversely, starting from Latin, it is surprising to observe that *species*, whose first meaning is "sight" or "vision" (cf. Lucretius, 4.236, 242), far from being always situated on the side of the *eidos* or model, refers no less frequently to image, spectre, and simulacrum, the *eidolon* [εἴδωλον], with Epicureanism having obliged it to reinterpret the cleavage (RT: *Dictionnaire étymologique de la langue latine: Histoire des mots* s.v. 2; cf. Lucretius, 1.125; see EIDÔLON). The choices in translation—beyond the contamination of different lexicons (Platonic, Aristotelian, Stoic, Epicurean . . .)—thus illustrate a characteristic feature of classical Latin philosophical translations: the superimposition of terms and the recourse to the Old Latin reserve, all the more "untranslatable" in the orbit of Romania as it will have been widely disseminated (see ESSENCE).

I. *Eidos, Species*: The Essential and the Apparent

In classical prephilosophical usage, *eidos* [εἶδος] and *idea* [ἰδέα] are polysemous terms ("form," "appearance," "structure," "category," "class"), from which Plato gave priority to certain meanings pressed into the service of his philosophical endeavors; thus the functions of intelligible forms in their various relations, given greater precision, are more easily graspable thanks to the semantic richness of the terms εἶδος-ἰδέα—structure and form: that which allows one to form categories and that which is given to be seen, that is, both the essential and the apparent, the most

profound and the most superficial (*Republic*, 5.479–80, and 10.132–35).

■ See Box 1.

The Latin *species* offers the same possibilities of articulating distinct levels and exploits equally the root of vision (the root-word *spex* is used as a second term in compounds conserved by the language of religion [*auspex-haruspex-exstipex*]); and yet Cicero alone imposed *species* coherently as a translation for *eidos*—at least in all of his works written after 46 BCE. Neither the Stoic Seneca nor, more strikingly, the Platonist Apuleius would retain that use of *species*, which for them had largely the meaning of "species" (in English), and they used instead *forma* and *exemplar*. Calcidius, finally, restricted the applications of *species* and resorted most frequently to *exemplum*. This can be observed in the limited corpus in which the doctrine of intelligible forms is exposed: Cicero's *De oratore*, Seneca's *Letters to Lucilius* 58 and 65, Apuleius's *Plato and His Doctrine*, and *Question 46* of Augustine's *Ideas*. One can draw as well on the two Latin translations of the *Timaeus*, that of Cicero and that of Calcidius.

In accounting for the diversity of the translations, one cannot neglect the history of philosophy, which is crucial on two distinct levels: that of the interpretation itself of Platonic doctrine and that of the dissemination accorded Aristotelian terminology by the Stoics. Nonetheless, a more attentive consideration of translation procedures and the semantic configurations implemented by them allows for a refinement of the observations one might make solely on the basis of the evolution of doctrines and the history of the language.

II. Cicero: The Distinction between *Forma* and *Species*

We shall first examine how Cicero constructed the equivalence *eidos-species*, then which configurations were exploited by his successors, thus better evaluating the coherence of the uses of *species* in the Ciceronian translation of *Timaeus*. We shall thus see that the choice of *species* entailed a polysemy so charged with philosophical problematics and was inscribed so much against the grain of certain uses dictated by the history of philosophy that, despite the authority of Cicero, it was not retained by those who, after Cicero, were to use and enrich the Latin philosophical lexicon.

A. Translating Plato: *Species*, model, and intelligible referent

It is in the text of *De oratore* (2.8–3.10) that one finds the first evidence of the use of *species* to evoke intelligible forms. *Species* (from the same family as Gr. *skeptomai* [σκέπτομαι], to look at) is used with the precise meaning of "model," or "vision" perceptible only by thought, *cogitata species*, which we see with our mind, *speciem animo videmus*. It is in the context that gives it its meaning: *species* is the Form of the beautiful that inhabits Phidias. With *species*, repeated three times, Cicero is no doubt preparing, by means of a more expressive Latin term, the technical translation of the Platonic *idea* by *forma*. Associated with *forma*, the word *species* ultimately designates that which allows one to underwrite dialectical procedure, the intelligible referent. Two of the principal functions of intelligible form are thus expressed by a single Latin word that would subsequently, in the *Academics* and the *Tusculan Disputations*, be used alone, without *forma*:

1

The *eidos* from Homer to Aristotle

➤ CONCETTO, Box 1, EIDÔLON, FORCE, PRAXIS, PRINCIPLE

Eidos is connected to the root *weid-*, which expresses the notion of seeing (*idein* [ἰδεῖν]) and in the perfect tense that of knowing (*oida* [οἶδα]; cf. the Sanskrit *Vedas*, "possession, acquisition" [RT: *Dictionnaire étymologique de la langue grecque*, s.v.]). It is found in Homer with the sense of "aspect, form" (*Iliad*, 2.58; *Odyssey*, 17.308; 454), where it already refers to a conformity between the outer and the inner (see BEAUTY, Box 1), Empedocles, and Democritus. It commonly designates, in the prose of the historians, for instance, the "characteristic" of something, its type (e.g., Herodotus, 1.203; Thucydides, 2.50), in medical vocabulary, the "constitution" (Hippocrates, *De natura hominis*, 9), in geometry, the "figure" (cf. Euclid, *Data*, 53, "duo eidê tôi eidei dedomena [δύο εἴδη τῷ εἴδει δεδομένα]," rendered in RT: LSJ as "two figures given in species").

It was Plato, then Aristotle, in a concerted displacement, who gave the word its philosophical configuration. The terminological meaning of *eidos* that emerges and predominates with Plato—"idea" or "Idea"—is to be understood first of all in opposition to *eidôlon* [εἴδωλον] (image, phantom), following the problematic of *mimêsis* [μίμησις], with the implementation of the three *eidê* of "beds" effected in *The Republic*, 10 (*trisin eidesi klinôn* [τρισὶν εἴδεσι κλινῶν], 597b 14; see MIMÊSIS). The god fabricates from what must indeed be termed the three "species" of beds the one that alone deserves, in Plato's words, the name of *eidos* or "idea": he makes "what the bed is (*ho esti klinê* [ὃ ἔστι κλίνη])," the bed-essence, unique and by nature (597c–d), a bed étantiquement [ontically] a bed (*ontôs* [ὄντως], 597d 1; see ESTI, III). The carpenter, for his part, makes not "the bed," but "a bed" among others (*klinên tina* [κλίνην τινά], 597a 2), which is only "as" *eidos* (*toulouton hoion* [τοιοῦτον οἷον], 597a 6). The painter, finally, an "imitator" of the carpenter, paints a carpenter's bed as it appears, a "third" bed (597a 3) in relation to the truth of the *eidos*: "it is that, the *eidôlon*" (598b 8). In a general manner, words are on the side of the *eidôlon*—the *nomothete* never works as anything but a carpenter, his eyes fixed on

the *eidos* (*Cratylus*, 389a, 390e); but it is the *eidos* that is known: the dialectic that rises unto the idea of the good ("tên tou agathou idean [τὴν τοῦ ἀγαθοῦ ἰδέαν]"; *The Republic*, 6.508e), moves from idea to idea ("eidesin autois di' autôn eis auta kai teleutai eis eidê [εἴδεσιν αὐτοῖς δι᾽ αὐτῶν εἰς αὐτά, καὶ τελευτᾷ εἰς εἴδη]"; 511c).

The Platonic *eidos* never ceased governing the idea, but remodeled (and this is what renders the "idea" so complex) by its Aristotelian reappropriation, which can be made perceptible by making explicit the new oppositions and new translations that it induces. The Aristotelian critique bears on the "separation" introduced by Plato: "Socrates did not produce either universals or definitions as separate (ta katholou ou chôrista epoiei oude tous horismous [τὰ καθόλου οὐ χωριστὰ ἐποίει οὐδὲ τοὺς ὁρισμούς]), but they (*hoi de* [οἱ δέ], i.e., the philosophers after Socrates), they separated them (*echôrisan* [ἐχώρισαν]), and called ideas (*ideas* [ἰδέας]) this type of entity" (*Metaphysics*, M.4.1078b 30–32; see HOMONYM, Box 1, and UNIVERSALS). To situate the *eidos* in its place, one has to render it simultaneously operative on different levels of intelligibility.

Physically, it becomes one of the four causes: it is as coupled with matter (*to ex hou* [τὸ ἐξ οὖ], what a thing is made of, for example, bronze for the statue) that the *eidos* intervenes ("cause in another sense is the form and the model" [allon de to eidos kai to paradeigma (ἄλλον δὲ τὸ εἶδος καὶ τὸ παράδειγμα)]; *Physics*, 2.3.194b 26); to those two first causes there come to be articulated the motor cause, first principle of movement and rest ("hê archê tês metabolês hê prôtê ê tês êremêseôs [ἡ ἀρχὴ τῆς μεταβολῆς ἡ πρώτη ἢ τῆς ἠρεμήσεως]," the father for the child, Polycletes for the statue—what we moderns designate customarily as "cause"), and the final cause (*to telos* [τὸ τέλος], *to hou heneka* [τὸ οὗ ἕνεκα], the reason for the sculpture; see PRINCIPLE). One thus moves from *eidos/eidôlon* (intelligible "idea"/perceptible copy) to *eidos/hulê* [ὕλη] ("form"/matter) as causes necessary for the description and existence of a single

and identical physical entity. *Eidos* and *hulê* are, in fact, analyzable as components: the *suntheton* [σύνθετον] (composite) or *sunolon* [σύνολον], an individuated and unique composite—for example, a bronze sphere—is a composite of *eidos*, designated as *morphê* [μορφή], "figure, configuration," namely: a sphere, and *hulê*, brass (*Metaphysics* Z.3.1029a 1–7; cf. 8.1033b 5–10); the *eidos* is then more essential or substantial than the matter since it is act, activity, entelechy, *energeia* [ἐνέργεια] and *entelecheia* [ἐντελέχεια], whereas it is potency, *dunamis* [δύναμις] (cf. 8.1050b 2: "the essence, that is, the form, is an act" [hê ousia kai to eidos energeia estin (ἡ οὐσία καὶ τὸ εἶδος ἐνέργεια ἐστιν)]).

The *eidos*, Aristotle specifies in the same passage of his *Physics*, is identical to the "affirmation which is that of the quiddity and its types" (ho logos ho tou ti ên einai kai ta toutou genê [ὁ λόγος ὁ τοῦ τί ἦν εἶναι καὶ τὰ τούτου γένη] (194b 27; see LOGOS, TO TI ÊN EINAI): as with Plato, we are here at the heart of ontology, but the pairing has been twice displaced, not only physically, but also logically. Indeed, at the same time as it plays physically the role of "form," the *eidos* plays logically the role of "species," differentiating itself this time not from "matter," but from "genus," genre, *genos* [γένος]. The *eidos* articulates what is essential in the essence; it allows a far closer approach to what is singular than *genos*; this specific sphere is more a sphere than a shape or figure, Socrates is more a man than a living being: in other words, by virtue of the well-named "specific" difference, the *toionde* [τοιόνδε], the "such," is closer to the *tode ti* [τόδε τι], the "this," closer to the essence or the primal substance that it contributes to defining (1033b 21–26; cf. *Categories*, 5.2b 22: "the species is more essence than the genus" [to eidos tou genous mallon ousia (τὸ εἶδος τοῦ γένους μᾶλλον οὐσία)]; see ESSENCE). Thus it is that in Aristotle's terms, the *eidos* can function as an ontological necessity, more essential and substantial than matter or genus, without having a separate existence.

Barbara Cassin

My opinion, then, is,—that there is no human production of any kind, so compleatly beautiful, than which there is not a "something" still more beautiful, from which the other is copied like a portrait from real life [*ut ex ore aliquo quasi imago exprimatur*], and which can be discerned neither by our eyes nor ears, nor any of

our bodily senses, but is visible only to thought and imagination [*cogitatione et mente*]. Though the statues, therefore, of Phidias, and the other images abovementioned, are all so wonderfully charming, that nothing can be found which is more excellent of the kind; we may still, however, suppose a something which is more exquisite, and more compleat. For it must not be thought that the ingenious artist, when he was sketching out the form of a Jupiter [*Jovis formam*], or a Minerva, borrowed the likeness from any particular object;—but a certain admirable semblance of beauty was present to his mind [*ipsius in mente insidebat* species *pulchritudinis eximia quaedem*], which he viewed and dwelt upon, and by which his skill and his hand were guided [*quam intuens in eaque defixus ad illius similitudinem artem et manum dirigebat*]. As, therefore, in mere bodily shape and figure [*in formis et figuris*] there is a kind of perfection, to whose ideal appearance every production which falls under the notice of the eye [*aliquid perfectum et excellens, cujus ad cogitatem* speciem *imitando referentur ea quae sub oculos ipsa cadunt*], is referred by imitation; so the semblance of what is perfect [*sic perfectae eloquentiae speciem animo uidemus*]. Oratory may become visible to the mind, and the ear may labour to catch a Likeness [*effigiem*]. These primary forms of things are by Plato [the father of science and good language] called "Ideas" [*has rerum formas appellat ideas ille*]; and he tells us they have neither beginning nor end, but are co-eval with reason and intelligence; while every thing besides has a derived, and a transitory existence, and passes away and decays, so as to cease in a short time to be the thing it was. Whatever, therefore, may be discussed by reason and method, should be constantly reduced to the primary form [*quicquid est igitur de quo ratione et via disputetur, id est ad ultimam sui generis formam speciemque redigendum*] or semblance of its respective genus.

(*De oratore*, 2.8–3.10)

The same *forma-species* connection would be rediscovered much later in Saint Augustine in the form of a strict equivalence: "Ideas igitur latine possumus vel formas vel species dicere, ut verbum e verbo transferre videamur" (We can thus render *ideas* in Latin either by *forms* or by *visions*, translating literally). Augustine continues in this famous passage, proposing a definition of the idea, inscribed in the divine intellect, which would remain classic at least until Malebranche:

Ideas are in fact principal forms or essential reasons [*sunt namque ideae principales formae quaedam vel rationes rerum*], fixed and immutable, not informed themselves, and thus eternal and permanent in their mode of being, subjectivated as they are in the divine intelligence [*stabiles atque incommutabiles, quae ipsae formatae non sunt, ac per hoc aeternae ac semper eodem modo sese habentes, quae in divina intelligentia continentur*]. And admitting in themselves neither origin nor extinction, one nonetheless defines as formed in accordance with them all that admits of origin and extinction, and all that is born and expires [*secundum eas tamen formari dicitur omne quod oriri et interire potest, et omne quod oritur et interit*].

(*Quaestio* 46, 2)

B. Translating Aristotle and the Stoics: *Forma*

The difficulty of distinguishing between *forma* and *species* at work in this text of the *Orator* can be read as an echo of a passage in the *Topics* (dating from 44 BCE), which allows one to understand at the same time what is at stake in the choice of *species*. Cicero, in point of fact, uses the pretext that the flexion of *species* in the oblique cases—and in the plural—is a bit awkward to refuse to use that word to translate the *eide* [εἴδη], which designate, in the *Topics*, elements of the analysis of definitions: that meaning is the one retained by Aristotle and the Stoics. Cicero proposes to use for this meaning not *species* but *forma*:

In division there are forms which the Greeks call *ideai;* our countrymen who treat of such subjects call them species [*formae sunt, quas Graeci* [εἴδη] *vocant, nostri, si qui haec forte tractant,* species *appellant*]. And it is not a bad name, though it is an inconvenient one if we want to use it in different cases. For even if it were Latin to use such words, I should not like to say *specierum* and *speciebus*. And we have often occasion to use these cases. But I have no such objection to saying *formarum* and *formis*; and as the meaning of each word is the same, I do not think that convenience of sound is wholly to be neglected [*Cum autem utroque verbo idemque significetur, commoditatem in dicendo non arbitror neglegendam*].

(*Topics*, 30)

The argument from euphony or usage may not be without weight, but it is remarkable that Cicero should reject the use of *species* in a context marked by the Aristotelian and Stoic dialectic. In other words, Cicero rejects the evolution of the uses of *eidos* to impose the meaning given it by Plato. This movement in reverse, which committed Cicero to restore all the semantic possibilities offered by *species*, is particularly palpable in the translation of *Timaeus*; the extent of the phenomenon will be best gauged, however, once one examines the specific lexical system put in place by Seneca in an analogous context.

III. Seneca: *Exemplar*, the Model in Art

In *Letter* 58, devoted to Platonic ontology, Seneca recalls the definition of *genus* and *species* by invoking Aristotle (58.9; on *genos*, see PEOPLE, in particular, III.A); it is thus not surprising that he does not use *species* to translate *idea*. Seneca thus rejects Cicero's linkage between *forma* and *species* to make the *eidos* explicit, whereas he draws on Cicero's authority at the beginning of the same letter (6) in using *essentia* as a translation for *ousia* [οὐσία]. Now the term he chose would commit the entire interpretation of his thought. Whereas in Cicero the role of Forms is present starting with the example of the artist, but is not reducible to that of a model, in Seneca, on the contrary, the use of *exemplar* to render Form privileges that sole function of the model. Thus the translation of *idea* as *exemplar* is immediately illustrated by the example of the painter:

And this "idea," or rather, Plato's conception of it, is as follows: "The 'idea' is the everlasting pattern of those things which are created by nature (*idea est eorum quae natura fiunt exemplar aeternum*). I shall explain this definition, in order to set the subject before you in a clearer light: Suppose that I wish to make a likeness of you (*imaginem tuam*); I possess in your own person the pattern of this picture (*exemplar picturae te habeo*), wherefrom my mind receives a certain outline, which it is to embody in its own handiwork. That outward appearance, then, which gives me instruction and guidance, this pattern for me to imitate, is the "idea" (*ita illa quae me docet et instruit facies, a qua petitur imitatio, idea est*).

(58.6)

It will be observed, from the elaboration of this example, that Seneca uses *exemplar* for the sensory model, whereas *facies* and *habitus* render that toward which the imitation tends, namely, intelligible form. Moreover, when he distinguishes a fourth ontological level, that of the form of the work executed by the artist, Seneca reserves *exemplar* for the model and *forma* for its copy:

The "idea" was Vergil's outward appearance, and this was the pattern of the intended work. That which the artist draws from this "idea" and has embodied in his own work, is the "form." Do you ask me where the difference lies? The former is the pattern; while the latter is the shape taken from the pattern and embodied in the work. Our artist follows the one, but the other he creates.

(Idea erat Vergilii facies, futuri operis exemplar: ex hac quod artifex trahit et operi suo imposuit, idos est. Quid intersit, quaeris ? Alterum exemplar est, alterum forma ab exemplari sumpta et operi inposita : alteram artifex imitatur, alteram facit.)

Not without difficulty, since a gloss continues to be necessary: *exemplar* is thus to designate at once the intelligible model, the *eidos,* and the sensory model, the *idea.* Exemplarity at the level of the intelligible is illustrated at the sensory level by a mimetic duplication, in Seneca as in Plato (cf., in particular, the example of the "beds" developed at the beginning of book 10 of *The Republic,* 596b–597e; see Box 1). It is striking that Seneca is constrained to render *exemplar* more precise by way of *facies,* thus massively reintroducing the visible: "A statue has a certain external appearance; this external appearance of the statue is the '*eidos.*' And the model or pattern itself has a certain external appearance, by gazing upon which the sculptor has fashioned his statue; this is the '*idea*' " (Habet aliquam faciem statua: haec est idos. Habet aliquam faciem exemplar ipsum, quod intuens opifex statuam figuravit: haec idea est). Thus *facies,* in turn, has a double—indeed, a triple—function, applicable to the sensory *exemplar* (Virgil's *facies*), as well as to the completed work, the statue, and the intelligible model: the *idos* has its aspect, its "physiognomy" or "face," and the *idea* has its aspect, its visibility. In using *facies* in this manner, not to translate, but to explain, Seneca reinforces the artificialist schema subtending the doctrine of ideas: it mobilizes as the most general of terms a word that refers to *facere,* the *making* of the artist, understood as an *imponere faciem,* to give form or shape (cf. Marcus Terentius Varro: "proprio nomine dicitur facere a facie, qui rei quam facit imponit faciem. Ut fictor cum dicit 'fingo', figuram imponit . . . , sic cum dicit 'facio' faciem imponit" [One says, properly speaking, to make (*facere*) from *facies* (fashion), for someone who imposes a form on the thing he

is doing. Just as the modeler, when he says, 'I am modeling,' imposes a shape, . . . so, when he says, "I am making," does he impose a fashion]; *De lingua Latina,* 6.78).

If the *exemplar* is not adequate to designate on its own an intelligible form, the term does nonetheless bring into relief the imitation in demiurgical creation, no doubt at the cost of an abusive reading of the myth presented in *Timaeus.* This emerges clearly in *Letter* 65, where Form is presented as a fifth sort of cause: "[To Aristotle's four causes] Plato adds a fifth cause, the pattern or model which he himself calls the 'idea'; for it is this that the artist-demiurge gazed upon when he created the work which he had decided to carry out" (His quintam Plato adicit exemplar, quam ipse idean vocat: hoc est enim, ad quod respiciens artifex id, quod destinabat, effect) (7).

In situating the artist and the god on the same level, Seneca gave priority to an "instrumental" conception of Form, which is defined in the process of an active imitation following the topical comparison of the creation of a statue (8). It is this interpretative perspective that gives its full pertinence to Seneca's choice of *exemplar:*

Neither is the pattern a cause, but an indispensable tool of the cause. His pattern is as indispensable to the artist as the chisel or the file; without these, art can make no progress.

(Exemplar quoque non est causa, sed instrumentum causae necessarium. Sic necessarium est exemplar artifici, quomodo scalprum, quomodo lima : sine his procedere ars non potest.)

(*Letter,* 65.13)

On the basis of the use of *exemplar,* a semantic configuration was initiated that was determined by the model of artistic activity.

■ See Box 2.

IV. Cicero and the Translation of *Timaeus:* The *Species/Exemplar* Distinction

This was the pitfall Cicero managed to avoid in his translation of the *Timaeus:* to that end, he uses *species* whenever there is a need to render what can be grasped by intellection alone. That coherent effort is palpable on three levels: on the one hand, the occurrences of *species* are not mechanically dictated by those of *eidos-idea*; on the other hand, sequences in which *species* figures contribute to produce an augmented nominal sense that brings into greater relief the intellection at work; finally, the distinction between *species* and *exemplar* favors the precision of the meaning of *species.*

The fact that *species* is not a word-to-word equivalent is evident from the first occurrence of the word: Plato's text (28a) distinguishes two phases, the time of the gaze that the artist-demiurge directs at what is conserved as identical and the time in which he achieves the form (*idea*) in his work; in his translation, Cicero condenses the time of the gaze and the apprehension of the form thanks to the use of *species* and thus anticipates the role of Forms in intellection.

ὅτου μὲν οὖν ἂν ὁ δημιουργὸς πρὸς τὸ κατὰ ταὐτὰ ἔχον βλέπων ἀεί, τοιούτῳ τινὶ προσχρώμενος παραδείγματι,

2

Apuleius: *Forma/exemplum/exemplar*

The model of art also inflected the vocabulary use of a Platonist like Apuleius in the succinct introduction of his brief work *Plato and His Doctrine*:

> Ideas, that is, the forms of all things, are simple and eternal, without, however, being corporeal; it is among them that the models of things present and future chosen by god are to be found; in these models, one cannot find more than a single image of each species and everything that is born has, like wax, its form and shape traced in accordance with the imprint of the models.

(Ideas vero, id est formas omnium, simplices et aeternas esse nec corporales tamen; esse autem ex his, quae deus sumpserit, exempla rerum quae sunt eruntve; nec posse amplius quam singularum specierum singulas imagines in exemplaribus inveniri gignentiumque omnium, ad instar cerae, formas et figurationes ex illa exemplorum inpressione signari.)

(1.6)

As in Seneca, *species* is used in its common meaning, whereas *forma-exemplum-exemplar* designate Form following a progression determined in this case by the quite concrete image of a slab of wax on which the model is imprinted. This convergence might suggest that the interpretation of Platonic doctrine, which was certainly not the same for the Stoic Seneca—however influenced he may have been by middle Platonism—as for Apuleius, was inflected in a manner indicated by choices in translation: the translations of Seneca and Apuleius make use of a vocabulary intent on being explicit, but the explicitation of *eidos* [εἶδος] as *exemplum* inflects the meaning, or, more precisely, reduces it. In wanting to transmit, one congeals; by giving priority to the example, one impoverishes the thought.

τὴν ἰδέαν καὶ δύναμιν αὐτοῦ ἀπεργάζηται, καλὸν ἐξ ἀνάγκης οὕτως ἀποτελεῖσθαι πᾶν.

(Thus each time that a creator fabricates something by resting his eyes on what remains always the same and taking as a model an object of this sort in order to reproduce its form and properties, all that he achieves by proceeding in this manner is necessarily beautiful.)

Quo circa si is, qui aliquod munus efficere molitur, eam speciem, quae semper eadem est, intuebitur atque id sibi proponet exemplar, praeclarum opus efficiat necesse est.

(When he who undertakes to achieve a work contemplates the form that remains always the same and takes it as a model, he necessarily accomplishes a masterpiece.)

In 39a–40a, one can observe the same type of displacement: the Forms comprised by the Living, "enousas ideas tôi ho estin zôion [ἐνούσας ἰδέας τῷ ὃ ἔστιν ζῷον]," become *formae,* whereas the Living is clearly rendered in its function as model by the group *species rerum.* It is equally remarkable that the use of *formae*, with a meaning close to *genera*, anticipates the description of the Forms contained by this world, namely, the four species.

ἥπερ οὖν νοῦς ἐνούσας ἰδέας τῷ ὃ ἔστιν ζῷον, οἷαί τε ἔνεισι καὶ ὅσαι, καθορᾷ, τοιαύτας καὶ τοσαύτας διενοήθη δεῖν καὶ τόδε σχεῖν. εἰσὶν δὴ τέτταρες, μία μὲν οὐράνιον θεῶν γένος, ἄλλη δὲ πτηνὸν καὶ ἀεροπόρον, τρίτη δὲ ἔνυδρον εἶος, πεζὸν δὲ καὶ χερσαῖον τέταρτον.

(Now as in the ideal animal the mind perceives ideas or species of a certain nature and number, he thought that this created animal ought to have species of a like nature and number.)

Quot igitur et quales animalium formas mens in speciem rerum intuens poterat cernere, totidem et tales in hoc mundo secumcogitavit effingere. Erant autem animantium genera quattuor.

(The number and the nature of the forms that the mind could discern by contemplating the Form [of all that exists], he decided to reproduce it in this world. There were four species of the living.)

If one now focuses on sequences containing *species*, one observes that the use of a (genitive) determiner renders more precise the role of *species*, which allows one to see mentally the object specified by the determiner. In 29a, the creator fixes his eyes on the eternal model, *to aidion (paradeigma)* [τὸ ἀίδιον (παράδειγμα)]; Cicero translates "speciem aeternitatis imitari":

εἰ μὲν δὴ καλός ἐστιν ὅδε ὁ κόσμος ὅ τε δημιουργὸς ἀγαθός, δῆλον ὡς πρὸς τὸ ἀίδιον ἔβλεπεν.

(If our world is beautiful and its creator is good, it is clear that the creator has fixed his eyes on what is eternal.)

(Atqui si pulcher est hic mundus et si probus ejus artifex, profecto speciem aeternitatis imitari maluit.)

This is confirmed by the fact that *aeternitas* by itself is sufficient, in the following sentence, to render the "eternal model," once the process of intellection has been put in place by *species*: "It is clear to everyone that the creator fixed his eyes on what is eternal [παντὶ δὴ σαφὲς ὅτι πρὸς τὸ ἀίδιον. Nonigitur dubium quin aeternitatem maluerit exsequi]."

These uses appear more characteristic still if they are situated parallel to "speciem optimi," which translates, while turning the adjective into a noun, "tou aristou idean [τοῦ ἀρίστου ἰδέαν]" in 46c (the best there is), and to "speciem rerum," which translates "tôi ho estin zôion [τῷ ὃ ἔστιν ζῷον]" (the Living) in 39e.

The gesture favoring the determining noun is a choice in translation that was not retained by Calcidius, as may easily be seen by comparing Cicero's text with his own in the four following passages, which were previously quoted and translated:

28: [Q]uocirca si is, qui aliquod munus efficere molitur, eam speciem quae semper eadem est, intuebitur atque id sibi proponet exemplar, praeclarum opus efficiat necesse est; quippe ad immortalis quidem et in statu genuino persistentis exempli similitudinem atque aemulationem formans operis effigiem honestum efficiat simulacrum necesse est. [In fashioning a representation of the work resembling and imitating an immortal model and conserving its original state, he necessarily achieves a work of beauty.]

29: Atqui si pulcher est hic mundus et si probus ejus artifex, profecto speciem aeternitatis imitari maluit. Namsi est—ut quidemest—pulchritudine incomparabili mundus, opifexque et fabricator ejus optimus perspicuum est, quod juxta sincerae atque immutabilis proprietatis exemplum mundi sit instituta molitio. [The construction of the world took place following the model of what is unaltered and unchangeable.]

39: Quot igitur et quale animalium formas mens in speciem rerum intuens poterat cernere, totidem et tales in hoc mundo secum cogitavit effingere atque ut mens, cujus visus contemplatioque intellectus est, idearum genera contemplatur in intelligibili mundo, quae ideae sunt illic animalia, sic deus in hoc opere suo sensili diversa animalium genera statuit esse debere constituitque quattuor. [when the mind ... contemplates the kinds of ideas in the intelligible world]

46: deus, cum optimi speciem, quoad fieri potest, efficit ... dei summam optimamque et primariam speciem molientis. [god implementing the first Form]

Whereas Cicero uses nouns to tighten the articulations governing the specific mode of intellection of the creator, Calcidius calls on adjectives and groups of qualifiers to specify what a model is. It is perhaps not a matter of indifference that in such passages, the term used three out of four times is *exemplum*, whereas the term *species* appears only once, qualified by the adjective *primaria*: systematic examination of Calcidius's translation and commentary reveals that the word *species* is reserved for what is apprehended by the intellect, whereas *exemplum* appears whenever, in intelligible form, it is the function of model that is being advanced. If that distinction, however, seems more or less to adhere to the one established by Cicero, it is not maintained with the same rigor. And yet it is in the distinction between uses of *exemplum* and *species* that the specificity of the Platonic reading of the myth of the Demiurge-Creator would appear to reside.

Thus, in the previously quoted translation from 28, Cicero designates as *species* that toward which the gaze of the creator tends, but uses *exemplar* to evoke the role played by the *species* in the process of imitation; similarly, in the following paragraph:

Rursus igitur videndum ille fabricator hujus tanti operis utrumsit imitatus exemplar, idne, quod semper

unumidem et sui simile, an id, quod generatum ortumque dicimus. Atqui si pulcher est hic mundus et si probus ejus artifex, profecto speciem aeternitatis imitari maluit.

(But one should further ask whether the artificer of such a work achieved it by imitating a pattern, that is, according to what is always identical and resembling itself, or according to what we call changing and created. If the world be indeed fair and the artificer good, it is manifest that he must have looked to that which is eternal.)

(29a)

The *exemplar* is what is imitated by the *fabricatoir* (*tektainomenos* [τεκταινόμενος]), whereas *species aeternitatis* is what is imitated by the *artifex probus* (*dêmiurgos* [δημιουργός]). Finally *species aeternitatis* is opposed to *generatum exemplum*.

This rigorously maintained distinction thus allows one to preserve on two distinct levels the description of the intelligible and the elaboration of its role in the sensory world: Calcidius made partial use of this distinction, but Seneca and Apuleius were unaware of it. Now, instead of invoking incomprehension or doctrinal inflection in their case, one might focus on the difficulties entailed by the choice of *species*. To do so it suffices to consider what the other uses of *species* were in philosophical discourse during Cicero's era. Cicero himself also employed the term to designate all that could not be an object of certainty, an appearance constraining one to be satisfied with the probable while the Stoics were intent on founding their theory of knowledge on true representations bearing their distinctive mark. But he also used it to designate the image of the gods, whose mental vision, according to the Epicureans, provides us, with certainty, proof that the gods are beatific and eternal. Although the *species dei* is a little explored aspect of Epicurean theology, it cannot be contested that the use of *species* in an Epicurean context is quite pertinent. This can be observed in the occurrences of the term in Lucretius, where *species* is used above all to designate appearance in as much as it gives to be seen, that is, in conformity with the Epicurean theory of knowledge insofar as it is the necessary condition of knowledge: the syntagm "naturae species ratioque," utilized on several occasions by Lucretius (*De rerum natura*, 1.148: "sight and the explanation of nature") provides a gripping encapsulation of it.

The fact that *species* is used, in the Ciceronian corpus, to reject the certainties of the Stoics, but also to evoke the very conditions of intellection—and to do so in a context not only of Platonism, but also of Epicureanism—suggests the formulation of the following hypothesis in the way of a conclusion: if *species* does indeed refer us back, in its Epicurean and anti-Stoic uses, to Hellenistic philosophy on the conditions of possibility of knowledge, Cicero's exploitation of it to translate Platonic Form can be explained by the frequently articulated wish to restore Plato's method to its true place, which would entail leaving inscribed in the language a question that would remain open. Like Plato, Cicero exploited in *species* all the heuristic potential contained in the term *eidos*. In so doing, he challenged the evolution of the uses of the Greek word fixed by the history of philosophy. His successors preferred to take that evolution into account in their choice as translators, which does not derive from the authority of Cicero.

Clara Auvray-Assayas

BIBLIOGRAPHY

Apuleius. *Works*. London: G. Bell and Sons, 1914.

———. *Opuscules philosophiques. Fragments*. Translated into French by J. Beaujeu. Paris: Les Belles Lettres, 1973.

———. *Apuleius: Rhetorical Works*. Translated and annotated by Stephen Harrison, John Hilton, and Vincent Hunink; edited by Stephen Harrison. Oxford: Oxford University Press, 2001.

Augustine, Saint. *Eighty-three Different Questions*. Translated by David L. Mosher. Washington, DC: Catholic University of America Press, 1982.

Cicero. *Cicero on the Ideal Orator (De Oratore)*. Translated, with introduction, notes, appendixes, glossary, and indexes, by James M. May and Jakob Wisse. New York: Oxford University Press, 2001.

Donini, Pier Luigi. "L'eclettismo impossibile. Seneca e il platonismo medio." In *Modelli filosofici e litterari. Lucrezio, Orazio, Seneca*, edited by P. L. Donini and G. F. Gianotti, 151–300. Bologna, It.: Pitagora Editrice, 1979.

Giomini, Remo. *Ricerche sl testo del "Timaeo" Ciceroniano*. Rome: A. Signorelli, 1967.

Lambardi, Noemi. *Il "Timaeus" Ciceroniano. Arte e tecnica del vertere*. Florence: Le Monnier, 1982.

Moreschini, Claudio. "Osservazioni sul lessico filosofico di Cicerone." *A. S. N. P.* (1979): 99–178.

Plato. *Timaeus*. Translated, with introduction, by Donald J. Zeyl. Indianapolis: Hackett, 2000.

Poncelet, Roland. *Cicéron, traducteur de Platon: L'expression de la pensée complexe en latin classique*. Paris: E. de Boccard, 1957.

Reynolds, Leighton Durham. *L. Annaei Senecae "Ad Lucilium Epistulae morales."* Oxford: Clarendon Press, 1965.

———. *The Medieval Tradition of Seneca's Letters*. London: Oxford University Press, 1965.

Varro, Marcus Terentius. *On the Latin Language*. Translated by Roland G. Kent. Loeb Classical Library. Cambridge, MA: Harvard University Press, 1951.

Waszink, Jan Hendrink. *"Timaeus" a Calcidio translatus commentarioque instructus*. Vol. 4 of *Plato Latinus*. Edited by R. Klibansky. London: Brill, 1962.

SPEECH ACT, PERFORMANCE

FRENCH	*acte de langage*
GERMAN	*Vollziehung*
GREEK	*epideixis* [ἐπίδειξις]
LATIN	*actus exercitus*

➤ *ACT*, ACTOR, AGENCY, DICHTUNG, ENGLISH, INTENTION, LOGOS, NONSENSE, PRAXIS, PROPOSITION, SACHVERHALT, SENSE, *SOPHISM*, TRUTH

The notion of a speech act is inseparable from J. L. Austin's work and his invention of the performative. The attention given to a category of utterances that undoes the true/false dichotomy (the "true/false fetish," as Austin calls it) in favor of a problematics of success and failure (felicity/infelicity) outlines a new field in which language, action, and intention compose a system, and invents a new vocabulary that sometimes leads to misunderstandings. No matter how contemporary it is, this invention, connected with the "linguistic turn," has led us to reconsider the movements or moments that, in the Greek and Latin traditions, are attached to language insofar as it acts and not insofar as it expresses. The problem to be solved is not, as in the Anglo-Saxon world, that of ethical utterances, but rather, in the context of Sophist *epideixis* [ἐπίδειξις], that of rhetorical

effectiveness, of culture as distinct from nature and the creation of the political. Then, in the Middle Ages, comes on the one hand the notion of *actus exercitus*—the revelation of a level of linguistic completeness in which the speech act, and no longer simply the combination of the parts of speech, intervenes; and on the other hand, the location of a remarkable attribute of sacramental utterances as "operative" utterances that "do what they signify."

I. *Epideixis*, Performance, and Performativity of the *Logos*

A. *Epideixis*, performance, and praise

Epideixis [ἐπίδειξις] is the word traditionally used, from Plato's dialogues to Philostratus's *Lives of the Sophists*, to characterize Sophistic discourse. The term is established by Plato, for example in *Hippias maior*, 282c and 286a, and *Hippias minor*, 363c, where it designates the continuous discourse of Prodicus, Hippias, and Gorgias in contrast to heuristic question-and-answer dialogue, seeking the truth about the object and grappling with the difficulties of the interlocutor, that characterizes Socratic dialectic. *Epideixis* is a long, continuous discourse whose effects are so calculated, even when improvised, that its author can only repeat it in the same form (*Gorgias*, 447c2–3). As Aristotle noted, the epidictic style is *graphikôtatê* [γραφικωτάτη], "the most specific to writing," because "its proper actualization is reading" (*Rhetoric*, 3.12; 1414a18–19). The best translation would therefore be "performance," "speech," or even "lecture," since the Sophists, who often came from Sicily or Magna Graecia, went on tour in foreign lands—that is, in the great Greek cities, Athens and Sparta.

With Aristotle (*Rhetoric*, 1.3), *epideixis* becomes more specific and is codified in a system of strict opposition: the epidictic genre, or "eulogy," is one of the three major genres in which all discourses are classified. "Deliberative" (*sumbouleutikon* [συμβουλευτικόν]) discourse is addressed to the assembly, in order to advise for or against something that concerns the future; "forensic" (*dikanikon* [δικανικόν]) discourse is addressed to the tribunal, to accuse or defend, and concerns the past. Epidictic, praise and blame, is addressed, Aristotle says, neither to a citizen nor to a judge, but to the spectator (*theôros* [θεωρός]); it concerns neither the future nor the past, but the present, and it is only "by following the present" ("kata ta huparchonta [κατὰ τὰ ὑπάρχοντα]," 1358b) that one can argue in it about the past or the future; it involves neither a decision nor a verdict, but simply the *dunamis* [δύναμις] (potentiality, power, talent) of the orator himself, regarding which the spectator is expected to express an opinion (1358b6). Finally, instead of referring everything to the useful and the harmful, as in the case of counsel, or to the just and the unjust, as in the case of the legal plea, the eulogy's only concern is "the beautiful and the shameful" ("to kalon kai to aischron [τὸ καλὸν καὶ τὸ αἰσχρόν]," 1358b28)—where the link between the aesthetic and the ethical is assumed (see BEAUTY, Box 1).

To understand the relation between the two senses of performance and eulogy better, we can start with etymology. *Deixis* [δεῖξις], from *deiknumi* [δείκνυμι], "show," is the act of designating without speech, pointing with one's index finger (see THEMIS). *Epideixis* refers to the art of "showing" (*deiknumi*) "before" (*epi* [ἐπί]): *epi* indicates first that one must be speaking before an audience, Aristotle's "spectators." Moreover, that is why *epideixis* can occur without speaking: thus Thales, the founding hero of philosophy (*archêgos* [ἀρχηγός], Aristotle, *Metaphysics*, A.3, 983b20), also founds chrematistics: avenging himself for a Thracian servant's scornful laughter, Thales, by taking monopoly control of the oil presses before a particularly abundant olive harvest, shows everyone that when he wishes, the philosopher can use his meteorological knowledge for economic ends, and thus performs an "epideixis heautou sophias [ἐπίδειξις ἑαυτοῦ σοφίας]"—a demonstration, proof, display of his wisdom, or rather of his competence (*Politics*, 1259a9–19, probably the only nonrhetorical use of the term in Aristotle's works). Thus *epideixis* is an opportunity to show what one can do by taking advantage of the propitious moments that only the present can offer (see MOMENT). Rhetorical *epideixis* is also an opportunity for such a demonstration. The epideictic orator uses what he exhibits as an example or a paradigm: by praising it, he "overrates" it, and shows "even more" (*epi*) thanks to it; simultaneously, he shows what he can do with regard to an object of any kind (Helen or Palamedes, Athens or Rome, a hair or a fly); he demonstrates himself and his talent "in addition" (*epi*). The eulogy thus constitutes the rhetorical performance par excellence—a performance in the athletic sense of the term.

B. The performativity of *epideixis*

It is the status of rhetoric itself that *epideixis* forces us to reconsider. It does not suffice to say that rhetoric, instead of "speaking of," undertakes to "speak to," nor to define it, as Plato would, as empirical or routine, "a worker for persuasion" ("peithous dêmiourgos [πειθοῦς δημιουργός]," *Gorgias*, 453a), or even, like Aristotle, who grants it the status of an art and science, as the "faculty of observing in any given case the available means of persuasion" ("peri hekaston tou theôrêsai to endechomenon pithanon [περὶ ἕκαστον τοῦ θεωρῆσαι τὸ ἐνδεχόμενον πιθανόν]," *Rhetoric*, 1.1355b25, trans. Roberts). We must reconsider the ontological status of persuasion or, as Jean-François Lyotard puts it, "extend the idea of seduction": "It is not the addressee who is seduced by the speaker. The latter, the referent, the meaning, are no less affected than the addressee by the

seduction exercised" (*Le différend*, 148.128, trans. Van Den Abbeele). And we have to understand that here we have a characteristic of the Greeks and a peculiarity of their discursive tradition that was obliterated by the great school of Platonic-Aristotelian philosophy. This power of language is explicit in the very paradigm of the eulogy, the most ancient that has come down to us, Gorgias's *Encomium of Helen*. In the latter, epidictic power is fully revealed: Helen is the most guilty of women because she has set the whole of Greece to war and violence, and yet Gorgias convinces us that Helen is innocence itself. The supplement to *deixis* constituted by *epideixis* succeeds in changing the object into its contrary: the phenomenon becomes the effect of the omnipotence of the *logos* [λόγος]. In so doing, Gorgias also provides the theory of his practice: "Speech is a great sovereign [*logos dunastês megas estin* (λόγος δυνάστης μέγας ἐστιν)] that with the smallest and most imperceptible of bodies achieves the most divine acts [*theiotata erga apotelei* (θειότατα ἔργα ἀποτελεῖ)]" (RT: DK 82B11 [8]; see LOGOS). The inverse model of Aristotle's *De interpretatione* (which establishes in opposition to Sophistic the "normal" system of our discourse; see SIGN) is thus located de facto: discourse, not phenomenon, causes the soul to suffer, or, as Gorgias puts it, "under the effect of discourse the soul undergoes a passion that is peculiar to it [idion ti pathêma dia tôn logôn epathen hê psuchê (ἴδιόν τι πάθημα διὰ τῶν λόγων ἔπαθεν ἡ ψυχή)]" (RT: DK 82B11 [9]). For instead of having to express the phenomenon adequately and convey it, discourse, in complete autonomy, produces it: "It is not speech that indicates the outside, but the outside that comes to reveal speech [ouch ho logos tou ektos parastatikos estin, alla to ektos tou logou mênutikon ginetai (οὐχ ὁ λόγος τοῦ ἐντὸς παραστατικός ἐστιν, ἀλλὰ τὸ ἐκτὸς τοῦ λόγου μηνυτικὸν γίνεται)]" (*Treatise on Non-Being*, RT: DK 82B3, 85). Gorgias, in his "game" of recreating a Helen who is now innocent, makes it clear that *epideixis* involves moving, not from being to speaking about being, as in ontology, but rather, in a logological mode, from speech to its effect. It is in this respect that the performance of rhetorical-sophistical discourse, of which *epideixis* is the emblem, is (to adopt Austin's expression) the art of "doing things with words."

■ See Box 1.

1

Gorgias's *Encomium of Helen*: From orthodoxy to the creation of values

➤ COMMONPLACE, DESCRIPTION, *WORLD*

Epideixis is all the more spectacular when it transforms, or even performs, the world, by producing new objects and new values. The whole art consists in making use of accepted values to propose new ones: Gorgias's *Encomium of Helen* (RT: DK 82B11) shows us, in its opening sentences, this passage from communion to invention, from liturgy to "happening."

The first vector is orthodoxy:

kosmos polei men euandria, sômati de kallos, psuchêi de sophia, pragmati de aretê, logôi de alêtheia; ta de enantia toutôn akosmia. andra de kai gunaika kai logon kai ergon kai polin kai pragma xhrê to men axion epainou epainôi timan, tôi de anaxiôi mômon epitithenai; isê gar hamartia kai amathia memphesthai te ta epaineta kai epainein ta mômêta. [κόσμος

πόλει μὲν εὐανδρία, σώματι δὲ κάλλος, ψυχῆι δὲ σοφία, πράγματι δὲ ἀρετή, λόγωι δὲ ἀλήθεια· τὰ δὲ ἐναντία τούτων ἀκοσμία. ἄνδρα δὲ καὶ γυναῖκα καὶ λόγον καὶ ἔργον καὶ πόλιν καὶ πρᾶγμα χρὴ τὸ μὲν ἄξιον ἐπαίνου ἐπαίνωι τιμᾶν, τῶι δὲ ἀναξίωι μῶμον ἐπιτιθέναι· ἴση γὰρ ἁμαρτία καὶ ἀμαθία μέμφεσθαί τε τὰ ἐπαινετὰ καὶ ἐπαινεῖν τὰ μωμητά.]

1. For the city-state, order is the excellence of its men; for the body, it is beauty; for the soul, wisdom; for something one makes, value; for speech, truth. Their contrary is disorder. Someone or something that is worthy of praise—a man, woman, discourse, work, city-state, thing—has to be honored by a eulogy, and someone who is unworthy of it has to be blamed, for blaming the praiseworthy and praising the blamable are equally wrong and equally ignorant.

The key words that today still define for us poetic and philosophical Greece are all there, distributed among two values, positive and negative, *kosmos* [κόσμος] and *akosmia* [ἀκοσμία], order and disorder, well-structured beauty—ornament, colors—and its absence, its lack, its defeat by chaos. The auditor-spectator is led to the point where words take on their meaning, exist together as a conventional system of meaning. The sense of truth is rooted in this communion, constituted by the continual creation of the values necessary for the very existence of the social bond. Here we are at the heart of the most efficacious, the most performative, because also the most economical, of orthodoxies: the common practice of language.

The second vector, in the sentences immediately following, is heterodoxy:

tou d' autou andros lexai te to deon orthôs kai elegxai . . . tous memphomenous Helenên, gunaika peri ês homophônos kai homopsuchos gegonen hê te tôn poiêtôn akousantôn pistis hê te tou onomatos phêmê, ho tôn sumphorôn mnêmê gegonen. egô de boulomai logismon tina tôilogôi dous tên men kakôs akouousan pausai tês aitias, tous de memphomenous pseudomenous epideixas kai deixas kai deixas talêthes pausai tês amathias. [τοῦ δ᾽ αὐτοῦ ἀνδρὸς λέξαι τε τὸ δέον ὀρθῶς καὶ ἐλέγξαι . . . τοὺς μεμφομένους Ἑλένην, γυναῖκα περὶ ἧς ὁμόφωνος καὶ ὁμόψυχος γέγονεν ἥ τε τῶν ποιητῶν ἀκουσάντων πίστις ἥ τε τοῦ ὀνόματος φήμη, ὃ τῶν συμφορῶν μνήμη γέγονεν. ἐγὼ δὲ βούλομαι λογισμόν τινα τῶι λόγωι δοὺς τὴν μὲν κακῶς ἀκούουσαν παῦσαι τῆς αἰτίας, τοὺς δὲ μεμφομένους ψευδομένους ἐπιδείξας καὶ δείξας καὶ δείξας τἀληθὲς παῦσαι τῆς ἀμαθίας.]

2. It is for the same man to say with rectitude what needs to be said, and to contradict those who blame Helen, a woman who combines in a single voice and a single soul the belief of the poets' audience and the sound of a name that reminds us of misfortunes. I want, giving logic to speech to put an end to accusations against a woman about whom we have heard so much calumny, to show that her detractors are wrong, to show the truth and end ignorance.

Gorgias—"I," all alone—is challenging a consensus that includes, "in a single voice and a single soul [*homophônos kai homopsuchos* (ὁμόφωνος καὶ ὁμόψυχος)]," all the poets and their audiences, and even the testimony deposited in language itself with the eponymy of Helen's name, constantly emphasized from Aeschylus (*helenas, helandros, heleptolis* [ἑλένας, ἕλανδρος, ἑλέπτολις], "destroyer of ships," "destroyer of men," "destroyer of cities," *Agamemnon,* 687–90) to Ronsard ("Her Greek name comes from ravish, kill, pillage, carry off," *Sonnets pour Hélène,* 2.9). The orator restores order in the *kosmos,* he restores *logismon* [λογισμόν] in the *logos,* and he is going to prove that Helen is an object to be praised, and not, as she has been since Homer, one to be blamed. The eulogy is thus based on the consensus implied in the first lines in order to recreate a new and, so to speak, contra-consensual consensus in the following lines. And that is exactly what happened: Gorgias launched into the world a new Helen who, through Isocrates and Euripides and on to Hofmannsthal, Offenbach, Claudel, and Giraudoux, is innocent and praiseworthy.

The *Encomium of Helen* thus illuminates two characteristics of eulogy in general. The first characteristic is that every eulogy that moves within the *doxa,* that manipulates the latter and the commonplace, is nonetheless, either virtually or in actuality, as here, paradoxical. It is the whole plan of the *Encomium of Helen,* codified as a norm in rhetorical manuals, that leads to this contradiction: the speaker praises her family line, her beauty, her qualities, and tells what she has done—or rather, since she is a woman, what she suffered: Helen is not guilty because she has nothing to do with the misfortunes and disasters, all of which were the result of divine decrees, men's violence, and the power of the discourses that forced her to do what she did—as if developing culpability sufficed to produce innocence.

The second specific characteristic, whose connection with the first is clear, is that every eulogy is at the same time a eulogy of the *logos,* that is, it is ultimately a eulogy of the eulogy. Gorgias's *Encomium of Helen* is once again the first and supreme illustration of this. It is in fact on the very power of the *logos* that Helen's innocence finally depends: Helen seduced by Paris's words is not guilty, for words are, literally, irresistible. This time we have to cite the whole passage:

(8) If what persuaded [Helen], deluded her mind, was speech, it is not difficult . . . to defend her against this accusation and to destroy the charge in this way: speech is a great sovereign which, by means of the smallest and most inconspicuous of bodies, achieves the most divine acts, for it has the power to end fear, produce joy, increase pity. I am going to show that this is in fact how it is. (9) And I shall have to show this to those who listen to me by also appealing to common opinion.

Then Gorgias analyzes the effects, in different areas of speech, and the deep causes of discursive tyranny, which are anchored in human temporality. In this way, he plays eulogy's game (*emon de paignion* [ἐμὸν δὲ παίγνιον], "my plaything," as the final words of the *Eulogy of Helen* bluntly put it), the game of this spectacle that is both codified and inventive, delivered by an orator who is playing with the consensus. "Appealing to opinion," taking banalities and accepted themes as his point of departure, Gorgias plays the *logos* to make them exist in a slightly different way, to produce them as different, to produce different ones. Or again: there is a moment in every eulogy where language overwhelms the object, where language performs a new object, where description and the commonplace open up. That is the moment of creation and, among other things, of the creation of values. It is also the moment of convergence between the criticism of ontology and the political institution.

BIBLIOGRAPHY

Cassin, Barbara. *Voir Hélène en toute femme.* Paris: Les empêcheurs de penser en rond, Institut d'édition Sanofi-Synthélabo / Éditions du Seuil, 2000.

Gorgias of Leontini. *Encomium of Helen.* Edited, introduced, and translated by D. M. MacDowell. London: Bristol Classical Press, 1982.

C. *Apodeixis* and *epideixis,* language that shows and language that works

Epideixis differs essentially from *apodeixis* [ἀπόδειξις]. *Apodeixis* is showing "on the basis of" what is shown, drawing on the object to show, drawing the object from the object itself: demonstration that is logical, mathematical, but also, and primarily, philosophical, including first philosophy. "Apodictic" involves saying what is, what is there, what manifests itself, or making it appear, unveiling it, making it visible by means of the discursive medium. Martin Heidegger rightly emphasizes the sequence of Aristotle's use of *apo-*: *apo-*dictic (the "de-monstrative") is based on *apo-*phantic (the "declarative"), which in Aristotle designates the very essence of language. For Aristotle, as Heidegger stresses, referring particularly to chapters 1 to 6 in *De interpretatione,* "to say, *legein,* is *apophainesthai,* 'to make visible' [*phainesthai*] on the basis of the very thing spoken of [*apo*]": "In discourse [*apophansis*], so far as it is genuine, *what* is said is drawn *from* what the talk is about"; that is why "phenomenology means *apophainestai ta phainomena*—to let that which shows itself be seen from itself in the very way in which it shows itself from itself" (*Sein und Zeit,* §7, pp. 32, 34, trans. McQuarrie, 56, 58).

■ See Box 2.

In the system of Aristotelian discourse, it is by opposition to *apodeixis,* which defines the "natural" relationship between word and thing, that we can understand the philosophically disturbing force of *epideixis.* Not only two discursive modalities but even two models of the world are opposed to each other: a physical model, in which it is a question of determining the principles of nature in accordance with demonstrations of truth (see TRUTH); and a cultural and political model, in which it is a question of performing, on occasion after occasion, the values in common that permit a city-state's constitution and ongoing consensus.

II. *Actus exercitus / actus significatus*

In the thirteenth century, the Latin expression *actus exercitus* (the act performed) was introduced into medieval Latin terminology in opposition to *actus significatus* (the act signified), in grammar as well as in logic. In both cases, the distinction made it possible to contrast, within language, simple or complex expressions that *signify* things, and those that make it possible to do something by means of language. In grammar, the initial question is that of completeness, since some utterances may be grammatically incomplete, and in particular lack a verb, the expression

---

2

Apodeixis in Aristotle

➤ ERSCHEINUNG

Apodeixis [ἀπόδειξις] is situated in two places in the Aristotelian corpus: within the *Analytics* and within the *Rhetoric.*

  Apodeixis and apodictic science constitute the very object of the *Analytics,* as is shown by its very first lines (*Prior Analytics,* 1.1, 24a11). Unlike the dialectical syllogism, which starts from accepted ideas (see DOXA), thus operating with probable premises, and the rhetorical enthymeme, which is never more than an abbreviated rhetorical syllogism, the domain of *apodeixis* is truth: it starts from true premises that are self-evident or already demonstrated, and "shows the cause and the why" (*Posterior Analytics,* 1.24, 85b23–24). There could in fact be no science of the sensible particular as such, any more than of definition (*Metaphysics,* Z.15, 1039b28). But *apodeixis,* following induction (*epagôgê* [ἐπαγωγή]), see *Posterior Analytics,* 1.18, 81a40–b2), is precisely the procedure that makes the particular known qua universal, and makes it possible, for example, to deduce that because Socrates is a man, Socrates is mortal (ibid., esp. 86a5–10; cf. 1.11, 77a5–9). Aristotle's demonstration and his procedure of moving analytically from sensation to induction and then to deduction thus provide the schema for philosophical science,

in the perennial nature of its tradition, down to Hegelian phenomenology, which, like philosophical science, draws the contingent toward the necessary and extracts universal truth from the particular.

  But *apodeixis* is not merely a procedure of transforming the phenomenon into a scientific object; it is also a technique of adhesion, and, in fact, the very heart of Aristotelian rhetoric.

  Rhetoric deals essentially with three objects: the parts of the discourse and their order, proofs and their sources, and style properly so called. With regard to the parts of the discourse and their order, Aristotle opposes the ridiculous practice of proliferating divisions, retaining only two of them: "It is necessary to say the thing you are talking about, and to demonstrate it [*eipein . . . kai tout' apodeixai* (εἰπεῖν . . . καὶ τοῦτ' ἀποδεῖξαι)]" (*Rhetoric,* 3.13, 1414a31–32). The first part, which corresponds to the dialectical "problem" (*problêma* [πρόβλημα], "what is put forward," 36), Aristotle proposes to call *prothesis* [πρόθεσις], "proposition"; the second is *apodeixis* proper, which he proposes to call also *pistis* [πίστις], from a term that means indissolubly, on the subjective side, "faith," "belief," "adhesion," and, on

the objective side, "proof," "confirmation." Thus the analysis rejoins the main object of rhetoric: the classification of proofs, *pisteis* [πίστεις]. The great dividing line passes, we recall, between "extra-technical" proofs, which come from outside and which one has to know how to "use," such as testimonies, and "technical" proofs, which are provided by the rhetorical method and by the orator himself, and which he has to "discover" (*Rhetoric,* 1.2, 1355b35–39). The latter are themselves of three kinds: they are to be sought in the character of the orator (on the side of the sender, we might say), in the listener's dispositions (on the side of the receiver), or, finally, in the *logos* itself (thus in the message), "since it shows or seems to show" (1356a4). Thus *apodeixis* corresponds to proof par excellence, that which constitutes the very body of the *logos* qua rhetoric.

  Art imitates nature and "partly completes what nature cannot bring to a finish" (Aristotle, *Physics,* 2.8, 199a17–18). Scientific demonstration and the system of rhetorical proof imitate nature and complete it insofar as they help the phenomenon to manifest itself, beyond its immediate apprehension, as true, universal, persuasive: they help us understand it and believe in it.

of the act, because they do not signify the act, but perform it. In logic, reflection bears on quantifiers and other logical terms that do not have a referent, that is, they do not refer to a thing or a concept, but have a function in the utterance by "acting" on the full terms. The notion of *actus exercitus* thus enabled thinkers to analyze, as in modern theories of speech acts, utterances that serve to act (counting, blessing, etc., in the examples below), in the framework of a theory of syntactical-grammatical completeness that is not based simply on formal criteria (grammaticality), but also on taking into account the speaker's intention to signify. Moreover (and this point is just as interesting in relation to contemporary thought), it enabled thinkers to include the emotive dimension of language in a new way, since it never converged, in the Middle Ages, with what had been said about it in the rhetorical tradition. It is interesting that the same notion enables us to analyze both utterances that are not assertive but performative, characterizing expressions that serve to carry out logical or linguistic operations (quantification, ostension, *deixis*, etc.), and utterances that, like interjections or verbal moods, are used to express non-conceptual mental states or affects, such as pain, hope, desire, and so on.

A. *Actus exercitus* and speech acts

The distinction between *actus exercitus* and *actus significatus* was introduced in the context of thirteenth-century grammarians' discussions of the completeness of utterances, more precisely in the commentaries on Priscian's *Institutiones*. Priscian says (*Institutiones grammaticae,* 17.10) that an adverb, *bene*, can have the value of a complete utterance if it is understood as "joined" either to an act previously carried out or to a previously made statement. Some authors glossed this passage by saying that the adverb can be referred either to an "act carried out"—for example, when one says "good," on seeing a master strike a pupil, the adverb would be the determinant of the act being carried out—or to an act signified by a verb. But in addition, we find, on the basis of the same example, a much more interesting use, which should be compared with the modern notion of a speech act. In the case of the master striking the pupil, the adverb not only helps to determine an unexpressed act (on the order of an ellipsis that could be constituted as the utterance "I think you are striking well," or "What you are doing is good," etc.), it can itself have the value of performing an act, because the utterance is tantamount to an encouragement to the person who is performing the act to continue to do so. Thus these two meanings of the expression *actus exercitus* are very different. Where the second is concerned, we can analyze many utterances that are considered to be complete even without a verb: they do not need an expressed verb that would express an act signified (*actus significatus*) because they constitute an "act performed" (*actus exercitus*); they are said to be "complete in relation to the act performed." Among these, we find examples of liturgical utterances such as "In the name of the Father, the Son, and the Holy Ghost," through which, says an anonymous grammarian, "I perform benediction": thus the act that is performed does not need to be signified.

There are two types of utterance. Through the first, we state something about another thing, such as "Socrates runs"; this type requires a verb to be complete. Through the second kind of utterance, something is done [*per quam aliquid exercetur*], as when one says "One, two, three" (an utterance, as is said elsewhere, that does not serve to signify the act of counting, but that enables the speaker to perform it); this utterance does not need an expressed verb, and it is made complete in the act performed: one does not need to say "I count one."

(Marbais, *Tractatus de constructione*)

The person counting does not intend to say something about numbers, or to designate himself as counting, but only to act by counting, says another author, with regard to the same example. The grammarians seek to provide a typology of the different kinds of act performed by distinguishing their formal properties. We will note here only two points.

First, utterances that are "complete in accord with the act performed" are not elliptical utterances: the latter are incomplete formally, but what is missing can always be expressed vocally (thus, if to the question "What is the supreme good in life?" we respond, "Dignity," the latter expression is a complete utterance in which, by anaphora, what is missing can be restored). This is not the case when an act is performed, as is indicated very clearly by the rule: "No word that performs an act of any kind is constructed with it, in fact *ecce* [behold] is not constructed with the act of designation, nor is the copulative or disjunctive conjunction constructed with the act of coordination or disjunction, nor *omnis* [everything] with the act of distribution. This would amount to a useless [*nugatio*] repetition and would not be comprehensible": it is a useless repetition because the same act would be both signified and performed.

Second, an important distinction that is very close to the one made by modern thinkers is introduced to distinguish between what might be called conventional and unconventional speech acts. In the first case, the acts "performed" are possible by virtue of the syntactical-semantic properties of expressions (*ex vi sermonis*); this is notably the case of vocative adverbs (*o!* to call someone), demonstratives (*ecce!* [here!] to show something), and interjections (*vae!* [woe!] to deplore something). In the second case, an act is performed by means of a given expression, solely because the speaker (*proferens*) intends to use the expression for that purpose, without it being particularly meant to have that function. A common and especially significant example is the expression *Aqua!* This noun, by itself, can be considered a complete utterance only because someone, in a particular situation where a fire has broken out, decides to use it to ask that someone get water. The notion of the speaker's intention to signify (*intentio proferentis*) is essential here: not only is such an utterance, even if it is not canonical (because it does not include a subject and a verb), totally acceptable, complete, and interpretable, but above all, it is much more adequate to expressing the intended sense (*intellectus intentus*) because through its very form it renders so clearly the urgency of the situation and the speaker's emotion or panic. Some authors qualify these utterances as "enclitic," perhaps because, like the particles designated by the same term that are not autonomous but require attachment to a principal word, such utterances can exist only when uttered and interpreted in a particular situation. This theory of the *actus exercitus* was developed chiefly among grammarians who accorded an essential place to the notion of intending to signify in the analysis of the formal properties of utterances. Among the Modists (second half of the twelfth century), who refused to take the speaker or the situation into account in order to arrive at a system of description that would be universal and thus scientific, the notion of *actus exercitus* was adopted only in the case of the vocative, which is the "term of the act performed" (e.g., *O Henrice!*—the noun is the end of the act of vocation carried out by the interjection), by opposition to the accusative, which is the "end of the act signified" (e.g., "I see a book": the noun is the end of the act of seeing).

B. *Actus exercitus* and logical operations

In logic, in the analysis of logical operators or signs of function, we find the same idea: that some constituents of language do not signify something but do something. Just as we say that the adverb *ecce* serves to perform *deixis*, we can say that "not" serves to perform negation, or *omnis* distribution, and not that they *signify* these operations (which the corresponding verbs or nouns--respectively, *negatio, negare*, or *distributio, distribuere*—are supposed to do). Logicians who adopt this analysis can thus distinguish very clearly between two types of expression: categorematic expressions, which are signs of things, and syncategorematic expressions, which are signs of mental operations. Other schools, seeking to attribute a type of signification to the latter (for example, by saying that they signify "relations between things"), obscure the distinction.

The distinction between *actus exercitus* and *actus significatus* should be compared with another distinction, used by grammarians and logicians, between expressions that signify in the way of a feeling (*per modum affectus*) and those that signify in the way of a concept (*per modum conceptus*) (see CONCEPTUS). The Parisian tradition of medieval logic tends to maintain that logical operations are "performed" by terms such as *non* or *omnis*, whereas the Oxford tradition opposes this view, emphasizing the idea that it is the speaker who performs these operations qua "principal agent," these signs being no more than the "instruments" of acts:

> Just as man or the soul is the principal agent in the operation of negation [est principale agens in operatione negandi] and the word "non" the instrument, in the same way a person who is beating someone with a stick is the principal agent of the act of beating, and the stick is the instrument; similarly, man or the soul is the principal agent in the distribution of the subject, and "all" is the instrument.

> (Bacon, *Summa de sophismatibus et distinctionibus*, 153–54)

Logical operations are "acts of the reason" that correspond to affects: for example, if I take two simple expressions that are mutually incompatible, I am affected by their disagreement, and I use the word "not" to express this disagreement ("This table is not square"). There are other affects that are also rendered by signifying expressions "in the mode of affect." Thus a disagreeable event that causes pain might be signified either in the mode of the concept ("I am suffering") or in the mode of pure affect ("Ow!"), or in an intermediary fashion, which is that of the interjection. (Authors differ in an interesting way concerning whether interjections signify a concept in the mode of affect, or an affect in the mode of the concept, the latter position being based on the conventional nature of interjections and their variability from language to language, which distinguishes them from exclamations, whereas the former seems to flow from their imperfect form, notably with respect to their pronunciation, which allows individual variations.) The relations between this "signification in the mode of affect" and expressions that allow us to perform an act are complex and theorized in different ways; the question is in particular whether these speech acts belong, qua "acts," to the sensitive faculty (which controls the emotions, the will, and thus action), or on the contrary to the rational faculty, insofar as they are realized by means of "language."

Furthermore, in logic, the distinction between a "signified act" and a "performed act" takes on a somewhat different but related value. Thus for William of Ockham, the copula is the sign of an act of the mind, the act that consists in predicating the concept of the subject with the concept of the predicate. The verb "predicate," and other verbs of the same kind ("verify," etc.), serve to "signify" the act that is "performed" by the copula. In "homo est animal," the predication is an *actus exercitus* and concerns particulars denoted by the subject and the predicate (taken in personal *suppositio*), whereas in "animal praedicatur de homine," the predication is an *actus significatus*, and concerns concepts (the terms being taken in simple *suppositio*). Ockham uses this distinction to explain the true sense of ambiguous or philosophically dubious propositions. Propositions whose terms seem to refer to universals (e.g., "homo est risibilis," "man is capable of laughter") are reformulated as predications of a superior type that can then be connected with the corresponding predication or predications "performed," whose terms denote only individuals (see PREDICATION and UNIVERSALS).

The distinction between *actus significatus* and *actus exercitus* was also used in the analysis of the paradoxes of self-reference, notably the liar paradox. In a proposition like "What I say is false" ("ego dico falsum"), there is a tension between what is "signified" and what is "performed," because the assertive content of the action is determined by the attribute "false" at the same time that the action is actually realized by uttering the proposition.

III. Speech Acts and Sacramental Theology

In the Middle Ages, reflections on speech acts are particularly developed in the area of sacramental theology. The very definition of a sacrament, "sacramentum id efficit quod significat/figurat" (the sacrament does what it signifies), is particularly explicit. The sacrament is a sign that has a twofold value, "cognitive" and "operative" or "factive," because it simultaneously signifies grace and confers it. Since it is composed of a matter (e.g., baptismal water) and a form (the formula "I baptize you," etc.), the question was what in this formula allows it to be efficacious—a question that is not independent of those raised in relation to magic formulas. The operativity of sacramental formulas was perceived by medieval theologicans as being dependent on a set of intrinsically connected factors: the formula itself (reflections on its constituents, the modes of the verbs, the enunciative markers), its meaning and its institution, the speaker (discussions of the role of the priest, the utterer of the formula, the agent in relation to the conferral of the sacrament, but not in relation to its effect), the intention to signify on the part of the priest and of those who receive the sacrament, and the situation (other elements of the sacramental rite). These reflections led to a clear perception of the distinction between constative utterances, called "cognitive" (*cognitiva, significativa*) and "operative" (*factiva, operativa*) utterances. Theologians were led to inquire into the characteristics of the latter, noting that they were not necessarily different in their form (we see the importance of the first person in some formulas, such as that of baptism, but "This is my body" is assertive in form), reflecting on the relative role played, in order to confer on them this operative character, the intention of the person who established these formulas, the intention of the person who utters them (the priest), and the intention of the person who receives them. The assertive form of the Eucharistic formula aroused discussions regarding the different truth-values of cognitive and operative utterances. Cognitive utterances are, as Thomas Aquinas says so well, true in relation to a state of affairs that preexists them, unlike operative utterances, which, by being pronounced, create this state of affairs. Duns Scotus, against the tradition of the thirteenth century, refused to think that the Eucharistic formula needed to be true in order to be operative, maintaining instead that it must first act before it becomes true through the transformation of the bread into the body of Christ. The distinction between "signified" and "performed," which is used to describe either the acts carried out by means of language, or linguistic or logical operations like quantification, is used in this context and applied to the *deixis* that is realized by the subject pronoun *hoc* (this) in the formula of Eucharistic consecration, "hoc est corpus meum" (This is my body). There are in fact numerous discussions of the interpretation of the deictic: according to some thinkers, it is reported speech, so that the priest is merely repeating Christ's words, and the *deixis* (*demonstratio*) is said *ut concepta* or *ut significata*; according to others, the priest actually shows the bread while uttering the formula (leading to difficulties in understanding how the proposition can at that point be true, since it is false that "this bread is the body of Christ"), and the *deixis* is said *ut exercita*.

There are other domains in medieval theology in which reflections on speech acts are carried on, but sacramental theology is peculiar in that there analyses take an eminently technical form, using the tools provided by the logic and grammar of the time. In different contexts, it is acknowledged that certain utterances make it possible to act on the world, to transform it, even to create it ("fiat lux"), or again, to act on others (e.g., prayers, praise, making vows, insults, and so on). Reflections on promises and oaths are particularly interesting: on the basis of the idea of "obligation," which is of juridical origin, the difference between,

for example, a promise and an ordinary utterance is clearly perceived. Duns Scotus emphasizes the distinction between "assertatory judgments" and the "promissory judgments" that oblige them to "make the truth be," that is, to act so that what they say becomes real. In the case of promises and oaths, as in that of sacramental formulas, opinions differ regarding whether the operativity of such utterances and their obligatory value have to do more with the speaker's intention or with the conventional content of the expressions actually uttered, a distinction that corresponds to that made by modern thinkers between "speaker's meaning" and "conventional meaning." We see that here, the moral dimension of the speech act is foreshadowed, as is shown, moreover, by treatises on the "sins of the tongue" (see TRUTH, IV).

IV. "Speech Acts," "Perform"

To properly understand the novelty constituted by the "speech act," we have to resituate it in its context: the invention of this new vocabulary enables us to account for unperceived linguistic phenomena and to mount a definitive challenge to the propositional model.

A. Language turn / linguistic turn

The contemporary problematics of speech acts has its origin, curiously, in the distinction between sense and nonsense, which is constitutive of the paradigm of analytic philosophy and was challenged by Austin (see NONSENSE). At first, analytical philosophy excluded certain judgments (such as moral judgments) from the field of language. According to either the criteria of Ludwig Wittgenstein's *Tractatus Logico-Philosophicus* (the proposition as a state of affairs) or those Moritz Schlick and Rudolf Carnap derived from it (empirical meaning), ethical or normative utterances are without meaning, and thus say nothing. Ethical propositions, for example, are nonsense, Wittgenstein says in the *Tractatus* (6.42, 67.421–22), insofar as one cannot draw factual descriptions from value utterances (6.41). Thus ethics is outside the world; this is what Wittgenstein calls its transcendental character, in a derivation from the Kantian term that became influential in contemporary Anglo-Saxon philosophy. The dichotomy between fact and value, world and morality, which determines the nonsense of ethical propositions, is a central element in early analytical philosophy. It is this dichtomy that defines the first "linguistic turn"—here we will call it a "language turn" rather than a "linguistic turn" because the point is to determine (by *The Bounds of Sense*, to borrow P. F. Strawson's famous title) the limits of language and thus to outline those of philosophy.

Ethics and value are excluded from the domain of facts, and thus from the domain of language—of language that has meaning, and is thus verifiable. Only a second "turn"—this time not in language but in linguistics—could reintroduce questions of value into questions of language, and reopen the field of language. The first turn did not in fact alter the Aristotelian criterion of truth: sentences are either true or false (in conformity with the reality of things or denying it), or they are nonsensical (outside language). Meaning is thus inseparable from truth understood in the classic sense of "correspondence." Philosophy has only to clarify ordinary language by eliminating the nonsense (metaphysical, normative, semantically deviant, paradoxical) that its unverified use can elicit. Starting in the 1920s, analytical philosophy gradually tried to "legitimate" nonsense, first maintaining the framework of the first analysis, and then simply exploding it: this is the "second analysis," that of the second linguistic turn.

B. The invention of speech acts

In a book published in 1923, *The Meaning of Meaning*, C. K. Ogden and I. A. Richards took the first step toward the second turn. They proposed an "emotive theory of ethics," adopted notably by A. J. Ayer: the concept of "good," if we consider that it is not the sum of its empirical determinations or of the various uses of the word, is "unique and unanalyzable." The specifically ethical use of the word "good" is thus supposed to be "purely emotive" (125), that is, it refers to no empirical datum and expresses only our emotive attitude toward the object we say is "good." This theory, though vague, has a twofold interest: it allows us to discern two rival functions in language, the symbolic function and the emotive function. The symbolic function is descriptive (statement), the emotive function is "the use of words to express and induce feelings or attitudes." Language is no longer envisaged in its cognitive dimension, but in its meaning: Ogden and Richards explicitly play on the multiple uses of the word "meaning"—linguistic signification and the intention of discourse (see SENSE, V.B.2).

Ogden and Richards, in their emotivist theory, also called noncognitivist, in fact remained close to the positivist project, whose divisions (cognitive/metaphysical) they replicated. There are similarities between their theory and Rudolf Carnap's description of the *Lebensgefühl* in "The Elimination of Metaphysics," where he asserts that the metaphysician is a musician or a poet without artistic talent (176–77). To be sure, as François Recanati says, "with the emotive theory of ethics, the domain of the non-cognitive recovered all the dignity it had lost" (Austin, *How to Do Things with Words*, postface). But this is still on the condition of being excluded from language (because it is nondiscursive). There remains another possibility: extending the boundaries of language, so as to make language itself an act. It is in this perspective that we must situate Austin's invention of performatives. His first texts deal with meaning, or rather, with the right way of raising the question of meaning. The question, "What is the meaning of a word?" was asked by Wittgenstein in the first words of the *Blue Book*. The meaning of an utterance, according to Wittgenstein, is its use ("meaning is use"). But Austin carried this idea to its logical conclusion. The use of language being founded—like any institutionalized human activity—on rules, and thus being normative in essence, it is language itself, in all its functions, that will be invested by what was, in early analytical philosophy, the order of nonsense.

Austin is the inventor of the theory of speech acts, even if the expression "speech act" is John Searle's. To understand his point of view, we have to see, for example, that moral judgments are speech acts: "It is not good to lie" and "It's cold" (said to someone who has left a window open) are each, in one way or another, utterances of blame, that is, moral acts, and not merely utterances that describe something—neither an empirical state of affairs, nor the taking of an "emotive" or psychological position regarding a state of affairs. Austin's most remarkable discovery is that speech acts are part of language and even represent the essence of language. His theory does not limit itself to inverting (as Ogden and Richards did) logical empiricism's act of drawing a dividing line between the sayable and the nonsayable, between sense and nonsense: it radicalizes it by extending the field of language and thus redefining what we mean by "language."

Let us recall Austin's point of departure, in the first lecture of *How to Do Things with Words*, the definition of performative utterances. Austin says he is beginning from a commonplace observation, but one to which attention has not yet been specifically been given. "It was for too long the assumption of philosophers that the business of a 'statement' can only be to 'describe' some state of affairs, or to 'state some fact,' which it must do either truly or falsely." Then, he goes on, philosophers showed (not without a certain dogmatism, unfortunately) that many statements were only pseudo-statements. Moreover, he suggests, one might classify more subtly the various types of nonsense. (That is practically what Carnap does in "The Elimination of Metaphysics.") But one must ask, "as a second stage," whether what has been taken for nonsense might be in some way a statement and thus reintegrated into the analysis of language.

We see that in the modern period, it is ultimately only with Austin that there is a break with the Aristotelian schema of language as apophantic, having as its primary task to describe the world as it is, and thus also with the model of the statement as description and with the concept of truth associated with it. There can be not only an act of uttering, but also an utterance (something said), without a state of affairs being described, and—this is the main discovery of ordinary language philosophy, and the center of the theory of performatives—without moving beyond the limits of language and the domain of truth. Thus not only the schema of description, but also that of signification and of the proposition, is put in question: the very idea of semantics.

However, Edmund Husserl, at the end of his sixth *Logical Investigation*, had already intuited the problem: he raises the question of the

> seemingly trivial, but, correctly regarded, most important and difficult point at issue whether the familiar grammatical forms used in our speech for wishes, questions, voluntary intentions—acts, generally speaking, we do not class as "objectifying" [*objektivierende Akten*]—are to be regarded as *judgments* concerning our acts, or whether these acts themselves, and not merely such as are "objectifying," can function as "expressed" [*ausgedrückte Akten*], whether in a sense-giving or sense-fulfilling fashion.

> (*Logical Investigations*, 2:9 §68)

In fact, sentences like "May Heaven help us!" and "Frank should take care of himself" (examples given by Husserl), being neither true nor false, should not even be statements, because, Husserl says, citing Bolzano, they say nothing *about their subject*, "but nonetheless they say something."

Here, Husserl is raising the philosophical problem specific to the very idea of a speech act, for since these utterances constituted by questions, expressions of desire, or commands—and blame—cannot be qualified as true or false, there must be a different way of qualifying them, and this forces us to abandon truth for veracity (or verdictiveness—*Wahrhaftigkeit*: *Logical Investigations*), if one wants these utterances to be part of language—and that other way of qualifying them is just what a theory of "speech acts" seeks to provide.

C. Performativity and approval

But how can an act be true or false? Austin proposes to replace the true/false opposition with an opposition between felicity and infelicity: a performative (e.g., a promise) is infelicitous, failed, if it is not accomplished under the right conditions, which Austin describes and classifies (for example, if I do not intend to keep my promise, or I am not entitled to perform the act). To be sure, one of Austin's ideas is to destroy what he calls "(1) the true-false fetish and (2) the fact-value fetish." But destroying them does not imply abandoning the concept of truth, only transforming it, enlarging it in order to be able to apply it to the new types of expression thus discovered:

> [My] doctrine is quite different from much that the pragmatists have said, to the effect that the true is what works, &c. The truth or falsity of a statement depends not merely on the meanings of words but on what act you were performing in what circumstances.

(Austin, *How to Do Things with Words*, 145)

"False is not necessarily used of statements only," Austin says at the end of his first lecture. And in his twelfth and last lecture, he describes the status of illocutionary acts, of which "state" is one:

The following morals are among those I wanted to suggest:

  a. The total speech act in the total speech situation is the *only actual* phenomenon which, in the last resort, we are engaged in elucidating.

  b. Stating, describing, &c., are *just two* names among a very great many others for illocutionary acts; they have no unique position.

  c. In particular, they have no unique position over the matter of being related to facts in a unique way called being true or false, because truth and falsity are (except by an artificial abstraction which is always possible and legitimate for certain purposes) not names for relations, qualities, or what not, but for a dimension of assessment.

(Austin, *How to Do Things with Words*, 148–49)

In short, it is language as a whole that is in question: if, as Austin has shown in his series of lectures, there exist speech acts, language is no longer merely descriptive ("objectivizing," to adopt Husserl's expression), it is action: "*By saying, in saying* something, we are doing something" (*How to Do Things with Words*, 12). But then truth is no longer adequation (between the description and the state of affairs), it is also an *act*, and an *approval*. That is what Austin has in mind when, cleverly parodying logicians, he replaces "truth" with "satisfaction" (see Quine, *Philosophy of Logic*: "Truth is the limiting case of

satisfaction"; for example, chap. 3). Approval and blame are thus speech acts "with moral bearing" among others: they represent and sum up the normative or ethical dimension of language. The very use of language and learning it are based on blame (the rejection of what I say as inadequate) and approval (the acceptance of what I say as satisfying the norms of the linguistic community). That is what Wittgenstein meant when he defined, in the *Philosophical Investigations*, language learning as a search for the approval of elders: "Here the teaching of language is not explanation, but training" ("Das Lehren der Sprache ist hier kein Erklären, sondern ein Abrichten," §5).

D. "Performative [utterance]," "intention," "speech act"

We might be tempted to say that a performative (for example, a promise) expresses an *intention* that could be defined or explained outside the field of language (what has been called, following Grice and Searle, a "communicative act") as if to accomplish a speech act were ultimately to express an intention. Austin himself guarded against any "intentionalist" interpretation of his theory of speech acts, because for him such an interpretation would be not only erroneous but also immoral. To say that the performative expresses an intention is to reduce it to the descriptive, and thus to destroy all of Austin's work; but it is also the end of all morality, for if in promising, for example, my promise does not commit me to anything (it is simply mistaken description of an internal action), then

> it is but a short step to go on to believe or to assume without realizing that for many purposes the outward utterance is a description, *true or false*, of the occurrence of the inward performance. The classic expression of this idea is to be found in the *Hippolytus* (l. 612), where Hippolytus says . . . "My tongue swore to, but my heart (or mind or other backstage artiste) did not." . . . It is gratifying to observe in this very example how an excess of profundity, or rather solemnity, at once paves the way for immorality. For one who says "promising is not merely a matter of uttering words! It is an inward and spiritual act!" is apt to appear as a solid moralist standing out against a generation of superficial theorizers. . . . Yet he provides Hippolytus with a let-out, the bigamist with an excuse for his "I do" and the welsher with a defence for his "I bet." Accuracy and morality alike are on the side of plain saying that *our word is our bond*.

(Austin, *How to Do Things with Words*, 9–10)

Despite Austin's warning, the intentionalist interpretation of speech acts has gained great influence. Its fecundity is connected with the generalization of the theory of speech acts and with the transition made by Searle from the performative utterance to the speech act (which French translators, thus reinforcing Searle's generalization, have chosen to render as "acte de langage" rather than "acte de parole").

■ See Box 3.

E. "Perform," "performance"

Austin's invention of performatives has brought out certain characteristics of the verb "perform" (which has no equivalent in French). The specific and philosophically interesting characteristics of performatives are in fact inseparable from

3

"Speech act": *Acte de langage / acte de parole*?

Unlike Austin, Searle refers to the Saussurean distinction between *langue* and *parole*, emphasizing the idea that speech acts are fully part of language: "An adequate study of speech acts is a study of *langue*" (*Speech Acts*, 17).

Searle uses the French term *langue*, which he thus considers untranslatable. It is remarkable that here Searle returns to the Saussurean distinction to extend Austin's theory, and it is no less remarkable that French translators of *Speech Acts* use this distinction to justify their translation of "speech acts" by *actes de langage* (notably in Ducrot's introduction to the French edition of Searle's work), long before the passage in which Searle mentions Saussure. However, we may wonder about the translation of some passages such as the one in which Searle says: "Speaking a language is performing speech acts" (16).

The French translation, "Parler une langue, c'est réaliser des actes de langage," erases the obvious connection between "speaking" and "speech," and transfers the parallel to "language" (*langue*) and "speech" (*langage*). For Ducrot, "speech acts" would thus have been just as well translated *actes de langue*, this translation being impossible only because it is ridiculous. But it might also seem unwise to appeal to Saussure in introducing the word *langage*, even if the latter is understood as *langue*, in a context in which there is much discussion of "language" in a sense that is not necessarily Saussurean.

It is clear that the translation *actes de langage* is partly justified by Searle's theory, which extends the speech act to the statement, to reference, and to predication: "Speaking a language is performing speech acts, acts such as making statements, giving commands, asking questions, making promises, and so on; and more abstractly, acts such as referring and predicating" (16).

But why immediately choose this translation, when Searle, in the same passage, speaks of "linguistic acts," which, in the French translation, thus seem oddly differentiated from *actes de langage* (speech acts), a more specific category? It is true that in French, "linguistic" is often translated by *linguistique*, whereas a more precise translation would be *langagier* (see IV.A here, on "the linguistic turn"). Moreover, in his book, Searle repeatedly stresses his "theory of language," which is thus artificially associated by the translation with "speech acts": to be sure, his philosophy of language is in fact a theory of speech acts, but that is what the book is to demonstrate, and the translation by *actes de langage* "begs the question," as Hume would say.

This translation, though justified in theory, is inadequate in practice and forced in the details of the text. However, theoretical validity wins out here, as is shown by the generalization, in linguistics and philosophy of language in France, of the expression *actes de langage*, which is certainly more easily assimilated by the French tradition. But doesn't this obvious fact rest on a misunderstanding?

BIBLIOGRAPHY

Searle, John. *Speech Acts*. London: Cambridge University Press, 1969. French translation by Hélène Pauchard: *Les actes de langage: Essai de philosophie du langage*. Paris: Hermann, 1972. 2nd ed. published in 2009.

---

this verb, which, Austin says, is "the usual verb with the noun 'action'" (*How to Do Things with Words*, 6). The performative utterance is used, not to describe an action, but to carry it out. The verb "perform" indicates an act. But this act is inseparable from the action itself; it is a "function" of the action, not one of its consequences (as would be, for instance, hurting someone by doing something). In this sense, "perform" is associated more with the notion of "act" than with that of "action" (and Austin's terminology recognizes this) and is particularly well adapted to the speech act. The difference between "perform" and *effectuer* or *accomplir*, its usual French translations, has to do with the pair *perform/performance*, performance being the act itself considered from a triple point of view: (1) its temporal development (cf. the progressive "the performing of an action"); (2) its achievement, its completion (see German *vollziehen*, which often translates "perform"); and (3) its success: if Austinian performatives may be felicitous or infelicitous, it is by reference to this aspect of every "performance." This triple dimension, which we also find, in a slightly different combination, in the word "achievement," sometimes makes the word particularly difficult to translate, as in this concluding passage in Cavell's "An Audience for Philosophy": "There is an audience of philosophy; but there also, while it lasts, is its performance" (*Must We Mean What We Say?* xxix)—performance being conceived simultaneously as activity, duration, accomplishment, and success.

Barbara Cassin (I)
Sandra Laugier (III)
Irène Rosier-Catach (II)

BIBLIOGRAPHY

Aristotle. *Rhetoric*. Translated by W. Rhys Roberts. In *Basic Works of Aristotle*, edited by R. McKeon. New York: Modern Library, 2001.

Ashworth, Elizabeth. "Aquinas on Significant Utterance: Interjection, Blasphemy, Prayer." In *Aquinas's Moral Theory*, edited by S. Macdonald and E. Stump, 207–34. Ithaca, NY: Cornell University Press, 1999.

Austin, John Langshaw. *How to Do Things with Words*. Cambridge, MA: Harvard University Press, 1962.

———. *Philosophical Papers*. Oxford: Clarendon, 1962.

Bacon, Roger. *Summa de sophismatibus et distinctionibus*. Edited by Robert Steele. Oxford: Clarendon, 1937.

Carnap, Rudolf. "The Elimination of Metaphysics through Logical Analysis of Language." Translated by A. Pap. In *Logical Empiricism at Its Peak: Schlick, Carnap and Neurath*, edited by S. Sarkar. New York: Garland, 1996.

Cassin, Barbara. *L'Effet sophistique*. Paris: Gallimard / La Pléiade, 1996.

Cavell, Stanley. *Must We Mean What We Say?* Cambridge: Cambridge University Press, 1969.

Grice, H. Paul. *Studies in the Way of Words*. Cambridge, MA: Harvard University Press, 1989.

Heidegger, Martin. *Being and Time*. Translated by John Macquarrie and Edward Robinson. New York: Harper, 1962.

Husserl, Edmund. *Logische Untersuchungen*. Berlin: Akademie Verlag, 2008. Translation by H. Findlay: *Logical Investigations*. London: Routledge and Kegan Paul, 1970.

Kennedy, George A. *The Art of Persuasion in Greece*. In *A History of Rhetoric*, vol. 1. Princeton, NJ: Princeton University Press, 1963.

Lyotard, Jean-François. *Le différend*. Paris: Minuit, 1983.

Marbais, Gosvin de. *Tractatus de constructione*. Edited by Irène Rosier. Nijmegen, Neth.: Artistarium, 1998.

Nuchelmans, Gabriel. "The Distinction *actus exercitus / actus significatus* in Medieval Semantics." In *Meaning and Inference in Medieval Philosophy*, edited by N. Kretzmann, 57–90. Boston: Kluwer Academic Publishers, 1988.

———. "Ockham on Performed and Signified Predication." In *Ockham and Ockhamists*, edited by E. P. Bos and H. A. Krop, 55–62. Nijmegen, Neth.: Ingenium, 1989.

Ogden, C. K., and I. A. Richards. *The Meaning of Meaning*. London: Routledge and Kegan, 1923.

Pernot, Laurent. *Rhetoric in Antiquity*. Translated by W. E. Higgins. Washington, DC: Catholic University of America Press, 2005.

———. *La rhétorique de l'éloge dans le monde gréco-romain*. 2 vols. Paris: Institut d'Études augustiniennes, 1993.

Quine, Williard van Orman. *Philosophy of Logic*. Cambridge, MA: Harvard University Press, 1970.

Recanati, François. *Literal Meaning*. Cambridge: Cambridge University Press, 2004.

Rorty, Richard, ed. *The Linguistic Turn*. Chicago: University of Chicago Press, 1992.

Rosier, Irène. "La distinction entre *actus exercitus* et *actus significatus* dans les sophismes grammaticaux du ms. Bibl. Nat. lat. 16618 et autres textes apparentés." In *Sophisms in Medieval Logic and Grammar*, edited by S. Read, 230–61. Dordrecht, Neth.: Kluwer, 1993.

———. *La parole comme acte*. Paris: Vrin, 1994.

Searle, John. *Speech Acts*. London: Cambridge University Press, 1969.

SPLEEN

FRENCH	*spleen*
GERMAN	*Überspanntheit*
GREEK	*splên* [σπλήν] (pl. *splênes* [σπλῆνες])
SPANISH	*esplín*

➤ *MALAISE*, and ACEDIA, ANXIETY, DOR, FEELING, GEFÜHL, GENIUS, INGENIUM, MADNESS, MELANCHOLY, *NOSTALGIA*, PATHOS, SAUDADE, SEHNSUCHT

Among the terms in European languages that have their origin in Greek *splên* [σπλήν], the English word "spleen" designates a moral sentiment and almost a style, the modern offspring of *acedia* and "melancholy." Its history takes one from the narrowly physical level to a psychological and moral semiology, opening on to a "malaise," the veritable symptom of a pathology of the culture, the spleen that accompanies modernization.

Splên [σπλήν] designates in Greek the organ of that name that is the seat of the humors necessary for the equilibrium of the body as a whole and, in the plural (*splenes* [σπλῆνες]), suffering of the spleen, hypochondria (RT: *Dictionnaire grec français*, s.v.; cf. the verb *spleniao* [σπληνιάω]). Its lexical neighbor *splagchna* [σπλάγχνα] designates entrails (of victims that one eats and examines in order to prophesy), the essential viscera of human survival (heart, liver, kidneys, lungs), thus also the heart or soul as seat of the affections and of character, and even the maternal breast (RT: *Dictionnaire grec français*, s.v.). In the Greek of the New Testament, *splagchna*, "heart," gave birth to *splagchna* (exceptionally *splagchnon* [σπλάγχνον]), "pity" (RT: *Dictionnaire étymologique de la langue grecque*, s.v. *splên*). In Spanish, the Academy of that language recognizes the claim of the form *esplín*, a rarity allowing one to connect with the English "spleen" and, above all, to underscore the Greco-Latin origin of this lexical field: thus did there surface, around 1740 (according to RT: *Diccionario de autoridades*) the term *splénico*, which, along with the use of *esplenetic* in Catalan and *esplenético* in Castillian, allows one to link this usage to the *esplén* of the Middle Ages.

The humor of the ancients, that produced by the spleen, is one of those "liquors nourished, maintained, and belonging to the physical condition, such as, in humans, blood, choler, phlegm, and bile, as well as excremental elements like urine, sweat, etc." (RT: *Diccionario de autoridades*). These humors are the product of the initial transformation of the meal (according to Avicenna, "[they are] a humid and liquid substance into which food is first converted"; RT: *Diccionario de autoridades*). An abundance of one of these humors governs the external manifestations of what becomes *genius*, a "condition" or "nature," that is, the basic temperament of each individual that can and should only be controlled: "Buen humor por vida mia /se purga todos los años [a good humor, in faith, should be purged every year]" (Moreto, *El lego del Carmen*, first day).

I. Shakespearean "Spleen" and Power over Others

The properly psychological sense of "spleen" appears in the English baroque, where, by way of Shakespeare's genius, the notion receives its status as a sign of the soul as well as of a virtue or quality linked to the nobleman or warrior. Shakespeare plainly takes into account the physical sense, which stems from the ancient theory of humors: "spleen," in fact, designates not only the flow of tears or other external humors already evoked, but also the bodily seat of feelings that turn around "spleen." "Spleen" is a quality of young bodies ("Quicken'd with youthful spleen and warlike rage"; *Henry VI*, part I, act IV, scene 6) that clash with the nobility of the sages ("You charge not in your spleen a noble person"; *Henry VIII*, act I, scene 2). Its dependence in relation to the realm of nature (which can be said to be external, but which is metaphorical of the discovery of a dangerous inner nature) makes of the feeling called spleen something not human, but primitive and legendary that dominates the soul and its strength ("Inspire us with the spleen of fiery dragons!"; *Richard III,* act V, scene 3).

Shakespeare bases himself on the physical and pathological ground of the humors ("unto a mad-brain rudesby full of spleen"; *The Taming of the Shrew*, act III, scene 2), but he above all bears witness to a specific psychopathology of the era, which perceived its own struggles over power in the mirror of the classics, as in the case of Julius Caesar, who dies a victim of the play of "political secretions" ("You shall digest the venom of your spleen"; *Julius Caesar*, act IV, scene 3). The connection between the physical and the moral is represented by the difficult balance of the mythical figure of Eros ("conceived of spleen, and born of madness; that blind rascally boy that abuses every one's eyes because his own are out, let him be judge how deep I am in love"; *As You Like It*, act IV, scene 1). Its effects are also abhorred ("That in this spleen ridiculous, appears, / To check their folly, passions solemn tears"; *Love's Labor's Lost*, act V, scene 2).

But the idiosyncrasy of Shakespeare is above all a function of the moral and social stature that he accords to spleen: it is a source of power over others. Cardinal Wolsey declares to his lady, "Madam, you do me wrong; / I have no spleen against you, / nor injustice for you or any" (*Henry VIII*, act II, scene 4), in order to emphasize that respect for the law is the logical limit of spleen, whose injustice may be inevitable ("the unruly spleen"; *Romeo and Juliet*, act III, scene 1). And all the more so in that spleen is accompanied by arrogance and pride: "You sign your place and calling, in full seeming, / With meekness and humility; but your heart / Is cramm'd with arrogancy, spleen, and pride" (*Henry VIII*, act II, scene 4).

Spleen is the trump card of the conqueror: "spleen and fury" compose Alcibiades's self-portrait (*Timon of Athens*, act III, scene 5). And it is modern warfare—as in the wars of religion evoked by Montaigne in his *Journal du voyage en Italie*—that amplifies the excess of its anger: "with swifter spleen than powder can enforce" (*King John*, act II, scene 1). This kind of offense, which inevitably incites to revenge, appears, in *Henry VI*, as a formidable quality of soldiers ("That robb'd my soldiers of their heated spleen"; *Henry VI*, part III, act II, scene 1), but also, in *Henry VI*, as a fatal inclination ("A weasel hath not such a deal of spleen / As you are tossed with"; *Henry VI,* part I, act II, scene 3), dangerous because it can govern "a hair-brain'd Hotspur" (act V, scene 2). That force becomes accursed in *Richard III* (act II, scene 4): "and frantic pitrage, end thy damned spleen." But it is always endowed by an ambivalence perceived by those in spleen's possession (thus valorous Achilles sulking in his tent, who writhes with laughter when Patrocles imitates the aged Nestor: "Give me ribs of steel! I shall split all / In pleasure of my spleen"; *Troilus and Cressida*, act I, scene 3). This is why spleen can ultimately be an object of desire (*Twelfth Night*, act III, scene 2) and exploration (*Troilus and Cressida*, act II, scene 2).

II. Baudelairean "Spleen" and Modern Sentiment

"Spleen" would make a return in a sense that—like *esplín* in Spanish—the Academy would describe as "tragic humor" (Breton de Los Herreros) and which characterizes the heart of proto-consumerist urban sensibility. The meaning of "spleen" as a modern feeling, that is, as a relation to society and the epoch, a sentiment composed of indefinite distance and pain, is the work of Baudelaire. *Les Fleurs du Mal* and *Le Spleen de Paris* constitute, in fact, the necesssary points of bearing for understanding this pathology of the century. Furor and anger would henceforth be oriented toward a nonlogical order, aberrant in relation to the sentiments and projects of individuals, which constitutes at the same time—underscoring its ambivalence—the occasion for all the new experiences of an age that defined itself through the instant and the ephemeral. "Spleen" then became a lifestyle rather than a moral or esthetic sensation. It manifested itself as extravagance (*Verschrobenheit*), and modern activity, "spleening"—an activity to be cultivated and not a fate to be undergone—had the value of a slight case of madness (*leicht Verrückt*). It was a matter then of neither an isolated (or nocturnal) event nor an "extraordinary state," but of a genuine and generalized style of life dominated by overexcitement (in current German: *Überspanntheit*).

It is precisely that irritation or complaint without object that gives its coloration to Baudelairean "spleen" (*Les Fleurs du Mal*, LXXV, "Spleen") and which appears on the scene as "Pluviôse, irritated with the entire city," where the melancholy of pure loss is given substance. The state is, in fact, not elaborated in joy—as in Bataille, for whom laughter will overflow "spleen" in a maniacal skidding off course—but undergone in a fall or vertigo of the new time whose instantaneity overwhelms categories and careers alike. The "spleen" of the period of the arcades of the new commerce (Benjamin's *Passagen-werk*) and the Commune is a dialogue in which the ancien régime offers a plaint at being lost forever

("The handsome jack of hearts and the queen of spades / chat, sinister, about their defunct loves").

The internalization of the cultural crisis opens onto a representation of intimacy as a desolate space impossible to contemplate, except in distress or an indulgence clinically designated by the rubric masochism: "I am a cemetery abhorred by the moon / . . . I'm an old boudoir full of wilted roses" (*Les Fleurs du Mal*, LXXVI, "Spleen"). From this topology there comes knowledge of a new suspension of time—an eternal present that affords no possibility of creative life: "Ennui, fruit of a mournful lack of curiosity, / Takes on the proportions of immortality." Such is the profile of the new stroller in the showcase-city, endlessly searching for signs in order to fill the awareness he has of his inner emptiness and to attain some pretext for enthusiasm. This king who walks about without anyone realizing it, this new consumer-citizen bears within him the paradoxes of the changed style of production and of life: "I am like the king of a rainy country, Rich, but impotent, young and yet quite old." The new phantasmagoria that we are told about by the Marx of merchandise-fetishism allows us access to hidden, repressed presences. The subject of "spleening" sees himself invaded by these signs that he must learn to decipher.

José Miguel Marinas

BIBLIOGRAPHY

Baudelaire, Charles. *The Flowers of Evil, and Other Poems*. Translated by Francis Duke. English and French edition. Charlottesville: University of Virginia Press, 1961.

Benjamin, Walter. *The Arcades Project*. Translated by Howard Eiland and Kevin McLaughlin. Cambridge, MA: Harvard University Press / Belknap Press, 1999.

Hume, David. *A Treatise of Human Nature*. Edited by David Fate Norton and Mary J. Norton. Oxford: Oxford University Press, 2000.

Moreto, Agustín. *El lego del Carmen*. Salamanca, Sp.: Anaya, 1970.

Shakespeare, William. *Complete Works*. Edited with an introduction and a glossary by Peter Alexander. London: Collins, 1951.

SPRECHGESANG (GERMAN)

ENGLISH	spoken song
FRENCH	*mélodie parlée, parler-chanter*

➤ *VOICE*, and AESTHETICS, DICHTUNG, LOGOS, STIMMUNG, TO TRANSLATE

Arnold Schoenberg created the neologism *Sprechgesang* in 1912 for compositional and aesthetic purposes and to signify a new manner of writing for the voice. *Sprechgesang* opposes two verbs: *sprechen*, "to speak," and *singen*, "to sing," and designates a vocal technique as well as a way of conceptualizing the vocal in the twentieth century. It was in *Pierrot lunaire* (1912), a melodrama for instrumental ensemble and voice, that the compound term, which would pose considerable difficulties for interpreters as well as for theorists and composers, would be found for the first time. It should be noted that although *Sprechgesang* is used only in the field of music, it has contaminated the entirety of studies and research in the realm of aesthetics, particularly with regard to literature and poetry.

Several abortive attempts at transposition reveal that *Sprechgesang*, invented by Schoenberg to put a halt once and for all to the vocal aesthetic of *bel canto* prevalent between the eighteenth and the end of the nineteenth centuries, constitutes a perfect case of untranslatability to the extent that the conjunction of speaking/singing in German has as a corollary that of vocalizing and vocality. Schoenberg's concern was not so much to fuse two categories of the *phônê* [φωνή] but to proceed in such manner that their fusion be representative of the transversal operations between questions of voice and variable forms of textuality and prosody. For Schoenberg the operation that consists in having a text sung is not necessarily dependent on a melodic musical structure. Voice calls for song, as though it were apostrophizing it, but the former is not necessarily dependent on the latter. Schoenberg regarded as trivial the reproach addressed to the composer of not doing justice to a text and "betraying" it vocally.

> When one has perceived this, it is also easy to understand that the outward correspondence between music and text, as exhibited in declamation, tempo, and dynamics, has but little to do with the inward correspondence, and belongs to the same stage of primitive imitation of nature as the copying of a model. Apparent superficial divergences can be necessary because of parallelism on a higher level. Therefore, the judgment on the basis of the text is just as reliable as the judgment of albumen according to the characteristics of carbon.
>
> ("The Relationship to the Text," in *Style and Idea*, 145)

Schoenberg sustained an atectonic ideal of the ambivalent relations between voice, song, and what he called in his *Berlin Diary*, 22 January 1912, "obligatory recitative." This is why *Pierrot lunaire* is the experimental site of an "unsayable" that, in the composer's mind, is to be, if possible, noted and interpreted by female speakers and not singers. The fusion of the inflections of the speaking and the singing voice is rooted in the theoretical premise that the voice is not a timbred entity with clearly defined contours. In *Sprechgesang* Schoenberg heard above all the irregularity of the vocal phenomenon, a skidding of one category over the other and, as a result, an abrupt aesthetic strangeness, the basis of a new harmony in which the sound of the voice is meaningful in itself. At the outset, Schoenberg noted in his preface to *Pierrot lunaire*, the task of the performer is "Maintaining the rhythm as accurately as if one were singing, i.e., with no more freedom than would be allowed with a singing melody; Becoming acutely aware of the difference between *singing tone* and *speaking tone* [emphasis in original]: singing tone unalterably stays on the pitch, whereas speaking tone gives the pitch but immediately leaves it again by falling or rising."

The expression *Sprechgesang* became a concept in its own right, affecting questions of declamation and textuality, beyond varieties of vocality put to work to declaim, say, speak, and sing the music of words. Such a matrix of musical writing, which renders intelligible not the words, assumed to undergo, vocally, mutations in diction, but the music itself, dislocates the homogeneity of the singing voice and pulverizes its lyric surface, the better to bring into relief the intermediary zones and limits of vocality. Schoenberg's project belongs to the hermeneutics of translation: in 1949, he himself, in a text titled "This Is My Fault" (*Style and Idea,* 145–47),

introduced the notion of translation to evoke the adventure of *Sprechgesang* at the time of *Pierrot lunaire*:

> In the preface to *Pierrot lunaire,* I had demanded that performers ought not to add illustrations and moods of their own derived from the text. In the epoch after the First World War, it was customary for composers to surpass me radically, even if they did not like my music. Thus when I had asked not to add external expression and illustration, they understood that expression and illustration were out, and that there should be no relation whatsoever to the text.

It is in the opposition between what Schoenberg designates by, on the one hand, the aesthetic and, on the other, the issue of craft that the question of translation inherent in the spoken and sung voice is to be understood.

Daniel Cohen-Levinas

BIBLIOGRAPHY

Schoenberg, Arnold. *Berliner Tagebuch*. Edited by Josef Rufer. Frankfurt: Propyläen-Verlag, 1974.
———. *Style and Idea: Selected Writings of Arnold Schoenberg*. Edited by Leonard Stein with translations by Leo Black. Berkeley: University of California Press, 1984.

SPREZZATURA

LATIN   *negligentia*

➤ *DÉSINVOLTURE*, and ART, BEAUTY, CIVILTÀ, GOÛT, *GRACE*, INGENIUM, LEGGIADRIA

The Italian word *sprezzatura*, which Baldassare Castiglione uses in his *Book of the Courtier* (1528), considering it as "new," characterizes a quality of the behavior required of the "courtier," that is, of man in his perfection according to the criteria defined by Castiglione, and falls under the rubric of the "je ne sais quoi." It has not, in fact, been absorbed into common usage and always refers to its specific literary origin.

> But having before now often considered whence this grace (*grazia*) springs, laying aside those men who have it by nature, I find one universal rule concerning it, which seems to me worth more in this matter than any other in all things human that are done and said: and that is to avoid affectation (*affettazione*) to the uttermost and as it were a very sharp and dangerous rock; and, to use possibly a new word, to practice in everything a certain *sprezzatura* that shall conceal design and show that what is done and said is done without effort and almost without thought.
>
> (trans. Leonard Eckstein, *Opdycke*)

This sentence, which can be read in chapter 26 of the *Book of the Courtier*, introduced into world literature a word that is untranslatable par excellence. To understand the reasons for that impossibility, one must analyze the richness of the meanings included in the term, and the value that it has in the work. The subject of the book is the joint quest, by certain members of the Court of Urbino at the beginning of the sixteenth century, for a definition of the "perfect courtier," the figure of the courtier being regarded as the very type of the ideal man. Now before even speaking in detail about the qualities that the courtier ought to know how to demonstrate in the various spheres of his existence, Castiglione posits from the outset a requirement that may seem a matter of mere form, but that nonetheless determines, in an absolute manner, the value of all the endeavors of the courtier, namely "grace" (*grazia*):

> The courtier must accompany his actions, gestures, habits, in short his every movement, with grace; and this you seem to regard as an universal seasoning, without which all other properties and good qualities are of little worth.

(ibid., chap. 24)

The domain in which grace is exercised is immense, and it partakes of theology, metaphysics, and aesthetics; Castiglione extends the exercise of grace to the domain of manners. After acknowledging the "gratuity" of grace when it is a gift of nature, he endeavors to define the art through which it may be acquired, the "very universal rule" one must follow in order to give "to what one does or what one says" the "seasoning of grace" (*condimento de la grazia*). This attempt is paradoxical: it consists in attempting to obtain through art, through obedience to rules, what is given by nature. Grace thus results from a difficult labor, a "suffering," "a constant preoccupation, which must never appear to be such, but which effaces itself, conceals design, and shows that what is done and said is done without effort and almost without thought" (ibid.): to do so is to demonstrate what Castiglione calls "a certain *sprezzatura*." In the contrary case, when art, as a reflective and voluntary activity, allows itself to be too visible, the result is not attained, grace fails one, and one is dealing with "affectation," affectation being at once the opposite of *sprezzatura* and what is closest to it, what it risks lapsing into at every moment.

Ancient rhetoric had opened the way in this case for Castiglione, which should come as no surprise, since *The Book of the Courtier* can be considered as a treatise on rhetoric extending from the realm of discourse to that of social behavior in general. Cicero, in *On the Orator*, speaking of the "simple" or "Attic style," characterized by *quaedam neglegentia diligens* (a certain diligent negligence), compares it to the elegance of certain women "without affectation," and he adds that "in both cases one does something to have more grace (*gratia*), but without it appearing to be the case" (*On the Orator*, XXIII, 76–78).

The word *neglegentia* puts us on the track of *sprezzatura*, a term that, we should note, Castiglione presents in the definitive version of his work as "possibly a new word," whereas in a prior version he said that "it was, however, already accepted by us with this meaning." Whatever the case, the composition of the word and its literal meaning are clear. The noun comes from the verb *sprezzare* (in Latin, *expretiare*, from *pretium*, with the negative *es*) and denotes the attitude of one who "scorns," that is, who assigns "little price" or even "no price at all" to someone or something. The good

courtier is thus one who seems to accord no value, no importance to what he says and does, and never betrays the slightest effort. He feigns natural ease, spontaneity, and conceals work, effort expended, art. "Art is to conceal art" ("Ars est celare artem").

What word in French is capable of rendering all the nuances of *sprezzatura* (the difficulty, moreover, being the same in other languages)? Chappuis, one of the first translators, at the end of the sixteenth century, speaks of *mépris* (scorn) or *nonchalance*, but those terms, in modern French, have taken on a range that makes their use unsatisfactory. The first has too harsh a meaning, and the second (to be compared with *nonchaloir* [to take minimally into account]) is currently too marked by a pejorative nuance implying a lack of energy and softness. The same holds for *négligence*, from the Latin *neglegere* (not to be concerned with), which carries the excessive connotations of its first meaning in French of "forgetting one's duties, a failing or error, especially in the religious sphere" (RT: *DHLF*). One might propose, in current French, *désinvolture* (A. Pons). Castiglione does indeed speak at a certain point of *sprezzata desinvoltura*, but it should be acknowledged that the word *desinvoltura* does not transmit the "deprecatory" nuance of the etymology, and refers rather to the "disenveloping" of manners, to their "disengaged" character.

The term *sprezzatura* has occasionally served, after Castiglione, to characterize within the aesthetic realm of mannerism, and particularly with regard to singing, a certain manner of taking one's distance in relation to the rules governing melody ("una certa sprezzatura di canto"). But if it continues to be used at present, it is always with explicit or implicit reference to Castiglione's book, with the result that the linguistic failure of the neologism is largely compensated for by the literary tribute paid to its "inventor."

Alain Pons

BIBLIOGRAPHY

Castiglione, Baldassare. *Il Libro del Cortegiano* [1528]. Translation by Leonard Eckstein: Opdycke. New York: C. Scribner and Sons, 1903. Translation and introduction by George Bull: *The Book of the Courtier*. Harmondsworth, UK: Penguin Books, 1976. Penguin edition first published in 1967.

D'Angelo, P. "'Celare l'arte.' Per una storia del precetto 'ars est celare artem.'" *Intersezioni* 6, no. 2 (1986).

Ferroni, Giulio. "'Sprezzatura' e 'Simulazione.'" In *La scena del testo*. Vol. 1 of *La Corte e il "Cortegiano."* Rome: Bulzoni, 1980.

Jam, Jean-Louis. "Sprezzatura." In *Dictionnaire raisonné de la politesse et du savoir-vivre du Moyen Âge à nos jours*. Paris: Éditions du Seuil, 1995.

STAND (TO), STANCE, STANDING

FRENCH   *se tenir, position, standing*
GERMAN   *stehen*

➤ *IDENTITY*, and ACTOR, BERUF, CONSCIOUSNESS, ENGLISH, I/ME/MYSELF, PERSON, STANDARD

English distinguishes clearly between qualitative identity, "sameness," which opts to identify several distinct entities as one and the same according to a given description, and an identificatory identity based on a "map" or network of questions. This identificatory discourse is currently witnessing the development, around Charles Taylor's fundamental work *Sources of the Self* (1989), of an interrelated series of powerful and privileged terms linked to personal responsibility: with "to stand," "stance," and "standing," we are witnessing a repositioning of selfhood and, simultaneously, an elaboration of terms that the play of adverbs, prepositions, idioms, and metaphors in English makes particularly difficult to translate.

I. An Untranslatable in the Nascent State

At the beginning of *Sources of the Self*, Charles Taylor writes,

> To know who I am is a species of knowing where I stand. My identity is defined by the commitments and identifications which provide the frame or horizon within which I can try to determine from case to case what is good or valuable, or what ought to be done, or what I endorse or oppose. In other words it is the horizon within which I am capable of taking a stand.

In considering this view of self-identity one might well take the crucial question to be whether "the ground where I stand is given to me. . . . [Or whether] I am free to choose where to take my stand." At first sight, no doubt, neither of these passages would appear to present any major problem of translation in moving from the English to, say, French. "To take a stand" would seem to go easily enough into *prendre position*; "to know where I stand" might be rendered as *savoir où je me tiens* or *où je me situe*; and, in the context, the sense of the expression "the ground where I stand" is perhaps best conveyed by *le terrain sur lequel je me trouve* or *le terrain que j'occupe*. On second thought, however, one may be struck by the way in which the unity that, in English, the terms "standing" and "stance" give to these different expressions is dispersed and redistributed by the French. (In this way French is more or less typical of all the modern Latin languages, whereas the German *stehen* provides roughly the same range of cognates as the English "to stand.")

In his discussion of the concepts of "the self" and "self-identity" Taylor lays great emphasis on the ways in which the modern world provides for many previously unknown possibilities of social mobility and exchange of one role for another and thus allows much more room for individual development and self-determination. Secondly, and not altogether unconnectedly no doubt, we can see developing from about the time of the Reformation onward, a growing insistence on the role of the individual in taking responsibility for his or her own actions and the values that he or she may stand for or represent. This concern with individual or "personal" responsibility for what an agent does as the author of his or her own actions lies (together, of course, with continuity of consciousness) at the heart of John Locke's attempt in his *Essay on Human Understanding* (bk. 3, chap. 27) to work out a systematic distinction between the identity of a man, qua human animal, and that of a person. "Person" for Locke is a "forensic term," that is to say that it is to human agents qua persons that we impute responsibility. And before Locke, of course, none other than Martin Luther himself proclaimed his

own responsibility for his own unmediated relationship to God in the words *Hier stehe Ich* (Here I stand) (*Verhandlungen mit D. Martin Luther auf dem Reichstage zu Worms*; see CONSCIOUSNESS, Box 3). It is true, no doubt, that Luther would not have used that language of identity with which Taylor is concerned and which, as he rightly says, has become common currency only over roughly the past fifty years (but a currency now so common, indeed, that it may risk a serious devaluation). But it is easy to imagine contexts in which, if anyone had asked Luther who he was, he might well have answered "I am he who stands here and can do no other."

II. Idiomatic Expressions and Metaphorical Networks

It may be, indeed, that the metaphor of standing (itself an expression not obviously transposable into French) carries with it something of a peculiarly Protestant flavor. To stand (on one's own feet) is to not lean upon anyone or anything; it is to be not propped up by someone or something else. To take a stand is to resist pressure to move (retreat) any further, it is to be independently or autonomously upright—"upright" itself being a term, whose particular manner of juxtaposing the notions of "being erect" (not "bowed down," "bent," or "blown over"; " 'undefeated' ") and of "moral probity" does not go straight over into French. "An upright man" might plausibly reappear as *un homme droit*, a man of whom, translating back into English, it would be natural to say that he was "straight" (cf. "He is as straight as an arrow"). However, one can, of course, be straight in a horizontal position, and to say of someone (or, indeed, of something) that he, she, or it is straight is to imply nothing whatsoever as to whether the person or thing is either literally or metaphorically standing on his/its own feet or not. But, it is important to note, he who "stands four-square," as it is said, and upon his own autonomous feet, does not necessarily "stand alone"; he may, on the contrary, "stand firm with" all those others who together are prepared to "stand up and be counted" as representatives of the values that they "stand for" and that they are ready to defend as they "take their stand" against the attacks of those who would discard them. In short, then, the English term "stand" is one that, together with a whole army of prepositional auxiliaries "standing ready" in the wings, as it were, is able to bring together a set of mutually supporting images of self-determination, autonomy, readiness to provide resistance or defense, uprightness, potential solidarity with others ("united we stand," "I stand with you/them"), and so on and so on.

Against the background of his own working out of a theme proposed by Harry Frankfurt in the latter's well-known "hierarchical account of identity," Taylor himself has been concerned to present a distinction between what might be called the ordinary or normal evaluative assessments that we all regularly make of one thing, one course of action, in relation to others and what he characterizes as deep or radical evaluation, that is to say the evaluative assessment by which one may pass in review one's existing range of first-order evaluations and, comparing them to other possible constellations of values, make a deep existential choice between them and in so doing determine or redetermine one's own self-identity. Taylor may be understood as seeking both to articulate and to understand the origins of a sense of identity according to which people—both individuals and, indeed, groups—have to be seen as having a large share of more or less autonomous responsibility for the acceptance or remaking of their own identity. Also, no doubt, in presenting identity understood in this way as constituting the proper basis of respect of both self and others, I do not in the least wish to suggest that this project cannot be set out in a language such as French. But when Taylor, who is himself bilingual, tries to do this, metaphors of standing and stance tend to be replaced by metaphors of frameworks of reference (*points de repère*) and of horizons, metaphors that, it is true, do occur in the English version, but that are not so immediately at home there. It may well be, of course, that both sets of metaphors are needed to give the full flavor of the concept of identity that Taylor is trying to articulate in the passage quoted at the beginning of this entry. It remains difficult not to lose the entire associative network serving to sustain that concept in translation.

Alan Montefiore

BIBLIOGRAPHY

Bransen, Jan. "Identification and the Idea of an Alternative of Oneself." *European Journal of Philosophy* 4, no. 1 (April 1996): 1–16.

Frankfurt, Harry. "Freedom of the Will and the Concept of a Person." *Journal of Philosophy* 68 (1971).

———. "Identification and Wholeheartedness." In *Responsibility, Character, and the Emotions*, edited by F. Schoeman, 159–76. Cambridge: Cambridge University Press, 1987.

Luther, Martin. *Verhandlungen mit D. Martin Luther auf dem Reichstage zu Worms.* Vol. 7 in *Weimarer Ausgabe (WA)* [*D. Martin Luthers Werke: Kritische Gesamtausgabe*]. 120 vols. Weimar, 1883–2009. First published in 1521.

Taylor, Charles. *Sources of the Self.* Cambridge, MA: Harvard University Press, 1989.

STANDARD

FRENCH   *règle, norme*
SPANISH *norma*

▶ *RULE*, *VALUE*, and ART, BEAUTY, CIVILTÀ, GOÛT, LAW [LEX, THEMIS], PRINCIPLE, SPREZZATURA, STAND, UTILITY, *VIRTUE*, WERT

Until the eighteenth century, the word "standard" allowed one to account for an elevated level of living in society or of good taste. Its translation into French was then *règle* (rule) or *critère*. But the concept's meaning increasingly shifted to designate a norm or principle allowing for a rectification of experience. "Standard" serves to define an experience regulated on the basis of an excellence or to measure deviations in relation to that excellence. Evaluation is of various aspects of social life, such as the multiplicity of modes of human conduct or the variety of tastes. "Standard" refers to a possible but tacit regulation of such experiences, far less rigorous and more regional than the prescription of the law.

"Standard" is first of all linked to an apprenticeship of civil life. It allows for a definition of forms of behavior ruled by politeness and for the admission of a sociability comprising habits, customs, and social solicitations. Shaftesbury, in *The Characteristics of Men, Manners, Opinions, Times* (3:179) of 1711, focuses on the acquisition by the young of a "standard of manners, breeding, gentility." This use of "standard" to improve the taste of individuals in the affairs of everyday life rediscovers the spirit of the term *norma* in Baltasar Gracián, generally translated in French as *règle*: proper taste presupposes a knowledge of the "rule for knowing what is worthy of esteem [*la norma de la verdadera satisfacion*]" (*Oraculo manual y arte de prudencia*, 157).

"Standard of taste" in Hume extends reflection of the norm or criterion of human conduct to the domain of the fine arts, whose evaluation is perpetually confronted with the radical diversity of sentiments at the very moment one is obliged to establish a rule of taste (*Selected Essays*, 136). Well-regulated taste presupposes the delicacy of critics or connoisseurs, which is a discernment of the actual qualities of the object by a mind that is attentive, without prejudice, and practiced. "Standard" expresses the possibility of an experience of art that is well read.

When "standard" designates the possibility of a well-regulated experience in domains that are as subject to the instability of human behavior as are styles of living and the fine arts, terms such as "rule" or "canon" can help to refine the most local dispositions of the standard: the affirmation of rules of politeness, of aesthetic canons. But "standard" also posits a unit of measurement. "Standard" is close to "measure" and can be translated in French as *norme*. In *The Theory of Moral Sentiments* (25, 247–49), Adam Smith develops a parallel between art and morality concerning standard. One can define two different types of norm for human conduct. An ideal norm, an idea of the perfection of an object or a conduct, is a spur to construe every evaluation on its imperfections. A usage-based norm, the common degree of excellence habitually attained in art or morality, allows one to actually consider the rank of a work or an action among others of the same type. A standard serves to evaluate a degree of proximity or distance, a lesser or greater deviation in relation to the posited norm.

The word "standard" serves to rectify experience and, to be effective, ought to be as forceful and readable as possible. The use of "standard" in John Stuart Mill's *Utilitarianism* satisfies that requirement: in order to ameliorate behavior, utilitarian philosophy takes cognizance of what constituted the major defect of all moral experience, "the absence of any distinct recognition of an ultimate standard" (3). The word "standard" is deployed against the horizon of the foundation defined by the utilitarian doctrine. It comes close to "principle."

Fabienne Brugère

BIBLIOGRAPHY

Gracián y Morales, Baltasar. *Oraculo manual y arte de prudencia.* Madrid: Catedra, 1997. First published in 1647.

Hume, David. "Of the Standard of Taste." In *Selected Essays*, edited by Stephen Copley and Andrew Edgar. Oxford: Oxford University Press, 1993. First published in 1777.

Mill, John Stuart. *Utilitarianism.* London: Everyman's Library, 1990. First published in 1863.

Shaftesbury, Anthony Ashley Cooper. *Characteristics of Men, Manners, Opinions, Times.* Hildesheim, Ger.: Olms, 1978. First published in 1711.

Smith, Adam. *The Theory of Moral Sentiments.* Oxford: Oxford University Press, 1976. First published in 1759.

STATE

State comes from the Latin *status*, which refers to the action of standing and one's manner of standing, posture, position, from *sto, stare* (to remain standing, immobile, firm), and from which we derive *statuo* (to establish, to reckon, to decide); we find the same root in the Greek *istêmi* [ἵστημι] (to stand, to place) and in the intransitive sense (for example, in the aorist *estên* [ἔστην], meaning "to stand up"), in the Spanish *estar* (to be; see SPANISH and *TO BE*), and of course the English "stand," the German *stehen*, and so on. The Greek *stasis* [στάσις] can thus refer both to political and moral stability, the state of a person, a city, a question (cf. Lat. *status quaestionis, status causae*, see *THING*), as well as sedition, uprising, and civil war when one part of the city "stands up" again another. "Stela," "statue," and "statute" are also related to "state," which we see can refer to a physical or moral way of being, and to the institution of institutions that is the state.

1. On state as a disposition and way of being, see *DISPOSITION, II,* STAND, SUBJECT.
2. The concept of state strictly speaking refers to a mode of organization of political power presupposing a specialized government that is separate from society and institutionalized. This is the dominant tradition in political philosophy, which, in agreement with the major theorists of public law, tends to reserve the word "state" for political forms created with the development of the modern doctrine of sovereignty. However, sometimes we speak of the state simply as what holds together a political community, regardless of the empirical elements that compose it: see POLIS, the "city" that is a state, society, nation, and none of these all at once; cf. *FATHERLAND,* POLITICS, *SOCIETY.*
3. On the relation between the state and the law, see RULE OF LAW; cf. LAW, RIGHT/JUST/GOOD.
4. We have opted to study here the modulation of the senses of "state" as it is carried in languages and national histories. Thus, the Italian *stato* and the English "state" do not articulate the relation between territory, power, political regime, and government in the same way. See DEMOS/ETHNOS/LAOS, STATE/GOVERNMENT, STATO; cf. *AUTHORITY, GOVERNMENT,* HERRSCHAFT, MACHT.
5. On the "welfare state," see ECONOMY, LIBERAL.

➤ *COMMUNITY,* NAROD, PEOPLE, *POWER*

STATE OF AFFAIRS

"State of affairs" is one of the possible translations of the German *Sachverhalt*, which refers in everyday language to "circumstances." But this translation focuses attention on the properties of the objects of experience at the expense of the propositional content of the object of judgment. The other translation of *Sachverhalt*, and just as common, is "propositional content," which obviously suffers from the reverse problem. See SACHVERHALT.

We are in the presence here of logical terminology related to the most general questions (object-word-mind and the definition of truth) that effects the shift from medieval Latin (DICTUM), coming out of Stoicism and its competition with Aristotelianism (see *lekton* under SIGNIFIER/SIGNIFIED, II), to nineteenth- and twentieth-century German terminology, and then to contemporary analytic English terminology, and for which French produces descriptive translations that make the problems clear.

See, on one hand, DICTUM, INTENTION, PROPOSITION, SENSE; on the other ERSCHEINUNG, *FACT,* GEGENSTAND, *IL Y A,* MATTER OF FACT, OBJECT, TATSACHE, *THING* [RES], *TO BE,* and finally TRUTH.

➤ *PROPOSITIONAL CONTENT*

STATE / GOVERNMENT

FRENCH	*état, gouvernement*
GERMAN	*Staat*
ITALIAN	*stato*

➤ *GOVERNMENT, STATE,* and DEMOS/ETHNOS/LAOS, LAW, POLIS, POLITICS, RULE OF LAW, STATO

If the English "state" is indeed the equivalent of *état* in French, of *Staat* in German, and of *stato* in Italian, the term "government," in English, is of a far broader use than *gouvernement* in French. "Government" refers simultaneously to the following: (1) the level at which the state is directed; (2) the political system in force in a state; (3) the whole constituted by the legislative, executive, and judiciary powers, and by the administration; and (4) the set of agents contributing to the action of the public powers that be. In the two last senses, the word will tend to be rendered by *état*.

The two primary meanings of "government" are close to the French use, for which *gouvernement* designates both officials in the executive branch and the regime, that is, the specific mode of organization under which a community (be it a republic, a democracy, or a monarchy) lives. The two additional meanings, however, are much closer to the notion of the state in the European sense: "the American government" would no doubt be *l'état américain* in French, and if one sought to translate into French what American conservatives mean when they denounce "big government," it may be said that undoubtedly their objection is to *trop d'état*. The preference in English for "government" to designate certain aspects of what the French call *état* has its source in the traditions of English law, which, despite Hobbes, never accorded the sovereign state the majesty granted it by the major authors of the Continent; in addition, the American use is all the more understandable in that, within the federal system of the American republic, the state is, in fact, a state in the federation: the United States do indeed have a government, but it is not clear that they constitute a state. Such nuances, however, are less clearcut at present than in the past, to the extent that political developments have imposed a uniform vocabulary to designate the different states that coexist in the international system.

■ See Box 1.

Philippe Raynaud

1

"Corporation"

In English, "corporation" has different connotations from those of French *corporation*, a function of the manner in which "public law" and "private law" are articulated in British juridical culture. A "corporation" is an artificial person or juridical entity distinct from the individuals composing it, and that can plainly survive them. The distinction between "public" and "private" corporations does not stem from the identity of the owners (a "public enterprise" in the French sense is not a corporation) but from the purposes for which they are constituted: a corporation will be public if it has political missions concerning the government, but inversely a private corporation can have a certain normative power in the creation of law. In this sense, the "states" of a federation can be seen as public corporations without being sovereign "states." The importance of corporations thus stems from the fact that they allow a relativization of the role of the state in the production of law.

STATO (ITALIAN), RAGION DI STATO (ITALIAN), REASON OF STATE

ENGLISH	state, Reason of State
FRENCH	état, Raison d'État
GERMAN	Staat
LATIN	status
SPANISH	estado

➤ *STATE,* and MACHT, PEOPLE, POLIS, POLITICS, *POWER,* STATE/GOVERNMENT, VIRTÙ

The political lexicon reveals the historic emergence of the modern state, also known as the nation-state. The word for that new political reality in the principal languages of Europe (*stato, état, estado,* "state," *Staat*), a vague and general term, gradually, starting in the sixteenth century, takes on a meaning that is itself new, supplanting rival terms. Was Machiavelli the first to use the Italian word *stato* in the politico-juridical sense that it has since retained, and was he the first theoretician of the modern state? The matter can be debated, but one cannot deny the interest—which is not only linguistic, but also political and philosophical—in examining the evolution of the word *stato* in the political writings of the Italian Renaissance, and of its transition from being a polysemous configuration to embodying a relative unity of meaning, with all the problems of translation flowing from it.

I. *Stato*: Power and Territory

In classical Latin, the word *status* expresses the fact of "holding oneself," posture, and is used metaphorically to mean the situation, the state of something or someone, in particular the "state of public affairs" at a given time, whence the formula *status rei publicae*—the word *res publica* designating, for the Romans, their idiosyncratic political institutions. But Cicero also uses the formula in a more general sense, that of a form of government, *res publica* designating in such cases a *regnum* as much as a *res publica* properly speaking.

Medieval Latin for the most part inherited this usage. *Status* means the good state, good order, prosperity of a specific community. In this sense, it is never employed alone, but as *status Ecclesiae, status regni*, or even *status rei publicae*, even if it is a matter of *regnum*.

In fifteenth-century Italy, the words *status* and *stato* pass from this vague sense of political situation to the more precise one of exclusive possession of a territory with the power to command its inhabitants. They refer to those who hold such possession and power, but the words also begin to be employed absolutely, to designate possession and power themselves, without specific reference to those who hold them. This core of meaning is shaded with all sorts of nuances, as may be seen from the political literature, particularly in Florence, in the fifteenth and early sixteenth centuries. This suppleness of meaning and diversity of use are particularly visible in Machiavelli.

In order to shed light on the analysis of these nuances, it can be said that, for Machiavelli as for his contemporaries (Guicciardini, for example), the word *stato* oscillates between two poles of meaning, with slippages from one to the other. On the one hand, it designates the political power exercised by a single person or group over a fixed set of people. It is then synonymous with a dominant position, and inseparable from the active subject of a command clearly separate from its object, which is passive. The word thus refers to the specific interest of those who govern: the *stato de Medici* is the power exercised over the city of Florence by members of the Medici family, and *stato* in this case has a meaning close to *governo*. Thus understood, the *stato* partakes of an *ars dominandi*, an art whose treatise par excellence is Machiavelli's *The Prince*, since the question it raises is that of knowing how to secure and preserve nonhereditary power. In chapter 2 of *The Prince*, for example, one reads: "se tale principe è di ordinaria industria, sempre si manterrà nel suo stato, se non è una estraordinaria et eccessiva forza che ne lo privi" (a prince of average powers will always maintain himself in his state, unless he be deprived of it by some extraordinary and excessive force). Or further still, in chapter 24: "E se si considerrà quelli signori che in Italia hanno perduto lo stato a'nostri tempi" (And if those seigniors are considered who have lost their states in Italy in our times). In both examples, *stato* clearly signifies "power."

Stato can also have a more material frame of reference as a term for the domain, territory, or population over which power is exercised: "Ma quando si acquista stati in una provincia" (But when *stati* are acquired in a province) (ibid., chap. 3). In chapter 4, one reads that the *baroni,* the feudal lords, "hanno stati sudditi proprii" (have their own *stati* and subjects). These *stati* are territories. The same holds in chapter 7, when Machiavelli speaks of Pope Alexander VI, who, wanting to satisfy the ambitions of his son Cesare Borgia, "non vedeva via di poterlo fare signore di alcuno stato che non fussi stato di Chiesa" (did not see his way to make him master of any *stato* that was not a *stato* of the Church). When one speaks in French of *États de l'Église*, the word *état* retains this older sense of territorial estate or realm.

In *The Prince* the two meanings of power and territory often come together. In the examples given in the preceding paragraphs, the prince *se manterrà nel suo stato* can translate as not only "will conserve his power" but also "will maintain himself on his lands." Sovereigns who have lost power have simultaneously lost their realm. One is inseparable from the other, but a translator is obliged to choose, unless she extricates herself by using indiscriminately the word "state." But one finds additional semantic difficulties when it is a matter of specifying the meaning, as in the aforementioned examples, of the word *stato*, namely, that of political power exercised over a human community. For *stato* can also mean "political regime" in the sense of "a type of organization of power." Thus the *stato popolare* is that in which the people, or a portion of the people, participates in the government of the city through different councils in which authority has not been confiscated by an individual or an oligarchy. In this case one speaks of a *stato stretto,* that is, one that is "tightened."

II. Machiavelli and the Notion of "State"

The thorniest question is whether there is a transition in Machiavelli from the meaning of "political power" or "concrete domain over which power is exercised" to that of an abstract and impersonal political and juridical structure in the modern sense of the word "state." In this case, the different powers constitutive of state structure are clearly distinguished from the person of those exercising them. In other words, the state is not identified with the government and its different modes of exercise but subsists even as regimes change, whether they be monarchical, aristocratic, or republican. The state preserves its own substance and exigencies, independently of the manner in which those exigencies are satisfied. In this regard, the first sentence of *The Prince* is frequently cited as marking the lexical birth of the modern state:

> Tutti li stati, tutti e'dominii che hanno avuto et hanno imperio sopra gli uomini, sono stati e sono o republiche o principati.

> (All states, all powers, that have held and hold rule over men have been and are either republics or principalities.)

Here Machiavelli seems to distinguish the notion of state, in the general sense of political structure of power, from that of regime or type of (republican or monarchical) constitution. But can it not be claimed that for Machiavelli, in this case, the *stati*, identified with *dominii*, are mere "facts," facts of power exercised over people in a given territory, and do not correspond to an "idea," which would be that of the "State" written with a capital "S"? One discovers the same ambiguity, the same occasion for interrogation, in numerous occurrences of the word *stato* in *The Prince* and in the *Discourses on the First Decade of Titus-Livius.* Two examples will suffice. When, in chapter 3 of *The Prince,* Machiavelli writes that the French *non si intendevano dello stato*, does he mean

that they did not have a sense of the State, or rather, more simply, that they did not know the art of conserving what was conquered, since the remark refers to Louis XII, who "lost Lombardy by not having followed any of the conditions observed by those who took possession of countries and wished to retain them"? Similarly, when he says, in a letter of 10 December 1513, to Francesco Vettori, concerning *The Prince*, that the "quindici anni, che io sono stato a studio all'arte dello stato, non gl'ho dormiti ne'giuocati" (the fifteen years that I devoted to the study of the art of the *stato* were not spent sleeping or amusing myself), is it a question of the art or science of the State, or rather of the art of winning and maintaining personal domination?

All these lexical uncertainties have been commented on abundantly, and it can be concluded that in his use of the word *stato*, Machiavelli did not greatly differ from his contemporaries. At most one can attribute to him an intuition (rather than a clear vision) of what the modern state would be. Nowhere does he define it, nor does he analyze its constitutive elements, as Bodin and Hobbes later would. He was interested in the phenomenon of pure political power; the conditions of its acquisition, exercise, and conservation, and rather than religious, moral, or juridical delimitation and structures of legitimation. This orientation explains his apparent indifference (at least in *The Prince*) to the institutional and juridical structure of the community subject to political power, with its attributions and limitations.

It is possible, however, to understand why Machiavelli has been turned into, if not the founder, then at least the forerunner of the conception of the nation-state. It is not by chance that republicans as well as partisans of absolute monarchy have invoked his authority. The idea of "the people," who, in *The Prince,* seem not to have an autonomous existence but to be mere objects submissive to power, makes its first appearance as a nation in the final chapter, which is a vibrant appeal to Italian unity. Moreover, when Machiavelli insists on the necessity of a national army and denounces the tutelary authority exercised by the Catholic Church, he reveals a lively sense of certain fundamental demands of the modern State: territorial unity, independence of the nation in relation to foreign powers ensured by a national army, and a refusal to submit political power to powers foreign or transcendent to it, specifically of a religious order. But if he undeniably has a sense of the general interest of the political community, he does not truly dissociate that interest from the personal interest of the individual or individuals exercising power: in the final analysis, what must be done for the prince to conserve his power is identified with what must be done for power itself—in its impersonal, "impartial" form, what we call the State—to be conserved. It is with the notion of *ragion di stato*, Reason of State, that this new sense of *stato* would clearly emerge.

III. *Ragion di Stato*

If, in the Italian political writings of the sixteenth century, *stato* long continued to be used with the diverse meanings encountered in Machiavelli, a clear distinction began to emerge between *stato* in the sense of *governo* and *stato* in a more abstract sense, designating everything concerning relations between individuals and social groups within a politically organized community. One speaks then of *subversione di tutto lo stato,* which is not reducible to that of the *governo.* When, in 1547, Giovanni Della Casa wrote of the *ragion di stato* (Francesco Guicciardini, in his *Dialogo del reggimento di Firenze* [1526], already had spoken of *ragione e uso degli stati*), one might wonder whether it was not still the interest of the *governo,* those who governed, that was in play in the political "argument." With the appearance of Giovanni Botero's book *Della ragion di Stato* (1589), the most representative of the abundant texts on "Reason of State" proliferating in Italy (and later throughout Europe in the late sixteenth and early seventeenth centuries), things become clear. For Botero the *stato* is "un dominio fermo sopra popoli, e agion di stato è notizia di mezzi atti a fondare, conservare ed ampliare un dominio cosi fatto" (a stable power over peoples, and Reason of State is the knowledge of the means suited to found, conserve, and augment such power), and he adds that *ragion di stato* (Reason of State) "suppone il prencipe e lo stato (quello quasi come artefice, questo come materia)" (presupposes the prince and the *stato* [the former being a kind of artisan and the latter his material substance) (Book I, chap. 1). The *stato* as *dominio* takes on a certain autonomy in relation to

the *governo* of the prince; it acts in its own interest when the political interest of governing officials is acted upon. What becomes an object of interest is no longer the *stato* of one prince or another, but the *stato* in and of itself; the State in its conditions of existence, in its proper functioning, and in its well-being. The concept of the impersonal, abstract, absolute state, unbound by any laws other than those it gives itself, is born. The paradox here is that the two authors who would definitively elaborate the political, juridical, and philosophical foundations of the modern state, Bodin and Hobbes, would not use or only rarely used words of the same family as *stato* in their lexicon, Bodin's work is called *The Six Books of the Commonwealth,* and Hobbes, in the introduction to *Leviathan*, speaks of "that great LEVIATHAN called a COMMON-WEALTH, or STATE (*in latine CIVITAS*)" and prefers the term "Common-Wealth," which is the English translation of the Latin *res publica,* and which Locke would use as well. One would have to wait a while for *État* and "State" to impose themselves.

■ See Boxes 1 and 2.

Alain Pons

1

Colonia and *imperium*

"Colony" and "empire" are words whose meanings have transformed over time as they have been translated between languages and therefore from one culture and its political system to another. The underlying shift in the twentieth century was from a positive to a negative connotation, reflecting the degree to which colonies are now regarded as negating the rights of indigenous peoples, and empires are seen as despotic systems in an age of democracy.

It was not always so. The Greek term for colony was originally *apoikia* [ἀποικία], or "settlement" (literally "people far from home"). Greek *apoikiai* [ἀποικίαι] were city-states established all over the Mediterranean of emigrants who retained their cultural ties with the *mētropolis* [μητρόπολις], or home city. Each colony, however, was politically autonomous and functioned as an independent *polis* [πόλις]. The Romans, for their part, used the Latin term *colonia* in two related ways: drawing upon the meaning of *colonus* as farmer, it designated a settlement, or farm estate, often granted to veteran soldiers in conquered territories, initially in regions relatively close to Rome intended to act as outposts to defend Roman territory. These settlements, however, could also include towns, which were assigned a comparably favored rank on the basis of their population of Roman citizens: Roman *coloniae* included Ostia (the first), London, Bath, York, Arles,

Köln, Narbonne, and Jerusalem, cities established at the farthest reaches of the empire (in various periods) to act in some degree as imperial garrisons. For this reason, Roman authors also used the term *colonia* to translate the Greek *apoikia* [ἀποικία]. However, the function of the *coloniae* as strategic outposts of the Roman Empire meant that later Greeks did not translate the word back the other way, rather employing the Latin *colonia* as an untranslatable term: *kolônia* [κολωνία]. It was this untranslatable Roman word with its particular political and strategic resonance that then entered French (fourteenth century) and English (sixteenth century) to designate plantations and settlements abroad. Modern European colonies were formed on the Roman political model, consisting of the founding of a settlement in a separate, usually overseas, locality that sought to expand the territory and duplicate or renew the culture of the parent country ("New" Amsterdam, England, Spain, York, etc.) while retaining allegiance to it and submitting to its overall political control. The model of sovereignty in this period meant that, in contrast to ancient Greece, individuals remained subjects of the crown wherever they might happen to be in the world. Although many early European colonies were colonies of settlement, these were generally restricted to temperate regions where Europeans could establish themselves more easily. Elsewhere,

other colonies were founded as trading posts (the Greeks, by contrast, distinguished between the *apoikiai* [ἀποικίαι] and their trading posts, which they called *emporiai* [ἐμπορίαι]), which gradually took on territorial scope: a primary example would be that of the East India Company, which expanded from the original outpost that became the city of Calcutta to control the whole of India. Such colonies, where trade, resource extraction, or port facilities were primary, are distinguished from settlement colonies by modern historians as "exploitation" colonies. However heterogeneous in form, they were all called colonies, with the Roman word consistently repeated across the various languages of the European empires (*kolonie* [Dutch], *colonie* [French], *Kolonie* [German], *colonia* [Italian], *colônia* [Portuguese], колония [Russian], *colonia* [Spanish]). After the American and Latin American revolutions of the eighteenth and early nineteenth centuries, the system, practice, and administration of colonies, "colonialism" (introduced into English in the mid-nineteenth century, into French at the beginning of the twentieth) increasingly lost the positive aura that had been retained from the Roman *coloniae* and by 1919 came to be used as a derogatory term by its opponents, with the implication that all colonialism represented a form of exploitation of subaltern peoples by too-powerful nations. "Colonialism" was soon used as a negative word in the discourse of the widespread opposition to colonial rule by the indigenous people of the colonies. This resistance is all generally termed "anticolonial" even if in practice the path of liberation tended to divide between relatively peaceful negotiation for exploitation colonies and violent warfare for settlement colonies, such as Algeria, where a significant presence of colonial settlers (*pieds noirs*) produced often apparently intractable situations. The old, more neutral sense of "colonial" survives today only in certain contexts, such as in the period designations "colonial architecture" or "colonial furniture."

In semantic terms, the Greek practice of autonomous colonies did not survive the creation of the Roman Empire: colony and empire ever since have retained an unbroken connection, even if it has often been one of tension and conflict. If colony comprises the individual settlement, empire involves the totality of settlements from the point of view of the metropolis, which is the center of imperial administration. There have been many empires throughout human history, but it is the Roman Empire, developed from the concept of the *imperium*, the supreme power of the ruler, that functions as the fundamental basis for the conceptualization of empire. What is significant here is that the idea of empire is the product of the supreme power of its ruler, and the language of command, *imperare*: the rule of the emperor and the territory over which that rule extends (cf. *translatio imperium*, the chronological succession of transfers of supreme power that form the basis of medieval and imperial histories). The first British Empire was simply that realm of dominion exercised after 1603 by James I over the British Isles, which he named Great Britain. The conventional land empire of contiguous or proximate territories, of which the Mongol was the largest historically, was supplemented in the colonial period by empires that were geographically dispersed, an aggregate of separate colonies held together by the new technology of ocean-going ships or, later, undersea telegraph cables. While the first British Empire was well established by the eighteenth century despite the loss of the American colonies, the defeat of the French in India (1757) and then Canada (1763) produced Napoleon's later attempt to compensate for their loss by reinstituting an empire through conquest of the European landmass. A new word was subsequently introduced to distinguish this "third way" of Napoleon's form of government between monarchy and republicanism: *impérialisme* (1832). It was not until the Second Empire of Napoleon III, however, that the word traveled into English as "imperialism" (1858) as a way of describing the French political system of an autocratic emperor creating an empire not through trade or emigration, but by the forcible appropriation of foreign territory through conquest (in the French case, consolidation of power in Algeria and invasions of or military missions to China, Cochinchina, Japan, the Levant, and Mexico).

Imperialism, which named the Napoleonic model of the French political system, was at this point actively rejected by British politicians and intellectuals (as well as by Karl Marx) as a form of despotism utterly alien to British traditions. Within twenty years, however, the allegedly untranslatable French concept of imperialism was to be shamelessly translated into British policy by Benjamin Disraeli, whose second (but first substantial) term of office began in 1874. Though the negative marker always endured for some, in public discourse it was gradually abandoned, together with the commitment to free trade, in favor of an imperialist policy of extending commerce through an actively acquisitive empire. In France "imperialism" was duly imported in its English form (1880) and initially referred to as *l'impérialisme anglais* (1900). These imports, exports, and insistence on the untranslatable difference of the French and English words for imperialism were markers of what continued to be regarded as a significant variation in the political organization of empire. Toward the end of the nineteenth century, British imperialism was conceived as a way of holding together an empire that was commonly seen as verging on the point of dissolution. The experience of the American War of Independence had encouraged the organization of the empire into units of semi-autonomous dominions: the British concept of a "Greater Britain," founded on a large number of settler colonies, including some that were entirely independent such as the United States, was distinct from most other European imperial powers in which imperialism involved the development of expansive concepts of "Greater France," "Greater Germany," and "Greater Italy"—and in the East, "Greater Japan"—in which the colonial territories were integrated administratively into the metropolitan mainland and considered as an integral part of the sovereign state. Such differences aside, at this point imperialism became the dominant world political system, an era best symbolized by the 1884 Berlin Conference in which the remaining territory of Africa was divided by agreement among Austria-Hungary, Belgium, Denmark, France, the United Kingdom, Italy, the Netherlands, Portugal, Russia, Spain, Sweden-Norway, and the Ottoman Empire (the United States was invited, but did not attend). While empire can describe a merely administrative arrangement for the government of diverse and diversely acquired territories, imperialism came to designate an ideology of empire that forged the identity of the originating imperial state, and whose interests lay in trade (importing raw commodities from their imperial possessions and reexporting them as manufactured goods), territorial control, and autonomy from the threat of other empires. (Some historians would argue that these were the underlying reasons for the First World War, and certainly increase of colonial territory was one war aim of all the main protagonists). Ideological justifications for empire were generally added to these material objectives—*la mission civilisatrice* (France), the rule of law (Britain), and conversion to Christianity (all European empires).

At the height of European imperial power, however, imperialism came under attack not only through resistance across the empire itself, but also from liberal and left-wing thinkers within Europe. Along with J. A. Hobson's *Imperialism* (1902), Henri Brunschwig's *Mythes et réalités de l'impérialisme colonial français* (1906), Rosa Luxemburg and Nikolai Bukharin's *Imperialism and the Accumulation of Capital* (1913), the most famous of these was Lenin's *Imperialism: The Highest Stage of Capitalism* (1916), which decisively transformed the public meaning of imperialism from positive back to negative once more, even in France. Ever since, even with the development of new forms of imperialism (such as the "economic imperialism" of the United States from the end of the nineteenth century, which in 1965 Kwame Nkrumah claimed continued among former European colonies after formal independence as "neocolonialism"), "imperialism" and "imperialist" have functioned as words of critique. With the exception of fascist ideologues in Germany, Italy, and Japan until the end of the Second World War, empire has been generally disavowed by states or politicians, and for the most part discussed in terms of something to be resisted and overcome (cf. Mao Tse Tung's "U.S. Imperialism Is a Paper Tiger," 14 July 1956, in *Selected Works*). It was Lenin who, following Hobson, made the connection between imperialism and finance capitalism so that imperialism and capitalism have since become almost synonymous in left discourse, and analyses of empire always establish their ground in economic critique. Lenin's argument was that the conjunction of the two represented a particular form of imperialism and that modern imperialism was therefore not to be usefully compared to, or translated into, the boundaries of the territorial expansion through conquest of historical empires in general Imperialism, he argued, was not translatable out of capitalism.

Although there were theories of colonization, colonialism can be defined largely as a practice Imperialism manifested itself as a

(continued)

(continued)

practice, but its meaning was grounded in a political concept of expansive power, seeking to turn heterogeneous colonies into a single political and economic system. Imperialism necessarily involves empires, therefore, but all empires do not necessarily invoke imperialism. As with "colony" and "colonialism," the meaning of "empire" and "imperialism" has shifted according to the political hegemony of their advocates or opponents.

Robert J. C. Young

BIBLIOGRAPHY

Baumgart, Winfried. *Imperialism: The Idea and Reality of British and French Colonial Expansion, 1880–1914.* Rev. ed. Translated by Winfried Baumgart with Ben V. Mast. Oxford: Oxford University Press, 1982.

Benton, Lauren. *A Search for Sovereignty: Law and Geography in European Empires, 1400–1900.* Cambridge: Cambridge University Press, 2009.

Brewer, Anthony. *Marxist Theories of Imperialism: A Critical Survey.* London: Routledge and Kegan Paul, 1980.

Brunschwig, Henri. *Mythes et réalités de l'impérialisme colonial français, 1871–1914.* Paris: A. Colin, 1906.

Burbank, Jane, and Frederick Cooper. *Empires in World History: Power and the Politics of Difference.* Princeton, NJ: Princeton University Press, 2010.

Hardt, Michael, and Antonio Negri. *Empire.* Cambridge, MA: Harvard University Press, 2001.

Harmand, Jules. *Domination et colonisation.* Paris: Flammarion, 1910.

Hobson, J. A. *Imperialism: A Study.* London: Allen and Unwin, 1938.

Koebner, Richard, and Helmut Dan Smith. *Imperialism: The Story and Significance of a Political Word, 1840–1960.* Cambridge: Cambridge University Press, 1964.

Lenin, V. I. *Imperialism: The Highest Stage of Capitalism: A Popular Outline.* Peking: Foreign Languages Press, 1965. First published in 1917.

Leroy-Beaulieu, Pierre-Paul. *De la colonisation chez les peuples modernes.* Paris: Guillaumin, 1874.

Luxemburg, Rosa, and Nikolai Ivanovich Bukharin. *Imperialism and the Accumulation of Capital.* Edited by K. J. Tarbuck. London: Allen Lane, 1972. First published in 1913.

Mao Tse-Tung. *Selected Works of Mao Tse-Tung.* 5 vols. Peking: Foreign Languages Press, 1965.

Nkrumah, Kwame. *Neo-Colonialism: The Last Stage of Imperialism.* London: Heinemann, 1965.

Osterhammel, Jürgen *Colonialism: A Theoretical Overview.* Translated by Shelley L. Frisch. Princeton, NJ: Marcus Wiener, 1997.

Semmel, Bernard. *The Liberal Ideal and the Demons of Empire: Theories of Imperialism from Adam Smith to Lenin.* Baltimore: Johns Hopkins University Press, 1993.

Veracini, Lorenzo. *Settler Colonialism: A Theoretical Overview.* Basingstoke, UK: Palgrave Macmillan, 2010.

Young, Robert J. C. *Postcolonialism: An Historical Introduction.* Oxford: Blackwell, 2001.

2

"Postcolonial," "Postcolonialism"

Few notions in recent theoretical parlance have aroused as much criticism as "postcolonial" and "postcolonialism." From the start their ambiguity, awkwardness and insufficiency as political concepts have been subject to critique. More than other terms conceived with and through specific movements and schools of thought, "postcolonialism" and "postcolonial" solicit a new definition with each and every iteration. Both terms have been sites of epistemological and ideological confrontation.

A mid-twentieth-century construct, the qualifier "postcolonial" was first used to mean "post-independence," with explicit historical reference to the aftermath of decolonization. But even in this chronological ascription "postcolonial" remains problematic, since the nature and reality of political "independence" can always be debated. If used indiscriminately, "postcolonial" risks homogenizing very different colonial histories and modes of accession to independence. In the shift from its use as a historical term to its use in critical, theoretical, and literary discourses, the adjective produced the noun "postcolonialism." It became untethered from specific moments in history, and began to circulate in discourses that moved more fluidly between colonial and postcolonial histories, and their complex cultural and social ramifications.

Robert J. C. Young has argued that tricontinentalism, a form of Third World activism brought to the fore by the 1966 Tricontinental Conference in Havana, is the direct antecedent of postcolonialism as a political concept: "In many ways the Bandung conference marks the origin of postcolonialism as a self-conscious political philosophy." (*Postcolonialism: A Very Short Introduction*, 17).

"Postcolonial" studies gained currency in the 1970s, at a moment when literary studies (especially in English) were confronted with the inability of nation-centered disciplines such as "English literature" (or "French literature," etc.), to address the important body of writing from former colonies, produced in European languages. The inadequacy of a simple equation of nation and language underlined the political and social insufficiencies of academic institutions, and drew attention to the multiple legacies of the colonial situation. The problem of naming literary fields and world literatures in light of the impact of colonization on culture, education, and the conditions of knowledge-production was foregrounded in postcolonial criticism. In France, the question of how to mark the postcolonial in academic fields remains particularly rife with controversy. The term *Francophonie*, which was adopted to designate extrahexagonal literatures of French expression, is often rejected on the grounds that it contains condescending undertones (cf. the writers' manifesto "Pour une littérature-monde en français," *Le Monde*, 16 March 2007). In Anglophone studies, where the designation of "Commonwealth literatures" gave way to "new literatures" that were in turn supplanted by "world literatures in English," an awareness of diverse writings in "English(es)" from formerly colonized nations and territories helped effect a shift in emphasis in the way the term "postcolonialism" was adduced—a shift from a strictly chronological and historical application to what might be described as a broadly critical and discursive usage. As the term was taken up in different fields it gave rise to an increasing number of debates and questions: How "post" was colonialism? Was there a difference in how the term signified depending on whether or not it was hyphenated? Was postcolonialism a historically circumscribed phenomenon or was it coextensive with ongoing forms of neo-imperialism? To what extent was it identified with the critique of Europe-centered epistemological assumptions? Had it become a disciplinary/theoretical locus with a momentum all its own, and whose dehistoricized adjectival usage required infinite linguistic and cultural translation?

Interestingly enough, the critics whose contributions to the analysis of colonial discourse were among the most notable—Edward W. Said, Gayatri Chakravorty Spivak, and Homi K. Bhabha—hardly used the term "postcolonial" in their seminal work of the late 1970s and early 1980s. And yet it was their articulations of Orientalism, the silencing of the subaltern, and colonial mimicry that gave substance to what came to be known as postcolonial theory, enabling it to challenge preexisting disciplinary boundaries. Arguably, the enduring force of postcolonial thought may be a product of the *non*existence of its disciplinary boundaries. Since "it" doesn't really exist as a discipline in and of itself, it works from without to split and suture discursive fields. It sutures, for example, "high theory" to the critique of colonial legacies; it carries an implicit endorsement of activist research and writing; and it fosters work that vigilantly attends to the way in which contemporary knowledge-systems are configured in specific geopolitical zones. This is perforce an anxiety-fraught exercise, for in requiring constant attention to manifestations of noninstitutional thought and systems, postcolonial theory sometimes assists (in politically problematic ways) in professionally institutionalizing them.

At their most effective, "postcolonial" and postcolonialism" can be identified with the politically engaged questioning of the primary historical meaning of "post" and with an enhanced understanding of what it means to colonize or to be colonized beyond the chronological definitions compounded by historians. From a postcolonial perspective, colonization is understood as an ongoing process that subsumes the exploitation of labor and resources; the history of social and political repression; and the imposition of values and systems of knowledge.

"Postcolonial" and "postcolonialism" represent something more like a critical tendency than a disciplinary category or distinct school of thought. The terms may be associated with heuristic practices; with readings that cut across literature, history, cultural studies, area studies, and economics. Because disciplinary categories themselves vary so much from one language and institutional context to another, postcolonial theory may be said to irrigate certain fields and to disappear in others. The difficulty that arises when translating "postcolonial" or "postcolonialism" is symptomatic of the terms' ability to unsettle the organization of academic disciplines. Equally symptomatic is the way in which the terms themselves have remained subject to political contestation. Given their sway in American and British academic contexts, they are suspected of becoming just another hegemonic form of thought, and as such, worthy of resistance. They have also come under attack for being used in conceptually unrigorous ways in a mainstream liberal arts education, which is to say used as loose synonyms for dominant social relations in almost any historical situation; for the subaltern status of certain minority groups within a nation, or for transnational cultural or religious practices as modes of resistance to the hegemonic pressures of the globalized economy. This expansion of intellectual, institutional, political, and ideological purview has, it is often thought, weakened the terms.

The untranslatability of "postcolonial" and "postcolonialism" may, paradoxically enough, be their greatest strength, for in becoming untranslatable they illuminate divergent concepts of the nation and national community; expose fault-lines in the modern nation-state; reveal the inherent violence of hegemonic intellectual and social practices; delegitimate assimilationism (and more specifically, the idea of a social contract based on the "integration" of all into one national model and language); and critique normalization in ways that have yet to be articulated in existing political and social idioms.

Émilienne Baneth-Nouailhetas

BIBLIOGRAPHY

Ashcroft, B., G. Griffiths, and H. Tiffin. *The Empire Writes Back: Theory and Practice in Post-colonial Literatures*. London: Routledge, 1989.

Bhabha, H. K. *The Location of Culture*. London: Routledge, 1994.

Forsdick, C., and D. Murphy. *Postcolonial Thought in the French-Speaking World*. Liverpool, UK: Liverpool University Press, 2009.

Roitman, Janet, ed. "Racial France." Special issue of *Public Culture* 63 (Winter 2011).

Said, E. *Orientalism: Western Conceptions of the Orient*. London: Penguin, 1991.

Spivak, G. *In Other Worlds: Essays in Cultural Politics*. New York: Methuen, 1987.

———. *The Post-Colonial Critic: Interviews, Strategies, Dialogues*. Edited by Sarah Harasym. New York: Routledge, 1990.

Young, Robert J. C. *Colonial Desire: Hybridity in Theory, Culture and Race*. London: Routledge, 1995.

———. *Postcolonialism: An Historical Introduction*. Oxford: Blackwell, 2001.

———. *Postcolonialism: A Very Short Introduction*, Oxford: Oxford University Press, 2003

———. *White Mythologies: Writing History and the West*. London: Routledge, 1990.

BIBLIOGRAPHY

Botero, Giovanni. *The Reason of State*. Translated by P. J. Waley and D. P. Waley. New Haven, CT: Yale University Press, 1956.

Chabod, Frederico. "Alcune questioni di terminologia: Stato, nazione, patria nel linguaggio del Cinquecentro." In *L'idea di nazione*. Bari: Laterza, 1967.

Della Casa, Giovanni. *Orazioni per esortare la Repubblica Veneta a entrare in lega co'l Papa e co'l Re di Francia contro l'imperator Carlo Quinto (1547–1548); Orazione a Carlo V imperatore per la restitutzione della città di Piacenza (1549–1550)*. In *Opere volgari di Monsignor della Casa*. Pavie, It.: Pio Andrea Viani, 1592.

Gilbert, Félix. *Machiavel et Guichardin. Politique et histoire à Florence au XVIe siècle*. Paris: Éditions du Seuil, 1996.

Guicciardini, Francesco. *Dialogue on the Government of Florence*. Edited and translated by Alison Brown. Cambridge: Cambridge University Press, 1994.

Hexter, J. H. "Il Principe e 'lo stato.'" *Studies in the Renaissance* 4 (1957).

Machiavelli, Niccolò. *Discourses*. 2 vols. Translated by Leslie J. Walker. New Haven, CT: Yale University Press, 1950.

———. *Florentine Histories*. Translated by Laura F. Banfield and Harvey C. Mansfield Jr. Princeton, NJ: Princeton University Press, 1988.

———. *The Prince*. Translated by Russell Price. Edited by Quentin Skinner and Russell Price. Cambridge: Cambridge University Press, 1988.

Mansfield, Harvey C. *Machiavelli's Virtue*. Chicago: University of Chicago Press, 1995.

Passerin D'Entrèves, Alessandro. *The Notion of the State*. Oxford: Clarendon Press, 1967.

Pocock, J.G.A. *The Machiavellian Moment: Florentine Political Thought and the Atlantic Republican Tradition*. Princeton, NJ: Princeton University Press, 2003.

Rubinstein, Nicolas. *Notes on the Word "Stato" in Florence before Machiavelli*. Toronto: University of Toronto Press, 1971.

Senellart, Michel. *Les arts de gouverner: Du "regimen" médiéval au concept de gouvernement*. Paris: Éditions du Seuil, 1995.

———. *Machiavélisme et raison d'etat*. Paris: Presses Universitaires de France, 1987.

Viroli, Maurizio. *From Politics to Reason of State: The Acquisition and Transformation of the Language of Politics, 1250–1600*. Cambridge: Cambridge University Press, 1992.

Vries, H. de. *Essai sur la terminologie constitutionnelle chez Machiavel ("Il Principe")*. Gravehenge, Neth.: Excelsior, 1957.

STILL, STILLE (GERMAN)

FRENCH   *calme, serein, silencieux; immobilité, sérénité, calme, silence*

➤ MOTIONLESS, SILENT, and AESTHETICS, CLASSIC, LEGGIADRIA,
   SECULARIZATION, SERENITY, SUBLIME

Because it unites three different semantic registers (spatial immobility, silence, and mystery) German *still* is privileged turf for untranslatability. Johann J. Winckelmann, who made it into the foundation of a central *topos* of classical aesthetics when he spoke of *"edle Einfalt und stille Größe* [noble simplicity and serene grandeur]," deliberately played on this ambiguity. In translating the notion of calm and serenity borrowed from French classicism as *Stille*, he created in German an aesthetic concept that is similarly untranslatable. *Stille*, the central characteristic of Greek beauty, refers for him not only to the physical motionlessness of the body but also to silence: Laocoön does not shout. This polysemy entails an entire theory of the sublime in art.

I. Initial Polysemy

The adjective *still* as well as the noun *Stille* have existed since Old High German. Already in that period their meaning was tripartite, referring at times to the realm of physical immobility (*still* means "without movement"), at others to the register of silence (without noise, without a word), or finally, by metaphorical extension, to that of secrecy and mystery (what is hidden, contained, concealed). Of those three senses it appears that the second is the most frequent. To those various meanings a mystical sense was already added in the medieval era. *Still* designates a state of serenity confident in the divine presence, a kind of *unio mystica*. Popularized by Luther through the expression "*die Stillen im Lande* [them that are quiet in the land]" (Ps. 35:20), the word *still* became a traditional motif of religious discourse, more specifically used, at the beginning of the eighteenth century, in Pietist circles and in the milieu of the Moravian Brothers. Ludwig von Zinzendorf frequently resorted to it. Nonetheless, the border between the various meanings remains hazy, which makes *Still* and its derivative terms difficult to translate.

II. A Central Concept of the German Classical Aesthetic

Winckelmann marks a major phase in the history of the word. In playing on the superimposition of meanings, on a fundamental untranslatability, he made of *still* a central aesthetic concept.

> The last and most eminent characteristic of the Greek works is a noble simplicity and serene grandeur (*eine edle Einfalt und eine stille Größe*) in gesture and expression. As the bottom of the sea lies peaceful (*ruhig*) beneath a foaming surface, a great soul lies sedate (*eine große und gesetzte Seele*) beneath the strife of passions in Greek figures.
>
> (Winckelmann, "Gedanken")

Stille becomes a major attribute of beauty. Its *locus* is ancient Greek art, but it can also be found in a rare few modern artists, such as Raffaello. In his use of the word, Winckelmann has recourse to two complementary strategies. He first of all plays with the ambiguities of German, effecting a slight displacement of meaning from the religious register of Pietistic *Stille* to the pagan space of ancient beauty. Even in greatest physical pain, Laocoön remains *still*, that is, at once serene, silent, and immobile, oscillating between sanctity and sublimity. In this way Winckelmann effects a secularization of the Pietistic notion of *Stille* while simultaneously imbuing Greek beauty with a strong spiritual dimension. This usage was taken up by a long tradition of writers: Herder, Hölderlin, Goethe. *Stille* became the attribute par excellence of classical man, the quintessence of Greekness—and did so until relatively recently, since the German philologist W. Rehm placed it in the very title of his great work on classicism, *Götterstille und Göttertrauer* (1951).

But *Stille* in Winckelmann was also nourished by a foreign linguistic source. A great reader of treatises of aesthetics of the seventeenth and eighteenth centuries, Winckelmann undertook to methodically forge a German lexicon of classicism by drawing on his European (and particularly French) library. His famous phrase "edle Einfalt, stille Größe" is, in fact, but the transcription of a commonplace of aesthetic literature, amply developed before him by C. A. Dufresnoy, R. de Piles, J.-B. Dubos, etc. In his manuscript collection, for example, he consigns such as it is the phrase *noble simplicité* in the French translation of a work by the son of Samuel Richardson. But Winckelmann was not satisfied with faithfully transcribing his sources. In translating the expression *grandeur sereine* as *stille Größe*, he confers on it a new density. In German *still* signifies not only "calm," "serene," "motionless," in the spatial realm, but also "silent" and "mute" in the vocal register. Winckelmannian calm invests the full range of speech. It designates fixity of muscles and suspension of voice. Whereas French is obliged to choose between *serein* and *silencieux*, Winckelmann knowingly plays on ambiguities in German that fuse the two registers. In rendering *sérénité* as *Stille*, he proliferates the semantic potentialities of calm and opens, in so doing, an extremely fruitful pathway to the theory of the sublime. It is, in fact, on the intrinsic ambiguity of the word *Stille* that his interpretation of the *Laocoön* is based: not only does Laocoön remain static in his effort, but he does not scream ("Gedanken"). This interpretation of the sublime is at the origin of a long debate on the role of the scream in art (Lessing, Hirt, etc.).

This deeply considered choice in translation, in fact, constitutes a foundational speech act. By making semantic potentialities that are separate in French converge in the concept of *Stille*, Winckelmann deliberately and genuinely created an untranslatable. It suffices, to be convinced of this, to read the French translations that, starting in 1756, sought to retranscribe *Stille*. Some choose immobility, others silence, and still others serenity. None renders all three. Winckelmann borrowed from French a concept that that language is incapable of translating back into French. The offshoot exceeds the matrix; the copy, the original. This irreversibility of translation should be seen as a forceful theoretical project. For Winckelmann it was a matter of bolting shut the German language, making it the depository of an original lexicon for classicism and, beyond that, of an inalienable aesthetic notion. Upon closer examination the *topos* "edle Einfalt, stille Größe" may owe its good fortune to a circumstance more profound than it appears to be: the invention, from a traditional theme of European classicism, of an autonomous concept that resists all translation.

Élisabeth Décultot

BIBLIOGRAPHY

Güthenke, Constanze. *Placing Modern Greece: The Dynamics of Romantic Hellenism, 1770–1840*. Oxford: Oxford University Press, 2008.

Rehm, Walther. *Götterstille und Göttertrauer*. Bern: A. Francke, 1951.

Stammler, Wolfgang. "Edle Einfalt." In *Wort und Bild*. Berlin: E. Schmidt, 1962.

Winckelmann, Johann Joachim. "Gedanken über die Nachahmung der griechischen Werke in der Malerei und Bildhauerkunst." In *Kleine Schriften*, edited by W. Rehm. Berlin: De Gruyter, 1968. Translation by Elfriede Heyer and Roger C. Norton: *Reflections on the Imitation of Greek Works in Painting and Sculpture*. La Salle, IL: Open Court, 1987.

STIMMUNG (GERMAN)

DANISH	*stemning*
FRENCH	*accord, ambiance, atmosphère, humeur, disposition, tonalité affective*

➤ DISPOSITION, and CLAIM, DASEIN, GEFÜHL, GEMÜT, PATHOS, SUBLIME, VOICE

The multiplicity of possible French translations for *Stimmung* is in itself evidence of the resistance to translation offered by the term, which is quite properly regarded as a crux for translators. The principal difficulty is a function of the fact that the German term (or the Swedish *stemming* in Kierkegaard), in the sense that it has enjoyed since the eighteenth century, rests on an analogy between the musical (tuning of instruments) and the psychological (a person's way of being in agreement, his or her mood), for which neither English nor the Romance languages have any real equivalent.

Stimmung is a noun stemming from the verb *stimmen*, "to express out loud," "to have one's say on a subject" (whence *Stimme*, "voice," also in the sense of a vote: *vox populi / Stimme des Volks*), "to tune," "to be on pitch," "to be in tune." Applied to musical instruments starting in the sixteenth century, *Stimmung* was also used for humans by the beginning of the eighteenth century.

It is, in fact, from the tuning of instruments, their being on pitch, that *Stimmung* comes, particularly for the violin and the organ:

das stimmen oder die stimmung der instrumente betrifft … hauptsächlich die geigen.

(the tuning or the being-in-tune of instruments concerns … principally violins.)

(Mattheson, *Der Volkommen Capellmeister*)

Nichts ist schwerer, als die reine stimmung einer orgel.

(Nothing is more difficult that the pure tuning of an organ.)

(Schubart, *Ideen zur einer Asthetik der Tonkunst*)

From there *Stimmung* was transposed to humans, with, for example, Goethe's *Stimmung des Nervensystems* (toning of the nervous system) and Diderot's *Le Rêve de d'Alembert*, where the *ton* signifies "tension" (*tonus,* from the Greek *tonos*

[τόνος]). In Herder, moreover, it will be observed that the metaphorical sense of *Stimmung* is not yet a matter of course, in a consideration of the Stoic idea of idiosyncrasy:

Jeder Mensch hat ein eigenes Maas, gleichsam eine eigene Stimmung aller sinnlichen Gefühle zueinander.

(Every individual has a measure that is his own, a certain harmony, so to speak, that is his own, of all his sensory [as opposed to intellectual] feelings.)

(Herder cited in Grimm, RT: *Deutsches Wörterbuch*)

This passage is precious in that it allows us to attend "live," as it were, the transposition of the musical sense to the aesthesiological—and even affective—sense. It is not without interest, moreover, to note that it was in the context of an analytics of the sublime that the term *Stimmung* seems to have made its true entry into the vocabulary of German philosophy, in Kant's *Critique of Judgement*:

Die Stimmung des Gemüts zum Gefühl des Erhabenen erfordert eine Empfänglichkeit desselben für Ideen.

(The proper mental mood for a feeling of the sublime postulates the mind's susceptibility to ideas.)

(trans. J. C. Meredith)

As was previously the case with J. Gibelin, A. Philonenko translates *Stimmung* into French as *disposition*, a possible, but debatable, translation, that does not allow one to draw a distinction in French between *Stimmung* and *Anlage* (whose apposite terms in English include "aptitude," "tendency," and "predisposition").

It is occasionally the case that the musical background, which is most often implicit, is explicitly evoked, as in Ernst Jünger's *Die abenteuerliche Herz*:

Es gibt ganz unvergleichliche Stunden, in denen der Mensch … sein Wesen wie ein Instrument in Stimmung bringt.

(There are truly incomparable hours, in the course of which man … is able to tune his very being as if it were an instrument.)

(in *Sämtliche Werke*, 9:173)

But it was only in the analyses of Heidegger (preceded by those of Max Scheler on sympathy) that the term *Stimmung*—notably in *Being and Time* (§29)—would become a key term in philosophical thought. On this question, consult F. Vezin's note in his French translation of *Sein und Zeit* (558ff.). "No sooner was it introduced than the word *Befindlichkeit* ["sensitivity to the situation" (R. Boehm and A. de Waelhens), "affection" (E. Martineau), "disposability" (F. Vezin)] was associated with *Stimmung* (disposition, mood) and the whole range of words in the *Stimmung* family" (*Sein und Zeit*, §29).

■ See Box 1.

In his Cerisy lecture, *Was ist das—die Philosophie?* (*What Is Philosophy?*), Heidegger relates *Stimmung* to the Greek *pathos* [πάθος], which he renders in French as *disposition*:

Nur wenn wir pathos [πάθος] als Stimmung (disposition) verstehen, können wir auch das thaumazein, das Erstaunen näher kennzeichnen.

1

Words of the *Stimmung* family according to M. Heidegger

In paragraph 29 of *Sein und Zeit,* Heidegger writes,

> Was wir ontologisch mit dem Titel Befindlichkeit anzeigen, ist ontisch das Bekannteste und Alltäglichste : die Stimmung, das Gestimmtsein. ... Dass Stimmungen verdorben werden und umschlagen können, sagt nur, dass das Dasein je schon immer gestimmt ist. Die oft anhaltende, ebenmässige und fahle Ungestimmtheit, die nicht mit Verstimmung verwechselt werden darf, ist so wenig nichts, dass gerade in ihr das Dasein ihm selbst überdrüssig wird. ... Die Stimmung macht offenbar, "wie einem ist und wird." In diesem "wie einem ist" bringt das Gesimmtsein das Sein in sein "Da."

> (What we indicate *ontologically* by the term "state-of-mind" is *ontically* the most familiar and everyday sort of thing: our mood, our Being-attuned. ... The fact that moods can deteriorate and change over means simply that in every case *Dasein* always has some mood. The pallid, even balanced lack of mood, which is often persistent and which is not to be mistaken for a bad mood, is far from nothing at all. Rather, it is in this that *Dasein* becomes satiated with itself. ... A mood makes manifest "how one is, and how one is faring." In this "how one is," having a mood brings Being to its "there.")

(trans. J. Macquarrie and E. Robinson)

And now two French versions:

Ce que nous indiquons ontologiquement sous le titre d'affection est la chose du monde la mieux connue et la plus quotidienne ontiquement: c'est la tonalité, le fait d'être disposé. ... Que des tonalités puissent s'altérer et virer du tout au tout, cela indique simplement que le *Dasein* est chaque fois toujours déjà intoné. L'atonie, c'est-à-dire l'indifférence persistante, plate et terne, que rien n'autorise à confondre avec de l'aigreur, est si peu insignifiante que c'est en elle justement que le *Dasein* devient à charge pour lui-même. ... La tonalité manifeste "où l'on en est et où l'on en viendra." Dans cet "où", l'être-intoné transporte l'être en son "Là."

(trans. E. Martineau, 113)

Ce que nous dénotons ontologiquement sous le terme technique de disponibilité est du point de vue ontique on ne peut plus connu et on ne peut plus quotidien: la disposition, l'état d'humeur. ... Or que veut dire que des dispositions de l'humeur puissent s'altérer et connaître des revirements, sinon qu'on chercherait en vain un cas où le *Dasein* ne soit déjà disposé? La morosité souvent persistante dans sa monotonie et sa grisaille, mais qui ne saurait se confondre avec la mauvaise humeur, est si peu rune que c'est justement en elle que le *Dasein* en arrive à n'en plus pouvoir de lui-même. ... La disposition révèle "comment on se sent," "comment on va." En ce "comment on va" » l'être disposé place l'être en son "là."

(trans. F. Vezin)

There appears here the "entire register of words belonging to the *Stimmung* family": *Gestimmtsein, stimmen, Ungestimmtheit, Verstimmung,* rendered respectively in French as: *tonalité, fait d'être disposé, (être) intoné, atonie, aigreur/disposition, état d'humeur, (être) disposé, morosité, mauvaise humeur.* That neither of the two French translations manages to capture the paronomasia of the German text shows the resistances offered by the term *Stimmung* to any attempt at translation.

The lapidary sentence in paragraph 31 of *Sein und Zeit*: *Verstehen ist immer gestimmtes* (Understanding always has its mood), has been translated into French either in a way quite unintelligible in its platitude as *Le comprendre est toujours déjà in-toné* (E. Martineau) or more expressively as *Entendre est inséparable de vibrer* (F. Vezin), a translation whose success one feels obliged to salute. However insurmountable the difficulties specific to the translation of *Stimmung* and its related terms may appear, the resources of French occasionally manage to escape the trap of woodenness.

BIBLIOGRAPHY

Heidegger, Martin. *Sein und Zeit.* Vol. 2 of *Heidegger Gesamtausgabe,* edited by F.-W. von Herrmann. Frankfurt: Vittorio Kolstermann, 1977. First published in 1927. English translation by John Macquarrie and Edward Robinson: *Being and Time.* London: SCM Press, 1962. French translation by Emmanuel Martineau: *Être et Temps.* Paris: Authentica, 1985. French translation by François Vezin: *Être et Temps.* Paris: Gallimard / La Pléiade, 1986.

(It is only if we understand *pathos* as *Stimmung* (disposition) that we can also characterize in a more precise way *thaumazein* (θαυμάζειν), astonishment.)

(trans. Jean T. Wilde and William Kluback)

One should, however, in this specific context, understand the *pathos* discussed by Plato and Aristotle with regard to astonishment as something other than "passion," and not decree as a rule that the French translation of *Stimmung* is "*disposition*," since the result would be to sacrifice the musical resonance of the German term. The expression *tonalité affective* (affective tone), to which French translators of Nietzsche and Heidegger occasionally resort, attempts to reconcile the two dimensions brought into contact by the term *Stimmung*.

■ See Box 2.

Pascal David

BIBLIOGRAPHY

Diderot, Denis. *Le Rêve de d'Alembert.* In *Œuvres philosophiques.* Paris: Garnier, 1964.

Heidegger, Martin. *What is Philosophy? [Was ist das —die Philosophie?].* Bilingual ed. Translated by Jean T. Wilde and William Kluback. New York: Twayne Publishers, 1958.

Heidegger, Martin. *Sein und Zeit.* Vol. 2 of *Heidegger Gesamtausgabe,* edited by F.-W. von Herrmann. Frankfurt: Vittorio Kolstermann: 1977. First published in 1927. Translation by Joan Stambaugh: *Being and Time.* Albany, State University of New York Press, 1996. French translation by François Vezin: *Être et Temps.* Paris: Gallimard / La Pléiade, 1986.

Jünger, Ernst. *Die abenteuerliche Herz.* Vol. 9 of *Sämtliche Werke.* Stuttgart: Klett-Cotta, 1979.

Kant, Immanuel. *Critique of Judgement.* Translated by J. C. Meredith. Oxford: Oxford University Press, 2007. Translation first published in 1952.

———. *Critique of Pure Reason.* Translated by Paul Guyer and Allen Wood. Cambridge: Cambridge University Press, 1998.

Mattheson, J. *Der Volkommen Capellmeister.* Hamburg: Herold, 1739.

Schubart, C.F.D. *Ideen zur einer Asthetik der Tonkunst.* Vienna: Degen, 1806.

2

Stockhausen and *Stimmung* in music

In music, the word *Stimmung* takes on a double meaning: as a practical term and as a distant analogy with the philosophical scheme subtending the question of *Stimmung*. Historically, Karlheinz Stockhausen was the first composer to have treated the voice according to an environment no longer partaking of a single vocal technique or aesthetic conception, but of a state characterized by the composer as atmospheric, by virtue of the terminological ambiguity of *Stimmung*. In 1968 he composed a work titled, precisely, *Stimmung* for six voices, a work that would become a kind of philosophical manifesto for musical production in the second half of the twentieth century.

In evoking the complex climate in which a musical work written for one or several voices evolves, composers use the German word *Stimmung*. The use of *Stimmung* as an expression capable of representing a notion exceeding the framework distributing voices by register is recent. It is owed to Stockhausen (born in Cologne in 1928), who, in 1968, voluntarily cast aside the traditional labels used to designate the full range of sound-based activities and phenomena. Stockhausen indicated explicitly that *Stimmung* owed nothing to *Stimme*, the voice. *Stimmung*, on the model of *Stimme*, is far removed from a logic of heights. It occupies a place that can be qualified as spectral by virtue of its radiating and molecular function in the musical realm—spectral music, which emerged at the end of the 1970s, explored the vibratory and acoustic dimensions of sound-phenomena in particular. It should for this reason be regarded as the very paradigm of the musical in the sense that it figures simultaneously the divagations of composition, its dual notations, and the injunction of the subject that it causes to resonate beyond the procedures involved in prior elaborations.

The paths of music for Stockhausen are consigned to the voice, insofar as it is an ambiguous drive, a site capable of simultaneously representing transversal categories of the musical. To give form to voice would amount to treating it as a raw material. By modifying the contours of a sound, note, or spectrum, one thus modifies the vocal envelope and, as a result, both timbre and perception. This is why Stockhausen speaks of a "composition of timbres" (cf. Cott, *Stockhausen: Conversations with the Composer*). Each sound is endowed with its own inner life, a fortiori the timbres of voices conceived as arrangements of spatial and temporal textures. This is why the composer takes delight in specifying that the word *Stimmung* conveys a significant and, no doubt, contradictory

ambivalence. It signifies, in point of fact, a chord, resonance, vocal form, and, a fortiori, a form of meaning of all vocal manifestations. It can in no way be reduced to voice as designated according to the barometer of registers and tessituras. In the beginning, the composer had wanted to "experiment on himself certain sets of sounds; I would see what happens each time I concentrate on a different part of my body" (ibid.). Stockhausen opted to shatter the concept of *Stimme*, deemed to be too reductive with regard to the deployment of timbres and spaces of the vocal phenomenon in its interiority. The piece was written to last one hour. It is entirely articulated on the founding principle of a single chord. The latter, conceived and composed as the harmonic spectrum of one sound (B-flat) never sung and never heard, is assumed to "timbrify" harmonic verticality, giving it an expansion beyond its frame, its voice, or any recognizable attack of pitch and rhythm. The procedure at work consists in an accumulation of compositional and formal analogies. Singers agree on that inaugural chord in search of a symbolic order. In German the verb "to agree" is *stimmen*. For Stockhausen, *Stimmung* will become "the action of coming to agreement"—as though the natural resonance of B-flat were in a situation allowing it to engender the form of the piece, following a generative procedure specific to the voice and its capacity to go beyond the question of intelligibility. *Stimmung* is not the art of the signifier or of signification. Every vocal timbre (two sopranos, a tenor, a baritone, a bass) stems from a polyphony of attacks and durations obliging the voice-material to organize a discourse without recognizable narrativity, no more than the syllabic substrate needed to maintain an assemblage of individuated voices. There are two *Stimmungen*, one of an acoustical nature, in order to cause the *Klang* (sound) to resonate and convey a series of onomatopoeic utterances, that are in turn subjected to the sovereignty of the harmonic deployment; the other of a temporal nature, in order to give that chain of nonsignifying onomatopoeic utterances the value of a petrification of the chronology of events. The *Stimmung* petrifies the place from which it springs. It casts it in a situation of entropy. The voice disappears behind this phenomenon of molecular atmospheric suspension transmuting the aerial materiality of voice into a quasi-aquatic—and even plasmatic—texture. Whence Stockhausen's quest for an original and originary *Stimmung*, prior to the speaking and singing voice. Each chord latches on to another as though it were the very texture into which

the time of the work was woven—or its form. Stockhausen insists that every *Stimmung* is organized around a single chord (or spectrum). Technically, the singers decline the first second, third, fourth, sixth, and eighth harmonics of a fundamental sound, which is itself treated spectrally since it is absent. Each chord "timbres" another, even as it retains its architectonic singularity. The word *Stimmung* is untranslatable because of the prolixity of the parameters it implements to designate a set of perceptible but nonrecognizable processes. Stockhausen seeks what he calls "an experiment without finality," a transition from what can be designated, to what acts without our knowledge. In that sense, one might say that the musical *Stimmung* is a composition of pure voices, which is not addressed to meaning, which rather attempts to suspend it, or even to interrupt it. *Stimmung* unbinds voice. In harkening to its origin, in this case its fundamental sound (B-flat), it resists the discursive temptation. "If you listen to *Stimmung*," Stockhausen writes, "you will see that there is nothing but a chord, and a single one, during the seventy-five minutes of the work's duration" (Cott, *Stockhausen: Conversations with the Composer*). On the other hand, and as though he wished to conjure away the risk of a fusion of voices or the magma, Stockhausen is careful to interpret the notion of *Stimmung* in his most precise (and even obsessional) writing configurations. Timbres and rhetorical figures of chordal setting—or, as one might say, "a vocal setting"—are scrupulously decrypted: "I noted them quite precisely, using the signs of international phonetics and assigning them numbers" (ibid.). One observed a reversal of functions. *Stimmung* slips ostensibly from the protean to a coded cartography, a grammar of timbres and their specific temporalities applicable to all instruments, but whose initial model remains the voice.

Danielle Cohen-Levinas

BIBLIOGRAPHY

Cott, Jonathan. *Stockhausen: Conversations with the Composer*. New York: Simon and Schuster, 1973. French translation by Jacques Drillon: *Conversation avec Stockhausen*. Paris: Jean-Claude Lattès, 1979.

Rigoni, Michel. *Stockhausen ... un vaisseau lancé vers le ciel*. Bourg-la-Reine, Fr.: Millénaire III Éditions, 1998.

Stockhausen, Karlheinz. *Stimmung, Partition für 6 Vokaslisken*. Vienna: Universal Edition, 1969.

———. *Stockhausen on Music: Lectures and Interviews*. Compiled by Robin Maconie. London: Marion Boyars, 1989.

STRADANIE [страдание] (RUSSIAN)

ENGLISH	suffering
FRENCH	*souffrance*
GREEK	*pathos* [πάθος]
LATIN	*passio*

➤ SUFFERING, and *LIBERTY*, *MALAISE*, PATHOS, RUSSIAN, SAMOST', SOBORNOST', SVOBODA, WORK

The Russian noun *stradanie* [страдание] stems from the common Slavic root *strad-*, which means principally suffering and passion; and yet *strada* [страда], from which Slavonic *stradati* [страдати] (suffering) is derived, signifies first of all, "effort, painful labor." Activity and intensity are thus linked to passion in *stradanie*—whence perhaps the preeminence of suffering, its moral and cognitive value, and its accent, in Russian, on spirituality.

I. *Stradanie*: An Active Passion

The root *strad-*, from which *stradanie* [страдание] comes, establishes a connection between suffering and passion: in Russian, Serbian, and Croatian, *strast'* [страсть] signifies "passion," whereas in Czech the word has retained its initial sense of suffering and affliction (RT: Herman, *A Dictionary of Slavic Word Families*, 493–94; Vasmer, *Ètimologicheskiĭ slovar' russkogo iazyka* [Etymological dictionary of the Russian language], 770–71). The idea that passion is essentially a form of suffering is present in both Greek *pathos* [πάθος] and Latin *passio* (RT: Herman, *Dictionary of Slavic Word Families*, 494). A. Kenny proposes that the Latin word, derived from the verb *pati* (to undergo, to suffer), initially designated suffering as submission (to an action or influence) and that it was only subsequently that the notion of submission to a particular kind of influence—in the sense of an intense affect—acquired the modern meaning of *passion* (Kenny, *Aristotle's Theory*, 28). The connotation of passivity has thus remained quite present in the French words *passif, patient, patience*, etc.

Similarly, the Latin verb *sufferre* possesses the passive sense of undergoing, which has been largely conserved in the modern verbs *souffrir* in French and "to suffer" in English, as well as in the nouns *souffrance* and "suffering." In contrast Slavonic *stradati* [страдати] (to suffer) is derived from *strada*, which first meant effort, then painful labor, before taking on the sense of torment (RT: Tsyganenko, *Ètimologiceskij slovar' russkogo jazyka* [Etymological dictionary of the Russian language], 456). In Slavonic *stradati* also has the meaning of "working painfully" and "seeking to obtain" (Vasmer, *Ètimologicheskiĭ slovar'*, 770). In modern Russian *strada* [страда] still signifies "painful labor during harvest." Thus *stradati* corresponds to the Latin *actio* (action) rather than *passio* (submission): this is similarly the case for the modern term *stradat'* [страдать], which means "to suffer" in contemporary Russian.

II. The Value of *Stradanie* in Russian Tradition

Another notable characteristic of *stradanie* resides in the elevated moral value that the Russian spiritual tradition attributes to suffering. As we are reminded by Fedotov, the first saints canonized by the Russian Orthodox Church, Boris and Gleb, died as victims of a political conflict in a feudal context, and precisely for that they are considered to be the greatest of the Russian Orthodox saints (Fedotov, *Russian Religious Mind*); they thus acquired the status of a particular kind of saint marked by the state of debasement and destitution that Paul called *kenosis*. Such saints are sufferers (*stradal'tsy* [страдальцы]): they are not martyrs of the faith, but "only men," just martyrs. Nonetheless, through their suffering itself, they deserve to be canonized:

> It is noteworthy that the Russian Church which loves the sufferers so much gives no outstanding place among her national saints to the martyrs who in the Greek, as well as in the Roman Church, always occupy first place both in the liturgical and popular cult.

> (Fedotov, *Russian Religious Mind*, 1:105)

In other words, the Russian spiritual tradition suggests that suffering "in itself," in its most extreme form—as nonresistance to death—is itself worthy of particular veneration.

The active character of *stradanie* and its moral value take on great importance in the novels of Dostoyevsky:

> Perhaps it is not only prosperity or well-being that man loves. Perhaps he passionately loves (*do strasti* [до страсти]) suffering (*stradanie*) as much as prosperity. I am sure that man never refuses genuine suffering (*stradanie*), that is, destruction and chaos.

> (Dostoyevsky, *A Writer's Diary*, quoted in Berdyayev, *Dostoyevsky*, 51)

Suffering, in all its meanings, typifies Dostoyevskian "man," characterized by his contradictory and painful passions, internal conflicts, and rich inner life catalyzed by the "ultimate questions" of life. It is suffering that allows Dostoyevsky to maintain a meliorist moral position.

In his book on Dostoyevsky, Berdyayev evokes both his moral and cognitive sense of *stradanie*:

> Dostoyevsky put his trust in the expiatory and revivifying force of suffering (*stradanie*). For him, life is essentially redemption, expiation of an individual's errors through suffering.

> (Berdyayev, *Dostoevsky*, 94)

From this point of view, *stradanie* represents a necessary aspect of the *svoboda* [свобода] (freedom) of the person (*ličnost* [личность]):

> Man is a responsible creature. His suffering is not innocent. . . . The road to freedom [*svoboda*] is that of suffering. There is always a temptation to liberate man from suffering by stripping him of his freedom. Dostoyevsky is an apologist of freedom. That is why he proposes that man accept suffering [*stradanie*] as an inevitable consequence of his freedom.

> (Ibid., 109)

The difficulties experienced in translating the Russian term *stradanie* are linked, on the one hand, to its meaning as active intensity and, on the other, to the exalted moral and cognitive value of suffering in Russian spirituality.

Zulfia Karimova
Andriy Vasylchenko

BIBLIOGRAPHY

Berdyayev, Nikolai. *Dostoevsky*. Translated by Donald Attwater. New York: Meridian Books, 1957.

Fedotov, George. *The Russian Religious Mind*. 2 vols. Cambridge, MA: Harvard University Press, 1944–46.

Kenny, Anthony. *Aristotle's Theory of the Will*. London: Duckworth, 1979.

STRENGTH, FORCE

FRENCH   *force*

➤ DYNAMIC, FORCE, and ACT, AGENCY, MOMENT, PATHOS, SOUL

"Strength" and "force," but also "vivacity" and "vividness," derive their meaning within a project already largely launched by Hobbes and Hume, and which Jeremy Bentham characterized as "psychological dynamics." "Strength" and "force" designate a mental or physical process in motion: both name the difference between the state of a psychical (or physical) system at a given moment and another state of what one wants to identify as the "same" system, totally or partially affected by that difference. No more than for Hume, a force is not, for John Stuart Mill, an "existing fact" but rather "a name for our conviction that in appropriate circumstances a fact would take place" (*A System of Logic*). He could have said the same thing about strength. However, the word "strength" remains quite close to the adjective "strong" and the verb "strengthen": its vitalist connotations are hospitable to the objectivity demanded by a calculation.

I. The Distinction between "Strength" and "Force"

A. Mathematical aspects of the two notions

"Strength" and "force" are all the more difficult to distinguish in French translation in that the subterfuges resorted to as a solution, such as *vigueur* or *violence*, have their cognate counterparts in English (vigor, violence), and they regularly accompany "force" or "strength" without being synonyms ("force and vigour" [Hume, *A Treatise of Human Nature*]; "force and violence" [ibid.]). French is constrained to speak uniformly of *force*, whereas English can use two terms concurrently to describe mental processes. Hume can even use the expression "strength and force of a body" (ibid.), without giving the impression of saying the same thing twice. No doubt, one speaks as easily of "force of mind" as of "strength of mind" (ibid., 418; Bentham, *Chrestomathia*, 5); of "force of the passion" (Hume, *A Treatise*, 427) as of "strength of the passion"; or of "force of imagination" (ibid., 319, 364, 385) as of "strength of imagination": but the intentions are different.

"Strength" is chosen to designate a tendency to increase or decrease without any calibration of degrees. "Strength" is always felt as being very close to the verb "strengthen." "Force" entails greater quantitative precision and discourse in terms of degrees. Hume speaks of "degrees of force" (*A Treatise*, 2, 5, 97, 103, 116, 119, 133, 138, 143), with all sorts of variants of forces superior, equal, or inferior to others (ibid., 150, 187, 194) rather than of "degrees of strength," and of "additional force" (ibid., 100, 184, 391, 420, 422, 426) rather than of "additional strength." In order to constitute his psychical dynamics, Hume borrows the word "force" from the natural philosophy and physics of his time, and "force," not "strength," signals that loan.

However, despite its arithmetical indetermination, "strength," more easily than "force," appears to express a geometrical sense, when forces balance out "obliquely" or, according to the law of the parallelogram, in conformity with a logic partaking of what would soon be called "vectorial calculus." Quite remarkable from this point of view is the change of terms when one passes from the first book of *A Treatise on Human Nature* to the second, which deals with the passions; the latter, which seeks to open a psychical space and attempts to develop a geometrical conception in their regard, resorts frequently to the term "strength" and expressions derived from it, like "as far as its strength goes" (*A Treatise*, 130, 278); on the other hand, the first book uses only "force" for mental processes, envisaged probabilistically (in sums of instances and cases [ibid., 130, 147, 163]), algebraically, or arithmetically (when it is a matter of the "addition of forces" [ibid., 130]).

The essays of Bentham on "psychical dynamics" confirm this point. "Force" is almost exclusively preferred to "strength" since it is a matter, if not of effecting a calculation, at least of attaining the conditions for doing so (*Chrestomathia*, 66, 68, 73, 283, 297, 303). Bentham is little inclined to Latinize his English, but if "strength" is geometrical in its connotations, and if the tendency of geometry, as noted in the *Chrestomathia*, is to be absorbed in an increasingly symbolic and algebraic discourse, one understands that the word "force" will emphatically take over.

B. The biological meaning of "strength"

"Strength," in addition, includes biological (and even vitalistic) aspects. One speaks of the "strength" of a body or a mind to emphasize its vital presence (Hume, *A Treatise*, 279, 299, 326, 365), even if it means appreciating the desire to excel in *strength* as an inferior ambition (*ibid.*, 300). Whereas "force" is implicated by the study of dynamics in a purely descriptive manner, in the way of objective observation, and inscribed in an artificial system of observation or measurement (ibid., 631), "strength," on the other hand, collaborates with the process, participates in it, regards it as a "strain," and posits itself as a manner of feeling it (Hume speaks willingly of "strength of conception" [ibid., 627]).

Force as a physical phenomenon is fundamentally related to a movement of transference: it can be "transported" (ibid., 176), "escorted" (142), or "transfused" (386); it "circulates" and is "exchanged" (109). Strength is more difficult to transport; it participates in another kind of movement, waxing and waning, which is rather sui generis. Thus the word "strengthen" almost always has the meaning of "firming up" from within rather than "reinforcing" from without. Hume speaks about resemblance that "*strengthens* a relation" (ibid., 112, 308, 349): in the same sense he writes, "strengthen the connection" 238). But it is always, in Hume, a supply of force that is qualified as new (131, 391, 421) and not some reinforcement of *strength*.

II. Adjacent Notions: "Vivacity," "Vividness," "Liveliness"

It is interesting to note with which notions "strength" and "force" are most often coupled in a philosophy that (like

Hume's) often uses concepts in pairs, without one term being strictly the equivalent of the other, but rather supplementing, specifying, displacing, and reorienting it.

One thus finds "force and evidence" (*A Treatise*, 31, 156, 197), an expression meaning not that evidence or proof is the same thing as force, but that the evidence or proof of an argument constitutes a kind of nonphysical force, partaking rather of "authority," which is often coupled with "weight" (ibid., 324). Hume speaks indifferently of the "force" of principles (ibid., 143, 198) or of their "authority" (31). "Forced" is paired with "unnatural" and denotes artifice (185).

Among these couplings, by far the most frequent is the linkage "force and vivacity" (ibid., 2, 85, 86, 96, 97, 98, 99, 119, 120, 122, 134, 138, 142, 143, 144, 148, 153, 184, 199, 215, 317, 354, 362, 365). If "force" is to be understood in a conceptual sense implying a link between mass and speed (whether or not it is squared), "vivacity" plainly signifies the speed required by dynamics. "Liveliness," often compared to "vivacity," is clearly differentiated from it, referring to a descriptive or phenomenological quality, whereas "vivacity," like "force," enters into a perspective of calculation: in the case of each of them one can add or subtract degrees (ibid., 19, 100, 112, 135, 137, 141, 354, 424). Vivacity, like force, can be divided, multiplied, accompanied (112, 142, 145, 208, 290). As for vividness, it is quite precisely what can be "quickened by some new impulse" (396).

French is tempted to translate with the single word *rapidité* the words "vivacity," "vividness," and "liveliness," but, in so doing, it effaces the difference between those terms, the first two of which are oriented toward speed, and the other toward life.

Jean-Pierre Cléro

BIBLIOGRAPHY

Bentham, Jeremy. *Chrestomathia*. Edited by M. J. Smith and W. H. Burston. Oxford: Clarendon Press, 1983.
Hume, David. *A Treatise of Human Nature*. Edited by David Fate Norton and Mary J. Norton. Oxford: Oxford University Press, 2000.
Mill, John Stuart. *A System of Logic*. Vol. 7 of *Collected Works of John Stuart Mill*, edited by J. M. Robson. Toronto: University of Toronto Press, 1963–91.

STRUCTURE, PATTERN, GESTALT

FRENCH	*structure*
GERMAN	*Struktur, Gestalt*
LATIN	*structura*

➤ AGENCY, ANALOGY, BEHAVIOR, CONCETTO, DISEGNO, *FORM*, GEISTESWISSENSCHAFTEN, LOGOS, *WORLD* [WELT, Box 1]

"Structure," a concept originating in architecture, designates the skeleton or armature, as opposed to the form or outer appearance. In the twentieth century, the use of "structure" has extended from linguistics and anthropology to the whole of the human sciences. Structuralism tends to conceive structure as an unvarying (but abstract or latent) network of relations. The hegemony of "structure" is in competition with the English "pattern" disseminated by psychologists and biologists. "Pattern" rejects the surface-structure opposition and designates a configuration that is less abstract, less rigid, and less permanent than structure. The German *Gestalt* (form) places the accent (like "structure") on form conceived as a set of relations, but shares with "pattern" a sense of the visual due to its roots in the psychology of perception.

I. *Structura*, Architectural Structure

In the nineteenth century, Viollet-le-Duc opposed (functional) architectural structure to exterior form and style. Latin *structura* (from *struere*, to dispose by layers, to dispose with order, to construct) designates: (1) the material or masonry of which walls are made (Vitruvius, *De generibus structurae* [On types of masonry], book 2, chap. 8); (2) the building itself, the edifice; (3) figuratively, the arrangement or disposition, for example, of words in the sentence to produce a rhythm ("verborum quasi structura" [so to speak, the masonry of the sentence]; Cicero, *Brutus*, 33). *Structura* thus designates the armature, the skeleton, what makes (a building, the human body) hold up as opposed to the appearance, the outer "form." Viollet-le-Duc (*Entretiens sur l'architecture*, 1863–76) defines Gothic architecture not by its style, but by an interplay of weights and thrusts, that is, by its functional structure. This is why Hubert Damisch sees in him the precursor of "structuralism" in the modern sense. The subordination of form to function by Viollet-le-Duc ("Everything is a function of structure") was taken up by the American architect L. H. Sullivan (*Form Follows Function*). It is opposed to the formal/stylistic approach given priority in the Germany of H. Wölfflin and A. Riegl and is clearly distinguished from the "nature" of the Gothic as defined by J. Ruskin, who, without failing to recognize the architectural structure, places more of an accent on the "moral elements" of Gothic design, notably on its capacity for infinite variety, its musical analogies, its naturalism ("The Nature of Gothic," in *The Stones of Venice*, 1853).

English continues to use "structure" regularly in the sense of building. This is notably the case in E. Panofsky's study *Gothic Architecture and Scholasticism*; only the back cover uses "architectural style" and "structure" in the abstract sense of Viollet-le-Duc. Similarly "the social structure" (in English, with the definite article) designates the "social edifice" and not *la structure sociale* in Lévi-Strauss's sense.

II. Structure, System, Model

In the twentieth century, "structure," for linguists and anthropologists, then for the full range of the human sciences, designated an abstract and invariant model, "the relational system latent within the object." The happy fate of "structure" in the human sciences of the twentieth century (whence "structuralism") stems from its use by linguists and anthropologists. Saussure did not use the word in his *Cours de linguistique générale*; it was C. Lévi-Strauss who popularized it (*Structures élémentaires de la parenté*, 1949; *Anthropologie structurale*, 1958, 1973), invoking the model and methods of Trubetskoy's phonology ("La Phonologie actuelle," 1933). For Lévi-Strauss, phonology succeeded in abandoning the study of conscious linguistic phenomena in order to focus on their underlying unconscious structure; it was interested not in isolated elements, but in relations between elements; it introduced the notion of system, revealed concrete phonological systems, and exposed their structure; it aimed at establishing, inductively or deductively, general laws (see in particular "The Structure of Myths," in Strauss's *Structural Anthropology*). While structuralism underscored above all the "relational" character of structure, it should also be noted that the Lévi-Straussian structure pursued the opposition between (deep) structure and (apparent) form; if structure is an "unconscious" or "latent" system, one can better understand Lacan's formula, "The unconscious is structured like a language." What is more problematic is the precise relation between structure, system, and model: is there an underlying structure to every system, or is the structure the shared invariant of all the systems whose diversity is only apparent or relative? On this point, Lévi-Strauss gives answers that appear to be contradictory. After affirming that "the fundamental principle is that the notion of social structure does not relate to empirical reality but to the models constructed from it" (*Structural Anthropology*), he nonetheless takes his distance from the formalism of V. Propp (1928):

[A]s opposed to formalism, structuralism refuses to oppose the concrete to the abstract, and to recognize in the latter a privileged value. *Form* is defined in opposition to a matter which is foreign to it. But structure has no distinct content; it is the content itself, apprehended in a logical organization conceived as a property of the real.

The use of "structure" by T. Todorov is closer to Propp's formalism:

Each work is thus considered [by poetics] only as the manifestation of an abstract and general structure, of which it is only one of the possible realizations. It is in this, that science is not concerned with actual literature, but with potential literature, in other words: with that abstract property which is the singularity of the literary fact: its *literarity*. The aim of this study [is] to propose a theory of the structure and functioning of literary discourse, a theory presenting a tableau of literary possibles, in such manner that existing literary works appear as particular and locally realized cases.

(*Introduction to Poetics*)

It was precisely the abstract and totalizing character (as well as the scientificity) of "structure," which made one lose sight of the concrete and individual texture of the text that Roland Barthes criticized: a sequence carved out of a Balzacian text, he maintained, has a basis that is "more empirical than rational, and it is useless to attempt to force it into a statutory order; its only logic is that of the "already-done" or "already-read"—whence the variety of sequences (some trivial, some melodramatic) and the variety of terms (numerous or few); here again, we shall not attempt to put them into any order. Indicating them (externally and internally) will suffice to demonstrate the plural meaning entangled in them" (*S/Z*). The plural text, infinitely dispersed, like the instability of particles of dust or the shimmering of meaning, traces a semantic field closer to that of "pattern" than of "structure."

Il s'agit, en effet, non de manifester une structure, mais autant que possible de produire une structuration. Les blancs et les flous de l'analyse seront comme les traces qui signalent la fuite du texte; car si le texte est soumis à une forme, cette forme n'est pas unitaire, architecturée, finie: c'est la bribe, le tronçon, le réseau coupé ou effacé, ce sont tous les mouvements, toutes les inflexions d'un *fading* immense, qui assure à la fois le chevauchement et la perte des messages.

(We are, in fact, concerned not to manifest a structure but to produce a structuration. The blanks and looseness of the analysis will be like footprints marking the escape of the text; for if the text is subject to some form, this form is not unitary, architectonic, finite: it is the fragment, the shards, the broken or obliterated network—all the movements and inflections of a vast "dissolve," which permits both overlapping and loss of messages.)

(Barthes, *S/Z*)

III. *Gestalt*, Form, Configuration

"Gestaltism," or the theory of form, places the accent on "totality," but remains principally restricted to psychology, even as the German word *Gestalt* remains restricted to a specialized lexicon.

Stemming from a past participle of *stellen*, "to put (together), to compose, to create," *Gestalt* (form, configuration) belongs to ordinary German usage, but has been used by psychologists, on the basis of the *Gestaltsqualität*, the "quality of form" of C. von Ehrenfels (1890), to designate the global form perceived as such, the whole or "totality" (*Ganzheit*) that is more than the sum of its parts. The examples most frequently cited are those of melody (which is more than the sum of the notes composing it) and optical illusions, in which global perception wins out over analytic perception. In that sense, disseminated by *Gestalttheorie*, *Gestalt* seems almost synonymous with structure. Here is the definition of that theory proposed by E. Clarapède in 1926:

It consists in no longer considering phenomena as a sum of elements that it would be above all a matter of isolating, analyzing, and dissecting, but as sets (*Zusammenhänge*) constituting autonomous units, manifesting internal solidarity, and having their own laws. It follows from this that the mode of being of each element depends on the structure of the set and the laws governing it.

(RT: *Vocabulaire technique et critique de la philosophie*)

Gestalt, nonetheless, insists more on the totality, and "structure" on the relational network; above all, *Gestalt* is distinguished from "structure" in the sense that it is perceived as such from the outset. It refers not to mathematical models, but to geometric figures. The link with (principally visual) perception explains its assignment to the fields of psychology and aesthetics.

In the 1930s, the theory and lexicon of *Gestalt* were disseminated in Anglophone countries by intellectuals of German origin like W. Koehler, one of the founders of the theory, K. Koffka, and R. Arnheim. Panofsky quotes Arnheim, and the analogy he sketched between the Gothic cathedral and Scholastic philosophy is based on the Gestaltist concept of "totality," assimilated to the Thomist concept of the *Summa*. For Panofsky, indeed, *Gestalt* psychology breaks with the nineteenth century, with its scorn for sense perception, and reconnects with Saint Thomas, who deemed the senses to be endowed with "a kind of reason" (sensus ratio quaedam est). Like the *Summa theologica*, the Gothic cathedral aspired to "totality," and its "structural design" offered a simplified and pared down synthesis of all the principal architectural "motifs" elaborated by the prior tradition (*Gothic Architecture and Scholasticism*). E. Gombrich frequently cites *Gestalt* psychology, notably the work of Koehler and Arnheim, while proposing to rectify and complete it with the help of Popper and information theory, putting the accent not on the simplicity of the form or configuration, but on an innate sense of order that makes us look for and identify symmetrical *patterns* in our environment and makes us particularly attentive to every deviation in relation to that symmetry (*The Sense of Order*).

Attempts at translating *Gestalt* into French have not supplanted the original. Alongside *théorie de la forme* (Guillaume, 1937), we also find *psychologie de la Gestalt*, *théorie de la Gestalt*, *gestaltisme*. In English, "configurationalism," proposed by Tichener in the 1920s, had even less success against Gestalt Psychology, Gestalt Theory, Gestaltism, Psychology of "Gestalt," and Gestalt School of Psychology.

IV. "Pattern," "Design," "Structure"

"Pattern" (Fr. *patron, modèle*) remains currently in common use in English, particularly for biologists and cognitivists, to designate arrangements or configurations, whether empirical, natural, or artificial, which are more concrete and more varied than structures.

The English "pattern" is the same word as French *patron*, derived from Latin *pater*, "father," whence *patronus*, "patron, protector, guide," and later "model" or "design" in embroidery, weaving, tailoring, etc. The concept remains, for the most part, linked to the decorative arts, which limits its capacity for abstraction. A "patterned material" is one with motifs, a "pattern book" a book of models (for architects), an assemblage of samples (for weavers or tailors). As R. Escarpit has well shown, a pattern is something that is recognized, that emerges from random surroundings, and the concept is linked to design (including the capacity to design or conceive patterns; "Du Pattern à la structure").

Five characteristics distinguish a pattern from a structure: (1) Pattern is associated with what is concrete, and with daily experience (Escarpit: "A pattern is not the elaboration of an experience, it is an experience"). (2) A pattern belongs to the surface of the object, it merges with it. In the case of lace, the pattern is inseparable from the material itself (Gombrich, *The Sense of Order*). The design of the pattern may not be immediately apparent (as in Islamic patterns in which the name of Allah is at first neither legible nor even visible for the Westerner, who initially sees only "pure" geometric arrangements; Gombrich, *The Sense of Order*), but it is difficult, indeed impossible, to speak of deep patterns, as one does of "deep structure" (Barthes, *S/Z*). (3) Pattern permits

variation. This may seem paradoxical since a pattern is originally what is able to be reproduced, but the field of decoration favors, along with identical repetition, variation—in color or otherwise—in relation to the original. Certain patterns, like moiré, appear to be mobile. English commonly refers to changing, shifting, flexible patterns (Gombrich, *The Sense of Order*). (4) Concordantly, pattern can integrate a temporal dimension, as sequence, rhythm, melody, or dance (Gombrich, *The Sense of Order*): it is thus lacking the ahistorical character attaching to structure, despite the efforts of Viollet-le-Duc or Lucien Goldmann to endow it with dynamism. (5) If pattern is opposed to the random, the chaos of the aleatory, it can nonetheless include it; there is no problem in speaking of random patterns. A work on paper by Jackson Pollock titled *Pattern* (ca. 1945, the Hirschhorn Museum, Washington), crazy pavements (whose paving stones are irregular in shape), and crazy quilts (in French . . . patchwork) are so many artificial patterns that give chaos, so to speak, its share and which, to that extent, resemble Brownian motion, the "eternal combat" of the atoms in Lucretius, or the disposition of the spots on a leopard: patterns and not structures. What appears here is the ambiguity of "design," both *dessin* and *dessein* in French, and which leaves unresolved the question of intentionality (see DISEGNO). The fact that there are patterns in the biological world is less the indication of an overarching divine "design" than that of the infinite variety of Darwinian "design" emerging from chaos: a sensibility attuned to Ruskin, moreover, will see no contradiction in those two uses of "design."

The use of "pattern" by scientists has itself grown in diversity and flexibility. Behaviorists used to speak rather schematically of behavior patterns and pattern reactions. This was also the case for sociologists. "Pattern" evokes "schema" in such cases. American "structuralist" anthropologist-linguists, like E. Sapir or T. A. Sebeok, use "pattern" and "structure" practically interchangeably (Sebeok, *Language in Culture and Society*). The concept was pressed into service anew in the 1970s, thanks to computer science and psychology, both of which speak of pattern recognition; it will be noted that once again the forms or patterns in question can be either natural or artificial. Currently a number of biologists play on the two terms "structure" and "pattern," through which they tend to designate respectively a framework determined by the intangible laws of physics and chemistry, and the visible and shimmering variety of forms assumed in the world of living creatures (e.g., Turing patterns—leopard spots, or butterfly wings—whose design is explained by the theory of the mathematician Alan Turing). The part played by chaos has been palpably reduced, and there has been a return, in biology, to a conception close to that of Lévi-Strauss in the human sciences, with the invariant of structure intuited or unveiled behind the appearance of change in the kaleidoscope or pattern (Ball, *The Self-Made Tapestry*).

We will conclude by observing that it is practitioners of literary studies who are responsible for the success of "structure," which belongs to "scientific Esperanto" (Escarpit, "Du Pattern à la structure"), for they thought they saw in it a hard-scientific concept, a mathematical model, whereas biologists and cognitivists continue to use "pattern," which comes from ordinary language, because the concept allows them, in a manner both familiar and almost poetic, to designate the relative order, the contingent, imperfect, and seductive symmetry of the reality of the senses, of living creatures, and of life itself.

Jean-Loup Bourget

BIBLIOGRAPHY

Ball, Philip. *The Self-Made Tapestry: Pattern Formation in Nature*. Oxford: Oxford University Press, 1999.

Barthes, Roland. *S/Z*. Translated by Richard Miller. New York: Hill and Wang, 1974.

Escarpit, Robert. "Du Pattern à la structure." *Le Discours social. Cahiers de l'Institut de littérature et de techniques artistiques de masse* 1 (1970): 16–22.

Gombrich, Ernst. *The Sense of Order: A Study in the Psychology of Decorative Art*. London: Phaidon Press, 1979.

Lévi-Strauss, Claude. *Structural Anthropology*. Translated by Monique Layton. Chicago: University of Chicago Press, 1976.

Panofsky, Erwin. *Gothic Architecture and Scholasticism*. Cleveland: Meridian Books, 1957.

Ruskin, John. "The Nature of Gothic." In *The Stones of Venice*. New York: Hill and Wang, 1964.

Sapir, Edward, and Morris Swadesh. "American Indian Grammatical Categories." *Word—Journal of the Linguistics Circle of New York* 2 (1946): 103–12.

Sebeok, Thomas A. "Structure and Content of Chermis Charms." In *Language in Culture and Society: A Reader in Linguistics and Anthropology*. Edited by D. Hymes. New York: Harper and Row, 1964.

Todorov, Tzvetan. *Introduction to Poetics*. Translated by Richard Howard. Minneapolis: University of Minnesota Press, 1981.

STYLE

Style, from the Latin *stilus*, which designates the nib of a quill and its sharpened point, originally figures as a concept within the language arts and currently refers more generally to the characteristic manner of an individual, genre, or era: the difference between manner and style, as a function of epoch, cultural region, and language, is treated under MANIERA. See also FAKTURA.

Style is at the intersection of a certain number of problematics:

I. Style and Rhetoric

"Style" is one of the current translations of the Greek *lexis* [λέξις] (from *legô* [λέγω]), "saying-thinking"; see LOGOS), which designates as well "word" (see WORD, II.B) and meaningful expression (see SIGNIFIER/SIGNIFIED, II). Cf. HOMONYM and PARONYM.

The "styles" of sixteenth- and seventeenth-century treatises of rhetoric render the three Latin *genera dicendi*—elevated, middle, and low. Under SUBLIME will be found a comparative reflection on the "grand style"; see also STILL.

On the rules of style, and in particular suitability (Greek *prepon* [πρέπον]), see MIMÊSIS, Box 6; see also COMMONPLACE.

On figures of style, see COMPARISON, COMMONPLACE, TROPE; cf. ANALOGY, HOMONYM.

II. Style and Art History

The categories serving to define and delimit "styles" in time in art history and aesthetics are not superimposable in different traditions, even when the words themselves coincide in different languages. See BAROQUE, CLASSIC, NEUZEIT, ROMANTIC.

III. Style and Mark of the Subject

"Style is the man himself," said Buffon—"the man one is speaking to," Lacan added ("Ouverture," *Écrits*). On the mark of the subject, linked to the invention of a style appropriate to its role, see MANIERA, but also ARGUTEZZA, CONCETTO, GENIUS, INGENIUM, SPREZZATURA, *WITTICISM*.

Cf. COMMONPLACE, SPEECH ACT.

➤ *ART*, WORK

SUBJECT

FRENCH	*sujet*
GERMAN	*Subjekt, Untertan*
GREEK	*hupokeimenon* [ὑποκείμενον], *hupostasis* [ὑπόστασις]
MODERN GREEK	*hupokeimeno* [ὑποκείμενο]
ITALIAN	*soggeto*
LATIN	*subjectum, suppositum, subjectus, subditus*
SPANISH	*sujeto, subdito, sugeto*

➤ SOUL and *CATEGORY*, CONSCIOUSNESS, GEMÜT, GOGO, I/ME/MYSELF, *LIBERTY*, MATTER OF FACT, OBJECT, PRÉDICABLE, PREDICATION, RES, *SELF*, SUPPOSITION, *TO BE*, TO TI ÊN EINAI

The English word "subject" (French, *sujet*) is used in a variety of senses that are, at first sight, difficult to articulate in philosophical terms. We can, however, identify three main groups of meanings, dominated by the ideas of subjectness (*subjectité* in French), subjectivity (*subjectivité*), and subjection (*sujétion*). The three notions are not completely distinct, and it is clear that various combinations of them are, to a greater or lesser extent, operative in most philosophical usages of the term.

The notion of subjectness is the richest of the three (the French word *subjectité* is a translation of the neologism *Subjektheit*, which was probably coined by Heidegger) and condenses several possible usages. It derives more or less directly from Aristotle's *hupokeimenon* [ὑποκείμενον] and basically provides a link between the logical subject ("of which" there can be predicates) and the physical subject ("in which" there are accidents). It also has a much broader meaning that is bound up with the etymology of *hupokeisthai* [ὑποκεῖσθαι] ("to be laid or placed somewhere," to serve as a base or foundation, to be proposed, accepted). This sense overlaps with the network of *thing* and *pragma* [πρᾶγμα], or *res* and *causa*, that intervenes no less frequently than the *subject* (in the sense of matter, object, or theme) that we find in the modern usage. In the same way we find the sense of cause, reason, or motive in the fourth part of Descartes's *Discourse on Method*. In his discussion of the existence of bodies, Descartes writes: "Nevertheless, when it is a question of metaphysical certainty, we cannot reasonably deny that there are adequate grounds for not being entirely sure of the subject. We need only observe that in sleep we may imagine in the same way that we have a different body" (*Philosophical Writings*, 1: 130). French still uses *sujet* in that sense in everyday speech (*Quel sujet vous amène?* ["What brings you here?"]; *avoir sujet de se plaindre* ["to have cause for complaint"]). Another meaning, expressed in English by the reduplicated "subject matter," signals membership of two categories and merits attention (the expression is also attested in the sixteenth century as "matter subject" and is, in fact, a translation of Boethius's *subjecta materia*, which itself reproduces Aristotle's *hupokeimenê hulê* [ὑποκειμένη ὕλη].) A third meaning makes "subject" synonymous with "object," as when we evoke the "subject" of a book or science.

The notion of subjectivity, on the other hand, makes "subject" the antonym of "object" when a more specific distinction has to be made between the sphere of the psyche or the mental, as opposed to that of objectivity (cf. the English "thinking subject," which is well attested in the seventeenth century).

Connotations of subjection are present in any usage of *sujet* that implies the idea of dependency or subjugation, or any form of domination that subjugates, compels or obliges; the first meaning of the English noun "subject" is "one who is under the dominion [= Latin: *dominium*] of a sovereign" or, in the adjectival form, "that is under the rule of a power" (fourteenth century). The articulation between this set and the first two remains problematic, despite the suggestions of ordinary language. Not everything that is *sous-mis* or "sub-mitted" (*subjectum*) is "subjected" (*subjectus*), nor is everything that is "submissive" (*soumis*); it is even clearer that "being placed beneath" should not be confused with "being subjected." Subjectivity is not the relative product of subjectness and subjection, even though a relationship of sub-position is present in both registers. The fate of the French term *suppost* (fourteenth century) and then *suppôt* (1611) provides a good illustration of these ambiguities. The term derives from the Latin *suppositum*, which is used in both grammar and logic as well as the natural sciences (physics, metaphysics, and psychology, to adopt the medieval classification of the sciences) in the sense of the Greek *hupokeimenon*; in its specifically French usage, the term *suppost* was, from the late fourteenth to the late seventeenth century, used in the sense of "vassal" or "subject of someone," or even in the sense of "subaltern." The spatial metaphor common to the fields of "sub-jectness" and "sub-jection" must not, however, lead us to trace the genealogy of subjectivity by identifying *subjectum* with *subjectus*. What is implicit in French or English is much less clear in German, where the "Aristotelean" *Subjekt* is not synonymous with *Untertan* and its derivatives *untertänig* (humble, submissive) and *Untertänigkeit* (submission, humble obedience), even though both *Subjekt* and *Untertan* can be translated into English as "subject" and into French as *sujet*. By the same criterion the notion of a "legal" or "political" subject or a subject with rights is difficult to accept in a context where "subject" is predestined to belong to the register of "submission"—one has only to think of the harmonics of the term "Islam," which, depending on how it is translated, can evoke either radical subjugation ("Muslims" = "those who submit") or "trusting abandonment of the self in God." The introduction of "subject" into philosophy is doubled with the avatars of *subjectum* and *subjectus*.

We will attempt to elucidate a set of problems that has determined the entire history of Western philosophy by alternating between two contrasting points of view. We will begin with the Latin use of *subjectum* in order to identify the medieval origins of the Moderns'"self-certainty," which is torn between the heritage of Aristotle and that of Augustine. We will then look at the contemporary critique of the unity and univocity of "the subject" inaugurated by Nietzsche in order to identify the roots of the conflicting expressions to which it now gives rise in the context of the "internationalization" of philosophical language. We will in both cases give a central role to the historical and hermeneutic reconstruction proposed by Heidegger and will demonstrate both its importance and its limitations.

I. *Hupokeimon*: Subject Degree Zero

"Subject" is Anglo-Latin, and *sujet* is Franco-Latin. No one term in Greek simultaneously supports the threefold idea of subjectness, subjectivity (see CONSCIOUSNESS), and subjection; there is no Greek word meaning "subject," just as there is none meaning "object," even though we encounter, and cannot but encounter, both terms in translations (see OBJECT).

The Latin *subjectum* was in fact originally a translation of the Greek *to hupokeimenon* [τὸ ὑποκείμενον], especially as used in the Aristotelian corpus, even though it is not only a translation of *hupokeimenon*, and even if other terms, such as *suppositum*, can capture other aspects of Aristotle's *hupokeimenon* in all circumstances (see Box 1, "Suppositum"/"Subjectum" in SUPPOSITION).

To hupokeimenon is never an expression of subjectivity. Nor is it an expression of subjugation, except for the quasi-sexual connotations that link it to the idea of "matter," *hulê* (ὕλη) as united with *eidos* (εἶδος) or *morphê* (μορφή), that is to say, the "form" it receives or to which it is subject, and with which it makes up a complete substance or *sunulon* (cf. *Metaphysics* Zeta VII 1029a—"Primary subject [*hupokeimenon prôton*] is in one way matter, in another shape-form, and in a third sense the composite of both of them [*to ek toutôn*]," with *De generatione animalium* I, 20. 729a 8–11: "What happens is what one would expect to happen. The male provides the 'form' and the 'principle' of the movement [*to t'eidos kai tên archên tês kinêseôs*]; the female provides the body and the matter [*to sôma kai tên hulên*]. Compare the coagulation of milk. Here, the milk is the body, and the fig juice or rennet is the principle that causes it to set." Sylviane Agacinski stresses that the gender hierarchy "is applied, by analogy, to the basic concepts of metaphysics, as when the philosopher states that "matter aspires to form in the same way that the female desires the male" (*Politique des sexes*, 44).

On the other hand, the term does cover and bring together two kinds of subject whose composition proves to be a necessary part of the very idea of subjectivity: the physical subject, which is a substrate for accidents that occur through changes, and the logical subject, which is a support for the predicates in a proposition. This suture, which is onto-logical in that it allows being and "being said" to coincide, as if by nature, is the mark of Aristotle's *ousia* [οὐσία].

■ See Box 1.

Following Bonitz (RT: *Index s.v. hupokeisthai*), we will take as our starting point all the senses in which Aristotle uses *hupokeimenon* and *hupokeisthai* [ὑποκεῖσθαι]. We can leave aside the local, or nonterminological, sense of "being there," as well as all the current meanings that Aristotle simply established, particularly when he posits something as the basis, principle, or premise for reflection (*positum*, *datum*). This leaves a complex of three usages. Bonitz describes it thus:

> We can identify three main genera in Aristotle's use of the words *hupokeisthai* and *hupokeimenon* in so much as *hupokeimenon* is either matter [*hê hulê*] that is determined by form, or *ousia*, in which passions and accidents are inherent, or the logical subject to which predicates are attributed; but as matter itself is also

1

Remnant (Italian *il resto*; Hebrew *she'-ar*; Greek *kataleimma*)

Theological term found in both the Old and New Testaments and taken to refer to the part of the nation of Israel that will be saved, as in Isaiah 10:22: "For although thy people be as the sand of the sea, yet a remnant of them shall be saved." Used by the Apostle Paul in a related context in the Letter to the Romans 11:5: "Even so then at this present time also there is a remnant according to the election of grace." The term plays a central role in the politico-theological reflections of Giorgio Agamben—principally in his books *The Remnants of Auschwitz* and *The Time That Remains*.

The passages from the Bible cited above present a number of interpretative dilemmas. It is Giorgio Agamben's attempts to solve them, as well as to develop a "paradigm" of the "remnant" that has given the term contemporary currency outside of its theological context. An initial question to be posed is why only a "remnant" of Israel will be saved. Is it because a purifying sacrifice is called for? Is it because only a part of Israel is worthy of salvation? Or is the idea to be understood in a different sense? In his discussions of the term, Agamben has stressed that "the remnant is a theologico-messianic concept" (*Remnants*, 162). This "theologico-messianic concept" is, obviously, concerned with salvation—a salvation that is to all appearances limited. Agamben, however, rejects this idea. "What is decisive," he writes, "is that . . . 'remnant' does not seem simply to refer to a numerical portion of Israel" (ibid., 163). "Remnant," for him, is to be understood in another sense than the conventional one of a remainder left over from some larger whole.

In *The Time That Remains* Agamben asks, "How should we conceive of this 'remnant of Israel?'" and offers as answer: "The problem is misunderstood from the very start if the remnant is seen as a numeric portion, as it has been by some theologians who understand it as that portion of the Jews who survived the eschatological catastrophe" (*Time That Remains*, 54–55, translation modified). This does not, however, resolve the problem

at hand, and Agamben is careful to stress that "it is even more misleading to interpret the remnant as outright identical to Israel" (ibid., 55). "A closer reading of the prophetic texts," he continues, "shows that the remnant is closer to being a consistency [*consistenza*] or figure that Israel assumes in relation to election or to the messianic event. It is therefore neither the whole, nor a part of the whole, but the impossibility for the part and the whole to coincide with themselves or with each other" (ibid., 55, translation modified). Agamben thus sees the "theologico-messianic concept" of the remnant as expressing a relation of part to whole that does not fall within the traditional lines drawn by dialectical thought and that has affinities with Adorno's "negative dialectics," Derrida's *différance*, and the Spinozist ideas of "immanence" and "multitude" that are important for Deleuze, Guattari, Negri, and Hardt. Like those ideas the remnant is located in a singular conceptual and strategic space as "the remnant is precisely what prevents divisions from being exhaustive" (ibid., 56).

Concerning divisions as it does, this "theologico-messianic concept" offers Agamben a paradigm for his idea of a "coming community." For Agamben the "remnant" "allows for a new perspective that dislodges our antiquated notions of a people and a democracy, however impossible it may be to completely renounce them. The people is neither the whole nor the part, neither the majority nor the minority. Instead, it is that which can never coincide with itself, as whole or as part, that which infinitely remains or resists each division and, with all due respect to those who govern us, never allows us to be reduced to a majority or a minority. This remnant is the figure, or the consistency [*la consistenza*], assumed by the people in the decisive moment—and as such, is the only real political subject [*l'unico soggetto politico reale*]" (ibid., 57, translation modified).

In Agamben's hands the remnant is a concept through which we can view how a totality conceives of itself and of its

component parts. At first sight the claim that "the only real political subject," "the true political subject," is a "remnant" may seem gnomic or paradoxical, but its sense lies in the idea that a true political subject is not merely a part of a totalizing whole. What is at issue is thus what Agamben calls "the problem of identities—ethnic or other. Such a thing as an ethnic identity will never truly exist because there will always remain a remnant" ("Das unheilige Leben," 20). This divided people becomes a paradigm for the idea that a people cannot and should not be thought of as pure, whole, or without remainder. A remnant is what results from every dialectical attempt at exhaustive identification and classification, every attempt to create a community that would completely subsume the singularity of its members. For this reason, remnant is a concept that Agamben applies not only to an entire people, but also to its individual members. For this reason he will claim that "the subject is a sort of remnant" (ibid.). The remnant is a response to the totalizing nature of dialectical thinking and its gradual elimination of differences. It is thus a paradigm for a conception of both part and whole.

Leland De la Durantaye

BIBLIOGRAPHY

Agamben, Giorgio. "Das unheilige Leben: Ein Gespräch mit dem italienischen Philosophen Giorgio Agamben." Interview with Hannah Leitgeb and Cornelia Vismann. *Literaturen* (Berlin) 2, no. 1 (2001): 16–21.

———. *Remnants of Auschwitz: The Witness and the Archive. Homo Sacer III*. Translated by Daniel Heller-Roazen. New York: Zone, 2002. *Quel che resta di Auschwitz. L'archivio e il testimone (Homo sacer III)*. Turin: Bollati Boringhieri, 1998.

———. *The Time That Remains: A Commentary on the Letter to the Romans*. Translated by Patricia Dailey. Stanford, CA: Stanford University Press, 2005. *Il tempo che resta. Un commento alla Lettera ai Romani*. Turin: Bollati Boringhieri, 2000.

related to the notion of *ousia*, the first and second genera are not differentiated by limits that are universally certain, and given that *einai* [*huparchein*, being in the sense of belonging to] and *legesthai* [*katêgoreisthai*, being said in the sense of being predicated of] are closely connected, the distinction between the second and third genera is little clearer.

(Bonitz, *Index Aristotelicus*, p. 798, col. 1)

Hupokeimenon's plurality of meanings is not, in other words, fixed or thematized in the same way that the meanings of "being" are fixed. (At best, we can read in *Metaphysics* Z, 13, 1038b: "περὶ τοῦ ὑποκειμένου, ὅτι διχῶς ὑπόκειται, ἢ τόδε τι ὄν, ὥσπερ τὸ ζῷον τοῖς πάθεσιν, ἢ ὡς ἡ ὕλη τῇ ἐντελεχείᾳ [There are two ways of being a subject (lit. 'subjected'), either as a possessor of thisness (as the animal is a subject for its properties) or as matter is a subject for actuality]." It is used, rather, to describe three types of relations: (1) relations between matter and form, to the extent that they combine to make up the *sunolon*, or the individual as a whole without parts; (2) relations between the individual, substance-subject of physics and what happens to it, its affections and accidents (an animal is subject to movement, or to being "white," "large," or "ill"); and (3) relations between the subject of the proposition and its predicates ("animal" as "white," "large," or "ill"). In the first two usages the subject can be variously described as matter (*hulê*), as the individual, the primary substance or essence (*tode ti* [τόδε τι] or *ousia prôtê* [οὐσία πρώτη]), but in the third there is no substitute for *hupokeimenon*. No other word can designate the subject of the proposition as such. The irreducible meaning is also the meaning that unifies the set (just as *kinêsis* [κίνησις] refers both to local movements and to movement in general; it therefore refers to all types of movement, such as growth) in a radically nondialectical conceptual structure. This is typical of Aristotle's classificatory thinking: the key species gives its name to the whole genus.

This description requires some qualification: the reason why subjectness is able to combine in the single word *ousia* both the sense of substance and that of subject is that *ousia* itself can also be a combination of the two. Just as primary essence is *malista* [μάλιστα], first of all, essence, so that which is first of all proper to essence (*malista idion tês ousias* [μάλιστα ἴδιον τῆς οὐσίας]) is, "although it remains, notwithstanding, numerically one and the same, its ability to be the recipient of contrary qualifications (*to tauton kai hen arithmôi on tôn enantiôn einai dektikon* [τὸ ταὐτὸν καὶ ἕν ἀριθμῷ ὄν τῶν ἐναντίων εἶναι δεκτικόν])" (*Categories* 6, 4a 10–11). A color cannot be both black and white and still remain one and the

same, but essence can. For example, an individual man (*ho tis anthrôpos* [ὁ τὶς ἄνθρωπος]), this singular man who remains one and the same, can sometimes be pale and sometimes black (*hote men leukos hote de melas gignetai* [ὁτὲ μὲν λευκὸς ὁτὲ δὲ μέλας γίγνεται]) (*Categories* 4a 19–20). This is not like the statement "he sits," which becomes false when "he rises," but "through a change which belongs to it in itself" (*kata tên hautês metabolên* [κατὰ τὴν αὑτῆς μεταβολὴν]) (*Categories* 4b 3). The accidents that are predicated upon *ousia* therefore arise from *ousia* itself; its subjectness qua material substance is one and the same as its subjectness qua logical subject, and it is precisely this that makes it the *hupokeimenon*.

Aristotle's various attempts to define *ousia* reveal a constant tension between the singular and the universal; it is the *eidos* or essence and the *to ti ên einai* (τὸ τί ἦν εἶναι) or "what-it-was-to-be-that-thing," which are in *Metaphysics* book Zeta (7, 1032b), referred to as *ousia prôtê*, and not the *tode ti* of the *Categories* (see TO TI ÊN EINAI). Now it is the definition given in the *Categories*, where essence is primarily the concrete singular, that determines the conflagration between logical subjectness and physical subjectness. We can deduce from this that the individual, being a subject in two senses, is a necessary (but obviously not sufficient) precondition for the later developments that generate "subjectivity" and "subjection."

■ See Box 2.

II. *Subjectum*: From *Hupokeimenon* to Self-Certainty

A. From subjectness to subjectivity

While the term "subjectivity" (*subjectivité*) appears to have been borrowed from the German *Subjektivität*, thanks to the diffusion of the adjective *subjetiv* in the Kantian sense,

---

2

The definition of the *ousia prôtê*

Οὐσία δέ ἐστιν ἡ κυριώτατά τε καὶ πρώτως καὶ μάλιστα λεγομένη, ἡ μήτε καθ' ὑποκειμένου τινὸς λέγεται μήτε ἐν ὑποκειμένῳ τινί ἐστιν, οἷον ὁ τὶς ἄνθρωπος ἢ ὁ τὶς ἵππος.

Est essence, quand on le dit au sens le propre, premier et principal, celle [ou ce] qu'on ne dit pas d'un sujet et qui n'est pas non plus dans un sujet, comme l'homme en question le chevel en question.

(A substance—that which is called a substance most strictly, primarily, and most of all—is that which is neither said of a subject nor in a subject, e.g., the individual man or the individual horse.)

(Aristotle, *Categories* 5, 2a 11–13)

Against the grain of received usage (as evinced in the English translation of Aristotle's *Categories*) "essence" is substituted for "substance" in the French translation for

ousia. This indicates that what is at stake here is the determination of that which is, which is not substance. "Substance" places undue emphasis on the physical (substance/accidents) and on the conjunction of logic and physics.

This definition, which is presented as both the primary definition of essence and, the definition of primary essence, is remarkable already in purely stylistic terms. Rather than stating directly that essence is *hupokeimenon* [ὑποκείμενον], it juxtaposes two negatives: "neither said of . . . nor is in"; essence is a *hupokeimenon* in two senses, as it is neither a predicate (or, more accurately, something predicable; see PRÉDICABLE and PREDICATION) nor an accident. We are actually dealing with a crudely knit juxtaposition, operated by means of the word *hupokeimenon*, that establishes the preeminence of essence/substance in both the physical and the logical sense. This sense of "primary

essences," as was noted in the previous example, comes through in the French and not in the English translation:

Tout le reste ou bien se dit de ces sujets (*êtoi kath' hupokeimenôn toutôn legetai* [ἤτοι καθ' ὑποκειμένων τούτων λέγεται]) ou bien est dans ces sujets eux-mêmes (*ê en hupokeimenais autais estin* [ἢ ἐν ὑποκειμέναις αὐταῖς ἐστίν]); de sorte que si ces essences premières n'étaient pas, impossible que quoi que ce soit d'autre soit.

Thus all the other things are either said of the primary substances as subjects (*êtoi kath' hupokeimenôn toutôn legetai* [ἤτοι καθ' ὑποκειμένων τούτων λέγεται]) or in them as subjects (*ê en hupokeimenais autais estin* [ἢ ἐν ὑποκειμέναις αὐταῖς ἐστίν]). So if the primary substances did not exist it would be impossible for any of the other things to exist.

(Ibid., 2b 4-6)

the psychological meaning of the term, which is dominant in ordinary usage, is the result of a series of transformations that began in the Middle Ages. According to Martin Heidegger, the most decisive of all is the mutation that transforms Aristotle's *hupokeimenon* into *subjectum*. According to the author of *Sein und Zeit*, the essential feature of the Cartesian initiative is the assertion that the *subjectum*, which is the *substans* of the Scholastics, in the sense of "that which is constant" (subsisting) and "real," is the basis of any psychology of the subject, or in other words the transition from the Latin *subjectum* to the modern sense of "subject," or, if we prefer, the transition from *subjectum* to *ego*, from subjectivity to I-ness (*égoité*). In volume 4 of his *Nietzsche*, Heidegger remarks: "Since Descartes and through Descartes, man, the human 'I' has in a preeminent way come to be the 'subject' in metaphysics. . . . Why is the human subject transposed into the 'I,' so that subjectivity here becomes coterminous with I-ness?" (4: 96). Heidegger's explanation for this phenomenon, which is based upon the structure of "the lying-before" (*vor-herige*) that he finds at the heart of the Cartesian notion of representation, gives Descartes the central role: he completes the transformation of *hupokeimenon* into *subjectum* by ballasting its "actuality" with the new dimension of perceptive activity:

> According to the metaphysical tradition from Aristotle onwards, every true being is a *hupokeimenon* [ὑποκειμένον]. This *hupokeimenon* is determined afterwards as *subjectum*. Descartes's thinking distinguishes the *subjectum* which man is to the effect that the *actualitas* of this *subjectum* has its essence in the *actus* of *cogitare* (*percipere*).
>
> (Heidegger, "Metaphysics as History of Being," in *End of Philosophy*, 31; trans. amended)

Heidegger's thesis is debatable. He claims that Descartes initiates a displacement that occurred either long before him or long after him and which does not in any case, directly or explicitly equate *subjectum* with *ego*. What is more, Heidegger's notion of "subjectivity" is too closely associated with the Lutheran notion of the certainty of salvation, which supposedly founds the certainty characteristic of "modern subjectivity" to be valid as a true genealogy of the subject.

■ See Box 3.

Consideration must also be given to other experiences demonstrating that the moment when *mens humana* has an exclusive claim on the term "subject," it belongs to a history that predates the "Cartesian" golden age of representation. Heidegger's analysis does, however, have one merit: it demonstrates the need for a distinction between subjectness and subjectivity. Heidegger sets us a task that his own text does not complete: describing in historicological terms what leads from one to the other, and that means taking the medieval contribution into account.

B. "Subjectum" in medieval psychology

In the Middle Ages philosophical theories of the subject were originally inscribed within the space of subjectness. The medieval notion of the *subjectum* is still, at least in problematic terms, Aristotle's notion of the *hupokeimenon*, or of a "subject" in the sense of a support or substrate for essential or accidental properties. In terms of the genealogy of the subject and subjectivity, however, medieval thought was for a long time characterized by a remarkable chiasmus that can be described as follows: the Middle Ages had a theory of the ego or I-ness (*égoité*), or a theory of the *subject* in the obvious philosophical sense of the term *mens*, but that theory did not require the implementation of the notion of a *subjectum*;

3
Hupokeimeno [ὑποκείμενο] in modern Greek

Aristotle defines matter as "the first *hupokeimenon* [ὑποκείμενον] of all the things from which they come and which belong to them not by accident" (*Physics* 1, 9, 192a 31–4). But while the term "subject" is an appropriate translation of *ousia* in the sense of "the ultimate subject of all predication," it is an inappropriate rendering of this text. *Hupokeimenon* is therefore often translated as "substrate," in keeping with the Scholastic tradition, which uses "substratum."

Like the English "subject" or the French *sujet*, the modern Greek [ὑποκείμενο] means both the grammatical and logical subject and "subjectivity." There is no adequate translation of "substrate." Théodorïs notes that "to the extent that 'subject' is, in our language, a worn-out and polysemic term, we are often obliged to resort to

something like 'substratum,' using the word *substructure* [*hupostrôma*]" (Introduction). This is why several modern Greek translations have been suggested. In his translation of the *Physics*, Kyrgiopoulos gives the impression of remaining close to the original by translating the term as "the primary subject (*hupokeimenon*) [ὑποκείμενον] in everything." Georgoulís suggests a periphrase: "that which is as lying beneath (*hôs hupokeimeno* [ὡς ὑποκείμενο]) all things." In his translation of Plotinus, Tzavaras sometimes uses the ancient Greek term, but he also adopts Georgoulís's suggestion and uses "that which lies below (κειμένη-απο-κάτω)"; he also extends that sense by using "substructure." While the modern Greek verb does indeed mean "to lie under something," and "to come under the authority of someone," the noun no

longer has the old meaning. The first translation simply uses the ancient Greek; the second resorts to a verbal form and uses the past participle of ὑπόκειμαι, which does not capture the ancient noun form; "substructure" forces the meaning, even though it does have the virtue of being a translation. These disagreements are an adequate demonstration of the difficulties involved in translating such an important term from Greek into Greek.

Lambros Couloubaritsis

BIBLIOGRAPHY

Aristotle. *The Complete Works of Aristotle*. 2 vols. Edited by Jonathan Barnes. Princeton, NJ: Princeton University Press, 1995.
Théodorïs, C. *Introduction to Philosophy* (in Greek). Paris: Éditions de Jardin, 1945. 2nd ed. 1955.

it also offered a complete theory of subjectness in grammar, logic, physics, and metaphysics but was reluctant to export it into psychology in the form of a theory of *mens humana*. The theory of *mens* did not, in other words, need to import the notion of *hupokeimenon*; conversely, the theory of the *subjectum* did not in itself claim to govern that of *mens*. And yet the two did intersect and were articulated several hundred years before the Cartesian theory of *ego cogito cogitatum*. It is impossible to reconstruct every stage in the process here. We can indicate the two poles that determine the very idea of subjectivity: on the one hand, a Trinitarian Augustinian model of the human soul based in part upon the idea of the circumincession (mutual in-dwelling) of the Persons of the Trinity and in part upon a non-Aristotelian notion of hypostasis (*hupostasis* [ὑπόστασις]; on the other, a non-Trinitarian Averroist model of subjectivity that is explicitly based on the Aristotelian notion of *hupokeimenon*. The two models are not intended to solve the same problem: the former is mainly concerned with the problem of consciousness and *self*-knowledge, while the latter is concerned with the *subject* of thought.

1. Averroism and the question of the "subject of thought"

It is with the translation of the *Long Commentary* on Book 3 of the *De anima* that the notion of subjectness really becomes part of the field of psychology. It represents an attempt to answer a specific question: what is the subject of thought? This question presupposes the validity of a model, Aristotle's analysis of sensation and the notions that make it possible: action (*energeia* [ἐνέργεια]), and actuality or the actualization of potentiality (*energein* [ἐνεργεῖν]). Aristotle's theory of sensation is not based upon the idea of a "feeling subject" that is affected by a sense of change but on the idea of sensation itself, defined as the joint action of a sense-object and a sense-organ (see SENSE 1.A, B). In Averroes it is this structure of the joint action that governs the question of the subject of thought. Just as sensation has two subjects, so thought, referred to here as *intentio intellecta* (see INTENTION), intelligible knowledge *in actu*, also has two subjects: (1) images (*intentiones imaginatae*), and (2) the so-called "material" intellect, which is divorced from the body and not numbered by it. The subject of thought is therefore twofold; only one of these subjects—the *ego* or the "me"—has anything to do with man.

According to Aristotle, cognizing through the intellect is like perceiving through the senses, and perceiving through the senses is accomplished through the intermediary of two subjects. The first is the subject [*subjectum*] through which what is sensed becomes true (the sensible that exists outside the soul), and the second the subject that ensures that what is sensed is an existing form (and this is the first perfection of the sensorial faculty). It follows that *intelligibilia in actu* must also have two subjects, one being the subject thanks to which they are true images, and the second, the subject that ensures that each *intelligibilia* exists in the [real] world. This is the material intellect. Indeed, to that extent there is no difference between the senses and the intellect, except in that the subject of what is sensed, and which makes it true, is external to the soul, whereas

the subject of the intellect, and which makes it true, is internal to the soul.

> (Averroës, *Commentary on De anima* III comm.
> 5 on *De anima* III 4 429a 21–24)

According to Averroës, man is not his intellect: if he has a role to play in intellection as such, it is thanks to his cognitive faculty (Ar. *al-quwwat al-mufakkira* [القوة المفكّرة], Lat. *vis cogitativa, vis distinctiva*), which supplies images or, rather, particular "intentions" (see INTENTION, Box 2) to the material intellect, a unique substance that is divorced from the human soul. Man is therefore not the subject of thought in the precise sense that the eye is the subject of vision. In a certain sense his subjective position is, rather, on the side of that which is seen. This is, in fact, the basic criticism that Aquinas makes of Averroës's noetics in the *De unitate intellectus contra averroistas*. The theory of the two subjects of intellection does not allow us to say that man—or, rather, the individual man ("that man there")—thinks, but only that its images are thought by a separate intellect.

> Assuming that one numerically identical species is both a possible form of intellect and simultaneously contained in images, that type of linkage would not be enough to allow this particular man to think. It is in fact clear that as, thanks to the intelligible species, something is *thought*, and as, thanks to the intellective power, something *thinks*, so something is felt thanks to the sensible species, just as something *feels* thanks to the sensible power. That is why the wall in which color is found, and whose sensible species *in actu* is vision, is something that is seen, and not something that sees; what sees is the animal endowed with the faculty of vision where the sensible species is found. Now the linkage between the possible intellect and the man in whom there are images whose species exist in the possible intellect is like that between the wall, in which color exists, and sight, in which the species of color exist. [If that linkage existed] just as the wall does not see, even though color is seen, it would follow than man does not think and that his images would be thought by the possible intellect. It is therefore impossible to defend the thesis that man thinks if we adopt the position of Averroës.

> (Aquinas, *De unitate intellectus contra averroistas*, ch. 3, §65)

Far from accepting Aquinas's counterargument, some thirteenth-century Latin Averroists radicalize the thesis that the subject, which has to be described as "thinking," as opposed to "imagined intentions," is not the individual man. Strictly speaking, thought does not have "man" as its subject because "thought is not a human perfection," but the "perfection of the intellect," and a separate material. Introducing the subject/object duality for the first time in this context, the Averroists (see Siger of Brabant, *In De Anima*, q. 9; ed. Bazán, 28, 79–82) go so far as to argue that thought does not need man in order to "sub-ject itself to him" in the strict sense. It only needs man, or rather fantasms, or, in the last analysis, a material body as an object and not as a subject. As an anonymous master writes: "As thought is not a human perfection, it needs man as an object . . . it needs a material body as an object, not as its subject" (cf. *Anonyme de Giele, Quaestiones de anima* II, q. 4; in Giele et al., *Trois commentaires*, 76, 91–96).

The thesis that the body is the object of the intellect enjoyed an exceptional longevity: we find it as late as the sixteenth century, when it is turned *against* Averroes in Pomponazzi's *De immortalitate animae* (1516). A follower of Alexander of Aphrodise's "materialism," Pomponazzi accepts the idea, which is doubly unacceptable for Averroism, that the body can be both the object *and the subject* of thought:

> According to its general definition, the soul is the action of a naturally organized body. The intellective soul is therefore the action of an organized natural body. Since the intellect is by virtue of its being the action of an organized natural organ, it therefore also depends, in all its operations, upon an organ, either as subject or as object. It is therefore never completely divorced from all organs.

> (Pomponazzi, *De immortalitate animae*, ed. Mojsisch, "Philosophische Bibliotek" 434, Hamburg: Meiner, 1990, ch. 4, p. 18)

For the Averroists of the thirteenth century, at least, it is clear that the existence of the ego and of the "fact of consciousness" certainly does not coincide with the assumption of man as *subjectum*. Man does not experience himself as the subject of thought; the "I" or "ego" does not experience itself as that which thinks or experiences thought. As the same *Anonyme de Giele* writes:

> You will say: I [and no other] feel and perceive that it is I who thinks. I reply: this is false. On the contrary, it is the intellect, which is naturally united with you as the motor (principle) and regulator of your body, that feels this, *lui ipse* [and no other], in exactly the same way that the separate intellect experiences that it has within it intelligibilia. You will say (again): I, the aggregate of a body and an intellect, feel that it is I who is thinking. I say: this is false. On the contrary, it is the intellect that is in need of your body as object (*intellectus egens tuo corpore ut obiecto*) that feels this and communicates it to the aggregate.

The heteronomy of the Averroist "subject" is very significantly illustrated by an episode in translation history that is worth recalling. We know that Averroes's *Long Commentary on the De Anima* is, given the current state of the corpus, fully accessible only in Latin, or in Michel Scot's tricky translation (the Arabic original having been lost). One of the most famous statements, in which Averroes appears to introduce the notion of the subject, is the passage on eternity and the corruptibility of the theoretical intellect—the ultimate human perfection. It asserts: "Perhaps philosophy always exists in the greater part of the subject, just as the man exists thanks to man, and just as the horse exists thanks to horse." What does the expression mean? Going against the very principles of Averroes's noetics, the Averroist Jean de Jandun understands it to mean that "philosophy is perfect in the greater part of its subject (*sui subiecti*)," or in other words "in most men" (*in maiori parte hominum*). There are no grounds for this interpretation. We can explain it, however, if we recall that

Averroes's Latin translator has confused the Arabic terms *mawḍū'* [مع ضو ع] (subject or substratum in the sense of *hupokeimenon*) and *mawḍi'* [مع ضو] (place). When Averroes simply says that philosophy has always existed "in the greater part of the place," meaning "almost everywhere," Jean understands him as saying that it has as its subject "the majority of men," as every man (or almost every man) contributes to a full (perfect) realization in keeping with his knowledge and aptitudes. "Subjectivity" does slip into Averroism here, but only because of a huge misunderstanding resulting from a translator's error. It therefore contradicts Averroes.

Appearances to the contrary notwithstanding, the moment when, thanks to Averroes's theory of the "two subjects" of thought, Aristotle's *hupokeimenon*, recycled as a *subiectum*, enters the field of psychology, has, as we can see, absolutely nothing to do with *mens humana*'s exclusive claim on the name "subject" (*subiectum* and *ego*, or "subjectivity" and "I-ness" [*égoïté*], therefore, take on exactly the same meaning). As we shall see, and by the same criterion, the attestation, in an originary experience, of the "fact of consciousness" was not, according to those who argued its case, originally bound up with the Aristotelian notion of subjectness.

2. The discovery of self-certainty

Confronted with the Averroist theory of the two subjects of thought, several medieval doctrines argue that the ego or the "I" can perceive itself, experience itself, and know itself, thanks, initially, to a kind of direct intuition. None of these doctrines, however, initially relates this apperception to the idea of self-apprehension as *subject*. The first thing they have in common tends to be an Augustinian denial of the specularity of the self-to-self relationship: "The mind [does not] know itself as in a mirror" (Augustine, *De Trinitate* X, 3, 5 BA 16, p. 128). Many medieval philosophers conclude from this theorem that, despite the claims of Aristotle and the Peripatetics, the soul cannot know itself in the same way that it can know other things, namely through representation or abstraction, and that it does not know itself either as another thing or as another soul. It knows itself as self-presence, and in, through, and as that self-presence. The absence of knowledge through representation is characteristic of both that which is present and that which is absent. Seeing is a more appropriate way of re-presenting that which is absent in its absence as though it were present. Self-presence is inadmissible. The soul can, Augustine goes on, therefore form an image of itself and can "love that image" but it cannot know itself in that way. To the contrary, Pierre Jean Olieu argues (*Impugnatio quorundam articulorum*, art. 19 f. 47ra) on similar grounds that it knows itself "through the infallible certainty of its being [*certitude infallibili sui esse*]": man knows from the outset "so infallibly that he exists and lives, that he cannot cast that into doubt [*scit enim homo se esse et vivere sic infallibiliter quod de hoc dubitare non potest*]." Even more so than the rejection of specularity, the dominant feature of the medieval Augustinian model of I-ness is the truly Trinitarian notion of circumincession. The primacy of circumincession explains why, in the Augustinian sphere, the notion of *hupokeimenon* does not have any particular role to play in the philosophical elucidation of the self-to-self relationship. The way in which the Greek *ousia* and *hupostasis* evolve in the Middle Ages is much more relevant.

a. The circumincession of Persons as a model for the theory of mind

The Augustinian theory of mind (*mens*) and mental actions does not depend solely upon the notions of essence and substance. It is entirely based on a notion derived from Trinitarian theology that was elaborated in order to explain how, to use Augustine's own terminology, a substance can be at once simple and multiple. This notion is what is usually known as the circumincession of Persons or perichoresis. Perichoresis means the mutual indwelling of the Persons of the Trinity. Their mutual immanence—which has two aspects: a *manence* (expressed in scholastic Latin by the term *circuminsessio*) and a dynamic and never-ending immanence (expressed by the term *circumincessio*)—excludes from the outset any recourse to the standard conception of the subject-substantial as a support for accidents. God cannot, in any strict sense of the term, be said to subsist in the same sense that a *substantia* subsists. That which subsists in the strict sense is that which is subjected to what is said to "be in a subject" ("ea quae *in aliquo subjectoesse* dicuntur," *De Trinitate* VII 4, 10, BA 15, p. 536). That which exists *in substantia* is not substance; it is an accident, such as color, which exists "*in subsistente atque subjecto copore*" and which, when it ceases to exist, "does not deprive the body of its bodily being." The relationship between God and His attributes cannot be like this: God is not the subject of his goodness (*nefas es dicere ut subsistat et subsit Deus bonitati suae*), which does not exist in him as in a subject (*tanquam in subiecto*). It is preferable to say of God that He is himself his goodness, that He is an essence rather than a substance, and that the Trinity is in the strict sense "a single essence"— Father, Son, and Spirit are considered to be three "hypostases" or, more accurately, three mutually indwelling Persons. The rejection of the *substantia / id quod est in subiecto* in Trinitarian theology is of crucial importance to the history of psychology. The doctrine of the Trinitarian image, which is central to Augustine's theory of the soul, in fact holds that the same structure of mutual immanence is found in the inner man. But if that is the case, the notion of *substantia*, in the sense of *subjectum*, has to be banished from the field of psychology, on pain of reducing mental acts to mere accidents that befall the mind. This is why Augustine, who was quite familiar with Aristotle's notion of *hupokeimenon*, eliminates the *subjectum* from his analysis of the triads of the inner man. The *hupokeimenon* is incompatible with the transposition of the theological notion of mutual immanence to psychology.

b. The application of the perichoretic model to the theory of "mens"

What we are calling the perichoretic model of the soul (even though Augustine himself obviously never uses the expression) is at work in the description of the two triads that the author of the *De Trinitate* invokes in order to distinguish between knowledge and self-consciousness, namely (a) *mens-notitia–amor* and (b) *memoria (sui)*, *intelligentia, voluntas*. The first analogy between the Trinity and the inner man subordinates self-consciousness to self-knowledge. The notions of *ousia* and *hupostasis* play an obvious role even at this level. Three theses articulate the perichoretic structure: the concept of *mens* necessarily implies its correlates: knowledge and the will; all three refer to substances: *mens* does so in the strict sense, while knowledge and the will do so in a broad sense insofar as, being acts, they differ from mere accidents; these three "substances," which are within one another, are simply "a single substance or essence."

■ See Box 4.

This structure allows the conceptualization of the transition from knowledge to self-consciousness: (1) the mind knows itself discursively and reflexively through the act of knowing; (2) this knowledge leads, directly and necessarily, to self-love; (3) in its self-love and self-knowledge, the mind becomes immediately self-conscious (*De Trinitate* IX, 2, 2–5, 8). In this analogy, which is still imperfect, between the inner man and the divine Trinity, *mens* represents the deity in his entirety, while the deity's acts correspond to the Persons of the Son and the Spirit.

In the second analogy (*memoria [sui]*, *intelligentia, voluntas*), in which the perichoretic model is more adequately applied, an immediate and intuitive self-consciousness precedes and founds reflexive knowledge. Because the terms of the triad, which are really distinct, form a unity (because the mind is one), we can say that *mens*, which is the substance or essence of the soul, represents the deity in his entirety, while *memoria*

4

Heidegger: Self-certainty and the certainty of salvation at the dawn of modernity

There is no room for the Middle Ages in the scenario Heidegger constructs in order to explain the certainty that will "take man to sovereignty within the real world." Everything obviously begins with the new Lutheran conception of *Er-lösung* and the problematic of the "certainty" of salvation (which is problematized from a different point of view by Max Weber in *The Protestant Ethic and the Spirit of Capitalism*).

Before all (i.e., in the medieval period), God the creator, and with him the institution of the offering and management of his gifts of grace (the Church), is in sole possession of the sole and eternal truth. As *actus purus*, God is pure actuality and thus the causality of everything real, that is, the source and place of salvation that, as blessedness, guarantees eternal permanence. By himself, man can never become, and be, absolutely certain of this salvation. On the other hand, through faith and similarly through lack of faith, man is essentially established in the attainment of salvation's certainty or forced to the renunciation of this salvation and its certainty. Thus a necessity rules, hidden in its origin, that man make sure of his salvation in some fashion in the Christian or in another sense (salvation; *sôtêria* [σωτηρία]; redemption; release).

(Heidegger, "Metaphysics as History of Being," 21)

corresponds to the Person of the Father, *intelligentia* to the Person of the Son, and *amor* to the Person of the Holy Spirit. When taken either separately or together, each of the three is equal to the others. Each of the three necessarily implies the other three, as all three are correlates. In the full Trinitarian structure the acts of *mens* are described as proceeding from the memory in the same way that, in God, the Son and the Holy Spirit proceed from the Father (*De Trinitate* X, 11, 18).

The language of *ousia* and *hupostasis* has a specific function: to demonstrate that there is a type of unity between acts of *mens*, which are actually distinct from one another, and *mens* itself. This intimate correlativity is irreducible to the relationship between accidents and substance. This is therefore, and by definition, a non-Aristotelian model designed to evade the notions of substance-subject and accidents, which are incompatible with the perichoretic structure of the soul. The invention of the "subjectivity" of which Heidegger speaks therefore requires the *subjectum* to intrude into the Augustinian structure. It requires what at first sight appears to be an unnatural encounter between *certitudo infallibilis sui esse* and the Aristotelian notion of a subject. That encounter allows self-certainty to be reformulated as a "subjective" certainty. That encounter presupposes in its turn a more sophisticated version of the subject/object distinction. We have two lines of investigation here.

c. The encounter between the Augustinian perichoretic model and the Aristotelian "subjectum"

The first, which seems self-evident, is the dichotomy between the subjective mode of being or presence and the objective mode of being or presence, between the *esse subjective* and the *esse objective* of an *intentio* or *conceptus*. This dichotomy does not, however, lead directly from subjectness to subjectivity. On the contrary, the idea that an intention or affect has a "subjective" existence merely likens mental states to the qualities of the soul or the accidents that befall it, and they are characterized by the relation of inherence. It therefore violates the principle of circumincession. It can be applied to acts (as in William of Ockham) or equated with the Averroist theory of the two subjects (as in Pierre d'Auriole) and remains closer to Aristotle's subjectness than to *certitudo sui esse*. Even though the opposition between objectness/objectity (*l'ob-jectité*) and sub-jectness is essential if a sub-jective notion of the ego is to emerge, it is not enough to guarantee that it will do so. We therefore have to turn to our second line of investigation.

Although it is always dangerous to give a date for the appearance of new theories in the Middle Ages, we can advance the hypothesis that one of the first people to witness the "subjective" mutation of sub-jectness was precisely the author of the formula *certitudo infallibilis sui esse*: Pierre Jean Olieu.

The Franciscan was reacting to a specific situation: the reformulation, which had become standard since the late thirteenth century, thanks to the notions of "act" and "object," of the Peripatetic doctrine that the intellect knows itself (1) in the same way that it knows other things, and (2) on the basis of its knowledge of those other things. This so-called Peripatetic formulation had in a sense already violated the

Augustinian principle stating that the *mens* cannot be regarded as the subject of acts that can be likened to mental accidents. Man is assumed to arrive at an understanding of his mind (*mens*) and of the nature of his ability to think (*naturae potentiae intellectivae*) on the basis of his acts (*per actus eius*) and the object of those acts (*per cognitionem objectorum*). This conjectural knowledge is the product of a process of reasoning that, taking objects as its starting point, works back to acts by postulating (a) that these acts subsist (*manant*) only because of the power that supplies their substrate (*ab aliqua potentia et substantia*), (b) that they therefore "exist in a subject" (*sunt in aliqui subjecto*), (c) which allows us to conclude that "we have a faculty that assures the subsistence" of those acts. Arguing against Augustine, the Peripatetics posit the existence of a "*potentia sub-jectiva*" in order to demonstrate the existence of "a subject of knowledge acts that are oriented towards objects." This conjecture, which looks to Moderns like a decisive step towards "subjectivity," is in reality what the Aristotelian model supplied: self-certainty. It actually says nothing about the ego or the I; it makes it possible to posit that my acts have a subject, but it does not establish that "I am" that subject. Nothing in the Peripatetic argument allows me "to be certain that I am, that I am alive and that I am thinking"; on the contrary, it merely posits that my acts "subsist thanks to a certain power and that they are inherent in a certain subject":

> If we carefully examine this way of thinking, we will see not only that it cannot be beyond doubt, but also that no one can use it to arrive at any certainty that he is what he is, that he is living, and that he is thinking, even though he can therefore be certain that these acts subsist by virtue of a certain power and that they reside in a certain subject.

> (*Si quis autem bene inspexerit istum modum, reperiet quod non solum potest in eo contingere aliqua dubietas, sed etiam quod nunquam per hanc viam possumus esse certi nos esse et nos vivere et intelligere, licet enim certi simus quod illi actus manant ab aliqua potentia, et sunt in aliquo subiecto.*)

(Impugnatio quorundam articulorum, art 19, f. 47ra)

In order to arrive at the self-certainty of the Moderns, we therefore have to take one more step: we must assume that I can intuit that I myself am the subject of my acts. We must, in a word, go back to Augustine's perichoretic conception of the soul and adapt the "peripatetic" language of subjectivity to it. This twofold manoeuvre brings about a forced synthesis and betrays both parties. The resultant thesis is, basically, neither Augustinian nor Aristotelian. But that is precisely why it is a farewell to "subjectness," or at least the precondition for that farewell. That is the step taken by Pierre Jean Olieu when he makes my perception of my acts depend upon "my prior perception of myself as subject of those acts." This leads him to formulate the theorem that "in the perception of my acts, the perception of the subject itself (= me) comes first according to the natural order of things." Expressions such as "*certitude qua sumus certi de supposito omnis actus scientialis*" or "*in hac apprehensione videtur naturali ordine praerie apprehensio ipsius suppositi*" signal the encounter between certainty and subjectivity that gives rise to the modern notions of subjecthood and subjective certainty. They also introduce one more basic feature: acts are likened to attributes or predicates of the subject-ego. Olieu is very clear about this: "Our acts are perceived by us only as predicates or attributes [*actus nostri non apprehenduntur a nobis nisi tamquam praedicata vel attributa*]." The subject is perceived first because "according to the natural order of things, the subject is perceived before the predicate is attributed to it as such." The "subjectivation" of the soul is now complete in every dimension, including the assumption of the linguistic or logical form of predication, which is reduplicated when Olieu introduces the word *ego* into linguistic communication. Although the term is unnecessary in Latin, Olieu in fact stresses that, when we wish to signal the existence within us of some mental state, "we put the subject first by saying '*I think that* or *I see that* [*quando volumus hoc aliis annunciare praemittimus ipsum suppositum dicentes: ego hoc cogito, vel ego hoc video*]." We could therefore describe this first medieval theorization of subjectivity as both "substantialist" and "attributivist." It entails the idea of self-intuition as "substance," or as subject and principle (*subjectum et principium*), as the "experiential and almost tactile sensation" (*sensus experimentalis et quasi tactualis*) that I am a permanent subject. We can further intuit, thanks to the same "inner sense," that my acts are so many "attributes" that are distinct from my substance. They subsist thanks to it and exist within a "becoming" mode:

> When we apprehend certain of our acts through an inner sensation, we make an almost experiential distinction between the substance whence they derive their subsistence and in which they exist, and the senses, or sensations themselves. This means that we perceive through our senses that they subsist prior to that substance and not by virtue of our senses, and that substance is substance, and that it alone is something stable that subsists in itself, whilst its acts are in a permanent state of becoming.
>
> (*Quando apprehendimus nostros actus quosdam interno sensu et quasi experimentaliter distinguimus inter substantiam a qua manant et in qua existunt et inter ipsos sensus, unde et sensibiliter percipimus quod ipsi manant et dependent ab ea, no ipsa ab eise, et quod ipsa est quiddam fixum et in se manens, ipsi vero actus in quodam continuo fierii.*)

Kant's description of the soul as it appears in rational psychology is, in any case, the full deployment of the theory outlined in the Middle Ages, thanks to a violent synthesis of two models that went on arguing over the theory of the soul until the fourteenth century: the Aristotelian model of sub-jectness, to which Heidegger restricts his analysis, and the Augustinian model of the circumincession of Persons (or hypostases), which, in this context, has been overlooked by almost all historians of the "subject."

■ See Box 5.

III. Subject: Subjectivity and Subjection

A. An untranslatable passage in Nietzsche

At the heart of the problems that are now raised by the use of the "subject" category—which has never been more central to philosophy, even though the twentieth century gave it a completely new orientation—there is a pun (intentional or otherwise) on two Latin etymologies: that of the neuter *subjectum* (which, like *suppositum*, has, ever since the Scholastics, been regarded by philosophers as a translation of the Greek *hupokeimenon*), and that of the masculine *subjectus* (equated with *subditus* in the Middle Ages). One gives rise to a lineage of logico-grammatical and ontological-transcendental meanings, and the other to a lineage of juridical, political, and theological meanings. Far from remaining independent of one another, they have constantly overdetermined one another, because, following Kant, the problematic articulation of "subjectivity" and "subjection" came to be defined as a theory of the constituent subject. That overdetermination can be overt, latent, or even repressed, depending on whether or not the language in question reveals its workings.

The best way to introduce these problems of modern philosophy is, perhaps, to read an astonishing passage from Nietzsche's *Beyond Good and Evil*. I cite the most authoritative French translation and include the German terms in parentheses.

5

The psychical trinity: I am, I know, I will

In the *Confessions*, Augustine uses the perichoretic model in his outline description of what might be termed the "psychical life" by invoking the triad of *esse, nosse, velle*. In this model Trinitarian relations permit a formal description of the interacting equalities that define the incomprehensible unity of the ego:

I am, I know, and I will. I am a being which knows and wills; I know both that I am and that I will.... In these three—being, knowledge, and will—there is one inseparable life, one life, one mind, one essence; and therefore, although they are distinct from one another, this distinction does not separate them.

(Augustine, *Confessions*, XIII, 11, 12)

In the description of the *mens-notitia-amor* triad, the doctrine of the circumincession of the persons of the Trinity is evoked even more directly in order to conceptualize the mutual in-dwelling of *mens* and its acts:

The mind, love, and knowledge ... each is a substance in itself, and all are found mutually in all, or each two in each one, consequently all are in all.... These three, therefore, are in a marvelous manner inseparable from one another; and yet each one of them is a substance, and all together are one substance or essence, while the terms themselves express a mutual relationship.

(Augustine, *On the Trinity*, IX, 5, 8)

Les philosophes ont coutume de parler de la volonté comme si c'était la chose la mieux connue au monde. . . . Un homme qui *veut* commande en lui-même a quelque chose qui obéit ou dont il se croit obéi (*befiehlt einem Etwas in sich, das gehorcht oder von dem er glaubt, dass es gehorcht*). Mais considérons maintenant l'aspect le plus singulier de la volonté, de cette chose si complexe (*vielfachen Dinge*) pour laquelle le peuple n'a qu'un mot: si, dans le cas envisagé, nous sommes à la fois celui qui commande *et* celui qui obéit (*zugleich die Befehlenden und Gehorchenden*), et si nous connaissons, en tant que sujet obéissant (*als Gehorchenden*), la contrainte, l'oppression, la résistance, le trouble, sentiments qui accompagnent immédiatement l'acte de volonté; si, d'autre part, nous avons l'habitude de nous duper nous-mêmes en escamotant cette dualité grâce au concept synthétique du "moi" (*uns über diese Zweiheit vermöge des synthetischen Begriffs "ich" hinwegzusetzen, hinwegzutäuschen*), on voit que toute une chaîne de conclusions erronées, et donc de jugements faux sur la volonté elle-même, viennent encore s'agréger au vouloir. . . . Comme dans la très grande majorité des cas, la volonté n'entre en jeu que là où elle *s'attend* à être obéi, donc à susciter un acte, on en est venu à croire, *fallacieusement,* qu'une telle conséquence était *nécessaire* (*so hat sich der Anschein in das Gefühl übersetz, als ob es da eine Notwendigkeit von Wirkung gäbe*). Bref, celui qui veut est passablement convaincu que la volonté et l'acte ne sont qu'un en quelque manière (*dass Wille und Aktion irgendwie Eins seien*). . . . "Libre arbitre," tel est le mot qui désigne ce complexe état d'euphorie du sujet voulant, qui commande et qui s'identifie à la fois avec l'exécuteur de l'action (*das Wort für jenen vielfachen Lust-Zustand des Wollenden, der befiehlt und sich zugleich mit dem Ausführenden als Eins setzt*) qui goûte au plaisir de triompher des résistances, tout en estimant que c'est sa volonté qui les surmonte. A son plaisir d'individu qui ordonne, le sujet voulant ajoute ainsi les sentiments de plaisir issus des instruments d'exécution (*Der Wollende nimmt dergestalt die Lustgefühle der ausführenden, erfolgreichen Werkzeuge*) qui sont les diligentes "sous-volontés" ou sous-âmes ("*Unterwillen" oder Unterseelen*) car notre corps n'est pas autre chose qu'un édifice d'âmes multiples (*ein Gesellschaftsbau vieler Seelen*). *L'effet, c'est moi* [in French in Nietzsche's text]: ce qui ce produit ici ne diffère pas de ce qui se passe dans toute collectivité heureuse et bien organisée: la class dirigeante s'identifie au succès de la collectivité (*dass die regierende Klasse sich mit den Erfolgen des Gemeinwesens identificiert*).

(Nietzsche, *Oeuvres philosophiques complètes,*
vol. 7, *Par-delà bien et mal,* §19)

In Hollingdale's English translation:

Philosophers are given to speaking of the will as if it were the best-known thing in the world. . . . A man who *wills*—commands something in himself which obeys or which he believes obeys. But now observe the strangest thing of all about the will—about this so complex thing for which people have only *one* word: insomuch as in

the given circumstance we at the same time command *and* obey, and the side which obeys know the sensations of constraint, compulsion, pressure, resistance, motions which usually begin immediately after the act of will; insomuch as, on the other hand, we are in the habit of disregarding and deceiving ourselves over this duality by means of the synthetic concept "I"; so a whole chain of erroneous conclusions and consequently of false evaluations of the will itself has become attached to the will as such. Because in the great majority of cases willing takes place only where the effect of the command, that is to say obedience, was to be *expected*, the *appearance* has translated itself into the sensation, as if it were here a *necessity of effect*. Enough: he who wills believes with a tolerable degree of certainty that will and action are somehow one. . . . "Freedom of will"—is the expression for that complex condition of pleasure of the person who wills, who commands and at the same time identifies himself with the executor of the command—who as such also enjoys the triumph over resistance involved but who thinks it was his will itself which overcame these resistances. He who wills adds in this way the sensations of pleasure of the successful executive agents, the serviceable "under-wills" or under-souls—"for our body is only a social structure composed of many souls"—to his sensations of pleasure as commander. *L'effet, c'est moi*: what happens here is what happens in every well-constructed and happy commonwealth: the ruling class identifies itself with the successes of the commonwealth.

It is not a matter here of challenging the choices made by the French translator (which would imply that we intended to propose alternatives) but to point out the problems they raise. We attach particular importance to the fact that Nietzsche's text itself contains some thoughts about "translation" inasmuch as it is a process of misrepresentation (*travestissement*) that has to be given a basic anthropological meaning. No less remarkable is the fact that, given the illusions of unity that are inherent in willing, the invocation of the political metaphor (if that is what it is . . .) goes hand in hand with the construction of a "French" phrase (which cannot be translated into French) that is a parodic version of the famous allegory of absolute monarchy attributed to Louis XIV ("*L'État, c'est moi*").

Two striking features of the French translation are to be noted. It systematically introduces the word *sujet* ("*sujet obéissant," "sujet voulant*") because it makes the metaphysical assumption that an *Etwas* remains the same throughout the actions of commanding and the effects of obeying and thus gets around the critique that Nietzsche's text is making, at this very moment, of the illusion of the I (*Ich*). It also plays on one of the connotations of the French *sujet* that is not present in the closest German philosophical equivalent (*das Subjekt*), and therefore uses a generic term to express the ambivalence of the real or imagined relations of subordination (*archein* [ἄρχειν] and *archeisthai*) that exist between the parts of the soul; in Nietzsche's view, they constitute the essence of the phenomenon of "will": *sujet obéissant* looks like a tautology, and *sujet voulant* almost like a contradiction. Or is it the other way around?

Far from being a mere curiosity, such a text brings us to the very heart of the linguistic tensions characteristic of the construction and use of the notion of *sujet*. Their essential characteristic derives from the Greek and Latin notions, which tend to produce two different paradigms for the interpretation of "subject," one specific to the neo-Latin languages (and especially French) and one specific to German. In one case the simultaneously logical-ontological and juridico-political connotations of *sujet* are—thanks to a sort of "historiological" word play on the meanings of *subjectum* and *subjectus*—exploited in a systematic investigation into the modalities of the "*assujettissement du sujet*" ("subjugation of the subject"). In the other case the relationship between the subject's mode of being and the register of law or power can be found exclusively in an ontology of freedom that contrasts it with nature, because the political dimension is immediately concealed by language or is, rather, relegated to the latent system. The two paradigms do not, of course, develop independently of one another, as they share the same classical references and because the more or less simultaneous translation of the works of European metaphysics is one of the main determinants of their history. In that respect it is striking that it should be the divergent readings of Nietzsche's work that bring this out.

B. Sovereignty of the subject: Bataille or Heidegger?

The first paradigm is exemplified by Georges Bataille, who was probably one of the first contemporary authors working in the French language to consciously exploit the possibility of inscribing a dialectical (or mystical) antinomy at the heart of anthropology by defining the subject in terms of its "sovereignty," or in other words its non-subjection. According to Bataille this is just a bad pun—even though his construct obviously relies upon it:

> If I have spoken of objective sovereignty, I have never lost sight of the fact that sovereignty is never truly objective, that it refers rather to deep subjectivity. . . . [In the world of things and their interdependencies] we perceive relations of force and doubtless the isolated element undergoes the influence by the mass [*la masse*], but the mass cannot *subordinate* [*subordonner*] it. Subordination presupposes another relation, that of object to subject. [Footnote: The custom of sovereigns saying "my subjects" introduces an unavoidable ambiguity: in my view the *subject* is the sovereign. The subject I am talking about is in no sense *subjected* [*assujetti*]]. The subject is the being *as he appears to himself from within. . . . The sovereign different from the others differs from them as the subject differs from the objective action of labour.* This unavoidable pun is unwelcome. I mean that the mass individual, who spends part of his time working for the benefit of the sovereign, *recognises* him; I mean that he *recognises himself* in him. The mass individual no longer sees in the sovereign the object that he must first of all be in his eyes, but rather the *subject*. . . . The sovereign, epitomizing the *subject*, is the one by whom and for whom the instant, the *miraculous* instant, is the ocean into which the streams of labour disappear.

> (Bataille, *La Part maudite* III, La Souveraineté, I, 4, in Œuvres *complètes* 8: 283–86; *The Accursed Share*, vol. 3, *Sovereignty*, pt. 1, ch. 4, 237–41; trans. amended)

The obstacle Bataille comes up against here may have influenced his decision to abandon his book. But it also provides Lacan, Althusser, and Foucault with their starting point when they transform the impasse into an opening.

The second paradigm is exemplified by Heidegger's suggestion that Nietzsche's doctrine of the "will to power" should be seen as part of the "history of being" characteristic of Western metaphysics. Nietzsche characterizes the subject that designates itself "I" (*Ich*) or "ego" as a grammatical fiction (see in particular the fragments from 1887–1889 published under the title *The Will to Power*). Heidegger, however, is trying to demonstrate that it "is grounded in the metaphysics established by Descartes," to the extent that, although he makes body rather than "soul" and "conscience" the substance of thought, he identifies the latter more closely than ever with subjectivity and makes the criterion of truth the definition of man as subject (Heidegger, *Nietzsche*, vol. 4, ch. 19, 123ff.). Heidegger's problem is how to determine, through a genealogical investigation into "metaphysics as the history of being," the preconditions for the moment of ontological conversion (which is closely linked to the mutation in the idea of truth itself) that made *subjectum*, which Latin philosophers regarded as a "translation" of Aristotle's *hupokeimenon*, not just the simple presupposition of the realization of an individual substance in a particular form, but "the" very power to think, from which all representations stem, and which reflects upon itself in the first person (*cogito me cogitare* is the key phrase attributed to Descartes by Heidegger). The "sovereignty of the subject" (*Herrschaft des Subjekts*), on which we are still dependent, is basically a creation of the Descartes of the *Meditations* and the *Principles of Philosophy*.

To begin to undo this tangle (and in doing so to elucidate at least part of the unsaid [*non-dit*] of late twentieth-century debates about the "philosophy of the subject" and the various critiques therefore), we must first restore Heidegger's construction of the history of Being as the history of successive generalizations of "subjectness" (*Subjektheit*, "I think") to the self-referentiality (or autonomy) of the transcendental subject and its retrospective attribution to Descartes and make it the starting point for the specifically modern attitude in philosophy. Despite Bataille's embarrassment about what he calls a pun, we must then reconstruct a *longue durée* semantics whose effects become ever more specific and conscious in the hands of his successors, whom it helps to unite, regardless of the obvious doctrinal disagreements. Let us begin with the first point.

C. The "Cartesian" subject: A Kantian invention

The expressions "Cartesian subject" and "Cartesian subjectivity" are so widely used and so often used to situate Cartesianism in a historical or comparative series (either in a French discourse or between French and other philosophical idioms) that it is worthwhile expounding in detail the prehistory of this construct, which is also a translation error. That error reveals the extraordinary conceptual work performed by the language itself (because of the syntactic differences between Latin, French, and German). The error is sufficiently powerful and suggestive to induce a retrospective understanding of Descartes's text and the issues at stake in his philosophy, and we can no longer ignore the issue. Thanks to Kant's reading of Descartes, we can see it as an early instance of resistance to the transcendental problematic but cannot divorce it from the language of "subjectivity." From that point of view, we cannot undo what Kant has done.

As J. Ritter judiciously reminds us, *Subjektivität* is already an important term in Baumgarten's *Aesthetics*. It refers to the field and quality of phenomena that, in the thinking, perceiving, and sentient being, are the effect not of the external objects that affect it but of its own dispositions (they are what Locke or Malebranche would call "secondary qualities"). Ritter's suggestion to the contrary notwithstanding, the use of *subjectum*, or rather *Subjekt*, in German does not, however, precede this abstract conceptual formation; it comes later. It is in fact only with the *Critique of Pure Reason* that *das Subjekt* (variously described as the "logical subject," the "empirical subject," the "rational subject," the "transcendental subject," or the "moral subject") becomes the key concept in a philosophy of subjectivity. Kant's philosophy therefore simultaneously "invents" the problematic of a thought whose conditions of access to both the objectivity of the laws of nature and the universality of ethical and aesthetic values lie in its own constitution (the so-called "Copernican revolution") and gives the name "subject" (i.e., the opposite of "object") to the generic individuality inherent in the interplay between the faculties of knowledge; for all finite minds that interplay constitutes "the world" and gives a meaning to the fact of acting in the world. Even if we take into account its remarkable forerunners (such as that identified by A. de Libera in the work of the "brilliant" twelfth-century Franciscan, Pierre Jean Olieu; see above), who were in all probability not known to Kant, the only intrinsic connection between the *Subjekt* created by Kant and the scholastic notion of the *subjectum* or *suppositum* is that implied by the idea of the Copernican revolution: the categories, or in other words, the most general modalities that the activity of judgment uses to attribute predicates to things, are no longer genera of being, but categories of the subject, constitutive of the object (and, in that sense, of experience in general: "transcendentals").

Why, in these conditions, did Kant retrospectively project this discovery on to a "precursor," namely Descartes? For over two hundred years he has lent credence to the idea that the subject is a Cartesian invention and has thus encouraged even the greatest thinkers to look for traces of a semantic mutation in terms that are almost never used by the philosopher of the *Meditations*. The answer lies, as so often, in the letter of the text itself. We will compare three passages from the *Critique of Pure Reason* ("Transcendental Deduction" and "Paralogisms of Pure Reason"). It has to be said that they are still not easy to translate.

1. Das: *Ich denke*, muss alle meine Vorstellungen begleiten können; denn sonst würde etwas in mir vorgestellt werden, was gar nicht gedacht werden könnte. . . . Also hat alles Mannigfaltige der Anschauung eine notwendige Beziehung auf das: *Ich denke*, in demselben Subjekt, darin dieses Mannigfaltige angetroffen wird. Diese Vorstellung aber ist ein Aktus der Spontaneität, sie kann nicht als zur Sinnlichkeit gehörig angesehen werden. Ich nenne sie die reine Apperzeption . . . weil

sie dasjenige Selbstbewusstsein ist, was, indem es die Vorstellung *Ich denke* hervorbringt, die alle anderen muss begleiten können, und in allem Bewusstsein ein und dasselbe ist, von keiner weiter begleitet werden kann.

(The *I think* must be able to accompany all my representations; for otherwise something would be represented in me which could not be thought at all. . . . Thus all manifold of intuition has a necessary relation to the *I think* in the same subject in which this manifold is to be encountered. But this representation is an act of *spontaneity*; i.e., it cannot be regarded as belonging to sensibility. I call it the *pure apperception* . . . since it is that self-consciousness which, because it produces the representation *I think*, which must be able to accompany all others and in which all consciousness is one and the same, cannot be accompanied by any further representation.

(Kant, *Critique of Pure Reason*, Transcendental Logic, §12, B 132)

2. *Ich,* als denkend, bin ein Gegenstand des inneren Sinnes, und heisse Seele. . . . Demnach bedeutet der Ausdruck: Ich, als ein denkend Wesen, schon den Gegenstand der Psychologie. . . . Ich denke, ist also der alleinige Text der rationale Psychologie, aus welchem sie ihre ganze Weisheit auswickeln soll. Man sieht leicht, dass dieser Gedanke, wenn er auf einen Gegenstand (mich selbst) bezogen werden soll, nichts anderes, als transzendentale Prädikate desselben, enthalten könne. . . . Zum Grunde derselben können wir aber nichts anderes legen, als die einfache und für sich selbst an Inhalt gänzlich leere Vorstellung: Ich; von der man nicht einmal sagen kann, dass sie ein Begriff sei, sondern ein blosses Bewusstsein, dass alle Begriffe begleitet. Durch dieses, Ich, oder Er, oder Es (das Ding), welches denkt, wird nun nichts weiter, als ein transzendentales Subjekt der Gedanken vorgestellt = x, welches nur durch die Gedanken, die seine Prädikate sind, erkannt wird.

(*I,* as thinking, am an object of inner sense, and am called "soul." Accordingly, the expression "I," as a thinking being, already signifies the object of a psychology. . . . *I think* is thus the sole text of a rational psychology, from which it is to develop its entire wisdom. One can easily see that this thought, if it is to be related to object (myself), can contain nothing other than its transcendental predicates. . . . At the ground of this doctrine we can place nothing but the simple and in content for itself wholly empty representation *I*, of which one cannot even say that it is a content, but a mere consciousness that accompanies every concept. Through this I, or He, or It (the thing), which thinks, nothing further is represented than a transcendental subject of thought = x, which is recognized through the thoughts that are its predicates.)

(Kant, *Critique of Pure Reason*, Paralogisms of Pure Reason, A 342, 343, 345–46)

3. Der Satz: *Ich denke*, wird aber hierbei nur problematisch genommen; nicht sofern er eine Wahrnehmung von einem Dasein enthalten mag (das kartesianische *cogito ergo sum*), sondern seiner blossen Möglichkeit nach, um zu sehen, welche Eigenschaften aus diesem so einfachen Satze auf das Subjekt desselben (es mag dergleichen nun existieren oder nicht) fliessen mögen. Läge unserer reinen Vernunftserkenntnis von denkenden Weser überhaupt mehr, als das *cogito* zum Grunde . . . so würde eine empirische Psychologie entspringen.

(The proposition "I think" is, however, taken here only problematically; not in so far as it may contain a perception of an existence (the Cartesian *cogito ergo sum*), but only in its mere possibility, in order to see which properties might flow from so simple a proposition as this for its subject (whether or not such a thing might now exist). If more than the cogito were the ground of our pure rational cognition of things in general . . . then an empirical psychology would arise.)

(Kant, *Critique of Pure Reason*,
Paralogisms of Pure Reason, A 347)

Leaving aside the remarkable alternation between the pronouns (*Ich, Er, Es*; see I/ME/MYSELF), we can see that Kant is doing one thing while claiming to do another. He attributes to Descartes a nominalization of the statement *cogito*, or "I think," so as to make it the name of a self-referential operation whereby thought takes itself as its own object; the full formula should be "I am thinking that I am thinking that I am thinking." It therefore designates the "something" or the "being" that both intends and is intended by thought as a *subject* (*subjectum*, which Kant transcribes as *Subjekt*) in the sense that classical metaphysics defines a subject as a pole or support for the attribution of predicates. Kant thereby suggests to his successors (Fichte, Hegel) that the only conceivable subject (*hupokeimenon*) is a subject that thinks itself and whose predicates are its thoughts. From the Cartesian point of view these two operations are contradictory, as we can see if we go back to the text of the *Meditations*. Strictly speaking, there is no nominalization of the simple phrase *cogito/ je pense* in Descartes (it first appears in Arnauld's *Des vraies et des fausses idées*), even though the way it reflects upon the properties of its own proper enunciation anticipates it. The transition to the metaphysical subject is, on the other hand, incompatible with the *cogito* in the strict sense (in the *Meditations* it is reduced to the existential proposition "*je suis, j'existe*"). The *cogito* is in fact inseparable from a first-person statement (*ego*), which Descartes contrasts with the "he/it" (*il/ille*) of God and the "this" (*hoc*) of his own body (in a problematic of identity or ego: "*Ce moi, c'est-à-dire mon âme, par laquelle je suis ce que je suis*"—"Thus this self (*moi*), that is to say the soul, by which I am what I am," *Discours de la méthode, Sixième Méditation; Philosophical Writings, 32*). "I think" is equivalent to "I am," which is then developed into "I am who I am," or in other words, my soul (*mens*) and not Him (God) or that (my body). We have here a misunderstanding—which has very serious implications as, reading through Kantian spectacles, the whole of transcendental philosophy, right down to Husserl and Heidegger, constantly criticizes

Descartes for having "substantialized the subject" in the very moment of its discovery. As we now know, transcendental philosophy reads Descartes as though he were a medieval thinker (Olieu) but has nothing to say about the philosophy of the Middle Ages.

The misunderstanding arises, basically, because Kant finds it difficult to situate in historical terms an idea that is revolutionary in philosophical terms and that is a concentrate of all the originality of his own "transcendental dialectic" and that differs from both the "subjectness" of Aristotelian metaphysics (*todi ti, hupokeimenon, ousia*) and the "ipseity" of the Cartesian "thing that thinks" (*ego ipse a me percipior*): that of the truth of the perceptive appearance inherent in thought. According to Kant, we cannot think (form concepts, subsume intuitions, etc.) without our inner sense being affected and without, therefore, giving rise to the illusion that there is an "inner reality" that is itself the object of thought: the thinking "self" recognizes itself in its logical function (unifying experience) to the extent that it constantly misrecognizes itself because it believes it can be known (as a phenomenon, literally a "that which appears" in the scene of representation: *erscheint*) (see ERSCHEINUNG). Now, in Kant, "substance" is no longer of the order of being or of the Thing "in itself." Substance is no more than the concept of that which remains permanent in phenomena. Kant therefore explains to us that the *subject*, which in itself (qua potentiality or logical faculty) is nothing substantial because it is in no sense phenomenal, constantly *appears to itself* in the modality of a substance as it thinks (itself) and because it thinks (itself). In the *Transcendental Deduction*, Kant writes: "I am conscious of myself not as I appear to myself, nor as I am in myself, but only that I am" (B 155). The "I," which is given only in a form that is inseparable from an "I think" statement, which also functions as its "proper," or in other words generic, name, can be apprehended (*en s'effectant lui-même*) only in an illusory mode. But this illusion or transcendental appearance (*Schein*) is the only thing that can deliver a primal truth and the only possible form of ground. In one sense it is the truth itself. "Subject" is the word that now denotes this astonishing unity of opposites. And Kant attributes to Descartes the metaphysical illusion he himself claims to have escaped. Descartes's "error" is testimony to the fact that the false lies at the heart of the true.

It does seem that we are dealing here exclusively with epistemological propositions and the experience of thought—and it should be noted that the enunciation's syntactic forms and the translations or transpositions play a determinant role. There is nothing to evoke openly a "practical" and, a fortiori, "political" dimension of the subject. This is not, however, certain when we look at two characteristics of the arguments we have just described. The first is that Kant's *subject* (the *Ich* or, to be more accurate, the *Ich denke*) is basically caught up in a relationship of ascription. The reflexivity ascribes to it, or it ascribes to itself, a representation that is both truth and error, recognition and misrecognition. The second is that this circle of apperception results in an injunction. It is not only tempting but necessary to compare this injunction with the very form of the categorical imperative: we are enjoined to free our own representation from phenomenalism (or, which comes down to the same thing, substantialism) in order to relate it to the idea of "pure" intellectual activity. Now as such an idea is meaningless in terms of nature, it is only as a correlate of freedom that it can acquire a meaning. This is the way the study of the "Paralogisms of Pure Reason" ends: the transcendental *subject* (the reflexive identity of the self or *Selbst*) is identified with the moral "personality" (*Persönlichkeit*): "a possible subject of a better world, which he has in its idea" (B 426).

In historical terms, one would like to be able to relate this substratum of Kant's thought to the "becoming a subject" of the revolutionary and postrevolutionary citizen, and especially to the establishment of the category of a "subject of law" (*Rechtssubjekt*) of which we do not, as yet, have a sufficiently clear idea. In a recent study, Yves-Charles Zarka notes in Leibniz, in contrast, a problematic of justice and equity that requires everyone to "put himself in the place of all," the emergence of the expression *subjectum juris*, in the sense of a "moral quality" that universalizes its bearer. But we also know that, even when he seems to come closest to defining the idea of it (as in the *Doctrine of Right* of 1795, where the divisions of right are deduced from the subjective relationship between the obligors and the obligees, Kant (and Hegel after him) never uses the expression *Rechtssubjekt*, which seems to appear only with the *Historical School of Law* (Savigny, Hugo, Puchta). These subjects (*Subjekte*), in "relation to whom" obligations can be conceptualized (and who "relate" those obligations to themselves) have strictly nothing to do with political *subjects* (*Untertan*, which Kant equates with the Latin *subditus*), who obey a sovereign (which may be the people, as constituted into a state). The encounter with the thematic of sovereignty and the law implicit in the idea of a liberation of the subject, and of the subject as one "he who frees himself," therefore remains repressed.

■ See Box 6.

D. Subjectivity à la française

It is, in contrast, possible to interpret the way in which contemporary philosophy—and especially contemporary French philosophy—understands the question of subjectivity: not as a question of essence, or as relating being to truth and appearance, or in the metaphysical opposition between nature and liberty, but as a political issue, a becoming or a relationship between forces that are "internal" to their conflict.

From the point of view of the history of ideas and words, we should obviously establish a certain number of intermediary links, but we can do no more than evoke them here. First and foremost, there is Rousseau. The two sides of his work and the corresponding turns of phrase leave traces everywhere. Think of the way *The Social Contract* establishes a strict correlation between the figures of the "citizen" who is a member of the sovereign (or, in other words, the author of the law) and the "subject," who finds freedom in absolute obedience to that same law thanks to the "total alienation" of individual wills that gives rise to a general will. That will founds a "collective ego" that is reflected in every individual consciousness (in *The Phenomenology of Mind*, Hegel makes explicit reference to Rousseau when he speaks of "*Ich, das Wir, und Wir, das Ich ist*"; see I/ME/MYSELF). Think too of the way in which Rousseau's autobiographical works associate the

theme of the authenticity of the ego with that of subjection (*l'assujettissement*):

> There is not a day when I do not recall with joy and emotion that unique and brief time in my life when I was completely me, when nothing prevented me from being truly myself and when I could say that I was alive. . . . I could not bear subjection [*assujettissement*], I was completely free, and more than free because I was subject [*assujetti*] only to my affections, and I did only what I wanted to do.
>
> (Rousseau, *Rêveries du promeneur solitaire* (dixième promenade))

We then have to take into account the revolutionary caesura, which not only has the effect of allowing the citizen (who is entitled to have political rights) to "take over" from the subject (*subjectus, subditus*) but also of allowing the subject (*subjectum*) to evolve into a citizen in the sense that his humanity is naturalized. This inscribes all anthropological differences (age, gender, culture, health, abilities, morality, etc.) in an "individual character," which determines the subject's social recognition, with which the subject identifies (to a greater or lesser extent) in the course of his education. Together with the Rousseauist theorem and the Hegelian or Nietzschean critiques that have been made of it, it is the historical and political precondition for Bataille's subversion of the relationship between sovereignty and subjectivity. Such (at least according to our hypothesis) is the genealogy of the identification of the *problem of subjectivity* with the *problem of subjection*, which will give a completely new meaning to the philosophical question of the subject (and at the same time our perception of its history).

Gilles Deleuze refers to this issue in his *Empiricism and Subjectivity*:

> It is the same difference [between the origin and the qualification of ideas] that Hume encounters under the form of an antinomy of knowledge: it defines the problem of the self [*moi*]. The mind is not subject: it is subjected. When the subject is constituted in the mind under the effect of principles, the mind apprehends itself as a self [*moi*], for it has been qualified. But the problem is this: if the subject is constituted only inside the collection of ideas, how can the collection of ideas be apprehended as a self, how can I say "I" under the influence of those same principles.
>
> (Deleuze, *Empiricism and Subjectivity*, 31)

Later (with Guattari), he carefully works upon the paradigms of servitude or slavery (*asservissement, servus*) and subjection or subjugation (*subjectus, subditus*) in order to explain the characteristic modernity of the capitalist subject:

> We distinguish machinic enslavement and social subjection as two separate concepts. There is enslavement when human beings themselves are constituent pieces of a machine . . . under the control and direction of a higher unity. But there is subjection when the higher unity constitutes the human being as a subject linked to a now exterior object. . . . It would appear, then, that the

6

Subject, thing, person

➤ ACTOR, *DROIT*, ESSENCE, LEX

Everyday language tends to assimilate the notion of "subject" to that of "person," and this appears to contradict interpretations of subjectness (*subjectité*) in terms of subjection or domination. Livy (*History of Rome*, VII, 2) traces *persona* back to the fourth century BC, and the term is basically political, referring to a "representation" that is assigned through a role. Thanks to this double metonymy, which moves from the mask worn by an actor to the role he is interpreting, and then to Cicero's definition of the magistrate as "spokesman" (*per-sona*) of the *civitas,* or one who "assumes the role" of the city ("*est proprium munus magistratus intelligere se gerere personam civitas* [It is . . . the particular function of a magistrate to realize that he assumes the role of the city]," *On Duties,* I, 34). This makes the magistrate nothing more than the voice of the law (conversely, the law is a "silent magistrate," *De Legibus*, III, 2). The *persona* is basically juridical; the first to hold it is the assembled Roman people, which, to the extent that it has a literal right to speak, is a de facto and de jure "person." Given that "*nul n'étant censé ignorer la loi* [ignorance of the law is no excuse]," a Roman citizen is a *persona*. The city is the supreme citizen or "supremely a persona" (*persona civitas*), and the magistrate is the persona of a person (*persona personae*). There therefore appears to be a hidden link between "person" and the dimension of subjection that is present in the notion of "subject." *Persona,* that is, provides the backdrop for the distinction between the free man (*caput*) and the slave (*servus*); it allows the distinction between autonomy and juridical hetermony. As the jurisconsult Gaius writes (ca. 135) "*Quaedam personae sui juris sunt, quedam allieno juris subjectae sunt* [some persons are *sui juris* (independent) and others are *alieni juris* (dependent on others)]" (*Institutes* I, 48). The history of "persona" is, in etymological terms, bound up with that of "role" (a political, juridical, social, or even ethical role) and with the emergence of "subjectivity"—subjection. In philosophical terms, however, "persona" is closely bound up with the phenomena of the translations and transpositions associated with the mutation of Aristotle's *hupokeimenon* [ὑποκείμενον] into *subjectum*.

Philosophical definitions of "person" first appear in the context of the controversies over Trinitarian theology that occurred in late antiquity. In chapter 3 of the *Contra Eutychen et Nestorium*, Boethius (84, 4–5) defines "person" as an "individual substratum endowed with a rational nature [*naturae rationabilis individua substantia*]." This definition provides the backdrop for the philosophical encounter between subjectness and personality. Yet Boethius uses not *hupokeimenon* but *hupostasis,* a term that is even more ambiguous and difficult to elucidate. In order to make the strange Trinitarian notion of "person" comprehensible to *Latini*, Aristotle's translator assumes that he first has to explain what the Greeks call *hupostasis*. The Latin word *persona*—which he regards as equivalent to the Greek *prosôpon* [πρόσωπον], even though the term refers to an optical model, to a visible representation such as the face of the law or the polis, rather than to a voice or to speech—does not, in his view, express what is at stake in the notion he is trying construct. And how indeed could a Latin speaker living in the 520s understand something of the Trinitarian mystery by using a term that evokes someone appearing on stage in a mask, the role that intervenes in the ethical formulation of "life choices" (in the sense in which Cicero writes: "*Ipsi autem* gerere *quam* personam *velimus a nostra voluntate profisicitur* [it is through a voluntary decision that we adopt the *role* we claim to be playing]"), or the death mask that wards off demons? The Greeks have the "much more expressive" (*longe signatus*) term *hupostasis,* which allows them to express the fundamental feature: the "individual subsistence of a nature [*naturae individuam subsistentiam*]" (Boethius).

Because of the initial hesitation over "substance" or "subsistence," Boethius's definition of "person" reveals the constituent features of the various medieval networks that use different combinations of "subject," *suppôt,* "thing," and "person."

The important thing here is the clarification of the distinction between subsistence and substance. Given that Boethius translates *ousia* as "essential," *ousiôsis* [οὐσίωσις] as *subsistentia,* and *hupostasis* as *substantia,* the first step is to make a systematic distinction between the three terms. This can be done by showing that an entity such as man has *ousia* or "essence" because he is; he has *ousiôsis* or "subsistence," because he is "in" no subject (is not, that is to say, an accident), and has *hupostasis* or "substance" because he is "subjected to others" who are not subsistencies (who are, that is, "accidents"). The second step is to demonstrate that that which is not accident, but which is a substrate for accidents, or in other words that which is a subsistence, "is" at the level of the universal, but "acquires substance," or in other words functions as a substance (as a substrate for accidents) in particulars ("*ipsae subsistentiae in universalibus quidem sint, in particularibus vero capiant substantiam*"). According to the Greeks, "substances subsisting in particulars" deserve to be called "substances" in the strict sense ("*iure subsistentias particulariter substantes* [ὑπόστασις] *appelaverunt*," ibid., 86, 35–8, 39). What Boethius calls a "hypostasis" or substance is therefore that which founds the particular existence of a nature, or which makes possible for its particularization and its existence, which are inseparable.

Quite apart from the way Aristotle's *hupokeimenon* mutates into *subjectum,* we must also make allowances for the way *hupostasis* mutates into *substantia,* if we are to understand the emergence of the personal dimension of subjectivity within the domain of Trinitarian theology. The history of the Latin reception of the Greek formula—"one essence in three hypostases"—provides the framework for a series of developments that are of great importance to the subjectness/subjectivity system. The replacement of the obscure term *substantia* by the word *res* or "thing" in the eleventh century is one of the hidden reasons for the philosophical debate between the realists and the nominalists. This also provided the framework for the first medieval reflections on the notion of *suppositum,* which affected grammar, logic, and theology alike. If we also recall that the formula "have *hypostasis* (in)," which Boethius translates into Latin as *habere substantiam (in)* was the pre-Scholastic way of expressing existence, we can see that this is also the theme that introduces ontology (the difference between essence and existence), which was initially part of Trinitarian theology's conceptual network.

From this perspective "subjective" is not the opposite of "objective" in the same way that "perceiving" is the opposite of "perceived," or that "inner world" is the opposite of "outside world." When we encounter the terms *subjectum* or *subjectivum* in medieval texts on psychology, we therefore have to take care not to interpret them in the sense of "subjective subject" or "ego-ness." Medieval philosophers were concerned with something very different, namely the substrate, *sub-jectum* or *suppôt* of thought. The way *subjectum* is used in the sphere of subjectness explains why authors such as Averroës give human thought two subjects. To ask what is the subject of thought is to raise questions about what it is that founds the *intentio intellecta* as an act *commun*. Averroës's answer—the imagination, which is a faculty situated in the body and numbered by it, and the "material" intellect, which is separate from the body and not numbered by it—is inscribed within what we would now call a "modular" psychology and therefore does not assimilate the *subjectum* to the *ego*.

BIBLIOGRAPHY

Boethius. *The Theological Tractates with an English translation*. Edited by H. F. Stewart and E. K. Rand.

Translated by H. F. Stewart, E. K. Rand, and S. J. Tester. Loeb Classical Library. Cambridge, MA: Harvard University Press, 1973.

Cicero. *On Duties*. Translated by M. T. Griffin and E. M. Atkins. Cambridge: Cambridge University Press, 1991.

Kantorowicz, Ernst. *Frederick the Second*. London: 1931.

Ullmann, Walter. *The Individual and Society in the Middle Ages*. Baltimore, MD: Johns Hopkins University Press, 1966.

modern State, through technological development, has substituted an increasingly powerful social subjection for machinic enslavement. . . . In effect, capital acts as the point of subjectification that constitutes human beings as subjects; but some, the "capitalists," are subjects of enunciation that form the private subjectivity of capital, while the others, the "proletarians," are subjects of the statement, subjected to the technical machines in which constant capital is effectuated.

(Deleuze and Guattari, *Thousand Plateaus*, 456–57)

Jacques Derrida discovers this constitutive amphibology from Rousseau onwards:

From then on, writing has the function of reaching subjects who are not only distant but outside the entire field of vision and beyond earshot.

Why subjects? Why should writing be another name for the constitution of subjects and, so to speak, of constitution itself? Of a subject, that is to say an individual held responsible (for) himself in front of a law and by the same token subject to that law?

(Derrida, *Of Grammatology*, 281)

He also finds it in connection with Levinas:

The subordination of freedom obviously means a subjection of the *subjectum,* but this is a subjection which, rather than depriving him of it, gives the subject both his birth and the freedom it orders in this way. It is indeed a subjection, not in the sense of internalization but, rather, in the sense of a coming-to-self of the subject [*une venue du sujet à soi*] in the movement in which he greets the Quite Other [*tout autre*] as the All Mighty [*Très-Haut*]. This subordination orders and gives [*ordonne et donne*] the subject's subjectivity.

(Derrida, *Adieu*)

But he also tries to force it to the point of implosion and, to adopt Artaud's neologism, to "derange the subjectile [*forcener le sujectile*]."

Writing at the same time as Bataille, Louis Althusser also emphasizes the paradox of sovereignty:

This God is a King-Subject, or in other words a King-Slave. Hegelian freedom frees the subject from his subjection and converts his servitude into a kingdom. The concept is the kingdom of subjectivity, or in other words the subject who has become a King. . . . Such is the circularity of freedom in the concept: it is the

conversion of servitude, the conversion of the subject into its kingdom.

(Althusser, "On Content," 90, trans. amended)

He sees this as the general mechanism whereby ideology "interpellates" individuals as subjects. The prototype is supplied by religious consciousness:

It then emerges that the interpellation of individuals as subjects presupposes the "existence" of a Unique and central Other Subject, in whose Name the religious ideology interpellates all individuals as subjects. . . . God then defines himself as the Subject *par excellence*, he who is through himself and for himself ("I am that I am"), and he who interpellates his subject, the individual subjected to him by his very interpellation, i.e., the individual named Moses. And Moses, interpellated-called by his Name, having recognized that it "really" was he who was called by God, recognizes that he is a subject, a subject *of* God, a subject subjected to God, *a subject through the Subject and subjected to the subject. The proof: he obeys him, and makes his people obey.*

(Althusser, "Ideology and Ideological State Apparatuses," 167)

It is Lacan and Foucault who deploy the specter of subjectivity as a process of subjugation most systematically. But they do so in diametrically opposed ways.

Lacan draws upon the old heritage of two French phrases that are at once paradoxical but absolutely idiomatic: "the ego is hateful" (Pascal) and "I is an other" (Rimbaud). What is the subject, according to Lacan? Nothing more than the sequential effects of the living individual's alienation by the "law of the signifier." While it has to be regarded as irreducible, the subject is never originary, but always already dependent. The subject exists only as an effect of the speech (*parole*) that constitutes it (and names it, to begin with) in a symbolic world of discourses and institutions that it cannot, by definition, master. This is how Lacan interprets the "misrecognition" that constitutes the unconscious. Because it is "subject [*soumis*] to the signifier" that irremediably cut it off from itself, the subject must forever oscillate between the illusion of identity—the narcissistic beliefs of a "imaginary capture" are resumed in the figure of the *ego*—and the unknown element in the conflict: the recognition of a question from the other (beginning with the other sex) as to what is most characteristic about it.

If desire is an effect in the subject of the condition—which is imposed on him by the existence of discourse—that his need pass through the defiles of the signifier . . . the subject [must] find the constitutive structure of his desire in the same gap opened up by the effect of signifiers in those who come to represent the Other for him, in so far as his demand is subjected to them.

(Lacan, *Écrits*, 525)

At best, analysis inverts the trajectory of the constitution of desire, which leads the subject to enunciate his own "lack of being" ("desire merely subjugates what analysis subjectifies," 520).

Foucault, for his part, found in the methods used to obtain admissions and confessions (which migrate from religion and the inquisition to psychology and psychiatry) a model for the relationship between subjectivity, appearance, and truth (*Madness and Civilization, History of Sexuality*). In Bentham's panopticism he finds an ideal diagram of all the "fictive relations" (which are materialized in the working of institutions of social normalization) in which "a real subjection is born mechanically" (*Discipline and Punish*, 202). On this basis, he drew up a program for an investigation into the "modes of objectification that transform human beings into subjects" and especially relations of power ("The Subject and Power," 326). But there is no power, either over the "self" or over "others," that does not involve the constitution of a knowledge (*un savoir*), and knowledge itself is not a purely theoretical activity: it is a social practice that produces objectivity. The question of the subject and that of the object, brought back to a twofold process of subjectivation and objectification, of the subordination (*assujettissement*) of the individual to rules and the construction of a self-to-self relationship that takes various practical modalities, are therefore not opposed to each another. They are two aspects of a single reality:

Foucault has now undertaken, still within the same general project, to study the constitution of the subject as an object for himself: the formation of procedures by which the subject is led to observe himself, analyse himself, recognize himself as a domain of possible knowledge. In short, this concerns the history of "subjectivity," if what is meant by that term is the way in which the subject experiences himself in a game of truth where he relates to himself.

(Foucault, "Foucault," 461)

These are the very words that were used in the *Transcendental Dialectic*, but their original meaning has been inverted. We can see that there is a circle of presuppositions; the *subject* is the set of subjecting or subjectifying structures (*dispositifs d'assujettissement ou de subjectivation*) that act objectively on the "subjectivity" of the individual. They presuppose, that is, the subject's "freedom," or ability to resist, and turn it against him. We are, in other words, talking about a power differential. It results in both a politics (trying to free the individual from certain disciplines and certain types of individualism) and an ethics (inventing "practices of freedom," "new power relations," and modes of *askesis* rather than of self-consciousness). Precisely because they are dispersed and conflicting, these propositions

transform our reading of Europe's philosophical past. Because they reveal the associations and metaphors that underlie Nietzsche's text, they allow us to make different use of the subjectivity defined in the *Critique of Pure Reason*. Had an internal relationship not been established between the subject (*subjectum, Subjekt*) and personal subjection, and therefore with the political, juridical, and theological power of which it is an effect and inverted image, we would not be able to recognize in the paradoxical combination of truth and transcendental appearance described in the "Paralogisms of Pure Reason" the sign of an originary difference (or *différance*) that concerns the ethics of internal obedience and *askesis* as much as the metaphysics of the mind and self-consciousness, if not more so. To conclude, they reopen the question of the active finitude specific to the Cartesian subject (or non-subject), which is, perhaps, not so much a "nature" or thinking "substance," or in other words a representation, as a "demand" (as Canguilhem puts it) for the right to say "I," "between infinity and nothingness," or between God and the body.

E. How should we translate French philosophers?

To conclude what is not so much a history of translations as that of the *split* that has occurred in philosophical language as each idiom works on the basis of its own relationship with the juridical, theological, and metaphysical heritage of European culture, we can ask two questions. First, can what we have termed a new "idiomatic French" grounding of the problematic of the subject in French be translated into other idioms? Second, does the philosophy that in the twentieth century provided the framework for its invention have any choice but to go on repeating its terms ad infinitum, or can it purely and simply break with it by adopting other paradigms (such as that of analytic individuality) and more or less adequately "Gallicizing" their discourse?

A few summary remarks must suffice here. The *sujétion-subjectivation* paradigm can obviously be translated into the other Romance languages, give or take a few minor differences in the current usage of *soggetto* and *suddito*, *sujeto* or *sugeto* and *subdeto*, as both Italian and Spanish have retained the doublet (even though the Spanish introduces a significantly variant spelling).

■ See Boxes 7 and 8.

Modern Greek, which has retained *hypokeimeno* for *subject*, has forged *hypokeimenotêta* for *subjectivité*, can translate *sujétion* and *assujettissement* by expressions such as *hypotagê* and *hypodoulôusê*, though there could be some confusion with servitude or slavery.

Strictly speaking, this discourse cannot be translated into German. The only possible translation of *sujétion* is *Unterwerfung* (*soumission*; "submission"), whereas *subjectivation* translates as *Subjektivierung*. A revelatory example is supplied by Habermas in his *Der philosophische Diskurs der Moderne* (1996), a collection of twelve lectures devoted mainly to contemporary French philosophy (Bataille, Derrida, and Foucault). Here are two samples:

Für Bataille öffnet sich mit dieser Idee der Entgrenzung eine ganz andere Perspektive als für Heidegger: die sich selbst überschreitende Subjektivität wird nicht

7

Subjectus/subjectum: the historial pun

➤ OIKONOMIA, POLIS, *POWER*, RIGHT/JUST/GOOD

The English "subject," the French *sujet,* the Spanish *sujeto,* and the Italian *soggetto* immediately reveal what the German *Subjekt* cannot evoke because of the differences between it and *Untertan.* They have a twofold etymology: *subjectum,* which is a support for individual properties, and *subjectus,* meaning "subject to" a law or power. "Subject" implies both presupposition and subjection, the answer to the question "what?" and the answer to the question "who?" It is my considered view that this linguistic fact has played a determining role in the development of Western philosophy, and I have, parodying certain French translations of Heidegger, spoken of a historial (*historial*) pun whose effects can be traced from Hobbes to Foucault, via Rousseau, Hegel, Nietzsche, and Bataille.

"Subject" was not originally one of the words with "antithetical" meanings that so fascinated Freud. But it has become one, and the result is that freedom and constraint now look like two sides of the same coin. The origins of this overdetermination are, inevitably, Greek, even though the structural analogy between the terms *hupokeimenon* (substrate or support) and *hupostasis* (meaning ground or substance until it became the Greek Fathers' technical term for the "persons" of the Trinity [*hupêkoos* (ὑπήκοος): "he who obeys the word," the servant, the disciple, or the vassal who pays tribute]) can have a retrospective effect on our imaginations. They have never been theoretical "neighbors." We have to turn to Latin or, in other words, to imperial and Christian Rome, and then to the history of the theologico-political and of a moral anthropology centered on obedience as the path to salvation.

The *subjectus* is a juridical figure with a history lasting seventeen hundred years, from Roman law to absolute monarchy. This raises the question of how we can go from an enumeration of the individuals who are subject to the power of an other, to a representation of the human race as a set of *subjects.* The distinction between independent and dependent persons was basic to Roman law. A text from Gaius is sufficient reminder of that:

> Next comes another division in the law of persons. For some persons are *sui juris* (independent) and others are *alieni juris* (dependent on others). Again, of those *alieni juris* some are *in potestas*, others *in manu,* and others *in mancipium.* Let us consider first persons *alieni juris,* for, knowing them, we shall at the same time know who are *sui juris.*

> (Gaius, *Institutes* I, 48–50)

It is the dialectical division of forms of subjection that gives us, *a contrario,* a definition of free men or masters. But the notions of *potestas, manus,* and *mancipium* are not enough for that division to create a link *between* subjects. What is needed is an *imperium.* The idea of a universal subjection therefore emerges with the empire (and in relation to the person of the emperor to whom citizens, and many noncitizens, owe *officium* or "service"). But that is still not a sufficient precondition: Romans must (if they have not already done so) submit to the *imperium* in the same way that conquered peoples "submit to the people of Rome" (the incipient confusion emerges in contradictory fashion when the personal status of "Roman citizen" extends to the entire empire). And, above all, the *imperium* must be theologically founded as a Christian *imperium,* as a spiritual power derived from and preserved by God, and reigning not over bodies but over (and in) souls.

Understood in this sense, the subject (the subject of law) is the absolute opposite of what will later be termed the *Rechtssubjekt* (a subject by right or with rights, *sujet de droit).* The *sujet de droit* has two main characteristics: he is a *subditus* but not a *servus.* To describe the subject as *subditus* is to say that he enters into a relation of obedience. Obedience is not only something that applies between a leader who has the power to coerce and those who are under his power; it also describes the relationship between a *sublimis* who is elected as commander and the *subditi* or *subjecti* who turn to him to hear what the law states. The ability or power (*pouvoir*) to coerce is distributed throughout a hierarchy of powers (*puissances*). Obedience is the principle that ensures that all who obey are members of the same body. Although it is concentrated at the top in the figure of a *principium/princeps,* it basically comes from below; insofar as they are *subditi,* subjects "will" their own obedience, which is inscribed within the economy of creation and salvation. The "loyal subject" (*fidèle sujet*) is of necessity a "faithful subject" or "believer" (*sujet fidèle*) who knows that all power comes from God.

Such obedience, in its theoretical unity and its innumerable forms, therefore implies the notion of a commandant (*archôn* [ἄρχων]), but being commanded (*archomenos* [ἀρχόμενος]) then implies—at least in a democratic *politeia*—the possibility of becoming a commander (this is Aristotle's definition of the citizen); alternatively, it is a domestic-style natural dependence. In that

perspective, the very idea of "free obedience" is a contradiction in terms. That a slave can "also" be free is a late (Stoic) idea that has to be understood as meaning that he who is a slave in this world can also be a master (of himself and his passions) in another world (a "cosmic" city of spirits); he can also be a citizen who is bound to others by reciprocal ties (*philia* [φιλία]: see LOVE). There is nothing here to suggest the idea of a freedom that resides in obedience or that results from obedience. For that to be conceivable, obedience must cease to pertain to the soul and must cease to be considered natural; it must be the supernatural part of an individual who understands the divine nature of order.

A constant distinction was made between the *subditus* and the *subjectus,* just as a distinction was made between the sovereignty of the prince or *sublimis* and that of a despotism (literally, the authority of a slave-master). But that basic distinction took several forms. Within the theological framework the subject is a believer, a Christian. This can also mean that because, in the last instance, he obeys his soul, he cannot be the sovereign's "thing" (to be used or abused as he wishes); the counterpart of his obedience is the prince's responsibility (duty) towards him. This way of conceptualizing the freedom of the subject is, in practice, extraordinarily ambivalent: it can be understood as meaning that his will to obey is assertive and active (just as the Christian can, through his works, "cooperate in salvation"), or that his will has been extinguished (which is why mystics seek to annihilate themselves in the contemplation of God, who is the only absolute sovereign). Autonomy is close to nothingness, and "property" to "expropriation."

It is understandable that when the "citizen" reappeared in the towns of the Middle Ages and the Renaissance, he was no longer reducible to the *zôion politikon* [ζῷον πολιτικόν]; Aquinas (who translates the expression as "social animal") makes a distinction between man's (supernatural) *christianitas* and (natural) *humanitas,* between the believer and the citizen. So what becomes of the "subject"? In one sense the subject becomes more autonomous (his subjection is an effect of a political order that integrates "civility" and "polity," and is therefore part of nature). But it becomes increasingly difficult to see the subject as a *subditus,* as the concept of his essential obedience comes

(continued)

(continued)

under threat. The contradiction explodes in the absolute monarchy, which stretches to breaking point the mystical unity of the "two bodies" of the temporal-spiritual sovereign. The same applies to the freedom of the subject. All that remains is a prince whose will is law, a "father of his subjects" who has absolute authority over them. "*L'État, c'est moi*," as Louis XIV is supposed to have said. But an absolute monarchy is state power, or in other words a power that is established and exercised through the law and an administration: its subjects are, if not "subjects by right" (*sujets de droit*), at least *de jure* subjects (*sujets en droit*) and members of a "republic" (or commonwealth, as Hobbes would say). All

the theorists of absolute monarchy explain that "subjects are citizens" (or, like Bodin [*La République* I, 6] that "all citizens are subjects, some of their freedom being diminished by the majesty of the man to whom they owe obedience; but not all subjects are citizens, as we have said of slaves"). Boethius inverts the terms of the argument and answers them by defining the power of the One as a "voluntary servitude." At the same time *raison d'état* means that freedom no longer has any supernatural meaning. The controversy over the difference (or non-difference) between absolutism and despotism went on throughout the history of the absolute monarchies. And the subject's condition is retrospectively identified with that of the slave. And from the viewpoint of the new citizen and his

revolution (which is also an essential factor in his idealization), subjection is identified with slavery.

BIBLIOGRAPHY

Balibar, Etienne. "Citoyen Sujet, Réponse à la question de Jean-Luc Nancy: 'Qui vient après le sujet?'" *Cahiers Confrontation* 20 (1989): 23–47.
"Citizen Subject." In E. Cadava et al., eds., *Who Comes after the Subject?* New York: Routledge, 1991.
Bodin, Jean. *Les Six Livres de la République*. Paris: Fayard, 1987. First published in 1583.
Kantorowicz, Ernst. *Frederick the Second*. London: 1931.
Ullmann, Walter. *The Individual and Society in the Middle Ages*. Baltimore, MD: Johns Hopkins University Press, 1966.

8

Sujeto, subdito, sugeto. The body of the subject: Montaigne and Saint Teresa

When we examine the process of the formation of the language of corporality and intimacy in Spanish, we should note the importance of the word *subjecto* or *sujeto*, which is very close to certain contemporary philosophical usages (Merleau-Ponty, Zubiri, Lacan), but also to the Montaigne of the *Journal de voyage en Italie*. The Spanish translation may help to bring this out. In this sense *sujeto* is closely related to the recognition of intimacy, to the experience of pain and, more generally, of the passions of one's own body. It applies to both the register of politics and the register of mysticism.

Sujeto enters the Spanish lexicon at some point in the mid-sixteenth century (see RT: Corominas and Pascual, *Diccionario crítico etimológico castellano e hispánico*). The Spanish *sujeto*, which derives from the Latin *subjicere*, has two meanings and refers both to "that thing underneath" and "one who is subject to an authority." But the difference between the two languages becomes apparent as Spanish prefers to derive the word from the radical *subdere*—which gives *subdita*—while *sujeto* is related to *suppositum* or, in other words, the materiality of the person and, ultimately, the body, with all its force or potentialities. The decisive moment for Castilian thought comes, however, when the terms begin to overlap.

Montaigne, writing in French, provides the essential contemporary account of the transition from the political to the intimate:

> Nous y passames un chasteau de l'Archiduc qui couvre le chemin, comme

> nous avons trouvé ailleurs pareilles clostures qui tiennent les chemins subjects et fermés.

> (We passed a castle belonging to the Archduke that overlooks the path, just as we found elsewhere similar fences that keep the roads subject and closed.)

> (Montaigne, *Journal du voyage en Italie*, 59)

This quotation exemplifies the transitive use of *sujeto*, which is a past participle designed to describe the act of squeezing or containing something from outside a passage or a pathway so as to prevent it from spilling out into the countryside. Leaving aside this technical sense, Montaigne describes other situations in which the first meaning of "subject"—the political subject—comes to the fore. But he also supposes (*suppositum* is the subject's other name) that it is possible to know an internal realm that is not divorced from the surrounding world and that finds in it the metaphors and signifiers that allow it to express itself. Travel is the path to intimacy. In his *Journal* Montaigne tries to appropriate certain words whose meaning has been altered in order to justify a new distribution of powers. "*Cuius regio eius religio*" is from now on the rule governing a process that Montaigne examines with an attention that is barely concealed by his air of nonchalance. *Subject* is an old word for a modern practice, for a strange practice that, for the first time, modifies what seemed to be part

of human nature or the unchangeable order of things. *Subject* is Montaigne's greatest discovery in Florence, and it seems to him to be as strange as the exotic animals (sables or black foxes) the Muscovite presented to the Pope. In his commentary on the Duke of Florence's policy towards his "subjects (of whom he must be wary)" Montaigne shows us the effort that was being made to naturalize a situation of conflict. And in Lucca, subjects are counted as "souls." "*Les seigneurs ont quelques chastelets, mais nulle ville en leur sujection* (ibid., 134) (The lords have several castles, but no city is subject to them)."

The specificity of Spanish allows *sugeto* to be displaced in the direction of a meaning that is directly linked to the disposition of both the body and the spirit. Cervantes provides an example: "*Es menester que me advirtáis si estais con sugeto de esucharme* (You must let me know if you are disposed to listen to me)," *Persiles* III 17. This semantic field includes a direct reference to the corporeal dimension of human beings, especially when they suffer some loss or are ill.

Autoridades's *Dictionary* (1726) gives this definition: "*se usa tambien por la actividad, vigor y fuerzas de la persona: y asi seulen decir del enfermo muy extenuado: No hai sugeto* [it is also used to refer to a person's activity, vigor, and strength, which is why it is said of someone who is ill and quite exhausted that there is no subject]." The last sense was in common use from the end of the sixteenth century onwards; the main evidence is supplied by quotations from so-called mystical or "spiritual" writers.

The Life of Saint Teresa gives twenty or so examples of the transitive *sujetarse* (to subject oneself, to restrict the discussion to a transliteration that has yet to acquire other cultural or psychoanalytic meanings). The beautiful thing about the text is that it gives a clear idea of a subject that is a product of work, of a "becoming-subject." Just as Montaigne saw paths that were "subject to" the walls of castles, the founder of the Avila convent was aware of the effort it took to become a subject—a subject of the law or, rather, of a novel and unwritten form of speech. This is why mysticism, which can be an experiment in writing that uses popular metrics, is of interest to the translator: Saint Teresa is trying not so much to say what cannot be said as to stay within the limits of what can be said. Theresa, an educated woman disguised (as she puts it) as an illiterate woman, exemplifies a very particular relationship with language. It is close to what Roland Barthes calls "logothesis," or the simultaneous invention of speech and a vital space. Its invention juxtaposes the two meanings of "subject": the political sense (henceforth, *subdito*) and the bodily sense (*sugeto*). Hence the surprising use of both *sugeto* and *yo*:

Padeciendo tan grandísimo tormento en las curas que me hicieron tan recias, que yo no sé cómo las pude sufrir; y en fin, aunque las sufrí no las pudo sufrir me sujeto.

(I . . . suffered the greatest tortures from the remedies they applied to me, which were so drastic that I do not know how I endured them. In fact, though I did endure them, my subject (that is to say my body) was not able to do it.)

(Teresa of Avila, *Life of Saint Teresa*, 35)

The same duality appears in the language of asceticism, as when Ignatius speaks of his penitence:

No es penitencia quitar lo superfluo de cosas delicadas o moles, ma es penitencia quando en el modo se quita de lo conveniente, y quanto más y más major, sólo que non se corrompa el subiecto, ni se siga enfermedad notable.

(Taking what is superfluous away from delicate and sweet things is not penitence. Taking away what is appropriate from our habit is penitence. In that case, the more we take away, the better,

provided that we neither injure the subject (body) nor risk serious illness.)

(Loyola, *Ejercicios spirituales*, 216)

This subject who scarcely suffers from illness, and this subject who can also be corrupted, are two examples of a new subject. What kind of subject is this, who signals its own existence without realizing it, or sends out signs pertaining to a different type of knowledge—the knowledge of the mystics to which Lacan refers: "This wisdom without wisdom passing all knowledge" (St. John of the Cross).

José Miguel Marinas

BIBLIOGRAPHY

Cervantes, M. de. *Les Épreuves et les Travaux de Persiles et Sigusmunda*. Paris: Gallimard, 1963.

Loyola, Ignace de. "Ejercicios Espirituales." In *Obras Completas*. Madrid: Biblioteca de Autores Cristianos, 1963.

Montaigne, M. de. *Diario del Viaje a Italia*. Edited by J. M. Marinas and C. Thiebaut. Madrid: Editorial Debate, 1994.

Teresa of Avila. *The Life of Saint Teresa*. Translated by J. M. Cohen. Harmondsworth, UK: Penguin, 1957.

zugunsten eines superfundamentalistischen Seinsgeschicks entthront und entmachtet, sondern der Spontaneität ihrer verfemten Antriebe zurückgegeben. Die Öffnung zum sakralen Bereich bedeutet nicht Unterwerfung unter die Autorität eines unbestimmten, in seiner Aura nur angedeuteten Schicksals; die Grenzüberschreitung zum Sakralen bedeutet nicht die demütige Selbstaufgabe der Subjektivität, sondern ihre Befreiung zur wahren Subjektivität.

(Habermas, *Der philosophische Diskurs der Moderne*, 251)

(For Bataille, a completely different perspective from Heidegger's is opened up with this idea of unbounding: The self-transcendent subject is not dethroned and disempowered in favour of a superfoundationalist destining of Being; rather spontaneity is given back its outlawed drives. Opening towards the sacral domain does not mean subjugation to the authority of an indeterminate fate only hinted at in its aura; transgressing boundaries toward the sacral does not imply the humble self-surrender of subjectivity, but liberation to true sovereignty.)

(Habermas, *Philosophical Discourse*, 214)

And later:

In seinen späteren Untersuchungen wird Foucault diesen abstrakten Machtbegriff anschaulich ausgestalten; er wird Macht als die Interaktion kriegführender Parteien

. . . schliesslich als die produktive Durchdringung und sujektivierende Unterwerfung eines leibhaften Gegenübers verstehen.

(Habermas, *Der philosophische Diskurs der Moderne*, 300)

(In his later studies, Foucault will fill out this abstract concept of power in a more tangible way; he will comprehend power as the interaction of warring parties . . . and ultimately as the productive penetration and subjectizing subjugation of a bodily opponent.)

(Habermas, *Philosophical Discourse*, 255)

As one can imagine, this linguistic obstacle is not without its effects on the reasons why Habermas finds the object, internal divisions, and aporias or limitations of the "French" philosophy of the subject to be both incomprehensible and unacceptable.

In English, finally, the situation is quite specific. The pun is fully present (*Subject/subject*). The *sujétion/subjectivation* paradigm can therefore be legitimately transposed and assimilated. It can be further developed in English. A single sentence from Hannah Arendt's *The Human Condition* proves the point:

Somebody began it [= his own life story] and is its subject in the twofold sense of the word, namely its actor and its sufferer, but nobody is its author.

(Arendt, *The Human Condition*, 184)

What does create a problem is, rather, the fact that philosophical anthropology has, since the classical age, been organized around notions such as "person," "self," and "agent" (see I/ME/MYSELF and AGENCY), and not "subject." The first meaning of "subject" is political and institutional ("The idea of the servant makes us think of the master; that of the subject carries our view to the price" [Hume, *A Treatise of Human Nature* II, 2, 2]; John Stuart Mill's famous work on the civil and political inequality of the sexes, which was published in 1869, is entitled *The Subjection of Women*). The naturalization of "French ideas" is, however, changing this situation (and raising the tension). The work of Judith Butler, which is inspired by Freud, Derrida, Althusser, and Foucault, provides a remarkable example. At the beginning of her *Psychic Life of Power* (1997), subtitled *Theories in Subjection* (the syntax is perfectly idiomatic but probably also contains an allusion to John Stuart Mill's famous essay), she cites the *Oxford English Dictionary*'s entry on *subjection*:

> The act or fact of being subjected, as under a monarch or other sovereign or superior power; the state of being subject to, or under the dominion of another. . . . The condition of being subject, exposed, or liable to. . . . The act of supplying a subject to a predicate.

> (*OED*, cited in *Psychic Life of Power*, 1)

She later discusses the correspondences between the terms, but sometimes inverts the values to which we are accustomed:

> No individual becomes a subject without first becoming subjected or undergoing "subjectivation" (a translation of the French *assujettissement*). . . . The term "subjectivation" carries the paradox in itself: *assujettissement* denotes both the becoming of the subject and the process of subjection—one inhabits the figure of autonomy only by becoming subjected to a power, a subjection which implies a radical dependency.

> (Butler, *Psychic Life of Power*, 11, 83)

This is, however, part of her own development of the question: *subjection* becomes the general (tropological) concept of power "turning back upon oneself, or even turning on oneself."

As for the reciprocal question—how can French get away from being French (in philosophical terms, of course)—we can state that it cannot be answered by means of injunctions, either hermeneutic or analytic. This is not to say that it cannot be answered by remaining inside the French frontier. In his *Mythe de l'intériorité*, Jacques Bouveresse basically suggests (see, in particular, 356ff. and 656ff.) that we have to make a detour via Wittgenstein, or in other words invert Nietzsche's critique of the "grammatical privilege" conferred upon the subject, so as to turn it into an instrument for analyzing the ways in which, in every language game, a speaker—a philosopher, perhaps—articulates statements containing expressions of self-referentiality with public acts of enunciation in such a way as to be recognized as the author of certain meanings or thoughts. The suggestion deserves consideration.

Étienne Balibar,
Barbara Cassin,
Alain de Libera

BIBLIOGRAPHY

Agacinski, Sylviane. *Politique des sexes*. Paris: Seuil, 1998.

Agamben, Giorgio. "Bataille e il paradosso della sovranità." In *Georges Bataille, il politico e il sacro*, edited by Jacqueline Risset. Naples: Liguori, 1987.

Althusser, Louis. "Ideology and Ideological State Apparatuses." In *Lenin and Philosophy, and Other Essays*. Translated by Ben Brewster. New York: Monthly Review Press, 1971.

———. "On Content in the Thought of G.W.F. Hegel." In *The Spectre of Hegel: Early Writings*. Edited with an introduction by François Matheron, translated by G. M. Goshgarian. London: Verso, 1997.

Arendt, Hannah. *The Human Condition*. Chicago: University of Chicago Press, 1998.

Aristotle. *Categories and On Interpretation*. Translated by J. L. Ackrill. Oxford: Clarendon Press, 1963.

Arnauld, Antoine. *On True and False Ideas*. Translated, with an introductory essay, by Stephen Gaukroger. Manchester: Manchester University Press, 1990.

Augustine, Saint. *Confessions*. Translated, with an introduction and notes, by Henry Chadwick. Oxford: Oxford University Press, 2008.

———. *On the Trinity. Books 8–15*. Edited by Gareth B. Matthews. Translated by Stephen McKenna. Cambridge: Cambridge University Press, 2002.

Averroës. *L'intelligence et la pensée: grand commentaire du De anima; livre III (429 a 10–435 b 25)*. Translated into French with an introduction and notes by Alain de Libera. Paris: Flammarion, 1998.

———. *Long Commentary on the De Anima of Aristotle*. Translated with introduction and notes by Richard C. Taylor with Thérèse-Anne Druart. New Haven, CT: Yale University Press, 2009.

Bataille, Georges. *The Bataille Reader*. Edited by Fred Botting and Scott Wilson. Oxford: Blackwell, 1997.

———. *Oeuvres complètes*. Vol. 8. Paris: Gallimard, 1976.

Benoist, Jocelyn. "La subjectivité." In *Notions de philosophie*, vol. 2. Edited by D. Kambouchner. Paris: Gallimard, 1995.

Boehm, Rudolf. *Das Grundlegende und das Wesentliche. Zu Aristoteles Abhandlung "Über das Sein und das Seiende," "Metaphysik Z."* The Hague: Nijhoff, 1965.

Boulnois, Olivier. *Etre et représentation: une généalogie de la métaphysique moderne à l'époque de Duns Scot, 13e–14e siècle*. Paris: Presses Universitaires de France, 1999.

Bouveresse, Jacques. *Le Mythe de l'intériorité: expérience, signification et langage privé chez Wittgenstein*. Paris: Éditions de Minuit, 1976.

Butler, Judith. *The Psychic Life of Power: Theories in Subjection*. Stanford, CA: Stanford University Press, 1997.

Canguilhem, Georges. "Le cerveau et le pensée." In *Georges Canguilhem, Philosophe, Historien des sciences*. Paris: Albin Michel, 1993.

———. *A Vital Rationalist: Selected Writings from Georges Canguilhem*. Edited by François Delaporte. Translated by Arthur Goldhammer. Introduction by Paul Rabinow. Critical bibliography by Camille Limoges. New York: Zone Books, 1994.

Copjec, Joan, ed. *Supposing the Subject*. London: Verso, 1994.

Deleuze, Gilles. *Empiricism and Subjectivity: An Essay on Hume's Theory of Human Nature*. Translated and with an introduction by Constantin V. Boundas. New York: Columbia University Press, 1991.

Deleuze, Gilles, and Félix Guattari. *A Thousand Plateaus: Capitalism and Schizophrenia*. Translated with a foreword by Brian Massumi. Minneapolis: University of Minnesota Press, 1987.

Derrida, Jacques. *Adieu to Emmanuel Levinas*. Translated by Pascale-Anne Brault and Michael Naas. Stanford, CA: Stanford University Press, 1999.

———. "Forcener le subjectile." In *Étude pour les dessins et portraits d'Antonin Artaud*. Paris: Gallimard, 1986. Translation by Mary Ann Caws: "Unsensing the Subjectile." In *The Secret Art of Antonin Artaud*, edited by Jacques Derrida and Paul Thévenin. Cambridge, MA: MIT Press, 1998.

———. *Of Grammatology*. Translated by Gayatri Chakravorty Spivak. Corrected ed. Baltimore, MD: Johns Hopkins University Press, 1998.

Descartes, René. *Œuvres*. 11 vols. Edited by Charles Adam and Paul Tannery. Paris: Vrin, 1996.

———. *Philosophical Writings*. Translated and edited by E. Anscombe and P. T. Geach. Indianapolis: Bobbs-Merrill, 1971.

———. *The Philosophical Writings of Descartes*. 3 vols. Translated by John Cottingham, Robert Stoothoff, and Dugald Murdoch. Vol. 3 including Anthony Kenny. Cambridge: Cambridge University Press, 1988.

Foucault, Michel. *Discipline and Punish: The Birth of the Prison*. Translated by Alan Sheridan. 2nd ed. New York: Vintage Books, 1995.

———. "Foucault." In *Dits et écrits 1954–1988*. Vol 4. Paris: Gallimard, 1994.

———. "The Subject and Power." In *Michel Foucault: Beyond Structuralism and Hermeneutics*. Edited by Hubert L. Dreyfus and Paul Rabinow. 2nd ed. Chicago: University of Chicago Press, 1983.

———. "What Is an Author?" Translated by Donald F. Bouchard and Sherry Simon. In *Language, Counter-Memory, Practice*, 124–27. Ithaca, NY: Cornell University Press, 1977.

Gaius. *The Institutes of Gaius*. Translated, with an introduction, by W. M. Gordon and O. F. Robinson; with the Latin text of Seckel and Kuebler. Ithaca, NY: Cornell University Press, 1988.

Giele, Maurice, Fernand Van Steenberghen, and Bernardo Bazán. *Trois commentaires anonymes sur le* Traité de l'âme *d'Aristote*. Louvain: Publications Universitaires, 1971.

Habermas, Jürgen. *The Philosophical Discourse of Modernity: Twelve Lectures*. Translated by Frederick G. Lawrence. Cambridge, MA: MIT Press, 1987.

Hans, James. *The Site of Our Lives: The Self and the Subject from Emerson to Foucault*. Albany: State University of New York Press, 1995.

Heidegger, Martin. *The End of Philosophy*. Translated by Joan Stambaugh. New York: Souvenir Press, 1975.

———. *Nietzsche*. 4 vols. Translated, with notes and an analysis, by David Farrell Krell. San Francisco: Harper and Row, 1979–1987.

Kant, Immanuel. *Critique of Pure Reason*. Translated by Paul Guyer and Allen Wood. Cambridge: Cambridge University Press, 1998.

Lacan, Jacques. *Écrits*. Paris: Seuil, 1966. Translation by Bruce Fink: *Écrits*. New York: W. W. Norton, 2007.

Libera, Alain de. "Exist-t-il une noétique averroïste? Note sur la réception latine d'Averroès au XIIIe siècle." In *Averroismus im Mittelalter und in der Renaissance*. Edited by F. Niewöhner and L. Sturlese, 51–80. Zurich: Spur Verlag, 1994.

———. *L'unité de l'intellect: commentaire du* De unitate intellectus contra Averroistas *de Thomas d'Aquin*. Paris: Vrin, 2004 .

Nancy, Jean-Luc. *L'impératif catégorique*. Paris: Flammarion, 1983.

Nietzsche, Friedrich. *Jenseits von Gut und Böse*. In *Werke: Kritische Gesamtausgabe*. Edited by Giorgio Colli and Mazzino Montinari. Berlin: De Gruyter, 1967–. Translation by R. J. Hollingdale: *Beyond Good and Evil*. New York: Penguin, 2003. Reprint. Translation by Walter Kaufmann: *Beyond Good and Evil*. New York: Vintage Books, 1989.

———. *The Will to Power*. Translated by Walter Kaufmann. New York: Random House, 1967.

———. *Zur Geneaologie der Moral*. In *Werke: Kritische Gesamtausgabe*. Edited by Giorgio Colli and Mazzino Montinari. Berlin: De Gruyter, 1967–. Translation by Walter Kaufmann: *On the Genealogy of Morals*. New York: Vintage Books, 1967.

Ogilvie, Bertrand. *Lacan. La formation du concept de sujet*. Paris: Presses Universitaires de France, 1987.

Puchta, Georg Friedrich. *Cursus der Institutionen*. Vol. 1. Edited by P. Krüger. Leipzig: Breitkopf and Härtel, 1893. First published in 1841.

Raffoul, François. *Heidegger and the Subject*. Translated by David Pettigrew and Gregory Recco. Atlantic Highlands, NJ: Humanities Press, 1998.

Ritter, Joachim. *Subjektivität*. Frankfurt: Suhrkamp, 1974.

Rousseau, Jean-Jacques. *Collected Writings*. 11 vols. Edited by Roger D. Masters and Christopher Kelly. Hanover, NH: University Press of New England, 1990–2005.

———. *Œuvres complètes*. 5 vols. Paris: Gallimard, 1959.

Siger of Brabant. *Quaestiones in tertium de anima. De anima intellectiva. De aeternitate mundi*. Edited by Bernardo Bazán. Louvain: Publications Universitaires, 1972.

Thomas Aquinas. *L'unité de l'intellect contre les averroïstes: suivi des textes contre Averroès antérieurs à 1270*. Translated, with an introduction and notes by Alain de Libera. Paris: GF-Flammarion, 1994. Translation by Ralph McInerny: *Aquinas against the Averroists: On There Being Only One Intellect*. West Lafayette, IN: Purdue University Press, 1993.

Tugendhat, Ernst. Ti kata tinos. *Eine Untersuchung zur Strucktur und Ursprung aristotelischer Grundbegriffen*. Freiburg: Karl Abert Verlag, 1958.

Zarka, Yves-Charles. "L'invention du sujet de droit." *Archives de philosophie* 60 (1997): 531–50.

Žižek, Slavoj. *Selected Writings*. Edited by Rex Butler and Scott Stephens. New York: Continuum, 2006.

———. *Subversions du sujet. Psychanalyse, philosophie, politique*. Paris: Presses Universitaires de Rennes, 1999.

SUBLIME

FRENCH	*sublime*
GERMAN	*Erhabene, erhaben*
GREEK	*hupsos* [ὕψος], *hupsêlos* [ὑψηλός]
LATIN	*sublimis*
SPANISH	*sublime*

➤ AESTHETICS, BEAUTY, COMPARISON, GENIUS, GOÛT, *IMAGINATION* [PHANTASIA], PATHOS, PLEASURE, *TO SENSE*

A profound and originary duality is concealed beneath the apparent uniformity of the vocabulary of the sublime. If, in English, French, Italian, and Spanish, the same term of Latin origin is currently used, with different ascriptions depending on whether it is an adjective or a noun, in aesthetic history the sublime wavers between Greek and Latin terms whose status differs grammatically and etymologically. Between the rhetorical tradition, stemming from Latin, and the philosophical tradition, stemming from Greek, there is a discontinuity. In the first tradition, "sublime" makes its appearance as an adjective, the synonym of "grave" and "elevated," but also of "vehement" and "terrible": a double sense that Cicero was already attributing to the grand style that Quintilian would name "genus sublime dicendi." In the second tradition, the sublime, far from characterizing only the "sublime style," is a noun designating in Longinus "a certain summit and eminence of discourse" ("akrotês kai exochê tis logôn" [ἀκρότης καὶ ἐξοχή τις λόγων]). "The sublime" is the term chosen by Nicolas Boileau to translate Longinus's *hupsos*, and it became, thanks to Edmund Burke in the middle of the eighteenth century, a principle systematically opposed to the beautiful: a principle whose theorization would accompany the birth of aesthetics in the eighteenth century.

I. Heterogeneity of the Ancient Tradition

A. *Sublimis*

Sublimis is an adjective in classical Latin whose meaning remains problematic. Its etymology has to be reconstructed: it is derived from *sub*, which indicates a displacement upward, and either from *limis*, "oblique, across," or, on the contrary, from *limen*, "limit, threshold." *Sub* does not designate in Latin merely a relation of inferiority, adjacency, or submission; it marks a displacement upward and is related to *super*, as the Greek *hupo* [ὑπό] is related to *huper* [ὑπέρ]. *Limis* (or *limus*) is an adjective characterizing an indirect and secretive manner of looking at something (as describes Athena, who is cross-eyed), or else a complex movement of elevation that is, in any event, not perpendicular to the ground. *Limen* is the noun favored by Sextus Pompeius Festus in the second century CE to explain the etymology of "sublime": the latter "comes from the upper threshold, because it is above us" (*Festus Grammaticus* [*De verborum significatu*], book 17, s.v.). Although Ernout and Meillet (RT: *Dictionnaire étymologique de la langue latine*, s.v.) reckon that this is a mere pun, one should not neglect the association established thereby between the sublime and the idea of a threshold. If the sublime constitutes a superseding, and even a transgression, it would be appropriate to evoke what might be called the "surliminal" rather than the subliminal, contrary to what is suggested by the entirely fortuitous and material association between sublime and subliminal. That term does indeed designate what remains beneath the threshold and was introduced by J. A. Ward in English at the end of the nineteenth century to translate the title of a book by J. F. Herbart, *Unter der Schwelle.*

The first meaning of *sublimis* is "who goes while rising" or "which holds itself aloft." Thus Ovid distinguishes man from other animals by evoking his "sublime face" ("os sublime," *Metamorphoses* 1.85), which rises toward the heaven and permits him to gaze at the stars. And "sublimem aliquem rapere" means "to abduct someone into the air" (like Zeus ravishing Ganymede). One thus cannot insist enough on the dynamic sense as well as the obliqueness, both of which are absent from the semantic register of *hupsos* [ὕψος].

The adjective *sublimis* came only late to characterize a rhetorical style: it is to be found in neither the *Rhetorica ad Herennium* nor the *De oratore* of Cicero. Thus the expression "genus sublime dicendi" receives its quarters of nobility only with Quintilian, after whom the sublime style referred to the grand style, that is, the grave but also vehement style of the rhetorical tradition (*Institutio oratoria,* 12.10). The rhetorical tradition, having as its Latin source the *Rhetorica ad Herennium* (between 86 and 83 BCE), generally distinguishes three styles. The function of the first style is to teach (*docere*); of the second, to delight (*delectare*) or counsel (*conciliare*); and of the third, to stir up and put in motion (*movere*), rather than to "move" in the emotional sense of the term. It was to this third style that Cicero and Quintilian would give pride of place, at least when it is used advisedly.

B. *Hupsos* and the treatise *On the Sublime*

Hupsos [ὕψος] is a noun, belonging to an ancient, rich, and well-constructed family of terms, all of which are derived from the adverb *hupsi* [ὕψι], "on high, upward": it commonly designates height, conceived as the spatial dimension opposed to width and length, and it subsequently took on the meaning of "summit, peak, or high point."

Its use was fixed by Longinus in a favored relation to simplicity of speech, force of conception, and greatness of mind. But *hupsos* is not the only term that can be rendered by "sublime" in the *Peri hupsous* [Περὶ ὕψους].

1. Longinus uses *megaloprepês* [μεγαλοπρεπής] (having an air of grandeur) when he evokes amplitude and majesty—rather than sobriety—of style.
2. He also uses *megethos* [μέγεθος], "greatness," and all sorts of compounds formed with the adjective *mega* [μέγα]: *megalêgoria* [μεγαληγορία], "greatness in speech"; *megalophrosunê* [μεγαλοφροσύνη], "greatness of mind, elevated conception"; *megalophuês* [μεγαλοφυής], "great nature"; *megalophuia* [μεγαλοφυία], "genius, nobility"; *megalopsuchia* [μεγαλοψυχία], "great soul."
3. The adjective *hadros* [ἁδρός], which Quintilian gives as the equivalent of *sublimis*, enters into the compound expression designating the first source of the sublime, "to peri tas noêseis adrepêbolon" [τὸ περὶ τὰς νοήσεις ἁδρεπήβολον] (8.1) and signifies literally "what attains its goal forcefully in thoughts."
4. Better still: Longinus uses the adjective *deinos* [δεινός] in a first sense (attested to by Homer) of "terrible, formidable," while the nouns *deinotês* [δεινότης] or *deinôsis* [δείνωσις], "vehemence, energy," serve him to designate the oratorical power of Demosthenes, that is, the very model of the sublime at its most concentrated and effective.

In addition, if one passes from terminology to thematic register as object of consideration, the network of citations subtending and at times overdetermining the theoretical text knows no end of instances of threatening death, parricidal rivalry, ravaging passion, horror at mutilated bodies, or terror at obstacles to be overcome: from this perspective, the hypothesis might be sustained that the meaning of *hupsos* would have been inflected or even revised in the sense of terror contributed by Burke in his *A Philosophical Enquiry into the Origin of Our Ideas of the Sublime and Beautiful.*

■ See Box 1.

When was the linkage between *sublimis* and *hupsos* established? It is not found in Quintilian, who gives as an equivalent of *sublimis* the adjective *hadros* [ἁδρός], until then rendered in Varro as *uber* (fertile, rich: *uber, -ris,* designates the teat or breast) or as *gravis* (having weight, that of the pregnant woman or that of authority) in the *Rhetorica ad Herennium* or in Cicero. He could certainly have used adjectives derived from *hupsi* available in Greek: *hupsagorês* [ὑψαγόρης] (who speaks loudly), of which there are four occurrences in the *Odyssey* (Quadlbauer, "Die genera dicendi bis"), and *hupsêlos* [ὑψηλός], "elevated," used by Longinus. But the real problem lies in the gap between an exclusively adjectival form and a nominal form of the word. In point of fact, the noun *sublimitas* in Quintilian or Pliny does not correctly render *hupsos*, since it does not designate the totality of what is sublime, but the mere fact of being sublime. The qualifying term tends to serve for description and evaluation, whereas the noun refers us to an essence. As much as Greek is concerned with the idea of the sublime and attempts to elucidate its genesis and status by surprising the sublime in its nascent state, so does Latin, a language of juridical and pragmatic efficacy, move toward determining one or several sublime characteristics, in order to define levels of discourse and perfect the prodigious rhetorical instrument constituted by the theory of styles.

We are the heirs to this heterogeneity of the ancient tradition: Is the unity of the sublime compatible with the diversity of its perceptible embodiments? Two symmetrical risks present themselves: either one presses abstraction to the point of rendering the sublime independent of all support and strips it of any capacity to attain presence, even negatively; or one defines a priori the character of the sublime and then tends to conflate its principle not only with one of its particularities, but also with a model that might be reproduced following a specific protocol. There have thus been at least three different ways of disposing of the sublime: by reducing it to a modality of the beautiful (its mere superlative), by assimilating it purely and simply to the terrifying, or, finally, by dissolving

1

Sublime *ekstasis*

The treatise *On the Sublime* retains even today a good measure of its mystery. We know neither its author (long assumed to be Dionysius Longinus, a Hellenistic philosopher, then Dionysius of Halicarnassus) nor, with any certainty, its date (which is no longer situated in the third century after Christ, but in the first, toward the era of Tiberius). The astonishment it arouses also stems from the sources it fuses: aside from the full range of the Greek tradition (Homer, Demosthenes, and Plato, but no less the lyricists, tragedians, and historians), and the Latin tradition (Cicero and the debates of the first century), the treatise cites "the lawgiver of the Jews" and Genesis—an occurrence almost unique in pagan literature—under the presumed influence of Philo of Alexandria. "Let there be light, and there was light; let there be land, and there was land" is an example, between two passages from Homer, of a presentation of the divine in all its power and dignity (*On the Sublime* 1.3–9, quoted in 9.9).

The "golden book," to take up Isaac Casaubon's expression, was genuinely known only in the modern age. It was published and translated during the second Renaissance, but it was Nicolas Boileau who first spread the fame of Longinus to a huge European audience. The celebrity of Longinus in the last quarter of the seventeenth century and the first two-thirds of the eighteenth century was such that the history of his interpreters tends to fuse with the vicissitudes of the concept of the sublime.

The definition of the sublime by Longinus puts the accent, as in the rhetorical tradition, on the effect that it produces. But it insists at the same time on what distinguishes that effect from the effects of persuasive discourse, which, according to Cicero's definition, aim simultaneously to instruct (*docere*), to delight (*delectare*), and to move (*movere*). The effect sought by the sublime essentially corresponds to *movere*, which Cicero, moreover, considered to be the most crucial effect in rhetorical discourse, one that won the agreement of the audience.

A sublime passage does not convince the reason of the reader, but takes him out of himself [*eis ek-stasis* (εἰς ἔκ-στασις)]. That which is admirable ever confounds our judgment, and eclipses that which is merely reasonable or agreeable. To believe or not is usually in our own power; but the Sublime, acting with an imperious and irresistible force, sways every reader whether he will or no. Skill in invention, lucid arrangement and disposition of facts, are appreciated not by one passage, or by two, but gradually manifest themselves in the general structure of a work; but a sublime thought, if happily timed, illumines an entire subject with the vividness of a lightning-flash, and exhibits the whole power of the orator in a moment of time.

(Longinus, *On the Sublime*, 1.4, trans. Russell)

The irresistible force of the sublime entails another characteristic that also distinguishes it from the discourse of persuasion: its universality. As opposed to rhetorical effects, which, according to Aristotle's definition, are often effective and are addressed to a majority of men, the sublime acts everywhere and on everyone: "In general we may regard those words as truly sublime which always please and please all readers" (*dia pantos . . . kai pasin* (διὰ παντὸς . . . καὶ πᾶσιν, 7.4). The question of universality thus opens onto another significant tradition for the philosophy of the sublime.

Barbara Cassin
Jacqueline Lichtenstein

it into the sphere of an absolute from which it would surface as a merely temporary mode of revelation.

II. Junction between the Greek and Latin Traditions: The German Exception

Boileau may not have invented the noun "the sublime." But he was undeniably the first to render *hupsos* as "the sublime"—a noun he even endowed with a capital initial—in the title of his translation of Longinus, *Traité du Sublime ou du merveilleux dans le discours* (1674). And he was the first to define "the sublime" by opposing it to "the sublime style":

One must then be aware that by Sublime, Longinus did not understand what the Orators call the sublime style, but that extraordinary and marvelous aspect which is striking in discourse and results in a work that captivates, ravishes, and transports. The sublime style always comes from great words; but the Sublime can be found in a single thought, a single figure, a single turn of phrase. A thing can be cast in the sublime style without, however, being Sublime, that is, without having anything extraordinary or surprising. For example, *The Sovereign Arbiter of nature with a single word formed light*. Here we are in the sublime style; it is not, however, Sublime; because there is nothing in it of the extreme-marvelous, and that one might not find [elsewhere]. But, *God said: Let there be light; and there was light*. This extraordinary turn of expression, which marks so effectively the obedience of the Creature to the orders of the Creator, is truly sublime and has something divine. One must thus understand by Sublime in Longinus, the Extraordinary, the Surprising, and, as I have translated it, the Marvelous in discourse.

(Boileau, preface to Longinus, *Traité du Sublime*, 70)

From France, the sublime moved on to all of Europe, notably to England, where Samuel Johnson declared it "a Gallicism, but now naturalized" (RT: *Dictionary of the English Language* [1755]). But the translation of *hupsos* by "the sublime," which seems a matter of course in the Romance languages, continues to pose problems in English. In the middle of the twentieth century, George Grube would render *Peri hupsous* as *Of Great Writing* (1957), recalling that W. Rhys Roberts, whose English version remains authoritative, confessed to regretting having been led by tradition to maintain that title (*Longinus on the Sublime* [1899]). It resulted in a "misconception which the existence of Burke's homonymous treatise . . . has done much to increase." More recently, Morpurgo-Tagliabue (*Demetrio*) has maintained that Burke's terrible-sublime would be closer to the *deinos* [δεινός] (vehement, terrible) of Demetrius than to the Longinian *hupsos*.

■ See Box 2.

In German, during the second half of the eighteenth century, *Erhaben* wins out over *sublim*, the use of which nonetheless persists and is revived, notably in Friedrich Nietzsche.

2

Sublime, privation, and "delight"

In opposition to John Locke, Edmund Burke proposed a distinction between pleasure stemming from the removal of pain and positive pleasure, just as, inversely, between pain produced by the disappearance of pleasure and positive pain. How is one to qualify relative pleasure stemming from a relation to pain, through a distancing and metamorphosis of the latter? Burke chose an already existent term, "delight," and ascribed to it a more restricted semantic range. "Delight" is the name of the sentiment that, according to him, accompanies the formation of the idea of the sublime. There is thus no simple pleasure, nor simple or relative pain.

It is most certain that every species of satisfaction or pleasure, how different soever in its manner of affecting, is of a positive nature in the mind of him who feels it. The affection is undoubtedly positive; but the cause may be, as in this case it certainly is, a sort of *Privation*. . . .

Whenever I have occasion to speak of this species of relative pleasure, I call it *Delight;* and I shall take the best care I can to use that word in no other sense. I am satisfied the word is not commonly used in this appropriated signification; but I thought it better to take up a word already known, and to limit its signification, than to introduce a new one, which would not perhaps incorporate so well with the language. . . .

WHATEVER is fitted in any sort to excite the ideas of pain and danger, that is to say, whatever is in any sort terrible, or is conversant about terrible objects, or operates in a manner analogous to terror, is a source of the *sublime;* that is, it is productive of the strongest emotion which the mind is capable of feeling. I say the strongest emotion, because I am satisfied the ideas of pain are much more powerful than those which enter on the part of pleasure. . . .

When danger or pain press too nearly, they are incapable of giving any delight, and are simply terrible; but at certain distances, and with certain modifications, they may be, and they are, delightful, as we every day experience. The cause of this I shall endeavour to investigate hereafter.

(Burke, *A Philosophical Enquiry into the Origin of Our Ideas of the Sublime and Beautiful*)

Sublim is inscribed in the great tradition of poetic and alchemical *Sublimierung* and is given new currency by Freudian *Sublimierung* in a way that leads to an interesting rivalry with Hegelian *Aufhebung*.

- See Box 3.

Bur *erhaben* is the term chosen by Johann Joachim Winckelmann, who casts it as a noun and insists in 1764 on its exclusively Apollonian character: "Apollo hat das Erhabene, welches im Laocoon nicht stattfand" (Apollo possesses the sublime, which was not to be found in Laocoon: *Geschichte der Kunst des Altertums*, 155). From Winckelmann, *das Erhabene* passed to Immanuel Kant, for whom it was palpably revised under the influence of the Burkean sublime and in the light of the transcendental. Criticizing the Kantian assimilation of the sublime to absolute greatness, Johann Gottfried Herder emphasized the relative character of the sublime and linked *erhaben* with *erhoben*, that is, "that which rises through its own forces or by external forces." *Das Erhabene* would thus be the mark less of absolute greatness than of elevation (*Kalligone*, part 3, "Vom Erhabenen und Ideal," 227–81), and its character would be immediately sensed as "sublimatory"; the negative aspect of the sublime (the dispossession it establishes through the effect of a shock, vertigo, or terror that must nonetheless be held at bay) would thus tend to be diminished. It can therefore be argued that from the Latinate tradition of "genus sublime dicendi," *das Erhabene* would retain the idea of elevation, but would reject that of vehemence.

III. The Sublime and the Critique of the Beautiful

It thus becomes necessary to rediscover the guiding thread that allows Burke and, following him, Kant to give its status and range to the sublime; all the seriousness of the sublime resides in the systematic critique it manages to impose with regard to the beautiful or, more precisely, in the radical suspension of its values. Whereas the beautiful creates calm satisfaction and is the object of a taste that entails the spontaneous and immediate application of certain rules whose formulation is possible, at least after the fact, the sublime is troubling and involves a stirring of the entire being. The beautiful "subsists" independent of any recognition; but the sublime does no more than exist, in the fragility of what must be perpetuated elsewhere than in itself in order to survive: it demands of me and breaches my being, being born in the experience of its discovery. On the one hand is the calling into play of social passions that attach us to more or less contingent objects of pleasure and love; on the other, the stirring of fundamental passions affecting the love of self, or what we would today call narcissism, in its triple—physical, psychological, and moral—dimension. As much, then, as the beautiful will appear to be endowed with "means," and to that extent, to be capable of being reproduced and of being the subject of academic instruction, just so will the sublime, for its part, appear to dispose only of favored "vehicles," whose use will remain random and perilous.

What are those vehicles? At times we apprehend the sublime in a destabilized world under pressure of greatness, ugliness, darkness, or simplicity. The beautiful then finds itself threatened in its form, in the pleasure it provides, its visibility, and its diversity. At other times, on the contrary, its collapse provokes a radical dispossession, and we experience more directly the sublime within us as a suspension of the ego. No doubt on such occasions we are more or less overwhelmed with enthusiasm (*enthousiastikon pathos* [ἐνθουσιαστικὸν πάθος], Longinus 7.2.7), astonishment (according to Burke), or respect (*Achtung*, Kant). But what is essential is that the

3

Sublimation according to Freud

Rather than adopt the Hegelian term *Aufhebung*—which, in certain respects, might have been equally suitable—for his purposes, Freud chose *Sublimierung* to designate the "capacity to exchange [an] originally sexual aim for another one, which is no longer sexual but which is psychically related to the first aim" ("Civilized Sexual Morality," trans. Strachey, 187). He postulated that in order to exchange sexual aims for nonsexual ones, the sexual drive "places extraordinarily large amounts of force at the disposal of civilized activity, and it does this in virtue of its especially marked characteristic of being able to displace its aim without materially diminishing in intensity." Subsequently, in 1932, Freud would specify that this modification of the libidinal aim would be accompanied by a change of object (*New Introductory Lectures*, 97).

Now, the term *Sublimierung*, which comes from the adjective *sublim*, before entering the vocabulary of the fine arts, had previously belonged to that of alchemy (borrowed from the Latin *sublimatio*), then to that of chemistry, where the word designated the process of "subjecting solids in a closed receptacle to heat in such manner that volatile elements rise to the upper part of the receptacle, where they become solids again and are stabilized" (RT: *Dictionnaire étymologique de la langue française*, s.v. *Sublimierung*). It was by way of an adoption of the figurative sense of the idea that *Sublimierung* made its reappearance, notably in Nietzsche. In *Human, All Too Human* (1876), the latter raises the following question: "How can something be born from its opposite, such as reason from the irrational, sensitivity from inertness, logic from illogicality, disinterested contemplation from avid desire, altruism from selfishness, truth from errors?" He replies by contrasting the respective approaches of the old metaphysics with more recent historical philosophy. The former "has until now avoided such difficulties by denying that one might engender the other and by assuming, in the case of things deemed to be superior, a miraculous origin, issuing immediately from the very essence and existence of the 'thing in itself.'" As for the latter, it was inspired by the natural sciences, and specifically by chemistry:

Finding that these are not at all opposites ... and that there is at the bottom of that opposition an error in reasoning: according to its explanation, there exists, in all rigor, neither unselfish behavior nor completely disinterested contemplation, each of them being but sublimations [*Sublimierungen*] in which the fundamental element appears to have almost vaporized and no longer betrays its existence to any but the most subtle observer.

(Nietzsche, *Human, All Too Human*, 1.1)

In *Daybreak*, Nietzsche pursued the same argument, evoked here under the rubric "The Chemistry of ideas and feelings."

The use made by Freud of the category of sublimation is deployed in a vast network of references that suffer, however, from ambiguities and absences such that Jean Laplanche and Jean-Bertrand Pontalis, the authors of the *Vocabulaire de la psychanalyse*, do not hesitate to conclude their article on the subject with these words: "The absence of a coherent theory of sublimation remains one of the gaps in psychoanalytic thought" (RT: *Vocabulaire de la psychanalyse*, s.v.). In relation to these references, moreover, sublimation is often defined negatively. It is thus clearly distinguished from the category of the sublime in the philosophy of art, from idealization, the ego-ideal, or *aphanisis* (the extinction of the capacity to experience sexual pleasure, according to Ernest Jones), and so on. On the other hand, other notions are more directly congruent with it. In point of fact, sublimation can be considered as a type of satisfaction occurring by way of desexualization, which, while continuing to have a libidinal source, has ceased being sexual in order to become social or cultural, and which, nonetheless, does not at all undergo the vicissitudes of a symptom. For Freud, such desexualization, which is directly related to his later thinking on narcissism, consists in the fact that the ego withdraws its power of attraction from the cathected sexual object in order to cathect a new object and aim that would be nonsexual. Thus sublimation, which Freud reduces to a form of derivation (*Ablenkung*, literally "deviation") and not suppression—or, even less, repression—has as its condition just such a desexualization (*Desexualisierung*), which itself requires the intervention of the ego or its mediation, in the context of the unifying power of Eros in the second topographical model.

It remains the case that in the eyes of many, Freud's theorization does not offer a convincing description of the qualitative leap through which sublimation moves from the sexual to the nonsexual. This, allows, for example, Melanie Klein to make of it a tendency to restore the "good object" destroyed by the aggressive drives, or François Roustang ("Sublimation") to locate its source in the anteriority and autonomy of fantasy in relation to the vicissitudes of the sexual drive.

Charles Baladier

BIBLIOGRAPHY

Freud, Sigmund. "Civilized Sexual Morality and Modern Nervous Illness." Translated by James Strachey. In *The Standard Edition of the Psychological Works of Sigmund Freud*, edited by J. Strachey, vol. 9. New York: W. W. Norton, 1989. First published in 1908.

———. *New Introductory Lectures on Psychoanalysis*. In *The Standard Edition of the Psychological Works of Sigmund Freud*, edited by J. Strachey, vol. 22. New York: W. W. Norton, 1989.

Nietzsche, Friedrich. *Human, All Too Human*. Translated by R. J. Hollingdale. Cambridge: Cambridge University Press, 1996. First published in 1878.

———. *Daybreak: Thoughts on the Prejudices of Morality*. Translated by R. J. Hollingdale. Cambridge: Cambridge University Press, 1997. First published in 1881.

Roustang, François. "Sublimation nécessaire et impossible." *Philosophie* 55 (1 Sept. 1997).

Saint Girons, Baldine. *Dictionnaire de la psychanalyse*. Paris: Encyclopaedia Universalis—Albin Michel, 1997.

reason for the impassioned effect be tied to the structure of the subject, which never stops transcending itself.

- See Box 4.

An illustration of this crucial triumph of the sublime over the beautiful is to be found in the movement of abstraction. It was thus in vain that Worringer, who intuited its future developments in 1908, failed to use the word *sublime*; he endlessly evoked its presence in a perspective close to that of Kant, for whom the two Egyptian examples of the sublime (the Pyramids and the inscription on the Temple of Isis) play a major role.

To whoever has just contemplated Egyptian monumental art and felt the extent to which its grandeur exceeds our capacity of apprehension . . . , the admirable works

---

4

On the introduction of the sublime in Kant

Kant removes the sublime from its preferred site, which, from antiquity on, was rhetoric. He does not even cite Longinus. On the other hand, he endorses the great discovery of the late seventeenth and the eighteenth century: that of the natural sublime associated with vast and irregular landscapes, specifically seascapes and mountain vistas. But he hesitates between two conceptions in presenting the sublime: the first, which became quite famous, insists on purely negative sensory stimulation; the second, barely noticed but more original, sought to develop a veritable asceticism of the sensibility, which forbade any projection of knowledge onto the spectacle contemplated.

1. No sensible form can contain the sublime properly so-called [*das eigentlich Erhabene*]. This contains only ideas of the Reason, which, although no adequate presentation is possible for them, by this inadequacy that admits of sensible presentation, are aroused and summoned into the mind. Thus the wide ocean, agitated by the storm, cannot be called sublime [*erhaben*]. Its aspect is horrible.

2. We must not think of [the sight of the ocean] as we ordinarily do, endowed as we are with all kinds of knowledge. . . . To call the ocean sublime [*erhaben*] we must regard it as poets do, merely by what strikes the eye; if it is at rest, as a clear mirror of water only bounded by the heaven; if it is restless, as an abyss threatening to overwhelm everything.

(Kant, *Critique of Judgment*, §23 and General Remark)

BIBLIOGRAPHY

Kant, Immanuel. *Critique of Judgment*. Translated by J. H. Barnard. 2nd rev. ed. London: Macmillian, 1914.

---

of the classical sculpture of antiquity . . . will not fail to appear like the products of a more childlike and inoffensive humanity, a humanity that has remained insensitive to the most powerful tremors. The term "beauty" itself will seem to him perfectly petty and inadequate.

(*Abstraction and Empathy*, trans. Bullock)

Closer to us, the most illustrious representatives of abstract expressionism, such as Barnett Newman or Mark Rothko, practice the same critique of the beautiful, while invoking the sublime and, quite remarkably, the Burkean sublime:

Without monsters and gods, art cannot enact our drama: art's most profound moments express this frustration. When they were abandoned as untenable superstitions, art sank into melancholy. It became fond of the dark.

(Rothko, "Romantics," 83)

One thus seems to arrive paradoxically at a unification of the category of the sublime. The difficulty remains, however, of thinking of its advent as problematical, not hypostatizing it, and according it the dimension of a mere principle—a principle of expropriation or overflow—while recalling its inherent value as stimulation. The sublime demands a reorganization of psychical life that offers a challenge to all of the productive faculties of man (power, knowledge, and will). The crucial matter thus becomes to analyze its bearing in each of those registers. In that perspective, it should not be reduced to the unrepresentable alone: the sublime will be identified with what seemed, until the moment of its advent, unthinkable, uninventable, and altogether beyond enjoyment.

Baldine Saint-Girons

BIBLIOGRAPHY

Axelsson, Karl. *The Sublime: Precursors and British Eighteenth-Century Conceptions*. Oxford : Peter Lang, 2007.

Burke, Edmund. *A Philosophical Enquiry into the Origin of Our Ideas of the Sublime and Beautiful*. Rev. ed. Oxford : Basil Blackwell, 1987.

Cicero. *On the Ideal Orator* [*De oratore*]. Translated with introduction, notes, appendixes, glossary, and indexes by James M. May and Jakob Wisse. New York: Oxford University Press, 2001.

Crowther, Paul. *The Kantian Sublime: From Morality to Art*. Oxford: Oxford University Press, 1991.

Demetrius. *On Style* [*De elocutione*]. Bilingual edition. Translated and edited by W. Rhys Roberts. New York: Arno Press, 1979.

Grube, George Maximilian Anthony. *Longinus: Of Great Writing*. Indianapolis, IN: Hackett, 1991. First published in 1957.

Herder, Johann Gottfried. *Kalligone*. In *Sämtliche Werke*, vol. 23, edited by B. Suphan. Berlin: Weidmann, 1877–1913.

———. *Selected Writings on Aesthetics*. Translated and edited by Gregory Moore. Princeton, NJ: Princeton University Press, 2006.

Kant, Immanuel. *Observations on the Feeling of the Beautiful and Sublime*. Translated by T. Goldthwait. Berkeley: University of California Press, 1981.

———. *Critique of the Power of Judgment*. Translated by Paul Guyer and Eric Matthews. Cambridge: Cambridge University Press, 2001.

Longinus. *On the Sublime*. Edited with introduction and commentary by D. A. Russell. Oxford: Clarendon, 1964. Translation by Nicolas Boileau: *Traité du Sublime*. Paris: Livre de Poche, 1995.

Mattioli, Emilio. *Interpretazioni dello Pseudo-Longino*. Modena, It.: Mucchi, 1988.

Monk, Samuel Holt. *The Sublime: A Study of Critical Theories in Eighteenth-Century England*. Ann Arbor: University of Michigan Press, 1960.

Morpurgo-Tagliabue, Guido. *Demetrio: Dello stile*. Rome: Ateneo, 1980.

Quadlbauer, Franz. "Die genera dicendi bis auf Plinius." *Wiener Studien* 71 (1958): 55–111.

Quintilian. *The* Institutio Oratoria *of Quintilian*. 4 vols. Translated by H. E. Butler. Loeb Classical Library. Cambridge, MA: Harvard University Press, 1953–59.

Rothko, Mark. "The Romantics Were Prompted." *Possibilities* 1, no. 1 (Winter 1947–48).

Russo, Luigi. *Da Longino a Longino, i luoghi del sublime*. Palermo, It.: Aesthetica edizioni, 1987.

Saint Girons, Baldine. *Fiat lux: Une philosophie du sublime*. Paris: Quai Voltaire, 1993.

———, ed. *Le paysage et la question du sublime*. Paris: Éditions du Seuil, 1997.

Winckelmann, Johann Joachim. *Geschichte der Kunst des Altertums*. Darmstadt, Ger.: Wissenschaftliche Buchgesellschaft, 1972.

Wood, Theodore E. B. *The Word "Sublime" and Its Context, 1650–1760*. The Hague: Mouton, 1972.

Worringer, Wilhelm. *Abstraction and Empathy: A Contribution to the Psychology of Style*. Translated by Michael Bullock. New York: International Universities Press, 1963.

Zelle, Karsten. *Die doppelte Ästhetik der Moderne*. Stuttgart: Metzler, 1995.

SUFFERING

"Suffering," from the Latin *suffere* ("to place beneath, to bear"), has become synonymous with physical or moral hardship. It is the accepted translation of the Russian *stradanie* [страдание], derived from *strada* [страда] ("work"), which assigns a redemptive value to suffering: see STRADANIE.

See also BERUF, *MALAISE, PASSION,* PATHOS, WORK.

➤ BOGOČELOVEČESTVO, ERLEBEN, PLEASURE, *SOUCI,* SVET

SUPPOSITION

FRENCH	*supposition*
GERMAN	*Supposition, Denotierung*
ITALIAN	*supposizione*
LATIN	*suppositio*
PORTUGUESE	*suposição*
SPANISH	*suposición*

➤ ANALOGY, CONNOTATION, ESSENCE, INTENTION, *NEGATION,* PARONYM, PREDICATION, REALITY, *REFERENCE,* SACHVERHALT, SENSE, SUBJECT, TROPE

Between the twelfth and the sixteenth centuries, translators into French of treatises of logic called on the word *supposition*, which served as a barely intelligible replica of the Latin *suppositio*, a key word of medieval philosophical semantics and assuredly one of the most difficult to understand, if not to translate, of the scholastic lexicon. A creation of logicians of the twelfth century, *suppositio* was situated at the intersection of three different disciplines: grammar, theology, and dialectic, all three of which gradually infused it with their own theoretical interests and specific problematics. Understood, if not formed, on the basis of *suppositum*, the noun originally designated the subject term of a proposition: to refer to, to be placed as the "henchman" (Fr. *suppôt*), the term *suppositum* designating the subject on which the statement bears, the subject matter of discourse in English, the *Subjektgegenstand* in German. With the *suppositum* thus understood being spontaneously associated with the "referent" of Saussurean linguistics, some translators have proposed the term "reference" as the technical equivalent of *suppositio*. That translation, without being inexact, nonetheless masks the complexity of the term's semantic field and collides with some formidable difficulties as soon as it is called on to measure up to the texts. It may, in any event, seem paradoxical to attempt to eschew the ambiguities of the Latin by using a French—or English—term, which is itself equivocal and, at the least, saturated, and whose various uses—Saussurian, Fregean (in translation), Russellian—are, at a minimum, discordant. This paradox is, in fact, an integral part of the genealogy of signification and reference.

"Supposition" offers a marvelous illustration, starting with French, of the difficulty confronting the various lexicons of European philosophies—difficulties of language, first of all, but ones soon compounded by those of philosophical idiolects. German, which disposes *Bezeichnung* for *significatio*, does not have a term for *suppositio*; it is thus obliged to use *Denotierung*—which is part of a conceptual opposition (*Denotierung/Konnotierung*) largely subsequent to the theory of *suppositio* and different from it, although issuing from it via complex and indirect paths—or the Franco-German

neologism *Supposition*, which is as opaque to a nonspecialist reader as the Latin that it translates. Italian and English, which have no need of a neologism—the Italian *supposizione* being common usage, and the English "supposition" documented since the fifteenth century—are engaged with the same range of meaning as French: all idea of reference is absent from it. The situation is similar for the Portuguese *suposição* or the Spanish *suposición*. Here it is the idea of hypothesis (*suppositio* being the exact duplicate of the Greek *hupothesis* [ὑπόθεσις]) or conjecture that come to the fore, rendering the "referential" aspect imperceptible. But there is a final problem beyond the difficulties of language: the temptation to neutralize the question of translation by voiding what the noncoincidence of "supposition" and "reference" explains of the noncoincidence of the Saussurian, Fregean, and Russellian uses (*signification, reference*; *Sinn, Bedeutung*; "meaning, denotation"). Whether one decides to render *supponere* by *supposer* (Fr.), "suppost" (Eng.), or *supponieren* (Ger.), rather than by *être mis pour*, "to stand for," or *denotieren* has its importance, but more important still is the philosophical reason for the bind in which interpreters find themselves and which is linked not *solely* to language but also to the very idea that scholastic Latin is alone in expressing and that relates to a semantic labor on the syntactical concept of the subject. In calling *suppositio* the semantic function of the subject term of a proposition—to be placed as a *suppôt* or auxiliary—medieval logicians were philosophizing "within the language," in this case, in Latin. It is the originally syntactico-semantic nature of the concept of *suppositio* that the European languages of philosophy have strained to translate and preserve. And it is that aspect that marks the point of discontinuity between medieval and contemporary semantics.

I. *Suppositio* as Supplement and Substitution

In his *Petite Logique* (*Introduction to Logic*), in which he combines vocabularies borrowed from both late Scholasticism (john of St. Thomas) and the *Logic* of Port Royal, Jacques Maritain proposes to render the term *suppositio* by *suppléance* and *valeur de suppléance*, intending thereby "the manner in which a term takes the place of, or becomes a substitute in discourse for, a thing," and he does not fear to translate *terminus supponit pro re* by "the term stands for [*supplée*] the thing." In this lexicon, the *suppositio* of a term is thus defined: "We shall say then that the *suppositio* of a term, which we may translate as its 'substitutive value,' is its function in discourse—the while its meaning remains the same—of taking the place of a thing. This substitution (of term for thing) is, considering the copula, legitimate" (Maritain, *Introduction to Logic*, chap. 1, §3C). In this perspective, the latter part of the definition ("This substitution [of term for thing] is, considering the copula, legitimate") does not mean that a substitution of term for thing gives rise to a true proposition in the nature of things themselves, but rather: "the sort of existence—actual (past, present or future), possible or 'imaginary'—denoted by the copula permits this substitution" (ibid). Even though they are partially adequate to the medieval use of the term *suppositio*, the words *suppléance* and *substitution* have never prevailed in modern translations. *Suppositio* says more, in point of fact, than the French *substitution* (the terms being synonymous only in the juridical expression *supposition d'enfants*, designating the fraudulent substitution of two newborns) or than the English "substitution" (which also presents, along with the adjective "supposititious," the meaning of "deceitfully substituted"). It is this supplementary meaning that we would determine here, at the border between medieval grammar and theology.

II. Significatio/Suppositio/Appelatio: "Signification"/"Reference"/"Denotation"

If the meaning of "referent" is rather well suited to the grammarian's sense of *suppositum* deposited in *suppositio*, it conveys only in part the various aspects implied by its theological sense. The theological *suppositum* is not, in fact, the *hupokeimenon* [ὑποκείμενον] of Aristotelian ontotheology, the "subject" understood as the support or substrate of essential or accidental properties, but rather the *hupostasis* [ὑπόστασις] of Greek Trinitarian theology, which became *Persona* in the West and which entertains with the *ousia* [οὐσία] an altogether different relation than that entertained by the Aristotelian subject-substance with essence. It is, in any event, thanks to theology and to the specific problems of Trinitarian semantics that the noun was given a linguistic use with a verb in the expression, of scarcely Latinate formation, *supponere pro*, charged with expressing the essential or "personal" semantic value—*supponere pro essentia* or *supponere pro persona*—of the terms figuring in the principal affirmations of the dogma. From these uses stems the distinction thematized in the terminist logic of the thirteenth century by the distinction between "simple" supposition (*suppositio simplex*) and "personal" supposition (*suppositio personalis*). If the English "to stand for" and the French *être mis pour* correspond more or less to that first sense of *supponere pro*, no expression is truly serviceable; on the other hand, when *suppositio* and *supponere* plus the accusative are opposed to *appositio* and *apponere* plus the accusative, it is a matter in such cases of expressing two kinds of properties, one semantic, the other syntactical, in a single syntactico-semantic function: the relation of a noun-subject to a substance, that of an adjective-predicate to a quality.

The field of *suppositio/supponere* is further complicated with turns of phrase such as *supponere verbo, supponere personam verbo,* or *supponere locutioni*, which render the identification of *suppositio* with reference still more difficult—unless it be taken into consideration that a predicated term does not "refer." Now, if it is true that medieval logicians frequently raise the question of knowing whether a predicated term or an adjective "supposes," it is clear that they do not strictly understand thereby what is normally understood as "referring." A term that "apposes" (*apponit*), "couples" (*copulat*), or "is coupled" (*copulatur*) does not "refer" any less than a term that "supposes," as is evidenced by the standard definition of *copulatio* in the thirteenth century: "Copulatio est termini adiectivi acceptio pro aliquo" (Coupling is the meaning of an adjectival term for any particular thing).

■ See Box 1.

Given the inelegance of the expression "to supposit for," "to refer to" would gain ground in the literature in English. An argument often advanced in favor of that translation is

---

1

Suppositum/subjectum

➤ SUBJECT, WORD ORDER

The term *suppositum* corresponds to a special case of a term originally meaning "support" or "auxiliary" and is used in grammar texts primarily to designate the referent of a pronoun: Priscian says, for instance, that one can raise the question of the substance of the support by way of the question *Quis ambulat?* (Who is walking?; *Institutiones*, 17.23). It can consequently be said that the pronoun, by virtue of the fact that it signifies a "pure substance" (*substantia mera*), that is, that it does not determine on its own the proper or common qualities of that substance, "may be applied to all referents" (*ad omne suppositum pertinent*; Pierre Hélie, ca. 1140), since each can say *ego* of itself. From the pronoun's referent, the transition is smooth to that of discourse, from the person or substance on which discourse bears ("*id de quo fit sermo*"; *Logica Porretani*) to the person about whom the statement speaks ("*suppositum locutioni*"). The use made in Trinitarian theology of the term *suppositum*, the equivalent of *persona*, for the three persons

of the Trinity, naturally reinforces the sense of referent. With regard to a given statement (e.g., *Pater genuit*) in theological texts, one will have to guess which person the subject refers to and which person it "supports" (*supponit pro*). That use of the term *suppositum* as referent will be maintained throughout the Middle Ages, not only in grammar but also and above all in terminist logic, which evolved in the second half of the twelfth century, since the referential function of a noun in a propositional context will precisely be called *suppositio* (a noun "supports" or "supposes for" an individual, a form, etc.). It is naturally the sense of referent of the *suppositum* that will cause the noun *suppositio* to signify a referential property of the nominal term.

Starting in the middle of the twelfth century, logicians in the Porretanian group (around Gilbert de La Porrée) explained that a noun has two functions: "(sup)posing substance" and "apposing quality" (*officium supponendi substantiam et apponendi*

qualitatem), a function it fulfills when it is respectively *subjectum* and *praedicatum*. There will thus be a slippage from a referential function to a syntactical function, whence the exclusive use by grammarians of the term *suppositum* for the latter. The expression *supponere verbo* (to be a subject for a verb) is in fact an abridgement of the original expression *supponere personam verbo* (to posit or determine the person connected to the verb). A distinction will be made between *supponere verbo*, referring to the person dictating the grammatical agreement, and *supponere locutioni*, referring to the actual or logical subject, which may be distinct from it. Thus, according to the grammarian Robert of Paris (at the end of the twelfth century), in "Socrates legit et ipsum legere est bonum" (Socrates is reading and the fact that he is reading is good), *ipsum legere* is the support for the verb, but it is the pronoun *ipsum* that serves as the support of the statement, what it is that is being spoken about.

The term *subjectum* (and words of the same family) goes back to an ancient use in logic: it will be noted that Boethius designated the subject as *subjectus terminus* (*subjectus, subjectum*) in contrast to the *praedicatus terminus* (*praedicatus, praedicatum*) and speaks as well of the *res subjectae* (things substrate) in the triad *res, intellectus, voces*. The Roman grammarians had neither a term nor a notion corresponding to the subject and used other terms when conveying the conditions of proper formation of a canonical statement (nominative, substance, etc.). The introduction of that notion in grammar, under the obvious influence of logic, occurred at the beginning of the twelfth century: discussing the function of the participle (in a context supplied by Priscian, *Institutiones* 17.18), a commentator introduced the noun *subjectum* (and the verb *subici*) as opposed to *praedicatum* (and *praedicari*) in the context of a discussion of the cause of the invention of the participle, which allows two acts to be construed together without need of a conjunction (*ego legens disputo*) and thus "to be predicates of the same subject."

One finds in the logicians' interesting discussions of the bearing (*inclusio*) of quantifiers, based on the distinction between grammatical subject and logical (or real) subject. Logicians generally decided that the grammatical subject ought to be in the nominative case but that the logical subject can be in an oblique case, as in the interesting example: *cuiuslibet hominis asinus currit*, which can be interpreted either as (1) for every man *x*, there exists an ass *y* such that *x* possesses *y* and *y* runs:

$$[\forall x \, [\exists y \, ((x \text{ possesses } y) \wedge (y \text{ runs}))]$$

Or as (2): there exists an ass *y* such that every man possesses it and it runs:

$$[\exists y \, [\forall x \, ((x \text{ possesses } y) \wedge (y \text{ runs}))].$$

In each interpretation, the two nouns are affected differently by the quantifier and thus possess distinct quantities and modes of reference. The terminology used is far from uniform: one finds *subjectum attributionis* versus *locutionis*, and *subjectum enuntiationis* versus *praedictionis*. The definitional criteria of each of the two subjects are variable, both grammatically and logically. The grammatical subject is not always in the nominative, since certain grammarians consider as *suppositum*, notably, the agent in the ablative of a passive verb or the oblique constructed with an impersonal verb. The subject can then be defined either on the basis of the criterion of word order, as what is constructed *a parte ante*, that is, before the personal verb, a criterion based on the idea of a (problematical) natural order of the sentence subject, verb, object; or on the basis of the criterion of referential identity (what the subject refers to and what the verb relates to are the same "person"); or even, on the basis of terminology borrowed from Aristotle's *Physics*, "that from which the movement or action expressed by the verb proceeds" (*illud a qui egreditur actio*). In logic, examples of the sort referred to above have been the object of lively debate, depending on whether one regards word order, manner of utterance, speaker's intention, or listener's judgment to be the determining factor in interpretation.

In the terms *suppositum/subjectum*, one finds all the ambiguity in grammar and in linguistics contained by our term "subject": from grammatical subject to theme, by way of the agent or logical subject. In addition, the distinction between the term and what it refers to is not always made; one has in mind, to be sure, the former when one refers to its case or gender, but one is dealing with the latter when it is defined as *id de quo fit sermo*, "that on which the discourse bears."

Irène Rosier-Catach

BIBLIOGRAPHY

Baratin, Marc. "Sur les notions de sujet et de prédicat dans les texts latins." *Archives et Documents de la SHESL* 10 (1994): 49–77.

de Rijk, Lambertus Marie. "Each Man's Ass Is Not Everybody's Ass: On an Important Item in 13th-Century Semantics." In *Studies in Medieval Linguistic Thought*, edited by K. Koerner et al., 220–30. Amsterdam: Benjamins, 1980.

Kneepens, Corneille H. "'Suppositio' and 'Supponere' in 12th-Century Grammar." In *Gilbert de Poitiers et ses contemporains*, edited by J. Jolivet and A. de Libera, 324–51. Naples: Bibliopolis, 1987.

Libera, Alain de. "Référence et champ: Genèse et structure des theories médiévales de l'ambiguïté (XIIe–XIIIe siècles)." *Medioevo* 10 (1984): 155–208.

Rosier, Irène. "L'introduction des notions de sujet de prédicat dans la grammaire médiévale." *Archives et Documents de la SHESL* 10 (1994): 91–119.

the equivalence established by a number of modern interpreters between the couple *significatio/suppositio* and the various linguistic formations that have been more or less precisely associated since Russell with the Fregean distinction between *Sinn* and *Bedeutung*.

significatio	*suppositio*
Sinn	*Bedeutung*
sens/signification	*référence*
meaning	denotation
sens	*dénotation*

Of those translations the most debatable is certainly "denotation," which, aside from rendering unintelligible such technical expressions of fourteenth-century logic as *denotatur supponere*, blurs—not to say effaces—the marked distinction in the thirteenth century between *suppositio* (def., *acceptio termini substantivi pro aliquo*) and *appelatio* (def., *acceptio termini pro re existente*).

▪ See Box 2.

In order to stabilize usage, it may be admitted that the least bad solution, for texts of the thirteenth century, is the tripartite choice:

significatio	*suppositio*	*appellatio*
signification	reference	denotation

This setup, however, would no longer be valid for a number of fourteenth-century texts, in which *appelatio* does not mean the denotation of existent things but rather the referral from a term to what it means in a secondary or connotative manner (see CONNOTATION) and for which it does not suppose. For Jean Buridan (*Sophismata*), for example, the term "white," in the proposition "Peter is white," is said "to suppose for a man" (Peter) and to "call"/*appeler* or "connote" the "quality" or "singular whiteness" (see TROPE) that is presently in him.

▪ See Box 3.

Given such variations, it seems preferable in all circumstances to restrict oneself to replicas of the original: the semiartificial Latin of a medieval logician was neither more

2

Denotation of supposition

The inappropriate nature of the translation of *suppositio* as "denotation" appears clearly if one notes that the two verbs "suppose" and "denote" are associated in a technical expression, *denotari supponere*, which plays a central role in the nominalist semantics of propositions. Rigorously speaking "denotation of supposition" is a semantic property of propositions, whether affirmative or negative, concerning the subject terms of those propositions insofar as they are denoted by them as supposing or not supposing something.

That notion, which seems to have appeared in the fourteenth century, is one of the foundations of the Ockhamist theory of the conditions of truth. An affirmative proposition "denotes that the subject-term of a proposition supposes for something." A negative proposition "denotes that the subject-term does not suppose for something, or supposes for something whose predicate is denied in truth." The thesis can be illustrated as follows. A negative proposition has two "causes of truth." The proposition "the white man is not" is true either because the man does not exist and for that reason is not white, or because he exists but is not white. Inversely, an affirmative proposition always denotes that the term supposes for something. If it supposes for nothing, the proposition is false. Given *P* (the affirmative proposition "the white man is a man"), if no man is white, *P* is false. In point of fact, the subject of *P* is taken meaningfully and personally, not because it supposes for something, but because it is "denoted to suppose for something." However, it supposes for nothing, whereas it is "denoted to suppose for something." *P* is thus indeed false. The notion of "denotation of supposition" can thus be read: for the proposition, in the active mode (*denotare*)—the proposition denotes (or does not) that its subject supposes for something; for the term, in the passive mode (*denotari*)—the subject is denoted (or not) to suppose for something. From this point of view, the inference "the term *T* supposes, therefore it supposes for something," which is accepted by many philosophers under the Fregean form of the "presupposition of reference," is not valid. Thanks to the notion of *denotare* / *denotari supponere*, one can, on the other hand, formulate the valid inference: "The term *T* supposes, therefore it is denoted to suppose for something or it is denoted not to suppose for anything."

BIBLIOGRAPHY

Ockham, William of. *Summa logicae*. 3 vols. Edited by Philotheus Boehner. St. Bonaventure, NY: Franciscan Institute, 1951–54. Translation by Michael J. Loux: *Ockham's Theory of Terms: Part I of the Summa Logicae*. Notre Dame, IN: University of Notre Dame Press, 1974. Translated by Alfred J. Freddoso and Henry Schuurman: *Ockham's Theory of Propositions: Part II of the Summa Logicae*. Notre Dame, IN: University of Notre Dame Press, 1980.

elegant nor less bizarre than the technical idiolect that modern translators are obliged to content themselves with.

III. The Different Schemas of Medieval Semantics

The vocabulary, from the thirteenth to the fourteenth century, would become steadily more precise. Without entering into the complicated details of the divisions and subdivisions of the *suppositio* or retracing the evolution of doctrines, one can, on the basis of a limited sample—Parisian and Oxonian semantics of the years 1230–60—show how, on the basis of the distinction between *significatio* and *suppositio*, diametrically opposed theories were elaborated. The Parisian masters of the 1230s generally admitted that a term like "man" in itself possesses two semantic properties: first, a *significatio* defined as *repraesentatio rei per vocem secundum placitum* (conventional representation of a thing by a vocal sound). Signification thus understood is an intensional property. The term "man" does not signify a plurality of singular extramental things but rather a certain common nature or participable intension (def., "an animate living being, a mortal endowed with sensation"). Second, the *suppositio* is founded on the *significatio*: it is an *acceptio ipsius termini iam significantis rem pro aliquo* (a sense of the term already signifying a thing for something else). In Saussurian terms, *res* can be considered here as a "signified," *aliquid* referring to one or several referents. The specificity of the original Parisian tradition is to admit in addition a *suppositio* said to be "natural," which is defined as follows by Peter of Spain (*Tractatus*):

> Natural supposition is the acceptance of a general term for all those things of which, by its original imposition it can be a sign; as the term "man," when it is taken by itself, denotes all men, including those who exist, those who will exist, and those who have existed.

> (Suppositio naturalis est acceptio termini communis pro omnibus a quibus aptus natus est participari, ut "homo" per se sumptus de natura sua supponit pro omnibus hominibus qui fuerunt et qui sunt et qui erunt.)

This clearly prepropositional "reference" is modified as soon as the term is inscribed in a phrastic context. Its *suppositio* becomes, in effect, in this case "accidental," that is, determined by the exigency of the predicate (ibid.):

> Accidental supposition is the acceptance of a general term for all those things its adjunct determines.

> (Accidentalis suppositio est acceptio termini communis pro eis pro quibus exigit adiunctum.)

In a proposition whose copula is in the future or the past, the exigency of the predicate, that is, that of the time whose vehicle is the copula, assures the "restriction" (*restrictio, coartatio*) of the supposition of the subject in the tense indicated by the verb. This position was globally rejected by several English masters. In 1245–50, Roger Bacon rejected the hypothesis of a *suppositio naturalis* and pitted against it a semantics whose terms presuppose only in a propositional context and—by their nature, that is, their imposition (see HOMONYM, IV and CONNOTATION, Box 2)—suppose only for presents (linguistic terms being normally imposed extensionally to present things). In this semantics, which can be called Oxonian, restriction thus does not have a role: the only problem is

3
Appellatio in medieval logic

The term *appellatio* presents quite different definitions in medieval logic. Behind the word's apparent unity several concepts are concealed, partaking of heterogeneous theories. The first sense attested to is the one which, in the thirteenth century, defined the *appellatio* of a common term, whatever it be, as the supposition of that term for existent things (*pro his qui sunt, pro existente, pro presentia supposita, pro suppositis actu existentibus,* etc.). This is the denotative sense. A second sense attributed *appellatio* to proper as well as common terms "when they designate an existent thing" (Peter of Spain maintains in this regard that the proper noun "Petrus" signifies, supposes, and names the same things, "since it signifies an existent thing"). Other theories, on the other hand, reserved *suppositio* for the subject term and *appellatio* for the predicate. The introduction of that syntactical criterion is characteristic of the fourteenth century. It appears, in particular, in the work of Walter Burley, who defined it as follows:

> Appellation is the property of a common term predicable on what is subordinated to it. Thus, just as supposition taken in the strict sense is the property of the subject insofar as it is related to the predicate, similarly appellation is the property of the predicate related to the subject or to what is subordinated to it.

(Est appellatio proprietas termini communis praedicabilis de suis inferioribus. Unde sicut suppositio stricte accepta est proprietas subiecti, prout comparatur ad praedicatum, ita appellatio est proprietas praedicati comparati ad subiectum sive ad inferius.)

(*On the Purity of the Art of Logic*, §2)

Independent of this syntactical redefinition of appellation, the fourteenth century also accomplished a revolution of a kind for which philosophical lexicography offers few comparable cases. In fact, where the logicians of the thirteenth century designated as *appellatio* what we call "denotation," Jean Buridan reserves *appellatio*, reconceived through his efforts, for what he calls "connotatives." With that, the denotation/connotation doublet was formed under the paradoxical aspect indicated above: that of a two-faced entity whose two halves are separated by several centuries. In Buridan, in fact, "connotation" is not opposed to "denotation." The term is absorbed into a different network, with "supposition" and "appellation" its only partners. Thus it is that in his *Summulae de dialectica* (4.5.1; his long commentary on the *Tractatus* of Peter of Spain), the logician from Picardy characterizes as "appellative" "any term that connotes something other than that for which it supposes," before explaining that only connotative terms have

an appellation: they alone indeed "call what they connote [*appellant illud quod connotant*]." What remains to be clarified is the meaning of the expression *appellare suam formam*. Buridan's analysis is precise: by *material termini*, one must understand that for which this term supposes; by *forma termini*, "the form of a term," one should understand "everything that it connotes." If one takes, for example, the word *dives* (rich), one sees that the term supposes for a man (*material termini*), but that it "calls/names a house, fields, livestock, and many another thing possessed by him." It is that set of things owned that constitutes the *forma termini*. To say that the term *dives*, inserted in a proposition, "calls forth its form" signifies that it "connotes" or is "appellative" of "all things" possessed by the individual for which it supposes.

BIBLIOGRAPHY

Buridan, Jean. *Sophisms on Meaning and Truth*. Translated with an introduction by Theodore Kermit Scott. New York: Appleton-Century-Crofts, 1966.
———. *Summulae de dialectica*. Translated by Gyula Klima. Yale Library of Medieval Philosophy. New Haven, CT: Yale University Press, 2001.
Burley, Walter. *On the Purity of the Art of Logic: The Shorter and the Longer Treatises*. Translated by Paul Vincent Spade. New Haven, CT: Yale University Press, 2000.

---

explaining how the supposition determined by the original imposition of a term *ad praesentia* can be extended in certain contexts to things past, future, or possible. This is what Bacon did in attributing to the verbal tense, past or future, and to the mode (*potest*) a function said to be of "amplification" (*ampliatio*).

If, as of the thirteenth century, the same term of *significatio* refers to models as distinct as the Parisian intensional thesis and the Baconian extensional thesis, it will be seen that the meanings of technical terms of medieval semantics should be approached, translated, and interpreted holistically within well-defined networks. In misconstruing them, the modern reader risks repeating, with regard to the fundamental concepts of various medieval semantics, the kind of forced synthesis that the Russell of *On Denoting* imposed on Frege's distinction between *Sinn* and *Bedeutung* (see SENSE).

IV. Buridan: The Logician's Supposition and the Grammarian's

In the fourteenth century, Buridan defined *suppositio* as follows:

Est autem suppositio prout hic accipitur acceptio termini in propositione pro aliquo vel pro aliquibus quo

demonstrato vel quibus demonstratis per ista pronomina "hoc" vel "haec" vel equipollentia illis, terminus vere affirmatur de isto pronomine mediante copula illius propositionis.

(*Sophismata*, chap. 3, soph. 5, remark 1)

J. Biard translated it into French as follows:

La supposition, telle qu'elle est prise ici, est l'acception d'un terme dans une proposition, pour quelque chose, ou pour quelques choses, telles que, si cette chose ou ces choses sont désignées par les pronoms "ce," "cet," "cette," ou des expressions équivalentes, le terme est affirmé véridiquement de ce pronom au moyen de la copule de cette proposition.

a translation that can be compared to D. Perler's German version:

Die Supposition ist die Verwendung eines Terminus in einem Satz für einen oder für mehrere Gegenstände, auf die mit einem Demonstrativpronomen hingewiesen wird. Von diesem Pronomen wird der Terminus mittels der Kopula wahrhaft ausgesagt.

and finally with T. Kermit Scott's translation into English:

> But supposition as it is here used is the taking of a term in a proposition for some thing or things, in such a way that if that thing or those things are indicated by the pronoun "this" or "these," or the equivalent, then that term is truly affirmed of this pronoun, by the mediation of the copula of the proposition.

In this analysis, the *suppositio* is said of the subject and the predicate and is deeply anchored in what today would be called *deixis* [δεῖξις]. What Buridan means is that in a proposition such as "the horse is running," the term "horse" "supposes for every horse that exists, since, whichever the horse one designates, it will (or would) be true to say: this is a horse." That clause allows one to distinguish the logician's point of view from that of the grammarian. For the grammarian, "the nominative is said to be a *suppôt* or auxiliary in relation to the verb because it confers its person on it." *Reddere personam verbo, supponere verbo*: such expressions are, according to Buridan, typical of grammatical metalanguage (see Box 1). They permit an understanding of the fact that for the grammarian, it is licit to say that the term "Chimera" *supposes* in the statement "a Chimera is running": this is because in this metalanguage, "Chimera" *supposes to the verb* "is running." The expression "a Chimera is running" is congruent in that it respects the rules of grammatical agreement. For the grammarian, a term that does not mean anything that might exist can thus "suppose," but *to the verb* (*supponere verbo*). On the other hand, for the logician, "Chimera" *does not suppose*. The term undoubtedly has a meaning, but since it can not be taken in the proposition "a Chimera is running" for something of which it can be said, with the help of a demonstrative (deictic), "this is a Chimera," it has no supposition. In the strict sense of the terms, it thus cannot be said that the term "Chimera" does not "denote" anything, only that it does not "suppose." Buridan's thesis is alleged to cut short all speculation over that for which an empty term supposes or would suppose: intentional object, *fictum*, or "homeless" (*heimatlos*) object in the style of Alexius Meinong (see REALITY). An empty term is one that does not suppose in the logical sense of the word *supponere*.

As can be seen, the evolution of doctrines of "supposition" tends to redistribute with increasing refinement, to the point of having them pass from the object-language to the metalanguage, the semantic and syntactical elements naively confused in the first formulations of the notion. It is this aspect that no translation in terms of "reference" can capture.

Alain de Libera

BIBLIOGRAPHY

Biard, Joël. *Logique et théorie du signe au XIVe siècle*. Paris: Vrin, 1989.

Brown, Stephen. "Medieval Supposition Theory in its Theological Context." In *Medieval Philosophy and Theology*, vol. 3, edited by Norman Kretzmann and Mark D. Jordan. Notre Dame, IN: University of Notre Dame Press, 1993.

Buridan, Jean. *Sophismata*. Critical edition by Fabienne Pironet: *Iohanni Buridani Summularum Tractatus nonus: De practica sophismatum (Sophismata)*. Turnhout, Belg.: Brépols, 2004. Translation by Joël Biard: *Sophismes*. Paris: J. Vrin, 1993. Translation and introduction by Theodore Kermit Scott: *Sophisms on Meaning and Truth*. New York: Appleton-Century-Crofts, 1966.

de Rijk, Lambertus Marie. *Logica Modernorum: A Contribution to the History of Early Terministic Logic*. Vol. 1, *On the Twelfth Century Theories of Fallacy*. Assen, Neth.: Van Gorcum, 1962.

———. *Logica Modernorum: A Contribution to the History of Early Terministic Logic*. Vol. 2, *The Origin and Early Development of the Theory of Supposition* (in two parts). Assen, Neth.: Van Gorcum, 1967.

Fedriga, Ricardo, and Mariateresa Fumagalli Beonio-Brocchieri. *Logica e linguaggio nel medioevo*. Milan: LED, 1993.

Lewry, Peter Osmond. "Oxford Logic 1250–1275: Nicholas and Peter of Cornwall on Past and Future Realities." In *The Rise of British Logic: Acts of the 6th European Symposium on Medieval Logic and Semantics*, edited by P. O. Lewry, 19–62. Toronto: Pontifical Institute of Medieval Studies, 1983.

Maritain, Jacques. *An Introduction to Logic*. Translated by I. Choquette. New York: Sheed & Ward, 1937.

Maurer, Armand. *Medieval Philosophy*. 2nd ed. Toronto: Pontifical Institute of Medieval Studies, 1982.

Michon, Cyrille. *Nominalisme: La théorie de la signification d'Occam*. Paris: Vrin, 1994.

Panaccio, Claude. *Les mots, les concepts et les choses: La sémantique de Guillaume d'Occam et le nominalisme d'aujourd'hui*. Paris: Bellarmin-Vrin, 1991.

———. "La philosophie du lanage de Guillaume d'Occam." In *Sprachtheorien in Spätantike und Mittelalter*, edited by Sten Ebbesen, 184–206. Tübingen: Gunter Narr, 1995.

Perler, Dominik. *Der Propositionale Wahrheitsbegriff im 14. Jahrhundert*. New York: Walter de Gruyter, 1992.

Peter of Spain. *"Tractatus" Called afterwards, "Summulae logicales."* Edited by L. M. de Rijk. Assen, Neth.: Van Gorcum, 1972. Translation by Joseph Patrick Mullally: *The Summulae Logicales of Peter of Spain*. Notre Dame, IN: University of Notre Dame Press, 1945.

Read, Stephen, ed. *Sophisms in Medieval Logic and Grammar: Acts of the Ninth European Symposium on Medieval Logic and Semantics*. Dordrecht, Neth.: Kluwer, 1993.

Sherwood, William of. *William of Sherwood's Introduction to Logic*. Translated with an introduction and notes by Norman Kretzmann. Minneapolis: University of Minnesota Press, 1966.

SVET [свет] (RUSSIAN)

ENGLISH	light, world
FRENCH	*lumière, monde*

➤ LIGHT, *WORLD*, and ACT, BOGOČELOVEČESTVO, DRUGOJ, ESSENCE, GOD, *GRACE*, MIR, NAROD, PLEASURE, POSTUPOK

The ambiguity of the root *svet* [свет], "light/world," is valid for all Slavic languages and is based on the ancient cosmology that characterizes the world as a space defined by light. Difficulties in translation appear when authors deliberately play on the semantic tension between *svet* (light) and *svet* (world). Another distinctive feature of the Slavic concept of light relates to the quasi-etymological consonance between *svet* (light) and *svjatost* [святость] (holiness), which is rooted in the Orthodox theology of uncreated light (*phôs* [φῶς]).

I. *Svet* as "Light" and *Svet* as "World"

The noun *svet* [свет] in modern Russian has conserved the ancient Slavonic sense of "light." But another sense of the same word is "world." The ambiguity of the root *svet*, "light/world," is a phenomenon common to Slavic languages: Polish *świat*, Ukrainian *svit* [світ], Czech *svět*, Serbo-Croatian *svijet* mean "world," whereas Polish *światło*, Ukrainian *svitlo* [світло], Czech *světlo*, Serbo-Croatian *svijetlo* mean "light" (RT: Herman, *Dictionary of Slavic Word Families*, 509). One finds an analogous ambiguity in Hungarian with *világ* (light, world) and in Romanian with *lumină* (light) and *lume* (inhabited world, people) from the Latin *lumen*, "light." In both cases, the ambiguity is attributed to a semantic borrowing modeled on the Slavic languages (ibid., 511), which is thus all the more noteworthy.

It is regularly admitted that "world" is a secondary meaning of *svet* (RT: Herman, *Slavic Word Families*, 511; Machek, *Etymologický slovník jazyka českého a slovenskeho* [Etymological dictionary of the Czech and Slovak languages], 488; Brückner, *Słownik etymologiczny języka polskiego* [Etymological dictionary of the Polish language], 535; Tsyganenko, *Ètimologiceskij slovar' russkogo jazyka* [Etymological dictionary of the Russian language], 412). According to V. Machek, this secondary meaning is due to the idiomatic expression *přijiti na svět* (literally, "to come to light"). This expression means "to arrive in a realm of light" and, at the same time, "to settle amidst the people and things of the place" (Machek, *Etymologický slovník*, 488). In Russian, *pojavit'sja na svet* [появиться на свет] (literally, "to appear in the light") means "to be born." The concept of *svet* as world seems to contain a visual intuition according to which to be, for something or someone, is essentially to be in the light, in the openness of space (cf. the ancient Greek *phôs* [φῶς—with a circumflex], "light," and *phos* [φώς—with an acute accent], "man." This concept of world/light—*svet*—succeeded in supplanting the more ancient concept of *mir* [мир] (world/peace) in a certain number of Slavic languages (for example, in Czech, Slovak, Polish, Ukrainian, Bulgarian), but not in Russian (see Herman, *Slavic Word Families*, 291; Machek, *Etymologický slovník*, 488).

II. *Svet* and *Svjat*

The other distinctive feature of this Slavic "light" is semantic proximity between the adjectives *svetlyj* [светлый], "luminous, radiant," and *svjatoj* [святой], "holy, sacred." Diachenko (RT: Diachenko, *Complete Church-Slavonic Dictionary*) concludes that the forms *sveti* and *svjat* are "philologically identical" (582). The elaboration of that identity is theological in nature:

> According to the most ancient beliefs, the sacred (*svjatoj*) is luminous (*svetlyj*) and white (*belyj* [белый]). This is because the very element of light is a divinity that does not tolerate any darkness, impurity, or, in its later sense, sin.

> (Ibid., 582)

But G. Diacenko's statement is not confirmed elsewhere. Thus, according to A. Brückner, *svet* (pre-Slavic *svet*) stems from Avestic *spaeta*, "white," whereas *svjatoj* (pre-Slavic *svet*) comes from Avestic *spenta*, "sacred," equivalent to Greek *hagios* [ἅγιος] and Latin *sanctus*. The connection between *spaeta* and *spenta* is thus not clear (Brückner, *Słownik etymologiczny*, 535, 537).

More plausibly, the idea of an etymological identity between *svet* and *svjat-* is simply a metaphysical invention, which is, moreover, quite appropriate. The consonance between light and holiness is amply corroborated in Orthodox theology, and its doctrine of powers or energies of God goes back to Dionysius the Areopagite. In Orthodox Christian thought divine power manifests itself in an act of grace offering each human being the possibility of *theôsis* [θέωσις] (see BOGOČELOVEČESTVO). Gregory Palamas (ca. 1296–1359) developed, following the church fathers, the distinction between the essence of God and the divine energies. This distinction was canonized as a dogma of the Eastern Church: the "Palamite" councils recognized the possibility of seeing God—in his energies or in his grace—with bodily eyes. Palamas characterizes the "divine energies" (*dunameis theou* [δυνάμεις θεοῦ]) as *phôs*, "light," or *ellampsis* [ἔλλαμψις], "illumination." This divine light, which a human being can labor to see, is not a creation of God but his mode of existence and real manifestation.

> Transcendent through his essence . . . God proceeds out of his essence. He continually emerges from that retreat and that exit, those "processions" or *dunameis*, are a mode of existing in which the Divinity can communicate itself to created beings.

> (Lossky, *Image and Likeness*)

■ See Box 1.

III. *Svet* and *Blagodat'* [благодать]

The divine light is thus in no way a metaphor but rather a real manifestation of God and a mode of his existence:

> It is the visible character of the divinity, the energies in which God communicates and reveals himself to those who have purified their hearts. . . . This uncreated, eternal, divine, and deifying light is grace, since the name of grace (*charis* [χάρις]) fits as well the divine energies, insofar as they are given to us and effect the work of our deification.

> (Lossky, *Image and Likeness*, 52–53)

The divine Light is the very substance of the Transfiguration: it is the real quality of "those who have purified their heart"—the saints.

It will not come as a surprise that linguistic intuition tends to link "light" (Russian *svet*) and holiness (Russian *svjatost'* [святость]). To be a saint is to be filled with grace, with divine light. The representation of holiness by means of a halo is characteristic of Eastern iconography and particularly, if the expression be permitted, of that of Slavic expression. Pavel Florensky, in chapter 5 of *The Pillar and Ground of the Truth*, cites copious testimony confirming the visible and visual character of the light emanating from the saints.

> The notion of the light of grace (*sveta blogodatnogo* [света благодатного]) is one of the few fundamental ideas of the entire liturgy, since that liturgy was composed by spiritual men, pneumataphora, who had undergone the experience of beatific knowledge (*blogodatnoe vedenie* [благодатное ведение]).

> (Florensky, *Pillar and Ground*, 69)

It should be remembered that the first meaning of *spenta*, "sacred," is "exuberant, overflowing with supernatural power," and that the first meaning of *svjat-* (pre-Slavic *svets*) refers to the pagan idea of supernatural gifts (RT: Benveniste,

1

The theology of light

In order to understand the theology of light of Palamas, one must begin with the distinction forged by Saint John of Damascus between the essence or nature of God (*ousia* [οὐσία], *phusis* [φύσις]) on the one hand, and "what is close to nature [*ta peri tên phusin* (τὰ περὶ τὴν φύσιν)]," on the other. To designate the second term, Palamas used the term *energeiai* [ἐνέργειαι], "energies," borrowed from the Cappadocians, simultaneously with the Dionysian term *dunameis* [δυνάμεις]. These "energies" do not designate voluntary acts, such as the Creation, but are a mode of being of God. God reveals himself in his powers or energies (*dunameis te kai energeiai* [δυνάμεις τε καὶ ἐνέργειαι]); however, as opposed to the essence of God, his powers are accessible to religious or mystical knowledge. Insisting on the absolute unknowability of the divine essence, Palamas regarded the word *ousia* as unsuitable for God: he preferred the term *huperousiotês* [ὑπερουσιότης], "superessence" (cf. de Andia, *L'Union à Dieu chez Denys l'Aréopagite*, 155), to the extent that God, as opposed to his creatures is not limited by his essence. Similarly, considering that traditional *dunameis* and *energeiai* were too abstract to name the living God, Palamas identified the visible being of God and created light (*phôs* [φῶς]). Thus rearticulating the ideas of the fathers in terms of his metaphysics of light, Palamas elaborated the edifice of traditional Orthodox theology (cf. V. Lossky, *In the Image and Likeness of God*). The notion of divine light or deifying grace, associated with the light of the Transfiguration seen by the apostles at Mount Tabor, was canonized by the Orthodox Church in the fourteenth century.

BIBLIOGRAPHY

de Andia, Y. *L'Union à Dieu chez Denys l'Aréopagite*, Leiden: Brill, 1966.

Le vocabulaire des institutions indo-européennes, 2:184). The "cultural baptism of paganism resulted in its transformation into "grace"; thus it was that against a Slavic backdrop, "holy" (*svjatoj*) became "luminous" (*svetlyj*) and "blessed" (*blagodatnyj* [благодатный], "full of grace"). This type of cultural baptism is a general phenomenon of European Christianity.

IV. Translating *Svet*, the Grace That Transfigures

Allusions to the *svet/svjat-* connection are part of the cultural heritage and do not imply, at least in the Russian tradition, a direct reference to the theology of light. Many such allusions are to be found in Dostoevsky. Light and holiness are for him, for example, the components of the respect owed to the *narod* [народ]: "There are in the people (*v narode est*) veritable saints (*svjatye*)—and what saints! Luminous themselves (*sami svetjat*), they illuminate (*osveščajut*) our common path [в народе есть . . . прямо святые, да еще какие: сами светят и всем нам путь освещают] (Dostoevsky, *Dnevnik pisatelia za 1876 god* [*A writer's diary of the year 1876*)]. In the translation, the consonance between *svetjat and osveščajut* (both derived from *svet*), on the one hand, and *svatje* (derived from *svjat-*), on the other, is lost. But plainly, the idea of a creative transformation, a transfiguration suited to the *narod* and represented by the image of light, is an important aspect of Dostoyevsky's thought (see NAROD). He thus writes, concerning the future of the *narod*:

Circumstances are going to change, things will go better, debauchery may even leave the people (*narod*), and the luminous principles (*svetlye načala*) within it will remain more unshakable and more holy (*svjatee*) than ever.

(А идеалы в нашем народе есть и сильные, а ведь это главное: поменяются обстоятельства, улучшится дело, и разврат, может быть, соскочит с народа, и светлые-то начала в нем останутся незыблемее и святее, чем когда-либо прежде.)

(Ibid., 43)

Light, perhaps more in Russian than in other languages, signals the spiritual, the ideal, the noble, the sacred. Whatever the case, the appeal to transfiguration via the image of the light of divine grace that is solicitous and divinizes, "*blogodatnyj svet* [благодатный свет]," has often been associated with the "Russian idea." Serge Troubetskoi, for example, writes in his article "The Light of Tabor and the Transfiguration of the Spirit" (1914):

Our creative, artistic and philosophical work has always needed not an abstract truth [see ISTINA], but one that is real and effective. . . . Intentionally or not, the greatest representatives of the genius of the Russian people (*narodnyj* [народный]) have always sought that light (*svet*) which cares for and transfigures from within the life of the body and the spirit.

(Troubetskoi, in M. A. Masline, ed., *Russkaja Ideja*, 242)

V. Strategies of Ambiguity

Other difficulties in translation emerge when authors play intentionally on the semantic tension between *svet*-light and *svet*-world. Vladimir Propp, in order to explain the complexity of the idea of the "other world [*tot svet* (тот свет)]" in fairy tales, writes:

The tale expresses things in a very naïve but perfectly precise manner: "There, the light (*svet*) is as it is with us. But the light (*svet*) changes, the forms of social organization change, at the same time as they do, 'the other world (*svet*)' changes."

(Propp, *Theory and History of Folklore*, 380)

To all appearances, the first occurrence of *svet* in this passage can also refer to the light of the other world just as well as to the other world itself, which renders the sentence "There, the *svet* is as it is with us" definitively ambiguous.

An even less translatable configuration of the meanings of *svet* is produced by Arsenij Tarkovskij in one of his poems:

There is no death in the world (*na svete* [на свете]). All are immortal, and everything is immortal. One mustn't be afraid of death, neither at seventeen nor at seventy. There is only the present (*jav'* [явь]) and light (*svet*), the shadows and death do not exist in this world (*na etom svete* [на этом свете]).

(Tarkovskij, *Zemle—zemnoye*, 85)

The key to this passage is maintaining as inexistent all the entities incompatible with *svet* (light) in *svet* (the world). The affirmation of the exclusive reality of *svet* is reinforced by the image of the world full of the grace that confers immortality. But the more the theological reality is veiled, the better it achieves its aim.

Zulfia Karimova
Andriy Vasylchenko

BIBLIOGRAPHY

Dostoyevsky, Fyodor. *The Unpublished Dostoevsky: Diaries and Notebooks (1860–1881)*. Edited by Carl R. Proffer. Translated by T. S. Berczynski et al. Ann Arbor, MI: Ardis, 1973–76.

Florensky, Pavel. *The Pillar and Ground of the Truth*. Translated and annotated by Boris Jakim. Princeton, NJ: Princeton University Press, 1997.

Lossky, Vladimir. *In the Image and Likeness of God*. Edited by John H. Erickson and Thomas E. Bird. Introduction by John Meyendorff. Crestwood, NY: St. Vladimir's Seminary Press, 1974.

Maslin, Mikhail. *Alexandrovi Aleksandrovič. Russkaja Ideja*. Moscow: Republica, 1992.

Propp, Vladimir. *Theory and History of Folklore*. Translated by Ariadna Y. Martin and Richard P. Martin et al. Edited, with an introduction and notes by Anatoly Liberman. Minneapolis: University of Minnesota Press, 1984.

Tarkovskij, Arsenij. *Zemle—zemnoe*. Moscow: Sovetskij Pisatel, 1966.

SVOBODA [свобода], VOLJA [воля] (RUSSIAN)

ENGLISH   liberty, freedom
FRENCH   *liberté, volonté*

➤ LIBERTY, WILL and DRUGOJ, I/ME/MYSELF, ISTINA, NAROD, PLEASURE, RUSSIAN, TRUTH, WILLKÜR

The two Russian terms *svoboda* [свобода] and *volja* [воля] are translated into French as *liberté* (freedom); *volja* also possesses the meaning of will. In addition *volja* designates a vast expanse without limits, e.g., a steppe; this sense reinforces the connotation of arbitrariness present in *volja* in the sense of freedom. The *svoboda/volja* opposition is interpreted with the help of those between "culture/nature" and "form/matter": *volja* is the matter of the person (*ličnost'* [личность]), whereas *svoboda* is its form and structure. *Svoboda*, in contrast to *liberum arbitrium*—the structure of free will—is always beyond norms and rules. In its existentialist sense (notably in Dostoyevsky), it is founded on the relation between self and fellow creatures, objects of love and hatred. For Russian thinkers, *svoboda*, understood as a victory over necessity, has always been a value in itself, whereas *volja*, manifesting the spontaneity of man, has rather served as a popular (and even populist) ideal.

I. The Semantic Fields of *Volja* and *Svoboda*

Volja [воля] comes from the old Russian verb *voliti* [волити], Sanskrit *varayati*, "he chooses himself, solicits, searches" (RT: *Etymological Dictionary of the Russian Language*). The term designates a psychological faculty of intention and desire, "will." It can also signify "the possibility of disposing, power." At the same time it means "the freedom to manifest something, a free situation, freedom, independence" (Preobrazhenski, *Dictionary of the Russian Language,* vol. 1). In addition, *volja* designates a vast expanse without limits (ibid.), of which the steppe is a paradigmatic case; this last sense is inherent in *volja* understood as "liberty."

The connotations of *volja* in the sense of "will" play a considerable role in the terminological field of *pleasure*. Thus the words *udovletvorenie* [удовлетворение] (satisfaction), and *udovol'stvie* [удовольствие] (pleasure), are derived from *volja* through the Old Russian lexeme *dov(o)l'*. The initial meaning is connected to satisfaction of the will (*volja*) to the point of satiety. In contemporary Russian one finds *dovlet'* [довлеть] (to suffice, to be sufficient), *dovol'nyj* [довольный] (who feels or expresses contentment, etc.); one finds as well the Ukrainian adverb *dovoli* [доволі] "quite enough." Thus *udovol'stvie* has the meaning of "joy of the sensations, the emotions, agreeable thoughts" (Preobrazhenski, *Dictionary of the Russian Language,* vol. 4). *Udovol'stvie* is not linked directly to the satisfaction of the desires or needs of the subject, as opposed to *udovletvorenie*. However, the etymological bond that attaches *udovol'stvie* to *volja* gives that word the nuance of abundance in relation to the will. The Russian term *svoboda* [свобода] (freedom) comes from the Slavic possessive pronoun *svoj* [свой], which means belonging to the person and is rendered, depending on the context by "(my, your, his, our, your, their) own"—as in Sanskrit *sva*, Latin *suus*, and Greek *swos* (RT: *Le vocabulaire des institutions indo-européennes*, vol. 1). Beyond that, *svoj* designates in contemporary speech (as in Old Slavonic and Russian) the member of a family, tribe, or community; *svoj* in this sense is the opposite of *čužoj* [чужой], "stranger." According to Vasmer's *Etymological Dictionary* (RT: *Ėtimologicheskiĭ slovar' russkogo iazyka* [Etymological dictionary of the Russian language]), pre-Slavic *svoboda* initially signified "belonging to a family or tribe," the "state of a free man." One also finds this sense of identity in Slavic terms of the same root *osoba* [особа] and *sobstvo* [собство] "the person," as in the contemporary *sobstvennost'* [собственность], "property."

In Old Russian, *svoboda* possesses a connotation of independence; it can signify a free colony. In ordinary language the modern use of *svoboda* is indistinguishable from that of *liberté* in French. But at the level of philosophical conceptualization, one finds the original connotations.

II. The Diglossic Opposition *Svoboda/Volja*

The formation of the modern concept of *svoboda* in Russian was accompanied by a semantic tension between the synonyms *svoboda* and *volja*. According to George Fedotov, at the time of the Moscovite state, the idea of *svoboda* (a leading term of the opposition) had a positive value solely in cultivated circles. The spirit of freedom (*svoboda*) manifested itself in attempts by the boyars to constrain the power of the czar. For the common man, on the contrary, *svoboda* had a purely negative value, synonymous with impunity and slackening. The popular ideal of *volja* (a lower-class term), however, signified the possibility of living while following only one's own will, in the margins of the limits imposed by the bonds of society.

> *Volja* finds its triumph either in a distancing from society, in the vast expanse of the steppe, or rather in power over society, in violence over men. . . . It is not opposed to tyranny, since the tyrant as well possesses *volja.* The brigand is the ideal of the Moscovite *volja,* just as Ivan the Terrible is the ideal of the czar. Since *volja,* like anarchy, is impossible in the cultural community, the Russian ideal of *volja* finds its manifestation in the cult of the desert, of nature in the wild, nomadic and bohemian life, wine, debauchery, the forgetting of oneself in passion—in criminality, rebellion, tyranny.

> (Fedotov, *Rossija i svoboda* [Russia and freedom])

These sociolinguistic remarks by Fedotov were written at the beginning of the 1940s, at the time of fascist and communist regimes that gave the *svoboda/volja* diglossic opposition political currency. For Fedotov *svoboda* refers to liberal and democratic: as an elevated term it was removed from connotations of arbitrariness and tyranny. "Personal freedom [*svoboda*] is not possible without respect for the freedom [*svoboda*] of the other" (ibid., 183). One can adduce here a passage from the *Two Treatises of Government* in which Locke states that man's original situation is a natural state or a "state of perfect freedom" (*Two Treatises of Government*, 287). According to Locke, "though this be a state of liberty, yet it is not a state of license" (288), since *liberty* includes obligations before God as before men. The two terms "freedom" and "liberty" are ordinarily both translated by *svoboda*, as they are translated by *liberté* in French, whereas "license," in the Russian edition of Locke is rendered by *svoevolie* [своеволие] (1988, 263), "the tendency to act by following one's whim or arbitrary caprice" (Preobrazhenski, *Dictionary of the Russian Language*, vol. 4). *Svoevolie*, which carries a negative charge, comes from the expression *svoja volja* [своя воля] (his own will); the adjective *svoevol'nyj* [своевольный] means "arbitrary, acting at whim"; thus the Russian translation of Locke's term "license" possesses a sense quite close to that of *volja* in Fedotov. *Volja*—as a debased term in the linguistic pair—designates an abuse of freedom.

III. *Svoboda* as Culture and Form, *Volja* as Nature and Matter

One says in Russian *svoboda slova* [свобода слова], "freedom of speech"; *svoboda pečati* [свобода печати], "freedom of the press"; *svoboda sovesti* [свобода совести], "freedom of thought"; *svoboda ličnosti* [свобода личности], "freedom of the individual." *Volja ličnosti* [воля личности] has the clear meaning of "individual will"; but the expressions *volja slova, volja pečati, volja sovesti* do not exist: *volja* as freedom does not allow a complement in the genitive. Indeed, *volja* cannot become partial or personal: it is a universal and indivisible reality, like the steppe, and has no owner. Even more, it is a homogeneous reality, opposed to every obligatory act and responsibility. It is pure formlessness, an indeterminate realm in which the defined character of things disappears—as in a Bakhtinian carnival.

The disorder and universalism of *volja* are opposed to the structural and specific character of *svoboda. Svoboda* is a cultural acquisition; it "presupposes an internal discipline" (Pomerants, "*Evropejskaja svoboda,*" 139); it is even the "inner form of the personality [*ličnost*]" (140) that renders the free act possible. The *svoboda/volja* opposition is thus interpreted by way of the opposition between culture and nature and, ultimately, via the traditional form/matter opposition. *Svoboda* is the form of the *ličnost* (the person or personality), just as, in classical philosophy, the soul is the form of the human being.

From this point of view, *volja* can no longer be identified with destruction. For Fedotov as a social ideal it takes on a destructive aspect, whereas *svoboda* obtains a positive value, specifically that of democratic "freedom." But at the level of the individual, *volja* rather represents a spontaneous, Dionysian origin of the human personality. Thus the Russian expression *davat' volju* [давать волю] signifies to give free rein (to one's emotions, thoughts, etc.), whereas *davat' svobodu* [давать свободу] means bestowing freedom (e.g., on a slave). The idiomatic equivalent in English succeeds in conveying the connotation of spontaneity: *davat' volju* is translated as "to give free play"—as in "giving free play to one's feelings" (as opposed to "curbing" them. *Volja* is the free play of the human personality; it can, to be sure, take a destructive turn, but it can also take on defined form—thanks to culture. "A balance between the freedom (*svoboda*) of civilization and natural freedom (*volja*) takes a different turn in each culture and in each era" (Pomerants, "*Evropejskaja svoboda,*" 141).

IV. *Svoboda* and *Drugoj* (Other People)

Russian thinkers frequently insist on the fundamental opposition between *svoboda* and the *liberum arbitrium* of an isolated subject. Our freedom (*svoboda*) is not the free will (*svoboda voli* [свобода воли], i.e., the freedom of choice (*svoboda vybora* [свобода выбора])" (Fedotov, *Rossija i svoboda*, 251). Similarly Berdyayev rejects the notion that *svoboda* can be understood as "freedom of choice, the possibility of turning left or right," (*Dream and Reality*, 72): such free will functions only in terms of responsibility and punishment, "from a juridical point of view, as criminology applied to human life." But "freedom [*svoboda*] has an entirely different bearing" (ibid., 72).

Svoboda reveals its structure in the novels of Dostoyevsky, whose characters are perpetually in intimate confrontations with Others (*drugoj* [другой], derived from *drug* [друг], "friend"), representing the entirety of the universe. The character must choose between the *caritas* of total responsibility for oneself and the universe, on the one hand, and the total diabolical destruction of "everything is permitted" (*vsedozvolennost'* [вседозволенность], derived from *volja*), on the other. The ground of *svoboda* is thus the relation between self and others, my fellow creatures, and ultimately objects of love and hatred. It is on that structure that the free act (*postupok*) [поступок] is ultimately based. Mikhail Bakhtin successfully integrated the existentialist notion of free choice in his philosophy of the act:

> My singularity as obligatory noncoincidence with everything that is not me always offers me the possibility

of a singular and irreplaceable act (*postupok*) in relation to everything that is not me.

(Bakhtin, Toward a Philosophy, 42)

According to Bakhtin, he who does not assume responsibility for himself and his situation toward Others cannot truly partake of being and is an impostor. It is solely in the responsible act toward others that freedom—the structure of the person—is achieved. Similarly, through love and friendship, freedom is an interpersonal structure: "I am not free unless you, too, are" (Berlin, *Russian Thinkers*, 107).

V. *Svoboda* and *Neobxodimost'* (Necessity)

Everything, however, that is imposed from without on the person—norms, rules, laws—becomes relative and conditional in that it restricts freedom. Paradoxically, *svoboda* as structure is anomic: it is nothing other than the elimination of necessity. Thus, according to Bakhtin, *svoboda* is an independence in relation to all laws, whether "political, criminal, or civil," that other men impose on the individual "against his private convictions" (*Toward a Philosophy*). But for all political thinkers—and not merely the anarchist Bakunin—*svoboda* as a triumph over necessity has always been a value in itself, whether understood as individual freedom (liberalism), communitarian freedom (of a Slavophile sort and *narodničestvo* [народничество]), or even as the freedom of workers (Marxism).

The feeling of *svoboda* has always been a value more appreciated than the rules of morality. "The truly free man (*svobodnyj* [свободный] creates his own morality," Herzen had already written in 1850 (Herzen, *Sobranie socinenij* [Collected works], 6:131). In elaborating the idea of *svoboda* as a triumph over necessity (*neobxodimost'* [необходимость]), religious thinkers (Solovyov, Vycheslavtsev, Lossky, Frank) developed the "ethic of love (*etika ljubvi* [этика любви])," which starts with the freedom of human action and contrasts with Kantian moral formalism. Berdyayev follows this ethical tradition:

Freedom is my independence and the inner determination of my person; it is my creative force, not the choice between the good and evil that are placed before me, but my own creation of evil and good.

(Berdyayev, *Dream and Reality*)

For Berdyayev, *svoboda* as a source of creation is the opposite of the "congealed and static moral order" (Berdyayev, *Destiny of Man*, 11), and, finally, of being (*bytie* [бытие]), of given and objectified reality. Moreover, man apprehends the truth (*istina* [истина]) solely if he is free:

It is in freedom and through freedom that one recognizes truth (*istina*). The truth (*istina*) that is imposed on me by asking me to renounce freedom (*svoboda*) is not at all truth (*istina*), but a temptation of the devil (*čertov soblazn* [чёртов соблазн]).

(Berdyayev, *Destiny of Man*, 73)

This existentialist doctrine, according to which every objective science is a source of necessity and thus of subjugation of man, takes on a tragic character in Shestov: "What is

sure is that having stretched a hand toward the tree of science, men have forever lost their freedom" (Shestov, *Athens and Jerusalem*, 135). After the Fall they conserved "only the freedom of choosing between 'good' and 'evil,'" whereas formerly "they had the possibility not of choosing between good and evil, but of deciding whether evil would or would not exist" (ibid.). According to Shestov true freedom is "the freedom of ignorance (*svoboda neznanija* [свобода незнания])" (198).

Despite the diversity of contemporary philosophical meanings of *svoboda*, the concept retains its anomic and anarchistic character. The expression *svoboda voli*, which renders the Latin *liberum arbitrium*, expresses an anomie even more violent than its literal translation as "freedom of the will."

VI. *Volja* in Ukrainian

Volja has the same double meaning in other Slavic languages. Thus, the Ukrainian word *volja* signifies "will" as well as "freedom." In Ukrainian *volja* and *svoboda* are synonyms; as in Russian *volja* is never used with a genitive. However, it does not have the connotation of a vast expanse without limits. In a classic poem of the beginning of the twentieth century, *Odno slovo* (A single word), Lesia Ukraïnka presents us with a deportee of the era of the Russian czarist empire living in a colony amid a northern tribe, in the middle of the vast expanse of Siberia. In studying the local language, he tries to explain the word "freedom" to the inhabitants of the region, since their language does not contain that term. The deportee suffers from the vanity of his efforts. Obsessed by constant moral suffering, he falls gravely ill—without any visible illness. Nearing death, he says to a young man of the region: "I am going to die from what has no name in your land, even if it exists *without limit* here. What might bring me back to life does not have a name either, but in any event it does not exist among you. If the word were nonetheless to exist, I would still be able to live; but it doesn't exist" (Ukraïnka, *Tvory v dvokh tomakh*). Whereas in Russian *volja* is limitless, in Ukrainian the word does not at all connote the infinite. On the contrary, it is *nevolja* [неволя] (slavery), the antonym of the *volja* that exists "without limits." The freedom of the individual is unique and inexpressible outside the limits of one's own culture; the vast unlimited expanse of a foreign country crushes freedom. The feeling of untranslatability is reinforced by an effect of preterition: the story is told by a young native of the country, without the words *volja* and *svoboda*. It is because of the untranslatable character of *volja* that Lesia Ukaïnka's deportee died: he felt useless outside his language, his culture, his freedom, even if plunged in the limitless expanse of the empire.

The fusion in *volja* of freedom and an expanse without limits thus seems a phenomenon specific to the Russian language alone, even as the extremely anomic character of *svoboda* is a phenomenon of Russian philosophy. Beyond the double meaning of *volja* as "will" and as "freedom," another translation difficulty of the terminological field of *svoboda* is related to the fact that *volja* as freedom often functions as a synonym of *svoboda*, whereas in diglossic contexts, on the contrary, it is opposed to it. In such contexts *volja*, which can be translated as "arbitrary" or with the expression "acting by whim," is fully as subversive for *svoboda* as constraint.

Svoboda is truly a fragile substance: it is as fearful of unlimited freedom (*volja*) as it is of necessity (*neobxodimost'*).

Andriy Vasylchenko

BIBLIOGRAPHY

Bakhtin, Mikhail. *Toward a Philosophy of the Act*. Translation and notes by Vadim Liapunov. Edited by Michael Holquist and Vadim Liapunov. Austin: University of Texas Press, 1993.

Berdyayev, Nikolai. *The Destiny of Man*. Translated by Natalie Duddington. New York: Harper, 1960.

———. *Dream and Reality: An Essay in Autobiography*. Translated by Katharine Lampert. New York: Macmillan, 1950.

Berlin, Isaiah. *Russian Thinkers*. London: Hogarth Press, 1978.

Fedotov, George. *Rossija i svoboda*. New York: Chalidze Publications, 1981.

Herzen, Alexander. *From the Other Shore*, translated from the Russian by Moura Budberg. *The Russian People and Socialism*, translated from the French by Richard Wollheim. Introduction by Isaiah Berlin. Oxford: Oxford University Press, 1979.

———. *Selected Philosophical Works*. Translated by L. Navrozov. Moscow: Foreign Languages, 1956.

———. *Sobranie sochinenii* [Collected works]. 30 vols. Moscow: Akademiia nauk, 1954–1966.

Locke, John. *Two Treatises of Government*. Edited by P. Laslett. Cambridge: Cambridge University Press, 1988.

Pomerants, Grigorij. "Evropejskaja svoboda i russkaja volja." *Druba narodov* 4 (1994).

Shestov, Lev. *Athens and Jerusalem*. Translated by Bernard Martin. Athens: Ohio University Press, 1966.

Ukraïnka, Lesia, *Tvory v dvokh tomakh* [Works]. Vol. 1. Kiev: Naukova Dumka, 1986.

TABLEAU

ENGLISH	picture, painting
GERMAN	*Malerei, Gemälde, Bild*
GREEK	*zôgraphêma* [ζωγράφημα], *pinax* [πίναξ]
ITALIAN	*quadro*
LATIN	*tabula*

➤ AESTHETICS, ART, BILD, DESCRIPTION, DISEGNO, HOMONYM, MIMÊSIS, PLASTICITY

Lord Shaftesbury gives a very precise tone to the issue when he affirms,

> But 'tis then that in Painting we may give to any particular Work the Name of Tablature, when the Work is in reality "a Single Piece, comprehended in one View, and form'd according to one single Intelligence, Meaning, or Design; which constitutes a real Whole, by a mutual and necessary Relation of its Parts, the same as of the Members in a natural Body."
>
> *(Historical Draught or Tablature of the Judgment of Hercules, in Characteristicks of Men, Manners, Opinions, Times, 3:349)*

The vocabulary of the different languages illustrates varying degrees of awareness of this material and formal autonomy.

I. *Zôgraphêma, Pinax, Tabula, Tableau*

"If on another hand, we compare the first names to these drawings (*grammasin* [γράμμασιν]) it is possible in the case of pictures (*zôgraphêmasin* [ζωγραφήμασιν]), to give them all the appropriate colors and forms, or not to provide them all and to make some omissions or some additions in their number and size." Without penetrating further into the rich vocabulary of this passage from Plato's *Cratylus* (431c), we can underscore the use of *zôgraphêma* [ζωγράφημα], which designates the painting insofar as it carries a representation—literally: the writing, the representation of the living creature—rather than the object-picture. *Zôgraphia* [ζωγραφία] signifies the painting and the art of painting at the same time, as a passage from *Phaedrus* confirms, in which Plato again compares writing to painting (275c).

The word *pinax* [πίναξ] will come later to designate the painting as object-picture. It no longer refers to the living model, but to the support. The term (which is related to the old Slavonic [pĭnĭ] [tree trunk, log]) at first refers to a plank (*Odyssey*, XII.67), a plate, or a platter (originally out of wood), and is later used in reference to tablets for tracing out signs (starting with the *Iliad*, VI.169) and to the geographic maps within which the Ionian astronomers started drawing "the face of the inhabited world" (to borrow the expression from J.-P. Vernant), and then to votive tablets and paintings. Ex-votos and pictures might seem at first to be fully interchangeable terms, insofar as most

Greek paintings referred to in literature were to be found in the picture galleries of temples, the pinacothecas beginning with the gallery described by Pausanias, and located in the north wing of the Propylaeas to the Athenian Acropolis.

But he also refers to the presence of paintings in private houses and to visits to the workshops of painters (Zeuxis, Protogenes, and Apelles). The many details that one can glean from the Millet collection (Reinach, *La Peinture ancienne*) are indications of the beginnings of the institutional conditions of painting, whose origins are certainly religious, but which tend toward a relative autonomy, since aside from the relative rarity of religious subjects and the frequent references to literature, the works are the result of commissions from the cities or the kings, or are carried out as part of a contest (thus the famous rivalry of Zeuxis and Parrhasios; cf. Pliny the Elder, *Natural History*, XXXV.64).

The first paintings seem to have been fragments of walls taken from buildings (starting with the Greeks apparently, although our evidence for this hypothesis is limited to Pliny's description of a brick fresco taken down in Rome, a fragment of which was given a matching frame [*Natural History*, XXXV.49]), which naturally led to the idea of a mobile painting, on a support made of stone, marble, terracotta, slate, or wood. There seems to be evidence for paintings on wood dating from the Pinacotheca of the Propylaea. Canvas seems to have been first used in theaters, starting with Agatharchos (thus the false curtain painted by Parrhasios that deceived Zeuxis after he had presented his grapes [cf. ibid., XXXV.64]). The emergence of painting on canvas is dated to the epoch of Nero, based on Pliny's account of a gigantic painting of the emperor that was destroyed by lightning (ibid., XXXV.51). The support on which the painting is posed becomes an autonomous fragment, transportable, exhibitable, and self-contained yet open to the possibility of a unified, organic composition. Most of the meanings of *pinax* passed into the Latin *tabula* (board, chessboard, *tabula votiva, tabula picta,* and so on) and its diminutive *tabella* (little board, writing tablet, *tabella picta*).

II. The Specificity of *Tableau* (Picture)

The lexical subtleties used to distinguish the frame and the painting enable the development of thinking. On the one hand, the issue is to discern the abstract limit of the painting (comparable to the contour of the figures). Whatever its size, the painting is differentiated from the frame, which, when it is present, represents a sort of "no man's land" between the world of the painting and the environment in which it is displayed. On the other hand, the issue is to illuminate the material and formal conditions specific to painting, the manner in which this medium manifests itself in reality. When Lord Shaftesbury writes (in French) his *Idée ou Raisonnement du tableau historique du Jugement d'Hercule suivant Prodicus* (published in English as *Historical Draught or Tablature of the Judgment of Hercules*) in 1712, its purpose is to propose a "scenario" to the painter Paolo de Matteis for an allegorical painting that the latter executes in the same year (*Hercules at the Crossroads*, Ashmolean Museum). The British philosopher takes the occasion to reflect on the pictorial medium: "Avant que d'entrer dans l'examen de notre Esquisse, ou *Tableau* projeté," one should know that "par le mot de *Tableau* nous désignons conformément au mot latin de *Tabula*." If Shaftesbury is in a position to give a precise definition to the object (materially different from the fresco, endowed with an organic character), this is not only because he is developing his conception of the plastic arts, but also because his work is further enabled by the necessity of speaking French in order to communicate with his Italian friend, since neither speaks the language of the other. One can see this *a contrario* in the awkward translation into English that the philosopher makes subsequently: "Before we enter on the Examination of our Historical Sketch, it may be proper to remark, that by the word Tablature (for which we have yet no name in English, besides the general one of Picture) we denote, according to the original word Tabula" (*Historical Draught or Tablature of the Judgment of Hercules*, in *Characteristicks of Men, Manners, Opinions, Times*, 3:348).

The subsequent history of the notion of the painting shows that the awareness of its specificity arises from reflections upon the conditions of its making (essentially, its planarity), but requiring some additional tightening of focus on the painting as the determinant of these qualities. Most of the classical definitions of painting, for example, by Raffaello Borghini (1584), Nicolas Poussin ("an imitation of everything under the sun, made up of lines and colors on some surface, whose purpose is delectation," in Letter to Fréart de Chambray, 1 March 1665, Rome) or by Roger de Piles ("the imitation of visible objects by means of form and colors," in *Course on Painting* [1708], p.8), refer back to the "general concept" of the painting, as Shaftesbury put it. Shaftesbury's own definition, on the other hand, introduces a specific concept. This same specific concept is found in Taine: "A painting is a colored surface upon which various tones and various degrees of light are distributed according to a certain choice; this is its intimate being" (*Philosophy of Art*). This definition will become the accepted scholarly one, as is evident in Maurice Denis's borrowings, in a famous injunction that is now the founding precept of many a visual artist:

> One should recall that a painting—before it is a warhorse, a naked woman, or some anecdote or another—is essentially a planar surface covered with colors that are assembled in a certain sequence.
>
> (*Art et Critique*, 23 and 30 August 1890, cited in *Le Ciel et l'Arcadie*)

This tightening of the concept no doubt reaches its culmination in what Denis says of Cézanne. After recalling Gauguin's ironic remark, "[N]othing resembles a daub (*croûte* in French) so much as a masterpiece," he adds, "Whether it is good or bad, Cézanne's canvas is definitely a painting" ("Cézanne," *L'Occident*, September 1907, cited in *Le Ciel et l'Arcadie*).

III. Approximate Equivalents to *Tableau* in the European Vocabulary

The English language, which contains "table" and "tablet" (as in a commemorative plaque), uses "tableau" only in the plural ("tableaux" or "tableaus") when speaking of a *tableau vivant*. An examination of the semantic potential contained within the lexical elements of the different European languages reveals extensive disparities. Only French and Italian (*quadro*, from the Latin *quadra* [square]) have a specific term at their disposal to refer to the object-picture—but one concentrates on the support, and the other on its limit (the frame).

▪ See Box 1.

1

Cadre, "Frame," "Framing," "Framework," *Corniche*, "Cornice"

The word *cadre* in French signifies both the limits that define the edges of the painted scene and (traditionally) the piece of wood around the stretcher, with the latter also possibly called the framing. In the seventeenth century, the word *corniche* (projecting ornament) was employed, as Poussin's famous letter attests, in which he asks Chantelou to add some ornamental *corniche* (*orner d'un peu de corniche*) to a painting he had sent to him, "for the painting needs it, so that when seen in all its parts, the projecting rays of viewing would be held inside and not scattered about outside, such that light refracted from nearby objects would not be confused pêle-mêle with depicted objects." In fact, the Italian word *cornice* is used to refer to both the frame and the framing (which can also be called *incorniciatura*), while *quadro* is used only for the frame in a figurative sense, for example, the historical framework. Poussin for that matter uses the Italianism *quadres* to speak of a fresco independently of the stucco *corniches* that frame it. "Frame" in English designates both the frame and its framing. In theoretical texts (by Arnheim, Schapiro, etc.), this word is most often synonymous with "limit," "boundary," or "border." Depending on the context, this last also signifies the framing, as in the text by Gombrich: "The frame, or the border delimits the field of force with its gradients of meaning increasing towards the centre" (*The Sense of Order*, 157). One should also note the Greek distinction, which Kant uses in section 14 of the *Critique of Judgment*, between *Ergon* (work) and *Parergon* (ornament, "that is to say that which is not an integral part of the entire representation of the object"), and that this latter category includes the frames of paintings (*Einfassungen der Gemälde*).

BIBLIOGRAPHY

Arnheim, Rudolph. *The Power of the Center*. Berkeley: University of California Press, 1982.

Gombrich, Ernst. *The Sense of Order*. Ithaca, NY: Cornell University Press, 1979.

Kant, Immanuel. *Critique of the Power of Judgment*. Translated by Paul Guyer and Eric Matthews. Cambridge: Cambridge University Press, 2001.

Poussin, Nicolas. *Lettres et propos sur l'art*. Paris: Hermann, 1964.

Schapiro, Meyer. "On Some Problems in the Semiotics of Visual Arts, Field and Vehicle in Image-Signs." *Semiotica* 1, no. 3 (1969): 223–42.

A greater richness of vocabulary does not necessarily entail a greater flexibility in comprehension. The German language has two series of terms for *tableau* at its disposal, but no specific term. On the one hand, there are the terms *Malerei* and *Gemälde*, both designating painting as art, as well as picture and the portrait, and both formed from the root *Mal* (stain, mark, sign). On the other hand, there is the term *Bild*, which signifies image, painting, picture, and figure. One should also note that blackboard, table, and tablet are all referred to by the word *Tafel* (also used in a figurative sense in the expression *ein Tafel der Zeit*, meaning "a chronology").

English also lacks any one specific term. It sometimes employs "painting," which, like *peinture* in French, has the technical sense of support for the paint (*painting in oils*), but also the figurative sense of "description." Sometimes "picture" denotes a generic object-picture (as in Mussorgsky's *Pictures from an Exhibition*), sometimes a particular denoted "image" (as in *The Picture of Dorian Gray* by Oscar Wilde). The nuances of the two terms are sharpened by their contextual overdetermination, especially in a philosophical text, as this passage from Nelson Goodman's *Languages of Art* (p. 5) illustrates:

> A Constable painting of Marlborough Castle is more like any other picture than it is like the Castle, yet it represents the Castle and not another picture—not even the closest copy. . . . [F]or a picture can represent another, and indeed each of the once popular paintings of art galleries represents many others.

Dominique Chateau

BIBLIOGRAPHY

Denis, Maurice. *Le Ciel et l'Arcadie*. Selected and edited by Jean-Paul Bouillon. Paris: Hermann, 1993.

Goodman, Nelson. *Languages of Art: An Approach to a Theory of Symbols*. 2nd ed. Indianapolis: Hackett, 1976.

de Piles, Roger. *Cours de peinture par principes*. Amsterdam: Arkstée and Merkus, 1766. First published in 1708.

Plato. *Cratylus*. Translated, with introduction and notes, by C.D.C. Reeve. Indianapolis: Hackett, 1998.

Pliny the Elder. *Natural History*. Vol. 10. With an English translation by H. Rackham. Loeb Classical Library. Cambridge, MA: Harvard University Press, 1962.

Poussin, Nicolas. *Lettres et propos sur l'art*. Paris: Hermann, 1964.

Reinach, Adolphe. *Textes grecs et latins relatifs à l'histoire de la peinture ancienne: Recueil Milliet*. Paris: Macula, 1985.

Shaftesbury, Anthony Ashley Cooper, Earl of. *Historical Draught or Tablature of the Judgment of Hercules*. Vol. 3 of *Characteristicks of Men, Manners, Opinions, Times*. 3 vols. Edited by Douglas den Uyl. Indianapolis: Liberty Fund, 2001. First published in 4th edition of *Characteristicks* in London by John Darby, 1727.

Taine, Hyppolite. *The Philosophy of Art*. Translated and revised by the author. London: Williams and Norgate, 1867. First published in several editions in French in 1865–82.

Vernant, Jean-Pierre. *The Origins of Greek Thought*. Ithaca, NY: Cornell University Press, 1982.

TALATTUF (ARABIC)

ENGLISH	felicitous ability
FRENCH	*habilité salutaire*
LATIN	*solertia, sapientia, sagacitas*

➤ *RUSE* and *GOD, HISTORIA UNIVERSALIS, INGENIUM, MÊTIS, PHRONÊSIS, PRUDENCE, WISDOM*

In the Qur'ān Allah is crafty and more able to wheel and deal than his adversaries (III, 54). He is also *laṭif* [لطف], an ambiguous word that can be translated, among other things, as graceful or charming (Fr. "*gracieux*"; cf. D. Gimaret, *Les noms divins en Islam*, 391–94). The notion of subtlety, *luṭf* [اللطف], links the two ideas: he steers things in the direction he wants to go, but he works softly and smoothly. The Brethren of Purity (or Brethren of Sincerity) in the second half of the tenth century applied the idea to the succession of generations of the living: the divine wisdom and the providence of God have cleverly arranged (*talaṭṭafa* [تلطّف]) for the permanence of the species, since an individual cannot exist forever (Epistles, IV, 1 [42], vol. 3). They take up an idea derived from Aristotle (*De Anima*, II, 4, 415a 29–b 7) but add to it the idea of ruse.

Averroës (who died in 1196) uses the verb to express the clever way that divine providence has ensured the continuity of the pure power and the pure act by placing between them the power according to place, the only one possessed by celestial bodies (*Epitome of Metaphysics*, 3rd ed. Jéhamy, 110). The verb also appears in a crucial passage of the *Decisive Treatise*: Allah "worked things out" so that those who are unable to accede to apodictic knowledge can partake of the truth through images (ed. L. Gauthier, 18, 4; ed. M. Geoffroy, § 38—the expression escaped the translators, who rendered it in French as "*faire la grâce de*" [have the grace of]). Maimonides (d. 1204) uses the term in the framework of a theology of history: God did not bring Israel directly to confront the peoples of Canaan but made a detour of forty years in the desert. The harsh life hardened the people who had become soft during their captivity in Egypt. It trained them in the warrior virtues and thus made them capable of conquering the promised land. In the same way, the law of Moses does not require a single leap from old habits to a pure cult of the spirit but is applied in degrees. (*Guide des égarés* [*Guide of the Perplexed*], III, 32, ed. Y. Joël, 383–86, Fr. trans. S. Munk, 249–54; cf. S. Pinès, *La Liberté de philosopher: De Maimonide à Spinoza*, [The freedom to philosophize: From Maimonides to Spinoza], 115–20). The notion of God's concessions to the weakness of human beings can be found in several of the Church Fathers: in relation to adaptation in Tertullian and later in Augustine, and in relation to condescension (*sugkatabasis* [συγκατάβασις]) in Justinian, John Chrysostomos, etc. If these refer to a basis, to a grace, the idea of ruse is nonetheless not explicitly addressed. The texts of the Brethren of Purity and of Averroës were unknown in Europe prior to the nineteenth century, but Maimonides was translated into Latin. The key word is rendered by expressions that link *solertia*, *sapientia*, and *sagacitas* (Latin trans. J. Buxtorf, 431). Hegel perhaps remembered

Maimonides's ideas when he formulated the concept of the "ruse of reason" (*List der Vernunft*), especially in the philosophy of history. History uses to its own ends passions that have no intention of serving it (*Leçons sur la philosophie de l'histoire* [*Lessons on the philosophy of history*], introduction, Glockner, ed., 11: 63, Fr. trans. J. Gibelin, 32ff.).

Rémi Brague

BIBLIOGRAPHY

Aristotle. *Arisṭūṭālis, fī al-nafs, "al-ārā' al-ṭabīʿīyah" al-mansūb ilá Flūṭarkhas, "al-Ḥāss wa-al-maḥsūs" li-Ibn Rushd, "al-Nabāt" al-mansūb ilá Arisṭūṭalis*. Translated into Arabic by Abd al-Raḥmān Badawī. Cairo: Maktabat al-Nahḍah al-Miṣrīyah, 1954.

Averroës. *On the Harmony of Religion and Philosophy* [*Kitāb faṣl al-maqāl*]. Translated by George F. Hourani. London: Luzac, 1961.

———. *Tafsīr mā baʿda al-ṭabīʿah*. Edited by Maurice Bouyges. Beirut, Lebanon: Impr. Catholique, 1938–1948; Translation by Charles Genequand: *Ibn Rushd's Metaphysics: A Translation with Introduction of Ibn Rushd's Commentary on Aristotle's Metaphysics, Book Lām*. Edited by Charles Genequand. Leiden, Neth.: Brill, 1984.

El-Bizri, Nader, ed. *Epistles of the Brethren of Purity: The Ikhwān al-Ṣafāʾ and Their Rasāʾil: An Introduction*. Oxford: Oxford University Press, 2008.

Gimaret, Daniel. *Les noms divins en Islam: Exégèse lexicographique et théologique*. Paris: Éditions du Cerf, 1988.

Hegel, Georg Wilhelm Friedrich. *Hegel's Lectures on the History of Philosophy*. 3 vols. Translated by E. S. Haldane and Francis H. Simson. London: Routledge and Paul, 1968.

Maimonides, Moses. *The Guide of the Perplexed* [*Dalālat al-ḥāʾirīn*]. Translated with an introduction and notes by Shlomo Pinès. Chicago, IL: University of Chicago Press, 1964.

Netton, Ian Richard. *Muslim Neoplatonists: An Introduction to the Thought of the Brethren of Purity, Ikhwān al-Ṣafāʾ*. London: Allen and Unwin, 1982.

Pinès, Shlomo. *The Collected Works of Shlomo Pinès*. Jerusalem: Magnes Press, Hebrew University, 1979–.

———. *Toldot ha-filosofyah ha-Yehudit meha-Rambam ʿad Ṣpinozah: Reshimot le-fi hartsaʾot*. Jerusalem: Mifʿal ha-shikhpul, Bet ha-hotsaʾah shel histadrut ha-studentim shel, 1976.

Shams al-Dīn, Abd al-Amīr, ed. *Al-falsafah al-tarbawīyah ʿinda Ikhwān al-Ṣafā min khilāli risāʾilihim: Dirāsah wa-taḥlīl*. Beirut, Lebanon: al-Sharikah al-ʿĀlamīyah lil-Kitāb, 1988.

TALENT

GREEK	talanton [τάλαντον]
ITALIAN	talento
LATIN	talentum
SPANISH	talento, talante

➤ *DESIRE*, and ART, GENIUS, GOÛT, INGENIUM, LOVE

The Latin word *talentum* first belonged in Greek to the vocabulary of weights, measures, and monies. The Old French *talent* belongs to the vocabulary of will and desire before taking on the meanings of "capacity" and "aptitude." Today, each of the three romance languages, Spanish, Italian, and French, has its own specific references for each of these different lexical units. In contemporary French, *talent* designates only gift or aptitude, whereas in addition to these, the Italian *talento* has retained the meanings of taste and inclination. In Spanish, *talento* referred to both desire and aptitude in the sixteenth century. It subsequently gained a doublet, *talante*, which remains closer to the Greek *etymon* and signifies desire and inclination. This obviated the semantic loss that in this case affected the French.

I. The Evolution of *Talent* in French

In Old French *talent* (like *talan* or *talen* in Provençal) had the meaning of desire, of inclination, of erotic attraction: *avoir en talent* meant to desire, to want to; *faire son talent d'une femme*, to take pleasure with a woman; *atalenter*, to please, to be right for, and to inspire desire; *atalentement*, fancy, love, affection for someone; *talentif* or *talentos*, seized with ardent desire; *maltalent*, ill-will, disaffection, a composite word that can still be found in Voltaire. In one of the *Lais* of Marie de France, a queen, irate at the rejection of her advances on the part of a young *chevalier*, declares, "I have often heard that you have no talent for women" (On m'a souvent répété que des femmes vous n'avez talent). This meaning, which predominated in the literature of the *trouvères* and the troubadours, was lost at the time of the Reformation and the beginning of the seventeenth century, and the word came to refer to capacity, aptitude, natural or acquired disposition: "Be a mason, then, if that is your talent" (Soyez plutôt maçon, si c'est votre talent) (Boileau).

In French the contemporary sense of *talent* came to replace the Old French meaning of "desire," whereas in Italian and Spanish both meanings persisted, thus attesting to how a metaphor with a common origin bifurcates in signification. Originally *talent*, borrowed from classical Greek through the Hellenic mode of speech of Marseilles, referred to the plate on a scale, then to the weight that would tip it, and then to the sum of gold or silver of a certain weight (somewhere between 20 and 27 kilos). Over time, the term was applied not only to decisions that rouse the will out of indifference and cause it to express a specific choice, but also to an attraction toward a person or a pleasure associated with an object choice. In the course of its semantic evolution, *talent* took on the meaning of "inclination" (*penchant*); both in the sense of a "feeling of love or sympathy for someone" and in the (older) sense of "decline" (*être sur son penchant*), with the latter containing a moralizing connotation, as in "ill-inclined" (*les mauvais penchants*).

The initial Greek usage acquired additional traction in Christian rhetoric, specifically in the Parable of the Three Servants. As told in Matthew (25:14), of the three servants entrusted by the master with some talents (a certain weight of gold or silver), two obtain interest, while the third buries his in the ground. The sense of "talent" as gift, which had remained current in ecclesiastical Latin *talentum* (in Saint Jerome, it refers to "the gift of God" or "grace," and for Calvin the "gift of the Holy Spirit"), was revived during the Renaissance and eventually replaced the earlier French meaning of bountiful desire and amorous attraction.

II. The Double Meaning in Modern Italian and Spanish

In addition to referring to aptitude, the modern Italian word *talento* retains the Old French sense of *talent*, especially when it is used in literary language. The word—which applies mostly to artistic activity—is to be understood in its ambiguous and composite sense of both "gift" and "particular taste," with the underlying assumption that disposition leads to inclination.

In the Castilian language of the sixteenth century, the word *talento* sometimes includes the sense of "desire" or "inclination," and sometimes refers to "capacity" or "natural gift." Thus Teresa of Avila speaks of *deseos y talentos* (desires and talents) that are required of those *postulants* who aspire to religious life (*Book of the Foundations*), and John of the Cross evokes *las inclinas y talentos de las personas* (the inclinations and talents of persons) ("Ascent of Mount Carmel"). These ties between *talentos* and *deseos* or *inclinaciones* clearly indicate that the first of these terms belongs to the register of desire. Nonetheless, the second sense of capacity and aptitude will appear during the same period. In his celebrated bilingual dictionary, *Tesoro de las dos lenguas española y francesa* (1607; last edition, 1675), César Oudin, interpreter to Henri IV and the first translator of *Don Quixote*, gives the following definition (with the punctuation of the time): "*Talent, m.* Talent qui valoit six cens escus, *item*, Inclination, valeur" (*Talent, masc.* Talent which is worth six hundred écus, *item*, inclination, value).

The etymological dictionary of J. Corominas points out that *talento* takes on the double meaning of "natural gift one should cultivate" and "disposition," "inclination," as well as "will." This last usage will become generalized through the "ecclesiastical tendency to consider good will more important than intelligence," but in the lexical form of *talante*, "borrowed directly from the Greek through the intermediary of the Latin vulgate." Whereas the meaning of "natural gift" will pass into the vulgar languages during the Renaissance and under the influences of the religious predicates of the Reformation and Counter-Reformation, but in the "semi-scholarly form of *talento*, borrowed from classical Latin." In relation to this latter term, such dictionaries as that of R. J. Dominguez (1878) and of the *Real Academia española* (1991) will henceforth ignore the sense of disposition, inclination, or desire. *Talento* is thus limited to the meaning of aptitude. And *talante* is used instead to indicate desire or inclination (an acceptation resembles the common expression in modern Spanish of *de buen* [o *mal*] *talante*, that is to say, "of good [or ill] will"). The dictionary of the Real Academia also indicates that *talento* has a meaning that does not belong to the French *talent*: that of "understanding" (*entendimiento*, Fr. *entendement*) or "power of the soul."

Charles Baladier
Bernard Sésé

BIBLIOGRAPHY

John of the Cross. "Ascent of Mount Carmel." In *The Collected Works of St. John of the Cross*, translated by Kieran Kavanaugh O.C.D. and Otilio Rodriguez. London: Thomas Nelson and Sons, 1966.

Lavis, Georges. *L'expression de l'affectivité dans la poésie lyrique française du Moyen âge, XIIe–XIIIe*. Paris: Belles Lettres, 1972.

Teresa of Avila. *The Book of the Foundations of St. Teresa of Jesus of the Order of Our Lady of Carmel*. Translated by David Lewis. New York: Benziger, 1913.

TATSACHE, TATHANDLUNG (GERMAN)

ENGLISH	fact
FRENCH	*fait*
GERMAN	*Faktum*
LATIN	*factum*

➤ *FACT* and *ACT*, CONSCIOUSNESS, ES, EXPERIENCE, GEGENSTAND, I/ME/MYSELF, MATTER OF FACT, OBJECT, PRAXIS, REALITY, SPEECH ACT, TRUTH

Tatsache originally was the term proposed by German translators in the eighteenth century to translate "fact," a concept used widely in English empirical philosophy. The term refers to real experience, to

an event, or to factual data, which are the only source of legitimacy for any true knowledge. Kant sought subsequently to free the term from its excessive dependence on the theses of empiricism and proposed a new definition: The fact or *Tatsache* became an object whose objective validity could be proven or, in the Kantian context, any concept that can correspond to an intuition in a possible experience. This change in meaning is clearly a function of the theory of knowledge that Kant sought to develop as an alternative to empiricism. Its translation would be unproblematic except that Kant opposes *Tatsache* to the term *Faktum*, two terms that English renders as fact. Fichte attempted to surmount the opposition between *Faktum* and *Tatsache*, which had led in Kant to difficulties around a priori synthetic judgment (whether or not it implies an intuition). Fichte had recourse to the neologism *Tathandlung*, based on the requirements of his own *Doctrine of Science*. The expression *Tathandlung*, whose correct translation in English (it is sometimes rendered as "fact/act"), as well as in other languages, is not generally agreed on, involves all of Fichte's philosophy. It is a term that also entailed a new definition of knowledge that would influence all those thinkers generally referred to as German Idealists.

I. From "Matter of Fact" to *Tatsache*: The English Influence and Kant's Intervention

The German term *Tatsache* is at its origin a direct transposition of the English expression "matter of fact." *Tatsache* took on the philosophical dimensions of "fact" in the middle of the eighteenth century, as part of the rapid and powerful propagation of English empiricism in Germany (cf. M. Puech, *Kant et la causalité* [Kant and causality]). In this context *Tatsache* refers to real experience, to observable empirical events, and thus, by virtue of the key theses of empiricism, it designates a fact of which there can be no doubt.

In the face of this definition, which he considered excessively dependent on the empiricist grounds on which it was developed, Kant greatly extended the meaning of the term:

> Ich erweitere hier, wie mich dünkt, mit Recht, den Begriff einer Thatsache über die gewöhnliche Bedeutung dieses Worts. Denn es ist nicht nötig, ja nicht einmal thunlich, diesen Ausdruck bloß auf die wirkliche Erfahrung einzuschränken, wenn von dem Verhältnisse der Dinge zu unseren Erkenntnisvermögen die Rede ist, da eine bloß mögliche Erfahrung schon hinreichend ist, um von ihnen bloß als Gegenständen einer bestimmten Erkenntnißart zu reden.
>
> (Here I extend the concept of a fact (*Tatsache*), as it seems to me right, beyond the usual meaning of this word. For when the issue is the relation of things to our cognitive capacities it is not necessary, indeed not even feasible, to restrict this expression merely to actual experience, since a merely possible experience is already sufficient for speaking of them merely as objects of a determinate kind of cognition.)
>
> (Kant, *Critique of the Power of Judgment*, trans. Guyer and Matthews, 332)

For Kant *Tatsache* no longer refers only to empirical reality but applies to any object possessing "objective validity," as is the case of geometric properties. In this context any concept that can correspond to an intuition becomes a "fact."

Gegenstände für Begriffe, deren objektive Realität (es sei durch reine Vernunft, oder durch Erfahrung und im ersteren Falle aus theoretischen oder praktischen Datis derselben, in allen Fällen aber vermittelst einer ihnen korrespondierenden Anschauung) bewiesen werden kann, sind (*res facti*) Thatsachen.

(Objects for concepts the objective reality of which can be proved (whether through pure reason or through experience, and whether in the first case through theoretical or practical data for reason, but in all cases by means of intuitions corresponding to the concepts) are (*res facti*) facts (*Tatsachen*).)

(Ibid.)

The fact thus becomes synonymous with valid knowledge (which, for critical philosophy, is a knowledge that binds a concept to an intuition) and can be determined in opposition to "matters of opinion" (*Meinen*) and "matters of belief" (*Glaube*).

Kant subjects what had previously been an empiricist notion of *Tatsache* to a semantic displacement that is clearly conditioned by his own new determination of knowledge: the validity of a notion does not derive from a basis in factual data or on empirical events but resides in any concept that can be constructed from a pure intuition. Because knowing is no longer the observing or ordering of facts but is constituted by a concept's being made figural or representable through its application to an intuition, the term *Tatsache* loses its original empirical signification in favor of becoming the construction or mark of valid knowledge.

II. *Faktum* and *Tatsache*: A Kantian Exception

Once the slippage of the meaning of the term *Tatsache* in the Kantian context has been acknowledged, its translation poses no problems except in relation to other terms. French translators felt compelled to translate *Faktum* as *fait* ("fact"). Before Kant the Latin *factum* was equivalent to *Tatsache* and thus to fact. But with Kant its use essentially evolved into the opposite of *Tatsache*. The *Faktum*, as opposed to the *Tatsache* "is not based on any intuition, either pure or empirical" (*Critique of Practical Reason*, 28). This *Faktum* makes its first appearance in the *Critique of Judgment* (it had not appeared in the *Foundation of a Metaphysics of Morals*); in addition, it needs to be distinguished from the *Faktum* of jurisprudence, thematized in the *Critique of Pure Reason* in the opposition between *Quid facti* ("questions of fact") and *Quid juris* ("questions of law"); in which *Faktum*, treated as unable to ground or justify moral law, is taken as the neutral foil to legal right, the morally entitled law produced by the Deduction of Freedom. (*Critique of Pure Reason*, 3: 99–100). This *Faktum* is associated with the consciousness of the moral law within us. "It is not an empirical fact (*Tatsache*) but the sole fact (*Faktum*) of pure reason which, by it, announces itself as originally lawgiving" (*Critique of Practical Reason*, 29).

Since in French it was difficult to render *Tatsache* and *Faktum* using two different terms, most translators indicated in parentheses or a footnote which of the two words was used in the original. This is an absolutely necessary distinction, since *Faktum* is a synthetic proposition not dependent on any intuition, whereas *Tatsache* is defined as that which requires a corresponding intuition. In introducing *Faktum*, Kant admits the existence of a synthetic a priori, apodictically certain proposition that does not depend on any intuition. This exception to a nodal thesis of critical philosophy, based on the assumption that any valid proposition requires an intuition, would pose problems for Kant's immediate successors (Reinhold, Maïmon, and Fichte). What was the status, they would ask, of a synthetic a priori proposition that does not rest on sensible intuition? Didn't this exception to the Kantian theory of knowledge reveal its limits, if not its limitations? For either truth is defined by the link between a concept and an intuition, without exception, as had been maintained in the *Critique of Pure Reason*, or the Kantian definition of truth as a link between a concept and an intuition was insufficient (see, for this argument, Fichte's "Foundations of the Entire Science of Knowledge" in *The Science of Knowledge*). The post-Kantians would choose the latter of these possibilities and question the Kantian determination of knowledge. Rather than simply considering them as exceptions, they would try to think through propositions that, although absolutely true, did not require any construction in time and space, were not based on any sensible intuition: in a word, propositions that did not express *Tatsachen*.

III. *Tatsache* and *Tathandlung*: Fichte's Intervention

Since valid knowledge cannot be reduced to the establishment of facts or to the construction of concepts through intuition, mathematics, and physics (the only valid forms of knowledge according to the *Critique of Pure Reason*), it requires another form of knowledge or way of knowing and must be developed and theorized by philosophy accordingly. As an opposite term to the Kantian *Tatsache*, Fichte would create his own neologism—*Tathandlung*—and present it as the only true *Faktum* of reason, the sole foundation of all knowing. How does one translate this expression? What does it mean? What is at stake in this opposition between *Tatsache* and *Tathandlung* to which, in the last analysis, all of Fichte's work is arguably reducible?

Historically, Fichte employs *Tathandlung* for the first time in 1793, in the *Recension des Aenesidemus* [Review of Aenesidimus]. It functioned here to ensure an unshakable foundation for philosophy: "*ein solcher muss nicht eben eine Thatsache, er kann auch eine Thathandlung ausdrucken*" (Such a principle [i.e., the principle of any and all philosophy] does not necessarily need to express a *Tatsache*; it can also express a *Tathandlung*). The *Grundlage der gesamten Wissenschaftslehre* [Foundations of the entire science of knowledge] of 1794 thematizes the *Tathandlung* from its opening lines, and Fichte will return to the fundamental opposition between *Tatsache* and *Tathandlung*, for instance in the *Versuch einer neuen Darstellung der Wissenschaftslehre* [Attempt at a new presentation of the science of knowledge]:

Es ist gar nicht so unbedeutend, als es einigen vorkommt, ob die Philosophie von einer ThatSache ausgehe, oder von einer ThatHandlung (d.i. von reiner Thatigkeit, die kein Object voraussetzt, sondern es selbst hervorbringt, und wo sonach das Handeln unmittelbar zur *That* wird.

(Accordingly, the question of whether philosophy should begin with a fact or with an Act (i.e., with a pure activity that presupposes no object but instead, produces its own object, and therefore with an acting becomes a deed) is by no means so inconsequential as it may seem to some people to be.)

> (Fichte, *Introductions to the Wissenschaftslehre and Other Writings, 1797–1800*, 51 [German edition *GA* 1, 4: 2210])

How can *Tathandlung* be translated from the German? There is virtually no concurrence in the French translations. As to the English, in their translation of the *Grundlage*, Peter Heath and John Lachs render the term simply as "act," and though legitimate, this has disadvantages. Most importantly, it gives no indication to the English reader that *Tathandlung* is a neologism entirely of Fichte's own making. Of course, the creation of composite expressions made by joining two existing terms is vastly more common in German than in French or English. Nonetheless Fichte himself underscored the idiosyncrasy of the term, which he intended as absolutely and unconditionally foundational to his whole doctrine of knowledge. Insofar as Fichte invents a word that he cannot find in the available lexicon, it would be desirable that any translation draw attention to the specificity of the term. For any translation to do justice to Fichte's term, it would be necessary to create an unusual expression (if not a new word), while taking care to avoid introducing connotations absent from the original German or defaulting to anachronistic applications of the term parasitic on recent usage. To respect Fichte's thinking, it is above all important to convey the redoubling of the act—the enactment of the act or action to the second power—expressed quite literally in *Tathandlung*. The two words that Fichte combines to create the expression, *Tat* (deed) and *Handlung* (action), are derived from verbs meaning "to do" (*tun*) and "to act" (*handeln*). *Tat* is taken from the past tense form of *Tun*, so the "deed" is literally the "did" (or the "done," but without the same emphasis on being finished or completed that this form conveys in English). This done-action or action-deed should convey a pure activity that presupposes no object but instead produces its own object and therefore with acting becomes a deed.

This notion of *Tathandlung* serves to characterize the specific actions of the self. Let us recall that for Fichte to philosophize is no longer to be interested in things, nor even in the relationship between knowledge and things—themselves defined in the Kantian manner as phenomena. To philosophize is to attempt to retrace the different actions through which the mind obtains knowledge. The issue is to restore through philosophical reflection the action immanent in every judgment. For Fichte two key acts can be theorized: the action through which the spirit posits something that is not itself (an act of opposition, or non-self, that works generically to designate the proposition set whose content is distinct from the positing subject), and the act of positing or "I = I." It is this latter form of positing that *Tathandlung* renders explicit. We can say of this notion of done-action or action-deed that the position of the "I" is the only proposition that contains both the positing of a reality and an action, in the sense in which the saying of "I" posits the "I" as an act and that act as existing. Within any other proposition there is a distance between the subject who makes the proposition and the object of the proposition. If I think, for example, that "the table exists" or that "the triangle has three sides," the act of positing and the object I posit are not identical. But, on the other hand, the "I" comes to exist in this very positing because there is no difference between the subject of the enunciation and the enunciated; the fact of enunciating suffices to realize the enunciation.

Contemporary analytic pragmatism may enable, *mutatis mutandis*, elucidation of this difficult notion of Fichte's. For pragmatic analysis does not analyze enunciations from the point of view of their propositional content (the information they deliver), but rather from the point of view of the act of their enunciation. As a result, any enunciation can be considered a speech-act. Within the vast ensemble of speech-acts, a relatively small group of enunciations has greater authority inasmuch as they are immediately and absolutely undeniable. Their opposite cannot be proposed without contradiction; the mere fact of their utterance would immediately invalidate the content of the enunciation. Such is the case with the proposition "I am speaking." No speaker would be able to say "I am not speaking" without denying the content of his proposition in the very act of saying it; whereas a proposition such as "you are speaking" or "he is speaking" can be empirically true or false but does not arrive as something whose opposite cannot be argued. Thus the "I," qua *Tathandlung,* functions as a performative utterance whose content derives from the very fact of saying it. The term *Tathandlung* aims then at showing how, in the determinate actions that constitute the "I," the affirmation of an act is the affirmation of the existence of the act.

The notion of *Tathandlung* as described here seems to have had, as such, no subsequent currency. One can find a few instances of the word in Novalis or Friedrich Schlegel, but only in reference to Fichte or as commentary on him. And yet, despite the abandonment of the term, one should still take into account the more general project crystallized by this neologism: to define knowing not on the basis of the content of a proposition but on the basis of a link between enunciative act and content of enunciation. Saying something without contradicting the fact of saying it is, in the end, the essence of the truth according to *Tathandlung*. Because this definition challenges traditional concepts of truth while backing off from the traditional Kantian determination of knowledge, it undoubtedly inaugurates the project that would eventually underlie German Idealism: theorizing a form of rationality that, though it be neither pure representational thought nor pure logic, would be no less a form of rationality or knowing as such. This is rationality that does not shy away from being called a science and that refuses to make of philosophy a discourse whose only meaning consists of declaring its own impossibility.

■ See Box 1.

Isabelle Thomas-Fogiel

1

Faktum, Faktisch, Faktizität

➤ ANXIETY, DASEIN, ERLEBEN, LEIB, PROPERTY

Fichte's neologism did not survive him. Instead, the Kantian term *Faktum*, which it had been meant to clarify and replace, was subject to significant transformations, first by its passage from German to another Germanic language—Danish—and then through the development of two derived terms: *faktisch* and *Faktizität*. These transplants and modifications expanded the scope and practical application of the "fact of pure reason" to religious and existential registers not hitherto included.

I. Faktum, from German to Danish: Kierkegaard

For Fichte the *Tathandlung*, signifying simultaneously event, product, and object of knowledge, refers to a form of history of the free and active subject. It is precisely this history that transforms the simple *Tatsache* into the *Tathandlung* of the originary subject. In his reflections on the object of faith, Kierkegaard simplifies and brings this development of thought to its conclusion by distinguishing two kinds of facts:

> Every historical fact is only a relative fact, and therefore it is entirely appropriate for the relative power, time, to decide the relative fates of people with respect to contemporaneity. More it is not, and only puerility and stupidity can make it the absolute by overestimation.

> (Kierkegaard, *Philosophical Fragments*, 99)

"The simple historical fact" is relative to those who exist at the same time, to its contemporaries—in order to establish it, one must either have been its contemporary or trust those who were. The "absolute fact" (*absolut Faktum*, ibid.), on the other hand, even if it takes place in time, is not relative to time insofar as it is "*declinable* in all instances of life" (ibid.) and remains constant despite the multiplicity of relations in time. These two facts are historical but can be distinguished from each other.

If the fact of which we speak were a simple historical fact, the historiographer's scrupulous accuracy would be of great importance. . . . The heart of the matter is the historical fact that the god has been in human form, and the other historical details are not even as important as they would be if the subject were a human being instead of the god.

> (Ibid., 103)

There is a third type of fact different from either of these, the "eternal fact" (*evigt Faktum*), on which Kierkegaard ironically remarks:

> Er hiint Faktum et evigt Faktum, saa er enhver Tid det lige nær; men vel at mærke ikke i Troen; . . . det er derfor kun en Accommodation til en mindre correct Sprogbrug, at jeg benytter det Ord : Faktum, der er hentet fra det Historiske.

> (If that fact is an eternal fact, then every age is equally close to it—but please note, not in faith, for faith and the historical are entirely commensurate, and thus it is only an accommodation to a less correct use of language for me to use the word "fact," which is taken from the historical.)

> (Ibid., 99)

If Kierkegaard can only use the word *Faktum* without recourse to another word, it is because the Scandinavian languages do not contain the doublet *Tatsache/Faktum*. But this apparent poverty of the Scandinavian lexicon is in fact an opportunity for Kierkegaard. If there is only one word to designate the historical fact and the absolute fact, it is because they are both historical as facts. The requirements of language overturn previously established classifications. In order to account for the absolute fact, there is no need to leap out of time into eternity, to conceive of an eternal fact, as did Kant and all the subsequent fathers of the Lutheran church. One needs instead to think through the paradox of a fact that is both historical and absolute, all the while adhering to the intelligence of a language. The *Faktum* of reason and the *Tathandlung* of Fichte are ironically consigned to the excesses of the historicity of the fact in relation to the a priori. Historical facts are not to be seen in the light of the a priori but in the light of religious fact, which is to say, in the light of an event that continues to occur. What is at issue is not a return to formal conditions, but the distinction between two types of fact, two meanings of the word "history."

II. *Faktisch* and *Faktizität*: Husserl and Heidegger

Under the influence of Kierkegaard, the young Heidegger sought to give a philosophical statute to this idea of the absolute fact, by opposing it to the concept of the positive fact—which led to the concept of *faktishes Leben* and of *Faktizität*:

> We think of the fact as a particular, as opposed to the genre or species. The

fact is thus on one side in relation to another. Facts are projected into a schema imposed on them, placed in an ordered relation. In this objectivizing concept of the factual, its relation to meaning becomes a false problem. . . . The factual must be understood as *expression*. Once one considers factual life in this manner, it no longer raises old false problems, of which individuation is also an example. The facts of life themselves are not sitting one next to another like stones.

> (Heidegger, *Gesamtausgabe*, 58: 256–57)

Like Fichte, Heidegger gives up on the positivity of fact in the hopes of untangling the *aporia* of fact and essence in Husserl.

In the *Ideen* 1 (§2–3), Husserl had indeed defined the fact (*Faktum*) in its difference from the essence (*Wesen*). The fact is what could be otherwise. The essence could not be otherwise. A true religion is called true only in its relation to the unvarying essence of religion: It remains just as relative, for it is not the religion that is true, it is a true religion. The historical relativity of facts is not opposed to the essence, which instead prescribes its meaning. But how is the essence itself to be discovered? The answer is a surprise: on the basis of the fact (*Faktum*) as example. The fact as relative gains its meaning only from the essence as absolute, but this absolute essence is drawn from the fact. What else can be said about the essence? It is accessible in its own mode of being given as is a fact. But if the essence contains nothing of the fact, how can it be given?

It is important to note that Heidegger transforms "fact/essence" into "factual/facticity." This transformation of gnosis into an existential problematic affects three essential points:

1. The contestation of objective formal logic. "This 'something or another' of factical experience . . . has nothing to do with the 'something or another' of formal logic (Heidegger, *Gesamtausgabe*, 58: 106–7, *Basic Problems of Phenomenology*, chap. 2, paragraph 24 B). "'Factical' does not mean naturally real or causally determined, nor does it mean real in the sense of a thing. The concept 'factical' may not be interpreted from certain epistemological presuppositions, but can be made intelligible only from the concept of the historical" (Heidegger, *Phenomenology of Religious Life*). Factical life, discovered through the destruction of the fact as construed by

formal objective logic, must therefore be thought of with the help of a different logic, which Heidegger calls "formal indicative."

2. The affirmation of a direct tie between fact and meaning. "The factual must be understood as *expression*" (*Gesamtsaugabe*, 58: 257, *Basic Problems of Phenomenology*); "That which concerns life reveals itself in a certain manner" (ibid. Part I, chap. 2, paragraph 11a; *Gesamtausgabe*, 58: 49–50); "Life . . . is what it is only as a form of concrete meaning" (*Basic Problems of Phenomenology*, app. A I.5; *Gesamtausgabe*, 58: 148). *Faktisch* life presents itself as an expression, this expression being what one usually calls a "situation," which holds the ties of meaning, the contexts of meaning, that shape the dimension in which the facts of life need to be considered. "The 'expressions' are always to be taken as a 'cluster of relations, of sense-complexes'" (*Gesamtausgabe*, 60: 134), and this is why "factive life is emotional, not theoretical" (App. B; *Gesamtausgabe*, 58: 220).

3. The ambivalence or mobility proper to factive life: the first and only fact is that life is at every moment in charge of itself. Life seeks to discharge this charge in a "ready-made" interpretation, or else it takes on the burden in the anxiety of the subject itself. In an explicit reference to Pascal, Heidegger says, "The mobility of factive life is to be interpreted, to first be described as *anxiety*" (*Gesamtausgabe*, 60: 93). But Saint Augustine also provides a reference: "*Molestia*—the endangerment of Having-of-Oneself" (Heidegger, *Phenomenology of Religious Life*, 182; *Gesamtausgabe*, 60: 244). This weight is specific to factive life, to life insofar as it is factive, that is to say, in its facticity: "The being-there of our own *Dasein* is what it is precisely and only in its temporally particular 'there,' its being 'there' for a while" (*Ontology*; *Gesamtausgabe*, 63: 29), whence the tendency of factive life to "indifference" or "self-sufficiency," as opposed to the tendency for "anxiety" in the "having-one's-self." Another opposition is also rooted in facticity, the opposition between proper and improper, between *eigentlich* and *uneigentlich*. One could say in a play on words that the question is whether life is actually "in fact."

The *Faktizität* of life is thus simultaneously a dimension of meaning, a lability induced by the facticity that weighs on life, and the demand for a logic other than the formal and objective. These analyses of the young Heidegger reappear in the vocabulary of *Being and Time* (§29 and §38):

Existence is not founded on anything, (it is thrown), it does not have an endpoint (it is understood factively, that is to say, at each instant), and this double movement describes the lability proper to factive life, a dimension of meaning that does not assign a final point to life and only roots itself in the primary fact that life has to do with itself before it has anything to do with something else. "Facticity is not the factuality of the *factum brutum* of something present-at-hand, but a characteristic of *Dasein*'s Being—one which has been taken up into existence, even if proximally it has been thrust aside."

(Heidegger, *Being and Time*, trans. Macquarrie and Robinson, 174)

The very precise meanings that Heidegger assigns to *Faktizität* and *faktisch,* and their imbrication in a series of complex oppositions in German (*Faktizität* versus *Tatsache,* versus *Faktum*, versus *Wesen*) make them especially difficult to translate. Optimally, one would devise a way to render the conceptual strangeness of these technical terms, which in German remain direct borrowings from Latin and thus outline a German history of the Latin *factum*.

Philippe Quesne

BIBLIOGRAPHY

Heidegger, Martin. *Being and Time*. Translated by John Macquarrie and Edward Robinson. London: SCM Press, 1962. Also translated by Joan Stambaugh. Albany: State University of New York Press, 1996.
———. *Grundprobleme der Phänomenologie*. Vol. 58 of *Gesamtausgabe*. Frankfurt: Klostermann, 1987.
———. *Ontologie, Hermeneutik der Faktizität*. Vol. 63 of *Gesamtausgabe*. Frankfurt: Klostermann, 1987. Translation by John van Buren: *Ontology: The Hermeneutics of Facticity*. Bloomington: Indiana University Press, 1999.
———. *Phänomenologie des Religiösen Lebens*. Vol. 60 of *Gesamtausgabe*. Frankfurt: Klostermann, 1987. Translation by Matthias Fritsch and Jennifer Anna Gosetti-Ferencei: *The Phenomenology of Religious Life*. Bloomington: Indiana University Press, 2004.
———. *Zur Bestimmung der Philosophie*. Vols. 56–57 of *Gesamtausgabe*. Frankfurt: Klostermann, 1987. Translation by Ted Sadler: *Towards the Definition of Philosophy*. London: Continuum, 2002.
Husserl, Edmund. *Ideas: General Introduction to Pure Phenomenology*. Translated by W. R. Boyce Gibson. New York: Collier Books, 1962.
Kierkegaard, Søren. *Philosophical Fragments: Johannes Climacus* [Philosofiske smuler]. Edited and translated by Howard V. Hong and Edna H. Hong. Princeton, NJ: Princeton University Press, 1985.

BIBLIOGRAPHY

Eisler, Rudolf. *Kant-Lexikon*. Hildesheim, Ger.: Olms, 2008.
Fichte, Johann Gottlieb. *Fichte: Early Philosophical Writings*. Edited and translated by Daniel Breazeale. Ithaca, NY: Cornell University Press, 1988.
———. *Fichte: Science of Knowledge*. Edited by Peter Heath and John Lachs. 2nd ed. Cambridge: Cambridge University Press, 1982.
———. *Gesamtausgabe der Bayerischen Akademie der Wissenschaften (GA)*. 42 vols. Edited by Reinhard Lauth, Hans Gliwitzky, Erich Fuchs, and Peter Schneider. Stuttgart-Bad: Cannstatt, 1962–2012.
———. *Introductions to the Wissenschaftslehre and Other Writings*. Translated and edited by Daniel Breazeale. Indianapolis, IN: Hackett, 1994.
———. *The Science of Rights* [Grundlage des Naturrechts nach Principien der Wissenschaftslehre]. Translated by A. E. Kroeger. New York: Harper and Row, 1970.

Franks, Paul. "Freedom, Tatsache and Tathandlung in the Development of Fichte's Jena Wissenschaftslehre." *Archiv für Geschichte der Philosophie* 79, no. 3 (1997): 310–23.
Kant, Immanuel. *Critique of Practical Reason*. Translated by Mary J. Gregor. Cambridge: Cambridge University Press, 1997.
———. *Critique of the Power of Judgment*. Translated by Paul Guyer and Eric Matthews. Cambridge: Cambridge University Press, 2001.
———. *Critique of Pure Reason*. Translated by Paul Guyer and Allen Wood. Cambridge: Cambridge University Press, 1998.
Puech, Michel. *Kant et la causalité. Étude sur la formation du système critique*. Paris: Vrin, 1990.
Thomas-Fogiel, Isabelle. *Critique de la représentation. Étude sur Fichte*. Paris: Vrin, 2000.
Tilliette, Zavier. *L'Intuition intellectuelle de Kant à Hegel*. Paris: Vrin, 1995.

TERM

FRENCH   *terme*
GERMAN   *Begriff*
GREEK   *horos* [ὅϱος]
LATIN   *terminus, nomen*

➤ *CONCEPT* [BEGRIFF, CONCEPTUS], INTENTION, LOGOS, MERKMAL, PRÉDICABLE, PREDICATION, PROPOSITION, SIGN, SUBJECT, *TO BE*, TRUTH, WORD

In the vocabulary of the Scholastic *Organon*, the Latin expression *terminus*, "term," designates an element of the *propositio*, the "proposition": this is what delimits a proposition, like the endpoint of a line. Rendering the Greek *horos* [ὅϱος] as *terminus* did not raise major issues of translation for a reader of medieval texts on logic. The various classical/modern avatars of the elementary constituents of a proposition in the original Aristotelian sense of the term serve as markers for changes in epistemes, corresponding to changes in the understanding of the very object of logic. Characteristic of the Aristotelian form of the enunciation/proposition is a structure that is sometimes called binary, in which two terms, respectively called the subject (Gr. *hupokeimenon* [ὑποκείμενον]) and the predicate (Gr. *katêgorêma* [ϰατηγόϱημα]) are linked or separated by a copula, itself affirmative/negative. This structure finds lexical form in the verb "to be" (which means that one has in fact three terms—subject, copula, predicate—in what would be more accurately called a ternary form, despite the affirmations of Kant or Hegel). In the classical period various rivals for the term "term" emerge, with the effect of moving away from the sense of enunciation/proposition and toward the idea of judgment. The principal rivals were "noun" (*nom*) and "concept" (*Begriff*). The fate of *terminus/horos* is an indication of the pendulum swing that starts in the Middle Ages and accelerates in the classical age, between two conceptions of the object of logic. "Noun" is a semiotic conception in which the terms are treated as signs (where *logica* is presented as a *scientia sermocinalis* [the science of discourse/language]). "Concept" is a more intentionalist than Thomist conception (even if Thomas remains the "great transmitter" of Scholastic language, from the Germany of the *Frühaufklarung* to present-day Germany). In the latter case terms are treated as concepts, making *logica* a "science of the secondary intentions that are added to the first intentions" (see INTENTION). This bears on the diverse "operations of the intellect"—the apprehension of simple quiddities, the composition/division of "terms" that contribute to a (propositional) judgment, and the forms of "reasoning" (Lat. *ratiocinatio remota*), understood as a syllogistic chain of judgments that are the products of the "second operation of the intellect." The fate of the Aristotelian "term" thus appears in the first analysis to be inherently caught up in a perpetual oscillation between sign and concept, between "nominalism" and "conceptualism." Yet its movement cannot be reduced to this simple oscillation. Other forces affect its semantic drift, from one translation to another. They include the Hegelian exposition—following in Kant's footsteps—of the ternary formal structure of the "Aristotelian" proposition, and the modern and contemporary critique of the "copula" whose confusion of functions is supposed to include, "on some occasions judgments of existence, on other occasions the inherence of a predicate within a subject, sometimes the membership of an individual in a class, at other times the inclusion of a class into a higher-order class, and sometimes the equivalence of a noun and its description, or the equivalence of a term and its definition" (Rougier, *La Métaphysique et le langage*). The history of the term "term" is also a history of the copula, and thus a history of the oppositions at work in the apophantic Aristotelian *logos*.

I. *Terminus* in Medieval Logic

In general, medieval authors followed the indications given by Aristotle in the *Prior Analytics* (24b 16–18): "I call the term that which resolves the premise [Ὅϱον δὲ ϰαλῶ εἰς ὃν διαλύεται ἡ πϱότασις], that is to say the predicate and the subject of its affirmation [οἶον τό τε ϰατηγοϱούμενον ϰαὶ τὸ ϰαθ' οὗ ϰατηγοϱεῖται]; whether joined by being or separated by non-being [πϱοστιθεμένου τοῦ εἶναι ἢ μὴ εἶναι]." This was translated by Boethius as: "Terminus vero voco in quem resolvitur propositio, ut praedicatum et de quo praedicatur, vel appositio vel divisio esse et non esse." The direction of *horos* [ὅϱος] is obvious (Fr. *obvie*): it is the limit, which delimits a proposition (*protasis* [πϱότασις] or *diastêma* [διάστημα]), like the endpoint of a line.

Aside from the obvious senses of "final term," "end" (*finis*), and "extremity," which explain the existence of periphrases such as *extra terminum* to designate the infinite, the word *terminus* has three meanings in medieval logic. Two of them are common:

1. the minimal syntactical/semantic unit that resolves a proposition: "the term is that which results from the analysis of a proposition, that is to say, a subject and predicate" (terminus est in quem resolvitur propositio ut subjectum et praedicatum) (Peter of Spain, *Tractatus*, 5–6);

2. the fundamental semantic unit in logic, as opposed to the noun or verb as grammatical units, which carries different couplets of difference depending on the competence of the logician: universal/particular, abstract/concrete, categorematic/syncategorematic, etc.

Finally a third use, rarer than the other two, makes the *terminus* a synonym for *definitio*; "the [objects] whose terms or definitions are different are themselves different" (quorum termini sive definitiones sunt differentes, ipsa quoque sunt differentia) (19–20). Aside from *terminus*, the lexicon of medieval logic also includes *extremum*. *Extremum* presents the same ambiguity as *subjectum*: most of the time, the referent of the word is that element through which the proposition can be analyzed and which is targeted by the vocable, but sometimes it is also or even only the object referred to by the proposition that is in question. This is especially the case in the various formulations of the rules regarding the truth of a proposition that stipulate that in "matters of nature" (*en matière naturelle*), "existence of the extremes is not required." The expression *existential extremorum* is thus partially equivalent to that of *constantia subjecti* (see SUBJECT, II). The only difference between the two is that the former extends to both the signified/referent of the subject as well as the predicate, while the latter is limited to only the signified/referent of the subject. A good example of this usage can be found in this passage from a sophism attributed to Robert Kilwardby (cf. "Omnis homo de necessitate est animal"; ms. Erfurt, *Amplon.* Q328, f. 8rb–10rb): "I say that the propositions 'every man is necessarily animal' [omins homo de necessitate est animal] and 'man is [an] animal' [homo est animal] are true, for in matters of nature the truth of a proposition does not require the existence of its terms in act [quoniam ad veritatem propositionis in naturali material non exigitur existential extremorum actu]. Indeed, the concepts of man and animal are naturally coherent [naturaliter coherentes]; thus, whether or not it is any one man in question, as long as the speech of *man* absolutely signifies that 'Man' is speaking, 'Animal' shall be understood to be within the speaker [dummodo hec vox "homo" hominem significet simpliciter in ipso intelligitur animal]."

Terminus appears in several thematic networks. The first contains the distinction among "written term"/"spoken term"/"mental term," which touches upon the Augustinian notion of "mental verb" on several points. Following the distinction between three kinds of propositions—written, spoken, mental—taken from the first (16a2–3: "the sounds made by the voice are symbols of states of mind [τὰ ἐν τῇ φωνῇ τῶν ἐν τῇ ψυχῇ παθημάτων σύμβολα]") and the last (24b 1–2: the affirmations and negations put forth by the voice [αἱ ἐν τῇ φωνῇ καταφάσεις καὶ ἀποφάσεις], are symbols of those in the mind [σύμβολα τῶν ἐν τῇ ψυχῇ]") chapters of *De interpretatione*, certain medieval logicians accepted the idea of "mental terms." This is the case, for example, of Boethius, who is said to have handed down the notion from Porphyrius. In his first *Commentary on the Perihermeneias*, he presents the set of ideas as a doctrine of the *Peripatos*, insisting on the existence of "nouns and verbs" manipulated "in the silence of the mind" (*In Aristotelis De interpretatione* [RT: *PL*, vol. 64, col. 407B]):

It is said that the peripatetics held that there are three kinds of discourse: one which is written with letter, one which is put forward with the voice, and the other which is articulated by the mind. If there are three kinds of discourse, there is no doubt that there are also three parts of discourse. Thus, since noun and verb are the principal parts of discourse, there are distinct written nouns and verbs, other spoken nouns and verbs, as well as those that one moves about silently in the mind.

(Dictum est tres esse apud Peripateticos orationes, unam quae litteris scriberetur, aliam quae proferretur in voce, tertiam quae conjungeretur in animo. Quod si tres orationes sunt, partes quoque orationes esse triplices nulla dubitatio est. Quare quoniam verbum et nomen principaliter orationes partes sunt, erunt alia verba quae scribantur, alia quae dicantur, aliae quae tacita mente tractentur.)

The notion of "mental nouns" and "mental verbs" is a first step in the direction of a "mental language," even if the Porphyro-Boethian thesis does not conform to all the requirements of a theory of "mentalese," such as that which William of Ockham seems to be the first to have proposed (cf. Panaccio, *Le Discours intérieur*).

A second network carried by *terminus* is the distinction, based on scattered sources in Priscien and Boethius, between categorema and syncategorema, often expressed in Paris, if not in Oxford (where the word *dictio* and its derivatives, such as *dictions officials*, official terms, are equally prevalent), as a distinction between "categoremic terms" and "syncategoremic terms." In this approach, called "terminist," the notions

of categoremic and syncategoremic terms are applied to various kinds of syntactic-semantic analyses. There is a modeling of the meaning of sentences by virtue of the relations of *inclusio* ("scope" in modern logic, in French, *champ* and *portée*) that exist between categorema and syncategorema or among syncategorema themselves. And there are theories of the "generation of discourse" (*generatio sermonis*) that seek to account not simply for the passage of thought to written or oral expression, but also for the formation of thought itself structured like a language. Some authors in this school use *signs* (*signa*) to designate the categoremas of quantity exclusively (see SIGN), the medieval form of quantifiers. Or they will use the term less restrictively to refer to all categoremas. These terminist distinctions, along with their discrepant applications, will reappear in Leibniz.

There is yet a third network carried by "term": that of the syntactic-semantic properties of categoremic terms understood within propositional contexts—the *proprietates terminorum*—whose analysis constitutes the most notable contribution of medieval logic to the history of logic. When they are inserted in a specific context, terms that carry signification acquire new semantic properties. Distinctions are drawn among the *suppositio* (reference; see SUPPOSITION), the *appellatio* (denotation or reference solely to that which exists), the *copulatio* (a syntactic-semantic property of verbs and adjectives), and the *relatio* (anaphora). As employed by medieval logicians, the *terminus* is radically set off from the *nomen* and the *verbum*, which are reserved for the use of grammarians. The Platonic theory of the primordial interconnections of nouns and verbs, which is authentically binary, is expelled from logic in favor of the falsely binary theory of Aristotle, founded on the pairing of subject-predicate + copula. Even if the distinction between substantive and adjective, apprehended ontologically, is present in the analysis of various types of *suppositiones*, the term has more in common with the sign than with the *nomen*. At least for a while, it does not precisely correspond to the concept (until Occam's redefinition of the concept as a natural sign as a term of a mental language and referential act). This primacy of the *terminus/signum* over the *terminus/intentio/conceptus* is evident by virtue of the fact that the authors, principally theologians or intentionalists (who put forth concepts as the elementary units of meaning within a theory of judgment), experience certain difficulties in taking full advantage of the novelties of the *Logica moderna*. The increasing power of the concept in relation to the term/sign and to the *nomen* marks the beginning of one of the great debates of the classical age. But an unfortunate ambiguity weighs down the lexicon from one end to the other. It goes back to the restricted use of "sign," starting in the Middle Ages, as an equivalent for syncategorema or operator. As a result, for adherents of the binary interpretation of the proposition, only subject and predicate could be considered "terms," while the copula was simply a "sign."

II. *Signum, Terminus, Nomen* in the Classical Age

The proximity of meanings among "sign," "term," and "noun" is everywhere evident in the philosophical practice of the classical age. In the following passage, for example, Leibniz defines signification as the relationship between *nomen* and *terminus*, the latter also identified with *notio*:

By "term" I do not mean a noun but rather a concept, that is to say, that which is signified by a noun, which could also be called "notion" or "idea."

(Per terminum non intelligo nomen sed conceptum seu id quod nomine significatur, possis et dicere notionem, ideam.)

(Specimen calculi universalis)

This highly conceptual iteration of terminism is specific to Leibniz. It is clearly a new synthesis of several philosophical instruments, drawn from rather different traditions, but which constitute the common ground of logical and linguistic positions that are themselves occasionally contradictory. Since different medieval criteria enable the distinction between categorema and syncategorema, Leibniz retains the functional criterion—the being or non-being of the subject or predicate—whence this other definition of term:

I call everything that exists on its own a TERM, that is, everything that can be a subject or predicate of a proposition; for example: *man, chimera.* . . . A term is either possible or impossible. But what is POSSIBLE is that which can be conceived distinctly, without contradiction.

(Ibid.)

Leibniz no longer speaks of "syncategorematic terms." He refers instead to syncategorema using the medieval term *signum* (see SIGN). The *signum* is thus considered a prefix of the *terminus* or of the entire *propositio*. One also comes across *signum* in the vocabulary of mathematics. The French algebraics of the School of Viète spoke of the "sign of affectation" "+" or "-" (cf. Vaulézard, *La Nouvelle algèbre de M. Viète*) When this use became impossible by its proximity to the logical acceptation, the authors subsequently employed the Latin *nota* or the French *marque* (see MERKMAL). These multiple overlays and contaminations are linked, up to a point, to effects of translation. It is necessary in French, for example, to put *terme* in quotation marks when translating passages of Porphyry's *Introduction* (or *Isagoge*) to the *Logical Categories* of Aristotle in order to avoid recourse to words like *chose* (thing), *nom* (name or noun), and *concept* (concept), all of which are absent from the original Greek. To not do so would run the risk of placing Porphyrian definitions of species and kind under the rubric of "realism," "nominalism," or "conceptualism."

The word *terme* is also often added to translations into French during the classical age to render the generality and indeterminacy of the Latin neuter pronoun or the substantive adjective. For example, when Descartes writes in the *Regulae*, "Item quaedam interdum sunt vere magis absoluta quam alia, sed nondum tamen omnium maxime," the most scrupulous translator cannot avoid, "Et aussi certains *termes* sont véritablement plus absolus que d'autres, mais pas encore les plus absolus de tous" (Fr. trans. Marion) (In addition, some terms are truly more absolute than others, but yet not the most absolute of all). This habit may run the risk of surreptitiously conferring a logical background or underpinning that the author may not have intended. But on the other hand, it has the advantage of neutralizing as much as possible the term *terme* in French, relative to its cognitive

interpretations. This is not the case in the German logical treatises, starting with Christian Thomasius and Christian Wolff. In recent translations from Latin to German, *terminus* is sometimes rendered as *Begriff*, which is partly justified by history (the importation of Latin vocabulary into the logic of the *Frühaufklärung*), but which poses certain problems of intelligibility. In the Leibniz sentence quoted above, it is impossible to identify *Begriff* with *terminus* at the lexical level, even though it may seem appropriate at the level of the informational content carried by the statement. For if one makes this identification along with the equivalence of *notio/ Begriff*, one ends up with the statement that "Per terminum (*Begriff*) non intelligo nomen sed conceptum (*Begriff*), seu id quod nominee significatur, possis et dicere notionem (*Begriff*) ideam" (By "term" [*Begriff*] I understand not the word but the concept [*Begriff*], that is, what is signified by the word, for which one could also say "notion" or "idea" [*Begriff*]).

One cannot properly understand the constitutive conditions of the German language without considering it within a very general slide from terminism in the direction of conceptualism. In the German logicians who still wrote in Latin, in particular in Jungius, the tripartite Scholastic division of the *terminus* into mental, written, and spoken terms gave way to a dualistic distinction, according to which the *oratio* is considered either as an internal or as an external reality in relation to the mind. No doubt because he inherits this distinction, Jungius has a tendency to abandon the *terminus* in favor of the *notio*. He makes the analysis of notions ("De notionibus") the first chapter of the *Logica*, reinterpreting the traditional plan that has been generally if not exclusively accepted since the commentary of Thomas Aquinas based on the three operations of mind:

1. "intelligentia indivisibulium sive incomplexorum" (the understanding of indivisible or non-complex things)
2. "compositio vel divisio intellectus" (the intellect's action of combining or dividing)
3. "discurrere ab uno in aliud" (to advance from one thing to another [i.e., to go from what is known toward what is unknown])

(Aristotelis libros posteriorum analyticorum expositio [Commentary on the *Posterior Analytics* of Aristotle], *Proemium*, 4)

In the *Logica Hamburgensis* of 1638, these three operations become "notio, enuntiatio et dianoia sive discursus" (*Prologus*, §1–7), which in an author so concerned with historical accuracy, clearly indicate that the understanding of the incomplexes (*termini*) should henceforth be interpreted as the science of notions. The *notiones* are also the object of a separate study, entitled *Disputationes noematicae*, for the ancients, including Aristotle himself did not sufficiently develop this part of the *Organon*, which should not consist only of the study of predicaments. One of the most common errors in relation to the *notiones/noemata* (the text of Jungius constantly reminds the reader of this identity) consists of neglecting the cognitive dimension of the foundation of logic, as is the case when the words used by logicians are taken as having direct reference to things. According to the thinker from Hamburg, this is the principal error of logicians (which is a reminder of the approach of the school of Ockham). For the nouns that occur in the phrases of calculation are the names of notions, and to claim otherwise would be to confuse the primary and secondary objects of logic.

The Latin word *terminus* still appears in the German of Thomasius, (e.g., in the *Einleitung zu der Vernunftlehre* [Introduction to the theory of reason]), although it is much less frequent or important than in Leibniz. It appears to be strictly limited to the technical vocabulary of syllogistics in the *Philosophisches Lexicon* of Johann Georg Walch: the expression *Ideen oder Termini* appears in the article "Syllogismus," itself completed by a short entry on "Termini Syllogismi." In Wolff's *Deutsche Logik*, the term has completely disappeared and been replaced with the concept of things (*von den Begriffen der Dinge*) and the usage of words (*von dem Gebrauche der Worte*) as if the elision of *terminus* resulted in the split of the first level of logic, which had traditionally been considered as one, into two different chapters (one more cognitive, the other more semantic).

Similar transformations occur in the corresponding passages from Latin to French and from Latin to English. But there are also differences, whether in relation to Hobbes's treatise on *computatio* or the *Logique* of Port-Royal. Whereas the very base of the edifice was contaminated by the *notiones* in Jungius, in these latter writers the whole construction is devoted to the mode of being of the idea in language, even if it does not build up a complete doctrine of the idea. For the idea enters into the signification of words, as "there would be a contradiction between saying that I know what I am saying when I say a word and my not conceiving of anything when pronouncing the very sound of the word" (*Logique*, I, I). As a general cognitive event, the Aristotelian-Thomistic "constituit intellectum" is clarified by the relation of the word to the idea. And the details of this relation account for the amphibology of signification, according to whether it is from one to one, from one to several, or from several to one.

- See Box 1.

If the term is thus excluded from the first part of logic for the sake of the sign, this does not mean that it is reintroduced into the second part as an element of the proposition. For the latter is analyzed according to grammatical

---

1

Signifying/the constitution of a thought: Aristotle, Thomas Aquinas, Port-Royal

➤ SENSE

In the *De interpretatione*, 3.16b 19–25, Aristotle writes,

> When uttered just by itself a verb is a name and signifies something.

[αὐτὰ μὲν οὖν καθ' αὑτὰ λεγόμενα τὰ ῥήματα ὀνόματά ἐστι καὶ σημαίνει τι.]

This line has been one of the fundamental starting points of a philosophy of signification. The passage bears principally on verbs: *rhêmata* [ῥήματα] must be considered a kind of noun (*onoma* [ὄνομα]) insofar as they too signify something. In fact, Aristotle continues, in a kind of parenthetical remark, meaning is produced when the speaker arrests his intellection:

> [T]he speaker arrests his thought and the hearer pauses.

[ἵστησι γὰρ ὁ λέγων τὴν διάνοιαν, καὶ ὁ ἀκούσας ἠρέμησεν.]

The Greek phrase is rendered into Latin by Boethius as follows:

> Ipsa quidem secundum se dicta verba nomina sunt et significant aliquid— constituit enim qui dicit intellectum, et qui audit quiescit.
>
> (*Aristoteles latinus*, II, 1–2)

Despite what the translation might lead one to think, the Latin commentary (RT: *PL*, vol. 64, cols. 309–10) indicates that Boethius took the dynamic metaphor of movement and rest quite seriously, and that he took his own *constituere* as a "fixing in place" or "stopping," which is rendered rather well in Ackrill's English translation, here reproduced with the phrase in its entirety:

> When uttered just by itself a verb is a name and signifies something—the speaker arrests his thought and the hearer pauses—but it does not yet signify whether it is or not.

See PROPOSITION.
When we use a noun, Aristotle specifies through paraphrase, the thinking of the listener is put into motion (*inchoat*) along with our enunciation (*prolatio*). When I say, for example, "Hippocentaurus," the thoughts of the listener start with the first syllable and come into full effect only when the word has been completely pronounced. Verbs and nouns have in common this power of generating a kind of anxiety, which is only released upon understanding their meaning. Signification is nothing more than this effect: the possibility of being able to rest (*conquiescere*) on something completed, of operating in consecutive order on the anxiety and repose of the listener. According to Boethius, the "constituit qui dicit intellectum" of *De interpretatione* sets out a process of meaning-analysis that applies equally to the utterance of a verb and to a proposition, for it is only when one has understood the entire proposition, "Socrates ambulat" (Socrates walks), for instance, that the listener can settle fully on a completed signification.

Thus in Boethius's commentary, a wide interpretation of the *constituit intellectum* comes to light, but this is not without problems of its own. Everything happens in fact as if the relative positions of the parts of the discourse enabled a double analysis, both ascending and descending, depending on whether one stresses the relations of words to meanings or the relation of utterances to the truth. In the first case, the relations of words to meanings, every *oratio* or part thereof is meaningful when it answers to the *constituit intellectum* (that which establishes the understanding of a thing). The basic atomic unit is thus the *nomen*, insofar as the subdivisions within a word itself are not meaningful. The horizon of signification, on the other hand, is more or less wide open as a result of the multiplicity of possibilities afforded by the infinite combinatorics in the composition of words. In the end, it can be said of an entire discourse that its completion has produced a thought process.

According to the second case, the relation of utterances to truth, what signifies is that which is capable of telling things as

(continued)

(continued)

they are, that is, saying if they are true or false. Here, the basic atomic element is the *propositio*, defined as the smallest part of the *oratio* that can carry the predicate of truth. A closer analysis still leads to the *terminus* as part of the *propositio*. But on this point, except for the specific case of Leibniz, the *terminus* is not generally qualified as true or false, such that the analysis of discourse into categorema and syncategorema remains a proto-analysis, or rather, in Carnap's words, a quasi-analysis. The concurrence of these two axes (*vox significativa, oratio/terminus, propositio vera*) has been the starting point for an extensive debate on the proper scope of the "constituit intellectum." Thomas Aquinas notes, for example, that the *nomen* cannot be rigorously considered as significant in itself according to the criterion of movement and repose of the mind. If, for example, the speaker says "*homo*" (man), the mind of the listener remains, so to speak, in suspense until he knows that what is being said is *de homine* (of or about man); and likewise, when he hears only the verb *currit* (to run), his mind will not come to rest until he knows the answer to the question "Who is being spoken about?" (Thomas Aquinas, *In Peri hermeneias*, L I, 1. V, 68). The criterion traditionally applied to signification thus seems paradoxically to preclude any philosophy of the sign in favor of a hypothetical *oratio perfecta* (a sentence that yields a complete understanding in the mind of the listener), unless it is itself supported by another supplementary distinction that establishes the orders of discourse. This is the path undertaken by Thomas. Referring to the division of the *intellectio* according to the three operations of the mind, he affirms that the *constituit intellectum* is only pertinent within the limits of an apprehension of the *intellectio* by the *concipere* (conception), but that it must be abandoned at the higher levels of the *divisio* (division) and *compositio* (composition), which the classical age will call "judgment." Just as the analysis of propositions through attention to terms is necessary to elucidate the concept of truth (even though the terms themselves are neither true nor false), so the grasping of meaning within a phrase does not entail any generalization in the use of the criterion of *constituit intellectum* that would apply only to their constituent parts. One can say that the *nomen* promotes signification (and this is true of all words that signify) as conception because at this level it effectively produces a state of rest. But at the same time it ignites anxiety in the subsequent sequence of the composition (*In Peri hermeneias*, LI, I. V, 69). Signification and conception thus have a deep historic tie, and Alberto Coffa seems to have been truly inspired when he suggested a correction to Quine's aphorism to say, "Meanings are what concepts became when wedded to the word" (*The Semantic Tradition*).

These remarks also serve to clarify the treatment of signification as developed in the logic of Port-Royal. We know that Arnauld and Nicole followed the classic Thomist tripartition of operations of mind, but that they claimed to enrich it in a fourth chapter inspired by Descartes and devoted to method. It would be highly unlikely for the whole edifice not to suffer from such an addition *in extremis*. As far as the tradition was concerned, this would in effect remove the structuring capacities of the three operations for rationality in general. And as far as modernity was concerned, it proceeded as if method had not been introduced by the author himself in the place of logic, in order to correct the excesses of his precepts and distinctions. But out of this double infidelity a new philosophical and Scholastic object would be born, giving rise to the conventionally accepted uses of *term* and *noun* or *name* in philosophy in the French language.

Jean-Baptiste Rauzy

BIBLIOGRAPHY

Aquinas, Thomas, Saint. *In Aristotelis libros Peri hermeneias et posteriorum analyticorum exposition, cum textu et recensione leonine*. Turin: Marietti, 1964. Translation by Jean T. Oesterle: *Aristotle: On Interpretation. Commentary by St. Thomas and Cajetan (Peri hermenias)*. Milwaukee: Marquette University Press, 1962.

Aristotle. *Categories and On Interpretation*. Translated by J. L. Ackrill. Oxford: Clarendon Press, 1963. French translation by J. Tricot: *Organon I: Catégories et sur l'Interprétation*. Paris: Vrin, 1989.

———. *Complete Works*. Edited by J. Barnes, Translated by J. Ackrill. Oxford: Oxford University Press, 1982.

———. *Aristoteles Latinus*, II, 1–2, *De interpretatione vel Periermenias*. Edited by L. Minio-Paluello. Bruges, Belg: Desclée de Brouwer, 1995.

Arnauld, Antoine, and Nicole Pierre. *La Logique ou l'art de penser*. Edited by P. Clair and F. Girbal. Paris: Presses Universitares de France, 1965. First published in 1662. Translation, with an introduction, by James Dickoff and Patricia James, and a foreword by Charles W. Hendel: *The Art of Thinking: Port-Royal Logic*. Indianapolis: Bobbs-Merrill, 1964.

Coffa, Alberto. *The Semantic Tradition from Kant to Carnap*. Cambridge: Cambridge University Press, 1991.

categories: nouns, pronouns, and verbs (cf. Hobbes, who defines the *propositio* as "a statement consisting of two coupled nouns [*oratio constans ex duobus* nominibus *copulates*]"; *Logica*, chap. 3, §2). Any search for the *terminus* as endpoint of the analysis of propositions will be in vain. The concurrence of the two traditional axes remains (*vox significativa, oratio/terminus, propositio vera*) but it is now split into two separate and largely asymmetrical functions: on the one hand a semantics whose closure is ensured metaphysically by the idea, on the other hand a relatively open syntax, whose role it is to expose the deep structure of enunciations. In French-language philosophy *terme* becomes a sort of free electron used here and there in multiple contexts, and which attests, at the very least in a negative way, to the different paths set out during the classical age toward the deconstruction of terminism.

III. Binary Form/Ternary Form; Kant, Hegel, Heidegger

As Kant knew nothing of the Middle Ages, he knew nothing of termism. His critical efforts were directed instead at the "modern" definition of the judgment/proposition as the representation of a relation between two *concepts* ("I was never satisfied with the definition that logicians give to judgment in general, when they say that it is the representation of the relation between two *concepts*" [*Critique of Pure Reason* §19]). His own concern was to introduce an innovation that one might call a first form of ternary judgment. His discovery is in effect the "medium," unknown to his predecessors, in other words, the relation of concepts to the "originary synthetic unity of apperception." The term "medium" has a long history; first and foremost it is the "middle term" of Aristotelian syllogistics. But the Kantian medium of judgment is not the middle term of a syllogism, it is not exactly a term enabling the passage from (two) premises to a conclusion. This "third" (Ger. *Drittes*) is neither another "concept," nor an "addition" (see PREDICATION) but rather, self-consciousness itself as a "principle of affinity" binding subject and predicate within a *single* judgment (A 766, B 794). One also finds a ternary schema in Hegel, this time pushed to its paroxysm, with the same intention of breaking with "classical" logic. The difference between the two readings lies in the fact that, for Hegel, the complete form of the proposition, what he calls the "universal form of reason" (*Wissenschaft der Logik*) does not consist in the simple judgment, but in the syllogism itself—albeit revised. By "syllogism" Hegel does not mean a chain of three predicative enunciations, but the "judgment according to its foundation." Thus a single enunciation that is "wholly contained within the universal proposition," as in the example used by Hegel of Socrates, "through the particularity of his being a man." In virtually any predicative syllogism one can speak of a "life" of "triplicity," which can be unpacked in terms of the "movement" of the middle term in its "unifying of the extremes." The "is" of the Hegelian proposition is thus not the "simple copula of judgment," the "*is* without spirit [*geistloses Ist*]" of classical logic (PREDICATION, Box 3), but is the "dialectical movement of the proposition

itself" (*Phänomenologie des Geistes*), in a word, it is the *Aufhebung*, "suppression, elevation, conservation" (see AUFHEBEN). It is actually rather amazing that Kant and Hegel (to different degrees) criticize or claim to move beyond binarism in the analysis of the proposition that originates in Aristotle. The "invention of the middle term" (*inventio medii*), as elaborated by Avicenna or Albertus Magnus in the context of reflections on natural prophecy has a number of resonances with the idea of a syllogism as a "judgment according to its fundament." But most importantly, the Aristotelian interpretation of the *propositio* is eminently ternary—something for which modern logicians have reproached it ever since Frege.

■ See Box 2.

On a more positive note, Heidegger (*Sein und Zeit*, §44) maintains that the Aristotelian proposition is not limited to uniting two concepts. In his view Aristotelian propositions are

---

2

Science, natural prophecy, and "invention of the middle term" according to Avicenna

➤ INGENIUM, Box 1

According to Avicenna, the practice of syllogisms requires an aptitude for discovering the middle terms that are necessary for deduction. This aptitude is the capacity to identify with active intelligence. It is present in varying degrees. Some have it to a degree sufficient to be able to obtain something of this activated intelligence without much effort or training. They also have a second capacity, which the *Avicenna Latinus* starts by calling *subtilitas* (subtlety) and then *intellectus sanctus in habitu* (intellect in habitus; see INTELLECT). This *subtilitas* renders the Arabic *hads* [الحدس] (Bakos translates it as "intellectual intuition" [Fr. *intuition intellectuelle*]; Van Riet as "flash of intellectual intuition" [Fr. *éclair d'intuition intellectuelle*]). It is the same word—*subtilitas*—which occurs later in the text to render the Arabic *ḏakā'* [الذكاء]. The Arabic text says that "Intellectual intuition [*hads*] is an action by which the mind discovers the middle term on its own, and that wisdom [*ḏakā'*] is the faculty (*quwwa* [قوة]; Lat. *virtus*) of intellectual intuition." The Latin version adds a further complication by stating "ingenium autem est actus rationis, cujus propria vi invenitur medius terminus; subtilitas autem est supra ingenium" (intellectual intuition is an act of reason; by reason's own power is the middle term discovered; subtlety, however, is above intellectual intuition)—whereas the Arabic says something that should be closer to "*subtilitas* est *virtus ingenii*" (subtlety/wisdom is the faculty of intellectual intuition). Returning to the original meaning of the Arabic, in the passages where *hads* [الحدس] was initially rendered as *subtilitas*, *ingenium* (intellectual intuition) would

have been the closer term. Étienne Gilson, following the Latin as written, says that *subtilitas* is superior to *ingenium*. And this, in fact, is what the Latins thought as well (as shown in Gilson's chart of "*Les sources gréco-arabes de l'augustinisme avicennisant*" [The greco-arabic sources of Avicennian Augustinianism]). Assuming that what is at stake in the Avicennian notion of natural prophecy (what we might today call "science") is an aptitude for discovering large numbers of middle terms, we see that men can be categorized according to a quantitative aptitude (the breadth of invention) and a qualitative one (the speed of invention). This natural inequality among men finds its lower limit in those who have no *ingenium* at all, and its upper limit in those whose *ingenium* applies to all questions (or at least most of them) and who can apply this *ingenium* rapidly. The *Avicenna latinus* thus describes the highest workings of intelligence in the form of the man whose spirit is so sufficiently purified and at one with the principles of intelligibility that it is as if he were inspired (*inspirata*); a person whose intelligence (*ingenium*) would seem to be on fire (*accendatur*). He obtains an answer to all of his questions from the intelligence at work; he knows everything in an instant (*subito*), or at least almost instantly (*pene subito*). The answers to his questions (the Latin mentions only *quaestiones*) are powerfully impressed upon him (*firmiter impressas*), and not just as a simple probability. He apprehends all the necessary middle terms in the correct order, not as some blind belief (*probata*) but as rational certainty (*intelligibilia*—the Latin a poor rendition

of the Arabic). Indeed, "belief does not entail rational certainty when it is applied to things that are known only if their causes are known." This state is one of the modes (or conditions) of prophecy; a *virtus sancta* (sacred virtue), the highest of all human faculties. The theory of Avicenna will be taken up by Albertus Magnus, who makes the Avicinnian natural "prophet" the prototype of the man of science, capable of "prediction" (Fr. *prévision*) in the sublunar world.

Alain de Libera

BIBLIOGRAPHY

Avicenna. *Liber de anima, seu sextus de naturalibus.* Edited by S. Van Riet. Leiden, Neth.: Brill, 1968–.

———. *Avicenna's Psychology: An English Translation of Kitāb al-najāt, book II, chapter VI.* Translated by F. Rahman. London: Oxford University Press, 1952.

Davidson, Herbert Alan. *Alfarabi, Avicenna, and Averroës, on Intellect: Their Cosmologies, Theories of the Active Intellect, and Theories of Human Intellect.* New York: Oxford University Press, 1992.

Elramani-Jamal, Abdelali. "De la multiplicité des modes de la prophétie chez Ibn-Sina." In *Études sur Avicenne*, edited by J. Jolivet and R. Rashed, 74–92. Paris: Les Belles Lettres, 1984.

Gilson, Étienne. "Les sources greco-arabes de l'augustinisme avicennisant." *Archives d'histoire doctrinale et littéraire du Moyen-Âge* 4 (1929–30): 74–92.

Torrell, Jean-Pierre. "La Question disputée. De prophetia de saint Albert le Grand. Édition critique et commentaire." In *Recherches sur la théorie de al prophétie au Moyen Âge, XIIe–XIVe siècle* 13 (1992): 11–204.

not predicative but apophantic: "the medium of apophantic propositions not being only *alêtheia*, but being itself as *alêthes ê pseudos*, from which basis such propositions are true as well as false." (Beaufret, "Hegel et la proposition speculative").

Alain de Libera

BIBLIOGRAPHY

Aquinas, Thomas, Saint. *In Aristotelis libros Peri hermeneias et posteriorum analyticorum exposition, cum textu et recensione leonine.* Turin: Marietti, 1964. Translation by Jean T. Oesterle: *Aristotle: On interpretation. Commentary by St. Thomas and Cajetan (Peri hermenias).* Milwaukee: Marquette University Press, 1962.

Aristotle. *De interpretatione vel Periermenias.* Edited by L. Minio-Paluello. *Aristoteles Latinus.* II, 1–2. Bruges, Belg.: Desclée de Brouwer, 1995.

Arnauld, Antoine, and Claude Lancelot. *La Grammaire générale et raisonnée.* Edited by H. E. Brekle. Stuttgart: Frommann, 1966. First published in 1660. Translation: *A General and Rational Grammar.* Menston: Scolar Press, 1968.

Arnauld, Antoine, and Nicole Pierre. *La Logique ou l'art de penser.* Edited by P. Clair and F. Girbal. Paris: Presses Universitares de France, 1965. First published in 1662. Translation, with an introduction, by James Dickoff and Patricia James and a foreword by Charles H. Hendel: *The Art of Thinking: Port-Royal Logic.* Indianapolis: Bobbs-Merrill, 1964.

Beaufret, J. "Hegel et la proposition speculative." In *Dialogue avec Heidegger,* vol. 2, *Philosophie modern.* Paris: Éditions de Minuit, 1973.

Boethius. *Commentaries on Aristotle's De interpretatione.* 2 vols. Edited by Karl Meister. New York: Garland, 1987.

Descartes, René. *Regulae.* In *Œuvres complètes.* Edited by C. Adam and P. Tannery, Paris: Vrin, 1996, French translation by J.-L. Marion: *Règles utiles et claires pour la direction de l'esprit en la recherche de la vérité.* The Hague: Nijhoff, 1977.

Hegel, G.W.F. *Phénoménologie de l'Esprit.* Edited by J. Lasson and completed by J. Hoffmeister. 4th ed. Leipzig: Meiner, 1937.

———. *Wissenschaft der Logik.* 3rd ed. Stuttgart: Frommann, 1959.

Hobbes, Thomas. *Logica.* Edited by William Molesworth. London, 1839.

———. *Part I of De Corpore* [*Elementorum philosophiae section prima de corpore*]. Translated by A. P. Martinich. New York: Abaris Books, 1981.

Jungius, Joachim. *Logica Hamburgensis.* Edited by Rudolf Meyer. Hamburg: J. J. Augustin, 1957. First published in 1638.

———. *Logicae Hamburgensis Additamenta.* Edited by W. Risse. Göttingen: Vandenhoeck and Ruprecht, 1977.

Kant, Immanuel. *Critique de la raison pure.* Translated by A. Tremesaygues and B. Pacaud. Paris: Presses Universitaires de France, 2001.

Kretzmann, Norman, Anthony Kenny, and Jan Pinborg. *The Cambridge History of Later Medieval Philosophy.* Cambridge: Cambridge University Press, 1982.

Leibniz, Gottfried Wilhelm. *Recherches générales sur l'analyse des notions et des vérités. 24 thèses métaphysiques et autres textes logiques et métaphysiques.* Paris: Presses Universitaires de France, 1998.

———. *Philosophical Essays.* Translated and edited by Roger Ariew and Dan Garber. Indianapolis: Hackett, 1989.

———. *Philosophical Papers and Letters.* Edited and translated by Leroy E. Loemker. 2nd ed., Dordrecht, Neth.: D. Reidel, 1969.

———. *Opuscules et fragments inédits de Leibniz.* Edited by Louis Couturat. Paris: Félix Alcan, 1903.

Nuchelmans, Gabriel. *Theories of the Proposition: Ancient and Medieval Conceptions of the Bearers of Truth and Falsity.* Amsterdam: North-Holland, 1973.

———. *Late-Scholastic and Humanist Theories of the Proposition.* Amsterdam: North-Holland, 1980.

———. *Judgment and Proposition from Descartes to Kant.* Amsterdam: North-Holland, 1983.

Panaccio, Claude. *Le Discours intérieur.* Paris: Éditions du Seuil, 1999.

Peter, of Spain. *Tractatus.* Edited by L. M. De Rijk. Assen, Neth.: Van Gorcum, 1972.

Rougier, L. *La Métaphysique et le langage.* Paris: Denöel, 1973.

Thomasius, Christian. *Einleitung zur Vernunftlehre.* Hildesheim, Ger.: Olms, 1968.

Vaulézard, J.-L. *La Nouvelle algèbre de M. Viète.* Paris: Fayard, 1986. First published in 1630.

Walch, Johann Georg. *Philosophisches Lexikon.* Leipzig, 1726.

Wille, Dagmar von. *Lessico filosofico della Frühaufklärung.* Rome: Ed. dell'Ateneo, 1991.

THEMIS [θέμις] / DIKÊ [δίκη] / NOMOS [νόμος] (GREEK)

ENGLISH   rule, juridical norm, principle, procedure, justice, law
FRENCH   *règle, prescription, jugement, justice, loi*
GERMAN   *Gottheit der Recht, Ordnung*

➤ *DESTINY* [KÊR], *JUSTICE*, LAW, LEX, RIGHT/JUST/GOOD, and FAIR, GOD, *LIBERTY*, *OBLIGATION*, PARDON, POLIS, PRAVDA, VIRTÙ, WILL

The vocabulary that organizes the theories and practices of justice in ancient Greece changes a great deal from Homer to Aristotle, with a succession of expressions for "rule" or "law" that includes *themis* [θέμις] (or the plural *themistes* [θέμιστες]), then *thesmos* [θεσμός]—both drawn from the root **dhe-*, "lay down," which refers to external sources of authority and divine power—and finally, starting in the fifth century, *nomos* [νόμος], "division," which signals a spatial notion of the city. These terms are always complements to *dikê* [δίκη] and, in the classical age, to its cognates (*to dikaion* [τὸ δίκαιον], "the just"; *dikaiosunê* [δικαιοσύνη], "justice"), which clearly refer to the situation of judgment; the meaning of the former is, in fact, a "sentence." The other values attached to the word, such as "justice" (as a principle or a virtue), are constructed out of this institutional signification: the law is established through procedure and does not preexist it. As a decision (be it divine or human) whose purpose is to put an end to a conflict dividing the community, *dikê* does not designate (at least before the distinctions drawn by Aristotle) a sphere of law considered to be autonomous, but rather refers to the political, moral, religious, and juridical norms that have been negatively affected by such conflicts.

I. *Themis, Dikê*, and Traditional Formulas

Translations of the terms *themis, dikê*, and their cognates, which encompass the notion of "justice" in Greek, are often hesitant and controversial for reasons that are not limited to the particularly open polysemy of each. The difficulty derives instead from the fact that ancient authors (before Plato and Aristotle) did not develop any terminological explanations, and the meanings of these concepts of law are only available through their repeated reuse of traditional syntagmatic formulas. It is this frozen quality of poetic diction (the only medium of a public reflection on the law) that explains that real juridical innovations resulted in a sudden change in terminology (whereas the vocabulary of law is generally more stable in other cultures).

In the epic poets (Homer, Hesiod, eighth century BCE), the law is apparently articulated through the couplet *themis/dikê* [θέμις/δίκη], that is to say, roughly, "rule, prescription" / "judgment." Later on, *dikê* (or rather the substantive adjective derived from this noun, "the just," *to dikaion* [τὸ δίκαιον]) is defined in its relation to other terms: in the seventh century BCE, the "codified rule" (for example, the "laws" of Dracon, around 621 BCE) is called the *thesmos* [θεσμός], a word from the same family as *themis*, which is absent, at least in this usage, from the epics; as *themis*, it refers back to the idea of a rule imposed from without, but it does not have the connotation of "tradition"—on the contrary, it often relates to new institutions. Starting at the end of the sixth century BCE in Athens (perhaps as part of the democratic reforms of Cleisthenes), *nomos* [νόμος] starts to be substituted for *thesmos*, before replacing it completely. In its political usage, *nomos*, unlike *thesmos*, seems to involve the idea of an order that is accepted by those who submit to it (cf. Ostwald, *Nomos*).

These radical changes correspond to differences in concepts and practices.

In his *Vocabulaire des institutions indo-européennes* (Vocabulary of Indo-European Institutions), Émile Benveniste examined the Homeric usages and compared them to languages related to Greek in order to expose the semantic kernels around which are organized the meanings of *themis* and *dikê* (RT: *Le vocabulaire des institutions indo-européennes*). Attached to the Indo-European root **dhe-*, "to put down, to place, to establish" (cf. Lat. *facere*, Fr. *faire*, Gr. *tithenai* [τιθέναι], "put down, make"), the feminine derivative *themis* marks the institution as the result of an act of external authority. It is the rule established by the gods, which Zeus, with his scepter, transmits to the kings (cf. *Iliad* 2.205ff., 9.97): "Coming face-to-face with Atrides Agamemnon / [Odysseus] relieved him of his fathers' royal scepter— / its power can never die—and grasping it tightly / off he strode to the ships of Argives armed in bronze (*Iliad* 2.214–17, trans. Fagles). These kings know the *themistes* [θέμιστες], that is to say, the collection of prescriptions that establish the rights and the duties of the individuals subject to them (the laws or sanctioned customs, the traditional sayings, the oracular proclamations). The application of these rules by the king is not simply automatic; it requires a decision, which may be good or bad, depending on whether it is linked to violence (*bia* [βία]): "When Zeus flings down his pelting, punishing rains—/ up in arms, furious, storming against those men / who brawl in the courts [*themistas* (θέμιστας)] and render crooked [*skolias* (σκολιάς)] judgments, / men who throw all rights to the winds with no regard / for the vengeful eyes of the gods" (*Iliad* 16.386–87, trans. Fagles, 16.457–61). The frequent use of the formulas "as is normally the case" (*hê themis estin* [ἣ θέμις ἐστίν]) or "it is not normal to . . ." (*ou themis esti* [οὐ θέμις ἐστί], followed by an infinitive) is based on this first meaning of a divine prescription guaranteed by the king.

Dikê refers to another order of activity (even if a *dikê* can also be described as "twisted," and even more often than the *themistes*). The word has the same root as the Latin *dicere*, "to say" (Fr. *dire*), and as the Greek *deiknunai* [δεικνύναι], "to show" (and comparisons to other Indo-European languages indicate that the latter meaning is the older one). Two interpretations are thus possible. If one starts from the "showing," the *dikê*, often accompanied by the epithet "right," would consist in designating a straight line, like a dividing line between two properties. This demonstration of visible evidence would be the original sense of "judgment," the meaning that *dikê* most often assumes during the archaic period (cf. Gagarin, *Early Greek Law*); on the other hand, if one wants to account for the passage using the sense of "saying" in Latin and with a word like *iudex* ("he who speaks the law"), then the supposed indexicality in the root will become a speech-act. Benveniste sees in *dikê* a formula that serves to "show what one should do," that "prescribes the norm" (RT: *Le vocabulaire des institutions indo-européennes*). From this comes one of the Homeric names for the judge: *dikaspolos* [δικασπόλος], or "he who guards over the formulas of the law."

■ See Box 1.

II. The Autonomization of the Sphere of Law

The classic question for interpretation is to determine when and under what conditions terms such as *themis* and *dikê*, which seem to have first referred to traditional forms validated by custom, acquired a fully juridical meaning. This required establishing at least some measure of autonomy for the sphere of law. The different interpretations have focused on two general historical lines of development that determined the juridical use of these words.

At the beginning of the twentieth century, *themis* and *dikê* were understood as embodying two forms of justice: the first, *themis*, was understood as applying to the archaic community of family (or "tribe"); the second, *dikê*, was considered to apply to an interfamilial justice on the way to becoming political organization. "That which is *themis*" is linked in its content to a "jurisdiction" internal to the tribe, whereas *dikê* as judgment (and not as simple arbitrage) requires an external authority (cf. Glotz, *La solidarité de la famille*; Gernet, *Recherches* and *Droit et société*; followed by RT: *Le vocabulaire*

1

Dikê

The word *dikê*, which is of the same family as *deiknunai*, "to show," has the primary meaning of "sentence" (as a "monstration" of the just, in an act of speech); from this derives *dikazein* [δικάζειν], "to judge." By extending this action to a procedure, it means "an action of justice" (from which comes "case argued, right claimed," in other words, the expected sentence given) and, more generally, "trial." In these institutional contexts, still linked to the temporal idea of a procedure that is meant to end in a decision, the word, unlike the Latin *ius*, does not designate a preexisting right that ought to be recognized. Instead, the rights are themselves defined by the judgment. The sense of "punishment," which it has in the fifth century (for example, in the expression *dikên didonai* [δίκην διδόναι], "to yield to what is due"), is derived from that of "verdict." When the word refers more abstractly to the principle of just action ("justice," as opposed to *hubris* [ὕβρις]), it is in fact still linked to procedure, providing it with a criterion of rectitude. In the classical period, this value is conveyed more by *dikaiosunê* [δικαιοσύνη] or *to dikaion* (in which *dikê* takes on a technical sense of "action of justice"). Another range of meanings derives from the notion of formula. It covers "usage" or habit, which occurs in archaic epic and in later archaizing prose (cf. *Odyssey* 11.218 for a "*dikê* of mortals," which prevents one from seizing the spirits of the dead). At stake is an imperative rule that determines the norms to follow. From here, one gets to the sense of "like" or "as" (Fr. *comme*) in comparisons taken on in the classical period by the accusative *dikên* [δίκην] accompanied by a genitive, as in *kunos dikên* [κυνὸς δίκην], "like a dog."

des institutions indo-européennes). This material and historical distinction does not, however, accord with what one reads in Homer and Hesiod, where the two terms are complementary, each with its own distinct function. Thus, the passage in the *Iliad* that refers to Zeus's rage at the kings "who had decided upon twisted *themistes*" (*Iliad* 16.387) is immediately followed by: "and who banished justice [*dikên*] without consideration for the vigilance of the gods" (16.388). Furthermore, the fully developed and most common form of the expression "who decided upon twisted *themistes*" is in fact "who decided *themistes* by means of twisted judgments [*dikai* (δίκαι)]" (or "rights," depending on the context). The core of the problem lies in establishing the relationship between these two uses of the same word, *dikê* (justice/judgments), in relation to the *themistes*.

Another weighty tendency of interpretation is to explain the development of archaic law in terms of the passage from orality to writing. According to this line of thought, there can be no law in the strict sense unless the rule can be identified as such, in its universal value and application ("whoever does *x* will be subject to *y*"), and unless it is independent of the traditional contexts of its enunciation, which are always specific and particular. This would only become possible with the institution of writing (which appeared in Greece in its alphabetical form in the first quarter of the eighth century, but became widespread later, at the same time that prose developed as distinct from oral poetry). In this context, the Homeric *themistes* and those in Hesiod cannot even designate an oral "code" (whose existence does not seem to be documented by other sources). They would be "norms of behavior," which the king, in a correct judgment, decides to apply (Gagarin, *Early Greek Law*). This stage would be considered as a "proto-legal" moment, in which the rules are not conceived as juridical rules, but in which there are recognized procedures (*dikai*) for the resolution of conflicts. On the cognitive level, this reconstruction, focused on the procedures and acts of language, leads one to defer until much later (in fact, not until Plato) the moment in which a general concept like "justice" not only can be extricated from each concrete situation in which speech about the law is uttered, but also and especially can be thematized in its universality (Havelock, *The Greek Concept of Justice*).

III. Reformulations and Displacements

A. Hesiod, or the expansion of norms

Though the general outlines of this framework can be accepted as stable (with a *dikê* that is first and foremost procedural in origin), one still needs to examine the workings of those Greek authors themselves on the notions and formulas that they inherited. The texts establish perspectives and theoretical positions antithetical to the received traditional terms. In an implicit and contradictory dialogue with the Homer of the *Iliad*, Hesiod reflects on the formulaic usage of the term *dikê* and proposes a new definition of the fundamental norm that governs the legitimacy of all norms or procedures in effect. According to the archaic poetic code, *dikê* is generally used in the plural, in the instrumental dative *dikais*, for "judgments": "deciding upon [*diakrinonta* (θιακρίνοντα)] prescriptions [*themistas* (θέμιστας)] by means

of straight and proper judgments [*itheîeisi dikêisin* (ἰθείῃσι δίκῃσιν)]" (*Theogony* 85–86)—or the opposite, "by means of twisted judgments" (*skoliêis . . . dikêis* [σκολιῆς . . . δίκης], *Works and Days* 221). The problem raised by this formulaic sentence concerns the criterion of rectitude that enables the king, in a pronouncement (*dikê*) adapted to a new situation, to apply a traditional prescription that is met by the general approval of his community. The goal of the right judgment is in fact to reestablish agreement where argument had taken over (law and politics are not differentiated). Other uses of *dikê*, this time in the singular, refer to the value or norm that is destroyed when judgments (*dikai*) are not correct: bad king-judges "banish justice [*dikên*]" (*Iliad* 16.388; cf. above).

Hesiod gives content to the norm of corrective judgment through his work on the poetic code. First, he seems to invent a formula that makes the expansion of the norm more explicit. The *Works and Days* opens with a request addressed to Zeus that defines the relation of the sovereign god to the king-judges: "You, with justice [*dikêi* (δίκῃ), in the dative singular], make judgments [*ithune themistas* (ἴθυνε θέμιστας)]. For my part, I will inform Perses of the confirmed truths" (9–10). A second-order corrective justice is superimposed over human justice in action. This statement presupposes that the king-judges themselves do not have at their disposal the principle of rectitude to inform their judgments. They must have recourse to a knowledge of Zeus and his justice, which only the poet can give them. This norm can be external, when a divine action is expected to reestablish it (in his other poem, the *Theogony*, Hesiod sets a framework for the validity of this norm when he makes Dikê the daughter of Zeus and a Titan, Themis; cf. below), or it can be internal as a criterion of just behavior (toward one's own: one's own family, people, inner circle, group of fellow citizens, or even the foreigners with whom one has contact). Its opposite, then, is *hubris* [ὕβρις], that is to say, transgression as "oppressive violence" (cf. Perpillou, *Recherches lexicales*). Morality and law are not distinguished (although Hesiod immediately asks that kings conform to "morality" in their judgments), and Aristotle will analyze this confusion in the uses of the expression *to dikaion* (the just) at the beginning of book 5 of the *Nicomachean Ethics*, in order to distinguish justice as properly juridical from the inclination to do what is just.

The debate that arises between the archaic Greek authors centers on the definition of this fundamental norm of behaviors and procedures. Hesiod does seem to take issue with Homer, for whom, in the *Iliad*, the correctness of a judgment is clearly evident (for example, in the judgment scene represented on Achilles's shield in book 18): the right and proper judgment is immediately praised by the community, which reunites as a result. The law, in Homer, can take care of itself, by respect for its own procedures. This implicit thesis has enormous influence over the course of the poem: the injustice of Agamemnon when he decides to take Achilles's captive Briseis for his own is apparent to all members of the Achaean warrior assembly; but this decision, which sets the whole account of the *Iliad* into motion, is necessary from a point of view that transcends the law and that, for Homer, is the very defining feature of reality, that is, Zeus's will to impose his own direction on history: as a result of this twisted judgment, he imposes both ruin on the Greeks and the capture of Troy (which in an eschatological perspective leads to the end of the "age of heroes").

Hesiod, on the other hand, constructs a reality in which the principle of justice plays a determining role. This requires him to deduce the necessity of this norm from a general conception of things. The personification of Dikê (absent from Homer) and her genealogy enable this principle to take its proper place in the hierarchy of beings. By making Dikê one of the Horai (along with Eunomia, "well-ordered politics," and Eirene, "peace"), that is, one of the daughters of the Titan Themis and the Olympian Zeus (*Theogony*, 901–2; this union also produces the Moirai, or Fates), who determine the quality and length of existence of mortals, Hesiod indicates two things. Dikê has to do with human beings, not with the gods; and her birth reconciles the two previously antagonistic generations: the Titans (Chronos, Themis, Ocean, Tethys, etc.), and the Olympian gods (Zeus, Poseidon, Hades, Hera, etc.) who had succeeded them in the course of total war. As Heinz Wismann ("Propositions") has underscored, the differential norms of the Titans and the gods are mediated by those of Man. The Olympian order is characterized by a fixed and constraining differentiation of the regions of reality to ensure peace in the divine world (according to a spatial representation of the city). This world needs to be reconciled with the vitality and fecundity of the world of the Titans. Human beings enable this reconciliation because, by definition, they are subject to excess, since their survival depends at every instant on overcoming nothingness through their work. Order is not given to them, as it is to the gods, but must be imposed on their activity, in the form of justice.

B. Solon, or the violence of the legislator

In Hesiod, the law as a procedure for decisions that guarantee a good distribution of vital resources is thus drawn from a natural order that is already given. In fact, its criterion of rectitude lies in taking into account the necessity of work, the consequence of a general theodicy—from which comes the ambiguity in Hesiod's text between *dikê* as procedure and *dikê* as principle. The opposite position, already evident in Homer, of a right to self-legitimization will be developed later, in another conceptual and social context, when the traditional *themistes* will give way to the *thesmoi* [θεσμοί],

identifiable juridical and political rules that are the objects of a new legislation, breaking with the past.

Solon, the archon of Athens in 594–593 BCE and the author of many new laws (*thesmoi*), no longer bases the authority of the laws on an external divine authority, but instead (cf. Blaise, "Solon") assumes the role traditionally ascribed to Zeus and claims to have reconciled the two opposites, *dikê* (understood in the institutional sense of "procedure") and *biê* [βίη] (violence: fr. 36 West). He is violent as a legislator: force is not a support or compensation for the law, it is internal to it, because of the law's constraining dimension. As for the content of the law, it is not deduced from something preexisting, but is a direct result of legislative activity itself. Solon (fr. 36 West 18–20) transforms the traditional saying that links the *themistes*, the prescriptions, to right justice (in the sense of "sentence") and states a paradox: "I have written the laws [*thesmoi*] as much for the bad as for the good, and I have adjusted the right judgment for each [*eutheian . . . dikên* (εὐθεῖαν . . . δίκην)]." The sentence establishes the written law, the individual case makes the rule; norms are created by accounting for diversity, and they gain legitimacy through their application, not by virtue of a principle that transcends them. This position would wither away if one translated *dikê* as "justice," without taking into account the procedure of judgment.

Even if we already recognize in the differences between Hesiod and Solon (who is, in a sense, already prefigured by Homer) some elements of the discussion that will subsequently pit the adherents of the law as something deduced from a more fundamental ontological reality against those who posit an autonomous legitimacy of the law, the framework of the discussion will change when the pole of the "rule" (as opposed to the *dikê* or its cognate *to dikaion*, "the just") will come to be represented, starting in the fifth century BCE, no longer by a word that is almost always used in the plural (the *themistes* or the *thesmoi*), but by a generic term, usually found in the singular: *nomos*.

▪ See Box 2.

Nomos is opposed by another term in the singular, *phusis* [φύσις], "nature": "The law [*nomos*] that tyrannizes men does violence [*biazetai* (βιάζεται)] to the nature of many

---

2

Nomos

The word *nomos* is derived from the root **nem-*, "to attribute, to distribute according to custom or propriety" (see RT: *Dictionnaire étymologique de la langue grecque*, s.v.). It has an older homonym (with the accent on the final syllable and not the first) that signifies "(out to) pasture," "nourishment" (cf. *nomeus* [νομεύς], "shepherd," *nomas* [νομάς], "pastoralist, nomad"). Accented on the first syllable, it has a meaning of "sharing" (cf. RT: *Le vocabulaire des institutions indo-européennes*, s.v., despite Ostwald,

Nomos). Not only is it a "habitual way of being" that would tend toward a meaning of "rule" ("law and order"); it also implies the idea of constraint: the notion of an "imposed division" is present from its very first uses (cf. Hesiod, *Works and Days* 276: if men, unlike animals, are subject to justice [*dikê*], this in fact results from a partition determined by Zeus, which establishes work as the means of subsistence, and not the devouring of other humans). The idea of an arrangement also appears in the use of *nome* in the

musical sense (as melody). With *nomos*, the rule becomes something that is admitted (and not "posed" like *thesmos*, which *nomos* supplants): the word in itself does not distinguish usage from custom, or from the law. The verb *nomizein* [νομίζειν] is derived from *nomos* and means "habitually using, recognizing, believing, thinking."

BIBLIOGRAPHY

Ostwald, Martin. *Nomos and the Beginnings of the Athenian Democracy*. Oxford: Clarendon, 1969.

things" (Plato, *Protagoras*, speaking as the sophist Hippias). In this statement, the law is posited in its autonomy for the first time, as a positive law, and as Hippias's statement points out, it can be contrasted with the norm that underlies it, with justice (through the idea of a tyrannical, i.e., unjust *nomos*). Plato will isolate the principle of a just, and hence natural, *nomos* by connecting it to the mind's faculty of intelligence (in the *Laws*, he derives *nomos* from *noos* [νόος], the "spirit," 4.714a). Aristotle will be the first to detach political (or juridical) justice from absolute (or moral) justice and thus move beyond the opposition between law and nature by turning them into two aspects of political justice whose existence as such depends on their realization in particular laws. The variability of the laws is thus naturalized: "The politically just [*to politikon dikaion* (τὸ πολιτικὸν δίκαιον)] is in part natural [*phusikon* (φυσικόν)] and in part legal [*nomikon* (νομικόν)]" (*Nicomachean Ethics* 5.10.1134b18–19).

IV. Justice and Equity: Aristotelian Distinctions

Book 5 of the *Nicomachean Ethics* is devoted to the just, *to dikaion*, and to justice, *dikaiosunê* [δικαιοσύνη]. Aristotle explores their multiple meanings (*pleonachôs legêtai* [πλεοναχῶς λέγηται], 5.2.1129a26). These meanings are pregnant with most of our modern distinctions, but with some distortions and differences in emphasis, which is why it is important to understand their exact significance.

A. Global and partial justice, distributive and corrective: Equality and proportion

Justice is first of all a virtue, *aretê* [ἀρετή], that is to say, an individual disposition (*hexis* [ἕξις]; cf. chap. 13). It is all the more fully developed (*teleia* [τελεία], 5.2.1129b30) in that it serves (*chrêsis* [χρῆσίς], 1129b31) in the relation between the self and itself, as well as between the self and other (*pros heteron* [πρὸς ἕτερον], 1130a4). It is also an *allotrion agathon* [ἀλλότριον ἀγαθὸν]: a good for the other, a good for someone else, an altruistic good (insofar as the goal is to promote and maintain the harmony of the political community [*politikê koinônia* (πολιτικῇ κοινωνία)]), but not a good for the foreigner. It has the same final purpose as the laws, and in a sense, it coincides with the obedience that is owed to them (1129b12–19). Aristotle thus returns to the ethico-political nexus of the old myth of Protagoras, in which Zeus adds to the technical gifts of Prometheus and grants to humans those excellent political qualities of *aidôs* [αἰδώς] (modesty, respect [as an awareness of others]) and of *dikê* so that they can live in peace (see VIRTÙ, Box 1). According to Aristotle, this is a total or global (*holê* [ὅλη]) justice that is dependent on the culture of the community, on education in the common interest (*peri paideian tên pros to koinon* [περὶ παιδείαν τὴν πρὸς τὸ κοινόν], 1130b26).

The new distinctions that will carry into the future concern partial justice (*kata meros* [κατὰ μέρος]) as a part of global justice (1130b30). Aristotle distinguishes between distributive justice, which regulates public participation and applies "to the distribution [*en tais dianomais* (ἐν ταῖς διανομαῖς)] of honors, riches, or other advantages to be split up among the members of the community" (1130b31–32) and so-called corrective justice "that directs or redresses." The latter supplies the meaning of *diorthôtikon* [διορθωτικόν]

(1131a1) as private relations (*en tois sunallagmasi* [ἐν τοῖς συναλλάγμασι]), whether based on free choice (a sale and a purchase) or not (as in clandestine cases, such as false witness or theft, or violent cases, such as defamation or armed robbery). These two parts of justice have as their goal not the legal, but the equal (*to ison* [τὸ ἴσον]).

What is not so obvious to us, if we are used to the formal universality of republican equality ("all men are born equal and with equal rights"), are the Aristotelian definitions of equality. For an equal distribution does not consist in giving the same share to each, but requires instead a proportional estimation (*axia* [ἀξία], 1131a26) of persons and of parts: "the just is an analogue" (*to dikaion analogon ti* [τὸ δίκαιον ἀνάλογόν τι], 5.3.1131a29; see LOGOS). Depending on the political regime, value can be defined in terms of liberty, wealth, birth, or excellence, but in each case equality is calculated as a geometric proportion establishing a one-to-one correspondence between persons and things. Injustice consists, then, not in a different distribution, but rather in a lack of proper proportion.

Corrective justice, by contrast, follows an arithmetic proportion (1132a1). It treats all persons as being of essentially equal value (*chrêtaios isois* [χρῆταιός ἴσοις], 1132a5). Yet upon closer analysis, its workings only serve to maintain proportion (in the case of a transaction) or to reestablish it (if there is a grievance), by averaging out loss and gain. The judge "equalizes" (*ho de dikastês epanisoi* [ὁ δὲ δικαστὴς ἐπανισοῖ], 1132a24). This is not so different, says Aristotle in a play on words, from the judge (*dikastês*) being someone who "cuts in two" (*dichastês* [διχαστής], 1132a32), that is, he returns the distribution to its prior state ("as before," 1132b20).

Proportionality as the only guarantor of equality: this is the Aristotelian position, and it is politically fundamental. Rather than start by considering all social atoms as identical, it starts with those differences without which there is no community. In order to enable exchanges and organization—a city, in short—distinct forms of competence and virtue are needed, as well as a common currency to make them commensurable (cf. all of *Nicomachean Ethics* 8). This is why, for example, money relates to *philia* [φιλία] (see LOVE, II.B.2). One can thus appreciate the difference in principle between the equality of the ancients and the equality of the moderns, and why some would advocate a return to antiquity (see LIBERAL).

B. The *epieikeia*, or soft rule

Aristotle proposed a form of justice to serve as a corrective to justice itself: the *epieikeia* [ἐπιείκεια] (a term formed from **eikô*, "resemble, appear to conform, to be suitable for"; see EIDÔLON, Box 1), which we have rendered as "equity" along the lines of the Latin *aequitas*, "equality," although it is as far as possible from formal equality. Equity redresses legal justice, not because the law is incorrect or erroneous, but because, by definition and structure, the law is general. "It is the imperfections [*lacunae*] that we are correcting [*epanorthoun to elleiphthen* (ἐπανορθοῦν τὸ ἐλλειφθέν)]" (5.14.1137b22), by acting "as if the legislator himself were there," by ruling "as he would have ruled if he knew the particular case" (1137b22–24; cf. also *Rhetoric* 1.1374b10). It is the rigidity of the law that needs redressing, by bending it like a soft rule(r): "In relation to the indeterminate, the canon is also indeterminate [*tou gar aoristou aoristos kai ho kanôn* (τοῦ γὰϱ ἀοϱίστου ἀόϱιστος ϰαὶ ὁ ϰανών)], like the lead in the canon of the architects of Lesbos." It moves and adapts to the curves of the stones like a *psêphisma* [ψήφισμα], a decree adapted to a particular affair (1137b28–31).

The inventive consideration of the individual and of difference (one will refer to "personality" and "circumstances") is thus inscribed at the very heart of the evaluation and reestablishment of equality.

■ See Box 3.

Pierre Judet de la Combe
Barbara Cassin

BIBLIOGRAPHY

Aristotle. *Nicomachean Ethics*. Translated and edited by Robert C. Bartlett and Susan D. Collins. Chicago, IL: University of Chicago Press, 2012.

Aubenque, Pierre. "La loi chez Aristote." *Archives de Philosophie du Droit* 25 (1980): 147–57.

Blaise, Fabienne. "Solon, Fragment 36W: Pratique et fondation des normes politiques." *Revue des Études Grecques* 108 (1995): 24–37.

Gagarin, Michel. *Early Greek Law*. Berkeley: University of California Press, 1986.

Gernet, Louis. *Droit et société dans la Grèce ancienne*. Paris: Sirey, 1964.

———. *Recherches sur le développement de la pensée juridique et morale en Grèce: Étude sémantique*. Paris: E. Leroux, 1917.

Glotz, Gustave. *La solidarité de la famille dans le droit criminel en Grèce*. Paris: A. Fontemoing, 1904.

Harrison, A.R.W. *The Law of Athens*. Oxford: Clarendon, 1968–71.

Havelock, Eric Alfred. *The Greek Concept of Justice: From Its Shadow in Homer to Its Substance in Plato*. Cambridge, MA: Harvard University Press, 1978.

Judet de la Combe, Pierre. "Les critères du jugement droit dans Travaux et les Jours d'Hésiode." *Droit et Culture* 29 (1995): 159–75.

Latte, Kurt. "Der Rechtsgedanke im archaischen Griechentum." In *Zur griechischen Rechtsgeschichte*, edited by E. Benecker, 77–98. Darmstadt, Ger.: Wissenschaftliche Buchgesellschaft, 1968.

Ostwald, Martin. *Nomos and the Beginnings of the Athenian Democracy*. Oxford: Clarendon, 1969.

Perpillou, Jean-Louis. *Recherches lexicales en grec ancien: Étymologie, analogie, représentations*. Louvain, Belg.: Peeters, 1996.

Reneault, Alain, and Lukas K. Sosoe. *Philosophie du droit*. Paris: Presses Universitaires de France, 1991.

Romily, Jacqueline de. *La loi dans la pensée grecque des origines à Aristote*. Paris: Les Belles Lettres, 1971.

Rudhardt, Jean. *Thémis et les Hôrai: Recherche sur les divinités grecques de la justice et de la paix*. Geneva: Droz, 1999.

West, M. L. *Iambi et elegi Graeci*. Oxford: Clarendon, 1971.

Wismann, Heinz. "Propositions pour une lecture d'Hésiode." In *Le métier du mythe: Lectures d'Hésiode*, edited by Fabienne Blaise, Pierre Judet de la Combe, and Philippe Rousseau. Villeneuve d'Ascq, Fr.: Presses Universitaires du Septentrion, 1996.

3

Equity in Nietzsche

The status of equity in Nietzsche is, of course, inseparable from his conception of justice, essentially developed over the period extending from *Human, All Too Human* (1878–79) to *Dawn* (1881). Justice—or equity—does not originate in a disinterested or unselfish act, but rather in a barter or exchange between equally powerful men who consider this preferable to a mutually damaging struggle (*Human, All Too Human*, 1.92; cf. *Genealogy of Morals*, 2.8). Properly speaking, equity is

> a development of justice that is born among those who do not sin against equality in the community: it is applied to cases where the law does not prescribe anything, in which a subtle sense of equilibrium intervenes, which takes the past into account, and whose maxim is to not do to others what you would not wish to have done to yourself.
>
> (*The Traveler and His Shadow*, §32, in *Human, All Too Human*)

Equity is thus defined primarily through the figure of the "equitable man," whose virtue consists in his ability to determine what is just (as to equality or inequality) when the law is mute or where the legal relations are unstable (cf. *Dawn* §112). Nietzsche takes up Aristotle's analyses (*Nicomachean Ethics*, 5.14.1137a31–1138a30) and gives them an "aristocratic" interpretation, which also grants a certain reciprocal indulgence to the "equals":

> *Aequum* means specifically: "it conforms to *our equality*." Equity levels out our little differences to reestablish the appearance of equality, and means that we forgive many things in ourselves that we shouldn't forgive.
>
> (*The Traveler and His Shadow*, §32, in *Human, All Too Human*)

Philippe Raynaud

BIBLIOGRAPHY

Nietzsche, Friedrich. *Dawn: Thoughts on the Presumptions of Morality*. Translated by Brittain Smith. Edited by Keith Ansell-Pearson. Stanford, CA: Stanford University Press, 2011.

———. *Human, All Too Human: A Book for Free Spirits*. Translated by R. J. Hollingdale. Cambridge: Cambridge University Press, 1996.

THING

I. *Chose: Causa, Res*

The French words *chose* and *cause* come from the same Latin word, *causa*, which is part of the juridical vocabulary and designates a case in which interests are at stake—simultaneously the trial, the object of the trial, and the parties concerned—all things that French also designates by *cause*. *Causa* is often joined with *ratio*, and then it takes on (or recovers, for some uses seem to have occurred earlier; see RT: *Dictionnaire étymologique de la langue latine*) the meaning of *cause* as "reason," "motive," "influence," what in French is called *cause* in the causal sense of the term (*à cause de*). Moreover, *causa* is often joined with *res* to designate the "matter" or the "facts of the case." *Causa* and *res*, which first meant "the family goods," "property," "wealth" (cf. Sanskrit *revā̄n*), and then "matter," "object," grow weaker and at the same time contaminate each other to designate together what we call *chose* (Ger. *Ding* and *Sache*, Eng. "thing," in which we also hear an old word for assembly or tribunal). On the other hand, the

Greek doublet *aition/aitia* [αἴτιον, αἰτία], which translates *causa* in both the legal and the causal sense, remains quite distinct from *pragma* [πρᾶγμα] (from *prattein* [πράττειν], meaning "act") and especially from *chrêma, chrêmata* [χρῆμα, χρήματα] (that which is used, wealth), which are the best equivalents of *res*.

We will begin by using the example of *res* in these ancient and modern systems to explore the word's polysemy and at the same time its extreme indetermination: see RES, Box 1 on Greek, RES, Box 2 on Arabic, and RES, Box 3 on all the etymologies of *res* and *Ding*, which refer to both the objective, solid consistency of Being (*ratum*) and thought and representation (Lat. *res/ratitudo*, Ger. *Ding/Denken*, Eng. "thing"/"think").

II. *Chose, Quelque Chose*, "Being," "Nothing"

1. On the extension of the term "thing," which applies to everything that exists, and even to everything that does not exist (thus we speak about "something" that does not exist, and in French, especially about *rien* (nothing), derived from the Latin accusative *rem*, see ESSENCE, *IL Y A, NOTHING*, OBJECT, REALITY, RES, SACHVERHALT, SEIN; cf. *NEGATION, PERSON, II.4, TO BE*). See also VORHANDEN for a determination of the thing as "subsisting" or "available." On the relationship between "thing" and "word," see SIGN and TRUTH, WORD; see also LOGOS, Box 4.
2. On the difference between "thing" and "person," see ANIMAL, I/ME/MYSELF, SUBJECT; cf. *LIFE/LEBEN, PERSON*.
3. On "the thing in itself" (*Ding an sich*), see ERSCHEINUNG, GEGENSTAND; cf. GERMAN.

➤ NATURE, WELT

| TIME / TENSE

FRENCH	*temps*
GERMAN	*Zeit, Wetter, Tempus*
LATIN	*tempus*

The French language has a particularly striking number of meanings attached to the word *temps*, each corresponding to a distinct and different word in the other European languages. First, there is *le temps qu'il fait*, which in English is the weather, and in German *das Wetter*. Second, there is *le temps qui passe*, which refers to time in English and *Zeit* in German. Third, *le temps des verbes* correlates to the tense of verbs in English and the *Tempus* in German. The Latin word *tempus*, from which the French word derives, had, interestingly enough, already applied to both chronology and grammar. It was also linked to meteorology: in addition to *tempestus*—whose first meaning is "opportune" and which translates the Greek *kairos* [καιρός]—starting with Ennius, the word *tempestas* refers to "the state of the atmosphere," and hence euphemistically to "bad weather" (Fr. *mauvais temps*), or tempest. Finally, the plural *tempora* designated portions of time, the "epochs" as well as the "seasons." Thus the Latin term encompassed all the usages of the Greek words *chronos* [χρόνος], "time," and *kairos*, "opportunity." The broad French usage attests to the term's ample range. See *ETERNITY, INSTANT*, MOMENT.

I. Objective Time and Subjective Time

1. Time is often analyzed by differentiating objective time, which can sometimes be physical and an object of mathematics, and at others historical and chronological, from a subjective time defined as time in relation to life and as duration. These two models, of the Greek *chronos* and *aiôn* [αἰών], of the Latin *tempus* and *aevum*, are in fact very intertwined and cannot be simply superimposed: see AIÔN.
2. On physical time, which is objective, measurable, and used as a measure itself, which Aristotle defines as "something of movement," see FORCE, MOMENT; cf. NATURE, *WORLD*. On its linear or cyclical representations, see also CORSO. On the measurement of musical time, see MOMENTE.
3. On subjective time and its representation specific to human existence, one can refer to DASEIN, ERLEBEN; cf. *DESTINY*, ESSENCE, *LIFE, MALAISE*.

II. Cut-Up Time; Present, Past, Future

1. There is some dispute as to the etymology of *tempus* (in linking *tempus* as weather and *tempus* as *tempe*). It is sometimes described in relation to the Greek *temnô* [τέμνω], to cut; see MOMENT, II.

   Whence the importance of the three instances that define time by cutting it up into present, past, and future, and the inflections suggested by the doublets that occur in certain languages (Ger. *Gegenwart* and *Anwesenheit*, *vergangen* and *gewesen*; Fr. *futur* and *avenir*); see PRESENT. On the preeminence of the present, see also ESTI, *IL Y A*.
2. The objectivity of these moments in time, linked to events and to narrative, is implied by history (see HISTORIA UNIVERSALIS, HISTORY, *PROGRESS*), and their subjectivity, which is sometimes upset or overturned, is linked to memory and forgetting (see MEMORY).
3. This objective partitioning (a "period piece" of furniture) and/or subjective partitioning is a characteristic of the notion of "epoch" (from the Gr. *epi* [ἐπί], on, and *ochê* [ὀχή], support, bearing, superimposed on *echein* [ἔχειν], to have to hold on to). A return to or reinvestment in the Greek meaning of "suspension" and "stop" characterizes the phenomenological method; see EPOCHÊ.

This way of cutting up also applies to the great periodizations of time, for example, in aesthetics—see BAROQUE, CLASSIC, ROMANTIC (and *STYLE*)—which vary somewhat in different cultures, and to the determination of the contemporary; see NEUZEIT.

III. Remarkable Instances of Time

Under the rubric of MOMENT, one can find a study of the expression of some singularities in the course of time, especially the Greek *kairos,* which designates the opportune moment. Its seizure and use properly belong to GENIUS, to INGENIUM (see also *WITTICISM*). See also, under JETZTZEIT, the irruption of a messianic present into the course of history, under *RÉVOLUTION*, a study of the ambiguity of change.

On the sudden, the instantaneous, and the immediate (Gr. *exaiphnês* [ἐξαίφνης]), which is tied to perception (see PERCEPTION), to evidence (see CONSCIOUSNESS, I/ME/MYSELF, and cf. *CERTITUDE*), to intuition (ANSCHAULICHKEIT; see also INTELLECTUS⋅ UNDERSTANDING, and cf. *INTUITION*), and which is subject to mediation (see AUFHEBEN), see also *INSTANT* and ETERNITY.

IV. The Expression of Time

1. On time in narrative, see ERZÄHLEN; for time in chronicle and history see GESCHICHTLICH, HISTORIA UNIVERSALIS, HISTORY (cf. above, II.2).

    On the enunciations of time in the grammar and syntax of languages, see ASPECT, ESTI.

2. We have paid special attention to the Danish philosopher Kierkegaard as an example of the idiomatic construction of a network of time within a language; see CONTINUITET, EVIGHED, MOMENT, Box 4, NEUZEIT, Box 1, PRESENT, Box 2, PLUDSELIGHED; cf. STIMMUNG.

➤ EREIGNIS, *TO BE*

| TO BE

I. "To Be": The "First Verb"

"To be" is, according to Friedrich Schleiermacher, the "first verb," and even it is "illuminated and colored by the language" ("Of the Different Methods of Translation," §239, Eng. translation in *The Translation Studies Reader*, 2nd ed. [Routledge]).

We have examined the following in particular:

a. the pecularities of Greek: ESTI; cf. TO TI ÊN EINAI;
b. the Spanish pair *ser/estar*, see SPANISH, to which add the Portuguese verb *ficar*, see FICAR; cf. HÀ;
c. the complexity of post-Kantian terminology: see SEIN.

II. The Different Senses of "Being"

We generally distinguish four main senses of being: existence, copula, veridical, identity. These senses involve several cross-cutting and complex divisions: essence/existence (quiddity/quoddity), object/subject, truth/falsehood/fiction.

A. Being-existence / being-essence

See under ESSENCE the study of the major ambiguities and translation that yield the divisions of *essence/substance/existence*.

On the fact of being, see OMNITUDO REALITATIS.

For the existential meaning, related to the object, see *IL Y A* [ES GIBT, ESTI, HÁ] cf. EREIGNIS; related to the subject, see DASEIN, ERLEBEN, EPOCHÉ; see also SUBJECT and cf. CONSCIOUSNESS.

On being in the sense of objective reality and in its relationship to "things," see GEGENSTAND, OBJECT, REALITY, RES (and under RES, especially the Greek *pragma* [πρᾶγμα], *chrêma* [χρῆμα], and the German *Ding, Sache*), SEIN⋅ VORHANDEN. Cf. *THING*.

On the ontological-theological identification of being with God, see I/ME/MYSELF, Box 4); cf. GOD.

Cf. *ACT*.

■ See Box 1.

B. Being-copula

See, besides ESTI: PRÉDICABLE, PREDICATION, Box 4, SUBJECT.

C. Being-veridical

See, besides ESTI, SACHVERHALT, TRUTH; see also SEIN, III. Cf. *APPEARANCE*, DOXA, ERSCHEINUNG, *FALSE, FICTION, LIE*.

D. Being-identity

See I/ME/MYSELF, Box 2, SELBST, SUBJECT (under which we discuss the Latin *persona*, especially SUBJECT, Box 5; cf. AGENCY). See also IMPLICATION.

Cf. *IDENTITY*.

➤ *EVENT*

1

Impotentiality

It is well known that Aristotle created the category of "potentiality" (*dynamis*) and opposed it to the category of "actuality." But the philosopher also invented a third modal notion, "impotentiality" (*adynamia*), and it may be that it alone explains the other two. In his *Metaphysics*, Aristotle undertook to define and distinguish potentiality and actuality. His argument was directed against the Megarians, who held that potentiality exists only in actuality. According to the Megarians, the cithara-player, for example, is capable of his art only during the moment in which he actually plays his cithara; at all other times he possesses no potentiality to set his art into effect. Wishing to vindicate the autonomous existence of skill (*techné*) and other potential beings, Aristotle posited the existence of impotentiality as a structural requirement of potentiality. "All potentiality is im-potentiality of the same [potentiality] and with respect to the same [potentiality] (*Metaphysics*, 1046.a.32), since "that which is potential can both be and not be, for the same is potential both to be and not to be" (ibid., 1050.b.10). Aristotle thus argued that the notion of potentiality constitutively requires that every potential to (do or be) be at the same time a potential not to (be or do), that every potentiality, in short, be also impotentiality. His reasoning can be simply summarized: if potentiality were always only potentiality to (be or do), everything potential would have always already been actualized; all potentiality would have always already passed over into actuality, and potentiality would never exist as such.

In his Freiburg lecture course of 1931, Martin Heidegger drew from these Aristotelian lines a single conclusion: all force (*Kraft*) is originally "un-force" (*Unkraft*). Giorgio Agamben is the contemporary thinker who has most incisively developed this thesis. Commenting on Aristotle, Agamben has written that "the 'potentiality not to' is the cardinal secret of the Aristotelian doctrine of potentiality, which transforms every

(continued)

(continued)

potentiality in itself into an impotentiality" (*Potentialities*, 52). Something can be capable of something else only because it is originally capable of its own incapacity, and it is precisely the relation to an incapacity that constitutes the essence of all potentiality: "in its originary structure, potentiality maintains itself in relation to its own privation, to its own *steresis*, its own non-Being. . . . To be potential means: to be one's own lack, *to be in relation to one's own incapacity*" (ibid., 15). But Agamben's analysis leads to a further conclusion, which concerns the passage from potentiality to actuality. Aristotle taught that "a thing is said to be 'potential' if, when the act of which it is said to be potential is realized, there will be nothing impotential" (*Metaphysics*, 1047a.24–26). Agamben notes that "usually, this sentence

is interpreted as if Aristotle had wanted to say, 'What is possible (or potential) is that with respect to which nothing is impossible (or impotential). If there is no impossibility, then there is possibility.' Aristotle would then have said a banality or a tautology" (*Potentialities*, 20). But another reading is possible. If impotentiality is understood as a structural condition of potentiality, then the sense of the affirmation changes greatly. "What Aristotle then says is, 'if a potentiality not to be originally belongs to all potentiality, then there is potentiality only where the potentiality not to (be or do) does not lag behind actuality but, rather, passes wholly into it *as such*'" (ibid., 21). Impotentiality is not effaced in the passage into actuality. On the contrary, actuality is itself nothing other than the full realization of impotentiality. Actuality shows itself as an impotentiality turned back upon itself: a potentiality

capable of *not* not being and, in this way, of passing into the act.

Daniel Heller-Roazen

BIBLIOGRAPHY

Giorgio Agamben. *Homo Sacer: Sovereign Power and Bare Life.* Translated by Daniel Heller-Roazen. Stanford: Stanford University Press, 1998.
———. *Potentialities: Collected Essays in Philosophy.* Edited and translated by Daniel Heller-Roazen. Stanford: Stanford University Press, 1999.
Heidegger, Martin. *Aristotle's Metaphysics Theta, 1–3: On the Essence and Actuality of Force.* Translated by Walter Brogan and Peter Warnek. Bloomington: Indiana University Press, 1995.
Schleiermacher, Friedrich. "On the Different Methods of Translating," translated by Susan Bernofsky. In *The Translation Studies Reader*, edited by Lawrence Venuti. London: Routledge, 2004.

| TO SENSE

I. *Sentir, Sentio, Sensus*

The meaning of the Latin verb *sentio, sentire* (from which the verb "to sense" is derived, by way of the French *sentir*) is presented in classical dictionaries along two major axes:

1. to perceive by or with the senses, or to experience;
2. to think, to notice, or to realize, to furnish an opinion (from the Latin *sententia,* partially corresponding to the Greek *doxa* [δόξα]), see PROPOSITION, SENSE, III, and DOXA.

It may be more comprehensive, however, to present a tripartite definition with respect to the term *sensus*: (1) perception; (2) intelligence; (3) signification.

The entry SENSE expands upon the origins and variations of this tripartite definition.

For the meaning of "signification," consult, beyond SENSE, the following: HOMONYM, LANGUAGE, LOGOS, SIGNIFIER/SIGNIFIED, TERM, TO TRANSLATE; cf. INTELLECTUS, INTENTION.

II. Sensation, *Sentiment*, Sensibility

1. For English terminology related to "sensitivity," see FEELING; cf. *PASSION*. For terminology related to morality, see MORAL SENSE; cf. COMMON SENSE.

   There is a difference among languages with the adjectives *sensitive/sensible*. In French the adjective *sensible* preserves both an objective and a subjective quality (for example, a sensitive person, a sensitive trait), whereas English privileges a link to the notion of signification or sense-making (sensible, related to the expression "to make sense"): see SENSE, Box 1), COMMON SENSE [*SENS COMMUN*]; cf. LOVE (particularly LOVE, Box 2).

2. Concerning the verb *sentir*, the French seemingly preserves only the first of the two registers given above in

section I, although the language generates here a certain ambiguous polysemy between:

  a. the modality of "sensation, Greek *aisthêsis* [αἴσθησις], see CONSCIOUSNESS (particularly CONSCIOUSNESS, Box 1), and SENSE, I, PERCEPTION;

  b. and the modality of *sentiment*.

     The difference between modalities does not rely on an opposition between "external" and "internal" feeling, but is rather due to the latter modality's effect on the soul and its communication with the passions; see GEMÜT, *PASSION,* PATHOS, STRADANIE.

3. The German doublet *Gefühl/Empfindung* does not divide along the lines of the French amphibology between sensation and sentiment, but rather introduces other connections and convergences, notably with the concept of moral sentiments; see GEFÜHL; cf. STIMMUNG.

4. French philosophy has developed a phenomenology of both the senses and of sensitivity that builds on (and is distinct from) a tradition of philosophical reflection on *le corps propre* from Descartes (his sixth meditation in *Meditations on First Philosophy*, and *Passions of the Soul*) and Malebranche to Maine de Biran, Bergson, and Merleau-Ponty. Privileged in this instance are states that unite the soul and the body, such as pain: see ERLEBEN, *FLESH,* LEIB, PATHOS, SOUL; cf. *MALAISE.*

The relative untranslatability of this discourse is ably demonstrated by Locke's reaction to Malebranche's *The Search after Truth.* In his personal annotations to the work, Locke expresses his incomprehension of what Malebranche means by the term *sentiment intérieur.* Conversely, French readers of Locke stumbled over the term "consciousness." See CONSCIOUSNESS, GEFÜHL.

▶ GOGO, *HEART, REASON*

TO TI ÊN EINAI [τὸ τί ἦν εἶναι] (GREEK)

ARABIC   *ḥaqīqa* [حقيقة], *māhiyya* [ماهية]
FRENCH   *la quiddité, l'essentiel de l'essence*
LATIN   *quidditas*

➤ *QUIDDITY*, and *ACT*, ASPECT, ESSENCE, ESTI, LOGOS, REALITY, RES, SEIN, SPECIES, *TO BE*

The Greek *to ti ên einai* could literally be taken to mean something like "the what it was to be" or "the what it was being." Few Aristotelian expressions fundamental for all of ontology raise as many issues as to their literal meaning. The most commonly accepted translation, "quiddity," is a perfectly opaque term operating as a mere signal, and is itself already symptomatic of this difficulty. The English "quiddity" (as well as the French *quiddité*) is just a modernized version of the Scholastic *quidditas*, itself a simplified and abbreviated form of the Latin *quod quid erat esse*, which can be found, for example, in the translation by Guillaume de Moerbecke of Aristotle's *Metaphysics* (cf. Thomas Aquinas, *In duodecim libros Metaphysicorum Aristotelis expositio*, nos. 1270, 1307–10, and passim). The undeniable progress of philology due to the great modern editions of Aristotle in the nineteenth century led to a slew of attempts at retranslation. It is impossible to choose between the translations without starting by (1) recognizing the specific structure of the question and differentiating it from the more general question of *ti esti?* [τί ἐστι;], "What is it? What is the essence of . . . ?"; (2) clarifying the syntax of Aristotle's formulation; and (3) taking a position on the meaning of the imperfect tense used with the verb "to be" in this expression. To these three approaches we have added Schelling's speculative interpretation as an illustration of all of these exegetical difficulties.

I. An Overly Translated Expression

Quidditas appears in the Latin translation of Avicenna (Avicenna Latinus, *Liber De philosophia prima, sive Scientia divina*), in which it serves for both *ḥaqīqa* [حقيقة] and *māhiyya* [ماهية]. This last term

> is formed from *ma*, "that which," and *hiya*, the third-person personal pronoun meaning "she is." It was

selected by . . . Al-Kindi to translate the Greek *to ti* [τὸ τί] in the putative *Theology* of Aristotle. In Avicennius, the term is a response to the question: *Mā huwa*, "What is it?"

> (Goichon, *La distinction*, 32; RT: *Lexique de la langue philosophique d'Ibn Sina*, no. 679)

Ḥaqīqa, built from the root *ḥqq*, which expresses "the general idea of reality, of truth," is usually rendered in medieval translations by *certitudo*.

■ See Box 1.

II. Determinants Internal to the Aristotelian Corpus

The first obstacle to grasping the meaning of the formula is posed by the difficulty of holding together the series of determinations that characterize it within the *corpus aristotelicum*.

If one asks what is in fact the *to ti ên einai* [τὸ τί ἦν εἶναι], several features emerge that combine to form a complex figure. First of all, the *ti ên einai* is what defines a thing: "*esti d' horos men logos ho to ti ên einai sêmainôn* [ἔστι δ' ὅρος μὲν λόγος ὁ τὸ τί ἦν εἶναι σημαίνων]" (*Topics* 101b38). Or, more precisely, in the *Metaphysics* (Z 4, 1029b13): "For each being, the *ti ên einai* is what is said to be of itself [*esti to ti ên einai hekastôi ho legetai kath' hauto* (ἐστὶ τὸ τί ἦν εἶναι ἑκάστῳ ὃ λέγεται καθ' αὑτό)]." In the "philosophical lexicon" that makes up book Δ of the *Metaphysics*—in reference, it seems, to Antisthenes and his doctrine of "proper definition" (*oikeios logos* [οἰκεῖος λόγος])—Aristotle invokes the *logos*, "which manifests the *ti ên einai* [*ho dêlôn to ti ên einai* (ὁ δηλῶν τὸ τί ἦν εἶναι)]." Antisthenes, for his part, according to Diogenes Laertius's account, was the first to define "discourse" as "that which manifests what it was, which is to say, what it is [*prôtos te horisato logon eipôn: logos estin ho to ti ên ê esti dêlôn* (πρῶτός τε ὁρίσατο λόγον εἰπών· λόγος ἐστὶν ὁ τὸ τί ἦν ἢ ἐστι δηλῶν)]" (*Lives and Doctrines of the Philosophers* 6.3).

It may be helpful to compare the expression—coined by Aristotle, but never justified or explained as such—to the Platonic formula of the *Phaedo* 78d: "*auto ho estin, auto hekaston ho estin* [αὐτὸ ὅ ἔστιν, αὐτὸ ἕκαστον ὅ ἔστιν]"—that very

---

1

On some translations

The difficulties of the Aristotelian expression are already apparent in the great variety of translations that have been proposed. Below is a mere sampling:

English

> "The answer to the question, what was it to be so-and-so" (W. D. Ross);
> "Essence" (W. D. Ross, H. Tredennick);
> "What it is to be something" (W. D. Ross);
> "The what it was to be," "the what it was for each to be" (E. Buchanan);

"What it is to be a thing/something/it" (J. Barnes, M. Furth);
"The-what-has-been" (P. Merlan).

French

"Quiddité" (P. Aubenque, J. Tricot);
"Le fait pour un être de continuer à être ce qu'il était" (E. Bréhier);
"L'essentiel de l'essence" (J. Brunschwig).

German

"Das, was war das Seyn, dass heist, das gedachte Wesen, vor der Wirklichkeit der Sache," "Der hervorbringende und

vorangehende Grund" (F. A. Trendelenburg);
"Das Sosein" (H. Seidl);
"Das Wesenswas" (H. Bonitz);
"Das, was es war, sein" (C. Arpe);
"Das jeweils zugehörige Sein" (F. Bassenge);
"Das vorgängige und durchgängige Was des Seins von Seiendem" (K. H. Volkmann-Schluck);
"Das Wesen als wesentliches Wassein" (W. Bröcker);
"Was es heisst, dieses zu sein" (M. Frede, G. Patzig).

thing that each thing is in its being, in its identity, its permanence, its stability.

Thus *to ti ên einai* seems to become an overdetermined form of *to ti esti* [τὸ τί ἐστι] (*Metaphysics* Z 4, 1027b28), a substantiation of the question that bears on the "definition," on the *kath' hauto* [καθ' αὐτό], the "by virtue of itself," of the *eidos* [εἶδος].

So, to understand the meaning and structure of *to ti ên einai*, it is crucial to start from the question *ti esti?* [τί ἐστι;] (What is [it] . . . ?), or from its nominalized version: *to ti esti* [τὸ τί ἐστι] (The what is [it] that . . .).

At any rate, this is what is suggested by the Aristotelian variations on the (still indeterminate) question *ti esti?* in the *Topics* (1.9.103b27–29, as translated into French by Jacques Brunschwig):

> Il est claire . . . qu'en désignant une essence [*ho to ti esti sêmainôn* (ὁ τὸ τί ἐστι σημαίνων)], on désigne tantôt une substance, tantôt une qualité, tantôt encore l'une des autres prédications [*hote men ousian sêmainei, hote de poion, hote de tôn allôn tina katêgoriôn* (ὁτὲ μὲν οὐσίαν σημαίνει, ὁτὲ δὲ ποιόν, ὁτὲ δὲ τῶν ἄλλων τινὰ κατηγοριῶν)].

> (It is clear . . . that by referring to an essence [*ho to ti esti sêmainôn* (ὁ τὸ τί ἐστι σημαίνων)], one sometimes refers to a substance, at other times to a quality, and sometimes to one of the other predications [*hote men ousian sêmainei, hote de poion, hote de tôn allôn tina katêgoriôn* (ὁτὲ μὲν οὐσίαν σημαίνει, ὁτὲ δὲ ποιόν, ὁτὲ δὲ τῶν ἄλλων τινὰ κατηγοριῶν)].)

In Aristotle, then, the ambiguity of the question "What is it?" is such that one could respond by "signifying" essence, substance (*ousia* [οὐσία]), or some other category. Previously in the same chapter, Aristotle had enumerated the "genres" or "types" of possible predications or categories, numbering ten: *ti esti, poson, poion, pros ti, pou, pote, keisthai, echein, poiein, paschein* [τί ἐστι, ποσόν, ποιόν, πρός τι, ποῦ, ποτέ, κεῖσθαι, ἔχειν, ποιεῖν, πάσχειν] (essence, quantity, quality, relation, location, time, position, state, action, passion). To the question "What is it?" (*ti esti?*), the relevant answer is one that indicates the primary or secondary *ousia*. A few lines later, it becomes clear that this polysemy of the question *ti esti?* is in turn only an echo of the polysemy of being, or rather, of *esti* [ἐστι]. It is clearly unnatural in modern European languages to answer a question like "What is it?" with "numerous," "large," "blue," "cold," "on the horizon"; but when, "about a white color over there," one says, "It is white, and it is a color [*to ekkeimenon leukon einai kai chrôma* (τὸ ἐκκείμενον λευκόν εἶναι καὶ χρῶμα)]," then one is in fact saying what it is (in response to the question "What is it?") while simultaneously referring to a quality ("*ti esti legei kai poion sêmainei* [τί ἐστι λέγει καὶ ποιὸν σημαίνει]," 103b31–33).

Thus it is possible to think that one of the first objectives of the complex formula *to ti ên einai* was to disambiguate the socratico-platonic question *ti esti?* as Plato had already attempted to do, by emphasizing that the "good" answer to the question about the essence of *x* is one that designates *auto ho esti*, that which is proper to and of itself (*kath' hauto*).

One can also say, and in a more rigorously Aristotelian manner, that a good answer to the question "What is it?" once narrowed and reformulated as *ti ên einai* is one that puts forward a well-articulated definition that can narrow down as much as possible the *x* in question, instead of simply giving it a name, even a proper name: "*esti d' horos men logos ho to ti ên einai sêmainôn* [ἔστι δ' ὅρος μὲν λόγος ὁ τὸ τί ἦν εἶναι σημαίνων]" (101b38). What we have here is a case of "*logos ant' onomatos* [λόγος ἀντ' ὀνόματος]," which is to say a "discourse," an "articulated utterance" (a "formula," says Brunschwig), which takes the place of a pure and simple name that would otherwise simply be in apposition to the object in question.

In his French translation of Aristotle's *Topics*, Brunschwig addressed the difficulties of settling on a translation of the term *to ti ên einai* in a "supplementary note," and explained his rendering of it as "that which is essential in essence [*l'essentiel de l'essence*]":

> Lorsqu'on demande *ce qu'est* [*ti esti*] telle chose ou tel être, un homme par exemple, on peut d'abord répondre en nomman son *genre*, en l'occurrence *animal*. La réponse est bonne; mais elle a la propriété de convenir aussi bien à d'autres êtres qu'à celui dont il s'agit. Si'l paraît souhaitable d'obtenir une réponse plus *ajustée*, il est nécessaire de serrer davantage la question, et c'est à ce besoin que répond la formulation *ti ên einai*. . . . Le redoublement du verbe *être* [*ên-einai*] a pour fonction, dans cette formule, d'écarter, parmi toutes les réponses possibles à une question posée, tout ce qui pourrait convenir à d'autres êtres qu'à celui dont il s'agit.

> (When one asks *what is it* [*ti esti*] about some thing or being, a man for example, one can start out by indicating his *genre*, in this case an *animal*. This is a good answer; but it also applies to beings other than the one in question. So if it seems desirable to obtain a more fitting answer, it becomes necessary to further narrow the question. The expression *ti ên einai* is meant to respond to this requirement. . . . The doubling of the verb *to be* [*ên-einai*] in this formulation is intended to eliminate all the possible answers to a particular question that might apply to beings other than the one concerned.)

(Topiques, 119–120 n. 3)

In other words, the *logos* (*horos* [ὅρος], *horismos* [ὁρισμός]) that expresses the *ti ên einai* is carefully distinguished from all that is predicated *kata sumbebêkos* [κατὰ συμβεβηκός] as accidental determination. By the same strict logic, this *logos* is distinguished from anything that relates to the universal or generic (as both Bonitz in his *Commentarius* and Trendelenburg in his article from the *Rheinisches Museum* [1828] had clearly indicated).

Brunschwig subtly illustrated the function of this "redoubling" in reference to perfectly common French turns of phrase:

> On n'a pas assez remarqué que le français possède des ressources d'un type tout à fait semblable, puisque, à côté de la formule simple "qu'est-qu'un homme?" et de la formule déjà dédoublée "qu'est-ce que c'est

qu'un homme?" il présente des formules dédoublées ("qu'est-ce qu'être un homme?") et même détriplées ("qu'est-ce que c'est qu'être un homme?"). Si l'on pouvait substantiver cette dernière expression, on obtiendrait à coup sûr le meilleur équivalent possible de *to ti ên einai*.

(It has not been sufficiently pointed out that the French language has perfectly similar resources, since in addition to the simple question *qu'est-ce qu'un homme?* [What is a man?] and an already double formula *qu'est-ce que c'est qu'un homme?* it also contains other doubled formulas, *qu'est-ce qu'être un homme?* and even tripled formulas, *qu'est-ce que c'est qu'être un homme?* [What is it (that which is) to be a man?]. If one could turn this last form into a substantive, it would be the closest possible equivalent to *to ti ên einai*.)

Despite the fact that his translations were not always consistent or very well explained, we are not far in this instance from what Léon Robin pointed out in his *La théorie platonicienne des idées et des nombres d'après Aristote* (The Platonic theory of ideas and numbers according to Aristotle):

We know that Aristotle, for his part, distinguished between *to ti esti* [τὸ τί ἐστι], which is the part of the definition that designates the genre [*Topics* 6.5.142b27ff.: *to de genos bouletai to ti esti sêmainein* (τὸ δὲ γένος βούλεται τὸ τί ἐστι σημαίνειν); cf. also 4.6.128a23–25] from *to ti ên einai* [τὸ τί ἦν εἶναι], which is *the unified whole of all elements of the definition*. The *ti ên einai* is proper to the definition itself, whereas the *ti esti* [τί ἐστι], in signifying the genre, extends beyond it.

(Robin, *La théorie platonicienne*, 27–28 n. 24 [emphasis added])

Another striking confirmation of this restriction or narrowing down of the question *ti ên einai?* in relation to the question *ti esti?* is to be found in the passage of *De anima* in which Aristotle emphasizes that the intellect, in its direct intellectual apprehension, is always "true," just as *aisthêsis* [αἴσθησις] is always true in relation to its proper sensible object. Both intellection and sense discover their proper object. Intellection is always true when it is "*tou ti esti kata to ti ên einai* [τοῦ τί ἐστι κατὰ τὸ τί ἦν εἶναι]" (the thinking of the definition in the sense of the essence). The translation by Bodéüs is basically correct, but it completely misses the point of the text: "When it grasps something in conformity with its essence"; Tricot translated it thus: "L'intellect, quand il a pour objet l'essence au point de vue de la quiddité, est toujours dans le vrai" (The intellect, when it has as its object the essence from the point of view of quiddity, is always within the truth).

III. The Structure of the Greek Expression

The second difficulty arises when one attempts to analyze the expression itself through its morphological and syntactic structure.

One should note at the outset that the *ti ên einai* constitutes in effect a nominal group, as it can be employed as follows:

a. in the plural: *Second Analytics* 93a13; *Metaphysics* Z 6, 1031b28;

b. as a predicate—without *to*—after *einai*: for example, *Metaphysics* Z 6, 1031b31: "*kaitoi ti kôluei kai nun einai enia euthus ti ên einai* . . . ? [καίτοι τί κωλύει καὶ νῦν εἶναι ἔνια εὐθὺς τί ἦν εἶναι . . . ;]" (*mais alors qui empêche, dès maintenant, que des êtres soient immédiatement leur propre quiddité . . . ?* [But what prevents beings from being immediately their own quiddity . . . ?], trans. Tricot); and

c. as a member of a coordinated group—for example, *Metaphysics* 983a26ff.: "*tên ousian kai to ti ên einai* [τὴν οὐσίαν καὶ τὸ τί ἦν εἶναι]" (*l'essence et la quiddité* [the essence and the quiddity]).

These examples clearly show that the entire phrase *ti ên einai* is nominalized by the neuter article *to*, not just the infinitive part of it.

In analyzing the expression, one must choose between two possibilities: (1) It is a question that has been made into a substantive (similar to the substantification of the question *ti esti*?); or (2) it is a complex variation in usage of the substantivized infinitive, *to . . . einai*, with a dative construction.

If one construes it in the manner suggested by Trendelenburg (*Ein Beitrag zur aristotelischen Begriffsbestimmung und zur griechischen Syntax*) as *to . . . einai*, then *ti ên* should become the predicative complement of *einai*: "the fact of being. . . ." But this interpretation is not convincing, because if this were correct, instead of the dative, one would expect here a relative construction and hence a different word order (for example, as "*to einai ho ên* [τὸ εἶναι ὃ ἦν]" or "*to ho ti ên einai* [τὸ ὃ τι ἦν εἶναι]"; cf. Aubenque, *Le problème de l'être chez Aristote*). It appears from William David Ross's translation that he takes *ti ên einai* as one single syntagm, since he interprets the *to ti ên einai* as a generalization based on phrases that apply to particulars, such as one found in *De partibus animalium* 649b22: "*oion ti ên autôi* [tôi haimati] *to haimati einai* [οἷον τι ἦν αὐτῷ (τῷ αἵματι) τὸ αἵματι εἶναι]" (Blood inasmuch as it is for it to be blood).

This analysis seems correct, and it is further confirmed by two linguistic features:

1. In the *Metaphysics* Z 17, 1041b6, one finds "oikia tadi dia ti? hoti huparchei ho ên oikiai einai [οἰκία ταδὶ διὰ τί; ὅτι ὑπάρχει ὃ ἦν οἰκία εἶναι]" (Why are these materials a house? Because that which was the essence of a house is present, the "quiddity" of the house belongs to them—or, more literally: Because there is present what it was for them to be a house). Here, *ho ên . . . einai* can be taken as an example capable of clarifying the formula *ti ên einai*. *Ho ên oikiai einai* is the subject of *huparchei*; within the relative clause, *ho* is the subject of *ên* and of the infinitive *einai*. This infinitive should be understood as a "final" infinitive (for the construction of *eimi* [εἰμί] + infinitive, cf. RT: *Ausführliche Grammatik der Griechischen Sprache*, 2:10: the infinitive can be the complement of verbs such as *eimi, pareimi* [πάρειμι], *pephukô* [πέφυκω], "when they signify: I am here for that, I am naturally capable of, the right one for, I have a natural capacity for, the natural quality of . . ."; these turns of phrase, which belong to everyday language, are very

pertinent to our formula). As for *oikiai* [οἰκίᾳ], this dative should be taken as a predicative dative with a "possessive" dative—*autois* [αὐτοῖς], being implied with the verb *huparchei*, and referring back to *tadi* [ταδί]. It is also possible that the syntax of *huparchei ho ên oikiai einai* was influenced by the common construction of a predicative dative with a noun in the dative (cf., for example, Plato, *Phaedo* 81a: "*huparchei autêi eudaimoni einai* [ὑπάρχει αὐτῇ εὐδαίμονι εἶναι]" (It belongs to her to be happy: cited by RT: *Ausführliche Grammatik der Griechischen Sprache*, 2:25).

2. In the *Metaphysics* Γ 4, 1007a21, one finds:

Holôs de anairousin hoi touto legontes ousian kai to ti ên einai. Panta gar anagkê sumbebêkenai phaskein autois, kai to hoper anthrôpôi einai ê zôiôi einai mê einai [ὅλως δὲ ἀναιροῦσιν οἱ τοῦτο λέγοντες οὐσίαν καὶ τὸ τί ἦν εἶναι. Πάντα γὰρ ἀνάγκη συμβεβηκέναι φάσκειν αὐτοῖς, καὶ τὸ ὅπερ ἀνθρώπῳ εἶναι ἢ ζῴῳ εἶναι μὴ εἶναι].

(En général, ceux qui raisonnent de cette manière anéantissent la substance et la quiddité. Il sont, en effet, dans la nécessité de dire que tout est accident et de dire que tout ce qui constitue essentiellement la quiddité de l'homme, ou la quiddité de l'animal, n'existe pas.)

(Trans. Tricot)

(In general, those who reason this way obliterate the substance and the quiddity. They are in fact obliged to say that everything is an accident, and to say that nothing exists that essentially constitutes of the quiddity of man or the quiddity of animal.)

(Et de façon générale, ceux qui disent cela détruisent l'essence, à savoir que quelque chose soit ce qu'il est. Car ils doivent nécessairement affirmer que tout arrive ensemble, et que être, pour un homme ou pour un animal, cela même qu'il est, n'est pas.)

(Trans. Cassin and Narcy)

(And in general, those who say this destroy the essence, which is to say that something is what it is. For they are forced to claim that everything occurs together, and that being itself, for a man or for an animal, is not.)

Here, the characteristic generalizing expression of *to ti ên einai* is illustrated by *to hoper anthrôpôi einai* (This is what being is for a man: based on the French translation by Cassin and Narcy, 129). Drawing on a range of French translations of *to hoper anthrôpôi einai* by Léon Robin, Monique Dixaut, Raphael Kühner, and Bernhard Gerth, the formula *to ti ên einai* is analyzed thus:

a. Implicit in the various constructions of the expression, there must be an underlying question (whose existence can only be imputed , since it never literally appears in Aristotle) along the lines of "*ti ên einai hekastôi?* [τί ἦν εἶναι ἑκάστῳ;]" (What was it for each entity to be?). To this, the answer (also assumed) would be:

"*ho ên oikiai einai* [ὃ ἦν οἰκία εἶναι]" (What it was [for] being a house; cf. *Metaphysics* 1041b6);

or:

"*to hoper anthrôpôi einai* [τὸ ὅπερ ἀνθρώπῳ εἶναι]" (What it was [that which was] to be [for a] man; cf. *Metaphysics* 1041b6);

or:

"*leukôi einai* [λεύκῳ εἶναι]" (To be [for] white; cf. *Metaphysics* 1031a20–22);

or still yet:

"*Kalliai* [Καλλίᾳ]" ([For] Callias); cf. *Metaphysics* 1022a27, "*hippôi* [ἵππῳ]" ([For a] horse); and cf. *Metaphysics* Z 6, 1031b30), "*sphairai ê kuklôi* [σφαίρᾳ ἢ κύκλῳ]" ([For a] sphere or [a] circle; cf. *De caelo* 278a3).

b. The interrogative phrase has been transformed into a substantivized and generalized formula, without an interrogative dimension, which itself assumes several variants:

"*to ti ên einai autôi, ekeinôi einai* [τὸ τί ἦν εἶναι αὐτῷ, ἐκείνῳ εἶναι]" (The what it was for him / this one to be; cf. *Historia animalium* 708a12; *Metaphysics* Z 6, 1031b6);

"*to ti ên einai hekastôi* [τὸ τί ἦν εἶναι ἑκάστῳ]" (The that which it was for each entity to be; cf., for example, *Metaphysics* 988b4, 1022a9, 1022a26);

"*to ti ên einai tôi toiôide sômati* [τὸ τί ἦν εἶναι τῷ τοιῷδε σώματι]" (The that which it was for such a body to be; cf. *De anima* 412b11);

"*to ti ên einai* [τὸ τί ἦν εἶναι]" (ibid.);

"*ti ên einai* [τί ἦν εἶναι]" (predicative form, cf. *Metaphysics* 1031b31).

IV. The Problem of the Imperfect Tense

Beginning with the Greek commentators, the imperfect *ên* [ἦν] has been interpreted in widely different ways. Alexander of Aphrodisias wrote in relation to the *Topics* (5.3, 132a1; RT: *CAG*, 2:2.42, *In Topica*, 1.4) that this use of the imperfect tense had no temporal dimensions. This interpretation is maintained today by Brunschwig (*Topiques*, trans. Brunschwig, 120), Horst Seidl, and others; yet one can wonder if this use of the imperfect, in referring to the present, is not directly linked to dramatic dialogue.

Ross seems to accept, with some hesitation, the interpretation that dates, via Schwegler, at least back to Trendelenburg, which sees in the use of the imperfect an expression of the "Aristotelian doctrine of the existence of the form, prior to its incorporation into a particular substance," its "designated" matter. Other interpretations, like Arpe's, specifically reject this interpretation as Platonic.

In order to understand this usage of the imperfect in the canonic formula, it is certainly possible to start from the use of *ên* in the passage cited above: "*oikia tadi dia ti? huparchei ho ên oikiai einai* [οἰκία ταδὶ διὰ τί; ὑπάρχει ὃ ἦν οἰκία εἶναι]" (Why are these materials are a house? Because there is present what it was for them to be a house). Here, the imperfect tense of the verb "to be," *ên*, is clearly the predicate of a relative proposition, and thus a standard predicate in a standard utterance. Like every predicate, *ên* needs to be attached to a referent term. Since Aristotle's question is posed in the present (cf. *tadi*), within a kind of mini-dialogue, it is the present of the utterance *huparchei* that provides the point of reference and orientation. The materials that will constitute the house in question possess *hic et nunc* what they already had prior to this *hic et nunc*, "before their incorporation in a designated matter," to use Ross's terms. In this way, the imperfect tense conveys a precise temporal reference. But in the general formula, nominalized by the neuter article *to*, in which *ên* is followed by the infinitve *einai*, *ên* no longer has a fixed point of orientation and hence does not refer to some specific past, any more than any particular name would do. As a result, the entire formula has acquired an omnitemporal value. One should note that it is not just the imperfect alone, as Seidl and Brunschwig believe, but the combination of *ên* with *einai* that results in this omnitemporal quality.

But in that case, how is this rendering of *to ti ên einai* different from that other ontological formula *to ti esti*, which also expresses omnitemporality? This latter expression is more directly tied to the *genos* [γένος] (cf. *Topics* 120b29a: "*to genos en tôi ti esti katêgoreitai* [τὸ γένος ἐν τῷ τί ἐστι κατηγορεῖται]," literally, "The genre is predicated in the that which it is," or "It is an essential predication"; cf. also *Topics* 142b27–28: "*to genos bouletai to ti esti sêmainein* [τὸ γένος βούλεται τὸ τί ἐστι σημαίνειν]," "The genre aims to signify the essence"). Aside from *to ti esti*, with its Platonic tone, Aristotle coined another expression whose purpose was to designate *eidos*, in the specific technical sense of *species* and not *genos*. Employing the grammatical model of the substantivized phrase *to ti esti*, he took care to adapt it to his own purposes. So, even though *ên* does not refer to the past in this new turn of phrase, the imperfect tense still evokes the fact that the *eidos* exists prior to its realization in matter. Aristotle relied on this linguistic fact to underscore this aspect of the *eidos*, and especially to indicate without any equivocation his interest in a purely non-Platonic meaning of *eidos*. On the other hand, one can deduce from the fact that the *to ti ên einai* is never employed in referring to the *genos* that the latter does not directly precede its own realization in matter, but does so only through the intermediary of the *eidos*.

We can conclude with some remarks relating to translation:

"Essence" can certainly be rejected as a translation of *to ti ên einai*: the term is too vague, and it works just as well for translating *to ti esti*.

"Quiddity," whose only purpose is to underscore this distinction between *to ti esti* and *to ti ên einai*, is both artificial and cryptic.

The German *das, was es war, sein* and the French *le fait pour un être de continuer à être ce qu'il était* (in English: "What it is for a being to continue to be what it was") should also be rejected, for the reasons listed above. The French translation as *l'essentiel de l'essence* (the essentiality of the essence), which clearly indicates the distinction from the *ti esti*, even if it diverges substantially from the Greek text, is to be preferred.

The English versions, "What it is to be something" and "What it is to be it," remain much closer to the structure of the Greek and, aside from omitting the imperfect tense, make clear that *to ti ên einai* applies to an individual being.

■ See Box 2.

Jean-François Courtine
Albert Rijksbaron

2

Schelling's interpretation

We give here as an example of interpretation, or better yet an exemplary interpretation, the main passages of *The Historical and Philosophical Introduction to the Philosophy of Mythology*, in which Friedrich Wilhelm Joseph Schelling works through *to ti ên einai* (*Sämtliche Werke*, 11:402–7). We have added, in brackets, some of the main Aristotelian references.

We should distinguish between being and that which being *is*. Every become-being is nothing but a determinate figure of being, and the closer it comes, in its materiality, to being in its entirety, the stronger will be the attraction it exerts on *that which is being*, and this latter will be in it as that which *is*. No matter whether the issue concerns being as such or being under a determinate figure, that which *is* is thus in the first place characterized by Aristotle by saying: its nature is *to ti ên einai*. And Aristotle uses the same expression to refer to the fourth cause, the first by rank [*Metaphysics* A 3, 983a27–28], but the last from the point of view of knowledge, for he considers it the limit of knowledge [*Metaphysics* Δ 17, 1022a8–9]. Despite the different interpretations to which this formula, specific to Aristotle, has given rise, the context within which it appears shows us that we were correct in maintaining that it must express not only what belongs to being, but that whose nature is *to be* being. Given that all the difficulty derives from the grammatical construction of the formula and that the analysis of this grammatical construction will help us more completely clarify the thing itself, we will start by examining its literal signification. . . . In fact, as far as the *content* or real meaning of the formula is concerned, there has in general been no possible doubt. We have always been guided by the passage in which it is noted: one could say that up to a point, the house is born of the house. The material house, constructed of stones and timbers, is born of the immaterial one, that which is only present as a concept, which was in the mind of the architect before the material house [*ek tês aneu hulês tên echousan* (ἐκ τῆς ἄνευ ὕλης τὴν ἔχουσαν), *Metaphysics* Z 17, 1032b12], where Aristotle adds that he calls "*ti ên einade*" the thing in question its immaterial *ousia* in the mind [*legô de ousian aneu hulês to ti ên einai* (λέγω δὲ οὐσίαν ἄνευ ὕλης τὸ τί ἦν εἶναι), *Metaphysics* Z 17, 1032b14]. But the question of the grammatical form of the expression remained

(continued)

(continued)

unresolved, particularly the imperfect tense. So it was tempting to maintain that the imperfect *was being* [ên (ἦν)] was based on the having-been-present of the form (the form having been in the mind of the sculptor prior to the statue), while the "being" refers back to the fact that the form is in the statue, that it was already previously. . . . Those who have followed us this far will not fail to realize that it would have been easy *for us* to provide an explanation of this sort: there needs to have been a unity prior to the separation of the three powers, none of which was being for itself; this unity is that which *was being*, and that which over the course of the reunification of the three powers enters into the resulting union and is its very soul. So it is not at all impossible to reconcile the imperfect with our presuppositions, insofar as we explain ourselves. Yet what still shocks us at the outset here is that, to a certain extent, the imperfect ἦν seems to fall on the good side, so to speak, while the present *being* falls on the lesser one. For example, the flesh and blood, and everything that constitutes the material side of man, can be crushed, destroyed, and obliterated, but that which *is* this material side (which for itself is nonbeing) cannot be destroyed. It *is* in a different sense than *was being*, and by its nature is eternal.

But the imperfect? It, too, is eternal, we will maintain, but this can only be explained by the extraordinary subtlety of the sense of the language that caused the Greeks to use the imperfect in identical or similar cases. For example, where we

would say: "What all the world desires is the good," Aristotle says: "*hou pantes ephientai, touto agathon ên* [οὖ πάντες ἐφίενται, τοῦτο ἀγαθὸν ἦν]" (It was [being] the good) [*Rhetoric* 1.24, 1363a8–9]. It was the good even before anyone desired it; it is not the good because everyone desires it, but it is desired because it was already being the good. And it is only through this confrontation that the good shone because of what it was. Likewise, the *ti esti* of each thing, that *which is* what each thing is (its *quid*), becomes *ti ên* when confronted with what it *is* (that by which it Is). It is thus that we answer that question, which had heretofore remained unclear, of the relation between the *ti esti* and the *ti ên einai*. . . . The painter who paints a portrait of Callias sees first of all *what* he is: dark or light in tone, hirsute or bald, etc., but none of this is Callias yet; there is nothing that is not shared by many others, and all of it put together would produce only a material resemblance; but the artist continues his explorations until he reaches that which *is* all of that, that for which everything else was mere presupposition, that which, properly speaking, was being—and it is only then that Callias himself is presented. When Aristotle explains himself most clearly and simply, he says: the *ti ên einai* is each thing according to which it is *Itself*, disengaged from all accident, from everything that has to do with *hulê* [ὕλη], from everything that is other. We can fully render the Aristotelian expression by saying that it means "*das, was das jedesmal Seyende* ist" (Fr. "*ce qui* est *l'à chaque fois étant*"). For Aristotle, the *eidos* is *actus*, and consequently not a simple *quid*, but rather the *quod* [*dass*] of the *quid* posed in

the being; the *eidos* is synonymous with *ousia*, insofar as it is for that which is the cause of being every time—in our terminology, "*das es* seyende" (Fr. "*ce qui l'*est"). . . . I can answer the question "What is Callias?" with a generic concept, and say, for example: he is a living being; but that which for him is the cause of being (in this case, of living) is no longer something general, but rather the *ousia*, not in its secondary, but in its primary and highest meaning, the *prôtê ousia* [πρώτη οὐσία]. And this is *proper* to each, belonging to *no other*, while the general is shared in common with others. . . . It is *each one* itself; in the living being, it is what we call the *soul* (Fr. *l'âme*), of which it is said that it is the *ousia*, the "energy" of an organic body. And as energy, the soul is the *quod* of any determinate body. . . . Being what is [what it is] or even further—if one thinks of it as anterior—what was being [what it was being], this is the fundamental concept, the nature of the fourth cause, that by which it rises up far above the simple being.

(Schelling, *Philosophische Einleitung*, trans. Christian Hubert, based on French trans. by Courtine and Marquet, 376–80)

BIBLIOGRAPHY

Schelling, Friedrich Wilhelm Joseph. *Philosophische Einleitung in die Philosophie der Mythologie oder Darstellung der reinrationalen Philosophie*. In *Sämtliche Werke*, edited by K.F.A. Schelling, 14 vols. Stuttgart: Cotta, 1856–61. French translation by J.-F. Courtine and J.-F Marquet: *Introduction à la philosophie de la mythologie*. Paris: Gallimard, 1998.

BIBLIOGRAPHY

Alexander of Aphrodisias. *In Topica*. Edited by M. Wallies. Commentaria in Aristotelem graeca 2.2.42. Berlin: Prüssische Akademie der Wissenschaften, 1883.

———. *On Aristotle Topics 1*. Translated by Johannes M. Van Ophuijsen. London: Duckworth, 2001.

Aquinas, Thomas. *Commentary on Aristotle's Metaphysics*. Translated by John P. Rowan. Rev. ed. Notre Dame, IN: Dumb Ox Books, 1995.

———. *In duodecim libros Metaphysicorum Aristotelis expositio*. In *Opera omnia*, vol. 8. Turin: Marietti, 1964.

Aristotle. *Aristoteles, Metaphysik*. Translated by H. Bonitz. 2nd ed. Hamburg: Felix Meiner, 1989.

———. *Aristotelis De anima libri tres*. Edited by F. A. Trendelenburg. Berlin: Weber, 1877.

———. *Aristotelis Politica*. Edited by W. D. Ross. 2nd ed. Oxford: Clarendon, 1962.

———. *Aristotle's De anima, Books II and III (with Certain Passages from Book I)*. Translated with introduction and notes by D. W. Hamlyn. Oxford: Clarendon, 1968.

———. *Aristotle's Metaphysics*. Revised text with introduction and commentary by W. D. Ross. 2 vols. Corrected ed. Oxford : Clarendon, 1966.

———. *Aristotle's Metaphysics*. Translated by H. Tredennick. Loeb Classical Library. Cambridge, MA: Harvard University Press, 1933–34.

———. *Aristotle's Posterior Analytics*. Translated by Jonathan Barnes. Oxford: Clarendon, 1975.

———. *Aristotle's Prior and Posterior Analytics*. Edited by W. D. Ross. 3rd ed. Oxford: Clarendon, 1965.

———. *De caelo*. Translated by J. L. Stocks. Oxford: Clarendon, 1922. French translation by P. Moraux: *Du ciel*. Paris: Les Belles lettres, 1965.

———. *De l'âme*. Translated by Richard Bodéüs. Paris: Garnier Flammarion, 1998.

———. *La décision du sens: Le livre Gamma de la* "*Métaphysique*" *d'Aristote*. Translation of *Métaphysique* Γ by Barbara Cassin and Michel Narcy. Paris: Vrin, 1989.

———. *Metaphysics: Books VII–X*. Translated by Montgomery Furth. Indianapolis, IN: Hackett, 1985.

———. *Die Metaphysik des Aristoteles*. Translated by A. Schwegler. 4 vols. Tübingen: Fues, 1847–48.

———. *La Métaphysique*. Edited and translated by J. Tricot. 2 vols. Paris: Vrin, 1964.

———. *On the Parts of Animals*. Translated with a commentary by James G. Lennox. Oxford: Clarendon, 2001.

————. *Topics: Books I and VIII*. Translated with commentary by Robin Smith. Oxford: Clarendon, 1997.

————. *Topiques, livres I–IV*. Edited and translated by Jacques Brunschwig. Paris: Les Belles Lettres, 1967.

Aubenque, Pierre. *Le problème de l'être chez Aristote*. Paris: Presses Universitaires de France, 1962.

Avicenna. *Liber De philosophia prima, sive Scientia divina*. Edited by S. van Riet. 3 vols. Louvain, Belg.: E. Peeters, 1977–83.

Bassenge, Friedrich. "Das τὸ τί ἐνὶ εἶναι, τὸ αγαθῷ εἶναι etc. und das τὸ τί ἦυ εἶναι bei Aristoteles." *Philologus* 104 (1960): 14–47.

Bonitz, Hermann. *Aristotelis Metaphysica, Commentarius*. Hildeshem, Ger.: Olms, 1960.

Bröcker, Walter. *Aristoteles*. Frankfurt am Main: V. Klostermann, 1935.

Buchanan, Emerson. "The Syntax and Meaning of τὸ τί ἦν εἶναι." *Greek, Roman and Byzantine Monographs* 2 (1962): 30–39.

Frede, Michael, and Günther Patzig. *Aristoteles "Metaphysik Z": Text, Translation and Commentary*. 2 vols. Munich: Beck, 1988.

Goichon, Amélie-Marie. *La distinction de l'essence et de l'existence d'après Ibn Sina (Avicenna)*. Paris: Desclée de Brouwer, 1936.

Hintikka, Jakkao, and Simo Knuuttila, eds. *The Logic of Being*. Dordrecht, Neth.: D. Reidel, 1986.

Kühner, Raphael. *Ausführliche Grammatik der Griechischen Sprache*. Hanover: Hahnsche Hofbuchhandlung, 1872.

Merlan, Philippe. "τὸ τί ἦν εἶναι." *Classical Philology* 61, no. 3 (1966): 188.

Owens, Joseph. *Aristotle's Gradations of Being in Metaphysics E–Z*. South Bend, IN: St. Augustine's Press, 2007.

————. *The Doctrine of Being in the Aristotelian Metaphysics: A Study in the Greek Background of Mediaeval Thought*. 3rd rev. ed. Toronto: Pontifical Institute of Mediaeval Studies, 1978.

Plato. *Plato's Phaedo*. Translated by G.M.A. Grube. Indianapolis, IN: Hackett, 1977.

Robin, Léon. *Aristote*. Paris: Presses universitaires de France, 1944.

————. *Greek Thought and the Origins of the Scientific Spirit*. New York: Knopf, 1928.

————. *La théorie platonicienne des idées et des nombres d'après Aristote*. Hildesheim, Ger.: Olms, 1963.

Trendelenburg, Friedrich-Adolf. "Das τὸ τί ἐνὶ εἶναι, τὸ αγαθῷ εἶναι etc. und das τὸ τί ἦν εἶναι bei Aristoteles: Ein Beitrag zur aristotelischen Begriffsbestimmung und zur griechischen Syntax." *Rheinisches Museum* (1828).

————. *Geschichte der Kategorienlehre*. Hildesheim, Ger.: Olms, 1979.

Tugendhat, Ernst. ΤΙ ΚΑΤΑ ΤΙΝΟΣ, *Eine Untersuchung zu Struktur und Ursprung aristotelischer Grundbegriffe*. Freiburg, Ger.: Karl Alber, 1958.

Volkmann-Schluck, Karl-Heinz. *Die Metaphysik des Aristoteles*. Frankfurt: Klostermann, 1979.

▌ TO TRANSLATE

FRENCH	*traduire*
GERMAN	*dolmetschen, übersetzen, übertragen, überliefern*
GREEK	*hermêneuein* [ἑρμηνεύειν], *metaballein* [μεταβάλλειν], *metaphrazein* [μεταφράζειν], *metapherein* [μεταφέρειν], *metagraphein* [μεταγράφειν], *metharmozein* [μεθαρμόζειν]
LATIN	*vertere, convertere, exprimere, reddere, transferre, interpretari, imitari, traducere*

➤ ANALOGY, COMPARISON, CONNOTATION, EUROPE, HEIMAT, HOMONYM, INTENTION, ITALIAN, LANGUAGE, LIGHT, LOGOS, MIMÊSIS, SENSE, SUPPOSITION, TROPE, WORD

"To translate," in the generally accepted sense of "passing from one language to another," derives from a relatively late French adaptation of the Latin verb *traducere*, which means literally "to lead across" and whose application is both more general and vaguer

than translation itself. We do well to keep in mind this initial, indefinite vagueness attached to the verbs we translate as the verb "to translate," verbs that always also designate something additional or something other than the passage from one language to another. We should keep in mind as well the determining role of Latin culture as it appropriated and adapted Greek culture in the construction of the Latin language. It takes at least two languages for any translation, but the Greeks, even when they spoke other languages, were willing to recognize only the *logos* [λόγος], their *logos*, the Greek language. Yet the lexicon of translation is partly Greek as well, since it derives from another foundational moment, the commission in Alexandria of a translation into Greek of the Old Testament, the Septuagint Bible, which joins together both interpretation and translation within *hermêneuein* [ἑρμηνεύειν] and in the hermeneutic gesture.

In different languages, particularly in Latin and German, a skein of recurring and varying tension runs through this lexicon of translation: between the precise and exact relations from one word to another (the *verbum e verbo* of the *interpres*) and the literary image (the *sensum* and *sensu* of the orator). The close proximity between translation, metaphor, and equivocation (the medieval *translatio*) is troubling for us. As a result, translation can both be appreciated as "treason," treachery, or betrayal, according to the Italian saying "*traduttore, traditore*," and, on the other hand, as the very essence of tradition (starting with that *translatio studii* that applies to the displacement of Greek, then Latin, then Christian knowledge right through to the *Überlieferung*, or transmission, that enabled Heidegger access to an authentic *Übersetzung*, or "translation." But as Schleiermacher explains, there are basically two, and only two, manners of translation: the exchange of supposedly equivalent linguistic values in the passage from one language to another according to the methods of an interpreting agency (*dolmetschen*) that "leaves the reader in peace as much as possible"; and the displacement of the reader in relation to his native language by virtue of the translation (*übersetzen*) such that they become foreign to each another, which is perhaps the best method for presenting it.

I. Greek Monolinguism: Hellenism or Barbarism

A. *Hellênizein*

One needs at least two languages in order to translate. But the Greeks, in A. Momigliano's expression (*Sagesses barbares*), were "proudly monolinguistic." Instead of speaking their language, they let their language speak for them. In this way, the polysemic value of the term *logos* [λόγος] allowed them to dispense with distinguishing between discourse and reason, between the language they speak and the language proper to man (see LANGUAGE, LOGOS, and GREEK, Box 4).

In a more definitive manner, *hellênizein* [ἑλληνίζειν] (after the adjective *hellên* [ἕλλην], "Greek") fixes under the same term the meanings of "speaking Greek" and "speaking correctly," or even, insofar as the corpus of rhetoric and the historico-political corpus are bound together here as one, to "behave as a free, civilized, and cultivated individual"—in short, as a person. To speak, to speak well, to think well, and to live well—these goals all nest together. Two occurrences in Plato reveal their interrelatedness. In the *Meno* (82b), the only criterion that Socrates applies to the young slave in order for him to come to understand the idea of the square root is that he "Hellenize": "*Hellên men esti kai hellênizei?*

[Ἕλλην μέν ἐστι καὶ ἑλληνίζει;]" (He is Greek and speaks our language?). Answer: Yes, he is "born to the household" (*oikogenês* [οἰκογενής]). In the *Protagoras*, the apprenticeship into Hellenism is indistinguishable from the apprenticeship into political competence and the practice of *isêgoria* [ἰσηγορία], that equality of speech that is a characteristic of Athenian democracy. (327e: In the city, all are teachers of virtue, just as everyone in the home teaches the child to speak Greek. "In the same way, if you asked who teaches *hellênizein*, you would not find anyone." See VIRTÙ, Box 1; cf. B. Cassin, *L'effet sophistique*, pt. 2, chap. 2).

Beginning with Aristotle, *hellênizein* or *hellênismos* [ἑλληνισμός] serves as a chapter heading in treatises on rhetoric (Aristotle, *Rhetoric*, 3.5: "On correction") or on grammar (Sextus Empiricus: "Is there an art of the Greek? [*Esti d'archê tês lexeôs to hellênizein* (Ἔστι δ' ἀρχὴ τῆς λέξεως τὸ ἑλληνίζειν)]"; *Adversus mathematicos*, 1.10). One has the choice of rendering the first sentence of the Aristotelian description as "The basis of expression is to express oneself in Greek" or as "The principle of style is in speaking correctly" (*Rhetoric*, 3.51407a20–21; on *lexis* [λέξις], see WORD, II.B and SIGNIFIER/SIGNIFIED).

In order for what one writes to be easily read or spoken aloud, one must simply respect the "natural order" (*pephukasi* [πεφύκασι]), the sequences set out by articles and conjunctions (that remain within the reach of memory in the same way as they are within hearing in the city) that respect semantic propriety (proper nouns, *idia* [ἴδια]; see PROPERTY), propriety of reference (by avoiding ambiguities and circumlocutions; see COMPARISON, HOMONYM), and propriety of grammar (the internal consistencies of genre and number). Speaking naturally, by following the accepted norms of clarity and precision—this remains the definition of Hellenism and of the classical "style": "whoever Hellenizes [*ho . . . hellênizôn* (ὁ . . . ἑλληνίζων)] is able to present the idea of things in a clear and distinct manner [*saphôs hama kai akribôs* (σαφῶς ἅμα καὶ ἀκριβῶς)], as in a conversation [*homilia* (ὁμιλία)] which signifies a band of warriors, companionship, society, commerce, relation—including sexual relation—the lessons of a master, discussion and the normal usage of a word" (*Adversus mathematicos*, 1.10.176–79). This concept cannot but provide support for a claim to universal legitimacy.

■ See Box 1.

B. The semantics of verbs that touch upon the operation of translation

If translation does not constitute a problem all unto itself, this is because the difference between languages is not taken into consideration as such. Instead, the place of translation is more of a gap or void. So it should come as no surprise that there is no Greek verb that signifies "translating" purely and simply, even if a certain number of them can be rendered that way.

One of the most explicit and general models of the difference between languages is sketched out by Plato in the *Cratylus*: it is presented as a simple matter of phonetic difference. As long as there is a competent nomothete capable of forming names that take into consideration the *eidos* [εἶδος] (the

form which is the name in itself, naturally appropriate to its object), then the matter itself is of little import, and the user will be the one to judge if the tool (*organon* [ὄργανον]) is of value:

> And the legislator, whether he be Hellene or barbarian, is not to be deemed by you a worse legislator, provided he gives the true and proper form of the name in whatever syllables—this or that country makes no matter.
>
> (*Cratylus*, 390a)

The verb that Catherine Dalimier chose to render as "translation," *apodidôi* [ἀποδιδῷ], literally signifies "to render to someone by right," "to restitute," "to give in exchange," "to transmit." It substitutes for the expression *tithenai eis ti* [τιθέναι εἰς τι] (389d, 390e), "to transpose, to impose" (the name in itself) "in" (syllables), as one imposes the form of a shuttle on a particular piece of wood: the terms definitely derive from another technical model. Most often, besides, the difference between languages is taken into account in the major philosophical texts only as a gap or void, as if by inadvertence. It is only implicit in the text or in a concept, and there is simply no term to specifically designate the operation of translation; thus, Aristotle's *De interpretatione* simply mentions that "just as all men have not the same writing, so all men have not the same speech sounds" (1.16a5–6; see SIGN, Box 1) and refers to the Stoics' "signified" as that which Sextus Empiricus defines as "what the barbarians don't understand when they hear the sound" (*Adversus mathematicos*, 8.11; see SIGNIFIER/SIGNIFIED, II.A).

The operation of translation is touched upon from many different points of view. Thus our verb *hellênizein*, when used transitively, can mean "learning Greek" (Thucydides, 2.68), to "Hellenize" a barbarian, or later—but essentially only in relation to the translation of the Bible—to "express in Greek," and thus to "translate" words or a text (in the second century CE, in Dion Cassius [55.3], in relation to what we would call the transliteration of "Noah" or "Jacob"; see Flavius Josephus, *Antiquities of the Jews*, 1.6.1). The same holds true for a number of composite verbs that incorporate *meta*, as indicating trans-port and trans-formation: *metapherein* [μεταφέρειν] (to transport, transpose, employ metaphorically, or report); *metaphrazein* [μεταφράζειν] (to paraphrase), and especially *metagraphein* [μεταγράφειν] ("to change the text," "to falsify" but also "to transcribe," "to copy"). These all designate literary operations of a poetic, rhetorical, or philological nature and only marginally take on the meaning of "translating" in classical Greek. (For *metaphrazein*, see Flavius Josephus, ibid. 9.14.2; for *metagraphein*, see Thucydides ["On being translated," 4.50.2] and Lucian, *How History Must Be Written*, 21, in which a purist claiming to be an inheritor of Thucydides purports to "transform Roman names [*metapoiêsai* (μεταποιῆσαι)]" and "to translate them into Greek [*metagrapsai es to hellênikon* (μεταγράψαι ἐς τὸ ἑλληνικόν)] such as Chronion for Saturn" or others even more ridiculous.)

The Aristotelian title *Peri hermêneias* is rendered as *De interpretatione*, as *Lehre vom Satz*, but never as "On Translation," and yet it is the phrase *hermêneuein*, meaning "interpreting, explaining, expressing," in the manner of one who puts his

1

What is a "barbarian" for a Greek?

➤ *AUTRUI*, COMPARISON, PEOPLE

Hellên and *barbaros* [βάρβαρος] are, as Koselleck puts it, "asymmetrical antonyms" (*Futures Past*, pt. 3, chap.1): the former is both a noun and a proper name as well, while the latter is only a common noun. *Barbarizein* [βαρβαρίζειν] is an onomatapoesis similar to "blah-blah-blah" (Fr. *blablater*; cf. Lat. *balbus*, stutter) and refers to a conjunction of linguistic, anthropological, and political features that make the "barbarian" altogether other from the self, a *heteros* [ἕτερος]—that make it unintelligible, perhaps even not altogether human.

In the rhetorical and grammatical corpus, "barbarism" refers to an effect of unintelligibility: for instance, in poetry, when one diverges from the proper meaning or common use (*to idiôtikon* [τὸ ἰδιωτικόν], *to kurion* [τὸ κύριον]) and uses "foreign" expressions instead (*xenika* [ξενικά]). Too many metaphors result in *ainigma* [αἴνιγμα]. a confusion of the signifier, and too many borrowings (*glossâi* [γλῶσσαι]) lead to *barbarismos* [βαρβαρισμός], gibberish, and the confusion of the signified (Aristotle, *Poetics*, 22.1458a18–31; see LANGUAGE, II.A). Diogenes Laertius went so far as to specify the difference, which is still current in classroom exercises, between "solecism" (*soloikismos* [σολοικισμός]), which is an error of syntax, and "barbarism," which is an error of morphology—which renders a word morphologically unrecognizable (7.44 and 59).

For the Greeks, the underlying problem was apparently to determine whether barbarianism (and hence Hellenism as well) is itself a fact of nature or a fact of culture (see BILDUNG, Box 1). Hence Antiphon uses the verb *barbarizein* to refer to those who make the distinction between Greek and barbarian into a natural distinction: "We make ourselves into barbarians in relation to each other [*barbarômetha* (βαρβαρώμεθα)] whereas by virture of nature itself, we are all naturally made to be barbarians and Greeks [ὁμοίως πεφύκαμεν καὶ βάρβαροι καὶ Ἕλληνες εἶναι]" (P. Oxy, 1364 + 3647, fr. A, col. 2, in Bastianini and Decleva-Caizzi; cf. Cassin, *L'effet sophistique*).

Similarly, Euripedes's *Orestes* contrasts a barbarian conception of Hellenism, which Orestes believes is a result of a natural difference, with a Greek conception of Hellenism, based on respect for legality, for the law, and maintained by Tyndareus (Cassin, ibid.), and Isocrates praises Athens for this advance:

> Our city has made the use of the word *Greek* no longer as a reference to the race [*mêketi tou genous* (μηκέτι τοῦ γένους)] but as a reference to the intellect [*alla tês dianoias* (ἀλλὰ τῆς διανοίας)], and we refer to those who play a part in our upbringing [*paideuseôs* (παιδεύσεως)] as Greeks, rather than to those who have the same nature [*phuseôs* (φύσεως)] as us.
>
> (*Panegyric*, 4.50)

But in either case, the question is in the end a political one: barbarians are those who submit to, or even seek out, despotism. If, according to Aristotle, "barbarians are more slave-like by nature [*doulikôteroi* (δουλικώτεροι)] than are the Greeks" (*Politics*, 3.14.1285a20; cf.1252b9, 1255a29), it is because, like the slave in his master's house, the barbarian is de facto ruled despotically (*despotikôs* [δεσποτικῶς]), according to the Persian model (every Persian, a slave to the great ruler, is "another's man") in contradistinction to the hegemonic (*hêgemonikôs* [ἡγεμονικῶς]) Greek model, which binds a leader (*hêgemôn* [ἡγεμών]) and a free man. This is what is at stake in the entire book 7.7 of *Politics*, which lays out a first theory of climate, in which the Greeks occupy a temperate middle zone between the thymic, passionate, and cold zones of Europe, in which life is free but disorganized, and a hot, dianoetic, and technical Asia, in which life is lived in submission. As for Greece, it is both passionate and intellectual; it is "capable of living in freedom within the best political institutions, and it has the capacity to give directions to all." An internal domination, the slavery of the slave, rests on an external domination, the slavery of the barbarians, who require a master, in a theoretical compact to which the modern era will no longer so easily subscribe (cf. Cassin, *Aristote et le logos*, pt. 1, chap. 3).

BIBLIOGRAPHY

Bastianini, Guido, and Fernanda Decleva-Caizzi. *Corpus dei papiri filosofici greci e latini*, pt. 1, vol. 1. Florence: L. S. Olschki, 1989.
Cassin, Barbara. *Aristote et le logos*. Paris: Presses Universitaires de France, 1997.
———. *L'effet sophistique*. Paris: Gallimard, 1995.
Koselleck, Reinhart. *Futures Past: On the Semantics of Historical Time*. Translated by Keith Tribe. Cambridge, MA: MIT Press, 1985.

thoughts into words (Plato, *Laws*, 966b) as well as one who serves as the interpreter for the gods (the poet, the rhapsodist, the seer), that is the most likely candidate for the retroversion of "translating" (starting with Xenophon, *Anabasis*, 5.44). At least this is what the future will hold (see below, II and III).

II. Greece in Rome: Translating/Adapting

In the classical Latin authors, the translation from Greek into Latin very barely satisfies modern criteria, and the process of translation itself is not clearly defined in the Latin language: the verbs *vertere, convertere, exprimere, reddere, transferre, interpretari, imitari* can all refer to what we would call "literal translation" as well as to looser adaptations of Greek models. The fact that we are unable to find a sharp distinction between literal translation and literary adaptation in these verbs rather clearly indicates that the question of translation is posed differently in the classical period than it would subsequently be raised starting with Jerome and the translation of sacred texts, when faithful rendering *verbum pro verbo* will become the very principle of translation: for the classics, translation consists of adhering to a meaning (*vis*) and not to a word (*verba*), and it is primarily an occasion for reflection on the creative modalities of the Latin language. At play in "translation" is the very reception of Greek culture in Rome, with all that entails.

A. Fluidity of meanings and contradistinctions

The uses of the verb *interpretari* in a single author reveal the fluidity of meanings that only contradistinctions can fix point by point. Thus Cicero has Varro say (*Academics*, 1.8) that he has imitated (*imitari*) rather than translated (*interpretari*) Menippus. Cicero himself specifies that he followed (*sequi*) Panetius rather than translating (*interpretari*) him in his treatise *On Duties* (2.60). But the same verb applies as much to the hermeneutic activities of the Stoics in relation to the mythic narratives (*On the Nature of the Gods*, 3.60) as to the interpretation of a philosophical doctrine (*On Moral Ends*, 2.34) or the adaptations of Greek works by the founders of Latin literature, such as Ennius did for *Sacred History* of Euhemerus (*On the Nature of the Gods*, 1.119).

None of the other verbs referred to above is sufficient to specifically designate the activity of translation: instead, each of them allows the Latin authors to define their work in relation to a Greek "model." The lexicon of translation can thus be understood only in relation to the tensions of literary polemics and within the specific context of Latin literature.

When Plautus uses the verb *vertere* to refer to his translation/adaptation of a Greek play, his usage is not neutral but instead underscores the difficulties that underlie the development of the literary Latin language (*The Comedy of Asses*, v. 11) In Greek, this play is called *The Donkey Driver*. It was written by Demophilus, and Maccus [Plautus] translated it into the barbaric language (*vortit Barbare*). "To translate into the barbaric tongue," that is to say, into Latin, is a provocative expression that Plautus also employs in *The Three Crowns* (v. 19), and it must be understood as a literary manifesto: that it is not a matter of submitting to the original language, the Greek, in relation to which everything else is the barbaric. On the contrary, in order to avoid the loss of meaning and end up with an incomprehensible language, one must write in one's own language and create one's own language. This is why Terence can contrast his comic rival's ability to translate well and his inability to write well:

> By translating well, but by writing poorly, he took good Greek comedies and made them into Latin ones that weren't.

> ([Q]ui bene vertendo et easdem scribendo male / ex graecis bonis latinas fecit non bonas.)

> (*The Eunuch*, v. 7–8)

B. Cicero and the sparkle of philosophical translation

The articulation between translating/adapting/creating sketched out by the Latin playwrights is explicitly taken up by Cicero, who defines his conception of philosophical translation in reference to the practices of the founders of Latin literature:

> Even if I were to translate [*vertere*] Plato or Aristotle literally, as our poets did with the Greek plays, I hardly think I would deserve ill of my fellow citizens for bringing [*transferre*] those sublime geniuses to their attention. . . . If I think fit, I will translate certain passages, particularly from those authors I just mentioned, when it happens to be appropriate, as Ennius often does with Homer and Afranius with Menander.

> (*On Moral Ends*, 1.7)

What is at work in this "transfer" from Greece to Rome is not some simple transport of booty, even if this dimension is always present in the background (see, e.g., *Tusculan Disputations*, 2.5: where it is expressed that it is necessary to tear away [*eripere*] Greece's philosophical preeminence in philosophy and transfer it to Rome): the verb *transferre*

also describes the displacement of meaning that is at work in the deployment of metaphor. By using the same verb for the activity of translation and the creation of metaphors, Cicero establishes the link in language between translating and writing; one has only to apply to translation what he has to say about the development of metaphor, undoubtedly starting from the Aristotelian reflections on metaphor as a process of enrichment of language, to define translation as a true creation:

> The third genre of ornament, the metaphorical use of a word, is born of necessity and constrained by need and inconvenience; it subsequently finds general application as a result of the pleasure and ease which it provides.

> (*On the Ideal Orator*, 3.155)

But this *rapprochement* has a broader scope as it is inscribed in language itself. The Greeks, who have no need to "translate," do not take advantage of this potential usage of *metapherein* (Plato uses it once to designate the transcriptions of proper names: *Crito*, 113a), and when Plutarch invokes the philosophical works of Cicero (*Life of Cicero*, 40), he uses the verbs *metaballein* [μεταβάλλειν] and *metaphrazein* to designate his "translations" in general and employs the term "metaphor" only in connection with isolated translations of terms that Cicero was unable to render through a word in its common form of usage. The work of polysemy that Cicero achieves through *transferre* is invisible to the Greek language because its referent is something only thought in Rome: to translate is to achieve a new splendor, a new brilliance that results from a use of language that is out of the ordinary, that results from borrowings instead of the familiar and proper usage: "these metaphors are a kind of borrowing [*mutationes*] which enable us to find elsewhere what we are lacking ourselves" (*On the Ideal Orator*, 156). The language of the other can thus provide what is lacking, but borrowings are only acceptable and provide appropriate ornamentation if they are fully reappropriated. To put metaphors (*verba translata*) to good use, "rather than suddenly appearing in some place that does not belong to them [*alienum locum*], they must appear to take up residence [*immigrasse*] in their own surroundings" (*Brutus*, 274). This is none other than an integration, a borrowing that does not arrive as a foreigner but makes itself at home. Seneca will also say that the "Latin grammarians give the [Greek] word *analogia* the right to the city [*civitas*]" (*Seneca's Letters to Lucilius*, 120.4). This idea of the reception of the Greek language, described as the integration into the body of citizens, validates the link established between translation and the use of metaphors by the verb *transferre*. It does not consist of a change from one language to another. It takes place within a single language, as a result of the transfer from Greece to Rome, as displacements and borrowings that create splendor: "[T]he metaphors draw attention to the discourse and illuminate it like so many shining stars" (*On the Ideal Orator*, 3.170). This is the sense in which Lucretius calls his poem a "translation" of the doctrine of Epicurus: "bringing to light the obscure discoveries of the Greeks" (1.136–137) and "composing sparkling verses on obscure subjects" (1.933)—bringing a new splendor and luminous intelligibility through translation by appeal to the senses. If "all metaphors are addressed directly to the senses, especially to the sense of vision, the most penetrating of them all" (*On the Ideal Orator*, 3.160), one can see that what is at stake in the transference by translation is precisely to achieve a form of immediacy in the form of the "living" language of Latin.

III. Translations of the Bible: The Lexicon of Translation and the Status of the *Hermêneus*

The translation of the Bible into Greek is not a counterexample to the monolinguism of the Greeks but rather an illustration of it. This translation is of Jewish inspiration rather than of Greek, born from the idea that Greek is de facto the language of culture par excellence, which enables it to render accessible the Book par excellence.

The body of literature that will be given the overarching title of *Biblia* [Βιβλία] in the twelfth century of the Common Era was translated into Greek first, though only in part, in Alexandria starting in the third century before Christ. It was a great novelty in the world of culture. These Greek "writings" (*graphai* [γραφαί]), which even today embody the Old Testament in the Greek Orthodox Church, served straightaway as the linguistic matrix for Christian doctrine, providing the concepts and expressions that course through the new phraseology. These texts provided the basis for most of the older versions of the Bible, right up to the translations of Cyril and Methodius (middle of the eleventh century) into old Slavonic. Competing Greek versions of the text appeared in the course of the second century, including an extremely literal one commissioned by the rabbis from the proselytizer Aquila. But this did not keep the former from serving as the exclusive source of the first Latin translations. Saint Jerome first proposed a series of scientific and literary revisions before deciding to directly translate the Hebrew texts of Jewish writings directly into Latin. The end result of his work of revision and translation was the Latin Vulgate, the official Bible of Roman Catholicism until the middle of the twentieth century. Jerome remained the champion of what he would himself call *hebraica veritas*. This conception even served as a model for Luther's German Bible. But in actuality, and despite his intent, a reign of *latina veritas* was the result of Jerome's labors instead. For centuries the Latin Vulgate would provide the textual basis for most translations into the so-called vernacular languages. Whatever the destiny of the Greek Bible itself, its appearance in classical antiquity signals an important moment in the very history of culture. Moses, in fact, lays down a challenge to Homer! And most of all, the objective foundations of the lexicon and of the discourse that have subsequently come to be known as "translation" are put irreversibly in place.

A. The Greek Bible of the Septuagint

Thus, in the third century before Christ, the peoples of *Iouda*, or the *Ioudaioi* ['Ιουδαῖοι], took up the translation of their *hagiai graphai* [ἅγιαι γραφαί], "holy writings," into Greek, starting first and foremost with the Law of Moses, *nomos* [νόμος]—or as they would say, their *nomothesia* [νομοθεσία], or "constitution." The *politeuma* [πολίτευμα], the "community within the city" that they formed in Alexandria, protected their difference of

nationality, and it would subsequently gain political recognition as well. Versions of the other books followed: spread out over two or even three centuries and probably completed by Christian writers. This was an event without precedent. The idiom of the Greeks, the language of thought that aspired to universality, now became the language of the Bible. Toward the end of the second century BCE, a widespread legend, first referred to in the *Letter of Aristeas*, would introduce "the book" (*hê biblos* [ἡ βίβλος]), as the law in question became Greek, as the extraordinary work of seventy or seventy-two scholars of *Iouda* at the request of the grand priest of Jerusalem. The order is said to have come from the royal librarian of Alexandria at the request of the second monarch of the Ptolemaic dynasty, Ptolemy Philadelphus (Ptolemy II). The latter wanted the books of the *Ioudaioi* included in the famous library of his sumptuous city. According to the same source, each of the translators translated the text in a rigorously consistent way, identical to the work of the other translators. In the middle of the second century CE, Christian authors circulated or forged the letter and set in place the Latin word *septuaginta*, "seventy." They made this into the general title of this collection of Greek writing that they had inherited and would henceforth be the only ones to use. The word is still in use today—although not without ambiguity, since the legendary role of the "seventy" applied only to the five books of Moses—as the title of the Greek Old Testament.

B. Translation, interpetation, inspiration, prophecy

The unprecedented event of the translation of the Law appealed immediately to the theoreticians of the local Judaic community, which was entirely hellenophonic. It was thus and at that moment that the conceptual field of translation became established in the Greek lexicon. The verb *hermêneuin* and the nouns, *hermêneia* [ἑρμηνεία] and *hermêneus* [ἑρμηνεύς] saw their respective meanings of "express" or "signify," "expression," "signification" or "interpretation," and "interpreter" become qualified to specifically signify "translate," "translation," and "translator." Other etymologically related and practically synonymous terms, such as *diermêneuein* [διερμηνεύειν] and *diermêneusis* [διερμήνευσις], were subject to the same process. The word *metagraphê* [μεταγραφή], "copy" or "transcription," came itself to signify "translation," and *metagraphein*, "to transcribe" or "to copy," became equivalent to "translate." The verb *metagein* [μετάγειν], to "deport," now applied to the text as "transferred into another language"; in other words, "translated" (*Prologue* by the translator of the *Siracides* around 100 BCE). Recourse was also taken to *metharmozein* [μεθαρμόζειν], "to arrange differently." Three great agents or Judaic witnesses of this semantic innovation succeeded one another between the second century BCE and the first century CE, all of them convinced that the translation of the Law was in response to an external political will. Around 180 BCE, the philosopher Aristobolus claimed that the "entire translation [*hermêneia*] of the Law" was realized under Ptolemy Philadelphus, but he insisted that there had been previous attempts at translation, ones that were fragmentary or flawed, which is impossible to verify anyway. His intention was to make more credible his own belief that Moses, the father of universal culture, was the original teacher of the Greek thinkers, especially of Plato and Pythagoreas, who would have learned directly from the Greek sources of "the Law" (text cited by Eusebius of Caesaria, *Praeparatio evangelica*, 13.12.1). Aristobolus was the first to demonstrate the use of *hermêneia* in the technical sense of "translation." A half-century later, and still in Alexandria, a lengthy piece of fiction appeared carried down in its entirety under the title *Letter of Aristeas*. This work decisively confirms the use of *hermêneia* as "translation," a term it immediately distinguishes from *metagraphê*, "transcription." It also contains the formulaic expressions *ta tês hermêneias* [τὰ τῆς ἑρμηνείας] and even *ta tês metagraphês* [τὰ τῆς μεταγραφῆς], the "work or works of translation" that one "executes" (*epitelein* [ἐπιτελεῖν]), or that one "achieves" (*telein* [τελεῖν]). As for the "translators," it would seem that they are still designated only by a participle of the verb *diermêneuein*.

The decisive setting up of the complete lexicon of translation is both certified and commented upon by the Alexandrian exegete and philosopher Philo in the first decades of the first century. The relevance, if not the legitimacy, of the act of translating the *hierai bibloi* [ἱεραὶ βίβλοι] (the sacred books) or simply *graphai* (writings) is demonstrated within the framework of a theological reasoning in which the mythological figure Moses plays the central part. Here are two essential texts:

1. For any time that Chaldeans who know the Greek language, or Greeks who know Chaldean [i.e., Hebrew] were to come upon the two versions [*graphai*] simultaneously, namely the Chaldaic and the translated version [*hermêneutheisê* (ἑρμηνευθείση)], they would look upon both of them with admiration and respect them as sisters, or rather as one and the same work in both substance and form, and they would call their authors not translators [*hermêneutheisê*] but hierophants and prophets to whose pure minds it had been granted to go along with the purest spirit [*pneuma* (πνεῦμα)] of Moses.

   ("A Treatise on the Life of Moses," 2.37)

2. For a prophet does not utter anything whatever of his own, but is only an interpreter [*hermêneus*] of another being who prompts and suggests to him all that he utters, at the very moment he is seized by inspiration [*enthousia* (ἐνθουσία)].

   ("The Special Laws," 4.49)

For Philo, the Greek translation of the writings is equally as "inspired" as the Hebrew original. The same holds true in his eyes for the interpretation of the sacred texts, which is limited to a small number of the elect, or the "initiates." To add force to his argument, he resorts to the register of the mysteries in the same manner as the Alexandrian writers in their explications of Homer's works. The schema that underlies his propositions is that of language (*logos*) as the interpreter (*hermêneus*) of thought or spirit (*nous* [νοῦσ]), whence his expression *ho hermêneus logos* [ὁ ἑρμηνεὺς λόγος], "the speech which translates our thought" (*De somniis*, 1.33). He uses the same schema in relation to the fact or process of divine revelation. The science and God's word (*logos*) have

their interpreter (*hermêneus*) in Moses. Philo designates the latter as *ho theologos* [ὁ θεολόγος] (*De proemiis et poenis*, 53; *De vita Mosis*, 2.115). Insofar as the divine *logos* expresses itself through the "holy laws [*nomoi hieroi* (νόμοι ἱεροί)]," Moses is their *hermêus*, or more precisely, *prophêtes* [προφήτης]. Yet he himself needs interpreters in his own image and of his stature, whence Philo's report of a chain of interpreters, "prophets," in which the translator and commentator hold the same rank, each "inspired." (We can compare this with Plato's *Ion*, in which the chain of enthusiasm goes from the muse or from the god to the poet and then to the rhapsodes, whose performances interpreted the interpreters [533c–535a]). Thus all the quantitative and qualitative divergences of the Greek version of the holy books are a priori justified and already fully recognized as authentic *graphai*. In some cases, the translator went to great lengths to repair the language of the works, occasionally going so far as to write what amounts to a new text. This is particularly evident for the book of Proverbs, entirely redrafted by a talented author of Greek wisdom. This is indeed the case of a *hermêneus* who is not so much a "translator" as an "interpreter" with literary and even musical connotations, since the book also contains poetry. But if there is translation nevertheless, it is insofar as the biblical message remains constant through its potency and deep articulations in relation and opposition to everything else. The semantic plenitude of the word *hermêneus* is thus assured.

C. Jerome, translator (*interpres*) or writer (*orator*)?

With Jerome (born in 347 CE near Emona, now Ljubljana in Slovenia, and died in Bethlehem in 420 CE), who was trained at a high level of humanism in Rome, the occidental destiny of the Christian Bible arrived at a decisive threshold. Very early on, he undertook to revise the text of the Latin scriptures, which appeared first in Africa around the beginning of the third century CE, then in Spain and in southern Gaul, and finally in Rome. Aside from the so-called Vulgate of Jerome, these writings are known as *Vetus Latina*, "old Latin," *Vetus edition, Antiqua translatio*, or *Vulgata editio*. Augustine called them *Italia*, "the Italian." Jerome considered all translations prior to his to be *vulgata editio*, or "commonly accepted editions," starting with the Septuagint (*Letters of St. Jerome*, letter 57, to Pammachius, para. 6). The variants of this *editio*, and especially the recensions, seemed to reflect a very ancient model of Greek related to a Hebrew family of texts that were found among the scrolls of Qumran.

This Bible made a significant contribution to the establishment of Christian Latin as distinct from classical Latin. The vocabularies of occidental languages that derive from Latin are deeply influenced by it. Shocked by the profusion of variants and its general literary impoverishment (at one point a *sermo humilis* had been the rule), Jerome wanted the Bible to be worthy of a Roman society that was rediscovering its classics. An extended stay in the East enabled him to perfect his knowledge of Greek and to properly learn Hebrew. He first used these skills with the encyclopedic accounts of Eusebius of Caesarea. Upon his return to Rome, he began to revise the Latin text of the Septuagint, limiting himself to stylistic corrections. In 386, he settled in Bethlehem permanently, where he discovered the *Hexapla of Origen*. His confrontation with this exhaustive synopsis in six columns raised profound questions regarding the truth of the text and its language. And he undertook the task of addressing them, limiting himself to the Hebrew canon of writings. He became increasingly open to Greek versions of the text other than the Septuagint, such as those of Aquila, Symmachus ben Joseph, and Theodotion. These were much closer to the Hebrew text that was already the official Jewish version than was the Alexandrian translation, the classic text for the Christians. Jerome thus adopted the Hebrew text as the only basis for the "revealed" truth, what he called *hebraica veritas*. This would be the third and final phase of his work as a translator, which lasted from 390 to 405. In his Latin translation of the Hebrew corpus, he was returning *ad fontes*, "to the sources." He put aside, although not completely, the other books contained in the Christian Bibles, generally known as deuterocanonic, which he called apocryphal. Beginning in the thirteenth century, the Latin Bible that derived from the work of Jerome was called the Vulgate. Its contents do not all come from Jerome. As in the case of most of the deuterocanonic books, it limits itself to adopting the older revision of the text of the *Vetus Latina*. The success of the long work of editing that the Vulgate embodies results from the fact that it answered the pressing need to have a standard text with a prestigious signator as well as being partly anonymous. It would thus remain the official Bible of the Roman Catholic Church until the middle of the twentieth century.

As a firm proponent of the *hebraica*, or *hebrea veritas*, Jerome saw the Hebrew language as the "matrix of all languages" (*matrix omnium linguarum*; *Book of Commentaries of the Prophet Sophonias*, 3.14–18), as the first language from which all others derive. As the originary language, Hebrew was thus at constant risk of having truth erode. Jerome was sympathetic to the pessimistic theory of history dear to Hesiod, which sees history as the progressive decay of humanity with perfect truth found only at its point of origin. So the Greek version of the Septuagint could only be a pale reflection of the Hebrew bible. Nonetheless, Jerome believed himself qualified to translate the holy books because his interventions occurred after the coming of the Christ, the historical principle of all truth. In regard to the technical framework that he formulates, his competence is far greater than that of the Septuagint, whose version, he admits, had "prevailed with good cause in the churches because it had been the first one . . . and the apostles had made use of it" (*Letters of St. Jerome*, letter 67, §11). But he justifies his rule of the *hebraica veritas* through the philosophy of language, influenced by Origen and Plato's *Cratylus*). Adopting the doctrine of the indivisible link between "being" in Greek, *on* [ὄν], and the "name," *onoma* [ὄνομα], he shows that this union is most forcefully achieved in the Hebrew language, the primordial idiom and the most apt to express and guarantee the truth. He comments upon it in these terms:

Just as there are twenty-two letters in Hebrew with which to write everything that is said, and that the human language is captured through the elementary functions of the letters, so too are there twenty-two books of the Bible, through which, as by the letters and basic rudiments the tender childhood of the just man is instructed in the divine doctrine.

(Prologue to the Book of Samuel
in the Book of Kings)

Thus, there was the need to have recourse to the Hebrew text in order to translate the Bible and to limit the translation to the Hebrew corpus as a remedy to both the excesses and deficiencies of the Septuagint. The "revealed" truth, which is one with the "name," in other words the formula itself, will thus be preserved. The books translated by Jerome will not be "corrupted by the transfer into a third vase [*in tertium vas transfusa*]." "Stored in a very clean jug as soon as they leave the press, they will retain all their taste" (Prologue to the books of Solomon).

For profane works and in his youth, Jerome claims to have applied the rules of Cicero or Horace, translating not "*verbum e verbo* but *sensum e sensu*," not "as a simple translator, but as a writer [*nec . . . ut interpres sed ut orator*]." He specifies that "I have not translated the words, but rather the ideas [*non verba sed sententias transtulisse*]" (*Letters of St. Jerome*, letter 57, §5 and §6). And he invokes those authors, starting with the Septuagint, who "translated according to the meaning [*ad sensum interpretati sunt*]," or some others, like Saint Hilary of Poitiers, who "captured the ideas in his own language by the law of the victor [*victoris jure transposuit*]" (ibid.). For the sacred texts, Jerome requires *verbum e verbo*. But what this means is that he does not want to lose a single word, for each and every one contains part of the divine "mystery" (*mysterium* or *sacramentum*). He is thus a "translator" and not a "prophet": "It is," he states, "the erudition and richness of the words that translate what one understands [*eruditio et verborum copia ea quae intelligit transfert*]" (Prologue to the Pentateuch). Even if he uses it, he rejects Aquila's Greek translation, done by a "meticulous interpreter [*contentiosus interpres*] who translates not only the words but also the etymologies" (*Letters of St. Jerome*, letter 57, §11)—in other words, Jerome rejects the servile forms of literality that evacuate the "mystery," the carrier of truth. In addition, he affirms that the *ad verbum*, or literal, version "sounds absurd" (ibid.). The hermeneutic way of putting *verbum e verbo* to use allows the talent—or even the genius—of the translator, in this case Jerome, to come into play without affecting the meaning or *mysterium*. It is even possible sometimes to "keep the euphony and propriety of the terms [*euphonia et proprietas conservetur*]" (ibid., letter 106, §55). This explains and justifies the literary qualities and even the audacities of Jerome's translation, which is certainly exempt of all servility.

Jerome's contemporary and correspondent Augustine rejected the rule of *hebraica veritas*. For him, the Greek text of the Septuagint is "inspired by the holy Spirit": it is the very best version in existence. This means that if there is an original truth, it is contained within this text. This Greek Bible had truly announced the Christ (e.g., by introducing the adjective *parthenos* [παρθένος], "virgin," to translate "young woman" in reference to the mother of the Emmanuel, in Isaiah 7:14), and the church made this translation its own. Augustine believed in the progress of humanity through history, culminating in its final stage, which the Christ had "completed." In addition, his position is directed by a concept of language that stems from the Stoic doctrine of the *res et signa* (the things and the signs; *On Christian Teaching*, bks. 1 and 2, passim). If *on* and *onoma* are fused, *res* and *signa* are separated. The unique and only *res* for Augustine is God, and *veritas* is just another way of saying God. Language, on the other hand, falls under *signa*, and writing is only a "sign" of a "sign": it cannot be identified with truth, which belongs to the order of the *res* (see SIGN, and below, IV).

IV. Medieval *Translatio*

In the Middle Ages, the term *translatio* encompassed different usages, all of which referred to a common idea of "displacement" or "transfer":

1. "transfer from one meaning to another" for one word, or "from the name of one thing to another" in a given language;
2. "transfer of a term from one language to an equivalent term in another," whence "translation" (see the difference with *etymologia* and *interpretatio*);
3. "transfer of culture or government from one epoch to another," "from one place to another" (*translatio studii, translatio imperii*).

A. Transfer of meaning

The notion of *translatio* is truly at the confluence of the arts of language (grammar, logic, rhetoric) and of theology. In its widest accepted meaning, the term *translatio* designates a transfer of meaning, a displacement of signification, from a proper usage to an improper usage. In a narrower acceptance, which one can find in grammar or rhetoric (in Quintilian or Donatus, for example), *translatio* is equivalent to *tropus*, defined as a change in signification for reasons of ornament or necessity (cf. Quintilian, *The Orator's Education*, 12.8–9) In an even narrower sense, *translatio* is equivalent to *metaphora*, which is one of the tropes; it entails using a word in some unusual and particular way, either because there is no proper word for this meaning or because this usage intensifies the meaning. The new use of the word is based on a perception of a resemblance between the thing that it properly signifies and the object to which it applies by transfer (e.g., when one says of some person: "he or she is a lion" because of his or her strength). The two first meanings apply equally to a single word as to a sequence of words; the third applies to a word in isolation. The terms *translatio* and *transumptio*, which had been distinct from each other in antiquity (e.g., with Quintilian), were, according to some medievalists, used interchangeably in the Middle Ages.

1. *Translatio*: Equivocation/ornament

In a very influential passage of his first chapter of the *Categories* of Aristotle, Boethius introduces the notion of *translatio*. He distinguishes two cases: (1) the transfer of meaning that occurs when one uses the name of one thing to designate another that has no name; this is done out of "penury of names" and results in equivocation, since the same name now applies to two different things; (2) the transfer of meaning that occurs for reasons of ornamentation and that does not result in equivocation (e.g., using *aurigia* [cart driver] to refer to the pilot of a ship, although this has its own proper

name: *gubernator*) "*Translatio nullius proprietatis est* [transfer is a property that belongs to no thing]," says Boethius, and this formula must be understood in relation to case (2): the transfer does not establish the property of a thing (since it does not receive its proper name by transfer) nor of a name (since the transferred usage does not constitute a stable or permanent property of the name). Abelard will also emphasize this latter point: the transfer occurs for some given length of time as part of a specific utterance and is to be understood in its context. He thus confirms that this does not lead to equivocation, since there is no new imposition of meaning, only an "improper" usage. He adds that this kind of *translatio* is a form of *univocatio* because there is only a single imposition, even if the term takes on an acceptation different from the original acceptation. The analysis of several of these variations in acceptation that are contextually determined, along with the idea of *univocatio*, forms the basis for elaborating the theory of supposition: one speaks of *translatio disciplinalis* for the specific ways terms are used in expressions of grammar (e.g., *homo est nomen* ["man" is a noun]), of logic (*homo est species* ["man" is a species]), or of poetry (*prata rident* [the prairies are laughing]). It is a matter of determining if the predicate is the reason for the particular acceptation or if it only actualizes some semantic potentialities already contained in the term. In the context of the medieval commentaries on Aristotle's *On Sophistical Refutations*, *translatio* is often analyzed as the second kind of equivocation: between the equivocation that is produced when two signifieds are equally present in the term (e.g., *canis*) and the contextually determined equivocation (e.g., *monachus albus*, "white monk" [Cistercian], where *albus* can only refer to the Cistercian in this particular context), one finds *translatio*, in which the two acceptations of a term are in a hierarchy "according to the anterior and the posterior [*secundum prius et posterius*]." One can see that the medieval commentaries are more precise than Aristotle's original text, which is difficult to interpret because of the absence of examples to illustrate this second kind; it seemed to concern the semantic variations due to use, when we make a habit of using a word in a sense that it did not originally have (166a–b16–17): "another manner, is when we have become used to expressing ourselves in a certain way"). In the thirteenth century, the notion of *analogia* would be developed within this second category, as when one acceptation is primary and all the others can be traced back to it according to a determinant relation (e.g., *sanum* relates first to the health of the animal, then later, and in relation to the first, to the urine, the potion, etc.).

2. The theological context

In a theological context, Augustine contrasted *signa propria* and *signa translata* (*De doctrina christiana*, 2.10.15); among the latter, he mentions the name "bull," which properly refers to the animal but also, by *usurpatio*, refers to the evangelist: the name properly refers back to a thing, which itself refers back to a second thing, and it thus signifies the second by transfer. In a different perspective, the *De trinitate*, §4 of Boethius, which takes up in part the *De trinitate*, §5 of Augustine, is the point of departure for a series of important reflections. In this text, Boethius speaks of the *mutatio* of categories when applied to the divinity: they are modified as a function of the subjects they are applied to, whence the adage "*talia sunt praedicamenta qualia subjecta permiserint* [the categories are such as their subjects permit them to be]"; when the predicates apply to something other than the divine reality, they can be substance or accidents; but they are modified when they apply to the divine ("*cum qui in divinam verterit predicationem cuncta mutantur que predicari possunt* [when one turns to divine predications, that which can be predicated finds itself completely changed]"). The adage is subject to two modifications in the context of the analysis of the propositions of Trinitarian theology. The first substitutes *predicata* for *praedicamenta* and gives it a semantic application: the value of predicates, when applied to divine reality, can change, even to the point of rendering false the utterance, says John of Salisbury in the first half of the twelfth century, and on the same occasion, Thierry de Chartres specifically talks of the "*verborum transsumptio.*" The second transformation consists in the inversion of the terms *subjecta* and *praedicata* ("*talia sunt subjecta qualia praedicata permittunt*" [subjects are such that predicates allow]) It is no longer an issue of showing the "improper" character because of the "transfer" of the discourse on God, but rather of setting out a general principle making the semantic and referential properties of the subject depend on the nature of the predicate (e.g., the predicate "engender," in "God engendered" [*Deus generat*] restricts the subject "God" to refer only to God the Father). Through this latter acceptation, the adage becomes the very principle of contextual semantics developed by the determinist logicians of the thirteenth century.

The notion of the transference of meaning was also influenced by the Dionysian tradition, starting with John Scotus Erigena, who took up the teaching of Pseudo-Dionysius. The term "metonomy" (translated as *transnominatio* in Erigena or as *denominatio* in John Sarrazin) is generally used here, and the trope by the same name likewise designates a transfer of sense based on different relations, especially from cause to effect, which makes it particularly useful in this context. Erigena chooses the term *translatio* (and its derivations) both for the transfer of categories and the transfer of names, and this usage would continue in all subsequent literature devoted to the divine names. He also speaks of *metaphora* when he considers types of relation and resemblance, but also relations of opposition and difference, which legitimize the transfer of names to God. These latter are affirmations that are called *per translationem*, which are improper and false, while the negations are proper and truthful.

The idea that names are attributed to God by a process of *translatio*, which results in an improper usage because it is different from the one assigned to the name by virtue of the first imposition, leads to the analysis of translated usages as examples of equivocation, *aequivocatio* (Abelard, and then the commentators on *De trinitate* of Boethius: Gilbert de Poitiers and Thierry de Chartres). At that time, one generally considered there to be "equivocity" between a noun or name applied to a created reality (which the name is proper to, having been first imposed upon it) and a noun applied to God. Toward the end of the twelfth century, several authors would think the opposite, that there is "univocity" in "God is just" and in "man is just" because in both expressions the word "just" signifies the same thing (whence the *univocatio*)

but *connote* different properties (the root of all justice and the effect of divine justice, respectively). So there is no incommensurability between the two kinds of discourse themselves, only a partial incommensurability, and the notion of *connotatio* permits the precise designation of this difference (see CONNOTATION). Alain de Lille, starting from the different theological sources mentioned previously and borrowing from the arts of language, specified the notion of *translatio* by distinguishing between the *translatio nominis* (transfer of the name) from the *translatio rei* (transfer of the thing). When one says *linea est longa* (the line is long), there is a transfer of both the word and the object it specifies; in *seges est leta* (the harvest is a happy one), there is only a transfer of the thing (the joy is transferred from a human, to which it properly belongs, to an inanimate object); in *monanchus albus*, there is a transfer of word only (only the name is transferred, as a "white monk" is not white), and only this latter mode comes into play in the *translationes in divinis* (see HOMONYM). In this way, Alain de Lille shows how language is subject to a general displacement when it is applied to God, a global distortion:

> Here, the words do not express existing realities. The terms are removed from their proper signification . . . here the nouns become pronouns, the adjectives become substantives, the verb does not apply in the usual way, the predicate has no subject, the subject has no content, here the affirmation is proper, the negation true, the words cannot be evaluated by the meaning they provide, but according to the meaning from which they originate, here syntax is not subject to Donatus's laws, metaphor (*translatio*) is a stranger to Cicero's rules.
>
> (Quoted in Dahan, *L'exégèse chrétienne*)

3. *Translatio* and analogy

The introduction of the notion of analogy in the thirteenth century reduces the scope of *translatio* (see ANALOGY). Analogy is introduced based on the second mode of equivocation of *On Sophistical Refutations*, the very same passage that had been previously considered a mode of *translatio* and following the same formula calling out the passage from *prius* to *posterius* ("healthy" refers first to health and then to urine, a constitutional walk, etc.). In theology, the question of ineffability is subdivided, starting with Pseudo-Dionysius, into two distinct parts: the first includes the case of "mystical" nouns, essential nouns, or nouns of perfection ("justice," "truth," etc.). The second applies to "symbolic" nouns (e.g., when one uses the name "lion"). The real philosophical and theological problem, according to Duns Scotus, applies to the former: to determine the relationship between divine justice and human justice, which will permit the analysis of the relation between the expression "God is just" and "man is just." *Translatio* or *metaphora* will be limited to "symbolic" nouns: purely linguistic questions that do not address resemblance or similarity between God and man (these are the dissimilar symbols, or metaphors without resemblance, of Pseudo-Dionysius). In order to determine the kind of "transfer," it is important to consider the location of the *per prius* that is transferred. Thus justice as a "thing" or "signified object" is found *per prius* in God, and secondarily *per posterius* in man (according to different modes of analysis, but, e.g., by virtue of a relation of participation).

But on the level of names or words, the relation is reversed, since the word "justice" applies *per prius* to the living creature (since names were first imposed on the things of this world, and then *per posterius*, "transferred" to God). On the basis of signification, such a noun applies "properly" to God, but it applies "improperly" on the mode of signification, since the latter is necessarily adequate for its user and thus inadequate to speak of unthinkable and ineffable realities (see SENSE, III.B.3). For a symbolic name like *leo*, there is no relation between the signified and the thing that the subject it is applied to signifies; the transfer, which is purely nominal (*translatio nominis*), is achieved by virtue of a property judged to be one of similarity and of a relation of proportionality (one says "God is a lion" by positing God/strength : lion/strength); for this reason, says Bonaventure, these are the only words that are truly "transferred names" (*nomina translativa*) (*In IV Sententiarum*, distinction 1.22, a. un., question 3 resp.). We should note that Albertus Magnus, on the other hand, considers that there is in fact a "transfer of thing" due to the fact that it is the property (strength) that is transferred from the lion to God. Whatever the case, these symbolic names are absolutely improper, both on the level of the signification and, as is the case with all names, on the level of the modes of signifying.

B. Transfer from one language to another: *translatio*/"translation"

The medieval grammarians and lexicographers sought to distinguish the different modes by which two terms can be set in relation to each other, on the condition that they have something in common. It is the recognition of what they have in common that allows one of them to serve as a gloss (*expositio*) of the other. One can see some of the difficulties they encountered by considering the following couplings of terms, where the equals sign points out an equivalence that is precisely what needs to be specified.

1. *deus* = *Dans Eternam Vitam Suis* (God = Giving Eternal Life to his Own): etymology called "by letters";
2. *episcopus* = *epi* + *skopos* [ἐπί + σκοπός]: analysis by composition;
3. *deus* = *theos* [θεός];
4. *homo* = *anthropos* [ἄνθρωπος];
5. *Iacob* = *Ioacobus*;
6. *sapientia* (wisdom) = *amor philosophiae* (love of philosophy).

The most common generic term for these equivalences is *expositio*. It is also used in logic to designate the logical structure of an utterance (e.g., *homo qui currit disputat*, "a man who runs discusses" = *homo qui currit et ille disputat*, "a man runs and he discusses"). In the same way, the *expositio* enables the recovery of multiple meanings or acceptations of a term, which may also explain its material form: the more difficult a word is to understand, the more one is tempted to capture it by a multiplicity of *expositiones* based on more commonly understood expressions, as in the case, in the *Catholicon* of John Balbi of Genoa, of the word *dues* (we find, among others, [1] and [3]).

The authors of the twelfth century distinguish two kinds of *expositions*. As for the first, "etymology (*etymologia*) is the *expositio* of a term by one or more better-known terms, based on the property of the signified object and the similarity of letters and sounds, and it (most often) occurs within a single language." It includes examples of type (1) but excludes (6) due to the absence of formal similarity. It can include the process of composition/derivation, although, as illustrated by example (2), which is fairly representative of what one finds in the dictionaries known as *Derivationes* (Hugh of Pisa, for example), the passage from one language to another is also authorized, since a Latin term is decomposed into Greek units. As for the second: "*Interpretatio* is the *expositio* or the *translatio* of a term into another language, whether or not there is similarity in sound." *Interpretatio* can be applied to (4). Depending on the author, the distinguishing criterion is either: in the same language / in another language; or: with a formal similarity / not necessarily with a formal similarity. Some authors distinguish between the two first notions of *translatio*, which occurs when a term is "transferred" from Greek to Latin—for example, *ego, tu, sui*, which are therefore "derived," according to John of Genoa. He then asks himself if there is always derivation (*derivatio*) whenever there is *translatio*, to which he replies in the negative: in the case of translation (3) or (5), one cannot say that there is derivation, since in both cases the *same noun* is subjected to a simple formal modification in passing from one language to another (*detorsio unius lingue in alteram*); each of the words in these copulas is thus the same in both its signification and its signifier. One can speak of derivation when this is not the case, as in the coupling (Latin) of *olor* (swan) "derived" from *olon* ("completely"; Gr. *holon* [ὅλον], "because the swan is COMPLETELY white," or in the case of *gigno* (to engender) from *gê* [γῆ] (earth). One should note that this problematic of the "unity of the noun," which originates from a theological context (it needed to be demonstrated that the Gospel was everywhere the same, even if it was written in various languages, see WORD), is also raised in relation to example (4) of *interpretatio*.

We can see from these remarks that it would be misleading to start from a problematic of *translation* when the heart of the matter is establishing the relationship between two words (or expressions). The function of all these *expositiones* is to account for the signification of words and/or to justify their formation, which explains how *etymologia* as a form of *veriloquium* (true talking) sometimes becomes the generic term applied to the different types we have encountered. Only with Roger Bacon did the notion of *etymologia* become defined by precise characteristics that are closer to modern criteria and clearly exclude what came to be called fantasy etymology (what Buridant, in "Les paramètres de l'étymologie médiévale," calls *ontological*, because of the kind of relationship between objects they depend on; cf. Rosier, "Quelques textes sur l'étymologie au Moyen Âge"). Thus we see that only some of these *expositiones* serve as translations, *translatio*, in the modern sense, for example, (3), (4), and (5).

■ See Box 2.

V. The German Tradition of Translation: *Dolmetschen/Übersetzen/Übertragen*

A. *Dolmetschen*: "To render in German" and "to translate"

It is often said that modern German was formed primarily through a translation: Luther's translation of the Bible.

2
Translatio studii: The constituent languages and traditions of philosophy in Europe

The theme of *translatio studii* constitutes a *topos* in medieval thought destined to illustrate how, at different moments, knowledge (*savoir*) "moved" from Greece to Rome and then from Rome to the Christian world. The concept was first developed by the defenders of Charlemagne and the empire as a defense of Capetian power. From the twelfth century on it reappeared at different times and under different forms, notably in the Scholastic setting, and then especially in the universities: the University of Paris was thus legitimized as the culmination of a long journey of knowledge, first from Greece to Rome, and finally as an essential component of the "identity of the French realm." One problem with this *topos* derives from the term *studium* itself when identified with knowledge or wisdom (*sapientia*): is this sacred knowledge or profane? Roger Bacon's approach was an original one. In discussing *translatio philosophiae*, he stated that "[i]t pleased God to give whatever wisdom he wanted, since all wisdom comes from God; he thus revealed it to philosophers, both to the faithful and the infidel alike" (*Opus Tertium*). This voyage of philosophy was necessarily a voyage through the languages, a *translatio linguarum*:

> God first revealed philosophy to his saints and gave them the laws. . . . It was thus primarily and most completely given in the Hebrew language. It was then renewed in the Greek language, primarily by Aristotle; then in the Arabic language, primarily through Avicenna; but it was never composed in Latin and was only translated/transferred [*translata*] based on foreign languages, and the best [texts] are not translated.
>
> (Bacon, *Opus Tertium*)

The improbable status of the Latin language is clearly apparent here. It is simultaneously a language of sacred knowledge, since it is one of the three languages of the cross, along with Hebrew and Greek, but it is not really a language of profane knowledge, since, according to Bacon, the "Latins" did not add anything to that domain, unlike the Greeks and the Arabs.

BIBLIOGRAPHY

Bacon, Roger. *Opus Tertium*. Edited by J. S. Brewer. London: Longman, 1859.

Jongkees, Adriaan G. "Translatio studii: Les avatars d'un thème médiéval." In *Miscellanea mediaevalia in memoriam Jan Frederick Niermeyer*, 41–51. Groningen, Neth.: J.B. Wolters, 1967.

Lusignan, Serge. "L'université de Paris comme composante de l'identité du royaume de France: Étude sur le thème de la translatio studii." In *Identité régionale et conscience nationale en France et en Allemagne du Moyen Âge à l'époque moderne*, edited by R. Babel and J.-M. Moeglin, 60–72. Sigmaringen, Ger.: Jan Thorbecke, 1997.

Luther designated the act of translating, constitutive of language and culture, as *dolmetschen*, and he often clarified it by substituting the verb *verdeutschen* ("to make German," to "Germanize," or as Philippe Büttgen translated it into French, "to put in German"). To explain *dolmetschen* by *verdeutschen* is to specify the method and purpose of translation: to make it understandable for the people, for "the mother at home and the ordinary man" ("Ein Sendbrief" [1530]), and to facilitate the mediation of cultures.

In our day, *dolmetschen* has remained close to "interpreting agency," that is to say, the oral and immediate translation of the interpreter-guide or the interpreter-translator. In *Truth and Method* by Hans-Georg Gadamer, "The Translator as Interpreter" ("*Der Übersetzer als Dolmetsch*") designates the intepreter-translator as part of a living dialogue. We should note nonetheless that within the domain of translation, the German language does not contain a term that in itself refers to interpretation as a necessary part of the understanding of meaning. *Dolmetschen* has simply been progressively replaced by *übersetzen*, and the two terms, which had started out as synonyms, have ended up being opposed to each other to the point of excluding *dolmetschen* from the philosophical vocabulary. Thus Schleiermacher sets them in radical opposition ("Über die verschiedenen Methoden des Übersetzens" [1813]): the two verbs designate two distinct manners of passing from one language into another and thus two perspectives on the activity of translation. Schleiermacher distinguishes authentic translation, which takes the signified content as its object and draws upon reflection (*übersetzen*) from simultaneous or immediate translation (*dolmetschen*), which is a simple exchange of linguistic values that are judged to be equivalent. This is why *dolmetschen* is rarely used in philosophy: Fichte, for example, used it occasionally to designate the interpretive activity of the preacher, the intermediary between human beings and the gods (*Fichtes Werke*, 7:600; 8:254), but never as part of a theoretical discussion. In contemporary philosophical language, both in the hermeneutic tradition (Gadamer) and in the analytic tradition, *übersetzen* is rendered as "to translate" (Quine, Davidson) or *traduire*.

B. *Übersetzen, übertragen*: "Translation" and "transposition"

The German language also includes a synonym of *übersetzen*, the verb *übertragen*. *Übersetzen* literally means "to transpose," whereas *übertragen* means "to transport." *Übertragen* is the more general term and designates all sorts of "transposition," "transfer," or "transmission," whereas today *übersetzen* is limited to the written transposition of discourse. Thus "to translate" is generally applied to *übersetzen*, while "to transpose" is used for *übertragen*. *Übertragung* can also designate "transfer" or even "metaphor." In Nietzsche, the verb is translated (into English) as "to transfer" ("On Truth and Lie"). In their normal usage, the terms are strictly equivalent, but they are distinguished from each other in the reflections and analytic writing of Heidegger and Gadamer, who used the nuances of this distinction in philosophical discourse.

C. *Übersetzen, übertragen, überliefern*: "Translation" and "transmission"

In fact, like "transmission" in general, *übertragen* can underscore the existing link between translation and transmission. In this sense, the two terms are complementary, as for Kant, for example. He writes in *Religion within the Bounaries of Mere Reason* (RT: Ak., 6:166):

> Indessen es ist nicht genug, es in Übersetzungen zu kennen und so auf die Nachkommenschaft zu übertragen.

> (It does not suffice to be acquainted with the book [the Bible] in translation and to transmit it to posterity in this form.)

It is this proximity that binds in French *traduction* and *tradition*.

It is in this same sense that Heidegger took up the philosophical problem of translating: *übersetzen* is to pass from one shore to another, the translator being the ferryman (*passeur*). *Übersetzen* signifies "translation" in the Latin sense of *traducere*, "to lead across." "To translate" is to bring a discourse across from one language into another, that is to say, to insert it into a different milieu, a different culture. Translation is not to be understood as a simple "transfer" or as a pure linguistic "version," but instead within the general development of the spirit. This idea, already present in Luther, would be taken up by Goethe, Herder, and Novalis, and in a general way by the first romantics that considered this exchange between languages as the condition of *Bildung* (Berman, *The Experience of the Foreign*). Schleiermacher's theory of the methods of translation, which favors the reader's encounter with the foreign, is likewise completely based on the analysis of this movement. "Translation" is thus considered as a "transplantation": to translate is "to transplant [*verpflanzen*] to a foreign soil the products of a language in the domains of the sciences and the arts of discourse, in order to enlarge the scope of action of these products of the mind" ("Über die verschiedenen Methoden"). F. Schlegel used similar formulas as early as 1798: "Each translation [*Übersetzung*] is either a *transplantation* [*Verpflanzung*] or a *transformation* [*Verwandlung*], or both at the same time" (*Kritische Friedrich-Schlegel Ausgabe*, 18:204, fr. 87). The same metaphor allows Benjamin to talk of a *Nachreife*, that is to say, a ripening of words past the point of their usefulness ("Die Aufgabe des Übersetzers").

1. *Über-setzen*: Trans-late

This is the classical perspective that Heidegger inherited when he affirmed that translation transposes the work of thought into the spirit of another language and thus transforms thought in a fruitful manner: this is why a translation "serves mutual comprehension in a higher sense. And each step in this direction is a blessing for the peoples" (Heidegger, author's prologue to Henri Corbin's French translation of *What Is Metaphysics?*). The "translation" of *Über-setzung* (*Über*-setzung, with the accent on the penultimate syllable) is thus, "trans-lation" (Über-*setzung*), the transposition of a thought into another universe of thought (Heidegger, *Off the Beaten Track*). The displacement of the stressed accent indicates the focus of the thought: to lead to the other side, to another context that will reveal its truth. Such a passage can be measured by what it passes over, "a bound over a trench," a "*Sprung über einen Graben*" (*Off the Beaten Track*), which becomes in Gadamer an "abyss" (*Kluft*; *Truth and Method*).

Thus, translation is no longer a simple transfer, but an inscription into another relation to the world or global form of comprehension of the world, according to the general structure of understanding. *Übersetzen* is thus not a "replacing" (*ersetzen*) but a "transposing" (*es setzt über*): there is a true "transfer," "transport" (Heidegger, *Parmenides*).

2. *Überliefern*: "Tradition" and "revealing"

If Heidegger's analysis of the term "translation" as "transmission" remains within the classical perspective, he nonetheless inflects it by introducing the dimension of truth. In translation as tradition (*tradieren*), Heidegger gives the idea of transmission (*Übertragung*) a particular form in which "to transmit" is called *überliefern*. By its connection to "tradition" (as Préau translates *Überlieferung*, without being able to render the full Heideggerian sense), the German language does not promote the relationship between translation and treachery (*Verrat*) that is imprinted so forcefully in the Italian expression *traduttore-traditore*. *Trahir* (to betray) is an adaptation of the Latin *tradere*, which signifies "to surrender," "to hand over," or "to bequeath," so that in French *trahir* also means "to reveal." The German connotation is different from the common usage in French and the Romance languages. If "translation" is "treason" or "betrayal" in French, it is because even a beautiful translation does not express the original text. The translation "abandons" the original. But by underscoring the tie to tradition, Heidegger instead conveys the *Übersetzung* of fundamental concepts into the historical languages, that is to say, the translation of a culture, touching upon the essence of language, as an *Überlieferung* (*The Principle of Reason*): *Übersetzung* as *Überlieferung* ensures a reprise, a taking over (*Übernahme*), which is a reception or "collection." In *Übersetzung/Überlieferung*, the transposition is a reappropriation, a deliverance, a liberation:

> [T]radition [*Überlieferung*] is what is proper to its name: a transmission, a handing over, a delivery [*ein Liefern*] in the Latin sense of *liberare*, a liberation. As a liberation tradition opens up and brings to light hidden treasures of what has never ceased from being, even if this light is only a first tentative dawn.

> (Heidegger, *Principle of Reason*)

There is thus an inflection despite the relation between *überliefern* and *tradere*, "to betray," "to hand over," "to reveal" (German has kept *tradieren* and *Tradition* as synonyms of *überliefern*, *Überlieferung*). For the connotations are different in French: if *livrer* can be traced back to its origin in *liberare* by Heidegger, to link *traduire* to *trahir* is to place it under the sign of infidelity and falsehood. But in following Heidegger's German, on the other hand, what translation reveals instead is the "truth," the "unconcealment." The French language seems less inclined to think of tradition as a revealing, whereas the German seems less inclined to think of tradition as treachery and betrayal.

The importance attributed to translation in contemporary German thought, and especially in Gadamer's hermeneutics (*Truth and Method*), is based on this approach. In effect, Gadamer sees "Heidegger's genius" in the analyses that lead back to the "natural meaning of words and to the wisdom that can be discovered in language" (*Philosophical Hermeneutics*). In this context, the rehabilitation of tradition is inseparable from the concept of translation. In *Truth and Method*, it is this notion that opens up the reflection on the "ontological turn taken by hermeneutics with language as its guide": not only is tradition usually transmitted to us through translation (*Truth and Method*), but it is essentially "translation." Tradition-translation transmits interpretations, that is to say, the understanding of the world that constitutes the framework in which the world reveals itself to us and in which the existential dimensions of comprehension are inscribed (Heidegger, *Being and Time*, para. 31). So to understand is both to receive and to translate what we have received. But this translation is *trans*-lation, a form of passage "beyond" that Gadamer calls the "fusion of horizons" (*Truth and Method*). From this point on, inscribed within an encompassing comprehension, translation carries with it a passivity that refers back to the idea of a comprehension that is always other. In effect, if translation liberates by submitting to tradition, and this liberation is also a betrayal, then one can understand how "*we understand in a different way, if we understand at all*" (*Truth and Method*). Heidegger made the same claim, although in a less radical fashion: explication does not

yield a better understanding, but just another one "all the while still encountering the same" (*Off the Beaten Track*). Difference and identity are the gap that translation straddles and that becomes an abyss for Gadamer. Here, translation, in its inevitable infidelity, becomes the revealer of truth.

Thus translation-tradition-treason loses the linguistic rigor on which it was based and becomes in Gadamer and later in Heidegger, the very revelation of the essence of language as a dimension of human accomplishment (cf. Escoubas, "De la traduction"). "To translate" becomes synonymous with "to think." In this context, it is in the very term in German that we can read the passage of translation from simple transfer to translation as an interpretation of the world (see WELTANSCHAUUNG).

■ See Boxes 3, 4, and 5.

Clara Auvray-Assayas
Christian Bernier
Barbara Cassin
André Paul
Irène Rosier-Catach

3

Duhem-Quine: On the underdetermination of theory and the indeterminacy of translation

1. The underdetermination of epistemological translation

In Pierre Duhem's work on the philosophy of science, *The Aim and Structure of Physical Theory*, one encounters the word "translation" in its original epistemological meaning. It allows Duhem to formulate a conception of the relation between experiment and theory, which profoundly influenced the epistemology of the twentieth century (see EPISTEMOLOGY). Starting with a critique of the notions of observation and the "experimental method," Duhem redefined the relation of scientific theory to facts using the idea of translation:

> The mathematical elaboration of a physical theory can be tied to observable facts only through a translation. In order to introduce experimental conditions into a calculation, one must make a *version* that replaces the language of concrete observation by the language of numbers; in order to make the results which the theory predicts into something observable, one needs a *theme* to transform a numerical value into an indication formulated in the language of experiment.

> (*Aim and Structure of Physical Theory*)

The interest of Duhem's thesis lies in the fact that it affirms that the nontransparency

and asymmetry inherent in each of these two translations is subject to indetermination. The first translation (version) is a mathematical translation upon concrete *things*, linked to methods of measurement: "The methods of measurement are the vocabulary which render translation possible in both directions" (ibid.). Duhem continues:

> But he who translates also betrays; *traduttore, traditore*; there is never a perfect fit [*adéquation*] between the two texts that a version makes correspond to each other.

Translation makes it possible to define the distance between theory and experiment, whose consequence for contemporary theories will be the underdetermination of theory in relation to experiment (the plurality or even empirical equivalence of theories that can account for the same facts), which will also lead to holism (the impossibility of assigning a specific experimental content to a theoretical point). From this, Duhem draws important methodological conclusions, which account for the posthumous reputation of *Aim and Structure* and its renown under the name of the Duhem-Quine thesis: an experiment cannot apply to an isolated hypothesis because there is a work of symbolization between a fact and its theoretical translation that is part of the work of theory: "a fact of practice does not translate into a single fact of theory," and

"an infinite number of theoretical facts can be taken as translations of the same fact of practice"(ibid.). Recourse to the idea of translation allows the formulation of an incommensurability between a fact and the theory applied to it.

Long before Popper, Duhem developed a critique of the inductive method. He took the transition from Kepler's laws to the Newtonian theory of gravitation as an example. Newton's theory is not an inductive generalization of Kepler's laws: on the contrary, it is incompatible with them. If Newton believed he had made a generalization based on Kepler's laws, it is because he *translated* those laws. "For them to acquire this fecundity, they needed to be transformed, to be translated symbolically" (ibid). Once Kepler's laws were "translated" into Newton's theoretical framework, they gained new meaning: "The translation of Kepler's laws into symbolic laws required the physicist to have already adopted a whole set of hypotheses" (ibid.). We can see the modernity of Duhem's approach: in the translation of the laws, the adoption of a new theory entails a change in usage and meaning of earlier concepts and facts within a new paradigm.

Duhem's use of the word "translation" to describe the process of scientific constitution

(continued)

(continued)

is thus neither metaphorical nor trivial: his affirmation of the nontransparency and asymmetry of any translation allows him to expose the indeterminacy between theory and experiment in a new light. *Aim and Structure* would have a considerable influence subsequently, both in epistemology through the ideas of paradigm and empirical influence (Kuhn, Feyerabend) and in the debates around Quine's thesis on the indeterminacy of translation, which radicalized Duhem's indeterminacy.

2. The indeterminacy of radical translation

The thesis on the indeterminacy of radical translation set out by the American philosopher W. V. O. Quine in 1960 in his book *Word and Object* played a central role in the development of philosophy of language, as well as in the philosophy of mind and the epistemology of the twentieth century. Quine attacked the idea of shared signification between different languages and affirmed that in a situation of radical translation (without prior contact and with nothing in common between his language and the local language) a linguist could develop contradictory manuals of translation that would be compatible with the facts; in other words, there would be *no basis* on which to determine whether the translator was right or wrong. The radicalness of this thesis and Quine's notion of a "conceptual schema" put his work at the center of the debate on relativism. It starts out with a "thought experiment": a linguist "on the ground" goes into the jungle to discover a completely unknown language. How will he produce a translation manual that makes correspondences between the terms of the foreign language and his own without a dictionary or interpreter? The linguist goes

for a walk with the native and sees a rabbit hop away in front of him. "*Gavagai*," exclaims the native. What does this expression mean? Quine's answer is to say that there is no sense in asking him, especially if one is wondering not only about the signification of the utterance but also what entity is designated by the word *Gavagai* (a stable object, a sense-datum, a spatiotemporal segment of rabbit-hood, an event—"he rabbits"; see SENSE).

The thesis of indeterminacy, with its critique of signification, is a "philosophical point," according to Quine: as soon as one leaves behind any linguistic community, synonymy becomes opaque. The point is also an anthropological one, since what is at stake in the question of synonymy is the very idea of a common core shared by several languages, such as one finds in Frege's classical formulations. Quine calls the belief in such a common core, which is expressed differently by each language, the *myth of meaning*. We can compare this thesis to the idea of paradigm as developed by T. S. Kuhn in *Structure of Scientific Revolutions* (1962), a work that is contemporary with Quine's. The question of the indeterminacy of translation is in fact the question of whether a form of thought, a meaning, or a reality can be held in common by all of humankind, or by all languages, even with different conceptual schemes. In a famous text, "On the Very Idea of a Conceptual Scheme," Donald Davidson applies his critique of relativism to what he calls the "conceptual relativism" of both Quine and Kuhn (see EPISTEMOLOGY). The idea of conceptual scheme extends the problem of translation between utterances to the commensurability of conceptions of the world, to conceptual schemas, and to *common sense* (see COMMON SENSE).

Translation is indeterminate, but not impossible; it is indeterminate because it is possible. "Indeterminacy means not that there

is no acceptable translation, but that there are many." Indeterminacy is the possibility of choice: "the freedom of conjecture, the field of free creation are both wide open" ("The Behavioral Limits of Meaning," Quine, unpublished conference paper of 1984). The choice is settled according to criteria that behavior and experience cannot settle or decide. This is true of the attribution of logic or rationality. Attributing binary logic to the native is not the result of discovering it in his language, even less so in his thought: it is an invention.

The thesis of indeterminacy means that one always translates *within* one's own language, *at home*. It consists of "catapulting oneself into the foreign language" with the momentum of one's own. According to Quine, we have *nothing* on which to be right or wrong. There is no *fact of the matter* (see MATTER OF FACT). This theme of radical skepticism paradoxically inscribes the question of the plurality of languages at the very heart of an analytic philosophy that has always tended to erase it.

Sandra Laugier

BIBLIOGRAPHY

Davidson, Donald. "On the Very Idea of a Conceptual Scheme." *Proceedings and Addresses of the American Philosophical Association* 47 (1973–74): 5–20.

Duhem, Pierre. *La théorie physique: Son objet, sa structure*. Paris: Marcel Rivière & Cie, 1914. Paris: Vrin, 1981. Translation by Philip P. Wiener: *The Aim and Structure of Physical Theory*. Princeton, NJ: Princeton University Press, 1991.

Quine, W.V.O. "Le mythe de la signification." In *La philosophie analytique*, 139–87. Paris: Minuit, 1962.

———. "On Empirically Equivalent Systems of the World." *Erkenntnis* 9 (1975): 313–28.

———. *Word and Object*. Cambridge, MA: MIT Press, 1960.

4

Qur'ān [قرآن]

The Qur'ān (or Koran, according to the usual English transliteration), the name of the Muslim holy book, comes from the verb *qara'a*, which means "to read," "to recite," or "to proclaim aloud." Muslims believe that it is the very word of God revealed to the prophet Muhammad and through him to humanity. The Qur'ānic text, which is often self-referential, declares (97:1): "We have indeed revealed this [message] in the Night of Power," an allusion to the "descent" of the word of God into this

world, which Islamic tradition (*hadith*) narrates as follows. It was a habit of Muhammad, before he declared himself a prophet, to go to the top of Jabal an-Nūr, one of the mounts near the city of Mecca, to spend many days in solitary meditation in a cave known as Hirā'. This was during the month called Ramadan. The "Night of Power" (or "Night of Destiny," as it is also translated) is a night during that month when he was visited in his solitude by the angel Gabriel, who commanded

him: "*Iqra!*" ("Read!"), using the very word that would give its name to the message he brought: "the Reading." After he had repeated three times in terror that he could not read (he was illiterate), Muhammad asked what he was supposed to read. Then the angel revealed to him the very first words of what would become the book of the Muslims: "Read! In the name of thy Lord and Cherisher, who created—created man, out of a (mere) clot of blood. Read! And thy

Lord is most Bountiful, He who taught (the use of) the Pen—Taught man that which he knew not" (96:1–6). After the experience was over, Muhammad ran home completely terrified and only gathered his spirits when his wife Khadija expressed her faith in him and in the truth of what he had been told by the angel: that he was the prophet of God chosen to proclaim His Qur'ān. The Message would then be revealed bit by bit during the twenty-three years that followed, during which the new religion founded upon it, Islam, started its expansion. It was only under the third caliph of Islam that the verses revealed by Muhammad and often known by heart by his followers were collected and put together into a book of 114 chapters classified by length, after the first one known as "The Opening."

As this narrative shows, at the core of Islamic belief is the notion that the Qur'ān is the miracle of a revelation by God to a simple man, Muhammad, and in a simply human language, Arabic, of a message He directly authored. Again, in self-referential statements, the Qur'ān declares that the evidence for its divine origin does not require

any miracle further than its "inimitability" (Qur'ānic verses are called *āyāt*, which means "miracles," or "signs"). Thus, chapter 17, verse 88 states: "Say: if the whole of mankind and Jinns were to gather together to produce the like of this Qur'ān they could not produce the like thereof, even if they backed up each other with help and support."

Does "inimitability" mean untranslatability, and what does the notion of a choice by God of a human language to carry His own word imply? These are important philosophical and theological questions. An early theological school in Islam, characterized by its rationalist outlook and known as Mu'tazilism, held the view that the Qur'ān is the word of God but created in a human language. One consequence of that view would be that the book, meant for human comprehension, is, de jure, fully understandable by human reason and translatable into all human languages. Conservative schools of thought would insist on the fundamental untranslatability of the word uttered by God Himself, parts of it being known solely by Him. Those schools would reluctantly accept translations of the Qur'ān only as a makeshift solution

because the majority of Muslim populations do not speak Arabic and use it merely as a liturgical language. One important aspect of the issue of translatability is the meaning of the "election" of the Arabic language: is there anything special in that language that called for its election or, on the contrary, does the Qur'ānic miracle consist precisely in the fact that this is simply a human language, equivalent to and translatable into any other human language?

Souleymane Bachir Diagne

BIBLIOGRAPHY

Ali, Abdullah Yusuf. *The Meaning of the Holy Qur'ān*. Brentwood, MD: Amana Corporation, 1992.

Asad, Muhammad. *The Message of the Qur'ān*. Bristol, U.K.: The Book Foundation, 2003.

Berque, Jacques. *Le Coran: Essai de traduction de l'Arabe annoté et suivi d'une étude exégétique par Jacques Berque*. Paris: Albin Michel, 2002.

Hamidullah, Muhammad. *Le Coran: Traduction intégrale et notes de Muhammad Hamidullah*. Paris: Le Club Français du Livre, 1959.

Irving, T. B., *The Qur'ān: The First American Version*. Brattleboro, VT: Amana Books, 1986.

5
No untranslatables!

There's nothing in Greek that can't also be said in Latin.

(Leonardo Bruni, *On Correct Translation*)

It was through the Italians that translation as a theoretical enterprise was revived in the Renaissance. This was in large part thanks to Leonardo Bruni, erstwhile chancellor of Florence and indefatigable translator of Greek into Latin at a particularly heady moment in the history of humanism: the early fifteenth century, two generations after that other indefatigable humanist (albeit one ignorant of Greek), Petrarch. Indignant over criticism of his translation of Aristotle's *Nicomachean Ethics*, Bruni threw himself into *De interpretatione recta* (*On Correct Translation*) in the mid-1420s. His anger at a churchman whose critique revealed misunderstanding not only of Greek but also of his own "mother tongue," Latin, produced a passionate statement about translation's importance to the modern Western world.

Bruni seems to be the first to have used *traductio* and *traducere* to mean "translation": words that would come to replace

interpretare, *vertere*, and *convertere*, as Remigio Sabbadini has noted, and thus words that insist on the act of transporting, and even transformation. Transformation is, in fact, at the heart of Bruni's meditations: the "best translator will turn his whole mind, heart, and will to his author, and in a sense be transformed by him" (*De interpretatione recta*). But after losing his identity, the translator must regain it, and he can only do so if he is absolute master of his own language, dominating all in his power ("Deinde linguam eam, ad quam traducere vult, sic teneat, ut quodammodo in ea dominetur et in sua totam habeat potestate"; ibid., chap. 11). In this act of transporting, nothing must be left behind, and all that is carried across must be transformed into the new tongue: "Don't go begging for words or borrowing them; leave nothing in Greek out of your ignorance of Latin. The translator must know with precision the exact value and efficacy of terms." Not to translate is to remain a beggar, a mendicant, trapped in the no-man's land between two languages and thus in exile. Bruni, utterly terrestrial and at war with the Scholastics who shoehorned Aristotle to fit their own theological and

pedagogical ends, was far more interested in a cultural patrimony whose greatest works looked not to otherworldly Christianity but defined and defended one's earthly homeland. Demosthenes's orations as he stood at the gate of Athens and exhorted the citizens to take a stand against Philip of Macedon were some of Bruni's earliest translations. Even Aristotle—despite his tutoring of Philip's son Alexander—becomes a supporter of civic identity and independence, the very independence Florence was struggling to maintain in the early fifteenth century.

But Aristotle (and along with him, Plato) becomes something else: a supreme and superb stylist, whose books possess "the splendor and clarity of a painting," in a comparison that harks back to Horace's *ut pictura poesis* from the *Ars poetica*. Bruni's Latin was not the medieval Latin of the Scholastics—and hence of Aristotle's prior translators. The closing chapters of the treatise are a tour de force, as Bruni lists examples of bad translations he had come across—sheer acts of "barbarism," he calls them—and enumerates

(continued)

(continued)

their many weaknesses. For one thing, these incompetent translators use words no one has ever used; thus "*oligarchica sophistica legislationis*"—a literally "Latinized" version of the Greek that means nothing in Latin. But the major reason for their "*ignorantia ruditatesque loquendi*"—their ignorance and rustic way of speech—is their lack of familiarity with Aristotle as a stylist: "and every writer has his own particular style" (*cum singulis fere scriptoribus sua quedam ac propria sit dicendi figura*; chap. 14). Bruni goes on to list Aristotle's stylistic traits, marveling at one point that "a philosopher, in the midst of the subtlest discussion, should take such care for the way he wrote" (chap. 24): he is full of ornaments, elegance, and dignity. Philosophy thus becomes indistinguishable from style, as the *way* one writes becomes just as important as *what* one writes, and the pilfering of antiquity for presentiments of the Christian revelation a misguided and misleading occupation. In so focusing on style, on what he calls the "*vim ac naturam verborum*"—the force and nature of words— Bruni recasts Aristotle and Plato alike as writers and orators. Rescued from the theologians, their words sparkle with the rhetorical and literary efficacy denied them by "barbarous" translators.

As Horace's *Ars poetica* attests, Romans generally felt their civilization to be distinctly secondary to the Hellenic world they had nonetheless vanquished. The cry of Aeneas's father, Anchises, in the sixth book of the *Aeneid* expresses Virgil's sentiment on the matter: "Others, I have no doubt, will forge the bronze to breathe with suppler lines . . . plead their cases better, chart with their rods the stars that climb the sky and foretell the times they rise" (6:976–80; Robert Fagles's translation); the Romans could excel in the art of government alone. Translate everything! is Bruni's response. In reveling over the "force and nature" of the Latin language, he turns Greek philosophy into Latin oratory and poetry, setting Plato and Aristotle alongside Sallust, Livy, and Cicero. It is thus through the act of translation that one recognizes the philosopher as an artist, an orator, a "stylist." Far from being diminished with respect to his status as a *philosophe*, Aristotle gains something, as the discourse of philosophy is considerably broadened, no longer prey to the clutches of theologians. Philosophy once again becomes powerfully transformative, as it had been with Plato, prompting its readers to reflect on how they live and how they speak. One is reminded that for Bruni translation itself is a transformative act, as the translator transforms himself into the author and the author's words are transformed into the translator's tongue. Bruni

closed the preface to his translation of Saint Basil's letter to his nephews with "*Et iam Basilium ipsum audiamus*" (and now let us listen to Basil himself), as though Basil himself stood before us and the translator had vanished. Except it is a Basil—one who wisely counsels his nephews to read the great works of pagan, Greek philosophy—who speaks in Latin.

Is not this dictionary, with its inclusion of "poetic" terms such as *sprezzatura* and *leggiadria*, "strength," "to stand," and thus terms from texts that are only marginally "philosophical" in the strictest sense, also a transformation of philosophical language into something broader: a way of speaking, or even a way of life? A philosophy for nonphilosophers?

Jane Tylus

BIBLIOGRAPHY

Bruni, Leonardo. *Sulla perfetta traduzione*. Translated and edited by Paolo Viti. Naples: Ligouri, 2004. Translation by James Hankins: *On Correct Translation*. In *The Humanism of Leonardo Bruni*, translated by Gordon Griffiths, James Hankins, and David Thompson. Binghamton, NY: Medieval and Renaissance Texts and Studies, 1987.

Sabbadini, Remigio. "Del tradurre i classici antichi in Italia." *Atene e Roma* 3 (1900): 201–17.

Virgil. *The Aeneid*. Translated by Robert Fagles. New York: Penguin, 2006.

BIBLIOGRAPHY

Aristotle. *De interpretatione*. Edited by Richard McKeon. In *The Basic Works of Aristotle*. New York: Random House, 2001.

Ashworth, Jenny. "Signification and Modes of Signifying in Thirteenth-Century Logic: A Preface to Aquinas on Analogy." *Medieval Philosophy and Theology* 1 (1991): 39–67.

Augustine, Saint. *On Christian Teaching*. Translated by R.P.H. Green. Oxford: Oxford University Press, 1999.

Benjamin, Walter. "Die Aufgabe des Übersetzers." In Vol. 2.1 of *Gesammelte Schriften*, edited by Rolf Tiedemann and Hermann Schweppenhäuser. Frankfurt: Suhrkamp Taschenbuch Wissenschaft. Translation: "The Task of the Translator." In vol. 1 of *Selected Writings*, translated by Marcus Bullock and Michael W. Jennings. Cambridge, MA: Harvard University Press / Belknap Press, 1996.

Berman, Antoine. *The Experience of the Foreign: Culture and Translation in Romantic Germany*. Translated by S. Heyvaert. Albany: State University of New York Press, 1992.

———. *La traduction et la lettre, ou, L'auberge du lointain*. Paris: Éditions du Seuil, 1999.

Bernofsky, Susan. *Foreign Words: Translator-Authors in the Age of Goethe*. Detroit, MI: Wayne State University Press, 2005.

Buridant, Claude. "Les paramètres de l'étymologie médiévale." *Lexique* 14 (1998): 11–56.

Cassin, Barbara. *Aristote et le logos*. Paris: Presses Universitaires de France, 1997.

———. *L'effet sophistique*. Paris: Gallimard, 1995.

———. "Le statut théorique de l'intraduisible." In Vol. 4 of *Encyclopédie philosophique universelle*, edited by J.-F. Mattéi, 998–1013. Paris: Presses Universitaires de France, 1998.

Cicero, Marcus Tullius. *Brutus, On the Nature of the Gods, On Divination, On Duties*. Translated by Hubert M. Poteat, with an introduction by Richard McKeon. Chicago: University of Chicago Press, 1950.

———. *On Academic Scepticism*. Translated with introduction and notes by Charles Brittain. Indianapolis, IN: Hackett, 2006.

———. *On Moral Ends*. Edited by Julia Annas, translated by Raphael Woolf. Cambridge: Cambridge University Press, 2001.

———. *On the Ideal Orator*. Translated by James M. May and Jakob Wisse. New York: Oxford University Press, 2001.

———. *Tusculan Disputations*. Translated by J. E. King. Cambridge, MA: Harvard University Press, 1945.

Dahan, Gilbert. *L'exégèse chrétienne de la Bible en Occident médiéval, XIIe-XIVe siècle*. Paris: Éditions du Cerf, 1999.

———. "Saint Thomas d'Aquin et la métaphore: Rhétorique et herméneutique." *Medioevo* 18 (1992): 85–117.

Dahan, Gilbert, Irène Rosier, and Luisa Valente. "L'arabe, l'hébreu, le grec et les vernaculaires." In *Sprachtheorien in Spätantike und Mittelalter*, edited by Sten Ebbesen, 184–206. Tübingen: Gunter Narr, 1995.

Davis, Paul. *Translation and the Poet's Life: The Ethics of Translating in English Culture, 1646–1726*. Oxford: Oxford University Press, 2008.

Duckworth, George, ed. *The Complete Roman Drama: All the Extant Comedies of Plautus and Terence, and the Tragedies of Seneca*. New York: Random House, 1942.

Escoubas, Éliane. "De la traduction comme 'origine' des langues: Heidegger et Benjamin." *Les Temps Modernes* 514–515 (May-June 1989): 97–142.

Eusebius of Caesarea. *Lettre d'Aristote à Philocrate*. Translated into French by A. Pelletier. Paris: Éditions du Cerf, 1962.

———. *Preparation for the Gospel*. Translated from a revised text by Edwin Hamilton Gifford. Oxford: Clarendon Press, 1903.

Fichte, Johann G. *Fichtes Werke*. 11 vols. Edited by Immanuel H. Fichte. Berlin: De Gruyter, 1971.

Gadamer, Hans-Georg. *Langage et verité*. Translated by Jean-Claude Gens. Paris: Gallimard, 1995.

———. *Philosophical Hermeneutics*. Translated by David E. Linge. Berkeley: University of California Press, 2008.

———. *Truth and Method*. Translated by Joel Weinsheimer and Donald G. Marshall. 2nd, rev. ed. London: Continuum, 2004.

Hartog, François. *Memories of Odysseus*. Translated by Janet Lloyd. Edinburgh: Edinburgh University Press, 2001.

Heidegger, Martin. *Being and Time*. Translated by John Macquarrie and Edward Robinson. New York: Harper and Row, 1962.

———. *Off the Beaten Track*. Edited and translated by Julian Young and Kenneth Haynes. Cambridge: Cambridge University Press, 2002.

———. *Parmenides*. Translated by André Schuwer and Richard Rojcewicz. Bloomington: Indiana University Press, 1992.

———. *The Principle of Reason*. Translated by Reginald Lilly. Bloomington: Indiana University Press, 1991.

———. *Qu'est-ce que la métaphysique?* Translated by Henri Corbin. Paris: Gallimard, 1938.

Hunt, Richard William. "The 'Lost' Preface to the *Liber derivationum* of Osbern of Gloucester." In *Collected Papers on the History of Grammar in the Middle Ages*, by Richard Hunt, edited by G. L. Busill-Hall, 145–50. Amsterdam: Benjamins, 1980.

Jerome, Saint. *The Letters of St. Jerome*. Translated by Charles Christopher Mierow, introduction and notes by Thomas Comerford Lawler. New York: Newman Press, 1963.

Kant, Immanuel. *Religion within the Boundaries of Mere Reason and Other Writings*. Translated by Allen Wood. Cambridge: Cambridge University Press, 1999.

Kirk, Robert. *Translation Determined*. Oxford: Clarendon Press, 1986.

Klinck, Roswitha. *Die lateinische Etymologie des Mittelalters*. Munich: W. Fink, 1970.

Koselleck, Reinhart. *Futures Past: On the Semantics of Historical Time*. Translated by Keith Tribe. Cambridge, MA: MIT Press, 1985.

Lefevre, André, ed. *Translating Literature: The German Tradition from Luther to Rosenzweig*. Assen, Neth.: Van Gorcum, 1977.

Libera, Alain de. "Logique et théologie dans la summa 'quoniam homines' d'Alain de Lille." In *Gilbert de Poitiers et ses contemporains*, edited by J. Jolivet and A. de Libera, 437–69. Naples: Bibliopolis, 1987.

Lusignan, Serge. *Parler vulgairement: Les intellectuels et la langue française aux xiiie et xive siècles*. 2nd ed. Paris: Vrin; Montréal: Presses de l'Université de Montréal, 1987.

Luther, Martin. "Ein Sendbrief D. M. Luthers. Von Dolmetzschen und Fürbit der heiligenn." In vol. 30, pt. 2 of *Dr. Martin Luthers Werke*. Weimar: Hermann Boehlaus Nachfolger, 1909. Translation: "An Open Letter on Translating (1530)." In vol. 35 of *Luther's Works*. 55 vols. St. Louis: Concordia Publishing House; Philadelphia: Fortress Press, 1960.

Momigliano, Arnaldo. *Sagesses barbares*. Paris: Gallimard, 1991.

Nietzsche, Friedrich. "Über Wahrheit und Lüge im aussermoralischen Sinne." In vol. 1 of *Kritische Studienausgabe*, edited by Giorgio Colli and Mazzino Montinari, 873–890. Berlin: De Gruyter, 1967–. Translation by Ladislaus Löb: "On Truth and Lie in an Extra-Moral Sense." In *Nietzsche: Writings from the Early Notebooks*, edited by Raymond Geuss and Alexander Nehamas. Cambridge: Cambridge University Press, 2009.

Philo of Alexandria. *The Works of Philo: Complete and Unabridged*, translated by C. D. Yonge. Peabody, MA: Hendrickson, 1993.

Plato. *Cratylus*. Translated by Benjamin Jowett. In *The Collected Dialogues of Plato*, edited by Edith Hamilton and Huntington Cairns. Princeton, N.J.: Princeton University Press, 1989. Translation by Catherine Dalimier: *Cratyle*. Paris: Garnier Flammarion, 1998.

———. *Meno*. Translated by W.K.C. Guthrie. In *The Collected Dialogues of Plato*, edited by Edith Hamilton and Huntington Cairns. Princeton, N.J.: Princeton University Press, 1989.

———. *Protagoras*. Translated by W.K.C. Guthrie. In *The Collected Dialogues of Plato*, edited by Edith Hamilton and Huntington Cairns. Princeton, N.J.: Princeton University Press, 1989.

———. *The Timaeus, and the Critias, or Atlanticus*. Translated by Thomas Taylor. 3rd ed. Princeton, N.J.: Princeton University Press, 1968.

Plutarch. *Fall of the Roman Republic: Marius, Sulla, Crassus, Pompey, Caesar, Cicero: Six Lives*. Translated by Rex Warner. Rev. ed. New York: Penguin, 1972.

Rochlitz, Rainer. "Le traduisible et l'intraduisible." In vol. 4 of *Encyclopédie philosophique universelle*, edited by J.-F. Mattéi, 1013–27. Paris: Presses Universitaires de France, 1998.

Rosier, Irène. "La grammatica practica du ms. British Museum V A IV. Roger Bacon, les lexicographes et l'étymologie." *Lexique* 14 (1998): 97–125.

———. "Prata rident." In *Langages et philosophie: Hommage à Jean Jolivet*, edited by A. de Libera, A. Elamrani-Jamal, and A. Galonnier, 155–76. Paris: Vrin, 1997.

———. "Quelques textes sur l'étymologie au Moyen Âge." *Lexique* 14 (1998): 221–29.

———. "Res significata et modus significandi. Les enjeux linguistiques et théologiques d'une distinction médiévale." In *Sprachtheorien in Spätantike und Mittelalter*, edited by Sten Ebeesen, 135–68. Tübingen: Gunter Narr, 1995.

Schlegel, Friedrich. *Kritische Friedrich-Schlegel Ausgabe*. Edited by E. Behler. Zürich: Schöningh, 1963.

Schleiermacher, Friedrich. "Über die verschiedenen Methoden des Übersetzens." In vol. 2, pt. 3 of *Friedrich Schleiermacher's sämmtliche Werke*, 207–45. Berlin: Reimer, 1838. Translation by André Lefevre: "On the Different Methods of Translating." In *Translating Literature: The German Tradition from Luther to Rosenzweig*, edited and translated by André Lefevre, 67–89. Assen, Neth.: Van Gorcum, 1977.

Seneca. *Seneca's Letters to Lucilius*. 2 vols. Translated by E. Phillips Barker. Oxford: Clarendon Press, 1932.

Sextus Empiricus. *Adversus mathematicos*. In *Esquisses Pyrrhoniennes*, translated by Pierre Pellegrin. Paris: Seuil-Points, 1997. Translation by R. G. Bury: *Outlines of Pyrrhonism*. Cambridge, MA: Harvard University Press, 1933.

Terence. *The Eunuch*. In *The Complete Comedies of Terence: Modern Verse Translations*. Translated by Palmer Bovie, Constance Carrier, and Douglass Parker. Edited and with a foreword by Palmer Bovie. New Brunswick, NJ: Rutgers University Press, 1974.

TORAH [תּוֹרָה] (HEBREW) / ŠARĪ'A [الشريعة] (ARABIC)

ENGLISH	law
FRENCH	*loi*
GERMAN	*Gesetz*
GREEK	*nomos* [νόμος]
LATIN	*lex*

➤ LAW [LEX], and *DESTINY, DUTY, EUROPE, GOD, SOLLEN, THEMIS, TO TRANSLATE, WILLKÜR*

In European philosophical discussion, the word "law," as it is developed in political philosophy, does not only derive from the Greek philosophers—Plato, Aristotle, the Stoics, Cicero—and the Roman jurists. It also has sources in the Bible, which have been the object of reflection by theologians such as Saint Augustine or Saint Thomas Aquinas. And it is an object for philosophical reflection as well, starting with Machiavelli's project to read the Bible judiciously (*Discourses on Livy*, 3.30), and continuing with Hobbes and Spinoza, right up to Kant. The idea of law comes to modern Europe through Luther's German translations (*Gesetz*) (RT: *Die Bibel nach der Übersetzung Martin Luthers*) or through the Authorized (King James) Version of the Bible. Both occur within a context already set forth by the Greek translation of the Septuagint (*nomos* [νόμος]) and the subsequent Latin translation known as the Vulgate (*lex*), with the focus of the discussion most often set by the value of the "law" in the Epistles of Paul. We shall attempt to explore the intersections of the different vocabularies of the law, starting from the Hebrew and the Arabic.

I. The Hebrew Vocabulary of the Law

In Hebrew, *torah* derives from the root YRH [ירה], which signifies "to throw," and in modern Hebrew, to "fire" with a firearm. It no doubt originally refers to "throws" of chance and their subsequent interpretation as expressions of divine will. The priests are known as the "keepers of the *torah*" (*tōfesëy hat-tōrāh* [תּוֹפְשֵׂי הַתּוֹרָה]; Jer 2:8). It is not a written text, but an oral teaching that applies to the domain of sacerdotal competence: ritual questions about, for example, the pure and the impure (Hg 2:11–13), or what is the appropriate kind of sacrifice to offer (Zec 7:2–3). This teaching is reputed to be given by YHWH himself. Obedience to the priests is required—one should act "according to the *torah* they will teach you (*yōrūḫā* [יורוך]), and according to the judgment (*mišpāṭ* [מִשְׁפָּט]) they will tell you" (Dt 17:11) The law is subsequently replaced during the exodus, thus becoming the Law of Moses, or more exactly, the Law of YHWH (1 Esd 7:10, etc.), transmitted through the intermediary of Moses. The word is subsequently expanded to the five books of the Pentateuch, and thence to the whole of the Bible, including the prophets and books of wisdom. It ends up encompassing the two aspects of the Law: the written Law and the oral Law, which was supposed to have been given in the Sinai. The meaning of "teaching" is taken up in the title of Martin Buber's translation, with Franz Rosenzweig, of the Pentateuch: *Die fünf Bücher der Weisung*. Franz Rosenzweig translates it as *Gesetzeslehre* (doctrine of law) (*Der Stern der Erlösung*, 3.1 §321).

Mitzvah [מִצְוָה] signifies "order, commandment." Initially, the word refers to every sort of injunction, but later comes to designate the precepts, both positive and negative, contained in the Torah. Efforts were made to distinguish them from each other and to enumerate them in an exhaustive manner; explanations were sought to explain all 613 precepts, and special attention was accorded the 365 negative precepts. In its extended sense, *mitzvah* can also designate the action that carries out a commandment, a meritorious action, and in the popular sense, a good deed.

Mišpāṭ comes from the root ŠPṬ [שׁפט], "to judge, to direct." The judgment is pronounced with authority by a director, a *šōfēṭ* [שׁוֹפֵט]—the "judge" in the sense of the book of Judges or "*suffète*," the highest Carthaginian magistrate. From this idea of "sentence" is derived the modern Hebrew meaning of "phrase" as well as the English sentence.

ḤOQ [חֹק] (plural, *huqqim* [חֻקִּים]) comes from the root ḤQQ [חק], "to engrave," from which derives "to inscribe" and then "to prescribe." The Hebrew word is related to the Arabic *ḥaqq* [حَقَّ], "the part that returns," or "truth." It refers to everything that is determinate and fixed. The feminine form *huqqāh* [חֻקָּה] can also designate the regularities of natural processes (Jer 5:24). These two latter terms took on technical meanings in the Talmud. *Mišpāṭ* designates those plausible seeming and easily universalized commandments (those that forbid idolatry, murder, incest, or rape). *Ḥoq*, on the other hand, designates those commandments whose meaning is not apparent (the ban on eating pork, or wearing fabrics that mix animal and vegetable fibers, etc.) (Talmud of Babylon, *Yoma* [VI], 67b). The justification of these latter commandments constitutes a genre of literature to which almost all Jewish thinkers have contributed—and even Christians, who call these commandments "ceremonial." A great variety of methods and arguments are employed: allegory, the idea of a divine condescension adapting itself to the customs of a particular period, a correspondence with celestial reality, a concern for counterbalancing idolatrous practices, etc.

The root HLḤ [הלך], which signifies "to go," was in use since ancient times, but the substantive *halāḫāh* [הֲלָכָה] (halakhah) is not in the Bible. It spells out the rules to follow, whether in practice or only theoretically: first some specific ordering principles, then a general code of conduct to adopt in Jewish life.

II. The Arabic Vocabulary of the Law

The Qur'ān contains few terms that can be translated as "law." Some precepts of legislative value are called "commandments" or "laws of God" (2:183/187 and 229–30; 4:17/13; 58:5/4; 65:1). The word that is used, *ḥadd* [حَدّ] (plural, *ḥudūd* [حدود]), suggests an idea of partition and delimitation, such that philosophers employ it to translate the Greek *horos* [ὅρος], in the sense of "definition." In Muslim law, the word has gained a specialized meaning of "legal punishments": stoning, crucifixion, mutilation, decapitation, flagellation.

Šarī'a [الشريعة] derives from the root ŠR' [ش ر ع], which has been linked to ŠRB, "to drink." The primary meaning is probably "the path leading to a source of water." A Bedouin's life depends on this kind of knowing, and the path that leads to water is the good path par excellence. In the Qur'ān, the verb *šara'a* [شرع] is employed in speaking of a divinity who imposes a code of conduct. Thus: "(Allah) has established [*šara'a*] for you, in matters of religion, what he prescribed to Noah" (42:13; cf. also 21).

A substantive noun, *šir'a* [شرعة], perhaps borrowed from the Ethiopian, indicates the path to follow. Thus: "We have given each of you a rule [*šir'a*] and a custom [*minhāǧ* [منهاج]]" (5:48)—this latter word is itself drawn from rabbinical Hebrew—this is the sense in which the Qur'ān has Allah say: "we placed you on a path proceeding from Order" (*ălā šarī'atin min al-'amri* [على شريعة من الأمر]) (45:18). The *šarī'a* has become the entire system of obligations and prohibitions drawn from a synthesis of the sources of Islamic law, in different proportions according to the main juridical schools (sometimes called "rites"): Qur'ān, traditions relating to the Prophet, customs of Medina, analogy.

The word has become more narrowly specialized to designate a law given by divinity, not a human law. To refer to these laws, philosophers have simply transcribed the Greek *nomos* [νόμος], in the form of *nāmūs* [ناموس] (plural, *nawāmīs* [نواميس]). The word thus serves to "translate" the title of Plato's *Laws*, or to designate apocrypha by the same title. When written in Arabic, medieval Judaism did not hesitate to pick up the word *šarī'a* to refer to Jewish law.

The primary meaning of *sunna* [سنة] (plural, *sunan* [سنن]) is "habit." In the Qur'ān, it refers to the customary behavior of Allah, especially in his punishment of the infidel of the past (8:38, etc.). Even before Islam, the word designated the normative custom, the precedent to refer to in judgment. With the constitution of an Islamic law, it designates the exemplary conduct of Allah, including his companions. *Sunna* can also refer to Allah's "habits." These take the place of the "laws" of nature, rendered unthinkable by the vision of the world of the *Kalām* [كلام] (the word of Allah) in its main current of interpretation, according to which things do not have a stable nature of their own, but are bundles of accidents held together at every instant by divine will alone. It was only later that the word came to refer to that tradition adopted by the main tendency of Islam, those who call themselves the people of the *sunna*, the "Sunnites."

Finally, there is also a series of terms designating the measures taken by governments without relying on religious law:

qānūn [قانون] (plural, *qawānīn* [قوانين]) is none other than the Greek *chanôn* [χανών] "rule"; *niẓām* [نظام] literally signifies "regulation" (Fr., *ordonnance*), and *marsūm* [مرسوم], "decree."

Rémi Brague

BIBLIOGRAPHY

Buber, Martin. *The Martin Buber Reader: Essential Writings*. Edited by Asher D. Biemann. New York: Palgrave Macmillan, 2002.

Buber, Martin, and Franz Rosenzweig. *Die fünf Bücher der Weisung*. Vol. 1 of *Die Schrift*. Cologne: Hegner, 1954–62.

———. *Die Schrift*. Stuttgart: Deutsche Bibelgesellschaft, 1992. Translation by Lawrence Rosenwald with Everett Fox: *Scswripture and Translation*. Bloomington: Indiana University Press, 1994.

Machiavelli, Niccolò. *Discourses on Livy*. Translated with an introduction and notes by Julia Conaway Bondanella and Peter Bondanella. Oxford: Oxford University Press, 1997.

McAuliffe, Jane Dammen. *The Cambridge Companion to the Qur'ān* [قرآن]. Cambridge: Cambridge University Press, 2006.

The Qur'an. Translated by M.A.S. Abdel Haleem. Corrected ed. Oxford: Oxford University Press, 2008.

Rosenzweig, Franz. *Der Stern der Erlösung*. Frankfurt: Suhrkamp Verlag, 1988. First published in 1921. Translation from the second edition of 1930 by William W. Hallo: *The Star of Redemption*. Notre Dame, IN: Notre Dame Press, 1985. First published in 1971.

TROPE

GERMAN   *Moment*

➤ ABSTRACTION, ANALOGY, COMPARISON, CONNOTATION, ESSENCE, IMPLICATION, MOMENT, PROPERTY, SUPPOSITION, UNIVERSALS

In classical language, the word "trope" designates a figure of rhetoric (Lat. *tropus loquendi*). This is the sense understood by Condillac in his *Art d'écrire* (Art of writing) and by Dumarais in his celebrated *Traité des tropes* (Treatise on tropes), VII, 2, when he writes that "one should not think that tropes"—in other words, figurative expressions—"were only invented out of necessity, because of the deficiencies and scarcity of proper names." In logic, the Greek word *tropos* [τρόπος] designates a mode (*modus*) in the sense of modal logic, that is to say, a syncategorematic expression that transforms an utterance into a modal expression, in other words: *necessary, possible, impossible, contingent* (the aletheic modes or "modalities" of *true* and *false* do not give rise to modal expressions). In modern philosophical usage, the word "trope" has a completely different meaning, unrelated to previous ones: it designates a specific instance (Fr. *instance*, Ger. *Einzelfall*) of a property or relation. Introduced in 1953 by the American philosopher D. C. Williams in the sense of the "occurrence of an essence" (in contrast to an earlier use of the term by Santayana as the "essence of an occurrence"), "trope" has become generally understood in contemporary Anglo-Saxon philosophy as the equivalent of the expression "abstract particular" employed by Stout in 1921. In English, "trope" is synonymous with what are called "concrete properties" (Küng, *Ontology and the Logistic Analysis of Language*), "quality instances"/"relation instances" (D. C. Long, "Particulars and Their Qualities"), "unit properties"/"unit relations" (Matthews and Cohen, "The One and the Many"), "quality bits"/"relation bits," "individualized forms," cases or aspects (Wolterstorff, *On Universals*), and "particularized qualities" (Wilson, *Statement and Inference*; Strawson, *Individuals* and *Subject and Predicate in Logic and Grammar*).

Williams's initiative, further extended by K. Campbell, is clearly unfortunate and all the more inexplicable in that the word "trope," in English just as in French, refers to a figure of speech. But today it would be impossible to go against this usage, given the currency of the expression in the philosophical literature. The only exception is in German, with the term *Moment*, which was introduced by Husserl in the mereological analysis of the notions of ontological dependence and independence (*Logical Investigations*, III), and which referred to the sense of "dependent part," as employed by B. Smith or K. Mulligan. With the ambiguity of the French meaning of *moment* added to the ambiguities in German, the substitution of this saturated term for the Franco-English "trope" fails to provide any decisive advantages. The reader of Husserl should still keep in mind that the Husserlian *moments* correspond to the "tropes" of Williams and Campbell.

I. Concrete Particular/Abstract Particular

In the theory advanced by Williams, tropes are "the first constituents of the real world or of any possible worlds": they are "the very alphabet of being." According to this analysis, Socrates is a concrete particular; the wisdom of Socrates—a "component" of Socrates—is an abstract particular, or "trope." The general wisdom of which any particular wisdom is a component or member forms an abstract universal. All creatures exactly identical with Socrates are part of or members of an abstract universal of a total "Socrateity" or "Socratesity." Humanity as a universal is not the class of concrete human beings, but abstract humanities. That is to say, it is not a class whose members are Socrates, Plato, and so on, but of the human trope within Socrates, the human trope in Plato, and so on. According to Williams, an individual is thus defined as a "sum of concurrent" or "co-present" tropes, that is to say, the wisdom of Socrates as a trope belongs to the "class of resemblance" of Wisdom. The proposition "Socrates is wise" [a est φ] thus signifies that the sum of tropes "concurrent to Socrates" includes a trope that is a member of the trope of "resembling wisdom." The relation of "concurrence," inherited from Whitehead and Keynes, corresponds to Russel's "compresence," Mill's "coinherence," Stout's "concrescence," and Goodman's "togetherness," and it is the "limit value" of localization; the relation of "precise or exact resemblance"; the "limit value" of resemblance traditionally known as "identity." The distinction between abstract universal and concrete universal allows the clear expression of the difference between instantiation and exemplification: Socrates is a concrete "instance" of Wisdom. The component wisdom is an "abstract" instance (= exemplification) of Wisdom. In the current theory of tropes, trope bundle theory individuals are considered as "bundles of tropes," "co-presence" and "exact resemblance" as second-order "bundling relations," and the notions of "individual," "particulars," and "universals" all follow Williams's mode of definition, using the notions of "compresence classes of tropes" and "similarity classes of tropes." The definition of an individual as a "mereological sum of a class of compresent tropes," set forth by Williams in 1953, has been the object of various critiques. The most widespread of these consists in claiming that a "class of compresence" cannot account for the individuality of an object, because as Martin puts it in "Substance Substantiated": "An object is not collectable out of its properties or qualities as a crowd is collectible out of its members."

According to Armstrong, every theory of tropes makes claims to the state of affairs (see SACHVERHALT): "States of affairs are required as part of the ontology of any trope theory."

II. A Loaded Genealogy

D. W. Mertz has proposed a genealogy of the notion of tropes going back to Plato, Aristotle, Boethius, Avicenna, Averroës, Thomas of Aquinas, Duns Scottius, Buridan, Suárez, Leibnitz, and Russel (in his early writings). This overview can be further specified—as far as Buridan (and Ockham) are concerned—by a certain interpretation of the distinction between absolute terms and connotative terms (see CONNOTATION). For Buridan, in fact, a term like "album" (a concrete accidental term according to common terminological usage) presupposes an individual, a singular composite of substance-quality, and connotes a singular quality that is "adjacent." A specific white, this white here, has all the characteristics that one expects from a trope. In the first sophism of chapter 4 of the *Sophismata*, Buridan specifically discusses the proposition that "Socrates and [this] white are the same thing," a *sophisma* that he proves thus: if he points to Socrates with his finger, it is true to say that "this is Socrates" and the same holds for "this same thing [*hoc idem*] is [this] white," thus "Socrates and [this] white are the same thing." This sentence makes it clearly understood that this white and Socrates, the individual possessing the same whiteness, are the same thing "by virtue of the "identity of reference" between "this is Socrates" and "this same thing is [this] white"— which Buridan calls *material termini*. Once he establishes the identity of Socrates and this white, that is to say, "once posited that Socrates *is* the same thing as [this] white," he goes so far as to infer, "by virtue of the matter" (= supposition, in opposition to the *forma termini* = connotation), that both "Socrates and this white exist . . . and even that they are beings, since Socrates consists of beings—given that he is made up of parts." In addition to this mereological of the individual (made up entirely of a substance and tropes), we can also add that the notion of "bundle" is present in the porphyrian idea of "gathering up proper characters" (*athroisma idiotêtôn* [ἄθροισμα ἰδιοτήτων]) referred to in the *Isagoge* to determine what makes an individual an individual. To state what constitutes the particular substance (literally, "the property of the subsistence") of an individual, the *Commentary on Categories* of Simplicius employs the expression *sundromê sumbebêkotôn* [συνδρομή συμβεβηκότων], "syndrome of accidents"— *concursus accidentium* in the Latin translation of Guillaume de Moerbeke. The source of Simplicius's theory is the porphyrian one, which integrates the Stoic "individual quality" (*idiôs poion* [ἰδίως ποιόν]) and Aristotle's ontological schema of subject-object, with the aid of the notions of "concurrence" (Fr. *concours*) (*sundromê* [συνδρομή]) and "description" (*hupographê* [ὑπογραφή]). The porphyrian and Simplician theory of the "syndrome of qualities" (*sundromê poiotêtôn* [συνδρομή ποιοτήτων]) is a mixture combining what D. M. Armstrong called the "substance-attribute view" with a "bundle theory" (these being, according to him, the two main types of theories of tropes); nonetheless, the properties that enter into the "syndrome" are not tropes, that is, abstract particulars, but

"common" properties. In this sort of theory, it is the bundling (Fr. *rassemblement*) that is particular, not what is bundled. The individual is first and foremost a primary substance in the Aristotelian sense of the term, constituted by an essential form, added to which is a "bundle of individualizing qualities," an object of "description."

In the twelfth century, Abelard will maintain that there are as many determinate species within the animal genre as there are different particular forms of rationality. By reducing the properties in common to differences all predicated on the species *de voce*, Abelard considers the specific differences of the sort that establish *de re* the singularity of individuals to be attributed to the name of the species. If the species seems to admit "bundled particulars," its ontology does not go so far as to define an individual as a "bundle of compresent particulars." Instead, it rejects the thesis claimed by "some" that (1) this particular man is not the result of accidents, whereas Socrates is; and (2) Socrates is the product of the ensemble of accidental properties not as a man, but as Socrates. Abelard mentions three versions of this theory, depending on whether the name "Socrates" is considered to designate all the accidental properties of Socrates, be they separable or inseparable, or only those accidental properties that are inseparable from Socrates, or only the "proper form" of the accidental properties of Socrates, which are called "Socraticity." Some maintain that all the accidental properties of Socrates, both separable and inseparable, are included in the name "Socrates," but that this name was "imposed" in such a way that whenever it is invoked, "Socrates" refers to all the accidental properties that Socrates possesses at that moment. Thus the meaning of "Socrates" "varies quite often," depending on the variability of accidental properties of Socrates. Abelard indicates that the adherents of this latter variant call the complete collection of the accidental properties of Socrates "Socraticity." For them, "Socraticity" is not a "single fact of nature," but a "composite individual." This medieval formulation of the doctrine of *individuum compositum* is no doubt the closest to the tropic theory of individuation.

Alain de Libera

BIBLIOGRAPHY

Abelard, Peter. "Glosses on Porphyry from His Logica 'ingredientibus.'" In *Five Texts on the Mediaeval Problem of Universals*. Indianapolis, IN: Hackett, 1994.
———. *Logica "ingredientibus."* In *Peter Abaelards philsophische schriften*. Edited by B. Geyer. Münster, Ger.: Aschendorff, 1919–27.
Armstrong, David M. *Universals: An Opinionated Introduction*. Boulder, CO: Westview Press, 1989.
Buridan, Jean. *Sophisms on Meaning and Truth* [Sophismata]. Translated by Theodore Kermit Scott. New York: Appleton-Century-Crofts, 1966.
Campbell, Keith. *Abstract Particulars*. Oxford: Blackwell, 1990.
———. *Logical Investigations*. Translated by J. N. Findlay. London: Routledge and Kegan Paul, 1970.
Chrudzimski, Arkadiusz. "Two Concepts of Trope." *Grazer philosophische Studien* 64 (2004): 137–55.
Küng, Guido. *Ontology and the Logistic Analysis of Language*. Dordrecht, Neth.: Reidel, 1967.
Long, D. C. "Particulars and Their Qualities." In *Universals and Particulars*, edited by M. J. Loux, 310–30. Notre Dame, IN: Notre Dame University Press, 1976.
Martin, Christopher B. "Substance Substantiated." *Australasian Journal of Philosophy* 58 (1980): 3–10.

Matthews, Gareth B. and Marc S. Cohen. "The One and the Many." *Review of Meta-physics* 21, no. 4 (June 1968): 630–55.

Maurin, A-S. *If Tropes*. Dordrecht, Neth.: Kluwer Academic Publishers, 2002.

Mertz, Donald W. *Moderate Realism and Its Logic*. New Haven, CT: Yale University Press, 1996.

Mulligan, Kevin, Peter Simons, and Barry Smith. "Truthmaker." *Philosophy and Phenomenological Research* 44 (1984): 287–321.

Simons, Peer. "Particulars in Particular Clothing: Three Trope Theories of Substance." *Philosophy and Phenomenological Research* 54 (1994): 553–75.

Smith, Barry, ed. *Parts and Moments: Studies in Logic and Formal Ontology*. Munich: Philosophia Verlag, 1982.

Stout, George Frederick. "The Nature of Universals and Propositions." In *The Problem of Universals*, edited by C. Landesman, 154–66. New York: Basic Books, 1971.

———. "Are the Characteristics of Particular Things Universal or Particular?" In *The Problem of Universals*, edited by C. Landesman, 178–83. New York: Basic Books, 1971.

Strawson, Peter F. *Individuals: An Essay in Descriptive Metaphysics*. London: Methuen, 1959.

———. *Subject and Predicate in Logic and Grammar*. London: Methuen, 1974.

Williams, D. C. "The Elements of Being." *Review of Metaphysics* 7 (1953): 3–18, 171–92.

———. "Of Essence and Existence and Santayana." *Journal of Philosophy* 51 (1953): 31–42.

Wilson, John Cook. *Statement and Inference, with Other Philosophical Papers*. 2 vols. Oxford: Clarendon Press, 1926.

Wolterstorff, N. *On Universals*. Chicago: University of Chicago Press, 1970.

▌TRUTH

FRENCH	*vérité*
GERMAN	*Wahrheit*
GREEK	*alêtheia* [ἀλήθεια], *orthotês* [ὀρθότης]
HEBREW	*ʾèmèt* [אֱמֶת], *ʾèmūnāh* [אֱמוּנָה]
LATIN	*veritas, adaequatio, aequalitas, concordia, convenientia*
RUSSIAN	*istina* [истина], *pravda* [правда]

➤ ISTINA, PRAVDA and *APPEARANCE*, BELIEF, DOXA, DUTY, EREIGNIS, *FALSE*, *FICTION*, HISTORY, *IMAGE*, IMPLICATION, *INTUITION*, *LIE*, LOGOS, MEMORY, MIMÊSIS, OBJECT, PREDICATION, PROPERTY, PROPOSITION, SACHVERHALT, SENSE, SUBJECT, *TO BE*

The European languages generally have only one word for "truth," with the notable exception of Russian, which distinguishes *istina* [истина] (which designates truth in its ontological and epistemological relation to being) and *pravda* [правда] (which is also translated as "truth" but which includes a notion of "justice") to designate truth as that which ought to be. These different terms (truth, *Wahrheit*, *vérité*, etc.) pose no significant problems of translation insofar as their semantic scope is more or less coextensive: they all carry a similar charge of signification that is simultaneously ontological, gnosiological, logical, and moral. These different languages have all incorporated a similar development of the notion of truth, first by freeing it from its initial poetic, religious, and juridical context, then by constituting it as a concept of philosophy, and subsequently by carrying it over to the field of science. After several centuries of this shared history, a generally agreed-upon definition has emerged: of truth as a "correspondence" between a thing and the mind, or *adaequatio rei et intellectus*. And yet our tradition is in this case particularly composite and heterogenous: three principal paradigms coexist within it, each of which can be traced separately through its etymology and semantics. The Hebrew paradigm *ʾèmèt* [אֱמֶת] is theological/juridical; it signifies "solid, durable, stable" based on faith

in the alliance between human beings and God and confidence in its promise, which makes the term semantically analogous to the English "truth." The Greek paradigm *alêtheia* [ἀλήθεια] constructs truth as an elimination of the hidden, of the forgotten (*alpha* privative, then *lanthanô* [λανθάνω], which signifies "being hidden" and at times "forgetting"—which is why Martin Heidegger constantly renders *alêtheia* as *Unverborgenheit*, "unconcealment"). The Latin paradigm *veritas*, which is the determining one for most modern vernacular languages, is normative: it designates the correct and the proper foundation of the rule; it is a juridical truth that "locks up" (Fr. *verrouille*—the etymological relationship is sometimes considered), that "guards" and "conserves" (like *Wahrheit*, based on *wahren* in German) a legitimate institution. These three paradigms do not necessarily exist in isolation from each other: thus the tradition of the New Testament, linked to the translations of the Bible, ties together the meanings of *ʾèmèt*, *alêtheia*, and *veritas* in truth understood as divine self-revelation, with the arrival of God the Son fulfilling the promise of the Father, in the institution of the church. But the differences between the three paradigms, forged in prephilosophical times but inherited by the philosophical treatment of truth, still give "truth" an analogical character that is often underestimated and enable us to illuminate some of its antinomies or instabilities.

I. The Different Paradigms

According to Pavel Florensky, who was one of the first to undertake a comparison of the paradigms of truth, *ʾèmèt* [אֱמֶת] is the imprescriptable promise of God. It is a "historical" notion that derives from theocracy; as for the truth of orthodoxy (*istina* [истина]), it is ontological, while *alêtheia* [ἀλήθεια] is gnosiological, and *veritas* is juridical. Nonetheless, according to the orthodox theologian, these notions can be conjugated as pairs:

> The Russian *istina* and the Hebrew *ʾèmèt* refer primarily to the divine content of truth, while the Greek *alêtheia* and the Latin *veritas* refer to its human form. On the other hand, the Russian and Greek terms have a philosophical character, while the Latin and Hebrew terms have a sociological character . . . in the Russian and Greek understanding, truth has an immediate relation to every person, whereas for the Romans and Hebrews, it is mediated by society.
>
> (Florensky, *Pillar and Ground*)

These observations, with their occasionally summary and cavalier formulations, call for further exploration.

A. *ʾÈmèt* and *ʾèmūnāh*

The Hebrew root ʾMN [אמן], the direct source of the exclamation *Amen!*, which has passed into all the Western liturgies, also yields two related words: *ʾèmūnāh* [אֱמוּנָה] and *ʾèmèt* (from **am(i)nt*). It is this latter word that the Septuagint most often rendered by *alêtheia*, "truth." The primary meaning of the Hebrew root seems to be "solid," not so much in a concrete sense of "hard" or "resistant," but more in the sense of "durable, stable"—with the temporal dimension of something one can count on into the future, like the German word *zuverlässig*. If one "plants a stake in a *nèʾèmān* [נֶאֱמָן] place" (Isa. 22:23), one can count on its still being there when one comes back. To he who "lives in heights, whose residence is a rocky fortress, his bread is given, his water is sure [*nè'ĕmānīm* (נֶאֱמָנִים)]" (Isa. 33:16): his shelter and sustenance are assured (cf. Jer. 15:18b). A *nè'ĕmān* illness is persistent, chronic (Deut. 28:59).

'*Ĕmèt* qualifies as that which will definitely occur in the future: a sure sign (Josh. 2:12), a leavening sure to rise (Jer. 2:21), a sure reward (Prov. 11:18). The travels of the servant that Abraham charged to get a wife for his son Isaac turns out to have been "a path of '*ĕmèt*" (Gen. 24:48) because God ensured that it ended in success (ibid. 24:21, 40:56). The "truth" in question has less to do with the adequacy of a representation than with the satisfaction of an expectation. It is not so much something beyond time as a guarantee of continuity beyond the distance it introduces. It is on the basis of this fundamental meaning that one can understand others such as "security," associated with "peace," or rather "integrity" (*šalōm* [שָׁלוֹם]) (Isa. 39:8; Jer. 33:6, etc.); the word can even take on the supposedly "Greek" meaning of correspondence between an account and reality (Gen. 42:16; Deut. 13:15, etc.).

The God of Israel is a historical god: at first, perhaps, a nomadic god living in a portable tent, then the god who marches at the head of his people—for example, to bring his people out of the Egyptian captivity—and who promises his help in alliance with them. He manifests himself as the one who can be relied on at any moment—this is perhaps the meaning of the famous self-definition: "I am / will be who I am / will be" (Exod. 3:14; see I/ME/MYSELF). He keeps his promises and is a sort of "God of truth" (Ps. 31:6). YHWH presents himself as rich in '*ĕmèt* (Exod. 34:6).

Another word that derives from the same root, '*ĕmūnāh*, has meanings similar to '*ĕmèt*, including that concrete sense of "firmness" that is said for example of Moses's hands in prayer (Exod. 17:12). It refers above all to the attitude that is worthy of confidence: the seriousness of someone who can be counted on, a conscientious attitude, honesty. Fidelity is first and foremost the faithfulness of God, who keeps his promises. The word is normally translated into Greek by *pistis* [πίστις], except in the psalms. In the Bible the word only rarely has the meaning of "faith of human beings in God" and not as something that is held as true but as something that one can lean on with confidence, that one can consider worthy of faith. Actually, this is only the case in one verse, but what a verse! The "just man who will live by his faith" [*bè-'ĕmūnātō* (בֶּאֱמוּנָתוֹ)] (Hab. 2:4) is placed at the very heart of Saint Paul—*ho dikaios ek pisteôs zêsetai* [ὁ δίκαιος ἐκ πίστεως ζήσεται]—as the opposing alternative to the law (Gal. 3:11, and cf. Rom. 1:17) and is subsequently inflected by Luther as the expression of the *sola fide*.

It is in playing on the meanings of the root 'MN that Isaiah can write: "If you do not have confidence [*ta'amīnū* (תַאֲמִינוּ)], you will not be able to hold on [*tē'āmēnū* (תֵאָמֵנוּ)]," which is first of all an invitation to maintain morale. The Vulgate (*credideritis . . . permanebitis*), Luther's (*gläubet . . . bleibet*), the Authorized Version ("believe . . . be established"), all remain literal. But the Septuagint (*pisteusête . . . sunête* [πιστεύσητε . . . συνῆτε]), followed by the *vetus Latina* (*credideritis . . . intelligetis*), enable the link between "believing" and "understanding." This gives a scriptural foundation to the dialectic of *fides* and *intellectus*—believing in order to

understand, understanding in order to know—that starts with Saint Anselm (*Cur Deus homo*, Dedication; *De l'incarnation du Verbe*, 1, PL, v. 158, col. 263d–264c) and extends to Hegel and beyond.

B. *Alêtheia*

1. Etymologies and synonyms: A position of enunciative strategy

The adjective *alêthes* [ἀληθής] appears earlier than the substantive; it is constituted by the negative particle *a*- and *lêthos* [λῆθος], *lathos* [λᾶθος], "escape from detection," and much later (in modern Greek) as "error," or *lêthe* [λήθη], "forgetting." When one looks for *alêthes*, "true," in Chantraine (RT: *Dictionnaire étymologique de la langue grecque*), one is also referred to *lanthanô* [λανθάνω], which signifies "remaining hidden," and even "forgetting." The *Odyssey* is often cited, when Odysseus, listening to the *Iliad* at Alcinous's palace, registered the bard "singing the famous deeds of fighting heroes" and "buried his handsome face, ashamed that his hosts might see him shedding tears [*enth' allous men pantas elanthane dakrua leibôn* (ἔνθ' ἄλλους μὲν πάντας ἐλάνθανε δάκρυα λείβων)]" (*Odyssey* 8:93); see MEMORY). *Lêthê* is a sister to Pain, Famine, and Suffering, and along with Lies and Falsehoods (*Pseudeas Logous* [Ψευδέας Λόγους]) and False Oaths (*Horkos* [Ὅρκος]), is daughter of Discord and Strife (*Eris* [Ἔρις]) and is considered one of the "children of night" (Hesiod, *Theogony*, v. 227, cf. 210–32). *Alêthês* (true, veridical) is said of "things and events that one does not hide," in opposition to "false" (*pseudês* [ψευδής]) (RT: *Dictionnaire étymologique de la langue grecque*), and thus as well in opposition to that which is "loyal, just, and fair" (*Iliad*, XIII: 433, with the image of the *chernêtis alêthês* [χερνῆτις ἀληθής], the painstaking "working widow," who struggles to properly balance the scales) (Homer, trans. Fagles, 502), and, after Homer, of persons who do not deceive, do not lie, oracles and dreams that come true in other words, everything that is "real and true" as opposed to "appearance" (*philos alêthês* [φίλος ἀληθής], "a true friend," [Euripides, *Oresteia*, Fr. trans. L. Méridier, Les Belles Lettres, "CUF," 1968, 424]).

The privative alpha, which indicates a specific form of negation that implies possibility rather than prohibition, involves a gesture of "de-concealment" (*Unverborgenheit* is the translation that Heidegger adopts; *hors de l'oubli*, "unforgetting," was Mallarmé's way of putting it in *Crise de vers*) that is a noticeable part of its meaning outside of any philosophical context. *Alêtheia* appears in epic narratives and poetry from Homer to Hesiod and Pindar in a manner that evokes the problematic of its construction: *alêthês* refers not to an accurate representation but to a strategy of utterance, in the interplay of the hero and his fame (*doxa* [δόξα]) or the poet with the Muse. In Homer the neuter plural form *alêthês* is placed next to declarative verbs (*alêthea muthêsasthai, agoreuein, eipein* [ἀληθέα μυθήσασθαι, ἀγορεύειν, εἶπειν], *Iliad*, VI: 382, *Odyssey*, III: 254, XIII: 254) to indicate that the questioner's request for information has been satisfied by a well-composed account. It is storytelling and the poetic act that give the hero his heroic character; his glory coincides with the power of his discourse, which triumphs over forgetting. This is what Hannah Arendt characterized in *The Human Condition* as the Greek solution to the fragility of human affairs.

And the privative etymology of *alêtheia* is always available for use in developing an argument. In the *Peri alêtheias* of Antiphon, the sophist and orator of the fifth century BCE (around 480–411), for example, nature is precisely "that which one cannot escape," as opposed to the conventional laws of the city (see *nomos* in THEMIS and LEX), and is thus founded "in truth"—which is why one has an interest in obeying nature, even when one is alone and without witnesses.

> If one breaks the laws of one's city, insofar as one gets away with it [*eian lathêi* (εἰὰν λάθη)] and keeps it out of sight of those who have agreed to the rules, one is free of both shame and punishment; but not if one does not get away [*mê lathôn* (μὴ λάθων)] and is caught. On the other hand, if one does violence to a natural law, even if it remains hidden from men [*lathêi* (λάθη)], the harm is no smaller; and if it becomes known, the harm is no greater. For the harm does not derive from opinion, but from the truth itself [*ou gar dia doxan . . . alla di' alêtheian* (οὐ γὰρ διὰ δόξαν . . . ἀλλὰ δι' ἀλήθειαν)].

> (POxy 1364 + 3647, fr. B, col. II;
> cf. B. Cassin *L'Effet sophistique*, esp. 168–71 and 273–78)

It is important to see that the usage of *alêthês* and of *alêtheia*, unlike our usage of "true" and "truth," does not immediately entail a corresponding real and observable referent. This is clearly the case in the three terms employed by Hesiod in the *Theogony*: *alêthês*, *pseudos* [ψεῦδος], and *etumos* [ἔτυμος]. For it is not *alêthês* but rather *etumos* that is paired with *pseudos*. The *pseudos* is constructed to mimic the "real" (*etumos*), as if it presented and duplicated all the opacity of the real, but not as embodying the "true" (*alêthês*). As Homer puts it to describe the manner in which Odysseus, upon his return to Ithaca, speaks to Penelope when he still does not want her to recognize him (Odyssey, XIX: 203): "*iske . . . homoia* [Gr. text]" (falsehoods all . . . ring of truth; trans. Fagles, XIX: 235–36). And as the Muses say to Hesiod:

> ἴδμεν ψεύδεα πολλὰ λέγειν ἐτύμοισιν ὁμοῖα·
> ἴδμεν δ', εὖτ' ἐθέλωμεν, ἀληθέα γηρύσασθαι.

> (We know how to speak many false things as though they were true; but we know, when we will, to utter true things.)

> (Hesiod, *Theogony*, v. 27–28, in *Homeric Hymns*)

Etumos, *etêtumos* [ἐτήτυμος], and *eteos* [ἐτεός] belong to the same family as the verb *etazô* [ἐτάζω], "examine, test" (which is also related to *hetoimos* [ἕτοιμος], "ready, available, imminent"). From Homer on, *etumos*, which is at the heart of the word "etymology" and supplies its eponymy, is used to indicate the register of the effective real. In Parmenides, *etêtumos*, an expressive elongation of *etumos* (the way "which exists and which is real [*tên d' hôste pelein kai etêtumon einai* (τὴν δ' ὥστε πέλειν καὶ ἐτήτυμον εἶναι)]," VIII: 18) is used to refer to the authenticity and effectiveness of the way of truth guaranteed by the goddess, attached to which is persuasion (*eupeitheos* [εὐπειθέος], I: 29; cf. II: 4); and *eteêi* [ἐτεῇ] will be a term in Democritus used to distinguish the effective reality of atoms and vacuum as opposed to their sense qualities, which are simply conventional, *nomôi* [νόμῳ] (68B 6–10; 9,

117 and 125 DK). One can see that *alêtheia* is not defined as completely separate from the "false" but includes within its condition relations to certain kinds of falsity: "negativity is not isolated, set apart from Being; it is the hem of reality. It is reality's inseparable shadow" (Marcel Detienne, *Masters of Truth*). The art of the ready-voiced Muses whose "words are well-suited" (*artiepeiai* [ἀρτιέπειαι]) (Hesiod, *Theogony*, v. 29) is an art of proper adjustment of words between each other, an art of the very structure of song and of "truth" as linked to the idea of structured rhythm (Hesiod, *Works*, v. 768, in which *alêtheia* designates the proper arrangement of works and days), and this art defines truth in harmony.

Nonetheless, *alêtheia* enters into a great variety of configurations that survive one within another in the practices of exegesis and palimpsest. These relations are unstable and vary between contradictions, external oppositions, or internal splittings, depending on the context, the poetic narrative, or categorical elaboration.

2. A plausible history of Greek truth: From *alêtheia* to *orthotês* and the analysis of propositions

Even today, the debate around the Greek conception of truth is a caricature: either Parmenides, Plato, and Aristotle are timeless Oxford fellows, and we measure their truth by the yardstick of our own, or else it is first and foremost a question of history, of change of scene, of appropriation and interpretation, and their truth astonishes us just as much as it is part of our own construction.

a. Parmenides and the path of co-belonging: the "Open without withdrawal"

Parmenides's *Poem*, written in the fifth century BC, gives the first impetus to what will become philosophy by giving dramatic figuration to the concepts of being and truth (fr. II). In the prologue, written in the manner of the grand epics of Homer and Hesiod, a young hero guided by the gods "travels a road [*hodos* (ὁδός)]"—far indeed does it lie from the steps of men, at the doors of Day and Night. The Goddess Justice (*Dike*; see THEMIS) welcomes him thus:

> χρεὼ δέ σε πάντα πυθέσθαι
> ἠμὲν ἀληθείης εὐπειθέος [εὐκυκλέος Simplicus]
>   ἀτρεμὲς ἦτορ
> ἠδὲ βροτῶν δόξας, ταῖς οὐκ ἔνι πίστις ἀληθής.

> (It is proper that you should learn all things, both the unshaken heart of well-rounded truth, and the opinions of mortals, in which there is no true reliance.)

> (Kirk, Raven, and Schofield, *Presocratic Philosophers*)

Or, with these Heideggerian words (Heidegger chooses the lesson of Simplicius: *eukukleos*):

> Du sollst aber alles erfahren / sowohl der unverborgenheit, der gutgegrundeten nichtzitterndes Herz / als auch der sterblichen Dafürhalten, dem fehlt das Vertrauenkönnen auf unverborgenes.

> (Heidegger, *Gesamtausgabe*, vol. 14)

> (But you should learn all: / the untrembling heart of unconcealment, well-rounded / and also the

opinion of mortals / who lack the ability to trust what is unconcealed.)

(Heidegger, "End of Philosophy")

Or else, in these more traditionally exact words:

You should be learned in all
Both of the untrembling heart of well-persuasive truth
And of what appears to mortals, where there is no true belief.

(Cassin, *Parmenides*)

Heidegger's translation seeks to convey the way in which being and thought belong to each other in the "clearing" (*Lichtung*; see LIGHT, Box 2), which is *alêtheia*: "It is not for the sake of etymology that I stubbornly translate the name *alêtheia* as "unconcealment" [Ger. *Unverborgenheit*, Fr. trans. J. Beaufret *état de non-retrait*] but for the sake of the matter which must be considered when we think adequately that which is called Being and thinking. Unconcealment is, so to speak, the element in which Being and thinking and their belonging together exist" ("End of Philosophy").

This step backwards in the direction of origin exhibits some of the characteristics of a meditation on immanence, which dismisses any "aiming at truth" from its claims. For one does not aim at *alêtheia*, one follows its path, which brings together the three dimensions of being, thinking, and saying. This triple unity at the heart of *alêtheia* is expressed in fragment II (v. 2 and following) as the relationship between truth and being: "The one that [it] is [*esti* (ἔστι)] and that it is impossible for [it] not to be, is the path of Persuasion (for she attends upon Truth)" (Kirk, Raven, and Schofield, *Presocratic Philosophers*, 291), and in fragment III for the identity between thinking and being: "for the same thing is there both to be thought of [*noein* (νοεῖν), "notice"] and to be" (ibid., 292), and in fragment VI for the identity between saying, thinking, and being: "What is there to be said and thought [*to legein to noein te* (τὸ λέγειν τὸ νοεῖν τε)] must needs be: for it is there for being" (ibid., 293) (these enigmatic textual fragments are par excellence open to being interpreted and translated in different ways).

But one can conclude that it is the Greek language itself that is deployed in and through the *Poem*: we can hear, in fragment after fragment, a subject, "what is" (*to eon* [τὸ ἐόν]), suddenly emerging from the impersonal verb *esti*, "to be," via a certain number of marked forms such as the infinitive and participle. In other words, in *alêtheia* it is a language that reveals and exploits its own structure, and it is to this self-deployment of language, in the narrative account of the road and the voyage, that the very act of ontology is entrusted (see ESTI).

Yet, and this is more legible in the second translation of the prologue,

We must acknowledge the fact that *alêtheia*, unconcealment in the sense of the opening of presence, was originally experienced only as *orthotês*, as the correctness of representations and statement.

(In Gesichtskreis dieser Frage muss anerkannt werden, dass die Alêtheia, die Unverborgenheit im Sinne der

Lichtung von Anwesenheit sogleich und nur als *orthotês*, als die Richtigkeit des Vorstellens und Aussagens erfahren wurde.)

(Heidegger, "*End of Philosophy*," 390)

No less fundamental and "always already," there is the system of opposition that conditions the mutation of *alêtheia*-opening into *veritas*-adequation, that is, the difference between the path of truth and the path of opinion (*brotôn doxai* [βροτῶν δόξαι], "the opinion of mortals," "what appears to mortals"; see DOXA).

b. Plato and the *orthotês* or the correctness of the gaze

Whatever the status of the world of mortals, be it the manifestation of beauty or deceiving confusion, all of Platonic thought and all of subsequent philosophy is structured by Parmenides's distinction between *alêtheia* and *doxa*. For one can or must today detach oneself from one world and aim at another: in the Platonic allegory of the cave, one must turn away from the appearances and opinions of this world that are represented by the projected shadows on the walls ("*tas skias* [τὰς σκιάς]," *Republic*, VII, 515a) and direct one's gaze to objects that are more "true" ("*ta tote horômena alêsthestera / tôn nun legomenôn alêthôn* [τὰ τότε ὁρώμενα ἀληθέστερα / τῶν νῦν λεγομένων ἀληθῶν]," ibid., VII, 515d 7/516a 2), which are the objects that project those shadows, or even leave the cavern to emerge in the full sunlight of "forms" or "ideas" so as to contemplate this new and only authentic "truth," in the sense of intelligibility, which derives from the Idea of the Good ["*autê kuria alêtheian kai noun paraschomenê* (αὐτὴ κυρία ἀλήθειαν καὶ νοῦν παρασχομένη)," ibid., VII, 517c 3; cf. VI, 508e 1–3]. Because of this duplication of worlds into the "world of appearances" and the (*real*) "world of truth" ("*die wahre Welt*" is Nietzsche's term in *Twilight of the Idols*, as in "How the 'true world' finally became a fable"), one must now strive to become a "philosopher," to seek to reach the idea, the very being of the existing through appearance: "outside the cavern, *sophia* is *philosophia*." Heidegger comments that

Everything depends on the *orthotês*, the correctness of the gaze. . . . Thus, the priority of *idea* and of *idein* over *alêtheia* results in a transformation in the essence of truth. Truth becomes *orthotês*, the correctness of apprehending and asserting. . . . As the correctness of the "gaze," it becomes a characteristic of human comportment toward beings.

(Heidegger, *Plato's Doctrine of Truth*, 155–82)

■ See Box 1.

c. Aristotle and adequation

There is no need for the Platonic duality of worlds for truth to become a task to undertake and an objective to attain. All that is required is for *alêtheia* of itself to be no longer thought of as the open paradise of co-belonging or of immanence, if one prefers to call it thus.

If Plato is the proper name of truth as transcendence, Aristotle is the proper name for truth in the modern sense, as the adequacy of utterances. The key text is the beginning of his treatise

1

The accuracy of the names *orthotês* and truth

➤ EIDÔLON, MIMÊSIS

The *Cratylus* is the turning point for a definition of truth as rectitude. In it *orthotês* [ὀρθότης] does not signify correct vision but rather the accuracy of names (*orthotês onamatôn* [ὀρθότης ὀνομάτων]): how one passes from naming to knowing. It hedges the question of the Parmenidian equivalence of saying and being and its unfolding in the sophistical thesis of the impossibility of uttering falsehoods (*Cratylus*, 429d).

The etymological fantasies and play on *alêtheia* break apart their belonging to each other. "It is the divine motion of existence (*hê gar theia tou ontos phora* [ἡ γὰρ θεία τοῦ ὄντος φορὰ]) that seems to be called out by this locution *alê theia* [ἄλη θεία]"; *alê* as wandering is the pure movement of the goddess, and Socrates finds himself becoming Heraclitean: "*on* [ὄν] and *ousia* [οὐσία] are 'ion' with an 'i' broken off; this agrees with the true principle, for being is (on) is also moving (ion)" (trans. by Benjamin Jowett).

The dialogue takes the form of an interrogation on the "correctness" or *orthotês* of names, whether it be, as Hermogenes first believes, that there is no "principle of correctness in names" (*xunthêkê kai homologia* [ξυνθήκη καὶ ὁμολογία]) "other than convention and agreement" (*nomôi kai ethei* [νόμῳ καὶ ἔθει]); or that there is instead a "natural" truth or correctness, which is thus approximately the same for Hellenes as for barbarians (383b), that consists in showing that the correct name indicates the nature of the thing (*onomatos . . . orthotês estin hautê hêtis endeixetai hoion esti to pragma* [ὀνόματος . . . ὀρθότης ἐστὶν αὕτη ἥτις ἐνδείξεται οἷόν ἐστι τὸ πρᾶγμα]) (428e); cf. 433d, and that a name is the representation (*dêlôma* [δήλωμα]) of a thing (433d), such that for Cratylus, logically, all names are correct, "at least, those that are names" (429b). Socrates examines several hypotheses: phonetic mimicry (423a–b), pictorial mimicry, and the ontological deficiencies of the image (beginning at 430b). In 430d, Socrates separates out the case of naming from the portrait, to which only *orthotês* can be applied. Naming requires another mode of assignment, *dianomê* [διανομή], which Socrates compares to the division between "man" and "woman" (431a). Thus

Socrates can introduce "right assignment" (*alêtheuein* [ἀληθεύειν]) and "wrong assignment" (*pseudesthai* [ψεύδεσθαι]) (431b), and as a result there may also be a wrong or inappropriate assignment of names and verbs (*xunthesis* [ξύνθεσις]) and of the sentences (*logoi* [λόγοι]) that are made up of them (431c). At issue is how to know things on the basis of their relations and affiliations (*di' allêlôn ge, ei pêi xungenê estin* [δι' ἀλλήλων γε, εἴ πῃ ξυγγενῆ ἐστιν]) without entering into a problematics of orthology and to show the "truth of what is" (*tên alêtheian tôn ontôn* [τὴν ἀλήθειαν τῶν ὄντων]) (438d–e). So, in the end, Socrates concludes, no matter what the correctness of names, the knowledge of things is not to be derived from names. No, they must be studied and investigated in themselves (*ouk ex onomatôn, alla polu mallon auta ex hautôn* [οὐκ ἐξ ὀνομάτων ἀλλὰ πολὺ μᾶλλον αὐτὰ ἐξ αὐτῶν]) (ibid., 439b). The accuracy of names, unlike correct vision, and despite all the pleasures of etymological play, does not give access to truth.

On Interpretation. Here he distinguishes between "things" (*pragmata* [πράγματα]) and "affections of the soul" (*pathêmata tês psuchês* [παθήματα τῆς ψυχῆς]) that resemble things, as well as "speech sounds" (*ta en têi phônêi* [τὰ ἐν τῇ φωνῇ]) that are both natural signs of these affections, in the case of animals, and conventional symbols in the case of human beings and their different languages. Three strata, or three places: things, the soul, language. As a result, there is no guarantee of transitivity, of full passage from one stratum to another (see SIGN). In fact, one can be mistaken (*pseudein* [ψεύδειν], *psuedesthai*): one can perceive inaccurately; one can speak falsely; in fact, one can seek to mislead, for example by lying (*pseudein* once again). The truth is like a target that one aims for but can miss (*hamartanein* [ἁμαρτάνειν]), whether on purpose or not.

Aristotle's great discovery, which provides the foundation for this new doctrine of truth, and on which classical Western thought is built, at least until Hegel, is to propose an analogous structure for being, which is given objectively, and for discourse, which is held subjectively. Being is analyzed in terms of "substance" (*ousia*, which comes to take the place of platonic *eidos* [εἶδος], and which is translated no less correctly as "essence") and of "accidents" (*sumbebêkota* [συμβεβηκότα], exactly the way a proposition is broken down into "subject" (*hupokeimenon* [ὑποκείμενον]) and "predicates" (*katêgoroumena* [κατηγορούμενα]). The substance is the subject, which is to say it is defined through the supposition, the assumption, and the reception (it is the same

verb: *hupokeisthai* [ὑποκεῖσθαι], "to stand under") of accidents like the predicates and itself is not supported or predicated by anything (see ESSENCE and SUBJECT).

This structural discovery, which as always is presented in the form of an observation and something evident, guarantees the possibility of a correspondence between the being as he appears and the discourse as it is proposed, and this is what will henceforth be called "truth." Truth is described in the same terms from Aristotle, the metaphysician of antiquity, to Tarksi, the modern logician. There is a clear line of filiation between the manner in which the goddess in Parmenides describes the lines of research into thought ("The one that [it] is and that it is impossible for [it] not to be, is the path of Persuasion (for she attends upon Truth)" fr. II, 3–5), through the Aristotelian definition of Truth ("To say of what is that it is not, or of what is not that it is, is false, while to say of what is that it is, and of what is not that it is not, is true." Aristotle, *Metaphysics*, Γ, 7, trans. W. D. Ross; cf. *Metaphysics* Θ, 10, 1051b 3–9: "It is not because we think truly that you are pale, that you are pale, but because you are pale we who say this have the truth" [trans. W. D. Ross]), up to Tarski's "semantic" turn: "The proposition 'the snow is white' is true if and only if the snow is white" for analytic propositions that are based on identity, and " 'it is snowing' is a true proposition if and only if it is snowing," for synthetic propositions that entail facts ("The Semantic Conception of Truth" and "The Concept of Truth in Formal Languages" in

Logics, Semantics, Metamathematics). But the term "correspondence" itself does not appear in Aristotle, nor in any of the proponents of the "correspondence theory of truth" of the twentieth century (the most plausible equivalent—*homoiôsis* [ὁμοίωσις], *homoiotês* [ὁμοιότης], "comparison, similitude, resemblance"—never defines truth; cf. Bonitz). Whatever the case, the most enduring definition of truth is traditionally referred back to Aristotle, formulated in the Latin of the Middle Ages as *veritas est adaequatio rei et intellectus*, "truth as the adequation of intellect and things," which should be simultaneously understood, as Heidegger emphasizes, as "adequation of intellect to the thing" and in a preexisting or primary reciprocity, "adequation of the thing to the intellect" (see Box 4).

As a matter of fact, we still think "truth" as Aristotelians. We continue to define ourselves as "animals endowed with *logos* [λόγος]," that is, language-reason. The entire logical apparatus of the *Organon* (both "instrument" and "organ" or second nature) consistently comes to the rescue of the *logos*, helping it tell the world as it is. First of all, when we speak, we *signify* something; we say something that has one single meaning, both for us and for others. The principle of non-contradiction is a principle of being ("it is impossible for the same to both belong and not belong to the same and according to the same, at the same time") that reveals and instantiates itself as a principle of discourse (it is impossible for the same

"word" to have and not have the same "meaning" simultaneously). It provides a foundation for being by starting with the identity of meaning and by forbidding any unmastered homonym (see PRINCIPLE and HOMONYM). After that, our utterances are structured into propositions of the type "S is P"—subject-copula-predicate—and thus also substance-accident (see SUBJECT). Finally, our reasoning is "logical," in particular "syllogistic." As a result we are able to engage in "discourse" about a world become legible, and that discourse is also a "calculus" (*logos*; see LOGOS), from which derive its claims to universality and to universal truth, which Leibniz expressed so clearly in his conception of a universal characteristic (*mathesis universalis*).

- See Box 2.

C. *Verus, veritas*

1. Etymologies

Unlike *alêtheia/alêthês*, the substantive *veritas* appears after the adjective *verus*. The adjective *verus* and its adverbial form *vero* existed previously; for a long time the substantive *veritas* only existed in its ablative forms. *Verus,-a,-um* relates to the series "veritable," "veridical," "veracity," Fr. *vrai*, and by extension "commonly used at all times," while verbs such as *verifico*, as used by Boethius, signify "presenting as true."

2

"True"/"better" or: What is relativism?

The *logos* of ontology is framed in the opening of *alêtheia* as the speaking of being, so that man, in Parmenides, as well as in Plato and Aristotle, is committed to this speaking; in the Heideggerian idiom he is the "shepherd of being." But this tradition is in tension with one of a sophistical sort, for whom discourse is not mimetic of the real or aimed at truth but rather produces the real. It is performative and performing, veracious as such: "every discourse proves to be" (this is one of the possible interpretations of the quote from Antisthenes, "*pas logos alêtheuei* [πᾶς λόγος ἀληθεύει]," *Proclus in Platonis Cratylum Commentaria*, ed. Pasquali, Tübner, chap. 37, scholie 385d). The sophist Gorgias, in his *Treatise on Non-being*, in fact analyzes the *Poem* of Parmenides as a performance of this genre, which is particularly effective because it succeeds in using language to produce this being that will be the object of all ontology. Instead of thinking of what lies on this side of the objective of truth, like the phenomenologists of today, like a received wisdom, one can instead think of it as an art of production (see SPEECH ACT).

This change of perspective translates into a change of vocabulary, which Plato impartially puts on display in the apology of Protagoras. Protagoras explains in what way

"man is the measure of all things" ("For I affirm," says Protagoras [*Theaetetus*, 166d], "that *Truth* [this is the title of Protagoras' treatise that remains] behaves just as I have written: each of us is the measure of what is and what is not"; see LEX, Box 1, "*Gnômon*"). It is no longer "truth" (*alêtheia*) that is at issue but the "true" (*alêthes*), and even the "more or less true": we have passed from the substantive to the adjective with its various degrees. And this more or less true turns out to be a "more or less good," implying a passage from a state that is less good to a better one: "It is imperative to bring about this change in states, for one is worth more than the other [*ameinôn gar hê hetera hexis* (ἀμείνων γὰρ ἡ ἑτέρα ἕξις)] . . . as the doctor effects this change with his drugs, the sophist with his speech" (ibid., 167a). Here is the crucial text:

Not that anyone ever made another think truly [ψευδῆ δοξάζοντά τις], who previously thought falsely [ἀληθῆ ἐποίησε δοξάζειν]. For no one can think what is not [τὰ μὴ ὄντα . . . δοξάσαι], or think anything different from that which he feels [οὔτε ἄλλα παρ' ἃ ἂν πάσχῃ]; and this is always true [ἀεὶ ἀληθῆ]. But as the inferior habit of mind [πονηρᾶς ψυχῆς ἕξει] has thoughts of kindred nature, so

I conceive that a good mind [χρηστὴ] causes men to have good thoughts; and these which the inexperienced call true [τινες τὰ φαντάσματα ὑπὸ ἀπειρίας ἀληθῆ καλοῦσιν], I maintain to be only better [βελτίω], and not truer than others [ἀληθέστερα δὲ οὐδέν].

(Plato, *Theaetetus*, 167a–b, trans. Jowett)

This position has been stigmatized as relativistic. It makes no distinction between *doxa* and *alêtheia*, being and appearance, and claims full justification in so doing (as Aristotle puts it so well: "because they maintain that it is sensation [*aisthêsin* (αἴσθησιν)] which is thought [*phronêsin* (φρόνησιν)] and that it is also alteration [*alloiôsin* (ἀλλοίωσιν)], they can claim that that which appears in sensation [*to phainomenon kata tên aisthêsin* (τὸ φαινόμενον κατὰ τὴν αἴσθησιν)] is necessarily true" (*Metaphysics*, Γ, 5, 1009b12–15). At any rate, it has nothing subjectivist about it. The truer is better, and is more useful for the individual, as well as the city (Plato, *Theaetetus*, 167c). This is why Protagoras, the expert in discourse, accepts without false modesty to be called "wise," or even better in the comparative form, "more wise" (ibid., 166e).

Most contemporary hypotheses propose that *verus*—and the words signifying true, *vrai, vérité, wahr, Wahrheit*—derive from an Indo-European root, **wer*, which would retainmeanings of "to please, pleasing, manifesting benevolence, gifts, services rendered, fidelity, pact." Chantraine (RT: *Dictionnaire étymologique de la langue grecque*) links it to the Homeric expression *êra pherein* [ἦρα φέρειν], "to please," as well as to *epiêra* [ἐπίηρα], *epiêros* [ἐπίηρος], and *epiêranos* [ἐπιήρανος], "agreeable" (*Odyssey*, 19, 343), just like the Latin *verus* (cf. *se-vere*: "without benevolence"), the German *war*, and the Russian *vera*, "faith," or *verit'* [верить], "to believe." Pokorny adds to this same theme the Greek *heortê* [ἑορτή], "religious feast, cult." And from the same basis have come terms signifying "guarantee, protect": French *garir* and later *garant*, German *Gewähren*, English *warrant, to grant*.

According to Chantraine, this root **wer* should be distinguished from another root *ver-*, whence *eirô* [εἴρω] in Greek, *verbum* in Latin ("word" in English, etc.), and words from the family of *vereor, revereor*, "to fear, to respect," *verecundia* (respectful fear). Alfred Ernout does not support this separation. We should recall that plays on the words *verum* and *verbum* were common, as Augustine mentions (*verbum = verum boare*, "proclaiming the truth," *Dialectics* 1, 1; see WORD). Pavel Florensky, following Georg Curtius (*Grundzüge der griechischen Etymologie*, 1873), also claims a single root for the ensemble of these derivations, including the Sanskrit *vratum*, "sacred act, vow, promise," the Greek *bretas* [βρέτας], "cult object, wooden idol" (Aeschylus, *Eumenides*, v. 258), and the Latin *verbum*. For Florensky the signification of *verus* must be considered as belonging first to the field of religious ritual and subsequently of juridical formulas: "strictly speaking, *verus* means protected or grounded in the sense of that which is the object of a taboo or consecration" (*Pillar and Ground*, 18).

2. From the juridical to the philosophical

Verus implies a rectification of an adversarial allegation considered to be fraudulent, as is indicated by the original opposition *verax/fallax-mendax*. It thus signifies the properly founded (in fact or in the rules of law): "*crimen verissimum*" a well-founded accusation (Cicero, *In Verrem*, 5, 158.) In texts of grammar and rhetoric, but also in juridical texts as well, *verus* and *veritas* signify the veracity of the rule, inasmuch as it can be distinguished from usage: "*Quid verum sit intellego; sed alias ita loquor ut concessum est*" (I know what is correct, but sometimes I avail myself of the variation in usage), (Cicero, *De oratore*, Loeb Classical Library); "*Consule veritatem: reprehendet; refer ad auris: probabunt*" (If you consult the strict rule of analogy, it will say this practice is wrong, but if you consult the ear, it will approve) (ibid., 158–69). The juridical connotation of the word *verus* (and thus of *veritas*) is retained and subsequently reinforced. In the glosses of the Middle Ages, *verus* signifies "legitimate" and the Latin sense of the word, "legal and authentic" or "conforming to existing law." One normally finds *verum est* in legal texts to certify that a new rule conforms to preexisting ones (*Digest*, 8, 4, 15).

It is this juridical dimension that produces the meaning of *verus* as "authenticated, authentic" (in contrast to "false," "imitative," "deceiving") and thus "real" as in "real cream" or "a genuine Rolex watch." The juridical here provides a foundation not only for the moral ("*Verum et simplex bonum quod non possit ab honestate sejungi*" [The true and simple Good which cannot be separated from honesty], Cicero, *Academica*, I, 2), but also for the ontological (which one can find in Cicero's translation [*Topica*, 35] of *etumologia* [ἐτυμολογία] by *veriloquium*). The association of *vera ratio* is particularly polysemic in consequence (see *ratio* under LOGOS) because of the equivocal status of *ratio* in its ascription as explication, cause, doctrine. Thus Lucretius introduces epicurean physics by "*animum nobis adhibe veram ad rationem*" (*De rerum natura*, II, 1023); *vera ratio* is simultaneously true reason, the true cause, and the manifestation of a new aspect of things ("*nove se species ostendere rerum*," ibid., II, 1025), in relation to a theory of causes ("*semina rerum*," ibid., II, 1059).

In turn, *veritas* first refers to the qualities of witnesses, which is not simply an issue of their sincerity but of their capacity to speak the truth: "*in tuam fidem, veritatem confugit*" (he seeks refuge in your good faith, in your truth and compassion) (Cicero *Pro Quinctio*, 10. trans. C. D. Yonge, 1903), "*veri testes*" (unimpeachable witnesses) (Cicero, *In Verrem*, 5, 165). This dimension of *truthfulness* in English has no French equivalent outside of *fiabilité*, which plays upon the register of confidence (see BELIEF, GLAUBE).

In this manner truth comes to be instituted, but not uncovered. *Veritas* qualifies an accreditative function, the power of having the last word, according to Roman law: "The judgment holds the thing to be true" (*res judicata pro veritate accipitur*) (*Digest*, 50, 17, 207). *Veritas* is performative: it does not designate a relation of adequacy between the utterance and reality but enacts the authority of judgment, the well-founded juridical utterance.

II. The Posterity of the Paradigms

A. 'Èmèt / alêtheia / veritas: Christian "revealed truth"

Alêtheia in Paul first takes on the meaning of 'èmèt: the "God of truth." This does not refer back to the idea of a supreme reality, but to veracity "in fulfilling his promises" (*eis to bebaiôsai tas epaggelias* [εἰς τὸ βεβαιῶσαι τὰς ἐπαγγελίας]) (Rom. 15:8). And if Paul speaks of the "truth of Christ" and of his "true word" (2 Cor. 11:10 and 6:6), it is to refer to his veracity. In return the "truth" asked of the Christians refers to sincerity (2 Cor. 7:14), uprightness in relation to divine expectations or requirements (cf. "those who rebel against truth," Rom. 2:8). Linked to truth are ideas of constancy (1 Pet. 5:12), solidity (1 Tim. 3:15), and plenitude (Col. 2:9), but always in relation to the imperatives of Genesis of the generative *fiat*. In 2 Thessalonians 2:11–12, one finds a revealing opposition between "belief in truth" and "belief in a lie."

It is only with the Epistle to the Galateans that the registers of 'èmèt and *alêtheia* become intermingled and that the evangelist is identified with truth and its revelation. Paul transforms the biblical notion of "the truth of the law" into "the truth of the evangelist" (Gal. 2:5 and 14) and points to the correspondence between the Revelation and his interpretation by stressing the contrast between the Evangelist, which is "power of God unto salvation" (Rom. 1:16) and the ineffectiveness of the law. John's *alêtheia* is completely defined by its Christological content. Thus the expression to "speak the truth," which in Paul is solely a matter of veracity (cf. Rom. 9:1) becomes in John the proclamation of true revelation (see LOGOS). Christ is truth as the fulfillment of Revelation and as the word of God the father. *Alêtheia* is defined along two axes: Revelation and Incarnation. Two texts are fundamental to this point of view: the prologue that describes the incarnation—the Christ is *"plêrês charitos kai alêtheias* [πλήρης χάριτος καὶ ἀληθείας]" (full of grace and truth) (John 1:14) and the text of the Last Supper—the words of Christ: *"Egô eimi hê hodos kai hê alêtheia kai hê zôê; oudeis erchetai pros ton patera ei mê di' emou* ['Εγώ εἰμι ἡ ὁδὸς καὶ ἡ ἀλήθεια καὶ ἡ ζωή· οὐδεὶς ἔρχεται πρὸς τὸν πατέρα εἰ μὴ δι' ἐμοῦ]" (I am the way, the truth, and the life: no man cometh unto the Father, but by me) (John 14:6).

Two expressions are taken from the Old Testament and given a meaning specific to John, to indicate the subjectivization of truth "in us." The Old Testament expression *"poien tên alêtheian* [ποιεῖν τὴν ἀλήθειαν]" (to wreak the truth) (2 Chron. 31:20), which signifies "keeping to obligations" and "being faithful to the Law," is reinterpreted by John in the sense of subjective faith: *"ho de poiôn tên alêtheian erchetai pros to phôs* [ὁ δὲ ποιῶν τὴν ἀλήθειαν ἔρχεται πρὸς τὸ φῶς]" (he that doeth truth cometh to the light) (John 3: 21, King James version). The formula "in truth" (*en alêtheiai* [ἐν ἀληθείᾳ]), which is found in the Old Testament (for example to "walk in truth," 1 Kings 2:4) and in Paul, sets up in John a dialectic of interiority: we are in truth, and we come "from the truth" (John 3:18–19) and truth "abides in us" (2 John 1–2). The work of faith entails the inhabitation of truth (living in truth).

It is Saint Augustine who gives the New Testament truth its specifically ontological determinations in his elaboration of the Trinity. He introduces a significant modification to the truth of John by applying the term of truth to God himself, and not just to Christ. He puts to use all the resources of *verus*, "true God," veracious God: *"Deus unus, solus, magnus, verus, verax, veritas* [one God, alone, great, true, truthful, the truth]" (*De Trinitate*, VIII, 2, 3). Augustinian "truth" extends itself in man in the concept of the interior "Master" and the intimacy of the "mental verb" in *De Trinitate*. According to *De Magistro*:

> It is not a speaker who utters sounds exteriorly whom we consult, but it is truth that presides within, over the mind itself. . . . And He who is consulted, He who is said to *dwell in the inner man*, He it is who teaches—Christ (*qui in interiore homine habitare dictus est Christus*).
>
> (Colleran, *Ancient Christian Writers*)

▪ See Box 3.

B. From 'ĕmèt̠ to "true" and from *verus* to *wahr*

1. From 'ĕmèt̠ to "true"

The history of "truth" is distinct from the history of *veritas/ verum* and follows a schema similar to that of 'ĕmèt̠. Etymologically, "true" derives from "tree" ("firm as a tree"). "True" (cf. Ger. *treu*), which has yielded "truth," is originally close to "faithful" (loyal, constant) and is related to "trust," entailing an idea of fidelity or solidity ("firmness"). As the expression "being true to a person" indicates, "truth" signifies first of all "confidence, trustworthiness" ("They had

---

3
Textual truth and allegory

➤ ANALOGY, COMPARISON, OIKONOMIA, SENSE

The Christian paradigm of truth implies a truth to the text: it is the register of the *oikonomia* [οἰκονομία] as "economy of salvation"; Tertullian translates *oikonomia* by *dispensatio*, and Augustine calls it *dispensatio temporalis*. The revelation is only such that it announces in advance, hidden behind the veil of actuality, another event of a higher order; the new is the accomplishment of the old and "completes the preludes" (*per adimpletionem*) (Tertullian, *Adversus Marcionem*, IV, 11). Tertullian invokes the "conspiracy between the meaning of the Scriptures and the deadlines of events and the order of time" (ibid., III, 23). He employs a Roman juridical term, *praescriptio* (the fact of having been written in advance), to characterize the mode of truth of the text, which is proven through the temporal continuity of the realization of the prophecies (ibid., V, 11). And Hilaire de Poitiers writes: *"Signata sunt omnia, et per spiritalem doctrinam resignanda* [all things are signified and must be unsealed through

the spiritual doctrine]" (*Commentary on Psalm 118*, 17).

This conception of the *oikonomia* conforms to Paul's allegories of hermeneutics and "typology" when he declares in 1 Corinthians 10:11 that everything that occurs in the New Testament was already *in figura* in the whole of antique law and that Christ was the "type" (*tupikôs* [τυπικῶς]) announced by the earlier figures, especially Moses and the prophets: *"Haec autem omnia in figura contingebant illis / Tauta de tupikôs sunebainen ekeinois* [ταῦτα δὲ τυπικῶς συνέβαινεν ἐκείνοις] / *Solches alles widerfuhr ienen zum Vorbilde* [Luther, Ger. translation]." Everything had already arrived as figures (*written down as warnings*): the events, the actions, and the persons of biblical history were thus "figures," "antetypes," or "prefigures" of the arrival of Christ—Adam himself being "a type of the one that was to come" (*tupos tou mellontos* [τύπος τοῦ μέλλοντος]) (Rom. 5:14, English Standard Version). Here allegory does not have only a simple semantic sense but an

ontological sense. It rests on what is. The *orthotês* does not designate correct vision but the correctness of names, a relation between things, not between words, and it involves the introduction of temporality. The *tupoi* [τύποι] are only identifiable through a double movement of retrospection-prospection that takes into account the fulfilled Revelation.

This new architecture of exegesis or articulation between the meaning of a text and the event, between the idea of "body" and of "letter," gives rise to the theology of the four senses of the Scripture, and beyond that, it provides the very paradigm of hermeneutics.

BIBLIOGRAPHY

Auerbach, Erich. "Figura." In *Scenes from the Drama of European Literature: Six Essays*. New York: Meridian Books, 1959. French translation by Marc André Bernier. Paris: Belin, collection "L'extrême contemporain," 1993.

Lubac, Henri de. *Medieval Exegesis*. Translated by Mark Sebanc. Grand Rapids, MI: W. B. Eerdmans, 1998.

been friends in youth, but whispering tongues can poison truth," Coleridge, *Christabel*, II). Like belief, it can be assimilated to faith (the suffix -*th* indicates the kinship of the two terms, according to the *Middle English Dictionary*) (see BELIEF, FAITH). The idea of dependability and loyalty ("trustworthiness") inherent in "trust/truth" leads to two new usages: on the one hand, conformity to an agreement, to a promise (cf. "faith") that can have a political meaning associating truth and normativity to sociality. In this case "truth" designates adherence to a norm or rule (agreement with a standard). On the other hand, truth is linked to sincerity, the inclination to tell the truth (veracity). For the liar, unlike the person in error, knows the truth. It is not enough to be in the truth or to know it; for social harmony one must also be disposed to say it or to agree to it.

The central problem is the duality of "truth": "sincerity" and "veracity." Thus "truthful" and "truthfulness," when said of a person, imply that "reliability" is not just a matter of faith but that faith itself is founded on an inclination to tell the truth. Similarly, "truly" moves from a moral sense ("faithfully, sincerely" as in the standard expression "yours truly") to a veridical sense. There is an amusing example in Austin, in his essay on "Truth":

Yet between stating, however truly, that I am feeling sick and feeling sick, there is a great gulf fixed.

(Austin, *Philosophical Papers*, 123–24)

One finds then, even in contemporary uses of the word "truth," an ambiguity proper to *verum*, in which the dimension of sincerity/reliability is prior to that of the veridical dimension.

2. From *veritas* to *wahr*

The paradigm of *verus-veristas* is not easy to separate from any epistemological dimensions, as is evident in the varied fates of the Indo-European root **wer*, from which derives, in addition to *vera* (in Russian, "belief"), the old French *garir*, in the sense of "certifying as true, designating as true," whence the participle *garant*. The evolution of these derived words inscribes *wahr* and *Wahrheit* in a semantic network from which emerge two directions, belief and salvation.

a. Belief

Wahr is often linked back, in composite words, to the idea of belief, in the sense of true belief, to take as true: *wahrsagen* (to predict), *wahr haben* (to admit, agree upon), *für wahr halten* (to hold as true, to believe). This is the term that Kant employs in the *Critique of Pure Reason*, "Transcendental theory of method," chap. 2, 3 ("On Opinion, Science, and Belief"): "*das Fürwahrhalten*" is a belief, as a modality of subjectivity, that can be divided into conviction (*Überzeugung*) or persuasion (*Überredung*) and that is capable of three degrees: opinion (*Meinung*), belief (*Glaube*), and science (*Wissenschaft*).

b. Safeguarding, conservation

Similarly *wahren, bewahren* in the sense of "to guard, to conserve" is linked to *Wahrung* in the sense of "defending one's interests" or "safeguarding." One might refer to Heidegger's use of this etymological and semantic relation in reference to Nietzsche:

Nietzsche reserves [*bewährt*] the rubrics "true" [*das Wahre*] and "truth" [*Wahrheit*] for what Plato calls "true being." . . . Holding [*wahren*] the "truth" is a representational holding-to-be-true [*Fürwahrhalten*]. . . . Truth is a condition for the preservation [*Bewahrung*] of will to power. Preservation [*Wahrung*] is of course necessary, but it is never adequate.

(Heidegger, *Nietzsche*: 3: 235–36)

In its sense of safeguarding, *wahr* makes no mention of any materiality. It deals with either the *real*, "actual, concrete" (*real Wert*, "real value"; *real Ich*, "the real and concrete me") or else with the *wirklich*, "effective," *Wirkung*, "effect, result," *Wirklichkeit* (the Hegelian translation of *energeia* [ἐνέργεια]); *wirklich* belongs to the paradigm of works, of labor. Here we find the ontological dimension of *verus*, as in the English usage of "real" (true in the sense of real: see REALITY).

3. "Real" and "true" / *wahr* / *vrai*, and the status of ontological truth

Two fundamentally different relations to ontology and the *ontos on* can be traced through the legacy of the paradigms of *alêtheia*/ὲμὲτ/*veritas*: the true as real and effective, or the true as authentic, nonimitative, or false (being such as it speaks itself). Two incompatible approaches to truth emerge, one corresponding to something said of things, the other to something said of speech.

It is not clear, as Austin put it so well, that the ordinary meanings of "real" and "true," which share the same intent, actually refer to an ontological questioning of reality.

"Real" is an absolutely normal word, with nothing newfangled or technical. . . . For instance, if we are going to talk about "real," we must not dismiss as beneath contempt such humble but familiar expressions as "not real cream."

(Austin, *Sense and Sensibilia*, 63–64)

In order to know what Austin calls "the Nature of Reality," one needs to examine the meaning of "real," "genuine," "authentic," as analogous to the sense of "true" in its nonveridical usage. There is a specific play between French and English and a complex relation between "real" and French *vrai*. "Real" is often translated into French as *vrai* (and in German as *wahr*) and not by *réel*. The English "real" is more common and less theoretical than the French *réel* or the German *real*. This is precisely why Austin claims in *Sense and Sensibilia* that "real" is "absolutely normal" and why he rejects the attachment of ontological over-investment to the term. "Real cream" would be rendered in French as *vraie crème* and "real color" (in hair color, for example) would be rendered as *couleur naturelle* or *véritable* (natural or true color). When one is dealing with expressions such as "not real cream," one is dealing with an "ersatz" or substitute (as in the case of a hair dye); a "not real color" in which "not real" hardly implies a large-scale illusion. "Real" poses no great problems for "reality" in expressions such as "a real Vuitton" or "a real idiot." But the problem can only be raised by Austin as a result of the flexibility of "real" (unlike the French *réel*), which brings it much closer to "true" and to a whole lexical field of terms, including "proper," "genuine," "live," "true," "authentic," "natural" (ibid., 71). This use of "real/true" separates questions of truth from questions of authenticity, making the latter the central question.

There is a significant difference between English usage, on the one hand, and French and German on the other. *Wahr* can be employed in the sense of "real, authentic," as can *vrai*. But Bolzano qualifies this sense of the inauthentic (*uneigentlich*) and claims that it only applies to the adjective, not to the noun: "*das Adjectiv 'wahr' werde auch im Sinne von 'wirklich,' 'echt' gebraucht*." But the English translator of Bolzano uses "real, genuine" as the equivalent of *wahr*, not "true." Following in the Aristotelian tradition, Bolzano points to the *derived* nature of this meaning of true, which is always a manner of translating or abbreviating one of the "primary" senses of *wahr* and *Wahrheit*, that is to say, it is part of a proposition. Even in what Bolzano calls "common usage," "true" is said primarily of utterances, not of things.

An additional problem derives from the fact that German establishes reference to the true within the very idea of perception. The verb *wahrnehmen*, "to perceive," is indeed constructed on *wahr* and literally means to "take as true." *Wahrnehmung* is thus the "grasp of the true" (see PERCEPTION, Box 3, "*Wahrnehmung*"). Thus in Husserl:

> It is clear that it belongs to the essence of perception that it perceives [*wahrnimmt*] some thing as its object, and consequently I can ask how the object is taken for real [*als was nimmt sie den Gegenstand für wahr*].

> (Husserl, *Introduction to Logic*)

Later on, Husserl proposes a curious construction relating to the false representation 2 x 2 = 5: "The representation does not conform to a corresponding perception, the represented does not reach the level of proper perception [*Wahrnehmung*] but of false perception [*Falschnehmung*]." Thus a false perception is a *Falschnehmung*, a direct grasp of the false. Part of German language philosophy insists in fact on the "truth" of perception based on a supposed "proper" meaning of *Wahrnehmung*. Brentano in particular speaks of internal perception as the only perception, "in the proper sense of the term," as the phenomena of external perception cannot be shown to be "real and true." "External perception is thus not, in the rigorous sense of the word, perception at all." Gandillac clarifies in a footnote that it is the etymological signification of *Wahrnehmung* that justifies the author's argument (*Psychology from an Empirical Point of View*). *Wahrnehmung* presents a problem of translation into French or English as soon as one plays on its construction based on *wahr*.

Thus German and French have a broader usage for *wahr/ vrai* than the English "true," but on the other hand, "real" in English has a broader and more "ordinary" usage. All of this is further complicated by the problems resulting from successive redefinitions of the relations of reality and truth since Aristotle. This is evident in the ambiguities of the term "realism," which is nonetheless easily transferable from one language to another but whose history and occasional incompatible meanings were developed in parallel to the terms "true"/*vrai*/*wahr*. Recent discussions of realism, especially in the United States, have focused on the notion of truth (especially Tarski's definition of it) without clearly separating the two issues.

It remains to be said that many common or colloquial expressions, in French as well as in English, play on the semantic slippages of *vrai* and "real," between the ontological sense and linguistic meanings. Thus in French, *c'est pas vrai!* does not mean it is false, but rather that it is not reality. In English, the opposite is the case: "get real!" means "come back down to earth," "accept the truth."

III. From Medieval to Classical Truth: Truth of the Matter, Rectitude, Adequation, Evidence, Certainty

The term *veritas* has three distinct standard acceptations during the Medieval period. The first, called the "Augustinian," is the "truth of the thing" (*veritas rei*); the second, called the "Anselmian," is truth as "the correctness grasped only by the intellect" (*rectitude sola mente perceptibilis*); and the third, generally credited to "Isaac" and Avicenna, is truth as "adequation of the thought to the thing" (*adequatio rei et intellectus*). All three uphold or, if need be, rectify, limit, or relativize the "logical" and predicative conception attributed to Aristotle. Within this network of meaning, one reformulation, called "Aristotelian," affects the first usage: truth as an "ontological disposition" (*dispositio rei in esse*), as a foundation of logical or "predicative" truth. Thomas Aquinas's *De veritate*, which contains a fairly exhaustive inventory of medieval elaborations, can serve as our guide.

A. The truth of the thing: Predicative and antepredicative

As Thomas presents it, the notion of "truth of the thing" is connected to an Aristotelian interpretation of truth as antepredicative before being logical. The three standard uses—Augustinian, Anselmian, Avicennian—clearly appear as the obligatory references starting with the first question of Thomas's *De veritate*. But in this system the first definition is supposed to look at "that which concerns the notion of truth and that which founds the true itself" (*illud quo praecedit rationem veritatis et in quo verum fundatur*), this truth that is called today "antepredicative" or "ontic." The tie between truth and existence, or rather beingness, is placed under the sign of Aristotle (*Metaphysics*, β, 1, 993b30) as an affirmation of the complete synonymity of "true" and "being" ("the true and the existent are completely the same thing" [*verum et ens sunt omnino idem*]). This is often alleged by the proponents of the theory of "making true" in the light of the dominant interpretation of the text, which is evident in the translations of Tricot ("*autant une chose a d'être, autant elle a de vérité*") or Reale ("*ogni cosa possiede tanto di verità quanto possiede di esse*").

■ See Box 4.

B. Truth and correctness: Anselm, or the two ways of "making true"

In his dialogue entitled *De veritate* (around 1080–85), especially in chapter 2, Anselm is determined to distinguish two types of truth and to define truth in relation to rightness or correctness (*rectitudo*). Anselm does not agree with the common usage according to which a discourse is said to be true when it signifies that what is actually exists. In that case truth would be found outside of the utterance, in things, whereas it is important that it be located within what it is, that is, in discourse itself. But truth cannot be immediately

4
Logical truth and antepredicative truth: On the Heideggerian reading of Θ, 10

➤ INTELLECTUS, *INTUITION*

In the Middle Ages the canonical Aristotelian thesis as it is expressed in the *Metaphysics*, Θ, 10, 1051b4–5 "He who thinks the separated to be separated and the combined to be combined has the truth, while he whose thought is in a state contrary to that of the objects is in error" (trans. W. D. Ross)—has now become *auctoritas* and circulates in a form similar to "saying the truth is to say that what is combined is combined and that what is separated is separated." The medieval version accentuates the "logical" aspect of the definition.

But for modern interpreters the primacy of the ontic truth (the truth of the thing) can lead to a very different reading. The Greek "*epseustai de ho enantiôs echôn ê ta pragmata* [ἔψευσται δὲ ὁ ἐναντίως ἔχων ἢ τὰ πράγματα]," rendered in Italian by G. Reale in the form of "*sarà, invece, nel falso, colui che ritiene che le cose stiano in modo contrario a come effettivamente stanno*" (Aristotle, *Metafisica*, trans. G. Reale, Milan: Rusconi, "Testi a Fronte," 1993, 429), which is closer to a beginning of considering the "state of affairs" (*Sachverhalt, état de choses*), claims to be closer to the authentic Aristotelian inspiration than the anachronistic "*nature des objets*" in the French translation of Tricot. The two translations are still based on the same supposition: the "primordial character of truth in things," the foundation of the theory that we call today the "correspondence theory of truth," which

Tricot stresses, following in the steps of Thomas Aquinas: "*compositio et divisio rei est causa veritatis et falsitatis in opinione et oratione*" (in *Metaph.*, 1899, 549). This "antepredicative" truth and its primacy are still at issue in the course held in 1926 in Marburg on the *Grundbegriffe der Antiken Philosophie*, in which Heidegger contrasts the Aristotelian conception of truth in Θ, 10 with that from E, 4 (truth as the "truth of proposition"), with the second based on the first. In regards to the truth in Θ, 10, Heidegger posits that it is known through "a simple dis-covering (or un-veiling) by a simple gaze (itself)." In the *Grundfragen der Philosophie, Ausgewählte "Probleme der Logik"* of 1937–38 (a course given in Freiburg in the winter semester), Heidegger attributes to Aristotle a concept of truth as "correspondence," "correction" (exactitude), or "adequation" between thought and being, all the while recalling that his concept of truth is based on the concept of truth as unconcealment or nonlatency of being from Θ, 10, "the ultimate resonance of the originary essence of truth" in the history of philosophy (cf. Heidegger, *Gesamtausgabe*, 45: 15, 97, 139, and 205). In *Metaphysics* Θ, 10, 1051a35ff., Aristotle explains that "the terms 'being' and 'non-being' are employed firstly with reference to the categories" and "secondly with reference to the potency or actuality of these or their nonpotency or nonactuality, and

thirdly in the sense of true and false" (trans. W. D. Ross). This passage, which is a prelude to the thesis of 1051b4–5, has been the object of different interpretations. Ross places the words *kuriôtata on* [κυριώτατα ὄν] in square brackets in the expression "*to de kuriôtata on alêthes ê pseudos* [τὸ δὲ κυριώτατα ὄν ἀληθὲς ἢ ψεῦδος]," and Tricot (p. 522) comments that "if one keeps these words, one must reattach them to [ἀληθὲς ἢ ψεῦδος], and not to [τὸ δὲ], because Aristotle did not intend to say that Being par excellence is the true and the false, when in his doctrine (as affirmed in E, 4, 1027b34), Being as true is only an affection of thought." Heidegger's interpretation is quite different. According to him, the adverb *kuriôtata*, which Schwegler rejected and Ross eliminated, should be maintained: Aristotle's thesis lies in this place, contrary to the claims of E, 4, that being as true exists in things in two forms, one of them relating to "composite realities" (= complex), expressed in judgments, and the other in "noncomposite realities" (= not-complex), expressed by the thought (*noein*), which is not a judgment. The true thesis of Aristotle on truth is thus that being in the sense of true (being) is, of all the meanings of "being," the most proper to it, that it is the truth of things and in things, that it is the "constant presence" on which the truth of thought, i.e., judgment, is based.

within discourse either, since, as Aristotle says, a specific utterance, made out of the same constituent parts, can be either true or false and can even be first one and then the other as a function of the state of affairs to which it refers. Anselm overcomes this difficulty by asking himself at what the affirmation had "been aimed" (*ad quid*). The statement has been made to signify that what-is is (or that what-is-not is not). But it has also has the capacity to signify that what-is is not, for if this were not the case, the statement could signify falsely. A statement that does what it ought to do (*facit quod debet*), in signifying what it has undertaken to signify (*significant quod accepit significare*) thus signifies "correctly" (*recte*) at a first level, just as the truth or rightness of a creature consists in doing what God has given him to do, that which he must do. This first correctness or truth is independent of any conformity with things and states of affairs.

Nonetheless, when the statement effectively signifies that what-is is, it doubly does what it ought to do, for it signifies both what it has undertaken to signify, as well as what it was designed to signify, that for which it was fashioned (*significant et quod accepit significare et ad quod facta est*). This second correctness and truth is normally what we call a true statement. The statement "it is day" is true at a first level when

it signifies that it is day (whether this is actually the case or not), for this is what it has naturally undertaken to do; it is true at a second level when it is in fact day, and the utterance is correctly used for the purpose for it was fashioned.

In statements that we would qualify as analytic, like "a human being is an animal" or "a human being is not a stone," the two truths of discourse are inseparable, since these utterances always and inextricably signify what they undertake to signify, as well as the truth of what they are meant to signify. The first correctness is immutable. It belongs naturally and permanently to the statement. The second correctness is mutable, accidental (since it occurs only when the state of affairs actually conforms to the meaning of the statement, and those states of affairs are subject to change) and impermanent, according to use.

Alia igitur est rectitudo et veritas enuntiationis, quia significat ad quod significandum facta est; alia vero, quia significat quod accepit significare. Quippe ista immutabilis est ipsi orationi, illo vero mutabilis. Hanc namque semper habet, illam vero non semper. Istam enim naturaliter habet, illam vero accidentaliter et secundum usum. Nam cum dico: dies est, ad significandum esse quod est, recte utor hujus orationis significatione, quia ad hoc facta est; et ideo tunc recte dicitur significare. Cum vero eadem oratione significo esse quod non est, non ea recte utor, quia non ad hoc facta est; et idcirco non recta tunc ejus significatio dicitur.

(A statement then is right and true either because it is correctly formed or because it fulfills its function of signifying correctly. The former belongs immutably to it, the latter is mutable. The former it always has, the latter not always. The former it naturally has, the latter accidentally and according to use. For when I say, "It is day" in order to signify what it is, I correctly use what the utterance means, because this is why it was fashioned, and therefore it then is correctly said to signify. But when by the same utterance I signify that what is not is, I do not use it correctly, because it was not fashioned for this purpose, and its signification is not then called correct.)

(St. Anselm, *De veritate*, 154–55)

At the moral level, the distinction between the two forms of correctness is only of value for rational beings, who are free and can thus recognize what they are fashioned to do, what they owe themselves to be, and to decide to do or not do what they are fashioned to do. The difference between man and God becomes the difference between the being who is because he is what it is his duty to be and the being who is because he is. The duty that defines man is a debt because in fulfilling it, man submits to a truth whose cause lies ultimately in God. In a similar manner true discourse conforms to what it signifies and pays off its initial debt because it has been fashioned to signify the true, and in this case it signifies it effectively and conforms to its original purpose.

C. Truth and adequation

The most celebrated definition of truth is "*adaequatio rei et intellectus.*" It is the canonical expression of truth as correspondence. One finds it for the first time, it would appear, in William of Auxerre (*Summa aurea* I, ed. J. Ribaillier, 1980, 1: 195, 228). It is also often attributed (from Thomas [*De veritate*, q.1a 1, c] through Heidegger [*Sein und Zeit*, § 44a, 214], to the Jewish philosopher Isaac Israeli (850–950). His *Book of Definitions*, written in Arabic, was translated into Latin by Gérard of Cremona (ed. H. Hirschfeld, *Festschrift . . . Steinschneider*, Leipzig, 1896, Hebrew, 131–41). A fragment of the original has been found (H. Hirschfeld, ed. *JQR*, no. 15 [1903]:

689–93 [= Latin, 318, 1–326, 32]). As it turns out, not only is the definition of truth as adequation not to be found, but the text contains another formula explicitly presented as defining the truth: "*ḥadd al-ḥaqq: huwa mā huwa aš-šay'*" (691, 6–8); *veritas est quod est res* (322, 10 and cf. 307; Hebrew 139, 14ff., and cf. 134, 9). The definition is not to be found in al-Kindī either (d. 870), who defines truth, or rather veracity (*ṣidq* [صدق]), as the fact of saying what-is is and what-is-not is not (*Definitions*, ed. Abu Rida, Cairo, 1950, 117). One should look to Avicenna (d. 1037) for the true and original context of the idea of adequation. One of his definitions of truth is: "the state of discourse or of thought which designates the state of the exterior thing, when this 'is' correspondent [*muṭābiq* (مطابق)] to that" (Shifā, *Metaphysics*, I, 8; Fr. trans. ed. G. C. Anawati, Cairo, 1960, 48, 6ff.). The Arabic participle suggests an image of two layers precisely covering each other, in the way two geometric figures can be superimposed. The Latin is more vague: "*Veritas autem quae adaequatur rei*" (*Avicenna latinus, Metaphysica*, ed. S. Van Riet, Louvain, 1977, 55). It is this idea of "correspondence" between discourse and the thing that William of Auvergne will attempt to express with the aid of other synonyms: *convenientia*, *concordia*, *aequalitas* (*De universo*, I, 3, XXVI, 795a). The term *adaequatio* will predominate in the subsequent medieval tradition and give rise to new distinctions, particularly between the *adaequatio* of discourse and the thing, which defines true (*verus*) discourse from false (*falsus*), as opposed to the *adaequatio* of the discourse to the intention of the sincere (*verax*) or nonsincere (*fallax*) interlocutor—see the text of Bonaventure referred to *infra*, in IV.A.2. Averroës builds on a definition that is already a classic: "the veridical [*ṣādiq* (صادق)] as is said in its definition, is 'the fact' that what is to be found in the soul 'is' according to what is outside the soul" (*Tahafot*, I, 188; ed. M. Bouyges, 103, 5ff.). The English translation of S. Van den Bergh (London, 1954, 60 and 179) introduces the terms "agreement" or "conformity," which are not explicit in the Arabic. The definition has remained a classic. The substantive "correspondence" (*mutābaqa* [المطابقة]) is to be found in the *Book of Definitions* of Gurgani (d. 1413, s.v. "*ḥaqq* [حق]," Flügel ed., Leipzig, 1845, 94).

■ See Box 5.

D. Truth, evidence, and certainty

For obvious reasons stemming from, among other things, the necessity of harmonizing the *auctoritates* (authorities), medieval thinkers started by searching for cross-references

---

5

Hoc est corpus meum, or how adequation is set in crisis by the performative

➤ ANALOGY, SIGN, SPEECH ACT, II, *TO BE*

Can the definition of logical truth as *adaequatio rei et intellectus*, rather than correctness, define the truth of all utterances or only of assertions? What is the status of truth with respect to different kinds of enunciations,

those, for example, of a performative kind? The analysis of the formula for the consecration of the Eucharist, *Hoc est corpus meum*, is an important place for such discussion in the Middle Ages.

The truth of the formula for Eucharistic conversion depends crucially on the reference one assigns to the pronoun *hoc*, the subject of the statement. If the demonstrative pronoun refers to "this bread is my body," the statement is false. If it refers to the body of Christ, the proposition is true, but it does not serve in the conversion, since Christ is then already present from the beginning of the utterance. Thomas Aquinas succeeds in finding a solution that relies on a distinction between two types of utterances: assertive statements and operative statements. He bases the distinction between them on the Aristotelian opposition between speculative and practical intellect. Thomas makes an original use of the adage taken from the first chapter of the *Peri hermeneias*, according to which words are signs of intellection (*voces sunt signa intellectuum*). He explains that there are two types of intellections or concepts. The concepts that pertain to the speculative intellect are drawn from things; they come from them because speculation is a contemplation of existing things. Thus, the truth of an assertive utterance depends for its adequation on a state of affairs that pre-exists it. If it conforms, the statement is true; otherwise it is false. Conversely, concepts belonging to the practical intellect precede the thing, since an artisan needs to have a model or concept of the object in his mind beforehand so the object can be made in its image. In this case the truth of an operative utterance can only be determined in reference to the thing it has created. Given the specificity of the utterance within which it occurs, the *hoc* cannot refer to a thing that exists prior to its utterance (the bread), but rather to the thing that the formula helps to create in the last instant of its being pronounced, that is, the very moment at which the conversion will take place. It turns out that using a pronoun is absolutely ideal because it possesses within itself an indeterminacy of reference that allows it to recruit bread and wine as substances that can become the body of Christ. Thomas thus draws out the particular

properties of performative utterances that enable them to determine truth or assign reference to the deictic function contained within them.

According to Duns Scotus, the truth of the Eucharistic utterance is not a condition of its operation. The utterance is pronounced, and it engenders a signification that enables it to realize what it has been commanded to realize by convention (in an original pact set in place at the moment of command). It is at this point "neutral" and does not carry veridical value. But once realized, *hoc est corpus meum* is true in that it refers to the body of Christ, which is present as a result of the conversion. So the utterance is operative insofar as it is neutral, not insofar as it is true. This constitutes a major reversal of previous analyses, which always sought to find a value for the *hoc* that would make it possible to say that the statement was true in order to explain how it could be operative.

In chapter 15 of *Logic or the Art of Thinking*, Arnauld and Nicole take up the problem of the signification of the word *hoc* in the formula. They consider it "a troublesome quarrel which the ministers made famous, on which they based their main argument establishing their metaphorical interpretation of Eucharist" (ibid., 71). And for them this argument is "more worthy of logic than theology." The whole mystery of the assertion, they point out, "arises not from the obscurity of terms, but from the change effected by Christ, which caused this subject *hoc* to have two different determinations at the beginning and at the end of the proposition" (ibid., 72). *Hoc* indicates only "the confused idea of a present thing," and the apostles added to the confused idea of a present thing the distinct idea of bread that Christ held in his hands, an idea "which was only prompted and not precisely signified by this term. . . . And so

when Christ uttered 'this,' which meant his body, the Apostles only had to subtract the distinct ideas of bread they had added. Retaining this same idea of a present thing, they conceived at the end of Christ's assertion that this present thing was *now* the body of Jesus Christ" (ibid.). The distinction between after and now indicates the movement of transformation that the verb "to be" accomplishes during the act of utterance. As the authors write somewhat later, in chapter 12, "This which is bread at this moment is my body at another moment" (ibid., 112). If one finds the medieval arguments in Arnauld and Nicole, new issues are here at stake. For the logicians of Port-Royal, the insistence on a distinction between literal and figural in temporal movement is part of an answer to those (i.e., the Protestants) who would reject the idea of a real transsubstantiation in the name of a purely symbolic interpretation of the proposition.

BIBLIOGRAPHY

Arnauld, Antoine, and Pierre Nicole. *Logic or the Art of Thinking*. Translated and edited by Jill Vance Buroker. Cambridge: Cambridge University Press, 1996.

Libera, Alain de, and Irène Rosier-Catach. "L'analyse scotiste de la formule de la consécration eucharistique." In *Vestigia, Imagines, Verba: Semiotics and Logic in Medieval Theological Texts (1150–1450). Acts of the 11th Symposium on Medieval Logic and Semantics*, 171–201. Turnhout, Belg.: Brepols, 1997.

———. "Les enjeux logico-linguistiques de l'analyse de la formule de la consécration eucharistique." *Cahiers de l'Institut du Moyen Âge Grec et Latin* 67 (1997): 33–77.

Rosier-Catach, Irène. "Éléments de pragmatique dans la grammaire, la logique et la théologie médiévales." *Histoire Épistémologie Langage* 20, no. 1 (1988): 117–32.

between standard uses of *veritas*. Three principal ways were explored in the Middle Ages and after:

1. Medieval thinkers sought to explain and to justify the content of the Augustinian definition by reversing the direction of the truth known as "adequation." Instead of the obvious sense of the *adaequatio rei et intellectus* as the adequation, conformity or conformation of human thought to the things of creation, the *adaequatio intellectus ad rem* becomes the *adaequatio rei ad intellectum*, the adequation or conformity of creation to its exemplary cause, the creative thought of the Divine. The adequation of the created to its model is defined as "certitude." Truth and certainty thus come together in the idea of determination, which will later be called objective, whereas here, at its origin, it is more ideal-real.

This reversal enables the reconciliation of two usages of the word *veritas* that are often opposed in the *sophismata* and the *disputationes*—the question as to whether truth resides in things or in thought, or else first in things and only then in thought, a set of questions that were commonplace in the philosophy and theology of the thirteenth and fourteenth centuries and were inherited from Anselm's *De veritate*.

■ See Box 6.

2. In the classical age, the thesis of adequation is passed on in various ways. In Spinoza the notion of *convenance* allows the axiomatic formulation that "a true idea must agree with [meet with, be suitable] that of which it is the idea," or more literally, with its "ideation": "*Idea vera debet cum suo ideato convenire*" (Benedictus de Spinoza,

6

Certainty and raison d'être (essential purpose)

➤ PRINCIPLE, RES

In keeping with the distinction between two meanings of the word *res* (see RES)— "*res a reor reris*," "*res a ratitudine*"—certain medieval theologians restrict "certainty" or "determination" (Ger. *Bestimmung*) to only those things called *a ratitudine*, which possess "being of essence" (*esse essentiae*) as paradigms (*ratio exemplaris*) of God, which render them naturally able to be produced in actual being. The *ratitudo* thus designates, in a fashion, the "certification" of a thing, an indication of its "authenticity." For Henry of Ghent, the "ratification" or "certification" of a thing determines both its beingness and its truth ("*quanto aliquid in se plus habet ratitudinis sive firmitatis, tanto plus habet entitatis, quare et veritatis*" [the more a thing has of ratification or certification, the more it has of beingness and consequently of truth], Henry of Ghent, *Summa*, art. 34, q. 2, fol. 212rS), as opposed to the inconstancy and inconsistency of fiction, as lacking an example in God (ibid., art. 21, q. 4, fol. 127rO). The ratification or "certitude" of a thing is sufficient reason for its creation: whatever does not have an example in God is nothing "in essence and in nature"; such a "thing" is not a "predicamental thing" (it does not belong to categorial being) and "cannot become effectively real," for God does not put into effect, "produce," "that which has no exemplary *raison d'être* in some creature or another." The exemplary reason is the *raison d'être*: an "authentic" thing is "a nature or absolute essence, endowed with an exemplary reason in God, *destined to exist in existence* through divine operation." The acceptation of truth as "a conformity of things with their essence, such as is thought by God" has been illuminated in a celebrated page of Heidegger:

> According to the traditional concept, truth [*veritas*] is the *adaequatio intellectus et rei*, the adequation of thought and thing [*die Angleichung von Denken und Ding*]; in the place of *adaequatio*, one also refers to *commensuratio* or *convenientia*, accordance or suitability [*Anmessung oder Übereinkunft*]. This definition of the essence of truth is ambiguous, with an ambiguity that already characterized the question of truth in the Middle Ages. . . . As an adequation, truth is part of a determination [*Bestimmung*] of the *ratio*, of the utterance [*der Aussage*], of the proposition [*des Satzes*]. A proposition is true insofar as it comes into line with things [*Wahr ist ein Satz, sofern er sich an die Dinge angleicht*]. But the definition of truth as adequation does not only apply to the proposition in its relation to things. It also applies to things, insofar as they are created and, referring back to the project of the creative spirit, conform to this project. Conceived this way, truth is the conformity of things to their essence, such as it is thought by God [*die Angemessenheit der Dinge an ihr von Gott erdachtes Wesen*].
>
> (Heidegger, *What Is a Thing?*)

BIBLIOGRAPHY

Heidegger, Martin. *What Is a Thing?* [Die Frage nach dem Ding]. Translated by W. B. Barton, Jr., and Vera Deutsch. Analysis by Eugene T. Gendlin. Chicago: Regnery, 1967.

Ethics, I, *De Deo, Axiomata*, VI: Wordsworth Classics of Literature, trans. W. H. White, A. H. Stirling, 29). In Locke, the matrix of joining/separating (for signs) and agree/disagree (for things) serves to repatriate truth to these sole propositions: truth is "nothing but the joining or separating of signs, as the things signified by them do agree or disagree one with another"—whence "the joining or separating of signs here meant is what by another name we call proposition. So that truth properly belongs only to propositions" (*An Essay Concerning Human Understanding*, IV, chap. 5, §2, ed. J. W. Yolton, London: Dent, 1974, 176–77). This purely predicative redefinition of truth constitutes, up to a certain point, a nominalist reading of Aristotle's thesis in the *Metaphysics*, Θ, 10, 1051b4-5, ("He who thinks the separated to be separated and the combined to be combined has the truth, etc."). As such, this is also what Leibniz rejects: if one looks for truth in signs, one ends up reducing truths not only to "mental or nominal" truths, "according to the species of signs," but also to "literal truths, which are indistinguishable from the paper truths or parchment ones, ordinary-ink truths or printers'-ink ones" (Leibniz, *New Essays*, 183). Via the voice of Philalethe, Leibniz in his *New Essays* takes up / translates Locke's thesis thus: truth would consist of "the joining or separating of signs according to how the things signified by them agree or disagree with one another." To which, via the voice of Théophile, he objects that "it would be better to assign truth to the relationships amongst the objects of the ideas—i.e., the items that the ideas are ideas *of*— by virtue of which one idea is or is not included within the other" (ibid., 182). This accent on the objects can be considered a step toward the common notion of "objective" truth, independent of our expressions and on the "good pleasure of men." The "relationship" in question "doesn't depend on languages and is something we have in common with God and the angels. And when God displays a truth to us, we come to possess the truth that is in his understanding, for although his ideas are infinitely more perfect and extensive than ours, they still have the same relationships that ours do," to which Leibniz adds that "truth should be assigned to these relationships. Then we are free to distinguish truths that *do not* depend on our good pleasure, from expressions, which we invent as we see fit" (IV, V, §2, ibid., 183).

3. In the modern period there have been attempts to combine the theme of *rectitudo* with that of *adaequatio*. To this end Anton Marty (1847–1914) defined truth (in Latin) as *adaequatio cogitantis et cogitati* (adequation of the judging [subject] to the [object] of judgment)—a formula in which *cogitare* has the same sense as *urteilen* (judging) and *cogitatum* has the same meaning as *Urteilsinhalt* (judgment-content). According to this definition, a judgment is correct if and only if "the judgment-content

of a judgment exists," which is to say if and only if "a co-existence of a process of judging and a corresponding state of affairs is actually the case [*wirklich gegeben* ist]" (*Untersuchungen*, 426). The *Urteilsinhalt* is "that which objectively grounds the correctness of our judgment" (*was die Richtigkeit unseres Urteilens objectiv begründet*). As the *Urteilsinhalt* is independent of the *Urteilsakt* (the act of judging) and from the *urteilende Person* (the person judging), the *Urteil* must "be directed towards this content" to be true (ibid., 404). Marty's thesis could be reformulated in more contemporary terminology as stating that the content of judgment is its truth-maker.

IV. Truth, Sincerity, Authenticity: Evolution of Antonyms

We can see how the process of truth's subjectification comes to be considered one of the distinctive markers of the modern period. This is particularly evident in the evolution in meaning of antonyms. Subjectification occurs in tandem with a redefinition of responsibility and of the implication of the individual. Instead of the Greek lack of differentiation among the false, the erroneous, and the deceitful, all included in the term *pseudos*, Latin proposes a double terminology: *fallax* is someone who is in error, while *mendax* is someone who lies. Modern terminology promotes confusion between truth value and moral value, as the semantic drift of certain key terms indicates. In French, for example, the word *sincère*, which appeared in 1475 and which derives from the Latin *sincerus*, "pure, uncorrupt," "of one growth" (formed, like *crescere*, on an Indo-European root that expresses ideas of "seed" and "springing forth"), is used in 1763 for "a state of consciousness which is effectively felt" (RT: *DHLF*, under heading "*sincère*"). Even more sincere than sincerity is "authenticity," which first appears in the juridical sense (*authentès* [αὐθέντης]) as indicating someone who acts on his own, *autos* [αὐτός], whether as an absolute master (Euripides, *The Suppliants*, v. 442) or as a murderer (Euripides, *Rhesus*, v. 117). The term subsequently assumes a resolutely moral sense that implies sincerity in relation to oneself. "Authenticity" comes to define the third age of ethics, after the age of excellence and the age of merit (Luc Ferry, *Homo Æstheticus*, Grasset, 1990, "*Les trois âges de l'éthique*," 329–46, trans. Robert de Loaiza: *Homo Aestheticus: The Invention of Taste in the Democratic Age*, 1993; see VIRTÙ).

A. From *pseudos* to *mendax*

1. *Pseudos*: falsehood, error, fiction

For us in the modern age, the most striking feature of the Greek *to pseudos* (adj. later *pseudês*) is the confounding in a single term of what we take pains to distinguish: on the one hand, what we consider under the rubric of lie and falsehood, of deception and feint, as opposed to sincerity and authenticity; and on the other hand, what we consider under the rubric of error and the fake, as opposed to the true and real. The substantive is derived from the verb *pseudô* [ψεύδω], "to deceive," which one finds first and foremost as a means, *pseudomai* [ψεύδομαι], "to cheat, to lie, to fail (an obligation), to betray," but one should also take note of the meaning of the passive constructions: "to be mistaken" with the genitive (*epseusthai tês alêtheias* [ἐψεῦσθαι τῆς ἀληθείας],

to be deprived of the truth) (Plato, *Republic*, 413a, trans. Benjamin Jowett), with the accusative (*pseusma pseudesthai* [ψεῦσμα ψεύδεσθαι], "to be mistaken") (Plato, Meno, 71d), with the dative (*pseusthênai gnômêi* [ψευσθῆναι γνώμῃ], "to be deceived in one's judgment") (Herodotus 7, 9), or with various prepositions (*en tini* [ἔν τινι], *peri tinos* [περί τινος], "to be mistaken about something," "to be mistaken in something") (RT: *Dictionnaire grec français*, and LSJ, s.v. ψεύδω). Dictionaries list "lie" and "lying" as the primary meanings, and for its etymology Chantraine proposes a radical **pseupsu*, a slightly enlarged form of the radical **bhes-*, "to blow," entailing a semantics of "blowing, the blowing wind, lying," which form the basis for the Greek *phêmi* [φημί] or Latin *fari*, "to say."

Perhaps what we call "fiction" will enable us to hold both ends of this chain. At the outset, as we have seen, the *pseudos* leads back to an enunciative strategy, similar to *alêtheia* but in opposition to it (cf. *supra*, I.B.1). We can hear its affirmative dimension in the complaints of the swineherd Eumaeus to Odysseus, unrecognizable in beggar's disguise (*Odyssey*, Bk 14, 124–25):

ἀλλ' ἄλλως κομιδῆς κεχρημένοι ἄνδρες ἀλῆται
ψεύδοντ', οὐδ' ἐθέλουσιν ἀληθέα μυθήσασθαι

(all' allôs komidês kechrêmenoi andres alêtai pseudont', oud' ethelousin alêthea muthêsasthai)

(Tramps in want of a lodging keep coming with their mouths full of lies, and not a word of truth.)

(trans. Samuel Butler)

(Random drifters, hungry for bed and board, lie through their teeth and swallow back the truth.)

(trans. Robert Fagles)

The *pseudos* is simultaneously error, mendacious accounts, and fiction. It is a construction, superimposed and out of sync, but not a counter-truth. The beggars do not lie about Odysseus and know nothing about him. Yet, based on this ignorance, they make up stories that enable them to hide who they really are, thus concealing the truth about themselves (cf. on these "two moments in the lie," Jean-Pierre Levet, *Le Vrai et le Faux dans la pensée grecque archaïque: étude de vocabulaire* [Truth and falsehood in archaic Greek thought: A study of vocabulary], Les Belles Lettres, 1976, 82–83).

The false, in its traditional and more philosophical usage, is in turn nothing more than a bad construction. *Pseudos* or *pseudês* becomes a pure and simple antonym to *alêthês* and *alêtheia* insofar as it implies combining elements that do not belong together. This is how Plato defines it in the *Thaetatus*: There is *pseudos* when there is a "permutation" of two entities in thought and one interchanges one thing for another (*antallaxamenos têi dianoiai phêi einai* [ἀνταλλαξάμενος τῇ διανοίᾳ φῇ εἶναι], *Thaetatus*, 189c), or when we make a bad "connection" between a perception and a thought ("*têi sunapsei* [τῇ συνάψει]," ibid., 195d; see DOXA), or when one "messes up" or "misses" (this is the primary sense of *hamartanein*, "to mistake") by taking one science for another, or a pigeon for a dove ("*anth' heteras heteran hamartôn labêi* [ἀνθ' ἑτέρας ἑτέραν ἁμαρτὼν λάβῃ]," ibid., 199b). The false is above all the result of a poor adjustment between beings and words. This is its definition in the *Cratylus* ("*hos an ta onta legêi hôs estin, alêthês; hos d' an hôs ouk estin, pseudês* [ὃς ἂν τὰ ὄντα λέγῃ ὡς ἔστιν, ἀληθής· ὃς δ' ἂν ὡς οὐκ ἔστιν, ψευδής]" [the discourse which says things as they are is true, that which says them as they are not, is false]) (*Cratylus*, 385b, cf. *Sophist*, 241b), and it is the definition of the *Sophist*, which puts forth the idea of a bad "synthesis," a poor "composition" of nouns and verbs (263d): "When other, then, is asserted of you as the same, and not-being as being [*thatera hôs ta auta kai mê onta hôs onta* (θάτερα ὡς τὰ αὐτὰ καὶ μὴ ὄντα ὡς ὄντα)] such a combination of nouns and verbs [*hê toiautê sunthesis ek te rhêmatôn gignomenê kai onomatôn* (ἡ τοιαύτη σύνθεσις ἔκ τε ῥημάτων γιγνομένη καὶ ὀνομάτων)] is really and truly false." This is, in the end, the classical logical definition of truth as correspondence since Aristotle (cf. *supra*, I.B.2.c).

We should keep in mind that the subjective intention to deceive makes no difference in the Greek terminology: the *pseudos* is part of the coherent and inseparable scope of *alêtheia*, which is simultaneously objective and subjective (truth of being, truth of propositions), and of *doxa* (appearance, opinion); but perhaps we find this all the more repugnant when we hear its echo in the French *fausseté* or the English "falsehood."

■ See Box 7.

2. *Falsus-fallax*, then *fallax-mendax*

Medieval reflections on the lie are based on Augustine (*De mendacio, Contra mendacium*). The most commonly retained definition is from the *Contra mendacium* (XII, 26): "*falsa vocis significatio cum intentione fallendi*" ("A lie is a false signification with will of deceiving," trans. H. Browne). This, however, is not a complete expression of Augustine's thought because for him the lie resides in the nonconformity between the "mouth of the heart" and the "mouth of the body." The liar expresses something other than what lies in his heart, with the intent of deceiving. It matters less whether what he says conforms to a state of affairs or not: he who swears that it is raining, if he truly thinks it, is not a liar, even if it is not raining. But he who says something is true while thinking the contrary, is lying, even if what he says is not a lie. Thus for Augustine it is the *sincerity* of the speaker that matters

---

7

Apatê

➤ ART (Box 2), *FICTION*, PLASTICITY, PROPERTY

There is nonetheless a Greek word, no less difficult to translate than *pseudos*, which implies an intention to deceive, as opposed to the simply false or untrue. It is *apatê* [ἀπάτη], which might be rendered through a series of words, themselves in chronological order—from Homer to later Greek—by "deception," "illusion," "fakery," "ruse," "artifice," "illusion," "pastime," "pleasure." The word's etymology is unknown, even though Aeschylus compares it to *atê* [ἄτη], "folly, fault, crime, the goddess of misfortune," in describing human insolence (*hubris* [ὕβρις]) (*Suppliants*, v. 111). There is a proliferation of verbs: *apataô* [ἀπατάω], to "cheat" or "deceive"; *exapataô* [ἐξαπατάω], to "completely deceive"; *proexapataô* [προεξαπατάω], to "completely deceive from the start." Gorgias enables us to understand the particular value of the *apatê*: "He who deceives [*ho . . . apatêsas* (ὁ . . . ἀπατήσας)] is more just than he who does not deceive, and he who is deceived [*ho . . . apatêtheis* (ὁ . . . ἀπατηθείς)] is wiser than he who is not deceived" (82 B 23 DK). "He who deceives is more just [*dikaioteros* (δικαιότερος)]," he says, "because he keeps to his promise, and he who is deceived is wiser [*sophôteros* (σοφώτερος)], because being easily pleased by discourse [*huph' hêdonês logôn* (ὑφ' ἡδονῆς λόγων)], he is not lacking in sensibility [*anaisthêton* (ἀναίσθητον)]." This fragment comes to us through Plutarch as being in reference to tragedy (*De gloria Atheniensium*, 5, 348). Thus

justice, the founding principle of the city, and wisdom, the basis of *paideia* [παιδεία], are tied to tragedy: *apatê* leads us to the entanglements of literature, pedagogy, and politics. This is a measure of the gulf between the entirely negative *pseudos* that philosophy attributes to the sophist (who, as Plato and Aristotle never cease to point out, deceives by falsely speaking, passing off the false for the true, imitating wisdom and philosophy), and this *apatê*, which results from discursive activity.

With sophism, *apatê* or illusion finds itself not only linked to justice and wisdom but even more radically, through the theater and aesthetic invention, to *aisthêsis* [αἴσθησις], to this very "sensibility" that characterizes our relationship to the world. *Apatê* is the tie between speaker and listener; it means that one recognizes the *pseudos* as *plasma* [πλάσμα], as "fiction," and that one becomes aware of the demiurgical power of the *logos* (see SPEECH ACT and LOGOS). But such a remark only becomes meaningful in contrast to the ontological use of language, implicated since Aristotle in what will become the phenomenological tradition. In *De anima*, the passage from things to words, from phenomena to the *logos*, is thematized and woven together, with the soul acting as guarantor of adequation. Indeed, as for the feeling of one's own sensations, the *idia* [ἴδια], for example, the visible-as-seen for sight (see SENSE, I), a sort of degree zero of sensation,

the soul cannot be deceived. Or more exactly, the *apatê* is *impossible*, in the sense of its being radically "improper" (*mê endechetai* [μὴ ἐνδέχεται], *non decet*), and this impossibility characterizes the immediacy of the aesthetic reception as a noetic reception: *peri ho mê endechetai apathênai* [περὶ ὃ μὴ ἐνδέχεται ἀπαθῆναι] (*De anima*, II, 418a12); *peri tauta ouk estin apathênai* [περὶ ταῦτα οὐκ ἔστιν ἀπαθῆναι] (*Metaphysics*, Θ, 10, 1051b31); "There can be no illusion about that" (cf. Cassin, *Aristote et le logos*, 140–47). Heidegger cannot but comment, playing the antepredicative against the *logos* and *De anima* against *De interpretatione*:

> The Greek conception of truth has been misunderstood. *Aisthêsis*, the sheer sensory perception of something, is "true" in the Greek sense. . . . Any *aisthêsis* aims at its *idia*, those entities which are genuinely accessible only *through* it and *for* it, and to that extent, this perception is always true.
>
> (Heidegger, *Being and Time*, § 7)

BIBLIOGRAPHY

Cassin, Barbara. *Aristote et le logos*. Paris: Presses Universitaires de France, 1997.
———. *L'Effet sophistique*. Paris: Gallimard, 1996.
Heidegger, Martin. *Being and Time*. Translated by Joan Stambaugh. Albany: State University of New York Press, 1996.

more than the *truth* of his utterances. The fact that language enables a disjunction between what is thought and what is signified thus constitutes an argument against the fact of language being an adequate instrument for access to knowledge: "For I am not questioning the fact that the words of truthful [*veracium*] people attempt and in some way profess to express the spirit of the speaker; and they would succeed, as everyone freely would admit, if it was forbidden for liars [*mentientibus*] to speak" (*De magistro*, XIII, 42).

Alexander of Hales distinguishes a *duplex veritas* as a pendant to a *duplex falsitas*, the *falsitas dicti*, the falsehood of what is said, and the *falsitas dicentis*, the "falsehood" of the speaker. As a result, according to Bonaventure, the outer speech can be considered in two modes: in comparison to the thing, the discourse (*sermo*) is said to be *verus* (as opposed to *falsus*) when there is adequation between the thing and the discourse (*adaequatio rei et sermonis*); but in relation to the intentions of the speaker, the discourse is said to be *verax* (as opposed to *fallax*) when there is adequation between the discourse and the intention (*adaequatio sermonis et intentionis*). As we see, the formula follows the wording of the truth as *adaequatio rei et intellectus*. The terms *verax* and *mendax* can also describe a discourse as well as a speaker. But in Thomas Aquinas it would seem that *verax* can only be applied to the speaker (the translation as "sincere" is not precisely correct, in that the term is simply "[he] who says the truth straightforwardly"). He thus very clearly distinguishes, in the line just described, between logical truth, by which something said is true (*adaequatio intellectus vel signi ad rem intellectam et significatam*), and moral truth, by which someone is said to be *verax*, and it is this latter that constitutes a virtue and whose infraction results in a lie (*Summa theologica*, 11, 11, q. 109, a. 1).

The reflections on lying reveal a development that will profoundly modify Augustinian thought. The first underscores the responsibility of the speaker in regards to his use of language; the others relate to the speaker's responsibility to the other. The Augustinian definition refers to *intentio fallendi* (an intention to deceive), while in fact it results from a "determination to speak falsely," as Alexander of Hales emphasizes, by reformulating it thus: "*falso vocis significatio cum voluntate falsum enuntiandi*" (a false utterance with the intention of uttering falsehood) (*Summa theologica*, p. 402, § 399). The speaker is expected to know the rules of language as fixed by convention; if he speaks in a way that does not reflect his intentions, or speaks in equivocal terms, or in formulae that are open to different interpretations from the intended meaning on the part of the listener, he is at fault. Thomas Aquinas puts this reformulation together in proposing an analysis of lies in three parts: (1) falsehood in matter, when the utterance is false; (2) falsehood in form, or the desire to utter the false (*voluntas falsum enuntiandi*); (3) falsity in effect, or the intention to deceive (*intentio fallendi*). Since it is beyond man's capacities to fully say or know the truth, the lie can only be defined as a *voluntary* deviation from the truth (*Summa theologica*, d. 39). In addition, the Augustinian vision of the lie as a discordance between intention and speech presents difficulties of its own, insofar as the intention itself is only accessible to God. But speech, and especially speech that carries an investment of commitment,

such as a vow that explicitly takes God for its guarantor, is uttered for the sake of a listener who does not have access to the intentions of the speaker, only to what he says. In this case is it the intention of the speaker (*intentio dicentis*) or the intention of the recipient (*intentio recipientis*) that creates the obligation? This problem becomes even more complex when the utterances are equivocal: one solution sets up a distinction between the judgment of the Church, which considers the obligation of a vow as a function of what is said, and the judgment of God, which is based on the profound intention and "the spark of conscience" (Bonaventure, *Book of Sentences III*, d. 39, a. III, q. 2).

3. Authenticity and the proper

The modern era prizes the authentic (Ger. *echt*, Eng. "genuine," based on Latin *genus* and Greek *gignesthai* [γίγνεσθαι], "to be born, to become"; see GENIUS, INGENIUM) and prizes authenticity as the task of the subject, an existential metasincerity of the self in relation to the self. This is in a way the impact of the "decentering of the subject"—whether it comes out of Marx (see PRAXIS), out of Freud (see ES, UNCONSCIOUS), out of structuralism (see STRUCTURE), or out of existentialism (see DASEIN)—on the intersecting requirements of logic and morality.

One can refer to the articles on PROPERTY and EREIGNIS and the deployment of the German *eigen* (from *eigen* to *Eigentlichkeit* and to *Ereignis*, from the "own particular" [Fr. *propre*] to "authenticity" and to "appropriating event") for the analysis of a fecund terminological nexus.

■ See Box 8.

V. Comparison of Some Singular Features of English and German in Contemporary Theories

There are three possible paths for expressing the adequation of language to the real in the philosophy of language and to translate the classical *adaequatio* into contemporary terminology: depiction (theory of the image/*Bild*), immanence (redundancy, disquotation), and adequation updated in ordinary language philosophy ("fitting").

A. Theory of the image: Wittgenstein

One of the most powerful paradigms of the representational theory is to be found in Wittgenstein's *Tractatus logico-philosophicus*, according to which propositions (*Sätze*) represent (*abbilden*) states of affairs (*Tatsache*). What is difficult to unpack is this relationship of representation, as soon as it is conceived in terms of an image, *Bild* (see BILD and REPRÉSENTATION). We make an picture of the world for ourselves (2.0212: "*ein Bild der Welt*"), and, more precisely, we picture facts (2.1: "*Wir machen uns Bilder der Tatsachen*"). *Bild* belongs both to the order of representation (*Darstellung, Abbildung*) and of modelling (2.12: *Modell*). It is precisely this link between the *Bild* and reality—the *Abbildung*—and its specific manner of attaining the real that cannot be expressed in language (2.1511: "*Das Bild is so mit der Wirklichkeit verknüpft; es reicht bis zu ihr* [that is how a picture is attached to reality; it reaches right up to it]").

The enigma of truth in the *Tractatus* is to be found in the definition of "logical form," common to the *Bild* and to reality (*Wirklichkeit*), which cannot be rigorously conceived

8

Mauvaise foi, a French affliction

➤ BELIEF, CONSCIOUSNESS, DASEIN, *FAITH*, GLAUBE, *MALAISE, NOTHING*

One of the most remarkable transpositions of the malaise engendered by the imperative of authenticity is Sartre's *mauvaise foi* ("bad faith"), a French rendition of Heideggerian idiom that in turn is difficult to transpose into other languages. For Jean-Paul Sartre, *mauvaise foi* is a structural and defining condition of man as being other than he is, as nonconjunctural: "How can he *be* what he is, when he exists as consciousness of being?" (*Being and Nothingness*, trans. Hazel Barnes, Simon and Schuster, 1992). Or, as we know of the waiter at the café: "from within, the waiter in the café cannot be immediately a café waiter in the sense that this inkwell *is* an inkwell, or the glass is a glass" (ibid., 102); and for my part, "if I represent myself as him, I am not he; I am separated from him as the object from the subject, separated *by nothing*, but this nothing isolates me from him. I cannot be he, I can only play *at being* him; that is, imagine to myself that I am he. And thereby I affect him with nothingness" (ibid.,103).

This is why the ideal of sincerity is a task impossible to fulfill, whose very meaning contradicts the structure of my consciousness. In fact, it is the impossibility of being what one is that is "the very stuff of consciousness." Thus, "in the final analysis, the goal of sincerity and the goal of bad faith are not so different" (ibid., 110). Indeed, sincerity aims at itself in the immanent present such that "bad faith is possible only because sincerity is conscious of missing its goal inevitably, due to its very nature." Bad faith differs from the lie in that "bad faith is *faith.*" Bad faith decides not to demand too much; it is in the end "a decision in bad faith on the nature of faith." In even more stringently Sartrean terms, "good faith seeks to flee the inner disintegration of my being in the direction of the in-itself which it should be and is not. Bad faith seeks to flee the in-itself by means of the inner disintegration of my being. But it denies this very disintegration as it denies that it is itself bad faith."

Contemporary consciousness has, at any rate, recognized itself in this type of analysis, which locates in *Da-Sein* the structural impossibility of sincerity.

as a "relation" to be defined or expressed: the tie between *Bild* and the *Abgebildet* cannot be uttered, only pointed to. But this showing is not exterior to language and to reality (the logical form that they share, *gemein*; cf. 2.2: "*Das Bild hat mit dem Abgebildeten die logische Form der Abbildung gemein* [a picture has logico-pictorial form in common with what it depicts]").

Truth turns out to be intimately dependent on the notion of *Abbildung*. For one to be able to call a proposition true or false, it must be a *Bild*. Truth (*Wahrheit*) and falsehood (*Falschheit*) are defined by the agreement or disagreement (*Übereinstimmung, Nichtübereinstimmung*) of its meaning (*Sinn*) with reality. Once again we come across the division between correctness and truth that the theory of the image is able to efface.

> 2.203 Das Bild stimmt mit der Wirklichkeit überein, oder nicht; es is richtig oder unrichtig, wahr oder falsch.
>
> (A picture agrees with reality or fails to agree; it is correct or incorrect, true or false.)
>
> 2.222 In der Übereinstimmung oder Nichtübereinstimmung seines Sinnes mit der Wirklichkeit, besteht seine Wahrheit oder Falschheit.
>
> (The agreement or disagreement of its sense with reality constitutes its truth or falsity.)

Although a theory of truth-as-correspondence is often attributed to Wittgenstein, based on this idea of *Übereinstimmung*, it nonetheless splits the correspondence into two clearly distinct questions, the issue of the *Abbildung* (the logical form of representation in language) and the question of *Übereinstimmung*, the agreement between the representation and the fact (which can be determined through comparison, *vergleichen*). Thus Wittgenstein sets up the dominant paradigm of analytic philosophy (which also comes out of Frege and his definition of sense as thought) in the association between meaning and truth. A proposition (*Satz*) is true (*wahr*) when it states what is the case, and for a proposition to have meaning is precisely for it to be able to be true or false.

> 4.024 Einen Satz verstehen, heisst, wissen was der Fall ist, wenn er wahr ist.
>
> (To understand a proposition means to know what is the case if it is true.)

This sentence has been interpreted, especially by Moritz Schlick and other members of the Vienna circle, as a verificationist definition of truth and signification, in terms of the empirical and concrete verification of the proposition. In reality, Wittgenstein's proposition is other: it seeks to show the link between meaning and reality by saying that only the *Satz* that says something (be it true or false) of reality is *sinnvoll*. The true, or the possibility of being true or false, thus defines both meaning and language, but also thought and spirit. The final consequence for truth is the bipolarity of the proposition. Even though they have opposite meanings, "p" and "not p" correspond to one single reality, so that negation does not correspond to anything in reality (4.021). The proposition "p" is thus seen as a nonassertive entity, neither affirmative nor negative (see BELIEF).

All of this contributes to redefining truth and correspondence in strongly realistic logico-linguistic terms, making thought and meaning dependent on the *possibility* of being true. Such a redefinition turns out to be tied to the impossibility of saying *in* the language (or demonstrating from outside it) the adequation between language and the real. Far from being a new avatar of correspondence (or of the metaphysics of adequation), the picture theory of the *Tractatus* definitively reveals its aporia.

One should also take note of Popper's reversal of Viennese verificationism in the *Logik der Forschung* (1934, Fr. trans. *Logique de la recherche*, and curiously translated into

English in 1959 as the *Logic of Scientific Discovery*). According to Popper, scientific theories cannot be verified (*verifizieren*) but only corroborated (*bewähren*): "*Theorien sind nicht verifizierbar; aber sie können sich bewähren*" (*Logik der Forschung*, 198). Against Carnap's advice Popper preferred to translate *bewähren* as "corroborate" rather than "confirm" or "retain." He saw *bewähren* as a process of testing by attempts at falsification (*Falsifizierung*), which had nothing to do with any "positive" or empirical confirmation (impossible as far as he was concerned) or with any issue of probability (*Wahrscheinlichkeit*). This translation of *Bewährung* by "corroboration" crystallizes the way Popper aimed to bring analytic philosophy into the English language. He would link the idea of empirical proof to his own method of testing through attempts at falsification (*bewähren* signifies both confirming and testing, as in the expression "a confirmed or proven player") and then separate it from verificationism. This led to numerous debates, but what disappeared in "corroboration" was the *wahr* in *bewähren*. Popper addressed this problem in *Conjectures and Refutations* by reelaborating the concepts of truth and verisimilitude ("truthlikeness"), all the while differentiating them from probability (*Wahrscheinlichkeit*). All of these discussions, reevaluations, and redefinitions were only made possible though the problematic but fecund passage of Viennese German–language epistemology into English at the time of the massive emigration of German and Austrian intellectuals (including Popper and Carnap) during the 1930s.

B. Redundancy, disquotation, immanence: Ramsey, Quine

Another option, in the face of the aporia of correspondence, would be to eliminate the predicate of truth. Frank P. Ramsey, following the *Tractatus*, sought to clarify the question of truth (and Wittgenstein's notion of the impossibility of expressing *in language* the adequation to the real) by proposing his "redundancy theory of truth." This theory is one of the first passes at "deflationism." The points in common between the different variants of deflationist theories of truth—disappearance theory of truth, no-truth theory of truth, minimalist theory of truth—are sufficiently important that one can group them together under the heading of "redundancy," as so many theories that maintain that the words "true" and "false" simply function in a statement as signs of assertion or negation. The foundation of redundancy theory (unfortunately translated into French as "*théorie redondante de la vérité*"—the "redundant theory of truth") used the meaning of the Latin *nugatio* ("useless repetition"). It was illustrated by Ramsey in 1927 (and subsequently by Ayer in 1935) that the phrase "it is true that Caesar was murdered" means no more than that "Caesar was murdered." "Deflationism" seems to be too vague a term to precisely qualify the thesis according to which the affirmation that a statement is true is nothing more than the affirmation of the statement. Another way of labeling the theory was the "disquotational theory of truth," but it remains a poor expression for this simple act of eliminating quotation marks. Whence Tarski's utterance, paradigmatic of the correspondence theory of truth: "The snow is white." According to Tarski's theory, "the snow is white" is true if and only if the snow is white. In Quine's analysis, since quotation (in quotation marks) is a name for a sentence that contains a name (*snow*, which is a name for snow): "By calling

the sentence true, we call the snow white." Quine concludes by stating that "the truth predicate is a device for disquotation." The quotation marks are made for being removed: "The truth predicate is a reminder that, despite a technical ascent to talk of sentences, our eye is on the world." (*Philosophy of Logic*, 97). This claim to an outside of language brings back something of the verificatory meaning of *esti* and of "existing" (see ESTI). This is why, according to Quine:

> Along with this seriocomic blend of triviality and paradox, truth is felt to harbor something of the sublime.
>
> (Quine, *From Stimulus to Science*)

C. Adequation revisited

1. Austin and "true"
A third option would be to rethink adequation by bringing it down to the level of ordinary language. Austin is equally critical of metaphysical doctrines of truth and its various epistemological and verificationist versions, and he goes after the idea of correspondence without sparing the *Tractatus*. Rather than taking on the idea of truth, he proposes to examine the true, and hence the usage of the word "true."

> We ask ourselves whether Truth is a substance (the Truth, the body of knowledge) or a quality inhering to truths, or a relation ("correspondence").... What needs discussing rather is the use, or certain uses, of the word "true."
>
> (Austin, *Philosophical Papers*, 117)

Rather than taking an interest in the truth, philosophers should, in his estimation, concern themselves with that which is at their level (cf. his formula "*Be your size*"): the usage of words. In a celebrated phrase (and following the traditional word order, cf. above), Austin adds that he places *verum* before *veritas*:

> "*In vino*," possibly "*veritas*," but in a sober symposium, "*verum*."
>
> (Ibid.)

If we limit ourselves to our usages of "true," we observe that we can neither reduce them to a correspondence with the real nor eliminate them, which means that we must conclude that the two analytic paradigms of truth—correspondence and redundance—cannot fully account for "true." The idea of a correspondence between every utterance and a determinate fact is illusory and leads one to think that each true utterance has "its own" corresponding fact: "for every cap the head it fits" (ibid., 123) Austin also points out that it is difficult to establish any purely internal and language-based criterion of truth: truth requires two elements. "It takes two to make a truth" (ibid., 124). On cannot eliminate the qualification "is true" nor consider "true" without a family of related qualifiers, about which it cannot be said that they are "logically superfluous": exaggerated, simplistic, vague, imprecise, general, or concise (ibid., 129).

2. After correspondence: "Fitting" / *es stimmt*
For Austin "true" designates only one of the possible ways of saying how words "fit the facts" of the world. "Fitting"

thus designates a concept of adequation that is no longer correspondence, in the sense of being exact or correct but that designates the appropriate or proper quality of the utterance for the occasion, thus coming back into contact with a dimension of the rhetoric of antiquity (Greek *prepon* [πρέπον], see MIMÊSIS, Box 6).

> There are various degrees and dimensions of success in making statements: the statement fits the facts always more or less loosely, in different ways on different occasions.
>
> (Austin, *Philosophical Papers*, 130)

This analysis of "true" is carried still further in *How to Do Things with Words*, in which Austin looks at the true within the framework of performatives in order to extend his conception to utterances known as "constatives," which describe a reality. "True" designates a general dimension of being proper, of what is appropriate to a particular circumstance. In that case "true" can also be said of a performative, since all of language is being considered under this aspect of convention.

> It is essential to realize that "true" and "false," like "free" and "unfree," do not stand for anything simple at all; but only for a general dimension of being a right or proper thing to say as opposed to a wrong thing, in these circumstances.
>
> (Austin, *How to Do Things with Words*, 145)

Such a conception of the true as "fitting" or appropriate is also proposed in the later Wittgenstein, with regard to certain relations of adequation between words and things, situations, and experiences that cannot be thought of in terms of correspondence (either logical or mental). This is what we understand by "the right expression," the words that are proper or convenient (*treffend, passend*)—that one looks for and does not necessarily find easily. But when one does find them, one says "*Das ist es*," "*ça y est*," "got it" to describe the thing or situation.

> Denke nur an den Ausdruck und die Bedeutung des Ausdrucks "das treffende Wort."
>
> (Just think of the expression, and the meaning of the expression: "the word that hits it off.")
>
> (Wittgenstein, *Philosophical Investigations*, II)

A feeling of adequation cannot be accounted for by a logic-based (Fr. *logiciste*) notion of meaning (see SENSE, III) but is essential to Wittgenstein's understanding of signification, as when one feels that a proper name just "fits" a person or a thing.

> Mir ist, als passte der Name Schubert zu Schuberts Werken und seinem Gesicht.
>
> (I feel as if the name "Schubert" fitted Schubert's works and Schubert's face.)
>
> (Ibid.)

To describe this feeling, Wittgenstein deploys an entire vocabulary: "*Es stimmt*" ("that's right"; Fr. *ça va*), "*Dies Wort passt, dies nicht*" ("*this* word fits, *that* doesn't"; Fr. *ce mot convient, l'autre non*) (ibid., 219). His entire effort in the second part of the *Investigations* is directed toward defining this specific "life experience" that conditions the usage of language and is the condition of its truth.

To understand what is at stake in this redefinition of the truth, one can compare it to certain reflections by Brentano and Husserl on truth, no longer conceived as a correspondence between thought and object but as an agreement, an adequation revisited: to be adequate (*übereinstimmen*), according to Brentano in *Wahrheit und Evidenz*, is not to be the same or similar but to be in agreement, to be suitable: *entsprechend sein, passend sein, dazu stimmen*. Husserl extends this questioning of the model of correspondence by differentiating *Übereinstimmung* from *Adäquation* (which causes problems for translation) (*Logical Investigations*, VI § 66). These reinterpretations of the scheme of adequation entail an extension of the scope, not the elimination of the concept of truth. The formulations of Wittgenstein and Austin have nothing to do with any "pragmatist" conception of truth, and even less with any relativistic one. Austin argues that there is a great difference between his conception of truth and the pragmatist doctrines. "This doctrine is very different from almost everything the pragmatists say, which is that the true is *what works*, etc." The characteristic that makes a statement appropriate, that Austin's doctrine and Wittgenstein's reflections seek to grasp, is determined by precise and enumerable criteria that cannot be collapsed into the success or effect of discourse, to what "works." There is a great difference between the verbs to "work" and to "fit," between the fuzziness of what "works" or functions and the rigor of the adjustments required. One can only be struck by the poverty of the French vocabulary when one tries to underscore or translate these differences.

Rémi Brague
Barbara Cassin
Sandra Laugier
Alain de Libera
Irène Rosier-Catach
Michèle Sinapi

BIBLIOGRAPHY

Anselm of Canterbury. *De veritate*. Translated by Ralph McInerny. In *Anselm of Canterbury: The Major Works*, edited by Brian Davies and G. R. Evans. Oxford: Oxford University Press, 2008.

Arendt, Hannah. *The Human Condition*. Chicago: University of Chicago Press, 1998.

Austin, J. L. *How to Do Things with Words*. Oxford: Clarendon Press, 1962.

———. *Philosophical Papers*. Oxford: Clarendon Press, 1962.

———. *Sense and Sensibilia*. Oxford: Clarendon Press, 1962.

Ayer, Alfred J. "The Criterion of Truth." *Analysis* 3 (1935).

Blackburn, Simon, and Keith Simmons, eds. *Truth*. Oxford: Oxford University Press, 1999.

Bolzano, Bernard. *Wissenschaftslehre*. Sulzbach: Seidel, 1837. *Theory of Science*. Edited by Rolf George. Oxford: Oxford University Press, 1972.

Cassin, Barbara. *L'Effet sophistique*. Paris: Gallimard, 1996.

———. *Parménide, "Sur la nature ou sur l'étant." La langue de l'être*? Paris: Seuil, 1998.

Clark, Maudemarie. *Nietzsche on Truth and Philosophy*. Cambridge: Cambridge University Press, 1990.

Colish, Marcia L. "The Stoic Theory of Verbal Signification and the Problem of Lies and False Statements from Antiquity to St. Anselm." In *Archéologie du Signe*, edited by L. Brind'Amour and E. Vance, 17–43. Toronto: Pontifical Institute of Medieval Studies, 1983.

Colleran, J. M. *Ancient Christian Writers*. Mahwah, NJ: Newman Press, 1950.

Detienne, Marcel. *The Masters of Truth in Archaic Greece*. Translated by Janet Lloyd. New York: Zone Books, 1996.

Ellenbogen, Sara. *Wittgenstein's Account of Truth*. Albany: State University of New York Press, 2003.

Engel, Pascal. *The Norm of Truth: An Introduction to the Philosophy of Logic*. Translated by Miriam Kochan and Pascal Engel. Toronto: University of Toronto Press, 1991.

Florensky, Pavel. *The Pillar and Ground of the Truth*. Translated and annotated by Boris Jakim. Princeton, NJ: Princeton University Press, 1997.

Frege, Gottlob. *Translations from the Philosophical Writings of Gottlob Frege*. 3rd ed. Edited and translated by P. Geach and M. Black. Oxford: Blackwell, 1980.

Heidegger, Martin. "The End of Philosophy and the Task of Thinking." Translated by Joan Stambaugh. In *Basic Writings*, edited by David Farrell Krell. New York: Harper and Row, 1977.

———. *An Introduction to Metaphysics*. Translated by Ralph Manheim. New Haven, CT: Yale University Press, 1959.

———. "'Logos,' 'Moira,' 'Alêtheia.'" In *Vorträge und Aufsätze*. 4 vols. Pfullingen, Ger.: G. Neske, 1978.

———. *Nietzsche*. 4 vols. Translated by David Farrell Krell. San Francisco: Harper and Row, 1979–1982.

———. "On the Essence of Truth." In *Basic Writings*, edited by David Farrell Krell. New York: Harper and Row, 1977.

———. "Plato's Doctrine of Truth." Translated by Thomas Sheehan. In *Pathmarks*, edited by W. McNeill. Cambridge: Cambridge University Press, 1998.

Hesiod. *Theogony*. In *The Homeric Hymns and Homerica*. Translated by Hugh G. Evelyn-White. London: W. Heinemann, 1914.

Husserl, Edmund. *Introduction to Logic and the Theory of Knowledge* [1906–1907]. Translation by Dallas Willard in *Early Writings in the Philosophy of Logic and Mathematics* (Hua vol. 5). Dordrecht, Neth.: Kluwer, 1993.

John XXI (Peter of Spain). *Syncategoreumata*. First critical edition with an introduction and indexes by L. M. de Rijk; with an English translation by Joke Spruyt. Leiden, Neth,: E. J. Brill, 1991.

Kirk, G. S., J. E. Raven, and M. Schofield. *The Presocratic Philosophers: A Critical History with a Selection of Texts*. 2nd ed. Cambridge: Cambridge University Press, 2007.

Leibniz, Gottfried Wilhelm. *New Essays on Human Understanding*. Cambridge: Cambridge University Press, 1996.

Lynch, Michael P., ed. *The Nature of Truth: Classic and Contemporary Perspectives*. Cambridge, MA: MIT Press, 2001.

Marty, Anton. *Untersuchungen zur Grundlegung der Allgemeinen Grammatik und Sprachphilosophie*. Vol 1. Halle, Ger.: Niemeyer, 1908.

Medina, Jose, and David Wood, eds. *Truth: Engagements across Philosophical Traditions*. Malden, MA: Blackwell, 2005.

Moody, Ernest A. *Truth and Consequence in Mediaeval Logic*. Westport, CT: Greenwood Press, 1976.

Nietzsche, Friedrich. *Twilight of the Idols, or, How to Philosophize with the Hammer*. Translated by Richard Polt. Introduction by Tracy Strong. Indianapolis, IN: Hackett, 1997.

Quine, W.V.O. *From Stimulus to Science*. Cambridge, MA: Harvard University Press, 1995.

———. *Philosophy of Logic*. Englewood Cliffs, NJ: Prentice Hall, 1970.

———. *Pursuit of Truth*. Cambridge, MA: Harvard University Press 1990.

———. *Word and Object*. Cambridge, MA: MIT Press, 1960.

Ramsey, Frank P. *The Foundations of Mathematics and Other Logical Essays*. Edited by R. B. Braithwaite. Preface by G. E. Moore. London: Routledge and Kegan Paul, 1965.

Rosier, Irène. "Les développements médiévaux de la théorie augustinienne du mensonge." *Hermès* 15–16: 87–99.

———. "Le serment et les théories linguistiques médiévales." *Memini: Travaux et documents publiés par la Société des études médiévales du Québec* 2 (1998): 3–28.

Smith, Barry. *Austrian Philosophy: The Legacy of Franz Brentano*. Chicago: Open Court Publishing, 1994.

Thomas, Yan. "Les artifices de la vérité: Note sur l'interprétation médiévale du droit romain." *L'Inactuel* 6 (Autumn, 1996): 81–99.

Vecchio, S. "Mensonge, simulation, dissimulation: Primauté de l'intention et ambiguïté du langage dans la théologie morale du bas Moyen Âge." In *Vestigia, Imagines, Verba: Semiotics and Logic in Medieval Theological Texts (1150–1450)*. Acts of the 11th Symposium on Medieval Logic and Semantics, 117–32. Turnhout, Belg.: Brepols, 1997.

Wittgenstein, Ludwig. *Philosophical Investigations*. Bilingual edition. Translated by G.E.M. Anscombe. Oxford: Blackwell, 2001.

———. *Tractatus Logico-Philosophicus*. Translated by D. F. Pears and B. F. McGuiness. London: Routledge and Kegan Paul, 1974.

UNCONSCIOUS, UNCONSCIOUSNESS

FRENCH   *inconscient, inconscience*
GERMAN   *unbewusst, Unbewusste; Unbewusstheit,*
          Unbewusstsein

➤ CONSCIOUSNESS, DRIVE, ES, I/ME/MYSELF, PERCEPTION, ROMANTIC, SOUL,
  SUBJECT

Unlike other terms from the vocabulary of psychoanalysis, the term
"unconscious" has never posed any particular problems of translation. French and English were already equipped to receive the
German noun *das Unbewusste* and to render it using the equivalent
terms "the unconscious" and *l'inconscient*. Similarly, *das Vorbewusste*
is translated without difficulty in French as *le préconscient* and in
English as "the preconscious." Does this mean that the "unconscious"
has effectively been understood exactly as Freud conceived it? It is
important to emphasize first of all that the term only really acquires
its meaning in his first topographical theory, which made a distinction among three systems: the unconscious, the preconscious, and
the conscious. This theory is unrivalled in its rigor in the psychology
of the end of the nineteenth century and the beginning of the twentieth century. It is perhaps precisely this rigor that causes problems
for translators. Thus, Freud is led to reject the term "subconscious,"
which was very much in vogue in France and in English-speaking
countries, or to put aside "unconsciousness" (*die Unbewusstheit*,
l'inconscient). The translation of *das Unbewusste* as "the unconscious"
is perhaps not sufficient to fully grasp its meaning. In order to understand what is at stake in this question, one has to tease out the
threads of several successive moments in its history.

I. "Non-Conscious Representations" and Unconsciousness

The problem of "non-conscious representations" is posed in the
wake of Leibniz and his "small perceptions." For Leibniz it is a
matter of affirming, against Descartes, that if the soul is always
thinking, it is not always conscious of its thoughts: "at every
moment there is in us an infinity of perceptions, unaccompanied by awareness or reflection; that is, of alterations in the soul
itself, of which we are unaware because these impressions are
either too minute and too numerous, or else too unvarying"
(*New Essays*, preface). These perceptions are said to be "insen-
sible," this adjective thus corresponding in classical language to
the future "unconscious" (cf. also Descartes, *Meditations on First
Philosophy*, 12–15). To be conscious is, in effect, to sense oneself
(from the Latin *sentire*).

The question that continuously haunts philosophical and
psychological debates is the question of degree. If full, complete consciousness has a status determined by clarity and
consciousness of self (which Leibniz calls awareness; see
CONSCIOUSNESS and PERCEPTION), how does one then go from
simple perception to insensibility? Kant took the Leibnizian
principle of continuity to its furthest consequences, and thus

proposed an infinite number of degrees between the fully
conscious and the unconscious, in a text that is part of a psychological, nontranscendental perspective:

> Just as between consciousness and the fully uncon-
> scious (psychological darkness) [*zwischen einem Be-
> wusstsein und dem völligen Unbewusstsein* (*psychologischer
> Dunkelheit*)], yet smaller degrees occur; therefore no
> perception is possible that shows a complete absence,
> e.g., no psychological darkness is possible that could
> not be regarded as a state of consciousness that simply
> is outweighed by another, stronger one, and thus it is in
> all cases of sensation.

(Kant, *Prolegomena to Any Future Metaphysics*, §21)

Ever faithful to Leibniz on this point, Kant therefore affirms, in *Anthropologie in pragmatischer Hinsicht*, that "the
field of *obscure* representations is the largest in the human
being" (*Anthropology from a Pragmatic Point of View*, 25).

Philosophically, there is a great deal at stake here, since
the adversary is not Descartes, but rather Locke, the founder
of empirical psychology, who cannot admit that a representation is unconscious (ibid., 23–24). We can also see that Kant
is in no way interested in clearing the way for a particular
topos, which would have specific laws (what *das Unbewusste*
will be for Freud), but simply in articulating the negative of
consciousness (*das Unbewusstsein*), that is, a "negative state
of consciousness": what darkness is to light. Translating this
as "unconsciousness" seems inevitable.

II. Substantivizing the Unconscious:
Romanticism and von Hartmann

With Romanticism, a wide range of terms were adopted in
German, English, and French, joining a privative prefix to
the lexical field of consciousness, such as *unbewusst*, "unconscious," and *inconscient*, and the nouns *Unbewusstheit*,
Unbewusstsein, "unconsciousness," and *inconscience*. The
substantivized adjective *das Unbewusste* was less common,
even though it is found, for example, in the opening lines
of a work by the Romantic philosopher and doctor Carl
Gustav Carus (1789–1869), in a first edition dating from
1846:

> The key to the knowledge of the nature of the conscious
> life of the soul is to be sought in the reign of the uncon-
> scious [*des Unbewusstseins*]. Hence the difficulty, if not
> impossibility, of understanding fully the secret of the
> soul. If it were absolutely impossible to find the uncon-
> scious [*das Unbewusste*] in consciousness, man would be
> left to despair of ever being able to attain knowledge of
> his soul, that is to say, knowledge of himself. But if this
> impossibility is merely apparent, then the first task of a

science of the soul will be to determine how man's mind can go down into these depths.

(Carus, *Psyche*, 1)

Generally speaking, and as this extract testifies, the importance of this trend is in the recognition that this unconscious realm has a positive quality: far from being the lowest degree of consciousness, the darkness of the unconscious is a guarantee of its richness and its truth value.

A third stage occurred when one work, *Philosophie des Unbewussten* by Edouard von Harmann (1870) definitively established the substantivized adjective *das Unbewusste* as a noun in its own right. Its title reveals how fully accepted and recognized the term was philosophically, since in this text *das Unbewusste* refers to the metaphysical basis of all things, which Schopenhauer had named *der Wille*, "the will." The choice of term is significant: in Schopenhauer the will is set in opposition to representation (*die Vorstellung*), which excludes the idea that there can be unconscious representations. The Freudian unconscious would itself be inseparably made up of affects and representations. Hartmann's work made a considerable impact and was soon translated into French (*Philosophie de l'inconscient*, translated by D. Nollen, 1877) and English (*Philosophy of the Unconscious*, translated by W. C. Coupland, 1884). Dictionaries, notably the French Littré (RT: *Dictionnaire de la langue française*), refer to this translation as full recognition of its use as a noun.

III. The Subconscious and Psychophysiology

Shortly before Freud there was a huge growth in scientific psychology from about the middle of the nineteenth century (in particular the *Grundzüge der physiologischen Psychologie* by Wilhelm Wundt or the works of Alexander Bain in England and Théodule Ribot in France), as well as research into multiple consciousness in somnambulism and hysteria. The intellectual context of these debates is no longer Romanticism but Positivism, which returns to the classical question of the degrees of consciousness. One can locate an effect of this vocabulary of the unconscious in the translation of texts in which the term was not present. Thus, in an early twentieth-century English translation of Leibniz's *La Monadologie*, the term "unconsciousness" is used to render the French *étourdissement*, which refers to the states of apparent death. The first sentence of paragraph 23 thus introduces into the translation a vocabulary of consciousness and unconsciousness that was altogether absent in Leibniz:

Therefore, since on awakening after a period of unconsciousness we become conscious of our perception, we must, without having been conscious of them, have had perceptions immediately before.

(Donc, puisque réveillé de l'étourdissement on s'aperçoit de ses perceptions, il faut bien qu'on en ait eu immédiatement auparavant, quoiqu'on ne s'en soit aperçu.)

(Leibniz, *Monadology*, 1902)

But it was the term "subconscious" (in French, *subconscient*; in German, *unterbewusst*) that came to designate that which

is just below the threshold of consciousness. In an article entitled "Consciousness and Unconsciousness," for example, the psychologist G. H. Lewes defended the thesis of the psychic nature of the *unconsciousness* and of the *subconsciousness* against the partisans of "unconscious cerebration," that is, of the purely reflex nature of unconscious mechanisms. But in any case, it is merely a question of complexity: "All of the arguments thus tend to show that between conscious, subconscious and unconscious states, the difference resides solely in the degrees of complication in the neural processes." In the field of psychopathology, Pierre Janet accords great importance to "subconscious acts" (*actes subconscients*), or "actions having all of the characteristics of a psychological fact except one, which is that the person who performs it is unaware of it at the very moment at which he or she performs it" (Janet, *L'automatisme psychologique*). These acts are due to "psychological weakness" (*faiblesse psychologique*), to the narrowing of the field of consciousness, which thus allows automatic acts to be expressed.

IV. The Freudian Moment

If we turn now to Freud, we can see that he himself uses the term "subconscious" (*subconscient*) in an article written in French in 1893, "Quelques considérations pour une étude comparative entre les paralysies motrices organiques et hystériques" ("Some Points for Comparative Study of Organic and Hysterical Motor Paralyses" in *The Standard Edition of the Complete Psychological Works of Sigmund* Freud, 160–72). Freud had been commissioned by Charcot to write this article, and we find him using the French terminology that was current at the time. It is from the *Interpretation of Dreams* on, however, and in the final chapter devoted to the "psychology of dream processes" (Strachey) that we find the first elaboration of the first topological theory, which is explained in the metapsychological article entitled precisely "Das Unbewusste" (1915). The unconscious—*das Unbewusste*—is therefore one of the three psychic systems. It follows its own laws (the primary process: condensation, displacement, etc.), which enable Freud to account for the formal particularities of dreams and the mechanisms for interpreting them. The *Vocabulaire de la psychanalyse* (Language of Psychoanalysis) summarizes neatly the characteristics of the "unconscious system" as follows:

a. Its "contents" are "representatives" of the instincts.
b. These contents are governed by the mechanisms specific to the primary process, especially by condensation and displacement.
c. Strongly cathected by instinctual energy, they seek to reenter consciousness and resume activity (the return of the repressed), but they can only gain access to the system *Pcs.-Cs.* in compromise-formations after having undergone the distortions of the censorship.
d. It is more especially childhood wishes that become fixated in the unconscious.

(Laplanche and Pontalis, *The Language of Psychoanalysis,* trans. Donald Nicholson-Smith, London: Hogarth, 1973)

Freud materializes this topological aspect by using abbreviations to refer to the different systems: *Ubw*, *Vbw*, *Bw* (in English *Ucs*, *Pcs* and *Cs*, and in French *Ics*, *Pcs*, *Cs*). This is a strange thing to do: the epistemology is on the face of it positivist, but Freud breaks away from any differentiation by degree (the differences between the *Pcs-Cs* and the *Ucs* are natural differences), and he appears to return to the Romantic proposition concerning the unconscious foundation of being. He only "appears" to, however, since on the one hand the unconscious "in itself" remains inaccessible, and on the other hand it is not endowed with any metaphysical attributes. We might well wonder whether the specificity of the unconscious "system" is duly conveyed by the term *das Unbewusste*, burdened as it is with the Positivist and Romantic double origin.

■ See Box 1.

An interesting example of the way in which Freud's "unconscious" was received in France can be found when we look at its fate in the first issues of the *Revue française de psychanalyse* (*RFP*), the official journal of the Société Psychanalytique de Paris, founded in 1926. The translations of Freud's texts are characterized by a scrupulous respect for the transition from the German *das Unbewusst* to the French *l'inconscient* and by the disappearance of the vocabulary of the "subconscious." There are traces nonetheless of the gap left by the word "subconscious." A significant example surfaces in Édouard Pichon's review of *Traité de psychologie* by Georges Dwelshauvers, a psychologist from the neo-Thomist school, an important school at the time. We find the following:

L'inconscient, ce n'est que l'insu. Il est toujours virtuellement sujet aux atteintes de la conscience.... Ainsi se complète pour moi la définition de l'inconscient: *l'ensemble des choses actuellement étrangères à la conscience du je, mais que cette conscience peut être éventuellement amenée à saisir sous l'espèce des siens états d'âme.*

(*RFP*, no. 2 [1928]: 369–70)

(The unconscious is only what is unknown. It is always virtually subject to the reach of consciousness.... For me, then, the definition of the unconscious is to be completed as follows: *the set of all things presently outside the consciousness of the self, but which can eventually be accessed as consciousness through states of feeling associated with self.*)

We see, then, that it was that much easier for French psychoanalysts to get rid of the subconscious since the term *inconscient* retained what was most essential, that is, the negative relationship to consciousness. Pichon, who was a good grammarian, must have been satisfied with a term that was constructed as a privative. Freud would perhaps have preferred a term that was not simply the negative of consciousness. We remain uneasy about the fact that English and French both lack a positive term to refer to this other psychic place. But is this not simply a linguistic problem?

Freud in effect chose the term *das Unbewusste* by default, no doubt because he was afraid of the many misunderstandings to which a term laden with dual Romantic and psycho-physiological history lent itself. Since German has no term that clearly designates the "systematic" character of the new unconscious any more than it has a term for its conceptual character, there are gaps of reference. This was no doubt what Jacques Lacan noticed when, in the introduction to a lecture on the unconscious delivered at a conference in Bonneval, he declared: "The unconscious is a concept forged from the trace of what is at work in constituting

---

1

Unconsciousness and the unconscious as a system

We find an interesting example of the linguistic and theoretical stakes of the unconscious as Freud understands it, and of his perspective on the term itself, in an article he wrote in English that was almost certainly translated into German by Hanns Sachs, although Freud would have proofread it. The article is "A Note on the Unconscious in Psychoanalysis" (Einige Bemerkungen über den Begriff des Unbewussten in der Psychoanalyse), originally published in the *Proceedings of the Society for Psychical Research* (1912). The final paragraph of this text presents the transition from the quality of that which escapes consciousness, simple *unconsciousness*, to the properly Freudian *unconscious*, characterized by its systematic dimension. The German text, curiously, does not take

into account this shift, nor do the first French translations, up to and including 1968. Ultimately, only the English and French (in its final version, that of the OCFIP) are in this respect faithful to Freud's theoretical operation.

Unconsciousness [*das Unbewusste*] seemed to us at first only an enigmatical characteristic of a definite psychical activity. Now it means more to us. It is a sign that this act partakes of the nature of a certain psychical category known to us by other and more important characteristics and that it belongs to a system of psychical activity which is deserving our fullest attention. The index value of the unconscious [*der Wert des Unbewussten als Index*] has far outgrown its importance as a property. The system

[*das System*] revealed by the sign that the single acts forming parts of it are unconscious [*unbewusst*] we designate by the name "the unconscious" ["*das Unbewusste*"], for want of a better and less ambiguous term [*in Ermangelung eines besseren und weniger zweideutigen Ausdruckes*]. In German, I propose to denote this system by the letters *Ubw*, an abbreviation of the German word *Unbewusst*. And this is the third and most significant sense which the term "unconscious" has acquired in psychoanalysis [*dies ist der dritte und wichtigste Sinn, den der Ausdruck "unbewusst" in der Psycho-analyse erworben hat*].

(Freud, *Standard Edition*, 12: 266; *Gesammelte Werke*, 8: 438–39) the subject. The unconscious is not a type that defines within psychic reality the circle of what has no attribute (or virtues) of consciousness" ("Position de l'inconscient," in *Ecrits*, Seuil, 1966, 830; "Position of the Unconscious," in *Ecrits*, trans. Bruce Fink, W.W. Norton, 2006, 716). And Lacan would in turn "invent" a term, not a translation but a transcription of the German into the French: the unconscious is "*l'une-bévue*" [lit. "one-slip"], or that which produces an unexpected meaning, not that which is outside of meaning, or which would contain the essence of all meanings (*Le Séminaire*, 24, *L'Insu qui sait de l'une bévue s'aile à mourre*, 1976–77, unpublished).

Alexandre Abensour

BIBLIOGRAPHY

Calich, José Carlos, and Helmut Hinz. *The Unconscious: Further Reflections*. London: International Psychoanalytic Association, 2007.

Carus, Carl Gustav. *Psyche: Zur Entwicklungsgeschichte der Seele*. Foreword by Friedrich Arnold. Darmstadt, Ger.: Wissenschaftliche Buchgesellschaft, 1975. First published in 1846. Translation by Renata Welch: *Psyche: On the Development of the Soul, Part One: The Unconscious*. New York: Springer, 1970.

Descartes, René. "First Meditation." In *Meditations on First Philosophy, with Selections from the Objections and Replies*. Edited and translated by John Cottingham. Rev. ed. Cambridge: Cambridge University Press, 1996.

Ellenberger, Henri F. *The Discovery of the Unconscious: The History and Evolution of Dynamic Psychiatry*. New York: Basic Books, 1970.

Ey, Henri, ed. *L'Inconscient* [6ᵉ Colloque de Bonneval, 1960]. Paris: Desclée de Brouwer, 1966.

Frankl, George. *The Social History of the Unconscious*. London: Open Gate, 1989.

Freud, Sigmund. *Gesammelte Werke*. 18 vols. Frankfurt am Main: Fischer, 1968–78.

———. *Nachtragsband (1885–1938)*. Frankfurt: Fischer, 1987.

———. *The Standard Edition of the Complete Psychological Works of Sigmund Freud*. 24 vols. Edited by James Strachey. London: Hogarth Press, 1953–66.

Hesnard, Angelo. *L'Inconscient*. Paris: Librairie Doin, 1923.

Janet, Pierre. *L'automatisme psychologique*. Paris: Odile Jacob, 1998. First published in 1894.

Kant, Immanuel. *Anthropologie in pragmatischer Hinsicht*. Edited by Königlich Preussischen Akademie der Wissenschaften. In *Kants Gesammelte Schriften*. Vol. 7. Berlin: De Gruyter, 1902–. Translation by Robert B. Louden: *Anthropology from a Pragmatic Point of View*. Edited by Robert B. Louden. Cambridge: Cambridge University Press, 2006.

———. *Prolegomena zu einer jeden künftigen Metaphysik, die als Wissenschaft wird auftreten können*. Edited by Königlich Preussischen Akademie der Wissenschaften. In *Kants Gesammelte Schriften*. Vol. 4. Berlin: De Gruyter, 1902–. First published in 1783. Translation by Gary Hatfield: *Prolegomena to Any Future Metaphysics That Will Be Able to Come Forward as Science; Selections from the Critique of Pure Reason*. Edited by Gary Hatfield. Rev. ed. Cambridge: Cambridge University Press, 2004.

Leibniz, Gottfried Wilhelm. *Discourse on Metaphysics, Correspondence with Arnauld, Monadology*. Translated by George Montgomery. Introduction by Paul Janet. Chicago: Open Court, 1902.

———. *New Essays on Human Understanding*. Edited and translated by Peter Remnant and Jonathan Bennett. Cambridge: Cambridge University Press, 1996.

Lewes, George Henry. "Consciousness and Unconsciousness." *Mind* 2 (1877): 156–67.

MacIntyre, Alasdair C. *The Unconscious: A Conceptual Analysis*. London: Routledge and Kegan Paul, 1958.

Münsterberg, Hugo, Théodule Ribot, Pierre Janet, Joseph Jastrow, Bernard Hart, and Morton Prince. *Subconscious Phenomena*. Boston: R. G. Badger, 1910.

Ribot, Théodule. *Les mouvements et l'activité inconsciente*. Paris: Cariscript, 1991.

Whyte, Lancelot Law. *The Unconscious before Freud*. New York: Basic Books, 1960.

UNDERSTANDING

FRENCH	*entendement*
GERMAN	*Verstand, Verstehen*
GREEK	*nous* [νοῦς]
ITALIAN	*intelletto*
LATIN	*intellectus*
SPANISH	*intendimiento, intelecto*

➤ BEGRIFF, CONSCIOUSNESS, GEMÜT, I/ME/MYSELF, INTELLECT, INTELLECTUS, *INTUITION*, LOGOS, PERCEPTION, *REASON*, *SENS COMMUN* [COMMON SENSE], SENSE, SOUL

Now philosophically obsolete (we speak rather of "reason," "mind," or "intelligence"), the term "understanding" was used to refer to the activity of the mind for two centuries in what corresponds to the classical period (seventeenth and eighteenth centuries), before disappearing, or rather, being transformed. As a translation of the Latin *intellectus*, it inherits a long conceptual history that contrasts it, as an act of intuition (Gr. *nous* [νοῦς]), with rational discursive acts (Gr. *dianoia* [διάνοια]), and it is defined in contradistinction to reason (Lat. *ratio*). But these words, being defined in terms of one another, exchange characteristics several times: the more prestigious one becomes ordinary, the ordinary one is reevaluated. The peculiar interest of these conceptual shifts derives from the clear impact of the different languages and conceptual schemes in virtue of which they redefine themselves. We can thus discern an analogy of distinctions between *nous/dianoia, intellectus/ratio, entendement/raison*, as well as, later, between *Verstand/Vernunft*, as long as we notice immediately that they are never interchangeable in their use. For between classical rationalism, which speaks French or Latin, and the thought of the Enlightenment, which is based on the English notion of human understanding, there is a conceptual break, just as there is between these two universes and that of German idealism. With the dilution of the latter, contemporary philosophy has reappropriated the term for a kind of grasp or comprehension: *das Verstehen*.

I. From *Ouïr* to *Entendre* and *Comprendre*

The reinterpretations of the word "understanding" rely on the resources of language and of individual languages. Arsène Darmesteter even used this complex term a century ago to illustrate the phenomena of semantic adjustments between words:

Take the group *ouïr, entendre*, and *comprendre*. *Ouïr* (Lat. *audire*) gradually falls out of usage towards the 16th–17th centuries and is replaced by *entendre*, which only had the figurative sense indicated by its etymology: *intendere* (*animum*); from the idea of *intelligere, entendre* changed its meaning to that of *audire*; but how could it be replaced in the sense of *intelligere*? The language went and found *comprendre*, which, to the meanings of *grasp* and *contain within itself* (*cumprehendere*), added that of *intelligere*.

(*La vie des mots*)

The medieval Latin *intellectus*, which Saint Thomas had etymologized as *inte-lectus intus-legere*, "to read in" by the vision of the intellect (see INTELLECTUS), was followed in vernacular European languages by *entendement* in French, which associates intellection with acuity of hearing and the mental grasp of words and things, by "understanding" in English, and finally *Verstand* in German, coming from *stehen* (to stand up), which is more clearly related to material representation—*vor-stellen/ver-stehen* (see Bréal, *Essai de sémantique*). Italian preserved *intellectus* with *intelletto*, which in a way transcends the displacements of the concept at the mercy of languages (*intendimento* remained rare, although Carl Friedrich Flögel's *Geschichte des menschlichen Verstandes*, from 1765, was translated in 1835 as *Istoria dell'intendimento umano*). Spanish, however, adopted *entendement* and dropped *intelecto/intendimiento*. The equivocity of the terms differs from language to language: *entendement* does not mean either "listening" or "agreement," whereas "understanding" can, for which German uses *Einverständnis*.

II. A Complex Prehistory:
Nous/Dianoia and Their Translations

Entendement, rather than *intellect*, is the standard French translation for *intellectus* (see INTELLECT); *intellectus* is the standard translation of *nous* [νοῦς] (see INTELLECTUS). We would be wrong, however, to believe that *entendement* is the standard translation of *nous* or that the Greek pairing of *nous/dianoia,* even mediated by the *intellectus/ratio,* can ever be translated into French by the pairing of *entendement/raison*.

The pairs are similar in that they all contrast something on the order of immediate intuition with something on the order of discursive rationality, as is suggested by *dia* and its implication of process. Thus, Plato distinguishes intellectual vision and intuition (*noêsis* [νόησις]) from discursive knowledge, *dianoia* [διάνοια] (*Republic*, 6.511d–e). Anaxagoras's

earlier usage was of a different scope, since there it involved a function of cosmic organization, a "governing intelligence" as Leibniz would translate it in his *Discourse on Metaphysics* (§20), referring to the *Phaedo* (97b–c: *nous . . . ho diakosmôn kai pantôn aitios* [νοῦς . . . ὁ διακοσμῶν καὶ πάντων αἴτιος]; see WORLD). *Nous* is characterized by the power of immediate contemplation of ideas: it is intuitive knowledge, whereas *dianoia* moves by way of hypotheses and demonstrations. Immediate knowledge is superior to mediated knowledge. In the "plain of truth," the souls of the gods (and any soul who seeks the appropriate nourishment) are in direct contact with ideas: "*dianoia* [*pensée*, Robin, Brisson] of a god, nourished by *nous* [*intellection* for Robin, *intellect* for Brisson] and knowledge [*epistêmê* (ἐπιστήμη)] without mixture . . . rejoices, and, contemplating the truths, is nourished and feels good" (*Phaedrus*, 247d).

However, no contemporary translator has had the thought of translating *nous* by *entendement*, either for Anaxagoras or Plato. How can we account for these distortions?

In part, they result from the fact that the paradigm brought into play by the Greek *nous* is neither that of hearing (*entendement*) nor of vision (*intuition*), but rather that of smell. In addition, with regard to the *entendement/raison* distinction, the word *raison* is preempted by *logos* and thus cannot be used to translate *dianoia* (see LOGOS).

■ See Box 1.

Despite its various determinations, there is a constant in what French translates as *entendement*: its intuitive and preeminent character in contrast to the discursive character of knowledge based on chains of reasons. It is interesting to

---

1

Scent: The origins of *nous*

Noos [νόος] (or *nous* [νοῦς]) is the complement of *thumos* in the description of the "mind" of the Homeric man; as Bruno Snell puts it, in terms that can only be inadequate: "*Thumos* means that which is the source of movements, reactions, and emotions; *noos*, that which gives rise to representations and ideas." Even though their semantic fields partially overlap (*noein* implies, as von Fritz shows, a situation with genuine emotional impact and engages the specific attitude of the individual), *noos* refers, according to Chantraine (RT: *Dictionnaire étymologique de la langue grecque*), to the "intelligence, the mind," insofar as it "perceives and thinks." *Noein* [νοεῖν] gives substance to the link between perception and thought, not in the sense of empiricism (in which nothing is in the mind that is not first in the senses) but rather in the suddenness, the immediacy of a perception. It is thus that *noein* is related to "to sense" in the sense of "to scent"— von Fritz mentions an almost Cratylian

etymology in English, which Chantraine does not even bother to consider, from the root "to sniff" or "to smell." It is true that Odysseus is "recognized" (*enoêsen* [ἐνόησεν], *Odyssey*, 18.301) under his rags by his old dog Argos, who then dies on his pile of manure. It is related, equally, to sight, "in the eyes" rather than "with" or "through" them (e.g., *Iliad*, 24.294), and describes in particular the way in which one "intuits" the god behind the man or not (*Odyssey*, 16.160). *Noein* also means "to put oneself in mind of" (to perceive, understand), "to have in mind" (to consider, project, to have good sense, to be intelligent and prudent). Perfectly congruently, *noein* (in contradistinction to *gignôskein* [γιγνώσκειν], 2.2 and 2.7) in Parmenides's poem expresses the immediate relation to being and saying, in the triad that constitutes the "Way of Being" (3, 6.1, 8.34–36). In later usage, allegedly intellectualized (Anaxagoras's *Nous*, the *noêsis noêseôs* [νόησις νοήσεως], or Aristotle's god, and up

to the *noêma* [νόημα] of rhetoric, "concept" or "meaning" rather than the word), this relationship to intuition, and more precisely to scent, is probably never forgotten.

Barbara Cassin

BIBLIOGRAPHY

Fritz, Kurt von. "Noos and Noein in the Homeric Poems." *Classical Philology* 38 (1943): 79–93.

———. "Nous, Noein, and Their Derivatives in Presocratic Philosophy (Excluding Anaxagoras)." *Classical Philology* 40 (1945): 223–42; and 41 (1946): 12–34. Reprinted in *The Pre-Socratics: A Collection of Critical Essays*, edited by Alexander Mourelatos. 2nd ed. Princeton, NJ: Princeton University Press, 1994.

Snell, Bruno. *Die Entdeckung des Geistes*. 2nd ed. Göttingen, Ger.: Vandenhoeck and Ruprecht, 1975. First published in 1946. Translation by Thomas G. Rosenmeyer: *The Discovery of the Mind*. New York: Dover, 1982.

note that the shift to vernacular European languages leads to an attenuation of the foundational Platonic distinction. We may see in effect that 1) The use of *entendement* is restricted to a single meaning; and 2) *entendement* ends up referring to the power of thinking in general.

III. From Human Understanding to Good Sense

The translation of *intellectus* by *entendement* is an interesting exception in relation to Romance languages such as Italian and Spanish, which use a calque (*intelletto, intelecto*). Although Descartes does not specifically identify *cogitatio* with *entendement*, but also associates it with *mens, animus, intellectus*, and *ratio* (*Méditation seconde*), he does adopt a rather ordinary distinction in the *Principes de philosophie* between "*perception de l'entendement*" and "*action de la volonté*" (art. 1, §32), which involves a more or less passive view of *entendement*, insisting on its finitude and the limits of its comprehension. From that point on, *entendement* mostly falls within the domain of logic and takes on the discursiveness of its procedures, distinguishing true from false. And thus, the difference between *entendement* (*intellectus* in philosophical Latin) and *raison* (*ratio*) becomes blurred. This tendency, which becomes cemented in Anglo-Saxon philosophy, has one notable exception, namely Spinoza, who harks back to the intuitive aspect proper to the medieval notion of *intellectus*. The four modes of knowledge described in his *Tractatus de emendatione intellectus* (*Treatise*, §19–24)—1) by hearsay or arbitrary sign, 2) by vague experience undetermined by the intellect (*entendement*), 3) by inference that is not adequate, and 4) adequately by the essence or proximate cause—establish a contintuity between the third and the fourth. The third allows us to formally infer the essence of one thing from that of another, and the fourth is this same inference extended intuitively in the knowledge of proximate causes. Spinoza's example shows how his *intellectus* (*entendement*) reconciles mathematical discursiveness and the intuition of the mind: the intellect may be able, on the basis of knowledge of a series of three numbers, to "invent intuitively without any operation" (*intuitive nullam operationem facientes*; ibid., §24) the fourth term.

In English, "understanding" does a better job than French or German of preserving the idea of comprehension; thus in Hobbes, it is the capacity "in a man, out of the words, contexture, and other circumstances of language, to deliver himself from equivocation, and to find out the true meaning of what is said" (*Human Nature*, chap. 5, §8). Similarly in Locke, although the more general sense of "power of perception" is dominant (*Essay*, bk. 2, chap. 21, para. 5), it can be analyzed as 1) perception of ideas in our minds, 2) perception of the meaning of signs, and 3) perception of the agreement or disagreement between our ideas. The semiotic dimension remains, even if the dichotomy between *understanding* and *will* tends to mask it. Furthermore, while Descartes, Spinoza, Malebranche, and Leibniz consider finite understanding by distinction with, but also with reference to, infinite understanding, for Locke it is rather a matter of a direct inspection of the understanding as a specifically human capacity, as the title of the *Essay* itself reveals. The same is true for Hume (*Enquiries concerning Human Understanding*, 1758). The understanding, in English, is decidedly *human*, and it is also as a finite power that it appears in Germany (see Tonelli, "La question des bornes"). We may note that Kant's teacher in Königsberg, Martin Knutzen, had Locke's essay translated into German by the orientalist Georg David Kypke, whose house Kant shared (*Anleitung des menschlichen Verstandes*, 1755). This inflection leads to a trivialization of the notion of understanding, which is thenceforth not only always human, *Menschenverstand*, but is also often qualified as "healthy," *gesunder Menschenverstand*; in other words, "good common sense." The insistence on the finitude of understanding leads to a defense of common sense, as is often the case among "popular" German philosophers. This is a far cry from the universally shared common sense mentioned by Descartes at the beginning of *Discours de la méthode*.

IV. *Verstand* or *Vernunft*, Understanding or Reason?

A new twist comes with Kant that leads to a devaluation of the understanding (*Verstand*) in favor of reason (*Vernunft*), even though one could take much of the *Critique of Pure Reason* (1781) as an analysis of understanding. Understanding is defined as the faculty of rules; it knows through concepts (discursively) and synthesizes the data of the senses into a unity. It is reason (*Vernunft*), however, the faculty of principles, that makes it possible to order them into a whole. The one is governed by the other. Kantian understanding is a superior faculty of the mind (see GEMÜT) that is synthetic and spontaneous even though it is only legitimately exercised with regard to sense data. That which performs the synthesis is the "transcendental I" (see I/ME/MYSELF), which unifies the categories or concepts of the understanding. Although the understanding is a "power of judgment" just as much as reason is, it is assigned to singular judgments rather than to reasoning. Although the post-Kantian idealists (Fichte, Schelling, Hegel) criticized Kant for his servitude to finite understanding and the proscription it entails against metaphysical knowledge, it is with Kant that the change takes place. The conception of the understanding as something finite, discursive, and analytic that draws distinctions (in contrast to reason, which is able to reach principles, synthesis, and syllogisms) is a legacy of German idealism, especially notable in Hegel (*Encyclopedia of the Philosophical Sciences*, §14). With the notion of intellectual intuition (*intellektuelle Anschauung*) championed by Fichte, but especially by Schelling, we move beyond the complementary pair of *Verstand/Vernunft* and return to the intuitive *intellectus* of the medievals (see Tilliette, *L'intuition intellectuelle*).

It is instructive to see how this reversal could, with regard to terminology, be used to the advantage of the enemies of idealism. Jacobi, the great attacker of rationalism, was thus able to pit reason (*Vernunft*) against understanding (*Verstand*), arguing that the latter cannot acquire unconditioned knowledge but must always depend on principles it cannot demonstrate. Reason, on the other hand, which Jacobi considers a faculty of reception (*Vernunft* being related to *vernehmen*, "to perceive" [see PERCEPTION]) is passive and open to revelation (Jacobi, preface, in *David Hume on Faith*).

In the context of the controversy over pantheism started by Jacobi, it is common to appeal to Spinoza to underwrite the intellectual intuition banished by Kant (Tilliette, *L'intuition intellectuelle*). The understanding is placed by Schlegel, however, above reason, which knows all things, insofar as it interprets (*deutet*), and thus allows for a historical recapitulation ("Transcendentalphilosophie").

V. Hear, Listen, Understand: Hermeneutic Understanding, *das Verstehen*

German romanticism rehabilitates "understanding," in a way, by effecting a radical redefinition. In the letter "On Philosophy," published in the *Athenäum* (1799), Friedrich Schlegel begins a reformulation of the understanding, which is characterized as being "the highest of human faculties," as against the recent usage of "contemporary philosophy," which privileged reason. The reversal called for by Schlegel expresses his rejection of absolute idealism:

> It is entirely natural that a philosophy which progresses towards the infinite rather than presenting that infinite, which mixes and binds everything together rather than completing the particular, should prize no part of the human mind so much as the power of attaching representations to each other [*im menschlichen Geiste, als das Vermögen, Vorstellungen an Vorstellungen zu knüpfen*] and should ceaselessly pursue the train of thought concerning infinitely numerous modes . . . everything takes on meaning for [the understanding], man sees each thing justly and truly [*alles wird ihm (dem Verstand) bedeutend, er sieht alles recht und wahr*].

Schlegel moves imperceptibly to a hermeneutic meaning of "understand," replacing the "power of knowing" that was understanding (*Verstand*) with "the act of understanding" (*Verstehen*): "An absolute understanding is denied by a philosophy which denies an absolute truth" ("Transcendentalphilosophie," §12). By shifting from the noun to the nominalized verb (*das Verstehen*), the understanding reclaims its link to interpretation, even though the analytic understanding of the classical age had broken it. Nevertheless, German retained the equivalence between *Sinn* and *Verstand* in expressions like "in the proper sense" (*im eigentlichen Verstand*) and "in the figurative sense" (*im bildlichen Verstand*) all through the eighteenth century, as in Chladenius or Herder. The abandonment of speculative claims on the part of idealism that had magnified the importance of reason (*Vernunft*) to the detriment of the understanding (*Verstand*) had the effect of a historicist reevaluation of the latter as "hermeneutic understanding," *Verstehen*. Schleiermacher's (1819) hermeneutics thus presents itself as the "art of understanding," *Kunst des Verstehens*. Wilhelm von Humboldt insists equally on this historical and linguistic dimension of understanding, which is related to the possibility of misunderstanding as to its shadow. Through Dilthey and his students (J. Wach, G. Misch) and then in Gadamer's hermeneutics (*Truth and Method*, 1960), *Verstehen* is distinguished from the formal procedures of method and explanation in order to defend an individual approach that is situated in a history and indefinitely revisable. Only English retained "understanding" throughout these inflections with its prior importance, while *Verstand*, *entendement*, and even *intelletto* have given way to other terms. The rise of cognitive science and artificial intelligence encourages the appeal to the terminology of intelligence (*Intelligence, Intelligenz*), whereas the critique of rationality, on the other side, gives preference to interpretation, to *Verstehen*.

Denis Thouard

BIBLIOGRAPHY

Apel, Karl Otto. *Understanding and Explanation: A Transcendental-Pragmatic Perspective*. Translated by G. Warnke. Cambridge, MA: MIT Press, 1984.

———. "Das 'Verstehen.' Eine Problemgeschichte als Begriffsgeschichte." *Archiv für Begriffsgeschichte* 1 (1955): 142–99.

Berner, Christian. "Understanding Understanding: Schleiermacher." In *The Edinburgh Encyclopedia of Continental Philosophy*, edited by Simon Glendinning. Edinburgh: Edinburgh University Press, 1998.

Bréal, Michel. *Essai de sémantique*. Paris: Hachette, 1924. First published in 1897.

Darmesteter, Arsène. *La vie des mots*. Paris: Champ Libre, 1979. First published in 1887.

Descartes, René. *Méditation seconde*. In *Meditationes*, vol. 7 of *Œuvres completes*, edited by Charles Adam and Paul Tannery. Paris: Cerf, 1904.

Hobbes, Thomas. *Human Nature*. In *The Elements of Law*, edited by J. C. Gaskin. Oxford: Oxford University Press, 1994. First published in 1651.

Jacobi, Friedrich Heinrich. *David Hume on Faith, or Idealism and Realism, a Dialogue* (1815). In *Main Philosophical Writings and the Novel "Allwill,"* translated by G. di Giovanni, 537–90. Montreal: McGill-Queen's University Press, 1994.

Locke, John. *An Essay concerning Human Understanding*. Edited by P. H. Nidditch. Oxford: Oxford University Press, 1975. First published in 1689.

Plato. *Phèdre*. Translated by Léon Robin. Paris: Les Belles Lettres, 1970. Translated by Luc Brisson. Paris: Garnier, 1989.

Schlegel, Friedrich. "Transcendentalphilosophie." In *Kritische Friedrich-Schlegel-Ausgabe*, vol. 12. Paderborn, Ger.: Schöningh, 1964. First published in 1801. Translation by Frederick C. Beiser: "Philosophical Lectures: Transcendental Philosophy." In *The Early Political Writings of the German Romantics*, edited by Frederick C. Beiser. Cambridge: Cambridge University Press, 1996.

———. "Über die Philosophie: An Dorothea." In *Kritische Friedrich-Schlegel-Ausgabe*, vol. 2. Munich: F. Schöningh, 1958. Translation by J. Schulte-Sasse: "On Philosophy, to Dorothea." In *Theory as Practice: A Critical Anthology of Early German Romantic Writings*, edited by J. Schulte-Sasse et al. Minneapolis: University of Minnesota Press, 1997.

Schleiermacher, Friedrich. *"Hermeneutics and Criticism" and Other Writings*. Translated by A. Bowie. Cambridge: Cambridge University Press, 1998.

Schneiders, W. "Vernunft und Verstand—Krisen eines Begriffspaares." In *Aufklärung und Skepsis: Studien zur Philosophie und Geistesgeschichte des 17. und 18 Jh.*, edited by Lothar Kreimendahl, 199–220. Stuttgart: Frommann-Holzboog, 1995.

Scholz, Oliver R. *Verstehen und Rationalität*. Frankfurt: Kostermann, 1999.

Spinoza, Baruch. *Treatise on the Emendation of the Intellect*. In *The Collected Works of Spinoza*, vol. 1, translated by E. M. Curley. Princeton, NJ: Princeton University Press, 1985.

Thouard, Denis. "Verstehen im Nicht-Verstehen: Zum Problem des Hermeneutik bei Humboldt." *Kodikas/Code. Ars Semeiotica* 21 (1998): 271–85.

Tilliette, Xavier. *L'intuition intellectuelle de Kant à Hegel*. Paris: Vrin, 1995.

Tonelli, G. "La question des bornes de l'entendement humain au XVIIIème siècle et la genèse du criticisme kantien." *Revue de Métaphysique et de Morale* 65 (1959): 396–427.

Wach, Joachim. *Das Verstehen*. Tübingen: Mohr (Siebeck), 1926.

Zovko, Jure. *Verstehen und Nichtverstehen bei Friedrich Schlegel*. Stuttgart: Frommann-Holzboog, 1990.

UNIVERSALS

GREEK   *to katholou* [τὸ καθόλου]
          to koinon [τὸ κοινόν]
LATIN   *universale*

➤ ABSTRACTION, ANALOGY, ESSENCE, LOGOS, MIMESIS, PRÉDICABLE, PREDICATION, RES, *TO BE*, TROPE

The term "universal" has a wide range of uses: one can speak of linguistic universals, logical universals, mental universals (in the sense of "translinguistic categories of thought"), or social universals. In its contemporary philosophical use, the "problem of universals" comes down to asking whether one should allow their ontology to include properties and *nonparticular* relations outside of individual substances. As an important confrontation point, although not the only one, between nominalism and realism, the problem of universals has a long history. A correct approach to the problem of universals, of its difficulties and its vocabulary, entails more than a description of current theories. It requires an archeological investigation back to the very source of the debate via Porphyry and Alexander. The "problem of Porphyry" is in fact conceptually saturated, by a distinction made upstream, as it were, by Alexander between the common (*to koinon* [τὸ κοινόν]) and the universal (*to katholou* [τὸ καθόλου]), and downstream by a distinction made by Ammonius between three "states" of the universal, popularized through the Scholastic triad of *ante rem/in re/post rem*. In his vocabulary, Porphyry's set of questions indicates the same level of saturation, formulated in the Stoic language of "incorporeals" (see SIGNIFIER/SIGNIFIED, II), which carries an opposition between Platonism and Aristotelianism, itself overlaid by a grid of readings initially set out by the Neoplatonic commentators of Aristotle, in order to determine the object (*skopos* [σκοπός]) of the *Categories*: words, things, or concepts. The history of the problem of universals thus presents itself, right up to the modern oppositions of nominalism, realism, and conceptualism, as the ongoing fusion of two sets of questions and two different lexicons, one Aristotelian-Stoic, the other Neoplatonic, with the latter replacing the former to such an extent as to entirely obscure the Stoic dimension of the problem.

I. The Questionnaire of Porphyry

The history of the "problem of universals" usually starts with Porphyry's celebrated questionnaire beginning at the second paragraph of the *Isagoge*.

> About genera and species—whether they subsist, whether they actually depend on bare thoughts alone, whether if they actually subsist they are bodies or incorporeal and whether they are separable or are in perceptible items and subsist about them—these matters I shall decline to discuss, such a subject being very deep and demanding another and larger investigation. Here I shall attempt to show you how the old masters—and especially the Peripatetics among them—treated from a logical point of view, genera and species and the items before us.
>
> *Introduction*, trans. Barnes

This set of questions, which Porphyry refrains from answering himself, has passed through various transpositions and simplifications over the course of time. By a sort of feedback of the traditional discussion of the subject (*skopos* [σκοπός]) of the *Categories* of the *Isagoge*, the Greek commentators, conveyed by the medieval ones, came to ask themselves whether the genera and species were words or voiced (*phônai* [φωναί]), concepts (*noêmata* [νοήματα]), things (*pragmata* [πράγματα]), or beings (*onta* [ὄντα]), which opens the way to those responses—vocalism or nominalism, conceptualism, realism—and their ongoing confrontation down through the centuries. In our day, the principal formulations set the partisans of "primitive natural classes" (Quinton) against the proponents of "Resemblance nominalism" (Price), or of "universals" in the strict sense (a thesis that is invoked, but without a representative), of "natural classes of tropes" (Stout), or "resemblance classes of tropes" (Williams)—and some philosophers try to combine the theory of tropes with the acceptance of universals (Wilson).

■ See Box 1.

The medieval debate on universals is often presented as an opposition between Platonism and Aristotelianism. Contemporary philosophers use the term "Platonism" to refer to transcendent realism, that is to say, any theory that admits the existence of universals or "uninstantiated properties"; and they assign to Aristotle the attempt to "bring universals back to earth," by attributing to him, as does Armstrong, the theory of *universals in things*, "whose Latin tag is *universalia in rebus*" (*Universals*). Rather than directly confronting the Platonic theory of Ideas and its Aristotelian critique, it would seem more fruitful to start from the construction of the problem by an author who, even more than Porphyry, set the framework for the questions, concepts, and strategies of argument: Alexander of Aphrodisias and his collection of *Quaestiones*. We will then follow the course of Alexander's theses through the Neoplatonic and medieval tradition and trace the genealogy of the distinction between the universals *ante rem/post rem/in re* to which the modern lexicon is deeply indebted.

II. Alexander's Construction: Community and Universality, *To Koinon* and *To Katholou*

Alexander's *Quaestio*, 1.11 consists of an "exegesis" of Aristotle's "*to de zôion to katholou êtoi outhen estin ê husteron* [τὸ δὲ ζῷον τὸ καθόλου ἤτοι οὐθέν ἐστιν ἢ ὕστερον]" (*De anima*, 1.1.402b7). Alexander's question is rendered by Sharples as "What is meant by the saying in the first book *On the Soul* [that] 'the living creature *that is* universal is either nothing or posterior'?" This question has been handed down in two versions: the shorter one, *Quaestio*, 1.11a, which proposes a single answer to the question (S2), and a longer one, *Quaestio*, 1.11b, which proposes two answers (S1 and S2) (402b7). The Arabic versions of the text include slightly discordant titles that draw our attention to the central problem of the Alexandrian theory and lexicon of the universal (the Arabic tradition includes two documents of 1.11a). In the inventory of Arabic Alexandrian texts drawn up by Abdurrahman Badawi, the two versions appear under the French title: *Traité d'Alexandre d'Aphrodise: Des choses communes et universelles, qu'elles ne sont pas des essences existentes* (Alexander of Aphrodisias: On common and universal things, which are not existing essences).

1

Six contemporary responses to the problem of universals

D. M. Armstrong sets out the six contemporary positions by considering how each would deal with the property of whiteness.

1. Primitive natural class view: The class of all the white things forms a natural class, a class with a reasonable degree of naturalness. That is all that can be said about what makes a white thing white.
2. Resemblance nominalism: The white things form a natural class in virtue of the objective fact that they all resemble each other to a certain degree.

Resemblance is an objective but unanalyzable fact.
3. Universals: All white things have an identical property in common (or a set of slightly different properties to correspond to the different shades of white).
4. Natural classes of tropes: Each white thing has its *own*, entirely distinct, property of whiteness. But the class of the whitenesses forms a primitive natural class.
5. Resemblance classes of tropes: Each white thing has its own property of whiteness. But the members of the class

of whitenesses all resemble each other more or less closely, resemblance being a primitive.
6. Tropes plus universals: Each white thing has its own property of whiteness. But these particular properties themselves each have a universal property of whiteness.

David Malet

BIBLIOGRAPHY

Armstrong, David. *Universals: An Opinionated Introduction*. Boulder, CO: Westview Press, 1989.

The problem posed by the title of the first Arabic version is clear, if not easy to resolve: is the expression "common things" when added to the original formula of *De anima* (1.1.402b7) ("the universal animal") itself a synonym? Or, to put it differently, should one distinguish between "universal" and "common" in Alexander? In short, should one distinguish between *to katholou* [τὸ καθόλου] and *to koinon* [τὸ κοινόν]?

A first part of the answer is provided by S2, which can be paraphrased thus:

S2 [1.11a, Bruns = 1.11b, Bruns]: Aristotle is correct in saying that the universal animal is "posterior," because he speaks of the universal in the sense of a "generic" universal, which is a concept engendered from individuals. On the other hand, this thesis cannot apply to the universal animal "in the sense of the common animal." To be fully rigorous, one must distinguish between *commonality* [Fr. *communauté*] and "universality." The latter is an "accident" that arrives from outside of "nature," from the fact that it is realized in a number of individuals. The former is not. In fact, a "nature" is in itself common. As soon as an individual exists, this nature—which is in itself common—also exists, even when only instantiated or realized in that individual, and reciprocally, an individual exists only "because" this nature is instantiated in it.

The distinction between *to katholou* and *to koinon* that S2 demands, and which has been discussed by various commentators, is fundamental for understanding the difference between the universal *in re* and the universal *post rem*, whose paternity historians like to attribute to Alexander.

■ See Box 2.

III. The Universal *In Re*

Even if the formula itself is the result of a series of reworkings, starting with Alexander, by the "Greek" commentators of Aristotle, which were further pursued by Avicenna and culminated in Albertus Magnus and the Scholastics, the

notion (but not the expression) of the "universal *in re*" can still be traced back to Aristotle himself. In fact, in *De anima*, he maintains that since the notion is the "form" of the thing, it is "necessarily inherent in any given matter if it is [real]": Ὁ μὲν γὰρ λόγος εἶδος τοῦ πράγματος, ἀνάγκη δ' εἶναι τοῦτον ἐν ὕλῃ τοιᾳδί, εἰ ἔσται (*De anima*, 1.1.403b2–3). No notion, no *logos* [λόγος]—for example, that of an animal, that is to say, an "animated essence endowed with sensation"— can *be*, which is to say *be* the *eidos* [εἶδος] of anything at all, if it is not realized in some matter. What Alexander adds to Aristotle is the idea that such a notion, even while it needs realization, is still distinct from the universal that corresponds to it, which is to say that it remains distinct from itself as a universal, by virtue of the fact that universality is for it a mere accident. Alexander's thesis is thus that the animal— or as Aristotle calls it, the *logos*-form of animal—only exists insofar as it is realized "in at least one individual," but that universality is not part of its "essence." Thus there is nothing "universal" in the notion of an *ousia empsuchos aisthêtikê* [οὐσία ἔμψυχος αἰσθητική], that is, in the notion of the animal (*to zôion* [τὸ ζῷον]). But this notion is not real; it only "exists"—as the *ousia* (essence) which it is—as realized in a body. Despite a few superficial dissonances, the Alexandrian lexicon of the universal is quite settled: the *logos*-form for an *ousia*, in itself a commonality—in other words, communicable to more than one—must be (and is in fact) realized in a matter (an individual) at least. Its realization in more than one accidentally confers the status of universal upon it. Such a *logos*-form for an *ousia* is, insofar as it is realized in more than one, what commentators and many modern philosophers would call a "universal *in re*." The concept that can be drawn by "abstraction" from the individual in which the *logos* is realized is what one calls a "universal *post rem*." It is this concept that Aristotle refers to in *De anima* (1.1.402b7) when he (problematically) qualifies it as "posterior" (*husteron* [ὕστερον]). In the terms of Alexander's language, the difference between the "universal *post rem*" and the "universal *in re*" can be defined by a weighty thesis that implies a certain difference between "being" and "existing" (in the sense of "being subject to oneself" [Fr. *se subjecter*, having hypostasis]:

2

The grasp of the universal according to Alexander of Aphrodisias

In the *Peri psuchês* Alexander presents the perception of the universal as follows (see ABSTRACTION):

[The intellect] that perceives (*labôn* [λαβών]) the form of something (*to eidos tinos* [τὸ εἶδός τινος]) apart from matter (*chôris tês hulês* [χωρὶς τῆς ὕλης]) possesses the common and the universal (*echei to koinon te kai katholou* [ἔχει τὸ κοινόν τε καὶ καθόλου]) since what grasps the form of man aside from material circumstances (*chôris tôn hulikôn peristaseôn* [χωρὶς τῶν ὑλικῶν περιστάσεων]) possesses the common man (*echei ton koinon anthrôpon* [ἔχει τὸν κοινὸν ἄνθρωπον]). Indeed, the differences between individual men in relation to each other (*pros allêlous diaphora* [πρὸς ἀλλήλους διαφορὰ]) is engendered by the fact of matter (*para tês hulês ginetai* [παρὰ τῆς ὕλης γίνεται]) since their forms, thanks to which they are men, are not at all different one from another. But [the intellect] that grasps what individuals have in common (*ho te to koinon to epi tois kath' hekasta sunidôn* [ὅ τε τὸ κοινὸν τὸ ἐπὶ τοῖς καθ' ἕκαστα συνιδών]) also perceives (*lambanei* [λαμβάνει]) the form apart from matter. In fact, this is what is common and identical (*to koinon te kai tauton* [τὸ κοινόν τε καὶ ταὐτόν]) to them.

Alexander, *Peri psuchês*, based on Bruns, ed.

BIBLIOGRAPHY

Alexandri Aphrodisiensis praeter commentaria scripta minora. De anima liber cum Mantissa. In *Supplementum Aristotelicum* 2.1. Edited by Ivo Bruns. Berlin: de Gruyter, 1961.

"the universals have 'being' [*einai* (εἶναι)] in thought and *hupostasis* [ὑπόστασις (*Quaestio*, 59, 7–8; *In topicorum Aristotelis libros*)]/[ὕπαρξις (*De anima*, 90)] in the particulars."

Alexander's distinction between *to katholou* and *to koinon*, and his formulation of the difference between "being in thought" (*epinoia* [ἐπίνοια]) as the product of an "abstraction" and "having hypostasis" in particulars are the epochal foundations of several important theories, the tracks of which can be followed to the end of the Middle Ages, and in some cases beyond. We will limit ourselves here to the two most important. The first is the distinction of "three types of universals." The second is the "indifference of the essence." The following section deals with the typology of universals.

IV. Universal *Ante Rem/Post Rem/In Re*

In their search for a "harmonic" or "concordant" reading of the two "great philosophies" of Aristotle and Plato, the Neoplatonic commentators of Aristotle and Porphyry formulated a scholastic division between three types of universals. In a sense, this division does not take into account the Alexandrian distinction between nature common in itself and universal by accident. But it is also clear that in another sense this division is required, even if tacitly, in order to be able to think that a "same entity" can assume different states of "being" in different substrates or "hypostases" without paradox or contradiction.

The first great source for the doctrine of the three types of universals is Ammonius, in his commentary on the *Isagoge*. Here one finds its two main features: the distinction between universals *pro tôn pollôn* [πρὸ τῶν πολλῶν] (anterior to the multiplicities), universals *en tois pollois* [ἐν τοῖς πολλοῖς] (in the multiplicities), and universals *epi tois pollois* [ἐπὶ τοῖς πολλοῖς] (posterior to the multiplicities); and the reuse of a metaphor, of the seal, the wax, and the imprinted image, which derives from the *Timaeus*, 50c–d (also mentioned by Aristotle in his critical account of Plato's doctrines in the *Metaphysics*, 1.6, 987b–988a with the help of the term *ekmageoin* [ἐκμαγεῖον], "seal," to explain the multiplication of the one in the many). The desired objective is clearly to reconcile the three points of view: the theological (in Plato), the physical (in both Plato and Aristotle), and the logical and noetic (in Aristotle). The universal *en tois pollois* provides a form of synthesis, based on a certain understanding of the middle term, between the Platonic theory of Ideas and the Aristotelian theory of abstraction.

■ See Box 3.

Ammonius's theory had a long afterlife. One finds it of course in the commentaries of David and Elias, but also in Simplicius—when he denounces "those certain people" who only see "the second sort of genres," who do not rise up to the level required for contemplating the transcendent (extrinsic) genres, and who believe that "common natures" only subsist in the singular; it could be found as well in the Syriac Christian Sergius de Rešʿayn (d. 22 April 536)—who clearly locates the genera and the species anterior to the multiples in the spirit of a *God* the "creator." But it is also the source of the mereological doctrine of the universal and of the whole by the Byzantine Eustratius of Nicaea, who presented it through the prism of the Alexandrian theory of homeomeric and nonhomeomeric wholes (cf. Alexander, *Problem*, 28); of the Avicennian doctrine of the three states of the universal; and through the latter to the Scholastic distinction imposed by Albertus Magnus and his contemporaries between *universale ante rem*, *in re*, and *post rem*.

Each different kind of universal that emerged from this system has had its own series of problems, but these concern the history of doctrines, not the languages of philosophy.

The Albertian triad has been subject to various adaptations. Although most authors until the end of the fifteenth century reproduced it unchanged, some of them focused on Avicenna's binary distinction between *logicalia* and *intellectualia* and a distinction between an abstract "logical" universal (or "universal of predication") and a separate

3
The Neoplatonic theory of the three states of the universal

Ammonius follows the "trajectory" of the universal from the Platonic Idea to the abstract concept as follows:

In order to clarify what the text [of Porphyry] means, let us present it by means of an example, for it is not true that [philosophers] designate simply and by chance some things as corporeal and some others as incorporeal. Rather, they do so according to a reasoning, and they do not contradict each other, as each of them says reasonable things. Let us imagine a ring, with an imprint [that represents] Achilles, for example, along with a multitude of sticks of wax; let us suppose that the ring is used to mark each piece of wax with its seal; now let us suppose that someone comes afterward and that he looks at all the pieces of wax and observes that [the marks] come from a single imprint: he himself will also have the mark imprinted in his discursive faculty [*dianoia* (διάνοια)]; we can thus say that the seal on the ring is "anterior to the multiplicity," that the mark in the

blobs of wax is "in the multiplicity," while the mark that is in the discursive faculty of the person who made the imprinted seals is "posterior to the multiplicity" and "posterior in the order of being." Well, this is what one needs to understand in the case of genera and species.

Ammonius, *In Porphyrii Isagogen*, based on Busse, ed.

The Syriac Christian commentator Sergius de Reš`ayn completes the process undertaken by Ammonius by transposing the universal anterior to the multiple into the "divine idea."

[This is how] species and genera of things are divided. Some are close to the creator, and they are called simple and primary. Others are in materials and they are called material and natural. Still others are in the intellect, and they are called last and intellectual. These are the teachings of Plato and the other members of the Academy regarding genera and species, which state that each and every thing which is naturally in the world is its own

or proper species and also has a proper species near its creator—a species that subsists by itself—through which [the thing in the world] has been imprinted and has come down here to existence. And when someone sees it, he takes its species into memory, and it subsists in his thought, such that this species exists in three ways, that is: near by the creator, in the thing itself, and in the memory of the person who has seen it, the one who knows it.

Sergius de Reš`ayn, *Treatise on Categories "to Philotheos,"* based on Fr. trans. by H. Hugonnard-Roche, §5

BIBLIOGRAPHY

Sergius de Reš`ayn. *Traité sur les Catégories "à Philotheos."* Translated into French by H. Hugonnard-Roche. In "Les Catégories d'Aristote comme introduction à la philosophie, dans un commentaire syriaque de Sergius de Reš`ainā." *Documenti e studi sulla tradizione filosofica medievale* 8 (1997): 339–63.

"theological" universal (or "universal of production") imbued with elements of Proclus's theory of "precontent" (*praehabere, praehabitio, praecontinentia*). This is the case of the Germans Dietrich of Freiberg (*De cognitione entium separatorum*, 10, 1–4) and Berthold de Moosburg (*Super elementationem theologicam Procli*, prop. I A); and it is also the case of some Oxonian realists of the fourteenth century, such as Wycliff (*Tractatus de universalibus*, II, 2), who opposed "logical" universals to "metaphysical" universals. In the fifteenth century, the "Albertists" of Cologne and Paris added a fourth type of universal, which allowed them to inscribe the ensemble of "modern" philosophies into a four-part structure inherited from Albertinian philosophical doxography. In this new arrangement, the nominalists, who proposed reducing all universals to the status of universal *post rem*, hold the role of a kind of "Epicurism" they called "literal" (*epiccurei litterales*).

If modern and contemporary philosophy has largely abandoned the thematic of the universal *ante rem*, modern forms of nominalism and realism have helped extend the perennial debate between Plato and Aristotle as orchestrated by antique and medieval commentary. The contemporary lexicon holds few problems for the (Continental) reader, outside of some expressions specific to English, with its own ellipses and shortcuts—such as the expressions "predicate nominalism" and "resemblance nominalism" (see Box 1), which are difficult to render into French (for example) without recourse to inelegant periphrases such as *nominalisme*

réduisant les universaux à des prédicats, or *nominalisme fondé sur la resemblance.* "Predicate nominalism" (directly transposed into French as *nominalisme du prédicat*) is defined as a doctrine that maintains that some individuals can be grouped together insofar as they have the same relation to the *token* (SIGN; cf. PROPOSITION, Box 4), either written or spoken of a same linguistic *type* ("some individuals, ordinary or relation instances, are *related to a shared entity—i.e. to a spoken or written token of a linguistic type*"; cf. Mertz, *Moderate Realism and its Logic*). "Concept nominalism" is understood as a doctrine that replaces the idea of "linguistic type" by that of "mental construct" in the role of type—and both doctrines agree on the rejection of universals, understood as properties common to several individuals, and "instantiated" or "exemplified" in them.

Alain de Libera

BIBLIOGRAPHY

Abelard, Peter. "Glosses on Porphyry from His *Logica 'ingredientibus.'*" In *Five Texts on the Mediaeval Problem of Universals.* Indianapolis, IN: Hackett, 1994.
———. *Logica "ingredientibus."* In *Peter Abaelards philosophische schriften.* Edited by B. Geyer. Münster, Ger: Aschendorff, 1919–27.
Ammonius. *Ammonii in Porphyrii Isagogen sive V Voces.* Edited by Adolf Busse. Berlin: G. Reimer, 1891. CAG, IV, 3.
Armstrong, David M. *Universals and Scientific Realism.* 2 vols. Cambridge: Cambridge University Press, 1978.
———. *Universals: An Opinionated Introduction.* Boulder, CO: Westview Press, 1989.
Bergman, Gustav. *Realism.* Madison: University of Wisconsin Press, 1967.

Boethius. *Boethius's "De topicis differentiis."* Translated by E. Stump. Ithaca, NY: Cornell University Press, 1978.

———. *Boethius's "In Ciceronis topica."* Translated by E. Stump. Ithaca, NY: Cornell University Press, 1988.

———. *In Porphyrii Isagogen commentarium editio duplex.* Edited by S. Brandt. Corpus scriptorum ecclesiasticorum latinorum, 38. Vienna, 1906.

———. "The Second Commentary on Porphyry." *In Five Texts on the Mediaeval Problem of Universals: Porphyry, Boethius, Abelard, Duns Scotus, Ockham.* Indianapolis, IN: Hackett, 1994.

Brakas, George. *Aristotle's Concept of the Universal.* Hildesheim, Ger.: Olms, 1988.

Ebbesen, Sten. "Philoponus, 'Alexander' and the Origins of Medieval Logic." In *Aristotle Transformed: The Ancient Commentators and Their Influences.* Edited by R. Sorabji. Ithaca, NY: Cornell University Press, 1990.

Küng, Guido. *Ontology and the Logistic Analysis of Language.* Dordrecht, Neth.: Reidel, 1967.

Libera, Alain de. *La Querelle des universaux: De Platon à la fin du Moyen Âge.* Paris: Éditions du Seuil, 1996.

———. *L'Art des généralités: Théories de l'abstraction.* Paris: Aubier, 1999.

Lloyd, A. C. *Form and Universal in Aristotle.* Liverpool, UK: Francis Cairns, 1981.

Loux, Michael, ed. *Universals and Particulars: Readings in Ontology.* Notre Dame, IN: University of Notre Dame Press, 1976.

Mertz, Donald W. *Moderate Realism and Its Logic.* New Haven, CT: Yale University Press, 1996.

Porphyry. *Introduction.* Translated with commentary by Jonathan Barnes. Oxford: Oxford University Press, 2003.

———. *Isagoge.* Translated into French by Alain de Libera and Alain-Philippe Segonds. Introduction and notes by Alain de Libera. Paris: Vrin, 1998.

———. *Isagoges translatio Boethii accedunt Isagoges Fragmenta M. Victorino interprete.* Edited by L. Minio-Paluello. *Aristotles Latinus,* I, 6–7. Bruges, Belg.: Descleê de Brouwer, 1966.

Price, H. H. *Thinking and Experience.* Cambridge, MA: Harvard University Press, 1953.

Quine, W.V.O. "On Universals." *Journal of Symbolic Logic* 12 (1947): 74–84.

Quinton, A. *The Nature of Things.* London, Routledge and Kegan Paul, 1953.

Sergius de Reš'ayn. *Traité sur les Catégories "à Philotheos."* Translated into French by H. Hugonnard-Roche. In "Les Catégories d'Aristote comme introduction à la philosophie, dans un commentaire syriaque de Sergius de Reš'ayn." *Documenti e studi sulla tradizione filosofica medievale* 8 (1997): 339–63.

Stout, G. F. "The Nature of Universals and Propositions." In *The Problem of Universals,* edited by C. Landesman, 154–66. New York: Basic Books, 1971.

Williams, D. C. "The Elements of Being." *Review of Metaphysics* 7 (1953): 3–18, 171–92.

Wilson, John Cook. *Statement and Inference, with Other Philosophical Papers.* 2 vols. Oxford: Clarendon Press, 1926.

Wolterstorff, N. *On Universals.* Chicago: University of Chicago Press, 1970.

Wycliffe. John. *Tractatus de universalibus.* Edited by I. J. Mueller. Oxford: Clarendon Press, 1985.

| UTILE

The French *utile* derives from the Latin *uti* ("to use"). This study traces a network of meanings via the English language, as inflected by Jeremy Bentham's invention of "utilitarian" as something different from "useful": see UTILITY; cf. FAIR, RIGHT/JUST/GOOD.

It should be compared to the network of "availability" which has recently been marked by the Heideggerian notion of *Vorhandenheit*: see VORHANDEN, and *DISPOSITION, I.*

➤ BEAUTY, ECONOMY, ENTREPRENEUR, PRAXIS, *VALUE, VIRTUE,* WORK

UTILITY, UTILITARIAN, UTILITARIANISM

➤ *UTILE,* and BEAUTY, ECONOMY, FAIR, *HAPPINESS,* RIGHT/JUST/GOOD, VALUE, VORHANDEN

One starting point for the widespread incomprehension among the French vis-à-vis the utilitarian philosophy of Jeremy Bentham, John Stuart Mill, and Henry Sidgwick can probably be found in a problem of translation. When the first French translators of Bentham and his friends sought an equivalent for the English neologism "utilitarian," which Bentham had created to describe his new philosophy of the general interest (in his *Introduction to the Principles of Morals and Legislation,* first appearing in 1780 and published in 1789), they invented a French neologism: *utilitaire* (1831). But by 1802, Bentham was aware of the perjorative sense that his term had gained through hostile reactions to his doctrine, and he proposed another term, utilitarien, in order to distinguish the technical term from everyday usage. But this new word met with no success or acceptance, and in 1922, the French word *utilitaire* was belatedly replaced with *utilitariste* to render the English "utilitarian," a term that has retained a pejorative connotation in addition to its philosophical content, and which is distinct from the more positive term "useful."

In French, *utilitarisme,* which had appeared in 1842, ultimately supplanted *utilitairianisme* (1845) or *utilitarianisme* (1872) to render the original English term "utilitarianism," but the expression *philosophie utilitaire* persisted, contributing to the misunderstanding of utilitarianism over the course of the nineteenth century. In his celebrated reference book *La Morale anglaise contemporaine, morale de l'utilité et de l'évolution* (1885), Jean-Marie Guyau described his objective as "the history and critique of *la morale utilitaire.*" Likewise Élie Halévy would write in 1901 (*La Formation du radicalisme philosophique,* vol. 1) that "to the spiritual philosophy of the rights of man (in France), corresponded (in England) the utilitarian philosophy [*philosophie utilitaire*] of the identity of interests."

I. "Utilitarian" and "Expedient"

It is fascinating to see how quickly the neologism "utilitarian" fell in public esteem and took on such a negative meaning. In *Hard Times* (1854), Dickens caricatured the "utilitarian" mentality as an attitude hardened toward moral feeling and concerned only with the facts, the eponymous "Gradgrindism" of the novel's main character. The problem is to understand whether this negative reading derives from the hostility of the spirit of the time—the rejection of burgeoning capitalism by romanticism, and subsequently by Marxism—or whether it derives from a weakness internal to utilitarianism that should then be subject to question. The philosophical meaning of the term, the criterion of benefit or harm based on "the greatest happiness for the greatest number, each one counting equally" (Bentham, *Introduction,* 1789), needs to be critically unpacked.

As Mill remarks at the beginning of *Utilitarianism,* the adjective "utilitarian" has come to designate only that which is instrumental or advantageous, that which dispenses with any concern for pleasure, for the beautiful, or for the "useless." The philosophy of utilitarianism has come to be identified with the shopkeeper and his or her short-term interest. "Freedom, equality, property and Bentham," proclaims Marx in *Capital.* In order to dispel this confusion and to defend utilitarianism against these accusations of immorality, Mill proposes to distinguish between "utilitarian" and "expedient." This latter term is identified with that pejorative sense of a pure means to an end, of short-term advantage, of an easy or effective means, of utility without any notion of morality. The simply expedient is a means to an end of which we may not necessarily approve, but that we accept because it functions efficaciously. Utility, on the other hand, is useful only in relation to a good end. Mill explains it thus:

> [The doctrine of] Utility is often summarily stigmatized as an immoral doctrine by giving it the name of Expediency, and taking advantage of the popular use of that term to contrast it with Principle. But the Expedient, in the sense in which it is opposed to the Right, generally means that which is expedient for the particular interest of the agent himself; as when a Minister sacrifices the interests of his country to keep himself in place. When it means anything better than this, it means that which is expedient for some immediate object, some temporary purpose, but which violates a rule whose observance is expedient in a much higher degree. The Expedient, in this sense, instead of being the same thing with the useful, is a branch of the hurtful.

> (*Utilitarianism*, chap. 2)

Utilitarianism, on the other hand, seeks a fundamental moral principle that can be used to define the morally right and wrong: the quantity of happiness that results from an action, from a decision, from a political system, from a redistribution of goods, material and social benefits, and so forth. In short, it proposes an objective and impartial method for evaluating justice and injustice, benefit and harm, in the place of criteria based on opinion, personal interest, or power. It takes the side of Socrates against Callicles.

II. "Utility" and "Usefulness"

So why the pejorative meaning? Why not link utility and the Good instead of saying that utility is a moral criterion only if it leads to a good end, only if it is *useful*? Because this would lead to an uncomfortable circularity, already observed by G. E. Moore (*Principa Ethica*, 1901), which is that in order to ground the distinction proposed by Mill, we would need to know what constitutes a good end in itself, independent of our immediate advantage: an independent criterion of the Good. This is precisely what utilitarianism rejects in defining the Good as utility or happiness. As Hume already wrote before Bentham,

> Usefulness is only a tendency to a certain end; and it is a contradiction in terms, that anything pleases as means to an end, where the end itself no wise affects us.

> ("An Enquiry Concerning the Principles of Morals,"
> §V, part 2)

From here we understand Hume's insistence on agreement and approval in defining utility, and his conclusion that "Everything that contributes directly to the happiness of society directly recommends itself to our approbation and well-meaning" (ibid.). This is the crucial point that Mill should have insisted upon if he had really wanted to release the utilitarian from the instrumental, and it is to Hume, in fact, that we owe the solution to our problem. What defines the useful as a good for the utilitarians and differentiates advantage from the useful is the general consensus, the approbation of universal suffrage, as Kant would say. Herein lies the essential point of the doctrine: utility, according to Hume, is collective; if it is not, then it is not utility:

> Usefulness is agreeable, and engages our approbation. This is a matter of fact, confirmed by daily observation. But, USEFUL? For what? For somebody's interest, surely. Whose interest then? Not our own only: For our approbation frequently extends farther. It must, therefore, be the interest of those who are served by the character or action approved of.

> (Ibid.)

The useful can only be understood in reference to the happiness and the reduction of pain for all, in relation to human happiness in general. This is why Bentham ultimately called the principle of utility the "principle of the greatest good for the greatest number, each counting equally." The utility of the British philosophers is thus not to be confused with the simply *expedient*—for it must lead to a good end, to that which has real value to us, to our happiness and satisfaction. It is not a matter of egotistical personal interest, but can be evaluated only by a general consensus, by what Halévy called an *identité des intérêts* (a community of interests or common interest). For the utilitarians, it is impossible to separate the individual from the whole. And it is precisely this universalist dimension that offers utilitarianism a way out of the confusions besetting its current usage.

The philosophical use of the term "utility" broadens its scope to mean that which procures a satisfaction for the greatest number. It thus loses any instrumental connotation or neutrality in relation to the desired end. Like Kantian morality, as a moral principle, it relies on a principle of impartiality. The happiness to be maximized is the happiness of all, with each and all treated in equal manner:

> The good of a specific individual, whoever he may be, has no more importance, from the point of view of the universe, if I can put it that way, than the good of any other individual, unless there are some special reasons to think that a greater Good is to be attained in one case rather than another.

> (Sidgwick, *The Method of Ethics*, bk. 3, chap. 13)

Catherine Audard

BIBLIOGRAPHY

Audard, Catherine, ed. *Antologie historique et Critique de l'utiliarisme*. 3 vols. Paris: Presses Universitaires de France, 1999.

Bentham, Jeremy. *Of Laws in General*. Edited by H.L.A. Hart. London: Athlone Press, 1970.

Halévy, Élie. *La Jeunesse de Bentham 1776–1789*. Vol. 1 of *La Formation du radicalisme philosophique*. Paris, 1901. Translation by Mary Morris: *The Growth of Philosophic Radicalism*. Boston, MA: Beacon Press, 1955.

Hume, David. "An Enquiry Concerning the Principles of Morals." In *Moral Philosophy*, edited and with an introduction by Geoffrey Sayre-McCord. Indianapolis, IN: Hackett, 2006.

Mill, John Stuart. *Utilitarianism*. Vol. 10 of *Collected Works of John Stuart Mill*, edited by J. M. Robson. Toronto: University of Toronto Press, 1985.

Rosen, Frederick. *Classical Utilitarianism from Hume to Mill*. London: Routledge, 2003.

Sidgwick, Henry. *The Methods of Ethics*. 7th ed. Preface by John Rawls. London: Hackett, 1981.

VALUE

"Value," like the French *valeur* or the German *Gewalt*, derives from the Latin *valere* ("to be strong, vigorous, in good health, well"; "to have force, to be able"; "to be worth"; cf. the salutation, *Vale*, in PLEASURE, Box 1), which is a translation of the Greek *dunasthai* [δύνασθαι] (see POWER). The German language contains a constellation of terms without equivalent, which includes *Wert* (worth), which connotes an "ought-to-be" (Fr. *devoir-être*; Ger. *werden* ["to become," Fr. *devenir*]) and *Geltung* (value) or *Gültigkeit* (validity) from *gelten* (to pay tribute). In German philosophy at the turn of the twentieth century, the different uses of "value" were developed in a systematic fashion. A rigorous distinction was made among terms, based primarily on the Kantian distinction between theoretical and practical philosophy (the Baden School) or on an attempted challenge to that distinction (Nietzsche's "conversion" of values, *Umwertung der Werte*), whose impact extended to attempts to establish a phenomenology of values (Max Scheler). The German network of meanings is thus an essential starting point; see WERT; cf. SOLLEN, WILLKÜR.

The difficulties around the term "value" derive from the diversity of domains in which "value" takes on its significance. In addition to WERT, which articulates the ensemble of these domains, one should refer to parts of the following entries.

I. Value and Virtue

"Value" comes under the lexicon of physical and moral personal qualities ("strength, bravery, courage"): see VIRTÙ (especially for the Greek *aretê* [ἀρετή], L. *virtus*, It. *virtù*). See also VIRTUE. On ethics as a system of values more generally, see DUTY, MORALS.

II. Value and Verity (Truth)

The central question is the articulation among "true," "valid," and "valuable," with the notion of "truth-value": see TRUTH, and PROPOSITION; see also *CROYANCE* [BELIEF, DOXA, GLAUBE]. On the separation of the spheres of ethics and knowledge, in particular, see WERT, IV.

III. Value and Meaning

On the relation between the meaning and value of a word, see SENSE (especially SENSE, III and SENSE, Box 4; cf. HOMONYM, SIGNIFIER/SIGNIFIED, *WITTICISM,* WORD.

IV. Value and Economy

See ECONOMY, ENTREPRENEUR, OIKONOMIA. On the relation between moral value and economic value, see more specifically BERUF, UTILITY; cf. SECULARIZATION, SOBORNOST'.

On the question of a thing, see RES (and RES, Box 1), VORHANDEN.

On the question of "surplus value," refer to WERT, Box 1.

V. Value and Aesthetics

On the question of values in color and timbre, see STIMMUNG. On the judgment of aesthetic value, see GOÛT, STANDARD, and especially AESTHETICS, ART, BEAUTY, INGENIUM, SUBLIME.

VERB

The word "verb" derives from the Latin *verbum*, which signifies "word, term, expression," based on an Indo-European root that led to the Greek *Fereô* [Ϝερέω] ("I will say"), the English "word," and the German *Wort*. Thus the translation of *verbum e verbo* refers to the translation "word to word"; see TO TRANSLATE, III.

1. On the manner of designating the minimal unit of language, on the differences between word, noun, and verb, as well as on the evolution in the meaning of the terms that designate them, see WORD; cf. LANGUAGE, LOGOS, SENSE, SIGN.
2. On the verb as a structuring element of a proposition and as a grammatical category, see ESTI, PROPOSITION; see also *CATEGORY,* PREDICATION, SUBJECT, *TO BE.*
   On the verb as an expression of time and aspect in particular, see ASPECT, PRESENT, TO TI ÊN EINAI; cf. MEMORY. See also ESTI for the present participle, ENGLISH for the gerund.
3. On the primacy of the verb as expression of action, linked to being and existence, see *ACT* and SPEECH ACT.
4. On the relation between *logos* [λόγος], *verbum, davar* [דָּבָר], verb, and divine word, see especially LOGOS, III.B; cf. *ALLIANCE,* GOD.

➤ DICHTUNG, *DISCOURSE, THING*

VERGÜENZA (SPANISH)

ENGLISH	shame, modesty
FRENCH	*vergogne, honte, fierté, honneur*
GREEK	*aidôs* [αἰδώς]
ITALIAN	*vergogna*
LATIN	*verecundia*

➤ *SHAME* and ART, CIVILTÀ, DESENGAÑO, FAIR, GENIUS, MIMÊSIS, NEIGHBOR, PHRONÊSIS, POLIS, RELIGIO, SPREZZATURA, THEMIS, VIRTÙ

In Spanish and in Italian, the terms *vergüenza* and *vergogna* have not fallen out of favor. Indeed, they are used in many different situations. In Spanish, the term has become oriented toward one's own dignity and self-esteem; but as the Spanish psychologist Eduardo Crespo reminds us, it must be understood as a collective sentiment, illustrated by the expression *vergüenza ajena* ("the shame of the other"), which refers to the shame one feels as a result of the behavior of another. Here we find one of the essential features of *aidôs* [αἰδώς], the Greek personification of modesty.

I. *Vergüenza/Vergogne*

The terms *vergüenza* (Sp.), *vergogna* (It.), and *vergogne* (Fr.) share the same Latin root, *verecundia*, "diffidence," "bashfulness," "modesty" or "decency"—which in imperial Latin means "shame in the face of the blameworthy." *Verecundia* is itself derived from the adjective *verecundus*, "respectful," "reserved"/"revered," "venerable." The latter comes from the verb *vereor* (or *vereri*): in religion, "to fear," "to revere," "to have respect or scruple for." *Vereor* belongs to a family of words that derive from the Indo-European root °*swer*-, meaning "pay attention," like the Greek *horan* [ὁρᾶν] (to look, pay attention, see).

Current French usage of *vergogne* is limited to the negative form: *sans*. The very obsolescence of the term is incorporated into its indication of a well-meaning disapproval bordering on irony. But what does he or she lack when one speaks of someone being or acting *sans vergogne*? In the adverbial form, one would say a lack of scruples and restraint; the attributive form adds a connotation of immorality: debauched (Fr. *dévergondé*). The definition of *vergogne* seems only to reside in the space of its opposite: *sans vergogne* is used exclusively as a figure of accusation or judgment.

One must take the path in exactly the opposite direction in Spanish. Before being *sin vergüenza*, one must first be *con vergüenza*. Persons *con vergüenza* are persons of honor, persons of their word. It is not so much that they keep their promises, but that they are bound by the word that they have given: they commit to *cumplire* and to *à ser cumplido*, "to carry out," "to accomplish a mission" (to fulfill their duties in relation to the community), and "to be fulfilled" (Fr. *s'accomplir*). In this context, the oath prevails over judgment. The motif of shame, at that point, derives from betrayal, the violation of a commitment that constitutes an affront to dignity. Self-accomplishment is a "compliment" to the group. The dignity of each is to the credit of the community, is a mark of its worth; on the other hand, to lack *vergüenza* is to attack the community, to injure it.

In French culture, the negative judgment is a reflection of immoderation, or the extreme nature of a person's conduct that is stigmatized. Here, the reaction of indignation translates or conjures with the rupture of an implicit contract based on norms and conventions (see MIMÊSIS, Box 6), whereas in Spanish the negative judgment is what guarantees and constructs relations of social solidarity.

To delve more deeply into the Spanish nuances, one can examine the expression *vergüenza ajena*, which, according to Eduardo Crespo, captures the feeling of shame that is experienced in the face of the incompetent or inadequate conduct of another person. The feeling of shame in this case has nothing to do with the subject's actions, for he or she has not done anything and cannot feel responsible or be held guilty. It is precisely because there is no direct relation to the person for whom one feels shame that the sentiment of *vergüenza* exhibits and constructs the tie. *Vergüenza* in this instance helps build a sense of community. The one who brings *vergüenza* (as in the related expression ¿*No te da vergüenza?* [Aren't you ashamed?]) does not stand accused or excluded from the community but is, rather, recalled to the duty of dignity.

▪ See Box 1.

II. *Aidôs* and the Gaze of the Other

The relation to the community expressed in the Spanish expression of *vergüenza ajena* is clearly transmitted in the Greek *aidôs* [αἰδώς], which *A Greek-English Lexicon* (RT: LSJ) translates as "reverence, awe, respect, shame, self-respect, sense of honor, regard" and also the so-called active sense, "that which causes shame or scandal," whence the plural form the "shameful parts" (Homer, *Iliad*, 2.262).

Although both terms can be translated as a sense of shame, *aidôs* is to be distinguished from *aischunê* [αἰσχύνη], "to shame or dishonor" (RT: LSJ). The family of the latter word also refers to deformity and ugliness (as opposed to beauty); *aischunô* [αἰσχύνω] has the primary meaning of "to dishonor," "to tarnish," or "to disfigure" (Homer, *Iliad*, 18.24), and Plato opposes *aischos* [αἶσχος] or *aischros* [αἰσχρός] to "beauty," *kalos* [καλός], in the *Symposium* (201a 4–5, 206c 4–5; see BEAUTY, Box 1). *Aischunê* is often tied to the body, and in the case of the female body, to modesty in the modern sense. *Aischunô* takes on the meaning of "blush," and in botany, *aischunomenê* [αἰσχυνομένη] means "the sensitive," as in the "sensitive plant" (whether *Mimosa pudica* [RT: *Dictionnaire grec-français*] or *Mimosa asperata* [RT: *Dictionnaire étymologique de la langue grecque*; RT: LSJ]). In this sense, it can even designate the feeling of shame that results from rape, and in the plural to the act of rape itself, the "the most extreme outrage" (for example, Isocrates, 64d [= *Panegyric*, 4.114]).

Both *aidôs* and *aischunê* move from the possibility of feeling shame to that which causes it, so that one could well translate the nuances of either term in the same author sometimes as "honor" and sometimes as "dishonor" (Thucydides, *History of the Peloponnesian War*, 2.51.5; 1.5.1). This fold in the structure of shame is illustrated by Phaedra, who does not know in which direction (honor or dishonor) *aidôs* will incline her love for Hippolytus: "Yet they are of two sorts, one pleasure being no bad thing, another a burden upon houses. If propriety [*kairos* (καιρός)—due measure or proportion: RT: LSJ] were always clear, there would not be two things designated by the same letters" (Euripides, *Hippolytus*, 385–87; for a different analysis, see Williams, *Shame and Necessity*). The Latin *pudor*, from *pudeo* (to be ashamed, to cause shame) has the same type of extension: "*ecqui pudor est?*" (where is your sense of shame?; Cicero, *In Verrem*, 4.18); "*vulgare alicujus pudorem*" (to broadcast someone's dishonor; Ovid, *Heroides*, 11.79). But unlike *pudor*, which, when used by itself is normally rendered by *aidôs*, the doublet *pudor/pudicitia* denotes "modesty"/"chastity": the syntagm *pudor et pudicitia* speaks to chastity, morality, and high morals (Cicero, *Orationes in Catilinam*, 2.25; on the Spartan conjunction of *aidôs-aischunê*, see Thucydides, *History of the Peloponnesian War*, 1.84.3).

1

The *sans vergogne* of Francis Ponge

Many uses of *vergüenza* resemble those of the Italian *vergogna*. Many invocations and exclamations in French are to be found in the lexical field of *honte*, and some of the common expressions from Spanish and Italian can be translated as *Quelle honte! C'est une honte!* (For shame! That's shameful!), but the meaning in French is most often considerably weakened. For in both Spanish and Italian, to call on *vergüenza* or *vergogna* is to bring pride into play. We would like to revive the French *vergogne* and give it back its meaning, a meaning that Francis Ponge was able to recover from disuse. Three examples suffice to show how the power of the term's signification can be reactivated.

As far as syntax, prose, or rhetoric goes, renewal is a matter of instinct, without shame [*sans vergogne*] (yet prudent, concerned only with the result, and with efficacy).

But first and foremost, one must insist that the experience of recent successes (and setbacks) in matters of literary or artistic fame has been most enlightening (Mallarmé, Rimbaud).

We have seen how daring in these areas *pays off*.

("My Creative Method," in *Méthodes*)

Some may reproach us for expecting our ideas to come from words (from the dictionary, from limericks, from rime, from who knows where . . .): well, yes we admit it, one has to use this process, to respect the material, to foresee how it will age, etc. . . . But we would answer that this is not the only way and we also ask that an unprepared contemplation, and a cynicism, a shameless [*sans vergogne*] honesty of relations, provide some of them as well.

(Ibid.)

[I]f you want to go off on a tangent, follow me—it may look pretentious—but it is so simple at the same time. You won't have to follow me very far. Just as far as this cigarette butt, for example, to pretty much anything, as long as it is considered honestly, which in the end is to say (without concern for everything we are told about the mind, about man) that it is considered shamelessly [*sans vergogne*].

("Tentative orale," in *Méthodes*)

This search for the "height of propriety in the use of terms" (*comble de la propriété dans les termes*) revitalizes the word "shame" (*vergogne*). Even if Ponge only uses the negative form *sans vergogne*, he lets it loose by placing

it in other systems of opposition; in a system of echoes and resonances (which he calls being "only concerned with the result"—from the Latin *resulto*, which in poetic usage "resounds,""rebounds as an echo"). In the first quotation, *sans vergogne* connotes spontaneity of instinct and invention, and it is linked once again, with daring and prudence, to the concept of being "without fear"—*verecundia, verecundus, vereri*. In the second quotation, *sans vergogne* implies the leveling of relationships, freed from the weight of literary and social convention, effectively liberated from an approach that takes the side of the human (or ideas) against the side of things. In the third quotation, considering anything (even a cigarette butt) *sans vergogne* means to look at it "honestly," as worthy of interest without regard to ontological hierarchies. The beauty of the paradox—and the sign of the inventiveness of the work—lies in the following: Ponge needs to *do away* with shame in order to bring into existence the "honorability" of the side he has chosen. By contrast, the Spanish and Italians must cultivate the positive side of "with"—as in (*avec*) *vergogne*—to translate their demands for dignity.

BIBLIOGRAPHY

Ponge, Francis. *Méthodes*. Paris: Gallimard, 1961.

For its part, *aidôs* defines the Homeric hero: the word (*aidomai* [αἴδομαι]) designates, according to RT: LSJ, "to stand in awe of," "to fear especially in a moral sense," "to have regard for a reputation for valor." In the French translation of *The Illiad* by Paul Mazon, Ajax rallies the Argives thus: "Amis, soyez des hommes, mettez-vous au coeur le sens de la honte [*aidô thesth' eni thumôi* (αἰδῶ θέσθ' ἐνὶ θυμῷ)]" (put a sense of shame in your hearts), followed by "Faites-vous mutuellement honte [*allêlous t' aideisthe* (ἀλλήλους τ' αἰδεῖσθε)]" (shame each other mutually, instill a sense of collective shame) (*Iliad*, 15.580–90). The 1900 Samuel Butler English translation renders these lines: "'My friends,' he cried, 'be men and fear dishonour [*aidô thesth' eni thumôi* (αἰδῶ θέσθ' ἐνὶ θυμῷ)]; quit yourselves in battle, so as to win respect from one another' [*allêlous t' aideisthe* (ἀλλήλους τ' αἰδεῖσθε)]." In the 1990 translation by Robert Fagles, shame is more clearly foregrounded as the rallying point of the call to battle: "'Shame, you Argives! All or nothing now— . . . Quick, better to live or die, once and for all, than die by inches, slowly crushed to death . . . by far inferior men!'"

Aidos and *Nemesis* (*Aidôs kai Nemesis* [Αἰδὼς καὶ Νέμεσις]) appear together in Homer (*Iliad*, 13.122) and Hesiod (*Works and Days*). *Aidôs* is comparable to an individual conscience, while *Nemesis* is comparable to a public conscience (for

example, the feeling of righteous indignation aroused especially by the sight of the wicked in undeserved prosperity). But perhaps one can say more correctly that in both shame-honor-respect and justice-vengeance, the look of the other is at issue more than the consciousness of self and that the other's look determines or insists upon a behavior or punishes a misbehavior (see CONSCIOUSNESS, Box 1 and THEMIS). We would support Van Windekens's (RT: *Dictionnaire étymologique complémentaire de la langue grecque*) etymological hypothesis, according to which *aideomai* [αἰδέομαι] would derive from **a-Fidomai* [**ἀ-Φιδομαι] of the same family as the Greek *Fidein* [Φιδειν], the Latin *videre*, and the French *voir*. *Aidôs* precisely identifies the definitive requirement of the hero, his "regard" for his *philoi* [φίλοι] and his *genos* [γένος].

Aidôs as "honor in the eyes of the other" leads to the pursuit of *kleos* [κλέος], "fame," and *timê* [τιμή], "honor as esteem," and more precisely (in Homer), that part of honor that men and gods accord to royal dignity and that is materialized in the *geras* [γέρας], the gift of honor, the prize due to the king (cf. RT: *Le vocabulaire des institutions indo-européennes*, vol. 2, chap. 5, "honor and honors"). The threat to *aidôs* is *hubris* [ὕβρις], "insolence, arrogance, excess, wantonness, outrage" (it can also be a heading for legal accusations; cf. RT: LSJ, s.v. *hubris* [2.3]: a term covering all the more serious injuries done to the person) and can apply to both the actor and the object. Thus the intrigue of the *Iliad* is entangled around the *hubris* of Agamemnon for his quarrel with Achilles over Chryseis and the intrigue of the *Odyssey* culminates in the *hubris* of the arrogant suitors (*Odyssey*, 4.627; "behaving with their old *hubris*"). *Hubris*, which a popular etymology connects with *huper* [ὑπέρ], "to be superior," consists for Aristotle "in doing and saying things that cause shame to the victim, not in order that anything may happen to yourself, or because anything has happened to yourself, but simply for the pleasure involved" (*Rhetoric*, 2.2.1378b23–25). *Hubris* is an indication of a bad or false superiority that men should avoid among themselves as well as when they face the jealous gods: it is an insult to the cosmic and human order.

It is against this background of the regulation of the world in common that one must interpret the myth of Protagoras: an assembly of citizens replaces the assembly of warriors. Even though they already have at their disposal the Promethean *technai* [τέχναι] as well as the *logos* [λόγος] of the arts and discursivity (see ART, LOGOS), humankind is still being killed off by animals or, if they gather in cities, people kill off each other. Fearing that the race would be wiped out, Zeus "sends Hermes to bring to men *aidôs* and *dikê* [δίκη] [in A. Croiset's French translation, *pudeur et justice*; in C.C.W. Taylor's English translation, "conscience and justice"] to serve as the organizing principles of cities and as the bonds of friendship" (Plato, *Protagoras*, 322c2–3). *Aidôs* and *dikê* together constitute the *aretê politikê* [ἀρετὴ πολιτική], the "excellence or virtue in politics," which, unlike technical competence, needs to be distributed equally among all: "and lay down on my authority a law [*nomon* (νόμον); see LEX] that who cannot share [*metechein* (μετέχειν)] in conscience and justice [*aidôs* and *dike*] is to be killed as a plague on the city" (Plato, *Protagoras*, 322d3–4). *Aidôs* is behavior, good comportment, self-restraint (the term is conveyed by *sôphrosunê* [σωφροσύνη] "moderation" 323a2; see PHRONÊSIS) provoked by the regard and expectations of the other. *Dikê*, before it came to signify "justice," referred to the rule, usage, procedure, everything that could "bring to light" (*deiknumi* [δείκνυμι]), public codes of conduct. Thus *aidôs* is the motivation to respect *dikê*, and *dikê* carries weight insofar as everyone experiences *aidôs*. The Protagorean combination is not concerned with ethical intention, and even less with the autonomy of the moral subject, but instead with a definition of politics as respect for the rules of public behavior—such that, as concludes Protagoras with no risk of moral scandal, the man that we know to be unjust, if he does not pretend in public to be just, is not showing his wisdom, his sincerity, or his moderation (*sôphrosunê*), but simply revealing his folly (*mania* [μανία], 323b–c).

Aristotle underscores this political dimension of *aidôs*. Insofar as politics is not to be confused with ethics (*Nicomachean Ethics*, 1.1; see PRAXIS), it is of important consequence that *aidôs* not be a virtue, nor an *aretê*, but a pathos [πάθος], an affection that involves the body, rather than a *hexis* [ἕξις], a state or disposition chosen by the soul (4.15.1128b10–11; see 2.6.1106b36–1107a1 for a definition of virtue as *hexis proairetikê* [ἕξις προαιρετική]). As a result, the distinction between *aidôs* and *aischunê* becomes increasingly fragile (cf. *Rhetorics*, 2.6 and J. Tricot's protestations in his notes to the *Nicomachean Ethics*, 4.15), in which he renders *aidôs* as the

French *modestie*, but it appears more than ever that *aidôs* hangs on the intersection of the gazes: as the proverb goes, "shame [*aidôs*] dwells in the eyes" (*Rhetoric*, 2.6.1384a33–36). This is why in the *Politics*, the "visible presence" (*en ophthalmois parousia* [ἐν ὀφθαλμοῖς παρουσία]) of the magistrates is recommended in the gymnasia, for the young as well as the old, because it "induces the true respect which is the form of fear proper to free men" [ἐμποιεῖ τὴν ἀληθινὴν αἰδῶ καὶ τὸν τῶν ἐλευθέρων φόβον] (*Nicomachean Ethics*, 7.12.1131a40); *a contrario*, the multitude, *hoi polloi* [οἱ πολλοί] "do not by nature obey the sense of shame, but only fear, and do not abstain from bad acts because of their baseness but through fear of punishment" [οὐδ' . . . διὰ τὸ αἰσχρὸν ἀλλὰ διὰ τὰς τιμωρίας] (ibid., 10.9.1179b20–31).

From *aidôs*, which is linked to the Latin *videre* (to see), to *vergüenza*, which is linked to the Greek *horan* (to see), we remain in the space of the gaze. But the structure of this space changes. As the public and private spheres diverge, the difference between what has been more recently labeled "shame civilization" and "guilt civilization" is recuperated (cf. Williams, *Shame and Necessity*). When the public space is primary, the *oikos* [οἶκος], the "home" or the "family," takes on the role of the private, specifically of privacy shielded from the public, or the properties proper to truth (see TRUTH, especially I.B, and PROPERTY). In serving thus to give structure to the relationship to the gods as well as that between persons, *aidôs* becomes constitutive of shame civilization. With the rise of subjectivity and the mediation of links between human beings and God, it is conscience (see CONSCIOUSNESS)—the eyes of the self and the eyes of God, not the eyes of the other—that gives structure to a form of the private that can be publicly presented: guilt civilization. But perhaps the notion of shame civilization is not refined enough to signify *aidôs*. The English word "shame," or the German *Scham*, derives from a root that means to "cover up" (see, for example, RT: *Comprehensive Etymological Dictionary of the English Language*). There can be little doubt that error and culpability were required when "the eyes of both of them were opened, and they realized they were naked" (Gen. 3:7)—Greek statuary did not conceal the pudenda. This is why *vergogne*, and to a lesser extent *vergüenza*, both of which preserve a connection to the Greek *aidôs* and the Latin *videre*, are vestigial remainders of a shame culture that continues to mutate.

Barbara Cassin
Vinciane Despret
Marcos Mateos Diaz

BIBLIOGRAPHY

Aristotle. *Nicomachean Ethics*. Translated by W. D. Ross, revised by J. O. Urmson. In *The Complete Works of Aristotle, The Revised Oxford Translation*, vol. 2, edited by Jonathan Barnes. Princeton, NJ: Princeton University Press / Bollingen, 1984.

———. *Rhetoric*. Translated by W. D. Ross. In *The Complete Works of Aristotle, The Revised Oxford Translation*, vol. 2, edited by Jonathan Barnes. Princeton, NJ: Princeton University Press / Bollingen, 1984.

Cairns, Douglas L. *Aidôs: The Psychology and Ethics of Honour and Shame in Ancient Greek Culture*. Oxford: Clarendon Press, 1995.

Cassin, Barbara. *L'effet sophistique*. Paris: Gallimard, 1996.

Cicero, Marcus Tullius. *In Verrem*. In *The Verrine Orations*, translated by Leonard Hugh Graham Greenwood. Loeb Classical Library. Cambridge, MA: Harvard University Press, 1953.

Crespo, Eduardo. "Emotions in Spain." In *The Social Construction of Emotions*, edited by R. Harré, 209–17. Oxford: Blackwell, 1986.

Euripides. *Hippolytus*. Translated by David Kovacs. Loeb Classical Library. Cambridge, MA: Harvard University Press, 1995.

Hesiod. *Theogony; Works and Days; Shield*. Translated by Apostolos N. Athanassakis. Baltimore, MD: Johns Hopkins University Press, 1983.

Homer. *The Iliad*. Translated by Robert Fagles. New York: Penguin Books, 1990.

———. *Iliade*. Translated by Paul Mazon. Paris: Collection des Universités de France, 1961.

———. *The Iliad of Homer*. Translated by Samuel Butler. New York: E. P. Dutton & Company, 1925. First published in 1900.

Ovid. *Heroides*. Translated by G. Showerman. Loeb Classical Library. Cambridge, MA: Harvard University Press, 1986.

Plato. *Protagoras*. Translated by C.C.W. Taylor, Oxford: Oxford University Press, 1996.

Williams, Bernard. *Shame and Necessity*. Berkeley: University of California Press, 2008.

VERNEINUNG (GERMAN)

ENGLISH   negation, denial, denegation

➤ *NEGATION* and ANXIETY, AUFHEBEN, CONSCIOUSNESS, DRIVE, ENTSTELLUNG, ES, SUBJECT, UNCONSCIOUS

Formed from the verb *verneinen* ("to say no [to a question], to answer in the negative," and by extension, "to deny, refuse"), the substantive *Verneinung* has come to designate, in psychoanalysis, a turn of phrase in which the analysand becomes conscious of a thought-content while simultaneously disowning what he is saying. To achieve this, the analysand employs a grammatical or logical denial of the content of the judgment he offers and attributes the undesirable thought to the other, the analyst. The classical Freudian example goes as follows: "You ask who this person in the dream can be. It's not my mother" ("Die Verneinung"; "Negation," 235). The French translations initially proposed, *dénégation* or *déjugement* (the terms used by Jean Hyppolite), erased the linguistic connection between the logical operation of negation and the conflictual relationship of the subject in relation to his own thought-content. But after lengthy discussions regarding the relations of psychoanalysis to German language philosophy, both Kantian and post-Kantian, the translation of *Verneinung* returned to "negation." As J. Laplanche reminds us in the French edition of the *Standard Works*, the *Œvres complètes* of Freud, there were more than ten different translations of the term by French psychoanalysts. The first dates from 1934 (H. Hoesli, *Revue française de psychanalyse* 7, no. 2: 174–77). The review *Le Coq Héron* published several others in 1975 (and 1976) for comparison.

I. The No and Negation in Psychoanalysis

The history of the translation of *Verneinung* is a function of the fact that psychoanalysis seeks to understand what is happening in relation to the instinctual drives when a subject uses logical categories. And in philosophy, one must take into account the fact that this same term is usually used as a synonym for "negation," a word that takes up the Latin term. In addition, modern metaphysics sometimes approaches the question of the status of the real in relation to thought through the certainty of the subject in his affirmations, making use of the same vocabulary by which Freud characterizes the various compromises that construct the subject as divided through the recognition of castration on the one hand, and on the other hand, by the subject's refusal of the same. For Freud, the subject is formed by the ways in which he compromises with everything that poses a threat to the omnipotence of his desires, whether he becomes set in the negation (*Verneinung*) of castration, in its denial (*Verleugnung*), or in its repudiation (*Verwerfung*) (Fr. *forclusion*), which lead, respectively, to neurosis, perversion, or psychosis.

Thus, the specific manner by which to deny the fact of castration is constitutive of the different modes of structure for the subject. At first glance it would seem that philosophy and psychoanalysis do not engage one another on the subject of *Verneinung*. The former speaks of logical inferences and of utterances relating to the world. The latter, on the other hand, approaches negation as a certain way of setting up a subjective division that applies to a subject of desire faced with a "lack of being" that sexual difference introduces into human reality. But on closer analysis the question of beliefs is a place of multiple encounters between psychoanalysis and philosophy in relation to negation.

For Freud "negation" and *Verneinung* are synonymous. He approaches the use of the expression "don't" (Ger. *nicht*, Fr. *ne pas*) by superimposing the linearity of discourse and the dissymetries of the system of the cure; in speaking, the analysand speaks to an Other. In a first moment, negation enables an accommodation, a distribution, between the self and the supposed Other, of what constitutes the subject. By attributing the thought to another through negation, the patient can come to terms with a thought-content that constructs him or her as a subject, all the while rejecting that construction. In a second phase, knowledge as such, even in its positive affirmation, can be caught up in that same system of alterity that sets negation to work: to know something, whether something of one's self or something outside the self, always consists of keeping at bay that which threatens us. Denial keeps that distance, as long as an Other can be assigned that which we cannot admit even as we express it. The theory of negation stands with the theory of knowledge, when understood as being carried along by drives. As one can see, it is precisely because the linearity of discourse carries with it a set of coordinates of a condition of language linked to the work of desires that Freud's *Verneinung* is distinct from an ontology of negation.

But in a third pass at an approach to negation, Freud in 1925 makes an incursion into the logic of judgment by referring to Aristotelian logic, which serves to articulate ontology and logic. By distinguishing the effect of the copula "to be" as joining or dis-joining subject and predicate, from the absolute meaning of "to be," it is possible to define two functions for negation in the implication of the subject in his or her judgments. To untie the bonds between subject and predicate through a judgment in the form of a negative attribution is to spit out or expel (*ausstossen*) something to an outside that is constituted as bad and as outside by this very act of expulsion. The negation of the judgment of existence, which rejects while it knows, is a way of coming back on this first exclusion of an outside. It is an important point: the *Verneinung* as refusal is less radical a refusal than the expulsion that sets up the excluded. It is a victory over the radical exclusion of some content that would cause too much pain if it were recognized as inside the self. But this victory comes at a high price: the intellectual recognition of content distances it from the self; for Freud, it serves to maintain the repression. One could even claim that it establishes the repression by leaving affect out of the new-found awareness. Negation does not establish just any repression: repression through consciousness occurs nearest the most menacing figures of alterity, in the immediate vicinity of that which a subject has been tempted to radically expel from the self. Negation is a second recourse, in the face of imminent threat—and in relation to a primary defense that consists of destroying the threat by expulsion—but negation requires the prior destruction of affect in the subject. Here Freud expresses himself "backwards": he says that negation shows how the "intellect separates itself from affect." But by dwelling on negation as a second recourse to an expulsion that sought to abolish a content through expulsion, he in fact establishes the reverse: negation restores that which had previously been abolished, but without reestablishing the affect or instinctual content of what it enables to come to consciousness. Negation does not illustrate how the intellect separates itself from affect, but rather that negation is an attempt by the subject to limit or offset the previous exclusion of a content. It is an attempt that establishes conscious thought without being able to reconcile the subject with his own experience. Negation does not suffice to account for repression, but it characterizes that form of repression that is linked to the establishment, in thought, of logic. Freud locates negation in the sequences of discourse and judgment, but he relates it to an experimental plan, somewhat like what Kant did when he left behind the formalism of onto-logic and reflected on the negative grandeurs, or more generally on the transcendental situations that our utterances and judgments return to. But in Freud, negation does not return to non-being.

The text of 1925 still does not make explicit the question of the relations between the lack inherent in desire and negation. Affirmative judgments of existence, according to Freud, are not a matter of finding an object in reality that corresponds to a desire, but to find it again, to regain it, which means that there is the possibility, already inscribed in the system of the psyche, of "not" regaining it. Admitting the absence (of the object that would be good to regain) would be another possible function of negation, which Freud does not address explicitly in this text, but which is nonetheless implicit in it. It is on this point that Lacan, making reference to Hyppolite, takes up the question again.

II. Philosophical and Psychoanalytic Readings of Negation

When Lacan asks Hyppolite whether the Freudian *Verneinung* has anything to do with Hegelian negativity, he returns to this possible relation between negation and non-being: in the first function of judgment, which unties the bonds between subject and predicate in such a manner that the bad is radically expelled to the outside, Lacan dwells on the effective workings of the death drive and wonders about its link with Hegelian negativity. He asks Hippolyte if the use of negation in language has something to do with the reality of death: whether there is a relation not only between negation and the lack internal to desire, but also between the destructiveness of desire and the negation that functions through

expulsion (*Ausstossung*). He stresses the death instinct, which was, of course, a notion found in Freud, but which Freud did not set in direct relation with an ontology of negation. Freud limited himself to considering the psychotic's compulsion to deny everything as a panic of negation, which at that point no longer plays the role of *Verneinung*, as a compromise between radical exclusion and the acceptance of a threatening thought-content. Lacan, on the other hand, asks the philosopher who specializes in Hegel to clarify such a possibility, which also means that the bridges between psychoanalysis and philosophy have been mended.

Hyppolite's reading is a subtle one: by translating *Verneinung* as *dénegation* (denegation) or *déjugement* (readjudication), he separates psychoanalysis from philosophy, since Hegelian negation has an ontological reach: death is active in reality, not just in the case of the desiring and thinking subject, but in the real taken as a universal whole. Freud relies on a distinction between affirmative judgment (*Bejahung*) and negative judgment (*Verneinung*), which is why he uses the latter as a general term, as the correlate and opposite of affirmation.

Curiously, Hyppolite does not give a direct answer to Lacan's question regarding the lack of desire in relation to Hegelian negativity. What he focuses on in Freud is the privileging of negation in relation to affirmation: in the relationship set up between the two functions of judgment, affirmation is the simple substitute for the logical unification of subject and predicate, that is to say, between a subject and a thought-content in psychoanalysis. Negation, on the other hand, is more than an impulse to untie the subject from the predicate, to expel something from the self. *Verneinung* is a subsequent *effect* (*Nachfolge*) of the *Ausstossung*. There is something creative about negation, something that produces out of a previous destruction. "A margin for thought can be generated, an appearance of being so in the guise of not being so" (Lacan, *Écrits*). Hyppolite clearly sees that the purpose of Freud's incursion into the theory of judgment is not to lead him back to Aristotle but to characterize the function of negation as a sublimating link between the two functions of the verb "to be." Affirming replaces unification. To deny is more than to destroy. Taking Hyppolite's formulation as a basis, one could say that for psychoanalysis the appearance of being, ontology, is conveyed by an instinctual process in which negation is the operator. Being and language are never alone in their own company.

It is all the more astounding that Hyppolite nonetheless brings together this instinctual function of negation and Hegelian negation, which is an ontological operator. Indeed, the latter occurs in being and experience, rather than in judgment. Hyppolite refers to an example in the *Phenomenology of Mind*: the struggle to the death for recognition invents a negation that modifies the absolute negation of animal desire. This first negation destroyed its object. The second negation, on the other hand, opens the way to the future by removing a situation of mastery and slavery from the risk of complete destruction. Hyppolite borrows the term "sublimation" from Freud and speaks of an "ideal negation," an idea that the philosopher obtains from the Freudian *Verneinung*, and which would avoid a real destruction. The relations between psychoanalysis and philosophy are thus more complex in the case of negation: Hyppolite starts from the idea of a revocation of judgment (*déjugement*), which serves to distinguish psychoanalysis from philosophy and which limits the scope of *Verneinung* to settling conflict internal to a subject. But in the end he draws on the idea of the sublimation of destruction to reinterpret Hegelian negativity.

Hyppolite starts out by distinguishing negativity from (de)negation. Nonetheless, he brings Freud and Hegel together on two points: first—and this is perhaps superficial—he calls the Freudian example in which the patient goes back on the first negation of a thought-content "negation of the negation" (Lacan, *Écrits*, 883). But this Freudian example is not a case of negativity, that mysterious sojourn that converts nothingness into being. What is at issue is how an intellectual acceptance of a previously denied content can still maintain the nonacceptance of that content. But this connection is made in order to introduce another observation: Hyppolite then connects the inventive character of Freudian *Verneinung*, which manages to limit a first exclusion, to the inventive character of negativity, which manages to limit the destruction at play in the work of the negative. The example he takes here is the passage from the absolute destruction of its object by animal desire according to Hegel, to the resource that in the "dialectic of master and slave" substitutes a situation of domination and slavery for the death of the adversary, enabling the possibility of a later invention of human existence. The negation of negation would be an ideal negation, as the *Verneinung* is an end result of expulsion, which limits the destructiveness of the Freudian death instinct.

The rapprochement between philosophical negativity and negation in psychoanalysis has one more consequence: the unilateral underscoring of the inventive aspect of negation in psychoanalysis, even though it is true that this negation differs from *Verwerfung* as the complete abolition of a content that cannot be recovered later. Yet it still does not eliminate the repression; it establishes it in a manner particularly difficult to transform in the therapeutic context of the transference: the destruction of part of the self derives sustenance from the activity of knowledge and the development of logical thought.

III. "Negation," *Verneinung, Verleugnung* in the Philosophical Problematics of Belief

Verneinung is the term employed in German to designate negation as applied to the form of attributive judgment (in Kant, for example) or to a proposition (for example, in Frege). So we can understand that Frege would entitle a text from 1921 *Die Verneinung*, as Freud would do in 1925, even though they were dealing with separate sets of problems. Frege is only interested in objective thoughts "independent of anyone thinking them," and the only negation that he is concerned with applies to a complete proposition: "It is the case that / It is not the case that. . . ." Freud, on the other hand, is interested in the way a subject carries on his thinking, so to speak, but he finds it in a counterpoint of affirmative and negative judgments, which brings him too to speak of *Verneinung*.

Kant bases his redefinition of formal logic into transcendental logic on a study of judgment: it is important for him to distinguish cases in which a judgment—either positive or negative—has an objective correlative from cases in which reason confuses a nothing with a something. He thus has recourse to the term *Verneinung* in its transcendental function as constitutive of a real object of knowledge. Thus, as early as 1763, he sees the importance of the concept of negative grandeur: an algebraic algorithm for finding the resultant of conflicting forces can be made to correspond to opposing judgments, one positive and the other negative. But since attention to judgment is for Kant only a stopping point on the path to transcendental and critical propositions, one can understand how *Verneinung* would be a synonym for "negation" in his terminology and that both words could apply either to a proposition as a whole or to one of its terms. This is the case, for example, when he opposes two pairs of antinomic judgments in relation to the world: the world is infinite or it is not infinite / the world is finite or infinite. What is important for Kant in relation to such pairs is to understand the difference between two cases. In one case negation divides the two alternative terms in a mutually exclusive way because the transcendental judgment, if it is correctly formed, has a real correlate. In another case the negation—whether it applies to a term or to the whole proposition—makes no distinction between the two alternative terms for the simple reason that there is no "case" at all, even if the formal appearance of the judgments seems to depict some "something" in this opposition of poorly formed propositions. Thus Kant usually uses *Verneinung*, but sometimes he has recourse to "negation"; and he accepts the difference between a negation that applies to a term and the negation that applies to a judgment (especially when he reflects on the question of knowing whether there are negations compatible with the idea of God), but he recognizes it as being of secondary importance compared to his transcendental concerns.

■ See Box 1.

When the authors we have referred to use other German verbs such as *leugnen, ableugnen, bezweifeln,* and *verneinen* in relation to negation, we can see in these different choices a concern to distinguish the different positions of consciousness of metaphysics when it comes to doubting the reality of the external world. Kant has recourse to the difference between doubting (*bezweifeln*) and denying (*leugnen*) to distinguish Descartes from Berkeley, that is to say, questioning idealism from dogmatic idealism. Schelling establishes the same distinction between *bezweifeln* and *leugnen* so as to oppose Descartes from both Berkeley and Malebranche together (*Einleitung*, 76–77).

Kant does not maintain these distinctions in the second edition of the *Critique of Pure Reason*, which claims to "refute idealism," instead of inscribing, as he did in the first edition, the theses on the real within the discourses on reason that constitute so many forms of belief. In that text, in effect, he affirmed that the existence of external reality could not be demonstrated but that it could be placed "out of doubt" (*ausser Zweifel*). One can understand, *a contrario*, that when psychoanalysis distinguishes between the positions of belief by which a human subject works out its relations to the real and to sexual difference—and hence indirectly to what philosophers call reality—it defines the work of negation in discourse in a far more explicit and precise fashion, by

---

1

The alternatives of *Verneinung* (Kant) and *Negativität* (Hegel)

Unlike Kant, Hegel never uses the term *Verneinung* but uses "negation" instead. This is consistent with his philosophical direction: he shows that the form of the proposition, specifically because it distinguishes between subject and object—whether to separate them or unify them—is ill suited to grasp the speculative element of thought. In effect, the latter consists in the destruction and internal critique of the propositional form of thought that occurs when negation affects each part of the proposition in turn, thereby critiquing the abstract hypothesis of their separation. It would seem that Hegel never gave his reasons for rejecting *Verneinung*, but his radical renunciation of the term is an integral part of his critique of the attributive proposition.

Such an abandonment is all the more remarkable in that it extends to the author's treatment of consciousness and all relations it has to itself, as well as to pure concepts of logic. In his critique of the moral vision of the world, one might well expect his descriptions of the tortuous displacement of moral consciousness in relation to itself, even including

its disguises (*die Verstellung*), to include terms like "misreading" (Fr. *méconnaissance*) or "misjudgment" (Fr. *déjugement*). But such is not the case. Only the terms "negation," *Negativität*, and *Aufhebung* are employed. The moral conscience "abolishes" its own conviction, without denial, misreading, or rejection. Even if the empirical positions of consciousness resemble those experiences in which consciousness revokes its judgment (Fr. *se déjuge*), to use Hyppolite's term, Hegel never comes back to *Verneinung* because his primary interest is to break down the separation of subject and predicate in judgment (whereas Kant relies on it in order to evaluate, depending on the case, the capacities for tying them together, to establish a position of existence by means of the transcendental synthesis). To this end, Hegel works on what starts to move in Being when "negation," in the *logos*, affects in turn the subject, the verb, the predicate, and the adverb (for example, the passage of the adverbial form *nichts*, "in no way," to the noun *das Nichts*, "nothingness," enables the stringing together of the first

categories in the *Science of Logic* [*Wissenschaft der Logik*], 66–67, §133, chap. 1). Even when he describes the arcana of self-consciousness, Hegel's intent is ontological. This is why he resolutely puts aside the verb *verneinen*. This is even more striking when he occasionally refers to specific Kantian expressions (*Phänomenologie des Geistes*, 565; *Phenomenology of Spirit*, 374) ("a whole nest" of thoughtless contradictions). In that very context Kant used the term *Verneinung* (*Kritik der reinen Vernunft*, A 573–75, B 601-3, in *Werkausgabe*, 4: 506–17). But in his reference to Kant and without explanation, Hegel replaces *Verneinung* by *Aufhebung*. For example, when he describes the permanent perversion (Fr. *travestissement*) of the moral consciousness, he employs the expression that Kant reserved for the illusory and tortuous reasonings regarding God, the ideal of pure reason. But at the same time, without explanation, he replaces *Verneinung*, which Kant had employed in that very passage, with "negation." With all due respect to Jean Hyppolite, the negation of negation is thus not a *Verneinung*.

---

distinguishing between "denying" (*verneinen*), "disavowing" (*verleugnen*), and "foreclosing" (*verwerfen*).

Monique David-Ménard

BIBLIOGRAPHY

Baudry, Francis. "Negation and Its Vicissitudes in the History of Psychoanalysis—Its Particular Impact on French Psychoanalysis." *Contemporary Psychoanalysis* 25, no. 3 (July 1989): 501–8.

Freud, Sigmund. "Die Verneinung." In *Gesammte Werke*. Vol. 14. Frankfurt: Fischer Verlag, 1948.

———. "Negation." In *The Standard Edition of the Complete Psychological Works of Sigmund Freud*. Vol. 19 (1923–1925): *The Ego and the Id and Other Works*. Edited by James Strachey. New York: Norton, 1989.

Hegel, Georg Wilhelm Friedrich. *Hegel's Science of Logic*. Translated by A. V. Miller. Atlantic Highlands, NJ: International Humanities Press, 1969.

———. *Phenomenology of Spirit*. Translated by A. V. Miller. Oxford: Clarendon Press, 1977.

Hyppolite, Jean. "Commentaire parlé sur la Verneinung de Freud." In *Écrits* by Jacques Lacan, 879–87. Paris: Seuil, 1966. Translation by Bruce Fink: *Écrits*. New York: W. W. Norton, 2007.

Kant, Immanuel. *Critique of Pure Reason*. Translated by Paul Guyer and Allen Wood. Cambridge: Cambridge University Press, 1998.

Lacan, Jacques. *Écrits*. Translated by Bruce Fink. New York: W. W. Norton, 2007.

Schelling, Friedrich. *Einleitung in die Philosophie*. Edited by W. E. Ehrhardt. Schellingiana 11. Stuttgart: Frommann-Holzboog, 1989. First published in 1830.

This, Bernard, and Pierre Thèves. *Die Verneinung. Nouvelle traduction. Étude comparée de quelques traductions disponibles. Commentaires sur la traduction en général. Le Coq Héron* 52 (1975).

———. *Die Verneinung II. Essai de remise en place du concept de dénégation.* Correspondance avec J. Laplanche et R. Lew. "*Die Verneinung* dans la théorie freudienne." *Le Coq Héron* 55 (1976).

———. *Die Verneinung III.* J. Rosenberg: "Kant avec Freud, la négation." R. Schutzwalder-Lochard. "De la réalité psychique." *Le Coq Héron* 60 (1977).

Thom, Martin. "Verneinung, Verwerfung, Ausstossung: A Problem in the Interpretation of Freud." In *The Talking Cure: Essays in Psychoanalysis and Language*. Edited by Colin MacCabe, 162–87. New York: St. Martin's, 1981.

Ver Eecke, Wilfried. *Denial, Negation, and the Forces of the Negative: Freud, Hegel, Lacan, Spitz, and Sophocles*. Albany: State University of New York Press, 2005.

VIRTÙ (ITALIAN)

ENGLISH	virtue
FRENCH	vertu
GERMAN	*Tugend*
GREEK	*aretê* [ἀρετή]
LATIN	*virtus, virtutes*

➤ *VIRTUE* and *DESTINY*, FORCE, GENIUS, GLÜCK, LEX, MORALS, PHRONÊSIS, PIETAS, SECULARIZATION, TALENT

The Italian *virtù*, constructed within the semantic field of the Greek *aretê* (excellence) and the Roman *virtus* (courage) as well as the Christian *virtutes* (virtues), takes on a new complexity with Niccolò Machiavelli and could be said to rise to the rank of concept. For Machiavelli, *virtù* must relate to two fundamental paradigms: the paradigm of virtue/fortune, as a principle of distinction between the new States, and the paradigm of virtue as decision and resolute action. In Machiavelli, the transition from the first to the second of these paradigms occurs through a transvaluation of the qualities traditionally associated with virtue, the result of which is to pass beyond these two paradigms in conceiving fortune as historical necessity. This necessity, to which abstract virtue must pay heed, is what Hegel in the *Phenomenology of the Spirit* will call "the way of the world" (*Weltlauf*). In relating *virtù* to temporality and historical necessity, Machiavelli moves away from the virtue of ancient philosophers, from Plato to the Stoics and to Augustine, to reconnect with the tradition of *virtus* of the Roman Republic, and he announces the relation between power and necessity that will be found in Spinoza, Hegel, and Nietzsche.

I. The Two Fundamental Paradigms: *Virtù/Fortuna* and *Virtù-Impetus*

It is only in his major writings after 1512, *The Prince* and *The Discourses*, that Machiavelli takes advantage of his experience as a diplomat and his familiarity with the work of Greek and Roman historians to speak of *virtù*, and to lay claim to the two fundamental paradigms that give it structure. Though he neither explicitly lays out the problematic nor pens the word itself, his missions to Cesare Borgia in 1502–3 and to Julius II in 1506 clearly helped to orient his thinking on the topic.

The first paradigm concerns Cesare Borgia and the distribution of virtue and fortune. The specific virtue of this model of the "new prince" for Machiavelli was to set the proper basis for his politics, but the model's success depended on chance—in this case, the life of the pope. Thus in *The Prince* (chap. 6), Machiavelli made Cesare Borgia the very model of the "virtuous man" who nonetheless is struck down by "extraordinary and extremely malign fortune." Still, Borgia's defeat was determined not only by the death of the pope, but also by his lack of foresight in allowing an enemy (Julius II) to then be elected pope. The relationship between virtue and fortune is constructed in an unstable equilibrium dependent on the success or failure of the enterprise.

In the course of his mission to Julius II, Machiavelli encountered the second paradigm of *virtù*, which is a matter of decisiveness, determination, and audacity. In an important letter to Giovan Battista Soderini, who was the nephew of the *gonfalonier* of Florence (published under the title *Ghiribizzi*, or "fantasies"), Machiavelli sketched out the principles of political decision-making. He asked himself how, in his conflict with his enemy Gianpaolo Baglioni, the pope was able to obtain by chance and without force that which he would probably only have succeeded in obtaining with difficulty through orders and arms. This is because, as Machiavelli says, men govern themselves according to different whims and talents. And since the times are unstable and changing, he who succeeds, whether he is good or bad, is the one who either best adapts his nature to the order of things (the role of *virtù*), or is lucky enough to live in times that correspond to his nature (the role of *fortuna*). As far as the first possibility is concerned, Machiavelli is quite skeptical. Since for him, human nature is something rigid and immutable, it is just as unlikely for there to be men capable of changing their natures according to the times as it is for there to be wise men capable of ruling the stars. So what is to be done? Human actions, wrote Machiavelli (*The Prince*, chap. 25), depend in equal parts on free will and fortune, the latter of which reveals its might most clearly where there is no clear virtue in place to resist it. In this respect, *virtù* is related to Greek *phronêsis* and to Roman *prudentia*, qualities that consist in taking precautionary measures, as when one erects dikes to protect against river flooding.

Machiavelli returns to the theorem of *Ghiribizzi* and concludes that if there are no qualities that are good in themselves, "it is better to be impetuous than cautious, because fortune is a woman who to be kept under must be beaten and roughly handled" (*The Prince*, chap. 25). In addition to virtue as prudence, there is virtue as *impetus*, in the decisive and deciding act. It is the "impulse and passion" of Julius II (*Discourses*, 3.9, trans. Thomsen). It is the principle according to which "fortune is more friendly to the one who attacks than to the one who defends" (*Florentine Histories*, 4.6, trans. Banfield and Mansfield). And it is the "extraordinary" act by which one obtains that which is beyond the reach of ordinary actions (*Discourses*, 3.36 and 44). The problem of fortune returns in the *Discourses* (3.9), providing further fodder to the partisans of Machiavelli's republicanism, who argue that republics have a better "fortune" than principalities, "since they are better positioned to adapt themselves to diverse circumstances." The issue of fortune returns one last time in the *Discourses* (3.21), linked to the counsel that a careful dose of cruelty and generosity can provide the proper mixture of personal virtue with the terror one needs to inspire if one wants to obtain respect.

II. The Transvaluation of Values from Antiquity

The second paradigm of *virtù* would seem to qualify the basic elements of political decision-making: preemptive prudence on the one hand, resolutive *impetus* on the other. Fortune acts as an independent variable relative to virtue (as shown throughout the *Discourses*). Virtue is all the stronger and fortune all the weaker when men act out of necessity and not out of choice (1.1). Good institutions lead to good fortune (1.11). Rome was able to benefit from the "fortune and virtue" of its consuls, and a well-organized republic should necessarily have a succession of able rulers (1.20). Machiavelli claims that the Romans were able to dominate more through their valor and ability (virtue) than through good fortune (2.1). And he constantly criticizes Italian princes who attribute the ruin of Italy to fortune rather than to their lack of virtue. The culmination of Machiavelli's thought is to be found in chapters 29 and 30 of the *Discourses*, in which he outlines a kind of pre-Hegelian philosophy of history, in which fortune no longer appears in opposition to virtue but rather seems to flow through it. Fortune blinds the minds of men who are opposed to her desires, but when she "wishes to effect some great result, she selects a man of such spirit and ability that he will recognize the opportunity which is afforded him." Machiavelli concludes that men can second-guess Fortune, but they cannot oppose her: "They may weave the threads, but they cannot break them. They should never abandon her though, because they can never know her aims, which she pursues by dark and devious means. Men should remain hopeful, never giving up no matter what troubles or ill fortune may befall them."

After arriving at a wager in the second paradigm that recalls the Virgilian adage *audaces fortuna iuvat* (Fortune favors the bold), Machiavelli's qualification of virtue reaches another adage, from Seneca this time: "fata volentem ducunt, nolentem trahunt" (The Fates lead the willing soul, but drag along the unwilling one). One must submit to this kind of necessity if one wants to succeed. But if fortune comes to the aid of *volentem*, what is the object of this will? What does it "intend"? What is its eidetic target? Since antiquity, virtue (whether it takes the form of the Greek *aretê* [see Box 1], the Roman *virtus*, or the Christian *virtutes*) has referred to a form of human action based on a teleological principle, whether it be Socratic wisdom, Epicurean pleasure (*hêdonê*), Stoic happiness (*eudaimonia*, *vita beata*), or those actions that, since Augustine, are meant to provide access to the City of God. With Machiavelli, however, the value of virtue or of good political conduct consists of love of country, affection for liberty, and state security. Regarding love of country, the object of the sagacious legislator and founder of a new state should be "to promote the public good, and not his private interests, and to prefer his country to his own successors" (*Discourses*, 1.9). The "exaltation and defense of country" is, according to Machiavelli, something that even the Christian religion endorses, despite its location of the ultimate good "in humility, lowliness, and a contempt for worldly objects" (2.2). As for Brutus's assassination of his sons, the crime is nonetheless an object of praise for Machiavelli (and thus an act of virtue) because it was committed "for the good of his country, and not for the advancement of any ambitious purposes of his own." Thus virtue is that "natural affection that each man should hold for his country" (letter of 16 October 1502), or (as he claims in a letter of 16 April 1527) the ability to esteem his fatherland more than his own soul, like those Florentine magistrates who dared oppose Pope Gregory IX in 1357–58 (*Florentine Histories*, 3.7, trans. Banfield and Mansfield).

Machiavelli's transvaluation of ancient values has contributed to the negative reputation of *The Prince* because it is proposed in the name of state security rather than of wisdom, pleasure, or happiness. In chapters 15 through 21 (summarized in *Discourses* 3.41), he condenses love of country and security of the State into the formula "safety of the country": "For where the very safety of the country [*salute della patria*] depends upon the resolution to be taken, no considerations of justice or injustice, humanity or cruelty, glory or shame, should be allowed to prevail. On the contrary, the only question that is valid is: What course will save the life and liberty of the country?" So it is as a function of the "safety of the country" that the "qualities" of traditional ethics change their meaning, as well as their relation to vice and virtue. Thus a prince should not shy from those vices without which he may not be able to safeguard the State. To follow what might seem to be the virtuous course could be his downfall, while taking the vicious one could ensure his security (*securità*) and well-being. The prince must then eschew liberality and not fear the infamy of cruelty if he wants to hold his subjects "united and faithful." He must not hold to his word if it would damage his rule. He must know how to be as wise as a fox or as strong as a lion depending on the circumstance, and he must act if necessary against faith, charity, humanity, and the respect of religion. Machiavelli does seem to deplore conduct that plays on appearance and reality, on simulation and dissimulation. It can ultimately lead to a kind of absolute relativism of political action (of the Jesuitical type), if it is not required by necessity. It is only out of necessity that the prince must adopt "a versatile mind, capable of changing according to the winds and changes of fortune . . . [he should not] swerve away from the good if possible, but [he should] know to resort to evil if necessity demands it" (*The Prince*, chap. 18).

■ See Box 1.

III. *Virtù* and the Public Sphere, between Rigorism and Utilitarianism

These chapters of *The Prince* effect the transition between the first paradigm and the second, because they qualify the value of an act that invariably relates to fortune in the assumption of power and is defined as a variable because of the choice involved, as *impetus* and as furor. But it does not involve, as it does in Kant, a universal value that holds for all circumstances. For on the one hand, if success in politics depends on the conjunction of the times in keeping with either the nature of man (on the side of fortune) or his capacity to adapt that nature to the times (on the side of virtue), then there are no good or bad qualities, nor absolutes of good and evil, and Hannibal's cruelty can be as much of a virtue as Scipio's humanity. On the other hand, this is not a form of absolute relativism, as in the Marquis de Sade, for the virtuous act must be linked to the common good, to the security of the State, to patriotic purpose (*The Prince*, chap. 26).

This reference to the public sphere locates Machiavellian virtue in a sort of conditional generality, equidistant from Kantian rigorism (which addresses the subject confronting the universality of law) and Sadean utilitarianism (which only concerns an individual through his particular interests). All of these parameters serve to define what one could call Machiavelli's "system," but it is a system that is far from coherent, stable, or linear, because it is affected by fluctuations, changes, and frequent contradictions. It is a function of two variables: first, the mixture of hope (desirable) and necessity (unavoidable); and second, the inscription of these thoughts not onto a peacetime logic (of better government, theories of justice, ideal or imaginary states, etc.), but onto a wartime logic, in times that are defined by the effective truth (*verità effettuale*) constituted by variation, circumstance, and accident. This is what Machiavelli calls the "quality of the times" (*qualità dei tempi*), which already points to a history being made, to the radical historicity of the world. It is thus within this system, with its instability, that it is necessary to evaluate the general significance of *virtù* in all of its various occurrences. This significance is refracted throughout a multiplicity of local and particular ascriptions as a result of context and what is called for by the argument.

■ See Box 2.

On a more general level, Machiavellian virtue radically distances itself from the ethico-philosophical Greco-Roman and Christian traditions. It is not something acquired through practice and exercise (*askêsis* [ἄσκησις]), nor by the lengthy and assiduous work of the self on the self (*cura sui*). It is not something that can be learned like an art (*technê* [τέχνη]), which has fed a debate from Socrates to the Stoics and Plutarch; nor is it a measure of moderation (*metron* [μέτρον]; see LEX, Box 1) between excessive extremes (as it is in Aristotle); nor is it even a simple rule for living (*technê tou biou* [τέχνη τοῦ βίου]). It is something that one either

1

Aretê: Excellence and purpose

➤ ART, GLÜCK, MORALS, PLEASURE, PRAXIS

Aretê [ἀρετή]: excellence, value, virtue, merit, consideration. . . . In ancient Greek, a single word, based on *aristos* [ἄριστος], the superlative of *agathos* [ἀγαθός], "good" (see also BEAUTY, Box 1), serves to designate all sorts of excellence that are thus bound together: excellence of the body ("value," in the sense of "valor" and "courage," which is linked to strength, beauty, and health—and is inseparable from the qualities of the heart and intelligence that already in Homer constitute the excellence of the hero [*Iliad* 15.642ff.], of the gods [ibid., 9.498], and even of women [*Odyssey* 2.206]), as well as the soul (with "virtue" defined as control of the self [*sôphronein aretê megistê* (σωφρονεῖν ἀρετὴ μεγίστη), Heraclitus 112], by respect [*to aideisthai* (τὸ αἰδεῖσθαι), Democritus 179], and by political and public virtues just as by ethical and private ones [Plato, *Republic* 6.500d, 9.576c16]), including the rewards of that excellence, the consideration and happiness that come with it (*Odyssey* 12.45; Hesiod, *Works and Days* 313). In a much broader context, the word refers to the "competence" of a workman as well as to the "performance" of a well-adapted organ that functions correctly. *Aretê* is thus the accomplishment or realization of purpose, whatever that may be, and for any being. *Aretê* always has an ontological dimension, even when it is translated as "virtue" in a moral sense. And if the value of human action can effectively be defined within moral systems according to some determinate teleological principle (wisdom, *sophia* [σοφία]; pleasure, *hêdonê* [ἡδονή], etc.), it is because every value as such is essentially the enactment of a *telos* [τέλος], of an end, of a proper aim, as in the notion of perfecting an art: *hê aretê teleiôsis tis* [ἡ ἀρετὴ τελείωσίς τις] (Aristotle, *Metaphysics* Δ.16, 1021b20, trans. Tredennick), "goodness is a kind of perfection" such that one can speak of a "perfect doctor" and, as even he points out, a "perfect thief."

In order to illustrate some of the difficulties of translation into a modern moral idiom, let us look at two classical texts whose intent is to define what we call "virtue," to determine whether it can be taught and to see it in practice, but whose breadth of examples forces us to considerably enlarge our framework of understanding.

In Plato's *Protagoras*, Protagoras claims to teach the *technê politikê* [τέχνη πολιτική], and Socrates doubts whether this is possible, because he doubts that virtue can be taught (320b). The two registers of art and ethics are indissolubly tied, and both fall under the rubric of *aretê*. Everything hinges on the comparison between competence in the *technai* [τέχναι] (for example, the *aretê tektonikê* [ἀρετή

τεκτονική], which can be translated as "architectural merit" or "excellence in building," 322d) and excellence in politics (*aretê politikê* [ἀρετή πολιτική], 323a), which opens up the question of "human excellence" (325a2) and "excellence" *tout court* (328e9). There is no satisfactory translation, even if "excellence" is the most common denominator, because no translation makes sense for every occurrence. If one wants to find out about technical competence, one consults the practitioners of an art—architects, for example, if one wants to build a rampart. But if one wishes to understand the practices of the Athenian assembly, which pertains to how to run the city well, then one listens to everyone, the blacksmith and the sailor, the rich man and the poor man, the nobleman and the commoner. For Socrates, the fact that the Athenians do not consider virtue to be teachable proves that they think there is nothing to teach. But for Protagoras, this is the proof—as illustrated in the celebrated myth of Zeus's equal distribution of *aidôs* [αἰδώς] and *dikê* [δική], respect and justice (see *aidôs* under VERGÜENZA and *dikê* under THEMIS), to all men in common—that political virtue, unlike technical competence, is shared simply and equally by all those who make up the city.

That, Socrates, is why the Athenians—as indeed everyone else—hold the view that when their deliberations require excellence at building [*peri aretês tektonikês* (περὶ ἀρετῆς τεκτονικῆς)] and other such practical skills [*ê allês tinos dêmiourgikês* (ἢ ἄλλης τινὸς δημιουργικῆς)], only a restricted group of men should contribute advice, and so they refuse to tolerate advice from anyone outside that group, as you say (naturally so, I would add); and that is why, on the contrary, when their deliberations involve *political excellence* [*politikês aretês* (πολιτικῆς ἀρετῆς)] and must be conducted entirely on the basis of justice and moderation [*dia dikaiosunês . . . kai sôphrosunês* (διὰ δικαιοσύνης . . . καὶ σωφροσύνης)], they quite naturally tolerate everyone. For they believe that all men must have this excellence in common [*tautês ge metechein tês aretês* (ταύτης γε μετέχειν τῆς ἀρετῆς)], since otherwise there would be no *cities*.

(Plato, *Protagoras*, 322d–323a,
trans. Hubbard and Karnofsky)

This breadth of meaning is equally evident in Aristotle, in the second book of his *Nicomachean Ethics*, in which he defines ethical virtue and the moral actions that correspond to it. In order to convey in what sort of

disposition of *habitus* (*poia hexis* [ποία ἕξις]), the *aretê ethikê* [ἀρετή ἐθική] consists, and before singularizing it as a mean between two extremes (*mesotês* [μεσότης]), he defines it as a virtue—and once again, "excellence" is the least misleading equivalent:

Every virtue or excellence [*pasa aretê* (πᾶσα ἀρετή)] *both* brings into good condition [*auto te eu echon apotelei* (αὐτό τε εὖ ἔχον ἀποτελεῖ)] the thing of which it is the excellence and makes the work of that thing be done well [*to ergon autou eu apodidôsin* (τὸ ἔργον αὐτοῦ εὖ ἀποδίδωσιν)]; e.g., the excellence of the eye [*hê tou ophthalmou aretê* (ἡ τοῦ ὀφθαλμοῦ ἀρετή)] makes both the eye and its work good [*spoudaion* (σπουδαῖον)]; for it is by the excellence of the eye that we see well [*têi gar tou ophthalmou aretêi eu horômen* (τῇ γὰρ τοῦ ὀφθαλμοῦ ἀρετῇ εὖ ὁρῶμεν)] . Similarly the excellence of the horse makes a horse both good in itself and good [*agathon* (ἀγαθόν)] at running and carrying its rider and at awaiting the attack of the enemy.

(*Nicomachean Ethics* 2.5.1106a15–21,
trans. Ross, 36–37)

Spoudaios [σπουδαῖος] (from *spoudê* [σπουδή], haste, effort, zeal, ardor, serious engagement) is opposed to *phaulos* [φαῦλος] (ugly, trivial, paltry, petty, sorry, poor), and is used as a term, in the *Politics* for instance, to distinguish good citizens from bad. Thus a single Greek expression carries a "physiological" meaning, such as "the excellence of the eye," and a "moral" meaning: "The excellence of the eye makes both the eye and its work good." Since excellence is thus the optimum of the *ergon* [ἔργον] proper to each thing, by rights and when unobstructed, we can understand that Aristotle's version of happiness is part and parcel with virtue, and that this conception is far from Kant's precautionary hopes for the sovereign good.

Barbara Cassin

BIBLIOGRAPHY

Aristotle. *Metaphysics*. In *Aristotle in 23 Volumes*, vols. 17–18, translated by Hugh Tredennick. Cambridge, MA: Harvard University Press, 1989.
———. *Nicomachean Ethics*. Translated by David Ross. Edited by Lesley Brown. Oxford: Oxford University Press, 2009.
Plato. *Protagoras*. Translated by B.A.F. Hubbard and E. S. Karnofsky. Chicago, IL: University of Chicago Press, 1984.

2

Virtù and virtus

The multiple uses of *virtù* and *virtus* reflect the various significations of *virtù* in the Roman semantic field in which *virtus*—as Joseph Hellegouarc'h has shown—is associated in turn with qualities of character: with generosity of spirit (*magnitudo animi*), with judgment (*consilium*), with wisdom (*sapientia*), and with prudence (*fortitudo, animus*) on the one hand, and with the capacity for governing on the other. In Machiavelli, virtue can in turn be associated with discipline and the stability of the military, with courage and the exploits of an army or its leader, with force (*dunamis*) and the proper disposition of affairs (the virtue of a city, people, or institution), with the excellence of great men and legislators of States, with political and military power, with generosity and prudence as capacities for foresight, for "seeing the problem from some distance" (*Discourses*, 1.18 and 3.28). This is in contrast to the disorder, the cowardice, the lack of foresight, the hesitation, the common behavior and half-measures that can be part of "humanity and patience," yet for conduct that fits the times, the impetuosity and fury of Julius II (*Discourses*, 3.9) is still to be preferred.

The model for this kind of virtue is classical virtue (*antiqua virtù*), the Spartan and especially Roman forms of virtue, which are opposed not so much to wealth and the vices that result from it, as in the ancient philosophers, but to corruption and its political consequences, like the weakening of, the insecurity of, the threats to, and the ruin of States. Machiavellian virtue is never an abstract principle: on the one hand, it always corresponds to real forms of behavior, to concrete and historically determined examples; on the other hand, these are carried by and subject to historical translations. This is the theory of *translatio imperii* (transfer of rule/authority): virtue as exceptional ability, says Machiavelli (in the introduction to book 2 of the *Discourses*), was first lodged in the "world" by the Assyrians, moved to Media, passed into Persia, from there to Rome, and subsequently to the peoples (of the North primarily) who still today "live in virtue." At any rate, as Cicero points out, there is no virtue except "in practice [*in usu*]" (*Republic* 1.2) and "in action [*in actione*]" (*De officiis* 1.19). In the face of this multiplicity of meanings, the translation of the word *virtù* in Machiavelli must take into account these two sets of coordinates, position in the system and situation in context, even if some will still prefer to always translate Machiavelli's *virtù* as "virtue" in English, *vertu* in French, and *Tugend* in German.

BIBLIOGRAPHY

Hellegouarc'h, Joseph Marie. *Le vocabulaire latin des relations et des partis politiques sous la République.* Paris: Les Belles Lettres, 1963.

has or does not have. *Virtù* does not exist outside of an act, a conduct, or a behavior that inflects time or tries to reorder its course. It is thus not the Stoic practice of individual subjectivation posited in a solitary relation of self to self, or of self to others and to society. It is a modification of the world made by public man through acts of taking and maintaining power or through increasing the size of the State. It is never linked to some form of natural or cosmopolitan universalism, but is inscribed as effective action in a historico-political context that gains legitimacy from civic and patriotic objectives or a commitment to preserving the State. In *The Prince*, the most significant act is the founding of a new State; in *Discourses*, it is a return to the basic and original foundations of the State.

The precedents for Machiavellian *virtù* should be sought not in the philosophers, but in the historians (Thucydides, Titus-Livy, Sallust, Plutarch, and especially Tacitus) who rely for their models on the Sparta of Lycurgus and Republican Rome (before the outbreak of civil wars and the establishment of the empire, in which, as they acknowledge, ancient virtue was lost). It was on the basis of the Roman models—revived by the English republicans of the seventeenth century and leading to the French equation of "virtue" with "republic" by Montesquieu, Rousseau, and Robespierre that the Anglo-Saxon "Cambridge" school (J.G.A. Pocock and Quentin Skinner) retracted the second paradigm of virtue as *impetus*. Virtue as *impetus* connotes the conduct of someone like Septimus Severus, a villain as an individual, but endowed, like Servius Tullius, with "great good fortune and virtue" (*Discourses*, 1.10), or Cleomenes in Sparta (*Discourses*, 1.9) or Agatocles in Syracuse (*The Prince*, chap. 8), neither of whom hesitated to employ extraordinary, violent measures to protect themselves from enemies and reestablish State power.

IV. Virtù and the Way of the World: Exemplum and Weltlauf

At the stylistic level, Machiavelli's use of *virtù* differs from the language of his diplomatic correspondence, where the term almost never appears. When he uses it in his major writing, he seems to want to elevate the political discourse to the "high" level of literary language, as if he had not so much "invented" his political subject as brought it back to the grand style of the history-writing of antiquity. His political analysis, previously limited in his diplomatic dispatches to deciphering current conditions and making conjectures about the future, is anchored by the use of *virtù* in the *exemplum*, which constitutes something that is not teachable, neither a warning, nor a precept, nor a piece of advice. The example consists of a history lesson that modern princes, in an era of corrupt morals and political institutions, are incapable of understanding or imitating.

Machiavellian virtue irrevocably marks the irruption of history and historicity into political discourse: ancient history as *exemplum*; contemporary history as an ensemble of occasions, circumstances, and accidents; history to come as a matter of intention and political will. Machiavelli's radical novelty lies in having transposed the sovereign virtue of the philosophers, in what Hegel, criticizing the "knights of virtue [*Ritter der Tugend*]" from the time of the Stoics to *Don Quixote* and Kant, called the "world process" (*Weltlauf*). As a result of this transposition, the previously irreconcilable opposition between abstract virtue and worldly event was suddenly annulled, voiding the "pompous discourse" of the supreme good, along with the waste of precious gifts. In this discourse, according to Hegel, the individual "puffs himself up and fills both his empty head, and that of others," with the verbiage of virtue as a value in itself, an "abstract unreal essence" (*The Phenomenology of Mind*, trans. Baillie, 172–74) separate from the world's processes and struggles. The virtue inscribed in the *Weltlauf* (and the virtue of Machiavelli) is that of the historians from antiquity, which is to say, a virtue referring to historic republican practices.

> Virtue in the olden time had its secure and determinate significance, for it found the *fullness of its content* and its solid basis in the *substantial life of the nation*, and had for its purpose and end *a concrete good that existed and lay at its hand*: it was also for that reason not directed against actual reality as a *general perversity*, and not turned *against a world process*.
>
> ("Virtue and the Course of the World,"
> in *The Phenomenology of Mind*, trans. Baillie, 174)

What Machiavelli calls "fortune" in his first paradigm is none other than the representation of what Hegel calls *Weltlauf*; immediate temporality within the immanence of a secularized time, and a brazen law of necessity according to which the man of virtue, the great man, "is what he does; of whom one must say that he wanted what he did just as he did what he wanted." Within the world process, virtue is no longer wisdom, pleasure, happiness, mastery of self, or any of the other principles that served to measure the value of acts in traditional ethics. It is an irruption into temporality, the abrupt encounter of human nature and history, the will to resolute action. Thus—and here is the second paradigm—virtue has become nothing but power, pure power, and power in its pure state, in Benedict de Spinoza's sense of the word:

> Virtue is human power [*virtus est ipsa humana potentia*] defined solely by man's essence . . . that is, . . . which is defined solely by the endeavor made by man to persist in his own being. Wherefore, the more a man endeavors, and is able to preserve his own being, the more is he endowed with virtue, and, consequently in so far as a man neglects to preserve his own being, he is wanting in power.
>
> (Spinoza, *The Ethics*, pt. 4, prop. 20, proof 20:1;
> trans. Elwes, 203)

According to Friedrich Nietzsche, it is with Socrates that *aretê* is written into a moral framework and into a system of "values" in the Heideggerian sense of the term. It is no longer the manifestation of an originary power, but is the evaluation of merit as a function of values (knowledge, rectitude, conviction) that are necessarily outside of it. Nietzsche's conception of values is the same as that which Callicles claims in Plato's *Gorgias* and which Socrates is quick to refute, specifically in the name of "values" such as moderation and the mastery of desires. The virtue of Callicles, the force and energies of intelligence in the service of passions, are, according to Nietzsche in the *Posthumous Fragments* of 1887–88, "virtue in the style of the Renaissance, *virtù*, virtue not embittered by morality" (Nietzsche, *The Will to Power*, trans. Kaufmann and Hollingdale). And in the *Tractatus politicus* that he was thinking of writing

during the same period, Nietzsche talks of the "politics of virtue, of how virtue is made to dominate." This politics of virtue is none other than Machiavellianism. "But," as Nietzsche says, "Machiavellianism *pur, sans mélange, cru, vert, dans toute sa force, dans toute son âpreté*, is superhuman, divine, transcendental, it will never be achieved by man, at most approximated" (ibid., 304). It is the virtue of the historians of antiquity, revisited by the Greco-Roman and Christian philosophers. As he says in the *Twilight of the Idols* in 1888, his "*cure* from all Platonism" has been Thucydides, "and perhaps the *Principe* of Machiavelli . . . by their unconditional will not to deceive themselves and not to see reason in *reality*—not in 'reason,' still less in 'morality'" (*Twilight of the Idols*, trans. Hollingdale).

Machiavelli's *virtù* revives the tradition that goes back to the *theia moira* (the unteachable divine element of Aristide, Themistocles, and Pericles), according to the definition that Socrates gives to virtue in the *Meno* (100a). It harks back to the Spartan *aretê* of Tyrtaeus (which indicates military valor, not caste membership, as in Homer) and the *aretê* of the Athenians in the speech that Thucydides attributes to Pericles in his funeral oration (*The Peloponnesian War*, bk. 2); and finally it reasserts its relationship to the history of republican virtue at the end of the Roman Republic and under the empire. But the real posterity of this virtue is to be found in Spinoza, Hegel, and Nietzsche, rather than among the "skeptics" with their relativism (from David Hume to François de La Rochefoucauld and Sade) or among the politicians with their realism (from Montesquieu to Rousseau and Robespierre). Without a doubt, Machiavellian virtue is nothing but power, the will to power, in the grip of time, with the "character of the times" (*qualità dei tempi*), and with that fortune that is just another name for the Hegelian *Weltlauf*.

The Machiavellian concept of *virtù* thus bears no relation to the "liberty" of ancient moral philosophy (the becoming free through practice and prudence; the proper measure of, government of, and concern for the self). It is related, rather, to historical necessity, with its constraints and submissions. For Machiavelli, *virtù* appears only where there is necessity. Free will, on the other hand, awakens the ambitions and desires that cause the downfall of the States (cf. *Discourses*, 1.5, 1.37). In the face of necessity, virtue lies in the collection of acts and decisions that increase the power of an individual or State. And this historical necessity has not waited for modern revolutions to bring it into the open, as Hannah Arendt would seem to think in her book *On Revolution*. Indeed, Machiavelli, Francesco Guicciardini, and their contemporaries experienced very early on the instability of the word, the changing times, the multiplicity of incidents and accidents, and the insecurity of States that followed the Italian wars after 1494. At some level, Machiavellian virtue, when confronted with the State logic of modern warfare, strangely resembles the attitude of the reformation in the face of salvation through grace—except that the *faith* of Luther and Calvin corresponded to what Machiavelli called *virtù*, whereas *grace*, in that century, corresponded to what Machiavelli called *fortuna*, fortune-necessity: the invincible force of the times, the brazen law of the world process, and the reasons and inscrutable ruses of history.

Alessandro Fontana

BIBLIOGRAPHY

Arendt, Hannah. *On Revolution*. New York: Viking, 1963.

Dumézil, Georges. *Servius et la fortune: Essai sur la fonction sociale de louange et de blâme et sur les éléments indo-européens du cens romain*. Paris: Gallimard, 1943.

Fontana, Alessandro. "Fortune et décision chez Machiavel." *Archives de Philosophie* 62 (1999).

Hegel, Georg Wilhelm Friedrich. *Phänomenologie des Geistes*. 1807. Translation by J. B. Baillie: *The Phenomenology of Mind*. London: Harper and Row, 1967.

Hyppolite, Jean. *Genesis and Structure of Hegel's "Phenomenology of Spirit."* Translated by Samuel Cherniak and John Heckman. Evanston, IL: Northwestern University Press, 1974.

Machiavelli, Niccolò. *Discourses on the First Decade of Titus Livius*. Translated by Ninian Hill Thomson. London: Kegan Paul, Trench and Co., 1883.

———. *Florentine Histories*. Translated by Laura Banfield and Harvey C. Mansfield. Princeton, NJ: Princeton University Press, 1988.

———. *The Historical, Political, and Diplomatic Writings of Niccolo Machiavelli*. Translated by Christian E. Detmold. Vol. 2. Boston, MA: J. R. Osgood, 1882.

———. *The Prince*. Edited by Quentin Skinner. Translated by Russell Price. Cambridge: Cambridge University Press, 1988.

Mansfield, Harvey C. *Machiavelli's Virtue*. Chicago, IL: University of Chicago Press, 1996.

Nietzsche, Friedrich. *Complete Works: The First Complete and Authorised English Translation*. Edited by Oscar Levy. 18 vols. New York: Russell & Russell, 1964.

———. *The Portable Nietzsche*. Selected and translated by Walter Kaufmann. New York: Penguin, 1976.

———. *The Twilight of the Idols*. Translated by R. J. Hollingdale. London: Penguin, 1990.

———. *Werke: Kritische Gesamtausgabe*. Edited by Giorgio Colli and Mazzino Montinari. Berlin: De Gruyter, 1967–.

———. *The Will to Power*. Translated by Walter Kaufmann and R. J. Hollingdale. New York: Vintage, 1967.

Pocock, J.G.A. *The Machiavellian Moment: Florentine Political Thought and the Atlantic Republican Tradition*. Princeton, NJ: Princeton University Press, 2003.

———. *Virtue, Commerce, and History: Essays on Political Thought and History, Chiefly in the Eighteenth Century*. Cambridge: Cambridge University Press, 1985.

Skinner, Quentin. *Machiavelli*. Oxford: Oxford University Press, 1981.

Spinoza, Benedict de. *The Ethics*. Translated by R.H.M. Elwes. New York: Dover, 1955. Translation originally published 1883.

Walker, Leslie J. *The "Discourses" of Machiavelli*. London: Routledge and Kegan Paul, 1950.

VIRTUE

In his clarifications to *The Spirit of the Laws*, Montesquieu writes, "Le mot de vertu, comme la plupart des mots de toutes les langues, est pris dans diverses acceptations: tantôt, il signifie les vertus chrétiennes, tantôt les vertus païennes, souvent une certaine vertu chrétienne, ou bien une certaine vertu païenne; quelque fois la force; quelque fois, dans quelques langues, une certaine capacité pour un art ou de certains arts. C'est ce qui précède ou ce qui suit ce mot qui en fixe la signification" (*Œuvres complètes*, Gallimard, 2:1169). (The word "virtue," like most words in every language, takes on different meanings: sometimes it refers to Christian virtues, sometimes to pagan virtues, often to a specific Christian or pagan virtue; sometimes to strength, and sometimes to special talents and abilities in the practice of an art or craft. The meaning of this word is determined by what precedes it or what follows it.) The French word derives from the Latin *virtus*, which refers to the physical and moral qualities that define the value of a man (*vir*). The polysemy of

"virtue" calls for a complex history of the term that does justice to the various strata of time and language. In particular the following should be noted:

1. The Greek *aretê* [ἀρετή] (excellence): see VIRTÙ, Box 1, where one can see this excellence conceived ontologically as an *energeia* [ἐνέργεια], as the actualization of a power or capacity; see also ART, I and PRAXIS; cf. *ACT, POWER, I, II*, and INGENIUM. On the relationship between the physical and the moral, see BEAUTY, Box 1; on the link to measure and moderation, see TRUTH, Box 2, and LEX, Box 1. Lastly, on *phronêsis* [φρόνησις] as practical wisdom, and the relationship between virtue and wisdom, see PHRONÊSIS and GLÜCK.

2. The Latin *virtus* (courage): see VIRTÙ, especially VIRTÙ, Box 2; cf. PIETAS, RELIGIO.

3. Christian virtues: see LOVE, cf. BERUF, *SERENITY*.

If the meaning given to "virtue" by Montesquieu—*l'amour des lois et de la patrie* ("the love of laws and the homeland")—which goes with a renunciation in relation to the self—does not derive directly from any of these other meanings, that is because it draws on another moment of the term's history: Machiavelli's elaboration of *virtù*. From Machiavelli on, the notion takes on a more distinctly political sense that will be taken up not only by Montesquieu but also by Hegel and Nietzsche: see VIRTÙ. Cf. DEMOS/ETHNOS/LAOS, *FATHERLAND*, LAW, POLIS, POLITICS, STATE/GOVERNMENT.

➤ DUTY, *GOOD/EVIL*, MORALS, SECULARIZATION, SOBORNOST', *VALUE*

VOCATION

The concept of "vocation" (based on the Latin *vocare*, "to call") is not simply a milder form of destiny, in the sense that a person could take charge of his or her fate (see *DESTINY*). Instead, it specifically addresses Martin Luther's notion of a *Beruf* (calling), as taken up and developed by Max Weber, whose French translations as *vocation* or *profession* have never proven themselves satisfying. See BERUF and *VOICE*.

➤ *ALLIANCE*, ECONOMY, ENTREPRENEUR, SECULARIZATION, WORK

VOICE

"Voice" (Fr. *voix*) derives from the Latin *vox* (the voice, the sound of the voice, word), which in turn, like the Greek *epos* [ἔπος] (speech, word, discourse, song), is formed from the Indo-European root **wekʷ⁻*, which indicates the voice's emissions as well as the religious and juridical force carried by them.

I. The Human Voice

1. The "voice," or at least the Latin *vox*, can serve to distinguish the human from the animal—as for the Greek *phônê* [φωνή], which can also be used in connection with animals and refers to the power and sharpness of the sound emitted, one needs to specify that it is

articulated and conveys meaning: see ANIMAL, LOGOS (especially LOGOS, II.B), SIGN, SIGNIFIER/SIGNIFIED, WORD (especially WORD, II.B.2) and also cf. HOMONYM.

2. It is linked to music and song: see SPRECHGESANG, STIMMUNG; see also ACTOR, DICHTUNG; cf. ERZÄHLEN.

On *epos* (Fr. *épopée*; cf. epic poem) as distinct from *muthos* [μῦθος] (speech, discourse, account, myth) and *logos* [λόγος] (speech, discourse, reason, proportion), see LOGOS, MIMÊSIS; cf. MÊTIS, *RÉCIT*.

3. It is also linked to destiny (Lat. *fatum*, from *fari*, "to say"); see DAIMÔN, Box 1, *DESTINY*, KÊR, SCHICKSAL, STIMMUNG, cf. BERUF, *VOCATION*.

4. Finally, it serves to speak and to lay claim to a right: see CLAIM and *DROIT*, RIGHT/JUST/GOOD.

II. Voice in Grammar

1. *Vox* is one of the most common ways of designating the "word" in Latin. See WORD; cf. LANGUAGE and PROPOSITION.

2. It is also one of the grammatical characteristics of the verb, along with tense, mode, and aspect; see ASPECT (especially as to the meaning of normal voice in Greek).

➤ *HUMANITY, RELIGION*

VORHANDEN / ZUHANDEN / VORHANDENHEIT / ZUHANDENHEIT (GERMAN)

ENGLISH	presence-at-hand / ready-to-hand / readiness-to-hand; extant, extantness / handy, handiness; occurrent/available
FRENCH	*subsistant / disponible, présence-subsistance / disponibilité, sous la main / à portée de la main*
SPANISH	*estar-ahí-delante / estar a la mano*

➤ UTILITY and ART, DASEIN, ES GIBT, ESSENCE, *IL Y A*, OBJECT, POETRY, PRAXIS, PRESENT, REALITY, RES, SEIN, *THING, TO BE*, WELT, WERT, *WORLD*

In Martin Heidegger's *Being and Time* the analysis of the surrounding world (Ger. *Umwelt*) opens with a contrast between two clearly defined modes of being: that which is present-at-hand, or extant (Ger. *Vorhanden*, Fr. *sous la main*), which is an object of simple consideration, and that which is ready-to-hand and available (Ger. *Zuhanden*, Fr. *à portée de la main*). While the former mode is merely deficient in relation to the second, both stand in contrast to *Dasein*, being-there (Fr. *être-là*). This triplicity is clearly fundamental and raises numerous problems of translation. Ontological determinations, we would suggest, should be considered in a more general framework in order to take into account the distinctions thematized by Lotze or Meinong. We will thus start by examining the first occurrences of *Vorhanden* in *Sein und Zeit* (Being and Time) and comparing a series of translations, most into French. We will then seek to disengage the doctrinal background that is the object of Heidegger's "destruction" before finally establishing the indispensable and irreducible polysemy of *Vorhandenheit*, which precludes any simple opposition between *Vorhanden* and *Zuhanden*.

I. The Multiple Senses of Being

The coupling of the adjectives *vorhanden/zuhanden* is not actually an invention of Heidegger's, but before Heidegger

the abstract substantive *Vorhandenheit* is rarely used, and, to our knowledge, the term *Zuhandenheit* not employed at all. Heidegger's purpose, in starting with the fairly common terms *vorhanden*, *Vorhandenheit* and then differentiating them from *zuhanden*, *Zuhandenheit*, is primarily to characterize a specific mode or manner of being. This is clearly evident in their first unmarked occurrence in *Being and Time*.

Let us start with the original text:

> "Seiend" nennen wir vieles und in verschiedenem Sinne. Seiend ist alles, wovon wir reden, was wir meinen, wozu wir uns so und so verhalten, seiend ist auch, was und wie wir selbst sind. Sein liegt im Daß- und Sosein, in Realität, Vorhandenheit, Bestand, Geltung, Dasein, im "es gibt." An welchem Seienden soll der Sinn von Sein abgelesen werden, von welchem Seienden soll die Erschließung des Seins ihren Ausgang nehmen? Ist der Ausgang beliebig, oder hat ein bestimmtes Seiendes in der Ausarbeitung der Seinsfrage einen Vorgang? Welches ist dieses exemplarische Seiende und in welchem Sinne hat es einen Vorrang?

> (Heidegger, *Sein und Zeit*)

The English translation by John Macquarrie and Edward Robinson goes as follows:

> But there are many things which we designate as "being" [*seiend*], and we do so in various senses. Everything we talk about, everything we have in view, everything towards which we comport ourselves in any way, is being; what we are is being, and so is how we are. Being lies in the fact that something is, and in its Being as it is; in Reality; in presence-at-hand; in subsistence; in validity; in *Dasein*; in the "there is." In *which* entities is the meaning of Being to be discerned? From which entities is the disclosure of Being to take its departure? Is the starting-point optional, or does some particular entity have priority when we come to work out the question of Being? Which entity shall we take for our example, and in what sense does it have priority?

From the point of view of our present investigation on *Vorhandenheit*, there is no significant difference between "presence-at-hand" (Macquarrie/Robinson) and "being-at-hand" (Stambaugh).[1]

This extended quote clearly describes what is at stake in the determination of manners of being: if, as is classically

---

[1] A note on translations of Heidegger in English: One of the main difficulties in standard English is that *Sein* (infinitive) is normally translated as "Being,"—that is to say, already a present participle. How then shall we distinguish between *Seiend* (*etant*, "being") and Sein (*etre*, "Being")? The solution adopted by Macquarrie and Robinson is to translate the present participle *seiend* using "entity"/"entities" (the difference between singular and plural in the English translation seems arbitrary), and to maintain Being for *Sein*. Two problems then arise: 1. The so-called ontological difference *Sein/seiend*, *etre/etant* is no longer recognizable in the word pair "Being"/"entity." 2. It is difficult to maintain the translation "entity" when Heidegger underlines the present participle and the presence of the present in it (cf. the first occurrence of "being" for *seiend*).

Stambaugh's translation proposes an alternative that more fully takes into account the present participle. She translates *seiend* by "in being," insisting on the progressive present. She maintains Being with a capital "B" for *Sein*. We are thus confronted with the manifold uses of "-ing" forms in English and the difficulties of nominalization in English.

the case, Being is understood in various senses (*to on lege-tai pollachôs* [τὸ ὂν λέγεται πολλαχῶς]), if we refer to various things as being (Ger. *seiend*, Fr. *étant*, both participles of verbs) and in different senses of the word, the question at issue is whether there is some sense that can serve as a guiding principle, or even better, if there is some exemplary being that can be privileged and thus serve as a model for reading the meaning of "Being."

How would we recognize such a being, if there is one? asks Heidegger. This fairly rough paraphrase of the text quoted above already shows that Heidegger formulates the question—and no doubt, very deliberately—in a more or less explicit reference to the doctrine of the analogy of Being, or even more precisely to the doctrine of the focal unity of senses of being (*pros hên legomenon* [πρὸς ἓν λεγό μενον]). It is through this doctrine that Heidegger addresses "the formal structure of the question of Being," starting in section I.2 of *Being and Time* (*Die Grundbegriffe der antiken Philosophie,* §55, in *Gesamtausgabe,* vol. 22). We will start by examining three existent French translations—but not for the purpose of a contest or choice between them:

1. Étant est tout ce dont nous parlons, tout ce à quoi nous pensons, tout ce à l'égard de quoi nous nous comportons, mais aussi ce que nous sommes nous-mêmes et la manière dont nous le sommes. L'être réside dans l'existence, dans l'essence, dans la réalité, dans l'être subsistant, dans la consistance, dans la valeur, dans l'être-là, dans l' "il y a." En quel étant faudra-t-il lire le sens de l'être, en quel étant l'exploration de l'être prendra-t-elle son point de départ? Le point de départ peut-il être arbitraire, ou quelque étant jouit-il d'une primauté dans le développement de la question de l'être? Quel est cet étant exemplaire et quel est le sens de sa primauté?

    (Trans. R. Boehm and A. de Waelhens, 22)

2. Nous appelons "étant" beaucoup de choses, et dans beaucoup de sens. Étant: tout ce dont nous parlons, tout ce que nous visons, tout ce par rapport à quoi nous nous comportons de telle ou telle manière—et encore ce que nous sommes nous-mêmes, et la manière dont nous le sommes. L'être se trouve dans le "que" et le "quid," dans la réalité, dans l'être-sous-la-main, dans la subsistance, dans la validité, dans l'être-là [existence], dans le "il y a." Sur quel étant le sens de l'être doit-il être déchifrée, dans quel étant la mise à découverte de l'être doit-elle prendre son départ? Ce point de départ est-il arbitraire, ou bien un étant déterminé détient-il une primauté dans l'élaboration de la question de l'être? Quel est cet étant exemplaire et en quel sens a-t-il une primauté?

    (Trans. E. Martineau, 29)

3. "Étant," nous le disons de beaucoup de choses et en des sens différents. Est étant tout ce dont nous parlons, tout ce que nous pensons, tout ce

à l'égard de quoi nous nous comportons de telle ou telle façon; ce que nous sommes et comment nous le sommes, c'est encore l'étant. L'être se trouve dans le fait d'être comme dans l'être tel, il se trouve dans la réalité, dans le fait d'être-là-devant, dans le fonds subsistant, dans la valeur, dans l'*existentia* (*Dasein*), dans le "il y a."

(Trans. F. Vezin, 30)

We can start with a few preliminary remarks. Unfortunately, the BW translation drops the quotation marks around the term "seiend." This immediately gives too much ontological intent to a remark that applies primarily to terms that are clearly "voices" (*voces*) that signify things (*pragmata*), as is the case in Aristotelian categories. The translation goes on to reinsert the classical terminology of essence and existence in speaking of an appreciably different distinction. Heidegger does not say that "being is to be found in existence, in essence" (Fr. *l'être réside dans l'existence, dans l'essence*). He says, "*Sein liegt im Daß- und Sosein*" (Being lies in the fact that something is, and in its Being as it is). He says, in what may be an implicit reference to Schelling and is most certainly a reference to Alexius Meinong, that being is or occurs in the *quod,* the "that" of the "that is" or the "that is the case" (*hoti esti* [ὅτι ἐστι]), and not only in the *quid,* the "what is?" or the "what is this?" (*ti esti* [τί ἐστι]): thus in the "that" as well as in the so-being or suchness (Ger. *Sosein,* Fr. *être-tel*).

The opposition between *Sein* and *Sosein* had already been thematized by Meinong as early as the *Theory of Objects* (*Über Gegenstandstheorie*, 1904), at the same time as he set out the principle of the independence of the so-being or suchness in relation to being in the sense of affirmation, of positing a fact or a state of things ("that is!" or "that is the case") (see SEIN, SACHVERHALT). F. Vezin misses part of the point of this first opposition by making the *Daßsein* into "the fact of being" (Fr. *le "fait d'être"*). But it is in the subsequent sentences that the slippages become more serious. In all three French versions the translators resolutely overtranslate, without concern for the context of the general problematic, which is nothing but a very first pass at the question of being, or rather of the meaning of "being," by way of the guiding thread of fundamental ontology.

▪ See Box 1.

II. Some Classical Concepts of Ontology in German Metaphysics

The original text spoke of *Realität, Vorhandenheit, Bestand, Geltung, Dasein, es gibt.* In his reference to *Realität*, we can assume (though this is doubtless the most difficult point to establish) that Heidegger is using the term in its classical sense (up to Kant), which he luminously presented in a course during the summer of 1927, *The Fundamental Problems of Phenomenology.* The term *Vorhandenheit* only gains its "technical" sense (which can be translated as "presence-at-hand") through its contrast to *Zuhandenheit*, that is to say, when it is an issue of opening up domains or regional ontologies. Here *Vorhandenheit* should be understood in its un-complicated sense, characterizing everything that is there, that is present—to provide an ordinary example, a book on

---

1

Existence, Arabic *wuǧūd*, and *Vorhandenheit*

Like Hebrew, Arabic does not use the copula in the present: the verb that serves its function in the past and in the future (*kāna* [كان], *yakūnu* [يكون]) has no existential meaning. To render the Greek *einai*, translators had recourse to the verb "to find" (Fr. *trouver*), which in the passive voice can mean "to find oneself there," "to be there." The grammatical noun (in Arabic grammar *maṣdar* [مصدر]) that corresponds is *wuǧūd* [وجود], "the fact of finding," or "the fact of being found." [Ibn] The Hebrew of the translators of the ibn Tibbon school has the exact equivalent, *nimṣā* [נמצא]. Al-Fārābī (d. 950) retains the memory of this derivation: "It may be that what they

understand by "being" [lit.: "found"], used by them [the Arabs] in an absolute sense, is that the thing becomes known by the place where it is found, that it can be used however one wants, and that it lends itself to whatever one demands of it." (Al-Fārābī's *Book of Letters* [Kitâb al-Hurûf], *Commentary on Aristotle's Metaphysics*, I, §80; Arabic text, edited with an introduction [in Arabic] and notes by Muhsin Mahdi. Beirut: Catholic Press, 1969; 110, I, 12–14). When Avicenna's writings in Arabic were translated into Latin, the translators recognized the origin of the term and rendered it by *esse, ens,* or *existentia*. The verb "to be," whose existential significance

had remained more or less latent in Greek, was able to deploy it to the full only at the end of a journey in which the Arabic leg is an important one. When Heidegger sought to find a term capable of embodying the thesis of being in traditional ontology, he chose *Vorhandenheit*, "being available" or "at hand" (for example, *Grundprobleme der Phänomenologie* [The fundamental problems of phenomenology], summer semester course, 1927, *Gesamtausgabe*, 24: 173). It is interesting to note that the concept he focuses on has a semitic prefiguration.

Rémi Brague

---

the bookshelf, as long as it was not borrowed (in which case it would be checked out, *nicht vorhanden*). A single example should suffice to illustrate this traditional usage, taken from the "German Metaphysics" of Christian Wolff: "*Wo etwas vorhanden ist, woraus man begreifen kann, warum es ist, das hat einen zureichenden Grund* [Wherever there exists something whose reason for being one can grasp, it has a sufficient ground]" (*Vernünftige Gedanken*, §30). The French translations of *être-subsistant, être-sous-la-main,* or *être-là-devant* are all overtranslations whose principal drawback is precisely their obscuring of the lexical and doctrinal background on the basis of which (as in the case of *endoxa* [ἔνδοξα] and the Aristotelian construction of aporia; see DOXA) Heidegger elaborates the question of the meaning of being. In the *Ideen* Husserl still used *Vorhanden* in its most common sense:

By my seeing, touching, hearing, and so forth, and in the different modes of sensuous perception, corporeal things with some spatial distribution or other are *simply there for me, "on hand"* in the literal or the figurative sense [*. . . sind für mich einfach da, im wörtlichen oder bildlichen Sinne "vorhanden" . . .*] whether or not I am particularly heedful of them and busied with them in my considering, thinking, feeling, or willing.

(Husserl, *Ideas Pertaining*, trans. Kersten)

The term *Bestand*, just like the term *Geltung*, needs to be taken in the sense it receives from Bolzano, through Lotze and Rickert, up to Meinong—but not further. It is truly misrepresented when a violent retrospection already imbues it with the meanings that it will later accrue through Heidegger's analysis of technique, and already translates *Bestand* into French as F. Vezin does, as some "*fonds subsistant*" ("standing reserve").

■ See Box 2.

III. The Vocabulary of Being in Lotze

What we have just described as an indispensable lexical/doctrinal context enables us to follow Heidegger's way of addressing the question of being—by starting with the concrete

and by subsequently overturning it. This can be read, for example, through Lotze's classical distribution of terms. When he questions the mode of being of Truth, Lotze seeks to distinguish between the specificity of *gelten* (to be valid or effective, or to have value) and of *es gilt* (it holds).

We all feel certain in the moment in which we think any truth, that we have not created it for the first time but merely recognized it; it was valid before we thought about it and will continue so [*auch als wir ihn dachten, galt er und wird* gelten]. . . . The truth which is never apprehended by us is valid no whit less than that small fraction of it which finds its way into our intelligence.

(Lotze, *Logic*, 212)

These precisions of definition allow Lotze to distinguish two types of reality/actuality. In a passage that is all the more remarkable because he draws explicitly on the German language and its specific resources, Lotze continues:

Finally it must be added that we ourselves, in drawing a distinction between the reality/actuality that belongs to the Ideas and laws and the reality/actuality that belongs to things, and by calling the latter Being [*der Wirklichkeit der Dinge als dem* Sein] and the former Validity [*Wirklichkeit als Geltung*], have so far merely discovered a convenient expression which may keep us on our guard against interchanging the two notions. The fact [*die Sache aber*] which the term validity expresses has lost none of that strangeness which has led to its being confused with Being.

(Ibid., 217–18)

Just prior to that passage, Lotze had listed four forms of *Wirklichkeit* (as distinguished through their verbs):

Wirklich nennen wir ein Ding welches ist, im Gegensatz zu einem andern, welches nicht ist; wirklich auch ein Ereignis welches geschieht oder geschehen ist, im Gegensatz zu dem, welches nicht geschieht; wirklich ein Verhältnis, welches *besteht*, im Gegensatz zu dem,

2

From Bolzano to Heidegger: The common meaning of *Bestand*

B. Bolzano, *Wissenschaftslehre*, I, §48:

The subjective idea [*subjektive Vorstellung*] is thus something real [*etwas Wirkliches*]; at the particular time at which it is present, it has a real existence [*wirkliches Dasein*] in the mind of the subject for whom it is present. As such, it also produces all sorts of *effects* [*Wirkungen*]. This is not true of the *objective* idea or *idea in itself* [*objective oder Vorstellung an sich*], which belongs to every subjective idea. I mean by it something [*etwas*] not to be sought in the realm of actuality [*das Reich der Wirklichkeit*], something that makes up the direct and immediate *material* [*Stoff*] of the subjective idea. This objective idea requires no *subject* to whom it is present, but would have being [*besteht*]—to be sure not as something existent, but nevertheless as a certain *something*—even if no single thinking being should apprehend it [*auffassen*]. And it is not multiplied when one or two or three or more beings think of it, as the subjective idea related to it then exists in plural number.

(Bolzano, *Theory of Science*, 78)

Objectness changes into the constancy of the standing-reserve, a constancy determined from out of Enframing [*Gestell*].

(Heidegger, "Science and Reflection," in *Question Concerning Technology*, 173)

If technique is "provocation" and "interpellation," it assures itself of that which is in respect of its own position and stability (*Stand*):

Whatever is ordered about in this way [being immediately at hand] has its own standing. We call it the "standing-reserve" [*Bestand*]. The word expresses here something more, and something more essential, than mere "stock." The name "standing-reserve" assumes the rank of an inclusive rubric. It designates nothing less than the way in which everything presences that is wrought upon by the challenging revealing. Whatever stands [*steht*] by in the sense of standing-reserve [*Bestand*] no longer stands over against us as object [*Gegenstand*].

(Heidegger, "Question Concerning Technology," in *Question Concerning Technology*, 17)

This collage of quotations is not meant to suggest that Bolzano's *Wissenschaftslehre* constitutes the backdrop to the introduction of *Sein und Zeit* but only that every supposedly immanent and violently self-interpretative translation runs the risk of creating its own misapprehensions. There is no question of "standing reserve" (*fonds subsistant*) in *Being and Time*, where *Bestand* is the specific mode of being of that which *besteht*, which consists or subsists, without existing, as is the case of an "idea in itself," of an ideality, a fiction, even a chimera, or an internally contradictory entity like a square circle. As Heidegger notes in the margins of his own copy of the book, *Dasein* here is also to be taken in its common meaning, in the sense that Kant for example spoke of the impossibility of an ontological proof of the *Dasein Gottes* (the existence of God), or the sense in which Bolzano spoke of the effective existence of the subjective idea in the one who conceives of something. This is a precision that E. Martineau incorporates in his French translation by adding the word "existence" between brackets to his translation as *être-là*. As for the last *es gibt*, we believe that it is meant to be understood in a technical sense prior to any of Heidegger's elaboration, in the way that Heidegger had treated it from his first course in Freiburg in 1919.

BIBLIOGRAPHY

Bolzano, Bernard. *Theory of Science*. Translated by Dailey Burnham Terrell. Dordrecht, Neth: Reidel, 1973.
Heidegger, Martin. *The Question Concerning Technology and Other Essays*. Edited and translated by William Lovitt. New York: Garland, 1977.

welches nicht besteht; endlich wirklich wahr nennen wir einen Satz, welcher *gilt*, im Gegenstand zu dem, dessen Geltung noch fraglich ist.

(Lotze, *Logik*, 512)

For we call a thing Real/Actual which is, in contradistinction to another which is not; an event Real which occurs or has occurred, in contradistinction to that which does not occur; a relation Real which obtains, as opposed to one which does not obtain; lastly, we call a proposition really true which holds or is valid as opposed to one of which the validity is still in doubt.

(Lotze, *Logic*, 208)

The point about Validity stems from Lotze's conviction that "the language of ancient Greece never found any term to express the reality of simple Validity as distinguished from the reality of Being, and this constant confusion has prejudiced the clearness of the Platonic phraseology" (ibid., 211).

Let us recall that in 1925–26 Heidegger had already cited Lotze's passage on Validity in relation to the four meanings of *Wirklichkeit* in a course in Marburg (*Logik, die Frage nach der Wahrheit*). The course was also an occasion for him to take some distance from it: "In an earlier research into the ontology of the Middle Ages, I myself returned to Lotze's distinction and used the expression 'actuality' for 'being,' but I no longer consider that correct."

Heinrich Rickert, who was a teacher of Heidegger, noted for his part in his celebrated *Logik des Prädikats*:

Ich nenne jetzt alles "seiend," was es überhaupt "gibt," oder was sich als "etwas" denken läßt, also auch das Gelten, den Sinn, den Wert, und das Sollen. . . . Wir haben also zunächst "Seiendes überhaupt" als den Begriff, unter den alles Denkbare fällt.

(Now I call "being" anything that "there is" in general, or anything that can be thought of as "something," and thus also validity, meaning, value, and that which ought to be. . . . So we take "being in general" to be the concept which subsumes everything that is thinkable.)

(Rickert, *Die Logik des Prädikats und das Problem der Ontologie*, 264)

We can take analyses of this sort (Lotze's or Meinong's on the one hand, or Rickert's on the other) as the background for the celebrated paragraph in *Sein und Zeit* in which Heidegger outlines different modes of being corresponding to different regional ontologies: *quod est* (the fact that something is) and Being as it is (*Daß- und Sosein*), Reality (*Realität*), presence-at-hand (*Vorhandenheit*), consistence and subsistence (*Bestand*), validity (*Geltung*), and existence (*Dasein*).

IV. *Vorhandenheit/Zuhandenheit*: The Play of Difference in Heidegger

The English translation by John Macquarrie and Edward Robinson suffers from the same lack of contextualization, and the direct consequence, once again, is overtranslation:

> There are many things which we designate as "being," and we do so in various senses. Everything we talk about, everything we have in view, everything towards which we comport ourselves in any way, is being; what we are is being; and so is how we are. Being lies in the fact that something is, and in its Being as it is; in Reality; in presence-at-hand; in subsistence; in validity; in Dasein; in the "there is."

In 1962 the first English translators, in a particularly unfortunate reference, were already claiming that the term *Dasein* was untranslatable (27n1). "The word *Dasein* plays so important a role in this work and is already so familiar to the English-speaking reader who has read about Heidegger, that it seems simpler to leave it untranslated." And yet if there were one and only one passage in *Being and Time* where it would be appropriate to translate *Dasein*, it would surely be that one!

Joan Stambaugh and J. Glenn Gray, in *Basic Writings, from* Being and Time *(1927) to the* Task of Thinking *(1964)*, proposed with more precision, "Being is found in thatness and whatness, reality, the objective presence of things, subsistence, validity, existence, and in the 'there is'" (47).

The very remarkable Spanish translation, *Ser y tiempo*, by Jorge Eduardo Rivera Cruchaga does not escape overtranslation either: "*El ser se encuentra en el hecho de que algo es y en su ser-así, en la realidad, en el estar-ahí (Vorhandenheit) en la consistencia, en la validez, en el existir, en el 'hay'*" (30).

The turn of phrase *estar-ahí* is proposed as a translation of *Vorhhandenheit/Vorhandensein* in counterpoint to the *ser-ahí* of José Gaos's translation (1951). The Gaos translation was intended to restore the *terminus technicus* "*Dasein*" in an apparently literal fashion, following the French *être-là* or the Italian *esserci*. Gaos had suggested translating *Vorhandenheit* as *ser ante los ojos*. In this he was followed by Jean Beaufret in his *Dialogue avec Heidegger*, speaking of *être devant / sous les yeux*. In this regard Beaufret's presentation remains especially illuminating: Beaufret recalls how Heidegger, in *Being and Time*, sought to follow an analytic of the everyday as a guiding thread to determine being's mode of being in its immediate presence for us, by looking to an analysis of the first objects that present themselves, not to *theôria* [θεωρία], but to that practical outlook (*praktische Umsicht*) that clarifies them in commerce (*Umgang*) with something whose reliability (*Verläßlichkeit*) is supposedly well established. This is the mode of being of *pragmata* [πράγματα], those ordinary things of this world that we deal with, or even better of *procheira* [πρόχειρα] (Aristotle, *Metaphysics* A, 2, 982b13):

> In this respect, as Jean Beaufret noted, things are essentially available to us [*disponible*]. Heidegger uses

the expression *zuhanden* "within reach" [*à portée de la main*]. . . . He opposes this term to *vorhanden* . . . which situates the same things beyond the horizon of their availability, where they generally first encounter us. Still present, but no longer a utensil, the thing as *Vorhandenes* is no longer . . . anything but the subject of predicates that apply to it when its use is no longer a preoccupation. . . . From the beginnings of philosophy, what characterizes the presence of things is that the *pragmata* are no longer anything other than *onta* [ὄντα], *beings étants* much more within view *sous les yeux* rather than within reach *à portée de la main*.

(Beaufret, *Dialogue avec Heidegger*, 3)

The Chilean translator justified his decision in the following terms:

> *Estar-ahí* . . . in German, *Vorhandensein* or also *Vorhandenheit*. . . . Gaos translates it as "*ser ante los ojos*" [to be in front of one's eyes]. This translation is not bad, and it affords a basis for following the young Heidegger's courses, but it doesn't seem excellent to me. First of all, because the expression "*ser ante los ojos*" doesn't say much in Spanish; it does not "speak" to us [*no dice nada en español, no nos "habla"*]. We would of course say "*estar delante, estar a la vista*" [to be there in front of us, to be in view]. I have preferred to translate *Vorhandensein, Vorhandenheit* as "*estar-ahí*" and sometimes for emphasis as "*estar-ahí-delante*." This is the Spanish way of saying what in classical German is meant by *Dasein*, which was the common translation of the Latin *existentia*. *Dasein* literally means "*estar-ahí*" (and never *ser-ahí*). What is fundamental about the idea of *Vorhandenheit* is simply that something "is there" [*está* without our necessarily being affected by it. Unlike *Zuhandenheit*, which we translate as "*lo que es o está a la mano*" that which is at hand], and which has some meaning for us, because there is something at stake [*lo que tiene un significato por nosotros, lo que nos importa porque en ello nos va algo*], *Vorhandenheit* is that which does nothing else but be there, which is, if you will, "pure presence" [*es lo que no hace más que estar-ahí; es, si se quiere, "pura presencia"*].

(Rivera Cruchaga, *Ser y tiempo*, 462)

One might perhaps object once again that this is a case of overtranslation. Perhaps it is, but with the difference that here the proposed translation extends Heidegger's own approach of reinterpreting *existentia*, or *Dasein* in its standard accepted use, in terms of *Vorhandenheit*.

Rivera Cruchaga justified his translation of *Zuhandenheit* in these terms:

> *Estar a la mano*: in ordinary German, the term *zuhanden* is used as an adjective to indicate that something is at hand [*encuentro a mano*], that it is available: Heidegger creates the neologism *Zuhandenheit* to express the particular manner of being of that with which we have a daily commerce, a mode of being. . . . The *Zuhandenes* is that which we handle [*lo que "traemos entre manos"*] without paying attention, so to speak, without any

form of objectification [*cas sin advertirlo y sin ninguna objetivación*].

(Rivera Cruchaga, *Ser y tiempo*, §69, note s.v., 467)

This is indeed well put, yet it seems to us impossible to be satisfied with a simple opposition of two modes of being that correspond to two attitudes—one purely theoretical and always secondary, abstract, and impoverishing, the other primary and "pragmatic—even if this opposition is often stressed by Heidegger in *Sein und Zeit*. It is indeed within the "pragmatic" horizons of preoccupied commerce that being is first discovered in its utensil dimension, as *zuhanden*, *à portée de la main*, within reach, at hand. But for its part, *Vorhanden*, according to Heidegger's quasi-genealogical account in *The Basic Problems of Phenomenology*, does not immediately lead to some form of seeing or to pure consideration, but rather to *poiêsis* [ποίησις]. It is in consideration of creative production that being is first apprehended as *Vorhandenes* (literally, *procheiron* [πρόχειρον]) and is thus referred to an "agent" in front of whom being comes "at hand" (*vor die Hand*) so to speak, for whom it is something handy (*ein Handliches*) (Heidegger, *Basic Problems of Phenomenology*, 143).

In Heidegger's genealogy of the notion of existence (*existentia*), this "return to the productive behavior of being [*Rückgang auf das herstellende Verhalten des Daseins*]" leads him to shed new light on fundamental ontological concepts (*eidos* [εἶδος], *morphê* [μόρφη], *to ti ên einai* [τὸ τί ἦν εἶναι]). He relates them no longer to a specific target or intentionality of perception but to a *Verhalten*, a "behavior" or primordial "posture" in relation to being. Such behavior can just as easily be called "pragmatic" or "poetic," since it is a matter of going beyond Aristotelian separations among *theôria*, *praxis* [πρᾶξις], and *poiêsis*. The *Vorhandenes*, in its "primitive" usage, can thus be understood not as *présent-subsistant* (the received French translation, meaning present-abiding), but as *vorhandenes Verfügbares* (Heidegger, *Basic Problems of Phenomenology*, 153), *present-sous-la-main disponible*—"available, present-at-hand."

Should we conclude from all of this that the distinction that seems to have been drawn so firmly in *Being and Time* is in fact a moving target and that we should put aside vain quarrels of translation and resign ourselves to arbitrary transpositions? Surely not. The principle of establishing an equivalent for a German term with a single univocal term in French or any other language is a falsely rigorous one. It runs the risk, especially in the case under consideration, of obscuring the complexity of Heidegger's gesture toward genealogy and phenomenological destruction. This gesture aims at rediscovering, beneath the sedimentations of traditional philosophical conceptualization, the living source from which the first conceptual elaborations were drawn, as well as their primary meanings. It is how *ousia* [οὐσία] (*Wesen*, essence) is led back to *Anwesen* (presence), and from thence to property, possession, and holding. It is how *Wirklichkeit* (the translation of *actualitas*) is led back to *Verwirklichung* (realization, effectuation) and to *Gewirktheit*, the effectuated (also translated as that which has been actualized), by which we understand the result of an operation.

V. Beyond the Division: The Circularity of *Vorhandenheit/Zuhandenheit*

Let us return once more to the passage in *The Basic Problems of Phenomenology* that previously drew our attention:

> Schon die Worterklärung von *existentia* machte deutlich, daß actualitas auf ein *Handeln* irgendeines unbestimmten Subjektes zurückweist, oder wenn wir von unserer Terminologie ausgehen, daß das Vorhandene seinem Sinne nach irgendwie auf etwas bezogen ist, dem es gleichsam *vor die Hand kommt*, für das es ein Handliches ist.

(Heidegger, *Grundprobleme der Phänomenologie*, 143)

> The verbal definition of *existentia* already made clear that *actualitas* refers back to an acting on the part of some indefinite subject or, if we start from our own terminology, that the extant (*das Vorhandene*) is somehow referred by its sense to something for which, as it were, it comes to *be before the hand*, at hand, to be handled.

(Trans. Albert Hofstadter, 101)

> L'explicitation littérale du terme d'*existentia* a déjà fait apparaître clairement que l'actualitas renvoie à l'agir (*Handeln*) d'un sujet indéterminé, ou encore, selon notre terminologie, que l'étant-subsistant (*das Vorhandene*) est, conformément à son sens, référé d'une certaine façon à un sujet devant lequel il *vient* pour ainsi dire *à portée de la main* (*vor die Hand*), pour lequel il est maniable.

(Trans. J.-F. Courtine, 130)

A passage like this one is obviously a challenge to translation, especially if one wants to retain the lexical play of *handeln*, *Vorhandene*, *vor die Hand*. But it becomes singularly opaque with the superimposition of the "well-known" distinction of *vorhanden/zuhanden*. At issue here is not the legitimacy of the distinction; Heidegger will maintain it for as long as the meaning of being is getting worked out in the framework of fundamental ontology. Yet one needs to take into account that the terms must have maintained their separate identities and that they should still be able to do so. Before becoming coupled to *Zuhandenheit*, *vorhanden* was used by Heidegger to unpack, or to interpret, the Greek and subsequent Latin work of ontological conceptualization, and this through a procedure of trans-lation (Fr. *tra-duction*, Ger. *Über-setzung*) in its literal sense. In this case, the *vorhanden*—beyond its opposition to the specific mode of being of the utensil, and in the broadest meaning of *Zeug*—can serve to designate anything that is present, more or less at hand, and capable metaphorically of coming to hand. Such is the case of *ousia* as Heidegger interprets it, reinvesting it with its primary and concrete meaning: property, real estate, "farmland." Here *ousia*—restored to its earlier, prephilosophical meanings of *Wesen* or *Anwesen*, in the sense of "goods, riches, possession, property"—is clearly "available," like wood in the forest, marble in the quarry, fruits on the trees, or grain in the barn. Here *ousia* carries with it a natural dimension but one that, according to Heidegger, can open up only within the framework of *technê* [τέχνη].

So we should not confuse the two meanings of *Vorhandenheit*. Its first meaning , which we cannot dare call its original or first meaning, still maintains—and this is the whole point of Heidegger's analysis of the term—an essential tie to action and handling. Its second meaning, which has been divested of its originally "technical" or pragmatic dimension by its philosophical usage, signifies only the "given," that which is there-present, present-subsistent. It is in relation to that second sense that it has been possible to speak (Granel, *Traditionis traditio*) of Heidegger's destruction of the ontology of *Vorhandenheit* or of *Vorhandenes* (whose second meaning is retained in the English "extant," "occurrent").

We can recognize a certain priority to the first meaning insofar as the *Vorhandenes* is literally "*vor der Hand*" ("at hand," *devant la main*), present, available as a "material." It is always already there (in the sense of *prouparchein* [προυπάρχειν]); it is "*das schon Dastehende*," which is there, which persists there (*estar-ahí*) (Heidegger, *Gesamtausgabe*, 25: 99). In this "first" meaning, *Vorhandenes*, which is always there (Fr. *là devant*), which does not need to be produced or brought out into presence, becomes confused with what lies at hand before us (*das Vorliegende*, Fr. *le pro-jacent*), the *hupokeimenon* [ὑποκείμενον]. Anteriority, permanence, stability, these are the constitutive features of *Vorhandenheit*. The *Vorhandenes* is, in fact, *vorfindlich*—it comes forward, it finds itself "there already" (Fr. *il y en a*). Availability (*Verfügbarkeit*) can be taken as the proper characteristic of *Vorhandenheit*, in its first meaning (ibid., 24: 153).

> The wood is a forest of timber, the mountain a quarry of rock; the river is water-power, the wind is wind "in the sails."
>
> (Heidegger, *Being and Time*, trans. Macquarrie and Robinson)

On the other hand, *Vorhandenes* in its second meaning is given a negative definition: it consists of deficient modes of preoccupation that include "abstaining from," "neglecting to," "refraining from." The fundamental feature of access to the *Vorhandenes* in this sense is the "*nur noch*": "to only," to refrain from any handling, to refrain from any use, to abstain from the practical attitude and only "consider" (*nur noch hinsehen*) (*Sein und Zeit*, 57).

VI. The Available World and the Workshop: Grounded Presence

One should not be surprised that the analysis of *Zuhandenheit* and of the *Zuhandenes* that begins as early as §15 of *Sein und Zeit* is conducted within the framework of a study of the being of beings such as it is initially encountered in the environment (*Umwelt*) and that it starts with the destruction of the concept of thing (*Ding*), guided by insistent references to the hand and to handling (*Handlichkeit*, 68–69). *Ding* is to be understood here as a metaphysical concept, a translation of *ens* rather than *res* (see RES).

As opposed to this metaphysical reduction of being as *pragmata* [πράγματα], *chrêmata* [χρήματα], *prokeimena* [προκείμενα] (so many Greek terms that can be translated

as *vorhanden* in its first meaning, as that which comes *vor die Hand*), in *Being and Time* Heidegger attempts to clear away the specific meaning of *Zeug* (the tool or instrument) such as it is experienced in the workshop (cf. §15–16), and, more generally, wherever there is work to be done, where the tool is to be put to work.

In 1925 (Heidegger, *Gesamtausgabe*, 20: 263) he introduces *Zuhandenheit* (*Zuhandensein*), as opposed to *Vorhandenheit*, to characterize the mode of being of instruments or tools, as distinct from the being of natural entities. The question (as will still be the case in *Sein und Zeit*, §15) is of being as it is initially encountered, as it first presents itself. In volume 20 (*Prolegomena*), the analysis clearly starts from the *Werkwelt*, the world of works and working (cf. also *Sein und Zeit*, 117, 172). Why is the *Werkwelt* given this importance? Precisely because of its *Begegnisfunktion*: it is through the *Werkwelt* that we encounter a person or thing. It enables the encounter with the ready-to-hand, with the immediately available: "*das Zuhandensein, besser die Zuhandenheit, das Zuhandene als Nächtsverfügbare.*" As for the *Vorhandenes*, as we have seen, it is always already there. We can better understand what Heidegger is aiming at if we go back again to the *Werkwelt*: the world of work refers us back to nature, to the world of nature (*Welt der Natur*), at least insofar as we think of it as a world that is available ("*Natur aber hier verstanden im Sinne der Welt des Verfügbaren,*" *Gesamtausgabe*, 20: 262). It is, then, in the very midst of "availability" that it becomes important to take note of a difference: the difference between the wood in the woodworker's shop, for instance, and the tools that are ready to hand. Thus the *Werkwelt* is not self-contained but open to nature as being available. In its very constitution working always refers back to "*das Werk selbst hat eine Seinsart des Angewiesenseins auf, der Schuh auf Leder, Faden, Nagel, Leder aus Häuten* [The work itself has a way of *being-dependent-on*, the shoe on leather, thread, nails, the leather from hides]" (*History of the Concept of Time*, 193). That form of being that refers to, that relies on, explains that Greek ontology, in its emphasis on the primacy of *Vorhandenheit*, passed over the phenomenon of the world. It is precisely because Greek ontology is developed in the context of working, of producing (or even better, of *poiêsis* [ποίησις]), that it is oriented toward nature (Heidegger, *Gesamtausgabe*, 24: 162) and misses the world, for if the world is "*daseinsmäßig*" (at the measure of the being-there), it is nonetheless inaccessible from the starting point of nature (ibid., 20: 231).

In the *Prolegomena*, Heidegger borrows Husserl's concept of "underpinning" (*Fundierung*) to clarify the primacy of the *Werkwelt*. The world of work, where the artisan is caught up in his work, "appresents" the ambient world close by, as well as the public world (in common) and the world of nature ("*die Welt der Natur*," in the sense of always already being there, as resource, as materiel, as available stock). One should posit that the world of preoccupation, the *Werkwelt*, underpins worldliness in general. *Weltlichkeit* reveals itself first as the worldliness of the ambient world: the phenomenon of the world reveals itself as and in the worldliness of the environment.

> We maintain that the specific world of preoccupation is the one by which the world as a whole is encountered.

We maintain that the world in its worldhood is built neither from immediately given things or sense data nor even from the always already present subsistence of nature, which consists of itself as one puts it [*aus dem immer schon Vorhandenen einer—wie man sagt—an sich bestehenden Natur*]. The worldhood of the world is grounded rather in the specific work-world [*Die Weltlichkeit der Welt gründed vielmehr in der spezifischen Werkwelt*]

(Heidegger, Prolegomena, 194; *Gesamtausgabe* (mod.) 20: 263)

We can thus say that *Vorhandenheit* and *Zuhandenheit* are co-originating, inasmuch as both are complementary modes of being that the *Werkwelt* necessarily opens up. *Vorhandenheit* and *Zuhandenheit* are the features that make a priori possible any "encounter with." Primacy is not a feature of *Zuhandenheit* but more fundamentally of the *Werkwelt*. The *Werkwelt*—the world-of-work, the world-of-labor: despite appearances it is not a composite term, the sort that the language of German philosophy is fond of. The world only opens itself through and for working. *Vorhandenheit* is not just thought of as a foil, as a simple correlate to the abstraction that results from an objectivizing intent entirely cut off from the world. Here the *Vorhandenes* is a co-constituent of the world of work, as a dimension of "nature," of "natural products," or of materials (*Sein und Zeit*, 70). What Heidegger characterizes as "founded presence" (*fundierte Präsenz*) is thus the *Zuhandenes*, without any real contradiction in relation to *Sein und Zeit*. If handiness (Fr. *l'à-portée-de-la-main*) is founded presence, this is always insofar as it presupposes a "taking care of," "concern for," "having to do with." The "givenness" for the factive being, which is in the world, is always the *Zuhandenes*, and certainly not the *Naturding*, which is apprehended through perception, the *Naturding* in its claim to be given as "in the flesh" (*Leibhaftigkeit*).

What is given? What gives? What is there (Ger. *Was "gibt es"*)? This could well be the question that leads ultimately from *Sein und Zeit* to *Zeit und Sein*.

Das echte zunächst Gegebene ist . . . nicht das Wahrgenommene, sondern das im besorgenden Umgang Anwesende, das im Greif- und Reichweite Zuhandene. Solche Anwesenheit von Umweltlichen, die wir Zuhandenheit nennen, ist eine fundierte Präsenz. Sie ist nicht etwas Ursprüngliches, sondern gründet in der Präsenz dessen, was in die Sorge gestellt ist.

The genuine immediate datum is thus . . . not the perceived but what is present in concerned preoccupation, the handy within reach and grasp. Such a presence of the environmental, which we call handiness, is a founded presence. It is not something original but grounded in the presence of that which is placed under care.

(Heidegger, *Gesamtausgabe* 20: 264; Eng. trans. Kisiel, *Concept of Time*, 194–95)

Presence (*Präzens*) is here to be understood as *Besorgtheitspräsenz*, the coming into presence whose origin and guiding thread lies in preoccupation and care. The insufficient attention that has

been paid to this double meaning of *Vorhandenheit* has made it possible to repeatedly deplore the absence of any ontology of nature or of natural reality in *Being and Time* (cf. Michel Haar, *Le chant de la terre*). One must not reduce all the ontological determinations elaborated in it (except of course for *Dasein*) to an "ontology of the workshop" or of "work" when, in fact, what is at stake in the complex play of *Vorhandenes* and *Zuhandenes* is to find a means of access to the phenomenon of the world.

Jean-François Courtine

BIBLIOGRAPHY

Beaufret, Jean. *Dialogue avec Heidegger*. 4 vols. Paris: Minuit, 1945. Translation by Marc Sinclair: *Dialogue with Heidegger*. Bloomington: Indiana University Press, 2006.

Bolzano, Bernard. *Wissenschaftslehre*. Sulzbach: Seidel, 1837. *Theory of Science*. Edited by Rolf George. Oxford: Oxford University Press, 1972.

Crowell, Steven, and Jeff Malpas, eds. *Transcendental Heidegger*. Stanford, CA: Stanford University Press, 2007.

Dreyfus, Hubert. *Being-in-the-World: A Commentary on Heidegger's Being and Time, Division I*. Cambridge, MA: MIT Press, 1990.

Granel, Gérard. *Traditionis traditio*. Paris: Gallimard, 1972.

Guignon, Charles B., ed. *The Cambridge Companion to Heidegger*. 2nd ed. New York: Cambridge University Press, 2006.

Haar, Michel. *Le chant de la terre: Heidegger et les assises de l'histoire de l'être*. Paris: L'Herne, 1985. Translation by Reginald Lilly: *The Song of the Earth: Heidegger and the Grounds of the History of Being*. Bloomington: Indiana University Press, 1993.

Heidegger, Martin. *Basic Writings, from Being and Time (1927) to The Task of Thinking (1964)*. Edited by David Farrell Krell. New York: Harper and Row, 1977.

———. *Being and Time*. Translated by Joan Stambaugh. Albany: State University of New York Press, 1996. Also translated by John Macquarrie and Edward Robinson. London: SCM Press, 1962.

———. *Die Grundbegriffe der antiken Philosophie*. In *Gesamtausgabe*. Vol. 22. Frankfurt: Klostermann, 1993. Translation by Richard Rojcewicz: *Basic Concepts of Ancient Philosophy*. Bloomington: Indiana University Press, 2008.

———. *Die Grundprobleme der Phänomenologie*. In *Gesamtausgabe*. Vol. 24. Frankfurt: Klostermann, 1975. Translation by Albert Hofstadter: *The Basic Problems of Phenomenology*. Introduction by Albert Hofstadter. Bloomington: Indiana University Press, 1982.

———. *Être et temps*. Translated into French by F. Vezin. Paris: Gallimard, 1986. *Être et temps*. Translated into French by E. Martineau. Paris: Authentica, 1985.

———. *Prolegomena zur Geschichte des Zeitsbegriffs*. In *Gesamtausgabe*. Vol 20. Frankfurt: Klostermann, 1979. Translation by Theodore Kisiel: *History of the Concept of Time: Prolegomena*. Bloomington: Indiana University Press, 1985.

———. *Sein und Zeit*. Tübingen: Niemeyer Verlag, 1963.

———. *Ser y tiempo*. Translated into Spanish by J. E. Rivera Cruchaga. Madrid: Trotta, 2003. *Ser y tiempo*. Translated into Spanish by J. Gaos. Madrid, 1951.

———. *Vorträge und Aufsätze*. 4 vols. Pfullingen, Ger.: G. Neske, 1978.

Husserl, Edmund. *Ideas: General Introduction to Pure Phenomenology*. Translated by W. R. Boyce Gibson. New York: Collier Books, 1962.

———. *Ideas Pertaining to a Pure Phenomenology and to a Phenomenological Philosophy: First Book: General Introduction to a Phenomenology*. Translated by F. Kersten. Dordrecht, Neth.: Kluwer, 1998.

Lotze, Rudolf Hermann. *Logik. Drittes Buch: Vom Erkennen*. Hamburg: Meiner Verlag, 1989. First published in 1912. Translation by Bernard Bosanquet: *Logic, in Three Books: Of Thought, of Investigation, and of Knowledge*. Charleston, SC: BiblioBazaar, 2009.

Rickert, Heinrich. *Die Logik des Prädikats und das Problem der Ontologie*. Heidelberg: Vorrede, 1930.

Wolff, Christian. *Vernünftige Gedanken von den Kräfften des menschlichen Verstandes*. In *Gesammelte Werke*. Vol. 1, Pt. 1. Hildesheim Ger.: Olms, 1965. First published in 1713. *Logic, or, Rational Thoughts on the Powers of the Human Understanding*. Hildesheim: Olms, 2003.

WELT (GERMAN)

DANISH	*verden, verdensalt*
DUTCH	*wereld*
ENGLISH	world
FRENCH	*monde*
GREEK	*kosmos* [κόσμος], *aiôn* [αἰών], *pan* [πᾶν], *ta panta* [τὰ πάντα]
LATIN	*mundus*
SWEDISH	*vårld*

➤ *WORLD* and AIÔN, DASEIN, ES GIBT, LEIB, NATURE, OLAM, OMNITUDO REALITATIS, *TO BE*, WELTANSCHAUUNG, *WHOLE*

Is there something like a predisposition to phenomenology or even to existentialism in the "Germanic" concept of the world? One that should be properly separated out from any strictly cosmological conception? If such is actually the case, it is nonetheless the seman- tic trajectory of the ancient Greek *kosmos* [κόσμος] (from Heraclitus to Saint Paul and Saint John, passing through Plato) seems to have prefigured the splitting of meaning, to be clearly found in Kant, between a cosmological sense corresponding to the universe and a cosmo-political, anthropological, or existential sense referring to a way of relating to both the universe and the community of human beings. Paradoxically, Kant himself emphasized, in an anthropologi- cal perspective, how the French word *monde* had rubbed off some of its connotations on the German word *Welt* in its cosmopolitan acceptations. *Welt* is further enriched, in the philosophical vocabu- lary of the twentieth century, through an impersonal verb, *welten*, *es weltet*, a word coined by Heidegger or at least endowed with new meaning by him.

I. "Germanic" Conception of the World?

It has been possible to detect a "Germanic" concept of the world underlying Heidegger's thought on the subject "be- cause the sense in which it is to be understood is suggested by the etymology of the terms" in Germanic languages, includ- ing the German *Welt*, the English "world," the Dutch *wereld*, Swedish *vårld*, the Danish *verden, verdensalt*, and so forth. The Germanic etymon is a compound word that combines an element signifying "man" (from the Latin *vir*) and a second element signifying "age" (cf. English "old"). The resulting meaning would be something like "where man finds himself as long as he is alive" (*ce dans quoi l'homme se trouve tant qu'il est en vie*) (R. Brague, *Aristote et la question du monde*, 27–28n37). We can note in passing that the seventeenth-century German word *Weltalter* ("age[s] of the world") is essentially redundant, since it can be taken apart as: Ger. *wer-alt* ("epoch," "world," "generation") + Ger. *Alter* ("age"), whence *age of ages of man*. As opposed to the cosmological concept of the world, which defines a whole of which I am but a tiny part, there is then perhaps a predisposition in the Germanic etymon leading in the direction of its phenomenological conception—that

within which the human being deploys his being, according to a triple determination: cosmological, anthropological, and ontological.

Etymologically, *Welt* maintains an optional relationship with time. This relationship is underscored by Schelling, the author of the *Weltalter* (Ages of the world), by means of a con- testable (albeit illuminating) etymological link between *Welt* and *währen* (to endure). This link is made at the end of lesson 14 of the *Philosophy of Revelation* in order to keep in place a speculative equivalence between world and time (the cosmic eon):

> Die Wahre Zeit besteht selbst in einer Folge von Zeiten, und ungekehrt, die Welt ist nur ein Glied der wahren Zeit, und insofern selbst eine Zeit, wie ja das Wort, das von w(ae)hren herkommt und eigentlich eine W(ae)hr ung, eine Dauer, anzeigt, und noch unmittelbarer das griechische aion beweist, das ebensowohl eine Zeit als die Welt.

> (True time itself consists of a series of times, but the world is only one element of true time. In this respect, as the very name *Welt* suggests, true time derives from *währen* (to endure) and thus indicates a *duration*, which the Greek *aiôn* reveals even more directly, as it can equally designate a time or the world.)

(Schelling, *Schellings Werke*, 6: 308, italics added)

Even if *Welt* does not come from *währen*, which is itself a term related to *wesen* and to the third root in the etymol- ogy of the verb "to be" (Sanskrit *vasami*, Germanic *wesan* ["to dwell, remain, to live"] [cf. Heidegger, *Introduction*]), Schelling has nonetheless instinctively sensed the essential co-belong- ing of the world and time in his reference to the Greek *aiôn* [αἰών] "cosmic eon," even if in an essentially Paulist sense (1 Cor. 7:31): "the form of this world [*kosmos* (κόσμος)] will pass away."

II. Mundus and Immundus

As in the case of Semitic languages, there are several words or expressions in ancient Greek to designate what we call the "world," depending on the aspect under consideration. Still, we should return to the concept of "world" that we are famil- iar with, which seems to have been barely examined, in order to appreciate the amount of speculative effort that it took to conceive of a totality that synthesized the two other Kantian categories of quantity, that is to say, the singular and the plu- ral. "Ancient Egyptian has no word for 'world,' nor do any of the languages of Mesopotamia" (Brague, *Wisdom of the World*, 10). In Greek, the *kosmos* is actively "produced" in fragment 30 of Heraclitus and was "installed definitively and without ambiguity in its meaning as 'world'" in Plato's *Timaeus* (ibid.; see also Kirk, Raven, and Schofield, *Presocratic Philosophers*,

197–200). The cosmic tends to gloss over the "cosmetic," the world of elegance, beauty, and order, as the opposite of the impure (the French *im-monde*). The Latin *mundus*, in the sense of the ensemble of celestial bodies, skies, universe of light, "seems to be the same word as *mundus*, 'finery,' which was chosen to designate the 'world,' no doubt in imitation of the Greek [κόσμος]." Thus, according to Amyot (*Vie de Dion*, X: 2, in Plutarch, *Vies parallèles*, 1559), the universe that obeys and is governed by the divinity "*est de faict et de nom* Monde, *qui autrement ne serait que désordre immonde*"—is in both name and actuality World (*monde*), which otherwise would only be a filthy mess (*immonde*).

■ See Box 1.

The meaning of *kosmos* will take a decisive turn in the Greek New Testament, and it will take its place alongside *mundus*, *Welt*, and *monde*, especially in Saint Paul (1 Cor. and Gal.) and Saint John: it comes to designate a way of being human, the ensemble of conditions and possibilities for terrestrial life, in the form of an attitude that turns away from God. The meaning of *kosmos* is no longer cosmological, but historical, even eschatological. "The *sophia tou kosmou* [σοφία τοῦ κόσμου], human wisdom as opposed to divine wisdom . . . *ho kosmos* [ὁ κόσμος], on its own is interchangeable with *ho kosmos outos* [ὁ κόσμος οὗτος], an expression interchangeable in turn with *ho aiôn outos* [ὁ αἰών οὗτος] (Bultmann, *Theology*, § 26, 254–59). It is also another name for philosophy: until the beginning of the nineteenth century, there was a discussion in German around *Weltweisheit*, the "wisdom of the world" (the cover page of Hegel's article of 1801 on *The Different between Fichte's and Schelling's Systems of Philiosphy* presents the author's credentials as *der Weltweisheit Doktor*, "the doctor in wisdom of the world"). Starting with the Greek-language versions of the New Testament, whose Hebrew origins specifically led them to set themselves apart from any Greek (pagan) sources, "world" comes to be understood as based on "this world" (this transitory world down below, with its existential attitude that entails turning away from God), and it takes on a negative connotation, even one of damnation, that brings it into almost direct opposition to *mundus* as the pure or the orderly. "World" paradoxically comes to connote that which the French refer to as *immonde*, literally "unworldly."

1

"Order for the city": The meaning of *kosmos*

➤ BEAUTY, DOXA, SPEECH ACT (Box 1), STRUCTURE

One could render the term *kosmos* by the Baudelairian syntagm of "order and beauty" and compare it to our modern "structure." Already in Homer the range of meaning resonates in every use of the term: thus the famous *toilette* of Hera, as she prepares herself for addling the mind of Zeus, in the seclusion and secrecy of her bedroom: ambrosia, oil, perfume, braids, dress, pin, belt, earrings, veil, and sandals, "she surrounds her body with *panta kosmon* [πάντα κόσμον]," all her finery, in other words, that glorious order which makes her woman's world (*Iliad*, XIV, 186)—the world that Sophocles in his *Ajax*, 293, defines as silence: *gunaixi kosmon hê sigê pherei* [γυναιξὶ κόσμον ἡ σιγὴ φέρει], "it is silence that brings women their finery / their world" (cf. Democritus 68 B 274 DK; even today we still think to say "just be beautiful and be quiet") (Fr. *sois belle et tais-toi*). And when Odysseus at Alcinous's house asks the bard Demodocus to "sing the *kosmos* of the wooden horse" (*Odyssey*, VIII, 492ff.), Victor Bérard's French translation refers to the "*histoire*," the Lattimore translation into English refers to it as "another part of the story," and Robert Fagles has Odysseus ask the bard to "shift his ground." At issue in the story is the construction-fabrication, the technique and the ruse, and the course of the world it determines. The goddess of Parmenides deploys both the "world of deception" in her speech (*kosmon . . . apatêlon* [κόσμον . . . ἀπατηλόν]) and the world of *doxa* [δόξα]

that men adhere to in their minds (*diakosmon* [διάκοσμον]), the "whole arrangement" of the world (VIII, 60), in the interweaving of a discursive arrangement and the order of the world. Finally, Gorgias brings to light the optimal form of organization that constitutes the *kosmos* and its corresponding excellences: "The order [*kosmos*] proper to a city is the excellence of its men; to a body, beauty; to a soul, wisdom; to a deed, excellence; and to a discourse, truth—and the opposites of these are disorder [*akosmia* (ἀκοσμία)]," Gorgias, Encomium of Helen, 82 B11 DK, §1).

In Heraclitus, cosmology does not triumph over cosmetics either: in fragment B 30 DK, which "produces" the *kosmos*, not only is fire required, but it is required in precise amounts ("This world-order [*kosmon*] did none of gods or men make, but it always was and is, and shall be: an everliving fire, kindling in measures and going out in measures [*metra* (μέτρα)]") (Kirk, Raven, and Schofield, *Presocratic Philosophers* §217, 198). And the world so "cosmologized," both elementary and measured, is also "the most beautiful" ("The most beautiful order of the world [*ho kallistos ho kosmos* (ὁ κάλλιστος ὁ κόσμος)]" is still a random gathering of things insignificant in themselves—Guy Davenport trans.). Thus in Plato's *Timaeus*, Critias is left with but one hypothesis to consider: "that this world is most beautiful [*ei men dê kalos estin hode ho kosmos* (εἰ μὲν δὴ καλός ἐστιν ὅδε ὁ κόσμος)] and that the demiurge is good" (29a 2–3). This equivalence of world and order

(*kosmos kai taxis* [κόσμος καὶ τάξις]) (Aristotle, *Metaphysics*, A, 984b16–17) is always at play: From the Pythagorean "harmony" to the *Timaeus* or the Aristotelian treatise *De caelo*, this identity is what makes it possible to physically describe or even to make mathematical calculations about the sky, celestial spheres, or the universe. But it also opens up the rhetorical and poetic sense of the *kosmos* as ornament (Aristotle, *Poetics*, 21, 1457b1–2: "a noun must always be either the ordinary word for the thing, or a strange word, or a metaphor, or an ornamental word [*kosmos*]," Bollingen Series 71, vol. 2), as well as an easy usage of the plural (Plato, *Protagoras*, 322c2–3: "the principles of organization of cities [*poleôn kosmoi* (πόλεων κόσμοι)] and the bonds of friendship").

Does the much praised beauty of the Greek world hang from this: that the *kosmos* always also involves the aesthetic?

Barbara Cassin

BIBLIOGRAPHY

Homer. *Iliad*. With an introduction, a brief Homeric grammar, and notes by D. B. Monro. 5th ed., rev. Oxford: Clarendon Press, 1958–1960.

———. *Odyssey*. Translated by Walter Shewring, introduced by G. S. Kirk. Oxford: Oxford University Press, 1998.

Kirk, G. S., J. E. Raven, and M. Schofield. *The Presocratic Philosophers: A Critical History with a Selection of Texts*. 2nd ed. Cambridge: Cambridge University Press, 1984.

"The 'world,' in the pejorative sense, flows in again unceasingly to the very midst of these islands which have been won from its expanse of miry waters" (Lubac, *Catholicism*, 272).

Once on this theological trajectory, *mundus* in the patristic and subsequent scholastic Latin will still designate a "totality," but the totality "of creation," the *ens creatum* that is thus distinct from God. In the modern era it is especially between Leibniz and Kant that the very concept of "world" will be defined. There is a branching out and differentiation of the concept in the overlap of languages (Latin, German, French).

III. World and Universe

■ See Box 2.

Leibniz's classical definition of the "world" does not admit of a plural form, according to the explicit terms of article 8 of the *Theodicy*:

2

"Whole" and "ensemble": *Pan* open / *holon* closed

➤ *IDENTITY*, UNIVERSALS

Ancient Greek has two main ways of saying the "whole": the adjective *pas* [πᾶς] and the noun *to pan* [τὸ πᾶν], or the adjective *holos* [ὅλος] and the noun *to holon* [τὸ ὅλον]. The difference is all the more difficult to grasp as it cannot be mapped onto the Latin distinction between *omnis* and *totos*. The word *holos* is basically to *pas* what *omnis* is to *totus* (RT: *Dictionnaire étymologique de la langue grecque*, see "*Holos*"), except for the fact, noted in even the most elementary grammars and indicated in the dictionaries as well, that "[πᾶς] *pas*, whole, each, corresponds to *omnis* and *totus*, while [ὅλος] *holos*, entire, only corresponds to *totus*" (Ragon, 39). Word order further complicates the semantics, since *pasa polis* [πᾶσα πόλις] is supposed to mean "any city," while *pasa hê polis* [πᾶσα ἡ πόλις] means "the whole city," and *hê pasa polis* [ἡ πᾶσα πόλις] "the city as a whole" (Fr. *l'ensemble de la ville*). In addition, there is an intensive form *hapas* [ἅπας], "the whole, completely," pl. *hapantes* [ἅπαντες], "all without exception, all together." Thus the LSJ (RT: LSJ) gives three ways of understanding *pas*, the collective pronoun: "when used of a number, *all*; when used of one only, *the whole*; of the several persons in a number, *every*." But the second translation holds equally for *holos*: "whole, entire, complete in all its parts" (LSJ, s.v. "*Holos*"). So how can one make the precise distinction between *to pan* and *to holon*?

Etymology gives an indication of the specificity of *to holon*, better rendered in English by "the whole" than by the French *totalité* or *ensemble*: *holos* is identical to the Sanskrit *sárva-*, "complete, intact," from which the Latin adjective *salvus* ("well, safe, unhurt") derives (cf. also the greeting *salve*, and the French *salut*) and which is also no doubt the source for "whole" and "holy" (Fr. *saint*), as well as "hale and healthy" (Fr. *sain*). *Holon* designates the whole as something more than the sum of its parts. Socrates takes the syllable *hê sullabê* [ἡ συλλαβή] (literally "com-position," or "com-prehension," or even "con-cept") as an example to illustrate the difference between *to holon*, ensemble rather

than totality, and *to pan*, the sum of the two elements S and O:

Socrates: Or would you say that a whole [*to holon*], although formed out of the parts, is a single notion different from all the parts [*ek tôn merôn gegonos hen ti eidos heteron tôn pantôn merôn* (ἐκ τῶν μερῶν γεγονὸς ἕν τι εἶδος ἕτερον τῶν πάντων μερῶν)]?

Theaetetus: Yes, that is what I should say.

Socrates: And would you say that all and the whole [*to holon tou pantos* (τὸ ὅλον τοῦ παντός)] are the same, or different?

(Plato, *Theaetetus*, 204a–b, trans. Benjamin Jowett)

We cannot help observing that this passage is immediately and irresistibly complicated by the play of the plural *ta panta kai to pan esth' hoti diapherei* [τὰ πάντα καὶ τὸ πᾶν ἔσθ' ὅτι διαφέρει], "Or would you say that a whole, although formed out of the parts, is a single notion different from all the parts?" [Fr. trans.: Diès: "*la totalité et la somme*"; Narcy: "*l'ensemble et le total*"] as well as by the intensive form "then in predicating the word 'all' of things measured by number we predicate at the same time a singular and a plural? [*to te pan kai ta hapanta* [(τὸ τε πᾶν καὶ τὰ ἅπαντα)]," 204d [Diès: "*la somme et la totalité*"; Narcy: "*le total et l'ensemble au complet*"]. Where French is concerned I would propose keeping the relation among the singular *pan* "*tout*," the plural *panta* "*total*" of the parts, and the plural *hapanta*, "*totalité*" or "*totalisation*" of the parts.

Aristotle takes up the example of the syllable, as opposed to the "heap" (*sôros* [σωρός]) to explain what makes the unity of a composite; what Socrates referred to as the *eidos* [εἶδος], as opposed to the letters that make up matter (*hulê* [ὕλη]), "causes the fact that it is a syllable" (*aition . . . tou einai . . . todi de sullabên* [αἴτιον . . . τοῦ εἶναι . . . τοδὶ δὲ συλλαβήν], (see TO TI ÊN EINAI). Aristotle calls *ousia* [οὐσία], "essence," which is to say *phusis* [φύσις], "nature" ("their substance would seem to be this nature, which is not

an element but a principle "(*hautê hê phusis ousia, hê estin ou stoicheion all' archê* [αὕτη ἡ φύσις οὐσία, ἥ ἐστιν οὐ στοιχεῖον ἀλλ' ἀρχή]) (*Metaphysics*, Z, 1041b25–32; see NATURE, PRINCIPLE). And he chooses to call *to sunolon* [τὸ σύνολον] what is usually understood as the "concrete thing" (or "complete substance," *LSJ*), the "formula taken with the matter" (or *eidos* with the *hulê*, *LSJ*), but which properly refers to the concrete "individual," Socrates himself or Callias, constituted by "the indwelling form" of what he refers to elsewhere as *ousia prôtê* [οὐσία πρώτη] or "primary substance (or essence)" (cf. Z, 11, 1037a29–33, *hê sunolê ousia* [ἡ συνόλη οὐσία]; see ESSENCE III.A.1 and SUBJECT, Box 1). Chapter 26 of book Δ very succinctly specifies the difference between *pan* and *holon*, for finite quantities that have a beginning, middle, and end: "those to which the position does not make a difference are called totals (*pan*), and those to which it does, wholes (*holon*)." Some things can be both wholes and totals, for instance, wax or a coat. "These are the things whose nature [*phusis*] remains the same after transposition, but whose form [*morphê* (μορφή)] does not" (ibid., 1024a3–6). But it is clearly the joining of body and soul, or that whole that is the body, which is *holistic par excellence*. (When a "part," such as a foot or hand, is removed, it is mutilated and no longer itself; they are "organs" only as homonyms: *Politics*, A, 2, 1253a20–21; cf. for example *De partibus animalium*, 645b14–17). We can see how the difference of *pan/holon* refers to the constitution of unity and of unicity, juxtaposition/organicity, and thus determines a powerful and lasting ontological modulation (cf. for example its application to *Dasein* in Martin Heidegger's *Sein und Zeit*, Niemeyer, §648, 244 and note 3).

The primacy and status of the *holon* is tied to the superiority of the finite over the infinite, of the closed over the open. With Parmenides (his being is *houlon* [οὖλον], "whole," and *tetelesmenon* [τετελεσμένον], "finished, completed," VIII, 38 and 42), but in

(continued)

(continued)

opposition to Anixamander, Atomism, and later Epicurus, Aristotle shapes an entire "classical" Greek tradition: the infinite *to apeiron* [τὸ ἄπειρον] "turns out to be the contrary of what it is said to be. It is not what has nothing outside it that is infinite, but what always has something outside it" (*Physics*, 6, 206b34–35, trans. R. P. Hardie and R. K. Gaye). The infinite is linked to matter, to privation, to the absence of *telos* [τέλος], to *dunamis* [δύναμις] (see FORCE and PRAXIS), and by definition it can neither be measured or known. The prevalence of the whole and holistic can function in every domain. In aesthetics, for example, it is of necessity the rule, and it is beautiful that tragedy represents a *holê praxis* [ὅλη πρᾶξις], an action that is complete of itself, with a beginning, middle, and end that is of a length that can be held in the memory (*Poetics*, 7). In logic it meets up with the problem of the "universal," *to katholou* [τὸ καθόλου] (which prior to Aristotle was no doubt written *kath' holou* [καθ' ὅλου], "on the whole" [RT: *LSJ*, "d'ensemble" [RT: *Dictionnaire grec français*]), which could be articulated analytically with *kath' hekaston* [καθ' ἕκαστον], "the particular," one by one, according to the distributivity of *pan* (cf. *Metaphysics*, Δ, 26, beginning; see UNIVERSALS), but which, unlike the latter, defines all objects of science. In politics we can see a strong dividing line separating

Platonism and Aristotelianism: the Platonic city is a *holon*, a hierarchical organism completely oriented toward a single goal, whereas democracy for Aristotle is a *pan* and even a *pantes hoi Athênaioi* [πάντες οἱ Ἀθηναῖοι], "all Athenians," in other words, a mass and mixture of citizens (cf. B. Cassin, "De l'organisme au pique-nique"; see POLIS).

But it is clearly in cosmology that this difference is thematized most powerfully, as in its original domain. The Stoics, who insisted so strongly on the organic and systematic, make it into a difference of doctrine: *to holon* designates the *kosmos*, the "world," while *to pan* designates both the world and the incorporeal emptiness that surrounds it, which it requires in order to dilate ("the whole [*pan*] is different from the universe [*holon*] for the Stoics. They call the "universe" the world [*holon men . . . ton kosmon* (ὅλον μὲν . . . τὸν κόσμον)], and "whole" the world with the void [*pan de meta tou kenou* (πᾶν δὲ μετὰ τοῦ κενοῦ)], RT: *SVF*, II, 523, cf. Goldschmidt, *Le système*, 27–28). Thus *to holon* is to be rendered as "the universe" (*universus*, literally "turned as a whole toward"): the choice of term is understandable. It lays emphasis on the unity of a common goal (see already, in Aristotle's *De caelo*, the characterization of the *holon* and of the parts as "according to the prevailing element" [*eis to auto pheretai to holon kai to morion* (εἰς τὸ αὐτὸ φέρεται τὸ ὅλον καὶ τὸ μόριον)], A, 3, 270a4). But the intersections and crossings of traditions

through translation, via Cicero (*Timeaus*, 6, where *pan* is rendered as *universitas*; of *De natura deorum*, I, 120 [*de universitate rerum . . . in eodem universo*], II, 29–32 [*mundum universum*], for example), via Lucretius, and through translations of translations, leads to an utter terminological imbroglio: thus in Lucretius *omne*, the infinite whole, and *summa* are both rendered at random, sometimes within the same passage, as "whole" (or "Whole") or as "universe," "ensemble," "space," etc. (compare, for example, the French translations by A. Ernout and J. Kany-Turpin for I, 706, 951–984, or II, 1044–1096). Small wonder, then, that at the dawn of the modern era, given all the confusion and regroupings of the differences of *pan/holon*, the world would be closed and the universe infinite (A. Koyré).

Barbara Cassin

BIBLIOGRAPHY

Cassin, Barbara. "De l'organisme au pique-nique. Quel consensus pour quelle cité?" In *Nos Grecs et leurs modernes*. Paris: Seuil, 1991.
Goldschmidt, Victor. *Le système stoïcien et l'idée de temps*. 4th ed., rev. and augm. Paris: Vrin, 1979.
Koyré, Alexandre. *From the Closed World to the Infinite Universe*. Baltimore, MD: Johns Hopkins Press, 1957.
Lucretius. *De rerum natura*. Edited and translated by Cyril Bailey. Oxford: Clarendon Press, 1947.
Ragon, Éloi. *Grammaire grecque*. Completely revised by A. Dain, J. de Foucault, and P. Poulain. 5th ed. Paris: J. de Gigord, 1957.

I call "World" the whole succession and the whole agglomeration of all existent things, lest it be said that several worlds could have existed in different times and different places. For they must needs be reckoned all together as one world or, if you will, as one Universe.

(Leibniz, *Theodicy*, "Essays on the Justice of God and the Freedom of Man in the Origin of Evil," I, 8, 128)

Baumgarten defines it thus in Latin, in 1743:

Mundus (universum, pan [πᾶν]) est series (multitudo, totum) actualium finitorum, quoe non est pars alteris.

(The world [universe, *pan* (πᾶν)] is the series (multitude, whole) of actual areas that is not part of another [i.e., that is not in turn part of a larger whole].)

(Baumgarten, *Metaphysica*, II, §354)

And Christian August Crusius, two years later, in German:

Eine *Welt* heißt eine solch reale Verknüpfung endlicher Dinge, welche nicht selbst wiederum ein Teil von einer andern ist, zu welcher sie vermittelst einer realen Verknüpfung gehörte.

(A *world* is a real connection of finite things, which itself is not part of another in turn, which it would belong to through any real connection.)

(Crusius, *Entwurf der notwendigen Vernunft*, §350)

Mundus will come to be defined as "*totum quod non est pars*," "a whole which is not a part [in turn]," as in *Sectio I*, entitled "*De notione mundi generatim*" (Of the notion of world in general) of Kant's *Dissertation* of 1770:

In compositio substantiali, quemodium Analysis non terminatur, nisi parte quœ non est totum, h.e. SIMPLICI: ita Synthesis non nisi toto quod non est pars.

(As the analysis of a substantial composite terminates only in a part which is not a whole, that is, in a *simple part*, so synthesis terminates only in a whole which is not a part, that is, the *world*.)

(Kant, *Dissertation*, section I, §1)

In section two of the same *Dissertation*, Kant enumerates the three "moments" that constitute the "world": *material, forma, universitas* (universality); this last defined as "*omnitudo compartium absoluta*," "the *absolute* totality of companion parts" (translated by Eckoff as "absolute allness of the appertaining parts"), which is, according to a celebrated formula, "the crucial test of philosophers":

Nam statuum universi in *æternum* sibi succedentium *numquam absolvenda series*, quomodo redigi possit in *Totum*, omnes omnino vicissitudines comprehendens, agere concipi potest.

(For it is scarce conceivable how the inexhaustible series of the state of the universe succeeding one another eternally be reducible to a whole comprehending all changes whatsoever.)

(Ibid., §2)

The fact that the "crucial" difficulty inherent in the concept of "world" thus defined lies in the third constitutive moment, which is the *universitas*, indicates that the problem of the "world" is none other than the problem of the *universe*, with whom it becomes henceforth confused—the "entire universe" (Leibniz), or "that continuous vicissitude which produces the beauty of the universe" (Malebranche, *Éclaircissements,* 3: 218; *Élucidations,* 665). In other words, the problem has less to do with the "world" and more to do with the *universitas mundi*—at least for the Latin author, Immanuel Kant.

IV. The German Adventures of "World"

The same does not hold true of Kant the German author, who in positing the equivalence of anthropology (or *Menschenkunde*) and *Weltkenntnis*, "knowledge of the world," draws out the existential meaning of *Welt* from German phraseology, which, unlike Latin, was his mother tongue. (We might also note the old French *toz li mon* in Commynes, in modern French *tout le monde,* "everyone," or the Creole *timoun* ["little world," "child(ren)"]; beginning in the sixteenth century *du monde* signifies "people" [Fr. *des gens*], and *kosmos* has the same meaning in modern Greek.)

Noch sind die Ausdrücke: die Welt *kennen* und Welt *haben* in ihrer Bedeutung ziemlich weit auseinander: indem der Eine nur das Spiel *versteht,* dem er zugesehen hat, der Andere aber *mitgespielt* hat.

(In addition, the expression "to *know*" the world and "to *have* the world" are rather far from each other in their meaning, since one only *understands* the play that one has watched, while the other has *participated* in it.)

(Kant, *Anthropology,* 4)

Michel Foucault translates the passage into French as follows:

Encore ces deux expressions: *connaître* le monde et *avoir* du monde sont-elles, quant à leur signification, passablement éloignées l'une de l'autre vu que dans un cas on ne fait que *comprendre* le jeu auquel on a assisté, tandis que dans l'autre on a *joué le jeu.*

(Kant, *Anthropologie,* Preface, in *AK,* 8: 120, Fr. trans. Foucault (modified), 11–12)

The translation of this passage into English poses particular difficulty. On one hand we are dealing with the thorny issue of idiomatic anachronism—does one say *"Welt haben"* in contemporary German with the same meaning that Kant had implied in the late eighteenth century? Does one ever say "having the world" in English, especially when it is being contrasted with "knowing the world"?—and on the other hand we are faced with an additional maneuver of translation (the Foucault), which has inadvertently complicated the thrust of the original. To parse this out, we can start with Kant's German. Kant's equivocation of anthropology (*Menschenkunde*) and world-knowledge (*Weltkenntnis*) places "knowing the world" (*Welt kennen*) squarely in opposition to the notion of "having the world" (*Welt haben*). As Kant subsequently makes clear, having the world requires an active engagement—one who has the world has played within it (*gespielt*)—while knowing the world is a separate form of passive engagement, perhaps akin to the attentive remove of ethnographic fieldwork, wherein the observer is attuned to the play of the natives without directly affecting their behavior. Thus, a basic dichotomy emerges, from which we can formulate a sense of Kant's implied meaning. Here, *Welt kennen* is the analytic mode of the dispassionate, academic observer, the one who does not enter into the action of the world but merely comprehends it as it plays out—who knows the world insofar as he or she would approach it, as from a distance, as critical object. *Welt haben*, by contrast, is an affair of contact and action. Like a certain *Dasein* in motion, to have the world is to engage with its sensorial splendor, to be materially involved in its goings-on, getting caught up in the mucky bits—being a body interacting with other bodies.

In this sense the contemporary French expression *"avoir du monde"* gains both philosophical ballast and justification in Foucault's translation. One uses the expression to denote a flood of people in one place, a surfeit of bodily contact; on the dance floor, at the parade, or in the train station at rush hour, *il y a du monde.* In such instances to inhabit the space of the real is manifestly to have contact with other bodies, to be pushed along among them, to be caught up in play. Thus, Foucault's casual shift from German's formal *"die Welt"* to French's partitive contraction *"du monde"* privileges the tangible and corporeal aspects of the experience of "having the world." And yet, his rendering of the opposite term seems to contribute to a new confusion. *Welt kennen* has become *connaître le monde*, obvious given the denotative equivalency of the two verbs, but slippery in their unequal connotations. In the literary French of the nineteenth century, "knowing the world" implies sexual experience, a certain fleshy materialism underfoot. This seems a far cry from Kant's anthropology, at a cold remove from carnal commerce. With this rendering Foucault inadvertently confounds the two modes. When he states that one mode has merely "understood the game" while the other has *joué le jeu*, it becomes difficult to separate "knowing" the world from "having" it. For as these notions are presented here, "knowing the world," the way, say, a dashing Flaubertian protagonist might, involves a fair amount of both knowledge and play. This encoded possibility of prior knowledge acquired through experience exceeds the binary initially established by Kant between aloof comprehension alone and comprehension achieved in the moment through the added level of physical involvement. Has Foucault blurred this separation deliberately? Likely no, but he has provided a great occasion for considering the troublesome density of connotation added to the signifier awaiting translation.

Thus, as we reflect on how to accurately render these terms in English, we should look beyond the French elaboration of *Welt kennen* and return to the messy world of bodies and crowds that helps to make *avoir du monde* such an evocative stand-in for *Welt haben*. We seek a term that simultaneously indicates play, presence, and embodiment. Heidegger achieved this magisterially, with all of the permutations of *Dasein*, but what is a translator of Kant to do? Can one mash up Kant and Heidegger together?—in English, can one be in the world, and have it too?

In Kant's diglossia, *mundus* carries a primarily cosmological meaning (= *universitas mundi*), whereas *Welt* is more oriented toward an anthropological and existential sense (with man as a *Weltbürger*, "a citizen of the world")—the irony of the story lies in the fact that, as Kant himself observes, it is the *French usage* of *monde* (from the French used at court, in diplomacy, and in culture) that left its mark on the German *Welt*, which would in some sense adopt the same distance from that point on, from the Latin *mundus* up to its usage in scholastic French and the *monde* in the classical age of France.

> *Welt haben*, heißt Maximen haben und große Muster nachahmen. *Es kommt aus dem Französischen.*
>
> (*Having the world* means to have maxims and to imitate the great models. *It comes from the French.*)

> (Kowalevski, *Die philosophischen Hauptvorlesungen*, 71)

We will refrain from following Michel Foucault and Henry Corbin in translating *Welt haben* by "having the ways of the world" (Fr. *avoir les usages du monde*), since Kant himself has drawn our attention to the literal transfer of the French *avoir du monde* into the German *Welt haben* (for the equivalences of *avoir du monde, savoir son monde, savoir-vivre et se conduire dans le monde* ["how to behave in good society"], see RT: Littré, *Dictionnaire de la langue française*, 5: 372, esp. meaning 19 ["the society of men, or a part of this society"], which quotes Mme. de Sévigné, Molière, Saint-Simon, and Jean-Jacques Pauvert).

It is when "world" ceases to entail a totality, a role now taken on by the concept of "universe," that different "worlds" can be distinguished from one another and as ways of relating to this world:

> Mais de quoi jouissais-je enfin quand j'étais seul? de moi, de l'univers entier, de tout ce qui est, de tout ce qui peut être, de tout ce qu'a de beau le monde sensible, et d'imaginable le monde intellectuel.
>
> (But what did I enjoy in the end when I was alone? Myself, the entire universe, everything that is, everything that can be, everything beautiful about the sensible world, everything imaginable about the intellectual world.)

> (Rousseau, *Troisième Lettre à M. de Malesherbes*, quoted in RT: *Dictionnaire de la langue française*, meaning 3 [the physical world, the sensible world])

The plural form of the world is not without consequence for the very meaning of the concept of the world, which can no longer be defined as *universitas mundi* in the light of the plurality of worlds, even if only possible or imaginary worlds (Leibniz, Fontenelle). Only "knowing the world," "*die Welt kennen*," is to refuse to become involved, to draw back and look upon something transformed into a spectacle, a scene that one can withdraw from at will, according to the Baroque topos (Shakespeare, Corneille) of the world as theater—right up to Descartes: "*ego, hoc mundi theatrum conscencurus, in quo hactenus spectator exstiti* [as for me, I was getting ready to mount that world stage of which I had previously only been a spectator]" (*Cogitationes privatae,* 10: 212).

Whence comes the distinction that will be established in the *Critique of Pure Reason* (A840–B868) between philosophy according to the *Schulbegriff* = *in sensu scolastico,* or scholastic concept intended for certain arbitrary ends, and philosophy according to the *Weltbegriff* = *in sensu cosmico,* that is, "what is necessarily of interest to each and everybody."

V. "Welt" and "Welten":
From the Noun to the Verb (Heidegger)

In Kant the discussion of *Welt* starts out from the French *monde* in its anthropological sense, and hence from the Latin *mundus*, especially in its Augustinian usage, and thus invites us to work our way back to the meaning of *kosmos* in the New Testament (especially John). This is the source of the equivalence posed or supposed by Heidegger, who proceeds in this connection to underscore the differences between the Greek *kosmos* in the Hellenistic sense, the Latin *mundus*, and the German *Welt*:

> Liegt das metaphysisch Wesentliche der mehr oder minder klar abgehobenen Bedeutung von κόσμος, *mundus*, *Welt* darin, daß sie auf die Auslegung des menschlichen Daseins *in seinem Bezug zum Seienden im Ganzen* abzielt.
>
> (Rather, what is metaphysically essential in the more or less clearly highlighted meaning of kosmos, *mundus*, world, lies in the fact that it is directed toward an interpretation of human existence [*Dasein*] *in its relation to beings as a whole*.)

> (Heidegger, "On the Essence of Ground," in *Pathmarks*, 121)

In the same text Heidegger will nonetheless adopt an unusual approach to the specificity of *Welt* and its connotations, and he prepares the reader through the discreet assonance of *walten/welten* ("to rule" / "to world")—i.e., to be deployed in the measure of a world [Fr. *se deployer à mesure d'un monde*]. "*Welt* ist *nie*, sondern *weltet* [World never *is*, but *worlds*]" (ibid., 126); Fr. "*le monde n'est jamais, le monde se mondifie*" (Fr. trans. H. Corbin, ibid., 142). The French comes close to Nerval (*Œuvres complètes*, Gallimard, "La Pléiade," 2: 848): "*Le monde amonde.*"

It was in fact in 1919 that Heidegger first took the risk of expressing *welten*, which in some way turns *Welt* into an unword (Fr: *déverbal*).

3
Umwelt: From ecology to the commerce of being

Popularized by ecology in the sense of "environment" (through the contrast between the terms of *Umweltschutz/ Umweltschmut-zung*: "environmental protection," "pollution"), *Umwelt* appears around 1800 in an ode of Baggasen, is then taken up by Campe (1811), and is borrowed from the German and transposed into the Danish *omverden* by Dahlerup

(1822); but it is Goethe's usage that sanctions the entry and adoption of the term in the German language. At that point its meaning is given as "*die den Menschen umgebende Welt* [the world around mankind]" (*Grimm*, s.v.): the prefix *um*, like the Latin *circum* or French *autour*, gives *Umwelt* the meaning of *umgebende Welt*, the world "around" (us).

But with Heidegger the prefix *um-* will take on intentional significance, in the locution *um zu*, "in order to," and will displace the meaningfulness of the world, insofar as we are "in cahoots" with it, into our daily commerce with being.

Outside of a specifically philosophical context, the term *Umwelt* can be taken up in German by the use of the French word *milieu*.

4
"Planetarity"

"Planetarity," as an English word, was first used in a paper I presented at Stiftung-Dialogik in Zurich, December 16, 1997, entitled "Imperatives to Re-Imagine the Planet," and later printed as *Imperatives to Re-Imagine the Planet/Imperative zur Neuerfindung des Planeten*, ed. Willi Goetschel, Vienna: Passagen, 1999. "Planetarity" was figured as a word set apart from notions of the planetary, the planet, the earth, the world, the globe, globalization, and the like in their common usage.

The untranslatability of "planetarity" rests on an old-fashioned argument. If we think dogmatically (to borrow Immanuel Kant's phrasing on the "dogmatic," in English translation) of "planetarity" as contained under another, prior concept of the object (the "planet"), which constitutes a principle of reason, and then determine it in conformity with this, we come up with contemporary planet-talk by way of environmentalism, referring usually, though not invariably, to an undivided "natural" space rather than a differentiated political space. This smoothly "translates" into the interest of globalization in the mode of the abstract as such. This environmental planet-speak is the planet as an alternate description of the globe, susceptible to nation-state geopolitics. It can accommodate the good policy of saving the resources of the planet.

My use of "planetarity," on the other hand, does not refer to any applicable methodology. It is different from a sense of being the custodians of our very own planet, although I have no objection to such a sense of accountability. (For that custodial sense a good epistemological preparation can be undertaken by way of Isabelle Stengers's *Cosmopolitics*.)

The sense of custodianship of our planet has led to a species of feudality without feudalism coupled with the method of "sustainability," keeping geology safe for good

imperialism, emphasizing capital's social productivity but not its irreducible subalternizing tendency. This is what translates and provides the alibi for *good* global capitalism.

On a different scale, Richard Dawkins–style DNA-ism is an attempt to translate planet-thought digitally. But "planetary" is bigger than "geological," where random means nothing, which no individual thought can weigh: "living organisms exist for the benefit of DNA rather than the other way around. . . . The messages that DNA molecules contain are all but eternal when seen against the time scale of individual lifetimes. The lifetimes of DNA messages (give or take a few mutations) are measured in units ranging from millions of years to hundreds of millions of years; or, in other words, ranging from 10,000 individual lifetimes to a trillion individual lifetimes. Each individual organism should be seen as a temporary vehicle, in which DNA messages spend a tiny fraction of their geological lifetimes" (Dawkins, *Blind Watchmaker*, 127). This, too, is a "dogmatic" thinking of planetarity.

If we think critically—via Kant again—only in reference to our cognitive faculties and consequently bound to the subjective conditions of envisioning planetarity, without undertaking to decide anything about its object, we discover that planetarity is not susceptible to the subject's grasp (see BEGRIFF). "The planet," I said in the original paper, "is in the species of *alterity*." I was iterating the older expression "in the species of eternity"—*sub specie aeternitatis*. The globe is on our computers. No one lives there. The "global" notion allows us to think that we can aim to control globality. The planet is in the species of alterity, belonging to another system; and yet we inhabit it, on loan. It is not really amenable to a neat contrast with the globe. I cannot say "the planet, on the other hand." When I invoke the planet,

I think of the effort required to figure the (im)possibility of this underived intuition. Since to be human may be to be intended toward the other, we provide for ourselves transcendental figurations ("translations?") of what we think is the origin of the animating gift of life: Mother, Nation, God, Nature. These are names (nicknames, putative synonyms) of alterity, some more radical than others.

If we think planet-thought in this mode of alterity, the thinking opens up to embrace an inexhaustible taxonomy of such names, including but not identical with the whole range of human universals: aboriginal animism as well as the spectral white mythology of postrational science. If we imagine ourselves as planetary subjects rather than global agents, planetary creatures rather than global entities, alterity remains underived from us; it is not our dialectical negation, it contains us as much as it flings us away—and thus to think of it is already to transgress, for, in spite of our forays into what we render through metaphor, differently, as outer and inner space, it remains that what is above and beyond our own reach is not continuous with us as it is not, indeed, specifically discontinuous.

We must persistently educate ourselves into the peculiar mindset of accepting the untranslatable, even as we are programmed to transgress that mindset by "translating" it into the mode of "acceptance."

Gayatri Chakravorty Spivak

BIBLIOGRAPHY

Dawkins, Richard. *The Blind Watchmaker*. New York: Norton, 1986.

Stengers, Isabelle. *Cosmopolitics*. Translated by Robert Bonono. Minneapolis: University of Minnesota Press, 2010.

In einer Umwelt lebend, bedeutet es mir überall und immer, es ist alles welthaft, "*es weltet*," was nicht zusammenfällt mit dem "*es wertet*."

(Living in an environment, it signifies to me everywhere and always, everything has the character of a world. It is everywhere the case that "*it worlds*" [*es weltet*], which is something different from "it values" [*es wertet*].)

(Heidegger, War Emergency Semester 1919, in *Definition of Philosophy*, 58)

As F.-W. von Herrman has noted (*Hermeneutik*, 43), *welten* is not properly speaking a neologism first used by Heidegger, for the verb, although no longer used, signified "leading the good life." Heidegger has thus not coined it but reinterpreted the verb and given it a much broader signification.

With *Being and Time*, *Welt*, "world," will become an existential, that is to say, an ontological structure of human existence. This is both a radicalization of the "anthropological" sense of the word (even though existential analysis would not consider itself to be a form of anthropology), such as it emerges in the New Testament and is separated out by Kant, and an emancipation of the concept of "world" in relation to that of "universe" as well. In a course from 1929/1930 (Heidegger, *Gesamtausgabe*, 29–30: §42, 261ff.), the stone is called *weltlos*, "without a world," the animal is *weltarm*, "poorly endowed with world," and the human being is *weltbildend*, "world image-making."

■ See Boxes 3 and 4.

Pascal David

BIBLIOGRAPHY

Baumgarten, Alexander Gottlieb. *Metaphysica*. Hildesheim, Ger.: Olms, 1982.

Brague, Rémi. *The Wisdom of the World: The Human Experience of the Universe in Western Thought*. Translated by Teresa Lavender Fagan. Chicago: University of Chicago Press, 2003.

Bultmann, Rudolf. *Theology of the New Testament*. Translated by Kendrick Grobel. New York: Scribner, 1951–1955. First published in 1948.

Crusius, Christian August. *Entwurf der notwendigen Vernunft—Wahrheiten, wiefern sie den zufälligen entgegengesetzt werden*. Hildesheim, Ger.: Olms, 1964. First published in 1745.

Descartes, René. *Cogitationes privatae*. In vol. 10 of *Oeuvres*. 11 vols. Edited by Charles Adam and Paul Tannery. Paris: Vrin, 1996.

Heidegger, Martin. *Die Grundbegriffe der Metaphysik*. In *Gesamtausgabe*. Vols. 29–30. Frankfurt: Klostermann, 1983. Translation by William McNeill and Nicholas Walker: *The Fundamental Concepts of Metaphysics: World, Finitude, Solitude*. Bloomington: Indiana University Press, 1995.

———. *Einführung in die Metaphysik*. Tübingen: M. Niemeyer, 1953. Translation by Gregory Fried and Richard Polt: *Introduction to Metaphysics*. New Haven, CT: Yale University Press, 2000.

———. *Pathmarks*. Edited by William McNeill. Cambridge: Cambridge University Press, 1998.

———. *Sein und Zeit*. In *Gesamtausgabe*, Vol 2. Frankfurt: Klostermann, 1977. Translation by Joan Stambaugh: *Being and Time*. Albany: State University of New York Press, 1996.

———. *Vom Wesen des Grundes*. In *Gesamtausgabe*. Vol 9. Frankfurt: Klostermann, 1976. Translation by Reginald Lilly: *The Principle of Reason*. Bloomington: Indiana University Press, 1991.

———. *Zur Bestimmung der Philosophie*. In *Gesamtausgabe*. Vols. 56–57. Frankfurt: Klostermann, 1987. Translation by Ted Sadler: *Towards the Definition of Philosophy*. London: Continuum, 2002.

Hermann, Friedrich Wilhem von. *Hermeneutik und Reflexion: der Begriff der Phänomenologie bei Heidegger und Husserl*. Frankfurt am Main: Klostermann, 2000.

Kant, Immanuel. *Anthropology from a Pragmatic Point of View*. Translated by Robert B. Louden. In *Anthropology, History, and Education*, edited by Günter Zöller and Robert B. Louden. Cambridge: Cambridge University Press, 2007.

———. *Dissertation, De mundi sensibilis atque intelligibilis form et principiis* [Dissertation on the form and principles of the sensible and intelligible world]. Translated by W. J. Eckoff (1894).

———. *Kant's Inaugural Dissertation and Early Writings on Space*. Translated by John Handyside. Westport, CT: Hyperion Press, 1979.

Kirk, G. S., J. E. Raven, and M. Schofield. *The Presocratic Philosophers: A Critical History with a Selection of Texts*. 2nd ed. Cambridge: Cambridge University Press, 1984.

Kowalevski, Arnold, ed. *Die philosophischen Hauptvorlesungen Immanuel Kants. Nach den neu aufgefundenen Kollegheften des Grafen Heinrich zu Dohna-Wundlacken*. Hildesheim, Ger.: Olms, 1965.

Leibniz, Gottfried Wilhelm. *Theodicy: Essays on the Goodness of God, the Freedom of Man and the Origin of Evil*. Translated by E. M. Huggard. La Salle, IL: Open Court, 1985.

Lubac, Henri de. *Catholicism: Christ and the Common Destiny of Man*. Translated by L. Sheppard and E. Englund. San Francisco: Ignatius Press, 1988.

Malebranche, Nicholas. *Éclaircissements sur la Recherche de la verité*. In *Œuvres complètes*. Vol. 3. Translated by Thomas M. Lennon and Paul J. Olscamp: *The Search for Truth* and *Elucidations of the Search after Truth*. Cambridge: Cambridge University Press, 1997.

———. *The Search after Truth*. Translated by Thomas M. Lennon and Paul J. Olscamp. In *Philosophical Selections*, edited by Steven Nadler. Indianapolis, IN: Hackett, 1992.

Richardson, William. *Heidegger: Through Phenomenology to Thought*. Preface by Martin Heidegger. 4th ed. New York: Fordham University Press, 2003.

Schelling, Friedrich Wilhelm Joseph von. *Philosophie der Offenbarung*. Edited by M. Frank. Frankfurt: Suhrkamp, 1977. First published in 1841–1842.

WELTANSCHAUUNG (GERMAN)

ENGLISH   worldview
FRENCH   *vision du monde, conception du monde*

➤ *WORLD* and AIÔN, ANSCHAULICHKEIT, *INTUITION*, LEIB, PERCEPTION, REPRÉSENTATION

The fact that *Weltanschauung* (Eng. "worldview," Fr. *vision du monde*) sometimes appears in untranslated form in French philosophical prose (as in Sartre's *L'Être et le néant* [Being and nothingness]) is an indication of this composite term's resistance to translation. The paternity of the term is sometimes attributed to Schelling ("Schelling, who was the first to coin the term *Weltanschauung*," Tilliette, *Schelling*, 1: 492) or to A. von Humboldt ("It seems that it was A. von Humboldt who ... coined the term *Weltanschauung*," Brague, *La Sagesse du monde*, 294n76). Although these attributions are erroneous, they are nonetheless instructive, for they attest to the various uses of the term that range from the intuition of the world to its interpretation.

In actual fact it would seem to have been Kant himself who first proposed the term *Weltanschauung* in §26 of the *Critique of Judgment*:

Denn nur durch dieses [*Vermögen*] und dessen Idee eines Noumenons, welches selbst keine Anschauung verstattet, aber doch der Weltanschauung, *als bloßer Erscheinung*, zum Substrat untergelegt wird.

(For it is only through this faculty and its idea of a noumenon, which latter, while not itself admitting of any intuition, is yet introduced as a substrate underlying the intuition of the world as mere phenomenon.)

(Kant, *Critique of Judgment*, 103)

(En effet c'est seulement par cette faculté et son idée d'un noumène, qui lui-même n'autorise aucune intuition, mais qui est toutefois en tant que substrat mis au fondement de l'intuition du monde [Weltanschauung] comme simple phénomène.)

(Fr. trans. A. Philonenko, 94; Fr. trans. J. Gibelin, 87)

In the French translations, as in the English ones by Meredith and J. H. Bernard (Hafner Library of Classics), the translators balked at translating Weltanschauung as, respectively, vision du monde or "world view."

The translation problem is complicated by the fact that in Kant's writings Weltanschauung does not necessarily have the meanings that it will subsequently assume in the philosophical literature. In his Marburg lectures from the spring of 1927, Heidegger undertook a preliminary reconstruction of the history of the term:

This expression is not a translation from Greek, say, or Latin. There is no such expression as kosmotheôria [κοσμοθεωρία]. The word "Weltanschauung" is of specifically German coinage (italics added); it was in fact coined within philosophy [das Wort ist eine spezifisch deutsche Prägung und zwar wurde es innerhalb der Philosophie geprägt]. It first turns up in its natural meaning in Kant's Critique of Judgment—world-intuition in the sense of contemplation of the world given to the senses or, as Kant says, the mundus sensibilis. . . . Goethe and Alexander von Humboldt thereupon use the word this way. This usage dies out in the thirties of the last century under the influence of a new meaning given to the expression "Weltanschauung" by the Romantics and principally by Schelling. . . . Thus the word approaches the meaning we are familiar with today, a self-realized, productive as well as conscious way of apprehending and interpreting the universe of beings [einer selbstvollzogenen, produktiven und dann auch bewußten Weise, das All des Seienden aufzufassen und zu deuten].

(Heidegger, The Basic Problems of Phenomenology, trans., intro., and lexicon by Albert Hofstadter, §2, 4–5 [with modifications])

Actually, one does indeed come across the term kosmothêoria [κοσμοθεωρία] but in modern Greek—and this as a translation or transposition of Weltanschauung! Heidegger goes on to describe the salient outlines of the semantic trajectory of Weltanschauung through a series of references: Hegel, Görres, Ranke, Schleiermacher, Bismarck, and finally Jaspers. In a lecture course given in 1936, Heidegger notes the extent to which the waning and deracination of the term has turned it into a slogan of the utmost platitude, even though it derived from the heights of German Idealism:

Es wird hier die "Weltanschauung" des Schweinezüchters zum maßgebenden Typus der Weltanschauung überhaupt gemacht.

(The world vision of the pig farmer has become the type and measure of the world vision altogether.)

(Heidegger, Schelling's Treatise)

An annotation (j) on the same page specifies in reference to Weltanschauung: "Das Wort ist nicht übersetzbar [the term is untranslatable]." After 1936 Heidegger would engage in a ferocious critique of the confusion, abetted by the phraseology of the Third Reich, between philosophy and Weltanschauung, reserving the latter for what it had become: an ideology. The semantic trajectory of Weltanschauung goes from an intuition of the world (the universe) to an ideology. Victor Klemperer provides further testimony in his study of the Lingua Tertii Imperii:

"Philosophie" . . . wird totgeschwiegen, wird durchgängig ersetzt durch "Weltanschauung." . . . "Weltanschauung" schon vor dem Nazismus verbreitet, hat in der LTI als Ersatzwort für "Philosophie" alle Sonntäglichkeit verloren und Alltags—, Metierklang bekommen.

(As a substitute for philosophy, the word "Weltanschauung," already prevalent before National Socialism, lost its solemnity and acquired an everyday, business-like ring.)

(Klemperer, Language)

Pascal David

BIBLIOGRAPHY

Brague, Rémi. La Sagesse du monde. Paris: Fayard, 1999. Translation by Teresa Lavender Fagan: The Wisdom of the World: The Human Experience of the Universe in Western Thought. Chicago: University of Chicago Press, 2003.

Heidegger, Martin. Die Grundprobleme der Phänomenologie. In Gesamtausgabe. Vol. 24. Frankfurt: Klostermann, 1975. Translation by Albert Hofstadter: The Basic Problems of Phenomenology. Introduction by Albert Hofstadter. Bloomington: Indiana University Press, 1982.

———. Schellings Abhandlung über das Wesen der menschlichen Freiheit. In Gesamtausgabe. Vol. 42. Frankfurt: Klostermann, 1988. Translation by Joan Stambaugh: Schelling's Treatise on the Essence of Human Freedom. Athens: Ohio University Press, 1985.

Kant, Immanuel. Critique of Judgment. Translated by James Creed Meredith. Oxford: Oxford University Press, 1978. Translation by Paul Guyer and Eric Matthews: Critique of the Power of Judgment, edited by Paul Guyer. Cambridge: Cambridge University Press, 2000. Translation into French by Alexis Philonenko: Critique de la faculté de juger. Paris: Vrin, 1993. Translation into French by Jean Gibelin: Critique du jugement. Paris: Vrin, 1946.

Klemperer, Victor. The Language of the Third Reich, Lingua Tertii Imperii: A Philologist's Notebook. Translated by Martin Brady. London: Athlone Press, 2000.

Tilliette, Xavier. Schelling: Une philosophie en devenir. 2 vols. Paris: Vrin, 1970.

WERT / GELTUNG (GERMAN)

ENGLISH	worth, value
FRENCH	valeur, validité
LATIN	valere

➤ VALUE and DUTY, ECONOMY, ES GIBT, MACHT, MORALS, SOLLEN, UTILITY, VIRTUE, WILLKÜR

Wert traces back to the Latin valere as do the etymologically related English terms "worth" and "value," the French valeur, and the German Gewalt. Its substantive form derives from the adjective wert, itself close to the verbs werdan and werden (to become), placing Wert in the semantic orbit of the ought-to-be (cf. SOLLEN). Gelten comes from the Gothic and Old High German geltan (which means "to pay tribute, to offer up as sacrifice"), as does *Geld* (money, cash; cf. gold, Fr. *l'or*). "*Es hat keinen Wert*" (it is of no value) refers back to a quality that is specific (or given) to the object being evaluated, while "*es gilt nicht*" signifies, for example, that a particular move in a game "does not count" or breaks the rules. Likewise the adjective *geltend* is used to describe legal tender or what is in effect (an act of jurisprudence, or a currency). *Geltung* can also signify the accepted use of a term or sign within a system of signification, and this "value" can also be given *Gültigkeit*, a pertinence or validity. The three terms *Wert*, *Geltung/Gelten*, and *Gültigkeit*, in their separate articulations, bring reflections on moral values into contact with ontology and the doctrine of judgment, in a configuration without equivalent in other languages.

In his polemical essay "Die Tyrannei der Werte" (The tyranny of values) Carl Schmitt considers the "philosophy of values" to be a "reaction to the crisis of nihilism of the nineteenth century" (46). This may well be the right dating and an accurate characterization of a reaction to the spread of positivism, but it does not address the philosophical reflection on value in a larger sense that entailed the problematization of *Wert* as critique of morality (even an axiology), as well as an analysis of what constitutes the validity (*Geltung*, *Gültigkeit*) of judgments in the form of a logical reflection. Schmitt sums up the essentials of the relation among *Wert*, *Geltung*, and *Gelten* in a way that is not without pertinence to philosophy, even if it falls short of qualifying as a truly philosophical definition: *Geltung* is the actualization of value (*Wert*), while *Gelten* is the process by which a value acquires its validity (52).

I. Nietzsche: The Evaluation of Values (*Werte*) and Their Validity (*Geltung*)

It was undoubtedly Nietzsche who introduced from the perspective of a critique of traditional morality and its foundations an incisive radicalization of the Kantian reflection on the limits of our instruments of knowledge. By reducing the entire rational process to a story in which one set of values replaces another, he implicitly stressed the importance of value:

> Skepticism regarding all moral values is a symptom of the fact that a new table of values [*Werttafel*] is in the process of emerging.
>
> (Die Skepsis an allen moralischen Werthen ist ein Symptom davon, daß eine neue moralische Werthtafel im Entstehen ist.)
>
> (Nietzsche, *Posthumous Fragments*, VIII 4 [56], Nov. 1882–Feb. 1883)

Values are, in effect, presented here as configurations that crystallize the developments to which they are consistently reduced:

> Pleasure and displeasure are the oldest symptoms of all judgments of value [*Werturteile*].
>
> (Lust und Unlust sind die ältesten Symptome aller Werthurtheile: nicht aber Ursachen der Werthurtheile!)
>
> (Ibid., VIII 1 [97], Autumn 1885)

The judgments themselves should be referred to more fundamental activities:

> Moral evaluation [*moralische Wertschätzen*] is an *exegesis*, a way of interpreting. The exegesis itself is a symptom of certain physiological conditions, likewise of a particular spiritual level of prevalent judgments: Who interprets?—Our affects.
>
> (*The Will to Power*, §254 [1885–1886], 148)

Moral values, he argues, compared to physiological evaluations, are false, as is the "metaphysical postulate" that leads us to establish a correlation between levels of value and levels of reality. The highest levels are no truer; they are simply the most symptomatic: "Whatever has proven itself useful [*nützlich*] from time immemorial is good: as a result, it may assert its validity [*Geltung*] as 'of the highest value,' as 'valuable in itself' [*wertvoll*]" (*Genealogy of Morals*, 14, First Essay, §3 *in fine*). The "utility" in question is part of the general economy of the will to power, that is to say, the permanent struggle among different affects, each seeking its maximum outpouring and release. Each affect is always "judging," constantly "evaluating" what it will accept and what it will refuse. From the ensemble of these conflicts, the state of our "health" can be seen as the psychophysiological result whose evanescent equilibrium can give us the illusion of a stability that we call "self," "identity," "value," and "truth." The only "truth" that we can attain is a state of health (or sickness) that enables us to affirm (or deny) our personal interpretation of the dynamic of drives, then taken as foundational of thought and cultural patterns. Values are thus nothing other than symptoms. Every belief in values is an illusion whose ends have nothing to do with morality. The successive scales of value thus take the form of a spiral, ascending or descending, necessarily finite in possibility—the form of the eternal return. The life of the emotional drives is completely "intellectual" in as much as it consists only of evaluations; it has no "foundation" outside itself. Consequently, the "conversion of all values" (*Umwertung aller Werte*) is not a "subversion of values" (*Umwälzung*) that leads to an ultimate unalienated life; it is simply a segment of the spiral of the eternal return. The "truth" of values is valid only as a function of the greater or smaller levels of risk assumed by the person that grants them this validity: the "giving virtue" (*die schenkende Tugend*) of the creator (in whichever system) lays claim to superiority by being the only one capable of achieving a balance between destruction and creation. Nietzsche does not abandon the field of values; in fact he postulates that it is impossible to even hope to escape it. The axiological horizon—which is also that of the "body"—is the only one given to us.

■ See Box 1.

II. Lotze: *Bestehen* and *Gelten*, *Geltung* and *Gültigkeit*

In his lecture course from the summer semester of 1919, *Phänomenologie und transzendentale Wertphilosophie* (Phenomenology and transcendental philosophy of value), Martin Heidegger credits Hermann Lotze with having reacted in the

1

Mehrwert

It is in *Capital* that Marx develops his theory of *Mehrwert*, or "surplus value" (the French expression *plus-value* is an Anglicization and was more precisely rendered as *survaleur* by Henri Lefebvre). Surplus labor (*surtravail*) is a given fact of any more or less developed civilization. In these societies it is simply a fact that work of any sort produces an excess that sustains persons other than the direct producers, as a kind of stocking of provisions. But the capitalist system of production was the first to make surplus labor into the direct source of profit. "Surplus value" is the result of the difference among the productive work time that reimburses fixed capital investment, raw materials, and salaries, and work time that produces pure and simple profit. This theory of "surplus value" leads to the conception according to which in a capitalist system use-value (*Gebrauchswert*) tends to give way to exchange-value (*Tauschwert*), as well as to the contested prediction of a "tendency to reduce the profit margin" engendered primarily by competition.

BIBLIOGRAPHY

Marx, Karl. *Capital: A Critique of Political Economy.* 3 vols. Translated by Ben Fowkes. New York: Vintage Books, 1977.

---

middle of the nineteenth century against the "absolute reification of the spirit promoted by naturalism" and "the reduction of all Being to corporeal matter, objectified events, matter and force" (Heidegger, *Towards the Definition of Philosophy*, 106–7). "His ubiquitous idea of the ought [*des Sollens*] and of value, and along these lines his interpretation of the Platonic ideas, which *are* not but instead *hold*, i.e., are valid as valuable, had a strong effect on the further development of philosophy, in the sense of a move away from naturalism and especially from psychologism" (ibid., 107). Heidegger sees a decisive motif in the development of modern value-philosophy in Lotze's doctrine of the primacy of practical Reason according to Fichte's interpretation, as "value-sensing" (*wertempfindenen*) (ibid). In his great work of 1864, *Mikrokosmos* (part 3, 500 and 510), Lotze had already introduced an opposition between *Bestehen* (to exist in the sense of "maintaining constancy") and *Gelten* (to have value in the sense of needing to be taken into account). In his *Logik* Lotze proceeds to make the following distinctions:

> For we call a thing Real which is, in contradistinction to another which is not; an event Real which occurs or has occurred; a relation Real which obtains [*besteht*], as opposed to one which does not obtain; lastly we call a proposition Really true which holds or is valid [*gilt*] as opposed to one of which the validity [*Geltung*] is still doubtful.

(Lotze, Logic, bk. 3, §316, 207)

Here *Gelten* and *Geltung* refer back to *Gültigkeit*, but the formal validity of a proposition does not necessarily entail its objective validity; to confuse *geltend* and *gültig* is reductive. The only effective reality of a proposition lies in the fact that it is valid and that its contrary is not. Likewise, our thoughts and representations, which are always in a perpetual becoming and not in a stable form of being, "arrive" and take place like events, and their content does not have effective being either but is "valid" (*gilt*). Thus there are three fundamental concepts, none of which can be reduced to something derived from one another: being, taking place, and holding or being valid. Worth is interpreted by Lotze in the manner

that Plato understood the ideas: a validity of truths that are eternally identical to themselves, independent of the existence of objects in the phenomenal world to confirm their relevance or of minds to think them. This intervention of Lotze's will have a significant impact on posterity, for example in the Austrian school: Meinong, for instance, will oppose (effective) being (*Sein*) and the "constancy" (*Bestehen*) of the habitual objects of knowledge (identity, difference, etc.). Lotze's theory will survive also in the neo-Kantianism of Baden under its normal appellation as "theory of the two worlds." This latter approach developed the consequences of Lotze's reinterpretation of the Platonic theory of ideas in all their breadth and complexity.

■ See Box 2.

III. Rickert: *Wert* and *Sollen*, the Primacy of Practical Reason

Taking his starting point in Windelband's reflections on negative judgment, Rickert shows that a factor that lies outside representation comes into play in any judgment: it is indeed impossible to judge without taking a position, either as an affirmation or as a rejection, on the established relation between a state of affairs and a predicate; thus "to know is to accept or reject" (*Der Gegenstand der Erkenntnis*, 58). Since what holds for judgment also holds more generally for the processes of knowing, what becomes primary is not the taking of a position in relation to a state of factual affairs but in relation to a value: for a fact does not require one to take a position; it can be simply accepted as such: "in all knowledge . . . it is a value [*Wert*] that is recognized" (ibid., 57ff.). And further, value is acknowledged as something psychologically given, a feeling that intervenes to such an extent that "in each judgment, I know at the instant of judging that I recognize something as eternally valid [*gilt*]" (ibid., 60). What is accorded "validity" (*Geltung*) can thus only be a value and not a being that I know only through the bias of representations. For it is according to their connections that I pronounce judgment and not on a being to which they refer. It is according to their connections that I accept or reject a value and this process in its turn is not raised by an objective necessity but by an ought-to-be (*Sollen*): "When I hear notes

2

Wertfreiheit

➤ UNDERSTANDING

The Weberian notion of "value-neutral" fact-finding has been translated into French as "axiological neutrality" (*neutralité axiologique*). (Julien Freund explained his position on the topic in his edition of Weber's essays devoted to the theory of science. Weber himself explained what he understood by the concept in "The Meaning of Value Neutrality in the Social and Economic Sciences" [*Der Sinn der "Wertfreiheit" der soziologischen und ökonomischen Wissenschaften*] (1917). In explicit reference to Rickert, Weber defends both the methodological utility of "axiological neutrality" and the problematics linked to values.

> Es sei daher nur daran erinnert, daß der Ausdruck "Wertbeziehung" lediglich die philosophische Deutung desjenigen spezifisch wissenschaftlichen "Interesses" meint, welches die Auslese und Formung des Objektes einer empirischen Untersuchung beherrscht. Innerhalb der empirischen Untersuchung werden durch diesen rein logischen Sachverhalt jedenfalls keinerlei "praktische Wertungen" legitimiert. Wohl aber ergibt jener Sachverhalt in Übereinstimmung mit der geschichtlichen Erfahrung, daß Kultur—und das heißt: Wertinteressen es sind, welche auch der rein empirisch-wissenschaftlichen Arbeit die Richtung weisen. Es ist nun klar, daß diese Wertinteressen durch Wertdiskussionen in ihrer Kasuistik sich entfalten können. Diese können dem wissenschaftlich, insbesondere dem historisch arbeitenden, Forscher vor allem die Aufgabe der "Wertinterpretation": für ihn eine höchst wichtige Vorarbeit seiner eigentlich empirischen Arbeit, weitgehend abnehmen oder doch erleichtern.
>
> (Weber, "Der Sinn der 'Wertfreiheit' der soziologischen und ökonomischen Wissenschaften"; *Gesammelte Aufsätze zur Wissenschaftslehre*. Hrsg. von Johannes Winckelmann. Tübingen 61985, S. 540)

(It should only be recalled that the expression "relevance to values" refers simply to the philosophical interpretation of that specifically scientific "interest" which determines the selection of a given subject-matter and the problems of empirical analysis. In empirical investigation, no "practical evaluations" are legitimated by this strictly logical fact. But together with historical experience, it shows that cultural (i.e., evaluative) interests give purely empirical scientific work its direction. It is now clear that these evaluative interests can be made more explicit and differentiated by the analysis of value-judgments. These considerably reduce, or at any rate lighten, the task of "value-interpretation"—an extremely important preparation of empirical work—for the scientific investigator and especially the historian.)

(Weber, "The Meaning of 'Ethical Neutrality' in Sociology and Economics," in *Methodology of the Social Sciences*, 22)

Scientific work that respects value-neutrality consists in the rational understanding of the point of view that gives direction to the actions of such-and-such social group or such-and-such historical individual, without engaging in judgment on the ethical validity of the point of view. But Weber never defines what value is; he limits himself to giving synonyms (ideal, ethical rule, etc.). As for the essentials, he adheres to the distinction made by Rickert in his work *Science of Nature and Science of Culture* between explaining (*erklären*) (the causes of a natural phenomenon) and understanding (*verstehen*) (the motives behind a cultural and historical event, the reasons for a human action).

BIBLIOGRAPHY

Rickert, Heinrich. *Science and History: A Critique of Positivist Epistemology* [Kulturwissenschaft und Naturwissenschaft]. Translated by George Reisman. Edited by Arthur Goddard. Princeton, NJ: Van Nostrand, 1962.

Weber, Max. *Economy and Society: An Outline of Interpretative Sociology*. Edited by Guenther Roth and Claus Wittich. Berkeley: University of California Press, 1978.

———. *From Max Weber: Essays in Sociology*. Translated, edited, and with an introduction by H. H. Gerth and C. Wright Mills. New York: Oxford University Press, 1980.

———. *The Methodology of the Social Sciences*. Translated and edited by Edward A. Shils and Henry A. Finche. Glencoe, IL: Free Press, 1949.

I must necessarily judge that I hear notes, which means that I am given an obligation [*ein Sollen*] along with the notes, that calls for an eventual judgment" (Wenn ich Töne höre, so bin ich genöthigt, so zu urteilen, sagt, dass mir den Tönen ein Sollen gegeben ist, das von einem eventuellen Urteil Zustimmung fordert und Zustimmung erhält) (ibid., 63). Thus, the truth of a judgment is not a quality that it possesses and that I should recognize, but a judgment that is true because I recognize a value in it.

We should therefore take care to distinguish between, on the one hand, the specific content of the judgment which is independent from all statements and psychical processes, and which we thus can call the "transcendental" logical sense, alongside the objective good which it clings to, and on the other hand, the subjective act of taking a position, with its own "immanent" meaning. The content of the judgment must be examined in relation to logic as well as in relation to the Form and its content. By "Form" we refer to the moment of validation [*Geltungsmoment*] in its conceptual isolation whereby content, itself logically indifferent, is elevated to the logical sphere and transformed for the first time into a logically valid [*gültig*] element of meaning.

(Wir müssen daher von dem eigentlichen Urteilsgehalt, der unabhängig von allen Sätzen und psychischen Vorgängen gilt, und den wir deshalb auch den "transzendenten" logischen Sinn nennen können, einerseits das objektive Gut, an dem er haftet, und andererseits den subjektiven Akt der Stellungnahme mit dem ihm "immanenten" Sinn sorgfältig scheiden. Der Urteilsgehalt ist von der Logik dann mit Rücksicht auf seine Form und seinen Inhalt zu untersuchen, wobei wir unter "Form" das theoretische Geltungsmoment in seiner begrifflichen Isolierung verstehen, durch welches der für sich logisch indifferente Inhalt in die logische Sphäre gehoben, also zum logisch gültigen Sinngebilde erst gemacht wird.)

(Rickert, "Über logische und ethische Geltung," in *Philosophische Zeitschrift*, Berlin, 1914)

Rickert reinterprets the "primacy of practical Reason" by making value (*Wert*) the *archi-lexeme* that includes moral values (*die Güter*, Fr. *les biens*) and the validity (*Geltung*) proper to all judgments on which knowledge depends. It is a "practical" procedure (*ein Sollen*) that recognizes a particular association of representations to be valid (*gilt*) and thus true. The ought-to-be must be understood before the "to be": "All our arguments depend on two statements: that judgment is not a representation and that 'being' gains meaning only as a component of a judgment" (Auf den beiden Sätzen, dass Urteilen nicht Vorstellen ist, und dass das "Sein" nur einen Sinn gewinnt als Bestandtheil eines Urtheils, beruhen all unsere Ausfuhrungen) (ibid., 84). Values can be inflected by taking the form of a truth, norm, or law. In the end, however, the criterion that enables one to distinguish an "unreal" value from an actual being is negation. To deny something real results in nothingness, not its opposite, unreality. By contrast, to deny a value results in a negative value (false, ugly, etc.).

IV. Lask: *Wert* and *Geltung,* the Separation of Spheres

Emil Lask, a disciple of Rickert, caused his teacher to revise his own conception of value. Starting in 1908, Lask opposed what he called the "ethicization" (*Ethisierung*) of notions of knowledge and judgment:

We call for a concept of value [*Wertbegriff*] in knowledge that is not an ethical one [*nichtethisch*], and we would also clearly distinguish it from scientific *life*, where, of course, practical reason has priority. At the same time, we raise the objection that making ethical value [*der ethische Wert*] the immediate correlate of objective worth [*das objektive gelten*] would be to give it a systematic standing which does not belong to it.

(Lask, "Does a 'Primacy of Practical Reason' Exist in Logic?" [1908] in *Néokantismes et Théorie de la connaissance*, 304 [trans. from Fr.])

Here, the highest position in the conceptual universe is not that of objective being but that of objective validity (*Geltung*). Ethical value is not endowed with objective validity:

What is encountered by the moral will, in the form of a demanding ethical value, is not a demand [*das Fordern*] in the sense of objective validity, but always some action whose doing is endowed with value. . . . Knowing *is* a behavior commanded by the objective validity of truth [*Wahrheitsgelten*]; moral will *has as its object* a commanded action.

(Ibid. [trans. from Fr.])

Lask introduces the distinction between the knowing subject (*Erkenntnissubjekt*) and the person (*Persönlichkeit*)

(responsible for an action ordered by a moral ought-to-be). This amounts to a distinction between the subjective correlate of the objective validity of truth—knowledge—and the fact of devoting oneself to science, an act that comes from the ethical: "the subjective sphere of the 'processes of knowledge' is completely independent of the personal ethical sphere" (ibid., 307). In making these distinctions, Lask does not leave the field of value, but simply dissociates his two orientations from its meaning. This is why, without breaking their ties to *Wert*, the terms *Geltung* and *Gelten* appear in his reflections on logic and its categories, as well as in his arguments about judgment. The nonethical concept of value is related to objective validity (*Geltung*), and when Lask claims that a being is a *Gelten*, his intent is to stress that our access to the predicate of being is from within a judgment and not from the point of real being. Since the sphere of judgment is part of the unreal sphere of the world, that is to say, the world ruled by validity (*Geltung*), we are complete "prisoners" of the sphere of *gelten*, which our knowledge obeys. The same holds true a fortiori for the ethical sphere, even if discussions of values (*Werte*) are more common there. In both spheres, no matter what, one finds notions of value, of validity, of ought-to-be, and of norm, but their usage no longer stipulates recourse to practical Reason. Logical value and ethical value become equivalent.

V. Scheler: Value and Feeling

Taking up the Husserlian notion of the vision of essence, Scheler extracts from the flux of experience that presents itself to consciousness contents that have no direct signification but that are nonetheless intentional acts. Thus, it is possible to apprehend qualities (such as the good, the agreeable, or the beautiful) without having an idea of their signification. In fact, the significations—of beauty, the good, etc.—are posterior to those actions at the heart of which one experiences such qualities (the exception is the quality of redness, which is experienced at the same time as its signification). Scheler insists on the importance of the intentional *feeling* (*intentionales Gefühl*; see GEFÜHL) that is not the same as an affective state and that leads directly to a content without the intermediary of a thought or representation. This content is the "material" base of the values apprehended by pure feeling. The world of values is grasped through pure feeling, by what Scheler calls the "emotional function" (*emotionale Funktion*). In addition, values are not experienced in a merely indistinct manner for there is a specific intuition of their hierarchy that depends on two other emotional acts, preference and repugnance (*Abscheu*) (this is not a matter of an empirical preference that relies on mere taste or idiosyncrasy, but of a "pure" preference attached only to values—a preference, for example, for beauty over the sacred, etc.). At a higher level than these acts of preference/repugnance is the level of love and hate (*Liebe*, *Haß*). Love guides and precedes actions of preference and repugnance. When one loves a person, one sees in that person qualities that reveal themselves little by little, by virtue of the love that one devotes to him or her. These acts of love and hate delimit the field of values accessible to a subject. The fact that a person strikes us as sympathetic (*sympatisch*)—or antipathetic—from the start shows that value presents itself independent of direct

3
Werturteilstreit: Value and interest

The controversy over "value judgments" that emerges at the turn of the twentieth century in Vienna with Carnap's positivistic reaction to the philosophy of values breaks out again at the end of the 1960s between Adorno and Karl Popper. In the later instance it takes the form of a dispute among a (European) continental movement, the Frankfurt school, and critical positivism (of Viennese inspiration). Aside from the political affiliations that set partisans of "revolution" (those committed to Marxism in its revised iterations) against those who adhere to an empirical and liberal "reformism," the conflict's stakes concern the methodological grounding of the social sciences. The adversaries of hermeneutics (in its broadest sense) contest, as always, any possibility of articulating utterances that apply to being.

They disqualify any ought-to-be as a naturalist fallacy, insisting that one cannot derive *ought* from *is*. To support this position they rely on Hume's *Treatise on Human Nature*, III, i.1. The defenders of the Frankfurt school, for their part, claim that the scientific status of the human sciences should be recognized and not rejected out of hand on the basis of criteria that apply only to the domains of the "empirico-analytic" sciences (mathematics, physics, biology). J. Habermas (cf. *Knowledge and Human Interests* and *Technology and Science as "Ideology"*) has echoed this controversy by attempting to substitute the notion of *interest* (Ger. *Interesse*) for the notion of value. He treats interest as a kind of anthropological invariant: to *homo faber* there corresponds a "technical" interest derived from work and

support, yet not without "material." What this means is that we cannot confuse values with goods (*Werte* with *Güter*). Values are extratemporal essences that can be grasped though emotional intuition. Nor can one confuse values with goals or purposes (*Zwecke* with *Ziele*). The goal is an intellectual representation of a real good, and it is based on an end that is entirely independent of a representation or intellectual act. The end consists of the expression of a value and an image of this value. Values are thus independent of ends, and these in turn are independent of goals. Values (as in the case of altruism) establish ends (as in the case of helping one's neighbor) that are in turn the basis for goals (for example, creating a neighborhood aid association).

Since values depend on an emotional act, it follows that they become in some sense imbued with history (the histories of the subject and of various collectivities—sociopolitical, cultural, and religious—at the heart of which this subject is to be found). This historical condition reopens the question of how to establish their validity (*Geltung*) and their "valuability" (*Gültigkeit*):

> It is therefore also possible that certain moral value-qualities will be comprehended for the first time in history, and that they will appear first, for example, in the feeling insight of a *single individual*. The evidential comprehension of such a quality and the fact that it represents a value higher than all those [values] known up to this point have nothing to do with the universality . . . of this comprehensibility or with the so-called "*universal validity*" of norms [*Normen*]. But it is necessary to distinguish three things: first, the factual *universal possession of dispositions to comprehend* certain values; second, what is morally valid [*gilt*] for a given group of people . . . ; third, those values whose recognition is universally "valid" [*gültig*] no

to which the empirico-analytic sciences adhere; to *Homo loquax*, a "practical" interest, derived from language, which becomes a principle of the historico-hermeneutic sciences. In early Habermas there is also the concept of "emancipatory" (*emanzipatorisch*) interest derived from the impulse to strive for freedom against the constraints of nature, as well as distinct sociopolitical forms of coercion that have preoccupied the "critical sciences" (ideology critique, psychoanalysis, etc.).

BIBLIOGRAPHY

Habermas, Jurgen. *Technik und Wissenschaft als "Ideologie."* Frankfurt am Main: Suhrkamp, 1968. Translation by J. Shapiro: "Technology and Science as 'Ideology.'" In *Toward a Rational Society*. Boston: Beacon Press, 1977.

matter if they are factually "universally valid" [*geltend*] or not.

> (Scheler, *Formalism in Ethics*, 273)

■ See Box 3.

Marc de Launay

BIBLIOGRAPHY

Albert, Hans, and Ernst Toptisch. *Werturteilstreit*. Darmstadt, Ger.: Wissenschaftliche Buchgesellschaft, 1969.

Aron, Raymond. *Introduction to the Philosophy of History: An Essay on the Limits of Historical Objectivity*. Translated by George J. Irwin. Boston: Beacon Press, 1961.

———. *La Philosophie critique de l'histoire: essai sur une théorie allemande de l'histoire*. Paris: Vrin, 1969.

Blosser, Philip. *Scheler's Critique of Kant's Ethics*. Athens: Ohio University Press, 1995.

Cohen, Hermann, Paul Natorp, Ernst Cassirer, Heinrich Rickert, Wilhelm Windelband, Emil Lask, and Jonas Cohn. *Néokantismes et théorie de la connaissance*. Paris: Vrin, 2000.

Heidegger, Martin. *Gesamtausgabe*. Frankfurt: Klostermann, 1987.

———. *Towards the Definition of Philosophy*. London: Athlone Press, 1998.

Lotze, Hermann. *Logik*. Edited by G. Gabriel. Hamburg: Felix Meiner, 1989. *Logic, in Three Books, of Thought, of Investigation, and of Knowledge*. Edited by Bernard Bosanquet. Oxford: Clarendon Press, 1888.

Nietzsche, Friedrich. *Genealogy of Morals*. Translated by Douglas Smith. Oxford: Oxford University Press, 1996.

———. *Nietzsche Briefwechsel, Kritische Gesamtausgabe*. Berlin: De Gruyter, 1975–.

———. *Werke, Kritische Gesamtausgabe*. Berlin: De Gruyter, 1967.

Rickert, Heinrich. *Der Gegenstand der Erkenntnis*. Tübingen: Mohr, 1927.

Scheler, Max. *Formalism in Ethics and Non-Formal Ethics of Values: A New Attempt toward the Foundation of an Ethical Personalism*. Translated by Manfred S. Frings and Roger L. Funk. 5th rev. ed. Evanston, IL: Northwestern University Press, 1973.

Schmitt, Carl. "Die Tyrannei der Werte." In *Säkularisation und Utopie*. Stuttgart: Kohlhammer, 1967.

Windelband, Wilhelm. *Beiträge zur Lehre vom negativen Urteil*. Tübingen: Mohr, 1921. First published in 1884.

WHIG, TORY

FRENCH   *libéral/conservateur*

➤ LIBERAL, and CIVIL SOCIETY, LAW, LEX, *LIBERTY*, POLITICS

The terms "Whig" and "Tory" have been conventionally used, respectively, to designate liberal and conservative tendencies in British politics (before the rise of the Labor Party at the end of the nineteenth century, which resulted in a change to previous political divisions). But these words possess a meaning at the same time more general and very English, which distinguishes them from the French terms *libéral* and *conservateur*. A Whig is not simply a liberal, but also a self-conscious heir to the English constitutional tradition, to the Rule of Law, and to the rights of Parliament. Likewise, a Tory is a conservative attached to certain kinds of social relations in which the authority of the aristocracy (Fr. *notables*) cannot be separated from its protectionist role. Such relations are bound to a specific interpretation of Anglican religious tradition. In addition to these political divisions, one can also speak of a Whig manner of writing political or intellectual history, or of the Tory legacy in the political doctrines of the nineteenth and twentieth centuries. After reviewing selected moments in the historical development of the Whig/Tory opposition, we will examine the central role that these two notions play in Hume's writings and their general impact on English-language political philosophy. We will conclude with some reflections on the status of these terms as untranslatables of British political thought, with special reference to their influence on Enlightenment notions of liberty and their role as political terms in colonial America.

I. "Whig" and "Tory" in English Politics

The historical origins of the words "Whig" and "Tory" are disputed, but the context in which they gained currency is well known, as are the negative meanings they initially carried. The adjectives "whig" and "tory" appeared during the emergence of the modern English political system, and their use became widespread during the crisis that resulted from the attempts of radical Protestants to exclude James of York (the future James II) from ascending to the British throne because of his Catholic and French sympathies. The adjective "whig" had already been used during the English Civil War in reference to Cromwell's Scottish partisans. A pejorative term of Gaelic origin, it referred, according to its most likely etymology, to thieves of horse and cattle. It also connoted attachment to the Presbyterian form of Protestantism and, by implication, to a penchant for rebellion. The term was applied to those whose antipapist convictions led them to advocate passing over the legitimate heir to the throne. The term "tory" was originally no less insulting since it referred to the Catholic rebels (the Irish "papist bandits") and was applied to those who defended the rights and claims of James. His accession to the throne in 1685 was followed by the Glorious Revolution of 1688, which removed him from the throne and replaced him with William of Orange, thus bringing about a redefinition of partisan differences. Most of the Tories abandoned their defense of absolutist doctrines and to some extent accepted the Whig interpretation of the British political system as a limited monarchy. But they remained attached to the notion of royal prerogative (which allows the monarch under certain circumstances to go against the laws of Parliament) and to all those parts of the English political

system that upheld traditional hierarchies. Tory became the party of the High Church and the provincial nobility, while Whig came to represent the more dynamic factions of the aristocracy allied with the middle classes to constitute a new dominant class, all the while relying on the support of the sensibilities of the most liberal currents of English Protestantism. The death of Queen Anne (1714) and the accession of George I to the throne marked the final ruin of the Stuarts and entailed the exile or discredit of those Tories who had remained faithful to them (the Jacobites). A long period of Whig supremacy in English politics ensued, a period in which Toryism was more of a sensibility than a true party (despite the presence of close to one hundred deputies in the House of Commons who identified themselves as Tories). The division Whig/Tory regained its importance at the end of the eighteenth century when William Pitt the Younger became the leader of a new Tory party, supported by both the gentry and the commercial classes. This led to the appearance of new Whigs with more progressive opinions who, under James Fox, set themselves up as the defenders of religious freedom and as advocates of various reforms of a quasi-democratic nature. The French Revolution provoked a rupture within the Whigs that was epitomized by the break between Edmund Burke and James Fox. While the English liberals siding with Fox saw the acts of the constitutional convention as the application of the principles of the Glorious Revolution (and as a way to inflect the English constitution in a more liberal direction), Burke saw the French Revolution as a radical subversion of tradition, and thus as something entirely hostile to Whig politics (which up until that point had been part of the continuous development of English freedoms). The conflict between England and revolutionary France led to a *rapprochement* of the more moderate Whigs and the new Tories around Pitt. What was left of the revolutionary heritage of the Whigs became absorbed into a new democratic culture that came in the wake of the French Revolution. After 1815 English politics increasingly took the bipartisan form with which we are familiar and which became dominant in the nineteenth century by virtue of the opposition between the liberal and conservative parties. These parties can legitimately be called the heirs of the Whigs and Tories (indeed the name "Tory" has remained in use for a long time to designate the conservative party).

II. "Court" and "Country"

The history of English politics cannot be completely accounted for by the story of the opposition between Whigs and Tories. Nor can the meanings of those two terms be reduced to a simple partisan division (just as the opposition between right and left in France can no more easily be reduced to the two sides of the parliamentary chamber). The long period of Whig supremacy, from 1714 to 1760, was in fact a period of fundamental transformation in the English political system, culminating in the Walpole ministry (1721–42). Intense controversies divided the Whiggery, many of them informed by Tory thinkers whose position could not be reduced to the simple defense of hierarchies. The Whig supremacy was in fact inseparable from the rise of a new figure, the prime minister, whose task it was to establish his position between the Houses of Parliament and the king. He could accomplish this task only by winning the support of part of the assemblies, while at the same time presenting himself as the agent of the crown. The simplest means of playing this game was to buy the support of members of parliament in various ways, ranging from corruption pure and simple to the creation and distribution of positions for the defenders of the ministers of the king. Since this form of politics, carried out with virtuosity by Walpole, was accompanied by a stable and relatively small oligarchy, relying on complex electoral laws that bypassed the older gentry, it is understandable that the system seemed to certain Whigs to be a betrayal of their principles. Walpole Whiggery thus helped revive an older Whig/Tory tension between the party of Country or Commonwealth, and the party of the Court. During Stuart times, the defenders of the rights of Parliament against the "papist" attempts at the subversion of the English Constitution were often called the Country Party, and its influence at the court was condemned. The same opposition made it possible to denounce the power of the executive "wielding two great instruments of corruption, of which the first was parliamentary patronage and the second public credit" (Pocock, *Virtue, Commerce, and History*). But even this argument can be subject to Whig or Tory interpretation, and it plays a central role both before and after the birth of liberal politics in England.

The Whig version of the "Country problem" redounded to the Old Whigs, who denounced Walpole's politics as a betrayal of the ideals of the Glorious Revolution. They rejected the foreign policy of the new oligarchy, which was favorable to a politics of peace, supporting an alliance with absolutist, Catholic France. John Trenchard and Thomas Gordon were the most well-known representatives of these new Old Whigs. Their text, *Cato's Letters*, published between 1720 and 1723, emerged as the classic expression of a sensibility imbued with civic humanism. At once liberal and republican, they cast civic virtue—always threatened by corruption—as the only sure guarantor of liberty.

The Tory version of this position found its best defender in the person of Henry Bolingbroke (1678–1751), who, after describing the decrepitude of the old parties of Great Britain (*A Dissertation upon Parties*), defended the idea that under these circumstances only a "patriot king" could overcome the divisions between parties and restore to the country the rights usurped by the ministers and the oligarchs (*The Idea of the Patriot King*).

These thinkers contributed to a current of civic humanism inaugurated by Machiavelli and taken up in England by James Harrington. It ranged across diverse political, social, and even religious contexts: the Deist Bolingbroke, for example, was the ally of writers and apologists for the High Church, and even of papists such as Atterbury and Pope. Meanwhile the Country party was supported both by the urban middle classes and the rural gentry (on all of these points, see Pocock, *Virtue, Commerce, and History*). The opposition between court and country thus transcended the traditional divisions between Whigs and Tories. It became a sign of the difficulties encountered by the new liberal world in asserting itself in the face of older republican ideals, themselves weakened by the crisis of absolutism and religious tradition.

Hume's work is important here, because it illustrates a deliberate choice in favor of the emerging liberal society (and the abandonment of republican models founded solely on virtue). Hume gave new meaning to the split between Whig and Tory despite his criticism of the unilateral quality of the doctrines defended by each of the two parties.

III. Hume's Synthesis

In his *Essays*, as in his *History of England*, Hume showed himself to be equally distant from Whig orthodoxy as from the traditional prejudices of the Tories. If he were indulgent toward the Stuarts and critical of English Protestantism, and only too aware that the "old English Constitution" was in many respects similar to those of the continental monarchies, he nonetheless appreciated the merits of the English political system, seeing it as favorable to liberty and to the development of the sciences. In the same spirit, he attempted to define a philosophical position midway between the "whig" principle of an original contract (that cannot account for the nature of political association), and the "tory" principle of passive obedience (which is incompatible with the interests of society properly understood). This impartiality is itself founded on an original interpretation of the English system: for Hume, the divisions between the "parties of Great Britain" derived from an internal dualism of the English Constitution, which combined monarchical and republican features and thus naturally produced (even as it limited) partisan division. The opposition between Whigs and Tories becomes, then, part of a sequence that starts with the Cavaliers and the Roundheads during the Civil War and leads to the divisions in Hume's time between a party of the court and a party of the nation. This opposition does not in and of itself undermine the system, because it rests on a compromise acceptable to both parties on the basics of the system in question:

> A Tory . . . may be defined in a few words, to be a lover of monarchy, though without abandoning liberty; and a partisan of the family of STUART. As a Whig may be defined to be a lover of liberty though not without renouncing monarchy; and a friend to the settlement in the PROTESTANT line.
>
> (Hume, *Political Essays*)

The opposition between the two parties took on new and somewhat confused meaning after the Revolution of 1688: just as the Whigs had often "proceeded with measures that could become dangerous for liberty" in order to better assure the Protestant succession, the Tories were led to oppose the Crown and to act like republicans after the change in dynasty. In addition, the development of the English regime (which translates into a certain predominance of the principle of liberty) is more favorable to Whig philosophy, as is evident in the decline of the Tories, even after they had abandoned their most shocking doctrines (like that of passive obedience).

IV. The Future of an Opposition

The central importance of the English system in the formation of liberal politics has been such that the opposed terms of "Whig" and "Tory," along with their different connotations, have been recognized and faithfully duplicated everywhere that there has been interest in the British experience.

The transformations of the British system since the end of the eighteenth century have, of course, modified the content of the notions of Whig and Tory. There is no longer room in the parliamentary government for a party that would support an active intervention by the monarch in the legislative process, and the executive power itself must remain in the hands of the prime minister at any given time. Even though one currently speaks more often of liberals and conservatives, the terms "Whig" and "Tory" have nonetheless been of use in interpreting new divisions in the traditional terms of English politics. One can call liberals with advanced and reformist ideas Whigs who are open to social reforms without being socialists properly speaking (in this sense, there was something "whiggish" about the New Labor party of Tony Blair). And "Tory" is a term with multiple meanings, suggesting a ruling class that is both guardian of tradition and protector of the weak, while remaining open to audacity and modernity. In literature, Coleridge's (1772–1834) romanticism tacks Tory, even if it includes radical elements. In the politics of the nineteenth century, the great man of the Tories was Benjamin Disraeli (1804–1881), who embodied a conservatism that both favored popular interests and supported the greatness of empire.

Beyond the play of politics and partisanship, the opposition between "Whig" and "Tory" (and the dissymmetry between the two notions) plays a certain role in the ways that political thought is framed in the English language. Political movements are classified according to distinctions whose origins lie in the English system of partisanship (liberal or conservative), and one often encounters in the best authors the idea that proper politics requires that there be a party of order and tradition and a party of progress and reform, and that their coexistence is a condition of a free political regime (see, for example, John Stuart Mill, *On Liberty*, chap. 2). The influence of Whig and Tory as modes of interpretation has been greatest on historical schools of thought. The dominant vision of English history (which stresses the continuity of English liberties since the mythical times of the "old constitution," and which sets up the limited monarchy of Great Britain and the Revolution of 1688 against absolute monarchy and the French Revolution) can be described as fundamentally Whig: it has inspired great historians, the most brilliant of whom is undoubtedly Thomas Macaulay (1800–1859). More generally, one can speak of a "whig interpretation of history," in the words of Herbert Butterfield, in reference to a history written from the point of view of the progress of the human spirit, which looks to the past for traces of the conflict between progressives and reactionaries in order to bring out the stages in that emancipation. In this sense, Whiggism is simply the English version of Enlightenment philosophy, which culminates in an interpretation of history whose continental equivalents could easily be found among authors such as Lessing or Condorcet. One should not be surprised to see that the endpoint of the Whig interpretation of history approximates versions of bourgeois progressivism. Marxism is both faithful to it (in its emphasis on the compatibility between political liberty and the interests of both the middle class and the market economy)

and unfaithful to it (in its critique of formal liberties). Contemporary authors tend to treat the ethnocentric character of Whig history with indulgent humor. In this spirit, J.G.A. Pocock, who has elucidated the subtleties of English politics better than anyone, estimates that there is no such thing as a pure Whig historian because his or her relation to the political paradigms holding sway in society is always a mixture of conservative and radical.

V. Translating "Whig" and "Tory" in France and the American Colonies

The terms "Whig" and "Tory" emerge as such quintessentially local terms for British politics that they stand as premier examples of national untranslatables. In France, one does not find the terms adopted in English very often, but their influence on definitions of liberty can be clearly discerned. Consider, for example, Voltaire's *Lettres philosophiques* (1734), which played a central role in France in the "invention" of English liberty as an alternative to the French regime. Despite what one might expect, Voltaire espoused an interpretation of the English regime that was not unlike Bolingbroke's, and thus rather clearly tory (see letter 8, in which he analyzes the sharing of power between parliament, the arbiter of the nation, and the umpire king). In *The Spirit of the Laws* (1748) Montesquieu hews closer to the classical whig theses, all the while showing in-depth how English liberty differs from that of the republics of antiquity. The Old Whigs, such as Trenchard and Gordon, had their own followers in France, where their implacable anti-Catholicism led the Baron d'Holbach to translate some of their writings. But it was arguably in America that whig politics came to have a truly creative influence on posterity, coming into its own as a political "translation" despite the fact that the English language remained the same. In the pre-Revolutionary period, the English colonies in America provided a highly receptive context for the republican problematic of the Old Whigs. As a consequence, their influence was determinative on the first phase of the Revolution (Bailyn, *The Ideological Origins of the American Revolution*; Pocock, *The Machiavellian Moment*) The epithet "Tory" was applied pejoratively to loyalists faithful to the British Crown, and, as a result, one of the great American parties adopted the name "Whig" before later becoming the Republican party of Lincoln.

Philippe Raynaud

BIBLIOGRAPHY

Bailyn, Bernard. *The Ideological Origins of the American Revolution*. 2nd ed. Cambridge, MA: Harvard University Press, 1992.

Bolingbroke, Henry Saint John. *Works*. 5 vols. Hildesheim, Ger.: Olms, 1968. First published in 1754.

Butterfield, Herbert. *The Whig Interpretation of History*. New York: Scribner's Sons, 1931.

Hume, David. *A History of England: From the Earliest Times to the Revolution in 1688*. New York: Harper & Brothers, 1878. First published in 1859.

———. *Political Essays*. Edited by Knud Haakonssen. Cambridge: Cambridge University Press, 1994.

Macaulay, Thomas Babington. *History of England from the Accession of James II*. 5 vols. New York: Dutton, 1953. First published 1848–61.

Mill, John Stuart. *On Liberty; with The Subjection of Women; and Chapters on Socialism*. Edited by Stefan Collini. Cambridge: Cambridge University Press, 1989.

Pocock, J.G.A. *The Machiavellian Moment: Florentine Political Thought and the Atlantic Republican Tradition*. Reprint. Princeton, NJ: Princeton University Press, 2003. First published in 1975.

———. *Politics, Language and Time: Essays on Political Thought and History*. Chicago: University of Chicago Press, 1989.

———. *Virtue, Commerce, and History: Essays on Political Thought and History, Chiefly in the Eighteenth Century*. Cambridge: Cambridge University Press, 1985.

Trenchard, John, and Thomas Gordon. *Cato's Letters or Essays on Liberty, Civil and Religious, and Other Important Subjects*. 4 vols. Indianapolis: Liberty Fund, 1995. First published 1720–23.

WHOLE

The French *tout* derives from the Latin *totus*, and applies to the object considered in relation to its extension and in its entirety, in the sense of *tout entier* (as a whole). Like *totus* on occasion, *tout* can be used in the distributive sense, in the sense of *chaque* (each), even though *omnis* has taken on that specialized function in Latin. The Greek language also has two ways of expressing the whole, *pas* [πᾶς] and *holos* [ὅλος], to which *omnis* and *totus* do not precisely correspond. *To holon* [τὸ ὅλον] like "the whole" in English, designates the integral and complete whole, but as something more than or other than just the sum of its parts: see WELT, Box 2.

The medieval Latin *totalis* (Nicole Oresme) refers to that which is complete, not lacking in anything, and thus opens the way to the translation of *to holon* as "totality." Totality (Ger. *Ganzheit*, *Gesamtheit*, *Allheit*, *Totalität*) is one of Kant's twelve categories and establishes the synthesis of unity and multiplicity: cf. *CATEGORY*, *JUSTICE*.

For the relationship among the words "world," "universe," and the "totality of the real," see WELT and OMNITUDO REALITATIS; see also MIR, NATURE, REALITY, SVET; cf. GOD.

On ways to think and express totality, see AUFHEBEN, COMBINATION AND CONCEPTUALIZATION, *CONCEPT*, HISTORIA UNIVERSALIS, MEMORY, STRUCTURE, UNIVERSALS.

➤ COMMUNITY, HUMANITY, SOCIETY

WILL

FRENCH *volonté*
GREEK   *thelêsis* [θέλησις], *orexis* [ὄρεξις], *boulêsis* [βούλησις]
LATIN   *appetitus, voluntas*

➤ AGENCY, *DESIRE*, HERRSCHAFT, I/ME/MYSELF, INTELLECTUS, INTENTION, LAW, *LIBERTY*, LOGOS, OBJECT, PATHOS, PHRONÊSIS, *REASON*, SUBJECT, SVOBODA, WILLKÜR

"Philosophers," wrote Nietzsche in *Beyond Good and Evil*, "are accustomed to speaking of the will as if it were the best-known thing in the world." But "the Historian cannot forget that it took mankind some eleven centuries of reflection after Aristotle to invent 'the will'" (R. A. Gauthier). How did this lexical and philosophical invention occur, with its considerable implications for medieval and modern thought?

I. The Medieval Invention of a Third Faculty: *"Thelêsis sive Voluntas"*

In an attempt to answer this question, one should start by taking the finished concept of will and examining its provenance. In *De fide orthodoxa*, John of Damascus gives a definition of *thelêsis* [θέλησις], which is translated as *voluntas* by Burgundio of Pisa and will subsequently serve to frame all of medieval thought on the will: the *thelêma*, or will, "is an appetite, both rational and vital, depending only on what is natural" (*De fide orthodoxa*, 2.22). Burgundio makes a choice of translation that will become an essential one and renders *thelêsis* by *voluntas*: "thelêsis, sive voluntas, est naturalis et vitalis et rationalis appetitus" (*thelêsis*, or will, is a natural, vital, and rational appetite). This definition will be taken up by medieval authors and become the authoritative version for Scholasticism: John of la Rochelle, Saint Bonaventure, and Thomas Aquinas will in turn define *voluntas* as an essentially rational appetite that naturally tends toward the Good. In this respect, will differs both from desire (*orexis* [ὄρεξις]) and from reason (*logos* [λόγος]), and designates a third faculty, an intermediate between the other two. Such a faculty was entirely lacking for the Greeks, as the German philologist Bruno Snell underscores:

> But the will, ever straining and champing at the bit, is a notion foreign to the Greeks; they do not even have a word for it. *Thelein* means "to be ready, to be prepared for something." *Boulesthai* is "to view something as (more) desirable." The former denotes a subjective preparedness, a kind of voluntary attitude devoid of specific commitment; the latter refers to a wish or plan (*boulê*) aimed at a particular object, i.e. a disposition closely related to the understanding and appreciation of a gain. But neither word expresses a realization of the will, the effective inclination of subject toward object.

(*The Discovery of the Mind*)

We should add the word *orexis* to this list, which refers to desire in its broadest sense, as well as the term coined by Aristotle to designate that state of mind that immediately precedes action: *proairesis* [προαίρεσις], "deliberate choice." None of these notions can be directly understood in terms of the medieval and modern concepts of *voluntas*.

But how does this concept emerge? What justifies its adoption? In which philosophical or theological context is it to be understood?

II. The Absence of a Problematics of Will in Aristotle and the Stoicism of Antiquity

The lack of an equivalent concept of will in ancient Greek thought can be established through a few examples. In Aristotle, the act of making a deliberate choice (*proairesis*) is not an indication of a power of self-determination analogous to the will, but refers to a judgment of the practical intellect that starts from a wish or recognition of a desired end (*boulêsis* [βούλησις]) and carries out a process of deliberation (*bouleusis* [βούλευσις]). It is a rational calculation of the means to achieve the end. Thus the choice itself is an act of the *nous* [νοῦς], which selects the means to that end, according to a rational process that yields a practical syllogism (*On the Movement of Animals*, 6.700b23). Many a misunderstanding has resulted from the translation of this doctrine in terms of will. Thus Thomas Aquinas, thinking he was following Aristotle, fixes on the *electio*, which chooses a modality of *voluntas* whose objective is its end. The same applies to the point of departure, the *boulêsis* or wish. Aristotle defines it as a desire penetrated by reason (*logistikê orexis* [λογιστικὴ ὄρεξις]) (*Rhetorics*, 1.10.1369a2), suggesting that what we have here is a precursor of *voluntas* or a quintessentially rational form of desire. This argument, however, is misleading, for *boulêsis* designates a modality of desire "accidentally" subject to reason; as a result, it can diverge from reason. One can always wish for the impossible, affirms Aristotle (*Nicomachean Ethics*, 3.2.1111b22: *boulêsis d' esti <kai> tôn adunatôn* [βούλησις δ' ἐστὶ <καὶ> τῶν ἀδυνάτων]). Here, it becomes apparent, we are as far as it gets from the medieval and modern concept of the will.

Similar problems arise in relation to the understanding and interpretation of one of the central concepts of Stoicism in antiquity: the accordance of assent (*sugkatathesis* [συγκατάθεσις]). Giving assent is an act of reason (*logos*), the basis for establishing a radical difference between human and animal. In the animal, as soon as the presentation occurs (*phantasia* [φαντασία]), the impulse to act (*hormê* [ὁρμή]) immediately follows. But in human being, reason (*logos*) must give its assent to the presentation for the impulse to follow, and freedom resides in this assent, as a judgment applied to a presentation, as the privileged role of reason. So assent is not a property of the will, but of judgment alone. At this point one can see the distortion that results from the imposition of the vocabulary of *voluntas* on the doctrine of *sugkatathesis*: "to these presentations which are accepted by the senses, so to speak, he [Zeno] adds the assent of the soul, which he considers up to us and voluntary [*in nobis positam et voluntariam*]" (Cicero, *Academica posteriora*, 1.11.40–42). Similarly, the central idea of Stoicism in antiquity, "that which is up to us" (*eph' hêmin* [ἔφ' ἡμῖν]), constitutes the very idea of moral responsibility, which is expressed from Seneca on in terms of will: anger depends on us, which is to say it is voluntary, insofar as we assent to it. We give in to anger of our own volition, and thus we are responsible for it ("*est enim voluntarium animi vitium*") (*De ira*, 2.2.2).

Of course, one could still inquire into the notion of *logikê hormê* [λογικὴ ὁρμή] in ancient Stoicism: doesn't this rational impulse of man, set into motion by assent, prefigure the will as *appetitus rationalis*? In other words, by making reason itself into an "active" faculty, didn't the Stoics come very close to the later notion of *voluntas*? Yet to be able to properly discuss the will, one must presuppose the existence of a faculty of the soul "distinct" from thought (*dianoia* [διάνοια]), from the intellect (*nous*), and from reason (*logos*), an autonomous and independent faculty that can on occasion be in opposition to reason and elect to go against it—which specifically excludes the psychological monism of Chrysippus, according to whom the human soul is not made of parts, but consists entirely of *logos*. As a result, nothing can assume the role of "will" as an independent faculty.

Things would change somewhat in the middle phase of Stoicism, which abandoned the thesis of the unity of the soul. In fact, the main innovation of Panaetius was to dissociate the rational part (*logikê* [λογική]) of the soul from the impulse (*hormê*), which would become in both human and animal an irrational drive. This *hormê* no longer fundamentally differs from Aristotle's desire (*orexis*), which will be translated into

Latin as *appetitus*. The immediate principle of action, for Panaetius, is thus not assent, insofar as it determines the logical impulse (*logikê hormê*), but rather this irrational impulse, which simply follows assent. This impulse has the specific feature of being, like *voluntas*, independent of reason. But insofar as it follows from assent, it still finds its source of freedom in the judgment of reason, and it is thus neither free in and of itself nor rational in essence. It remains to interrogate the notion of *thelêsis* [θέλησις] in Epictetus: the word appears frequently in his work, along with the verb *thelein* [θέλειν], and is largely synonymous with *boulesthai* [βούλεσθαι], to the point that one can agree with Voelke's claim that "no other Stoic writing in Greek uses these verbs as frequently" (*L'idée de volonté dans l'ancien stoïcisme*). For example, Epictetus affirms that the single criterion of wisdom consists in the following: "Be willing at length to be approved by yourself (*thelêson aresai autos pote seautôi* [θέλησον ἀρέσαι αὐτός ποτε σεαυτῷ])," which is to say, "be willing to appear beautiful to God (*thelêson kalos phanêtai tôi theôi* [θέλησον καλὸς φανῆται τῷ θεῷ])" (*Discourses*, 2.18, Long trans.). Yet Voelke is forced to admit that "the will in Epictetus does not have a clearly defined and specific function" (*L'idée de volonté dans l'ancien stoïcisme*). In addition, for Epictetus, as for the Stoics of antiquity, there is no such thing as an independent notion of free will, for freedom is a determination of judgment, and is consequently completely intellectual. Epictetus even goes so far as to claim that "the soul of man is nothing else aside from his judgments" [ἀνθρώπου ψυχὴν οὐδὲν ἄλλο ἢ δόγματα] (*Discourses*, 4.5.26).

III. The Christian Problematic of the Will: Saint Augustine

Should one look then to the Christian tradition of the church fathers for the first appearance of the concept of "will" in its modern sense? Should one follow Hannah Arendt and see in Saint Augustine the "first philosopher of the will"? Nothing is less certain.

Just as one could speak of a "Roman voluntarism" (Pohlenz, *Die Stoa*, I) one could speak of Augustine's "voluntarism" since all activities, including perception and cognitive activity in general, are for him imbued with will. In order to see, he maintains, one must want to see, which is to say that the sensory organ of vision fixes upon a visible object through attention. This is also the case for rational knowledge: in this respect there is not a single motion of the soul that is not engendered by the will: "*voluntas est animi motus*" (*De duabus animabus*, 10.14). So can one still speak of a "primacy of the will" in Augustine, as is the case, for example, in Duns Scotus or Descartes? Undoubtedly not, insofar as the will for Augustine is not a distinct faculty independent of desire in general and love in particular: "*voluntatem nostram, vel amorem seu dilectionem quae valentior est volunta*" (our own will, or love, or affection, which is a stronger will) (*De Trinitate*, 15.21.41, Haddan trans.). Love, or the affection by which the soul takes joy and rejoices in God (*fruitio*), is only the will in all its power, which means that inversely, will is a weaker form of love or desire. This is why Augustine can compare love to the weight that strains the will and impels it toward its object, just as weight drags down bodies toward the center of the earth: "My love is my weight: wherever I go my love is what brings me there" (Augustine, *Confessions*, book 13, 9, 10). And since the notion of affection is indissociable from the notion of love, one could also say that "*delectatio quasi pondus est animae*" (*De musica*, 6.11.29); such an affection is the union of the heart and its object, according to the saying of Matthew the Evangelist that Augustine likes to quote: "*ubi enim erit thesaurus tuus ibi erit et cor tuum*" (6.21). Thus will is not an abstract faculty, indeterminate as to its object, but is essentially determined as love by its *dilectio Dei*. It is love itself reaching toward God to rejoice, and reaching to the things of creation only to use them from the point of view of God himself. In that sense, sin does not stem from the will's desire for evil, since evil is nothing, but results from inverting the hierarchy of goods by "enjoying" the things of creation rather than simply *using* them in relation to the supreme and uncreated good, God himself. Thus for Augustine the will is only this capacity to be open to God and to take joy in him, to attain that point through love and beatitude where God fills the soul and leaves no room for anything else. This is why all precepts and commandments come down to a single one: to desire God, to join with him passionately, in other words to love him; any act that comes from this love of God is necessarily and infallibly good. Everything comes down to love: "*Dilige, et quod vis fac*" (love, and then what you will, do; *In Epistulam Johannis ad Parthos*, 7.8).

It is true that for Augustine, will is the deepest of the three human faculties. It puts memory and intellect to work and ultimately "unites them one to another," since it is thanks to the will that "these three elements are united [*coguntur*] in a single whole, and this union [*coactus*] endows that whole with the name of thought [*cogitatio*]" (*De Trinitate*, 10.2.6). But if the will is the deepest faculty of the soul, and since the fact that it unites the two others gives it its real name (Augustine derives *cogitatio* from *cogere*, "to collect or compress with force"), this is only because love holds them together. Since love is the universal bond, those united by love, writes Augustine, are "strangely wedded together by the bond of love" (*cohaerunt enim mirabiliter glutino amoris*) (10.8.20). And thus love, the true bond, is the best and proper name for the will.

It is difficult to see how this Augustinian doctrine of the will would prefigure a finished concept of the will as an essentially rational appetite (differing in this regard from the Thomistic problematic). Complicating things further is the fact that Augustine is also taken to be the "inventor" of the problematic of free will. He writes: "*nihil tam in nostra potestate quam ipsa voluntas est*" (nothing is so much under our control than the very will itself), which allows him to conclude that "because it is within our power, it is free for us" (*De libero arbitrio*, 3.3.27). It is this doctrine of free will that will have the greatest philosophical traction, along with the problem of the reconciliation of free will and grace. Yet here too, we should stress Augustine's originality in relation to the Scholastic treatments of will. For the free will is nothing without freedom, that is to say, without restoring the integrity of the will divided against itself by sin (*Confessions*, 8.9.21), a restoration of integrity that results from grace. This unity of the will with itself, which results in the will not only wishing for the good but also being capable of effectively achieving the good, is none other, once again, than love. Only love frees. Only love confers integrity on the will rendered impotent by sin, and gives it its strength, its permanence,

and its "rest" (*De Trinitate*, 11.5.9). True freedom is thus none other than love itself.

IV. The Emergence of the "Completed" Concept of Will and the Controversy of Monothelism

If the concept of will in Saint Augustine still remains largely indeterminate (will "deserves the name of love, of concupiscence, of passion"; *De Trinitate*, 11.2.5) or underdetermined in relation to its "completed" version in Scholasticism—one could also say that it is overdetermined since the will for Augustine is but a modality of love. This leaves unanswered a number of questions that we are addressing: where does the canonical determination of the will as "*appetitio rationalis sive intellectualis*" make its first appearance? As part of what philosophical or theological debate? Within which intellectual context does the concept (which has since become classic) of the will as an autonomous faculty, equally independent of desire and the intellect, first emerge and find form?

In our attempt to answer such questions, we need to return to our point of departure. We had found in John of Damascus a first instance of the concept of the will that will become the classical notion from the twelfth and thirteenth centuries on, reaching Descartes, Malebranche, and Leibniz virtually unchanged. In fact, along with this canonical definition of the will, a definition of free will emerged (*autexousion* [αὐτεξούσιον]), traceable to John of Damascus and accorded an extended afterlife:

> In the case of creatures without reason, as soon as appetite [*orexis* (ὄρεξις)] is aroused for something, straightway there arises an impulse [*hormê* (ὁρμή)] to action. For irrationality is the tendency of creatures without reason who are ruled by their natural appetites [*phusikê orexis* (φυσικὴ ὄρεξις)]. Hence, neither the names of *thelêsis* nor *boulêsis* are applicable to the appetite of creatures without reason. For *thelêsis* is rational, free, and natural desire, and in the case of man, the natural appetite is under his rule [*autexousiôs* (αὐτεξουσίως)].

> John of Damascus, *De fide orthodoxa*, 945 b–f

The Latin translator Burgundio of Pisa will in fact translate *autexousiôs* as "free will." However, we still need to take further philological and historical steps if we are to understand the provenance of this concept of "will," and determine whether John of Damascus might himself have received his definition from elsewhere. Here it is compelling to follow the hypothesis put forward by R.-A. Gauthier in a relevant article ("Saint Maxime Confesseur et la psychologie de l'acte humain") that demonstrates how John of Damascus found direct and literal inspiration for his definitions from an author of the seventh century, Maximus the Confessor, specifically from his two texts *Dispute with Pyrrhus* (645) and the first *Letter to Martin* (645–646). This philological discovery is not simply a matter of historical interest; it allows us to identify the context in which the notion of the will may well have first come to light.

The context in question concerns the heresy of monothelism. It consists in the affirmation that Christ had only one (divine) will—that of God the Father—and that, as a consequence, when Christ at Gethsemane prays, "Father, all things are possible unto thee; take away this cup from me" (King James Version), he is expressing the point of view of humankind and not his own. This thesis was condemned by the church insofar as it ignored the union of both human and divine natures in Christ. To counter the monothelist heresy, Maximus the Confessor proposed two complementary truths: (1) as a man, Christ possesses a human will that he expresses in the prayer quoted above; (2) nonetheless, this will is not capable of sin, as it is always in accordance with the will of God the Father. This is the basis for a distinction in Maximus between two types of will: natural will (*thelêma phusikon* [θέλημα φυσικόν]), corresponding to that human will that Christ must possess, and gnomic will (*thelêma gnômikon* [θέλημα γνωμικόν]), corresponding to that will capable of sinning that must be denied to him.

In this way, Maximus the Confessor "invents" a naturally righteous will, arrayed alongside a fallible will, one that is erratic, prone to sinning, capable of wishing for the good and then turning away from it. The righteous will, by contrast, is naturally and rationally directed only to the good. In Gautier's commentaries, "The *thelêsis* is no longer a desire that is subject to reason by accident, but a desire that is rational by nature, it is a faculty (*dunamis*) carried on its own *élan*, before any intervention by consciousness, in the direction of that same universal good of nature that consciousness is made for knowing." The choice between good and evil that belongs to the gnomic will is now no longer an intellectual act (as was decision [*proairesis*] in Aristotle), but an act of free will (*autexousion*), as Maximus had also affirmed.

We should emphasize two essential points: first of all, what is perhaps the first expression of the medieval and modern conception of the will is elaborated in a theological context, specifically in a Christological one. It is only insofar as humans are understood as "following God" or rather "following Christ" that a will as a rational power distinct from desire and ordered toward the good can be attributed to them. In other words, it is the notion of "God's will" that seems decisive in attributing to humans (through the intermediary of Christ) an appetite that is "rational in essence." Second, this "technical" concept of will (which will subsequently become the philosophical concept), although it is developed in a theological and Christological context, will become secularized bit by bit over time. By the beginning of the modern times, with Francis Bacon and Descartes, the will becomes this infinite capacity in man (if it is considered "formally in itself") that is not directed at any predetermined object, but can aim at any object in general. Entirely abstract, indeterminate in its object, the will can reach toward a possible object and thus become the ideal instrument in the service of science and technique in the light of a project of domination of the world, in which man considers himself "the lord and master of nature." This concept, theological in origin, will still serve in modern times to elaborate political concepts of sovereignty or of the general will.

This provenance is perhaps not without consequence for philosophy.

■ See Box 1.

Claude Romano

1

The emergence of a new vocabulary to describe the will

The contemporary philosophy of action has set out to address a number of problems left unsolved by the moderns, but the big question that remains is whether a unified field theory of action in humans and animals is desirable, or whether priority should be given to the reasons for action that give acts their meaning or that explain the causes of an action's appearance. The terms in play are largely determined by doctrinal positions, so we cannot avoid outlining their principal articulations. The "hermeneutic" approach (Ger. *hermeneutisch*, Fr. *herméneutique*) conceives of action as the direct expression of the will by an agent capable of practical reason (Ricoeur, *Philosophy of the Will*; Taylor, "What Is Human Agency?"). As for the "causal" approach (Ger. *kausal*, Fr. *causale*), it defines an action as a causal relation among mental states—beliefs and desires—and behavior (Davidson, *Essays on Action and Events*; Searle, *Intentionality*). The definitional stakes of the

vocabulary of action illustrate how current debates recall some of the issues that were at stake in the medieval debates, with the practical register taking the place of the religious. This is particularly clear with respect to the concept of desire. Should one distinguish between desire as a "non-motivated appetite" and desire as a "motivated pro-attitude," a state at which the subject arrives through decision and deliberation (Nagel, *The Possibility of Altruism*; Schueler, *Desire*; Dancy, *Practical Reality*)? (The category of "pro-attitudes" encompasses every form of conative thought, and includes desires, intentions, urges, and wishing along with moral views and aesthetic principles insofar as these are guides toward actions of a specific kind [Davidson].) Or would it not be better to introduce a category independent of "second-order desire" that enables the subject to hold to a set of preferences among desires of the first order (Frankfurt, "Freedom of the Will")?

The notion of will is at the heart of this debate. Does this term derive from the domain of judgment or from an autonomous faculty for forming and putting intentions to work? Some philosophers close to the Aristotelian tradition do not see a complete and separate faculty, but rather, the result of reasoning based on an ensemble of pro-attitudes and beliefs or propositional attitudes. Donald Davidson justifies his "rational and interpretive" conception of actions by their reasons, as well as by a "causal" conception in which a given cerebration yields a corresponding movement and its accompanying effects on the world. The "reason to act" formed from the desires and beliefs of the agent is normally a representation that tends to produce a behavior that realizes it. The principal difficulty of this perspective stems from the possibility of *akrasia* [ἀκρασία], which Aristotle had already tried to address, that is to say, the incontinence

(continued)

(continued)

or "weakness of the will." In this case, the subject acts contrary to what he thinks best. If, in the analysis proposed above, the intention of the subject coincides with his reasons to act, then how can he de facto form an intention that is incompatible with his rational judgment? Davidson addresses this difficulty by distinguishing between two types of judgment at work in action: the "prima facie" judgment relative to a group of objectives, and the "unconditional judgment" not subject to circumstance, which expresses the absolute preferences of the subject. The irrationality of the subject results from the non-coincidence between his reasons for action and the attitudes that in fact determine his behavior.

A second type of approach declares the independence of the will in relation to beliefs and desires, and makes intentions into an irreducible propositional attitude (Bratman, *Intentions, Plans, and Practical Reason*). This analysis aims at underscoring the difference between the existence of simple preferences (which determine desires) and the fact of deciding to act in some particular fashion, or to form a specific intention. It points out that the motivational characteristics of desire and of intention are not identical—and that they do not tally with the distinction between the two types of desire invoked above. While desire constitutes a premise of practical reason at best, the relation between intention and reasoning is a more complex one. It is formed after practical reasoning is finished and puts an end to further deliberations; but it can also be formed without prior practical reasoning at all. This is

the case of intentions that form themselves "in action"—and the term "intention in action" (Fr. *intention en action*) tends today to supplant the classical term of "volition" (Searle). Finally, intentions "on the future" constitute the element in which planning takes place. The notion of intention in this context takes on a clear "executive" meaning since the intention can cause a given behavior without any mediation from a primary reason for action.

This realist analysis of the will leads to the specification of intention in its double role as "guide" for behavior and "rational control" of action. The naturalist philosophers have drawn a specialized vocabulary and new themes of argument from the computational theories of *monitoring* and from the neurosciences. The ideas of "internal model," of "inverse model," and of "perceptual feedback" have been discussed in relation to philosophical problems like the anchoring of intentions in the environment and the justification of action in its motor accomplishments (Israel et al., "Executions, Motivations, and Accomplishments"; Pacherie, "The Content of Intentions"). These works have helped articulate the differences between multiple levels of consciousness and voluntary action (Proust, "Awareness of Agency").

Contemporary thinking about the will, according to the terms of Pierre Livet, is determined "to abandon neither the linguistic pole nor the motor pole" (Livet, "Modèles de la motricité et théorie de l'action"). What results from this constraint is a palpable lexical tension destined to simultaneously maintain the general comprehensibility of terms while inflecting them with innovative characteristics,

in expressions such as "non-conceptual content of action" or "motor representation."

Joëlle Proust

BIBLIOGRAPHY

Bratman, M. E. *Intentions, Plans, and Practical Reason*. Cambridge, MA: Harvard University Press, 1987.

Dancy, Jonathan. *Practical Reality*. Oxford: Oxford University Press, 2000.

Davidson, Donald. *Essays on Actions and Events*. Oxford: Clarendon Press, 1980.

Frankfurt, Harry. "Freedom of the Will and the Concept of a Person." *Journal of Philosophy* 67, no. 1 (1971): 5–20.

Israel, David, John Perry, and Syun Tutiya. "Executions, Motivations, and Accomplishments." *Philosophical Review* 102, no. 4 (1993): 515–40.

Livet, Pierre. "Modèles de la motricité et théorie de l'action." In *Les neurosciences et la philosophie de l'action*, edited by J. L. Petit, 341–61. Paris: Vrin, 1997.

Nagel, Thomas. *The Possibility of Altruism*. Oxford: Oxford University Press, 1970.

Pacherie, Elisabeth. "The Content of Intentions." *Mind & Language* 15, no. 4 (2000): 400–432.

Proust, Joëlle. "Awareness of Agency: Three Levels of Analysis." In *The Neural Correlates of Consciousness*, edited by T. Metzinger, 307–24. Cambridge, MA: MIT Press, 2000.

Ricoeur, Paul. *Philosophie de la volonté*. Paris: Aubier, 1988.

Schueler, George. *Desire: The Role of Practical Reason and the Explanation of Action*. Cambridge, MA: MIT Press, 1995.

Searle, John. *Intentionality*. Cambridge: Cambridge University Press, 1983.

Taylor, Charles. "What Is Human Agency?" In *Philosophical Papers*, vol. 1, *Human Agency and Language*, 15–44. Cambridge: Cambridge University Press, 1985.

BIBLIOGRAPHY

Arendt, Hannah. *The Life of the Mind*. Vol. 2, *Willing*. New York: Harcourt Brace Jovanovich, 1978.

Aristotle. *Nicomachean Ethics, Books VIII and IX*. Translated by M. Pakaluk. Oxford: Oxford University Press, 1999.

Augustine, Saint. *Confessions*. Translated by F. J. Sheed. Indianapolis, In: Hackett, 1993.

———. *On the Trinity*. Books 8–15. Edited by Gareth B. Matthews, translated by Stephen McKenna. Cambridge: Cambridge University Press, 2002.

Bobzien, Susanne. *Determinism and Freedom in Stoic Philosophy*. Oxford: Clarendon Press, 1998.

Burns, J. Patout. *The Development of Augustine's Doctrine of Operative Grace*. Paris: Études augustiniennes, 1980.

Epictetus. *Discourses*. Translated by George Long. London: George Bell and Sons, 1888.

———. *The Discourses and Manual, Together with Fragments of His Writings*. Translated by P. E. Matheson. Oxford: Clarendon Press, 1916.

Gauthier, René-Antoine. *Introduction to L'Ethique à Nicomaque*. Louvain, Belg.: Publications Universitaires de Louvain, 1970.

———. "Saint Maxime Confesseur et la psychologie de l'acte humain." *Recherches de théologie ancienne et médiévale* 21 (1954): 51–100.

Gilbert, Neal Ward. "The Concept of Will in Early Latin Philosophy." *Journal of the History of Philosophy* 1, no. 1 (1963): 17–35.

Gilson, Etienne. *The Christian Philosophy of Saint Augustine*. Translated by L.E.M. Lynch. New York: Random House, 1960.

John of Damascus. *De fide orthodoxa: Versions of Burgundio and Cerbanus*. Edited by Eligius M. Buytaert. St. Bonaventure, NY: Franciscan Institute, 1955.

Long, Anthony A., and David Sedley, eds. *The Hellenistic Philosophers*. Cambridge: Cambridge University Press, 1987.

Lottin, Odon. "La psychologie de l'acte humain chez saint Jean Damascène et les théologiens du XIIIe siècle occidental." *Revue thomiste* 36 (1931): 631–61.

Maximus the Confessor. *The Disputation with Pyrrhus of Our Father among the Saints*. Translated by Joseph P. Farrell. South Canaan, PA: St. Tikhon's Seminary Press, 1990.

Pohlenz, Max. *Die Stoa*. Göttingen: Vandenhoeck and Ruprecht, 1948.

Snell, Bruno. *The Discovery of the Mind: The Greek Origins of European Thought*. Translated by T. G. Rosenmeyer. Oxford: Blackwell, 1953.

Thomas Aquinas. *Summa theologica*. Translated by Laurence Shapcote of the Fathers of the English Dominican Province, revised by Daniel J. Sullivan. 2nd ed. Chicago: Encyclopædia Britannica, 1990.

Vernant, Jean-Pierre, and Pierre Vidal-Naquet. *Myth and Tragedy in Ancient Greece*. Translated by Janet Lloyd. New York: Zone Books, 1988.

Voelke, André-Jean. *L'idée de volonté dans le stoïcisme*. Paris: Presses Universitaires de France, 1973.

WILLKÜR, FREIE WILLKÜR (GERMAN)

ENGLISH	free will, (free) choice, free power of choice
FRENCH	arbitre, libre arbitre
LATIN	(liberum) arbitrium

▶ LIBERTY [ELEUTHÊRIA], and DESTINY, DUTY, MORALS, *POWER*, SOLLEN, WILL

The cluster of terms used to translate the Kantian notion of *(freie) Willkür*—"(free) will, choice," "free power of choice"; *(libre) arbitre* (Fr.)—provides a remarkable example of what philosophical philology can contribute to the understanding of a concept operative within a given theory. In German there are strong morphological and semantic reasons for linking *die Willkür* to *der Wille* (the free choice and the will). There are also theoretical reasons for this link when this (free) choice is further qualified as explicitly "free" as *freie Willkür*. In Kantian terms *freie Willkür* (free power of choice) expresses the highest exercise of reasoning; the "freedom" associated in Kant with the highest "autonomy of the will." More generally, however, the German *Willkür* carries additional morphological and etymological applications. One important usage, distinct from its relation to free will and choice, is "arbitrariness" or "caprice," or *Willkür*, as linked to the "arbiter." This meaning complicates the translation of Kant's terminology. The problem arises of how to bring to another language what Kant manages in his own by linking *frei* (free/autonomous) to *Willkür* (both arbiter and free choice). The existing English translations of both Kant's *freie Willkür* and *Willkür/willkürlich* rarely make explicit the link between *Willkür* as morphologically/etymologically related to "caprice" and "arbitrariness." Often they opt for the highest form of free will indicated by the expression "free power of choice." This, however, entails relinquishing the philological richness of the German in which *freie Willkür* (free power of choice) retains its capricious potential (it is *liberum* but nonetheless an *arbitrium*).

It is only via other translations of Kant's *(freie) Willkür* that the other side of *Willkür* can again be recuperated. In French translation this recuperation is especially apparent. In this case, the concept is rendered not as freedom of the will but as *libre arbitre,* a free or independent arbitrator (which suggests the discretion of an arbiter and therefore an uncertain outcome, neither determined nor necessary). This said, the French translations of *Willkür* can also be problematic since they often use the expression *libre arbitre* for both *Willkür* and *freie Willkür,* thereby obscuring the way in which the Kantian doctrine of freedom distinguishes between an already free choice (*Willkür/arbitre*) and a free power of choice (*freie Willkür/libre arbitre*).

I. *Willkür* in French Translation: Terminological and Philosophical Problems

A. The problem of translation

The difficulty raised by the French translation of *Willkür* was pointed out as early as 1853, by J. Barni, who was faced with the need to translate it in his introduction to the French translation of Kant's *Metaphysics of Morals*. Barni wrote the following in a note:

> The (French) word *arbitre*, which I use to translate the German word *Willkür*, is normally only used along with a qualifying adjective, such as *libre arbitre, franc arbitre,* etc.; but I cannot use *libre arbitre* here, for I will use it to translate *freie Willkür*, and so I am forced to use the word *arbitre* by itself. Any other expression would either not serve as well or is completely unavailable, because I need to hold all related words in reserve to render other distinctly defined Kantian expressions. Later, when I can do so without inconvenience, I will translate *Willkür* as *volonté* (will).

> (Barni, trans., in Kant, *Éléments métaphysiques de la doctrine du droit*)

Is it possible for the Kantian doctrine of freedom to hold up against the inevitable confusion that arises from the impossibility of differentiating the "freedom" of *Willkür* from the more pointed *freie Willkür*? Does one solve the problem by rigorously adhering to *arbitre* for *Willkür*, while retaining *libre arbitre* for *freie Willkür* (the rule adopted by J. and O. Masson in their edition of Kant's *Œuvre* as part of the Bibliothèque de la Pléiade)? The French attempts to render *Willkür* foist a long history of confrontations between Pelagius and Augustine, Erasmus and Luther, Molina and Jansenius, back onto Kant's understanding of the term. These confrontations inform subsequent philosophical debates pertaining to Cartesianism, including its critiques and modifications by Spinoza, Malebranche, and Leibniz. Ultimately they amount to imposing a doctrinal debate on Cartesianism that is extraneous to it, obscuring Kant's intentions and originality, especially the manner in which they were meant to be taken within his own doctrinal system.

The translation problem of *freie Willkür* that we encounter in Kant, namely how and when (in French) to apply the qualifier *arbitre* to *Willkür*, or for that matter how to mark the notion of *frei* (*libre,* free) in relation to *arbitre*, leads us back to a longstanding tension between philosophy and theology in the history of rationalism. The problem is one of understanding the freedom of individual choice in what is known as *liberum arbitrium* both in relation to the will and to understanding, judgment, reason, action, and God. To clarify this problem one must first restore the coherence of the Kantian doctrine to its French translation by relating *Willkür* to *Wille* through the element of freedom, and by drawing on *arbitre libre* to convery *freie Willkür*. The problem of translation, which at first might have seemed to be merely tangential, turns out to be of vital concern to the integrity of the concept itself. What is at stake is not just the validity of Kantian metaphysics but its value: that which animates it and makes it live. We are talking about the point where Kantian metaphysics seeks to justify itself, that is, in the two domains where the *arbitre* must be qualified as free: that of morals (law and virtue) and that of the relationship to evil. In both cases these justifications are made from the point of view of "practical reason."

B. Lexicography, etymology

1. The arbiter and the arbitrary (*l'arbitre* and *l'arbitraire*)

Let us dwell a bit longer on some of the insights into *l'arbitre* and *Willkür* that can be gleaned from major French-language dictionaries. From Émile Littré's RT: *Dictionnaire de la langue française* to the RT: *DHLF*, essentially two meanings come to the fore. The first, which would eventually become classic, appeared early in the seventeenth century as "the person who judges when there is disagreement" (later this becomes "the authority whose decision is to be respected"). The second, which is specifically philosophical, even metaphysical (for Littré), from the thirteenth century onward, refers to "the power of the will to choose between several options without external influence." This sense is further defined as "the faculty of making a determination for oneself, with only the will for cause" (RT: *Dictionnaire de la langue française*), or as "the faculty of making a decision by the will alone, without constraint" (RT: *DHLF*). The philosopher will note the immediate politicization of the classical meaning: the arbiter as absolute master. The substantive form of the adjective, the "arbitrary," refers more to the pleasure of the prince than to his good will, drawing the *arbitre* more in the direction of the irrational and capricious (together with all the associations these terms entail), as well as toward despotism. In its more purely philosophical ascription, the term *arbitre* must first be determined as *franc* or *libre* (unfettered or free). Once it is, it will be detached from power and transferred to the faculty of the will, itself defined as a capacity for choice without external influence or any form of determinism. The source of the "metaphysical" dimension of the *arbitre* (as evoked by Littré) derives from the fact that it is free only by virtue of the will. It is then an eminently classical philosophy of the will (the predestined place of true freedom) that takes over the idea of *arbitre* in the notion of *libre arbitre*. And we are perhaps in a better position to address the following question enabled by close attention to *Willkür*: Was Kant in fact breaking with classical philosophy, particularly its culmination in Leibniz's comment in his *Critical Thoughts on the General Part of the Principles of Descartes* ("On Article 39"): "To ask whether our will is endowed with freedom is the same as to ask whether our will is endowed with will. Free and voluntary signify the same thing" (trans. Loemker in *Philosophical Papers and Letters*, 9).

2. *Willkür*

Dictionaries of current accepted usage underscore the emphasis in German on the sense of the arbiter as arbitrary or capricious (as in the expression *nach Willkür handeln* [to act according to a caprice of the will, or according to its freedom]). This sense dominates the meaning of the adjective *willkürlich* (shifting from "without external motives" to "despotic"), and does so even more explicitly in *Willkürherrschaft* (a tyrannical regime, despotic, subject to the whim and pleasure of the ruler). Furthermore—and this is essential to our discussion—from the *Grimm* to the *Duden* the lesson of the etymology of *Willkür* teaches that the doubling of the *Will* with *Kür* leads to a redundancy of meaning significant in itself. That aspect of free choice that is completed in a decision by the will (and that takes on pejorative meanings of the unmotivated and the despotic from the middle of the eighteenth century), becomes the dominant one. *Kür* refers back to the verb *kiesen* (in the past-tense *kor*, with the past participle *gekoren*), which has the same sense as *wählen* (to choose), a meaning that is still retained, for example, in the "free program" in gymnastics, which are in effect called *Kür*, as in the *Kurfürst*, who is the elector prince. The unity of meaning is fully achieved when, through further etymological study, one takes into account that *wollen* (to will) has not only the

same root as *wählen* but also the same root as *wohl* (see WERT), which is combined in so many German terms to mean the well and the good; fulfilled or in a state of contentment, and related feelings of pleasure. It is surely this same possession of the power to choose, linked to the gratifying experience of sensible pleasures or happiness, that finds expression in Kant's definition of *Willkür* in his introduction to the *Metaphysics of Morals*:

> The faculty of desire in accordance with concepts, insofar as the ground determining it to action [*Bestimmungsgrund*] lies within itself and not in its object, is called *a faculty to do or to refrain from doing* [*zu tun oder zu lassen*] *as one pleases* [*nach Belieben*]. Insofar as it is joined with one's consciousness of the ability to bring about its object by one's actions it is called *choice* [*Willkür*].

> (*The Metaphysics of Morals*, trans. M. J. Gregor [German added within text; emphasis added to English])

The specific feature of *Willkür* lies indeed in the decision to act (in the sense of being "free to . . . ," being—supposedly—"master of . . ."), *nach Belieben*, that is, according to one's will and desires in whatever way seems "good" to us, as one "pleases." These directives of the will (*arbitre*) are linked to the satisfaction of our senses and feelings. Let us return to our initial question: from what does the word *frei* liberate the *Willkür* when the latter comes to be defined within the term *freie Willkür*? A good way to gain access to this metaphysics of *Willkür* is to examine German grammar more closely, focusing on the full play of *Will* within *Willkür*.

C. Grammar: Freedom and temporality

1. *Ich will*, preterite-present

Grammatically speaking, *ich will* (I want) is the first-person present indicative of the verb *wollen* (to want) in its use as an auxiliary mode, characterized specifically by the *past* form of its *present* —what grammarians call the preterite-present. Germanic languages contain a whole family of preterite-presents; they form a small, anomalous group in which the present tense shows the form of the strong preterite (the preterite being actions completed in the past, as in the French *passé simple*). Preterite-present verbs signify completed actions situated in the nonpast that are temporalized as present tense.

In addition to *ich will* from *wollen*, the list of verbs with a similar temporal modal function include the following:

- *ich kann*, from *könne* ("power to do" in the sense of "being capable of" and thus of "knowing how to" ([Fr. *savoir-faire*]), which links it to *Kunst*, to art in all its forms;
- *ich darf*, from *dürfen* (still as the "power to do," but this time in the sense of "being authorized," of having permission within the framework and limits of a "right");
- *ich mag*, from *mögen* ("to like" or even "to love"), but in relation to another sense of power: *möglich* (the power of being possible) or *Möglichkeit* (having the possibility).

- *ich soll*, from *sollen* ("ought" in the sense of "ought-to-be"), which very generally relates to the register of order (to make happen), in particular to obligation, especially an obligation that comes from a *Schuld* (a debt to be repaid or a fault to be redeemed);
- *ich muß*, from *müssen* (here again an "obligation," but in the sense of "needing to," in the register of necessity, generally in submission to a constraint, of a "de-fault" [French wordplay on *dé-faut*], of a lack that must be filled, of a need);
- and finally, *ich weiß*, from *wissen* ("to know" in the sense of being acquainted with or knowing what something is [Fr. *connaître*]), which also brings us back to *können* (Fr. *savoir-faire*, see first entry in this list) by passing through its other form, *kennen*.

Preterite-present verbs share the fact that they are imbued with an awareness of time. They contain, implicitly, the recollection of the subject's essential temporality (of action, including the very act of knowing itself). As auxiliaries (see ASPECT and PRESENT), they open past determinations to future expectations (uncertainties, promises, hypothetical projections). This family of preterite-presents is the element in which Kant's reflections live and breathe. In his critical philosophy what he calls the "interest of reason" is constantly being articulated in terms of these modal verbs. They saturate both the letter and spirit of his German. Salient examples may be found in a series of questions posed in the *Critique of Pure Reason* that encapsulate Kant's philosophical anxiety: *was* kann *ich wissen?* (what *can* I know?), *was* soll *ich tun?* (what *should* I do?), *was darf ich hoffen?* (what hope am I *permitted?*) (*Critique of Pure Reason*, B 833).

What story would "*ich will*" tell us if we asked it to unpack everything contained in its past form of the present, which in fact stretches toward its future? *Ich will* in German extends to a sense of "out of my present-day desire." It refers to the decision to update or not to update positions as a result of sampling, tasting, testing, and comparing the multiple "objects" of experience, determining the pleasure or displeasure such objects afford. The Kantian "choice" in its typical usage is signified precisely as a choosing faculty defined in the context of a *Begehrungsvermögen* (power of desire). It connotes actions that are the result of a representation or that arise from expectation of either an anticipated pleasure or a dreaded displeasure. It also implies decision-making that takes place in the ambiguous space between "what one can do" and "what one ought to do."

2. The persistence of the past

What Kant seems to stress when he qualifies the will as *frei*, is the *wollen* of the *Will-kür*; the power to "choose" (*wählen* as reiterated in *-kür*), released from all experience, from all circumstances in which diverse impulses and stimuli constrain behavior. Will is thus freed from everything impinging on it from the outside, including the sense of exteriority as such and the succession of time, with its inexorable flow. In the final analysis, how could the will be free if it continued to be a choosing in

the thrall of time's passage? If to be free is to be *dominos compos sui* (master of oneself, master of one's own mind), what power would the will have over itself if in the passage of time there were no present but only a past that imposes form and content? As Kant often reminds us, "that which belongs to time past is no longer within the power of the acting subject" (*AK*, 5:94–95, 97).

Under the semblance of a "freedom of choice," reinforced by the German sense of *freie Willkür*, we understand Kantian "freedom" in all its rigor. In the terms set out in the introduction to the *Critique of Pure Reason* (B 1–3), freedom of the will is none other than the return of the will to an a priori order. But before we turn to the doctrinal implications of this provisional conclusion, it is worth lingering one last moment on what might be the effect on that family of modal auxiliaries when *freie Willkür* is liberated as *frei* from its *wollen*, which is to say from its *wählen*, and thus as a correlative also frees the present of this *wollen-wählen* from all that is indicated and endures in the form of *ich will*: the persistence of the past, the marks of a legacy, the weight of an empirical history. A whole chain of effects follows from the way in which modalities of freedom are signified within the preterite-present. Especially important are those instances in which the Kantian lesson finds its most memorable articulation, that is, where Kant tell us (and thereby legitimizes the recognition of freedom and its purview), that man wants what he ought, and thus what he can do (cf. *Critique of Practical Reason*, in *AK*, 5:159: "that one *can* do it because our own reason recognizes this as its command and says one *ought* to do it"; or *Anthropology from a Pragmatic Point of View*, in *AK*, 7:148: "what [the human] wills *at the order of his morally commanding reason* he *ought* to do and consequently *can* do").

Here, in the most direct way, *Wollen, Sollen*, and *Können* are bound together in solidarity. It is a solidarity that reminds us that every choice made in the *Wollen*, which is in fact a *Wählen*, is inscribed within the framework set up by all the various modal auxiliaries, insofar as each of them, in its present indicative, expresses the conclusion of a past. When the *Wollen* is freed from choice as determined by the past, isn't the *Sollen* liberated as well? Isn't the weight of debt lifted from its own obligation (*ich soll* does in fact mean "I have incurred a debt")? Isn't *Sollen* then released from its obligation to reimburse or repay the legacy of a fault in the form of original sin? What we discover is a will no longer subject to the "legal clause" that refers it back to a reductive motivation that sustains the illusion that it is independent and "quits" with the obsession with acquittal. The same solidarity also implies that *Können* can now be liberated from the long, painstaking process that makes it a *Kunst* or a *Kennen* (*ich kann* does in fact mean "I have finished learning, and now I know how to do it"). "Power" is freed from the skill and measure required for *savoir-faire* in relation to things and to men. So now we have an *arbiter* freed from the pragmatic clause that makes "techno-practical" intelligence the determinant of will, autonomous only insofar as it is instructed and trained.

Pierre Osmo

BIBLIOGRAPHY

Allison, Henry E. *Idealism and Freedom: Essays on Kant's Theoretical and Practical Philosophy*. Cambridge: Cambridge University Press, 1996.

Castillo, Monique. *Kant*. Paris: Vrin, 1997.

Delbos, Victor. *La philosophie pratique de Kant*. 3rd ed. Paris: Presses Universitaires de France, 1969.

Guyer, Paul. *Kant and the Experience of Freedom: Essays on Aesthetics and Morality*. Cambridge: Cambridge University Press, 1993.

Kant, Immanuel. *Critique of Practical Reason*. Edited and translated by Mary J. Gregor. Cambridge: Cambridge University Press, 1997.

———. *Éléments métaphysiques de la doctrine du droit*. Introduction by J. Barni. Paris: A. Durand, 1863.

———. *The Metaphysics of Morals*. Edited and translated by Mary J. Gregor. Cambridge Texts in the History of Philosophy. Cambridge: Cambridge University Press, 1996.

———. *Practical Philosophy*. Edited and translated by Mary J. Gregor. Cambridge: Cambridge University Press, 1996.

———. *Gesammelte Schriften (AK)*. 29 vols. Edited by the Preussischen Akademie der Wissenschaften. Berlin: De Gruyter, 1900–.

Leibniz, Gottfried Wilhelm von. *Critical Thoughts on the General Part of the Principles of Descartes*. In *Philosophical Papers and Letters*, translated and edited by Leroy E. Loemker. 2nd ed. Dordrecht, Neth.: Reidel, 1969.

Roviello, Anne-Marie. *L'Institution kantienne de la liberté*. Brussels: Ousia, 1984.

WISDOM

I. The Twofold Meaning of Wisdom

1. *Sapientia* translates the Greek *sophia* [σοφία] and retains that term's twofold practical and theoretical orientation: the *sophos* [σοφός] is first a clever man, an expert, before he is a scientist. He is a life-model before he is a master of the sciences: see ART, MÉTIS.

   This happy conjunction that characterizes both Greek *sophia* and Latin *sapientia* can malfunction: the distinction drawn by Plato, and clearly marked by Cicero, between the *sophistês* [σοφιστής], the "sophist" who claims to know everything, and the *philosophos* [φιλόσοφος], the "philosopher" who is a lover of wisdom, also marks the dividing line between theory and practice, *scientia* and *sapientia*: see PRAXIS; cf. SOPHISM. On the relation between wisdom and philosophy in the various traditions, see EUROPE.

   The characteristic of the sage, which is connected with the key role played by Stoicism (cf. LOGOS and GLÜCK), nonetheless remains the conjunction of the greatest possible wisdom in the epistemological sense (science, knowledge) and also in the practical-ethical sense (prudence and/or detachment). But modern languages generally distinguish between theoretical wisdom and practical wisdom and retain for wisdom only the practical-ethical meaning: see, in addition to GLÜCK and LOGOS, PHRONÊSIS, PRUDENTIAL, *SOUCI*, VERGÜENZA.

2. More broadly, on practical-ethical wisdom, see CONSCIOUSNESS, DUTY, MORALS, *VIRTUE* [VIRTÙ, WERT].

   On knowledge and science, see EPISTEMOLOGY, GEISTESWISSENSCHAFTEN, *REASON* (particularly GERMAN, INTELLECT, INTELLECTUS, UNDERSTANDING).

On the relation between wisdom and ordinary life, see CLAIM, COMMON SENSE, ENGLISH.

On the relation between human wisdom and divine wisdom, see *ALLIANCE*, DEVIL, *INTUITION*, LIGHT, LOGOS, SVET.

II. The French Terms *Sagesse* and *Goût*

The French word *sage* (wise, good) is derived from classical Latin *sapidus*, "that which has taste, tasty," formed from the verb *sapere*, which means "to have taste, sense," but also "to have intelligence or judgment, appreciate," and finally "to be acquainted with something, understand, know." *Sapientia* (*sagesse*, "wisdom") was thus initially connected with taste, with the ability to assess, with discernment—and Thomas Aquinas is still aware of the etymology: "Doctrina per studium acquiritur, sapientia autem per infusionem habetur" (Doctrine is acquired by study, but wisdom is acquired by infusion; *Summa theologica*, 1.1a6): see GOÛT, and cf. SENSE.

➤ *CROYANCE*, *CULTURE*, *EXPERIENCE*, MADNESS, MENSCHHEIT, PATHOS, TRUTH

WITTICISM

A witticism is an instantaneous linguistic invention that is linked to the specific occasion in which it is used (see MOMENT, II), and that both engages and at the same time eludes its author.

Every age and every linguistic region has its own means of determining the value and the relevant traits of a witticism. INGENIUM discusses the elements of a comparison among, in the first place, the Greco-Latin, classical, humanist, and baroque traditions, in which a witticism is above all the sign of a natural gift (*euphuia* [εὐφυΐα]); the French *esprit* in the second place (see also FRENCH); and finally the Anglo-Saxon tradition of "wit" and of the *Witz* (from *wissen* [to know]).

The first tradition privileges the rhetorical and political aspect of the witticism: for Greek and Latin, see COMPARISON (the Greek word for a witty remark is *asteion* [ἀστεῖον], from *astu* [ἄστυ], "the town"; cf. COMPARISON, Box 1 for a treatment of this metaphor), and, for witticism in Italian (and still hewing to this tradition), ARGUTEZZA, CONCETTO; cf. CIVILTÀ and SPREZZATURA. For the emphasis on invention and cunning, see MÉTIS and the play on words described by Ulysses (MÉTIS, Box 1). Likewise, in Arabic, see INGENIUM, Box 1; cf. TALAṬṬUF.

The second tradition stresses the break in logic, and the relation to nonsense; see NONSENSE and *ABSURD*. English is particularly rich in nuance: wit, humor, joke, pun (see INGENIUM, Box 2).

The contemporary thematization of witticisms is linked to Freud, for whom *Witz*, along with dreams, stands out as one of the privileged roads to the unconscious (see UNCONSCIOUS). The Freudian *Witz* is discussed both in INGENIUM, IV, and in NONSENSE, IV, and in its relation to the signifier when adopted by Lacan, under SIGNIFIER/SIGNIFIED, V.

➤ GEMÜT, GENIUS, LOGOS, MANIERA, SOUL, WORD

WORD

FRENCH	*mot*
GERMAN	*Wort*
GREEK	*onoma* [ὄνομα], *rhêma* [ῥῆμα], *lexis* [λέξις]
ITALIAN	*parola*
LATIN	*vox, verbum, dictio, locutio, muttum, pars orationis, vocabulum*
PORTUGUESE	*palavra*
ROMANIAN	*cuvânt*
RUSSIAN	*slovo* [слово]
SPANISH	*palabra*

➤ HOMONYM, LANGUAGE, LOGOS, PRÉDICABLE, PREDICATION, PROPOSITION, SENSE, SIGN, SIGNIFIER/SIGNIFIED, SUBJECT, TERM, *THING*

All European languages have a term that refers to an element of the language felt spontaneously to be distinct, grammatically and/or semantically, and that corresponds to the English term "word": Italian *parola*, Spanish *palabra*, Portuguese *palavra*, French *mot*, German *Wort*, Russian *slovo* [слово], etc.

This pleasing unanimity glosses over several questions, however. The first is knowing whether the word is a universal category. It is not in fact certain that in all languages there is a signifying unit perceived as autonomous by its speakers. Furthermore, even if we confine ourselves to the Greco-Roman tradition, this unit was constituted for its speakers in a way that was not independent of the process of the formation of its grammar. Finally, the designation of such a unit has been the object of so many political and religious debates over the centuries that its modern form was not established until the end of the seventeenth century.

In addition to this, whether we distinguish the minimal unit that is a word on the basis of criteria that are grammatical (morphology, function) or semantic, different words to say "word" are related to, or in competition with, each other, not only from one language to another but also within the same language, to the extent that there is sometimes no generic term, or no longer any generic term, to designate a "word." Thus, in Aristotle's *De intepretatione*, the word is made up of the pair *onoma-rhêma* [ὄνομα-ῥῆμα], "noun-verb," which constitutes *logos* [λόγος], so that when medieval commentators introduce *dictio* (the "word") as a generic term covering both *nomen* and *verbum*, it appears as a distortion.

Moreover, the terms that are continually reinvested from within other perspectives are particularly difficult to translate, terms such as *onoma* (word/name), *verbum* (word/verb), and at the confluence of several different traditions, *lexis* [λέξις] (speech, style, expression, articulate vocal sound, word) or *vox* (voice, word).

I. A Linguistic Entity? The Word as a Result of Grammar Formation

In Greek and in Latin, everyday language did not contain a term devoted specifically and monosemically to a linguistic entity that corresponded to the word and that was endowed with its general properties (Fruyt and Reichler-Béguelin, "La notion"; Lallot, "Le mot"). It was the predominance of parts of speech in the process of forming a grammar that placed the segmentation into words at the center of how language was discussed (see Auroux, *Histoire des idées linguistiques*, vol. 2). In the Hellenic graphic tradition, the norm was the *scriptio continua*, and the regular separation of words by a space did

not appear until later in the Byzantine era. As for the designation "word," which since Plato had been confused with that of "name," *onoma* [ὄνομα], from the Hellenistic period onward it was expressed by the term *lexis* [λέξις]: "word" was understood at that time to mean "part of speech." It was only with the grammarians in the Alexandrine tradition that the word came to be characterized as an autonomous segment with a single stress and meaning (see Lallot, "Le mot"). For Latin, it would seem that it was Varro (1 BCE) who named the word *verbum* (whose etymology was *verum boare*, "to proclaim what is true") in his *De lingua latina*.

Nevertheless, the polysemy of the word *verbum* was omnipresent for this author, who assigned it several meanings (Di Pasquale, "La notion"). This polysemy (see below) was evident in the first French-Latin dictionary, Jean Nicot's *Thresor de la langue françoyse tant ancienne que moderne* (1606), where the entry "Mot: *dictio, verbum*" contains a list of expressions in which the occurrence of the word *mot* is translated alternately as *verbum, dictio, oratio, vox, vocabulum, tessera*: "haec vox dominus," "dictum breviter," "prisca vocabula," "oratio capitalis," "vigiliarum tesserae," "pervetusta verba." This polysemy, which is still very much present in modern dictionaries through collocations, is as much indicative of the questions linked to the designation of the word as it is of the difficulties of translating the different terms that name it.

■ See Box 1.

II. The Word in Greek, Grammatical and Semantic Issues

A. *Onoma/rhêma*: "Word," "noun," "verb"

In Greek grammatical terminology, *onoma* and *rhêma* [ῥῆμα] refer to the basic constituent elements of *logos* ("statement, phrase"; see LOGOS), the noun and the verb. These are the preferred terms of *merismos* [μερισμός], the separation of the sentence into functionally different constituent parts. But this pair has a history, and the terms *onoma* and *rhêma* preexist their conjunction.

1. *Onoma* and *rhêma*: Two possible designations for "word"

The term *onoma* is intimately associated with the oldest and most elementary awareness of the referential function of language: language gives names to things, it is a nomenclature that has the world as its referent. Even though at this stage it is still not a question of "parts of speech," the elements of nomenclature are prototypically *substantives*, that is, nominal types of words that are applied to concrete—"substantial"—objects around us: it is quite likely that in the first instance these are proper names of people (Socrates, Zeus—it is important to note the Greek use of the definite article, so they would say *ho Sôkratês* [ὁ Σωκράτης], literally "the Socrates" or "the Zeus"; see SUBJECT). During this roughly pre-Platonic stage, *onomata* [ὀνόματα] in the plural refers to the "vocabulary" of a language, and the singular, *onoma*, to a "word" (proper noun, common noun, adjective, or verb). As for the other kinds of "words" (articles, pronouns, conjunctions, prepositions, particles, etc.), we can see that for Aristotle, in any case (*Poetics*, 20), all of this "small matter" of the language is classified, like syllables, as *phônai asêmoi* [φωναὶ

1

The word is not a universal category

The word poses a problem as a universal category. We know that it is extremely difficult for Western grammarians to deal with agglutinative and polysynthetic languages from the vantage point of the Western model of the dictionary of words, which presupposes a segmentation into units. In the cases where grammars were constituted independently of the Western model, the system of writing played a fundamental role. So in languages with logographic writing, such as Chinese, the unit is iconic and does not always correspond to a fixed acoustic image (the number "5" can be expressed as "five," *cinq*, *fünf*, etc.). In Chinese, two ideograms correspond partially to the word: the ideogram that translates the notion of word or term, the character *ci*, was only recently imported (after 1920), whereas the unit of analysis remains the character *zi* (Alleton, "Terminologie de la grammaire chinoise"). In certain cases, two systems can coexist, such as when the parts of speech derived from the Greco-Latin model are superimposed on the traditional units. The Japanese tradition thus has two terms: *kotoba* in everyday language, and *tango* as a grammatical term. Japanese presents a duality of the basic units, at present visualized through notation: the referential part (called either *kotoba* or *shi*, depending on the era) is notated as an "ideogram," and the syntactic or enunciative part (*teniha* or *ji*, depending on the era) is notated using syllables. The grammatization of Japanese by Western languages, in this case by the translation of Dutch grammars from the beginning of the nineteenth century, produced terms for the parts of speech that reduplicated those of the Japanese tradition. The terms ending in *-shi* correspond to the parts of speech (*dôshi*, verb) and translate the Dutch *woord*: those containing the Chinese root *-go* correspond to the functional groups (*shugo*, subject). Moreover, *-go* refers to lexical units: *tango*, "simple word"; *fuku-go*, "complex word" (Tamba, "Approche du signe et du 'sens'").

In the Greco-Roman tradition, the word was finally accepted as a unit by grammarians, by theologians, and by everyday language during the first few centuries of the Common Era. This did not, however, resolve the problems of designating this unit. If we confine ourselves to the Romance languages, we notice that there are in fact three terms that contribute to the naming of the word: *mot*, *verbe*, and *parole*. Romanian is an exception, since it is the only Romance language that does not have an equivalent of *parole*, and the word for mot is *cuvânt*, which comes from the Latin *conventus*, "assembly." The semantic shift from "assembly" to "conversation" then to "word" is apparent in other Balkan languages, such as ancient Bulgarian, Albanian, and Serbian, in which *kuvent* means "assembly," "conversation." Romanian also uses (at a more stylistic and familiar level) the noun *vorb ă*, meaning "speech," "way of speaking." In modern Greek, there is a very common word, *kouventa* [κουβέντα], also derived from the Latin, which means both "conversation" and "spoken word," "word." *Mot*, *parole*, and *verbe* were all present in their Latin forms, *muttum*, *parabola*, and *verbum*, as names for a unit of language, and one of these terms, in a given vernacular, would become the established term meaning word. We should also mention here historical, political, or religious reasons, and one would have to make a detour through the various etymologies.

BIBLIOGRAPHY

Alleton, Viviane. "Terminologie de la grammaire chinoise." *Travaux du Groupe Linguistique Japonaise* 1 (1975): 12–23.

Tamba, Irène. "Approche du signe et du 'sens' linguistique à travers les systèmes d'écriture japonais." *Langages* 82 (1986): 83–100.

ἄσημοι], "vocal sounds that have no meaning" and in this respect is quite distinct from *onoma*, the first vocal sound to be recognized as "signifying" (*sêmantikê* [σημαντική]) in the ascending hierarchy that goes from the phoneme to speech in general.

This generic meaning of *onoma* would continue in Greek, including in the writings of the grammarians, well beyond the grammatical specification of the term that we will go on to discuss (so we can find in Galen [17A], who was certainly aware of the grammar of his time, the second century CE, the expression, the "*onoma 'illainein'*" [τὸ ἰλλαίνειν ὄνομα], which is remarkable once we understand that that *illainein* is a verb).

Alongside *onoma*, a synchronically unmotivated term inherited in its prototypical sense of "proper noun" from a distant Indo-European past, the Greek language in its ancient period came up with a postverbal derivation with a very clear formation, *rhêma*, first attested in the sixth century BCE. As an integral part of the family of *rhêtôr* [ῥήτωρ], "orator"; *rhêsis* [ῥῆσις], "speech"; etc., *rhêma* is the action noun with a *-ma* ending derived from a root **wera-/*wre-*, meaning "to speak," "to say" (see Gr. Γερέω, "I will say," Lat. *verbum*, Ger. *Wort*, Eng. "word," etc.). As its formation suggests, *rhêma* seems initially to have designated something "said," a complex expression or a simple word, no doubt noted first of all for its semantic range, and then, in a more banal sense, any "word" as an instrument used to say something (an expression such as *kata rhêma apaggeilai* [κατὰ ῥῆμα ἀπαγγεῖλαι], "to report word for word" [Aeschines, *Peri tês parapresbeias*, 2.122] illustrates well this aspect of the materiality of saying), so in this respect it is explicitly opposed to "acts" and to "truth." Plato uses *rhêma* widely and does so at times in this loose sense of an unspecialized linguistic indicator (see *Timaeus*, 49e, where he refers to the demonstrative *tode* [τόδε]), which is more or less equivalent to *onoma*, and with which he alternates freely in the same contexts (*Laws*, 906c 3; see also in this same free variation, the composite noun *prosrhêma* [πρόσρημα] [*Politics*, 276b 4, *Phaedrus*, 238b 3], which refers initially, no doubt, to a form of salutation; see *chaire* [χαῖρε], "salute" [*Charmides*, 164e 1]).

2. Platonic pairs

We might conclude from the above that in Plato's time the Greek language invented, by different routes, two interchangeable words for "word" as an instrument of linguistic expression: *onoma* and *rhêma*. Although it is not essentially incorrect, this conclusion does not do full justice to the semantic richness of the pair *onoma/rhêma*. It is precisely in Plato that we can observe how the two terms, far from sinking into banality and a lack of differentiation, each develop in opposition to one other (in the Saussurean sense) its own semantic potentiality and produce a very unusual pair.

We can distinguish three types of contexts in which the pair regularly appears with a formulaic regularity that deserves our attention:

A. Typically "Cratylian" contexts, in which *rhêma* is opposed to *onoma* as the "etymological expression" is opposed to the "name" it accounts for, formally and semantically. So *Dii philos* [Διΐ φίλος], "dear to Zeus," is the underlying *rhêma* of the *onoma Diphilos* [Δίφιλος], "Diphilus" (399b 7, 421 1). This feature appears as a local analysis of the opposition between *onoma* as name (a single term that designates) and *rhêma* as expression (a syntagm with a predicative content), an opposition that is clear in the *Republic*, 463e, where *onomata* are names of relations ("father," "mother," etc.), and *rhêma* is a time-honored expression, such as "things are going well."

B. Contexts that have a rhetorical connotation. Here, the pair *onomata te kai rhêmata* [ὀνόματα τε καὶ ῥήματα] (sometimes in inverse order) refers to the variety of forms of linguistic expression that the masters of spoken language, orators (*Apology*, 17c 1; *Symposium*, 198b 5, see 199b 4; *Theaetetus*, 184c 1, see 168c) or poets (*Republic*, 601a 5), are capable of exploiting to aesthetic ends, whereas Socrates, who had no technical training, is content to speak with the words (*onomata*) that he happens to have been provided with (*eikêi legomena tois epituchousin onomasin* [εἰκῇ λεγόμενα τοῖς ἐπιτυχοῦσιν ὀνόμασιν]; *Apology*, 17c 2). Influenced by what we observed in group A, translators readily translate the pair as "words and expressions." A plausible alternative would be to consider that in the contexts in group B, we are dealing with a more-or-less redundant expression of the kind, "ways and customs": Plato can be seen, then, to have freely exploited the combination of two terms of weakly contrasting values in order to create an expression that "imitates" in its very superfluity the use of language it attempts to describe.

C. Contexts in which the pair *onoma-rhêma* is closely associated with *logos*. We can probably distinguish between two varieties here:
1. Typical of this variety is the first definition of *logos* in *Theaetetus* (206d 2): "make one's thought [*dianoia* (διάνοια)] manifest with one's voice using *rhêmata* and *onomata*." Although there is no question in this passage of a rhetorical *logos*, and although the paired expression certainly has no aesthetic connotation here, we could be very close to group B (see LOGOS). We would place in this section the passage from *Letter 7*, 342b, where the noun (*onoma*) *kuklos* [κύκλος], "circle," is opposed to the *logos*, "definition" of the circle, "composed of *onomata* and *rhêmata*" (see 343b 4), namely "that of which the extremities are always equidistant from the centre." There is clearly no question here of aesthetics, but it would be no less risky, as regards the *logos* of "circle," to claim to be able to say precisely what is *onoma* and what is *rhêma*—the French translators of the Belles Lettres edition (A. Diès for the *Theaetetus* and J. Souilhé for the *Letter 7*) are certainly making a bold statement in translating them as "nouns" and "verbs."

2. Although it is similar to the two passages quoted in C1 in that the *logos* is said there to be "composed of *onomata* and *rhêmata*," the famous passage from the *Sophist* 262a–e is decisively different on one point: *onomata* and *rhêmata* each have their own distinct definition and exemplification. The sui generis combination that is a "first and minimal" *logos*, such as "man learns," owes its singularity to the fact that it connects an *onoma* that designates an agent (*prattôn* [πράττων]), for example, "lion," "stag," or "horse," to a *rhêma* that designates an action (*praxis* [πρᾶξις]), for example, "walks," "runs," or "sleeps." *Onoma* and *rhêma* each have here, without question, an inalienable specificity of minimal, noninterchangeable constituent elements of the predicative statement, and they are prototypically represented by what grammar will call, with the help of the very terms Plato uses, *onoma* and *rhêma*, a "noun" and a "verb." We have to stress that this in no way implies that in the *Sophist onoma* and *rhêma* refer exclusively to the grammatical categories of "noun" and "verb": the only thing we can say is that *onoma* here designates a propositional constituent, typically a noun that is liable to function as a subject, and *rhêma* designates a propositional constituent, typically a verb that is liable to function as a predicate. That being the case, no single word can provide a satisfactory translation of these two terms. This in itself matters little, but what is important is that Plato was able to analyze a simple affirmative proposition in terms of its two fundamental constituent elements and to find in his language two terms capable of designating each one of these. The innovation of the *Sophist* would prove to be exceptionally productive.

3. Nouns and verbs

a. The Aristotelian polarity

Aristotle, for whom the functional pair appears to be a successful outcome of the analysis of *logos* as a simple affirmative statement, enriches the definitions of the two constituent terms and makes their relationship more symmetrical. In the *Peri hermêneias* (16a 19), *onoma* is defined as "a vocal sound, which has a conventional meaning, without reference to time, and no part of which has any meaning when it is taken separately" [φωνὴ σημαντικὴ κατὰ συνθήκην ἄνευ χρόνου, ἧς μηδὲν μέρος ἐστὶ σημαντικὸν κεχωρισμένον]. In the following chapter (16b 6), *rhêma* is defined as "that which adds to its own meaning the meaning of time, and it always indicates something that is affirmed by something" [τὸ προσσημαῖνον χρόνον, οὗ μέρος οὐδὲν σημαίνει χωρίς, καί ἐστιν ἀεὶ τῶν καθ' ἑτέρου λεγομένων σημεῖον]. *Rhêma* is thus clearly identified as conveying a predicative function and is functionally opposed to the substratum, or subject (*hupokeimenon* [ὑποκείμενον]). The insistence on the nonsignifying nature of the parts that *onoma* and *rhêma* can be broken down into has the effect of not allowing these terms to be applied to segments of more than one word: in "the little horse is white," the constituent subject "the little horse" is not a noun nor is the constituent predicate "is white" a verb, since they each can be broken down into separate signifying parts. What was only implicitly explained in the *Sophist* thus becomes an intrinsic part of the definition of each of the terms: *onoma* is a single word that can occupy the subject position, typically a substantive noun, and *rhêma* is a single word that can occupy the predicate position, typically a verb. The latter is distinguished from the former by its capacity to "signify time as well": clearly one thinks here of the system of verbal inflection, which produces, among other things, temporally specific forms. Even though Aristotle from his own logical perspective refines his analysis by further restricting the application of *rhêma* to the verbal forms of the present (see PARONYM, Box 2) and that of *onoma* to the nominal nominative (which effectively corresponds to the form that the noun takes in the subject position), it is clear that he laid the foundations of a specifically grammatical understanding of "noun" and "verb."

b. Parts of speech

Stoic dialectics undoes the self-evident nature of the polarity between *onoma* and *rhêma* as it was defined by Plato and Aristotle, since *onoma* and *rhêma* are now seen as two of the five parts of speech presented in place of the vocal sound (*topos peri phônês* [τόπος περὶ φωνῆς]) and form part of the investigation concerning the signifier (see SIGNIFIER/SIGNIFIED).

Rhêma is defined by Diogenes Laertius (*Lives of Eminent Philosophers*, 7.58) as "an element of speech which cannot be declined, signifying a non-composite predicate" [στοιχεῖον λόγου ἄπτωτον σημαῖνον ἀσύνθετον κατηγόρημα], or by others as "an element of speech which cannot be declined, signifying what can be formed with one or several subjects, for example: (I) write, (I) say" [στοιχεῖον λόγου ἄπτωτον, σημαῖνόν τι συντακτὸν περὶ τινος ἤ τινων, οἷον γράφω, λέγω] (ibid.). In accordance with how Aristotle characterizes it, *rhêma* is here clearly presented as signifying a predicate—in other words, a morphological entity that, having no case, is opposed to the noun and its satellites; more precisely, in relation to the composite predicate "eats the mouse," which includes an oblique case, *rhêma* signifies the noncomposite predicate "eats." *Rhêma* thus seems to be the part of speech that signifies *a part* of what enables complete predication. The verb, since we need to call it by its name, is understood here by its subtraction as the part that has no case of a composite predicate (its definition also allows it to include the case of an intransitive verb that would constitute a predicate by itself).

In the same context, *onoma* means "proper noun," which is defined as "a part of speech designating a particular quality, like *Diogenes, Socrates*" and is distinct from *prosêgoria* [προσηγορία], the "appellative," which for its part is defined as "a part of speech signifying a common quality, like *man, horse*" (Diogenes Laertius, ibid.). After the initiative taken by Chrysippus, there is in Stoic dialectics no longer any generic term meaning a noun, whether proper or common.

Among grammarians, and most particularly Apollonius Dyscolus, the noun and the verb are considered, of all eight parts of the sentence (*merê logou* [μέρη λόγου]), to be "the most essential," "the most important," or even, "the most lively." Without a noun or a verb, indeed, no phrase is "complete" ("*sugkleietai* [συγκλείεται]"; Apollonius Dyscolus, *Syntax*, 1.14).

The other parts of the sentence fulfill auxiliary functions and are all related to the functions that the noun and the verb perform.

In the ordered list of parts of the sentence, the noun precedes the verb. Following on from Apollonius Dyscolus (*Syntax*, 1.16), the Alexandrine grammatical tradition—for example, Dionysius of Halicarnassus (*De compositione verborum*, 5)—almost unanimously justifies the precedence of the noun over the verb by the physical primacy of the body over its dispositions or of a substance over its accidents.

Among grammarians, *onoma* and *rhêma* are given new technical definitions, but the symmetry of these definitions means that they preserve the memory of the pair invented by Plato and incorporate the criterion of time introduced by Aristotle. In the *Technê grammatikê* of Dionysius Thrax, *onoma* is defined (chap. 12) as a "part of the sentence that has a case, designating a concrete entity, for example 'stone', or abstract, for example, 'education,'" and *rhêma* (chap. 13) as a "word [*lexis*, see below] that has no case, which includes tense, person and number, and which expresses the active or the passive." The personal inflection of a verb, which has no case, corresponds to the inflection of a noun, which has a case, and the verb opposes its temporal variation and diathetic flexibility to the stability of the entities reflected by the nouns. In Alexandria, the Stoic legacy is partially rejected: *onoma* restores the generic value that Chrysippus had taken away from it—"the appellative [*prosêgoria*] is classed as a kind of noun [*onoma*]" (*Technê grammatikê*, chap. 11). On the other hand, Apollonius Dyscolus remains faithful to the Stoic definition of the noun in terms of quality (*poiotês* [ποιότης]) and not of substance (*ousia* [οὐσία]) (ibid., chap. 12). The pair quality-substance is used to contrast the noun to the pronoun; for him a noun and a pronoun do not have the same attributes; indeed, a noun does not involve *deixis* [δεῖξις] but instead signifies quality, whereas a pronoun does have *deixis* but only signifies substance. One could say, then, that strictly speaking pronouns are "substantives" par excellence, whereas nouns are "qualifiers." Whereas all that "I," "this," etc. do is to point to a substance without describing it, "Socrates," "man," "big," "Greek," etc. in their own way each give some qualitative indication, whether the quality in question is given as something "proper" to a substantial individual (Socrates), as "common" to a class of substantial individuals (man), or as predicating a substance of which it will designate an "added" attribute—*epitheton* [ἐπίθετον]—(large), etc.

By including predicable terms, we might be concerned that *onoma* comes dangerously close to *rhêma*. For a grammarian, the protection against this danger resides in morphology: defined by the case inflection and having nothing to do with personal inflection, the noun could in no way be confused with the verb, which is also endowed with personal inflection and has no case inflection. So, for better or worse, the meanings of the two terms that Plato was the first to join together as a pair become stabilized in grammatical theory, but their values are still multiple and fluid.

B. *Lexis*

1. The evolution of the meaning of *lexis*

The gains made in the reflection on language that gave the specialized meanings of "noun" and "verb" to *onoma* and *rhêma* paradoxically deprived Greek of two potential designations of "word." Even though *onoma*, as we mentioned, could on occasion continue to designate a word once it had been given its specialized meaning of "noun," we can legitimately ask whether or not Greek grammatical vocabulary produced a specific term for "word." The answer is yes: in grammatical texts, the word for "word" is *lexis*, and this perfectly stable term remains the designation for "word" in modern Greek (demotic, *lexi*).

But *lexis* has a singular history that should also be mentioned. As an action noun derived from the root *leg-*, "to say," this term refers in principle to saying, as opposed to doing (*praxis*), (for example, Plato, *Republic*, 396c), but also as opposed to "the said." This latter distinction is stipulated by Plato as well, for instance in *Republic* 392c, where *lexis* is opposed to *logos* as the form of a linguistic expression is opposed to the content expressed—or the style opposed to the thought, if one prefers. This semantic orientation is clearly confirmed by Aristotle, who makes a distinction between *dianoia*, "thought," or the "faculty of saying . . . the appropriate thing," and *lexis*, "expression," or "manifestation, interpretation [of the thought] by means of its being put into words" (*tên dia tês onomasias hermêneian* [τὴν διὰ τῆς ὀνομασίας ἑρμηνείαν]; *Poetics*, 6.1450b 14–15), whose "figures," *schêmata tês lexeôs* [σχήματα τῆς λέξεως], refer both to an actor's vocal schema for asking or demanding and to the varieties of an enthymeme or the morphology of an expression. This same opposition structures the argument of *Rhetoric*, which makes a distinction between "what is to be said," the *dianoia*, and "how it is to be said," the *lexis* (3.1.1403b 15). The meaning of *lexis* as "style" will continue in Greek well beyond the appearance of its meaning of "word": in the entire Alexandrine and Byzantine tradition, *lexis pezê* [λέξις πεζή], like its Latin calque *sermo pedestris*, will be the technical designation for prose, as opposed to metrical expression, *lexis emmetros* [λέξις ἔμμετρος].

In Aristotle, *On Sophistical Refutations* forces us to widen the meaning of the term, so it is closer to the Saussurean signifier than to style. Aristotle in fact makes a distinction between two tropes of refutation: those that are "*exô tês lexeôs* [ἔξω τῆς λέξεως]" (*extra dictionem*, "outside expression," "independent of speech"), which are designed to dispel the errors of reasoning produced in particular by the confusions between the different meanings of being; and those that are "*para tên lexin* [παρὰ τὴν λέξιν]" (*in dictio*, "tied to expression," "part of speech"), which are designed to dispel the confusions produced by the very materiality of language (homonymy and amphiboly, composition, separation, accentuation, morphology of expression: 4.165b 23–27). In the examples he uses to support his argument, we can see that what comes under *lexis* is what we would nowadays call the signifier, via the play of audible meanings in the sounds of the language (thus, *sigônta legein* [σιγῶντα λέγειν] is an amphiboly that can be understood both in the sense of 'to speak of mute things,' neuter plural, and 'to speak by being silent,' masculine singular: 4.166a 12–14; 10.17a 7–10.17b 2; 19.177a 20–26). But these illusions are highlighted in order to be dispelled with the aid of the tools of the categories and of grammar (see HOMONYM).

■ See Box 2.

The Stoics, who invented the analysis of language in terms of signifier/signified/referent, thematize this relationship between *lexis* and signifier and define *lexis* as one of the three moments of the signifier that may or may not present a meaning (see SIGNIFIER/SIGNIFIED, and below, 2). Nothing is said, however, either by Aristotle or the Stoics, of the dimension of *lexis*, and articulate vocal sound could correspond equally to a syllable, a word, or a succession of words. It is not easy to explain precisely how, from there, the shift in meaning occurred that led grammarians to define *lexis* as referring to "the smallest part of the sentence constructed" (*meros elachiston tou kata suntaxin logou* [μέρος ἐλάχιστον τοῦ κατὰ σύνταξιν λόγου]; Dionysus Thrax, *Technê grammatikê*, chap. 11). It is possible, as Baratin has suggested ("Les origines stoïciennes"), that grammarians, while retaining the intermediary position that the Stoics had assigned to *lexis* (between an inarticulate sound and a statement as a site of meaning), also used the term to refer to an intermediary unit, the word, as a compound of syllables devoid of signification and as a unit in a signifying sentence. While remaining faithful in part to the Stoic analysis, this new meaning of *lexis* had the unquestionable advantage for the grammarians of Alexandria, philologists that they were, of finding a concrete application and a functional usefulness for this term in the field of textual studies. The word, as a minimal signifier resulting from the segmentation of *logos*, constituted a precious empirical entity that ancient grammar would make into its object par excellence. Its definition, even in the *Technê* of Dionysus mentioned earlier, explains that *lexis* (word) and *meros logou* (part of a sentence) are strictly interchangeable and alternate in free variation.

We can thus see how, after having allocated to the terms *onoma* and *rhêma* the designation of specific parts of speech that could, at least in some instances for the latter, refer to the word, the Greek language ended up taking *lexis* as a truly generic name for the word as a minimal signifying unit. It would later on derive the name for a collection of words from it, *lexikon* [λεξικὸν] (*biblion* [βιβλίον]), the ancestor of our "dictionary," which itself is derived from *dictio*, the Latin calque for *lexis*. The most ancient collections of words, simply entitled *Lexeis* [Λέξεις], "words," or *Glôssai* [Γλῶσσαι], "strange words," did not at all claim to be exhaustive but were lists of words that were, for one reason or another, marginal to the reference idiom (obsolete words, dialect words, etc.). (On *glôssa* [γλῶσσα], see Aristotle, *Poetics*, 1457b 4; *glôssarion* [γλώσσαριον], "glossary," is a late derivation.)

2. The tripartite Stoic division into *phônê, lexis,* and *logos* and the change of perspective in relation to Aristotle

We have to give a particular mention here to the Stoic reinvestment of Aristotelian terms, which are placed in a new order. This blurring, which is the sign of a doctrinal will, is the only way we can understand the terminological complexity of someone like Boethius, for example, who superimposes or assimilates these different usages.

For the Stoics, *lexis* is the second of the three stages of the signifier (see SIGNIFIER/SIGNIFIED; on this, see Diogenes Laertius, *Lives of Eminent Philosophers*, 7.56–57). The first stage is the *phônê*: it is both a generic term, since the signifier is

2

Schêma tês lexeôs and the *schêma* in grammar

➤ COMPARISON, *FORM, IDEA,* SPECIES, TROPE

Schêma [σχῆμα], documented in Greek from 5 BCE onward, is a nominal derivation constructed from the root σχε/ο- of the verb *echein* [ἔχειν], "to hold," "to have," and intransitively, "to stand," "to be in such and such a condition": semantically, *schêma* is related to the intransitive value of the verb and so refers primarily to the "way one stands." This basic meaning took on many more specific and diverse meanings during the fifth and sixth centuries: it is variously translated according to the context as "stature," "posture or pose," "look," "style," "configuration," "figure (including geometrical)," "form." *Schêma*, one of the Greek names for "form," refers usually to a complex configuration; in geometry, it is a closed figure.

In Aristotle, we see quite a wide variety of applications of *schêma* in the domain of language: configurations of the mouth allow the air to be shaped into distinct sounds, characteristic morphological features of certain classes of signifiers, the modulation of an utterance to assist modal differentiation, and syntactic and rhetorical configurations. Several of these meanings are conveyed by the syntagm *schêma tês lexeôs* [σχῆμα τῆς λέξεως], which can be translated literally as "figure of expression." Post-Aristotelian rhetoric would retain *schêma* to refer generically to any unusual turn of phrase: via the intermediate stage of the Latin translation *figura*, the *schêma* of Greek orators would become the *figure* of classical rhetoric.

Grammatical theory, which we can see being formed as of 2 BCE, would retain, alongside a diverse and loosely specified usage of *schêma* as the name for a form, three clearly technical kinds of usage:

– In inflectional morphology, *schêma* forms the basis of a family of words describing the phenomenon of the variation of meaning of inflected words: at the heart of this family, *metaschêmatismos* [μετασχηματισμός], literally "trans-formation," applies principally to the case variation of nominals and to the variation in person of verbs;
– In lexical morphology, *schêma*, "figure," refers to the *simple or compound* status of a word. Three *schêmata* can be distinguished: the simple (for example, *Memnôn* [Μέμνων]), the compound (for example, *Aga-memnôn* ['Αγα-μέμνων]), and the derivation of a compound (for example, *Aga-memnon-idês* ['Αγα-μεμνον-ίδης]). Why *schêma* was applied to this particular type of morphological feature is not clear: commentators would later on (for want of a better reason?) suggest that the greater or lesser complexity of the word gives it the "look" of a type, comparable to the poses (*schêmata*) of a statue;
– In syntax, based on the rhetorical meaning of "figure" as an unusual turn of phrase, *schêma* would acquire the specialized meaning of "deviant turn of phrase in relation to the syntactic norm." As an anomalous turn of phrase that is in theory incorrect, *schêma* can, however, become an acceptable part of the language whenever an ennobling origin can be assigned to it, which can be found either in a dialect (an Attic figure, a Boeotian figure, etc.), or in a renowned author (a Pindaric figure, a Sophoclean figure, etc.). One commentator combines the defining characteristics of syntactic *schêma* in a striking expression: a *schêma* is, he says, an "excusable error."

studied in treatises *Peri phônês (On Sound)*, and the basic signifier as a physical body, that is, air that is percussed as an effect of an animal impulse (*hormê* [ὁρμή]) or of a human reflection (*dianoia*), which goes from the sender to the receiver. Thus specified, the *phônê* is not as such articulate (it can be animal, and then it is an *êchos* [ἦχος], a "noise" that is not written), and it certainly does not carry meaning. The second stage is then the *lexis*, which is a *phônê eggrammatos* [φωνὴ ἐγγράμματος], a sound (this time, *phônê* tends to be translated as "voice") that lends itself to writing, and the "letters" that make it up (*stoicheia* [στοιχεῖα]) are a guarantee of articulation (*enarthron* [ἔναρθρον]; ibid., 7.57): for example *hêmera* [ἡμέρα], "day" (ibid., 7.56). It is *lexis* that is properly human, but it is quite remarkable that it should be defined as not necessarily carrying meaning (*asêmos* [ἄσημος]): *blituri* [βλίτυρι], an onomatopoeia imitating the sound of a vibrating string, is as much a "lexical item," or *lexie*, as "day." In fact, only the *logos*, the final stage of the "vocal sound endowed with meaning impelled by a reflection" (*phônê sêmantikê apo dianoias ekpempomenê* [φωνὴ σημαντικὴ ἀπὸ διανοίας ἐκπεμπομένη]; ibid.), is at once a voice that is articulate and that carries meaning; for example, *hêmera esti* [ἡμέρα ἐστι], the statement from a sentence implying, by means of a conjugation, something like an event, "it is day." The summary at the end is clear: "The *phônê* differs from the *lexis* in that the *phônê* can be a noise, whereas the *lexis* is always something articulate. The *lexis* differs from the *logos*, because the *logos* always has meaning (*aei sêmantikos* [ἀεὶ σημαντικός]), whereas the *lexis* can be devoid of meaning (*kai asêmos* [καὶ ἄσημος]), for example, *blituri*, but never the *logos* (ibid., 7.57). This can be illustrated by the following diagram:

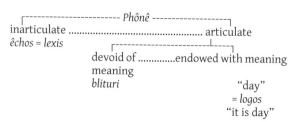

Claude Imbert remarks that "the Stoic terms seem to have been deliberately chosen to contradict Aristotelian semantics" ("Théorie de la représentation"). It is not the word as such, whether a noun or a verb, that constitutes the signifying unit, as it does at the beginning of *De interpretatione*, but rather the statement—obviously an entirely different way of apprehending the world, in terms of events and not of substances or in terms of a narrative of action and not of predicative syntax; in short, an entirely different "phenomenology."

First of all, the Stoic *phônê* is not the Aristotelian *phônê*. Aristotle defines *phônê* in *De anima* as "a certain noise [*psophos* (ψόφος)] produced by an animate being" (2.8.420b 5; see *De historia animalium*, 1.1 and 4.9): this "noise" applies to man as well as to an animal, and the definition goes from noise to voice by means of a certain number of physical dichotomies, each determining a category of exemptions (the sound made by an animate being—not flutes; produced by a movement of the air inside—not fish, but dolphins; striking the trachea-artery—not a cough). This definition appears to be compatible initially with the Stoic definition until it intersects with another kind of prerequisite, presented as self-evident by means of a simple "and," which I will quote here for emphasis:

> Not all sound emitted by an animal is a voice, as we have said (since we can make a noise with our tongue or by coughing), but what strikes has to be animate and accompanied by a certain representation [*meta phantasias tinos* (μετὰ φαντασίας τινός)], since the voice is of course a semantic noise [*sêmantikos gar de tis psophos estin hê phônê* (σημαντικὸς γὰρ δέ τις ψόφος ἐστὶν ἡ φωνή)].

(Aristotle, De anima, 420b 29–33)

The "voice" in Aristotle is a kind of noise that already involves articulation (it is said to be *dialekton* [διάλεκτον; 420b 18], with the same property, precisely the property of articulation, as the *lexis* of the Stoics) and meaning (it is said to be *hermêmeia* [ἑρμηνεία; 420b 19 ff.], having this time the same particularity, meaning, as their *logos*). So the three levels that the Stoics chose to keep distinct are collapsed here, three levels that in Aristotle gravitate toward, so to speak, this last one the "end" and the "good," which, beyond animal impulse, constitutes meaning for man: "A living being has . . . hearing so that meaning can be conveyed to him, and a tongue so that he can convey meaning to someone else" (ibid., 435b 19–25). We might say that all the Stoics did, in the end, was to move Aristotle's sequence forward a notch, giving the name *phônê*, "vocal sound," to what he had chosen to call *psophos*, "noise." What it involves, however, is a shift in the very direction of the hierarchies: noise can be, and even must be, envisaged independently of meaning. Whereas the Aristotelian *lexis*, particularly in *On Sophistical Refutations*, was at first an analytical tool and involved initially through the definition of homonymy in a relationship to the signified, the Stoic *logos* is conceived, conversely, in terms of the category of the signifier, as a particular kind of *lexis*. At the same time, the requirement of fullness of meaning that defines *logos* means that the most relevant unit has no longer to do with the word, whether it is *onoma* or *lexis*.

III. The Words Designating "Word" in Latin

A. *Dictio, locutio, pars orationis, verbum, vocabulum, vox*: Distinctions and polysemies

In Latin, the word is understood as form, as the combination of form and meaning, and, finally, as a linguistic category.

As form, the term for word is *vox*. This term, which originally meant "voice," "phonic matter" (and it retains this meaning at all times), becomes the object of all sorts of classifications, depending on whether the *vox* is *articulate*

or *confused*, can or cannot be *written*, etc. When it applies to linguistic entities, *vox* is used to designate their form and, insofar as the word is the natural frame of reference for etymological, semantic, and morphological analysis, *vox* signifies the form of the word: so Varro contrasts the *vox* and the *significatio* of the word (*De lingua latina*, 9.38–39; 10.77), *vox* being "what is made up of syllables," "what is heard," as opposed to what the word means. *Vox* thus also refers at the same time to the different forms that appear as the variables of a same word or as the inflected forms of a declined or conjugated word: *Aemilius* is a word, but this form itself is the nominative and all of the oblique corresponding forms (*Aemiliu, Aemilii, Aemilio*, etc.) are *discrimina vocis*, variable forms of this word. Varro's text (ibid., 8.10) clearly suggests a dissociation between the notions of *word* and of *form*, insofar as a *single* word can have *several* forms if it is inflected. *Vox* is thus one of the forms of word, but at the same time refers, in the concrete reality of its realizations, to a particular word (*Aemilius*, or *Aemilium, Aemilii*, etc.).

Identified in this way with the word, and unlike its synonyms *forma* and *figura*, which are less determinate, *vox* is even used by Varro to signify the word in relation to the thing (ibid., 10.69 and 72). This use is also attested in Quintilian (*De institutione oratoria*, 1.5.2) and is occasionally found in the texts of the grammarians. However, it remains an exception in relation to the two original terms used to designate the word, *verbum* and *vocabulum*.

The first characteristic of *verbum* in Varro is that it is presented as being at the heart of a process of signification, between *vox*, which is the means by which the *verbum* signifies, and *res*, which is what the *verbum* signifies (*De lingua latina*, 10.77, and see 9.38–39, where *verbum* is defined as the combination of a *vox* and a *significatio*).

These two terms are polysemic at all times. *Verbum* in fact also signifies "verb," beginning with Varro and then constantly among grammarians. Another specialized use appears with Saint Augustine, in the *De dialectica*, with a very particular distinction between *verbum*, or a word "when it is spoken for itself," that is, when it "only refers to itself," and *dictio*, or a word when it is used "to signify something else."

■ See Box 3.

Vocabulum alternates in Varro's work with *verbum*, with no apparent nuance (see for example *De lingua latina*, 6.1 or 9.1), and pairs up with *res* in the contrast of the word and the thing. *Vocabulum* is itself also polysemic, but whereas *verbum* signifies the verb, *vocabulum* signifies the noun, exactly opposed to *verbum* (ibid., 8.11, 9.9). At the other end of the history of the Latin language, Priscian suggests moreover that *nomen*, a term normally used to signify a noun, could also be used as a generic term for "word." So there would have been a perfect parallelism between *vocabulum* and *nomen*, both able to correspond to both noun and word, but with *vocabulum* signifying primarily a word and secondarily a noun, and *nomen* the other way around (this use of *nomen* is, however, only documented by Priscian). Another specialized use of *vocabulum* appears in the texts of the grammarians, where this term is sometimes cited as representing a specialized category of common nouns, those which designate concrete objects, as opposed to abstract common nouns (see Dositheus

3

Verbum, dicibile, dictio, res: St. Augustine, *De Dialectica*, 5.8

Haec ergo quattuor distinct teneantur: verbum, dicibile, dictio, res. Quod dixi verbum, et verbum est et verbum significant. Quod dixit dicibile, verbum est, nec tamen verbum, sed quod in verbo intellegitur et animo continetur, significat. Quod dixi dictionem, verbum est, sed quod jam illa duo simul id est et ipsum verbum et quod fit in animo per verbum significat. Quod dixi rem, verbum est, quod praeter illa tria quae dicta sunt quidquid restat significat.

(These four terms must be kept distinct: *verbum, dicibile, dictio, res*. What I call *verbum* both is a word and means "word." What I call *dicibile* is a word but does not signify "word," but what is understood in the word and what is contained in the soul. What I call *dictio* is a word, but signifies together the two preceding meanings, that is, the word and what is produced in the soul by the word. What I call *res* is a word and signifies everything else, that is, everything not signified by the three preceding words.)

The young Augustine, in his *De dialectica*, introduces a four-term system: *verbum, dicibile, dictio, res*. The passage quoted makes clear the distance he takes in relation to Stoic dialectics: Augustine considers that it is the simple term, and not the statement, that is "the meeting point between the signifier and the signified." The *verbum* is a sign of a thing (*verba sunt signa rerum*), and the sign is what is offered to the senses and, in addition, shows something to the soul (*signum est quod se ipsum sensui, et praeter se aliquid animo ostendit*). The *verbum* is the word understood insofar as it refers to itself, thus independently of its relation of meaning to something else, and this sense becomes manifest in a metalinguistic context. The word "autonym" is sometimes used in this respect. This does indeed correspond to something of this kind, but on condition that one does not give too restricted a definition of the signified of autonym. Augustine's *verbum* corresponds to a use that is a mention; that is, it does have its signified but is not used to manifest this signified. This usage of *verbum* is not attested among grammarians. The *dicibile* is the mental content associated with the word, which Augustine sometimes says is anterior to the utterance of the word, sometimes simply contained within the word, and sometimes even what is given to be understood in the

mind or soul of the listener. The *dictio* is the word insofar as it is uttered to signify something: it is a *verbum* taken in its relation to a *dicibile*. The *res* is everything that is not yet either expressed by a word nor conceived by the mind, whether or not there is a word that can signify it. So if a grammar teacher takes the first word of the *Aeneid*—*arma*—and asks about its grammatical category, he takes it in itself as a *verbum*, whereas in the line by Virgil, it is a *dictio*, used to signify arms. These same arms, insofar as they were in fact borne, could be pointed at and are in that case neither *verba*, nor *dicibilia*, nor *dictiones*, but *res*. Augustine is keenly aware of the distinction between the linguistic level and the metalinguistic level: all of the terms—*verbum*, dicibile, *dictio* and *res*—are *verba* when they are part of statements that refer to themselves, but *dictiones* when they are understood in terms of their relation to the mental content that corresponds to them and things. The rest of *De dialectica* attempted to examine the value of words that are used in argumentation, either understood in and of themselves or in terms of their relation to what they signify. These relations can be seen from the original point at which they are established (the discussion about whether the nature of this connection is natural or not) or according to the way in which they work in synchrony, with all of the potential for discordance because of the equivocality and obscurity that can affect them.

One question for French translators is knowing whether to use *mot* for *verbum* or for *dictio*: Baratin and Desbordes (*L'analyse linguistique*) chose the first solution, even though in *De dialectica verbum* sometimes appears to be equivalent to the simple signifier: they translate *dictio* as *dit* [thing said] in order to keep the close connection with the mental content of *dictio*, the *dicibile*. It is not possible to translate *res* as "referent" because this term is relational: while *res* can be the *res* of a sign, it is not necessarily so. In the *De doctrina Christiana*, the term *res* gathers together all the elements of the world, with signs constituting a subset. Shortly before the passage cited earlier, Augustine defined the thing as "everything that is perceptible to the senses or to the intellect, or which escapes perception" (*Res est quidquid vel sentitur vel intelligitur vel latet*). In the passage cited, *res* are all the things which are not in some relation to a signifier—just like actual weapons if they are considered

as material objects, and not as things that can be signified by the word "arm" (whether this is understood as *verbum*, and does not refer to them in speech, or whether it is understood as *dictio*, and is used to signify these arms) or that can be the mental contents associated with this word. In the English translation, Darrell Jackson translates *verbum* as *word*, notably in the initial definition in chapter 5 ("verbum est uniuscujusque rei signum" [a word is a sign of any sort of thing]), but when it is a question of the four-term system, he keeps them in the Latin (which gives for the Latin sentence "Quod dixit verbum, et verbum est et verbum significat" [see above], and for the translation: "'verbum' both is a word and signifies a word"). In his Italian translation, Mariano Baldassarri interprets the passage in light of Stoic dialectics, which introduces some confusion, since he makes *sêmainon* [σημαῖνον] correspond to both *signum* and *verbum* (equivalent to the signifier alone) but also posits *verbum* as equivalent to *phônê*; he interprets *dictio* as *lexis sêmantikê* [λέξις σημαντική], *dicibile* as *lekton* [λεκτόν], and *res* as *tughkanon* [τυγχάνον]. These problems of translation ultimately depend on the weight assigned to the Stoic influence in the writing of *De dialectica*.

BIBLIOGRAPHY

Augustine, Saint. *De dialectica*. Edited by Jan Pinborg. Translated by B. Darrell Jackson. Dordrecht: Reidel, 1975. *I principii della dialettica*. Translated by Mariano Baldassarri. Como: Noseda, 1985.

Baratin, Marc. "Les origines stoïciennes de la théorie augustinienne du signe." *Revue des etudes latines* 59 (1981): 260–68.

Baratin, Marc, and Françoise Desbordes. *L'analyse linguistique dans l'Antiquité classique*. Paris: Klincksieck, 1981.

———. "Sémiologie et métalinguistique chez saint Augustin." *Langages* 65 (1982): 75–88.

Long, A. A. "Stoic Linguistics, Plato's Cratylus, and Augustine's *De Dialectica*." In *Language and Learning: Philosophy of Language in the Hellenistic Age*, edited by Dorothea Frede and Brad Inwood, 36–55. Cambridge: Cambridge University Press, 2005.

Munteanu, Eugen. "On the Object-Language/Metalanguage Distinction in St. Augustine's Works: *De Dialectica* and *De Magistro*." In *History of Linguistics I: Traditions in Linguistics Worldwide*, edited by David Cram et al., 65–78. Amsterdam: Benjamins, 1996.

Magister in RT: *Grammatici latini*, 7:390, l. 16), or inanimate objects (see Diomedes in RT: *Grammatici latini*, 1:320, l. 23).

Perhaps in order to clarify a terminology suffering from these phenomena of polysemy (this is Quintilian's interpretation, at least in relation to *verbum* [*De institutione oratoria*, 1.5.2]), these different terms were subsequently supplanted by *dictio*, which appears in the sense of "word" after Varro.

The fundamental characteristic of *dictio* is that it is made up, like *verbum*, of a signifier and a signified: Diomedes (ibid., 7:436, l. 10) defines this term as "vox articulate cum aliqua significatione" (an articulate vocal sound with a meaning). Similarly Priscian, while readily acknowledging that a *dictio* can have only one syllable, makes a careful distinction between the syllable, as a signifier without a signified, and the *dictio*, which has a signified (RT: *Grammatici latini*, 3:3, ll. 13–18). The use of *dictio* by St. Augustine in *De dialectica* is based on this same contrast.

Dictio can, however, also be contrasted with *sensus*, that is, to the signified alone: when it is a question of accounting for the phenomena of syllepsis (agreements with more than one meaning), for example, in the case where the subject of a plural verb is *pars* (part), a singular that we would call collective (in an expression such as "part of them are cutting out pieces . . ."), Priscian remarks that the verb "relates not to the *dictio*, but to the *sensus*, that is, to what we understand by the word in the singular" (RT: *Grammatici latini*, 3:201, ll. 22–23). To relate the verb to the *dictio* would have consisted in matching it to the form of the word *pars*, which is singular, to get to the signified "singular," whereas relating it to the *sensus* consists in starting with the meaning "part" and then inferring that it can apply to a plurality of persons, so it therefore contains the signified "plural."

There is a sort of parallelism between the disjunction of word and form in Varro, and the disjunction between a word and its sense in Priscian (a single word, but more than one sense, that which corresponds to the form and another).

Dictio, moreover, can be understood within a hierarchical perspective as the constituent part of a much larger whole. This is how Diomedes explains the relationship between the *dictio* and the *oratio* (statement)—by emphasizing that the statement is a construction of which the *dictio* is the unit ("*dictio . . . ex qua instruitur oratio et in quam resolvitur*" [the word . . . from which the statement is formed and in which this statement is resolved (that is, is analyzed)]; ibid., 1:436, l. 10). Priscian likewise notes that the *dictio* is the "pars minima orationis constructae" (the smallest part of the constructed statement).

The most frequent expression, however, for designating the word as a constituent of a much larger whole is *pars orationis*. The meaning of the whole that is referred to here, *oratio*, is not obvious. For Varro, *oratio* can apply to the language in its entirety (*De lingua latina*, 8.1 or 44, etc.), and in this sense, the *partes orationis* are the main divisions of the language, the "categories of words." But elsewhere *oratio* also means "statement," and it is indeed in this sense that Priscian, just like all the grammarians, understands the *partes orationis*, as the "constituent parts of the statement." However one understands it, *pars orationis* signifies the word as a set of traits (*accidentia*) such as gender, number, person, tense, etc. in a system in which each set of traits is in contrast to the others, just as the noun is in contrast to the verb or to the pronoun.

One last term appears as a way of saying word: *locutio*, already documented in Quintilian (*De institutione oratoria*, 1.5.2), but its uses in this sense are rare and isolated.

B. The double meaning of *vox* in the Middle Ages

1. The semantic understandings: Aristotle, the Stoics, Boethius

Vox is used among Latin grammarians, along with *verbum*, *vocabulum*, and *dictio*, to designate the word. All through the Middle Ages, the term *vox* will keep the two meanings Boethius gives to it, that is, "vocal matter" and "vocal sound endowed with signification," which for him are merged because of the two sources that are in the background of his commentaries on the *Peri hermêneias* (*Commentarii in librum*). The term *vox*, at the start of the second commentary, is defined on the one hand in Aristotelian terms: the *vox* is the result of the tongue striking the air and is produced with some intended meaning. But elsewhere, Boethius uses *vox* to translate *phônê* on the basis of the Stoic tripartite division *phônê*, *lexis*, *logos* (see above, II.B.2), which he renders as *vox*, *locutio*, *interpretatio*. The hiatus is clear: signification is present in the first definition, whereas in the economy of the Stoic system, signification does not take place at the level of the *phônê-vox*, rather only at the third level, with the second level, as we saw earlier, being one of articulation (the fact of being made up of letters or of discrete sounds: thus, *blituri* is a *lexis* but not a *logos*).

With Boethius, the problem resurfaces and becomes even more confused once we move on to the question of the parts. What he understands by the expression *partes locutionis*, because of the translation of the Stoic Greek *lexis* as *locutio*, is the *merê lexeôs* [μέρη λέξεως] of Aristotle's *Poetics* (elements, syllables, conjunctions, articles, nouns, cases, verbs, *orationes*), and by *partes interpretationis* (because of the equivalence of *logos* and *interpretatio*), the *merê logou* of Aristotle's *Peri hermêneias* (noun, verb, *oratio*), although he also talks about *partes orationis*, taking *oratio* in the stricter sense of "minimal statement" (noun, verb). Later tradition will generally leave this lack of precision aside and will focus on how Boethius uses these terms, not on his definitions. Indeed, in his commentaries on logic, Boethius uses *vox* to refer to any articulate expression, which can be meaningful or not and may, if it *is* significant, have been the object of an imposition and thus signify *ad placitum*, or may signify "naturally" (see SIGN). It is this term that forms part of the triad *vox*, *intellectus*, *res* in the first chapter of the *Peri hermêneias*. *Sermo* is sometimes used when it is a question of mentioning or talking about a word ("*hic sermo homo*," "*hic sermo lexis*"; Boethius, *Commentarii in librum*). Elsewhere, however, *vox* alternates with other terms, notably at the beginning of the commentary on the *Categories*, a work which, according to Boethius, deals with "*de primis vocibus* [the first *voces*]" (RT: *PL*, vol. 64, col. 161A), "*sermonibus prima rerum genera significantibus* [*sermones* signifying the first types of things]" (col. 162B), and in the same context we find the term *vocabula* (col. 162D).

■ See Box 4.

When *De anima* (2.8.420b 5ff.) began to be reread at the beginning of the thirteenth century, particularly with

4

Vocales and *Nominales*

The question of the origin of the term *Nominales*, used in the eleventh century, has given rise to an interesting debate. Were the *Nominales* partisans of a particular position on universals, which considered genera and species to be names (*nomina*), or were they defenders of the so-called theory of the *unita nominis*, the unity of the name? According to this latter theory, the three vocal expressions (*voces*) *albus, alba, album* constitute one and the same name (*nomen*), and based on this assertion, certain theologians have maintained that the three complex statements or expressions "Christ is going to be born," "Christ is born," "Christ will be born" correspond to one and the same enunciable (*enuntiabile*), which constitutes the eternal and sole object of faith (see DICTUM). The debate was not settled, nor was the question of knowing whether Abelard was dubbed the "prince of Nominals [*Princeps Nominalium*]" (Walter Map, 1181) by virtue of his position on universals. The interesting point regarding universals is that the *Nominales* are in reality the successors of the *Vocales*, and that strictly speaking, Roscelin de Compiègne and Abelard are *Vocales*, and indeed, for them, genera and species are *voces*. The first accounts of the existence of this current of thought, which appeared around 1060–70, show that it was originally concerned with a discussion about how to engage in dialectics, that is, how to read and interpret Porphyrius's *Isagoge* and Aristotle's *Categories*, and thus about the primary object of these texts and of dialectics: in other words, did Porphyrius and Aristotle aim to deal with vocal sounds or things (*de rebus de vocibus agere*) (see Iwakuma, "*Vocales* or Early Nominalists")? Boethius's position is not clear: in the *Categories* (RT: *PL*, vol. 64, col. 160A), he maintains that Aristotle's aim was to talk about *voces*, but he also describes the categories as "first names of things" (*de primis rerum nominibus*; col. 159C), and also says

that species "are in certain sense names of names" (*nomina nominum*; col. 176D). In the commentaries on the *Isagoge*, he agrees with *Porphyrius* in saying that predicables are *res*. Those who, like Roscelin, maintain that universals are *voces* (the *sententia vocum*) are until the middle of the twelfth century called *Vocales*. Abelard clearly seems uncomfortable with the imprecision of the term *vox*. He attempts to make a distinction between *vox* as physical matter, and *vox* as an expression that conveys meaning (*Super Porphyrium*) and will in the end keep the term *vox* in the first sense, and for the second use the term *sermo*: "there is another position on the universals, which is more in accordance with reason; it attributes community neither to things (*res*) nor to sounds (*voces*); according to its advocates, they are *sermones*, whether they are singular or universal" (*Logica "Nostrorum petitioni sociorum"*). In his French translation (*Abélard ou la philosophie dans le langage*), Jolivet translates *sermo* as *terme* (term), but in his commentary also uses *mot* (word) and *nom* (name), which is justified by certain passages in Abelard (*nomen sive sermo*, he says on the same page). It is perhaps out of concern for originality that he chose *sermo* rather than *nomen*, but perhaps also because he considered that other expressions than those which grammatically speaking are nouns, such as verbs, could be universals (*Super Porphyrium*). So it is no longer *voces* but *sermones* that are now universals, insofar as they are vocal expressions that convey meaning. It is likely that it is Abelard's critiques of the universal as *vox*, along with the alternation between *vox* and *nomina* in Boethius, that led to the term *nomen* being retained and that ultimately motivated the transition from *Vocales* to *Nominales* around the middle of the twelfth century (see Marenbon, "Vocalism, Nominalism"). Whatever the primary motivation was for using the term *Nominales*, it is clear

that the theses attributed to the *Nominales* are not restricted to a position on universals (in logic) or on the *unita nominis* (in theology) but concern other questions as well, on propositions, on the relationship of the parts to the whole, and so on. Theologians from the middle of the thirteenth century will remember the *Nominales* exclusively as the defenders of the theory of the unity of the enunciable. Only Albert the Great will talk about the *Nominales* as supporting a thesis about universals, according to which they exist within the intellect, and this transition constitutes an essential link between the *Nominales* of the twelfth century, and those of the fourteenth to fifteenth centuries, a period in which the term refers unequivocally to Nominalists (see Kaluza, *Les querelles doctrinales à Paris*).

BIBLIOGRAPHY

Abelard, Peter. *Abélard ou la philosophie dans le langage*. Translated by J. Jolivet. Paris: Éditions du Cerf, 1994.
———. *Logica "Nostrorum petitioni sociorum."* Edited by B. Geyer. Münster: Aschendorff, 1933.
———. *Super Porphyrium*. Edited by B. Geyer. Münster: Aschendorff, 1919.
Courtenay, William. "*Nominales* and Nominalism in the Twelfth Century." In *Lectionum varietates: Hommage à Paul Vignaux*, edited by Jean Jolivet, Zénon Kaluza, and Alain de Libera, 11–48. Paris: Vrin, 1991.
Iwakuma, Yukio. "*Vocales* or Early Nominalists." *Tradition* 47 (1992): 37–111.
Kaluza, Zénon. *Les querelles doctrinales à Paris: Nominalistes et réalistes aux confins du XIVe et du XVe siècles*. Bergamo: Lubrina, 1988.
Libera, Alain de. *Querelle des universaux: De Platon à la fin du Moyen Age*. Paris: Éditions du Seuil, 1996.
Marenbon, John. "Vocalism, Nominalism and the Commentaries on the Categories from the Earlier Twelfth Century." *Vivarium* 30 (1992): 51–61.
Tweedale, Martin M., ed. and trans. *Scotus vs. Ockham: A Medieval Dispute over Universals*. 2 vols. Lewiston, NY: Mellen, 1999.

Avicenna's commentary, the questions that arose centered immediately on the imprecision of the terms *vox* and *vocare*. Given that *vox* is both the "vocal" sound made by animals that have lungs, a trachea, etc. and the same sound inasmuch as it is associated with a representation ("*cum imaginatione aliqua*"; 420b 29) (it is a sound that signifies, *sonus significativus*), the question of knowing whether animals *vocant* (this is glossed by *habent vocem*) or whether this activity is particular to man is literally untranslatable, since the verb refers to the two meanings of the noun (according to the classical

etymology: *vox a vocando dicitur* [*vox* is the term for what is expressed with a voice]). The answer to the question also depends on the status of the *imaginatio* for animals and on the role that the *imaginatio* plays in the vocals sounds made by animals in relation to instinct (see PHANTASIA and LANGUAGE). Along with Avicenna, some consider that the emission of *voces* (Avicenna's Latin text has *soni*) is confused for animals, in the sense that even if two vocal productions are numerically distinct, they are specifically distinct—in other words, all dogs bark, but each bark does not correspond to an individual mental *imago* (see the *Quaestio de voce* by Albert the Great). For Dante, when Ovid in the *Metamorphoses* talks about fish "that speak [*loquentibus*]," he is talking figuratively, since the act of fish or birds is not in fact a language (*locutio*) but rather an "imitation of the sound of our voice" (*imitatio soni nostre vocis*), "an imitation in the sense that we make sounds, and not in the sense that we speak" (*vel quod nituntur imitari nos in quantum sonamus, sed non in quantum loquimur*; *De vulgari eloquentia*, 2). So for him, the answer is clear: man alone was endowed with the ability to speak (*loqui*) ("*Et sic patet soli homini datur fuisse loqui*"; ibid.). It is worth noting again the terms *locutio* and *interpretatio* in the translation of *De anima*: "*Jam enim respiranti congruit natura in duo opera, sicut lingua in gustum et locutionem, quorum quidem gustus necessarium est, unde et pluribus inest, interpretatio autem est propter bene esse*" (For here nature uses the air that is inhaled for two purposes, just as it uses the tongue for tasting and for speech, the former use, for tasting, being indispensable, and therefore more widely found, while expression of thought is a means to wellbeing; Aristotle, *De anima*, 420b 16–20). *Locutio*, according to an anonymous commentator, is what allows man to "express what is within him by means of his speech [*sermo*]" (*Lectura in librum "De anima"*). He then posits an equivalence, glossing the second part of the sentence, between *interpretatio*, *sermo*, and *loquutio* (*sic*), to which he attributes this same definition. This distinction exists, however, in Greek, *intepretatio* translating *hermêneia*, a faculty that is not specific to man and that certain birds have, according to *De partibus animalium* (2.17.660a 35-b 1). This passage from *De anima* will become an oft-cited adage in universities (see LANGUAGE).

Medieval logicians were in general agreement about a minimal system in terms of a hierarchy that starts with *sonus* and to which successive differences are applied. The *sonus* (sound) is simply what is perceived by the ear. It can be vocal (*vox*) or not (*non vox*). The *vox* can be meaningful or not. The meaningful vocal sound can signify *ad placitum* or *naturaliter* (see SIGN, Box 3). The *dictio* is a *vox significativa ad placitum*, no part of which can signify separately, as opposed to the *oratio*, whose parts are meaningful. In the *Peri hermêneias*, Aristotle opposed the noun and the verb, on the one hand, with the *logos*, on the other, using a single criterion: the former have parts that are not meaningful, and the latter is made up of parts that are meaningful. The Latin authors later introduced the generic term *dictio* as a means of joining together the noun and the verb and distinguishing them from *oratio*, which allows them to oppose a simple signifying unit to a "complex" signifying unit. In practice, however, *vox* will be synonymous with *dictio* in the sense of "simple word." It is worth noting that *vox*, unlike *dictio* but like *nomen*, can be constructed with a genitive and thus becomes a relative term (see for example Roger Bacon, *De signis*, §148: "*rebus corruptis utimur vocibus illarum significative*" [when things are destroyed, we use (lit.) the vocal sounds of these things (that is, the ones which refer to them) in a way which signifies]). The *terminus* is a word insofar as it fulfills a function in a proposition, and "categorematic terms" are distinguished from "syncategorematic" terms, leading to the two types of treatises that constitute the so-called terminist logic, or *logica modernorum* (see TERM).

2. *Dictio* within speculative grammar

While *dictio* and *vox* were used almost interchangeably, as we have seen, to signify a word, the Modists, or *Modistae*, philosopher grammarians of the second half of the thirteenth century, proposed an original theory that articulates these two terms in a precise way on the basis of a double articulation of language. In this sense, no term in our modern languages can translate exactly what *dictio* meant for the Modists.

The theory of the Modists is based on a reflection on the process of the imposition of words, which is conceived in two stages. The process begins with *vox*, sound matter. Since it is endowed with a property that confers upon it an aptitude to signify (*ratio significandi*), at the end of the process of the first imposition *vox* becomes *dictio*. In a second stage, *dictio* is endowed with a property that confers upon it an aptitude to consignify (*ratio consignificandi*), and at the end of this process of second imposition, or articulation, *dictio* becomes *pars orationis* or *constructibile*. Strictly speaking, *dictio* is the signifier (matter) in that it is associated with the signified (form) that corresponds to the things as it is conceived, then signified (*res significata*). All of these terms correspond to the same *res* and are thus the same *dictio* (for example, "to suffer," "suffering," "ouch," etc.). In this context, *dictio* is untranslatable and corresponds to a sort of arch-word, or lexeme, or signifying unit that conveys a signified, although it would be difficult to imagine a single "vocal" vehicle that could carry the identical meaning that all of these expressions have. It is only once it is specified as a grammatical category (for example, as a verb) with its own grammatical properties, the means by which it can signify, that the linguistic unit is complete and able to be part of a statement: only then is it *constructibile*. The distinction between the two processes of imposition is justified on both an ontological and a psychological level. For the first time, and rather ephemerally as it happens, the two types of properties of the linguistic unit—the semantic properties and the morphosyntactic properties—are distinguished in this way: *dictio* corresponds only to the first, and *constructibile* to the second (See SENSE, III.B.3, and Box 3).

The notion of word as a minimal unit of meaning and of construction seems unavoidable and was not challenged until the nineteenth century. It was with comparative grammar that the idea of signifying units that are less than a word was first introduced, some expressing a meaning (*roots, sémantèmes*, Ger. *Bedeutungslaute*), others expressing a relationship (*morphemes*, Ger. *Beziehungslaute*), which are themselves separated into inflections and affixes. Realizing that this distinction is not valid for all language, linguists preferred to use a single term for all of the signifying units making up a word (Eng. "morpheme," "formative"; Fr. *morphème, formant*, or even, in Martinet, *monème*), which correspond, depending on the theory, either to *signifiers* (physical entities) or to *signs*. Moreover, the problem, which Aristotle and his commentators had already confronted with examples such as *tragelaphus* (goat-stag) or *respublica*, was that of the minimal signifying units which appear to be greater than the word, since they are made up of other minimal signifying units, and the consequent difficulty of separating them out from the sentence. One solution was proposed based on the notion of choice: for the speaker, *tragelaphus* or "pineapple," say, each correspond, just as "table" does, to one single choice and not to several consecutive choices. In the same way, the syntagm has been recognized as a minimal unit of construction after breaking the sentence down, since a syntagm can be made up of several words of morphemes that do not necessarily appear to be joined together in the linear chain of speech. In the same way again, the prospect of translation becoming an automatic process led French structuralist linguists at the beginning of the 1960s to define the units of segmentation of the written chain, which could also be units of translation. They therefore had to coin new terms to define syntactic units that are greater than the word being understood, not only from the point of view of their internal mode of construction, but also in terms of their relationship to the rest of the statement. All of these new names introduced (*lexies* in Bernard Pottier, *synapsies* in Émile Benveniste, *synthèmes* in André Martinet, and so on) reflect an unprecedented questioning of the criteria of identification, of construction, and of classification of minimal units and are based on precise theoretical choices (see Léon, "Conceptions du mot"). Attempts to eliminate the word and to treat it as one syntagm among others, in order to assimilate the different processes of combination, have ultimately been called into question. In recent linguistics, attention has turned once again to the word, and to its specificities as a unit (that is, as the site of realization of phonological or morphological phenomena), which is distinct from the sentence (the constrained, non-motivated, non-free nature of the combination of its constituent elements, and so on). What is more, the segmentation into words remains, in the Western tradition, inseparably bound up with certain practical ends: teaching, classifying, translating, and making dictionaries.

IV. The Terms for "Word" in French

A. *Mot*

Latin (RT: Du Cange, *Glossarium mediæ et infimæ latinitatis*) and etymological dictionaries (RT: Ménage, *Dictionnaire etymologique, ov Origines de la langue françoise*; RT: Ernout and Meillet, *Dictionnaire étymologique de la langue latine*; RT: von Wartburg, *Französisches etymologisches Wörterbuch*) all agree that the word *mot* comes from the Low Latin *muttum* (word, grunt), derived from the verb *muttire* meaning "to say mu," that is, both (a) to make a grunt, or an inarticulate sound like cattle, or humans deprived of the power of speech (*mute, mutus*), and (b) to breath a word, to make an articulate statement. This etymology, which might seem paradoxical, is, however, part of the tradition in that it accumulates two types of etymology anticipated by Isidore of Seville: onomatopoeia and antiphrasis. The recourse to onomatopoeia in etymology was a common practice from the Middle Ages to the Renaissance (see Buridan, *L'étymologie*). It constituted the privileged site and example of the principle of a fit between designation and signification, insofar as the signification reduplicated the designation, and motivated it by giving it a meaning. Moreover, the contradictory meaning of "to say mu," both an inarticulate sound and an articulate statement, can be compared to the etymology by antiphrasis, or opposition, that the ancients were fond of: so, for example, *lucus* (wood) was said to be derived from *lucendo* (light), because

there is no light in a wood (*lucus a non lucendo* [a clearing because one cannot see clearly]).

If we postulate more simply that *muttum* means "sound emitted" (RT: Bloch and von Wartburg, *Dictionnaire étymologique de la langue française*; RT: *DHLF*), we see that, in Low Latin, the first attested uses of the word *mot* were always negative, meaning "not to make a sound": *ne muttum quidem audet dicere* (he does not dare say a word); *ne mu quidem audere facere* (to not even dare to say *mu*). This is also true of the first attested uses of the word *mot* in Old French, in the *Song of Roland* in the eleventh century: "N'i ad paien qui un sul mot respondet" (Not one pagan replied with a single word), or "N'i a celui qui mot sont ne mot tint" (There was no-one who made the sound or the ring of a word). We might also think of the French exclamation *motus*, urging someone to remain silent (in present-day French one also says *ne mot dire* (not to say a word). *Mot* is said to have evolved into its meaning of *parole* (spoken word) through its contact with verbs such as *dire* (to say), *sonner* (to sound), *tinter* (to ring), *respondre* (to reply), and *mot* became the signifying unit we use today through the expression *mot à mot* (word for word), suggesting as early as the twelfth century a segmentation of language.

B. *Verbe*

Verbe comes from the Latin *verbum*, which shares the same Indo-European root with terms from a dialect region of Indo-European.

Compared to the Latin *verbum*, which has three meanings, the meaning of *verbe* in French is more restricted. Firmin Le Ver's first Latin-French dictionary (RT: *Firmini Verris dictionarius*) thus contains three entries for *verbum*: (1) a conversation among several people, (2) the son of God, the second person of the Holy Trinity, and (3) a part of speech that has tense and mood. The last two meanings of *verbe* are attested in French from the twelfth century as a part of speech, *tel fist personel del verbe impersonal*, and as the word of God, *Deu verbe* (1120), which will become *le Verbe* (the Word), the second person of the Trinity, God incarnate, from the sixteenth century.

C. *Parole*

Parole comes from the Greek *parabolê* [παραβολή], which Latin borrows as *parabola*, documented since Seneca. It was when the Septuagint was being written (the first Hebrew-to-Greek translation of the Old Testament) that its translators gave two meanings to *parabolê*: "comparison" and "allegory," using the Greek *parabolê* to translate the Hebrew *mashal* [מָשָׁל], which did have these two meanings. This double meaning was adopted by the Christian Latin writers Tertullian and Jerome, and the term *parabola*, as well as its derivations, would spread throughout the everyday language of Christianity between the fifth and eighth centuries, with the meaning "fable," "tale" and would then finally assume the meaning of "speech," "way of speaking." In almost all Romance languages it therefore replaced the Latin *verbum* as a term designating the word; *verbum* would remain in these languages, but it would be reserved for technical, theological, and grammatical uses.

D. *Verbe/parole*

The Low Latin *parabola* was used to designate the word in Romance languages (with the exception of Romanian) because of how frequently this term was used in sermons and also because people were loath to use *verbum*, which was reserved for *Verbe*, the translation of the Greek *Logos* [Λόγος], the Word of God in John's Gospel (see LOGOS). In French, *parole* was used until the sixteenth century in a nonreligious sense. But as a result of the wars of Religion and the advent of French as the national language with the creation of the Académie française in 1635, *Parole* began to compete with *Verbe* as a translation of the incarnation of God in religious texts during the sixteenth and seventeenth centuries. In the Geneva Bible of 1669 we thus find the following commentary: "the Greek *ho Logos*, which in vulgar language is called *le Verbe*, and which is more conveniently translated as *la Parole*." But it was the term *Verbe*, first used in the *Œuvres chrestiennes* of Desportes (around 1600), that would replace *Parole*, first in religious literature and then gradually in the translations of the Bible (Le Maistre de Sacy, 1678), where it would finally become the accepted term.

This was a transitional period from a linguistic and religious point of view. In the sixteenth century, French prevailed over Latin as a means of expression in literature and theology. The debate was complicated by the religious disputes between Protestants and Catholics, who supported opposing positions. Protestants called for the use of French as the ecclesiastical language, and Catholics firmly held on to Latin in the liturgy and the translations of the Bible. In the sixteenth century, *parole* became a word that was appropriated by Protestants, who called their ministers *ministres de la Parole de Dieu* (ministers of the Word of God). *La Parole* was even used to refer to Protestantism ("The king . . . has proclaimed a general abolition whereby the prisons have been opened for all those who were prisoners for the word [*parole*]. This is the term we use instead of saying religion"; É. Pasquier, *Lettres*, 4.5). For Calvin, the Word (*Parole*) was the incarnation of God: "Therefore, as all revelations from heaven are duly designated by the title of the word of God, so the highest place must be assigned to that substantial Word, the source of all inspiration, which, as being liable to no variation, remains for ever one and the same with God, and is God" (*Institutes of the Christian Religion*, 71); "Christ is that Word become incarnate" (ibid.). It was thus no surprise that it was *Verbe* that would prevail during the Counter-Reformation.

The transition was apparent in the first monolingual dictionaries of the seventeenth century. *Verbe* was thus defined as *Parole* in the Richelet dictionary, RT: *Dictionnaire françois* (1680): "This word is used in terms of *Theology and Holy Scripture*, and means *Jesus-Christ*, the second person of the Trinity. It also means *la parole*"; see also the RT: *Dictionnaire de l'Académie française* (1694): "Jesus-Christ is called *la parole éternelle, la parole incréée, la parole incarnée* [the eternal word, the unbegotten word, the word incarnate] although one more commonly says *le Verbe*." The Word of God (*Verbum Dei*) refers in both dictionaries to the Holy Scripture.

E. Mot/Parole

In the seventeenth century, as a result of the establishment of French as the language of the state and the national language (see Collinot and Mazière, *Un prêt-à-parler*), the production of the Port-Royal *Grammaire générale et raisonnée* (1660), and the appearance of the first monolingual dictionaries, French came of age as a language and as a rival to Latin.

Parole was the scientific term referring to the faculty of language. It was the only entry in the *Dictionnaire des arts et des sciences de l'Académie française* (1694) to the exclusion of *mot* and *verbe*: "The articulation that the sound produced by the air passing through the trachea receives from the tongue and the throat," a definition copied from the way Aristotle defined *phônê* [φωνή], the "voice," that is, the noise produced by an animate being (*De anima*, 2.8.420b 5–29; see above, *vox*, III.A).

In the first monolingual dictionaries, even though *mot* and *parole* were defined the one by the other—"*Mot: parole* of one or more syllables. *Parole*: articulated *mot* of one or more syllables" (RT: Furetière, *Dictionnaire universel*)—*mot* became the unit of language, and *parole* the unit of speech.

So, following Furetière's definition, *mot* was clearly defined as a linguistic unit required by the dictionary and by the grammars that classified words as parts of speech. As for *parole*, it referred more generally to the language "used to explain thought, and that man alone is capable of speaking" (ibid.). Likewise, in the RT: *Dictionnaire de l'Académie française*, the first collocations referred to *mot* as a unit of language—"French word, Latin word, Greek word, Barbarian word"—whereas *parole* was a unit of speech: "mot prononcé" (spoken word). Finally, in RT: Richelet (*Dictionnaire françois*), it is the unit of language as a *distinct* unit that is foregrounded for *mot*: "Everything that is spoken and written separately . . . To transcribe word for word [*mot pour mot*]"; while *parole* was defined as "speech and explanation of thought by using sound and voice."

Nonetheless, the norm advocated during the seventeenth century by no means dispelled the different meanings of *mot* and *parole*, and present-day dictionaries retain many traces of this historically determined polysemy (see also LANGUAGE).

Marc Baratin
Barbara Cassin
Irène Rosier-Catach
Frédérique Ildefonse
Jean Lallot
Jacqueline Léon

BIBLIOGRAPHY

Aeschines. *The Speeches of Aeschines with an English translation by Charles Darwin Adams*. Cambridge, MA: Harvard University Press, 1919.

Allan, Keith. *The Western Classical Tradition in Linguistics*. London: Equinox, 2007.

Apollonius Dyscolus. *De constructione*. Edited by Gustav Uhlig. *Grammatici graeci* 2.2. Leipzig: Teubner, 1910. Translation by Fred W. Householder: *The Syntax of Apollonius Dyscolus*. Amsterdam: Benjamins, 1981.

Aristotle. *De anima*. Translated by R. D. Hicks. Cambridge: Cambridge University Press, 1907.

———. *Poetics*. In Vol. 2 of *The Complete Works of Aristotle*, edited by Jonathan Barnes. Princeton, NJ: Princeton University Press / Bollingen, 1984.

Aurous, Sylvain, ed. *Histoire des idées linguistiques*. Vol. 2, *Le développement de la grammaire occidentale*. Liège, Belg.: Mardaga, 1992.

Baratin, Marc. "Les origines stoïciennes de la théorie augustinienne du signe." *Revue des Études Latines* 59 (1981): 260–68.

Boethius. *Commentarii in librum Aristotelis Peri hermêneias*. 2nd ed. Edited by C. Meiser. Leipzig: Teubner, 1880.

Buridan, C., ed. *L'étymologie de l'Antiquité à la Renaissance. Lexique* 14 (1998).

Calvin, John. *Institutes of the Christian Religion*. Translated by Henry Beveridge. Peabody, MA: Hendrickson Publishers, 2008.

Cassin, Barbara. "Homonymi et signifiant." In *L'effet sophistique*. Paris: Gallimard, 1995.

———. "Who's Afraid of the Sophists? Against Ethical Correctness." Translated by Charles T. Wolfe. *Hypatia* 15, no. 4 (2000): 102–20.

Collinot, André, and Francine Mazière. *Un prêt à parler: Le dictionnaire*. Paris: Presses Universitaires de France, 1997.

Diogenes Laertius. *Lives of Eminent Philosophers*. Translated by R. D. Hicks. 2 vols. Cambridge, MA: Harvard University Press, 1972.

Dionysius Thrax. *Technê grammatikê*. Edited by Gustav Uhlig. *Grammatici graeci* 1.1. Leipzig: Teubner, 1883. Translation by Thomas Davidson: *The Grammar*. St. Louis: Studley, 1874.

Di Pasquale, M.-L. "La notion de mot dans le *De lingua Latina* de Varron." *Lalies* 10 (1992): 135–41.

Frede, Dorothea, and Brad Inwood, eds. *Language and Learning: Philosophy of Language in the Hellenistic Age*. Cambridge: Cambridge University Press, 2005.

Frede, Michael, and John M. Rist. "Principles of Stoic Grammar." In *The Stoics*, edited by John M. Rist, 27–75. Berkeley: University of California Press, 1978.

Fruyt, Michèle, and Marie-José Reichler-Béguelin. "La notion de 'mot' en latin et dans d'autres langues indo-européennes anciennes." *Modèles Linguistiques* 12 (1990): 21–46.

Imbert, Claude. "Théorie de la représentation et doctrine logique dans le stoïcisme ancient." In *Les Stoïciens et leur logique*, edited by Jacques Brunschwig. Paris: Vrin, 1978.

Juilland, Alphonse, and Alexandra Roceric. *The Linguistic Concept of Word: Analytic Bibliography*. The Hague: Mouton, 1972.

Lallot, Jean. "Le mot dans la tradition grammaticale et prégrammaticale en Grèce." *Lalies* 10 (1992): 125–34.

Lectura in librum "De anima." Edited by R. A. Gauthier. Grottaferrata, Italy: Collegii S. Bonaventurae ad Claras Aquas, 1985.

Léon, Jacqueline. "Conceptions du mot et débuts de la traduction automatique." *Histoire, Épistemologie, Langage* 23, no. 1 (2001): 81–106.

Long, A. A. "Stoic Linguistics, Plato's Cratylus, and Augustine's *De Dialectica*." In *Language and Learning: Philosophy of Language in the Hellenistic Age*, edited by Dorothea Frede and Brad Inwood, 36–55. Cambridge: Cambridge University Press, 2005.

Manetti, Giovanni. *Theories of the Sign in Classical Antiquity*. Translated by Christine Richardson. Bloomington: Indiana University Press, 1993.

Nicot, Jean. *Le thresor de la langue françoyse tant ancienne que moderne*. Paris: D. Douceur, 1606.

Padley, G. A. *Grammatical Theory in Western Europe, 1500–1700*. 2 vols. Cambridge: Cambridge University Press, 1985–88.

WORD ORDER

➤ ASPECT, COMBINATION AND CONCEPTUALIZATION, *DISCOURSE*, EUROPE, FRENCH, LOGOS, PREDICATION, PROPOSITION, SIGN, SIGNIFIER/SIGNIFIED, SPEECH ACT, WORD

Terms and word order are part of ordinary language. They are used in the informal description of languages and in particular serve to identify differences among languages. Thus German differs from French in its vocabulary (its words) and in the word order in utterances. Grammar and then linguistics have provided concepts to characterize the formal nature of what they designate. Here we will provide an analysis of the phenomena grouped under the rubric "word order," presented as a rational reconstruction (I. Lakatos, *Proofs and Refutations*).

We will first review the problematics that emerges from grammatical reflection on the phenomenological diversity of languages

when we consider the placement of functional constituents in the sentence. Then we will set forth a few elements for the critique of this problematics, which contemporaries see as a kind of vulgate. Finally, we will abandon the notion of word order and propose the concept of construction, as it is defined in one of the contemporary schools of the generative paradigm (construction grammars) to analyze the pertinence of the placement of constituents in the utterance.

From this point of view, it can be maintained that the lexical unit (the concept making it possible to analyze what the term "word" designates) and construction are entities of the same type, signs (lexical signs and syntagmatic signs, according to the terminology of the grammatical framework of Head-driven Phrase Structure Grammar [HPSG]), which allows us to extend the notion of arbitrariness, in Saussure's sense, to the architecture of the utterance, and to overdetermination, in Lacan's sense. The linguistic analysis completed, we conclude that, if word order gives rise to an untranslatable, this untranslatable has the same etiology as the one to which words may give rise.

I. The Vulgate on Word Order

A. The fixed order of French

Word order seems at first to be what distinguishes French from Latin. Sentence (1) has the same meaning, that is, the same propositional content, as sentences (2):

(1) *Le père aime le fils*

(2) (a) *Pater filium amat*
   (b) *Amat pater filium*
   (c) *Filium pater amat*
   (d) *Pater amat filium*
   (e) *Amat filium pater*
   (f) *Filium amat pater*

We say that the order is "fixed" in French because (1) can be translated by (2) in Latin, but also because (1) is not equivalent to (3):

(3) *Le fils aime le père*

and because the order of (1) is not open to any variation, which is shown by the agrammaticality (signaled in the examples by the asterisk *) of the sentences in (4):

(4) (a) **Le père le fils aime*
   (b) **Aime le père le fils*
   (c) **Aime le fils le père*
   (d) **Le fils le père aime*

Moreover, the possibility of varying the order of the constituents in Latin is further increased if we take into consideration two facts: the order of a noun and its determinant can vary within the noun group (henceforth NG); and the members of a given group cannot form a continuous sequence. In (5), the determinant (*suum*) is to the left or the right of the determined noun (*filium*); in (6), the determinant is separated from the noun that it determines by constituents that do not belong to the NG that they constitute (they are separated, in this case, by the NG subject *pater*):

(5) (a) *Pater suum filium amat*
   (b) *Pater filium suum amat*

(6) *Suum pater filium amat*

We synthesize the observation by saying that French is a fixed-order language and Latin a free-order language. We have succeeded, after long controversies, in explaining this differential. It is because French does not have a case-based morphological system that it resorts to a fixed word order: French exploits the opposition between preverbal placement and postverbal placement to identify the nominal terms fulfilling the functions of subject and object. On the other hand, the reason that several word orders are available in Latin is that this language has an inflectional system of morphology that marks cases: thus in (2), the NGs *filium* and *pater*, whatever place they occupy in relation to *amat*, are identified as forms bearing, respectively, the affixed marks of the accusative and the nominative, and thus as terms performing distinct functions. From this analysis we draw the following proportion: word order is to French as case is to Latin. If case-based inflection is a system of marks, then word order is a system of marks. They are grammatical functions that are marked, in one case by morphological means, and in the other by means of a relative order.

- See Box 1.

B. The free word order of Latin

We have to return to this notion of Latin's "free" word order. Latin permits six orders realized in the sentences in (2). But it is acknowledged that among these six orders, one is unmarked: the order SOV (Subject Object Verb, to adopt the vocabulary of modern typologies), illustrated by the following sentence:

(7) *Pater filium amat*

In particular, we maintain that this order is pragmatically neutral. The latter analysis assumes that if the six sentences of (2) share the same propositional content, they differ in their pragmatic value. The orders exhibited by the other five sentences are associated with values that have long been known as expressivity, emphasis, or insistence. We can render these values by means of glosses that, in French, appeal precisely to constructions of the utterance that are distinct from the one that presides over the canonical sentence proposed in (1):

(8) (a)   *Amat pater filium*
    (a')   *Il l'aime, le père, son fils*
    (b)   *Filium pater amat*

    (b')   *Son fils, le père l'aime*
    (b'') *C'est son fils que le père aime*
    (b''') *C'est son fils qu'aime le père*

The word order in Latin is free, that is, not constrained insofar as the marking of functions in the syntactical dimension is concerned, but it is neither aleatory nor without meaning. We can synthesize the observation by positing the following generalization, which condenses the content of a vulgate shared by the grammatical and stylistic traditions:

(9) The order of words constitutes a mark. Depending on the languages, it has a role as a syntactical mark or a role as a pragmatic mark.

C. The division of labor

If we project generalization (9) into a grammatical apparatus, we are led to understand that the different dimensions of organization distinguished in languages can enter into relationships of equivalence. What morphology marks in language A is marked by word order in language B. What is marked syntactically in language C is marked by intonation in language D. For example, contemporary theories acknowledge that whether or not the subject NG (the fact that the grammatical subject NG is also the logical subject) has a thematic character is marked in Italian by word order, in English by intonation, and in Japanese by morphology.

Thus in (10), the grammatical subject NG is not a logical subject: it is postverbal in Italian, accent-bearing (with correlative disaccentuation of the verbal group) in English, and marked by the particle *ga* (which is opposed to a "thematic" particle *wa*) in Japanese:

(10) (a) *Mi si è rotta la macchina*
     (b) *My car broke* down
     (c) *Watashino   kuruma   ga   koshoo   sheiteimas*
        (I   car   particle   breakdown   verb)

This image of grammar is now common in linguistics, particularly in grammatical approaches that include the pragmatic dimension (cf., for example, K. Lambrecht, *Information Structure and Sentence Form*), but also in reflections on translation. Foucault bases his (enthusiastic) critical assessment of Klossowski's translation of the *Aeneid* on the following premise:

> The Latin sentence . . . can be governed simultaneously by two prescriptions: that of syntax, which declinations

---

1

A "Natural and Perfect Order"

In Simone Delesalle and Jean-Claude Chevalier's book *La linguistique, la grammaire et l'école*, we find a synthetic presentation of the debate that brings out the problematics of word order in the seventeenth and eighteenth centuries. We can also consult Ulrich Ricken, *Grammaire et Philosophie au siècle des Lumières* (1978), which identifies two central points in this debate: (a) the relation between word order and thought, and (b) the evaluation of languages in relation to each other, the French order being considered perfect because it is natural. In the initial analyses of Claude Lancelot's *Port-Royal Grammar* (1975), language is compared with "thought," which is supposed to constitute the reference: "The natural order, in conformity with the natural expression of our thoughts, consists in a judgment expressed with regard to a concept, the substantive subject coming first" (S. Delesalle and J.-C. Chevalier, *La Linguistique*, 40), because the substance has to precede the accident. "We can say that at this stage of the analysis [at Port-Royal] the resemblance between the order of French and the natural order of thought is itself so natural and so integrated that it does not need to be explained, much less justified" (ibid., 4).

make sensible; and another, purely plastic one that is revealed by a word order that is always free but never gratuitous. . . . Whereas in French syntax prescribes the order and the sequence of words reveals the precise architecture of the system.

("Les mots qui saignent," 425)

D. The terms and content of the relation of order

The term "word" in "word order" covers two types of units: lexical units considered in the constitution of groups, and groups considered in the constitution of the utterance. When we speak of "word order" we are thus speaking about the order of the constituents in the different groups and about the order of the groups in the utterance.

Furthermore, the notion of order covers three types of phenomena. The first is constituted by the relations of placement relative to a term: for example, the French subject NG is preverbal (to the left of the inflected verb). If it appears to the right of the verb, then we speak of "inversion." The second is constituted by the fixed placement of certain constituents. For example, the subordinating word necessarily appears at the head of the subordinate clause in Latin; Latin has, from this point of view, at least one rule of fixed order. Finally, the third phenomenon groups together relations of adjacency. In a language like French, the parts of a given group are adjacent; one cannot mix the parts of several syntagmas in the sequence, as one can in Latin; in (6), the subject NG is interpolated between the two parts of the object NG. In French, the relation of adjacency brings together terms that enter into a relation of grammatical dependency that contemporary linguistics has constructed under the name of "syntagma." It is not true that in all languages the relations of dependency coincide with relations of adjacency in the sequence.

II. Critique of the Vulgate

In relation to the details of the organization of languages, neither generalization (9) nor the relationships of equivalence between the means of expression that it produces are empirically correct. These propositions are defective mainly because of the idealization they presuppose and because, by immediately constituting word order as a mark, they cannot envisage recognizing in it a purely formal type of organization. In the following we will limit ourselves to the syntactical dimension (reduced to the coding of functional relations between the verbal head and its arguments) and the pragmatic dimension; we will leave completely aside the semantic and prosodic dimensions.

- See Box 2.

A. The accumulation of values

According to generalization (9), word order is used to mark either grammatical functions or pragmatic distinctions. If the analysis we have given of the contrast between (1) and (2) is correct, we might expect word order not to be available in French to mark pragmatic distinctions, because it is used to mark grammatical functions. But that is not what we see. In French, the order of constituents in the utterance also serves as a support for the expression of pragmatic values.

We have seen that utterance (1) (*Le père aime son fils*) exhibits the sole possible order in the sentence, namely the SVO order. This order characterizes the canonical construction of the sentence. We can schematize the spatial organization, or, to adopt a terminology traditional in the linguistics of Germanic languages, the topological organization of construction by a tree-representation (11), in which the order among groups is explicitly represented:

(11)

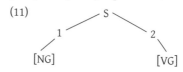

2

Weil's thesis: Syntax, word order, and the order of thought

The thesis that Henri Weil published in 1844 and that was republished by M. Bréal in 1869 marks a break with the problematics inherited from the eighteenth century and introduces a certain number of ideas that prefigure those that we take as the basis of our analysis. A synthetic presentation of this thesis will be found in Simone Delesalle and Jean-Claude Chevalier, *La linguistique, la grammaire et l'école* (37–90, 179–94), and it is put into a contemporary perspective in Françoise Kerleroux, "Discordances d'une langue à une autre, d'une langue à elle-même."

a. According to Weil, syntax and word order constitute distinct orders. We find the same principle of partitioning in contemporary grammars that treat relations of

constituence and relations of dependency (which cover functional relations) as a module of rules (or constraints) distinct from the module bringing together the rules that govern the linearization of constituents (rules or constraints of "linear precedence"). Gerald Gazdar et al., *Generalized Phrase Structure Grammar*, is the standard reference work.

b. Weil posits, alongside the development of syntax, a development of thought (*marche de la pensée*) in which the notion of *thought* refers to a pragmatic-enunciative dimension, and which he conceives as a universal organization. In this organization he distinguishes the "initial element" and the "end" of the sentence. This

conception is still alive in contemporary functionalist approaches (cf., for example, P. Downing and M. Noonan, eds., *Word Order in Discourse*). There are thus two principles of order: a purely syntactical principle and a pragmatic-enunciative principle.

c. Weil relates the order that we observe in actual utterances to a "mutual relationship" between the different developments. We make the same distinction between two principles of order in what we will call "construction": we will distinguish between the topological organization of the utterance, and constraints of a pragmatic-discursive nature bearing on the places (or fields) defined by topology.

The construction figured by the tree in (11) is far from being neutral from the pragmatic point of view. We see, in fact, that the NG that appears under branch 1 (or the left field of the sentence, by opposition to branch 2, which describes the right field) is, in an actual utterance, rarely an NG that introduces a new referent of discourse, that is, a referent that does not belong to the shared universe of discourse and that the content of the utterance makes it possible to identify. We can show this fact by contrasting the answers to a question of the following type:

(12) *Qu'est-ce qui se passe?*

This type of question calls for an answer bearing on a situation whose characteristics are completely new, in particular the participants. We see that an utterance belonging to the canonical construction, like (13a), is not the most appropriate form of answer; in ordinary usage, one would answer with the utterances (13b) or (13c):

(13) [*Qu'est-ce qui se passe?*]
 (a) *Un chien aboie*
 (b) *Il y a un chien qui aboie*
 (c) *C'est un chien qui aboie*

The utterance (13a) is well formed syntactically: no syntactical constraint prevents an indefinite NG from appearing in the left field of the sentence or from being a grammatical subject. If (13a) is not appropriate in the context defined by question (12), we have to seek the reason in the pragmatic value attached to the canonical construction in general and to its left field in particular.

The existence of turns of phrase like (13b) or (13c) (two split constructions that are called "presentational") and their appropriate character in the context of (12) constitute another indication that (11) is not pragmatically neutral. For an NG that introduces a new referent of discourse, the right field of the sentence is favored. It is the "genius" of the two presentational constructions (split into *il y a . . . qui*, and *c'est . . . qui*) to make the NG, a dog (*chien*), which introduces a completely new referent, appear in the right field of the matrix sentence (*il y a un chien* or *c'est un chien*): we note that the main informational content of the utterance is provided by the subordinate clause *qui aboie*. In other words, the cleavage uses for discursive ends not so much the fixed nature of the grammatical order SVO as the rigidity of the matching between a pragmatic value and a field in the construction of the sentence of which (11) describes the topological organization.

We can analytically dissociate grammatical distinction (the expression of functions) and pragmatic distinction (the expression of the informational value of an NG), but the support for this double system of values is one and the same. It is the topological organization figured by the tree in (11) that constitutes this support. Thus the word order in actual utterances can accumulate a double system of values. That is the case in French: the order of constituents is simultaneously syntactical and pragmatic.

B. Morphology and the value of word order

According to the view of grammar that underlies generalization (9), morphology and word order are in a relationship of complementarity: if one language has a rich morphology (used to distinguish grammatical functions), we would expect word order, freed of the responsibility of marking functions, to be available for the expression of pragmatic distinctions. However, German constitutes a clear counterexample for this expectation. German is a language that includes both a rich case-morphology and phenomena of strict fixation in word order. Moreover, this fixity is not associated with the expression of any value in any interpretive dimension (semantic or pragmatic).

Three kinds of order are characteristic of the German sentence. The untensed verb (participle, infinitive) occupies the final position in the sentence; (14) illustrates the rule with a past participle (*gesehen*):

(14) Adam saw a rose
 (a) *Adam hat eine Rose gesehen*
 (b) **Adam hat gesehen eine Rose*

The tensed form of the verb (in the examples above, the auxiliary *hat*) can occupy only two places: either the absolutely final position in a subordinate clause (15), or the second position in an independent clause (16):

(15) I believe that Adam saw a rose
 (a) *Ich glaube, dass Adam eine Rose gesehen hat*
 (b) **Ich glaube, dass Adam hat eine Rose gesehen*

(16) Adam saw a rose
 (a) *Eine Rose hat Adam gesehen*
 (b) **Eine Rose Adam gesehen hat*

Finally, the initial field (which German grammarians call the *Vorfeld*) can be occupied by only one constituent:

(17) Adam saw a rose yesterday, or, Yesterday, Adam saw a rose
 (a) *Eine Rose hat Adam gestern gesehen*
 (b) *Gestern hat Adam eine Rose gesehen*
 (c) **Gestern eine Rose hat Adam gesehen*

This constituent can be any element dependent on the verb, whatever its function and category (18a, b), but it can also be a conjunction (18c, d), as is shown by these two verses by Goethe (in "Erlkönig"), which we have segmented into sentences:

(18) (a) *Ich liebe dich*
 (b) *Mich reizt deine schöne Gestalt*
 (c) *Und bist du nicht willig*
 (d) *So brauche ich Gewalt*
   (I love you, / your fair face pleases me / and if you're not willing / then I'll use force)

Thus we must dissociate the two characteristics of fixed word order and the "richness" of case morphology: the existence of a rich morphology does not necessarily imply a free order of the constituents. The only generalization that a language like German allows us to make is that a rich morphological repertory, when it is used to mark functional distinctions, can enable dependent elements to avoid subjection to fixed placement, either among themselves or in relation to the constituent on which they depend.

The three rules of word order in German are associated neither with functional marking nor with the expression of a given semantic or pragmatic value. Their only value is to create demarcations in the topological space itself: they delimit distinct fields in the utterance.

C. Word order is arbitrary

The fact of appearing to the left or the right of another term is in itself an insignificant characteristic. For example, the fact that the object is placed to the right or to the left of the verb plays no role in the definition of what the grammatical function of the object of the verb is. The same goes for all grammatical functions (subject, complement, addition) or semantic functions (argument, modifier, determinant). The fact of occupying a fixed place in the utterance and even the fact that two constituents must necessarily be contiguous are also in themselves insignificant. For example, appearing at the beginning, in the middle, or at the end of a sentence in no way affects the functioning of the French possessive determinant in relation to its Latin equivalent, which is not subject to this constraint [cf. (5) above]. In other words, there is nothing natural about word order. This point is important, because it constitutes word order as an arbitrary characteristic of languages. This outcome is commonly recognized by specialists in syntax. Among typologists inspired by functionalism, there is still some debate as to whether the chronology of psycholinguistic processes of encoding and decoding might constitute a factor determining word order, at least at the level of the utterance.

Many languages, in fact, allow us to make the following observation:

(19) Thematic constituents precede rhematic constituents.

A thematic constituent is one that refers to the referent about which it provides information; a rhematic constituent is one that conveys new information.

In languages that have the notion of a subject, the subject is generally thematic and the verb (and its dependencies) is rhematic. For example, the distribution of pragmatic values in the canonical construction of French [cf. (11) above] falls under this generalization. The same seems to be partially true of German: the utterances in (17) can be analyzed as illustrating the generalization formulated in (19), but not those in (18c, d), because the initial field is occupied by constituents that have no descriptive content. Thus the hypothesis has been put forward that (19) could be the effect of a cognitive principle according to which it is natural to present the theme of the discourse first, so that it functions as an anchor-point for information or elaborations conveyed by discourse. In other words, the linearization of the informational constituents might reflect the chronology of psycholinguistic operations.

However, experiments on encoding and decoding have provided no decisive empirical support for this hypothesis. Moreover, there is a direct counterexample: some languages have the inverse order—the rhematic constituents precede the thematic constituents. This is the case for languages like Ojibwa, Nandi, or Toba Batak (Amerindian, Afro-Asiatic, and Austronesian languages, respectively). These are languages in which the verb appears in the first position in the sentence (so-called VSO languages). This correlation suggests that the relative order between theme and rheme is not determined by an external principle that prevails in the language. In other words, a generalization like (19) cannot be considered proof of the motivation of the order of constituents by an external process, but rather as the effect of the coding, by the grammars of languages, of pragmatic distinctions. Word order is thus arbitrary in the same sense and on the same grounds as the relationship between signifier and signified in the morpheme: it is not motivated by any external principle. In section III we will examine more closely this comparison between word order and morphemes.

D. Critique of the founding paradigm of the vulgate

The vulgate regarding word order is essentially based on the comparison between Latin and French illustrated above by the contrast between (1) and (2). It has given rise to a series of variants using other pairs of languages (Russian and English, English and Finnish, etc.), to the point of becoming a cliché in contemporary linguistic arguments. But this contrast is deceptive: in fact, it draws attention exclusively to the fact that the dependent elements are not subject to placement constraints with regard to each other or to the constituent on which they depend. We have just seen that the placement of elements depending on the verb (which constitutes the major syntactical phenomenon in many languages) is distinct from the placement of constituents in the utterance. From a contrast like (1)-(2) we can therefore draw no conclusion regarding the order of constituents in the utterance in general.

III. Word Order and Construction

Word order is a reflection, in utterances, of the topological organization of the language. Figure (11) offers a representation of the topology of the phrastic field; figure (21) below situates the phrastic field within the topological organization of the utterance. Recently it has been discovered that the value attached to each field is variable. It varies depending on the construction. Thus a single field can be associated with distinct values. We will illustrate this point by considering the pragmatic values associated with the prephrastic field. Here we will grant, in accord with theories of the informational component (K. Lambrecht, *Information Structure and Sentence Form*), that there are two types of pragmatic value to be distinguished: the old (pragmatically presupposed) or new (asserted) nature of a bit of information, on the one hand, and the degree of accessibility of the referents of discourse (generally introduced by an NG), on the other hand.

■ See Box 3.

A. A single topological organization and two pragmatic values

French has two constructions that are designated by the conventional names of "left dislocation" (*dislocation gauche*) and "topicalization." Several properties distinguish them from each other; the most obvious is the fact that the prephrastic constituent is repeated by a pronoun in the case of dislocation, and that there is no repetition in topicalization:

(20) (Dislocation)
  (a) *Marie, (je pense que) je l'ai vue*
    [*The constituent "Marie" is repeated by the anaphoric pronoun "l"*]
    (*Topicalization*)

3
How should we deal with the order of constituents?

In grammars that make use of the notion of construction, there are three ways of dealing with the order of constituents: (a) by orderly trees, (b) by the constraints of linear precedence, or (c) by positing a topological organization (O. Bonami, "DI/ DP, linéarisation, arbres polychromes").

For the defense and illustration of the topological approach, see, among others, Andreas Kathol, *Linear Syntax*, and Jean-Marie Marandin, "Sites et constructions dans la théorie de la syntaxe," and the references cited therein. For a presentation of the concept of construction,

see Charles Fillmore, Paul Kay, and Mary C. O'Connor, "Regularity and Idiomaticity in Grammatical Constructions," *Language* 64, no. 3 (1988): 501–38, and Arnold M. Zwicky, "Dealing Out Meaning: Fundamentals of Syntactic Constructions," *Berkeley Linguistic Society*, 20 (1994): 611–25.

(b) *À Marie, (je pense que) je répondrai par la négative*
[The constituent "Marie" is not repeated in any way]

It has been shown, and we will accept here, that the two constructions make use of the same topological organization, which we can schematize as follows:

(21)   Utterance
           (1)   (2)
    Prephrastic Field   Phrastic field

Even though the word order is identical, the pragmatic value attached to the constituent that occupies the prephrastic field is different in the dislocated construction (20a) from what it is in the topicalized construction (20b).

The prephrastic constituent of left dislocation introduces a referent that must already be identified (in particular, the information contributed by the sentence cannot serve to identify it) and that necessarily functions as a theme. This constraint has an impact on the type of NG that can appear in this prephrastic field. It can be neither an NG reduced to a bare quantifier (22a) nor an indefinite NG with a specific or existential interpretation (22b):

(22) (a) **Beaucoup, je les vois*
     (b) **Un chien, je le vois*

If an indefinite NG is possible, it can be interpreted only in a generic way:

(23) (a) *Un enfant, ça se soigne*
     (b) *Q: As-tu vu des enfants sur ta route ?*
         A: Des enfants, je n'en ai vu aucun

The constraint is quite different for topicalization, as is shown by the fact that the NG reduced to a bare quantifier and the indefinite NG with an existential interpretation are permissible in the prephrastic field:

(24) (a) *À beaucoup, on a donné de mauvais conseils*
     (b) *À un clochard, Pierre a même donné cent francs*

The prephrastic constituent of the topicalized construction is not subject to any constraint of identifiability external to the utterance and it is not necessarily a theme.

In (20), the constituents *Marie* and *à Marie* occupy the same field, but they are not associated with the same pragmatic values. Neither the lexicon nor the placement in the sentence varies; what varies is the complex of properties that allow a constituent to appear at a greater or lesser distance

from the verb with which it is interpreted. It is this complex that contemporary modelings call a construction. A construction is the given of a matching between several dimensions: syntactical, semantic, pragmatic, and topological. If the matching is arbitrary, we might expect that it will differ from one language to another. That is confirmed by the comparison with English.

B. Left dislocation and topicalization in English

It happens that English has two constructions almost identical with those that we have just defined for French, whose names we retain. Their syntactical and topological properties are identical, as is shown by the two sentences below:

(25) (a) Mary, (I think) I saw her
     (b) *To Mary, (I think) I'll say no*

We would expect each of these constructions to assign a different value to the prephrastic constituents, as in French. And that is the case. But what is remarkable is that these values are different from those in French. The prephrastic constituent of the topicalized English construction must introduce an identifiable and thematic referent of discourse, unlike the constituent in the corresponding French construction, which is neither thematic nor necessarily identified, as is shown by the contrast between (26) and (27). In (26), the group "in London" can be (pragmatically) inferred from "in England":

(26) Q: Are you planning to settle in England?
     A: Yes, in London, I've bought a studio.

(27) Q: *Tu penses t'installer en Angleterre?*
     A: **Oui, à Londres, j'ai acheté un studio.*

On the other hand, the prephrastic constituent in the English dislocated construction is thematic and identifiable, as in French. But the same resources of identifiability cannot be mobilized in both languages. The constituent of the English sentence can be identified thanks to a relation of the part-whole (metonymic) type, with a theme belonging to the universe of discourse, which is not the case in French:

(28) (a) Mary made three groups. The first one, she gave them algebra. The two others, she gave them permission to leave.
     (b) **Marie a fait trois groupes. Le premier, elle leur a fait faire des exercices d'algèbre. Les deux autres, elle leur a donné quartier libre.*

Inversely, in French the identification of a referent of discourse by means of a metonymic relation is possible in the context of a topicalized construction:

(29) *Marie a fait trois groupes. Au premier, elle a donné des exercices d'algèbre. Aux deux autres, elle a donné quartier libre.*

C. The singularity of constructions

We have gradually abandoned the notion of word order. Under this rubric, tradition designates a set of relations that are definable in the sequence (relative placement, fixity, adjacency), as we have shown in the previous sections. But the crucial relations of order are the ones that constitute the topological organization of the language. We have just seen that it is a given field that is the support for a given value, syntactical or pragmatic, and that the association of a value with a field is carried out in the context of a construction. It follows that the notion of word order has a limited descriptive and theoretical pertinence. What constitutes the pertinent entity is the construction.

At the same time, a parallelism between word and construction has taken shape. Words and constructions are entities that associate several dimensions belonging to either the signifier or the signified. The signifier of construction implements a topological organization. The specific character of a construction is to associate a syntactical, semantic, or pragmatic value with the fields that it distinguishes. We have just seen that the association of a given value (in our example, a pragmatic value) with a field is arbitrary. We were able to show that this association is oppositive: the two French split constructions, *il y a un NG qui V* or *c'est un NG qui V*, do not assign the same pragmatic values to the NG (K. Lambrecht, *Information Structure and Sentence Form*). In other words, what characterizes the word insofar as it is a sign also characterizes the construction. This common character can be explained by borrowing a generalization formulated by Jacques Lacan:

> Every linguistic symbol that can be easily isolated is not only inseparable from the whole, but is intersected and constituted by a whole series of incoming elements, oppositional overdeterminations that situate it in several registers simultaneously.
>
> (*Le Séminaire*, Book I, *Les Écrits techniques de Freud*)

Construction appears as a linguistic individual, and like all individuals, it has general characteristics that make it "inseparable from the whole" and irreducibly specific characteristics. In one or in several languages, constructions share common ways of functioning; topicalization shares with relativization the same mechanism of distancing. It is the same mechanism in English and in French. The same goes for words: the way a verb functions transitively is identical in French and English. The irreducibly specific character of constructions can be seen in the fact that there are no synonymous constructions, just as there are no synonymous words.

IV. Word Order and Translation

We can now come to the question of the untranslatable and characterize the untranslatable that arises from "word order" in relation to the untranslatable that arises from words.

According to the hypothesis put forward by construction grammars, the grammar of a language is composed of two repertories: a lexical repertory (infinite) and a repertory of constructions (finite). The elements of these two repertories are of the same type: they are signs marked by arbitrariness, in the sense in which the principle of matching the different dimensions that constitute them does not refer to an external principle. From this we can conclude that the untranslatable arising from word order is of the same nature as that arising from words. Just as a word in a language A has no exact equivalent in a language B, we predict that a construction in a language A has no exact equivalent in a language B. If that view is correct, it allows us to understand that there is no place for a study of a phenomenon such as word order by comparing language A and language B, because this phenomenon cannot be detached and isolated from the instance of each of its constructions.

If constructions, like words, are multidimensional entities subject to arbitrariness and overdetermination, the problem of the translation of constructions is posed in the same terms as that of the translation of words. If the translation of words is "abridging and partial" (Cassin, "Présentation: Quand lire, c'est faire"), the translation of constructions is as well, and for the same reason: the unique assemblage that characterizes a construction in language A (its internal constitution and its place in the grammatical system) is destroyed and must be reconstructed in language B.

Beyond the referential equivalence, every choice regarding the translation of a word has consequences for the metaphorical sequences, the models of assonance, and the morphological figures into which it may enter in language A and into which its equivalents can enter in language B. Similarly, every choice regarding the translation of a construction has consequences for the network of discursive relations and the rhetorical arrangement that constitute the text in which it occurs. Each time, we have to choose, not a word order, but a construction, that is, a set of constraints connected with a form of utterance, constraints that bear on the expression of a content and on the type of relation that the utterance can entertain with other utterances in the text (for an example, see F. Kerleroux and J.-M. Marandin, "L'ordre des mots").

Françoise Kerleroux
Jean-Marie Marandin

BIBLIOGRAPHY

Bonami, Olivier. "DI/DP, linearization, arbres polychromes: Trois approaches de l'ordre des mots." *Linx* 39 (1998): 43–70.

Carnie, Andrew. *Syntax: A Generative Introduction.* 2nd ed. Malden, MA: Blackwell, 2007.

Cassin, Barbara. "Présentation: Quand lire, c'est faire." Pp. 9–68 in *Parménide: Sur la nature ou sur l'étant.* Paris: Éditions du Seuil, 1998.

Delesalle, Simone, and Jean-Claude Chevalier. *La linguistique, la grammaire et l'école: 1750–1914.* Paris: Colin, 1986.

Downing, Pamela, and Michael Noonan, eds. *Word Order in Discourse.* Amsterdam: Benjamins, 1995.

Emonds, Joseph E. *Discovering Syntax: Clause Structures of English, German, and Romance.* New York: De Gruyter, 2007.

Fillmore, Charles, Paul Kay, and Mary Catherine O'Connor. "Regularity and Idiomaticity in Grammatical Constructions." *Language* 64 (1988): 501–38.

Foucault, Michel. "Les mots qui saignent." Pp. 424–27 in vol. 1 of *Dits et Écrits*. Paris: Gallimard, 1994.

Gazdar, Gerald, et al. *Generalized Phrase Structure Grammar*. Cambridge, MA: Harvard University Press, 1985.

Kathol, Andreas. *Linear Syntax*. Oxford: Oxford University Press, 2000.

Kerleroux, Françoise. "Discordances d'une langue à une autre, d'une langue à elle-même." *Le Gré des langues* 6 (1993): 5–27.

Kerleroux, Françoise, and Jean-Marie Marandin. "L'ordre des mots." Pp. 277–302 in *Cahier Jean-Claude Milner*. Edited by Jean-Marie Marandin. Paris: Verdier, 2001.

Koktova, Eva. *Word-Order Based Grammar*. Berlin: De Gruyter, 1999.

Lacan, Jacques. *Le Séminaire*. Book I: *Les Écrits techniques de Freud*. Edited by Jacques-Alain Miller. Paris: Éditions du Seuil, 1975. Translation by John Forrester: *Freud's Papers on Technique, 1953–1954*. Edited by Jacques-Alain Miller. Vol. 1 in *The Seminar of Jacques Lacan*. Cambridge: Cambridge University Press, 1988.

Lakatos, Imre. *Proofs and Refutations: The Logic of Mathematical Discovery*. Edited by John Worrall and Elie Zahar. Cambridge: Cambridge University Press, 1976.

Lambrecht, Knud. *Information Structure and Sentence Form: Topic, Focus, and the Mental Representations of Discourse Referents*. Cambridge: Cambridge University Press, 1994.

Marandin, Jean-Marie. "Sites et constructions dans la théorie de la syntaxe." In *Cahier Jean-Claude Milner*, edited by Jean-Marie Marandin. Paris: Verdier, 2001.

———. "Contours as Constructions." *Constructions* 1 no. 10 (2006): 1– 28.

Ricken, Ulrich. *Sprache, Anthropologie, Philosophie in der französischen Aufklärung: Ein Beitrag zur Geschichte des Verhältnisses von Sprachtheorie und Weltanschauung*. Berlin: Akademie, 1984. Translation by Robert W. Norton: *Linguistics, Anthropology, and Philosophy in the French Enlightenment: Language Theory and Ideology*. New York: Routledge, 1994.

Virgil. *The Aeneid*. Rev. ed. 2 vols. Translated by H. Rushton Fairclough. The Loeb Classical Library. Cambridge, MA: Harvard University Press, 1969. Translation by Robert Fagles: *The Aeneid*. Introduction by Bernard Knox. New York: Viking, 2006. French translation by Pierre Klossowski: *L'Énéide*. Marseille: André Dimanche, 1989.

Weil, Henri. *De l'ordre des mots dans les langues anciennes comparées aux langues modernes: Question de grammaire générale*. Reprint. Paris: Didier, 1991. First published in Paris by Joubert in 1844. Translation by Charles W. Super: *The Order of Words in the Ancient Languages Compared with That of the Modern Languages*. Boston: Ginn, 1887.

Zwicky, Arnold M. "Dealing Out Meaning: Fundamentals of Syntactic Constructions." *Proceedings of the Berkeley Linguistics Society* 20 (1994): 611–25.

WORK

FRENCH	*travail, œuvre*
GERMAN	*Arbeit, Werk*
GREEK	*ponos* [πόνος], *ergon* [ἔργον]
LATIN	*labor, opus*

➤ ART, BERUF, *CULTURE*, ECONOMY, ENTREPRENEUR, ESSENCE, *PERFORMANCE*, PLASTICITY, STRADANIE, *THING*, UTILITY, *VOCATION*

The human activity that falls under the category of "work," at least in some of its uses, is linked to pain (the French word *travail* derives from the Latin word for an instrument of torture), to labor (Lat. *labor* [the load], Eng. "labor"), and to accomplishment, to the notion of putting to work (Gr. *ergazomai* [ἐργάζομαι], Lat. *opus*, Fr. *mise en œuvre*, Eng. "work," Ger. *Werk*), which is not necessarily the opposite of leisure but can be its partner. With Hegel, work (Ger. *Arbeit*) becomes a philosophical concept, but it designates self-realization

(whether the course of history or the life of God) rather than a reality that is exclusively or even primarily anthropological.

That form of human activity that is specifically human can be designated from two distinct points of view: stress is placed either on the tedious, "laborious," or even painful, or else on accomplishment. The first sense of "labor" reverts to the Indo-European term for agricultural laborer (*laboratores*), and was used in opposition to the warrior (the *bellatores*) or the preacher (*oratores*). These three terms have their structural analogy in Roman mythology, with the Capitoline triad of Jupiter-Mars-Quirinius.

The tedious character of work, its "negativity" in the analysis of philosophers such as Hegel and Marx, comes out clearly in the French word *travail*, from the vulgate Latin *tripalium* (first documented in the year 578 as *trepalium*), which was a "torture instrument formed from three stakes whose purpose was to immobilize recalcitrant animals" (as in the "travail" of the horse smithy) or to torment slaves. *Travailler* is to take pains to do something (from the Greek *ponos* [πόνος], which designates all fatiguing exercises, in the plural, as in the example of the labors of Hercules). It is this sense that is underscored in a verse from La Fontaine's fable "Le Laboureur et ses enfants" (The Laborer and his children): "Travaillez, prenez de la peine" (Work, and take pains to do it). This usage entered the French language to such an extent that it became the preferred expression for designating the exhausting activity of turning over the soil. The biblical heritage is felt in the notion of working "with the sweat of one's brow." "Labor" also refers to the pains of childbirth. These last two uses are linked in the Bible (Gen. 3:16–19).

It is only with Hegel, in the preface to the *Phenomenology of the Spirit* (1807) that work becomes a philosophical concept, which is at first not anthropological (since it is applied to the "life of God") in the expression "the work of negativity" (*Arbeit des Negativen*), itself picking up "the serious, pain, and patience." Nonetheless, the German *Arbeit* points toward an entirely different area of meaning, related to the Greek *orphanos* [ὀρφανός], the Latin *orbus* (deprived of), the German *Erbe* (inheritance), as well as *Armut* (poverty). To be an orphan is to be a child subject to harsh physical activity in order to provide for one's own needs. This is the source of the reluctance of Ernst Jünger, author of *Der Arbeiter*, to have his work translated into French:

> If I was reluctant for so long to have *Der Arbeiter* (Fr. *Le Travailleur*) translated into French, it stems in the first place from a pure problem of etymology. *Arbeiter* comes from *arbeo*, the gothic word "inheritance." *Travailleur* comes from *tripalium*, an "instrument of torture." *From the outset, there is a risk of a fundamental contradiction which could only increase in the translation.*
>
> (Hervier, *The Details of Time: Interviews with Ernst Jünger* [emphasis added])

The meaning of this human activity is nonetheless not exhausted by reference to its painful character. At least in some of its aspects, it can be seen as the accomplishment, the institution of a work (Gr. *ergon* [ἔργον], Lat. *opus*, Fr. *œuvre*, Ger. *Werk*). In his *Second Treatise on Civil Government* (chap. 5), Locke distinguishes between the "labor" of his body and the

1

"Labor," "work" / *Arbeit*

"Labor" and "work" form one of the many pairs of English words whose origins lie in the Norman Conquest. "Labor" derives from the Norman French and refers back to the exercise of mental or corporal faculties, especially when it is difficult or painful. "Work" is more humble. It derives from the Anglo-Saxon and simply designates everything one does or the act of doing it. "Labor" has been employed in Marxist discourse because it connotes suffering and difficulty. In America, the pragmatists adopted the happier word "work" in their discussions.

As in French, the German language does not make this distinction. *Arbeiten*, like *travailler*, refers equally to labor and to work. In a lecture on "Hegel's Legacy," given at Northwestern University in 1998, Jürgen Habermas developed an argument first published in English in 1973 under the title *Labor and Interaction*. But in the changed circumstances of 1998, *Arbeit* would now be translated as "work," such that Habermas's discourse, instead of sounding like that of a European Marxist, comes more into line with contemporary American pragmatism.

John McCumber

2

Œuvre: A complex network of terms

Œuvre is part of a vast family of words connected with the Indo-European root **op-*, "productive activity." In Latin, for example, we find, alongside *ops, opis* ("abundance," whence *copia* [resources, wealth], which yields French *copie* [large quantity, reproduction]; see MIMÊSIS), *opus, operis* (to designate "work" and its product, the "œuvre" [whence *opifex* (worker, craftsman)] and *officium* [function, office, duty]), and the feminine *opera* (activity, care).

Another noun root, **werg*, designates action, whence the Greek words *ergon* [ἔργον] (task, work), *energeia* [ἐνέργεια] (action, activity)—see PRAXIS, Box 1, and FORCE, Box 1—*organon* [ὄργανον] (tool, organ), and the Germanic *werk* (Eng. "work," Ger. *Werk*). We must add two heterogeneous families of

➤ *FACT, FICTION, IL Y A,* OBJECT, REALITY, *THING,* VORHANDEN

Latin words around *labo*: *labare* (to slip, collapse; cf. Fr. *lapsus*), whence *labor* (work as a "load" under which one bends) and *tripalium* (from *palus* [pillory, post]), which connotes our work as torment.

I. *ŒUVRE* AND WORK OF ART

Modern uses of *œuvre* link the term to artistic and literary production. In this sense, a literary *œuvre* is the result of a "doing" or "making," as in a Greek *poeien* [ποιεῖν] (see DICHTUNG, ERZÄHLEN, *POETRY;* cf. SPEECH ACT). *Œuvre* is also used in the critical and technical discourses around the creation of art and the nature of art and artists, see ART, BEAUTY, MIMÊSIS, TABLEAU; cf. AESTHETICS, LOGOS.

II. *ŒUVRE*, ACT, THING

An *œuvre* can also be seen as an exercise of power or will, a coalescence of forces. This vein opens onto the ontological dimension of implementation, power, and act (*dunamis* [δύναμις], *ergon* [ἔργον], *energeia* [ἐνέργεια]), explored in ACT, I, and additionally in FORCE and PRAXIS, ESSENCE, and SPECIES; cf. NATURE, WELT. Thinking in these terms raises the question of work as the result of human practice(s), explored in ACT, II, as well as in PRAXIS and ACTOR, BERUF ; cf. ENTREPRENEUR, MORALS. In counterpoint, the notion of God's work is addressed in *GRÂCE*, II. A final consideration, that of the work as physical embodiment, as a "thing" itself, is examined in RES, in particular RES, Box 1.

"work" of his hands, as properly belonging to each man as his own, but without clearly thematizing the distinction, and within the context of an analysis that paradoxically tends to erase rather than accentuate it insofar as the word "labor" becomes a generic term absorbing the distinction.

In *The Human Condition*, Hannah Arendt takes up this distinction, but in the opposite sense from Locke's analyses, as being "somewhat reminiscent" of the classical Greek distinction between *ponein* [πονεῖν] (to take pains to, to make the effort to) and *ergazesthai* [ἐργάζεσθαι] (to accomplish, to set to work; *mise en œuvre*), which is also used to distinguish slaves from artisans. The free man, on the other hand, is defined by his leisure, Greek *scholê* [σχολή] (whence the English word "school"), Latin *otium*, whose *neg-otium* (cf. Fr. *négoce*) is a privation. One should be careful not to confuse leisure (*otium*) with idleness (Lat. *otiositas*), or even with simple "free time" that corresponds to a "chronometric leisure" that Valéry opposes to "interior leisure" (*The Outlook for Intelligence*).

■ See Boxes 1 and 2.

Pascal David

BIBLIOGRAPHY

Arendt, Hannah. *The Human Condition*. Chicago: University of Chicago Press, 1958.

Hegel, Georg Wilhelm Friedrich. *Phenomenology of Spirit*. Translated by A. V. Miller. Oxford: Clarendon Press, 1977.

Hervier, Julien. *The Details of Time: Conversations with Ernst Jünger*. Translated by Joachim Neugroschel. New York: Marsilio Publishers, 1995.

Jünger, Ernst. *Der Arbeiter: Herrschaft und Gestalt*. Stuttgart: Klett-Cotta, 1981.

Locke, John. *Two Treatises of Government*. Edited by P. Laslett. Cambridge: Cambridge University Press, 1988.

Valéry, Paul. *The Outlook for Intelligence*. Volume 10 of *The Collected Works of Paul Valéry*. 15 vols. Edited by Jackson Mathews. Princeton, N.J.: Princeton University Press, 1956–75.

WORLD

The term refers to a totality of belonging, a set of objects that have the same mode of being (the "world of the senses," the "intelligible world," the "sublunar world"), unlike a simple "summa" of objects. In Greek, as well as in Latin, it can have a "laudatory" meaning, that of a well-organized totality (see WELT, Box 1 on the meaning of *kosmos*). The Russian constellation, where "world" is always only one of a number of possible meanings, linked to "light" or to "peace," is explored under MIR and SVET; cf. PRAVDA, RUSSIAN, SOBORNOST'.

The German WELT is the point of departure that introduces the division, particularly apparent in Kant, between a cosmological sense (*mundus* as "universe") and an anthropological sense.

Finer distinctions can be made among the following:

1. A cosmological sense; see also NATURE.
2. An ontological sense, linked to the representation of the whole and of totality; see WELT, Box 2; see also OMNITUDO REALITATIS; cf. *WHOLE*.
3. A theological sense (*mundus*, *saeculum*; cf. the scriptural expressions: "to come into the world, to leave the world"); see OLAM, SECULARIZATION.
4. A chronological sense (*aiôn* [αἰών]), as in *Weltalter* (historical time or period); see AIÔN, and *TIME*; cf. HISTORIA UNIVERSALIS.
5. A sociological and anthropological sense, as in *Umwelt* (world, environment, milieu); see WELT, Box 3.
6. An existential sense, as in the world of experience, mundanity (*Weltlichkeit*, *in-der-Welt-sein*); see DASEIN, LEIB, Box 1, WELTANSCHAUUNG.

➤ ERLEBEN, GOD, *IL Y A*, OBJECT, REALITY, RES, SEIN, VORHANDEN

WUNSCH (GERMAN)

ENGLISH   wish
FRENCH   *désir, souhait*

➤ *DESIRE* and CONSCIOUSNESS, DRIVE, ES, I/ME/MYSELF, INTENTION, LOVE, *MALAISE*, PLEASURE, SEHNSUCHT, UNCONSCIOUS, WILL

The German term *Wunsch* is, like *Trieb* (drive, instinct), at the heart of Freudian conceptualization, as it designates the fulfillment of desire (which is literally "filled," *erfüllt*) by the formations of the unconscious (dream, fantasy, symptom, lapsus, etc.). While the English "wish" is a near relative to *Wunsch*, close in meaning and deriving from the same root (the Sanskrit *wunskjan*), the French language has no obvious equivalent. The two words closest in meaning are *souhait*, which is a weaker term than *wunsch*, and *désir*, which is both stronger and more active and has the additional disadvantage of being used to translate a number of other terms that regularly surface in Freud's writings with different meanings. The French reception of Freud has been marked by the decision to adopt *désir* as the standard translation, obscuring the automatic quality of the mechanism described by Freud. This translation has also masked

the wealth of terms that Freud used to account for multiple facets of human desire. There is nothing in Freud's writings that resembles the theory of desire that Lacan believes he can find in them, even if he does so through the intermediary of Hegel as interpreted by Kojève and the latter's readings of Heidegger. Lacan's *désir* is much closer to Hegel's *Begierde* (contentiously translated as "recognition," "appetite," or "desire," and assumed to refer to a conscious state) than to the Freudian notion of *Wunsch* (assumed to refer to an unconscious psychic mechanism).

I. The Meaning of *Wunsch* in Freud

The particular conceptual meaning Freud gives to *Wunsch* can be traced back to his *Project for a Scientific Psychology* (1895) and especially to *The Interpretation of Dreams* [*Die Traumdeutung*, 1899], whose most celebrated thesis is the definition of the dream as a *Wunscherfüllung*, translated into English as "wish-fulfillment," but into French as "*réalisation de désir*" or as "*accomplissement de souhait*." The difficulty is a double one: establishing the precise meaning of *Wunsch* and addressing the multiplicity of terms in Freud's work that can all be translated by *désir* in French: *Begierde* (appetite, recognition, desire, conscience), *Begehren* (to desire, to crave, to covet), *Begehrung* (longing), *Lust* (lust, pleasure, delight, inclination), *Gelüste* (hankering, longing), *Sehnsucht* (longing, yearning, desire), *Gier* (avarice, craving), *Verlangen* (to demand, to call, to want).

In Freud *Wunsch* refers to an unconscious and automatic psychological mechanism linked to the necessities of living. It is to be understood in relation to an *experience of satisfaction*. In the chapter of *Die Traumdeutung* specifically called "Zur Wunscherfüllung" (on wish-fulfillment, Fr. *sur la réalisation du désir*), Freud clearly explains the link between the experience of satisfaction and desire. He makes a hypothesis about a "psychic apparatus" whose purely reflexive functioning becomes more complicated as a result of a "necessity of life" that imposes its own requirements on the organism:

> A hungry baby screams or kicks helplessly. But the situation remains unaltered, for the excitation arising from an internal need is not due to a force producing a *momentary* impact but to one which is in continuous operation. A change can only come about if in some way or other (in the case of the baby, through outside help) an "experience of satisfaction" can be achieved which puts an end to the internal stimulus. An essential component of this experience of satisfaction is a particular perception (that of nourishment, in our example) the mnemic image of which remains associated thenceforward with the memory trace of the excitation produced by the need. As a result of the link that has thus been established, the next time this need arises a psychical impulse will at once emerge which will seek to re-cathect the mnemic image of the perception and to re-evoke the perception itself, that is to say, to re-establish the situation of the original satisfaction. An impulse of this kind is what we call a wish; the reappearance of the perception is the fulfillment of the wish; and the shortest path to the fulfillment of the wish is a path leading

direct from the excitation produced by the need to a complete cathexis of the perception.

(Freud, *Interpretation of Dreams*, in *Standard Edition*, 5: 565–66)

We see how *Wunsch*, like *Trieb*, has a technical meaning in Freud. The psychological mechanism to which the two terms refer are for that matter very close to each other. Freud mentions repeatedly that desire is the driving force (*Triebkraft*) without which the dream would not take form. At issue is *Wunsch* as the "sole psychical motive force for the construction of dreams" (*einziger psychischer Triebkraft für den Traum*) (*Gesammelte Werke*, 2–3: 574, *Standard Edition*, 5: 568). Freud, however, defines *Wunsch*, as we saw in the passage above, as an "excitation arising from an internal need [that] is not due to a force producing a *momentary* impact but to one which is in continuous operation." *The Interpretation of Dreams* takes up the formulae from the *Project for a Scientific Psychology* and also anticipates the later definition of the drive. Thus, we can see *Wunsch* as an instinctual mechanism with its own specific characteristics: the hallucinatory reliving of an experience of satisfaction. Insofar as what is proper to desire lies in its link to a perception, one can understand how the study of dreams would permit a better understanding of its nature. But above all, it is the unconscious dimension of desire that needs to be taken into account. How does one apply the wish-fulfillment rule of desire to painful dreams or nightmares? The answer derives from the division of psychic life into two agencies: one (the unconscious) seeks to obtain pleasure through the fulfillment of a desire that is subsequently experienced as painful in the second agency (the preconscious-conscious). Thus nothing could be further from the Freudian *Wunsch* than an ontological model of desire, whose origin would be found in the Platonic *erôs* and whose tracks could be followed in the Augustinian *amor Dei*: that is to say, a force inscribed in the being of man that leads him, if he knows how to follow it, toward an object that would offset his essential lack. Here desire becomes a mark of human imperfection and a trace of the perfection that man aspires to. But Freudian desire is based on an unconscious mechanism over which man has no mastery. What is more, this desire translates the fundamental maladjustment of the human psychic process: unconscious desire is indestructible and always follows the "shortest path," the most dangerous one, since it concentrates all of its energies on simple perception.

II. The Translation of *Wunsch* into French

Is it correct to translate *Wunsch* as *désir* in French? Here questions of terminology and the weight of the Lacanian theory of desire converge. This was the standard translation right up until the team of the *Œuvres complètes de Freud/Psychanalyse* (OCF/P) made its own determination (cf. Bourguignon et al., *Traduire Freud*). In an attempt to take into account the diversity of Freudian terms that touch upon the domain of desire, and in an effort to establish a precise and systematic language, the OCF/P chose to translate *Wunsch* by *souhait* (and reserved *désir* for *Begierde*). But *Wunsch* means something stronger than *souhait*. Whereas *souhait* translates the Latin *votum*, *Wunsch* is mentioned in the

sixteenth century (cf. Johann Fries, *Novum dictionariolum puerorum latinogermanicum*, Zurich, Froschover, 1556) as a translation of *appetitio* (along with *Begird*), *desideratio* (with *Begird* and *Verlangen*), and *desiderium* (with *Lust*, *Begird*, and *Verlangen*). And this meaning has not become any weaker over time. When Goethe writes, "*In deinem Herzen muß eben der Wunsch keimen*," he clearly wants to say that "desire must stir in your heart" and not some weaker wish or *souhait*. Furthermore, the idea of an unconscious *souhait* seems harder to accept than an unconscious desire. A *souhait* presumes the active participation of the person who wishes. It would be difficult to think of oneself as the plaything of a *souhait* the way one can be subject to a desire. So there can be some justification in translating *Wunsch* as "desire."

III. Multiple Desires in the Freudian Text

Freud makes full use of the wealth of the German lexicon to account for the different levels of human desire: *Begierde* (or *Begehren*), *Lust*, *Gelüste*, *Verlangen*, and *Sehnsucht*. *Verlangen* (which literally means "extending out an arm to reach" or more colloquially "at arm's reach") is the most general term, the form of "desire" par excellence. Freud uses the term *Gelüste* (formed from *Lust*, but retaining only its meaning of desire, not of pleasure) for the strong longings that made it necessary to erect the two fundamental totemic interdictions: do not kill the totem animal and do not have sexual intercourse with members of the totem clan. As Freud wrote, parricide and incest "must be the oldest and most powerful human desires [*Gelüste*]" (*Totem und Tabu*, in *Gesammelte Werke*, 9: 42). Can neurosis, the essential object of Freudian theory, be understood as the cultural transformation of *Gelüste* into *Wunsch*, or of *desire* into *wish*, by means of the effect of repression? In interpreting dreams, then, we would recover the unconquerable power of desire behind the mechanism of wish.

We find the same mechanism at work in *Sehnsucht*, a term deemed untranslatable into French that contains the sense of a violent, painful desire for a distant or unattainable object. In *The Interpretation of Dreams* this is the term used for the longing to go to Rome, a desire so strong, and an object so distant, that for a long time it could only be expressed as the *Wunsch* of a dream. Freud writes: "In another case I note the fact that although the wish that excites the dream is a contemporary wish it is nevertheless greatly reinforced by memories of childhood. I refer to a series of dreams which are based on the longing [*Sehnsucht*] to go to Rome" (*Traumdeutung*, in *Gesammelte Werke*, 2–3, p. 199).

The fact remains that only *Wunsch* was subject to rigorous definition and thus raised to the status of concept: so it is in relation to this core meaning that the other terms are deployed, terms that have retained meanings closer to common usage and the literary tradition. It is in this sense that Lacan thought it legitimate to show that the work of Freud was much more a theory of desire than an anthropology of desires that would entail, as Kant established, precise definitions of the multiple terms afforded by the German language:

Desire [*Begierde*] (*appetitio*) is the self-determination of a subject's power through the representation of something in the future as an effect of this representation. . . .

Desiring without exercising power to produce the object is *wish* [*Wunsch*]. Wish can be directed toward objects that the subject feels incapable of producing, and then it is an *empty* (idle) wish [*leerer Wunsch*]. The empty wish to be able to annihilate the time between the desire [*Begehrten*] and the acquisition of the desired object is *longing* [*Sehnsucht*].

(Kant, *Anthropology from a Pragmatic Point of View*, Bk. 3, § 73, R. B. Louden, ed. Cambridge Texts in the History of Philosophy, 149 [German added])

- See Box 1.

Alexandre Abensour

BIBLIOGRAPHY

Bourguignon, André, Pierre Cotet, Jean Laplanche, and Robert François. *Traduire Freud*. Paris: Presses Universitaires de France, 1989.

Freud, Sigmund. *Gesammelte Werke*. 18 vols. London: Imago, 1940–1952. Translation under the general editorship of James Strachey, in collaboration with Anna Freud, assisted by Alix Strachey and Alan Tyson: *The Standard Edition of the Complete Psychological Works of Sigmund Freud*. 24 vols. London: Hogarth Press, 1957–1974.

———. *The Interpretation of Dreams I. Standard Edition*, Vol. 5. *The Interpretation of Dreams II. Standard Edition*, Vol. 6.

Hegel, Georg Wilhelm Friedrich. *Phänomenologie des Geistes*. Hamburg: Meinert, 1988.

Kojève, Alexandre. *Introduction à la lecture de Hegel*. Edited by R. Queneau. Paris: Gallimard, 1947.

Lacan, Jacques. *Écrits*. Paris: Seuil, 1966. Translation by Bruce Fink: *Écrits*. New York: W. W. Norton, 2007.

1

"Desire" according to Jacques Lacan

➤ AUFHEBEN, DASEIN

Lacan's interpretation of desire according to Freud leads him to make a rigorous distinction between *Wunsch* and *désir*: "Il faut s'arrêter à ces vocables de *Wunsch*, et de *Wish* qui le rend en anglais pour les distinguer du désir. . . . Ce sont des vœux" (We must pause at the term *Wunsch* and its English translation "wish" to distinguish them from the French *désir* [desire]. . . . Their French equivalent is *vœu*) (Lacan, *Écrits*). Whereas Freud makes *Wunsch* a special case of *Trieb*, Lacan makes desire into a general structure of the drives (Fr. *pulsions*): "This desire, in which it is literally verified that the desire of man is alienated in the desire of the other, structures in fact the drives discovered in the analysis." But this interpretation reproduces on Freud the very operation that A. Kojève had already carried out on Hegel during his celebrated seminars at the *École pratique des hautes études* from 1933 to 1939, which were faithfully attended by Lacan. In his commentary "Autonomy and Dependence of Self-Consciousness: Mastery and Slavery" (IV § A), Kojève gives desire a scope it does not have in Hegel. For Kojève, desire (with a capital D in Queneau's compilation) is at the heart of the process of subjectivation: "The (conscious) Desire of a being is what constitutes that being as a 'myself.' . . . The very being of man, the self-conscious being, therefore, implies and presupposes Desire." But, Kojève specifies, "by itself, this Desire only constitutes the sentiment of self" (*Reading of Hegel*, 3–4). How does one pass on to the specifically human stage of self-consciousness? By the desire of desire: "For there to be Self-Consciousness, Desire must be directed toward a non-natural object, toward something that goes beyond given reality. Now, the only thing that goes beyond given reality is Desire itself" (ibid., 5). From this comes Kojève's interpretation of the "struggle for recognition," which is for him a "desire for recognition": "Man's humanity 'comes to light' only in risking his life to satisfy his human Desire—that is, his Desire directed toward another Desire. Now, to desire a Desire is to want to substitute oneself for the value desired by this Desire" (ibid., 7).

How does Hegel address this? "Desire" is the translation of the German word *Begierde* in Hegel's text, a term that clearly implies a relation to an object. But which object? For Hegel it is life that is at issue: life presents itself as the other of consciousness: "self-consciousness is thus only assured of itself through sublating [*aufheben*] this other, which is presented to self-consciousness as an independent life; self-consciousness is Desire [*Begierde*]" (*Phänomenologie des Geistes*, 174). The satisfaction of desire in the object (cast not as *Wunscherfüllung* but as *Befriedigung der Begierde*) does not cancel the desire but instead reproduces it. For Hegel, consciousness can only be satisfied in an object that does not cancel it, that is to say, in an object that "effects the negation"—in other words, in another self-consciousness. "Self-consciousness attains its satisfaction only in another self-consciousness" (ibid., 175). But it would seem that in the course of this analysis, and contrary to Kojève's interpretation, "desire" never goes beyond the sphere of "life," of the immediate, of independence, of the "object," whereas the "I" [*Ich*] that is according to Hegel the "object of its own notion [of self-consciousness], is in point of fact not 'object'" ("Ich, das der Gegenstand seines Begriffs ist, ist in der Tat nicht Gegenstand"; ibid., 177). The struggle for recognition, the dialectic of master and slave, entails a stage superior to that of life (with its implication of a death-risk) and thus superior also to desire itself.

If Freud's *Wunsch* may be translated as a *vœu* (promise, vow, wish), there is no term in Freud that corresponds to this ontological desire fabricated by Lacan, who used Heideggerian *Dasein* to interpret Hegel.

BIBLIOGRAPHY

Kojève, Alexandre. *Introduction à la lecture de Hegel*. Edited by R. Queneau. Paris: Gallimard, 1947. Translation by J. Nichols: *Introduction to the Reading of Hegel: Lectures on the Phenomenology of Spirit*. Edited by A. Bloom. New York: Basic Books, 1969.

Lacan, Jacques. *Écrits*. Paris: Seuil, 1966. Translation by Bruce Fink: *Écrits*. New York: W. W. Norton, 2007.

Reference Tools

Listed here are some of the reference works (encyclopedias, dictionaries, complete works, and other resources) that were used or cited in the writing of the articles.

Ak. *Kants gesammelte Schriften*. By Immanuel Kant. Edited by Königliche Preussische Akademie der Wissenschaften. Berlin: Georg Reimer, 1902–13.

CAG *Commentaria in Aristotelem Graeca*. Edited by the Preussische Akademie der Wissenschaften. 23 vols. Berlin: De Gruyter, 1882–1909.

CCSL *Corpus christianorum: Series latina*. Turnhout, Belg.: Brepols, 1953–.

CLE *Carmina latina epigrafica*. By Franz Bücheler. Amsterdam: Hakkert, 1972.

CSEL *Corpus scriptorium ecclesiaticorum latinorum*. Vienna: Österreichische Akademie der Wissenschaften, 1886–.

DHLF *Dictionnaire historique de la langue française*. Edited by Alain Rey. 3 vols. Paris: Le Robert, 1992.

DK *Die Fragmente der Vorsokratiker*. By Hermann Diels and Walther Kranz. 5th ed. 3 vols. Berlin: Weidmann, 1934–37.

GW *Gesammelte Werke* [Collected Works]. By Sigmund Freud. 18 vols. London and Frankfurt: Imago and Fischer, 1940-52; vol. suppl. *Nachtragsband (1855–1938)*. Frankfurt: Fischer, 1987.

LIMC *Lexicon iconographicum mythologiae classicae*. 8 vols. Zurich: Artemis, 1981–2009.

LSJ *A Greek-English Lexicon*. By Henry G. Liddell, Robert Scott, and Henry Jones. 9th ed. Oxford: Clarendon Press, 1925–40. Supplement, edited by E. A. Berber, 1968.

PG *Patrologiae cursus completus: Series graeca*. Edited by Jacques-Paul Migne. 161 vols. Paris, 1857–66.

PL *Patrologiae cursus completus: Series latina*. Edited by Jacques-Paul Migne. 221 vols. Paris, 1844–64.

SVF *Stoicorum veterum fragmenta*. By Johannes von Arnim. Leipzig, 1903–5. Republished in 4 vols. Stuttgart: Teubner, 1964. Italian translation and bilingual ed. by R. Radice: *Stoici antichi: Tutti i frammenti*. Milan: Rusconi, 1998.

TGF *Tragicorum graecorum fragmenta*. By Stefan Lorenz Radt. Göttingen, Ger.: Vandenhoeck and Ruprecht, 1985.

Allgemeines Handwörterbuch der philosophischen Wissenschaften. By Wilhelm Traugott Krug. Stuttgart: Frommann, 1969.

The Anchor Bible Dictionary. Edited by David Noel Freedman. 6 vols. New York: Doubleday, 1992.

Ancient Greek Accentuation: Synchronic Patterns, Frequency Effects, and Prehistory. By Philomen Probert. New York: Oxford University Press, 2006.

Ancilla to "The Pre-Socratic Philosophers: A Complete Translation of the Fragments in Diels, 'Fragmente der Vorsokratiker.'" Edited and translated by Kathleen Freeman. Cambridge, MA: Harvard University Press, 1957.

Anglo-Ukrajins'kyj filosofs'kyj slovnyk [English-Ukrainian philosophic dictionary]. By Nina Polichtchuk and Vasyl Lisovyj. Kiev: Lybid', 1996.

Aperçu d'une histoire de langue grecque. By Antoine Meillet. 8th ed. Paris: Klincksieck, 1975. First published 1965.

Archives d'histoire doctrinale et littéraire du Moyen Âge. Paris: Vrin, 1926–.

Attic Greek Prose Syntax. Edited by Guy Cooper. Ann Arbor: University of Michigan Press, 1998–2002.

Ausführliche Grammatik der Griechischen Sprache. By Raphael Kühner and Bernhard Gerth. Vol. 2, *Satzlehre*. Hanover: Hannsche Buchhandlung, 1976.

Axular-en hiztegia: Euskara, español, français. Español-euskara; français-euskara. By Luis Villasante. Arantzazu, Sp.: Jakin, 1973.

The Basque Language. By Luis Michelena. Translated by Gloria Castresana Waid. Bilbao, Sp.: Basque American Foundation, 1987.

Die Bibel nach der Übersetzung Martin Luthers. Stuttgart: Deutsche Bibelgesellschaft, 1985.

The Bible: Authorized King James Version. Oxford: Oxford University Press, 2008.

Black's Law Dictionary, Centennial Edition (1891–1991). St. Paul, MN: West Company, 1998.

Bol'shaja Sovetskaia Èntsiklopedija. Edited by A. M. Prokhorov. 3rd ed. 31 vols. Moscow: Sov. Èntsiklopedija, 1970–78. Translated as: *Great Soviet Encyclopedia*. 31 vols. New York: Macmillan, 1979.

Le bon usage: Grammaire française. By Maurice Grévisse. 13th ed. Revised by A. Goosse. Brussels: Duculot, 1993. First published in 1936.

The British Moralists on Human Nature and the Birth of Secular Ethics. By Michael B. Gill. Cambridge: Cambridge University Press, 2006.

The Cambridge Dictionary of Philosophy. Edited by Robert Audi. Cambridge: Cambridge University Press, 1995.

A Catholic Dictionary. Edited by D. Attwater. New York: Macmillan, 1941.

Characteristicks of Men, Manners, Opinions, Times. By Anthony Ashley Cooper, third earl of Shaftesbury. Edited by Philip Ayres. Reprint, Oxford: Clarendon Press, 1999. First published 1711.

A Companion to the Philosophy of Mind. Edited by Samuel Guttenplan. Oxford: Blackwell, 1994.

A Compleat English Dictionary. By Nathan Bailey. 8th ed. Leipzig: Frommann, 1792.

Complete Church-Slavonic Dictionary. By G. Diachenko. N.p.: Firebird Publications, 1993.

A Comprehensive Etymological Dictionary of the English Language. By Ernest Klein. 2 vols. New York: Elsevier, 1971.

A Concise German Etymological Dictionary. By Maurice O'C. Walshe. London: Routledge and Kegan Paul, 1952.

Contemporary Philosophy of Mind. By Georges Rey. Oxford: Blackwell, 1997.

Cours de linguistique générale. By Ferdinand de Saussure. Paris: Payot, 1979. Translation by R. Harris: *Course in General Linguistics*. Edited by C. Bally and A. Sechehaye with A. Riedlinger. LaSalle, IL: Open Court, 1986.

Des mots à la pensée: Essai de grammaire de la langue française. Paris: Éditions d'Artey, 1911–40.

Deutsche Encyclopädie oder allgemeines Real Wörterbuch aller Kunste und Wissenschaften von einer Gesellschaft Gelehrten. 25 vols. Frankfurt: Varrentrapp Sohn and Wenner, 1778–1807.

Deutsches Wörterbuch. By Jacob and Wilhelm Grimm. Leipzig: Hirzel, 1854. Reprint, Munich: Deutscher Taschenbuch, 1984.

Deutsche Wortbildung. By Ludwig M. Eichinger. Tübingen: Narr, 2000.

Diccionario crítico etimológico castellano e hispánico. Edited by Joan Corominas and José A. Pascual. New ed. 6 vols. Madrid: Gredos, 1984–91. First published in 1961.

Diccionario de autoridades. By Real Academia Española. Madrid, 1726. Reprint in 3 vols., Madrid: Gredos, 1990.

Diccionario de construcción y regimen de la lengua castellana. By Rufino Cuervo. Bogotá: Instituto Caro y Cuervo, 1994. First published in 1886.

Diccionario del español actual. By Manuel Seco, Olimpia Andrés, and Gabino Romas. Madrid: Aguilar Lexicografía, 1999.

Diccionario del uso del español. By Maria Moliner. Madrid: Gredos, 1980.

Diccionario etimologico romano. By Alexandre Cioranescu. La Laguna, Sp.: Biblioteca Filologica Universidad de la Laguna, 1958–61.

Diccionario general vasco = Orotariko euskal hiztegia. By Luis Michelena. Bilbao, Sp.: Real Academia de la Lengua Vasca, 1987–.

Diccionario nacional ó gran diccionario clásico de la lengua española. By Ramón Joaquin Domínguez. 14th ed. Madrid: Bernat, 1878. First published in 1849.

Diccionario retana de autoridades de la lengua vasca. Edited by Manuel de la Sota et al. Bilbao, Sp.: La Gran Enciclopedia Vasca, 1976–.

Dicionário etimológico da linga portuguesa. José Pedro Machado. Reedition. Lisbon: Livros Horizonte, 1990. First published in 1952.

Dicionário inglês-português, português-inglês. By Leonel Vallandro. 10th ed. Rio de Janeiro: Globo, 1987.

Dicţionar explicativ al limbii române [Explanatory dictionary of the Romanian language]. Bucarest: Éditions de l'Académie, 1975.

Dicţionar universal al limbii române [Universal dictionary of the Romanian language]. By Lazàr Sàineanu. Craiova, Rom.: Scrisul Românesc, 1926.

Dictionarium Britanicum; or, A More Compleat Universal Etymological English Dictionary Than Any Extant. By Nathan Bailey. London: T. Cox, 1730.

A Dictionary of Art Terms: Painting, Sculpture, Architecture, Engraving and Etching, Lithography and Other Art Processes. By Reginald George Haggar. New York: Hawthorn, 1962.

A Dictionary of Christian Spirituality. Edited by Gordon S. Wakefield. London: SCM, 1983.

A Dictionary of Linguistics and Phonetics. Edited by David Crystal. 6th ed. Malden, MA: Blackwell, 2008.

A Dictionary of Marxist Thought. By Tom Bottomore. Cambridge, MA: Harvard University Press, 1983.

Dictionary of Philosophy. Edited by Dagobert D. Runes. 16th rev. ed. New York: Philosophical Library, 1960.

A Dictionary of Slavic Word Families. By Louis Jay Herman. New York: Columbia University Press, 1975.

A Dictionary of the English Language. By Samuel Johnson. London, 1755.

Dictionnaire critique de la langue française. By Jean-François Féraud. 2nd ed. Marseille, 1788.

Dictionnaire critique de la sociologie. By Raymond Boudon and François Bourricaud. 2nd ed. Paris: Presses Universitaires de France, 2000.

Dictionnaire critique du marxisme. Edited by Georges Labica and Gérard Bensussan. Paris: Presses Universitaires de France, 1982.

Dictionnaire de l'Académie Française. 9th ed. Paris: Fayard, 2011. First published in 1694.

Dictionnaire de la langue française. By Émile Littré. 4 vols. Paris: Hachette, 1873.

Dictionnaire de la langue française du seizième siècle. By Edmond Huguet. 7 vols. Geneva: Slatkine, 1999. First published 1925–73.

Dictionnaire de l'ancienne langue française, et de tous ses dialectes du IXe au XVe siècle. By Frédéric Godefroy. 1881–1902. 10 vols. Reprint, New York: Kraus, 1961.

Dictionnaire de musique. 1768. By Jean-Jacques Rousseau. In *Œuvres complètes*, vol. 5. Paris: Gallimard / La Pléiade, 1995. Translation by William Waring: *A Dictionary of Music.* London, 1779.

Dictionnaire de philosophie politique. By Philippe Raynaud and Stéphane Rials. Paris: Presses Universitaires de France, 1996.

Dictionnaire de psychanalyse. Edited by E. Roudinesco and M. Plon. Paris: Fayard, 1997.

Dictionnaire de psychiatrie. Edited by Jacques Postel. Paris: Larousse-Bordas, 1995.

Dictionnaire des arts de peinture, sculpture et gravure. By Claude-Henri Watelet and Pierre-Charles Lévesque. 5 vols. Paris, 1792.

Dictionnaire de spiritualité: Ascétique et mystique; Doctrine et histoire. Edited by M. Viller et al. 16 vols. Paris: Beauschesne, 1932–.

Dictionnaire de théologie catholique. Edited by Alfred Vacant, Eugène Mangenot, et al. Paris: Letouzey and Ané, 1923–50.

Dictionnaire de Trévoux: Dictionnaire universel français et latin. 3 vols. and supp. Trévoux, Fr.: Estienne Ganeau, 1704.

Dictionnaire d'étymologie daco-romaine, éléments latins. By Alexandru de Cihac. Frankfurt: Saint-Goar, 1870.

Dictionnaire du judaïsme. Paris: Albin Michel, 1998.

Dictionnaire étymologique complémentaire de la langue grecque. By Albert J. Van Windekens. Louvain, Belg.: Peeters, 1986.

Dictionnaire étymologique de la langue française. By Oscar Bloch and Walther von Wartburg. 6th rev. ed. Paris: Presses Universitaires de France, 1975.

Dictionnaire étymologique de la langue grecque. By Émile Boisacq. Heidelberg: Winter-Klincksieck, 1938.

Dictionnaire étymologique de la langue grecque. By Pierre Chantraine. New ed. Paris: Klincksieck, 1999.

Dictionnaire étymologique de la langue latine: Histoire des mots. By Alfred Ernout and Antoine Meillet. Edited by Jacques André. 4th ed. Paris: Klincksieck, 2001.

Dictionnaire étymologique du français. By Jacqueline Pioche. Paris: Le Robert, 2000.

Dictionnaire étymologique, ov Origines de la langue françoise. By Gilles Ménage. 2 vols. Reprint, Geneva: Slatkine, 1973. First published in 1694.

Dictionnaire français-anglais, anglais-français. 2nd ed. Paris: Dictionnaires Le Robert / Collins, 1987.

Dictionnaire français-grec. By Charles Alexandre, Joseph Planche, and Charles-Auguste Defauconpret. Paris: Hachette, 1859.

Dictionnaire françois: Contenant les mots et le choses, plusieurs nouvelles remarques sur la langue françoise. By Pierre Richelet. 2 vols. Reprint, Hildesheim, Ger.: Olms, 1973. First published in 1680.

Dictionnaire général de la langue française du commencement du dix-septième siècle jusqu'à nos jours. Paris: Delagrave, 1890.

Dictionnaire grec-français. By Anatole Bailly. Rev. ed. Edited by L. Séchan and P. Chantraine. Paris: Hachette, 1994.

Dictionnaire grec moderne–français. By Hubert Pernot. Paris: Garnier, 1970.

Dictionnaire hébreu-français. By Nathaniel Sander and Isaac Trenel. Reprint, Geneva: Slatkine, 1982. First published in 1859.

Dictionnaire philosophique. By Voltaire. Paris: Flammarion, 1964. Translation by P. Gay: *Philosophical Dictionary*. New York: Basic Books, 1962. First published in 1764.

Dictionnaire portatif de peinture, sculpture et gravure. By Antoine-Joseph Pernety. Paris: Bauche, 1757.

Dictionnaire universel, contenant généralement tous les mots français tant vieux que modernes, et les termes de toutes les sciences et des arts. By Antoine Furetière. Reprint in 3 vols., Paris: Le Robert, 1978. First published in 1690.

Duden: Deutsches Universalwörterbuch. 3d ed. Mannheim, Ger.: Dudenverlag, 1996.

Duden: Das Herkunftswörterbuch. Vol. 7, *Etymologie der deutschen Sprache*, edited by Günther Drosdowski et al. 4th ed. 12 vols. Mannheim, Ger.: Dudenverlag, 2007.

The Encyclopedia of Philosophy. Edited by Paul Edwards. 8 vols. New York: Macmillan, 1972.

Encyclopedia: Selections. By Denis Diderot and Jean Le Rond d'Alembert. Translated by Nelly S. Hoyt and Thomas Cassirer. Indianapolis, IN: Bobbs-Merrill, 1965.

Encyclopédie méthodique: Architecture. By Antoine Quatremère de Quincy. 3 vols. Paris: Panckoucke-Plomteux, 1788–1825.

Encyclopédie ou Dictionnaire raisonné des sciences, des arts et des métiers. Edited by Denis Diderot and Jean Le Rond d'Alembert. Paris, 1751–80. 35 vols. Stuttgart: Frommann, 1966. Facsimile of the original.

Encyclopédie philosophique universelle. Edited by André Jacob. Paris: Presses Universitaires de France, 1990.

English-Basque Dictionary. By Gorka Aulestia and Linda White. Reno: University of Nevada Press, 1992.

English-German, German-English Dictionary. By Karl Wildhagen. Edited by Will Heraucourt. 12th ed. 2 vols. Wiesbaden, Ger.: Brandstetter, 1962–63.

English-Greek and Greek-English Dictionary of Law Terms / Angloellêniko & Hellênoangliko lexico nomikón horôn. By Chares Karatzas and Helena Zompola. Athens: Nomiki Bibliothiki, 2003.

English-Russian Comprehensive Dictionary. Edited by Oleg P. Benyukh. New York: Hippocrene, 1995.

Entciklopediceskij slovar' [Encyclopedic dictionary]. 35 vols. St. Petersburg: Brockhaus-Efron, 1890–1902.

Ėtimologiceskij slovar' russkogo jazyka [Etymological dictionary of the Russian language]. By Galina Tsyganenko. 4 vols. Kiev: Radians'kasokla, 1970.

Ėtimologicheskiĭ slovar' russkogo iazyka [Etymological dictionary of the Russian language]. By Max Vasmer. 4 vols. Moscow: Progress, 1986–87.

Ėtimologicheskiĭ slovar' slavianskykh jazykov [Etymological dictionary of Slavic languages]. By Oleg Nikolaevitch Trubachev. Moscow: Nauka, 1978.

Études sur l'étymologie et le vocabulaire du vieux slave: Seconde partie. By Antoine Meillet. 2nd ed. 2 vols. Paris: Champion, 1961.

Etymological Dictionary of Greek. By R.S.P. Beekes. Leiden, Neth.: Brill, 2009.

Etymological Dictionary of Latin and the Other Italic Languages. By Michiel Vaan. Leiden, Neth.: Brill, 2008.

An Etymological Dictionary of the English Language. By Walter W. Skeat. New ed. Oxford: Clarendon Press, 1974. First published 1910.

An Etymological Dictionary of the French Language. By A. Brachet. Translated by G. W. Kitchin. 3rd ed. Oxford: Clarendon Press, 1882.

An Etymological Dictionary of the German Language. By Friedrich Kluge. Translated by John Francis Davis. London: Bell, 1891.

An Etymological Dictionary of the Latin Language. By F.E.J. Valpy. London: Baldwin, 1838.

Etymological Dictionary of the Russian Language. By Aleksandr Grigor'evich Preobrazhenskiĭ. Reprint, New York: Columbia University Press, 1951. Originally published as *Ėtymologiceskij slovar' russkogo jazyka*. 2 vols. Moscow, 1910–14.

Etymologický slovnik jazyka ceského a slovenskeho [Etymological dictionary of the Czech and Slovak languages]. By Václav Machek. Prague: Nakladatelství Česoslovenské Akademie Věd, 1957.

Etymologičny slovnyk ukraïns'koï movy [Etymological dictionary of the Ukranian language]. Kiev: Naukova Dumka, 1985.

Etymologie: Herkunftswörterbuch der deutschen Sprache. By Konrad Duden. Edited by G. Drosdowski, P. Grebe, et al. Mannheim, Ger.: Dudenverlag, 1963.

Etymologisches Wörterbuch der deutschen Sprache. By Friedrich Kluge. 22nd ed. Berlin: De Gruyter, 1989.

The Etymology of the Words of the Greek Language in Alphabetical Order. By F.E.J. Valpy. London: Longman, Green, Longman and Roberts, 1860.

Filosofskij èntsiklopedieskij slovar' [Philosophic encyclopedic dictionary]. By E. F. Gubsky et al. Moscow: Infra-M, 1997.

Firmini Verris dictionarius: Dictionnaire latin-français de Firmin Le Ver, 1440. Edited by Brian Merrilees and William Edwards. Turnhout, Belg.: Brepols, 1994.

Die Fragmente zur Dialektik der Stoiker. By Karlheinz Hülser. 4 vols. Stuttgart: Frommann-Holzboog, 1987–88.

"Fragments." By Aeschylus. Translated by Herbert Weir Smyth. Edited by Hugh Lloyd-Jones. In vol. 2 of *Works*. Loeb Classical Library. Cambridge, MA: Harvard University Press, 1963.

Die französischen Wörter "langue" und "langage" im Mittelalter. By Hans Georg Koll. Paris: Minard-Droz, 1958.

Französisches etymologisches Wörterbuch. By Walther von Wartburg. Basel, Switz.: Zbinden, 1959.

Französisches etymologisches Wörterbuch: Eine Darstellung des galloromanischen Sprachschatzes. By Walther von Wartburg. 25 vols. Bonn: Klopp, 1928–2003.

A General and Bibliographical Dictionary of the Fine Arts. By James Elmes. London, 1826.

Geschichtliche Grundbegriffe: Historisches Lexikon zur politisch-sozialen Sprache in Deutschland. Edited by Otto Brunner, Werner Conze, and Reinhard Koselleck. 8 vols. Stuttgart: Klett, 1972–92.

Gesamtausgabe [Collected works]. By Martin Heidegger. Frankfurt: Klostermann, 1975–.

Glossarium mediæ et infimæ latinitatis. By Charles Du Fresne Du Cange. 1678. 10 vols. Paris: Librairie des Sciences et des Arts, 1937–38.

Goethes Werke (Hamburger Ausgabe). By Johann Wolfgang von Goethe. Edited by Erich Trunz. 14 vols. Munich: Beck, 1981.

Grammaire de l'ancien français. By Gérard Moignet. Paris: Klincksieck, 1973.

A Grammar of the Homeric Dialect. By David Binning Monro. 2nd rev. ed. Oxford: Clarendon Press, 1891.

Grammatici latini. Edited by Heinrich Keil. 8 vols. Hildesheim, Ger.: Olms, 1981. First published in 1857–80.

Grande dizionario della lingua italiana. Edited by Salvatore Battaglia. Milan: Unione Tipografico-Editrice Torinese, 1961.

Grand vocabulaire française … par une société de gens de letters. 2nd ed. 30 vols. Paris: C. Pankouke, 1767–74.

Great Soviet Encyclopedia. Edited by A. M. Prokhorov. 20 vols. New York: Macmillan, 1979.

A Greek-English Lexicon of the New Testament and Other Early Christian Literature. Edited by Frederick W. Danker. Chicago: University of Chicago Press, 2000.

The Greek Language. By Leonard R. Palmer. London: Faber and Faber, 1980.

Greek Lexicon of the Roman and Byzantine Periods from B.C. 146 to A.D. 1100. By Evangelinus Apostolides Sophocles. Cambridge, MA: Harvard University Press, 1914. Facsimile edition: Hildesheim: Olms, 1975.

Griechisches etymologisches Wörterbuch. By Hjalmar Frisk. 3 vols. Heidelberg: Winter-Universitätsverlag, 1960–72.

Guide for Translating Husserl. By Dorion Cairns. The Hague: Nijhoff, 1973.

Hamner's German Grammar and Usage. By Martin Durell. 4th ed. New York: McGraw-Hill, 2002.

Handbuch der literarischen Rhetorik. By Heinrich Lausberg. 2nd ed. Munich: Max Hueber, 1973.

The Hellenistic Philosophers. Edited by Anthony A. Long and David Sedley. Cambridge: Cambridge University Press, 1987.

Histoire littéraire de la France, où l'on traite de l'origine, du progrès, de la décadence et du rétablissement des sciences parmi les Gaulois et parmi les Français … par des religieux bénédictins de la Congrégation de Saint-Maur. Edited by Antoine Rivet et al. 12 vols. Paris: Chez Osmont, 1733–63.

Historical Dictionary of Ancient Greek Philosophy. Edited by Anthony Preus. Lanham, MD: Scarecrow, 2007.

Historical Dictionary of Ethics. Harry J. Gensler and Earl W. Spurgin. Lanham, MD: Scarecrow, 2008.

Historical Dictionary of Kant and Kantianism. By Helmut Holzhey and Vilem Mudroch. Lanham, MD: Scarecrow, 2005.

Historical Dictionary of Medieval Philosophy and Theology. Edited by Stephen F. Brown and Juan Carlos Flores. Lanham, MD: Scarecrow, 2007.

A Historical Dictionary of Psychiatry. By Edward Shorter. Oxford: Oxford University Press, 2005.

An Historical Greek Grammar, Chiefly of the Attic Dialect. 1897. Edited by Antonius Jannaris. Reprint, Hildesheim, Ger.: Olms, 1968.

Historisches Lexikon zur politisch-sozialen Sprache in Deutschland. 8 vols. Stuttgart: Klett, 1972–92.

Historisches Wörterbuch der Philosophie. Edited by Joachim Ritter and Karlfriend Gründer. New ed. Basel, Switz.: Schwabe, 1971–2007.

Historisches Wörterbuch der Rhetorik. Edited by Gert Ueding. Darmstadt, Ger.: Wissenschaftliche Buchgesellschaft, 1994.

The Holy Bible. New International Version (NIV). Colorado Springs, CO: Biblica, 2011. BibleGateway.com, http://www.biblegateway.com/versions/New-International-Version-NIV-Bible.

Les idées reçues: Sémiologie du stéréotype. By Ruth Amossy. Paris: Nathan, 1991.

Idee w Rosji: Leksykon Rosyjsko-Polsko-Angielski [Ideas in Russia: Lexicon in Russian-Polish-English]. Edited by Andrej de Lazari. Warsaw: Sepmer, 1999.

Index aristotelicus. By Hermann Bonitz. Berlin: Reimer, 1870. Reprint, Berlin: Akademik-Verlag, 1955.

An Index to Aristotle in English Translation. By T. W. Organ. Princeton, NJ: Princeton University Press, 1949.

Index zu Heideggers "Sein und Zeit." By Hildegard Feick. 3rd ed. Tübingen: Niemeyer, 1980. First published in 1961.

Indogermanisches etymologisches Wörterbuch. By Julius Pokorny. 2nd ed. 2 vols. Bern: Francke, 1989.

An Inquiry into the Original of Our Ideas of Beauty and Virtue in Two Treatises. By Francis Hutcheson. Reprint, Hildesheim, Ger.: Olms, 1971. First published in 1725.

Introduction to Contemporary Epistemology. By Jonathan Dancy. Oxford: Blackwell, 1985.

A Kant Dictionary. By Howard Caygill. Oxford: Blackwell, 1995.

Kant-Lexikon. By Rudolf Eisler. Hildesheim, Ger.: Olms, 2008. First published in 1930.

Korais Printed and Electronic Greek-English Dictionary. Edited by Geôrgios Kokkinakês. Patras, Gr.: Ekdoseis Panepistêmiou Patrôn, 2008.

A Latin Dictionary: Founded on Andrews' Edition of Freund's Dictionary. By E. A. Andrews. Edited by Charlton T. Lewis and Charles Short. Rev. ed. Oxford: Clarendon Press, 1966.

A Latin Grammar. By B. L. Gildersleeve. New York: University Publishing Co., 1875.

Leksikologija i slovoobrazovanie drevnerusskogo jazyka [Lexicology and word formation of the Old Russian language]. Moscow: Nauka, 1966.

Lessico filosofico della Frühaufklärung. By Dagmar von Wille. Rome: Edizioni dell'Ateneo, 1991.

Léxico del marginalismo del siglo de oro. By José Luis Alonso Hernández. Salamanca, Sp.: University of Salamanca, 1977.

Lexicon philosophicum, quo tanquam clave philosophiae fores aperiuntur. By Rudolph Goclenius. Reprint, Hildesheim, Ger.: Olms, 1964. First published in 1613.

Lexicon of Presocratic Philosophy. 2 vols. Athens: Academy of Athens, 1994.

Lexicon totius latinitatis. By Eigidio Forcellini. Padua, 1940.

Lexiko tês neas Hellênikês glôssas [Dictionary of the modern Greek language]. By Georgios Babiniotis. 2nd ed. Athens: Kentro Lexikologias, 2002.

Lexique de la langue philosophique d'Ibn Sina. By Amélie-Marie Goichon. Paris: Desclée de Brouwer, 1937.

Linguae vasconum primitiae. By Bernat Dechepare. Edited by P. Altuna. Critical ed. Bilbao, Sp.: Real Academia de la Lengua Vasca, 1980.

La littérature européenne et le Moyen-Âge latin. By Ernst Robert Curtius. 1948. Reprint, Paris: Presses Universitaires de France, 1956.

Le Littré: Dictionnaire de la langue française en un volume. By Emile Littré. Paris: Hachette, 2000.

Les matérialismes philosophiques. By Jean-Claude Bourdin. Paris: Kimé, 1997.

Materialy dlia slovaria drevnerusskogo iazyka [Material for a dictionary of Old Russian]. By Izmail Ivanovich Sreznevskiĭ. 3 vols. Moscow: Znak, 2003.

Mega lexikon olês tês Hellênikês glôssês [A large lexicon of the entire Greek language]. By Dêmêtrios Dêmêtrakos. 15 vols. Athens: Asêmakopoulos, 1964.

The MIT Encyclopedia of Cognitive Science. Edited by Robert A. Wilson and Frank Keil. Cambridge, MA: MIT Press, 1999.

Modern Greek–English Dictionary. By Achilleus Kyriakides. Athens: Anesti Constantinides, 1909.

Najstarije slavensko filosofsko nazivlje [Slavic philosophical terminology]. By Anto Knezevic. Zagreb, Cro.: Hrvatski Filozofsko Drustvo, 1991.

Der Neue Brockhaus. Edited by Friedrich Arnold Brockhaus. 7th ed. 5 vols. Mannheim, Ger.: Brockhaus, 1991.

The New Catholic Encyclopedia. Washington, DC: Catholic University of America Press, 2002.

The New Oxford Annotated Bible with the Apocryphal/Deuterocanonical Books: New Revised Standard Version. Edited by Michael D. Coogan. 3rd ed. New York: Oxford University Press, 2007.

Le nouveau dictionnaire des auteurs. By Robert Laffont and Valentino Bompiani. 3 vols. Paris: Laffont, 1994.

Nouveau dictionnaire des sciences du langage. Edited by Oswald Ducrot and Jean-Marie Schaeffer. Paris: Éditions du Seuil, 1995.

Nouveau dictionnaire du voyageur, français-allemand-latin. Geneva: Perachon, 1732. First published in 1708.

Le nouveau petit Robert. Edited by Josette Rey-Debove and Alain Rey. Paris: Dictionnaires Le Robert, 2002.

Nova gramática do português contemporâneo. By Celso Cunha and Lindley Cintra. 15th ed. Lisbon: da Costa, 1999.

Novo dicionário da língua portuguesa. By Aurélio Buarque de Holanda. Rio de Janeiro: Nova Fronteira, 1986.

The NRSV Concordance Unabridged: Including the Apocryphal/ Deuterocanonical Books. By John R. Kohlenberger III. Grand Rapids, MI: Zondervan, 1991.

Œuvres. By René Descartes. Edited by C. Adam and P. Tannery. 11 vols. Paris: Vrin, 1996.

The Origins of European Thought about the Body, the Mind, the Soul, the World, Time and Fate: New Interpretations of Greek, Roman and Kindred Evidence, also of Some Basic Jewish and Christian Beliefs. By Richard Broxton Onians. 1st paperback ed. Cambridge: Cambridge University Press, 1988. First published in 1951.

The Oxford Companion to the Mind. Edited by Richard L. Gregory. Oxford: Oxford University Press, 1987.

The Oxford Dictionary of English Etymology. Edited by C. T. Onions. Oxford: Oxford University Press, 1966.

Oxford-Duden German Dictionary: German-English, English-German. By W. Scholze-Stubenrecht and J. B. Sykes. 3rd ed. Oxford: Oxford University Press, 2005.

The Oxford English Dictionary. Edited by John Simpson and Edmund Weiner. 2nd ed. 20 vols. Oxford: Clarendon Press, 1989.

The Oxford English-Hebrew Dictionary. Edited by N. Doniach and A. Kehane. Oxford: Oxford University Press, 1998.

Oxford Latin Dictionary. Edited by P.G.W. Glare. New York: Oxford University Press, 1996.

Petit dictionnaire français–grec moderne et grec moderne–français. By André Mirambel. Paris: Maisonneuve et Larose, 1980.

Philosophical Arguments. By Charles Taylor. Cambridge, MA: Harvard University Press, 1995.

Philosophical Dictionary: English-Greek and Greek-English. By Constantine Cavarnos. Belmont, MA: Institute for Byzantine and Modern Greek Studies, 2006.

Philosophisches Lexicon. Johann Georg Walch. Hildesheim, Ger.: Olms, 1968.

Polnyj tserkovno-slavianskij slovar' [Complete church Slavonic dictionary]. By Grigorij Diačenko. Moscow: Tipografia Vilde, 1899.

Portuguese: An Essential Grammar. By Amélia P. Hutchinson and Janet Lloyd. 2nd ed. New York: Routledge, 2003.

The Practice of Conceptual History: Timing History, Spacing Concepts. By Reinhard Koselleck. Translated by T. Presner, K. Behnke, and J. Welge. Stanford, CA: Stanford University Press, 2002.

Praktycna psyxologija v konteksti kul'tur [Applied psychology in a cultural context]. Kiev: Nika-Tsentr, 1998.

Précis d'accentuation grecque. By Michel Lejeune. Paris: Hachette, 1945.

Précis de grammaire. By Dominique Maingueneau. 3rd ed. Paris: Armand Colin, 2004.

Prepodobnyj Maksim Ispovednik i vizantijskoe bogoslovie [Saint Maximus the Confessor and the Byzantine liturgy]. By S. Epifanovic. Kiev, 1915.

The Pre-Socratic Philosophers: A Companion to Diels, "Fragmente der Vorsokratiker." By Kathleen Freeman. Cambridge, MA: Harvard University Press, 1946.

Les Présocratiques. Edited by Jean-Paul Dumont. Paris: Gallimard / La Pléiade, 1988.

Psixologija ličnosti [Psychology of personality]. Edited by Pavel Gornostaj and Tatiana Titarenko. Kiev: Ruta, 2001.

The Qur'an. Translated by M.A.S. Abdel Haleem. Corrected ed. Oxford: Oxford University Press, 2008.

Remarks on John Locke by Thomas Burnet; with Locke's Replies. Edited by George Watson. Doncaster, UK: Brynmill, 1989.

Repertorium reale pragmaticum juris publici et feudalis imperii romano-germanici. By Heinrich Gottfried Scheidemantel. Leipzig, 1782–95.

Routledge Encyclopedia of Philosophy. Edited by Edward Craig. London: Routledge, 1998.

Russian Etymological Dictionary. By Terence Wade. London: Bristol Classical, 1996.

Sachwörterbuch der Litteratur. By Gero von Wilpert. Stuttgart: Kröner, 1955.

Le slave commun. By Antoine Meillet. 2nd rev. ed. Paris: Champion, 1965.

Slovar' russkogo iazyka [Dictionary of the Russian language]. By A. P. Evgen'eva. Moscow: Russkii Iazyk, 1981–.

Slownik etymologiczny jezyka polskiego [Etymological dictionary of the Polish language]. By Alexander Brückner. Warsaw: Wiedza Powszechna, 1957.

Standard French-English, English-French Dictionary. New ed. Paris: Larousse, 1994.

Stéréotypes et clichés: Langue, discours, société. By Ruth Amossy. Paris: Nathan, 1997.

Syntaxe grecque. By Jean Humbert. 3rd rev. ed. Paris: Klincksieck, 1997.

Tesoro de la lengua castellana o española. By Sebastián Covarrubias. Edited by M. de Riquer. Reprint, Barcelona: Alta Fulla, 1998. First published in 1611.

Tesoro de las dos lenguas española y franscesca. By César Oudin. Reprint, Paris: Ediciones Hispano-Americanas, 1968. First published in 1607.

Theologisches Wörterbuch zum neuen Testament. Edited by Gerhard Kittel and Gerhard Friedrich. 9 vols. Stuttgart: Kohlhammer, 1933–73. Translation by Geoffrey W. Bromiley: *Theological Dictionary of the New Testament*. Edited by Geoffrey W. Bromiley. 10 vols. Grand Rapids, MI: Eerdmans, 1964–76.

Thesaurus linguae latinae. Stuttgart: Teubner, 1900–1906.

Thresor de la langue française tant ancienne que moderne. By Jean Nicod. Reprint, Paris: Picard, 1960. First published in 1606.

Tolkovyï slovar' zhivogo velikorusskogo iazyka [Explanatory dictionary of the living language of Great Russia]. By Vladimir Ivanovich Dal'. 4 vols. Moscow: Russkiï Iazyk, 1978–80.

Traduction œcuménique de la Bible. By the Société Biblique Française. 9th ed. Paris: Éditions du Cerf, 2000.

Traité d'accentuation grecque. By Joseph Vendryès. Paris: Klincksieck, 1904.

De verborum significatu quae supersunt. By Sextus Pompeius Festus. Edited by Wallace M. Lindsay. Stuttgart: Teubner, 1997.

Versuch einer allgemeinen deutschen Synonymik. By Johann August Eberhard. Reprint, Hildesheim, Ger.: Olms, 1971. First published in 1795.

Versuch eines vollständingen grammatisch-kritischen Wörterbuches der hochdeutschen Mundart. By Johann Christoph Adelung. 5 vols. Leipzig: Breitkopf, 1774–86.

Vocabolario Toscano dell'arte del disegno. By Filippo Baldinucci. In vols. 2–3 of *Opere*. Milan, 1809. First published in 1681.

Vocabulaire de la langue espagnole classique (XVI et XVIIème siècles). By Bernard Sesé and Marc Zuili. Paris: Nathan, 2001.

Vocabulaire de la psychanalyse. Edited by Jean Laplanche, Jean-Bertrand Pontalis, and Daniel Lagache. Reprint, Paris: Presses Universitaires de France, 2007. First published in 1967. Translation by Donald Nicholson-Smith: *The Language of Psycho-Analysis*. New York: W. W. Norton, 1973.

Vocabulaire de sciences cognitives. Edited by O. Houdé, D. Kayser, O. Koenig, J. Proust, and F. Rastier. Paris: Presses Universitaires de France, 1998.

Le vocabulaire des institutions indo-européennes. By Émile Benveniste. 2 vols. Paris: Éditions de Minuit, 1969. Translation by Elizabeth Palmer: *Indo-European Language and Society.* Coral Gables, FL: University of Miami Press, 1973.

Vocabulaire de théologie biblique. Edited by Xavier Léon-Dufour et al. 2nd ed. Paris: Éditions du Cerf, 1970. Translated as: *Dictionary of Biblical Theology* under the direction of Joseph Cahill. Updated 2nd ed. London: Chapman, 1995.

Vocabulaire technique et critique de la philosophie. By André Lalande. 19th ed. Paris: Presses Universitaires de France, 1999.

Vocabulario filosofico. By Juan Zaragüeta. Madrid: Espasa-Calpe, 1955.

Volksthümliches Wörterbuch der deutschen Sprache, mit Bezeichnung der Aussprache und Betonung für die Geschäfts- und Lesewelt. By Theodor Heinsius. 4 vols. Hanover: Hahn, 1818–22.

Webster's Spanish-English Dictionary. Springfield, MA: Merriam-Webster, 2002.

Webster's Third New International Dictionary of the English Language, Unabridged. Edited by Philip Babcock Gove. Springfield, MA: Merriam-Webster, 2002.

Werke, Kritische Gesamtausgabe. By Friedrich Nietzsche. Edited by G. Colli and M. Montinari. Berlin: De Gruyter, 1967–.

Wörterbuch der deutschen Sprache. By Daniel Sanders. Reprint, Hildesheim, Ger.: Olms, 1969. First published in 1860.

Index

vrai (French), and the status of ontological truth, 1167–68

Vulgate, 1143, 1144–45; contribution of to the establishment of Christian Latin as distinct from classical Latin, 1144–45; reintroduction of philosophically charged terms in, 298; and the rule of *hebraica veritas,* 1145

wahr (German): and belief, 1167; and safeguarding, conservation, 1167; and the status of ontological truth, 1167–68

Weber, Max, 76, 111, 227, 412, 433, 448, 449, 607, 609, 706, 801, 830, 1076; on domination, 436; on secularization and the disenchantment of the world, 934–35; on the spirit of capitalism, 267; use of *Beruf,* 103–5, 106, 1208; use of *Ethik,* 698; use of *Sinn,* 964; use of *Wirtschaft,* 244–45; on values, 1228; and *Vergemeinschaftung/Vergesellschaftung* distinction, 137

welfare, 402; and the French *salut public,* 402; and the German *Wohlfahrt,* 402, 429

Welt (German), 1217; etymology of, 1217; and the Greek *kosmos,* 1217, 1217–19; and the Latin *mundum,* 1219; translation of, 1221–22; and universe, 1219–21; and *welten,* 1222, 1224

Weltanschauung (German), 512, 1224–25

Weltlauf (German), 1206–7

Wert (German), 1225–26; etymology of, 1225

Wesenschau (German), 360

Whig and Tory, 1231; in English politics, 1231; Hume's synthesis of, 1232; role of the opposition of in the ways that political thought is framed in the English language, 1232–33; and the tension between the party of Country and the party of Court, 1231–32; translation of in France and the American colonies, 1233

whole, 1234

will, 1234; the absence of a problematics of in Aristotle and Stoicism, 1234–35; the Augustinian doctrine of the, 255–56, 1235–36; contemporary thinking about the, 1237–38; the emergence of the "completed" concept of the and the heresy of monotheism, 1236–37; the

"enslaved will," 256; and the Latin *liberum arbitrium,* 255–56, 575; and the Latin *servum arbitrium,* 256; and the medieval invention of a third faculty, 1234

Willkür (German), 1239; and emphasis on the sense of the arbiter as arbitrary or capricious, 1240; etymology of, 1240; French translation of, 1239–40; Kant's *(freie),* 1239, 1241

Winckelmann, Johann Joachim, 15, 107, 112, 673, 1094; and the notion of the "beautiful soul" *(schöne Seele),* 87; reference of to *historia,* 445–46; use of *nachahman,* 671, 672; use of *Stille,* 622, 1060–61

Wirkung (German), 347

Wirtschaft (German), 243, 244–45; etymology of, 245

wisdom: and the French *sagesse* and *goût,* 1242; twofold meaning of, 1242

wit (English), 485; and humor, 487, 488; and mind, 487; and the pleasure of using language, 487

Wittgenstein, Ludwig, 7, 20, 21, 143, 272, 273, 295, 464, 474, 715, 775, 820, 924, 966, 1044; antipsychological precepts of, 93; and behaviorism as a reflection on the nature of the linguistic given, 96; on consciousness, 185; and critique of the mental, 1022–24; and definition of language, 1045; and elimination of "attitude" and mind from belief, 100; on the feeling of certainty, 102; interest of in counting, 590; and the linguistic turn, 257, 262, 263; on nonsense, 717–21, 1043; the originality of *praxis* of, 831–32, 1009; private language argument of, 725; and the *Sinn/Bedeutung* distinction, 962; on the symbol as use endowed with meaning, 66–67; and theory of the image, 1175–78; use of *Geschmack,* 414; use of *Satz,* 870, 874; use of *übereinstimmen,* 144

witticism, 1242

Witz (German), 485, 487, 488; according to Freud and his translators, 489

Wohlfahrt (German), 402, 429

Wolff, Christian, 109, 152, 180, 302, 355, 374, 648, 886, 1120; and adoption

of *cosmologia* as a title, 325; and definition of happiness, 400; and elision of the Latin *terminus,* 1121; "reality," "possibility," and "quiddity" in the work of, 734–36; and theory of consciousness as a general faculty of knowledge, 174; use of *Begriff,* 90, 327; use of *Bewusstsein,* 181, 183; use of *Empfindung,* 356–57

word, 859, 1243; Augustine's *verbum, dicibile, dictio, res,* 1250; the French vocabulary of, 1254–55; as a grammatical unit, 1244; the Greek *lexis,* 1243; the Greek *onoma,* 1243–44; the Greek *onoma/rhêma,* 1244–45; the Greek *rhêma,* 1244; the Latin vocabulary of, 1243, 1249–54; as a result of grammar formation, 1243

word order, 1256; and the accumulation of values, 1258–59; arbitrariness of, 1260; and the division of labor, 1257–58; the fixed of French, 1256–57; the free of Latin, 1257; left dislocation and topicalization in English, 1261–62; left dislocation and topicalization in French, 1260–61; morphology and the value of, 1259–60; and the order of constituents, 1261; the singularity of constructions of, 1262; the terms and content of the relation of, 1258; and translation, 1262; and Weil's thesis, 1258

work, 1263–64; and the English "labor," 1264; and the English "work," 1264; etymology of, 1264

world, 1265

Wort (German), 593

wuǧūd (Arabic), 1211

Wunsch (German), 1265; meaning of in Freud, 1265–66; translation of into French, 1266

Xenophon, 194, 399, 442, 567, 728–29, 760, 787, 1141

zaoum (Russian), 336

Zivilisation (German), 112, 118–19

Zivilisationsprozess (German), 713

Žižek, Slavoj, 36, 710

zôê (Greek), 280; and *bios,* 281

zôion (Greek), 34, 34–35; etymology of, 34